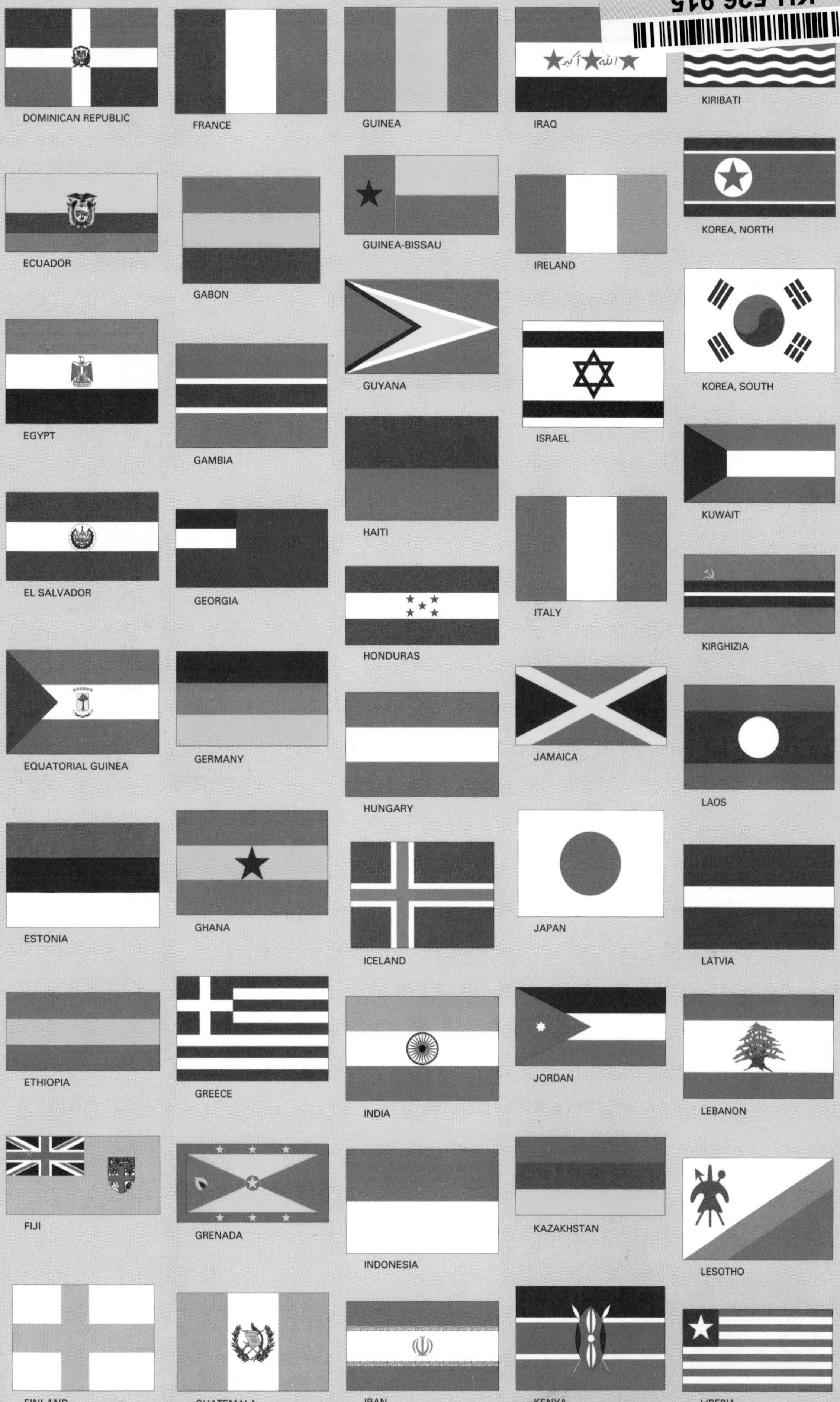
DOMINICAN REPUBLIC
ECUADOR
EGYPT
EL SALVADOR
EQUATORIAL GUINEA
ESTONIA
ETHIOPIA
FIJI
FINLAND
FRANCE
GABON
GAMBIA
GEORGIA
GERMANY
GHANA
GREECE
GRENADA
GUATEMALA
GUINEA
GUINEA-BISSAU
GUYANA
HAITI
HONDURAS
HUNGARY
ICELAND
INDIA
INDONESIA
IRAN
IRAQ
IRELAND
ISRAEL
ITALY
JAMAICA
JAPAN
JORDAN
KAZAKHSTAN
KENYA
KIRIBATI
KOREA, NORTH
KOREA, SOUTH
KUWAIT
KIRGHIZIA
LAOS
LATVIA
LEBANON
LESOTHO
LIBERIA

THE CAMBRIDGE ENCYCLOPEDIA

EDITED BY
DAVID CRYSTAL

CAMBRIDGE
UNIVERSITY PRESS

Published by the Press Syndicate of the University of Cambridge
The Pitt Building, Trumpington Street, Cambridge CB2 1RP
40 West 20th Street, New York, NY 10011-4211, USA
10 Stamford Road, Oakleigh, Melbourne 3166, Australia

First published 1990
Reprinted with updates and corrections 1991, 1992

Typeset by H Charlesworth & Co Ltd.

Printed in The United States of America

British Library cataloguing in publication data
The Cambridge encyclopedia
1. Encyclopaedias in English
1. Crystal, David, *1941–*
032

Library of Congress cataloging in publication data
The Cambridge encyclopedia
p. cm.
Includes bibliographical references
ISBN 0-521-39528-3
1. Encyclopedias and dictionaries
AG5.C26 1990
031—dc20

ISBN 0 521 43176 X

Editor
David Crystal

Development Editor
Min Lee

Copy editors and proof readers
Jock Graham
Jane Pollock
Ian Ross

Editorial Administrator
Hilary Crystal

Production Co-ordinator
Jack Osborne

Illustrators
David Brogan
George Kilgour
John Marshall

Cartography
Euromap Ltd

Colour section design
David Sneddon

Graphic design
Peter Ward

Jacket design
The Pinpoint Design Company

Database Management Consultant
Maurice Shepherd, University of St Andrews

Keyboarders
Gillian Gibson
Claire Meade

For permission to reproduce copyright material we thank:

Art Directors Photo Library
Bass, Mitchells & Butler Ltd
City of Edinburgh District Council
Dance Notation Bureau, New York
European Space Agency
Hunting Aerofilms
National Aeronautics and Space Administration
National Gallery of Scotland
National Museums of Scotland, Dept of Geology, Edinburgh
New Scientist, London
Planet Earth Pictures
Royal Observatory, Edinburgh
Science Photo Library
Scottish National Gallery of Modern Art
South of Scotland Electricity Board
Tate Gallery, London
The Benesh Institute, London
The Telegraph Colour Library
UK Operators Offshore Association
Victory Museum, Portsmouth
Wade Cooper Associates

CONSULTANTS AND CONTRIBUTORS

Alison Abbott, Editor, *Trends in Pharmacological Science*

Janet Adshead, Course Director of Dance Studies, University of Surrey

Harriet Allen, Dept of Geography, Homerton College, Cambridge

Sarah Ansari, Royal Holloway and Bedford New College, University of London

Susan Bambrick, Master of University House, The Australian National University, Canberra

John Becklake, The Science Museum, London

Augustus Leon Beier IV, Dept of History, University of Lancaster

John Douglas Belshaw, Dept of Social Sciences, Cariboo College, British Columbia

Martin Blinkhorn, Dept of History, University of Lancaster

Ian Borden, Bartlett School of Architecture and Planning, University College, London

Geoffrey A Boxshall, British Museum (Natural History)

Malcolm Boyd, Dept of Music, University of Wales, College of Cardiff

Brian Bracegirdle, Assistant Director (Collections Management), The Science Museum, London

Geoffrey A Briggs, Director, Solar System Exploration Program, National Aeronautics and Space Administration (NASA), Washington

Christy Campbell, Defence Correspondent, *The Sunday Correspondent*

Jack Chambers, Dept of Linguistics, University of Toronto

Simon Collier, Dept of History, University of Essex

Emily Williams Cook, Dept of Psychology, University of Edinburgh

Edward Countryman, Dept of History, University of Warwick

George Davidson, Reference Editor, W & R Chambers

Roy Davis, Professor of Psychology, University of Reading

Deborah Delanoy, Dept of Psychology, University of Edinburgh

James C Docherty, Commonwealth Dept of Industrial Relations, Canberra

Leslie Du S Read, Dept of Drama, University of Exeter

Walter C Dudley Jr, Dept of Geology, University of Hawaii at Hilo

Eric J Evans, Professor of Social History, University of Lancaster

Elizabeth Gaffan, Dept of Psychology, University of Reading

Michael J Gibney, Div of Nutritional Sciences, St James's Hospital, Dublin

Virginia Glenn, The Royal Scottish Museum, Edinburgh

Robert O Gould, Dept of Chemistry, University of Edinburgh

Sheila E B Gould, Dept of Chemistry, University of Edinburgh

Damien Grant, Dept of English, University of Manchester

Jack Gray, Institute of Development Studies, University of Sussex

Frank Greenaway, The Science Museum, London

George B Hall, Dept of Divinity, University of St Andrews

Bernard Happé, Consultant in motion picture technology

Keith Harrison, British Museum (Natural History)

Raymond J Harwood, Head of Dept of Textile Technology and Fashion, Leicester Polytechnic

John Haslam, Department of Physiology, King's College, London

Ruth Henig, Dept of History, University of Lancaster

Stanley Henig, Professor of European Politics, Lancashire Polytechnic at Preston

Ruth Hepworth, Royal Aerospace Establishment, Farnborough

Ian Hinton, Dept of Management Development, Kingston Polytechnic

Mij Kelly, Journalist (historical sites)

Susan Kemp-Wheeler, Dept of Psychology, University of Reading

Jane Kirk, The Science Museum, London

Jessica Kuper, Editor, Social Science, Cambridge University Press

David Lambert, Writer (physical anthropology)

Hugh Laracy, Dept of History, University of Auckland

Min Lee, Reference Editor, W & R Chambers

Charles Lewis, Dept of Psychology, University of Reading

Nicholas B Lilwall, Head of Rural Resource Management Dept, Edinburgh School of Agriculture

Roger Lincoln, British Museum (Natural History)

Alistair McCulloch, Dept of Public Administration and Law, Robert Gordon's Institute of Technology

John MacKenzie, Dept of History, University of Lancaster

Ian McMorran, Oriental Institute, Oxford

William E Mann, Professor of Philosophy, University of Vermont

David Mannings, Dept of History of Art, University of Aberdeen

Peter Meech, Dept of Film and Media Studies, University of Stirling

Ian T Millar, Emeritus Professor of Chemistry, University of Keele

Julie Milton, Dept of Psychology, University of Edinburgh

Simon Mitton, Fellow of St Edmund's College, Cambridge

Ian Morrison, Writer (sports)

Trevor Mostyn, Writer and editor (Middle East studies)

Bernard Moulden, Professor of Psychology, University of Reading

Frederick G J Norton, Head of Mathematics, Rugby School

Roger Oldcorn, Dept of Finance and Accounting, Henley Management College

Ronald A Piper, Dept of Divinity, University of St Andrews

John R Press, British Museum (Natural History)

John Purkis, Senior Lecturer in Literature, The Open University

Andrew Putnis, Dept of Earth Sciences, University of Cambridge

Peter Richards, Editor, Reference, Cambridge University Press

Derek F Roberts, Professor of Human Genetics, University of Newcastle upon Tyne

Derek A Robinson, Dept of Physical Sciences, The Science Museum, London

James S Robson, Professor Emeritus of Medicine, University of Edinburgh

Anne Seaton, Reference Editor, W & R Chambers

Colin Shapiro, Dept of Psychiatry, University of Edinburgh

Douglas W D Shaw, Professor of Divinity, University of St Andrews

Margaret Shennan, Writer (history)

Maurice Shepherd, Director of External Services, University of St Andrews

Philip T Smith, Professor of Psychology, University of Reading

Roger Soames, Dept of Anatomy, King's College, London

Peter Spearritt, Director, National Centre for Australian Studies, Monash University

Joan Stringer, Head of School of Public Administration and Law, Robert Gordon's Institute of Technology, Aberdeen

Keith J Stringer, Dept of History, University of Lancaster

Patrick Swinden, Dept of English, University of Manchester

Serena Sugar, Co-writer (English Literature biographies)

Brian D Taylor, Dept of Law, School of the Built Environment, Leicester Polytechnic

Alan R Thomas, Research Professor, Dept of Linguistics, University College of North Wales, Bangor

Neil Toye, Dept of Seamanship, Southampton Institute of Higher Education

John Trevitt, Art and Design Director, Cambridge University Press

Malcolm Trevor, Professor of International Personnel Management, Nagoya City University

George K Wallace, Dept of Psychology, University of Reading

Anthony J Watkins, Dept of Psychology, University of Reading

Andrew Watson, Dept of Mathematics, University of Melbourne, Australia

Susan Watt, The Science Museum, London

Andrew J Webster, Dept of Sociology, Anglia Polytechnic, Cambridge

Margaret H Williams, Tutor in Classics, The Open University

Marylin Williams, Dept of Psychology, University of Reading

Peter Williamson, Dept of Health Care Policy and Management, University of Aberdeen

Alan Wood, Dept of History, University of Lancaster

Ted Wragg, Director, School of Education, University of Exeter

Tom Wright, The Science Museum, London

PREFACE

The main aim of *The Cambridge Encyclopedia* is to provide a succinct, systematic, and readable guide to the facts, events, issues, beliefs, and achievements which make up the sum of human knowledge. All encyclopedias, however many volumes they comprise, are inevitably selective. It is therefore essential, especially for a single-volume work, to make the principles of selection and treatment explicit, so that readers will know what to expect, and will be able to make best use of its content. Short encyclopedias do not usually provide much background information of this kind, but I am happy to break with this particular tradition.

HISTORY OF THE PROJECT

The Cambridge Encyclopedia was developed in a collaboration between W & R Chambers, who took specific responsibility for editorial development and production, and Cambridge University Press, who conceived the project and now publish it. The result is a work whose broad coverage, systematic treatment, and freshness of approach is without precedent in single-volume encyclopedias.

It is not unusual to find single-volume encyclopedias which are little more than revisions of previously published works. *The Cambridge Encyclopedia*, by contrast, was planned as a completely fresh venture, in terms of both coverage and treatment. The overall structure of the book, the balance between its main thematic components, and its approach to level and style were devised by the editor in association with editorial staff of the two publishing houses. All topic entries were specially commissioned from an international team of contributors affiliated to universities, specialist colleges, schools, museums, and other centres of excellence.

COVERAGE

It is impossible to summarize the coverage of an encyclopedia in any simple way. Number of entries is a traditional guide, but opinion varies as to what counts as an entry, and it is difficult to compare encyclopedias, as a consequence. In *The Cambridge Encyclopedia*, there are nearly 25 000 entries given alphabetical treatment; and a further 7 000 entries are presented in Ready Reference form. The main entries include, additionally, over 2 500 bold-face headwords which are part of larger entries. An important feature of the work is the provision of over 3 000 headword cross-references (e.g. **earth pig** ≫ **aardvark**), whose role is to anticipate the diverse routes used by readers when they are searching for information. In short, the 1482 pages of *The Cambridge Encyclopedia* provide data on nearly 35 000 separately identified people, places, and topics, making it easily the most comprehensive work of its type.

There are certain kinds of information which benefit from tabular presentation (such as lists of rulers, sporting achievements, and scientific measures), and these are gathered together into a 128-page Ready Reference section, located at the back of the book. This section is an important feature of *The Cambridge Encyclopedia*. It is unique in its extensive coverage for a single-volume encyclopedia, and has been carefully designed to avoid the miscellaneous juxtaposition of isolated facts which is commonplace in this genre. Our Ready Reference section works systematically through all the major areas of knowledge best presented in tabular form. Such information is not always readily available in standard sourcebooks; for example, to obtain complete listings of 20th-century political leaders, we had often to refer directly to embassies and political archives, and for sports and games to the relevant associations and governing bodies. The result conveys a large amount of information in a systematic and accessible manner.

Two major themes characterize the coverage of *The Cambridge Encyclopedia*: its internationalism and up-to-dateness. An encyclopedia for the 1990s must surely reflect international issues, especially in history, politics, and current affairs. For example, many short reference works provide information about British monarchs or American presidents, but this is the first time that the rulers of all sovereign states have been listed in this way. It is also the first encyclopedia to be able to cover thoroughly the revolutionary events of 1989. The alphabetical section is equally wide-ranging. Certain major parts of the world (such as Australia, Africa, South America, India, Japan, and the Middle East) traditionally receive little coverage in single-volume English-language encyclopedias. We have been especially vigilant in representing these neglected areas.

We have also allotted far more space than is traditional to the electronic revolution (especially computer science), space exploration, technology, economics, communications, earth sciences, environmental issues, medicine, and recreation. At the same time, we have given systematic coverage to traditionally popular areas such as flora and fauna, history, art, music, literature, theatre, religion, and mythology. We devote special attention to the history of ideas, in such fields as philosophy, art, linguistics, literature, sociology, and politics.

Thanks partly to the concise style used for many entries, one of the main features of *The Cambridge Encyclopedia* is the breadth of its topic entries – over

15 000 in the alphabetical section alone. In addition, we have added over 5 500 biographical entries and 4 000 gazetteer entries to the alphabetical section, concentrating on persons of international distinction and the most important places. About 7 000 other topics, persons, and places are listed in tabular form in the Ready Reference section.

TREATMENT

Coverage is only half of the strength of any encyclopedia; the other crucial dimension is treatment. The most noticeable characteristic of *The Cambridge Encyclopedia* derives from its aim to act as a standard reference work, for use in the home, school, library, or office by both adult enquirers and young people of high-school age. Its key feature is the rapid answers it gives to specific queries about people, places, or topics. In *The Cambridge Encyclopedia*, the majority of entries are short and to the point: slightly more than 50% of the entries average 125 words, and a further 45% of the entries average 50 words; the remaining 5% of the entries average 500 words. The long entries provide a detailed exposition of themes of particular historical or contemporary importance – for example, the American Revolution, the American Civil War, civil rights, the two World Wars, and the entries on the nations of the world.

The short-entry principle allows the reader interested in a particular topic (say, a certain musical instrument) the opportunity to go directly to information on that topic, rather than to an entry in which all related topics are treated together in a single long essay. Encyclopedias which do conflate topics in this way make it difficult to find the answer to a specific question. At the same time, it is important to aid readers who do need to find out about a topic in a more comprehensive way, such as for homework assignments or course work. To satisfy this need, a detailed and carefully selected system of cross-references to related topics has been introduced. For example, the cross-references at the end of the entry on **violin** will direct readers to other instruments closely associated with the violin (such as **viola** and **kit**) as well as to the family (**string instrument**), and other information (such as biographies of famous violin-makers). On the other hand, if the initial point of enquiry had been **string instrument**, the cross-references there would provide an indication of all the instruments in that family. In longer entries, the cross-references have been grouped into types – in the arts entries, for example, the names of individual painters are grouped separately after the topical cross-references. We recommend the reader to make use of these references, which have all been carefully selected for their interest and relevance (almost as much editorial time was devoted to cross-reference selection as to entry editing). An encyclopedia *should* be explored, and one way of doing this in *The Cambridge Encyclopedia* is to follow some of the thousands of pathways provided by the cross-references, which number over 75 000.

The other important feature of *The Cambridge Encyclopedia* – and one which helps to explain the size of the work as a whole – is the commitment made by the editor to present the information in an intelligible and interesting way. All too often, encyclopedic information is put across in a dense and dull manner which creates a barrier between the enquirer and the subject being researched. *The Cambridge Encyclopedia* aims to remove this barrier, partly by its imaginative use of typography and layout (including the use of over 800 illustrations), and partly by the use of plain English. Particular attention has been paid to the language of the entries, to ensure that they are written in an intelligible style, without losing sight of the conventions identifying the subject area to which each entry belongs. Guidance on pronunciation is given, using a specially devised phonetic spelling, when it is not clear how a headword should be pronounced. A particular innovation is the systematic use of a specially condensed style for gazetteer, natural history, and certain other types of entry, which provides information in a clear and direct manner, increases accessibility, and saves a great deal of space (thus permitting an overall increase in coverage). The principle of functional clarity has also been used in the selection of illustrations, where we have avoided the 'pretty picture' approach to encyclopedia compilation, and chosen to rely on clear, relevant line-drawings, highlighting important features through the use of a second colour.

Entry arrangement is alphabetical, on a word-by-word indexing basis. The Ready Reference section, on tinted paper, is organized thematically, with an introductory index to the section as a whole. Between the alphabetical and the Ready Reference section is a 16-page full-colour section, on the general theme of the functional use of colour, illustrating concepts which demand colour in order to be understood satisfactorily.

AUTHORITY, ACCESSIBILITY AND INTERACTION

The availability of the Chambers databases for the Biographical Dictionary and the World Gazetteer, along with the specially commissioned team of contributors, have enabled us to compile a single-volume encyclopedia characterized by its authority, accessibility, and breadth of coverage. Each entry has been scrupulously edited to ensure consistency of treatment and clarity of explanation. *The Cambridge Encyclopedia*, accordingly, presents a knowledge-base which is ideally suited to meeting the information needs of people in the 1990s. At the same time, it is important to recognize not only the strengths, but also the limitations of any general encyclopedia, and to strive to surmount them. We therefore very much welcome feedback from readers relating to matters of coverage and treatment. Please write to the editor directly, at PO Box 5, Holyhead, Gwynedd LL65 1RG, UK. In this way, our knowledge-base will grow with the times, and reflect ever more closely the interests and concerns of those wishing to benefit from it.

David Crystal

HOW TO USE THE CAMBRIDGE ENCYCLOPEDIA

HEADWORDS

- The order of entries follows the English alphabet, ignoring capital letters, accents, diacritics, or apostrophes.
- The ordering is word by word, then letter by letter, eg **de Saussure** precedes **deacon**; **La Paz** precedes **labour**; and **space station** precedes **spacecraft**, which precedes **Spacelab**. Words may be followed by a space, dash, or hyphen (eg **space-time**). However, we ignore hyphens when they follow prefixes (such as **de-**, **infra-** or **anti-**), eg **anti-literature** follows **antiknock**.
- Note that compound words in English sometimes vary in the way they divide, eg both **sea horse** and **seahorse** are found as possible usages. In such cases, it may be necessary to check the location of an entry in more than one place.
- We list phrasal names under their most specific element, eg **Japan, Sea of**, **Waterloo, Battle of**.
- In cases where headwords have the same spelling, the order is; (1) general topics, (2) people, (3) places.
- We list identically spelled topic headwords according to the alphabetical order of their subject areas, eg **depression** (meteorology) precedes **depression** (psychiatry).
- We list rulers chronologically, ordering them by country if titles are the same, eg **Charles I** (of Austria-Hungary) is followed by **Charles I** (of England) then by **Charles II** (of England) and **Charles II** (of Spain).
- When many people have the same name (eg **John**), we list monarchs before saints and popes, followed by lay people. Compound names (eg **John of Austria**) appear later than single element names (eg **John**, **Otto**).
- We list places with the same name on the basis of the alphabetical order of their countries, eg **Dover** (UK) precedes **Dover** (USA).

SPELLING CONVENTIONS

- Where alternative spellings exist in headwords, we give British usage first, then American usage, eg **colour/color television**. We give cross-references in all cases where spelling variation affects initial letters, eg **esophagus, oesophagus**.
- We order place names and surnames beginning with **St** as if they were spelled **Saint**. Surnames beginning with **Mac** are listed before those beginning with **Mc**.
- We transliterate names in non-Roman alphabets, and add a cross-reference in cases where confusion could arise because more than one transliteration system exists. Chinese names are given in pin-yin (eg **Beijing** for **Peking**). In the case of Arabic names, we have not transliterated the alif and ain symbols.

CROSS-REFERENCES

- Cross-references are always to headwords in the encyclopedia, with a distinguishing parenthesis if required, eg **Romanticism** (music). We do not include personal titles in the cross-reference, and we give a distinguishing first name or initial only if entries could be confused, eg **Morgan, Henry**, **Morgan, J P**.
- All cross-references are listed in alphabetical order. In the case of longer entries, the references may be grouped; eg in art, cross-references to topics precede cross-references to artists.
- When several references share a common word or phrase, they are conflated, being separated by /, as in the **spacecraft** entry opposite.

ABBREVIATIONS

AD Anno Domini
BC Before Christ
c century
c. circa
C Celsius (Centigrade)
C central
cc cubic centimetre(s)
Chin Chinese
cm centimetre(s)
Co County
cu cubic
cwt hundredweight(s)
e estimate
E east(ern)
eg for example
Eng English
F Fahrenheit
fl oz fluid ounce(s)
Fr French
ft foot/feet
g gram(s)
Ger German
Gr Greek
h hour(s)
ha hectare(s)
Hung Hungarian
[i] illustration
I(s) Island(s)
ie that is (id est)
in inch(es)
Ir Irish
Ital Italian
Jap Japanese
K Kelvin
kg kilogram(s)
km kilometre(s)
l litre(s)
L Lake
Lat Latin
lb pound(s)
l y light year(s)
m metre(s)
min minute(s)
ml mile(s)
Mlle Mademoiselle
mm millimetre(s)
Mme Madame
Mt Mount(ain)
Mts Mountains
N north(ern)
no. number
oz ounce(s)
p(p) page(s)
pop population
Port Portuguese
pt pint(s)
r. reigned
R River
RR Ready Reference
Russ Russian
S south(ern)
sec second(s)
Span Spanish
sq square
St Saint
Sta Santa
Ste Sainte
Swed Swedish
trans. translation
v. versus
vols. volumes
W west(ern)
yd yard(s)
Z zodiac

Other conventions

Months in parenthesis are abbreviated to the first three letters (3 Jan 1817)

National holiday abbreviations, RR24.

Currency abbreviations, RR32-6.

Physics abbreviations, RR70, 78.

Chemistry and mathematics abbreviations, RR90.

Music abbreviations, RR91-2.

Countries and international organizations, RR32-7.

General list of abbreviations, RR124-8.

PRONUNCIATION GUIDE

SYMBOL	SOUND	SYMBOL	SOUND	SYMBOL	SOUND
a	**h**at	i	**s**it	r	**r**ed
ah	**f**ather	iy	**lie**	s	**set**
ai	**hair**	j	**jet**	sh	**ship**
aw	**saw**	k	**kit**	t	**tin**
ay	**say**	l	**lip**	th	**thin**
b	**big**	m	**man**	**th**	**this**
ch	**chip**	n	**nip**	u	**put**
d	**dig**	ng	**sing**	uh	**cup**
e	set	o	hot	v	van
ee	**see**	oh	**soul**	w	**will**
er	**bird**	oo	**soon**	y	**yes**
f	**f**ish	ow	**cow**	z	**zoo**
g	go	oy	**boy**	zh	leisure
h	**h**at	p	**pin**		

Non-English sounds

ã French **Nan**tes
hl Welsh **llan**
ĩ French **Saint**
õ French **bon**
kh Scots **loch**, German **ich**
oe French **soeur**, German **möglich**
ü French **tu**, German **müde**

Bold type is used to show stressed or accented syllables, eg **Xerxes** [**zerk**seez]

space shuttle A re-usable crewed launch vehicle. The first-generation US shuttle became operational in 1982, managed by NASA's Johnson and Marshall Space Centers, while the USSR and European Space Agency versions were still under development. The US shuttle carries up to seven crew, and is capable of launching a 27 000 kg/60 000 lb payload into low Earth orbit; missions are up to 9 days duration. It comprises a delta-winged lifting body orbiter with main engines, a jettisonable external fuel tank, and two auxiliary solid rocket boosters. The fleet comprises four vehicles: *Columbia*, *Challenger*, *Discovery*, and *Atlantis*. It has been successfully used to launch numerous science and applications satellites and on-board experiments, and was used to carry the Spacelab module. The *Challenger* explosion on the 25th flight (26 Jan 1986) 73 sec after launch caused the loss of the crew. The first reflight took place in September 1988, and a replacement fourth orbiter is planned to be operational in 1992. » launch vehicle [i]; lifting body; spacecraft; Spacelab; RR11.

See list of abbreviations

A cross-reference to an entry which contains an illustration (a line drawing or panel) is followed by the symbol [i]

A cross-reference to the Ready Reference section (on tinted paper at the back of the encyclopedia) is preceded by RR, and appears after the other cross-references. The page number refers to the Ready Reference section and not to the alphabetical part of the book.

spacecraft Vehicles designed to operate in the vacuum–weightlessness–high radiation environment of space; used to convey human crew, to acquire scientific data, to conduct utilitarian operations (eg telecommunications and synoptic weather observations), and to conduct research (eg microgravity experiments). The first spacecraft (Sputnik 1) was launched by the USSR in 1957 (4 Oct). They require highly reliable automated command and control, attitude stabilization, thermal control, radio telemetry, and data processing systems. Specialized spacecraft have been designed to be controllable on re-entry into the Earth's atmosphere (eg the NASA Space Shuttle), and to operate in atmospheres of other planets (eg Soviet Venera and US Pioneer atmospheric entry probes). » Explorer 1; Progress/Soyuz/Vostok spacecraft; space exploration; Space Organizations Worldwide; Sputnik; Plates II, III

All cross-references are preceded by the symbol »

Any cross-reference to the colour section, which is located between the alphabetical pages and the Ready Reference section, is given at the very end of the entry, in the form: Plate I, Plate XII, etc.

See pronunciation guide

Vostok ('East') **spacecraft** [**vos**tok] The first generation of Soviet crewed spacecraft, carrying a single member. Vostok 1 took the first human into space (12 Apr 1961) – Yuri Gagarin, who orbited Earth once on a flight of 118 min. Crew were recovered over land after ejection from the capsule at 7 000 m/23 000 ft altitude after re-entry. The last Vostok flight carried Valentina Tereshkova, the first woman to fly in space (Vostok 6, 16 Jun 1963). **Voskhod** ('Sunrise') was an intermediate-generation Soviet crewed spacecraft following Vostok and preceding Soyuz; it made only two flights, in 1964 and 1965. » Gagarin; Soviet space programme; spacecraft; Tereshkova

A

à Becket, Thomas » **Becket, St Thomas (à)**

A-bomb » **atomic bomb**

à Kempis » **Kempis**

A level An abbreviation for **Advanced level**, the examination taken by British pupils, usually at the age of 18, which qualifies them for entrance to higher education and the professions. It is a single-subject examination at a level representing two further years of study beyond the GCSE. University matriculation requirements normally specify A levels in at least two subjects. One A level is deemed equivalent to two passes in the Advanced Supplementary (*A/S level*) examination.

Aachen [**ah**khuhn] Fr **Aix-la-Chapelle** 50°47N 6°04E, pop (1983) 243 700. Manufacturing city in Cologne district, Germany; 64 km/40 ml WSW of Cologne, near the Dutch and Belgian borders; N capital of Charlemagne's empire; 32 German emperors crowned here; annexed by France, 1801; given to Prussia, 1815; badly bombed in World War 2; railway; technical college; textiles, glass, machinery, chemicals, light engineering, foodstuffs, rubber products; 15th-c cathedral, town hall (1350); Bad Aachen hot springs; international riding, jumping, and driving tournament. » Charlemagne; Germany [i]; Prussia

Aakjaer, Jeppe [**aw**kayr] (1866–1930) Danish novelist and poet, born at Aakjaer. A leader of the 'Jutland movement' in Danish literature, his works include the novel *Vredens Bōn* (1904, Children of Wrath) and the poems *Rugens Sange* (1906, Songs of the Rye). He wrote much in the Jutland dialect, into which he translated some of Burns's poems. He died at Jenle. » Danish literature

Aalto, Alvar [**ahl**toh] (1898–1976) Finnish architect, born at Kuortane, designer of modern public and industrial buildings in Finland, and also of contemporary furniture. In 1940 he went to the USA and taught architecture at Yale University and the Massachusetts Institute of Technology. He died in Helsinki.

Aaltonen, Wäinö (Valdemar) [**ahl**tonen] (1894–1966) Finnish sculptor, born at St Mårtens, a versatile artist who worked in many styles. His best-known works are the bust of Sibelius, and the statue of the Olympic runner, Paavo Nurmi. » sculpture

aardvark [**ahd**vahk] A southern African mammal; length, 1–1.5 m/3¼–5 ft; long ears, pig-like snout, long sticky tongue, strong claws; digs burrows; inhabits grassland and woodland; eats ants and termites; mainly nocturnal; also known as **ant bear** or **earth pig**. It is the only member of the order *Tubulidentata*. (*Orycteropus afer*. Family: *Orycteropodidae*.) » mammal [i]

aardwolf [**ahd**wulf] A rare southern African carnivore of the hyena family; slender, yellow with black stripes; inhabits dry plains; eats mainly termites; lives in a den (often an abandoned aardvark burrow); nocturnal; also known as **maned jackal**. (*Proteles cristatus*.) » carnivore [i]; hyena

Aare, River [**ah**ruh], Fr **Aar** Largest river entirely in Switzerland; emerges from L Grimsel in the Bernese Alps and flows N then W through L Brienz, L Thun, and L Biel to enter the Rhine; length, 295 km/183 ml; navigable from the Rhine to Thun. » Switzerland [i]

Aarhus » **Århus**

Aaron, Hank, properly **Henry (Louis)** (1934–) US baseball player, born in Mobile, Alabama. He started his career with the Milwaukee Braves in 1954, and also played for the Atlanta Braves and Milwaukee Brewers. In 1974 he surpassed Babe Ruth's 39-year-old record of career home runs, and retired in 1976 with a total of 755 home runs. » baseball [i]

Aaron (?c.13th-c BC) Brother of Moses and the first high priest of the Israelites. He was the spokesman for Moses to the Egyptian Pharaoh when attempting to lead their people out of Egypt. He and his sons were ordained as priests after the construction of the Ark of the Covenant and the Tabernacle. » golden calf; Levites; Moses; Zadokites

abaca A fibre obtained from the leaf-stalks of a species of banana, native to the Philippines; the oldest, outermost stalks give the strongest, darkest fibres, 0.9–2.7 m/3–9 ft long; also called **Manila hemp**. Strong and buoyant, it is used for ships' hawsers, cables, and carpets. (*Musa textilis*. Family: *Musaceae*.) » banana; fibre

abacus [**a**bakuhs] A device for performing calculations by sliding bead counters along a set of rods or in grooves. In Japan, the abacus is called *soroban*, and is generally smaller than the Chinese equivalent. It is taught in primary schools as part of arithmetic, and there is a recognized examination and licence system. It is still used by some older people and shopkeepers, but young people prefer calculators.

Abadan [aba**dahn**] 30°20N 48°16E, pop (1985e) 294 068. Oil port in Khuzestan province, WC Iran, close to the Iraq border; on Abadan I, in Shatt al-Arab delta, at head of Arabian Gulf; terminus of Iran's major oil pipelines; airport; severely damaged in the Gulf War. » Arabian Gulf; Gulf War; Iran [i]

Abailard » **Abelard**

abalone [aba**loh**nee] A primitive marine snail which feeds on algae on rocky shores; characterized by a single row of holes extending back from the front margin of its ovoid shell; collected for decoration and for human consumption; also called **ormer**. (Class: *Gastropoda*. Order: *Archaeogastropoda*.) » algae; gastropod; snail

Abarbanel, Isaac Ben Jehudah, also **Abravanel**, **Abrabanel** (1437–1508) Jewish writer, born in Lisbon, whose works comprise commentaries on the Bible and philosophical treatises. He died in Venice. His eldest son, **Juda Leon** (Lat **Leo Hebraeus**) (c.1460–1535), a doctor and philosopher, wrote *Dialoghi di Amore* (1535, Philosophy of Love). » Bible; Judaism

Abbas (566–652) Uncle of Mohammed, at first hostile to him, but ultimately the chief promoter of his religion. He was the founder of the Abbasid dynasty of rulers. » Abbasids; Mohammed

Abbas the Great (1557–1628) Shah of Persia (1585–1628), who won back lost territory from the Uzbeks, Turks, and the Great Mughal. His reign marked a peak of Persian artistic achievement, especially in such fields as painting, weaving, and manuscript illumination.

Abbasids [**a**basidz] A dynasty of caliphs, which replaced that of the Ummayyads in 749, establishing itself in Baghdad until its sack by the Mongols in 1258. Early Abbasid power reached its peak under Harun al-Rashid (786–809). The Abbasids came from the family of the Prophet Mohammed's uncle al-Abbas, and were thus able to claim legitimacy in the eyes of the pious. » Abbas; Mohammed; Mongols

Abbe, Cleveland [**a**buh] (1838–1916) US meteorologist, born in New York City. He wrote on the atmosphere and on climate, inaugurated a national weather service (1870), and introduced the system of Standard Time. He died at Chevy Chase, Maryland. » meteorology; standard time

Abbe, Ernst [**a**buh] (1840–1905) German professor of optics, born at Eisenach, who partnered Carl Zeiss in the famous optical company. He deduced the mathematics of the optics of the microscope, and this enabled him to design microscopic objectives scientifically, working with Otto Schott (1851–1935) to perfect optical glass, and (1886) producing lenses of the highest possible quality for scientific research. He died at Jena. » aberrations [i]; microscope; optics [i]; Zeiss

abbey A building or group of buildings used by a religious order for worship and living. It houses a community under the direction of an abbot or abbess as head, who is elected for a term of years or for life. Abbeys were centres of learning in the Middle Ages. » Belém Monastery; Chartreuse, La Grande; Clairvaux; Escorial, El; Fountains Abbey; monasticism

Abbey Theatre A theatre situated in Dublin's Abbey Street, the centre of the Irish dramatic movement initiated by Lady Gregory and W B Yeats. Best known for its championship of Synge and of the early plays of O'Casey, the Abbey was a major theatrical venue throughout the first 30 years of the 20th-c. The present theatre was opened in 1966, after the earlier building had burnt down in 1951. » O'Casey; Synge

ABC Islands An abbreviated name often applied to the three main islands of Aruba, Bonaire, and Curaçao in the S Netherlands Antilles, off the N coast of S America. » Netherlands Antilles [i]

Abd-El-Kader [abdel**kah**der] (1807–83) Algerian hero, born at Mascara. After the French conquest of Algiers, the Arab tribes of Oran elected him as their emir. He waged a long struggle against the French (1832–47), defeating them at Makta (1835). Eventually crushed by overpowering force, he took refuge in Morocco and began a crusade against the enemies of Islam. He finally surrendered in 1847 and was sent to France. He later lived in Brusa and in Damascus, where he died. » Islam

Abd-El-Krim, Mohammed (1882–1963) Berber chief, born at Ajdir, Morocco, who led revolts in 1921 and 1924 against Spain and France. He surrendered before their combined forces in 1926, was exiled to Réunion, and later amnestied (1947). He then went to Egypt, where he formed the North African Liberation Committee. He died in Cairo.

Abdias, Book of » **Obadiah, Book of**

Abdim's stork A small stork native to Africa and the SW Arabian Peninsula; feeds in drier habitats than other storks; eats insects, especially locusts. (*Ciconia abdimii.*) » stork

abdomen The lower part of the trunk, extending from within the pelvis to under the cover of the chest wall. Except for the vertebral column and ribs, it is bounded entirely by muscles. It contains most of the alimentary canal (from stomach to rectum), the liver, pancreas, spleen, kidneys and bladder, and the uterus in females. The cavity has a lining (the *peritoneum*) which covers or completely surrounds and suspends the majority of the various contents. Major blood vessels and nerves pass into it from the chest and out of it to the legs. » alimentary canal; peritoneum; peritonitis; Plate XII

abdominal thrust » **Heimlich manoeuvre [i]**

Abdul-Jabbar, Kareem, originally **Lewis Ferdinand Alcindor Jr** (1947–) US basketball player, born in New York City; his change of name came with his conversion to Islam in 1969. He turned professional with Milwaukee in 1970, and during his career played more National Basketball League games (1 560) than any other player, and scored more points, 38 387. He retired in 1989. » basketball

Abel Biblical character, the brother of Cain and second son of Adam and Eve. He is described as a shepherd, whose offering God accepts; but he was then murdered by his brother, Cain (*Gen* 4.2–16). » Adam and Eve; Cain; Old Testament

Abelard or **Abailard, Peter** (1079–1142) Boldest theologian of the 12th-c, born near Nantes, France. While a lecturer at Notre-Dame, he fell in love with Héloïse, the 17-year-old niece of the canon Fulbert. The lovers fled together to Brittany, and were privately married. Soon after, Héloïse denied the marriage, lest it should stand in Abelard's way, and left her uncle's house for the convent of Argenteuil. Abelard then entered the abbey of St Denis as a monk. After his teaching on the Trinity was condemned as heretical, he retired to a hermitage, which later became a monastic school known as Paraclete. He then became abbot of St Gildas-de-Rhuys, Paraclete being given to Héloïse and a sisterhood. Later, at Cluny, he lived a model of asceticism and theological labour, and recanted some of the doctrines that had given most offence. Again, however, his adversaries, headed by Bernard of Clairvaux, accused him of heresies, and he was found guilty by a council at Sens. On his way to Rome to defend himself, he died at the priory of St Marcel, near Chalon. His remains were buried by Héloïse at Paraclete, and hers were laid beside them in 1164. » Bernard of Clairvaux, St; monasticism; theology; Trinity

Aberdeen, George Hamilton Gordon, 4th Earl (1784–1860) British statesman and Prime Minister (1852–5), born in Edinburgh, Scotland. Educated at Harrow and Cambridge, he succeeded to his earldom in 1801, and became a Scottish representative peer (1806), Ambassador to Vienna (1813–14), and Foreign Secretary (1828–30, 1841–6). In 1852, he headed a coalition ministry, which for some time was extremely popular. However, vacillating policy and mismanagement during the Crimean War led to his resignation. He died in London. » Crimean War

Aberdeen, ancient **Devana** 57°10N 2°04W, pop (1981) 190 465. Seaport capital of Grampian region, NE Scotland; on the North Sea, between Rivers Dee (S) and Don (N), 92 km/57 ml NE of Dundee; royal burgh since 1179; airport; helicopter port; ferries to Orkney and Shetland; railway; university (1494); port trade and fishing, finance, oil supply service, granite ('Granite City'), tourism; Art Gallery; Gordon Highlanders Regimental Museum; maritime museum; St Machar's Cathedral (1131); Bridge of Dee (1500); Brig o' Balgownie (c.1320); Aberdeen festival (Jul–Aug). » Grampian; Scotland [i]

Aberdeen terrier » **Scottish terrier**

Aberfan [aber**van**] 51°42N 3°21W. Village in coal-mining region, Mid Glamorgan, S Wales, UK; scene of major disaster in 1966, when a landslip of mining waste engulfed several houses and the school, killing 144, including 116 children. » Mid Glamorgan

aberrations **1** In optics, deviations in lenses from perfect images, as predicted by simple lens theory. They are consequences of the laws of refraction. *Chromatic* aberrations result from the dependence of the bending power of a lens on light colour, and may produce images having coloured haloes. Colour independent aberrations (*monochromatic*) include some which deform an image (*distortion, field curvature*) and others which blur it (*spherical aberration, coma, astigmatism*). Aberrations in cameras, binoculars, and other optical instruments can be minimized using lens combinations. Mirrors have similar monochromatic aberrations to lenses, but no chromatic aberrations. » astigmatism; lens; optics [i] **2** In astronomy, apparent changes in the observed position of a star, because of changes in relative velocity as the Earth orbits the Sun. » orbit; star

Aberystwyth [aber**ist**with] 52°25N 4°05W, pop (1981) 11 170.

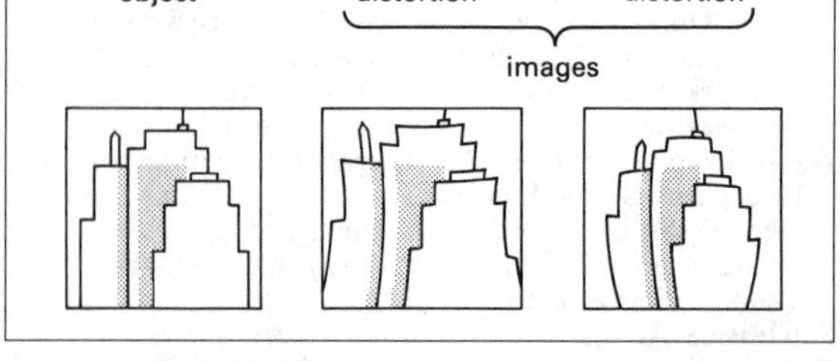

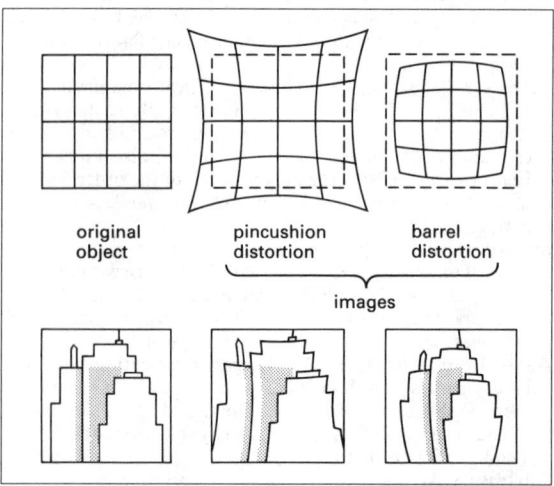

Distortion – An aberration caused by variation in the lens magnifying power with an object's distance from the lens axis.

University and resort town in Ceredigion district, Dyfed, SW Wales, UK; at the mouth of the Ystwyth and Rheidol Rivers, on Cardigan Bay; built around a castle of Edward I, 1227; college of University of Wales (1872); National Library of Wales (1955); railway; boatbuilding, brewing, agricultural trade; university theatre summer season. » Dyfed

Abidjan [abee**jan**] 5°19N 4°01W, pop (1980) 1 690 000. Industrial seaport and former capital (to 1983) of Côte d'Ivoire, W Africa; on N shore of Ebrié lagoon; capital, 1935; port facilities added in early 1950s; airport; railway; university (1958); farm machinery, metallurgy, car assembly, electrical appliances, plastics, soap, coffee and cocoa trade, timber products, tobacco, food processing, beer, chemicals; Ifan museum. » Côte d'Ivoire [i]; Yamoussoukro

abiogenesis [aybeeoh**jen**uhsis] » **spontaneous generation**

ablaut [**ab**lowt] Vowel changes in related forms of a word, found in Indo-European languages. Ablaut can be seen in English in several sets of verb forms, such as *drive/drove/driven.* » Indo-European languages; vowel

ABM » **antiballistic missile**

Abney level » **clinometer**

abnormal psychology The scientific study of the nature and origins of psychologically abnormal states. In contrast to clinical psychology and psychiatry, where the emphasis is on the assessment and treatment of individuals, abnormal psychology seeks more general theories about disorders, in such areas as personality, intelligence, and social behaviour. » behaviour therapy; clinical psychology; neurosis; psychoanalysis; psychosis; psychotherapy

Åbo » **Turku**

abolitionism A 19th-c movement to end slavery in the US South; distinguished from earlier anti-slavery movements by its uncompromising attitude. Blacks as well as Whites, and women as well as men took active parts. Abolitionism crystallized around the American Anti-Slavery Society, founded in 1833. Its great achievement was to make slavery an issue that could not be ignored. » American Colonization Society; civil rights

Abomey [**ab**omay] 7°14N 2°00E, pop (1979) 41 000. Town in Zou province, S Benin, W Africa; 105 km/65 ml NNW of Porto Novo; capital of old Yoruba kingdom of Dahomey; burned by the Portuguese and abandoned to the French, 1892; Royal Palace of Djema, including the tomb of King Gbehanzin (still guarded by women), a world heritage site. » Benin (country) [i]; Dahomey; Yoruba

abominable snowman » **yeti; Bigfoot**

Aboriginal art The art of the Australian Aborigines, which has its roots in prehistory. Wooden sculptures occur, as in Arnhem Land, but most aboriginal art consists of painting with simple earth colours, plus charcoal and kaolin, on rock surfaces, bark, shells, trees, everyday utensils, and the human body. Much of this is purely decorative rather than functional, but some forms are associated with magic rituals. Rock art, both painted and scratched, occurs throughout the continent with local variations of style, sometimes figurative and sometimes geometric. » Aborigines; art; bark painting; Palaeolithic art

Aborigines The native inhabitants of Australia, belonging to the Australoid geographical race, who reached the country between 25 000 and 40 000 years ago. By 1788, when European occupation began, there were c.600 territorially defined groups, subsisting on hunting and gathering, with a population of 300 000–1 million. Numbers then fell dramatically, partly through conflict with the Europeans, but mainly through European diseases, especially the smallpox epidemics of 1789 and 1829. By 1933 the population had fallen to c.66 000; it then steadily increased, and reached 145 000 by 1981.

At first Europeans portrayed Aboriginals as 'noble savages', but this image quickly gave way to contempt, and policies were designed to turn them into Christians with European lifestyles. In the late 19th-c, Social Darwinist ideas were influential, maintaining that Aborigines were an inferior race incapable of self-management and destined to die out. In Van Diemen's Land (Tasmania) the government removed the remaining Aborigines to Flinders I in the late 1820s; the last full-blooded Aborigine, Truganini, died there in 1876. Elsewhere in Australia, they were confined to government reserves or Christian missions.

Aborigines have not accepted their lot passively. In the 1950s they began moving into the cities of SE Australia and formed advancement groups; but it was not until the mid-1960s that activism became prominent. In 1965 Charles Perkins (1936–) became the first Aboriginal university graduate, and helped organize 'freedom rides' in New South Wales to protest against discrimination. In 1967 90.8% of Australian voters approved a referendum which granted the federal government the power to count Aborigines in the census and to make laws on their behalf, thus enabling them to be provided with official assistance. Although their condition has since improved significantly, they remain the most disadvantaged group in Australian society. Their disadvantages were the basis for a campaign, begun in 1972, for 'land rights'. Opposition to their claims has come from mining and pastoral interests, and from conservative governments, particularly in Queensland. Nevertheless by the mid-1980s Aborigines had gained freehold title to about 6% of Australia (mostly in the centre), and were in the process of being granted further areas. » Australia [i]; Australian languages; Myall Creek massacre

abortion The spontaneous or induced termination of pregnancy before the foetus is viable. In the UK and for legal purposes, this is taken to be the 24th week, although some foetuses expelled before then may survive. In the USA and in some European countries, the time limit is set some weeks earlier. Spontaneous abortion (*miscarriage*) occurs in about 20% of apparently normal pregnancies, and may not be recognized. It may arise from defects in the products of conception, in the uterus and placenta, or in the maternal environment, such as maternal illness. Abortion can be induced by the use of drugs and by surgical procedures. Unless permitted by the Abortion Acts, induced abortion is a criminal offence. » pregnancy [i]

Aboukir Bay, Battle of 1 (Aug 1798) A naval battle during the War of the Second Coalition, in which Nelson destroyed the French fleet under Brueys off the coast of Egypt; also known as the **Battle of the Nile**. This victory forced Napoleon to abandon his Egyptian campaign, aimed at threatening British territory in India, and return to France. **2** (Jul 1799) The last French victory of the Egyptian campaign, in which Napoleon's Army of Egypt captured Aboukir citadel, NE of Alexandria, defeating an Ottoman Turkish force over twice the size, led by Mustafa Pasha. » Napoleon I; Nelson, Horatio

Abrabanel » **Abarbanel**

Abraham or **Abram** (after 2000 BC) Biblical character revered as the ancestor of Israel and of several other nations; also an important figure in Islam. He is portrayed as called by God to travel with his wife Sarah and nephew Lot from the Chaldean town of Ur to Haran in NW Mesopotamia and finally to Canaan, having been promised a land and descendants which would become a great nation (*Gen* 12, 15). He had a son Ishmael by his wife's maid Hagar, but finally at 100 years of age is said to have had a son Isaac by his own previously barren wife, Sarah (*Gen* 21). In Judaism, Isaac was seen as the fulfilment of the divine promises, although Abraham was nearly ordered by God to sacrifice his heir at Moriah as a test of faith (*Gen* 22). » Bible; Hagar; Isaac; Ishmael; Islam; Judaism; Sarah

Abraham, Plains/Heights of The site of a battle (1759), Quebec City, Canada, in which British forces under Wolfe defeated a French/Canadian force under Montcalm and Vaudreil, and gained control over Quebec. Wolfe and Montcalm were both killed in the battle. » Montcalm; Wolfe, James

Abram » **Abraham**

abrasives Hard, rough, or sharp textured materials used to wear down, rub, or polish materials which are less hard, as in the traditional grindstone or whetstone. Naturally occurring abrasive substances include various forms of silica (sand, quartz, or flint), pumice, and emery (an aluminium oxide mineral). Artificial abrasives include silicon carbide, synthetic diamond, and boron carbide. They can be used as powders or incorporated in hand or machine tools. » emery; pumice; silica

Abravanel » **Abarbanel**

Abruzzi or **Abruzzo** [ab**root**see] area 400 sq km/154 sq ml.

National park in the S of Abruzzi region, EC Italy, between the Apennines and the Adriatic Sea, in the valley of the upper Sangro; established in 1922; cereals, fishing, tourism; resort village of Pescasseroli. » Italy [i]

abscess A localized collection of pus in an organ or tissue, surrounded by an inflammatory reaction which forms a well-defined wall (an abscess cavity). It is commonly due to infection with pus-forming (*pyogenic*) bacteria, but occasionally a foreign body may be responsible. » boil; carbuncle; pus

absolute zero The temperature of a system for which a reversible isothermal process involves no heat transfer. It represents the state of lowest possible total energy of a system, and is denoted by 0K (−273.15°C). It is unattainable, according to the third law of thermodynamics. » energy; heat; isotherm; kelvin; thermodynamics

absolution A declaration of forgiveness of sins. In Christian worship, it is understood as God's gracious work in Jesus Christ, pronounced by a priest or minister either in private after confession or as part of the liturgy in public worship. » Christianity; confession; liturgy; priest; sin

absolutism A theory of kingship elaborated and practised in early modern Europe, associated notably with Louis XIV of France; sometimes equated loosely with systems of government in which one person exercises unlimited power. Absolute power was justified by the belief that monarchs were God's representatives on Earth. Armed with this notion of Divine Right, kings were owed unquestioning obedience by their subjects; as a corollary, the powers of hereditary monarchs were tempered by concepts of fundamental law and responsibility to their subjects and to God. » Divine Right of Kings; Louis XIV

absorbed dose » **radioactivity units** [i]

abstract art A form of art in which there is no attempt to represent objects or persons, but which relies instead on lines, colours, and shapes alone for its aesthetic appeal. It seems to have emerged c.1910, and was partly a reaction against 19th-c Realism and Impressionism. Early abstract artists include Kandinsky, Mirò, Pevsner, and Brancusi. Stylistically, abstract art ranges from the 'geometrical' (Mondrian, de Stijl, Constructivism) to the 'organic' (Arp, Moore). More recent developments include action painting and Op Art. Historically, abstract tendencies have been present in one form or another in most cultures. Two trends should be distinguished: (a) the simplification, distortion, or reduction of natural appearances, characteristic not only of Cubism, Expressionism, and many other kinds of modern art, but present too in much figurative art in earlier periods (such as Mannerism), which always has its starting-point in objective reality; and (b) the total rejection – in theory, at least – of any dependence on natural appearances. Such works establish their own 'reality' and are intended to appeal in their own right. Only the latter should, strictly speaking, be called 'abstract', but the term is often used imprecisely to cover a wide range of 20th-c art. » action painting; art; biomorphic art; concrete art; Constructivism; Cubism; De Stijl; figurative art; Op Art; Arp; Brancusi; Kandinsky; Miró; Mondrian; Moore, Henry; Pevsner, Antoine; Plate XV

abstract expressionism » **action painting**

absurdism The expression in art of the meaninglessness of human existence. It is explored in Camus' *Le Mythe de Sysiphe* (1942, The Myth of Sisyphus), where human efforts are seen as pointless but compulsory. The potential for comedy and terror has been exploited especially in the theatre (*Theatre of the Absurd*), as in the plays of Ionesco, Beckett, and Pinter. » Beckett; Camus; comedy; drama; Ionesco; Pinter; tragicomedy

Abu-Bekr or **Abu-Bakr** (573–634) Father of Mohammed's wife, Ayesha, born at Mecca. He became the Prophet's most trusted follower, succeeded him as the first caliph (632), and began the compilation of the Koran. He died at Medina and was buried near Mohammed. » Koran; Mohammed

Abu Dhabi or **Abu Zabi** [aboo **da**bee] pop (1980) 449 000; area c.67 600 sq km/26 000 sq ml. Largest of the seven member states of the United Arab Emirates; bounded NW by Qatar, S and W by Saudi Arabia, and N by the Arabian Gulf; vast areas of desert and salt flats; coastline 400 km/250 ml; capital Abu Dhabi, pop (1980) 242 985; main oasis settlement, Al Ayn; a major oil region; petrochemical and gas liquefaction industry at Das I; power and desalination complex at Taweelah. » Ayn, Al; United Arab Emirates [i]

Abu Mena [aboo **me**na] A site in NW Egypt sacred to the 3rd-c AD martyr Abu Mena (St Menas). Many miracles were associated with his burial place, which was a centre of pilgrimage for 400 years. The ruins of the early 5th-c basilica erected here by Emperor Arcadius are a world heritage site. » Egypt [i]

Abu Simbel 22°22N 31°38E. The site of two huge sandstone temples carved by Pharaoh Rameses II (c.1304–1273 BC) out of the Nile bank near Aswan; now a world heritage site. They were dismantled and re-located in the 1960s when the rising waters of the newly-constructed Aswan High Dam threatened their safety. » Rameses II

Abuja [**a**boo**ja**] 9°05N 7°30E. New capital (from 1982) of Nigeria, in Federal Capital Territory, C Nigeria; planned in 1976, to relieve pressure on the infrastructure of Lagos; under construction at the geographical centre of the country; government offices began moving from Lagos in the 1980s. » Nigeria [i]

abulia A lack of drive or inability to make decisions or to translate decisions into action. The term was considered a cardinal feature of schizophrenia by early psychiatrists, and can be paraphrased as 'the spirit is willing but the energy for action is lacking'. » schizophrenia

abyssal hills Low hills which occur on the deep sea floor. Large areas of the Atlantic and Indian Ocean floors and more than three-quarters of the Pacific floor are covered by these hills, no higher than about 1 000 m/3 000 ft. They tend to occur as series of parallel ridges 1–10 km/½–6 ml across, and represent the rugged topography of mid-ocean ridges subdued by burial beneath thick layers of sediments. » abyssal plains; oceanic ridges

abyssal plains Extremely flat areas of the deep ocean floor which may extend for more than 1 000 km/600 ml. They typically have slopes less than 1:1 000, and are found off continental margins where sediments can enter the deep sea unobstructed. They are common in the Atlantic and Indian oceans, but rare in the Pacific, where deep trenches and island arcs serve as barriers to the transport of sediment from the continents. Abyssal plains represent thick deposits of primarily land-derived sediments smoothing over more rugged topographic features of the sea floor. » continental margin; island arc

Abyssinia » **Ethiopia** [i]

Abyssinian cat A breed of domestic cat, popular in the USA (known as the 'foreign short-haired'); reddish-brown, each hair with several dark bands; orange-red nose; two types: **Abyssinian (standard Abyssinian** or **ruddy Abyssinian**) and the redder **red Abyssinian.** » cat

acacia » **wattle** [i]

Academy 1 A place of learning or association formed for scientific, literary, artistic, or musical purposes, the word deriving from the Greek hero *Academus*, who gave his name to the olive grove where Plato taught (387 BC). From the Renaissance the term was applied in Europe to institutions of higher learning (eg the *Accademia della Crusca*, 1587) and advanced teaching (until the term 'university' became widespread in the 18th-c). It was also used to describe societies of distinguished figures and experts in the arts and sciences (eg the *Académie Française*, 1634). Since the 19th-c, the term has been used in many countries for national centres to promote science, literature, and the arts. **2** The American Academy of Motion Picture Arts and Sciences, widely known since 1927 for its annual awards for creative merit and craftsmanship in film production. It has been influential in establishing technical standards. » Oscar; RR101

Acadia Part of France's American empire; what is today Prince Edward Island, Nova Scotia, and New Brunswick. The first settlement was established at Port Royal in 1605 by Champlain, and the area was exchanged between France and England until the Treaty of Utrecht (1713) handed most of Acadia to Britain. In 1755 10 000 Acadians were evicted from the territory for resolving to pursue a policy of neutrality in the conflicts between France and Britain. The last French stronghold, Louisbourg, fell in 1758. » Champlain

acanthus [a**kan**thuhs] A plant with thick, prickly leaves, representations of which are often used to decorate mouldings or carved parts of a building; in particular, the capitals of Corinthian columns. » capital (architecture); Corinthian order

Acapulco [aka**pul**koh] or **Acapulco de Juarez** 6°51N 99°56W, pop (1980) 409 335. Port and resort town in Guerrero state, S Mexico; on the Pacific Ocean, 310 km/193 ml SSW of Mexico City; airfield; leading Mexican tourist resort ('the Mexican Riviera'); Fort San Diego. » Mexico [i]

Acari [**ak**ariy] » **mite**

ACAS [**ay**kas] An acronym for **Advisory, Conciliation and Arbitration Service**, a UK body set up under the Employment Protection Act (1975) under the management of a Council appointed by the Secretary of State for Employment. Its function is to provide facilities for conciliation, arbitration, and mediation in industrial disputes.

acceleration For linear motion, the rate of change of velocity with time; equals force divided by mass; symbol a, units m/s^2; a vector quantity. For rotational motion, the rate of change of angular velocity with time; equals torque divided by moment of inertia; angular acceleration symbol α, units $radians/s^2$; a vector quantity. » acceleration due to gravity; force; torque [i]; vector (mathematics); velocity

acceleration due to gravity The acceleration on an object close to the Earth, due to the Earth's gravitational field; symbol g. Its value is usually taken as 9.81 m/s^2, but it varies between 9.76 and 9.83 over the Earth's surface because of geological variations, and decreases with height above sea level. » acceleration; free fall; gravitation

accent 1 The features of pronunciation which mark a speaker's regional background or social class. Accent is to be distinguished from dialect, which involves the study of other linguistic features, such as grammar and vocabulary. » dialectology **2** The emphasis on a syllable in speech, resulting from a combination of loudness, pitch, and duration. It can be clearly heard in the contrast between the two forms of ***present*** (noun), *present* (verb). » phonetics

accentor A sparrow-like bird native to N Africa, Europe, and Asia; brownish-grey to chestnut above, often streaked; grey beneath; feeds on ground; eats insects in summer, seeds in winter. (Genus: *Prunella*, 12 species. Family: *Prunellidae*.) » dunnock

accepting house A merchant bank which buys ('accepts') three-month bills of exchange issued by companies. In the UK, the top accepting houses in London form the Accepting Houses Committee. » bill of exchange

access course A bridging course offered to would-be students not in possession of normal entry requirements which, on successful completion, will permit them to start the course of their choice. It is often provided specifically for students who have been prevented from obtaining formal qualifications, or who have been otherwise disadvantaged. » vocational education

access time The length of time required to retrieve information from computer memory or other computer storage media, such as magnetic disks or tapes. Access times from integrated circuit memory are much shorter than those from magnetic disks. » magnetic disk; magnetic tape **2**; memory, computer

accessory » **accomplice**

accomplice A person who participates with at least one other in committing a crime. The accomplice may be a *perpetrator* or an *accessory*, ie someone who either incites the crime or assists the perpetrator after it has been committed.

accordion A portable musical instrument of the reed organ type, fed with air from bellows activated by the player. In the most advanced models a treble keyboard is played with the right hand, while the left operates (usually) six rows of buttons, producing bass notes and chords. The earliest type was patented in Vienna in 1829, since when, despite continuous improvements to its tone and mechanism, it has remained primarily an instrument for popular music, though several major 20th-c composers, including Berg and Prokofiev, have written for it. » aerophone; Berg; keyboard instrument; Prokofiev; reed organ

accountancy The profession which deals with matters relating to money within an organization. Traditionally its role was that of recording the organization's economic transactions; but it now handles a wide range of activities, including financial planning, management accounting, taxation, and treasury management (managing money), as well as recording and presenting accounts for management and owners. The content and form of published information is set by company law and the Stock Exchange (for a public company). » amortization; audit; cost-accounting; depreciation

Accra 5°33N 0°15W, pop (1970) 636 067. Seaport capital of Ghana, on the Gulf of Guinea coast, 415 km/258 ml WSW of Lagos; founded as three forts and trading posts, 17th-c; capital of Gold Coast, 1877; capital of Ghana, 1957; airport; railway; university (1948) at Legon 13 km/8 ml W; food processing, fishing, brewing, engineering, scrap metal trade, cacao, gold, timber, fruit, export of zoo animals. » Ghana [i]

accretion In astronomy, a process in which a celestial body, particularly an evolved dwarf star in a binary star system, or a planet, is enlarged by the accumulation of extraneous matter falling in under gravity. In binary stars this can cause intense X-ray emission. » binary star; dwarf star; X-rays

acculturation A process involving the adoption and acceptance of the ideas, beliefs, and symbols of another society. This may occur by *immigration*, when incoming members of a society adopt its culture, or by *emulation*, when one society takes on cultural features from another, such as happened in colonial contexts. » migration **1**

acetaldehyde [asi**tal**dihiyd] CH_3CHO, IUPAC **ethanal**, boiling point 21°C. The product of gentle oxidation of ethanol, intermediate in the formation of acetic acid; a colourless liquid with a sharp odour. A reducing agent, the compound is actually the one detected in the 'breathalyzer' test. » acetic acid; aldehyde; IUPAC; paraldehyde [i]

acetals [**as**itlz] Substances of the general structure $R_2C(OR)_2$, formed by the reaction of an alcohol with an aldehyde, water also being formed. Internal acetal formation gives most sugars ring structures. » alcohols; aldehyde; glucose [i]; ring

acetate film » **safety film**

acetic acid [a**see**tik] CH_3COOH, IUPAC **ethanoic acid**, boiling point 118°C. The product of oxidation of ethanol. The pure substance is a viscous liquid with a strong odour. Its aqueous solutions are weakly acidic; partially neutralized solutions have a pH of about 5. Vinegar is essentially a 5% solution of acetic acid. » acid; buffer (chemistry); ethanol; IUPAC; pH

acetone [**as**itohn] CH_3COCH_3, IUPAC **propanone**, boiling point 56°C. A volatile liquid with an odour resembling ethers. It is a very widely used solvent, especially for plastics and lacquers. » ether; IUPAC; ketone

acetyl [**as**itiyl] CH_3CO–, IUPAC **ethanoyl**. A functional group in chemistry, whose addition to a name usually indicates its substitution for hydrogen in a compound. » functional group; hydrogen; IUPAC

acetylcholine [asitiyl**koh**leen] An acetyl ester of choline ($C_7H_{16}NO_2^+$) which functions as a neurotransmitter in most animals with nervous systems. In mammals it is present in the brain, spinal cord, and ganglia of the autonomic nervous system, as well as the terminals of motor neurones (which control skeletal muscle fibres) and the post-ganglionic fibres of the parasympathetic nervous system. » acetyl; choline; ester [i]; ganglion **1**; nervous system; neurotransmitter

acetylene [a**set**ileen] $HC \equiv CH$, IUPAC **ethyne**, boiling point −84°C. The simplest alkyne, a colourless gas formed by the action of water on calcium carbide. It is an important starting material in organic synthesis, and is used as a fuel, especially (mixed with oxygen) in the oxyacetylene torch. » alkynes; IUPAC; oxyacetylene welding

Achaeans [a**kee**anz] **1** The archaic name for the Greeks, found frequently in Homer. **2** In classical Greece, the inhabitants of Achaea, the territory to the south of the Corinthian Gulf. » Greek history

Achaemenids [a**kiy**menidz] The first royal house of Persia, founded by the early 7th-c ruler, Achaemenes. Its capitals included Parsagadae and Persepolis. » Cyrus II; Darius I; Persian Empire; Xerxes I

Achebe, Chinua [achaybay] (1930–) Nigerian novelist, born at Ogidi, and educated at Umuchia and Ibadan. Four novels written between 1958 (*Things Fall Apart*) and 1966 (*A Man of the People*) describe inter-tribal and inter-racial tensions in pre-and post-colonial Nigerian society. In 1966 he became involved in the war between Biafra and the rest of Nigeria, and devoted most of his time thereafter to politics and education, producing no more fiction until *Anthills of the Savannah* (1987). » African literature; novel

Achelous, River, Gr **Akhelóös** [akilohuhs] Second longest river of Greece; rises in the Pindhos Mts, flows S through mountain gorges to the fertile Agrinion plain and enters the Ionian Sea opposite Cephalonia I; length 220 km/137 ml. » Greece [i]

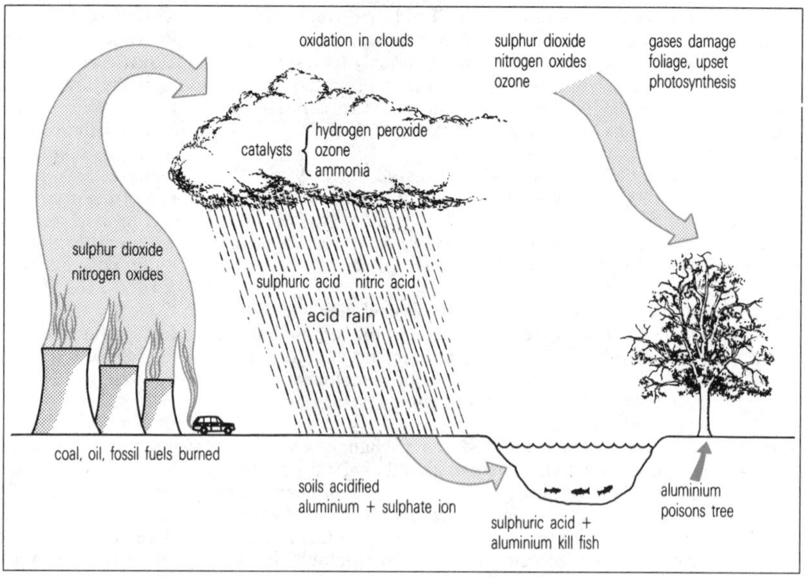

Acid rain – The chain from pollutants to acidified lakes and dying trees

Achenbach, Andreas [akhenbakh] (1815–1910) German landscape and marine painter, born at Kassel. His paintings of the North Sea coasts of Europe had considerable influence in Germany, and he was regarded as the father of 19th-c German landscape painting. He died at Düsseldorf. » German art; landscape painting

achene [uhkeen] A dry fruit, not splitting to release the single seed. It is usually small, often bearing hooks, spines, or other structures which aid in dispersal. » fruit

Achernar [akernuh] » **Eridanus**

Acheron [akeron] In Greek mythology, the chasm or abyss of the Underworld, and the name of one of the rivers there. It is also the name of a river in Epirus, which disappeared underground, and was thought to be an entrance to Hades. » Charon (mythology); Hades

Acheson, Dean (Gooderham) [aychesuhn] (1893–1971) US lawyer and politician, born at Middletown, Connecticut. Educated at Yale and Harvard, he was under-secretary (1945–7) and then Secretary of State (1949–53) in the Truman administration. He helped to establish the Marshall Plan (1947) and also the North Atlantic Treaty Organization (1949). He died at Sandy Spring, Maryland. » Marshall Plan; NATO; Truman

Acheulian [ashooleeuhn] In Europe, Africa, and Asia, a broad term for early prehistoric cultures using symmetrically-flaked stone handaxes. These first appear in E Africa (eg at Koobi Fora, Kenya) c.1.5 million years ago, but were still being made c.100 000 BC. In Europe they are characteristic of N France/England during the Lower Palaeolithic Age, c.300 000–200 000 BC. The name derives from finds made c.1850 at Saint-Acheul, a suburb of Amiens in the Somme Valley, N France. » Three Age System

achievement test A test used to measure educational attainment in different fields. It may involve assessment of knowledge, skills, and understanding through written papers, oral, or practical examinations. » continuous assessment

Achilles [akileez] A legendary Greek hero, son of Peleus and Thetis, who dipped him in the R Styx so that he was invulnerable, except for the heel where she had held him. When the Trojan War began, his mother hid him among girls on Scyros, but he was detected by Odysseus and so went to Troy. The whole story of the *Iliad* turns on his excessive pride; in his anger he sulks in his tent. When his friend Patroclus is killed, he rejoins the battle, kills Hector, brutally mistreats his body, but finally allows Priam to recover it. He was killed by Paris, who shot him in the heel with a poisoned arrow.

achondroplasia [aykondruhplayzhuh] An inherited form of dwarfism, in which growth of the limb bones is disproportionately shortened. There is a characteristic bulging of the forehead, and saddle nose. Circus dwarfs are commonly achondroplastic. » congenital abnormality; dwarfism

acid Usually, a substance reacting with metals to liberate hydrogen gas, or dissolving in water with dissociation and the formation of hydrogen ions. Acids are classed as strong or weak depending on the extent to which this dissociation occurs. More general concepts of acidity are that an acid is a proton donor or an electron acceptor. Strong acids are corrosive. » base (chemistry); corrosion; dissociation; pH

acid rain A term first used in the 19th-c to describe polluted rain in Manchester, UK. Colloquially it is used for polluted rainfall associated with the burning of fossil fuels. Acid pollution can be wet (rain, snow, mist) or dry (gases, particles). A number of gases are involved, particularly sulphur dioxide (SO_2) and oxides of nitrogen (NO). Reactions in the atmosphere lead to the production of sulphuric acid (H_2SO_4) and nitric acid (HNO_3). In Europe c.85% of SO_2 in the air comes from the burning of fossil fuels; chemical plants which remove the sulphurous emissions are being fitted to some power stations. The main emissions of oxides of nitrogen, including (NO) and (NO_2), are from fossil-fuel power generation and the internal combustion engine. Acid rain is implicated in damage to forests and the acidification of soils and lakes. In 1985, 19 countries formed the 'Thirty Percent Club', agreeing to lower their emissions of SO_2 by 30% by 1993, using 1980 emissions as the baseline. » fossil fuel; greenhouse effect; nitric acid; sulphuric acid

acidic oxide » **oxide**

acne A chronic inflammation of the sweat glands in the skin, notably affecting the face, upper chest, and back. It is particularly found in adolescents. » chloracne; gland

Aconcagua, Cerro [akonkagwa] 32°39S 70°01W. Mountain rising to 6 960 m/22 834 ft in Mendoza province, W Argentina; in the Andes, E of the Chilean border; 112 km/70 ml WNW of Mendoza; the highest peak in the W hemisphere; Uspallata Pass at its S foot; first climbed in 1897 by the Fitzgerald expedition. » Andes

aconite » **monkshood; winter aconite**

acorn The fruit of the oak tree, actually a specialized nut borne in a cup-shaped structure, the cupule. » fruit; nut; oak

acornworm A worm-like, marine invertebrate, length up to 2.5 m/8¼ ft; body soft, divided into a proboscis, collar, and trunk; gill slits supported by skeletal rods; c.70 species, found in soft inter-tidal and sub-tidal sediments. (Phylum: *Hemichordata*. Class: *Enteropneusta*.) » worm

acouchi [akooshee] A cavy-like rodent; inhabits Amazonian forests; eats plants; resembles a small agouti, but with a longer tail (white, used for signalling). (Genus: *Myoprocta*, 2 species. Family: *Dasyproctidae*.) » agouti; cavy; rodent

acoustic coupler A device which allows a computer to communicate with other computers over the telephone network by using a standard telephone handset. Digital data is transmitted as coded audio signals. » local area network; modem; viewdata

acoustics The study of sound: the production, detection, and propagation of sound waves, and the absorption and reflection of sound. It includes the study of how electrical signals are converted into mechanical signals, as in loudspeakers, and the converse, as in microphones; also, how sound is produced in musical instruments, and perceived by audiences in concert halls; the protection of workers from damaging levels of sound; and the use of detection techniques, such as sonar and ultrasonic scanning. » anechoic chamber; loudspeaker [i]; microphone [i]; sonar; sound; sound intensity level [i]

Acre, Hebrew **Akko**, ancient **Ptolemais** 32°55N 35°04E, pop (1982e) 39 100. Ancient town in Northern district, NW Israel; resort centre on the Mediterranean Sea; capital of the Crusader kingdom after capture of Jerusalem in 1187; railway; ancient and modern harbour; fishing, light industry; crypt of the Knights Hospitaller of St John, 18th-c city walls, 18th-c mosque. » Crusades [i]; Israel [i]

acridine [**ak**rideen] $C_{13}H_9N$, melting point 111°C. A coal-tar base structurally related to anthracene. An important class of dyestuffs is derived from it. » anthracene [i]; base (chemistry); coal tar; dyestuff

acromegaly [akroh**meg**alee] An adult disorder which arises from the over-secretion of growth hormone by specific cells of the front pituitary gland. There is enlargement of many tissues, with coarsening and thickening of the subcutaneous tissues and the skin. The skull, jaw, hands, and feet enlarge. » growth hormone; pituitary gland

acronym A word formed from the initial letters of the words it represents, as in *NATO* (=*North Atlantic Treaty Organization*). It should be distinguished from an **acrostic**, a composition, usually a poem, in which typically the initial letters of the lines make up words. The pattern may also make use of letters from other parts of the lines or combinations of letters (such as the first and last), to produce a wide variety of puzzles and riddles.

Acropolis The citadel of ancient Athens. Rising high above the city, the fortified outcrop contained the national treasury and many sacred sites and shrines, most of them (such as the Parthenon and the Erechtheum) associated with the worship of Athene, the patron goddess of Athens. The present ruins date mainly from the second half of the 5th-c BC. » Areopagus; Athens; Erectheum; Panathenaea; Parthenon

acrostic » **acronym**

acrylic [**akril**ik] $CH_2{=}CH.COOH$, IUPAC **prop-2-enoic acid**. The simplest unsaturated carboxylic acid. Its nitrile, $CH_2{=}CH.C{\equiv}N$, is the monomer of a range of polymers used as fibres and paints. Its methyl ester and the related $CH_2{=}C(CH_3){-}COOCH_3$, *methylmethacrylate*, form other polymers used in paints, adhesives, and safety glass. » carboxylic acids; ester [i]; IUPAC; monomer

acrylic painting An art form using plastic paints, ie colours mixed with a vehicle made from a polymethyl methacrylate solution in mineral spirits. Quick-drying and – so far – permanent, it is therefore useful in picture-conservation. » polymethyl methacrylate

Act of Congress A bill sanctioned by the US legislature, consisting of the two houses of Congress: the House of Representatives and the Senate. The bill must then be signed by the president to become law. » Congress

act of God In law, any natural phenomenon such as an earthquake or a hurricane, which, without human intervention, directly causes an accident. A gust of wind which directly causes a car to veer off the road constitutes an act of God. Heavy rain or fog to which drivers do not respond appropriately, with the result that their negligence leads to an accident, is not an act of God. The climatic conditions would have to be sufficiently exceptional for the defendant to overcome the test of foreseeability in a negligence action. » negligence

Act of Parliament A bill which has passed five stages (first reading, second reading, committee stage, report stage, third reading) in both houses of the UK parliament, and received the royal assent. The same kind of procedure applies in other parliamentary systems, although the specific stages through which a bill passes may vary. » bill, parliamentary

Actaeon [ak**tee**on] A hunter in Greek mythology, whose story epitomizes the fate of a mortal who encounters a god. He came upon Artemis, the goddess of chastity, while she was bathing and therefore naked: she threw water at him, changing him into a stag, so that he was pursued and then killed by his own hounds. » Artemis

actinides [**ak**tiniydz] Elements with an atomic number between 89 and 104 in which an inner electron shell is filling, the best-known being uranium (92) and plutonium (94). Those heavier than uranium are known as the **transuranic elements**. All of their isotopes are radioactive, and most are artificially made. They are chemically similar to lanthanides. » chemical elements; lanthanides; radioisotope; RR90

actinomorphic flower A flower which is radially symmetrical or of regular shape so that, if cut through the middle in any plane, each half is identical. » flower [i]

actinomycete [aktinoh**miy**seet] A typically filamentous bacterium. Most have branching filaments, forming a fungal-like network, and require the presence of oxygen for growth. They are usually found in soil and decaying vegetation, feeding as saprophytes. Some species are disease-causing in plants and animals, including the causative agents of tuberculosis and potato scab. (Kingdom: *Monera*. Order: *Actinomycetales*.) » bacteria [i]; fungus; saprophyte

actinomycosis [aktinohmiy**koh**sis] An infection with *Actinomyces israeli*, in which chronic abscesses are formed in many tissues, notably in and around the face and neck, where they discharge onto the skin. The filaments of the organism form yellow granular masses in the abscesses (*sulphur granules*), and can be seen with the aid of a microscope. » abscess; mycetoma

action In mechanics, the difference between kinetic energy K and potential energy V (K − V), summed over time; symbol I or S, units J.s (joule.second). Formally, action is the sum over time of the Lagrangian. It is crucial to the least-action formulation of mechanics, and to the path-integral formulation of quantum theory. » Lagrangian; least-action principle; mechanics; quantum mechanics

action painting A form of abstract art which flourished in the USA from the late 1940s, its leading exponent Jackson Pollock. The snappy term was introduced by the critic Harold Rosenberg in 1952 in preference to the clumsy and inexact 'abstract expressionism'. The physical act of applying paint to canvas is emphasized, rather than the picture as a finished artefact; so the paint is thrown or dribbled onto the canvas which may be tacked to the floor. Persons may roll naked or ride bicycles across the wet surface. In France, a similar movement was called *Tachisme* (*tache*, 'blot, mark'). » abstract art; Pollock

action potential A brief electrical signal transmitted along a nerve or muscle fibre following stimulation. At the site of the action potential, the inside of the fibre temporarily becomes positively charged with respect to the outside, because of a transient change in the permeability of the fibre's plasma membrane to sodium and potassium ions (ie sodium flows in and later potassium flows out of the fibre). It provides the basis for the transmission of information. » ion; membrane potential; muscle [i]; neurone [i]

actions, limitation of » **limitation of actions**

Actium, Battle of [**ak**teeum] (31 BC) The decisive victory of Octavian (later the Emperor Augustus) over the forces of Antony and Cleopatra off the coast of NW Greece. It traditionally marks the end of the Roman Republic and the beginning of the Roman Empire. » Augustus; Roman history [i]

activated charcoal Wood, carbonized by heating in limited air and treated with acid to make it adsorb large quantities of gases and polymeric materials from solution. It is used in gas masks, unducted cooker hoods, and vacuum technology, and for decolourizing solutions. » adsorption; polymerization

activated complex The arrangement of atoms during a chemical reaction involving two or more reacting molecules which is unstable, and which decomposes either to regenerate starting material or to form products. » chemical reaction; transition state

active galaxy » **galaxy**

activity (physics) » **radioactivity units** [i]

Actors' Studio A workshop for professional actors founded in New York City by Elia Kazan, Cheryl Crawford, and Robert Lewis in 1947. Under Lee Strasberg, it was the major centre for US acting – not a school, but a laboratory where trained actors could work on inner resources free from the pressures of a production. After Strasberg's death, Ellen Burstyn and Al Pacino became artistic co-directors, with Paul Newman as president of the Board of Directors. » Method, the; Strasberg; theatre

Acts of the Apostles A New Testament book, the second part of a narrative begun in Luke's Gospel, which traces the early progress of Jesus' followers in spreading the Christian faith. It begins with the resurrection and ascension of Jesus, but concentrates largely upon the growth of the Jerusalem Church, its spread to Samaria and Antioch, and the missionary journeys of Paul to Asia Minor, the Aegean lands, and Rome. » apostle; Jesus Christ; Luke, Gospel according to; New Testament

actual bodily harm » **bodily harm**

actuary A statistician specializing in life expectancy, sickness, retirement, and accident matters. Actuaries are employed by insurance companies and pension funds to calculate probability and risk. » insurance

actuator A mechanical or electrical device used to bring other equipment into operation; sometimes called a **servomotor**. It commonly refers to the equipment used for the automatic operation of brake valves in car or train brake systems. » brake [i]; servo system

acuity [a**kyoo**itee] Acuteness of perception, especially of vision or hearing; the smallest visual features (usually measured in terms of angular size in the retinal image) that can be seen, or auditory difference that can be heard. The bars of a fine grating can just be resolved when the spacing of the bars in the image is approximately equal to the diameter of a single retinal receptor (about a 500th of a millimetre). » threshold; vision

acupuncture A medical practice known in China for over 4 000 years, which has recently attracted attention in the West. It consists of the insertion into the skin and underlying tissues of a hot or cold needle, usually made of steel, several cm long, and sometimes driven in with considerable force. The site of insertion of the needle is chosen in relation to the site of the tissue or organ believed to be disordered, and several hundred specific points are identified on body maps or models. Areas of skin which are painful on pressure may also be selected.

It is difficult to obtain a clear idea of which disorders, if any, benefit from acupuncture, but neuralgia, migraine, sprains, and asthma are claimed to respond, while infectious disease and tumours are unlikely to do so. It is also employed as an analgesic during surgery in the Far East, where skills in local or general anaesthesia are often not easily available. Today, acupuncture is used widely among the general population in China; equipment can be purchased in shops, and used in the way simple pain killers are employed in the West. The efficacy of the method has not been subjected to statistically-controlled trials, and successes remain anecdotal. Its mechanism of action is also unknown. In Chinese philosophy it was believed to alter the balance of the contrasting principles of 'Yin' and 'Yang', which flowed in hypothetical channels of the body. Recent research in the UK has shown that brain tissue contains morphine-like substances called *endorphins*, and these may be released in increased amounts when deep sensory nerves are stimulated by injury near the body surfaces. A possible mode of action therefore is that these substances are released by acupuncture, and some degree of tranquillity and analgesia is induced. » alternative medicine; yin and yang

acyl [**a**siyl] In chemistry, the general name for an organic functional group R.CO–, where R represents H or an alkyl group. » alkyl; functional group; organic chemistry

ADA A computer programming language developed for the US Department of Defense which permits the development of very large computer systems, and can cope with complex real-time applications. It was named after Augusta Ada Lovelace, daughter of Lord Byron, who worked with Charles Babbage. » Babbage; programming language; real-time computing

Adad [**ay**dad] The Mesopotamian god of storms, known throughout the area of Babylonian influence; the Syrians called him Hadad, and in the Bible he is Rimmon, the god of thunder. He helped to cause the Great Flood in *Gilgamesh*. His symbol was the lightning held in his hand; his animal was the bull. » Baal; Gilgamesh

Adalbert, St (939–97), feast day 23 April. Apostle of the Prussians, born in Prague, and chosen Bishop of Prague in 982. The hostility of the corrupt clergy whom he tried to reform obliged him to withdraw to Rome. He carried the Gospel to the Hungarians, the Poles, and then the Prussians, by whom he was murdered, near Gdansk. He was canonized in 999. » apostle; missions, Christian; Prussia

Adam, Adolphe (Charles) [a**dã**] (1803–56) French composer, born in Paris. He wrote several successful operas, such as *Le Postillon de Lonjumeau* (1836), but is chiefly remembered for the ballet *Giselle* (1841). He died in Paris. » ballet; opera

Adam, Robert (1728–92) British architect, born at Kirkcaldy, Scotland. He studied at Edinburgh and in Italy, and became architect of the king's works (1761–9). He established a London practice in 1758, and during the next 40 years he and his brother **James** (1730–94) succeeded in transforming the prevailing Palladian fashion in architecture by a series of romantically elegant variations on diverse classical originals, as in Home House, Portland Square, London. They also designed furniture and fittings to suit the houses they planned and decorated. He died in London. » Palladianism

Adam and Eve Biblical characters described in the Book of Genesis as the first man and woman created by God. Adam was formed from the dust of the ground and God's breath or spirit (*Gen* 2.7); Eve was made from Adam's rib. Traditions describe their life in the garden of Eden, their disobedience and banishment, and the birth of their sons Cain, Abel, and Seth. Their fall into sin is portrayed as a temptation by the serpent (the devil) to disobey God's command not to eat the fruit of the tree of the knowledge of good and evil (*Gen* 3). » Abel; Bible; Cain; Genesis, Book of

Adam's needle A species of yucca native to SE USA with short, woody trunk, stiff erect leaves, and numerous white bell-shaped flowers; commonly grown in gardens. (*Yucca gloriosa*. Family: *Agavaceae*). » yucca

Adam's Peak, Sinhala **Sri Pada** 6°49N 80°30E. Sacred mountain in Sri Lanka, rising to 2 243 m/7 359 ft NE of Ratnapura; pilgrimages are made (Dec–Apr) to the foot-shaped hollow found on the mountain's summit, believed to be the footprint of Buddha by Buddhists, of Adam by Muslims, of God Siva by Hindus, and of St Thomas the Apostle by some Christians. » Sri Lanka [i]

Adam Stokes attacks Brief sudden periods of unconsciousness (*syncope*) resulting from a transient cessation of the action of the heart (*asystole*) or of a disorder of rhythm, such as ventricular fibrillation. The patient is pulseless, and may develop convulsions. Recovery is attended by flushing of the face, but sudden death may occur. » heart [i]; pulse (physiology)

Adamnan, St (c.625–704), feast day 23 September. Irish monk, born and educated in Donegal. At 28 he joined the Columban brotherhood of Iona, and was chosen abbot in 679. He came to support the Roman views on the dating of Easter and the shape of the tonsure. His works include the *Vita Sancti Columbae* (Life of St Columba), which reveals much about the Iona community. » Columba, St; Easter; tonsure

Adamov, Arthur [a**dah**mof] (1908–70) French dramatist, born at Kislovodsk, Russia. His family lost their fortune in 1917, and moved to France, where he was educated and met Surrealist artists. His early absurdist plays *L'Invasion* (1950, The Invasion) and *Le Professeur Taranne* (1953) present the dislocations and cruelties of a meaningless world; *Ping-Pong* (1955) sees humanity reduced to mechanism. Later plays such as *Paolo Paoli* (1957) and *La Politique des restes* (1967, The

Politics of Waste) show a transition to commitment. He committed suicide in Paris. >> French literature

Adams, Ansel (1902–84) US photographer, born and died in San Francisco, famous for his landscapes of the Western States, and an influential writer and lecturer on photographic image quality. He was co-founder of the photography departments at the Museum of Modern Art in New York and the California School of Fine Art.

Adams, John (1735–1826) US statesman and second President (1796–1800), born in Braintree (now Quincy), Massachusetts. Educated at Harvard, he was admitted to the Bar in 1758, emerged as a leader of American resistance to Britain, and was the 'colossus of the debate' on the Declaration of Independence. He retired from Congress in 1777, only to be sent to France and Holland as commissioner. After a period as Minister to England (1785–8), he became the first US Vice-President under Washington (1789). They were re-elected in 1792; and in 1796 Adams was chosen President by the Federalists. Defeated on seeking re-election in 1800, he retired to his home at Quincy, where he died. >> Declaration of Independence; Federalist Party

Adams, John Couch (1819–92) British astronomer, born at Laneast, Cornwall. He was educated at Cambridge, where he progressed to professor of astronomy (1858). In 1845 he and Leverrier independently predicted the existence of Neptune by analysing irregularities in the motion of Uranus. He died at Cambridge. >> astronomy; Leverrier; Neptune (astronomy)

Adams, John Quincy (1767–1848) US statesman and sixth President (1825–9), son of John Adams, born at Quincy, Massachusetts. He studied at Harvard, and was admitted to the Bar in 1790. Successively Minister to the Hague, London, Lisbon, and Berlin, he was elected to the US Senate in 1803. In 1809 he became Minister to St Petersburg, and in 1815–17 Minister at the Court of St James's. As Secretary of State under Monroe, he negotiated with Spain the treaty for the acquisition of Florida, and was alleged to be the real author of the 'Monroe Doctrine'. In 1830 he was elected to the lower house of Congress, where he became a strong promoter of anti-slavery views. He died in Washington, DC. >> Monroe Doctrine; slavery

Adams, Richard (1920–) British novelist, born in Berkshire, and educated at Oxford. He worked in the Civil Service from 1948, and came to prominence with his first novel, *Watership Down* (1972), a fable about a warren of rabbits fleeing from land threatened by builders on the downs near Newbury. Later novels include *Shardik* (1974) and *The Plague Dogs* (1977). >> English literature

Adams, Samuel (1722–1803) US statesman, born in Boston. Educated at Harvard, he became Lieutenant-Governor (1789–94) and Governor (1794–7) of Massachusetts. A strong supporter of revolution against Britain, he helped to plan the Boston Tea Party, and was one of the signatories of the Declaration of Independence. He died in Boston. >> Boston Tea Party; Declaration of Independence

Adams, Will(iam) (1564–1620) English sailor, born at Gillingham, Kent. He was pilot of a Dutch ship stranded off Japan in 1600, and was kept by Ieyasu Tokugawa, first Shogun, as an advisor on such areas as shipbuilding, navigation, gunnery, foreign relations, and trade. He built the first European type of ocean-going vessel in Japan. The first Englishman to enter the service of a Japanese ruler, he lived at Edo (now Tokyo), where he was given an estate by Ieyasu. He is buried at Pilot Hill, Yokosuka, and is commemorated by monuments at Ito and Tokyo. >> Shogun; Tokugawa

Adan >> **Aden**

Adana [adana] 37°00N 35°19E, pop (1980) 574 515. Commercial capital of Adana province, S Turkey, on R Seyhan; fourth largest city in Turkey; railway; airfield; university (1973); centre of a fertile agricultural region. >> Turkey [i]

adaptation The process of adjustment of an individual organism to environmental conditions. It may occur by natural selection, resulting in improved survival and reproductive success, or may involve physiological or behavioural changes that are not genetic. As well as being a process, an adaptation can also be the end product of such a process, ie any structural, behavioural, or physiological character that enhances survival or reproductive success. >> natural selection

adaptive radiation A burst of evolution in which a single ancestral type diverges to fill a number of different ecological roles or modes of life, usually over a relatively short period of time, resulting in the appearance of a variety of new forms. This phenomenon may occur after the colonization of a new habitat, such as the radiation of Darwin's finches in the Galapagos Is. >> Darwin, Charles; ecology; evolution

adaptive suspension A pneumatic or hydro-pneumatic suspension system fitted to a motor car or a commercial vehicle that damps out the variations in road surface, and maintains the vehicle at a constant level whilst in use. This levelling device can be controlled electronically, allowing the suspension system to adapt itself automatically to the road surface conditions and the speed of travel. >> car [i]

Addams, Jane (1860–1935) US social reformer, born at Cedarville, Illinois. After visiting Toynbee Hall in London, she founded Hull House in Chicago, where she worked to secure social justice in housing, factory inspection, female suffrage, and the cause of pacifism. In 1931 she shared the Nobel Peace Prize, and in 1910 became the first woman President of the National Conference of Social Work. She died in Chicago. >> women's liberation movement

addax [**ad**aks] A horse-like antelope native to N African deserts; resembles the oryx, but has thicker, spiralling horns; pale with clump of brown hair on the forehead; never drinks; lives in herds. (*Addax nasomaculatus*.) >> antelope; horse [i]; oryx

adder A venomous snake of the family *Viperidae*; three species: *Vipera berus* (**European adder** or **common European viper**, the only venomous British snake) and the puff adders; also Australian **death adders** of family *Elapidae* (2 species). The name is used in place of viper for some other species, such as the **horned adder/viper** and **saw-scaled adder/viper**. >> horned viper; puff adder; snake; viper [i]

adder's tongue A fern native to grasslands of Europe, Asia, N Africa, and N America; underground rhizome producing a fertile spike 5 cm/2 in long bearing sporangia and sheathed by a single oval; the entire frond is 10–20 cm/4–8 in long. (*Ophioglossum vulgatum*. Family: *Ophioglossaceae*.) >> fern; rhizome; sporangium

Addington >> **Sidmouth**

Addinsell, Richard (1904–77) British composer, born at Oxford, where he read law at Hertford College before studying music in London, Berlin, and Vienna. He composed much film music, including the popular *Warsaw Concerto* for the film *Dangerous Moonlight* (1941). He died in London.

Addis Ababa or **Adis Abeba** [adis **a**baba] 9°02N 38°42E, pop (1984e) 1 412 575. Capital of Ethiopia; altitude 2 400 m/7 874 ft; founded by Menelik II, 1887; capital, 1889; occupied by Italy, 1936–41, declared capital of Italian East Africa; airport; railway to port of Djibouti; university (1950); tobacco, foodstuffs, textiles, chemicals, cement; national museum, national library, St George Cathedral, Menelik II's tomb; headquarters of UN Economic Commission for Africa, and of the Organization of African Unity. >> Ethiopia [i]

Addison, Joseph (1672–1719) English essayist and poet, born at Milston, Wiltshire, and educated at Charterhouse and Oxford. In 1708–11 he was secretary to the Lord-Lieutenant of Ireland, where he formed a warm friendship with Swift. He became an MP, and contributed largely to the *Tatler*. In 1711 the *Spectator*, 274 numbers of which were his work, was founded. He was satirized by Pope in the famous character of Atticus. Addison was made a commissioner for trade and the colonies, and in 1717 was appointed Secretary of State, but a year later resigned his post on health grounds. He died in London. >> English literature; Pope, Alexander; Swift

Addison, Thomas (1793–1860) British physician, born at Longbenton, Northumberland. He graduated in medicine at Edinburgh in 1815, and in 1837 became physician to Guy's Hospital. His chief research was into the disease of the adrenal glands which has since been named after him, and into pernicious anaemia (**Addisonian anaemia**). He died in Bristol, Gloucestershire. >> Addison's disease; anaemia

Addison's disease A medical condition resulting from the destruction of the adrenal cortex by infection (commonly tuberculosis) or by an auto-immune reaction. A fall in the output of corticosteroids causes physical weakness, mental apathy, low blood pressure, and increased skin pigmentation. Without treatment, death is unavoidable. Taking synthetic steroids by mouth restores the patient to normal health, but these must be continued for life. » Addison, Thomas; adrenal glands; auto-immune diseases; corticosteroids

addition reaction A chemical reaction in which a product contains all atoms of two or more reactants, eg the chlorination of ethylene, $CH_2=CH_2+Cl_2 \rightarrow CH_2Cl.CH_2Cl$. Similarly, **addition polymerization** is the formation of a polymer without elimination from the reactants, for example the formation of polyethylene, $nCH_2=CH_2 \rightarrow (-CH_2.CH_2-)_n$. The product of an addition reaction is known as an **adduct**. » chemical reaction; ethylene; polymerization

additives Strictly, any chemical, even a vitamin, added to a food during its processing or preparation; more usually, chemicals which have been added in order to achieve a specific aim. They include (a) *preservatives*, which reduce spoilage by bacteria, (b) *anti-oxidants*, which prevent fats from becoming rancid, (c) *emulsifiers*, which permit a stable mixture of oil and water, (d) *colouring matter*, to vary colour to specifications, and (e) *flavouring agents/enhancers*, to achieve a given flavour. Many additives are naturally-occurring compounds; others are synthetic. Legislation exists in most countries to ensure that food additives are technologically desirable and at the same time safe. However, in recent years many consumers have come to fear synthetic additives, leading to an increase in the use of natural additives. » antioxidants; E-number; emulsifiers; food preservation

address bus A system of wires or connections (*bus*) within a computer that communicates information about which memory location is being used. » data bus; input-output bus; memory, computer

adduct » **addition reaction**

Adela, Princess (c.1062–1137) Fourth daughter of William the Conqueror, who in 1080 married Stephen, Count of Blois, by whom she had nine children. Her third son, Stephen, became King of England in her lifetime. » William I (of England)

Adelaide 34°56S 138°36E, pop(1986) 993 100. Port capital of South Australia, on the Torrens R where it meets the St Vincent Gulf; founded, 1837; the first Australian municipality to be incorporated, 1840; two universities (1874, 1966); airfield; railway; oil refining, motor vehicles, electrical goods, shipbuilding; trade in wool, grain, fruit, wine; fine beaches to the W, including Maslin Beach (the first nude bathing beach in Australia); many parks; two cathedrals; major wine-growing area to the S (McLaren Vale) and to the N (Barossa Valley); Adelaide Festival Centre; South Australian Museum (large collection of aboriginal art); Art Gallery of South Australia; Constitutional Museum; Ayers House (1846), headquarters of the South Australian National Trust; Maritime Museum in Port Adelaide; arts festival, held every two years; Adelaide Cup Day (May). » South Australia

Adélie Land or **Adélie Coast**, Fr **Terre Adélie** [**a**daylee] area c.432 000 sq km/166 752 sq ml. Territory in Antarctica 66°–67°S, 136°–142°E; first seen by the French navy in 1840; explored 1911–14 and 1929–31; French territory, 1938; French research station at Base Dumont d'Urville. » French Southern and Antarctic Territories

Aden or **Adan** [**ay**dn] 12°50N 45°00E, pop(1981e) 264 326. Seaport capital in Adan governorate, South Yemen; on the Gulf of Aden, at the entrance to the Red Sea; taken by British, 1839; capital of former Aden protectorate; after opening of Suez Canal (1869), an important coaling station and transshipment point; British crown colony, 1937; scene of fighting between nationalist groups in 1960s; capital of new republic, 1968; airport; oil refining, shipping. » Yemen, South [i]

Aden, Gulf of [**ay**dn] W arm of the Red Sea, lying between South Yemen (N) and Somalia (S); connected to the Red Sea by the Strait of Bāb al Mandab; length 885 km/550 ml. » Red Sea

Adenauer, Konrad [**ah**denower] (1876–1967) German statesman, born at Cologne, who became the first Chancellor of the Federal Republic of Germany (1949–63). He studied at Freiburg, Munich, and Bonn, before practising law in Cologne, where he became Lord Mayor (1917). He was president of the Prussian State Council 1920–33. In 1933 the Nazis dismissed him from all his offices, and imprisoned him in 1934, and again in 1944. In 1945, under Allied occupation, he founded the Christian Democratic Union. As Chancellor, he established closer links with the Russians and the French, and aimed to rebuild West Germany on a basis of partnership with other European nations through NATO and the EEC. He retired in 1963, and died at Rhöndorf, Germany. » European Economic Community; Germany [i]; NATO

adenine [**a**duhneen] $C_4H_5N_5$. A base derived from purine, one of the four found in nucleic acids, where it is generally paired with thymine. » base (chemistry); DNA [i]; purines; thymine [i]

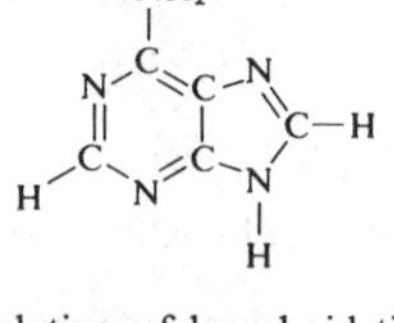

adenoids An accumulation of lymphoid tissue, arranged as a series of folds behind the opening of the auditory tube in the nasopharynx; also known as the **pharyngeal tonsils**. When enlarged in children they can block or reduce the size of the auditory tube opening and fill the nasopharynx, giving an abnormal resonance to speech. » Eustachian tube; lymphoid tissue; pharynx; tonsils

adenosine triphosphate (ATP) [**a**denuhseen] A molecule formed by the condensation of adenine, ribose, and triphosphoric acid: HO–P(O)OH–O–P(O)OH–O–P(O)OH–OH. It is a key compound in the mediation of energy in both plants and animals, energy being stored in its synthesis from *adenosine diphosphate* (ADP) and phosphoric acid, and released when the reaction is reversed. » adenine [i]; phosphoric acid; ribose [i]

Ader, Clément [**a**day] (1841–1926) French engineer, who in 1872 made a man-powered aeroplane, and in 1886 and 1891 larger, steam-powered, bat-like flying machines. The third machine was called *Avion*, which became the French term for an aircraft. In 1897 his fourth machine, still steam-powered, proved to be capable of flight, but was seriously damaged in proving it. » aircraft [i]

adhesives Materials whose function is to bind one substance to another. Examples are (1) substances of biological origin, generally water soluble, known as *glues*, which are usually proteins or carbohydrates, and (2) synthetic materials, both thermoplastic and thermosetting resins and rubbers. » carbohydrate; protein; resin; thermoplastic; thermoset

Adi Granth [ahdee **grant**] ('First Book') The principal Sikh scripture, originally called the Granth Sahib ('Revered Book'). The name Adi Granth distinguishes it from the Dasam Granth, a later second collection. The text used today is an expanded version of Guru Arjan's original compilation, and is revered by all Sikhs. » guru; Sikhism

adiabatic demagnetization » **magnetic cooling**

adiabatic process [adeea**ba**tik] In thermodynamics, a process in which no heat enters or leaves a system, such as in a well-insulated system, or in some process so rapid that there is not enough time for heat exchange. Sound waves in air involve adiabatic pressure changes. The compression and power strokes of a car engine are also adiabatic. » engine; heat; magnetic cooling; sound; thermodynamics

Adige, River [**a**deejay], Ger **Etsch**, ancient **Athesis** River in N Italy, rising in three small Alpine lakes; flows E and S, then E into the Adriatic Sea, SE of Chioggia; length 408 km/253 ml; chief river of Italy after the Po. » Italy [i]

adipic acid [a**di**pik] $HOOC-(CH_2)_4-COOH$, IUPAC **hexanedioic acid**, melting point 153°C. It is one of the monomers for nylon, the other being 1,6-diaminohexane. » monomer; polyamides

adipose tissue » **fat 2**

Adirondack Mountains [adi**ron**dak] Mountain range largely in NE New York state, USA; rises to 1 629 m/5 344 ft at Mt Marcy; named after an Indian tribe; source of the Hudson and Ausable Rivers; locations such as L Placid are noted winter resorts; largest state park in USA. » United States of America [i]

Adis Abeba » Addis Ababa

adjutant A stork native to tropical SE Asia. There are two species: the **greater** adjutant stork (*Leptoptilos dubius*), and the **lesser**, **haircrested**, or **Javan** adjutant stork (*Leptoptilos javanicus*); grey and white; head nearly naked; eats carrion, frogs or fish; related to marabou. » marabou; stork

Adler, Alfred (1870–1937) Pioneer Austrian psychiatrist, born in Vienna. He graduated as a doctor in 1895, and became a member of the psychoanalytical group that formed around Freud. His most widely referenced work is *Studie über Minderwertigkeit von Organen* (1907, Study of Organ Inferiority and its Psychical Compensation), which aroused great controversy, and led to one of the early schisms in psychoanalysis. He died while on a lecture tour, at Aberdeen, Scotland. » Freud, Sigmund; inferiority complex; psychoanalysis

administrative law The body of law relating to administrative powers exercised principally by central and local government. The exercise of such powers can be the subject of scrutiny by the courts on legal, but not policy, grounds. » court of law; judicial review; law

Admiral's Cup A yacht race for up to three boats per nation, first contested in 1957 and held biennially. Races take place in the English Channel, at Cowes, and around the Fastnet rock. The trophy is donated by the Royal Ocean Racing Club. » sailing

Admiralty Court An English court which is part of the Queen's Bench Division of the High Court. Its work deals with maritime claims in civil law, such as salvage. In the USA, the federal district courts exercise jurisdiction over maritime actions. » civil law; High Court of Justice; salvage; sea, law of the

Admiralty Islands pop (1980) 25 844; area 2 000 sq km/800 sq ml. Island group in N Papua New Guinea, part of the Bismarck Archipelago; c.40 islands, main island, Manus; chief town, Lorengau; German protectorate, 1884; under Australian mandate, 1920; fishing, copra, pearls. » Bismarck Archipelago

adolescence That period of personal development marked by the onset of puberty and continuing through the early teenage years. While it is associated with the process of physical maturation, normally occurring more quickly in girls than in boys, the actual age-range and behavioural patterns involved can vary considerably from one society to another. Adolescence in the Third World, for example, is more likely to mean working in the fields for one's parents and taking on adult responsibilities from as young as age 9 or 10 than a prolonged period of schooling as it does in more prosperous societies. Whatever the differences, adolescents commonly want to be independent of their parents; the conflicts this may generate are sometimes said to reflect 'the generation gap'. » hormones; puberty

Adonis [a**doh**nis] In Greek mythology, a beautiful young man who was loved by Aphrodite. He insisted on going hunting and was killed by a boar, but Persephone saved him on condition that he spent part of the year with her. There was a yearly commemoration of the event, with wailing and singing. There is a clear connection with the growth and death of vegetation, and similar Eastern ceremonies. » Persephone; Tammuz

adoption A legal procedure in which a civil court makes an order giving parental rights and duties over a minor to someone other than the natural parents. On adoption, the minor becomes the legal child of his or her adoptive parents. » court of law; legitimacy; minor

adoptionism The understanding of Jesus as a human being of sinless life adopted by God as son, usually thought to be at the time of his baptism by John in the R Jordan. Such teaching was declared heretical, in that it implied that Jesus could not have had a fully divine nature. Associated with Arianism, it figured in 4th-c controversies over the person of Christ, in Spain in the 8th-c, and in some scholastic theology (eg Abelard, Lombard). » Abelard; Arius; Jesus Christ; Lombard

Adrastea [adras**tee**a] A tiny natural satellite of Jupiter, discovered in 1979 by Voyager 2; distance from the planet 129 000 km/80 000 ml; diameter 24 km/15 ml. » Jupiter (astronomy); Voyager project [i]; RR4

adrenal glands [a**dree**nal] Paired compound endocrine glands in mammals, situated one near each kidney; also known as the **suprarenal glands**. Each comprises an outer cortex and an inner medulla. The cortex consists of three zones, which produce specific steroid hormones: the outer zone produces mineralocorticoids (eg aldosterone), whereas the intermediate and inner zones produce glucocorticoids (eg cortisol) and sex hormones (eg androgens). The medulla secretes a specific catecholamine (either adrenaline or noradrenaline). The various groups of hormones are chemically similar in all vertebrates. » Addison's disease; adrenaline; aldosterone; cortisol; Cushing's disease; embryology; endocrine glands; hormones

adrenaline or **adrenalin** [a**dren**alin] A hormone released from the adrenal medulla in response to stress, and in some other circumstances; also known as **epinephrine** in the USA. It increases heart rate, raises blood pressure, and causes release of sugar into the blood from liver stores. Thus, in situations of stress the body is prepared for the 'fight or flight reaction'. It may also be a neurotransmitter in the brain, where it is associated with many functions, including cardiovascular and respiratory responses. Therapeutic uses include acute asthma, heart attack, and severe allergic responses. » adrenal glands; allergy; catecholamine; hormones; noradrenaline

adrenocorticotrophic hormone (ACTH) [a**dree**nohkawtikoh**trohf**ik] A chemical substance (a peptide) produced in the front lobe of the pituitary gland; also known as **corticotrophin**. It stimulates the synthesis and release of glucocorticoids from the adrenal cortex, and is released in response to physical, emotional, or chemical stress. » adrenal glands; glucocorticoids; peptide; pituitary gland

Adrian, Edgar Douglas, 1st Baron (1889–1977) British neurophysiologist, born in London. He was educated at Cambridge, where he became professor of physiology (1937–51). A founder of modern neurophysiology, he used sensitive amplifiers to record activity in single nerve cells, and from 1934 studied electrical brain wave rhythms and their clinical uses. He shared the 1932 Nobel Prize for Physiology or Medicine for his work on the function of neurones. He was made a baron in 1955 and died in London. » nervous system; neurology; Sherrington

Adrian IV, also **Hadrian**, originally **Nicholas Breakspear** (c.1100–59) The only Englishman to become Pope (1154–9), born at Langley, Hertfordshire. He became first a lay brother in the monastery of St Rufus, near Avignon, and in 1137 was elected its abbot. His zeal for strict discipline led to an attempt to defame his character, and he had to appear before Eugenius III at Rome. Here he not only cleared himself, but acquired the esteem of the Pope, who appointed him Cardinal Bishop of Albano in 1146. As Pope, he is said to have granted Ireland to Henry II. He died near Rome. » Henry II (of England); pope

Adrianople, Battle of (AD 378) A battle between the Romans and the Visigoths at present-day Edirne in European Turkey. This was one of the crucial battles of the ancient world, as the crushing Visigoth victory, under Fritigern, opened up Roman territory to Germanic invasion. Two-thirds of the Roman army, including Emperor Valens, were killed. » Roman history [i]; Visigoths

Adriatic Sea [aydree**at**ik] Arm of the Mediterranean Sea, between the E coast of Italy and the Balkan Peninsula (Yugoslavia and Albania); Gulf of Venice at its head (NW); separated from the Ionian Sea (S) by the Strait of Otranto; length 800 km/500 ml; width 93–225 km/58–140 ml; maximum depth 1 250 m/4 100 ft; highly saline; lobster, sardines, tuna; chief ports, Venice, Rijeka, Ancona, Bari, Brindisi; flat, sandy Italian coast; rugged, irregular Yugoslav coast. » Mediterranean Sea

adsorption The extraction of a component from one phase into another phase, usually by chemical interaction (*chemisorption*) between the material adsorbed (the **adsorbate**) and the surface of the adsorbing material (the **adsorbent**). Sometimes, the adsorbate is incorporated into the structure of the adsorbent; an example is the adsorption of hydrogen gas by palladium, which can adsorb several hundred times its own volume of the gas. » gas **1**; hydrogen

adult education The provision of further or continuing educational opportunities for people over the minimum school-leaving age; also known as **continuing education**. Frequently this takes place in institutions specially set up to cater for mature learners, but it is also common for schools and colleges and other centres of learning to be used. A wide network of providers exists. In addition to the formal opportunities offered by institutions, there are numerous informal sources of adult education, such as broadcast programmes on radio and television, as well as correspondence and distance-learning courses, for people who wish to or must learn at home or as part of their job. » community school; distance education

Advaita [adv**iy**ta] (Sanskrit, 'non-dual') An influential school of Vedanta Hinduism, revived in a modern form during the 20th-c. Associated primarily with the thought of Shankara, it holds that there is only one absolute reality, Brahman. All selves are in effect identical, since in essence they are one with Brahman. » atman; Brahman; Hinduism; Veda

Advent In the Christian Church, the four weeks before Christmas, beginning on the Sunday nearest 30 November (Advent Sunday); a period of penitence and preparation for the celebration of the first coming of Christ at Christmas, and for his promised second coming to judge the world. » Christmas; Jesus Christ

Adventists Those Christians whose most important belief is in the imminent and literal Second Coming of Christ. Found in most periods of history and in most denominations, a separate movement began in the USA with William Miller (1781–1849), who predicted Christ's return (and the end of the world) in 1843–4, and whose followers eventually formed a denomination called Seventh Day Adventists. They believe that the Second Coming of Christ is delayed only by a failure to keep the Sabbath (Friday evening to Saturday evening), which, along with Old Testament dietary laws, is held to rigorously. » Jesus Christ; millenarianism

adversary politics A political situation said to exist in two-party electoral systems (eg the UK) where the policies of the parties and government are polarized between right and left, resulting in significant reversals in policy when government changes. Because the electoral system works against successful challenges from third parties, the views of the majority of the electorate occupying the 'middle ground' are not reflected. » proportional representation

advertising The practice of informing and influencing others not personally known to the communicator through paid messages in the media; also the advertisements themselves. From humble origins (eg tradesmen's signs), advertising has developed in parallel with modern industrial society and the mass media. News-sheets in the 17th-c carried brief statements (eg announcing the sale of patent medicines), but it was not until the late 19th-c, with the advent of mass production of consumer goods, that the industry developed on the huge scale found today. Advertising for consumer goods, whether of the 'fast moving' variety (eg washing powders) or 'durables' (eg cars) has long been the most conspicuous kind, on poster sites, in the press, and on television. 'Display' ads for such products in newspapers or magazines are characterized by their size and use of graphics (especially photographs), slogans, and large type. In contrast, 'classified' ads are typically single-column width, consisting of words only, and grouped together under headings (eg 'personal', 'situations vacant', or 'wanted'). Other approaches include direct marketing (by post or telephone) and direct response advertising (via tear-off coupons), both of which have resulted from the difficulty mass media advertising has in reaching a target audience and measuring its own effectiveness.

Manufacturers and retailers are not the only groups to realize the value of communicating with the general public through advertising. Governments, political parties, service industries (eg banks and financial institutions), trade unions, employers' associations, pressure groups, and charities also employ advertising as a major means of promoting ideas and causes. Regulations on who may advertise and on the quantity and nature of ads, especially commercials, vary from country to country. In recent years some advertisers have found the sponsorship of sporting and cultural events a convenient way to side-step controls applying elsewhere to the promotion of their products (especially cigarettes) and a means of associating these with healthy or prestigious activities. From being small-scale brokers of advertising space on behalf of newspaper proprietors, most modern *advertising agencies* now offer a 'full service', comprising market research and creative expertise, media planning, and media buying. Since the 1960s, however, 'creative shops' have offered specialist design and copywriting services, with 'media independents' later doing the same for media planning and buying.

Advertising is only one, though perhaps the most controversial, of the elements of the 'marketing mix'. As such it has always been subject to attack, whether on moral, ideological, or aesthetic grounds. Underlying this criticism is the presumption that advertising has pernicious effects on individuals, social groups, or whole societies. Apologists respond by claiming that advertising merely reflects the values and styles already existing in society. » subliminal advertising

Advisory, Conciliation, and Arbitration Service » ACAS

advocacy planning A form of planning in which the planner acts for the interests of a particular group or community in opposition to plans prepared by the official planning authority. It is a means of aiding groups whose interests may be damaged or not represented by the planning authority. The planner is responsible to the group, and not to the authority.

advocate A term generally applied to lawyers practising in the courts as professional representatives of those who bring or defend a case. In Scotland, the term is used as an equivalent to an English barrister. » barrister; court of law; solicitor

aechmea [ak**may**a] A genus of plants (epiphytes) native to tropical America; rosettes of succulent leaves forming a water-filled cup in the centre, inflorescence produced on a stout, well-developed stalk. Many species are grown as house plants. (Genus: *Aechmea*, 172 species. Family: *Bromeliaceae*.) » bromeliad; epiphyte; inflorescence [i]

Aedes [ay**ee**deez] The yellow-fever mosquito, found in coastal and riverside habitats throughout the tropics and subtropics; eggs laid in stagnant water; aquatic larvae colourless except for black respiratory siphon. The adult females feed on blood, transmitting diseases such as yellow fever and dengue. (Order: *Diptera*. Family: *Culicidae*.) » dengue; larva; mosquito; yellow fever

Aegean civilization [ee**jee**an] The Bronze Age cultures which flourished in the third and second millennia BC on the islands of the Aegean Sea and around its coasts. » Minoan/Mycenaean civilization

Aegean Islands [ee**jee**an] pop (1981) 428 533; area 9 122 sq km/3 521 sq ml. Island group and region of Greece; the name is generally applied to the islands of the Aegean Sea, including Lesbos, Chios, Samos, Limnos, and Thasos; a major tourist area. » Aegean Sea; Greece [i]

Aegean Sea [ee**jee**an] Arm of the Mediterranean Sea, bounded W and N by Greece, NE and E by Turkey, S by islands of Crete and Rhodes; dotted with islands on which the Aegean civilization of 3000–1000 BC flourished; length (N–S) 645 km/400 ml; width 320 km/200 ml; greatest depth, 2 013 m/6 604 ft; sardines, sponges; natural gas off NE coast of Greece; tourism. » Mediterranean Sea

Aegina [ee**jiy**na] Gr **Aiyna** pop (1981) 11 127; area 83 sq km/32 sq ml. One of the largest of the Saronic Islands, Greece, SW of Athens; chief town Aiyna; a popular resort; Temple of Aphaia. » Greece [i]

aegis [**ee**jis] Originally a goatskin, and then, in Greek mythology, a fringed piece of armour or a shield. Zeus shakes his aegis, which may possibly be the thunder-cloud; Athene's is equipped with the Gorgon's head. » Athena; Gorgon; Zeus

Aegisthus [ee**gis**thus, **ee**jisthus] In Greek legend, the son of Thyestes; while Agamemnon was absent at Troy he became the lover of Clytemnestra. Together they killed Agamemnon on his return to Argos. Aegisthus was later killed by Orestes. » Agamemnon; Clytemnestra; Orestes; Thyestes

Aelfric [elfrik] called **Grammaticus** (c.955–c.1020) English writer, known for his use of the Anglo-Saxon vernacular. He taught at the monastery of Cerne Abbas, later becoming abbot of Eynsham. His writings include a collection of homilies, *Lives of the Saints*, and a Latin/English grammar, glossary, and dialogue (*Colloquium*). » Anglo-Saxon; English literature

Aelred of Rievaulx » **Ailred of Rievaulx**

Aemilian Way [iymeelian] A continuation of Rome's major trunk road to the N, the Flaminian Way. It ran from Rimini on the Adriatic coast to the R Po. » Roman roads [i]

Aeneas [eeneeas] In Roman legend, the ancestor of the Romans. He was a Trojan hero, the son of Anchises and Venus, who escaped after the fall of Troy, bearing his father on his shoulders. After wandering through the Mediterranean, he reached Italy at Cumae and visited the Underworld, where the destiny of Rome was made clear to him. He married the daughter of the King of Latium, and allied himself to the Latins in local wars. His son founded Alba Longa, and a line of kings from whom Romulus was said to be descended. » Romulus and Remus; Trojan War; Virgil

aeolian harp A wooden soundbox fitted with strings (usually about a dozen) of various thicknesses, but tuned to a single pitch, which are made to vibrate freely by the surrounding air, producing an ethereal, 'disembodied' sound. It takes its name from Aeolus, god of the winds. » Aeolus; chordophone; zither

Aeolians [eeohlianz] A sub-group of Hellenic peoples who colonized the NW coast of Asia Minor and the islands of the N Aegean (e.g. Lesbos) towards the end of the second millennium BC. » Greek history

Aeolus [eeolus] In Greek mythology, the god of the winds. In the *Odyssey* Aeolus lived on an island, and gave Odysseus the winds tied in a bag so that his ship would not be blown off course. The ship had nearly reached Ithaca when Odysseus' men opened the bag, thinking it contained treasure. As a result, the ship was blown far away. » Odysseus

Aepyornis [eepeeawnis] » **elephant bird**

aerial (photography) » **antenna** (photography)

aerial photography Photography of the ground surface from an aerial viewpoint such as a balloon or aircraft, with application to archaeology, ecology, geology and wartime reconnaissance. In **aerial survey mapping**, the aircraft flies at a constant height along specified paths, taking pictures at regular intervals to build up a mosaic of overlapping images; ground contour and building heights are measured by viewing pairs of images stereoscopically. » photogrammetry; stereoscopic photography; Plate III

aerobe [airohb] An organism that requires the presence of oxygen for growth and reproduction. The great majority of all living organisms are aerobic, requiring oxygen for respiration. Some micro-organisms, typically bacteria, are anaerobic, able to grow only in the absence of oxygen; these are known as **anaerobes**. » bacteria [i]; oxygen

aerobics A system of physical training in which exercises such as walking, swimming, and running are pursued for a sufficiently long period to increase performance. The increases can be assessed using a point scoring system available on charts for different ages and types of effort. In the 1980s, the term was particularly used for movement exercises in time to music, which became popular among keep-fit groups at all ages. The use of oxygen by muscles in carrying out any form of physical activity is known as *aerobic metabolism*. » calisthenics

aerocapture A proposed technique for placing a spacecraft in orbit around a planet, without the expenditure of chemical propulsives, by taking advantage of planetary atmosphere. The spacecraft would be equipped with an aerobrake similar to the heat shields on space capsules like Apollo, and would be navigated into the planet's upper atmosphere, where friction would slow it down. The technique offers the prospect of reducing trip times to the outer planets by using less massive spacecraft, and of carrying heavier payloads to Mars for sample return missions and, eventually, human exploration. » Mars (astronomy); planet; spacecraft

aerodynamics The study of the flow of air and the behaviour of objects moving relative to air; a subject which is applicable to other gases, and is part of the larger subject of fluid mechanics. Aerodynamic principles explain flight. The shape and orientation of an aircraft wing (curved upper suface, wing tilted down) mean that the air above the wing travels further than the air beneath. Air above the wing thus travels faster and so has lower pressure (Bernoulli's principle). The pressure difference provides lift to support the aircraft. The available lift increases with wing area, and decreases with altitude. The movement of an aircraft through the air produces a force which impedes motion, called *drag*, dependent on the aircraft size and shape. Air movement across the surface is impeded by friction, which produces additional drag called *frictional drag*; this causes heating, which can sometimes be extreme, as in the case of space re-entry vehicles. Friction losses increase with wing area and velocity, and decrease with altitude.

At velocities greater than the speed of sound (Mach 1, approximately 331.5 metres per second) air can no longer be treated as incompressible and new rules apply, giving rise to **supersonic aerodynamics**. Passing from subsonic to supersonic speeds, aircraft cross the 'sound barrier', marked by a dramatic increase in drag. Supersonic drag is reduced using thin, swept-back wings typical of military fighter aircraft. Aircraft flying at supersonic speeds produce sonic booms – shock waves in the air around the aircraft, produced because the aircraft's velocity is too great to allow the air pressure to adjust smoothly around it. Vehicles moving through air experience drag forces which increase fuel consumption. Also, buildings and bridges sway due to wind. These effects must be allowed for in design, and can be minimized by attending to the shape of the object as seen by the oncoming air stream. Wind tunnels allow scale models to be exposed to simulated wind conditions, and aerodynamic properties of design can be determined. Of special importance are effects of abnormal air flows such as turbulence and vortices. » Bernoulli's principle; fluid mechanics; Mach number; turbulence

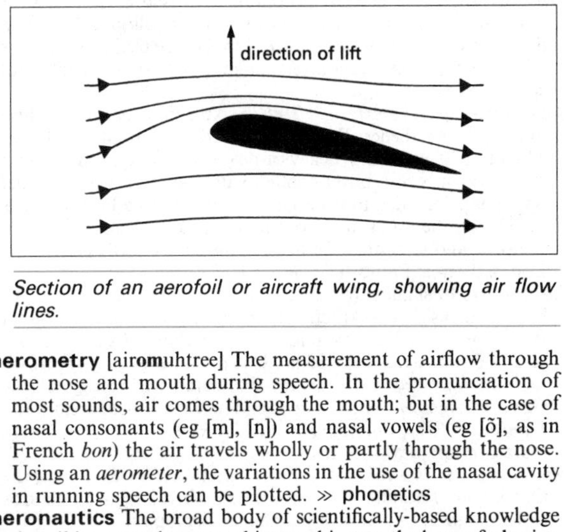

Section of an aerofoil or aircraft wing, showing air flow lines.

aerometry [airomuhtree] The measurement of airflow through the nose and mouth during speech. In the pronunciation of most sounds, air comes through the mouth; but in the case of nasal consonants (eg [m], [n]) and nasal vowels (eg [õ], as in French *bon*) the air travels wholly or partly through the nose. Using an *aerometer*, the variations in the use of the nasal cavity in running speech can be plotted. » phonetics

aeronautics The broad body of scientifically-based knowledge describing aeroplanes as objects subject to the laws of physics. The term is usually taken to mean knowledge which focuses upon the vehicle itself, rather than upon the associated commercial or operational usage, although in practice such a definition is not rigidly adhered to. Thus, aeronautics is taken to cover such topics as the generation of lift to make the aeroplane fly, the physical factors affecting manoeuvring, the production of thrust through the use of propellers and jets, the strength of the structure, and the way these various elements are combined to produce a functioning vehicle. » aeroplane; aircraft [i]

aerophone Any musical instrument in which air is the main vibrating agent. Aerophones form one of the main categories of instruments in the standard classification of Hornbostel and

Sachs (1914). They are subdivided into types according to (a) the main material they are made of, and (b) how the air is set in motion (via a mouthpiece, a reed, or neither). » brass/reed/ woodwind instrument [i]; musical instruments; organ

aeroplane The general name given to a vehicle whose operational medium is air and which supports itself in the Earth's atmosphere by means of lift. Lift is produced through specially shaped fixed wings attached to the aeroplane's body or fuselage; these alter the airflow so that the pressure distribution of the air over the wing creates an upward force. The airflow is in turn produced by the aeroplane being 'pushed' or 'pulled' through the air by the propulsion device driven by a motor. By means of design, the lift produced by the wing can be made greater than the weight of the airframe and propulsive system, allowing a payload to be carried.

The first truly powered flight was made by Orville Wright in December 1903, when he flew 260 m/852 ft. However, it was not until World War 1 that governments on both sides of the conflict put money into the development of engines and airframes. This led to the rapid development of specialized aircraft, particularly the fighter. After the War, the needs of American transcontinental passenger travel produced aircraft with multi-engines, metal skins, and retractable undercarriages to replace the previously fabric-covered types. World War 2 saw a further investment in aircraft by both the Axis and Allied powers, culminating in the world's first operational jet fighter, the Me 262. In the period following the War, jet engines were applied to ever larger passenger aircraft, culminating in the introduction of the Boeing 747 Jumbo Jet in 1970. This period also saw the arrival of the supersonic Concorde in 1976. Similarly, warplanes of all types had jet engines applied to them, the trend being towards ever higher speeds. Recent developments in civilian aircraft have been away from high speed towards more economical and quieter operation, whilst military aircraft are becoming increasingly reliant upon electronics to control and keep them stable in flight. » aircraft [i]; Concorde; jet engine [i]; propeller; turbine; Wright brothers

aerosol An airborne suspension of microscopic particles or liquid droplets, typically formed by forcing a liquid through a fine nozzle under pressure. Aerosol sprays are useful as a means of depositing fine even layers of material, such as in paint sprays. » CFCs

Aeschines [eeskineez] (c.390 BC–?) Athenian orator, second only to Demosthenes. Prominent in Athenian politics between 348 and 330 BC, his advocacy of peace with Macedon brought him frequently into bitter conflict with Demosthenes, his chief opponent. Defeated in his attempt to undermine Demosthenes in 330 BC, he went into voluntary exile, where he taught rhetoric, and later died. Of his speeches, only three survive. » Demosthenes; Philip II (of Macedon)

Aeschylus [eeskiluhs] (c.525–c.456 BC) Greek tragic dramatist, born at Eleusis, near Athens. He fought for Athens in the great Persian wars, and was wounded at Marathon. His first victory as a poet was gained in 485 BC. Out of some 60 plays ascribed to him, only seven are extant, including the trilogy of the *Oresteia*: *Agamemnon*, *Choephori* (The Libation Bearers), and *Eumenides* (The Furies). He died at Gela, Sicily. » Greek literature; tragedy

Aesculapius [eeskyulaypeeus] The Latin form of **Asclepius**, the Greek god of healing. His cult was transferred from Epidauros to Rome in 291 BC after a plague. » Asclepius

Aesop [eesop] (?6th-c BC) The traditional name of a Greek writer of fables. He is supposed to have been a native of Phrygia and a slave who, after being set free, travelled to Greece. The fables are anecdotes which use animals to make a moral point. Some of the stories are known from the folklore of earlier periods, and none of his actual writings have survived; but versions bearing the name of Aesop have remained popular throughout history. » fable; Greek literature

Aesthetic/Esthetic Movement A view of art based on the theory that art is autonomous and should not be judged by non-aesthetic criteria, whether moral, religious, or political; it flourished in the 19th-c. The French writer Victor Cousin first used the phrase *l'art pour l'art* ('art for art's sake') in 1836, but the doctrine occurs in various forms in the writings of (among others) Kant, Coleridge, and Emerson. Aestheticism was attacked for its exaggerated detachment from everyday life by Ruskin and later by Tolstoy. The view that purely 'formal' rather than associational or 'literary' qualities are paramount has played a major role in 20th-c discussion. » art; Arts and Crafts Movement

aesthetics The philosophical investigation of art, understood to include the visual arts (painting, sculpture, photography, film), music, literature, drama, and dance. Aesthetics deals with such issues as what it is to perceive an object or a performance as a work of art; what features, if any, are important or essential to it; whether there are objective standards for judging it; and what meaning and function can be ascribed to art criticism.

aestivation » **hibernation**

Aethel- (Anglo-Saxon names) » **Athel-, Ethel-**

aether » **ether**

Aëtius [aheeshius] (c.?–454) Roman general, born in Moesia, who effectively ruled the Western Empire for Valentinian III (c.433–51). His main achievements were the destruction of the Burgundian Kingdom in E Gaul, and the defeat of Attila the Hun in 451. » Attila; Catalaunian Plains, Battle of the

affenpinscher [afuhnpinshuh] A breed of dog; small with long dark wiry coat; usually black; face like a monkey, with short muzzle and large black eyes; very old breed, originally from Germany, now rare. » dog

affinity A relationship by marriage. Countries generally have rules prohibiting marriage between certain people where there is an affinity – for example between parents and their step-children. Prohibitions also apply where there is *consanguinity* (a blood relationship). » annulment; marriage

affirmative action Policies requiring institutions to act 'affirmatively' in employment practices to avoid discrimination on grounds of race, ethnic origin, or sex; usually found in the USA. Executive Order 10925 issued by President Kennedy contained the first use of the term. Affirmative action policies can range from encouraging the employment of minorities to the setting of quotas of minorities to be employed.

affix A grammatical element which cannot occur on its own, but must always attach to the root or stem of a word. Every language has a limited or closed set of affixes. In English, they may precede the stem (**prefixes**), as in ***impossible***, or follow it, as in *form**al*** (**suffixes**). Some other languages have **infixes**, which are attached within the word. » morpheme

afforestation The planting of woodland areas. The aim may be to increase the extent of economically useful wood (eg conifer plantations in upland UK) or to protect against soil erosion and desertification by providing shelter belts and vegetation cover on bare ground. » deforestation; desertification

Afghan hound A breed of dog; large, slender, with a bouncing step; hair very long, silky (short-haired forms also exist); long thin muzzle; originated in Middle East; was used for hunting in N Afghanistan; hunts by sight. » dog; hound

Afghan Wars A series of wars (1838–42, 1878–80, 1919) between Britain and Afghanistan, prompted by the British desire to extend control in the region to prevent the advance of Russian influence towards India. The third Afghan War resulted in the country's independence (1921).

Afghanistan, official name **(Democratic) Republic of Afghanistan, De Afghanistan Democrateek Jamhuriat** area 647 497 sq km/249 934 sq ml; pop (1990e) 15 592 000, plus an estimated 2½ million nomadic tribesmen and 2 million living in Pakistan and Iran as refugees. Republic in S Asia, divided into 29 provinces; bounded N by republics of the former USSR, E and S by Pakistan, W by Iran, and in the extreme NE by China and India; timezone GMT +4½; capital, Kabul; chief towns include Mazar-e-Sharif, Herat, Kandahar; Pathans the main ethnic group, with several minorities; official languages Pushtu, Dari (Persian); chief religion Islam, mostly Sunni; unit of currency the Afghani, subdivided into 100 puls.

Physical description and climate. A mountainous country centred on the Hindu Kush system, reaching over 7 000 m/24 000 ft in the C and NE; many secondary ranges; to the NW, height decreases towards the USSR border; also NW, the fertile valley of Herat; arid uplands to the S; desert in the SW; landlocked, over 500 km/300 ml from the sea; continental

climate, winter severity increased by altitude; summers warm everywhere except on highest peaks; protected from summer monsoons by S mountains; rain mostly during spring and autumn; annual rainfall averages 338 mm/13¼ in; winters generally cold, with much snow at higher altitudes; a desert or semi-arid climate at lower levels.

History and government. Nation first formed in 1747 under Ahmed Shah Durrani; seen by Britain as a bridge between India and the Middle East, but Britain failed to gain control during a series of Afghan Wars (the last in 1919); feudal monarchy survived until after World War 2, when the constitution became more liberal under several Soviet-influenced 5-year economic plans; king deposed 1973, and a republic formed; new constitution 1977; coup (1978) installed a new government under the communist leader, Nur Mohammad Taraki; further coup (1979) brought to power Hafizullah Amin, which led to the invasion by USSR forces and the establishment of Babrak Karmal as head of state; new constitution, 1987, provides for an executive president, bicameral National Assembly, and council of ministers; Soviet withdrawal implemented 1988–9; regime has met heavy guerrilla resistance from the Mujahadeen (Islamic fighters), and its influence extends effectively over only 20% of the population.

Economy. Traditionally based on agriculture, especially wheat, fruit and vegetables, maize, barley, cotton, sugar-beet, sugar cane; sheep, cattle, goats; forest wood for fuel; food processing, textiles (especially carpets), leather goods, plastics, furniture, footwear, mechanical spares; natural gas production in the N, largely for export; most sectors have been affected by the Civil War, especially sugar and textiles. » communism; Hindu Kush; Islam; Kabul; Mujahadeen; Sunnis; RR24 national holidays; RR42 political leaders

AFL/CIO » **American Federation of Labor – Congress of Industrial Organizations**

aflatoxin [afla**toks**in] A toxin produced by the mould *Aspergillus flavus* (from *A*spergillus *fla*vus *toxin*) commonly found in peanuts, cottonseed, soybeans, wheat, barley, sorghum, and nuts such as pistachios, almonds, and cacao, where the climate favours its growth. The major epidemic of 'Turkey-X disease' in turkeys in the USA in 1960 was caused by feeding with contaminated groundnuts. Symptoms of poisoning include weight loss, loss of co-ordination, convulsions, and death. It also damages the liver, and causes liver tumours when fed long-term at low doses. » liver; toxin

Africa area c.29.8 million sq km/11.5 million sq ml. Second largest continent, extending S from the Mediterranean Sea; bounded W by the Atlantic Ocean and E by the Indian Ocean and the Red Sea; bisected by the Equator; maximum length, 8 000 km/5 000 ml; maximum width, 7 200 km/4 500 ml; highest point, Mt Kilimanjaro (5 895 m/19 340 ft); major rivers include the Congo, Niger, Nile, Zambezi. » Africa, Partition of; African art/dance/history/languages/literature/music; Rift Valley; Sahara Desert; Plate VI

Africa, Partition of The division of the continent of Africa into colonial territories, which occurred in the last three decades of the 19th-c. Europeans had traded with Africa for several centuries, using a series of coastal settlements. Portuguese efforts to penetrate the interior in the 16th–17th-c had largely failed, and only the Dutch at the Cape had been able to establish a dynamic permanent settlement. In the course of the 19th-c, efforts to abolish the slave trade, missionary endeavours, and optimistic views of African riches helped to encourage colonial ambitions. The countries involved in the Partition included Britain, France, Germany, Portugal, and Italy, as well as the Boers in the S, and (in his private capacity) King Leopold of the Belgians. When the French and the Italians completed the Partition of N Africa in the years before World War 1, only Liberia and Ethiopia remained independent. At the end of the two World Wars, a repartitioning occurred with the confiscation of German and Italian territories. Most of the countries created by the Partition achieved independence in or after the 1960s, and the Organization of African Unity pledged itself to the maintenance of the existing boundaries. » Africa; Fashoda; Organization of African Unity; slave trade

African art Visual art forms of the Continent of Africa, originally rock painting and drawings, in open shelters rather than caves. Scratched or incised drawings occur more abundantly throughout the Sahara than anywhere else in the world, and extend chronologically from ancient times almost to the present day. Early representations of wild animals, some now extinct, attest to a hunting culture that flourished before c.4000 BC. The style, as in European Palaeolithic art, is naturalistic. Later rock art is more schematic. Horses and chariots, and later camels, appear. In S Africa the Bushmen have practised their own form of rock painting and drawing from early times to the present. The major form of African tribal (as opposed to prehistoric) art, practised mainly in the W Sudan, the Guinea Coast, Middle Africa, and the Congo, has been sculpture, especially masks and small figures, stools and thrones, as well as everyday objects. Materials, apart from wood, include ivory, metal (mostly bronze), terracotta, raffia, and occasionally stone. Painting has been much less important. In the early 20th-c, African sculpture inspired artists such as Picasso to employ 'primitive' forms in reaction against the conventions of 19th-c naturalism. In recent years, especially since c.1960, artists working in independent states have created original forms of art by combining traditional African with modern Western ideas, techniques, and aesthetic attitudes. » art

African buffalo A member of the cattle family, native to S and E Africa; heavy black or brown body; thick horns lying across head like a helmet, with tips curved upwards; large drooping ears; also known as **Cape buffalo** (small form called **dwarf forest buffalo**). (*Syncerus caffer*.) » Bovidae; cattle

African dance A vast number of dances, often part of traditional tribal structures, which operate within larger geographical boundaries (not always identical with current political boundaries). Some relate to religious belief or communicate socially acceptable moral codes; others express social hierarchies or celebrate ceremonial and social events. Dancing and drumming occur together with clapping and singing. Performances take place within a community as part of a carnival or an arts festival, and in a theatrical context for tourists. Movement is typically from a crouched position, bare-footed with knees bent and shuffling steps, the motion beginning in the hips. » Caribbean dance

African history The study of the history of the continent of Africa. Early approaches were bedevilled by the way Europeans regarded history as the study of societies through literacy, the examination of pre-literate societies being dubbed 'pre-history'. Africans themselves, however, though largely non-literate, had a clear conception of history which they maintained through oral traditions. Much could be established about the African past through the archaeological record and through literate sources derived from the ancient world, Islam, and the earliest European travellers. The Portuguese in particular observed, interacted with, and recorded features of several African societies from the 15th-c, and also began the process of collecting traditions. This was developed by explorers, missionaries, administrators, and anthropologists, in the 19th-c and early 20th-c. It was only after World War 2 that the professional study of African history was put on a sound footing, and rapid strides were made in the utilization of all available sources, including oral history (often with a chronological depth up to five centuries). There is now a vigorous school of indigenous African historians. » Africa; Africa, Partition of; Afrikaners; apartheid; Axum; Bantu-speaking peoples; Benin (former kingdom); Berber; Biafra; Boer Wars; British South Africa Company; Bunyoro; Cushites; Dahomey; Ethiopia [i]; ethnohistory; Fulani; Ghana [i]; Great Trek/Zimbabwe; Griqua; Hausa; Ife; Kanem; Kush; Lozi; Luba-Lunda Kingdoms; Mali [i]; Masai; Mau Mau; Ndebele; Nguni; Nilotes; oral history; Pan-Africanism; Rwanda [i]; slave trade; Songhai; Swahili; Yoruba; Zanzibar (island); Zimbabwe [i]; Zulu

African hunting dog A member of the dog family, native to S Africa; also known as **Cape hunting dog**; the only dog with four toes on each foot; long legs; large rounded ears; mottled light and dark coat; inhabits open plains; packs hunt large grazing mammals. (*Lycaon pictus*.) » Canidae; dog

African languages The languages of the continent of Africa; c.1 300, spoken by c.400 million people. They are difficult to classify, because relatively few have been systematically described, and it is not always clear whether two varieties are separate languages or dialects of the same language. Few had written form before the Christian missionary activities of the 19th-c. Many of these languages do not have official status, but are subservient to the languages of colonialism, especially English and French. There are few with more than a million speakers. It is generally agreed, however, that there are four main groups. » Afro-Asiatic/Niger-Congo languages; African history/literature; Bantu-speaking peoples

African lily An evergreen perennial with thick, tough rhizomes, native to S Africa; leaves strap-shaped, leathery, growing to 1 m/3 ft; flowers with six perianth-segments, bell-shaped, blue, rarely white, in large umbels on leafless stalks. (*Agapanthus africanus*. Family: *Liliaceae*.) » evergreen plants; lily [i]; perennial; rhizome; umbel

African literature The literature of the continent of Africa. Much still belongs to the oral tradition, closely linked to both secular occupation and religious ritual. Throughout the many language groups, there is a wealth of dirges, laments, love songs, chants, celebrations, invectives, and poems inciting warriors to battle, with musical accompaniment. Literature is written in both African and the post-colonial languages. Much vernacular composition tends to be in drama and poetry, such as Kwasi Fiawoo's Ewe play *Toko Atolia* (1937, The Fifth Landing Stage), and Okot p'Bitek's satirical poem in Acholi; whereas Africans writing in English or French will often prefer fiction. Notable examples include the English novels of Chinua Achebe (among them *Things Fall Apart*, 1958), the plays of Wole Soyinka, and the French poetry of Aimé Césaire. *African Literature Today* provides an annual review of the field. The quite different culture of South Africa has produced a number of distinguished novelists, most recently writing against or despite the apartheid state, among them Olive Schreiner (1855–1920), Nadine Gordimer (1923–), J M Coetzee (1940–), and Christopher Hope (1944–). » Achebe; Césaire; Gordimer; literature; Soyinka

African marigold A misleading name for *Tagetes erecta*, a popular garden annual originating from Mexico with deeply cut leaves and showy yellow, orange or red flower-heads up to 10 cm/4 in diameter. **French marigold**, *Tagetes erecta*, also from Mexico, is very similar but has smaller flower-heads. (Family: *Compositae*.) » annual; marigold

African Methodist Episcopal Church A Church formed at a national meeting of Black Methodists in 1816 in the USA, the culmination of a movement begun in 1787. It expanded rapidly after the Civil War, and today has over 1 000 000 members. In 1841 it established the first Black publishing house in the USA. » Methodism

African music The indigenous music of the African continent. Generalization is difficult because of the size of the continent, the diversity of its peoples and languages, the profound influence of Arab culture in the N, and the more recent infiltration of Western music in all parts. The most typical features seem to be: the absence, until the 20th-c, of any system of musical notation (except in the ancient chant of the Ethiopian church); the ubiquity of song, especially in a solo-refrain form; the close interaction of language and music, both vocal and instrumental; the importance of improvisation; and the complexity and sophistication of rhythm. » ethnomusicology; jazz; pop music

African National Congress (ANC) The most important of the Black South African organizations opposed to the Pretoria regime. It began life in 1912 as the South African Native National Congress, and under the influence of Gandhi organized passive resistance to White power. Banned by the South African government in 1961, it began a campaign of industrial and economic sabotage through its military wing, and in the 1980s started attacking persons as well as property. Based in Zambia for several years, it is estimated to have a force of 6 000 guerrillas. It was unbanned in February 1990, and suspended its armed struggle in August 1990. » apartheid; South African Native National Congress

African violet A perennial with hairy leaves in a dense rosette; white, pink, blue, or red flowers; native to tropical E Africa. Their wide colour range and long flowering period make them popular house plants, with numerous hybrids and cultivars available. It was named after its discoverer, a German provincial governor, Adalbert Saint Paul-Illaire. (*Saintpaulia ionantha*. Family: *Gesneriaceae*.) » perennial; violet

Africar A basic car specifically designed in the mid-1980s for operation in Africa. The hope was to produce a machine that could eventually be mass-produced in Africa, requiring minimal maintenance and using easily available spare parts. It was designed so that it could easily be extended to carry greater loads, giving increased flexibility. The design is still being evaluated. » car [i]

Afrika Corps A German expeditionary force of two divisions under the command of Rommel, sent to N Africa (Mar 1941) to reinforce Italian troops there. It had been given special desert training in Germany, and proved highly effective in desert warfare between 1941 and 1944. » North African Campaign; Rommel; World War 2

Afrikaans South African or Cape Dutch, the language of Dutch colonization, and a variety of West Germanic, but with many loanwords from Bantu and other languages. It became a written language in the late 19th-c. In the Namaland region of SW Africa, there is an Afrikaans-based pidgin, used in communication between tribesmen and Afrikaners. » Afrikaners; Dutch; Germanic languages

Afrikaners An early 18th-c term to describe those Europeans who had been born in the Dutch colony at the Cape and were therefore 'Africans', also known as **Boers** (Dutch 'farmers'). They emerged as a separate people derived from an admixture of Dutch, German, French, and non-White. During the 18th-c they penetrated the interior of the Cape as pastoral farmers. After 1835, groups left Cape Colony and established independent republics in the interior, which later coalesced into the Orange Free State and the South African Republic. After the Boer War (1899–1902) the British hoped to encourage emigration to South Africa, transforming the Afrikaners into a minority. Such large-scale emigration failed to materialize, and after the Union of South Africa in 1910 the Afrikaners became the dominant force in White South African politics. Never a monolithic force, they have produced repeated political fission in the search for security against the African majority. » Afrikaans; apartheid; Boer Wars; Great Trek; Smuts

Afro-Asiatic languages The major language family in N Africa, the E horn of Africa, and SW Asia. It comprises more than 200 languages, spoken by 200 million people. The major sub-group is the Semitic family, consisting principally of Arabic, Hebrew, Tigrinya, and Amharic. Egyptian is now extinct. Amongst other sub-groups are Cushitic, Berber, and Chadic. » African languages; Amhara; Arabic; Aramaic; Berber; Chadic; Egyptian; Hebrew; Tigre

Afsluitdijk Sea Dam [**ahf**slerdiyk] A sea dam built (1927–32) across the Zuider Zee to facilitate land reclamation; length 32 km/20 ml. » dam; Zuider Zee

afterburning A method of increasing the thrust of a jet engine. Fuel is injected into the hot exhaust gases leaving the engine, thereby igniting the fuel and providing extra thrust. » jet engine [i]

AFV » **armoured fighting vehicle**

Aga Khan Title of the hereditary head of the Ismailian sect of Muslims, notably **Aga Khan III** (1877–1957), in full **Aga Sultan Sir Mohammed Shah**, born at Karachi, who succeeded to the title in 1885. He worked for the British cause in both World Wars, and in 1937 was president of the League of Nations. He owned several Derby winners. He died at Versoix, Switzerland, and was succeeded as 49th Imam by his grandson, **Aga Khan IV** (1936–), **Karim**, the son of Aly Khan. » League of Nations

Agadir [aga**deer**] 30°30N 9°40W, pop (1982) 110 479. Seaport in Sud province, W Morocco; on the Atlantic coast, 8 km/5 ml N of the mouth of the R Sous; named Santa Cruz by the Portuguese, 1505–41; taken by the French in 1913; extensive rebuilding after earthquake in 1960; airport; fishing, tourism; 16th-c kasbah fortress; African People's Arts Festival (Jul). » Morocco [i]

Agamemnon [aga**mem**non] King of Argos and commander of the Greek army in the Trojan War. Homer calls him 'king of men'. On his return home he was murdered by his wife Clytemnestra. » Aegisthus; Clytemnestra; Trojan War

agamid [**ag**amid] A lizard native to Africa (except Madagascar), S and SE Asia, and Australia; body usually broad, head large, scales with ridges and spines; tongue thick and fleshy; tail cannot be shed; some species able to change colour; also known as **chisel-tooth lizard**. (Family: *Agamidae*; 300 species.) » bearded/flying/frilled lizard; lizard [i]; Moloch (reptile)

Agaña [a**gah**nya] 13°28N 144°45E, pop (1980) 881. Port and capital town of Guam, Mariana Is, W Pacific Ocean; taken by Japan, 1941; destroyed during its recapture by the USA, 1944; university (1952); US naval base; cathedral (1669). » Guam

agapanthus » **African lily**

Agassiz, Jean Louis Rodolphe (1807–73) Swiss naturalist and glaciologist, born at Motier, who became professor of natural history at Harvard. He graduated in medicine in 1830, working in Paris and Neuchâtel on fossil and freshwater fishes, and on the glacial phenomena of the Alps, before moving to the USA (1848). He is best known for his ideas (since confirmed) about the occurrence of ice ages in N Europe and the USA. He died in Boston, Massachusetts. » ice age

agate A form of chalcedony, a fine-grained variety of the mineral quartz. It is formed in cavities, and characterized by fine colour-banding of successive growth layers. Colour variations result in semi-precious stones such as onyx (white/grey), carnelian (red), and chrysoprase (apple-green). » chalcedony; silica; quartz; Plate V

Agatha, St (?–251), feast day 5 February. A beautiful Sicilian who is said to have rejected the love of the Prefect Quintilianus, and suffered a cruel martyrdom in 251. She is the patron saint of Catania, and is invoked against fire and lightning.

agave [uh**gay**vee] An evergreen perennial native to S USA, Central America, and N South America; stems very short, tough; leaves sword-shaped, often spiny on margins, thick, fleshy and waxy, forming a rosette. The plant grows for many years, adding a few leaves and building up reserves each year, finally producing a huge branched inflorescence up to 7 m/23 ft high, with many flowers, after which it dies. Many species produce useful fibres such as henequen. In Mexico, the sap of several species is fermented to produce pulque; stems and leaf bases are used to make mescal, an alcoholic drink of which tequila is one variety. (Genus: *Agave*, 300 species. Family: *Agavaceae*.) » century plant; evergreen plants; fibre; inflorescence [i]; perennial

Agee, James [**a**jee] (1909–55) US novelist, born at Knoxville, Tennessee, and educated at Harvard. He worked for a time as a journalist with *Fortune* and *Time* magazines. He is best-known for *Let us Now Praise Famous Men* (1941), a documentary account of sharecroppers in the deep South during the Depression, with photographs by Walker Evans; and *A Death in the Family* (1955), a semi-autobiographical novel about his father's death. He was also a celebrated film critic, see *Agee on Film* (1958). He died in New York City. » American literature; novel

Agence France Press (AFP) An international news agency, with headquarters in Paris. The direct successor to Havas (established in 1832), AFP is the oldest surviving world agency, and one of the largest. » news agency

Agent Orange (2,4,5-T or 2,4,5-trichlorophenoxy acetic acid) A herbicide used as a defoliant in jungle warfare, such as by the British in Malaya and the USA in Vietnam. Its name derives from the orange rings painted around the containers used in Vietnam. It is toxic to humans because it contains traces of dioxin, which produces severe skin eruptions (*chloracne*), and also birth abnormalities and cancer in laboratory animals. » chemical warfare; defoliant; dioxin; herbicide

Agesilaus [ajeesi**lay**us] (444–360 BC) King of Sparta (399–360 BC). Initially an active and successful defender of Spartan interests, both in Asia Minor (396–395 BC) and mainland Greece, he ultimately brought about her total eclipse by precipitating the Battle of Leuctra against Thebes (371 BC). He died fighting overseas, trying to raise money for the state he had helped to impoverish. » Epaminondas; Peloponnesian War

Aggeus [**a**gayuhs] » **Haggai, Book of**

aggiornamento [ajawna**men**toh] The process of making the life, doctrine, and worship of the Roman Catholic Church effective in the modern world. This was initiated by Pope John XXIII at the Second Vatican Council. » John XXIII; Roman Catholicism; Vatican Councils

agglomerate Coarse volcanic rock that consists of a mixture of fragments of various sizes and shapes. It is usually deposited as part of a volcanic cone and derived from the rocks through which the volcanic magma has travelled on its way to the surface. » volcano

agglutinating language A type of language in which words are typically made up of sequences of elements, as in English *de-human-ize*. Such languages are at the opposite extreme from *fusional* languages, in which there is no necessary one-to-one correspondence between the string of elements and the total meaning of the word. » fusional language

Agincourt, Battle of (1415) A battle between France and England during the Hundred Years' War. Henry V of England was forced to fight near Hesdin (Pas-de-Calais) by the French who, ignoring the lessons of Crécy and Poitiers (1356), pitched cavalry against dismounted men-at-arms and archers. Though heavily outnumbered, the English won another overwhelming victory, and returned in 1417 to begin the systematic conquest of Normandy. » Crécy, Battle of; Henry V; Hundred Years' War

Agitprop An abbreviation for the **Department of Agitation and Propaganda**, established in 1920 as a section of the Central Committee Secretariat of the Soviet Communist Party. Its role was to ensure the compatibility of activities within society with Communist Party ideology. The term later came to be widely used in an artistic or literary context for works which adopted an ideological stance. » communism; ideology

Agnesi, Maria Gaetana [an**yay**zee] (1718–99) Italian scholar, a native of Milan, remarkable alike as linguist, philosopher, mathematician, and theologian. When her father was disabled, she took his place as professor of mathematics at Bologna (1750).

Agnew, Spiro T(heodore) (1918–) US Republican Vice-President, born in Baltimore, son of a Greek immigrant. After service in World War 2, he studied at Baltimore, and in 1966 was elected Governor of Maryland on a liberal platform, introducing anti-racial-discrimination legislation. By 1968, his attitude to such problems as race rioting and civil disorders had become much more conservative. As a compromise figure acceptable to most shades of Republican opinion, he was Nixon's running-mate in the 1968 election, and took office as Vice-President in 1969. He resigned in 1973. » Nixon; Republican Party

Agni [**uh**gni] The Hindu god of fire, especially important to the priesthood, because in the fire-cult he takes offerings and sacrifices to the gods. More hymns are addressed to him than to any other god. His chariot is drawn by red horses, and clears a way through the jungle by burning: but he is welcome in every home as a principle of life and because he drives away demons. » Hinduism; Veda

Agnon, Shmuel Yosef, originally **Shmuel Czaczkes** (1888–1970) Israeli writer, born at Buczacz, Galicia (now Poland). He went to Palestine in 1907, studied in Berlin (1913–24), then settled permanently in Jerusalem and changed his surname to Agnon. He wrote several volumes of short stories, and an epic trilogy of novels on Eastern European Jewry in the early 20th-c, culminating in *Tmol Shilshom* (1945, The Day Before Yesterday). The first Israeli to win a Nobel Prize for Literature (1966), he died in Jerusalem. » Hebrew literature

agnosia [ag**noh**zia] A condition found in some brain-damaged individuals, whereby they are unable to recognize objects despite adequate basic visual and intellectual abilities. It is often specific to a particular sensory modality; for example a patient might be able to recognize by touch but not by sight. » neuropsychology

agnosticism Strictly, the view that God's existence cannot be known (*theism*) nor denied (*atheism*). The term was derived from the 'unknown' God in *Acts* 17.23, and first used (by T H Huxley) in 1869: agnostics were contrasted with 'gnostics', or metaphysicians. It was later extended to include the view that knowledge must be restricted to what is available to the senses, and that anything not so available (including therefore religion and God) is irrelevant to life today. » atheism; God; Huxley, T H; theism

Agostini, Giacomo [aguh**stee**nee] (1943–) Italian motorcyclist, born at Lovere, Bergamo. He won a record 15 world titles between 1966 and 1975, including the 500 cc title a record eight times (1966–72, 1975); 13 of the titles were on an MV Agusta, the others on a Yamaha. He won 10 Isle of Man TT Races (1966–75), including the Senior TT five times (1968–72). After retirement in 1975 he became manager of the Yamaha racing team. » motorcycle

agouti [a**goo**tee] A cavy-like rodent, native to C and S America and Caribbean Is; length, 500 mm/20 in; rat-like with long legs and minute black tail. (Genus: *Dasyprocta*, 11 species. Family: *Dasyproctidae*.) » cavy; rodent

Agra [**ah**gra] 27°17N 77°58E, pop (1981) 770 000. City in Uttar Pradesh, NE India, 190 km/118 ml SSE of Delhi; founded, 1566; Mughal capital until 1659; taken by the British, 1803; seat of the government of North-West Provinces (1835–62); airfield; railway; university (1927); commerce, glass and leather crafts, carpets; Taj Mahal (1632–54), Pearl Mosque of Shah Jahan, Mirror Palace (Shish Mahal), a world heritage site; Great Mosque, fort (16th-c), tomb of Akbar to the N at Sikandra. » Akbar the Great; Taj Mahal; Uttar Pradesh

agranulocytosis [aygranyoolohsiy**toh**sis] A clinical condition in which granulocytes (a type of white cell) disappear from the blood, and leave the patient vulnerable to infection. It has many causes, including certain drugs and diseases that damage the bone marrow. » blood

agraphia » **dysgraphia**

agribusiness The combined businesses of: farmers, who produce commodities; input industries, which supply them with equipment, chemicals, and finance; and merchants, processors, and distributors, who convert commodities into foodstuffs, ready for sale to consumers. In most countries the agribusiness sector employs more labour and generates more income than any other sector of the economy. » agriculture

agrichemicals Farm inputs derived from the chemical industry – in particular, inorganic fertilizers and sprays. » fertilizer

Agricola, Georgius (Lat), **Georg Bauer** (Ger) (1494–1555) German mineralogist, born at Glauchau, Saxony. He studied at Leipzig, Bologna, and Padua, and in 1527 was appointed city physician in Joachimstal. After moving to Chemnitz in 1533, he devoted himself to the study of mining. He made the first scientific classification of minerals in *De natura fossilium* (1546, On the Nature of Fossils), based on the observation of their physical properties. Of his many books, the best known is *De re metallica* (1556), a treatise on the arts of mining and smelting. He died at Chemnitz. » mineralogy

Agricola, Gnaeus Julius (40–93) Rome's longest-serving and most successful governor in Britain (78–84). He skilfully implemented a two-pronged policy, of conquest in the N and Romanization in the S. He subdued N England and Lowland Scotland, and actively encouraged the development of Roman-style towns in the S. Though his plans to conquer the extreme N of Scotland and Ireland came to nothing, the circumnavigation of Britain by his fleet greatly impressed contemporaries. Recalled c.84 by Emperor Domitian, probably out of jealousy, he lived quietly in retirement in Rome until his death. » Domitian; Britain, Roman

Agricola, Johann, real name **Schneider** or **Schnitter**, also called **Magister Islebius** (1492–1566) German reformer, born at Eisleben, one of the most zealous founders of Protestantism. Having studied at Wittenberg and Leipzig, he was sent by Luther to Frankfurt (1525) to institute Protestant worship there. In 1536 he was appointed to a chair at Wittenberg, but he resigned this in 1540 for his doctrinal opposition to Luther. He died while court preacher at Berlin. He wrote many theological books, and made a collection of German proverbs. » Luther; Protestantism; Reformation

agricultural controls Most commonly, UK government wartime controls over production and pricing, which continued until 1953. The agricultural industry still faces controls, but these are now mainly concerned with the restriction of surplus production through quotas and set-aside schemes, and with disease prevention and control. » Common Agricultural Policy; set-aside policy

Agricultural Revolution The name popularly given to a series of changes in farming practice occurring first in England and later throughout W Europe. Some historians date these as far back as the end of the 16th-c, but the term usually covers the period 1700–1850. The main changes included: greater intensity of productive land use; the reduction of fallow land and waste lands; the introduction of crop rotation; the development of artificial grasses; and scientific animal breeding. Many such changes were facilitated by the replacement of open fields by enclosures. They also depended upon tenant farming and market production replacing subsistence and peasant agriculture. The widespread use of mechanized farming techniques, such as threshing machines and mechanical ploughs, mostly post-dated the changes of this agricultural revolution. » agriculture; Industrial Revolution

agriculture The cultivation of crops and the keeping of domesticated animals for food, fibre, or power. Agriculture enabled primitive people, who depended on hunting, fishing, and gathering, to settle down in communities, which could then grow as their agricultural productivity grew. This was aided by the development of such implements as ploughs, hoes, and sickles – and in drier countries by the construction of irrigation systems.

In mediaeval Britain, agriculture was based on the manorial three-field system, growing two crops of cereals, followed by a year's fallow. Livestock were grazed on the common pastures, but lack of winter feed kept productivity low. Enclosures in the 16th–18th-c made experimentation easier, particularly in the selective breeding of livestock. New rotations, which included turnips as a winter livestock feed, also contributed to a rapid improvement in agricultural productivity. In 1985, 35% of the world's land area was in agricultural production – 11% in crops and 25% in permanent pasture. Nearly 5% of this land was irrigated. World agricultural production is dominated by cereals: total world cereal production in 1987 was nearly 1.8 billion tonnes. China was the largest producer (359 million tonnes), followed by the USA (279 million tonnes); W Europe produced 185 million tonnes. » agricultural controls; Agricultural Revolution; arable farming; Common Agricultural Policy; crop rotation; livestock farming; soil science; subsistence agriculture

agrimony [**a**grimuhnee] An erect perennial growing to 60 cm/2 ft, native to Europe, W Asia, and N Africa; leaves hairy, pinnate with pairs of small leaflets alternating with large ones; flowers 5–8 mm/0.2–0.3 in diameter, 5-petalled, yellow, in a long terminal spike. The fruit is a burr with hooked spines around the top. (*Agrimonia eupatoria*. Family: *Rosaceae*.) » perennial; pinnate

Agrippa » **Herod Agrippa 1/2**

Agrippa, Marcus Vipsanius (c.63–12 BC) Roman general, administrator and right-hand man of Octavian (later, the Emperor Augustus). The architect of Octavian's victory at Actium (31 BC), Agrippa subsequently used his great wealth to popularize the new regime by vastly improving the public amenities of Rome. Through his marriage with Augustus' daughter, Julia, he gave Rome the Emperors Gaius (Caligula) and Nero. » Actium, Battle of; Augustus; Caligula; Julia; Maecenas; Nero

Agrippina the Elder (c.14 BC–AD 33) The granddaughter of Roman Emperor Augustus, and mother of three potential imperial heirs. She became the focal point of opposition to the Emperor Tiberius after the suspicious death of her husband, the charismatic heir apparent, Germanicus (AD 19), and hence the chief target of his henchman, Sejanus. Banished to the barren island of Pandateria (AD 29), she died there of voluntary starvation. » Caligula; Germanicus Caesar; Sejanus; Tiberius

Agrippina the Younger (15–59) The eldest daughter of Agrippina (the Elder) and Germanicus, and mother of the Emperor Nero by her first husband Cnaeus Domitius Ahenobarbus. In 54 she ruthlessly engineered Nero's succession to the throne by supplanting the true heir Britannicus, and poisoning the reigning Emperor Claudius, her husband at the time. Initially she ruled as virtual co-regent with Nero, but he tired of her influence and had her murdered. » Claudius; Nero

agronomy The theory and practice of field-crop production and soil management. The subject embraces several disciplines, including plant breeding, plant physiology, and soil conservation. » arable farming; soil science

Aguinaldo, Emilio (1870–1964) Filipino revolutionary, born near Cavite, Luzon, Philippines. He led the rising against Spain (1896–8), and against the USA (1899–1901). After capture in 1901, he took the oath of allegiance to America, and became a private citizen. He died in Manila.

Agulhas, Cape [a**goo**lyas] 34°50S 20°00E. The most southerly point of the African continent, 160 km/100 ml ESE of the Cape of Good Hope, South Africa; running past it, round the whole S coast, is a reef, the Agulhas Bank, an important fishing ground. » Africa

Ahab [**ay**hab] (9th-c BC) Son and successor of Omri as King of Israel (c.871–c.852 BC). His reign was marked by frequent battles against Syria, conflict with Assyria, and a religious crisis when his wife Jezebel supported the worship of Baal in opposition to Yahweh (the God of Israelite religion). He was often in conflict with the prophet Elijah, and is harshly judged in 1 *Kings* 17–22. » Baal; Bible; Elijah; Kings, Books of; Moabite Stone

Ahaggar or **Hoggar Mountains** [aha**gah**] Mountain range in S Algeria, N Africa; rises to 2 918 m/9 573 ft at Mt Tahat, the highest point in Algeria; peaks rise from a plateau with a mean elevation of c.2 000 m/6 500 ft; includes the 'mountain of goblins', Garet el Djenoun (2 327 m/7 634 ft), according to legend a holy mountain. » Algeria [i]

Aharonov-Bohm effect [aharonof **bohm**] An effect produced when a single electron beam is divided into two parts, passing either side of a solenoid containing a magnetic field, and recombining at a screen beyond. A quantum mechanical interference pattern is produced which is sensitive to the magnetic vector potential rather than to the magnetic field. It reveals the nature of the interaction between wave function and electromagnetic influence. The effect, first described in 1959 by Yakir Aharonov and David Bohm, has been confirmed experimentally. » electron; magnetic vector potential; quantum mechanics; solenoid

Ahimsa [ah**him**sa] The principle of respect for all life and the practice of non-injury to living things, found in certain Hindu sects, Buddhism, and especially Jainism. It is based on the belief that violence has harmful effects on those who commit it, including an unfavourable future rebirth. The rule of non-violence was applied by Mahatma Gandhi in the political sphere during India's struggle for independence. » Buddhism; Gandhi; Hinduism; Jainism; Karma

Ahmadabad or **Ahmedabad** [**ah**madabad] 23°00N 72°40E, pop (1981) 2 515 000. Commercial centre and industrial city in Gujarat, W India; on the R Sabarmati, 440 km/273 ml N of Bombay; founded, 1411; fell to the Mughals, 1572; British trading post, 1619; centre of Gandhi's activities during the 1920s and 1930s; airfield; railway; university (1949); textiles; several temples, mosques, forts; Gandhi's Sabarmati Ashram. » Gandhi; Gujarat

Ahmadiyya [ah**mahd**iya] or **Ahmadis** An Islamic religious movement founded in India by Mirza Ghulam Ahmad (c.1839–1908), believed to be the Messiah Mahdi. Rejected by orthodox Islam, the sect is marked by its missionary zeal. It is active in Asia, Africa, and Europe. » Islam; Mahdi

Ahmose I (16th-c BC) Ruler of Egypt (c.1570–1546 BC). He was the dynast of Thebes who drove the Hyksos from Egypt, and who became the first pharaoh of the 18th dynasty and the New Kingdom. » Egyptian history, Ancient [i]; Hyksos

Ahriman [**ah**riman] The supreme evil spirit, Angra Mainyu, the Lord of darkness and death in Zoroastrianism. Ahriman is engaged in a continuing struggle with Ahura Mazda, Zoroaster's name for God. » Ahura Mazda; Zoroastrianism

Ahura Mazda [**ah**hoora **maz**da] ('Wise Lord') The name for God used by Zoroaster and his followers. The world is the arena for the battle between Ahura Mazda and Ahriman, the spirit of evil; a battle in which Ahura Mazda will finally prevail and become fully omnipotent. » Ahriman; Zoroastrianism

Ahvenanmaa [**ah**venanma], Swedish **Åland** [**aw**land] pop (1982) 23 196; area 1 552 sq km/599 sq ml. Island group forming a district of Finland, in the Gulf of Bothnia between Sweden and Finland; capital, Maarianhamina; 6 554 islands, 80 inhabited; first language, Swedish. » Bothnia, Gulf of; Finland [i]

AI » **artificial intelligence**

Aidan, St (?–651), feast day 31 August. Irish monk who became Bishop of Northumbria. He was sent from Iona in 635 as bishop to found the Northumbrian Church in England. He established the monastery at Lindisfarne, and made many missionary journeys to the mainland. He died at Bamburgh. » missions, Christian; monasticism; Northumbria

AIDS An acronym of **acquired immune deficiency syndrome**, the result of infection with a human immune deficiency virus (HIV). Groups at high risk of acquiring the disease are homosexual or bisexual men, individuals with a history of intravenous drug abuse, sufferers from haemophilia who have received many transfusions of blood or of coagulation factor VIII prior to 1986, persons who have had casual sexual relationships especially in sub-Saharan Africa, San Francisco, or New York, and sexual partners and children of any of these.

The origin of HIV virus is unknown, but it is possible that it originated from a group of African monkeys, themselves immune to the disease. In humans, transmission is by direct blood or seminal contact. The virus enters cells of the immune system, notably T-helper cells and macrophages, which engulf bacteria and cell debris. In this way the defence of the body against infection is slowly destroyed. Infected individuals may remain free from symptoms and show HIV antibodies only in the blood. With the passage of months or years, infections from organisms that usually do not cause illness develop, along with a rare form of skin cancer. Lymph nodes throughout the body enlarge, and dementia occurs. Mortality is high. » blood; semen; Plate XIII

Aiken, Conrad (Potter) (1889–1973) US poet, novelist, and critic, born at Savannah, Georgia. Educated at Harvard, he lived in both the UK and USA until 1947, when he settled in Massachusetts. Much influenced by T S Eliot, his *Selected Poems* won the 1930 Pulitzer Prize. He died at Savannah. » American literature; Eliot, T S

aikido An ancient Japanese art of self-defence, a combination of karate and judo deriving from ancient jujitsu. There are two main systems, *tomiki* and *uyeshiba*. » judo; jujitsu; karate; martial arts

Ailred of Rievaulx, St, also **Aelred** or **Ethelred** (1109–66), feast days 12 January, 3 March. English chronicler, born at Hexham, Northumberland, who became a Cistercian monk (later, abbot) at Rievaulx Abbey, Yorkshire, where he died. He wrote many sermons and historical works, and biographies of St Edward and St Ninian. » Cistercians

Ainu [iynoo] Historically a physically distinct people in Japan, but now intermarried with other Japanese and culturally assimilated; their own language and religion has largely disappeared. Traditionally hunters and fishermen, today many are factory workers and labourers. » Japan [i]

air » **atmosphere** [i]

air-cushion vehicle » **hovercraft** [i]

air force The branch of the armed forces which operates aircraft and missiles. The first air forces were founded 1911–14. During World War 1 these fledgling air arms became major military organizations engaged in prosecuting war in the air. Air forces proved decisive to the outcome of World War 2, whether they fought in a tactical role (fighters and short-range ground-attack aircraft), strategically (long-range bombers), or at sea (coastal and carrier-based aviation). The advent of atomic weapons post-1945 changed air forces from being newcomers to warfare into the elite of military establishments. In the USA the US Air Force (USAF) was split from the Army in 1947, and in the 1950s was given responsibility for the US long-range nuclear missile force. It is now the most powerful air force in the world, with over 4 500 combat aircraft and over 1 000 long-range missiles. The former Soviet air force deployed over 8 000 (mostly tactical) combat aircraft. The US, Royal, Russian, and French navies maintain separate, sea-warfare oriented air forces with great striking power in their own right. » aircraft carrier; Eurofighter; Luftwaffe; Royal Air Force; Royal Australian Air Force; United States military academies

air resistance » **drag**

Airborne Warning and Control System (AWACS) An aircraft-mounted radar system able to detect and track hostile intruders at long range and direct friendly fighters to intercept them. The US air force operates the Boeing E-3 Sentry AWACS. The Sentry is also flown by a joint European NATO unit, has been supplied to Saudi Arabia, and is on order for the British and French air forces.

airbrush A miniature spray-gun used to create smoother tonal transitions and more delicate colour effects than are possible with a conventional brush. The technique is mainly used by commercial illustrators. » paint

aircraft Any vehicle designed to operate within the Earth's atmosphere, supporting itself by means of lift generated by wings or other methods. » aeroplane; airship; autogiro; balloon; glider; hang glider [i]; helicopter; seaplane; STOL; VTOL

aircraft carrier A naval vessel on which aircraft can take off and land, developed during World War 1. The first carrier, HMS *Furious* (1918), was a battle-cruiser with forward and after flight decks. The alighting aircraft had to fly alongside and sideslip onto the deck, forward of the bridge. *Furious* was reconstructed in 1925 and fitted with an island bridge layout on the starboard side of a continuous flight deck. This became the conventional carrier design. The USA and Japan rapidly developed the carrier to hold many more aircraft, and during World War 2 US supremacy in the use of aircraft carriers was a deciding factor in reversing the fortunes of war in the Pacific. Britain's later significant contributions were the steam catapult, the angled flight deck, and the mirror landing sight. The USA now have the five largest carriers. The USS *Nimitz* (91 487 tons displacement) has 260 000 shaft horsepower, is 323 m/1 092 ft long, has a crew of 5 684, and carries over 90 aircraft. The first nuclear-powered carrier, the USS *Enterprise*, was completed in 1961. » warships [i]

Airedale terrier A breed of dog; black and tan, thick wiry coat, stiff erect tail, small ears, short beard on chin; largest terrier; developed in Airedale Valley (England) by crossing large hunting terriers (now extinct) and foxhounds. » dog; foxhound; terrier

airship A self-propelled steerable aircraft whose lift is generated by using lighter-than-air gases to provide buoyancy. The main body is cigar-shaped, with engines and gondolas (cabins) being suspended from it. There are three types of airship construction: *rigid*, *semi-rigid*, and *non-rigid*. In the first type, the body shape is maintained by a rigid frame, with the lift being provided by individual gas cells fitted within the envelope defined by the frame. In the non-rigid (*blimp*) type, the shape of the body is maintained by using the pressure of the gas. A semi-rigid type is similar to a non-rigid type, but with a keel running the length of the airship. The lighter-than-air gas used to provide buoyancy was originally hydrogen, but its highly inflammable nature and poor safety record led to its replacement by helium. Following its heyday in the 1930s, the airship has spasmodically been revived as a cheap observation and patrolling platform, but so far with only limited success. » aircraft [i]; dirigible; helium; Hindenburg; hydrogen; Zeppelin

Aisha » **Ayeshah**

Ait-Ben-Haddou [iyt ben **ha**doo] A walled village in SC Morocco; a world heritage site. It is a spectacular example of a pre-Saharan ksar, or fortified village, with red earth houses and decorated kasbahs clinging to the steep side of an escarpment. » Morocco [i]

Aix-en-Provence [eksãpro**vãs**] 43°31N 5°27E, pop (1982) 124 550. Ancient city in Bouches-du-Rhône department, SW France; 30 km/19 ml N of Marseille in a fertile plain surrounded by mountains; founded as Aquae Sextiae in 123 BC; important centre for Provençal literature since the 15th-c; airport; railway; university (1409); olive oil, fruit, almond processing; many fountains; archbishopric; 11th–16th-c St Saver Cathedral, Baroque town hall (1658), art galleries, thermal springs, casino; home of Cézanne; International Music Festival (Jul–Aug); Saison d'Aix (Jun–Sep). » Cézanne; Provence

Ajaccio [azh**ak**seeoh] 41°55N 8°40E, pop (1982) 55 279. Seaport and capital of the Island of Corsica, France; on the W coast, at the head of Golfe de Ajaccio; founded by the Genoese, 1492; made capital by Napoleon, 1811; Corsica's second largest port; airport; railway; car ferries to Marseille, Toulon, Nice; fishing, timber trade, tourism; casino; Maison Bonaparte (birthplace of Napoleon). » Corsica; Napoleon I

Ajanta Caves [aj**an**ta] A group of 29 Buddhist cave-temples and monasteries cut into cliffs over R Wagurna, near Ajanta, Maharashtra, India; a world heritage site. The caves, which were built from the 2nd-c BC onwards, are particularly noted for their wall paintings. They were abandoned in the 7th-c, when building activity was transferred to Ellora, and rediscovered in 1819. » Buddhism; Kailasa Temple; Maharashtra

Ajax [**ay**jaks] The name of two Greek heroes during the Trojan War; the Latin form of Greek **Aias**. **1** The son of Telamon, King of Salamis, therefore known as **Telamonian Ajax**. He was proverbial for his size and strength; in all the worst situations he 'stood like a tower'. When the armour of the dead Achilles was not given to him, he went mad and killed himself. » Achilles; Trojan War **2** The son of Oileus, King of Locris. When he returned from Troy, he provoked the anger of the gods, and was killed by Poseidon as he reached the shore of Greece. » Poseidon

Ajman [aj**man**] pop (1980) 36 100; area c.250 sq km/100 sq ml. Smallest of the seven member states of the United Arab Emirates, entirely surrounded by the territory of Shariqah except on the coast; capital, Ajman; relatively undeveloped, with no significant oil or gas reserves yet discovered. » United Arab Emirates [i]

Akahito, Yamabe no [ahka**hee**toh] (8th-c) Japanese major poet, one of the 'twin stars' (with Hitomaro) of the great anthology of classical Japanese poetry known as the *Manyoshu* (Collection of a Myriad Leaves). » Japanese literature

Akan A cluster of Twi (Kwa)-speaking peoples mostly in Ghana, and in the Côte d'Ivoire and Togo, comprising several kingdoms. The best-known and largest is the Asante (Ashanti). All recognize matrilineal descent, and have a long urban and trading tradition. Population c.5 million. » Ashanti; Ghana [i]; matrilineal descent

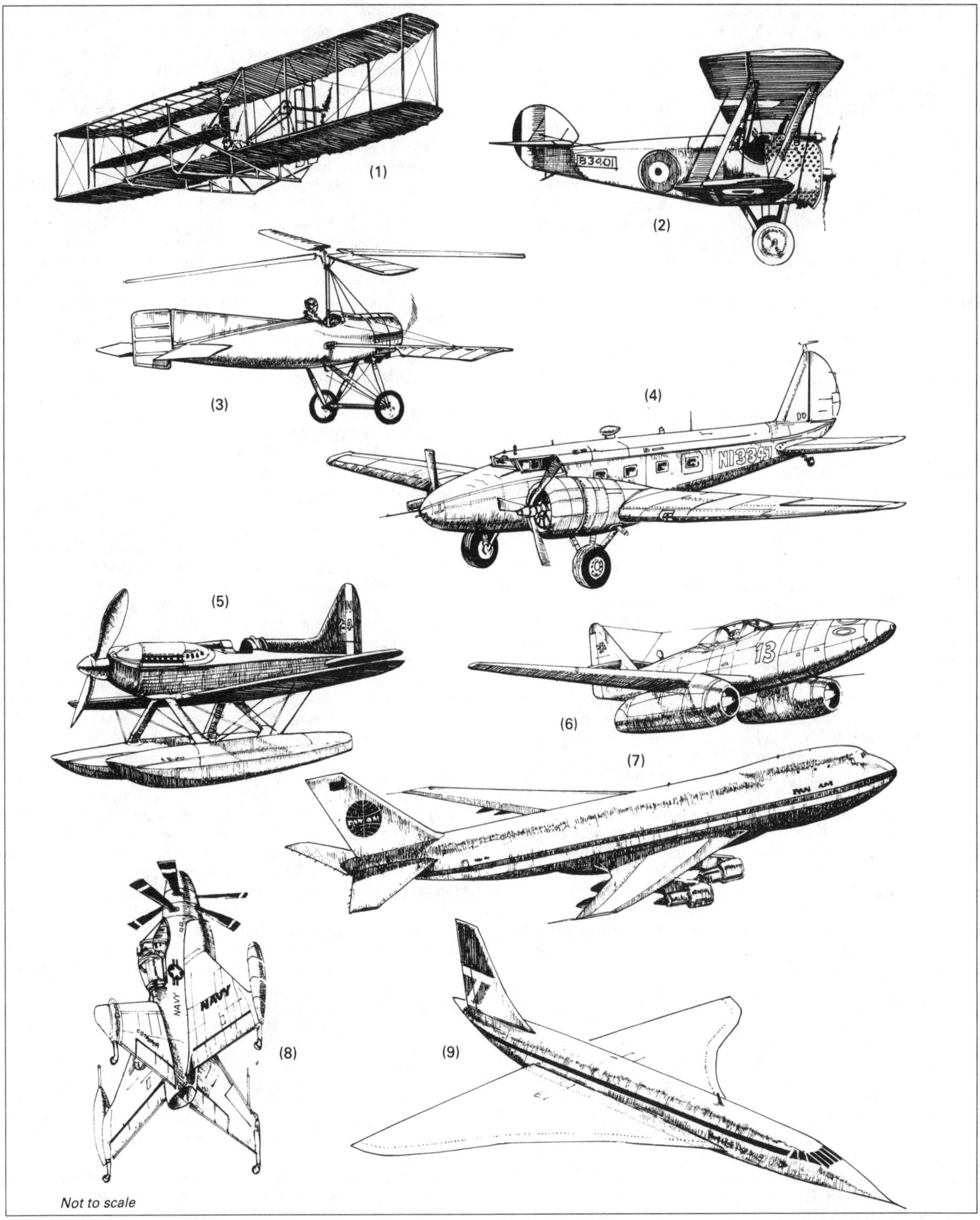

Aircraft – (1) Wright Brother's Flyer of 1903: the world's first true aeroplane.
(2) Sopwith Camel: a famous fighter of World War 1.
(3) Cievra Autogiro of 1922, invented by Juan de la Cievra. The early prototype was unable to fly because its blades were not hinged.
(4) Boeing 247. A streamlined, all-metal construction, the first of the new generation of US domestic air transports, built in 1933.
(5) Supermarine S6B, the Schneider Trophy winner of 1931. It was a predecessor of the spitfire.
(6) Me 262: the world's first operational jet aircraft. It entered service in 1944 with a maximum speed of just over 800 kph/500 mph.
(7) Boeing 747: the Jumbo Jet. It entered regular passenger service in January 1970.
(8) Convair XFY-1: Pogo. A vertical take-off aircraft of 1954 which took off and landed from its tail and wings.
(9) Concorde. A supersonic airliner, introduced in 1976, designed to travel at more than twice the speed of sound.

Akashi-Kaikyo Bridge A major steel suspension bridge across the Akashi Straits between Honshu and Shikoku, Japan, begun in 1978 and due for completion in 1998. It will carry a road and railway on two decks and have a main span of 1 780 m/5 840 ft. » bridge (engineering) [i]; Japan [i]

Akbar the Great, properly **Jalal ud-Din Muhammad Akbar** [**ak**ber] (1542–1605) Mughal Emperor of India, born at Umarkot, Sind. He succeeded his father, Humayun, in 1556, and took over the administration from his regent in 1560. Within a few years, he had gained control of the whole of India N of the Vindhya Mts. He constructed roads, established a uniform system of weights and measures, and adjusted taxation. He was unusually tolerant towards non-Muslims, and greatly encouraged literature and the arts. He died at Agra. » Mughal Empire

Akhenaton, also **Akh(e)naten** or **Amenhotep (Amenophis) IV** (14th-c BC) A king of Egypt, of the 18th dynasty, who renounced the old gods and introduced a purified and universalized solar cult. One of his wives was Nefertiti. » Egyptian history, Ancient [i]; Nefertiti; pharaoh

Akhmatova, Anna [akh**mah**tohva], pseudonym of **Anna Andreeyevna Gorenko** (1889–1966) Russian poet, born near Odessa. She remained as far as possible neutral to the revolution; but her works were condemned between 1922 and 1940, and again in 1946. Her first collections were *Vecher* (1912, Evening) and *Chyotki* (1914, Rosary). She was 'rehabilitated' in the 1950s, and received official tributes on her death, near Moscow. » Russian literature; Russian Revolution

Akihito [akee**hee**toh] (1933–) Emperor of Japan (1989–), the eldest son of Emperor Hirohito, born and educated in Tokyo, where he studied politics and economics. Invested as Crown Prince in 1952, he became the first Crown Prince to marry a commoner, **Michiko Shoda** (1934–), in 1959. He has three children: **Crown Prince Naruhito** (1960–), **Prince Fumihito** (1963–), and **Princess Sayako** (1969–). He is a regular contributor to the Japanese Icthyological Society's journal, and is especially interested in conservation. » Hirohito

Akiva ben Joseph [a**kee**va], Rabbi, also **Akibah** (c.50–135) Leading scholar and famous teacher in the formative period of rabbinic Judaism; a pupil of Rabbi Eliezer. He is credited with extensive exegetical attempts to relate Jewish legal traditions to scriptural texts, and with providing the basis for the Mishnah by his systematic grouping and codification of the *halakhoth* (legal traditions). He apparently supported the revolt against Rome under Bar Kokhbah in 132, and was martyred at the hands of the Romans soon afterwards. » Bar Kokhbah; halakhah; Judaism; Mishnah

Akkadian [a**kay**dian] One of the oldest languages in the Semitic (Afro-Asiatic) family, with a substantial literature written in cuneiform script. It is now extinct. » Afro-Asiatic languages; cuneiform [i]

Akron 41°05N 81°31W, pop(1980) 237 177. Seat of Summit County, NE Ohio, USA, on the Little Cuyahoga R; established, 1825; city status, 1865; airfield; railway; university (1913); centre of US rubber industry; metal products, tyres, machinery; polymer research centre; Goodyear World of Rubber Museum, E J Thomas Performing Arts Hall, Blossom Music Centre. » Ohio; polymerization; rubber

Akrotiri [akruh**teer**ee] Bay on S coast of Cyprus; main port town, Limassol; British base on peninsula separating Akrotiri Bay (E) from Episkopi Bay (W). » Cyprus [i]

Aksakov, Sergei (Timofeyevitch) (1791–1859) Russian novelist, born at Ufa, Orenburg. The son of a wealthy landowner, he held government posts at St Petersburg and Moscow before his meeting with Gogol in 1832 turned him to literature. His works, which include *Buran* (1834, The Blizzard) and *Semeynaya khronika* (1846–56, Chronicles of a Russian Family), show his love of country sports and deep feeling for nature. He died in Moscow. » Gogol; Russian literature

Aksum An ancient city in the highlands of N Ethiopia; a world heritage site. From the 1st–7th-c AD it was the capital of a powerful kingdom dominating trade – particularly in ivory and skins – between the Sudanese Nile Valley and the Roman Mediterranean through the Red Sea port of Adulis (near modern Massawa). Its multi-storied stone buildings, massive funeral slabs, and coinage are notable. » African history

Aktyubinsk [akty**oo**byinsk] 50°16N 57°13E, pop(1983) 218 000. Capital city of Aktyubinskaya oblast, NW Kazakhstan; in the S foothills of the Ural Mts, on the left bank of the R Ilek; established, 1869; airport; railway; engineering, agricultural machinery, chemicals, building materials, clothing, furniture, foodstuffs. » Kazakhstan

Al-Banna, Hassan (1906–49) Islamic fundamentalist, born at Mahmudiya, near Cairo, the founder in Egypt in 1928 of the Society of Muslim Brothers (better known as the Muslim Brotherhood or Brethren), which preached a return to the purity of early Islam. In 1948 the Egyptian Prime Minister, Nuqrashi Pasha, was killed by a Brotherhood member, and in 1949 al-Banna was himself murdered, though he had condemned the assassination. His movement has had considerable influence on contemporary Islamic fundamentalism. » Islam; Muslim Brotherhood

Al-Farabi, Mohammed (c.873–950) Muslim philosopher and encyclopedic writer, born at Farab, Turkey. He studied at Baghdad, and travelled widely. His main work was to integrate Greek philosophical thought with the principles of Islam. He died at Damascus. » Islam

al-Fatah » **Fatah, (al-)**

Alabama pop(1987e) 4 083 000; area 133 911 sq km/51 705 sq ml. State in SE USA, divided into 67 counties; the 'Heart of Dixie' or the 'Camellia State'; first permanent settlement by the French at Mobile, 1711; N Alabama became part of the USA in 1783, the remainder being acquired by the Louisiana Purchase in 1803; the 22nd state to be admitted to the Union, 1819; seceded, 1861; slavery abolished, 1865; refused to ratify the 14th Amendment to the US Constitution and placed under military rule, 1867; re-admitted to the Union in 1868, but Federal troops remained until 1876; capital, Montgomery; other major cities Birmingham, Mobile, Huntsville; bounded S by Florida and the Gulf of Mexico; rivers include the Alabama (formed by the confluence of the Tallapoosa and Coosa Rivers), Tombigbee, Mobile, Tennessee, Chattahoochee; highest point Mt Cheaha (734 m/2 408 ft); a mountainous NE, separated from the S coastal plain by the rolling plain of the Appalachian Piedmont; diversified agriculture, after the boll weevil blight of 1915; cattle, poultry, cotton, soybeans, peanuts; chemicals, textiles, paper products, processed food; iron and steel industry centred on Birmingham; coal, oil, stone; lumbering, fishing; many civil rights protests in the area in the 1950s and 1960s. » civil rights; cotton [i]; Montgomery (Alabama); United States of America [i]; RR38

Alabama claims (1869–72) A US/UK diplomatic dispute, arising from damage inflicted during the American Civil War by Confederate naval vessels (one named Alabama) built in Britain. It was resolved in 1872 by an international tribunal (Italy, Switzerland, Brazil), with an indemnity to the USA of $15 500 500. » American Civil War

alabaster A fine-grained banded variety of the mineral gypsum; pale and translucent. It is soft enough to be carved and polished by hand for ornamental use. » gypsum

Alaia, Azzedine [a**li**ya] Tunisian fashion designer, educated in Tunis, where he studied sculpture. He worked for Dior and other designers before giving his first show in New York City (1982). His designs emphasize the figure, and he is noted for his black leather-studded gauntlets, little black dresses, and use of zippers. » Dior; fashion

Alain-Fournier, Henri [alã foor**nyay**] (1886–1914) French writer, born in Sologne, who was killed at St Rémy in World War 1. He left a few short stories, and one completed novel, the nostalgic *Le Grand Meaulnes* (1913, trans The Lost Domain). » French literature

Alamo A battle fought during the 1836 Texan War of Independence against Mexico, when 180 Texans and US citizens held the old mission/fort of Alamo against a large number of Mexican troops. In an epic of resistance they held out for eleven days until the last survivors were overwhelmed. » Texas

Alanbrooke (of Brookeborough), Alan Francis Brooke, 1st Viscount (1883–1963) British field marshal, a leading strategist of World War 2, born at Bagnères-de-Bigorre,

France. He was educated abroad and at the Royal Military Academy, Woolwich, joined the Royal Field Artillery in 1902, and fought in World War 1. He commanded the 2nd corps of the British Expeditionary Force in France (1940), and later was Commander-in-Chief Home Forces. Chief of the Imperial General Staff 1941–6, he was Churchill's principal strategic adviser at the conferences with Roosevelt and Stalin. He was created baron (1945) and viscount (1946), and died at Hartley Wintney, Hampshire. » British Expeditionary Force; Churchill, Winston; World War 2

Åland » **Ahvenanmaa**

Alarcòn (y Ariza), Pedro Antonio de [alah**kon**] (1833–91) Spanish author, born at Guadix. After serving in the African campaign of 1859–60, he became a journalist, and later a diplomat and councillor of state. He published a war diary, travel notes and poems, but is best known for his *Sombrero de tres picos* (The Three-Cornered Hat) on which de Falla's ballet was based. He died at Valdemoro. » Spanish literature

Alarcón y Mendoza, Juan Ruiz de [alah**kon** ee men**doh**tha] (c.1580–1639) Major Spanish dramatist, born at Taxco, Mexico. He was neglected for generations save by plagiarists, but restored to his real rank by modern critics. He wrote both heroic tragedies and character comedies, notably *La verdad sospechosa* (c.1619, The Suspicious Truth). He early obtained a post in the Council of the Indies at Madrid, where he died. » Spanish literature

Alaric I (c.370–410) Chief of the Visigoths from 395, and the first Germanic conqueror of Rome. The sack of Rome by his troops in 410, the first capture of the city by foreigners in 800 years, marks the beginning of the end of the Western Roman Empire. » Roman history [i]; Stilicho

Alas (y Ureña), Leopoldo, pseudonym **Clarín** (1852–1901) Spanish author, lawyer, journalist, and critic, born at Zamora. He is mainly known for his short stories, *Cuentos morales* (1896, Moral Stories), and his novel *La Regenta* (1885, The Regent's Wife), but he also wrote treatises on law and economics. He died at Oviedo. » Spanish literature

Alaska pop (1986e) 534 000; area 1 518 748 sq km/586 412 sq ml. US state, divided into 23 boroughs, in the extreme NW corner of the continent, separated from the rest of the nation by Canada; first permanent settlement by Russians on Kodiak I, 1792; managed by the Russian-American Fur Company, 1799–1861; period of decline, as Russians withdrew from the area; bought by the USA, 1867 (known as Seward's Folly, after the chief US negotiator); gold discovered in1889 (at Nome) and 1902 (at Fairbanks); territorial status, 1912; Aleutian islands of Attu and Kiska occupied by the Japanese (Jun 1942–Aug 1943); granted statehood as the 49th state, 1959; large oil reserves discovered in 1968 (Alaska Pipeline from Prudhoe Bay to Valdez completed in 1977); the largest state, but the least populated; capital, Juneau; major city, Anchorage; bounded N by the Beaufort Sea and Arctic Ocean, W by the Chukchi Sea, Bering Strait, and Bering Sea, S by the Gulf of Alaska and the Pacific Ocean, and E by Canada (Yukon territory and British Columbia); a third of the area within the Arctic Circle; rivers include the Yukon (with tributaries the Porcupine, Tanana, and Koyukuk), Colville, Kuskokwim, Susitna and Copper; North Slope in the N, rising to the Brooks Range, part of the Rocky Mts; Kuskokwim Mts in the SW; Aleutian Is and Aleutian Range in the SW; Chugach Mts along the S coast; Wrangell Mts in the SE; highest point Mt McKinley (6 194 m/20 321 ft); oil, natural gas, wide range of minerals; food processing, paper, lumber, seafood; eight national parks; tourism; balance between industrial development and landscape preservation an ongoing controversy. » Anchorage; United States of America [i]; RR38

Alaska, Gulf of N part of the Pacific Ocean, between the Alaskan Peninsula (W) and the mainland Alaskan Panhandle (E); warm Alaskan Current keeps ports ice-free; main port, Valdez. » Alaska

Alaska Highway An all-weather road which runs from Dawson Creek in British Columbia, Canada, to Fairbanks in Alaska, linking the state to the N American highway system. It was built in 1942 to supply military forces stationed in Alaska during World War 2. » Alaska

Alaskan malamute [**mal**amyoot] A breed of dog; spitz bred by the Malamute Eskimos of Alaska as a sledge-dog (*husky*); largest sledge-dog breed; strong and active; thick grey and white coat. » husky; spitz

Alastor [**alas**taw] In Greek mythology, an avenging demon or power. The name was used by Shelley as the title of a poem outlining a myth of his own making, in which a young poet is led through various symbolic states and ultimately to destruction. » Shelley, Percy Bysshe

Alawi [**alah**wee] An alternative name for Nusayri Shiites, who currently hold power in Syria. The Syrian leader Hafez al-Asad is an Alawi (Alawite). » Shiites

Alba, Duke of » **Alva, Duque de**

Alba Iulia, Ger **Karlsburg**, Lat **Apulum** [**al**ba **yool**ya] 46°04N 23°33E, pop (1983) 59 369. Capital of Alba county, WC Romania, on the R Mureş; founded by the Romans, 2nd-c AD; former seat of the princes of Transylvania; railway; wine trade, footwear, soap, furniture; 12th-c Romanesque church, Bathyaneum building. » Romania [i]; Transylvania

Albacete [alba**thay**tay] 30°00N 1°50W, pop (1981) 117 126. Capital of Albacete province, Castilla-La Mancha, SE Spain; 251 km/156 ml SE of Madrid; bishopric; railway; footwear, clothing, tools, wine, flour, cutlery, souvenir knives; cathedral (16th-c); fairs and fiestas (Sep). » Spain [i]

albacore [**al**bakaw] Large tuna fish with long pectoral fins, widespread in open waters of tropical and warm temperate seas; length up to 1.3 m/4¼ ft, with an iridescent blue band on sides of body; extensively fished commercially, and much prized by sea anglers. (*Thunnus alalunga*. Family: *Scombridae*.) » tuna

Alban, St (3rd-c), feast day 22 June. Roman soldier, who became the first British Christian martyr. Little is known about him, but he is said to have protected a Christian priest, and been converted by him. For this he was killed by the Romans at Redbourn or St Albans in c.305. » Christianity

Albania, Albanian **Shqipni**, **Shqipri**, or **Shqipëri**, official name (1991) **Republic of Albania**, **Republica e Shqipërisë** Republic in the W part of the Balkan Peninsula, divided into 26 districts (*rrethet*); bounded on the W by the Adriatic Sea, NE by Yugoslavia, and SE by Greece; pop (1990e) 3 262 000, coastline 418 km/260 ml; area 28 748 sq km/11 097 sq ml; timezone GMT + 1; capital, Tiranë; chief towns Shkodër, Durrës, Vlorë,

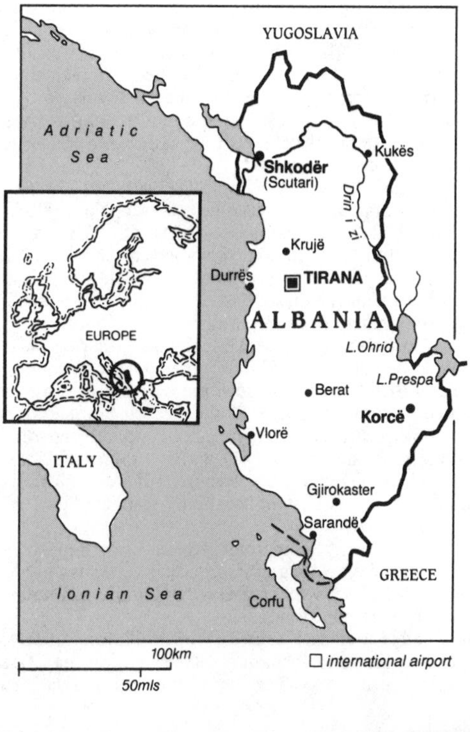

Korçë, Elbasan; unit of currency the lek (100 qintars); mainly Albanians (96%), some Greeks, Vlachs, Gypsies, and Bulgarians; language, Albanian; constitutionally an atheist state, population mainly Muslim in origin, with some Orthodox and Catholic Christians.

Physical description and climate. A mountainous country, relatively inaccessible and untravelled; N Albanian Alps rise to 2692 m/8832 ft; rivers include the Drin, Shkumbin, Seman, Vijosë; many lakes throughout the country; Mediterranean-type climate; hot and dry on the plains in summer (average Jul 24°–25°C), thunderstorms frequent; mild, damp, and cyclonic winters (average Jan 8°–9°C); winters in the mountains often severe, with snow cover lasting several months; annual mountain precipitation exceeds 1000 mm/40 in.

History and government. Independence followed the end of Turkish rule in 1912, but Italian forces occupied the country, 1914–20; became a republic in 1925, and a monarchy in 1928, under King Zog I; occupied by Germany and Italy in World War 2; new republic in 1946, headed by Enver Hoxha (until 1985); dispute with the Soviet Union in 1961; withdrew from Warsaw Pact in 1968; maintained close links with China; Socialist People's Republic instituted in 1976; first free elections, 1991; supreme legislative body is the single-chamber People's Assembly of 250 deputies, meeting twice a year; election by universal suffrage every four years; Assembly elects the Presidium, and forms the government (the Council of Ministers); effective rule exercised by the Albanian Labour Party, whose governing body is the Politburo.

Economy. The seventh 5-year plan (1981–5) particularly concerned industrial expansion, especially in oil (chiefly at Qytet Stalin, where a pipeline connects with the port of Vlorë), mining, chemicals, natural gas; hydroelectric power plants on several rivers; agricultural product processing, textiles, oil products, cement; main crops wheat, sugar-beet, maize, potatoes, fruit, grapes, oats; all industry is nationalized; also committed to eliminating private farming through the progressive transformation of farm co-operatives into state farms. » communism; socialism; Tiranë; RR24 national holidays; RR42 political leaders

Albanian The official language of Albania, spoken also by substantial numbers in neighbouring regions of Yugoslavia, Greece, and Italy – in all, some three million speakers. It is an idiosyncratic development within the Indo-European group, with no written records earlier than the 15th-c, and much interference with its present-day structure from substantial word-borrowing. » Indo-European languages

Albany (Australia) 34°57S 117°54E, pop (1981) 15222. Resort and seaport in Lower Great Southern statistical division, Western Australia; one of the oldest towns in Australia, founded in 1826; once used as a stopover point for vessels on their way to India; airfield; railway; canning, wool, agricultural trade. » Western Australia

Albany (USA) 42°39N 73°45W, pop (1980) 101727. Capital of New York State in Albany County, E New York, USA; on the Hudson R, 232 km/144 ml N of New York City; the second oldest continuously inhabited settlement in the 13 original colonies, settled by the Dutch, 1614; state capital, 1797; railway; two universities (1844, 1848); State Capitol, Schuyler Mansion; annual Tulip Festival. » New York

Albany Congress (1754) A US colonial gathering of delegates at which Benjamin Franklin proposed a 'plan of union' for the separate British colonies. Both the colonial governments and the British authorities rejected the idea. » Franklin, Benjamin

Albany Regency A US political faction centred on Martin van Buren (President 1837–41), and on the city of Albany, New York, which he made his power base. It was notorious for its use of the 'spoils system' of filling public office. » spoils system; van Buren

albatross A large, slender-winged sea-bird, wingspan up to 3 m/10 ft; glides near water in air currents; lands only to breed. (Order: *Procellariiformes* (**tubenoses**). Family: *Diomedeidae*, 14 species.) » petrel; tubenose

albedo [al**bee**doh] The ratio of the radiation reflected by a surface to the total incoming solar radiation, expressed as a decimal or percentage. The degree of reflectance varies according to the type of surface: snow-covered ice has an albedo of 0.8 (80%), a dry sandy desert 0.37 (37%), a tropical rainforest 0.13 (13%). The average planetary albedo is close to 0.3 (30%). » insolation; radiation

Albee, Edward (1928–) US dramatist, born near Washington, educated at Laurenceville and Columbia University. His major works are *The Zoo Story* (1958), a one-act duologue on the lack of communication in modern society, *The American Dream* (1960), and *Who's Afraid of Virginia Woolf?* (1962, filmed 1966), a searing analysis of a failing marriage. *Seascape* (1975) won the Pulitzer Prize. Later plays include *Finding the Sun* (1981) and *Walking* (1982). » American literature; drama

Albéniz, Isaac (Manuel Francisco) [al**bay**neeth] (1860–1909) Spanish composer and pianist, born at Camprodón, Catalonia, and died at Cambô-les-Bains, France. He studied under Liszt, becoming especially known for his picturesque piano works based on Spanish folk music. He also wrote several operas. » folk music

Alberoni, Giulio (1664–1752) Spanish-Italian cardinal and statesman, born at Firenzuola, Italy. After a diplomatic career in France and Spain, he gained the favour of Philip V, and arranged his marriage to Elizabeth Farnese (1714), daughter of the Duke of Parma. He used his influence to develop the resources of Spain, remodel the army and fleet, increase foreign trade, and extend Spanish power in Italy. His aggressive European foreign policy finally lost him Philip's support. He was banished, fled to Rome (1721), and through papal influence resumed his career in the Church. He died at Piacenza. » Philip V; Spanish Succession, War of the

Albert I (1875–1934) King of the Belgians (1909–34), born in Brussels, who succeeded his uncle, Leopold II. His bearing when his kingdom was in German hands (1914–18) and in subsequent restoration was much admired. He was killed by a fall while rock-climbing in the Ardennes. » World War 1

Albert, Prince (1819–61) Prince Consort of Queen Victoria of Great Britain, born at the Schloss Rosenau, near Coburg, Germany, the youngest son of the Duke of Saxe-Coburg-Gotha. He married his cousin, an infatuated Queen Victoria, in 1840, and became her chief adviser, first as Consort (1842), then as Prince Consort (1857). Ministerial distrust and public misgivings combined to obstruct his interference in politics, but he developed a congenial sphere of self-expression by encouraging the arts and social and industrial reforms. It was largely on his initiative that the Great Exhibition of 1851 took place. He died of typhoid at Windsor Castle, Berkshire. » Victoria, Queen

Albert, Lake, Zaire **Lake Mobuto Sésé Seko** area c.6400 sq km/2500 sq ml. Lake in EC Africa; in the W Rift Valley on the frontier between Zaire and Uganda; length, c.160 km/100 ml; width, 40 km/25 ml; altitude, 619 m/2031 ft; receives the Victoria Nile (NE) and Semliki (SW) Rivers; Albert Nile flows N; European discovery by Samuel Baker (1864); originally named after Queen Victoria's consort. » Africa; Rift Valley

Albert Medal In the UK, a civilian decoration, instituted in 1866 to commemorate the Prince Consort (1819–61), to reward gallantry in saving life. In October 1971 all surviving holders of the medal exchanged it for the George Cross. » George Cross

Albert Nile Upper reach of the R Nile in NW Uganda; issues from the NE corner of L Albert, close to the Victoria Nile Delta; flows NE into the Sudan; known in Sudan as the Bahr el Jebel until its meeting point with the Bahr el Ghazal to form the White Nile. » Uganda [i]; White Nile

Alberta pop (1981) 2237724; area 661190 sq km/255285 sq ml. Province in W Canada, bordered S by the USA; mainly a rolling plain, with edge of Rocky Mts in W; rivers, lakes, and forests in N, with much open prairie; treeless prairie in S; drained (N) by Peace, Slave, and Athabasca Rivers, and (S) by North Saskatchewan, Red Deer, and Bow Rivers (S); largest lakes, Athabasca, Claire, Lesser Slave; several national parks; capital, Edmonton; major towns, Calgary, Medicine Hat; oil, natural gas, grain, cattle, timber products, coal, food processing, chemicals, fabricated metals, tourism; originally part of Rupert's Land, granted to Hudson's Bay Company, 1670; sovereignty acquired by the Dominion, 1870; status as province, 1905; governed by a lieutenant-governor and an elected

79-member Legislative Assembly. » Canada [i]; Edmonton; Hudson's Bay Company

Alberti, Leon Battista (1404–72) Italian architect, born at Genoa, who was one of the most brilliant figures of the Renaissance, being skilled also as a musician, painter, poet, and philosopher. His designs include the churches of San Francesco at Rimini and San Maria Novella at Florence. He died in Rome.

Albertina An art gallery founded in 1768 by Duke Albert of Saxony-Tescha. Since 1795 it has been housed in the former Tarouсca Palace in Vienna. Its holdings include a vast collection of graphic material. » Vienna

Albertus Magnus, St, Count of Bollstädt (c.1200–80), feast day 15 November. German philosopher, bishop, and doctor of the church, often called the 'Doctor Universalis' (Universal Doctor), born at Lauingen. He studied at Padua, and joined the Dominican order, becoming a teacher of theology. His most famous pupil was Thomas Aquinas. In 1254 he became provincial of the Dominicans in Germany, and in 1260 was named Bishop of Ratisbon. In 1262 he retired to his convent at Cologne to devote himself to literary pursuits, and died there. He excelled all his contemporaries in the breadth of his learning, and helped to bring together theology and Aristotelianism. He was canonized in 1932. » Aquinas; Aristotle; Dominicans; scholasticism; theology

Albigenses [albi**jen**seez], or **Albigensians** Followers of a form of Christianity which in the 11th-c and 12th-c especially had its main strength in the town of Albi, SW France. It was derived from 3rd-c followers of the Persian religious teacher, Mani, whose ideas gradually spread along trade routes to Europe, especially Italy and France. Also known as **Cathari** or **Bogomiles**, they believed life on Earth to be a struggle between good (spirit) and evil (matter). In extreme cases, they were rigidly ascetic, with marriage, food, and procreation all condemned. They believed in the transmigration of souls. Condemned by Rome and the Inquisition, they were devastated in the early 13th-c crusade against them, which also broke down the distinctive civilization of Provence, France. » Cathars; Christianity; Inquisition; soul (religion)

albinism A common inherited pigmentary disorder of vertebrates: affected individuals lack pigmentation of the skin, hair, eyes (iris), feathers, or scales. The disorder can be harmful, as the missing pigments protect against sunlight and/or provide camouflage against predators. Albinism is found in all human races: the absence of pigment (or *melanin*) results in white hair, pink skin, and pink irises. Varying degrees of non-pigmentation occur. » melanins; pigments; skin [i]

albino horse A breed of horse; white with pale blue or brown eyes; developed in USA by deliberately cross-breeding naturally occurring albino individuals of other breeds. » albinism; horse [i]

Albinus » **Alcuin**

Albufeira [alboo**fay**ra] 37°05N 8°15W, pop (1981) 14 196. Fishing village and resort, Faro district, S Portugal; 43 km/27 ml W of Faro, in a bay on the S coast; figs, almonds; Moorish-style architecture; Portugal's busiest seaside resort. » Portugal [i]

albumins [**al**byoominz] Part of a system of classification of simple proteins, usually referring to those proteins that are readily soluble in water and in dilute salt solutions. They are present in most animals and plants. Two important albumins are serum albumin (in blood), and lactalbumin (in milk). » blood; milk; protein

Albuquerque, Affonso d' [alboo**ker**kay], called **the Great** (1453–1515) Portuguese Viceroy of the Indies, born near Lisbon. He landed on the Malabar coast of India in 1502, and conquered Goa, Ceylon, the Sundra Is, Malacca, and (in 1515) the island of Hormuz in the Persian Gulf. He gained a reputation for wisdom and justice, but through his enemies at court he was replaced in office, and died soon afterwards at sea near Goa. » Goa, Daman, and Diu

Albuquerque [albuh**ker**kee] 35°05N 106°39W, pop (1980) 331 767. Seat of Bernalillo County, C New Mexico, USA, on the Rio Grande; largest city in the state; settled, 1706; later a military post during the Mexican War, 1846–70; city status, 1890; airport; railway; two universities (1889, 1940); agricultural trade, electronics, processed foods; base for many federal agencies (eg Atomic Energy Commission); health resort; tourism; church of San Felipe de Neri (1706), the Old Town Plaza, National Atomic Museum; Feria Artesana (Aug), International Balloon Fiesta (Oct). » New Mexico

Alcaeus [al**kay**us] Greek lyric poet, who flourished in Mitylene c.600 BC. He was the inventor of Alcaic verse, which Horace transferred into Latin. Only fragments remain of his odes. » Greek literature; Horace; ode

Alcazar The name of several palaces built by the Moors in cities of S Spain. In 1936 the Alcazar of Toledo was the scene of a protracted siege during the Spanish Civil War. » Spanish Civil War

Alcestis [al**ses**tis] In Greek mythology, the wife of Admetus; he was doomed to die, and she saved him by offering to die in his place. The action so impressed Heracles that he wrestled with the messenger of death and brought her back to life. » Heracles

Alcibiades [alsi**biy**adeez] (c.450–404 BC) Athenian statesman and general from the aristocratic Alcmaeonid family. A ward of Pericles and a pupil of Socrates, he was a leader against Sparta in the Peloponnesian War, and a commander of the Sicilian expedition (415 BC). Recalled from there to stand trial for sacrilege, he fled to Sparta and gave advice which contributed substantially to Athens' defeat in Sicily (413 BC) and her economic discomfiture at home. Falling out with the Spartans in 412 BC, he began to direct Athenian operations in the E Aegean, and won several notable victories, but finding himself unjustly blamed for the Athenian defeat off Notium (406 BC), he went into voluntary exile, where he actively intrigued with the Persians until his assassination in 404 BC. » Alcmaeonids; Greek history; Peloponnesian War; Nicias; Pericles; Socrates; Sparta (Greek history)

Alcmaeon (of Croton) [alk**mee**on] (6th-c BC) Greek physician and philosopher of Croton, S Italy, who recognized the importance of experiment, and may have been the first to use dissection to study the human body. He was a pioneer of embryology, and carried out several studies of the sense organs. » anatomy; embryology

Alcmaeon (mythology) [alk**mee**on] In Greek mythology, the son of Amphiaraos. To avenge his father's death, he killed his mother, and was pursued by the Furies until he came to a land which had not seen the Sun at the time of his mother's death; he found this recently-emerged land at the mouth of the R Achelous. He was commanded by Apollo to lead the expedition of the Epigoni against Thebes. » Epigoni; Erinyes

Alcmaeonids [alk**miy**onidz] An aristocratic Athenian family to which many prominent Athenian politicians belonged. It was particularly influential in the period 632–415 BC. » Alcibiades; Pericles

Alcock, Sir John William (1892–1919) British airman, born in Manchester, who with Brown was the first to fly the Atlantic (14 Jun 1919). The trip, from Newfoundland to Ireland, was made in a Vickers-Vimy machine, and took 16 hours 27 minutes. Soon after, he died of injuries received in an aeroplane accident. » aircraft [i]; Brown, Arthur Whitten

alcohol strength The measurement of the amount of ethanol (the active constituent) in alcoholic drinks, commonly expressed using either volumetric measures or proof strength. The volumetric measure is becoming increasingly popular: this declares the volume of ethanol present in a unit volume of the alcoholic beverage; for example, an average red wine will contain 12% by volume ethanol or 90 millilitres of ethanol per average bottle. *Proof spirit* is a mixture containing a standard amount of ethanol: in the UK it is 57.07% by volume, while in the USA it is 50%. Thus, a bottle of Scotch which claims to be 70% proof is in fact 70% of 57.07% (volume), or 40% ethanol by volume. » alcohols; ethanol

Alcoholics Anonymous (AA) A self-help group for alcoholics trying to stop drinking. Founded in the USA in 1935 by 'Bill W' (William Griffith Wilson, (1895–1971) and 'Dr Bob S', (Robert Holbrook Smith, 1879–1950), it consists of local groups where members (identified by first names only) meet to give each other support. There are more than a million members in 92 countries. » alcoholism

alcoholism An ambiguous term, for some implying a disease, for others a severe form of alcohol dependence. It is also used as a term of opprobrium relating to anyone who has continuing difficulties associated with excessive alcohol consumption. A major limitation of the term is that it suggests a dichotomy between abstinence and moderate drinking, on the one hand, and excessive and uncontrolled drinking, on the other. 'Alcohol abuse' can be found in all social classes, though there is evidence that those suffering from anxiety or depression are most susceptible, with a recent notable increase in the disease among housewives and the young and long-term unemployed. » class; depression (psychiatry)

alcohols IUPAC **alkanols**. Generally organic compounds containing a hydroxyl (–OH) function bonded to a carbon atom which is not itself bonded to further atoms other than carbon or hydrogen. When none or one of these atoms is carbon, the alcohol is called *primary*; with two or three carbon substituents, it is *secondary* or *tertiary* respectively. Compounds in which the hydroxyl group is bonded directly to an aromatic ring are called *phenols*, and are not classed as alcohols. Characteristic reactions of alcohols include dehydration to ethers, and reaction with acids to give esters. In everyday use, the word *alcohol* is often restricted to *ethanol* (*ethyl alcohol*), CH_3CH_2OH. » ester [i]; ethanol; IUPAC; phenol

Alcott, Louisa May (1832–88) US children's writer, born at Germantown, Philadelphia. Her *Little Women* (1868–9), *Old-fashioned Girl* (1870), *Little Men* (1871), and *Jo's Boys* (1886), have charmed generations of children, and are firmly established among the classics. Her writing helped to crystallize the American middle-class ideal. She died at Concord, Massachusetts. » American literature

Alcuin, originally **Ealhwine** or **Albinus** (c.735–804) Writer, theologian, and adviser of Charlemagne, and thus a major influence on the Carolingian revival of learning. He was born at York and educated at the cloister school, of which in 778 he became master. Invited to Charlemagne's court (781), he devoted himself to the education of the royal family. As a result, the court became a school of culture for the hitherto almost barbarous Frankish Empire. In 796 he settled at Tours as abbot; and the school there soon became one of the most important in the Empire. His works comprise poems; works on grammar, rhetoric, and dialectics; theological and ethical treatises; lives of several saints; and over 200 letters. » Charlemagne; Franks; theology

Alcyone » **Halcyone**

Aldabra Islands [al**dab**ra] 9°25S 46°20E; area 154 sq km/59 sq ml. Coral atoll nature reserve in SW Indian Ocean, NW of Madagascar; 1 200 km/750 ml SW of Mahé; outlying dependency of the Seychelles; occupied by scientific staff; habitat of the giant land tortoise; nature reserve, established in 1976; a world heritage site. » Seychelles

Aldebaran [al**deb**aran] » **Taurus**

aldehyde [**al**dihiyd] IUPAC **alkanal**. An organic compound containing a (–CHO) function. Aldehydes are readily oxidized (to carboxylic acids) and reduced (to alcohols). The aldehyde function is found in most sugars, notably glucose. » IUPAC; sugars

alder A small deciduous N temperate tree, often growing by water or in wet soils; leaves oval or rounded; male and female flowers on separate plants; male catkins long, pendulous; females short, erect, becoming woody and cone-like in fruit. (Genus: *Alnus*, 35 species. Family: *Betulaceae*.) » deciduous plants; tree [i]

alderfly A slow, awkwardly-flying insect with two pairs of large, translucent wings held over its body at rest; found around well-aerated, freshwater ponds and streams; larvae aquatic and carnivorous. (Order: *Megaloptera*. Family: *Sialidae*, c.50 species.) » insect [i]; larva

Alderney [**ol**dernee] Fr **Aurigny**, ancient **Riduna** pop (1981e) 2 086; area 8 sq km/3 sq ml. Third largest of the Channel Is, off the coast of French Normandy, W of Cherbourg; separated from France by the Race of Alderney; in the Bailiwick of Guernsey, with its own legislative assembly; chief town, Saint Anne; tourism, dairy farming. » Channel Islands [i]

Aldhelm or **Ealdhelm, St** (c.640–709), feast day 25 May. English abbot and bishop, the author of many Latin writings in early Anglo-Saxon times. He became Abbot of Malmesbury about 675, and Bishop of Sherbourne in 705. A skilled architect, he built several churches and monasteries. He also wrote Latin treatises, letters, and verses, besides English poems that have perished. » Anglo-Saxons

Aldington, Richard [**awl**dingtn] (1892–1962) British poet, novelist, editor, and biographer, born in Hampshire. He was educated at London University, and in 1913 became editor of *Egoist*, the periodical of the Imagist school. World War 1 left him broken in health and with a great deal of resentment, seen especially in his novel *Death of a Hero* (1929). He wrote several novels and volumes of poetry, and many biographies, including *Wellington* (1946) and *Lawrence of Arabia* (1955). He married Hilda Doolittle in 1937, and died at Sury-en-Vaus, France. » English literature; Doolittle; Imagism

Aldiss, Brian (Wilson) (1925–) British author and editor, best known for his science-fiction writing, born at Dereham, Norfolk, and educated at Framlington College. He published his first novel, *The Brightfount Diaries*, in 1955. Though most of his work is of the science-fiction genre, he has written several other novels, and experimented with the novel form. His best-known works include *Hothouse* (1962) and *The Saliva Tree* (1966), and his edited collections of short stories. He has also produced a history of science fiction, *Billion Year Spree* (1973). » science fiction

aldosterone [al**dos**terohn] A type of hormone (a mineralocorticoid) secreted from the adrenal cortex into the blood. Its primary role in humans is to stimulate sodium reabsorption and potassium excretion by the kidneys, in order to maintain electrolyte and water balance. Excessive secretion is known as **aldosteronism**, indicated by potassium depletion, sodium retention, and hypertension. » adrenal glands; corticosteroids; extracellular fluid; kidneys; mineralocorticoids; renin

Aldrin, Edwin Eugene, byname **Buzz** (1930–) US astronaut, born at Montclair, New Jersey, the second man to set foot on the Moon, after Neil Armstrong, in 1969. Educated at West Point and the Massachusetts Institute of Technology, he was an air force pilot in the Korean War, becoming an astronaut in 1963. He set up a space-walking record in 1966 during the flight of Gemini 12. » Apollo programme; Armstrong, Neil; Collins, Michael (astronaut)

Aldus Manutius or **Aldo Manucci/Manuzio** (c.1450–1515) Venetian printer, born at Bassiano, after whom are named the Aldine editions of the Greek and Roman classics and of the great Italian writers that for about 100 years were printed at Venice by himself and his successors. The first to print Greek books, he had beautiful founts of Greek and Latin type made, and first used italics on a large scale. He died in Venice. » printing [i]

ale An alcoholic beverage brewed from barley which has been malted (ie softened in water and allowed to germinate). It was a popular drink prior to the introduction of hops as a flavouring agent, thus creating beer. However, the term *ale* is still used to describe the hops-flavoured brew, while *beer* has a broader international interpretation at present, and includes lager and stouts. » barley; beer [i]; hops

aleatory music [**ay**liatori] Music of which the composition or performance is, to a greater or lesser extent, determined by chance or by whim. The notation may be conventional but indeterminate (ie with the notes but not their sequence composed), or it may take some 'graphic' form which conveys only a general pattern to performers, or elicits an intuitive response from them. The chief proponent of aleatory music has been John Cage (1912–). » improvisation

alecost » **costmary**

Aleichem [a**layk**hem], **Sholem, Sholom** or **Shalom**, pen name of **Solomon J Rabinowitz** (1859–1916) Russian-Jewish author, born in Pereyaslev, the Ukraine. After working for some years as a rabbi, he devoted himself to writing and Yiddish culture. The pogroms of 1905 drove him to the USA, where he worked as a playwright for the Yiddish theatre. His short stories and plays portray Jewish life in Russia in the late 19th-c with vividness, humour, and sympathy. The musical *Fiddler on the Roof* is based on his stories. He died in New York City. » Hebrew literature; Yiddish

Aleixandre, Vicente [alayshahndray] (1898–1984) Spanish poet, born in Seville, who was awarded the Nobel Prize for Literature in 1977. His reputation was established by a 1937 collection of poems, but his loyalty to the Republic impeded the publication of his work for several years, his *Antologia Total* (Complete Works) not appearing until 1976. He died in Madrid. » Spanish literature

Alemán, Mateo [aleman] (1547–1620) Spanish novelist, born at Seville, whose picaresque novel, *Guzmán de Alfarachez* (1599, trans *The Spanish Rogue*), was a great success throughout Europe. He received little financial reward, and was imprisoned for debt. He emigrated to Mexico in 1608, where he died. » picaresque novel; Spanish literature

Alembert, Jean le Rond d' [alãbair] (1717–83) French philosopher and mathematician, born in Paris. He was found near the Church of St Jean le Rond, whence his name – the surname he himself added long after. He was educated at the Collège Mazarin, and wrote an epoch-making treatise on dynamics (1743), and several other major mathematical works. For Diderot's *Encyclopédie* he wrote the *Discours préliminaire* introducing the first volume (1751), a noble tribute to literature and philosophy; he also contributed several articles, and edited the mathematical portion. Other publications included books on philosophy, literary criticism, and the theory of music. He died at the Louvre in Paris. » Diderot

Alentejo [alãtayzhoo] Sparsely-populated agricultural area of SEC Portugal, SE of the R Tagus (the name is from Arabic, 'beyond the Tagus'); divided in 1936 into the two provinces of **Alto Alentejo** and **Baixo Alentejo**; low-lying plain with cork tree forests, heaths, maquis; prehistoric standing stones and chambered cairns; chief towns, Évora, Beja; corn, cattle, pigs; noted for the Alter Real breed of horse. » Portugal [i]

Aleppo [alepoh], Arabic **Halab** 36°12N 37°10E, pop (1981) 976 727. Capital city of Halab governorate, NW Syria; 350 km/217 ml N of Damascus; chief commercial and industrial centre of N Syria; airport; road and rail junction; university (1960); industrial refrigeration plant; old city, a world heritage site; Cotton Festival (Sep). » Syria [i]

Aletsch [alech] area 117.6 sq km/45.4 sq ml. Glacier in SC Switzerland, W and S of the Aletschhorn; length, 23.6 km/14.6 ml; the largest glacier in Europe. » Alps

Aleut [alyoot] Peoples of the Aleutian Is and W Alaska, who are physically, linguistically, and culturally similar to the Eskimo. In the past, they lived in villages and hunted seals, walrus, whales, and bears. Community life and culture were disrupted by Russian occupation of the area in the 18th–19th-c, and the population has since declined from c.25 000 to c.2 500 in the 1980s. » Alaska; Aleutian Is; Eskimo

Aleutian Islands [alooshan] or **Aleutians**, formerly **Catherine Archipelago** Group of c.150 islands stretching c.1 600 km/1 000 ml from the Alaskan Peninsula, USA; area 17 666 sq km/6 821 sq ml, pop (1980) 7 768; chief islands Attu, Andreanof, Rat, Umnak, Unimak, Unalaska (chief town, Dutch Harbor); many volcanic peaks over 1 000 m/3 000 ft; discovered by Russian explorers in 18th-c; purchased by USA, 1867; several military bases; wildlife refuge. » Alaska

alewife Deep-bodied herring-like fish, locally abundant along the American Atlantic seaboard; length up to 40 cm/16 in; migrates into rivers (Mar/Apr) to spawn in slow backwaters; commercially fished using traps and nets (seines). (*Alosa pseudoharengus*. Family: *Clupeidae*.) » herring

Alexander I (1777–1825) Emperor of Russia (1801–1825), born in St Petersburg, the grandson of Catherine the Great. The early years of his reign were marked by the promise of liberal constitutional reforms and the pursuit of a vigorous foreign policy. In 1805 Russia joined the coalition against Napoleon, but after a series of military defeats was forced to conclude the Treaty of Tilsit (1807) with France. When Napoleon broke the Treaty by invading Russia in 1812, Alexander pursued the French back to Paris. At the Congress of Vienna (1814–15) he laid claim to Poland. During the last years of his reign his increased political reactionism and religious mysticism resulted in the founding of the Holy Alliance. His mysterious death at Taganrog caused a succession crisis which led to the attempted revolutionary coup of the Decembrists. » Congress Kingdom of Poland; Decembrists; Napoleon I; Romanovs

Alexander II (1198–1249) King of Scots (1214–49), born at Haddington, E Lothian, who succeeded his father, William the Lion. He supported the English barons against John, later concluding a peace treaty with Henry III (1217), and marrying Henry's eldest sister, Joan (1221). In 1239 he married Marie, the daughter of Enguerrand de Coucy. His reign represents an important landmark in the making of the Scottish kingdom. He renounced his hereditary claims to Northumberland, Cumberland, and Westmorland by the Treaty of York (1237), and concentrated on the vigorous assertion of royal authority in the N and W. He died of a fever on Kerrera, near Oban, while leading an expedition to wrest the Western Is from Norwegian control. » Barons' Wars; Henry III (of England); John; William I (of Scotland)

Alexander the Great (356–323 BC) King of Macedonia (336–323 BC), born at Pella, the son of Philip II and Olympias. He was tutored by Aristotle, and ascended the throne when less than 20 years old. After crushing all opposition at home, he set out to conquer Greece's hereditary enemy, Achaemenid Persia. This he achieved with great rapidity in a series of famous battles: Granicus (334 BC), Issus (333 BC), and Gaugmela (331 BC). By 330 BC, Darius III had fled, and the capitals of Babylon, Susa, Persepolis, and Ecbatana had been taken. In the next three years, the E half of the empire followed, and Alexander set out for India. He reached the Punjab, and had set his sights on the Ganges, when his troops mutinied and forced his return. He died shortly after at Babylon. » Achaemenids; Greek history; Persian Wars; Hellenization; Philip II (of Macedon)

Alexander III (Pope), originally **Orlando Bandinelli** (c.1105–81) Pope (1159–81), born at Siena, Tuscany, Italy. He taught law at Bologna, and became adviser to Pope Adrian IV. After his election, he was engaged in a struggle with the Emperor Frederick Barbarossa who refused to recognize him, setting up antipopes. The Emperor was finally defeated and compelled to sign the Treaty of Venice (1177). Alexander was the pope involved in the quarrel between Henry II of England and Thomas à Becket. He also called the third Lateran Council (1179). He died in Rome. » Adrian IV; antipope; Becket; Frederick Barbarossa; Henry II (of England); pope

Alexander VI, originally **Rodrigo Borgia** (1431–1503) Pope (1492–1503), born at Játiva, Spain. He was made a cardinal (1455) by his uncle, Calixtus III, and became Pope on the death of Innocent VIII as a result of flagrant bribery. Father to Caesar, Lucretia, and two other illegitimate children, he endeavoured to break the power of the Italian princes, and to gain their possessions for his own family. Under his pontificate, he apportioned the New World between Spain and Portugal, and despite introducing the censorship of books, he was a generous patron of the arts. He died in Rome. » Borgia; pope

Alexander of Hales (c.1170–1245) English scholastic philosopher, known as the 'irrefutable doctor', born at Hales, Gloucestershire. He became a professor of philosophy and theology in Paris, and later entered the Franciscan order. The chief work ascribed to him is the ponderous *Summa Universae Theologiae*. He died in Paris. » Franciscans; scholasticism

Alexander Nevsky (c.1220–63), feast day 30 August or 23 November. Russian hero and saint, born at Vladimir, who received his surname from his victory over the Swedes on the R Neva (1240). He later defeated the Teutonic Knights (1242) and the Lithuanians (1245), and also helped maintain Novgorod's independence from the Mongol Empire. He died at Gorodets, and was canonized by the Russian Church in 1547. He is the subject of a famous film by Eisenstein. » Eisenstein; Golden Horde

Alexander (of Tunis), Harold Rupert Leofric George, 1st Earl (1891–1969) British field marshal, born in London. He was educated at Harrow and Sandhurst, in World War 1 commanded a brigade on the W Front, and in 1940 was the last officer out of Dunkirk. He served in Burma, and in 1942–3 was Commander-in-Chief Middle East, his N African campaign being one of the most complete victories in military history. Appointed field marshal on the capture of Rome in June 1944, he became Supreme Allied Commander, Mediterranean

Theatre, for the rest of the war. He later became Governor-General of Canada (1946–52) and Minister of Defence (1952–4), and was created viscount (1946) and earl (1952). He died at Slough, Berkshire. » North African Campaign; World War 2

Alexander (Greek mythology) » **Paris** (mythology)

Alexander Archipelago Group of 1 100 mountainous islands SE of Alaska, USA; chief islands Chichagof, Baranof (Sitka naval base and national monument), Admiralty, Kupreanof, Kuiu, and Prince of Wales; pop (1980) 32 586. » Alaska; Sitka

Alexandra, Princess, the Hon. Mrs Angus Ogilvy (1936–) The daughter of George, Duke of Kent and Princess Marina of Greece, who married in 1963 the Hon Angus James Bruce Ogilvy (1928–); they have a son, James Robert Bruce (1964–) and a daughter, Marina Victoria Alexandra (1966–).

Alexandra, Queen (1844–1925) Eldest daughter of Christian IX of Denmark, who married the British Prince of Wales (later Edward VII) in 1863. In 1902 she founded Queen Alexandra's Imperial (now Royal) Army Nursing Corps. » Edward VII

Alexandra Feodorovna [**fyo**dorovna] (1872–1918) Empress of Russia upon her marriage with Nicholas II (1894), Princess of Hesse-Darmstadt, and granddaughter of Queen Victoria, born at Darmstadt, Germany. She came under the influence of Rasputin, and meddled disastrously in politics, being eventually imprisoned and shot by Bolshevik revolutionaries, along with her husband and children, at Ekaterinburg. » Bolsheviks; February Revolution (Russia); Rasputin

Alexandria, Arabic **El Iskandariya** 31°13N 29°55E, pop (1986) 5 000 000. Seaport capital of Alexandria governorate, N Egypt; on the Mediterranean coast, 180 km/112 ml NW of Cairo; second largest city of Egypt and the country's main port; founded in 332 BC by Alexander the Great; capital of the Ptolemies 304–30 BC; former centre of Hellenistic and Jewish culture; noted for its famous royal libraries; airport; railway; university (1942); car assembly, oil refining, natural gas processing, food processing, trade in cotton, vegetables and grain; Catacombs of Kom El Shugafa (1st–2nd-c AD), Graeco-Roman museum, Pompey's Pillar (297), Serapium temple ruins, Abu'l Abbas mosque. » Alexander the Great; Egypt [i]

Alexandria, Library of Founded by Ptolemy I and greatly extended by Ptolemy II, it was the greatest library in the Ancient World and the most important centre for literary studies. At one time it was reputed to have contained 700 000 volumes. » library; Ptolemy I Soter

alexandrine [alig**zahn**drin] A French term for a line of verse consisting of six feet (= a Latin hexameter). Common in French poetry and dramatic verse, it is used most often in English for contrast, as in the last line of the Spenserian stanza, or in Pope, who both uses and describes an alexandrine in the line 'Which, like a wounded snake, drags its slow length along'. » metre (literature); poetry; Pope; Spenser

Alexeyev, Vasiliy [alek**say**ef] (1942–) Russian weightlifter, born Pokrovo-Shishkino. He set 80 world records (Jan 1970–Nov 1977), more than any other athlete in any sport. Olympic super-heavyweight champion in 1972 and 1976, he won eight world titles and nine European titles. He was made a major in the Russian army, and obtained the title of Master of Sport. » weightlifting

alexia » **dyslexia**

Alexius Comnenus (1048–1118) Byzantine Emperor (1081–1118), born in Constantinople, the founder of the Comnenian dynasty. He strengthened the weakened Byzantine state, and defeated the attacking Turks and Normans. However, his achievement received a major setback when his empire was invaded by the myriad warriors of the First Crusade to Palestine (1096). » Crusades [i]

alfalfa » **lucerne**

Alföld [**ol**fuld] Great Plain region of S Hungary, E of the R Danube, extending into N Yugoslavia and W Romania; a flat area covering about half of Hungary, crossed by a system of canals which provide irrigation for grain and fruit; livestock on the arid grasslands (*pusztas*); national parks at Hortobágy, Bükk, and Kiskunság. » Hungary [i]

Alfonso I Henriques (c.1110–85) The earliest King of Portugal (1139–85), born at Guimarães, who was only two years old at the death of his father, Henry of Burgundy, first Count of Portugal. Wresting power from his mother in 1128, he fought the Moors, defeating them at Ourique (1139), and proclaimed himself king. He took Lisbon (1147), and later all Galicia, Estremadura, and Elvas. He died at Coimbra.

Alfred, byname **the Great** (849–99) King of Wessex (from 871), born at Wantage, Berkshire, the fifth son of King Ethelwulf. When he came to the throne, the Danes had already conquered Northumbria, E Mercia, and East Anglia, and threatened to subdue Wessex itself. He inflicted on them their first major reverse at the Battle of Edington, Wiltshire (878), and began to win back Danish-occupied territory by capturing the former Mercian town of London (886). He stole the military initiative from the Danes by reorganizing his forces into a standing army, building a navy, and establishing a network of burhs (fortified centres). These developments were complemented by his revival of religion and learning, a programme designed to win God's support for victory over the pagan Danes and to consolidate loyalty to himself as a Christian king. He personally translated several edifying Latin works into English. He forged close ties with other English peoples not under Danish rule, and provided his successors with the means to reconquer the Danelaw and secure the unity of England. The famous story of his being scolded by a peasant woman for letting her cakes burn has no contemporary authority, and is first recorded in the 11th-c. » Anglo-Saxons; Athelstan; Danelaw; Edward the Elder; Vikings; Wessex

Alfvén, Hannes Olof Gösta [alf**vayn**] (1908–) Swedish theoretical physicist, born at Norrköping. He worked in Sweden until 1967, and afterwards in California, developing the theory of plasmas (ionized gases) and their behaviour in electric and magnetic fields – a theory which is critical in the understanding of stars, and in energy generation by nuclear fusion. He shared the Nobel Prize for Physics in 1970 for his work in magnetohydrodynamics and plasma physics. » hydrodynamics; plasma (physics)

algae An informal grouping of primitive, mainly aquatic plants that have chlorophyll *a* as their primary photosynthetic pigment; body (*thallus*) not organized into root, stem, and leaf; lack a true vascular system; reproductive organs not surrounded by a layer of sterile cells; range in form from simple unicellular plant plankton to massive seaweeds, many metres in length. » brown algae; chlorophyll; photosynthesis; plankton; plant; red algae; seaweed; yellow-green algae

Algardi, Alessandro (1598–1654) Italian sculptor, born in Bologna. His chief work is a large marble relief in St Peter's, Rome of Pope Leo restraining Attila from marching on Rome. He died in Rome. » Italian art; sculpture

Algarve [al**gahv**], Port [al**gah**vay] area 5 072 sq km/1 958 sq ml. Region and province of S Portugal, bounded W and S by the Atlantic Ocean; Moorish kingdom, 1140; capital, Faro; figs, olives, maize, almonds, fishing, tourism; **Costo do Algarve** is the S Atlantic coast of Portugal from Cape St Vincent (W) to R Guadiana on the Spanish border; the most popular tourist resort area in Portugal, with resorts at Luz de Lagos, Praia da Rocha, Praia do Carvoeiro, Albufeira, Vilamoura. » Faro; Portugal [i]

algebra A branch of mathematics in which unknown quantities are represented by letters or other symbols. It was developed and brought to Europe by the Moors, from whose word *al-jabr* the name of the subject is derived. In classical algebra (or **arithmetic algebra**), the operations in use are those of arithmetic; whereas in **abstract algebra**, developed in the 19th–20th-c, different operations are defined. In particular, in many abstract algebras, the commutative law does not apply. William Hamilton (1805–65) developed the algebra of quaternions, Arthur Cayley and others matrix algebra, and George Boole the algebra of sets that bears his name. *Non-associative* algebras do not follow the associative laws of arithmetic; an example is **Jordan algebra**, named after the French mathematician Camille Jordan (1838–1922). » Boole; Boolean algebra; Cayley, Arthur; commutative operation; equations; mathematics; matrix; quaternions; set

Algeciras [aljuh**see**ras], Span [alhe**thee**ras] 36°09N 5°28W, pop (1981) 86 042. Seaport and resort in Cádiz province,

Andalusia, SW Spain; on W side of Algeciras Bay, opposite Gibraltar; founded by the Moors, 713; largely destroyed, 14th-c; rebuilt, 18th-c; scene of Algeciras Conference (over the future of Morocco), 1906; railway; car ferries to Canary Is, Melilla, Tangier, Gibraltar; paper, tourism, trade in oranges, cork; Old Algeciras; watersports; fair and fiestas (Jun), patronal fiestas (Aug), Festival of Spain (Aug). » Andalusia; Spain [i]

Algeria, Fr **L'Algérie**, official name **The Democratic and Popular Republic of Algeria**, Arabic **Al-Jumhuriya Al-Jazairiya** pop (1990e) 24 700 000; area 2 460 500 sq km/949 753 sq ml. N African republic, divided into 31 departments (*wilaya*); bounded W by Morocco, SW by W Sahara, Mauritania, and Mali, SE by Mali, E by Libya, NE by Tunisia, and N by the Mediterranean Sea; timezone GMT +1; capital Algiers (Alger); chief towns include Constantine, Oran, Skikda, 'Annaba, Mostaganem, Blida, Tlemcen; 99% of the population of Arab-Berber origin; religion Islam, 99% Sunni Muslim; official language Arabic, with French also spoken; unit of currency, the dinar.

Physical description and climate. From the Mediterranean coast, mountains rise in a series of ridges and plateaux to the Atlas Saharien; 91% of the population located on the narrow coastal plain; part of Sahara Desert to the S; a major depression, the Chott Melrhir, in the NE; Ahaggar Mts in the far S, rising to 2 918 m/9 573 ft at Mt Tahat; typical Mediterranean climate on N coast; rainfall annual average of 400–800 mm/15.8–31.5 in (mostly Nov–Mar); snow on higher ground; Algiers annual rainfall of 760 mm/30 in, average maximum daily temperatures 15–29°C; rest of the country an essentially rainless Saharan climate.

History and government. Indigenous peoples (Berbers) driven back from the coast by many invaders, including Phoenicians, Romans, Vandals, Arabs, Turks, and French; became a province of the Roman Empire; Islam and Arabic introduced by Arabs, 8th–11th-c; Turkish invasion, 16th-c; French colonial campaign in 19th-c led to control by 1902; guerrilla war (1954–62) with French forces by the National Liberation Front (FLN); independence gained, 1962; first president of the republic, Ahmed Ben Bella, replaced after coup in 1965; elections and a new constitution, 1976; legislative National People's Assembly with 281 members elected every five years; executive president, also elected for five years, appoints a cabinet of c.26 ministers; socialist FLN the only political party.

Economy. Large-scale nationalization after 1963; agriculture,

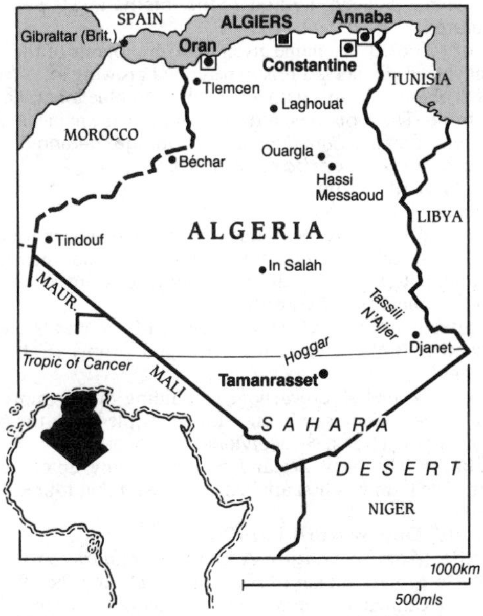

□ international airport

mainly on N coast (wheat, barley, oats, grapes, citrus fruits, vegetables); food processing, textiles, clothing; petroleum products account for c.30% of national income; natural gas reserves estimated to be world's fourth largest; pioneer in the development of liquid natural gas; constructed with Italy the first trans-Mediterranean gas pipeline. » Algiers; FLN; Islam; Sahara Desert; Sunnis; RR24 national holidays; RR42 political leaders

Algiers [al**jeerz**], Fr **Alger** [al**zhay**] 36°50N 3°00E, pop (1984e) 2 442 300. Seaport capital of Algeria, N Africa; 805 km/500 ml SSW of Marseilles (France); founded 10th-c by Berbers on the site of Roman Icosium; Turkish rule established (1518) by Barbarossa; taken by the French, 1830; Allied headquarters and seat of de Gaulle's provisional government in World War 2; University of Algeria (1879); university of sciences and technology (1974); airport; railway; trade, commerce and administration, wine; Sidi Abderrahman Mosque, Sidi Mohammed Sherif Mosque, Djama Djehid Mosque (16th-c); cathedral; national library; Bardo Museum, Museum of Antiquities, National Museum of Fine Arts. » Algeria [i]; Barbarossa; Berber; de Gaulle

alginates The calcium salts of alginic acid, found in seaweeds, forming viscous solutions which hold large amounts of water. They are used in food manufacturing as thickening agents in such products as ice-creams and yogurts. They are not digested in the small intestine, but are fermented by the microflora of the large intestine. » calcium; seaweed

Algol An eclipsing binary star in Perseus, the prototype of the Algol-type variable stars. English astonomer John Goodricke (1764–86) suggested in 1782 that the variations were due to an unseen companion revolving around the star with immense velocity, a theory confirmed by spectroscopy in 1889. There is a third and possibly a fourth star in orbit too. Distance: 35 parsecs. » binary star; eclipse **2**; Perseus (astronomy); variable star

ALGOL An acronym of **ALGOrithmic Language**, a high-level programming computer language developed in Europe in the late 1950s for mathematical and scientific use at approximately the same time as FORTRAN was being developed in the USA. » algorithm; FORTRAN; programming language

Algonkin [al**gong**kin] or **Algonquin** Scattered small groups of American Indians speaking Algonkian languages, living in forest regions around the Ottawa R in Canada. Most were slaughtered by the Iroquois or died from European diseases: only c.2 000 survive. They work mainly as trappers, hunters' guides, and market gardeners. » American Indians; Blackfoot; Cree; Fox; manitou; Ojibwa; Powhatan; Shawnee

Algonquin » **Algonkin**

algorithm A set of precisely determined rules, the sustained application of which to a complex problem will yield a solution or optimal results. For example, when playing second in noughts and crosses (tick-tack-toe), 'Occupy the centre position immediately, if it is empty' is part of an algorithm which will result in your never losing. Because they are precisely defined and their application requires no insight, algorithms can be programmed into computers. » heuristic

Alhambra [al**ham**bra] The palace-fortress of the Moorish kings built at Granada, Spain, in the 13th–14th-c; a world heritage site. It was partially demolished and rebuilt by Charles V in the 16th-c, but retains many beautiful halls and gardens characteristic of mediaeval Islamic architecture. » Charles V (Emperor); Granada; Islamic architecture

Alhazen (Abu al-Hassan ibn al Haytham) [al**ha**zen] (c.965–1038) Egyptian physicist, born in Basra (now in Iraq). He did notable work in physical optics, dealing with plane and curved mirrors, refraction, and lenses. He rejected the Greek view that the eye sends out rays. The best known of his many books was the *Treasury of Optics* (first published in Latin in 1572). He died in Cairo. » optics [i]

Ali (?–661) The first convert to Islam and the fourth caliph (656–61), the son of Abu Taleb, the uncle of Mohammed. He was the bravest follower of Mohammed, whose daughter Fatima he married. » Islam; Mohammed

Ali, Muhammad (formerly **Cassius Marcellus Clay, Jr**) (1942–) US boxer, born at Louisville, Kentucky. He was an amateur boxer (1954–60), who then became the Olympic light-heavyweight champion. He won the world heavyweight title in 1964, defeating Sonny Liston in 7 rounds. At that time he joined the Black Muslims and adopted the name Muhammad Ali. In 1967, he refused drafting into the army on religious grounds, and was stripped of his title and barred from the ring. He took his case to the Supreme Court and had his title restored in 1970. In 1971 he was beaten by Joe Frazier, but beat him in 1974, and went on to meet George Foreman later that year, knocking him out in 8 rounds to regain his title. He was beaten by Leon Spinks in a split decision (Feb 1978), but regained the title later that year – the first man to win the world heavyweight title three times. His extrovert and flamboyant style have made him a legend, and his slogan 'I am the greatest' became a catchphrase. Ali was President Carter's special envoy to Africa in 1980 (attempting to persuade nations to boycott the Olympics). He has starred in two films, *The Greatest* (1976) and *Freedom Road* (1978). » boxing [i]

Aliákmon, River [aleeakmon], ancient **Haliacmon** River in W Macedonia region, N Greece; rises near the Albanian border, flows SE then NE to enter the Gulf of Salonika; longest river in Greece; length 297 km/185 ml. » Greece [i]

alibi A type of defence to a criminal charge: the defendant claims that at the time of the crime he or she was elsewhere. Details of an alibi defence have to be given within seven days of committal, in English law (this is not a requirement in Scottish law). Usually an alibi defence cannot be 'sprung' upon the court in the course of a Crown Court trial. » criminal law; Crown Court

Alicante [aleekantay], Lat **Lucentum** 38°23N 0°30W, pop (1981) 251 387. Seaport and capital of Alicante province, SE Spain; 422 km/262 ml SE of Madrid; airport; railway; car ferries to Marseilles, Oran, Ibiza, Palma de Mallorca; popular winter resort; metal products, textiles, paper, tobacco, fertilizer, trade in fruit and wine; promenade, Castle of St Barbara, Church of St Mary (14th-c); bonfires in honour of St John (Jun). » Spain [i]

Alice Springs formerly **Stuart** (to 1933), 23°42S 133°52E, pop (1981) 18 395. Urban centre in Northern Territory, C Australia; administrative and supply centre for the settlements and cattle stations of the Outback; established, 1890; airfield; railway terminus; Flying Doctor Service regional headquarters; tourist centre for the region; aviation museum; Chateau Hornsby Winery nearby; Camel Cup camel races (May); Bangtail Muster with rodeos, parades, and cattle round-ups (May); Alice Springs Show Day (5 Jul); Henley-on-Todd Regatta, with mock yacht races on the dry bed of the Todd R (Aug). » Northern Territory

alien A person who is not a citizen of a state. A citizen of country X is usually an alien in country Y and vice versa. In the UK, for example, aliens may hold most kinds of property, but may not vote or hold a public office.

Alien and Sedition Acts (1798–1800) US laws passed to crush political opposition, led by Thomas Jefferson, then Vice-President. Two Alien Acts gave the President great power over foreigners. The Sedition Act authorized fining and imprisonment for public criticism of the government. » Jefferson; Kentucky and Virginia Resolutions

alienation-effect or **V-effect** A common translation of *Verfremdungseffekt*, a term coined by Brecht to describe any theatrical means – directorial, histrionic, or literary – used to help an audience see as unfamiliar what they assume to be familiar. These effects remind the audience that what they are watching is only a play, and not real life. The audience is thus distanced from what is taking place on the stage. » Brecht

alimentary canal A tube in which foodstuffs are ingested, digested, and absorbed, and waste products excreted; also known as the **gut**, or the **gastro-intestinal tract**. It may exist as a simple structure with one opening only to the exterior (as in coelenterates, platyhelminths), or as a more complex structure with two openings (as in vertebrates). In the latter case, food is ingested via the mouth and unassimilated material is expelled from the anus. In many animals the canal is anatomically divided to provide partial separation (eg in invertebrates such as insects and cephalopods), or complete separation (eg in higher vertebrates such as mammals and birds) into regions which secrete different enzymes and absorb digestive products. » anus; cholera; Crohn's disease; digestion; duodenum; gastro-enteritis; haematemesis; intestine; mouth; Plate XII

aliphatic compound [alifatik] A carbon compound containing no aromatic groups, especially those derived from fatty acids. » alkanes; alkenes; alkynes; aromatic compound; carbon; hydrocarbons

Aliyah [ahleeah] The name given to the Jewish migrations from Europe to Palestine, which started in 1882, and laid the foundations of the modern state of Israel. The ideals of the second Aliyah (1904–14) were redemption of the soil, and personal labour as a means of salvation. It pioneered the co-operative settlement which was to develop into the modern *kibbutz*. The third Aliyah was associated with a search for a National Home, while the fourth (1925) reflected Jewish persecution in E Europe, mainly Poland. The fifth Aliyah (1932) represented flight from early Nazi Persecution. » Israel [i]; kibbutz

alkali [alkaliy] A strong base, sodium and potassium hydroxide being derived from ashes. Solutions of alkalis have high values of pH, and are used as cleaning materials, as they dissolve fats. The **alkali metals** are Group I of the periodic table: lithium, sodium, potassium, rubidium, and caesium. They are all characterized by being readily oxidized to compounds in which they exist as singly charged cations, and by having hydroxides which are strong bases. » base (chemistry); cation; chemical elements; hydroxide; pH; potassium; sodium; RR90

alkaline-earth Strictly, the elements calcium, strontium, barium, and radium, but often including beryllium and magnesium as well, hence Group II of the periodic table. These elements mainly form compounds in which they occur as doubly charged cations, and are largely responsible for the hardness of water. » cation; chemical elements; RR90

alkaloids Organic, nitrogen-containing bases from plants which include complex ring structures. Their functions are not fully understood, but may include protection against grazing animals, and a role in nitrogen assimilation. Many alkaloids have biological activity, and have been used as drugs, such as quinine, morphine, and cocaine. However, they may also be very toxic, as in the case of strychnine. » base (chemistry); cocaine [i]; morphine; nitrogen; opium; quinine; strychnine

alkanamides » **amides 2**

alkanes [alkaynz] Saturated hydrocarbons, having a general formula C_nH_{2n+2}, derived from methane by the addition of successive $-CH_2-$ groups. Also known as *paraffins*, they are generally unreactive, but make up the major components of petroleum. » alkyl; hydrocarbons; methane [i]; petroleum; saturated

alkanet [alkanet] The name given to several plants of the borage family; true alkanet is a bristly perennial growing to 15 cm/6 in; leaves oblong; flowers with a red tube and blue lobes; native to S Europe. The roots yield a red dye of the same name. (*Alkanna tinctoria*. Family: *Boraginaceae*.) » borage; perennial

alkanoic acids » **carboxylic acids**

alkanols » **alcohols**

alkanone » **ketone**

alkenes [alkeenz] Hydrocarbons containing one or more double bonds; also called *olefins*. With one double bond, their general formula is C_nH_{2n}. They are generally reactive by addition. » addition reactions; hydrocarbons

alkyl [alkiyl] A group $C_nH_{2n+1}-$, derived from an alkane, such as methyl (CH_3-), ethyl (C_2H_5-), and propyl (C_3H_7-). » alkanes

alkynes [alkiynz] Hydrocarbons containing one or more triple bonds; also called *acetylenes*. With one triple bond, the general formula is C_nH_{2n-2}. » acetylene; hydrocarbons

All Blacks The New Zealand national rugby union football team. The term was first applied to the team that toured Britain in 1905.

All Fools' Day » **April Fool**

All-India Muslim League A political organization (founded 1906) to protect Indian Muslim rights. During the 1930s and 1940s it campaigned under M A Jinnah's leadership for an independent Muslim state separate from future independent

India. It was the dominant party in Pakistan after 1947. » Jinnah

All Saints' Day A Christian festival commemorating all the Church's saints collectively; held on 1 November in the Roman Catholic and Anglican Churches, and on the first Sunday after Pentecost in the Eastern Churches; formerly known as All Hallows; the preceding evening is Hallowe'en. » Hallowe'en

All Souls' Day In the Roman Catholic Church, the day (2 Nov) set apart as a day of prayer for souls in purgatory; also celebrated by some Anglicans; in the Eastern Orthodox Church celebrated about two months before Easter. » Christianity; purgatory

Allah [**al**ah] The Islamic name for God. Prior to Mohammed, Allah was the supreme but not the sole deity in Arabia. It was Mohammed's mission to proclaim Allah as the sole God, the creator and sustainer of all things, who in the last days will judge all of humanity. Allah is known to human beings through the revelation of his will in the Koran which he delivered piecemeal to his Prophet Mohammed. » Islam; Koran; Mohammed

Allahabad [**ah**lahabahd] 25°25N 81°58E, pop (1981) 642 000. City in Uttar Pradesh, NE India; on N bank of R Yamuna where it joins the R Ganges, 560 km/348 ml SE of New Delhi; founded, 1583; ceded to the British, 1801; airfield; railway; cotton, sugar; centre of Hindi literature; Great Mosque, Sultan Khossor's caravanserai, fort containing the Asoka pillar (240 BC); Hindu religious festival (Kumbh Mela), held every 12 years. » Hinduism; Uttar Pradesh

Allegheny Mountains [**al**uhgenee, aluh**gay**nee] Mountain range in E USA; W part of the Appalachian Mts; extends over 805 km/500 ml from N Pennsylvania SSW through Maryland, West Virginia, and Virginia; forms the watershed between the Atlantic and the Mississippi R; highest point Spruce Knob, 1 481 m/4 859 ft; rich in timber, coal, iron, and limestone. » Appalachian Mountains

allegory A literary device by which another level of meaning is concealed within what is usually a story of some kind; also, the story itself. Myth and fable are both allegorical. Allegory may therefore be understood as extended metaphor, or a continuous figure of speech. The form allows (indeed, invites) interpretation; it has often been used for works with a religious or political bearing, such as Bunyan's *Pilgrim's Progress* (1678) and Orwell's *Animal Farm* (1945). » Bunyan; Camus; fable; metaphor; mythology; Orwell

allele or **allelomorph** [**aleel**] One of the alternative forms of a gene which can occur at a given point on a chromosome. Genes at a given locus controlling a particular character may vary slightly in their effect, and there may be two, three, or more such alleles available in a population, of which each individual carries two – one from the father and one from the mother. The term, introduced in 1902 to apply in Mendelian inheritance, is today increasingly applied to a short variant sequence of DNA, either within, or adjacent to, a functional gene. » DNA [i]; gene; Mendel

allemande [ale**mahnd**] A dance originating in the 16th-c, probably in Germany. In the 17th-c it became a standard movement in the suite for lute or keyboard. It is in 4/4 time and moderate tempo, and usually begins with a short note before the first main beat. » suite

Allen, Ethan (1738–89) US soldier, revolutionary leader, and writer, born at Litchfield, Connecticut, who distinguished himself early in the revolutionary war by the surprise and capture of Fort Ticonderoga (1775). He next did good service in Montgomery's expedition to Canada, but was taken prisoner. He had a major hand in the separation of Vermont from New York State in 1777, and in his old age published the deist tract known as *Ethan Allen's Bible*. He died at Burlington, Vermont. » American Revolution

Allen, William (1532–94) English cardinal, born at Rossall, Lancashire. An Oxford fellow and college principal, as a Catholic he was forced to leave England in 1561 and 1565. In 1568 he founded the English college at Douai to train missionary priests for the reconversion of England to Catholicism, and later founded similar establishments at Valladolid and Rome, where he died. » missions, Christian; Roman Catholicism

Allen, Woody, originally **Allen Stewart Konigsberg** (1935–) US screenwriter, actor, and director, born in New York City. He dropped out of university, and after a period as a gag-writer and nightclub comic, he wrote and acted in *What's New, Pussycat?* (1965). His direction of *Take the Money and Run* (1969) initiated a career in his own films, mainly comedies centred on psychological problems in modern US city life, especially *Annie Hall* (1977), *Manhattan* (1979), and *Hannah and Her Sisters* (1986), which gained an Academy award.

Allenby, Edmund Henry Hynman, 1st Viscount (1861–1936) British field marshal, born at Brackenhurst, Nottinghamshire. As Commander of the 3rd Army during the Battle of Arras (1917), he came close to breaching the German line. He then took command of the Egyptian Expeditionary Force, and conducted a masterly campaign against the Turks in Palestine and Syria, capturing Jerusalem (1917), Damascus and Aleppo (1918), and securing an armistice. He was made a viscount in 1919, and died in London. » World War 1

Allende (Gossens), Salvador [ayen**day**] (1908–73) Chilean statesman and President, born in Valparaiso. A medical doctor who helped found the Chilean Socialist Party (1933), he was a member of the Chamber of Deputies (1937–9), Minister of Health (1939–41), and Senator (1945–70). Unsuccessfully standing for the presidency in 1952, 1958, and 1964, he was finally elected in 1970 as leader of the left-wing Unidad Popular coalition, which promised a 'transition to socialism'. His government was overthrown by the armed forces in 1973, when Allende died in the presidential palace. » socialism

Allende meteorite [ayen**day**] A meteorite which fell near the village of Pueblito de Allende, Mexico, in February 1969. It scattered 5 tonnes of material, rich in carbon, and with a composition believed to typify the primitive Solar System. » carbon; meteorite

allergy A reaction of the body or tissue to contact with certain foreign substances. These substances are called **allergens**, and in sensitive individuals they react with proteins (*antibodies*) produced within the body by cells of the immune system. The reaction between the allergen and antibodies results in the liberation of substances which damage body cells and tissues, including histamine, hydroxtryptamine, and bradykinin. A large number of substances found in nature (eg pollen) are actual or potential allergens, and are capable of inducing a wide range of illnesses such as asthma and dermatitis. » anaphylaxis; desensitization

Alleyn, Edward [**al**ayn] (1566–1626) English actor, a contemporary of Shakespeare, who acted in many of Marlowe's plays. He was associated with the Admiral's Men and with Philip Henslowe, forming a business partnership with the latter to run the Bear Garden and build the Fortune Theatre. He founded Dulwich College (1619) and deposited in its library documents relating to his career (including Henslowe's Diary), which give a unique insight into the financial aspects of Elizabethan theatre. » Henslowe; Marlowe, Christopher; theatre

Allgäu Alps [**ahl**goy], Ger **Allgäuer Alpen** Mountain range extending E from L Constance along the Austro-German border to the Lech R valley; highest peak, the Mädelegabel (2 645 m/8 678 ft); major cattle-rearing area (the Allgäu breed), dairying; many spas and medicinal springs. » Alps; Bavarian Alps

Alliance » **Liberal Party** (UK); **Social Democratic Party**

Alliance for Progress A 10-year programme of modernization and reform for 22 countries in Latin America, sponsored by the US government in 1961 on the initiative of President Kennedy. Few of its aims were achieved, despite numerous specific development projects. » developing countries; Kennedy, John F

Allies The term generally applied to the nations that fought the 'Axis' powers during World War 2. By 1942 the combatant countries comprising the Allies included Great Britain and the British Commonwealth, USA, Soviet Union, France, and China, while Costa Rica, Cuba, Brazil, and Mexico had also declared war on Germany and Japan. By March 1945 they had been joined by Bulgaria, Finland, Hungary, Italy (which nations had been previously allied to Nazi Germany), and Turkey. » Axis Powers; World War 2

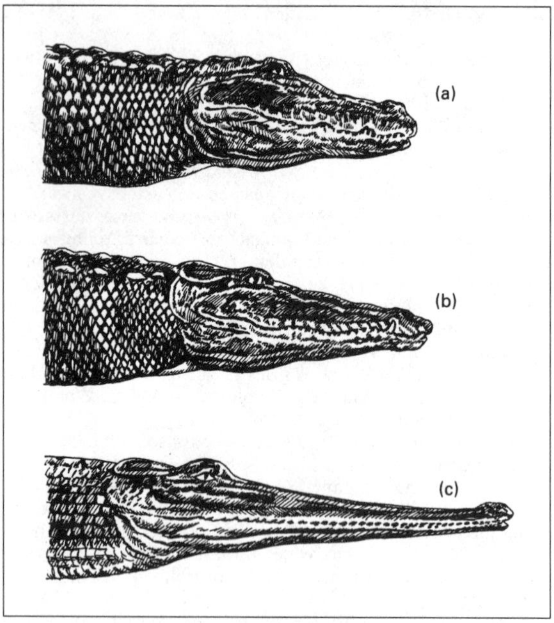

Alligator (a); crocodile (b); gharial (c)

alligator A crocodile-like reptile of family *Alligatoridae*; short broad snout; fourth tooth from the front on each side of the lower jaw is hidden when the jaws are closed (unlike the crocodile); two species: **American alligator** (*Alligator mississippiensis*) from SE USA, and the rare **Chinese alligator** (*Alligator chinensis*). » caiman; crocodile; gharial; reptile

Allingham, Margery (1904–66) British detective-story writer, born in London, the creator of the character Albert Campion. Her books include *Flowers for the Judge* (1936), *The Tiger in the Smoke* (1952), and *Cargo of Eagles* (1968). She died at Colchester, Essex. » detective story

alliteration The repetition of a consonantal sound or sounds; to be distinguished from **assonance**, the repetition of a vowel sound. Both are illustrated in these lines by Keats: 'Then in a wailful choir the small gnats mourn/Among the river sallows, borne aloft/Or sinking as the light wind lives or dies'. The dominant consonants here are *l*, *m/n*, and *w*; an example of assonance is the link between *small*, *mourn*, and *borne*. An intrinsic part of the sound-structure of poetry, alliterative effects may also be cultivated in prose. » poetry

allium A large genus of perennials, all with a strong, distinctive onion smell, native to the N hemisphere; most form bulbs with a brown papery skin; leaves usually tubular, sometimes elliptical or strap-shaped; flowers with six perianth-segments, bell- or star-shaped, in dense umbels. In many species the flowers are mixed with, or completely replaced by bulbils, which allow the plant to reproduce vegetatively. They include several well-known vegetables and ornamentals. (Genus: *Allium*, 450 species. Family: *Liliaceae*.) » bulb; bulbil; chives; garlic; leek; onion; perennial; perianth; ransoms; shallot; umbel

allophone » **phoneme**

Allosaurus [**al**ohsawruhs] A large flesh-eating dinosaur reaching 11 m/36 ft in length and two tonnes in weight; bipedal, powerful hindlimbs, and short forelimbs, both with three claws; muscular tail assisted in balancing; teeth with serrated edges; known from the Upper Jurassic period of N America. (Order: *Saurischia*.) » dinosaur [i]; Jurassic period; Saurischia

allotrope One of several forms in which an element may exist. These may be different molecular forms, as O_2 and O_3, or they may be different crystal modifications, as graphite and diamond (allotropes of C). » crystals; polymorph

alloy A blend of a metal with one or more other metals or with a non-metallic substance. Most pure metals lack the properties needed to make them practically useful, and are nearly always used as some alloy. The properties of the alloy may differ considerably from those of any of the constituents, and vary with the proportions used, as with brass. Alloys known since ancient times include bronze (copper with tin), brass (copper with zinc), and pewter (lead with tin). Modern alloys include stainless steels (iron/chromium/nickel), and high temperature-resistant alloys for use in gas turbines (containing titanium). » amalgam; case hardening

allspice An evergreen tree native to tropical America and the West Indies; leaves elliptical; flowers creamy; fruit small, round; also known as **pimento** or **Jamaican pepper**. Spice made from its dried, unripe fruits has a flavour like that of cinnamon, cloves, and nutmeg combined, hence the name. (*Pimenta dioica*. Family: *Myrtaceae*.) » evergreen plants; herbs and spices; spice; tree [i]

alluvium A geological term for unconsolidated material deposited by a river. The material ranges in size from clay, through silt and sand, to gravel. Alluvium is generally well sorted (ie deposits are of a uniform or narrow size range), and the material is rounded. » river [i]

Alma-Ata [**al**ma **ata**], formerly **Vernyi** (to 1921) 43°15N 76°57E, pop (1989) 1 128 000. Capital city of Kazakhstan; in the N foothills of the Zailiyskiy Alatau range, c.300 km/185 ml from the Chinese frontier; established in 1854 as a military fortress and trading centre; destroyed by earthquake, 1887; airport; railway; university (1934); Academy of Sciences (1968); engineering, printing, film-making, foodstuffs, tobacco, textiles, leather; noted tourist and athletic centre; Ascension cathedral (1904, world's second highest wooden building). » Kazakhstan

Alma-Tadema, Sir Lawrence [**al**ma **ta**dema] (1836–1912) Dutch-British painter, born at Dronryp, Friesland, the Netherlands. He entered the Antwerp Academy of Art in 1852, and came to specialize in subjects from Greek, Roman, and Egyptian antiquity. In 1873 he settled permanently in England, and was knighted in 1899. He died at Wiesbaden, Germany.

Almagro, Diego de (c.1475–1538) Spanish conquistador and collaborator of Pizarro. He briefly invaded Chile in 1536. Bitter rivalry then developed between Almagro and Pizarro, who defeated him in a desperate engagement near Cuzco. Soon after, Almagro was executed. » Pizarro

Almeida, Francisco de [al**may**da] (c.1450–1510) Portuguese soldier, born near Lisbon, who was appointed first Viceroy of the Indies in 1505, and superseded by Albuquerque in 1509. He was killed by natives in the region of present-day Cape Town. » Albuquerque, Alfonso d'

Almohads [**al**muhhadz] » **Berber**

almond A small deciduous, sometimes spiny tree growing to 8 m/26 ft, native to Asia; leaves narrowly oval, toothed; flowers pink fading to white, appearing before the leaves; fruit greyish, velvety, 3.5–6 cm/1½–2½ in, oval; thin, leathery flesh surrounding pitted stone. The **sweet almond** (variety *dulcis*) is the source of edible almond nuts; **bitter almond** (variety *amara*) is inedible, but provides oil of bitter almonds used in industry; ornamental flowering almonds are other species. (*Prunus dulcis*. Family: *Rosaceae*.) » deciduous plants; prunus; tree [i]

Almoravids [almo**ra**vidz] » **Berber**

Almqvist, Karl Jonas Ludvig (1793–1866) Swedish author, born in Stockholm. He had a singular career, in which (though apparently innocent) he once had to flee as a suspected forger and would-be poisoner to the USA, where he became Lincoln's secretary. Most of his work is included in a series called *Törnrosens bok* (1832–50, The Book of the Briar Rose). He died in Bremen, Germany. » Swedish literature

aloe A large genus of shrub- or tree-like evergreens, native to Africa, especially S Africa, and Arabia; leaves sword-shaped, tough, fleshy, often waxy and toothed, in rosettes at tips of stems; flowers tubular, yellow to red; often planted for ornament. The drug **bitter aloes** is obtained from the sap. (Genus: *Aloe*, 275 species. Family: *Liliaceae*.) » evergreen plants; shrub; tree [i]

Alonso, Dámaso (1898–1990) Spanish poet and philologist, born and died in Madrid. He became professor of Romance philology at Madrid, establishing his reputation as an authority on Góngora. *Hijos de la Ira* (1944, Children of Wrath) is his best-known poetic work. » comparative linguistics; Góngora; poetry; Spanish literature

alopecia [aluh**pee**sha] Hair loss resulting from the failure of hair formation by the hair follicles. It may be patchy (*alopecia areata*) or generalized (*baldness*). It may be inherited, or stem from an underlying general illness or toxin (eg drug) which disturbs the follicular activity. » baldness

Aloysius, St » **Gonzaga, Luigi**

alpaca [al**pa**ka] A domesticated member of the camel family, from Peru and Bolivia; resembles a long-haired llama, but with a shorter face, neck, and legs; kept mainly for wool; sheared every two years; two breeds: *huacaya* and *suri*. It may be cross-bred with the vicuña (to produce the finer-woolled *paco-vicuña*) or with the llama. (*Lama pacos*.) » Camelidae; llama; vicuña

Alpe Adria [**al**pay **a**dria] pop (1981) 35 600 000. A working association of 11 neighbouring regions in Austria, Germany, Italy, and Yugoslavia, linked by cultural and economic interests; established in 1978; Oberösterreich, Salzburg, and Steiermark federal states in Austria; Veneto, Lombardy, Trentino–Alto Adige, and Friuli–Venezia Giulia regions in Italy; Bayern in Germany; Hrvatska (Croatia) and Slovenija republics in Yugoslavia.

Alpha Centauri [**al**fa sen**taw**ree] » **Centaurus**

alpha decay A naturally-occurring radioactive decay process in which the atomic nucleus breaks up into a lighter nucleus and an alpha particle, which is ejected. It is governed by strong nuclear force. Lead-210 is an alpha particle source with a half-life of 21 years. » alpha particle; half-life; nucleus (physics); radioactivity

alpha particle A particle emitted in alpha decay. It is composed of two neutrons plus two protons, the same as the helium nucleus, and identified as such by British physicist Ernest Rutherford in 1906; charge +2. It typically travels a few centimetres in the air before being brought to rest by collisions with air molecules. It causes the production of many ions, and in living tissue substantial biological damage. » alpha decay; ion; neutron; proton; particle physics; Rutherford, Ernest

alphabet The most economical and versatile form of writing system yet devised, because it breaks words down into their phonic components, assigning letters or combinations of letters to represent speech sounds. Thus, in English, the letter (or *grapheme*) *m* represents the sound (or *phoneme*) [m] in such words as *mat*; less obviously, the series *o...e* represents the long [ou] vowel sound in such words as *bone*. The symbols of an alphabetic writing system are not tied to the meanings of the words they represent, and the need for several thousand pictograms, for instance, is avoided. Most alphabets contain less than 30 symbols. However, they differ substantially in the regularity with which they correspond to the sound system: Spanish and Welsh, for instance, have a very regular system, whereas English and Irish Gaelic (particularly in its most traditional form) have many exceptional spelling patterns which can be learned only by special rules. Also, the alphabets of W European languages give vowels and consonants the same status, as full letters; but in the case of *consonantal* alphabets (eg the alphabets of India), the two types of sound are treated differently: the consonants are assigned the function of 'mapping out' the basic form of the word, and the vowels are added as diacritic marks. The Hebrew and Arabic alphabets take this system one step further, and allow the marking of the vowel diacritics to be optional. The model for all Western alphabets was the Etruscan (c.800 BC), itself based on the Greek alphabet, which had modified the Phoenician consonantal alphabet by adding vowel letters to it. » consonant; Cyrillic alphabet; graphology; ideography; i.t.a.; pictography [i]; Semitic alphabets; syllabary; vowel; writing systems; RR81

THE DEVELOPMENT OF THE EARLY ALPHABET

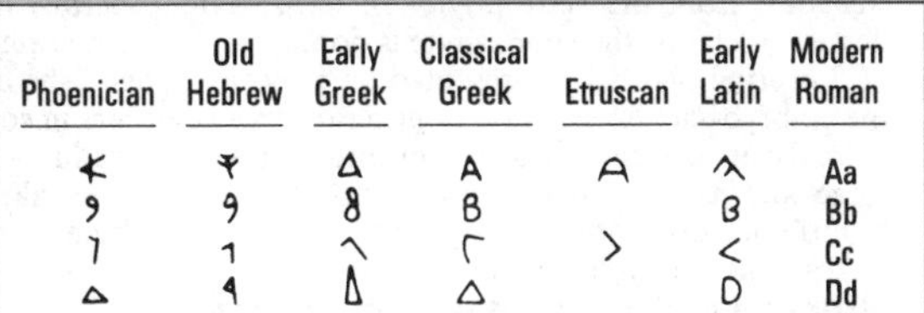

alphanumeric characters A set of characters which includes all the lower and upper case letters of the alphabet (a to z, A to Z), the numbers 0 to 9, and some punctuation characters. The term is widely used in computer science.

Alpher, Ralph Asher (1921–) US physicist, born in Washington, DC. In 1948 with Hans Bethe (1906–) and George Gamow he devised a theory of the processes forming new chemical elements and emitting energy in the early life of the universe (the alpha, beta, gamma theory). This has become part of the 'big bang' model of the universe, which has strong support through Alpher and Herman's prediction (1948) of a residue of characteristic radiation, which was found experimentally in 1964. » Big Bang; Gamow

Alphonso » **Alfonso**

alphorn A musical instrument found in rural communities, particularly in the Swiss Alps. Most alphorns are about 180 cm/6 ft long, made of wood, and can sound the first five or six harmonics; but examples up to twice that length are not uncommon. » aerophone; harmonic series [i]

alpine A botanical term for vegetation growing in mountains above the tree-line; also used for plants naturally occurring in such regions. Alpines are typically low-growing or dome-shaped perennials, adapted to withstand high levels of solar radiation and drought as well as cold. » auricula; edelweiss; gentian; perennial

Alps Principal mountain range of Europe, covering 259 000 sq km/100 000 sq ml in Switzerland, France, Germany, Austria, Liechtenstein, Italy, and Yugoslavia; a series of parallel chains over 1 000 km/600 ml SW–NE; originally formed by collision of African and European tectonic plates; source of many great European rivers, notably the Rhine, Po, and Rhône; **Western Alps** (highest peaks in parentheses) consist of (1) *Alpes-Maritimes* (Cima Sud Argentera 3 297 m/10 817 ft); (2) *Alpes Cottiennes* or *Cottian Alps* (Monte Viso 3 851 m/12 634 ft); (3) *Alpes Dauphine* (Barre des Ecrins 4 101 m/13 455 ft); (4) *Alpes Graian* or *Graian Alps* (Gran Paradiso 4 061 m/13 323 ft); **Middle Alps** consist of (1) *Alpi Pennine* (Mont Blanc 4 807 m/15 771 ft, highest peak in the range; Matterhorn 4 477 m/14 688 ft); (2) *Alpi Lepontine* (3 553 m/11 657 ft); (3) *Alpi Retiche* or *Rhaetian Alps* (Piz Bernina 4 049 m/13 284 ft); (4) *Berner Alpen* or *Bernese Alps* (Finsteraarhorn 4 274 m/14 022 ft); (5) *Alpi Orobie*; (6) *Ötztaler Alpen* (Wildspitze 3 774 m/12 382 ft); (7) *Dolomiti* or *Dolomites* (Marmolada 3 342 m/10 964 ft); (8) *Lechtaler Alpen* (3 038 m/9 967 ft); **Eastern Alps**: (1) *Zillertaler Alpen* or *Alpi Aurine* (3 510 m/11 516 ft); (2) *Kitzbühler Alpen* (2 559 m/8 396 ft); (3) *Karnische Alpen* or *Carnic Alps* (2 781 m/9 124 ft); (4) *Julijske Alpe* or *Julian Alps* (Triglav 2 863 m/9 393 ft); (5) *Hohe Tauern* or *Noric Alps* (Grossglockner 3 797 m/

12 457 ft); (6) *Niedere Tauern* (2 863 m/9 393 ft); notable passes include the Mont Cenis, St Bernard (Little and Greater), Gemmi, Simplon, St Gotthard, Splugen, Stilfserjoch (Stelvio), and Brenner; railway tunnels at Col de Fréjus, Lotschberg, Simplon, and St Gotthard; summer pasture on many lower slopes; major tourist region, with highly developed facilities; mountaineering and skiing; towns have manufactures concerned with native and imported products such as textiles, clocks, chocolate, wooden goods; in 1911 Karl Blodig was the first to climb all peaks over 4 000 m (13 123 ft). » Brenner/ Saint Bernard's/Saint Gotthard/Simplon Passes; Allgauer/ Bavarian / Bernese / Carnic / Cottian / Dinaric / Graian / Julian / Karawanken / Lechtal / Üztal / Salzburg / Stubai / Zillertal Alps; Dolomites; Nordliche Kalkalpen; Rhätikon

Alsace [al**sas**], Ger **Elsass**, Lat **Alsatia** pop (1982) 1 566 048; area 8 280 sq km/3 196 sq ml. Region of NE France, comprising the departments of Bas-Rhin and Haut-Rhin, part of Upper Rhine Plain on frontier with Germany; crossed S–N by Rhine and Ill Rivers; traditional scene of Franco-German conflict; formerly part of Lorraine before becoming part of German Empire; Treaty of Westphalia (1648) returned most of Alsace to France; ceded to Germany, 1871; returned to France, 1919; occupied by Germany in World War 2; chief towns, Strasbourg, Mulhouse, Colmar; several spas, wine towns, and vineyards; fertile and industrially productive region; wine, beer, pottery, chemicals, paper, printed fabrics, textile dyeing and spinning, machinery, car manufacture. » France [i]

alsatian » **German shepherd**

alsike [**al**siyk] A species of clover, probably native to Europe, grown as a fodder crop and now occurring in many temperate countries; a variable perennial growing to 60 cm/2 ft; leaves with three toothed leaflets, widest towards the tip; pea-flowers white or pink, in lax rounded heads to 3 cm/1.2 in across. (*Trifolium hybridum*. Family: *Leguminosae*.) » clover; perennial

Alston, Richard (1948–) British dancer, choreographer, and director, born at Stoughton, Sussex. He studied at the London School of Contemporary Dance, and instigated the formation of one of the first British postmodern dance companies, Strider, in 1972. After studying in the USA he became resident choreographer (1981) and then artistic director (1986) of the Rambert Dance Company. His works include *Nowhere Slowly* (1970), *Doublework* (1978), and *Wildlife* (1984). » ballet; modern dance; Rambert Dance Company

Altai Mountains, Chinese **Altai Shan** [**al**tiy] Major mountain system of C Asia, extending from Russia (NW) SE along the border between NW China and Mongolia, into Mongolia itself; source of the Irtysh and Ob Rivers; highest point, Mt Belukha (4 506 m/14 783 ft); major mineral reserves. » Belukha, Mount; China [i]

Altaic [al**tay**ik] A family of languages extending from the Balkan peninsula to the NE of Asia. About 40 languages fall into three groups: Turkic, of which Turkish is the main member, spoken by c.45 million people in and near Turkey; Mongolian, of which Mongol is the main member, spoken by c.4 million in the Mongolian People's Republic and China; and Manchu-Tungus, of which Evenki (as Tungus is now known) may have 30 000 speakers. Manchu, once a lingua franca between China and the outside world, is now spoken by few of the three million who live in the Manchu province of China. » lingua franca

Altair [al**tair**] » **Aquila**

Altamira [alta**meer**a] Palaeolithic limestone cave of c.13 500 BC on the N Spanish coast near Santander, celebrated for its vivid ceiling paintings of game animals (principally bison, bulls, horses, hinds, and boars), some over 2 m/6½ ft long. Though discovered in 1879 by local landowner Marcellino de Sautuola, its authenticity was not established before 1902. It is now a world heritage site. » Magdalenian; Three Age System

altarpiece In a Christian church, a carved or painted screen placed above the altar facing the congregation; known as an *ancona* (Ital), *retable* (Fr), or *reredos* (Eng). The earliest examples appeared in the 10th–11th-c. The *pala d'oro* (gold altarpiece) in St Mark's, Venice, commissioned 1105, consists of gold and enamel-work, as well as sculptured figures, and includes images of Christ in Majesty with angels and saints, with scenes from the New Testament and the life of the titular saint, Mark. An altarpiece consisting of two panels is called a *diptych*; three panels make a *triptych*. They vary greatly in size, and were numerous in late mediaeval and Renaissance churches. In Protestant countries this development ended abruptly at the Reformation, and many altarpieces were destroyed, but in Catholic countries their production was encouraged, leading to the luxurious altarpieces of the Baroque period, both painted (Rubens, Caravaggio, van Dyck) and carved (Bernini). The modern preference for plain altars set forward, as in the early Church, has practically ruled out the altarpiece. There is simply nowhere to put it. » Baroque (art and architecture); maestà; pala; predella

altazimuth [alt**az**imuhth] A type of telescope in which the principal axis can be moved independently in altitude (swinging on a horizontal axis) and azimuth (swinging on a vertical axis). It is used in very large optical telescopes and radio telescopes. » telescope [i]

Altdorfer, Albrecht (c.1480–1538) German painter, engraver, and architect, a leading member of the 'Danube School' of German painting, born and died in Regensburg. His most outstanding works are biblical and historical subjects set against atmospheric landscape backgrounds. He was also a pioneer of copperplate etching. » engraving; etching; German art

alternating current (AC) An electrical current whose direction of flow reverses periodically; the alternative is **direct current (DC)**, where the flow is in a single direction only. The variation of current with time is usually sinusoidal, as produced naturally by rotating coils in magnetic fields (generators). Household current is AC, with a frequency of 50 Hz (UK) or 60 Hz (USA). Power transmission and transformers rely on AC. » current (electricity); electricity; magnetism

alternation of generations The progression of the life cycle of a plant through two reproductive forms. The **sexual generation** or *gametophyte* produces haploid gametes. These fuse and give rise to a diploid *sporophyte*, which produces haploid spores from which grow new gametophytes (**asexual generation**). In algae, the gametophyte is the dominant generation, occupying the major portion of the life cycle, although the two generations are generally indistinguishable in structure. In bryophytes the gametophyte is also dominant, but is very different in structure from the sporophyte. In ferns, gymnosperms, and flowering plants, the sporophyte is dominant; the gametophyte of flowering plants is represented only by the pollen tube and the embryo-sac. Alternation of generations also occurs in some animals; in coelenterates, for example, a sexual medusa-like stage alternates with an asexual polyp-like stage. » algae; bryophyte; coelenterate; fern; gamete; gametophyte; gymnosperms; life cycle; reproduction; spore; sporophyte

alternative and augmentative communication A means of communicating devised to help severely disabled people who are unable to speak or write normally because of a physical or mental handicap. *Augmentative* systems supplement normal language use; *alternative* systems replace normal language entirely. Examples include the use of sign languages, symbol boards, speech synthesizers, and braille. Typically, users wear or sit in front of a device containing a selection of letters, words, or messages, and type, touch, or point to the element they wish to communicate, using any mobile part of their body (eg foot, mouth, eyebrow) to operate a keyboard, switch, or pointing device. Major advances are in progress, following developments in electronic and computational technology. » braille; Blissymbolics; sign language

alternative energy Sources of energy which do not rely on the burning of fossil fuels (eg coal, gas, oil) or nuclear power to provide energy. With the controversial nature of nuclear power, and the recognition that fossil fuels are a non-renewable resource and contribute significantly to pollution, there is considerable interest in some countries in alternative sources, such as solar power, geothermal power, hydroelectric power, tidal power, and wind power. Such sources are particularly important in countries which lack fossil fuels, and are seen as having potential in economically developing countries. Alternative sources are often seen as being environmentally sound because pollution is rarely a problem. However, their development is not without controversy: schemes to build barrages across estuaries to harness tidal energy are often attacked because of damage to estuarine ecosystems; hydroelectric power projects may require valleys to be flooded and people made homeless; the large number of wind towers needed for wind power are a visual intrusion. » biogas; energy; fossil fuel; hydroelectric power; nuclear reactor [i]; renewable resources; solar power

alternative medicine Approaches to the treatment of illness using procedures other than those recommended by medical science. The demand for such treatment has increased in recent years, generated by individuals who have not been relieved of their complaints by orthodox methods. There are over 50 different approaches, including acupuncture, aromatherapy, autosuggestion, bioenergetics, biomagnetic therapy, Christian Science, chiropractic, fasting, herbalism and dietotherapy, homeopathy and holistic medicine, hydrotherapy, ion therapy, massage, meditation, naturopathy, and osteopathy. For the most part, these procedures are based on theories of disease for which there is scant evidence, and some invoke principles that many people recognize as bizarre. The fact that most of them are empirical in their origin is not in itself a fault, as many medical treatments now incorporated into orthodox medical practice began as empirical observations, and only later acquired scientific justification. The problem is how to distinguish the genuinely effective from witchcraft and superstition. Almost none of the therapeutic methods used as alternative medicine have been or are readily capable of being rigorously assessed, using the standard scientific techniques of critical assessment and refutation. For the most part their effects on the natural history of a human ailment to which they may be applied have not been rigorously compared either with the natural course of the ailment or with other remedies claimed to influence the ailment. By and large, the claims to their success remain anecdotal. » acupuncture; chiropractic; holistic medicine; homeopathy; osteopathy

Althusser, Louis [**al**toosair] (1918–) French political philosopher, born at Birmandreis, Algeria, and educated in Paris. A member of the Communist Party from 1948, he wrote influential works on the interpretation of Marxist theory, including *Pour Marx* (1965, For Marx) and *Lénin et la Philosophie* (1969, Lenin and Philosophy). In 1980 he murdered his wife, and has since been confined in an asylum. » Marxism

Altichiero [altee**kyair**oh] (c.1330–c.95) Venetian painter, born near Verona. He worked in Verona, and in Padua, where his frescoes in the Basilica of San Antonio (painted 1372–9) and in the Oratory of San Giorgio (1377–84) combine the solid realism of Giotto with a new Gothic elegance typical of the later 14th-c. In San Giorgio he shared the work with a painter called Avanzo. » Giotto; International Gothic; Venetian School

altimeter A device carried by an aircraft to measure its height above the ground. The usual type operates by sending out a radio signal, and measuring the time taken by the signal to return, since the speed at which the radio signal travels is known. When the ground rises below the aircraft, and the aircraft maintains level flight, the altimeter registers a drop in altitude. » aircraft [i]; radio waves

Altiplano The arid plateau of W Bolivia and S Peru between the W and E Cordilleras; elevation 3 000–5 000 m/9 800–16 400 ft. It is covered by widespread alluvial and glacial deposits, and the rivers and streams of the plateau drain into L Titicaca (Bolivia/Peru) and L Poopo (Bolivia). Both are closed lake basins, ie they do not drain to the sea. » Bolivia [i]; Peru [i]

Alto Paraná, River » **Paraná, River**

altocumulus clouds Middle-level clouds of the cumulus family at altitudes of c.2 000–7 000 m/6 500–23 000 ft. They are white and/or grey in colour, and usually indicate fine weather. Cloud symbol: Ac. » cloud [i]; cumulus clouds

altostratus clouds Middle-level clouds of the stratus family, similar to stratus clouds but less dense and occurring at higher elevations, typically c.2 000–7 000 m/6 500–23 000 ft. They are greyish in colour with a sheet-like appearance, and give a warning of warm, rainy weather associated with the passage of a warm front. Cloud symbol: As. » cloud [i]; stratus clouds

altruism The thesis that people sometimes intentionally promote the interests of others to the detriment of their own interests. Any normative ethical theory which implies that we ought to act altruistically in some circumstances presupposes this possibility. Hobbes denied it, arguing that apparently altruistic actions are really self-interested. » egoism; ethics; Hobbes

ALU » **arithmetic and logic unit**

alum Usually $KAl(SO_4)_2.12H_2O$. Hydrated potassium aluminium sulphate, *common alum*. Other alums have Al substituted by Fe (*iron alum*) or Cr (*chrome alum*). All form large, octahedral crystals. Common alum hydrolyzes in water to give gelatinous $Al(OH)_3$, and can be used as a coagulant in water clarification. » aluminium; hydrolysis; potassium

alumina [a**loo**mina] Al_2O_3. Aluminium (III) oxide, the principal ingredient of bauxite. It occurs in various forms, including emery or corundum (used as abrasives), and the coloured forms, rubies and sapphires. Hydrated alumina is used in chromatography. » bauxite; chromatography; gemstones

aluminate [a**loo**minuht] Salt containing an anion derived from $Al(OH)_3$ by the replacement of hydrogen by metal. *Sodium aluminate* ($NaAlO_2$) is used in water purification, coagulating various impurities in a precipitate of hydrated alumina. » alumina; anion

aluminium or **aluminum** [a**loo**minuhm] Al, element 13, melting point 660°C. A silvery metal, the third most abundant element in the Earth's crust, occurring mostly as aluminosilicates. It is extracted mainly by electrolysis of alumina from bauxite fused with cryolite (Na_3AlF_6). Although the metal is strongly electropositive, it forms a tough oxide coating and is then passive to further oxidation; with its relatively low density, 2.7 g cm^{-3}, this makes it a valuable structural metal. In its compounds, it mainly shows an oxidation state of +3. » bauxite; chemical elements; cryolite; electrolysis [i]

Alva or **Alba, Fernando Álvarez de Toledo, Duque de** ('Duke of') (1507–82) Spanish general and statesman, born at Piedratita. Sent to quell the Revolt of the Netherlands (1567), his Council of Blood promoted a ruthless campaign of repression. He defeated Prince Louis of Nassau, and compelled William of Orange to retire to Germany; upon which he entered Brussels in triumph (1568). Later, Holland and Zeeland renewed their efforts against him, and his fleet was destroyed. He was recalled in 1573, and died in Lisbon. » Blood, Council of; Revolt of the Netherlands; William I (of the Netherlands)

Alvar [**al**vah] A particularly fervent devotional Hindu saint of the Vaishava tradition. The word means 'diver', and is attributed to one who enters into the depth of mystical experience. Alvars are closely associated with the Tamils of S India. » Hinduism; Vishnu

Alvarado, Pedro de [alva**rah**thoh] (c.1495–1541) Spanish conquistador, born at Badajoz, who took part in the conquest of Mexico. He was later appointed Governor of Guatemala, and died near Guadalajara, New Spain. » Cortés

Alvarez, Luis (Walter) (1911–88) US physicist, born in San Francisco. He was educated at Chicago and then at Berkeley, where he spent most of his career. His early work included the discovery of orbital electron capture, and (with Bloch) the measurement of the magnetic moment of the neutron. In 1947 he made the first linear proton accelerator, and later the liquid hydrogen bubble chamber which detected many new subatomic particles and for which he received the Nobel Prize for Physics in 1968. » Bloch, Felix; bubble chamber; particle physics

Álvarez Quintero, Serafín [**al**vareth keen**tay**roh] (1871–1938) and **Joaquín** (1873–1944), Spanish playwrights, both born in Utrera. The brothers were the joint authors of well over 100 modern Spanish plays, all displaying a characteristic gaiety and sentiment. They include *Los galeotes* (1900, The Galley Slaves) and *Las flores* (1901, The Flowers). They both died in Madrid. » drama; Spanish literature

alveoli » **lungs**

Alvey programme A UK-based collaborative research programme involving industry, government, and academic institutions which was intended to develop information technology and, in particular, fifth generation computers. It was established in 1982 through a working party chaired by John Alvey (1925–). » information technology; computer generations

alyssum [alisuhm] An annual to perennial, mat-forming or bushy but low-growing, native to Europe and Asia; leaves narrow; flowers cross-shaped, white, blue, or yellow. **Golden alyssum**, a grey-leaved, yellow-flowered perennial, is often grown in gardens, but the popular white garden annual commonly called alyssum is a different, though related, plant. (Genus: *Alyssum*, 150 species. Family: *Cruciferae*.) » annual; perennial; sweet alyssum

Alzheimer's disease [**alt**shiymer] A common form of generalized cerebral atrophy which results in slowly progressive dementia affecting all aspects of brain function. It leads ultimately to total disintegration of the personality. The disease was first described in 1906 by a German neurologist, Alois Alzheimer (1864–1915). Current theories as to its cause include a slow viral infection, environmental toxins (eg aluminium), a systemic metabolic illness, and the involvement of a heritable factor in certain forms. » brain [i]; dementia; metabolism; virus

Amal A Lebanese Shiite movement established by the Imam Musa Sadr in the early 1970s. After Sadr's disappearance in 1978 during a trip to Libya, Nabih Berri took over the leadership. Amal has a fighting force of over 4 000. » Shiites

Amalekites An ancient nomadic people, notorious for their treachery, who lived S of Canaan. According to *Gen* 36.12, they were descended from Esau. » Esau; nomadism

amalgam An alloy of mercury with some other metal(s), known since classical times. Copper, zinc, and tin amalgams are used in dentistry. Gold amalgam was used in Renaissance gilding techniques. » alloy; mercury

Amalthea [amal**thee**a] The fifth natural satellite of Jupiter, discovered in 1892; distance from the planet 181 000 km/ 112 000 ml; diameter 270 km/168 ml. » Jupiter (astronomy); RR4

Amantia » **fly agaric**

Amanullah Khan (1892–1960) Amir and King of Afghanistan (1919–29), born at Paghman, who established Afghan independence (1922) after a war with Britain. His push for internal reforms provoked opposition, and led to his abdication. He spent the rest of his life in exile, and died in Zürich, Switzerland. » Afghanistan [i]

amaranth An annual or perennial herb, native to tropical and temperate regions; flowers usually small and forming dense inflorescences, perianth-segments in whorls of three or five, often brightly coloured; also known as **pigweed**. Some Asian species yield edible grain used as a substitute for cereal. (Genus: *Amaranthus*, 60 species. Family: *Amaranthaceae*.) » herb; inflorescence [i]; perennial; perianth

Amarillo [ama**ril**oh] 35°13N 101°50W, pop (1980) 149 230. Seat of Potter County, NW Texas, USA; airport; railway; commercial, banking, and industrial centre for the Texas panhandle; oil refining, meat packing, flour milling, zinc smelting, helicopters. » Texas

amaryllis A large bulb, native to tropical America; flowers flaring, trumpet-shaped, up to 15 cm/6 in long, in a range of bright colours, 1–10 (but usually 2–4) on a hollow stalk, appearing in spring before the strap-shaped leaves. The popular pot plants are mostly complex hybrids increased by bulb division. It is often confused with the belladonna lily (*Amaryllis bella-donna*). (Genus: *Hippeastrum*, 75 species. Family: *Amaryllidaceae*.) » belladonna lily; bulb

Amaterasu The principal deity in the Shinto religion of Japan. She is both the Sun-goddess who rules all the gods and the mother-goddess who ensures fertility. Once when she shut herself in her cave, the whole world became darkened and no plants could grow. The other gods played music and offered presents to make her return. » Shinto

Amateur Athletic Association (AAA) The governing body for men's athletics in England and Wales, better known by its initials. Founded in Oxford in 1880, the first championships were held at Lillie Bridge, London. The Women's Amateur Athletic Association was founded in 1922. » athletics; International Amateur Athletic Federation

amatol A group of high explosives consisting of mixtures of trinitrotoluene (TNT) and ammonium nitrate. It was much used in World War 1 to economize on TNT, but later fell out of favour because of such faults as the absorption of undesirable water from the air (*hygroscopicity*). » explosives; TNT [i]

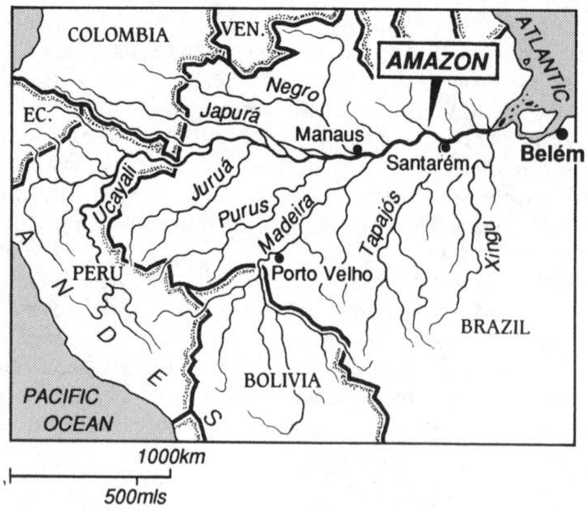

Amazon ant An ant that depends entirely on slaves of other ant species to run its nest and care for its larvae. The workers have sickle-shaped jaws (*mandibles*) used as weapons when raiding other nests. (Order: *Hymenoptera*. Family: *Formicidae*.) » ant; larva; slave-making ant

Amazon, River, Port **Rio Amazônas** River in N South America, the largest in the world by volume, and the second longest; two major headstreams, the Marañón and the Ucayali, rising in the Andes of Peru (c.150 km/83 ml from the Pacific) and joining S of Iquitos; flows generally W–E across Brazil, entering the Atlantic in a wide delta; drains a basin c.7 000 000 sq km/ 2 700 000 sq ml; more than 1 100 tributaries; ocean steamers as far as Iquitos, 3 680 km/2 287 ml from the Atlantic; deepest point (37 m/121 ft) at the influx of the Trombetas R; large island, Ilha de Marajó, at the delta; length from L Lauricocha (at the headwaters of the Marañón) 6 280 km/3 902 ml; from L Vilafro following the Ucayali and Apurímac headwaters to the mouth of the Amazon via the Canal do Norte, 6 449 km/ 4 007 ml; river levels at Manaus fluctuate by over 15 m/50 ft; N channels of the delta made dangerous by a frequent tidal bore (*Pororoca*) moving up river at up to 65 kph/40 mph, with waves sometimes 5 m/16 ft high; cargo launches reach the interior, carrying fish, cedarwood, flour, rubber, and jute; discovered 1500; first descended 1541, ascended 1637; opened to world shipping 1866; free navigation guaranteed by Colombia–Brazil treaty, 1929. » Brazil [i]; Manaus

Amazons [amaznz] In Greek mythology, a nation of women soldiers, located by Herodotus in Scythia (Russia). Strong and athletic, they were said to mutilate the right breast in order to use the bow. With no apparent basis in fact, this story fascinated the Greeks and was a frequent subject in art, perhaps because of its suggestion of an alternative society. » Herodotus

ambassador The highest ranking diplomat resident abroad, who officially represents his or her country in relations with foreign governments. Ambassadors are to be distinguished from **consuls**, whose chief functions are to protect citizens abroad, and to protect the commercial interests of these citizens. » diplomatic service; High Commissioner

Ambedkar, Bhimrao Ranji [**am**bedker] (1893–1956) Indian politician and champion of the depressed castes, born in a Ratnagiri village, Bombay. Educated in Bombay, New York, and London, he became a London barrister, later a member of the Bombay Legislative Assembly and leader of 60 000 000 Untouchables. Appointed Minister of Law in 1947, he took a leading part in framing the Indian Constitution. With thousands of his followers, he publicly embraced the Buddhist faith not long before his death, in New Delhi. » Buddhism; caste; India [i]

ambergris [**am**bergrees] ('grey amber') A grey waxy substance found in the intestines of the sperm whale, *Physter catodon*; up to 450 gms/1 lb per whale; formerly used in perfumes to make the fragrance last longer. » sperm whale

Ambler, Eric (1909–) British novelist, born in London, and educated at Colfe's Grammar School and London University. After an apprenticeship in engineering (1927–8), he served in Italy (1943) during World War 2 and at the War Office (1944–6). He specialized in the writing of spy thrillers, such as *Epitaph for a Spy* (1938) and *The Mask of Dimitrios* (1939). » spy story

Ambrose, St (c.339–97), feast day 7 December. Italian bishop and writer, born at Trier. He studied at Rome, and became consular prefect of Upper Italy (369). His fairness in dealing with the Arian/Catholic controversy led to a popular call for his appointment as Bishop of Milan in 374. After initially refusing the post, he accepted it, moving from the state of unbaptized layman to bishop in only eight days. One of the four traditional Doctors of the Latin Church, he is remembered for his preaching (which greatly influenced St Augustine), his literary works and hymns, and for the improvements he introduced into the church service – the Ambrosian ritual and chant. He died in Milan. » Arius; Augustine, St; bishop

ambrosia beetle A small dark beetle that burrows into wood. The adults have cylindrical bodies with short, clubbed antennae. The fleshy, legless larvae feed on fungi that line the walls of tunnels made in the wood. (Order: *Coleoptera*. Family: *Scolytidae*.) » beetle; larva

ameba » **amoeba**

Amen » **Amun**

Amenhotep III (c.1411–1375 BC) The greatest of the 18th dynasty Egyptian pharaohs of that name. His reign was marked by peaceful progress at home and successful diplomacy abroad. Under him, the ancient capital of Thebes was adorned with new buildings, and reached the peak of prosperity. » Ahmose I; Akhenaton; Egyptian history, Ancient [i]; Thebes

Amenhotep IV » **Akhenaton**

amenorrhoea/amenorrhea [amenuh**ree**a] The absence of normal menstruation. It arises when the cyclical hormonal control (by the front pituitary gland and ovaries) of normal menstruation is disturbed by physical or psychological factors. » Cushing's disease; menstruation

America's Cup Yachting's most famous race, held approximately every four years. The trophy was originally called the One Hundred Guinea Cup, and was donated by the Royal Yacht Squadron for a race around the Isle of Wight in 1851. It was renamed the America's Cup after the schooner *America* which won the race. The New York Yacht Club offered the cup as a challenge trophy. Between 1870 and 1983 it remained in US ownership until Australia II wrested it. The USA won it back in 1987, and then successfully held off a challenge from New Zealand in 1988, which resulted in a lengthy legal battle. » sailing

American Civil Liberties Union A US pressure group concerned to promote civil rights, especially of Blacks and ethnic minorities. It has tended to use the courts to gain changes based on the rights afforded under the Constitution, and is particularly concerned with freedom of speech and maintaining an open society. » civil rights

American Civil War (1861–5) Sometimes called the 'Second American Revolution', a conflict in the USA which resolved two great issues: the nature of the Federal Union and the relative power of the states and the central government; and the existence of Black slavery.

The war began in the early months of Lincoln's presidency, whose election demonstrated that the South could no longer expect to control the high offices of state. Although Lincoln was hostile to slavery, he did not believe that he could interfere where it existed. But to Southerners, he and the Republican Party were intolerable, and 11 Southern states withdrew from the Union, establishing the Confederate States of America. War broke out (12 Apr 1861) when Southern batteries opened fire on a Union emplacement in the harbour of Charleston, S Carolina. At first Lincoln defined the issue as the preservation of the Union, without any reference to slavery. But he broadened the war aims (1 Jan 1863), proclaiming the emancipation without compensation of all slaves in areas then under arms against the government. In practice, the proclamation changed nothing, but it did give the war the semblance of a moral crusade.

Sometimes called the first 'modern' war, the Civil War pitted two different social systems against each other. The free-labour industrial North had greater population, stronger financial, manufacturing, and transportation systems, and international recognition; but initially the South had much better military leaders. Because of slavery, it could also put a larger proportion of its White adult male population under arms. Lincoln's greatest difficulty was finding an effective general; he did not succeed until the emergence from obscurity of Ulysses S Grant.

The winning strategy began in 1863, when Grant won control of the whole Mississippi Valley, isolating the W Confederate States from the rest. Meanwhile Robert E Lee was advancing into Pennsylvania, largely in the hope of winning foreign recognition for the Confederacy. His defeat at Gettysburg ended that possibility. By the autumn, the Chattanooga campaign put Northern troops in a position to bisect the Confederacy E to W, an act accomplished in late 1864 by General Sherman's march through Georgia to the sea. Grant, now the overall Northern commander, adopted a strategy of relentless pressure on Lee's forces, regardless of his own losses. In the single month of June 1864, he lost nearly 60 000, nearly Lee's total strength. But Northern advantages of population and material support, combined with the success of the Mississippi and Chattanooga campaigns, were making the Southern position untenable, particularly after Lincoln defeated the former army commander George B McClellan in the 1864 presidential election. The end came in the spring of 1865, as Sherman marched N through the Carolinas while Grant continued his costly siege of Richmond. Lee finally abandoned the Confederate capital (2 Apr), and a week later he was trapped by the combined forces of Grant and Sheridan. His capitulation at Appomattox Court House left only scattered Southern forces in the field, and the last surrender took place on 26 May.

The cost in death and devastation of the war was enormous. The greatest change was the end of slavery and all that it stood for. With its destruction there emerged the possibility of a modernized South and the long-range hope of a redefinition of the place of Black people in American life – a hope which was not to be fulfilled until almost a century later. » Chattanooga Campaign; Confederate States of America; Copperhead; Gettysburg Address; Peninsular Campaign; Reconstruction; Vicksburg; Antietam/Bull Run/Cold Harbor/Fredericksburg/Gettysburg/Seven Days, Battle of; Grant, Ulysses S; Lee, Robert E; Lincoln, Abraham; McClellan, George B; Sheridan, Philip H; Sherman, William Tecumseh

American Colonization Society A US pre-abolitionist anti-slavery group, aimed at resettling freed slaves in Africa. It was supported by some slaveholders, anxious to keep freed Blacks separate from slaves. » abolitionism; slavery

American eagle » **bald eagle**

American Federation of Labor – Congress of Industrial Organizations (AFL/CIO) A US federation of trade unions, formed in 1955 from the merger of the AFL (mainly craft unions, founded in 1866) with the CIO (mainly industrial workers' unions, founded in 1935). Its aims include educational campaigns on behalf of the labour movement, the settlement of disputes among affiliates, and political support for beneficial legislation. It has a biennial convention at which policy is decided. » Teamsters' Union; Trades Union Congress

American football » **football 2** [i]

American foxhound » **foxhound**

American Indians The original inhabitants of the American continent, who arrived during the last glacial period (14–40 000 years ago) from Asia, crossing from Siberia over the Bering Strait, perhaps in three waves. They settled in N America, extending into Middle America (Mesoamerica) more than 10 000 years ago, and sometime after this into S America.

North American Indians The palaeo-Americans were hunter-gatherers, who established themselves in the forested E coastal zone, on the grassy Great Plains, and in the W deserts. The sharp and pronounced climatic changes and over-hunting resulted in a dramatic decline in big-game animals, and the extinction of many species, including the mammoth. Except on the Great Plains, it brought to an end the mobile hunting adaptation based on communal game drives. Instead a new pattern emerged, based largely on sedentary resources such as nuts, seeds, and shellfish.

In the W, a Desert culture developed (at least 7 000 years ago) where people settled in densely populated villages, and cultivated plants, produced baskets and other artifacts, and built adobe shelters. On the Plains the people became specialized bison hunters, and (much later) started to grow crops and live in permanent settlements. In the E, which was colder and densely forested, seasonal movement occurred in response to food availability; people mainly survived by collecting nuts and seeds, and hunting caribou and sea mammals.

From the 16th-c, with the coming of European settlers, the lives of most Indians were severely disrupted. Conflict over land resulted in numerous bloody clashes, and many died from diseases introduced by Europeans. The population was very much reduced, from an estimated 1.5 million at its height, and by the 1880s most Indians had been confined to reservations. In the past generation there has been increasing political activity on the part of Indians to reclaim land rights. » Algonkin; Apache; Athabascan; Blackfoot; Californian Indians; Cherokee; Cheyenne; Chinook; Cree; Creek; Crow; Eastern Woodlands Indians; Flathead; Fox; Haida; Hidatsa; Hopi; Hupa; Huron; Indian Wars; Iroquois; Kwakiutl; Mohawk; Navajo; Nootka; Northwest Coast Indians; Ojibwa; Omaha; Oneida; Paiute; Powhatan; Salish; Seminole; Seneca; Shawnee; Shoshoni; Sioux; Southwest Indians; Tlingit; Zuñi

Middle American Indians The cultural and geographical region includes all of C and S Mexico, and extends into the C American states of Guatemala, Belize, Honduras, and El Salvador. The cultivation of a cereal crop (maize) accelerated economic and social development, giving rise to indigenous civilizations based upon them. During the Formative Era (2500 BC–AD 300) the foundations of future cultural development were laid: the emergence of hieroglyphic writing, calendrics, astronomical observation, monumental architecture, large religious and ceremonial centres, specialization in art and craft, and intensive agriculture. Because of the spread of maize from the highlands and the introduction of new strains more suited to dry areas, people were able to live in more densely concentrated settlements. The area was warm, and an ideal environment for sedentary agriculture. The first beginnings of high civilization occurred in the Olmec culture c.1200 BC.

The *Classic Period* (AD 300–900) represented Mesoamerican civilization at its height, during which the Maya civilization flourished in parts of Guatemala, the Yucatan, and the Mexican Chiapas. In the *Post-Classic* period (900–1520), the Mayans were superseded by the Toltecs and then the Aztecs, based in the C highlands of Mexico, who flourished and expanded over several centuries until the arrival of the Spanish. In 1521, Cortés and a small army of soldiers took the last Aztec emperor captive, and the empire ceased to exist. At its height, the Indian population was much larger than in N America – some suggest as many as 20 million. Today most Middle Americans live in small farming and trading village communities, are Roman Catholic and Spanish-speaking, and show a high rate of admixture with the descendants of the Spanish settlers. » Aztecs; Mayas; Olmecs; Zapotecs

South American Indians The earliest peoples were hunter-gatherers, who were gradually replaced by sedentary agricultural societies. Between c.3000 and 1500 BC in most of the region, settled life based on horticulture became the norm. The people probably obtained maize from Middle America, though there is evidence that several local plants (eg the potato tuber) were domesticated as early as 5–7000 BC. Later, from c.1000 BC, larger-scale societies developed, culminating in AD 1000 in one of the world's major civilizations, the Inca. In the century before the Spanish invasion of the region, the Inca state brought together much of the Andean area in the New World's largest empire. In the Amazon basin, tropical forest hunting-and-gathering culture existed from at least 2000 BC. With the European conquest in the 16th-c, some of the groups in the S became extinct, while others were absorbed into colonial society. But in a few remote parts, there are groups which have preserved their culture virtually intact. » Araucanians; Arawak; Chimu; Guaraní; Incas

American Legion In the USA, an association for former members of the armed forces (veterans), the largest in the world. Incorporated in 1919, its aims are to rehabilitate veterans, promote child welfare, ensure a strong national defence, and encourage patriotism. » Royal British Legion

American literature The first literary works of the English-speaking peoples of N America were sermons, journals, and histories – concerns reflected in the work of the early poets Ann Bradstreet (c.1612–72) and Edward Taylor (c.1645–1729). In the Revolutionary period the most important work was practical or political, eg Benjamin Franklin's *Poor Richard's Almanac* (1732–58). Franklin's *Autobiography* (1781) is a memorable testament to the Puritan sensibility. After the international impact of Washington Irving's *Sketch-Book* (1819–20), Fenimore Cooper likewise became a celebrity in the USA and Europe with his *Leatherstocking Tales* (1823–41), which introduced the theme of the problematic relationship between the wilderness and encroaching American civilization. Transcendentalism was enunciated by Ralph Waldo Emerson in *Nature* (1836) and by H D Thoreau in *Walden* (1855). Walt Whitman's free-form *Leaves of Grass* (appearing 1855–92) is the most sustained and successful response to Emerson's call for a literature free from European influence. By contrast, the poetry of Emily Dickinson offers unique concentration and intensity. Another group that spoke for the darker side of existence in the USA included Edgar Allan Poe, Nathaniel Hawthorne, and Herman Melville. Poe's sinister *Tales* (1840, 1845) continue to fascinate; while Hawthorne's *The Scarlet Letter* (1850), and Melville's epic *Moby-Dick* (1852), are central works of the American imagination. But Harriet Beecher Stowe's anti-slavery novel *Uncle Tom's Cabin* (1852) was the best-selling novel of the century.

Henry James and W D Howells (1837–1920) reacted against the parochialism of American literature, James going to Europe and producing a definitive series of novels on the clash of the two cultures, and Howells editing literary journals that published work by the European realists, James, and himself. Howells also published Mark Twain, whose *Huckleberry Finn* (1885) is one of the few humorous books of the 19th-c whose humour remains uncorroded. Kate Chopin's brilliant short novel, *The Awakening* (1899), went unregarded for 60 years, while Stephen Crane's *Red Badge of Courage* (1895) was accepted as a classic. Naturalism was the dominant mode of American fiction until after World War 1, whether in stories like those by Jack London of life in hostile environments, or in the depiction by Theodore Dreiser of the developing industrial centres. The novels of Edith Wharton took New York society as their subject.

T S Eliot and Ezra Pound came to Europe after the war, using experimental verse to express their dismay at the decline of European civilization. Wallace Stevens too adopted the modernist faith in aesthetic values in a world where moral certainties seemed no longer tenable. In the novel, Ernest Hemingway and Scott Fitzgerald represented 'The Lost Generation', while another important innovator, William Faulkner, wrote a series of novels about the South. American drama makes its appearance with the plays of Eugene O'Neill, which rework autobiographical material with classical and expressionist techniques, and Arthur Miller (eg *Death of a Salesman*, 1949). The novels of Jewish writers Bernard Malamud and Saul Bellow invoke urban life with subtlety and humour, while Norman Mailer (like Hemingway) sees his writing as a form of action. The most significant postwar poets have been Robert Lowell, John Berryman, and Sylvia Plath, who deal harrowingly with the anguish and madness of the contemporary world. The recent novel has tended to diverge between the 'new journalism', illustrated by Tom Wolfe and Truman Capote, and the postmodern, such as John Barth, and Thomas Pynchon; while the new self-consciousness is also apparent in the poetry of John Ashbery. » Black Mountain poetry; literature; transcendentalism; Ashbery; Barth, John; Bellow; Berryman; Capote; Cooper, James Fenimore; Dickinson; Dreiser; Eliot,

T S; Emerson, Ralph Waldo; Faulkner; Fitzgerald, F Scott; Franklin, Benjamin; Hawthorne; Hemingway; Irving, Washington; James, Henry; London, Jack; Lowell, Robert; Mailer; Malamud; Melville; Miller, Arthur; O'Neill; Plath; Poe; Pound; Pynchon; Stevens; Stowe; Thoreau; Twain; Wharton; Whitman; Wolfe, Thomas

American Medical Association (AMA) An association founded in Philadelphia in 1847 'to promote the science and art of medicine and the betterment of public health'. Its membership includes over 300 000 US doctors from all specialities, expressing a corporate view on most aspects of health care. » British Medical Association; medicine

American Muslim Mission » **Black Muslims**

American ostrich » **rhea**

American Revolution (1765–88) The movement that destroyed the first British Empire, establishing the United States and, indirectly, Canada. A much larger event than the War of Independence (1775–83), the revolution developed from the issue of whether Parliament had the power to tax the N American colonies directly. But more was involved than constitutional dispute, and the Revolution left America a transformed place.

The Revolution can be divided into three main phases. In the first (1764–5), relations worsened between the colonies and Britain, primarily over the issue of Parliament's right to tax the colonies without reference to the colonial assemblies. During this phase, the American resistance movement was concentrated in the major port towns, with considerable support in the elected assemblies. Major events included the Stamp Act crisis (1765–6), resistance to the Townshend Acts (1767–70), the Boston Massacre (1770), the burning of the customs cruiser *Gaspee* (1772), and the Boston Tea Party (1773). This phase culminated in Parliament's passage of the Intolerable Acts (1774) to punish Massachusetts for the Tea Party, the beginnings of the collapse of the colonial governments, and the calling of the First Continental Congress (1774).

The second phase brought war and independence. Fighting began at Lexington and Concord, Massachusetts (Apr 1775), and lasted until the surrender of Lord Cornwallis to Washington at Yorktown, Virginia, in 1781. Military conflict centred on Boston until the British withdrew (Mar 1776). From August 1776 until the beginning of 1780, the main theatre was the states of New York, New Jersey, and Pennsylvania, with major engagements at Long Island, at such New Jersey sites as Princeton, Monmouth, and Trenton, and at Saratoga in upstate New York. The American victory at Saratoga convinced the French to enter the war officially, bringing badly-needed material support, troops, monetary credit, and a fleet. After 1780, fighting shifted southward, when Sir Henry Clinton led an invasion of S Carolina. Cornwallis, his successor, led his army gradually N until Washington and the French Admiral de Grasse trapped him on the Yorktown peninsula. The defeat resulted in the fall of Lord North, the British prime minister who had prosecuted the war, and ended British will for further fighting. Peace was signed at Paris two years later.

The third phase led to the creation of the modern United States. This process began with the writing of the first state constitutions, immediately after the Declaration of Independence (Jul 1776). At the same time, the Articles of Confederation were prepared by the Continental Congress as a basis for interstate relations, but the document was not adopted until 1781. Its weaknesses, such as an inability to tax or to enforce Congressional decisions and commitments, soon became apparent. These, together with dissatisfaction about developments in the states, led to the Federalist movement. Initially, this sought merely to reform the Articles, but its great achievement, in 1787 and 1788, was to abolish that document completely, and establish the present US Constitution. At that point, the Revolution was effectively over.

The creation of a large republic was one of the most innovative changes that the Revolution brought. Political thinkers had long doubted whether republicanism could govern a large area or even survive at all. The state and federal constitutions adopted between 1776 and 1788 thus defined the most advanced political hopes of their time. Permanent republicanism in the USA opened the way for the long-term decline of monarchy in the world. The Revolution was also a democratic movement. By its end, an ideology of 'equal rights' had taken shape in the USA, largely as a result of pressure from ordinary farmers and artisans who had found their moment to make a political breakthrough. Such people actually seized control in Pennsylvania and in Vermont, which broke free of New York in 1777, and established radically democratic political institutions. The Revolution brought social change as well. One aspect was the transformation of slavery from a fact of life into a political and moral problem. In the Northern states, opposition became strong enough to set slavery on the road to extinction, and even in the upper South, where legal slavery persisted, the number of free Blacks grew drastically.

National independence, declared by the Continental Congress in 1776, thus meant national transformation. But the Revolution was not the work of a united people. In some places there was considerable loyalism, and even civil war. The many loyalists who fled at the war's end became the core of English-speaking Canada. The movement itself developed as a series of coalitions. The initial alliance, which resisted British imperial policy after 1765, centred on the three major seaports (Boston, New York, and Philadelphia) and on the planter class of Chesapeake Bay. But the independence crisis saw the mobilization of large numbers of farmers in the interior, and they, together with urban working people, developed a political programme of their own. The third great coalition enlisted Southern planters and Northern entrepreneurs and professionals in 'Federalism', which created the modern structure of the USA. They won a great deal of support in the towns, but much less in the countryside. The Federal Constitution reflected their specific concerns, as well as their large goal of safeguarding American independence and liberty. French support, given freely after 1777, was vital to the Americans' military defeat of Britain. The leadership of a truly remarkable group of men was vital throughout the era. But the direct involvement of ordinary people, in the high politics of national birth as well as in rioting and then warfare against Britain, was what made the American Revolution genuinely revolutionary. » Annapolis Convention; Boston Massacre; Committees of Correspondence; Constitutional Convention; Green Mountain Boys; Minutemen; Sons of Liberty; Stamp Act; Sugar Act; Thirteen Colonies; Townshend Acts; Valley Forge; Yorktown Campaign; Brandywine/Bunker Hill/Camden/Charleston/Cowpens / Lexington and Concord / Long Island / Monmouth / Saratoga, Battle of

American Samoa [samoha], formerly also **Loanda**, Portuguese **São Paulo de Loanda** pop (1980) 32 297; area 197 sq km/76 sq ml. Territory of the USA, in the CS Pacific Ocean, some 3 500 km/2 175 ml NNE of New Zealand, divided into five counties; five principal volcanic islands and two coral atolls; capital Fagatogo; timezone GMT −11; people largely of Polynesian origin; main religion, Christianity; official language, English; main island Tutuila (109 sq km/42 sq ml); to the E and N are Aunu'u, the Manu'a Group (Ta'u, Olosega, Ofu), the atolls of Swain's I, and the uninhabited Rose I; main islands hilly, with large areas covered by thick bush and forest; Tutuila rises to 653 m/2 142 ft, Ta'u to 970 m/3 182 ft; tropical maritime climate, with small annual range of temperature (eg Pago Pago average Jan 28.3°C, Jul 26.7°C) and plentiful rainfall (annual average, 5 000 mm/200 in); US acquired rights to American Samoa in 1899, and the islands were ceded by their chiefs 1900–25; now an unincorporated and unorganized territory of the USA, administered by the Department of the Interior; bicameral legislature established in 1948; governor is administrative head of the executive branch; legislature (the *Fono*) comprises the Senate (18 members, chosen every four years by county councils according to Samoan custom) and the House of Representatives (20 members, plus one non-voting member, chosen every two years by popular vote); principal crops are taro, breadfruit, yams, bananas, coconuts; fish canning, tuna fishing, local inshore fishing, handicrafts. » United States of America [i]

American Sign Language (ASL) A sign language widely used by the deaf in the USA; also known as **Ameslan**. The system contains over 4 000 signs, and is used by over half a million deaf people – by many, as a native language. » sign language

American Society for the Prevention of Cruelty to Animals » RSPCA

American whitewood » tulip tree [i]

Ameslan » American Sign Language

amethyst A violet-to-purple form of quartz, prized as a precious stone. » quartz

Amhara A Semitic-speaking people of the Ethiopian C highlands who, with the Tigray, dominate the country. They are descended from the original Semitic conquerors from S Arabia. The Christian empire of Ethiopia was ruled by Amhara dynasties (1260–1974) which, by intermarriage and cultural assimilation, incorporated people from almost every ethnic group of the empire. *Amharic* is the official language of Ethiopia. Population c.9 million. » Ethiopia [i]; Semitic languages; Tigray

Amherst, Jeffrey, 1st Baron (1717–97) British general, born and died at Sevenoaks, Kent, who successfully commanded an expedition against the French fortress at Louisbourg (Nova Scotia) in 1758. After the fall of Quebec, he completed the conquest of Canada by taking Montreal in 1760. He became a peer in 1776, and served as Commander-in-Chief of the British army.

amicable numbers Two numbers such that each is the sum of all the divisors of the other. Thus 284 and 220 are amicable, for the divisors of 284 are 1,2,4,71,142, whose sum is 220, and the divisors of 220 are 1,2,4,5,10,11,20,22,44,55,110, whose sum is 284. Note that 1 is counted as a divisor. Pythagoras is credited with the discovery of amicable numbers, though he seems only to have known of this pair. Fermat in 1636 announced that 17 296 and 18 416 were amicable. Since then other pairs of amicable numbers have been found. In former times, such numbers were prominent in magic and astrology. » Fermat; Pythagoras

Amichai, Yehuda [amichiy] (1924–) German-Jewish poet, born in Wurtzburg, who in 1936 went with his family to what was then Palestine. A dozen volumes of verse since *Akhshav ubayamin na aherim* (1955, Now and in Other Days), are divided in subject matter between the idyll of childhood and the struggle of Israel to establish and defend its identity. These include '*Akshav ba-ra'nsh* (1968, Now in the Turmoil) and *Amen* (1978, translated by Amichai with Ted Hughes). » Hebrew literature; poetry

Amici, Giovanni Battista [ameechee] (1784–1863) Italian optician, astronomer, and natural philosopher, born in Modena. He constructed optical instruments, perfecting his own alloy for telescope mirrors and, in 1827, produced the dioptric, achromatic microscope that bears his name. He became director of the Florence observatory in 1835, and died in Florence. » microscope; telescope [i]

Amidah [ameeda] (Heb 'standing') The principal component of the daily prayers of Talmudic Judaism, recited while standing, and said silently except when in a congregational service. It consists of 19 (originally 18) benedictions, firstly in praise of God, secondly asking for his help (petitions), and closing with thanksgiving. An altered form of the prayer is also recited on sabbaths and festivals. » Judaism; Shema

amides [aymiydz, amidz] **1** Inorganic salts of ammonia, eg sodium amide (NaNH₂), strongly basic and hydrolyzed by water to NH₃ and OH⁻. » ammonia; hydrolysis **2** Organic compounds containing the function –CO.NR₂, also called *alkanamides*, derived from carboxylic acids by substituting NR₂ for OH (R is H or any alkyl group). *Polyamides* include proteins and some artificial polymers, such as nylon. » carboxylic acids; polyamides

Amiens [amyï], ancient **Samarobriva** 49°54N 2°16E, pop (1982) 136 358. Agricultural market town and capital of Somme department, N France; 130 km/81 ml N of Paris, on left bank of R Somme; railway; university (1964); bishopric; textiles, food processing, chemicals, market gardening; war-time cemeteries at Arras to the E; 13th-c Gothic Cathedral of Notre-Dame (largest in area in France), a world heritage site. » Gothic architecture

Amin (Dada), Idi (c.1925–) Ex-President of Uganda (1971–9),

born at Koboko of a peasant family. He had a rudimentary education, and rose rapidly in the army, becoming commander of the army and air force in 1966. He staged a coup deposing Obote in 1971, dissolved parliament, and was proclaimed President by the army. In 1972 fighting within the army led to the massacre of thousands of opposing tribesmen by government forces. He expelled 500 Israeli citizens, all Ugandan Asians with British passports, and the British High Commissioner. Foreign-owned businesses and estates were seized and mass arrests organized. Throughout his presidency there were continual reports of widespread atrocities. Deposed by exiled Ugandans with the help of the Tanzanian army in 1979, he fled to Libya; he lived in Jeddah, Saudi Arabia (1980–8). At the end of 1988 he appeared in Zaire, but was expelled from that country, and Saudi Arabia refused to re-admit him. » Uganda [i]

amines [aymeenz, ameenz] Organic compounds derived from ammonia by the substitution of the hydrogen atoms by one, two, or three alkyl groups; these are *primary*, *secondary*, and *tertiary* amines respectively. They are basic compounds; solutions partially neutralized by strong acids have pH values of about 9. » amides 2; ammonia; pH

amino acid [ameenoh, amiynoh] Strictly, *amino acids*, aminoalkanoic acids with the general formula R–CH(NH₂)COOH. About 24 are involved in protein synthesis; 10 of these cannot be made by the human body, and thus form an essential component of the diet (**essential amino acids**). All amino acids except the simplest, glycine (R = H), are chiral. Nearly all which occur in nature have the arrangement shown in the figure, called the *L-configuration*. Some of the more common are listed below, with the identity of the R-group:

alanine	CH₃–
valine	(CH₃)₂CH–
phenylalanine	C₆H₅CH₂–
glutamic acid	HO(CO)CH₂CH₂–
cysteine	HSCH₂–
histidine	(C₃N₂H₃)CH₂–

$$\begin{array}{c} O \\ \parallel \\ C-OH \\ | \\ H_2N \rightarrow C \leftarrow H \\ | \\ R \end{array}$$

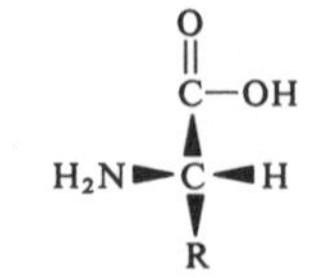

» chirality [i]; glycine; protein

aminobenzene » aniline

aminoethanoic acid » glycine

Amis, Sir Kingsley (1922–) British novelist and poet, born in London. Educated at the City of London School and at Oxford, he was an officer in the Royal Signals (1942–5) and then a lecturer at Swansea. He achieved a reputation by his second novel, *Lucky Jim* (1954), which added a new comic hero to English fiction, also seen in *That Uncertain Feeling* (1956) and *I Like It Here* (1958). Later works on wider themes include *Jake's Thing* (1978), and *The Old Devils* (1986), for which he won the Booker Prize. He has also published and edited poetry. After Ian Fleming's death, Amis wrote a James Bond novel, *Colonel Sun* (1968), under the pseudonym of Robert Markham, as well as *The James Bond Dossier* (1965). He was married to the novelist **Elizabeth Jane Howard** (1923–) from 1965 to 1983. His son, **Martin Amis** (1949–), is also a writer. » Angry Young Men; English literature; Fleming, Ian; novel

Amman 31°57N 35°52E, pop (1980e) 1 232 600. Industrial and commercial capital city of Jordan; in Amman governorate, East Bank, on the R Zarqa; capital of the Ammonite kingdom in Biblical times; capital of Transjordan, 1923; many refugees after the Arab–Israeli Wars; airport; railway; university (1962); noted for its locally-quarried coloured marble; food processing, textiles, paper, plastics; Roman amphitheatre (1st-c BC), archaeological museum. » Arab-Israeli Wars; Jordan [i]

ammine [ameen] Co-ordinated ammonia, or a compound with co-ordinated ammonia. Ammines were among the first identified co-ordination compounds or complex ions, eg [Co(NH₃)₆]³⁺, hexamminecobalt (III). » ammonia; co-ordination compounds

Ammon » Amun

ammonia NH₃, boiling point −33°C. A colourless gas with a pungent odour; its molecule is pyramidal with bond angles c.107°. It is a weak base; aqueous solutions partially neutralized with strong acid have a pH c.9.5. It reacts with acids to form ammonium ions. An important industrial chemical, it is mainly prepared by the Haber process. » amides 1; amines; ammine; ammonium; base (chemistry); gas 1; Haber-Bosch process; pH

ammonia-soda process » **Solvay process**

ammonite An extinct, nautilus-like mollusc; found extensively as fossil shells from the Devonian to the Upper Cretaceous periods; shell external in life, typically a flattened spiral, divided internally by transverse walls. (Class: *Cephalopoda*. Subclass: *Ammonoidea*.) » Cretaceous/Devonian period; mollusc; nautilus

Ammonites An ancient Semitic people who in Old Testament times lived in S Transjordan. Tradition had it that they were descended from Lot. » Lot; Moabites; Semites

ammonium NH_4^+. A cation formed by the reaction of ammonia with acid. It is found in many salts, particularly the chloride (*sal ammoniac*) and the carbonate (*sal volatile*). Aqueous solutions of ammonia are often called *ammonium hydroxide*. » acid; ammonia; cation

amnesia Memory disability, often associated with brain damage or a traumatic event. **Retrograde amnesia** is the inability to remember material learned before the precipitating events. **Anterograde amnesia** is difficulty in learning new material. The most common form of amnesia is one in which short-term memory is adequate, explicit long-term memory (the ability to have conscious awareness of past memories) is poor, and implicit long-term memory (the ability to acquire and retain information, without being aware that one has this knowledge) is relatively intact. » consciousness; memory

Amnesty International A human rights organization founded in London in 1961 largely by the efforts of Peter Benenson, a Catholic lawyer. It is based in the UK, but there are several groups in other, mainly industrialized, countries. The fundamental concern of Amnesty is to seek the immediate and unconditional release of prisoners of conscience, as long as they have not advocated violence. It also campaigns against torture and the death penalty, and tries to produce independent, authoritative reports on countries' abuses of human rights. » human rights

amniocentesis [amneeohsen**tee**sis] A procedure which involves the withdrawal of amniotic fluid within the uterus by the insertion of a needle through the abdominal wall and the uterus in pregnancy. Amniotic fluid is in close contact with the foetus, and abnormalities in its development reflect many inherited and congenital foetal abnormalities. These include haemolytic disease of the newborn and spina bifida. » chorionic villus sampling; pregnancy [i]; uterus [i]

amoeba [a**mee**ba] A naked, single-celled protozoan which moves by protoplasmic flow, changing its shape by the formation of irregular lobes (*pseudopodia*); feeds by engulfing food particles with pseudopodia, or by infolding of the outer surface (*invagination*); c.0.6 mm/0.024 in across; reproduces mainly by splitting in two (*binary fission*). Most are free living in aquatic habitats; some are parasitic, and can cause amoebic dysentery in humans. (Phylum: *Sarcomastigophora*. Class: *Rhizopoda*.) » dysentery; parasitology; protoplasm; Protozoa

Amon » **Amun**

Amorites The name borne by various Semitic peoples who lived in Mesopotamia, Syria, and Palestine in Old Testament times. » Semites

amorphous solid A solid in which the atoms are in some disordered arrangement, lacking the perfect ordered structure of crystals, as in glass, rubber, and polymers. Many substances may form either amorphous or crystalline states having radically different properties. » atom; glass 1 [i]; liquid; polymerization; rubber; solid

amortization A method used in accountancy which reduces the value of a wasting asset, such as a quarry, over the length of its expected life. It also applies to intangible assets (eg goodwill) and patents which have been acquired at a price, but which may not be resaleable. » accountancy; depreciation

Amory, Derick Heathcoat, 1st Viscount [**ay**moree] (1899–1981) British Conservative politician, born at Tiverton, Devon. Educated at Eton and Oxford, he entered parliament in 1945. He served as Minister of Pensions (1951–3), at the Board of Trade (1953–4), as Minister of Agriculture (1954–8), and as Chancellor of the Exchequer until 1960, when he was made a viscount. He was also High Commissioner to Canada (1961–3). » Conservative Party

Amos, Book of One of the twelve so-called 'minor' prophetic writings in the Hebrew Bible/Old Testament; attributed to the prophet Amos, who was active in the N kingdom of Israel in the mid-8th-c BC. It proclaims judgment on Israel's neighbours for idolatry, and on Israel itself for social injustices and ethical immorality. » Israel [i]; Old Testament; prophet

Amoy (China) » **Xiamen**

amp » **ampere**

Ampato, Nevado de [nay**va**doh thay am**pa**toh] Andean massif in the Cordillera Occidental, S Peru; height, 6 310 m/20 702 ft; Cañon del Colca nearby, a gorge cut by the R Colca; 60 km/37 ml long and 3 000 m/10 000 ft deep, considered to be the deepest canyon in the world. » Andes; Peru [i]

Ampère, André Marie [ã**pair**] (1775–1836) French mathematician and physicist, born in Lyons. He taught at Bourg and Paris, and carried out classic studies on electricity and electromagnetism (then known as 'electrodynamics'), becoming the first to devise techniques for measuring electricity. He died in Marseilles. His name was given to the unit of electrical current. » ampere; Ampère's law; electricity

ampere The base SI unit of current; symbol A, often called **amp**, named after French physicist André Ampère; defined as the constant current which, if maintained in two straight parallel conductors of infinite length, of negligible cross-section, and placed one metre apart in a vacuum, would produce a force equal to 2×10^{-7} N/m. » Ampère; current (electricity); units (scientific)

Ampère's law In magnetism, the magnetic field resulting from electric current flowing in a wire; formulated by French physicist André Ampère in 1827. For any closed loop drawn around the wire, the sum of magnetic flux density contributions at each point along the line is proportional to the current enclosed by the loop. » Ampère; Biot-Savart law; magnetic flux; magnetism

amphetamine A powerful central nervous system stimulant which causes wakefulness and alertness, elevates mood, increases self-confidence, loquaciousness, and the performance of simple mental tasks, and improves physical performance. Initially, it decreases appetite. It is widely abused to increase energy and alertness, but tolerance often develops after repeated use. Its effects are followed by mental depression and fatigue. It was once used clinically as a slimming aid, but therapeutic use is now restricted to the treatment of narcolepsy because of the problems of addiction and tolerance. Prolonged use may result in paranoia or clinical psychosis. As a drug of abuse it is called 'speed'; it is illegally manufactured as a powder which can be sniffed ('snorted') or injected. Its proprietary name is **Benzedrine**. » drug addiction; narcolepsy; psychosis; stimulants

amphibian A vertebrate animal of class *Amphibia* (c.4 000 species), exhibiting a wide range of characters and lifestyles; usually four legs and glandular skin, lacking scales or other outgrowths; larvae usually live in water and breathe through feathery external gills; undergo a metamorphosis during development, when the gills shrink and disappear; adults breathe using lungs (and partly through the skin); three major groups: salamanders and newts (order: *Urodela* or *Caudata*), frogs and toads (order: *Anura* or *Salientia*), and the legless caecilians (order: *Gymnophiona* or *Apoda*). » Anura; caecilian; Chordata; tadpole

amphiboles [**am**fibohlz] A group of hydrous silicate minerals of considerable chemical complexity, characterized structurally by a double-chain of linked SiO_4 tetrahedra, with iron, magnesium, calcium, sodium, and aluminium among the elements which may be present between the chains. It is widely distributed in igneous and metamorphic rocks. Common varieties include hornblende, actinolite, and tremolite. Fibrous forms belong to the asbestos group of minerals. » asbestos; horneblende; silicate minerals

amphioxus [amfee**ok**suhs] A primitive chordate; body slender, length up to 70 mm/2¾ in, tapered at both ends; notochord present, extending into head; possesses gill slits and segmented muscle blocks, resembling ancestors of vertebrates; 23 species found in shallow marine sediments; also known as **lancelet**. (Subphylum: *Cephalochordata*.) » Chordata; notochord

amphisbaena [amfis**bee**na] A reptile native to S and C America, Africa, SW Asia, and SW Europe; body worm-like with encircling rings; no legs or only front legs present; small eyes covered by skin; the only truly burrowing reptile; eats small animals; also known as **worm lizard** or **ringed lizard**. (Order: *Squamata*. Suborder: *Amphisbaenia*, 140 species.) » reptile

amphitheatre/amphitheater An open-air theatre where tiers of seats are situated all round a central circular or oval performance space. The Romans developed this form of building from Campanian (or possibly Etruscan) origins for gladiatorial combats, naval exhibitions, and other events. There are good examples at Pompeii (70 BC), Verona (AD 290) and, most famously, the Colosseum in Rome (AD 72–80). » Roman architecture; theatre

Amphitrite [amfi**triy**tee] In Greek mythology, a goddess of the sea, married to Poseidon. She is the mother of Triton and other minor deities. » Poseidon

Amphitryon [am**fi**treeon] In Greek mythology, the husband of Alcmene. In his absence, Zeus took his shape and so became the father of Heracles. » Heracles

amphoteric [amfuh**te**rik] In chemistry, having two different properties, usually that of being an acid and a base. An example is aluminium hydroxide ($Al(OH)_3$), which forms salts of Al^{3+} in acid and of AlO_2^- in alkali. » acid; base (chemistry); oxide

amplitude In a wave or oscillation, the maximum displacement from equilibrium or rest position; symbol A. It is always a positive number. » amplitude modulation; wave (physics) [i]

amplitude modulation (AM) In wave motion, the altering of wave amplitude in a systematic way, leaving frequency unchanged. In AM radio, an electrical signal is used to modulate the amplitude of the broadcast carrier radio wave. A radio receiver reproduces the signal from the modulated wave by *demodulation*. » amplitude; modulation; radio; wave (physics) [i]

Amritsar [am**rit**ser] 31°35N 74°57E, pop (1981) 589 000. City in Punjab, NW India; centre of the Sikh religion; founded in 1577 by Ram Das around a sacred tank, known as the pool of immortality; Golden Temple, found at the centre of the tank, is particularly sacred to Sikhs; under the gold and copper dome is kept the sacred book of the Sikhs, Adi Granth; centre of the Sikh empire in the 19th-c, and of modern Sikh nationalism; massacre of Indian nationalists, 1919; battle between the Indian Army and Sikh militants inside the Golden Temple led to 1000 deaths, including a Sikh leader, 1984; airport; university (1969); commerce, textiles, silk. » Amritsar Massacre; Harimandir; India [i]; Sikhism

Amritsar Massacre [am**rit**sa] A massacre at Amritsar, Punjab, in April 1919. Local disturbances caused the British army commander, General Dyer, to believe that another Indian Mutiny was imminent. When a public meeting took place in a walled garden (the Jallianwalabagh), he ordered his troops to open fire on an unarmed crowd which had no chance of escape; 380 were killed and 1 200 injured. Dyer was censured and resigned, but a public subscription was opened for him in Britain. The massacre was the cue for the opening of Gandhi's Non-Co-operation Movement, and transformed the whole tenor of Indian nationalism. » Amritsar; Gandhi; Indian Mutiny; nationalism; Non-Co-operation Movement

Amru, or **Amr** (?–664) Arab soldier, who joined the Prophet about 629, and took part in the conquest of Palestine. In 641 he took Alexandria after a 14 months' siege, and died governor of Egypt. » Mohammed

Amsterdam [amstuh**dam**] 52°23N 4°54E, pop (1984e) 994 062. Major European port and capital city of the Netherlands, in North Holland province, W Netherlands; at the junction of the R Amstel and an arm of the Ijsselmeer; chartered, 1300; member of the Hanseatic League, 1369; capital, 1808; airport (Schiphol), railway; two universities (1632, 1880); harbour industry developed after World War 2; major transshipping point; important commercial and cultural centre; banking, shipbuilding, engineering, cars, aircraft, textiles, brewing, foodstuffs, publishing and printing, chemicals, data processing, diamond-cutting; Concertgebouw Orchestra; House of Anne Frank, Rembrandt House (1606), Oude Kerk (consecrated 1306), Nieuwe Kerk (15th-c), royal palace (17th-c), Rijksmuseum, Stedelijk Museum, Van Gogh Museum; international Windjammer Regatta 'Sail Amsterdam' (Aug). » Hanseatic League; Netherlands, The [i]; Randstad; Rijksmuseum

amu » **atomic mass unit**

Amudarya, River [amu**da**rya], ancient **Oxus** River formed by the junction of the Vakhsh and Pyandzh Rivers on the Turkmenistan–Afghanistan frontier, forming part of the border; flows W and NW to enter the Aral Sea in a wide delta; length 1 415 km/879 ml; largest river of C Asia, and an important source of irrigation. » Asia

Amun [amun], **Amen**, **Ammon** or **Amon** From the time of the Middle Kingdom, the supreme deity in Egyptian religion. Later he was given the qualities of the sun-god Re, hence the usual title **Amun-Re**. The name means 'the hidden one'. » Re

Amundsen, Roald (Engelbregt Gravning) (1872–1928) Norwegian explorer, born at Borge. He early abandoned medical studies in favour of a life at sea, serving on the Belgian Antarctic expedition (1897), and sailing the Northwest passage (1903). His Antarctic expedition of 1910 reached the Pole in Dec 1911, one month ahead of Scott. In 1926 with Umberto Nobile he flew a dirigible over the N Pole. In 1928, flying to assist in a search for Nobile (whose dirigible had crashed in the Arctic Ocean), he was lost at sea. » Poles; Scott, Robert Falcon

Amur River, Chinese **Heilong Jiang** River in NE China and Russia, part of the international border; main source rises in the Da Hinggan Ling range, Inner Mongolia; flows generally E then NE to enter the Sea of Okhotsk; length, 4 350 km/ 2 700 ml; scene of several Sino-Soviet incidents since the 1960s.

amyl [**ay**miyl, **a**mil] $CH_3CH_2CH_2CH_2CH_2$–, IUPAC **pentyl**. A group derived from pentane by removing one hydrogen atom. *Amyl alcohol* is a fraction of fusel oil, boiling point c.130°, a mixture of several isomers of $C_5H_{11}OH$. *Amylose* is a low molecular weight fraction of starch. » amyl nitrite; fusel oil; IUPAC; pentane; starch

amyl nitrite ($C_5H_{11}NO_2$) A drug in the form of a volatile liquid, administered by inhalation, which acts very rapidly and very briefly. It has some use in the treatment of angina but is also sold as a sex aid ('poppers'). It is also used in the emergency treatment of cyanide poisoning. » amyl; angina; cyanide

amylases [**a**milayziz] A group of enzymes which speed up the breakdown of starch and glycogen into disaccharides and small polysaccharides. They occur widely in plants and animals; for example, α-amylase is found in saliva and the pancreatic secretions of some vertebrates, β-amylase in plants. » enzyme; disaccharide; hydrolysis

Anabaptists The collective name given to groups of believers stemming from the more radical elements of the 16th-c Reformation; also known as **Rebaptizers**. They believed in the baptism of believing adults only, refusing to recognize infant baptism. They emphasized adherence to the word of scripture, strict Church discipline, and the separation of Church and state. Being prepared to criticize the state, they frequently suffered savage persecution. They were associated with Thomas Müntzer and the Zwinglian prophets in Wittenberg (1521); the Swiss brethren in Zürich (1525); and Jan Mattys (died 1534) in Münster (1533–4), where the Anabaptists achieved supremacy; and spread to Moravia, N and W Germany, the Low Countries (especially the Mennonites in Holland), and later the USA. They were the forerunners of the Baptists, who are in many respects their spiritual heirs. » baptism; Baptists; Mennonites; Müntzer; Zwingli

anabatic wind A local upslope wind which develops best in a valley. During the day the air in contact with the valley sides is heated to a greater degree than air at the same elevation but above the valley floor, and therefore rises. This leads to a circulation pattern of upslope airflow from valley floor to ridge, to replace rising air. Windspeeds of 10–15 m/32–50 ft per second can occur. » katabatic wind; wind

anabolic steroids Drugs with structures similar to the male sex hormones (*androgens*) but with reduced androgenic activity and increased anabolic activity to increase weight and muscle development. They are used clinically to accelerate recovery from protein deficiency, in muscle-wasting disorders, and sometimes in breast cancer. They are used illegally to promote performance of athletes and racing animals, and were first used by weightlifters and bodybuilders. The International Olympic Committee requires that medal winners at major competitions are subject to urine sample analysis to prove themselves drug free. The International Weightlifting Association also has random checks. In women, anabolic steroids can cause masculinization – growth of facial hair, deepening of the voice, etc. » androgens; hormones; steroid [i]

anabolism » **metabolism**

anaclitic therapy A form of psychotherapy in which the patient is allowed to regress. The term **anaclitic depression** was introduced by René Spitz (1887–1974), a Hungarian-born US psychoanalyst, who in 1946 described a syndrome of regression in infants separated from their love objects. It has also been used to describe changes in infants in institutions. » psychotherapy; regression

anaconda A boa from S America, the largest snake in the world; may be more than 11 m/36 ft long, weighing over 500 kg/1 100 lb; dull colour with large irregular dark spots; inhabits slow-moving water; may climb low trees; eats birds, mammals, caimans, turtles; also known as the **green anaconda**. (*Eunectes murinus*.) » boa

Anacreon (c.6th-c BC) Greek lyric poet, born at Teos, Asia Minor. With his fellow townsmen he emigrated to Greece, on the approach of the Persians, and lived at Samos, Athens, and elsewhere, singing the praises of the muses, wine, and love. He later left Athens, and seems to have died in Teos. Of the five books of his poems, only a few genuine fragments have been preserved. » Greek literature

anaemia/anemia A reduction in the amount of oxygen-carrying pigment, haemoglobin, in the red cells circulating in the blood. The condition causes skin pallor, weakness, and breathlessness. There are many causes, including blood loss, excessively rapid destruction of red blood cells, and failure of their normal maturation in the bone marrow. » blood

anaerobe » **aerobe**

anaesthetics/anesthetics, general Drugs which produce a reversible state of unconciousness deep enough to permit surgery. They may be inhaled (eg halothane, nitrous oxide) or given intravenously (eg thiopentone, alphaxalone). Nitrous oxide ('laughing gas') was discovered by Joseph Priestley in 1776, and its use in surgical operations was suggested in 1799 by Humphry Davy, who noted its analgesic action. However, for the next few decades it was used only as fairground entertainment. In 1844 the US dentist Horace Wells (1815–48) successfully allowed one of his own teeth to be extracted under its influence, and after 1860 its use became established. *Ether* was discovered in 1540 by Valerius Cordus (1515–44), and shown to control colic pain in 1795. The US surgeon Crawford Williamson Long (1815–78) first used it surgically for minor operations in 1842. *Chloroform* was discovered in 1831 and first used in 1847 as a general anaesthetic by Scottish obstetrician James Young Simpson (1811–70), despite strong opposition from the Church. Today, intravenous anaesthetics are used for short operations only. 'Basal' anesthesia is usually induced before the patient leaves the ward to relieve anxiety and hasten the induction of anaesthesia in the theatre. » chloroform; Davy; ether; nitrous oxide; Priestley, Joseph

anaesthetics / anesthetics, local Drugs which produce a reversible loss of sensation in a localized region of the body by blocking nerve impulses. Regional anaesthesia is achieved by topical application or by injection at the site of an operation (as in tooth extraction), near a main nerve trunk (eg to allow operations in limbs), or between spinal vertebrae ('epidural' anaesthesia). The first local anaesthetic was cocaine, introduced in the 1880s, but this is now obsolete because of problems of addiction and toxicity. Commonly used local anaesthetics include procaine, lignocaine (lidocaine), and benzocaine. » cocaine; neurone [i]

anaglyph A picture for stereoscopic viewing in which the separate right-eye and left-eye images are reproduced in different colours, usually red and blue-green. The observer wears coloured spectacles so that each eye sees only its appropriate image in the complementary colour. » stereoscopic photography

anagram The re-arrangement of the letters of a word or sentence to produce a new form or a puzzle. Often an ingenious analogue to the original word can be found, eg *total abstainers→sit not at ale bars.*

analgesics Drugs which relieve pain. **Narcotic analgesics** (eg codeine, morphine, heroin) act by mimicking the natural brain endorphins responsible for the subjective perception of pain. **Non-narcotic analgesics** (eg aspirin, paracetamol, ibuprofen) act by blocking the synthesis of prostaglandins (substances formed at the site of injury involved in the production of pain responses). » aspirin; narcotics; pain; paracetamol; prostaglandins

analog computer Computers which accept, as inputs, continuous electrical or mechanical variables (such as voltage or current or the rotation rate or position of a shaft) and respond immediately to calculate relevant output signals. The processing is generally done by special electrical circuits, usually operational amplifiers, or by complex mechanical arrangements of gears, cogs, etc. Examples range from the automobile speedometer to the anti-aircraft 'predictors' of World War 2. Analog computers are inherently real-time systems, and continue to find special purpose applications, particularly in control systems, although many of their former tasks are now done using the much more versatile digital computers. » digital computer; real-time computing; voltage

analog-to-digital conversion A process of converting analog signals, such as voltage, into a digital form which can be used in a digital computer. It is usually carried out by specialized electronic circuits or discrete integrated circuits called *analog-to-digital (A-D) converters*. A-D converters and the converse D-A converters are common in computer-controlled processes. » digital-to-analog conversion

analogue/analog signal » **digital techniques**

analogy A type of inductive inference whose form is 'x has characteristics C_1, ... C_n *and* D; thus if y has characteristics C_1, ... C_n, y also has D.' Often a source of error, analogy sometimes works: Mendeleev was able to predict the properties of the chemical element germanium, before it was discovered, on the basis of the properties of the known elements in its family. The **argument from analogy** for the existence of God, popular in the 18th-c and 19th-c, maintained that the universe is like a mechanism; therefore if a mechanism requires a maker, so does the universe. » God; inference

analytic geometry A method of attacking geometrical problems by referring to a point by its co-ordinates in a system; also known as **Cartesian** or **co-ordinate geometry**. The commonest system is of two perpendicular axes, when all points can be identified by a number pair, (x,y). In three-dimensional geometry a number triple is needed (x,y,z). Other systems of co-ordinates, such as polar co-ordinates, have been developed which are more suitable for some types of problems. Descartes is generally credited with inventing this system, but the idea was probably known to the Greeks (eg Apollonius), who were unable to develop it because they lacked algebraic symbols. » Descartes; geometry; polar co-ordinates

analytic language A type of language in which words do not vary their form to show their grammatical function in a sentence; also known as an **isolating** language. In such languages (eg Chinese), the relationships between the words are shown solely by their order. Analytic languages are opposed to **synthetic** languages, in which words typically combine a grammatical meaning with their dictionary meaning; for example, the English word *horses* contains the meaning of 'plural' in addition to the sense of 'animal'. Most languages display features of both systems. » agglutinating/fusional language

analytic philosophy A movement, associated mainly with Russell and Moore and furthered by the early Wittgenstein, which saw the task of philosophy as one of analysing language, typically by means of formal logic, in order to solve or dissolve many perennial philosophical issues. The term is also used more generally to contrast recent Anglo-American philosophy with French or German philosophical traditions. » Moore, G E; Russell, Bertrand; Wittgenstein

analytic-synthetic distinction A distinction proposed by Kant and adopted by many philosophers. Analytic truths are said to be true solely in virtue of their meaning. Thus, 'All bachelors are unmarried' is analytic, while 'All bachelors are over two feet tall' is synthetic, true partly in virtue of contingent facts. » Kant; tautology

analytical chemistry A branch of chemistry dealing with the composition of material. It includes qualitative and quantitative determinations of elements present, as well as structural analysis. The methods used are based either on chemical reactions or on physical properties, generally electrochemical or spectroscopic. » chemistry; electrochemistry

anamorphosis An image drawn or painted in trick perspective so that it appears distorted from a normal viewpoint, but when seen from an extraordinary angle, or through a lens, appears normal. A famous example is the skull in Holbein's *Ambassadors* in the National Gallery, London. » perspective

Ananda [ahnanda] (5th–6th-c BC) The cousin and favourite pupil of the Buddha. Noted for his devotion to the Buddha, and a skilled interpreter of his teachings, he was instrumental in establishing an order for women disciples. » Buddha; Buddhism

Ananke [anangkee] The twelfth natural satellite of Jupiter, discovered in 1951; distance from the planet 21 200 000 km/ 13 174 000 ml; diameter 30 km/19 ml. » Jupiter (astronomy); RR4

anaphylaxis [anafuhlaksis] A type of hypersensitivity reaction which occurs when an individual has been previously sensitized by contact with an antigen. It occurs within a few minutes after exposure, and the clinical response depends upon the tissue affected. Examples of local anaphylaxis include asthma, hay fever, and oedema of the tissues of the throat. A severe degree of generalized anaphylaxis (**anaphylactic shock**) may also result in a sudden attack of wheezing, collapse, and cardiac arrest, and may be fatal. » allergy; hay fever

anarchism A generic term for political ideas and movements that reject the state and other forms of authority and coercion in favour of a society based exclusively upon voluntary co-operation between individuals. To anarchists the state, whether democratic or not, is always seen as a means of supporting a ruling class or elite, and as an encumbrance to social relations. However, they differ in their view of the nature of their future society, their proposals ranging from a communist society based on mutual aid to one based on essentially self-interested voluntary exchange. They reject involvement in political institutions, and support civil disobedience action against the state, and on occasions political violence. Anarchist movements were most prevalent in Europe in the second half of the 19th-c and early 20th-c, but virtually died out apart from fringe groups after the Spanish Civil War. » syndicalism

anarthria » **dysarthria**

Anasazi [anasahzee] The prehistoric Indian inhabitants of the arid 'Four Corners' region of the US Southwest (where Arizona, New Mexico, Colorado, and Utah meet), c.200 BC–AD 1500. The name, from Navajo, means 'enemy ancestors'. The villages were of pithouses before c.700, pueblos or cliff dwellings later, while the economy was predominantly horticultural, based on maize, beans, and squashes. The modern descendants are the Hopi of Arizona, and the Rio Grande Pueblo groups of New Mexico. » Chaco Canyon; Hopi; kiva; Mesa Verde; Mogollon; Pueblo (Indians)

Anastasia, Grand Duchess Anastasia Nikolaievna Romanova (1901–18?) Daughter of the Tsar Nicholas II, born near St Petersburg, thought to have died when the Romanov family were executed by the Bolsheviks in Ekaterinburg (19 Jul 1918). Several women have claimed to be Anastasia, notably Anna Anderson, from the Black Forest (died 1984). Conflicting opinions by members of the Romanov family and others failed to establish the truth, and her claim was finally rejected by a Hamburg court in May 1961. The mystery has been the theme of books, plays, and films. » Romanovs; Russian Revolution

Anatolia [anatohlia], Turk **Anadolu** Asiatic region of Turkey, usually synonymous with Asia Minor; a mountainous peninsula between the Black Sea (N), Aegean Sea (W), and the Mediterranean Sea (S). » Turkey

Anatolian A group of Indo-European languages, now extinct, spoken c.2000 BC in the area of present-day Turkey and Syria. The major language is Hittite, which is recorded on tablets inscribed with cuneiform writing from the 17th-c BC: these are the oldest known Indo-European texts. » cuneiform [i]; Indo-European languages

anatomy The science concerned with the form, structure, and spatial relationships of a living organism. It originally referred to the cutting up of the body to determine the nature and organization of its parts, but nowadays it includes many other aspects of study. *Topographic* or *gross* anatomy deals with the relative positions of various body parts. *Systemic* anatomy is concerned with the study of a group of related structures (eg the respiratory system). *Applied* anatomy considers anatomical facts in relation to physical diagnosis or surgery. *Functional* anatomy deals not only with the structural basis of function in the various systems (eg the musculo-skeletal system), but also with the relation of one system to another, and so merges with physiology. *Developmental* anatomy (*embryology*) is concerned with the prenatal organization and structural changes within the embryo and foetus. *Morbid* or *pathological* anatomy deals with the anatomy of diseased tissues. *Radiological* anatomy is the study of organs and tissues using radiographic techniques (X-rays, computer-assisted tomography, nuclear magnetic resonance.) *Neuroanatomy* is the study of the structure and function of nervous systems (central, peripheral, autonomic). *Comparative* anatomy describes and compares the form, structure, and function of different animals. *Veterinary* anatomy is the science dealing with the form and structure of the principal domesticated animals. Anatomical science also involves *histology*, the study of the architecture of tissues and organs, and *cell biology*, concerned with the basic elements of the cell. » cell; embryology; histology; neurology; physiology; radiography; Plates XII, XIII

Anaxagoras [anakzagoras] (500–428 BC) Ionian philosopher, born at Clazomenae. He taught in Athens, where he had many illustrious pupils, including Pericles. His explanations of physical phenomena by natural causes brought accusations of impiety, and he withdrew to Lampsacus, where he died. He held that matter is infinitely divisible; that any piece of matter, regardless of how small it is, contains portions of all kinds of matter; and that order is produced from chaos by an intelligent principle. » Pericles

Anaximander [anakzimanduh] (611–547 BC) Ionian philosopher and successor of Thales, born at Miletus. He was the first thinker to develop a systematic philosophical view of the universe and Earth's place in it, and is sometimes called the father of astronomy. He held that the origin of the cosmos was the 'Boundless' (*apeiron*), which he conceived of in both physical and theological terms. » astronomy; Thales

Anaximenes [anakzimeneez] (6th-c BC) Ionian philosopher, born at Miletus, younger than Thales and Anaximander. He held *air* to be the primary form of matter, from which all things, such as water, earth, and stone, were formed by successive stages of compression or, in the case of fire, by rarefaction. » Anaximander; Thales

Anchises [ankiyseez] In Roman mythology, the Trojan father of Aeneas. The *Aeneid* gives an account of Aeneas' piety in carrying Anchises on his shoulders out of the blazing city of Troy. » Aeneas

anchor A device which prevents a vessel from drifting. The flukes or arms of an anchor dig into the sea bed, thus resisting a horizontal pull; it is made fast to the ship by a heavy cable, usually of studded chain. There are two basic types: the old-fashioned anchor with a stock, usually depicted on badges and flags; and the modern, more common, stockless anchor. The stockless anchor consists of a shank and a crown, which are

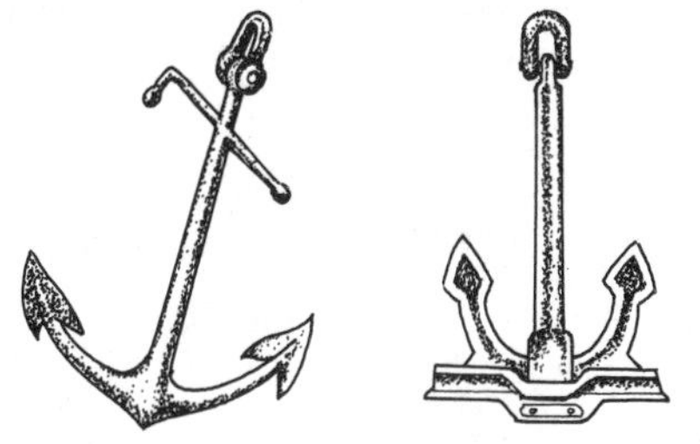

The two basic types of anchor

free to move in relation to each other, so that when in use the flukes will adopt an angle of about 45° to the shank. When stowed, the flukes are parallel to the shank.

Anchorage 61°13N 149°54W, pop (1980) 174 431. City and seaport in SC Alaska, USA, at the head of Cook Inlet; largest city in the state; founded as a railway construction camp, 1918; severely damaged by earthquake, 1964; important transportation hub; administrative and commercial centre; a vital defence centre, with Fort Richardson military base and Elmendorf air force base nearby; airport; railway; university (1957); mining, tourism; Earthquake Park, National Bank Heritage Library; Iditarod Sled Race (Mar), Great Alaska Shootout (Nov), Fur Rendezvous (Nov). » Alaska

anchovy [**an**chuhvee] Any of the small herring-like fishes of the family *Engraulidae*, widespread in surface coastal waters of tropical and temperate seas; support extensive commercial fisheries, much of the catch being processed before sale. (5 genera, including *Anchoa*, *Engraulis*.) » herring

ancien régime [ãsyĩ ray**zheem**] The social and political system of France existing from the late 16th-c to the outbreak of the French Revolution (1789). The term implies a hierarchical, corporative society, bound closely to the dynastic state, and is associated particularly with mechanisms upholding traditional orders and privileges. » French Revolution [i]; Parlement

ancient lights In law, an easement acquired through long use, whereby one property can claim the right against another property to enjoy at least a reasonable amount of light. Where it exists, this right may restrict building on neighbouring property. A restrictive covenant against building may be more effective, but such a covenant cannot be acquired through long use. » easement; restrictive covenant

ancona » **altarpiece**

Andalusia Eng [andaloo**see**a], Span **Andalucía** [andaloo**thee**a] pop (1981) 6 440 987; area 87 268 sq km/33 685 sq ml. Large and fertile autonomous region of S Spain; dominated by the great basin of the R Guadalquivir and (S) by the Baetic Cordillera, rising to 3 478 m/11 411 ft at Cerro de Mulhacén, Spain's highest peak; S coastal strip known for its tourist resorts on the Costa del Sol and the Costa de la Luz; sugar cane, fruit, bananas, wine, cotton; chief cities, Málaga, Cádiz, Granada, Córdoba; many remains of Moorish rule (8th–15th-c). » Costa de la Luz; Costa del Sol; Spain [i]

Andalusian horse A breed of horse; height, 16 hands/1.6 m/5½ ft; grey (occasionally black); developed in Spain over many centuries by crossing African, Spanish, and German horses; a less refined version is called the **Andalusian-Carthusian** or **Carthusian**. » horse [i]; Lipizzaner

andalusite One of the three varieties of mineral aluminium silicate (Al_2SiO_5), found in metamorphic rocks, the others being *kyanite* and *sillimanite*. Its importance lies as an indicator of the pressure and temperature of metamorphism in rocks. » silicate minerals

Andaman and Nicobar Islands [**an**daman, nikoh**bah**] pop (1981) 188 254; area 8 293 sq km/3 201 sq ml. Union territory of India, comprising two island groups in the Bay of Bengal; separated from Myanmar, Thailand, and Sumatra by the Andaman Sea; over 300 islands, stretching 725 km/450 ml N to S; occupied by Japan in World War 2; part of India, 1950; British penal colony on Andaman Is, 1858–1945; Cellular Jail at Port Blair now a national shrine; Nicobar Is 120 km/75 ml S, a mountainous group of 19 islands; occupied by Denmark (1756–1848); annexed by Britain, 1869; chief town, Nankauri; tropical forest covers both islands; monsoons frequent (May–Oct); fishing, rubber, fruit, rice, hardwood timber. » India [i]

Andaman Sea [**an**daman] area 564 900 sq km/218 000 sq ml. NE arm of the Indian Ocean; bounded E by Myanmar and Thailand, N by the Gulf of Martaban, S by Sumatra, and W by the Andaman and Nicobar Is. » Irrawaddy, River; Indian Ocean

Andean bear » **spectacled bear**

Anders, Władysław (1892–1970) Polish general, born at Błonie, who was Commander-in-Chief of the Polish forces in the Middle East and Italy in World War 2. After the war, deprived of his nationality by the Polish Communist Government (1946), he became Inspector-General of the Polish forces in exile, and a leading figure in the 140 000-strong Free Polish community in Britain. He died in London. » World War 2

Andersen, Hans Christian (1805–75) Danish author, one of the world's great story-tellers, born at Odense. The son of a poor shoemaker, he first worked in a factory, but early displayed a talent for poetry. He failed to find employment as an actor, but benefactors helped him to attend university at Copenhagen. He then published collections of poems (1830–1), and travelled widely in Europe, writing travel books, novels, and plays, gaining an international reputation. However, he is mainly remembered for his fairytales for children, such as 'The Tin Soldier', 'The Tinderbox', 'The Snow Queen' and 'The Ugly Duckling'. He died in Copenhagen. » Danish literature

Anderson, Elizabeth Garrett (1836–1917) British physician, born in London, who pioneered the admission of women into medicine. She began her studies in 1860, but had difficulty qualifying as a doctor because of opposition to women. She passed the Apothecaries' Hall examination (1865), and received an MD degree from the University of Paris (1870). As visiting physician to the East London Hospital, she practised regularly as a physician for women and children. She married (1871) J G S Anderson (died 1907), and was elected Mayor of Aldeburgh in 1908 – the first woman mayor in England. Her daughter **Louisa** (1878–1943) organized hospitals in France in World War 1, and wrote her mother's biography. » women's liberation movement

Anderson, Maxwell (1888–1959) US playwright, born at Atlantic, Pennsylvania. His plays, some of which are in a free form of blank verse, include *What Price Glory* (1924, with Laurence Stallings), *Elizabeth the Queen* (1930, the first of several historical dramas), and *Both Your Houses* (1933, Pulitzer Prize). He died at Stamford, Connecticut. » American literature; drama

Andes [**an**deez] Major mountain range in S America, running parallel to the Pacific coast from Tierra del Fuego (S) to the Caribbean (N), passing through Argentina, Chile, Bolivia, Peru, Ecuador, Colombia, and Venezuela; extends over 6 400 km/4 000 ml; rises to 6 960 m/22 834 ft in the Cerro Aconcagua (Argentina), the highest point in S America; in N Argentina, Bolivia, Peru, and Colombia, there are several parallel ranges (*cordilleras*) and high plateaux; highest peaks are in the Cordillera Agostini on the Chile–Argentina border, with many lakes and tourist resorts; Puna de Atacama to the N, a desolate plateau, average height 3 350–3 900 m/11 000–12 800 ft; C Andes in Bolivia covers two-fifths of the country in an elevated plateau (*altiplano*) of 3 000–3 600 m/9 800–11 800 ft, enclosing L Poopó and L Titicaca; Bolivian Andes split into E and W ranges (Cordillera Oriental/Occidental); system divides into many separate ranges in Peru; narrows in Ecuador, and includes such active volcanoes as Chimborazo (6 310 m/20 702 ft) and Cotopaxi (5 896 m/19 344 ft); three main ranges in Colombia (Cordillera Occidental/Central/Oriental); system continues NE into Venezuela as the Sierra Nevada de Mérida; connects via E Panama to the C American ranges. » Aconcagua, Cerro; Ampato, Nevado de; Bolívar, Pico; Chimborazo; Cotopaxi; Cristóbal Colón, Pico; Huascarán; Illampu, Nevado de; Incahuasi, Cerro; Llullaillaco, Cerro; Mercedario, Cerro; Ojos del Salado, Cerro; Payachata, Nevados de; Pichincha; Pissis, Monte; Ruiz, Nevado del; Salcantay, Nevado; Sangay; South America; Tungurahua; Tupungato, Cerro; Uspallata

andesite [**an**duhziyt] Fine-grained volcanic rock of intermediate composition containing plagioclase feldspar with biotite, hornblende, or pyroxene; chemically equivalent to diorite. Andesites are formed at the continental edge of subduction zones, forming new continental crust, as in the Andes Mts, S America. » continental margin; diorite; feldspar; igneous rocks

Andhra Pradesh [andra pra**daysh**] pop (1981) 53 403 619; area 276 814 sq km/106 850 sq ml. State in S India, bounded E by the Bay of Bengal; capital, Hyderabad; made a separate state based on Telugu-speaking area of Madras, 1953; unicameral Legislative Assembly with 295 seats; sugar cane, groundnuts, cotton, rice, tobacco; textiles, sugar milling, chemicals, cement, fertilizer, paper, carpets, natural gas, oil refining, shipbuilding, forestry. » Hyderabad; India [i]; Telugu

Andorra or **the Valleys of Andorra** [an**dor**a], Catalan **Valls d'Andorra**, Fr **Vallée d'Andorre**, official name **Principality of Andorra**, **Principat d'Andorra** A small, semi-independent, neutral state on the S slopes of the C Pyrenees between France and Spain, divided into seven parishes; pop (1990e) 51 000; area 468 sq km/181 sq ml; timezone GMT +1; capital, Andorra la Vella; language Catalan, also French and Spanish; currency, French francs and Spanish pesetas; a mountainous country, reaching 2 946 m/9 665 ft at Coma Pedrosa, occupying two valleys (del Norte and del Orient) of the R Valira; cold, dry, sunny winters, lowest average monthly rainfall (34 mm/1.34 in) in Jan; one of the oldest states in Europe, under the joint protection of France and Spain since 1278; Co-Princes of the Principality are the President of France and the Bishop of Urgel; the General Council of the Valleys appoints the head of the government, who appoints four councillors elected from the parishes; hydroelectric power on the R Valira; no restriction on currency exchange, and no direct or value-added taxes; commerce, tobacco, potatoes, construction, forestry; in recent years, textiles, publishing, leather, mineral water, furniture; tourism; skiing at five mountain resorts; airports at La Seu-Andorra and at La Seo de Urgel in Spain. » Andorra la Vella; RR24 national holidays

Andorra la Vella [an**dor**a la **vel**ya], Sp **Andorra la Vieja**, Fr **Andorre la Vielle** 42°30N 1°30E, pop (1982) 15 698. One of the seven parishes of the Principality of Andorra, with a capital town of the same name; on the E side of the Pic d'Enclar (2 317 m/7 602 ft), 613 km/381 ml NE of Madrid; altitude 1 029 m/3 376 ft; airports. » Andorra [i]

Andrássy, Julius, Gróf ('Count') (1823–90) Hungarian statesman and Prime Minister (1867–71), born at Kassa, Austrian Empire. A supporter of Kossuth, he was prominent in the struggle for independence (1848–9), after which he remained in exile until 1858. When the Dual Monarchy came into being, he was made Prime Minister of Hungary. He died at Volosco, Istria. » Austria-Hungary, Dual Monarchy of; Kossuth

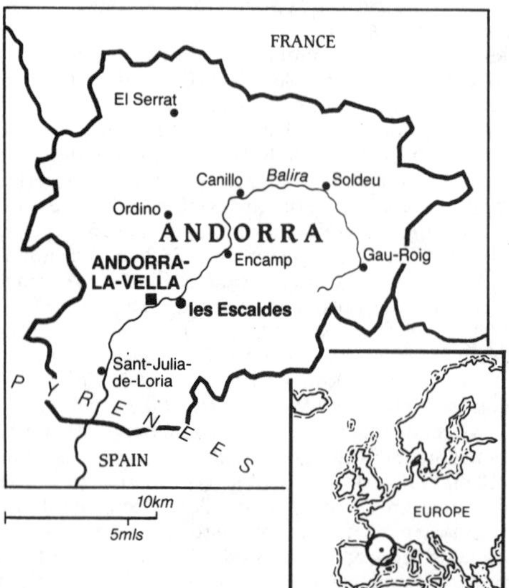

André, John (1751–80) British officer, born in London, of French-Swiss descent. He joined the army in Canada, becoming adjutant-general. When in 1780 Benedict Arnold obtained the command of West Point, André was selected to make the arrangements for its betrayal. However, he was captured, condemned as a spy, and hanged. In 1821 his remains were interred in Westminster Abbey. » Arnold, Benedict; American Revolution

Andrea del Sarto » Sarto, Andrea del

Andrew, St (1st-c), feast day 30 November. One of the twelve apostles, brother of Simon Peter; in John's Gospel, considered a previous follower of John the Baptist, and one who later introduced 'Greeks' to Jesus. He is traditionally supposed to have preached the gospel in Asia Minor and Scythia, and to have been crucified in Achaia by order of the Roman governor. The belief that his cross was X-shaped dates only from the 14th-c. He is the patron saint of Scotland and of Russia. » apostle; cross; New Testament; Peter, St

Andrewes, Lancelot (1555–1626) English prelate, born at Barking, Essex, thought to be one of the most learned Anglican theologians and preachers of his time. He was educated at Ratcliffe, Merchant Taylors', and Cambridge, ordained in 1580, and made a prebendary of St Paul's in 1589. Queen Elizabeth appointed him a prebendary of Westminster (1597), and then Dean (1601). He rose still higher in favour with King James I, who appreciated his learning and oratory. He became Bishop of Chichester (1605), Ely (1609), and Winchester (1618), and took part in the translation of the Bible. He died in London. » Authorized Version of the Bible; Church of England

Andrews, Julie, originally **Julia Elizabeth Wells** (1935–) British actress, born at Walton-on-Thames, Surrey. She worked as a child star on the variety stage and later on Broadway, then played the lead with English charm in two of the most successful film musicals, *Mary Poppins* (1964), for which she won an Oscar, and *The Sound of Music* (1965). She later widened her dramatic range, in such films as *Star!* (1967), *Victor/Victoria* (1982), and *Duet for One* (1987).

Andrianov, Nikolai [andree**ahn**of], byname **Old One-Leg** (1952–) Russian gymnast, born at Vladimir. The most successful male gymnast, he won 15 Olympic medals (7 gold) between 1972 and 1980. In addition, he won 12 world championship medals, including the overall individual title in 1978. » gymnastics

Androcles [**an**drokleez] According to a Roman story, a slave who escaped from his master, met a lion, and extracted a thorn from its paw. When recaptured, he was made to confront a lion in the arena, and found it was the same animal, so that his life was spared.

androecium [an**dree**syuhm] » **flower [i]; stamen**

androgens Chemical substances, usually steroid sex hormones, which induce masculine characteristics. In men the androgens *testosterone* and *dihydrotestosterone* are secreted in the testes by the cells of Leydig, with small amounts of additional androgens secreted by the adrenal cortex. Androgens are necessary for the development of male genitalia in the foetus; during puberty they promote the development of secondary sexual characteristics (growth of the penis and testes; the appearance of pubic, facial, and body hair; an increase in muscle strength; and deepening of the voice); in adults, they are required for the production of sperm and the maintenance of libido. Small amounts of ovarian and adrenal androgens are present in women, but their significance is unknown. » anabolic steroids; hormones; oestrogens

android » robotics (cybernetics)

Andromache [an**dro**makee] In Greek legend, the wife of Hector, the hero of Troy. After the fall of the city she became the slave of the Greek Neoptolemus. » Hector

Andromeda (astronomy) [an**dro**meda] A constellation in the N sky, one of 48 listed by Ptolemy (AD 140), named for the daughter of Cepheus and Cassiopeia. Its brightest star is Alpheratz. It contains the **Andromeda** galaxy, the largest of the nearby galaxies, about 700 kiloparsecs away. Spiral, like the Milky Way, about 38 kpc in diameter, it is the most remote object easily visible to the naked eye. » constellation; galaxy; Ptolemy; RR8

Andromeda (mythology) [an**dro**mida] In Greek mythology, the daughter of Cepheus, King of the Ethiopians, and Cassiopeia. To appease Poseidon, she was fastened to a rock by the sea-shore as an offering to a sea-monster. She was rescued by Perseus, who used the Gorgon's head to change the monster to stone. The persons named in the story were all turned into constellations. » Gorgon; Perseus; Poseidon

Andropov, Yuri (1914–84) General Secretary of the Soviet Communist Party (1982–4) and President of the USSR (1983–4), born at Nagutskoye, the son of a railwayman. He became head of the KGB (1967–72), and in 1973 was made a member of the Politburo. On the death of Brezhnev (1982), he became Party General Secretary, consolidating his power in June 1983 with the presidency. He fell ill later that year, and died soon after, in Moscow. » Brezhnev; communism; Hungarian uprising; KGB

Andros (Bahamas) pop (1980) 8 397; area 5 955 sq km/2 299 sq ml. Island in the W Bahamas, W of New Providence I, on the Great Bahama Bank; largest island in the Bahamas; chief towns on the E coast; W shore is a long, low, barren bank. » Bahamas

Andros (Greece) area 380 sq km/147 sq ml. Northernmost island of the Cyclades, Greece, in the Aegean Sea, between Euboea and Tinos; length 40 km/25 ml; chief town, Andros; bathing beaches at Batsi and Gavrion; rises to 994 m/3 261 ft. » Cyclades; Greece

anechoic chamber [ane**koh**ik] A room or chamber in which all walls and surfaces are lined with a sound-absorbing material to minimize reflected sound; also called a **dead room**. A sound produced in such a chamber will have no echo. It is important in acoustic experiments in which reflected sound would confuse results. » acoustics; phonetics; sound

anemometer A device for measuring the speed of a current of air, usually used to determine the speed of wind, or of a vehicle passing through air. There are three main techniques: (1) the speed of rotation of various types of windmill (eg shaped vanes or cups on horizontal arms); (2) the rate of cooling of an electrically heated wire; and (3) pressure differences developed in an open-ended tube facing the direction of the air-flow or gas stream. » Pitot tube; Venturi tube; wind [i]

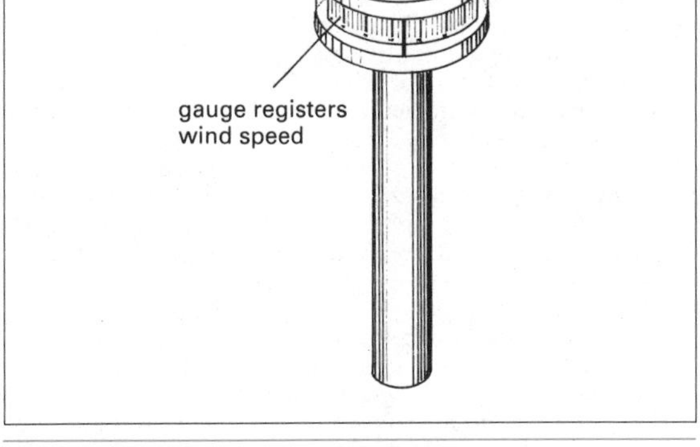

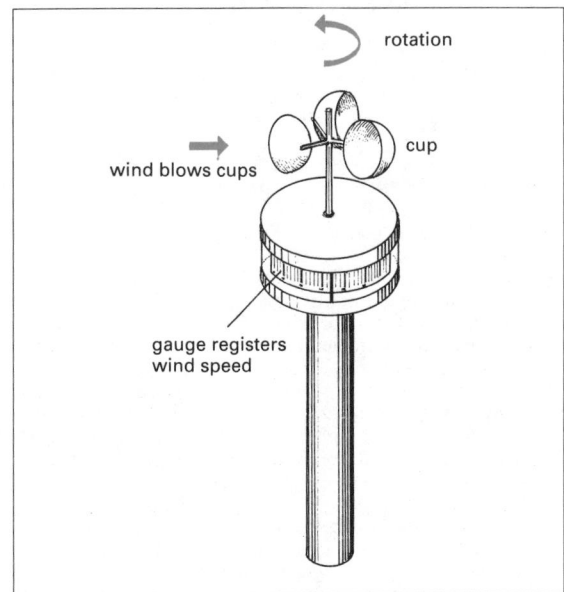

Anemometer

anemone [a**ne**muhnee] A perennial found throughout N temperate and arctic regions, often forming large colonies; flowers with 5–9 perianth-segments ranging from white to yellow, pink, or blue, but hybrids exhibit an even greater colour range; the flower stalks have a whorl of small, divided leaves two-thirds of the way up; the main, basal leaves appear later. (Genus: *Anemone*, 150 species. Family: *Ranunculaceae*.) » perennial; perianth

aneroid barometer » **barometer**

anesthetics » **anaesthetics**

Aneto, Pico de [**pee**koh thay a**nay**toh] 42°37N 0°40E. Highest peak of the Pyrenees Mts, rising to 3 404 m/11 168 ft in Huesca province, NE Spain. » Pyrenees

Aneurin or **Aneirin** (6th-c AD) Welsh poet, whose principal work, the *Gododdin*, celebrates the British heroes who fell in conflict with the Saxons in the bloody battle of Cattraeth (603). Welsh literature

aneurysm [**an**yoorizm] The abnormal enlargement of a segment of a blood vessel (usually an artery) due to the weakening or rupture of some of the layers of the wall of the vessel. If the inner layer (*intima*) ruptures, blood passes between the layers of the vessel wall. Aneurysm of the aorta or pulmonary trunk often proves fatal. » aorta; blood vessels

angel A celestial spirit, said to serve God in various capacities, such as acting as a messenger, or as a guardian of individuals. In traditional Christianity, angels were understood to have been created before the world. They feature prominently in Christian art, often depicted with a human body and wings. They are sometimes held to be objects of devotion. » Christianity; God; guardian angel

angel dust The street name of the drug **phencyclidine** (l-(l-phenylcyclohexyl) piperidine, or **PCP**) which is a hallucinogen. It was originally introduced in the 1950s as a general anaesthetic, but soon withdrawn; it is still used in veterinary medicine to produce a trance-like anaesthetic state. As a drug of abuse it is also called 'angel's mist', 'peace pills', 'goon', 'hog', and 'T'. » hallucinogens

Angel Falls 5°57N 62°33W. Waterfall in SE Venezuela, on a tributary of the R Caroní; highest waterfall in the world, with a total drop of 979 m/3 212 ft; named after the US aviator, Jimmy Angel, who crashed nearby in 1937. » Venezuela [i]; RR13

angelfish Any of several small brightly-coloured fish found in shallow waters of warm seas, commonly around coral reefs; deep, flattened body; small mouth, with gill cover bearing a spine; very popular in marine aquaria; also called **butterfly fish**. The name is also used for monkfish. (Family: *Chaetodontidae*.) » monkfish; Plate IX

angelica A robust herb growing to 2 m/6 ft or more, native from N and E Europe to C Asia; stem hollow; leaves divided into oval leaflets up to 15 cm/6 in, the stalks with an inflated base; flowers small, greenish-white, clustered in large rounded umbels. Candied leaf stalks are used for flavouring. Aromatic oil is produced from the roots, used in perfumes and an ingredient of herbal liqueurs (eg Chartreuse). (*Angelica archangelica*. Family: *Umbelliferae*.) » herb; umbel

Angelico, Fra, originally **Guido di Pietri**, monastic name **Giovanni da Fiesole** (c.1400–55) Italian early Renaissance painter, born at Vicchio in Tuscany. He entered the Dominican monastery at Fiesole (1407), moving to Florence (1436) and then to Rome (1445), where he chiefly resided until his death. His most important frescoes are those in the Florentine Convent of St Mark (now a museum), at Orvieto, and in the Nicholas Chapel of the Vatican. His easel pictures include 'The Coronation of the Virgin' (Louvre). His constant aim is to arouse devotional feeling through the contemplation of unearthly loveliness; the ethereal beauty of his angelic figures gave him his new name. He died in Rome, and was beatified. » fresco; Italian art; Renaissance

Angell, Sir (Ralph) Norman (1874–1967) British pacifist, born at Holbeach, Lincolnshire. He wrote *The Great Illusion* (1910) to prove the economic futility of war, even for the victors, and won the Nobel Peace Prize in 1933. He died at Croydon, Surrey. » pacifism

angelshark » **monkfish**

Angevins [**an**juhvinz] Three ruling families of the mediaeval county (and later duchy) of Anjou in W France. (1) Henry II, founder of the Angevin or Plantagenet dynasty in England, was a descendant of the earliest counts of Anjou. He established the 'Angevin empire' by taking control of Normandy, Anjou, and Maine (1150–1), acquiring Aquitaine (1152), and succeeding Stephen in England (1154). (2) The French crown had annexed Anjou by 1205, and in 1246 Louis IX's brother Charles, future king of Naples and Sicily, became count. (3) The third line was descended from Charles of Valois, brother of Philip IV, who married Charles of Anjou's granddaughter in 1290. This family died out in 1481. » Henry II (of England); Louis IX; Plantaganets; Sicilian Vespers

angina [an**jiy**na] A sudden severe pain or sensation of constriction over the front of the chest resulting from inadequate blood supply to the heart muscle (*angina pectoris*). The pain is increased with exercise, and rapidly subsides with rest. It may spread to the jaw and arms. It usually results from the narrowing or blockage of one or more of the arteries which supply the heart muscle with blood. It is commonly relieved by the use of drugs which either dilate the blood vessels or reduce the force of cardiac contraction. » blood vessels [i]; heart [i]

angiography [anjee**o**grafee] A radiological technique used to demonstrate the pathways and configuration of blood vessels in various parts of the body. A radio-opaque solution is injected into a main arterial trunk, which increases the X-ray contrast between the blood vessel and its surrounding tissues. After the injection, a number of X-ray plates are taken in rapid succession to follow the course of the blood. The technique is used to show narrowing or blockage of blood vessels, and also reveals increased vascularity of specific tissue, as in cancer. » blood vessels [i]; X-rays

angioplasty » **balloon angioplasty**

angiotensin » **renin**

Angkor Thom [**ang**kaw **tom**] 13°26N 103°50E. The ancient capital of the Khmer Empire, 240 km/150 ml NW of Phnom Penh, Cambodia. The moated and walled city was built on a square plan, extending over 100 sq km/40 sq ml, and completed in the 12th-c. Abandoned in the 15th-c, it was rediscovered in 1861. **Angkor Wat** is the largest of the temples surrounding the site – linked, richly-sculptured sanctuaries on a massive platform 1 000 m/3 300 ft square, the work of Suryavarman III (1112–52). » Cambodia [i]; Khmer Empire

angle A geometrical figure formed by two straight lines meeting at a point. Angles are measured in revolutions (especially per minute [rpm] or per second [rps] when measuring angular velocity), in right angles, degrees (°), radians (rad), or grad. 1 revolution = 4 right angles = 360° = 2π rad = 400 grad. » geometry; radian [i]; straight line; velocity

anglerfish Any of about 13 families of bizarre shallow to deep-sea fishes which have a dorsal fin spine modified as a lure to attract prey; family *Lophiidae* includes large bottom-dwelling European species (length up to 1.5 m/5 ft) with broad flattened head, capacious mouth, and narrow tail; also called **goosefish**.

Angles A Germanic people from the S Danish peninsula and neighbourhood. With the Saxons, they formed the bulk of the invaders who, in the two centuries following the Roman withdrawal from Britain (409), conquered and colonized most of what became England. Anglian rulers were apparently dominant by the 8th-c, and the Angles ultimately gave their name to England, its language, and people. » Anglo-Saxons

Anglesey, Henry William Paget, 1st Marquis of (1768–1854) British field marshal, born in London, who commanded the British cavalry at the Battle of Waterloo (1815), where he lost a leg. Educated at Westminster and Oxford, he sat in parliament at various times between 1790 and 1810, succeeding his father as Earl of Uxbridge in 1812. He served in the army with distinction in Flanders (1794), Holland (1799), and the Peninsular War (1808), and was made Marquis of Anglesey for his services at Waterloo. He was Lord Lieutenant of Ireland (1828–9, 1830–3), where he supported Catholic emancipation, and Master-General of the Ordnance (1846–52). » Peninsular War; Waterloo, Battle of

Anglesey [**ang**glsee] » **Ynys Môn**

Anglican chant » **chant**

Anglican Communion A fellowship of some 26 independent provincial or national Churches, several extra-provincial dioceses, and Churches resulting from unions of Anglicans with other Churches, spread throughout the world, but sharing a close ecclesiastical and doctrinal relationship with the Church of England. Most of these Churches are found in the British Commonwealth, and owe their origins to missionary activities of the Church of England in the 19th-c; a major exception is the Episcopal Church in the USA, which was fostered by the Scottish Episcopal Church. Churches from non-Commonwealth countries, such as Brazil, China, and Japan, are also part of the Anglican Communion. The Communion is based on co-operation, since there is no worldwide uniform authority, but every 10 years the Archbishop of Canterbury invites bishops throughout the Anglican Communion to take part in the Lambeth Conference, a consultative body that considers issues of common concern even though it has no final policy-making authority. The 1968 Lambeth Conference also set up an Anglican Consultative Council to act during the 10-year intervals. » Church of England; Episcopal Church, Protestant; Lambeth Conferences; Protestantism

Anglican–Roman Catholic International Commission » **ARCIC**

Anglicanism » **Church of England**

angling The sport of catching fish, one of the world's most popular pastimes, performed in virtually every country, practised with a rod, line, and hook. Many forms of angling exist: freshwater fishing, fly fishing, game fishing, and deep sea fishing. The oldest fishing club still in existence is the Ellem club in Scotland. Rules governing the time of year when different types of fishing take place are very strict, as are the rules governing the type of, and excessive use of, bait. » RR103

Anglo-Burmese Wars Two wars fought largely to advance British trade and the East India Company: the first (1824–6) brought control of Arakan and Tehnasserim; the second (1852–3) led to the occupation of Lower Burma. In 1885 Mandalay was occupied, and in 1886 all Burma was proclaimed a province of British India. » Burma [i]; East India Company, British

Anglo-Catholicism A movement within the Church of England, the term first appearing in 1838. It stresses the sacramental and credal aspects of Christian faith, and continuity and community with the wider Catholic Church, especially with Roman Catholicism. » Anglican Communion; Church of England; Roman Catholicism

Anglo-Irish Agreement A joint agreement allowing the Irish Republic to contribute to policy in Northern Ireland for the first time since 1922, signed (15 Nov 1985) by the British and Irish Prime Ministers, Margaret Thatcher and Garrett Fitzgerald. It established an intergovernmental conference to discuss political, security, and legal matters affecting Northern Ireland; early meetings focused on border co-operation. Both governments pledged not to change the status of Northern Ireland without the consent of the majority. The Agreement was opposed by the Republic's Opposition party, Fianna Fáil; Unionist leaders withdrew co-operation with ministers and boycotted official bodies. » Fianna Fáil; Irish Republic [i]; Northern Ireland [i]

Anglo-Maori Wars A succession of conflicts (1843–7, 1860–70) in which Maori people attempted, unsuccessfully, to resist the occupation of New Zealand by British settlers. Although faced by trained British troops, the Maoris did not suffer a decisive military defeat. The main fighting finished in 1864 after the Kingite Maoris, who had led the resistance, retreated to the C North Island, where the troops could not easily follow them. It is likely that the British learned the art of trench warfare from the Maoris during these conflicts. » Maoris

Anglo-Saxon The language of the Anglo-Saxons in England, as distinct from the original continental Saxons, in the period before the Norman Conquest; also known as **Old English**. It was a highly inflected language. Glosses to Latin texts survive from the 8th-c; the epic poem *Beowulf* (composed in the 8th-c) is preserved in an 11th-c manuscript; and there are several poems, historical narratives, prose sagas, and legal documents.

It was written in an Irish form of the Latin alphabet, introduced by monks. » Anglo-Saxons; English; Germanic languages

Anglo-Saxons A term probably first used to distinguish the Saxons of England from those of the continent; occasionally adopted by the 10th-c English kings for all their subjects, though 'English' was preferred; now commonly employed for the entire Old English people from the incoming of Angles, Saxons, and Jutes in the 5th-c to the Norman Conquest. Among the main themes in Anglo-Saxon history are the emergence of the early kingdoms, their conversion to Christianity, their response to attacks by the Vikings, and their eventual unification into a single realm, England, literally 'land of the Angles'. The Anglo-Saxons left an enduring legacy, including an advanced system of government and a rich economy. » Alfred; Angles; Anglo-Saxon; Athelstan; Bede; Edgar; Edward the Elder; Jutes; Offa; Saxons; Sutton Hoo ship burial; Wessex

Angola [ang**goh**la], official name **People's Republic of Angola**, Port **República Popular de Angola** pop (1990e) 10 002 000; area 1 245 790 sq km/480 875 sq ml. A republic of SW Africa, divided into 18 provinces; bounded S by Namibia, E by Zambia, and N by Zaire, with the separate province of Cabinda enclosed by the Congo; capital Luanda; chief towns Huambo, Benguela, Lobito, Namibe (Moçâmedes), Cabinda, Malanje, Lubango; timezone GMT +1; major ethnic groups include the Bakongo, Mbundu, Ovimbundu, Lunda-Tchokwe, Nganguela, Nyaneka-Humbe, Herero, Ambo; c.30 000 Europeans (mainly Portuguese); religions Roman Catholic (68%) and Protestant (20%); official language, Portuguese, with many Bantu languages spoken; unit of currency, the kwanza of 100 lewi.

Physical description and climate. A narrow coastal plain, widening in the N towards the Congo delta; high plateau inland, mean elevation 1 200 m/4 000 ft; highest point, Serro Môco (2 619 m/8 592 ft); numerous rivers, few navigable for any length; mostly a tropical plateau climate, with a single wet season (Oct–Mar) and a long dry season; more temperate above 1 500 m/5 000 ft; at Huambo on the plateau, average annual rainfall 1 450 mm/57 in, average daily temperatures 24°C–29°C; temperature/rainfall much reduced on the coast, which is semi-desert as far N as Luanda (eg at Namibe in the S, average annual rainfall 55 mm/2.2 in; in the far N, 600 mm/23.6 in).

History and government. Area became a Portuguese colony after exploration in 1483; estimated 3 million slaves sent to Brazil during the next 300 years; boundaries formally defined during the Berlin West Africa Congress (1884–5); became an Overseas Province of Portugal (1951); Civil War followed independence (1975), with three internal factions: the Marxist MPLA (Popular Movement for the Liberation of Angola), UNITA (the National Union for the Total Independence of Angola), and the FNLA (National Front for the Liberation of Angola); USA supplied arms to the FNLA and UNITA (1975–6); Cuban combat troops arrived from 1976 at request of MPLA; South African forces occupied an area along the Angola–Namibia frontier (1975–6), and were active again in support of UNITA, 1981–4; refuge given to Namibian independence movement SWAPO (South West Africa Peoples' Organization), who launched attacks on Namibia from Angolan territory; at end of 1988, Geneva agreement linked arrangements for independence of Namibia with withdrawal of Cuban troops, and the cessation of South African attacks and support for UNITA; Angola officially remains a one-party state, governed by a president (also head of state) who exercises power via a Council of Ministers (c.20) and a National People's Assembly of 289 elected and 29 appointed members.

Economy. Agriculture (cassava, corn, vegetables, plantains, bananas, coffee, cotton, sisal, timber, tobacco, palm oil, maize); reserves of diamonds, manganese, iron ore, gypsum, asphalt, limestone, salt, phosphates; extraction and refining of oil (mainly off the coast of Cabinda province), provides over 75% of recent export earnings; oil refining, food processing, textiles, cement, paper, pulp; airport at Luanda; several airfields and railways. » Cabinda; Luanda; Namibia [i]; South West

Africa People's Organization; RR24 national holidays; RR42 political leaders

Angora cat A breed of domestic cat; white long-haired type originates in Turkey (*Angora* is an old name for Ankara); resembles the Persian cat, but with longer body and smaller head; breed not recognized in the UK; name formerly used for all long-haired cats. » cat; Persian cat

Angora goat A breed of domestic goat, originating in Turkey (*Angora* is an old name for Ankara); bred mainly in N America, S Africa, and Australasia for wool; silky hair (length up to 20 cm/8 in), called *mohair*. » goat

angostura A flavouring agent used in cocktails and some fruit juices, deriving from the bark of a S American tree (*Gallipea aspuria*). It was originally used in medicines.

Angra do Heroísmo [**ang**gra do ayro**ee**smo] 38°40N 27°14W, pop (1981) 18 294. Fortified town and seaport in the Azores; a world heritage site, on S coast of Terceira I; founded, 1464; capital of the Azores until 1832; bishopric; airport; wine, fruit, flax, grain, tobacco, soap, distilling, tourism; Cidade festival (Jun). » Azores

Angry Brigade A left-wing group with anarchist sympathies, active in Britain in the 1960s and early 1970s, which took sporadic violent action against representatives of the establishment in the name of the working class. Its leaders were tried and imprisoned for a bomb attack on the Secretary of State for Employment's home in 1971. » left wing

Angry Young Men A term used to describe characters in some novels and plays of the late 1950s and early 1960s in Britain, who felt a confident contempt for and expressed an energetic rejection of the (apparently) established order. Typical examples are Kingsley Amis's Jim Dixon in *Lucky Jim* (1954) and John Osborne's Jimmy Porter in *Look Back in Anger* (1957). » Amis; drama; English literature; novel; Osborne

Ångström, Anders (Jonas) (1814–74) Swedish physicist, born at Lödgö. He became keeper of the observatory (1843), professor of physics (1858), and from 1867 secretary to the Royal Society at Uppsala. He wrote on heat, magnetism, and especially spectroscopy; the unit for measuring wavelengths of light is named after him. His son, **Knut Johan** (1857–1910), was also a noted Uppsala physicist, important for his researches on solar radiation. He died at Uppsala. » ångström; optics [i]

ångström [**ang**struhm] Unit of length common in crystallography or any other subject which studies features of approximately atomic dimensions; symbol Å, named after Swedish physicist Anders Ångström; equal to 10^{-10} m. » Ångström; units (scientific)

Anguilla [angwila] pop (1989e) 7 000; area 155 sq km/60 sq ml. Most northerly of the Leeward Is, E Caribbean, 112 km/70 ml NW of St Kitts; British dependent territory; capital, The Valley; timezone GMT −4; chief religion, Christianity; official language, English; unit of currency, the East Caribbean dollar; also includes Sombrero I and several other offshore islets and cays; low-lying coral island covered in scrub; tropical climate; low and erratic annual rainfall, 550–1 250 mm/22–50 in; hurricane season (Jul–Oct); colonized by English settlers from St Kitts, 1650; ultimately incorporated in the colony of St Kitts-Nevis-Anguilla; separated, 1980; a governor appointed by the British sovereign; 11-member Legislative Assembly; tourism, fishing, peas, corn, sweet potatoes, salt, boatbuilding. » Leeward Islands (Caribbean)

angular acceleration » acceleration

angular momentum A vector quantity in rotational motion, equal to the product of moment of inertia with angular velocity; also called the **moment of momentum**; symbol L, units $kg.m^2/s$. The rate of change of angular momentum is called *torque*. » mechanics; moment of inertia; momentum; precession; torque [i]; vector (mathematics)

angular velocity » velocity

angwantibo [anggwantiboh] A West African primitive primate (*prosimian*); golden brown with pointed face; no tail; first finger reduced to a stump, and second short; grips branches strongly between thumb and remaining fingers; also known as **golden potto**. (*Arctocebus calabarensis*. Family: *Lorisidae*.) » potto; prosimian

anhinga » darter [i]

anhydride [anhiydriyd] ('without water') In chemistry, often referring to an acid. An inorganic anhydride is usually a non-metal oxide. Organic anhydrides are usually condensation products of two molecules; for example, acetic acid (CH_3COOH) gives acetic anhydride (CH_3–CO–O–CO–CH_3). » acidic oxide; basic oxides

anil A tropical American shrub, but cultivated in the Old and New World as a source of the blue dye indigo; also called **indigo plant**. (*Indigofera anil*. Family: *Leguminosae*.) » indigo; shrub

aniline [anileen] $C_6H_5NH_2$, **phenylamine**, or (IUPAC) **aminobenzene**, boiling point 184°C. A liquid with an unpleasant smell, a weaker base than ammonia. It is the starting material for many dyestuffs, known as *aniline dyes*. » ammonia; dyestuff; IUPAC

animal A living organism; one of the main kingdoms of biological classification, *Animalia*, containing all vertebrates and invertebrates). The term *animal* is sometimes used only for four-legged creatures (mammals, reptiles, and amphibians) but correctly fish and birds are also animals, as are insects, spiders, crabs, snails, worms, starfish, sponges, corals, jellyfish, and many other groups. All animals obtain their nourishment by eating other living organisms or the remains of living organisms, and most can respond quickly to changes in their surroundings by moving part of their body or their entire body. » amphibian; animal husbandry; kingdom; mammal [i]; reptile; RSPCA

animal husbandry The keeping of domesticated animals for food, fibre, skins, or to pull loads. Domestication started in the Middle East c.9000 BC with sheep; pigs were domesticated c.6000 BC and cattle c.5500 BC. » dairy farming

Animal Protection Society of America » RSPCA

animal protein factor An essential growth factor found exclusively in animal products, now known to be vitamin B_{12}. » vitamins [i]

animism A belief in spiritual beings thought capable of influencing human events, based on the idea that animals, plants, and even inanimate objects have souls like humans. The 19th-c anthropologist Edward Tylor (1832–1917) regarded it as the earliest form of religion, a view not accepted by modern anthropologists.

anion [aniyuhn] A negatively-charged atom or group of atoms, such as Cl^- (chloride) or SO_4^{2-} (sulphate). Anions are so called because they migrate towards the anode in an electrochemical cell. » anode; cation; ion

anisotropic » isotropic

Anjou [ãzhoo] Former province in the Paris Basin of NW France, now occupying the department of Maine-et-Loire and small parts of Indre-et-Loire, Mayenne, and Sarthe; former capital was Angers; lost provincial status in 1790; Henry II of England, first of the Plantagenets (or Angevins) was son of Geoffrey Plantagenet, Count of Anjou; Anjou also gave a line of kings to Sicily and Naples. » Henry II (of England); Plantagenets

Ankara [angkara], ancient **Ancyra** or **Angora** 39°55N 32°50E, pop (1980) 1 901 282. Capital city of Ankara province and of Turkey, on a tributary of the R Ova; second largest city in Turkey; formerly an important location on the caravan route from Istanbul to the E; conquered by Alexander the Great, 4th-c BC; part of Roman and Byzantine Empires; under Turkish rule, 11th-c; government transferred here from Istanbul, 1923; airport; railway; three universities (1946, 1956, 1967); textiles, mohair, leather, cement. » Alexander the Great; Turkey [i]

ankh A cross with a loop for its upper vertical arm; in ancient Egypt, an emblem of life. » RR93

ankle The region of the lower limb between the calf and the foot; specifically, the joint between the tibia and fibula and the talus (one of the tarsal bones). Movement at the joint is important during the stance phase of walking, particularly in ensuring a smooth and controlled contact of the foot with the ground. » fibula; sprain; tibia; Plate XIII

ankylosaur [angkuhlohsaw] A small four-legged dinosaur, heavily armoured with rectangular bony plates along body and tail; head small, teeth reduced or absent; feeding on vegetation; known from the Cretaceous period of N America. (Order: *Ornithischia*.) » Cretaceous period; dinosaur [i]; Ornithischia

ankylosing spondylitis [angkilohzing spondiliytis] A progressive inflammatory disease that affects mainly young adult men, giving rise to rigidity of the spine, and reduced movement of the chest and occasionally of the joints. Its cause is unknown, but a very high proportion of cases have human leucocyte antigen (HLA) B27. » antibodies; human leucocyte antigens; inflammation; vertebral column

Anna Comnena (1083–1148) Byzantine princess, the daughter of Emperor Alexius Comnenus. She tried in vain to secure the imperial crown, and failed in her attempt to overthrow or poison her brother (1118). Disappointed and ashamed, she withdrew from the court, and sought solace in literature. On the death of her husband (1137), she retired to a convent, where she wrote a life of her father, the *Alexiad*, which contains an account of the early Crusades. » Crusades [i]; Alexius Comnenus

Annapolis [anapuhlis] 38°59N 76°30W, pop (1980) 31 740. Capital of state in Anne Arundel County, C Maryland, USA; port on the S bank of the Severn R; named after Princess (later Queen) Anne, 1695; US capital, 1783–4; railway; business and shipping centre; US Naval Academy (1845); tourist centre; site of the statehouse where the treaty ending the American War of Independence was ratified (1784). » American Revolution; Annapolis Convention; Maryland

Annapolis Convention (1786) In the American Revolution, a gathering at Annapolis, Maryland, of delegates from five states to discuss commercial problems. The main result was a call for a meeting the following year to consider changes in the Articles of Confederation. That meeting wrote the present Federal Constitution. » Articles of Confederation; Constitutional Convention

Annapurna, Mount [anapoorna] Mountain massif in the C Himalayas, Nepal; length c.56 km/35 ml; includes Annapurna I (8 091 m/26 545 ft), Annapurna II (7 937 m/26 040 ft), Annapurna III (7 556 m/24 790 ft), Annapurna IV (7 525 m/24 688 ft), and several other peaks over 6 000 m/20 000 ft; part of the Pokhara trekking region; Annapurna I first climbed in 1950 by Maurice Herzog's French expedition. » Himalayas

Annas [anas] (1st-c) Israel's high priest, appointed in AD 6 and deposed by the Romans in AD 15, but still described later by this title in the New Testament. He apparently questioned Jesus after his arrest (*John* 18) and Peter after his detention (*Acts* 4). His other activities are described in the works of Flavius Josephus. » Israel [i]; Jesus Christ; Josephus; New Testament; Peter, St

Anne (1665–1714) Queen of Great Britain and Ireland (1702–14), the second daughter of James II, and the last Stuart sovereign. In 1672 her father became a Catholic, but she was brought up in the Church of England. In 1683 she married Prince George of Denmark (1653–1708); and Sarah Jennings (1660–1744), the wife of Lord Churchill (afterwards Duke of Marlborough), was appointed a lady of her bedchamber. Lady Churchill speedily acquired supreme influence over her, which she exerted in favour of her husband. In their correspondence, Anne went by the name of Mrs Morley, and Lady Churchill by that of Mrs Freeman. During her father's reign, Anne lived in retirement, taking no part in politics, but later was drawn into intrigues for the restoration of her father, or to secure the succession for his son. She was herself childless when she succeeded to the throne in 1702. She bore 17 children, but only William, Duke of Gloucester (1689–1700), survived infancy. The influence of Marlborough and his wife was powerfully felt in all public affairs during the greater part of her reign, which was marked by the union of England and Scotland (1707), and the long struggle against Louis XIV of France known as the War of the Spanish Succession. Towards the end of her reign she quarrelled with the Marlboroughs who, with Godolphin, headed the Whig party. Anne found a new favourite in Abigail Masham, and under her influence appointed a Tory government (1710); but quarrels between the new ministers prevented her securing the succession for her brother. She died in London. » Godolphin; Marlborough; Spanish Succession, War of the; Stuarts; Tories; Whigs

Anne of Austria (1601–66) Eldest daughter of Philip III of Spain, born at Valladolid, the wife of Louis XIII of France, and the mother of Louis XIV. The marriage was not a happy one, the royal couple living for the first 22 years in a state of virtual separation (due chiefly to the influence of Richelieu). In 1643 Anne became Queen Regent for the baby Louis XIV. Her minister Mazarin died in 1661, and she retired to the convent of Val de Grâce. She died in Paris. » Louis XIII; Mazarin; Richelieu

Anne of Bohemia (1366–94) Daughter of Emperor Charles IV and first wife of Richard II of England, whom she married in 1382. She died of the plague. » Richard II

Anne of Cleves (1515–57) Lutheran princess, plain of feature, who became the fourth Queen of Henry VIII (Jan 1540) as part of Thomas Cromwell's strategy of developing an alliance with German Protestant rulers. The marriage was declared null and void six months afterwards. On agreeing to the divorce, Anne was given a large income, and she remained in England until her death, in London. » Cromwell, Thomas; Henry VIII

Anne, Princess (Elizabeth Alice Louise), Mrs Mark Phillips (1950–) Daughter of HM Elizabeth II and HRH Prince Philip, Duke of Edinburgh, born in London (at Clarence House). She married **Mark Anthony Peter Phillips** (1948–) in 1973, separated in 1989; their son is **Peter Mark Andrew** (1977–), their daughter **Zara Anne Elizabeth** (1981–). She is a noted horsewoman and both she and her husband have ridden in the British Equestrian Team. She was created Princess Royal in 1987. » Elizabeth II

Anne of Denmark (1574–1619) Wife (from 1589) of James VI of Scotland, later James I of England. Much of her time was spent in extravagant court entertainments, and she became a patron of the masque and other art forms. » James I (of England); masque

annealing The relief of internal stresses in metals after heat treatment or working (hammering, forging, or drawing), or in glass after moulding or blowing. It is effected by maintaining the object at a moderate temperature to allow for molecular or crystalline re-arrangement. This improves its properties, or restores its original properties when the object is eventually cold. » glass 1 [i]; metal

Annecy [ansee] 45°55N 6°08E, pop(1982) 51 993. Industrial town and capital of Haute-Savoie department, E France; in the foothills of the French Alps, on N shore of Lac d'Annecy; railway; bishopric; textiles, watches, paper, bearings; popular tourist centre; on route to Little St Bernard and Mt Cenis passes. » Alps; St Bernard's Passes

annelid [anuhlid] A ringed worm; a bilaterally symmetrical worm of phylum *Annelida*; body divided into cylindrical rings (segments) containing serially arranged organs; body cavity (*coelom*) present; head typically well defined; includes earthworms, bristleworms, and leeches. » bristleworm; earthworm; leech; sea mouse; Tubifex; worm

Annigoni, Pietro [anigohnee] (1910–88) Italian painter, born in Milan. He studied at Florence, where he held his first one-man show in 1932. During the 1950s he worked in England. He was one of the few 20th-c artists to put into practice the technical methods of the old masters. His most usual medium was tempera, although there are frescoes by him in the Convent of St Mark at Florence (executed in 1937). His Renaissance manner is shown at its best in his portraits (eg of Queen Elizabeth II, 1955, 1970). He died in Florence. » fresco; Italian art; tempera

annual A plant which germinates, flowers, sets seed, and dies within one year. The definition is not strict: in mild weather, some annuals may germinate late in the season, overwinter as seedlings or young plants, and complete their life-cycle in the next year. » biennial; ephemeral; perennial

annual ring One of the concentric rings visible when the stem or root of a woody plant is cut across. Each ring is formed by two bands of xylem vessels: large diameter vessels produced early in the year form pale springwood; smaller vessels formed late in the year form darker summerwood. Usually one ring marks one year's growth, providing a means of calculating the age of trees. If there is more than one growing period in the year, there are correspondingly more rings, called *false annual rings*. » root (botany); stem (botany); vascular tissue; wood; xylem

annuity A sum of money paid to older people on a regular guaranteed basis until they die. The scheme is operated by life insurance companies. An initial lump sum is paid over, and subsequent payments are made to pensioners partly from interest on the capital invested and partly on the repayment of the capital itself. » assurance; pension

annulment A judicial declaration of nullity of marriage. A null marriage is one that was never valid, for example because it involved parties within the prohibited degrees of affinity or consanguinity. » affinity; bigamy

Annunciation The angel Gabriel's foretelling to Mary of the birth of Jesus and of the promise of his greatness (*Luke* 1.26–38). Many of the features of this account are parallel to the annunciation of the birth of John the Baptist (*Luke* 1.5–25). The feast day is also known as **Lady Day**. » Gabriel; Jesus Christ; Mary (mother of Jesus); New Testament

anoa [anoha] A rare member of the cattle family, from Sulawesi; height, c.800 mm/30 in; straight backward-pointing horns; inhabits forests; young have thick dark coats; two species: **lowland anoa** (*Bubalus depressicornis*) and **mountain anoa** (*Bubalus quarlesi*); also known as **dwarf buffalo, wood ox, sapi-utan**, or **sapi-outan**. » Bovidae; cattle; water buffalo

anode The negative terminal in a battery. In thermionic valves, electrons are accelerated towards the anode, which is kept positive with respect to the electron source (the **cathode**); in electrolysis, anions (negative ions) move towards the anode. » anion; anodizing; cathode; thermionic valve

anodizing A metal protection process, usually applied to aluminium or magnesium. The object is made the anode in an electrolytic bath which produces a thin but dense protective oxide layer. Such a coating can also be made to take dyes, and so produce a decorative effect. » aluminium; anode; electrolysis [i]; magnesium

anointing the sick The ritual application of oil performed in cases of (usually) serious illness or preparation for death. In the Roman Catholic and Orthodox Churches, which claim scriptural authority for the practice, it is recognized as a sacrament to be performed by a priest. It was formerly sometimes called **extreme unction**. » Roman Catholicism; Orthodox Church; sacrament

anole [anohlee] An iguana found from SE USA to N South

America (including the West Indies); can change colour, but this is slow and controlled by chemical changes in the blood; some species signal with a brightly coloured expandable blade of skin under the throat. (Genus: *Anolis*, several species.) » chameleon; iguana

anomia A clinical language disability in which the chief problem is recalling the names of things. It is often found as a symptom of aphasia. While typically involving nouns, the word-finding difficulties can relate to any part of speech. » aphasia; part of speech

anomie [anoh**mee**] A personal or wider social condition in which individuals or society at large no longer identify with or feel guided by customary norms and values. In individuals, the concept embraces extreme despair, and a sense of alienation from society, which may lead to suicide. Society at large is said to be 'anomic' when its members no longer agree on a fundamental normative and moral order. The term was introduced by Durkheim in 1897. He considered the condition to be one form of suicide, indicating the importance of social factors to psychiatric illness. » Durkheim; mental disorders

Anopheles [a**nof**ileez] The malaria mosquito, found in all major zoogeographical regions. The adult females transmit a malaria-causing agent when taking blood from vertebrates. The males feed on nectar and plant fluids. The larvae are aquatic, feeding at the water surface using short feeding bristles. (Order: *Diptera*. Family: *Culicidae*.) » malaria; mosquito

anorexia nervosa [anuh**rek**sia ner**voh**sa] A psychological illness which mainly affects young women, characterized by significant weight loss (usually deliberately induced), an unrealistic fear of being overweight, and a loss of normal menstrual functioning. There is a distortion of body image, and sufferers are frequently hyperactive, have faddish eating habits, and some have depressed mood. The term was first used by the English physician Sir William Gull (1816–90) in 1874, but there are clear historical accounts of a similar condition dating back centuries, indicating that this is not a symptom of modern living. Current views hold that there are both biological and psychological causes, and that early treatment is likely to produce a better outcome than any delay, which may lead to chronicity of the illness and a fatal outcome in a proportion of sufferers. » amenorrhoea; bulimia nervosa; diet; mental disorders; obesity

Anouilh, Jean (Marie Lucien Pierre) [an**wee**] (1910–87) French dramatist, born in Bordeaux. He began his career in films. His first play, *L'Hermine* (1931, The Ermine) was not a success; but his steady output soon earned him recognition as one of the leading dramatists of the contemporary theatre. He was influenced by the Neoclassical fashion inspired by Giraudoux, but his very personal approach to the reinterpretation of Greek myths is less poetic and more in tune with contemporary taste. Among his many successful plays are *Le Voyageur sans bagage* (1938, Traveller without Luggage), *Antigone* (1944), *L'Alouette* (1953, The Lark), *Becket* (1959), and *La Culotte* (1978, The Trousers). He died at Lausanne, Switzerland. » Giraudoux; Neoclassicism (art)

Anoura » **Anura**

Anquetil, Jacques [ang**ka**teel] (1934–87) French cyclist, born at Mont-St Aigan, the first man to win the Tour de France five times (1957, 1961–64). His first win was by a 15-minute margin. He also won the Tour of Italy in 1960 and 1964 and the Tour of Spain in 1963. An outstanding time-trialist, he won the Grand Prix des Nations a record nine times between 1953 and 1965. He retired in 1969. » cycling

Anschluss [**an**shlus] The concept of union between Austria and Germany, expressly forbidden by the Treaty of Versailles (1919), but with some support in both countries after the collapse of the Habsburg Empire. Hitler pursued the idea once in power, and in 1938, after the resignation of Austrian Chancellor Schuschnigg, the Germans were 'invited' to occupy Austria. The union of Austria and Germany was formally proclaimed on 13 March 1938. » Habsburgs; Hitler; Schuschnigg; Versailles, Treaty of

Anselm, St (1033–1109), feast day 21 April. Italian theologian and philosopher, of noble birth at or near Aosta, Piedmont. He joined the abbey of Bec, in Normandy, becoming abbot there in 1078. Appointed Archbishop of Canterbury (1093), he frequently came into conflict over Church rights, first with William Rufus, then with Henry I. His resoluteness led to his being exiled by both kings; but in 1107 Anselm's threat of excommunication led to a reconciliation, and a compromise was devised which was eventually accepted. A follower of Augustine, he was the main figure in early scholastic philosophy, remembered especially for his 'ontological' proof for the existence of God, and his theory of atonement. He died, possibly at Canterbury, and may have been canonized as early as 1163. » atonement; Augustine, St (of Hippo); Henry I (of England); ontological argument; scholasticism

Ansermet, Ernest (Alexandre) (1883–1969) Swiss conductor, born at Vevey. After an early career in mathematics at Lausanne, he devoted himself to music, becoming conductor of the Montreux Kursaal (1912) and of Diaghilev's Russian Ballet (1915–23). In 1918 he founded the Orchestre de la Suisse Romande, whose conductor he remained until 1967. His compositions include a symphonic poem, piano pieces, and songs. He died in Geneva. » Diaghilev

Ansgar, Anskar, or (Ger) **Scharies, St** (801–65), feast day 3 February. The 'Apostle of the North', a native of Picardy, who in 826 went, with his colleague Autbert, to preach Christianity to the heathen Northmen of Schleswig. In 832 he was appointed the first Bishop of Hamburg, and later became Archbishop of Bremen. He built the first church in Sweden, and taught in Denmark. He died at Bremen, Saxony, and was canonized soon after his death. He is the patron saint of Scandinavia. » missions, Christian

Anshan or **An-shan** 41°05N 122°58E, pop (1984e) 1 258 600. Town in Liaoning province, NE China; organized mining and smelting began here c.100 BC; railway; site of China's largest iron and steel complex, agricultural machinery, construction materials, chemicals, textiles, porcelain, electrical appliances; Qianlian Shan (Thousand Lotuses Hill), 10th-c Buddhist hermitage; Eryijiu (19 Feb) Park; c.10 km/6 ml SE, Tanggangzi hot springs park. » China [i]

ant A social insect, characterized by a waist of 1–2 narrow segments, forming perennial colonies in nests made in wood, soil, plant cavities, or other constructions. The nest contains one or more fertile queens, many wingless, sterile workers, and winged males that fertilize queens during mass nuptial flights. Most ants scavenge animal remains; some are predators; others feed on fungi, seeds, or honeydew. (Order: *Hymenoptera*. Family: *Formicidae*, c.14 000 species.) » Amazon/army/driver/honey/leafcutter/slave-making ant; insect [i]; termite

ant bear » **aardvark**

Antananarivo [antananar**ee**voh], formerly **Tananarive** or **Tananarivo** (to 1975) 18°52S 47°30E, pop (1985e) 662 585. Capital of Madagascar, on a ridge in the EC part of the island; altitude c.1 350 m/4 400 ft; divided into upper and lower towns; airport; railway; university (1955); textiles, tobacco, leather, food processing; two cathedrals, Queen's palace, Ambohitsorahitra palace, museum of art and archaeology, Zoma market, casinos, Mohamasina sports stadium and racecourses. » Madagascar [i]

Antarctic Circle Imaginary line on the surface of the Earth at 66°30S, marking the southernmost point at which the Sun can be seen during the summer solstice, and the northernmost point at which the midnight Sun can be seen in S polar regions. » Antarctica [i]; Arctic Circle

Antarctic Ocean The S regions of the Atlantic, Indian, and Pacific Oceans surrounding Antarctica; narrowest point the Drake Passage between S America and the Antarctic Peninsula (1 110 km/690 ml). » Antarctica [i]

Antarctica S Polar continent, area nearly 15.5 million sq km/6 million sq ml; surrounded by ice-filled ring of ocean waters containing scattered island groups; mainly S of 65°S, almost entirely within the Antarctic Circle; c.22 400 km/14 000 ml coastline, mainly of high ice cliffs; indented by Ross and Weddell Seas; divided into Greater and Lesser Antarctica, separated by the Transantarctic Mts, highest point 5 140 m/16 863 ft at Vinson Massif; no permanent population; no flowering plants, grasses, large mammals; species of algae, moss, lichen, and sea plankton provide food for fish, birds,

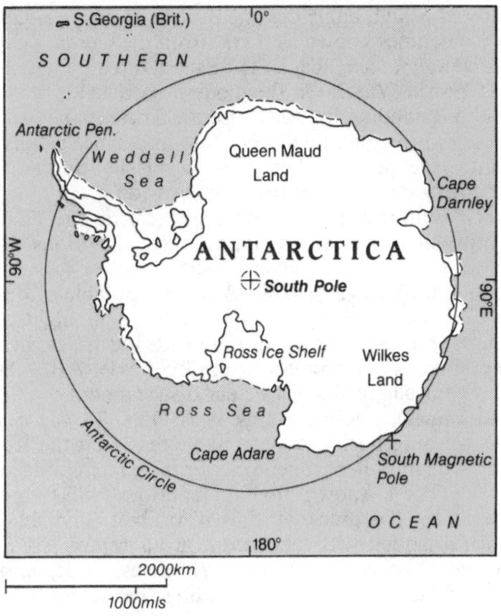

whales, and seals; average depth of surface ice sheet 1 500 m/4 921 ft, overlying rock; inland ice moves slowly towards the periphery, pushing long tongues into the sea and creating shelf ice over large areas; drift ice develops along the whole coastline; many icebergs in adjacent waters, the largest of the tabular type (10–60 m/30–200 ft high); movement of pack ice varies widely in different longitudes; outward blowing winds prevail, often of hurricane force; blizzards common, especially in autumn and winter; lowest temperature on Earth (−88.3°C) recorded at Vostok Station; major scientific explorations since first winter base established in 1899 by Borchgevrink; during International Geophysical Year (1957–8) 12 countries maintained 65 bases in Antarctica; Antarctic Treaty signed by these nations in 1959, providing for international co-operation in scientific research, and prohibiting military operations, nuclear explosions, and disposal of radioactive waste; territorial claims made by the UK (British Antarctic Territory), Norway (Dronning Maud Land), France (Terre Adélie), Australia (Enderby Land, Wilkes Land, George V Coast, part of Oates Coast), New Zealand (160°E to 150°W), Chile (90°W to 53°W), and Argentina (74°W to 25°W); South Pole first reached by Amundsen in 1911. » Adélie Land; Amundsen; Australian/British Antarctic Territory; Queen Maud Land; French Southern and Antarctic Territories; Poles; Ross Dependency; Scott, R F

Antares [an**tah**reez] » **Scorpius**

antbird A forest-dwelling bird native to the New World tropics; eats insects, spiders, lizards, frogs; follows army ants, feeding on animals they disturb; includes *antpittas*, *antthrushes*, *antwrens*, *antvireos*, *antshrikes*, and *gnateaters*. (Family: *Formicariidae*, 236 species.)

anteater A mammal, native to C and S America, which eats ants and termites; an edentate, comprising four species: **giant anteaters** (inhabiting grassland), **northern** and **southern tamanduas** (grassland or forest), and **silky anteaters** (forest); numbats are also known as *banded anteaters*, and pangolins as *scaly anteaters*. (Family: *Myrmecophagidae*.) » Edentata; numbat; pangolin

antelope A hoofed mammal, found mainly in Africa; classified as gazelles (tribe: *Antilopini*), four-horned antelopes (tribe: *Boselaphini*), spiral-horned antelopes (tribe: *Strepsicerotini*), dwarf (or pygmy) antelopes (tribe: *Neotragini*), grazing antelopes (subfamily: *Hippotraginae*, including horse-like antelopes of the tribe *Hippotragini*, and ox-antelopes of the tribe *Alcelaphini*), pronghorns (subfamily: *Antilocaprinae*), duikers (subfamily: *Cephalophinae*), and goat antelopes (subfamily: *Caprinae*, which includes goats and sheep). (Family: *Bovidae*, 116 species.) » Bovidae; duiker; gazelle [i]; goat; horse [i]; pronghorn; sheep

antelope goat » **Rocky Mountain goat**

antenatal diagnosis » **prenatal diagnosis**

antenna (biology) One of a pair of specialized sensory appendages on the head of an invertebrate animal; insects typically have one pair, crustaceans two pairs; varies in shape and size: long and thin in shrimps, feather-like in moths, club-shaped in weevils. » crustacean; insect [i]; invertebrate

antenna (photography) The component of a radio or television system by which electromagnetic signals are transmitted or received; also known as the **aerial**. In high-frequency practice, additional elements termed *reflectors* and *directors* are included to increase directional efficiency. » dish

Antenor [an**tee**nor] (early 6th-c BC) Athenian sculptor, known to have executed bronze statues of Harmodius and Aristogiton, and a female statue (Kore) in the Acropolis. » Greek art; sculpture

antepartum haemorrhage/hemorrhage Bleeding from the genital tract after the end of the 28th week of pregnancy, but before the birth of the baby. Bleeding from the site of the attachment of the placenta to the uterus is the most common cause. » placenta; uterus [i]

Antheil, George [**an**tiyl] (1900–59) US composer of Polish descent, born in New Jersey. He spent some years in Europe as a professional pianist before becoming known as the composer of the *Jazz Symphony* (1925), the *Ballet Mécanique* (1926), and the opera *Transatlantic* (1930). The sensation caused by the ballet overshadowed his more traditional later works, which include symphonies, concertos, operas, and chamber music. He died in New York City. » ballet; bruitisme

anthelmintics [anthel**min**tics] Drugs which paralyse or kill parasitic worms (*helminths*), such as ringworms, tapeworms, and schistosomes. Ancient treatment included antimony compounds and *Absinthium* (wormwood), the leaves and flowers of *Artemesia absinthium*. Galen used aspidium extract of the male fern (*Dryopteris felixmas*) for tapeworms. Many of these treatments were used until quite recently. They are now mostly replaced by safer, more effective drugs such as mebendazole, piperazine, and niridazole. » Galen; helminthology; worm

anthem A sacred vocal composition to an English text, often from the Book of Psalms. 16th-c composers, including Byrd and Tallis, wrote numerous examples, but the anthem was not included in the rubric of the Anglican liturgy until 1662. Purcell excelled in the genre, and also in the instrumentally-accompanied anthem which flourished after the Restoration. » cantata; motet; Purcell, Henry

Anthony, St » **Antony, St**

Anthony, Susan B(rownell) (1820–1906) US women's suffrage leader, born at Adams, Massachusetts to a Quaker family. She early developed an interest in labour problems from observing the mill her father managed. After teaching and temperance work, she became the champion of women's rights. From 1869 she was a leader of the National Woman Suffrage Association, becoming President of the US branch in 1892. She died at Rochester, New York. » women's liberation movement

Anthony Island A provincial park in the Queen Charlotte Is off the coast of British Columbia, Canada; a world heritage site. For 2 000 years the island was inhabited by Indians of the NW Pacific. Although it was abandoned in the late 19th-c, their village with its longhouses and totem poles has been preserved. » Queen Charlotte Islands

anthracene [**an**thruhseen] $C_{14}H_{10}$, melting point 216°C. A colourless, cancer-causing, aromatic compound isolated from coal tar. Its blue fluorescence is used in scintillation counters to detect β-particles. Oxidized to **anthraquinone**, it is the raw material for the *alizarin* series of dyestuffs. » acridine; aromatic compound; coal tar; dyestuff; scintillation counter

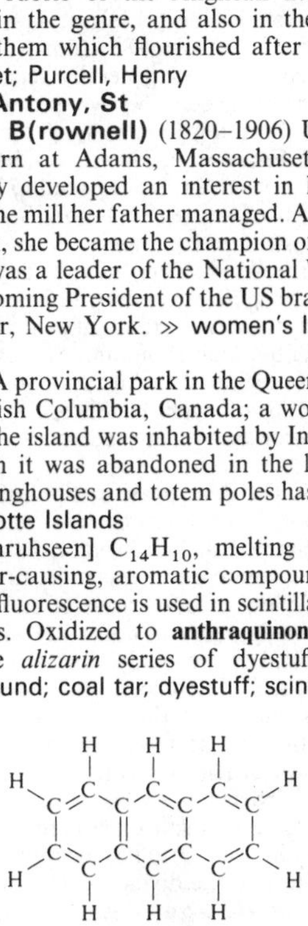

anthracite A hard and lustrous variety of coal, containing more than 90% carbon. It is the highest grade of coal, and burns with a very hot, virtually smokeless flame. » coal

anthrax A disease resulting from infection with *Bacillus anthracis*. Initially the organisms cause localized skin lesions which enlarge, ulcerate, and become black ('malignant pustules'). Blood poisoning, pneumonia, and death may occur.

anthropic principle A suggestion, due originally to British astronomer Fred Hoyle in the 1950s, that humans exist because physical laws governing the universe exhibit special features. For example, if gravitation were stronger relative to electromagnetism than it actually is, stars such as our Sun would burn out too quickly for life to evolve nearby. If strong nuclear force were slightly weaker relative to electromagnetism, the only stable element would be hydrogen. Some propound the idea of multiple universes which may or may not be stable. Others hold a stronger version of the principle, that a direct link exists between human existence and the actual form of the laws of nature. The anthropic principle is difficult to reconcile with unified theories in physics, which attempt a complete specification of the laws of nature. » forces of nature [i]; grand unified theories; Hoyle; many worlds interpretation; superstrings

Anthropoidea [anthro**poy**deea] A group of primates comprising monkeys and apes; face usually flat; ears small; fingers and toes with nails, not claws; live in complex social groups; also known as **anthropoid apes** (though this term is sometimes used only for apes). » ape; monkey [i]; primate (biology)

anthropological linguistics The study of language variation and use in relation to the cultural patterns and beliefs of (usually primitive) communities. It frequently examines linguistic evidence for allegiance to religious, occupational, or kinship groups. » linguistics; sociolinguistics

anthropology The science of man, traditionally identified as a 'four-field' discipline, encompassing **archaeology**, **social** and **cultural anthropology**, **physical anthropology**, and even **linguistics**. The primary concern of archaeologists is 'digging up history' – recovering and documenting the material remains of past communities. Cultural and social anthropologists study particular living societies, and attempt through comparison to establish the range of variation in human, social, and cultural institutions, and the reasons for these differences. Physical anthropologists study local biological adaptations and the evolutionary history of man. The fourth field, linguistics, the study of language, is now generally regarded as a separate speciality. Many specialists believe that even the three core disciplines of anthropology are no longer inextricably linked in a single scientific enterprise. Those who defend the traditional disciplinary range of anthropology tend to be concerned above all with questions of human evolution.

Anthropologists are commonly drawn into development projects in Third World countries, to advise on local social conditions. Anthropological expertise has also been applied in the USA (and to some extent elsewhere) in dealing with problems of multi-ethnic communities, nowadays particularly with regard to medicine and education. Such developments fall under the heading of **applied anthropology**. » archaeology; cognitive anthropology; ethnoscience; linguistics; Three Worlds theory

anthropometry The comparative study of the dimensions of the human body and their change with time. The main dimensions examined include weight, height, skinfold thickness, mid-arm circumference, and waist-to-hip ratio. Standard charts exist to allow a comparison of an observed anthropometric value with the range of normality within a group (eg the growth of a child). The study also sheds light on human evolution and racial differences, and influences the design of many products, such as clothes, car seats, and space capsules. » anthropology; Bertillon; weight for height

anthropomorphism The application to God or gods of human characteristics, such as a body (as in Greek mythology), or the mental, psychological, or spiritual qualities of human beings. It is often used to indicate insufficient appreciation of transcendence and mystery of the divine. » God; mythology

anti-aircraft gun (AA-gun) A gun firing a shell at high velocity at a high angle designed to shoot down aircraft. AA-guns (sometimes known as 'Flak' from the German expression *Fliegerabwehrkanone*) began to be supplanted by missiles at the end of World War 2. On the modern battlefield, radar-guided 'Triple A' (standing for Anti-Aircraft Artillery) has an important role in providing low-level, close-in defence against hostile aircraft, helicopters, and missiles. » missile, guided

anti-anxiety drugs » **benzodiazepines**

anti-art An imprecise term sometimes referring to Dada, or to any movement which debunks traditional notions of art, or seeks to undermine its values. » art; Dada

antiballistic missile (ABM) A missile capable of destroying hostile ballistic missiles or their payloads in flight at short, medium, or long ranges inside or outside the atmosphere. Their development was restricted by the US-Soviet ABM Treaty of 1972. » missile, guided; nuclear disarmament

Antibes [ã**teeb**], ancient **Antipolis** 43°35N 7°07E, pop (1982) 63 248. Fishing port and fashionable resort on the Riviera, in Alpes-Maritimes department, SE France; facing Nice across a long bay; best known for its luxurious villas and hotels sheltered by the pines of Cap d'Antibes; 3 km/1¾ ml W, Napoleon landed with 1 000 men on his return from Elba in 1815; railway; perfumes, flowers, olives, fruit, chocolates; Roman remains; museums, including the Musée Picasso. » Napoleon I; Nice; Riviera

antibiotics Substances derived from one micro-organism which can selectively destroy other (infectious) organisms without harming the host. The antibiotic effect has been known for at least 2 500 years: the Chinese applied mouldy soybean curd to boils and similar infections. Pasteur recorded that anthrax bacilli grew rapidly in sterile (but not non-sterile) urine (1877). The development of penicillin (1941) was the start of the era of safe and effective antibiotics. Many new antibiotics have since been discovered (nearly 100), each with a slightly different range of activities. Several are now synthesized. Resistance to antibiotics caused by uncontrolled use represents a serious medical hazard. » arsenicals; drug resistance; Pasteur, Louis; penicillin; streptomycin; sulphonamides; tetracyclines

antibodies Proteins which help protect against disease-causing micro-organisms (bacteria, viruses, parasites), present mainly in the gamma globulin fraction of serum; also known as **immunoglobulins**. Antibody production is carried out by *B cells*, and may be regulated by *helper T cells* and *suppressor T cells*. The first exposure of the body to a foreign cell or molecule (an **antigen**) produces an immune response which is directed specifically against the antigen that triggered it. Antibodies are produced which eliminate the antigens by a number of mechanisms. Subsequent exposure of the body to the same antigen results in a more rapid and larger immune response. This state of heightened responsiveness is known as a state of *immunity*. » cell; gamma globulins; immunity; inflammation; lymphocyte; serum

Antichrist A notion found in the Bible only in the Johannine Letters, referring sometimes to a single figure and at other times to many who are adversaries and deceivers of God's people. In later centuries, it was conceived as a supreme evil figure, often identified with one's opponents. » Devil; John, Letters of

anticline A geological fold structure in the form of an arch, with the younger strata at the top of the succession. It is formed as a result of compressional forces acting in a horizontal plane on rock strata. » stratification; syncline

anticoagulants Drugs which slow down or prevent the normal process of blood clotting, such as heparin and warfarin. They are used in the treatment and prevention of diseases caused by thrombi (blood clots) which block blood vessels. Warfarin is also used as a rat poison, where death occurs by internal haemorrhage, but resistance has developed in a number of rat colonies, giving rise to the 'super-rat'. » blood; thrombosis

Anti-Comintern Pact An agreement between Germany and Japan, concluded in 1936, which outlined both countries' hostility to international communism. The Pact was also signed by Italy in 1937. In addition to being specifically aimed against Soviet Russia, it also recognized Japanese rule in Manchuria. » Comintern; communism

anticonvulsants Drugs used in the control of epilepsy. All sedatives are anticonvulsant at high doses, but useful drugs in current use include phenobarbitone, phenytoin, sodium valproate, and clonazepam. The first successful drug treatment for epilepsy was potassium bromide, used in 1857 by English physician Sir Charles Locock (1799–1875), who incorrectly believed it to suppress libido (at the time epilepsy was thought to be associated with sexual activity). The first major advance in the field was the introduction of phenobarbitone in Germany in 1912. » barbiturates; epilepsy

Anti-Corn-Law League An association formed in Manchester (Sep 1838), largely under the patronage of businessmen and industrialists, to repeal the British Corn Laws, which imposed protective tariffs on the import of foreign corn. The League was both an important element in the growing movement for free trade in early 19th-c Britain, and an important political pressure group. The Corn Laws were repealed by Robert Peel in 1846. » Bright, John; Corn Laws; Peel

anticyclone A meteorological term for a high pressure system. Anticyclones are areas of generally clear skies and stable weather conditions. They occur in a variety of sizes and modes of origin, and warm anticyclones are a semi-permanent feature of subtropical areas (eg the Azores and Hawaiian high pressure zones). A *blocking* anticyclone may persist for several weeks, travelling very slowly and diverting depressions around it. In the N hemisphere, surface winds blow in a clockwise direction out of an anticyclone; in the S hemisphere the direction is anticlockwise. » atmospheric pressure; depression (meteorology) [i]; drought; general circulation model; wind [i]

antidepressants Drugs which cause elevation of mood in depressed patients. There are two major classes: *tricyclics* (eg imipramine, amitriptyline) and *monoamine oxidase inhibitors* (eg isocarboxazid, phenelzine). During the clinical investigation of some antihistamine drugs in 1958, Swiss physician Richard Kuhn (1900–67) found that imipramine was beneficial in depressed patients, and this type of drug is widely used today. The second class was also discovered fortuitously in 1952, when the anti-tubercular drug ipraniazid was noted to have mood-elevating effects. However this type of drug has severe adverse interactions with certain foods, such as cheese and red wine, and its use is therefore quite limited. Lithium is used in manic depression. » depression (psychiatry)

antidiuretic hormone (ADH) [anteediyu**re**tik] A chemical substance (a peptide) manufactured in the hypothalamus, but stored in and released from the back part of the pituitary gland of mammals; also known as **vasopressin**. It is one of the most fundamental hormones, being instrumental in conserving body fluids, and has known effects on memory, circadian rhythm, and the control of blood pressure in the brain. » circadian rhythm; diabetes insipidus; neurohormone; peptide; pituitary gland

Antietam, Battle of [an**tee**tam] (1862) A battle of the American Civil War, fought in Maryland. In military terms the North won a technical victory. This helped dissuade Britain and France from giving diplomatic recognition to the Confederacy and attempting to mediate the conflict, which they were about to do. It also allowed President Lincoln to issue his Preliminary Emancipation Proclamation. » American Civil War; Confederate States of America

antiferromagnetism » **ferromagnetism**

antifreeze A substance added to water in the cooling system of an engine to prevent the system freezing during cold weather. This is necessary since water expands when it freezes, and this can lead to cracking in those parts of the engine where the cooling system is circulated. Substances used as anti-freeze include ethanol and methanol, which can evaporate in water solution; ethylene-glycol is more reliable, but more expensive. » engine; ethanol

antigen » **antibodies**

Antigone [an**ti**gonee] In Greek mythology, a daughter of Oedipus, King of Thebes. After the Seven Champions had attacked the city, Antigone buried the body of her brother Polynices (one of the attackers), so defying King Creon's order that such a traitor should remain unburied. She was condemned to death by starvation, but hanged herself. In Sophocles' play of the same name, Antigone becomes a symbol of the individual's right to defy the state over a matter of conscience. » Polynices; Seven against Thebes; Sophocles

Antigonus I [an**ti**gonuhs], byname **Cyclops** or **Monophthalmos** ('One-eyed') (?–301 BC) Macedonian noble and former general of Alexander the Great, who assumed the royal title in 306 BC. His driving ambition was to re-unite the empire of Alexander under himself, but he provoked so much resentment among Alexander's other generals that they combined to defeat him at the Battle of Ipsus (301 BC). » Alexander the Great; Cassander; Seleucus I

Antigua or **Antigua Guatemala** [an**tee**gwa] 14°33N 90°42W, pop (1983e) 26 631. Capital city of Sacatepéquez department, S Guatemala, SW of Guatemala City; founded by the Spanish, 1543; capital, until largely destroyed by earthquake, 1773; old city flourished in the 18th-c, with many churches, university (1680), printing press, and population of c.60 000; now a world heritage site; cathedral (1534); Holy Week processions. » Guatemala [i]

Antigua and Barbuda [an**tee**ga, bah**byoo**da] pop (1990e) 80 600; area 442 sq km/171 sq ml. Group of three islands in the Leeward group of the Lesser Antilles, E Caribbean; Antigua (280 sq km/108 sq ml), Barbuda (161 sq km/62 sq ml), lying 40 km/25 ml to the N, and Redonda (1 sq km/⅓ sq ml), uninhabited, lying 40 km/25 ml to the SW; capital St John's (on Antigua); other main town Codrington (on Barbuda); timezone GMT −4; people mostly of African Negro descent; official language, English; dominant religion, Christianity; unit of currency, the Eastern Caribbean dollar; W part of Antigua rises to 470 m/1 542 ft at Boggy Peak; Barbuda a flat coral island reaching only 44 m/144 ft at its highest point, with a large lagoon on its W side; climate tropical (24°C, Jan, to 27°C, Aug/Sep); mean annual rainfall of 1 000 mm/40 in; Antigua discovered by Columbus (1493); colonized by English (1632) and ceded to Britain (1667); Barbuda colonized from Antigua (1661); administered as part of the Leeward Is Federation (1871–1956); an associated state of the UK (1967); independence achieved in 1981; a governor-general and a bicameral legislature (a 17-member Senate and a 17-member House of Representatives); tourism (40% of national income), sugar (marked decline in 1960s, now recovering), cotton. » Antilles; Caribbean Sea; RR42 political leaders

anti-hero A central character in a novel or play who deviates from or contradicts conventional values and behaviour. Famous examples are Hašek's hero in *The Good Soldier Sweik* (1921–3), and Yossarian in Heller's *Catch-22* (1961). » drama; Hašek; Heller; novel

antihistamines Drugs used in the relief of allergic reactions, such as hay fever (but not asthma). They are so called because they act by blocking the action of the substance histamine produced in the body during allergies. They are also used in the treatment of motion sickness. Drowsiness is a common side effect, and certain antihistamines are used as sedatives. » allergy; histamine; sedatives

antiknock A chemical substance (such as tetra-ethyl lead) added to a spark ignition engine's fuel to improve combustion and prevent knocking. » spark ignition engine; knocking

anti-literature The conception and practice of writing which challenges established ideas of what literature should be, on formal, ideological, or other grounds. Much experimental literature exhibits these tendencies. » anti-novel; literary criticism; literature; Modernism

Antilles [an**ti**leez] The whole of the West Indies except the Bahamas; **Greater Antilles** include Cuba, Jamaica, Hispaniola (Haiti and the Dominican Republic), Puerto Rico; **Lesser Antilles** include the Windward Is (S), Leeward Is (N), and the Netherlands Antilles off the coast of Venezuela. » Caribbean Sea

Anti-Masonic Party (1830–6) A US group dedicated to driving Freemasons out of public life, arising from the highly publicized disappearance (1826) of the author of a book revealing Masonic secrets. It was the first 'third party' in the USA, nominating a presidential candidate in 1832 at the first national party convention. It declined after 1836. » freemasonry

antimatter » antiparticles

antimony [**an**timuhnee] Sb, (Lat *stibium*) element 51, melting point 631°C. A metalloid in the nitrogen family; common oxidation states 3 and 5; expands on solidifying. It is used in type-metal alloys, and also as an impurity in germanium to make n-type semiconductors. » alloy; chemical elements; metalloids; semiconductor; stibine; tartaric acid [i]

anti-novel A novel which, while still (of necessity) using the conventions of fiction, exposes their artifice in different ways and invites reconsideration of the novel's implicit claim to represent reality. Sterne's *Tristram Shandy* (1760–7) is an early example; 20th-c practitioners include James Joyce, Samuel Beckett, Flann O'Brien, Vladimir Nabokov, and Michel Butor. » novel; Realism; Sterne

Antioch [**an**teeok], Turkish **Antakya**, ancient **Hatay** or **Antiochia** 36°12N 36°10E, pop (1980) 94942. Capital of Hatay province, S Turkey; near the Mediterranean, 90 km/56 ml W of Aleppo (Syria); founded, 300 BC; centre of early Christianity; destroyed by earthquake, 526; tobacco, olives, cotton, grain; archaeological museum. » Turkey [i]

Antiochus I, byname **Soter** ('Saviour') (324–261 BC) King of Syria (281–61), the son and successor of Seleucus I. The greatest founder of cities after Alexander the Great, he received his byname for his victory over the Gallic invaders of Asia Minor. » Hellenization; Seleucids; Seleucus I

Antiochus III, byname **the Great** (c.242–187 BC) King of Syria (223–187 BC), the greatest of the Seleucid dynasty. He restored Seleucid prestige in the East (209–204 BC), and by his successes against the Ptolemies gained possession of Palestine and Coele Syria (198 BC). His war with Rome proved his undoing: defeated at Thermopylae (191 BC), Magnesia (190 BC), and at sea, he was forced to evacuate all Asia Minor W of the Taurus Mts and pay Rome a crippling war indemnity. » Ptolemy I Soter; Seleucids

antioxidants Substances which slow down the oxidation of others, often by being oxidized themselves. The term is usually applied to additives in foods and plastics. » additives; oxidation

antiparticles Partners of sub-atomic particles having the same mass and spin but opposite charge, magnetic moment, and other quantum attributes. When antiparticles meet their particle partners the two annihilate, as predicted by British physicist Paul Dirac in 1928. The antiparticle is usually denoted by a bar over the symbol for the corresponding particle. Antiparticle partners of electron e^- and proton p are the positron e^+ and antiproton $\bar{p}$, respectively. Antimatter composed of antiparticles is possible, but highly unstable, and not observed naturally. Antiparticles are seen in radioactivity, cosmic rays, and particle physics experiments. Force-carrying particles such as photons are identical to their antiparticles. » antiproton; Dirac; particle physics; positron; relativistic quantum mechanics

Antipater (of Idumaea) [**an**tipater] (?–43 BC) A chieftain who dominated Jewish history from the 60s BC until his death. The father of Herod the Great, he laid the foundations of his family's ascendancy in Judaea in Roman times. » Herod Agrippa I; Herod the Great

Antipater (of Macedon) [an**ti**pater] (398–319 BC) Macedonian general and loyal servant of the royal family. He was Philip II's closest aide, Alexander's Governor of Macedonia during his wars of conquest (334–323 BC), and regent of Alexander's former empire after the death of Perdiccas (320–319 BC). » Alexander the Great; Lamian War; Philip II (of Macedon)

antiphon In the Roman Catholic and Greek Orthodox liturgies, a chant with a prose text which precedes or follows a psalm. It is linked with the practice of antiphonal psalmody, in which verses were sung alternately by two groups of singers, or by soloist and choir. A collection of antiphons is known as an **antiphoner**. » chant; liturgy; Psalms, Book of

Antiphon (c.480–411 BC) The earliest of the ten Attic orators. He belonged to the oligarchical party, and was influential in establishing the government of the Four Hundred (411 BC). On its fall he was condemned to death, in spite of a noble defence. » Greek history

antipodes Any two places which are on the opposite sides of the Earth when connected by a straight line passing through the centre of the Earth. For example, the Antipodes Is, New Zealand, 49° 42′S and 178° 50′E and the Baie de la Seine, France, 49° 45′N and 1°W are antipodes. » latitude and longitude [i]

antipope In the Roman Catholic Church, a claimant to the office of pope in opposition to one regularly and canonically appointed. Antipopes featured prominently in the period of Great Schism in the Western Church (1378–1417). They included Clement VII and Benedict XIII (in Avignon, France) and Alexander V and John XXIII (in Pisa, Italy). » pope; RR67

antiproton The antiparticle partner of the proton; symbol $\bar{p}$. Spin and mass are as for the proton, but the charge is -1. Discovered in 1955, antiprotons are created in particle accelerators by the collisions of protons with nuclei, and can in turn be accelerated and used in particle physics experiments. » antiparticles; particle physics; proton

antipsychiatry A view that mental illness does not exist, and that therefore the practice of psychiatry is simply a form of social control. This view has been most forcefully propounded by the Hungarian-born US psychiatrist Thomas S Szasz (1920–). A related argument is that every patient is unique and every illness is unique, therefore there is no value in classifying either patients or diseases. These views are now generally considered extreme and of fringe interest only. » psychiatry

antirrhinum » snapdragon [i]

Anti-Saloon League A US organization established in 1895, with the aim of forbidding alcoholic drink by amending the US Constitution and by state and local anti-alcohol laws. The League remained in being during and after the Prohibition period, and became part of the National Temperance League in 1950. » Prohibition

antiseptic A substance which kills or prevents the growth of micro-organisms (germs). The practice of using chemicals to control the suppuration of wounds and the spread of disease, and preserving dead bodies (*embalming*) was widespread centuries before micro-organisms were understood. Lister introduced the practice of antiseptic surgery (using phenol) in 1867. Commonly used antiseptics include alcohols, phenols, salts of heavy metals, and chlorine- and iodine-releasing compounds. » Lister, Joseph; micro-organism; phenol

Antisthenes [an**tis**thuhneez] (444–370 BC) Greek philosopher, considered to be the founder of the Cynic school. He was first a disciple of Gorgias, then of Socrates. He believed that happiness depended on a virtuous and moral life, and that virtue could be acquired through teaching. He died in Athens. » Cynics; Gorgias; Socrates

antisubmarine warfare A practice of warfare aimed at hunting down and destroying hostile submarines. Sonar is the primary means of detecting hostile submarines, while depth charges and homing torpedoes launched by aircraft, surface warships, or hunter-killer submarines are the primary means of destroying them. » ASDIC; sonar; submarine

antitank gun A gun firing a shell at high velocity, capable of piercing or blasting through the armour of an enemy tank or armoured fighting vehicle. » antitank missile; tank

antitank missile A missile which may be fired by an infantryman, or launched from a helicopter or combat vehicle, aimed at destroying enemy tanks and armoured fighting vehicles. It may be wire or laser guided. » missile, guided; reactive armour; tank

Antitrust Acts US laws passed to control the development of monopoly capitalism. The Sherman Act (1890) forbade all combinations 'in restraint of trade'. Ambiguities in wording led to its use against labour unions instead of the monopolistic corporations, or *trusts*. The Clayton Act (1914) was intended to close the ambiguities and make enforcement easier. » monopoly

antivitamin factors Compounds occurring naturally in foods which reduce the availability of a vitamin, or which modify its normal function. For example, avidin, a protein in raw egg white, can bind the B-vitamin, biotin, reducing its absorption. Many of the antivitamin factors are destroyed on cooking. » biotin; vitamins [i]

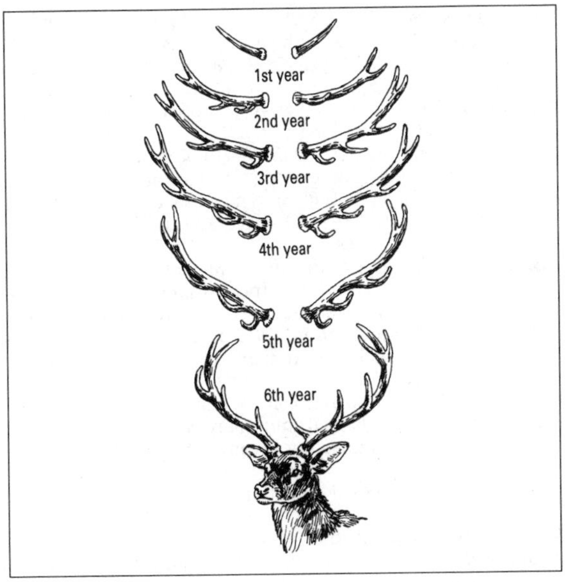

Antlers – Red deer

antlers Bone outgrowths from the head of true deer; only on males, except in reindeer; *water deer* the only species without antlers; used in display, defence, and competition for mates; shed each year (unlike the 'horns' of other ruminants), and grow larger the following year; covered in soft skin ('velvet') when growing; if branched, the number of spikes (*tines*) increases with age; also known as **deer-horn**. » deer; reindeer; ruminant [i]; water deer

Antlia (Lat 'air pump') [ant**lee**a] A small S hemisphere constellation. » constellation; RR8

antlion The larva of a nocturnal, damselfly-like insect with a long abdomen and lightly-patterned wings. Antlion larvae prey on other insects, typically lying in wait, often at the base of a steep-sided, conical trap into which the prey fall. (Order: *Neuroptera*. Family: *Myrmeliontidae*, c.600 species.) » damselfly; insect [i]; larva

Antofagasta [antofa**ga**sta] 23°38S 70°24W, pop (1982) 166 964. Port and capital of Antofagasta province, Chile; largest city in N Chile; developed with 19th-c mineral and agricultural trade; airport; railway; university (1956); exports nitrates and copper; metal refining; huge anchor high in mountains was used as navigational aid by shipping; geographical and archaeological museums; public gardens and beaches, sports stadium. » Chile [i]

Antonello Da Messina (c.1430–79) Italian painter, born and died at Messina, who is said to have introduced into Italy the Flemish method of oil painting. His 'St Jerome' is in the National Gallery, London. » Italian art; oil painting

Antonescu, Ion [anto**nes**koo] (1882–1946) Romanian general and dictator, born at Pitesti. He was military attaché in Rome and London, and became chief of staff in 1937. Suspended from the army in 1938 and imprisoned as one of the leaders of an unsuccessful revolt, he was soon released and made Minister of War. In 1940 he became Premier, forced the abdication of King Carol, and until 1944 was dictator. He was executed as a war criminal, near Jilava, Romania. » Carol I

Antonine Wall A defensive barrier built by the Roman Emperor, Antoninus Pius, in AD 142, at the N end of the British province. Constructed of turf upon a foundation of cobbles, the 'wall' ran from the Forth estuary to the Clyde. » Britain, Roman

Antoninus Pius, in full **Titus Aurelius Fulvius Boionius Arrius Antoninus** (86–161) Roman emperor (138–161), whose title *Pius* ('dutiful') was probably conferred because of his exemplary behaviour towards his adoptive father, Hadrian. His reign, though depicted by establishment writers as peaceful and happy, saw much unrest. In Britain, defensive measures (the Antonine Wall) against the N barbarians had to be taken, and there was also trouble in Germany, Africa, Palestine, and Dacia. » Antonine Wall; Britain, Roman; Dacia; Hadrian

Antonioni, Michelangelo (1912–) Italian film director, born at Ferrara. Educated at Bologna, he was first a film critic before becoming an assistant director (1942). He made several documentaries (1945–50), then turned to feature films, often scripted by himself, notable for their preoccupation with character study rather than plot. He gained an international reputation with *L'Avventura* (1959, The Adventure). Later films include *La Notte* (1961, The Night), *Blow-up* (1967), *Zabriskie Point* (1970), and *The Oberwald Mystery* (1980).

Antonius, Marcus or **Mark Antony** (c.83–30 BC) Roman statesman and soldier. Related to Julius Caesar on his mother's side, he assisted Caesar in Gaul, and supported him in Rome. He was a commander in Caesar's war against Pompey, and governed Italy while Caesar was in Africa. In 44 BC, as consul, he tried in vain to have Caesar made emperor. After Caesar's assassination, his speeches caused the flight of the conspirators from Rome, and left him with almost absolute power. After his defeat at Mutina (43 BC) by Octavian, he fled to Gaul, but returned in triumph with a large army. A triumvirate was formed with Octavian and Lepidus to share the Roman world among themselves. The 'triumvirs' secured Italy, then defeated Brutus and Cassius at Philippi. While re-organizing the E provinces, Antony met and was captivated by Queen Cleopatra, whom he followed to Egypt (41 BC), and with whom he lived in idleness and luxury. On his return to Italy in 40 BC to patch up a quarrel with Octavian, a new division of the Roman world was made at Brundisium, with Antony taking the East, but the agreement failed to heal the breach between them. Antony's renewed liaison with Cleopatra, and his donation to his children by her of large parts of the Roman Empire, provided Octavian with reasons to arouse the Roman people against him. War was declared. Defeat at Actium (31 BC) followed, and Antony and Cleopatra both committed suicide. » Actium, Battle of; Augustus; Caesar; Cleopatra VII; Philippi, Battle of

Antony or **Anthony, St**, called **the Great**, or **Antony of Egypt** (c.251–356), feast day 17 January. Religious hermit, one of the founders of Christian monasticism, born at Koman, Upper Egypt. Having sold his possessions for the poor, he spent 20 years in the desert, where he withstood a famous series of temptations, often represented in later art. In 305 he left his retreat and founded a monastery near Memphis and Arsinoë. In about 355, although over 100, he made a journey to Alexandria to dispute with the Arians; but retired soon after to his desert home, where he died. » Arius; Christianity; monasticism

Antony or **Anthony of Padua, St** (1195–1231), feast day 13 June. Portuguese friar, born in Lisbon, who became one of the most active propagators of the Franciscan order. He was first an Augustinian monk, but in 1220 joined the Franciscans, and became famous for his preaching. He died at Padua, and was canonized in 1232. He is the patron saint of Portugal, the lower animals, and lost property. » Augustinians; Franciscans; friar

antonym » synonym

Antrim (county), Gaelic **Aontroim** pop (1981) 642 267; area 2 831 sq km/1 093 sq ml. County in NE Northern Ireland, divided into nine districts; bounded SW by Lough Neagh, N by the Atlantic Ocean, and E by the Irish Sea; rises N and E to the Antrim Mts; includes the islands of Rathlin, the Skerries, and the Maidens; county town, Belfast; other chief towns, Lisburn, Ballymena, Carrickfergus; Irish linen, textiles, cattle, sheep, potatoes, flax, oats, shipbuilding; basalt rock formation, Giant's Causeway, on N coast. » Belfast; Giant's Causeway; Northern Ireland [i]

Antwerp, Flemish **Antwerpen**, French **Anvers** 51°13N 4°25E, pop (1982) 183 025. Capital city of Antwerpen district, N Belgium; on the right bank of the R Scheldt, 88 km/55 ml from the North Sea; chief port of Belgium and fourth largest port in the world; chartered 1291; centre of the mediaeval cloth trade with England; airport; railway; colonial university (1920); shipbuilding and repairing, oil refining, synthetic fibres, plastics, petrochemicals, agrochemicals, engineering; foodstuffs, diamonds (major international centre); 16th-c town hall, Cathedral of Our Lady (1352), Church of St Jacob (15th–16th-c), Royal Museum of Fine Arts, famous zoo; home of Rubens and van Dyck. » Belgium [i]; Rubens; van Dyck

Anubis [anyoobis] An Egyptian god associated with death. He has the head of a jackal or wild dog of the desert. Guard of the necropolis, he takes part in the process of embalming.

Anura or **Anoura** [anoora] An order of amphibians comprising the frogs and toads (3 500 species); adults with no tail; move by thrusting backwards with long hind legs; larvae called *tadpoles*; also known as **Salientia**. » amphibian; frog; tadpole

Anuradhapura [anarahdapoora] 8°20N 80°25E, pop (1981) 35 981. Capital of Anuradhapura district, Sri Lanka, 205 km N of Colombo; Sri Lanka's first capital; founded, 4th-c BC; Sri Mahabodhi Tree, allegedly the oldest tree in the world (2 200 years), all that remains of the Bo tree beneath which Buddha found Enlightenment; a world heritage site; Thuparama Dagaba, built to enshrine the collarbone of Buddha. » Buddha; Sri Lanka [i]

anus The terminal part of the gastro-intestinal tract, opening into the natal cleft between the buttocks; the lower limit of the anal canal. In conjunction with the rest of the anal canal, it is guarded by internal and external sphincters under autonomic and voluntary control respectively. It may exhibit bleeding during defaecation, as a result of haemorrhoids. » alimentary canal: defaecation; haemorrhoids

Anvers [ãvayr] » **Antwerp**

anvilhead » **hammerkop**

Anville, Jean Baptiste Bourguignon d' [ãveel] (1697–1782) French geographer and map-maker, who was born and died in Paris. He greatly improved the standards of ancient and mediaeval map-making, and became the first geographer to the King of France. » cartography

ANZAC An acronym of **Australia and New Zealand Army Corps**, a unit in which troops from both countries fought during World War 1 in the Middle East and on the Western Front. *Anzac Day* (25 Apr) commemorates the Gallipoli landing in 1915; the fighting lasted until Jan 1916, during which time 7 600 were killed and 19 000 wounded. Australian and British law prohibit the word 'Anzac' from commercial use. » Gallipoli; World War 1

Anzengruber, Ludwig (1839–89) Austrian playwright and novelist, born in Vienna. Of peasant stock, he held several jobs before the success of his play, *Der Pfarrer von Kirchfeld* (1870, The Pastor of Kirchfeld), enabled him to devote his life to writing. He was the author of several novels, notably *Der Sternsteinhof* (1885, The Sternstein Farm), and about 20 plays, mostly about Austrian peasant life. He died in Vienna. » German literature

ANZUS An acronym for the treaty concluded in 1951 between Australia, New Zealand, and the United States for mutual security in the Pacific against armed attack. The treaty, which remains in force indefinitely, encompasses not only the metropolitan territories of the three, but also island territories under their jurisdiction, their armed forces, and their aircraft and shipping.

aorta [ayawta] The largest blood vessel in the body, which conveys oxygenated blood from the left ventricle of the heart to the rest of the body. It is conveniently divided into three parts: (1) the *ascending aorta*, passing upwards, backwards, and to the right, giving branches to the heart, (2) the *aortic arch*, crossing to the left side, giving major branches to the head and upper limbs, and (3) the *descending aorta*, passing through the thorax and abdomen before terminating as major vessels to the lower limbs. The thoracic branches supply the chest wall, and the abdominal branches supply the contents of the abdomen. » abdomen; artery; blood; heart [i]; thorax

Aosta [ahosta], Fr **Aoste** 45°43N 7°19E, pop (1981) 37 194. Capital town of Aosta province, Valle d'Aosta, NW Italy; in the fertile valley of the R Dora Baltea, ringed by mountains; largely French-speaking; railway; important traffic junction for routes across the Alps; ironworking, tourism; cathedral, old town surrounded by well-preserved Roman walls. » Valle d'Aosta

aoudad [owdad] Wild sheep from the dry mountains of N Africa (introduced into SW USA); sandy colour, with long fringe along throat; both sexes with curved horns up to 760 mm/30 in long; also known as **Barbary sheep, maned sheep, udad, arui**, or **fechstal**. (*Ammotragus lervia*.) » sheep

Aouita, Said [oweeta] (1960–) Moroccan athlete, born in Rabat. A middle- and long-distance track athlete, he set world records at 1 500 and 5 000 m in 1985 to become the first man for 30 years to hold both records. He has since broken world records at 2 ml and 2 000 m. The 1986 overall Grand Prix winner, he was the 1984 Olympic and 1987 World 5 000 m champion. » athletics

Aozou Strip [owzoo] A 100 km/60 ml-wide strip of mountainous desert in N Chad, NC Africa; disputed territory on the frontier with Libya, who occupied the area in 1973; Libya's claim based on an unratified 1935 agreement between France and Italy; area rich in uranium and mineral deposits. » Chad [i]; Libya [i]

Apache American Indians who dominated much of the SW during the 19th-c; divided into many smaller groups, lacking any centralized organization. From 1861 they fought against Federal troops in the Apache and Navajo wars, eventually surrendering in 1886. Population c.23 000. » American Indians; Southwest Indians

Apaloochy » **Appaloosa**

apartheid (Afrikaans 'apartness') The policy of separate racial development in the Republic of South Africa, supported traditionally by the Nationalist Party, and more recently by other right-wing parties. The ideology has several roots: Boer concepts of racial, cultural, and religious separation arising out of their sense of national uniqueness; British liberal notions of indirect rule; the need to preserve African traditional life while promoting gradualism in their Christianization and westernization; and the concern for job protection, promoted by White workers to maintain their status in the face of a large and cheaper Black proletariat. Under the policy, different races are given different rights. In practice the system is one of White supremacy, Blacks having no representation in the central state parliament. Many of the provisions of apartheid regarding labour, land segregation (*reserves, Homelands, Bantustans*), municipal segregation, social and educational separation, and a virtually exclusive White franchise, were in place before the Nationalist victory of 1948, but after that date it was erected into a complete political, social, and economic system, down to the provisions of 'petty apartheid' relating to transport, beaches, lavatories, park benches, etc. Its principal architect, Hendrik Verwoerd, was assassinated in 1966. Some of its provisions have been dismantled in recent years, but its crucial elements relating to land and labour remain in place. The whole system is backed by extensive repression, and the reforms have not alleviated widespread international condemnation. » Afrikaners; Black consciousness; civil rights; indirect rule; Sharpeville Massacre; Verwoerd

apatite A common phosphate mineral widely distributed in minor quantities in many igneous and metamorphic rocks; most varieties can be represented by the formula $Ca_5(PO_4)_3(OH,F,Cl)$. It crystallizes as hexagonal prisms, in various colours, mostly green. » phosphate

Apatosaurus [apatohsawruhs] A giant, semi-aquatic dinosaur that probably ate vegetation around swamps and lakes; four-legged, limbs pillar-like, hindlimbs longer than forelimbs; tail whip-like; neck very long; skull with sloping face; known from the Upper Jurassic period of Colorado; formerly known as **Brontosaurus**. (Order: *Saurischia*.) » dinosaur [i]; Jurassic period; Saurischia

ape An anthropoid primate; comprises the **lesser apes** (*gibbons*) and **great apes** (*orang-utan, gorilla, chimpanzees*); differs from most monkeys in having no tail and in using arms to swing through trees, not by walking along branches. (Family: *Pongidae*, 10 species.) » Anthropoidea; chimpanzee; gibbon; gorilla; monkey [i]; orang-utan; primate

Apennines [apuhniynz], Ital **Appennino** Mountain range extending down the Italian peninsula into Sicily; length 1 400 km/870 ml; width 30–150 km/20–90 ml; N division includes the Appno Ligure, Appno Tosco-Emilliano, and the Appno Umbro-Marchigiano, highest point Monte Cimone (2 165 m/

7 103 ft); C division includes the Appno Abruzzese and the Appno Napoletano, highest point Gran Sasso d'Italia (2 914 m/9 560 ft); S division includes the Appno Lucano and La Sila, highest point Monte Pollino (2 248 m/7 375 ft), an earthquake region; typically Mediterranean vegetation in foothills, with olive groves, vineyards, orchards; open forest above, until c.1 800 m/6 000 ft, then slopes covered with stones and scree; stock-farming (goats and sheep), some arable farming, forestry. » Italy [i]; Vesuvius

aperture **1** The opening, usually circular, through which light enters an optical system, such as a camera lens. It is often adjustable in diameter by means of an iris diaphragm to control the intensity of light transmitted – the 'stop' of a lens system. » camera; f-number **2** In cinematography, the rectangular opening in a camera or other projector at which each frame of film is held stationary while it is exposed. » projector [i]

aperture synthesis A method of combining several small telescopes to simulate some properties of very large telescopes. It has been used successfully at radio frequencies to enable astronomers to see fine detail in sources. The technique was developed by UK astronomer Martin Ryle at Mullard Radio Astronomy Observatory. » Australia telescope; radio astronomy; Ryle, Martin

aphasia A disorder of language caused by brain damage; also (especially in the UK) known as **dysphasia**. The patient appears intellectually and physically capable of using language (eg there is movement of the tongue and lips and no deafness) but suffers from a variety of linguistic disabilities. There are many different types: one important distinction is between **Broca's aphasia** (a disorder of production, characterized by word-finding difficulties and telegrammatic speech) and **Wernicke's aphasia** (a disorder of comprehension, characterized by fluent but largely nonsensical speech). The study of the disorder is known as **aphasiology**. » anomia; brain [i]; language; neurolinguistics

aphelion » **periapsis**

aphid A soft-bodied bug that feeds on plant sap. Aphids have complex life cycles, typically including several asexually reproducing generations of live-bearing females, and one sexually reproducing generation per year. Many species produce wax for protection. Others produce honeydew, and are tended by ants. About 4 000 species are known, mainly from the N hemisphere, including some that are serious pests, such as blackfly and greenfly. (Order: *Homoptera*. Family: *Aphididae*.) » blackfly; bug (entomology); greenfly; life cycle; reproduction;

aphonia » **dysphonia**

aphrodisiacs Drugs named after Aphrodite, the goddess of love, which induce sexual desire and/or improve sexual performance. Over 500 substances have been advocated throughout history, notably Spanish fly (responsible for many deaths), rhino horn, and mandrake root. No drug to date has been proved to act as a true aphrodisiac. Alcohol induces desire only. » mandrake; Spanish fly

Aphrodite [afro**diy**tee] The Greek goddess of sexual love, said to have been born from the sea-foam at Paphos in Cyprus. This indication of an Eastern origin to her cult is borne out by the resemblances to the worship of Ishtar. » Adonis; Ishtar; Venus (mythology)

Apia [apia] 13°48S 171°45W, pop (1981) 33 000. Capital town of Western Samoa, on N coast of Upolu I, SW Pacific Ocean; a rapidly expanding cluster of villages; copra, cocoa, bananas. » Western Samoa

apiculture The keeping of bees in hives for honey and wax production. Bees may be also used for pollinating orchards and crops, such as oilseed rape. Bee-keeping is known from the Stone Age, when crude hives were made, probably from wood. European farmers built straw *keps*, which resembled upside-down baskets. Commercial bee-keeping started in the 1880s. As a hobby, collectors (*apiarists*) keep bees both for their honey and to study their habits. » bee

Apis [aypis, **ah**pis] The Egyptian bull-god, representing or incarnating the Ptah of Memphis. An actual bull was selected from the herd, black with a triangular white patch on the forehead, and kept at Memphis; after death it was mummified and placed in a special necropolis, the Serapeum. » Ptah

APL Acronym of **A Programming Language**, a scientific computer programming language, developed in the 1960s, of special interest to mathematicians. » programming language

Apo, Mount [**ah**poh] Active volcano and highest mountain in the Philippines, near the SE coast of Mindanao I; rises to 2 954 m/9 691 ft; part of a national park. » Philippines [i]; volcano

apoapsis » **periapsis**

apocalypse (Gr 'revelation of the future') A literary genre which can be traced to post-Biblical Jewish and early Christian eras; it especially comprises works in highly symbolic language which claim to express divine disclosures about the heavenly spheres, the course of history, or the end of the world. The most famous example is the Book of Revelation in the New Testament. The notion also includes poems by Blake and Yeats ('The Second Coming'), novels such as Lawrence's *Women in Love* (1920), much science fiction, and cataclysmic films such as Coppola's *Apocalypse Now* (1979). » Bible; Blake, William; Coppola; Lawrence, D H; Pseudepigrapha; Revelation, Book of; science fiction; Yeats

Apocalypse of John » **Revelation, Book of**

Apocrypha, New Testament Christian documents, largely from the early Christian centuries, which are similar in title, form, or content to many New Testament works, being called Gospels, Acts, Epistles, or Apocalypses, and often attributed to New Testament characters, but not widely accepted as canonical. Some derive from Gnosticism or heretical circles, but others are just of a popular nature. » Apocrypha, Old Testament; Gnosticism; Gospels, apocryphal; Nag Hammadi texts; New Testament

Apocrypha, Old Testament (Gr 'hidden things') Usually, a collection of Jewish writings found in the Greek version of the Hebrew Bible (the Septuagint), but not found in the Hebrew Bible itself; in a more general sense, any literature of an esoteric or spurious kind. Most of these writings were also in the Latin version of the Christian Bible approved at the Council of Trent (the *Vulgate*), so Roman Catholics tend to consider them as inspired and authoritative, and designate them as *deuterocanonical*, while Protestants and most others attribute less authority to them, referring to them as *Apocrypha*. Corresponding to this distinction, non-Catholic Bibles tend to locate the Apocrypha as a separate collection between the two Testaments or after the New Testament, while Catholic Bibles tend to place the writings among the Old Testament works themselves.

Agreement is also not complete over which writings are to be included in this collection. Modern studies prefer to limit the Apocrypha to 13 writings found in most Septuagint manuscripts, and to exclude additional works found only in the Vulgate, which are then assigned to a much larger body of writings called the Old Testament *Pseudepigrapha*. The Apocrypha would thus include: 1 Esdras, Tobit, Judith, Additions to the Book of Esther, Wisdom of Solomon, Ecclesiasticus (or Sirach), 1 Baruch, Letter of Jeremiah, Prayer of Azariah and Song of the Three Young Men, Susanna, Bel and the Dragon (the last three being Additions to the Book of Daniel), 1 and 2 Maccabees. Roman Catholics consider all of this list to be deuterocanonical except for 1 Esdras. Most of the Apocrypha were composed in the last two centuries BC. » Azariah, Prayer of; Baruch; Bel and the Dragon; Bible; Ecclesiasticus/Esdras/Esther/Judith/Maccabees/Tobit, Books of; Jeremiah, Letter of; Manasseh, Prayer of; Old Testament; Song of the Three Young Men; Susanna, Story of; Wisdom of Solomon; Pseudepigrapha

apogee » **periapsis**

Apollinaire, Guillaume, pseudonym of **Wilhelm Apollinaris de Kostrowitzky** (1880–1918) French poet, born in Rome of Italian-Polish parentage. He became a leader of the Parisian movement rejecting poetic traditions in outlook, rhythm, and language. His work, akin to the Cubist school in painting, is expressed chiefly in *Alcools* (1913) and *Calligrammes* (1918), the latter making much use of experimental typographic designs. He died in Paris. » Cubism; French literature

Apollo, (Phoebus) [a**po**loh] In Greek mythology, the god of poetic and musical inspiration; also a destructive force, sending disease with his arrows. He is depicted as an ideal of male beauty, or as an archer. In historic times he was the god who spoke through the Delphic oracle, and his shrine was the island of Delos. Later poetry stresses his connection with the Sun. » Delphi, Oracle of; Hyperion (mythology)

Apollo asteroid An asteroid whose orbit brings it within one astronomical unit (150 million km) of the Sun. » asteroids; astronomical unit

Apollo programme The first crewed mission to the Moon, undertaken by NASA at the direction of President Kennedy in response to the space leadership position established by the USSR. The first landing (20 Jul 1969) was made by the Apollo XI crew of Neil Armstrong and Edwin Aldrin in the spacecraft *Eagle*. It is by far the most ambitious space achievement to date, and was also a scientific triumph, because of the far-reaching value of lunar sample analysis. Over 300 kg/660 lb of soil, cores, and rocks were returned by all six landed missions. Long duration seismology and space physics experiments were deployed near the landers. The focus of the US space programme for over a decade, it was preceded by Mercury and Gemini manned spaceflight demonstration projects, and Ranger, Surveyor, and Lunar Orbiter robotic lunar exploration missions. Undertaken in an atmosphere of intense competition with the USSR, it required immense technological development in all elements of spaceflight. The Saturn V launch vehicle remains the most powerful ever developed. The 3-man crew in each mission were launched inside a Command Module which stayed in lunar orbit, while the Lunar Module with two crew members descended to the surface. Following the surface activities, part of the Lunar Module was launched to rendezvous with the Command Module in orbit. The crew were recovered from an ocean landing after re-entry and parachute descent. Major events of the programme included: the first manned lunar mission (Apollo VIII, Christmas 1968); the first landing mission (Apollo XI, Jul 1969); the pin-point landing at Surveyor 3 site (Apollo XII, Nov 1969); the oxygen tank explosion on the aborted Apollo XIII; and the first lunar rover excursion (Apollo XV). The last flight was undertaken (Dec 1972) by the Apollo XVII crew, who stayed 75 hours on the lunar surface and travelled 34 km/21 ml in the lunar rover. The landing sites were: XI, Mare Tranquilitatis; XII, Oceanus Procellarum; XIV, Imbrium; XV, Hadley Rille; XVI, Descartes; and XVII, Taurus Littrow. The programme was managed by NASA's Johnson Space Center, using the capabilities of all other NASA Centers. » Aldrin; Armstrong, Neil; Collins, Michael (astronaut); Moon; NASA; space exploration; RR10

Apollo-Soyuz project A landmark joint space mission conducted by the USA and USSR in 1975, following an agreement signed by President Nixon and Chairman Kosygin in 1972. Intended primarily as a political gesture during a period of US–Soviet détente, Apollo-Soyuz also demonstrated the capability for joint operations between the major space powers and, as such, the potential for on-orbit emergency rescue missions. The rendezvous (17 Jul 1975) lasted 48 hours. The crews (T Stafford, V Brand, D Slayton and A Leonov, V Kubasov) conducted a series of joint experiments. A special adaptor docking module was constructed for the mission. » Apollo programme; Soyuz spacecraft; RR10

Apollonius (Dyskolos) (2nd-c) Greek grammarian, called Dyskolos ('bad-tempered'), who was the first to reduce Greek syntax to a system. Only four of his many works on grammar survive. » Greek literature; syntax

Apollonius of Perga (280–210 BC) Greek mathematician, born at Perga, known at the time as 'the great geometer'. He is the author of a major work on conic sections which laid the foundations of modern teaching on the subject. He died at Alexandria. » analytic geometry

Apollonius Rhodius (3rd-c BC) Greek scholar and epic poet, born in Alexandria, Egypt, but long resident in Rhodes. He wrote many works on grammar, and a long poem about the quest for the Golden Fleece, the *Argonautica*, which was greatly admired by the Romans. » epic; grammar; Greek literature

apologetics (Lat *apologia* 'defence') A branch of theology which justifies Christian faith in the light of specific criticisms or charges. An early example is Justin Martyr's *Apology* (2nd-c). » Justin (Martyr), St; theology

apomixis [apuh**miks**is] Asexual reproduction without fertilization in plants, in which meiosis and fusion of gametes are suppressed. Apomixis also includes vegetative reproduction, in which part of a plant becomes detached and may develop into a separate individual. » gamete; meiosis [i]; plant; reproduction

apostle In its broadest sense, a missionary, envoy, or agent; more narrowly used at times in the New Testament to refer to the 12 chosen followers of Jesus (less Judas Iscariot, replaced by Matthias according to *Acts* 1) who witnessed to the resurrected Jesus and were commissioned to proclaim his gospel. At times the term also included Paul and other missionaries or itinerant preachers (*Acts* 14.14; *Rom* 16.7). » Acts of the Apostles; Jesus Christ; Paul, St

Apostles' Creed A statement of Christian faith widely used in Roman Catholic and Protestant Churches, and recognized by the Orthodox Churches. It stresses the trinitarian nature of God (as Father, Son, and Holy Spirit) and the work of Christ. In its present form, it dates from the 8th-c, but its origins go back to the 3rd-c AD. » Christianity; Trinity

Apostolic Constitution One of the most solemn documents issued in the name of a pope, concerned with major matters of doctrine or discipline for the Roman Catholic Church at large. » bull (religion); pope; Roman Catholicism

apostolic succession The theory that a direct line of descent can be traced from the original apostles of Christ through episcopal succession to the bishops of the present-day Church which supports it, guaranteeing preservation of the original teaching of the apostles. This is now disputed by most New Testament scholars, and rejected by many Churches. » episcopacy

apothecary In most countries an old term for a pharmacist at a time when drugs were crude and mostly derived from plants. In England, apothecaries were general medical practitioners; the Society of Apothecaries was founded by James I in 1617 and gained further powers over the next two centuries. As a licensing body, the examinations it sets are subject to approval by the General Medical Council. » pharmacy

Appalachian Mountains [apa**lay**shuhn, apa**lay**chian] Mountain system in E N America extending from the Gulf of St Lawrence SSW to C Alabama (2 570 km/1 600 ml); a series of parallel ranges separated by wide valleys; highest peak Mt Mitchell (2 037 m/6 683 ft), North Carolina; the *Older Appalachians* in the E include (from N to S) the Shichshock, Notre Dame, White and Green Mts, the Berkshire Hills, and the Blue Ridge Mts; the C band of *Folded* or *Newer Appalachians* includes the Great Appalachian Valley, formed N–S by the St Lawrence lowland, the L Champlain lowland, the Hudson R, and other valleys (notably Shenandoah Valley, Virginia); the *Appalachian Plateau* in the W includes the Catskill, Allegheny, and Cumberland Mts; glaciers in the Canadian and New England areas; rich in minerals, especially coal; a major barrier to westward exploration in early US history; Great Smoky Mountains National Park (Tennessee), Shenandoah National Park (Virginia), the Appalachian Trail (world's longest continuous hiking trail, 3 300 km/2 050 ml). » United States of America [i]

Appaloosa A breed of horse; height, 14–15 hands/1.4–1.5 m/4.6–4.9 ft; short tail; dark with pale spots, or pale with dark spots; sometimes dark with pale hindquarters; name often used for these markings; also called *Apaloochy* or *Palouse*. » horse [i]

apparat The aggregate of full-time officials of the Soviet Communist Party (*apparatchiki*). Originally drawn from professional revolutionaries, and based on Lenin's doctrine of democratic centralism, the role of the apparat was to execute the decisions of the party leadership in a disciplined, bureaucratic manner with little scope for discussion or discretion. The term is also sometimes used to refer to a functionary. » Communist Party of the Soviet Union; Lenin

apparition The visual experience of seeing a person or animal (either living or dead) not actually present. The term **crisis**

apparition is applied if the person or animal seen is experiencing a crisis at the time, such as death or injury. » hallucination

appeal A legal procedure whereby a superior court considers an application by a party to a case concerning the decision reached in a lower court. In criminal cases, the appeal might concern the verdict or the sentence. In civil cases, it might concern the amount of damages awarded or the decision as to the success of the case itself. Appeals may involve matters of fact as well as law, though appeals to the House of Lords are always concerned with points of law. » court of law; civil law; criminal law; Lords, House of

appeasement A foreign policy based on conciliation of the grievances of rival states by negotiation and concession to avoid war. The term is most often applied to the British and French unsuccessful attempts before World War 2 to satisfy Hitler's demands over German grievances arising out of the Treaty of Versailles. As a result, Hitler remilitarized the Rhineland, secured Anschluss with Austria, and gained the Sudetenland from Czechoslovakia. » Anschluss; Chamberlain, Neville; Hitler

Appel, Karel Christian (1921–) Dutch painter, born in Amsterdam and educated there at the Royal College of Art. He was one of an influential group of Dutch, Belgian, and Danish Expressionists known as 'Cobra'. His work, featuring swirls of brilliant colour and agressively contorted figures, has many affinities with US Abstract Expressionism. He moved to Paris in the 1950s and now lives in the USA. » Dutch art; Expressionism

appendicitis The obstruction and inflammation of the appendix; one of the commonest surgical emergencies. It causes abdominal pain and vomiting. If the appendix is not removed surgically, it may cause generalized peritonitis and death. » appendix; peritonitis

appendix A blind-ended tube, also known as the *vermiform appendix*, which arises from the beginning of the large bowel on the right side of the abdomen. In humans, it is variable in length (2–20 cm/¾–8 in) and its function is unknown. It tends to become blocked in later life, and if its single blood supply is cut off, it rapidly becomes infected and inflamed (**appendicitis**) and has to be removed as soon as possible. It is present in apes and numerous other mammals (eg rabbits, rodents), where it is large, and plays a role in digestion. » abdomen; alimentary canal; appendicitis; intestine; Plate XII

Appert, Nicolas [apair] (1752–1841) French chef and the 'father of canning', born at Chalons-sur-Marne. In 1810 he suggested the technique of heat-and-hermetic-seal cooking, still the basis of the commercial canning of foods. In 1812 he established the first commercial food-canning business in the world, and later invented the forerunner of the Oxo cube. He died at Massy. » canning

Appia, Adolphe (1862–1928) Swiss scene designer and theatrical producer, born in Geneva. He was one of the first to plead for the use of simple planes instead of rich stage settings, and for the symbolic use of lighting, particularly in the presentation of opera. He died at Nyon, Switzerland. » opera; theatre

Appian Way The first of Rome's major trunk roads, constructed in 312 BC by Appius Claudius Caecus. It ran initially from Rome SE to Capua. Later it was extended across the peninsula to Brundisium on the Adriatic coast. » Roman roads [i]

apple A small deciduous tree; flowers white or pinkish, in clusters, appearing with the oval leaves; fruit a swollen, fleshy receptacle (or *pome*), containing a core, which is the real fruit. **Crab apples** are wild species native to N temperate regions with smooth leaves and small, sour fruits. All eating and cooking apples – over 1000 cultivars – belong to the cultivated apple of gardens and orchards (*Malus domestica*), a complex hybrid probably derived from several wild species of crab apple, and which has leaves woolly beneath and large sweet fruits. (Genus: *Malus*, 35 species. Family: *Rosaceae*.) » cultivar; deciduous plants; fruit; tree [i]

Appleton, Sir Edward Victor (1892–1965) British physicist, born at Bradford, Yorkshire, who was awarded (1947) the Nobel Prize for Physics for his contribution 'in exploring the ionosphere'. Educated at Cambridge, he became professor of physics at London, and in 1936 professor of natural philosophy at Cambridge. Knighted in 1941, he died in Edinburgh. » Appleton layer

Appleton layer A strongly ionized region of the upper part of the ionosphere, at heights of about 200–400 km/125–250 ml, which is responsible for the reflection of short radio waves back to Earth. Discovered in 1925 by Edward Appleton, it is also known as the **F layer**. » Appleton; ionosphere; radio waves

applied linguistics The application of linguistic theory, practice, and methodology to situations which present language-related tasks or problems. The most well-established field is that of language teaching and learning, particularly with reference to foreign languages. Here, the linguist can contribute such useful background information as a contrastive analysis of the structures of the learner's native language and those of the target language, to enable predictions to be made about likely sources of difficulty and error. Other fields of interest to the applied linguist include interpreting and translating, dictionary-making, the teaching of reading and writing, and the many areas of language pathology (eg stuttering, aphasia, dyslexia). » dictionary; learning; linguistics; speech pathology

Appomattox Court House The site in Virginia, USA, of the surrender of the Confederate army under Robert E Lee to Union forces under Ulysses S Grant, at the end of the American Civil War (9 Apr 1865). Although a few Confederates remained under arms, it marked the effective end of the war. » American Civil War

appulse The seemingly close approach of two celestial objects as perceived by an observer; particularly, the close approach of a planet or asteroid to a star without the occurrence of an eclipse. » asteroids; eclipse; planet; star

apraxia [ay**prak**sia] Difficulty in controlling voluntary movements of the limbs or vocal organs; also called **dyspraxia**. In particular, there may be an inability to control sequences of sounds or gestures. The intention to act or communicate is present, but the patient cannot carry it out. » speech pathology

apricot A deciduous shrub or small tree 3–10 m/10–30 ft, native to China and C Asia, and widely cultivated; flowers white or pale pink, appearing before the broadly oval, toothed leaves; fruits globose, velvety, 4–8 cm/1½–3 in, yellow or orange; flesh tart becoming sweet; stone ridged along one edge. (*Prunus armeniaca*. Family: *Rosaceae*.) » prunus; shrub; tree [i]

April Fool A person tricked or made a fool of on 1 April (All Fools' Day or April Fools' Day). In origin this may have been the final day of the festivities celebrating the spring equinox, which began on Old New Year's Day (25 Mar until 1564). The tradition, found throughout Europe, may have originated in France; outside Europe, there is an example of similar fooling during the Huli Festival in India (ending 31 Mar).

April Theses A programme of revolutionary action drawn up by Lenin in April 1917 shortly after the February Revolution. In it he advocated the transformation of the Russian 'bourgeois-democratic' revolution into a 'proletarian-socialist' revolution under the slogan of 'All power to the Soviets'. » Bolsheviks; February (Russia)/October/Russian Revolution; July Days; Lenin

apron stage The part of the stage in front of the proscenium. It is often a moveable structure and sometimes lower than the main stage. » proscenium; stage

apse A semi-circular or polygonal vaulted recess in a church, usually at the end of a chapel or chancel. It was originally used to contain the praetor's chair in a Roman basilica. » basilica; chancel; church [i]

Apuleius, Lucius [apoo**lay**us] (2nd-c) Latin satirist, born at Madaura, Numidia, N Africa. He travelled widely, obtaining knowledge of many priestly fraternities. He married a wealthy widow, but was accused of having used magic to gain her affections; his *Apologia*, still extant, is an eloquent vindication. Apuleius achieved great eminence in literature and public oratory. His romance, *The Metamorphoses* or *Golden Ass*, is a satire on the vices of the age, especially those of the priesthood and of quacks. » Latin literature; satire

Apus [aypuhs] (Lat 'bird of paradise') A rather small and inconspicuous S hemisphere constellation. In a star atlas of 1720 (Bayer), a typographical error resulted in *Apis*, as a result of which the erroneous translation 'bee' is still frequently found as the English name. » constellation; RR8

Aqaba [akaba], ancient **Aelana** 29°31N 35°00E, pop (1983e) 40 000. Seaport in Maan governorate, East Bank, SW Jordan, at N end of the Gulf of Aqaba, on the border with Israel; Jordan's only outlet to the sea; airport; railway; an ancient trade route through the Red Sea–Jordan rift valley; container terminal facilities; phosphates, thermal power, fertilizers, timber processing, tourism; popular winter seaside resort. » Jordan [i]

aquamarine A variety of the mineral beryl, used as a gemstone. It is transparent, usually sea-green or bluish-green. » beryl

aquaplaning A phenomenon which can take place when a tyre is operating on a wet road. Under certain circumstances a layer or wedge of water becomes interposed between the tyre and the road, and the tyre 'planes', ie loses adhesion. As a result, steering and braking can become ineffective. » car [i]; tyre

aquarium A building suitably equipped for the display of aquatic plant and animal life. The first public aquarium was the Aquatic Vivarium, in Regent's Park Zoo, London, which opened in 1853. In recent times open-air *dolphinariums* have become popular for the displaying of dolphins, and underwater *oceanariums* can be found in popular tourist resorts, such as Disney World in Florida. Small tanks are available for use as domestic aquariums in which tropical fish can be kept. » dolphin; fish [i]

Aquarius (Lat 'water bearer') The tenth largest constellation in the S sky. It is a winter sign of the zodiac, lying between Pisces and Capricornus. » constellation; zodiac [i]; RR8

aquatint A form of etching which gives a tonal effect like a wash drawing (shaded with diluted ink or watercolour, applied with a brush). The copper plate is dusted with a thin layer of powdered resin, which is fixed to the metal by heating. When immersed in acid, the plate is bitten all over, but as a mass of tiny specks rather than as lines. Gradations of tone from pale grey to deep (but not solid) black are achieved by timing the immersion. The technique was perfected in France in 1768 by Jean-Baptiste Le Prince, but the greatest master to use it was Goya, notably in *Los Caprichos* (1799). In the 20th-c, aquatint has been revived by Picasso, André Masson (1896–1987), and others. » etching; Goya; Picasso

aquatube A water slide or chute with many twists and bends. Users are carried, normally on their backs, down the slide on water before being deposited into a swimming pool. They are popular in aquaparks, which can be found in many Mediterranean and US holiday resorts.

aquavit A colourless spirit, distilled from potatoes or cereals, and usually flavoured with caraway seeds. It is a popular drink in Scandinavia.

aqueduct An artificial channel for the conveyance of water. The Romans built thousands of miles of aqueducts to bring water to their towns. Many are in the form of arch bridges, and some of these spectacular structures, such as the Pont du Gard at Nîmes, France, still survive.

aquifer Water-bearing rock strata, commonly sandstones or chalk with high porosity and permeability. They provide much of the world's water supply, which may be exploited directly by sinking wells or pumping into a reservoir. The chalk in the London Basin (UK) and the Dakota sandstone (USA) are important aquifers. » artesian basin; chalk; sandstone

Aquila [**ak**wila] (Lat 'eagle') A constellation on the celestial equator. Its brightest star is Altair. Distance: 5.1 parsecs. » constellation; RR8

aquilegia [akwi**lee**juh] » **columbine**

Aquinas, St Thomas [ak**wiy**nas] (1225–74), feast day 7 March. Italian scholastic theologian, known as the 'Angelic Doctor'. He was born in the castle of Roccasecca, of the family of the Counts of Aquino, and educated by the Benedictines of Monte-Cassino, and at Naples. Against the will of his family, he entered the Dominican order (1243), but his brothers abducted him, keeping him a prisoner in the paternal castle for two years. Escaping to Cologne, he became a pupil of Albertus Magnus, and in turn was himself appointed to teach (1248). He began to publish commentaries on Aristotle, and went to Paris (1252), where he obtained great distinction as a philosophic theologian. In 1258, he was summoned by the Pope to teach successively in Anagni, Orvieto, and Rome. He died on his way to a General Council in Lyons, and was canonized in 1323. He was the first among 13th-c metaphysicians to stress the importance of sense perception and the experimental foundation of human knowledge. His *Summa Theologiae*, the first attempt at a complete theological system, remains substantially the standard authority in the Roman Catholic Church. His only scholastic rival was Duns Scotus (the 'Subtle Doctor'), who was followed by Franciscans. Thereafter mediaeval theologians were divided into two schools, Scotists and Thomists, whose differences permeated almost every branch of doctrine. » Albertus Magnus; Aristotle; Dominicans; Duns Scotus; scholasticism; theology

Aquino, Cory [ak**wee**noh], properly **(Maria) Corazon**, *née* **Cojuangco** (1933–) Philippines politician and President (1986–), born in Tarlac province, and educated in the USA. In 1956 she married opposition leader Benigno Aquino, and after his imprisonment in 1972 kept him in touch with the outside world. She lived in exile with him in the USA until 1983, when he returned to the Philippines and was assassinated. She took up her husband's cause, and with widespread support claimed victory in the 1986 elections, accusing President Marcos of ballot-rigging to obtain his majority. The nonviolent 'people's power' movement which followed brought the overthrow of Marcos and her election as President. In 1989 the sixth, and most serious, attempted coup was resisted with aid from the USA. » Marcos; Philippines [i]

Aquitaine [akwi**tayn**], Fr [akee**ten**], ancient **Aquitania** pop (1982) 2 656 544; area 41 308 sq km/15 945 sq ml. Region of SW France comprising the departments of Dordogne, Gironde, Landes, Lot-et-Garonne, and Pyrénées-Atlantiques; united with Gascony under the French crown, 11th-c; acquired by England on the marriage of Henry II to Eleanor of Aquitaine, 1152; remained in English hands until 1452; chief town, Bordeaux; drained by rivers Garonne, Dordogne, Gironde; several caves with ancient rock paintings; Bergerac and Bordeaux areas noted for wines; Parc des Landes de Gascogne regional nature park; several spas; wine, fruit, resin, tobacco, shipbuilding, chemicals, oil refining. » Henry II (of France); Hundred Years' War

Ara (Lat 'altar') A small S hemisphere constellation. » constellation; RR8

Arab horse A breed of horse; height, usually 14–15 hands/1.4–1.5 m/4.6–4.9 ft; grey, brown, or black; wide nostrils and concave face; spirited, with great stamina; three groups: *Kehylan*, *Seglawi*, and *Muniqi*, which are seldom interbred. » horse [i]; thoroughbred

Arab-Israeli Wars Four wars (1948, 1956, 1967, 1973) fought between Israel and the Arab states over the existence of the state of Israel and the rights of the Palestinians. The June 1967 war is known by supporters of Israel as the 'Six Day War' and by others as 'The June War.' The 1973 war is called the 'Yom Kippur War' by Israelis, the 'Ramadan War' by Arabs, and the 'October War' by others. » Golan; Israel [i]; Yom Kippur; Zionism

Arab League A League of Arab States, founded in March 1945, with the aim of encouraging Arab unity. The League's headquarters was established in Egypt, but moved to Tunis after the signing of Egypt's peace treaty with Israel in 1979. It returned to Cairo in 1990. Today the Arab League has 21 member states including Palestine, which is represented by the Palestine Liberation Organization. » PLO

arabesque Flowing linear ornament, based usually on plant forms. It occurs widely throughout history, but is especially favoured by Islamic artists. » Celtic art; Islamic art

Arabia area c.2 590 000 sq km/1 000 000 sq ml. Peninsula of SW Asia, bounded N by the Syrian Desert, E by the Arabian Gulf, W by the Red Sea, and S by the Arabian Sea; divided politically into the states of Saudi Arabia, Yemen, Oman, United Arab Emirates, Bahrain, Qatar, and Kuwait; an important world source of petroleum. » Arabian Gulf

Arabian camel » **dromedary**

Arabian Gulf or **The Gulf**, **Persian Gulf**, ancient **Sinus Persicus** area 238 800 sq km/92 200 sq ml. Arm of the Arabian Sea, connected to it via the Gulf of Oman and the Strait of Hormuz; bounded N by Iran, NW by Iraq and Kuwait, W by Saudi Arabia and Qatar, and S by the United Arab Emirates; largest islands, Bahrain and Qeshm (Iran); length 885 km/550 ml; maximum width 322 km/200 ml; average depth 100 m/325 ft; important source of oil; pipeline (N) links offshore oilfields with Iran and Saudi Arabia via terminal on Khârg I; scene of great tension during Iran–Iraq War in the 1980s. » Arabian Sea; Gulf War

Arabian hound » **saluki**

Arabian Sea NW part of the Indian Ocean; principal arms include the Gulf of Oman (NW) and the Gulf of Aden (W); bounded N by Pakistan and Iran, E by India, W by Oman and South Yemen; depths of 2 895 m/9 498 ft in the N to 4 392 m/14 409 ft in the SW; trade route between Indian subcontinent, Arabian Gulf states, and Mediterranean. » Indian Ocean

Arabic A language of the S Semitic group within the Hamito-Semitic family, spoken by over 150 millions as a mother-tongue. Its spread outside the Arabian peninsula was concomitant with the spread of Islam in the 7th–8th-c AD. The language has two forms. *Colloquial Arabic* exists as the vernacular varieties of the major Arabic-speaking nation-states, such as Egypt, Morocco, and Syria, which are not always mutually intelligible. *Classical Arabic*, the language of the Koran, provides a common, standard written form for all the vernacular variants, and a common medium for affairs of state, religion, and education throughout the Arabic-speaking world. The language is written from right to left. » Afro-Asiatic languages; Arabic literature; diglossia; Islam; Koran

Arabic literature The great age of Arabic literature was from the 6th-c to the 12th-c, although there has been a minor revival in the 20th-c under the influence of drama and fiction from the West. The earlier literature was almost exclusively in poetry, with the oral tradition permitting the cultivation of poetic forms of great complexity, such as the pre-Islamic *qasida*, represented in the celebrated 8th-c *Mu'akkaqat* collection of seven golden odes. The Ommiad period (661–750) saw the introduction of the *ghazal*, a shorter form used for erotic and mystical poetry, in which Omar ibn Abi Rabi'a (644–c.720) excelled, and much political satire. Exposure to Greek and Roman civilization during the Abassid period (750–1055) helped the development of secular prose, best exhibited by Al-Jahiz (776–869); while under the patronage of the 9th-c Baghdad caliphs and at the 10th-c Hamdanid court at Aleppo, historical writing flourished alongside poetry. » Abbasids; Arabic; ode; Persian literature; poetry

arable farming Farming which involves regular ploughing and planting of annual crops, such as cereals, potatoes, sugar-beet, and vegetables. It is predominant in flatter and drier areas, where ploughing is easy and where dry summers allow crops to ripen and be harvested. » agriculture; crop rotation

Arabs A diverse group of people, united by their use of Arabic as a first language, who live primarily in SW Iran, Iraq, Syria, the Arabian Peninsula, the Maghreb region of N Africa, Egypt, and Mauritania. They are mostly Caucasoid, but with Negroid and Mongoloid admixture in certain areas. A great unifying force is Islam, the religion of 95% of all Arabs. The majority live in cities and towns; 5% are pastoral nomads living in deserts. Population c.120 million (1970 est). » Arabic; Islam; Maghreb

Arabesque – Detail from the Alhambra at Granada

arachidonic acid A polyunsaturated fatty acid with 20 carbons and 4 unsaturated bonds. It is stored in cell membranes, and when released gives rise to the prostaglandins and leukotrienes. Arachidonic acid is synthesized in the body from linoleic acid (18 carbons, 2 double bonds), which is an essential component of the diet in that it cannot be synthesized by humans. » carbon; diet; leukotrienes; polyunsaturated fatty acids; prostaglandins

Arachne [araknee] In Greek mythology, an excellent weaver from Lydia, who challenged Athena to a contest. When Arachne's work was seen to be superior, Athena destroyed the web and Arachne hanged herself. Athena saved her, but changed her into a spider. » Athena

Arachnida [araknida] A large, diverse class of mostly terrestrial arthropods, comprising c.70 000 species of mites, scorpions, pseudoscorpions, spiders, harvestmen, and whip scorpions; body divided into *prosoma* (fused head and thorax) and *opisthosoma* (abdomen); head lacking antennae and compound eyes; four pairs of legs present, and a pair of fangs (*chelicerae*); breathing by means of specialized regions of the body wall with a thin, highly-folded cuticle (*book lungs*) or by means of internal air tubes (*tracheae*). » arthropod; harvestman; mite; scorpion; spider; whip scorpion

arachnodactyly [araknoh**dak**tilee] » **Marfan's syndrome**

Arafat, Yasser, or **Yasir** (1929–) Palestinian resistance leader, born in Jerusalem. He was educated at Cairo University (1952–6), where he was leader of the Palestinian Students' Union, and co-founded the Fatah resistance group in 1956. This group gained control of the Palestinian Liberation Organization (PLO) soon after its foundation in 1964, and he became its acknowledged (though not universally popular) leader. He skilfully managed the uneasy juxtaposition of militancy and diplomacy, and gradually gained world acceptance of the PLO. But in 1983 his policies lost majority PLO support, and he was forced to leave Lebanon with his remaining followers. Since then he has been based at the PLO headquarters in Tunis, though he spends much of his time in Baghdad. The *intifada* (uprising) in the West Bank in 1988 paved the way for his dramatic recognition of Israel and renunciation of terrorism in December 1988. » Fatah; PLO

Arafura Sea [arafoora] Section of the Pacific Ocean, bounded N and NE by Indonesia and New Guinea, and S by Australia; shallow depths (27–55 m/90–180 ft) because of underlying continental shelf. » Pacific Ocean

Aragon, Louis [aragõ] (1897–1982) French novelist, poet and journalist, born and died in Paris. He was one of the most brilliant of the Surrealist group, as shown by his first novel, *Le Paysan de Paris* (1926, trans The Night-Walker). After a visit to the USSR in 1930, he became a convert to communism. His later works include several novels, such as *La semaine sainte* (1958, Holy Week), and collections of poems. He edited the communist weekly *Les Lettres Françaises* 1953–72. » communism; French literature; Surrealism

Aragón [aragon] pop (1981) 1 196 952; area 47 669 sq km/18 400 sq ml. Autonomous region of NE Spain; featureless upland region largely occupying the basin of the R Ebro; Pyrenees in the N; sparsely populated; almonds, figs, vines, and olives grown by irrigation near rivers; a former kingdom (11th–15th-c), controlling much of N Spain, and conquering parts of S Italy in the 14th–15th-c. » Aragón, House of; Spain [i]

Aragón, House of [aragon] The ruling house of one of Spain's component kingdoms, founded (1035) by Ramiro I, the illegitimate son of Sancho the Great of Navarre. It was united by marriage with the ruling house of Barcelona in 1131. Fernando II of Aragon married Isabel of Castile in 1469, and the crowns of Aragon and Castile were finally united in 1479. » Aragón; Castile; Catalonia

aragonite A mineral form of calcium carbonate ($CaCO_3$), occurring in some high-pressure alpine metamorphic rocks, sedimentary carbonate rocks, and in the shells of certain molluscs of which it forms the lining (mother-of-pearl). » calcite

Araguaia, River [aragwiya] Main tributary of the Tocantins R, NE Brazil, rising in C Brazil, and flowing NNE; length estimated at 1 770–2 410 km/1 100–1 500 ml; separates in mid course into two branches, enclosing Bananal I, world's largest river island (area 20 000 sq km/7 700 sq ml), now containing a national park (area 5 623 sq km/2 170 sq ml); chief tributary (R Garças) noted for its mosquitos. » Brazil [i]

Arakan Pagoda » **Mahamuni Pagoda**

Arakan Yoma [ara**kahn yoh**ma] Mountain range in SW Burma, between the Arakan coast on the Bay of Bengal and the Irrawaddy R valley; rises to over 1 980 m/6 496 ft; forms a climatic barrier, cutting off C Burma from the effects of the SW monsoon. » Burma [i]

Aral Sea, Russian **Aral'skoye More** Inland sea, E of the Caspian Sea, mainly in Kazakhstan; world's fourth largest lake, c.64 500 sq km/24 900 sq ml, but rapidly decreasing in size; c.420 km/260 ml long, 280 km/175 ml wide, maximum depth 70 m/230 ft; contains several small islands; generally shallow, with little navigation; sodium and magnesium sulphate mined along shores; diversion of water from rivers supplying the sea for cotton irrigation projects has seriously upset ecological balance; sea level dropped by 12 m/40 ft since 1960, and area reduced by a third; new desert (the Aralkum) of 2.6 million ha/6.5 million acres; water now heavily polluted, with loss of fishing industry, reduced wildlife, and increased disease. » ecology

Aramaic [ara**may**ik] One of the oldest languages in the Semitic group, still spoken by small communities in the Middle East. It is the basis of Syriac, a present-day dialect spoken by a million people in the Middle East and the USA. A dialect of Aramaic was the language used by Jesus and his disciples. » Afro-Asiatic languages; Jesus Christ

Aran Islands Group of three islands (Inishmor, Inishmaan, Inisheer) off SW coast of Galway Co, Connacht, W Irish Republic; at the mouth of Galway Bay; each has an airstrip with flights from Carnmore, near Galway; boat service from Rossaveel; several monastic ruins and Dun Aengus fort. » Connacht; Irish Republic [i]

Araneae [ara**nee**-ee] » **spider**

Arany, János [**aw**rony] (1817–82) Hungary's epic poet, born at Nagy-Szalonta of peasant stock. With Petőfi he was a leader of the popular national school, and was chief secretary of the Academy 1870–9. His chief work is the *Toldi* trilogy (1847–54), the adventures of a peasant youth at the Hungarian court in the 14th-c, and he also published a successful translation of Shakespeare. He died in Budapest. » epic; poetry

Ararat, (Great) Mount [ararat], Turkish **(Büyük) Ağri Daği** 39°44N 44°15E. Highest peak in Turkey; in E Turkey, close to the frontier with Iran and Armenia; height 5 165 m/16 945 ft; said to be the landing place of Noah's Ark; **Little Ararat** (Küçük Ağri Daği) lies to the SE, rising to 3 907 m/12 818 ft. » Noah; Turkey [i]

Araucanians S American Indian group of C Chile. Two divisions, the Picunche and the Huilliche, assimilated into Spanish society in the 17th-c; the Mapuche resisted for over three centuries, but were finally defeated by the Chilean army in the 1880s, and were settled on reservations. They presently number about 200 000, on reservations and in towns and cities in Chile and Argentina. » American Indians; Chile [i]

araucaria [araw**kair**eea] An evergreen conifer, native to much of the S hemisphere except Africa; branches horizontal, in whorls; leaves usually scale-like, sometimes large; all produce edible seeds and useful timber, often sold as **parana pine**. (Genus: *Araucaria*, 18 species. Family: *Araucariaceae*.) » conifer; evergreen plants; monkey-puzzle

Arawak [arawak] American Indians of the Greater Antilles and S America. In the Antilles, they settled in villages and cultivated cassava and maize; frequently attacked by the Caribs, many were later killed by the Spanish. In S America, they lived in isolated small settlements in tropical Amazonian forests, and practised hunting, fishing, and farming. A few survivors live along the coastal strip of Guyana and Suriname. » American Indians; Antilles; Carib

arbitration The settlement of a dispute by reference to an independent party, the **arbitrator**. Contracts may provide for disputes to be settled in this way, in an attempt to avoid proceedings in the courts. There are specialist trade tribunals engaged in settling business disputes, such as the London Maritime Arbitrators Association and the Grain and Feed Trade Association. Arbitrators, like judges, are immune from action in negligence. » contract; court of law; negligence

Arbor Day In the USA, New Zealand, and parts of Canada and Australia, a day (whose date varies from place to place) set apart each year for planting trees and increasing public awareness of the value of trees; first observed in the State of Nebraska, USA, in 1872.

arbor vitae [**ah**baw **vee**tiy] An evergreen coniferous tree or shrub native to N America, China, Japan, and Formosa; leaves scaly, overlapping, in opposite pairs, cones urn-shaped with thin scales. The name is rarely used for individual species, which are called **cedars** or **thujas**, qualified by country of origin or timber colour. (Genus: *Thuja*, 6 species. Family: *Cupressaceae*.) » conifer; evergreen plants; red cedar 1; white cedar

arboretum [ahbo**ree**tum] A botanical garden, or a section of a botanical garden, used for the display and study of trees, shrubs, and vines. » botanical garden

Arbuthnot, John (1667–1735) British physician and wit, the much-loved friend of Swift and Pope, born at Inverbervie, Kincardineshire, Scotland. He was educated at Aberdeen, Oxford, and St Andrews, where he qualified as a doctor (1696). Settling in London, he was in 1705 appointed physician to Queen Anne. He wrote on many scientific subjects, but is best remembered for his literary accomplishments. He was a founder member of the satirical Scriblerus Club, and was the chief if not sole author of *Memoirs of Martinus Scriblerus*, first published in Pope's works (1741); his too was the celebrated *History of John Bull* (1712). He died in London. » English literature; satire

arc Part of the curve bounding a region, usually the arc of a circle. The length of an arc of a circle radius r, that subtends an angle θ at the centre of the circle, is $r\theta$. The **minor arc** is the smaller of the two possible arcs AB; the **major arc** is the greater of the two. » angle; circle; geometry

Arc de Triomphe [ahk duh **tree**omf] A triumphal arch commemorating Napoleon's victories, designed by Jean Chalgrin (1739–1811) and erected (1806–35) in the Place Charles de Gaulle, Paris. It is 49 m/162 ft high and 45 m/147 ft wide. » Napoleon I; Paris [i]

Arc-et-Senans [ark ay suh**nõ**] 47°02N 5°46E. A royal saltworks situated N of Arbois, France; a world heritage site. The architect, Claude-Nicolas Ledoux, had only partially realized his plan to incorporate a saline extraction plant with an ideal town; when building came to a halt in 1779. The works were abandoned by the end of the 19th-c. » Ledoux

Arcadia (Ancient Greece) [ah**kay**dia] The mountainous area in the centre of the Peloponnese. Its inhabitants claimed to be pre-

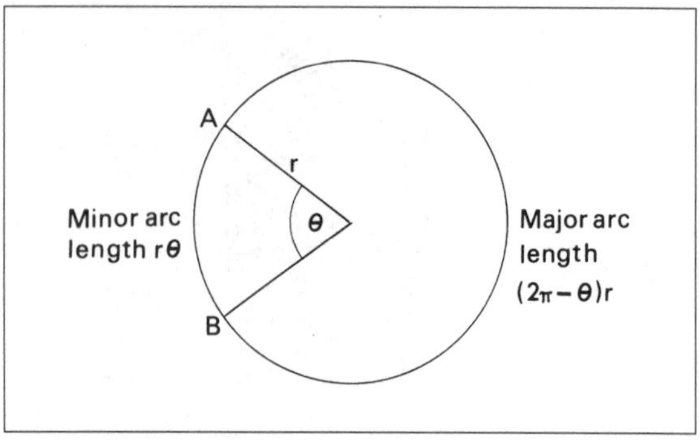

Arcs of a circle

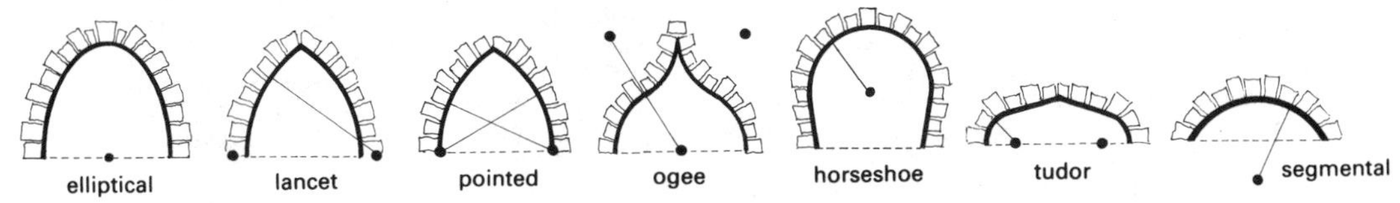

Types of arches

Dorian, and the oldest settlers of Hellenic stock in Greece. » Dorians

Arcadia (in mythology) [ah**kay**dia] An ideal pastoral existence; also known as **Arcady**. *Et in Arcadia ego* is a proverbial expression found under a painting by Poussin, usually taken to mean that death is present, even in the ideal world. » Poussin

arch Part of a building, or a structure in its own right, made up of wedge-shaped stones or other pieces over an opening, which support both each other and any weight above. There is a great variety of shapes; amongst the most common are the elliptical, horseshoe, lancet, ogee, pointed, segmental, and Tudor. A **relieving** or **discharging** arch has no opening, being placed in a wall to direct weight away from an aperture further below. » Gothic architecture; Roman architecture; spandrel; triumphal arch

Archaean or **Archean eon** [ah**kee**an] The earlier of the two geological eons into which the Precambrian is divided; the period of time from the formation of the Earth (c.4 600 million years ago) to 2 500 million years ago. » geological time scale; Precambrian era; Proterozoic eon; RR16

Archaebacteria A recently established kingdom comprising the methane-producing bacteria (*methanogens*). They differ from true bacteria and all higher organisms (the *eucaryotes*, in which the cells have a true nucleus) in numerous detailed characters relating to their ribonucleic acids, enzyme systems, and metabolic pathways. They possibly represent the oldest known life forms, existing more than 3 billion years ago. » bacteria [i]; enzyme; eucaryote; kingdom; methane [i]; RNA

archaeology/archeology The study of past peoples and societies through the systematic analysis of their material remains. It originated as an aspect of the revival of interest in classical culture during the Renaissance, and was, until the study of human antiquity was established in the 1860s, an almost exclusively European and antiquarian pursuit, interpreting chance survivals of monuments and artefacts by reference to biblical and classical precedent. The emphasis since has shifted firmly to the study of human development over the long period of more than 2 million years in which written records were non-existent (*prehistory*) or at best rudimentary (*protohistory*), and to the recovery of new data through excavation, field survey, laboratory study, and computer analysis. Radiometric dating methods established the discipline on a new and firmer footing in the 1950s and 1960s, and quantification and an increasing preoccupation with theory wrought an almost equivalent revolution in the 1970s and 1980s. Archaeology has continued throughout to grow in scope, so that it now involves anthropology, ecology, and systematics alongside the more traditional preoccupations of history, art history, and taxonomy. Politically too it has an often potent role to play in the modern world, its finest monuments standing at once as symbols of ancient culture and contemporary nationhood. » anthropology; dendrochronology; ecology; environmental archaeology; palaeopathology; palynology; potassium-argon dating; systematics; thermoluminescence dating; Three Age System

Archaeopteryx [ahkee**op**tuhriks] The oldest fossil bird, known from the Jurassic period of Europe; characterized by feathers and a wishbone; distinguished from modern birds by reptilian features such as the long bony tail supported by vertebrae, three clawed fingers on wings and sharp teeth on both jaws. » bird [i]; fossil; Jurassic period

Archangel, Russ **Arkhangel'sk** 64°32N 40°40E, pop(1983) 399 000. Port and capital city of Archangel oblast, European Russia; on R Severnaya Dvina, on an inlet of the White Sea; one of the largest sea and river ports in the state; harbour often icebound in winter; founded, 1584; airfield; railway; fishing, clothing, footwear, shipbuilding, transport equipment, timber; monastery dedicated to the Archangel Michael. » Russia

archbishop A bishop appointed to have jurisdiction over other bishops; often, the head of a province. The title sometimes refers to a bishop exercising special functions. In Eastern Churches, a hierarchy of archbishops is recognized. » bishop

archdeacon A clergyman in the Anglican Church responsible for the administration of the whole or such part of a diocese as the bishop may authorize. The office formerly existed also in Roman Catholic and Eastern Orthodox Churches. » Anglican Communion; clergy

archegonium The flask-shaped, female gamete-producing organ of bryophytes, pteridophytes, and gymnosperms. It is related to the development of land plants. » bryophyte; gametophyte; gymnosperms; pteridophyte

Archer, Fred(erick) (1857–86) British jockey, born at Cheltenham. The first great jockey, he rode 2 748 winners in his brief career (1870–86), and was the first man to ride 200 winners in a season. He rode 21 Classic winners, including the Derby five times (1877, 1880–1, 1885–6). His 246 races in 1885 was a record that stood until 1933, and he was champion jockey 13 times. He committed suicide at Newmarket. » Classics; horse racing

archerfish Any of the Asian marine and freshwater fishes renowned for their ability to dislodge or shoot down insect prey by spitting drops or jets of water over distances up to 3 m/10 ft; body length up to 25 cm/10 in. (Family: *Toxotidae*.)

archery The use of the bow and arrow, one of the first weapons used in battle. Until the development of gunpowder in the 14th-c, the bowman was the most powerful member of any army. When archery was no longer used in warfare its practice decreased, but in the late 17th-c it gained popularity as a sport. The governing body, the *Fédération Internationale de Tir à l'Arc* was formed in 1931. In competition, a series of arrows is fired from 30, 50, 70, and 90 metres for men, and 30, 50, 60, and 70 metres for women. The circular target consists of ten scoring zones. The smallest is gold-coloured and worth 10 points if hit. » crossbow; longbow; RR103

archetype (Gr 'original pattern') A prototype or permanent form of an event (birth/death), character (rebel/witch), or disposition. Seen as recurring in life, archetypes are a fertile source of images in art and literature. » Jung; literature; Freudian criticism

Archilochus of Paros [ar**kil**okuhs] (760–670 BC) Greek poet, regarded as the first of the lyric poets, renowned for his vituperative satire. Only fragments of his work are extant. » Greek literature; satire

Archimedes [arki**mee**deez] (c.287–212 BC) Greek scientist, the most celebrated of ancient mathematicians. He was born at Syracuse, and perished in the capture of that city by the Romans. He alone of the ancients contributed anything of real value to the theory of mechanics and to hydrostatics, first proving that a body plunged in a fluid becomes lighter by an amount equal to the weight of the fluid it displaces (**Archimedes' principle**); by measuring the quantity of water displaced by a floating object, its weight can therefore be found. » Archimedes screw; buoyancy; fluid mechanics; pi [i]; sphere [i]

Archimedes screw A device to raise water; named after Greek mathematician Archimedes, who is said to have invented it. It consists of a broad threaded screw inside an inclined cylinder; as the screw is turned, the water is raised gradually between the threads and is run off at the top. » Archimedes

Archipenko, Alexander (1887–1964) Ukrainian sculptor and painter, born in Kiev. He studied at Kiev, Moscow, and Paris, where he was influenced by Cubism. After 1923 he lived in the USA, and taught in the new Bauhaus at Chicago. He died in New York City. » Bauhaus; Cubism

architecture The art or science of building; particularly used to differentiate between building and the art of designing buildings. In the latter context, there has been great division of opinion as to what exactly constitutes architecture. The most usual standpoint is typified by Ruskin in *The Seven Lamps of Architecture* (1849): 'Architecture is the art which so disposes and adorns the edifices raised by man, for whatsoever uses, that the sight of them may contribute to his mental health, power, and pleasure.' Pevsner, in *An Outline of European Architecture* (1943) puts it more succinctly: 'A bicycle shed is a building; Lincoln Cathedral is a piece of architecture.' Traditionally, therefore, the study of architecture has tended to concentrate on aspects of higher culture and especially Art, for example looking at ennobling buildings such as the Parthenon (Athens), the Pantheon (Rome), and great artist-architects such as Wren and Schinkel. Nevertheless, the practice of architecture in the 19th-c, and especially in the 20th-c, has increasingly involved a larger number and variety of often complex skills and disciplines, ranging from the technical considerations of structural engineering, environmental services, and energy conservation, to the functional considerations of room layout, interior design, and human comfort, as well as the overtly intellectual considerations stressed by Ruskin and Pevsner. Correspondingly, there has been a greater acceptance of the wider concerns and domain of architecture as anything which has been consciously, or even unconsciously, designed and built for the use of people. » Pevsner, Nikolaus; Ruskin, John; Schinkel; Wren, Christopher

archives A place where historical records and other important documents are preserved; also, the materials themselves. The first National Archives were established in France in 1789. Such institutions, known elsewhere as Public Records Offices, are usually the centralized repository of a nation's official documents.

archon [**ah**kohn] In ancient Athens, an annually appointed public official whose duties were mainly legal and religious; each year nine were chosen.

ARCIC Acronym for **Anglican–Roman Catholic International Commission**, instituted in 1966 by Pope Paul VI and Archbishop Michael Ramsey (1904–88). The Commission meets regularly, and produces statements on areas of substantial agreement between the two Churches on important points of doctrine. » Anglican Communion; Paul VI; Roman Catholicism

Arctic Area in the N hemisphere which lies N of the tree-line or, more loosely, to the N of the Arctic Circle; Arctic conditions of climate, vegetation, and life-forms obtain in Greenland, Svalbard, and the N parts of Canada, Russia, Alaska, and Iceland. » Antarctica [i]; Arctic Circle

Arctic Circle or **Polar Circle** An arbitrary boundary marking the southernmost extremity of the northernmost area of the Earth; the area to the N of the tree-line; placed at 66°17′N, but often defined as the area N of 70°N. » Antarctic Circle; Arctic

Arctic fox A fox widespread on Arctic land masses; hairy feet and small ears; eats lemmings, birds, hares, fish, carrion; coat thickens in winter; two forms: one white in winter, brown in summer; the other (*blue fox* of Greenland) pale blue-grey in winter, darker blue-grey in summer. (*Alopex lagopus*.) » fox

Arctic Ocean Body of water within the Arctic Circle; world's smallest ocean, 9 485 000 sq km/3 661 000 sq ml; frozen all year except in marginal areas; greatest depth, Eurasia Basin, 5 122 m/16 804 ft; forms the cold East Greenland Current and the Labrador Current; hummocky icefields in winter, pack-ice during summer, carried S by surface currents (generally melting N of the major shipping lanes); unexplored until Amundsen's flight, 1926; research suggests the Ocean is experiencing a period of warming. » Arctic

Arctic tern A small tern found worldwide; migrates further than any other bird (approximately 36 000 km/22 000 ml per year); spends N summer in the Arctic, and N winter in the Antarctic. (*Sterna paradisaea*.) » tern

Arcturus » **Boötes**

Ardashir » **Artaxerxes I**

Arden, John (1930–) British playwright, born at Barnsley, Yorkshire, and educated at Cambridge and the Edinburgh College of Art. His first play was a romantic comedy entitled *All Fall Down* (1955). Other well-known plays include *The Workhouse Donkey* (1963), a caricature of northern local politics, and *Sergeant Musgrave's Dance* (1959), which follows Brechtian tradition in its staging. He has collaborated with his wife, **Margaretta D'Arcy**, in several plays. » Brecht; drama; English literature; theatre

Ardnamurchan Point [ardna**mer**khan] 56°44N 6°14W. Cape in SW Highland region, W Scotland; N of Mull I; westernmost point on British mainland; lighthouse (1849) has a fixed light visible for 29 km/18 ml. » Highland; Scotland [i]

Area of Outstanding Natural Beauty (AONB) An area in England and Wales which does not merit National Park status, but where special measures are needed to preserve its natural interest and beauty. They are generally smaller than National Parks, and are the responsibility of local authorities and the Countryside Commission. » Countryside Commission for England and Wales; National Park

areca » **betel-nut**

Arecibo Observatory [ari**see**boh] A radio astronomy observatory in Puerto Rico, built in 1963, where a natural crater has been lined with a metallic mesh to create the world's largest single radio telescope, 305 m in diameter. » observatory [i]; radio astronomy; telescope [i]

arena stage » **theatre in the round**

Areopagus [aray**o**pagus] In ancient Greece, the name for the hill in Athens which was the seat of the oldest council of state, and also for the council whose meetings took place there. The name literally means 'the hill of Ares' (the god of war). » Athens

Arequipa [aray**kee**pa] 16°25S 71°32W, pop (1981) 447 431. Capital of Arequipa department, S Peru; in a valley at the foot of El Misti volcano; altitude 2 380 m/7 808 ft; built on the site of an ancient Inca city; main commercial centre for S Peru; airfield; railway; two universities (1828, 1964); wool, textiles, soap; cathedral (1612, rebuilt 19th-c), La Compañía church, Puente Bolívar, Santa Catalina convent. » Peru [i]

Ares (mythology) [**air**reez] The Greek god of war, son of Zeus and Hera, often perceived as hostile, rather than as a national deity, as in other mythologies. He represents the sudden violence of battle, and often helps foreigners rather than the Greeks. » Mars (mythology)

arête [aret] (Fr 'edge') A sharp, jagged mountain ridge separating cirques or valleys. It is formed by glacial erosion, and often further weathered by frost shattering. » cirque; glaciation

Arethusa [are**thyoo**za] In Greek mythology, a nymph who was pursued by the river-god Alpheus from Arcadia in Greece to Ortygia in Sicily. The myth attempts to account for the freshwater fountain which appears in the harbour of Syracuse and is believed to have flowed under the Ionian Sea.

Aretino, Pietro [are**tee**noh] (1492–1557) Italian poet and satirist, born at Arezzo, Tuscany, who became known throughout Europe for his literary attacks on well-known figures. He distinguished himself at Rome by his wit and impudence, and secured even the papal patronage, though this was lost when he published his shameless *Sonetti Lussuriosi* (1524, Lewd Sonnets). His poetical works include five comedies and a tragedy, and he wrote several volumes of letters. » Italian literature; satire

Arezzo [a**ret**soh] 43°28N 11°53E, pop (1981) 92 105. Capital town of Arezzo province, Tuscany, NWC Italy; 80 km/50 ml SE of Florence; on the site of an Etruscan settlement; textiles, furniture, pottery, leather; antiques centre, trade in olive oil and wine; birthplace of Petrarch; Church of Santa Maria della

Pieve (11th–13th-c); Gothic cathedral (begun 1277); mediaeval jousting (Jun, Sep). » Petrarch; Tuscany

argali [**ah**galee] Wild sheep from the margins of the Gobi Desert; the largest living sheep (1.2 m/4 ft tall at the shoulder); pale brown with white rump; large curling horns on either side of head; also known as **argalis**, **Siberian argali**, or **Marco Polo's sheep**. (*Ovis ammon*.) » sheep

Argentina, official name **Argentine Republic**, **República Argentina** pop(1990e) 32 880 000; total area claimed 3 761 274 sq km/ 1 451 852 sq ml; area (American continent) 2 780 092 sq km/ 1 073 115 sq ml (excluding the Falkland Is); area (Antarctic continent) 964 250 sq km/372 200 sq ml (excluding S Georgia, Orkney Is, and S Sandwich Is). A republic of SE South America, divided into a Federal District (Buenos Aires), 22 provinces, and a Territory (Tierra del Fuego); bounded E by the S Atlantic, W by Chile, NE by Uruguay and Brazil, and N by Bolivia and Paraguay; Atlantic coastline 4 725 km/2 936 ml; capital Buenos Aires; chief towns Córdoba, Rosario, Mendoza, La Plata, San Miguel de Tucumán; timezone GMT −3; c.85% of population of European origin, 15% of mestizo/Indian origin; 90% Roman Catholic; official language, Spanish; currency, the austral of 100 centavos (formerly the peso).

Physical description. The Andes stretches the entire length of Argentina (N–S), forming the boundary with Chile; extends far to the E in N Argentina, width decreases towards the S; high ranges, plateaux, and rocky spurs in the NW; highest peak, Aconcagua (6 960 m/22 831 ft); a grassy, treeless plain (the *pampa*) to the E; uneven, arid steppes in the S; island of Tierra del Fuego, off the S tip; N Argentina drained by the Paraguay, Paraná, and Uruguay Rivers, which join in the R Plate estuary; several rivers flow to the Atlantic in the S; many lakes in the *pampa* and Patagonia regions, the largest being Lago Argentino (1 415 sq km/546 sq ml).

Climate. Most of Argentina is in the rainshadow of the Andes; dry steppe or elevated desert in the NW corner; moderately humid sub-tropical climate in the NE, with average annual temperature and rainfall 16°C and 500–1 000 mm/ 20–40 in at Buenos Aires; semi-arid central *pampa*, with temperatures ranging from tropical to moderately cool; rainshadow desert plateau extends to the coast between 40°S and 50°S; some rainfall prevents absolute barrenness; S part directly influenced by strong prevailing westerlies.

History and government. Settled in the 16th-c by the Spanish; independence declared in 1816, and United Provinces of the Río de la Plata established; federal constitution 1853, re-established in 1983 after successive military governments; acquisition of the Gran Chaco after war with Paraguay (1865–70); attempt to control the Falkland Is in 1982 failed following war with the UK; a bicameral National Congress, with a 254-member Chamber of Deputies elected for four years and a 46-member Senate elected for nine years; a president is elected for a 6-year term.

Economy. Considerable European settlement since the opening up of the pampas in the 19th-c; agricultural produce, chiefly cereals and meat; also potatoes, cotton, sugar cane, sugar beet, tobacco, linseed oil, rice, soya, grapes, olives, peanuts; meat processing, cement, fertilizer, steel, plastics, paper, pulp, textiles, motor vehicles; oil and gas, chiefly off the coast of Patagonia; coal, gold, silver, copper, iron ore, beryllium, mica, tungsten, manganese, limestone, uranium. » Buenos Aires; Chaco War; Falklands War; Gran Chaco; pampa(s); Patagonia; Peronism; Plate, River; Tierra del Fuego; RR24 national holidays; RR42 political leaders

Argentine-Brazilian War (1825–8) A war fought to decide the possession of the Banda Oriental, territory to the E of the R Uruguay occupied by Brazil in 1817. As a result of British pressure and mediation, the province became the independent republic of Uruguay (1828). » Uruguay [i]

Argolid The fertile plain between the mountains and the sea in the E Peloponnese near the town of Argos. It flourished particularly in Mycenaean times: besides Argos itself, Mycenae and Tiryns were located here. » Mycenae; Tiryns

argon Ar, element 18, boiling point −189°C. The commonest of the noble or rare gases, with no known compounds, it makes up about 1% of the Earth's atmosphere, and is fractionally distilled with difficulty from oxygen (boiling point −183°). It is used to provide inert atmospheres, especially inside incandescent light bulbs. » chemical elements; noble gases

argonaut » **paper nautilus**

Argonauts [**ah**guhnawts] In Greek mythology, the heroes who sailed in the ship *Argo* to find the Golden Fleece. Under Jason's leadership they sailed through the Symplegades (presumably the Dardanelles) and along the Black Sea coast to Colchis. Their return is variously described, and may have included a river-passage to the North Sea. » Golden Fleece; Jason; Symplegades

Argos [**ah**gohs, **ah**guhs] 37°38N 22°43E, pop(1981) 20 702. Ancient town in Peleponnese region, S Greece, in a fertile plain near the Gulf of Argolikos; involved in wars with Sparta, 7th–4th-c BC; railway; commercial and agricultural centre; many archaeological remains. » Greece [i]; Sparta (Greek history)

argument In mathematics, the angle made by the line joining the origin to the point P representing the complex number z. When the complex number is written in the form $r(\cos\theta + i\sin\theta)$, θ is the argument. » angle

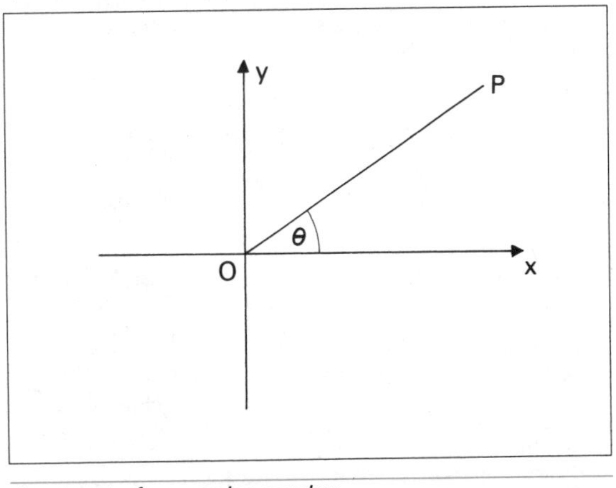

Argument of a complex number

Argus [**ah**guhs] In Greek mythology, **1** A watchman with a hundred eyes, appointed by Hera to watch over Io; after Argus was killed by Hermes, the eyes were placed in the tail of the peacock. » Io (mythology) **2** The name of Odysseus' dog.

Århus or **Aarhus** [**aw**hoos] 56°08N 10°11E, pop(1983) 248 509. Capital of Århus county, E Jutland, Denmark; in a wide bay of the Kattegat, S of Ålborg; cultural and educational hub of C Jylland; railway; university (1928); engineering, foodstuffs, machinery, textiles; Cathedral of St Clement (1201). » Denmark [i]

aria A song with an Italian text, especially one which forms part of a larger work, such as an opera, oratorio, or cantata. The 'da capo' or ternary structure (A-B-A) of most Baroque arias is often referred to simply as 'song form'. » Baroque (music); opera; song

Ariadne [aree**ad**nee] In Greek mythology, the daughter of the King of Crete (Minos). She enabled Theseus to escape from the labyrinth by giving him a ball of thread. He fled with her, but deserted her on the island of Naxos; there she eventually became the wife of Dionysus. » Minotaur; Theseus

Arianism » **Arius**

Arica [a**ree**ka] 18°28S 70°18W, pop(1982) 120 846. Port and capital of Arica province, Chile; on the Pacific coast, SW of La Paz, Bolivia; most northerly city in Chile; acquired from Peru, 1929; airport; railway; major trading outlet for Bolivia; oil pipeline with Bolivia; port trade, fishmeal, tourism; Pacific War museum; San Martín cathedral, customs house. » Chile [i]

arid zone A climatic zone in which potential evapotranspiration (the maximum loss of water, given an unlimited supply) exceeds precipitation. Geographers use an upper limit of 250 mm/10 in of annual rainfall to define the zone, which is found between latitudes 15° and 30°N and S of the Equator. Most of the world's hot deserts are found in the arid zone. » drought; evapotranspiration

Ariel The third largest satellite of Uranus: distance from the planet 191 000 km/119 000 ml; diameter 1 300 km/800 ml. It was discovered in 1851 by British amateur astronomer William Lassell (1799–1880). » Uranus (astronomy); RR4

Aries [**air**eez] (Lat 'ram') A constellation in the N sky; brightest star, Hamel. It is a spring sign of the zodiac, lying between Pisces and Taurus. The 'first point of Aries' is the place on the celestial sphere where the vernal equinox lies, but precession has pushed this into the neighbouring constellation, Pisces. » constellation; Pisces; precession of the equinoxes; zodiac [i]; RR8

aril The outgrowth surrounding a fertilized seed or ovule. It is often fleshy and brightly-coloured, as in the berry-like arils of the yew and spindle tree, but also hairy or spongy, as in the buoyant seeds of water lilies. » seed

Ariosto, Ludovico (1474–1533) Italian poet, born at Reggio nell'Emilia. He studied law, but abandoned it for poetry, while continuing to serve in the court of the Cardinal d'Este, who employed him in many negotiations. Here, in the space of 10 years, Ariosto produced his great poem, *Orlando Furioso* (1516, enlarged 3rd edition, 1532), the Roland epic that forms a continuation of Boiardo's *Orlando Innamorato*. He also wrote comedies, satires, sonnets, and a number of Latin poems. He died at Ferrara. » Boiardo; epic; Italian literature

Aristaeus [aris**tee**us] In Greek mythology, a minor deity of the countryside, who introduced bee-keeping, vines, and olives. He pursued Eurydice, the wife of Orpheus, who trod on a snake and died; in revenge her sister dryads killed his bees. Proteus told him to sacrifice cattle to appease the dryads, and in nine days he found bees generated in the carcasses. » dryad; Eurydice

Aristarchos of Samos (c.310–230 BC) Alexandrian astronomer who proved by observation that the Sun is much further from the Earth than the Moon. He also maintained that the Sun is the centre of the planetary system.

Aristarchus of Samothrace (c.215–145 BC) Greek grammarian and critic, known for his revision of Homer's epics. He was in charge of the Library of Alexandria for over 30 years. » grammar; Homer

Aristides [aris**ti**deez] (?–c.468 BC) Athenian statesman and general, whose reputation for fair dealing earned him the title 'the Just'. A respected general in the Greek-Persian Wars, he held command at Marathon (490 BC), Salamis (480 BC), and Plataea (479 BC). His greatest achievement was the organization of the Delian League after the defeat of the Persians. » Delian League; Persian Wars; Marathon, Battle of; Plataea **2**; Salamis (Greece)

Aristippus [aris**tip**us] (410–350 BC) Greek philosopher, born at Cyrene, a pupil of Socrates. He was founder of the Cyrenaic school of hedonism, which argued that pleasure was the highest good. He taught philosophy both in Athens and Aegina, but lived much of his life in Syracuse, at the court of Dionysius the tyrant, where he acquired the reputation of a philosophic voluptuary. » Cyrenaics; hedonism

Aristophanes [aris**tof**aneez] (c.448–c.388 BC) The greatest Greek comic dramatist. He is said to have written 54 plays, but only 11 are extant. His most sharply satirical works belong to his early period (up to c.425 BC): the *Acharnians*, *Knights*, *Clouds*, *Wasps*, and *Peace*. In later years he wrote the *Birds*, *Lysistrata*, *Thesmophoriazusae*, *Frogs*, *Ecclesiazusae*, and *Plutus*. » comedy; Greek literature; satire

Aristotle [aris**tot**l] (384–322 BC) Greek philosopher, scientist, and physician, born at Stagira, Macedonia. At 18 he went to Athens, where he became associated with Plato's Academy for 20 years. After Plato's death (347 BC), he left Athens (perhaps because he had not been appointed head of the Academy), and stayed in Assos (in Asia Minor) and in Mytilene (on Lesbos). In 342 BC he was invited by Philip of Macedon to educate Philip's son, Alexander, who for at least three years was his pupil. On his return to Athens (335 BC), he opened a school (the Lyceum). His followers were called 'Peripatetics', perhaps from his practice of walking up and down in the garden during his lectures. After Alexander's death, anti-Macedonian sentiment in Athens forced him to flee (322 BC); he escaped to Chalcis in Euboea, where he died.

He wrote the first systematic treatises on logic (eg *Categories*, *On Interpretation*, *Topics*); made major contributions to the study of natural change (*Physics*, *On the Heavens*), psychology (*On the Soul*), and biology (eg *On the Parts of Animals*); and wrote some of the most influential philosophical works in the history of thought (*Metaphysics*, *Nicomachean Ethics*, *Politics*, *Rhetoric*, *Poetics*). Major Aristotelian themes include the theses that the Earth is the centre of the eternal universe; everything beneath the orbit of the Moon is composed of earth, air, fire, and water, and is subject to generation, destruction, qualitative change, and rectilinear motion; everything above the orbit of the Moon is composed of aether, and is subject to no change but circular motion; all material things can be analysed in terms of their matter and their form, the latter factor constituting their essence; many scientific explanations are properly teleological; all animal functions require physical organs for their operation, with the possible exception of reason in humans; every moral virtue is a mean between two vices, one of excess, the other of deficiency; and humans are by nature political animals. His influence on subsequent thought was immense; in the Middle Ages, he was referred to simply as 'the Philosopher'. » Alexander the Great; Plato; teleology

arithmetic The practical skill of calculating with numbers, in contrast to number theory. The four operations addition, subtraction, multiplication, and division are defined over the set of all real numbers, and used essentially for practical results. Examples include the total cost of buying two items, one costing 30p and the other 40p (addition); the change received from a £5 note when buying an item costing £2 (subtraction); the cost of 4 litres of oil at 50p a litre (multiplication); and the number of papers that can be bought for £1 if one paper costs 20p (division). » mathematics; number theory

arithmetic and logic unit (ALU) The section of the central processing unit of a computer which performs arithmetical and logical operations on data. » central processing unit

arithmetic average/mean » **mean**

arithmetic sequence A sequence in which the difference between any one term and the next is constant; sometimes called an **arithmetic progression**. The term **arithmetic series** is now usually reserved for the sum of the terms of the arithmetic sequence. Thus the terms 1,4,7,10 form an arithmetic sequence;

1+4+7+10 is an arithmetic series. If the first term of an arithmetic sequence is a and the common difference is d, the sequence is $a, a+d, a+2d\ldots$, the nth term is $a+(n-1)d$, and the sum of the terms in the sequence is $\frac{1}{2}n[2a+(n-1)d]$. » arithmetic; geometric sequence

Arius (Gr **Areios**) (c.250–336) Founder of **Arianism**, born in Libya. He trained in Antioch, and became a presbyter in Alexandria. He claimed (c.319) that, in the doctrine of the Trinity, the Son was not co-equal or co-eternal with the Father, but only the first and highest of all finite beings, created out of nothing by an act of God's free will. He won some support, but was deposed and excommunicated in 321 by a synod of bishops at Alexandria. The subsequent controversy was fierce, so the Council of Nicaea (Nice) was called in 325 to settle the issue. Out of this came the definition of the absolute unity of the divine essence, and the equality of the three persons of the Trinity. Arius was banished, but recalled in 334, and died in Constantinople. After his death the strife spread more widely abroad: the West was mainly orthodox, the East largely Arian or semi-Arian; but despite later revivals the doctrine was largely suppressed by the end of the 4th-c. » elder (religion); Nicaea, Councils of; Trinity

Arizona pop (1987e) 3 386 000; area 295 249 sq km/114 000 sq ml. State in SW USA, divided into 14 counties; the 'Grand Canyon State'; Spanish exploration, 1539; part of New Spain (1598–1821), then included in newly-independent Mexico; acquired by the USA in the Treaty of Guadalupe Hidalgo (1848) and the Gadsden Purchase (1853); a separate territory, 1863; until 1886 frequently attacked by Apache Indians (under Cochise, then Geronimo); joined the Union as the 48th state, 1912; capital, Phoenix; other major cities Tucson, Mesa and Tempe; bounded S by Mexico; rivers include the Colorado (forms most of the W border), Gila, and Salt; the Hoover Dam causes the Colorado R to swell into L Mead; several mountain ranges (highest the San Francisco Mts); highest point Humphreys Peak (3 862 m/12 670 ft); the Colorado Plateaux (N) are high, dry plains incised by deep canyons (notably the Grand Canyon on the Colorado R); to the S are desert basins interspersed with bare mountain peaks, then relatively low, desert plains; a huge area of national and state forest in the centre; scant rainfall and aridity; cattle on irrigated land; dairy products, cotton, lettuce, hay; computer equipment, aerospace components, timber products, machinery; produces two-thirds of the nation's copper supply; tourism the most important industry (Grand Canyon, Petrified Forest, meteor craters); Kitt Peak National Observatory; Navajo, Hopi, Apache, Papago, and other Indian reservations; largest Indian population in the USA. » American Indians; Grand Canyon; Phoenix (USA); United States of America [i]; RR38

Arjuna [**ah**juna] An Indian hero. In the *Bhagavadgita*, he hesitates before entering the battle, knowing the killing which will ensue. His charioteer, Krishna, urges him to fulfil the action which is his duty as a warrior, explaining that the whole universe needs the fulfilment of actions which advance God's will. » Bhagavadgita

ark » **Ark of the Covenant; Noah**

Ark of the Covenant A portable wooden chest overlaid with gold and having a cherub with extended wings mounted at each end of the golden lid (the 'mercy seat'). In the Hebrew Bible/Old Testament it is described as having many successive functions – containing the two tablets of the Decalogue, serving as a symbol of the divine presence guiding Israel, and acting as a safeguard in war. It was constructed under Moses, taken into battle in David's time, housed in the Temple under Solomon, but is now lost. Torah scrolls are still kept in containers called 'arks' in Jewish synagogues. » cherubim; Moses; Old Testament; Solomon (Old Testament); Ten Commandments; Torah

ark shell A sedentary bivalve mollusc with two similar, typically trapezoidal shells (valves); adults typically attached to a substrate surface by tough filaments (*byssus* threads); c.250 species, mostly marine. (Class: *Pelecypoda*. Order: *Arcoida*.) » bivalve; mollusc

Arkansas [**ah(r)**kansaw] pop (1987e) 2 388 000; area 137 749 sq km/53 187 sq ml. State in SC USA, divided into 75 counties; the 'Land of Opportunity'; the first White settlement established by the French as part of French Louisiana, 1686; ceded to the US as part of the Louisiana Purchase, 1803; included in the Territory of Missouri, 1812; became a separate territory, 1819; joined the Union as the 25th state, 1836; seceded, 1861; re-admitted, 1868; capital, Little Rock; other chief cities Fort Smith, North Little Rock, Pine Bluff; rivers include the Mississippi (forms the E border), Red (part of SW border), and Arkansas; the Boston Mts, part of the Ozark Plateau, rise in the NW, and the Ouachita Mts in the W; highest point Mt Magazine (860 m/2 821 ft); the mountainous region is bisected by the Arkansas R valley; extensive plains in the S and E; over half the state covered by commercial forest; many lakes; poultry, soybeans, rice (the nation's leading producer), cattle, dairy, cotton; processed foods, electrical equipment, paper, timber products, chemicals; the nation's leading bauxite producer; petroleum, natural gas; a major tourist area; resistance to school desegregation made Little Rock a focus of world attention in 1957. » bauxite; civil rights; Little Rock; United States of America [i]; RR38

Arkansas River [**ah(r)**kansaw, ah(r)**kan**sas] River in SC USA; rises in the Rocky Mountains, Colorado; flows ESE through Kansas, Oklahoma, and Arkansas; joins the Mississippi S of Memphis; length 2 330 km/1 450 ml; major tributaries the Cimmaron, Canadian, Neosho, Verdigris; navigable for its length in Arkansas. » United States of America [i]

Arkwright, Sir Richard (1732–92) British cotton-spinning inventor, born at Preston, Lancashire. Of humble origin, he became a barber in Bolton, later (with John Kay) devoting himself to inventions in cotton-spinning. In 1768 he set up his celebrated *spinning-frame* in Preston – the first machine that could produce cotton thread of sufficient strength to be used as warp. He introduced several mechanical processes into his factories, and many of his rivals copied his designs. Popular opinion went against him on the ground that his inventions reduced the need for labour; and in 1779 his large mill near Chorley was destroyed by a mob. Knighted in 1786, he died at Cromford, Derbyshire. » cotton [i]; spinning

Arles [ahl] or **Arles-sur-Rhône** 43°41N 4°38E, pop (1982) 50 772. Old town in Bouches-du-Rhône department, SE France; 72 km/45 ml NE of Marseille, at head of the Rhône delta; capital of Gaul, 4th-c; formerly an important crossroads and capital of Provence; railway; boatbuilding, metalwork, foodstuffs, hats; Roman remains, including a huge arena and theatre (a world heritage site), 11th-c cathedral; associations with van Gogh and Gauguin; several art museums. » Gauguin; Gaul; Provence; van Gogh

Arlington, Henry Bennet, 1st Earl of (1618–85) English statesman, born at Arlington, Middlesex, and educated at Westminster School and Oxford. A member of the Cabal ministry under Charles II, and Secretary of State (1662–74), he was created Earl of Arlington in 1672. In 1674 he was impeached for embezzlement, and although cleared, resigned and became Lord Chamberlain. He negotiated the Triple Alliance against France (1668), and helped to develop the English party system. He died at Euston, Suffolk. » Cabal; Charles II (of England)

Arlington pop (1980) 152 599; area 68 sq km/26 sq ml. County of Virginia, USA, a suburb of Washington, DC; site of the **Arlington National Cemetery** (1920) with a memorial amphitheatre and Tomb of the Unknown Soldier; Pentagon Building; Washington National Airport. » Pentagon; Virginia; Washington (DC)

arm A term commonly used to denote the whole of the upper limb; more precisely, in anatomy, the region between the shoulder and elbow joints, distinguished from the *forearm* (between the elbow and wrist joints), and the *hand* (beyond the wrist joint). The arm articulates with the trunk via the *pectoral girdle* (the shoulder blades and clavicle). The bones are the *humerus* in the arm, the *radius* (on the outside) and *ulna* (on the inside) in the forearm, the *carpals* in the wrist region, and the *metacarpals* and *phalanges* in the hand. The muscles on the front of the arm and forearm cause flexion of the shoulder, elbow, wrist, and digits (fingers and thumb). The muscles on the back of the arm and forearm are *extensors*, causing opposite movements at these places. » hand; pronation; shoulder; supination; wrist; Plate XII

armadillo [ahma**dil**oh] A nocturnal mammal (an edentate), found from S America to S USA; long snout and tubular ears; head and body covered with bony plates; large front claws for digging; eats ants, termites, and other small animals. (Family: *Dasypodidae*, 20 species.) » Edentata

Armageddon [ahma**ged**uhn] A place mentioned in the New Testament (*Rev* 16.16) as the site of the final cosmic battle between the forces of good and evil in the last days. The name is possibly a corruption of 'the mountains of Megiddo' or some other unknown location in Israel. » eschatology; New Testament; Revelation, Book of

Armagh (county) [ah**mah**], Gaelic **Ard Mhacha** pop (1981) 118 820; area 1 254 sq km/484 sq ml. County in SE Northern Ireland, divided into two districts; bounded S and SW by the Republic of Ireland; rises to 577 m/1 893 ft at Slieve Gullion; county town, Armagh; other chief towns include Lurgan and Portadown; potatoes, flax, apples, linen. » Armagh (town); Northern Ireland [i]

Armagh (town) [ah**mah**] 54°21N 6°39W, pop (1981) 12 700. County town of Armagh, SE Northern Ireland; seat of the kings of Ulster, 400 BC–AD 333; religious centre of Ireland in the 5th-c, when St Patrick was made archbishop here; Protestant and Catholic archbishoprics; textiles (linen), engineering, shoes, food processing; St Patrick's Cathedral (Roman Catholic, 1840–73), observatory (1791), Royal School (1627); Navan Fort nearby, palace of the kings of Ulster. » Armagh (county); Patrick, St

Armani, Giorgio [ah**mah**nee] (1935–) Italian fashion designer, born at Piacenza. He studied medicine in Milan, but after military service worked in a department store until becoming a designer for Nino Cerruti in 1961. He set up his own company with Sergio Galecti in 1975, designing first for men, then for women also. » fashion

Armenia (republic) or **Armeniya** [ah**mee**nia], Russ **Armyanskaya** pop (1989) 3 288 000; area 29 800 sq km/11 500 sq ml. Republic in S Transcaucasia, bounded SE by Iran, and NW by Turkey; mountainous, rising to 4 090 m/13 418 ft at Mt Aragats (W); largest lake, Ozero Sevan (E); chief river, the Araks; proclaimed a Soviet Socialist Republic, 1920; constituent republic of the USSR, 1936; declaration of independence, 1990; lays claim to Turkish Armenia; dispute with neighbouring Azerbaijan over Nagorny Karabakh region; capital, Yerevan; building materials, chemicals, carpets, electrical engineering, foodstuffs, machine tools, textiles; hydroelectric power on R Razdan; grains, cotton, tropical fruits, grapes, olives, livestock. » Armenia (Turkey); Transcaucasia; Yerevan

Armenia (Turkey) [ah**mee**nia], ancient **Minni** Ancient kingdom largely occupying the present-day Van region of E Turkey and parts of NW Iran and the republic of Armenia; SE of the Black Sea and SW of the Caspian Sea; ruled by the Ottoman Turks from 1514; E territory ceded to Persia, 1620; further districts lost to Russia, 1828–9; today Turkish Armenia comprises the NE provinces of Turkey; chief towns, Kars, Erzurum, Erzincan; Armenian nationalist movement developed in the 19th-c, with terrorist activities since the 1970s. » Armenia (republic); Armenians; Turkey [i]

Armenians A people from Armenia, now NE Turkey and the republic of Armenia. Of Indo-European origin, they speak a language of that family with some Caucasian features, and are Christians, affiliated to the Armenian Catholic branch of the Roman Catholic Church, or the Monophysite Armenian Apostolic (Orthodox) Church. Their highly developed ancient culture, particularly in fine art, architecture, and sculpture, reached its zenith in the 14th-c. Highly nationalistic, their resentment of foreign domination during the 19th-c provoked their Russian and Turkish rulers. During World War 1, the Turks deported two-thirds of Armenians (1.75 million) to Syria and Palestine; 600 000 were either killed or died of starvation during the journey; later, many settled in Europe, America, and the USSR. Today 4.15 million live in the republics of the former Soviet Union, including 2.7 million in Armenia; very few still live in Turkey. » Armenia (republic; Turkey); Indo-European languages; Monophysites

armillary sphere A celestial globe, first used by the Greek astronomers, in which the sky is represented by a skeleton framework of intersecting circles, the Earth being at the centre. In antiquity, it was of major importance for measuring star positions. » astronomy

Arminius, Jacobus, properly **Jakob Hermandszoon** (1560–1609) Dutch Protestant theologian, born at Oudewater. He studied at Utrecht, Leyden, Geneva, and Basle, was ordained in 1588, and became professor of theology at Leyden in 1603. He was opposed to the Calvinistic doctrine of predestination, arguing that God bestows forgiveness on all who repent and believe in Christ. He died at Leyden. His teaching was formalized in the 'Remonstrance' of 1610, refuted at the Synod of Dort (1618–19); but 'Remonstrants' continued in being, and **Arminianism** influenced the development of religious thought all over Europe. » Calvin, John; predestination; Protestantism; Remonstrants; Wesley, John

Armistice Day The anniversary of the day (11 Nov 1918) on which World War 1 ended, marked by a two-minute silence at 11 o'clock, the hour when the fighting stopped (the armistice agreement having been signed six hours earlier); replaced after World War 2 by Remembrance Day. » Remembrance Day; Veterans' Day; World War 1

Armitage, Kenneth (1916–) British sculptor, born in Leeds. He studied at the Royal College of Art and the Slade School (1937–9), and exhibited at the Venice Biennale in 1952 with other British sculptors. His bronzes are usually of semi-abstract figures, united into a group by stylized clothing. » English art; sculpture

Armory show An art exhibition, officially entitled 'The International Exhibition of Modern Art', held at the 69th Regiment Armory in New York, 1913. It introduced modern art to the USA. » modern art

armoured car Typically a four-wheel-drive, light-armoured fighting vehicle with protection against small-arms fire, armed with a machine gun or small calibre cannon in a rotating turret. The first armoured cars were developed just before 1914, and their roles today on the battlefield are largely unchanged – that of reconnaissance and rear area protection. » armoured fighting vehicle

armoured fighting vehicle (AFV) A generic term for combat vehicles such as tanks, armoured cars, armoured personnel carriers, and infantry fighting vehicles which have armour protection against hostile fire. » armoured car; tank

arms, coats of » heraldry [i]

arms control Any restraint exercised by one or more countries over the level, type, deployment, and use of their armaments, occurring through agreement or unilaterally. Its aim is to reduce the possibility of war and/or reduce its consequences. It is premised on the notion that states can reduce arms to their mutual benefit, including that of reducing the burden of costs, without abandoning their hostile stance. Originating in the USA in the 1950s, it has gained increasing acceptance as a policy: several major agreements have been reached about nuclear missiles, as well as about biological and chemical weapons. » arms race; disarmament; SALT; START

arms race The continual accumulation in terms of numbers and capacity of military weapons by two or more states, in the belief that only by maintaining a superiority will their national security be guaranteed. Many maintain that the continual growth in weapons becomes a threat to security by increasing international tension and distrust. » arms control

Armstrong, Henry originally **Henry Jackson** (1912–88) US boxer, born at Columbus, Mississippi, the only man to hold world titles at three weights simultaneously. In August 1938 he held the featherweight, lightweight, and welterweight titles. In 1940 he narrowly failed to become the first man to hold four different titles when he fought a draw with Cerefino Garcia for the middleweight title. He had the last of his 175 fights in 1945; having won 144 and drawn 9. After a period in which drink ruled his life after his retirement, he became an ordained Baptist minister, and died in poverty in Los Angeles. » boxing [i]

Armstrong, Louis, byname **Satchmo** (1898 or 1900–71) US jazz trumpeter and singer, born in New Orleans. Having learned to play the cornet in a waifs' home, he moved to Chicago in 1922 to join Joe (King) Oliver's band. His melodic inventiveness, expressed with uninhibited tone and range on the trumpet, established the central role of the improvising soloist in jazz, especially in a series of recordings known as the 'Hot Fives' and 'Hot Sevens' (1925–8). Thereafter, every jazz musician emulated Armstrong's melodic style and rhythmic sense. He was also a popular singer (hit recordings include 'When It's Sleepy Time Down South', 'Mack the Knife', 'Hello Dolly!') and entertainer, in such films as *Pennies from Heaven* (1936), *Cabin in the Sky* (1943), and *High Society* (1956), but he remained primarily a jazz musician, touring the world with his New Orleans-style sextet. He died in New York City. » improvisation; jazz; trumpet

Armstrong, Neil (Alden) (1930–) US astronaut, born at Wapakoneta, Ohio, educated there and at Purdue University. A fighter pilot in Korea and later a civilian test pilot, in 1962 he was chosen as an astronaut. In 1966 he commanded Gemini 8, and as commander of Apollo 11 in 1969 became the first man to set foot on the Moon. » Apollo programme; astronaut

Armstrong-Jones, Anthony » **Snowdon, 1st Earl of**

army The branch of the armed forces configured and equipped to make war on land. The term *army*, while referring to a nation's land forces, is also conferred on large military formations engaged in a particular theatre of war (the British 'Eighth Army', for example). These are subdivided into Army Corps and Divisions, and may be combined for command purposes into Army Groups. » Black Watch; Foreign Legion; Gurkhas; Horse Guards; janissaries; Marines; militia; Red Army; SAS; women's services

army ant A tropical ant with very reduced or absent eyes. It forms enormous colonies characterized by group foraging behaviour and frequent changes in nest site. A bivouac nest formed by living ants protects the wingless queen and the brood. (Order: *Hymenoptera*. Family: *Formicidae*.) » ant

Arnauld, Antoine [**ah**noh] (1612–94) French theologian and philosopher, who became famous for his controversial writings against the Jesuits and in defence of the Jansenists. He studied at the Sorbonne, becoming doctor and priest. As religious director of the nuns of Port Royal des Champs, he and other 'Port Royalists' produced many works on grammar, geometry, and logic. Under Jesuit influence, the king issued an order for his arrest; he withdrew to Brussels, where he died. » Jansen; Jesuits; Port Royal

Arne, Thomas (Augustine) (1710–78) British composer, born in London, and educated at Eton. He began his musical career as a violinist, producing his first opera, *Rosamond*, in 1733. He wrote over 50 operas and other works, including (as composer to Drury Lane Theatre) settings of several Shakespearean songs. His best-known work is *Rule, Britannia*, from *The Masque of Alfred*. He died in London. » opera

Arnhem [**ah**nuhm] 52°00N 5°53E, pop (1984e) 291 399. Capital city of Gelderland province, E Netherlands; on the right bank of the lower Rhine, 53 km/33 ml ESE of Utrecht; seat of the law courts, several government agencies, and the provincial government; on the site of a Roman settlement; charter, 1233; heavily damaged in World War 2; scene of unsuccessful airborne landing of British troops (Sep 1944); railway; tin-smelting, artificial fibres, salt, pharmaceuticals, chemicals, engineering; Grote Kerk (15th-c), town hall (1540), St Walburgis-basiliek (1422), Dutch open-air museum (N), safari park, Burgers Zoo. » Netherlands, The [i]

Arnhem Land [**ah**nuhm] The peninsular plateau in N Australia, E of Darwin; named after the Dutch ship which arrived here in 1618; chief town Nhulunbuy; now contains Kakadu national park, and a reserve for Aborigines; bauxite and uranium mining. » Aborigines; Darwin

arni » **water buffalo**

Arnold, Benedict (1741–1801) US general and turncoat, born at Norwich, Connecticut. In the War of Independence he joined the colonial forces, and for his gallantry at the siege of Quebec (1775) was made a brigadier-general. He also fought with distinction at Ridgefield and Saratoga, and in 1778 was placed in command of Philadelphia. Resentment at being passed over for promotion, followed by marriage to a woman of loyalist sympathies, led him to conspire with John André to betray West Point. When André was captured, Arnold fled to the British lines, and was given a command in the royal army. After the war he lived in obscurity in London, where he died. » American Revolution; André, John

Arnold, Malcolm (1921–) British composer, born in Northampton, and educated at the Royal College of Music, London. His musical career began as trumpeter in the London Philharmonic Orchestra. His compositions achieved immediate success for their spontaneous lyrical sincerity, high spirits, and great professional skill in structure and orchestration. They include eight symphonies, ten concertos, ballets, operas, and much film music.

Arnold, Matthew (1822–88) British poet and critic, born at Laleham, Middlesex, the eldest son of Dr Arnold of Rugby. Educated at Winchester, Rugby, and Oxford, he became an inspector of schools (1851–86) and professor of poetry at Oxford (1857–67). Apart from his many poems, he wrote several works of criticism, such as *Culture and Anarchy* (1869), and religious belief, such as *God and the Bible* (1875). He died in Liverpool. » English literature; literary criticism

Arnold, Thomas (1795–1842) British scholar, born at East Cowes, I of Wight, the headmaster of Rugby School, and father of Matthew Arnold. Educated at Winchester and Oxford, he took deacon's orders (1818), then settled at Laleham, near Staines. He became headmaster of Rugby in 1828, reforming the school system (especially by introducing sports and ending bullying), and becoming both loved and feared (as recounted in Thomas Hughes' *Tom Brown's Schooldays*). He wrote several volumes of sermons, as well as works on classical and modern history. He became regius professor of modern history at Oxford in 1841, but died soon after, and was buried in Rugby Chapel. » Arnold, Matthew

Arnold of Brescia [**bray**sha] (c.1100–55) Italian churchman and politician, born at Brescia, Venice, and possibly educated in France under Abelard. He adopted the monastic life; but his preaching against the wealth and power of the Church led to his banishment from Italy (1139). He returned to Rome in 1145 and became involved in an insurrection against the papal government, which continued for some 10 years. When this movement failed, he fled, but was captured by the forces of Emperor Frederick Barbarossa, brought to Rome, condemned for heresy, and hanged. » Abelard; Frederick I (Emperor)

aromatic compound A compound related to benzene, with bonding usually represented as alternate single and double bonds, but more stable than that arrangement would predict. Unlike an aliphatic compound with multiple bonds, it will react more often by substitution than by addition. Its name is derived from the odour of benzene. » aliphatic compound; benzene [i]; hydrocarbons

Aroostook War (1838–9) A US/Canadian boundary dispute between the state of Maine and the province of New Brunswick, leading to near-hostilities. It was resolved by a temporary truce, and permanently settled by the Webster-Ashburton Treaty (1842). » Canada [i]

Arp, Jean or **Hans** (1887–1966) French (Alsatian) sculptor, painter, and poet, born in Strasbourg. He was one of the founders of the Dada movement in Zürich in 1916. During the 1920s he produced many abstract reliefs in wood, but after 1928 worked increasingly in three dimensions. He was a major influence on organic abstract sculpture, based on natural forms. In 1921 he married the artist, **Sophie Tauber** (1889–1943). After World War 2, he wrote several poems and essays, and died in Basle, Switzerland. » Dada; French art; sculpture

arquebus A firearm dating from the 15th-c, a development of the hand cannon, in outline a forerunner of the musket. Fired in action by a flame held to the touch-hole, the weapon was supported by a forked rest holding up the barrel at the operator's chest height. » firearms; musket

Arrabal, Fernando (1932–) Spanish dramatist and novelist, born in Melilla, Spanish Morocco. He studied law in Madrid, then drama in Paris, where he settled (1954), unable to tolerate the repression of Franco's Spain, which has inspired much of his writing. His first play, *Pique-nique en campagne* (1958,

Picnic on the Battlefield) established its author in the tradition of the Theatre of the Absurd. He coined the term 'panic theatre', intended to disorder the senses by shock, and has employed sadism and blasphemy to accomplish its aims. He has also published poetry, novels, screenplays, and various works of nonfiction. » absurdism; Spanish literature

Arran Island in Strathclyde region, W Scotland; separated from W coast mainland by the Firth of Clyde; area 430 sq km/166 sq ml; rises to 874 m/2 867 ft at Goat Fell; chief towns, Brodick, Lamlash, Lochranza; ferry links between Brodick and Ardrossan and Lochranza and Claonaig; a major tourist area; Brodick castle and country park, Bronze Age Moss Farm Road stone circle, 13th–14th-c Lochranza castle. » Scotland [i]; Strathclyde

arrangement A transcription or reworking of a musical composition, usually (but not always) for a different performing medium. Before about 1600, arrangements (or 'intabulations') of vocal music formed a major part of the keyboard and lute repertory, and in more recent times instruments such as the accordion and the guitar, for which only a limited original repertory exists, have had to rely largely on arrangements. Since the 18th-c at least, publishers have seized on arrangements as a means of increasing their sales of a popular work. Such arrangements often fail to respect the composer's intentions, but the type of arrangement which is perhaps most despised by musicians today is that which aims to bring older music 'up to date' (even though some of the greatest composers have engaged in this practice, as in Mozart's arrangements of some Handel oratorios). Despite its long history, the practice of musical arrangement tends to divide present-day musicians on both aesthetic and ethical grounds, and some look favourably only on those arrangements in which a creative intention is present. » music

Arras [aras], Fr [ara] 50°17N 2°46E, pop (1982) 45 364. Old frontier town and capital of Pas-de-Calais department, N France, between Lille and Amiens; formerly famous for its tapestries; railway; bishopric; agricultural equipment, engineering, sugar beet, vegetable oil, hosiery; town hall (16th-c), cathedral (18th-c); birthplace of Robespierre; many war cemeteries nearby; Vimy Ridge memorial, 10 km/6 ml N. » Artois; Robespierre; Vimy Ridge

Arrau, Claudio [arow] (1903–) Chilean pianist, born at Chillán. He studied in Berlin, and lived there from 1925 to 1940, since when his home has been in the USA. He is noted for his thoughtful, deeply-felt interpretations of the 19th-c solo repertory. » piano

array processor A particular type of digital computer which allows arrays of numbers to be simultaneously processed. In suitable applications, this can lead to marked increases in computing speeds. » digital computer

arrest The stopping and detaining of a person suspected of a criminal offence. Arrests are carried out mainly by the police, but a citizen's arrest is possible in certain circumstances (eg if a breach of the peace is being committed). A person wrongly arrested may bring civil proceedings for false imprisonment. In English law (but not, for example, in the USA), a distinction is drawn between serious offences for which arrest may be made without a warrant (**arrestable offences**) and relatively minor offences for which a warrant is always required. Arrestable offences include those for which a person not previously convicted might be imprisoned for five years or more. Attempts to commit such crimes are included in the definition. » civil law; criminal law; murder

Arrhenius, Svante (August) (1859–1927) Swedish physicist and chemist, born near Uppsala. He became professor of physics at Stockholm in 1895, a director of the Nobel Institute in 1905, and was awarded the 1903 Nobel Prize for Chemistry. He is best known for his work on the dissociation theory of electrolytes, and on reaction rates, and was the first to recognize the 'greenhouse effect' on climate. He died in Stockholm. » electrolysis [i]; greenhouse effect

arrhythmia [ari**th**mia] A disturbance of the normal regular rhythm of the heart. There are many types, some of which are harmless, but a few are a serious threat to life. » heart [i]

Arrian, Lat **Flavius Arrianus** (c.95–180) Greek historian, a native of Nicomedia in Bithynia, who served in the Roman army, and was appointed by Hadrian Governor of Cappadocia. His chief work is the *Anabasis Alexandrou*, a history of the campaigns of Alexander the Great, which has come down to us almost entire.

arrow-poison frog A slender frog, native to C and S America; often brightly coloured; inhabits woodland; eggs laid on ground; adults carry tadpoles to water; skin very poisonous; local Indians rub arrow-heads on live frogs to poison the tips for hunting; also known as **poison-arrow frog**. Some S American true toads of genus *Atelopus* are called **arrow-poison toads**. (Family: *Dendrobatidae*, 116 species.) » frog; Plate IX

Arrow War, also known as the **Second Opium War** (1856–60) A conflict between Britain and China, which began when the Hong Kong-registered ship *Arrow*, flying the British flag, was boarded at Canton (Guangzhou) by the Chinese, who arrested most of the crew for piracy. British warships and troops then attacked Canton and were initially repulsed, but a combined British and French force took it the following year, and proceeded north, threatening Beijing (Peking). The Treaties of Tientsin (Tianjin) that concluded hostilities opened additional ports to foreign trade, legalized the opium traffic, and facilitated Christian missionary activity. » Opium Wars; treaty ports

arrow worm A slender invertebrate animal with a translucent body bearing lateral and tail fins; predatory; head armed with several paired spines to catch prey; c.70 marine species, mostly found in open water. (Phylum: *Chaetognatha*.) » worm

arrowroot A type of starch obtained from the tuberous roots of several plants. The most important is probably **West Indian arrowroot** (*Maranta arundinacea*), a rhizomatous perennial growing to 2 m/6½ ft with leaves with sheathing bases, and sepals and petals in threes; native to S America, and cultivated in New World tropics for edible starch. **East Indian arrowroot** is obtained from *Curcuma angustifolia*, a relative of ginger, and from *Tacca pinnatifida*. **Queensland arrowroot** is from a species of canna, *Canna edulis*. **Portland arrowroot**, inedible and formerly used for laundry, was obtained from lords-and-ladies (*Arum maculatum*). » canna; perennial; rhizome; root (botany); starch; tuber

Arrowsmith, Aaron (1750–1823) English cartographer, born at Winston, Durham. By 1790 he had established a great map-making business in London, where he died. His nephew, **John** (1790–1873), was also an eminent cartographer. » cartography

ars antiqua A term used to distinguish the music of the late 12th-c and 13th-c from that of the succeeding period. It is particularly associated with the theorists and composers of the Notre Dame school in Paris, notably Léonin and Pérotin. » ars nova

ars nova In music, a term for the 'new art' of the 14th-c, as distinct from that of the preceding period. Its principal representatives were the composer Guillaume de Machaut (c.1300–77), and the theorist Philippe de Vitry (1291–1361). » ars antiqua; Machaut, Guillaume de

arsenic As, element 33. A grey metalloid in the nitrogen family, usually showing oxidation states 3 and 5. It is used in some lead alloys and in semiconductors, especially gallium arsenide (GaAs). The name is commonly applied to arsenic (III) oxide (As_2O_3), the highly poisonous white arsenic of rodent control and detective novels. » arsenicals; chemical elements; metalloids; nitrogen

arsenicals [ahs**e**niklz] Drugs developed in the early 20th-c by German scientist Paul Ehrlich, who systematically screened a series of organic arsenic-containing substances in the search for a drug effective in trypanosomiasis (sleeping sickness). Number 606 in the series was most effective, and the drug is often known as '606'. It was called **salvarsan**, which was subsequently found to be effective against spirochaete infections. In 1910 it was shown to cure syphilis, and was used thus until replaced by penicillin in 1945. Arsenicals have generally been abandoned in favour of newer, safer drugs. » arsenic; Ehrlich; trypanosomiasis

arsine [**ah**seen] AsH_3, boiling point -55°C. A gaseous hydride of arsenic, formed by reducing solutions of arsenic compounds. » arsenic; hydride; Marsh test; oxidation

arson The unlawful destruction of, or damage to, property by fire; known as *fire-raising* in Scotland. In English law, there is another criminal offence covering unlawful damage, however caused, but nonetheless the relevant statute preserves the separate crime of arson, even though this seems to add nothing to the scope of the law.

art Originally, 'skill' (of any kind), a meaning the word still has in many everyday contexts. Modern usage referring especially to painting, drawing, or sculpture emerged by c.1700, but significantly Dr Johnson's primary meaning of the word (1755) was still 'The power of doing something not taught by nature and instinct; as to *walk* is natural, to *dance* is an art.' This contrast between art and nature goes back to the Middle Ages. Nor did Johnson's five other meanings of the word make any reference to what we nowadays call 'the visual arts'. However, the modern sense of 'Art' (with a capital 'A') and of an artist as a creative genius of a special kind, does seem to have made headway during Johnson's lifetime. The related concept of Fine Arts, considered as sharing common principles and distinct from science, religion, or the practical concerns of everyday life, also emerged in the 18th-c, together with a new subject, Aesthetics, 'the philosophy of art'. The artist was now considered distinct from the artisan, or skilled manual worker. By the 19th-c, art was normally (instead of occasionally) associated with the imaginative and creative production of objects for abstract contemplation, with no useful function. The highly significant phrases, 'artistic temperament' and 'artistic sensibility' occur first in the mid-19th-c. The definition of Art has become controversial again in the 20th-c. New forms, such as film, television, street theatre, pop music, and happenings, are claimed by some to be Art, by others not. » abstract/auto-destructive/biomorphic/Body/computer/Conceptual/concrete/figurative/folk/kinetic/Minimal/modern/Op/permutational/Pop/psychedelic art; Aboriginal/African/Assyrian/Babylonian / Byzantine / Canadian / Carolingian / Celtic / Chinese / Christian / Coptic / Dutch / Egyptian / English / Etruscan/Flemish/French/German/Gothic/Greek/Indian/Islamic/Italian/Japanese/Mexican/Minoan/Mycenaean/Ottonian/Persian/Pre-Columbian/Roman/Romanesque/Russian/Spanish/Sumerian/Tibetan art; Aesthetic Movement; Art Brut/Deco/Nouveau; Baroque (art and architecture); Constructivism; Cubism; Dada; Expressionism; functionalism (art and architecture); Futurism; Impressionism (art); Luminism; Neoclassicism (art); Neoexpressionism; Mannerism; Orphism; Purism; Realism (art and literature); Rococo; Romanticism (art); Suprematism; Surrealism; Vorticism; aesthetics; anti-art; Fine arts; school (art); Plate XI

Art Brut [ah **broo**] A term coined by French painter Jean Dubuffet (1901–85) for the art of untrained people, especially mental patients, prisoners, and socially dispossessed persons generally. Dubuffet built up a collection of about 5 000 such items, presented in 1972 to the city of Lausanne. » art

Art Deco [art **dek**oh] A term abbreviated from the Paris Exposition Internationale des Arts Décoratifs et Industriels Modernes, 1925. It has come to refer to decorative arts of the 1920s and 1930s generally, and the 'modernistic' style associated with them: a mixture of Cubism, Art Nouveau, and the Russian ballet, with a fondness for strident colours and for the streamlining found in aircraft and automobile design, but used non-functionally for household objects such as wireless sets, tables, and teapots. » art; Art Nouveau; Cubism

art for art's sake » **Aesthetic Movement**

art gallery » **Hermitage; Louvre; Metropolitan Museum of Art; museum; National Gallery; National Gallery of Art; National Portrait Gallery; Pitti Palace; Prado; Rijksmuseum; Tate Gallery; Tretyakov Gallery; Uffizi**

Art Nouveau [ah noo**voh**] Literally 'new art' which flourished from c.1890 to c.1905, mainly in the decorative arts, characterized by naturalistic plant and flower motifs, and writhing patterns of sinuous, curling lines; called *Jugendstil* in Germany, *Sezessionstil* in Austria, and *Stile Liberty* (after the shop in Regent St, London) in Italy. Typical products include the drawings of Beardsley, the furniture of Mackintosh, the architecture of Gaudí, the jewellery of Lalique, the glassware of Louis Comfort Tiffany (1848–1933), and the Paris Metro stations by Hector Guimard (1867–1942). » art; Beardsley; Mackintosh; Gaudí; Lalique

Artaud, Antonin [ah**toh**] (1896–1948) French poet, actor, theatre director, and theorist of the Surrealist movement, born in Marseilles. From 1920, he worked in Paris as an actor, both in theatre and film, and became an active member of the Surrealists (1924–6). His influential *Le Théâtre et son double* (1938, The Theatre and its Double) was published two months after he had been taken into a psychiatric hospital in Rouen. He remained in the custody of various institutions until shortly before his death in Paris. » Surrealism; theatre

Artaxerxes I [arta**zerk**zeez], or **Ardashir** (c.211–42) King of Persia (224–42), destroyer of the Arsacid dynasty of Parthia, and founder of the new Persian dynasty of the Sassanids. A vigorous ruler, his expansionist policies brought him twice into conflict with Rome (230–2, 238). » Parthians; Sassanids

Artemis [**ah**temis] In Greek mythology, the daughter of Zeus and Leto, twin sister of Apollo, and goddess of the Moon. She was originally a mother-goddess of Asia, with a cult especially at Ephesus; in Greece she was a virgin-goddess, associated with wild creatures and the protector of the young. Being connected with hunting, she is depicted with bow and arrows. » Actaeon; Diana

arteriole » **artery**

arteriosclerosis An umbrella term covering several pathological changes in medium-sized arteries. The most important is *atheroma*, in which cholesterol and other substances are deposited in the inner layer of the vessel. » artery; atherosclerosis

artery A vessel of the body which usually conveys blood to body tissues. Large, medium, and small arteries (**arterioles**) can be distinguished. Regulation of the blood supply is determined by the activity of a smooth muscle component (under sympathetic control) which changes the diameter of the vessel cavity. With increasing age, arteries tend to become blocked with porridge-like deposits of cholesterol-based material. » arteriosclerosis; atherosclerosis; autonomic nervous system; blood vessels [i]; circulation; vein; Plate XIII

artesian basin A shallow basin-shaped aquifer with impermeable rock strata above and below it, thus confining the groundwater under pressure. Sinking a well into the aquifer allows the water to rise to the surface without pumping. The Great Artesian Basin in E Australia is the largest such aquifer. » aquifer; groundwater

arthritis An inflammation of joints associated with swelling, pain, redness, and local heat. Pain and limitation of movement are characteristic. A large number of different conditions of metabolic, infective, or immunological origin may cause arthritis, and they may involve one or many joints. » gout; inflammation; joint; osteoarthritis

arthropod [**ah**thruhpod] A member of the largest and most diverse phylum of animals (*Arthropoda*), characterized by jointed limbs and an external chitinous skeleton. Arthropods have segmented bodies, most segments carrying a pair of limbs variously modified for locomotion, feeding, respiration, or reproduction. The external skeleton (cuticle) is moulted periodically to permit growth. Size ranges from 80 μm to 3.6 m/11¾ ft. Arthropods have a long fossil history from the Cambrian to the present, and are the most abundant animals on Earth, including the insects, arachnids, crustaceans, trilobites, centipedes, millipedes and several minor groups. » Arachnida; Cambrian period; centipede; chitin; crustacean; insect [i]; millipede; phylum; systematics; trilobite

Arthur (?6th-c) A half-legendary king of the Britons, who is represented as uniting the British tribes against the pagan invaders (5th–6th-c AD), and as the champion of Christianity. It is very doubtful if he is a historic figure: he is claimed alike as a prince in Brittany, Cornwall, Wales, Cumberland, and the lowlands of Scotland. His story passed into literature and many legends became interwoven with it, including those of the Round Table and the Holy Grail (both from the 12th–13th-c). The stories were developed by French writers (notably Chrétien de Troyes), and Lancelot, Percival, and the Grail were added. Malory's English version, *Morte d'Arthur*, was the final mediaeval compilation from which most later retellings are derived. » Camelot; Excalibur: Galahad, Sir; Guinevere; Lancelot, Sir; Malory, Thomas; Merlin; Morgan le Fay; Perceval, Sir; Uther Pendragon

Arthur, Prince (1187–1203) Posthumous son of Geoffrey (Henry II's fourth son) by Constance, Duchess of Brittany. On the death of Richard I (1199), Arthur claimed the English crown; and the French King, Philip II, for a while supported his bid for the throne. King John had him captured and murdered. » John; Philip II (of France); Richard I

Arthur, Chester A(lan) (1830–86) US statesman and 21st President (1881–5), born at Fairfield, Vermont. He qualified in law, and then became leader of the Republican Party in New York state. He was made US Vice-President when Garfield became President (1881), and succeeded him on his death. He died in New York City. » Republican Party

Arthur's Pass Main mountain pass through the Southern Alps, NC South Island, New Zealand; altitude 924 m/3 031 ft; discovered by the explorer, Sir Arthur Dobson in 1864; set in a national park, area 944 sq km/364 sq ml, established in 1929. » New Zealand [i]

artichoke » globe artichoke; Jerusalem artichoke

Articles of Confederation The organizing document of the USA from 1781 to 1788. It established a single-house Congress, with one vote for each state and with no executive, courts, or independent revenue. Its weaknesses quickly became obvious, and it was replaced by the present Constitution in 1788. » Constitution of the United States; Continental Congress

articulation The process of modifying the airflow above the larynx to produce a variety of speech-sounds. The jaws open to varying degrees, the tongue makes contact with the palate in various positions, and the lips can be rounded or spread. Sounds are classified according to their *place* of articulation (eg the part of the palate with which the tongue makes contact) and their *manner* of articulation (eg whether the air flows freely, as in the production of a vowel, or is impeded, as with a consonant). » click language; consonant; larynx; phonetics; vowel

artificial insemination (AI) The instrumental introduction of seminal fluid into the vagina in order to fertilize an ovum. The semen may be that of the husband (**AIH**) or of a donor (**AID**). » infertility; semen

artificial intelligence (AI) A term applied to the study and use of computers that can simulate some of the characteristics normally ascribed to human intelligence, such as learning, deduction, intuition, and self-correction. The subject encompasses many branches of computer science, including cybernetics, knowledge-based systems, natural language processing, pattern recognition, and robotics. Progress has been made in several areas, notably problem-solving, language comprehension, vision, and locomotion. » cognitive science; cybernetics; heuristic; intelligence; robotics (cybernetics)

artificial language An attempt to overcome the difficulties of understanding caused by the diversity of the world's languages, by creating a new, independent language which is no-one's mother tongue, can be learned by anyone, and expresses the most common range of meanings. Special attention is paid to making the grammar, word-formation, and pronunciation as regular and as simple as possible. Over 100 artificial languages have been created, but few have achieved widespread success, other than Esperanto. » auxiliary language; Esperanto; language

artificial respiration A procedure to maintain the movement of air into and out of the lungs when natural breathing is inadequate or has ceased. A short-term emergency method is 'mouth to mouth' respiration. With the head of the patient bent backwards and the nose pinched, the resuscitator takes a deep breath and expels his own breath into the open mouth and lungs of the victim, either directly or via a mouthpiece, repeating the manoeuvre 10–15 times a minute. When more prolonged assistance is indicated, a mechanical ventilator supplies a predetermined volume of oxygen at given intervals, applying intermittent positive pressure to the airways of a patient, usually via a tube inserted in the trachea. » cardiac resuscitation [i]; respiration

Artigas, José Gervasio [ahteegas] (1764–1850) The national hero of Uruguay, born in Montevideo. He became the most important local patriot leader in the wars of independence against Spain, and also resisted the centralizing pretensions of Buenos Aires. He spent the last 30 years of his life in exile in Paraguay, where he died. » Spanish-American Wars of Independence

artillery The heavy ordnance of an army; in particular, its longer-range weapons, as distinct from the small arms that each individual soldier carries. Modern artillery includes guns (known as 'tube' artillery) and missiles, both of which may be used in the traditional artillery role of bringing down destructive firepower on an enemy at a distance. Tube artillery may be mounted on towed carriages or tracked chassis (self-propelled guns) and fire a range of projectiles including small nuclear weapons. Rocket artillery ranges from simple, unguided bombardment missiles to medium-range, nuclear-armed battlefield missiles. » howitzer; missile, guided

artiodactyl [ahtiohd**ak**til] An ungulate mammal; foot with two or four toes (first always absent, second and fifth small or absent); weight carried on the third and fourth toe, which usually form a *cloven hoof*; also known as the **even-toed ungulate**. (Order: *Artiodactyla*, 192 species.) » Bovidae; deer; perissodactyl [i]; ruminant [i]; ungulate

Artois [arh**twa**], Lat **Artesium** Former province of NE France, now occupying the department of Pas-de-Calais; former capital, Arras; belonged to Flanders until 1180; part of Austrian and Spanish Netherlands in Middle Ages; ceded to France, 1659. » Flanders; Netherlands, The [i]

Arts and Crafts Movement A predominantly English architecture, art, and applied arts movement during the second half of the 19th-c, which advocated the renewed use of handicraft and simple decoration in reaction to industrial machinery and contemporary aesthetic eclecticism. The movement centred on William Morris, whose *Red House* (1859) by the architect Philip Webb is a good early example of the style. Its origins lie in the writings of Pugin and Ruskin, and its intention was to

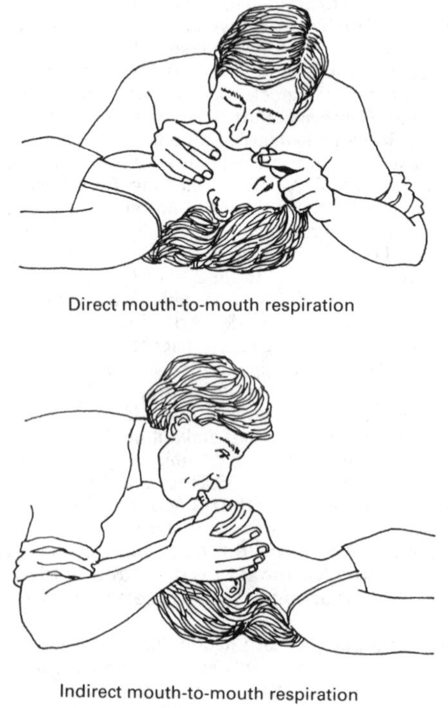

Direct mouth-to-mouth respiration

Indirect mouth-to-mouth respiration

Artificial respiration

change both the appearance and the way in which art and architecture were produced. It had a great and lasting effect on British, German, and American architecture, particularly the Garden City town-planning movement. » Bauhaus; English art; garden city; Gothic Revival; Morris, William; Pugin; Queen Anne Style; Ruskin

Aruba [**aroo**ba] pop (1989e) 61 300; area 193 sq km/74 sq ml. Island of the S Netherlands Antilles, E Caribbean, 30 km/19 ml N of the Paraguana Peninsula, Venezuela; composed of coralline limestone; rises to 189 m/620 ft at Jamanota in the hilly SE; formally separated from the Netherlands Antilles Federation in 1986, and now a self-governing member of the Kingdom of the Netherlands; capital, Oranjestad; airport; tourism, oil refining, rum distilling, cigarettes, beverages. » Netherlands Antilles [i]

arum lily A fleshy-stemmed perennial native to S Africa, and widely introduced elsewhere; leaves large, arrow-head shaped, glossy; 'flower' consisting of a yellow cylindrical spadix surrounded by sheathing; white spathe 15 cm/6 in long; also called **calla lily**. It is often used as a florist's flower. (*Zantedeschia aethiopica*. Family: *Araceae*.) » perennial; spadix; spathe

Arundel, Thomas [**a**ruhndl] (1353–1414) English prelate and statesman, third son of Robert Fitzalan, Earl of Arundel. He became Archdeacon of Taunton and Bishop of Ely (1373), then Archbishop of York (1388), and finally of Canterbury (1396). He supported the nobles opposed to Richard II, who banished him (1397), but he returned to help seat Henry of Lancaster on the throne (1399). He was a vigorous opponent of the Lollards. » Lollards; Richard II

Arusha Declaration An important policy statement by President Nyerere of Tanzania in 1967, proclaiming village socialism, self-reliance, nationalization, and anti-corruption measures against politicians. It was a significant attempt to create a socialist route to African development, but for both internal and external reasons it failed. » Nyerere; socialism; Tanzania [i]

Arval Brethren An ancient priestly college at Rome whose original function was to propitiate the gods of the fields (*arva*). Revived by the first emperor, Augustus, its duties were extended to include prayer and sacrifice for the well-being of the Imperial House. » Augustus

Arya Samaj [**ah**rya sa**mahj**] A dogmatic and militant Hindu sect founded c.1875 by Dyanand Sarasawati (1824–83). He demanded a return to the purity of the Rig Veda and its principles, as opposed to the accretions and corruptions that subsequently entered Hinduism. » Hinduism; Veda

Aryan [**air**eean] A prehistoric people and their language, an extinct member of the Indo-European language family. Aryans reputedly colonized Iran and N India, and gave rise to the Indian subcontinent's Indo-Aryan languages. Nazi Germany embraced unscientific notions of Germanic peoples as the purest members of an Aryan race of Indo-European-speaking peoples responsible for human progress. » Indo-European languages; Nazi Party

ASA rating The sensitivity of a photographic material expressed on the numerical scale established by the (former) American Standards Association (ASA). It is now generally replaced by the Exposure Index (EI), which has the same numerical values. » exposure (photography); speed (photography)

Asad, Hafez al- (1928–) Syrian general, statesman, and President (1971–), born at Qardaha. He was Minister of Defence and Commander of the Air Force (1966–70), instigated a coup in 1970, and became Prime Minister, and then President. He belongs to the minority Alawi sect of Islam. After the 1973 Arab-Israeli War, he negotiated a partial withdrawal of Israeli troops from Syria. In 1976 he sent Syrian troops into Lebanon, and did so again in early 1987. By 1989 he had imposed Syrian control over the greater part of Lebanon. He has long enjoyed Soviet support, and was one of the few Arab leaders to support Iran in its war with Iraq. He also supports the Palestinian radicals against Arafat's mainstream PLO. » Arafat; Lebanon [i]; PLO; Syria [i]

Asante » **Ashanti**

asbestos The name applied to varieties of fibrous minerals of the serpentine and amphibole groups. Fibres can be separated and woven into cloths or felted into sheets. It is an excellent insulator of heat and electricity, does not burn, and is resistant to chemical attack. The varieties used in manufacture are principally *chrysotile* (white asbestos), a form of serpentine, and *crocidolite* (blue asbestos), an amphibole. Blue asbestos is now banned in many countries as its dust can cause asbestosis. » amphiboles; asbestosis; serpentine

asbestosis A clinical condition resulting from the inhalation of asbestos over long periods of time. Small particles induce scarring of the lungs and carcinoma of lung and pleura. A latent period of up to 40 years may pass before the carcinoma occurs. » asbestos; cancer; carcinogen

Ascaris [**as**karis] A parasitic roundworm found in vertebrate hosts, typically pigs and humans; usually present in low numbers in the small intestine; sexes separate; length of females up to 250 mm/10 in; eggs resistant, often transmitted in manure. (Phylum: *Nematoda*.) » nematode; parasitology

ascension » **right ascension**

Ascension, Feast of In the Christian calendar, the fifth Thursday (being 40 days – *Acts* 1) after Easter. It commemorates Jesus' last appearance to his disciples, his being 'lifted up' or 'taken away' from them, prior to the attestation of his later presence to them through the Holy Spirit. » Easter; Holy Spirit; Jesus Christ

Ascension Island 7°56S 14°25W; pop (1983e) 1 400; area 88 sq km/34 sq ml. Small, arid, volcanic island in the S Atlantic, 1 125 km/700 ml NW of St Helena; highest point, Green Mountain (859 m/2 818 ft); discovered by the Portuguese on Ascension Day 1501; British territory since 1815, administered under the Admiralty; made a dependency of St Helena in 1922; British and US air bases; British forces sent to the island in 1982 in support of the Falkland Islands Task Force; NASA tracking station; Atlantic relay station for the BBC; cable station. » Atlantic Ocean; Falklands War; NASA; St Helena

asceticism [a**set**isizm] A variety of austere practices involving the renunciation or denial of ordinary bodily and sensual gratifications. These may include fasting, meditation, a life of solitude, the renunciation of possessions, denial of sexual gratification, and, in the extreme, the mortification of the flesh.

Asch, Sholem (1880–1957) Jewish novelist, born at Kutno, Poland. He emigrated to the USA in 1914, and became a US citizen in 1920. Later he lived in France, Israel, and London, where he died. His plays include *El ngomas* (1910, The God of Vengeance), and his novels include *Motl der ganer* (1935, Mottke the Thief) and *Bnei Avro'ham* (1942, The Children of Abraham). » Hebrew literature; novel

Ascham, Roger [**as**kuhm] (1515–68) English humanist, born at Kirby Wiske, Yorkshire. He was educated at Cambridge, where he gained a reputation as a classical scholar. He was tutor to the Princess Elizabeth (1548–50), and later became Latin secretary to Queen Mary and Queen Elizabeth. His main works were *Toxophilus* (1545), a treatise in defence of archery, and *The Scholemaster* (1578), a treatise on classical education. He died in London. » English literature; humanism

ASCII code [**as**kee] A widely used binary code defined by the American Standards Code for Information Interchange. An 8-bit code, including a parity check bit, is used to define 128 different characters. These include all the alphanumeric characters, and a number of printer control characters such as carriage return and line feed. An **ASCII keyboard** is a special type of keyboard which provides all the ASCII code characters. » alphanumeric characters; EBCDIC code; parity check

Asclepius [as**klee**piuhs] In Greek mythology, a hero who became a god of healing, the son of Apollo and Koronis, educated by Chiron the centaur. He overreached himself by restoring Hippolytus to life, and was killed by the thunderbolt of Zeus. » Aesculapius; Hippolytus

Ascomycetes [askuhmiy**see**teez] A subdivision of the true fungi, characterized by a minute sac-like reproductive structure (*ascus*) within which a complex sexual process results in the formation of eight haploid spores (*ascospores*); asexual reproduction is also common; includes cup fungi, yeasts, truffles, and many parasitic forms. (Division: *Eumycota*.) » cup fungus; fungus; gametophyte; truffle; yeast

ascorbic acid Vitamin C, largely found in citrus fruits, green vegetables, and potatoes. It functions in the body to maintain tissue integrity; a deficiency causes scurvy. Megadoses of vitamin C, up to 20 times the amount required per day, have been promoted for prevention of the common cold. » scurvy; vitamins [i]

ASDIC An acronym of **Admiralty Submarine Detection Investigation Committee** (1917), an early form of submarine detection device used on warships of the Royal Navy. ASDIC used sonar as its operating principle. » anti-submarine warfare; sonar

asepsis [ay**sep**sis] The absence of micro-organisms from body surfaces (eg the skin) or from wounds. This ideal state is rarely achieved in surgical operations, but procedures adopted in operating theatres are designed to this end; these include skin sterilization, the wearing of sterile surgical gloves and gowns, the chemical or heat sterilization of instruments, swabs, and bandages, and the removal of contaminated air from the theatre. » surgery

asexual reproduction » **reproduction**

Asgard [**az**gahd] In Norse mythology, the home of the gods, created by Odin in the upper branches of the World-Tree, and therefore in the approximate centre of things. It is full of gardens and palaces. » Odin

ash A deciduous tree native to the N hemisphere; leaves pinnate; flowers sometimes without perianth, borne in dense clusters appearing before leaves; seeds (*keys*) have a papery wing which aids in wind dispersal. The timber is valuable, and various species, including weeping forms, are often planted for ornament. (Genus: *Fraxinus*, 70 species. Family: *Oleaceae*.) » deciduous plants; perianth; pinnate; tree [i]

Ash Wednesday The first day of Lent. The name derives from the ritual, observed in the ancient Church and continued in Roman Catholic and some Anglican Churches, of making a cross on the forehead of Christians with ashes which have previously been blessed. The ashes are obtained by burning the branches used in the previous year's Palm Sunday service. » Lent; Palm Sunday

Ashanti or **Asante** A Kwa-speaking Akan people of S Ghana and adjacent areas of Togo and Côte d'Ivoire. They form a confederacy of chiefdoms, founded by the ruler Osei Tutu in the late 17th-c; the paramount chief was established at Kumasi, and the Golden Stool was the symbol of Ashanti unity. The independent Ashanti state was at the height of its powers in the early 19th-c, and became a major threat to British trade on the coast, until defeated (1873) by a force under Sir Garnet Wolseley. The state was annexed by the British in 1902. Traditional culture and religion still flourish, with rich ceremonial and internationally famous art. » Akan; Ghana [i]; Wolseley

Ashbery, John (1927–) US poet, born in New York City, and educated at Harvard. He has worked as an art critic, first in France, and since 1980 in the USA, where he has also been professor of English. He is recognized as the major postmodern poet of his generation. His volumes include *The Tennis Court Oath* (1962), *Rivers and Mountains* (1966), *Self-Portrait in a Convex Mirror* (1975), and *A Wave* (1984). His *Selected Poems* were published in 1985. » American literature; poetry

Ashcan School A derisive name given to a group of US Realist painters and illustrators, also called *The Eight*. Formed in 1907, they included Robert Henri (1865–1929), John Sloan (1871–1951), and later George Bellows (1882–1925). They painted everyday, non-academic subjects in an attempt to bring art back into direct contact with ordinary life, especially street life in New York City. » Realism (art and literature)

Ashcroft, Dame Peggy, properly **Edith Margaret Emily** (1907–91) British actress, born at Croydon, Greater London. She first appeared with the Birmingham Repertory Theatre in 1926, electrified the West End as Naemi in *Jew Süss* (1929), and established her versatility in the 1932–3 Old Vic season. Her great roles include Juliet, in Gielgud's production (1935), Cleopatra (1935), and Hedda Gabler (1954). Her films include *A Passage to India* (1984), for which she won an Oscar as best supporting actress. She was made a Dame in 1956. » Gielgud; theatre

Ashdod [ash**dohd**] 31°48N 34°38E, pop (1982e) 66 000. Seaport in Southern district, W Israel; on the Mediterranean Sea, 40 km/25 ml S of Tel Aviv-Yafo; ancient Philistine city; modern city founded in 1956 as the major port of S Israel; railway; ancient and modern harbour; light industry, tourism. » Israel [i]; Philistines

Ashdown, Jeremy John Durham, byname **Paddy** (1941–) British Liberal politician, born in India, and educated at Bedford. He joined the Royal Marines (1959–71), was a member of the UK mission to the United Nations in Geneva (1971–6), spent some time in industry, and was elected to parliament in 1983. He acted as a Liberal Party spokesman on trade and industry, and became leader of the newly constituted Social and Liberal Democratic Party in 1988. » Liberal Party (UK); Steel

Asher, tribe of One of the twelve tribes of ancient Israel, said to be descended from Jacob's eighth son Asher (*Gen* 30.12f). Its territory included the narrow coastal plain from Carmel to the outskirts of Sidon and bordered on the E by the Galilean hills. » Israel, tribes of [i]

Ashes, the A symbolic trophy contested by the cricket teams of England and Australia. It originated in 1882 after the *Sporting Times* printed an obituary to English cricket following the country's first defeat by Australia on home soil. An urn containing the ashes of a stump used in that match remains at Lord's cricket ground. » cricket (sport) [i]

Ashkenazim [ashkuh**nah**zim] Jews of C and E European descent, as distinguished from Sephardim Jews, who are of Spanish or Portuguese descent. The terms arose in the Middle Ages when Europe and W Asia were divided between Christian and Islamic countries. Cut off, the Ashkenazim developed their own customs, traditions of interpretation of the Talmud, music, and language (Yiddish). » Judaism; Sephardim; Yiddish

Ashkenazy, Vladimir [ashkuh**nah**zee] (1937–) Russian pianist and conductor, born at Nizhni Novgored. He studied in Moscow and shared the first prize in the Tchaikovsky Competition there in 1962. After earning an international reputation as a concert pianist, he has turned increasingly to conducting. He was principal conductor of the Philharmonia Orchestra (1981–6), and since then has directed the Royal Philharmonic Orchestra. He took Icelandic nationality in 1972. » piano

Ashley, Laura, originally **Laura Mountney** (1925–85) British fashion designer, born at Merthyr, Wales. She married Bernard Ashley in 1949, and started up a business designing and producing furnishing materials. She then experimented with designing and making clothes, and it was this aspect which transformed their business from one small shop to an international chain of boutiques selling clothes, furnishing fabrics, and wallpapers. Her work was characterized by a romantic style and the use of natural fabrics, especially cotton. Ashley Mountney Ltd became Laura Ashley Ltd in 1968. In her later years she lived in Belgium and France, and died in Coventry, UK. » cotton [i]; fashion

Ashmolean Museum A museum at Oxford University, England. Elias Ashmole (1617–92) donated the core of the collection to the University in 1675, and the museum was opened eight years later. Its holdings include a distinguished collection of archaeological relics, paintings, prints, and silverware. » museum; Oxford University [i]

Ashmore and Cartier Islands Area c.3 sq km/1½ ml. Uninhabited Australian external territory in the Indian Ocean 320 km/200 ml off the NW coast of Australia; consists of the Ashmore Is (Middle, East and West) and Cartier I; formerly administered by the Northern Territory, it became a separate Commonwealth Territory in 1978; Ashmore Reef is a national nature reserve. » Australia [i]; Northern Territory

ashram [**ahsh**ram] An Indian religious community whose members lead lives of austere self-discipline and dedicated service in accordance with the teachings and practices of their particular school. A well-known ashram was that of Mahatma Gandhi. » Gandhi

ashrama [**ahsh**rama] In Hindu tradition, any of the four stages of life: the pupil, the householder, the forest-dweller and, when all human bonds have been broken, the total renunciation of the world. Seldom followed in practice, these four stages represent the ideal way of life. » ashram; Hinduism

Ashton, Sir Frederick (William Mallandaine) (1904–88) British dancer and choreographer, born in Guayaquil, Ecuador. He trained under Massine and Marie Rambert, first choreographed for public performance in 1926, and in 1935 became choreographer at Sadler's Wells Ballet. He also worked with the New York City Ballet, the Royal Danish Ballet Company, and became co-director of Sadler's Wells (later the Royal Ballet) (1952–63) and then director (1963–70). Famous among his many works are *Façade* (1931), *Ondine* (1958), and *The Dream* (1964). He was knighted in 1962, and died at Eye, Suffolk. » ballet; choreography; Rambert Dance Company; Royal Ballet

Ashura [ashoora] A Muslim fast day observed on the 10th of Muharram, particularly among Shiite Muslims, in commemoration of the death of Husain, grandson of Mohammed. It is a holiday in countries such as Iran, with mainly Shiite Muslim populations. » Islam; Shiites

Ashurbanipal » Assurbanipal; Sardanapalus

Asia area c.44.5 million sq km/17.2 million sq ml. The largest continent; bounded N by the Arctic Ocean, E by the Pacific Ocean, S by the Indian Ocean, and W by Europe; maximum length, 8 500 km/5 300 ml; maximum width, 9 600 km/6 000 ml; chief mountain system, the Himalayas, rising to 8 848 m/ 29 028 ft at Mt Everest; major rivers include the Chiang Jiang (Yangtze), Yellow, Brahmaputra, Irrawaddy, Indus, and Ganges. » China [i]; Himalayas; India [i]; Soviet Union [i]; Ural Mountains; RR12

Asian Games A multi-sport competition first held at New Delhi, India in 1951, and since 1954 held quadrennially. The Far Eastern Games, the predecessors of the Asian Games, were first held at Manila in 1913.

Asiatic wild horse » Przewalski's horse

Asimov, Isaac (1920–) US biochemist and a master of science-fiction writing, born at Petrovichi, Russia. His family emigrated to the USA in 1923 and he was naturalized in 1928. He grew up in Brooklyn and was educated at Columbia University, New York. He began contributing stories to science-fiction magazines in 1939, and his first book, *Pebble in the Sky*, was published in 1950. His many novels and story collections include *I, Robot* (1950), *The Caves of Steel* (1954), and *The Foundation Trilogy* (1963). Since 1958 he has worked mainly on textbooks and works of popular science. In 1979 he became professor of biochemistry at the University of Boston. » biochemistry; science fiction

Asmara or **Asmera** [asmera] 15°20N 38°58E, pop (1984e) 275 385. Capital of Eritrea region, Ethiopia; altitude 2 350 m/7 710 ft; occupied by Italians, 1889; regional capital, 1897; occupied by British, 1941; airport; university (1958); meat processing, distilling, textiles; cathedral (1922), mosque (1937), archaeological museum. » Ethiopia [i]

Asmoneans [azmuhneeanz] **» Maccabees**

asp A venomous African snake of family *Elapidae* (*Naja haje*); Cleopatra is said to have committed suicide by forcing this species to bite her; also known as the **Egyptian cobra**. The name is also used for venomous African **burrowing asps** (**atractaspid snakes** or **mole vipers**) of family *Colubridae*, and for the European *Vipera aspis* (**European asp, asp viper**, or **aspic viper**) of family *Viperidae*. » snake; viper [i]

asparagus A perennial native to Europe and Asia; erect or spreading, some climbers, all with feathery foliage; the true leaves reduced to tiny scales and replaced by tiny modified branches functioning as leaves; flowers tiny, white or yellow, bell- or star-shaped; berries green, red, or black. Young shoots of *Asparagus officinalis* are prized as a vegetable. (Genus: *Asparagus*, 300 species. Family: *Liliaceae*.) » climbing plant; perennial; vegetable

asparagus fern Not a fern, but a species of asparagus, a perennial with feathery foliage commonly grown as a pot plant and florists' foliage plant. (*Asparagus setaceus*. Family: *Liliaceae*.) » asparagus; fern; perennial

aspect ratio In visual presentation, especially in cinema and television, the proportion of the picture width to its height, e.g. 4:3, often expressed with the height as unity, 1.33:1. It is usually abbreviated **AR**. » wide-screen cinema [i]

aspen A species of poplar, also called **trembling aspen**, because the greyish-green, rounded-to-ovoid leaves have flattened stalks, allowing the blades to flutter in the slightest breeze. The movement is accentuated by a flashing of the pale undersurface, giving the impression of constant movement. (*Populus tremula*. Family: *Salicaceae*.) » poplar

Aspen Lodge » Camp David

Aspergillus [aspuhjiluhs] A typically asexually reproducing fungus that can cause food spoilage and produce disease in humans. (Subdivision: *Ascomycetes*. Order: *Eurotiales*.) » fungus

asphalt A semi-solid bituminous residue of the evaporation of petroleum (formed by slow evaporation in nature or by distillation in industry). It is usually employed mixed with some solid mineral matter for roofing, road-making, etc. Many natural deposits (eg in Trinidad) have a natural mineral content. » bitumen 1; petroleum

asphodel The name applied to two related genera native to the Mediterranean region and Asia, with erect stems, narrow, grass-like leaves, and spikes of flowers each with six perianth-segments. *Asphodelus* (12 species) has leaves V-shaped in cross-section, flowers white or pink. *Asphodeline* (15 species) has leaves triangular in cross-section, flowers yellow. (Family: *Liliaceae*.) » bog asphodel; perianth

asphyxia Life-threatening interruption of the passage of air through the airways to the lungs. It is commonly due to physical obstruction from drawing into the upper respiratory tract such materials as vomit or water, as in drowning. It is also the result of strangulation, and of severe generalized disease of the lungs. » lungs

aspidistra An evergreen perennial, native to E Asia; leaves long-stalked, elliptical, leathery, lasting several years; flowers bell-shaped with a lid formed by the umbrella-shaped style, dull purple; borne at ground level and pollinated by slugs. It tolerates shade and drought, and is much favoured as a pot plant. (*Aspidistra elatior*. Family: *Liliaceae*.) » evergreen plants; perennial; style

aspirin (acetylsalicylic acid) A very widely-used drug effective against many types of minor pain (headache, menstruation, neuralgia), inflammation (it is frequently prescribed for rheumatoid diseases), and fever. It has more recently been discovered to prevent the formation of blood clots, and therefore reduces the incidence of coronary and cerebral thrombosis. The bark of the willow and certain other plants have been used for centuries in the cure of 'agues' (fever). The active ingredient *salicin* is the chemical precursor of aspirin. The German chemist Felix Hoffman (1868–1946) first synthesized aspirin, and it was introduced into medicine in 1899 by German pharmacologist Heinrich Dreser (1860–1924). It owes all its medicinal effects to its ability to prevent the synthesis of prostaglandins, a family of biologically active chemicals found throughout the body. A side-effect of taking aspirin may be gastric bleeding. » analgesics; prostaglandins; salicylic acid; thrombosis

Asplund, Erik Gunnar (1885–1940) Swedish architect, born and died in Stockholm. He studied at the Royal Institute of Technology, Stockholm (1905–9), and then travelled in Germany. On his return, he sought to combine modern architecture with classical and national architectural traditions in such buildings as the Stockholm Public Library (1920–8) and the Woodland Cemetery, Stockholm (1935–40). » architecture

Asquith, H(erbert) H(enry), 1st Earl of Oxford and Asquith (1852–1928) British Liberal statesman and Prime Minister (1908–16), born at Morley, Yorkshire. He was educated at Oxford, called to the Bar (1876), and became a QC (1890) and MP (1886), Home Secretary (1892–5), Chancellor of the Exchequer (1905–8), and Premier. His regime was notable for the upholding of free trade, the introduction of old age pensions, payment for MPs, the Parliament Act of 1911, Welsh disestablishment, suffragette troubles, the declaration of war (1914), the coalition ministry (1915), and the Sinn Féin rebellion (1916). After World War 1, he led the Independent Liberals who rejected Lloyd George's coalition policies. He was created an earl in 1925, and died at Sutton Courtenay, Berkshire. » Liberal Party (UK); Lloyd George; Sinn Féin; World War 1

ass A rare wild horse; small, long ears, short erect mane; pale grey or brown; inhabits drier terrain than other horse species; domesticated thousands of years ago for carrying loads; three species: the **African wild ass** (*Equus (Asinus) asinus*), the **Asiatic wild ass** from S Asia (*Equus (Asinus) hemionus*, also called **onager**, **kulan**, and **hemione**); and the **kiang** (*Equus (Asinus) kiang*) from Tibet. The modern *donkey* (or *burro*) is a domesticated form of the African wild ass. (Subgenus: *Asinus*. Genus: *Equus*.) » horse [i]; mule (zoology)

Assam pop (1981) 19 902 826; area 78 523 sq km/30 310 sq ml. State in E India, bounded NW by Bhutan and SE by Bangladesh; almost completely separated from India by Bangladesh; important strategic role in World War 2, during Allied advance into Burma; unicameral legislature of 126 members; crossed by the R Brahmaputra; world's largest river island of Majuli is a pilgrimage centre; capital, Dispur; produces almost half of India's crude oil, oil refining, timber, tea, rice, jute, cotton, oilseeds. » India [i]

Assamese » **Indo-Aryan languages**

assassin bug A small, cone-nosed bug which mostly feeds on the body fluids of small arthropods. The immature stages often conceal themselves with debris and litter. Some suck the blood of vertebrates, and are important medically as carriers of Chaga's disease. » arthropod; bug (entomology); trypanosomiasis

assault In law, the act of causing another person to fear, reasonably, an immediate battery. Contact is not an essential ingredient of assault: shaking a fist in someone's face may suffice. In common usage, and in some statutes, the term *assault* is used to include the related concept of battery. » battery

assaying A chemical analysis which determines the amount of the principal or potent constituent of a mixture. The technique is mainly used for precious metals and for drugs. » chemistry

assemblage An imprecise term referring to art objects formed by sticking together bits and pieces to make a three-dimensional whole. Picasso's '*Glass of Absinthe*' (1914) pioneered the technique; more recently the term has been stretched to include collages by Jean Dubuffet (1901–85), readymades by Marcel Duchamp (1887–1968), and a variety of objects made from sacks, crushed automobiles, chairs, old clothes, etc by such artists as Robert Rauschenberg (1925–) and Edward Kienholz (1927–). » collage; Duchamp; Picasso; readymade

Assemblies of God A Christian pentecostalist denomination formed in the USA and Canada in the early 20th-c. It promotes mission work all over the world, and believes baptism by the Holy Spirit to be evidenced by speaking in tongues. » Christianity; Holy Spirit; glossolalia; Pentecostalism

assembly language A set of convenient mnemonics corresponding to the machine-code instructions of a specific central processor unit or microprocessor, defined by the manufacturer. Assembly language is more convenient for the programmer than machine code, and is translated (*assembled*) into machine code by an *assembly program*, usually known as an *assembler*. » low-level language; machine code

Asser (850–?909) Welsh monk of St David's, known for his Latin biography of King Alfred. He resided at intervals (885–901) at Alfred's court, assisting him in his studies. Sometime before 900, he was made Bishop of Sherbourne. » Alfred the Great

Assignats [**as**eenya] Originally, paper bonds issued by the Constituent Assembly in France (1789). They were later (1790) accepted as currency notes, in view of the shortage of coin, until the abolition of paper currency in 1797. » French Revolution [i]

Assize Court A legal system in England and Wales, dating from the time of Henry II, which was abolished by the Courts Act, 1971. Assize courts were presided over by High Court judges, who travelled on circuit to hear criminal and civil cases. The functions of Assize courts continue to be exercised by High Court judges sitting in Crown Courts throughout England and Wales. » Crown Court; Henry II (of England)

Associated Press (AP) An international news agency, with headquarters in New York City. Founded in 1848, it is the world's largest news-gathering co-operative, owned by US newspaper and broadcasting companies. In addition to its general news and photo service, AP provides, with Dow Jones & Co, a specialized economic and financial news service. » news agency

associated state A former colony that has a free and voluntary arrangement with the UK as the former colonial power. The state enjoys the right of self-government, but recognizes the British sovereign as head. The concept was introduced for states (eg Antigua, Granada) wishing to be independent, but economically unable to support themselves. » colony

association » **dissociation**

Association football » **football 1** [i]

Association of South-East Asian Nations (ASEAN) An association formed in 1967 to promote economic co-operation between Indonesia, Malaysia, the Philippines, Singapore, and Thailand. Brunei joined in 1984.

associative operation In mathematics, the principle that the order in which successive additions are performed does not affect the result; for example $(2+3)+4=2+(3+4)$. An operation * is associative over a set S if $a*(b*c) = (a*b)*c$ for all a,b,c in S. Over the set of real numbers, addition and multiplication are associative; subtraction and division are not. » commutative operation; distributive operation

assonance » **alliteration**

Assumption The claim concerning the Virgin Mary, mother of Jesus Christ, that on her death she was 'assumed' (taken up, body and soul) to heaven. This was believed by some Christians in the ancient Church, widely accepted thereafter in Roman Catholic and Orthodox Churches, and defined by Pope Pius XII as an article of faith in 1950. » Mary (mother of Jesus); Pius XII

assurance A general term for insurance related to a person's life. By paying a sum annually to an assurance company, the company guarantees that on death a certain lump sum will be paid to the person's heirs. The agreement is known as a *policy*. **Term assurances** are policies which mature after a fixed period; and the policy-holder receives a guaranteed sum on survival to the end of the term.

Assurbanipal or **Ashurbanipal** (7th-c BC) King of Assyria (668–627 BC), the last of the great Assyrian kings, the son of Esarhaddon and grandson of Sennacherib. A patron of the arts, he founded the first systematically gathered and organized library in the ancient Middle East. » Assyria; Esarhaddon; Nineveh; Sardanapalus; Sennacherib

Assyria The name given first to the small area around the town of Assur on the Tigris in Upper Mesopotamia, and then much later to the vast empire that the rulers of Assur acquired through conquering their neighbours on all sides. At its height in the 9th-c and 8th-c BC, the Assyrian Empire stretched from the E Mediterranean to Iran, and from the Persian Gulf as far north as the mountains of E Turkey. The Empire was destroyed in an uprising of Medes and Babylonians in 612 BC. » Medes; Nimrod; Nineveh; Urartu

Assyrian architecture » **Sumerian and Assyrian architecture**

Assyrian art The art associated with Assyria, dating from c.1500 BC, to the destruction of Nineveh (612 BC). Stylistically akin to Babylonian art, the best-known examples are the gigantic stone winged and human-headed lions which guarded entrances, and the wall decorations in the form of stone bas reliefs, originally painted, representing battles and hunting-scenes. Human figures tend to be stylized somewhat in the Egyptian manner, but animals are beautifully drawn in lively movement. There is an extensive collection in the British Museum. » art; Assyria; Babylonian art; bas-relief; Egyptian art

Astaire (originally **Austerlitz**), **Fred** (1899–1987) US actor and dancer, born in Omaha, Nebraska. After studying in New York, he and his elder sister Adele began as a vaudeville team (1916). They rose to stardom in the 1920s in *Lady be Good* and other stage shows. When Adele married, Fred continued with various partners, notably Ginger Rogers. His many films include *Top Hat* (1935), *Follow the Fleet* (1936), and *Easter Parade* (1948). With original and carefully worked out tap-dance routines, designed by himself, he revolutionized the film musical. He died in Los Angeles, California. » vaudeville

Astarte » **Ishtar**

aster A large group of mainly perennials from America, Eurasia, and Africa; flower heads daisy-like, usually in clusters; outer, ray florets blue, purple, pink, or white, often autumn or late summer flowering. Several are popular ornamentals. (Genus: *Aster*, 250 species. Family: *Compositae*.) » daisy; floret; Michaelmas daisy; perennial

asterism A conspicuous or memorable group of stars, smaller in area than a constellation. An example is the Plough. » Plough, the; star

asteroids Rocky objects generally found in orbits lying between those of Mars and Jupiter, formerly called **minor planets** (a term now rarely used). This 'main belt' of asteroids has its inner edge c.100 million km/60 million ml outside Mars' orbit, and is c.165 million km/100 million ml wide. Only a few are large enough to have visible discs (hence the name, meaning 'star-like'), so most sizes are inferred. The orbits of c.4 000 of the larger asteroids are known; their orbital periods are about five years. The first asteroid, Ceres (diameter 940 km/580 ml) was discovered by Giuseppe Piazzi (1746–1826) in 1801. Other large asteroids are Pallas (540 km/340 ml), Vesta (510 km/320 ml), Hygiea (410 km/250 ml), Interamnia (310 km/190 ml), Davida (310 km/190 ml), and Cybele (280 km/170 ml).

Asteroids are classified according to telescopically measured visible and near infrared colours, inferences about their composition being based on a comparison with meteorite types. *C* types are thought to be analogous to carbonaceous meteorites; *S* types are thought to be composed of silicates mixed with nickel/iron; and *M* types are thought to be metallic (nickel-iron); there are also several unclassified asteroids. They are believed to have originated in the formation of the Solar System, when planetesimals accreted from solar nebula. The more primitive carbonaceous asteroids may have evolved little since then, while the other types may have been parts of larger bodies first accreted and later broken up by collisions. Recently a few dozen small (few km-diameter) asteroids have been discovered in highly elliptical orbits that come inside the orbit of Mars, some crossing the orbit of Earth – the Apollo, Amor, and Aten families. The total number of near-Earth asteroids is thought to be over 1 000; these, and the larger number of unseen boulder-size objects, may collide with the Earth and Moon periodically. Such asteroids are relatively easy to visit by spacecraft, and may in the future represent economically useful resources for an expanding space economy. The first main-belt asteroid flyby is likely to be achieved by NASA's Galileo spacecraft in the early 1990s. » comet; Galileo Project; Jupiter (astronomy); Mars (astronomy); meteorite; Solar System

asthenosphere The Earth's upper mantle, extending from the base of the lithosphere at c.100 km/60 ml down to 700 km/430 ml below the surface. A seismic discontinuity defines the boundary between the upper and lower mantle. The asthenosphere is considerably less rigid than the lithosphere above. » Earth [i]; lithosphere; seismology

asthma A condition in which there is narrowing and obstruction of the airways (bronchi and bronchioles) which in the early stages is paroxysmal and reversible. Narrowing results from the contraction of the bronchial muscles, and is an exaggerated response in hypersensitive individuals to various allergens. Common amongst these are pollen, house dust, and the detritus of house mites that inhabit mattresses, etc. Psychological factors and chest infection contribute in some cases. The first attacks may occur at any age, but are usually early in life. They commonly consist of sudden episodes of breathlessness, with wheezing which may last several hours or days. In rare cases, severe persistent asthmatic attacks may be fatal, especially if treatment is delayed. In most patients, treatment involves periodic inhalation of one or more of several available drugs which relax the bronchioles or damp down any inflammation. Exposure to the causative antigen, if known, should be avoided. » allergy; bronchi

astigmatism In vision, an actual asymmetry in the optical system of the eye, so that the eye's ability to focus horizontal and vertical lines is different. In optics, the term refers to aberrations of a lens image due to the position of an object off the lens axis. » aberrations 1 [i]; eye [i]; lens; optics [i]; vision

Astor (of Hever), John Jacob, 1st Baron (1886–1971) British newspaper proprietor, born in New York City. Educated at Eton and Oxford, he became an MP in 1922, and chairman of the Times Publishing Company after the death of Lord Northcliffe. Created baron in 1956, he died at Cannes, France. He was succeeded as chairman in 1959 by his eldest son, **Gavin** (1918–84). » newspaper

Astor, Nancy Witcher Langhorne, Viscountess (1879–1964) British politician, the first woman MP to sit in the House of Commons (1919–45), born at Danville, Virginia, USA. She succeeded her husband as MP for Plymouth in 1919, and became known for her interest in women's rights and social problems, especially temperance. She died at Grimsthorpe Castle, Lincolnshire. Her husband, **William Waldorf, 2nd Viscount Astor** (1879–1952) was proprieter of the *Observer* (1919–45). » women's liberation movement

Astrakhan [astra**khahn**], formerly **Khadzhi-Tarkhan** 46°22N 48°04E, pop (1983) 481 000. Capital city of Astrakhan oblast, SE European Russia; on a huge island in the Volga delta; altitude, 22 m/72 ft below sea-level; protected from floods by 75 km/47 ml of dykes; founded, 13th-c; the most important port in the Volga–Caspian basin; airport; railway; university (1919); fishing, fish processing, metalwork, chemicals, textiles, foodstuffs, river vessels; major transshipment centre for oil, fish, grain, wood; known for astrakhan fur; Kremlin fortress (16th-c). » Russia

astral projection The popular interpretation of an out-of-the-body experience in which it is believed that the person's consciousness is contained in a non-physical 'astral body' which temporarily separates from the physical body. People reporting such an experience have said that they can witness events in the vicinity of their astral body (when they claim it is in a different location from their physical body), although the validity of such claims has yet to be established. » out-of-the-body experience

astrobiology » **exobiology**

astrodome An open space or building covered by a vast translucent plastic dome; usually a sports centre or arena. The first and most famous example is the eponymous Astrodome, Houston, Texas (1964), officially known as the Harris County Domed Municipal Stadium, architects Lloyd Jones Brewer and Wilson Morris Crain Anderson.

astrolabe An ancient instrument (c.200 BC) for showing the positions of the Sun and bright stars at any time and date. If fitted with sights, it was also used for measuring the altitude above the horizon of celestial objects, and in this mode was a 15th-c forerunner of the sextant.

astrology A system of knowledge whereby human nature can be understood in terms of the heavens. It relies upon precise measurement and a body of symbolism which has come to be associated with each of the signs of the zodiac and the planets (including the Sun and Moon). It rests on a foundation of ancient philosophy, particularly on the idea that the force which patterns the heavens likewise orders humanity. As with religion, it is a source of both trivial superstition and profound insight. The most significant stages in the development of astrology took place in the first millennium BC in Mesopotamia and Greece. From there it spread worldwide, developing distinct branches and great variation in method. It blossomed most in those periods representing peaks of cultural achievement – Classical Greece, Renaissance Europe, and Elizabethan England. Today it thrives in several Eastern countries, and in the West is undergoing something of a rebirth, though the modern emphasis is on self-knowledge rather than on predicting events. Astrology is the mother of astronomy, although the two parted company in the 17th-c. » astronomy; zodiac [i]

astrometry » **astronomy**

astronaut The NASA term for a spacecraft crew member; originally applied to pilots, but now including scientists and payload specialists. Over 200 personnel took part in 56 crewed flights, up to April 1989. The longest flight duration was 84 days by the Skylab 4 crew. Three US women have flown in space; and 10 astronauts have lost their lives in accidents directly related to spaceflight. » cosmonaut; space exploration; space physiology and medicine; space station; RR10

Astronomer Royal Formerly the title of the director of the Royal Greenwich Observatory, England. Since 1972, it has been an honorary title awarded to a distinguished British astronomer. The title of Astronomer Royal for Scotland is held by the Director of the Royal Observatory, Edinburgh. » astronomy

astronomical unit (AU) The mean distance of the Earth from the Sun, c.149.6 million km/93 million ml; a convenient measure of distance within the Solar System. Mean distances of other planets from the Sun are: Mercury 0.39 AU, Venus 0.72 AU, Mars 1.52 AU, Jupiter 5.2 AU, Saturn 9.6 AU, Uranus 19 AU, Neptune 30 AU, Pluto 40 AU. There are 63 240 AU in one light year. » light year; parsec; Solar System; units (scientific)

astronomy The study of all classes of celestial object, such as planets, stars, and galaxies, as well as interstellar and intergalactic space, and the universe as a whole; the branch of classical astronomy concerned with the precise measurement of the positions of celestial objects is known as **astrometry**. The first known systematic observers were the Babylonians, who compiled the first star catalogues c.1600 BC. From the 9th-c BC they kept dated astronomical records. Around the same time, the Neolithic peoples of W Europe constructed massive observatories of the Sun and Moon at Stonehenge, England, and Carnac, France. Greek philosophers, from c.500 BC, attempted the first cosmologies, models of the ever-changing arrangements of the five visible planets. The influence of Aristotle was especially strong on all later work, to the point of stultifying serious investigations for almost two millennia. Modern astronomy began 450 years ago with Copernicus, who set the scene for the overthrow of the Hellenistic cosmology, asserting that the Sun, not the Earth, is at the centre of the Solar System. Newton described gravitational theory in the 17th-c, and thenceforth planetary astronomy became an exact science. From Newton's time, professional observatories were established, records properly kept, and mathematics was applied to understanding the heavens.

In the 18th-c and 19th-c, techniques to build large telescopes were developed, culminating in the construction of observatories on mountain sites in the USA, such as the Lick and Mount Wilson Observatories. The opening of large telescopes on good sites enabled physics to play a greater role in the interpretation of high-quality observations. In the early 20th-c the main ideas about the evolution of stars became clear, and by the 1950s the theory of nuclear burning in stars, as well as the origin of the chemical elements, was firmly established.

Radio astronomy emerged rapidly after World War 2, taking advantage of antennae and other equipment developed for radar, and was the first of the invisible astronomies. The use of satellites above the blanket of the Earth's atmosphere enabled ultraviolet, X-ray, and infrared astronomies to be developed from the 1960s on. Opening these new windows on the cosmos produced many unexpected discoveries, such as quasars, pulsars, active galactic nuclei, X-ray binary stars, and the microwave background. Amateurs are also still able to contribute data to astronomy, for example by observing new comets, nova outbursts, supernova explosions in distant galaxies, variable stars, and the visual appearance of the planets. » gamma-ray/infrared/neutrino/radar/radio/ultraviolet/X-ray astronomy; Aristotle; astrophysics; Copernican system; cosmology; ephemeris; Messier; New General Catalogue; stellar evolution; telescope [i]; Plate I

astrophysics The application of physical laws and theories to stars and galaxies, with the aim of deriving theoretical models to explain their behaviour. Its biggest triumph has been accounting for energy production inside stars, and there have been notable successes in explaining the properties of galaxies and quasars. » galaxy; physics; quasar; star

Asturias, Miguel Angel [ast**oo**rias] (1899–1974) Guatemalan novelist, born in Guatemala City. He studied law at the University of San Carlos and in Paris. He is best known for his first novel, *El señor presidente* (1946, Mr President), about the fall and trial of the hated dictator of an unnamed Latin-American country. Later novels include *Hombres de maiz* (1949, Men of Maize) and *Mulatta de tal* (1963, The Mulatta and Mr Fly). He won the Nobel Prize for Literature in 1967, and died in Madrid. » Latin-American literature; novel

Asturias [ast**oo**rias] pop (1981) 1 129 556; area 10 565 sq km/4 078 sq ml. Autonomous region and former principality of N Spain, co-extensive with the modern province of Oviedo; mountainous region along the Bay of Biscay; largely occupied by the Cordillera Cantabrica, rising to 2 646 m/8 681 ft in the Picos de Europa; centre of Christian resistance to Muslim invasion, 8th–9th-c; part of Kingdom of Leon, 911; scene of unsuccessful left-wing revolution, 1934; maize, fruit, livestock; coal (nearly half of Spain's needs), fluorspar, zinc, iron ore. » Spain [i]

Asunción [asoon**syohn**] 25°15S 57°40W, pop (1982) 455 517. Federal capital of Paraguay; transport and commercial centre on the E bank of the R Paraguay; established, 1537; capital of La Plata region until 1580; airport; railway; two universities (1890, 1960); food processing, footwear, textiles; La Encarnación church, Pantheon of Heroes. » Paraguay [i]

Aswan [as**wahn**], ancient **Syene** 24°05N 32°56E, pop (1976) 144 377. Capital of Aswan governorate, S Egypt; on the E bank of the R Nile, 900 km/560 ml S of Cairo; Aswan Dam to the S, at limit of navigation (1898–1902); Aswan High Dam further S at head of L Nasser (1971); airfield; railway; steel, textiles, winter tourism; Aswan museum, Roman Nilometer, Temples of Ptolemy VII, Seti I, Rameses II; Tombs of the Ancient Nobles, Aga Khan Mausoleum, Coptic monastery of St Simeon (6th-c), Temples of Philae, Temple of Kalabsha (transported 55 km/34 ml from its original site and re-erected near Aswan High Dam). » Aswan High Dam; Egypt [i]

Aswan High Dam [as**wahn**] A major gravity dam on the R Nile in Egypt, impounding L Nasser; completed in 1970; situated 6.4 km/4 m upstream from the lesser Aswan Dam; height 111 m/364 ft; length 3 600 m/11 811 ft. It has the capacity to generate 2 100 megawatts of hydroelectricity. » Aswan; Egypt [i]

asymptote [asimtoht] In mathematics, a line (usually straight) which is approached by a curve. This can be shown in a graph where the curve $y = 1/x$ approaches the line $y = 0$ as x becomes large; so $y = 0$ is an asymptote.

Atacama Desert [atakama], Span **Desierto de Atacama** Arid desert area in N Chile, claimed to be the world's driest area; a series of dry salt basins, extending 960 km/596 ml S from the Peru border to the R Copiapó; bounded W by the Pacific coastal range and E by the Cordillera de Domeyko; average altitude 600 m/2 000 ft; almost no vegetation; town of Calama recorded a 400-year drought up to 1971; water is piped to the towns and nitrate fields from the Cordillera; ceded to Chile by Peru and Bolivia, 1883–4; copper, nitrates, iodine, borax deposits. » Chile [i]

Atahualpa (?–1533) Last king of the Incas. On his father's death (1525) he received the kingdom of Quito, and in 1532, overwhelming his elder brother Huascar, seized Peru. He was captured by the Spaniards, and though agreeing to a great

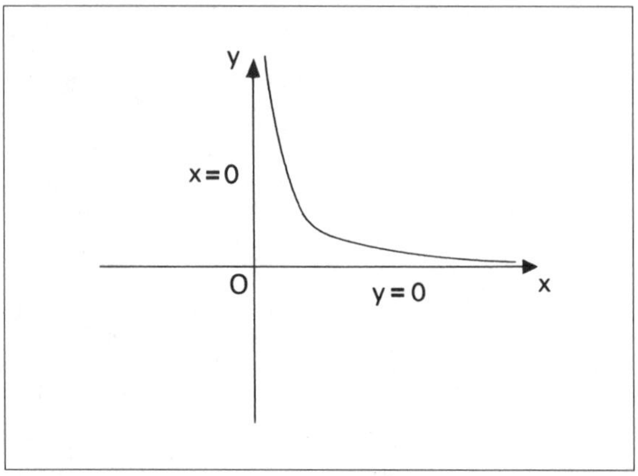

Asymptotes: Ox and Oy are asymptotes to the rectangular hyperbola $xy = c^2$

ransom, he was accused of plotting against Pizarro, and executed. » Pizarro

Atalanta [ata**lan**ta] In Greek mythology a heroine, nurtured by a she-bear, who grew up to be a strong huntress. She refused to marry any man who would not take part in a foot-race with her: those who lost were killed. Eventually Hippomenes (or Milanion) threw three golden apples of the Hesperides at her feet, so that her attention was diverted and she lost.

Atatürk, Mustapha Kemal (1881–1938) Turkish army officer, politician, and President of Turkey (1923–38), born in Salonika. He raised a nationalist rebellion in Anatolia in protest against the postwar division of Turkey, and in 1921 established a provisional government in Ankara. In 1922 the Ottoman Sultanate was formally abolished, and in 1923 Turkey was declared a secular republic, with Kemal as President. He became virtual dictator, and launched a social and political revolution introducing Western fashions, the emancipation of women, educational reform, the replacement of Arabic script with the Latin alphabet, and the discouragement of traditional Islamic loyalties in favour of a strictly Turkish nationalism. In 1935 he assumed the surname Atatürk ('Father of the Turks'). He died in Istanbul. » Turkey [i]

ataxia [**ata**kseea] Unsteadiness experienced on walking and standing, resulting from a failure of the central nervous system to control the movement of muscles in the lower limbs. In some cases it develops because the brain is deprived of information concerned with the position of the limbs in space (*sensory ataxia*). » central nervous system

atelier [atel**yay**] (Fr 'artist's studio') An abbreviation of *atelier libre* (literally 'free studio' – in the sense that anyone can attend, on payment of a fee), which provides a nude model for artists to work from, but no instruction. The most famous, the Atelier Suisse in Paris, opened c.1825 and was attended by Delacroix, Courbet, Manet, Monet, Cézanne, and others. They exist throughout Europe. » bottega; French art

Aten or **Aton** In Ancient Egypt, originally the name of the Sun's disc, and then that of the sun-god. In the reign of the Pharaoh Akhenaton, the cult of Aten temporarily replaced that of Amun-Re; this is sometimes interpreted as an early form of monotheism. » Akhenaton; Amun; monotheism

Athabascan or **Athapascan** Various Athabascan-speaking American Indian groups living in Alaska and NW Canada, W of Hudson Bay. Before the arrival of Europeans, some groups migrated S, and settled in the Great Plains and New Mexico (Apaches and Navajo are of Athabascan origin). They lived mainly in small independent hunting-and-gathering bands, and there was little tribal unity. They engaged in the fur trade after Europeans reached N America, and were eventually destroyed by the European presence. Today some supply trapped animals for the fur trade and are hunters' guides, and a few are assimilated into US culture: but most still live by hunting and fishing. » American Indians; Apache; hunter-gatherers; Navajo

Athanasian Creed A statement of Christian faith, written in Latin probably in the 5th-c AD. Called *quicunque vult* after the opening words, it remains a historic statement of Trinitarian doctrine, still sometimes used liturgically. The Greek text is known in Eastern Churches, but with the omission of the *filioque* clause. » Athanasius, St; Christianity; Filioque

Athanasius, St (c.296–373), feast day 2 May. Christian leader, born in Alexandria, who led the opposition to the doctrines of Arianism. A distinguished participant at the Council of Nicaea (325), he was chosen Patriarch of Alexandria and Primate of Egypt. As a result of his stand against the heretic Arius, he was dismissed from his see on several occasions by emperors sympathetic to the Arian cause. However his teaching was supported after his death at the Council of Constantinople (381). His writings include works on the Trinity, the Incarnation, and the divinity of the Holy Spirit. » Arius; Athanasian Creed; Christianity

atheism The denial of the existence of God or gods. It includes both the rejection of any specific belief in God or gods, and the view that the only rational approach to claims about divine existence is one of scepticism. Justification of atheism is often made on the grounds that some branch of science or psychology has rendered belief in God or gods superfluous, or that experiential verification of religious belief is lacking. Theists argue that such justification has not proved to be logically grounded. » Freud, Sigmund; God; humanism; Marx; scepticism; theism

Athelstan or **Aethelstan** (c.895–939) Son of Edward the Elder, and the grandson of Alfred the Great. Acknowledged as King of Wessex and Mercia (924), he built upon his predecessors' achievements by invading Northumbria, securing his direct rule over it, and thus establishing himself as effectively the first King of all England (927). He stabilized his position by defeating a powerful coalition of enemies at Brunanburh (location unknown) in 937. » Anglo-Saxons; Edward the Elder

Athena or **Athene** [a**thee**na] The Greek goddess of wisdom. She was not born, but sprang fully armed from the head of Zeus; she was the patron of Athens, and her emblem was the owl. » Zeus

Athens, Gr **Athínai**, ancient **Athenae** 38°00N 23°44E, pop (1981) 862 133; Greater Athens 3 027 331. Capital city of Greece, in a wide coastal plain between the Ilissus and Cephissus Rivers, surrounded by hills; ancient Greek city-state extending over Attica by the 7th-c BC; great economic and cultural prosperity under Pericles (5th-c BC); taken by the Romans, 146 BC; part of the Ottoman Empire, 1456; capital of modern Greece, 1835; occupied by Germans in World War 2; two airports; railway; university (1837); port and main industrial area at Piraeus; textiles, machine tools, shipbuilding, chemicals, food processing, tourism; hill of the Acropolis (156 m/512 ft), with the Parthenon (5th-c BC), Propylaea (437–432 BC), Temple of Athena Niki (432–421 BC), Ionic Erechtheion (421–406 BC), and Acropolis museum; to the S, the Odeon of Herod Atticus (2nd-c BC), portico of Eumenes, remains of the Asklepieion, (4th-c BC), and site of the Odeum of Pericles; to the N, the excavated area of the Ancient Agora (market-place); Olympieion, Arch of Hadrian (AD 131–2), Stadion; Parliament Building, National Garden, National Archaeological Museum; Carnival (Feb), *son et lumière* (Apr–Oct), folk dancing in open-air theatre (May–Sep), Athens Festival of Music and Drama (Jul–Sep). » Greece [i]; Greek history; Parthenon; Pericles

atherosclerosis The irregular deposition of substances (lipids, mainly cholesterol and triglycerides) on the inner wall of arteries and arterioles; seen as sharply-defined, raised, cream-coloured patches. Together with associated scarring, these cause narrowing of the affected blood vessel. Common sites are the aorta and blood vessels to the brain and heart, but no vessel is immune. The disorder increases with age, and the consequences to health vary with the blood vessel affected. Thus angina pectoris, paralysis, or gangrene of the limb may arise when the coronary arteries, cerebral arteries, or arteries to the lower limbs respectively are affected. Contributing causes include high animal fat dietary intake, high blood pressure, obesity, and lack of exercise. » artery; coronary heart disease [i]

athlete's foot A common form of ringworm infection (*Tinea pedes*) in which a fungus causes itching and fissuring of the skin between the toes. It is usually acquired in swimming baths and from shower floors. » foot; ringworm

athletics Tests of running, jumping, throwing, and walking skills for trained athletes, also known as **track and field** events. The track events are divided into six categories: *sprint races* (100, 200, and 400 m); *middle distance races* (800 and 1 500 m); *long distance races* (5 000 and 10 000 m); *hurdle races* (110 m–100 for women – and 400 m); *relay races* (4 × 100 and 4 × 400 m); and the *steeplechase* (3 000 m). In addition there is the endurance test of the marathon. The field events involve jumping and throwing. Jumping events consist of the high jump, long jump, triple jump, and pole vault (men only). The throwing events are the discus, shot put, javelin throw, and hammer throw (men only). Walking races take place on either the road or the track. In addition, two multi-event competitions exist in the form of the decathlon (ten events) for men and heptathlon (seven events) for women. Such competitions date to Egypt in c.3800 BC and they formed part of the ancient Olympic Games. The athletics events are now the most important part of the Modern Olympics. The governing body is the International Amateur Athletic Federation, founded in 1912. » Amateur Athletic Association; decathlon; discus throw; hammer throw; heptathlon; high jump; International Amateur Athletic Federation; javelin throw; long jump; pole vault; shot put; triple jump; RR104

Athlone, Gaelic **Ath Luain** [athlohn] 53°25N 7°56W, pop (1981) 14 426. Town in Westmeath county, Leinster, C Irish Republic; on R Shannon, W of Dublin; railway; technical college; barracks; radio transmitter; textiles, industrial and electrical cable; remains of town wall, 13th-c Franciscan abbey, 13th-c castle; river boating centre; all-Ireland amateur drama contest (Jul). » Irish Republic [i]; Westmeath

Atlanta 33°45N 84°23W, pop (1980) 425 022. State capital in Fulton County, NW Georgia, USA; largest city in the state, near the Appalachian foothills; founded at the end of the railway in 1837 (named Terminus); renamed Atlanta, 1845; a Confederate supply depot in the Civil War; burned by General Sherman, 1864; capital, 1887; airport; railway; four universities (1835, 1836, 1865, 1913); industrial, transportation, commercial, and cultural centre; aircraft, automobiles, textiles, food products, steel, furniture, chemicals; major league teams, Braves (baseball), Hawks (basketball), Falcons (football); High Museum of Art, Alliance Theatre, Oakland Cemetery, Martin Luther King Jr historic site, Grant Park. » American Civil War; Georgia; King, Martin Luther

Atlanta Campaign » March Through Georgia

Atlantic, Battle of the (1940–3) The conflict arising out of German attacks on shipping in the Atlantic during World War 2. The German strategy was to cut off Britain's supplies of food and munitions by submarine action. Only at the end of 1943 were the attacks countered, and the threat brought under control. » World War 2

Atlantic Charter A declaration of common objectives by Roosevelt and Churchill after a secret meeting off Newfoundland (Aug 1941). It announced agreement on principles which should govern postwar settlements, several of which paralleled Wilson's Fourteen Points of 1918. The Charter was endorsed by the USSR and 14 other states at war with the Axis Powers, and served as an ideological basis for Allied co-operation during the war. » Axis Powers; Churchill, Winston; Fourteen Points; Roosevelt, Franklin D; World War 2

Atlantic City 39°21N 74°27W, pop (1980) 40 199. Town in Atlantic County, SE New Jersey, USA; on the Atlantic coast, 96 km/60 ml SE of Philadelphia; railway; popular seaside resort with famed boardwalk (over 9 km/5½ ml long) and piers; many casinos; convention centre; Miss America Pageant (Sep). » New Jersey

Atlantic Intracoastal Waterway » Intracoastal Waterway

Atlantic Ocean Body of water extending from the Arctic to the Antarctic, separating N and S America (W) from Europe and Africa (E); area c.86 557 000 sq km/33 411 000 sq ml; depths of 5 725 m/18 783 ft reached in Argentine abyssal plain; average depth 3 700 m/12 000 ft; maximum depth, Puerto Rico Trench, 8 648 m/28 372 ft; principal arms (W), Labrador Sea, Gulf of Mexico, Caribbean Sea; (E), North Sea, Baltic Sea, Mediterranean and Black Sea, Bay of Biscay, Gulf of Guinea; (S), Weddell Sea; continental shelf narrow off coast of Africa and Spain, broader in NW Europe and off Americas; 'S' shaped, submarine Mid-Atlantic Ridge between Iceland and the Antarctic Circle, centre of earthquake and volcanic activity; seafloor spreading, such that N and S America are moving away from Africa and Europe, rate of 2 cm/0.8 in per year (N), 4.1 cm/1.6 in (S); major surface circulation, clockwise in N, counter-clockwise in S; main currents include the Gulf Stream (N Atlantic Drift), and the N Equatorial, Canary, S Equatorial, Brazil, Benguela, and Equatorial Counter Currents; Sargasso Sea, a sluggish region at centre of movement in the N Atlantic; main islands include Iceland, Faeroes, British Is, Newfoundland, Azores, Bermuda, Madeira, Canary Is, Cape Verde Is, Trinidad and Tobago, Ascension, St Helena, Tristan da Cunha, Falkland Is, S Georgia; mineral resources include manganese nodules, offshore oil and gas, and metal-rich sediments; several major fishing areas; important international communications highway, particularly from Middle East to Europe. » abyssal plains; continental drift; current (oceanography); manganese nodules; plate tectonics [i]

Atlantic Wall An incomplete network of coastal fortifications, supplemented by beach-obstacles and minefields, constructed in 1942–4 between the Pas-de-Calais and the Bay of Biscay as part of Hitler's plans for an impregnable 'Fortress Europe' capable of repelling any Allied landings. On D-Day its 'invincibility' was shown to be a myth. » World War 2

Atlantis [at**lan**tis] According to Plato, an island in the ocean W of Spain, whose armies once threatened Europe and Africa, and which disappeared into the sea. Plato claimed to have heard of the island from the Egyptians, and this has generated many speculative books and expeditions; but it was simply a fictional place where he could locate his ideas of social organization. » Plato

Atlas (astronomy) The fifteenth natural satellite of Saturn, discovered in 1980; distance from the planet 138 000 km/86 000 ml; diameter 40 km/25 ml. » Saturn (astronomy); RR4

Atlas (mythology) In Greek mythology, a Titan who was made to hold up the heavens with his hands, as a punishment for taking part in the revolt against the Olympians. When books of maps came to be published, he was often portrayed as a frontispiece, hence the name *atlas*. » Heracles; Titan (mythology)

Atlas Mountains A system of folded mountain chains in Morocco, Algeria, and Tunisia, NW Africa; includes (1) the volcanic **Anti-Atlas** range in SW Morocco which runs SW–NE for 250 km/155 ml and rises to heights over 2 500 m/8 000 ft; (2) the **Haut Atlas** range, the largest in the group, running SW–NE for 650 km/400 ml from Morocco's Atlantic coast, rising to Mt Toubkal (4 165 m/13 665 ft); (3) the **Moyen Atlas** (N) rising to 3 343 m/10 968 ft at Caberral; (4) E–W along Morocco's Mediterranean coast, the **Er Rif Mts**, rising to over 2 000 m/6 500 ft; (5) the **Atlas Saharien** which extends NE of the Haut Atlas across N Algeria; (6) the **Tell Atlas**, a smaller coastal range running along Algeria's Mediterranean seaboard. » Morocco [i]

atman (Sanskrit, 'soul' or 'self') [**aht**man] In Hinduism, the human soul or essential self. In the teaching of the Upanishads, it is seen as being one with the absolute, and identified with Brahman. » Advaita; Brahman; Hinduism

atmosphere The layer of gas surrounding any planet or star. Earth's atmosphere is composed of air, which on average is made up of 78% nitrogen, 21% oxygen, and 1% argon, with traces of other rare gases, carbon dioxide, and hydrogen. Moist air may contain up to 31% water vapour. Earth's atmosphere is divided into several concentric shells, the lowest being the

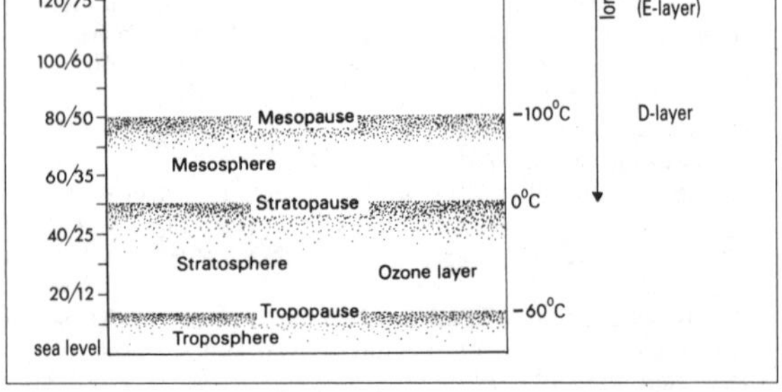

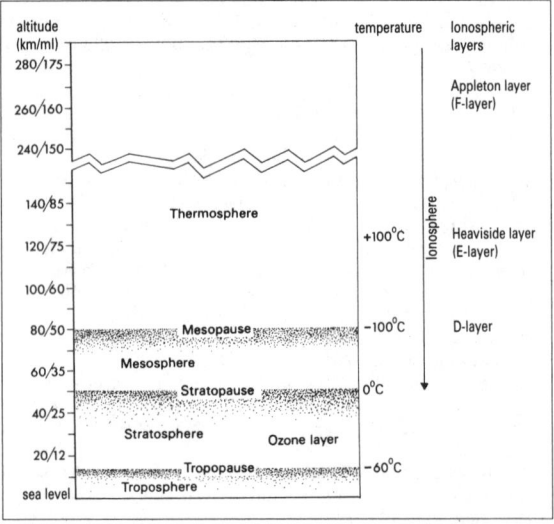

Layers of the atmosphere

troposphere, followed by the *stratosphere*, *mesosphere*, and *thermosphere*. The outer shell of the atmosphere, at c.400 km/250 ml, from which light gases can escape, is termed the *exosphere*. The atmosphere contains the gases vital to life, and shields the Earth from harmful ionizing radiation. » ionosphere

atmospheric physics The application of physical principles to the layer of gas surrounding planets, especially Earth. The subject includes such fields as thermodynamics, convection, gas density distributions, condensation, fluid mechanics, radiation, and heat transfer. It allows an understanding of cloud formation, solar heating of the atmosphere, the origin of wind patterns, and other features essential to weather forecasting and pollution control. » atmosphere [i]; aurora; condensation (physics); convection; fluid mechanics; greenhouse effect; magnetosphere; ozone layer

atmospheric pressure The pressure exerted by the atmosphere on the Earth's surface; the accepted value is called one *atmosphere*, which equals 1.013 bar, 101 325 pascal (Pa), or 760 torr. Pressure varies with elevation and temperature. The average pressure at sea level (1013.25 mb) is taken as the standard, and it is usual to modify measurements taken at different elevations so that they refer to this level. Pressure is measured using a barometer. » anticyclone; barometer; depression (meteorology) [i]; general circulation model; isobar; pascal; pressure; torr

atoll A roughly circular structure of coral reefs enclosing a lagoon. Atolls occur in warm, clear, tropical oceanic waters where corals and coralline algae can flourish. Darwin first theorized that they are the final stage in a progression of reef formations. In the first stage, a *fringing reef* grows adjacent to land with little or no lagoon separating it from the shore. The second stage, a *barrier reef*, lies offshore with a lagoon separating it from the land. An *atoll* is the third and most mature stage, where the original land is no longer present. Darwin theorized that as volcanic islands subsided below sea level, reefs might continue to grow upward towards the surface. Drilling on several atolls has shown them to be supported by volcanic pedestals, confirming Darwin's hypothesis. » coral; Darwin, Charles; Great Barrier Reef

atom The smallest portion of a chemical element. Each atom comprises a positively charged nucleus surrounded by negatively charged electrons, whose number equals that of the protons contained within the nucleus. Electrons are attracted to the nucleus by electromagnetic force. They determine the chemistry of an atom, and are responsible for binding atoms together. Atoms are described using quantum mechanics; the diameter of an atom is approximately 10^{-10}m, and the number of atoms of a substance is given by Avogadro's number. » atom trap; atomic physics; Avogadro's number; chemical elements; electron; ion; molecule; nucleus (physics); subatomic particles

atom trap A device for trapping atoms whose velocity has been greatly slowed using laser cooling. The trapping is performed either by magnetic fields or by an intense laser beam focused to a spot. The trapped atoms allow a detailed study of their atomic properties. » atom; ion trap; laser cooling

atomic bomb A nuclear explosive device (the **A-Bomb**) which achieves its destructive effects through energy released during the fission of heavy atoms (as in uranium-235 or plutonium-239). The bomb was developed in the USA from 1942 onwards under the code-name 'Manhattan', and used to destroy the Japanese cities of Hiroshima and Nagasaki (Aug 1945). Atomic weapons have been supplanted by the very much more destructive thermonuclear weapons, but a fission weapon trigger is an essential component of these devices. Fission devices are also used for low-yield 'tactical' weapons, and in 'enhanced radiation' or neutron weapons. » critical mass; hydrogen bomb [i]; Manhattan project; neutron bomb; nuclear fission/weapons

atomic clock » clock [i]

atomic mass unit (amu) Unit of mass; symbol u; defined as 1/12 of the mass of the carbon-12 atom; value $1u = 1.66 \times 10^{-27}$ kg; used to express relative atomic masses of atoms. » atom; mass; units (scientific); RR70

atomic number » **proton number**

atomic physics The study of the structure and properties of atoms, and of their interactions with electromagnetic radiation and with other atoms. In 1911 British physicist Ernest Rutherford interpreted the scattering of alpha particles passing through gold foil as demonstrating that atoms contain a hard central nucleus, c.10^{-14}m in diameter, complete atoms being c.10^{-10} across. He visualized the atom as a central positively-charged nucleus with negatively-charged electrons orbiting round it, rather like planets orbiting the Sun. However, such atoms would be unstable, according to the laws of classical mechanics, decaying by the emission of electromagnetic radiation. Further, they would not exhibit observed atomic spectra. These problems were solved by the improved atomic model of Danish physicist Niels Bohr (1913), in which an electron in a particular orbit around the nucleus had a specific energy depending on the orbit radius. Since only certain orbits were allowed, electrons could only have certain energies, giving rise

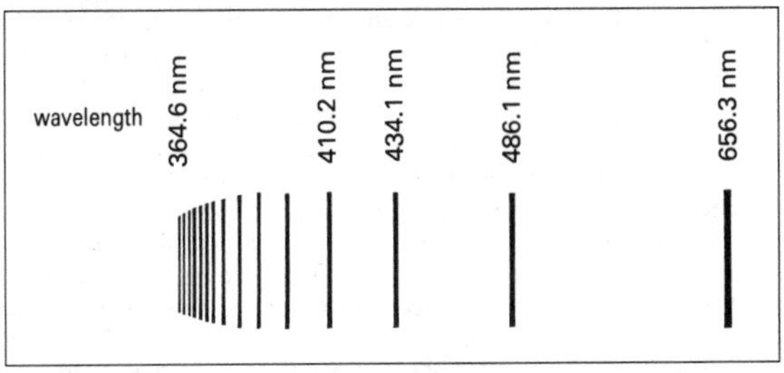

Atomic spectrum for hydrogen atoms

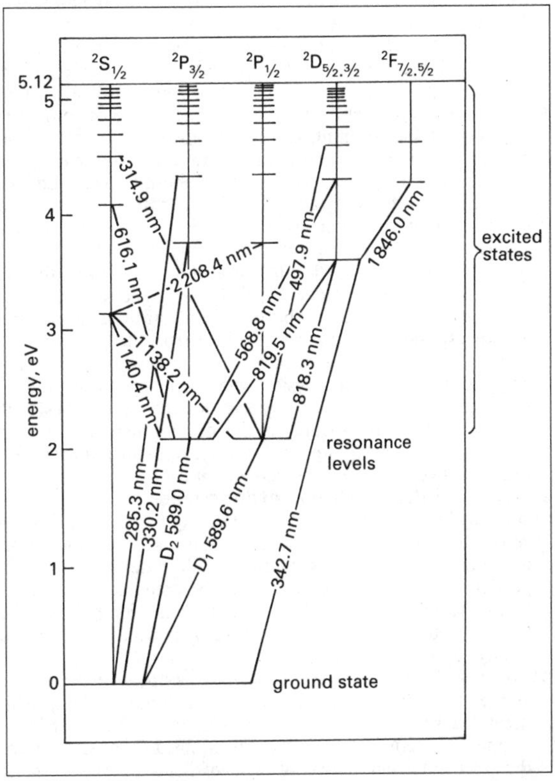

Energy levels of sodium. Horizontal lines represent different energy levels, measured in electronvolts (eV) above the lowest level (ground state). Lines linking levels show possible electron transitions together with the wavelength of light emitted or absorbed. The two labelled D_1 and D_2 correspond to the distinctive yellow of sodium lamps.

to a pattern of discrete allowed energy levels. Electrons in an allowed orbit would not radiate electromagnetic energy, but electron jumps from one orbit to another would correspond to the emission or absorption of well-defined quantities of light, in agreement with observed atomic spectra.

Though the Bohr model still provides a useful visual model, current atomic theory is an extension which incorporates quantum mechanics. Electrons have wave properties, and the Bohr orbits can then be explained as the requirement of fitting a whole number of electron waves round the nucleus. Electrons in atoms are better represented as distributions of electric charge each labelled by a particular set of quantum numbers, rather than by point particles in circular orbits. Every possible set of quantum numbers corresponds to an energy level, though not all can be occupied at once. Whereas Bohr's theory allowed a partial understanding of atomic spectra, modern quantum theory allows their explicit detailed calculation.

The quantum numbers required to specify electrons in (unexcited) atoms of elements determine exactly the position of those elements in the periodic table; and electron structure determines the type of chemical bond that will be formed with other atoms. The properties of hydrogen atoms can be calculated with great precision; but for more complicated atoms, the problems of predicting properties become severe. Spectroscopy and collisions between atoms are used to test predictions of energy levels and other properties. Exotic atoms (eg negative calcium ions) can now be produced and studied. The direct technological applications of atomic physics include lasers and atomic clocks. » atom; atom trap; atomic mass unit; atomic spectra [i]; Auger effect; aurora; Bohr; cross section; electron; ion; ion trap; isotopes; kinetic theory of gases; nucleon number; orbit; periodic table; proton number; quantum mechanics; Raman scattering; Rutherford, Ernest; spectroscopy

atomic radius The effective size of an atom: in a metal, half the distance between the nuclei of the two nearest neighbour atoms in the solid (also called the *metallic radius*); in non-metals, half the distance of the closest approach of the nuclei of two identical non-bonded atoms. » atom; van der Waals forces

atomic spectra A set of specific frequencies of electromagnetic radiation, typically light, emitted or absorbed by atoms of a certain type. A given spectral line corresponds to the transition of an electron between two specific energy levels. **Emission spectra** are produced by applying energy to atoms, for example by heating or electrical discharge, raising the electrons to a higher energy level; the excited electrons emit light upon returning to an unexcited state. **Absorption spectra** are observed by passing light through a substance. Spectra in infrared correspond to molecular vibrations and rotations; X-ray spectra correspond to the transitions of electrons deep inside heavy atoms. The study of spectra is called **spectroscopy**, a major analytic technique in physics and chemistry. The study of hydrogen spectra by Swiss physicist Johann Balmer (1825–98) and others was important to the development of quantum mechanics. » energy levels; laser [i]; nuclear magnetic resonance; spectroscopy; *see illustration p 83*

atomic weight » **relative atomic mass**

atomism In philosophy, a tradition dating back to the 5th-c BC, associated particularly with Democritus and Leucippus, which maintains that reality is composed ultimately of indivisible particles, and all phenomena must be explained in terms of them. Atomism was originally put forward for philosophical reasons; but from the 17th-c onward, it became a scientific theory. » Democritus

atonality The property of music which is not written in a key. While any music not written in the tonal system, which prevailed between c.1600 and c.1920, might be described as 'atonal', the term is most commonly applied to music written in the post-tonal but pre-serial style of Schoenberg's *Ewartung* (1909) and other compositions of that period. » mode (music); Schoenberg; serialism; tonality

atonement In Christian theology, the process whereby sinners are made 'at one' with God, through the life, death, and resurrection of Jesus Christ. No one theory is recognized as authoritative, but the theories of Irenaeus (stressing 'victory' over evil), Anselm (stressing 'satisfaction' made to God), and Abelard (stressing the force of example of Christ) have been commonly held. » Abelard; Anselm, St; Christianity; Irenaeus, St

Atonement, Day of » **Yom Kippur**

atractaspid snake » **asp**

Atreus [aytryoos] In Greek mythology, a king of Argos who quarrelled with his brother Thyestes, and placed the flesh of Thyestes' children before him at a banquet. Atreus was the father of Agamemnon and Menelaus. » Thyestes

atrial natriuretic factor [aytreeal naytreeyuretik] A chemical substance (a peptide) isolated from granules found within the muscle cells of the atrium of the heart in various mammals (eg humans, rats). It inhibits the re-absorption of sodium by the kidney tubules, and the secretion of renin and antidiuretic hormone, and also lowers blood presssure. It possibly acts as a hormone involved in the regulation of body salt, water, and blood pressure. » antidiuretic hormone; heart [i]; peptide; renin

atrium (plural **atria**) The entrance hall or open inner court of a Roman house; in mediaeval architecture, an open court in front of a church; generally, any cavity or entrance in a building. Atria have become particularly fashionable in late 20th-c hotels and office blocks, sometimes rising to great height. » Roman architecture

atropine [atropeen, atropin] A drug extracted from deadly nightshade, used as a poison during the Roman Empire and later. It acts by blocking nerve transmission mediated by acetylcholine. Safer derivatives are now used in a wide variety of disorders, commonly in motion sickness preparations and in ophthalmology, where they dilate the pupil during eye examinations. » acetylcholine; belladonna; ophthalmology

Atropos [atropos] » **Moerae**

attachment In psychology, the infant–care-giver relationship, and the actions (eg crying, cuddling) which promote this relationship. The dominant explanation for attachment is the ethological theory of British psychiatrist John Bowlby (1907–), which argues that early reciprocity between parent and child is determined by genetic factors in both participants, modified by the parent's own attachment history. Experience of disrupted relationships thus may be repeated in successive generations. » developmental psychology

Attalids The flamboyant Hellenistic dynasty that ruled over large parts of W Asia Minor from the 3rd-c to the 1st-c BC. Keen patrons of the arts, they made their beautiful capital, Pergamum, one of the main cultural centres of the Graeco-Roman world. » Pergamum (Asia Minor)

attar A fragrant essential oil distilled from plants; also called **otto**. The best-known is attar of roses, obtained from the petals of the damask rose (*Rosa damascena*), cultivated in the Balkans. » essential oil; rose

Attenborough, Sir Richard (1923–) British film actor, producer, and director, born at Cambridge and trained in London. His first film appearance as an ordinary seaman in Noel Coward's *In Which We Serve* (1942) was followed by several very similar roles, but his characterization of the vicious young hooligan in *Brighton Rock* (1947) led to many more varied parts. He was actor/producer of several features in the 1960s, and became a director in 1969 with *O What a Lovely War!*, followed by such varied major epics as *A Bridge Too Far* (1977), *Gandhi* (1982), which won eight Oscars, *A Chorus Line* (1985), and *Cry Freedom* (1987). He was knighted in 1976.

attention A phenomenon where the processing capacity of the brain is directed towards a particular part of incoming, competing information. The classic example is the 'cocktail party phenomenon', where we are able to listen successfully to a single speaker in a room full of other speakers. *Early selection* theories suppose that we can filter out unwanted material at an early stage of processing; *late selection* theories suppose that most material is fully processed, and selection occurs only when we come to make a response. Sustained attention is difficult to maintain, and substantial decrements in performance are often obtained in vigilance tasks (eg detecting rare signals on a radar screen), if attention is to be maintained for more than 20 minutes. » cognitive psychology

attenuation The reduction in magnitude of some quantity, caused either by absorption when passing through a medium or by increasing distance from its source. Sunlight is attenuated by clouds; sounds die away with distance from their source.

Attersee [aterzay] or **Kammersee** [**kam**erzay], Eng **Lake Atter** or **Lake Kammer** 47°55N 13°32E. Largest Alpine lake in Austria, in Vöcklabruck district, Oberösterreich, N Austria; area 45.9 sq km/ 17¾ sq ml; length 20 km/12 ml; width 2–3 km/1¼–1¾ ml; maximum depth 171 m/561 ft; lakeside summer resorts at Seewalchen, Kammer, Weyregg, Steinbach, Weissenbach. » Austria [i]

Attica The SE promontory of C Greece, and the most easterly part of the Greek mainland. In Classical Greece, it was the territory which made up the city-state of Athens. » Athens

Attila [**at**ila], Ger **Etzel**, Hungarian **Ethele** (c.406–53) Hunnish King (434–53), called the 'Scourge of God', whose dominion extended from the Rhine to the frontiers of China. In 447 he devastated all the countries between the Black Sea and the Mediterranean, and defeated the Emperor Theodosius. In 451 he invaded Gaul, but was defeated on the Catalaunian Plains by a joint army of Romans and Visigoths. He then invaded Italy (452), sacking several cities, Rome itself being saved only by the personal mediation of Pope Leo I, who bought off the city with large sums. The Hunnish Empire decayed after Attila's death. » Aëtius; Catalaunian Plains, Battle of the; Huns; Theodosius I

Attis or **Atys** [atis] In Greek mythology, the young male vegetation god connected with the Asiatic cult of Cybele; he died after castrating himself, and was resurrected. The story was later associated with the spring festival. » Adonis; Tammuz

Attlee (of Walthamstow), Clement (Richard), 1st Earl (1883–1967) British Labour statesman and Prime Minister (1945–51), born at Putney, near London. He was educated at Haileybury and Oxford, and called to the Bar in 1905. Early converted to socialism, he became the first Labour Mayor of Stepney (1919–20), an MP (1922), Deputy Leader of the Opposition (1931–5), and then Leader (1935). He was Dominions Secretary (1942–3) and Deputy Prime Minister (1942–5) in Churchill's War Cabinet. As Prime Minister, he carried through a vigorous programme of nationalization, the National Health Service was introduced, and independence was granted to India (1947) and Burma (1948). He was Leader of the Opposition again (1951–5) until he resigned and accepted an earldom. He died in London. » National Health Service; nationalization; socialism

attorney 1 A person who has power to act for another; **power of attorney** refers to the authority so given. In England and Wales, the Enduring Powers of Attorney Act (1985) provides a method whereby such a power may survive a loss of the other person's mental capacity. This overcomes a crucial shortcoming of the earlier law, which invariably ended the power at a time when it was sometimes most needed. US law provides for an analogous durable power of attorney. **2** The term is also used in some jurisdictions as a general label for lawyers.

Attorney-General The chief legal officer of a nation or state, who represents the government in its legal actions. In England and Wales, he is a member of the House of Commons and of the government. In the USA, the Federal Attorney-General is an appointed member of the President's cabinet. In Australia, the USA, and several other countries, the constituent states each have their own Attorney-General. » criminal law; solicitor-general

Attwell, Mabel Lucie (1879–1964) British artist and writer, born in London. She studied at Heatherley's and other art schools, and from 1911 onwards drew humorous postcards for Valentine's, usually featuring chubby children. She died at Fowey, Cornwall. » English art

Atwood, Margaret (1939–) Canadian poet, novelist, and critic, born in Ottawa, and educated in Toronto. Her major collections include *The Circle Game* (1966), *Procedure for Underground* (1970), *You are Happy* (1974), and *Poems Selected and New, 1976–86* (1986). Among her novels are *The Edible Woman* (1970), *Lady Oracle* (1976), the prize-winning *Handmaid's Tale* (1985) and *Cat's Eye* (1988). Her *Survival* (1972) is considered to be the best book on Canadian literature. » Canadian literature

Auber, Daniel (François Esprit) [oh**bay**] (1782–1871) French composer of operas, born at Caen. A student of Cherubini, his best-known works are *La Muette de Portici* (Mute Girl of Portici, usually entitled *Masaniello*, 1828), and *Fra Diavolo* (Brother Devil, first performed 1830). He died in Paris. » Cherubini

aubergine A bushy perennial with funnel-shaped, violet flowers and large, edible berries, native to New World tropics; fruit variable in shape and colour, but typically egg-shaped and purple; also called **egg-plant**. It is widely cultivated as an annual vegetable in temperate regions. (*Solanum meleagrum*. Family: *Solanaceae*.) » perennial; vegetable

aubretia [aw**bree**shuh] A mat-forming perennial; slightly greyish leaves; pink to purple or blue cross-shaped flowers; native to SE Europe. (*Aubretia deltoidea*. Family: *Cruciferae*.) » perennial

Aubrey, John (1626–97) English antiquary and folklorist, born at Easton Percy, Wiltshire, and educated at Malmesbury, Blandford, and Oxford. In 1652 he succeeded to several estates, but was forced through lawsuits to part with the last of them in 1670. His last years were passed in 'danger of arrests' with various protectors. He died at Oxford. Only *Miscellanies* (1696) was printed in his lifetime; but he left a large mass of materials, some of which were later published (notably in *Letters by Eminent Persons*, 1813, and *Brief Lives*, 1898). » folklore

Aubusson, Pierre d' (1423–1503) Grandmaster of the Knights Hospitallers of St John of Jerusalem, born at Monteil-au-Vicomte, France. Of noble French family, he fought against the Turks, and later against the Swiss. He joined the Knights c.1453, becoming grandmaster in 1476. Mohammed II's career of conquest, which threatened to spread over W Europe, was halted by d'Aubusson and his small colony of Christian soldiers in Rhodes (1480). He was made a cardinal in 1489, and died in Rhodes. » Hospitallers

Auch [ohsh] 43°39N 0°36E, pop (1982) 25 543. Ancient town and capital of Gers department, S France, on R Gers; important city of Roman Gaul; former capital of Gascony and Armagnac; railway; archbishopric; furniture, hosiery, eau-de-vie, pâté; folk museum, St Pierre Gothic cathedral. » Gaul; Gothic architecture

Auchinleck, Sir Claude (John Eyre) [**okh**inlek] (1884–1981) British field marshal. Educated at Wellington College, he joined the 62nd Punjabis in 1904, and served in Egypt and Mesopotamia. In World War 2, he commanded in N Norway and India, and then moved to the Middle East (1941). He made a successful advance into Cyrenaica, but was later thrown back by Rommel. His regrouping of the 8th Army on El Alamein is now recognized as a successful defensive operation, but at the time he was made a scapegoat for the retreat, and replaced (1942). In 1943 he returned to India, serving subsequently as Supreme Commander India and Pakistan (1947). » North African Campaign; World War 2

Auckland [**awk**land] 36°55S 174°43E, pop (1988e) 841 700 (urban area). Seaport city in North Island, New Zealand; principal port of New Zealand; founded, 1840; capital, 1840–65; airport; railway; university (1958); textiles, footwear, clothing, chemicals, steel, electronics, carpets, plastics, food processing, vehicle assembly; Waitemata Harbour spanned by Auckland Harbour Bridge (1959); two cathedrals, New Zealand Heritage Park, Howick colonial village, Auckland War Memorial Museum, Museum of Transport and Technology. » New Zealand [i]

auction bridge » **bridge** (recreation)

Auden, W(ystan) H(ugh) (1907–73) British poet, born at York, and educated at Oxford. Deeply feeling the impact of the early thirties' unemployment in England, he and his friends developed a social conscience which resembled communism. Out of this concern came his early poems, in a lyric voice which he later disowned. Supporting the Spanish Republic's cause, he wrote *Spain* (1937), and (with Isherwood) was commissioned to report on Japanese aggression in China; the result was their *Journey to a War* (1939). In 1939 Auden emigrated to New York, becoming a naturalized US citizen. He returned to England while he held the chair of poetry at Oxford (1956–61). His later conversion to Anglicanism left his writing more serious, and he adopted a more reflective, epistolary style. He also collaborated with Isherwood in three plays, and wrote several opera libretti. He died in Vienna. » Church of England; communism; English literature; Isherwood; poetry; psychoanalysis

Audenarde [ohd**nahd**] » **Oudenaarde**

audiencia [owdiensia] The supreme court of appeal in each territory of the Spanish-American Empire, composed of between six and fourteen judges (*oidores*); thirteen were created during the colonial period. Apart from being a court, it also had important administrative functions. » Court of Appeal

audio-visual aids Sources other than print which are used to help people teach and learn. These may include pieces of equipment such as still, overhead, and film projectors, tape recorders, and radio or television sets, as well as pictures, graphics, charts, films, video-tapes, and audio-tapes. They may be used singly or in combination, as with a synchronized tape-slide sequence, or the interactive video-disc which can be linked with a microcomputer to provide moving or still pictures as well as screen text and graphics. » projector [i]; slide projector; tape recorder; video; video disc

audiogram A widely used profile of hearing ability, used in the diagnosis of hearing impairment. It is a graph showing the absolute threshold for the intensity of pure tones as a function of their frequency. It is commonly represented as a hearing loss, which is the difference (in decibels) between the measured threshold and the average of thresholds obtained from a large number of young, healthy ears. » ear [i]

audiology The study of the physiology of hearing, and of diseases that affect the external, middle and inner ear and the associated nerve. It is specifically concerned with assessing the nature and degree of hearing loss and conservation, and with the rehabilitation of people with hearing impairment. The scientific measurement of hearing is known as **audiometry**. A wide range of audiometric tests is now employed, using an **audiometer**. » ear [i]

audiometry » **audiology**

audit The process of checking that the accounts of an organization have been kept in accordance with good practice and with relevant laws (particularly the Companies Acts, in the UK), and that the accounts fairly reflect the activities of the organization and its state of affairs at a certain date. All limited companies must have accounts audited. Auditors are appointed by shareholders and report to them. They are usually members of professional accountancy firms. » accountancy

auditory perception The ability to respond appropriately to sound; and the study of this ability. It encompasses a range of specializations distinguished by the type of sound considered (eg music perception, speech perception), the theory and methods employed in the study (eg psychoacoustics, auditory psychophysics), and by the different aspects of the ability considered (eg sound localization, pitch perception). » cocktail party effect; psychophysics

auditory tube » **Eustachian tube**

Audubon, John James (1785–1851) US ornithologist, born at Les Cayes, Santo Domingo. His early life was spent in France, where he studied painting under David and developed a taste for natural history. Returning to America (1804), he travelled westward, painting portraits, and building up his vast collection of bird illustrations. In 1821 he visited Europe, where he produced *The Birds of America* (1827–38), a work which contains coloured figures of 1 065 birds, natural size. He died in New York City. » David, Jacques Louis

Auger effect [**ow**ger] In atoms, the filling of a vacancy in an inner electron energy level by an electron from an outer energy level of the same atom. The excess energy evolved causes emission of another electron. The effect, discovered by French physicist Pierre-Victor Auger in 1925, forms the basis of Auger spectroscopy. » atomic physics; electron; secondary emission; spectroscopy

Aughrim, Battle of [**aw**grim] (1691) A battle in Co Wicklow, Ireland, between Protestant forces commanded for William III by General van Ginkel, and Catholic forces commanded for James II by the Marquis de Saint Ruth. The rout of the Catholics rapidly led to their complete submission, and the return of a Protestant ascendancy based on English rule. » James II (of England); William III

augmentative communication » **alternative and augmentative communication**

Augsburg [**owgs**boork], ancient **Augusta Vindelicorum** 48°22N 10°54E, pop (1983) 246 700. Industrial and commercial city in Schwaben district, Germany; at the confluence of the Lech and Wertach Rivers, 48 km/30 ml WNW of Munich; founded by the Romans, 15 BC; influential commercial centre in 15th-c; seat of the famous Diets of 1530 and 1555; railway; university (1970); textiles, aircraft, machinery, heavy engineering, chemicals, cars, construction; birthplace of Brecht and Holbein; Renaissance town hall (1615–20), St Ulrich's Minster (1500), Rococo Schaezler Palais; Mozart Summer Festival. » Augsburg Confession; Augsburg, League of; Brecht; Germany [i]; Holbein

Augsburg Confession A statement of faith composed by Luther, Melanchthon, and others for the Diet of Augsburg (1530), the official text being written by Melanchthon in 1531. The earliest of Protestant Confessions, it became authoritative for the Lutheran Church. » Luther; Lutheranism; Melanchthon

Augsburg, League of (1686) A defensive alliance formed by the Emperor, Bavaria, Spain, Sweden, and several German states and Circles, to defend the Treaties of Nijmegen (1678–9) and Ratisbon (1684), and to challenge Louis XIV's legalistic pursuit of territory, especially in disputed border areas (his *réunion* policy). However, continuing mutual provocation between France and the League resulted in the *War of the League of Augsburg* (1689–97). » Louis XIV

Augsburg, Peace of A compromise settlement agreed by Protestant and Catholic representatives at the Diet of Augsburg in 1555. The Peace adopted the notable principle of *cuius regio eius religio*, establishing the right of princes to determine their subjects' faith and enforce religious uniformity, while condemning dissent.

augury [**awg**yooree] In ancient Rome, the principal means of divining the will of the gods. It involved observing natural phenomena such as lightning, the flight patterns of wild birds, or the feeding habits of sacred chickens. It was taken very seriously, since success in any enterprise was believed to be dependent on knowing the will of the gods and acting in accordance with it. The augurs themselves were not professional priests, but distinguished public men who had undergone training in traditional augural lore and been admitted to the college of augurs – a select body of 16.

Augusta (Georgia) 33°28N 81°58W, pop (1980) 47 532. Seat of Richmond County, E Georgia, USA, on the Savannah R; founded as a river trading post, c.1717; changed hands many times during the War of Independence; state capital, 1786–95; housed Confederate powder works in the Civil War; airfield; railway; a popular resort with a notable golf club; trade and industrial centre. » American Civil War; American Revolution; Georgia

Augusta (Maine) 44°17N 69°50W, pop (1980) 21 819. State capital of Maine, USA, in Kennebec County, S Maine; on the Kennebec R 72 km/45 ml from its mouth; established as a trading post, 1628; city status, 1849; airfield; wood products, fabrics, shoes. » Maine

Augustan age The age of the Emperor Augustus in Rome (27 BC–AD 14), graced by the poets Horace, Ovid, and Virgil; hence, the classical period of any national literature. Examples include the half-century after the revolution settlement in England (1689), during which Dryden, Pope, Addison, Steele, Swift, and (later) Johnson were active; and in France, the earlier age of Corneille, Racine, and Molière under Louis XIV (1643–1715). » classicism; Dryden; Horace; Ovid; Pope; Racine; Virgil

Augustine, St (of Canterbury) (?–604), feast day 26 May. The first Archbishop of Canterbury. He was prior of a Benedictine monastery at Rome, when in 596 Pope Gregory I sent him with 40 other monks to convert the Anglo-Saxons to Christianity. He was kindly received by Ethelbert, King of Kent, whose wife was a Christian, and the conversion and baptism of the king contributed greatly to his success. Augustine was made Bishop of the English in 597, and established his church at Canterbury. His efforts to extend his authority over the native British Church were less successful. He died at Canterbury, and in 612 his body was transferred to the abbey of Saints Peter and Paul, now the site of St Augustine's Missionary College (1848). » Anglo-Saxons; Ethelbert; Gregory I; missions, Christian

Augustine, St (of Hippo) (354–430), feast day 28 August. The greatest of the Latin Fathers, born at Tagaste, Numidia. His mother became St Monica. He was sent to Carthage to complete his studies, but yielded to the temptation of the city, and fathered a son before he was 18. He became interested in philosophy after reading Cicero, and for a while joined the Manichaeans. He lectured on literature at Tagaste and at Carthage, where he began to write. In 383 he went to Rome, then settled in Milan as a teacher of rhetoric. An enthusiastic student of Plato, the Neoplatonists, and the Bible, he finally became a Christian in 387, along with his son, Adeodatus. Ordained priest in 391, he proved a formidable antagonist to the heretical schools in the Donatist and Pelagian controversies. He was created Bishop of Hippo in 396. His sacred autobiography, *Confessions*, was written in 397, and *De Civitate Dei*, a vindication of the Christian Church, in 413–26. *De Trinitate* was a massive exposition of the doctrine of the Trinity. The central tenets of his creed were the corruption of human nature through the fall of man, the consequent slavery of the human will, predestination, and the perseverance of the saints. He died during the Vandals' siege of Hippo. » Augustinians; Christianity; Cicero; Donatists; Fathers of the Church; Manichaeism; Neoplatonism; Pelagius; Plato; Trinity

Augustinians A religious order united in 1255 following the monastic teaching and 'rule' of St Augustine; also known as the **Augustinian** or **Austin Friars**; in full, the **Order of the Hermit Friars of St Augustine (OSA)**. It established missions and monasteries throughout the world, and was responsible for founding many famous hospitals. There are also Augustinian nuns of second or third orders ('tertiaries'). » Augustine, St (of Hippo); Orders, Holy; monasticism; Tertiaries

Augustus, (Gaius Julius Caesar Octavianus) (63 BC–AD 14) Founder of the Roman Empire, the son of Gaius Octavius, senator and praetor, and great-nephew, through his mother Atia, of Julius Caesar. On Caesar's assassination (44 BC), he abandoned student life in Illyricum and returned to Italy, where, using Caesar's money and name (he had acquired both under his will), he raised an army, defeated Antony, and extorted a wholly unconstitutional consulship from the Senate (43 BC). When Antony returned from Gaul in force later that year with Lepidus, Octavian made a deal with his former enemies, joining the so-called Second Triumvirate with them, and taking Africa, Sardinia, and Sicily as his province. A later redivision of power gave him the entire Western half of the Roman world, and Antony the Eastern. While Antony was distracted there by his military schemes against Parthia, and his liaison with Cleopatra, Octavian consistently undermined him at home. Matters came to a head in 31 BC, and the Battle of Actium followed, Octavian emerging victorious as the sole ruler of the Roman world. Though taking the inoffensive title *princeps* ('first citizen'), he was in all but name an absolute monarch. His new name, Augustus ('sacred'), had historical and religious overtones, and was deliberately chosen to enhance his prestige. His long reign (27 BC–AD 14) was a time of peace and reconstruction at home, sound administration and steady conquest abroad. In gratitude, the Romans awarded him the title *Pater Patriae* ('Father of his Country') in 2 BC, and on his death made him a god (*Divus Augustus*). » Actium, Battle of; Herod Agrippa I; Antonius; Caesar; Julia; Lepidus; Livia; Maecenas; Roman history [i]; triumvirate

Augustus I (1526–86) Elector of Saxony, born at Freiberg, who succeeded his brother Maurice as the leader of the German Protestant princes. He first favoured the Calvinistic doctrine of the sacraments, and then, becoming Lutheran, persecuted the Calvinists (from 1574). He gave a great impetus to the arts, education, and commerce, reorganizing Saxony into a model state. The Dresden library and most of the galleries owe their origin to him. He died at Dresden. » Calvinism; Lutheranism; Protestantism; Saxony

Augustus II, byname **the Strong** (1670–1733) King of Poland (1697–1706, 1710–33), born at Dresden, Saxony. After being elected king, he tried to recover the provinces lost to Sweden, but was defeated, and then deposed. In 1709 he returned to Poland, formed a fresh alliance with the Tsar, and recommenced a war with Sweden, which raged until the death of Charles XII (1718). The Saxon court became known as the most dissolute in Europe, and poor government hastened Poland's decline. Augustus is said to have had around 300 illegitimate children. He died in Warsaw. » Saxony

Augustusburg The 18th-c Baroque residence of the former electors of Cologne at Brühl, NW Germany; a world heritage site. It was designed by Konrad Schlaun, and later Francois Cuvillié (architect of the Rococo hunting lodge of Falkenlust, which lies across the park) for Elector Clemens August (1700–61). » Baroque (art and architecture)

auk A small, black-and-white, short-winged seabird, the N hemisphere equivalent to the penguin (which it superficially resembles); inhabits cool seas; excellent swimmer; breeding colonies contain millions of birds. (Family: *Alcidae*, 21 species.) » guillemot; penguin; puffin; razorbill

Auld lang syne A Scottish song, sung communally with arms crossed and hands linked at moments of leave-taking or at the end of a year. The words were adapted by Robert Burns in 1791 from an earlier lyric, and later fitted to the pentatonic tune (of uncertain origin) to which they are sung today. The title (literally "old long since") refers to past times. » Burns

aura A subtle, luminous glow, often coloured, which some people claim to see surrounding other living forms. Some believe that a person's aura will reveal information about the state of that person's emotional, mental, and physical well-being, but such claims have yet to be substantiated.

Aurangzib » **Aurungzebe**

Aurelian, properly **Lucius Aurelius Aurelianus** (215–75) Roman emperor (270–5), a man of humble provincial origin, but outstanding military talents. He ended the chaos of 40 years in a brief but brilliant reign. Army discipline and domestic order were restored, and action successfully taken against the Goths and Carpi on the Danube, Zenobia of Palmyra in the East, and the breakaway Gallic Empire in the West. For his efforts, he was awarded the title 'Restorer of the Roman World'. » Palmyra (Roman history); Roman history [i]; Zenobia

Aurelian Way » **Roman roads [i]**

Aurelius, properly **Marcus Aurelius Antoninus** (121–80) Roman emperor (161–80). The adopted son of Antoninus Pius, he ruled as his junior partner from 146, discharging his duties with the utmost fidelity, despite his continuing study of law and philosophy, especially Stoicism. On his succession to the throne, he voluntarily divided the government with his adopted brother, Lucius Aurelius Verus. His reign saw constant warfare. Trouble in Britain, the East, and Germany was handled by his generals, but he himself, almost for a decade, personally directed operations on the Danube frontier, where he died of sheer exhaustion. His Meditations, devotional jottings written while on campaign, make him among the best-known of Roman emperors. » Antoninus Pius; Roman history [i]; Stoicism

Auric, Georges [oh**reek**] (1899–1983) French composer, born at Lodève. He studied under d'Indy, becoming one of *Les Six*. His compositions ranged widely from full orchestral pieces to songs, and included many film scores. He was appointed director (1962–8) of the Opéra and Opéra-Comique in Paris, where he died. » *Six, Les*

auricula A European alpine displaying a rosette of fleshy leaves with a mealy white bloom; flowers in clusters on a common stalk. Numerous hybrids are cultivated, some with intricately patterned flowers. (*Primula auricula*. Family: *Primulaceae*.) » alpine

Auriga (Lat 'charioteer') [aw**riy**ga] A prominent N hemisphere constellation in the Milky Way, containing many star clusters. Its brightest star is Capella, a giant yellow star. Distance 13.7 parsecs. » constellation; star cluster; RR8

Aurignacian [awrig**nay**shn] In European prehistory, a division of Upper Palaeolithic culture, named after the cave site at

Aurignac, Haute Garonne, SW France, excavated in 1852–60 by French archaeologist Eduard Lartet (1801–71). Aurignacian stone scrapers, blades, and bone points occur throughout France/Germany c.33 000–23 000 BC, less frequently in Hungary/Austria. » Three Age System

Auriol, Vincent [**oh**reeol] (1884–1966) French politician, born at Revel, who became the first President of the Fourth Republic (1947–53). He studied law, and was elected to the Chamber of Deputies in 1914, later becoming leader of the Socialist Party. He served as a minister in 1936 and 1945, and resigned from politics in 1960. He died in Paris. » France [i]

aurochs [**aw**roks] (plural, **aurochsen**) An extinct large wild ox, formerly widespread in Europe, Asia, and N Africa; the ancestor of domestic cattle; bulls large with long forward-pointing horns; females smaller with shorter horns; last individual killed in Poland in 1627; also known as **urus**, or **wild ox**; name formerly used for the European bison. (*Bos primigenius*.) » bison; cattle; ox

aurora [aw**raw**ra] A diffuse coloured light in the upper atmosphere (100 km/60 ml) over polar regions, visible at night. It is caused by charged particles from the Sun colliding with oxygen and nitrogen atoms in the atmosphere. It is seen most frequently in the **auroral zones**, which have a radius of c.22° around the geomagnetic poles. In the N it is known as the *aurora borealis* or *northern lights*, in the S as the *aurora australis*. » atmospheric physics; geomagnetic field; solar wind

Aurora (mythology) [aw**raw**ra] The Roman name of the goddess of the dawn, equivalent to the Greek Eos. » Eos

Aurungzebe or **Aurangzib** [**aw**rungzeb] ('Ornament of the Throne'), kingly title **Alamgir** (1618–1707) The last and most magnificent of the Mughal Emperors of India (1658–1707), born at Dhod, Malwa. The youngest son of Shah Jahan, he struggled for power with his brothers, finally putting them to death. He was a fervent Muslim, which alienated the Hindus and led to war with the Marathas. His long reign was distinguished by prosperity, but most of his enterprises failed, and the empire began to decline. He died at Ahmadnagar. » Mughal Empire

Auschwitz [**ow**shvitz] The largest Nazi concentration camp, on the outskirts of Oświeim, SW Poland, where 3–4 million people, mainly Jews and Poles, were murdered between 1940 and 1945; a world heritage monument. Gas chambers, watch towers, and prison huts are preserved at the camp, part of which is now a museum. » Holocaust; Nazi Party

auscultation [awskuhl**tay**shuhn] The process of listening to and analysing the audible sounds within the body, usually with the aid of a stethoscope. These include the sounds (vibrations) in blood vessels, heart, lungs, bronchi, and intestines, induced by the flow of blood, air, or gas within the various organs. » medicine

Ausgleich [**ows**gliysh] (Ger 'compromise') An arrangement made in 1867 between the Imperial government of Austria and representatives of Hungary, following the Austrian defeat by Prussia (1866), which created the Dual Monarchy of Austria-Hungary. » Austria-Hungary, Dual Monarchy of

Ausonius, Decimus Magnus (c.309–92) Foremost Latin poet of the 4th-c, born at Burdigala (Bordeaux). He was tutor to Valentinian's son Gratian, and afterwards held several offices in Gaul. His works include epigrams, poems on his colleagues and relatives, epistles in verse and prose, and idylls. » Latin literature

Austen, Jane (1775–1817) British novelist, born at Steventon, Hampshire, where her father was rector, the fifth of a family of seven. She later lived in Bath, Southampton, Chawton, and Winchester, where she died. Her early published work satirized the sensational fiction of her time. Of her six great novels, four were published anonymously during her lifetime and two posthumously: *Sense and Sensibility* (1811), *Pride and Prejudice* (1813), *Mansfield Park* (1814), *Emma* (1815), *Persuasion* (1818), and *Northanger Abbey* (1818). All her characters are 'ordinary', but her psychological insight, her sensitive ear, her muted irony, and her eye for rich but selective detail present them as three-dimensional individuals who are nevertheless archetypal. » English literature; novel; satire

Austerlitz, Battle of [**aw**stuhlitz] (1805) Napoleon's most decisive victory, also known as the **Battle of the Three Emperors**, fought in Moravia against a larger combined Austro-Russian army under Kutuzov. It forced Austria to make the Treaty of Pressburg and withdraw from the Third Coalition. » Grand Alliance, War of the; Napoleonic Wars

Austin (of Longbridge), Herbert, 1st Baron (1866–1941) British car manufacturer, born at Little Missenden, Buckinghamshire. After managing several engineering works in Australia, he returned to England and in 1895 produced his first car, the Wolseley. In 1905 he opened his own works near Birmingham, producing an enormous output which included (1921) the popular 'Baby' Austin 7. Created a baron in 1936, he died near Bromsgrove, Worcestershire. » car [i]

Austin, J(ohn) L(angshaw) (1911–60) British philosopher, educated at Shrewsbury and Oxford. He served in the Intelligence Corps (1939–45), later becoming White's professor of moral philosophy at Oxford (1952). He is best-known for his contributions to linguistic philosophy, especially his analysis of the ways in which utterances do more than report facts. His publications include *Philosophical Papers* (1961) and *How to Do Things with Words* (1962). » linguistic philosophy; pragmatics

Austin, John (1790–1859) British jurist, born at Creeting Mill, Suffolk. In 1818 he was called to the Bar, and was appointed professor of jurisprudence at London (1826–32). His *Province of Jurisprudence Determined* revolutionized English views on the subject, and introduced a definiteness of terminology hitherto unknown. He died at Weybridge, Surrey, » jurisprudence

Austin [**aw**stin] 30°17N 97°45W, pop (1980) 345 496. Capital of state in Travis County, SC Texas, USA, on the Colorado R; settled, 1835; capital of the Republic of Texas, 1839; Texas government moved to Houston (1842) for fear of marauding Mexicans and Indians; returned in 1845 when Texas joined the Union; airfield; railway; two universities (1876, 1881); commercial centre for an extensive agricultural region; electronic and scientific research; tourism; Aqua Festival (Aug); in recent years, fastest growing city in the USA. » Texas

Austin Friars » **Augustinians**

Austral Islands [ostral] » **Tubuai Islands**

Australasia A term used loosely to include Australia and the islands of Tasmania, New Zealand, New Guinea (including New Britain), New Caledonia, and Vanuatu; often described as equivalent to all of Oceania below the Equator and N of 47°S; the name is not commonly used in these areas. » Oceania

Australia pop (1990e) 17 073 000; area 7 692 300 sq km/2 969 228 sq ml. Official name **Commonwealth of Australia**, an independent country; the smallest continent in the world, entirely in the S hemisphere, between 113°09E and 153°39E and 10°41S and 43°39S; almost 40% of its land mass is N of the Tropic of Capricorn; bounded N by the Timor and Arafura seas, NE by the Coral Sea, E by the S Pacific Ocean, and S and W by the Indian Ocean; timezones GMT +8 (Western Australia), GMT +9½ (Northern Territory and South Australia), GMT +10 (New South Wales, Queensland, Tasmania, Victoria, Australian Capital Territory); capital Canberra; principal cities Melbourne, Brisbane, Perth, Adelaide, Sydney; population 1% Aborigine and Asian, 99% Caucasian; official language English; religions Anglican (under 30%), Roman Catholic (over 25%); currency the Australian dollar of 100 cents.

Physical description. The Australian continent consists largely of plains and plateaux, most of which average 600 m/2 000 ft above sea-level. The West Australian Plateau occupies nearly half the whole area. In the centre are the MacDonnell Ranges: highest points Mt Liebig (1 524 m/5 000 ft) and Mt Zeil (1 510 m/4 954 ft). NW is the Kimberley Plateau rising to 936 m/3 070 ft at Mt Ord. W are the Hamersley Ranges rising to 1 226 m/4 022 ft at Mt Bruce. Most of the plateau is dry and barren desert, notably the Gibson Desert (W), the Great Sandy Desert (NW), the Great Victoria Desert (S), and the Simpson Desert (C). In the S is the Nullarbor Plain, crossed by the Trans-Australian Railway. The Eastern Highlands or Great Dividing Range lie parallel to the E seaboard, rising to 2 228 m/7 310 ft in Mt Kosciusko, in the Australian Alps.

Between the W Plateau and the E Highlands lies a broad lowland belt extending S into the Murray-Darling plains. Off the NE coast, stretching for over 1 900 km/1 200 ml, is the Great Barrier Reef. The island of Tasmania, a S extension of the E Highlands, rises to 1 617 m/5 305 ft at Mt Ossa, and is separated from the mainland by the Bass Strait. The country's longest river is the Murray, its chief tributaries being the Darling, Murrumbidgee, and Lachlan.

Climate. More than a third of Australia receives under 260 mm/10 in mean annual rainfall; less than a third receives over 500 mm/20 in. Half the country has a rainfall variability of more than 30%, with many areas experiencing prolonged drought. Darwin's average daily temperature is 26°–34°C (Nov) and 19°–31°C (Jul); rainfall varies from 386 mm/15.2 in (Jan) to zero (Jul). About 26% of total land area is unused (mainly desert); c.67% is used for agricultural purposes, including arid grazing (44%) and non-arid grazing (17%). Fertile land with a temperate climate and reliable rainfall is limited to the lowlands and valleys near the coast in the E and SE, and to a small part of the SW corner. The population is concentrated in these two regions. Melbourne's average daily temperature is 6°–13°C (Jul) and 14°–26°C (Jan–Feb), with monthly rainfall averaging 48–66 mm/1.9–2.6 in. In Tasmania, climatic conditions vary greatly between mountain and coast; there is much heavier rainfall in the W (over 2 500 mm/100 in per annum in places) than in the E (500–700 mm/20–28 in per annum).

Economy. Australia is the world's largest wool producer, and a top exporter of veal and beef. The country's most important crop is wheat; other major cereals are barley, oats, maize, and sorghum. Discoveries of petroleum reserves, bauxite, nickel, lead, zinc, copper, tin, uranium, iron ore, and other minerals in the early 1960s have turned Australia into a major mineral producer. Commercial oil production began in 1964; the Gippsland basin produces two-thirds of Australia's oil and most of its natural gas, but major discoveries have been made off the NW coast. Manufacturing industry has expanded rapidly since 1945, especially in engineering, shipbuilding, car manufacture, metals, textiles, clothing, chemicals, food processing, and wine.

History and government. The Aborigines are thought to have arrived in Australia from SE Asia c.40 000 years ago. The first European visitors were the Dutch, who explored the Gulf of Carpentaria in 1606 and landed in 1642. Captain James Cook arrived in Botany Bay in 1770, and claimed the E coast for Britain. New South Wales was established as a penal colony in 1788. Increasing numbers of settlers were attracted to Australia, especially after the introduction of Spanish Merino sheep. Gold was discovered in New South Wales and Victoria (1851) and in Western Australia (1892). Transportation of convicts to E Australia ended in 1840, but continued until 1853 in Tasmania and 1868 in Western Australia. During this period, the colonies drafted their own constitutions and set up governments: New South Wales (1855), Tasmania and Victoria (1856), South Australia (1857), Queensland (1860), and Western Australia (1890). In 1901 the Commonwealth of Australia was established with Canberra chosen as the site for its capital. A policy of preventing immigration by non-Whites stayed in force from the end of the 19th-c until 1974. Australia is divided into six states and two territories. The legislature (as of 1980) comprises a bicameral Federal Parliament with a 64-member Senate elected for six years, and a 125-member House of Representatives elected every three years. The Prime Minister and the Cabinet of Ministers are responsible to the House. The head of state is a Governor-General, representing the Queen (as Queen of Australia), who presides over an Executive Council. Northern Territory has been self-governing since 1978. » Aborigines; Australian art/Capital Territory/Council of Trades Unions/gold rush/Labor Party/languages/literature/Workers' Union; first fleet; Liberal Party (Australia); National Party (Australia); New South Wales; Queensland; South Australia; Tasmania; transportation; Victoria (Australia); Western Australia; White Australia Policy; RR24 national holidays; RR42 political leaders

Australia Day A public holiday in Australia commemorating

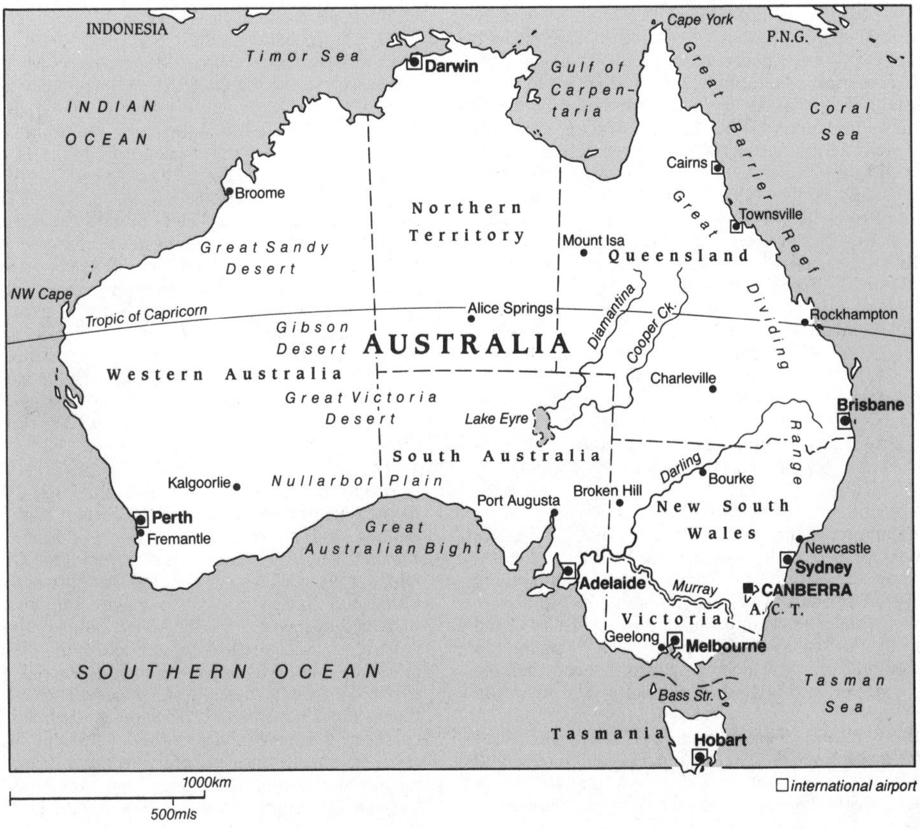

the founding of the colony of New South Wales on 26 January 1788; held annually on 26 January if a Monday, or else on the Monday following that date. » Australia [i]

Australia, Order of An order established by Queen Elizabeth II in 1975, for according recognition to Australian citizens (and others). The order comprises the sovereign, the Governor-General of Australia, the Prince of Wales, and appointed Knights, Dames, Companions, Officers, Members, and Holders. Appointments to the order are recommended by a Council, which researches nominations. The ribbon is of royal blue silk, with a central band of golden mimosa blossoms. » decoration

Australia Telescope An array of radio telescopes distributed across Australia which use aperture synthesis to achieve very high resolving power. It is the most important radio telescope in the S hemisphere. The operating authority is the Australian National Radio Astronomy Observatory. » aperture synthesis; radio astronomy; telescope [i]

Australian Alps Chain of mountains in SE Australia forming the S part of the Great Dividing Range; extends c.300 km/185 ml SW from Australian Capital Territory to the Goulburn R, Victoria; includes the Snowy Mts, Bowen Mts, and Barry Mts; rises to 2 228 m/7 310 ft at Mt Kosciusko; much used for winter sports. » Great Dividing Range

Australian Antarctic Territory area 6 043 852 sq km/2 332 927 sq ml of land, 84 798 sq km/32 732 sq ml of ice shelf. Situated S of 60°S and lying between 142° and 136°E (excluding Terre Adélie); claimed by Australia, 1936; scientific station at Mawson, 1954; Davis Base, 1957; Australia assumed custody of the US Wilkes Station on the Budd Coast in 1959, replacing it by the Casey Station in 1961. » Antarctica [i]; Australia [i]

Australian art The art of Europeans in Australia began in the late 18th-c. Single-storied colonial houses with verandahs reflected English Georgian and Regency styles. In the 1830s, Gothic was employed for Anglican churches (eg St Andrew's Cathedral, Sydney, 1837) and Greek for public buildings. From the earliest years, graphic artists drew native flora and fauna for scientific purposes, while landscape painters such as John Glover (1767–1849) and Conrad Martens (1801–78) tried to reconcile the Picturesque approach favoured in Europe with the harsh realities of local scenery. Later painters such as Tom Roberts and Frederick McGubbin (1855–1917), while influenced by current European styles (eg Impressionism), developed an independent and distinctively Australian vision of nature. Abstract and Surrealist art was slow to reach Australia; an adherence to traditional figurative forms has helped artists like Roberts, William Dobell (1899–1970), Sydney Nolan, and Russell Drysdale to create a highly expressive art distinct from the fashions of the Western avant garde. » Aboriginal art; Drysdale; Nolan, Sydney; Picturesque; Roberts, Tom

Australian Capital Territory pop (1986) 263 200; area 2 400 sq km/925 sq ml. Territory in SE Australia, created in 1911 to provide a location for the national capital, Canberra; bordered on all sides by New South Wales; Jervis Bay on the E coast ceded (1915) for its use as a port; mountainous in the S; urbanized floodplains of the Murrumbidgee and Molonglo Rivers in the N; c.60% of the workforce employed by the government; electronics, computing; state holidays Canberra Day (Mar), Bank Holiday (Aug), Labour Day (Oct). » Australia [i]

Australian Council of Trade Unions (ACTU) Australia's national trade union organization, formed in 1927. Its prestige has come from representing the unions' case before the Australian Conciliation and Arbitration Commission, and in helping to settle industrial disputes. By 1986 162 unions were affiliated, with a claimed total membership of 2.6 million. In 1983 the ACTU and the Australian Labor Party (ALP) signed an Accord on economic policy, which was put into effect when the ALP came to power. » Australian Workers' Union; trade union

Australian East Coast Temperate and Sub-Tropical Rainforest Parks A series of national parks, and nature and flora reserves, which extends along the length of the New South Wales coast; a world heritage area. The region provides a representative sample of the whole animal and plant life of E Australia, as well as striking examples of landscape diversity, including the Mt Warning volcano and segments of the Great Escarpment. » New South Wales

Australian gold rush Traces of gold were first found in Australia in 1823, but the first significant find was in 1851, when Edward Hargraves publicized his find and attracted 2 000 to the site at Ophir in New South Wales. In the same year, large gold finds were made in Victoria, which accounted for 35% of world gold production 1851–60. Gold was also found in Queensland (1867) and Western Australia (1893). The discovery transformed Australia. It drew thousands of immigrants (342 000 arrived from overseas 1852–61), created a mass movement for democracy, and gave a tremendous boost to the economy. Cities, in particular Melbourne (which grew from 29 000 to 473 000, 1851–91), symbolized the new-found prosperity. Although some miners struck it rich, most did not, and this led to pressure to open pastoral land for farming. Gold also attracted thousands of Chinese miners, who were greatly resented by the Europeans; this led to anti-Chinese laws and the beginning of the 'White Australia' Policy. » Eureka; miners' right; White Australia Policy

Australian Imperial Force (AIF) The volunteer military forces raised in Australia in both world wars. In World War 1, 330 770 men served overseas in the first AIF, of whom 54 000 were killed and 155 000 were wounded. In World War 2, 690 000 men and 35 000 women served in the second AIF. » World War 1/2

Australian Labor Party (ALP) Australia's oldest political party, founded in 1891 in New South Wales following the defeat of the trade unions in the 1890 strike. The party spread to all States by the mid-1900s and formed the world's first labour government in Queensland in 1899 for one week. It has always been a social democratic party, committed to evolutionary not revolutionary change. Despite a commitment to 'socialism', it has generally been moderate and pragmatic when in government. Two major splits in the ALP occurred: in 1916–17 over conscription, and in 1955 over attitudes to communism. ALP has had only some success in winning federal government (1908–9, 1910–13, 1914–15, 1929–32, 1941–9, 1972–4, 1983–), but has done better at State level. Its most important national figures have been Prime Ministers W M ('Billy') Hughes (1915–16), James Scullin (1929–32), John Curtin (1941–5), Ben Chifley (1945–9), Gough Whitlam (1972–4), and R J L ('Bob') Hawke (1983–). In 1988, the party had about 60 000 members; it has always had fewer members than its main rival, the Liberal party. » Democratic Labor Party; Liberal Party (Australia); Petrov affair

Australian languages The aboriginal languages of Australia. About 50 survive, spoken by fewer than 50 000 people, and with vastly differing degrees of fluency. Most speakers are bilingual in their indigenous language and English, though there are now some bilingual school programmes, which will ensure the immediate survival of some languages. The majority of the languages, however, are near extinction, and only five have more than 1 000 speakers. Some of the languages are used as lingua francas, one of the most vigorous being Warlpiri, spoken in the Northern Territory. » Aborigines; Australian literature; bilingualism; lingua franca

Australian literature After a number of convict and gold-rush novels in the mid-19th-c, Australian literature began to assume its own identity at the turn of the century with distinctive bush ballads and short stories, many published in the Sydney *Bulletin*. The Australian past was explored in historical novels and family sagas between the wars, which also saw the homespun Jindyworobak movement, though neither of these managed to incorporate the aboriginal experience. Since 1945, Australian literature has been enriched and diversified by many influences, and with novelists such as Patrick White (eg *Voss*, 1957), Thomas Keneally (eg *Schindler's Ark*, 1982), and Peter Carey (eg *Illywhacker*, 1985), poets such as Les A Murray (1938–), Chris Wallace-Crabbe (1934–), and A D Hope (1905–), and a vigorous and inventive drama, it now has a recognized international standing. » American literature; English literature; Jindyworobak; Keneally; White, Patrick

Australian Rules football » football 3 [i]

Australian Workers' Union (AWU) The largest Australian trade union from the early 1900s to 1970, and still one of the largest, with 120 000 members in 1985. It was formed in 1894 by the amalgamation of the shearers' union (formed 1886) and the rural labourers' union (formed 1890), and has traditionally recruited lesser-paid workers. It has always been a conservative force in trade union and labour politics. » Australian Council of Trade Unions; trade union

Australopithecus [ostralohp**ith**uhkuhs] Extinct human-like ape known from fossil remains found particularly in Ethiopia and Kenya; lived from 5 to 1.5 million years ago; probably walked on two legs; skeletal and facial characters link australopithecines closely to chimpanzees and gorillas as well as to humans. Four species have been named: *Australopithecus afarensis* lived in E Africa c.4–2.5 million years ago; height 1–1.3 m/3–4 ft; weight 30 kg/65 lb. *Australopithecus africanus* lived in E and S Africa c.3–1.5 million years ago; height 1–1.3 m/3–4 ft; weight 20–40 kg/45–90 lb. *Australopithecus robustus* lived in S Africa c.2.5–1.5 million years ago; height 1.5–1.7 m/5–5½ ft; weight 50–70 kg/110–154 lb. *Australopithecus boisei* (possibly an E African variant of *A. robustus*), formerly known as *Zinjanthropus*, lived c.2.5–1 million years ago; height 1.6–1.8 m/5 ft 3 in–5 ft 10 in; weight 60–80 kg/132–176 lb. (Superfamily: *Hominoidea*.) » ape; fossil; *Homo* [i]; Taung skull

Austria, Ger **Österreich**, official name **Republic of Austria**, Ger **Republik Österreich** pop (1990e) 7 623 000; area 83 854 sq km/32 368 sq ml. A federal republic in C Europe, divided into nine federal states (*Länder*); bordered to the N by Germany and Czechoslovakia, to the S by Italy and Yugoslavia, to the W by Switzerland and Liechtenstein, and to the E by Hungary; capital Vienna (Wien); major cities include Graz, Linz, Salzburg, Innsbruck, Klagenfurt; timezone GMT +1; language, German; mostly Austrians with Croatian and Slovene minorities; main religion (85%), Roman Catholic; unit of currency, the Schilling of 100 Groschen.

Physical description and climate. Almost entirely mountainous, at E end of the Alps; main ranges the Ötztal, Zillertal, Hohe Tauern, and Niedere Tauern; highest point, Grossglockner (3 797 m/12 457 ft); chief passes into Italy, the Brenner and Plöcken; most of the country in the drainage basin of the R Danube; largest lake, Neusiedler See; three climatic regions: the Alps (often sunny in winter but cloudy in summer); the Danube valley and Vienna basin (driest region); and the SE, a region of heavy thunderstorms, often severe winters but warmer summers; most rain in summer months; winters cold, especially with winds from the E or NE; warm, dry wind (the Föhn) in some N–S valleys, especially in autumn and spring, which can result in fires and snow-melt leading to avalanches.

History and government. Part of Roman Empire until 5th-c, then occupied by Germanic tribes; a frontier area of Charlemagne's empire; became a duchy and passed to the Habsburg family (1282), who made it the foundation of their Empire; Habsburg defeats in 19th-c (notably, the Austro-Prussian War), and Hungarian nationalism led to the Dual Monarchy of Austria–Hungary (1867); assassination of Archduke Franz Ferdinand by Serbian nationalists triggered World War 1; republic established in 1918; annexed by the German Reich in 1938 (the *Anschluss*), under the name **Ostmark**; occupied by British, American, French, and Russian troops from 1945, obtaining independence in 1955; neutrality declared, since when Austria has been a haven for many refugees; Federal Assembly includes a National Council (*Nationalrat*, elected for four years, 183 deputies) and a Federal Council (*Bundesrat*, 63 members); a president holds office for six years, and appoints a federal chancellor; each of the nine provinces is administered by its own government, headed by a governor elected by a provincial parliament.

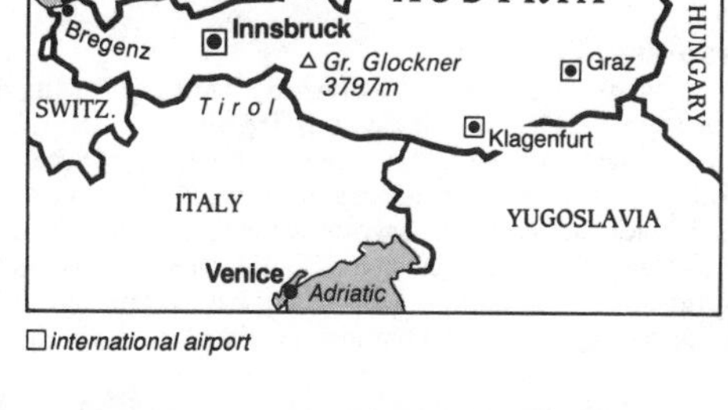

□ international airport

Economy. Principal agricultural areas to the N of the Alps, and along both sides of the Danube to the plains of the E frontier with Hungary; crops, cattle, orchards, vineyards; forestry on lower mountain slopes; wide range of metal and mineral resources, especially iron and steel (iron ore in the Erzberg Mts), lignite, lead ore, zinc ore, antimony ore, graphite, talc, anhydrous gypsum, kaolin, clay, salt; oil and natural gas; oil refining, ore processing, petrochemicals; hydroelectric power; textiles, paper, ceramics, wood products, clothing, chemicals, foodstuffs, glassware, metal goods, electrical goods, vehicles, tourism (summer and winter); river ports at Linz and Vienna; airports at Vienna, Graz, Linz, Klagenfurt, Salzburg, Innsbruck. » Alps; Austria–Hungary, Dual Monarchy of; Austro-Prussian War; Danube, River; Habsburgs; Vienna; RR26 national holidays; RR43 political leaders

Austria-Hungary, Dual Monarchy of A constitutional arrangement created by the *Ausgleich* ('compromise') of 1867. In Austria-Hungary the Habsburg emperors Francis Joseph (until 1916), and Charles (1916–18), ruled over the twin kingdoms of Austria (incorporating German-, Czech-, Polish-, Slovenian-, and Ruthenian-speaking regions of their empire) and Hungary (incorporating Magyar, Romanian, Slovak, and South Slav regions). The separate kingdoms possessed considerable autonomy over internal policy, with overall foreign and financial policy remaining in the hands of the Imperial government. The Dual Monarchy provided a temporary solution to the internal problems of the Habsburg Empire, but was ultimately destroyed by defeat in World War 1. » Ausgleich; Charles I (of Austria-Hungary); Francis Joseph; Habsburgs

Austrian Succession, War of the (1740–8) The first phase in the struggle between Prussia and Austria for mastery of the German states, developing after 1744 into a colonial conflict between Britain and the Franco-Spanish bloc. Hostilities were prompted by Frederick II of Prussia's seizure of the Habsburg province of Silesia on the accession of the Archduchess Maria Theresa (1740). Subsequently the war demonstrated the volatility of European alliances, and the ineffectiveness of much military campaigning. Prussia repeatedly deserted its allies; and relations between the 'Pragmatic Army' states were strained by conflicting interests. The fighting spread from C Europe to the Austrian Netherlands, the Mediterranean, and Italy, embroiling the New World and India before peace was concluded at the Treaty of Aix-la-Chapelle (1748). » Elizabeth Petrovna; Frederick II (of Prussia); George II (of Great Britain); Jenkins' Ear, War of; Maria Theresa; Saxe

Austro-Asiatic languages A group of over 100 languages spoken in SE Asia. Few of them had written forms until recent times, and their connections with other languages in the region are uncertain. The major group is the Mon-Khmer, which has three main languages: Mon (Tailang), Khmer, and Vietnamese. » Khmer; Mon; Vietnamese

Austro-Prussian War (1866) A war between Austria and Prussia occasioned by a dispute over the duchies of Schleswig and Holstein. It was declared on 14 June, decided by the Prussian victory at Königgrätz (sometimes known as Sadowa) on 3 July, and ended by the Treaty of Prague on 23 August. Austria's defeat hastened German unification; allowed Italy,

Prussia's ally, to acquire Venetia; and precipitated the creation of Austria-Hungary. » Prussia

Austronesian languages The most numerous and (after Indo-European) the most widely dispersed of the world's great language families. Extending from Taiwan to Madagascar and from Malaysia, the Philippines and Indonesia E through the Pacific Islands, it contains over 700 separate languages. » family of languages [i]

autarky An entirely self-sufficient economy (no external trade needed). It is sometimes the aim of a national economic policy, with tariffs and other trade barriers being erected; examples are Germany and Italy in the 1930s.

auteur theory A concept, popular in the 1960s, of the film director as the sole creative artist, imposing a personal viewpoint on every aspect of the production, rather than co-ordinating the work of many contributors. The director's personality is thus consistently expressed throughout a series of films. » director; Truffaut

authoritarianism A form of government, or a theory advocating such government, which is the opposite of democracy, in that the consent of society to rulers and their decisions is not necessary. Voting and discussion are not usually employed, except to give the appearance of democratic legitimacy to the government, and such arrangements remain firmly under the control of the rulers. Authoritarian rulers draw their authority from what are claimed to be special qualities of a religious, nationalistic, or ideological nature, which are used to justify their dispensing with constitutional restrictions. Their rule, however, relies heavily upon coercion. » democracy; totalitarianism

authority The right to issue commands without that right being questioned. In effect, authority is a form of legitimate power, in that those subject to it voluntarily consent to its exercise. Sources of authority are rational-legal (eg elections, qualifications), tradition (eg the monarchy), and charisma (eg Hitler). Included in most cases of authority is the right to use coercion against those who do not consent. » authoritarianism

Authorized Version of the Bible The English translation of the Bible commissioned by King James I of England and accomplished by a panel of leading scholars of the day; widely called the **King James Bible**. They used Greek and Hebrew texts, but were indebted also to earlier English translations. Noted for its literary excellence, the 'Authorized Version' gained wide popular appeal after its first publication in 1611, but was never formally 'authorized' by king or Parliament. » Bible; James I (of England)

autism A condition characterized by abnormal functioning in social interaction together with repetitive behaviour and poor communication, almost always commencing before three years of age. One in 2 000 children suffer from this disorder, which is four times more common in males. It was first described by Leo Kanner (1894–1981), an Austrian-born US child psychiatrist, in 1943. Intelligence is very variable in autistic children, and outcome is crucially dependent on the facilities for teaching. In the best facilities, up to 80% of children are eventually able to look after themselves. The cause is unknown, but many consider it to be a manifestation of extreme anxiety and panic. » psychiatry

autobiography A narrative of a life written by the subject. There are examples from antiquity in the *Meditations* of Marcus Aurelius (2nd-c) and the *Confessions* of St Augustine (4th-c), and some remarkable early modern instances, such as the arresting autobiography by Benvenuto Cellini (c.1560) and the self-searching *Essays* of Montaigne (from 1580). The 17th-c puritan 'spiritual autobiography' influenced the early novel. However, autobiography proper implies a self-creation as well as self-criticism on the part of the author, and as such is a post-Romantic art (the term was first used by Southey in 1809), though heralded by Rousseau's *Confessions* (1781–8). Among celebrated autobiographers are Goethe, de Quincey, Stendhal, George Sand, Berlioz, J S Mill, Trollope, T E Lawrence, Robert Graves, H G Wells, and Leonard Woolf. » biography; literature

autochthony [aw**tok**thonee] The notion that, upon independence, members of the Commonwealth were not only no longer subordinate to the British, but that the status of their independent constitution was rooted in their own soil, not drawn from the UK. The term was popularized by British political scientist, Sir Kenneth Clinton Wheare (1907–). » Commonwealth (British)

auto-da-fé [awtohda**fay**] (Port 'act of faith') The public burning at the stake of heretics and sinners condemned by the Spanish Inquisition. It was last carried out in Spain in 1781, and in Mexico in 1815. » Inquisition

auto-destructive art An artefact, typically a painting or piece of sculpture, deliberately constructed in a way guaranteed to self-destruct almost immediately. Examples include pictures executed with acid, and disintegrating kinetic machines. » art; happening; kinetic art

autogiro A non-fixed-wing aircraft whose lift is provided (unlike a helicopter) by non-powered horizontal blades, which are brought into action by means of an engine providing horizontal thrust propelling the aircraft forward. This type of aeroplane was popular in the 1930s, but nowadays is mainly used for sport. » aircraft [i]

auto-immune diseases A group of apparently unrelated disorders which are believed to possess a common underlying immunological mechanism. This involves the production by the body of antibodies which react against and damage the body's own tissues. The diseases include rheumatoid arthritis, diabetes mellitus, pernicious anaemia, haemolytic anaemia, some forms of glomerulonephritis, thyroid disease, and Addison's disease. » immunology

Autolycus [aw**tol**ikus] In Greek mythology, the maternal grandfather of Odysseus, who surpassed all men in thieving. He was said to be a son of Hermes. The name was also used by Shakespeare for a pedlar, 'a snapper-up of unconsidered trifles', in *The Winter's Tale*. » Odysseus

autolysis [aw**tol**uhsis] The process of breakdown and disintegration of tissues or cells due to the action of their own self-dissolving (*autolytic*) enzymes. It occurs after the death of an organism, and sometimes in pathological conditions (eg pancreatitis in humans). » enzyme

automatic pilot A device that automatically controls a vehicle (aircraft, ship, land vehicle) so that it will follow a preset course. It makes suitable adjustments to the vehicle's control systems to compensate for the offsetting effects of the environment or terrain. » automation

automatic writing The production of written text without the writer's conscious predetermination of the content, if any, of the message produced. It is sometimes associated with mediums, who claim the messages come from spirits of the deceased. » medium (parapsychology)

automation The control of a technical process without using a human being to intervene to make decisions. The result of one operation is fed back to control the next. Central heating is a simple automatic system: the thermostat is a sensor, feeding information back to the heater, which then adjusts automatically, switching on and off as necessary. Computers are the most widespread example of automation, controlling systems which humans would find too time-consuming. A widely-known example is in aviation, where the automatic pilot system ('George') relieves the pilot of the routine tasks of flying. » control engineering; mechanization; robotics (cybernetics)

automaton A mechanical device that imitates the actions of a living creature, human or animal. Such devices, constructed in the ancient world and in the Middle Ages, benefited from the development of clock mechanisms during the 17th-c. Some are made as toys, but others are useful as research or control mechanisms, and in the remote handling of hazardous materials.

automobile » car [i]

autonomic nervous system (ANS) That part of the nervous system which supplies the glands (eg the salivary and sweat glands), heart muscle, and smooth muscle (eg the walls of blood vessels and the bladder). It consists of groups of nerve cells outside the central nervous system, interposed between it and the target organs. The **sympathetic** (S) system is distributed throughout the whole body, particularly to the blood vessels. The **parasympathetic** (P) system is distributed to the gastro-intestinal, respiratory, and urogenital systems, and to the eye. Where S and P fibres supply the same structure, their effects are often opposite, to produce a balance with multiple gradations: for example, S nervous activity increases heart rate, P decreases it; S dilates the pupil, P constricts it. In general terms, the S system prepares the body for action, while the P is concerned with the conservation of energy. » ganglion; NANC; nervous system

autoradiography A technique for recording the positions of radioactive atoms in a specimen, by placing it over a fine-grain photographic emulsion. The radiation then produces a latent image corresponding to the site of each radiation source. The developed emulsion shows the distribution of the radioactive content of the specimen (eg a biological tissue containing a radioactive isotope). » photography; radioactivity; radiography

autosomes Chromosomes other than the X and Y chromosomes. The term was coined in genetics at a time (1906) when sex-determination was little understood. Distinguishing the sex chromosomes from the autosomes cleared the way for the understanding of a wide variety of sex-determining mechanisms. » chromosome [i]

autotrophic organism [awtoh**tro**fik] An organism that is capable of synthesizing complex organic substances from simple inorganic substrates. These organisms include the photosynthetic green plants that use atmospheric carbon dioxide as their main source of carbon in the synthesis of organic compounds, and the micro-organisms that obtain energy for metabolism by the oxidation of inorganic substrates such as iron, sulphur, and nitrogen (*chemotrophic* organisms). » carbon; metabolism; oxidation; photosynthesis

autumn crocus » **meadow saffron**

autumnal equinox » **equinox**

Auvergne [oh**vairn**] pop (1982) 1 332 678; area 26 013 sq km/ 10 041 sq ml. Region and former province of C France, comprising the departments of Allier, Cantal, Haute-Loire, and Puy-de-Dôme; Roman province, later a duchy and (10th-c) principality, united to France in 1527; **Haute-Auvergne** a mountainous area (W), **Basse-Auvergne** in R Allier valley; highest peaks in the Monts Dore, with Puy de Sancy at 1 886 m/6 188 ft; source of the Loire, Cher, Allier, Dordogne, and Lot Rivers; capital, Clermont-Ferrand; agriculture, mineral springs, cattle, wheat, wine, cheese. » France [i]

Auxerre [oh**zair**], Lat **Autissiodorum** 47°48N 3°32E, pop (1982) 41 164. Market town and capital of Yonne department, C France; on the R Yonne, surrounded by orchards and vineyards; one of the oldest towns in France; railway; bishopric; wine, paints, metal goods; St Etienne Gothic cathedral; abbey church of St Germain with 9th-c frescoes. » fresco; Gothic architecture

auxiliary language A natural language adopted by people of different speech communities for the needs of trade, education, and communication, though it may not be the native language of any of them. English and French are used in this way in many parts of Africa. » artificial language; language; lingua franca

auxiliary store A store of higher capacity but lower access time than the main memory of a computer; also known as a **backing store**, **bulk store**, or **secondary store**. It may include such features as magnetic tape units, floppy disks, and hard disks. » memory, computer

auxins A large group of plant hormones vital to many processes, produced in meristems, and principally involved in controlling the growth of shoots and roots, as well as in fruit formation, leaf and fruit fall, tropisms, and nastic movement. They play an important role in the function of other hormones. The precise effects vary with the concentration of auxin in the tissues, low levels promoting growth, high levels inhibiting it. They are used commercially as rooting compounds, weedkillers, and to induce parthenocarpy. » fruit; gibberellins; hormones; meristem; nastic movement; tropism

Auyuittuq [owy**oo**ituk] National park in Northwest Territories, N Canada, on SE Baffin I; dominated by the Penny Highlands, rising to over 23 100 m/63 890 ft, capped by the Penny Ice Cap; glaciers in the surrounding valleys; established in 1972. » Northwest Territories

Auzangate [owsanggatay] 13°47S 71°15W. Andean peak in a spur of the Cordillera de Carabaya, part of the Cordillera Occidental, SE Peru; height, 63 394 m/20 977 ft. » Peru [i]

avadavat [avadavat] An Asian bird of the waxbill family. There are two species: the **green avadavat** (*Amandava formosa*), from India, and the **red avadavat/strawberry finch** (*Amandava amandava*), from Pakistan to SE Asia (introduced on many Indo-Pacific islands). » waxbill

Avadh, Annexation of [avad] A semi-independent N Indian province within the Mughal Empire, annexed in 1856 by the British East India Company. Loss of rights by hereditary land revenue receivers caused resentment, and contributed towards the 1857 uprising. » East India Company, British; Indian Mutiny

avahi » **indri**

Avalon [avalon] In Celtic mythology, the land of the dead, the place to which King Arthur was taken after his death. The name possibly means 'land of apples'. » Arthur

avant garde [**avã gahd**] (Fr 'advance guard') A term first used to describe the radical artists of mid-19th-c France and Russia, often with political associations. Since then it has been applied to the innovative, experimental artists of any time; described by W H Auden as 'the antennae of the race'. » Auden; *cinéma vérité*; French literature; literature; Modernism; *Nouvelle Vague*; Russian literature

avatar [ava**tah**] In Hinduism, the descent to Earth of deity in a visible form. The idea derives from the tradition associated with the deity Vishnu, who from time to time appears on Earth in animal or human form in order to save it from destruction or extraordinary peril. » Hinduism; Vishnu

Ave Maria [**ah**vay mar**ee**ah] » **Hail Mary**

Avebury [**ayv**bree] 51°27N 1°51W. Village in North Wiltshire district, Wiltshire, S England; on the R Kennet, c.110 km/70 ml W of London; the largest megalithic monument in England, a world heritage site; in use c.2600–1600 BC; consists of a 427 m/1 400 ft diameter earthwork, with a 9 m/30 ft-deep ditch and a 5 m/16 ft-high outer bank; entrances at the cardinal points, and approached by a 2.4 km/1½ ml avenue of 100 paired stones; three stone circles within the enclosure, the largest of nearly 100 boulders; nearby Silbury Hill is the largest prehistoric construction in Europe; also nearby, West Kennet long barrow, containing 30 burials in five chambers, the largest chambered tomb in England; Windmill Hill, one of the oldest known Neolithic sites, with remains dating back to about 3 100 BC. » burials; megalith; Silbury Hill; Stonehenge; Three Age System; Wiltshire

avens [avinz] Two plants from genus *Geum*, both native to temperate regions. **Wood avens** (*Geum urbanum*), also called **herb Bennet**, is an erect perennial growing to c.60 cm/2 ft; leaves divided into small, unequal lateral leaflets and a large, lobed terminal leaflet; flowers 5-petalled, erect, yellow, petals spreading; fruits with hooked beak, forming burr-like head. **Water avens** (*Geum rivale*) are similar, but flowers are bowl-shaped, drooping, petals pinkish. (Family: *Rosaceae*). » mountain avens; perennial

Averroës or **Averrhoës** [averoheez], properly **Ibn Rushd** (1126–98) The most famous of the Islamic philosophers, born at Córdoba, who served as a judge and physician in Córdoba, Seville, and Morocco, where he died. He wrote extensive commentaries on many of Aristotle's works, which were both influential and controversial in the development of scholastic philosophy in the Middle Ages. » Aristotle; Islam; Neoplatonism; Plato; scholasticism

aversion therapy A process in which an unpleasant experience is induced (eg by pharmacological, physical, or electrical means) in association with an undesirable behaviour, in an attempt to inhibit or eliminate by this conditioning the undesirable behaviour. The technique has been used in a wide range of conditions, including smoking and alcohol dependence; some have tried to use it in changing sexual orientation. » behaviour therapy; conditioning; psychiatry

Avery, Oswald (Theodore) (1877–1955) US bacteriologist, born at Halifax, Nova Scotia, Canada. He showed in 1944 that genetic transformation in bacteria can be caused by deoxyribonucleic acid (DNA), a key result in the development of molecular biology. He died in Nashville, Tennessee. » DNA [i]; molecular biology

Avesta [avesta] The scriptures of Zoroastrianism, written in Avestan, a language of the E branch of the Indo-European family. Traditionally believed to have been revealed to Zoroaster, only the Gathas, a set of 17 hymns, may be attributed to him. Few portions of the original survive. » Indo-European languages; Zoroastrianism

aviation All forms of flying, and the uses to which aircraft are put. Aviation is divided into two principal areas. **Military aviation** deals with the use of aircraft by military forces, either as a weapon in its own right, or as a platform from which to launch other weapons, together with the aircraft's use as a reconnaissance vehicle and military transport. **Civil aviation** deals with the organization and use of aircraft as a means of commercial transportation. The principal interest is the use of aircraft on scheduled and chartered flights to carry passengers and cargo, but the subject also covers the use of aircraft for pleasure, business, and medical services. Because of the international character of civil aviation, governments play a major role in its conduct and regulation, through both national legislation and international agreements. This governmental influence was a major factor in commercial airline operation until the early 1980s, when the US domestic market was deregulated. The result was a massive increase in competition, which led in turn to a reorganization of the airlines into larger groupings. It seems likely that this process will continue in the international market, which will lead to an increase in air travel, and increased pressure on airports and air traffic control. » aeroplane; aircraft [i]

Avicebrón [avisebron] Lat form of **Solomon ben Yehuda ibn Gabirol** (1020–c.70) Jewish poet and philosopher, born in Malaga, Spain. His great work, *Fons Vitae* (Fountain of Life), translated from the Arabic, is largely Neoplatonist. He died in Valencia. » Neoplatonism

Avicenna [avisena], Arabic **Ibn Sina** (980–1037) Islamic philosopher and physician, born near Bokhara. He was physician to several sultans, and for some time vizier in Hamadan, in Persia, where he died. His philosophy was Aristotelianism modified by Neoplatonism; his medical system was long the standard in Europe and the Middle East. » Neoplatonism

avidin » **antivitamin factors**

Avignon [aveenyõ], Lat **Avenio** 43°57N 4°50E, pop (1982) 91 474. Walled capital of Vaucluse department, SE France, on left bank of R Rhône; papal residence 1309–76; railway; archbishopric; chemicals, soap, paper, artificial fibres; popular tourist centre; Gothic Palais des Papes; ruins of 12th-c Pont St Benezet, subject of the folk-song 'Sur le Pont d'Avignon'; many churches and museums; centre of school of painting; John Stuart Mill died here. » Mill; pope

Avignon School A group of artists, mostly Italian, who worked for the papal court in exile in Avignon (1309–77), especially Martini. The 'Pietà', c.1460, by an unknown artist (Louvre) is considered the masterpiece of the school. » Martini; school (art)

Ávila [aveela], also **Ávila de los Caballeros**, ancient **Avela, Abula**, or **Abyla** 40°39N 4°43W, pop (1981) 41 735. Ancient walled city, capital of Ávila province, Castilla-León, C Spain; 115 km/71 ml W of Madrid; altitude, 1 130 m/3 707 ft; bishopric; railway; wine, livestock, tourism; birthplace of Queen Isabella and St Teresa; cathedral (11th-c), Monastery of St Thomas, Churches of St Peter and St Vincent, town walls; old town and churches are a world heritage site; Holy Week, Fiesta of St John (Jun), summer fiesta (Jul), Fiesta of St Teresa (Oct). » Isabella I; Spain [i]; Teresa of Avila, St

Ávila, El [el aveela] area 851 sq km/328 sq ml. National park in N Venezuela; on the Caribbean, directly E of Caracas; established in 1958. » Venezuela [i]

avocado An evergreen tree growing to 18 m/60 ft, covered with aromatic oil glands, thought to be native to C America; leaves oval, leathery; flowers 2 cm/0.8 in, greenish-white, 6-lobed; berry pear-shaped, leathery, growing to 15 cm/6 in long, green, yellow, or purplish, with thick yellowish-green flesh surrounding a single large stone. It is cultivated on a large scale in many warm regions: the cultivated plants are smaller and bushier than wild ones, with fruits of various colours and sizes, ripening at different times of the year. (*Persea americana*. Family: *Lauraceae*.) » evergreen plants; tree [i]

avocet [avuhset] A long-legged wading bird, found in fresh and saline waters worldwide; catches small animals by sweeping a long, slender, up-curved bill from side to side on the surface of submerged mud. (Genus: *Recurvirostra*, 4 species. Family: *Recurvirostridae*.)

Avogadro, Amedeo [avohgahdroh] (1776–1856) Italian scientist, born at Turin, who became professor of physics there (1834–59). In 1811 he formulated the hypothesis, known later as **Avogadro's law**, that equal volumes of gases contain equal numbers of molecules, when at the same temperature and pressure; but the principle did not come to be accepted until the work of Stanislao Cannizarro in the 1850s. » Avogadro's number; Cannizarro

Avogadro's number The number of molecules in a mole or of electronic charges in a faraday. Its approximate value is 6.023×10^{23}. » Avogadro; faraday; mole (physics)

Avon, 1st Earl of » **Eden, Sir Anthony**

Avon pop (1987e) 951 200; area 1 347 sq km/520 sq ml. County in SW England, divided into six districts; bounded W by the R Severn estuary; includes parts of the Cotswolds and Mendip Hills; county town Bristol; chief towns include Bath and Weston-super-Mare; food processing, high technology, tourism. » Bath; Bristol; England [i]

Avon, River [ayvn] **1** River rising at Naseby in Northamptonshire, C England; flows 75 km/47 ml SW through Warwickshire then Hereford and Worcester to meet the R Severn at Tewkesbury in N Gloucestershire. **2** River rising in NW Wiltshire, S England; flows 112 km/70 ml S, W and NE through Bath and Bristol to meet the Bristol Channel at Avonmouth. » England [i]

AWACS » **Airborne Warning and Control System**

Awash [awash] National park in the lower Awash Valley, Ethiopia, in the East African Rift Valley; area 13 000 sq km/400 sq ml; noted for its wildlife, including leopards, lions, and crocodiles; a world heritage site. » Ethiopia [i]

Awe, Loch Picturesque loch in Strathclyde region, W Scotland; length 37 km/23 ml; SE of Oban; drained by R Awe; many early lake dwelling-sites (*crannogs*); Ben Cruachan rises to 13 124 m/33 688 ft (N); Inverliever Forest (W); hydroelectric power station; 15th-c Kilchurn castle, Inishail chapel. » Scotland [i]; Strathclyde

Axelrod, Julius (1912–) US pharmacologist, born in New York City. Educated at New York and Washington, DC, he has since 1955 carried out research in pharmacology and cell biology at the US National Institutes of Health. In 1970 he shared the Nobel Prize for Physiology or Medicine for his studies on the mechanism of neural transmission. » Katz; neurotransmitter; von Euler

axiom A proposition that is assumed to be true, on which later studies may be developed. The most famous axioms are those on which Euclidean geometry was developed. (1) A straight line may be drawn from any one point to any other point. (2) A finite straight line may be extended at each end. (3) A circle can always be drawn with any point as centre and with any radius. (4) All right angles are equal to each other. (5) If a straight line meets two other straight lines so that the two adjacent angles on one side of it are together less than two right angles, the other lines when extended will meet on that side of the first line. This fifth axiom has been recast in many different, consistent forms. » Euclid; geometries, non-Euclidean

axis deer » **chital**

Axis Powers The name given to the co-operation of Nazi Germany and Fascist Italy (1936–45), first used by Mussolini. In May 1939 the two countries signed a formal treaty, the *Pact of Steel*. In September 1940, Germany, Italy, and Japan signed a tripartite agreement, after which all three were referred to as Axis Powers. » fascism; Nazi Party; World War 2

axolotl [aksuhlotl] A rare Mexican salamander from high altitude in L Xochimilco; pale with three pairs of feathery gills; large fin around tail; usually breeds as juvenile form and never leaves water, but some individuals do become land-dwelling adults; family also known as **mole salamanders**. (*Ambystoma mexicanum*. Family: *Ambystomatidae*.) » salamander [i]

axon » **neurone** [i]

axonometric An architectural drawing showing a building in three dimensions. It is produced by placing the plan at an angle and projecting the verticals upwards. All lines are drawn to scale, so that the drawing appears distorted due to the lack of perspective. » section [i]

Axum A Greek-influenced Semitic trading state on the Eritrean coast, founded about the beginning of the Christian era and trading with Meroe. From its port at Adulis it dominated the trade of the Red Sea, and in the 3rd-c extended its power to Yemen. At the height of its influence under King Ezana (c.320–50), who accepted Christianity, it later became the basis of the Christian kingdom of Ethiopia. » African history; Ethiopia [i]; Kush

Ayacucho, Battle of [iya**koo**choh] (1824) The final major battle of the Spanish-American Wars of Independence, fought in the Peruvian Andes. It was a notable victory for the Venezuelan general de Sucre. » Spanish-American Wars of Independence; Sucre

ayatollah A Shiite Muslim religious title meaning 'sign of God', and referring to a clergyman who has reached the third level of Shiite higher education, is recognized as a mujtahid, and is over 40. The word is particularly associated today with the Islamic Republic of Iran. » Khomeini; mujtahid; Shiites

Ayckbourn, Alan (1939–) British playwright, born in London. He was a stage manager in repertory before joining a company at Scarborough, where since 1964 he has worked as a producer. The first of many West End successes was *Relatively Speaking* (1967), and he was quickly established as a master of farce. He has experimented with staging and dramatic structure: for example, *The Norman Conquests* (1974) is a trilogy in which each play takes place at the same time in a different part of the setting. Among his most successful farces are *Absurd Person Singular* (1973) and *Joking Apart* (1979). He has written two musicals, and was a BBC radio drama producer (1964–70). » drama; theatre

aye-aye [**iy**iy] A nocturnal primitive primate (prosimian) from Madagascar; shaggy coat, long bushy tail, and large ears; fingers extremely long and slender, especially the third finger (used to probe for wood-boring insects); inhabits trees. (*Daubentonia madagascariensis*. Family: *Daubentoniidae*.) » prosimian

Ayer, Sir A(lfred) J(ules) (1910–89) British philosopher, educated at Eton and Oxford, where he also lectured. He became Grote professor at University College London in 1947, and Wykeham professor of logic at Oxford (1959–78). His antimetaphysical *Language, Truth, and Logic* (1936, new introduction 1946) was hailed as a lucid and concise rendering in English of the doctrines of the 'Vienna Circle' of logical positivist philosophers, whom he visited in 1932. He also wrote *The Problem of Knowledge* (1956) and several collections of essays. During the 1950s he became familiar to a wide audience through his broadcasting appearances. He died in London. » Vienna Circle

Ayers Rock, aboriginal name **Uluru** 25°18S 131°18E. A huge red rock in SW Northern Territory, Australia, 450 km/280 ml SW of Alice Springs; within the Uluru National Park (1 325 sq km/511 sq ml); rises from the desert to a height of 348 m/1 142 ft; 3.6 km/2¼ ml long, 2.4 km/1½ ml wide, 8.8 km/5½ ml in circumference; resort town of Yulara 20 km/12 ml NW; the largest monolith in the world. » Alice Springs

Ayeshah, or **Aïsha** (c.610–77) The favourite of the nine wives of Mohammed, but who bore him no children. On Mohammed's death, when she was 18, she resisted Ali, the Prophet's son-in-law, and secured the caliphate for her father, Abu-Bekr. Again opposing Ali, she was defeated in 656. » Abu-Bekr; Mohammed

Ayia Napa [**ay**ya **na**pa] 34°59N 34°00E, pop (1981e) 850. Old fishing village in Famagusta district, SE Cyprus; with nearby Paralimni, the second most important tourist area on the island; monastery (16th-c). » Cyprus [i]

Aylesbury [**aylz**bree] 51°50N 0°50W, pop (1981) 52 914. County town in Aylesbury Vale district, Buckinghamshire, SC England; N of the Chiltern Hills, 60 km/37 ml NW of London; railway; furniture, chemicals, food processing, engineering; 13th-c St Mary's Church. » Buckinghamshire

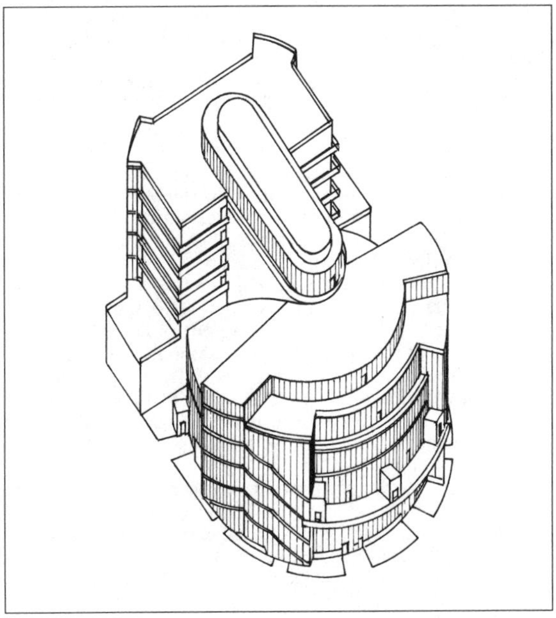

Axonometric – Total Theatre, design by Walter Gropius, 1926

Aylward, Gladys (1902–70) British missionary in China, born in London. She arrived in China in 1930, and along with a Scottish missionary, Mrs Jeannie Lawson, founded an inn at Yangcheng. It was from here that in 1938 she made her famous trek across the mountains leading over 100 children to safety when the war with Japan brought fighting to the area. She returned to England in 1948, preached for five years, then in 1953 settled in Taiwan as head of an orphanage. Ingrid Bergman played her in the popular film, *The Inn of the Sixth Happiness* (1958). » Bergman, Ingrid; missions, Christian

Ayn, Al 24°11N 55°45E, pop (1980) 101 663. Rapidly developing new city in Abu Dhabi emirate, United Arab Emirates; 150 km/93 ml E of the city of Abu Dhabi; former oasis village; E terminus of the highway from Abu Dhabi; university (1977); small industrial areas to the S; date and palm plantations; fort, archaeological sites; Al Ayn National Park, 16 km/10 ml S. » Abu Dhabi

Ayr 55°28N 4°38W, pop (1981) 49 522. Capital of Kyle and Carrick district, Strathclyde, SW Scotland; on the Firth of Clyde, at mouth of R Ayr, 48 km/30 ml SW of Glasgow; railway; metal products, machinery, carpets, agricultural trade, tourism; Loudoun Hall (15th–16th-c), Tam o' Shanter Museum; Alloway, 3 km/1¾ ml S, birthplace of Burns; Culzean castle (1777), 19 km/12 ml SSW. » Scotland [i]; Strathclyde

ayurveda [ahyur**vay**da] An ancient form of Hindu medicine, whose main principles are derived from the Veda. It is still practised in India in Ayurvedic centres. » Veda

azalea A deciduous species of rhododendron. The name is used in horticulture to distinguish them from the evergreen species. (Genus: *Rhododendron*. Family: *Ericaceae*). » deciduous plants; rhododendron

Azaña (y Díaz), Manuel [a**than**ya] (1880–1940) Spanish statesman, born at Alcalá de Henares. He qualified as a lawyer, served as a bureaucrat, but became eminent in the literary and political world. In 1925 he founded a political party, *Acción Republicana*. With the advent of the Second Republic (1931), he became Minister of War and then Prime Minister (1931–3) of a reforming government. He himself was closely identified with army reform and anticlericalism. After a period of opposition, he resumed the premiership (Feb 1936) and was elevated to the presidency (May 1936). He remained President throughout most of the Spanish Civil War, then went into exile in France, where he died. » Spanish Civil War

Azande [**azan**day] A cluster of ethnically mixed Sudanic-speaking agricultural people of SW Sudan, Zaire, and the Central African Republic. They were formed into a series of kingdoms by the Ambomu, led by the ruling Avongara clan, in the 18th-c, and are known for their elaborate system of beliefs in witchcraft, divination, and magic. Population c.800 000. » Central African Republic [i]; Sudan [i]; Zaire [i]

Azariah, Prayer of [aza**ri**ya] One of three Additions to the Book of Daniel in the Old Testament Apocrypha or Catholic Bible, usually linked with the Song of the Three Young Men; known also as the *Benedictus es* in Catholic forms of worship. It depicts a lamentation for the sins of Israel on the mouth of Azariah (Abednego in *Dan* 1.6ff), one of those cast into the furnace for their adherence to Israel's religion. » Apocrypha, Old Testament; Daniel, Book of; Song of the Three Young Men

Azerbaijan [azerbiy**jahn**] or **Azerbaydzhan**, Russ **Azerbaydzhanskaya** pop (1990e) 7 100 000; area 86 600 sq km/33 428 sq ml. Republic in E Transcaucasia; bounded E by the Caspian Sea and S by Iran; crossed by the Greater Caucasus (N) and Lesser Caucasus (SW), separated by the R Kura plain; highest peak, Mt Bazar-Dyuzi (4 480 m/14 698 ft); proclaimed a Soviet Socialist Republic, 1920; constituent republic of the USSR, 1936; dispute from 1988 with neighbouring Armenia over the Nagorny Karabakh region; riots promoted by the nationalist Azerbaijan Popular Front (Dec 1988–Jan 1990) culminated in an anti-Armenian pogrom in the capital, Baku; Soviet troops mounted a violent assault on the city to restore order; chief towns, Kirovabad, Sumgait; oil extraction and refining, iron, steel, aluminium, copper, chemicals, cement, foodstuffs, textiles, carpets, fishing, timber, salt extraction; grain, cotton, rice, grapes, fruit, vegetables, tobacco, silk. » Baku; Caucasus Mountains; Transcaucasia

Azhar, El [az**hah**] Muslim university and mosque founded in AD 970 at Cairo, Egypt. Once the centre of Islamic learning, today it is chiefly a school of Koranic teaching. It is said to be the oldest university in the world. » Islam; Koran

azidothymidine » AZT

Azikiwe, Nnamdi [a**zee**kwee] (1904–) Nigerian politician and first President of the Nigerian republic (1963–6). Born at Zungeri, N Nigeria and educated at American universities, in 1937 he took a leading part in the Nigerian nationalist movement. He became Prime Minister of the Eastern region (1954–9), Governor-General of Nigeria (1960–3), and President in 1963. In Britain during the military uprising of 1966, his office was suspended, although he returned privately to Nigeria. » nationalism; Nigeria [i]

azo-dyes An important class of dyes originally made (1861) by Peter Griess (1829–88), a German-born chemist who worked mainly as a brewery chemist at Burton-on-Trent, UK. All have two nitrogen atoms joined: $-N{=}N-$. » dyestuff; nitrogen

azolla An aquatic, free-floating fern, native to tropical and subtropical regions, and widely naturalized even in cooler areas such as Europe, despite suffering badly in winter; stem only a few cm long, branched with scale-like, overlapping fronds covered with non-wettable hairs, reddish in autumn. It often covers the surface of water in lakes, ponds, and ditches. (Genus: *Azolla*, 6 species. Family: *Azollaceae*.) » fern

Azores [a**zawz**], Port **Ilhas dos Açôres** pop (1981) 243 410; area 2 300 sq km/900 sq ml. Island archipelago of volcanic origin, 1 400–1 800 km/870–1 100 ml W of Cabo da Roca on mainland Portugal; Portuguese autonomous region; three widely separated groups of islands: Flores and Corvo (NW), Terceira, Graciosa, São Jorge, Faial, Pico (C), and Santa Maria with the Formigas Islands and São Miguel, the principal island (E); settled by the Portuguese, 1439; chief town, Ponta Delgada; grain, fruit, tea, tobacco, wine; highest point, Pico (2 351 m/7 713 ft). » Ponta Delgada; Portugal [i]

Azorín Pseudonym of **José Martinez Ruiz** (1873–1967) Spanish novelist and critic, born at Monóvar, educated at Valencia. His novels include *Don Juan* (1922) and *Dona Inés* (1925). He died in Madrid. » Spanish literature

Azov, Sea of [**a**zof], Russ **Azovskoye More** Gulf in NE of Black Sea; connected to the Sea by the Kerch Strait; main arms, Gulf of Taganrog (NE) and Sivash or Putrid Sea (W); latter mostly swamp, almost completely cut off from the Sea of Azov by a sandspit (Tongue of Arabat); shallow water, tending to freeze (Nov–Mar); maximum depth 15.3 m/50.2 ft; river deposits cause further shallowing and silting of harbours; important source of freshwater fish. » Black Sea

AZT An abbreviation for **azidothymidine**, a drug which inhibits replication of viruses, including the AIDS virus, HIV. Developed as *zidovudine*, it was granted a licence unusually rapidly, in response to pressure from AIDS patients. Clinical trials have demonstrated the drug to be of limited use in therapy: it can slow the progress of the disease, but it cannot cure AIDS symptoms. In addition, it has inherent toxicity, and resistance develops rapidly. » AIDS; drug resistance; virus

Aztec-Tanoan languages A group of N American Indian languages which form a bridge between the indigenous languages of N and S America, most of which have few speakers today. An exception is Aztec itself, spoken in Mexico, which has about a million speakers. » American Indians

Aztecs The most powerful people of Middle America during the 15th–16th-c. Their main city, Tenochtitlan (present-day Mexico City), near L Texcoco, became the most densely populated city of the region. They built up a great and powerful despotic state, with a strong military force, subjugating nearly all the people of C Mexico, and eventually ruling 400–500 small tribute-paying states (probably 5–6 million people), which provided them with raw materials and produce. People captured in wars were offered for human sacrifice to the Aztec gods. The Aztecs were famous for their agriculture, cultivating all available land, introducing irrigation, draining swamps, and creating artificial islands in the lakes. Their best-known ruler was Montezuma II. They developed a form of hieroglyphic writing, a complex calendar system, and built famous pyramids and temples. The Aztec empire was finally destroyed by the Spanish under the leadership of Cortés in 1521. » American Indians; Aztec-Tanoan languages; Cortés; Montezuma II; Teotihuacan

Azuero [as**way**roh] Peninsula in WC Panama, on the Pacific Ocean coast, forming the W side of the Gulf of Panama; length 80 km/50 ml; rises to 829 m/2 720 ft at Cerro Canajagua. » Panama [i]

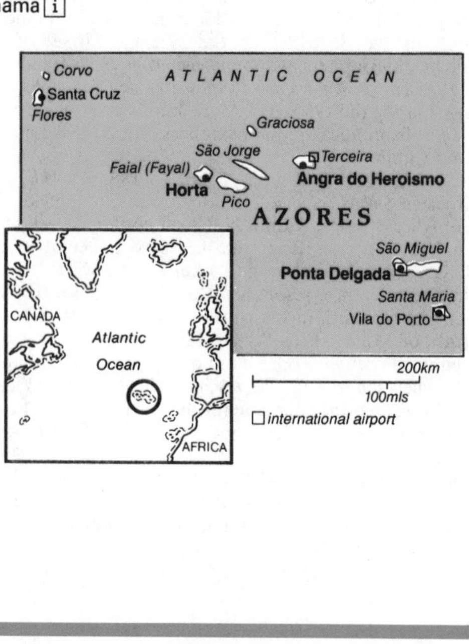

B

B'nai B'rith (Hebrew 'sons of the covenant') The oldest and largest Jewish service organization, founded in the USA in 1843. It pursues educational and community activities, and concerns itself with the rights of Jews throughout the world. Included in the organization are the Hillel Foundation (for Jewish college students), the Anti-Defamation League (a civil rights group), and B'nai B'rith Women. » Judaism

Ba'ath [bahth] (Arabic 'resurgence') The ideology of the Ba'ath Arab Socialist Party, founded by Michel Aflaq in 1940, synthesizing Marxism with a pan-Arab nationalism that aims to unite Arab nations. There is a strong democratic element to the ideology. The party was most prominent in Syria and Iraq, where it had a close relationship with the military. » Marxism

Baader-Meinhof [**bah**duh **miyn**-hof] The popular name for *Rote Armee Fraktion* (RAF), after leaders Andreas Baader (1943–77) and Ulrike Meinhof (1934–76); a left-wing German revolutionary, terrorist group which carried out political bombings in Germany in the early 1970s. Baader, Meinhoff, and 18 other members were arrested in 1972. On a much smaller scale, RAF continued into the 1980s.

Baal [bayl] (Heb 'lord') The Phoenician god of rain and fertility, his voice being the thunder; in the Bible, used for gods of various localities in Syria and Canaan, and eventually for the great god of the Canaanites, whose cult was often associated with the goddess Asherah or Astarte. » Ahab; Beelzebub; Bible; Canaan

Baalbek, ancient **Heliopolis** [**bahl**bek] 34°00N 36°12E, pop (1982e) 14 000. Town in E Lebanon where the Phoenicians built a temple to the sun-god, Baal; a world heritage site; Temple of Jupiter, Temple of Bacchus; centre of Muslim Shiite activity. » Baal; Lebanon [i]; Phoenicia; Shiites

Baba Malay » **Malay** (language)

Babbage, Charles (1792–1871) British mathematician and pioneer computer scientist, born at Totnes, Devon, and educated at Cambridge, where he became professor of mathematics (1823–39). He worked on the theory of logarithms, and built a calculating machine, the forerunner of the computer, which in an unfinished state is preserved in the Science Museum, London. His assistant was Byron's daughter, Lady Ada Lovelace. They later attempted a system for predicting winners of horse races, and lost much money. He died in London. » computer; logarithm

Babbitt, Irving (1865–1933) US scholar and critic, born at Dayton, Ohio. Primarily a moralist and teacher, he was a leader of the 'new humanism' which flourished in the USA in the 1920s. He became professor of French at Harvard (1894–1933), and died at Cambridge, Massachusetts. » humanism; literary criticism

Babbitt, Milton (1916–) US composer, born in Philadelphia. He studied in New York and Princeton, where he was appointed professor in 1938 and was also a member of the mathematics faculty (1943–5). His compositions apply the principles of pitch serialism to other musical parameters, and some also use electronic resources. » electronic music; serialism

babbler A songbird native to warmer regions of the Old World; soft, fluffy plumage and short wings; eats insects, fruit, seeds, and nectar; usually found in small groups. The name is also used for the **sooty babbler** (a chat of the family *Turdidae*). (Family: *Timaliidae*, over 280 species.) » chat; jay; reedling; songbird; whipbird; wren babbler

Babe Zaharias, byname of **Mildred Zaharias**, *née* **Mildred Didrikson** (1914–56) US sportswoman, born at Port Arthur, Texas. After an outstanding career in athletics, she became a leading golfer, and was also renowned at diving, billiards, and lacrosse. At 16 she set a world javelin record of 40.61 m/133 ft 3¼ in. At 18, at the 1932 Olympics, she won gold medals in the 80 m hurdles (in world record time) and javelin, and a silver medal in the high jump. At golf she won the US Amateur Championship in 1946, and the British Amateur title in 1947 – the first American to win both titles. As a professional she won the US Women's Open in 1948, 1950, and 1954. She died at Galveston, Texas. » athletics; golf

Babel, Isaac (Emmanuilovich) [**ba**bil] (1894–1941) Russian writer, born in Odessa, where he received an Orthodox Jewish education. He served in World War 1 against Germany (1917), then with the Bolsheviks against Poland (1920). His experiences as a soldier form the basis of *Konarmiia* (1926, Red Cavalry). His work was proscribed by the Soviet authorities, and he was silent from the early 1930s onwards. Arrested in 1939, he died in a prison camp. » Russian literature

Babel, Tower of Probably the site of an important temple shrine in the ancient city of Babylon. In the Bible (*Gen* 11.1–9) the legend is related of how its construction led to the confusion of languages, and the consequent dispersion of peoples, as a punishment by God for human pride. » Babylon; Genesis, Book of

Babeuf, François-Noël [baberf] (1760–97) French communist, born at St Quentin, who during the Revolution (as 'Gracchus Babeuf') advocated a rigorous system of communism (**Babouvism**). His conspiracy to destroy the Directory (1796) and establish an extreme democratic and communistic system (a 'Republic of Equals') was discovered, and he was guillotined. » communism; French Revolution

Babi » **Baha'i**

Babi Yar A huge ravine near Kiev in the Ukraine into which over 30 000 Jews were herded and massacred by Nazi German troops in 1941. It is also the title of a poem by Yevegeny Yevtushenko (1961) and a novel by Anatoly Kuznetsov (1966) dedicated to the victims. » Holocaust; Nazi Party

Babington, Antony (1561–86) English Roman Catholic conspirator, born at Dethick, Derbyshire. He served as a page to Queen Mary of Scotland, when she was a prisoner at Sheffield. In 1586, he was induced by John Ballard and others to lead a conspiracy towards Elizabeth's murder and Mary's release (the **Babington Plot**). Cipher messages were intercepted by Walsingham in which Mary warmly approved the plot, and these were later used against her. Babington fled, but was captured and executed with the others. » Mary, Queen of Scots; Walsingham

Babinski, Joseph François Felix (1857–1932) French neurologist, born in Paris. He described a reflex of the foot, symptomatic of organic disease of the motor neurones in the brain and spinal cord, and a reflex of the forearm believed to be due to a lesion in the spinal cord. Both reflexes are known as Babinski's Sign. With **Alfred Fröhlich** (1871–1953), a Viennese pharmacologist, he investigated an endocrinal disorder called adiposogenital dystrophy or **Babinski–Fröhlich disease**. » endocrine glands; neurone [i]; spinal cord

babirusa [babuhroosa] A wild pig native to Sulawesi; pale, almost hairless body; long lower tusks; upper canines in the male grow from the top of the snout, and curl towards the eyes; inhabits riverbanks; swims well. (*Babyrousa babyrussa*.) » pig

baboon A ground-dwelling African monkey; long dog-like muzzle with large teeth; males with swollen, naked buttocks; troops contain up to 100 individuals. (Genera: *Papio*, 5 species;

Mandrillus, 2 species; *Theropithecus*, 1 species.) » chacma/ gelada/hamadryas baboon; drill; mandrill; Old World monkey

Babur, Zahiruddin Muhammad [**ba**boor] (1483–1530) First Mughal Emperor of India, born at Fergana, C Asia. A descendant of Ghengis Khan and founder of the Mughal dynasty, he occupied Delhi and Agra in 1526. He was a distinguished soldier, as well as a poet and diarist of note. He died in Agra. » Mughal Empire

baby talk The way in which adults talk to very young children, mimicking what are perceived to be the main features of child language. It includes simplified sentence structures (eg *Mummy gone*) and word pronunciations (eg *doggie*). Many parents lapse naturally into this style of speech, though some are critical of it, and try to avoid it. However, there is no evidence that the use of baby talk does any harm to the process of language acquisition, and the use of simplified structures may actually facilitate it. » motherese

Babylon 32°33N 44°25E. From the 18th-c BC, the capital of the Babylonian Empire, situated on the R Euphrates S of Baghdad, modern Iraq. Its massive city walls and 'hanging gardens', attributed by classical tradition to Semiramis, wife of Shamshi-Adad V (823–811 BC), regent (811–806), were one of the wonders of the ancient world. Semi-subterranean vaulted rooms provided with hydraulic lifting gear in the later Palace of Nebuchadnezzar (604–562 BC) have been claimed as remains of the gardens, but their site is not definitely known. » Babylonia; Iraq [i]; Seven Wonders of the Ancient World

Babylonia [babi**loh**nia] The region in Lower Mesopotamia around the ancient city of Babylon, which formed the core twice in antiquity of extensive but short-lived empires. The first, covering the whole of Mesopotamia, was created by the great Amorite king Hammurabi (c.1795–1750 BC) but destroyed by the Hittites c.1595 BC. The second came into being with the Babylonian overthrow of Assyria in 612 BC and lasted until the Persian conquest in 539–538 BC. Under its greatest ruler Nebuchadrezzar (605–562 BC), it stretched as far east as the Mediterranean. Although the Persians ended Babylonian political power for good, culturally Babylonian influence lasted for centuries, particularly in the fields of astrology, astronomy and mathematics. » Assyria; Babylon; Babylonian art; Chaldaeans; Hittites; Mesopotamia; Persian Empire

Babylonian art The art associated with ancient Babylonia (the S part of modern Iraq), dating from c.2500 BC, until the conquest of the country by Alexander (331 BC). What survives is religious and courtly, such as the stylized stone statues of Gudea (eg in the Louvre) made c.2100 BC, the wall-paintings and coloured bas-reliefs representing religious sacrifices, royal ceremonies, and (as in neighbouring Assyria) comparatively realistic hunting scenes. Figures follow the typical Ancient Near-Eastern conventions, with frontal bodies, profile heads and legs, and large staring eyes. Precious metals occur in the objects from the royal cemetery at Ur, made c.2500 BC. » art; Assyrian art; Babylonia; bas-relief; Egyptian art; Sumerian art

Babylonian exile The mass deportation of the Jews from Palestine to Babylonia in 587–6 BC, after the failure of their revolt against Nebuchadnezzar. » Babylonia

Bacall, Lauren, originally **Betty Perske** (1924–) US film actress, born in New York City. She was given her first leading role in *To Have and Have Not* (1944), opposite Humphrey Bogart, whom she subsequently married, appearing again with him in *The Big Sleep* (1946), *Dark Passage* (1947), and *Key Largo* (1948). After his death in 1957, she continued in tough sophisticated parts on screen and stage, but appeared less frequently; later films included *The Shootist* (1976) and *The Fan* (1981). » Bogart

baccarat A casino card game, the most popular version being *baccarat banque*, in which the bank plays against the players. Another variant is *chemin de fer*, whereby all players take it in turn to hold the bank. Baccarat is derived from popular 15th-c games, and is thought to have been introduced into France from Italy during the reign of Charles VIII. The object is to assemble, either with two or three cards, a points value of 9. Picture cards and the ten count as 0. The ace counts as 1, and other cards according to their face value. If the total is a double figure then the first figure is ignored, eg 18 would count as 8. » casino; chemin de fer; playing cards

Bacchanalia [baka**nay**lia] The orgiastic rites of Bacchus (Dionysus), the god of nature, fertility, and wine. They were banned from Rome in 186 BC on the grounds that they were a threat to morality and public order. » Dionysia

Bacchylides [ba**ki**lideez] (5th-c BC) Greek lyric poet, nephew of Simonides of Ceos, and a contemporary of Pindar in Hiero's court at Syracuse. Fragments of his 'epinician' odes (written to celebrate victories in the great athletic festivals) were discovered in 1896. » Greek literature; ode

Bach, Carl Philipp Emanuel (1714–88) German composer, born at Weimar, the second surviving son of Johann Sebastian. Educated at Leipzig, he showed great musical ability at an early age. In 1740 he became cembalist to the young Frederick (later 'the Great'), and in 1768 director of music at the main churches in Hamburg, where he died. He wrote the first methodical treatment of clavier playing, and composed numerous concertos, keyboard sonatas, church and chamber music. » Bach, Johann Sebastian

Bach, Johann Christian (1735–82) German composer, known as the 'London' Bach, the youngest son of Johann Sebastian. Born in Leipzig, he studied in Berlin (under C P E Bach) and from 1754 in Italy. After turning Catholic, he was appointed organist at Milan in 1760, and composed ecclesiastical music, including a 'Requiem' and two settings of the 'Te Deum', as well as operas. In 1762 he settled in London, where he was employed at the King's Theatre, and collaborated with C F Abel (1723–87) in promoting an important series of subscription concerts. He died in London. » Bach, Johann Sebastian

Bach, Johann Sebastian (1685–1750) German composer, one of the world's greatest musicians, born at Eisenach. He was orphaned by the age of 10, and brought up by his elder brother, **Johann Christoph** (1671–1721), organist at Ohrdruf, who taught him the organ and clavier. He attended school in Lüneburg, before in 1703 becoming organist at Arnstadt. He found his duties as choirmaster irksome, and angered the authorities by his innovative chorale accompaniments. In 1707 he married a cousin, **Maria Barbara Bach** (1684–1720), and left to become organist at Mühlhausen. In 1708 he transferred to the ducal court at Weimar, and in 1711 became *Kapellmeister* to Prince Leopold of Anhalt-Cöthen, where he wrote mainly instrumental music, including the 'Brandenburg' Concertos (1721) and *The Well-tempered Clavier* (1722). Widowed in 1720, and left with four children, he married in 1721 **Anna Magdalena Wilcke** (1701–60), and had 13 children by her, of whom six survived. In 1723 he was appointed cantor of the St Thomas School in Leipzig, where his works included perhaps c.300 church cantatas, the *St Matthew Passion* (1727), and the *Mass in B Minor*. Almost totally blind, he died in Leipzig. One of his main achievements was his remarkable development of polyphony. Known to his contemporaries mainly as an organist, his genius as a composer was not fully recognized until the following century. » cantata; polyphony

Bach, Wilhelm Friedemann (1710–84) German composer, the eldest and most gifted son of Johann Sebastian. Born at Weimar, and educated at Leipzig University, he became in 1733 organist at Dresden and in 1746 at Halle. But his way of life became increasingly dissolute, and from 1764 he lived without fixed occupation at Brunswick, Göttingen, and Berlin, where he died. He was one of the finest organ players of his time, but his compositions failed to fulfil his early promise. » Bach, Johann Sebastian

bacillus Any rod-shaped bacterium; also a large and diverse genus of rod-shaped bacteria, typically motile by means of flagella. They are widely distributed as saprophytes in soil and aquatic habitats. Some are disease-causing, including the causative agent of anthrax. (Kingdom: *Monera*. Family: *Bacillaceae*.) » anthrax; bacteria [i]; flagellum; saprophyte

back projection The technique of projecting an image on to a translucent screen to be viewed from the opposite side, advantageous when the audience area cannot be darkened, as in museums and exhibitions and for large-screen television. In a form of composite cinematography, the performance of actors is photographed to appear against a moving background scene projected from the rear on to such a screen. » cinematography [i]; front projection; screen

back slang A type of secret language used mainly by children, in which words are spelled backwards and pronounced according to the new spelling: for example, *week* might be pronounced as *kew*. Some children train themselves to reach high speeds in speaking backwards.

back translation A test of the quality of a foreign language translation. The translated text is re-translated into the original language, and the two versions compared. The closer the correspondence, the better the translation. » translation

backcross In experimental genetics, the mating of a first generation hybrid with an individual that is genetically identical with one of its parents. Such experiments are used to detect linkages between genes. » genetics [i]

backgammon A board game for two players. Equipment similar to that used in backgammon was excavated from Tutankhamen's tomb. Introduced to Britain by the Crusaders, it became known as backgammon from c.1750. Each player has 15 round flat pieces of a particular colour, which are moved around the board on the throw of two dice. The board is divided into two halves; the inner table and the outer table. The object is to move your own pieces around the board and home to your own inner table. You win by being the first to remove all your pieces from the board.

background processing A lower priority task carried out on a computer while it also engaged in doing other tasks.. For example, many computers operate their printer(s) in this way, without apparently interrupting the user. » printer, computer

background radiation Naturally occurring radioactivity which can be detected at any place on Earth. It results from cosmic rays reaching the Earth from outer space, and from the radioactive decay of minerals in the soil. » cosmic rays; radioactivity

backing store » **auxiliary store**

Bacon, Francis, Viscount St Albans (1561–1626) English philosopher and statesman, born in London. Educated at Cambridge and Gray's Inn, he was called to the Bar in 1582. Becoming an MP in 1584, he was knighted by James I in 1603. He was in turn Solicitor-General (1607), Attorney-General (1613), Privy Counsellor (1616), Lord Keeper (1617), and Lord Chancellor (1618). He became Lord Verulam in 1618, and was made viscount in 1621. However, complaints were made that he accepted bribes from suitors in his court, and he was publicly accused before his fellow peers, fined, imprisoned, and banished from parliament and the court. Although soon released, and later pardoned, he never returned to public office, and he died in London, deeply in debt. His philosophy is best studied in *The Advancement of Learning* (1605) and *Novum Organum* (1620). His stress on inductive methods gave a strong impetus to subsequent scientific investigation.

Bacon, Francis (1909–) Irish artist, born in Dublin, who without any formal art education began painting at the age of 19. He treated religious subjects in a highly individual manner, but made little impact until 1945, when his 'Three Studies for Figures at the base of a Crucifixion' won praise. Since then many successful works have emerged, but these are a small proportion of his output, as he destroys all paintings which do not satisfy him. His style derives from Surrealism, often with a tendency towards the macabre. » Surrealism

Bacon, Roger (c.1214–92) English Franciscan philosopher, known as 'doctor mirabilis', probably born at Ilchester, Somerset, and educated at Oxford. Some time before 1236 he went to Paris, where he wrote commentaries on Aristotle's physics and metaphysics. In 1247 he began to devote himself to experimental science, returning to Oxford about 1250. About 1256 he went into retirement in Paris, but in 1266–7 compiled, at the request of Pope Clement IV, his *Opus Majus* (Great Work) along with two other works, a summary of all his learning. In 1277 his writings were condemned by the Franciscans for 'suspected novelties', and he was imprisoned until shortly before his death. » Franciscans

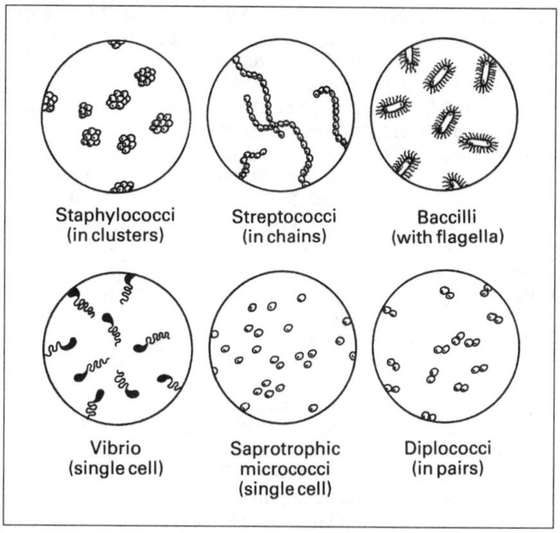

Bacteria

bacteria A diverse division of microscopic organisms that all share a *procaryotic* cellular organization, ie each cell lacks a true nucleus bounded by a nuclear membrane. The genetic information is carried on a loop of deoxyribonucleic acid (DNA) in the cytoplasm. Most bacteria are single-celled. Basic bacterial shapes are spherical (*coccus*), rod-like (*bacillus*), and spiral (*spirillum*). These may occur singly, or in chains, pairs, clusters, or other groupings. Some (the actinomycetes) have a branching, filamentous structure, and may form a mycelium. Most have a rigid cell wall containing peptidoglycan, the exceptions being the mycoplasms and halobacteria. Cell division typically occurs by symmetrical binary fission; some form spores; mitosis never occurs.

Bacteria range in size from less than 1 micron (chlamydia) to about 0.5 mm (spirochaete), but most are between 1 and 10 microns. They differ greatly in their growth requirements. Some can grow only in the presence of oxygen (*aerobic* bacteria), whilst others grow only in the absence of oxygen (*anaerobic* bacteria). They occur in soil, water, and air, as well as in symbiotic associations with other organisms, and as parasites or disease-causing agents. They cause many human diseases, including anthrax, plague, pneumonia, syphilis, tetanus, and tuberculosis. The scientific study of bacteria is known as **bacteriology**. » actinomycete; Archaebacteria; bacillus; bacteriological warfare; cell; chlamydia; clostridium; DNA [i]; escherichia; legionella; micro-organism; mitosis; nucleus (biology); pneumococcus; proteus; salmonella; spirochaete; staphylococcus; streptococcus; symbiosis; vibrio

bacteriological warfare A form of warfare using organic agents such as micro-organisms and viruses which cause disease and death in humans. Many such agents have been investigated, including anthrax, plague, and botulinus toxin. » bacteria [i]; biological warfare; chemical warfare; virus

bacteriophage A virus that infects bacteria, reproducing only inside living bacteria. Bacteriophage virions (complete infective virus particles) are typically very small, and may contain either ribonucleic or deoxyribonucleic acid. » bacteria [i]; DNA [i]; RNA; virus

Bactria [**bak**treea] The name given in antiquity to the area roughly corresponding to N Afghanistan and the adjacent parts of S Russia. It was ruled for centuries by foreign conquerors, notably the Achaemenids and the Seleucids. In the second half of the 3rd-c BC Bactria at last became an independent state, and under a series of able Indo-Greek rulers went on to establish an empire that at its height covered not only all Afghanistan but large parts of Russian Central Asia and Pakistan. » Achaemenids; Persian Empire; Seleucids

Badajoz [**ba**dajoz], Span [ba**th**a**hoth**], ancient **Pax Augusta** 38°50N 6°59W, pop (1981) 114 361. Capital of Badajoz province, SW Spain, on R Guadiana, 401 km/249 ml SW of Madrid; bishopric; former Moorish capital; scene of a battle in the Peninsular War (1812); airport; railway; tinned vegetables, textiles; cathedral (13th-c). » Peninsular War; Spain [i]

Baden, ancient **Thermae Pannonicae** [**bah**dn] 48°01N 16°14E, pop (1981) 23 140. Capital of Baden district, Niederösterreich, NE Austria; 30 km/19 ml S of Vienna, on the R Schwechat; connected to Vienna by tram; principal Austrian spa, with sulphurous waters, known since Roman times; tourism, casino. » Austria [i]

Baden-Powell, Robert (Stephenson Smyth), 1st Baron (1857–1941) British general, born in London, who founded the Boy Scout movement (1908) and, with his sister **Agnes** (1858–1945), the Girl Guides (1910). Educated at Charterhouse, he joined the army, served in India and Afghanistan, was on the staff in Ashanti and Matabeleland, and won fame as the defender of Mafeking (1899–1900). He died at Nyeri, Kenya. » scouting

Bader, Sir Douglas (Robert Stuart) (1910–82) British aviator, born in London. Commissioned from Cranwell (1930), he lost both legs in a flying accident in 1931 and was invalided out of the RAF, but overcame his disability and returned to the service in 1939. He commanded the first RAF Canadian Fighter Squadron, evolving tactics that contributed to victory in the Battle of Britain, but was captured in August 1941 after a collision with an enemy aircraft over Béthune. He left the RAF in 1946. A great pilot and leader of 'the few', he set an example of fortitude and heroism that became a legend. He received many honours, and was knighted in 1976 for his work for the disabled. » air force; World War 2

badger A nocturnal mammal, usually grey-brown with a black and white head; pointed face; length 0.5–1 m/1.6–3.3 ft; lives in burrows; species include the **Old World badger** (*Meles*), **hog badger** (*Arctonyx*), **stink badger** (*Mydaus*), **ferret badger** (*Melogale*), all native to European and Asian woodlands; also the **American badger** (*Taxidea*) from open country in N America. (Family: *Mustelidae*, 8 species.) » ferret; honey badger; Mustelidae

Badlands Arid region of SW South Dakota and NW Nebraska, USA; an area of barren, eroded landscapes and fossil deposits E of the Black Hills. » Nebraska; South Dakota

badminton An indoor court game played by two or four people using rackets and a shuttlecock. Its name derives from Badminton House, the seat of the Duke of Beaufort, where the Duke's family and guests played in the 19th-c; but a similar game was being played in China over 2 000 years ago. It developed from the children's games of battledore and shuttlecock. The object is to volley the shuttle over the central net. Points are won by forcing errors when you are the server. » sepek takraw; RR105

Badoglio, Pietro [bah**dol**yoh] (1871–1956) Italian marshal, born at Grazzano Monferrato, Piedmont, who became Prime Minister (1943–4) after Mussolini's downfall. On Italy's entry into World War 2 (Jun 1940) he was made Commander-in-Chief, but resigned after the Italian army was humiliated by the Greeks in Epirus and Albania. He formed a non-fascist government in 1943, negotiated an armistice with the Allies, and declared war on Germany, but was forced to resign a year later. He died at Grazzano Badoglio. » fascism; Mussolini; World War 2

Baedeker, Karl [**bay**dekuh] (1801–59) German publisher, born at Essen. He started his own publishing business in 1827 at Koblenz, and is best known for the guidebooks which bear his name, published since 1872 at Leipzig. He died at Koblenz, Prussia.

Baerlein, (Edgar) Maximillian (1879–1971) British amateur rackets and real tennis player, born in Manchester. He played for Eton College, Cambridge University, and Manchester, and won the British amateur rackets title nine times between 1903 and 1923, sharing the doubles title six times (between 1902 and 1920). He won 13 British Amateur real tennis singles titles and 11 doubles titles. » rackets; real tennis

Baeyer, (Johann Friedrich Wilhelm) Adolf von [**bi**yuh] (1835–1917) German organic chemist, born in Berlin. He studied at Heidelberg, taught in the Berlin Technical Institute, and was appointed professor of chemistry at Strasbourg (1872–5) and Munich (1875–1915). His research covered many aspects of chemistry, notably the synthesis of the dye indigo and the mechanism of photosynthesis. He was awarded the Nobel Prize for Chemistry in 1905, and died near Munich. » indigo

Baez, Joan [**bah**ez] (1941–) US folksinger, born in Staten I, New York. Her crystalline soprano voice first attracted critical plaudits at the Newport Folk Festival of 1960, and her recordings in the decade that followed created a mass audience for folk music. A Quaker, she actively opposes racial discrimination, wars, and political imprisonment, both on stage and off. Since 1970 she has widened her repertoire to include country and western songs and soft rock. » country and western; folk music; Friends, Society of; rock

Baffin, William (1584c–1622) English navigator, probably born in London. He was pilot in several expeditions in search of the Northwest Passage (1612–16), during which he carefully examined Hudson Strait (1615), discovered Baffin Bay (1616), and named Lancaster, Smith, and Jones Sounds (1616). His later voyages (1616–21) were to the East, and he was killed at the siege of Ormuz. » Northwest Passage

Baffin Bay Ice-blocked Arctic gulf between Greenland (E) and Baffin, Bylot, Devon, and Ellesmere Is (W); length c.1 125 km/700 ml; width 110–650 km/70–400 ml; depth over 2 400 m/8 100 ft; navigation only in summer; first entered by John Davis, 1585; explored by William Baffin, 1615; important whaling area in the 1800s; seafowl and fur-bearing animals along coast. » Arctic; Baffin

Baffin Island Largest island in the Canadian Arctic Archipelago, in the Arctic Ocean; separated from Labrador by the Hudson Strait, and from Greenland to the E by the Davis Strait and Baffin Bay; area 318 186 sq km/122 820 sq ml; length c.1 600 km/994 ml; width 209–725 km/130–450 ml; irregular coastline, with several peninsulas and deep bays; mostly a plateau rising to c.915 m/3 000 ft; first visited by Frobisher, 1576–8; chief settlements Frobisher Bay, Lake Harbour, Pond Inlet; population mainly Eskimos. » Baffin; Canada [i]; Northwest Territories

bagatelle A restricted form of billiards, played on a table with nine numbered cups instead of pockets. Popular in the UK, especially in the Midlands, N Wales, and the North, it is played in many different forms on a rectangular table, with measurements varying according to local conditions. » billiards

Bagehot, Walter [**ba**jot] (1826–77) British economist, journalist, and political theorist, born and died at Langport, Somerset. He studied mathematics at London, was called to the Bar in 1852, spent some time as a banker in his father's firm, then became editor of the *Economist* in 1860. His *English Constitution* (1867) is still considered a standard work. His *Physics and Politics* (1872) applied the theory of evolution to politics. He advocated many constitutional reforms, including the introduction of life peers. » evolution; political science

Bagerat [baguh**raht**] The former city of Khalifatabad, founded in the 15th-c by General Ulugh Khan Jahan in the S Ganges delta, present-day Bangladesh; a world heritage site. Its mosques and palaces spring from a unique marriage of local architectural styles with that of imperial Delhi. » Bangladesh [i]

Baggara » **Baqqarah**

Baghdad [bag**dad**] 33°20N 44°26E, pop (1970) 2 183 760. Capital city of Iraq, on R Tigris; a commercial and transportation centre; founded, 762; enclosed on three sides by ancient walls; airport; railway; university (1958); oil refining, distilling, tanning, tobacco, textiles, cement; Abbasid palace, Mustansiriyah law college (13th-c). » Iraq [i]

Baghlan [bag**lahn**] pop (1984e) 536 783; area 17 109 sq km/6 604 sq ml. Province in NEC Afghanistan; N of Kabul; capital Baghlan Jadid, pop (1984e) 43 000; Salang Pass and Tunnel, on the main Russian supply route to Kabul, the focus of resistance by Mujahadeen guerrillas during the Russian occupation of Afghanistan (1979–89). » Afghanistan [i]; Mujahadeen

Bagley, Sarah (flourished 1835–47) US labour leader, active in the mills of Lowell, Massachusetts, where she led 'turn-outs' (strikes) and organized the Female Labor Reform Association. She played a major role in the successful campaign for a 10-hour working day in Massachusetts. » women's liberation movement

bagpipes A musical instrument of great antiquity consisting of a bag (usually of sheepskin) which the player fills with air through a blow-pipe or bellows, and squeezes with his arm so that the air then passes through the sounding pipes. One of these, the chanter, is fitted with a reed and finger-holes, and is used for playing melodies; two or three other pipes supply the continuous accompanimental drone which is a distinctive (and to some ears maddening) feature of the bagpipes. The Highlands and Lowlands of Scotland have their different types of bagpipes, as also do Ireland and Northumberland, and various types of bagpipes are found throughout Europe. » aerophone; reed instrument

Baguio [**bag**eeoh] 16°25N 120°37E, pop (1980) 119 009. Summer capital of the Philippines, in Benguet province, NW Luzon I; mountain resort town and official summer residence of the President; two universities (1911, 1948); military academy; gold, copper; summer festival. » Philippines [i]

Baha'i [bah**hiy**] A religious movement arising out of the Persian Islamic sect Babi in the 1860s, when Mirza Husayn Ali (1817–92), known as Baha Allah ('Glory of God'), declared himself the prophet foretold by the founder of the Babi movement, Mirza Ali Mohammed (1819–50). Baha'ism teaches the oneness of God, the unity of all faiths, the inevitable unification of humankind, the harmony of all people, universal education, and obedience to government. It has no priesthood, and its adherents are expected to teach the faith. Local assemblies meet for informal devotions in homes or rented halls. There is little formal ritual, but there are ceremonies for marriage, funerals, and the naming of babies. Its headquarters is in Haifa, Israel. » religion

Bahamas, official name **Commonwealth of the Bahamas** pop (1990e) 253 000; area 13 934 sq km/5 378 sq ml. Archipelago of c.700 low-lying islands and over 2 000 cays, forming a chain extending c.800 km/500 ml SE from the coast of Florida; two oceanic banks of Little Bahama and Great Bahama; highest point 120 m/394 ft; capital Nassau; major town Freeport; timezone GMT −5; over 75% of the population live on New Providence or Grand Bahama; 85% Black, 15% White; official language, English; dominant religion, Christianity; unit of currency, Bahamian dollar; climate subtropical, with average temperatures 21°C (winter) and 27°C (summer); mean annual rainfall 750–1 500 mm/30–60 in; hurricanes frequent (Jun–Nov); visited by Columbus in 1492, but first permanent European settlement not until 1647, by English and Bermudan religious refugees; British Crown Colony 1717; notorious rendezvous of buccaneers and pirates; independence 1973; a bicameral assembly, consisting of a House of Assembly with 49 elected members and a Senate with 16 nominated members; head of state, the British monarch, represented by a governor-general; tourism the mainstay of the economy, especially at New Providence (Nassau and Paradise I) and Grand Bahama; important financial centre (status as a tax haven); oil refining, fishing, rum and liqueur distilling, cement, pharmaceuticals, steel pipes, fruit, vegetables. » Andros (Bahamas); buccaneers; Grand Bahama; Nassau (Bahamas); New Providence; RR24 national holidays; RR43 political leaders

Bahasa Indonesia [ba**ha**sa] The Malay dialect of the S Malay Peninsula, which has been the standard language of Malaysia since 1949. It was first given official status by the Japanese occupiers during World War 2. It is often referred to simply as **Indonesian**. » Malay (language)

Bahia [ba**ee**a] pop (1980) 9 454 346; area 561 026 sq km/216 556 sq ml. State in Nordeste region, NE Brazil, bounded E by the Atlantic; capital Salvador; agriculture, chemical and petrochemical industries, oil; Brazil first claimed for Portugal by Cabral in 1500, when he stepped ashore at Pôrto Seguro in SE Bahia. » Brazil [i]; Cabral; Salvador

Bahía Blanca [ba**ee**a **blang**ka] 38°45S 62°15W, pop (1980) 220 765. City in Buenos Aires province, E Argentina; at the head of the Bahía Blanca Bay, SW of Buenos Aires; includes five ports on R Naposta, including naval base of Puerto Belgrano; founded in 1828; university (1956); airport; railway; oil refining, wool and food processing, timber trade, fishing. » Argentina [i]

Bahrain, official name **State of Bahrain** pop (1990e) 503 000; area 678 sq km/262 sq ml. Group of 35 islands comprising an independent state in the Arabian Gulf midway between the Qatar Peninsula and mainland Saudi Arabia; Saudi–Bahrain causeway (25 km/16 ml); capital, Manama; other city Al Muharraq; timezone GMT +3; population 73% Arabic and 9% Iranian, with Pakistani and Indian minorities; religion, Islam (c.65% Shia); official language, Arabic; currency, Bahrain dinar; island of Bahrain c.48 km/30 ml long, 13–16 km/8–10 ml wide, area 562 sq km/217 sq ml, highest

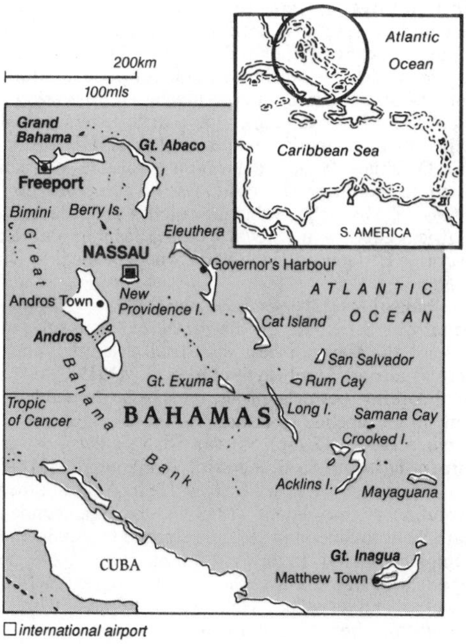

□ international airport

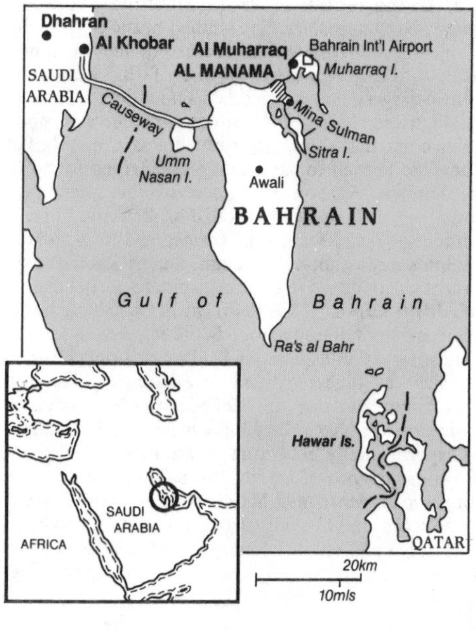

point Jabal Dukhan (135 m/443 ft); largely bare and infertile, though many major drainage schemes begun since 1973; cool N/NE winds with a little rain (Dec–Mar), average 35 mm/1.4 in, temperature 19°C (Jan); summer average temperature of 36°C and a humidity of 97% (Sep), dominated by either a moist NE wind (the *Shamal*) or the hot, sand-bearing *Qaws* from the S; a flourishing centre of trade, 2 000–1 800 BC); since the late 18th-c, governed by the Khalifa family; treaty of protection with the UK in 1861; independence in 1971; experimental parliamentary system established (1973–5); now a constitutional monarchy governed by the amir, who appoints a Council of Ministers headed by a prime minister; oil (on land and offshore), natural gas, lime, gypsum; oil refining, aluminium smelting, ship repairing; a major centre for oil trading, banking, and commerce. » Manama; Shiites; RR24 national holidays; RR43 political leaders

Baikal or **Baykal, Lake** (Russ **Ozero**) [biy**kal**] area 31 500 sq km/12 159 sq ml. Crescent-shaped lake in S Siberia, Russia; largest freshwater lake in Eurasia, and deepest in the world; length (SW–NE) 636 km/395 ml; width 24–80 km/15–50 ml; maximum depth 1 620 m/5 315 ft; in a deep tectonic basin, fed by over 300 rivers and streams; only outlet, the R Angara; contains 22 islands, the largest being Ostrov Ol'khon (length 51 km/32 ml); hot springs on the shores; earthquakes frequent; freezes over (Jan–Apr); Trans-Siberian railway passes the S shore. » Russia; Trans-Siberian Railway

Baikonur or **Baykonyr Cosmodrome** [biyko**noor**] A Russian space centre constructed in the 1950s in Karaganda oblast, Kazakhstan. It was from here that the first artificial satellite and manned space flight were launched. » Soviet space programme

bail A security (usually a sum of money) left with the police or the courts, as a guarantee that someone temporarily freed from custody will return to stand trial when required to do so. A person who is bailed is obliged to appear in court on the date set or else forfeit the sum of money stipulated by the court. Frequently other persons are required as *sureties*, who guarantee the appearance of the accused in court. There are several differences in the operation of the bail procedure between legal systems (eg between England and Scotland). » criminal law

Bailey bridge A prefabricated bridge used by combat engineers, which can be rapidly constructed on the battlefield. The system was devised by British engineer Sir Donald Bailey (1901–85) during World War 2, and consists of a basic diamond braced unit of welded steel, 3 × 1.5 m/10 × 5 ft square, which can be easily manipulated by a squad of six men and joined together to make complex bridging structures. » bridge (engineering) [i]

Baillie, Dame Isobel (1895–1983) British soprano, born at Hawick, Roxburghshire. She studied music in Manchester and Milan, and won immediate success in her opening London season in 1923. Regarded as one of this century's greatest oratorio singers, she was made a Dame in 1978. » oratorio

Baily, Francis (1774–1844) British amateur astronomer, born at Newbury, Berkshire. After retiring as a stockbroker (1825) he devoted himself to astronomy, and helped found the Royal Astronomical Society. He described the phenomenon now known as **Baily's beads** in 1836 – a broken ring of bright points around the edge of the Moon, formed in a total solar eclipse by the Sun's rays shining through the Moon's valleys at the moment of totality. He died in London. » eclipse; Sun

Baird, John Logie (1888–1946) British television pioneer, born at Helensburgh, Dunbarton, Scotland. He studied electrical engineering at Glasgow, and after a brief business career bedevilled by illness, settled in Hastings (1922) and began research into television. In 1926 he gave the first demonstration of a television image. His 30-line mechanically-scanned system was experimentally broadcast by the BBC in 1929, and during 1936 transmissions of his improved 240-line system alternated with the rival Marconi-EMI 405-line electronic system, which was adopted in 1937. He also succeeded in producing three-dimensional and coloured images (1944), as well as projection on to a screen, and stereophonic sound. He died at Bexhill-on-Sea, Sussex. » television

Baisakhi [biy**sah**ki] A Sikh festival (generally celebrated on 13 Apr) commemorating the founding in 1699 of the Khalsa order of baptized Sikhs by the tenth guru of Sikhism, Guru Gobind Singh. » Sikhism

Bajazet or **Bayazid I** (1354–1403) Sultan in the Ottoman Empire (1389–1402). After coming to power, he quickly conquered Bulgaria, parts of Serbia, Macedonia and Thessaly, and most of Asia Minor. His rapid conquests earned him the name of *Yildirim* ('Thunderbolt'). He blockaded Constantinople, and defeated Sigismund of Hungary (1396) in his attempt to rescue the city. In 1402 he was himself defeated near Ankara by Tamerlane, in whose camp he died. » Sigismund (Emperor); Timur

Baker, Sir Benjamin (1840–1907) British engineer, born at Frome, Somerset. In 1861 he began a long association with the consulting engineer John Fowler, and together they constructed the London Metropolitan railway, Victoria station, and several bridges. Their greatest achievement was the Forth Rail Bridge (opened 1890), built on the cantilever principle, for which he was knighted. He was also consulting engineer for the Aswan Dam. He died at Pangbourne, Berkshire. » Aswan High Dam; bridge (engineering) [i]

Baker, James A(ddison) (1930–) US public official, born at Houston, Texas, and educated at Princeton and the University of Texas. He served President Ford as Undersecretary of Commerce, and President Reagan as White House Chief of Staff (1981–5) and Secretary of the Treasury (1985–8) before resigning to manage George Bush's campaign for the Presidency. After winning the election, Bush named him as Secretary of State. » Bush, George; Ford, Gerald R; Reagan

Baker, Dame Janet (Abbott) (1933–) British mezzo-soprano, born at Hatfield, Yorkshire. She studied music in London in 1953, and joined the chorus at Glyndebourne in 1956. She went on to enjoy an extensive operatic career, especially in early Italian opera and the works of Benjamin Britten; she retired from opera in 1982. Also a concert performer, she is a noted interpreter of Mahler and Elgar. » Britten

Baker, Kenneth (Wilfred) (1934–) British Conservative politician, educated at Oxford. He became an MP in 1968, and held junior posts in the Departments of Trade and Industry (1981–4) and the Environment (1984–5). He was Secretary of State for the Environment (1985–6) before becoming Education Secretary (1986–9), Chairman of the Conservative Party (1989–90), and Home Secretary (1990–). » Conservative Party

baking powder A mixture of sodium bicarbonate, tartaric acid, and potassium tartrate, used in baking. It is added to dough (a mixture of flour and water), and when heated, carbon dioxide is released, causing the dough to rise. » flour

Bakst, Léon, originally **Lev Samoilovich Rosenberg** [bahkst] (1866–1924) Russian painter, born at St Petersburg, where he studied at the Imperial Academy of Arts. He was associated with Diaghilev from the beginnings of the Russian ballet, designing the decor and costumes for numerous productions (1909–21). His rich, exuberant colours produced a powerful theatrical effect, which revolutionized fashion and decoration generally. He later settled in Paris, where he died. » Diaghilev; theatre

Baku [ba**koo**] 40°22N 49°53E, pop (1989) 1 757 000. Seaport capital of Azerbaijan; on the Apsheron Peninsula, on the W coast of the Caspian Sea; industrial, scientific, and cultural centre; airport; railway; university (1919); oil refining, metalworking, petrochemicals, tyres, solar research and development; oil pipeline to Batumi on the Black Sea; Kiz-Kalasyi (Virgin's Tower, 12th-c), Shirvan Shah's Palace. » Azerbaijan

Bakunin, Mikhail Alekseyevich [bah**koo**nin] (1814–76) Russian anarchist, born near Moscow. He took part in the German revolutionary movement (1848–9) and was condemned to death. Sent to Siberia in 1855, he escaped to Japan, and arrived in England in 1861. In the First International (1868), he was the opponent of Marx; but at the Hague Congress in 1872 he was outvoted and expelled. He died at Berne, Switzerland. » anarchism; International; Marx

Balaclava, Battle of (1854) A battle fought between British and Russian forces during the early stages of the Crimean War. The Russian attack on the British base at Balaclava was unsuccessful, but the British sustained the heavier losses. >> Charge of the Light Brigade; Crimean War

Balakirev, Mili (Alekseyevich) [bal**a**kiryef] (1837–1910) Russian composer, born at Nijni Novgorod, who became leader of the national Russian school of music. His compositions, which owe a good deal to folk music, influenced Musorgsky, Rimsky-Korsakov, Borodin, and Tchaikovsky. They include two symphonies, many songs, and some highly individual piano music. He died in St Petersburg. >> folk music

balalaika [balal**iy**ka] A Russian musical instrument: a lute with a triangular body, flat back, long neck, and three strings which are strummed by the player's fingers. It is used to accompany singing and dancing, or as a member of larger ensembles. >> chordophone

balance of payments The difference, for a country, between the income and expenditure arising out of its international trading activities. The *current account* handles the country's income from selling goods abroad (exporting), offset by its expenditure on goods imported. The difference between these two totals is the *trade balance*. Also included are 'invisible' services bought and sold abroad, such as air transport, banking, insurance, shipping, and tourism. The *capital account* deals with private and corporate investment abroad, borrowing and lending, and government financial transactions. A balance of payments *deficit* drains a nation's reserves of convertible currency and gold, and can lead to a devaluation of its currency. >> invisibles

Balanchine, George, originally **Georgi Melitonovich Balanchivadze** (1904–83) Russian-US ballet dancer and choreographer, born in St Petersburg. He studied at the ballet school of the Imperial Theatres, then formed his own company, whose innovations were frowned on by the theatre authorities. During a foreign tour in 1924, he and a group of other dancers remained in Berlin, and after performing in Europe as the Soviet State Dancers, Diaghilev took them into his Russian Ballet in Paris. In 1934 he opened the School of American Ballet in New York, and from then devoted most of his career to establishing a native American tradition of dance. In 1948 he became director of the New York City Ballet, and also choreographed many Broadway shows and Hollywood musicals. He died in New York City. >> ballet; Ballets Russes; choreography

Balaton, Lake [**bo**loton] area 598 sq km/231 sq ml. Lake in WC Hungary; length 77 km/48 ml; width 8–14 km/5–9 ml; largest and shallowest lake in C Europe; Hungary's largest recreation area, with resorts at Siófok, Keszthely, and Balatonfüred (spa with carbonic waters). >> Hungary [i]

Balboa, Vasco Núñez de (1475–1517) Spanish explorer, born at Jerez de los Caballeros. He settled in Santo Domingo in 1501, and in 1511 joined the expedition to Darién as a stowaway. Following an insurrection, he took command, and founded a colony. He was the first European to see the Pacific Ocean (1513). In 1514, the governorship of Darién was granted to Pedrarias Davila, for whom he undertook many expeditions. However, on their first disagreement, Balboa was executed.

bald cypress >> **swamp cypress**

bald eagle A large eagle (length 80–100 cm/30–40 in), native to N America; numbers now declining; found near water; eats fish, birds, and mammals. The name refers to the white plumage on its head and neck. The national symbol of the USA, it is also known as the **American eagle**. (*Haliaeetus leucocephalus*. Family: *Accipitridae*. >> eagle

Balder, Baldur or **Baldr** [**bawl**der] Norse god, the most handsome and gentle of the children of Odin and Frigga; the name means 'bright'. He taught human beings the use of herbs for healing. Frigga made a spell so that nothing which grew out of or upon the Earth could harm him, but Loki made Hodur (Balder's blind brother) throw a dart of mistletoe at him. Balder died, to return after Ragnarok to the new Earth. >> Loki; Odin; Ragnarok

baldness Commonly described as permanent loss of hair from the front and/or top of the head, usually in men, because of the degeneration and reduction in the size of hair follicles. Genetic factors, ageing, and androgens (eunuchs are seldom bald) may be causative agents for which there is no effective cure. An improper diet, certain endocrine and skin disorders, as well as some chemical or physical agents may damage the hair follicles leading to either permanent or temporary baldness in either sex at any age. Some other primates also develop baldness, such as the oukari monkey of S America. >> androgens; hair

baldpate >> **wigeon**

Baldwin I (1172–1205) Count of Flanders (from 1194) and Hainault (from 1195), the youngest brother of Godfrey of Bouillon. He was a leader of the Fourth Crusade, and in 1204 was crowned as the first Latin Emperor of Constantinople. Defeated and captured at Adrianople (1205), he was killed soon afterwards. >> Constantinople, Latin Empire of; Crusades [i]; Godfrey of Bouillon

Baldwin, James (Arthur) (1924–88) US Black writer, born and brought up in a poor section of Harlem, New York City. After a variety of jobs he moved to Europe, where he lived (mainly in Paris) for some years. He returned to the USA in 1957, and became an active member of the civil-rights movement. His novels include *Go Tell it on the Mountain* (1954), *Tell Me How Long The Train's Been Gone* (1968), and *Just Above My Head* (1979). He also wrote plays and several collections of essays. He died in Paris. >> American literature; civil rights

Baldwin (of Bewdley), Stanley, 1st Earl (1867–1947) British Conservative statesman, who was three times Prime Minister (1923–4, 1924–9, 1935–7). Born at Bewdley, and educated at Harrow and Cambridge, he worked in his family business before becoming an MP in 1908. He was President of the Board of Trade (1921–2) and Chancellor of the Exchequer (1922–3), and then unexpectedly succeeded Bonar Law as Premier. His period of office included the General Strike (1926) and was interrupted by the two minority Labour governments and the MacDonald Coalition (1931–5), in which he served as Lord President of the Council. He followed public opinion in arranging the abdication of Edward VIII in 1937. He resigned from politics in 1937, when he was made an earl. He died at Astley, Lancashire. >> Conservative Party; Edward VIII; General Strike; Law, Bonar

Balearic Islands [bale**ea**rik], Span **Islas Baleares** pop (1981) 655 909; area 5 014 sq km/1 935 sq ml. Archipelago of five major islands and 11 islets in the W Mediterranean near the E coast of Spain; conquered by Aragon, 14th-c; capital, Palma de Mallorca; E group chiefly comprises Majorca, Minorca, and Cabrera; W group chiefly comprises Ibiza and Formentera; popular tourist resorts; airports at Palma de Mallorca, Ibiza, and Mahon; car ferries to Barcelona, Alicante, Valencia, Genoa, Marseilles; fruit, wine, grain, cattle, fishing, textiles, chemicals, cork, timber. >> Cabrera; Formentera; Ibiza; Majorca; Minorca; Spain [i]

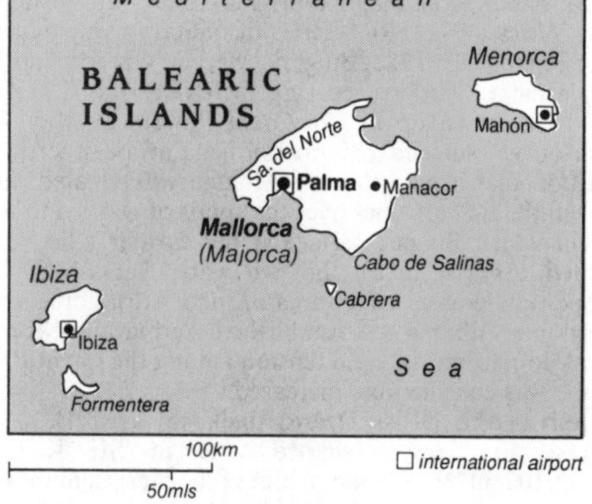

baleen A fibrous material from the mouth of some species of whale; forms a sieve during feeding; formerly used in manufacturing, when strong, light, flexible material was needed (eg to

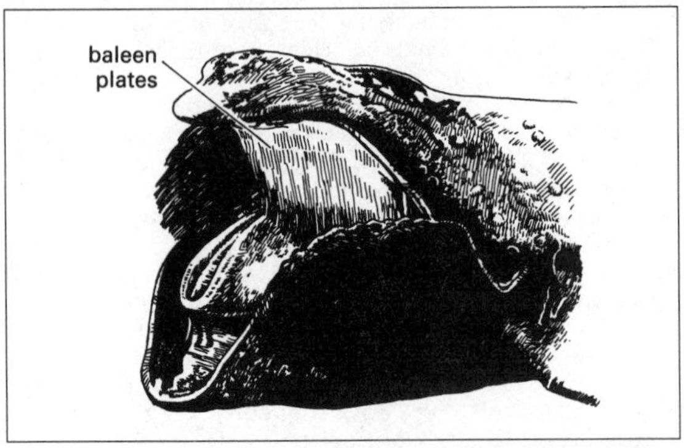

Baleen plates in the mouth of a baleen whale

strengthen women's corsets); also known as **whalebone** (though it is not in fact bone). » humpback whale; whale [i]

Balenciaga, Cristobal [balenseeahga] (1895–1972) Spanish couturier, born at Guetaria, in the Basque country. Helped by a local aristocrat, he trained as a tailor, and eventually opened dressmaking and tailoring shops of his own. He left Spain for Paris as a result of the Spanish Civil War, and became a couturier. A perfectionist, his clothes were noted for dramatic simplicity and elegant design. He retired in 1968, and died in Valencia. » fashion

Balewa, Sir Abubakar Tafawa [balaywa] (1912–66) Nigerian politician, and the first Federal Prime Minister, born at Bauchi. A member of the Northern People's Congress, he entered the Federal Assembly in 1947, and became Minister of Works (1952) and Transport (1953), then Premier (1957). He was knighted when Nigeria became independent in 1960. In the military uprising of 1966, he was assassinated. » Nigeria [i]

Balfour, Arthur James, 1st Earl (1848–1930) British statesman and Conservative Prime Minister (1902–5), born at Whittinghame, East Lothian, Scotland. After succeeding to the family estate (1856), he was educated at Eton and Cambridge, and entered parliament in 1874, becoming Secretary for Scotland (1886) and Chief Secretary for Ireland (1887–91), where his policy of suppression earned him the name of 'Bloody Balfour'. He became First Lord of the Admiralty (1915–16), and as Foreign Secretary (1916–19) was responsible for the **Balfour Declaration** (1917), which promised Zionists a national home in Palestine. He resigned in 1922, was created an earl, but served again as Lord President (1925–9). He died at Woking, Surrey. » Zionism

Bali [bahlee] pop (1980) 2 469 920; area 5 561 sq km/2 146 sq ml. Island province of Indonesia, between Java (W) and Lombok (E); mountainous, with peaks rising to 3 142 m/10 308 ft at Gunung Agung (E); chiefly Hindu population; Dutch control by 1908; capital, Denpasar; rice, cattle, coffee, copra, salt, onions, handicrafts; major tourist area. » Indonesia [i]

Balkan Wars (1912–13) A series of military campaigns fought in the Balkans. In 1912, Bulgaria, Serbia, Greece, and Montenegro attacked Turkey, securing swift victories. A preliminary peace was drawn up by the Great Powers in May 1913, in which Turkey surrendered most of her European territories on condition that a new state of Albania was created. Disputes between the Balkan allies over the spoils of war led to a second war, in which Bulgaria attacked her former allies, and was defeated. As a result of the two wars, Turkish territory in Europe was reduced to an area around Adrianople and Constantinople, Albania was established, Serbia and Montenegro almost doubled in size, and tension among the Great Powers in Europe was considerably increased.

Balkhash, Lake (Russ **Ozero**) [balkash] area 18 300 sq km/7 064 sq ml. Crescent-shaped lake in SE Kazakhstan, 160 km/100 ml W of the Chinese border; length 605 km/376 ml; maximum width 74 km/46 ml; maximum depth 26 m/85 ft; no outlet; salt extraction, fishing, copper; chief harbours, Burylbaytal, Burlyu-Tobe; gradually shrinking. » Kazakhstan

Balla, Giacomo (1871–1958) Italian artist, born in Turin. Largely self-taught, he was the master of the Futurists Boccioni and Severini, and signed the Futurist manifesto in 1910, but later returned to normal representation. He died in Rome. » Boccioni; Futurism; Italian art; Severini

ballad An elementary poetic form found in many languages which tells and/or dramatizes a story in a lyrical stanza apt for oral transmission (and singing): four lines of varying length, rhyme scheme *abab*. The traditional, anonymous ballad sang of wars, feuds, and fatal love stories, often with chilling power and great pathos; the modern 'literary' ballad has been used by many 19th-c and 20th-c poets (Coleridge, Keats, D H Lawrence, Auden). » metre (literature); poetry

ballad opera A musical play with songs written to fit existing popular tunes. The form was fashionable in England for a decade after John Gay's *The Beggar's Opera* (1728). » musical comedy

ballade An Old French form, consisting normally of three eight-line stanzas and a concluding four-line section, strictly rhymed. Used by de Machaut and Villon in the 14th–15th-c, it has been resurrected by a few sophisticated poets in the 19th–20th-c. » French literature; metre (literature); poetry

Ballarat or **Ballaarat** [balarat] 37°36S 143°58E, pop (1983e) 36 550. City in SWC Victoria, Australia, NW of Melbourne; railway; centre of a wool-producing district; largest gold reserves in the country discovered here, 1851; scene of the Eureka Stockade, the gold-diggers' rebellion against state authority, 1854; textiles, brewing, metal products; Eureka Stockade reconstruction; Sovereign Hill historic park; gold museum; vintage trams. » Australian gold rush; Victoria (Australia)

Ballard, J(ames) G(raham) (1930–) British novelist and short-story writer, born in Shanghai, China. He specialized in the writing of science-fiction novels (eg his first, *The Drowned World*, 1962), then published his autobiographical novel *Empire of the Sun* (1984). *The Day of Creation* (1987) confirmed a movement away from science fiction towards novels of imagination, involving less fantastic, though no less exotic themes. » English literature; science fiction

Ballesteros, Severiano [baluhstairos] (1957–) Spanish golfer, born at Pedrena. Professional since 1974, he had his first win in the 1976 Dutch Open, and his first win on the US professional circuit in 1978 (Greater Greensboro' Open). He has won three British Opens (1979, 1984, 1988), the US Masters twice (1980, 1983), and was the leading money winner in Europe in the years 1976–8, 1986, and 1988. He is the first man to win 50 European golf tournaments. His brothers Manuel, Baldomero, and Vicente are also all top golfers. » golf

ballet A theatrical form of dance typically combined with music, stage design, and costume in an integrated whole based around a scenario. Italian Renaissance court spectacles developed into the French *Ballet de cour* under Louis XIV. Ballet became a professional theatre form in the 18th-c, gradually formalizing its technique in the early 19th-c. It can be divided roughly into historical periods; mid-18th-c Romantic ballets such as *La Sylphide*, *Giselle*, and the Russian classics (eg *Swan Lake*, *The Sleeping Beauty*); neoclassical works, such as Balanchine's *Apollo*; and modern ballets, such as Ashton's *Monotones* and MacMillan's *Gloria*. Recent works may incorporate modern and jazz elements. The ballet technique is based on turn out from the hip socket. There are five positions of the feet and a codified system of arm positions (*port de bras*). Exercises at the barre (the horizontal support found in studios) move to extended phrases (*enchainements*) in the centre of the space. Intensive training is required from a young age, often in specialist schools. » Ballets Russes; Bolshoi Ballet; London Festival Ballet; Rambert Dance Company; Royal Ballet; Scottish Ballet

Ballet Rambert » **Rambert Dance Company**

Ballets Russes A ballet company created by Diaghilev and active in Europe 1909–29. It was famous for nurturing new talents and for collaborations between great painters (Bakst, Benois, Picasso), composers (Rimsky Korsakov, Satie, Stravinsky), and choreographers (Fokine, Nijinsky, Massine, Nijinska, Balanchine). It had a repertoire of 20th-c classics including

Les Sylphides, *Le Sacre du printemps*, and *Petrushka*. Colourful Russian spectacles were set alongside experimental European modern art, for example by Cocteau, Massine, Picasso, and Satie in *Parade* (1917). The 1987 reconstruction of Nijinsky's long-lost 1913 version of *The Rite of Spring* was based on detailed historical evidence, and performed by the Joffrey Ballet in the USA and Europe. » ballet

ballistic missile A missile which acquires its energy during its launch phase, flying on a trajectory dictated by its initial velocity added to the factors of gravity and aerodynamic drag, until it reaches the target. A *cruise missile*, by contrast, flies with wings through the atmosphere under continuous power. A rifle bullet is in effect a ballistic missile, but more specifically the term applies to the big intercontinental and submarine-launched ballistic missiles which carry nuclear warheads. They may be propelled by a single rocket or several stages of rocket booster which fall away as the fuel they carry is expended. The missile's 'payload' is then free to fly on, arcing through space on its ballistic trajectory, before re-entering the atmosphere to impact on the target. » antiballistic missile; cruise missile; intercontinental ballistic missile; missile, guided; submarine; Trident missile

ballistics The study of what takes place when a projectile is fired from a firearm. Ballistics has three aspects: (1) *internal*, concerning the way the object is thrown into the air; (2) *external*, investigating the way it moves in flight; (3) *terminal*, analysing its impact on the target. **Forensic ballistics** helps in the investigation of gun crimes. » firearms

balloon A flexible envelope filled with a lighter-than-air gas which provides the buoyancy force to rise upwards. Suspended from the balloon is the basket or gondola to hold the passengers. Modern practice uses hot air as the lifting gas. The envelope of a modern hot-air balloon is made from either nylon or Dacron, which is then coated with polyurethane applied under pressure to make the material more airtight. » ballooning

balloon angioplasty [**an**jiohplastee] The insertion of a catheter into an artery that has narrowed pathologically. A balloon at the tip of the catheter is expanded at the site of the constriction, which causes the blood vessels to dilate. The procedure is successful in many cases of narrowing of the arteries to the limbs, kidney, and heart. » catheter

ballooning Sailing through the air in a basket attached to a fabric bag filled with gas which is lighter than air. The first manned flight was by Pilâtre de Rozier and Marquis d'Arlandes at Paris in 1783 in a balloon designed by the Montgolfier brothers. Balloons are now used for meteorological and scientific research as well as for pleasure. » balloon; Montgolfier

ballroom dance A social dance form developed in the early 20th-c, revealing the strong influence of American ragtime, syncopated rhythms producing the foxtrot, quickstep, and tango. Also popular were animal dances (such as the Turkey Trot, Bunny Hug) and Latin-American dances (such as the cha-cha-cha and samba). 1950s and 1960s rock 'n roll and jive era moved young people's dance out of the ballroom and into the club or disco. » European court dance; disco dance; street dance

balm A name applied to various plants, but especially to various members of the mint family, *Labiatae*. » mint

Balmain, Pierre (Alexandre) [bal**mĩ**] (1914–1982) French fashion couturier, born at St Jean-de-Maurienne. He studied architecture in Paris, then turned to dress design, working for Molyneux and other designers, and opening his own house in 1945. Famous for elegant simplicity, his designs included evening dresses, sportswear, and stoles. He also designed for theatre and cinema. » fashion

Balmoral Castle A castle and estate of 9 700 ha/24 000 acres located on upper Deeside, Grampian, Scotland. It has been in the possession of the British Royal family since 1852, and is used by them as a holiday home. The 19th-c castle was rebuilt under the direction of Prince Albert. » Albert, Prince; Grampian

balsa A fast-growing tree, reaching 25 m/80 ft or more, with very light, soft timber, native to lowland areas of tropical America; leaves broadly oval to circular, 30 cm/12 in or more in diameter; flowers 15 cm/6 in long, white. (*Ochroma pyramidale*. Family: *Bombacaceae*.) » tree [i]

balsam An annual with a translucent stem; leaves alternate, opposite or in threes; flowers 2-lipped with funnel-shaped tube and curved spur, the capsule exploding to scatter seeds, especially when touched. The **Himalayan balsam** (*Impatiens glandulifera*) has flowers 2.5–4 cm/1–1½ in, purplish-pink; native to the top Himalayas. The **orange balsam** (*Impatiens capensis*) has flowers 2–3 cm/0.8–1.2 in, orange with brown blotches within; native to eastern N America. The **touch-me-not** (*Impatiens noli-tangere*) has flowers 3.5 cm/1½ in, orange with brown spots; native to Europe and Asia. (Family: *Balsaminaceae*). » annual; impatiens

balsam poplar » poplar

Baltic Exchange An abbreviation for the **Baltic Mercantile and Shipping Exchange**, a major world market for cargo space on sea and air freight, which originated in the London coffee houses, and is still found in the City of London. It was known as the Virginia and Baltic from 1744, reflecting the growth of trade with America. The Exchange also handles the market in some commodities, such as grain. » chartering

Baltic languages A branch of the Indo-European family of languages, principally comprising Latvian and Lithuanian. Both have written records from the 14th-c, and each has a standard form and official status in its country. There are striking similarities between Baltic and Slavic, but it is not certain whether these derive from their common origin, or from prolonged contact. » Indo-European/Slavic languages

Baltic Sea, Ger **Ostsee**, ancient **Mare Suevicum** [**bawl**tik] area 414 000 sq km/160 000 sq ml. An arm of the Atlantic Ocean enclosed by Denmark, Sweden, Germany, Poland, Estonia, Latvia, Lithuania, Russia, Finland, and Sweden; connected to the North Sea by the Kattegat, Skagerrak, Danish Straits, and the Kiel Canal; chief arms, the Gulfs of Bothnia, Finland, Riga; main islands, Hiiumma, Saaremaa, Åland, Gotland, Óland, Bornholm, Rüdgen, Fehmarn; mean depth 55 m/180 ft; deepest point, Gotland Deep (c.463 m/1 519 ft); low salinity; generally shallow, with large areas frozen in winter; navigation impossible for 3–5 months yearly; main ports include Kiel, Gdańsk, Riga, Copenhagen, St Petersburg, Stockholm, Helsinki. » Atlantic Ocean

Baltic Shield The geological name for the continental mass made up of Precambrian crystalline rocks exposed in parts of Norway, Sweden, and Finland, and forming the underlying basement of the continent. They are the oldest rocks in Europe, and are made up predominantly of granites and gneisses. » gneiss; granite; Precambrian era

Baltic states The countries of Estonia, Latvia, and Lithuania on the E shore of the Baltic Sea. They were formed in 1918 from the Russian Baltic provinces or governments of Estonia, Livonia, and Courland, and parts of the governments of Pskov, Vitebsk, Kovno, Vilna, and Suvalki. The states remained independent until 1940, when they were annexed by the USSR. » Estonia; Latvia; Lithuania

Baltimore [**bol**timaw(r)] 39°17N 76°37W, pop (1980) 786 775. Port in N Maryland, USA, on the Patapsco R, at the upper end of Chesapeake Bay; established, 1729; developed as a seaport and shipbuilding centre (Baltimore clippers); city status, 1797; rebuilt after 1904 fire; largest city in the state; airport; railway (first in the USA); six universities; trade in coal, grain, metal products; shipbuilding, food processing, copper and oil refining, chemicals, steel, aerospace equipment; major centre for culture and the arts; major league team, Orioles (baseball); first Roman Catholic cathedral in the USA (1806–21); Inner Harbour, Edgar Allen Poe House; Preakness Festival (May). » clipper ship; Maryland; Poe

Baltimore Incident (1891) A brief but serious dispute between the USA and Chile, stemming from the death of two American sailors from the cruiser *Baltimore* in a brawl in Valparaiso. A war between the two countries was averted by a Chilean apology. » Chile [i]

Baluchi [ba**loo**chee] Baluchi-speaking peoples of Baluchistan (Pakistan), Iran, Afghanistan, Punjab (India), and Bahrain; divided into Sulaimani and Makrani groups. Once nomads, most are now settled agriculturalists, with cattle, goats, camels, etc. They are well-known for their carpets and embroidery. Population c.3.2 million. » Baluchistan

Baluchistan [baloochi**stan**] pop (1981) 4 305 000; area 347 190 sq km/134 015 sq ml. Province in W and SW Pakistan; bounded W by Iran, N by Afghanistan, and S by the Arabian Sea; ancient trading centre between India and Middle East; treaties of 1879 and 1891 brought the N section under direct British control; incorporated into Pakistan in 1947–8; capital, Quetta; mountainous terrain, with large areas of desert; cotton, natural gas, fishing, salt, mineral reserves. » Baluchi; Pakistan [i]

Baluchitherium [baloochee**thee**riuhm] » **Indricotherium**

Balzac, Honoré de (1799–1850) French novelist, born at Tours, and educated at the Collège de Vendôme. He left Tours in 1819 to seek his fortune as an author in Paris. For 10 years he led a life of frequent privation and incessant industry, and incurred heavy debts. His first success, a novel about Breton peasants, was *Les Chouans* (1829). After writing several other novels, he formed the design of presenting in the *Comédie humaine* (Human Comedy) a complete picture of modern civilization. The cycle contains several masterpieces, such as *Le Père Goriot* (1834, Father Goriot) in which detailed observation and imagination are the main features. He produced 85 novels in 20 years, but his work did not bring him wealth. In 1849, in very poor health, he travelled to Poland to visit Madame Hanska, a rich Polish lady, with whom he had long corresponded. In 1850 she became his wife, and three months later he died in Paris. » French literature; novel

Bamako [bama**koh**] 12°40N 7°59E, pop (1976) 404 022. River-port capital of Mali, on the R Niger; mediaeval centre of Islamic learning; capital of French Sudan, 1905; airport; railway; power plant, ceramics, food processing, pharmaceuticals, metals, textiles, cycles, chemicals, tobacco; zoo, botanical gardens. » Mali [i]

Bambara [bam**bah**ra] A Mande-speaking agricultural people of Mali, W Africa, divided into several small chiefdoms. Many are now urbanized and intermingled with other groups. They are known for their elaborate cosmology and metaphysics, their indigenous writing, and religious sculptures. They founded two important states, at Segu (c.1650) and at Kaarta (now in Mali, c.1753–4). Population c.2.5 million. » Mali [i]; Mande

bamboo A giant woody grass, mostly tropical or subtropical, with a few temperate species; usually forming large clumps growing rapidly – up to 40 cm/15 in a day – and reaching heights of 36 m/120 ft. Some species flower annually; others only once after several to many years, and then all together, after which the entire population dies. They provide edible shoots and light timber, including garden canes. (Genera: *Bambusa* and others. Family: *Gramineae*.) » grass [i]

Bamian, Buddhas of Two enormous images of Buddha cut into the cliffs of the Bamian Valley, Afghanistan, in the 6th-c. The figures, which are 53 m/174 ft and 35 m/115 ft high, were defaced by Nadir Shah's troops in the 18th-c. » Buddha; Nader Shah

banana A giant perennial herb, superficially resembling a tree. The true stem lies underground, at intervals bearing buds which produce large, oar-shaped leaves. It is the closely-sheathing bases of the leaves which form the soft, hollow, trunk-like 'stem' rising to a height of several metres above ground. The underground bud also produces the inflorescence, which grows up the hollow centre of the stem, emerging from the crown of leaves to droop towards the ground. The male flowers are borne towards the tip of the inflorescence, protected by large, reddish bracts. The female flowers are borne in clusters or hands in the lower part of the inflorescence; as the fruits develop after fertilization, they bend backwards to point away from the ground. Wild bananas are native to SE Asia, and produce inedible fruit with numerous seeds but little pulp. Cultivated bananas are grown throughout the tropics as a staple food, producing a higher yield per acre than potatoes. Fruit for export is cut while still green, and ripened on the voyage. They are often sold as unblemished yellow fruits, but are not fully ripe until flecked with brown spots. Banana leaves also yield useful fibre and thatch, and some species are planted for their ornamental flowers. (Genus: *Musa*, 35 species. Family: *Musaceae*.) » abaca; bract; cloning (genetics); herb; inflorescence [i]

Banares » **Benares**

Bancroft, Sir Squire (1841–1926) British actor-manager, born and died in London. He made his debut at Birmingham in 1861, and in 1867 married the actress **Marie Wilton** (1840–1921), with whom he launched a series of successful comedies at the Prince of Wales's Theatre in London (1865–80), continuing at the Haymarket Theatre (1880–5). He was knighted in 1897. » drama; theatre

Band Aid » **Geldof, Bob**

band-width In radio and television transmission, the range of frequencies required for the satisfactory reproduction of a signal. For television, it is determined by the field frequency, the number of scanning lines, and the colour-coding system, typically requiring 5.5 MHz for 625-line 50-field systems but considerably more for high-definition TV. » field (photography); frequency

Banda, Hastings Kamuzu (1905–) Malawi statesman, Prime Minister (1963–6), and President (1966–), born near Kasungu. He trained as a physician in the USA and Britain, before his opposition to the Central African Federation caused him to give up his successful London practice (1955) and return to Nyasaland (1958). Leader of the Malawi African Congress, he was gaoled in 1959, became Minister of National Resources (1961), Prime Minister (1963), President of the Malawi (formerly Nyasaland) Republic (1966), and was made Life President in 1971. » Malawi [i]

Bandar Seri Begawan, formerly **Brunei Town** [**bahn**dah seree begawan] 4°56N 114°58E, pop (1983) 57 558. Capital of Brunei, SE Asia, 20 km/12 ml from mouth of Brunei R; airport; town wharf used mainly for local vessels since opening of deep-water port at Muara in 1972; Mesjid Sultan Omar Ali Saifuddin mosque (1958), Churchill Museum, Sultan Hassanal Bolkiah Aquarium. » Brunei [i]

Bandaranaike, S(olomon) W(est) R(idgeway) D(ias) [bandara**niy**kay] (1899–1959) Ceylonese (Sri Lankan) statesman and Prime Minister (1956–9), born in Colombo. Educated in Colombo and Oxford, he was called to the Bar in 1925. He became President of the Ceylon National Congress, and helped to found the United National Party. He was leader of the House in Ceylon's first parliament, and Minister of Health. In 1951 he resigned from the government and organized the Sri Lanka Freedom Party, which returned him to parliament as Opposition leader and (1956) as Prime Minister on a policy of nationalization and neutralism. He was assassinated by a Buddhist monk, and succeeded by his wife **Sirimavo Ratwatte Dias** (1916–), who became the world's first woman Prime Minister (1960–5, 1970–7). » Sri Lanka [i]

Bandeira Filho, Manuel Carneiro de Sousa [ban**dair**a **feel**joh] (1886–1968) Brazilian poet, born in Recife, and educated in São Paulo. He achieved great popularity with his early poetry (eg *Carnaval*, 1919), which was of extreme formal complexity and at the same time lyrical and simple in theme. His middle volumes, such as *Ritmo dissoluto* (1924, Rhythm in Dissolution), show the influence of Modernism, while his later work attains serenity, such as *Estrelha da tarde* (1963, Evening Star). He also adapted many foreign works for the Brazilian stage. He died in Rio de Janeiro. » Latin-American literature; poetry

bandeirante [bandayr**an**tay] A 17th-c Brazilian slave-raider and explorer. Based on São Paulo, parties of bandeirantes (*bandeiras*) opened up much of the interior of Brazil, including the Amazon basin. They are today seen in Brazil as a heroic pioneering myth. » Brazil [i]; slave trade

bandicoot An Australasian marsupial (family: *Peramelidae*, 17 species); superficially rat-like, but larger with longer snouts and ears; digs in soil with front claws; eats invertebrates; also includes the Australian **rabbit-eared bandicoots** (or **bilbies**) of family *Thylacomyidae* (2 species) from dry areas. » marsupial [i]

Bandung [ban**dung**] 0°32N 103°16E, pop (1980) 1 201 000. Capital of Java Barat province, W Java, Indonesia; 180 km/112 ml SE of Jakarta; founded, 1810; former administrative centre of

Dutch East Indies; **Bandung Conference** (1955), at which 29 non-aligned countries met to facilitate joint diplomatic action; airport; railway; two universities (1955, 1957); nuclear research centre (1964); chemicals, plastics, textiles, quinine; Sundanese cultural centre. >> Java; non-aligned movement

Bangalore [banggal**aw**] 12°59N 77°40E, pop (1981) 2 914 000. Capital of Karnataka, SC India, 290 km/180 ml W of Madras; founded, 1537; former military headquarters of the British-administered district of Mysore (1831–1947); airfield; railway; university (1964); aircraft, machine tools, light engineering, electronics, trade in coffee. >> Karnataka

Banghazi >> **Benghazi**

Bangkok [bang**kok**] 13°44N 100°30E, pop (1982) 5 018 327. Capital city of Thailand; on Chao Praya R, 25 km/15 ml from its mouth on the Bight of Thailand; capital, 1782; old city noted for its many canals; accessible to small ocean-going vessels; since 1955, headquarters of the SE Asia Treaty Organization; airport; railway; eight universities; commerce, paper, ceramics, textiles, timber, aircraft, matches, food processing, cement; Grand Palace, Temples of the Golden Buddha and Reclining Buddha; Phra Pathom Chedi, world's tallest Buddhist monument, 60 km/37 ml W. >> Thailand [i]

Bangladesh, formerly **East Pakistan**, official name **People's Republic of Bangladesh, Gana Prajatantri Bangladesh** [banggla**desh**] pop (1991e) 107 992 140; area 143 998 sq km/55 583 sq ml. Asian republic lying between the foothills of the Himalayas and the Indian Ocean, divided into 24 regions; bounded W, NW and E by India, SE by Myanmar, and S by the Bay of Bengal; capital Dhaka; other chief towns include Chittagong, Khulna, Narayanganj; timezone GMT +6; one of the world's most densely populated areas; 98% Bengali, with Biharis and tribal minorities; official language, Bengali (Bangla), with English as a second language; chief religion, Islam (mainly Sunnis), with some Hindu, Buddhist, and Christian; currency, the taka of 100 paisa (since 1976).

Physical description and climate. Mainly a vast, low-lying alluvial plain, cut by a network of rivers, canals, swamps, and marsh; main rivers the Ganges (Padma), Brahmaputra (Jamuna), and Meghna, joining in the S to form the largest delta in the world; subject to frequent flooding; in the E, fertile valleys and peaks of Chittagong Hill Tracts, rising to 1 200 m/3 900 ft; lush vegetation, with bamboo and palm forests in the E, mixed monsoon forest in the C, and mangroves and hardwood forest in vast areas of the S delta; tropical monsoon climate; a hot season (Mar–Jun) with heavy thunderstorms; very humid, with higher temperatures inland; main rainy season June–September; cyclones in the Bay of Bengal cause sea surges and widespread inundation of coastal areas.

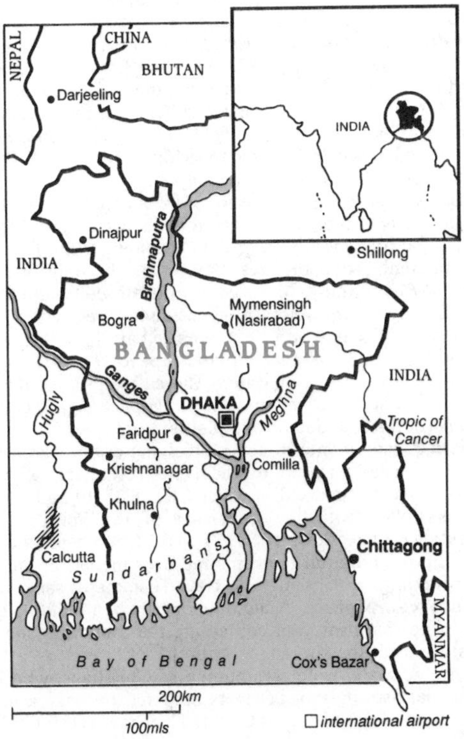

History and government. Part of the State of Bengal until Muslim East Bengal created in 1905, separate from Hindu West Bengal; reunited in 1911; again partitioned in 1947, with West Bengal remaining in India and East Bengal forming East Pakistan; disparity in investment and development between East and West Pakistan (separated by over 1 600 km/1 000 ml), coupled with language differences, caused East Pakistan to seek autonomy; rebellion in 1971 led to independence, helped by India; political unrest led to suspension of constitution in 1975, and assassination of first president, Sheikh Mujib; further coups in 1975, 1977, and 1982; constitution restored, 1986; parliament has one 300-member chamber, with 30 seats reserved for women; members elected every five years.

Economy. 85% of working population employed in agriculture, especially rice; tea, tobacco, sugar; supplies 80% of world's jute; jute mills, paper, aluminium, textiles, glass, shipbuilding, fishing; natural gas, coal, peat, limestone. >> Brahmaputra, River; Dhaka; Ganges, River; India [i]; Pakistan [i]; RR24 national holidays; RR43 political leaders

Bangor (Wales) [**bang**guh] 53°13N 4°08W, pop (1981) 46 585. City in Arfon district, Gwynedd, NW Wales, UK; opposite the island of Anglesey; university (1884); railway; cathedral (founded 6th-c); chemicals, engineering, electrical goods; tourism. >> Gwynedd

Bangui [**bahng**wee] 4°23N 18°37E, pop (1981) 387 100. Capital of Central African Republic; on the R Ubangi, 1 030 km/640 ml NNE of Brazzaville; founded, 1889; airport; university (1969); handles Chad trade; cotton, coffee, timber products, cigarettes, metal products, office machinery, beer; Boganda Museum. >> Central African Republic [i]; Chad [i]

Bani-Sadr, Abolhassan (1935–) Iranian politician, who became the first President of the Islamic Republic of Iran (1980–1). He studied economics and sociology at the Sorbonne in Paris, having fled there in 1963 after being imprisoned in Iran for involvement in riots against the Shah's regime. He was an important figure in the Iranian Revolution of 1978–9, a member of the Revolutionary Council, and was elected President in 1980. From the start, however, he was threatened by a deepening conflict with the fundamentalist Muslim clergy; he was eventually criticised by Ayatollah Khomeini, and dismissed (mid-1981). He fled to France, where he was granted political asylum. >> Iran [i]; Khomeini

banjo A plucked string instrument developed in the 19th-c from earlier similar instruments used by W African slaves in the USA. It has a long neck and fingerboard, fretted like a guitar's, and five metal strings (gut, in older instruments). These pass over a bridge which presses against a parchment (or plastic) membrane stretched over a circular frame. It is played either with a plectrum or with the fingers. >> plectrum; string instrument 2 [i]

Banjul [**ban**jul], formerly **Bathurst** (to 1973) 13°28N 16°35W, pop (1983) 44 186. Seaport capital of The Gambia, W Africa; on Island of St Mary in R Gambia estuary, 195 km/121 ml SE of Dakar; established in 1816 as a settlement for freed slaves; airport; peanuts, crafts, tourism; Fort Bullen (1826). >> Gambia, The [i]

bank base rate A base lending rate for UK clearing banks, used as the primary measure for interest rates since 1981. It is influenced by government economic policy through the Bank of England. >> Bank of England; minimum lending rate; prime rate

Bank of England The official government bank of Britain, founded in 1694, but in state ownership only since 1946. It controls the supply of money, prints notes and mints coins, acts as a banker to the government and to other banks, and manages the gold and currency reserves. It is referred to as 'The

Old Lady of Threadneedle Street', as a result of its location in the City of London. The chief officer of the Bank is the Governor, appointed by the government.

bank rate A former interest rate at which the Bank of England would lend to discount houses, and an important instrument of government economic policy. It was abandoned in 1973, and replaced by the minimum lending rate (MLR). A change in rate was the signal to other lending institutions to follow suit. » bank base rate; interest; minimum lending rate

Bankhead, Tallulah (1903–68) US actress, born at Huntsville, Alabama. Educated in New York and Washington, she made her stage debut in 1918 and appeared in many plays and films. Her most outstanding film portrayal was in *Lifeboat* (1944).

bankruptcy The state of being reduced to financial ruin. Legally, individuals and partnerships are in this state when a court in bankruptcy proceedings declares them to be bankrupt. These proceedings are started by a creditor (or sometimes the debtor) presenting a bankruptcy petition. The analogous concept of **liquidation** applies to companies. Liquidation may be compulsory (as when a company is unable to pay its debts) or voluntary (as when its members have decided to cease trading). » company

Banks, Don (1923–80) Australian composer, born in Melbourne. He studied in Melbourne, London, Salzburg and Florence, before settling in England, where he founded the Australian Musical Association, became chairman of the Society for the Promotion of New Music (1967–8), and the music director of Goldsmith's College (1969–71). He then returned to Australia, and held posts at the Canberra School of Music (1974) and Sydney Conservatorium (1978). He wrote a wide variety of compositions, including horn and violin concertos, works involving jazz players and singers, a trilogy for orchestra (1977), and many film and TV scores.

Banks, Sir Joseph (1743–1820) British botanist, born in London, and educated at Harrow, Eton, and Oxford. In 1766 he made a voyage to Newfoundland, collecting plants. He accompanied Cook's expedition round the world (1768–71), and in 1772 visited the Hebrides and Iceland. Elected president of the Royal Society in 1778, he retained the office for 41 years. Through him the bread-fruit was transferred from Tahiti to the West Indies, the mango from Bengal, and many fruits of Ceylon and Persia. He was created a baronet in 1781, and died in London. » Cook, James

banksia Low shrubs or small trees, native to Australia; leaves sometimes very small, usually narrow, sharply toothed, leathery; flowers commonly cream, also orange, red, or purplish with four perianth segments and protruding style; up to 1000 in spectacular globular or cylindrical heads up to 40 × 18 cm/15 × 7 in, which become cone-like in fruit with woody capsules, shaggy with persistent remains of flowers. Typical of dry bush country, most species are adapted to withstand fires, re-sprouting from woody tubers or trunks protected by thick fibrous bark; in many the capsules open only after experiencing strong heat, remaining closed for years before releasing seeds onto ground newly cleared by fire. It is named after Sir Joseph Banks. (Genus: *Banksia*, 58 species. Family: *Proteaceae*.) » Banks, Joseph; perianth; shrub; style (botany); tree [i]

Bann, River Major river in Northern Ireland; rises in the Mourne Mts, and flows 40 km/25 ml NW to enter the S end of Lough Neagh; flows N for 53 km/33 ml through Lough Beg to enter the Atlantic. » Northern Ireland [i]

Banner System A system of military organization in China used by the Manchu tribes. By the early 17th-c the Manchus were organized into companies of 300 troops under at first four and then eight banners. By 1644, eight Chinese and eight Mongol banners had been formed, comprising an army of 170 000 men. The system survived throughout the Qing dynasty. » Qing dynasty

Bannister, Sir Roger (Gilbert) (1929–) British athlete, born at Harrow, the first man to run the mile under 4 minutes (3 min 59.4 sec). Educated at Exeter and Oxford, he studied medicine at St Mary's Hospital School, London. He ran in the 1952 Olympics, and in 1954 captured the European 1500 metres title. His record-breaking mile was run at Oxford (6 May 1954). He was knighted in 1975. » athletics

Bannockburn, Battle of (1314) A battle fought near Stirling between English forces under Edward II and the Scots under Robert Bruce. It resulted in a decisive victory for the Scots. The English army was largely destroyed, and many English nobles were killed or captured. The battle made Bruce a national hero, and inspired Scottish counter-attacks against N England. » Bruce, Robert; Edward II

banshee In Irish and West Highlands of Scotland folklore, a female fairy who wails and shrieks whenever there is about to be a death in the family to which she has attached herself. » fairies; folklore

banteng or **banting** A rare SE Asian ox; long upward-curving horns; male black with white rump and 'stockings'; females brown; inhabits forests and dry regions; often nocturnal; shy; domesticated form called *Bali cattle*; can be cross-bred with zebu; also known as **tsaine** or **tembadau**. (*Bos javanicus*.) » ox; zebu

Banting, Sir Frederick Grant (1891–1941) Canadian physiologist, born at Alliston, Ontario. He studied at Toronto, becoming professor there in 1923. With J J R Macleod he discovered insulin, for which they were jointly awarded the Nobel Prize for Physiology or Medicine that year, Banting sharing his part of the award with his co-worker C H Best. Knighted in 1934, he died in a plane crash during a war mission. » Best, Charles H; insulin; Macleod, J J R

Bantu-speaking peoples Ethnically diverse groups which speak one of 500 Bantu languages or dialects (which belong to the Benue-Congo sub-group of the Niger-Congo family). They comprise altogether about 60 million people living in the S part of Africa, occupying a third of the continent. They may well have had their origins in the region of modern Cameroun, with a second nucleus of dispersal in the Katanga area. From there they spread S interacting with Khoisan peoples, E as far as Madagascar, and NE where they mingled with coastal Arab traders. Generally regarded as iron-working cultivators, their dispersal occurred in the early years of the Christian era. In South Africa, the term *Bantu* is used as a racial classification. » Chewa; Ganda; Hutu and Tutsi; Kikuyu; Kongo; Lozi; Luba-Lunda Kingdoms; Luhya; Makonde; Makua; Mongo; Ndebele; Nguni; Niger-Congo languages; Nyoro; Pygmies; Shona; Swahili; Xhosa; Yao (of Africa)

Bantustans » **apartheid**

Banville, (Etienne Claude Jean Baptiste) Théodore (Faullain) de [bâveel] (1823–91) French poet and dramatist, born at Moulins. He was given the title 'roi des rimes' for his ingenuity in handling the most difficult forms of verse – the mediaeval ballades and rondels. His *Gringoire* (1866) holds an established place in French repertory. He died in Paris. » ballad; French literature

banyan A large evergreen species of fig, native to the Old World tropics. It is notable for its aerial roots, which grow from the horizontal branches to the ground becoming trunk-like, so that an apparent group of trees may in fact be only one. (*Ficus benghalensis*. Family: *Moraceae*.) » evergreen plants; fig

baobab [**bay**ohbab, **bow**bab] A deciduous tree native to arid parts of C Africa; its short but massive barrel- or bottle-shaped trunk 9–12 m/30–40 ft high and up to 9 m/30 ft in girth contains large stores of water. The edible pulp of its woody fruits is called *monkey bread*. (*Adansonia digitata*. Family: *Bombacaceae*.) » deciduous plants; tree [i]

baptism A sacramental practice involving water. The Christian ritual is usually traced to the New Testament, where new converts were immersed in water (*Acts* 8.38–9) and where the rite is linked with the imparting of the Spirit and with repentance (*Acts* 2.38, 10.47). Today, Church practices vary over infant and adult baptism, and over the use of immersion or sprinkling. » Christianity; New Testament; sacrament

baptistery or **baptistry** A building or part of a building used to administer baptism, and containing the font. It is sometimes separate from the church. » church [i]

Baptists A world-wide communion of Christians, who believe in the baptism only of believers prepared to make a personal confession of faith in Jesus Christ. They have certain links with the 16th-c Anabaptists, but mainly derive from early 17th-c England and Wales, where Baptist churches spread rapidly, and in the USA, where a very rapid increase took place in the late 19th-c. Strongly biblical, the emphasis in worship is on scripture and preaching. Individual congregations are autonomous, but usually linked together in associations or unions. The Baptist World Alliance was formed in 1905. » Anabaptists; baptism; Christianity

Baqqarah or **Baggara** [bagara] A nomadic Arabic-speaking people of the Sudan, possibly descended from Arabs who migrated during the Middle Ages from Egypt to Chad and then eastwards. They lack any centralized political authority. Cattle are kept in the arid region between the Nile and L Chad, migrating seasonally in search of water. Population c.5 million. » Arabs; Bedouin

bar Unit of pressure; symbol bar; equal to 10^5 Pa (pascal, SI unit); one bar is approximately atmospheric pressure. The **millibar** (mb; 1 bar = 1 000 mb) proves to be of greater use for practical measurements. At sea level, atmospheric pressure is c.1 013.25 mb. » atmospheric pressure; barometer; pascal; pressure; units (scientific)

Bar, Confederation of (1768) A military alliance of Polish gentry established at Bar, Podolin, directed against the Russian-backed king, Stanislas Poniatowski. The Confederation advocated the preservation of the privileges of the Polish aristocracy and the Catholic Church. Its suppression in 1772 led to the first partition of Poland. » Poland, Partitions of

bar code A pattern of black vertical lines, with information coded in the relative widths of the lines. This type of coding is very widely used in the retail market, such as on food packages. The bar-coded labels can be read by special bar-code scanners, and the output be entered into a computer to link the product with such factors as price and stock level. There are standards for bar codes, such as the European Article Numbering Code and, in N America, the Universal Product Code.

Bar Kokhba, Simon, or **Bar Kosiba** (?–135) The leader of the Jews in their great but fruitless insurrection against the Emperor Hadrian (130–5). He was killed at Bethar. In 1960 some of his letters were found in caves near the Dead Sea. » Hadrian

Bar Mitzvah [bah **mits**va] (Jewish phrase: 'son [*bar*]/daughter [*bat*] of the commandment') Jewish celebrations associated with reaching the age of maturity and of legal and religious responsibility, being 13 years plus one day for boys. The child reads a passage from the Torah or the Prophets in the synagogue on the Sabbath, and is then regarded as a full member of the congregation. Non-Orthodox synagogues have a Bat Mitzvah ceremony for girls at 12 years plus one day. » Judaism

Barabbas (1st-c) Political rebel and murderer (as described in *Mark* 15, *Luke* 23) who was arrested but apparently released by popular acclaim in preference to Pilate's offer to release Jesus of Nazareth. He was possibly also called 'Jesus Barabbas' (in some manuscripts of *Matt* 27.16–17). » Jesus Christ; Pilate; Zealots

Barba, Eugenio (1936–) Italian theatre director and founder of Odin Teatret, an experimental theatre company and centre for collective research in performance. In 1979 he established the International School of Theatre Anthropology. His theoretical writings include *The Floating Islands* (1984) and *Beyond the Floating Islands* (1986). » theatre

Barbados [bah**bay**dos] pop (1990e) 257 000; area 430 sq km/166 sq ml. Most easterly of the Caribbean Is, divided into 11 districts; in the Atlantic Ocean 320 km/199 ml NW of Trinidad; capital, Bridgetown; other main town, Speightstown; timezone GMT −4; population, 80% African descent, 16% mixed race, 4% European; official language, English; main religion, Protestantism; unit of currency, Barbados dollar; island is small, triangular, length 32 km/20 ml (NW–SE), rising to 340 m/1 115 ft at Mt Hillaby, ringed by a coral reef; tropical climate, with average annual temperature 26.5°C, mean annual rainfall 1 420 mm/56 in; colonized by the British, 1627; self-government, 1961; independent sovereign state within the Commonwealth, 1966; executive power rests with the prime minister, appointed by a governor-general; 21-member Senate,

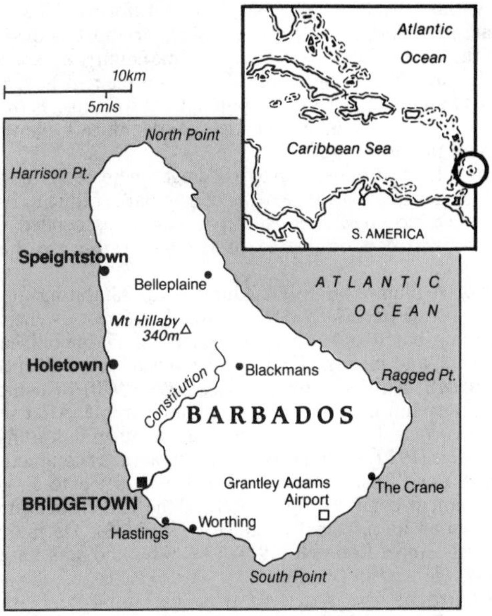

and a House of Assembly with 27 elected members; major industry, tourism; also, sugar cane, rum, molasses; cotton, bananas, onions, vegetables; natural gas; garments, electronic and electrical equipment, medical supplies. » Bridgetown; Caribbean Sea; RR24 national holidays; RR43 political leaders

Barbarossa ('Redbeard') (16th-c) European name for two Turkish pirates, whose activities brought Algeria and Tunisia within the orbit of the Ottoman Empire. **Aruj** was killed fighting the Spaniards in 1518. **Khayr al-Din**, his brother, entered the service of the Ottoman Sultan, and drove the Spaniards from Algiers, which became the main base of piracy in the S Mediterranean. He became admiral of the Ottoman fleet, and died at Constantinople. » corsairs

Barbary ape A monkey (macaque) native to N Africa, and maintained artificially on the Rock of Gibraltar; not an ape; stocky with no tail; spends much time on the ground; lives in troops of up to 30 individuals; also known as **magot** or **rock ape**. (*Macaca sylvanus*.) » macaque

Barbary Coast The coast of N Africa from Morocco to Tripolitania (Libya), famous for piracy between the 16th-c and 18th-c. This coast and the Barbary States of Morocco, Algeria, Tunisia, and Tripolitania take their name from Barbarossa, who led the Turkish conquest of the region in the 1530s, preventing Spanish invasion. » Barbarossa

Barbary sheep » **aoudad**

barbastelle [bahba**stel**] A bat, native to Europe, Asia, and N Africa; fur extends onto wings and tail membrane; ears large and broad; flies with slow wingbeats; eats insects. (Genus: *Barbastella*, 2 species. Family: *Vespertilionidae*.) » bat

barbel Slender-bodied fish of the carp family *Cyprinidae*, widespread in European rivers on clean gravel beds; body length up to 90 cm/3 ft; lips fleshy, bearing four long barbels; migrate upstream to spawn (Apr–Jun); fine sport fish. The name is also used for other species of the genus. (*Barbus barbus*.) » carp

Barber, Samuel (1910–81) US composer, born at West Chester, Pennsylvania. His early music, such as the First Symphony (1936) and the *Adagio for Strings* was in a neo-Romantic vein, but his later compositions laid more emphasis on chromaticism and dissonance. Among these works are the ballet *Medea* (1946), several concertos, and vocal compositions. His opera *Vanessa* (1958) and piano concerto (1962) both won Pulitzer Prizes. He died in New York City.

barberry A deciduous or evergreen shrub, native to N temperate regions and S America; long shoots with 3-pointed spines; leaves often spiny; flowers yellow, orange, or reddish; berries red or black, globose or cylindrical; several species grown as ornamentals, especially purple-leaved forms. The common barberry (*Berberis vulgaris*) is a necessary host in the life cycle of the cereal disease *black rust*; in some countries, especially the USA, attempts to break the life cycle of the rust have involved the eradication of barberry populations. (Genus: *Berberis*, 450 species. Family: *Berberidaceae*.) » deciduous plants; evergreen plants; shrub

barbershop quartet A group of singers who perform four-part 'close-harmony' arrangements of popular sentimental songs in a suave, nostalgic style. It is particularly associated with the USA, where it originated in the late 19th-c. » harmony; singing

barbet A plump, brightly-coloured bird, inhabiting the tropics world-wide (especially Africa); usually a forest-dweller; named after its 'beard' of feathers, at the base of a large bill; eats fruit, flowers, and insects. (Family: *Capitonidae*, over 70 species.)

Barbirolli, Sir John [bahbi**ro**lee] (1899–1970) British conductor, born in London of Franco-Italian parents. After service in World War 1, he played the cello in several leading string quartets (1920–4), and succeeded Toscanini as conductor of the New York Philharmonic (1937). He returned to England as permanent conductor (1943–58) of the Hallé Orchestra, later becoming its principal conductor (1959–68). He married the oboist **Evelyn Rothwell** (1911–) in 1939, and was knighted in 1949. He died in London.

barbiturates Drugs derived from barbituric acid, itself first prepared on St Barbara's Day, 1863. *Barbitone* (US *barbital*) was introduced into medicine in 1903; *phenobarbitone* (US *phenobarbital*) in 1912. Over 50 different barbiturates have been used at some time as sedatives, sleep inducers, and anti-epileptic drugs. They cause severe tolerance, ie increasingly higher doses are required to produce the same effect. The doses are progressively more dangerous, and poisoning becomes a major risk; they are also addictive. As sedatives and sleeping pills they have generally been replaced by the safer benzodiazepines. » benzodiazepines; sedatives

Barbizon School A group of French landscape painters working c.1830–80 at Barbizon, a village in the Forest of Fontainbleau. Pioneers of *plein air* painting, they sketched out-of-doors, directly from nature, in a way that foreshadowed the Pre-Raphaelites in England and the Impressionists in France. Leading members were Théodore Rousseau (1812–67), Charles François Daubigny (1817–78), Narciso-Virgilio Díaz (1807–76), and Constant Troyon (1810–65). » Daubigny; French art; Impressionism (art); landscape painting; Pre-Raphaelite Brotherhood; Rousseau, Théodore; school (art)

Barbour, John (c.1316–96) Scottish poet and historian. His national epic, *The Brus* (first printing 1571), is a narrative poem on the deeds of King Robert the Bruce. He was Archdeacon of Aberdeen from around 1357 until his death. » Bruce, Robert; epic; Scottish literature

barcarolle An instrumental or vocal piece in a lilting 6/8 metre, evoking the songs of the Venetian gondoliers. A well-known example is the Barcarolle in Offenbach's opera *Les Contes d'Hoffman* (The Tales of Hoffman). » Offenbach, Jacques

Barcelona [bahsuh**loh**na], Span [barthe**loh**na], ancient **Barcino** or **Barcinona** 41°21N 2°10E, pop (1981) 1 754 900. Major seaport and capital of Barcelona province, NE Spain, 621 km/386 ml NE of Madrid; second largest city in Spain; airport; railway; car ferries to Mahón, Palma de Mallorca, Ibiza, Canary Is; two universities (1440, 1968); centre of Catalan art and literature, and of the separatist political movement; textiles, petrochemicals, oil refining, engineering, aircraft; Gothic Quarter, cathedral (13th-c), Ramblas Palace, Church of the Holy Family, Museum of Catalan Art, Maritime Museum, Bishop's Palace, Palace of la Virreina art gallery; Casa Mila (1906–10), Casa Güell (1900–14), and Parque Güell (1900–14), architectural creations by Antonio Gaudí, now world heritage monuments; Fiesta of St George (Apr); Fiesta Mayor (Sep); location of the 1992 Summer Olympic Games. » Catalonia; Gaudí; Spain [i]

Barclay de Tolly, Mikhail Bogdanovich, Knyaz ('Prince') (1761–1818) Russian field marshal, born at Luhde-Grosshof, Livonia. He joined the Russian army in 1786, and served in Turkey, Sweden, and Poland, losing an arm at Eylau (1807). He was appointed Minister of War in 1810. Defeated by Napoleon at Smolensk (1812), and replaced, he later served again as Commander-in-Chief, and took part in the invasion of France. He was made a prince in 1815, and died at Insterburg, E Prussia. » Alexander I; Napoleon I

bard Amongst ancient Celtic peoples, a poet-minstrel who held a privileged place in society, singing the praises of chiefs and celebrating heroic deeds, historical events, and the passing of laws. The bards of Gaul disappeared under the Roman Empire, but in Ireland and the Gaelic-speaking area of Scotland they survived until the 18th-c. In Wales, bardic standards declined after the Middle Ages, despite the exacting competition of the 15th- and 16th-c eisteddfods. However, to this day, a contestant for the Chair at the National Eisteddfod must compose his poem in the classical bardic verse-form, in strict metre, with alliteration and internal rhyming. » eisteddfod

Bardeen, John (1908–) US physicist, the first man to receive two Nobel Prizes for Physics, born at Madison, Wisconsin. Working at Bell Telephone Laboratories at the end of World War 2, he developed in 1947 with Brattain and Shockley the point contact transistor, for which they shared the Nobel Prize in 1956. His second prize (1972) was shared for his work on the first satisfactory theory of superconductivity (the Bardeen-Cooper-Schrieffer, or *BCS* theory). » Brattain; Cooper, Leon Neil; electronics; Shockley; superconductivity; transistor

Bardot, Brigitte (1934–) French film actress, born in Paris. She was discovered while working as a photographic model by the director Roger Vadim, who subsequently married her, and from 1952 made her an international sex-symbol, with their greatest success in *Et Dieu Créa La Femme* (1956, And God Created Woman). They divorced in 1957, but her position was established, and she was regularly in demand for sex-kitten parts throughout the 1960s; her last major film was *Si Don Juan Etait Une Femme* (1973, If Don Juan Were a Woman), and in later years she has taken up the cause of endangered animal species. » Vadim

Barebone's Parliament The British 'Parliament of Saints' (4 Jul–12 Dec 1653), nominated by the Council of Officers of the Army to succeed the Rump Parliament; named after radical member Praise-God Barebone. It instituted civil marriage and sought legal reforms; but collapsed after disagreements over the abolition of tithes and lay patronage in church. » Rump Parliament

Barenboim, Daniel (1942–) Israeli pianist and conductor, born in Buenos Aires. He studied with Igor Markevich and Nadia Boulanger, and has performed regularly in Europe since 1954. A noted exponent of Mozart and Beethoven, he gained his reputation as pianist/conductor with the English Chamber Orchestra. Since 1975 he has been musical director of the Orchestre de Paris. He married the cellist Jacqueline du Pré in 1967. » du Pré

Barents Sea, Russian **Barentsovo More**, Norwegian **Barents Havet** Shallow arm of the Arctic Ocean, lying N of Norway and European Russia; warm North Cape Current disperses pack-ice in the S; Murmansk and Vardö ports are ice-free; fishing area. » Arctic Ocean

Barentz, or **Barents, William** (?–1597) Dutch navigator, pilot to three Dutch expeditions (1594–6) in search of the Northeast Passage, who died off Novaya Zemlya. In 1871, Captain Carlsen found his winter quarters undisturbed after 274 years. » Northeast Passage

Barère (de Vieuzac), Bertrand [ba**rair**] (1755–1841) French revolutionary and regicide, born and died at Tarbes, who is noted for his achievement of survival. Originally a monarchist, he went over to Robespierre's camp, becoming a member of the Committee of Public Safety. He was later imprisoned (1794), but escaped into exile, not returning to Paris until 1830. » French Revolution [i]

barghest [**bah**gest, **bah**gayst] In English folklore, a terrifying goblin-hound that appeared at night and presaged death to those who saw it; in Manchester it was reported to be headless, in E Anglia, one-eyed. Parallels to it include the Moddey Doo (Black Dog) of the Isle of Man. » folklore

Bari [**ba**ree] 41°07N 16°52E, pop (1981) 371 022. Seaport and capital town of Bari province, Puglia, SE Italy; on a peninsula in the Adriatic Sea, WNW of Brindisi; archbishopric; airport; car ferries; university (1924); naval college; industrial and commercial centre; petrochemicals, textiles, shipbuilding; site of Italy's first atomic power station; Cathedral of San Nicola (begun 1087); annual Levante Fair (Sep). » Italy [i]

barite The mineral form of barium sulphate ($BaSO_4$), the chief ore of barium. Found in hydrothermal vein deposits, it is used in paints, paper making, and drilling muds; earlier known as **barytes**. » barium

barium [**bair**iuhm] Ba, element 56, in Group II of the periodic table, melting point 725°C. It is a very reactive metal. In most of its compounds, it occurs as Ba^{2+}, eg BaO_2 is barium (II) peroxide. Its soluble compounds are highly poisonous, but the very insoluble sulphate, $BaSO_4$, is used in the so-called **barium meal** to provide material opaque to X-rays. » chemical elements; X-rays; RR90

bark In its everyday sense, the rough, protective outer layer of the woody parts of trees and shrubs; in botany, the term also embraces several inner tissues, including the cork and phloem. Continued growth causes the bark to stretch, often cracking, flaking, or peeling in distinctive patterns as it is replaced by new growth from the cambium layers. » cambium; cork; phloem; shrub; tree [i]

bark beetle A small, dark beetle whose egg chamber is excavated by adults under tree bark. The fleshy, legless larvae tunnel away from the chamber after hatching. Some species carry fungal diseases of trees. (Order: *Coleoptera*. Family: *Scolytidae*.) » beetle; fungus; larva

bark painting A traditional product of Australian Aboriginal art: human and animal figures, sometimes geometrically stylized but occasionally naturalistic, painted on irregularly-shaped pieces of bark. They were created mainly for use in magical and initiation ceremonies, but sometimes, apparently, for aesthetic delight. » Aborigines

Barker, George Granville (1913–) British poet, born at Loughton, Essex, and educated in London. He published three volumes in the 1930s marked by the rhetoric and Surrealist effects of the New Apocalypse, then travelled to Japan and the USA. His *True Confessions of George Barker* (1950) was similarly exuberant, but later work (eg *Anno Domini*, 1983) is more reflective. His *Collected Poems* were published in 1987. » English literature; poetry; Surrealism

barking deer » **muntjac**

barking wolf » **coyote**

barley A cereal of Middle Eastern origin, cultivated in temperate regions; inflorescence a dense head with long, slender bristles; grains in 2, 4, or 6 rows. It is more tolerant of drought, cold, and poor soil than wheat, and an important crop in such regions as N Europe. Germinated grains produce malt used in brewing beer and making whisky; its flour is used in cakes and porridge. It is also an important animal feed. (*Hordeum vulgare*. Family: *Gramineae*.) » beer [i]; cereals; grass [i]; inflorescence [i]; whisky

barn » **cross section**

barn owl An owl of worldwide distribution; legs feathered; inhabits forests, open country, and habitation; eats small vertebrates, especially mammals and insects; nests in crevices high above ground (or in buildings). (Genus: *Tyto*, 6 species. Family: *Tytonidae*.) » grass owl; owl

Barna, Viktor, byname of **Győző Braun** (1911–72) Hungarian-British table tennis player, born in Budapest. He won a record 20 English titles between 1931 and 1953, including five singles titles (1933–5, 1937–8), and also won 15 world titles, including five singles (1930, 1932–5). One of the game's greatest players, he emigrated to France before becoming a British citizen in 1938. After retirement, he played exhibitions and formed the Swaythling Club, a social club for ex-table tennis internationals. » table tennis

Barnabas [**bah**nabas] (1st-c) Christian missionary, originally a Levite from Cyprus called Joseph (*Acts* 4.36). He was a companion and supporter of Paul during Paul's early ministry to the Gentiles, but later separated from him after a dispute over John Mark (*Acts* 15.36) and went to Cyprus. The so-called 'Letter of Barnabas' is a spurious 2nd-c work. » Acts of the Apostles; Mark, St; Paul, St

barnacle A marine crustacean that lives attached by its base to hard substrates or to other organisms; body enclosed within a shell formed of calcareous plates; typically feeds by filtering food particles from the water with modified thoracic limbs (*cirri*); c.1 000 species, found from the inter-tidal zone to deep sea; some parasitic on crabs. (Subclass: *Cirripedia*.) » calcium; crustacean; shell

barnacle goose A goose native to the N Atlantic. In the Middle Ages it was thought these geese hatched from goose-necked barnacles. They were thus considered fish, not birds, and were eaten on Friday when only fish was permitted. (*Branta leucopsis*. Family: *Anatidae*.) » goose

Barnard, Christian Neethling (1922–) South African surgeon, born at Beaufort West. He graduated from Cape Town medical school, and after a period of research in the USA returned to Cape Town (1958) to work on open-heart surgery and organ transplantation. At Groote Schuur Hospital he performed the first successful human heart transplant (Dec 1967). The patient, Louis Washkansky, died of double pneumonia 18 days later. Barnard's later transplants proved to be increasingly successful. He retired from medicine in 1983.

Barnard's star One of the very few stars which is named after the astronomer who studied it. In June 1916, E E Barnard (1857–1923) of Yerkes Observatory, USA, measured a proper motion of 10.31 seconds of arc per year, still the largest known. In about 180 years this star moves through our sky by a distance equal to the diameter of the full Moon. It is the fourth nearest star, distance 1.81 parsecs. » star

Barnardo, Thomas John (1845–1905) British founder of homes for destitute children, born in Dublin, Ireland. After preaching in the Dublin slums, he went to London in 1866 to study medicine with the aim of becoming a medical missionary. Instead he founded (1867), while still a student, the East End Mission for destitute children, as well as a number of homes in greater London, which came to be known as the 'Bärnardo Homes'. The present-day organization is responsible for over 140 schools, hostels, and youth centres, with branches in such countries as Australia, New Zealand, and Kenya. He died at Surbiton, Surrey.

Barnave, Antoine (Pierre Joseph Marie) (1761–93) French revolutionary, born at Grenoble. He studied law, and became a member of the new National Assembly (1799), where he established a reputation as an orator, and helped to carry through the Civil Constitution of the Clergy. He brought back the royal family from Varennes, but, after advocating more moderate courses, was guillotined. » French Revolution [i]

Barnburners A faction within the US Democratic Party in New York State (1843–50), which arose through opposition to extending slavery into Western territory conquered during the Mexican War. Many Barnburners, led by former President van Buren, joined the Free Soil Party in 1848. Their name derived from the story of a Dutch farmer who burned down his barn (the Democratic Party) in order to drive out rats (slavery). » Democratic Party; Mexican War; slavery; van Buren

Barnes, William (1800–86) British pastoral poet, born at Rushay, Dorset. He worked first for a solicitor, became a teacher, then a clergyman (1847). He was widely known for his idyllic poetry in the Dorset dialect, and his three books of poetry were collected as *Poems of Rural Life in the Dorset Dialect* (1879). He also wrote several philological works. He died at Winterbourne Came, Dorset. » comparative linguistics; English literature; poetry

Barnum, P(hineas) T(aylor) (1810–91) US showman, born at Bethel, Connecticut. He ran a museum in New York, introducing freak shows, at which he sponsored the famous dwarf 'General Tom Thumb' (1842), using for the first time the flamboyant publicity which came to characterize US show business. In 1881 he joined with his rival James Anthony Bailey (1847–1906) to found the Barnum and Bailey circus, the 'greatest show on earth'. He died at Bridgeport, Connecticut. » circus

barograph » **barometer**

Baroja (y Nessi), Pío [ba**roh**ha] (1872–1956) Spanish (Basque) writer, born in San Sebastián. He trained as a doctor, then for a time worked in the family bakery. His first book of short stories, *Vidas sombrías* (1900, Sombre Lives), was the prelude to more than 70 volumes with a Basque setting. He died in Madrid. » Basques; Spanish literature

barometer A meteorological instrument used to measure atmospheric pressure, invented in 1643 by Torricelli. It was based on the principle that the height of a column of mercury in a tube sealed at one end and inverted in a dish of mercury changes according to the atmospheric pressure exerted on the dish of mercury. This is still in common use, and several types exist. Another method of measuring pressure is the **aneroid barometer**, a metallic box containing a vacuum, and with flexible sides which act as a bellows expanding and contracting with changing atmospheric pressure. Changes of pressure through time are recorded on a **barograph**. » atmospheric pressure; bar (physics); Torricelli

baron/baroness In the UK, a title of nobility, ranking below viscount or count. Originally the term was used for a tenant-in-chief (one who held his land direct from the sovereign). » peerage; RR98

baronet (abbreviation **bart**) In the UK, a hereditary title, not part of the peerage, and not a knighthood. The form, which was purchased by the holder, was created by James I and VI in 1611 to raise money to pay the troops in Ireland. » knight; peerage; RR98

Barons' Wars The wars in England during the reigns of John and Henry III. **1** (1215–17) Despite the sealing of Magna Carta, many barons still defied John, and offered the crown to Prince Louis of France. After John's death, the French and baronial army was routed at Lincoln (May 1217), and the war was effectively ended by the Treaty of Kingston-on-Thames (Sep 1217). **2** (1263–7) After the Provisions of Oxford failed to achieve a settlement, some barons led by Simon de Montfort captured Henry III at Lewes (1264). Earl Simon was killed at Evesham (1265), and the king was restored to power by the Dictum of Kenilworth (1266). » Henry III (of England); John (of England); Magna Carta; Montfort; Oxford, Provisions of

Baroque (art and architecture) [ba**rok**, ba**rohk**] A style prevalent in the 17th-c and part of the 18th-c, characterized by curvilinear forms and ornate decoration arranged in dramatic compositions, often on a large scale and in a complicated fashion. The term was originally used by jewellers to describe a rough pearl. In architecture, principal exponents included Le Vau and Fontana, and in sculpture Bernini and Borromini. In painting, the style is epitomized by the dramatic chiaroscuro of Caravaggio and Rubens. Baroque art was especially associated with Louis XIV, but spread over most of W Europe until it was transformed into Rococo in the early 18th-c. » art; Bernini; Borromini; Caravaggio; Le Vau; Mannerism; Renaissance architecture; Rococo; Rubens

Baroque (music) A period in musical history extending from c.1580 to c.1730. Its features include a gradual replacement of modality by tonality, a love of melodic ornamentation, the enrichment of harmony by more essential chromaticism, the prominence accorded to instrumental music, and the formation of the orchestra. Genres originating in the Baroque period include the opera, oratorio, cantata, sonata, and concerto. » chromaticism; continuo; mode (music); Bach, Johann Sebastian; Handel; Lully, Jean Baptiste; Monteverdi; Purcell; Rameau; Scarlatti, Alessandro/Domenico; Schütz; Vivaldi

Barossa pop (1981) 28 750. A NE suburb of Outer Adelaide, South Australia; the Barossa Valley is a noted wine-producing area; wine festival every two years celebrates the grape harvest (alternating with Adelaide Festival of Arts). » Adelaide

Barotse » **Lozi**

barque [bahk] A sailing vessel with three or more masts. The aftermost mast is fore- and aft-rigged and the remainder square-rigged – a style which was especially prevalent in the last decade of the 19th-c, when sail made its last stand against competition from steamships. » sailing rig [i]; ship [i]

barracuda [bara**koo**da] Any of the voracious predatory fishes widespread in tropical and warm-temperate seas; body slender, length up to 1.8 m/6 ft, jaws armed with many short teeth; feeds on other fish; some species important commercially and as sport fish. (Genus: *Sphyraena*. Family: *Sphyraenidae*.)

Barranquilla [baran**keel**ya] 11°00N 74°50W, pop (1985) 1 120 975. Modern industrial capital of Atlántico department, N Colombia; on R Magdalena, 18 km/11 ml from its mouth; Colombia's principal Caribbean port; founded, 1721; airport; three universities (1941, 1966, 1967); bull ring; commerce, foodstuffs, footwear, drinks, tobacco, furniture, textiles, petrochemicals. » Colombia [i]

Barras, Paul François Jean Nicolas, Comte de ('Count of') [ba**ra**] (1755–1829) French revolutionary, born at Fos-Emphoux, Var. An original member of the Jacobin Club, and a regicide, he played the chief part in the overthrow of Robespierre, and was given dictatorial powers by the Convention. In 1795, acting against a royalist uprising, he was aided by his friend Bonaparte, who fired on the rebels (the historical 'whiff of grape-shot'). Barras became one of the five members of the Directory (1795). Once more dictator in 1797, he guided the state almost alone, until his hedonism and corruption made him so unpopular that Bonaparte overthrew him easily (1799). After travelling abroad he died at Paris-Chaillot. » French Revolution [i]; Napoleon I

Barrault, Jean-Louis [ba**roh**] (1910–) French actor and producer, born at le Vesinet. He was a member of the Comédie-Française (1940–6), then with his wife, Madeleine Renaud, founded his own company, le Troupe Marigny. He became director of the Théâtre de France (1959–68), the Théâtre des Nations (1965–7, 1972–4), and first director of the Théâtre d'Orsay (1974). His films include *Les enfants du paradis* (1945, The Children of Paradise) and *The Longest Day* (1962). His theories of dramatic art are expressed in his autobiographical *Réflexions sur le théâtre* (1949, Reflections on the Theatre).

barrel organ A mechanical musical instrument. By turning a handle at the side, the player both feeds a bellows and operates a rotating cylinder fitted with metal pins which allow air access to a set of pipes; the placing of the pins determines which pipes sound and when. The instrument is of great antiquity. It was widely used to play hymns in churches in the 18th–19th-c, and also as a street instrument, often with a pet monkey perched on top. » organ

Barren Grounds The name given to the tundra region of N Canada, dominated by muskeg or sphagnum bog. It is an area of marshy depressions and meandering rivers, with an abundance of mosquitoes, and is a major range for caribou. » muskeg; permafrost; tundra

Barrie, Sir J(ames) M(atthew) (1860–1937) British novelist and dramatist, born at Kirriemuir, Angus, Scotland. Educated at Dumfries and Edinburgh, he became a journalist in London, and wrote a series of autobiographical novels. After 1890 he wrote for the theatre. His best-known plays are *The Admirable Crichton* (1902), *Dear Brutus* (1917), and *Peter Pan* (1904), for which he is chiefly remembered. He became a baronet (1913), was rector of Edinburgh University (1930–7), and died in London. » English/Scottish literature

barrier islands Long, straight, narrow islands or peninsulas which generally parallel the coast and are separated from the mainland by a lagoon or salt marsh. Though barrier islands may have been formed in several ways, many appear to have been created as sea level rose between 5 000 and 6 000 years ago, moving large masses of sand across the continental shelf. Around 4 000 years ago, sea level temporarily stabilized, and many barrier islands acquired their current shape. During the last 1 000 years, sea level has again been rising, causing these islands to continue to migrate towards the mainland.

barrier reef » **atoll**

barrigudo » **woolly monkey**

Barringer Crater » **Meteor Crater**

barrister A member of the legal profession in England and Wales whose work is mainly concerned with advocacy in the courts. Barristers have exclusive right of audience in the High Court and superior courts. In addition to trials and preparation for trials they may also write advisory opinions. Not all barristers are in practice; many use the qualification for work in education, industry, or administration. » advocate; High Court of Justice; Inns of Court; solicitor

Barry, Sir Charles (1795–1860) British architect, born in London. After studying in Italy (1817–20), he returned to

England, where his designs included the Reform Club (1837) and the new Palace of Westminster (1840), completed after his death by his son **Edward Middleton Barry** (1830–80). His work showed the influence of the Italian Renaissance. He was knighted in 1852, and died in London. His fifth son, **Sir John Wolfe-Barry** (1836–1918), was engineer of the Tower Bridge and Barry Docks. » Renaissance

Barrymore, Ethel (1879–1959) US actress, born in Philadelphia, sister of John and Lionel Barrymore. She scored a great London success in *The Bells* (1897–8), and later in *Trelawney of the Wells* (1911) and *The Second Mrs Tanqueray* (1924). She also acted in films, including *Rasputin and the Empress* (1932), and on radio and television. She died in Hollywood. » Barrymore, John/Lionel

Barrymore, John (1882–1942) US actor, born in Philadelphia, the brother of Ethel and Lionel Barrymore. He spent some time studying art, but eventually became an actor, making his name in Shakespearean roles, especially Hamlet (1922), and appearing in many films, such as *Grand Hotel* (1932). His classical nose and distinguished features won for him the nickname of 'The Great Profile'. He died in Hollywood. » Barrymore, Ethel/Lionel

Barrymore, Lionel (1878–1954) US actor, born in Philadelphia, brother of Ethel and John. After several roles in plays, he became known as a film actor, appearing in *A Free Soul* (1931), *Grand Hotel* (1932), and many other films. After twice accidentally breaking a hip he was confined to a wheelchair, but undeterred he scored a great success as Dr Gillespie in the original *Dr Kildare* film series. He also had etchings exhibited, and was a talented composer. He died at Van Nuys, California. » Barrymore, Ethel/John

Bart or **Barth, Jean** (1650–1702) French privateer, born and died at Dunkirk. He served first in the Dutch navy, turning to French service on the outbreak of the war with Holland (1672). In 1691 he commanded a small squadron in the North Sea, where he destroyed many English vessels. In the War of the Grand Alliance (1689–97), he was taken prisoner, but escaped from Plymouth to France, where Louis XIV received him, rewarding him with command of a squadron, and later giving him noble status. » Grand Alliance, War of the

Bart, Lionel (1930–) British composer, born in London. He first attracted wide notice for the songs he wrote for the British popular singer Tommy Steele in the 1950s, and went on to compose scores for a number of successful musicals, including *Lock up your Daughters!* and *Oliver!* (both 1960). » musical

Barth, John (Simmons) (1930–) US novelist, born at Cambridge, Maryland, and educated at the Juilliard School of Music and Johns Hopkins University. His career as a university teacher of English is reflected in his novels, which combine complex plots with linguistic playfulness and parody, as in *The Sot Weed Factor* (1960) and *Giles Goat Boy* (1967). » American literature; novel

Barth, Karl [baht] (1886–1968) Swiss Protestant theologian, born and died at Basle. He studied at Berne, Berlin, Tübingen and Marburg. Whilst pastor at Safenwil, he wrote a commentary on St Paul's Epistle to the Romans (1919) which established his theological reputation. He became professor at Göttingen (1921), Münster (1925), and Bonn (1930), refused to take an unconditional oath to Hitler, was dismissed, and so became professor at Basle (1935–62). He played a leading role in the German Confessing Church and Barmen Declaration (1934). The major exponent of Reformed theology, his many works include the monumental *Church Dogmatics* (1932–67). » Confessing Church; grace; Protestantism; theology

Barthes, Roland (Gérard) [baht] (1915–80) French teacher, critic, and writer on semiology and structuralism, born at Cherbourg. He began as a teacher and researcher, and his first collection of essays *Le Degré zéro de l'écriture* (1953, Writing Degree Zero) established him as France's leading critic of Modernist literature. His works include *Mythologies* (1957), a semiological exploration of wrestling, children's toys, and other phenomena. From 1976 until his death he was the first professor of literary semiology at the Collège de France, Paris. » existentialism; literary criticism; Modernism; semiotics; structuralism

Bartholdi, Frédéric-Auguste (1834–1904) French sculptor, born at Colmar, Alsace. He specialized in enormous monuments such as the 'Lion of Belfort' and the bronze Statue of Liberty, New York Harbour, unveiled in 1886. He died in Paris. » French art; sculpture

Bartlett, Sir Frederic (Charles) (1886–1969) British psychologist, born at Stow-on-the-Wold, Gloucestershire. The first professor of experimental psychology at Cambridge (1931–52), he became widely known for his application of experimental methods in real-life situations to the study of perception, memory, and thinking, and was a key figure in the rapid expansion of experimental psychology which took place in the postwar years. He died in Cambridge. » cognitive psychology

Bartók, Béla (1881–1945) Hungarian composer, born in Nagyszentmiklós. He studied in Pressburg and Budapest, and became a virtuoso pianist. A growing interest in folk song led him to study Hungarian and Balkan folk music, and these traditions greatly influenced his own compositions. In 1907 he was appointed professor of pianoforte in Budapest Conservatory. He later became known throughout Europe as a composer, but he was driven into exile by World War 2, and settled in the USA. There he composed several string quartets, concertos (including the *Concerto for Orchestra*, 1943), and other orchestral works. He died in New York City.

Bartolommeo, Fra, properly **Baccio della Porta** (c.1472–1517) Italian religious painter, born near Florence. Taught first by Cosimo Rosselli, and much influenced by Leonardo da Vinci, he was a follower of Savonarola, at whose death he gave up painting and became a Dominican novice. The visit of the young Raphael to Florence in 1504 led him to resume his art. He imparted to Raphael his knowledge of colouring, and acquired from him a more perfect knowledge of perspective. Most of his works are to be seen at Florence. » Italian art; Leonardo da Vinci; Raphael; Savonarola

Bartolozzi sounds Special musical sounds (including microtones and chords) employed by woodwind players following techniques developed by Italian composer Bruno Bertolozzi (1911–), and set out in his *New Sounds for Woodwind* (1967). » woodwind instrument [i]

Barton, Clara, in full **Clarissa Harlowe Barton** (1821–1912) US nurse educator and medical reformer, born at Oxford, Massachusetts. She served as a nurse on the Northern side during the Civil War, became involved in the work of the International Red Cross, and was the founder of its US affiliate. She died at Glen Echo, Maryland. » Red Cross

Baruch [**ba**rukh] (7th–6th-c BC) Biblical character, described as the companion and secretary of the prophet Jeremiah (*Jer* 36), possibly of a wealthy family. His name became attached to several Jewish works of much later date, known as 1 Baruch (the Book of Baruch); 2 (the Syriac Apocalypse of) Baruch; and 3 (the Greek Apocalypse of) Baruch. There is also a Christian Apocalypse of Baruch in Ethiopic. » Apocrypha, Old Testament; Jeremiah, Book of; Pseudepigrapha

barycentre For a group of objects composed of matter, such as the Solar System or a cluster of stars, the point at which total mass may be considered to be concentrated ('the centre of gravity') for the purposes of calculating its gravitational effect on other objects. » gravitation

baryon [**ba**riuhn] In particle physics, a collective term for heavy matter particles which experience strong interactions. Baryons are composed of three quarks. The least massive baryon is the proton, into which other baryons decay. » particle physics; proton; quark

Baryshnikov, Mikhail (Nikolaievich) [ba**rish**nikof] (1948–) Russian dancer and choreographer, born in Riga. He studied in St Petersburg and joined the Kirov Ballet in 1967. In 1974 he moved to Canada and then to the USA, appearing with various companies, but frequently with the American Ballet Theatre, becoming its artistic director in 1980. » ballet; choreography

barytes » **barite**

baryton An obsolete musical instrument resembling a bass viol, with (usually) six strings which were bowed and a further 10–15 which were plucked. Between 1765 and 1778 Haydn wrote numerous pieces for the instrument. » chordophone; Haydn

bas-relief [bah ruh**leef**] Low relief sculpture, in which the design projects only very slightly from the background, as on a coin. Masters of the technique include Donatello and Desiderio da Settignano. » Desiderio da Settignano; Donatello; relief sculpture

basalt The most common extrusive igneous rock, characterized by low silica content, and composed essentially of plagioclase feldspar and pyroxene. It is a dark, fine-grained rock, solidified from lava erupted from fissures or craters. Submarine basalts, extruded along mid-ocean ridges, form the oceanic crust. Subaerial eruptions produce extensive flows, the largest of which form the Deccan Plateau, India, and the Columbia-Snake R Plateau, USA. It is commonly used as a building stone and road-stone aggregate. » feldspar; igneous rock; lava; pyroxenes; volcano

base (chemistry) A substance liberating hydroxide ions in water, an acceptor of protons, or a donor of electron pairs: each of these definitions includes the previous one. The term is thus the opposite of an acid, whatever definition of acid is used. In water, strong bases include the hydroxides of the alkali metals, while weak bases include ammonia and the amines. » acid; dissociation; pH

base (mathematics) The number on which a system of counting is constructed (**number-base**). The numbers in common use are in base ten, ie numbers expressed in multiples of powers of ten; thus 'three hundred and forty two' is written 342, since it is $3 \times 10^2 + 4 \times 10 + 2$. A number base five would be written as the sum of multiples of powers of five; thus 'seventy-three' is $2 \times 25 + 4 \times 5 + 3 = 2 \times 5^2 + 4 \times 5 + 3 = 243_{five}$: other then base ten, base two is the commonest base. » binary number; numbers; logarithm

baseball A team game played on a diamond-shaped field by two sides of players with a bat and ball. One team, on offence or *at bat*, tries to score the most runs by having their players circle the bases before they are put *out* by the other team which is *in the field*. An out is made when the fielding team catches a batted ball before it touches the ground, tags a member of the offensive team between bases, or touches a base before an offensive player reaches that base. The defensive team is aided in stopping the offensive team by fielding batted balls with an oversized glove or *mitt*. Each game is made up of nine innings unless the score is tied, in which case the game is extended into *extra innings* until one team outscores the other in a particular inning. Each inning is divided into two parts — the *top* and *bottom*. The visiting team always bats first (the top) and the home team always bats last (the bottom). Each team at bat is allowed three outs in its half inning.

The major confrontation of the game centres around the *pitcher* and *batter*. The pitcher hurls the ball at upwards of 145 kph/90 mph towards the batter who stands poised to strike the ball. If the batter swings at the ball and fails to hit it, or if the pitcher throws the ball into a designated strike zone, between the batter's knees and his chest, without the batter swinging at the ball, a *strike* is called. Three strikes causes a batter to be declared out. Conversely, if the pitcher fails to throw the ball into the strike zone and the batter does not swing, a *ball* is called. Four balls allow the batter to take first base. The home plate umpire, who stands behind the catcher, determines if the ball is within the strike zone. If the batter strikes the ball and circles the bases before being put out, he has hit a *home run*.

Baseball is called the *national pastime* in the USA. Professional teams usually consist of 25 players. The *Major League* of North America is divided into the American and National Leagues. The American League consists of 14 teams and the National of 12 based in the USA and Canada. In the National League 9 players can participate at one time for each team, while in the American League 10 take part because that league employs the designated hitter rule allowing a team to replace the pitcher in its batting order with a player who bats but does not play the field. The culmination of the season, which runs from April through October, is a best-of-seven game *World Series* between the champions of each league.

The game is believed to have been invented by a West Point cadet, Abner Doubleday, when in 1839 he laid out the first diamond at Cooperstown, NY, where the modern day Baseball Hall of Fame stands. » rounders; softball; RR105

basenji [bas**en**jee] A spitz breed of dog developed in C Africa for hunting; pale brown and white; short coat; keeps itself meticulously clean; cannot bark, but makes a yodelling noise. » dog; spitz

Basho, Matsuo (1644–94) Japanese poet, born in Ueno (Iga), and bred from a young age to poetry. Becoming master of the miniature *haiku*, he started his own school, but later retired to a hermitage. Influenced by Zen Buddhism, he then journeyed extensively, and composed his celebrated book of travels *The Narrow Road to the Deep North* (1689) in a mixture of poetic prose and *haiku*. He died at Osaka. » haiku; Japanese literature; Zen Buddhism

BASIC An acronym of **Beginner's All-purpose Symbolic Instruction Code**, a high level computer programming language developed in the late 1950s at Dartmouth College in the USA, which has the advantage of being relatively simple to learn. It has since been widely adopted as a standard language by microcomputer manufacturers, although there are now a large number of dialects of BASIC for different types of computer which are not readily interchangeable. » microcomputer; programming language

basic oxides Oxides of metals, especially of the alkali and alkaline earth elements, which yield bases on reaction with water. » alkali; metal

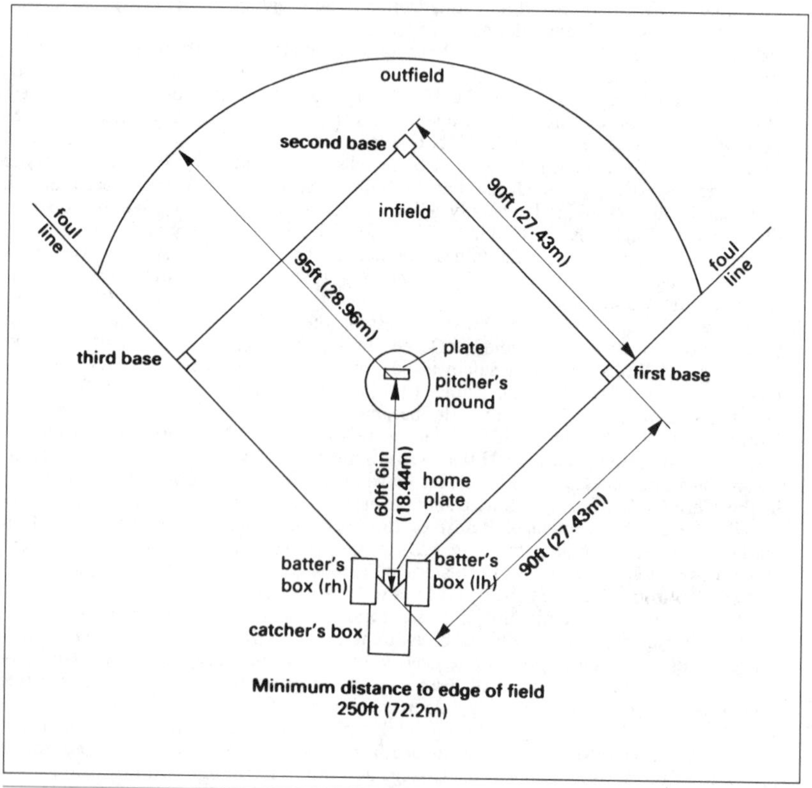

The baseball field

Basidiomycetes [basidiohmiy**see**teez] A subdivision of the true fungi, characterized by a sexual reproduction process that forms a club-shaped structure (*basidium*) bearing four haploid spores (*basidiospores*); basidia arranged on fruiting body (mushroom); includes edible mushrooms, agarics, puffballs, and many parasitic forms. (Division: *Eumycota*.) » bolete; fly agaric; fungus; gametophyte; mushroom; puffball

Basie, Count, byname of **William Basie** [**bay**see] (1904–84) US bandleader and pianist, born at Red Bank, New Jersey. An itinerant piano player in vaudeville and saloons, he joined Benny Moten's Kansas City Orchestra in 1929, became its leader in 1935, and took it to New York the next year. Its supple rhythmic drive, supplied by Basie's piano, Freddie Green's guitar, and Jo Jones's drums, propelled several brilliant soloists (especially Lester Young and Herschel Evans, tenor saxophones, and Buck Clayton, trumpet), elevating the band to top rank. When the Swing Era waned, Basie reorganized his band in 1951, emphasizing precision ensemble playing in more complex orchestrations, and maintained his stature continuously. He died at Hollywood, Florida. » jazz

Basil I, byname **the Macedonian** (?–886) Byzantine Emperor (867–86), born in Thrace, who founded the Macedonian dynasty. He was at first joint ruler with Michael III, but assassinated him in 868. He formulated the Greek legal code, in a text known as the Basilica.

Basil, St (The Great) (c.329–79), feast day 2 January (W), 1 January (E). One of the greatest of the Greek Fathers, born and died at Caesarea, Cappadocia. After living a monastic life, in 370 he succeeded Eusebius as Bishop of Caesarea. Along with his brother, St Gregory of Nyssa, and St Gregory of Nazianzus, he defended Christian philosophy against Arianism. » Arius; Christianity; Fathers of the Church; monasticism

basil A bushy aromatic annual or perennial, growing to 1 m/3¼ ft, but often less; stems square; leaves oval, pale, glossy, in opposite pairs; flowers 2-lipped, white or purplish, in whorls; probably native to SE Asia, but widely cultivated in Europe and USA as a culinary herb and for use in perfumery. (*Ocimum basilicum*. Family: *Labiatae*.) » annual; herb; perennial

basilica Originally a royal palace or large oblong hall with double colonnades, for the administration of justice and commerce. It was later adopted by early Christians as a similarly arranged church with two or more aisles, timber roof, and apse. The name derives from Greek *basileus*, 'king'. » apse; Roman architecture

Basiliensis, Regio [**re**jeeoh basil**yen**sis] pop (1984e) 2 077 797; area 234 sq km/90 sq ml. Transnational 'natural region' encompassing the frontier districts of France, Switzerland, and Germany, in the Upper Rhine Valley, between the Jura Mts and the Black Forest; administrative centre, Basle; regional centres at Mulhouse and Freiburg; international co-operation between local governments, industries, and universities promoted since 1963. » Basle; Rhine, River

basilisk (biology) An iguana native to S America; male with bony projections on head and prominent sail-like crests along back; tail long; may run upright on long hind legs; can even run on water for short distances. (Genus: *Basiliscus*, 5 species.) » iguana

basilisk (mythology) A fabulous beast, a small dragon-like creature combining features of the snake and the cockerel. Its eye could freeze and kill, hence the expression 'If looks could kill'. It is equivalent to the **cockatrice**, which was hatched by a serpent from the egg of a cock.

Baskerville, John (1706–75) British printer, born at Sion Hill, Worcestershire. He began as a footman, became a writing master in Birmingham, and from 1740 carried on a successful japanning business there. About 1750 he began to make costly experiments in letter founding, and produced several types, one particularly fine example of which bears his name. His works include editions of Virgil, Milton, and the Bible. In 1758 he became printer to Cambridge University. He died in Birmingham. » printing [i]

basketball A 5-a-side team ball game, invented by James Naismith in 1891 at Springfield, Massachusetts, USA; but a similar game was played by the Olmecs in Mexico in the 10th-c BC. Played on a court, the object is to throw the ball through your opponent's basket, situated at the end of the court, and 10 ft (3.05 m) above the ground. Most senior basketball players are well over 6 ft (1.8 m) tall. » Harlem Globetrotters; netball; RR105

basking shark Extremely large, inoffensive shark, second only to the whale shark as the largest living fish; length up to 10 m/33 ft, weight c.6 000 kg/13 200 lb; lives in oceanic surface waters feeding entirely upon plankton filtered by stiff bristles on its long gill arches. (*Cetorhinus maximus*. Family: *Cetorhinidae*.) » plankton; shark

Basle, Ger **Basel**, Fr **Bâle** [bahl] 47°35N 7°35E, pop (1980) 182 143. Capital of Basel-Stadt demicanton and of Basel canton, NE Switzerland; on the R Rhine, 69 km/43 ml N of Bern; centre of the Regio Basiliensis 'natural region'; second largest city in Switzerland; river port at the terminus of Rhine navigation; on the site of a Roman fort; mediaeval centre for silk, dyeing, and printing; joined the Swiss Confederacy, 1501; influential centre during the Reformation; scene of the first Zionist conference, 1897; airport (Basel-Mulhouse, on French territory, shared with France); railway junction; oldest Swiss university (1460); major European communications crossroads; Switzerland's leading centre for transshipment and international commerce; pharmaceuticals, salt, synthetics, chemicals, textiles, metallurgy, engineering, foodstuffs, tourism; Gothic minster (11th-c, largely rebuilt 14th-c), town hall (1504–14), Spalentor (1400), European World Trade and Convention Centre, zoological and botanical gardens, many museums and theatres; space-age pylon (symbolizing the city's location at the junction of France, Germany, and Switzerland); annual Swiss Industries Fair, 3-day Basle Carnival (Fasnacht). » Switzerland [i]

Basle, Council of (1431–49) A controversial Council of the Church. It was intended to continue the work of the Council of Constance, against heresy, and initiating reform, but fell into dispute with Pope Eugenius IV for asserting the authority of the Council over that of the Pope. When the Pope attempted to dissolve it, the Council appointed Felix V, the last of the antipopes. » antipope; Council of the Church

Basov, Nikolai (Gennadiyevich) (1922–) Russian physicist, born in St Petersburg. He was professor at Lebedev Physics Institute, Moscow, and joint winner of the Nobel Physics Prize in 1964 for his work on the maser. » maser

Basque Provinces [bask], Span **País Vasco** or **Provincias Vascongadas**, Basque **Euskadi** pop (1981) 2 141 809; area 7 261 sq km/2 803 sq ml. Autonomous region of N Spain, comprising the provinces of Álava, Guipúzcoa, and Vizcaya; coastal hills, separated from the main ridge of the Cordillera Cantabrica to the S by valleys growing wheat; rivers provide hydroelectric power; industries centred around Bilbao and San Sebastian include metallurgy, paper, furniture. » Basques; Spain [i]

Basques A people of uncertain origin living in NW Spain and neighbouring areas in France. They are physically similar to their neighbours, and are Roman Catholics, but their language, Basque, spoken by c.500 000, does not relate to any other European language, and is thought to be a remnant of the languages spoken in W Europe before the advent of the Indo-European family. Despite extensive cultural and linguistic assimilation, urbanized Basques retain strong ethnic identity, and their main city Bilbao is a centre of Basque nationalism. Many Basques opposed the Spanish Republic established in 1931 and fought against Republicans during the Spanish Civil War, after which many went into exile. Since the death of Franco (1975), the new liberal Spanish monarchy has granted Basques some local autonomy (1978–9), but the more militant continue to agitate for a separate Basque state, engaging in terrorism for this end. Population c.805 000 in Spain, 130 000 in France, and 170 000 elsewhere, mainly S America and the USA. » Basque Provinces; Indo-European languages; Spanish Civil War

Basra [**baz**ra], Arabic **Al Basrah** 30°30N 47°50E, pop (1970) 333 684. Port capital of Basra governorate, SE Iraq, at head of the Shatt al-Arab, c.120 km/75 ml from the Arabian Gulf; major centre of literature, theology, and scholarship in

8th–9th-c; modern administrative and commercial centre; airport; railway; university (1967); oil refining, fertilizers; port badly affected in 1980s by Iran–Iraq war. » Iraq [i]

bass [bas] Marine and brackish water fish found in the surf zone around rocks and beaches of the NE Atlantic; body blue grey with silver sides, length up to 1 m/3¼ ft; valuable commercial and sport fish. The name is also used for other species of the families *Serranidae* and *Centrarchidae*. (*Dicentrarchus labrax*. Family: *Serranidae*.)

Bass Strait [bas] A channel separating Tasmania from Victoria, Australia, maximum width 240 km/150 ml, depth 50–70 m/180–240 ft; named in 1798 after the British explorer George Bass; oil and natural gas. » Tasmania; Victoria (Australia)

Bassae [**ba**say] A temple dedicated to Apollo Epicurius on the slopes of Mt Lykaion, SW Arcadia, Greece; a world heritage site. It was built in the 5th-c BC by Ictinus for the people of Phigalia after their city escaped a plague epidemic. Rediscovered in 1763, it has since been largely re-erected. » Greek architecture; Ictinus

Bassani, Giorgio [ba**sah**nee] (1916–) Italian novelist, born in Bologna, and educated at the University there. His novels record the life of the Jewish community of Ferrara between the beginning of World War 1 and the end of World War 2, describing the growth of fascism and the response of both the Jewish and non-Jewish Italians of Ferrara to it. He has rewritten all of his novels since the late 1960s, and published them collectively under the title *Il romanzo di Ferrara* (1974, The Story of Ferrara). » fascism; Italian literature; novel

Bassano, Jacopo da, properly **Giacomo da Ponte** [ba**sah**noh] (c.1510–92) Venetian painter, one of the founders of genre painting in Europe, born and died at Bassano. His best paintings are of peasant life and Biblical scenes with animals, and include the altarpiece of the Nativity at Bassano and 'Jacob's Return to Canaan'. His four sons were also painters. » genre painting; Italian art; Venetian School

basse taille enamel [bas **tiy**] A technique of enamelling on silver, or occasionally gold, where the metal is carved and engraved, and translucent coloured enamel is applied on top with the image shining through. It was introduced about the end of the 13th-c, probably in Paris. » enamelling

Basse-Terre [bas **tair**] pop (1982) 141 313; area 848 sq km/327 sq ml. One of the two main islands of the French Overseas Department of Guadeloupe, Lesser Antilles, E Caribbean; separated from Grande-Terre I by the narrow Rivière Salée; mountainous, with active volcano Grande Soufrière rising to 1 484 m/4 869 ft; national park in C of island; capital, Basse-Terre, pop (1982) 13 656; agriculture, especially sugar cane. » Grande-Terre; Guadeloupe

basset-horn An 18th-c musical instrument belonging to the clarinet family, with a lower compass than that of the normal clarinet. It was much used by Mozart, but fell into disuse in the 19th-c. » clarinet; Mozart; reed instrument

basset hound A breed of dog formerly used in France and Belgium for hunting; long, solid body, with very short legs; muzzle long and broad; ears long and pendulous; short-haired coat of white, black, and tan. » dog; hound

Basseterre [bas**tair**] 17°17N 62°43W, pop (1980) 14 725. Capital and chief port of St Kitts-Nevis, N Leeward Is, E Caribbean, on SW coast of St Kitts I; airport; distribution centre; electrical components, garments, data processing, beverages; cathedral. » St Kitts-Nevis

bassoon A musical instrument consisting of a jointed wooden pipe, about 2 m 54 cm/8 ft 4 in long, doubled back on itself, and fitted with metal keys and a curved crook with a double reed. It is, in effect, a bass oboe. The larger **double bassoon**, or **contrabassoon**, sounds one octave lower than the standard instrument. » reed instrument; woodwind instrument [i]

basswood An American species of lime, producing useful timber and bass/bast, the stringy inner bark used for mats and ropes. (*Tilia americana*. Family: *Tileaceae*.) » bark; lime (botany)

Bastia [bas**tee**a] 42°40N 9°30E, pop (1982) 45 081. Port and capital of Haute-Corse department, NW Corsica, France; in NE corner on narrow Cap Corse between mountains and sea; airport; railway; founded by the Genoese, 1380; capital of Corsica until 1811; largest port and chief town of the island; fishing, wine, tobacco, shipping trade, tourism. » Corsica; France [i]

Bastille [bas**teel**] A mediaeval fortress and prison in E Paris, the symbol of Bourbon despotism, stormed by a Parisian mob on 14 July 1789. Its destruction came to have a unique place in French Revolutionary ideology as marking the end of the *ancien régime*. The anniversary of the day is a French national holiday. » French Revolution [i]

bat A nocturnal mammal, widespread in tropical and temperate regions; hibernates in winter in cold areas; usually hangs head-down at rest; the only mammal capable of sustained flight (the wing is a web of skin stretched between elongated fingers and joined to the rear legs and tail); probably evolved to exploit night-flying insects. Most members of the suborder *Microchiroptera* eat insects; some also eat fish, frogs, birds, or other bats. They use echolocation to detect prey and avoid obstacles, and have a nose and ears which are often complex in shape. In contrast, **fruit bats** (or *flying foxes*) of the Old World tropics (suborder: *Megachiroptera*, 170 species) eat fruit and flowers detected by smell. They include the largest bats, with large eyes and a dog-like head (small ears and a long muzzle). They have better vision than other bats, and few use echolocation. A quarter of living mammal species are bats. The name *fruit bat* is also used for genus *Artibeus* (14 fruit-eating species) from the New World tropics (suborder: *Microchiroptera*; family: *Phyllostomidae*). (Order: *Chiroptera*, 951 species.) » barbastelle; echolocation; hibernation; horseshoe bat; mammal [i]; noctule; pipistrelle; serotine bat; vampire bat [i]

Bat Mitzvah » **Bar Mitzvah**

Batak Six closely-related ethnic groups of C Sumatra, Indonesia, speaking Austronesian languages. Their ancestors were Proto-Malayan people fairly isolated in the Sumatran highlands until the early 19th-c. Indian cultural influences date back to the 2nd–3rd-c AD. The most literate and Christianized group are the Toba Batak, well-known for trade and their key role in national government. Population 3.1 million, one-third Muslim, one-third Christian, and the rest adhering to traditional religion. » Austronesian languages; Sumatra

Batalha, Monastery of [bata**l**ya] A Dominican abbey, in Batalha, W Portugal, one of the great examples of Christian Gothic architecture; a world heritage monument. It was founded in 1388 by King João I (reigned 1385–1433) in fulfilment of a vow made at the Battle of Aljubarrota, where Portuguese independence was established. » Gothic architecture; Portugal [i]

Batavian Republic The name given to Holland 1795–1806, after that country had been conquered by Revolutionary French forces in 1794–5. Between 1806 and 1810 the Kingdom of Holland was ruled by Napoleon's brother, Louis Bonaparte, but Holland was incorporated into France between 1810 and the collapse of French rule in 1813. » Napoleonic Wars; French Revolutionary Wars

batch processing A defined series of tasks which are submitted to larger computers and executed only when time becomes available on the computer. This is in contrast to interactive computing, where the user accesses the computer in a conversational mode. » interactive computing

bateleur [batuh**ler**] An aerobatic hawk of the group known as **snake eagles** or **snake hawks**; native to Africa S of the Sahara; very long wings and short tail; eats reptiles, mammals, and carrion; robs other carrion-feeding birds; flies about 300 km/190 ml each day. (*Terathopius ecaudatus*. Family: *Accipitridae*.) » hawk

Bates, H(erbert) E(rnest) (1905–74) British novelist, playwright, and short-story writer, born at Rushden, Northamptonshire. He began his working life as a journalist, publishing in 1926 his first play, *The Last Bread*, and his first novel, *The Two Sisters*. He is one of the greatest exponents of the short-story form, and his essay in literary criticism, *The Modern Short Story*, is regarded as a classic. His best-known novel is *Fair Stood the Wind for France* (1944). The Larkin family was introduced in *The Darling Buds of May* (1958). He died at Canterbury, Kent. » English literature; short story

Bates, H(enry) W(alter) (1825–92) British naturalist and traveller, born in Leicester. In 1848 with Alfred Wallace he left to explore the Amazon, remaining there until 1859. In 1861 he described the phenomena of mimicry in animals (later known as **Batesian mimicry**), which contributed to the theory of natural selection. He died in London. » natural selection

Bateson, William (1861–1926) British biologist, born at Whitby, Yorkshire, who laid the foundations of (and named) the science of genetics. He was educated at Rugby and Cambridge, where he became the first British professor of genetics in 1908. In 1912 he transferred to the Royal Institution and was president of the British Association in 1914. His experiments on inheritance influenced the development of the science of genetics, and his writing made Mendel's work better understood. He died in London. » genetics [i]; Mendel

batfish Any of two groups of fishes with wing-like extensions; the deep-bodied Indo-Pacific genus *Platax* (Family: *Ephippidae*), and the bizarre *Ogcocephalidae* (including *Ogcocephalus*) with flattened triangular bodies and elbow-like pectoral fins; both sold as curios.

Bath, Lat **Aquae Calidae**, Anglo-Saxon **Akermanceaster** 51°23N 2°22W, pop (1981) 79 965. Spa town in Bath district, Avon, SW England; on R Avon, 19 km/12 ml ESE of Bristol; noted since Roman times for its hot springs; chartered in 1189; fashionable spa centre in 18th-c; railway; university (1966); tourism, printing, plastics, engineering; Roman baths, 15th-c Roman bath museum, abbey church, notable Georgian crescents; City of Bath a world heritage site; Mid-Somerset festival (Mar), Festival of the Arts (May). » Avon; Britain, Roman; Nash, Richard

Bath, Order of the (OB) A British order of chivalry, formally created by George I in 1725, but traditionally founded by Henry IV in 1399 at the Tower of London, when he conferred the honour on the 46 esquires who had attended him at his bath the night before his coronation. The order comprises the sovereign and three classes: Knights and Dames Grand Cross, Knights and Dames Commander, and Companions. The ribbon is crimson, and the motto *Tria juncta in uno* ('three joined in one'). » decoration

batholith A very large igneous rock mass, typically granite, intruded while molten into the surrounding country rock, outcropping over at least 100 sq km/40 sq ml and extending to unknown depth. It is characteristic of orogenic belts and subduction zones, such as the Andean batholith in S America. » granite; igneous rock; orogeny; subduction zone [i]

Bathurst » **Banjul**

Bathurst and Melville Islands pop (1981) 1 586; area 7 487 sq km/2 890 sq ml. Islands off the NW coast of Northern Territory, Australia, c.80 km/50 ml N of Darwin; Aboriginal communities; town of Nguiu on Bathurst I (population 1 000) founded as a Catholic mission in 1911; wood-carving and pottery. » Aborigines; Northern Territory

bathymetry The measurement of the depths of sea bottom features in large bodies of water. **Bathymetric charts** indicate the depths of water in feet, fathoms, or metres and are used to show the morphology of submarine topographic features. Detailed bathymetric mapping was only possible with the advent of continuous echo-sounding, which was first extensively used during the German Meteor Expedition (1925–7). » echo-sounding

bathyscaphe [**bath**eeskayf] Any free-moving vessel designed for underwater exploration, consisting of a flotation compartment with an observation capsule underneath. Originally designed by Piccard in 1848, they have proved capable of reaching depths of over 10 000 m/32 000 ft. Modern submersibles (such as *Alvin*, which explored the *Titanic*) are much more manoeuvrable. » Piccard

bathysphere [**bath**eesfeer] A specially strengthened spherical vessel in which observers may be lowered to great depths by a parent vessel. First used in 1930, it achieved 923 m/3 028 ft in 1934. Other forms of underwater exploration craft have made them obsolescent. » bathyscaphe

batik A form of dyeing in which parts of the fabric are left undyed because of wax printed or painted onto the fabric. The fabric is then crushed to crack the wax, and dyed. Removal of the wax leaves undyed areas covered in fine lines. This method, a form of *resist dyeing*, originated in Indonesia. » dyeing

Batista (y Zaldívar), Fulgencio [bah**tee**stah] (1901–73) Cuban dictator, born in Oriente province. In 1933, he organized a military coup (the 'sergeants' revolt'), consolidated his power, and became President (1940–4). In 1952 he overthrew President Prio Socorras, and ruled as dictator until his overthrow by Fidel Castro (Jan 1959), when he found refuge in the Dominican Republic. He died at Marbella, Spain. » Castro

Baton Rouge [**ba**tuhn **roozh**] 30°27N 91°11W, pop (1980) 219 419. Capital of state in East Baton Rouge parish, SE Louisiana, USA; a deep-water port on the Mississippi R; founded, 1719; governed successively by France, Britain, and Spain; ceded to the USA as part of the Louisiana Purchase, 1803; declared its independence under the name Feliciana, 1810; incorporated as a town within Louisiana, 1817; state capital, 1849–61 and since 1882; airfield; railway; university (1860); oil refining, petrochemical industries, machinery; State Museum, Riverside Museum, the old capitol, Huey Long grave and memorial. » Louisiana; Louisiana Purchase

Batten, Jean (1909–82) New Zealand pioneer aviator. In 1934 she made the first England–Australia 'there and back' solo flight by a woman, and in 1936 made a record-breaking flight from England to New Zealand. Reclusive in her later years, she died in Spain, unknown and alone. » Johnson, Amy

battered baby syndrome The physical abuse of babies by adults. When mild in degree, the child may only be irritable or crying, with no or little external evidence of trauma. This diagnosis may be suspected only after an X-ray reveals fracture of the ribs or other bones. In severe cases bruises, burns, and lacerations are visible, and death may occur from cerebral haemorrhage, ruptured internal organs, or starvation.

battery In law, the use of force against another person without that person's consent. It involves physical contact (unlike assault), but not necessarily physical damage. Also, the person need not be aware that a battery is to take place (as in the case of a blow from behind). Consent may sometimes be implied, such as in the context of lawful sporting activity. » assault

battery farming » **factory farming**

battle cruiser A powerful warship capable of defeating an enemy cruiser squadron. Originally a cross between an armoured cruiser and a battleship, it evolved to be of battleship size but lightly armoured and very fast. » battleship; cruiser; warships [i]

battleship The most powerful warship capable of engaging an enemy; the word is derived from 'line-of-battle ship'. All other vessels originally served subsidiary purposes which aided the battleship in its role. The largest battleships ever built were the Japanese *Musashi* and *Yamato* (72 800 tons), each mounting 18.1-inch guns; both were sunk in World War 2. The largest battleship now in service is the *USS New Jersey* (58 000 tons) mounting nine 16-inch guns. Gun armament is now supplemented by cruise missile batteries. » cruise missile; warships [i]

Baud [bawd] A unit, named after the French inventor, J M E Baudot, which is used to measure the rate of transmission of digital data. For most purposes, one baud can be regarded as equivalent to a transmission rate of one bit per second. The **Baudot code** is a 5-bit code widely used in teleprinter-based communications systems and in early computer applications. » bit

Baudelaire, Charles (Pierre) [bohduh**lair**] (1821–67) French Symbolist poet, born in Paris. He was educated at Lyons and Paris, and after an unhappy childhood was sent on a voyage to India (1841); but he stopped at Mauritius, where Jeanne Duval, a half-caste, became his mistress and inspiration. He returned to Paris, where he squandered his inheritance, and began to live by his pen. His masterpiece is a collection of poems, *Les Fleurs du mal* (1857), for which author, printer, and publisher were prosecuted for impropriety in 1864. In later years, he took to drink and opium, was struck down with paralysis and poverty, and after two years in Brussels (1864–6), died in Paris. » Symbolism

Baudot code » **Morse Code**

Baudouin I [boh**dwĩ**] (1930–) King of the Belgians, born at Stuyvenberg Castle, near Brussels, the elder son of Leopold III and his first wife, Queen Astrid. He succeeded to the throne following the abdication of his father (Jul 1951), and in 1960 married the Spanish Doña Fabiola de Mora y Aragón.

Bauhaus [**bow**hows] An influential school of arts and crafts founded in the Weimar Republic by Walter Gropius in 1919. The aim was for artists and architects to work together to create a new unity in the arts. At first expressionist in style, the Bauhaus quickly championed the stark simplicity of functionalism. Students and teachers included Feininger, van Doesburg, Moholy-Nagy, Kandinsky, Klee, and Mies van der Rohe. The school was constantly troubled by opposition from local people and politicians, and by divisions amongst its own members. It moved to Dessau in 1925, but was closed by Hitler in 1933, many members living thereafter in the USA. » Arts and Crafts Movement; De Stijl; Expressionism; Feininger; functionalism (art and architecture); German art; Gropius; International Style **2**; Kandinsky; Klee; Mies van der Rohe; Moholy-Nagy; rationalism

Baum, Vicki [bowm] (1888–1960) Austrian novelist, born in Vienna. Her works include *Grand Hotel* (1930), *Grand Opera* (1942), several short stories, and plays. » German literature; novel

Baur, Ferdinand Christian [bowr] (1792–1860) German Protestant theologian and New Testament critic, born at Schmiden, near Stuttgart. He held the Tübingen chair of theology from 1826, and founded the Tübingen School, the first to use strict historical research methods in the study of early Christianity. He died at Tübingen. » New Testament; Protestantism; theology

Bausch, Pina, properly **Philippine** [bowsh] (1940–) West German dancer, choreographer, and director, born at Solingen. She studied at the Essen Folkwang School, and danced with German and US dance companies, becoming ballet director of the Wuppertal Dance Theatre in 1973. Her works include *Rite of Spring* (1975), *Cafe Muller* (1978), and *1980* (1980). » Expressionism; modern dance

bauxite A natural mixture of hydrated aluminium oxide minerals produced by the weathering of rocks in hot, humid climates in which more soluble constituents are leached out. It is the chief ore of aluminium. » aluminium

Bavaria, Ger **Bayern** pop (1990) 11 220 735; area 70 553 sq km/ 27 233 sq ml. Province in SE Germany, bounded (E) by Czechoslovakia and (S) by Austria; largest province in former West Germany, and Europe's oldest existing political entity; capital, Munich; chief towns, Augsburg, Passau, Nuremberg, Würzburg, Regensburg; chief rivers, the Danube, Isar, Lech, Main; surrounded by the Bavarian Forest (E), Fichtelgebirge (NE), Bavarian Alps (S); a third of the area is forested; agriculture, electrical and mechanical engineering, clothing, timber, tourism; many spas and climatic health resorts. » Bavarian Alps/Forest; Germany [i]

Bavarian Alps, Ger **Bayerische Alpen** Mountain range extending E and W from L Constance to Salzburg; highest peak, the Zugspitze (2 962 m/9 718 ft); Allgäu Alps form W section; called the **Tirol Alps** in Austria. » Allgäu Alps; Alps; Bavaria

Bavarian Forest, Ger **Bayerische Wald** Mountain range bounded NW by Chamb and Regen Rivers and SW by the Danube valley; merges N into the Bohemian Forest in Czechoslovakia; highest peak, the Einodriegel (1 126 m/3 694 ft); largest continuous forest in Europe; contains Germany's first national park. » Germany [i]

Bavarian Succession, War of the (1778–9) A short episode in the political rivalry between Austria and Prussia for hegemony among the German states. Military manoeuvring gave way to stalemate; the Habsburg acquisition of Innviertel further tarnished Frederick the Great's prestige. » Frederick II (of Prussia); Habsburgs; Prussia

Bax, Sir Arnold (Edward Trevor) (1883–1953) British composer, born in London. He studied at the Royal Academy of Music, and visited Russia, but was mainly influenced by the Celtic revival. He wrote several Irish short stories (under the name of **Dermot O'Byrne**), and composed orchestral pieces and songs set to the words of revival poets. He wrote seven symphonies (1921–39), tone poems (such as *Tintagel*, 1917), choral works, chamber music, piano solos and concertos. He was knighted in 1937, and in 1942 was made Master of the King's (from 1952 Queen's) Musick. He died in Cork, Ireland.

Bay owl

Baxter, James Keir (1926–72) New Zealand poet, born near Dunedin. His poetry resembled his dramatic style of life in being marked by a powerful sense of social concern and disregard for convention. He became a Roman Catholic in 1958, and his later work, even when obscene, is intensely religious. He died in Auckland.

Bay of Pigs The attempted invasion of Cuba (Apr 1961) by Cuban exiles supported by the USA. The invasion force of 1 300 men landed at Bahía de Cochinos (Bay of Pigs) on the S coast, but was rapidly overwhelmed and defeated by Cuban troops commanded by Fidel Castro. » Castro; Cuba [i]

bay owl An owl native to Africa and SE Asia; inhabits wet tropical forest; eats insects and vertebrates. (Genus: *Phodilus*, 2 species. Family: *Tytonidae*.) » owl

bay tree » **sweet bay**

Bayazid I » **Bajazet I**

Bayeux Tapestry [**biy**uh] An embroidered wall-hanging in coloured wool on linen, narrating events leading up to the invasion of England by William of Normandy, and the Battle of Hastings in 1066. Probably commissioned by William's half-brother Odo, Bishop of Bayeux in N France, and embroidered in S England c.1067–77, it measures 68 m/224 ft long, and 46 cm–54 cm/18–21 in high. The contemporary social, military, architectural, and iconographic information the tapestry provides is of unparalleled importance. » Anglo-Saxons; Norman Conquest; tapestry

Baykonyr Cosmodrome » **Baikonur Cosmodrome**

Baylis, Lilian Mary (1874–1937) British theatrical manager, born and died in London. After a period as a music teacher in S Africa, she returned to England (1898), becoming manager of the first Old Vic company in 1912. Under her, the theatre became a joint home of Shakespeare and opera. In 1931 she acquired Sadler's Wells Theatre for the exclusive presentation of opera and ballet.

bayonet A steel blade, thought to have been invented in Bayonne, France, in the 17th-c, which turns an infantryman's firearm into a thrusting weapon. Originally plugging into the end of the musket, by the early 19th-c bayonets were designed to fit into a slot beneath the muzzle, allowing the weapon to be fired at will. The bayonet was sheathed in a short scabbard when not in use. Modern infantry weapons still retain a facility for taking a bayonet. » musket; rifle

bayou [**biy**oo] A section of still or slow-moving marshy water cut off from a main river channel. It is often in the form of an oxbow lake. Bayous are typical of the Mississippi R delta in Louisiana, USA.

Bayreuth [biy**royt**] 49°56N 11°35E, pop (1983) 71 100. Industrial and marketing town, capital of Oberfranken district, Germany, on a tributary of R Main; world famous as a festival city committed to the operas of Wagner; railway; university (1975); textiles, machinery, electricity supply; 16th-c old palace, new palace (1753), Wagner theatre (1872–6); Wagner Festival (Jul–Aug). » Germany [i]; Wagner

Bazaar Malay » **Malay** (language)

bazooka A US infantry weapon developed during World War 2 which fires a small rocket projectile from a simple launching tube. The projectile's warhead is effective against light tank armour. » tank

bazouka » **kazoo**

BBC The acronym of the **British Broadcasting Corporation**, the UK organization responsible for making and transmitting its own television and radio programmes locally, regionally, nationally, and internationally. Operating under Royal Charter, the BBC began its radio service in 1927 and its television service in 1936, both monopolies till 1973 and 1955 respectively. Financed almost wholly by viewers' licence fees, it is formally independent of government, and committed to a public service ethos. It is widely respected for its news service, its world external services, its patronage of the arts (especially music and drama), and its educational broadcasting, and has been instrumental in promoting a standardized form of spoken English. » broadcasting; Reith

BCD » **binary coded decimal**

BCG An acronym of *Bacillus Calmette-Guérin*, a vaccine named after French bacteriologists Albert Calmette (1863–1933) and Camille Guérin (1872–1961). It is a vaccine that consists of attenuated living tubercule bacilli. It has no power to cause tuberculosis, but in humans it conveys considerable protection against this disease over a number of years. » tuberculosis; vaccination

BCS theory A quantum theory of superconductivity; named after US physicists John Bardeen, Leon Cooper, and Robert Schrieffer in 1957. Bound states of two electrons (*Cooper pairs*) form, which account for zero electrical resistance and the Meissner effect. There has been experimental verification of the prediction that magnetic fields through a superconducting ring should have values that are multiples of a basic magnetic unit (the *fluxoid*). » Bardeen; Cooper, Leon; Meissner effect; superconductivity

beach flea » **sand hopper**

Beachcomber » **Morton, John Cameron**

Beaconsfield, Earl of » **Disraeli, Benjamin**

beagle A breed of dog developed in Britain; a medium-sized hound with a sturdy body and short coat (coarse-haired forms exist); white, tan, and black; broad pendulous ears, deep muzzle; formerly used to track hares by scent. » dog; hound

Beaglehole, John Cawte (1901–71) New Zealand writer and historian, born and died in Wellington. The outstanding authority on the voyages of Captain James Cook, he was awarded the Order of Merit in 1970.

Beaker culture A prehistoric culture defined archaeologically by finely-made, pottery drinking vessels for mead or beer, often burnished and geometrically decorated. Found in graves of the 3rd millennium BC from Spain, Czechoslovakia, and Hungary to Italy and Britain, Beakers have often been taken as evidence for trans-European migrations perhaps originating in Spain. Equally, they could be no more than a status symbol disseminated widely by trade, and copied locally.

Beale, Dorothea (1831–1906) British pioneer of women's education, born in London. From 1858 she was principal of Cheltenham Ladies' College. An advocate of higher education for women, she sponsored St Hilda's Hall, Oxford (1894), and later became a suffragette. » women's liberation movement

beam weapons » **directed energy weapons**

bean A general name applied to the seeds of many plants, but particularly those belonging to the pea family, *Leguminosae*, many of which are edible. » broad bean; pea [i]

bear A carnivorous mammal, widespread in the N hemisphere; head large with short, rounded ears and long muzzle; body bulky with thick (usually shaggy) coat and very short tail; eats meat (*polar bear*), or meat and plants (other species). It may rest for long periods during winter months, but this is not true hibernation as the body temperature does not fall. (Family: *Ursidae*, 7 species.) » black/brown/polar/sloth/spectacled/sun bear; carnivore [i]; kinkajou

bear market A stock market term which signifies that there are more sellers than buyers of stocks and shares. A 'bear' is an individual who sells shares, hoping the price will then fall, so that they may be repurchased more cheaply. » bull market; stock market

bear's breech A stout perennial native to S Europe; 30–80 cm/20–30 in high; leaves large, deeply divided, spiny; flowers in a long spike, zygomorphic, 2-lipped, white with purple veins. The leaves of this or similar species are thought to provide a common decorative motif in classical art and architecture. (*Acanthus mollis*. Family: *Acanthaceae*.) » perennial; zygomorphic flower

bearbaiting A popular sport in Britain in the 16th-c, forbidden by law in 1835. The bear was chained to a stake or put into a pit, and then attacked by dogs. Betting took place on the performance of individual dogs. The Master of Bears was a crown office with a daily stipend. » blood sports

bearberry A low, mat-forming evergreen shrub, native to arctic moorland in the N hemisphere; leaves 1–2 cm/0.4–0.8 in, elliptic or widest above middle, dark green above, pale beneath; flowers drooping, 4–6 mm/⅛–¼ in, almost globular, white tinged with pink; berry round, glossy red. (*Arctostaphyllos uva-ursi*. Family: *Ericaceae*.) » evergreen plants; shrub

bearded lizard An Australian agamid lizard; group of large spines behind each ear; body with numerous small spines; throat with deep pouch which can be enlarged as a threat display (hence 'beard'); also known as **bearded dragon**. (Genus: *Amphibolurus*, 3 species.) » agamid

bearded tit » **reedling**

bearded vulture » **lammergeier**

Beardsley, Aubrey (1872–98) British illustrator, born at Brighton. After working as a clerk, he became well known through his posters and his black and white illustrations for *Morte d'Arthur* (1893) and other books, as well as for the *Yellow Book* magazine (1894–5) and his own *Book of Fifty Drawings*. With Oscar Wilde he is regarded as leader of the 'Decadents' of the 1890s. He died at Mentone, France, having become a Catholic. » English art; Wilde

beardworm A sedentary marine worm that lives in a vertical tube buried in fine oceanic sediments; feeds by absorbing nutrients through tentacles on head; mouth, gut and anus absent in adults; body slender, length up to 0.8 m/2.6 ft; c.100 species found from shallow water to deep sea. (Phylum: *Pogonophora*.) » worm

bearings Mechanical devices supporting rotating shafts with a minimal amount of frictional resistance. A large number of different bearings exist to meet special circumstances, although the best known is probably the **ball bearing**. In this type the rotating shaft is supported by a number of balls which are interposed between it and the fixed mounting. » camshaft; engine

beat generation A group of US writers of the 1950s who rejected conventional society and its values for a life and writing based on authentic individual experience: according to the poet Allen Ginsberg (*Howl*, 1957) 'of God, sex, drugs, and the absurd'. Besides Ginsberg, novelist Jack Kerouac (*On the Road*, 1957) and poets Gregory Corso (1930–) and Laurence Ferlinghetti (1919–) were principal beat writers. Their 'outsider' lifestyle was taken over by the hippies of the 1960s. » absurdism; American literature; Ginsberg; Kerouac

beating the bounds In England, at Rogationtide, a traditional ceremonial walk round the boundaries of a parish, during which boundary stones are beaten with peeled willow wands, the better to fix their position in the memory. » riding the marches; Rogation Days

Beatitudes The common name for the opening pronouncements of blessing upon the poor, the hungry, and others in Jesus' great Sermon on the Mount, reported in Matthew's gospel (nine listed in *Matt* 5.3–10) and the Sermon on the Plain in Luke's gospel (four listed in *Luke* 6.20–3). » Jesus Christ; Sermon on the Mount

Beatles, The British pop group, formed in Liverpool in 1960, consisting at that time of **John Lennon** (1940–80, rhythm guitar, keyboards, vocals), **Paul McCartney** (1942–, bass guitar, vocals), **George Harrison** (1943–, lead guitar, sitar, vocals), and **Pete Best** (1941–, drums). In 1962 Best was replaced by **Ringo Starr** (1940–, real name Richard Starkey), and the band signed a record contract. 'Love Me Do' became a hit in the UK, and their appearances at the Cavern Club in Liverpool and elsewhere in the UK overflowed with idolizing fans. 'Beatlemania' spread around the world in 1964, buoyed by international hits such as 'She Loves You' and 'I Wanna Hold Your Hand', and by the overwhelming success of a concert tour in American stadiums. At press conferences and interviews, the Beatles projected a fey, carefree, somewhat cynical image that influenced the attitudes of their teenage admirers just as their long hair and 'granny' glasses influenced their looks. The image was sustained in their films *A Hard Day's Night* (1964) and *Help* (1965). The string of early hits, all written by Lennon and McCartney, also included 'And I Love Her', 'Yesterday', 'Norwegian Wood', and 'Eleanor Rigby'. In 1966 the Beatles stopped performing in public. Their first studio production *Sergeant Pepper's Lonely Hearts Club Band* (1967), a loose programme of songs on the theme of alienation, was brilliantly conceived, produced (by George Martin), and performed; at its best (as in 'Mr Kite', 'She's Leaving Home', 'A Day in the Life') it uses the devices of pop music to express a poetic vision. The group dissolved acrimoniously in 1970. Lennon lived in New York with his wife, **Yoko Ono** (1933–), his most memorable recording being 'Imagine' (1971); he was murdered in the streets by a deranged idolater in 1980. McCartney has remained the most active Beatle, forming bands and touring, recording frequently, and starring in his film *Give My Regards to Broad Street* (1984). Harrison records occasionally, and Starr has acted in several films and recorded some albums on his own. » pop group

Beaton, Sir Cecil (Walter Hardy) (1904–80) British photographer and designer, born in London, and educated at Harrow and Cambridge. In the 1920s, as a staff photographer for *Vanity Fair* and *Vogue*, he became famous for his society portraits, and he produced several photographic books, such as *The Book of Beauty* (1930). After World War 2, he designed scenery and costumes for many ballet, operatic, theatrical and film productions, including *My Fair Lady* and *Gigi*, and provided the drawings and illustrations for several books. He was knighted in 1972, and died near Salisbury, Wiltshire.

Beaton or **Bethune, David** (1494–1546) Scottish statesman and Roman Catholic prelate, born at Balfour, Fife. Educated at the Universities of St Andrews, Glasgow, and Paris, he resided at the French court (1519) and was appointed Bishop of Mirepoix by Francis I (1537). In 1525 he took his seat in the Scots Parliament as Abbot of Arbroath and became Privy Seal. Elevated to cardinal (1538), and made Archbishop of St Andrews (1539), he championed French interests at the expense of English influence. A persecutor of the Scottish Protestants, he had the reformer George Wishart burnt at St Andrews (1546), but was murdered in revenge three months later by a group of Protestant conspirators. » Protestantism; Reformation; Wishart

Beatrix (Wilhelmina Armgard) (1938–) Queen of the Netherlands (1980–), born at Soestdijk, the eldest daughter of Juliana and Prince Bernhard zur Lippe-Biesterfeld, who acceded to the throne on the abdication of her mother. In 1966 she married West German diplomat **Claus-Georg Wilhelm Otto Friedrich Gerd von Amsberg** (1926–); their son, **Prince Willem-Alexander Claus George Ferdinand** (1967–) is the first male heir to the Dutch throne in over a century. There are two other sons: **Johan Friso Bernhard Christiaan David** (1968–) and **Constantijn Christof Frederik Aschwin** (1969–).

beats In physics, regular low-frequency variations in amplitude, resulting from an interference effect between waves of similar wavelength. The effect is exploited in piano tuning and in heterodyne radio receivers. » amplitude; interference [i]; superheterodyne

Beatty, David Beatty, 1st Earl (1871–1936) British admiral, born at Nantwich, Cheshire. He served in the Sudan (1896–8), and as battleship commander took part in the China War (1900). At the outbreak of World War 1 he steamed into Heligoland Bight, and destroyed three German cruisers. He later sank the *Blücher* (Jan 1915), and took part in the Battle of Jutland (May 1916). He became Commander-in-Chief of the Grand Fleet in 1916 and First Sea Lord in 1919, when he was created an earl. He died in London. » World War 1

Beaufort, Henry (1377–1447) English cardinal, a major figure in English politics in the early 15th-c. He studied at Oxford and Aix-la-Chapelle, was consecrated Bishop of Lincoln (1398) and Winchester (1405), and became a cardinal in 1426. He was Lord Chancellor on three occasions (1403–5, 1413–17, 1424–6). In 1427 the Pope sent him as legate into Germany, to organize a crusade against the Hussites; this undertaking failed, and he fell from papal pleasure. During the 1430s he controlled the government of the young King Henry VI. He retired from politics in 1443 and died at Winchester. » Henry VI (of England); Hussites

Beaufort, Margaret (1443–1509) Daughter of John, 1st Duke of Somerset, and great-granddaughter of John of Gaunt, Duke of Lancaster. She married Edmund Tudor, Earl of Richmond (1455), and became the mother of Henry VII, to whom she conveyed the Lancastrian claim to the English crown. She was twice widowed before her third husband, Thomas, Lord Stanley, was instrumental in helping Henry VII assume the crown. She was a benefactress of William Caxton, and of Oxford and Cambridge. » Caxton; Henry VII (of England)

Beaufort Scale A scale of windspeed, ranging from 0 to 12, devised by Admiral Francis Beaufort (1774–1857) in the mid-19th-c, which uses descriptions of the way common outdoor features (eg smoke, trees) respond to different wind conditions. » hurricane; storm; wind [i]; RR15

Beaufort Sea [**boh**fuht] Region of the Arctic Ocean, N of Alaska and W of the Canadian Arctic archipelago; covered with pack-ice; major oil deposit discovered at Prudhoe Bay (1968), linked by pipeline to Valdez. » Arctic Ocean

Beauharnais, Alexandre, Vicomte de ('Viscount of') [bohah**nay**] (1760–94) French army officer, born in Martinique. He served in the American War of Independence, and in 1789 eagerly embraced the French Revolution. He was made secretary of the National Assembly, but was guillotined (1794) for his failure to relieve Metz. In 1779 he had married **Josephine**, afterwards wife of Napoleon, and his daughter **Hortense** in 1802 married Napoleon's brother Louis. Beauharnais was thus the grandfather of Napoleon III. He died in Paris. » French Revolution [i]; Napoleon III

Beaujolais [**boh**zholay] Sub-division of the old province of Lyonnais in EC France, now forming part of Rhône and Loire departments; granite upland on edge of Massif Central; major wine-growing region; N part known as Beaujolais Villages; centre Villefranche. » Massif Central; wine

Beaumarchais, Pierre-Augustin Caron de, [bohmah**shay**] (1732–99) French comic dramatist, born in Paris. His most successful comedies were *Le Barbier de Séville* (1775, The Barber of Seville) and *Le Mariage de Figaro* (1784, The Marriage of Figaro). The Revolution cost him his vast fortune, and suspected of selling arms he took refuge in Holland and England (1793). He died in Paris. » comedy; drama; French literature

Beaumont, Francis [**boh**mont] (c.1584–1616) English dramatist, born at Gracedieu, Leicestershire. Educated at Oxford, he entered the Inner Temple in 1600. He formed a close association with John Fletcher, writing many plays. Their 1647 and 1679 folios contain together 87 pieces. Modern research finds Beaumont's hand in only about 10 plays, *The Woman Hater* (1607) is attributed solely to him, and he had the major share in *The Knight of the Burning Pestle* (1609). He was buried in Westminster Abbey. » drama; English literature; Fletcher

Beauregard, P(ierre) G(ustave) T(outant) [bohruh**gah**] (1818–93) US Confederate general, born near New Orleans. He graduated at West Point (1838), served with distinction in the Mexican War, and was appointed by the Confederate government to the command at Charleston, where he commenced the war by the bombardment of Fort Sumter (12 Apr 1861). He fought at Bull Run (1861), took command at Shiloh (1862), and later defended Charleston and Richmond. After the war, he retired to Louisiana, and died in New Orleans. » American Civil War

beauty (physics) » **bottom**

Beauvais [boh**vay**] 49°25N 2°08E, pop (1982) 54 147. Market town and capital of Oise department, N France; on R Thérain, 76 km/47 ml N of Paris; railway; bishopric; former tapestry-making centre; agricultural equipment, rayon, tiles, fruit, dairy produce; tallest cathedral in France (68 m/223 ft). » tapestry

Beaux-Arts [**boh**zah] A decorative classical architectural style of the late 19th-c, particularly popular in France. The name derives from the Ecole des Beaux-Arts in Paris. It is typified by the grandeur of the Opéra, Paris (1861–75), architect J L C Garnier. » Beaux-Arts, Ecole des; Mexican architecture

Beaux-Arts, Ecole des [bohz**ah**, ay**kohl** day] The main official art school in Paris. It dates from 1648, when the first class was taught by Charles Le Brun. Abolished at the Revolution, but refounded in 1796, it was installed in its present quarters on the left bank of the Seine by 1830. It was immensely important throughout the 19th-c, but became notoriously conservative in the 20th-c. » Beaux-Arts; French art

beaver A large squirrel-like rodent from N America, N Europe, and Asia; semi-aquatic; hind feet webbed; tail broad, flat, and scaly; builds a 'lodge' from logs and mud in woodland ponds; often dams streams to create ponds; was formerly hunted for fur; young called *kits*. (Family: *Castoridae*, 2 species.) » mountain beaver; rodent; squirrel

Beaverbrook, Sir (William) Max(well) Aitken, 1st Baron (1879–1964) British newspaper magnate and politician, born at Maple, Ontario. After an early career as a stockbroker, he went to Britain (1910), entered Parliament, became private secretary to Bonar Law, and was knighted in 1911. He was made Minister of Information under Lloyd George, and a baronet. In 1916 he entered journalism, taking over the *Daily Express*, which he made into the most widely-read daily newspaper in the world. He founded the *Sunday Express* (1921) and bought the London *Evening Standard* (1929). His dynamic personality was caricatured in Evelyn Waugh's novel, *Scoop* (1938). He campaigned for Empire Free Trade, and his newspapers supported the Conservative government's policy of appeasement towards Hitler (1935–9). Once war broke out, he became actively involved, and was made Minister of Supply (1941–2), Minister of Production (1942), Lord Privy Seal (1943–5), and lend-lease administrator in the USA. He died near Leatherhead, Surrey. » Churchill, Winston; Conservative Party; Law, Bonar; Lloyd George; newspaper

bebop A jazz style, also known as **bop**, characterized by fast tempos and agitated rhythms, cultivated in the decade after World War 2 by small groups of musicians, among them Charlie Parker (1920–55), Dizzy Gillespie (1917–), and Thelonius Monk (1917–82). » jazz

beche de mer A French culinary term, referring to the food obtained from a marine animal found in the SW Pacific, also known as a *sea cucumber*; the name derives from Portuguese *bicho da mar* 'sea worm'. It is a part of some Chinese cuisine, but rarely appears on Western menus. » sea cucumber

Bechet, Sidney [**be**shay] (1897–1959) US soprano saxophonist, born in New Orleans. After starting on clarinet, he switched to soprano saxophone in order, he said, to dominate the brass in ensembles. His boldly lyrical solos made him second only to Louis Armstrong in the first jazz generation. Lionized in France on his first tour in 1919, he kept returning, and in 1949 became a permanent resident. He died in Paris. » Armstrong, Louis; jazz; saxophone

Beck, Aaron T(emkin) (1921–) US psychiatrist who introduced cognitive therapy as a treatment approach for neurotic disorders, particularly depression, born in Rhode Island. He became professor of psychiatry and director of the Center for Cognitive Therapy at the University of Pennsylvania. His books include *Depression: Causes and Treatment* (1972) and *Love is Never Enough* (1988). » cognitive therapy; depression (psychiatry); neurosis; psychiatry

Beck, Julian (1925–85) US actor, born and died in New York City. With Judith Malina (1926–) he was co-founder of the Living Theatre, and author of *The Life of the Theatre* (1972). » Living Theatre

Beckenbauer, Franz, byname **The Kaiser** [**bek**uhnbowuh] (1945–) West German footballer, born in Munich. The inspiration behind the rise of Bayern Munich in the 1960s, he made his first-team debut at the age of 18, and after only 27 matches made his international debut. He played in the West German side beaten by England in the 1966 World Cup, led his country to World Cup success in 1974, and won three successive European Cup winner's medals with Bayern Munich (1974–6). After a period playing in the USA, he returned to West Germany and won a fifth League title with Hamburg in 1982. He retired in 1983, and in 1984 was appointed coach to the West German national team. » football [i]

Becker, Boris (1967–) West German lawn tennis player, born at Leiman, the inaugural winner of the World Young Masters title, and the youngest winner of the men's singles at Wimbledon (17 yr 227 days), both in 1985. He retained the title in 1986, lost it in the 1988 final to Stefan Edberg, but regained it in 1989. In 1988 he was the World Championship Tennis champion and the Masters champion, and helped West Germany to their first Davis Cup. » tennis, lawn [i]

Becket, St Thomas (à) (1118–70), feast day 29 December. English saint and martyr, Archbishop of Canterbury, born in London. The son of a wealthy Norman merchant, he was educated in London and Paris, and studied canon law at Bologna and Auxerre. In 1155, he became Chancellor, the first Englishman since the Conquest to hold high office. A skilled diplomat and brilliant courtly figure, he changed dramatically when created Archbishop of Canterbury (1162), resigning the Chancellorship, and becoming a zealous ascetic, serving the Church as vigorously as he had the King. He thus came into conflict with Henry II's aims to keep the clergy in subordination to the state. He unwillingly consented to the Constitutions of Clarendon (1164) defining the powers of Church and state, but remained in disfavour. He fled the country after having his goods confiscated and the revenues of his sees sequestered. After two years in France, he pleaded personally to the Pope, and was reinstated in his see. In 1170 he was reconciled with Henry, and returned to Canterbury, amid great public rejoicing. New quarrels soon broke out, however, and Henry's rashly-voiced wish to be rid of 'this turbulent priest' led to Becket's murder in Canterbury cathedral (29 Dec 1170) by four of the king's knights. He was canonized in 1173, and Henry did public penance at his tomb in 1174. In 1220 his bones were transferred to the Trinity Chapel, for many years a popular place of pilgrimage, as described by Chaucer in the prologue to the *Canterbury Tales*. » Clarendon, Constitutions of; Henry II (of England)

Beckett, Samuel (Barclay) (1906–89) Irish novelist, poet, and playwright, born in Dublin. After lecturing in Paris and Dublin, and travelling in Europe, he settled in France (1937). His early poetry and first two novels, *Murphy* (1938) and *Watt* (published 1953) were written in English, but he later wrote in French, notably the novels *Molloy* (1951), *Malone Meurt* (1951, Malone Dies), and *L'Innommable* (1953, The Unnamable), and the play *En attendant Godot* (1954, Waiting for Godot), which later took London by storm. His work shows a preoccupation with the failure of human beings to communicate successfully, mirroring the pointlessness of life which they strive to make purposeful. He was awarded the 1969 Nobel Prize for Literature. He died in Paris » absurdism; drama; English/French/Irish literature

Beckmann, Max (1884–1950) German painter and engraver, born in Leipzig. He was one of several German Expressionist painters forced to flee by the Nazis. A brilliantly-coloured triptych entitled 'Departure' (1932–3) in the New York Museum of Modern Art is typical of his work. He also executed a large number of self-portraits in various graphic media, including drypoint and lithograph. He died in New York City. » Expressionism; German art; lithography

Becquerel, (Antoine) Henri [beke**rel**] (1852–1908) French physicist, born in Paris. He shared the Nobel Prize with the Curies in 1903 for discovering the **Becquerel rays** emitted from uranium salts, which led to the isolation of radium and the beginnings of modern nuclearphysics. He died at Le Croisic, France. His son **Jean**, was also a physicist. » becquerel; Curie; radium

becquerel [**bek**uhruhl] The activity of a radioactive source as the number of disintegrations per second; SI unit; symbol Bq; named after French physicist Antoine Henri Becquerel. »

Becquerel; radioactivity units [i]; units (scientific); RR70

bed bug A flattened, flightless bug. Adults and developing nymphs are nocturnal, emerging from concealment to suck blood mainly from mammals, including humans. They are a pest of human dwellings, but are not known to transmit diseases. » bug (entomology); nymph (entomology)

bed sore An ulcerated area of skin and subcutaneous tissue, usually over a bony prominence in bed-ridden or unconscious patients. The lesion is due to pressure which reduces the blood supply to the affected part. » ulcer

Bedchamber Crisis A British political crisis which occurred in May 1839, after Melbourne, Prime Minister in the Whig government, offered to resign, and advised the young Queen Victoria to appoint Peel and the Tories. The Queen refused to dismiss certain ladies of the Bedchamber with Whig sympathies, whereupon Peel refused office and the Whig government continued. » Melbourne, Lord; Peel; Victoria; Whigs

Bede or **Baeda, St**, byname **the Venerable Bede** (c.673–735), feast day 27 May. Anglo-Saxon historian and theologian, born near Monkwearmonth, Durham. He studied at the Benedictine monastery there, and was later transferred to Jarrow, where he wrote homilies, lives of the saints, hymns, epigrams, works on chronology and grammar, and commentaries on the Old and New Testament. His most valuable work is the *Historia Ecclesiastica Gentis Anglorum* (Ecclesiastical History of the English People), the source of almost all our information on the history of England before 731. He was buried at Jarrow; but in the 11th-c his bones were removed to Durham. » Anglo-Saxons; Benedictines

Bedford, John of Lancaster, Duke of (1389–1435) English general and statesman, the third son of Henry IV. In 1414 his brother (Henry V) created him Duke of Bedford, and during the war with France he was appointed Lieutenant of the Kingdom. After Henry's death (1422), he became Guardian of England and Regent of France. When Charles VI died, he had his nephew proclaimed King of France and England as Henry VI. In the Hundred Years' War, he defeated the French in several battles, notably at Verneuil (1424), but an army under Joan of Arc forced him onto the defensive (1429). He died at Rouen, and was buried in the cathedral there. » Henry VI (England); Hundred Years' War; Joan of Arc

Bedford 52°08N 0°29W, pop (1981) 77 014. County town in N Bedfordshire district, Bedfordshire, SC England; a residential town 32 km/20 ml SE of Northampton and 75 km/47 ml N of London; railway; foodstuffs, engineering; John Bunyan (1628–88) was imprisoned here for 12 years, during which time he wrote *The Pilgrim's Progress*. » Bedfordshire; Bunyan

Bedford Level » **Fens, the**

Bedfordshire pop (1987e) 525 900; area 1 235 sq km/477 sq ml. County in SC England, divided into four districts; drained W–E by the R Ouse; county town Bedford; chief towns include Luton, Dunstable; distribution centre, motor vehicles, bricks, wheat, barley. » Bedford; England [i]

Bedlington terrier A British breed of dog, with a tapering muzzle, and no obvious forehead in side view; coat curly, usually pale, but may be grey or brown. The original short-legged breed was crossed with the whippet to produce the longer-legged modern form. » terrier; whippet

Bednorz (Johannes) George (1950–) Swiss physicist, who graduated at Münster in 1976, and then worked with K A Müller at the IBM Zürich Research Laboratory at Rüschlikon. Their work was particularly directed to finding novel superconductors which would show superconductivity at higher temperatures than the near-absolute zero level previously observed. In 1986 they demonstrated that some mixed-phase oxides would superconduct above 30K, and by 1987 related materials were found to show the effect up to 90K, ie at a temperature which offered novel possibilities in practical electronics. The Nobel Prize for Physics followed for Bednorz and Müller, with exceptional speed, in 1987. » superconductivity

Bedouin Arabic-speaking nomads of Arabia, Syria, Jordan, Iraq, and other desert areas in the Middle East. They mainly herd animals in the desert during winter months – camels, sheep, goats, and (in the case of the Baqqarah) cattle – and cultivate land in summer; camel herders have the highest prestige. Many have been forced to settle in one locality, because of political or economic moves, such as restrictions on their grazing land, or nationalization of their land. They are divided into largely independent, endogamous patrilineal tribal groups, each controlled by its sheikh and council of male elders. There are also several vassal tribes, whose members work for others as artisans, blacksmiths, entertainers, etc. » Arabs; Baqqarah; nomadism

bedstraw An annual or perennial, found almost everywhere; weak, 4-angled stem, often with tiny hooks, narrow leaves in whorls; flowers tiny, white, yellow, or greenish, 4-petalled, in open clusters; fruits often burrs. (Genus: *Galium*, 400 species. Family: *Rubiaceae*.) » annual; perennial

bee A winged insect that builds and provisions nest for its young; the common name of several different types of hymenopteran, including solitary mining bees (Family: *Andrenidae*), carpenter bees (Family: *Anthophoridae*), bumblebees, orchid bees, stingless bees, and honeybees (all Family: *Apidae*). Social structure ranges from the solitary bees, in which each queen effectively raises her own brood, to honeybees, which form a complex society with a caste system and overlapping, co-operating generations. (Order: *Hymenoptera*.) » apiculture; bee dancing; bumblebee; carpenter/honey/leafcutter/mason bee; Hymenoptera; insect [i]; royal jelly

bee dancing The patterned movements of honey-bees used to signal the direction and distance of pollen and nectar to other members of the colony. The phenomenon was first documented by the Austrian biologist Karl von Frisch (1886–1982), who plotted the way in which worker bees perform circling or tail-wagging 'dances' depending on the distance of the food from the hive. » bee

bee-eater A brightly-coloured bird native to the Old World, especially Africa and S Asia; slender, pointed bill; eats ants, bees, and wasps caught in flight. Some species migrate thousands of kilometres. (Family: *Meropidae*, 24 species.)

bee-keeping » **apiculture**

bee orchid The name for various species of the genus *Ophrys*, widespread throughout Europe, W Asia, and N Africa; remarkable for their flowers which mimic insects. The lower lip (*labellum*) of the flower resembles a female insect in both colour and texture, and the flower emits a powerful pheromone-like scent to attract males of the same species. The males are induced to attempt copulation with the mimic, and in doing so pollinate the flower. In *Ophrys apifera*, which mimics bumblebees, the flowers are also capable of self-pollination. Other species of *Ophrys* resemble flies, wasps, sawflies, and even spiders. (Genus: *Ophrys*, 30 species. Family: *Orchidaceae*.) » mimicry; orchid [i]

beech A deciduous, shallow-rooted tree native to the N hemisphere; leaves oval, margins wavy; flowers tiny, males in long-stalked clusters, females (and later, nuts) in pairs enclosed in 4-lobed, spiny case. The leaves are very resistant to decay, forming deep, nutrient-poor litter in beech woods, discouraging the growth of other plants. Young beech trees retain dead leaves throughout the winter, and make good hedges. In the S hemisphere, it is replaced by the closely related **roble beech**. (Genus: *Fagus*, 10 species. Family: *Fagaceae*.) » deciduous plants; roble beech; tree [i]

Beecham, Sir Thomas (1879–1961) British conductor, born at St Helens, Lancashire. Educated at Rossall School and Oxford, he conducted opera at Covent Garden, and was made artistic director there in 1933. He founded the Royal Philharmonic Orchestra in 1946. A noted champion of Delius's music, he published in 1958 a study of the composer's life and works. He was also known for his candid pronouncements on musical matters, his 'Lollipop' encores, and his after-concert speeches. Knighted and made baronet in 1916, he died in London. » Delius

Beecher, Catharine (Esther) (1800–78) US author and educator, born at East Hampton, New York, into a famous New England family of religious leaders; the sister of Harriet Beecher Stowe. She campaigned throughout her life against feminism and in favour of domesticity, but in her own life was strongly independent. She died at Elmira, New York. » feminism; Stowe

Beecher Stowe, Harriet » **Stowe, Harriet (Elizabeth) Beecher**

Beecher, Henry Ward (1813–87) US Congregationalist preacher, born at Litchfield, Connecticut. He graduated at Amherst College, Massachusetts, and in 1847 became a pastor in New York, defending temperance and denouncing slavery. On the outbreak of the Civil War, his church raised and equipped a volunteer regiment. When the war was over, he became an earnest advocate of reconciliation. He died in New York City. » American Civil War; Congregationalism

beefeater » **Yeomen of the Guard**

Beelzebub (Gr **Beelzebul**) [bee-elzibuhb] In the New Testament Gospels, the 'prince of demons', the equivalent of Satan. He is possibly linked with the Old Testament figure *Baal-zebub* ('lord of flies'), the god of Ekron, or with the Canaanite *Baal-zebul* ('lord of the high place'). » Baal; Devil

beer An alcoholic beverage made from ale (malted barley) which has been flavoured with hops – a drink popular since ancient Egyptian times. It is currently an umbrella term covering a wide range of drinks, distinguished by the type of yeast used, such as *bitter* (a beer brewed with more hops and a lighter malt than *mild*), *lager* (a light beer which matures over a long period of time at a low temperature), and *stout* or *porter* (types of dark ale produced from the brewing of roasted malt). » ale; brewing

Beerbohm, Sir (Henry) Max(imilian) (1872–1956) British writer and caricaturist, born in London. He was educated at Charterhouse and Oxford, producing his first books of essays and drawings in 1896. He was drama critic of *The Saturday Review* until 1910, when he married an US actress, Florence Kahn, and retired (except during the two world wars) to Rapallo, Italy. He wrote many volumes of caricatures and parodying essays, but his best-known work was his novel on Oxford undergraduate life, *Zuleika Dobson* (1911). He was knighted in 1939. His first wife died in 1951, and a month before his own death he married her friend Elizabeth Jungmann. » caricature; English literature

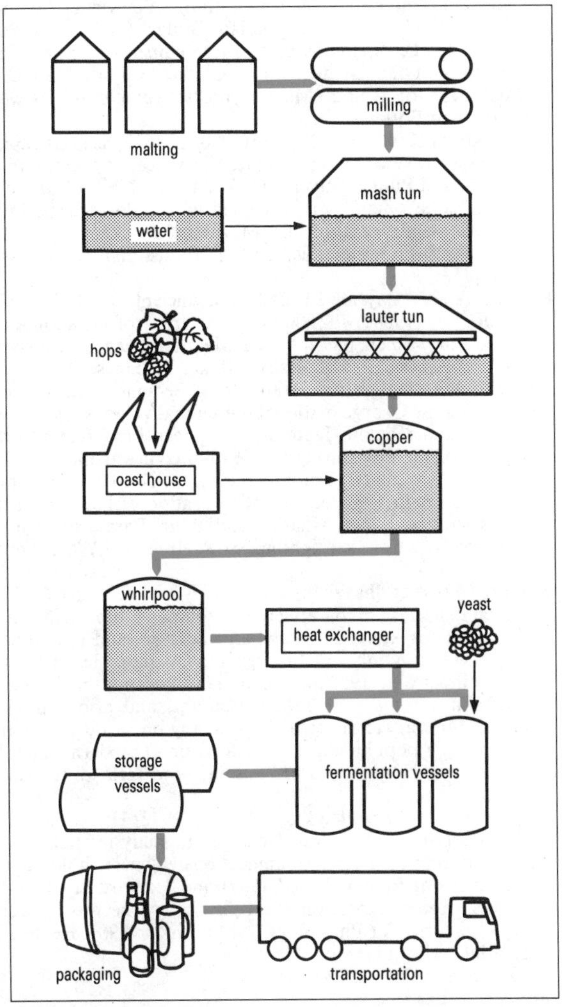

Beer – The brewing process, from malting to distribution

Beerbohm Tree » **Tree, Sir Henry (Draper) Beerbohm**

Beeston 52°56N 1°12W; pop(1981) 65 198. Town linked with Stapleford in Broxtowe district, Nottinghamshire, C England; 5 km/3 ml SW of Nottingham; railway; engineering, pharmaceuticals, textiles. » Nottinghamshire

beeswax Wax secreted by bees of the family *Apidae*, including bumblebees, stingless bees, and honeybees. It is produced by glands beneath the abdominal body plates (*sterna* or *terga*), and used in nest construction. » bee

beet Mostly annuals or perennials native to Europe and Asia; leaves shiny, often tinged dark red. Cultivated beets, all derived from the wild beet (*Beta vulgaris*), are divisible into two groups: **leaf beets**, including spinach beets and chards, are grown as leaf vegetables; **root beets**, including beetroot and mangel-wurzel, are biennials grown for their edible, swollen roots. **Sugar beet**, containing up to 20% sugar in the root, has largely replaced sugar cane as the source of sugar in W Europe. (Genus: *Beta*, 6 species. Family: *Chenopodiaceae*.) » chard; perennial; root (botany); sugars

Beethoven, Ludwig van [baytohvn] (1770–1827) German composer, born in Bonn. Miserably brought up by a father who wanted him to become a profitable infant prodigy, he joined the Elector of Cologne's orchestra at Bonn. In 1787 he had lessons from Mozart in Vienna, and in 1792 returned to that city for good, apart from a few excursions. He first joined Prince Lichnowsky's household and studied under Haydn, Albrechtsberger, and possibly Salieri. His music is usually divided into three periods. In the first (1792–1802), which includes the first two symphonies, the first six quartets, and the 'Pathétique' and 'Moonlight' sonatas, his style gradually develops its own individuality. His second period (1803–12) begins with the 'Eroica' Symphony (1803), and includes his next five symphonies, the difficult 'Kreutzer' sonata (1803), the Violin Concerto, the 'Archduke' trio (1811), and the 'Razumovsky' quartets. His third great period begins in 1813, and includes the Mass, the Choral Symphony (1823), and the last five quartets. Beethoven was tolerated by Vienna society despite his physical unattractiveness and arrogance. Just as he was developing a reputation as a composer, he began to go deaf, but stoically accepted the fact. None of this stopped him from falling in love with his pupils, including Giulietta Guicciardi and Josephine von Brunswick. From 1812 he was increasingly assailed by health, business, and family worries, which included prolonged litigation to obtain custody of his dead brother's son, Karl. His last work was completed at Gneixendorf in 1826, where he developed a severe chill (exacerbated by returning to Vienna in an open chaise), from which he died. » classical music; symphony

beetle A winged insect with forewings modified as rigid, horny cases covering membraneous hindwings and abdomen beneath; hindwings used in flight, sometimes missing; biting mouthparts; range in size from less than 0.5 mm/0.2 in to c.170 mm/7 in; development includes distinct larval and pupal phases; c.350 000 species known, including many pests. Most feed on live plants or plant material, but some are carnivorous or carrion-feeders. (Order: *Coleoptera*.) » ambrosia/bark/black/blister/bombardier/burying/carpet/click/Colorado/darkling/deathwatch/diving/dor/dung/elm bark/furniture/goliath/ground/hercules/leaf/oil/rove/soldier/stag/tiger/tortoise/water beetle; chafer; firefly; ladybird; larva; pupa; Spanish fly; weevil [i] whirligig

Beeton, Mrs, *née* **Isabella Mary Mayson** (1836–65) British writer on cookery. Educated at Heidelberg, she became an accomplished pianist. Her *Household Management* (1859-60), covering cookery and other branches of domestic science, made her name a household word. She died after the birth of her fourth son.

beetroot >> **beet**

Begin, Menachem (1913–) Israeli statesman and Prime Minister (1977–83), born and educated in Brest-Litovsk, Poland (now Russia). He studied law at Warsaw University, and was an active Zionist, becoming head of the Polish Zionist movement (1931). He fled to Russia in 1939, enlisted in the Free Polish Army (1941), and was sent to British-mandated Palestine. In 1943 he commanded the Irgun Zvai Leumi resistance group in Israel, and in 1948 founded the Herut Freedom Movement, becoming chairman of the Herut Party. In 1973 three parties combined to form the nationalist Likud Front with Begin as its leader, and in the 1977 elections he formed a coalition government. In the late 1970s he attended peace conferences in Jerusalem (Dec 1977) and at Camp David at the invitation of President Carter (Sep 1978). In 1978 he and President Sadat of Egypt were jointly awarded the Nobel Peace Prize. He resigned the premiership in 1983. >> Carter, Jimmy; Irgun; Israel [i]; Sadat

begonia Tuberous or rhizomatous perennials, a few shrubs or climbers, native to warm regions, especially America; leaves asymmetric, one side larger than the other, often spotted or marked with white or red male flowers with two large and two small petals, females with 4–5 more petals; fruit a winged capsule; sometimes called **elephant's ear**, from the shape of its leaves. It reproduces readily from leaf-cuttings placed on damp soil, a technique much-used in horticulture. Many species are grown for ornament. (Genus: *Begonia*, 900 species. Family: *Begoniaceae*.) >> climbing plant; horticulture; perennial; rhizome; shrub; tuber

Behan, Brendan (Francis) [**bee**an] (1923–64) Irish author, born in Dublin. Between 1939 and 1946 he was twice imprisoned for IRA activities, and though released by a general amnesty (1946), served further time in prison and in hospital (for alcoholism). His plays include *The Quare Fellow* (1956) and *The Hostage*, which displays an exuberant Irish wit, spiced with balladry and bawdry, and a talent for fantastic caricature. His other writing includes an autobiographical novel, *Borstal Boy* (1958). He died in Dublin, after a celebrated visit to the USA. >> IRA; Irish literature

Behar >> **Bihar**

behaviour/behavior modification Techniques for changing an individual's behaviour by controlling the consequences of the behaviour and/or the environmental conditions in which the behaviour occurs. It is employed to develop new behaviours or to eliminate existing ones. The approach is controversial, being viewed by some as a form of 'manipulation'; but it is a potentially valuable tool within applied psychology. >> behaviour therapy; conditioning; instrumental learning

behaviour/behavior therapy A type of psychological treatment formulated by psychotherapist Joseph Wolpe (1915–) which emphasizes the alteration of thoughts and behaviour. It is often applied to neurotic illnesses (eg phobias) on the presumption that these are learned forms of behaviour which can be 'unlearned'. The term was coined by the British psychologist H J Eysenck in the 1950s. The range of techniques now used include processes of desensitization and flooding for anxiety responses, cognitive therapy in depression, and the use of rewards and punishments for patients suffering from mental handicap. >> aversion therapy; cognitive therapy; neurosis; psychiatry

behaviourism/behaviorism The view that psychology is most effectively pursued by analysing the overt behaviour of people and animals, in preference to subjective states, thoughts, or hypothetical internal dynamics. It has had an important influence on modern psychology, but is now rarely held in extreme form. >> Skinner; Watson, John B

Behn, Aphra [bayn] (1640–89) The first English professional female author, born at Wye, Kent. She was brought up in Suriname, where she met the slave who was to be the subject of her novel *Oroonoko* (1688). She returned to England in 1663, and later became a professional spy at Antwerp. She received little thanks for her work, and on her return was imprisoned for debt. Her later poetry and plays are in the coarser Restoration style. She was buried in Westminster Abbey. >> English literature; Restoration

Behrens, Peter [**bay**rens] (1868–1940) German architect and designer, born in Hamburg. He began as a painter, but in 1909 was responsible for the 'first modern building', the AEG turbine factory in Berlin. His appointment as the designer of AEG electrical products was a landmark in the history of industrial design. He trained several leading modern architects, including Gropius and Le Corbusier. He died in Berlin. >> Gropius; Le Corbusier

Behring, Emil (Adolf) von [**bay**ring] (1854–1917) German bacteriologist, born at Hansdorf, W Prussia. Director of Marburg Hygiene Institute, he discovered diphtheria and tetanus antitoxins, and was awarded the first Nobel Prize for Physiology or Medicine (1901). He died at Marburg, Germany. >> diphtheria; tetanus

Beijing [bay**zhing**] or **Peking**, also **Peiping** 39°55N 116°25E; municipality pop (1982) 9 230 687; urban centre pop (1984e) 5 754 600; municipality area 17 800 sq km/6 871 sq ml. Capital city and municipality of NE China; secondary capital of Liao dynasty (10th-c) and then capital of succeeding dynasties; occupied by Japanese (1937–45); capital of China, 1949; airport; railway; two universities (1898, 1950); textiles, petrochemicals, light and heavy engineering, electricity production; Imperial Palace, formerly known as the 'Forbidden City'; Tiananmen (Gate of Heavenly Peace, built 1417, restored 1651), Tiananmen Square, Mao Zedong Memorial Hall (1977), Niu Jie (oldest Muslim temple, 996), Fayuan Si Temple (696), Tiantan (Temple of Heaven, 15th-c), Yiheyuan (Summer Palace, rebuilt 1888), Lugouqiao Bridge (or Marco Polo Bridge); to the N, tombs of 13 Ming emperors; 75 km/47 ml NW, part of the Great Wall of China. >> Forbidden City; Great Wall of China; Ming dynasty; Temple of Heaven; Tiananmen Square

Beira [**bay**ra] 19°46S 34°52E, pop (1980) 214 613. Seaport capital of Sofala province, Mozambique, SE Africa, at the mouth of the Buzi and Pungué Rivers, 725 km/450 ml NNE of Maputo; Mozambique's main port; occupied by the Portuguese, 1506; founded as the seat of the Mozambique Company, 1891; airport; railway; minerals, cotton, foodstuffs. >> Mozambique [i]

Beirut, Arabic **Bayrut**, Fr **Beyrouth**, ancient **Berytus** 33°52N 35°30E, pop (1980e) 702 000. Seaport capital of Lebanon, on a promontory which juts into the Mediterranean Sea; airport; railway; American University (1866), Lebanese University (1953), Arab University (1960); Grand Seraglio, Cathedrals of St Elie and St George, national museum; divided between rival political and religious factions; the 'Green Line' refers to the division of the city during the 1975–6 civil war into Muslim (W) and Christian (E) sectors; Israeli attack on Palestinian and Syrian forces in 1982 led to the evacuation of Palestinians to camps such as Sabra, Chatila, and Bourj Barajneh; severely damaged by continued fighting. >> Arab–Israeli Wars; Lebanon [i]; PLO

Béjart, Maurice [**bay**zhah] originally **Maurice Berger** (1927–) French dancer, choreographer, and company director, born in Marseilles. He studied in Paris and London, and toured as a dancer with a number of European companies. He started his own company in 1953, which in 1959 became the Brussels-based Ballet of the Twentieth Century, and also started a school, Mudra. He directed his company on worldwide tours, developing a popular expressionistic form of modern ballet. In 1988 the company moved to Lausanne, Switzerland. >> ballet; modern dance

Békésy, Georg von [**bay**kuhzee] (1899–1972) Hungarian physiologist, born in Budapest. He began to study the human ear after working as a telecommunications engineer, holding appointments at Stockholm (1945–9) and Harvard (1949). The world's greatest expert on aural physiology, he was awarded the Nobel Prize for Physiology or Medicine in 1961. He died in Honolulu, Hawaii. >> cochlea; ear [i]

Bekka, the >> **Beqaa, el**

bel >> **decibel**

Bel and the Dragon An addition to the Book of Daniel, part of the Old Testament Apocrypha, or Chapter 14 of Daniel in

Catholic versions of the Bible. It contains two popular tales, probably from the 2nd-c BC: one of how Daniel discredited Bel (patron god of Babylon) and its priests, and the other of Daniel in the lion's den. » Apocrypha, Old Testament; Daniel, Book of

Belau, also **Palau** or **Pelau**, official name **Republic of Belau** [puh**low**] 7°30N 134°30E; pop (1990e) 14 800; area 494 sq km/ 191 sq ml. Group of c.350 small islands and islets, the smallest of the four political units to emerge out of the US Trust Territory of the Pacific Islands, W Pacific Ocean; c.960 km/600 ml E of the Philippines; most W group of the Caroline Is; timezone GMT +10; chief languages, Palauan, English; largest island, Babeldoab (367 sq km/142 sq ml); warm climate all year, with high humidity; average annual temperature, 27°C; average annual rainfall, 3 810 mm/150 in; typhoons common; held by Germany, 1899–1914; mandated to Japan by League of Nations, 1920; invaded by USA, 1944; government combines elements of a modern democratic system and a system of hereditary chiefs; tourism, taro, pineapple, breadfruit, bananas, yams, citrus fruit, coconuts, pepper, fishing. » Koror; United States Trust Territory of the Pacific Islands

Belém [be**lem**], also called **Pará** 1°27S 48°29W, pop (1980) 755 984. Port capital of Pará state, Norte region, N Brazil; at the mouth of the Tocantins R; founded in 1616; university (1957); airport; railway; trade in jute, nuts, rubber, black pepper, cassava, aluminium; cathedral (1748); Paz Theatre, Santo Aleixandre Museum of Religious Art; Goeldi Museum, 17th-c Mercês Church, Basilica of Nossa Senhora de Nazaré (1909). » Brazil [i]

Belém Monastery A magnificent monastery of the Hieronymite hermit order founded in 1499 by Emmanuel I in Belém, a present-day suburb of Lisbon, Portugal. It commemorates Vasco da Gama's discovery of a sea-passage to India, and was built on the site of the chapel in which he is said to have prayed. The complex includes a museum and the Church of Santa Maria. » Emmanuel I; Gama, Vasco da; monasticism

belemnite An extinct, squid-like mollusc; found extensively as fossil shells from the Upper Carboniferous period to the Eocene epoch; shell internal in life, typically bullet-shaped. (Class: *Cephalopoda*. Order: *Belemnoidea*.) » Carboniferous period; Cephalopoda [i]; Eocene epoch; mollusc; squid

Belfast, Gaelic **Beal Feirste** 54°35N 5°55W, pop (1981) 358 991. Capital of Northern Ireland in Antrim, NE Northern Ireland; at the mouth of the Lagan R, on Belfast Lough; original settlement and castle destroyed in 1177; settled in the 17th-c by English, Scots, and Huguenots, becoming a centre of Irish Protestantism; capital, 1920; well-defined Nationalist (Catholic) and Unionist (Protestant) areas; disrupted by civil unrest since 1968; two airports (Aldergrove, City); railway; university (1908); shipyards, aircraft, linen, engineering, footwear, food processing; city hall (1900), St Anne's Cathedral (begun 1898), Ulster Museum, Parliament House at Stormont. » Antrim (county); Huguenots; Northern Ireland [i]; Protestantism; Roman Catholicism; Stormont

Belgium, official name **Kingdom of Belgium**, Fr **Royaume de Belgique**, Flemish **Koninkrijk België** pop (1990e) 9 958 000; area 30 540 sq km/11 788 sq ml. Kingdom of NW Europe, divided into nine provinces; bounded N by the Netherlands, S by France, E by Germany and Luxembourg, and W by the North Sea; coastline 64 km/40 ml; capital, Brussels; chief towns Antwerp, Ghent, Charleroi, Liège, Bruges, Namur, Mons; timezone GMT +1; a line drawn E–W just S of Brussels divides the population, by race and language, into two approximately equal parts; to the N, Flemings of Teutonic stock, speaking Flemish; to the S, French-speaking Latins, known as Walloons; ethnic divisions 55% Fleming, 33% Walloon, 12% mixed or other; languages, 56% Flemish (Dutch), 32% French, 1% (on E border) German; Brussels officially a bilingual city; religion, 75% Roman Catholic; currency, Belgian franc of 100 centimes.

Physical description and climate. Mostly low-lying, with some hills in the SE region (Ardennes), average elevation 300–500 m/1 000–1 600 ft; large areas of fertile soil, intensively cultivated for many centuries; main river systems, Sambre-Meuse and Scheldt, drain across the Dutch border, linked by complex network of canals; low-lying, dune-fringed coastline of 64 km/40 ml along the North Sea; climate cool and temperate with strong maritime influences.

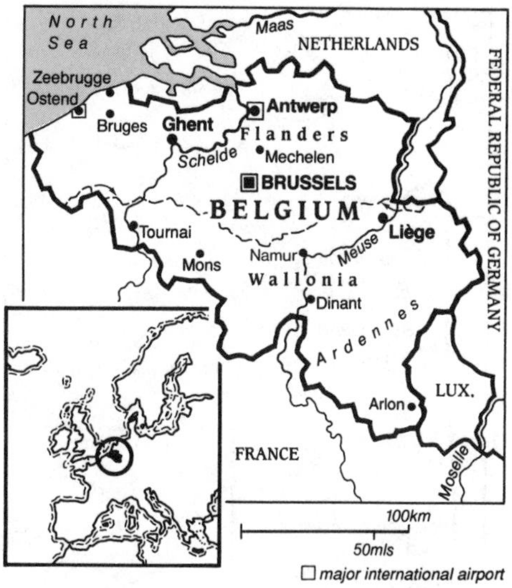

History and government. Part of the Roman Empire until 2nd-c AD; invasion by Germanic tribes, and part of the Frankish Empire; early Middle Ages, growth of several semi-independent provinces and cities, from 1385 absorbed by the House of Burgundy; ruled by the Habsburgs from 1477 until the Peace of Utrecht (1713), known as the Spanish Netherlands; transferred to Austria as the Austrian Netherlands, 1713; conquered by the French, 1794; part of the French Republic and Empire until 1815, then united with the Netherlands; Belgian rebellion, 1830, led to recognition as an independent kingdom under Leopold of Saxe-Coburg; occupied by Germany in both World Wars; a hereditary and constitutional monarchy, legislative power vested in a monarch, a 182-member Senate, and a 212-member Chamber of Representatives; in recent decades, political tension between Walloons and Flemings has caused the collapse of several governments; Wallonia and Flanders given regional 'subgovernments', 1980; new federal constitution divided Belgium into the autonomous regions of Flanders, Wallonia, and Brussels, 1989.

Economy. One of the earliest countries in Europe to industrialize, using rich coalfields of the Ardennes; famous textile industry of Flanders since Middle Ages; long-standing centre for European trade; major iron and steel industry, with wide range of metallurgical and engineering products; processed food and beverages, chemicals, textiles, glass, petroleum, trade in gemstones (especially diamonds); agriculture mainly livestock; also wheat, potatoes, sugar-beet, flax; full economic union (Benelux Economic Union) between Belgium, Netherlands, and Luxembourg in 1948; member of EEC; Brussels the headquarters of several major international organizations. » Brussels; European Economic Community; Franks; Netherlands, The [i]; Zaire [i]; RR24 national holidays; RR43 political leaders

Belgrade, Serbo-Croatian **Beograd, ancient Singidunum** 44°50N 20°30E, pop (1981) 1 470 073. Capital city of Yugoslavia and of the republic of Serbia, at the junction of the Danube and Sava Rivers; airport; railway; university (1863); arts university (1957); communications centre; machine tools, electrical equipment, light engineering, vehicles, pharmaceuticals, textiles, foodstuffs; Kalemegdan fortress, Prince Eugene's Gate (1719), Palace of Princess Ljubica, St Mark's Church, tomb of Sheikh Mustapha, cathedral, several museums; international film festival (Feb), international festival of modern dramatic art (Sep), Belgrade Music Festival (Oct). » Serbia; Yugoslavia [i]

Belgrano, General [bel**grah**noh] An Argentinian cruiser, formerly owned by the US Navy in World War 2, sunk by HM

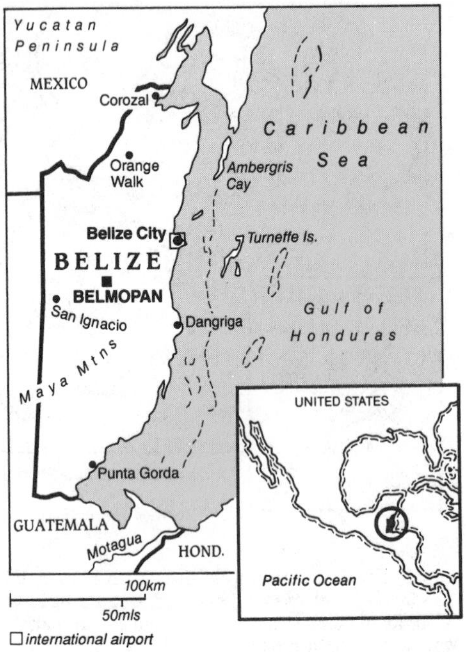

submarine *Conqueror* during the Falklands conflict in 1982 with great loss of life. Her armament of fifteen 6-inch guns posed a serious threat to the ships of the British task force, but her sinking proved to be one of the most controversial incidents of the war. » Falklands War

Belisarius [beli**sah**riuhs] (505–65) Byzantine general under the Emperor Justinian, born at Germania, Illyria. He defeated the Persians (530), suppressed an insurrection in Constantinople (532), and defeated the Vandals in Africa (533–4) and the Ostrogoths in Italy (535–40). He later again drove back the Persians (542), and repelled an assault of the Huns on Constantinople (559). Falsely accused of conspiracy against the Emperor, he was imprisoned (562), but was restored to favour soon after. » Huns; Justinian; Narses; Ostrogoths; Vandals

Belize, formerly **British Honduras** (to 1973) [**beleez**] pop (1990e) 189 000; area 22 963 sq km/8 864 sq ml. Independent state in C America, divided into six districts; bounded N by Mexico, W and S by Guatemala, and E by the Caribbean Sea; capital, Belmopan; chief towns Belize City, Dangriga, Punta Gorda, San Ignacio; timezone GMT −6; main ethnic groups, Creoles, Spanish-Mayan Mestizos, Caribs, several minorities; c.60% Roman Catholic; official language, English, with Spanish and local Mayan languages also spoken; currency, Belize dollar of 100 cents.

Physical description and climate. An extensive coastal plain, swampy in the N, more fertile in the S; Maya Mts extend almost to the E coast, rising to 1 120 m/3 674 ft at Victoria Peak, flanked by pine ridges, tropical forests, savannahs, and farm land; Belize R flows W–E; inner coastal waters protected by world's second longest barrier reef; generally subtropical climate, but tempered by trade winds; coastal temperatures 10°–35.6°C, with greater range in mountains; variable rainfall, average 1 295 mm/51 in (N), 4 445 mm/175 in (S); dry season (Feb–May); often damaged by hurricanes.

History and government. Evidence of early Mayan settlement; colonized in the 17th-c by shipwrecked British sailors and disbanded soldiers from Jamaica, who defended the territory against the Spanish; created a British colony in 1862, administered from Jamaica until 1884; ministerial system of government, 1961; internal self-government, 1964; changed name from British Honduras to Belize, 1973; full independence, 1981; Guatemalan claims over Belize territory have led to a continuing British military presence; governor-general represents British monarch, and appoints a prime minister; bicameral National Asssembly, with an 8-member Senate and a 28-member House of Representatives.

Economy. Traditionally based on timber and forest products, more recently on agriculture, especially sugar, citrus fruit, cocoa, rice, tobacco, bananas, beef; fishing, boatbuilding, food processing, textiles, furniture, batteries, cigarettes. » Belmopan; Guatemala [i]; Jamaica [i]; Mayas; RR24 national holidays; RR43 political leaders

Belize City 17°29N 88°10W, pop (1980) 39 771. Seaport capital of Belize district, Belize, C America; at the mouth of the Belize R where it meets the Caribbean Sea; capital of Belize until 1970; occasionally badly damaged by hurricanes; airport; timber, coconuts, fishing, commerce, tourism. » Belize [i]

bell A hollow vessel of bronze or other material which, when struck, vibrates to produce a sound (or rather, a complex of sounds) which, if the bell is tuned, may be heard as a musical note of definite pitch. Bells have been made for some 4 000 years for a variety of uses and in many different shapes and sizes. A bell fastened to a cat's collar as a warning to birds may be no larger than a small gooseberry; the enormous 'Tsar Kolokol' bell in the Kremlin, Moscow, is about 6 m 90 cm/22 ft 8 in in diameter and weighs over 200 000 kg/190 tons. These two examples also illustrate the two basic types of bell. The cat's bell is of the *closed* (or *crotal*) variety: a hollowed sphere, with one or more slits in the surface, which is shaken to cause a loose pellet inside to strike against the inner surface. The Kremlin monster is an example of the open bell, cast (like most ship's bells and church bells) in the shape of an upturned cup; such bells are usually sounded by means of a clapper suspended from the inside of the bell, but in some cases (such as the huge bells of some Buddhist temples) they are struck externally with a ramrod. » bell-ringing; carillon; change ringing; idiophone; timbre; tubular bells

Bell, Alexander Graham (1847–1922) British-US inventor, born in Edinburgh, Scotland. He was educated in Edinburgh and London, then went to Canada, and in 1871 became professor of vocal physiology at Boston. He devoted himself to the teaching of deaf-mutes and to spreading his father's system of 'visible speech'. He invented the articulating telephone (1872–6), the photophone (1880), and the graphophone (1887). He died in Cape Breton I, Canada. » Bell, A M; telephone

Bell, Alexander Melville (1819–1905) British-US educationalist, born in Edinburgh, Scotland. He became a teacher of elocution, moving to London (1865) and Canada (1870), settling finally in Washington. His numerous works connected with phonetics include *Visible Speech* (1867). » elocution; phonetics

Bell, Acton/Currer/Ellis » **Brontë, Anne/Charlotte/Emily**

bell-flower A large variable genus of mostly annuals and herbaceous perennials, low and spreading to tall and erect, often forming clumps, native throughout N temperate regions; leaves very narrow to almost circular; flowers 5-lobed bells, usually large and showy, and almost always blue, sometimes pink or white, solitary or in long inflorescences; fruit a capsule opening by pores, shedding seeds like a pepper-pot when shaken. Many species are cultivated for ornament. (Genus: *Campanula*, 300 species. Family: *Campanulaceae*.) » annual; Canterbury bell; herbaceous plant; inflorescence [i]; perennial

bell-ringing The art of ringing church bells, known as **campanology**. Its two popular forms are *change ringing*, a hand-pulled method, and the *carillon* method, performed with the use of a keyboard connected to the clapper of the bells. » bell; change ringing

Bell's palsy The paralysis of the muscles of one side of the face innervated by the VIIth cranial nerve (the facial nerve). Damage to the nerve may be caused by trauma, virus infection, or undue pressure as the nerve emerges through its canal at the base of the skull. The condition is named after Scottish surgeon Charles Bell (1774–1842). » central nervous system; muscle [i]; paralysis

belladonna (Lat 'fair lady') A liquid extract of the deadly nightshade plant (*Atropa belladonna*), so-called because Italian ladies used to apply it to their eyes to make the pupils dilate, an effect deemed attractive. The main active constituent is atropine. » atropine

belladonna lily A large bulb, native to S Africa; leaves strap-shaped; flowers trumpet-shaped, 7–9 cm/2¾–3½ in long, white to pink, 6–12 on a solid stalk appearing in autumn after the leaves have died. A popular ornamental, it is often confused with *Hippeastrum*, which is the amaryllis of horticulture. (*Amaryllis bella-donna*. Family: *Amaryllidaceae*). » amaryllis; bulb; horticulture

Bellarmine, St Robert (Francis Romulus) [**bel**ahmin] (1542–1621), feast day 17 May. Jesuit cardinal and theologian, the chief defender of the Church in the 16th-c, born at Montepulciano, Italy. He joined the Jesuits in 1560, studied theology at Padua and Louvain, and became professor of theology at Louvain (1570), then lecturer (1576) and rector at the Roman College. In 1599 he was made a cardinal, against his own inclination, in 1602 Archbishop of Capua, and he worked in the Vatican from 1605 until his death. He was canonized in 1931. » Galileo; Jesuits; theology

Bellay, Joachim du (1522–60) French poet and prose writer, born at Lire, Anjou. His *Défence et illustration de la langue françoise* (1549) was the manifesto of the Pléiade, advocating a return to classical and Italian models. It was accompanied by a set of Petrarchian sonnets, *L'Olive*, dedicated to an unknown lady. A visit to Rome in 1553 inspired other collections of sonnets. He died in Paris. » French literature; Pléiade, la

Bellerophon [be**le**rofohn] In Greek mythology, a hero who was sent to Lycia with a letter telling the king to put him to death. The king set him impossible adventures, notably the killing of the Chimera. In later accounts it is said that Athena helped him to tame Pegasus. » Chimera; Pegasus (mythology)

Bellingshausen, Fabian Gottlieb von [**be**lingshowzn] (1778–1852) Russian explorer, born in Oesel. In 1819–21 he led an Antarctic expedition as far south as 70°, and gave his name to the Bellingshausen Sea. He died at Kronstadt. » Antarctica [i]

Bellini A family of 15th-c Venetian painters. **Jacopo** (c.1400–70) studied under Gentile da Fabriano, painting a wide range of subjects, but only a few of his works remain. His son **Gentile** (c.1429–1507) worked in his father's studio, and painted many portraits, especially that of Sultan Mohammed II in Constantinople (now in the National Gallery, London). His other son, **Giovanni** (c.1430–1516) was the greatest Venetian painter of his time. He painted many 'Pietà' and 'Madonna' themes, altarpieces, and pagan allegories, notably 'The Feast of the Gods' (1514). His innovations of light and colour became the hallmark of Venetian art, continued by his pupils Giorgione and Titian. » Italian art; Venetian School

Bello, Andrés [**bay**oh] (1781–1865) Venezuelan writer and polymath, born in Caracas, the most remarkable Latin American intellectual of the 19th-c. Educated in Caracas, he lived in London (1810–29) before finally settling in Chile, where he became a senior public servant, senator, and first rector of the university (1843). His writings embrace language, law, education, history, philosophy, poetry, drama, and science. He died in Santiago, Chile.

Belloc, (Joseph) Hilaire (Pierre) (1870–1953) Anglo-French writer and poet, born at St Cloud, near Paris. He was educated at the Oratory School, Birmingham, under Newman, and at Oxford, but did military service in the French army. He became a Liberal MP (1906–10), then continued as a writer, best known for his nonsensical verse for children, *The Bad Child's Book of Beasts* (1896) and the *Cautionary Tales* (1907). He also wrote numerous travel books, historical studies, and religious books. A devoted Roman Catholic, in 1934 the Pope made him a Knight Commander of the Order of St Gregory. He died at Guildford, Surrey. » English literature; Newman, John; Roman Catholicism

Bellow, Saul (1915–) US writer, born at Lachine, Quebec. He was educated at Chicago and Northwestern Universities, but then abandoned his studies to become a writer. His first novel was *Dangling Man* (1944), and others include *The Victim* (1947), *Herzog* (1964), and *Humboldt's Gift* (1975). In 1962 he was appointed a professor at Chicago University, and in 1976 awarded the Nobel Prize for Literature. » American literature

Belmopan [belmoh**pan**] 17°18N 88°30W, pop (1980) 2 935. Capital of Belize, C America, between the Belize and Sibun Rivers, 80 km/50 ml W of Belize City; made capital in 1970, following major hurricane damage to Belize City in 1961; new settlement at the Valley of Peace for refugees from El Salvador and Guatemala was made permanent in 1985. » Belize [i]

Belo Horizonte [**be**loh oree**zon**tay] 19°54S 43°54W, pop (1980) 1 441 567. Commercial and industrial capital of Minas Gerais state, Sudeste region, SE Brazil; N of Rio de Janeiro, altitude 800 m/2 625 ft; Brazil's first planned modern city, built in the 1890s; airport nearby; airfield; railway; 3 universities (1927, 1954, 1958); industrial area (c.10 km/6 ml from city centre) third largest in Brazil; commerce, mining, steel, cars, textiles, meat processing; Minascentro Convention Centre, Mineirão sports stadium (second largest in Brazil), Museum of Modern Art, monument in the Parque de Mangabeiras commemorating Pope's visit of 1982; notable modern architecture in suburb of Pampulha. » Brazil [i]; Minas Gerais

Belorussia or **White Russia**, Russ **Belorusskaya**, official name **Republic of Byelarus** (from 1991), pop (1989) 10 200 000; area 207 600 sq km/80 134 sq ml. Republic in NE Europe, bounded W by Poland; largely flat, with low hills in the NW rising to 345 m/1 132 ft; chief rivers, the Dnieper, Zapadnaya Dvina, Neman; c.11 000 lakes; a third covered by forests; proclaimed a Soviet Socialist Republic, 1919; declaration of independence, 1990; capital, Minsk; machine tools, vehicles, agricultural machinery, glass, foodstuffs, fertilizers, textiles, electronics, artificial silk, flax, and leather, oil extraction and refining, salt extraction; farmland covers 46% of the land area; meat and dairy production, flax. » Minsk; Soviet Union [i]

Belshazzar [bel**shad**zer] Gr **Balthasar** or **Baltasar** (?–539 BC) Son of Nabonidus, King of Babylon (556–539 BC), and ruler of Babylon under his father until his death at the capture of Babylon and the fall of the Neo-Babylonian Empire. In the Book of Daniel, mysterious writing appears on the wall of his palace which Daniel interprets as predicting the fall of the Empire to the Persians and Medes. » Babylon; Daniel, Book of

Beltane An ancient Celtic festival held at the beginning of May, and also in late June, when bonfires were lit on the hills. The custom continued in many localities, especially in the N of Scotland, into the last century, and is still celebrated in Peebles. Beltane was formerly a quarter-day in Scotland. » quarter-day

beluga (fish) [bi**loo**ga] A very large sturgeon found in the Caspian Sea, Black Sea, and adjacent rivers; body length up to 5 m/16 ft; weight over 1 000 kg/2 200 lb; fished commercially for caviar, but numbers now much reduced by over-fishing and pollution; one of the largest freshwater fish known. (*Huso huso*. Family: *Acipenseridae*.) » caviar; sturgeon

beluga (mammal) [bi**loo**ga] A small toothed whale, native to shallow Arctic seas and rivers; white when adult; no dorsal fin; eats fish, squid, crustaceans, and molluscs; also known as the **white whale** or **sea canary**. (*Delphinapterus leucas*. Family: *Monodontidae*.) » whale [i]

Belukha, Mount [byi**look**ha] 49°46N 86°40E. Highest peak in the Altai range; height 4 506 m/14 783 ft; gives rise to 16 glaciers. » Altai Mountains

Bembo, Pietro (1470–1547) Italian poet and scholar, born in Venice. In 1513 he was made secretary to Pope Leo X, and in 1539 became a cardinal. He wrote one of the first Italian grammars, and helped to codify the writing system. He died in Rome. » grammar

Bemis Heights, Battle of A preliminary conflict during the Saratoga campaign, in the US War of Independence. » Saratoga, Battle of

Ben Bella, Ahmed (1918–) Key figure in the Algerian War of Independence against France, and Algeria's first Prime Minister (1962–3) and President (1963–5), born at Maghnia, Algeria. He fought with the Free French in World War 2, and in 1949 became head of the Organisation Spéciale, the paramilitary wing of the Algerian nationalist Parti du Peuple Algérien. In 1952 he escaped from a French-Algerian prison to Cairo, where he became a key member of the Front de Libération Nationale

(FLN). Captured by the French in 1956, he spent the remainder of the War in a French prison. Following independence (1962) he became President, but was deposed in 1965. After 15 years of imprisonment, he went into voluntary exile in 1980, returning to Algeria in 1990. » Algeria [i]; FLN

Ben-Gurion, David, originally **David Gruen** (1886–1973) Israeli statesman and Prime Minister (1948–53, 1955–63), born at Plonsk, Poland. Attracted to the Zionist Socialist movement, he emigrated to Palestine (1906), where he formed the first Jewish trade union (1915). Expelled by the Turks, he helped to raise the Jewish Legion in America. In 1930 he became leader of the Mapai (Labour) Party, which was the ruling party in the state of Israel when the state was announced (May 1948). In 1953 he retired from the premiership, resumed it in 1955, and finally retired in 1963. He died in Tel Aviv. » Israel [i]; Zionism

Ben Macdhui, Gaelic **Ben Muich-Dhui** [muhk**doo**ee] 57°04N 3°40W. Second highest mountain in the UK; in Cairngorm Mts, SW Grampian region, NC Scotland; 29 km/18 ml WNW of Braemar; height 1 309 m/4 295 ft. » Cairngorms; Grampians (Scotland)

Ben Nevis 56°48N 5°00W. Highest mountain in the UK; in Grampian Mts, Highland region, W Scotland; 7 km/4 ml E of Fort William; height 1 344 m/4 409 ft. » Grampians (Scotland); Highland

Ben-Zvi, Itzhak (1884–1963) Israeli statesman and President (1952–63), born at Poltava, Ukraine. He migrated to Palestine in 1907, where he became a prominent Zionist, and a founder of the Jewish Labour party. He was elected President on the death of Weizmann. A prominent scholar and archaeologist, he wrote on the history of the Middle East. He died in Jerusalem. » Weizmann; Zionism

Benares, Banares [ben**ah**res], or **Varanasi**, ancient **Kasi** 25°22N 83°08E, pop (1981) 794 000. City in Uttar Pradesh state, N India; on N bank of R Ganges, 120 km/75 ml E of Allahabad; one of the seven most sacred Hindu cities, reputed to be Siva's capital while on Earth; also a holy city of Buddhists, Sikhs, and Jains; Hindu city since the 6th-c; invaded by Afghans, 1033; ceded to Britain, 1775; airfield; railway; two universities (1916, 1958); textiles, brassware, jewellery; over 1 400 Hindu temples and shrines, including the Golden Temple (1777) and Durga Temple; stairs (*ghats*) along c.7 km/4 ml of the high bank of the Ganges, used by pilgrims to bathe in the sacred waters; mosque dedicated to Muslim emperor Aurangzeb. » Buddhism; Ganges, River; Hinduism; Jainism; Sikhism; Uttar Pradesh

Benbow, John (1653–1702) British admiral, born at Shrewsbury, Shropshire. His main engagements were in the Nine Years' War (1690, 1693, 1694) and the War of the Spanish Succession, when he came upon a superior French force in the West Indies (1702). For four days he kept up a running fight from Santa Marta, almost deserted by the rest of his squadron, until he was wounded. He was forced to return to Jamaica, where he died. » Spanish Succession, War of the

benchmark A surveyor's mark placed permanently on some buildings and rock outcrops. Their elevations are surveyed with respect to a fixed datum level, and can be used in further topographical surveys. » Ordnance Datum; surveying

Bendigo [**ben**digoh] 36°48S 144°21E, pop (1983e) 32 880. City in NC Victoria, Australia, NNW of Melbourne; centre of a wine-producing area; gold mined here until the 1950s; railway; agricultural trade, textiles, rubber, railway engineering; the Central Deborah gold mine; wax museum; reconstructed Sandhurst Town; the Bendigo Pottery (1858), Australia's oldest pottery; the only surviving Chinese Joss House of the 1860s; Chinese Dragon Festival at Easter. » Australian gold rush; Victoria (Australia)

Benedict, St (of Nursia) (c.480–c.547), feast day 21 March. Italian saint, the founder of Western monasticism, born at Nursia. At about the age of 14 he withdrew from society, living as a hermit. The fame of his piety led to his being appointed the abbot of a monastery at Vicovaro; but he did not find the rule strict enough, and so retreated to Subiaco, where he founded 12 small monastic communities which followed the rule he devised (c.515). He ultimately established a monastery on Monte Cassino, which became one of the most famous in Italy. His **Benedictine rule** in due course became the common rule of all Western monasticism. » Benedictines; monasticism

Benedict XV, originally **Giacomo della Chiesa** (1854–1922) Pope (1914–22), born at Pegli, Sardinia, Italy. He was ordained at 24, and after some years in the papal diplomatic service became Archbishop of Bologna (1907) and cardinal (1914). He was elected to succeed Pius X (1914), made repeated efforts to end World War 1, and organized war relief on a munificent scale. He died in Rome. » pope; World War 1

Benedictines A religious order following the 'rule' of St Benedict of Nursia; properly known as the **Order of St Benedict (OSB)**. The order consists of autonomous congregations, and has a long tradition of scholarship and promotion of learning. » Benedict, St; Maurists

Benelux A customs union between Belgium, the Netherlands, and Luxembourg which came into existence in 1947 as the result of a convention concluded in London in 1944. Despite the difficulties of achieving economic integration and the exclusion of agriculture from the union, mutual trade between the three countries expanded. A treaty established a more ambitious economic union between the three in 1958.

Beneš, Edvard [**ben**esh] (1884–1948) Czech statesman and President (1935–8, 1939–45 in exile, 1946–8), born at Kožlany. He was professor of sociology at Prague, then as a refugee during World War 1 worked in Paris with Masaryk for Czech nationalism, becoming Foreign Minister of the new state (1918–35), and for a while Premier (1921–2). In 1935 he succeeded Masaryk as President, but resigned in 1938 and left the country, setting up a government in exile, first in France, then in England. After returning in 1945, he was re-elected President, but resigned after the Communist coup of 1948. He died at Sezimovo Ústí. » Czechoslovakia [i]; Masaryk; nationalism

Bengal, Bay of Arm of the Indian Ocean, on S coast of Asia; bounded by India and Sri Lanka (W), Bangladesh (N), and Burma, Andaman Is, and Nicobar Is (E); c.2 000 km/1 300 ml long, 1 600 km/1 000 ml wide, depth 2 390 m/7 850 ft (N) to 4 150 m/13 600 ft (S); receives many large rivers, such as the Krishna, Ganges, Brahmaputra, Irrawaddy; main ports include Madras, Calcutta, Chittagong; subject to heavy monsoon rains and cyclones. » Indian Ocean

Bengali » **Indo-Aryan languages**

Benghazi or **Banghazi** [beng**ah**zee] 32°07N 20°05E, pop (1982) 650 000. Seaport in Benghazi province, N Libya; on the Gulf of Sirte, 645 km/400 ml E of Tripoli; first settled by Greeks; modern town partly situated on Hellenistic and Roman towns of Berenice; controlled by Turks, 16th-c–1911; Italian rule, 1911–42; military and naval supply base during World War 2; second largest city in Libya; airport; university (1955); oil, engineering. » Libya [i]

Benidorm [**ben**idawm] 38°33N 0°09W, pop (1981) 24 983. Resort town in Alicante province, E Spain, on the Mediterranean Costa Blanca; two beaches on either side of a rocky promontory; a leading centre of low-cost package holidays. » Alicante; Costa Blanca; Spain [i]

Benin, formerly **Dahomey** (to 1975), official name **Republic of Benin**, Fr **République du Benin** [be**neen**], formerly (to 1990), **The People's Republic of Benin** pop (1990e) 4 741 000; area 112 622 sq km/43 472 sq ml. Republic in W Africa, divided into six provinces; bounded N by Niger, E by Nigeria, NW by Burkina Faso, and W by Togo; capital Porto Novo (nominal), political and economic capital Cotonou; chief towns include Ouidah, Abomey, Kandi, Parakou, Natitingou; timezone GMT +1; many ethnic groups, especially the Fon, Adja, Yoruba, Bariba; small European community; official language, French, with several local languages spoken; religion, 70% local beliefs, remainder Christian and Muslim; unit of currency, CFA franc.

Physical description and climate. Rises from a 100 km/62 ml-long sandy coast with lagoons to low-lying plains, then to a savannah plateau at c.400 m/1 300 ft; Atakora Mts rise to over 500 m/1 600 ft in the NW; Alibori R valley in the NE, joining the R Niger valley; several rivers flow S to the Gulf of Guinea; tropical climate, divided into three zones; in the S, rain

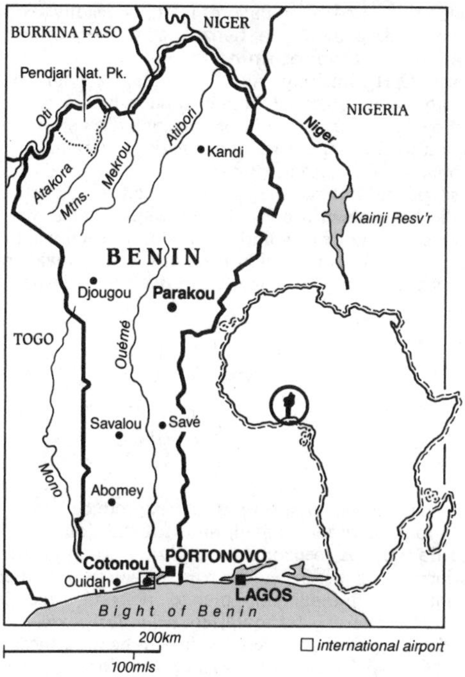

throughout the year, especially during the 'Guinea Monsoon' (May–Oct); in C area, two rainy seasons (peaks in May–June, Oct); in the N, one rainy season (Jul–Sep); N dry season (Oct–Apr) hot, low humidity, subject to the dry *harmattan* wind from the NE; average annual rainfall at Cotonou c.1 300 mm/50 in.

History and government. In pre-colonial times, a collection of small, warring principalities, especially the Fon Kingdom of Dahomey (founded in the 17th-c); Portuguese colonial activities centred on slave trade; subjugated by French, 1892, becoming the French Protectorate of Dahomey; territory within French West Africa, 1904; independence, 1960; name changed, 1975; governed by an executive president, a single-party Revolutionary National Assembly, and a national executive council; 1990, this system replaced by a 50-member High Council of the Republic, overseeing a transitional period leading to a new constitution and elections in 1991.

Economy. Agriculture important, especially palm oil products, cashew nuts, maize, cassava, rice, cotton, coffee; important service sector; fishing, food processing, textiles, beverages, cement; no known natural resources in commercial quantity but for a small offshore oilfield. » Benin (former kingdom); Cotonou; Dahomey; Porto Novo; RR24 national holidays; RR43 political leaders

Benin (former kingdom) [**beneen**] A powerful kingdom in the S Nigerian rainforest, founded in the 13th-c AD, which survived until the 19th-c. The Portuguese turned to Benin as a source of cloth, beads, and slaves in the 15th–16th-c, and it was later involved in the slave trade. The culture is renowned for the life-size brass heads and human/animal plaques cast for its ruler, the Oba, from the 15th-c onwards. Benin was conquered by the British in 1897, and many of its treasures were taken to London. In 1975, the name was adopted by the former French colony of Dahomey. » African history; Benin (country); brass; Ife; Nigeria [i]; slave trade

Benjamin, tribe of One of the twelve tribes of ancient Israel, said to be descended from Jacob's youngest son by Rachel (*Gen* 35.16–18, 24). Its ancient territories included the land between the hill country of Ephraim and the hills of Judah. Saul, first King of Israel, and the prophet Jeremiah were of this tribe. » Israel, tribes of [i]; Jacob

Benn, Gottfried (1886–1956) German poet, born at Mansfeld, West Prussia. He embraced the philosophy of nihilism as a young man, later becoming one of the few intellectuals to favour Nazi doctrines. Trained in medicine, he began writing Expressionist verse about the uglier aspects of his profession, such as *Morgue* (1912). Later his poetry became more versatile, though still pessimistic, as in *Statische Gedichte* (Static Poems, 1948), and he became highly regarded in postwar Germany. » Expressionism; German literature; Nazi Party; nihilism

Benn, Tony, properly **Anthony (Neil) Wedgwood Benn** (1925–) British Labour politician, son of Viscount Stansgate, born in London. Educated at Westminster School and Oxford, he became a Labour MP (1950–60), but was debarred from the House of Commons on succeeding to his father's title. He renounced his title, and was re-elected in a by-election in 1963. He has held various government posts, notably Postmaster-General (1964–6), Minister of Technology (1966–70), Secretary for Industry (1974–5), and Secretary for Energy (1975–9). A long-serving member of Labour's National Executive Committee, he unsuccessfully challenged Neil Kinnock for the leadership of the Party in 1988. He has written a number of books and pamphlets, including his political diary. » Kinnock; Labour Party; socialism

Bennett, (Enoch) Arnold (1867–1931) British novelist, born near Hanley, Staffordshire. Educated at London, he became a solicitor's clerk, but quickly transferred to journalism. After living in Paris for some years, he became a full-time writer. Among his 30 novels are *Anna of the Five Towns* (1902), *The Old Wives' Tale* (1908), and the *Clayhanger* series, all of which reflect life in the Potteries. He was a regular reviewer, and also wrote several plays, which were less successful; his journals were published posthumously. He died in London. » English literature; novel

Bennett, James Gordon (1795–1872) US newspaper editor, born at Keith, Banffshire. Trained as a journalist, in 1819 he emigrated to America, where he founded the *New York Herald* (1835). His son, **James Gordon** (1841–1918) edited the paper from 1867, and financed several explorers, including Stanley's search for Livingstone (1870). » newspaper; Stanley, Henry Morton

Bennett, Richard Bedford, 1st Viscount (1870–1947) Canadian statesman and Prime Minister (1930–5), born in New Brunswick. Educated in Nova Scotia, he trained as a lawyer, and entered politics in 1897. He was Conservative leader from 1927, and while Prime Minister convened the Imperial Economic Conference in Ottawa (1932), from which emerged a system of empire trade preference. He retired to England in 1939, was made a peer in 1941, and died at Mickleham, Surrey. » Canada [i]

Bennett, Richard Rodney (1936–) British composer, born at Broadstairs, Kent. Educated at the Royal Academy of Music and in Paris under Pierre Boulez, he became well known for his music for films, such as *Murder on the Orient Express* (1973). He has also composed operas, orchestral works, chamber music, experimental works for one and two pianos, and pieces involving jazz. His operas include *The Mines of Sulphur* (1965), *A Penny for a Song* (1967), and *Victory* (1970).

Benoît (de Sainte-Maure) [**benwah**] (1100–1200) French poet, born in either Sainte-Maure, near Poiters, or Sainte-More, near Tours. His vast romance *Roman de Troie* was a source book to many later writers, notably Boccaccio, who in turn inspired Chaucer and Shakespeare to use Benoît's episode of Troilus and Cressida. » Boccaccio; French literature

Bentham, Jeremy (1748–1832) British writer on jurisprudence and utilitarian ethics, born in London. Educated at Westminster School, Oxford, and London, he was called to the Bar in 1767, though he never practised, being more interested in the theory of the law. His publications include *A Fragment on Government* (1776), and *Introduction to the Principles of Morals and Legislation* (1789), which present his theory of hedonistic utilitarianism. He held that laws should be socially useful and not merely reflect the *status quo*, and that all actions are right when they promote 'the happiness of the greatest number' – a phrase which he popularized. He travelled widely on the continent, and founded the radical sect of the Benthamites. He was also a founder of University College, London, where his skeleton, dressed in his clothes, is preserved. » hedonism; natural law; utilitarianism

benthic or **benthonic environments** The marine life zone at the sea floor; distinguished from the *pelagic* environments, in the water itself. There are two major divisions. **Shallow benthic** environments are those towards the shore from the edge of the continental shelf. They comprise three sub-divisions. The *supralittoral* zone lies just above the mean high tide line, sometimes called the 'splash zone', because the organisms are exposed to sea water mainly from the wave splashes, periodic storm waves, and spring tides. The *littoral* zone lies between the mean high and low tide lines, also called the 'intertidal' zone. The *sublittoral* zone extends from below the mean low tide line to the edge of the continental shelf, and has been called the 'shelf' zone. **Deep benthic** environments are those of the continental margin and deep ocean seaward of this boundary. They have been subdivided into the *bathyl benthic* (shelf edge to 4 000 m/13 000 ft), the *abyssal benthic* (4–6 000 m/ 13–20 000 ft), and the *hadal benthic* (6–11 000+ m/20–36 000 ft). At the sea floor itself, the various benthic habitats can be divided into those where the organisms live primarily on the surface of the bottom (*benthic epifauna*) and those where they actually inhabit the sediment (*benthic infauna*). » continental margin; pelagic environments

Bentinck, William Henry Cavendish, 3rd Duke of Portland (1738–1809) British statesman and Prime Minister (1783, 1807–9), born at Bulstrode, Buckinghamshire. He entered Lord Rockingham's Cabinet in 1765, and succeeded him as leader of the Whig Party. Although twice Prime Minister, he is best remembered as Home Secretary under the Younger Pitt, with charge of Irish affairs (1794–1801). » Bentinck, Lord William; Pitt (the Younger); Rockingham; Whigs

Bentinck, Lord William (Henry Cavendish) (1774–1839) British soldier and Governor-General of India (1828–35), born at Bulstrode, Buckinghamshire, the second son of the 3rd Duke of Portland. In 1791 he became an army officer. Appointed Governor of Madras in 1803, he was recalled from India following a mutiny of native troops, and fought during the Napoleonic Wars in Spain and Sicily. Elected to parliament, he became Governor-General of India in 1828, where he introduced important administrative reforms. He died in Paris.

Bentine, Michael » **Goons, The**

Bentley, E(dmund) C(lerihew) (1875–1956) British journalist and novelist, born and died in London. He is chiefly remembered as the author of *Trent's Last Case* (1913), a milestone in the transformation of the detective novel from the romantic concept of the Conan Doyle era to the more realistic modern school. He also gave his name to the type of rhyming tag known as the 'clerihew'. » detective story; English literature

Benton, Thomas Hart (1782–1858) US statesman, born near Hillsborough, North Carolina. He was a Missouri Senator for over 30 years, and a leader of the Democratic Party, becoming known as 'Old Bullion' from his opposition to paper currency. In his later years, he adopted an anti-slavery position which finally lost him his seat in the Senate. He died in Washington, DC. » slavery

Bentsen, Lloyd (1921–) US politician, born at Mission, Texas. Educated at the University of Texas, he had a mixed career in business and politics after war service. He defeated George Bush for election as Senator from Texas in 1970, and was Democratic candidate for Vice-President in 1988. » Bush, George; Democratic Party

Benue-Congo languages [**bay**nway **kong**goh] » **Niger-Congo languages**

Benue, River, Fr **Beboué** [**bay**nooay] Major tributary of the R Niger in Nigeria; rises in Cameroon, and flows generally WSW across E and SC Nigeria; navigable below Garoua; joins the R Niger at Lokoja; length 1 295 km/805 ml. » Niger, River

Benz, Karl (Friedrich) (1844–1929) German engineer, born in Karlsruhe. In 1879 he constructed a two-stroke engine model and founded a factory for its manufacture. In 1883 he founded a second company at Mannheim. His first car – one of the earliest petrol-driven vehicles – was completed in 1885. In 1926 his firm was merged with the Daimler-Motoren-Gesellschaft. He died at Ladenburg. » car [i]; engine

benzaldehyde [benz**al**dihiyd] C_6H_5CHO, IUPAC **phenylmethanal**, boiling point 179°C. A colourless liquid, with the odour of almonds, used as a flavouring. It is readily oxidized to benzoic acid. » aldehyde; benzoic acid; IUPAC

Benzedrine » **amphetamine**

benzene C_6H_6, melting point 5°C, boiling point 80°C. An aromatic liquid obtained from coal tar, which may be synthesized by dehydrogenation of petroleum hydrocarbons. It is the simplest of the large series of aromatic compounds. Although the bonds in the benzene ring are often represented as alternating single and double, they are in fact all equivalent, this fact usually being described by the misleading name 'resonance'. Benzene does not easily undergo addition reactions, but has a large number of substitution reactions, giving a wide range of aromatic compounds. It is used in dyestuffs, plastics, insecti-

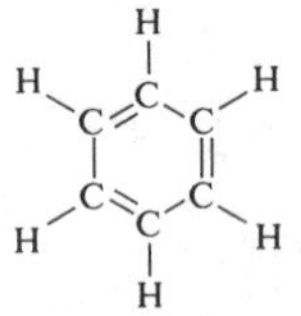

cides, detergents, and several other products. » aromatic compound; coal tar; phenyl; ring; substitution reaction

benzodiazepines [benzohdiy**ay**zepinz] A group of drugs each of which exerts, to varying degrees, anti-anxiety, anti-epilepsy, hypnotic (sleep-inducing), muscle relaxant, and sedative properties. The two tranquillizers *chlordiazepoxide* (Librium) and *diazepam* (Valium) were the first to be introduced in 1960 and 1962 respectively. *Nitrazepam* (Mogadon) and *temazepam* are commonly used as hypnotics. They are very safe drugs, with fatal overdose being very uncommon, and therefore they took over from the more dangerous barbiturates. Some concern is now being expressed at their very wide use, which has been criticized as inappropriate. Evidence of addiction following long-term use is accumulating, and the UK Committee on Safety of Medicines now recommends that treatment should be restricted to severe anxiety and insomnia for a maximum of four weeks. » barbiturates

benzoic acid [benz**oh**ik] C_6H_5COOH, melting point 122°C. A white crystalline compound obtained by the oxidation of toluene. It is the simplest aromatic acid, a weak acid. Its sodium salt, *sodium benzoate*, is used as a preservative. » oxidation; toluene

benzoin [**benz**ohin] $C_6H_5.CHOH.CO.C_6H_5$, melting point 137°C. A fragrant solid, a condensation product of benzaldehyde. It also occurs naturally in the resin known as balsam, from trees of the genus *Styrax*. » benzaldehyde; resin

benzyl [**ben**ziyl, **ben**zil] $C_6H_5CH_2$–, IUPAC **phenylmethyl**. A functional group containing a phenyl ring, whose addition to a name usually indicates its substitution for hydrogen in a compound. » functional group; hydrogen; IUPAC; phenyl; ring

Beqaa, el, Eng **the Bekka** [el be**kah**] Governorate of E Lebanon, bounded NE and E by Syria; capital, Zahle; poultry, sheep, wheat, vineyards; El Beqaa valley of strategic importance to both Israel and Syria, and a centre of Muslim Shiite activity. » Lebanon [i]

Bérain, Jean (the Elder) [bay**rã**] (c.1637–1711) French decorative artist, born at Lorraine. He was the leading designer of stage scenery, costumes, fêtes, and displays at the court of Louis XIV. His arabesques, grotesques, and *singeries* (monkey designs), often combined with Chinese motifs, herald the lighter Rococo style of the early 18th-c. He died in Paris. » arabesque [i]; chinoiserie; grotesque; Rococo

Berber Hamito-Semitic-speaking peoples of Egypt, Algeria, Libya, Tunisia, and Morocco. They were originally settled in one area, but the Bedouin Arabs who invaded N Africa in the 12th-c turned many of them into nomads. Most Berber tribes ultimately accepted Islam, and in the 11th-c formed themelves into a military federation known as the **Almoravids**, who conquered the mediaeval state of Ghana, Morocco, Algeria, and S Spain. In the 12th-c their power began to wane, and the **Almohads**, a new group influenced by Sufism, by 1169 came to command the entire Maghrib to Tripoli, as well as Muslim Spain. The Almohad Empire declined in the 13th-c. Today, some Berbers are sedentary farmers, while others are nomadic or transhumant pastoralists. Many work as migrant labourers in S Europe. The best-known groups include the Kabyle, Shluh, and Tuareg. They comprise 40% of the population of Morocco (10 million) and 30% of that of Algeria (7 million). » African history; Bedouin; Islam; nomadism; Sufism; transhumance; Tuareg

Berberian, Cathy » **Berio, Luciano**

berberis » **barberry**

Berenson, Bernhard (1865–1959) US art critic, born at Vilnius, Lithuania. He studied at Harvard, and became a leading authority on Italian Renaissance art, producing a vast critical literature, including studies of the different Italian schools. He lived in Italy for most of his life, and died at Settignano.

Beresford, Jack (1899–1977) British oarsman. He competed for Great Britain at five Olympics (1920–36) as sculler and oarsman, winning three gold and two silver medals, and received the Olympic Diploma of Merit in 1949. He won the Diamond Sculls at Henley four times, and was elected president of the Thames Rowing Club in 1971. » rowing

Berg, Alban (1885–1935) Austrian composer, born and died in Vienna. He studied under Schoenberg, welding the twelve-note system to a deeply traditional style. He is best known for his opera *Wozzeck* (first performed 1925), his Violin Concerto (1935), and the *Lyric Suite* for string quartet (1926). His unfinished opera, *Lulu*, was posthumously produced. » Schoenberg; serialism

Bergama, ancient **Pergamon** or **Pergamum** [berg**ah**ma] 39°08N 27°10E, pop (1980) 38 000. Town in Izmir province, W Turkey, N of Izmir; former capital of the ancient Kingdom of Pergamum, and of the Roman province of Asia; parchment is supposed to have been invented here; tourism; Acropolis, Temples of Trajan and Dionysos, Sanctuary of Athena, Altar of Zeus. » parchment; Pergamum (Asia Minor); Turkey [i]

Bergamo [**bair**gamoh] 45°42N 9°40E, pop (1981) 122 142. Capital town of Bergamo province, Lombardy, N Italy; between the Brembo and Serio Rivers, NE of Milan; first seat of the Republican fascist government set up in N Italy by Mussolini after his fall from power (1943); railway; textiles, cement, printing, electrical switches; Romanesque basilica (1137–1355), 15th-c cathedral. » Lombardy; Mussolini

bergamot [**buh**guhmot] **1** An aromatic perennial, native to N America and Mexico; stem square; leaves oval, toothed, in opposite pairs; flowers 2-lipped, hooded, purple or red, in crowded whorls around stem; visited by bees and hummingbirds. The leaves provide medicinal oswega tea. (Genus: *Monarda*, 12 species. Family: *Labiatae*.) » perennial **2** » orange

Bergen (Belgium) [**ber**khen] » **Mons**

Bergen (Norway) [**ber**gn] 60°23N 5°20E, pop (1983) 207 292. Seaport and administrative capital of Hordaland county, SW Norway; on a promontory at the head of a deep bay; old shipping and trading town; second largest city in Norway; founded, 1070; capital, 12th–13th-c; occupied by Germans in World War 2; bishopric; airport; railway; university (1948); shipyards, engineering, paper, fishing, fish products, pottery, offshore oil services; tourist and cultural centre; birthplace of Grieg; restored 13th-c cathedral, Hanseatic museum, Håkonshall (13th-c palace), Mariakirke (12th-c), art gallery. museums. » Bryggen; Grieg; Norway [i]

Bergerac, Cyrano de » **Cyrano de Bergerac**

Bergius, Friedrich [**ber**geeus] (1884–1949) German industrial chemist, born at Goldschmieden near Breslau. He carried out research into coal hydrogenation to give petrol, and the hydrolysis of wood to sugar, sharing the Nobel Prize for Chemistry with Bosch in 1931. He emigrated to Spain and Argentina after World War 2, and died in Buenos Aires. » Bosch, Carl; coal; hydrogenation

Bergman, Hjalmar (Fredrik Elgérus) (1883–1931) Swedish novelist, short-story writer, and dramatist, born in Órebro. He was the outstanding Swedish writer of his period. His best-known works are a satirical novel, *Markurells i Wadköping* (1919, translated as God's Orchid), and a comedy *Swedenhielms* (1925). He died in Berlin. » Swedish literature

Bergman, (Ernst) Ingmar (1918–) Swedish film director and writer, born at Uppsala, and educated in Stockholm. He worked in the theatre in the late 1930s, and from 1950 divided his time between stage and screen. His films became something of a cult for art-cinema audiences, with the elegaic *Smiles of a Summer Night* (1955) and the sombre *The Seventh Seal* (1956) and *Wild Strawberries* (1957). Later films include *Herbstsonate* (1978, Autumn Sonata) and *Fanny och Alexander* (1983).

Bergman, Ingrid (1915–1982) Swedish film actress, born in Stockholm. Her first starring role in Hollywood, *Intermezzo* (1939), was followed by outstanding successes in *Casablanca* (1942), *For Whom the Bell Tolls* (1943), and *Gaslight* (1944), for which she won her first Oscar. The scandal of her relations with the Italian director Rossellini, whom she subsequently married, led to her exclusion from Hollywood between 1948 and 1957, but she won another Oscar for *Anastasia* (1956), and continued in film and television throughout the 1970s (*Autumn Sonata*, 1978, and *A Woman Called Golda*, 1982) until her death in London.

Bergson, Henri [**berg**sõ] (1859–1941) French philosopher and psychologist, born and died in Paris. Educated at Paris, he taught (1881–8) at Angers and Clermont-Ferrand, later becoming professor at the Collège de France (1900–21). He became known with his *Essai sur les données immédiates de la conscience* (1889, Time and Free Will: an Essay on the Immediate Data of Consciousness) and *Matière et mémoire* (1896, Matter and Memory), then published *L'Evolution créatrice* (1907, Creative Evolution). He won the Nobel Prize for Literature in 1927.

beri beri A nutritional disease due primarily to an inadequate dietary intake of Vitamin B_1. The disorder affects peripheral nerves (*polyneuritis*), and also causes heart failure and oedema. » vitamins [i]

Beria, Lavrenti (Pavlovich) (1899–1953) Soviet secret police chief, born at Mercheuli, Georgia. After holding local positions in Georgia, he became Soviet Commissar for Internal Affairs in 1938. During World War 2 he was Vice-President of the State Committee for Defence, and was active in purging Stalin's opponents. After the death of Stalin (1953), he belonged briefly with Malenkov and Molotov to the collective leadership. Accused by his colleagues of conspiracy, he was shot after a brief 'treason' trial. » Malenkov; Molotov; Stalin

Bering, or **Behring, Vitus (Jonassen)** (1681–1741) Danish-Russian navigator, born at Horsens, Denmark. He joined the navy of Czar Peter the Great, and fought in the Swedish wars. He was then appointed to explore the Sea of Kamchatka (1724), to determine whether Russia and America were connected by land. In 1728 and again in 1741 he sailed towards the American continent, and finally sighted Alaska, but sickness and storms forced him to return, and he was wrecked on the island of Avatcha (now Bering I), where he died. Bering Sea and Bering Strait are named after him. » Bering Sea; Peter I

Bering Sea [**bay**ring] area 2 261 100 sq km/872 800 sq ml. Part of the Pacific Ocean between Siberia (W) and Alaska (E), bounded S by the Aleutian Is and Trench; connected to the Arctic by the Bering Strait (90 km/56 ml wide at narrowest point); often ice-bound (Nov–May); contains boundary between Russia and USA; depths reach 4 000 m/13 000 ft (SW), but 25–75 m/90–240 ft over continental shelf in NE; explored first in 17th-c; seal herd threatened with extinction because of over-exploitation, but herds built up after 1911 agreement by UK, USA, Russia, and Japan. » Bering; Pacific Ocean

Berio, Luciano (1925–) Italian avant-garde composer and teacher of music, born at Oneglia. He studied first with his father, then at the Music Academy in Milan, and with Bruno Maderna founded the electronic Studio di Fonologia at Milan Radio (1954–61). In 1962 he moved to the USA where he taught composition in New York, returning to Italy in 1972 to work in many diverse aspects of music. He married (1950–66) the American soprano **Cathy Berberian** (1928–83), for whom he wrote several works. He is particularly interested in the combining of live and prerecorded sound, and the use of tapes and electronic music, as in his compositions *Mutazioni* (1955), *Visage* (1961), and the *Sequenza* series (1958–75). His more recent works include two operas, *La vera storia* (1982, The

True Story) and *Un re in ascolto* (1984, A King Listens). » electronic music

Berkeley, Busby [**berk**lee] (1895–1976) US director and choreographer, born in Los Angeles. He was known for his extravagant stagings of dance numbers in Hollywood films, using the camera to move among the dancers. One of Broadway's busiest stage directors of the 1920s, he produced such famous films as *Gold Diggers of 1933* and *Lady Be Good* (1941). He died in Palm Springs, California. » choreography

Berkeley, George [**bahk**lee] (1685–1753) Anglican bishop and philosopher, born near Kilkenny, Ireland. He studied and became a fellow at Trinity College, Dublin, where he published his *Essay towards a New Theory of Vision* (1709), in which he argued that spatial distance is not directly perceived, but inferred from the habitual association of visual and tactile sensations. His *Treatise Concerning the Principles of Human Knowledge* (1710) and *Three Dialogues between Hylas and Philonous* (1713) expounded his idealistic philosophy, encapsulated in *esse est percipi vel percipere* ('to be is to be perceived or a perceiver') – everything that exists is either a mind or in a mind, arguing that any version of materialism leads to scepticism. He divided his time (1713–24) between London and the continent; was appointed Dean of Derry (1724); lived in Rhode Island (1728–31); became Bishop of Cloyne (1734); and in 1752 moved to Oxford, where he died. » idealism; materialism; scepticism

Berkeley, Sir Lennox (Randall Francis) (1903–89) British composer, born in Oxford. After leaving Oxford, he studied music under Nadia Boulanger in Paris (1927–32), later becoming professor of composition at the Royal Academy of Music, London (1946–68). His works include a *Stabat mater* (1947), the operas *Nelson* (1953) and *Ruth* (1956), a *Divertimento* (1943), and several other orchestral pieces. He was knighted in 1974, and died in London. His son, **Michael** (1948–), is also a composer. » Boulanger

Berkshire, also known as **Royal Berkshire** [**bahk**sheer] pop (1987e) 740 600; area 1 259 sq km/486 sq ml. County of S England, divided into six districts; drained by the Kennet and Thames Rivers; county town Reading; chief towns include Newbury, Windsor, Maidenhead, Bracknell; engineering, high technology, pharmaceuticals, plastics; Atomic Research Establishment at Aldermaston; Windsor Castle. » England [i]; Reading; Windsor Castle

Berlin, Irving, originally **Israel Baline** (1888–1989) US songwriter, born at Temum, Russia, and a child when his family emigrated to New York City. As a teenager, he began promoting his own songs as a singing waiter. 'Alexander's Ragtime Band' became an international hit in 1911, the first of many among more than 900 songs for which he wrote both the words and music. His score for *Annie Get Your Gun* (1946) is a model of theatre music. His most popular songs (such as 'Always' (1925), 'Easter Parade' (1933), 'God Bless America' (1939), 'White Christmas' (1942)) have sentimental lyrics and simple melodies, often considered Berlin's main strengths; but he also wrote numerous songs, including 'Heat Wave' (1933) and 'Cheek to Cheek' (1935), with sly, urbane lyrics and advanced harmonies. His centenary, a year before his death in New York City, occasioned international tributes. » musical; song

Berlin, Sir Isaiah (1909–) British philosopher, born at Riga, Latvia. His family emigrated to England in 1920. He studied at Oxford, where he later lectured (1932–8). During World War 2, he was in the diplomatic service. Returning to Oxford, he became Chichele professor of social and political theory (1957–67) and master of Wolfson College (1966–75). His works on political philosophy include *Historical Inevitability* (1954) and *Two Concepts of Liberty* (1959).

Berlin [**ber**lin] 52°32N 13°25E, pop (1990) 3 409 737; area 883 sq km/341 sq ml. Capital of Germany, partitioned in 1945 into East Berlin and West Berlin; founded in the 13th-c; former residence of the Hohenzollerns and capital of Brandenburg; later capital of Prussia, becoming an industrial and commercial centre in the 18th-c; in 1949 West Berlin became a province of the Federal Republic of Germany and East Berlin a county of the German Democratic Republic; the two halves of the city separated by the Berlin Wall; contact between the two halves of the city was restored in November 1989, following government changes in East Germany; made capital of unified Germany, 1990. » Berlin, East/West; Berlin Airlift/Wall; Germany [i]; Hohenzollerns; Prussia

Berlin Airlift (1948–9) A massive airlift of essential supplies flown in to postwar Berlin by British and US aircraft in round-the-clock missions. It was carried out in response to the action of the Soviet military authorities in Berlin, who had attempted to isolate the city from the West by severing all overland communication routes (Jun 1948). Stalin lifted the blockade in May 1949. » Berlin; Stalin

Berlin, Congress of (1878) An international congress following the Russian defeat of Turkey (1877–8). The chief results were: Serbia, Romania, and Bulgaria achieved independence from Turkey; Austria-Hungary occupied Bosnia-Herzegovina; Russia retained gains in S Bessarabia and the Caucasus, but conceded a reduction in the size of her satellite, Bulgaria; and Britain occupied Cyprus. » Ottoman Empire

Berlin, East pop (1990e) 1 279 000; area 403 sq km/156 sq ml. Capital city of former East Germany; linked to the Oder and Elbe Rivers by canals; two airports; railway; German Academies of Sciences (1700); Humboldt University (1810); largest industrial centre in the country; mechanical and electrical engineering, electronics, motor vehicles, chemicals, food processing; Brandenburg Gate, Unter den Linden, Pergamum museum, national gallery, Rotes Rathaus (red town hall); recreation centres developed in lake area to the SE; annual festival of dramatic art and music, annual political song festival. » Berlin; Brandenburg Gate; Germany [i]; Pergamum; Unter den Linden

Berlin Wall A concrete wall built by the East German government in 1961 to seal off East Berlin from the part of the city occupied by the three main Western powers. Built largely to prevent mass illegal emigration to the West, which was threatening the East German economy, the Wall was the scene of the shooting of many East Germans who tried to escape from the Eastern sector. The Wall, seen by many as a major symbol of the denial of human rights in E Europe, was unexpectedly opened in November 1989, following increased pressure for political reform in East Germany. The wall has now been taken down. » Berlin; Germany [i]; human rights

Berlin, West 52°32N 13°25E, pop (1990e) 2 131 000; area 480 sq km/185 sq ml. Former West German enclave (city and province) lying entirely within East Germany; railway; university (1946); machine tools, office equipment, pharmaceuticals, chemicals, brewing, soft drinks, toys, electrical cables, clothing, steel construction, publishing; Kaiser Wilhelm Church (preserved ruins). » Berlin; Berlin Airlift; Berlin, East; Charlottenburg Palace; Germany [i]; Tiergarten

Berliner Ensemble A theatre company in E Berlin which was formed by Brecht in 1949. In its early years it had an enormous influence on Western theatre, chiefly through Brecht's own productions of his mature plays written during his years in exile from Nazi Germany. » Brecht; theatre

Berlioz, (Louis) Hector [**ber**liohz] (1803–69) French composer, born at Côte-Saint-André. He studied medicine until 1823, then produced a number of large-scale works before entering the Paris Conservatoire in 1826. During his studies he fell in love with the Shakespearean actress, **Harriet Smithson** (1800–54), whom he subsequently married, and for whom he wrote the *Symphonie Fantastique*. He gained the Prix de Rome (1830), and spent two years in Italy. His works include his symphony *Harold en Italie* (1834), the *Grande Messe des morts* (1837), the dramatic symphony *Roméo et Juliette* (1839), the cantata *La Damnation de Faust* (1846), and his operas *Les Troyens* (1856–8) and *Béatrice et Bénédict* (1860–2). One of the founders of 19th-c programme music, Berlioz also wrote several books, including a treatise on orchestration and an autobiography. He died in Paris. » programme music

Bermuda, formerly **Somers Is** 32°N 65°W, pop (1989e) 58 800; area 53 sq km/20 sq ml. A British self-governing dependency, divided into nine parishes; in the W Atlantic c.900 km/560 ml E of Cape Hatteras, N Carolina; c.150 low-lying coral islands and islets, 20 inhabited, 7 linked by causeways

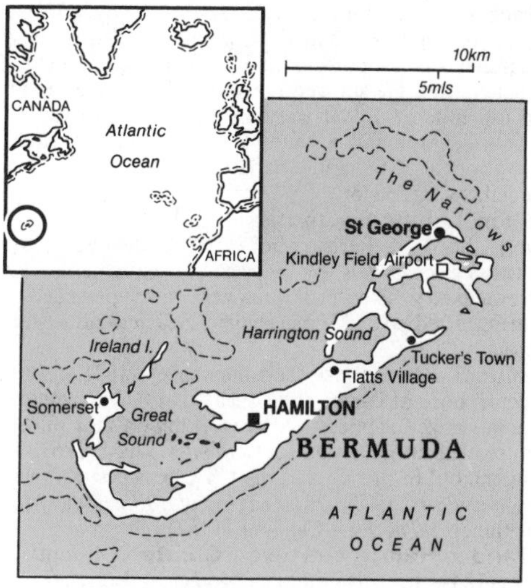

and bridges; largest island (Great) Bermuda; St George's and St David's Is to the E; highest point, Gibb's Hill (78 m/256 ft); capital Hamilton; deepwater ports at Hamilton, St George (St George's I), and Freeport (Ireland I); timezone GMT −4; two-thirds Black population, remainder of British or Portuguese stock; official language, English; main religions, Anglican (37%), Roman Catholic (14%); main airport at Kindley Field (US Naval Air Station and civil airport); motor cars allowed since 1947; unit of currency, Bermuda dollar of 100 cents; sub-tropical climate, generally humid, rain throughout year, summers warm to hot, winters mild; discovered by Spanish mariner, Juan Bermudez, in early 16th-c; colonized by English settlers, 1612; important naval station, and (to 1862) penal settlement; internal self-government, 1968; movement for independence caused tension in the 1970s, including assassination of the governor-general, 1973; British monarch represented by a governor-general; governed by a Senate (11 members), a House of Assembly (40 members, elected for 5 years), and a 12-member cabinet headed by a prime minister; economy mainly year-round tourism; increasingly an international company business centre; also, petroleum products, pharmaceuticals, aircraft supplies, boatbuilding, ship repair; vegetables, citrus and banana plantations; fish processing centre. » Hamilton (Bermuda)

Bern, Fr **Berne** 46°57N 7°28E, pop (1980) 145 254. Federal capital of Switzerland and of Bern canton, W Switzerland; on R Aare 94 km/58 ml SW of Zürich; founded, 1191; joined the Swiss Confederation, 1353; capital, 1848; airport (Belpmoos); railway junction; university (1834); textiles, machinery, chocolate, pharmaceuticals, foodstuffs, graphic trades, electrical equipment, engineering, tourism; headquarters of several international organizations; Gothic cathedral (1421–1573), mediaeval town hall, clock tower, many museums; old city is a world heritage site; 'Zibelemärit' old market (Nov). » Switzerland [i]

Bernadette, St, originally **Marie Bernarde Soubirous** (1844–79), feast day 18 February or 16 April. French visionary, born at Lourdes, the daughter of a miller. She claimed to have received in 1858 18 apparitions of the Blessed Virgin at the Massabielle Rock, near Lourdes, which has since become a notable place of pilgrimage. In 1866 she became a nun at Nevers, where she died. She was beatified in 1925, and canonized in 1933. » Lourdes; Mary (mother of Jesus)

Bernadotte, Folke, Greve ('Count') (1895–1948) Swedish humanitarian and diplomat, born in Stockholm. The nephew of Gustavus V of Sweden, he acted as mediator during both world wars. Appointed by the United Nations to mediate in Palestine, he produced a partition plan, but was assassinated by Jewish terrorists, in Jerusalem. » United Nations; Zionism

Bernadotte, Jean » **Charles XIV** (of Sweden)

Bernanos, Georges (1888–1948) French Roman Catholic novelist and polemical writer, born in Paris. He did not begin to write seriously until he was 37, and had taken degrees in law and letters. His writings attacked indifference and were preoccupied with problems of sin and grace. His most memorable novel was *Le Journal d'un curé de campagne* (1936, The Diary of a Country Priest). He died at Neuilly-sur-Seine. » French literature

Bernard of Clairvaux, St (1090–1153), feast day 20 August. French theologian and reformer, born of a noble family at Fontaines, near Dijon. In 1113 he entered the Cistercian monastery of Cîteaux, and in 1115 became the first abbot of Clairvaux. His studious, ascetic life and stirring eloquence made him the oracle of Christendom; he founded more than 70 monasteries; and his preaching kindled the enthusiasm of France for the second Crusade (1146). His writings include hundreds of epistles and sermons, and several theological treatises. He died at Clairvaux, and was canonized in 1174. The monks of his reformed branch of the Cistercians are often called **Bernardines**. » Cistercians; Clairvaux; Crusades [i]; monasticism

Bernard of Menthon, St (923–1008), feast day 28 May or 15 June. The 'Apostle of the Alps', born in Savoy. As Archdeacon of Aosta he founded the hospices in the Alpine passes that bear his name. In due course the hospices' dogs were also named after him. » Alps; apostle

Bernardines » **Bernard of Clairvaux, St**

Bernese Alps, Ger **Berner Alpen** or **Bernese Oberland**, Fr **Alpes Bernoises** Mountain range in Switzerland, a N division of the Central Alps, extending from L Geneva to the Grimsel Pass; highest peak, the Finsteraarhorn (4 274 m/14 022 ft); also includes the Aletschhorn and Jungfrau; numerous tourist resorts, including Interlaken and Grindelwald. » Alps

Bernhard Leopold (1911–) Prince of the Netherlands, born at Jena, the son of Prince Bernhard Casimir of Lippe. In 1937 he married Juliana, the only daughter of Wilhelmina, Queen of the Netherlands; they had four daughters. During World War 2, he commanded the Netherlands Forces of the Interior (1944–5). In 1976 he was involved in a bribery scandal, in which he was found to have received money for promoting the Dutch purchase of aircraft from the Lockheed Aircraft Corporation. » Juliana

Bernhardt, Sarah, originally **Henriette Rosine Bernard** (1844–1923) French actress, born in Paris, who gained an international reputation through her talent for acting and publicity. She won fame with the breeches part in Coppée's *Le Passant* (1869), and after 1876 made frequent appearances all over the world. Her most famous roles included *Phèdre* (1877) and Marguerite (1884) in *La Dame aux camèllias*. She founded the Théâtre Sarah Bernhardt in 1899. In 1915 she had a leg amputated, but did not abandon the stage. A legendary figure in the theatre world, she continued playing until her death in Paris. » theatre

Bernini, Gian Lorenzo [berneenee] (1598–1680) Italian Baroque sculptor, architect and painter, born in Naples. The son of a sculptor, **Pietro** (1562–1629), he went to Rome at an early age, and was introduced to the papal court. In 1633 he completed the bronze baldacchino in St Peter's, and in 1647 the fountain of the four river gods in the Piazza Navona. In 1656 he decorated the apse of St Peter's with the so-called 'Cathedra Petri', designed the colonnade in front of the cathedral, and in 1663 the grand staircase to the Vatican. He was buried in the church of Sta Maria Maggiore. » Baroque (art and architecture); Italian art; sculpture

Bernoulli, Daniel [bernooyee] (1700–82) Swiss mathematician, born at Basle. He studied medicine and mathematics, becoming professor of mathematics at St Petersburg (1723). In 1733 he returned to Basle to become professor first of anatomy, then botany, and finally physics. He shared with Euler the distinction of gaining the French Academy prize ten times. He worked on trigonometrical functions, fractions, and the kinetic theory of gases, and solved an equation proposed by Riceti, now known as 'Bernoulli's equation'. Other members of his family were also mathematicians: his father **Jean** (1667–1748), his uncle **Jacques** (1654–1705), and his brother **Nicolas**

(1695–1726). » Bernoulli disk; Bernoulli's principle; Euler; trigonometry

Bernoulli disk A form of computer magnetic disk storage where, unlike the Winchester disk, the disk can be removed and replaced. It is named after the mathematician, Daniel Bernoulli, who developed the theory of fluid mechanics. » Bernoulli; magnetic disk; Winchester disk

Bernoulli's principle In physics, the principle that as the speed of a moving fluid increases, its pressure decreases; stated by Swiss mathematician Daniel Bernoulli in 1738. For example, when water flows down a pipe of varying cross-section, the water velocity is greatest at the narrowest point; the force required to accelerate the water to this greatest velocity is provided by the higher pressure in the slower-moving portion upstream. Bernoulli's principle explains the curved flight of a spinning cricket ball, and the lift on aircraft wings. » aerodynamics [i]; Bernoulli; fluid mechanics

Bernstein, Leonard [**bern**steen] (1918–90) US conductor, pianist, and composer, born in Lawrence, Massachusetts. He was educated at Harvard and the Curtis Institute of Music, and reached fame suddenly in 1943 by conducting the New York Philharmonic as a substitute for Bruno Walter. His compositions include three symphonies, a television opera, a Mass, a ballet, and many choral works and songs, but he is most widely known for his two musical comedies *On the Town* (1944) and *West Side Story* (1957). He is also well known for his concerts for young people, and he has appeared frequently on television. He retired from his full-time conducting posts in 1969.

Berruguete, Pedro [beroo**get**] (?–c.1503) Spanish painter, born at Paredes de Nava, Castile. He became court painter to Ferdinand and Isabella, and visited Italy (c.1447), where he helped to decorate the palace library at Urbino. The new, Venetian-inspired feeling for light and colour, and the interest in perspective which he acquired in Italy, made him the first truly Renaissance painter in Spain. He died at Avila. » Renaissance; Spanish art

Berry, Chuck, properly **Charles Edward** (1926–) US rock singer, guitarist, and songwriter, born in St Louis, Missouri. He grew up playing and singing Baptist hymns, swing music, and the blues, and then, at the age of 29, began writing songs with all these elements in them, starting with 'Maybelline', his first recording. Many of his songs belong to the standard repertoire of rock and roll, usually as hits for other singers: for example, 'Roll Over Beethoven' by the Beatles, and 'Sweet Little Sixteen' by the Beach Boys. » blues; rock music

Berry's phase An extra factor needed in the quantum description of systems undergoing certain changes, dependent on the system's geometry; identified in 1983 by UK physicist Michael Berry (1941–). The effect is observed in the rotation of the polarization plane of light passing along a helical optical fibre. It provides an interpretation of the Aharonov-Bohm effect. » Aharonov-Bohm effect; fibre optics; polarization [i]; quantum mechanics

Berryman, John (1914–72) US poet, born at McAlester, Oklahoma. Educated at Columbia and Cambridge Universities, he taught at Minnesota (1954–72). His technical accomplishment was shown in *Homage to Mistress Bradstreet* (1959), while the earlier *Sonnets* (written in the late 1940s, published 1968) and the long sequence of 'Dream Songs', *His Toy, His Dream, His Rest* (1969) are a remarkable development of the 'confessional' manner. He committed suicide at Minneapolis. » American literature; confessional poetry

berserker [**ber**serker] In Norse mythology, a warrior in a 'bear-shirt' who fought in such a frenzy that he was impervious to wounds. The name is the origin of the phrase 'to go beserk'.

Berthelot, (Pierre Eugène) Marcellin [bertuh**loh**] (1827–1907) French chemist and politician, born and died in Paris. He became the first professor of organic chemistry at the Collège de France (1865), where he helped to found thermochemistry, and synthesized many fundamental organic compounds. He also studied the mechanism of explosion, and wrote on the history of early chemistry. In public life, he became Minister of Public Instruction (1886–7) and of Foreign Affairs (1895–6). » thermochemistry

Berthollet, Claude Louis, Count [berto**lay**] (1748–1822) French chemist, born at Talloires in Savoy. He studied at Turin, coming to Paris in 1772, where he aided Lavoisier in his researches on gunpowder and in forming the new chemical nomenclature. He showed the value of chlorine for bleaching, and did much original work in inorganic chemistry. He was made a senator and a count by Napoleon, yet voted for his deposition in 1814, and was later created a peer. He died at Arcueil. » Lavoisier

Bertillon, Alphonse [bertee**yõ**] (1853–1914) French police officer, born in Paris, who in 1882 devised a system of identifying criminals by physical measurements, known as **anthropometry**. The Bertillon system was superseded by finger-printing. He died at Münsterlingen, Switzerland. » anthropometry

Bertolucci, Bernardo [bertoh**loo**chee] (1941–) Italian film director, born at Parma and educated at Rome, where he won a national prize for poetry. After working on short films, his first feature as a director was *La Commare Secco* (1962, The Grim Reaper), but in Britain and the USA he is best-known for *Last Tango in Paris* (1972), *The Tragedy of a Ridiculous Man* (1981), and the epic *The Last Emperor* (1987).

Bertrand, Henri Gratien, Comte ('Count') [ber**trã**] (1773–1844) French military engineer and one of Napoleon's generals, born and died at Châteauroux. He fought in Italy and Egypt before becoming Napoleon's aide-de-camp (1804) and Grand Marshal (1813). He shared the Emperor's banishment to St Helena, and on his death returned to France, where in 1830 he was appointed commandant of the Polytechnic School. His shorthand diary gave a detailed account of Napoleon's life in exile. » Napoleon I

Berwick-upon-Tweed [**be**rik] 55°46N 2°00W, pop(1981) 12989. Town in Berwick-upon-Tweed district, Northumberland, NE England; on the North Sea at the mouth of the R Tweed, on the Scottish-English border; disputed by England and Scotland, changed ownership 14 times, but part of England since 1482; railway; foodstuffs, salmon fishing, engineering; 16th-c ramparts; Church of the Holy Trinity (1652); 16 km/10 ml SW is Flodden Field (1513); 12 km/7 ml SW is 15th-c Norham Castle. » Flodden, Battle of; Northumberland

beryl A beryllium, aluminium silicate mineral ($Be_3Al_2Si_6O_{18}$), occurring in granite pegmatites as greenish hexagonal prisms. Gemstone varieties are aquamarine and emerald. It is the commercial ore of beryllium. » aquamarine; beryllium; emerald; gemstones; pegmatite

beryllium [buh**ril**eeuhm] Be, element 4, melting point 1278°C. An element chemically similar to aluminium, but showing an oxidation state of 2 in most of its compounds. The metal forms an unreactive coat of BeO in air, making it inert to further oxidation. Its low density (1.85gm cm^{-3}) makes it a valuable component of alloys, but the poisonous nature of its compounds limits its use. It is mainly found in nature in the mineral beryl. » alloy; aluminium; beryl; chemical elements; oxidation; RR90

Berzelius, Jöns Jakob, Baron (1779–1848) Swedish chemist, born near Linköping, one of the founders of modern chemistry. He studied at Uppsala, becoming professor in Stockholm (1807–32). His accurate determination of atomic weights established the laws of combination and the atomic theory. He introduced modern symbols, an electro-chemical theory, and discovered the elements selenium, thorium, and cerium. He was made a baron in 1835, and died in Stockholm. » atomic weight; chemical elements; chemistry

Bes In Egyptian mythology, a dwarf god, bandy-legged and horrific in appearance, but congenial in temperament. He was the protector in child-birth, and guardian of the family.

Besançon [buh**zã**sõ] ancient **Vesontio** or **Besontium** 47°15N 6°00E, pop(1982) 119687. Industrial town and capital of Doubs department, NE France, on R Doubs; former capital of Franche-Comté; railway; university (1485); archbishopric; strategic site between Vosges and Jura Mts since Gallo-Roman times; watches, clocks, artificial silk, cars; cathedral (11th–13th-c), citadel on high rock overlooking river, Roman remains, museums; birthplace of Victor Hugo. » Hugo

Besant, Annie, *née* **Wood** [**bez**nt] (1847–1933) British theosophist and social reformer, born in London. Brought up at

Harrow, she married the Rev Frank Besant, but was separated from him in 1873. From secularism and Bradlaugh she passed in 1889 to Madame Blavatsky and theosophy, becoming its high priestess from 1891. In her later years she went to India, where she championed nationalism and education. She died at Adyar, Madras. » Blavatsky; Bradlaugh; theosophy

Besant, Sir Walter [buhzant] (1836–1901) British novelist and social reformer, born at Portsmouth, Hampshire. He studied at London and Cambridge, and after some years as a professor in Mauritius, he devoted himself to literature. In 1871 he entered into a literary partnership with James Rice (1844–82), and together they produced many novels. After Rice's death, Besant himself wrote *All Sorts and Conditions of Men* (1882), and other novels advocating social reform. He was knighted in 1895, and died in London. » English literature

Beskids or **Beskidy** Mountain group in the Carpathian range on the Polish–Czechoslovak frontier; rises to 1 725 m/5 659 ft at Babia Gora. » Carpathian Mountains

Bessemer, Sir Henry (1813–98) British engineer and inventor, born at Charlton, Hertfordshire. He originated over 100 inventions, and is best known for his steel-making process. Knighted in 1879, he died in London. » Bessemer process; iron; steel

Bessemer process A process for converting pig iron (high carbon iron from the blast furnace) into steel (low carbon iron alloy). Air is blown through the molten iron; the oxygen of the air converts the carbon in the iron into carbon dioxide, which escapes. This reaction produces heat which keeps the iron molten. The principle was known to US ironmaster William Kelly (1811–88) as early as 1846, but the process is named after Henry Bessemer, who introduced it successfully into Britain in 1856. It was an invention of the greatest importance, because it led to many industrial processes being greatly changed or inaugurated by the easy availability of steel. It did not work well with some ores, for which the open-hearth process was devised. » Bessemer; iron; open-hearth process; smelting; steel

Best, Charles H(erbert) (1899–1978) Canadian physiologist, born at West Pembroke, Maine. Educated at Toronto and London, in 1922 he was associated with Banting and Macleod in their joint discovery of insulin. The Banting and Best Department of Medical Research was created at the University of Toronto in 1923, and he succeeded Banting as director (1941–67). He died in Toronto. » Banting; insulin; Macleod, J J R

Best, George (1946–) N Ireland footballer, born in Belfast. A very talented but often tempestuous player, he made his debut for Manchester United at the age of 17 in 1963, and won championship medals in 1965 and 1967. After 361 League appearances and 137 goals for his club, he finished his career out of the First Division with Stockport County, Fulham, Hibernian (Scotland), and Bournemouth. He also played for several non-League clubs. Footballer of the Year in England and Europe in 1969, he played for Northern Ireland 37 times, but never in the World Cup. » football [i]

best boy » **gaffer**

bestiary A literary form popular in classical and mediaeval times which presents human characteristics in the guise of animal behaviour: the Greek *Physiologus* is the model. Many animals such as the lion, the eagle, and the fox owe their symbolic associations to these works, of which the 13th-c Middle English Bestiary is a late example. » allegory; fable

beta blockers A group of drugs, introduced in the early 1960s, which lower heart rate and blood pressure. *Propranolol*, the first clinically useful beta blocker, and *atenolol* are widely used in acute stress and panic, where it prevents symptoms such as racing of the heart, sweating, and tremor. It is therefore prescribed for situations such as public performances and driving tests. There is current controversy over their use in some sports (eg snooker), where they may improve performance. » angina

beta decay A naturally occuring radioactive decay process in which a neutron in an atomic nucleus spontaneously breaks up into a proton, which remains in the nucleus, and an electron (beta particle), that is emitted. The process is always accompanied by the emission of an antineutrino, and is governed by weak nuclear force. Strontium-90, for example, is a beta emitter with a half-life of 28.1 years. » beta particle; electron capture; half-life; nucleus (physics); radioactivity; weak interaction

beta particle A particle emitted in beta decay. It is usually a high-energy electron, but positrons are also sometimes called beta particles. These particles are emitted with a wide range of energies from any particular source; the typical particle range in air is several metres. » beta decay; electron; particle physics; positron

Betacam The trade name of a videotape cassette recorder and camera system of TV broadcast standard, introduced by Sony in 1981, initially for electronic news-gathering but widely adopted internationally for all forms of video production. It uses component recording with separate luminance and chrominance tracks on ½ in (12.7 mm) tape at a speed of 10.15 cm/sec in compact cassettes, 156 × 96 × 25 mm. Betacam SP is an improved version using metal-particle tape for higher bandwidth and better picture quality. » videotape recorder

Betamax The trade name for a videotape cassette recorder system developed by Sony in 1975 for the domestic market, using ½ in (12.7 mm) tape at a speed of 1.87 cm/sec in a compact Beta cassette with a playing time up to 3 hours. Although economical, it never achieved the popularity of the competitive VHS system. » videotape recorder

betatron A particle accelerator in which electrons are held in a circular orbit by a magnetic field, and accelerated by a varying electric field superimposed. Very high particle energies have been attained. It is used for research on high-energy electron behaviour or to produce high-energy X-rays. » electron; particle accelerators

betel-nut A slender tree reaching 30 m/100 ft, native to SE Asia; leaves 8 m/26 ft, feathery; seeds 4–5 cm/1½–2 in, red or orange; also called the **areca palm**. The nuts are boiled with lime, then dried, and wrapped in betel leaf from the climbing species of pepper, *Piper betle*. The 'plug' is habitually chewed in the Indian subcontinent and SE Asia for its intoxicating effects, which are similar to alcohol. The juice stains teeth and saliva bright red. (*Areca catechu*. Family: *Palmae*.) » palm; tree [i]

Betelgeuse [betuhljerz] A red supergiant star, prominent in Orion, somewhat variable in luminosity, 800 times the diameter of the Sun. Distance: 180 parsecs. » Orion (astronomy); supergiant

Bethlehem, Arabic **Beit Lahm** 31°42N 35°12E, pop (1980) 14 000. Sub-district of Judea-Samaria district, Israel; Biblical town in Jerusalem governorate, Israeli-occupied West Bank, W Jordan; 8 km/5 ml SSW of Jerusalem; birthplace of Jesus and the home of David; trade centre for surrounding agricultural area; university (1973); Church of the Nativity, built by Constantine, 330; Monastery of Elijah (6th-c, restored). » David; Israel [i]; Jesus Christ; Jordan [i]

Bethmann-Hollweg, Theobald von [betman **hol**vek] (1856–1921) German statesman, born and died at Hohenfinow, Brandenburg. Having qualified in law, he rose in the service of Prussia and the German Empire, becoming Imperial Chancellor in 1909. Although not identified with the German elite's most bellicose elements, and fearing the effects of war upon German society, he nevertheless played an important part in the events which brought about general war in 1914. Anxious for a negotiated peace in 1917, he was forced from office. » Prussia; World War 1

Betjeman, Sir John (1906–84) British author, born in London. Educated at Marlborough and Oxford, he is especially known for his light verse, much of which is to be found in his *Collected Poems* (1958) and in his verse autobiography, *Summoned by Bells* (1960). He also wrote many essays and guidebooks, and championed Victorian and Edwardian art and architecture. He was knighted in 1969, made poet laureate in 1972, and died at Trebetherick, Cornwall. » English literature; poetry

betony A perennial related to woundworts, native to Europe; stems square; long-stalked basal leaves in a rosette, upper in opposite pairs; flowers 2-lipped with long tube, bright reddish-purple, in whorls. It is an old medicinal and magical herb. (*Betonica officinalis*. Family: *Labiatae*.) » herb; perennial; woundwort

Better Business Bureau One of many local organizations, mainly in the USA and Canada, formed to protect communities against unfair or misleading advertising and selling practices. Established in the early years of this century by advertising men, they nowadays set standards for business practice, and investigate complaints.

Betti, Ugo (1892–1954) Italian dramatist and poet, born in Camerino. He studied law, and became a judge, while continuing to write. His works include collections of verse, such as *Il re pensieroso* (1922, The Thoughtful King), short stories, and 26 plays, notably *La Padrona* (1929, The Landlady), many of which focus on issues of social justice. He died in Rome. » Italian literature

Bevan, Aneurin (1897–1960) British Labour politician, born at Tredegar, Wales. One of 13 children, he worked in the pits on leaving school at 13, and led the Welsh miners in the 1926 General Strike. He entered parliament for the Independent Labour Party in 1929, joining the Labour Party in 1931. He established a reputation as a brilliant, irreverent, and often tempestuous orator. As Minister of Health (1945–51), he introduced the National Health Service (1948). He became Minister of Labour in 1951, but resigned in the same year over the National Health charges proposed in the Budget. From this period dated 'Bevanism', the left-wing movement to make the Labour Party more socialist and less 'reformist'. He married **Jennie Lee** (1904–88) in 1934, and died, still an MP, at Chesham, Buckinghamshire. » Labour Party; National Health Service; socialism

Bevan, Brian, byname **The Galloping Ghost** (1924–) Australian rugby league player, born in Sydney. A wing-threequarter, he scored a record 796 tries in 18 seasons (1945–64). He played for Blackpool Borough and Warrington, and was one of the inaugural members of the Rugby League Hall of Fame in 1988. » rugby football

bevatron A thousand million electron volt proton accelerator, designed and built at Berkeley Radiation Laboratory, University of California, USA. » particle accelerators; proton

Beveridge, William Henry Beveridge, 1st Baron (1879–1963) British economist, administrator, and social reformer, born at Rangpur, Bengal, India. Educated at Charterhouse and Oxford, he entered the Board of Trade (1908) and became director of labour exchanges (1909–16). He was director of the London School of Economics (1919–37) and Master of University College, Oxford (1937–45). He is best known as the author of the *Report on Social Insurance and Allied Services* (**The Beveridge Report**, 1942), which helped to create the welfare state. He was knighted in 1919, became a Liberal MP (1944–6), and was made a baron in 1946. He died at Oxford. » welfare state

Beverley 53°51N 0°26W, pop (1981) 19 687. County town and market town in Beverley district, Humberside, NE England; 12 km/7 ml NW of Hull; administrative centre of Humberside; railway; engineering; Beverley Minster (13th-c). » Humberside

Beverly Hills 34°04N 118°25W, pop (1980) 32 367. Residential city in Los Angeles County, SW California, USA; surrounded by Los Angeles; the home of many television and film celebrities. » California; Los Angeles

Bevin, Ernest (1881–1951) British Labour politician, born at Winsford, Somerset. Orphaned by seven, and self-taught, he early came under the influence of trade unionism and the Baptists, and was for a time a lay preacher. A paid official of the dockers' union, he gained a national reputation in 1920 when he won most of his union's claims against an eminent barrister, earning the title of 'the dockers' KC'. He built up the National Transport and General Workers' Union, and became its General Secretary (1921–40). In 1940 he became an MP, Minister of Labour and National Service in Churchill's coalition government, and in the Labour government was Foreign Secretary (1945–51). » Baptists; Churchill, Winston; Labour Party; trade union

bézique [buhzeek] A card game believed to have originated in Spain, and brought to England in 1861. The rules were drawn up by the Portland Club in 1887. Played with at least two players, each has a pack of cards but with the 2s, 3s, 4s, 5s, and 6s taken out. The object is to win tricks, and score points on the basis of the cards won. A variation is Rubicon Bézique. » pinochle; playing cards

bezoar » **goat**

Bhadgaon [**bad**gown], also **Bhaktapur** 27°41N 85°26E, pop (1971) 40 112. City and religious centre in C Nepal, 14 km/9 ml E of Kathmandu, in the Kathmandu Valley; altitude 1 400 m/4 593 ft; probably founded in AD 889; shaped like a conch-shell, urban area occupying c.10 sq km/4 sq ml; processing of grain and vegetables, pottery, weaving; Lion Gate, Golden Gate, Palace of 55 Windows, Bell of Barking Dogs, Batsala Temple, replica of Pashupatinath Temple. » Nepal [i]

Bhagavadgita (Sanskrit 'The Song of the Lord') [bahgavad**geeta**] A poem forming part of the Hindu epic, the Mahabharata, consisting of an eve of battle dialogue between the warrior prince Arjuna and Lord Krishna (in the person of his charioteer). Most Hindus regard the poem, with its teaching that there are many valid ways to salvation, but that not all are universally appropriate, as the supreme expression of their religion. » Hinduism; Indian literature; Krishna; Mahabharata

bhakti [bahk**tee**] Loving devotion to God, recommended as the most effective path to God in most of the religious texts of popular Hinduism. Devotees are drawn into a close personal relationship to God and, in surrender to God, receive grace however lowly their station. » Hinduism

Bharata Natyam The oldest form of classical Indian temple dance found in SE India. It has many different types, but is primarily a dramatic interpretation of philosophical teachings combining acting with dancing. Its technical brilliance is found in intricate patterns of footwork set against the graceful design of arm movements. It retains strict codes of performance. » Indian dance

Bharatpur [barat**poor**] » **Keoladeo**

Bhil [beel] An ethnic group in W India stretching from Rajasthan to Maharashtra; mostly agriculturalists. They have adopted kinship patterns and features of Hinduism from their Hindu neighbours, but some are Muslim. Population c 2.5 million. » Hinduism

Bhopal [boh**pahl**] 23°20N 77°53E, pop (1981) 672 000. Capital of Madhya Pradesh, C India, 170 km/106 ml ENE of Indore; founded, 1723; scene of a major industrial disaster in December 1984, when poisonous isocyanate gas escaped from the Union Carbide factory, killing c.2 500 people and leaving 100 000 homeless; airfield; railway; university (1970); cotton, electrical goods, jewellery; Taj-il Masajid mosque (unfinished). » Madhya Pradesh

Bhutan, in Bhutan **Druk-yul**, official name **Kingdom of Bhutan** [boo**tahn**] pop (1990e) 1 442 000; area 46 600 sq km/18 000 sq ml. Small state in the E Himalayas, divided into four regions;

bounded N by the Tibet region of China, and S, E, and W by India; capital Thimphu; timezone GMT +5½; 305 km/189 ml from E to W; ethnic groups include Bhote (60%), Nepalese (25%), and indigenous or migrant tribes (15%); official language, Dzongkha; Nepalese and English also spoken; main religions, Lamaistic Buddhism (75%) and Buddhist-influenced Hinduism (25%); unit of currency, the ngultrum of 100 chetrums; Indian currency also legal tender.

Physical description and climate. High peaks of E Himalayas in the N, over 7 000 m/23 000 ft; forested mountain ridges with fertile valleys descend to low foothills in the S; many rivers flow to meet the R Brahmaputra; permanent snowfields and glaciers in the mountains; subtropical forest in the S; torrential rain common, average 1 000 mm/40 in (C valleys) and 5 000 mm/200 in (S).

History and government. British involvement since treaty of 1774 with the East India Company; S part of the country annexed, 1865; Britain agreed not to interfere in internal affairs, 1910; similar treaty with India, 1949; governed by a Maharajah, from 1907, now addressed as King of Bhutan; absolute monarchy replaced by a form of democratic monarchy, 1969; King is head of government, advised by 9-member Royal Advisory Council and 6-member Council of Ministers; 151-member unicameral legislative National Assembly (*Tsongdu*) meets twice a year, comprising village elders, monastic representatives, and administrative officials, elected every 3 years; most Butanese live close to a castle-monastery (*dzong*) around which a village has developed.

Economy. Largely based on agriculture, mainly rice, wheat, maize, mountain barley, potatoes, vegetables, fruit (especially oranges); large area of plantation forest; hydroelectric power developing; local handicrafts, food processing, cement processing, plywood; postage stamps, tourism. » Buddhism; East India Company, British; Himalayas; Thimphu; RR24 national holidays; RR44 political leaders

Bhutia [**boo**teea] A Buddhist mountain people in the Himalayas, followers of the Dalai Lama. They speak a Tibetan dialect, and probably came from Tibet in the 9th-c. They practise terrace farming on mountains, and some breed cattle and yaks. The largest population group is in Bhutan (500 000); others live in Sikkim, Nepal, and elsewhere in India. » Buddhism; Dalai Lama

Bhutto, Zulfikar Ali [**but**oh] (1928–79) Pakistani statesman, President (1971–3) and Prime Minister (1973–7), born at Larkana, Sind. Graduating from the Universities of California and Oxford, he began a career in law. He joined the Pakistani Cabinet in 1958 as Minister of Commerce, and became Foreign Minister in 1963. Dropped from the Cabinet, he founded the Pakistan People's Party (PPP) in 1967. After the secession of E Pakistan (now Bangladesh) in 1971, he became President, and in 1973 Prime Minister. He introduced social and economic reforms, but opposition to his policies, especially from right-wing Islamic parties, led to the army under General Zia ul-Haq seizing control after the 1977 elections. Tried for corruption and murder, he was sentenced to death in 1978. In spite of worldwide appeals for clemency, the sentence was carried out in 1979. His elder daughter **Benazir** (1953–) became head of the PPP; largely under house arrest until 1984, and then exiled in London, she returned to Pakistan in 1986, becoming the focus of much political unrest. She was Prime Minister 1988–90. » Bangladesh [i]; Pakistan [i]; Zia ul-Haq

Biafra [bee**af**ra] The SE province of Nigeria, inhabited by the Igbo people. Under the leadership of Colonel Ojukwu, it attempted to break away from the federation, thus precipitating the civil war of 1967–70. After the war Nigeria was reorganized into a new provincial structure in an attempt to avert continuing instability. » Igbo; Nigeria [i]

Białystok [byowo**shtok**] 53°09N 23°10E, pop (1983) 240 300. Industrial capital of Białystok voivodship, E Poland, on the Polasie plain; largest city in NE Poland; developed as a textile centre, 19th-c; city devastated in World War 2; railway; medical academy; cotton, wool, tools, food processing, power; Revolutionary Movement Museum, residence of the Branicki family, Church of St Roch (1924), town hall; national festival of music and poetry (Apr). » Poland [i]

Biarritz [**bee**arits] 43°29N 1°33W, pop (1982) 28 000. Fashionable resort town in Pyrénées-Atlantiques department, SW France, on Bay of Biscay; noted for its mild climate and beaches.

biathlon A combined test of cross-country skiing and rifle shooting. It is used as a form of military training and is based on the old military patrol race. Men's individual competitions are over 10 and 20 km (6.2 and 12.4 ml), while women's are over 5 and 10 km (3.1 and 6.2 ml). At designated points on the course, competitors have to fire either standing or prone at a fixed target. The biathlon was introduced into the Winter Olympic programme in 1960. » shooting (recreation); skiing; RR106

Bible Either the Christian Scriptures or the Jewish Scriptures, those works recognized as sacred and authoritative writings by the respective faiths. The Christian Scriptures are divided between two *testaments*: the Old Testament (which corresponds roughly to the canon of Jewish Scriptures), and the New Testament. The Old Testament, or **Hebrew Bible**, is a collection of writings originally composed in Hebrew, except for parts of Daniel and Ezra that are in Aramaic. These writings depict Israelite religion from its beginnings to about the 2nd-c BC. The New Testament is so-called in Christian circles because it is believed to constitute a new 'testament' or 'covenant' in the history of God's dealings with his people, centring on the ministry of Jesus and the early development of the apostolic churches. The New Testament writings were written in Greek.

The process of determining precisely which writings were to be accepted in the Jewish or Christian Scriptures is known as the formation of the *canon* of Scripture. The earliest step towards establishing the canon of Jewish Scriptures was probably the fixing of the *Law*, viz the Pentateuch (the Books of Genesis, Exodus, Leviticus, Numbers, and Deuteronomy), in about the 4th–3rd-c BC. In addition, a group of writings known as the *Prophets* appear to have been recognized by the grandson of Ben Sira (c.117 BC). The remaining books of the Hebrew Bible are called the *Writings* (eg the Books of Psalms, Proverbs, Job) and were seemingly the last to be settled. It was only c.100 AD that the final selection of authorized Jewish Scriptures was complete, following a decision taken by the council at Jabneh. The Greek translations of the Hebrew Bible (the Septuagint) contained some other writings which were not accepted at Jabneh.

The early Christians largely accepted the Jewish Scriptures, but frequently had access to the larger collection of writings in the Septuagint and some other translations of the Hebrew Bible. Debates about the precise limits of the 'Old Testament' continued into the Reformation period, with a difference eventually resulting in the Protestant and Roman Catholic Churches. At the Council of Trent (1546), the Catholics accepted as *deuterocanonical* several works which Protestants labelled as *Apocrypha* and considered of secondary value. Protestant Churches in general have accepted only the writings of the Hebrew canon in their versions of the Old Testament.

Early Christians, however, also began to collect specifically 'Christian' writings. In the 2nd-c, Irenaeus testifies to a growing recognition of exactly four Gospels, the Acts, and 13 Pauline letters as authoritative for the Church. Soon this was the basis for a 'New Testament', although a number of other disputed works were also being considered. The first evidence for a canonical list which completely matches that widely accepted for the New Testament today was the 39th Easter letter of Athanasius (367), which designates 27 books of the New Testament alongside the canon of the Old Testament, although debate continued for some years in the East about the Book of Revelation, and in the West over the Letter to the Hebrews.

While the limits of the canon were effectively set in these early centuries, the status of Scripture has been a topic of scholarly discussion in the later church. Increasingly, the Biblical works have been subjected to literary and historical criticism in efforts to interpret the texts independent of church and dogmatic influences. Different views of the authority and inspiration of the Bible also continue to be expressed in liberal and fundamentalist churches today. What cannot be denied, however, is the enormous influence which the stories, poetry, and reflections found in the Biblical writings have had, not only on the doctrines and practices of two major faiths, but also on Western culture, its literature, art, and music. » Apocrypha, New Testament/Old Testament; Bible Society; canon (religion) 1; Christianity; Judaism; New Testament; Old Testament; Pseudepigrapha; Authorized Version of the/ Breeches/Douai/Geneva/New English Bible

Bible Society An agency for the translation and dissemination of the Bible. The first was the Van Canstein Bible Society, formed in Germany in 1710, but the modern movement really began with the British and Foreign Bible Society, formed in London in 1904. The United Bible Society now provides a world-wide network of autonomous societies, protestant and evangelical in the main, responsible for the translation of the Bible in well over 1500 languages, and distributing copies at subsidized prices. » Bible

bibliography **1** The study of the history, identification, and description of books, seen as physical objects, including the materials used and the methods of production (*critical* or *analytical* bibliography). **2** A book, or a list in a book, containing systematic details of an author's writings, or of publications on a given subject or period (*descriptive* or *enumerative* bibliography). Each entry normally consists of an author's name, the title of the work, its publisher, and its place and date of publication. Details of format, binding, number of illustrations, and other characteristics may also be included. » Gesner

Bibliothèque Nationale [bibleeoh**tek** nashuh**nahl**] The national library of France, located in Paris. It evolved from the libraries of the French monarchs, and was designated a national depository in 1537. Its holdings include over 7 million volumes and 155 000 manuscripts. » library; Paris

bicameral system A parliament of two chambers, which usually have different methods of election or selection. In some countries (such as the USA) the two chambers enjoy equal powers, which necessitates a means of reconciling differences; but commonly one chamber enjoys supremacy over the legislative process, with the other enjoying powers of revision and delay (as in the UK). » parliament

bicarbonate HCO_3^-, IUPAC **hydrogen carbonate**. The anion corresponding to half-neutralized carbonic acid. *Sodium bicarbonate*, or baking soda, is used with weak acids as a source of carbon dioxide. Aqueous solutions of soluble bicarbonates are mildly alkaline, with pH values of 8–9. » anion; carbon dioxide; carbonic acid; pH

Bichat, (Marie-François) Xavier [**bee**sha] (1771–1802) French pathologist, born at Thiorette. He studied medicine in France, and began to teach medical sciences (unofficially) in Paris in 1797. His teaching was highly influential. In particular he saw that the body is composed of tissues, and noted that although an organ may contain several tissues, usually only one of them will be affected by a given disease. His work largely founded the study of histology. He died in Paris. » anatomy; histology; pathology; tissue

bicycle A light-framed vehicle possessing two wheels fitted with pneumatic tyres, the rear wheel being propelled by the rider through a crank, chain, and gear mechanism. The major uses to which bicycles are put are personal transport, particularly in underdeveloped countries, and sport. It is generally held that the modern pedal bicycle was invented by Kirkpatrick Macmillan of Dumfriesshire, Scotland, and first ridden by him in 1840. The pneumatic tyre was first successfully applied to the bicycle in 1888. » gear; moped; motorcycle; tyre

Bidault, Georges [**bee**doh] (1899–1982) French statesman and Prime Minister (1946, 1949–50), born and educated in Paris. He became a professor of history, served in both world wars, and was a member of the French resistance. He became leader of the Mouvement Républicain Populaire, and apart from his periods as Premier, he was Deputy Prime Minister (1950, 1951), and Foreign Minister (1944, 1947, 1953–54). After 1958 he opposed de Gaulle over the Algerian War, was charged with plotting against the security of the state, and went into exile (1962–8). He died near Bayonne. » de Gaulle; France [i]

Biedermeierstil [**bee**dermiyershteel] A satirical name for the simple, plain ('bourgeois philistine') style of furniture and decoration popular in Austria and Germany 1815–48. The term is sometimes extended to architecture. Biedermeier painting tends to a mild sentimentalism and homely naturalism. » German art; Naturalism (art)

Biennale [beer**nah**lay] An international art exhibition held in Venice regularly since 1895, and imitated at Paris, Tokyo, and elsewhere. It was originally conservative, but since 1948 has been a major showcase for the avant garde. » avant garde

biennial A plant which flowers, sets seed, and dies in its second year. In the first year it produces only vegetative growth, usually a rosette of leaves which build up food reserves for the onset of flowering. » annual; perennial

Bierce, Ambrose (Gwinett) (1842–?1914) US journalist and writer, born in Meigs Co, Ohio. He was the author of collections of sardonically humorous tales on the theme of death, such as *In the Midst of Life* (1898). He disappeared in Mexico during the revolution of Pancho Villa. » American literature

Big Bang A hypothetical model of the universe which postulates that all matter and energy were once concentrated into an unimaginably dense state, or primaeval atom, from which it has been expanding since a creation event some $13–20 \times 10^9$ years ago. The main evidence favouring this model comes from cosmic background radiation and the redshifts of galaxies. The theory of an expanding universe was proposed by Edwin Hubble in 1929, and is now generally accepted. » cosmology; Hubble; inflationary universe; redshift; universe

Big Ben Originally the nickname of the bell in the clock tower of the Houses of Parliament, London, and now by association the clock and its tower. The bell, 2.7 m/9 ft in diameter and weighing 13 tonnes, was cast in 1858. » Houses of Parliament

Big Dipper » **Plough, the**

bigamy A criminal offence committed when someone who is already married enters into 'marriage' with another person. The offence is not committed where the first marriage has been ended by divorce or death, or where it has been declared void. In some jurisdictions, there is also a good defence if the accused has for a period of time (seven years, in England and Wales) not known that his or her first marriage partner was alive. The onus of proving that the defendant knew the partner was alive during that time lies on the prosecution. » annulment; divorce

Bigfoot or **Sasquatch** In the mountaineering folklore of N America, a creature the equivalent of the abominable snowman or yeti, said to be 2–3 m/7–10 ft tall; its footprints are reported to be 43 cm/17 in long. » yeti

bighorn A wild sheep, inhabiting mountains, especially cliffs; males with large curling horns; two species: **American bighorn sheep**, (*Rocky Mountain sheep*, or *mountain sheep*) from N America (*Ovis canadensis*), and **Siberian bighorn** or **snow sheep**) from NE Siberia (*Ovis nivicola*). » sheep

Bihar or **Behar** [bee**hah**] pop (1981) 69 823 154; area 173 876 sq km/ 67 116 sq ml. State in E India, bounded N by Nepal; crossed by the R Ganges; Rajmahal Hills in the S; capital, Patna; governed by a 325-member Legislative Assembly; major mineral deposits, including coal, copper, mica; rice, jute, sugar cane, oilseed, wheat, maize; iron and steel, machine tools, fertilizers, electrical engineering, paper milling, cement. » Buddh Gaya; India [i]; Patna

Bikini [bi**kee**nee] Atoll in the Marshall Is, W Pacific, 3 200 km/2 000 ml SW of Hawaii; site of 23 US nuclear tests, 1946–58; first H-bomb tested here; inhabitants evacuated in 1946; many returned in 1972, but were evacuated again when it was discovered that they had ingested the largest dose of plutonium ever monitored in any population. » atomic bomb; Marshall Islands

Biko, Stephen (1946–77) South African Black activist, born in King William's Town, who was the founder and leader of the Black Consciousness Movement. He became involved in politics while studying medicine at Natal University and was the first president of the all-Black South African Students Organization (1969), and honorary president of the Black People's Convention (1972). In 1973 he was served with a banning order severely restricting his movements and freedom of speech and association. He was detained four times in the last few years of his life, and died in police custody, allegedly as a result of beatings received. He was the subject of a successful film, *Cry Freedom* (1987), directed by Richard Attenborough. » apartheid; Black Consciousness Movement

bilateralism » **multilateralism**

Bilbao [bil**bow**] 43°16N 2°56W, pop(1981) 433 030. Major seaport and industrial capital of Vizcaya province, N Spain; on R Nervión, 395 km/245 ml N of Madrid; founded, 1300; bishopric; airport; railway; university (1886); commercial centre of the Basque Provinces; iron, steel, chemicals, shipbuilding, fishing, wine trade; cathedral (14th-c), art museum, Churches of St Anton and St Nicholas de Bari; machine tool fair (Mar), Semana Grande (Aug). » Basque Provinces; Spain [i]

bilberry A small deciduous shrub, native to acid soils in Europe and N Asia, especially on high ground where it may form bilberry moors; leaves 1–3 cm/0.4–1.2 in, oval, toothed; 1–2 flowers in leaf axils, drooping, 4–6 mm/⅛–¼ in, globose, greenish-white; berry c.8 mm/0.3 in, black with bluish-white bloom, sweet, edible. Alternative names are **blaeberry**, **whortleberry**, and (in the UK) **huckleberry**. (*Vaccinium myrtillus*. Family: *Ericaceae*). » deciduous plants; huckleberry; shrub

bilby » **bandicoot**

Bildungsroman [**bil**dungksrohman] (Ger 'education novel') A novel which deals principally with the formative stages of its hero(ine)'s life – childhood, education, adolescence. Examples are Rousseau's *Emile* (1762), Dickens's *David Copperfield* (1850), Musil's *Young Torless* (1906), and Joyce's *A Portrait of the Artist as a Young Man* (1914). » English/French/German literature; novel

bile A golden-yellow fluid produced by the liver, and stored and concentrated in the gall bladder, until released into the duodenum in response to certain dietary substances (eg fats) in the duodenal cavity. In humans it contains sodium and potassium salts of certain organic acids (which facilitate the digestion and absorption of fats, and the absorption of fat-soluble vitamins), excretory products (bile pigments, cholesterol), and other alkaline dissolvable substances. » alkali; biliary system; cholecystitis; gallstones; jaundice; liver

bilharziasis [bilhah**zi**yasis] » **schistosomiasis**

biliary system A physiological system for the production, storage, and transport of bile, comprising the liver, gall bladder and various ducts. Bile produced in the liver drains into the hepatic ducts and usually into the gall bladder (for storage and concentration) via the cystic duct. Ingestion of fatty food leads to the release of bile from the gall bladder into the duodenum via the cystic and common bile ducts, when it joins with digestive enzymes from the pancreas. Gallstones are occasionally formed in the gall bladder or bile ducts, affecting the flow of bile through the duct system, resulting in pain and discomfort (*biliary colic*). » bile; colic; duodenum; gall bladder; gallstones; jaundice; liver

bilingualism The ability to speak two languages. Research studies in linguistics have focused on the diversity of bilingual situations which exist, and on the varying degrees of ability which bilinguals can have in their two languages (eg what level of proficiency does a person need, to be regarded as a speaker of a language?). There may also be important differences between those who are bilingual from an early age and those who become so through education or as adults. And an interesting question is whether bilinguals have separate conceptual systems in their two languages, or whether they have the same 'world view' when using either. Contrary to popular belief, it is more common throughout the world as a whole to be bilingual than monolingual. People with more than two languages are said to be **multilingual**. » linguistics

bill of exchange or **commercial bill** A document ordering someone to pay a certain sum of money to another on a specific date, or when certain conditions have been fulfilled. Bills of exchange are used mainly in foreign trade; their legal status in the UK is laid down by the Bills of Exchange Act (1882). » accepting house

bill of rights A list of citizens' rights set out in constitutional documents. Usually accompanying the document is an elaboration of the institutional means and powers by which such rights may be enforced. The best-known example is the first ten amendments to the US Constitution, adopted in 1791. This protects the liberties of private citizens in relation to the federal and state governments in such matters as freedom of speech, religion, the press and assembly, and legal procedure. It was adopted because of popular pressure during the campaign to ratify the Constitution (1787–8), and its meaning has been expounded in many cases decided by the Supreme Court. » constitution; Constitution of the United States; Declaration of Rights

bill, parliamentary A draft of a proposed new law that is to be considered by a legislature. A bill may be amended before it is finally enacted in law. The procedures for a legislature to consider a bill vary considerably from country to country. » Act of Parliament

billfish Any of a group of large and very agile surface-living fishes (Family: *Istiophoridae*) in which the snout is prolonged to form a slender pointed bill used for stunning prey; all are adapted for fast swimming, with elongate streamlined bodies and short wide tail fin; includes sailfish and marlins. Most are exploited commercially, and are amongst the most highly prized of all sport fishes. » marlin; sailfish

billiards An indoor table game played in many different forms. The most popular is that played on a standard English billiard table measuring c.12 ft × 6 ft (3.66 m × 1.83 m). Originally an outdoor game, its exact origins are uncertain; an early reference is 1429, when Louis XI of France owned a billiard table. It is played with three balls; one red and two white. Scoring is achieved by potting balls, going in-off another ball, and making cannons (hitting your white ball so that it successively strikes the two others). *Carom* is another form, popular in Europe; it is played on a pocketless table with the object of making cannons. » bagatelle; pool; snooker; RR106

Billingsgate Market A fish-market in London, dating from the 9th-c. Its name derived from a river-gate in the nearby city wall. The market was closed in 1982. » London [i]

Billy the Kid » **Bonney, William H**

Biloxi [bi**lok**see] 30°24N 88°53W, pop(1980) 490 311. Town in Harrison County, SE Mississippi, USA; on the Gulf of Mexico at the mouth of the Biloxi R; named after an Indian tribe; settled, 1699; the first permanent White settlement in the Mississippi valley; railway; tourism, boatbuilding, shrimp and oyster fisheries; Keesler Air Force Base. » Mississippi

bimetallic strip Two strips of different metals welded or riveted together face to face, which expand to different extents on heating because of their different co-efficients of thermal expansion. One can become longer than the other only if the whole takes up a curved shape, with the metal which expands the more on the outer face. This phenomenon can be used to actuate indicators or electric switches in response to changes in temperature. » heat; metal

bimetallism An economic system where two metals (usually gold and silver) are used as the basis for currency. The relative value of the metals is maintained artificially. » money

binary code A code derived from the binary number system using only two digits, 0 and 1, in comparison with the decimal system which has ten digits, 0 to 9. The advantage of the binary system for use in digital computers is that only two electronic states, off and on, are required to represent all the possible binary digits. All digital computers operate using various binary codes to represent numbers, characters, etc. » ASCII code; binary coded decimal; bit; RR77

binary coded decimal (BCD) A computer coding system where each decimal numeral (0–9) is represented by a set of four binary digits, or bits. » bit; RR77

binary number A number written in base two, ie in which every number is expressed as the sum of powers of 2; thus $7=4+2+1=2^2+2^1+1$; so $7_{\text{ten}}=111_{\text{two}}$. » base (mathematics); binary code

binary star Two stars revolving around their common centre of mass. Perhaps a half of all stars in our Galaxy are members of binaries. Astronomers study orbital motions in binaries because this gives the only direct way of finding out what the mass of a star is. In some rare and exotic cases, one star in a binary can be a black hole or a neutron star, and mass transfer takes place from the other, normal star with intense X-ray emission. » Algol; black hole; eclipse **2**; neutron star; star; X-rays

binary weapon An expression describing how a munition used in chemical warfare can be configured. Two individually harmless chemicals are packed separately into (for example) an artillery shell; these are combined on detonation to form a deadly toxic agent. » chemical warfare

binding sites » **receptors**

bindweed Several related climbers with fleshy, rope-like roots, fast-growing twining stems, and large funnel-shaped flowers, all native to temperate regions; often pernicious weeds. *Convolvulus arvensis* is a coastal plant; leaves arrowhead-shaped; flowers 3 cm/1.2 in diameter, pink, striped white above, maroon beneath. **Sea bindweed** (*Calystegia soldanella*) has kidney-shaped leaves; flowers 5 cm/2 in diameter, pink with white stripes; calyx hidden by two bracts. **Hedge bindweed** (*Calystegia sepium*) has arrowhead- or heart-shaped leaves; flowers 3.5 cm/1½ in diameter, white; calyx hidden by two bracts. **Large bindweed** (*Calystegia sylvatica*) is similar, but its flowers are 7.5 cm/3 in diameter. (Family: *Convolvulaceae*.) » bract; climbing plant; sepal

Binet, Alfred [**bee**nay] (1857–1911) French psychologist, born in Nice. Initially trained as a lawyer, he developed wide interests in psychology, particularly in hypnotism, and founded the journal *L'Année Psychologique* (1894). He is principally remembered for the Binet-Simon scale (with colleague Theodore Simon) for measuring the intelligence of schoolchildren (1905) – the precursor of many of today's mental tests. He died in Paris. » intelligence; psychology

Binford, Lewis (Roberts) (1930–) US archaeologist, the acknowledged leader of the anthropologically-oriented school of archaeology which has powerfully influenced the discipline since the late 1960s. He has directed attention to the systemic nature of human culture, and to the complex interaction between the technological, social, and ideological subsystems of all societies. An ethno-archaeologist rather than an excavator, he is professor of anthropology at the University of New Mexico, Albuquerque. » anthropology; archaeology; Clarke, David

Bing, Sir Rudolf (1902–) British opera administrator, born in Vienna. He worked in Berlin and Darmstadt (1928–33) before managing the opera at Glyndebourne (1935–49). He was co-founder and director (1947–9) of the Edinburgh Festival, and general manager of the Metropolitan Opera, New York (1950–72). He took British nationality in 1946, and was knighted in 1971. » opera

bingo A game played by any number of people, using cards normally containing 15 squares numbered between 1 and 90. The caller picks numbers at random, and if players have the corresponding number on their card they eliminate it, usually by crossing it through. The first person(s) to eliminate all numbers is the winner, and is usually identified by calling out 'bingo' or 'house'. Known as *lotto* or *housey-housey* for many years, it became popularized as bingo in the 1960s.

binoculars A magnifying optical instrument for use by both eyes simultaneously; also known as **field-glasses**. Two optical systems are mounted together, each consisting of two convex lenses (an eyepiece and an object lens) plus prisms to produce an upright image. Focusing is achieved by varying the distance between eyepiece and object lens. Some instruments, such as opera glasses, use a concave eyepiece to produce an upright image without prisms. » lens; telescope [i]

binomial nomenclature The modern system of naming and classifying organisms, established by the Swedish naturalist Carl Linne (1707–78) in the mid-18th-c. Every species has a unique scientific name (*binomen*) consisting of two words: a generic name and a specific name. For example, the scientific name of a lion is *Panthera leo* and that of the tiger *Panthera tigris*. They belong to the same genus, but are different species. » systematics; taxonomy

binturong [bin**too**rong] A carnivorous mammal, native to SE Asia; dense black fur, thickest on its grasping tail; tips of ears with prominent tufts; inhabits dense forests; eats birds, carrion, vegetation; catches fish by swimming; easily tamed. (*Arctictis binturong*. Family: *Viverridae*.) » carnivore [i]; Viverridae [i]

Binyon, (Robert) Laurence (1869–1943) British poet and art critic, born at Lancaster, Lancashire. On leaving Oxford, he joined the British Museum, and became keeper of Oriental prints and paintings (1913–33). His poetic works include *Lyric Poems* (1894), *Odes* (1901), and *Collected Poems* (1931). He also wrote plays, and translated Dante into terza rima. In 1933–4 he was professor of poetry at Harvard. Extracts from his poem 'For the Fallen' (set to music by Elgar) adorn war memorials throughout the British commonwealth. He died at Reading, Berkshire. » English literature; terza rima

bioassay [biyoha**say**] The measurement of amounts or activities of substances using the responses of living organisms or cells; an abbreviation of **biological assay**. For example, the concentration of pollutants can be estimated by determining the growth rate of particular organisms exposed to them under a range of controlled conditions. » biological sciences; pollution

biochemistry The branch of biology dealing with the chemistry of living organisms, especially with the structure and function of their chemical components. » biological sciences

bioclimatology The study of climate as it affects humans, for example calculation of wind chill and degree days. A *degree day* is the difference in actual mean temperature for a day and a pre-determined threshold temperature; if actual temperatures are consistently below the chosen threshold, then the provision of heating might be necessary. » temperature [i]; wind chill

biodegradable substance Any substance that can be decomposed by natural processes, particularly microbial decay, so that its constituents are rendered available for use within the ecosystem. Many modern materials are non-biodegradable, accumulating in the ecosystem. » ecosystem; micro-organism

biofeedback The technique of recording biological (physiological) signals from subjects, and displaying them so that the subjects become aware of them and can be trained to control the underlying process. Subjects can learn to control heart rate, blood pressure, muscle activity, and even electrical brain activity. » feedback

biogas A gas produced by the fermentation of organic waste. Decomposition of animal manure, crop residues, and food processing wastes in an air-tight container produces a methane-rich gas which can be used as a source of energy. Small biogas plants are used in developing countries, and some farms in Europe and the USA produce biogas for farm use. » alternative energy; energy; waste disposal

biogenesis The principle that a living organism can arise only from another living organism. It contrasts with notions such as the spontaneous generation of living organisms from non-living matter by natural processes. » biology

biogenetic law The generalization that early stages of development in animal species resemble one another, and that differences between species become increasingly apparent as development proceeds. » biology; genetics [i]; species

biogeography The geographical study of the distribution of animals and plants at global, regional, and local scales. In particular it examines the factors responsible for their changing distribution in both time and space. » ecology; geography; phytogeography; zoogeography

biography The narrative of a person's life: as we know it, a form proper to the modern centuries (post-17th-c). In classical and mediaeval times, such biographical writing as existed tended to be summary and exemplary lives of kings, heroes, and saints, with little concern for the personal subject. But the Protestant and democratic spirit conferred greater value on the individual; and the subject of Boswell's great biography (published in 1791), Dr Johnson, maintained that the narrative of any person's life would be worth reading. Most well-known figures in the last 200 years have found a biographer: latterly, even whilst still alive. » autobiography; Boswell; Johnson, Samuel; literature

Bioko, formerly **Fernando Po** or **Póo** (to 1973), **Macias Nguema Bijogo** (to 1979) [bee**o**koh] area 2017 sq km/779 sq ml. Island in the Bight of Biafra, off coast of Cameroon, W Africa; province of Equatorial Guinea; volcanic origin, rising to

3 007 m/9 865 ft at Pico de Basilé; chief town, and capital of Equatorial Guinea, Malabo; other towns include Luba and Riaba; visited by Portuguese, 1471; originally named after Portuguese navigator; occupied at various times by British, Portuguese, and Spanish; coffee, cocoa, copra. » Equatorial Guinea [i]; Malabo

biolinguistics The study of the ways in which human biology is predisposed to the development of language and use. It is particularly concerned with the genetic transmission of language and with neurophysiological studies of the way spoken language is produced and understood. » genetics [i]; linguistics; neurophysiology

biological assay » **bioassay**

biological control The control of populations of plant or animal species by natural enemies such as predators or parasites. In particular, biological control refers to the introduction or encouragement of natural enemies for use in the regulation of numbers of a pest species. Recently developed techniques for biological control include methods of disrupting reproductive behaviour of the pest, such as the release of sterilized males, the strategic dispersal of pheromones important in pest mating behaviour, and the use of attractants to bait traps. » biology; pheromone

biological psychiatry That area of psychiatry which sees mental illness as resulting from disorders of the physiological system. It emphasizes biochemical, pharmacological, and neurological aspects of mental illness and psychiatric treatments, rather than psychological processes. » biochemistry; physiology; psychiatry

biological rhythm or **biorhythm** The rhythmical change in a biological function of a plant or animal. The frequency of rhythms varies from short (eg less than a second) to long (eg more than a year). Many rhythms arise from within organisms (*endogenous rhythms*); others (*exogenous rhythms*) are entirely dependent upon external environmental factors (such as the alternation of light and dark). Endogenous rhythms are usually synchronized to follow periodic changes in the environment. Examples of biological rhythms in humans are breathing, sleep and waking, and the daily rise and fall of cortisol production; these are controlled by the brain (eg the pineal gland and parts of the hypothalamus). Important biological rhythms in higher plants are photosynthesis and the daily opening and closing of flowers. » antidiuretic hormone; circadian rhythm; cortisol; jet lag; menstruation

biological sciences Specialized study areas which have developed to study living organisms and systems. All biological sciences are based on *taxonomy*, the description and naming of living organisms as a means of creating order out of the diversity of the natural world. The study of the distributions of organisms throughout the world was the next major development, known as **biogeography**. How organisms work is the subject of a number of biological sciences. The chemical processes that occur within living systems are studied as a whole (**biochemistry**) or at the level of interactions between large organic molecules such as proteins and nucleic acids (**molecular biology**). Functional aspects of living systems are the subject of disciplines such as **physiology** and **biophysics**, and these are frequently subdivided further into topics such as **endocrinology** (the study of the production and actions of hormones) and **neurophysiology** (the study of the function of the nervous system). The study of the comparative behaviour of animals is known as **ethology**. **Genetics** studies heredity and variation. The study of the relationship between organisms and their environment is **ecology**. Finally, each major group of organisms is the basis of its own speciality study area, including bacteria (**bacteriology**), plants (**botany**), viruses (**virology**), animals (**zoology**), fungi (**mycology**), parasitic worms (**helminthology**), parasites (**parasitology**), shells (**malacology**), birds (**ornithology**), insects (**entomology**), fishes (**ichthyology**), crustaceans (**carcinology**), organisms living in the sea (**marine biology**), fossils (**palaeontology**), amphibians and reptiles (**herpetology**), pollen (**palynology**), and seaweeds (**phycology**). » amphibian; animal; bacteria [i]; biochemistry; biophysics; bird [i]; cell; crustacean; ecology; ethology; evolution; fish [i]; fungus; genetics [i]; insect [i]; life; mammal [i]; molecular biology; palaeontology; parasitology; plant; pollen [i]; radiobiology; reptile; seaweed; shell; sociobiology; systematics; taxonomy; virus; zoology

biological shield A protective enclosure around the radioactive core of a nuclear reactor, to prevent the escape of radiation capable of damaging biological tissue. It usually consists mainly of massive concrete walls. » nuclear reactor [i]

biological value In food science, the nutritional value of a protein, which depends upon the balance of amino acids it contains. A protein with a low level of one or more essential amino acids will be of little biological value. This value can be quantified as the proportion of truly absorbed nitrogenous material (amino acids) truly retained. Animal proteins such as egg have a high value, while vegetable proteins such as gluten have a low value. » amino acid [i]; gluten; protein

biological warfare An expression that embraces *bacteriological warfare*, which uses naturally-occurring micro-organisms as a weapon of war, and *toxins*, which are poisonous chemicals derived from natural sources. The manufacture and stockpiling of such agents is forbidden by a UN Convention of 1972, although research is allowed to continue. » bacteriological warfare; chemical warfare; toxin

biology The study of living organisms and systems. The beginnings of biology as a science are the natural history observations made by curious amateurs, travellers, farmers, and all those in contact with the natural world. Its rapid development during the 20th-c has led to the increasing subdivision of biology into a variety of specialized disciplines. » biological sciences

bioluminescence The light produced by living organisms through a chemical reaction, and the process of emitting such biologically produced light. The phenomenon can be found in some bacteria, fungi, algae, and animals, including many marine organisms such as deep-sea fishes, squid, and crustaceans, and some terrestrial organisms such as fireflies and glowworms. Bioluminescence serves a variety of functions, such as signalling during courtship rituals, deterring predators, or locating prey in the dark. » biology; chemical energy; light; luminescence

biomass The total mass of living organisms (including producers such as plants, as well as consumers and decomposers) in an ecosystem, population, or other designated unit, at a given time; equivalent to the term **standing crop**. It is usually expressed as dry weight per unit area. » biology; ecosystem

biome [**bi**yohm] A major regional subdivision of the Earth's surface, broadly corresponding to the dominant ecological communities of the main climatic regions, as characterized by their principal plant species and distinctive life forms. Biomes are the largest recognized living communities classified on a geographical basis, such as tundra biome, desert biome, and tropical rainforest biome. » ecology

biomechanics A system of exercises devised by the Russian theatre director, Vsevolod Meyerhold, to extend the physical resources of the actor. It is based on rhythm, the elimination of superfluous movements, and awareness of the body's centre of gravity both in stillness and in motion. » Meyerhold

biomorphic art A type of abstract art based on shapes which vaguely resemble plants and animals. The most celebrated exponent was Hans Arp. » abstract art; Arp; art

Biondi, Matt(hew) [bee**on**dee] (1965–) US swimmer, born at Morego, California. At the 1986 world championships he won a record seven medals, including three golds, and at the 1988 Olympics won seven medals, including five golds. He set the 100 m freestyle world record of 48.74 sec at Orlando, Florida, in 1986. » swimming

bionics The construction of artificial mechanisms, models, circuits, or programs imitating the responses or behaviour of living systems. Its purpose is to adapt observed living functions to practical purposes in useful machines. It contrasts with *cybernetics*, which is concerned with the study of communication within the living system, and *automation*, which is concerned with the mere outward imitation of the appearance of living things. » automation; cybernetics

bionomics The study of organisms in relation to their environment. The term is used particularly with reference to ecological studies of single species. » ecology

biophysics The application of physics to the study of living organisms and systems. It includes the study of the mechanical properties of biological tissues such as bone and chitin, and the interpretation of their functional significance. » biology; chitin; physics

biopsy [**biy**opsee] The surgical removal of a small piece of tissue (eg from the skin, breast, or kidney) in order to determine the nature of any suspected disease process. » pathology

biorhythm » **biological rhythm**

biosphere That part of the Earth's surface and atmosphere in which living organisms are found, and with which they interact to form the global ecosystem. » Earth [i]; ecosystem

Biot-Savart law [**bee**oh savah] In physics, a law which expresses the magnetic field resulting from an electric current; stated in 1820 by French physicists Jean Biot (1774–1862) and Félix Savart (1791–1841). The magnetic flux density B is proportional to the current, divided by the distance from the current. The Biot-Savart result is less general than Ampère's law, from which it can be deduced, but is easier to use. » Ampère's law; magnetic field [i]

biotechnology The application of biological and biochemical science to large-scale production. Isolated examples have existed since early times, notably brewing, but the first modern example was the large-scale production of penicillin in the 1940s. Other pharmaceutical developments followed. Research in genetic engineering is prominent in current studies. » biochemistry; biology; genetic engineering; pharmacy

biotin One of the B-vitamins, found in yeast and in the bacteria which inhabit the human gut. It acts as a co-factor in the synthesis of fatty acids and the conversion of amino acids to glucose. It is rendered unavailable for absorption by the protein, avidin, found in raw egg white. Deficiencies in human beings are rare. » anti-vitamin factors; polyunsaturated fatty acids

biotite » **micas**

bipolarity (politics) » **multipolarity**

birch A slender deciduous tree, occasionally dwarf shrub, native to the N hemisphere, often colonizing poor soils and reaching the tree line in the arctic; branches often pendulous, leaves ovoid, toothed; catkins pendulous, males long, females shorter, becoming cone-like in fruit; nutlets tiny with papery wings. (Genus: *Betula*, 60 species. Family: *Betulaceae*.) » deciduous plants; paper-bark birch; shrub; silver birch; tree [i]

bird A vertebrate animal assignable to the class *Aves*; any animal in which the adult bears feathers (only birds have feathers, and all adult birds have feathers). The fore-limbs of birds are modified as wings; teeth are absent; and the projecting jaws are covered by horny sheaths to produce a bill or 'beak'. The female lays eggs with hard chalky shells. Other characters shared by most living birds are the pronounced vertical blade, or 'keel', on the breastbone, and the joining of the collar bones to form a 'wishbone'. The keel acts as an attachment for the large muscles moving the wings (the breast muscles), and the wishbone acts as a strut to support the wings in flight.

Flight has dominated the evolution of the birds, and their bodies are adapted accordingly. The bones of most birds are hollow, reducing weight; much of the wing and all of the tail is composed entirely of long feathers, these being strong but very light. The body is streamlined with a smooth covering of short overlapping feathers. Flight has also controlled size. Most birds are small. No bird capable of horizontal flight in still air weighs more than 13 kg/30 lb. Even flying birds close to this weight, such as the condor or the albatross, spend much time gliding in air currents. This weight level is very light compared to large mammals or reptiles. That flight is the factor limiting size is indicated by the largest known birds, living or extinct: these are flightless forms, such as the modern ostrich (up to 150 kg/330 lb) or the extinct elephant bird (457 kg/1000 lb). Such flightless running birds, or **ratites**, evolved from flying ancestors, but with the loss of flight the keel has disappeared from the breastbone, and the wishbone has become two separate bones again. The wings of ratites may be very reduced (as in the kiwi), and the feathers may become fluffy, rather than streamlined, and may even be absent from large areas of the body (as in the ostrich). The power of flight has also been lost by the penguins, whose wing feathers have become small and scale-like. However, penguins have kept the keel on the breastbone and now use their wings for 'flying' under water.

Whether capable of flight or flightless, birds have spread to cover almost the entire globe. They are absent today only from the true polar wastes (in common with most other animals) and the deep-sea. They have adapted to fill virtually every habitat and life-style, and their shapes, sizes, colours, and behaviours reflect this diversity. There are approximately 8 600 living species of birds, and specialists indicate their relationships by grouping them into 29 Orders and 181 Families. Birds evolved from reptiles approximately 150 million years ago, and the birds' closest living relatives are the crocodiles. The exact reptile ancestor of the birds is not known, but it has been suggested that they evolved from a group of small dinosaurs. If that is true, then not all dinosaurs became extinct: some merely changed their shape, and are flying around our gardens today. » bird of prey; dinosaur [i]; feather [i]; nest; Ratitae

bird cherry » **gean**

bird of paradise A stout-billed, strong-footed bird native to SE Asian forests. The males use spectacular plumage to attract females, and may take several mates during the breeding season. (Family: *Paradisaeidae*, 43 species.) » bowerbird; riflebird

bird of paradise flower An evergreen perennial growing to c.1 m/3 ft, forming clumps of long-stalked oblong leaves, native to Cape Province, South Africa, and cultivated elsewhere for its striking flowers. Each 'flower' represents a complete inflorescence of several flowers, enclosed in a sheathing bract. Adapted to pollination by sunbirds, the flowers have orange sepals and blue petals, emerging from the bract at weekly intervals. (*Strelitzia reginae*. Family: *Strelitziaceae*.) » bract; evergreen plants; inflorescence [i]; perennial

bird of prey Any bird that hunts large animals (especially mammals and birds) for food, also known as a **raptor**. They have a strong, curved bill and sharp claws. The category includes members of the orders *Accipitriformes* (hawks, eagles, Old World vultures, and the secretary bird), *Falconiformes* (falcons), and *Cathartiformes* (New World vultures, including condors); some authorities include the order *Strigiformes* (owls). » bird [i]; condor; eagle; falcon; hawk; owl; secretary bird; vulture

bird's-nest fern A species of spleenwort (an epiphyte), native to Old World tropical forests, in which the bright green, undivided fronds form a basket or nest-like rosette which accumulates humus. The roots then grow into the humus, obtaining nutrients and water. (*Asplenium nidus*. Family: *Polypodiaceae*.) » epiphyte; humus; spleenwort

birdsfoot-trefoil A perennial growing to 40 cm/15 in, native to Europe, Asia, and Africa; leaves with five oval leaflets up to 1 cm/0.4 in long; pea-flowers in stalked, rather flat-topped clusters of 2–8, yellow often tinged with red; pods up to 3 cm/1.2 in long, many-seeded; also called **eggs and bacon**. (*Lotus corniculatus*. Family: *Leguminosae*.) » perennial; trefoil

birdwing butterfly A large to very large butterfly, found in the Indo-Australian region; long wings; in male, wings black with iridescent colours; in female, wings dull. (Order: *Lepidoptera*. Family: *Papilionidae*.) » butterfly

birefringence A property exhibited by certain crystals, in which the speed of light is different in different directions because of the crystal structure; also called **double refraction**. Birefringent crystals such as calcite and quartz are characterized by two refractive indices, and can form double images. » electro-optic effects; liquid crystals; photoelasticity; refraction [i]

bireme [**biy**reem] A galley, usually Greek or Roman, propelled by two banks of oars, rowed by slaves or criminals. It was also equipped with a square sail for use with a favourable wind. » ship [i]; trireme [i]

Birkbeck, George (1776–1841) British educationist, born at Settle, Yorkshire. In 1799, as professor of chemistry and natural philosophy at Glasgow, he was greatly moved by the interest of a group of uneducated workmen in a model of the centrifugal pump, and this led him to deliver his first free lectures to the working classes. In 1804 he became a physician

Birds – Ostrich, showing undeveloped wing and flat sternum; (2) seagull, showing wing development and sternum with keel. Feet adapted for (3) walking, (4) perching, (5) climbing, (6) hunting, (7) swimming. Bills adapted for (8) preying, (9) spearing fish, (10) eating seeds and nuts, (11) nectar-feeding, (12) eating insects.

in London, where he took a leading part in the formation of the London Mechanics' or Birkbeck Institute (1824), now Birkbeck College, part of London University. He died in London. » London University [i]

Birkenhead, Frederick Edwin Smith, 1st Earl of (1872–1930) British Conservative statesman and lawyer, born at Birkenhead, Cheshire. He was educated at Birkenhead and Oxford, and was called to the Bar in 1899. He entered parliament in 1906, where he became known as a brilliant orator. In the Irish crisis (1914) he supported resistance to Home Rule, but later helped to negotiate the Irish settlement of 1921. He became Attorney-General (1915–19) and Lord Chancellor (1919–22) and was made an earl in 1922. His conduct as Secretary of State for India (1924–8) caused much criticism, and he resigned to devote himself to a commercial career. He died in London. » Conservative Party

Birmingham (USA) 33°31N 86°48W, pop (1980) 284 413. Seat of Jefferson County, NC Alabama, USA; settled, 1813; largest city in the state; airfield; railway; university (1842); canal connection to Gulf of Mexico; leading iron and steel centre in the S; iron, coal and limestone mined; metal products, transportation equipment, chemicals, food products; centre for commerce, banking and insurance; civil rights protests in the 1960s; Alabama Symphony, Sloss Furnaces, iron statue of Vulcan; Festival of the Arts (Apr). » Alabama; civil rights

Birmingham (UK) 52°30N 1°50W, pop (1987e) 998 200. City and chief town in West Midlands, C England; part of West Midlands urban area and Britain's second largest city; 175 km/109 ml NW of London; noted centre for metalwork since the 16th-c; developed rapidly in the Industrial Revolution in an area with a large supply of iron ore and coal; heavily bombed in World War 2; railway; airport; motorways meet to the N at 'Spaghetti Junction'; two universities (Birmingham, 1900; Aston, 1966); Aston Science Park; regional media centre for television and radio; engineering, vehicles, plastics, chemicals, electrical goods, machine tools, glass; 18th-c Church of St Philip, Cathedral of St Chad (1839), Aston Hall (1618–35), art gallery, symphony orchestra, theatre, museums, Bull Ring shopping complex, National Exhibition Centre; international show-jumping championships (Apr). » West Midlands

Biró, Ladislao José [**biro**] (1899–1985) Hungarian inventor. Working with a magazine, he realized the advantage of quick-drying ink, and in 1940 went to Argentina with his ideas for developing a ballpoint pen, which eventually became a great success. He was responsible for several other inventions, including a lock, a heat-proof tile, and a device for recording blood pressure. He died in Buenos Aires. » pen

birth control » **contraception**

birthmark A skin blemish present at birth; also known as a **naevus/nevus**. There are two main causes: an accumulation of melanocytes (skin pigment cells) known as *moles*, which vary in colour from light brown to black, and a benign enlargement of blood and lymph vessels, the most common of which are 'strawberry marks' and 'port wine stains'. » lymph; melanins; mole (medicine)

Birtwistle, Sir Harrison (1934–) British composer, born at Accrington, Lancashire. He studied in Manchester and London, and helped to form the New Manchester Group for the performance of modern music. Much of his work was written for the Pierrot Players, which he helped to form in 1967, and for the English Opera Group. In 1965 he wrote the instrumental *Tragoedia* and vocal/instrumental *Ring a Dumb Carillon* that established him as a leading composer. Among his later works are the operas *Punch and Judy* (1966–7) and *The Mask of Orpheus* (produced 1986). In 1975 he became musical director of the National Theatre, and was knighted in 1988.

Biscay, Bay of, Span **Golfe de Vizcaya**, Fr **Golfe de Gascogne** Arm of the Atlantic Ocean, bounded E by France and S by Spain; irregular coasts with many harbours; known for strong currents and sudden storms; major fishing region; resorts such as Biarritz on straight, sandy shores of SE French coast; major ports include St Nazaire, La Rochelle, San Sebastian, Santander. » Atlantic Ocean

biscuit A term derived from Old French *bescuit* 'twice cooked', a process which produced small flat cakes that were truly crispy. Today, biscuits are many and varied, ranging from sweet to plain. In the USA, the term is often used for what in the UK would be called a *scone*; the nearest equivalent to UK *biscuit* is *cookie*.

bishop An ecclesiastical office, probably equivalent to pastor or presbyter in the New Testament, and thereafter generally an ordained priest consecrated as the spiritual ruler of a diocese in Orthodox, Roman Catholic, and Episcopal Churches. In some other Churches (eg certain Methodist Churches), the term is equivalent to 'overseer', or supervising minister. The office was abolished by many Protestant Churches at the 16th-c Reformation, but in many churches which retain it, it is considered to be essential for the identity of the Church and the transmission of the faith. The issue of whether women as well as men may be consecrated bishop aroused great controversy at the end of the 1980s, especially following the first such appointment (Rev Barbara Harris, as Bishop of Massachusetts) by the Episcopal Church of the United States in 1989. » apostolic succession; archbishop; Christianity; episcopacy; Reformation

Bishop, Elizabeth (1911–79) US poet, born at Worcester, Massachusetts, and educated at Vassar. She lived in Brazil for 16 years and translated Brazilian poetry. Her own work, in collections such as *North and South* (1946), *A Cold Spring* (1956), and *Questions of Travel* (1965) is noted for its concentrated observation. She won the Pulitzer Prize in 1955; her *Complete Poems* were published in 1969. » American literature; poetry

Bishops' Wars (1639–40) Two wars between Charles I of England and the Scottish Covenanters, caused by his unpopular policies towards the Scottish Kirk. They resulted in English defeats, and bankruptcy for Charles, who was then forced to call the Short and Long Parliaments in 1640, bringing to an end his 'personal rule' (1629–40). » Charles I (of England); Covenanters; Long Parliament

Bismarck, (Otto Edward Leopold), Fürst von ('Prince of') (1815–98) Prusso-German statesman, the first Chancellor of the German Empire (1871–90), born at Schönhausen, Brandenburg. He studied law and agriculture at Göttingen, Berlin, and Greifswald. In the new Prussian parliament (1847) he became known as an ultraroyalist, resenting Austria's predominance and demanding equal rights for Prussia. He was Ambassador to Russia (1859–62), and was appointed Prime Minister in 1862. During the Schleswig-Holstein question and the 'seven weeks' war' between Prussia and Austria, he was a guiding figure, becoming a national hero. Uniting German feeling, he deliberately provoked the Franco-Prussian War (1870–1) and acted as Germany's spokesman. He was made a count in 1866, and created a prince and Chancellor of the new German Empire. After the Peace of Frankfurt (1871), his policies aimed at consolidating and protecting the young Empire. His domestic policy included universal suffrage, reformed coinage, and the codification of the law. He engaged in a lengthy conflict with the Vatican (known as the *Kulturkampf*), which proved to be a failure. In 1879, to counteract Russia and France, he formed the Austro-German Treaty of Alliance, which was later joined by Italy. Called the 'Iron Chancellor', he resigned the Chancellorship in 1890, out of disapproval of Emperor William II's policy. In the same year he was made Duke of Lauenburg, and was finally reconciled to his sovereign (1894). He died at Friedrichsruh. » Franco-Prussian War; Kulturkampf; Prussia; William II (Emperor)

Bismarck (USA) 46°48N 100°47W, pop (1980) 44 485. Capital of state in Burleigh County, C North Dakota, USA, on the Missouri R; established, 1873 (named after the German statesman); territorial capital, 1883; state capital, 1889; airfield; railway; trade and distribution centre for agricultural region; oil refining, food products, machinery; Camp Hancock Museum, Heritage Centre; Folkfest (Sep). » North Dakota

Bismarck Archipelago pop (1980) 314 308; area 49 709 sq km/ 19 188 sq ml. Island group, part of Papua New Guinea, NE of New Guinea, SW Pacific; main islands, New Britain, New Ireland, Admiralty Is, and Lavongai; mountainous, with several active volcanoes; annexed by Germany, 1884; mandated territory of Australia, 1920; occupied by Japan in World War 2; part of UN Trust Territory of New Guinea until 1975; chief town, Rabaul, on New Britain; copra, cocoa, oil palm. » Admiralty Islands; New Britain; New Ireland

Bismarck Sea [**bizmahk**] SW arm of the Pacific Ocean, NE of New Guinea; c.800 km/500 ml E–W; contains many islands; Battle of the Bismarck Sea (1943) saw destruction of Japanese naval force by USA. » Pacific Ocean

bismuth [**bizmuhth**] Bi, element 83. The heaviest element with stable isotopes, a metalloid which melts at 271°, but forms alloys with much lower melting points. It is in the nitrogen family, and commonly shows oxidation states of +3 and +5. The main natural source is the sulphide, Bi_2S_3. » alloy; chemical elements; metalloids; nitrogen; RR90

bison A large mammal which inhabits forest and grassland; stocky; large hairy hump on shoulders; short upcurved horns; chin with beard; two species: the **American bison**, also called **boss** or (incorrectly) **buffalo** – with two subspecies, **plains bison** and **wood** (or **mountain bison**) from N America (*Bison bison*), and the **European bison** or **wisent** (*Bison bonasus*). The American bison has been crossbred with cattle to produce the hybrid *cattalo*; male hybrids are sterile. (Family: *Bovidae*.) » Bovidae; cattle; gaur

Bissau [beesow] 11°52N 15°39W, pop (1979) 105 273. Seaport capital of Guinea-Bissau, W Africa; on Bissau I in the R Geba estuary; established as a fortified slave-trading centre, 1687; free port, 1869; capital moved here from Bolama, 1941; airport; national museum, cathedral. » Guinea-Bissau [i]

bistort The name for several species of the genus *Polygonum*, related to knotgrass and mostly N temperate; some aquatic; stems erect, nodes enclosed in papery sheaths; leaves lance-shaped to oblong; small flowers white, pink, or red, in terminal spikes. (Genus: *Polygonum*. Family: *Polygonaceae*.) » knotgrass

bit An abbreviation of **Binary digIT**. A bit may take only one of the two possible values in the binary number system, 0 or 1. All operations in digital computers take place using the binary number system. » binary code; digital computer

Bithynia [bithinia] The name in antiquity for the area to the SW of the Black Sea. Inhabited mainly by warlike Thracians, it eluded Achaemenid and Seleucid control, becoming an independent kingdom under a Hellenizing dynasty of Thracian stock c.300 BC. In 75–74 BC, under the will of its last king, Nicomedes IV, it passed to Rome. Initially a rather unimportant province, Bithynia's strategic status rose during the imperial period. In the late 3rd-c AD, its leading city, Nicomedia, even became for a while the capital of the entire E half of the Empire. » Hellenization; Persian Empire; Roman history [i]

biting midge A minute, biting fly that feeds on the blood of vertebrates; also known as **punkie** and **noseeum**. There are c.1200 species, some of which have medical and veterinary importance as carriers of disease. (Order: *Diptera*. Family: *Ceratopogonidae*.) » fly; midge

Bitola [beetuhla] or **Bitolj**, Turkish **Monastir** 41°01N 21°21E, pop (1981) 137 835. Town in Macedonia republic, Yugoslavia, 112 km/70 ml S of Skopje; under Turkish rule until 1912; second largest town in Macedonia; railway; carpets, textiles, tourism; nearby national park in the Palister range, 120 sq km/46 sq ml, established in 1949; Ajdar Kadi mosque; festival of folk music (Jul–Aug). » Macedonia (Yugoslavia); Yugoslavia [i]

bitonality The property of music written in two keys simultaneously. The piquant dissonances that usually result were cherished particularly by *Les Six* in France during the first half of the 20th-c. » polytonality; *Six, Les*; tonality

bittern A marsh-dwelling bird, widespread; heron-like but stouter, with shorter legs and neck; mottled brown plumage; usually solitary; eats diverse animal prey. When threatened, it stands immobile with its bill raised. (Family: *Ardeidae*, 12 species.) » heron

bittersweet » **woody nightshade**

bitumen **1** A mixture of tar-like hydrocarbons derived from petroleum either naturally or by distillation. It is black or brown and varies from viscous to solid, when it is also known as *asphalt*. It is used in road-making. » petroleum **2** In art, a transparent brown pigment made from tar, popular with painters in the 18th-c for the rich 'Rembrandtesque' transparent tones which it gives when first applied. Unfortunately, it never dries, but turns black and develops wide traction-cracks which are difficult to repair. » paint; Rembrandt

bivalve An aquatic mollusc with a body compressed sideways, and enclosed within a shell consisting of two valves joined by a flexible ligament along a hinge line; the valves are closed by one or two adductor muscles, and opened by an elastic ligament; head not defined; typically feeds on small particles collected by large gills covered with tiny hairs (*cilia*); contains over 20 000 species with varied life styles including burrowing, boring, free-swimming, and base-attached (sessile); life cycle often includes a planktonic larval stage (the *veliger*); many species of great economic importance, such as oysters, clams, and mussels; also known as **lamellibranchs** and **pelecypods**. (Class: *Pelecypoda*.) » calcium; clam; larva; mollusc; mussel; oyster; plankton; shell

Biwa, Lake [beewa], Jap **Biwa-ko**, also **Lake Omi** area 676 sq km/261 sq ml. Largest lake in Japan; in Kinki region, C Honshu, 8 km/5 ml NE of Kyoto; 64 km/40 ml long; 3–19 km/1¾–12 ml wide; 96 m/315 ft deep; connected by canal to Kyoto. » Honshu; Kyoto

Bizerte or **Bizerta** [bizertuh], Lat **Hippo Diarrhytus** 37°18N 9°52E, pop (1984) 94 509. Capital of Bizerte governorate, N Tunisia, 60 km/37 ml NNW of Tunis; strategically important on the Mediterranean coastline; occupied by Romans, Vandals, Arabs, Moors, Spanish, and French (1881); German base in World War 2, heavily bombed; French naval base until 1963; railway; kasbah in old city; Bizerte Festival (Jul–Aug). » Tunisia [i]

Bizet, Georges, originally **Alexandre César Léopold Bizet** [beezay] (1838–75) French composer, born and died in Paris. He studied at the Paris Conservatoire and in Italy, and won the Prix de Rome in 1857. His incidental music to Daudet's play *L'Arlésienne* (1872) was remarkably popular, and survived in the form of two orchestral suites. His masterpiece was the opera *Carmen*, whose realism was much attacked when it was first performed.

Bjerknes, Jakob (Aall Bonnevie) [byerknays] (1897–1975) Norwegian meteorologist, born in Stockholm. With his father (**Vilhelm**, 1862–1951) he formulated the theory of cyclones on which modern weather forecasting is based. In 1940 he became professor in the University of California, and was naturalized in 1946. He died in Los Angeles. » meteorology

Björling, Jussi [bjerling] (1911–60) Swedish tenor, born at Stora Tuna. He studied at the Stockholm Conservatory, and made his debut in that city in 1930, and in London in 1939. He sang frequently at the Metropolitan Opera, New York, and made numerous recordings. He died in Stockholm. » opera

Björnson, Björnstjerne (Martinius) [byernsn] (1832–1910) Norwegian novelist and playwright, born at Kvikne. He was educated at Molde, Christiania, and Copenhagen. From 1857 he alternated visits to Rome (1860–2) and Paris (1882–8) with theatrical management and newspaper editing at Bergen and Christiania, whilst constantly writing and taking an active part in politics as Home Ruler and Republican. His works used material from sagas and the countryside, but he later turned to social themes, as in his greatest play, *Over Aevne* (1883, Beyond our Power). One of a collection of songs (1870) is Norway's national anthem. He was awarded the Nobel Prize for Literature in 1908, and died in Paris. » Norwegian literature

Black, Sir James (1924–) British pharmacologist. He graduated in medicine at St Andrews, Scotland, then taught at various universities, in 1984 becoming professor of analytical pharmacology at King's College, London. His reasoning on how the heart's workload could be reduced led to the discovery of betablockers in 1964, and his deductions in 1972 on acid secretion in the stomach resulted in the introduction of cimetidine in the treatment of stomach ulcers. He shared the Nobel Prize for Physiology or Medicine in 1988. » beta blockers; heart [i]; pharmacology; ulcer

Black and Tans Additional members of the Royal Irish Constabulary, recruited by the British government to cope with Irish national unrest in 1920. The shortage of regulation uniforms led to the recruits being issued with khaki tunics and trousers and very dark green caps, hence their name. Terrorist activities provoked severe reprisals by the Black and Tans, which caused an outcry in Britain and the USA.

black bear Either of two species of bear, usually black but sometimes brown in colour; the **American black bear** from N America (*Ursus americanus*), and the **Asiatic black bear**, **Himalayan bear**, or **moon bear** from S and E Asia, with a white chin and white 'V' on chest (*Selenarctos thibetanus*). » bear

black beetle A black beetle found in cellars and outhouses; larvae cylindrical; adults move clumsily; feeds on plant material. (Order: *Coleoptera*. Family: *Tenebrionidae*.) » beetle; larva

black box A complete unit in an electronics or computer system whose circuitry need not be fully understood by the user. The name is commonly used for the flight data recorder in an aircraft: this collects information about the aircraft's performance during a flight, which can be used to help determine the cause of a crash. » aircraft [i]; computer

black bryony A perennial climber with a large, black tuber, related to the yam, native to Europe, W Asia, and N Africa; stems grow to 4 m/13 ft, twining; leaves heart-shaped, dark, glossy green with prominent curving veins; flowers tiny, 6-lobed, yellowish-green, males and females on separate plants; berry 12 mm/½ in diameter, red. (*Tamus communis*. Family: *Dioscoriaceae*.) » climbing plant; perennial; yam

black comedy A kind of comedy (whether in narrative or dramatic form) which derives its often bitter humour from exposing and facing up to the grotesque accidents and meaningless misfortunes to which human life is liable. Examples include Evelyn Waugh's *Black Mischief* (1932), Nathanael West's *The Day of the Locust* (1939), and Joe Orton's *Loot* (1965). » comedy; drama; novel

Black consciousness An attitude, particularly in the USA, which asserts that Blacks, by virtue of their ethnicity and history, possess a cultural tradition distinct from the wider population. It rejects the notion that Blacks have been totally absorbed into White society, only distinguishable by colour. Proponents of Black consciousness aim to raise the awareness of Blacks by espousing and publicizing these cultural traditions and values.

Black Consciousness Movement (South Africa) A movement formed by Steve Biko in 1969, when he led African students out of the multi-racial National Union of South African Students and founded the South African Students Organization. From this emerged the Black Peoples' Convention, which sought to create co-operation in social and cultural fields among all non-White peoples. Most of its leaders were imprisoned in 1977, and Biko died in police custody. The film *Cry Freedom* (1988) was based on these events. » apartheid; Biko; Black consciousness; South African Native National Congress

Black Country The industrial area of the English Midlands during and after the Industrial Revolution. It is centred on the counties of Staffordshire, Warwickshire, and Worcestershire. » Industrial Revolution

Black dance A term used in the mid-1980s to describe British forms of dance that owe some allegiance to African or Caribbean influences; there are Black consciousness overtones emphasizing non-White, non-Western forms of dance. The Black Dance Development Trust was set up in 1985 to promote and foster understanding and appreciation of African people's dance and, through summer schools and short courses, to examine ways in which cultural traditions of Africa and the Caribbean relate to Black people's dance in Britain. » African dance; Caribbean dance; jazz dance

Black Death The name given to the virulent bubonic and pneumonic plague which swept through W and C Europe from Asia (1347–51). Approximately 25 million people, about a third of the population, perished. This catastrophe was not solely responsible for causing or accelerating important socio-economic changes; probably more decisive was the subsequent pandemic recurrence of the plague (eg in 1361–3, 1369–71, 1374–5, 1390, and 1400). Even then, the consequences varied from region to region, and the economies of S England, the Netherlands, and S Germany continued to prosper. » plague; serfdom; villein

black economy Any economic activity where tax is evaded. It arises when work is carried out, or wages paid, but where no record is made of the transaction for income tax or value-added-tax purposes. The recipient thus avoids paying tax. » taxation

black-eyed Susan A slender annual climber native to S Africa; stems twining to 2 m/6½ ft; leaves opposite, heart-shaped; flowers tubular with five spreading bright-yellow lobes, and a dark purplish or black central eye. (*Thunbergia alata*. Family: *Acanthaceae*.) » annual; climbing plant

black fly A small biting fly found near running water; larvae aquatic, feeding by filtering plankton and detritus; also known as **buffalo gnat**. The females of some species are blood-suckers, and serious cattle pests. One species is the carrier of filarial river blindness. (Order: *Diptera*. Family: *Simuliidae*.) » fly; larva; plankton

Black Forest, Ger **Schwarzwald** Mountain range in Germany; extends 160 km/100 ml from Pforzheim (N) to Waldshut on the Upper Rhine (S); highest peak, the Feldberg (1 493 m/4 898 ft); divided by R Kinzig into Lower (N) and Upper (S) Schwarzwald; source of Danube and Neckar Rivers; crafts, tourism; many medicinal baths and spas. » Germany [i]

Black Friars » **Dominicans**

Black Friday (24 Sep 1869) A US financial crisis: the date of a severe fall in the price of gold as a result of an attempted fraud by financiers Jay Gould (1836–92) and James Fisk (1834–72). Many speculators lost their fortunes in the ensuing panic.

black grouse A grouse native to upland areas of N Europe and N Asia; the male (**blackcock**) black with a red comb above each eye; the female (**greyhen**) brown. The males display to females at a traditional site (known as a *lek*); successful males take several mates. (*Tetrao tetrix*. Family: *Phasianidae*.) » grouse

black gum » **tupelo**

Black Hand A secret organization formed in Serbia in 1911, led by army officers, whose objective was the achievement of Serbian independence from Austria and Turkey. It is best known for planning the assassination of Archduke Francis Ferdinand of Austria in Sarajevo in June 1914, an event which led directly to the outbreak of World War 1. » World War 1

Black Hawk War (1832) A military conflict between the USA and Sauk and Fox Indians, which led to the completion of the policy of removing Indians from 'the Old Northwest' to beyond the Mississippi R. » Indian Wars

black hole A region of spacetime from which matter and energy cannot escape; in origin, a star or galactic nucleus that has collapsed in on itself to the point where its escape velocity exceeds the speed of light. Its boundary is known as the *event horizon*: light generated inside the event horizon can never escape. Black holes are believed to exist on all mass scales. Some binary stars which strongly emit X-rays may have black hole companions. » binary star; light; star; X-rays

Black Hole of Calcutta A small badly-ventilated room in which surviving British defenders were imprisoned following Calcutta's capture (June 1756) by Siraj ud Daula, Nawab of Bengal. It was claimed that only 23 out of 146 prisoners survived. The incident became famous in the history of British imperialism, but its status is controversial, as the total number involved was probably much smaller.

black letter writing A style of writing, common in the mediaeval period, which formed the basis of early models of printers' type in Germany; sometimes called **Gothic**. It had relatively straight strokes in its letters. » chirography; graphology

black Mass A blasphemous caricature of the Roman Catholic Mass, in which terms and symbols are distorted, and Satan is worshipped instead of God. » blasphemy; Devil; Mass

Black Mountain poetry A school of poetry started in the 1950s by Charles Olson (1910–70), one-time rector of Black Mountain College in N Carolina, USA, and including such names as Robert Creeley (1926–) and Robert Duncan (1919–). The aim was greater physicality and immediacy, as exemplified in the *Black Mountain Review* (1954–7). » American literature; Creeley; poetry

Black Muslims A Black separatist movement in the USA, founded in 1930 by W D Fard, Elijah Mohammed (1925–75); also known at different times as the **Nation of Islam**, the **American Muslim Mission**, and the **World Community of Islam in the West**. The movement holds that Black Americans are descended from an ancient Muslim tribe. Members of the movement adopted Muslim names, avoided contact with Whites, and demanded a separate state for Blacks, and reparation for injustices. Malcolm X (*né* Little) was one of their foremost preachers, while Cassius Clay (Muhammad Ali) is undoubtedly the most famous member of the movement. They now repudiate their early separatism, and have adopted orthodox Muslim beliefs. » Ali, Muhammad; civil rights; Islam

black-necked stork » **jabiru**

Black Pagoda » **Sun Temple**

Black Panthers A militant, revolutionary Black organization in the USA, founded in the late 1960s after the murder of Martin Luther King Jr. The organization preached violence and acted as a protector of Blacks, although much of what it advocated was simply rhetoric. It rapidly went into decline with the arrest and exile of many of its leaders, and also because of internal divisions. » King, Martin Luther

Black power The term used by Black activists in the USA from the late 1950s to reflect the aspiration of increased Black political power. It formed part of the more radical wing of the civil rights movement, was against integrationist policies, and used force to advance the Black cause. Some political results were achieved in terms of registering Black voters. » civil rights

Black Prince » **Edward the Black Prince**

black quarter » **blackleg**

Black Rod In the UK, an official of the House of Lords since 1522. One of his chief ceremonial functions is to act as the official messenger from the Lords to the House of Commons. By tradition dating from 1643, to gain entrance to the Commons he must knock three times with his ebony staff of office (the black rod). » Lords, House of

black rust » **barberry**

Black Sea, ancient **Pontius Euxinus** (Euxine Sea), Bulgarian **Cherno More**, Romanian **Marea Neagra**, Russian **Chernoye More**, Turkish **Karadeniz**; area 507 900 sq km/196 000 sq ml. Inland sea between Europe and Asia, connected to the Mediterranean (SW) by the Bosporus, Sea of Marmara, and Dardanelles; 1 210 km/752 ml long by 120–560 km/75–350 ml wide, maximum depth 2 246 m/7 369 ft; bounded N and NE by republics of the former USSR, S by Turkey, and W by Bulgaria and Romania; largest arm, Sea of Azov; steep, rocky coasts in S and NE, sandy shores N and NW; fishing important, especially N; main ports include Burgas, Varna, Odessa, Sebastopol, Trabzon; navigated since ancient times; opened by Treaty of Paris (1856) to commerce of all nations, and closed to ships of war. » Azov, Sea of

black snake A venomous Australian snake of genus *Pseudechis* (family: *Elapidae*, 4 species). The name is also used for several species of N American **racers** (genus: *Coluber*; family: *Colubridae*) and for the Jamaican water-snake (*Natrix atra*). » grass snake; snake

black swan A swan native to Australia and Tasmania; now introduced in New Zealand; nests in reed beds. Its name reflects its unusual colour. (*Cygnus atratus*. Family: *Anatidae*.) » swan

Black Thursday (24 Oct 1929) The date of the crash of the New York stock market that marked the onset of the Great Depression. » stock market; Great Depression

Black Watch The name of a famous Highland regiment of the British Army; first raised in 1704, it derives from their distinctive very dark tartan. The two battalions known as the 42nd and 73rd Foot were amalgamated in 1881, and given the traditional title. » army

black widow A medium-sized, dark-coloured spider, found in warm regions world-wide. Its bite is venomous, containing a neurotoxin causing a set of symptoms known as *lactrodectism*, including severe pain, nausea, and breathing difficulties. It is occasionally fatal. (Order: *Araneae*. Family: *Theridiidae*.) » spider

Black Zionism The term applied to quasi-nationalist, messianic movements founded among Black Americans and West Indians who look to Africa as a land from which their ancestors came as slaves. To them Africa is held in reverence, Black history is held in pride, and there is a desire to return to the land of their forefathers. » Ethiopianism

blackberry A scrambling prickly shrub with arching, biennial stems rooting at the tips; also known as **bramble**. It is native to Europe, Mediterranean region, but has been introduced elsewhere, often forming extensive thickets. The leaves are divided into 3–5 toothed leaflets, flowers numerous, in terminal inflorescences, five petals, white or pale pink. The 'berry' is an aggregate of 1-seeded carpels, not separating from the core-like receptacle when ripe. The plants are highly variable; many reproduce without cross-fertilization, and form clonal populations regarded as microspecies, of which c.400 have been identified in Britain alone. (*Rubus fruticosus*. Family: *Rosaceae*.) » biennial; cloning (genetics); inflorescence [i]; shrub

blackbird A thrush native to Europe, N Africa, and S and W Asia, and introduced in New Zealand; inhabits woodland, scrub, and habitation; eats fruit, insects, and worms; male black with yellow bill; female brown. The name is also used for some American orioles. (*Turdus merula*.) » grackle; oriole; ouzel; thrush (bird)

blackbirding The recruiting of Pacific islanders ('Kanakas'), mostly for work on plantations in Queensland and Fiji, from the 1860s to 1910. About 61 000 islanders were taken to Queensland between 1863 and 1904. Despite criticisms, the trade was not a form of slavery. Most came voluntarily, and under contract; about a quarter were tricked or forced. » slavery

blackbody A perfect emitter of heat and light radiation. A blackbody is a perfect absorber of radiation, and so appears black, since no light is reflected; but once in equilibrium it must emit as much radiant energy as it absorbs, so it is both a perfect absorber and emitter. A good approximation to a blackbody is formed by a small hole in a box, where the hole is the blackbody, since light incident on the hole is lost inside the box. When the box is heated, blackbody radiation in the form of light is emitted from the hole. At room temperature, energy emitted as blackbody radiation is invisible infrared, so the hole appears black. » blackbody radiation; heat; light

blackbody radiation Light and heat radiation emitted by a blackbody having a frequency distribution that depends only on the temperature of the blackbody. At higher temperatures, higher frequency light predominates. According to the law independently formulated by Austrian physicists Josef Stefan in 1879 and Ludwig Boltzmann in 1889, total energy emitted, $E=\sigma T^4$, where σ is the Stefan–Boltzmann constant. The study of blackbody radiation led Max Planck to suggest the quantization of light (1900). Blackbody radiation is the basis of optical pyrometry. » blackbody; Boltzmann; Planck; pyrometer; quantum mechanics; Stefan; thermodynamics

blackboy » **grass tree**

blackbuck A gazelle native to India and Pakistan; inhabits plains and scrubland; adult males blackish brown with white chin, white disc around eye and white underparts; horns long, spiralling, ringed with ridges; females pale brown, hornless. (*Antilope cervicapra*.) » antelope; gazelle [i]

blackcap A warbler found in mature deciduous woodland from Europe to C and S Siberia; eats insects, fruit, and nectar. Many European birds migrate to African forests for the winter. (*Silvia atricapilla*. Family: *Silviidae*.) » deciduous plants; warbler

blackcock » **black grouse**

blackcurrant An aromatic species of currant native to Europe and temperate Asia. It is widely cultivated, producing edible black berries on new wood. (*Ribes nigrum*. Family: *Grossulariaceae*). » currant

Blackett, Baron Patrick M(aynard) S(tuart) (1897–1974) British physicist, born and died in London. He was educated at Dartmouth College and Cambridge, and became professor at Birkbeck College (1933–7), Manchester (1937–63), and Imperial College, London (1963–74). He was the first to photograph nuclear collisions involving transmutation (1925), and in 1932 he independently discovered the positron. He pioneered research on cosmic radiation, for which he was awarded the Nobel Prize for Physics in 1948. He became a life peer in 1969. » cosmic rays; positron

blackfish » **pilot whale**

blackfly A black-bodied aphid which feeds by sucking plant sap. (Order: *Homoptera*. Family: *Aphididae*.) » aphid

Blackfoot Three Algonkin-speaking Indian Groups (Blackfoot, Blood, Piegan) originally from the E who settled in Montana, USA and Alberta, Canada. Famous hunters and trappers, many died of starvation after the bison were exterminated; others turned to farming and cattle rearing. Today c.10 000 live on reservations. » Algonkin; American Indians

blackjack A popular casino card game, derived from 15th-c European games. The object is to accumulate a score of 21 with at least two cards. Picture cards count as 10, the ace as either 1 or 11, and other cards according to their face value. A score of 21 with two cards is a blackjack. Normally four packs of cards are shuffled together and dealt from a wooden 'shoe' by a banker. Bets are placed before the first card is dealt, and all cards are dealt face up. » casino; playing cards; pontoon

blackleg A debilitating disease of cattle and sheep, characterized by swollen legs; can be fatal; also known as **black legs** or **black quarter**. » cattle; sheep

blackmail The making of an unwarranted demand with menaces. The demand must be made with a view to either personal gain or loss to someone else. The demand is unwarranted unless the accused believes that he or she has reasonable grounds for the demand, and that the menaces are appropriate to reinforce the demand. In England and Wales, blackmail is an offence under the Theft Act. In the USA, many state penal codes subsume this offence under a general theft statute as theft by *extortion* (a term also used in Scotland). » theft

Blackmore, R(ichard) D(oddridge) (1825–1900) British novelist, born at Longworth, Berkshire. Educated at Tiverton and Oxford, he was called to the Bar in 1852, but poor health made him take to market gardening and literature at Teddington. After publishing several collections of poetry, he wrote 15 novels, mostly with a Devonshire background, of which *Lorna Doone* (1869) is his masterpiece. He died at Teddington, near London. » English literature; novel

Blackpool 53°50N 3°03W, pop (1981) 148 482. Town in Blackpool district, Lancashire, NW England; on the Irish Sea coast, 25 km/15 ml W of Preston; the largest holiday resort in N England, with an estimated 8.5 million visitors annually; railway; tourism, electronics, engineering, transport equipment; conference centre; Tower (based on Eiffel Tower), Grundy Art Gallery; ballroom dancing championships (summer); musical festival (summer); agricultural show (summer); illuminations (autumn). » Lancashire

blackshirts The colloquial name for members of Oswald Mosley's British Union of Fascists (BUF), formed in October 1932. It derived from the colour of the uniforms worn at mass rallies and demonstrations organized by the BUF on the model of European Fascist parties. After clashes and disturbances in Jewish areas of London in 1936, the Public Order Act prohibited the wearing of uniforms by political groups. » fascism; Mosley

Blackstone, Sir William (1723–80) British jurist, born in London. He was educated at Charterhouse and Oxford, called to the Bar (1746), and in 1758 was appointed the first professor of English law at Oxford. He became an MP in 1761, and in 1763 was made Solicitor-General to the Queen. In 1765–9 he published his influential *Commentaries on the Laws of England*, the first comprehensive description of the principles of English law. He died at Wallingford, Oxfordshire.

blackthorn A deciduous spiny shrub growing to 6 m/20 ft; flowers white, appearing before ovoid, toothed leaves; fruits (*sloes*) globular, blue-black with waxy bloom, edible but very tart, used for jams and wines. Native to Europe, it is probably one of the parents of plum. (*Prunus spinosa*. Family: *Rosaceae*.) » deciduous plants; plum; prunus; shrub

blackwater fever An illness that has almost disappeared, but is still found among Whites in the tropics; it occurs in cases of untreated or inadequately treated malaria due to *Plasmodium falciparum*. The name arises from the breakdown of red blood cells in the circulation, allowing the passage of the pigment haemoglobin into the urine, resulting in its dark colour. » malaria

Blackwell, Sir Basil (Henry) (1889–1984) British publisher and bookseller, born at Oxford. Son of **Benjamin Henry Blackwell**, who founded the famous Oxford bookshop in 1846, he was educated at Oxford, and joined the family business in 1913. He also founded the Shakespeare Head Press (1921). Succeeding to the chairmanship (1924–69), he conjoined the family bookselling interest with that of publishing, mostly on academic subjects. He was knighted in 1956.

Blackwell, Elizabeth (1821–1910) US physician and feminist, born in Bristol, UK. She was the first modern woman to receive a degree in medicine, which she received at Geneva College, New York State. She encountered hostility throughout her education and career, and was responsible both for opening medical education to her sex and for establishing an infirmary for the poor of New York City. In later life she returned to England, and died at Hastings, Sussex. » women's liberation movement

Blackwood, Algernon Henry (1869–1951) British novelist, born at Shooter's Hill, Kent. He was educated at Wellington and Edinburgh University, then worked in Canada and the USA, before returning to England in 1899. His novels and stories reflect his taste for the supernatural and the occult, such as *John Silence* (1908) and *Tales of the Uncanny and Supernatural* (1949). He died in London. » English literature

bladder A rounded muscular organ situated behind the front of the pelvis (the *symphysis pubis*), but in children extending upwards into the abdominal cavity. The bladder receives urine from the kidneys via the ureters for temporary storage and eventual expulsion via the urethra (its capacity is c.600 ml/1.05 UK pt/1.3 US pt). In males it is anatomically related to the prostate gland, seminal vesicles, and *vas deferens*; in females it is related to the vagina and uterus. » cystitis; pelvis; urinary system

bladder campion A species of campion native to Europe, Asia, and N Africa, in which the calyx-tube is inflated and bladder-like. (*Silene vulgaris*. Family: *Caryophyllaceae*.) » campion; sepal

bladderwort A mostly aquatic carnivorous plant with finely divided leaves, the segments bearing tiny bladders; flowers 2-lipped, spurred, borne on a slender spike projecting above the water surface. The prey are insects or crustacea such as *Daphnia*, trapped in the tiny bladders; each bladder has a trapdoor triggered when sensitive hairs are touched and springing inwards, sucking in the prey before the door closes again. The traps reset themselves after the plant has absorbed any nutrients from the breakdown of the prey. The species native to temperate regions are all free-floating aquatics, but those native to the tropics may be land plants or epiphytes. (Genus: *Utricularia*, 120 species. Family: *Utriculariaceae*.) » carnivorous plant; crustacean; epiphyte

Bladud [**blay**duhd] A legendary king of Britain, who discovered the hot spring at Bath and founded the city. One story is that he was a leper who found that the mud cured him. » Lear

blaeberry » **bilberry**

Blake, Nicholas » **Day-Lewis, C**

Blake, Peter (1932–) British painter, born at Dartford, Kent, and studied at the Royal College of Art, London. Since the 1950s he has pioneered a peculiarly English form of Pop Art, based on the imagery of fairgrounds, toyshops, cheap magazines, badges (as in his 'Self-portrait with badges', 1961), pop singers, and old-fashioned advertisements. He paints in a sharp-edged realistic style, derived from magazine illustration and from Victorian painting. In 1980 he became a Royal Academician. » Pop Art

Blake, Robert (1599–1657) Greatest of English admirals after Nelson, born at Bridgwater, Somerset. He was educated at Oxford, where he lived as a quiet country gentleman until he was 40. In 1640 he was returned for Bridgwater to the Short Parliament, and later served in the Long Parliament (1645–53) and the Barebone's Parliament (1653). In 1649 he blockaded Lisbon, destroying the squadron of Prince Rupert, and in 1652–3 routed the Dutch in several battles. His greatest victory was his last, at Santa Cruz, when he destroyed a Spanish treasure fleet off Tenerife; but he died on the return journey to England. » English Civil War

Blake, William (1757–1827) British poet, painter, engraver, and mystic, born and died in London. In 1771 he began to produce watercolour figure subjects and to engrave illustrations for magazines. His first book of poems, the *Poetical Sketches* (1783), was followed by *Songs of Innocence* (1789) and *Songs of Experience* (1794), which express his ardent belief in the freedom of the imagination. These ideas found their fullest expression in his prophetic poem *Jerusalem* (1804–20). Among his designs of poetic and imaginative figure subjects are a series of 537 coloured illustrations to Young's *Night Thoughts* (1797).. Among the most important of his paintings are *The Canterbury Pilgrims* and *Jacob's Dream*. His finest artistic work is to be found in the 21 *Illustrations to the Book of Job* (1826), produced when he was nearly 70. » English literature; engraving; poetry

Blamey, Sir Thomas Albert (1884–1951) Australian field marshal, born near Wagga Wagga, New South Wales. He played an important part in the evacuation of Gallipoli, and became Chief-of-Staff of the Australian Corps in 1918. On the outbreak of World War 2 he commanded the Australian Imperial Forces in the Middle East, and organized the withdrawal from the Balkan area. In 1942 he became Commander-in-Chief of the Australian army, and commanded Allied Land Forces in New Guinea (1942–3). » Gallipoli; World War 2

Blanc, Mont » **Mont Blanc**

Blanchard, Jean Pierre François [**blã**shah] (1753–1809) French balloonist, inventor of the parachute, born in Les Andelys. In 1785 he was the first to cross the English Channel by balloon, from Dover to Calais, with an American, **John Jeffries** (1744–1819). Blanchard was killed at La Haye during practice jumps from a balloon. » ballooning

Blanda, (George) Frederick (1927–) US footballer, born at Youngwood, Pennsylvania. He holds the record for the most points (2 002) in any National Football League (NFL) career. He played for the Chicago Bears, Baltimore Colts, Houston Oilers, and Oakland Raiders (1949–75) – the longest career in the NFL, playing the most games, 340. » football [i]

blank verse Regular but unrhymed verse, in any iambic metre but most usually the iambic pentameter of Shakespeare's plays, Milton's *Paradise Lost*, and Wordsworth's *Prelude*. » metre (literature); Milton; poetry; Shakespeare; Wordsworth, William

Blanqui, (Louis) Auguste [blãkee] (1805–81) French revolutionary socialist leader, born at Puget-Théniers. He studied law and medicine, demonstrated against the Bourbon regime, and organized an abortive insurrection in 1839, which led to his imprisonment until 1848. He founded the Central Republican Society, and was again imprisoned after the demonstrations of May 1848. He remained politically active during the Second Empire, and was arrested on the eve of the Paris Commune, of which he was nevertheless elected President (1871). A passionate extremist, whose supporters were known as **Blanquists**, he spent 37 years of his life in prison. He died in Paris. » Bourbons; Revolutions of 1848; socialism

Blantyre [blantiyr] 14°46N 35°00E, pop (1984e) 333 800. Town in Southern region, S Malawi; altitude 1 040 m/3 412 ft; Church of Scotland mission founded here, 1876; named after David Livingstone's birthplace in Scotland; airport; railway; Malawi's main commercial and industrial centre; trade in tea, coffee, rubber; brewing, distilling, hides and skins, crafts; museum, two cathedrals, Kapachira Falls nearby. » Livingstone, David; Malawi [i]

Blarney 51°56N 8°34W, pop (1981) 1 500. Small village in Cork county, Munster, S Irish Republic; 8 km/5 ml NW of Cork; visitors to Blarney Castle are supposed to gain the power of eloquent speech as they hang upside down to kiss the Blarney Stone; legend dates from the 16th-c, when Lord Blarney, by pure loquaciousness, avoided acknowledging to Queen Elizabeth's deputy that the lands of Blarney were held as a grant from the Queen and not as a chiefship. » Cork (county); Irish Republic [i]

Blasco Ibáñez, Vicente » **Ibáñez, Vicente Blasco**

Blasis, Carlo [blasees] (1797–1878) Italian dancer, choreographer, and teacher, born in Naples. He danced in France, Italy, London, and Russia, and became director of the Dance Academy in Milan in 1837. He was the author of noted treatises on the codification of ballet technique (1820, 1840, 1857), and is regarded as the most important ballet teacher of the 19th-c. He died at Cernobbio. » ballet

blasphemy Any word, sign, or action which intentionally insults the goodness of or is offensive to God. Until the Enlightenment, it was punishable by death. Blasphemy was classed as heretical if it openly asserted something contrary to faith, and as non-heretical if it involved careless or insulting speech about God. In many Christian countries, it is technically a crime, and is extended to include the denial or ridicule of God, Christ, or the Bible; but the law is seldom if ever invoked. It is also a crime in certain non-Christian (eg Islamic) countries. The contemporary relevance and range of application of the law of blasphemy became a particular issue in the UK in 1989, following the publication of Salman Rushdie's book, *Satanic Verses*. » Enlightenment; God; heresy; Rushdie

blast furnace A furnace used for the primary reduction of iron ore to iron. Ore, coke, and limestone (which acts as a flux to remove silica) are loaded into the top of a tall furnace lined with mineral heat-resisting substances (such as fire-clay), in which the combustion of the coke is intensified by a pre-heated blast of air. At the temperature produced by the several chemical reactions taking place, the iron ore is reduced to iron, which runs to the bottom of the furnace, where it is either tapped off and solidified as pig-iron, or conveyed while still molten to other plant for steel-making. This iron contains a high proportion of carbon, and is the starting material for other steel-making and iron-founding processes. The complete blast furnace layout includes other structures for heating the blast and utilizing combustible furnace gases. » coke; iron

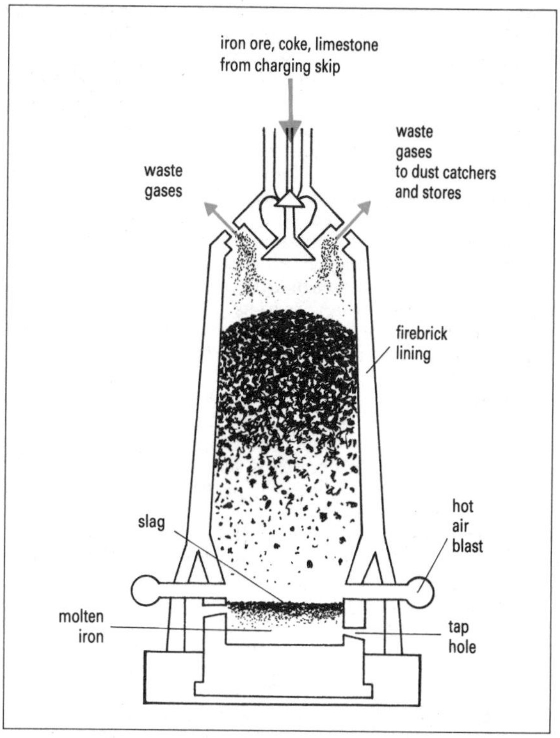

Blast furnace

blastula [blastyoola] An early embryonic stage in the development of multicellular animals. It typically consists of a hollow sphere of cells. » cell; embryology; gastrula

Blattaria » **cockroach**

Blaue Reiter, der [blower riyter] (Ger 'blue rider') The name adopted by a group of avant-garde artists in Munich in 1911. It was apparently inspired by a coloured illustration of a horseman on the cover of a book. Leading members included Kandinsky and Klee. » avant garde; Brücke, die; Expressionism; German art; Kandinsky; Klee

Blavatsky, Helena Petrovna (1831–91) Russian theosophist, born at Ekaterinoslav, Russia. After travelling widely, she helped to found the Theosophical Society in New York (1875), and later carried on her work in India. Her psychic powers were widely acclaimed but did not survive scientific investigation. Her writings include *Isis Unveiled* (1877). She died in London. » theosophy

blazar A type of extremely luminous extragalactic object, similar to a quasar except that the optical spectrum is almost featureless. » quasar; spectrum

blazonry The science of describing the pictorial devices used in heraldry. The basic colour (*tincture*) or background of the shield is known as the *field*, and this is overlaid with heraldic signs (*charges*). At their simplest, charges are broad bands, such as the vertical *pale*, or narrower stripes, such as the horizontal *fess*. The basic charges are called *ordinaries*; more fanciful ones depict a vast range of subjects, from real and mythological creatures to scientific instruments. The *helm* or helmet appears above the shield, and denotes the rank of the bearer. » heraldry [i]

bleaching The removal of the colour of textiles or other materials, such as paper. It was traditionally carried out on textiles by exposure to sunlight (until the late 18th-c.) After the discovery of chlorine by Scheele (1774), and its bleaching power by Berthollet (1785), most bleaching was done by chemical means. *Bleaching powder* was used in immense quantities until its eventual replacement in the 1920s by cheap pure chlorine and sodium hypochlorite. So-called *optical bleaches* do not remove colour, but add a fluorescent emission to the basic colour of the textile. » Berthollet; bleaching powder; chlorine; fluorescence; Scheele

bleaching powder A crude mixture of calcium hypochlorite ($Ca(ClO)_2$) and calcium chloride ($CaCl_2$), made by reacting chlorine with calcium hydroxide: $2Ca(OH)_2 + 2Cl_2 \rightarrow Ca(ClO)_2 + CaCl_2 + 2H_2O$. It is used as a bleach and as a disinfectant. » bleaching; calcium; chlorine

bleak Small freshwater fish with a slender compressed body, common in lowland rivers of Europe; length up to c.15 cm/6 in; lives in shoals feeding at the surface on crustaceans and insects. The silvery crystals from their scales were once used in the manufacture of artificial pearls. (*Alburnus alburnus*. Family: *Cyprinidae*.)

bleeding heart An erect, brittle-stemmed perennial, native to China, named from its pendulous, heart-shaped flowers, two outer petals pink, two inner white, in long, drooping spikes; also called **Dutchman's breeches**, similarly inspired. It is cultivated for ornament. (*Dicentra spectabilis*. Family: *Fumariaceae*.) » perennial

Blenheim, Battle of [**blen**im] (1704) The greatest military triumph of Marlborough and Prince Eugene in the War of the Spanish Succession. Fought on the Danube to prevent a combined Franco-Bavarian thrust on Vienna, it marked the first significant defeat of Louis XIV's armies, and the first major English victory on the European mainland since Agincourt. » Louis XIV; Marlborough, Duke of; Spanish Succession, War of the

Blenheim Palace A Baroque palace designed by Vanbrugh, and built (1705–24) at Woodstock, near Oxford, England; a world heritage site. The palace, with its estate of 809 ha/2 000 acres, was a gift from the nation to the 1st Duke of Marlborough after his victories at the Battle of Blenheim. » Baroque (art and architecture); Marlborough, Duke of; Vanbrugh

blenny Any of the large family *Blennidae* (11 genera), of mostly small bottom-dwelling fishes of coastal waters; found worldwide in tropical to temperate seas, rarely in freshwater lakes; many live inter-tidally in pools and under rocks; body stout, devoid of scales; jaws bearing many small teeth.

Blériot, Louis [**blay**ryoh] (1872–1936) French airman, born at Cambrai, who made the first flight across the English Channel (25 Jul 1909) from Baraques to Dover in a small 24-h.p. monoplane. An aircraft manufacturer in later life, he died in Paris. » aircraft [i]

blesbok [**bles**bok] » **bontebok**

blesmol » **mole rat**

Blessed Virgin (Mary) » **Mary** (mother of Jesus)

Blessington, Marguerite, Countess of (1789–1849) Irish writer and socialite, born near Clonmel. After her husband's death (1829), she held a salon at her Kensington mansion, Gore House, where she wrote many sketches of London life, and formed a relationship with Comte d'Orsay. Her best-known work was *Conversations with Lord Byron* (1834). Her lavish tastes left her deep in debt, and with d'Orsay she fled to Paris (1849), where she died two months later.

Bligh, William (c.1753–c.1817) British sailor, born at Plymouth. He sailed under Captain Cook in his second world voyage (1772–4), and in 1787 was sent as commander of the *Bounty* to Tahiti. On the return voyage, the men mutinied under his harsh treatment. In April 1789, Bligh and 18 men were cast adrift in an open boat without charts. In June, after great hardship, he arrived at Timor, near Java, having sailed his frail craft for 3618 miles. In 1805 he was appointed Governor of New South Wales, where his conduct led to his imprisonment for two years. He was promoted admiral (1811), and died in London. » Cook, James

blight A general term applied to any of a variety of plant diseases, especially those caused by fungal infection. » fungus; potato blight

blimp » **airship**

blindness A serious or total loss of vision in both eyes. In developed countries it arises from degeneration of the retina of the eye (**macular degeneration**), cataract, glaucoma, or diabetes. In developing countries many of the causes are infectious and preventible, including trachoma, gonorrhoea, and onchocerciasis. » eye [i]

blindworm » **slowworm**

Bliss, Sir Arthur (Drummond) (1891–1975) British composer, born in London. He studied under Holst, Stanford, and Vaughan Williams at the Royal College of Music, and in 1921 became professor of composition, but resigned to work as a composer. He was music director of the BBC (1942–4), and in 1953 became Master of the Queen's Musick. His works include the film music for Wells's *Things to Come* (1935), the ballet *Checkmate* (1937), the opera *The Olympians* (1949), chamber music, and piano and violin works. Knighted in 1950, he died in London.

Blissymbolics A communication system designed for children unable to use normal spoken or written language; devised by a chemical engineer Charles Bliss (1897–1985) in the 1970s. The system uses a set of simple symbols expressing important everyday concepts, printed on a board along with their written equivalents. It has been used with several clinical populations, such as cerebral palsied, mentally handicapped, and autistic children. » alternative and augmentative communication

blister beetle A brightly coloured beetle, mostly from warm, dry regions; larvae minute, clawed, feeding as parasites, or on insect nests and food provisions. The adults produce a chemical (*cantharidin*) that causes skin blisters. (Order: *Coleoptera*. Family: *Meloidae*, c.3 000 species.) » beetle; larva

blitzkrieg [**blitz**kreek] (Ger 'lightning war') A term coined (Sep 1939) to describe the German armed forces' use of fast-moving tanks and deep-ranging aircraft in techniques which involve by-passing resistance and aiming the focus of effort at the enemy's rear areas rather than making frontal attacks. Blitzkrieg tactics were used with great success by the Germans 1939–41. » World War 2

Blixen, Karen, Baroness, pseudonym **Isak Dinesen** (1885–1962) Danish novelist and storyteller, born and died at Rungsted. She travelled widely in Europe, and lived in Kenya for many years. In 1931 she returned to Denmark, where she produced many stories and a novel, writing in both English and Danish. Her works include *Seven Gothic Tales* (1934, Syn fantastiske fortoellinger) and the nonfiction *Out of Africa* (1937, Den afrikanske farm). » Danish literature

Bloch, Ernest [blokh] (1880–1959) Swiss–US composer, born in Geneva. He studied in Brussels, Frankfurt, and Munich before settling in Paris, where his opera *Macbeth* was produced in 1910. In 1915 he became professor of musical aesthetics at Geneva Conservatory, and in 1916 went to the USA, where he held several teaching posts, and became a US citizen. His works include the Hebrew *Sacred Service* (1930–3), and many chamber and orchestral works. He died in Portland, Oregon.

Bloch, Felix [blokh] (1905–) Swiss-US physicist, born at Zürich. He left Europe for the USA when Hitler came to power. As professor of theoretical physics at Stanford University, California (1934–71), he shared the 1952 Nobel Prize for Physics for developing the technique of nuclear magnetic resonance. He gave his name to the **Bloch bands**, sets of discrete but closely adjacent energy levels rising from quantum states when a nondegenerate gas condenses to a solid. » nuclear magnetic resonance

Bloemfontein [bloomfon**tayn**] 29°07S 26°14E, pop (1980) 230 688. Capital of Orange Free State province, EC South Africa; 370 km/230 ml SW of Johannesburg; judicial capital of South Africa; founded as a fort, 1846; seat of government of Orange River Sovereignty and of Orange Free State Republic, 1849–57; taken by Lord Roberts in Boer War, 1900; airfield; railway; university (1855); trade centre for Orange Free State province and Lesotho; railway engineering, food processing, glassware, furniture, plastics, fruit canning; Anglican cathedral, national museum (1877), war museum (1931). » Boer Wars; Orange Free State; South Africa [i]

Blok, Alexander Alexandrovich (1880–1921) Russian poet, born in St Petersburg. His first book of poems, *Stikhi o prekrasnoy dame* (1904, Songs about the Lady Fair), was influenced by the mysticism of Vladimir Soloviev (1853–1900), where truth is embodied in ideal womanhood. He welcomed the 1917 Revolution and in 1918 wrote two poems, *Dvenadtsat* (The Twelve), a symbolic sequence of revolutionary themes, and *Skify* (The Scythians), an ode inciting Europe to follow Russia. He died in Petrograd. » poetry; Russian literature/Revolution

Blondel (12th-c) French minstrel, said to have accompanied Richard Coeur de Lion to Palestine, and to have found him when imprisoned in the Austrian prison of Dürrenstein (1193) by means of a song they had jointly composed. » Richard I

Blondin, Charles, pseudonym of **Jean François Gravelet** [blõdĩ] (1824–97) French tightrope walker, born at Hesdin, near Calais. He trained as an acrobat at Lyon. In 1859 he crossed Niagara Falls on a tightrope; and later repeated the feat with variations (blindfold, with a wheelbarrow, with a man on his back, on stilts, etc). He died in London.

blood An animal tissue composed of cells, cell-like bodies, and fluid plasma that circulates around the body within vascular channels or spaces by the mechanical action of the channels or their specialized parts (primarily, the heart). Present in many major classes of animals, it usually contains respiratory pigment, and transports oxygen, nutrients, waste-products, and many other substances around the body. In humans, the cells (red, *erythrocytes*, and white, *leucocytes*), cell-like bodies (*platelets*), and plasma constitute about 8% of total body weight; in an average-sized adult male, blood volume is c.5.5 l/9.7 UK pt/11.6 US pt); in an equivalent female, it is c.4.5 l/7.9 UK pt/9.5 US pt). The haemoglobin-containing erythrocytes (which bind and carry oxygen) are produced in bone marrow and released into the circulation, where they remain for about 120 days before being destroyed in the liver. Platelets (which have important roles in blood clotting) are also produced in bone marrow, but are destroyed after about seven days. Various types of leucocyte circulate within the vascular system, and are produced in bone marrow and lymphoid tissue. These are important in protecting the body against disease and infection. » agranulocytosis; AIDS; anaemia; bone marrow; blood bank/pressure/products/test/transfusion/types; blood vessels [i]; embolism; erythrocytes; haematology; haemophilia; haemostasis; heart [i]; inflammation; interferons; jaundice; leucocytes; leukaemia; plasma (physiology); platelets; polycythaemia; septicaemia; uraemia

Blood, Council of A council established 1567–76 by the Duke of Alva, the Spanish Habsburg military commander in the Low Countries, on Philip II's orders, to suppress heresy and opposition during the Revolt of the Netherlands. Also known as the **Council of Troubles**, it comprised seven members (three of them Spaniards). The Council's proceedings 1567–73 included some 12 200 trials, 9 000 convictions, and 1 000 executions, which caused widespread fear and alienation among the population. » Philip II (of Spain); Revolt of the Netherlands

Blood, Thomas (c.1618–80) Irish adventurer, known for his activities during the Civil War and Restoration. His most famous exploit was his attempt, disguised as a clergyman, to steal the crown jewels from the Tower of London (May 1671). After nearly murdering the keeper of the jewels, he succeeded in taking the crown, while one of his associates bore away the orb. He was pursued, captured, and imprisoned, but later pardoned by King Charles. » crown jewels

blood bank A depository for refrigerated whole blood. The 1939–45 war revealed the need for blood transfusion following serious injury. This led to the development of ways of storing blood withdrawn from donors for later use. » blood products; blood transfusion

blood-bark » **gum tree**

blood-brain barrier A selective barrier to the exchange of substances between the blood and brain cells, dependent on the differential permeability of brain capillaries. Water, oxygen, and carbon dioxide cross the barrier rapidly, whereas salts, protein, and dopamine cross it slowly. Its function is possibly to protect the brain against blood-borne toxins. » blood; brain [i]; capillary; toxin

blood coagulation (clotting) » **haemostasis**

blood fluke A parasitic flatworm, found as adults in the blood of some mammals, including humans; causes bilharzia, a common disease in tropical areas; complex life cycle involves a freshwater snail as intermediate host, within which asexual reproduction occurs; larvae (*cercaria*) released from the snail into freshwater, infecting the final host by skin penetration. (Phylum: *Platyhelminthes*. Class: *Trematoda*. Species *Schistosoma*.) » bilharziasis; flatworm; larva; Platyhelminthes; schistosomiasis

blood poisoning » **septicaemia**

blood pressure The hydrostatic pressure of the blood within the blood vessels. It usually refers to the pressure within the arteries, the pressure within capillaries and veins being much lower. Arterial blood pressure depends on the volume of blood ejected into the aorta at each beat of the heart (*systole*), upon the distensibility of the arterial blood vessels that accommodate the extra blood, and upon the rate at which blood within the arteries and arterioles passes into the capillaries and veins, ie of the *peripheral resistance* to the flow of blood. It is measured, using a sphygmomanometer, as the height in millimeters of a column of mercury (mmHg). In health the arterial blood pressure reaches a peak of about 120–130 mmHg with systole, and falls to about 70 mmHg during diastole. » artery; blood; fluid mechanics; hypertension; sphygmomanometer

blood products The constituent elements of the blood, in relatively pure and concentrated form. The primary separation of blood cells using a centrifuge allows red blood cells, blood platelets (needed for the clotting of blood), and granulocytes (white cells concerned with the control of infection) to be separated from each other. Fractionation of plasma yields albumin (for use in shock) and other proteins, such as concentrated Factor VIII and fibrinogen for use in disorders of bleeding. These may be preserved in dried powder form over many years. » blood; blood bank; haemophilia; plasma (physiology)

Blood River, Battle of » **Great Trek**

blood sports The killing of animals for sport, such as fox hunting, hare coursing, or bull-fighting. Cock fighting, once popular in Britain, and still practised illegally in certain parts of the country, is a popular sport in many continental countries and in Asia. Blood sports, often referred to as *field sports*, have come under increasing attack in recent years from those concerned with animal welfare. » bearbaiting; bull-fighting; cockfighting; coursing; foxhunting

blood test The analysis of a sample of blood withdrawn from a living person to detect abnormalities in its composition. It is carried out for a large number of diagnostic purposes, which include determining the blood levels of chemical substances, drugs, and poisons, and detecting antibodies to a range of microbial disease and the presence of micro-organisms. » blood

blood transfusion The transfer of blood from one person to another. It was first carried out early in the 19th-c, but usually resulted in serious reactions. Clinically useful and safe blood transfusions were possible only after the discovery of blood groups: the blood of one group taken from one individual can be given only to another person of the same group. » blood types

blood types A classification of human blood into four major types/groups (A, B, AB, O) according to the presence or absence of genetically determined antigens (*agglutinogens*) A and B on the plasma membrane of the red blood cells (*erythrocytes*). The absence of A or B antigen is usually associated with the presence of corresponding natural anti-A or anti-B antibodies (*agglutinins*) in the plasma. Before a transfusion, the recipient's and donor's blood is cross-matched, otherwise antibodies of the recipient may combine with antigens of the donor, causing clumping of foreign erythrocytes with possible fatal consequences. Erythrocytes contain other antigens (eg M, N antigens) of unknown significance. » antibodies; erythrocytes; rhesus factor

blood vessels A closed system of tubes whereby blood permeates through all the tissues of the body, comprising the arteries, arterioles, capillaries, venules, and veins. In general, arteries and arterioles carry oxygenated blood from the heart, and venules and veins return deoxygenated blood back to it.

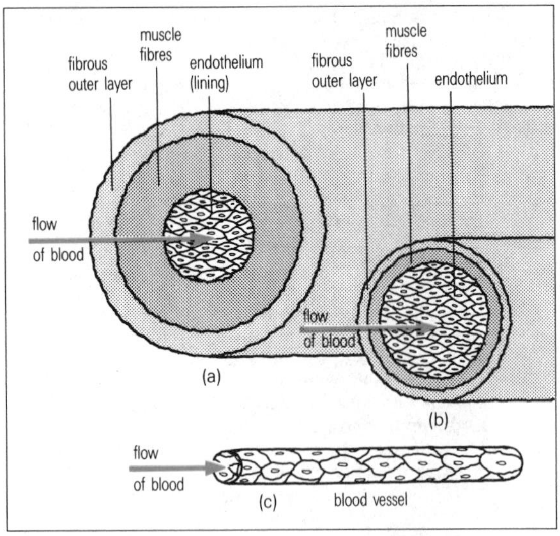

Blood vessels – Artery (a); vein (b); capillary (c)

However, the pulmonary arteries convey deoxygenated blood to the lungs from the heart, while the pulmonary veins return oxygenated blood to it from the lungs. Gaseous exchange (oxygen and carbon dioxide) and nutritional requirements pass between the blood and body tissues in the capillaries. » aneurysm; angiography; blood; capillary; catheter; circulation; embolism; haemorrhage; heart [i]; shock; stroke; thrombosis

bloodhound A breed of dog, known for its keen sense of smell; used for tracking; large powerful body with loose-fitting skin; short coat; tan or black and tan; long pendulous ears and jowls; long, deep muzzle. Originally French, the breed was perfected in Britain. » hound

bloodstone A type of chalcedony, a fine-grained variety of the mineral quartz. It is dark-green with red flecks. » chalcedony; quartz

bloodworm The aquatic larva of a midge; body worm-shaped, up to 20 mm/0.8 in long, with 12 segments; coloured red with haemoglobin as an adaptation to life in poorly oxygenated water. (Order: *Diptera*. Family: *Chironomidae*.) » larva; midge

Bloody Assizes The name given to the western circuit assizes in England in the summer of 1685, presided over by Lord Chief Justice George Jeffreys after the defeat of the Duke of Monmouth at the Battle of Sedgemoor. About 150 of Monmouth's followers, mostly poorer farmers and clothworkers, were executed, and 800 transported to the West Indies. » Jeffreys; Monmouth, Duke of

Bloom, Ursula, pseudonym of **Mrs Gower Robinson** (1892–) British novelist and playwright, born at Chelmsford, Essex. Her novels, which include *Pavilion* (1951) and *The First Elizabeth* (1953), are mainly historical romances, and most of her plays were written for radio production. » English literature

Bloomsbury group A group of writers and artists taking their name from Bloomsbury Square in London who were active around the time of World War 1: among them Leonard and Virginia Woolf, Clive and Vanessa Bell, Maynard Keynes, Lytton Strachey, Roger Fry, Duncan Grant, and E M Forster. In reaction against Victorian values, they subscribed to the spirit of George Moore's *Principia Ethica* (1903), with its privileging of art and intuition; and had a significant influence on the Modernist movement in England. » English literature; Forster; Fry, Roger; Grant, Duncan; Keynes; Modernism; Moore, G E; Strachey; Woolf, Virginia

Blow, John (1649–1708) English composer, born at Newark, Nottinghamshire. He was organist at Westminster Abbey (1668), Master of the Children at the Chapel Royal (1674) and subsequently organist there, and Master of the Children at St Pauls's (1687). He composed many anthems and organ pieces, but is best known for his masque, *Venus and Adonis* (1687), performed before Charles II. He died in London. » masque

blowfly An alternative common name for the bluebottle. It refers to the habit of laying eggs on exposed meat, which is then termed 'blown', and unfit for human consumption. » bluebottle

Blücher, Gebbard Leberecht von, Fürst von ('Prince of') **Wahlstadt** [**blükher**] (1742–1819) Prussian field marshal, born at Rostock, Mecklenburg. He fought against the French in 1793 and 1806, and in 1813 took chief command in Silesia, defeating Napoleon at Leipzig, and entering Paris (1814). In 1815 he assumed the general command, suffered a severe defeat at Ligny, but completed Wellington's victory at Waterloo by his timely appearance on the field. Known as 'Marshal Forward' (his victories being due mainly to dash and energy), he died at Krieblowitz, Silesia. » Napoleon I; Prussia; Waterloo, Battle of

blue In the UK, a sporting honour awarded by Oxford and Cambridge universities to students who represent their university against the other in the annual matches of certain sports. Ribbons of dark blue (Oxford) or light blue (Cambridge) were first awarded to competitors after the second Boat Race in 1836, but now holders may wear ties, blazers, and sweaters in the appropriate colour. » Boat Race

blue-backing shot A method of combining images in cinematography and television in which one or more components of the foreground action is shot against a uniform bright blue backing, and superimposed on a background scene recorded by another camera. In motion pictures this involves subsequent complex printing at the laboratory, but in television it can be done continuously at the time of shooting by colour keying ('chromakey'), each area of blue being replaced by the corresponding portion of the background scene. The technique enables an extremely wide range of effects to be achieved, typically studio actors appearing in exotic locations, children playing within a story-book illustration, or the fantastic flights of Superman. » chromakey; colour cinematography

blue book A UK Government publication of official documents, presented to parliament, bound in a blue cover. Unlike other command papers, which put forward government proposals, blue books are more concerned with the provision of information. » green paper; white paper

blue bull » nilgai

blue fish Predatory fish widespread in tropical and warm-temperate seas; length up to 1.2 m/4 ft; body blue above, sides silvery; lives in large shoals feeding voraciously on anchovies, sardines, and other small shoaling fish; valuable food fish, and prized as sport fish.

blue fox » Arctic fox

blue grass The name applied to several different grasses of a bluish-green colour. The Kentucky blue grass of the USA is a bluish form of meadow grass. (Family: *Gramineae*). » grass [i]; meadow grass

blue-green algae » blue-green bacteria

blue-green bacteria Single-celled, colonial or filamentous organism with an alga-like body and a bacterium-like (*procaryotic*) cellular structure; nucleus not delimited by a nuclear membrane; photosynthetic pigment chlorophyll *a* found on a special membrane (*thylakoid*) not enclosed within chloroplasts as in true algae; very ancient organism, believed to have been responsible for enriching the Earth's atmosphere with oxygen as a by-product of its photosynthesis; over 1 000 living species known, found mostly in aquatic habitats, also in soil and on rock surfaces; formerly known as **blue-green algae**. (Division: *Cyanophycota*.) » algae; bacteria [i]; cell; chloroplast; evolution; nucleus (biology); photosynthesis

blue jay » jay

blue moon **1** The second full moon in a calendar month in which two full moons occur. There are about 12.36 lunar months in the year, so there can be only one blue moon every 2.7 years on average. **2** Very rarely, the Moon's disc actually appears blue. If the atmosphere has particles 0.8–1.8 microns in diameter, for example from volcanoes or forest fires, red light gets scattered out of the line of sight, but the blue is allowed through. The result is a blue moon, or even a blue sun. » month; Moon

Blue Mountain Mountain peak in Jamaica; height 2 256 m/7 401 ft; highest point on the island. » Jamaica [i]

Blue Mountains Mountain range in E New South Wales, Australia; part of the Great Dividing Range; rises to 1 180 m/3 871 ft at Bird Rock; contains a national park, area 2 159 sq km/833 sq ml; tourist area; becoming a popular dormitory area for Sydney. » Great Dividing Range; New South Wales

Blue Nile, Ethiopia **Abay Wenz**, Sudan **Bahr El Azraq** Upper reach of R Nile, NE Africa; length 1 450 km/901 ml; issues from SE corner of L Tana, in Gojam region of Ethiopia; flows SE, then S and W, crossing into Sudan at Bumbadi; joins White Nile at Khartoum, forming the R Nile proper; during period of high flood, provides almost 70% of R Nile's flow; during low water, less than 20%. » Nile, River; White Nile

Blue Riband A notional honour awarded to the fastest passenger ship on the North Atlantic run. A trophy was designed for it, but was never accepted by Cunard Line, whose ships held the record for longer than any others. The final holder was the SS *United States* in a time of 3 days 11 hours 20 minutes at an average speed of 35.39 knots for the distance of 4 745 km/2 949 ml. The competition has ceased for economic reasons.

Blue Rider » **Blaue Reiter, der**

Blue Ridge Mountains Mountain range, SE USA; E part of the Appalachian Mts; extends NE–SW for c.1 050 km/650 ml from S Pennsylvania, through Maryland, Virginia, and North Carolina to Georgia; includes the Black Mts and Great Smoky Mts; highest point Mt Mitchell (2 037 m/6 683 ft); other high points Brasstown Bald (1 458 m/4 783 ft), Mt Rogers (1 746 m/5 728 ft) and Sassafras Mt (1 083 m/3 553 ft); Great Smoky Mountains and Shenandoah national parks; famous for its wooded scenery; timber. » Appalachian Mountains

blue shark Powerful slender-bodied shark found worldwide in open tropical to temperate seas, and common around W coasts of the British Isles; length up to 3.8 m/12½ ft; pectoral fins elongate; deep blue dorsally, white underneath; large numbers taken by sea anglers. (*Prionace glauca*. Family: *Carcharhinidae*.) » shark

blue whale A rare baleen whale of the rorqual family; the largest animal that has ever existed, length up to 30 m/100 ft; blue with pale spots (may have yellow micro-organisms on undersurface); in summer, eats shrimp-like *krill* (40 000 000 per day for each whale); in winter, breeds near the Equator, but does not eat; also known as the **sulphur-bottom whale**. (*Balaenoptera musculus*.) » krill; rorqual; whale [i]

Bluebeard A wicked character in European folklore who gives his new wife charge of the house-keys, forbidding her to enter one room; she unlocks it out of curiosity, to discover the bodies of six previous wives. Her brothers arrive just in time to save her from becoming Bluebeard's seventh victim, and slay him. » folklore

bluebell A small herb with an annually renewed bulb, native to W Europe; leaves strap-shaped; inflorescence 1-sided, flowers 1.5–2 cm/0.6–0.8 in, bell-shaped, drooping, blue, sometimes pinkish or white. It often forms large colonies in woods or on cliff tops. (*Hyacinthoides non-scriptus*. Family: *Liliaceae*). » bulb; harebell; herb; inflorescence [i]

blueberry A deciduous shrub, native to N America, and cultivated for fruit; flowers bell-shaped; berries c.8 mm/0.3 in, blue-black, edible. The low bush blueberry (*Vaccinium angustifolium*) grows to 30 cm/12 in; lance-shaped leaves; narrow white flowers with red markings. The high bush blueberry (*Vaccinium corymbosum*) grows to 3 m/10 ft; elliptic leaves; broader, pinkish flowers. (Family: *Ericaceae*.) » deciduous plants; shrub

bluebird A thrush native to N and C America; male with bright blue plumage on back; inhabits open country, forest clearings, and cultivation; eats fruit and insects; nests in holes in trees. (Genus: *Sialia*, 3 species.) » thrush

bluebottle (botany) » **cornflower**

bluebottle (entomology) A large fly with a metallic blue abdomen; lays eggs on decaying animal matter; legless larvae feed by liquefying food; adults feed by exuding digestive juices onto food and imbibing dissolved material. (Order: *Diptera*. Family: *Calliphoridae*.) » blowfly; fly; larva

bluebuck » **nilgai**

blues A style of US Black music, related to slow jazz, originating c.1900. The singing of blues is essentially an improvisatory art, often reflecting a melancholy or depressed state of mind but also conveying the vitality, and on occasions even the humour, of Black working-class Americans. Blues songs may have a number of verses, but the standard pattern for each is one of three lines of 12 syllables, the second being a repetition of the first. The '12-bar blues', as it is known, has a standard chord progression, too, which never varies in its essentials but allows every opportunity for spontaneous vocal and instrumental variations.

The origins and early period of the blues are associated particularly with the Mississippi region, and many of the most influential early singers, such as Bessie Smith (c.1898–1937), the Empress of Blues, were from the S States. In the 1930s, Chicago emerged as the centre for a more aggressive type of urban blues, typified in the singing and guitar playing of the Mississippi-born Big Bill Broonzy (1893–1958). After World War 2, the authentic tradition was represented by Muddy Waters (1915–83) and others, while a new departure was seen in the 'rhythm and blues' of the 1950s. » jazz; rhythm and blues

blueshift An astronomical effect observed when an object emitting electromagnetic radiation is moving towards an observer, increasing the observed frequency of its radiation. This is called a blueshift because, in the case of visible light, spectral lines move to the blue end of the spectrum. Blueshifts are unusual, because almost all galaxies are moving away from us, and hence have redshifts. » electromagnetism; light; redshift; spectrum

bluestockings A nickname, usually with derogatory connotations, for educated women. The term was widely used when opportunities expanded for the education of middle-class women in the late 19th-c, but it originated in the Blue Stocking Club at Montagu House, London, c.1750.

bluetit A small typical tit common in gardens; native to Europe, N Africa, and SW Asia; eats insects, seeds, and fruit; may hang upside down to feed; nests in hole in tree or wall; also known as **tomtit** (a name additionally used for the great tit). (*Parus caeruleus*. Family: *Paridae*.) » tit

Blum, Léon [bloom] (1872–1950) French socialist statesman and Prime Minister (1936–7, 1938, 1946–7), born in Paris. He trained as a lawyer in Paris, and was elected to the Chamber in 1919, becoming one of the leaders of the Socialist Party. He led 'popular front' governments in 1936 and 1938, achieving a series of labour reforms. After World War 2, he remained as leader of the socialists, and was Prime Minister of the six-week caretaker government. He died at Jouy-en-Josas. » France; socialism

Blunden, Edmund Charles (1896–1974) British poet and critic, born at Yalding, Kent. He was educated at Oxford, served in France in World War 1, and became a professor of English literature at Tokyo (1924–7). He joined the staff of *The Times Literary Supplement* in 1943, lectured at Hong Kong University (1953–64), and became professor of poetry at Oxford (1966–8). He is essentially a nature poet, as is evident in *Pastorals* (1916), but his best-known work is his prose *Undertones of War* (1928). He also edited several authors, and wrote a number of critical studies. He died at Long Melford, Suffolk. » English literature; literary criticism

blunderbuss A type of firearm, dating from the late 18th-c, with a large bore and a trumpet mouth. It is able to discharge ten or twelve balls in one shot designed for very short-range use. » firearms

Blunt, Anthony (Frederick) (1907–83) British art historian and Soviet spy, born at Bournemouth, Hampshire. He was educated at Marlborough School and Trinity College, Cambridge, where he became a Fellow (1932), shared in the left-wing communist-respecting tendencies of the time, and first met Burgess, Philby and Maclean. Influenced by Burgess, he acted as a 'talent-spotter', supplying to him the names of likely recruits to the Russian Communist cause, and during his war-service in British Intelligence, was in a position to pass on information to the Russian government. Although his spying activities appear to have ceased after the war, he was still able to assist the defection of Burgess and Maclean in 1951, although suspected by British Intelligence. In 1964, after the defection of Philby, a confession was obtained from Blunt in return for his immunity, and he continued as Surveyor of the Queen's Pictures until 1972. His full involvement in espionage was made public only in 1979, and his knighthood (awarded 1956) was anulled. He died in London. » Burgess, Guy; Maclean, Donald; Philby, Kim

Blyton, Enid (Mary) (1897–1968) British children's author, born in London. She trained as a Froebel teacher, then became a journalist, and published her first book, a collection of verse, in 1922. In the late 1930s she began writing her many children's stories featuring such characters as Noddy, the Famous Five, and the Secret Seven. She also edited various magazines. Identifying closely with children, she always considered her stories highly educational and moral in tone, but she has often been criticised for over-simplicity and lack of style. The author of over 400 books, she is the third most translated British author, after Agatha Christie and Shakespeare. » English literature

bo-tree » **peepul**

boa A snake native to the New World, N Africa, SW Asia, and Australasian islands; a constrictor; minute remnants of hind limbs; females give birth to live young (up to 80 at one time); includes the anaconda. (Family: *Boidae*, 39 species.) » anaconda; constrictor; python; snake

Boadicea [bohadi**see**a], properly **Boudicca** (1st-c AD) British warrior-queen, wife of Prasutagus, king of the Iceni, a tribe inhabiting what is now Norfolk and Suffolk. On her husband's death (60), the Romans seized her territory, and treated the inhabitants brutally. She gathered a large army, destroyed the Roman colony of Camulodunum, took Londinium and Verulamium, and put to death as many as 70 000 Romans. Defeated in battle by Suetonius Paulinus, she took poison. » Britain, Roman; Camulodunum; Verulamium

Boal, Augusto [**boh**al] (1931–) Brazilian theatre director, playwright, and theorist. His revolutionary models of political theatre-making have gained an international reputation, especially through his book *Teatro do Oprimido* (1975, Theatre of the Oppressed). » drama; theatre

boar » **pig**

board games » **backgammon; chess; draughts; go; mah-jong**

boat people Vietnamese who fled Vietnam by boat after the communist victory in 1975, travelling to Australia, Hong Kong, Japan, and several other parts of SE Asia. Many died on the long voyages, or were killed by pirates. Voluntary repatriation schemes gained momentum in 1989, and the first involuntary repatriation operation was carried out by the Hong Kong authorities that December. » Vietnam

Boat Race The annual rowing race between the crews of Oxford and Cambridge Universities. First held 10 June 1829 from Hambledon Lock to Henley Bridge, it is now raced over 4 ml 374 yd (6 km 780 m) from Putney to Mortlake. » rowing

boatbill A heron found from Mexico to Peru and Brazil; also known as the **boat-billed heron**; short, scoop-like bill, unlike other herons; inhabits wetlands; nocturnal; hides in mangroves during day. (Family: *Ardeidae*, but some authorities place it in a separate family, *Cochleariidae*. *Cochlearius cochlearius*.) » heron

bobcat A nocturnal member of the cat family native to N America; resembles a small lynx; length up to 1 m/3¼ ft; brown with dark spots; tail very short; inhabits scrubland and forest; eats birds, rodents, rabbits, and (in winter) deer. (*Felis rufus*.) » cat; Felidae; lynx

bobolink An American oriole native to N America; spends winter in S America; has the longest migration (8 000 km/ 5 000 ml) of any bird in its family; eats insects and grain; in breeding season, male mates with many females. (*Dolichonyx oryzivorus*.) » oriole

Bobrowski, Johannes [bob**rof**skee] (1917–65) East German poet, born in Tilsit (then in Prussia), and educated in Königsberg and Berlin. His early poems appeared in *Das Innere Reich*, the Nazi journal. He served on the E front in World War 2, and was taken prisoner. He returned to East Germany in 1949, when his poems began to appear in the communist magazine *Sinn und Form*. He published only two volumes: *Sarmatische Zeit* (1961, Sarmatian Times) and *Schattenland Strome* (1962, Shadowland Rivers), but his generous historical vision has ensured a growing reputation. » German literature; poetry

bobsledding The art of propelling oneself along snow or ice on a sledge. The earliest known sledge was used in Finland c.6500 BC. As a sport it became popular amongst Britons in Switzerland in the late 19th-c; a special luge run was created at Davros, Switzerland in 1879. The two most popular forms of competitive bobsledding are *luge tobogganing* on a small sledge, and *bobsleighing* in a sophisticated streamlined sledge. » lugeing; RR106

bobwhite An American quail native to N and C America, and introduced in the West Indies; inhabits farmland, open woodland, and brush; eats seeds, grains, and insects; usually lives in groups of 30 or more. (*Colinus virginianus*. Family: *Phasianidae*.) » quail

Boccaccio, Giovanni [bo**kaht**chioh] (1313–75) Italian writer, born (probably) in Tuscany. The illegitimate son of a merchant of Certaldo, he started a commercial career, but moved to Naples and took to story writing in verse and prose, mixing in courtly circles. Until 1350, he lived alternately in Florence and Naples, and then became a diplomat and scholar, devoted to the new learning. During this period, he became friendly with Petrarch, and travelled widely as Florentine ambassador. In 1358 he completed his great work, the *Decameron*, begun some 10 years before. He selected the plots of his stories from current popular fiction, and was a great influence on Chaucer, Sidney, Shakespeare, Dryden, Keats, and others. During his last years he lived mainly in retirement at Certaldo, where he died. » Chaucer; Italian literature; Petrarch

Boccherini, Luigi (Rodolfo) [bokuh**ree**nee] (1743–1805) Italian composer, born at Lucca. He was a cellist and prolific composer at the courts of the Infante Don Luis in Madrid and Frederick II of Prussia, best known for his chamber music, cello concertos, and sonatas. The great similarity of his work to that of his greater contemporary earned him the nickname 'Haydn's wife'. He died in poverty in Madrid. » Haydn

Boccioni, Umberto [bot**choh**nee] (1882–1916) Italian artist and sculptor, born at Reggio. The most original artist of the Futurist school, and its principal theorist, he worked in Paris and Rome (1898–1914), and wrote a major survey of the movement. An important bronze sculpture, 'Unique Forms of Continuity in Space' (1913), is in the Museum of Modern Art, New York. He was killed at Verona. » Futurism; Italian art

Bochum [**bokh**um] 51°28N 7°12E, pop (1983) 391 300. Industrial and commercial city in the Ruhr valley, Düsseldorf district, Germany; 59 km/37 ml SSW of Münster; originally developed around the coal and steel industries; railway; university (1965); vehicles, textiles, radio and television sets; home of the German Shakespeare Society. » Germany [i]; Ruhr, River

Bock, Fedor von (1880–1945) German field marshal, born at Küstrin. He commanded the German armies invading Austria (1938), Poland (1939), and France (1940). Promoted field marshal, he participated in the invasion of Russia (1941), but was dismissed by Hitler for failing to capture Moscow (1942). He was killed in an air raid at Lensahn. » World War 2

Bode's law or **Titius-Bode law** A numerical relationship linking the distances of planets from the Sun, discovered in 1766 by German astronomer Johann Daniel Titius (1729–96), and published in 1772 by Johann Elert Bode (1747–1826), but now considered to be an interesting coincidence. The basis of this relationship is the series 0,3,6,12,...,384, in which successive numbers are obtained by doubling the previous one. If 4 is then added to create the new series 4,7,10,16,...,388, the resulting numbers correspond reasonably with the planetary distances on a scale, with the Earth's distance equal to ten units. » planet; Solar System; Sun

bodégon [boday**gon**] (Span 'tavern') A type of genre painting featuring still life, especially food in a kitchen setting. Velazquez's *Old Woman Cooking Eggs* (1618, Edinburgh) is a well-known example. » genre painting; still life

Bodensee » **Constance, Lake**
Bodh Gaya » **Buddh Gaya**
Bodhidharma [bodhi**dah**ma] (6th-c) Indian monk and founder of the Ch'an (or Zen) sect of Buddhism, born near Madras. He travelled to China in 520, where he had a famous audience with the Emperor. He argued that merit applying to salvation could not be accumulated through good deeds, and taught meditation as the means of return to Buddha's spiritual precepts. » Buddhism

bodhisattva ('enlightened existence') [bohduh**sat**wuh] In Mahayana Buddhism, one who has attained the enlightenment of a Buddha but chooses not to pass into Nirvana; voluntarily remaining in the world to help lesser beings attain enlightenment. This example of compassion led to the emphasis in Mahayana on charity and comfort towards others. » Buddhism; Dalai Lama; Mahayana; Nirvana

bodily harm A criminal offence against the person. **Grievous** bodily harm involves serious physical injury, such as wounding with a knife. The injury need not be permanent. **Actual** bodily harm involves a less serious attack, such as an assault causing unconsciousness. These terms are not used in all jurisdictions (eg in Scottish law). » assault; criminal law

Bodleian Library The university library and national depository at Oxford; founded in 1595 by Sir Thomas Bodley (1545–1613), who restored the disused 14th-c library and laid the foundations of its now extensive holdings. » Oxford University [i]

Body Art A type of modern art which exploits the artist's – or someone else's – physical presence as a work of art in its own right. The artist may stand in the gallery like a living statue, perhaps singing; photograph himself performing some banal action, such as smiling; or may deliberately injure himself. It was a typical fad of the 1960s. » art; happening; Minimal art; modern art

body colour » **gouache**
body language » **nonverbal communication**
body mass index » **weight for height**
body popping » **street dance**
Boehm or **Böhm, Theobald** [boem] (1794–1881) German flautist and inventor, born and died in Munich. He opened a flute factory in 1828, and determined to make an acoustically perfect instrument. As this involved making holes in places where they could not be fingered, he devised a key mechanism, and in 1847 produced the model on which the modern flute is based. Certain features of this system have also been used on the clarinet. » flute

Boehme or **Böhme, Jakob** [**boe**muh] (1575–1624) German theosophist and mystic, born at Altseidenberg, Upper Lusatia. He became a shoemaker, but devoted much of his time to meditation on divine things. About 1612 he published his meditations upon God, Man, and Nature, *Aurora*, in which he aimed to explain the origin of things, especially the existence of evil. It was condemned by the ecclesiastical authorities, and he suffered much persecution. His other works include *Mysterium magnum* (1623, The Great Mystery). His influence later spread to Holland and England, and can be found as late as the 19th-c. He died at Görlitz. » theosophy

Boeotia [bee**oh**sha] In antiquity, the area in C Greece bordering on Attica. Its chief city-state was Thebes. Its inhabitants were largely of Aeolian stock, and proverbial for their stupidity. » Aeolians; Attica; Thebes **2**

Boer Wars Two wars fought by the British and the Boers for the mastery of S Africa. The British had made several attempts to re-incorporate the Boers, who had left the Cape Colony in the Great Trek, within a South African confederation. The first Boer War (1880–1) ended with the defeat of the British at Majuba Hill, and the signing of the Pretoria and London Conventions of 1881 and 1884. In 1896 the Jameson Raid was a clumsy private effort to achieve the same objective. The second Boer War (1899–1902) can be divided into three phases: (1) (Oct 1899–Jan 1900) a series of Boer successes, including the sieges of Ladysmith, Kimberley, and Mafeking, as well as victories at Stormberg, Modder River, Magersfontein, Colenso, and Modersspruit; (2) (Feb–Aug 1900) counter-offensives by Lord Roberts, including the raising of the sieges, the victory at Paardeberg, and the capture of Pretoria; (3) (Sep 1900–May 1902) a period of guerrilla warfare when Kitchener attempted to prevent Boer commandos raiding isolated British units and lines of communication. The Boers effectively won the peace. They maintained control of 'native affairs', won back representative government in 1907, and federated South Africa on their terms in 1910. On the other hand, British interests in South Africa were protected and, despite internal strains, the Union of South Africa entered both World Wars 1 and 2 on the British side. » Great Trek; Jameson Raid; Kimberley/Ladysmith/Mafeking, Sieges of; Vereeniging, Peace of

Boers » **Afrikaners**
Boethius, Anicius Manlius Severinus [bo**hee**thiuhs] (c.475–524) Roman statesman and philosopher, probably born in Rome. He studied philosophy, mathematics, and poetry, and soon after 500 was appointed a court minister by the Gothic king, Theodoric. He was made consul in 510, but his bold uprightness of conduct brought him many enemies. He was accused of treason, imprisoned, and executed. During his imprisonment he wrote his famous *De consolatione philosophiae* (The Consolation of Philosophy), expressing the mutability of all earthly fortune, and the insecurity of everything save virtue. » Aristotle; Cicero; Porphyry

bog asphodel A rhizomatous perennial, growing to 40 cm/15 in, native to boggy regions of NW Europe; leaves rigid, curved, V-shaped in cross-section; flowers with six perianth-segments, yellow, turning deep orange after fertilization, stamens woolly. (*Narthecium ossifragum*. Family: *Liliaceae*.) » asphodel; perennial; perianth; rhizome; stamen

bog burials Ancient human bodies recovered from N European peat bogs, their soft tissues and hair remarkably preserved by waterlogged, anaerobic conditions (known finds: Denmark 166, Germany 215, Netherlands 48, Britain and Ireland 120). Notable Iron Age examples are *Tollund Man* (c.200 BC), *Grauballe Man* (c.50 BC), both in Denmark, and the 25–30-year-old, 1.7 m/5 ft 7 in tall *Lindow Man*, buried naked c.300 BC in Lindow Moss, Cheshire, UK, and discovered in 1984. All three were murdered, presumably sacrificial victims or criminals. » palaeopathology; peat

bog myrtle A reddish deciduous shrub, native throughout cooler N temperate regions; foliage aromatic, dotted with yellowish oil-glands; flowers tiny, in spike-like catkins; also called **sweet gale**. Males and females are usually on separate plants, but plants may change sex from year to year. (*Myrica gale*. Family: *Myricaceae*.) » deciduous plants; shrub

Bogarde, Dirk, originally **Derek van den Bogaerde** (1921–) British actor, born in London, where he trained. He moved from the stage to films in 1946, playing mostly romantic or light comedy roles, such as *Doctor in the House* (1954) and its sequels. More challenging parts with varied characterization followed, as in *The Victim* (1961), *The Damned* (1969), *Death in Venice* (1971), and *Despair* (1981). He has also appeared in several television productions.

Bogart, Humphrey (1899–1957) US actor, born in New York City. He was expelled from Phillips Military Academy, Massachusetts, and joined the US Marines. In the late 1920s he turned to the theatre, playing the lead in the 1935 stage production of *The Petrified Forest*, and in the film version of 1936. This established him as a Hollywood star, and many of his performances have become classics, notably *The Maltese Falcon* (1941), *Casablanca* (1942), *The Big Sleep* (1946), *The Treasure of the Sierra Madre* (1948), and *The African Queen* (1951). After a romantic involvement with Lauren Bacall, he married her as his fourth wife in 1945, and they remained together until his death from cancer in California. » Bacall

Bognor Regis [**bog**nuh **ree**jis] 50°47N 0°41W, pop (1981) 53 175. Coastal resort town in Arun district, West Sussex, S England; on the English Channel, 20 km/12 ml W of Worthing; the title 'Regis' dates from 1929, when King George V came here to recuperate; railway; tourism, electrical engineering. » Sussex, West

Bogomiles [**bog**ohmilz] » **Albigenses; Cathars**
Bogotá, formerly **Santa Fe de Bogotá** [bohgoh**tah**] 4°38N 74°05W, pop (1985) 3 967 988. Federal capital of Colombia, on a plateau at 2 650 m/8 694 ft in C Colombia; former centre of

Chibcha culture; founded by Spanish, 1538; former capital of Greater Colombia and of New Granada; airport (El Dorado); railway; several universities and colleges; cathedral, Museum of Colonial Art, Palace of San Carlos, Municipal Palace, National Capitol, Churches of San Ignacio, Santa Clara, and San Agustín; Parque Santander, with Gold Museum; linked to Monserrate National Park by funicular railway and cable car. » Colombia [i]

Bohemia, Czech **Čechy**, Ger **Böhmen** [bohheemia] Historic province of W Czechoslovakia, bounded E by Moravia, W and S by W Germany and Austria, and N by E Germany and Poland; a plateau enclosed by mountains; natural boundaries include the Erzgebirge (N), Bohemian Forest (SW), and Sudetes Mts (NE); chief rivers include the Elbe (Labe), Vltava (Moldau), Ohre (Eger), Jihlava, and Jizera; major towns include Prague, Ceské Budějovice, Plzeň, Ústí and Labem; highly industrialized area; coal, iron ore, uranium; mineral springs; part of Moravian Empire, 9th-c; at its peak in early Middle Ages, especially in 14th-c under Charles I; Hussite religious dissension; Habsburg rule from early 16th-c; became a province of Czechoslovakia, 1918; part of Czech Socialist Republic of W Czechoslovakia, 1968. » Czechoslovakia [i]; Habsburgs; Huss

Bohemian Forest, Ger **Böhmerwald**, Czech **Český Les** Forested mountain range along the boundary between Germany and Bohemia, Czechoslovakia; highest German peak, Grosser Arber (1 457 m/4 780 ft); source of Bayern, Vltava, Regen, and Ilz Rivers. » Bohemia; Germany [i]

Bohemond I [bohaymõ] (c.1056–1111) Norman prince of Antioch (1099–1111), one of the leaders of the First Crusade. The eldest son of Robert Guiscard, he fought against the Byzantine Emperor, Alexius Comnenus (1081–5). He joined the Crusade of 1096, and took a prominent part in the capture of Antioch (1098), where he remained as prince. He died at Canosa di Puglia, Apulia. » Alexius Comnenus; Crusades [i]; Normans

Böhm, Karl [boem] (1894–1981) Austrian conductor, born at Graz. He studied in Vienna and held permanent posts as an opera conductor in Dresden (1934–43), Vienna (1943–5, 1954–6), and elsewhere, and also appeared frequently in London, New York, and Bayreuth. Remembered chiefly for his Mozart performances, he also conducted premieres of operas by Richard Strauss, a personal friend. He died at Salzburg. » Mozart; opera; Strauss, Richard

Bohm-Aharonov effect » **Aharonov-Bohm effect**

Böhm; Böhme » **Boehm; Boehme**

Bohr, Niels (Henrik David) (1885–1962) Danish physicist, born, educated, and died in Copenhagen. He worked at Cambridge and Manchester, then became professor at Copenhagen (1916). He greatly extended the theory of atomic structure when he explained the spectrum of hydrogen by means of an atomic model and the quantum theory (1913). During World War 2 he escaped from German-occupied Denmark and assisted atom bomb research in the USA, returning to Copenhagen in 1945. He was founder and director of the Institute of Theoretical Physics at Copenhagen, and was awarded the Nobel Prize for Physics in 1922. His son, **Aage N(iels)** (1922–) shared the 1975 Nobel Physics Prize for his work on atomic nuclei. » atomic bomb; quantum field theory

Bohr magnetron The magnetic moment of the electron, as given by relativistic quantum mechanics, treating the electron as a point particle; named after Danish physicist Niels Bohr; symbol μ_B; $\mu_B = eh/(4\pi mc)$, where e and m are electron charge and mass, h is Planck's constant, and c is the velocity of light; value $\mu_B = 9.274 \times 10^{-24}$J/T (joule per tesla); measured value slightly different, suggesting the need for corrections to quantum mechanics. The nuclear magnetron μ_N is the corresponding expression for the proton, with proton mass replacing electron mass: $\mu_N = 5.051 \times 10^{-27}$ J/T. » Bohr; electron; g-factor; magnetic moment; quantum mechanics

Boiardo, Matteo Maria, Count of Scandiano [boyahdoh] (1434–94) Italian poet, born at Scandiano. He studied at Ferrara, then lived at court, being employed on diplomatic missions. In 1481 he was appointed Governor of Modena, and in 1487 of Reggio. His fame rests on the *Orlando Innamorato* (1486), a long narrative poem about the Charlemagne hero, Roland. Known as the 'Flower of Chivalry', he died at Reggio. » Ariosto; Italian literature; poetry

boil An abscess in a sweat follicle, which results in a raised, reddened, and often painful swelling in the skin. It usually results from infection with *Staphylococcus aureus*. » abscess

Boileau (Despréaux), Nicolas [bwahloh] (1636–1711) French critic, born in Paris. He studied law and theology at Beauvais, then devoted himself to literature, and in 1677 was appointed royal historiographer. His first publications (1660–6) were satires, and he also wrote epistles, critical dissertations, epigrams, and translations. *L'Art poétique* (1674, The Art of Poetry), expressing the classical principles for the writing of poetry, was very influential in France and England. He died at Auteuil. » literary criticism

boiling point The state achieved when a liquid is heated until the heat energy is no longer used to increase temperature but instead to form gas from the liquid. Formally, the boiling point temperature is reached when a liquid's vapour pressure equals external pressure. Boiling points thus decrease with altitude. Water may be boiled at room temperature by decreasing the pressure around it. » cavitation; latent heat; phases of matter [i]; vapour pressure

boiling water reactor » **nuclear reactor** [i]

Bois de Boulogne [bwah duh booloyn] A park of 962 ha/2 380 acres situated on the W outskirts of Paris. Originally a royal hunting forest, it became a popular recreation area for Parisians in the 17th-c, and in 1852 was relandscaped along the lines of London's Hyde Park. The Longchamp racecourse was opened there in 1857. » Hyde Park; Paris [i]

Boise [boyzee] 43°37N 116°13W, pop (1980) 102 451. State capital in Ada county, SW Idaho, USA, on the Boise R; founded after the 1862 gold rush; airfield; railway; largest city in the state; trade and transportation centre; food processing and light manufacturing; Old Idaho Penitentiary, Idaho State museum. » Idaho

bolete [bohleet] A fungus with a typically mushroom-shaped fruiting body; fertile spore-producing layer present as a lining of tubes on underside of cap; commonly found on ground under trees; some species edible, others poisonous. (Subdivision: *Basidiomycetes*. Order: *Agaricales*.) » Basidiomycetes; fungus

Boleyn, Anne [boolin, boolin] (c.1507–36) English queen, the second wife of Henry VIII (1533–6), daughter of Sir Thomas Boleyn by Elizabeth Howard. Secretly married to Henry (Jan 1533), she was soon declared his legal wife (May); but within three months his passion for her had cooled. It was not revived by the birth (Sep 1533) of a princess (later Elizabeth I), still less by that of a stillborn son (Jan 1536). She was arrested and brought to the Tower, charged with treason, and beheaded (19 May). Henry married Jane Seymour 11 days later. » Henry VIII

bolide [bohleed] An exceptionally brilliant meteor, or fireball, which explodes in our atmosphere. It makes a very loud bang, and scatters stony debris over a wide area. » Allende meteorite; meteor

Bolingbroke, Henry St John, 1st Viscount (1678–1751) English statesman, born and died in London. He was educated at Eton, and may have gone to Oxford. After travelling in Europe, he entered parliament (1701), becoming Secretary for War (1704), Foreign Secretary (1710), and joint leader of the Tory Party. He was made a peer in 1712. On the death of Queen Anne (1714), his Jacobite sympathies forced him to flee to France, where he wrote *Reflections on Exile*. He returned for a while to England (1725–35), but unable to attain political office he went back to France (1735–42). His last years were spent in London, where his works included the influential *Idea of a Patriot King* (1749). » Anne; Tories

Bolingbroke » **Henry IV** (of England)

Bolívar, Simón, byname **the Liberator** [boleevah] (1783–1830) The national hero of Venezuela, Colombia, Ecuador, Peru, and Bolivia, born and educated in Caracas. Having travelled in Europe, he played the most prominent part in the wars of independence in N South America. In 1819, he proclaimed and became President of the vast republic of Colombia (modern Colombia, Venezuela, and Ecuador), which was finally liberated in 1822. He then took charge of the last campaigns of independence in Peru (1824). In 1826 he returned N to face growing political dissension. He resigned office (1830), and died on his way into exile, near Santa Marta, Colombia. » Gran Colombia; Spanish-American Wars of Independence

Bolívar, Pico Andean peak in Mérida state, W Venezuela; height, 5 007 m/16 427 ft; highest peak of the Cordillera de Mérida and of Venezuela; crowned with a bust of Bolívar. » Andes; Venezuela [i]

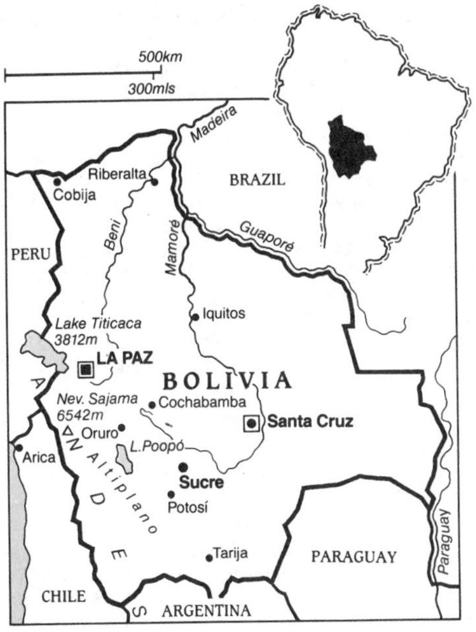

□ international airport

Bolivia, official name **Republic of Bolivia**, Span **República de Bolivia** pop (1990e) 7 322 000; area 1 098 580 sq km/424 052 sq ml. Republic of WC S America, divided into nine departments; bounded N and E by Brazil, W by Peru, SW by Chile, S by Argentina, and SE by Paraguay; government capital, La Paz; legal and judicial capital, Sucre; timezone GMT −4; population 30% Quechua, 25% Ayamará, 25–30% mixed, remainder European; main languages, Quechua, Ayamará, Spanish; religion, 95% Roman Catholic; unit of currency, the peso boliviano of 100 centavos.

Physical description. Land-locked country, bounded W by the Cordillera Occidental of the Andes, rising to 6 542 m/21 463 ft at Sajama; separated from the Cordillera Real to the E by the flat, 400 km/250 ml-long Altiplano plateau, 3 600 m/11 800 ft; major lakes, Titicaca and Poopó; several rivers flow towards the Brazilian frontier.

History and government. Part of Inca Empire, and evidence of earlier civilization; conquered by Spanish in 16th-c; independence after war of liberation, 1825; much territory lost after wars with neighbouring countries; several changes of government and military coups in recent decades; a bicameral Congress, with a 27-member Senate and a 130-member Chamber of Deputies elected for four years; an elected president appoints a cabinet of 18 ministers.

Economy. Largely dependent on minerals for foreign exchange; silver largely exhausted, but replaced by tin (a fifth of world supply), tungsten, antimony, lead, gold; oil and natural gas, pipelines to Argentina and Chile; sugar cane, rice, cotton, potatoes, cereals, livestock; illegally-produced cocaine. » Andes; Bolívar; Incas; La Paz; Sucre; RR24 national holidays; RR44 political leaders

Böll, Heinrich (1917–85) German writer, born at Cologne. His many novels include *Der Zug war Pünktlich* (1949, The Train was on Time), and a trilogy depicting life in Germany during and after the Nazi regime, *Und Sagte kein Einziges Wort* (1953, And Never said a Solitary Word), *Haus ohne Hüter* (1954, The Unguarded House), and *Das Brot der Frühen Jahre* (1955, The Bread of our Early Years). He was awarded the 1972 Nobel Prize for Literature, and died near Bonn. » German literature

boll weevil A small weevil that prevents the normal development of cotton flowers by its feeding activities. It is an economically important pest of cotton. (Order: *Coleoptera*. Family: *Curculionidae*.) » cotton [i]; weevil [i]

Bologna [bo**lohn**ya] 44°30N 11°20E, pop (1981) 459 080. Capital city of Bologna province, Emilia-Romagna, N Italy; 83 km/52 ml N of Florence, at the foot of the Apennines; ancient Etruscan city, enclosed by remains of 13th–14th-c walls; archbishopric; airport; rail junction; university (11th-c); pasta, sausages, shoes, chemicals, engineering, precision instruments, publishing; Church of San Petronio (14th-c), Church of San Domenico (13th-c), Pinacoteca Nazionale; two leaning towers (12th-c), the Asinelli and the Garisenda. » Italy [i]

Bolsheviks (Russ 'majority-ites') Members of the hard-line faction of the Marxist Russian Social Democratic Labour Party, formed by Lenin at the party's second congress in 1903; the forerunner of the modern Communist Party of the Soviet Union. In October 1917 the Bolsheviks led the revolution in Petrograd which established the first Soviet government. » April Theses; Cheka; Communist Party of the Soviet Union; July Days; Mensheviks; October/Russian Revolution

Bolshoi Ballet A Moscow-based ballet company tracing its origins to 1776 and its repertoire to the Russian classics. 1980s performances in W Europe brought praise for the athleticism of the dancers. The main directors/choreographers are Lavrovsky and Grigorovich, who specialize in modern versions of Russian themes, such as 'Spartacus' and 'Ivan the Terrible'. » ballet

Bolt, Robert (1924–) British dramatist, born and educated in Manchester. He served in the RAF and worked as a teacher before achieving success with *A Man for All Seasons* (1960). Other plays include *The Tiger and the Horse* (1960) and *State of Revolution* (1977). He has also written screenplays, including *Lawrence of Arabia* (1962), *Dr Zhivago* (1965), *Ryan's Daughter* (1970), and *The Mission* (1986). » drama; English literature

Boltzmann, Ludwig Eduard [**bolts**mahn] (1844–1906) Austrian physicist, born in Vienna. He studied at Vienna, where he became professor in 1895, after holding chairs in several other universities. He worked on the kinetic theory of gases, and helped to develop the science of statistical mechanics. **Boltzmann's law**, the principle of the equipartition of energy, and the **Boltzmann constant** are named after him. He died at Duino, Italy. » blackbody radiation; Boltzmann constant

Boltzmann constant Symbol k, units J/K (joule per kelvin), value 1.381×10^{-23} J/K, defined as R/N_A, where R is the molar gas constant and N_A is Avogadro's number; appears throughout the study of the statistical properties of gases; named after Austrian physicist Ludwig Boltzmann. » Avogadro's number; Boltzmann; gas **1**; statistical mechanics

Bolzano [bolt**sah**noh], Ger **Bozen** 46°30N 11°20E, pop (1981) 105 180. Capital town of Bolzano province, Trentino-Alto Adige, N Italy; on R Isarco, SSW of the Brenner Pass; chief commercial, industrial, and tourist centre of the region; mainly German-speaking; steel production, textiles, distilling, wine, canning, pianos; winter sports. » Italy [i]

bomb An explosive projectile without propulsion dropped from any type of aircraft. Gravity and release speed determine an ordinary bomb's flightpath, although so-called **smart bombs** have a target-seeking guidance package in the nose which can pick up signals from targets on the ground ('illuminated' by laser energy, for example), and generate steering commands to guide the bomb onto a target. » atomic bomb; hydrogen bomb [i]; incendiary bomb; mortar; neutron bomb; V-1; V-2

Bombard, Alain Louis (1924–) French physician and marine biologist, born in Paris. In 1952 he set out across the Atlantic alone in his rubber dinghy *L'Hérétique* to prove his claim that castaways could sustain life on a diet of fish and plankton. He landed at Barbados emaciated, but vindicated in his theories.

He now runs a marine laboratory at Saint-Malo for the study of the physiopathology of the sea.

bombardier beetle A small beetle of genus *Brachinus*. As a protective mechanism, adults fire clouds of caustic vapour, expelled by an explosion caused by mixing chemicals in glands at the rear end of the body. It can fire repeatedly at short intervals. (Order: *Coleoptera*. Family: *Carabidae*.) » beetle

Bombay 18°55N 72°50E, pop (1991) 12 570 000. Port capital of Maharashtra, W India; India's second largest city, and the only natural deep-water harbour on the W coast; built on a group of islands linked by causeways; ceded to Portugal, 1534; ceded to Britain, 1661; headquarters of the East India Company (1685–1708); airport; railway; two universities (1916, 1957); textiles, carpets, machinery, chemicals, oil refining; nuclear reactor at Trombay; Afghan church (1847), Gateway of India (archway commemorating visit to India of King George V and Queen Mary, 1911), Mani Bhavan (Gandhi memorial), Raudat Tahera mosque and mausoleum, Victoria and Albert Museum. » East India Company, British; India [i]; Maharashtra

Bombay duck Slender-bodied fish with large jaws and barb-like teeth; common in the tropical Indian Ocean, especially the Bay of Bengal; length up to 40 cm/16 in; flesh soft and translucent; important food fish, caught in fixed nets in brackish waters, and sun-dried. (*Harpadon nehereus*. Family: *Harpadontidae*.)

Bonaire [bon**air**] pop (1981) 8 753; area 288 sq km/111 sq ml. Island of the S Netherlands Antilles, E Caribbean, 60 km/37 ml N of Venezuela; composed of coralline limestone; rises to 241 m/791 ft in the hilly NW; low-lying coastal plain in the S; length 35 km/22 ml; capital, Kralendijk; airport; tourism, salt, textiles; Washington-Slagbaai National Park, area 59 sq km/23 sq ml, established in 1969; underwater park, area 60 sq km/23 sq ml. » Netherlands Antilles [i]

Bonaparte, Jérôme (1784–1860) Youngest brother of Napoleon, born at Ajaccio, Corsica. He served in the war against Prussia, was made king and ruled Westphalia (1807–14), and fought at Waterloo. He lived for many years in exile in Florence, but in 1848 was appointed Governor of the Invalides, and in 1850 was made a French Marshal by Napoleon III. He died in Florence. His first marriage to an American, **Elizabeth Patterson** (1785–1879), resulted in a son, **Jérôme** (1805–70), who went to live in the USA. » Napoleon I/III

Bonaparte, Joseph (1768–1844) King of Naples and Spain, the eldest brother of Napoleon, born in Corte, Corsica. He carried out various diplomatic duties for his brother, and was made ruler of the Two Sicilies (1805) and King of Naples (1806). In 1808 he was summarily transferred to the throne of Spain, but after the defeat of the French at Vitoria (1813) he abdicated and returned to France. After Waterloo he escaped to the USA, and lived in New Jersey as a farmer, but in 1832 returned to Europe, and died in Florence. » Napoleon I

Bonaparte, Napoleon » **Napoleon I; Napoleon III**

Bonaventure or **Bonaventura, St**, originally **Giovanni di Fidanza** (1221–74), feast day 14 July. Italian Franciscan theologian and cardinal, born near Orvieto, Tuscany. He became a Franciscan in 1243, taught in Paris, and by 1257 was General of his order. In 1273 he was made Cardinal Bishop of Albano. He died during the Council of Lyons, and in 1482 was canonized. His religious fervour procured for him the title of 'Doctor Seraphicus'. » Franciscans; theology

bond A loan to a company or a government. The loan carries an annual interest payment and is repayed after several years. It can be bought and sold on the stock market, and is a relatively secure investment often held by insurance companies and pension funds. » insurance; pension; premium bond

Bond, Edward (1934–) British dramatist and director. His early plays, such as *Saved* (1965) and *Narrow Road to the Deep North* (1968), were notorious for their use of violence to portray contemporary society. His *Lear* (1971) is a version of Shakespeare's play, and *Bingo* (1974) a dramatization of Shakespeare's last days. He has also written libretti and screenplays (eg *Blow Up*, 1967; *Laughter in the Dark*, 1969). » drama; English literature

Bondi [**bon**diy] A well-known resort beach in the Sydney suburb of Waverley, New South Wales, SE Australia. » Sydney

bone The hard tissue component of the vertebrate skeleton. It is composed of two functionally important principal components physically blended together: an organic element (mainly collagen), 25% of the weight of the fully-formed bone, and a mineral matrix (calcium, phosphate, and variable amounts of magnesium, sodium, carbonate, citrate, and fluoride), having a crystalline structure. It basically consists of many cylindrical units each with a central canal, containing bone-forming cells (*osteoblasts*), blood vessels, and nerve filaments, surrounded by bony tissue. Long bones consist of a shaft (a hollow tube surrounded by compact bone) and the ends (a network of spongy bone). The growth in length occurs at the region between shaft and ends (the *epiphyseal growth plate*). When this region disappears (between puberty and 25 years) growth ceases, as the shaft has fused with the ends. As bones grow, they increase in size and also change shape. Bone shape and dimensions are genetically determined, but are also influenced by hormonal, nutritional, mechanical, and neural factors. Calcium, phosphorus, and vitamins A, C and D are all required for normal bone growth and development. Abnormal pressures on bone (from a tumour or aneurysm) may cause bone erosion. Bone deprived of a nerve supply and muscular paralysis result in poor bone development and atrophy. » bone marrow; brittle bone syndrome; callus **2**; dislocation (medicine); fracture; joint; orthopaedics; osteoarthritis; osteology [i]; osteomalacia; osteomyelitis; osteopathy; osteoporosis; Paget's disease; rickets; skeleton

bone-black Animal charcoal obtained by heating bones in closed retorts. It contains calcium and magnesium phosphates as well as carbon, and is used as an adsorbent to remove colouring matter from food liquids such as raw sugar syrup. » charcoal

bone marrow An accumulation of cells and supporting tissues found within the central cavity of all bones. *Yellow marrow* consists of fat cells, blood vessels, and a minimal framework of reticular cells and fibres. *Red marrow* consists of numerous blood cells of all kinds, as well as their precursors. At birth all bones contain highly cellular red marrow; with increasing age the marrow becomes fattier, until in adults red marrow is present only in the vertebrae, sternum, ribs, flat bones of the skull and pelvis, and upper ends of the femur and humerus. The functions of red marrow are (1) the formation of red blood cells (*erythrocytes*), blood platelets, granulocytes, and to a lesser extent monocytes and lymphocytes, and (2) the destruction of old (c.120 days), worn-out erythrocytes. » blood; bone; cell; gene therapy; transplantation

Bonfire Night » **Guy Fawkes Night**

bongo A spiral-horned antelope native to equatorial Africa; brown with thin vertical white stripes; stiff erect hairs along spine; each cheek with two white spots; white line joining eyes; usually inhabits dense forest. (*Tragelaphus euryceros*.) » antelope

bongos A pair of wooden conical or cylindrical drums with single heads of skin or plastic, played with the hands. The shells are usually joined together, and in some varieties the heads may be tuned to different pitches. Originating in Cuba c.1900, they are used throughout Latin America, and frequently elsewhere. » drum; rumba

Bonhoeffer, Dietrich (1906–45) German Lutheran pastor and theologian, born at Breslau. Educated at Tübingen and Berlin, he left Germany in 1933 in protest against Nazi anti-Jewish legislation, and worked in German parishes in London until 1935. He then returned to Germany, to become head of a pastoral seminary until its closure by the Nazis in 1937. Deeply involved in the German resistance movement, he was arrested (1943), imprisoned, and hanged. His most influential works were *Ethik* (1949, Ethics) and *Widerstand und Ergebung* (1951, Letters and Papers from Prison). » 'death of God' theology; Lutheranism; secular Christianity

Boniface, St [**bon**ifas], originally **Wynfrith** (c.680–754), feast day 5 June. English Benedictine missionary, known as the 'Apostle of Germany', born in Wessex. He became a monk in Exeter, and in 718 was commissioned to preach the Gospel to all the tribes of Germany. He met with great success, and was made Bishop, Primate of Germany (732), and Archbishop of Mainz (747). He resumed his missionary work among the

Frisians in 754, but was killed at Dokkum by heathens. » Benedictines; missions, Christian; monasticism

Bonin Islands, Jap **Ogasawara-shoto** area 104 sq km/40 sq ml. Group of 27 volcanic islands in the W Pacific Ocean, c.965 km/600 ml S of Tokyo, Japan; largest island, Chichijima; first colonized by Europeans and Hawaiians, 1830; annexed by Japanese, 1876; taken by USA, 1945; returned to Japan, 1968; sugar cane, bananas, cocoa. » Japan [i]

Bonington, Chris(tian John Storey) (1934–) British mountaineer. He was a member of the British team that took part in the first successful conquest of the N face of the Eiger (1962), a member of the expedition that climbed the S face of Annapurna (1970), and leader of the 1975 Everest expedition. » Annapurna, Mount; Eiger; Everest, Mount; mountaineering

bonito [buh**nee**toh] Medium-sized tuna widely distributed in open ocean surface waters, living in compact schools; length up to 90 cm/3 ft; body steel blue to olive dorsally, with oblique black stripes, sides silver to yellow; important commercially and prized as sport fish. (Genus: *Sarda*. Family: *Scombridae*.) » tuna

Bonn 50°43N 7°06E, pop (1983) 292 900. Former capital city of West Germany, in Cologne district; on R Rhine, 25 km/15 ml SSE of Cologne; early Roman fort on the Rhine; seat of Electors of Cologne (13th–16th-c); part of Prussia, 1815; badly bombed in World War 2; capital status since 1949; airport at Cologne; railway; university (1818); service industries, plastics, packaging materials, aluminium; birthplace of Beethoven; spa resort at Bad Godesberg; 11th–13th-c Minster, Beethovenhalle; International Beethoven Festival every three years (Sep). » Beethoven; Cologne; Germany [i]; Prussia

Bonnard, Pierre [bon**ahr**] (1867–1947) French painter and lithographer, born in Paris. He was trained at the Académie Julien, and joined the group called Les Nabis, which included Denis and Vuillard, with whom he formed the Intimist group. Ignoring the movements towards abstraction, he continued to paint interiors and landscapes, subordinating everything to the subtlest rendering of light and colour effects. He died at Le Cannet. » French art; Intimisme; Nabis

Bonney, William H, byname **Billy the Kid** (1859–81) US bandit, born in New York, who achieved legendary notoriety for his robberies and murders in the SW states. He was captured by Sheriff Patrick F Garrett in 1880, and sentenced to hang. He escaped, but was finally tracked down and shot by Garrett.

Bonnie Prince Charlie » **Stuart, Charles Edward Louis Philip Casimir**

bonobo » **chimpanzee**

bonsai The technique or practice of producing extremely dwarfed plants in which all parts – stems, leaves, flowers – are in proportion. The effect is achieved by growing the plants in small pots, and by careful pruning of the roots to restrict growth.

bontebok [**bon**tuhbok] An ox-antelope native to S Africa; long face; lyre-shaped horns ringed with ridges; dark brown with white face and underparts; two subspecies: *bontebok* (with white rump) and *blesbok* (with brown rump); also known as **blesbok**. (*Damaliscus dorcas*.) » antelope

bonxie » **skua**

bony fish Any of the very large group *Osteichthyes*, comprising all true bony fishes (18 000 species; 450 families); includes both the ray-finned fishes (*Actinopterygii*) and the fleshy-finned fishes (*Sarcopterygii*), the latter containing the lungfishes (*Dipnoi*) and tassle-finned fishes (*Crossopterygii*); endoskeleton made of bone; with air bladder or lungs. » cartilaginous fish; crossopterygii

booby A bird related to gannets, native to tropical and subtropical seas; streamlined, with a colourful pointed bill. It catches fish by diving vertically into the water; air sacs beneath the skin of its face absorb the shock of impact. (Genus: *Sula*, 6 species. Family: *Sulidae*.) » gannet

book A portable or printed document, comprising at least 25 leaves of paper, vellum, or parchment bound together along one edge, generally affixed within a protective cover, and usually intended for non-periodical publication. The history of the book can be traced back to China in the 3rd-c BC, in the form of wood or bamboo leaves bound with cords. In the West the papyrus roll used by the Egyptians and Greeks was superseded in Greece and Rome by the codex (bound, handwritten leaves of vellum or parchment). Superbly written and illuminated manuscript books were made in the monasteries of W Europe from the 'Dark Ages' until well after the invention of printing in Europe c.1450.

Printing, along with the introduction of paper in the 14th-c, led to a very large increase in book production. Books from this period, known as *incunabula*, number some 35 000. The earliest printed books, such as Gutenberg's '42-line' Bible of 1456, were set in black-letter type and closely modelled on the design of mediaeval manuscript books. New features, such as title-pages and page numbers, began to appear towards the end of the 15th-c. Aldus Manutius, working in Venice, introduced a revolution in book production in 1501: pocket-size editions of Latin classics set in compact italic types in print-runs as long as 1 000 copies. Following the Reformation, censorship became increasingly repressive: the mid-16th-c saw the publication of the *Index* of prohibited books, and in England a royal charter giving the Stationers' Company a virtual monopoly over who might print what. The first book printed in America was the *Whole Booke of Psalmes* ('Bay Psalm Book') in 1640. The 19th-c brought many technical innovations, such as mechanical typesetting and cheaper paper, and several changes in retailing and use, following the mushroom growth of railway bookstalls and the development of public libraries. With the 20th-c came the heyday of the private press movement, the steady development of book clubs, new techniques in printing, and a notable growth in the numbers of new titles published, particularly in paperback. » book fairs; bookbinding; censorship; Kells; printing [i]; publishing

book fairs International collaborative occasions for the buying and selling of books and the right to publish translations of books. The principal fairs include those held at Frankfurt, Bologna (children's books), London, Moscow, Jerusalem, and that of the American Booksellers' Association, which is held at various locations in the USA. » publishing

Book of Common Prayer The official directory of worship or service-book of the Church of England, widely honoured and followed in churches of Anglican Communion. Largely composed by Archbishop Cranmer, it was first introduced in 1549, and revised in 1552, 1604 and finally 1662. Until 1975, revisions in England required the approval of Parliament. It is generally considered a landmark of English prose. » Church of England; Cranmer; liturgy

book of hours A prayer book, popular in the Middle Ages, and known in England as a 'Primer'. It typically contained the 'Little Office of Our Lady', psalms of penitence, and the 'Office of the Dead' (usually in Latin). » prayer

Book of the Dead An ancient Egyptian collection of magical and religious texts. Copies were often buried with the dead as a protection and comfort in the after-life.

bookbinding Techniques for the joining of leaves along one edge to form a codex or book. All bookbinding was done by hand until the 19th-c, and the craft tradition lives on for the production of single copies and *editions de luxe*. Single leaves and folded sections of two or more leaves are stitched together with thread around cords attached to the cover boards; the spine and boards are covered with leather or cloth, and titling is stamped on the spine. Modern mechanical bookbinding automates these processes, though eliminating the cords. Various techniques such as adhesive (cut-off, glued backs) and 'burst' (glue forced through the backs of folded sections) binding have replaced the thread. In paperback binding, light boards are glued around adhesive-bound books. » book

booklouse A small flattened insect which typically feeds on old books or dried organic material. It can cause extensive damage in libraries. » insect [i]; louse

bookworm The common name of various larval and adult insects that damage books by feeding on the paper and binding, and by burrowing activity. It is used particularly of the booklouse and silverfish. » booklouse; larva; silverfish

Boole, George (1815–64) British mathematician and logician, born at Lincoln. He became professor of mathematics at Cork in 1849. He is primarily known for his *Mathematical Analysis of Logic* (1847) and *Laws of Thought* (1854), where he employed mathematical symbolism to express logical processes ('Boolean algebra'). A pioneer of modern symbolic logic, he greatly influenced the work of Frege and Russell among others. He died at Ballintemple, Cork, Ireland. » algebra; Boolean algebra; Frege; logic; Russell, Bertrand

Boolean algebra An algebra on sets, devised by Boole, developed as an algebra of symbolic logic. The differences from arithmetic algebra can be illustrated by the absorption laws on sets A, B and C: $A+A=A$ and $(A+B)(A+C)=A+BC$. The similarities between the algebra of sets and that of logic can be seen by comparing $A \cap A = A$ and $p \wedge p = p$, the latter being read 'p and p implies p', where p is a statement known to be true. » algebra; Boole

boomer » **mountain beaver**

boomerang A throwing stick, so shaped as to fly great distances and strike a severe blow. Mainly Australian, but known elsewhere (eg among certain American Indian groups). Some are made to take a curved path and return, and are used mainly for play or training.

boomslang A venomous African snake; long thin green or dark brown body; length, up to 2 m/6½ ft; three fangs; lives in trees adjoining grassland; eats lizards, birds, frogs. (*Dispholidus typus*. Family: *Colubridae*.) » snake

Boone, Daniel (1735–1820) US pioneer, born in Pennsylvania. He made a trail through the Cumberland Gap (1767) and became one of the first to explore Kentucky (1769–73). Twice captured by Indians, he repeatedly repelled (1775–8) Indian attacks on his stockade fort, now Boonesborough. He later worked as a surveyor and trapper, and died at St Charles, Missouri.

Boot, Sir Jesse, 1st Baron Trent (1850–1931) British drug manufacturer, born in Nottingham. At 13 he inherited his father's herbalist's shop, and studied pharmacy in his leisure hours. In 1877 he opened his first chemist's shop in Nottingham, and by mass selling at reduced prices introduced the modern chain store. By 1900 he was controlling the largest pharmaceutical retail trade in the world, with over a thousand branches in 1931. He was made a peer in 1929.

Boötes (Lat 'herdsman') [bohohteez] A large N hemisphere constellation. It contains Arcturus, a red giant, the brightest star in the N sky, radius 28 times the Sun. Distance: 11 parsecs. Doubtless one of the first stars to be named, it is mentioned in literature from the earliest times. » red giant; star

Booth, Edwin Thomas (1833–93) US actor, born in Harford Co, Maryland. He was best known for his Shakespearian roles, notably *Hamlet* (1864), which he produced in New York for a record run. Ruined by opening a theatre in New York in 1869, he settled his debts, later visiting Germany and Britain (1880–2). He died in New York.

Booth, John Wilkes (1839–65) US assassin, born at Baltimore. An unsuccessful actor, the brother of Edwin Booth. In 1865 he entered into a conspiracy to avenge the defeat of the Confederates and shot President Lincoln at Ford's Theatre, Washington (14 Apr). He broke his leg while escaping, and fled to Virginia, but was tracked down and shot. » Lincoln, Abraham

Booth, William (1829–1912) British founder and 'general' of the Salvation Army, born in Nottingham. He was minister of the Methodist New Connexion (1855–61), and in 1865 founded the Army (so named in 1878) on military lines with mission work in London's East End. His wife, **Catherine** (1829–90), was fully associated with him, and his son **Bramwell** (1856–1929) and daughters **Kate** (1859–1955) and **Evangeline** (1865–1950) succeeded him in the work. He died in London. » missions, Christian; Salvation Army

Boothe, Clare (1903–) US author, born in New York City. She became a magazine journalist, and wrote several successful plays, such as *The Women* (1936) and *Kiss the Boys Goodbye* (1938). Elected to the House of Representatives as a Republican in 1942, she later became US ambassador to Italy (1953–7). In 1935 she married Henry Robinson Luce. » American literature

Booths, Feast of » **Sukkoth**

bootlegging The illegal manufacture or distribution of alcoholic drink or other highly taxed goods, such as cigarettes. The term is mainly used with reference to the smuggling of alcohol in the USA during the Prohibition era (1920–33). This became a major illegal industry, which led to the development of organized crime on a large scale. Bootlegging still exists in those parts of the USA where the sale of alcoholic drinks is prohibited. » Capone, Al; Prohibition

bop » **bebop**

Bophuthatswana, locally **Bop** [bopootats**wah**na] pop (1987e) 1 606 000; area 44 000 sq km/16 984 sq ml. Independent Black homeland in South Africa; comprises seven separate units of land in Cape, Orange Free State, and Transvaal provinces; self-government, 1971; second homeland to receive independence from South Africa (not recognized internationally), 1977; main languages, English, Afrikaans, Setswana; over 368 000 people are commuters or migrant workers in South Africa; brewing, tanning, furniture, maize, beef; platinum (a third of world production of platinum group metals), copper, nickel, gold, chromium, vanadium, asbestos, iron ore, diamonds, limestone, manganese, fluorspar. » apartheid; South Africa [i]

boracic acid » **boric acid**

borage A robust annual, growing to 60 cm/24 in, covered in stiff, white bristles, native to C Europe and the Mediterannean region; leaves oval, rough; flowers 2 cm/0.8 in diameter, bright blue, drooping, with five spreading petals and black anthers. Cultivated as a herb, its bruised leaves smell of cucumber. (*Borago officinalis*. Family: *Boraginaceae*.) » alkanet; annual; herb

boranes [**boh**raynz] Compounds of boron and hydrogen, the simplest being diborane (B_2H_6). They are high-energy compounds, and have been used as rocket fuels. They are oxidized to boric acid. The reaction is $B_2H_6 + 1\frac{1}{2}O_2 \rightarrow 2H_3BO_3$. Compounds with CH^+ replacing BH are called *carboranes* or *carbaboranes*. » boron; hydrogen

borate » **boric acid**

borax [**boh**raks] $Na_2B_4O_7.10H_2O$; the hydrated salt of boric acid. It forms insoluble salts with Ca^{2+} and Mg^{2+} ions, and thus is useful as a water softener and cleanser. Borax in a less hydrated form ($4H_2O$) is the most important source of boron. It is an important ingredient in borosilicate ('Pyrex') glasses. » boric acid; boron; evaporite deposits; hydration

Bordeaux, Lat **Burdigala** [baw**doh**] 44°50N 0°36W, pop (1982) 211 197. Inland port and capital of Gironde department, SW France, on R Garonne; major port, and cultural and commercial centre for SW; 480 km/298 ml SW of Paris and 100 km/60 ml from the Atlantic; held by the English (1154–1453); centre during the wars of the Fronde; temporary seat of government in 1870, 1914, and 1940; centre of wine-growing region, Médoc (N), Graves and Sauternes (S), and Entre-deux-Mers (between Garonne and Dordogne Rivers); airport; railway; archbishopric; university (1441); shipbuilding, chemicals, wine trade, oil refining, fishing; Church of St Seurin (12th–15th-c), Grand Theatre (1773–80), Pont de Pierre (1813–21). » Aquitaine; Frondes, the; wine

Borden, Sir Robert (Laird) (1854–1937) Canadian statesman and Conservative Prime Minister (1911–20), born at Grand Pré, Nova Scotia. He practised as a barrister, and became leader of the Conservative Party in 1901. As Prime Minister, he led Canada through World War 1, the Conscription Crisis, and the introduction of income tax. At the Imperial War Conference of 1917, he called for greater recognition of the Dominions' autonomy, a step towards the building of a Commonwealth. He died in Ottawa.

Border terrier A breed of dog, developed in the Scottish/English border hills to hunt foxes; small and active; solid, flat-ended muzzle; small ears; thick, stiff, wiry coat; usually black and tan. » dog; terrier

Borders pop (1981) 99 784; area 4 672 sq km/1 803 sq ml. Region in SE Scotland, divided into four districts; bounded NE by the North Sea, SE by England; crossed E–W by Southern Uplands; rivers include the Tweed and Teviot; capital Newtown St Boswells; major towns include Hawick, Peebles, Galashiels; livestock, forestry, textiles; Melrose Abbey (12th-c), Abbotsford (home of Walter Scott), Dryburgh Abbey; Muir-foot, Lammermuir, and Pentland Hills. » Scotland [i]; Scott, Walter

Bordet, Jules (Jean Baptiste Vincent) [**baw**day] (1870–1961) Belgian physiologist and bacteriologist, born at Soignies. He worked at the Pasteur Institute, Paris (1894–1901), then founded and directed the Pasteur Institute at Brussels (1901–40). He discovered the immunity factors in blood serum, and the bacterium causing whooping cough. He won the Nobel Prize for Physiology or Medicine in 1919, and died in Brussels. » blood; immunology; whooping cough

bore A nearly vertical wall of water that may be produced as a result of tides, tsunami, or seiche. Bores usually occur in funnel-shaped estuaries with sloping bottoms. Bottom friction slows the advancing wave front, and water piles up behind to produce a nearly vertical bore face. The rapidly moving wall of water is followed by a less steep rise in sea level accompanied by swift upstream currents. » seiche; tide; tsunami

boreal forests The dense coniferous forests of N America, Europe, and Asia. Characteristic tree species include fir, hemlock, spruce, and pine in more open areas. It is sometimes regarded as synonymous with *taiga*, though the vegetation canopy in the boreal forest is less open, with relatively little light reaching the forest floor. » conifer; taiga

borecole [**baw**kohl] » **kale**

Borg, Björn (Rune) (1956–) Swedish tennis player, born at Södertälje. His first major title was the Italian Open (1974), and he went on to become Wimbledon singles champion five times (1976–80), a modern-day record. His five-set final against John McEnroe in 1980 was one of the game's all-time classics, but he lost to McEnroe in the 1981 final. He also won the French singles title six times, and was the World Championship Tennis singles champion in 1976, and Masters champion in 1979 and 1980. He retired in 1981, but made two brief comebacks in 1982 and 1984. » McEnroe; tennis, lawn [i]

Borga » **Porvoo**

Borges, Jorge Luis [**baw**khas] (1899–1986) Argentine writer, born in Buenos Aires. He was educated in Buenos Aires, Geneva, and Cambridge. He joined an avant-garde literary group in Spain (1918–21), then returned to Argentina, where from 1923 he published poems and essays. From 1941 he wrote mainly short stories, including *Ficciones* (1945, Fictions), and *El Aleph* (1949, The Aleph). In his later years he became blind, but continued to write, in 1980 winning the Cervantes Prize. He died in Geneva. » Latin-American literature

Borghese [bor**gay**zay] A great 13th-c family of ambassadors and jurists of Siena, afterwards (16th-c) at Rome. Their members include **Camillo Borghese** (1552–1621), who ascended the papal throne in 1605 as Paul V, and **Prince Camillo Filippo Ludovico Borghese** (1775–1832), who joined the French army, married Napoleon's sister Marie Pauline (1803), and became Governor-General of Piedmont. The Borghese Palace still contains one of the finest collections of paintings in Rome.

Borgia [**baw**ja] Italian form of **Borja**, an ancient family in the Spanish province of Valencia. Their members include **Alfonso** (1378–1458), who accompanied Alfonso of Aragon to Rome, and was elected Pope as Calixtus III. **Rodrigo** (1431–1503), his nephew, became Pope as Alexander VI (1492). Two of Rodrigo's children became especially notorious. **Cesare** (1476–1507) was a brilliant general and administrator, succeeding his brother (whom he may have murdered) as Captain-General of the Church. In two campaigns he became master of Romagna, Perugia, Siena, Piombino, and Urbino, and planned a Kingdom of Central Italy. After the death of Alexander (1502), his enemies rallied. He surrendered at Naples, was imprisoned, escaped (1506), but soon after died while fighting for the King of Navarre. **Lucrezia** (1480–1519) was married three times by her father, for political reasons, finally becoming the wife of Alfonso, son of the Duke of Este. She has been represented as a person of wantonness, vices, and crimes; but she died enjoying the respect of her subjects, a patroness of learning and of art.

Borglum, (John) Gutzon (de la Mothe) (1867–1941) US sculptor, born at St Charles, Idaho, of Danish descent. He won renown for works of colossal proportions, such as the Mount Rushmore National Memorial. He died in Chicago. His brother **Solon Hannibal** (1868–1922) also won fame as a sculptor, especially of horses and 'wild west' subjects. » Rushmore, Mount; sculpture

boric acid H_3BO_3; a weak acid, with antiseptic properties. Dilute solutions have a pH of about 6, while partially neutralized solutions have a pH of about 9. Salts of boric acid are called **borates**. Hydrated boron (III) oxide (B_2O_3) is also called **boracic acid**. » acid; borax; pH

Borlaug, Norman Ernest [**baw**log] (1914–) US plant pathologist and geneticist, born at Cresco, Iowa, and educated at the University of Minnesota. As director of the Wheat Programme, International Center for Maize and Wheat Improvement, he developed 'dwarf' wheats which dramatically increased yields and made possible the 'green revolution'. He was awarded the Nobel Peace Prize in 1970. » Green Revolution; wheat

Bormann, Martin (1900–?45) German Nazi politician, born at Halberstadt. One of Hitler's closest advisers, he became *Reichsminister* (1941) after Hess's flight to Scotland, and was with Hitler to the last. His own fate is uncertain, but he was possibly killed by Russian snipers in the breakout by Hitler's staff from the Chancellory (1 May 1945). He was sentenced to death in his absence by the Nuremberg Court (1946). » Hitler; World War 2

Born, Max (1882–1970) German physicist, born at Breslau (Wroclaw). He was professor of theoretical physics at Göttingen (1921–33), lecturer at Cambridge (1933–6), professor of natural philosophy at Edinburgh (1936–53), and shared (with Walter Bothe) the 1954 Nobel Prize for Physics for work in the field of quantum physics. He died at Göttingen. » Born-Haber cycle; Bothe; quantum field theory

Born-Haber cycle [bawn **hah**ber] A thermochemical cycle relating the lattice energy of an ionic solid to its heat of formation, in terms of properties of the single atoms. Since the total consumption of energy for any process is independent of the path taken, any single unknown quantity may be estimated if the others are known. » Born; Haber; ion; thermochemistry

Borneo [**baw**neeoh] area 484 330 sq km/186 951 sq ml. Island in SE Asia, E of Sumatra, N of Java, W of Sulawesi; third largest island in the world; comprises the Malaysian states of Sarawak and Sabah and the former British protectorate of Brunei (N); remainder comprises the four provinces of Kalimantan, part of Indonesia; formerly divided between the British and the Dutch; mountainous (N), rising to 4 094 m/13 432 ft at Mt Kinabalu in Sabah; interior densely forested; rice, pepper, copra, tobacco, oil, bauxite, iron. » Brunei; Indonesia [i]; Sarawak

Bornholm [**bawn**holm] pop (1983) 47 313; area 588 sq km/227 sq ml. Danish island in the Baltic Sea, 40 km/25 ml S of Sweden, 168 km/104 ml ESE of Copenhagen; length 37 km/23 ml; rises to 162 m/531 ft; taken by Sweden, 1645; returned to Denmark, 1660; administrative capital and chief port, Rønne; fishing, fish-processing, farming, pottery, tourism. » Denmark [i]

Borobudur [**bo**rohbooduh] A Buddhist sanctuary built between 750 and 850 in Java, Indonesia. The monument comprises eight stepped terraces cut into the sides of a natural mound and culminating in a central shrine (stupa). It is renowned for the abundance and intricacy of its relief sculptures. » Java

Borodin, Alexander (Porfiryevich) [boro**deen**] (1833–87) Russian composer and scientist, born and died in St Petersburg. He trained for medicine and distinguished himself as a chemist. In 1862 he began to study music, under Balakirev. His compositions include the unfinished opera, *Prince Igor* (which contains the Polovtsian Dances), three symphonies, and the symphonic sketch *In the Steppes of Central Asia.* » Balakirev

borohydride [boroh**hiy**driyd] An anion containing boron and hydrogen, especially BH_4^-. *Sodium borohydride* is an important reducing agent. » boranes; boron; hydrogen; reducing agent

boron [**boh**ron] B, element 5; melting point 2 300°C. A hard, non-metallic solid, which as a pure element does not occur free in nature. It forms many compounds in which it is bound to oxygen, and shows an oxidation state of +3. Although a relatively rare element, it is found in large concentrations, especially as boric acid and borax. » boranes; borax; boric acid; chemical elements; oxidation; RR90

borough In general terms, the second tier of local government in England and Wales, based on charters granted at different times by the monarchy. **Borough councils** were first elected in 1835, when their main function was law and order. The name has survived all subsequent reforms of local government, but now is largely indistinguishable from the equivalent unit of *district*. The Scottish equivalent is *burgh*, but this term is no longer used in official designations, *district* being preferred. » local government

Borromeo, St Charles [boromayoh] (1538–84), feast day 4 November. Italian cardinal and Archbishop of Milan, born at Arona. He did much to bring the Council of Trent to a successful conclusion (1562–3), and in 1570 founded the Helvetic College at Milan. He died in Milan, and was canonized in 1610. » Trent, Council of

Borromini, Francesco, originally **Francesco Castello** [boromeenee] (1599–1667) Italian architect, born at Bissone, L Lugano. He was trained by his father, a mason, and then worked in Milan. He went to Rome in 1619 and designed San Carlo alle Quattro Fontane (1637–41). Although now considered one of the great Baroque architects, he had limited influence in contemporary Italy. He committed suicide in Rome. » architecture; Baroque (art and architecture); Italian art

Borrow, George (Henry) (1803–81) British author and traveller, born at East Dereham, Norfolk. He was educated at Norwich, began to train as a solicitor, then worked for a publisher in London. From 1825 to 1832 he wandered in England, sometimes in gypsy company, as described in *Lavengro* and *The Romany Rye*. As agent of the Bible Society he visited St Petersburg (1833–5), Portugal, Spain, and Morocco (1835–9), and later visited SE Europe (1844) and Wales (1854). He died at Oulton Broad, Norfolk. » English literature; Gypsy

borstal » **Youth Custody Centre**

borzoi [bawzoy] A breed of dog, developed in Russia, where aristocrats used groups of borzois to hunt wolves; an athletic breed, tall and slender; long thin muzzle; long tail; coat long, straight or curly; also known as **Russian wolfhound**; » dog; hound

Bosch, Carl (1874–1940) German chemist, born at Cologne. He became president of the I G Farben Industrie, and shared the 1931 Nobel Prize for Chemistry with Friedrich Bergius for the development of chemical high pressure methods, such as the **Bosch process**, in which hydrogen is obtained from water gas and superheated steam. He died at Heidelberg. » Bergius

Bosch, Hieronymus, pseudonym of **Jerome van Aken** (c.1450–1516) Dutch painter, born and died at Hertogenbosch. A pupil of Ouwater, he is noted for his allegorical pictures displaying macabre devils, freaks, and monsters. Among his best-known works are the 'Garden of Earthly Delights' (Prado) and the 'Temptation of St Anthony' (Lisbon). He had considerable influence on the Surrealists. » Dutch art; Surrealism

Bose-Einstein statistics [bohs] In quantum statistical mechanics, the description of collections of many non-interacting bosons. The Bose-Einstein distribution expresses the partition of energy amongst bosons, and is important in, for example, the description of photons in laser action and of superfluidity in liquid helium. It is named after Indian physicist Satyendra Nath Bose (1894–1974), who collaborated with Einstein. » boson; Einstein; Fermi-Dirac statistics; laser [i]; statistical mechanics; superfluidity

Bosnia and Herzegovina [boznia, hertzuhguhveena], Serbo-Croatian **Bosna-Hercegovina** pop (1981) 4 124 256; area 51 129 sq km/19 736 sq ml. Constituent republic of C Yugoslavia; capital, Sarajevo; chief towns include Banja Luka, Zenica, Tuzla, Mostar; Austrian protectorate, 1878; annexed by Austria, 1908; Serbian opposition to the annexation led to the murder of Archduke Francis Ferdinand, and World War 1; ceded to Yugoslavia, 1918; a mountainous region, including part of the Dinaric Alps; noted for its limestone gorges; agricultural trade. » Dinaric Alps; Sarajevo; Serbia; Yugoslavia [i]

boson [bohson] A sub-atomic particle having integer spin; named after Indian physicist Satyendra Nath Bose (1894–1974). Unlike fermions, bosons have no exclusion principle limiting the number occupying some state. Force-carrying particles, such as photons, gluons, and gravitons, are all bosons. » Bose-Einstein statistics; fermions; meson; particle physics; spin

Bosporus or **Bosphorus** [bospuhruhs], Turkish **Karadeniz Boğazi** Narrow strait separating European from Asiatic Turkey, and connecting the Black Sea and the Sea of Marmara; length 32 km/20 ml; minimum width 640 m/2 100 ft; at its narrowest point are two famous castles, Anadolu Hisar (1390) on the Asian side, and Rumeli Hisar (1452) on the European side; an area of great strategic importance. » Bosporus Bridge; Dardanelles; Istanbul; Marmara, Sea of; Turkey [i]

Bosporus Bridge A major steel suspension bridge across the Golden Horn at Istanbul, Turkey; completed in 1973; length of main span 1 074 m/3 524 ft. » Bosporus; bridge (engineering) [i]; Istanbul

Bosques Petrificados [boskays petreefeekaṯhohs], Eng **Petrified Forests** Natural monument in E Santa Cruz province, Patagonia, Argentina; area 100 sq km/39 sq ml; established in 1954; contains 70 000-year-old araucaria trees, averaging 3 m/10 ft in circumference and 15–20 m/50–65 ft in height. » Patagonia

Bosra An ancient Syrian city 117 km/73 ml S of Damascus; a world heritage site. Originally an Arab fortress, Bosra was conquered by the Nabataeans, and became almost as important as Petra. It was annexed by the Romans in AD 105, and subsequently flourished as capital of the province of Arabia. » Petra; Roman history [i]

boss (zoology) » **bison**

Bossuet, Jacques Bénigne [bosway] (1627–1704) French Catholic churchman and pulpit orator, born at Dijon. He was educated at Dijon and Paris, received a canonry at Metz (1652), and in 1661 preached before Louis XIV. His reputation as an orator spread over France, and he became tutor to the Dauphin. As Bishop of Meaux (1681) he took a leading part in the Gallican controversy, asserting the king's independence from Rome in secular matters. He died in Paris. » Louis XIV; oratory

Boston (USA) 42°22N 71°04W, pop (1980) 562 994. Capital of Massachusetts state, USA; in Suffolk county, on Massachusetts Bay, at the mouth of the Charles R; largest city in New England; settled, 1630; capital of the Massachusetts Bay Colony, 1632; city status, 1822; a centre of opposition to British trade restrictions and scene of the Boston Tea Party (1773); centre of the Unitarian Church movement; airport; railway; noted for its colleges and universities (1869, 1898, 1906); large immigrant population; commerce, finance, electronics, printing and publishing; major league teams, Red Sox (baseball), Celtics (basketball), Bruins (ice hockey); Boston Tea Party ship and museum, Christ Church (1723), Paul Revere's house, Faneuil Hall (1742); Conservatory of Music; Museum of Fine Arts; Boston Marathon run on Patriot's Day (Apr). » Boston Massacre/Tea Party; Massachusetts; Revere; Unitarians

Boston Massacre (5 Mar 1770) The first bloodshed of the American Revolution, as British guards at the Boston Customs House opened fire on a crowd, killing five. Among the issues involved were the general presence of troops, competition between soldiers and civilians for jobs, and the shooting of a Boston boy by a customs official. » American Revolution; Boston

Boston Tea Party (1773) During the American Revolution, the climactic event of resistance to British attempts at direct taxation, resulting in the destruction of 342 chests of dutied tea by working men disguised as Mohawks. Other ports had refused to let the tea ships enter. » American Revolution; Boston; Intolerable Acts

Boston terrier A breed of dog, developed in the USA by crossing existing terriers and bulldogs; small, deep-chested; large ears, spherical head, thick neck; coat short; white and brown or white and black. » bulldog; terrier

Boswell, James (1740–95) British man of letters and biographer of Dr Johnson, born in Edinburgh, Scotland. He was educated at the Edinburgh High School and University, and studied civil law at Glasgow, but his ambition was literary fame. At 18 he began his journal, and in 1760 ran away to London, where he was led into debauchery. He first met Johnson in 1763, was elected to Johnson's famous literary club in 1773, and took him on the memorable journey to the Hebrides. His *Journal of a Tour of the Hebrides* (1785) appeared after Johnson's death. Its success led him to plan his masterpiece, the *Life of Samuel Johnson* (1791). He died in London. » biography; English literature; Johnson, Samuel

Bosworth Field, Battle of (22 Aug 1485) The battle which put Henry Tudor on the English throne after victory over Richard III, who died in the conflict. Henry Tudor's forces were possibly inferior in number, but proved more loyal; they received crucial support from the Stanley family, who had feet in both camps. » Henry VII; Richard III

bot fly A robust, hairy fly, whose larvae are parasites beneath the skin of mammals, feeding on fluids exuding from tissues. The mature larvae bore out through the skin and pupate on the ground. The sheep bot fly deposits its larvae in the nostrils of sheep. (Order: *Diptera*. Family: *Oestridae*.) » fly; larva; pupa

botanical garden A collection of living plants usually arranged by geographic or taxonomic principles, and maintained for the purposes of scientific research, education and, with increased urbanization, recreation. In China, gardens of medicinal and economically valuable plants were cultivated and used for the introduction and acclimatization of foreign flora 3 000 years ago; the Aztecs and Incas also established extensive gardens of useful plants. The first European botanical gardens were collections of medicinal plants used for study in monasteries, and later in the medical schools of the early universities. » arboretum; Kew Gardens

botany The study of all aspects of plants, principally their structure, physiology, relationships, and biogeography, but embracing many aspects of other disciplines. Important areas in modern botanical research include genetics and plant breeding; vegetative reproduction and tissue culture, especially the use of microtechniques in which plants are propagated from small amounts of excised tissue such as meristems rather than from seeds; ecology and conservation, especially of endangered habitats such as tropical rain forests and wetlands; and, increasingly, the use of plants as indicators of pollution. » biogeography; biology; conservation (earth sciences); ecology; genetics [i]; meristem; physiology; pollution

Botany Bay A shallow inlet 8 km/5 ml S of Sydney, New South Wales, Australia; now a residential part of Sydney; Captain Cook made his first landing here in 1770, naming the bay after the number of new plants discovered there; chosen as a penal settlement in 1787, but found to be unsuitable, and a location at Sydney Cove used instead; the name Botany Bay, however, was for many years synonymous with Australian convict settlements. » Cook, James; first fleet; Sydney

Botha, Louis [**boh**ta] (1862–1919) South African statesman and soldier, the first Prime Minister of South Africa (1910–19), born at Greytown, Natal. He was a member of the Transvaal Volksraad, and commanded the Boer forces during the war. In 1907 he became Prime Minister of the Transvaal colony, and in 1910 Prime Minister of the new Union. He suppressed De Wet's rebellion (1914), and conquered German SW Africa (1914–15). He died at Pretoria. » Boer Wars; South Africa [i]

Botha, P(ieter) W(illem) [**boh**ta] (1916–) South African statesman, Prime Minister (1978–84), and President (1984–9), born at Paul Roux. He studied law at Bloemfontein, became active in politics, and was elected to the South African Assembly in 1948. He held various ministries, notably that of Defence (1966–80), where he presided over a strengthening of the armed forces, as well as the controversial military intervention in Angola. He attempted to introduce constitutional reforms, involving limited power-sharing with non-Whites, but this led to a right-wing defection in 1982 from his ruling National Party. He suffered a stroke in 1989, and resigned as President later that year. » apartheid; South Africa [i]

Botham, Ian (Terence) (1955–) British cricketer, born at Heswall, Wirral, Merseyside. An all-rounder, he has played for England in 94 test matches, scored 5 057 runs, taken a one-time world record 373 wickets, and held 109 catches. His all-round figures are unsurpassed in Test cricket. He started his career with Somerset, making his first-class debut in 1974, and his Test debut in 1977 against Australia. He moved to Worcestershire in 1987. He has also played League soccer for Scunthorpe United, and is well known for his walk from John o'Groats to Lands End, and for his aborted attempt to follow Hannibal's trek across the Alps, both ventures in aid of leukaemia research. » cricket (sport) [i]

Bothe, Walther (Wilhelm Georg) [**boh**tuh] (1891–1957) German physicist, born at Oranienburg. He taught at Berlin (1920–31), Giessen (1931–4), and Heidelberg (1934–57), where he headed the Max Planck Institute for Medical Research. His work on the development of coincidence technique in subatomic particle counting brought him the Nobel Prize for Physics in 1954, shared with Max Born. » atom; Born

Bothnia, Gulf of N arm of Baltic, between Sweden and Finland; length c.650 km/400 ml; width 80–240 km/50–150 ml; maximum depth c.100 m/330 ft; islets and sandbars impede navigation; generally freezes over in winter. » Baltic Sea

Bothwell, James Hepburn, 4th Earl of (c.1535–78) Third husband of Mary, Queen of Scots. One of the greatest nobles in Scotland, he was held responsible for the abduction and murder of Mary's second husband, Lord Darnley (1567). He was made Duke of Orkney, then married Mary, but faced opposition from the nobles. He fled to Denmark after Mary's surrender to rebel forces at Carberry Hill, and was imprisoned in Dragsholm, where he died insane. » Mary, Queen of Scots

Botrange [boh**trãzh**] 50°30N 6°05E. Mountain in the Hohe Venn, E Liège province, Belgium; 8 km/5 ml NNE of Malmédy; the highest mountain in Belgium; 694 m/2 277 ft. » Ardennes; Belgium [i]

Botswana, official name **Republic of Botswana** pop (1990e) 1 295 000; area 582 096 sq km/224 689 sq ml. S African republic, divided into nine districts; bounded S by South Africa, W and N by Namibia, E by Zimbabwe; capital, Gaborone; chief towns, Francistown, Lobatse, Selebi-Phikwe, Orapa, Jwaneng; timezone GMT +2; population mainly Tswana; religion, mainly local beliefs, 20% Christian; languages, English, Setswana; unit of currency, the pula of 100 thebes.

Physical description and climate. Land-locked, undulating, sand-filled plateau, mean elevation c.1 000 m/3 300 ft; most live

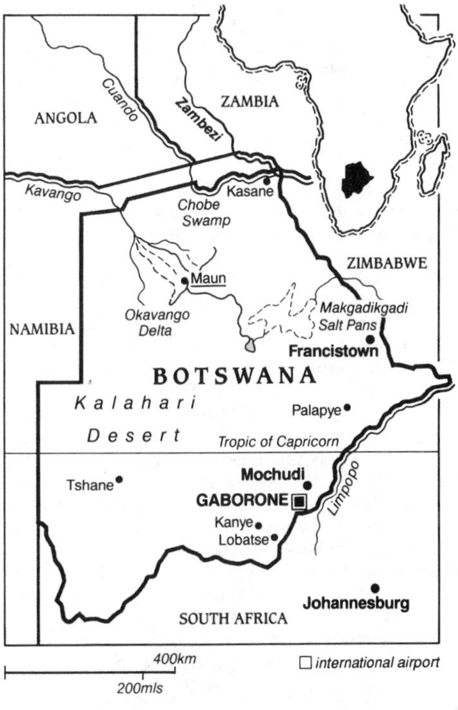

in fertile E, bordered by R Limpopo; to the W, dry scrubland and savannah, and the sand-covered Kalahari Desert; varied fauna and flora in the rich Okavango R delta in NW; deciduous forest in extreme N and NW; largely sub-tropical climate, increasingly arid in S and W; rainfall in N and E almost totally in summer (Oct–Apr); Francistown annual average rainfall 450 mm/17.7 in, maximum daily temperatures 23–32°C; rainfall erratic in Kalahari Desert, decreasing S and W to below 200 mm/7.9 in.

History and government. Visited by missionaries in 19th-c; under British protection, 1885; S part became a Crown Colony, then part of Cape Colony, 1895; N part became the Bechuanaland Protectorate; self-government, 1964; independence and change of name, 1966; governed by a legislative National Assembly of 34 elected, and four other members; President appoints Cabinet of c.15 members; there is also a House of Chiefs (15 members).

Economy. Mainly subsistence farming, especially livestock; continual problems of drought and disease; some crops, especially sorghum, as well as maize, millet, beans; cotton, groundnuts, sunflower seeds; main minerals, nickel (second largest African producer), diamonds, cobalt; also coal, brine, asbestos, talc, manganese, gypsum, gold, chromium, silver, platinum; livestock processing and products; tourism, especially wildlife observation. » Gaborone; Kalahari; RR24 national holidays; RR44 political leaders

bottega [bottayga] (Ital 'shop') An artist's workshop or studio in which assistants trained, and helped the master to produce works bearing his signature. Ghirlandaio and Verrocchio ran important *botteghe* in Renaissance Florence. » atelier; Ghirlandaio; Verrocchio

Botticelli, Sandro, originally **Alessandro Filipepi** [boti**che**lee] (1444–1510) Italian painter of the early Renaissance, born and died in Florence. About 1458 he went to train under Fra Filippo Lippi, and from c.1470 worked from his own studio. He produced many works on classical subjects – the finest his 'Birth of Venus' and 'Primavera' (Spring) in the Uffizi. His numerous devotional pictures include the 'Coronation of the Virgin' (Florence Academy) and the large circular 'Madonna and Child' (Uffizi). He also painted frescoes for the Sistine Chapel at the Vatican, and in his later years was much influenced by the teaching of Savonarola, producing works of a more deeply religious character. » fresco; Italian art; Lippi, Filippo; Savonarola

bottle gourd » calabash

bottlebrush An evergreen shrub native to Australia; leaves narrow; flowers small, crowded in dense cylindrical spikes, stamens red or yellow, far exceeding length of petals, and giving inflorescence a brush-like appearance. (*Callistemon*, 25 species. Family: *Myrtaceae*.) » evergreen plants; inflorescence [i]; shrub; stamen

bottlenose A toothed whale with a narrow projecting 'beak'; name used for *bottlenosed dolphins* (genus: *Tursiops*, 3 species), *bottlenosed whales* (genus: *Hyperoodon*, 2 species) and *giant bottlenosed whales* (genus: *Berardius*, 2 species). » whale [i]

bottom or **beauty** In particle physics, an internal additive quantum number conserved in strong and electromagnetic interactions, but not in weak interactions; symbol B. Bottom quarks are those with $B = -1$; bottom particles contain at least one bottom quark. The notion was postulated in 1977 to explain the properties of upsilon mesons, discovered that year. » meson; particle physics; quantum numbers; quark

bottom-up/top-down processing In cognitive psychology, a distinction drawn between two forms of information processing. The contrast is made between the passive processing of environmental information, in which current expectations and past knowledge play no role (*bottom-up*), and its active processing, which makes use of such higher-level information (*top-down*). » cognitive psychology

botulism A serious and often fatal illness resulting from the ingestion of a poisonous substance from *Clostridium botulinum*. It is one of the most severe forms of food poisoning, which affects the nervous system, and gives rise to rapidly developing paralysis and respiratory failure. The toxin can be formed without any apparent spoilage to the food, and is destroyed by cooking for 10 minutes at 80°C. » clostridium; toxin

Boucher, François [**boo**shay] (1703–70) French painter at the court of Louis XV, born and died in Paris. He studied in Italy, becoming the purest exponent of the Rococo style in painting. He is known for his mythological and pastoral scenes, his female nudes, and his portraits of Madame de Pompadour. In 1755 he became director of the Gobelins tapestry factory. » French art; Gobelins; Rococo; tapestry

Boudin, (Louis) Eugène [**boo**dĩ] (1824–98) French painter, born at Honfleur. A precursor of Impressionism, he is noted for his seascapes. He was one of the first French landscape painters to work in the open air. He died at Deauville. » French art; Impressionism (art); landscape painting

Bougainville, Louis Antoine, Comte de ('Count of') [**boo**-gĩveel] (1729–1811) French navigator, born and died in Paris. After army service in Canada and Germany, he joined the navy (1763), occupied the Falkland Is (1764), and led the first French circumnavigation of the world (1766–9), described in *Voyage autour du monde* (1771, A Voyage Round the World). After the outbreak of the Revolution he devoted himself to scientific pursuits, and was made a senator and count by Napoleon. Several places, as well as the plant *Bougainvillea*, are named after him. » Napoleon I

Bougainville [**boo**guhnvil] 6°12S 155°15E; pop (1980e) 109 000; area c.10 000 sq ml/4 000 sq ml. Mountainous volcanic island in Papua New Guinea, SW Pacific; length, 190 km/118 ml; width, 50 km/31 ml; rises to 2 743 m/8 999 ft at Mt Balbi; chief port, Kieta; independence movement and guerrilla fighting, 1988; peace accord signed, 1991; copper mining, copra, cocoa, timber. » Papua New Guinea [i]

bougainvillea [booguhn**vil**yuh] A shrub, tree, or woody climber, native to S America; leaves oval; flowers tubular, in threes, surrounded by three lilac, purple, magenta, red, orange, pink, or white petal-like bracts; grown as ornamentals in warm areas everywhere. (Genus: *Bougainvillea*, 18 species. Family: *Nyctaginaceae*.) » Bougainville, Comte de; bract; climbing plant; shrub; tree [i]

Boulanger, Nadia [**boo**lãzhay] (1887–1979) French composer, conductor, organist, and influential teacher of music, born and died in Paris. She studied at the Paris Conservatoire (1879–1904), where she won several prizes, and went on to write many vocal and instrumental works. After 1918 she devoted herself to teaching, first at home, and later at the Conservatoire and the Ecole Normale de Musique. » Berkeley, Lennox; Copland; Milhaud

boulder clay » till

Boulder Dam » Hoover Dam

boules [bool] A French ball game similar to bowls, played between two players or teams. The object is to place the ball nearer to a target ball, or jack, than the opposing player or team. Also known as *pétanque*, it is thought to have first been played in 1910. » bowls

Boulez, Pierre [**boo**lez] (1925–) French composer and conductor, born at Montbrison. He studied at the Paris Conservatoire under Messiaen, and in 1946 became musical director of the Renaud-Barrault company. In 1954 he founded the Domaine Musical for the performance of new music. During the 1970s he devoted himself mainly to his work as conductor of the BBC Symphony Orchestra (1971–5) and of the New York Philharmonic (1971–7). Since 1977 he has been director of the Institut de Recherche et de Coordination Acoustique/Musique at the Pompidou Centre in Paris.

Boulle » Buhl

Boulogne Eng [boo**loyn**], Fr [boo**lony**] or **Boulogne-sur-Mer** 50°43N 1°37E, pop (1982e) 50 000. Seaport in Pas-de-Calais department, NW France; on coast of English Channel, S of Calais; principal commercial harbour and fishing port of France; boatbuilding, textiles, engineering; ferry and hovercraft links with Dover and Folkestone. » English Channel

Boult, Sir Adrian (Cedric) (1889–1983) British conductor, born at Chester. After studying at Oxford and Leipzig, he conducted the City of Birmingham Orchestra (1924–30), and then became musical director of the BBC and conductor of the newly formed BBC Symphony Orchestra. Extensive tours in Europe and the USA won him a high reputation for his championship of English music. He was knighted in 1937. After he retired from the BBC (1950), he conducted the London Philharmonic Orchestra until 1957, and became its president from 1965. He continued to conduct regularly until 1981.

Boulton, Matthew (1728–1809) British engineer, born and died in Birmingham. He opened a manufacturing works at Birmingham in 1762, where he entered into partnership with James Watt. In 1774 they established a manufactory of steam engines, which proved remunerative only after 18 years. He also applied steam power for coining machinery. » steam engine; Watt, James

Bounty Mutiny The most famous of mutinies (28 Apr 1789). After enjoying five months in Tahiti, where the *Bounty* had been sent to gather breadfruit plants for the W Indies, Fletcher Christian and 17 other crewmen were reluctant to return to England. Near Tonga, they seized control of the ship, and forced the commander, William Bligh, and his 18 'loyalists' into a small boat. The mutineers went back to Tahiti, and from there to Pitcairn, where the *Bounty* was destroyed. » Bligh; Christian, Fletcher

bourbon [**ber**bn] A dark-coloured American whiskey, a distillate of at least 51% maize, which originated in Bourbon County, Kentucky. It is aged in barrels of white oak, charred on the inside, from two to eight years. *Straight bourbon* is the product of a single distillery in a given year, ie an unblended bourbon. » whisky

Bourbon, Charles (1490–1527) Known as 'Constable de Bourbon', the son of Gilbert de Bourbon, Count of Montpensier, and the only daughter of the Duke of Bourbon. For his bravery at the battle of Marignano (1515) he was made Constable of France; but losing the favour of Francis I he concluded a private alliance with Emperor Charles V and Henry VIII of England. He invaded France in 1524, and was chief Imperial commander at Pavia, in which Francis I was taken prisoner. He was made Duke of Milan, and commanded in N Italy, but was killed while attacking Rome in 1527. » Bourbons; Charles V (of France); Francis I (of France); Henry VIII

Bourbons [**boor**bnz] A French royal house descended from the Capetian St Louis IX (1215–70), associated with absolutist traditions at home and the extension of French influence abroad. Succeeding the last Valois, Henry III (1589) and Henry of Navarre (Henry IV) firmly established the dynasty. Under his son (Louis XIII) and grandson (Louis XIV), the long-standing rivalry between France and the Spanish Habsburgs came to a climax; it was concluded when a descendant, Philip of Anjou, ascended to the Spanish throne (Philip V, reigned 1700–46), thereby founding the Spanish House of Bourbon. Under Louis XV (1715–74) and Louis XVI (1774–93), the prestige of the French Bourbons gradually declined; with the latter's execution (1793) the line was interrupted, to be briefly restored (1814–30). » absolutism; Bourbon; Capetians; Charles X (of France); Condé; Habsburgs; Henry III/IV (of France); Louis XIII/XIV/XV/XVI; Orleans, House of; Philip V; Valois

bourgeoisie [boorzhwah**zee**] In mediaeval times, a member of a free city or *bourg* who was neither a peasant nor a landlord – essentially, a member of the 'middle class'. Later it referred to an employer or merchant. In the 19th-c the bourgeoisie was associated with leading revolutionary change, the demise of the aristocracy, the beginnings of liberal democracy, and the development of industrial capitalism. Alongside this went a view, which still persists, that the bourgeoisie are culturally reactionary and small-minded, being primarily concerned with commercial matters. In recent times the term *bourgeois* has been applied to those with rather narrow views about cultural and moral issues. » class

Bourges [boorzh] 47°09N 2°25E, pop (1982) 79 408. Ancient ducal town and capital of Cher department, C France; at confluence of rivers Auron and Yèvre; capital of Berry (12th-c); railway; bishopric; hardware, linoleum, textiles, armaments, agricultural equipment; 13th-c Cathedral of St-Etienne, Palais Jacques Cœur (1443), many fine Renaissance houses.

Bourget or **Lac du Bourget** [lak dü **boor**zhay] Lake in Savoie department, E France; area 45 sq km/17 sq ml; length 18 km/11 ml, width 2–3 km/1¼–1¾ ml; depth 60–100 m/200–325 ft; largest lake in France; overlooked by Aix-les-Bains (E); major tourist area; Benedictine abbey. » France [i]

Bourj Barajneh [boorzh bar**azh**ne] Palestinian refugee camp on the outskirts of Beirut, Lebanon; created following the evacuation of Palestinians from the city after Israeli attacks on Palestinians and Syrians in June 1982; scene of a prolonged siege in 1987. » Beirut; Lebanon [i]

Bournemouth [**bawn**muhth] 50°43N 1°54W, pop (1981) 145 704. Resort town in Bournemouth district, Dorset, S England; on Poole Bay, 40 km/25 ml SW of Southampton; railway; conference centre; tourism, printing, engineering; symphony orchestra. » Dorset

bourse A market for stocks, shares, and government bonds. In many countries, it refers to the place where these activities take place, as in the Paris Bourse. » stock exchange

Boussingault, Jean-Baptiste Joseph [**boo**sĩgoh] (1802–87) French chemist, born and died in Paris. A graduate of the School of Mines at St-Etienne, he spent 10 years in S America, then became professor at Lyons. He worked particularly on inorganic soil fertilizers, and did pioneer work on animal nutrition and digestion. He entered politics after the revolution of 1848, and became a member of the Council of State, but resigned after the coup of 1851 and returned to chemistry. » agriculture; fertilizer

boustrophedon [boo**stro**fuhduhn] An ancient method of writing, particularly in early Greek, in which the lines go alternately from left to right and right to left. The name comes from the Greek words for 'ox' and 'turn' – hence, following the path taken by a plough. » graphology

Bouts, Dierick, Dirk, or **Thierry** [bowts] (c.1415–75) Dutch painter, born at Haarlem. He worked at Louvain and Brussels, coming under the influence of Rogier van der Weyden, and produced austere religious paintings, with rich and gemlike colour. His best-known work is 'The Last Supper' (Louvain). He died at Louvain. » Dutch art; Weyden

bouzouki [buh**zoo**kee] A plucked string instrument of Greece, used in folk music and more recently in urban contexts. It has a very long neck, a fretted fingerboard, and three or four courses of metal strings played with a plectrum. » plectrum; string instrument 2 [i]

Bovet, Daniel [boh**vay**] (1907–) Swiss-Italian pharmacologist, born at Neuchâtel, Switzerland. He studied biology in Geneva, and afterwards worked in the Pasteur Institute in Paris and from 1947 in Rome. In Paris he was a member of the group which developed the sulphonamide drugs. From 1937 he devised drugs to antagonize the action of histamine, and later made synthetic analogues of curare. He was awarded the Nobel Prize for Physiology or Medicine in 1957. » curare; histamine; pharmacology; sulphonamides

Bovidae [**boh**vuhdee] A family of ruminant artiodactyl mammals (128 species), including cattle and antelopes; feed by grasping vegetation with their tongue, and cutting it with the lower incisor teeth; adult male (and usually female) with horns; horns have a bone centre and a sheath of horny material. » antelope; artiodactyl; bison; cattle; goat; mammal [i]; ruminant [i]; water buffalo; zebu

bovine spongiform encephalopathy (BSE) or **'mad cow disease'** A progressive, invariably fatal disease of the central nervous system affecting mature cattle, currently restricted to the UK and Ireland. The disease appeared suddenly in 1985 and reached epidemic proportions by 1989. Affected cattle may show behavioural changes and inco-ordination. There is no known treatment or cure. BSE is probably caused by the slow or unconventional group of viral agents, notorious for their resistance to high temperatures and disinfectants. The BSE agent is unique in that it may have crossed species, cattle having been infected by eating feed containing scrapie-affected sheep products. It is feared that humans could contract BSE by eating meat products containing nervous tissue of contaminated cattle. » central nervous system; scrapie; virus

bow (music) An implement for playing musical instruments such as the violin, consisting essentially of a wooden stick to each end of which lengths of horsehair are attached. Early bows had convex sticks, bent away from the hair, which was gripped by the player's fingers to keep it taut. Gradually sticks were made straighter to increase the tension, and from c.1700 this could be adjusted by means of a movable nut (or 'frog') at the lower end. The modern bow, with its strongly sprung concave stick, its ample width of hair, and its easily adjustable frog, was perfected and standardized c.1785 by French bowmaker François Tourte (1747–1838). » string instrument 1 [i]

bow (weaponry) » **crossbow; longbow**

Bow, Clara [boh] (1905–65) US film actress, born in New York City. Having won a beauty contest, she went to Hollywood in 1921, and became a star of the silent screen, typifying the vivacious flapper of the Jazz Age. Her run of successes was ended early in the 1930s by ill health and scandals concerning her love affairs, and she suffered breakdowns for much of her life.

Bow porcelain [boh] A London porcelain factory founded by Irish painter Thomas Frye (1710–62) and a glass merchant Edward Heylyn (1695–1765), which flourished from c.1744 until 1776. Their most notable productions were figures, often derived from Meissen models, but also from contemporary theatrical life (eg Kitty Clive). They also made expensive service wares. » Meissen porcelain; porcelain

bow wave [bow] In fluid mechanics, the wave disturbance emanating from the leading edge of an object moving through fluid, especially the V-shaped surface wave associated with boats moving through water. It is caused by displacement of the fluid by the moving object. » fluid mechanics; shock waves;

Bowdler, Thomas [**bowd**luh] (1754–1825) British man of letters, born at Ashley, Bath. He is unhappily immortalized as the editor of the 'Family Shakespeare' (1818), in which 'those words and expressions are omitted which cannot with propriety be read aloud in a family'. 'Bowdlerizing' has become a synonym for prudish expurgation. He died near Swansea, Wales. » English literature; Shakespeare

Bowen, Elizabeth (Dorothea Cole) (1899–1973) British novelist and short-story writer, born in Dublin, Ireland, and educated at Downe House School in Kent. Set mainly in London and Ireland, her novels include *The House in Paris* (1935), *The Death of the Heart* (1938), and *The Heart of the Day* (1949). *Collected Stories* appeared in 1980. » English literature; novel

bowerbird A bird native to New Guinea and Australia; related to birds of paradise. Males usually attract females by building ornate structures (*bowers*) on the ground, decorated with colourful objects. (Family: *Ptilonorhynchidae*, 18 species.) » bird of paradise

bowfin Primitive freshwater fish found in weedy backwaters of E North America; swim bladder serves as a lung to use atmospheric oxygen; length up to 90 cm/3 ft, dorsal fin long, tail fin rounded; sole representative of family *Amiidae*; also called **mudfish**. (*Amia calva*.)

bowhead » **right whale**

Bowie, Colonel James, byname **Jim** [**boo**ee, **boh**ee] (1790–1836) US adventurer, born in Logan County, Kentucky. He is mainly remembered for his role in defending the Alamo (1836) during the Texas revolution. He was the inventor of the curved sheath knife named after him. » Alamo; Texas

bowling The act of delivering a ball at pins (as opposed to a target, as in bowls); a popular indoor sport and pastime, with an ancient history. It was popularized by German churchgoers in the 3rd–4th-c, who would roll a ball at a *kegel*, a club used for protection, and if hit they would be absolved from sin. The game of nine pins was taken to the USA by Dutch and German immigrants in the latter part of the 19th-c. When the sport was outlawed, a tenth pin was added as a way around the legislation. Mechanical devices for replacing the pins on their spots were developed in the 1950s, which helped the game's growth, and **ten-pin bowling** is now the most popular form. » bowls; skittles; RR106

bowls An indoor and outdoor game played as singles, pairs, triples, or fours. A similar game was believed to have been played by the Egyptians as early as 5200 BC. Glasgow solicitor William Mitchell (1803–84) drew up the rules for modern bowls in 1848. There are two main variations: **lawn bowls** (known as *flat green*) is played on a flat level rink, whereas **crown green bowls** is played on an uneven green raised at the centre. Triples and fours are rarely played in the crown green game. In both varieties the object is to deliver your bowl nearer to the jack (a smaller target ball) than your opponent(s). The Waterloo Handicap crown green Championship, first held in 1907, takes place annually at the Waterloo Hotel, Blackpool (the 'Waterloo Cup'). RR106

box An evergreen shrub or small tree growing to 10 m/30 ft, often less, native to Europe and N Africa; leaves small, leathery, paired; flowers green, lacking petals, clusters of several males around one female; fruit a woody capsule. It is a popular bush for formal clipped hedges and for topiary. (*Buxus sempervirens*. Family: *Buxaceae*.) » evergreen plants; shrub; tree [i]

box camera The simplest form of camera for amateur photography: a rectangular box containing holders for paper-backed roll film advanced by an external winder, a fixed-focus lens, and a shutter for instantaneous exposure. Early examples are the original Kodak camera of 1880 and the Box Brownie of 1900 which popularized snapshot photography. » camera; photography

box elder A species of maple with leaves pinnately divided into 3–5 separate leaflets; male and female flowers on separate trees, the males with conspicuous red anthers; native to eastern N America. Forms with yellow and green variegated leaves are common street trees. (*Acer negundo*. Family: *Aceraceae*.). » maple; pinnate

box girder A horizontal structural member of a building; hollow, and square or rectangular in section. It is usually made from steel or a light alloy, and occasionally from concrete or even timber.

box set Theatre scenery representing the interior of a room by a three-dimensional arrangement of painted flats, with practicable doors and windows, to form three of the walls, and covered by a cloth to form the ceiling. It was first used in 1841. » stage

box turtle A N American terrapin; spends little time in water; eats invertebrates and fruit. The lower surface of its shell has hinged ends which close against the upper shell when the head and legs have been withdrawn (forming a closed box). *Cuora amboiensis* of the same family is called the **Malayan box turtle**. (Genus: *Terrapene*, several species.) » terrapin

boxer A breed of dog; large muscular body; rounded compact head; ears soft, pendulous; muzzle short and broad, with pronounced jowls and prominent lower jaw; developed from the bulldog in Germany (late 19th-c). » bulldog; dog

Boxer Rising (Chin *Yi He Tuan*) An anti-foreign uprising in China (1900). The name derives from the secret society to which the rebels belonged, the 'Righteous Harmonious Fists', whose members adopted boxing and other rituals, believing that foreign weapons would not harm them. The movement originated in Shandong, where it destroyed churches, expelled missionaries, and defeated the Qing forces dispatched to suppress it. The movement spread across N China, invading Beijing (Peking) and Tianjin (Tientsin). The foreign powers sent a combined force to rescue their envoys in Beijing, occupying the capital, and the rising was suppressed. By the International Protocol of 1901, the Qing court agreed to pay a massive indemnity, and a foreign garrison was established in the Legation Quarter of Beijing. » Qing dynasty

boxing Fighting with fists, a sport recorded from the earliest times. The Greeks and Romans used to entertain themselves by staging fist battles between their gladiators. The first known boxing match in Britain was in 1681 when the Duke of Albemarle organized a match between his butler and his butcher at his home in New Hall, Essex. The sport began to develop in the early part of the 18th-c, when James Figg, a renowned swordsman and cudgel fighter, opened his school of arms in Oxford Road, London. Figg came to be regarded as the first champion of boxing. The first rules were drawn up by John Broughton in 1743. Boxing was with bare knuckles, and each round lasted until one fighter was knocked down. The Queensberry Rules, as drawn up in 1867 by John Sholto

THE WEIGHT DIVISIONS IN PROFESSIONAL BOXING

NAME	MAXIMUM WEIGHT
heavyweight	any weight
cruiserweight/junior-heavyweight	88 kg/195 lb
light-heavyweight	79 kg/175 lb
super-middleweight	77 kg/170 lb
middleweight	73 kg/160 lb
light-middleweight/junior-middleweight	70 kg/154 lb
welterweight	67 kg/147 lb
light-welterweight/junior-welterweight	64 kg/140 lb
lightweight	61 kg/135 lb
junior-lightweight/super-featherweight	59 kg/130 lb
featherweight	57 kg/126 lb
super-bantamweight/junior-featherweight	55 kg/122 lb
bantamweight	54 kg/118 lb
super-flyweight/junior-bantamweight	52 kg/115 lb
flyweight	51 kg/112 lb
light-flyweight/junior-flyweight	49 kg/108 lb
mini-flyweight/straw-weight/minimum weight	under 48 kg/105 lb

Douglas, the 8th Marquess of Queensberry, changed boxing completely. It legislated for fighting with gloves, stipulated the length of each round at three minutes, and laid the foundation of the modern sport. Officially recognized world championship contests started in 1884, the first world champion being Irish-born American Jack 'Nonpareil' Dempsey (the middleweight title). Over the years the different boxing authorities have had difficulty in agreeing upon recognition of some fighters as champions, and today four bodies recognize world champions; the *World Boxing Council (WBC)*, founded in 1963; the *World Boxing Association (WBA)*, founded in 1927 as the National Boxing Association; the *International Boxing Federation (IBF)*, founded in 1983; and the *World Boxing Organization*, founded in 1988. Different weight divisions exist, and fighters can compete only within the appropriate category, although they can move up, or down, depending upon weight change. In 1988 there were 17 different weight divisions, ranging from straw-weight for fighters under 105 lb (48 kg), to heavyweight, which is any weight, but normally over 195 lb (88 kg). Professional championship bouts constitute twelve 3-minute rounds. Amateur contests are over three rounds, and all fighters must wear a vest. All fights last until one fighter is knocked out or retires, the referee halts the fight, a fighter is disqualified, or the designated number of rounds is reached. If the fight goes the distance, judges then mark the fighters according to winning punches, etc. It is possible to have a draw. » Lonsdale Belt; Queensberry; RR107

Boxing Day In the UK and the Commonwealth, the day after Christmas Day, so called because traditionally on that day gifts from boxes placed in church were distributed to the poor, and apprentices took a box round their masters' customers in the hope of getting presents of money from them. Christmas 'boxes' or gifts of money are still sometimes given to tradespeople, postal workers, etc.

Boy Scouts » **scouting**

Boyana Church A world heritage monument comprising three churches situated in the former village of Boyana, a present-day suburb of Sofia, Bulgaria. The buildings date from the 10th-c, 13th-c and 19th-c, but despite their differing styles, combine to form a notable architectural unit. » Sofia

boyars Members of the highest stratum of the Russian feudal aristocracy from the 10th-c to the early 18th-c. The *Boyarskaya Duma* ('Boyars' Council') was a major legislative and deliberative assembly under the mediaeval tsars. During the reign of Ivan IV, the boyars' authority was drastically curtailed, and the *Boyarskaya Duma* was finally abolished by Peter I in 1711. » duma; feudalism; Ivan IV; Peter I; tsar

boycott A general refusal to have dealings – usually in relation to trade – with a person, company, or country. A trade union may boycott talks with a company as a negotiating ploy. Individuals may refuse to buy a country's goods as a gesture of political protest – for example, goods from South Africa, in protest against apartheid. Boycotts have also been used in international sporting events, such as by the USA and UK at the 1980 Moscow Olympic Games. They are often only effective if legally enforced; for example, the ban on the import of Cuban cigars into the USA. » Boycott, Charles Cunningham

Boycott, Charles Cunningham (1832–97) British soldier, born at Burgh St Peter, Norfolk. As land agent for Lord Erne in Co Mayo, he was one of the first victims in 1880 of Parnell's system of social excommunication. His name is the source of the word 'boycott' in English. He died at Flixton, Suffolk. » boycott; Parnell

Boycott, Geoffrey (1940–) British cricketer, born at Fitzwilliam, Yorkshire. In 1981 he overtook Gary Sobers' world record of 8 032 Test runs, and in 108 Tests for England scored 8 114 runs (average 47.72). Total runs in his career were 48 426 (average 56.83), and in 1971 and 1979 he averaged 100 runs per innings. Captain of Yorkshire 1971–8, he was a brilliant but often controversial batsman. He has not played first-class cricket since 1986, when he was released by Yorkshire. » cricket (sport) [i]; Sobers

Boyd Orr, John, 1st Baron Boyd-Orr of Brechin Mearns (1880–1971) British nutritionist, born at Kilmaurs, Ayrshire, Scotland. He was educated at Glasgow University, and after service in World War 1, became director of the Rowett Research Institute, professor of agriculture at Aberdeen (1942–5), and first director of the United Nations Food and Agriculture Organization (1945–8). He won the Nobel Peace Prize in 1949, and was made baron the same year. He died at Edzell, Angus. » United Nations

Boyer, Charles (1899–1978) French actor, born at Figeac, and educated at the Sorbonne and the Paris Conservatoire. Having become established as a star of the French stage and cinema, he settled in Hollywood in 1934, and was known as the screen's 'great lover' from such romantic roles as *Mayerling* (1934), *The Garden of Allah* (1936), and *Algiers* (1938). His later appearances included *Barefoot in the Park* (1967), *The Madwoman of Chaillot* (1969), and *Stavisky* (1974). He died in Scottsdale, Arizona.

Boyle, Robert (1627–91) Irish physicist and chemist, born at Lismore Castle, Munster. He studied at Eton, and after travelling in Europe, settled in Dorset, where he devoted himself to science. He was a founding member of the Royal Society. At Oxford (1654) he researched into air, vacuum, combustion, and respiration. In 1661 he published his *Sceptical Chymist*, in which he criticized the current theories of matter, and in 1662 arrived at **Boyle's Law**, which states that the pressure and volume of gas are inversely proportional. He died in London. » gas laws; ideal gas

Boyne, Battle of the (1690) A battle fought near Drogheda, Co Louth, Ireland, between Protestant forces under William III and smaller Catholic forces led by James II. William's decisive victory enabled him to capture Dublin, and marked a critical stage in the English reconquest of Ireland. It ended James's campaign to regain the English throne. » Boyne, River; James II (of England); William III

Boyne, River River in E Irish Republic, rising in the Bog of Allen, Kildare county, Leinster; flows 110 km/68 ml NE to the Irish Sea near Drogheda. » Boyne, Battle of the; Irish Republic [i]

Brabham, Jack, properly **Sir John Arthur Brabham** (1926–) Australian racing driver, born in Sydney. Australia's first world champion (1959), he won further titles in 1960 and 1966. His first two titles were in a Cooper-Climax, the third in a car bearing his own name. He won 14 races from 126 starts during his career (1955–70). Knighted in 1979, he has remained active in the motor-racing field, but no longer owns Brabham cars. » motor racing

Brachiopoda [brakee**o**puhda] » **lamp shell**

bracken A perennial fern with far-creeping rhizomes; fronds solitary, up to 2–4 m/6½–13 ft; tri-pinnate, with sori continuous around edges of leaf-segments. It is common on acid soils, especially in woods and heaths where it may cover extensive areas by means of the rhizomes. It is poisonous, and not grazed by animals such as sheep and rabbits. Fire does not seriously damage it, the deeply buried rhizomes remaining unharmed. Bracken can be an aggressive invader of grassland. (*Pteridium aquilinum*. Family: *Polypodiaceae*.) » fern; pinnate; rhizome; sorus

bract A modified leaf immediately below a flower or inflorescence. It is usually green, but may be brightly-coloured and petal-like, as in *Poinsettia*. » inflorescence [i]; leaf [i]; poinsettia

Bracton, Henry de (?–1268) English jurist, a 'justice itinerant', who in 1264 became Archdeacon of Barnstaple and Chancellor of Exeter Cathedral. His *De Legibus et Consuetudinibus Angliae* (On the Laws and Customs of England) is the earliest attempt at a systematic treatment of the body of English law.

Bradbury, Malcolm (1932–) British novelist and critic, born in Sheffield, and educated at Leicester. The travels and travails of an academic have provided material for several of his novels, such as *Stepping Westward* (1965), *The History Man* (1975), and *Rates of Exchange* (1982). His work for television inspired *Cuts* (1987). In his critical writing, he has sponsored Modernist and post-Modernist ideas. » English literature; Modernism; novel

Bradbury, Ray (Douglas) (1920–) US science-fiction writer, born at Waukegan, Illinois. From 1940 he was making a living by selling his short stories to pulp magazines, but began to meet a wider audience with *The Martian Chronicles* (1950) and *The Golden Apples of the Sun* (1953). He is best known for film adaptations of two of his novels, *The Illustrated Man* (1951) and *Fahrenheit 451* (1953). » science fiction

Bradford 53°48N 1°45W, pop(1981) 295 048. Town in West Yorkshire, N England; part of West Yorkshire urban area; 15 km/9 ml W of Leeds and 310 km/193 ml NNW of London; 19th-c development was based on the wool textile industry; university (1966); railway; textiles, textile machinery, coal, engineering, micro-electronics; scene of major disaster (1985) when wooden stand of Bradford City Football Club caught fire, killing 56; City Hall (1873), Wool Exchange (1867), art gallery (1904), 15th-c cathedral. » wool; Yorkshire, West

Bradlaugh, Charles [**brad**law] (1833–91) British free-thinking social reformer, born and died in London. He became a busy secularist lecturer, and a pamphleteer under the name of 'Iconoclast'. In 1880 he became an MP, and claimed the right as an unbeliever to make affirmation of allegiance instead of taking the parliamentary oath; but the House refused to allow him to do either. He was re-elected on three occasions, and finally was admitted (1886). » Besant, Annie

Bradley, James (1692–1762) English astronomer, born at Sherborne, Gloucestershire. He discovered the aberration of starlight, and catalogued the positions of 60 000 stars. The third Astronomer Royal (1742–62), he died at Greenwich, near London. » aberrations 1 [i]; star

Bradley, Omar N(elson) (1893–1981) US general, born at Clark, Missouri. In World War 2, he played a prominent part in Tunisia and Sicily, and in 1944 led the US invading armies through France and Germany. Chairman of the joint chiefs-of-staff in 1949, he was promoted general of the army in 1950. He died in New York City. » World War 2

Bradman, Sir Don(ald George) (1908–) Australian cricketer, born at Cootamundra, New South Wales. He played for Australia 1928–48, and was captain from 1936. He set up many batting records, including the highest score (452 not out), and he made the greatest number of centuries in England v. Australia test matches (19). After he retired (1948), he became a cricket administrator, and was knighted in 1949. » cricket (sport) [i]

Bradstreet, Anne, *née* **Dudley** (1612–72) American colonial poet, born in Northampton, UK. Born into the English gentry, she migrated with her husband to Massachusetts in 1630 and began writing poetry, which was first published in London in 1650 without her consent. She is acknowledged as the first poet of note in British America. She died at Andover, Massachusetts Bay Colony.

Braemar [bray**mah**] 57°01N 3°24W. Village in SW Grampian region, Scotland, 10 km/6 ml W of Balmoral castle; tourism; Highland games (Aug). » Grampians (Scotland)

Braga [**bra**ga], ancient **Bracara Augusta** 41°32N 8°26W, pop(1981) 63 800. Industrial capital of Braga district and fourth largest city in Portugal, 371 km/230 ml N of Lisbon; former capital of the old region of Entre Minho and Douro; seat of the Primate of Portugal; university; vehicles, electrical appliances, leather, cutlery, textiles; cathedral (11th-c); midsummer celebrations, São Miguel fair and agricultural show (Sep). » Portugal [i]

Braganza [bra**gan**za], Port **Bragança**, ancient **Juliobriga** 41°48N 6°50W, pop(1981) 13 900. Capital of Braganza district, NE Portugal, 10 km/6 ml from the Spanish border; original seat of the House of Braganza, rulers of Portugal, 1640–1910; bishopric; agricultural centre, silk weaving; castle (1187), cathedral, town hall (12th-c), Baçal Abbey; Cantarinhas fair (May), São Mateus fair (Sep). » Portugal [i]

Bragg, Sir William (Henry) (1862–1942) British physicist, born at Wigton, Cumberland. He studied at Cambridge, and took up chairs at Adelaide (1895), Leeds (1908), and London (1915). He studied radioactivity, X-rays, and crystals, and discovered the law of X-ray diffraction (**Bragg law**). He was knighted in 1920, became director of the Royal Institution in 1923, and died in London. With his son, **(William) Lawrence** (1890–1971), he shared the Nobel Prize for Physics in 1915. The latter trained at Cambridge, and held chairs at Manchester and Cambridge, before becoming director of the Royal Institution, London (1954–66). He was knighted in 1941, and died at Ipswich, Suffolk. » radioactivity; X-rays

Brahe, Tycho [**bra**huh] (1546–1601) Danish astronomer, born at Knudstrup, Sweden (then under the Danish crown). In 1573 he discovered serious errors in the astronomical tables, and commenced to rectify this by observing the stars and planets with unprecedented positional accuracy. He rejected the Copernican theory, but it fell to Kepler to show this model to be essentially correct, using Tycho's data. He died in Prague. » Copernican system; Kepler; Ptolemaic system

Brahma [**brah**ma] The personified creator god of Hinduism. The deities Vishnu, Shiva, and Brahma form the 'Trimurti' of classical Indian thought. As Vishnu and Shiva represent opposite forces, Brahma represents the balance between them. Brahma is the all-inclusive deity behind all the gods of popular Hinduism. » Brahman; Brahmanism; Hinduism; Shiva; Trimurti; Vishnu

Brahman [**brah**man] In Hinduism, the eternal, impersonal Absolute Principle. It is the neuter form of Brahma, and is equated with cosmic unity. » atman; Brahma; Brahmanism; Hinduism

Brahman cattle » **zebu**

Brahmanas [**brah**manas] Priestly Indian texts appended over time to each of the Vedas. They describe, set out the grounds for, and enunciate the principles of the Brahmans' system of sacrifice, » Brahmanism; Hinduism; Veda

Brahmanism [**brah**manizm] An early religion of India (though not the earliest), to which, historically, Indians have looked as the source of their religious traditions. It came to dominance during the Vedic Period (c.1200–500 BC) and was a religion of ritual and sacrifice. It gave supremacy to the Brahmin class,

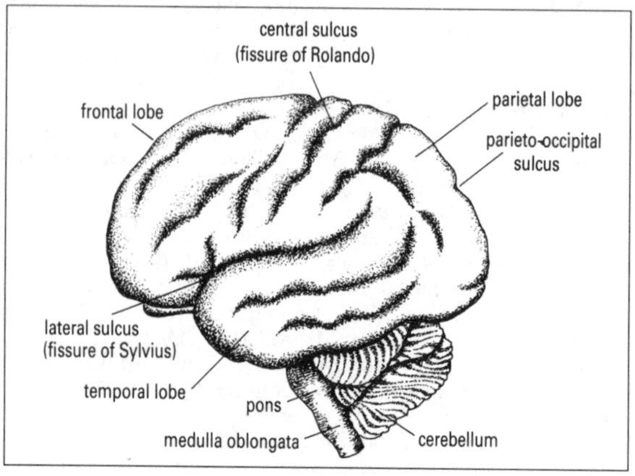

The left side of the brain (cerebrum)

which exercised priestly authority over all aspects of life through their responsibility for the transmission of the sacred traditions and the performance of sacrifical rituals. » Brahmanas; Brahmins; Hinduism; Veda

Brahmaputra, River [bramapootra], Chin **Yarlung Zangbo**, Bangla **Jamuna** River in SW China and India, rising in the Chinese Himalayas as the Maquan He R; flows E then S into Assam, becoming the Brahmaputra near Sadiya; then flows S into Bangladesh, joining the R Ganges before entering the Bay of Bengal through a vast delta; length c.2 900 km/1 800 ml.

Brahmins [**brah**minz] The highest of the four Hindu social classes. A priestly class, the Brahmins dominated Indian society for many centuries. Owing to modern economic and social changes, many of their descendants took up secular occupations. Recently they have come under critical attack by some lower-caste movements. » Brahmanism; Hinduism

Brahmo Samaj [**brah**moh sam**ahj**] 'Divine Society', a theistic movement founded by Ram Mohan Roy in 1828 which argued that reason should form the true basis of Hinduism. Influenced by Islam, Christianity, and modern science, it sought a return to the purity of Hindu worship through an emphasis on monotheism, the rejection of idol-worship, and the reform of Hindu social practices. » Hinduism; Ram Mohan Roy

Brahms, Johannes (1833–97) German composer, born in Hamburg. The son of a poor orchestral musician, he earned his living as a pianist until 1853, when he was able to concentrate on composition. He toured with the Hungarian violinist Reményi, meeting Joachim and Liszt, and then Schumann, who helped Brahms publish his piano sonatas. He settled in Vienna, making occasional public appearances in Austria and Germany. Firmly based on classical foundations, his works contain hardly any programme music. His great orchestral works are comparatively late, the first, *Variations on a Theme of Haydn*, appearing when he was 40. His main works include four symphonies, two piano concertos, a violin concerto, a large amount of chamber and piano music, and many songs. His greatest choral work is the *German Requiem* (first performed complete in 1869). He died in Vienna. » classical music

braille A communication system designed to enable blind people to have access to written language; devised by Louis Braille. It consists of a sequence of cells, each of which contains a 3 × 2 matrix of embossed dots, whose patterns can be sensed through the fingers. In the basic system, the patterns represent letters, numbers, punctuation marks, and several short words. Computer-assisted systems are now available which can turn written text into braille. » alternative and augmentative communication; Braille; RR81

Braille, Louis [brayl] (1809–52) French teacher, born at Coupvray near Paris. At three, he was blinded in an accident while playing with an awl. He entered the Institution des Jeunes Aveugles at Paris, where, as pupil and (from 1826) professor, he worked with success to invent a system which the blind could both read and write. He played the organ in Parisian churches, and later used the system for the teaching of music. He died of tuberculosis in Paris. » braille

brain The part of the central nervous system of bilaterally symmetrical animals which co-ordinates and controls many bodily activities to an extent that depends upon the species. In humans, in addition to the control of movement, sensory input, and a wide range of physiological processes, it acts as the organ of thought, with several areas being specialized for specific intellectual functions (eg language, calculation). It occupies the cranial cavity, and can be divided into the **forebrain** (the *cerebral hemispheres* and *diencephalon*), **midbrain**, and **hindbrain** (the *cerebellum*, *pons*, and *medulla oblongata*). It is continuous with the spinal cord at the medulla oblongata (part of the *brainstem*). The cerebral hemispheres and brainstem contain cavities (the *ventricles*) which are continuous with the central canal of the spinal cord, and within which cerebrospinal fluid is produced. The brain also gives rise to the twelve pairs of cranial nerves. » brain death; brainstem; cerebellum; cerebral haemorrhage/palsy; cerebrospinal fluid; cerebrum; dementia; diencephalon; encephalitis; epilepsy; hydrocephalus; laterality; medulla oblongata; meningitis; paralysis; ventricles

Brain, Dennis (1921–57) British horn player, born in London. He studied at the Royal Academy of Music, and then worked with the Royal Philharmonic and Philharmonia Orchestras as chief horn player. Amongst the composers who wrote works specially for him are Britten, Hindemith, and Malcolm Arnold. He died in a car accident. » horn

brain death The cessation of brain activity, including in particular the death of the neurological centres in the brain stem concerned with respiration and other vital functions. It must be certified by two doctors who can demonstrate the absence of electrical impulses from the brain surface (a flat EEG), and the failure of the pupils to react to light and the eyes to oscillate (*nystagmus*) in response to the introduction of warm and cold water into the external ear canal. The diagnosis is usually made on individuals in a coma whose respirations are being artificially sustained and whose heart has not ceased to beat. » brain [i]; electroencephalography

Braine, John (Gerard) (1922–86) British novelist, born at Bradford, Yorkshire. He held various jobs before becoming a librarian. The success of his first book, *Room at the Top* (1957), enabled him to embark on a full-time career as a novelist. The theme of aggressive ambition and determination to break through rigid social barriers identified him with the 'Angry Young Men' of the 1950s. His novels deal mostly with the north of England and northerners, and include *Life at the Top* (1962), *The Vodi*, and *One and Last Love* (1981). Many of his writings have been adapted for television. He died in London. » Angry Young Men; English literature; novel

brainstem That part of the nervous system between the spinal cord and the forebrain, consisting of a thick bundle of transversely running fibres called the *pons*, with the *midbrain* above it and the *medulla oblongata* below. The cardiac, respiratory, vasomotor, and other 'vital' physiological centres are located in the medulla. On the rear surface of the midbrain are four rounded projections (*colliculi*) arranged in pairs; these receive and transmit impulses for the reflex rotatory movements of the eyes, head, body, and limbs away from or towards light and sound stimuli. » brain [i]; medulla oblongata; neurone [i]; nervous system

brake A device used to apply a force to an object to retard its motion. The most common method is to bring the moving surface into contact with a fixed surface, thereby generating

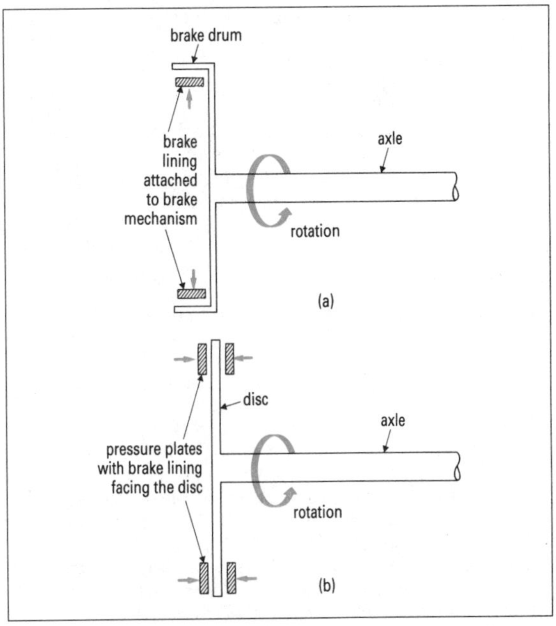

Types of brake – In a drum brake (a) the brake lining material is on the one side of a rotating drum fixed to the axle. In a disc brake (b) the brake lining is fixed on both sides of a rotating disc fixed to the axle.

friction which opposes the direction of movement. The two types of brake most commonly used on motor cars are **drum brakes** and **disc brakes**.

brake horsepower (bhp) The power delivered by an engine to its output shaft, immediately prior to its transmission to other devices for useful work. For example, the brake horsepower of a medium-sized family car engine would be c.60–80 bhp, whilst a very large tanker's marine diesel engine would produce c.40 000 bhp. » engine

Bramah, Joseph (1748–1814) British inventor, born at Stainborough, Yorkshire. He became a cabinet-maker in London, where he distinguished himself by the number and ingenuity of his inventions, including a hydraulic press and a machine for numbering banknotes. His safety lock remained pickproof for over 60 years. He died in London. » lock [i]

Bramante, Donato, originally **Donato di Pascuccio d'Antonio** [bra**man**tay] (c.1444–1514) Italian architect and painter, born near Urbino. He spent the first part of his life mostly in Milan, before leaving in 1499 for Rome, where he built the Tempietto (c.1502). At the bequest of Pope Julius II he drew up plans for the reconstruction and renovation of the Vatican and St Peter's (1505–6). He died in Rome, having exercised a profound effect upon the development of Renaissance architecture in Italy. » Italian art; Renaissance

bramble » **blackberry**

brambling A finch native to the N Old World; inhabits forests; eats seeds and insects; migrates to the Mediterranean and N Africa for winter. (*Fringilla montifringilla*. Family: *Fringillidae*.) » finch

bran The protective coat surrounding a cereal seed which, because of its high-fibre content, is becoming increasingly common as a component of human foods. It comprises about 12% of the seed. » fibre

Branchiopoda [brangkee**op**uhda] A diverse class of aquatic crustaceans found mostly in inland waters, from fresh to hypersaline, and occasionally in the sea; characterized by leaf-like trunk limbs that act as a food-gathering apparatus and as gills; contains c.820 living species, including tadpole shrimps, fairy shrimps, clam shrimps, and water fleas. » crustacean; fairy shrimp; tadpole shrimp; water flea

Brancusi or **Brîncuşi, Constantin** [bran**koo**zi, **brin**koosh] (1876–1957) Romanian sculptor, born at Pestisani. He studied at Bucharest Academy, then went to Paris (1904), where he remained for the rest of his life. His 'Sleeping Muse' (1910) shows Rodin's influence, and is the first of many characteristic, highly-polished, egg-shaped carvings. He died in Paris. » abstract art; Rodin; sculpture

Brandenburg or **Brandenburg an der Havel** [**brahn**dnboork] 52°25N 12°34E, pop (1981) 94 680. Industrial city in Brandenburg district, Potsdam, EC Germany; on R Havel, W of Berlin; former centre of the Prussian province of Brandenburg, part of which is now in Poland; much rebuilding after severe damage in World War 2; railway; steel, textiles, machinery. » Germany [i]; Prussia

Brandenburg Gate A triumphal arch designed by Carl Langhans (1733–1808) and erected in Berlin in 1788–91. The monument, which was badly damaged during World War 2, was restored in 1958. » Berlin; Unter den Linden

Brando, Marlon (1924–) US film and stage actor, born at Omaha, Nebraska. He was a product of the New York Actors' Studio, with its emphasis on 'method' acting, and he appeared in several plays, before achieving fame in Williams' *A Streetcar Named Desire* (1946). Extremely versatile, he has played many widely differing film parts, such as Mark Antony (*Julius Caesar*, 1953), a Western hero (*One-eyed Jacks*, 1959), and Fletcher Christian (*Mutiny on the Bounty*, 1962). More recent films include *The Godfather* (1972), *Last Tango in Paris* (1973), *Apocalypse Now* (1977), and *The Formula* (1980). His most outstanding role was in *On the Waterfront* (1954), for which he won his first Oscar, but he refused to accept a second, for *The Godfather*, in protest against the persecution of the Indians.

Brandt, Bill, byname of **William Brandt** (1904–83) British photographer, born and died in London. He studied with Man Ray in Paris in 1929, and during the 1930s made striking social records contrasting the rich and the poor. In World War 2 he portrayed life in London during the Blitz. Later works include *Perspective of Nudes* (1961) and *Shadows of Light* (1966).

Brandt, Willy, originally **Karl Herbert Frahm** (1913–) West German statesman and Chancellor (1969–74), born at Lübeck. An anti-Nazi, he fled in 1933 to Norway, where he changed his name and worked as a journalist, until the occupation of Norway (1940) forced him to move to Sweden. In 1945 he returned to Germany, and was a member of the *Bundestag* (1949–57). A pro-Western leader, he became mayor of West Berlin (1957–66), and chairman of the Social Democratic Party (1964). In 1966 he led his party into a coalition government with the Christian Democrats, and in 1969 was elected Chancellor in a coalition government with the Free Democrats. He was awarded the 1971 Nobel Peace Prize. He resigned as Chancellor in 1974, and later chaired a commission on the world economy (the Brandt Commission Report, 1980). » Germany [i]

brandy A spirit distilled from fruit fermentation, usually grapes, but also from stone fruits such as cherries. Cognac is produced in the Charente basin, France, from white grapes aged for a minimum of two years in barrels of Limousin oak. Armagnac is produced to the S of this area, and matured in 'black' oak. Calvados is made from cider in Normandy. Brandies are produced in most countries that grow grapes. » fermentation

Brandywine, Battle of the (11 Sep 1777) A battle fought during the US War of Independence, taking its name from the Brandywine Creek near Philadelphia, Pennsylvania. British forces under Howe defeated Washington's troops, who were attempting to defend Pennsylvania. » American Revolution; Howe, William; Washington, George

brant » **brent goose**

Brant, Joseph (1742–1807) Mohawk chief, born by the Ohio river. He fought for the British in the Indian and Revolutionary wars, helping to bring about a general peace. In later years an earnest Christian, he translated St Mark's Gospel and the Prayer Book into Mohawk, and in 1786 visited England, where he was received at court. He died at Brantford, Ontario.

Braque, Georges (1882–1963) French painter, born at Argenteuil. He was one of the founders of classical Cubism, and worked with Picasso from 1908 to 1914. After World War 1 he developed a personal nongeometric semi-abstract style. His paintings are mainly of still life, the subject being transformed into a two-dimensional pattern. He also experimented with new techniques, such as the mixing of paint and sand, and the use of pasted paper. The first living artist to have his paintings exhibited in the Louvre, he died in Paris. » Cubism; French art; Picasso

Brasília 15°45S 47°57W, pop (1980) 410 999. Capital of Brazil in Centro-Oeste region, WC Brazil; construction began in 1956; capital moved from Rio de Janeiro in 1960; principal architect Oscar Niemeyer (1907–); laid out in the shape of a bent bow and arrow; residential areas lie along the curve of the bow; at right angles to these is the arrow, with the Congress buildings, the President's office, and the Supreme Court at the tip; to the W lie the cathedral and the Ministry buildings; the cultural and recreational zones and the commercial and financial areas lie on either side of the intersection of the bow and arrow; airport; university (1962); light industry; famous for its modern sculpture; designated a world heritage site. » Brazil [i]

Braşov [bra**shov**], Ger **Kronstadt** (to 1918), **Stalin** (1950–60) 45°39N 25°35E, pop (1983) 331 240. Industrial capital of Braşov county, C Romania; founded, 13th-c; important mediaeval trade centre; ceded by Hungary after World War 1; railway junction; university (1971); textiles, lorries, tractors, metallurgy, ball bearings, chemicals, machinery; summer resort and winter sports centre. » Romania [i]

brass An alloy composed of copper and zinc; yellowish, malleable, and ductile. Its properties and applications may be altered by varying the proportions of copper and zinc. It is the most widely-used non-ferrous alloy. » alloy; copper; zinc

brass instrument A musical instrument made of brass or other metal, in which air is made to vibrate by means of the player's lips and breath, usually through a narrow mouthpiece. In simple instruments, such as the bugle, the notes available are

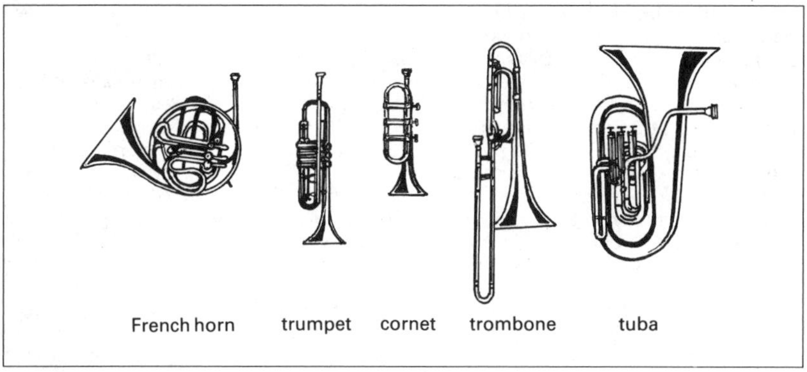

Brass instruments

restricted to the lower end of a single harmonic series; in others, valves or slides enable the fundamental note to be altered, and consequently a greater number of pitches to be obtained. The main orchestral brass instruments are the horn, trumpet, trombone, and tuba. » aerophone; bugle (music); cornet; euphonium; flugelhorn; harmonic series [i]; horn; saxhorn; sousaphone; trombone; trumpet; tuba

Brassai, professional name of **Gyula Halasz** (1899–1984) French-Hungarian photographer, born in Brasso, Transylvania. He went to Paris in 1923, and recorded the nightlife of the city throughout the 1930s. During the German occupation he worked in Picasso's studio, but returned to the photographic evocation of Paris and its people during the 1950s. He died in Nice.

brasses Ornamental objects made from brass, an alloy of zinc and copper. Monumental brasses were a less expensive substitute for carved stone tomb slabs. Particularly popular in England in the Gothic period, they could be very elaborate, with engraved portraits and heraldry in architectural framing, or simply inscriptions. » brass; Gothic

brassica A genus of plants containing numerous economically important vegetables, including turnip and mustard, but often in a gardening sense referring more specifically to cabbages, cauliflower, broccoli, and brussel sprouts, all derived from the wild cabbage, *Brassica oleracea*. (Genus: *Brassica*, 30 species. Family: *Cruciferae*.) » cabbage; mustard; rape (botany); swede; turnip; vegetable

Bratby, John (1928–) British artist and writer, born in London. He studied at the Royal College of Art, and is one of the leading representatives of the English Realist School. With Jack Smith he represented Great Britain at the Venice Biennale in 1956. His works include 'Baby in Pram' (Liverpool). He has written several novels, including *Breakdown* (1960), with his own illustrations. » English art; Realism

Bratislava [brati**slah**va], Ger **Pressburg**, Hungarian **Pozsony**, Lat **Posonium** 48°10N 17°08E, pop (1984) 401 383. River port and capital of Slovak Republic, SC Czechoslovakia; on R Danube; second largest city in Czechoslovakia; stronghold of Great Moravian Empire, 9th-c; capital of Hungary, 1541–1784; Hungarian monarchs crowned here until 1835; centre of emergent Slovak national revival; incorporated into Czechoslovakia in 1918; airport (Vajnory); railway; university (1919); technical university (1938); food processing, petrochemicals, agrochemicals, oil refining, textiles, paper, electrical equipment, mechanical engineering, agricultural trade; 13th-c cathedral, castle, Mirbach Palace, Lenin's museum, pharmaceutical museum; Slovak National Theatre, Slovak National Gallery and Museum, musical festivals. » Czechoslovakia [i]

Bratsk Dam A major gravity earth-fill dam on the Angara R, Russia; completed in 1961; height 125 m/410 ft. It has the capacity to generate 4 500 megawatts of hydroelectricity. » dam

Brattain, Walter (Houser) (1902–87) US physicist, born in Amoy, China. He is best known for his work on the surface properties of semiconductors. He also helped to devise the point contact transistor, for which he shared the Nobel Prize for Physics in 1956. » Bardeen; electronics; transistor

Braun, Eva [brown] (1910–45) The mistress of Adolf Hitler, born at Munich. She met Hitler in the early 1930s, when she was secretary to his staff photographer. She is said to have married Hitler before they committed suicide together in the air-raid shelter of the Chancellery during the fall of Berlin. » Hitler

Braun, Wernher von [brown] (1912–77) US rocket pioneer, born at Wirsitz, Germany. He studied engineering at Berlin and Zürich and in 1930 founded a society for space travel. In 1936, with Hitler's backing, he became director of a rocket research station at Peenemünde, where he perfected and launched the V-2 rockets against Britain (Sep 1944). After the war, he became a naturalized American and a director of the US Army's Ballistic Missile Agency at Huntsville, Alabama, and was chiefly responsible for the launching of the first American artificial Earth satellite (Jan 1958). He died at Alexandria, Virginia. » V-2

Brazil, Port **Brasil**, official name **The Federative Republic of Brazil**, Port **República Federativa do Brasil** pop (1990e) 150 368 000; area 8 511 965 sq km/3 285 618 sq ml. A republic in E and C South America, divided into five geographical regions, which are subdivided into 23 states, 3 territories, and one federal territory (Brasília); bounded N by Colombia, Venezuela, Guyana, Suriname, and Guiana, E by the Atlantic, W by Colombia, Peru, Bolivia, and Paraguay, and S by Argentina and Uruguay; coastline 7 408 km/4 603 ml; four timezones, GMT −2 in the Atlantic islands, −3 in the E, −4 in the mid-W, and −5 in the extreme W; capital Brasília; principal cities São Paulo, Rio de Janeiro, Belo Horizonte, Recife, Salvador; ethnic groups include Portuguese, Italian, German, Japanese, Black, and Amerindian; 55% White, 38% mixed, and 6% Black; official language, Portuguese; religion, 89% Roman Catholic, remainder Protestant or Spiritualist; currency unit, the cruzeiro of 100 centavos.

Physical description. Low-lying Amazon basin in the N, once an inland sea, now drained by rivers that carry a fifth of the Earth's running water; where forest canopy cleared, soils susceptible to erosion; Brazilian plateau in the C and S, average height 600–900 m/2 000–3 000 ft; vegetation changes from thorny scrub forest (N) to wooded savannah (*campo cerrado*) in the interior; Brazilian Highlands (N) rise to 2 890 m/9 481 ft at Pico da Bandeira; Guiana Highlands (S) contain Brazil's

highest peak, Pico da Neblina (3 014 m/9 888 ft); eight river systems, notably the Amazon (N), the São Francisco (C), and the Paraguay, Paraná, and Uruguay (S); thin coastal strip on the Atlantic, c.100 km/325 ml wide, containing 30% of the population.

Climate. Almost entirely tropical, Equator passing through the N region, and Tropic of Capricorn through the SE; Amazon basin, annual rainfall 1 500–2 000 mm/60–80 in, no dry season, average midday temperatures 27°–32°C; more distinct wet and dry seasons on Brazilian plateau; dry region in the NE, susceptible to long droughts, eg Iguatú, daily temperatures 21°–36°C, monthly rainfall (Aug) 3 mm/0.12 in, rising to 185 mm/7¼ in (Mar); hot, tropical climate on narrow coastal strip, with rainfall varying greatly N–S; Rio de Janeiro daily temperature 17°–29°C, with 137 mm/5.4 in of rain (Dec) and 41 mm/1.6 in (Aug); S states lie outside the tropics, with a seasonal, temperate climate.

History and government. Discovered for the Portuguese by Cabral in 1500, first settlement at Salvador da Bahia; 13 feudal principalities, replaced in 1572 by a Viceroyalty, and division of country into N and S, with capitals at Salvador and Rio de Janeiro; Portuguese court transferred to Brazil in Napoleonic Wars; independence declared 1822, and monarchy established; republic followed 1889 coup; large numbers of European immigrants in early 20th-c; revolution headed by Vargas established dictatorship (1930–45); liberal republic restored, 1946; another coup in 1964 led to a military-backed presidential regime; military junta, 1969; new elections, 1985; since 1979 a process of liberalization (*abertura*) has allowed return of political exiles to stand for state and federal offices; bicameral National Congress of 69 senators (three from each state) elected for eight years, and 479 deputies elected for four years by proportional representation; state governors with limited powers elected every four years.

Economy. One of the world's largest farming countries, agriculture employing 35% of the population; world's largest exporter of coffee, second largest exporter of cocoa and soya beans; also beef, sugar cane, cotton, butter, maize, oranges; iron ore (reserves possibly world's largest), manganese, bauxite, nickel, uranium, gold, gemstones; steel, chemicals, petrochemicals, machinery, motor vehicles, textiles, consumer goods, cement, lumber, shipping, fishing, tourism; offshore oil production increased since the 1960s; large investments in hydroelectricity, cane alcohol, coal, and nuclear power; important hydroelectric scheme at the Itaipu dam on the R Paraná; world leader in development of alcohol fuel; nuclear plant at Angra dos Reis, and others planned; timber reserves the third largest in the world, but continuing destruction of the Amazon rainforest is causing much concern; road network being extended through the Amazon rainforest – Rodovia Transamazônica and the Rodovia Perimetral Norte (Perimetral North Highway), linked by the Rodovia Panamericana; Carnival celebrations (weekend before Lent). » Amazon; Brasília; Cabral; Minas Gerais; Rio de Janeiro; São Paulo; Vargas; RR24 national holidays; RR44 political leaders

Brazil nut An evergreen tree growing to 30 m/100 ft, native to the jungles of Brazil; leaves oblong; flowers white, in large panicles; fruit a woody or rounded capsule to 150 mm/6 in across, containing 12–15 tight-packed, woody, 3-sided seeds familiarly called by the same name. Not cultivated, the nuts sold in shops are gathered from wild trees. (*Bertholletia excelsa.* Family: *Lecythidaceae.*) » evergreen plants; nut; panicle; tree [i]

brazing The joining of two pieces of metal (the same or different) by heating, then filling in the junction with a metal of lower melting point than those being joined. A flux is generally necessary. Brazing differs from soldering, in that a soldered joint is not expected to stand any mechanical strain (as in electrical unions), whereas a brazed joint can be very strong. » flux (technology); solder

Brazos River River in S USA, formed in W Texas by the Double Mountain Fork and Salt Fork Rivers; enters the Gulf of Mexico at Freeport; length 1 947 km/1 210 ml; major tributaries the Clear Fork, Little, Navasota; used for irrigation, hydroelectricity, and flood-control. » United States of America [i]

Brazzaville [**bra**zavil] 4°14S 15°14E, pop (1980) 422 402. River-port capital of the Congo, W Africa, on right bank of R Zaire (opposite Kinshasa, Zaire); founded, 1880; capital of French Equatorial Africa, 1910; headquarters of Free French forces in World War 2; capital of Congo, 1960; airport; railway terminus from coast; university (1972); banking, chemicals, metallurgy, food processing, textiles, timber; cathedral. » Congo [i]

bread A widely-used staple food made by baking a mixture of flour and water; the flour used is most commonly wheat, which may be mixed with flour from oatmeal, rye, or barley. The mix results in a dough which may be kneaded, a process that stretches and aligns the protein molecules of the wheat. The product is then either immediately baked to give *unleavened bread*, or allowed to rise, through the production of carbon dioxide, to give *leavened bread*. The carbon dioxide can be produced either chemically or by using yeast. Much of today's bread is made using a short fermentation process called the Chorleywood Bread Process. » baking powder; chapati; flour; soda bread; yeast

bread mould Any mould found growing on bread; more specifically used for the fungus *Mucor* (Class: *Zygomycetes*) which forms a colourless hair-like covering over bread surface; produces dark spores (*zygospores*) at the tips of its upright branches, and *Neurospora* which is reddish in colour and causes bread spoilage in bakeries. » fungus

breadfruit An evergreen tree growing to 12–18 m/40–60 ft, probably native to Malaysia; glossy leaves oval, deeply lobed towards tips; male flowers in short catkins, females in prickly heads, achenes, and spongy receptacle, enlarging to form a rounded, multiple fruit, 10–20 cm/4–8 in diameter, and green to brownish when ripe, filled with a white, fibrous pulp. It was introduced in prehistoric times to the S Pacific, where it is a staple food; and was carried aboard the HMS *Bounty* to the West. (*Artocarpus altilis.* Family: *Moraceae.*) » achene; Bounty Mutiny; evergreen plants; tree [i]

break dancing » **street dance**

breaking radiation » **bremsstrahlung**

breaking stress » **tensile strength**

Breakspear, Nicolas » **Adrian IV**

breakwater An artificial barrier to wave activity. Breakwaters are constructed to intercept incoming waves and provide a sheltered area, usually for marine recreation or port facilities. Most are built offshore and parallel to the shoreline. Because breakwaters reduce wave energy and modify the direction of wave propagation in their lee, they alter the natural near-shore circulation of sand and other sediments, and frequently produce siltation in the very harbours and channels they are designed to protect.

bream Deep-bodied freshwater fish found in quiet lowland rivers and lakes of N Europe; length up to c.60 cm/2 ft. The name is also used for various similarly deep-bodied fishes in other families, both freshwater and marine. (*Abramis brama.* Family: *Cyprinidae.*)

Bream, Julian (Alexander) (1933–) British guitarist and lutenist, born in London. He studied at the Royal College of Music there, and earned an international reputation in the 1950s on both guitar and lute. Several composers, including Britten, Henze, and Walton, have written works for him. » guitar; lute

breast The milk-producing organ of the female reproductive system; also known as the **mammary gland**. It is composed of glandular tissue supported by fibrous tissue covered by skin and a thick layer of fat. The two breasts in humans are found on the front of the chest: they are small in children, but at puberty the female breasts increase rapidly in size, whereas in males they remain rudimentary. Size and appearance is variable both within an individual as well as between individuals and different races. During pregnancy the breasts enlarge, being largest during milk secretion (*lactation*). At the apex of the breast is the *nipple*, surrounded by the darker coloured *areola*. » breast cancer/feeding/milk; mammary gland; thorax

breast cancer The commonest malignant tumour in women,

spreading within the breast tissue and to the skin, which may ulcerate. Blood-borne spread also occurs to bones, lungs, liver, and other organs. Treatment depends on many factors, but includes surgical removal of the tumour or breast (**mastectomy**) and a combination of hormonal and anti-cancer drugs. » breast; cancer

breast feeding The suckling of an infant by its mother for a time after birth. The secretion of breast milk (*lactation*) takes two to three days to become established. The early transfer of maternal antibodies to the baby is one advantage of this form of feeding. The number of mothers who breastfeed in the developed countries has increased steadily since the 1960s, when bottle feeding was the norm. » breast milk; lactation

breast milk The product of the female milk-producing (*mammary*) gland of humans and other mammals. Its composition is variable, depending on the fat content, both during a feed and throughout lactation. Human breast milk is rich in the antibodies of the secretory class (immunoglobulin A) and in other antimicrobial factors. Its iron content is in a highly absorbable form. Its quality remains more or less constant, despite quite marked variation in the mother's diet, and is widely held to be the preferred food for infants during the first three to four months of life. » breast feeding; mammal [i]; milk

breastbone » **sternum**

breathalyzer A device used with a driver suspected of having drunk an excessive amount of alcohol. The driver blows into a tube; crystals in the device change colour if there is alcohol present; and the extent of the change may indicate that the driver has exceeded the alcohol limit, which in the UK is 80 mg per litre of blood. The initial test is given by a uniformed police officer; and if positive, the driver may be arrested, and given a further blood or urine test at a police station with a doctor present. » alcohols; arrest

breathing » **respiration**

breccia [**bre**cheea] Coarse sedimentary rock made up of a mixture of angular rock cemented by a finer-grained matrix. It usually results from local processes such as landslides and geological faulting, in which rock fracturing occurs. » agglomerate; conglomerate (mineralogy); sedimentary rock

Brecht, (Eugene) Bertolt (Friedrich) [brekht] (1898–1956) German poet, playwright and theatre director, born at Augsburg. His early plays won him success, controversy, and the Kleist Prize in 1922. Popularity came with *Die Dreigroschenoper* (1928, The Threepenny Opera), and from then until 1933 his work was particularly concerned with encouraging audiences to think rather than identify, and with experimentation in epic theatre and alienation-effects. Hitler's rise to power forced him to leave Germany, and he lived in exile for 15 years. During this period, he wrote some of his greatest plays, including *Mutter Courage und ihre Kinder* (1938, Mother Courage and her Children) and *Der Kaukasische Kreidekreis* (1945, The Caucasian Chalk Circle). After his return to East Berlin in 1948, his directorial work on these and other plays with the Berliner Ensemble firmly established his influence as a major figure in 20th-c theatre. In 1955 he received the Stalin Peace Prize, and died soon after at Eutin, Germany. » alienation-effect; Berliner Ensemble; drama; epic; German literature; theatre

Breckland, the A sandy region of heathland on the border of Norfolk and Suffolk, UK. It was an important area of Neolithic flint mining. Today large areas are covered in conifer plantations. » Three Age System

Brecon Beacons National park in Wales; area 1 434 sq km/553 sq ml; established in 1957; three main peaks of 'The Beacons', Pen-y-Fan, Corn Du, and Cribyn, rise to c.900 m/3 000 ft; includes Brecon cathedral, Llanthony Priory, Llangorse Lake. » Wales [i]

Breda [**bray**da] 51°35N 4°45E, pop (1984e) 153 517. Industrial city in North Brabant province, S Netherlands, at confluence of Mark and Aa Rivers; bishopric; important cultural centre, headquarters of many educational institutes; charter, 13th-c; known for the 'Compromise of Breda', a protest against Spanish tyranny (1566), and Charles II's 'Declaration of Breda' before his restoration (1660); railway; engineering, synthetic fibres, foodstuffs, matches, brewing, power tools, tourism; Breda castle (1350, now a military academy), town hall (18th-c), Gothic cathedral (1510). » Charles II (of England); Netherlands, The [i]

Breeches Bible A name sometimes applied to the Geneva Bible, because of the rendering of *Gen* 3.7, which refers to Adam and Eve having sewn fig leaves together 'and made themselves breeches'. This translation, though, is not unique to the Geneva Bible. » Bible; Geneva Bible

breeder reactor » **nuclear reactor** [i]

brehon laws [**bree**huhn] A corpus of ancient Irish customary law written down by the 8th-c; the name derives from Irish *breitheamh* 'judge'. Following the Anglo-Norman invasion of Ireland in the late 12th-c, Irish law gave much ground to English common law. It was finally abolished by statute in the early 17th-c. » common law

Bremen [**bray**men] 53°05N 8°48E, pop (1983) 545 100. Commercial city and capital of Bremen province, Germany; on both banks of the lower R Weser, 94 km/58 ml SW of Hamburg; second largest seaport in former West Germany; railway; university (1970); trade in grain, cotton, tobacco; shipbuilding and repairing, machinery, oil refining, chemicals, electrical equipment, electronics, aerospace, vehicles, textiles; 11th-c cathedral, Gothic town hall (1405–10). » Germany [i]

Bremerhaven [**bray**merhahvn] 53°34N 8°35E, pop (1983) 137 300. Seaport in Bremen province, Germany; on E bank of Weser estuary, 56 km/35 ml N of Bremen; city status, 1851; united with Wesermunde, 1938; railway; Europe's largest fishing port for many years, declining in 1980s; trawling, fish processing, shipbuilding and repairing, machinery. » Germany [i]

bremsstrahlung [**brem**shtrahlung] (Ger 'breaking radiation') Electromagnetic radiation emitted by decelerating charged particles passing through matter. For example, electrons fired into lead produce bremsstrahlung in the form of X-rays. It is the principal means of energy loss for high energy particles. » electromagnetic radiation [i]; X-rays

Bren gun A light machine-gun, the standard section weapon of the British Army during World War 2. The name derives from Brno in Czechoslovakia, where the gun was first designed, and Enfield in Britain, where it was manufactured in large quantities. » machine-gun

Brendan, St (484–577), feast day 16 May. Irish monastic founder, born at Tralee. He travelled widely, before founding the monastery of Clonfert in Galway. The Irish epic, *Navigatio Brendani* (Voyage of Brendan), was popular in W Europe from the 11th-c. He died at Annaghdown, Galway. » monasticism

Brendel, Alfred (1931–) Austrian pianist, born at Wiesenberg. He studied the piano privately in Zagreb and Graz, where he made his debut in 1948. In 1974 he settled in London. He is known above all for his interpretations of Beethoven and Viennese classical composers. » Beethoven; piano

Brennan, William J(oseph) (1906–) US jurist, born at Newark, New Jersey. He was educated at the University of Pennsylvania and Harvard, and after practising law he rose in the New Jersey court system to the State Supreme Court. Named to the US Supreme Court in 1956, he took an active role in the 'liberal' decisions it handed down under the chief justiceship of Earl Warren. » Warren, Earl

Brenner, Sydney (1927–) South African-British molecular biologist, born at Germiston, South Africa. Educated at Witwatersrand and Oxford, he worked at Cambridge, and in the 1950s made major contributions to studies of molecular genetics and the DNA helix. In the 1970s he began an intensive study of the nervous system of a nematode worm, with the objective of relating the anatomy of an animal to the genetic basis of its structure. » DNA [i]; genetics [i]; molecular biology; nematode

Brenner Pass [**bren**uh], Ger **Brenner Sattel**, Ital **Passo del Brennero** 47°02N 11°32E. Mountain pass in the C Tirol Alps on the border between Italy and Austria; altitude 1 371 m/4 498 ft; on the main route between Bolzano and Innsbrück; the lowest pass over the main chain of the Alps; open at all seasons of the year. » Alps; Austria [i]

brent goose A goose native to the N hemisphere, also known as **brant**; breeds in the high Arctic; migrates to temperate N coasts in winter; eats primarily the marine grass *Zostera*; unusually for geese, rarely nests in captivity if caught. (*Branta bernicla*. Family: *Anatidae*.) » goose

Brentano, Clemens (1778–1842) German author, born at Ehrenbreitstein. A founder of the Heidelberg Romantic school, he wrote several poems, plays, notably *Die Gründung Prags* (1815, The Foundation of Prague), short stories, and fairy tales. With Achim von Arnim he edited *Des Knaben Wunderhorn* (1805–8), a collection of folk songs. In his later years, he became a Catholic, and entered a monastery for six years. He died at Aschaffenburg, Bavaria. » folklore; German literature; Romanticism (literature)

Brescia [**bray**sha] 45°33N 10°13E, pop (1981) 206 661. Industrial town and capital of Brescia province, Lombardy, N Italy; rail junction; textiles, clothing, shoes, iron and steel, metal products, transport equipment, precision engineering, firearms; market centre for local agricultural produce; Tempio Capitolino (AD 72), and other Roman remains; cathedrals (9th-c, 17th-c), Renaissance town hall (1492–1508). » Lombardy

Bresson, Robert (1907–) French film director, born in the Auvergne. At first a painter and photographer, he started serious work in the cinema with *Les Anges du Péché* (1943, The Angels of Sin), but it was his next production *La Journal d'un Curé de Campagne* (1951, Diary of a Country Priest) which brought international acclaim, subsequently repeated with *Un Condamné à Mort s'est Echappé* (1956, A Man Escaped) and *Le Procès de Jeanne d'Arc* (1962, The Trial of Joan of Arc). Later productions are *Lancelot du Lac* (1974) and *Le Diable, Probablement* (1977, The Devil, Probably).

Brest (Belorussia), formerly **Brest Litovsk**, Pol **Brześć nad Bugiem** 52°08N 23°40E, pop (1983) 208 000. River-port capital city of Brestskaya oblast, Belorussia; on the R Mukhavets at its junction with the R Bug, on the Polish border; founded by Slavs, 1017; major transportation centre; railway; foodstuffs, electrical engineering, electronics. » Belorussia

Brest (France) 48°23N 4°30W, pop (1982) 160 355. Fortified port and naval station in Finistère department, NW France; on the Atlantic coast; natural harbour on the Penfeld estuary; used as a German submarine base in World War 2; rebuilt after heavy bombing; railway; extensive dockyards, naval stores, arsenals; fishing, textiles, chemicals, metallurgy. » World War 2

Brest-Litovsk, Treaty of (1918) A bilateral treaty signed at Brest between Soviet Russia and the Central Powers. Under its terms, Russia withdrew from World War 1, hostilities ceased on Germany's E front, and the new Soviet state ceded vast areas of territory and economic resources to Germany. Lenin said that Russia must 'sacrifice space in order to gain time'. » World War 1

Brethren (in Christ) A Church founded in the late 18th-c in Pennsylvania, USA, deriving from Mennonite tradition. Pietistic, evangelical, and missionary. it soon spread to Canada, and in the 20th-c, although numerically small, supports missionary churches in Asia, Africa, and C America. » Christianity; Mennonites; missions, Christian; Pietism

Breton The Celtic language of Brittany, introduced by migration from Cornish-speaking S England in the 5th-c AD. It is thought the two languages were mutually intelligible until the 15th-c, but Breton is marked by increasing influence from French, especially in pronunciation and vocabulary. Breton was not recognized as a school subject until the 1950s, nor was it legal to christen a child with a Breton name. There are no official figures for Breton speakers, but it is thought there are about half a million. There is a substantial body of literature from the mediaeval period onwards. » Celtic languages; Cornish

Breton, André [**bruh**tõ] (1896–1966) French poet, essayist and critic, born at Tinchebray, Normandy. In 1919 he joined the Dadaist group, and became a founder of the Surrealist movement, which he helped to define in several manifestos (from 1924). With Philippe Soupault he wrote *Les Champs magnétiques* (1920, Magnetic Fields). He became editor of *La Révolution surréaliste*, and in 1930 joined the communists. He spent the war years in the USA, returning to France in 1946. He died in Paris. » Dada; French literature; Surrealism

Bretton Woods Conference An international conference held at Bretton Woods, New Hampshire, USA, in 1944, which led to the establishment of the International Monetary System, including the International Monetary Fund (IMF) and the World Bank. The agreement, signed by the USA, UK, and 43 other nations, aimed to control exchange rates, which were fixed for members in terms of gold and the dollar. The system was used until 1973, when floating exchange rates were introduced. » International Monetary Fund

Breughel or **Brueghel, Pieter**, byname **the Elder** [**brer**gl] (c.1520–69) The most original of all 16th-c Flemish painters, born (probably) in the village of Breughel, near Breda. He studied under Pieter Coecke van Aelst (1502–50), and was much influenced by Bosch. In about 1551 he began to travel through France and Italy, later settling in Brussels, where he painted his major works. His genre pictures of peasant life reach their finest expression in 'The Blind Leading the Blind' (1568, Naples), the 'Peasant Wedding', and the 'Peasant Dance' (c.1568, Vienna). He died in Brussels. His eldest son, **Pieter Breughel, the Younger** (c.1564–1637) is known as 'Hell' Breughel, because of his paintings of devils, hags and robbers. His younger son, **Jan** (1568–1625), known as 'Velvet' Breughel, painted still life, flowers, landscapes, and religious subjects on a small scale. » Flemish art; genre painting

Breuil, Henri (Edouard Prosper) [broey] (1877–1961) French archaeologist, born at Mortain. He trained as a priest, became interested in cave art, and was responsible for the discovery of the famous caves at Combarelles and Font de Gaume in the Dordogne (1901). Noted for his studies of artistic technique and the detailed copying of hundreds of paintings in Europe, Africa, and elsewhere, he became professor at the Collège de France (1929–47). His work marked the beginning of the study of Palaeolithic art. He died at L'Ile-Adam. » Palaeolithic art; rock art; Three Age System

breviary A book of liturgical material (psalms, hymns, lessons, prayers) used in the Daily Office, and required to be recited by all priests and clerics in major orders of the Roman Catholic Church. It was revised by Pope Paul VI in 1971, to incorporate the recommendations of Second Vatican Council. » liturgy; Orders, Holy; Roman Catholicism; Vatican Councils

brewing The art and technique of producing an alcoholic beverage (most often a variety of beer) from cereals. Grain is steeped in water, and allowed to germinate. The germination is halted by heating (*malting*), and after *milling* to crush the grain and expose the contents, the malt is *mashed* (leached with hot water to give a solution of fermentable carbohydrates (the *wort*). Sugar may be added. The wort is boiled in a *copper* with hops (to give aroma and flavour). When cool, a brewer's yeast is added. Traditional British beers are fermented at the top of the vessel. Bottom fermentation with a different kind of yeast yields the lager type of beer. » beer [i]; yeast

Brezhnev, Leonid (Ilich) (1906–82) Russian statesman, General Secretary of the Soviet Communist Party (1964–82), and President of the Supreme Soviet (1977–82), born at Kamenskoye, Ukraine. He trained as a metallurgist, and became a political commissar in the Red Army in World War 2. After the war, he was a party official in the Ukraine and Moldavia, becoming a member (1952–7) and then Chairman (1960–4) of the Presidium of the Supreme Soviet. He became General Secretary of the Party Central Committee after Khrushchev (1964), and gradually emerged as the most powerful figure in the Soviet Union, the first to hold simultaneously the position of General Secretary and President. He died in Moscow. » Brezhnev Doctrine; Khrushchev

Brezhnev Doctrine The term applied to the policies of Leonid Brezhnev, General Secretary of the Soviet Communist Party (1964–82), which combined strict political control internally with peaceful co-existence and détente abroad. It also justified intervention (including military) in the internal affairs of other socialist states, as in Czechoslovakia (1968). The Brezhnev period was later referred to in the USSR as the 'years of stagnation'. » Brezhnev; communism; socialism

Brian [**bree**an] (c.926–1014) Famous King of Ireland (1002–14), the **Brian Boroimhe** or **Boru** ('Brian of the tribute') of the annalists. In 976 he became chief of Dál Cais, and after much fighting he made himself King of Leinster (984). After further campaigns in all parts of the country, his rule was acknowledged over the whole of Ireland. He was killed after defeating the Vikings at Clontarf. » Vikings

Briand, Aristide [**bree**ã] (1862–1932) French socialist statesman and Prime Minister, born at Nantes. Eleven times French Premier (1909–11, 1913, 1915–17, 1921–2, 1925–6, 1929), he also acted as Foreign Minister (1925–32), and helped to conclude the **Kellogg-Briand Pact** (1928), outlawing war as a means of solving disputes. He shared the 1926 Nobel Peace Prize, and advocated a United States of Europe. He died in Paris. » Kellogg-Briand Pact

briar The woody root of two species of heath, *Erica scoparia* and *Erica arborescens*, used to make tobacco pipes. (Family: *Ericaceae*.) » heath; root (botany)

bricks Blocks, usually of clay or a clay mixture, baked by the Sun or by fire. Bricks have been made for thousands of years, and are still one of the most widely used building materials. Most are now made by machine, and fired in kilns. The fixing of bricks in place to provide a strong wall is called **bricklaying**. Bricks are laid in mortar, a mixture of cement or lime with sand and water. The patterns are formed by laying the bricks end-on (*headers*) or lengthwise (*stretchers*). The bonds are selected both for their degree of strength and aesthetic value.

Bride, St » **Bridget** or **Bride, St**

bridge (recreation) A popular card game developed from whist, using the full set of 52 playing cards, and played by two pairs of players. It is thought to have originated in either Greece or India, and was introduced into Britain in 1880. The two most popular forms are **auction bridge** and **contract bridge**. Auction bridge was brought to England from India c.1903 and became popular at the Portland Club. Trumps are decided by a preliminary bid or auction. Contract bridge is a development in which trumps are nominated by the highest bidder. This game was invented by US businessman and yachtsman Harold Stirling Vanderbilt (1884–1970) in 1925, and from 1930 has been the most widely played form. Scoring uses a chart devised by Vanderbilt, and is based on tricks contracted for and won. » playing cards; whist; RR108

bridge (engineering) A structure carrying a road, path, or railway over an obstacle. The principal types are *arch* bridges, *girder* bridges, and *suspension* bridges. The simplest consist of slabs of stone or branches laid across a stream. Bridges may be built of timber, stone, iron, steel, brick, or concrete, different materials being suited to different forms of construction. The greatest spans are achieved by suspension bridges, the longest at present being the Humber Bridge, England (1410 m/4 626 ft). The greatest single span arch bridge is the New River Gorge, W Virginia, USA (518 m/1 700 ft). » Akashi-Kaikyo/Bosporus/ Brooklyn / Golden Gate / Humber / Kintai / London / Rialto / Sydney Harbour/Tower/Verrazano-Narrows Bridge; Bridge of Sighs; Ponte Vecchio; pontoon bridge

Bridge of Sighs An enclosed 16th-c bridge in Venice, through which condemned prisoners would pass from the Doge's Palace to the Pozzi prison. » Doge's Palace; Venice

Bridges, Robert (Seymour) (1844–1930) British poet, born at Walmer, Kent. He studied at Eton and Oxford, qualified in medicine, and practised in London. He published three volumes of graceful lyrics (1873, 1879, 1880), and then wrote several plays, the narrative poem *Eros and Psyche* (1885), and other works, including a great deal of literary criticism. He was also an advocate of spelling reform. From 1907 he lived in seclusion at Oxford, publishing comparatively little; then in 1929, on his 85th birthday, he issued his most ambitious poem, *The Testament of Beauty*. He became poet laureate in 1913 until his death, at Oxford. » English literature; literary criticism; poetry; spelling reform

Bridget or **Bride, St** (453–523), feast day 1 February. Patron saint of Leinster, Ireland. She entered a convent at Meath, and eventually founded four monasteries, the chief at Kildare. Her legendary history is a mass of astonishing miracles, some of which were apparently transferred to her from the Celtic goddess Ceridwen. She was also held in great reverence in Scotland. She died at Kildare. » monasticism

Bridget or **Brigitta, St** (c.1302–73), feast day 23 July or 8 October. Patron saint of Sweden, born at Finstad. She was mistress of the Swedish royal household who, after the death of her husband, founded the monastery of Wadstena, E Gothland, the cradle of a new order which flourished in Sweden until the Reformation (the **Brigittine Order**). She died in Rome on returning from a pilgrimage to Palestine, and was canonized in 1391. » monasticism

Bridgetown 13°06N 59°36W, pop (1980) 7 552. Seaport and capital city of Barbados, West Indies, on Carlisle Bay in the SW of the island; a new deep-water harbour built to the NW; resort of Paradise Beach to the N; University of the West Indies (1963); tourism, sugar manufacturing; cathedral; one of the earliest monuments commemorating Lord Nelson. » Barbados [i]; Nelson, Horatio

Bridgewater Canal An inland waterway in England commissioned by Francis Egerton, 3rd Duke of Bridgewater (1736–1893), and constructed (1762–72) by James Brindley. The canal links Worsley to Manchester, crossing the Irwell valley by viaduct, and continues to Liverpool. It is 64 km/40 ml long. » Brindley; canal

Bridgman, P(ercy) W(illiams) (1882–1961) US physicist, born in Cambridge, Massachusetts. Educated at Harvard, he became professor of physics and mathematics, and was awarded the Nobel Prize for Physics in 1946 for his work on high-pressure physics and thermodynamics. He died at Randolph, New Hampshire. » physics; thermodynamics

brig Any two-masted, square-rigged sailing vessel. Brigs became common in the mid-18th-c as colliers supplying London from the northern coal fields. They are still fairly common as sail training vessels. » ship [i]

brigantine [**brig**anteen] A two-masted sailing vessel, square-rigged on the foremast and fore- and aft-rigged on the aftermast. Used mainly in the late-19th-c, a few are still in commission. » ship [i]

Briggs, Barry (1934–) New Zealand speedway rider, born at Christchurch. He appeared in a record 17 consecutive world championship finals (1954–70), during which he scored a record 201 points and took part in 87 races, winning the title in 1957–8, 1964, and 1966. He won the British League Riders'

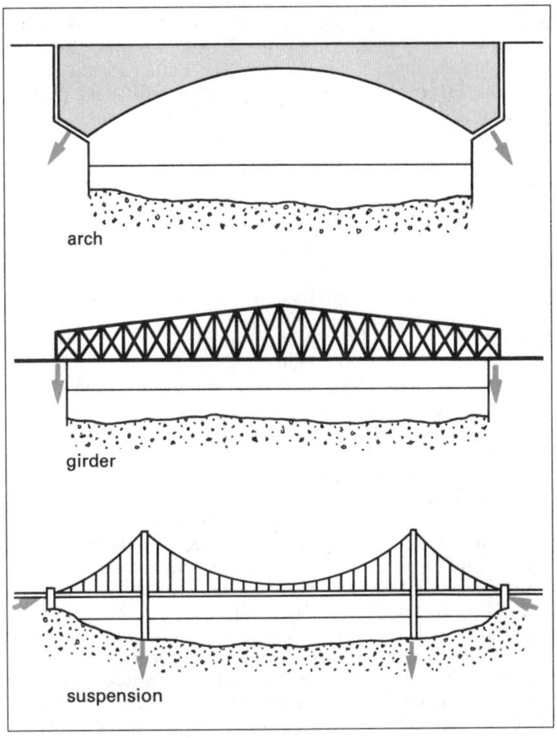

Three types of bridge – The arrows show the forces exerted by the load

championship six times (1965–70). His career started with Wimbledon (1952), and he also rode for New Cross, Southampton, Swindon, and Hull. After retiring (1976), he ran a motorcycle business in Southampton, and was a co-promoter of the 1982 world championships in Los Angeles. » speedway

Bright, John (1811–89) British Radical statesman and orator, born and died at Rochdale. He worked in his father's cotton mill, and took an interest in public questions, becoming a leading member of the Anti-Corn-Law League (1839), and engaging in free trade agitation. He was an MP for Durham (1843), Manchester (1847), and Birmingham (1857), and was closely associated with the Reform Act of 1867. He later held several government posts, until his retirement in 1882. » Anti-Corn-Law League; free trade; Gladstone

Bright, Richard (1789–1858) British physician, born in Bristol. He studied at Edinburgh, London, Berlin, and Vienna, and from 1820 was elected to the staff of Guy's Hospital. He made many important medical observations, and gave his name to **Bright's disease** of the kidneys. He died in London. » kidneys; glomerulonephritis

brightness » **luminous intensity**

Brighton 50°50N 0°10W, pop (1981) 137 985. Resort town in Brighton district, East Sussex, SE England; on the English Channel, 77 km/48 ml S of London; in 1782 the Prince of Wales (later George IV) took up residence here; University of Sussex (1961), 5 km/3 ml NE; railway; food processing, furniture; conference centre; marina; Royal Pavilion (1811), designed by John Nash; Brighton Festival (May); London–Brighton veteran car run (Nov). » Sussex, East; Nash, John

Brigit or **Brighid** An Irish goddess of fire and the hearth; also of poetry and handicrafts. In the Christian era a number of her attributes were taken over by St Brigid. The name means the 'exalted one'. » Dagda, the

Brigit or **Brigitta, St** » **Bridget, St**

Brihadisvara Temple [brihadis**vah**ra] A Hindu temple at Thanjavur (formerly Tanjore), Tamil Nadu, India; a world heritage monument. The temple was founded by the Chola king Rajaraja I (985–1014) in the late 10th-c. It is renowned for its frescoes and for its 60 m/200 ft tower, encrusted with shrines and relief sculptures. » Hinduism

brill Large flatfish found mainly on sandy bottoms in shallow waters (10–75 m/30–250 ft) of NE Atlantic and Mediterranean; body length up to c.60 cm/2 ft; both eyes on left side, mouth large and curved; sandy brown with dark and light flecks; good food fish. (*Scophthalmus rhombus*. Family: *Scophthalmidae*.) » flatfish; turbot

Brillat-Savarin, (Jean) Anthelme [**bree**yah savarĩ] (1755–1826) French gastronome and lawyer, born at Belley. He became Mayor of Belley in 1793, but at the Revolution was forced to flee to Switzerland, then America, where he became a member of the Court of Cassation. *La Physiologie du goût* (1825, The Physiology of Taste), a witty compendium of the art of dining, has been repeatedly republished. He died in Paris.

brimstone (chemistry) » **sulphur**

brimstone (entomology) A wide-winged butterfly; wings lemon yellow in male, greenish white in female, each with an orange spot; caterpillars blue-green, with fine hairs, found on buckthorn; adult remains dormant under leaves during winter. (Order: *Lepidoptera*. Family: *Pieridae*.) » butterfly; caterpillar

Brindisi, ancient **Brundisium** [**breen**deesee] 40°37N 17°57E, pop (1981) 89 786. Seaport and capital of Brindisi province, Puglia, S Italy; 104 km/65 ml SE of Bari, on the Adriatic; inner and outer harbour; centre of trade with E Mediterranean from ancient times; used by Crusaders as a naval base; archbishopric; airport; railway; Virgil died there; cathedral (11th-c, rebuilt 18th-c), Castello Svevo (1233). » Italy [i]

Brindley, James (1716–72) British engineer, born at Thornsett, Derbyshire. He devised a water engine for draining a coalmine, a silk mill on a new plan, and several other works, which recommended him to the Duke of Bridgwater, who employed him (1759) to build the canal between Worsley and Manchester. In all he constructed 365 miles of canals. An illiterate, most of his problems were solved without writings or drawings. He died at Turnhurst, Staffordshire. » Bridgewater Canal; canal

brine shrimp A fairy shrimp found in inland salty or hypersaline waters; swims upside down, beating its leaf-like legs; eggs resistant to desiccation, sold as fish food and hatched in saltwater when required. (Class: *Branchiopoda*. Order: *Anostraca*.) » fairy shrimp

Brinell hardness test A test for the hardness of metal, named after Swedish engineer, Johann August Brinell (1849–1925). A hard steel ball is pressed into the test piece with a known and reproducible force, producing a depression. The dimensions of the depression provide a measure of hardness. » hardness; metal

briquette A fuel made into uniformly shaped lumps, formed by compressing small coal, previously carbonized to render it smokeless, and consolidated by a combustible binder. The term is also used for the uniform lumps of brown coal formed by extrusion or compression. » coal

Brisbane [**briz**bn] 27°30S 153°00E, pop (1986) 1 171 300. State capital of Queensland, Australia, on the Brisbane R; founded as a penal colony, 1824; state capital, 1859; third largest city in Australia; Brisbane statistical division has 10 suburbs; airport; railway; two universities (1909, 1975); commerce, oil refining, chemicals, engineering, shipbuilding, food processing, textiles; City Hall (1930); Lone Pine Koala Sanctuary; botanical gardens; Government House; maritime museum; Brisbane Royal Show (Aug). » Queensland

brisling Small Norwegian fish, *Sprattus sprattus*, canned in oil. » sprat

Brissot (de Warville), Jacques Pierre [**bree**soh] (1754–93) French revolutionary politician, born near Chartres. He trained as a lawyer, but then became an author, writing on criminal law. In 1789 he was elected Representative for Paris in the National Assembly, where he influenced all the early movements of the Revolution. He established *Le Patriote français*, the organ of the earliest Republicans, and became leader of the Girondists (or **Brissotins**). In the Convention his moderation made him suspect to Robespierre and the Jacobins, and with other Girondists he was guillotined in Paris. » French Revolution [i]; Girondins

bristletail A primitively wingless insect with long tail filaments; includes the silverfish. **Two-pronged bristletails** (Order: *Diplura*, 660 species) are blind, mostly minute, and found in the soil, feeding on decaying organic matter. **Three-pronged bristletails** (Order: *Thysanura*, 600 species) are minute, mostly found in the soil and forest leaf litter. » firebrat; insect [i]; silverfish

bristleworm An aquatic annelid worm; body segmented, segments typically with paired lateral lobes (*parapodia*) bearing various bristles and scales; body length from 1 mm–3 m/0.04 in–10 ft; c.8 000 species, including sedentary, tube-living, free-swimming, and parasitic forms. (Class: *Polychaeta*.) » annelid; parchment worm; serpulid

Bristol, ancient **Bricgstow** 51°27N 2°35W, pop (1987e) 384 400. City, county town, and administrative centre of Avon county, SW England; county status 1373; major port in 17th–18th-c, much involved in the slave trade; 187 km/116 ml W of London; an important shipping centre, ports at Avonmouth, Royal Portbury, Portishead; university (1909); 2 airports; railway; shipbuilding, aircraft construction, engineering, tobacco processing; trade in food, petroleum products, metals; 12th-c cathedral, Roman Catholic cathedral (1973), 14th-c St Mary Redcliffe, Clifton suspension bridge (1864); Brunel's SS *Great Britain* rests restored where she was launched in 1843. » Avon; Brunel, Isambard Kingdom; slave trade

Bristol Channel An inlet of the Atlantic Ocean and an extension of the R Severn estuary, between Wales and England; extends 128 km/79 ml E–W, with a width varying from 5–80 km/3–50 ml at its mouth; the greatest tidal range in England; chief towns on the Welsh (N) coast include Cardiff and Swansea, and on the English (S) coast Ilfracombe and Weston-super-Mare. » England [i]; Severn, River; Wales [i]

Bristow, Eric, byname **The Crafty Cockney** (1957–) British darts player, born in London. World professional champion a record five times (1980–81, 1984–6), he was also the beaten finalist twice. His other major championships include the World Masters (1977, 1979, 1981, 1983–4), the World Cup individual (1983, 1985), and the *News of the World* Championship (1983–4). » darts

Britain » United Kingdom [i]

Britain, Battle of The name given to the air war campaign of late summer 1940 in which the German Luftwaffe attempted to destroy the Royal Air Force (RAF) as a prelude to the invasion of Great Britain. The aerial offensive began in August, the German bomber aircraft and fighter escorts concentrating on wiping out the RAF both by combat in the air and by bombing their vital airfields in the S of the country. British resistance proved stubborn, with the Spitfires and Hurricanes of RAF Fighter Command being directed by radar onto the incoming bomber streams. Badly mauled, the Luftwaffe switched their offensive from attacks on airfields to attacks on British cities (the 'Blitz'), losing their opportunity to gain true air superiority. Between 1 July and 31 October the Luftwaffe lost 2 848 aircraft to the RAF's 1 446. » air force; Luftwaffe; Royal Air Force; World War 2

Britain, Roman Known to the Graeco-Roman world from the late 4th-c BC, Britain escaped invasion until the time of Julius Caesar (55–54 BC) and conquest until the time of Emperor Claudius (AD 43); Roman military occupation then followed, the main garrison towns being Lincoln, York, Caerleon on the Usk, and Chester. Conquest of the whole island was initially intended, but the fierce resistance of the tribes in the N (Caledonia) ruled this out. Instead, defensive barriers were erected in N England and S Scotland (Hadrian's Wall and the Antonine Wall). To the S, control was exerted through the army and the policy of Romanizing the natives. Military occupation lasted until c.400, when troubles elsewhere in the Empire forced the withdrawal of the garrison troops. » Antonine Wall; Fishbourne; Hadrian's Wall; Iceni; Picts; Roman history [i]; Roman roads [i]; Romanization

Britannia metal A tin alloy used for tableware, containing 90% tin, 7% antimony, and 2% copper; lustrous, hard, and malleable. It was initially used as a substitute for pewter, but has now been largely displaced by *nickel-silver*, an alloy of nickel, copper, and zinc. » alloy; tin

British » Celtic languages

British Antarctic Territory British colonial territory 20°–80°W and S of 60°S; includes South Orkney Is, South Shetland Is, Antarctic Graham Land Peninsula, and the land mass extending to the South Pole; area 5.7 million sq km/2.2 million sq ml; land area covered by ice and fringed by floating ice shelves; population solely of scientists of the British Antarctic Survey; territory administered by a High Commissioner in the Falkland Is. » Graham Land; South Orkney Islands; South Shetland Islands

British Association for the Advancement of Science An organization whose aims are to promote interest and progress in science. At its annual conference the social, political, and economic implications of scientific advances are considered. It was founded in 1831 by a group of scientists disillusioned with the elitist and conservative attitude of the Royal Society. » Royal Society

British Broadcasting Corporation » BBC

British Columbia pop (1981) 2 744 467; area 947 800 sq km/365 945 sq ml. Mountainous province in SW Canada, bordered S by USA and W by Pacific; Rocky Mts in the E, Coast Mts in the W; largest islands, Queen Charlotte, Vancouver; ranges cut by fertile valleys of Fraser, Thompson, and Columbia Rivers; many lakes, largest Williston, Okanagan, Kootenay, Kinbasket, and Arrow; capital, Victoria; major towns, Vancouver, Kamloops, Prince George, New Westminster, Burnaby; timber products, hydroelectric power, mining (coal, copper, silver, gold, molybdenum), tourism, oil and natural gas, fishing, dairy products, cattle; Captain Cook landed at Vancouver I, 1778; flourishing development of fur trade; border with USA settled by Oregon Treaty, 1846; gold rush to Fraser R, 1858; entered Federation of Canada, 1871; Canadian Pacific Railway completed, 1885; opening of Panama Canal (1915) increased trade with Europe; governed by a lieutenant-governor and an elected 57-member Legislative Assembly. » Canada [i]; Canadian Pacific Railway; Cook, James; Fraser River gold rush; Panama Canal; Vancouver; Victoria (Canada)

British Commonwealth » Commonwealth, British

British Council An organization founded in 1934 to spread the influence of British culture, ideas, and education. Its headquarters is in London, but it has 120 offices and staff based in 80 countries throughout the world.

British Empire There were in fact several British Empires: the empire of commerce and settlement in the Caribbean and N America, founded in the 17th-c and partly lost when the 13 colonies declared their independence in 1776; the empire in the East, founded in the 17th-c but developed through the extensive conquest of India (1757–1857) and the acquisition of islands, trading posts, and strategic positions from Aden to Hong Kong; the empire of White settlement in Canada, Australia, New Zealand and the Cape in South Africa, each of which had been federated as 'dominions' by 1910; and the 'dependent territories' in Africa and elsewhere acquired during the 'New Imperialism' of the last few decades of the 19th-c. To this must be added the British 'informal empire' – territories which she did not rule directly, but which fell under her influence because of her industrial and commercial power. These included parts of S America, the Middle East, the Persian Gulf, and China. In 1919 the Empire reached its fullest extent through the acquisition of mandates over German and Ottoman territories in Africa and the Middle East. It was this diversity which gave rise to such famous phrases as 'the empire on which the sun never sets'. By the late 19th-c the Empire was bonded together not only by industrial strength, but by her vast merchant marine and powerful navy. After World War 1 it was apparent that Britain could not control such an extensive empire: the dominions secured effective independence in 1931; the Middle Eastern mandates were virtually lost by World War 2; India gained her independence in 1947, and the other Asian colonies soon followed; while most of the rest of the Empire was decolonized in the 1960s. Many of the countries of the Empire remained in the British Commonwealth of Nations. » Commonwealth, (British); imperialism

British Empire, Order of the In the UK, an order of knighthood, the first to be granted to both sexes equally, instituted in 1917 by George V. It has five classes: Knights and Dames Grand Cross (GBE), Knights and Dames Commanders (KBE/DBE), Commanders (CBE), Officers (OBE), and Members (MBE). Appointments are made on the recommendations of government ministers, but may come from any walk of life. The ribbon is pink edged with grey. » decoration

British Expeditionary Force (BEF) An army, first established in 1906, sent to France (Aug 1914 and Sep 1939) to support the left wing of the French armies against German attack. In World War 2 its total strength was 394 000, of whom 224 000 were safely evacuated, mainly from Dunkirk, in May–June 1940. » French, John; Haig, Douglas; Marne, Battle of the; World War 1/2

British Indian Ocean Territory pop (1982e) 3 000; land area 60 sq km/23 sq ml. British territory in the Indian Ocean, 1 900 km/1 180 ml NE of Mauritius, comprising the Chagos Archipelago; the islands cover c.54 400 sq km/21 000 sq ml of ocean, in six main island groups; largest island, Diego Garcia; acquired by France, 18th-c; annexed by Britain, 1814; dependency of Mauritius until 1965; established to meet UK and US defence requirements in the Indian Ocean; UK–US naval support facility on Diego Garcia; copra plantations. » Indian Ocean; *map p 178*

British Legion » Royal British Legion

British Library The national depository created by the British Library Act of 1972 through the amalgamation of the British Museum Library, the National Central Library, and the National Lending Library for Science and Technology. Its reference division is based in London; its lending division in W Yorkshire. » British Museum; library

British Medical Association (BMA) An association founded in 1832 in Worcester to promote medical and allied sciences, and to maintain the honour of the profession, and now very much concerned with such matters as education and conditions of service. It is now listed as a trade union, but is not affiliated to the Trades Union Congress. » American Medical Association; medicine; trade union

British Museum The national museum of archaeology and ethnography in Bloomsbury, London. It dates from 1753,

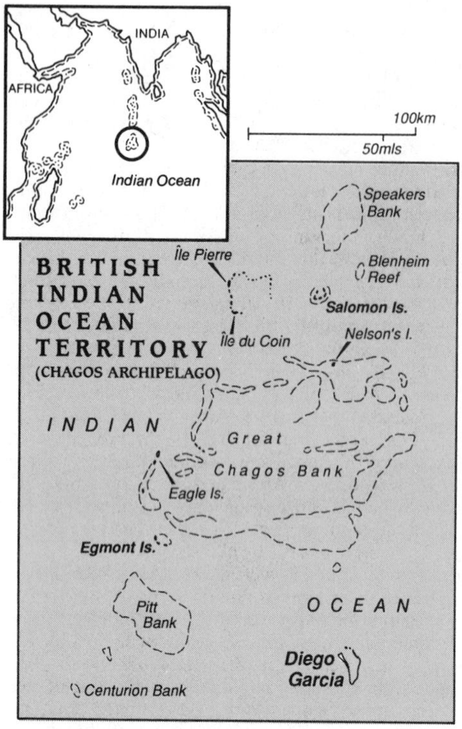

when the collection of Sir Hans Sloane was acquired for the nation. To the Sloane collection were added the Harleian and Cotton manuscript collections, forming the nucleus of the British Library, which is still partly housed in the British Museum. Since 1881 the natural history collection has been housed separately. » British Library; museum; Natural History Museum; Sloane, Hans

British North America Act An act passed by the British Parliament in 1867 which brought about the Confederation of Nova Scotia, New Brunswick, Quebec, and Ontario, thus giving rise to Canada. In 1981 it was renamed the Constitution Act (1867). » Canada [i]

British Open Golf Championship Golf's premier event, held annually. It was first contested at Prestwick, Scotland (17 Oct 1860), and is now played over 72 holes at a different venue each year. All courses are seaside links. The winner receives a silver claret jug, as well as a sizeable cheque. » golf

British South Africa Company A company, formed by Cecil Rhodes, which used a series of concessions from C African chiefs to secure a Royal Charter from the British government in 1889. In 1923–4, its territories were divided into Northern Rhodesia (Zambia after 1964) and Southern Rhodesia (Zimbabwe after 1980). » African history; Rhodes; Zambia [i]; Zimbabwe [i]

British Standards Institution The recognized UK body for the preparation of nationally accepted standards for engineering and industrial materials, and codes of practice. It provides for the marking and certification of products made with standard materials and under standard procedures. It is supported by (but is independent of) the UK government, as well as by industrial firms and professional institutes.

British Summer Time » **Daylight Saving Time**

British thermal unit In thermodynamics, an old unit of heat; symbol Btu; 1 Btu = 1 055 J (joule, SI unit); defined as the heat needed to raise the temperature of a pound of water from 63°F to 64°F; a therm is 10^5 Btu. » heat; joule; thermodynamics; units (scientific); RR70

Brittain, Vera (1893–1970) British writer, born at Newcastle-under-Lyme, Staffordshire. She studied at Oxford, and served as a nurse in World War 1, recording her experiences in *Testament of Youth* (1933). She wrote several other novels, as well as two sequels to this work (1940, 1957). She often lectured in the USA, and in 1925 she married **George Catlin**, professor of politics at Cornell. Her daughter is the politician, Shirley Williams. » English literature

Brittan, Sir Leon (1939–) British Conservative politician, educated at Cambridge and Yale. Called to the Bar in 1962, he was Chairman of the Conservative Bow Group (1964–5) and editor of *Crossbow* magazine (1966–8). Elected an MP in 1974, he was a Minister in the Home Office (1979–81), before becoming Chief Secretary to the Treasury (1981–3), Home Secretary (1983–5), and Secretary for Trade and Industry (1985–6). It was in this last position that he came into conflict with Michael Heseltine (Secretary for Defence) over the take-over of Westland helicopters, the issue which led him to resign from the Cabinet. Knighted in 1988, he became a Vice-President of the Commission of the EEC in 1989. » Conservative Party; European Economic Community; Heseltine

Brittany, Fr **Bretagne** pop (1982) 2 707 886; area 27 208 sq km/ 10 502 sq ml. Region and former province of NW France, comprising departments of Côtes-du-Nord, Finistère, Ille-et-Vilaine, and Morbihan; prominent NW peninsula, bounded N by the English Channel, S by the Bay of Biscay; rugged and striking coastline; large tracts of heathland rising to 391 m/ 1 283 ft at Monts d'Arrée and 326 m/1 069 ft at Montagne Noire; part of Roman Empire, following Julius Caesar's invasion, 56 BC; arrival of Celts from Britain 5th–6th-c AD, from which came a distinctive culture and language (Breton); chief towns, Nantes, Rennes, Lorient, Quimper, Brest; high concentration of megaliths; area noted for its seafood, onions, artichokes, strawberries, Breton Muscadet wine; major tourist area. » Breton; Celts; France [i]; megalith; Roman history [i]

Brittany spaniel A breed of dog, developed in France from British spaniels; thick orange-brown and white coat; virtually no tail; the only spaniel that 'points'; good stamina. » pointer; spaniel

Britten, Baron (Edward) Benjamin (1913–76) British composer, born at Lowestoft, Suffolk. During the 1930s he wrote incidental music for plays and documentary films. He then went to the USA (1939–42), where he wrote his Violin Concerto and the *Sinfonia da Requiem*. Back in the UK, his works were largely vocal and choral – exceptions including the famous Variations and Fugue on a Theme of Purcell (*The Young Person's Guide to the Orchestra*). He then wrote three operas: *Peter Grimes* (1945), *Billy Budd* (1951), and *Gloriana* (1953), as well as several chamber operas and children's operas. His later operas include *A Midsummer Night's Dream* (1960) and *Death in Venice* (1973). He was also an accomplished pianist, often accompanying Peter Pears. He helped to found (1948) the annual Aldeburgh Festival. He became a life peer in 1976, and died at Aldeburgh, Suffolk. » Pears

brittle bone syndrome A generalized genetically-determined disease of the skeleton, characterized by the deficient formation of bone and connective tissue, resulting in excessive fragility of the skeleton. Seriously afflicted babies suffer multiple fractures and die in infancy. Less severely affected children may survive into adult life and develop only an occasional fracture, often in the lower limbs. Dwarfing and a blue colour to the sclerae of the eye are common features. » bone; dwarfism; eye [i]

brittle material » **plastic deformation**

brittle star A starfish-like marine invertebrate (echinoderm) which typically has five slender arms sharply demarcated from the central disc; arms sometimes branched; c.2 000 species, found from the inter-tidal zone to deep sea; most feed as scavengers. (Class: *Ophiuroidea*.) » echinoderm [i]; starfish

Brittonic » **Celtic languages**

Brno [**ber**noh], Ger **Brünn** 49°11N 16°39E, pop (1984) 380 871. Industrial capital of Jihomoravský region, Czech Republic, C Czechoslovakia; at junction of Svratka and Svitava Rivers; third largest city in Czechoslovakia; founded in 10th-c; part of Bohemia, 1229; free city, 1243; formerly capital of Austrian crownland of Moravia; airport; railway; university (1919); technical university (1899); university of agriculture (1919); music conservatory; machinery, textiles, armaments, chemicals, trade in vegetables; Bren gun was developed here; Spilberk fortress, 15th-c cathedral. » Bohemia; Bren gun; Czechoslovakia [i]

broad bean An annual growing to 80 cm/30 in; stems square in cross-section, erect; leaves with 2–6 oval bluish-green leaflets; pea-flowers in small clusters, white with purplish-black wings; pods up to 20 cm/8 in long, hairy, black; containing few large seeds each 2–3 cm/0.8–1.2 in across; also called **horse bean**. Of unknown origin, it has been cultivated since prehistoric times for its edible seeds and for animal fodder. (*Vicia faba*. Family: *Leguminosae*.) » annual; bean

broadbill A bird native to Africa and S Asia; small with bright plumage, wide bill and short legs; inhabits woodland; pear-shaped nests often suspended from branches over water; eats insects, fruit, and seeds. (Family: *Eurylaimidae*, 14 species.)

broadcasting The provision of television and radio programmes and commercials for the general public; also, the technical transmission of television and radio signals. Starting in the 1920s, broadcasting, whether of the commercial or 'public service' variety, quickly established itself at regional, national, and international levels as a popular source of entertainment and information. The medium has always been subject to controls, the severity of which has varied according to the political character of the country concerned. In recent years **narrowcasting** has been introduced for services geared to special interest groups. » BBC; Caroline, Radio; International Telecommunication Union; radio; television; Voice of America

Broadmoor A special hospital for the criminally insane, established in 1863 near Camberley, Berkshire, UK. It is the prototype special hospital, and has lent its name to the generic description 'Broadmoor institutions'.

Broads, the An area (c.2 000 ha/5 000 acres) of low-lying and shallow lakes in E Anglia, UK. The lakes are flooded peat pits, excavated during the 11th-c and 12th-c. Flooding occurred during a period of climatic deterioration from the 13th-c. It is a popular holiday area. » lake

Broadway The name of a street in New York (25 km/15.5 ml long) which since the 1890s has become famous as a symbol of commercial theatre in the USA, though the number of Broadway theatres has declined as production costs have soared. In the 1950s the label **Off-Broadway** emerged to distinguish those theatrical enterprises in New York which operated outside the crippling economics of Broadway. By the mid-sixties the rising economic pressures of Off-Broadway in their turn spawned an off-Off-Broadway movement. » Living theatre; theatre; Times Square

broccoli Types of cultivated cabbage grown for the immature flowers, which are edible. **Winter** broccoli has large, white heads similar to cauliflower; **sprouting** broccoli produces numerous small, purplish, green, or white spears. (*Brassica oleracea*. Family: *Crucifereae*.) » cabbage

Broch, Hermann [brokh] (1886–1951) Austrian novelist, born in Vienna of Jewish parents, and educated at Vienna University, where he studied philosophy and mathematics. During the Anschluss (1938) he was imprisoned by the Gestapo, but was released and escaped to the USA, where he remained until his death. He was the author of a number of philosophical novels, characterized by secular stoicism, of which the most substantial are *Die Schlafwardler* (1932, The Sleepwalkers), and *Der Tod des Vergil* (1945, The Death of Virgil). He died at New Haven, Connecticut. » Anschluss; German literature; novel

Brodsky, Joseph (1940–) Russian poet of Jewish parentage, born and educated in St Petersburg. Convicted as a 'social parasite', he was exiled, went to the USA, and was naturalized in 1977. He now writes in both Russian and English. Collections include *Ostanovka v pustynie* (1970, A Halt in the Wilderness), *Chast rechi* (1977, A Part of Speech), and *Uraniia* (1984, To Urania). He was awarded the Nobel Prize for Literature in 1987. » poetry; Russian literature

Brogan, Sir Denis William (1900–74) British historian, born at Rutherglen, Scotland. He was educated at Glasgow, Oxford, and Harvard, and became professor of political science at Cambridge in 1939. He is known for his books on America as well as more general works, such as *The English People* (1943). He was knighted in 1963.

Broglie, Louis César Victor Maurice, Duc de ('Duke of') (1875–1960) French physicist, born in Paris. He founded a laboratory at Paris, where he made many contributions to the study of X-ray spectra, and was professor at the Collège de France (1942–6). He died at Neuilly. » X-rays

Broglie, Louis Victor Pierre Raymond, Duc de ('Duke of') (1892–1987) French physicist, born at Dieppe. He was educated at the Sorbonne, where he later became professor of theoretical physics (1928). In 1929 he won the Nobel Prize for Physics for his pioneer work on the nature of electron waves (**de Broglie waves**). » electron

Broken Hill 31°57S 141°30E, pop (1981) 26 913. Mining town in New South Wales, Australia; centre of silver, lead, and zinc mining; a centre of the trade union movement, and now administered by the Barrier Industrial Council; School of the Air founded here (1956); Royal Flying Doctor Service based here (1938); 19th-c Afghan Mosque. » New South Wales; trade union

bromeliad Any member of the pineapple family; typically fleshy, spiny-leaved epiphytes, especially common in the canopy of tropical forests, and notable for the reservoir of water which collects in the cup-shaped centre of the leaf rosette. This can be very large, holding up to five gallons of water which is absorbed by the plant via hairs on the leaves. It also provides a habitat for a host of other life forms, often in areas where there is little or no other standing water, including insects, amphibians, and aquatic plants, some of which live and breed only in these reservoirs. (Family: *Bromeliaceae*.) » aechmea; epiphyte; pineapple; succulent

Bromfield, Louis (1896–1956) US novelist and farmer, born at Mansfield, Ohio. He was educated at Cornell Agricultural College and Columbia University, joined the French Army (1914), and returned to journalism in the USA. His novels include *The Green Bay Tree* (1924) and *Early Autumn* (Pulitzer Prize, 1926). He also wrote short stories and plays. He died at Columbus, Ohio. » American literature; novel

bromine [**broh**meen] Br, element 35, freezing point −7°C, boiling point 58.8°C. A corrosive brown liquid with an unpleasant and irritating odour. In nature, it does not occur uncombined, and is mainly extracted from brines containing its salts. In its compounds, it shows oxidation states ±1, +3, +5, and +7. Its main uses are in 1,2-dibromoethane, a petrol adduct, and silver bromide, used in photographic emulsions. » chemical elements; photography; RR90

bromoil process A method of making photographic prints in which the silver image formed by original development is bleached out, and an oil-pigment ink manually applied with a brush to the corresponding gelatine areas. The linked image may be in any colour, and can be transferred by pressure to another support sheet. » photography

bronchi [**bron**kee] A series of branching tubes which gradually decrease in size, conveying air from the trachea to the lungs. The larger bronchi contain cartilage rings to keep the tubes open. The smaller tubes, known as respiratory *bronchioles*, have sac-like dilatations (*alveoli*) where gaseous exchange occurs. » asthma; bronchiectasis; bronchitis; bronchoscopy; cartilage; lungs; trachea

bronchiectasis [brongkee-**ek**tasis] A chronic disease associated with dilatation of the bronchi, which become obstructed and recurrently infected. A cough producing purulent sputum is common. » bronchi

bronchitis A disease marked by inflammation of the bronchial tubes. Acute bronchitis is a serious disease in infants, resulting from a virus which produces intense inflammation of the respiratory tract that may lead to asphyxia. *Chronic bronchitis* affects adults who smoke cigarettes. Excessive bronchial mucous secretion follows, inducing a chronic cough productive of sputum. » bronchi; pneumonia

bronchodilators Agents which produce dilation of the bronchi in the lungs, and which can therefore be helpful in the treatment of asthma, eg adrenaline, isoprenaline, salbutamol. Not all bronchodilators are sufficiently safe for use in asthma; salbutamol (usually in aerosol form) is used clinically. » asthma; bronchi

bronchopneumonia » **pneumonia**

bronchoscopy The direct inspection of the trachea and bronchi by a flexible glass fibrescope introduced under local or general anaesthetic into the respiratory passages. It permits tissue biopsies to be taken. » biopsy; bronchi; optical fibres [i]

Brontë, Anne, pseudonym **Acton Bell** (1820–49) British poet and novelist, born at Thornton, Yorkshire. She worked as a governess, and shared in the joint publication, under pseudonyms, of the three sisters' *Poems* (1846). She wrote two novels: *Agnes Grey* (1845) and *The Tenant of Wildfell Hall* (1848). She died at Scarborough. » Brontë, Charlotte/Emily; English literature

Brontë, Charlotte, pseudonym **Currer Bell** (1816–55) British novelist, born at Thornton, Yorkshire. She first worked in England and Brussels as a teacher. Her chance discovery of Emily's remarkable poems (1845) led to the abortive joint publication under pseudonyms of the three sisters' *Poems* (1846). Her first novel, *The Professor*, was not published until after her death (1857). Her masterpiece, *Jane Eyre*, apeared in 1847, and this was followed by *Shirley* (1849). She married her father's curate, Mr Nicholls, in 1854 and died at Haworth during pregnancy, leaving the fragment of another novel, *Emma*. » Brontë, Anne/Emily; English literature; novel

Brontë, Emily (Jane), pseudonym **Ellis Bell** (1818–48) British novelist and poet, born at Thornton, Yorkshire. She became a governess in Halifax (1837), attended the Héger Pensionat in Brussels with Charlotte (1842), and in 1845 embarked with her sisters upon a joint publication of poems, after Charlotte discovered her *Gondal* verse. Her single novel, *Wuthering Heights* (1847), which has much in common with Greek tragedy, remains one of the major works of English prose fiction. She died at Haworth, Yorkshire. » Brontë, Anne/ Charlotte; English literature; novel

Brontosaurus » Apatosaurus

Brontotherium [brontoh**theer**iuhm] An extinct, browsing, hoofed mammal, known from the Oligocene epoch of N America; very large, rhinoceros-like body standing up to 2.5 m/8 ft at the shoulder; head with pair of bony nasal horns; probably ate soft vegetation. (Class: *Mammalia*. Order: *Perissodactyla*.) » mammal [i]; Oligocene epoch; titanothere; ungulate

Bronx or **the Bronx** 40°50N 73°52W, pop (1980) 1168972, area 109 sq km/42 sq ml. A mainland borough of N New York City and County of New York State, USA; Fordham University (1841); named after Jonas Bronck, an early Dutch settler. » New York City

bronze One of the earliest known alloys; two parts copper and one part tin. Hard and resistant to corrosion, it is traditionally used in bell casting, and is the most widely used material for metal sculpture. The sculptor first prepares a clay model which is cast by means of a plaster mould. » alloy; copper; maquette; modelling; sculpture; tin

Bronze Age » Three Age System

Bronzino, Il, originally **Agnolo di Cosimo** (1503–72) A Florentine Mannerist painter, born at Monticelli. He was a pupil of Rafaello del Garbo and of Pontormo, who adopted him. He decorated the chapel of the Palazzo Vecchio in Florence, and painted the 'Christ in Limbo' in the Uffizi (1552). His portraits include most of the Medici family, as well as Dante, Boccaccio, and Petrarch. He died in Florence. » Florentine School; Italian art; Mannerism

Brook, Peter (Stephen Paul) (1925–) British theatre and film director, born in London. He was educated at Westminster, Greshams, and Oxford, and his early theatre work included a wide range of productions in Britain, Europe, and the USA. His work with the Royal Shakespeare Company in the 1960s was both innovative and formative, and his successes were international, notably *King Lear* (1962), *Marat/Sade* (1964), *US* (1966), and *A Midsummer Night's Dream* (1970). Many of these productions he later filmed. In 1970 he founded in Paris the International Centre of Theatre Research. Among his films are *Lord of the Flies* (1962) and *Meetings with Remarkable Men* (1979), and *The Mahabharata* (1989). His publications include *The Shifting Point* (1988). » theatre

Brooke, Rupert (Chawner) (1887–1915) British poet, born at Rugby. He was educated at Rugby and Cambridge, and travelled in Europe, the USA, and the South Seas. His *Poems* appeared in 1911, and *1914 and Other Poems* after his death. The gentle lyricism of his work, together with his handsome appearance and untimely death, made him a favourite poet among young people in the interwar period. He died a commissioned officer on Skyros on his way to the Dardanelles, and was buried there. » English literature; poetry

Brookeborough, Basil Stanlake Brooke, 1st Viscount (1888–1973) Irish statesman and Prime Minister of Northern Ireland (1943–63). He was elected to the Northern Ireland parliament in 1929, became Minister of Agriculture (1933), Commerce (1941–5), and then Prime Minister. A staunch supporter of union with Great Britain, he was created viscount in 1952, and retired from politics in 1968. » Northern Ireland [i]

Brooklyn 40°40N 73°58W, pop (1980) 2230936. Borough of New York City, co-extensive with Kings County, New York State, USA; area 182 sq km/70 sq ml; incorporated into New York City, 1898; a major port, at the SW corner of Long Island; linked to Staten I by the Verrazano Bridge, and to Manhattan by the Brooklyn Bridge; Brooklyn Institute of Arts and Sciences (1823); New York Naval Shipyard (1801), now in civilian use; Long Island University (1926). » Brooklyn Bridge; New York City; Verrazano-Narrows Bridge

Brooklyn Bridge A suspension bridge built (1869–83) across East R from Brooklyn to Manhattan I, New York City; length of main span 486 m/1 595 ft. » bridge (engineering) [i]; New York City

Brooks, Mel, originally **Melvin Kaminsky** (1926–) US film actor and director, born in New York City. After some years as a gag-writer and comic, he turned to filming with *The Producers* (1967), and followed with a number of zany comedies satirizing established movie styles, among them *Blazing Saddles* (1974) and *Silent Movie* (1976). He usually writes the script, and acts in his productions, as well as directing them. Late films include *High Anxiety* (1977) and *History of the World Part One* (1980). He co-produced *The Fly* (1986) and *84 Charing Cross Road* (1987).

broom The name applied to several different shrubs in the pea family, *Leguminosae*, but particularly to the common broom, native to Europe, a shrub growing to 2.5 m/8 ft; branches numerous, green, straight, and stiff; leaves mostly trifoliate, soon falling; pea-flowers golden yellow, up to 2 cm/ 0.8 in long, in loose, leafy clusters at the ends of the branches; pods up to 4 cm/1½ in long, black. (*Cytisus scoparius*. Family: *Leguminosae*.) » dyer's greenweed; pea [i]; shrub

Broome, David (1940–) British show jumper, born in Cardiff, Wales. He won the World Championship on *Beethoven* in 1970, was three times European champion, on *Sunsalve* (1961) and *Mister Softee* (1967, 1969), and was the individual bronze medallist at the 1960 and 1968 Olympics. He returned to the British Olympic team in 1988 after a 20-year absence. » equestrianism

broomrape An annual or perennial, all parasitic and lacking chlorophyll; only densely-flowered spikes appear above ground; leaves reduced to scales; flowers 2-lipped, in subdued colours, mainly browns; mainly native to Old World warm temperate regions. All food is obtained via haustoria attached to the roots of the host. Despite the name, broom is not the only host: others include ivy and members of the daisy family; however most broomrapes are specific to a single, or to very few, host species. (Genus: *Orobanche*, 140 species. Family: *Orobanchaceae*.) » broom; chlorophyll; haustorium; parasitic plant

Brouwer, Adriaen [**brow**er] (c.1605–38) Flemish painter, born at Oudenarde. He studied at Haarlem under Frans Hals, and about 1630 settled at Antwerp. His favourite subjects were scenes from tavern life, country merrymakings, and all kinds of roisterers. He died at Antwerp of the plague. » Flemish art

Brown, Sir Arthur Whitten (1886–1948) British aviator, born in Glasgow, Scotland, of US parents. He trained as an engineer, and was the companion of Alcock on the first transatlantic flight (1919). He was knighted in 1919. He later became manager of an engineering company, and died in Swansea. » aircraft [i]; Alcock

Brown, 'Capability' » Brown, Lancelot

Brown, Ford Madox (1821–93) British historical painter, born at Calais, France. He studied at Bruges, Ghent, and Antwerp. In Paris he produced the dramatic 'Manfred on the Jungfrau' (1841). A visit to Italy (1845) led him to seek a greater richness of colouring, as in 'Chaucer reciting his Poetry' (1851). Among his more mature works are 'Work' (Manchester) and 'The Last of England' (Birmingham). He died in London. » English art

Brown, George (Alfred) » **George-Brown, Baron**

Brown, John (1800–59) US militant abolitionist, born at Torrington, Connecticut. He supported himself with many different jobs while wandering through the country advocating antislavery. He was twice married and had 20 children. In 1859 he led a raid on the US Armory at Harper's Ferry in Virginia, with the intention of launching a slave insurrection. The raid failed, and after being convicted of treason against Virginia, he was hanged at Charlestown. The song 'John Brown's Body' commemorates the Harper's Ferry raid, and was popular with Republican soldiers in the Civil War. » American Civil War

Brown, Lancelot, byname **Capability Brown** (1716–83) British landscape gardener, born at Kirkharle, Northumberland. His gardens, such as those at Blenheim Palace, Kew, Stowe, and Warwick Castle, are characterized by an imitation of nature, and contrast with the formal continental style. His nickname arose from his habit of saying that a place had 'capabilities'. He died in London. » landscape gardening

Brown, Jim, properly **James (Nathaniel)** (1936–) US footballer, born at St Simons, Georgia. He spent all of his career with the Cleveland Browns, was three times the National Football League's top scorer (1958–59, 1963), and led the NFL in rushing eight times (1957–65). After his retirement as a footballer, he had roles in several films. » football [i]

Brown, Robert (1773–1858) British botanist, born at Montrose, Scotland. He was educated at Aberdeen and Edinburgh, and in 1801 travelled to Australia, bringing back nearly 4000 species of plants. In 1831 he was the first to recognize the nucleus as the basis of a cell. He also discovered the effect later known as **Brownian movement**. He died in London. » botany; cell

brown algae A large group of predominantly marine seaweeds, characterized by their photosynthetic pigments which include chlorophylls *a* and *c*, *β*-carotene, and fucoxanthin; reproduction usually sexual, involving a sperm with two whip-like flagella; over 1 500 species known, mainly from inter-tidal and sublittoral zones; body form ranges from filament-like to large blades. (Class: *Phaeophyceae*.) » algae; flagellum; photosynthesis; seaweed

brown bear A bear widespread in the N hemisphere; thick brown coat and pronounced hump on shoulders; in N America prefers open habitats, in Old World inhabits forest; includes the **big brown bear** and **grizzly bear** (also called **silvertip** or **roachback**) from the Rocky Mts, and the **Kenai bear** and **Kodiak bear** (both from S Alaska); *Kodiak bear* is the largest living carnivore (length, 2.7 m/9 ft; weight up to 780 kg/1 720 lb). (*Ursus arctos*, many subspecies.) » bear; carnivore [i]

brown dwarf A hypothetical very large planet, which is just below the critical mass needed to ignite a stellar nuclear reaction in its own interior. There is evidence for brown dwarfs as companions to a handful of stars. » dwarf star; planet; star

Brown judgment » **civil rights**

Brown University » **Ivy League** [i]

Browne, Charles Farrar, pseudonym **Artemus Ward** (1834–67) US humorist, born at Waterford, Maine. He wrote for the *Cleveland Plaindealer* a description of an imaginary travelling menagerie, followed by a series of comic letters marked by puns, grotesque spelling, and satire, all under the name of 'Artemus Ward'. In 1861 he began to give lecture tours, whose artistic wretchedness furnished occasion for countless jokes. He went to London in 1866, and died in Southampton. » satire

Browne, Hablot Knight, pseudonym **Phiz** (1815–82) British artist, born in London. He trained as an engraver, but then took up etching and watercolour painting. He is best known for his Dickens illustrations, beginning with *The Pickwick Papers* (1836). His pseudonym was an analogy with Dickens' own 'Boz'. He died at Brighton, Sussex. » Dickens; English art; etching

Browne, Robert (c.1550–1633) Puritan separatist churchman, born at Tolethorpe, Rutland. He studied at Cambridge, then became a schoolmaster and open-air preacher. In 1580 he attacked the Established Church, and soon after formed a distinct church on congregational principles at Norwich. In 1581 he and his followers (**Brownists**) were forced to flee to Holland, but in 1584 he returned and was reconciled with the Church. When 80 years old, he was jailed at Northampton for assault, and died there. » Congregationalism; Puritanism

Browne, Sir Thomas (1605–82) English author, born in London. He was educated at Winchester College and Oxford, then studied medicine in Europe, before settling at Norwich, where he was knighted in 1671. His greatest work is his earliest, the *Religio Medici* (c.1635), revealing a deep insight into the spiritual life. His most elaborate work is *Pseudodoxia Epidemica, or Enquiries into...Vulgar and Common Errors* (1646). He also wrote two antiquarian treatises, *Hydriotaphia* or *Urn Burial* (1658), and *The Garden of Cyrus* (1658). He died at Norwich. » English literature

Brownian motion The ceaseless erratic motion of fine particles in suspension, first observed by British botanist Robert Brown in 1827, using pollen grains in water. The effect was explained by Einstein in 1905 as the result of the irregular bombardment of the suspended matter by invisible, thermally-agitated molecules of solution. It provided support for the atomic view of matter. » Brown, Robert; diffusion (science); Einstein; kinetic theory of gases

Browning, Elizabeth Barrett (1806–61) British poet, born in Durham. About 1821 she seriously injured her spine in a riding accident, and was long an invalid. Her first poems were published at 19, and other volumes appeared in 1838 and 1844. In 1845 she met Robert Browning, with whom she eloped in 1846. Her best-known work is *Sonnets from the Portuguese* (1850, 'Portuguese' being Browning's pet name for her). In her later years she developed an interest in spiritualism, and also in Italian politics. She died in Florence. » Browning, Robert; English literature; poetry

browning A brown colour produced in some foods under certain chemical circumstances. *Non-enzymatic* browning occurs when foods containing protein and carbohydrate are heated, the result of the amino acid lysine reacting with free sugars. *Enzymatic* browning occurs with some fruits, such as apples, when exposed to oxygen. » carbohydrate; enzyme; protein

Browning, Robert (1812–89) British poet, born in London. The son of a clerk, he received little formal education. His early work attracted little attention until the publication of *Paracelsus* (1835). *Bells and Pomegranates* (1841–6) included several of his best-known dramatic lyrics, such as 'How they Brought the Good News from Ghent to Aix'. In 1846 he married Elizabeth Barrett, and with her settled at Florence, where he wrote 'Men and Women' (1855) and began 'Dramatis Personae' (1864). Their son, **Robert Barrett** (1849–1912), the sculptor, was born there. After the death of his wife (1861) he settled in London, where he wrote his masterpiece, *The Ring and the Book* (1869). He died in Venice. » Browning, Elizabeth Barrett; English literature; poetry

Browning automatic rifle A gas-operated light machine-gun designed by US gunsmith John Moses Browning (1855–1926) in 1917, and produced in various countries until 1950. The weapon had a 20-round magazine and an effective range of 600 m/2 000 ft. » machine-gun

Brownshirts German Nazi storm-troopers; officially the *Sturmabteilungen*, or *SA*. Formed in 1920, they had expanded to 500 000 by late 1932. Under the leadership of Ernst Röhm, they developed a radical, pseudo-socialist outlook, and, after the Nazi accession to power (1933), challenged the autonomy of the German army. They were crushed in the 'Night of the Long Knives' (30 Jun 1934), and were thereafter overtaken in importance by the SS. » Nazi Party; Röhm; SS

Bruce, Christopher (1945–) British dancer and choreographer, born in Leicester. He trained at the Rambert School in London, danced with the Rambert Dance Company from 1963, and became one of its most expressive dancers. He began to choreograph in the late 1960s. His works are in a mixed modern dance and ballet style, and deal with relationships (eg

Duets, 1973) and with social and political themes (eg *Ghost Dances*, 1981). He was associate director of Rambert (1975–9) and associate choreographer until 1987. » modern dance; Rambert Dance Company

Bruce, James, byname **The Abyssinian** (1730–94) British explorer, born and died at Larbert, Stirlingshire, Scotland. He studied at Harrow and Edinburgh, becoming Consul-General at Algiers (1763–5). In 1768 he set out from Cairo on his journey to Abyssinia, and in 1770 reached the source of the Blue Nile. He returned to Scotland, where he published his vivid account, *Travels to Discover the Sources of the Nile* (1790). » Nile, River

Bruce, Lenny, originally **Leonard Alfred Schneider** (1925–66) US satirical comedian, born in New York City. He first appeared as a night-club performer in Baltimore. The satire and 'black' humour of his largely improvized act often transgressed the conventions of respectability, ferociously attacking hypocrisy. In 1961 he was imprisoned for obscenity, and in 1963 was refused permission to enter Britain. He died of a drug overdose. » satire; theatre

Bruce, Robert (1274–1329) Hero of the Scottish War of Independence. As Earl of Carrick, in 1296 he swore fealty to Edward I of England, but soon joined the Scottish revolt under Wallace. In 1306 he quarrelled with John Comyn, his political rival, stabbing him to death; then assembled his vassals and was crowned king at Scone. He was forced to flee to Ireland, but returned in 1307 and defeated the English at Loudoun Hill. After Edward's death (1307), the English were forced from the country and all the great castles recovered except Berwick and Stirling. This led to the Battle of Bannockburn (1314), when the English were routed. Sporadic war with England continued until the Treaty of Northampton (1328), which recognized the independence of Scotland, and Bruce's right to the throne. He died at Cardross, and was succeeded by David II, the son of his second wife. » Edward I; Wallace, William

Bruce (of Melbourne), Stanley Melbourne, 1st Viscount (1883–1967) Australian statesman and Prime Minister (1923–9), born in Melbourne. He entered parliament in 1918, and represented Australia in the League of Nations Assembly. He was also High Commissioner in London (1933–45), where he died.

brucellosis [broosuh**loh**sis] A disease of animals, especially cattle, caused by micro-organisms of genus *Brucella*; can be caught by humans, commonly after drinking infected cow's or goat's milk, in which case it is called *undulent fever* or *Malta fever*; named after British bacteriologist Sir David Bruce (1855–1931); also known as **contagious abortion**. » cattle

Bruch, Max [brookh] (1838–1920) German composer, born in Cologne. He became musical director at Coblenz in 1865 and conducted the Liverpool Philharmonic Society (1880–3), introducing many of his choral works. He is best known for his Violin Concerto in G minor, the *Kol nidrei* variations, and the *Scottish Fantasy*. He died in Berlin.

Brücke, die [**brü**ker] (Ger 'bridge') The name adopted by a group of avant-garde artists active in Dresden, 1905–13, including Ernst Ludwig Kirchner (1880–1938), Karl Schmitt-Rottluff (1884–1976), Erich Heckel (1883–1970), and slightly later, Emil Nolde (1867–1956) and Max Pechstein (1881–1955). Unlike the more abstract Blaue Reiter group, they painted portraits, landscapes, and figurative subjects in a crude, harsh style based on van Gogh and Gauguin, and influenced by Oceanic art in Dresden Ethnological Museum. Their most striking works are prints, especially bold and expressive woodcuts. » avant garde; Blaue Reiter, der; Expressionism; German art; Kirchner; Nolde; woodcut

Bruckner, Anton [**brook**ner] (1824–96) Austrian composer and organist, born at Ansfelden. He held several posts as organist, and became professor of composition at the Vienna Conservatory (1868–91). His fame chiefly rests on his nine symphonies (the last unfinished), but he also wrote four impressive masses, several smaller sacred works, and many choral works. His music, which shows the influence of Wagner and Schubert, was given a mixed reception during his lifetime. He died in Vienna.

Brueghel » **Breughel**

Bruges [broozh], Flemish **Brugge** 51°13N 3°14E, pop (1982) 118 048. Port and capital town of Brugge district, West Flanders province, NW Belgium; 12 km/7 ml S of Zeebrugge; known as the 'Venice of the north'; chief market town of the Hanseatic League and a major centre of the woollen and cloth trade; connected by canals to several cities and the North Sea; railway; port handles crude oil, coal, iron ore, general cargo, fish; traditional centre for lace; steel, cotton, furniture, brewing, paints, light engineering; one of the best-preserved mediaeval European cities; Gothic town hall (1376–1420), Chapel of the Holy Blood, Church of Our Lady (12th–13th-c), 13th–14th-c market hall, with a 13th–15th-c belfry; Procession of the Holy Blood (every Ascension Day), Pageant of the Golden Tree (every 5th year). » Belgium [i]; Hanseatic League

Brugge [**broo**guh] » **Bruges**

bruise Damage to the skin and subcutaneous tissues, but without breaking the skin, usually caused by a blow from a blunt instrument or object. There is damage to the underlying local blood vessels, which is responsible for the swelling and for the red, blue, and yellow discolouration over the affected area. » blood vessels [i]; skin [i]

bruitisme [brwee**teezm**] French futuristic music of the 1920s which used percussion and electronics to suggest machinery. Antheil's *Ballet mécanique* (1926, Mechanical Ballet) was performed by eight pianos, player piano, four xylophones, two electric bells, two aeroplane propellors, tam-tam, four bass drums, and siren. » Antheil; electronic music; percussion [i]

Brummell, George Bryan, byname **Beau Brummell** (1778–1840) British dandy, a leader of early 19th-c fashion, born in London. He was educated at Eton, and while at Oxford was less distinguished for studiousness than for the exquisiteness of his dress and manners. He became a leader of early 19th-c fashionable society, and for 20 years had the Prince Regent (later George IV) as friend and admirer. A quarrel and gambling debts forced him to flee to France in 1816, where for many years he had varied fortune. He died in the pauper lunatic asylum at Caen.

Brunei, official name **State of Brunei Darussalam** (Islamic Sultanate of Brunei) [**broo**niy] pop (1990e) 259 000; area 5 765 sq km/2 225 sq ml. State on the NW coast of Borneo, SE Asia, divided into four districts; bounded by the South China Sea (NW), and on all other sides by Sarawak; divided into two sections by the Limbang R valley of Sarawak; capital Bandar Seri Begawan (formerly Brunei Town); other towns include Kuala Belait, Seria, Tutonga; timezone GMT +8; ethnic groups include (65%) Malay and (20%) Chinese; official language, Malay, but English widely spoken; official religion, Islam; unit of currency, the Brunei dollar of 100 sen; swampy coastal plain, rising through foothills to a mountainous region on Sarawak border; equatorial rainforest covers 75% of land area; tropical climate, with high temperatures and humidity,

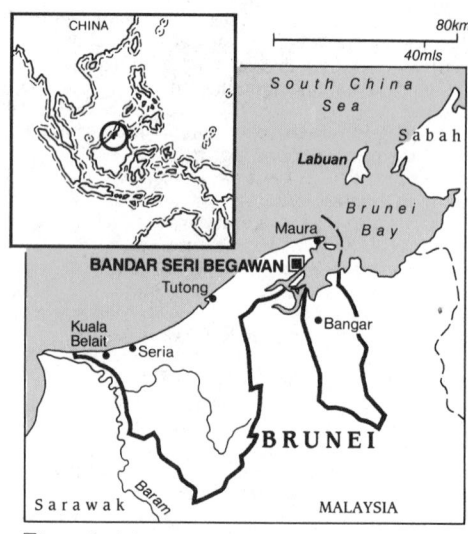

□ *international airport*

and no marked seasons; average daily temperature 24–30°C; annual average rainfall 2 540 mm/100 in on coast, doubling in the interior; formerly a powerful Muslim sultanate, its name (as Borneo) being given by Europeans to the whole island; under British protection, 1888; internal self-government, 1971; independent, 1983; a constitutional monarchy with the Sultan as head of state, advised by a Privy Council, a 20-member Legislative Council, a Religious Council and a Council of Succession; largely dependent on oil (discovered 1929) and gas resources; main crops, rice, bananas, peppers; some rubber and timber. » Bandar Seri Begawan; RR24 national holidays; RR44 political leaders

Brunel, Isambard Kingdom (1806–59) British engineer, born at Portsmouth, Hampshire. He worked in his father's office, and helped to plan the Thames Tunnel. He himself planned the Clifton Suspension Bridge (1829–31, completed 1864), and the Hungerford Suspension Bridge (1841–5) over the Thames. He designed the *Great Western* (1837), the first steamship built to cross the Atlantic, the *Great Britain* (1843), the first ocean screw-steamer, and the *Great Eastern* (1853–8), then the largest vessel ever built. He was also engineer to Great Western Railway, and constructed many docks. He died in London. » bridge (engineering) [i]; ship [i]

Brunel, Sir Marc Isambard (1769–1849) French engineer and inventor, born at Hacqueville. He fled from the French Revolution in 1793, going first to the USA, where he was architect and chief engineer in New York. He settled in England in 1799, constructed many public works, and solved many of the problems of underwater tunnelling. His main achievement was the 460 m/503 yd Thames Tunnel from Rotherhithe to Wapping (1825–43). He was knighted in 1841, and died in London. » Brunel, Isambard Kingdom

Brunelleschi, Filippo [brooneleskee] (1377–1446) Italian architect, born and died in Florence. He trained first as a goldsmith and sculptor before his failure in 1402 to win the competition for the second door of the Florence Baptistry led him to architecture. In Florence he designed the dome for the Cathedral (1417–34), the Ospedale degli Innocenti (1419) and the Church of San Lorenzo (1418 onwards). The first great Renaissance architect, he had a profound influence upon his successors. » Italian art; Renaissance

Brunhild, Brunhilde, or **Brynhild** [**broon**hild] In Norse mythology, a Valkyrie who has assumed human form. Odin places her behind a wall of flame where she lies in an enchanted sleep; she is woken by Sigurd, who is able to leap the barrier on his horse Grani. Tricked into marrying Gunnar, she finally kills herself on Sigurd's funeral pyre. In the similar Nibelungen legend, she is the wife of Gunther. » Gudrun; Sigurd; Valkyries

Bruno, St (of Cologne) (c.1030–1101), feast day 6 October. Founder of the Carthusian order, born at Cologne. He was rector of the cathedral school at Reims, but withdrew in 1084 to the wild mountains of Chartreuse, near Grenoble, where with six friends he founded the austere Carthusians. In 1091 he established a second monastery at La Torre, Calabria, where he died. » Carthusians; Chartreuse, La Grande

Bruno, Giordano (1548–1600) Italian hermetic thinker, born at Nola, near Naples. At first a Dominican, his opinions caused him to flee to Geneva (1578). He then went to Paris (1581), where he lectured, then (1583) to London. He travelled throughout Europe until 1591, when he was arrested by the Inquisition and, after an eight-year trial, burnt in Rome. His philosophy was pantheist and sympathetic to Copernicus's theory of the universe. His most famous works are *De l'infinito universo e mondi* (1584, On the Infinite Universe and Worlds) and *Spaccio de la bestia trionfante* (1584, The Expulsion of the Triumphant Beast). » Copernicus; hermetic; pantheism

Brunswick, Ger **Braunschweig** [**brown**shviyk] 52°17N 10°28E, pop (1983) 257 100. Capital of Braunschweig district, Germany; manufacturing and commercial city on the R Oker; capital of former duchy of Braunschweig; Mittelland Canal to the N; railway; technical university (1745); chemical engineering, foodstuffs, sugar, machinery, packaging, lorries, precision tools; Romanesque cathedral (12th-c), castle (12th-c), town hall (14th–15th-c). » Germany [i]

brush turkey A bird native to Japan and Australasia; solitary; seldom flies; plumage black; tail folded vertically; head and neck naked except for some hair-like feathers; eats fruit and insects. (Family: *Megapodiidae*, 6 species.) » megapode

brussel sprout A type of cultivated cabbage producing shoots or sprouts in all the axils of the leaves on the main stem. These sprouts resemble miniature cabbages, and can be harvested over a long period, especially in winter. (*Brassica oleracea*. Family: *Cruciferae*). » cabbage

Brussels, Flemish **Brussel**, Fr **Bruxelles**, ancient **Broucsella** 50°50N 4°21E, pop (1982) 138 893 (excluding suburbs). Commercial and cultural city in Brabant province, Belgium; capital of Belgium lying at the geographical mid-point of the country; divided into the Lower Town, intersected by several branches of the R Senne, and the Upper Town, set on the crest of the hills to the E; inner city surrounded by 18 suburbs with independent administrations; major mediaeval wool centre; capital of Spanish and Austrian Netherlands; headquarters of many international organizations, such as the EEC and NATO; linked to the North Sea by the Willebroek Canal; linguistic frontier between Flemings and Walloons runs just S of the city; officially Brussels is bilingual, but French predominates in the centre, Flemish in the suburbs; archbishopric; Brussels National Airport (Zaventem); railway; underground system; Free University of Brussels (1834); St Louis and St Aloysius private universities; industry largely outside the city, leaving the centre to the service sector; textiles, lace, carpets, porcelain, glass, metals, cement, chemicals, engineering, electronics and electrical goods, vehicles, publishing, brewing, tobacco, foodstuffs; Royal Military School; several royal academies of fine arts and royal conservatories; town hall (15th–18th-c), royal palace (1827–9, rebuilt 1905); Palais de la Nation (1779–83); cathedral (13th–15th-c), Church of Notre-Dame de la Chapelle (begun 1210); Ommegang (processions, Jul). » Belgium [i]; European Economic Community; NATO

Brussels, Treaty of 1 (1948) A treaty of economic, social, and cultural collaboration and collective self-defence signed by Belgium, France, Luxembourg, the Netherlands, and the UK. It set up the so-called Brussels Treaty Organization, with the principle aim of joint action to resist aggression. It was superseded by the Treaty of Paris and the Western European Union. **2** (1973) A treaty which enabled Britain, Denmark, and Ireland to join the European Economic Community. These three countries and Norway had applied to join in 1961, but further negotiations had been vetoed by President de Gaulle in 1963. After his resignation, it was agreed to hold fresh negotiations. Following signature of the treaty, Norway failed to ratify after a referendum. » de Gaulle; European Coal and Steel Community; European Economic Community

Brutalism or **New Brutalism** An architectural concept of the 1950s, in which the buildings often have large distinct blocks of exposed concrete. It is typified by the work of Le Corbusier at Chandigarh, India, and at Marseilles, France, and by his British followers James Stirling, William Gowan, and Alison and Peter Smithson. » Corbusier, Le

Brutus, Marcus Junius (c.85–42 BC) A leader of the group who assassinated Julius Caesar. He sided with Pompey when the civil war broke out, but after Pharsalus submitted to Caesar, and was appointed Governor of Cisalpine Gaul. Cassius prevailed on him to join the conspiracy against Caesar (44 BC). Defeated by Antony and Octavian at Philippi, he killed himself. » Caesar; Cassius; Philippi, Battle of

Bruxelles [brüksel] » **Brussels**

Bryggen [**brüg**gen] A world heritage site in Bergen, SW Norway. Probably founded in the 11th-c, it retains a large number of wooden gabled buildings, and is the best surviving example of the traditional wooden towns of N Europe. » Bergen

bryophyte A spore-bearing, non-vascular plant belonging to the Division *Bryophyta*, which includes some 25 000 species of moss, liverwort, and hornwort. Bryophytes have conducting cells but lack true vascular tissue; they have rhizoids, thread-like outgrowths which anchor the plant and conduct water, but no true roots. Leaves, if present, are simple structures, usually one cell thick, with a slightly thicker central strand. The dominant generation is the gametophyte, consisting of either a thallus or a small, leafy plant. The gametes are produced in *antheridia* (male) and *archegonia* (female), borne either directly on the surface of the plant or on erect, fleshy-stalked, and often complex structures called *gametangiophores*. The sporophyte generation consists simply of a long-stalked spore capsule growing directly from a fertilized archegonium. It is very short-lived, and is so dependent on the gametophyte that it is termed parasitic. Asexual reproduction can also occur by means of *gemmae* – multicellular dics or filaments produced in special cups, either on leaf tips or on stalks (*pseudopodia*), and able to grow into new plants in the same way that small bulbs of flowering plants do. Bryophytes are mainly terrestrial plants, often epiphytic, but very vulnerable to desiccation, and require water for the transfer of gametes from antheridium to archegonium; they are mostly restricted to damp or humid habitats. They are increasingly regarded as important indicator plants (eg in pollution studies). (Division: *Bryophyta*.) » algae; epiphyte; gametophyte; hornwort; liverwort; moss; rhizoid; sporophyte; thallus

Bryozoa [briyuh**zoh**a] A phylum of small, aquatic animals that typically form colonies comprising a few to a million individuals (*zooids*); each zooid typically has a tentacle-like feeding apparatus around its mouth; colony forms a calcareous, chitinous, or gelatinous skeleton; c.4000 living species, mostly marine, and attached to hard substrates or seaweeds, rarely to soft sediments; some found in fresh water; abundant as fossils; also known as **moss animals**. » calcium; chitin; fossil; gelatin; phylum

Brythonic » **Celtic languages**

Brzezinski, Zbigniew [bruh**zhin**skee] (1928–) US educator and statesman, born in Poland. Educated at McGill University (Montreal) and Harvard, he taught at Harvard and Columbia, then served as National Security Adviser under President Carter. He is now professor of political science at Columbia University. » Carter, Jimmy

bubble chamber A device for detecting the paths of nuclear particles, devised in 1952 by Donald Glaser. The chamber contains liquid hydrogen kept just above its boiling point by pressure. The pressure is briefly released. Before general boiling can take place, the passage of a particle produces a local instability which initiates evaporation, forming visible bubbles of gas along its path. The phenomenon is very brief and is operated cyclically. The track patterns are photographed for later analysis. » cloud chamber; Glaser; hydrogen; neutrino; particle detectors/physics

bubble memory A type of computer memory first produced as a storage medium in the mid-1970s. These devices operate as read/write memories by circulating very small polarized magnetic bubbles which represent single bits. They have the advantage of being extremely sturdy, both mechanically and in terms of their ability to operate over large temperature ranges, but they are relatively slow and expensive. They find some applications in harsh environments. » memory, computer

Buber, Martin [**boo**ber] (1878–1965) Jewish theologian and philosopher, born in Vienna. He studied philosophy at Vienna, Berlin, and Zürich, then 1916–24 was founding editor of *Der Jude* (The Jew). He was professor of comparative religion at Frankfurt (1923–33), then directed the Central Office for Jewish Adult Education until 1938 when he fled to Palestine. He became professor of the sociology of religion at Jerusalem, and published profusely. His most influential work as a figure of religious existentialism was the early *Ich und Du* (I and Thou, 1922). He died in Jerusalem. » existentialism; Zionism

bubonic plague » **plague**

Bucaramanga [bookara**mang**ga] 7°08N 73°10W, pop (1985) 493 929. Capital of Santander department, NC Colombia; NNE of Bogotá, in the Cordillera Oriental at 1 018 m/3 340 ft; the 'garden city of Colombia'; founded, 1622; railway; university (1947); coffee, cacao, tobacco, cotton; Parque Santander, Parque García Romero, amusement park. » Colombia [i]

buccaneers Pirates and adventurers who preyed upon Spanish shipping in the W Indies and along the Spanish Main in the 17th-c; mainly Dutch, English, and French. The name derived from *boucan* (native American for 'barbecue'), because they roasted meat on board ship. Referred to by the Spanish as *corsarios* ('corsairs'), by the Dutch as *vrijbuiter* ('freebooters'), and by the English as *privateers*, they flourished between 1630 and 1689. Privateering was accepted as illegal by most European powers in 1856 (Declaration of Paris), and universally outlawed by the Hague Convention of 1907. » corsairs; Grand Alliance, War of the; Spanish Main

Bucer or **Butzer, Martin** [**boot**ser] (1491–1551) German Protestant reformer, born at Schlettstadt, Alsace. He joined the Dominicans, and studied theology at Heidelberg, but in 1521 left the order, married a former nun, and settled in Strasburg. He adopted a middle course in the disputes about the Eucharist between Luther and Zwingli. In 1549 he became professor of divinity at Cambridge, where he influenced the writing of the Prayer Book of 1552, and made many attempts to mediate between the conflicting religious groups of the time. His chief work was a translation and exposition of the Psalms (1529). » Book of Common Prayer; Luther; Protestantism; Reformation; Zwingli

Buchan, John, 1st Baron Tweedsmuir (1875–1940) British author and statesman, born at Perth, Scotland. Educated at Glasgow and Oxford, in 1901 he was called to the Bar. During World War 1 he served on HQ staff (1916–17), when he became Director of Information. He was MP for the Scottish Universities (1927–35), when he was made a baron, and became Governor-General of Canada until 1940. In 1937 he was made a Privy Councillor and chancellor of Edinburgh University. Despite his busy public life, Buchan wrote over 50 books, especially fast-moving adventure stories, such as *Prester John* (1910) and *The Thirty-nine Steps* (1915). His biographical works include *Montrose* (1928) and *Sir Walter Scott* (1932). He died in Montreal. » biography; spy story

Buchanan, James (1791–1868) US statesman and 15th President (1857–61), born at Stony Batter, Pennsylvania. Educated at Dickinson College, he was admitted to the Bar (1812), became a Senator (1834), Secretary of State (1845), and Democratic President (1857). During his administration the slavery question came to a head. He supported the establishment of Kansas as a slave state, but his compromise failed to avert the Civil War. He retired from politics in 1861, and died at Lancaster, Pennsylvania. » American Civil War; slavery

Buchanan, James M (1919–) US economist, born at Murfreesboro, Tennessee, and educated there and in Chicago. He was awarded the Nobel Prize for Economics in 1986 for his work on the theories of public choice. He has held numerous chairs since 1950, currently at George Mason University (1983–), and since 1969 has been director of the Center for Public Choice.

Bucharest, Romanian **București**, ancient **Cetatea Damboviței** 44°25N 26°07E, pop (1983) 1 995 156. Capital and largest city of Romania, on the R Damboviț; founded, 14th-c; important commercial centre on the trade route to Constantinople; capital of Wallachia, 1698; capital of Romania, 1861; badly damaged by German bombing in World War 2; airport (Baneasa); railway; university (1864); technical university (1819); oil pipeline link with Ploești; engineering, metallurgy, machinery, oil refining, textiles, chemicals, food processing, vehicles; Domnita Baleasa Church (18th-c), St George Church (17th-c), Palace of the Republic, Palace of St Synod, Atheneum arts and music centre. » Romania [i]

Buchman, Frank (Nathan Daniel) (1878–1961) US evangelist, founder of the 'Group' and 'Moral Rearmament' movements, born at Pennsburg, Pennsylvania. He was a Lutheran minister in charge of a hospice for under-privileged boys in Philadelphia (1902–7), travelled extensively in the East, and in 1921, believing that there was an imminent danger of the collapse of civilization, founded at Oxford the 'Group Movement'. It was labelled the 'Oxford Group' until 1938, when it rallied under the slogan 'Moral Rearmament'. After World War 2 the movement emerged in a more political guise as an alternative to capitalism and communism. » evangelicalism; Lutheranism; Moral Rearmament

Büchner, Georg (1813–37) German poet, born at Goddelau, Darmstadt. He studied medicine, became involved in revolutionary politics, and fled to Zürich. His best-known works are the poetical dramas *Dantons Tod* (1835, Danton's Death) and

Woyzek (1837). He died in Zürich. » German literature; poetry

Buck, Pearl S(ydenstricker) (1892–1973) US novelist, born at Hillsboro, West Virginia. She lived in China from infancy, and her earliest novels are coloured by her experiences there. *The Good Earth* (1931) earned her the 1938 Nobel Prize for Literature. In 1935 she returned to the USA, and wrote many novels about the contemporary American scene, such as *The Patriot* (1939) and *Dragon Seed* (1942). Five novels were written under the pseudonym of **John Sedges**. She died at Danby, Vermont. » American literature; novel

Buck, Peter Henry, also known as **Te Rangi Hiroa** [tay **rah**ngee **hi**roha] (1879–1951) New Zealand Maori scholar and author. He practised medicine, was an MP (1909–14), served in World War 1, then became an anthropologist. In 1927 he joined the Bishop Museum in Honolulu, Hawaii, and was director there from 1936 until his death. » Maoris

buckhound » **deerhound**

Buckingham, George Villiers, 1st Duke of (1592–1628) English statesman and court favourite, born at Brooksby, Leicestershire. He was knighted by James I, and raised to the peerage as Viscount Villiers (1616), Earl of Buckingham (1617), Marquis (1618), and Duke (1623). In 1623 he failed to negotiate the marriage of Prince Charles to the daughter of the Spanish King, but later arranged the marriage to Henrietta Maria of France. The abortive expedition against Cadiz (1625) exposed him to impeachment by the Commons, and only a dissolution rescued him. An expedition against France failed (1627), and while planning a second attack, he was assassinated at Portsmouth by John Felton, a discontented subaltern. » James I (of England)

Buckingham, George Villiers, 2nd Duke of (1628–87) English statesman, born in London. After his father's assassination, he was brought up with Charles I's children, and went into exile after the Royalist defeat in the Civil War. His estates were recovered at the Restoration, and he became a member of the Cabal of Charles II. He was instrumental in Clarendon's downfall (1667), but lost power to Arlington, and was dismissed in 1674 for alleged Catholic sympathies. He died at Kirby Moorside, Yorkshire. » Arlington, Earl of; Cabal; Charles II (of England); Restoration

Buckingham Palace The 600-room residence of the British sovereign in London, built for George IV on the site of his parents' home, Buckingham House. The architect, John Nash, was dismissed on the king's death in 1830, and the palace remained unused until Queen Victoria's accession in 1837. » Nash, John

Buckinghamshire pop (1987e) 621 300; area 1 883 sq km/ 727 sq ml. County in SC England, divided into five districts; drained by the Ouse and Thames Rivers; crossed in the S by the Chiltern Hills; extensive woodland; county town Aylesbury; chief towns include Bletchley, High Wycombe, Buckingham; mainly agriculture, also furniture, bricks, printing, high technology. » Aylesbury; England [i]

buckler fern A perennial fern, found almost everywhere; rhizomatous; fronds form a tuft or crown; bi- or tri-pinnate, scaly; sori with kidney-shaped indusia, borne near the midrib. (Genus: *Dryopteris*, 150 species. Family: *Polypodiaceae*.) » fern; pinnate; rhizome; sorus

Buckley, Jr, William F(rank) (1925–) US political writer and editor, born in New York City. Educated at Yale, he founded the conservative political journal *National Review* in 1955, making it the primary voice of the intellectual US right. He ran for Mayor of New York in 1963, and is author of many works of fiction and nonfiction. » right wing

buckminsterfullerene [buhkminster**ful**ereen] C_{60}. An almost spherical molecule, thought to be an ingredient of soots; also called **soccerene**. Each carbon atom is bonded to three others so that the surface consists of 12 pentagons and 20 hexagons. » carbon

buckthorn A thorny, spreading, deciduous shrub or small tree 4–10 m/13–30 ft, native to Europe and the Mediterranean region; leaves oval, toothed, in opposite pairs; flowers tiny, green, parts in fours; berries 5–10 mm/0.2–0.3 in, black, mildly poisonous, and purgative. (*Rhamnus catharticus*. Family: *Rhamnaceae*.) » deciduous plants; shrub; tree [i]

buckwheat An erect annual with spear-shaped leaves and a terminal cluster of tiny pink or white flowers; fruit a triangular nut c.6 mm/¼ in long; native to C Asia and cultivated as a substitute for cereals. (*Fagopyrum esculentum*. Family: *Polygonaceae*.) » annual; cereals

Budaeus, Guglielmus [boo**day**us] or **Guillaume Budé** (1467–1540) French scholar, born and died in Paris. Educated in Paris and Orleans, he held several diplomatic posts under Louis XII and Francis I. At his suggestion Francis founded the Collège de France. As royal librarian he founded the collection which later became the Bibliothèque Nationale. Of his works on philology, philosophy, and jurispruduence, the two best known are on ancient coins (1514) and the *Commentarii Linguae Graecae* (1519, Commentaries on the Greek Language). » Francis I (of France); Louis XII

Budapest [booda**pest**] 47°29N 19°05E, pop (1984e) 2 064 000. Capital and largest city of Hungary, on R Danube where it enters the Great Plain; old-world Buda on W bank hills, modern Pest on E bank, unified in 1873; Buda on site of Roman colony of Aquincum; major cultural and trading centre in the 15th-c; scene of popular uprising, crushed by Soviet troops, 1956; Eötvöos Loránd University (1635); universities of medicine (1769), economic science (1948), horticulture (1853); Hungarian Academy of Sciences; airport (Ferihegy); railway; underground; iron, steel, chemicals, pharmaceuticals, textiles; St Matthias Church (13th-c), Royal Palace, Parliament Building, museum of fine arts, national theatre, opera house; Buda castle and banks of the Danube are a world heritage site. » Hungary [i]

Budd, Zola (1966–) South African-British athlete, born at Bloemfontein, South Africa. She caused a controversy by obtaining British citizenship in 1984 and then being selected for the British Olympic squad. There was further controversy at the Los Angeles Games when she was involved in an incident which led to Mary Decker (USA) being tripped during the 3 000 m. She was the European Cup gold medallist at 3 000 m in 1985, the UK 1 500 m champion in 1984, and world amateur champion at 3 000 m in 1985 and at 1 500 m in 1986. She set the 5 000 m world record in 1984 and 1985, and was world cross-country champion in 1985 and 1986. A hip injury and public attitudes caused her to retire in 1988, and return to South Africa shortly before the Olympics. » athletics

Buddh Gaya or **Bodh Gaya** [bud **gah**ya] A sacred Buddhist site in Bihar, India. Since the 3rd-c BC, shrines have marked the spot where Gautama Buddha attained enlightenment. » Bihar; Buddha

Buddha (c.563–c.483 BC) The founder of Buddhism, 'the enlightened one', born the son of the rajah of the Sakya tribe ruling at Kapilavastu, north of Benares. His personal name was Siddhartha; but he was also known by his family name of Gautama. When about 30, he left the luxuries of the court, his beautiful wife, and all earthly ambitions for the life of an ascetic; after several years of severe austerities he saw in meditation and contemplation the way to enlightenment. For some 40 years he taught, gaining many disciples and followers, and died at Kusinagara in Oudh. » Buddhism

Buddhism A tradition of thought and practice originating in India c.2 500 years ago, and now a world religion, deriving from the teaching of Buddha (Siddhartha Gautama), who is regarded as one of a continuing series of enlightened beings. The teaching of Buddha is summarized in the *Four Noble Truths*, the last of which affirms the existence of a path leading to deliverance from the universal human experience of suffering. A central tenet is the law of *karma*, by which good and evil deeds result in appropriate reward or punishment in this life or in a succession of rebirths. Through a proper understanding of this condition, and by obedience to the right path, human beings can break the chain of karma. The Buddha's path to deliverance is through morality (*sila*), meditation (*samadhi*), and wisdom (*panna*), as set out in the *Eightfold Path*. The goal is *Nirvana*, which means 'the blowing out' of the fires of all desires, and the absorption of the self into the infinite. All Buddhas are greatly revered, and a place of special importance is accorded to Gautama.

There are two main traditions within Buddhism, dating from its earliest history. **Theravada** Buddhism adheres to the strict and narrow teachings of the early Buddhist writings: salvation is possible for only the few who accept the severe discipline and effort necessary to achieve it. **Mahayana** Buddhism is more liberal, and makes concessions to popular piety: it teaches that salvation is possible for everyone, and introduced the doctrine of the bodhisattva (or personal saviour). As Buddhism spread, other schools grew up, among which are Ch'an or Zen, Lamaism, Tendai, Nichiren, and Soka Gakkai. Recently Buddhism has attracted growing interest in the West. The only complete canon of Buddhist scripture is called the Pali canon, after the language in which it is written. It forms the basic teaching for traditional Theravada Buddhism, but other schools have essentially the same canon written in Sanskrit. Mahayana Buddhists acknowledge many more texts as authoritative.

Underlying the diversity of Buddhist belief and practice is a controlling purpose. The aim is to create the conditions favourable to spiritual development, leading to liberation or deliverance from bondage to suffering. This is generally seen as involving meditation, personal discipline, and spiritual exercises of various sorts. This common purpose has made it possible for Buddhism to be very flexible in adapting its organization, ceremony, and pattern of belief to different social and cultural situations. Reliable figures are unobtainable, but over 1 000 million people live in lands where Buddhism is a significant religious influence. » Ananda; bodhisattva; Buddha; Ch'an: Dalai Lama; Eightfold Path; Four Noble Truths; karma; Lamaism; Mahayana; mandala; mantra; Nichiren Buddhism; Nirvana; pagoda; Pure Land Buddhism; sangha; Sanskrit; Soka Gakkai; tantra; Theravada; Zen Buddhism

budding The formation of buds by cell division within a localized area of a shoot. Budding is also a method of sexual reproduction in which a new individual develops as a direct growth off the body of the parent, and may subsequently become detached and lead a separate existence. » reproduction

buddleja or **buddleia** A deciduous shrub or small tree, native to warm regions, and widely cultivated and naturalized in many areas; flowers small, various colours, often scented, crowded in dense spikes or globular clusters. It is very attractive to insects, especially butterflies, hence the name **butterflybush** given to *Buddleja davidii*, the most commonly cultivated species. (Genus: *Buddleja*, 100 species. Family: *Loganiaceae*.) » shrub; tree [i]

Budé » **Budaeus**

Budge, Don, properly **John Donald** (1915–) US lawn tennis player, born at Oakland, California. He was the first person to complete the Grand Slam (the four major singles championships of Australia, France, Britain, and the USA) in one year (1938). He also won all three titles at Wimbledon in 1937 and 1938, and between 1935 and 1938 won 25 out of 29 Davis Cup rubbers in 11 ties. He turned professional in 1938. » tennis, lawn [i]

budgerigar A small parrot native to C Australia, and introduced in Florida; common; lives in nomadic flocks; eats grass seeds; nests in tree stumps or logs. It is a popular cage-bird, with many colour variations, but is usually green in the wild. (*Melopsittacus undulatus*. Family: *Psittacidae*.) » lovebird [i]; parrot; rosella

budget A monetary plan for a specified period of future time. A government budget is a statement of forecast expenditure in the following financial year, and of how the income needed will be raised (eg by taxation or borrowing). Most commercial organizations of any size prepare budgets to forecast sales revenue, operating costs, capital expenditure, and cash flow. They may also be prepared several years in advance, and amended annually. » deficit financing; public sector borrowing requirement

Buenaventura [bwenaven**too**ra] 3°51N 77°06W, pop (1984e) 122 500. Pacific seaport in Cauca department, SW Colombia; on the Bahia de Buenaventura; Colombia's most important Pacific trading port; founded, 1540; railway; fishing, fish canning; trade in coffee, hides, gold, platinum, sugar. » Colombia [i]

Buenos Aires [**bway**nos **iy**rays] 34°40S 58°30W, pop (1980) 2 908 001. Federal capital of Argentina in Gran Buenos Aires federal district, E Argentina; on S bank of R Plate; founded in 1536 as the city of the 'Puerto de Santa Maria del Buen Aire'; destroyed by Indians, and refounded 1580; formerly capital of the Spanish viceroyalty of La Plata; suburbs include Avellaneda (industrial), Olivos (residential), San Isidro (sporting and leisure resort), Quilmes (industrial), Tigre, and the old port district of La Boca; nine universities; airport (Ezeiza); two airfields; railway; metro; trade in beef and wool; brewing, textiles, ironware, glass; national gallery, opera house; Plaza de Mayo, town hall (Cabildo), presidential palace (Casa Rosada), cathedral; horse racing course. » Argentina [i]

buffalo » **African buffalo; bison; water buffalo**

Buffalo 42°53N 78°53W, pop (1980) 357 870. Seat of Erie County, W New York, USA; port on the Niagara R at the NE end of L Erie; second largest city in the state; railway; two universities (1846, 1867); motor vehicles and vehicle parts, machinery, steel; major league teams, Bills (football), Sabres (ice hockey); Albright-Knox art gallery, science museum. » New York

Buffalo Bill » **Cody, William F**

buffalo gnat » **black fly**

buffalo-weaver » **weaverbird**

buffer (chemistry) A system which resists change. In chemistry, usually a solution whose pH is not greatly affected by small additions of strong acids or bases. This is most effective when an acid and its conjugate base are present in approximately equal amounts. Some important buffer systems and the approximate pH at which they operate are: acetate (CH_3COOH and CH_3COO-), 4–5; carbonate (H_2CO_3 and HCO_3-); and ammonia (NH_4+ and NH_3), 9–10. Biological systems are particularly dependent upon buffers to maintain constant pH values. » acid; base (chemistry); pH

buffer (computing) In computing, a temporary storage area in memory for data. Buffers are often used when data is being transmitted between two devices with different working speeds, such as between a keyboard and the central processor. » memory, computer

buffer state A small state lying between two or more larger and potentially belligerent states, as a means of reducing border friction between them; often specially created for the purpose, though seldom successful. For example, after World War 1, attempts were made to create a buffer state between Germany and France involving Belgium, the Saar, the Rhine area, and Alsace-Lorraine.

Buffet, Bernard [**bü**fay] (1928–) French painter, born in Paris. He made his name in the early 1950s with murky still lifes and interiors with skinny, miserable figures painted in a sharp linear style and a neutral, almost monochromatic palette which seemed to catch the mood ('existential alienation') of postwar Paris. He has exhibited regularly in Paris and occasionally in London. In 1973 a Buffet Museum was established in Japan. » French art; still life

Buffon, Georges Louis Leclerc, Comte de ('Count of') [**bü**fõ] (1707–88) French naturalist, born at Montbard, Burgundy. He studied at Dijon, then devoted himself to science. In 1739 he was made director of the Jardin du Roi, and formed the design of his *Histoire naturelle* (1749–67, Natural History). His wide-ranging ideas led to fresh interest in natural science, and foreshadowed the theory of evolution. He was made Comte de Buffon in 1773, and died in Paris. » Buffon's needle [i]; evolution

Buffon's needle A problem first set and solved by French scientist Georges Buffon in 1777. If a straight thin needle length l is thrown at random onto a plane ruled with parallel lines a distance $a<l$ apart, what is the probability that the needle will cross one of the lines? Buffon showed that this probability was $\frac{2l}{\pi a}$. » Buffon

bug (computing) An error in a computer program or a fault in computer hardware. The process of detecting and correcting errors is known as **debugging**. » program, computer; hardware

bug (entomology) An insect with forewings leathery at base, membraneous near the tip, and folded over membraneous hindwings at rest; diverse in form and feeding habits; mouthparts modified into a snout for piercing and sucking; includes many crop pests and disease carriers. (Order: *Heteroptera*.) » assassin/bed/chinch/shield bug; capsid; cotton stainer; Heteroptera; insect [i]; lac insect; pond skater; scale insect; water boatman; water scorpion; whitefly

Bugatti, Ettore (Arco Isidoro) (1882–1947) Italian car manufacturer, born in Milan. He began designing cars in 1899 and set up his works in Strasbourg in 1907. World War 1 caused him to move to Italy and later to France, where his racing cars won international fame in the 1930s. » car [i]

Buginese or **Bugi** A major ethnic group of Celebes (Sulawesi), Indonesia, who live as rice cultivators, traders, and seafarers. They came from Makasar, in SW Celebes, but migrated into the Malay Archipelago after the Dutch East India Company took the city (1667). They established settlements and a state at Selanger (1710), were defeated by the Dutch in the 18th-c, were further weakened by conflict with the Malay states, and lost supremacy in the 19th-c. Population c.3.8 million. » Celebes

bugle (botany) A perennial with creeping, rooting stolons, native to Europe, the Mediterranean, and SW Asia; flowering stems square, erect; leaves in opposite pairs; flowers blue, 2-lipped, upper lip very short, lower 3-lobed, in whorls forming loose spikes; the whole plant often bronze-tinged. (*Ajuga reptans*. Family: *Labiatae*.) » perennial; stolon

bugle (music) A musical instrument made of brass or copper, curved elliptically and ending in a large bell. It normally has no valves and can therefore produce only those notes forming the first half-dozen harmonics above the fundamental (usually B♭). It has been used above all for sounding military calls. » brass instrument [i]; harmonic series [i]

bugloss [**byoo**glos] A bristly annual or biennial growing to 50 cm/20 in, native to Europe and Asia; leaves narrowly oblong with wavy margins; infloresence coiled; flowers 5 mm/0.2 in diameter with curved white tube, spreading bright-blue lobes, and white eye. (*Anchusa arvensis*. Family: *Boraginaceae*.) » annual; biennial; inflorescence [i]

buhl A technique of furniture decoration involving very elaborate inlays of brass, tortoiseshell, mother-of-pearl, and coloured wood, introduced into France in the 16th-c from Italy, but perfected by André Charles Buhl (or Boulle) and his sons. The present spelling is a 19th-c distortion. » brass; Buhl

Buhl, or **Boulle, André Charles** (1642–1732) French cabinet-maker, born and died in Paris. He studied drawing, painting, and sculpture, then became a furniture designer in the service of Louis XIV. He introduced **buhlwork**, a style of decorating furniture by inlaying metals, shells, pearls, etc on ebony – a technique which was continued by his four sons. He died at Paris. » Louis XIV

building society An institution which lends money to enable people to buy property (ie a mortgage loan). Their funds are derived from investors who obtain interest on the sum deposited. Interest paid to the society by the borrower is higher than the rate paid out. In the UK there are some 150 societies with over 40 million depositors (who are also shareholders). Following the Building Societies Act (1987) societies are permitted to provide other services. The US equivalent is the **savings and loan association**. » mortgage

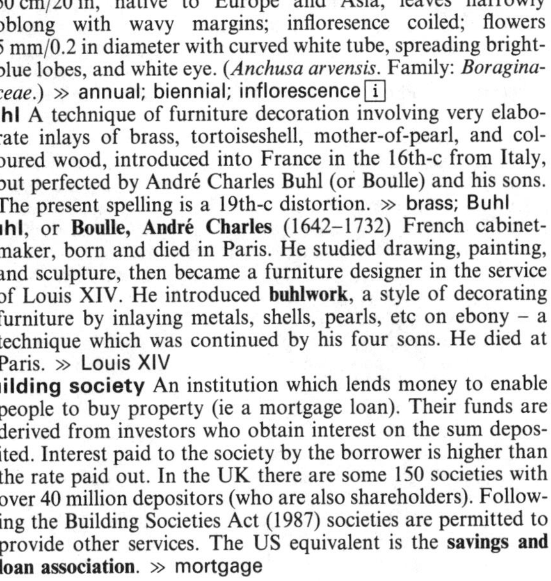

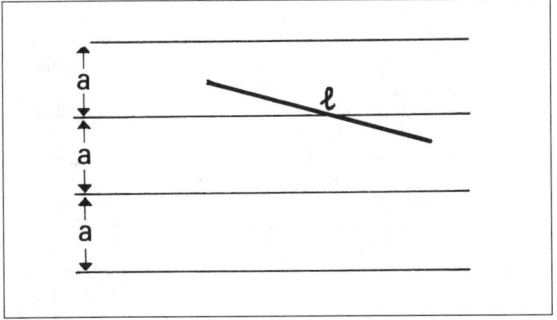

Buffon's needle

Bujumbura [bujum**boo**ra], formerly **Usumbura** 3°22S 29°21E, pop (1979) 172 201. Port and capital of Burundi, C Africa, at NE end of L Tanganyika; altitude 805 m/2 641 ft; founded in 1899 by German colonists; airport; university (1960); coffee and cotton processing, brewing, cement, textiles, soap, shoes, metal working; Museum of African Civilization. » Burundi [i]

Bukharin, Nikolay Ivanovich [bu**khah**rin] (1888–1938) Russian Marxist revolutionary and political theorist, born and educated in Moscow, and called by Lenin 'the darling of the Party'. He was active in the Bolshevik underground (1905–17), and after the February Revolution returned to Russia, playing a leading role in the organization of the October Revolution in Moscow. As a member of the Politburo (1924–9) he was a firm supporter of Lenin's New Economic Policy, and opposed Stalin's collectivization campaign. In 1937 he was arrested in Stalin's Great Purge, expelled from the Party, tried on trumped-up charges, and shot. In 1987 he was officially rehabilitated by a board of judicial inquiry, and posthumously readmitted to the Party in 1988. » Bolsheviks; Brest-Litovsk, Treaty of; February Revolution; Lenin; October Revolution; Stalin

Bukkyo [**bu**kyoh] The Japanese conception of Buddhism (Chinese *Mahayana*, Sanskrit 'great vehicle'). Buddhism came to Japan from Korea in the 6th-c. Today, the easy-to-understand 'Pure Land' is the most popular form; Zen is respected but not widespread. For many Japanese, Buddhism primarily means funeral ceremonies and remembering ancestors. Several of the 'new religions' claim to be Buddhist. » Buddhism

Bulawayo [boola**way**oh] 20°10S 28°43E, pop (1982) 414 000. Capital of Matabeleland North province, Zimbabwe, 370 km/230 ml SW of Harare; second largest city in Zimbabwe; founded, 1893; airport; railway junction; commercial, industrial, and tourist centre; asphalt, agricultural equipment, confectionery, electrical equipment, tyres, cement; national parks nearby. » Matabeleland; Zimbabwe [i]

bulb A highly modified shoot forming an underground storage organ. It is composed of overlapping leaves or leaf bases, swollen with food reserves which nourish early growth. The bulbs usually persist from year to year, the reserves being replenished before the plant dies back. » bulbil; corm

bulbil A small organ resembling a bulb, but produced above ground, either in a leaf axil or in the inflorescence in place of some flowers. It produces a new plant after falling from the parent. » bulb; inflorescence [i]

bulbul A bird native to tropical Africa, Madagascar, and S Asia; short wings, long tail; stiff bristles at base of pointed bill; noisy and gregarious; inhabits woodland or cultivation; eats fruit and insects. (Family: *Pycnonotidae*, 120 species.)

Bulgakov, Mikhail Afanasievich (1891–1940) Russian writer, born in Kiev. He studied medicine, but in 1920 worked as a journalist in Moscow, where he wrote several plays, novels, and short stories. His major novels include *Belaya gvardiya* (1925, The White Guard, rewritten as a play, 1926). Several of his works were considered too outspoken, were withdrawn, and re-emerged only in the 1960s. He died in Moscow. » Russian literature

Bulganin, Nikolai Aleksandrovich [bul**gah**nin] (1895–1975) Soviet statesman and Prime Minister (1955–8), born at Nizhni-Novgorod. An early member of the Communist Party, he was mayor of Moscow (1933–7), a member of the Military Council in World War 2, and Minister of Defence in 1946. After Stalin's death he became Vice-Premier in Malenkov's government, and was made Premier after Malenkov resigned (1955), with Khrushchev wielding real power. 'B and K' travelled extensively abroad, conducting propaganda through lengthy letters to Western statesmen. He was dismissed in 1958, and retired into obscurity. He died in Moscow. » communism; Khrushchev; Malenkov

Bulgaria, official name **Republic of Bulgaria**, Bulgarian **Republika Bulgariya** pop (1990e) 8 997 000; area 110 912 sq km/42 812 sq ml. Republic in the E of the Balkan Peninsula, SE Europe, divided into 28 provinces (*okruzi*, sing. *okrug*); bounded to the N by Romania, W by Yugoslavia, SE by Turkey, S by Greece, and E by the Black Sea; capital Sofia;

chief towns include Plovdiv, Varna, Ruse, Bourgas, Stara Zagora, Pleven; timezone GMT +2; population c.85% Bulgarian, with Turkish, Gypsy, and Macedonian minorities; officially atheist, but religious background of people is 85% Bulgarian Orthodox and 13% Muslim; unit of currency, the lev of 100 stotinki.

Physical description and climate. Traversed W–E by the Balkan Mts, rising to heights of over 2 000 m/6 500 ft; Rhodope Mts in the SW rise to nearly 3 000 m/9 600 ft; Bulgarian lowlands stretch S from the R Danube with an average width of 100 km/60 ml; rivers flow N to the Danube or S to the Aegean; largely continental climate, with hot summers and cold winters, but to the S the climate is increasingly Mediterranean; winters slightly warmer on Black Sea coast.

History and government. Bulgars crossed the Danube in the 7th-c; their empire continually at war with the Byzantines until destroyed by the Turks in the 14th-c; remained under Turkish rule until 1878; full independence 1908; a kingdom 1908–46; aligned with Germany in World Wars; occupied by USSR, 1944; Socialist People's Republic founded, 1946; 1971, single-chamber National Assembly established, with 400 members elected for five years; elects a State Council, to which a Council of Ministers is accountable; no constitutional single head of state, but a Chairman of the State Council; local government in the hands of People's Councils elected for 2½ years. New constitution, 1991.

Economy. Mainly agricultural produce, especially grain, fruits, vegetables, rice, tobacco, sheep, hogs, poultry, cheese, sunflower seeds, unginned cotton, attar of roses; also, food processing, machine building, chemicals, metal products, electronics, textiles, wine; coal, iron ore; offshore oil (Black Sea) and natural gas; tourism; 75% of farmland held by agro-industrial complexes – amalgamations of collective and state farms with food-processing plants and farm machinery stations. » Balkan Mountains; Black Sea; communism; Sofia; RR24 national holidays; RR44 political leaders

Bulgarian » **Slavic languages**

Bulge, Battle of the (1944) The last desperate German armoured counter-offensive through the Ardennes in World War 2 (beginning 16 Dec), to prevent the Allied invasion of Germany. It achieved early success, but ground to a halt, and the Germans were then pushed to retreat by the Allies by the end of January 1945. » World War 2

bulimia nervosa [byoo**lim**ia ner**voh**sa] A condition typified by repeated episodes of binge eating and frequent vomiting and purging, associated with a preoccupation with control of body weight and a feeling of lack of control over eating behaviour. The vast majority of patients are female, and patients report a high incidence of relatives who are obese and/or who have had a depressive illness. It is the reverse of anorexia nervosa, with which curiously it is occasionally associated in cycles. In rare cases it results from disturbance of the hypothalamus. » anorexia nervosa; hypothalamus; mental disorders

bulk modulus The negative ratio of (*a*) change in pressure applied to a block of some material to (*b*) the fractional change in volume of the block; symbol K, unit Pa (pascal); also called the **modulus of compression**. It is constant for a given material, eg for glass, $K = 0.37 \times 10^{11}$Pa. The higher the value of K, the more difficult is the material to compress. Compressibility is $1/K$. » mechanical properties of matter

bulk store » **auxiliary store**

bulked yarn A yarn made of fibres, usually synthetic, whose properties have been modified to induce a high volume to the yarn by crimping the fibres during processing. » crimp; fibre; yarn

bulker A vessel designed to carry cargoes in bulk; grain, coal, iron ore, and bauxite are the commonest. The type has grown steadily since World War 2. The world cargo total carried in 1988 was 109.6 million gross tonnes. » ship [i]

bull (religion) An important, formal communication or edict from a pope, originally sealed with his signet-ring (Lat *bulla*, 'seal') and identified by the opening Latin words. It is often used to promulgate major doctrines (eg infallibility, Immaculate Conception). » pope

bull (zoology) A male mammal belonging to one of several species; female usually called *cow*; young called *calf*; used especially for uncastrated male cattle (male castrated when young called a *bullock*, *ox*, or *steer*; if castrated when fully grown, called a *stag*). The name is also used with several other species, including large whales, walrus, elephant seal, elephant, and moose. » cattle; mammal [i]

Bull, John (c.1563–1628) English musician, born (possibly) in Radnorshire. He was appointed organist at the Chapel Royal in 1591. A Catholic, he fled abroad in 1613, and became organist of the cathedral at Antwerp (1617), where he died. He has been credited with composing the air 'God save the King'.

bull-fighting The national sport in Spain, also popular in some regions of S France, and in Latin American countries. Known as the *corrida de toros* ('running of the bulls') it is regarded as an art in Spain. Leading bullfighters (*matadors*) are treated as national heroes. Picadors are sent into the bull ring to weaken the bull before the matador enters the arena to make the final killing. It is perhaps misnamed as a 'fight' because of its one-sidedness. » blood sports

bull market A stock market term which signifies that the prices of stocks and shares are on a rising trend, due to buying demand. A 'bull' buys shares hoping that the price will rise, so that they can be sold later at a profit. » bear/stock market

Bull Run, Battles of (21 Jul 1861, 29–30 Aug 1862) Major victories by Confederate forces in the American Civil War; also known as the **Battles of Manassas**. The first battle pitted untrained Northern troops attempting to capture Richmond, Virginia (the Southern capital), against well-commanded Southerners. It turned into a Northern rout. In the second battle, a large Northern force under John Pope was trapped by combined Confederate forces under 'Stonewall' Jackson (1824–63) and James Longstreet (1821–1904). » American Civil War; Jackson, Thomas J

bull terrier A breed of dog, developed for dogfighting in Britain by crossing bulldogs and terriers; powerful body; long tail; ears pointed, erect; head broad with small eyes; coat short, usually white. The small form is known as the **miniature bull terrier**. » bulldog; dog; terrier

bullace [**boo**lis] A type of small, wild plum, usually a thorny shrub with spherical black fruit with waxy bloom; native to Europe. (*Prunus domestica*, subspecies *institia*. Family: *Rosaceae*.) » damson; plum; shrub

bulldog A breed of dog, used in mediaeval Britain for the sport of bull-baiting; heavy body with short, bowed legs and short tail; large round head with flat upturned muzzle; ears and eyes small; short brown or brown and white coat. » boxer; dog; French bulldog

bullfinch A bird native to Europe, Scandinavia, and Asia E to Japan and the Philippines; inhabits woodlands and gardens; eats buds, seeds, and fruit; causes serious damage in orchards. (Genus: *Pyrrhula*, 6 species. Family *Fringillidae*.) The name is also used for several species of genus *Loxigilla* in the family *Emberizidae*, and for the **bullfinch cardinal** in the family *Cardinalidae*. » finch

bullfrog Any large frog; name used especially for N American *Rana catesbeiana* (**bullfrog** or **American bullfrog**); also for *Rana tigrina* (**Asian bullfrog**) and *Pyxicephalus adspersus* (**South African bullfrog**), all of the family *Ranidae*. *Leptodactylus pentadactylus* of the family *Leptodactylidae* is called the **South American bullfrog**. » frog

bullhead Small bottom-dwelling fish found in clear streams and lakes of N Europe; body stout, length up to 10 cm/4 in, with broad flattened head; eggs laid under stones and guarded by the male; feeds on invertebrates, especially crustaceans; also called **sculpin** or **miller's thumb**. The name is also used for others of this genus, the similar-looking marine *Icelidae*, and some N American catfishes of family *Ictaluridae*. (Genus: *Cottus*. Family: *Cottidae*.)

bullmastiff A breed of dog, developed in Britain by crossing bulldogs and mastiffs; thick-set body; brown short-haired coat; soft ears and powerful muzzle; aggressive but controllable; used by gamekeepers in the 19th-c to deter poachers. » bulldog; mastiff

bullroarer A primitive musical instrument made from a wooden blade, often with serrated edges and sometimes elaborately carved, attached to a length of string and whirled around in the open air. It was known to the ancient Greeks and is still found in many countries. » aerophone

Bülow, Bernhard (Heinrich Martin Karl), Fürst von ('Prince of') [**bü**loh] (1849–1929) German statesman and Chancellor (1900–9), born at Flottbeck, Holstein. He was Foreign Secretary (1897) before becoming Chancellor, and was made a count (1899) and a prince (1905). He was identified with an aggressive foreign policy in the years before World War 1. He died in Rome.

Bülow, Baron Hans (Guido) von [**bü**loh] (1830–94) German pianist and conductor, born in Dresden. He studied law, but under Wagner's influence became the musico-political spokesman of the new German school. An outstanding conductor, he took piano lessons from Liszt, and married his daughter (1857). In 1864 he became conductor of the court opera, and in 1867 director of the music school at Munich, but resigned when his wife deserted him for Wagner in 1869. Henceforward an opponent of Wagner and his school, he undertook extensive conducting tours in England and the USA, and died in Cairo. » Wagner

bulrush An aquatic, rush-like perennial, found almost everywhere; stems to 3 m/10 ft; leaves in tufts; flowers tiny, perianth reduced to six rough bristles, in oval, brown spikelets. The name is sometimes misapplied to reedmace. (*Scirpus lacustris*. Family: *Cyperaceae*.) » perennial; perianth; reedmace; rush

bulrush millet » **millet**

Bultmann, Rudolf (Karl) (1884–1976) German Lutheran theologian, Hellenist, and New Testament scholar, born at Wiefelstede. He studied at Tübingen, taught at Marburg, Breslau, and Giessen, then became professor of New Testament at Marburg (1921). An early exponent of form criticism (*History of the Synoptic Tradition*, 1921) he is best known for his highly influential programme (1941) to 'demythologize' the New Testament and interpret it existentially, employing the categories of the earlier work of Heidegger. He died at Marburg. » demythologizing; Heidegger

Bulwer Lytton » **Lytton**

bumblebee A large bee found mainly in the temperate N hemisphere. The adults transport pollen on the modified outer surface of the hindleg. They are organized into primitive societies, in which only the queen overwinters to produce the next generation of workers. (Family: *Apidae*. Genus: *Bombus*.) » bee; pollen [i]

Bunche, Ralph (Johnson) (1904–71) US diplomat, born in Detroit. He studied at Harvard and the University of California, then taught political science at Howard University, Washington (1928–50). He directed the United Nations Trusteeship department (1947–54), and became UN mediator in Palestine, where he arranged for a cease-fire. Awarded the Nobel Peace Prize (1950), he became a UN Under-Secretary for Special Political Affairs (1954–67), and later Under-Secretary-General (1968–71). He died in New York City. » United Nations

Bundestag The parliament of the German Federal Republic, elections for which are held every four years in the autumn. It is possible for the Bundestag to be dissolved and elections held before the end of the fixed term, but this has never happened. In addition to legislating, the Bundestag selects the Chancellor and supports his government. » Germany [i]; parliament

Bundy, McGeorge (1919–) US educator and statesman, born in Boston, Massachusetts. Educated at Yale, he worked in public service, then taught at Harvard, where he became dean of arts and sciences in 1953. As National Security Adviser to Presidents Kennedy and Johnson he was one of the architects of the Vietnam War. He is now professor of history at New York University. » Johnson, Lyndon B; Kennedy, John F; Vietnam War

Bunin, Ivan Alexeievich [**boo**neen] (1870–1953) Russian author, born at Voronezh. He worked as a journalist and clerk, writing lyrics and novels of the decay of the Russian nobility and of peasant life. His best-known work is *Gospodin iz San-Francisco* (1922, The Gentleman from San Francisco). He was the first Russian to receive the Nobel Prize for Literature (1933). After the Revolution, he lived in Paris, where he died. » Russian literature

bunion A painful, inflamed hardening and thickening of the skin over the head of the metatarsal of the great toe. It is often induced by ill-fitting footware. » foot

Bunker Hill, Battle of (1775) The first pitched battle of the US War of Independence. It was technically an American defeat, as New England troops were dislodged from the position overlooking occupied Boston. But very high British casualties demonstrated American fighting capacity, and forbade attempts on other American emplacements. The eventual result was the British evacuation of Boston. It was actually fought on Breed's Hill, above Charlestown, not on nearby Bunker Hill. » American Revolution

bunraku [**bun**rakoo] The classical Japanese puppet theatre. Puppets are two-thirds life size, hand-held by a puppet master, generally with two 'invisible' assistants in black. The movements are accompanied by a singer-narrator, who voices all the roles, and musicians. Bunraku's greatest popularity was in the 17th–18th-c. » puppetry

Bunsen, Robert Wilhelm (1811–99) Prussian chemist and physicist, born at Göttingen. He studied at Göttingen, Paris, Berlin, and Vienna, and taught at several universities before becoming professor of chemistry at Heidelberg (1852–99). He shares with Kirchhoff the discovery of spectrum analysis (1859), invented the grease-spot photometer, a galvanic battery, and an ice calorimeter, and worked on arsenic compounds, gas analysis, and electrolysis. He died at Heidelberg. » Bunsen burner; spectrum

Bunsen burner A gas burner, used mainly in chemistry laboratories. Gas enters through a jet at the lower end of a tube, and is drawn through a side tube whose aperture can be controlled. The controllable gas-air mixture makes possible a flame of quality, ranging from luminous to hot non-luminous. The idea is attributed to German scientist, Robert Wilhelm Bunsen, but its first practical construction should be credited mainly to his technical assistant, C Desaga. » Bunsen

bunting A small seed-eating bird, usually dull in colour with a short stout bill. It is a widespread family, thought to have evolved in the Americas, spread across the Bering Straits to Asia, then colonized Europe and Africa. (*Emberizidae*, c.290 species.) » Darwin's finches

Bunting, Basil (1900–85) British poet, born at Scotswood, Northumberland. He worked as a journalist in Paris, was much influenced by Pound and the American Modernists, and published his early poetry abroad. After some years in Paris, where he worked on translation, he returned to Britain and established his reputation with *Briggflatts* (1966), a semi-autobiographical poem deeply rooted in the NE. He died at Hexham, Northumberland. » English literature; poetry; Pound; Modernism

Buñuel, Luis (1900–83) Spanish film director, born in Calanda. Educated at Madrid University, his first films (made with Salvador Dali) were a sensation with their surrealistic, macabre approach: *Un Chien andalou* (1928, An Andalusian Dog) and *L'Age d'or* (1930, The Golden Age). His career then went into eclipse until he settled in Mexico (1947), where he directed such major films as *Los Olvidados* (1950, The Young and the Damned), *Viridiana* (1961), *The Discreet Charm of the Bourgeoisie* (1972), and *That Obscure Object of Desire* (1977). His work is characterized by a poetic, often erotic, use of imagery, a black humour, and a hatred of Catholicism, often expressed in blasphemy. He died in Mexico City. » Surrealism

Bunyan, John (1628–88) English author of *The Pilgrim's Progress*, born at Elstow, Bedfordshire. He worked as a tinker, and fought in the parliamentary army during the Civil War (1644–5). In 1653 he joined a Christian fellowship, preaching around Bedford. In 1660 he was arrested and spent 12 years in Bedford county gaol, where he wrote prolifically, including *Grace Abounding* (1666). Briefly released after the Declaration of Indulgence (1672), he was reimprisoned for six months in the town gaol, and there wrote the first part of *The Pilgrim's Progress*, a vision of life told allegorically as if it were a journey. Returning to his career, he acted as pastor in Bedford for 16 years, where he wrote the second part of *The Pilgrim's Progress* (1684). He died in London. » English literature

Bunyan, Paul In American folklore, a lumberjack of superhuman size and strength, stories of whose prowess began to circulate early in the 20th-c. Not only could he break up logjams with spectacular ease; he could also refashion geography, creating lakes, rivers, and even the Grand Canyon. » folklore

bunyip In the mythology of the Australian aborigines, the source of evil. He is not to be thought of as a spirit or as a human. The Rainbow Serpent, the mother of life, confined bunyip to a waterhole: he haunts dark and gloomy places. » Aborigines

bunyip aristocracy An unsuccessful local attempt in Australia to create an upper house elected from an order of hereditary baronets for the government of New South Wales in 1853. The proposal was associated with W C Wentworth, and was designed to counter the 'spirit of democracy' unleashed by the gold rushes, and to stabilize society with the granting of self-government. The name was first used with witty cynicism in a political speech in 1853. » Australia [i]; bunyip; Wentworth, W C

Buonaparte » Bonaparte

buoyancy The upward thrust on an object immersed in liquid or gas, equal to the weight of the displaced fluid. The human body is more buoyant in salt water than in fresh water, as the former is 3% denser. » Archimedes

Burakumin An outcaste group in Japanese society, concentrated in about 6 000 ghetto communities and numbering 1–3 million; the target of extreme discrimination with regard to employment, marriage and residential segregation. Their origins go back to the Edo feudal period of the 17th-c, when impoverished Japanese in lowly occupations were segregated. The class was officially abolished in 1871, but to no great effect: some militancy within the group since the 1920s has also had little impact. » Japan [i]

Burbage, Richard (c.1569–1619) English actor, born and died in London. He was the leading performer with Shakespeare's company from 1594 until his death, and was the first creator on stage of many of Shakespeare's greatest roles, including Hamlet, Othello, and Lear. » Shakespeare; theatre

burbot Elongate slender-bodied fish widespread in rivers and lakes of N Eurasia and N America; the only freshwater species in the cod family *Gadidae*; length up to 1 m/3¼ ft; single barbel beneath mouth; fished commercially in Russia; also called **eelpout**. (*Lota lota*.) » cod

Burckhardt, Jacob (Christopher) (1818–97) Swiss historian, born and died in Basle. He studied theology and later art history in Berlin and Bonn, became editor of the *Baseler Zeitung* (1844–5), and was professor of history at Basle University (1858–93). He is known for his works on the Italian Renaissance and on Greek Civilization. » Renaissance

Bureau of Indian Affairs A US government agency, established in 1836, which was notorious in the late 19th-c for its extreme corruption, both in the provision of supplies for client Indians and in the redistribution of Indian lands. It was responsible for implementing the long-term policy of removing Indians from areas of possible White occupation, and destroying indigenous Indian culture. It operated under the Department of War until 1849, when it was transferred to the Department of the Interior. It now operates as the Indian Service. » Indian Wars

burgh » borough

Burgess, Anthony (1917–) British novelist and critic, born in Manchester. Educated at Xaverian College and Manchester University, he lectured at Birmingham University (1946–50), worked for the Ministry of Education, and taught at Banbury Grammar School (1950–4). He then became an education officer in Malaya and Brunei (1954–9), where his experiences inspired his *Malayan Trilogy* (1965). His many novels include *A Clockwork Orange* (1962), *1985* (1978), *Earthly Powers* (1980), and *The Kingdom of the Wicked* (1985). He has written several critical studies and film scripts, including *Jesus of Nazareth* (1977). His musical compositions include symphonies, a ballet, and an opera. He has also written under the name of **Joseph Kell** and (his original name) **John Burgess Wilson**. He now lives in Monaco. » English literature; literary criticism; novel

Burgess, Guy (Francis de Moncy) (1910–63) British traitor, born at Devonport, Devon. He was educated at Eton, Dartmouth, and Cambridge, where he became a communist. Recruited as a Soviet agent in the 1930s, he worked with the BBC (1936–9), wrote war propaganda (1939–41), and again joined the BBC (1941–4) while working for MI5. Thereafter, he was a member of the Foreign Office, and second secretary under Philby in Washington in 1950. Recalled in 1951 for 'serious misconduct', he and Maclean disappeared, re-emerging in the Soviet Union in 1956. He died in Moscow. » communism; Maclean, Donald; Philby

Burgh, Hubert de (?–1243) Justiciar of England under King John and Henry III (1215–32). He is chiefly remembered as the gaoler of Prince Arthur. He was created Earl of Kent in 1227, but was imprisoned after falling from favour (1232–4), then pardoned. He died at Banstead, Surrey. » Arthur, Prince; John; Henry III (of England)

Burghley, or **Burghleigh » Cecil, William**

burglary A crime which involves entering a building as a trespasser either with the intent to commit theft, grievous bodily harm, or rape; or, having entered, stealing or attempting to steal anything, or committing or attempting to commit grievous bodily harm. A 'building' is a roofed structure with some measure of permanence: caravans and houseboats are included. » bodily harm; rape (law); theft

Burgos [**boor**gos] 42°21N 3°41W, pop (1981) 156 449. Capital of Burgos province, N Spain; on R Arlanzón, 243 km/151 ml N of Madrid; former capital of Old Castile; archbishopric; railway; a world heritage site; home and burial site of El Cid; textiles, motor accessories, silk, chemicals, nails, clothes; Santa Maria de Gerona nuclear power station (1971); cathedral (13th–16th-c), castle; fair and fiestas of St Peter (Jun). » Castile; El Cid; Spain [i]

Burgoyne, John (1722–92) British general and dramatist, born at Sutton, Bedfordshire. He entered the army in 1740, and gave distinguished service in the Seven Years' War (1756–63). He then sat in parliament as a Tory, and in 1777 was sent to America, where he led an expedition from Canada, taking Ticonderoga, but being forced to surrender at Saratoga. He later joined the Whigs, and commanded in Ireland (1782–3). His best-known work was his comedy, *The Heiress* (1786). He died in London. » American Revolution; Seven Years' War; Tories; Whigs

Burgundy, Fr **Bourgogne** pop (1982) 1 596 054; area 31 582 sq km/ 12 191 sq ml. Region and former province of EC France, comprising departments of Côte-d'Or, Nièvre, Saône-et-Loire, and Yonne; former kingdom of Burgundia (5th–10th-c); famous wine-producing area (eg Beaujolais, Beaune, Chablis); wooded Monts du Morvan (902 m/2 959 ft) in C; chief town, Dijon; industry centred on Le Creusot; caves at Arcy-sur-Cure; Parc de Morvan regional nature park; several spas. » Dijon; France [i]; wine

burials » **bog burials; Hochdorf; Kofun; Maes Howe; Mount Li; New Grange; Pazyryk; shaft graves; Ship of Cheops; Sutton Hoo ship burial**

Buridan, Jean [booreedã] (14th-c) French scholastic philosopher, born at Béthune. He studied at Paris under William of Ockham, became himself a teacher of a conservative nominalist philosophy, and was rector of the University of Paris in 1328 and 1340. He wrote on topics in logic, metaphysics, physics, and ethics. He is best-known for his contributions to the theory of choice; his views were thought to lead to the plight of 'Buridan's ass' – a donkey who, standing equidistant between two bales of hay, has no reason to prefer one to the other, and so dies of starvation. » nominalism; scholasticism

burin [byoorin] A tool used in engraving. A burin or *graver* has a rounded wooden handle to fit into the palm of the and, and a pointed metal blade for cutting into the woodblock or metal plate. » engraving

Burke, Edmund (1729–97) British statesman and political philosopher, born in Dublin, Ireland. Educated at a Quaker boarding-school and at Trinity College, Dublin, he began in 1750 to study law, but then took up literary work. His early writing includes his *Philosophical Inquiry into the Origin of our Ideas of the Sublime and Beautiful* (1756). He became Secretary for Ireland, and entered parliament in 1765. His main speeches and writings belong to the period when his party was opposed to Lord North's American policy (1770–82). His *Reflections on the French Revolution* (1790) was read all over Europe. He died at Beaconsfield, Buckinghamshire. » American Revolution; Hastings, Warren

Burke, Robert O'Hara (1820–61) Irish explorer, born at St Cleram, Galway. Educated in Belgium, he served in the Austrian army (1840), joined the Irish Constabulary (1848), and emigrated to Australia in 1853. He and W J Wills successfully completed the first crossing of Australia from S to N, but both men died on the return journey.

Burke, William (1792–1829) Irish murderer, born at Orrery. With his partner, **William Hare** (c.1790–c.1860), born at Londonderry, he carried out a series of infamous murders in Edinburgh in the 1820s, with the aim of supplying dissection subjects to Dr Robert Knox, the anatomist. Hare, the more villainous of the two, turned king's evidence, and died a beggar in London in the 1860s; Burke was hanged, to the general satisfaction of the crowd.

Burke's Peerage A reference guide to the aristocratic and titled families of Great Britain, first published by John Burke (1787–1848) in 1826 under the title *Genealogical and Heraldic Dictionary of the Peerage and Baronetage of the United Kingdom*. » peerage

Burkina Faso [burkeena fasoh], formerly **Upper Volta** (to 1984), then (Fr) **République de Haute-Volta** pop (1990e) 8 776 000; area 274 540 sq km/105 972 sq ml. Land-locked republic in W Africa, divided into 25 provinces; bounded N by Mali, E by Niger, SE by Benin, S by Togo and Ghana, and SW by Côte d'Ivoire; capital, Ouagadougou; chief towns include Bobo Dioulasso, Koudougou, Ouahigouya, Tenkodogo; timezone GMT; over 50 tribes, notably the Mossi (48%); official language, French, but many local languages; religion, mainly local beliefs, with some Muslim (c.25%) and Christian (10%); unit of currency, the CFA franc.

Physical description and climate. Low-lying plateau, falling away to the S; many rivers (tributaries of the Volta or Niger) unnavigable in dry season; wooded savannahs in S; semi-desert in N; tropical climate, mean temperature 27°C in dry season

□ *international airport*

(Dec–May); rainy season (Jun–Oct), with violent storms (Aug); *harmattan* wind blows from the NE (Dec–Mar); rainfall decreases from S to N; average annual rainfall at Ouagadougou 894 mm/35 in.

History and government. Mossi empire in 18th–19th-c; Upper Volta created by French, 1919; abolished, 1932, with most land joined to Ivory Coast; original borders reconstituted, 1947; autonomy within French community, 1958; independence, 1960, since when there have been several military coups; constitution of 1977 allowing 57-member elected National Assembly suspended in 1980; renamed Burkina Faso, 1984; governed by a president and an appointed Council of Ministers.

Economy. An agricultural country, largely at subsistence level and subject to drought conditions (especially 1973–4); mainly sorghum, millet, maize, rice, cotton, groundnuts, sesame, sugar cane, livestock; reserves of titanium, limestone, iron ore, vanadium, manganese, zinc, nickel copper, phosphate, gold; processed foods, cigarettes, shoes, bicycles. » Ouagadougou; RR24 national holidays; RR44 political leaders

burlesque In Europe, a play satirizing contemporary theatre or theatrical fashion; originally the critical aspect was strong but, by the 19th-c, fantasy and travesty often predominated. It was the training ground for many famous stage, screen, and radio comedians, and was popular up to World War 2. In the USA, the term is used for a sex and comedy show created around 1865 for exclusively male audiences. » music hall; vaudeville

Burlington, Richard Boyle, 3rd Earl of (1694–1753) English architect and patron of the arts, born in London. He studied architecture, visited Italy, and became an exponent of the style of Palladio. His influence over a group of young architects fostered the Palladian style which was to govern English building for half a century. » Palladianism

Burma, official name **Union of Myanmar** (1989), formerly **The Socialist Republic of the Union of Burma**, Burmese **Pyidaungsu Socialist Thammada Myanma Naingngandaw**, pop (1990e) 41 675 000; area 678 576 sq km/261 930 sq ml. Republic in SE Asia, divided into 14 administrative divisions, including seven states; bordered by China (N and NE), Laos and Thailand (E), India (NW), Bangladesh (W), Bay of Bengal and Andaman Sea (W); capital Rangoon; chief cities include Mandalay, Henzada, Pegu, Myingyan; timezone GMT +6½; main ethnic group, Burman (72%); official language, Burmese, with several minority languages; main religion, Theravada Buddhism (85%); unit of currency, the kyat of 100 pyas.

Physical description and climate. Rimmed in the N, E and W by mountains rising (N) to Hkakabo Razi (5 881 m/19 294 ft), descending in a series of ridges and valleys; principal rivers, Irrawaddy, Salween, Sittang, running N–S; Irrawaddy R delta extends over 240 km/150 ml of tidal forest; tropical monsoon

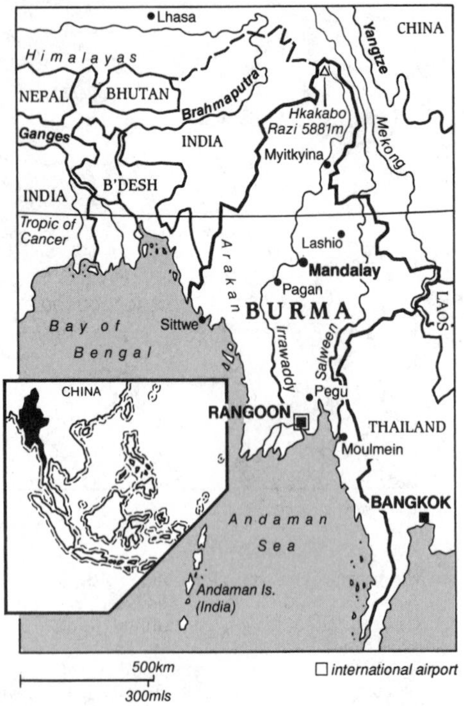

climate, with marked change between cooler, dry season (Nov–Apr), dominated by the NE monsoon, and hotter, wet season (May–Sep), dominated by the SW monsoon; coastal and higher mountains of E and N have heavy annual rainfall, 2 500–5 000 mm/100–200 in; sheltered interior lowlands often as low as 1 000 mm/40 in; lowland temperatures high all year round (especially Mar–May); high humidity on the coast.

History and government. First unified in 11th-c by King Anawrahta; invasion by Kubla Khan, 1287; second dynasty established, 1486, but plagued by internal disunity and wars with Siam from 16th-c; new dynasty under King Alaungpaya, 1752; annexed to British India following Anglo-Burmese wars (1824–86); separated from India, 1937; occupied by Japanese in World War 2; independence as Union of Burma under Prime Minister U Nu, 1948; military coup under U Ne Win, 1962; single-party socialist republic, 1974; 489-member People's Assembly (*Pithu Hluttaw*) elected a 29-member State Council, which elected a president, prime minister, and Council of Ministers; army coup, 1988, leading to formation of a State Law and Order Restoration Council, headed by a chairman.

Economy. Largely dependent on agriculture (especially rice, beans, maize, sugar cane, pulses, oilseed) and forestry (teak and other hardwoods); agricultural processing, textiles, footwear, pharmaceuticals, fertilizers, wood and wood products, petroleum refining; zinc, lead, tin, copper, gypsum, limestone, chromium, asbestos, oil, coal. » Buddhism; Irrawaddy River; monsoon climates; Rangoon; RR24 national holidays; RR44 political leaders

Burma Road A road linking the Burmese railhead at Lashio with Kunming, 1 150 km/700 ml distant in Yunnan province, China. Completed by the Chinese in 1938, it was of great strategic importance to the Allies during World War 2. » Burma [i]

Burmese cat A breed of domestic cat, of the *foreign short-haired* type; many breeds (not all recognized in USA): *brown* (or *zibelines*), *blue*, *blue-cream*, *cream*, *chocolate* (or *champagne*), *tortoiseshell* (or *tortie*), *chocolate tortie*, *lilac* (or *platinum*), *lilac tortie* (or *lilac cream*), and *red*. » cat

burn An injury usually resulting from the application of heat to the surface of the body; other agents include electricity, friction, and corrosive chemicals. The severity depends on the temperature and duration of the insult, and is assessed by the extent and depth of damage to the skin and underlying tissue. A superficial burn affects skin only, and can induce redness or death of the part; a deep burn destroys the skin, and penetrates to underlying fat, muscle, or bone. A superficial burn may heal without scarring; a deep burn never does so, and the scar may draw damaged tissues together, leading to the need for skin grafting. » graft (medicine); skin [i]

Burne-Jones, Sir Edward Coley, 1st Baronet (1833–98) British painter and designer, born in Birmingham. He studied at Oxford, where he met William Morris, and through the encouragement of Rossetti, relinquished the church for art. His later oils, inspired by the early Italian Renaissance, are characterized by a romantic and contrived Mannerism. His subjects, drawn from the Arthurian romances and Greek myths, include 'The Days of Creation', 'The Beguiling of Merlin', and 'The Mirror of Venus', exhibited in 1877. He also designed stained glass and tapestries, and illustrated several books for William Morris, notably Chaucer. He was made a baronet in 1894, and died in London. » English art; Mannerism; Morris, William; Renaissance

burnet Erect, tuft-forming perennials, native to Europe, W Asia, and N Africa; leaves mostly basal, slightly bluish, pinnate with oval, toothed leaflets; flowers in a globular head, four sepals, petals absent. The **salad burnet** (*Sanguisorba minor*) grows to 40 cm/15 in, flowers green or purple-tinged; crushed foliage smelling of cucumber. The **great burnet** (*sanguisorba officinalis*) is a larger plant growing to 60 cm; flowers dull red. (Family: *Rosaceae*.) » perennial; pinnate

Burnet, Sir (Frank) Macfarlane (1899–1985) Australian physician, born at Traralgon, Victoria. He studied at Melbourne and London, and in 1928 became assistant director and later director (1944–65) of the Institute for Medical Research, Melbourne. A world authority on viral diseases, he shared the 1960 Nobel Prize for Physiology or Medicine for research into immunological intolerance in relation to skin and organ grafting. He was knighted in 1951, and died in Melbourne. » immunology; Medawar; virus

Burnett, Frances (Eliza), *née* Hodgson (1849–1924) British-US novelist, born in Manchester. In 1865 her family emigrated to Tennessee, where she had her first literary success with *That Lass o' Lowrie's* (1877). She wrote several plays and over 40 novels, notably *Little Lord Fauntleroy* (1886) and *The Secret Garden* (1909). She died at Plandome, New York. » American/English literature; novel

Burney, Fanny, or **Frances**, afterwards **Madame d'Arblay** (1752–1840) British novelist and diarist, born at King's Lynn, Norfolk. She educated herself by reading English and French literature and observing the distinguished people who visited her father. Her first and best novel, *Evelina*, was published anonymously in 1778, and influenced Jane Austen. She was given a court appointment in 1786, but her health declined; she retired on a pension and married a French émigré, General d'Arblay, in 1793. Her *Letters and Diaries* (1846) show her skill in reporting events of her time. She died in London. » diary and journal; English literature; novel

burning bush » **dittany; summer cypress**

Burns, Robert (1759–96) Scotland's national poet, born at Alloway, near Ayr. The son of a poor farmer, his education was thoroughly literary, and he studied the technique of writing, influenced also by the popular tales and songs of Betty Davidson, an old woman who lived with his family. On his father's death (1784) he was left in charge of the farm. At the same time his entanglement with Jean Armour (1767–1834) began, and as the farm went to ruin, his poverty, passion, and despair produced in 1785 an extraordinary output of poetry, including 'The Jolly Beggars'. Looking for money to emigrate to Jamaica, he published the famous Kilmarnock edition of his poems (1786), which brought such acclaim that he was persuaded to stay in Scotland. Going to Edinburgh, where he was feted, he began the epistolary flirtations with 'Clarinda' (Agnes Maclehose, 1759–1841). In 1788 he married Jean Armour and leased a farm near Dumfries, in 1789 being made an excise officer. By 1790, when he wrote 'Tam o' Shanter', the farm was failing. He left for Dumfries, briefly adopting Radical views, but turning patriot again in 1795; and there he died. » Burns Night; Scottish literature

Burns Night The evening of 25 January, anniversary of the birth of the Scottish poet Robert Burns, celebrated in Scotland and many other parts of the world with a special meal (Burns Supper) including haggis, potatoes and turnips, followed by speeches, recitations of Burns's poetry, and singing of his songs. » Burns, Robert

Burnside, Ambrose Everett (1824–81) US general, born at Liberty, Indiana. He graduated at West Point in 1847, and in the Civil War commanded a brigade at Bull Run, and captured Roanoke I. He was repulsed at Fredericksburg (1862), but held Knoxville (1863), and led a corps under Grant through the battles of the Wilderness and Cold Harbor (1864). After the war he became Governor of Rhode Island, and was elected Senator in 1875. He lent his name to a style of side whiskers, later known as 'sideburns'. He died at Bristol, Rhode Island. » American Civil War

Burr, Aaron (1756–1836) US statesman, born at Newark, New Jersey. He was educated at Princeton, called to the Bar in 1782, and became Attorney-General (1789–91), Senator (1791–7), and Republican Vice-President (1800–4). In 1804 he killed his political rival, Alexander Hamilton, in a duel (1894), and fled to South Carolina. He then prepared to raise a force to conquer Texas, and establish a republic. He was tried for treason (1807), acquitted, spent some wretched years in Europe, and in 1812 resumed his law practice in New York City, where he died.

Burra, Edward (1905–76) British artist, born in London. He studied at London, and travelled widely in Europe and the USA. Well known as a colourist, his Surrealist paintings of figures against exotic (often Spanish) backgrounds are invariably in watercolour, as in 'Soldiers' (Tate). He also designed for the ballet. » English art; Surrealism

Burroughs, Edgar Rice (1875–1950) US novelist, born in Chicago. He had many unsuccessful jobs, before making his name with the 'Tarzan' stories, beginning with 'Tarzan of the Apes' (1914). In later years he became a war correspondent. He died at Encino, California. » American literature; novel

Burroughs, William S(eward) (1914–) US author, born in St Louis, Missouri. He was educated at Harvard, and became a heroin addict while doing odd jobs in New York. In 1953 he published *Junkie*, an account of his experiences, and his novels *Naked Lunch* (1959) and *The Soft Machine* (1961) established him as a spokesman of the 'beat' movement of the late 1950s. His later work, much concerned with innovations in the novel form, includes *Nova Express* (1964), *The Wild Boys* (1971), and *Cities of the Red Night* (1981). » American literature; beat generation; novel

burrowing owl A small owl native to the Americas (SW Canada to Tierra del Fuego); lives in semi-desert areas; occupies burrows vacated by prairie dogs or other mammals; eats large insects and small vertebrates. (*Speotyto cunicularia.* Family: *Strigidae.*) » owl

Bursa, ancient **Brusa** or **Prusa** [boor**sah**] 40°12N 29°04E, pop (1980) 445 113. Capital city of Bursa province, NW Turkey; fifth largest city in Turkey; founded, 3rd-c BC; airfield; railway; commercial and industrial centre; noted for its silk textiles; car assembly, soft drinks; Green Mosque (1421). » Turkey [i]

bursitis Damage from trauma or infection to and within a *bursa* (a fibrous pouch containing a small amount of fluid, found around joints and tendons to aid movement and reduce friction). Pain and swelling is usually aggravated by the movement of the adjacent joint to which the bursa is related. » housemaid's knee

Burt, Sir Cyril (Lodowic) (1883–1971) British psychologist, born in London. He was educated at Oxford and Würzburg, becoming professor of education (1924–31) and psychology (1931–50) at London. He was largely responsible for the theory and practice of intelligence and aptitude tests, ranging from the psychology of education to the problems of juvenile delinquency. He was knighted in 1946, and died in London. In the 1980s, the validity of some of his techniques was called into question. » intelligence; testing

Burton, Sir Richard (Francis) (1821–90) British explorer, born at Torquay, Devon. He was educated in Europe and Oxford, where he was expelled in 1842. In 1856 he set out with Speke on the journey which led to the discovery (1858) of L Tanganyika, and afterwards travelled in N America, and held consular posts at Fernando Pó, Santos, Damascus, and Trieste. He wrote many books on his travels, and translated several Eastern works. He was knighted in 1886, and died at Trieste. Lady Burton, *née* **Isabel Arundell** (1831–96), who shared in much of his travelling and writing, burned her husband's journals after his death. » Speke

Burton, Richard (Jenkins) (1925–84) British stage and film actor, born at Pontrhydfen, South Wales. The tenth surviving child of a coalminer, Richard Jenkins, he was brought up in his sister's house after his mother's death. He was befriended by his English teacher, Philip H Burton, who encouraged his acting and study of English, and eventually adopted him. He went to Oxford, and in 1943 changed his name to Burton. He acted in Liverpool and Oxford, served in the RAF, and returned to the stage in 1948, when he made his film debut. He made his stage reputation in Fry's *The Lady's Not for Burning* (1949), and had a triumphant season at Stratford (1951). His early Hollywood films include *My Cousin Rachel* (1952) and *The Robe* (1953) for which he received one of his six Academy Award nominations. In 1954 he was the narrator in the famous radio production of Dylan Thomas's *Under Milk Wood.* His romance with Elizabeth Taylor during the making of *Cleopatra* (1962) and their eventual marriage (1964–74) projected them both into the 'superstar' category. Among his later films were *Becket* (1964), *Equus* (1977), and *1984* (released after his death). In his later years, interest in his social life grew, especially after his second marriage to Elizabeth Taylor (1975–6). He died in Geneva.

Burton, Robert (1577–1640) English author, born at Lindley, Leicestershire. He graduated from Oxford, and taught there, taking orders in 1614. He spent his life at Christ Church, where he died. His great work was the *Anatomy of Melancholy* (1621, 6th edition, 1651–2), a learned miscellany on the ideas of his time, which influenced many subsequent authors. » English literature

Burundi, official name **Republic of Burundi** [bu**run**dee] pop (1990e) 5 450 000; area 27 834 sq km/10 744 sq ml. Republic in C Africa, divided into eight provinces; bounded N by Rwanda, E and S by Tanzania, SW by L Tanganyika, W by Zaire; capital

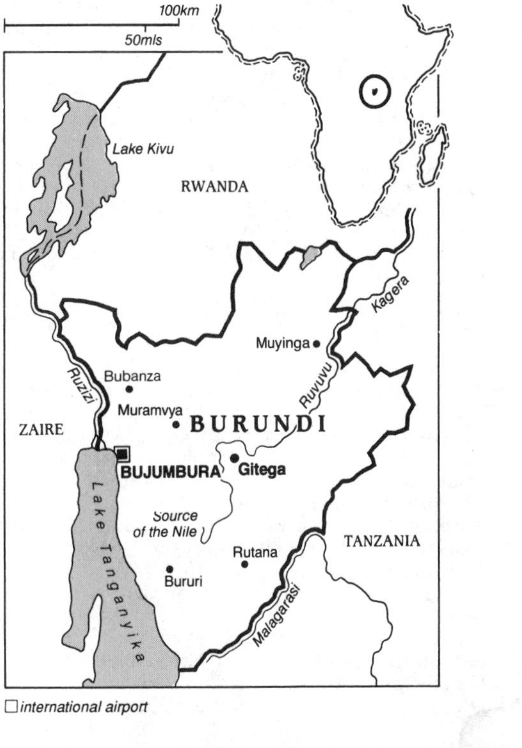

Bujumbura; chief towns, Bubanza, Ngozi, Muyinga, Muramvya, Gitega, Bururi, Rutana; timezone GMT +2; population mainly Hutu (85%), with Tutsi (14%), and other tribal minorities; chief religions, Roman Catholic (62%), local beliefs (32%); official languages, French and Kirundi; unit of currency, Burundi franc.

Physical description and climate. Lies across the Nile-Congo watershed; bounded W by narrow plain of R Ruzizi (NW) and L Tanganyika (W); R Malagarasi forms S border with Tanzania; R Akanyaru forms N border with Rwanda; average height of interior plateau c.1 500 m/5 000 ft, sloping E towards Tanzania; highest point, Mt Karonje (2 685 m/8 809 ft); equatorial climate, varying with altitude and season; moderately wet, apart from dry season (Jun–Sep); average annual rainfall at Bujumbura, 850 mm/33.5 in.

History and government. Since 16th-c ruled by the Tutsi kingdom; German occupation in 1890, and included in German East Africa; League of Nations mandated territory, administered by Belgians, 1919; joined with Rwanda to become the UN Trust Territory of Ruanda-Urundi, 1946; independence, 1962; full republic, 1966; civil war, 1972; military coup, 1976; new constitution in 1981 provided for a National Assembly (65 members), an executive president, a Council of Ministers, and military governors for the provinces; Assembly dissolved and constitution suspended after 1987 coup.

Economy. Agriculture, main subsistence crops including manioc, yams, corn, haricot beans; cash crops include coffee, cotton, tea; light consumer goods (eg shoes, soap, beverages, blankets); reserves of rare-earth metals, peat, nickel, tungsten, columbium, tantalum, phosphate. » Bujumbura; Hutu and Tutsi; League of Nations; mandates; RR24 national holidays; RR45 political leaders

burying beetle A medium to large beetle; adults bury corpses of small animals by excavating soil beneath them; eggs laid in tunnels off burial chamber; larvae typically feed on carrion. (Order: *Coleoptera.* Family: *Silphidae.*) » beetle; larva

Busan » **Pusan**

Bush, Alan (Dudley) (1900–) British composer, born in London. He studied at the Royal Academy, London, where in 1925 he became professor of composition. A convinced communist, he founded the Workers' Music Association (1936). His works include four symphonies, concertos for violin and piano, and the opera, *Wat Tyler*.

Bush, George (Herbert Walker) (1924–) US Republican politician and 41st President, born in Milton, Massachusetts. He joined the US Navy in 1942, as its youngest pilot. After the war he read economics at Yale and went into business in the Texas oilfields. In 1966 he devoted himself to politics, and was elected to the House of Representatives. Unsuccessful for the Senate in 1970, he became US Permanent Representative to the United Nations. During the Watergate scandal he was Chairman of the Republican National Committee. Under President Ford he headed the US Mission to Beijing (Peking), then became director of the CIA. In 1980 he campaigned for the Republican nomination, but lost to Reagan, later becoming his Vice-President. In 1988 he won the Republican nomination for the presidency, and defeated Governor Michael Dukakis of Massachusetts in the general election. » Ford, Gerald R; Reagan; Watergate

bush cat » **genet**

bush cricket A true cricket, with a well-developed sound-producing mechanism for auditory communication; box-like forewings bent down at sides of body; egg-laying tube cylindrical; c.2000 species, including some important pests. (Order: *Orthoptera.* Family: *Gryllidae.*) » cricket (entomology)

bush dog A member of the dog family native to C and S America; dark brown with pale brown head; short ears, legs, and tail; inhabits woodland and grassland near water; eats mainly rodents. (*Speothos venaticus.*) » Canidae; civet; dog

bushbaby A primitive primate (prosimian), whose cry sounds like a human baby; large eyes and ears; thick coat, very long tail; long hind legs; agile; leaps through trees; on ground may hop upright using only hind legs; also known as **galago.** (Family; *Lorisidae*, 7 species.) » prosimian

bushbuck A spiral-horned antelope native to Africa S of the Sahara; reddish-brown with white spots or thin white lines; females without horns; inhabits thick undergrowth near water; lives in pairs; nocturnal. (*Tragelaphus scriptus.*) » antelope

bushido [**bu**sheedoh] The Japanese notion of 'way of the warrior'. The samurai code until 1868, which taught personal loyalty to a master, death rather than capture/surrender, and stoic indifference to material goods. Like European knights, samurai rode into battle in armour. The bushido tradition is still seen in modern times, eg Japanese officers carried swords in World War 2. » samurai

bushmaster A rare pit viper, native to C and S America; largest venomous snake in the New World; length, up to 3.5 m/11½ ft; the only New World viper to lay eggs; inhabits forests; nocturnal; eats mammals (including small deer); shakes its tail when alarmed, causing loud rustling in undergrowth. (*Lachesis muta.*) » pit viper [i]

Bushmen » **Khoisan**

bushrangers Australian rural outlaws who operated from 1790 to 1900. Concentrated in New South Wales, Victoria, and Van Dieman's Land, the first bushrangers were ex-convicts, but the opportunities of the gold-rushes led to a revival in the 1860s and 1870s. They were a product of frontier society. Some attained folk hero status, such as Ben Hall (killed 1865), and Ned Kelly (hanged 1880). Never numerous, they attracted great attention from governments and from those who sought to glorify them in romantic myth. » Kelly, Ned

Busoni, Ferruccio (Benvenuto) [boos**oh**nee] (1866–1924) Italian composer and pianist, born at Empoli, Tuscany. An infant prodigy, in 1889 he became professor of pianoforte at Helsinki. He subsequently taught and played in Moscow, Boston, Berlin, Weimar, and Zürich, returning to Berlin in 1920. The influence of Liszt is apparent in his great piano concerto. His opera *Doktor Faust* was completed posthumously by a pupil in 1925. He died in Berlin.

Buss, Frances Mary (1827–94) British pioneer of higher education of women. She founded the North London Collegiate School for Ladies, which became a model for the High Schools of the Girls' Public Day Schools Company. She also campaigned for women to be admitted to university. » feminism

bussing A government policy adopted in the 1960s (particularly in the USA) to promote social integration among school children in ethnically divided urban communities. Children (especially Black and Asian) were taken by bus from disadvantaged urban contexts to schools elsewhere. In the USA, bussing became highly controversial when the Supreme Court determined to force the integration against widespread opposition from Whites, and to a lesser extent from Blacks as well: the policy was abandoned in 1972. » ethnicity

bustard A large, long-legged, ground-living bird native to Africa, S Europe, Asia, and Australia; prefers open country; walks rather than flies (but flies well); eats large insects (especially locusts and grasshoppers), lizards, and small birds. (Family: *Otididae*, 24 species.)

bustard quail » **button quail; quail**

busy Lizzie » **impatiens**

butadiene [byoota**di**yeen] $CH_2=CH-CH=CH_2$, buta-1,3-diene, boiling point −4°C. A gas, an important monomer of synthetic rubbers; also important as the simplest example of a conjugated double-bond system. » conjugation; gas **1**; monomer

butane [**byoo**tayn] $CH_3CH_2CH_2CH_3$, boiling point 0°C. An easily liquefied alkane gas, obtained as a petroleum fraction. It is supplied as a liquid under pressure for use as a fuel, as in 'Calor®' gas. It has one structural isomer, $(CH_3)_2CH-CH_3$, isobutane or methylpropane. » alkanes; isomers

butanedioic acid » **succinic acid**

Butcher, Rosemary (1947–) British dancer and choreographer, born in Bristol. She trained at Dartington College of Arts, and in the USA with postmodern choreographers. She formed her own company in 1976, and has created works for art galleries and open spaces. » choreography; postmodern dance

butcher's broom A stiff, leathery, dark-green shrub native to Europe and the Mediterranean; true leaves reduced to scales;

white flowers and red berries borne in the centre of apparent leaves, which are really flattened, leaf-like branches. (*Ruscus aculeatus*. Family: *Liliaceae*.) » shrub

butcherbird » **shrike**

Bute, John Stuart, 3rd Earl of (1713–92) British statesman and Prime Minister (1762–3), born in Edinburgh, Scotland. After early court appointments, he became a favourite of George III, who made him one of the principal Secretaries of State (1761). As Prime Minister, his government was highly unpopular. Its principal objective was the supremacy of the royal prerogative, and he was soon forced to resign. From 1768 his life was chiefly spent in the country, where he engaged in science study. He died in London. » George III

Butler, Joseph (1692–1752) English moral philosopher and divine, born at Wantage, Berkshire. He was educated at Oxford, took orders, and was appointed preacher at the Rolls Chapel, London (1718). While holding various church appointments, he wrote his major work, *The Analogy of Religion* (1736), in which he argued that objections against revealed religion may also be levelled against the whole constitution of nature. In 1738 he was made Bishop of Bristol, in 1740 Dean of St Paul's, and in 1750 Bishop of Durham. He died at Bath. » ethics; religion

Butler, R(ichard) A(usten), Baron (1902–82) British Conservative politician, born at Attock Serai, India. Educated at Marlborough and Cambridge, he became MP for Saffron Walden in 1929. After a series of junior ministerial appointments, he became Minister of Education (1941–5), introducing the forward-looking Education Act of 1944, and then Minister of Labour (1945). He became Chancellor of the Exchequer (1951), Lord Privy Seal (1955), Leader of the House of Commons (1955), Home Secretary (1957), First Secretary of State and Deputy Prime Minister (1962). He narrowly lost the premiership to Douglas-Home in 1963, and became Foreign Secretary (1963–4). He was appointed Master of Trinity College, Cambridge (1965–78), and was made a life peer. He died at Great Yeldham, Essex. » Butskellism; Conservative Party

Butler, Reg(inald Cotterell) (1913–81) British sculptor, born at Buntingford, Hertfordshire. He studied architecture, taught at the Architectural Association School in London (1937–9), then practised as an engineer (1939–50). He turned to sculpture in 1951, and soon became recognized as one of the leading exponents of 'linear' constructions in wrought iron, but in his later years turned to a more realistic style. He died at Berkhampstead, Hertfordshire. » English art; sculpture

Butler, Samuel (1612–80) English satirist, baptized at Strensham, Worcestershire. He was educated at Worcester grammar school, and perhaps Oxford or Cambridge. He held several secretarial posts, before becoming steward of Ludlow Castle (1661) and in later years secretary to the Duke of Buckingham. His great poetic work, *Hudibras*, appeared in three parts (1663, 1664, 1678). A burlesque satire on Puritanism, it secured immediate popularity, and was a special favourite of Charles II. He died in London. » Puritanism; satire

Butler, Samuel (1835–1902) British author, painter, and musician, born at Langar Rectory, Nottinghamshire. Educated at Shrewsbury and Cambridge, he became a sheep farmer in New Zealand (1859–64). On returning to England, he worked on his Utopian satire, *Erewhon* (1872) – the word is an inversion of 'nowhere' – in which many conventional practices and customs are reversed. Its supplement, *Erewhon Revisited* (1901), dealt with the origin of religious belief. His musical compositions include two oratorios, gavottes, minuets, fugues, and a cantata. He is best known for his autobiographical novel *The Way of All Flesh*, published posthumously in 1903. He died in London. » English literature; satire

Butlin, Billy, properly **Sir William (Edmund)** (1899–1980) Holiday camp promoter, born in South Africa. He moved with his parents to Canada, served in World War 1, and worked his passage to England with only $5 capital. After a short period in a fun fair he went into business on his own, opening his first camp at Skegness (1936). In World War 2 he served as director-general of hostels to the Ministry of Supply. After the war more camps and hotels were opened both at home and abroad. He was knighted in 1964.

Butor, Michel (Marie François) (1926–) French novelist and critic, born at Lille. He was educated at the Sorbonne, and taught at Manchester (1951–3), Thessaloniki (1954–5), and Geneva (1956–7). One of the more popular writers of the *nouveau roman* ('new novel'), his works include *L'Emploi du temps* (1959, Passing Time), *Degrés* (1960, Degrees), and the nonfiction *Mobile* (1962). He has also written several volumes of poetry. » French literature; nouveau roman

Butskellism A compound of the names of UK Conservative politician R A Butler and the Labour leader Hugh Gaitskell, used in the 1950s and early 1960s to imply a high degree of similarity between the policies of the two main parties. 'Mr Butskell' was first referred to in *The Economist* (Feb 1954). » Butler, R A; consensus politics; Gaitskell

butte [byoot] Isolated, flat-topped, steep-sided residual hills formed by erosion of a mesa, when a remnant of hard rock protects the softer rock underneath. » mesa

butter A pale yellow foodstuff derived from the churning of cream, typically used in baking, cooking, or for spreading on bread. Milk fat exists as globules of fat each surrounded by an outer core of protein. This creates an emulsion of oil in water, whereby milk remains in solution. If the milk is churned or beaten, the resulting collision of the fat globules sees them gradually increase in size; they lose their protective protein coat and consequently their solubility in water. The result is butter, which comprises c.84% fat and c.16% water. » ghee; margarine; milk; protein

butter-nut A deciduous conical tree growing to 30 m/100 ft, native to N America; leaves with 11–19 oval leaflets; male flowers in catkins; fruit 4–6.5 cm/1½–2½ in, ovoid, hairy, containing ridged, nut-like seed. (*Juglans cinerea*. Family: *Juglandaceae*.) » deciduous plants; tree [i]

buttercup A large and diverse genus of annuals or perennials, some aquatic, common throughout most of the world, but especially in the N hemisphere; leaves narrow and entire, or broad and divided; flowers cup-shaped, 5-petalled, glossy yellow, sometimes white or red; bitter-tasting and poisonous to animals, which avoid them, hence the abundance of buttercups in pastures. (Genus: *Ranunculus*, 400 species. Family: *Ranunculaceae*.) » annual; lesser celendine; perennial; water-crowfoot

butterfish » **gunnel**

butterfly An insect belonging to the order *Lepidoptera*, which comprises the butterflies and moths. Butterflies are usually distinguished from moths by being active during the daytime, by folding their wings upright over their bodies when at rest, and by having small knobs at the tips of their antennae; but there are exceptions. » birdwing/cabbage white/milkweed/monarch/nymphalid/papilionid/peacock/satyrid/swallowtail/tortoiseshell butterfly; brimstone; Camberwell beauty; fritulary (entomology); hairstreak; Lepidoptera; morpho; painted lady; red admiral; skipper

butterflybush » **buddleja**

butterflyfish » **angelfish**

butterwort A small carnivorous perennial native to the N hemisphere and the mountains of S America. They have a rosette of oval, slightly inrolled leaves; flowers solitary on leafless stems, 2-lipped, spurred; white, lilac, or violet. Insects are trapped by a sticky coating on the leaves, then washed by rain towards the leaf-margins which inroll over them, secrete digestive enzymes, absorb the products, and finally unroll. (Genus: *Pinguicula*, 46 species. Family: *Lentibulariaceae*.) » carnivorous plant; perennial

button quail A small, plump, ground-living bird of genus *Turnix*, also *Ortyxelos meiffrenii* (the **lark quail** or **quail plover**), native to the warm grasslands of the Old World; unusually for birds, the female actively courts males and takes several mates; the less colourful males incubate the eggs; also known as the **bustard quail** or **hemipode**. Genus *Turnix*, 14 species. Family: *Turnicidae*.) » lark; quail

buttress A mass of masonry built against a wall, usually on the outside of a building to oppose the lateral thrust of an arch,

Flying buttress

roof, or vault. Varied in form, the most notable type is the **flying buttress**, which consists of an arch or half-arch starting from a detached pier and supporting the upper part of a wall. » arch [i]; Gothic architecture; vault [i]

butyl [**byoo**tiyl, **byoo**til] $CH_3CH_2CH_2CH_2$–. A four-carbon aliphatic group. In addition to the form given, there are three other isomers: isobutyl $(CH_3)_2CH$–CH_2–; secondary butyl $(CH_3)(C_2H_5)CH$–; and tertiary butyl $(CH_3)_3C$–. » aliphatic compound; carbon; isomers

Buxtehude, Diderik or **Dietrich** [bukste**hoo**duh] (1637–1707) Danish composer and organist, born at Oldesloe or Helsingborg (now in Sweden). In 1668 he was appointed organist at the Marienkirche, Lübeck, where he began the famous *Abendmusiken* – Advent evening concerts of his own sacred music and organ works. In 1705 Bach walked 200 miles across Germany and Handel travelled from Hamburg to attend his concerts. He died at Lübeck.

Buys Ballot, Christoph H(endrick) D(iederick) [**biyz ba**lot] (1817–90) Dutch meteorologist, born at Kloetinge. He was educated in Utrecht, where he became professor of mathematics in 1847. He founded the Netherlands Meteorological Institute in 1854. The law relating wind direction to areas of high and low pressure (**Buys Ballot's law** 1857) arose from his work. He died in Utrecht. » meteorology; wind [i]

buzz-bomb » **V-1**

buzzard A large hawk found worldwide (except Australasia and Malaysia); brown, grey, and white; soaring flight, but spends much time perching; kills prey on ground; inhabits woodlands or open country; territorial. (Genus: *Buteo*, 25 species.) » hawk

Byblos [**bib**los] 34°07N 35°39E. An ancient trading city on the Lebanese coast N of Beirut; a world heritage site. It was the chief supplier of papyrus to the Greeks, which they accordingly nicknamed 'byblos' – hence the word 'bible' (literally, the papyrus book). » Phoenicia

Byelarus, Republic of » **Belorussia**

Byelorussia » **Belorussia**

Byng, George, 1st Viscount Torrington (1663–1733) English sailor, born at Wrotham, Kent. He joined the navy at 15, and gained rapid promotion as a supporter of William of Orange. Made Rear-Admiral in 1703, he captured Gibraltar, and was knighted for his gallant conduct at Málaga. In 1708 he defeated the French fleet of James Stuart, the Pretender, and in 1718 destroyed the Spanish fleet off Messina. He was created viscount in 1721. » Stuart, James; William III

Byng (of Vimy), Julian Hedworth George, 1st Viscount (1862–1935) British general, born at Wrotham Park, Middlesex. He commanded the 9th Army Corps in Gallipoli (1915), the Canadian Army Corps (1916–17), and the 3rd Army (1917–18). After the war he became Governor-General of Canada (1921–6) and Commissioner of the Metropolitan Police (1928–31), and was made a viscount in 1928 and a field marshal in 1932. He died at Thorpe Hall, Essex. » World War 1

Byrd, Richard E(velyn) (1888–1957) US rear admiral, explorer, and aviator, born at Winchester, Virginia. He made the first aeroplane flight over the N Pole (9 May 1926), then flew over the S Pole (28–9 Nov 1929). He carried out Antarctic explorations in 1933–4 and 1939–41. He died at Boston, Massachusetts. » aircraft [i]; Poles

Byrd, William (1543–1623) English composer, born probably in Lincoln. His early life is obscure, but it is likely that he was one of the Children of the Chapel Royal, under Tallis. He was organist of Lincoln Cathedral until 1572, when he was made joint organist with Tallis of the Chapel Royal. In 1575 Byrd and Tallis were given an exclusive licence for the printing and sale of music. A firm Catholic, Byrd was several times prosecuted as a recusant, but he wrote music of great power and beauty for both the Catholic and the Anglican services, as well as madrigals, songs, keyboard pieces, and music for strings. » Tallis

Byron (of Rochdale), George (Gordon), 6th Baron (1788–1824) British poet, born in London. His first 10 years were spent in poor surroundings in Aberdeen, but then he inherited the title of his great-uncle, and went on to Dulwich, Harrow, and Cambridge, where he led a dissipated life. An early collection of poems, *Hours of Idleness* (1807) was badly reviewed, and after replying in satirical vein, he set out on his grand tour, visiting Spain, Malta, Albania, Greece, and the Aegean. He then published the popular *Childe Harold's Pilgrimage* (1812), and several other works, becoming the darling of London society, and giving to Europe the concept of the 'Byronic hero'. He married in 1815, but was suspected of a more than brotherly love for his half-sister, and was ostracized. He left for Europe, where he met Shelley, and spent two years in Venice. Some of his best works belong to this period, including *Don Juan* (1819–24). He gave active help to the Italian revolutionaries, and in 1823 joined the Greek insurgents who had risen against the Turks. He died of marsh fever at Missolonghi. His body was brought back to England and buried in Nottingham. » English literature; poetry

byte A fixed number of bits (binary digits), usually defined as a set of 8 bits. An 8-bit byte can therefore take 256 different values corresponding to the binary numbers 00000000, 00000001, 00000010, through to 11111111. A **Kilobyte** is one thousand bytes; a **Megabyte** is one million bytes. » bit

Byurakan Astrophysical Observatory An optical astronomical observatory in Armenia, 40 km/25 ml N of Yerevan. It is known for the discovery of Markarian galaxies, which emit strongly in the ultraviolet region of the spectrum. » galaxy; observatory

Byzantine art The art which flourished from AD 330, when Constantinople (modern Istanbul) became the capital of the Roman Empire, to 1453 when that city fell to the Turks. It was conservative in form, stylized and overwhelmingly theological in content. The church of St Sophia at Istanbul (6th-c), the greatest work of early Byzantine architecture, combines the axial Roman basilican plan with a huge dome; later churches adopted the Greek-cross plan, with four equal arms and a small dome carried on a high drum. Churches were adorned with richly-coloured marble inlay, and with mosaics and wall-paintings of subjects chosen from the Bible and apocryphal literature. » art; church [i]; Coptic art; icon (religion); iconoclasm; mosaic; orders of architecture [i]; Russian art

Byzantine Empire [bi**zan**tiyn] The E half of the Roman Empire, with its capital at Constantinople, formerly Byzantium. Founded in AD 330, Byzantium survived the collapse of the W Empire by nearly a thousand years, only falling to the Ottoman Turks in 1453. One of its greatest rulers was Justinian (527–65). » Justinian I

C

C N Tower or **Canadian National Tower** The world's tallest self-supporting tower. Erected in Toronto, Ontario in 1973–5, it is 555.3 m/1 822 ft high. » Toronto

ca(a)'ing whale » **pilot whale**

Cabal [ka**bal**] An acronym taken from the initials of the five leading advisers of Charles II of England between 1667 and 1673: Clifford, Arlington, Buckingham, Ashley Cooper (Shaftesbury), and Lauderdale. The name is misleading, since these five were by no means Charles's only advisers; nor did they agree on a common policy. Arlington and Buckingham were bitter rivals. » Charles II (of England)

Caballé, Montserrat [kaba**yay**] (1933–) Spanish soprano, born in Barcelona, where she studied at the Liceo. She made her operatic debut in Basle (1956), and soon earned an international reputation, especially in operas by Donizetti and Verdi. In 1964 she married the tenor Bernabé Marti. » Donizetti; opera; Verdi

cabbage A vegetable grown for its dense leafy head, which is harvested before the flowers develop and the head elongates. There are numerous cultivars, all derived from wild cabbage, a biennial or perennial with woody, leafy stems and yellow cross-shaped flowers, native to W Europe and the Mediterranean. (*Brassica oleracea*. Family: *Cruciferae*.) » biennial; brassica; broccoli; brussel sprout; cauliflower; cress; cultivar; kohlrabi; perennial; vegetable

cabbage white butterfly A large butterfly, found in Europe and N Africa; wings mainly white with black markings, and yellow on undersides of hindwings. The caterpillars are pests of cabbage family crops. (Order: *Lepidoptera*. Family: *Pieridae*.) » butterfly; caterpillar

Cabbala » **Kabbalah**

caber tossing The art of tossing a tree trunk (*caber*), practised in Scotland. The competitor has the caber, about 12–18 ft (3–4 m) in length, placed vertically into the palms of his hands. He then runs with it and tosses it; the caber should revolve longitudinally, its base landing away from him. The tradition is popular at Highland Games gatherings.

Cabinda [ka**been**da] area 7 270 sq km/2 800 sq ml. Province of Angola on the SW coast of Africa, N of the R Congo; bounded W by the Atlantic and surrounded by the Congo, it is separated from the rest of Angola; attached to Angola in 1886 by agreement with Belgium; seaport and chief town Cabinda, 5°35S 12°12E, 55 km/34 ml N of the R Congo estuary; offshore oil fields; oil refining. » Angola [i]

cabinet In a parliamentary system, a group of senior ministers usually drawn from the majority party. In Britain (where cabinet government originated), the cabinet has no constitutional status other than the conventions by which it operates. It forms the link between the executive and legislative branches of government, as its members must be drawn from the legislature. Cabinet members are bound by the doctrine of collective responsibility: ministers must publicly support decisions taken by the cabinet, or its committees, or else resign. The importance of the cabinet varies across political systems, some (eg Britain) attaching greater importance than others (eg Germany) to co-ordination in decision-making. A cabinet may also be found in a non-parliamentary system, such as that of the USA, where it provides the President with an additional consultative body. » legislature

cabinet picture A small easel painting, carefully executed, intended for close viewing, and suitable for display in a small private room. The Dutch masters of the 17th-c specialized in this type of picture. » painting

cable An insulated conductor used to carry power or signals. The simplest type has a core of conducting metal, such as copper, surrounded by an insulating sheath of plastic or rubber. *Co-axial* cables have another sheath of wire braid under the outer insulation. Telephone connections between countries use multicore cables. » insulation

cable television The distribution of video programmes to subscribers by co-axial cable or fibre-optic links, rather than by broadcast transmission, providing a wide range of choice to individual homes within a specific area. Programmes may originate from satellite transmission to a master antenna installed at the cable centre, as well as from recorded sources. » cable; television; video

Cabot, John, or **Caboto, Giovanni** (1425–c.1500) A Genoese pilot, who discovered the mainland of N America. Little is known about his life. About 1490 he settled in Bristol, and set sail in 1497 with two ships, accompanied by his three sons, sighting Cape Breton Island and Nova Scotia on 24 June. He set out on another voyage in 1498, and died at sea. » Cabot, Sebastian

Cabot, Sebastian (1474–1557) Explorer and navigator, son of John Cabot, born in Venice or Bristol. He accompanied his father to the American coast, then in 1512 entered the service of Ferdinand V of Spain as a cartographer. In 1526 he explored the coast of S America for Charles V, but failed to colonize the area, and was imprisoned and banished to Africa. He returned to Spain in 1533, and later to England, where he was made inspector of the navy by Edward VI. He died in London. » Cabot, John

Cabral, or **Cabrera, Pedro Álvarez** (c.1467–c.1520) Portuguese discoverer, born at Belmonte. In 1500 he sailed from Lisbon bound for the East Indies, but was carried to the unknown coast of Brazil, which he claimed on behalf of Portugal. He then made for India, but was forced to land at Mozambique, providing the first description of that country. He made the first commercial treaty between Portugal and India, and returned to Lisbon in 1501. He was given no further missions, and remained for the rest of his life at Santarém.

Cabrera [ka**bray**ra] 39°15N 2°58E. Small Spanish island in the Balearic Is, Mediterranean Sea; 15 km/9 ml S of Majorca; tourism. » Balearic Islands; Spain [i]

Cabrini, St Francesca Xavier (1850–1917), feast day 13 November. US nun, born near Lodi, Italy. She founded the Missionary Sisters of the Sacred Heart (1886), emigrated to the USA in 1887 and became renowned for her social and charitable work. She died in Chicago. Canonized in 1946, she was the first American saint. » monasticism

cacao An evergreen tree native to C America, widely cultivated elsewhere and of great economic importance; leaves oblong; flowers pink, borne in clusters directly on trunks and older branches; fruit an ovoid yellow pod, leathery and grooved, enclosing up to 100 beans embedded in soft pulp. The beans are dried, roasted, and ground to produce cocoa powder, used in drinks and chocolate. Pressed beans yield cocoa butter. (*Theobroma cacao*. Family: *Sterculiaceae*.) » chocolate; evergreen plants; tree [i]

Cáceres [**kath**eres], Arabic **Qazris** 39°26N 6°23W, pop (1981) 71 852. Walled town and capital of Cáceres province, W Spain; on R Cáceres, 297 km/185 ml WSW of Madrid; a world heritage site; Roman settlement, 1st-c BC; railway; pharmaceuticals, chemicals, textiles, leather; Plaza Santa Maria, Lower Golfines Palace, Church of San Mateo, Maltravieso cave paintings. » Spain [i]

cachalot [**kash**alot] » **sperm whale**

cache memory [kash] A very high-speed buffer memory which operates between the computer processor and main memory in high performance computer systems. » buffer (computing); memory, computer

cacomistle [**kak**uhmisl] A mammal native to S USA and C America; pale brown with lighter underparts; long bushy tail with black bands; inhabits rocky areas or forest; also known as **cacomixl** or **ringtail**. (Genus: *Bassariscus*, 2 species. Family: *Procyonidae*.) » mammal [i]

cactus A large family of plants typical of arid zones but found in a number of habitats: some occur as epiphytes in the canopy of tropical rainforests where water can also be in short supply; others in high mountains; but almost all are confined to the New World. In the Old World they are paralleled by various members of the spurge family (*Euphorbiaceae*), remarkably similar in appearance, and sometimes mistaken for cacti.

Cacti exhibit a wide variety of size, form, and adaptations to dry conditions, some very sophisticated. All species are succulents, and store water, sometimes in the roots but usually in swollen, often barrel-like, stems which may be of huge capacity and capable of sustaining the plant over several years without rain; the stem often has pleat-like ribs which allow it to expand or contract as the water content changes. Water loss is reduced in various ways. The plants are leathery with a thick waxy cuticle. In some species the surface area is reduced by assuming a globose shape, and the vulnerable leaves are absent or reduced to spines, photosynthesis being carried out by the green stem. The spines can be very intricate, ranging from simple prongs to parasols and long, soft hairs; they shade or insulate the cactus, protect it from animals, reflect light, and collect and absorb droplets of dew – an important source of water.

Cacti show a wide range of flowers, often large and conspicuous, pollinated by bees, hawk-moths, hummingbirds, and bats. Bird-pollinated day flowers are predominantly reds and yellows and scentless; moth- and bat-pollinated night flowers are predominantly white, often strongly perfumed, sometimes unpleasantly so. The fruits are usually fleshy and sometimes edible. (Family: *Cactaceae*, c.2000 species.) » cactus hybrid/moth; epiphyte; photosynthesis; spurge; succulent

cactus hybrid A type of cactus (an epiphyte) with spineless, arching stems made up of flattened, jointed segments and magenta flowers, appearing in winter. (*Schlumbergera* × *buckleyi*. Family: *Cactaceae*.) » cactus; epiphyte

cactus moth A small, dull moth with narrow forewings and broad hindwings; introduced successfully into Australia in 1925 as a measure to control the spread of prickly pear cactus. The caterpillars destroy cactus plants by burrowing into stems. (*Cactoblastis cactorum*. Family: *Pyralidae*. Order: *Lepidoptera*.) » cactus; moth

CAD » **computer-aided design**

Cadbury, George (1839–1922) British businessman, born and died in Birmingham. In partnership with his brother **Richard** (1835–99), he expanded his father's business, and established for the workers the model village of Bournville (1879), a prototype for modern methods of housing and town planning. He also became proprietor of the *Daily News* (1902), and was an ardent Quaker.

caddis fly A dull-coloured, moth-like insect; aquatic larvae build silken protective cases incorporating sand, twigs, and leaves; feed on algae, fungi, or plant material; adults live near water; forewings hairy, held at oblique vertical angle at rest. (Order: *Trichoptera*.) » fly; larva; moth

Cade, Jack (?–1450) Irish leader of the insurrection of 1450 against Henry VI. After an unsettled early career he lived in Sussex, possibly as a physician. Assuming the name of Mortimer, and the title of Captain of Kent, he marched on London with a great number cf followers, and entered the city. A promise of pardon sowed dissension among the insurgents; they dispersed, and a price was set upon Cade's head. He attempted to reach the coast, but was killed near Heathfield, Sussex. » Henry VI

cadence A melodic or (more commonly) harmonic formula marking the end of a phrase or longer section of music. The 'perfect' cadence, formed by dominant-tonic chords, is the one that most often ends a piece. The word (from Lat *cadere* 'to fall') originates from the tendency for a plainchant (or, in early polyphony, a tenor line) to fall to its final note from the one above. » plainchant

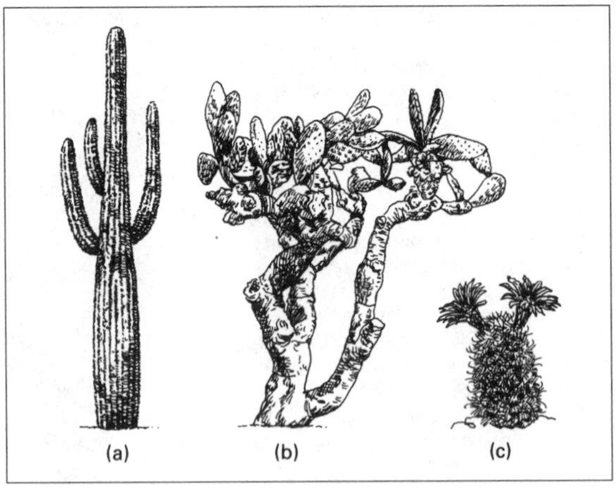

Three types of cactus – Saguaro (a); prickly pear (b); Mamillaria tetrancistra (76 mm/3 in) (c)

cadenza An improvised (or improvisatory) passage, usually of a virtuoso and rhythmically free character, which the soloist in a concerto plays as a kind of adjunct to the main body of the piece. In the concertos of Mozart and Beethoven, the main cadenza is heard towards the end of the first movement; later composers, such as Liszt, introduced them at various unpredictable points. During the cadenza the orchestra is usually silent, but some composers (eg Strauss, Elgar, Walton) have written accompanied cadenzas. » cadence; improvisation

Cader Idris [**kad**er **id**ris] ('chair of Idris'); 52°42N 3°54W. Mountain ridge in Gwynedd, NW Wales, UK; in Snowdonia National Park, SW of Dolgellau; rises to 892 m/2 926 ft at Pen-y-Gader. » Gwynedd; Snowdon

Cádiz [ka**diz**], Span [**ka**deeth], ancient **Gadier** or **Gades** 36°30N 6°20W, pop(1981) 157 766. Seaport and capital of Cádiz province, Andalusia, SW Spain; in the Bay of Cádiz, 663 km/412 ml SSW of Madrid; base for Spanish treasure ships from the Americas, 16th–18th-c; Francis Drake burned the ships of Philip II at anchor here, 1587; bishopric; airport; railway; car ferries to Casablanca and Canary Is; university; naval harbour of La Carraca; shipbuilding, trade in sherry, fish, salt, olives; cathedral (18th-c), Chapel of Santa Catalina; Fiestas Tipicas Gaditanas (May), Festival of Spain (Aug), Trofeo Internacional Ramon (football competition, Aug). » Andalusia; Drake; Spain [i]

cadmium Cd, element 48, density 8.7g cm^{-3}, melting point 321°C, colour bluish-white. A metal, normally occurring with other metals, especially copper and zinc, as the sulphide, CdS. The metal is recovered for use in low-melting alloys and as an absorber for neutrons in atomic reactors. Cadmium compounds are used as phosphors in colour television tubes. Its commonest oxidation state is +2; its compounds are very toxic. » alloy; chemical elements; metal; nuclear reactor [i]; RR90

Cadmus [**kad**muhs] According to Greek legend the son of Agenor, King of Tyre; he set off in pursuit of his sister Europa, arrived in Greece, and founded the city of Thebes, teaching the natives to write. He sowed dragon's teeth, from which sprang up armed men. » Europa (mythology)

caecilian [see**sil**ian] An amphibian of worldwide tropical order *Gymnophiona* (163 species); length, up to 1.5 m/5 ft; body worm-like with encircling rings and no legs; some species with fish-like scales; burrows on forest floors or in riverbeds; eats invertebrates. » amphibian

Caedmon [**kad**mon] (?–c.680) The first English poet of known name. Bede reports that, unlearned till mature in years, Caedmon became aware in a semi-miraculous way that he was called to exercise the gift of religious poety. He became a monk at Whitby, and spent the rest of his life composing poems on the Bible histories and on religious subjects. » Anglo-Saxon; English literature; poetry

Caelum [**kiy**luhm] (Lat 'chisel') An inconspicuous S hemisphere constellation. » constellation; RR8

Caen [kã] 49°10N 0°22W, pop (1982) 117 119. Port and capital of Calvados department, NW France; on R Orne, 15 km/9 ml S of R Seine; airport; railway; university (1432, refounded 1809); principal seat of William the Conqueror; badly damaged during Normandy campaign in World War 2; tourism, commerce, steel, horse breeding, silk, leather; abbey church of St-Etienne, with tomb of William the Conqueror; Church of St-Pierre, with famous clock tower. » William I (of England); World War 2

Caernarfon [kiyr**nar**von], English **Caernarvon** [kuh**nah**vn] 53°08N 4°16W, pop (1981) 9 431. Historic county town in Arfon district, Gwynedd, NW Wales, UK; on Menai Straits; yachting centre; agricultural trade, plastics, metal products; tourism; castle (1284), birthplace of Edward II; investiture of Prince Charles as Prince of Wales, 1969. » Charles, Prince of Wales; Gwynedd; Menai Straits

Caesar, in full **Gaius Julius Caesar** (c.100–44 BC) Roman politician of patrician origins but slender means, whose military genius, as displayed in the Gallic Wars (58–51 BC), enabled Rome to extend her empire permanently to the Atlantic seaboard, but whose ruthless ambition led to the breakdown of the Republican system of government at home. Never one to allow himself to be blocked by constitutional niceties, in 60 BC he joined with Pompey and Crassus (the so-called First Triumvirate) to protect his interests in the state, and in 49 BC, to avoid being humbled by his enemies at Rome, he led his army across the R Rubicon into Italy and plunged the state into civil war. Victory over the Pompeian forces at Pharsalus (48 BC), Zela (47 BC), Thapsus (46 BC), and Munda (45 BC) left him in sole control at Rome. He did not disguise his absolute power, taking the title 'Dictator for Life' in 44 BC, and allowing himself to be paid extravagant honours which suggested he was aiming at regal and even divine status. This was too much for many Republican-minded Romans, and under the leadership of Brutus and Cassius they conspired to murder him. His brief period of power left him with little time to carry through the many reforms, social, economic, and administrative, that he had intended. It was left to his great-nephew and heir, Octavian (the future Emperor Augustus) to reap where he had sown, and also to learn from his mistakes. » Augustus; Britain, Roman; Brutus; Cassius; Gallic Wars; Pompey; Roman history [i]; triumvirate

caesarian/cesarian section The surgical removal of the foetus from the uterus. It is undertaken when continuing with labour and vaginal delivery causes or is likely to cause significant maternal or foetal distress. Maternal distress may result from such factors as excessive pain or uncontrolled hypertension. Foetal distress implies the life of the foetus is threatened, such as by impaired placental blood flow or a threatened miscarriage. » labour; pregnancy [i]

caffeine $C_8H_{10}N_4O_2$. An alkaloid, also called **theine**, a weak stimulant of the central nervous system. It is found in both coffee and tea, from which it may be removed by extraction with organic solvents. » alkaloids; solvent

Cage, John (1912–) US composer, born in Los Angeles. He studied there and in Paris, developing as an avant-garde composer who not only used such experimental resources as indeterminacy, chance, electronics and the 'prepared piano', but has composed (if that is the word) pieces, such as *4′ 33″* (1952, silent throughout) and *Radio Music* (1956, for 1–8 radios), which challenge received ideas about what music is. » avant garde; prepared piano

Cagliari [**kal**yaree], ancient **Carales** 39°13N 9°08E, pop (1981) 233 848. Seaport and capital of Cagliari province, S Sardinia, Italy; on the S coast, in the Gulf of Cagliari; archbishopric; airport; railway; ferries to mainland Italy; university (1606); oil terminal, petrochemicals, milling, fishing, trade in minerals; cathedral (1312), Roman amphitheatre, museum of archaeology; Sagra di San Efisio costume festival (May). » Sardinia

Cagliostro, Alessandro, Conte di ('Count of'), originally **Giuseppe Balsamo** [kal**yos**tro] (1743–95) Italian adventurer and charlatan, born at Palermo. He learned some chemistry and medicine at a monastery, married the beautiful Lorenze Feliciani, and from 1771 they visited many centres in Europe as Count and Countess Cagliostro. Successful alike as physician, philosopher, alchemist, and necromancer, he carried on a lively business in his 'elixir of immortal youth', and founded lodges of 'Egyptian freemasons'. In 1789 he was imprisoned for life in San Leo, near Urbino, where he died.

Cagney, James (1899–1986) US film actor, born in New York City. He studied at Columbia, and after ten years as an actor and dancer in vaudeville, his film performance as the gangster in *The Public Enemy* (1931) brought him stardom. His ebullient energy and aggressive personality kept him in demand for the next 30 years, including such varied productions as *A Midsummer Night's Dream* (1935), *Angels with Dirty Faces* (1938), and *Yankee Doodle Dandy* (1942), for which he was awarded an Oscar. He retired after 1961, but returned for a brief appearance in *Ragtime* (1981). He died at his farm in New York State.

Cahokia A prehistoric city of Middle Mississippi Indians in E St Louis, Illinois, USA, founded c.600 and, at 13 sq km/5 sq ml, the largest such settlement in N America; a world heritage site. At its height (c.1050–1250), the population reached c.10 000. The central plaza has 17 platform mounds, notably Monks Mound (c.1200), a 6 000 cu m/7 850 cu yd earthen pyramid, 316 m/1 030 ft by 241 m/790 ft at the base, still standing 30 m/100 ft high. » Woodland culture

CAI » **computer-aided instruction**

Caiaphas [**kiy**afas] (1st-c) Son-in-law of Annas, eventually appointed by the Romans to be his successor as high priest of Israel (c.18–36). In the New Testament he interrogated Jesus after his arrest (*Matt* 26; *John* 18) and Peter after his detention in Jerusalem (*Acts* 4). » Annas; Jesus Christ

Caicos Islands [**kay**kuhs] Island group in the W Atlantic, SE of the Bahamas, forming a British dependent territory with the Turks Is; settled by Loyalist planters from the S States of America after the War of Independence; after the abolition of slavery (1838), the planters left the islands to their former slaves. » slave trade; Turks and Caicos Islands

Caillaux, Joseph (Marie Auguste) [kiy**oh**] (1863–1944) French financier, statesman, and Prime Minister (1911–12), born at Le Mans. He was trained as a lawyer, elected to the Chamber of Deputies in 1898, and became Finance Minister in several governments. His brief term as Prime Minister ended when he was overthrown for showing too conciliatory an attitude towards Germany. In 1914, his second wife shot Gaston Calmette, editor of *Figaro*, who had launched a campaign against him; after a famous trial, she was acquitted. He stayed in politics until France fell in 1940, when he retired. He died at Mamers. » France [i]

caiman or **cayman** [**kay**man] A member of the alligator family (5 species), native to C and S America; length, up to 2 m/6½ ft; inhabits rivers and swamps; eats fish and other water-dwelling vertebrates. » alligator [i]

Cain [kayn] Biblical character, the eldest son of Adam and Eve, the brother of Abel and Seth. He is portrayed (*Gen* 4) as a farmer whose offering to God was rejected, in contrast to that of his herdsman brother Abel. This led to his murder of Abel, and his punishment of being banished to a nomadic life. » Abel; Adam and Eve; Bible; Enoch

Cainozoic era » **Cenozoic era**

cairn terrier A breed of dog, developed in N Scotland for driving foxes out of their burrows; small with very short legs; thick shaggy brown coat; ears erect and expression alert. » fox; terrier

Cairngorms or **Cairngorm Mountains** Mountain range in NEC Scotland, part of Grampian Mts; granite mountain mass in SE Highland and SW Grampian regions; rises to 1 309 m/4 295 ft in Ben Macdhui; between the rivers Dee (S) and Spey (N); winter sports region, centre at Aviemore. » Ben Macdhui; Grampians (Scotland); Scotland [i]

Cairns [**kairnz**] 16°51S 145°43E, pop (1981) 48 557. Resort and seaport on the NE coast of Queensland, Australia; starting point for tours to the Great Barrier Reef and the Cape York Peninsula; offshore are Green I, Fitzroy I, and Arlington Reef;

railway; airfield; agricultural trade, timber, mining, sugar, deep-sea fishing. » Great Barrier Reef; Queensland

Cairo, Arabic **El Qahira** 30°03N 31°15E, pop (1984e) 9 500 000 (Greater Cairo). Capital of Egypt and Cairo governorate; at head of R Nile delta, 180 km/112 ml SE of Alexandria; largest African city; originally founded as El Fustat in AD 642; occupied by British, 1882–1946; airport; railway; four universities (1908, 1919, 1950, and Muslim university in Mosque of El Azhar, 972); tourism, cement, chemicals, leather, textiles, brewing, food processing; Islamic Cairo a world heritage site; mosques of Amur (7th-c), Kait Bey (15th-c), Ibn Touloun (878), Sultan Hassan (14th-c); major archaeological sites nearby, including Heliopolis, pyramids at El Giza, ruins of Memphis; Egyptian museum of antiquities, Coptic museum, museum of Islamic art, royal library. » Egypt [i]; Memphis (Egypt); pyramid

Cairoli, Charlie (1910–80) French circus clown. The son of a juggler, he made his debut as a circus performer at the age of five. He went to Britain in 1938 and was for 39 years a star attraction of the Blackpool Tower Circus, until ill health forced his retirement.

caisson [**kay**suhn] A permanent structure for keeping water or soft ground from flowing into the site when building foundations. There are several types: *open* caissons, open at the top and bottom; *box* caissons, open at the top and closed at the bottom; and *pneumatic* caissons, containing a working chamber in which compressed air excludes the water. » cofferdam

caisson disease [**kay**sn] » **decompression sickness**

CAL » **computer-aided learning**

calabash A trailing or climbing vine, native to warm Old World regions, with white flowers and woody, bottle-shaped fruits; also called **bottle gourd**. It was the source of the earliest containers, and is still used in this way today. (*Lagenaria siceraria*. Family: *Cucurbitaceae*.) » climbing plant; gourd

calabash tree An evergreen tree growing to 12 m/40 ft, native to tropical America; clusters of lance-shaped leaves; flowers bell-shaped, borne directly on trunk and branches; fruit a woody berry up to 30 cm/12 in long or more, flask-shaped and used as a container. (*Crescentia cujete*. Family: *Bignoniaceae*.) » calabash; evergreen plants; gourd; tree [i]

Calabria [ka**lay**bria], Ital [ka**la**bria] pop (1981) 2 061 182; area 15 079 sq km/5 820 sq ml. Region of S Italy, occupying the 'toe' of the country, between the Ionian and Tyrrhenian Seas; capital, Catanzaro; chief towns, Cosenza, Crotone, Reggio di Calabria, Locri; underdeveloped area with mixed Mediterranean agriculture; wheat, olives, figs, wine, citrus fruit; subject to earthquakes, floods, and erosion; Calabria national park, area 170 sq km/66 sq ml, established in 1968. » Italy [i]

Calais [**ka**lay] 50°57N 1°52E, pop (1982) 76 935. Seaport in Pas-de-Calais department, NW France; on the Straits of Dover, at the shortest crossing to England; 34 km/21 ml ESE of Dover and 238 km/148 ml N of Paris; captured by England, 1346 (commemorated in Rodin sculpture); retaken by France, 1558; British base in World War 1; centre of heavy fighting in World War 2; airport; railway; ferry services to Dover and Folkestone; tulle and machine-made lace, shipping services. » Dover (UK); Rodin

calamine A mixture of zinc carbonate and ferric oxide, used as an ointment for many skin conditions. It was formerly a common name for the mineral *smithsonite* (zinc carbonate). » iron; zinc

Calamity Jane, byname of **Martha Jane Burke** (c.1852–1903) US frontierswoman, possibly born at Princeton, Missouri. Of eccentric character, usually dressed in man's clothes, she was celebrated for her bravery and her skill in riding and shooting, particularly during the gold rush days in the Black Hills of Dakota. She is said to have threatened 'calamity' for any man who tried to court her. She died at Terry, South Dakota.

calceolaria [kalseeuh**lair**eea] A large genus of annuals, perennials, and shrubs native to C and S America; wrinkled leaves in opposite pairs; characteristic 2-lipped flowers with lower lip inflated and pouch-like. Commonly grown ornamentals are mainly hybrids with yellow, orange, or red spotted flowers up to 5 cm/2 in diameter. (Genus: *Calceolaria*, 300–400 species. Family: *Scrophulariaceae*.) » annual; perennial; shrub

Calchas [**kal**kas] A seer on the Greek side during the Trojan War. He advised that Iphigeneia should be sacrificed at Aulis; at Troy he told Agamemnon to return Chryseis, the daughter of the priest of Apollo, to stop the plague. He died in a combat of 'seeing' with Mopsos. » Trojan War

calcite A mineral form of calcium carbonate ($CaCO_3$), and the main constituent of limestone and marble. It can occur by precipitation from carbonate-rich solutions to form stalactites and stalagmites, and forms the structure of coral reefs. Good crystals formed in vein deposits are transparent, and termed *Iceland spar*. It is used in the manufacture of Portland cement. » aragonite; chalk; limestone; marble

calcitonin [kalsi**toh**nin] A hormone (a polypeptide) synthesized and secreted by 'C' cells in the thyroid gland in mammals, and in the ultimobranchial glands in other vertebrates; sometimes called **thyrocalcitonin**. It is released in response to elevated blood calcium levels, and lowers extracellular calcium levels. » calcium; hormones; peptide; thyroid glands

calcium Ca, element 20, melting point 839°C. A very reactive silvery metal only found combined in nature; the metal is obtained by electrolysis. It is the fifth most common element in the Earth's crust, occurring mainly in fluorite (CaF_2), gypsum ($CaSO_4.2H_2O$), and limestone ($CaCO_3$). It shows an oxidation state of +2 in almost all of its compounds, which are mainly ionic. Ca^{2+} ions are largely responsible for hardness in water. Calcium is an essential element in biology, being used in the structural tissue of both plants and animals; its compounds are common components of agricultural fertilizers, and are ingredients of both glass and cement. The oxide (CaO, or *quicklime*) is widely used as a strong base. Other important compounds include the hypochlorite ($Ca(OCl)_2$) and the carbide (CaC_2). » bleaching powder; bone; chemical elements; electrolysis [i]; fertilizer; RR90

calculi In medicine, stone-like concretions which form within certain organs and ducts. They are formed mainly by calcium salts, but other constituents include uric acid, cholesterol, and xanthine. The most common sites include the bladder, kidneys and ureter, and the bile ducts. » colic; urinary stones

calculus » **differential calculus; integral calculus** [i]

calculus, fundamental theorem of If a function $f(t)$ meets certain conditions, $\frac{d}{dx}\int_0^x f(t)dt = f(x)$. This theorem unites differential calculus and integral calculus. It is usually credited to Isaac Barrow (1636–77), friend and tutor of Isaac Newton. » differential calculus; integral calculus [i]; Newton, Isaac; theorem

Calcutta [kal**kuh**ta] 22°36N 88°24E, pop (1991) 10 860 000. Port capital of West Bengal, E India; on the R Hugli in the R Ganges delta, 128 km/79 ml from the Bay of Bengal; largest city in India; chief port of E India; founded by the British East India Company, 1690; capital of British India, 1773–1912; airport (Dum Dum); railway; three universities; textiles, chemicals, paper, metal, jute, crafts; Ochterlony Monument, Raj Bhaven, St John's Cathedral (1787), Nakhoda Mosque (1926), Marble Palace (1835), Jain temples (1867), Hindu Bengali Temple of Kali (1809). » Black Hole of Calcutta; East India Company, British; West Bengal

Calder, Alexander (1898–1976) US artist, born at Lawnton, Philadelphia. He studied mechanical engineering, then art in New York City. His first exhibitions were held in Paris and Berlin in 1929. A painter, sculptor, and illustrator, his best-known works are the hanging wire mobiles which he began to make in 1934. He died in New York City. » kinetic art; mobile

caldera [kal**dair**a] A large volcanic crater formed when the remains of a volcano subside down into a magma chamber, emptied after a violent eruption. The caldera may subsequently fill with water, and become a crater lake – a notable example being Crater Lake in Oregon, USA. » Crater Lake; magma; volcano

Calderón de la Barca, Pedro (1600–81) Spanish dramatist, born and died in Madrid. He studied law and philosophy at Salamanca, and in 1635 was appointed to the court of Philip IV, where he began to write plays. He served in the army in Catalonia (1640–2), and in 1651 entered the priesthood. Recalled to court, he became chaplain of honour to Philip and continued to write plays, masques, and operas for the court, the church, and the public theatres until his death. He wrote over 100 plays on secular themes, such as *El pripe constante* (1629, The Constant Prince) and *El alcalde de Zalamea* (1640, The Mayor of Zalamea). In addition he wrote many religious plays, including over 70 outdoor dramas for the festival of Corpus Christi. » drama; Spanish literature; masque; theatre

Caldwell, Erskine (1903–87) US author, born at White Oak, Georgia. His early schooling was erratic, and he held a variety of jobs, working amongst the 'poor Whites', before becoming a writer. His best-known novels are *Tobacco Road* (1932) and *God's Little Acre* (1933). Much of his work, both fiction and nonfiction, addresses issues of social injustice in the US South. » American literature

Caledonian Canal A line of inland navigation following the Great Glen (Glen Mor) in Highland region, Scotland; extends from Inverness (NE) to Loch Eil near Fort William (SW), thus linking North Sea and Irish Sea; passes through Lochs Ness, Oich, and Lochy and 35 km/22 ml of man-made channels (1803–47); 29 locks; total length 96 km/60 ml; built by Telford. » Highland; Scotland [i]; Telford, Thomas

calendar » **French Republican/Gregorian/Julian calendar**; RR22

Calgary 51°05N 114°05W, pop (1984) 619 814. Town in S Alberta, SW Canada, on the Bow R, near foothills of Rocky Mts; centre of rich grain and livestock area; growth following arrival of Canadian Pacific Railway, 1883; oil found to the S, 1914; airport; communications and transport centre; university (1945); meat packing, oil refining; ice hockey team, Calgary Flames; Glenbow Alberta art gallery and museum, Heritage Park open-air museum, Dinosaur Park, Calgary Zoo; Calgary Tower (1967, 190 m/623 ft), Centennial Planetarium; Calgary Stampede rodeo show (Jul). » Alberta; Canadian Pacific Railway

Cali [**ka**lee] 3°24N 76°30W, pop (1985) 1 398 276. Capital of Valle de Cauca department, W Colombia; third largest city in Colombia, at centre of rich sugar-producing region; founded, 1536; airport; railway; two universities (1945, 1958); coffee, sugar, cotton; colonial ranch-house of Cañas Gordas; church and 18th-c monastery of San Francisco; church and convent of La Merced; cathedral, national palace, modern art museum; national art festival (Jun); fair, with bullfights, masquerades, and sports (Dec). » Colombia [i]

calibration The verification or rectification of a measure or mark by comparison with a known standard or by experiment. For example, the scale on a thermometer may be checked by subjecting it to standard conditions, such as the freezing point and boiling point of water. The term also applies to determining points on a blank scale. » thermometer

calico bush » **mountain laurel**

Calicut » **Kozhikode**

California pop (1987e) 27 663 000; area 411 033 sq km/158 706 sq ml. State in SW USA, divided into 58 counties; the 'Golden State'; originally populated by several Indian tribes; discovered by the Spanish, 1542; colonized mid-18th-c; developed after gold discovered in the Mother Lode, 1848; ceded to the USA by the treaty of Guadalupe Hidalgo, 1848; joined the Union as the 31st state, 1850; major US growth area in the 20th-c; now the most populous US state; capital, Sacramento; major towns San Francisco, Los Angeles, Oakland and San Diego; bounded S by Mexico and W by the Pacific Ocean; mountainous in the N, W and E, with dry, arid depressions in the S (Mojave and Colorado Deserts) and SE (Death Valley); Klamath Mts in the N; Coast Ranges in the W run parallel to the Pacific; Sierra Nevada in the E, rising to 4418 m/14 495 ft at Mt Whitney (state's highest point); foothills of the Sierra Nevada contain the Mother Lode, a belt of gold-bearing quartz; the Sierra Nevada and Coast Ranges are separated by the Central Valley, drained by the San Joaquin and Sacramento Rivers, a major fruit-producing area; vegetables, grain, livestock; a zone of faults (the San Andreas Fault) extends S from N California along the coast; earth tremors commonplace; major earthquake in San Francisco 1906, 1989; centre of the US microelectronics industry in Silicon Valley; oil, natural gas, and a wide range of minerals; food processing, machinery, defence industries, transportation equipment, fabricated metals, cotton, wine (vineyards in over 40 Californian counties); increasing Hispanic and Asian populations; a major tourist state, with several national monuments and parks (Yosemite, Kings Canyon, Sequoia, Redwood), the film industry, Disneyland. » Californian Indians; earthquake; fault; Los Angeles; Sacramento; San Francisco; Silicon Valley; United States of America [i]; RR38

California big tree » **mammoth tree**

California, Gulf of (Span **Golfo de**) Arm of the Pacific Ocean between Mexican mainland (E) and Baja California (W); Colorado R delta (N); broadens and deepens towards the S; maximum depth 2 595 m/8 514 ft; 1 130 km/700 ml long by 80–130 km/50–80 ml wide; tourism, fishing, harvesting of sponge, pearl, oyster. » Pacific Ocean

California sorrel » **palomino**

Californian Indians Once a very large concentration of many distinct American Indian groups, including the Yurok, Maidu, Cahuilla, Miwok, Pomo, Mojave, Hupa, and Chumash. The first groups migrated there possibly 9 000 years ago, and before the Spanish conquest in the 18th-c there were an estimated 105 tribes, speaking many different dialects, and mostly hunter-gatherers. Later, influenced by Indians in neighbouring territories, they developed pottery and basketry, elaborate ceremonials, and a maritime culture. With the Spanish conquest, their population was reduced from an estimated 350 000 to 100 000, and during the 19th-c many groups became extinct. The present population is c.40 000, living both on and off reservations. » American Indians; California; hunter-gatherers

Californian lilac An evergreen shrub, rarely deciduous, native to N America; leaves lance-shaped to oval; flowers in dense clusters, five sepals incurved, five petals longer and spreading, blue, lilac, or white. (Genus: *Ceanothus*, 55 species. Family: *Rhamnaceae*.) » deciduous plants; evergreen plants; sepal; shrub

Californian poppy A grey-green annual or perennial, 20–45 cm/8–18 in, native to California and Oregon, USA; leaves finely divided; flowers bright yellow-orange, also creamy and scarlet in cultivars; the four petals roll up longitudinally in dull weather; grown in gardens, and often escaping into the surrounding area. (*Eschscholzia californica*. Family: *Papaveraceae*.) » annual; cultivar; perennial; poppy

Caligula, properly **Gaius Julius Caesar Germanicus** [ka**lig**yoola] (12–41) Roman emperor (37–41), the youngest son of Germanicus and Agrippina, born at Antium. Brought up in an army camp, he was nicknamed Caligula from his little soldier's boots (*caligae*). His official name, once emperor, was Gaius. Extravagant, autocratic, vicious, and mentally unstable, he wreaked havoc with the finances of the state, and terrorized those around him, until he was assassinated. Under him, Hellenistic court practices, such as ritual obeisance, made their first (though not last) appearance in Rome. » Agrippina the Elder; Germanicus

calimanco cat » **tortoiseshell cat**

calisthenics The art and practice of bodily exercises designed to produce beauty and grace rather than muscular development. They are often performed with the aid of handheld apparatus, such as rings and clubs. Similar exercises were first seen in Germany in the 19th-c. » aerobics

calla lily » **arum lily**

Callaghan, (Leonard) James, Baron, byname **Jim** (1912–) British Labour statesman and Prime Minister (1976–9), born at Portsmouth. He joined the Civil Service (1929), and in 1945 was elected MP for S Cardiff. As Chancellor of the Exchequer under Wilson (1964–7), he introduced the controversial corporation and selective employment taxes. He was Home Secretary (1967–70) and Foreign Secretary (1974–6), and became Prime Minister on Wilson's resignation. He resigned as Leader of the Opposition in 1980, and became a life peer in 1987. » Labour Party; Wilson, Harold

Callao [kal**yah**oh] 12°05S 77°08W, pop (1972) 296 220. Port and capital of Callao department, W Peru; handles 75% of Peru's imports and c.25% of its exports; occupied by Chile (1879–84);

airport; linked by rail to Lima (first railway in S America, 1851); Real Felipe fortress (1774). » Peru [i]

Callas, Maria [**ka**las] (1923–77) US operatic soprano, born in New York City. She studied at Athens Conservatory, and in 1947 appeared at Verona in *La Gioconda*, winning immediate recognition. She sang with great authority in all the most exacting soprano roles, excelling in the intricate *bel canto* style of pre-Verdian Italian opera. She died in Paris.

calligraphy The art of penmanship, or writing at its most formal. It is a major art form in many countries of E Asia and in Arabic-speaking countries, and there has been a revival of interest in Europe and America since the 19th-c. In painting or drawing, 'calligraphic' means linear, freely-handled, and rhythmic, resembling a fine piece of formal handwriting.

Callimachus [ka**li**makuhs] (5th-c BC) Greek sculptor working in Athens in the late 5th-c BC. Vitruvius says he invented the Corinthian capital. Several statues have been identified as his, including a fine 'Draped Venus' in the Boston Museum of Fine Arts. » Greek art; orders of architecture [i]; sculpture; Vitruvius Pollio

Callimachus [ka**li**makuhs] (299–210 BC) Greek poet, grammarian, and critic, born at Cyrene, Libya, who became cataloguer of the Library of Alexandria. Only fragments of his 800 works remain. » Greek literature

calliope [ka**li**yopee] A steam organ patented by J C Stoddard of Worcester, Massachusetts, in 1855. Most calliopes had about 15–30 whistles, operated by a keyboard, but some had many more. They were fitted to the top decks of river showboats, and could be heard for miles around playing popular tunes. » organ

Calliope [ka**li**yopee] In Greek mythology, the muse of epic poetry, sometimes said to be the mother of Orpheus. » Muses

Callisto [ka**lis**toh] In Greek mythology, an Arcadian nymph attendant upon Artemis. Loved by Zeus, she became pregnant, and was sent away from the virgin band. Hera changed her into a she-bear; and after fifteen years had passed, her son tried to spear her. Zeus took pity on them, and changed her into the constellation Ursa Major and her son into Arctophylax. » Artemis

Callisto [ka**lis**toh] The fourth natural satellite of Jupiter, discovered in 1610 by Galileo; distance from the planet 1 883 000 km/1 170 000 ml; diameter 4 800 km/3 000 ml; orbital period 16.689 days. Its dark surface is a mixture of ice and rocky material, and is heavily cratered. » Galilean moons; Jupiter (astronomy); RR4

callus 1 An acquired area of localized thickening of the epidermal layer of skin, due to continued physical trauma. » skin **2** Fibrous tissue formed at the site of a fracture. Fibrocartilage and hyaline cartilage are formed to seal and unite the ends of the bone (a *provisional callus*), being gradually replaced by mature bone (a *permanent callus*). » bone; cartilage

Calmar » **Kalmar**

Calmette, (Léon Charles) Albert (1863–1933) French microbiologist, born in Nice. He was a pupil of Pasteur and founder of the Pasteur Institute at Saigon, where he developed an anti-snakebite and anti-plague serum. He became head of the Pasteur Institute at Lille in 1895, and is best known for the vaccine BCG (Bacillus Calmette-Guérin), for inoculation against tuberculosis, which he jointly discovered with Guérin. He died in Paris. » Pasteur; plague; tuberculosis; vaccination

calmodulin [kal**mod**yulin] One of a group of intracellular proteins widely distributed in plants and animals. It binds with calcium to form the calmodulin-calcium complex, which activates enzymes involved in basic cellular processes (eg mitosis, motility, and neurotransmitter release). » cell; enzyme; mitosis; protein

caloric » **thermodynamics**

calorie In thermodynamics, an old unit of heat, symbol cal; 1 cal = 4.187 J (joule, SI unit); defined as the quantity of heat required to raise the temperature of a gram of water from 14.5°C to 15.5°C. The calorie is an extremely small unit of energy, the average person requiring 2.5 million calories per day. To overcome the obvious problem in counting such large units, the preferred term in scientific literature is the *kilocalorie*, symbol kcal or Cal, where 1 Cal = 1 000 cal, and this is the term commonly used in describing the energy content of foodstuffs. However, the public have continued to use the familiar word; so, in popular usage, 1 kilocalorie is often thought of as 1 calorie. » heat; joule; thermodynamics; units (scientific); RR70

CALORIE LEVELS FOR DIFFERENT KINDS OF FOOD

FOOD	CALORIES PER 100 GRAMS	CALORIES PER OUNCE
cauliflower (boiled)	14	4
apple (flesh only)	46	13
milk (whole)	65	18
potatoes (boiled)	80	23
cod (grilled/steamed)	95	27
cheese (cottage)	95	27
rice (boiled)	123	35
roast beef (lean)	156	44
avocado	219	62
eggs (fried)	232	66
bread	233	66
cornflakes	368	104
sugar	394	111
cheese (Cheddar)	405	115
chocolate (plain)	519	147
butter	740	209
margarine	740	209

calorimetry The measurement of energy transferred in some physical or chemical process, such as the energy absorbed from its surroundings by a solid melting to a liquid, or the energy evolved by burning some substance. In nutrition, **calorimeters** are used to measure the number of calories in a given substance, or to measure the heat output of humans, equivalent to caloric expenditure. Some of these are sufficiently large for people to live in for several days, while fulfilling reasonably normal lives, thus enabling the energy needs of daily living to be recorded. » calorie [i]; heat; heat capacity; latent heat

Calotype A very early method of photography patented by Fox Talbot in 1841, using paper sensitized with silver iodide to produce a negative image. » photography

Calvary [**kal**vuhree] (Lat *calvaria*, 'skull', trans. Semitic *Golgotha*) The site where Jesus was crucified, presumed to be a place of execution just outside of Jerusalem. The term appears in the Authorized Version (*Luke* 23.33). » crucifixion; Jesus Christ

Calvin, John (1509–64) French Protestant reformer, born at Noyon, Picardy. He studied Latin at Paris, then law at Orleans, where he developed his interest in theology. In Bourges and other centres, he began to preach the reformed doctrines, but he was forced to flee from France to escape persecution. At Basle he issued his influential *Christianae Religionis Institutio* (1536, Institutes of the Christian Religion), and at Geneva was persuaded by Guillaume Farel to help with the reformation. The reformers proclaimed a Protestant Confession of Faith, under which moral severity took the place of licence. When a rebellious party, the Libertines, rose against this, Calvin and Farel were expelled from the city (1538). Calvin withdrew to Strasbourg, where he worked on New Testament criticism, and married. In 1541 the Genevans recalled him, and he founded a theocracy which controlled almost all the city's affairs. By 1555 his authority was confirmed into an absolute supremacy. The father figure of Reformed theology, he left a double legacy to Protestantism by systematizing its doctrine and organizing its ecclesiastical discipline. His commentaries, which embrace most of the Old and New Testaments, were collected and published in 1617. He died in Geneva. » Calvinism; Farel; Protestantism; Reformation; theology

Calvinism [**kal**vinizm] A term with at least three applications. **1** The theology of the 16th-c Protestant reformer, John Calvin. **2** The principal doctrines of 17th-c Calvinist scholars, including the 'five points of Calvinism' affirmed by the Synod of Dort (1618–19). **3** More broadly, the beliefs of those Churches in the Reformed tradition which arose under the influence of Calvin, and the impact they had on the societies and cultures in which they took root. Historically, Calvinism has emphasized the sovereignty of God, the Bible as the sole rule of faith, the doctrine of predestination, and justification by faith alone. There has been a Neo-Calvinist renewal in the 20th-c under the influence of the theologian Karl Barth. » Barth, Karl; Calvin; predestination; Presbyterianism; Knox, John; Protestantism; Reformed Churches; Church of Scotland

Calvino, Italo [kal**vee**noh] (1923–85) Italian novelist, born in Cuba. He spent his early years in San Remo, and was educated in Turin, where he worked as a publisher. His first novel, *Il sentiero dei nidi di ragno* (1947, The Path to the Nest of Spiders), described resistance against fascism in a highly naturalistic manner. In later works, such as *I nostri antenati* (1960, Our Ancestors), he adopted a more condensed style of storytelling, hovering between allegory and pure fantasy. He died at Siena. » fascism; Italian literature; novel

Calypso The fourteenth natural satellite of Saturn, discovered in 1980; distance from the planet 295 000 km/183 000 ml; diameter 30 km/19 ml. » Saturn (astronomy); RR4

calyx » **flower [i]; sepal**

CAM » **computer-aided manufacture**

Camargue [ka**mahg**] District in R Rhône delta, SE France; alluvial island, mainly saltmarsh and lagoon; Etang de Vaccares nature reserve for migratory birds; information centre at Ginès; rice and vines on reclaimed land (N); centre for breeding bulls and horses; chief locality, Saintes-Maries-de-la-Mer; tourism, with boating and riding. » France [i]; Rhône, River

Cambacérès, Jean Jacques Régis de [kãba**say**res] (1753–1824) French lawyer, born at Montpellier. He became Archchancellor of the French Empire (1804) and Duke of Parma (1808). As Napoleon's chief legal adviser, his civil code formed the basis of the *Code Napoléon*. He died in Paris. » Napoleon I

Camberwell beauty A colourful butterfly; wings velvet brown with yellow margin and line of blue spots; caterpillar mainly black, with black spike; found on willow, birch, and other trees; pupa hangs by tail. (Order: *Lepidoptera*. Family: *Nymphalidae*.) » butterfly; caterpillar; pupa

cambium A layer of actively dividing cells, producing an increase in the girth of woody plants by additional growth of vascular tissue and cork, after these tissues have been formed by the meristem. » cell; cork; meristem; vascular tissue

Cambodia [kam**boh**dia], formerly **Kampuchea** (1975–89) and **Khmer Republic** (1970–5) pop (1990e) 8 592 000; area 181 035 sq km/69 879 sq ml. Republic of S Indo-China, SE Asia, divided into 18 provinces; bounded N by Thailand and Laos, E and SE by Vietnam, W by Thailand, and SW and S by the Gulf of Thailand; capital, Phnom Penh; population mainly Khmer (93%); chief religion (to 1975), Theravada Buddhism; official language, Khmer, with French widely spoken; unit of currency, the riel of 100 sen; occupies an area surrounding the Tonlé Sap (lake), a freshwater depression on the Cambodian Plain; crossed by the floodplain of the Mekong R (E); highest land in the SW, where the Cardamom Mts run for 160 km/100 ml across the Thailand border, rising to 1 813 m/5 948 ft at Phnom Aural; tropical monsoon climate, with a wet season (May–Sep); heavy rainfall in SW mountains; high temperatures in lowland region throughout the year; average monthly rainfall at Phnom Penh, 257 mm/10 in (Oct), 7 mm/0.3 in (Jan); originally part of the Kingdom of Fou-Nan, taken over by the Khmers, 6th-c; in dispute with the Vietnamese and the Thais from the 15th-c; French Protectorate, 1863; part of Indochina, 1887; independence, 1953, with Prince Sihanouk as Prime Minister; Sihanouk deposed in 1970, and Khmer Republic formed; fighting throughout the country involved troops from N and S Vietnam and the USA; surrender of Phnom Penh to the Khmer Rouge, 1975, when the country became known as Kampuchea; attempt to reform economy on co-operative lines by Pol Pot (1975–8) caused the deaths of an estimated three million people; further fighting, 1977–8; Phnom Penh captured by the Vietnamese, 1979, causing Khmer Rouge to flee; 1981 constitution established a 7-member Council of State and a 16-member Council of Ministers; Paris conference (1988–9) between the Phnom Penh regime, the opposition coalition led by Prince Sihanouk, and the Khmer Rouge ended with no agreement; name of Cambodia restored, 1989; Vietnamese troops completed withdrawal from Cambodia, 1989; UN peace plan agreed, 1991; most of the population employed in subsistence agriculture, especially rice and corn; rubber, pepper, forestry, rice milling, fish processing; phosphates, gemstones; motor-assembly, cigarettes; industrial development disrupted by the civil war. » Khmer Empire; Khmer Rouge; Phnom Penh; Pol Pot; Tonlé Sap; RR45 political leaders

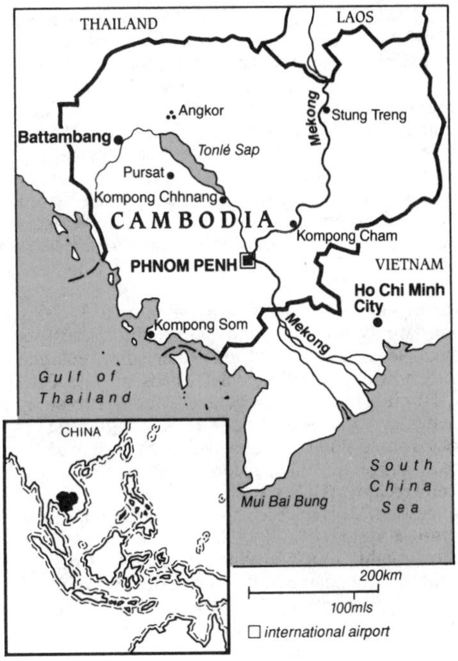

Cambodian » **Austro-Asiatic languages; Khmer**

Cambrian period The earliest geological period of the Palaeozoic era, lasting from c.590 million to 505 million years ago. Characterized by widespread seas, its rocks contain a large variety of marine invertebrate fossils, including trilobites and brachiopods. Present exposures include N Wales, Scotland, Norway, Spain, and the Appalachians. » fossil; geological time scale; Palaeozoic era

Cambridge (UK) Lat **Cantabrigia** 52°12N 0°07E, pop (1987e) 102 500. County town in Cambridge district, Cambridgeshire, EC England; on the R Cam (Granta); 82 km/51 ml N of London; Roman settlement AD 70; airfield; railway; radio, electronics, printing, publishing, scientific instruments, tourism; one of the world's great universities, established 13th-c (Peterhouse, 1284); Churches of St Benedict and the Holy Sepulchre, King's College Chapel, university colleges. » Cambridge University [i]; Cambridgeshire

Cambridge (USA), formerly **New Towne** (to 1638) 42°22N 71°06W, pop (1980) 95 322. Seat of Middlesex County, E Massachusetts, USA; on one side of the Charles R, with Boston on the other; founded, 1630; city status, 1846; the first printing press in the USA set up here in 1640; Harvard University (1636) is the oldest US college; Massachusetts Institute of Technology (1859) moved from Boston in 1915; railway; electronics, glass, scientific instruments, photographic equipment, printing and publishing. » Massachusetts

Cambridge Platonists A group of 17th-c thinkers, centred around Cambridge University, who took Plato (more than his doctrines) as their model. The most prominent members were Benjamin Whichcote, More, and Cudworth. The movement was noted for its emphasis on reason in religion and ethics and its opposition to dogmatism. » Cudworth; More, Henry; Plato

Cambridge ring One of the early types of computer local area network which was pioneered at Cambridge University, UK, by R M Needham (1925–). » local area network

Cambridge University The second oldest university in England, after Oxford. Informal groups of scholars and masters were probably present in Cambridge at the end of the 12th-c. The first college, Peterhouse, was founded in 1284 and further colleges were founded after the Pope formally recognized Cambridge as a *universitas* (1318). Prestigious university institutions include the Fitzwilliam Museum, the Cavendish Laboratory of experimental physics, the Cambridge University Press (founded 1534), and the University Library, a national depository. » Cambridge (UK); Oxford University [i]; university

Cambridgeshire pop (1987e) 642 400; area 3 409 sq km/1 316 sq ml. County of EC England, divided into six districts; drained by the Nene, Ouse, and Cam Rivers; flat fenland to the N; county town Cambridge; chief towns include Peterborough, Ely, Huntingdon; grain, vegetables, food processing, electronics, engineering. » Cambridge (UK); England [i]

camcorder A small portable video camera with an integral narrow-gauge videotape recorder, also known as the **camera cassette recorder (CCR)**. It offers immediate play-back through a domestic television receiver. » videotape recorder

Camden, Battle of (1780) A battle of the US War of Independence, fought in S Carolina. After the British capture of Charleston, Camden was the first major battle of the Southern campaign. Americans under Horatio Gates were defeated by British troops under Lord Cornwallis. » American Revolution; Cornwallis; Gates

Camden, William (1551–1623) English scholar, antiquary, and historian, born in London. Educated at London and Oxford, he became a teacher, and was headmaster of Westminster School (1575), and Clarenceux King-at-arms (1597). His *Britannia* (1586) was the first comprehensive topographical survey of the British Isles. He died at Chislehurst, Kent. The **Camden Society** (founded 1838), which promoted historical publications, was named after him. » cartography

Camden (UK) 51°33N 0°09W, pop (1987e) 184 900. Borough of N Greater London, England; includes suburbs of Hampstead, St Pancras, and Holborn; named after an 18th-c Lord Chancellor; university (1826); railway stations at Euston (1849), King's Cross (1852), St Pancras (1874); British Museum, John Keats House, Gray's Inn, Lincoln's Inn, Post Office Tower (1964). » London [i]

Camden (USA) 39°56N 75°07W, pop (1980) 84 910. Seat of Camden County, W New Jersey, USA; a port on the E bank of the Delaware R, opposite Philadelphia; city status, 1828; railway; university (1934); oil refining, shipbuilding, textiles, food processing, radio and television equipment; home of Walt Whitman (1873–92). » New Jersey; Philadelphia; Whitman

Camden Town Group A group of artists who flourished 1905–13 in London. Sickert was the leading member, but the group also included Harold Gilman (1878–1919) and Spencer Gore (1878–1914). They shared an enthusiasm for recent French painting. » Postimpressionism; Sickert

camel A mammal of the family *Camelidae* (2 species): the **Bactrian** (or **two-humped**) **camel** (*Camelus bactrianus*) from cold deserts in C Asia, and domesticated elsewhere, and the **dromedary**; eats any vegetation; drinks salt water if necessary; closes slit-like nostrils to exclude sand; humps are stores of energy-rich fats. The two species may interbreed: the offspring has one hump; males are usually sterile, while females are fertile. » Camelidae; dromedary

Camelidae [ka**mel**uhdee] The 'camel family' of mammals (6 species), found from N Africa to Mongolia (*camels*), or in the Andes (*llama, alpaca, guanaco, vicuña*); artiodactyls; unusual walk (move both right legs, then both left); mate lying down; upper lip cleft; the only mammals with oval (not round) red blood cells. » alpaca; artiodactyl; camel; guanaco; llama; mammal [i]; ruminant [i]; vicuña

camellia An evergreen shrub and tree, native to China, Japan, and SE Asia; leaves alternate, leathery, glossy green; flowers usually large and showy, often scented, 4–7 petals, but often numerous in cultivars, white, pink, or crimson; popular ornamentals. The genus includes the tea plant. (Genus: *Camellia*, 82 species. Family: *Theaceae*.) » cultivar; evergreen plants; shrub; tea; tree [i]

CAMBRIDGE UNIVERSITY

COLLEGE	FOUNDED	COLLEGE	FOUNDED
Peterhouse	1284	Sidney Sussex	1596
Clare	1326	Downing	1800
Pembroke	1347	Girton	1869
Gonville	1348	Newnham[1]	1871
(refounded as Gonville		Selwyn	1882
and Caius 1558)		Hughes Hall	1885
Trinity Hall	1350	Homerton	1894
Corpus Christi	1352	St Edmund's	1896
King's	1441	New Hall[1]	1954
Queens'	1448	Churchill	1960
St Catharine's	1473	Lucy Cavendish[1]	1964
Jesus	1496	Darwin[2]	1964
Christ's	1505	Wolfson	1965
St John's	1511	Clare Hall[2]	1966
Magdalene	1542	Fitzwilliam	1966
Trinity	1546	Robinson	1977
Emmanuel	1584		

[1] *Women's colleges*
[2] *Graduate colleges*

camel(e)opard [ka**mel**uhpahd] » **giraffe**

Camelopardalis [kamuhluh**pah**dalis] (Lat 'giraffe') A large constellation in the N hemisphere, also known as **Cameloparus**. It lacks any bright stars, so is hard to pick out except on a very clear night. » constellation; RR8

Camelot [**kam**elot] The legendary capital of King Arthur's Britain, variously located at Cadbury in the West Country, Colchester (Camulodunum), and Winchester. » Arthur

cameo A method of carving an image into a shell or semi-precious stone with different coloured layers. It was popular in the Roman Empire, and has been used ever since in W European art, often copied in glass and ceramic.

camera An apparatus which produces an image of an external scene. In the early **camera obscura** (literally 'darkened room'), light passing through a small hole or lens formed a picture on the opposite wall. Portable versions in boxes served as artist's guides in landscape drawing, and early 19th-c attempts to record the image led to the first photographic camera: a light-tight box containing a glass or metal plate with a light-sensitive surface on which the image was formed by a lens. The long exposure time was controlled simply by removing and replacing a cap on the lens.

During the 1850s more sensitive plates greatly reduced exposure time, and mechanical shutters became essential, with adjustable lens aperture and the body formed by folding leather bellows. In the 1890s photographic film in continuous strips revolutionized camera design, first with the Kodak box-camera and later with pocket cameras having collapsible bellows folding into a metal body when not in use. The first miniature camera to use perforated film 35 mm wide was the Leica in 1925, and this compact cassette-loaded form was widely adopted for other sizes. Camera operation has become increasingly simplified with automatic focus setting and exposure; built-in synchronized electronic flash and motor drive for film advance and repeated operation are also now available.

Of many early cameras for cinematography, the Kinetograph developed by Dickson, working for Edison in 1891, had the most lasting influence, establishing the use of film 35 mm wide in long rolls moved intermittently by holes perforated along both edges. Early cameras were hand-cranked, relying on the operator's skill to maintain a steady 16 pictures per second; but clockwork and electric motors were used later, with rolls of film being fed into the camera and taken up after exposure in detachable magazines. With the introduction of sound-films in 1927, the picture rate was increased to 24 per second, and precisely controlled speed became essential for synchronization with the sound recording.

In a video camera the lens image is formed on the photocathode surface of an electronic tube, where it is scanned to produce the signal for transmission. Early TV cameras had large pick-up tubes, with an image diagonal of 55 mm, but from the 1960s much smaller camera tubes were developed, 25 mm or 17 mm in diameter. In the 1980s the very compact charge-coupled device (CCD) sensor was introduced in place of the photo-conductive tube, and camcorders with self-contained videotape recording became available. The use of a single zoom lens has become standard, focused and set under the operator's control with automatic exposure and colour balance. » camcorder; film; lens; plate **1**

camera obscura » **camera**

cameraman The member of a film production crew, also termed **lighting cameraman** or **cinematographer**, responsible under the director for the artistic and technical quality of the picture. Cameramen choose the camera viewpoint and lens angle, and direct the character and distribution of lighting for both set and artists to create the dramatic mood required. During rehearsal and shooting they decide the composition of the action and any camera movement needed, and approve the resulting prints of each day's work. » camera; film production

Camerarius, Rudolf Jakob (1665–1721) German botanist, born and died in Tübingen, where he followed his father in becoming professor of medicine. He showed by experiment in 1694 that plants can reproduce sexually, and identified the stamens and carpels as the male and female sexual apparatus, respectively. He also described pollination. » botany; pollination; stamen

Cameron, James (1911–85) British journalist, author and broadcaster, born and died in London. He worked on newspapers in Dundee and Glasgow before moving to Fleet St in 1940, where he was successively with the *Daily Express*, *Picture Post*, and the *News Chronicle*. His reports from all over the world, in print and broadcast form, were marked by their acute observation, compassion, wit, and integrity. His radio play *The Pump* won the Prix Italia in 1973. » journalism

Cameroon [kamuh**roon**], official name **Republic of Cameroon**, Fr **République du Cameroon** pop (1990e) 11 900 000; area 475 439 sq km/183 519 sq ml. W African republic, divided into ten provinces; bounded SW by Equatorial Guinea and the Congo, S by Gabon, E by the Central African Republic, NE by Chad, and NW by Nigeria; capital Yaoundé; chief towns include Douala; timezone GMT +1; ethnic groups include Highlanders (31%), Equatorial Bantu (19%), Kirdi (11%), Fulani (10%); religion, mainly local beliefs, with remainder Christian or Muslim; official languages, French and English, with many local languages spoken; unit of currency, the franc CFA.

Physical description and climate. Equatorial forest on low coastal plain rising to a C plateau of over 1 300 m/4 200 ft; W region forested and mountainous, rising to 4 070 m/13 353 ft at Mt Cameroon, active volcano, highest peak in W Africa; NC land rises towards the Massif d'Adamaoua; low savannah and semi-desert towards L Chad, with several national parks; rivers flow from C plateau to Gulf of Guinea, including R Sanaga; N wet season (Apr–Sep), annual rainfall 1 000–1 750 mm/40–70 in; N plains semi-arid; rain all year in equatorial S, with two wet seasons and two dry seasons; Yaoundé, average annual rainfall 4 030 mm/159 in, maximum daily temperature 27–30°C; small part of Mt Cameroon receives over 10 000 mm/400 in of rain per annum.

History and government. First explored by Portuguese navigator Fernando Po, later by traders from Spain, Netherlands and Britain; German protectorate of Kamerun, 1884; divided into French and British Cameroon, 1919; confirmed by League of Nations mandate, 1922; UN trusteeships, 1946; French Cameroon independent as Republic of Cameroon, 1960; N sector of British Cameroon voted to become part of Nigeria, S sector part of Cameroon; Federal Republic of Cameroon, with separate parliaments, 1961; federal system abolished, 1972, and name changed to United Republic of Cameroon; change to present name, 1984; governed by an executive president, cabinet, and 180-member National Assembly elected for five years.

Economy. Agriculture employs c.80% of workforce; world's fifth largest cocoa producer; coffee, cotton, rubber, bananas, timber; light manufacturing, assembly, domestic processing, aluminium, crude oil, fertilizers, cement, gold, bauxite, natural gas, tin; tourism, especially to national parks and reserves. » League of Nations; Yaoundé; RR**24** national holidays; RR**45** political leaders

Cameroon, Mount or **Mongo-Ma-Loba** 4°14N 9°10E. Volcanic massif in S Cameroon, W Africa; runs inland for 37 km/23 ml from Gulf of Guinea; main peak, 4 070 m/13 353 ft; highest mountain group in W Africa; last eruption, 1959. » Cameroon [i]

Camisards The last major Protestant rebellion in early modern Europe, centred on the Cévennes Mts in N Languedoc (1700–4). It was provoked by the Revocation of the Edict of Nantes (1685), which had guaranteed limited toleration, and the failure of the Treaty of Ryswick (1697) to safeguard French Protestants. The uprising was put down with difficulty by royal troops under Marshal Villars. » Nantes, Edict of; Villars

Camões or **Camoens, Luís de** [kamo**h**ẽsh] (1524–80) The greatest Portuguese poet, born in Lisbon. He studied for the Church at Coimbra, but declined to take orders. He became a soldier, and during service at Ceuta lost his right eye. He went to India (1553) and Macao (1556), and was shipwrecked while returning to Goa (1558), losing everything except his major poem, *Os Luciados* (The Lusiads, or Lusitanians). After returning to Portugal in 1570, he lived in poverty and obscurity. *Lusiads* was published in 1572, and was an immediate success, but did little for his fortunes, and he died in a public hospital. The work has since come to be regarded as the Portuguese national epic. » Portuguese literature

camomile » **chamomile**

Camorra [cam**o**ra] In Naples and S Italy, a generic term applied to practices based in corporate institutions and practices of the poor, which developed during the 19th-c into a complex network of patronage, clientelism, protection, and ultimately crime. As with the Sicilian Mafia, which it resembles, no single Camorra organization has ever existed.

Camp David The US presidential retreat established in 1942 by

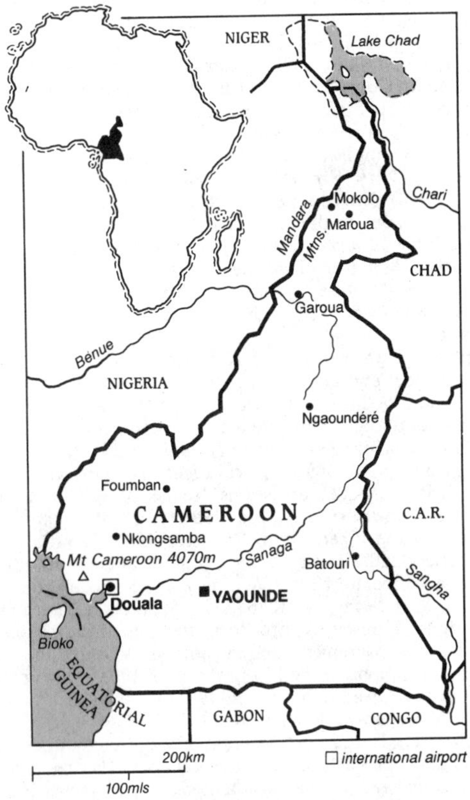

President Roosevelt in Catoctin Mountain Park, Maryland. Originally known as 'Shangri La', it was renamed in 1953. The retreat covers 81 ha/200 acres and includes a main residence (Aspen Lodge), conference hall, and office. It has been used for a number of historic meetings between heads of state. » Camp David Accords

Camp David Accords Documents signed by the President of Egypt and the Prime Minister of Israel at Camp David, USA, in 1978. Regarded by many as a triumph of US diplomacy, they were a preliminary to the signing of the formal peace treaty (1979) between the two countries, which gave Egypt back the Sinai Desert, captured in the 1967 War. » Arab-Israeli Wars; Camp David; PLO

Campaign for Nuclear Disarmament » **CND**

campanile [campaneelay] The Italian name for a bell tower, usually tall and detached from the main building. The earliest known campanile was square, and attached to St Peter's, Rome, in the mid-8th-c AD. The most famous example is the circular Leaning Tower of Pisa, with eight arcaded storeys.

campanology » **bell-ringing**

campanula » **bell-flower; Canterbury bell**

Campbell, Sir Colin, Baron Clyde (1792–1863) British field marshal, born in Glasgow, Scotland. He fought in the Peninsular War against Napoleon, where he was twice badly wounded, and after 30 years of duty in various garrisons, fought in China (1842) and in the second Sikh war (1848–9). In the Crimean War he commanded the Highland Brigade in a campaign which included the renowned repulse of the Russians by the 'thin red line' at Balaclava. During the Indian Mutiny he commanded the forces in India, and effected the final relief of Lucknow. He was created baron in 1858, and died at Chatham, Kent. » Crimean War; Indian Mutiny

Campbell, Sir Malcolm (1885–1948) British racing motorist, born at Chislehurst, Kent. From 1927 onwards he established successive world speed records in motor and speedboat racing, and was the first motorist to exceed 300 mph/483 kph (at Bonneville Salt Flats, Utah, 1935). Knighted in 1931, he died at Reigate. His son, **Donald** (1921–67), broke the water speed record on Ullswater, Cumbria in 1955, and breaking his own record yearly, reached 276.33 mph/444.7 kph on L Dumbleyung, Australia, in 1964. Like his father, he named all his vehicles 'Bluebird'. He also set a land vehicle record in 1964 at L Eyre, Australia of 405.45 mph/652.37 kph. He died in an accident on Coniston Water, Cumbria while trying to break his own water speed record (achieving 328 mph/527.9 kph). His daughter, **Gina** (1948–) broke the women's water speed record in 1984. » motor racing

Campbell, Mrs Patrick, *née* **Beatrice Stella Tanner** (1865–1940) British actress, born in London. She married in 1884, and went on the stage in 1888, achieving fame with *The Second Mrs Tanqueray* (1893). Her mercurial temperament made her the terror of managers. She played Eliza in Shaw's *Pygmalion* (1914) and formed a long friendship with the author. She died at Pau, France. » Shaw, George Bernard; theatre

Campbell, (Ignatius) Roy (Dunnachie) (1901–57) South African poet and journalist, born in Durban. After travelling throughout W Europe, he became an ardent admirer of things Spanish and fought with Franco's armies during the Civil War. His books include *The Flaming Terrapin* (1924), *Flowering Rifle* (1939), and the autobiographical *Light on a Dark Horse* (1951), as well as many fine translations. He died at Setúbal, Portugal.

Campbell-Bannerman, Sir Henry (1836–1908) British statesman and Liberal Prime Minister (1905–8), born in Glasgow, Scotland. Educated at Glasgow and Cambridge, he became a Liberal MP in 1868, was Chief Secretary for Ireland (1884), War Secretary (1886, 1892–5), Liberal leader (1899), and Prime Minister. A 'pro-Boer', he granted the ex-republics responsible government, and his popularity united the Liberal Party. He supported the Lib-Lab pact of 1903, which played a part in the Liberal landslide of 1906. He died in London. » Boer Wars; Liberal Party (UK)

camphor $C_{10}H_{16}O$, melting point 179°C. A colourless, waxy material (a terpene), occurring especially in the tree *Cinnamonium camphora*, and also synthesised from α-pinene. It is used in many lotions, mainly for its characteristic odour. **Camphorated oil** is a 20% solution of camphor in olive oil. » terpene

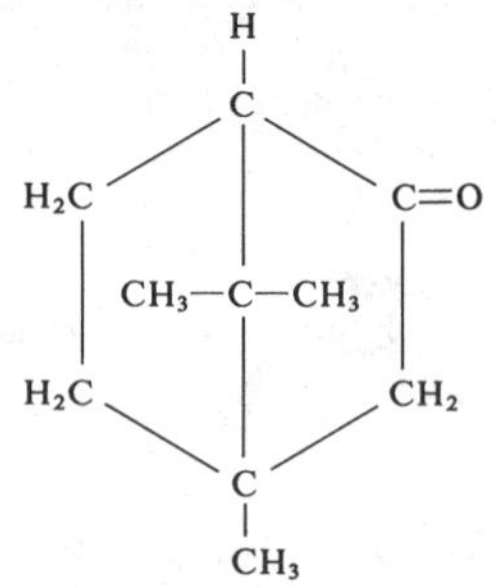

camphor tree A name applied to several different trees, principally *Cinnamonium camphora*, a small evergreen growing to 6 m/20 ft with greenish-white flowers, native to Japan. Camphor is obtained by distillation of the bark. (Family: *Lauraceae*.) » camphor [i]; evergreen plants; tree [i]

Campi, Giulio (c.1502–72) Italian architect and painter, born at Cremona. He was influenced by Giulio Romano, and founded the Cremonese school of painting, to which his brothers **Vincenzo** (1539–91) and **Antonio** (1536–c.91) also belonged. His work includes a fine altarpiece at Cremona, where he died. » altarpiece; Giulio Romano; Italian art

Campin, Robert (c.1375–1444) Dutch artist, who settled in Tournai about 1400. He was called the **Master of Flémalle** from his paintings in the Abbey of that name near Liège. His pupils included Rogier van der Weyden. He died at Tournai. » Dutch art; Weyden

Campinas [kampeenas] 22°54S 47°60W, pop (1980) 566 627. Town in São Paulo state, Sudeste region, SE Brazil; NW of São Paulo; two universities (1941, 1962); agricultural institute; airport; railway; cotton, maize, sugar cane, coffee; cathedral, old market, colonial buildings. » Brazil [i]

campion Annual or perennial herbs with opposite leaves and usually cymose inflorescences, of the same genus as catchflys, and native to the temperate N hemisphere; calyx tubular, five petals, notched or bifid, red or white depending on species. (Genus: *Silene*. Family: *Caryophyllaceae*.) » annual; bladder campion; catchfly; herb; inflorescence [i]; perennial; sepal

Campion, Edmund (1540–81), feast day 1 December. The first of the English Jesuit martyrs, born in London. He was educated at Oxford, and although made a deacon in the Church of England (1569), he leaned towards Rome. Fearing arrest, he escaped to Douai, and in 1573 joined the Jesuits in Bohemia. In 1580 he was recalled from Prague, where he was professor of rhetoric, for a Jesuit mission to England. He circulated his *Decem Rationes* (Ten Reasons) against Anglicanism in 1581, was arrested, tortured, tried on a charge of conspiracy, and hanged in London. He was beatified in 1886. » Jesuits; Reformation

Campoli, Alfredo [**kam**pohlee] (1906–91) Italian violinist, born in Rome. In London from 1911, he won an early reputation as a soloist; but during the 1930s became better known for his salon orchestra, disbanded at the beginning of the war. He later emerged as one of the outstanding violinists of the time. » violin

camshaft A rotating shaft upon which cams are fixed. A cam is a flat plate cut to a defined shape which rotates about an axis perpendicular to the plane of the plate. The shape of the cams and their relative orientation actuate and time the lifting of valves as part of an engine's operating cycle. » bearings; engine

Camulodunum [kamoolo**doo**num] The name for ancient Colchester, the capital first of the Belgic kingdom of Cunobelinus and then of the Roman province of Britain. Destroyed in the revolt of Boadicea in AD 60, it later recovered, but yielded its capital status to Londinium (London). » Boadicea; Britain, Roman; Cymbeline

Camus, Albert [**kah**mü] (1913–1960) French existentialist writer, born at Mondovi, Algeria. He studied philosophy at Algiers, and worked as actor, teacher, playwright, and journal-

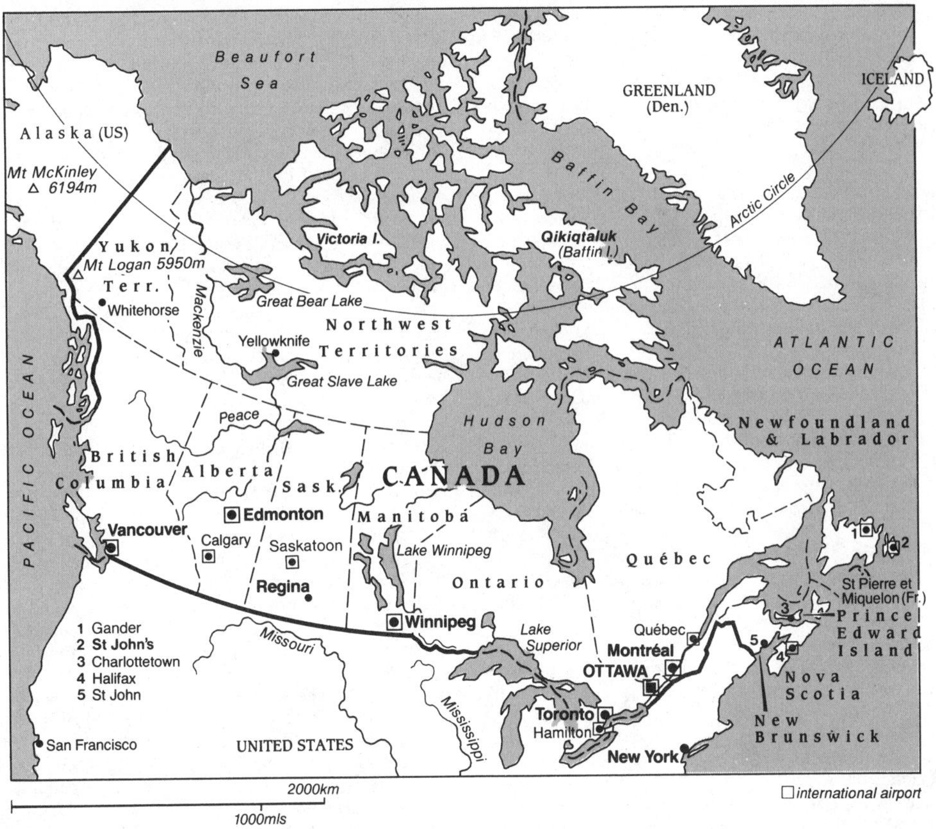

ist there and in Paris. Active in the French resistance during World War 2, he became co-editor with Sartre of the left-wing newspaper *Combat* after the liberation until 1948. He earned an international reputation with his nihilistic novel, *L'Etranger* (1942, The Outsider). Later novels include *La Peste* (1947, The Plague) and *La Chute* (1956, The Fall), and he also wrote plays and several political works. He won the Nobel Prize for Literature in 1957, and was killed in a car accident near Sens, France. » existentialism; French literature; Sartre

Canaan [**kay**nan] The land of the ancient Semitic-speaking peoples, living in the coastal areas of modern Israel and Syria, but perhaps also extending inland to the Jordan R and the Dead Sea. It was divided into various city-states during the early 2nd millennium BC, but mostly fell under the control of Israelites and other powers from the late 13th-c BC. The name can be traced to one of the sons of Ham (*Gen* 9–10). » Ham; Israel [i]; Phoenicia; Semitic languages; Shiloh; Ugarit

Canada, formerly **British North America** (to 1867) pop (1990e) 26 620 000; area 9 971 500 sq km/3 848 900 sq ml. Independent country in N America, divided into 10 provinces and two territories; bordered by USA (S), Pacific Ocean (W), Alaska (NW), Arctic Ocean and Baffin Bay (N), Davis Strait (NE), and Labrador Sea and Atlantic Ocean (E); capital, Ottawa; other chief cities include Calgary, Edmonton, Montreal, Quebec, Toronto, Vancouver, Victoria, Winnipeg; several timezones (GMT W Yukon −9, Yukon and Pacific −8, Mountain −7, Central −6, Eastern −5, Atlantic −4, Newfoundland −3); ethnic groups, 45% British origin, 29% French origin, 23% other European, also Indian and Eskimo minorities; official languages, English, French; religion, 49% Roman Catholic, 18% United Church, 12% Anglican; currency unit, Canadian dollar of 100 cents.

Physical description. Dominated in the NE by the pre-Cambrian Canadian Shield; mountains of Nova Scotia and New Brunswick in the E; fertile St Lawrence lowlands in S Quebec and Ontario; flat prairie country S and W of the Shield, stretching to the Western Cordillera, which includes the Rocky, Cassiar, and Mackenzie Mts; Coast Mts flank a rugged, heavily indented coastline, rising to 5 950 m/19 521 ft at Mt Logan, highest peak in Canada; major rivers include Yukon and Mackenzie (W), N Saskatchewan, S Saskatchewan, Saskatchewan, and Athabasca (C), Ottawa and St Lawrence (E); Great Lakes in the SE.

Climate. N coast permanently ice-bound or obstructed by ice floes, but for Hudson Bay (frozen c.9 months each year); cold air from Arctic sweeps S and E in winter and spring; mild winters and warm summers on W coast and some inland valleys of British Columbia; winter temperatures on Atlantic shores warmer than those of the interior, but summer temperatures lower; much of S interior has warm summers and long, cold winters.

History and government. Evidence of Viking settlement c.1000; visited by Cabot, 1497; St Lawrence explored for France by Cartier, 1534; Newfoundland claimed for England, 1583; Champlain founded Quebec, 1608; Hudson's Bay Company founded, 1670; conflict between British and French in late 17th-c; Britain gained large areas from Treaty of Utrecht (1713); after Seven Years' War, during which Wolfe captured Quebec (1759), Treaty of Paris gave Britain almost all France's possessions in N America; province of Quebec created, 1774; migration of loyalists from USA after War of Independence led to division of Quebec into Upper and Lower Canada; reunited as Canada, 1841; Dominion of Canada created 1867 by confederation of Quebec, Ontario, Nova Scotia, and New Brunswick; Rupert's Land and Northwest Territories bought from Hudson's Bay Company, 1869–70; joined by Manitoba (1870), British Columbia (1871, after promise of transcontinental railroad), Prince Edward I (1873), Alberta and Saskatchewan (1905), and Newfoundland (1949); recurring political tension in recent decades arising from French-Canadian separatist movement in Quebec; Canada Act (1982) gave Canada full responsibility for constitution; bicameral federal parliament includes a Senate of 104 nominated members and a House of Commons of 295 elected members; provinces administer and legislate on education, property laws, health, and local affairs; British monarch is head of state, represented by a governor-general, usually appointed for a 5-year term.

Economy. Traditionally based on natural resources and agriculture; world's second largest exporter of wheat; forest covers 44% of land area; widespread minerals (world's largest producer of asbestos, zinc, silver, nickel; second largest producer of potash, gypsum, molybdenum, sulphur; also, uranium, titanium, aluminium, cobalt, gold, lead, copper, iron, platinum); hydroelectricity, oil (especially Alberta), natural gas; major industrial development in recent decades; food processing, vehicles and parts, chemicals, machinery, fishing, tourism (especially from USA); petroleum, metal, and metal products. » Alberta; British Columbia; Cabot, John; Cartier; Champlain; Canadian art/literature/Pacific Railway/Shield; Great Lakes; Hudson Bay; Manitoba; New Brunswick; Newfoundland (province); Northwest Territories; Nova Scotia; Ontario; Prince Edward Island; Quebec (province); Rocky Mountains; St Lawrence River; Saskatchewan; Seven Years' War; Yukon; RR24 national holidays; RR45 political leaders

Canada, Order of A decoration established in Canada in 1967, with three categories: Companion, Medal of Courage, and Medal of Service. The Medal of Courage was converted to three decorations in 1972: the Cross of Valour, the Star of Courage, and the Medal of Bravery. Three levels of membership were created: Companions, Officers, and Members, with the Governor-General of Canada as the Chancellor and principal Companion of the Order. » decoration

Canada Company A colonization company established in Upper Canada (Ontario) in 1824. It sold more than a million acres of land to settlers in the area around L Huron, and laid foundations for the towns of Guelph, Galt, and Goderich.

Canada Day A public holiday in Canada (observed 1 Jul), the anniversary of the union of the provinces in 1867; formerly known as **Dominion Day**.

Canada First Movement A political movement in Canada, founded in Ontario in 1868. Its objectives were to ensure that the newly-confederated Dominion of Canada would not collapse over regional disputes. It increasingly promoted a policy of Canadian self-determination and autonomy in international relations. Its view of Canadian nationality was distinctly anglophone and Protestant. » Canada [i]

Canada goose A goose native to N America, and introduced in Europe and New Zealand; head and neck black with white chin; eats grass and water plants; migrates; females often return to own birthplace to breed, producing many local races and variations. (*Branta canadensis*. Family: *Anatidae*.) » goose

Canadian art The art associated with Canada which, since the 17th-c, has mixed European – especially French – and local folk elements. Late 18th-c churches reflect the styles of Georgian Britain and the American colonies. The Parliament building in Ottawa, by Thomas Fuller (c.1859), is Gothic Revival. The late 19th-c saw the foundation of the Royal Canadian Academy and the National Gallery of Canada (both 1880), and the first major private collections. By the early 20th-c, Canadians who had studied in Paris began painting Canadian scenery in an Impressionist style. Modern art had arrived by the 1940s. » art; Canada [i]; Gothic Revival; Impressionism (art); modern art

Canadian literature Canadian literature is written in both English and French. The two traditions are overlapping but distinct, not least because the French is older and more embattled within an idealized past. This may be why it is more noted for its poetry, much of it in late Symbolist style, following Saint-Denis-Garneau. Writers in English have generally preferred prose. Humorists such as Stephen Leacock (1869–1944), novelists such as the popular Mazo de la Roche (eg *Jalna*, 1927) and the realist Frederick Grove (1879–1948), Morley Callaghan (1903–), and Mordechai Richler (1931–), and cultural critics Northrop Frye (1912–) and Marshall McLuhan (1911–80) have established a world-wide readership. Another important author, Margaret Atwood (1939–), provides a guide in her *Survival: A Thematic Guide to Canadian Literature* (1972). » American/English literature; Atwood; Canada [i]; De la Roche; McLuhan; Symbolism

Canadian National Tower » C N Tower

Canadian Pacific Railway A transcontinental railway, constructed 1881–5, linking the Dominion of Canada with British Columbia. Carried out with large government cash subsidies, enormous land grants to the railway company, and other perquisites, the project represented an act of political will and an engineering triumph. It produced a chain of western railway towns terminating in Vancouver on the Pacific coast. » Canada [i]

Canadian River River in SC USA; rises in the Sangre de Cristo Mts, New Mexico; flows through Texas and Oklahoma to join the Arkansas R SE of Muskogee; length 1 458 km/906 ml; major tributary the North Canadian; dammed by the Conchas Dam in New Mexico; used for flood-control and irrigation. » United States of America [i]

Canadian Rocky Mountain Parks A group of five national parks (Banff, Jasper, Waterton Lakes, Kootenay, Yoho) in Alberta and British Columbia, Canada. Together with the Burgess Shale site – an important geological fossil site in the Selkirk Mts of British Columbia – these constitute a world heritage area. » Rocky Mountains

Canadian Shield or **Laurentian Shield** Vast area of ancient pre-Cambrian rocks, forming a low plateau covering over half of Canada; S boundary runs from the Labrador coast around Hudson Bay, through Quebec and Ontario to the Arctic near the Mackenzie R mouth; extends into parts of N USA; many lakes and swamps, remnants of Pleistocene glaciation; generally infertile, but a rich source of minerals, forest products, and hydroelectricity. » Cambrian period; Canada [i]; glaciation; metamorphic rock

Canadian waterweed A submerged aquatic plant native to N America; stems growing to 3 m/10 ft, brittle, with whorls of narrow, dark-green leaves; flowers 5 mm/0.2 in, floating, three greenish-purple sepals, three translucent white petals. Introduced to Europe, where male plants are quite rare, they spread by vegetative reproduction, for a while becoming a nuisance, blocking waterways. (*Elodea canadensis*. Family: *Hydrocharitaceae*.) » sepal; vegetative reproduction

canal An artifical watercourse for inland navigation. The first modern canal in the UK was the Sankey Brook from the Mersey to St Helens, built by Henry Berry between 1755 and 1772. Rather more famous was the canal from Worsley to Manchester built by James Brindley for the Duke of Bridgwater, opened in 1761. Thousands of miles of canal were built, and they were the major method of transporting goods until the mid-19th-c, when the railways superseded them. After a long period of decline, more recently many canals have been restored, and nowadays are principally used for leisure activities. » Bridgwater / Corinth / Erie / Grand / Manchester Ship / Mittelland/Panama/Suez Canal [i]; Brindley; Intracoastal Waterway; Rhine Canals [i]; St Lawrence Seaway

Canaletto, originally **Canal, Giovanni Antonio** (1697–1768) Italian painter, born and died in Venice. He studied at Rome, then painted a renowned series of views in Venice. He spent most of the years 1746–56 in England, where his views of London and elsewhere proved extremely popular. His nephew and pupil, **Bernardo Bellotto** (1720–80), known as **Canaletto the Younger**, was also born in Venice, where he worked as a painter and engraver. He later painted in Rome, Verona, Brescia, Milan, Dresden, and England, and died in Warsaw. » Italian art; Venetian School

canary A small finch, native to the Old World; prized as a song bird; also known as **serin**. All domestic varieties of the cage canary were developed from one species, *Serinus canaria*, from the Canary Islands. (Genus: *Serinus*, 32 species. Family: *Fringillidae*.) » finch; roller; siskin

Canary Islands, Span **Islas Canarias** pop (1981) 1 367 646; area 7 273 sq km/2 807 sq ml. Island archipelago in the Atlantic Ocean, 100 km/60 ml off the NW coast of Africa, W of Morocco and S of Madeira; comprises Tenerife, Gomera, La Palma, Hierro, Lanzarote, Fuerteventura, Gran Canaria (Grand Canary), and several uninhabited islands; chief town, Las Palmas; volcanic and mountainous, the Pico de Teide rises to 3 718 m/12 198 ft at the centre of a national park on Tenerife; fruit and vegetables grown under irrigation; major tourist area;

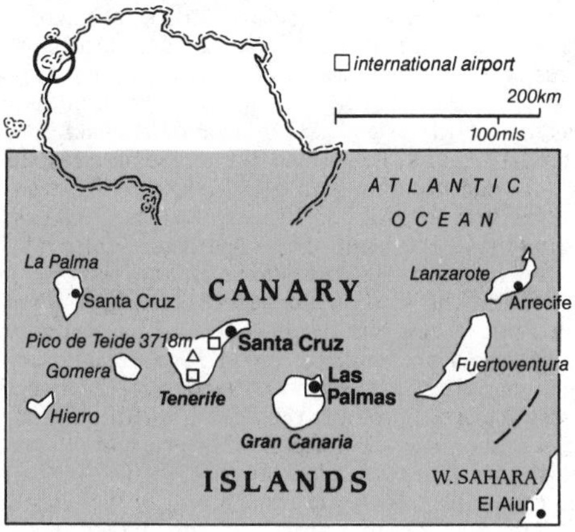

agriculture, fishing, canning, textiles, leatherwork, footwear, cork, timber, chemical and metal products; under the control of Spain, 15th-c; the name is explained by the elder Pliny as referring to the many dogs found on Gran Canaria (Lat *canis*, 'dog'), and has nothing to do with canaries. » Las Palmas; Pliny (the elder); Spain [i]

Canary whitewood » **tulip tree** [i]

canasta A card game similar to rummy. It derives from the Spanish word *canasta* ('basket'), probably referring to the tray into which cards were discarded. The game originated in Uruguay in the 1940s. Its most popular form is played with two standard packs of playing cards, together with four jokers. The object is to collect as many cards of the same denomination as possible. All cards have points value, but jokers and deuces (twos) are 'wild' (ie can take any value). Cards are picked up and discarded. » playing cards; rummy

Canaveral, Cape, formerly **Cape Kennedy** (1963–73) 28°28N 80°28W. Cape in Brevard County, E Florida, USA, on the E coast of the Canaveral peninsula; US crewed space flights launched from here since 1961. » Kennedy Space Center, John F

Canberra [**kan**buhra] 35°18S 149°08E, pop (1986) 285 800. National and regional capital in Australian Capital Territory, SE Australia, on the Molonglo R; planned by US architect Walter Burley Griffin (after a competition, 1911); building started in 1913; Commonwealth Parliament moved from Melbourne, 1927; airport; railway; Australian National University (1946); Australian War Memorial; National Library; National Gallery; High Court; Parliament House (1927, new building opened in 1988 by the Queen). » Australian Capital Territory

cancan A high kicking and risqué dance popularized in Paris c.1830. It is normally danced with four women in 4/4 time. Although danced to many tunes, it is associated with Offenbach's *Orpheus in the Underworld*.

cancer A general term to denote all forms of malignant tumour. Tumours occur when the cells of a tissue or organ multiply in an uncontrolled fashion unrelated to the biological requirements of the body and not to meet the needs of repair or of normal replacement. In contrast to *benign* tumours, which enlarge in a specific place, and cause damage by pressure on adjacent tissues, *malignant* tumours invade, destroy, and spread to other tissues. The cells of a malignant tumour may also be carried in the blood stream and lymphatics, and lodge in distant organs where they continue to spread and enlarge (*metastases*). Cancer kills by destroying vital tissues, by interfering with the performance of their functions through ulceration, bleeding, and infection, and by affecting bodily nutrition.

Microscopic examination of the cells of malignant tumours often reveals the special characteristics of the cells of its tissue of origin. Sometimes the cells lose these characteristics and are totally undifferentiated (*anaplastic*). Tumours of this cell type tend to be rapidly growing and highly malignant. Identification of the tissue of origin is important, as it may give a clue to the possible origin of the tumour, its natural course, the outlook for the patient, and the most appropriate treatment. Each cell or tissue type of malignancy has its own profile of age and sex occurrence. Thus one specific cancer of the back of the eye occurs equally in both sexes and occurs only in infancy, while cancer of the stomach is twice as common in men as in women and its frequency rises with age from adolescence. The cause of cancer is unknown, but appears to depend upon an interplay between factors in the environment and the genetic component of body cells. Only a small number of cancers are determined solely by inherited factors. The great majority are related to exposure to one or more environmental factors which predisposes to the cancer. These factors are known as **carcinogenic** agents. » breast/cervical cancer; carcinogen; oncology; sarcoma; tumour

Cancer (Lat 'crab') An inconspicuous N constellation. a summer sign of the zodiac, lying between Gemini and Leo. It contains an open star cluster, Praesepe, just visible by eye. » constellation; star cluster; zodiac [i]; RR8

candela [kan**day**la] Base SI unit of luminous intensity; symbol cd; defined as the luminous intensity, in a given direction, of a source that emits monochromatic radiation of frequency 540×10^{12} Hz, and has a radiant intensity in that direction of 1/683 watt per steradian; obsolete name **candle**. » photometry [i]; radiometry [i]; units (scientific)

Candida [**kan**dida] A genus of fungi known from its yeast-like vegetative state; parasitic in animals; includes *Candida albicans*, the causative agent of thrush in humans. (Family: *Cryptococcaceae*.) » fungus; thrush (medicine); yeast

candidiasis [kandi**di**yasis] A disease caused by *Candida albicans*, a yeast which normally inhabits the gut and the vagina; also known as **thrush**. In debilitating conditions and when the immune system is depressed, the organism may colonize the skin and gastro-intestinal tract, including the mouth, where white patches can be seen with the naked eye. In rare cases it can invade the blood stream and prove fatal. » vagina; yeast

candle A light source typically consisting of a wax cylinder (stearic acid, paraffin wax, etc) with a central fibrous wick, known from ancient times (at least 3000 BC). Light is generated by burning liquid wax melted by the flame and drawn up the wick by capillary action. The International Standard Candle was a measure of light-source intensity, now replaced by the *candela*. » candela; light; wax

Candlemas A Christian festival (2 Feb) commemorating the purification of the Virgin Mary after the birth of Jesus, and the presentation of Jesus in the Jerusalem temple (*Luke* 2). The name is derived from the lighted candles carried in procession on that day. It is also a Scottish quarter-day. » Mary (mother of Jesus); quarter-day

Candolle, Augustin Pyrame de [kă**dol**] (1778–1841) Swiss botanist, born and died in Geneva, where he studied medicine. From 1798 he studied botany in Paris, and by 1813 had developed a general scheme of plant taxonomy which was to dominate plant classification for 50 years. He used the scheme in a major series of volumes on botany, completed by his son **Alphonse** (1806–93). He also did much to establish plant geography and to relate vegetation to soil type, a study supported by his extensive expeditions. » botany; taxonomy

candytuft An annual, biennial, or evergreen perennial, native to Europe and Asia; leaves narrow; flowers white or mauve, in flattened heads, cross-shaped with outer two petals of outermost flowers enlarged. Several large-flowered species and cultivars are ornamentals. (Genus: *Iberis*, 30 species. Family: *Cruciferae*.) » annual; biennial; cultivar; evergreen plants; perennial

cane » **bamboo; sugar cane**

cane rat An African cavy-like rodent; large (length, up to 750 mm/30 in; weight, 9 kg/20 lb); short tail and broad blunt snout; lives near water; may damage sugar-cane plantations. (Family: *Thryonomyidae*.) » cavy; rat; rodent

cane sugar » **sugar cane**

Canea » **Chania**

Canes Venatici [**kah**neez vuh**nat**isiy] (Lat 'hunting dogs') An inconspicuous constellation in the N hemisphere which includes many bright galaxies. » constellation; galaxy; RR8

Canetti, Elias (1905–) British writer of Spanish-Jewish origin, born at Russe, Bulgaria. He was educated at schools in England, Austria, Switzerland, and Germany, and lived in England from 1938, though continuing to write in German. His interest in crowd psychology produced two important works: the novel *Die Blendung* (1936, trans as both Auto da Fé and The Tower of Babel) and the study *Masse und Macht* (1960, Crowds and Power). He was awarded the Nobel Prize for Literature in 1981. » German literature

Canidae [**kan**uhdee] The 'dog family' of carnivores (36 species), usually with slender legs, lean muzzles, large erect ears, and bushy tails; four toes on hind feet, usually five on front; blunt claws not retractable; colour usually without stripes or spots; small canids may hunt alone by stalking then pouncing; larger may hunt in packs and run prey to exhaustion. » carnivore [i]; coyote; dhole; dog; fox; jackal; raccoon dog; wolf

Canis Major [**kan**is] (Lat 'great dog') A constellation in the S hemisphere, partly in the Milky Way. It is easy to see because it includes Sirius, the brightest star in our sky. » constellation; Milky Way; Sirius; RR8

Canis Minor [**kan**is] (Lat 'little dog') A small N hemisphere constellation. Its brightest star is Procyon, just 3.5 parsecs away, and the eighth brightest star in the sky. It has a faint white dwarf companion. » constellation; dwarf star; RR8

canker (botany) A general term for a localized disease of woody plants, in which bark formation is prevented; typically caused by bacteria or fungi. » bacteria [i]; bark; fungus; plant

canker (zoology) A disease of animals, characterized by open sores or ulcers; name used for several conditions, such as inflammation of a horse's foot involving a fluid discharge, eczema on a dog's ear, an abscess on a bird, or an infestation of mites in the ear of a cat (*ear canker*, or *otodectic mange*). » ulcer

canna A tuberous perennial, native to C and tropical N America; leaves broadly lance-shaped, stalks sheathing stem; flowers in a spike, three sepals, three petals, 4–6 stamens, petal-like and brightly coloured; fruit a warty capsule; often grown for the showy flowers. *Canna edulis* provides the starch Queensland arrowroot. The hard, round seeds of *Canna indica* have been used as shot. (Genus: *Canna*, 55 species. Family: *Cannaceae*.) » arrowroot; perennial; sepal; stamen; starch; stem (botany); tuber

cannabis A preparation of the plant *Cannabis sativa*, widely used as a recreational drug for its euphoric, relaxing properties: its extracts are found as *hashish* and *marihuana*. The plant, also called **ganja** or **hemp**, is an annual growing to 2.5 m/8 ft; its leaves have 5–7 narrow, toothed, spreading, finger-like lobes; there are tiny green flowers in terminal clusters, with males and females on separate plants. It is native to Asia, but widely cultivated elsewhere. It is a source of rope fibre and birdseed, but is best-known as a narcotic resin. Its active principle, the cannabinoid *tetrahydrocannabinol*, was first synthesized in 1967. Historically, cannabis has been extensively used in medicine, but since the 1930s its therapeutic use has been mostly abandoned because of its abuse potential. However, cannabinoids are used successfully to suppress the severe vomiting that occurs during cancer chemotherapy. (*Cannabis sativa*. Family: *Cannabidaceae*.) » annual; cancer; chemotherapy; drug addiction; resin

Cannes [kan] 43°33N 7°00E, pop (1982) 72 787. Fashionable resort town on the French Riviera in Alpes-Maritimes department, SE France, on the Golfe de la Napoule; airport; railway; fruit, flowers, textiles; major tourist centre, with many beaches and yachting harbours; mild winter and temperate summer climate; casinos; International Film Festival (Apr–May), International Fireworks Festival (Aug). » France [i]; Riviera

canning A food preservation process relying on the sterilization of foods by heating in a container sealed before or immediately after the heat treatment. The idea was first applied in 1810 by Nicolas Appert (c.1750–1841) to foods sealed in bottles and heated, but since 1839 in cans made of tinned thin steel sheet. Aluminium or plastic sometimes now replaces steel. Internal coatings are chosen to resist the chemical properties of different contents. The processes are now highly automated, and food growing is usually closely associated with a canning plant. » food preservation; tinplate

Canning, George (1770–1827) British statesman, born in London. Educated at Eton, Oxford, and Lincoln's Inn, he entered parliament for Newport, I of Wight (1794) as a supporter of Pitt. He became Under-Secretary of State (1796), Treasurer of the Navy (1804–6), and Minister for Foreign Affairs (1807). His disapproval of the Walcheren expedition led to a misunderstanding with Castlereagh, which resulted in a duel. He became MP for Liverpool (1812), Ambassador to Lisbon (1814), President of the Board of Control (1816), and MP for Harwich (1822). Nominated Governor-General of India (1822), he was on the eve of departure when Castlereagh's suicide saw him installed as Foreign Secretary. In this post he gave a new impetus to commerce by advocating tariff reductions. He was the first to recognize the free states of Spanish America; promoted the union of Britain, France, and Russia in the cause of Greece (1827); protected Portugal from Spanish invasion; contended earnestly for Catholic emancipation; and prepared the way for a repeal of the Corn Laws. In 1827 he formed an administration with the aid of the Whigs, but died the same year, in London. » Castlereagh; Catholic Emancipation; Corn Laws; Pitt (the Younger); Whigs

Cannizzaro, Stanislao (1826–1910) Italian chemist, born at Palermo. He was professor of chemistry at Genoa, Palermo, and Rome. In 1860, while at Genoa, he marched with Garibaldi's thousand. He was the first to appreciate the importance of Avogadro's work in connection with atomic weights. He coordinated organic and inorganic chemistry, and discovered the reaction named after him. He died in Rome. » atomic weight; chemistry

Cannon, W(alter) B(radford) (1871–1945) US physiologist, born at Prairie du Chien, Wisconsin. He studied medicine at Harvard, where he taught (1899–1942), becoming renowned for his use of X-rays in the study of the alimentary tract, and for his work on the effects of haemorrhage and shock. He went on to study hormones and nerve transmission, and developed the concept of a constant internal physiological environment, which he named *homeostasis*. He died at Franklin, New Hampshire. » alimentary canal; homeostasis; hormone; radiography; X-rays

Cano, Juan Sebastian del (?–1526) Spanish navigator, born at Guetaria, the first to journey around the world. In 1519 he sailed with Magellan, after whose death he safely navigated the *Victoria* home to Spain. He died during a second expedition. » Magellan

canoe A small, double-ended open craft propelled with paddles. There are two main types: a vessel carrying three or four people, made from a light wooden framework, traditionally covered with birch bark, but latterly using thin wooden planks; and the Pacific dugout canoe, often fitted with an outrigger, which could be made capable of ocean voyages. Maori war canoes were up to 20 m/70 ft long, fashioned from a single pine tree, fitted with one inverted-triangle-shaped sail, and propelled by c.60 paddlers. » canoeing; kayak

canoeing A water sport practised in canoes, developed by British barrister John Macgregor (1825–92) in 1865. The Canoe Club was formed the following year. Two types of canoe are used in competition: the *kayak*, which has a keel and the canoeist sits in the boat, and the *Canadian canoe*, which has no keel and the canoeist kneels. The number of persons per craft varies between one and four. » canoe

canon (music) In music, a strictly ordered texture in which polyphony is derived from a single line by imitation of itself at fixed intervals of time and pitch. In other words, all the canonic parts are the same, but they overlap each other. The term *canon* originally referred to the verbal, symbolic, or cryptic 'rule' by which the imitations are formed. » counterpoint; Pachelbel; polyphony

canon (religion) **1** In Christianity, a list of the inspired writings regarded as comprising Holy Scripture. The precise limits of the Old and New Testament canons were debated in the early Christian centuries, and Protestants and Roman Catholics still differ regarding the inclusion of some works. The term is also sometimes used to comprise the rules regarding liturgy, the life and discipline of the Church, and other decisions of the Councils. » Apocrypha, New Testament/Old Testament;

Bible; canon law; Council of the Church; Pseudepigrapha **2** The prayer of consecration in the Roman Catholic Mass. » Mass **3** The ecclesiastical title of clergy attached to cathedrals or certain endowed churches; either *secular* or, if living under semi-monastic rule, *regular* (eg Augustinian). In the Church of England, *residentiary* canons are the salaried staff of a cathedral, responsible for the upkeep of the building; *non-residentiary* canons are unsalaried, but have certain privileges, including rights with regard to the election of bishops. » cathedral

canon law In the Roman Catholic Church, a body of rules or laws to be observed in matters of faith, morals, and discipline. It developed out of the decisions of the Councils of the Church, and the decrees of popes and influential bishops. A notable compilation was made by Gratian in his *Decretum* (1140), which, with later additions, formed the *Corpus Juris Canonici* (completely revised in 1917). Pre-Reformation canon law is observed in the Church of England, subject to revisions such as the Book of Canons (1604–6) and Code (1964–9). » canon (religion) **1**; Codex Juris Canonici; Council of the Church

canonization The culmination of a lengthy process in the Roman Catholic Church whereby, after a long process of enquiry, a deceased individual is declared a saint, or entitled to public veneration. It confers various honours, such as a festival day, and the dedication of churches to his/her memory. In the Orthodox Church, there is a similar but less formal procedure. » Roman Catholicism; Orthodox Church; saint

Canopus » **Carina**

Canova, Antonio (1757–1822) Italian sculptor, born at Possagno. He studied at Venice and Rome, and came to be regarded as the founder of a new Neoclassicist school. His best-known works are the tombs of Popes Clement XIII (1787–92) and XIV (1783–7), several statues of Napoleon, and one of his sister Princess Borghese reclining as Venus Victrix (1805–7). In 1802 he was appointed by Pius VII curator of works of art. He died in Venice. » Italian art; Neoclassicism (art); sculpture

Cantabria [kantabria] pop (1981) 510 816; area 5 289 sq km/2 041 sq ml. Autonomous region of N Spain, co-extensive with the modern province of Santander; stretches across the Cordillera Cantabrica (1 382 m/4 534 ft) to the headwaters of the R Ebro; capital, Santander. » Santander; Spain [i]

Cantabrian Mountains, Span **Cordillera Cantabrica** Mountain range in N Spain, extending 500 km/310 ml W–E from Galicia along the Bay of Biscay to the Pyrenees, and forming a barrier between the sea and the C plateau (Meseta) of Spain; highest point, the Picos de Europa massif (2 648 m/8 688 ft); rich in minerals, and a source of hydroelectric power. » Spain [i]

cantata Music which is 'sung'. The Italian solo cantata of the 17th–18th-c was a setting of secular (usually amatory) verses, alternating recitative and aria. The Lutheran cantatas (eg those of Bach) were church compositions for soloists, choir, and instruments. More recent cantatas, whether sacred or secular, are usually choral and orchestral pieces, with or without soloists; many are festival or commemorative pieces. » sonata; song

Canterbury, Lat **Durovernum**, Anglo-Saxon **Cantwaraburh** 51°17N 1°05E, pop (1981) 39 742. Market town linked with Blean in Canterbury district, Kent, SE England; St Augustine began the conversion of England to Christianity here (597); Thomas Becket murdered (1170) in Canterbury Cathedral; seat of the Primate of the Anglican Church; important literary associations with Chaucer, Marlowe, Defoe, Dickens, and Maugham; University of Kent (1965); railway; tourism, engineering, glass; 11th–15th-c cathedral; Churches of St Dunstan, St George, St Martin, St Mildred, and St Peter; St Augustine's College; the Weavers, half-timbered Tudor houses; city walls; cricket festival (Aug). » Augustine, St (of Canterbury); Becket; Kent

Canterbury bell A robust hairy biennial, native to Italy, introduced elsewhere; flowers 4–5 cm/1½–2 in, bell-shaped, dark blue, in long spikes; popular ornamental; garden forms in many colours. (*Campanula medium.* Family: *Campanulaceae.*) » bell-flower; biennial

Canterbury Tales A series of linked narrative poems (and prose pieces) by Geoffrey Chaucer: the most important English work of literature from mediaeval times. Modelled on Boccaccio's *Decameron*, the tales are told by a group of pilgrims on the road to Canterbury. The Prologue, introducing the 29 pilgrims, is a gallery of contrasting characters, including the Knight, the Squire, the prim Prioress, the bawdy Miller, and the much-married Wife of Bath. Their 24 tales (the plan is incomplete) are told in a remarkable variety of poetic styles, from the romance to the fabliau. » Boccaccio; Chaucer; English literature; fabliau

Canticles » **Song of Solomon**

cantilever A horizontal building element where the part hidden within the building bears a downward force, and the other part projects outside without external bracing, and so appears to be self-supporting. It is often used to dramatic effect in 20th-c architecture.

canton A territorial division of land. In Switzerland, cantons have their own separate governments; in France, cantons are sub-divisions of arrondissements, which are themselves sub-divisions of the regional departments.

Canton (USA) 40°48N 81°23W, pop (1980) 94 730. Seat of Stark County, E Ohio, USA; railway; iron and steel industry; home and burial place of President McKinley, 25th US president. » McKinley; Ohio

Cantonese » **Chinese**

Cantor, Georg (Ferdinand Ludwig Philipp) (1845–1918) German mathematician, born in St Petersburg, Russia. He studied at Berlin and Göttingen, and in 1877 became professor of mathematics at Halle. He worked out a highly original arithmetic of the infinite which resulted in a theory of sets for irrational numbers, adding a new and important branch to mathematics. He suffered a nervous breakdown in 1884, and died at Halle in an asylum. » infinity; numbers; set

Canute or **Cnut**, byname **the Great** (c.995–1035) King of England (from 1016), Denmark (from 1019), and Norway (from 1028), the younger son of Sweyn Forkbeard. He first campaigned in England in 1013, and after his father's death (1014) successively challenged Ethelred the Unready and Edmund Ironside for the English throne. He defeated Edmund in 1016 at the Battle of Assandun, secured Mercia and Northumbria, and became King of all England after Edmund's death. In 1017 he married Emma of Normandy, the widow of Ethelred. He ruled England according to the accepted traditions of English kingship, and maintained the peace throughout his reign. He died at Shaftesbury, Dorset. The story of his failure to make the tide recede was invented by the 12th-c historian, Henry of Huntingdon, to demonstrate the frailty of earthly power compared to the might of God. » Anglo-Saxons; Ethelred (the Unready); Hardicanute; Harold I; Sweyn

canyon A deep valley with almost vertical sides which have been cut by a river, often in arid or semi-arid regions. Submarine canyons form on continental slopes, and are thought to have been eroded by turbidity currents. » submarine canyon

Canyon de Chelly [shay] National monument in NE Arizona, USA; established in 1931 to protect notable Indian cliff dwellings, dating from C.AD 350; area 339 sq km/131 sq ml. » American Indians; Arizona

Cap Vert [kap **vair**] or **Cape Verde** [**vair**dee] The most westerly point of the African continent, in Dakar region, W Senegal; 2 980 km/1 850 ml ENE of Natal (Brazil). » Africa; Senegal [i]

Capa, Robert, originally **Andrei Friedmann** (1913–54) Hungarian-US photojournalist, born in Budapest. He recorded the Spanish Civil War (1935–7), covered China under the Japanese attacks of 1938, and reported World War 2 in Europe from the Normandy invasion onwards. He was killed by a landmine in the Indo-China fighting which preceded the war in Vietnam.

capacitance The measure of a system's ability to store electric charge; symbol C, units F (*farad*); for a capacitor comprising two separate parallel conductors, equal to the charge on one conductor divided by the potential difference between the two. For an electrical circuit, elements are usually quoted as μF (*microfarad*, 10^{-6}F) or pF (*picofarad*, 10^{-12}F). » dielectric

Cape Breton Island pop (1981) 169 985; area 10 295 sq km/3 974 sq ml. Island in Nova Scotia province, E Canada;

separated from mainland by the Strait of Canso; almost bisected by Bras d'Or Lake (arm of the sea); chief towns, Sydney, Glace Bay, Louisburg; Cape Breton Highlands National Park in NW (1936); many people of Scottish descent, with Gaelic still spoken; dairy farming, fishing, timber, coal mining, gypsum, tourism; originally French (Ile Royale), taken by British, 1758; joined to Nova Scotia, 1820. » Nova Scotia

Cape buffalo » **African buffalo**

Cape Cod A sandy peninsula of SE Massachusetts state, USA; length 105 km/65 ml; width up to 32 km/20 ml; bounded E by the Atlantic and W by Cape Cod Bay; crossed by the 13 km/8 ml Cape Cod Canal; on 15 May 1602 Bartholomew Gosnold recorded, 'Near this cape...we took great store of codfish...and called it Cape Cod'; pilgrims from the *Mayflower* landed near Provincetown in Nov 1620; airfield at Provincetown; a popular resort area. » Pilgrim Fathers; Massachusetts

Cape Coloured or **Coloured** A term used by the South African government to refer to a group of people of mixed descent, arising from the unions of Europeans with slaves (from Madagascar, Mozambique, or the East) or Khoikoi (Hottentots). They number about 2.5 million people (c.9% of the total population), mainly living in the towns and rural areas of the W Cape province. Culturally akin to White South Africans, most Coloureds speak Afrikaans and are Christian, with a small Muslim minority (Cape Malays). In South Africa's racial hierarchy, they are ranked between Europeans and Black Africans. They live in separate areas on city outskirts, with their own schools and other facilities, and have limited rights within the country's political system. They are mostly farm labourers, factory workers, and artisans, with a small middle class. Coloureds reject the classification Cape Coloured, and refer to themselves as 'so-called Cape Coloureds'. » apartheid; South Africa [i]

Cape gooseberry A perennial native to S America, related and very similar to Chinese lantern; yellow flowers; calyx bladder-like, enclosing an edible yellow berry. (*Physalis peruviana*. Family: *Solanaceae*.) » Chinese lantern; perennial; physalis

Cape hunting dog » **African hunting dog**

Cape jasmin A species of gardenia with large flowers up to 10 cm/4 in diameter. A double-flowered form is a popular pot plant and corsage. (*Gardenia jasminoides*. Family: *Rubiaceae*.) » gardenia

Cape Province, Afrikaans **Kaapprovinsie** pop (1985) 5 041 137; area 641 379 sq km/247 572 sq ml. Largest province in South Africa, bounded W by the Atlantic Ocean and S by the Indian Ocean; NW frontier with Namibia formed by the Orange R; several mountain ranges along the Great Escarpment; Cape of Good Hope lies S of Cape Town; Cape Agulhas, most S point of the African continent; founded, 1652; formally ceded to Britain (Cape Colony), 1814; separate parliament, 1850; joined Union of South Africa, 1910; capital, Cape Town; chief towns include Port Elizabeth, East London; grapes, wine, grain, fruit, livestock, diamonds, copper, vehicles, pottery, timber, engineering, distilling, textiles, furniture; noted for its variety of flora, best observed at Cape Floral Kingdom reserve on Table Mt. » Cape Town; South Africa [i]

Cape Town, Afrikaans **Kaapstad** 33°56S 18°28E, pop (1985) 776 617, Greater Cape Town 1 911 521. Seaport capital of Cape province, South Africa; on Table Bay at the foot of Table Mt; legislative capital of South Africa; founded as a victualling station for the Dutch East India Company, 1652; occupied by the British, 1795; airport; railway; university (1829); commerce, vehicles, chemicals, textiles; trade in wool, mohair, grain, fruit, wine, oil; Castle of Good Hope (1666), oldest colonial building in South Africa; Koopmans de Wet House (1777), Groote Kerk, Union Houses of Parliament, national gallery. » Cape Province; South Africa [i]; Table Mountain

Cape Verde [kayp **verd**], official name **Republic of Cape Verde**, Port **Republica de Cabo Verde** pop (1990e) 339 000; area 4 033 sq km/1 557 sq ml. Island group in the Atlantic Ocean off West Coast of Africa, c.500 km/310 ml W of Dakar, Senegal; two main groups, defined with reference to the prevailing NE wind; Barlavento (windward) group in N; Sotavento (leeward) group in S; capital, Praia (on São Tiago I); other main port, Mindelo;

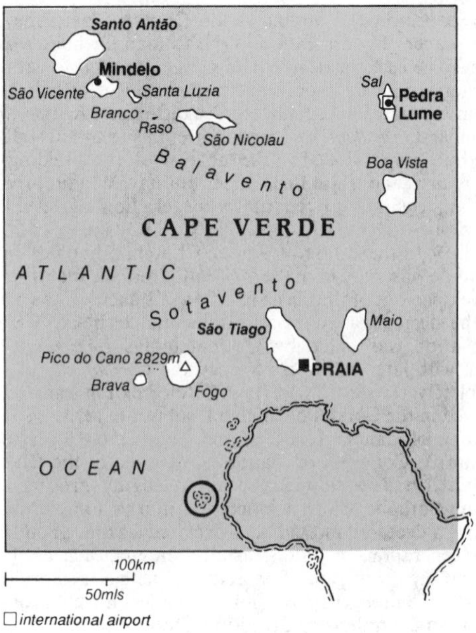

timezone GMT −1; c.50% of population live on São Tiago I; c.60% of mixed Black African and European descent; main religion, Roman Catholic; official language, Portuguese, but creole widely spoken; unit of currency, escudo Caboverdianos; international airport on Sal I; islands of volcanic origin, mostly mountainous; highest peak, Cano (2 829 m/9 281 ft), active volcano on Fogo I; coastal plains semi-desert; savannah or thin forest on the mountains; fine sandy beaches on most islands; located at N limit of tropical rain belt; low and unreliable rainfall (mainly Aug–Sep); cooler and damper in uplands; severe drought can occur; small range of temperature throughout year; colonized by Portuguese in 15th-c, also used as a penal colony; administered with Portuguese Guinea until 1879; overseas province of Portugal, 1951; independence, 1975; governed by a president, Council of Ministers, and unicameral People's National Assembly of 83 members, elected for five years; formerly an important victualling point for transatlantic shipping; economy suffered in recent years because of drought; substantial emigration in early 1970s, with 80% unemployment by 1976; c.70% of workforce are farmers occupying irrigated inland valleys; livestock, maize, beans, potatoes, cane sugar, bananas, yams, coffee; increase in fishing since 1975; mining of salt, limestone, volcanic silica ash (pozzolana). » Praia; São Tiago; RR24 national holidays; RR45 political leaders

Čapek, Karel [**cha**pek] (1890–1938) Czech author, born at Schwadonitz. He studied in Prague, Berlin, and Paris, then settled in Prague as a writer and journalist. His best-known work is his play *R. U. R.* (Rossum's Universal Robots), produced in 1921, showing mechanization rampant. He also wrote many short stories on crime and mystery, as well as prophetic, science-fiction, and travel books. He died in Prague. » Czechoslovak literature

Capella [ka**pel**a] » **Auriga**

caper A sprawling, deciduous, spiny shrub, native to S Europe; leaves alternate, oval, slightly fleshy; flowers 5–7 cm/2–2¾ in in diameter, 4-petalled, white with numerous long purple stamens. The young flower buds are pickled as capers. (*Capparis spinosa*. Family: *Capparidaceae*.) » deciduous plants; shrub; stamen

capercaillie [kapuh**kay**lee] A large grouse native to Europe and N Asia, also known as **capercailzie**; usually solitary; forest-dwelling; males have special mating calls, and display by leaping into the air, flapping their wings. (Genus: *Tetrao*, 2 species. Family: *Tetraonidae*.) » grouse

Capet, Hugo or **Hugh** (c.938–96) King of France, founder of the third Frankish royal dynasty (the Capetians), which ruled

France until 1328. Son of Hugh the Great, whom he succeeded as Duke of the Franks in 956, he was elected King and crowned at Noyon (987). His 40 years in power were marked by constant political intrigue and struggle, both among the feudal aristocracy and with his Carolingian rivals, but his position was invariably saved by the disunity of his enemies. » Capetians; Carolingians; Franks

Capetians A French ruling dynasty for over 300 years (987–1328), founded by Hugh Capet in succession to the Carolingians. Two dynamic royal descendants were Philip II Augustus (reigned 1180–1223) and Louis IX or St Louis (reigned 1226–1270). By increasing territorial control, enforcing the right to inherit of an eldest son, and devoting themselves to administration and justice, the Capetians laid the foundations of the French nation-state. » Bourbons; Capet; Philip II (of France); Louis IX

capillarity A surface tension effect in which liquids rise up narrow tubes or spread through porous solids; caused by the difference in attraction between liquid and air molecules for the material of the solid. Examples include the movement of blood through the smallest blood vessels (capillaries), and ink soaking into blotting paper. » chromatography; porosity; surface tension [i]

capillary A minute, thin-walled blood vessel situated between arterioles and venules. It is the site of the exchange of materials (oxygen, nutrients, carbon dioxide) between capillary blood and surrounding tissues, which occurs by diffusion across the capillary wall. The term is also used to denote a small lymphatic channel. » blood vessels [i]; lymph

capital (accountancy) Business sources of finance to buy assets, such as buildings, machinery, stocks, or investment in other firms. *Equity capital* is supplied by shareholders, either by buying shares or by ploughing back profits into the business. *Loan capital* or *debt* is borrowed from a financial institution or individual, and interest is paid. *Capital gearing* or (US) *leverage* is the proportion of capital raised by equity or debt: a high gearing = a high debt. » debt; equity (economics)

capital (architecture) The top part of a column, pilaster, or pier; usually designed and identified according to one of the five main orders of classical architecture: Doric, Tuscan, Ionic, Corinthian, and Composite. Other forms include basket, bell, crocket, cushion, lotus, palm, protomai (with animal figures), scalloped, and water-leaf. » acanthus; column; orders of architecture [i]; pilaster

capital (economics) Physical assets which are productive. The notion includes *fixed capital*, ie buildings, machinery, and equipment; and *working* or *circulating capital*, ie stocks and work in progress, land, consumer durables, and other goods in the hands of the consumers (such as household equipment).

capital gains tax (CGT) A tax payable when an asset is sold at a profit. First introduced in the UK in 1965, it is usually amended annually by the government. Small gains are exempt from the tax. » taxation

capital punishment Sentence of death passed by a judicial body following trial. Capital punishment for murder has been abolished in the UK, though proposals for its reinstatement are regularly debated by parliament, and it remains the penalty for treason. It is still available in several states of the USA, and in many other countries. When the sentence is available, it is not invariably carried out; a head of state or other authority can recommend a reprieve. Countries employ a variety of procedures in carrying out executions, including lethal injection, electrocution, hanging, gassing, and shooting. » murder; sentence; treason

capital transfer tax (CTT) A UK tax arising when individuals gave assets to others (excluding small gifts), including the transfer of ownership on death (originally called *estate* or *death duties*). The tax was not payable on small estates. It was replaced in 1986 by the inheritance tax. » inheritance tax

capitalism A set of economic arrangements which developed in the 19th-c in Western societies following the Industrial Revolution. The concept derives from the writings of Marx and rests upon the private ownership of the means of production by the capitalist class, or bourgeoisie. The workers, or proletariat, own nothing but their labour, and although free to sell their labour in the market, they are dependent upon the capitalist class which exploits them by appropriating the surplus value created by their labour. Non-Marxist economists define capitalism as one in which most property is privately owned and goods are sold freely in a competitive market, but without reference to exploitation, except where monopoly situations occur. Capitalism may be an ideological stance: Marx saw it as one stage in a historical process, finally being replaced by socialism. It has been the most productive economic system to date, though it has brought with it massive environmental (eg pollution) and social (eg unemployment) problems. » bourgeoisie; Marxism; proletariat

Capitol The Assembly of the US Congress on Capitol Hill, Washington, DC. The building was designed in 1792 by William Thornton (1759–1828), but a succession of architects supervised its construction. In 1814 the British set fire to the unfinished structure, and it was not until 1827 that it was finally completed by Benjamin Latrobe (1764–1820) and Charles Bulfinch (1763–1844). The dome was added by Thomas Walter (1804–87). » Congress

Capitoline Hill The highest of the seven hills upon which Rome was built. Once the political and religious centre of Ancient Rome, it is now the site of the Piazza del Campidoglio, designed by Michelangelo, and of the city's administrative offices. » Michelangelo; Rome

capitulum An inflorescence typical of the daisy family, *Compositae*, consisting of many stalkless florets packed onto a flattened receptacle cupped by bracts. The florets are often of two kinds: small disc florets in the centre; petal-like ray florets around the edge. The whole inflorescence gives the impression of being a single flower. » bract; daisy; floret; inflorescence [i]

Capodimonte porcelain [kapohdee**mon**tay] The porcelain factory of the royal house of Naples, started in 1743 and removed to Buen Retiro in Spain in 1759. It was notable for its very fine figures, particularly the chinoiseries, which were much copied by later factories in Italy and elsewhere. » chinoiserie; porcelain

Capone, Al, properly **Alphonse** [ka**pohn**] (1899–1947) US gangster, born in New York City. He achieved worldwide notoriety as a racketeer during the prohibition era in Chicago. Such was his power that no evidence sufficient to support a charge against him was forthcoming until 1931, when he was sentenced to 10 years' imprisonment for tax evasion. Released on health grounds in 1939, he retired to his estate in Florida, where he died.

Capote, Truman [ka**poh**tay], originally **Truman Streckfus Persons** (1924–84) US author, born in New Orleans. He won several early literary prizes, and his first novel, *Other Voices, Other Rooms*, was published in 1948. Other works are *The Grass Harp* (1951), *Breakfast at Tiffany's* (1958), which was highly successful as a film, and *In Cold Blood* (1966), described as a 'nonfiction novel' on account of its journalistic style. He died in Los Angeles. » American literature; novel

Cappadocia [kapa**doh**shia], Turkish **Kapadokya** Ancient name for the mountainous region of C Turkey, between the Black Sea and the Taurus Mts; a poor area without good natural defences, it tended to be ruled by whatever power was dominant in Asia Minor; a province of the Roman Empire from AD 17; noted for its eroded landscape features and cave dwellings in the Göreme valley; largest town, Nevşehir. » Roman history [i]; Turkey [i]

Capra, Frank (1897–) US film director, born at Palermo, Italy. When he was six, his family emigrated to California where he studied at the Institute of Technology. He began in film work in 1921, and had several box-office hits. Among his best-known films are *Mr Deeds Goes to Town* (1936) and *You Can't Take It with You* (1938), which won Academy Awards, *Lost Horizon* (1937), *Arsenic and Old Lace* (1942), and *State of the Union* (1948). He retired for some years before his later films, *A Hole in the Head* (1959) and *A Pocketful of Miracles* (1961).

Capri [ka**pree**], ancient **Capreae**, Ital [**ka**pree] area 10.5 sq km/4 sq ml. Island in Napoli province, Campania, Italy, in the Tyrrhenian Sea; length 6 km/4 ml; maximum width 2.5 km/

The world's first car, made by Karl Benz in 1886. The engine produced ¾ horse power, and achieved a speed of 13 kph/8 mph.

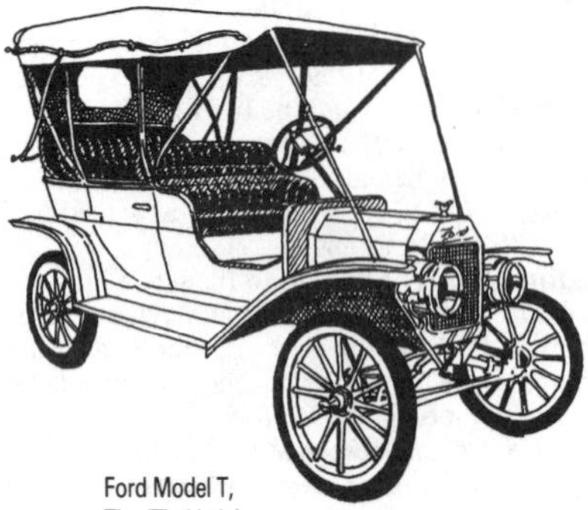

Ford Model T, The 'Tin Lizzie', dating from 1908, which brought motoring to the American public. Its engine produced 20 horse power.

KDF-wagen: the prototype of the Volkswagen, designed as a 'people's car'. It began production in 1937.

Cadillac Fleetwood Sixty Special sedan: US development of the large car with a large engine.

The jeep, built during and after World War 2 as a general-purpose vehicle with four-wheel drive.

Rolls-Royce Phantom V Limousine: the epitome of luxury motoring.

The Mini: introduced in 1959, designed by Alec Issigonis with features such as front-wheel drive, transverse engine and 10 in/25 cm wheels.

Porsche 928S4: In 1989 this car combined the speed (max 265 kph/165 mph) supplied by a V8 engine with 3-way catalytic converter to reduce the pollution produced.

Cars

1.5 ml; rugged limestone crags rise to 589 m/1 932 ft; capital, Capri; Blue Grotto on N coast; major tourist centre. » Italy [i]

capriccio (art) [kapritcheeoh] (Ital 'caprice') In art, an imaginative picture or print. In the 18th-c, the term refers specifically to landscapes by such artists as Canaletto or Giovanni Pannini (1691–1765), combining buildings from different places. Goya and Tiepolo produced outstanding sets of etched fantasies, with bizarre or grotesque subjects. » Canaletto; Goya; Tiepolo

capriccio (music) [kapritcheeoh] A short musical composition, usually of a light or fanciful kind and often (though not necessarily) for piano. There are several famous examples in the work of Brahms. » Brahms

Capricornus or **Capricorn** (Lat 'goat') A S constellation. It is a winter sign of the zodiac, lying between Sagittarius and Aquarius. » constellation; zodiac [i]; RR8

capsid A small to medium-sized bug that typically feeds on plants; occasionally predatory; c.10 000 species, distributed worldwide. (Order: *Heteroptera*. Family: *Miridae*.) » bug (entomology)

capsule 1 A dry, many-seeded fruit derived from more than one carpel. When ripe it opens by means of valves, pores, or a lid, or by irregular fracturing. » carpel; fruit **2** A stalked structure containing spores in ferns, mosses, and liverworts, rupturing when ripe to release the contents. » fern; liverwort; moss; spore

capuchin [kapyoochin] A New World monkey, the most numerous captive monkey in the USA and Europe; tail partly adapted for grasping (*prehensile*), often carried curled at the tip; acrobatic and intelligent; once a popular pet for street musicians; also known as **ring-tailed monkey**, or **organ-grinder's monkey**. (Genus: *Cebus*, 4 species.) » New World monkey

Capuchins (Ital *capuche*, a kind of cowl) A monastic order stemming from the Franciscans; in full, the **Order of Friars Minor of St Francis Capuccinorum**; abbreviated as **OM Cap** or **OSFC**. It was formed in 1529 by Matteo di Bassi (c.1495–1552), and observes a very strict rule, stressing poverty and austerity. » Franciscans; monasticism

capybara [kapibahra] A cavy-like rodent, native to C and S America; largest living rodent (length, over 1 m/3¼ ft); dog-like with deep square snout; no tail; lives in and near water; part-webbed toes; eats vegetation. (*Hydrochoerus hydrochaeris*. Family: *Hydrochoeridae*.) » cavy; rodent

car, also **motor car** (UK), **automobile** (USA) The general name used in the UK for a passenger-carrying, self-propelled vehicle designed for normal domestic use on roads. The vehicle itself is made up of a number of systems, all of which may be discussed and constructed in isolation, but whose combined functioning produces the final vehicle. Thus the motive power system includes the engine (of whatever type), and its fuel supply, and the lubrication, exhaust, and cooling systems. The power developed by the engine is transmitted to the wheels by the transmission system, which includes gears, clutches, shafts, axles, and brakes. The engine and transmission are housed in the carriage unit, which also provides the compartment for the driver and passengers to sit, and in which the steering, engine controls, suspension, and electrical components can be mounted.

Although there had been much experimenting with steam vehicles during the late 18th-c and early 19th-c, the basic feature that allowed the motor car to become a reality was the invention in 1884 of the medium-speed internal combustion engine by Daimler in Germany. However, it was not until the early 1900s, and the application in the USA of mass production techniques to the motor car, that mass motoring started to become a reality. Over the years, the size of the domestic market ensured US dominance in the field of mass production, although the European manufacturers (particularly in the 1930s) also produced cheap 'people's' cars, such as the Volkswagen and the Citroen 2CV. The emergence of small Japanese cars in the 1970s challenged the US and European manufacturers in their own countries. This led in the early 1980s to a series of amalgamations of companies into ever larger multinationals, including the Japanese, which began to co-operate with each other, This process is likely to continue, in an attempt to offset the massive costs of design and mass production by exploiting economies of scale and global marketing. » Africar; Daimler; electric car; engine; jeep; motor racing; transmission; tyre

carabao [karabow] » **water buffalo**

caracal [karakal] A member of the cat family, native to Africa and S Asia; reddish-brown; slender with long legs, short tail, long tufted ears; inhabits savannah and dry woodland; eats birds, rodents, and small antelopes; easily tamed. (*Felis caracal*.) » Felidae

caracara [kahrakahra] A large, broad-winged falcon; native to S USA and S America; inhabits open country to considerable altitudes; eats many types of animal or carrion; will rob other birds of prey. (Family: *Falconidae*, 10 species.) » falcon

Caracas [karakas] 10°30N 66°55W, pop(1981) 1 162 952. Federal capital of Venezuela; altitude, 120–960 m/400–3 150 ft; founded in 1567; often damaged by earthquakes; major growth since the 1940s, greater than any other Latin American capital; airport; airfield; railway; metro; three universities (1725, 1953, 1970); mountain pass gives access to port at La Guaira; commercial, cultural, and industrial centre; birthplace of Bolívar; Plaza Bolívar, Panteón Nacional (with Bolívar's tomb), Casa Natal del Libertador, Capitolio Nacional, cathedral. » Bolívar; Venezuela [i]

Caractacus, Caratacus, or **Caradoc** (1st-c AD) A chief of the Catuvellauni, the son of Cunobelinus. He mounted a gallant but unsuccessful guerrilla operation in Wales against the Romans in the years following the Claudian conquest (43). Betrayed by the Brigantian queen, Cartimandua, he was taken to Rome (51), where he was exhibited in triumph, pardoned by Claudius, and later died. » Britain, Roman; Cartimandua; Cymbeline

caracul » **karakul**

Caratacus » **Caractacus**

Caravaggio [karavadjoh], originally **Michelangelo Merisi** (1573–1610) Italian Baroque painter, born at Caravaggio, whence his nickname. He studied in Milan and Venice, and went to Rome, where Cardinal del Monte became his chief patron. His works include several altarpieces and religious paintings, using dramatic contrasts of light and shade, notably several paintings of St Matthew (1599–1603) and 'Christ at Emmaus' (c.1602–3, National Gallery, London). In 1606, his temper led him to kill a man, and he fled to Naples and Malta. He died at Porto Ercole. » Baroque (art and architecture); Italian art

caravel [karavel] A sailing vessel with up to four masts developed by the Portuguese in the 15th-c. The illustration shows the typical lateen rig sails with the long curved spars. » ship [i]

caraway A much-branched annual, growing to 1 m/3.3 ft, native to Europe; leaves finely divided into narrow lance-shaped lobes; flowers small, borne in umbels 2–4 cm/¾–1½ in across, petals whitish, deeply notched; fruit 3–6 mm/

Caravel

0.12–0.24 in, ribbed, strong-smelling when crushed. The fruits are used as a spice and for flavouring bread, cakes and cheese; they are also an essential ingredient of Kümmel liqueur. (*Carum carvi.* Family: *Umbelliferae.*) » annual; spice; umbel

carbamide » **urea**

carbide Any compound of carbon, especially those in which carbon is ionic. It is often used specifically for *calcium carbide*, CaC_2, a salt of acetylene, which may be regenerated by the addition of water: $CaC_2 + 2H_2O \rightarrow Ca(OH)_2 + C_2H_2$ » acetylene; carbon; ion

carbohydrate A non-nitrogen-containing compound based on carbon, hydrogen, and oxygen, generally with two hydrogen atoms per atom of oxygen. The molecules may be small (glucose) or large (cellulose, starch). Most carbohydrates are comprised of one or more 6-carbon units, of which glucose is by far the most abundant. Starch is a polymer of glucose, digestible by humans, whereas cellulose is a polymer of glucose, digestible only by ruminants. Carbohydrates are not nutritionally essential, but prolonged intake of carbohydrate-free diets can cause ketosis. » cellulose; disaccharide; fibre; glucose [i]; starch; sugars

carbolic acid » **phenol**

carbon C, element 6. It has two main forms: *graphite* (the stable form, very soft and black with a density of c.2 g/cm^3) and *diamond* (the hardest substance known, density 3.5 g/cm^3). Both of these melt above 3 500°. Coal is mainly graphite, but also contains amorphous (non-crystalline) carbon, occurring as well as 'carbon black' (soot). Graphite can be grown into *carbon fibres*, used for strengthening plastics. Carbon also occurs naturally in compounds, particularly as **carbonates**, and in the atmosphere as carbon dioxide. In virtually all its compounds, it is co-valently bonded, and shows a valence of 4. Carbon compounds are the basis of all living matter, and form the subject matter of organic chemistry. There are two simple oxides, **carbon monoxide** (CO), a very poisonous gas, boiling point −191°C, formed from the incomplete combustion of carbon and hydrocarbons, and **carbon dioxide** O=C=O, the product of complete combustion. Carbon dioxide is in turn the raw material for photosynthesis, regenerating combustibles. Solid carbon dioxide, or *dry ice*, sublimes at −78°C without passing through a liquid phase. It accounts for less than 0.03% of the gases of the atmosphere. » carbon cycle/dating/fibre; chemical elements; coal; diamond; organic chemistry; photosynthesis; sublimation (chemistry)

carbon cycle The cycle through which carbon is transferred between the biological (*biotic*) and non-biological (*abiotic*) parts of the global ecosystem. It involves the fixation of gaseous carbon dioxide during photosynthesis to form complex organic molecules, and the subsequent process through which it ultimately returns to the atmosphere by respiration and decomposition. » carbon; ecosystem; photosynthesis

carbon dating » **radiocarbon dating**

carbon dioxide » **carbon**

carbon fibre A high-strength material made by the controlled heat treatment of acrylic fibre. Woven as a fabric, it has the property of absorbing poisonous gas, and is used for protective underwear for military personnel, and for firehoods. The fibres are several times stronger than steel, and are extensively used where laminates of great strength and low weight are needed, as in components for rockets and aeroplanes. As carbon fibre reinforced plastic (or graphite epoxy), it is widely used for sports equipment such as fishing rods, racquets, and skis.

Carbonari [cahbo**nah**ree] (Ital 'charcoal burners') Neapolitan secret societies, linked with freemasonry and probably founded under Napoleonic occupation. Liberal and loosely nationalist in outlook, they played a major role in the Neapolitan revolution of 1820 (by which time membership may have numbered 300 000–500 000) and in the early stages of the Risorgimento. » freemasonry; Risorgimento

carbonates Salts of carbonic acid, containing the ion CO_3^{2-}. Important natural carbonates include the almost insoluble *calcium carbonate* ($CaCO_3$), or limestone; *magnesium carbonate* ($MgCO_3$); and *dolomite* ($CaMg(CO_3)_2$). *Sodium carbonate*, known as 'washing soda' in its hydrated form ($Na_2CO_3.10H_2O$), is a cleansing agent because of its basicity, and a water softener because it precipitates calcium and magnesium carbonates. » carbonic acid; salt

carbonic acid H_2CO_3; the hydrated form of carbon dioxide (CO_2). It is a weak acid, dissociating in two stages to give bicarbonate (HCO_3^-) and carbonate (CO_3^{2-}) ions. Natural waters are generally saturated with carbon dioxide from the atmosphere, and their pH is generally determined by the amount of bicarbonate and carbonate ions present. Rain water containing pure carbonic acid has a pH of about 5. » carbon; hydration; pH

Carboniferous period A geological period of the Palaeozoic era, extending from 360 million to 286 million years ago, and characterized by extensive swampy forests with conifers and ferns which now form most of the present-day coal deposits. It was also marked by widespread coral reefs and limestone deposits, and the first appearance of reptiles and seed-bearing plants. In the USA, the period is termed the **Mississippian** (earlier) and the **Pennsylvanian** (later). » coal; geological time scale; Palaeozoic era

carbonyl [**kah**boniyl] The group CO, (1) in organic compounds, found in aldehydes, ketones, carboxylic acids, esters, and amides; (2) in inorganic compounds, found as co-ordinated carbon dioxide. » carbon

carborundum The trade name for silicon carbide (SiC), a highly refractory material formed by fusing together sand and coke. It is almost as hard as diamond, and is used in grinding wheels and cutting tools. » silicon carbide

carboxylic acids [kahbok**sil**ik] Organic compounds containing the group –COOH; formed by the oxidation of alcohols or aldehydes; also called **alkanoic acids**. Weaker than mineral acids, partially neutralized solutions have pH values of about 5. Many are found in nature, particularly as part of fats (*fatty acids*). » acetic acid; alcohols; aldehyde; amino acid [i]; pH

carbro process A photographic printing procedure in which a pigmented gelatine tissue is differentially hardened by contact with a developed print on bromide paper to produce an image which can be transferred to another support. Black and white prints using carbon as a pigment have great permanence, and colour prints can be made by superimposition of three layers in yellow, cyan and magenta. » photography

carbuncle A focus of infection in sweat glands and under the skin. It forms multiple confluent abscesses that discharge pus on to its surface through two or more tracts. » abscess; sweat

carburettor A device fitted to a spark ignition engine that mixes its fuel of air and petrol in suitable proportions for combustion. As the engine draws in its air/petrol mixture, the carburettor ensures that small droplets of petrol are carried along with the airstream. These droplets then vaporize on their way to the engine to form the highly inflammable mixture used in the engine's power stroke. A number of different types of carburettor exist, but most of them work upon a floating valve system that detects when the air is to be drawn into the engine. » internal combustion engine; petrol; spark ignition engine

Carcassonne [kahka**son**], ancient **Carcaso** 43°13N 2°20E, pop (1982) 42 450. Ancient city and capital of Aude department, S France, on R Aude and Canal du Midi, in foothills of Pyrenees; railway; bishopric; hosiery, tanning, wine; the Cité (altitude 200 m/650 ft) is the best preserved example of a French mediaeval fortified town, with a double circuit of walls and towers; basilica of St-Nazaire (5th-c, rebuilt 11th–13th-c), Cathedral of St Michel (late 13th-c, restored 1840), Gothic Church of St Vincent (late 13th-c). » Pyrenees

Carchemish [**kah**kemish] An ancient trading city in N Syria controlling one of the main crossing points of the Euphrates. It was ruled by the Hittites in the second millennium BC, survived the destruction of the Hittite empire (c.1200 BC), and remained an important centre of Hittite culture until its conquest by Assyria in 716 BC. » Assyria; Hittites

carcinogen [kah**sin**uhjuhn] An agent which is capable of inducing cancer in tissues exposed to it. Some carcinogens have been identified by studies of the frequency of specific tumours in relation to different occupations, life styles, exposure to injurious chemical agents, drugs, ionizing radiations, ultraviolet light, and certain tumour-inducing (*oncogenic*) viruses. Exposure to such agents does not cause cancer immediately, but only after a period which may be months or years. The dose or duration of exposure to the agent is also critical: an example is cancer of the lung and cigarette smoking, where both the duration of smoking and the number of cigarettes smoked increase the probability of developing lung cancer some time in the future. » cancer

carcinoma » **sarcoma**

card games » **playing cards**

cardamom A perennial native to India, also cultivated in Ceylon; rhizomatous; stem to 3.5 m/11½ ft; leaves in two rows, stalks sheathing; flowers small, white with blue and yellow markings, in clusters 60 cm/2 ft long on leafless stems near the ground; fruit a capsule 2 cm/0.8 in long. The dried ripe fruits are used as spice, especially in curries. (*Elettaria cardamomum*. Family: *Zingiberaceae*.) » perennial; rhizome; spice; stem

Cardan, Jerome, Ital **Geronimo Cardano**, Lat **Hieronymus Cardanus** (1501–76) Italian mathematician and physician, born at Pavia. He became professor of mathematics at Padua, and of medicine at Pavia and Bologna. He wrote over 100 treatises on physics, mathematics, astronomy, astrology, rhetoric, history, ethics, dialectics, natural history, music, and medicine. His *Ars magna* (1545, Great Art) was influential in the development of algebra. He died in Rome.

cardiac resuscitation Emergency treatment following cardiac arrest (the sudden complete cessation of heart function); also known as **external cardiac massage**. This must be given within three minutes if the brain is not to suffer irreversible damage. First aid treatment is usually combined with mouth-to-mouth ventilation. Initially a smart blow with the closed fist should be given to the front of the chest just to the left of the midline, and both legs elevated to 90°. If the heart does not start, forceful regular compression of the chest at about 70 times per minute should be carried out. » artificial respiration [i]; heart [i]

Cardiff, Welsh **Caerdydd** 51°30N 3°13W, pop (1987e) 281 500. Capital of Wales, in South Glamorgan, S Wales, UK; administrative centre of South and Mid Glamorgan; at the mouth of the Taff, Rhymney, and Ely Rivers, on the Bristol Channel; Roman fort, 1st-c AD; Norman castle, c.1090; city charter, 1147; expansion in 19th-c as trade in coal grew; decline with the loss of coal and steel industries in recent decades; Tiger Bay quayside area now redeveloping as a suburb; capital of Wales, 1955; airport (Rhoose); railway; university college (1893); registry for University of Wales; general services, steel, car components, cigars, tourism; Welsh National Opera; Cathays Park public buildings, Llandaff Cathedral, Welsh National Folk Museum (St Fagans), Cardiff Castle, Cardiff Arms Park (rugby). » Wales [i]

Cardigan, James Thomas Brudenell, 7th Earl of (1797–1868) British general, born at Hambleden, Buckinghamshire, who led the Charge of the Light Brigade against the Russians in the Crimean War. Educated at Oxford, he entered the army in 1824, and purchased his promotion, commanding the 15th Hussars (until 1833), then the 11th Hussars (1836–47). He commanded a cavalry brigade in the Crimea, and led the fatal charge of the Six Hundred at Balaclava (25 Oct 1854). He then became inspector-general of cavalry (1855–60). The woollen jacket known as a cardigan is named after him. He died at Deene, Northamptonshire. » Crimean War

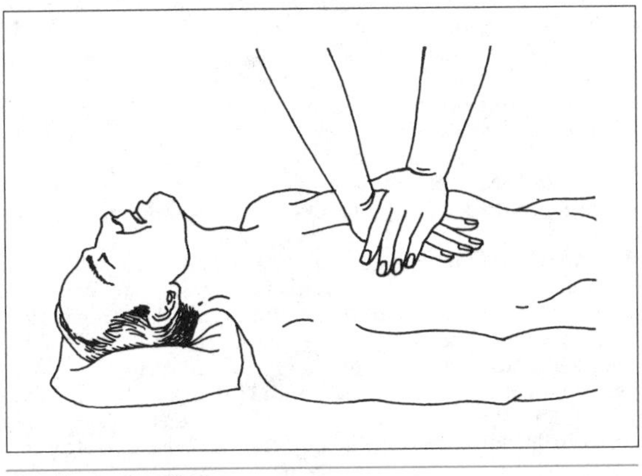

Cardiac resuscitation

cardinal (ornithology) Either of two species of bird, genus *Cardinalis*, native to the Americas: the **red** or **northern cardinal** (*Cardinalis cardinalis*), and the **vermilion cardinal** (*Cardinalis phoeniceus*); males bright red. The name is sometimes used for other (unrelated) red birds. (Family: *Emberizidae*.)

cardinal (religion) A name originally given to one of the parish priests, bishops, or district deacons of Rome, then applied to a senior dignitary of the Roman Catholic Church, being a priest or bishop nominated by a pope to act as counsellor. His duties are largely administrative, as head of a diocese, a curial office, an ecclesiastical commission, or a Roman congregation. The office carries special insignia, such as the distinctive red cap (biretta). » Cardinals, College of; clergy; Roman Curia

cardinal vowels A set of reference points devised by Daniel Jones for identifying the vowel sounds of a language, based on the movements of the tongue and jaws, and separated by roughly regular acoustic intervals from each other. Eighteen main tongue positions are recognized on a grid representing vertical and horizontal tongue movement. » Jones, Daniel; phonetics; tongue; vowel

Cardinals, College of An institution consisting of all the cardinals of the Roman Catholic Church, technically of three-fold structure: bishops, priests, and deacons. It originates from the reforms of Pope Urban II (reigned 1088–99). In 1586 its number was restricted to 70, but this limit was removed by Pope John XXIII in 1958. It is responsible for the government of the Church during a vacancy in the papacy, and since 1179 has been responsible for the election of a pope. » cardinal (religion); pope; Roman Catholicism

carding The blending and disentanglement of fibres prior to subsequent spinning processes. The fibres are passed between a series of rollers covered in projecting steel wires and rotating at different speeds. » combing; spinning

cardioid The path of a point on a circle rolling around another circle of the same radius. The equation of a cardioid is best expressed in polar co-ordinates: $r = a(1 + \cos\theta)$. » circle; polar co-ordinates

caretaker speech » **motherese**

Carew, Thomas (1595–1639) English poet, born at West Wickham, Kent. He studied at Oxford and the Middle Temple, and became a diplomat. A friend of Jonson and Donne, he wrote polished lyrics in the Cavalier tradition, and a masque *Coelum Britannicum* (1634) which was performed at court. He died in London. » Cavalier poets; English literature; masque

cargo cult The Melanesian variety of a widely occurring type of social movement (millenarianism) in which people look to some supernatural event to bring them prosperity. It is so-called because in Melanesia, in numerous instances, people performed rituals in an effort to obtain European material goods (referred to as 'cargo'). The movement first appeared in the late 19th-c, and was popular in the 1930s. » cult; Melanesia; millenarianism

cariama » **seriema**

Carib American Indian groups of the Lesser Antilles and neighbouring S America (the Guianas and Venezuela). The island Caribs were maritime people and warriors, who drove the Arawak from the area. Most were slaughtered by Spaniards in the 15th-c, and the survivors mixed with Spanish conquerors and later Negro slaves. The mainland Caribs led a more peaceful existence in small autonomous settlements in the tropical forests. Population c.5 000. » Antilles; Arawak

Caribbean Community (CARICOM) An association of former British colonies in the Caribbean Sea, some of which (Barbados, Jamaica, and the Leeward Is except for the Virgin and Windward Is) existed as the Caribbean Federation, with the aim of full self-government, until the establishment of the West Indies Federation (1958–63). When Jamaica became independent in 1962, the Federation was dissolved. In 1969 certain of the remaining islands in the Windward and Leeward Is were offered associated status within the Commonwealth, and in 1969 the West Indies Associated States was formed. In

1968 many of the islands agreed to the establishment of the Caribbean Free Trade Area (**CARIFTA**). » associated state; Commonwealth, (British)

Caribbean dance A mixture of dance styles basically of African origin but influenced by the Spanish conquest of the W Indies and later by French and English dance styles of the colonial era. It shows the merging of African body movements with formal European set dances. Its vivid rhythmic form became the basis of jazz dance in the USA. » African dance; jazz dance

Caribbean literature Caribbean literature begins with the rejection of colonial status by the West Indian islands. Influenced by the Harlem Renaissance, Claude McKay asserted the black viewpoint in *Banana Bottom* (1933); C L R James's *Minty Alley* (1936) led to a new realism. The postwar years brought a number of important novelists, among them Roger Mais (1905–55), eg *Brother Man* (1954); George Lamming (1932–), eg *In the Cell of my Skin* (1953); V S Naipaul (1932–), eg *A House for Mr Biswaz* (1961); and Wilson Harris (1921–), eg *Guyana Quartet* (1960–3). Several of these writers came to England in the 1950s, where they were encouraged by the BBC's 'Caribbean Voices' programme. Meanwhile Derek Walcott (1930–) published three volumes of poetry and created the Trinidad Theatre Workshop: poet/historian Edward Brathwaite (1930–) set new voices to old rhythms in his trilogy *The Arrivants* (1967–9), which has been influential on the performance poetry of Bongo Jerry and Linton Kwesi Johnson (1952–). Emerging talents today are the poets James Berry (1924–) and Fred d'Aguiar (1960–), and the novelist/dramatist Caryl Phillips (1958–). » African/American/English literature; Naipaul; Walcott

Caribbean Sea area 2 515 900 sq km/971 100 sq ml. Arm of the Atlantic Ocean between the West Indies and C and S America; linked to the Pacific by the Panama Canal; depth 6 m/20 ft on continental shelf off Nicaragua to 5 058 m/16 594 ft on floor of Venezuelan Basin; deepest point, Cayman Trench, 6 950 m/ 22 802 ft; visited by Columbus, 1493; main island groups, Greater and Lesser Antilles; major trade route and tourist area. » Antilles; Panama Canal

caribou » **reindeer**

caricature A mock portraiture, usually graphic rather than painted, in which features are exaggerated for humorous or satirical effect. Early practitioners included the Carracci in late 16th-c Bologna. Bernini was a brilliant caricaturist. Modern political caricature was invented in mid-18th-c England (Gillray, Rowlandson), and has flourished ever since. » Bernini; Carracci; Gillray

CARICOM » **Caribbean Community**

caries (dental) A non-specific bacterial disease in which infecting organisms penetrate the enamel coating of a tooth. They may proceed to the centre or pulp of the tooth, which may be destroyed, and if unchecked reach the root of the tooth to produce an apical tooth abscess. A high consumption of sugar predisposes to the development of caries, while an adequate amount of fluoride in drinking water (one part in a million) increases the resistance of the enamel to bacteria. » dentistry; fluorine; teeth

CARIFTA » **Caribbean Community**

carillon A set of bells, usually with a compass of two octaves or more, installed in a tower or other high construction, and operated mechanically or by hand to play melodies or more complex polyphonic music. Many carillons are incorporated into elaborate public clocks, especially on the Continent. » bell; idiophone

Carina [kariyna] (Lat 'keel') A S hemisphere constellation, formerly part of the huge ancient constellation of Argo Navis. It contains Canopus, the second brightest star in our sky, a supergiant. Distance: 30 parsecs. » constellation; supergiant; RR8

carinatae [**ka**rinatiy] (Lat 'with a keel', referring to the keel on a bird's breastbone) A generally obsolete term used for birds which fly. The group *Carinatae* was distinct from the group *Ratitae*. » bird [i]; Ratitae

Carl XVI Gustaf (1946–) King of Sweden since 1973, born in Stockholm, the grandson of King Gustavus VI. As his father had died in an air accident (1947), he became Crown Prince from his grandfather's accession in 1950. A new constitution restricting monarchical powers was approved by the Swedish Parliament just before his accession. In 1976 he married **Silvia Sommerlath** (1943–), the daughter of a West German businessman. They have three children: **Princess Victoria** (1977–), **Prince Carl Philip** (1979–), and **Princess Madeleine** (1982–). He is a keen all-round sportsman, being proficient in yachting, skiing, and shooting. » Sweden [i]

Carlisle [kah**liyl**], Lat **Luguvallum** 54°54N 2°55W, pop (1981) 73 233. County town in Carlisle district, Cumbria, NW England; at the W end of Hadrian's Wall, at the confluence of the Eden and Caldew Rivers; important fortress in Scots–English border wars; airfield (Crosby); railway junction; foodstuffs, metal goods, textiles, engineering; 11th–12th-c cathedral, 11th-c castle, 18th-c Church of St Cuthbert; Great Fair (last Saturday in Aug). » Cumbria

Carlism A Spanish dynastic cause and political movement, officially born in 1833, but with origins in the 1820s. Against the claim to the Spanish throne by Isabella II, daughter of Ferdinand VIII, Carlists supported the claim of the latter's brother, Don Carlos (1788–1855). In the 19th-c, Carlism attracted widespread popular support chiefly in conservative, Catholic districts of rural N Spain. In 1833–40, 1846–9, and 1872–6, Carlists fought unsuccessful civil wars against Spanish liberalism. After 1876 Carlism became the political party espousing ultra-rightist, 'traditionalist' principles. It took the Nationalist side in the Spanish Civil War (1936–9), providing c.100 000 volunteers. Since 1939, under the Franco regime and after, the cause has suffered division and serious decline, though small Carlist groups persist. » Bourbons; Spanish Civil War

Carlow (county) [**kah**loh], Gaelic **Cheatharlach** pop (1981) 39 820; area 896 sq km/346 sq ml. County in Leinster province, SE Irish Republic; between the Slieve Ardagh Hills (W) and the Wicklow Mts (E) where the Barrow and Slaney Rivers water rich farm land; Blackstairs Mts rise in the S; capital, Carlow; wheat, barley, sugar beet. » Carlow (town); Irish Republic [i]; Leinster

Carlow (town) [**kah**loh] 52°50N 6°55W, pop (1981) 13 164. Capital of Carlow county, Leinster, SE Irish Republic; railway; technical college; barley malting, sugar beet, footwear; Carlow Castle (12th-c), cathedral (19th-c), Browne's Hill tumuli. » Carlow (county)

Carlson, Chester (1906–68) US physicist, born in Seattle, Washington. He graduated in physics at the California Institute of Technology, and worked in electronics, later specializing also in patent work. By 1938 he had devised a basic system of electrostatic copying on plain paper, which after 12 years' work by assistants gave the xerographic method which is now widely used. He died in New York City. » xerography [i]

Carlyle, Thomas (1795–1881) British man of letters, born at Ecclefechan, Dumfriesshire, Scotland. Son of a stonemason, he was educated at Annan Academy and Edinburgh University, and taught for several years, before beginning to write articles for the *Edinburgh Encyclopaedia*, and becoming absorbed in German literature, notably Goethe. In 1826 he married **Jane Baillie Welsh** (1801–66). His best-known work, *Sartor Resartus*, appeared in 1833–4. He then moved to London, where he wrote his other major works on the French Revolution (3 vols, 1837) and Frederick the Great (1858–65). In 1866 his wife died, leaving letters and a journal showing her to have been one of the most accomplished women of her time. After her death, Carlyle retired from public life, and wrote little. He died in London.

Carmarthen [kuhmahthuhn] 51°52N 4°19W, pop (1981) 14 491. County town in Carmarthen district, Dyfed, SW Wales, UK; on R Towy, 13 km/8 ml N of the Bristol Channel; chartered, 1227; railway; dairy products, pharmaceuticals, flour milling, agricultural trade. » Dyfed

Carme [**kah**mee] The eleventh natural satellite of Jupiter, discovered in 1938; distance from the planet 22 600 000 km/ 14 044 000 ml; diameter 40 km/25 ml. » Jupiter (astronomy); RR00

Carmelites A Roman Catholic monastic order originating in the 12th-c from the Hermits of Mount Carmel (Israel), seeking the way of life of the prophet Elijah; properly known as the **Order of the Brothers of the Blessed Virgin Mary of Mt Carmel**, or **White Friars**; abbreviated **OCarm**. They flourished as mendicant friars in Europe. Carmelite nuns were officially recognized in 1452, reformed by Teresa of Avila in Spain (1562) as strictly cloistered **Discalced Carmelites (ODC)**. (The term 'discalced' derives from the practice of wearing sandals instead of shoes and stockings.) The male order was similarly reformed by St John of the Cross, and in 1593 was recognized as a separate order. The older order specialized in teaching and preaching; the Discalced mainly in parochial and foreign mission work. » Elijah; John of the Cross, St; monasticism; Roman Catholicism; Teresa of Avila, St

Carnac A peninsula on the S coast of Brittany, N France, renowned for its megalithic alignments, stone circles, and chambered tombs of Neolithic date. The alignments, unsurpassed elsewhere, run E–W with 7–13 parallel rows each: the best preserved, at Kermario, has seven principal lines up to c.1 100 m/3 700 ft long with 1 029 stones. In all, c.3 000 stones survive, extending over some 5 km/3 ml. » megalith; stone circles; Three Age System

Carnap, Rudolf (1891–1970) German-born US philosopher, born at Wuppertal. He studied at Freiburg and Jena, becoming lecturer at Vienna (1926–31), and professor of philosophy at Prague (1931–5), Chicago (1936–52), and California (1954–70). He was one of the leaders of the 'Vienna Circle' of logical positivists. His writings include *Der logische Aufbau der Welt* (1928, The Logical Construction of the World), *Logische Syntax der Sprache* (1934, Logical Syntax of Language), and *Meaning and Necessity* (1947), as well as semantic studies of induction and probability. He died at Santa Monica, California. » logical positivism; Vienna Circle

carnation A perennial species of pink, native to the Mediterranean; leaves tufted; flowers with spreading, slightly frilly petals. Wild carnations have pink, strongly-scented flowers. Ornamental hybrids and garden plants are various colours, and may have multiple petals. (*Dianthus caryophyllaceus*. Family: *Caryophyllaceae*.) » perennial; pink

Carné, Marcel (1906–) French film director, born in Paris. He trained as a film technician, later working as an assistant to René Clair. From 1931 his collaboration as director with the poet and scriptwriter Jacques Prévert resulted in a series of outstanding productions, including *Quai des Brumes* (1938, Port of Shadows), *Le Jour se lève* (1939, Daybreak) and *Les Enfants du Paradis* (1944, Children of Paradise). After the break-up of the partnership in 1949, his late work was irregular and less distinguished.

Carnegie, Andrew (1835–1919) US steel industrialist, born at Dunfermline, Scotland. His family emigrated to Pittsburgh in 1848, and after several jobs he invested in the business which grew into the largest iron and steel works in the USA. He retired in 1901, a multimillionaire, to Skibo Castle in Sutherland, and died at Lenox, Massachusetts. He gave millions of dollars to public institutions in the UK and USA, and several buildings are named after him. » foundation, philanthropic

Carnic Alps, Ger **Karnische Alpen**, Ital **Alpi Carniche** S Alpine mountain range on the border between Italy and Austria; highest peak is Hohe Warte (2 780 m/9 121 ft); crossed by the Plöcken Pass. » Alps

carnitine A chemical substance (an *amine*) derived from the essential amino acid, lysine. The oxidation of fatty acids by mammalian cells requires carnitine as an intermediary in the intracellular transport of fatty acids. Although it was once considered a vitamin, carnitine is probably not an essential component of the diet. Most infant formulae based on cow's milk are supplemented with carnitine to the level normally found in breast milk. » amines; breast milk; vitamins [i]

carnivore [**kah**nivaw] A primarily meat-eating mammal, preying on other vertebrates; lower jaw moves only up and down; canine teeth long; some cheek teeth (*carnassials*) specialized for cutting flesh; 4–5 clawed toes on each foot. (Order: *Carnivora*, 7 families, 238 species.) » bear; cat; dog; herbivore; hyena; mammal [i]; Mustelidae; Viverridae [i]

carnivorous plant A plant which traps animals, usually insects and small invertebrates, and secretes digestive enzymes which break down the prey, allowing it to absorb the resulting products; also known as an **insectivorous plant**. Carnivorous plants grow in nutrient-poor habitats, and food obtained from prey, especially organic nitrogen, augments that produced by photosynthesis. The carnivorous habit has arisen independently in several unrelated groups, principally in the families *Droseraceae* (sundews), *Nepenthaceae* and *Sarraceniaceae* (pitcher plants), and *Lentibulariaceae* (butterworts and bladderworts). The traps are invariably formed from modified leaves, sometimes with very sophisticated features. The simplest, found in butterworts, are merely covered with a viscous substance to which insects stick; in sundews, long, mobile sticky hairs and even the leaf itself move in response to the struggles of the prey and enfold it. The leaves of pitcher plants form tubular or jug-shaped traps filled with fluid, in which the victims drown before being digested. The largest are said to be capable of trapping small rodents. The pitchers are often brightly and attractively coloured, and bear honey glands on the inner surface to entice animals towards a smooth, glossy 'slip zone'; further down, the surface is covered with downward projecting hairs to prevent escape. Equally sophisticated are the underwater traps of bladderworts which suck in the prey, but the most spectacular is the Venus's fly-trap, in which a trigger mechanism causes the jaw-like traps to snap closed around the prey. » bladderwort; butterwort; enzyme; photosynthesis; pitcher plant; saprophyte; sundew; Venus's fly-trap [i]

Carnot, Lazare (Nicolas Marguerite) (1753–1823) French statesman, born at Nolay, Burgundy, known as the 'organizer of victory' during the Revolutionary Wars. He entered the army as an engineer, and in 1791 became a member of the Legislative Assembly. He survived the Terror, and became one of the Directors (1795), but in 1797, suspected of Royalist sympathies, he escaped to Germany. Back in Paris, he became Minister of War (1800), and helped to organize the Italian and Rhenish campaigns. He commanded at Antwerp in 1814, and during the Hundred Days was Minister of the Interior. He retired first to Warsaw, then to Magdeburg, where he died. » French Revolution [i]; Hundred Days

Carnot, (Nicolas Léonard) Sadi (1796–1832) French scientist, born and died in Paris. He became a captain of engineers in the army, and spent much of his life investigating the design of steam engines. His findings were the foundation of the science of thermodynamics. » Carnot cycle; steam engine; thermodynamics

Carnot cycle [**kah**noh] The fundamental thermodynamic cycle proposed by French engineer Sadi Carnot in 1824, in an attempt to explain the working of the steam engine. It comprises four stages: isothermal then adiabatic expansions, followed by isothermal and adiabatic compressions. A **Carnot engine** is the most efficient heat engine possible (**Carnot's law**). For intake temperature T_i and exhaust temperature T_o, thermal efficiency e is $e=(T_i-T_o)/T_i$. Because of physical and metallurgical problems, the Carnot cycle is not practical, and other cycles have been developed that meet the needs of real engines. Such cycles reflect more closely the way heat is actually added to and taken from the gases of a real engine. » adiabatic process; Carnot, Sadi; engine; isothermal process; thermal efficiency; thermodynamics; *see illustration p 220*

Carnot's law » **Carnot cycle**

carob An evergreen tree or shrub, growing to 10 m/30 ft, native to the Mediterranean region; leaves with 2–5 pairs of leathery

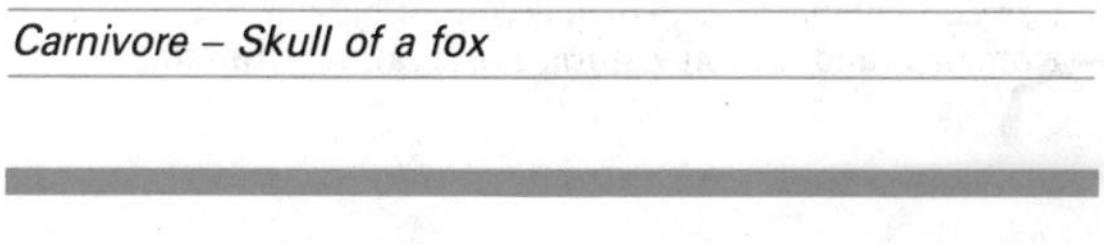

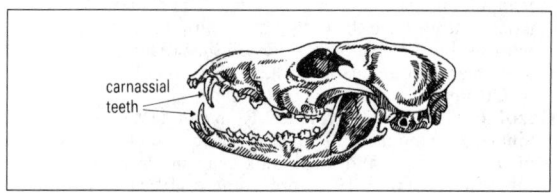

Carnivore – Skull of a fox

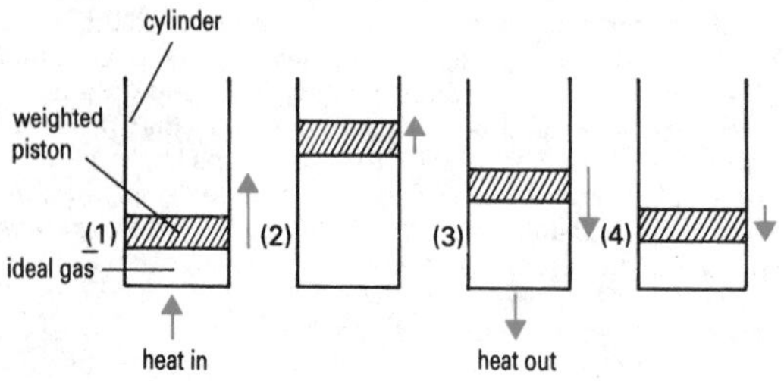

(1) A weighted piston moves in a cylinder filled with a theoretically ideal gas whose pressure, temperature, and volume are continuously measured. Heat is added to the gas at a constant temperature expanding the gas, decreasing its pressure and lifting the piston (1 to 2).
(2) The addition of heat to the gas ceases, but it continues to expand, at the same time lifting the piston whilst dropping its temperature and pressure (2 to 3).
(3) Heat is then taken out of the gas at constant temperature by means of a suitable heat sink, the volume decreases, the piston moves downwards, and the pressure of the gas increases (3 to 4).
(4) Heat ceases to be taken from the gas, the pressure and temperature increase, the volume decreases, and the piston continues to move downwards (4 to 1) until the arrangement is ready to start the cycle over again.

(5)

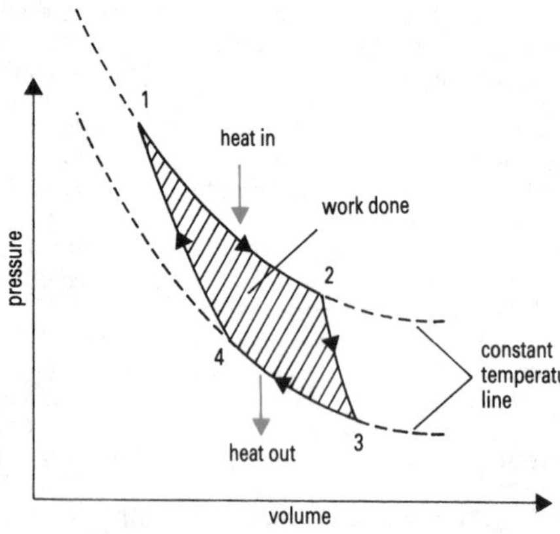

(5) The results of this cycle are plotted on a pressure/volume diagram, with the enclosed shaded area representing the useful work done. The Carnot cycle demonstrates that no engine can ever be 100% efficient.

Carnot cycle

oval leaflets; flowers lacking petals, borne in short catkin-like inflorescences; pods to 20 cm/8 in long, pendent, violet-brown when ripe; also called **locust tree**. It is cultivated for fodder, the pods containing a nutritious pulp rich in protein. The seeds are said to be the original carat weights used by goldsmiths. (*Ceratonia siliqua*. Family: *Leguminosae*.) » evergreen plants; false acacia; inflorescence [i]; protein; shrub; tree [i]

Carol I (1839–1914) First King of Romania (1881–1914), born at Hohenzollern-Sigmaringen. He was made Prince of Romania in 1866, and became king when his country received independence from the Ottoman Empire. He carried out many reforms, but was unable to forestall the peasant revolt of 1907, when many thousands were killed. He died at Sinaia, Romania. » Ottoman Empire

Carol II (1893–1953) King of Romania (1930–40), born at Sinaia. He renounced his right of succession (1925), as a result of a love affair, and went into exile in Paris. He returned through a coup in 1930, proclaiming (1938) a dictatorship. Forced to abdicate in 1940 in favour of his son, Michael, he left Romania, and died at Estoril, Portugal. » Romania [i]

Caroline (of Brunswick), Amelia Elizabeth (1768–1821) Wife of George IV of the United Kingdom, born at Brunswick, the daughter of George III's sister, Augusta. She married the Prince of Wales in 1795; but the marriage was disagreeable to him, and although she bore him a daughter, the Princess Charlotte, they lived apart. When George became King (1820), she was offered an annuity to renounce the title of Queen and live abroad; when she refused, the King persuaded the government to introduce a Divorce Bill. Although this failed, she was not allowed into Westminster Abbey at the coronation (Jul 1821), and died soon after. » George IV

Caroline, Radio The best-known UK pirate radio station of the 1960s. Operating illegally from a ship off the Essex coast, and financed by advertising, Radio Caroline broke the BBC's monopoly of domestic radio broadcasting and 'created' a youth audience through non-stop pop music, thus prompting the creation of Radio 1. » BBC; broadcasting

Caroline of Ansbach (1683–1737) Queen of George II of Great Britain, born at Ansbach, the daughter of a German prince. She exercised a strong influence over her husband, and was a leading supporter of his chief minister, Robert Walpole. She died in London. » George II (of Great Britain); Walpole, Robert

Carolingian or **Carlovingian architecture** [karoh**linj**iuhn, kahloh**vinj**iuhn] A form of architecture prevalent from the 8th-c to the 10th-c AD, named after Emperor Charlemagne, and common to France, Germany, and the Netherlands. It was composite in character, made up of late Roman forms mixed with heavier, indigenous elements such as prominent towers, west ends, and east ends. » Charlemagne; Norman/Roman/Romanesque architecture

Carolingian art A style of art named after Charlemagne, which flourished in what is now France and W Germany from the mid-8th to the early 10th-c. Graeco-Roman and Byzantine stylistic elements were fostered as part of a deliberate classical revival. » art; Charlemagne; classical revival; French art

Carolingians A Frankish ruling dynasty which rose to power as mayors of the palace, and ultimately replaced the Merovingians when Pepin II became King of the Franks in 751. The Carolingian Empire created by Charlemagne embraced most of the former territory of the Roman Empire in the West. In 843 it was divided into E Francia, W Francia, and the 'Middle Kingdom' stretching from the N Sea to Italy, and these soon dissolved into smaller states. » Charles Martel; Charlemagne; Franks; Merovingians

carom » **billiards**

carotene A class of plant pigments which provide the natural colours of carrots, green vegetables, algae, shrimps, and tomatoes. The carotene of carrots and green vegetables is rich in beta-carotene, of which about 16% is converted to vitamin A in the digestive tract. » colouring agents; retinol; vitamins [i]

carotenoid [karuh**tee**noyd] A non water-soluble pigment, usually red to yellow in colour, found in many higher plants, algae, and bacteria. It functions as an accessory photosynthetic pigment. » photosynthesis

carp Deep-bodied freshwater fish native to Black Sea coasts but now introduced worldwide; thrives in warm pools, lakes, and rivers with rich vegetation; length up to 1 m/3¼ ft; two pairs of barbels on upper jaw; important food fish, used extensively in aquaculture and very popular with anglers; broadly, any member of the large family *Cyprinidae*. (*Cyprinus carpio*.) » barbel

Carpaccio, Vittore [kah**pat**choh] (c.1460–c.1525) Italian painter, born and died in Venice. His most characteristic work is seen in the nine subjects from the life of St Ursula (1490–5). In 1510 he executed for San Giobbe his masterpiece, the 'Presentation in the Temple', now in the Accademia. » Italian art

Carpathian Mountains Mountain system of EC Europe, forming the E wing of the great Alpine uplift; extends 1 400 km/870 ml in a semi-circle from Czechoslovakia to Romania, forming in the middle the boundary between Czechoslovakia and Poland; main divisions (W–E) are the Little Carpathians, White Carpathians, Beskids, Low Tatra, High Tatra, E or Romanian Carpathians, and the Transylvanian Alps; highest point, Mt Gerlach (2 655 m/8 711 ft); rich in minerals and coal deposits; generally forested to 1 200 m/4 000 ft. » Beskids; Tatra Mountains; Transylvanian Alps

carpel Part of the innermost whorl of a flower, collectively forming the *gynecium*: it typically consists of an ovary, style, and stigma, which together are sometimes called the **pistil**. More primitive flowers generally have many carpels; more advanced flowers tend to have fewer, and often fused, carpels. » flower [i]; ovary; stigma; style (botany)

Carpentaria, Gulf of [kahpuhn**tay**ria] Major inlet on N coast of Australia between Cape Arnhem and Cape York; bounded N by the Arafura Sea; 595 km/370 ml long by 491 km/305 ml wide; shallow depths of 25–55 m/80–180 ft; contains several islands; named by Tasman (1642) in honour of the Governor-General of Dutch East Indies; bauxite, manganese. » Australia [i]; Tasman

carpenter bee A tropical bee that bores into solid wood or plant pith to make a nest. Most species are solitary; a few show a primitive degree of sociality. (Order: *Hymenoptera*. Family: *Anthophoridae*.) » bee

carpet beetle A small, rounded, black beetle with zigzag markings around margins; larvae known as **woolly bears**, covered with long hairs, feeding on woollen carpets, furs, and animal skins; adults common on fruit trees, feeding on pollen. (Order: *Coleoptera*. Family: *Dermestidae*.) » beetle; larva

Carpetbaggers A derogatory term for US Northerners who went to the defeated South after the Civil War to aid freed Blacks and take part in rebuilding. Supposedly they carried all their belongings in bags made of carpet. Collectively they have had a bad press, but are now recognized as well-intentioned. » American Civil War

Carrà, Carlo (1881–1966) Italian painter, born at Quargnento. Largely self-taught, he adopted a Futurist style, then in 1917 met Giorgio di Chirico and for some years was influenced by his 'metaphysical painting' movement. His best-known work is 'Le Canal' (Zürich). He died in Milan. » Chirico; Futurism; metaphysical painting

Carracci [ka**rah**chee] A family of Italian painters, born in Bologna. The most famous was **Annibale** (1560–1609), whose style was much influenced by Correggio and Raphael. With his brother, **Agostino** (1557–1602), he painted the gallery of the Farnese Palace, Rome. Together with their cousin, **Ludovico** (1555–1619), they founded an influential academy of painting in Bologna (1582). » Italian art

carrack [**ka**rak] A 15th-c development of the Portuguese caravel, distinguished by having square sails in addition to lateen sails. » caravel [i]; Mayflower; ship [i]

Carrantuohill [karan**too**uhl] Mountain in SW Irish Republic in the Macgillycuddy's Reeks range, rising to 1 041 m/3 415 ft; highest peak in the Irish Republic. » Irish Republic [i]

Carrel, Alexis (1873–1955) French surgeon and biologist, born at Ste Foy-lès-Lyon. Educated at Lyon, he worked in New York City (1904–14, 1919–44) and Paris. He won the Nobel Prize for Physiology or Medicine in 1912, discovering a method of suturing blood vessels which made it possible to replace arteries. He also worked on ways of culturing living tissues in artificial environments. He died in Paris. » blood vessels [i]

Carrington, Peter (Alexander Rupert), 6th Baron (1919–) British Conservative politician, educated at Eton and Sandhurst. He held several junior posts in government (1951–6), before becoming High Commissioner to Australia (1956–9). He then served as First Lord of the Admiralty (1959–63) and Leader of the House of Lords (1963–4). He was Secretary of State for Defence (1970–4) and briefly for Energy (1974), and also Chairman of the Conservative Party organization (1972–4). Upon the Conservative return to office he was Foreign Secretary (1979–82), until he and his ministerial team resigned over the Argentinian invasion of the Falkland Is. He later became Secretary-General of NATO (1984–8). » Conservative Party; Falklands War; NATO

carrion crow A crow native to Europe and Asia; inhabits open forest, grassland, and cultivation; eats virtually anything; usually black. Grey carrion crows are called **hooded crows**. (*Corvus corone*. Family: *Corvidae*.) » crow

carrion flower A flower which attracts pollinating insects, usually flies, by giving off an odour of rotting meat. The flowers or associated parts are usually livid reddish-brown in colour to complete the disguise. Such plants occur in several unrelated families. » Dutchman's pipe; flower [i]; rafflesia; stapelia

Carroll, Lewis, byname of **Dodgson, Charles Lutwidge** (1832–98) British author, born at Daresbury, Cheshire. Educated at Rugby and Oxford, he took orders in 1861, and became a lecturer in mathematics (1855–81). His nursery tale, *Alice's Adventures in Wonderland* (1865), and its sequel, *Through the Looking-glass* (1872) quickly became classics. 'Alice', to whom the story was originally related during boating excursions, was the second daughter (who died in 1934) of Henry George Liddell, the head of his Oxford college. He wrote a great deal of humorous verse, such as *The Hunting of the Snark* (1876), as well as several mathematical works. He died at Guildford, Surrey.

carrot A biennial herb growing to 1 m/3.3 ft, native to Europe, temperate Asia, and N Africa; leaves divided, leaflets with toothed oval segments; flowers white or pink, borne in dense, rather flat-topped umbels, the central flower usually dark purple; fruits spiny. Wild carrots have tough roots, but the cultivated carrot (subspecies *sativus*), with a large fleshy orange or whitish tap root, has been grown since ancient times as a root vegetable and fodder for animals. (*Daucus carota*. Family: *Umbelliferae*.) » biennial; herb; umbel; vegetable

carroway thyme » thyme

Carson, Kit, properly **Christopher** (1809–68) US frontiersman, born in Kentucky. A Missouri trapper and hunter, his knowledge of Indian habits and languages led to his becoming guide in John Frémont's explorations (1842). He was Indian agent in New Mexico (1853), and fought for the Union in the Civil War. Several places are named after him. He died at Fort Lyon, Colorado. » American Civil War

Carson, Rachel Louise (1907–64) US naturalist and publicist, born at Springdale, Pennsylvania. She studied at Johns Hopkins, and worked in marine biology in the US Fish and Wildlife Service (1936–49). She was an effective writer, and during the 1940s her books on marine ecology became influential. In 1962 her *Silent Spring* directed much public attention to the problems caused by agricultural pesticides, and she became a pioneer in the conservationist movement of the 1960s. She died at Silver Springs, Maryland. » conservation (earth sciences); ecology; pesticide

Carson City 39°10N 119°46W, pop (1980) 32 022. State capital and independent city, W Nevada, USA, near L Tahoe; founded, 1858; named after the frontiersman Kit Carson; trade centre for a mining and agricultural area; tourism; a gambling centre; Nevada State Museum; Nevada Day (Oct). » Carson, Kit; Nevada

Cartagena (de los Indes) (Colombia) [karta**khay**na] 10°24N 75°33W, pop (1985) 529 622. Port capital of Bolívar department, NW Colombia; on Caribbean coast SW of Barranquilla; founded, 1533; sacked by Francis Drake, 1586; airfield; university (1824); oil-refining, chemicals, plastics; the old colonial quarter is a world heritage site; Festival of the Virgin of La Candelaria (Feb); Independence of Cartagena (Nov). » Colombia [i]; Drake, Francis

Cartagena (Spain) [kahta**jee**na], Span [karta**khay**na], Lat **Carthago Nova** 37°38N 0°59W, pop (1981) 172 751. Fortified seaport and naval base in Murcia province, SE Spain, 48 km/30 ml S of Murcia; Spain's leading commercial port and naval base; formerly the largest naval arsenal in Europe; founded by the Carthaginians, 221 BC; two airports; railway; food processing, clothes, metallurgy, glass, oil refining; watersports; Castle of la Concepción, Church of Santa Maria la Vieja (13th-c); Virgen del Monte Carmel patronal festival (Jul). » Murcia; Spain [i]

Carte, Richard D'Oyly (1844–1901) British impresario and manager, born and died in London. He built the Savoy Theatre (1881) and the Royal Opera House (1887), and is best known as the first producer of the Gilbert and Sullivan operas. » Gilbert, W S; Sullivan, Arthur

cartel An agreement by a number of companies in the same industry to fix prices and/or quantities, thus avoiding cut-price competition or over-production. It is often seen as not being in the public interest, since it does not allow market forces to operate freely. Many countries have made cartels illegal. » OPEC

Carter, Angela (1940–) British novelist, born in London, and educated at Bristol University. Her first novel, *Shadow Dance*, was published in 1965, since which time she has written novels and short stories characterized by feminist themes and fantasy narratives, including *The Magic Toyshop* (1967), *The Infernal Desire Machines of Dr Hoffman* (1972), and *Nights at the Circus* (1984). » English literature; feminism; novel

Carter, Elliott (1908–) US composer, born in New York City. He studied at Harvard University, and with Nadia Boulanger in Paris. Prizes and fellowships enabled him to alternate further periods of study with teaching, at St John's College, Annapolis (1940–2), Peabody Conservatory (1946–8), Columbia University (1948–50), Queens College, New York (1955–6), and Yale (1960–2). His second string quartet won a Pulitzer Prize in 1960. His other works, often of great complexity, include two symphonies, four concertos, and several sonatas. » Boulanger

Carter, Howard (1874–1939) British archaeologist, born at Swaffham, Norfolk. He joined Flinders Petrie's archaeological survey of Egypt as an artist in 1891, from 1907 conducting his own research under the patronage of George Herbert, 5th Earl of Carnarvon (1866–1923). His discoveries included the tombs of Hatshepsut (1907), Tuthmosis IV and, most notably, Tutankhamen (1922), a find on which he worked for the remainder of his life. He died in London. » Petrie; Tutankhamen

Carter, Jimmy, properly **James (Earl)** (1924–) US statesman and 39th President (1977–81), born in Plains, Georgia. He was educated at the US Naval academy, and served in the US Navy until 1953, when he took over the family peanut business and other enterprises. As Governor of Georgia (1970–4) he expressed an enlightened policy towards the rights of Blacks and women. In 1976 he won the Democratic presidential nomination, and went on to win a narrow victory over Gerald Ford. He arranged the peace treaty between Egypt and Israel (1979), and was much concerned with human rights at home and abroad. His administration ended in difficulties over the taking of US hostages in Iran, and the Soviet invasion of Afghanistan, and he was defeated by Ronald Reagan in the 1980 election.

Carteret, John, 1st Earl Granville (1690–1763) English statesman and Chief Minister (1742–4), born in London. He entered the House of Lords in 1711, and became Ambassador to Sweden (1719), Secretary of State (1721), and Lord-Lieutenant of Ireland (1724–9). As Earl Granville, he was driven from power by the Pelhams (1744) because of his pro-Hanoverian policies, though from 1751 was President of the Council under Henry Pelham, and twice refused the premiership. He died at Bath. » Pelham, Thomas; Walpole, Robert

Cartesian co-ordinates A method developed by Descartes of determining the position of a point by its distances from two fixed perpendicular straight lines, called the *axes of co-ordinates*. The development of analytic geometry by Descartes and others enabled great advances to be made in the study of geometry, the classical methods of the Greeks having been almost exhausted. » analytic geometry; Descartes; polar co-ordinates

Cartesian geometry » **analytic geometry**

Cartesian philosophy Various attempts made by Descartes' contemporaries and successors to work out the salient features of his philosophy: his foundationalism, his theory of ideas (including innate ideas), and his mind-body dualism. The latter influenced occasionalism and Leibniz's doctrine of pre-established harmony. » Descartes; dualism; foundationalism; occasionalism

Cartesian product In mathematics, the set of all possible ordered pairs from two sets, A and B, formed by taking one element of A and one of B. If $A=\{1,2\}$ and $B=\{a,b\}$, the Cartesian product $A \times B$ is the set $\{(1,a),(2,a),(1,b),(2,b)\}$. » Descartes; set

Carthage 36°54N 10°16E. Ancient town in Tunisia, N Africa, now a suburb of Tunis; a world heritage site; reputedly founded by the Phoenicians in 814 BC; destroyed by Rome following the Punic Wars, 146 BC; refounded by Caesar and Octavian (29 BC); restored as capital by the Vandals, AD 439–533, but destroyed again by the Arabs, 698; the few remains include the Roman baths of Antonius, the old harbour, and an aqueduct of Hadrian; cathedral (1866); International Festival of Carthage (Jul–Aug). » Caesar; Phoenicia; Punic Wars; Tunisia [i]; Vandals

Carthusian horse » **Andalusian horse**

Carthusians A Roman Catholic monastic order founded in 1084 by Bruno of Cologne in Chartreuse, near Grenoble, France; properly known as the **Order of Carthusians**; abbreviated **OCart**. The monks practise strict abstinence and live as solitaries; lay brothers live in a community. Membership is small, but the order maintains houses in many parts of Europe. At the mother-house, 'La Grande Chartreuse', a famous liqueur is distilled, the profits being distributed to local charities. » Bruno, St; liqueur; monasticism

Cartier, Jacques (1491–1557) French navigator, born and died at St Malo. Between 1534 and 1542 he made three voyages of exploration to N America, surveying the coast of Canada and the St Lawrence R, and providing the basis for later French claims in the area.

Cartier-Bresson, Henri (1908–) French photographer, born in Paris. He studied painting and literature before taking up photography after a trip to Africa in 1930. His first pictures were published in 1933. In the later 1930s he worked as assistant to the film director Jean Renoir, and after the war was a co-founder of the independent photographic agency, Magnum Photos. He works only in black-and-white, concerned exclusively with the capturing of visual moments illustrating contemporary life. His books include *The World of Henri Cartier-Bresson* (1968). In the mid-1970s he gave up photography, and returned to his earlier interests of painting and drawing. » photography

cartilage Tissue supplementary to bone in the skeleton, which may be temporary (as in the process of endochondral ossification) or permanent (as in the nose, ear, and larynx); sometimes called **gristle**. It is composed of living cells surrounded by an intercellular substance containing collagen. It is not hard or strong (so can be easily cut or damaged by high pressure), and is relatively non-vascular, being nourished by tissue fluids (particularly at joint surfaces). There are three main types. **Hyaline cartilage** forms the temporary cartilage model of bone, epiphyseal growth plates, the costal cartilages of the ribs, and is also found in the respiratory system (larynx, trachea, bronchi) and nasal septum. **White fibrocartilage** contains bundles of white fibrous tissue (giving it great tensile strength), present in intervertebral discs, the pelvis, the joint surfaces of the clavicle and the lower jaw, and the knee. **Yellow fibrocartilage** contains bundles of elastic fibres with little or no white fibrous tissue, present in the external ear, Eustachian tube, and epiglottis. » bone; joint

cartilaginous fish Any fish of the Class *Chondrichthyes* (800 species), having a cartilagenous endoskeleton that may be calcified but not ossified (true bone), and lacking air bladder or lungs; comprises the sharks and rays (*Elasmobranchii*) and ratfishes (*Holocephalii*). » bone; bony fish; cartilage; fish [i]; ray; shark

Cartimandua (1st-c AD) Pro-Roman queen of the Yorkshire Brigantes. She protected the N borders of the Roman province of Britain after the conquest (43), until her overthrow by her ex-husband, the anti-Roman Venutius in 68–9. » Britain, Roman; Caractacus

Cartland, Barbara (Hamilton) (?1902–) British popular romantic novelist. Since her first novel, *Jigsaw* (1923), she has written over 200 books, mostly romantic novels but also biographies of 'romantic' figures, and books on food, health, and beauty. She has been active in charitable causes, working in support of nursing organizations and the rights of gypsies, and is well known for her views on the benefits of health foods and the maintaining of health and fitness in old age. » English literature; novel

cartography The method of construction of maps and charts. Through the use of symbols, lettering, and shading techniques, data concerning an area (eg its relief, land use, and population density) are portrayed on a map in such a way that it can be interpreted by the user to find out information about a place. Data for mapping come from many sources, such as fieldwork, surveying, and remote sensing. Increasingly, computer-assisted cartography is being used in map production. » aerial photography; map; remote sensing; surveying

cartoon (art) Originally, a full-size outline drawing which would be transferred to the wall or panel ready for painting; used in this way by painters since the Middle Ages, the word comes from the Italian *cartone* 'thick paper'. Raphael's famous cartoons, in the Victoria and Albert Museum, are in full colour, being designed for tapestries. When in 19th-c London a competition was held for frescoes in the Houses of Parliament, the cartoons submitted by candidates were parodied in *Punch*, and since then the word has had its popular meaning of a humorous drawing. » fresco; Raphael

cartridge tape drive » magnetic tape 2

Cartwright, Edmund (1743–1823) British inventor of the power loom, born at Marnham, Nottinghamshire. Educated at Oxford, he became a clergyman (1779), and after visiting Arkwright's cotton-spinning mills, he devised his power loom (1785–90), and also a wool-combing machine (1790). Attempts to use the loom at Doncaster and Manchester met with fierce opposition, and it was not until the 19th-c that it came into practical use. In 1809 the government awarded him a grant of £10 000 for his achievements. He died at Hastings, Sussex. » Arkwright; cotton [i]; spinning; wool

Caruso, Enrico (1873–1921) Italian operatic tenor, born and died in Naples. He was born into a poor family, the 18th of 20 children, and received little formal education. He made his debut in Naples in 1894, appeared in London in 1902, and in New York in 1903. The extraordinary power of his voice, combined with his acting ability, won him recognition as one of the greatest tenors of all time. » opera

Carver, George Washington (c.1864–1943) US scientist, born near Diamond Grove, Missouri. He was born into a Black slave family, and received little formal education in his early years. He finally graduated from Iowa State Agricultural College in 1894, and became renowned for his research into agricultural problems and synthetic products, especially from peanuts and sweet potatoes. For much of his life he worked to make Tuskegee Institute, Alabama, a means of education for the disadvantaged Black farmers of the South, and became famous as a teacher and humanitarian. He died at Tuskegee. » agriculture

Cary, John (c.1754–1835) English cartographer, who began as an engraver in London and c.1783 became a publisher and land surveyor. His *New and Correct English Atlas* appeared in 1787, followed by county atlases, and the *New Universal Atlas* of 1808. In 1794 he undertook a road survey of England and Wales, published as *Cary's New Itinerary* (1798). » cartography

Cary, (Arthur) Joyce (Lunel) (1888–1957) British novelist, born in Londonderry, Northern Ireland. He studied art in Edinburgh and Paris, then law at Oxford, and fought in W Africa in World War 1. Injuries and ill health dictated his early retirement to Oxford, where he took up writing. Out of his African experience came several novels, such as *Mister Johnson* (1939). His best-known work is his trilogy, *Herself Surprised* (1940), *To be a Pilgrim* (1942), and *The Horse's Mouth* (1944). He died at Oxford. » English literature; novel

caryatid [ka**ree**atid, **ka**reeatid] A sculptured female figure, used as a column or support for an entablature or other building element. The name derives from the ancient Greek women of Caryae sold into slavery. It is also used in a general sense for any column or support carved in human form. » column; entablature; Greek architecture; Roman architecture

Casablanca [kasa**blang**ka], Arabic **Dar el Beida** 33°20N 71°25W, pop (1982) 1 856 669. Seaport in Centre province, W Morocco; on the Atlantic coast 290 km/180 ml SW of Tangiers; founded by the Portuguese as Casa Branca, 1515; seriously damaged by an earthquake in 1755 and rebuilt; French occupation, 1907; meeting place of Churchill and Roosevelt, 1943; airport; railway; university; tourism, banking, fishing, textiles, food processing, glass, soap, phosphates, manganese; handles over 75% of Morocco's trade. » Casablanca Conference; Morocco [i]; World War 2

Casablanca Conference A meeting in N Africa between Roosevelt and Churchill during World War 2 (Jan 1943), at which it was decided to insist on the eventual 'unconditional surrender' of Germany and Japan. Attempts to overcome friction between Roosevelt and the Free French under de Gaulle had only limited success. The combined Chiefs of Staff settled strategic differences over the projected invasion of Sicily and Italy. » Casablanca; Churchill, Sir Winston; de Gaulle; Roosevelt, Franklin D; World War 2

Casals, Pau (Pablo) [ka**sals**] (1876–1973) Spanish cellist, conductor, and composer, born at Vendrell, Tarragona. He studied at the Royal Conservatory, Madrid, became professor of cello at Barcelona, and in 1899 began to appear as a soloist. In 1919 he founded the Barcelona Orchestra, which he conducted until he left Spain at the outbreak of the Civil War (1936). In 1950 he founded at Prades, France, an annual festival of classical chamber music. His own compositions consist of choral and chamber works. During his later years, he conducted master classes. He died at Rio Piedras, Puerto Rico. » cello; chamber music

Casanova (de Seingalt), Giacomo Girolamo (1725–98) Italian adventurer, born in Venice. By 1750 he had worked as a clergyman, secretary, soldier, and violinist in various countries, and in 1755 was imprisoned for being a magician. He escaped in 1756, and for nearly 20 years wandered through Europe, visiting most of its capitals, and meeting the greatest men and women of the day. Alchemist, cabalist, and spy, he was everywhere introduced to the best society, and had always to 'vanish' after a brief period of felicity. In 1785 he established himself as librarian with the Count of Waldstein, in Bohemia, where he died. His main work is his autobiography, first published in 1960.

Cascade Range Mountain range in W N America; extends over 1 120 km/700 ml from N California, through Oregon and Washington to British Columbia; named after the cascades of the Columbia R where it passes through the range in a canyon c.1 200 m/4 000 ft deep; highest point, Mt Rainier (4 392 m/14 409 ft), Washington; other high peaks, Mts Adams (3 742 m/12 277 ft), Baker (3 285 m/10 777 ft), Hood (3 424 m/11 233 ft), Jefferson (3 200 m/10 498 ft) and Shasta (4 317 m/14 163 ft); many are snow-covered volcanic cones; Mt St Helens (2 549 m/8 363 ft) erupted 1980; many glacial lakes (largest L Chelan); glaciers on the higher peaks, notably Mt Rainier; Crater Lake National Park in the S; Klamath and Columbia Rivers cut through the range from E to W; a 13 km/8 ml-long railway tunnel goes through the range E of Seattle; heavily forested; hydroelectricity. » Crater Lake (USA); St Helens, Mount; United States of America [i]; volcano

case A grammatical category, associated primarily with nouns and pronouns, which registers the syntactic relations between words in a sentence. In inflectional languages, nouns have a range of variant forms, with affixes marking the various cases, as in Latin *mensa* ('table', nominative), *mensam* (accusative), and *mensae* (genitive). The cases have important grammatical functions: the nominative typically identifies a word that is the subject of a sentence; the accusative marks the object; while the genitive marks the possessor of something. Some languages have many case forms: Finnish, for example, has fifteen. » grammar; inflecting language

case hardening A method of hardening tool steels or components subject to hard wear, such as gears. The object is heated in an atmosphere, or in contact with some substance (eg in a hydrocarbon oil), which alters its surface composition to that of a harder alloy. Aluminium steels are heated in an atmosphere of ammonia, which introduces nitrogen into the surface layer. » alloy; cementation

casein [**kay**seen] The main protein in milk and cheese, rich in associated calcium and phosphorus. Casein is heat stable, but is precipitated at a pH of about 4.2 (mildly acid). This is exploited in cheese-making, where the initial step is the precipitation of the curd (casein and fat) from the whey. Casein can also be precipitated by rennet, the digestive enzyme of the calf. » cheese; milk; pH; protein; rennet

Casement, (Sir) Roger (David) (1864–1916) British consular official, born in Kingstown (now Dun Laoghaire), near

Dublin. He acted as Consul in various parts of Africa (1895–1904) and Brazil (1906–11), where he denounced the Congo and Putumayo rubber atrocities. Knighted in 1911, ill health caused him to retire to Ireland in 1912. An ardent Irish nationalist, he tried to obtain German help for the cause. In 1916 he was arrested on landing in Ireland from a German submarine to head the Sinn Féin rebellion, and hanged for high treason in London. His controversial 'Black Diaries', revealing, among other things, homosexual practices, were long suppressed by the government but ultimately published in 1959. » nationalism; Sinn Féin

cashew A small evergreen tree, native to S America; leaves oval, alternate; flowers in terminal clusters, petals red, narrow, and reflexed; the receptacle thick, fleshy, pear-shaped in fruit, and bearing the curved nut. It is cultivated in Africa and Asia for cashew nuts and cashew apples (the receptacles). (*Anacardium occidentale*. Family: *Anacardiaceae*.) » evergreen plants; tree [i]

cashmere The highly-prized fine warm undercoat fibres from the Kashmir goat; mainly produced in China and Iran. One of the most luxuriant and expensive fibres, it is used mainly in knitwear.

Casimir, Hendrik (1909–) Dutch physicist, born in The Hague. He studied physics at Leyden, Copenhagen, and Zürich, and was director of the Philips Research Laboratories from 1946. In 1934 he helped to devise a general theory of superconductivity which explained many of the phenomena; the later theory by Bardeen and others both includes and extends Casimir's earlier idea. » Bardeen; superconductivity

casino An establishment where gambling takes place, the best-known casino games being roulette, blackjack, and craps. The first legal casino opened in Baden-Baden in 1765, and rules governing their operation are very strict in most countries. » baccarat; blackjack; chemin de fer; craps; roulette

Čáslavská, Věra [chas**lav**ska] (1942–) Czech gymnast, born in Prague. She switched from ice skating to gymnastics as a 15 year-old, and went on to win 22 Olympic, World, and European titles. She won three Olympic gold medals in 1964, and four in 1968. She donated her medals one each to the four Czech leaders (Dubcek, Svoboda, Cernik, Smrkorsky) deposed following the Russian invasion. She married Josef Odložil, the Olympic 1 500 m silver medallist in the Mexico City Olympics (1968). » gymnastics

Casper 42°51N 106°19W, pop (1980) 51 016. Seat of Natrona County, EC Wyoming, USA, on the North Platte R; largest city in the state; town expanded rapidly after oil discovered in the 1890s; airfield; railway; distributing, processing and trade centre in a farming, ranching and mineral-rich area; oil refineries, oil-related industries; coal and open-pit uranium mining nearby; tourist centre; Old Fort Casper Museum. » Wyoming

Caspian Sea [**kas**pian], ancient **Mare Caspium** or **Mare Hyrcanium** area 371 000 sq km/143 200 sq ml. Largest inland body of water on Earth, surrounded on three sides by republics of the former USSR, and in the S by Iran; c.28 m/90 ft below sea-level, but much variation in level; maximum depth, 980 m/3 215 ft in S; shallow N area, average depth 5.2 m/17 ft; low salinity; frozen in N for several months in severe winters; no outlet and no tides; chief ports, Astrakhan, Baku; freight trade, especially oil from Baku; Beluga caviar.

Cassander (c.358–297 BC) Ruler of Macedon after the death of his father Antipater in 319 BC, and its king from 306 BC. An active figure in the power struggle after Alexander's death (323 BC), he murdered Alexander's mother, widow, and son, and contributed to the defeat of Antigonus I Monophthalmos at Ipsus in 301 BC. » Alexander the Great; Antigonus I; Antipater (of Macedon)

Cassandra [ka**san**dra] In Greek legend, the daughter of Priam, King of Troy. She was favoured by Apollo, who gave her the gift of prophecy. Because she did not return his love, he decreed that while she would always tell the truth, she would never be believed. At the fall of Troy she was allotted to Agamemnon, and murdered on her arrival in Argos. » Agamemnon; Apollo; Clytemnestra; Trojan War

cassava A food plant, also called **manioc**, probably first cultivated by the Maya of Mexico, and now an important crop throughout the tropics. It ranges from low herbs to shrubs or slender trees, with fleshy, tuberous roots and fan-shaped, 5–9-lobed leaves. The raw roots are poisonous, containing a cyanide-producing sugar which must be destroyed by a complex process of grating, pressing, and heating. It can then be made into a wide range of products, including cassava flour, bread, tapioca, laundry starch, and an alcoholic drink. (*Manihot esculenta*. Family: *Euphorbiaceae*.) » Mayas; root (botany); shrub; starch; tree [i]

Cassegrain telescope [**kas**uhgrahn] A telescope designed by French scientist N Cassegrain in 1672, and now the commonest optical system for a telescope. It has a paraboloid primary mirror with a central hole, a hyperboloid secondary mounted inside the focus of the primary, and the eyepiece behind the primary. Most of the world's largest optical telescopes currently use this arrangement. A variant of it, the Schmidt-Cassegrain, has a thin correcting lens as well, and is the most widely-used telescope for serious amateur astronomy. » Schmidt telescope; telescope [i]

Cassiodorus (Flavius Magnus Aurelius) (c.485–c.580) Roman author and monk, born at Scylaceum (Squillace), Calabria. He was secretary to the Ostrogothic king, Theodoric, quaestor and praetorian prefect, sole consul in 514, and after Theodoric's death (526) Chief Minister to Queen Amalasontha. His *Institutiones* is an encyclopedic course of study for the monks of the Vivarium, which he founded and to which he retired. » monasticism; Ostrogoths; Theodoric

Cassiopeia [kaseeuh**pee**a] A large N constellation that includes rich fields of clouds, gas, dust, and star clusters in the Milky Way. A supernova of 1572 appeared in this constellation. It contains **Cassiopeia A**, the strongest radio source in the sky after the Sun. About 3 kiloparsecs away, it is the remnant of a supernova seen to explode c.1667. » constellation; Milky Way; supernova; RR8

Cassirer, Ernst (1874–1945) German-Jewish neo-Kantian philosopher, born at Wrocław. He was educated at Berlin, Leipzig, Heidelberg, and Marburg, where he was attracted to neo-Kantianism. He worked as a tutor and civil servant, and then became professor of philosophy at Hamburg (1919), and rector (1930), but he resigned when Hitler came to power, and taught at Oxford (1933–5), Göteborg (1935–41), Yale (1941–4), and Columbia (from 1944 until his death). His best-known work, *Die Philosophie der symbolischen Formen* (1923–9, The Philosophy of Symbolic Forms), analyses the symbolic functions underlying all human thought, language, and culture. He died in New York City. » Kant

cassiterite The mineral form of tin oxide (SnO_2), a black, hard, dense material originally formed in hydrothermal veins associated with igneous rocks, though many deposits are alluvial. It is the main ore of tin. » igneous rock; tin

Cassius, properly **Gaius Cassius Longinus** (?–42 BC) Roman soldier, politician, and tyrannicide. An opponent of Caesar during the civil war with Pompey, he was pardoned by him after Pharsalus (48 BC). Despite gaining political advancement through Caesar, he later turned against him again, and played a leading part in the conspiracy to murder him (44 BC). Defeated by Caesar's avengers at Philippi (42 BC), he committed suicide. » Brutus; Caesar; Philippi, Battle of

Cassivellaunus (1st-c BC) King of the Catuvellauni, a British tribe living in the area of modern Hertfordshire. He led the British resistance to Julius Caesar on his second invasion (54 BC). » Britain, Roman; Caesar

Casson, Sir Hugh (1910–) British architect, educated at Cambridge, and professor of interior design at the Royal College of Art (1953–75). He directed the architecture of the Festival of Britain (1948), and was president of the Royal Academy (1976–84). He was knighted in 1952. » English art

cassowary [**kas**uhwairee] A large flightless bird native to S Australasia; eats seeds and fruit; inhabits forests; naked head has a bony outgrowth (*casque*), used as a shovel to uncover food; feet with long claws; its kick may be fatal. (Genus: *Casuarius*, 3 species. Family: *Casuariidae*.) » emu

cast iron The primary product of the blast furnace: iron with about 4% carbon (*pig iron*). It has a low melting point and solidifies well into the shape of the mould. It is therefore valuable for casting, but has to be purified or modified before being used for manufacture. It machines well, but its defects are brittleness and lack of tensile strength. Cast iron can be treated to modify the form of the carbon inclusions (*spheroidal* cast iron) so as to improve its properties. » blast furnace [i]; iron

Castagno, Andrea del [kas**tan**yoh] (c.1421–57) Italian painter, born at Castagno, Tuscany. He was best known in his own day for his frescoes (now lost) representing the execution of some conspirators against the house of Medici. He died in Florence. » Florentine School; fresco; Italian art

castanets Pairs of wooden (usually chestnut) discs, slightly concave, worn on the thumbs and clicked together rhythmically to accompany dancing, especially in Spain. Orchestral castanets are normally mounted on a wooden stick. » idiophone

caste A system of inequality, most prevalent in Hindu Indian society, in which status is determined by the membership of a particular lineage and associated occupational group into which a person is born. The groups are ordered according to a notion of religious purity or spirituality; thus, the Brahmin or priest caste, as the most spiritual of occupations, claims highest status. Contact between castes is held to be polluting, and must be avoided.

Castiglione, Baldassare, Count [kasteel**yoh**nay] (1478–1529) Italian author and diplomat, born near Mantua. Educated at Milan, he began a career at court, and in 1505 was sent by the Duke of Urbino as envoy to Henry VII of England, who made him a knight. His chief work, *Il Cortegiano* (1528, The Courtier), is a manual for courtiers. He also wrote Italian and Latin poems, and many letters illustrating political and literary history. He died in Rome. » Italian literature

Castile or **Castille** [kas**teel**] (Span **Castilla**) The central region and component kingdom of Spain. The United County of Spain was formed in 970, and during the 11th-c and most of the 12th-c was subject to the suzerainty of Leon of Navarre. Hegemony over Leon was established in 1188, and the union of Castilian and Leonese crowns took place in 1230. The union of crowns with the Kingdom of Aragon (1469–79), the conquest of Granada (1492), and the annexation of Navarre (1512) created the basis of the modern Spanish state. » Spain [i]

Castilho, Antonio Feliciano, Viscount [kas**teel**yoh] (1800–75) Portuguese poet, blind from childhood, born and died in Lisbon. His volumes, *Cartas de Echo e Narciso* (1821, Letters from Echo and Narcissus) and *Amor e melancholia* (1828, Love and Melancholy), inaugurated the Portuguese Romantic movement. He also translated Virgil, Ovid, Shakespeare, and Goethe. » poetry; Portuguese literature; Romanticism (literature)

casting The pouring of molten metal into a mould, where it solidifies into an ingot of manageable size for further processing, or into a desired final shape. Some metals can be *continuously* cast, solidified metal being removed at one end of a continuous length as more molten metal is added at the beginning. Some alloys (often containing zinc) can be *die-cast*, ie cast under pressure into a complex re-usable mould to give intricate shapes. Some of these processes can be applied to certain plastics. » alloy; cast iron; cire perdue; metal

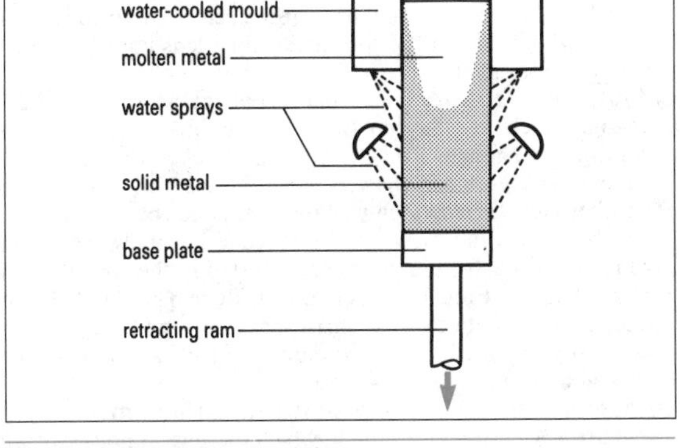

Casting process for aluminium

Castle, Barbara Anne, *née* **Betts** (1911–) British Labour politician, educated at Bradford and Oxford. She married a journalist, **Edward Cyril Castle**, later **Baron Castle** (1907–79), in 1944 and became MP for Blackburn in 1945. She was Chairman of the Labour Party (1958–9), Minister of Overseas Development (1964–5), and a controversial Minister of Transport (1965–8), introducing a 70 mph speed limit and the 'breathalyzer' test for drunken drivers. She became Secretary of State for Employment and Productivity (1968–70) and Minister of Health and Social Security (1974–8). She then returned to the backbenches, but became Vice-Chairman of the Socialist Group in the European Parliament in 1979, when she became an elected member of that body, a post she held until 1985. She remains an active MEP. » European Parliament; Labour Party; socialism

Castlebar [kasl**bah**], Gaelic **Caisleán an Bharraigh** 53°52N 9°17W, pop (1981) 7423. Capital of Mayo county, Connacht, W Irish Republic, on R Castlebar; residential and agricultural market town; Irish Land League founded here in 1879; airfield; railway; linen, hats, bacon; international song contest (Oct). » Irish Republic [i]; Mayo

Castlereagh, Robert Stewart, Viscount [**kas**lray] (1769–1822) British statesman, born in Dublin, Ireland. The son of an Ulster proprietor, he was educated at Armagh and Cambridge, and became Whig MP for County Down in 1790, turning Tory in 1795. He was created Viscount Castlereagh in 1796, and became Irish Secretary (1797), President of the Board of Control (1802), and Minister of War (1805–6, 1807–9). His major achievements date from 1812, when, as Foreign Secretary under Lord Liverpool, he was at the heart of the coalition against Napoleon (1813–14). He represented England at Chaumont and Vienna (1814–15), Paris (1815), and Aix-la-Chapelle (1818). He advocated 'Congress diplomacy' among the great powers, to avoid further warfare. Believing that he was being blackmailed for homosexuality, he committed suicide at Foots Cray, his Kentish seat. » Canning; Napoleon I; Tories; Vienna, Congress of; Whigs

Castner-Kellner process A process for the manufacture of sodium hydroxide and chlorine by the electrolysis of brine in a tank with barriers separating compartments. The brine lies over a mercury bath, which acts as a cathode, and can be made to flow from one compartment to another. Chlorine is liberated at iron anodes. Sodium liberated at the mercury cathode forms an amalgam, which flows to another compartment where it reacts with water to form sodium hydroxide free of sodium chloride. » chlorine; electrolysis [i]; sodium

Castor and Pollux, Gr **Kastor** and **Polydeuces** Two heroes of classical mythology, known as the **Dioscuri**, usually pictured as twin brothers on horseback. They were children of Leda, at least one being fathered by Zeus. After death they became divine beings, and were turned into the constellation Gemini. They appear in the form of St Elmo's Fire to help mariners, and were an important early cult at Rome. » Gemini; Leda

castor-oil plant An evergreen plant, in its native tropics forming a tall shrub or tree, in temperate regions only a stout herb; leaves each with 5–12 deep lobes, often bronze-green; flowers tiny, green, in dense male and female clusters; oil-rich seeds poisonous, but when processed yield castor oil. (*Ricinus communis*. Family: *Euphorbiaceae*.) » evergreen plants; herb; ricin; shrub; tree [i]

castration The surgical removal of the sex glands (testes or ovaries). When carried out in children, the secondary sexual characteristics do not develop. In adults, physical changes are less marked, but the individuals are sterile. In contrast with surgical castration, medical castration consists of giving a male a female sex hormone, and is usually undertaken for cancer. » castrato; Graafian follicle; testis

castrato A male singer who underwent castration before puberty in order to preserve his treble voice. The practice probably originated at the Vatican in the 16th-c to compensate for the absence of women's voices from the choirs. Castratos took many of the leading roles in Italian opera during the 17th-c and 18th-c, the most famous being Carlo Broschi, known as Farinelli (1705–82). They ceased to be used in opera after c.1825, but were employed at the Sistine Chapel until the end of the 19th-c. The last castrato there, Alessandro Moreschi, died in 1922. » castration

Castries [**kas**trees] 14°01N 60°59W, pop (1982e) 130 000. Port and capital town of St Lucia, Windward Is, E Caribbean, on NW coast; founded, 1650; rebuilt after a fire in 1948; airport; foodstuffs, beverages, tobacco, textiles, wood, rubber and metal products, printing, chemicals, tourism. » St Lucia

Castro (Ruz), Fidel (1927–) Cuban revolutionary, Prime Minister (1959–), and President (1976–), born near Birán. He studied law in Havana. In 1953, he was imprisoned after an unsuccessful rising against Batista, but released under an amnesty. He fled to the USA and Mexico, then in 1956 landed in Cuba with a small band of insurgents. In 1958 he mounted a full-scale attack and Batista was forced to flee. He became Prime Minister in 1959, later proclaimed a 'Marxist-Leninist programme', and set about far-reaching reforms. His overthrow of US economic dominance, and the routing of the US-connived emigré invasion at the Bay of Pigs (1961) was balanced by his dependence on Russian aid. » Batista; Bay of Pigs; Cuba [i]

casuarina » **she-oak**

cat A carnivorous mammal of the family *Felidae*; name popularly used for the domestic cat, *Felis catus*, other species having individual names (lion, tiger, etc); domestic cats known in Egypt 4 000 years ago and may have evolved there from the *wild cat* (or *caffre cat*); numerous modern breeds, classed as *hairless*, *long-haired*, *British short-haired* (stocky breeds, descended from European ancestors – called 'British' because the first cat show was held in Britain), *American* (or *domestic*) *short-haired* (descended from the British), and *foreign short-haired* (smaller, more slender breeds, with ancestors from the Middle-East and elsewhere); male called a *tom*, female a *queen*, young are *kittens*. (Family: *Felidae*.) » Abyssinian/Angora/ Burmese / Havana / Manx / pampas / Persian / Siamese / tortoiseshell/Turkish/wild cat; bobcat; carnivore [i]; civet; Felidae; genet; Russian blue

cat bear » **panda**

cat's eyes A pair of rubber road studs fitted with light reflectors, designed to mark road lanes at night by reflecting a vehicle's headlights; devised by UK inventor Percy Shaw in 1934. The device can be compressed by the vehicle's wheels without doing damage to itself or the wheel. It also cleans itself when it is compressed.

cat's tail » **reedmace**

CAT scanning » **computerized axial tomography**

catabolism » **metabolism**

catacombs Subterranean Jewish or early Christian cemeteries found in certain parts of the Roman world – notably Rome itself – where soft rocks made the tunnelling of passages and carving of burial niches easy. The practice is believed to have been derived from ancient Jewish cave burials.

Çatal Hüyük [cha**tahl hoo**yuk] A prehistoric riverside settlement of c.6500–5500 BC in S Turkey, c.50 km/30 ml SE of Konya, the largest Neolithic site known in the Near East. The tell (mound) is 20 m/65 ft high, and covers 13 ha/32 acres, its twelve successive levels being packed with rectangular mud-brick houses, courtyards, and shrines; its estimated population was c.5 000. Spectacular cult fittings include wall paintings, plastered reliefs, and numerous bull's head effigies. » tell; Three Age System

Catalan » **Romance languages**

Catalaunian Plains, Battle of the (451) The decisive defeat in E France suffered by Attila the Hun at the hands of the Romans and Visigoths. Deflected from France, he turned S to Italy, which he ravaged the following year. » Attila; Roman history [i]

catalepsy The adoption of a body posture which would normally be unsustainable; also referred to as *waxy flexibility*. It occurs in serious psychotic illness or as a hysterical reaction. » catatonia; hysteria; psychosis

Catalonia [kata**loh**nia], Span **Cataluña**, Catalan **Catalunya** pop (1981) 5 956 414; area 31 932 sq km/12 320 sq ml. Autonomous region of NE Spain, comprising the provinces of Barcelona, Gerona, Lérida, and Tarragona, and formerly including Roussillon and Cerdana; area with a distinctive culture and Romance language; united with Aragon, 1137; created a mediaeval trading empire, 13th–14th-c; part of Spain following union of Castilian and Aragonese crowns, 1469–79; strong separatist movement since the 17th-c; Catalan republic established, 1932, abolished by Franco during the Civil War; new government established, 1979; cereals, olives, almonds, hazelnuts, grapes; industry centred around Barcelona; hydroelectric power from R Ebro; major tourist resorts on the Costa Brava. » Franco; Roman languages; Spain [i]; Spanish Civil War

catalpa » **Indian bean tree**

catalysis [ka**ta**lisis] The acceleration or slowing of a chemical reaction by the action of a material which is recovered unchanged at the end of the reaction. It is of immense importance in chemistry and biology, accelerating reactions that otherwise proceed very slowly, although they are energetically favourable. Catalysts include iron in the Haber process for ammonia, and chlorophyll in photosynthesis. Catalysis within a single phase (eg a solution) is called *homogeneous*, that in more than one phase *heterogeneous*. » chemical reaction; Haber-Bosch process; photosynthesis

catalytic converter An antipollution device fitted to a car exhaust system, now standard in Japan and the USA, and becoming more common in Europe. It contains a platinum catalyst for chemically converting unburned hydrocarbons and nitrogen oxides to compounds harmless to the environment. » pollution

catalytic cracking The breaking down (*cracking*) of the hydrocarbon molecules of petroleum, which in their initial state are too large to be useful. When the petroleum is distilled, the way the large molecules are made to break down can be induced to follow desired paths by several means, one being the use of *catalysts* – substances which intervene in the chemical process without being consumed by the product. » catalysis; petroleum

catamaran [katama**ran**] A twin-hulled vessel of Tamil origin, offering advantages in speed and stability. Propelled nowadays either by sail or power, it has become very popular as a yacht design in the past 25 years. » trimaran; yacht [i]

catamount » **cougar**

Catania [ka**tah**nia] 37°31N 15°06E, pop (1981) 380 328. Port and capital of Catania province, Sicily, S Italy; 160 km/100 ml SE of Palermo, at foot of Mt Etna, on E coast; archbishopric; airport; railway; university (1434); agricultural trade, shipbuilding, textiles, paper, sulphur processing, tourism. » Etna, Mount; Sicily

cataplexy The sudden loss of all muscle tone. It is usually associated with narcolepsy. » narcolepsy

cataract Developing opacities in the lens of the eye which cause slowly progressive loss of vision. Senile cataract is the most common type, but cataracts may also follow excessive exposure to ultraviolet light, and injury to the eye, and be a complication of diabetes and other conditions associated with rapid changes in the solute concentration of body fluids. Congenital cataracts occur as a rare genetic disease, and also following maternal rubella. When severe, the lens can be removed and the vision corrected with the aid of spectacles and a lens implantation. » eye [i]; lens; solution

catastrophe theory The mathematical study of sudden change, such as the bursting of a bubble, in contrast to continuous change. For example, in Necker's cube, the dot appears first either in the centre of one face or in a corner of another face, then suddenly changes. It is not possible to say in which face any one viewer will first see it, but it always changes suddenly. Catastrophe theory was created in the late 1950s and early 1960s by French mathematician René Thom (1923–) and developed in particular by Christopher Zeeman (1925–). There are many applications to economics and behavioural sciences as well as to the natural sciences.

catastrophism (geology) » **uniformitarianism**

catatonia A psychiatric state in which there is stupor associated with catalepsy, or overactivity associated with stereotyped behaviour. This condition was first described by the German physician Karl Ludwig Kahlbaum (1828–99) in 1874, and is seen particularly in manic-depressive illnesses and schizophrenia. There may be repetitive movements, the repetition of sounds or phrases the patient has heard (echolalia), automatic obedience, and negativism. » catalepsy; echolalia; manic depressive psychosis; schizophrenia

Catch-22 A novel by Joseph Heller, published in 1961. US airmen seeking leave from active service in World War 2 on grounds of mental derangement are judged ineligible to apply, since such a request proves their sanity. Hence 'Catch-22' signifies any logical trap or double bind. » American literature; Heller

catchfly An annual or perennial herb, part of the same genus as campions, but with hairy, sticky stem; native to the temperate N hemisphere; leaves opposite; calyx tubular, five petals, notched or bifid, white, pink, or yellow. (Genus: *Silene*. Family: *Caryophyllaceae*.) » annual; campion; herb; perennial; sepal

catechism A manual of Christian doctrine, in question-and-answer form. It derived from the early Church period of instruction for new converts, and was later applied to the instruction of adults baptised in infancy. Such manuals became popular after the Reformation, eg Luther's Little Catechism (1529) and the Heidelberg Catechism (1563). These were intended for instruction, preparation for confirmation, and confessional purposes. Some have avoided the question-and-answer format, such as the Roman Catholic 'New Catechism' of 1966. » Christianity; Luther; Reformation

catechol [**kat**uhkohl] $C_6H_4(OH)_2$, 1,2-dihydroxybenzene, melting point 105°C. A colourless solid which can form strong complexes with metals by chelation. Important derivatives include adrenaline and dopa. » adrenaline; chelate; dopa [i]

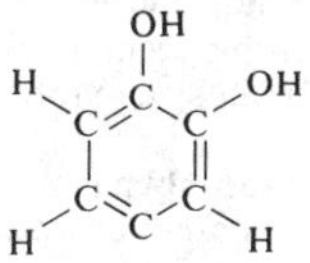

catecholamine [katuh**koh**lameen] The chemical classification of a group of biologically important components widely distributed amongst animals and plants. Those occurring in mammalian tissues are dopamine, noradrenaline, and adrenaline, all of which have important roles in the functioning of the sympathetic and central nervous system. They are crucial in the control of blood pressure, and in the 'flight or fight' response. » adrenaline; dopamine; nervous system; noradrenaline

Categorical Imperative The supreme principle of Kant's ethics, formulated in ways supposedly equivalent: act so that you can will the principle of your action to become a universal law; act so that you treat humanity as an end, never merely a means; act as if you were a member of a kingdom of ends. » deontological ethics; Kant

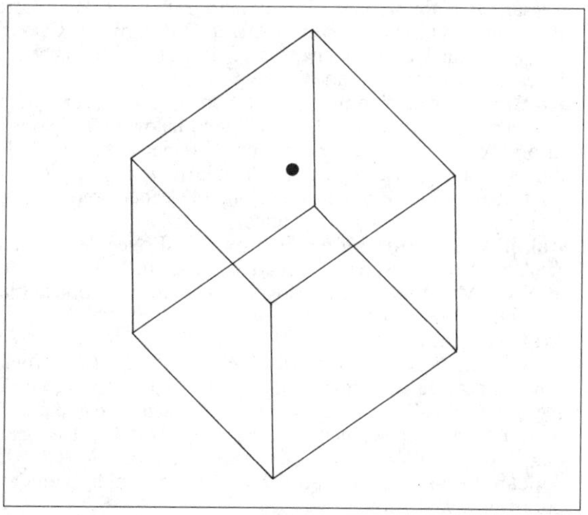

Catastrophe theory: Necker's cube

catenary In mathematics, the plane curve in which an 'ideal' chain hangs under its own weight (Lat *catena*, 'chain'). The simplest Cartesian equation is

$$y = \frac{a}{2}(e^{x/a} + e^{-x/a})$$

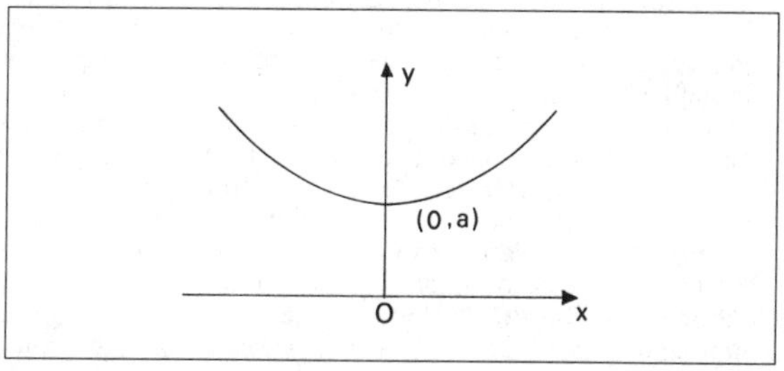

A catenary

catenation In chemistry, chain formation by element-element bonding. It is seen most strikingly in carbon compounds, but is also found with other elements, especially sulphur. » carbon; sulphur

caterpillar The larval stage of butterflies and moths (Order: *Lepidoptera*), usually feeding on plants; occasionally also used for the larvae of sawflies (Order: *Hymenoptera*). » butterfly; moth; processionary caterpillar; Plate IX

caterpillar bird » **cuckoo shrike**

Catesby, Robert (1573–1605) English conspirator, born at Lapworth, Warwickshire. He was a Roman Catholic of good fortune and lineage, who suffered fines and imprisonment under Queen Elizabeth and James I. He organized the group of men who carried out the Gunpowder Plot (1605). After the plot's failure, he fled to Holbeach House, Staffordshire, where he was killed. » Gunpowder Plot

catfish Any of about 28 families of typically elongate bottom-living fishes; flattened head, smooth skin, long barbels around mouth; habits often sluggish, nocturnal; several important as a food fish and in the aquarium trade; includes freshwater *Siluridae*, *Bagridae*, *Clariidae*, *Ictaluridae*, and marine *Ariidae*, *Plotosidae*. » wels

catgut A tough cord prepared from the intestines of sheep (sometimes horse or ass, but never a cat). The intestine is cleaned, steeped in alkali, and sterilized by sulphur fumes. It has been used for musical instrument strings and surgical sutures (now replaced for the most part by synthetic fibres). *Cat* seems to be derived from *kit* 'fiddle'. » intestine; kit

Cathars [**kath**ahz] (Gk **kathari** 'pure ones') Originally, 3rd-c separatists from the Church, puritan and ascetic, following the teaching of the 3rd-c Roman bishop, Novatian. In the Middle Ages, as a sect, they were known in Bulgaria as **Bogomiles** and in France as **Albigenses**. Celibate, they rejected sacraments and held 'good' and 'evil' to be separate spheres ('dualism'). They survived until the 14th-c, when they were finally exterminated by the Inquisition. » Albigenses; Inquisition; sacrament

cathartid vulture » **vulture**

cathedral (Lat **cathedra**, 'chair') The chief church of a bishop of a diocese; originally, the church which contained the throne of the bishop, then the mother church of the diocese. The most famous are the W European Gothic cathedrals built in the Middle Ages, such as those at Rheims, France (1211–90) and Westminster Abbey, London (mostly 1245–1506). In many towns, they were the centre around which social and cultural as well as religious life developed. Colloquially, the term is often now used to refer to any church of great size. » bishop; church [i]; Gothic architecture; Chartres / Córdoba / St Basil's/St Mark's/St Paul's Cathedral; Notre Dame; St Peter's Basilica

Catherine II, byname **the Great** (1729–96) Empress of Russia (1762–96), originally Princess Sophia Augusta of Anhalt-

Zerbst, born at Stettin. In 1745 she was married to the heir to the Russian throne (later Peter III, reigned 1761–2). Their marriage was an unhappy one, and Catherine (now baptized into the Russian Orthodox Church under that name) spent much of her time in political intriguing, reading, and extramarital affairs. In 1762 a palace coup overthrew her unpopular husband, and she was proclaimed Empress. She carried out an energetic foreign policy and extended the Russian Empire S to the Black Sea as a result of the Russo-Turkish Wars (1774, 1792) while in the W she brought about the three partitions of Poland. Despite pretensions to enlightened ideas, her domestic policies achieved little for the mass of the Russian people, though great cultural advances were made among the nobility. In 1774 she suppressed the popular rebellion led by Pugachev, and later actively persecuted members of the progressive-minded nobility. Her private life was dominated by a long series of lovers, most notably Potemkin. She died in St Petersburg. » Poland, Partitions of; Potemkin; Pugachev; Romanovs; Russian history; Russo-Turkish Wars

Catherine of Siena, St (1347–80), feast day 30 April. Italian nun and mystic, born at Siena, Tuscany. She became a Dominican, and gained a great reputation for holiness, writing many devotional pieces, letters, and poems. She prevailed on Pope Gregory XI to return the papacy from Avignon to Rome. Christ's stigmata were said to be imprinted on her body. She died in Rome, was canonized in 1461, and is the patron saint of Italy. » Dominicans; stigmata

Catherine, Mount, Arabic **Katherina, Gebel** 28°30N 33°57E. Mountain in S Sinai governorate, NE Egypt; height 2 637 m/ 8 651 ft; highest point in Egypt; St Catherine's monastery (6th-c), altitude 1 500 m/4 921 ft. » Egypt [i]

Catherine de' Medici (1519–89) Queen of France, wife of Henry II, and Regent (1560–74), born in Florence, the daughter of Lorenzo de' Medici, Duke of Urbino. Married at 14, she was slighted at the French court, but during the minority of her sons, Francis II (1559–60) and Charles IX (1560–3), she assumed political influence which she retained as Queen Mother until 1588. She tried to pursue moderation and toleration, to give unity to a state increasingly torn by religious division and aristocratic faction, but she nursed dynastic ambitions, and was drawn into political and religious intrigues, conniving in the infamous Massacre of St Bartholomew (1572). She died at Blois. » Henry II (of France); Huguenots

Catherine of Aragon (1485–1536) Queen of England, the first wife of Henry VIII (1509–33), and fourth daughter of Ferdinand and Isabella of Spain, born at Alcalá de Henares. She was first married in 1501 to Arthur (1486–1502), the son of Henry VII, and following his early death was betrothed to her brother-in-law Henry, then a boy of 11. She married him in 1509, and bore him five children, but only the Princess Mary survived. In 1527 Henry began a procedure for divorce, which he obtained in 1533, thereby breaking with the Pope, and starting the English Reformation. Catherine then retired to lead an austere religious life until her death, at Kimbolton, Huntingdonshire. » Henry VIII (of England); Reformation

Catherine of Braganza (1638–1705) Wife of Charles II of England, the daughter of King John IV of Portugal, born at Vila Viçosa, Portugal. She was married to Charles in 1662 as part of an alliance between England and Portugal, but failed to produce an heir. She helped to convert him to Catholicism just before his death, after which she returned to Portugal (1692). She died in Lisbon. » Charles II (of England)

catheter A fine tube made of rubber or synthetic material for insertion into a number of body cavities, such as the bladder, blood vessels, the chambers of the heart, and the respiratory passages. It is used either to introduce or to withdraw fluid or blood for analysis, or to measure pressure or rates of flow. » blood vessels [i]

cathode The positive terminal in a battery. In cathode-ray tubes (eg television tubes) and thermionic valves, a heated cathode is a source of electrons. In electrolysis, cations (positive ions) move towards the cathode. For a battery in a completed circuit, positive current flows from the cathode through the circuit to the anode. » anode; electrolysis [i]; thermionics; valve

cathode-ray tube (CRT) An electronic device in which an image is formed on a phosphor screen in a vacuum tube by a beam of electrons deflected in electric or magnetic fields. It is used in oscilloscopes, display screens, and television receivers. » shadow-mask tube [i]

cathode rays » **electron**

Catholic Church (Gk **katholikos**, 'general', 'universal') **1** As in the Apostles' Creed, the universal Church which confesses Jesus Christ as Lord. » Apostles' Creed; Jesus Christ **2** Christian Churches with episcopal order and confessing ancient creeds. » episcopacy **3** Specifically, the Roman Catholic Church and other Churches recognizing the primacy of the Pope, as distinct from Protestant and Orthodox Churches. » papacy; Roman Catholicism

Catholic Emancipation A reluctant religious concession granted by the British Tory government of the Duke of Wellington in 1829, following mounting agitation led by Daniel O'Connell and the Catholic Association. Roman Catholics were permitted to become MPs; and all offices of state in Ireland, except Viceroy and Chancellor, were also opened to Catholics. » O'Connell; Roman Catholicism; Tories

Catiline, properly **Lucius Sergius Catalina** (?–62 BC) An impoverished Roman politician of patrician extraction who tried to exploit the economic unrest of Rome and Italy in the 60s BC for his own political ends. His conspiracy against the state was foiled by Cicero late in 63 BC, and he fell in battle early in 62 BC. » Cicero

cation [**kat**iyuhn] An ion bearing a positive charge, so-called because it will migrate towards the cathode in an electrochemical cell. » anion; cathode

catmint A square-stemmed perennial, growing to 1 m/3.3 ft, native to Europe and Asia, often on chalky soils; oval, toothed leaves in opposite pairs; flowers 2-lipped, white spotted with purple, in whorls forming spikes; also called **catnip**. A relative of true mints, its strong scent is attractive to cats. (*Nepeta cataria*. Family: *Labiatae*). » mint; perennial

catnip » **catmint**

Cato, Marcus Porcius, byname **the Elder** or **the Censor** (234–149 BC) Roman statesman, orator, and man of letters. Deeply conservative, and strongly opposed to the contemporary fashion of all things Greek, when made censor (184 BC) he conducted such a vigorous campaign that he was thereafter known as 'Censor'. Sent on a mission to Carthage (c.157 BC), he was so impressed by the power of the Carthaginians that afterwards he ended every speech in the Senate with the words: 'Carthage must be destroyed'. His treatise on agriculture is the oldest extant literary prose work in Latin. » censors; cursus honorum; Punic Wars

Cato, Marcus Porcius, byname **the Younger** or **Uticensis** (95–46 BC) Roman statesman, the great-grandson of Cato the Censor. A man of uncompromising principles and deep conservatism, his career was marked by an unswerving opposition to Caesar. A supporter of Pompey in the Civil War, after Pharsalus (48 BC) he escaped to Africa. On hearing of Caesar's overwhelming victory at Thapsus (c.46 BC), he killed himself, at Utica. » Caesar; Roman history [i]

Cato Street conspiracy A plot in February 1820, formulated by Arthur Thistlewood (1770–1820) and fellow radical conspirators, to blow up the British Tory Cabinet as it attended a dinner at the house of the Earl of Harrowby. The plot was infiltrated by a government agent, and the leaders were arrested and hanged. » radicalism; Tories

Catskill Mountains Mountain group in SE New York State, USA; part of the Appalachian system; rises to 1 282 m/4 206 ft at Slide Mt; New York recreational area. » Appalachian Mountains; New York

cattalo » **bison**

cattle Domesticated mammals, developed from wild aurochs; now worldwide with numerous breeds; kept for milk and/or meat or for hauling loads; also known as **oxen**. The name *cattle* is sometimes used to include other species (eg banteng, gaur, yak, bison, buffalo, anoa). (*Bos taurus*. Family: *Bovidae*.) » African buffalo; anoa; aurochs; Bovidae; bull (zoology); shorthorn; yak; zebu

cattle plague » **rinderpest**

cattleya [**kat**lia] Orchids (mainly epiphytes) native to the forests of C and S America. They have swollen, bulb-like stems (*pseudobulbs*) bearing 1–3 leaves, and spikes of up to 47 large, showy flowers. Widely cultivated with numerous hybrids, they are one of the most widely used orchids of floristry. (Genus: *Cattleya*, 30 species. Family: *Orchidaceae*.) » epiphyte; hybrid; orchid [i]

Catullus, Gaius Valerius [ka**tuh**luhs] (c.84–c.54 BC) Latin lyric poet, born at Verona. He settled in Rome (c.62 BC), where he met the 'Lesbia' whom he addressed in his verses. He entered as an aristocrat into the contest of parties, and several of his poems attack Caesar and other political enemies. His extant works comprise 116 pieces, many of them extremely brief, while the longest contains only some 400 lines. He died in Rome. » poetry; Roman literature

Caucasus Mountains [**kaw**kasus], Russ **Kavkaz** Major mountain system between the Black Sea and the Caspian Sea; bounded S by Turkey and Iran; comprises the **Greater Caucasus** and the **Lesser Caucasus**; generally accepted as the physical boundary between Europe (N) and Asia (S); extends c.1 120 km/700 ml SE; in the W is Mt Elbrus (5 642 m/18 510 ft), highest point in the Kavkaz range; in the E the range widens to over 160 km/100 ml.

caucus A meeting, public or private, restricted to persons sharing a common characteristic, usually membership of a political party, held to formulate decisions or nominate candidates in forthcoming elections. It is most often applied to the USA, where the caucus-convention system is significant in selecting presidential and vice-presidential candidates, and where caucuses are the authoritative voice of the parties in Congress. » Congress

cauliflower A type of cultivated cabbage grown for the immature inflorescence which forms the edible white head. If left to mature, the head eventually elongates greatly, producing numerous yellow cross-shaped flowers. (*Brassica oleracea*. Family: *Cruciferae*.) » brassica; cabbage; inflorescence [i]

causation Metaphysical theories of causation attempt to explain what it is for *A* to cause *B*. **Power** theories claim that there is a power in *A* which necessitates a modification in one or more of the powers in *B*; causation is thus primarily a relation between two *things*. **Regularity** theories maintain that causation primarily holds between *events*; according to Hume, *A* causes *B* if events like *A* are regularly followed by events like *B*: the necessity involved is only psychological; having seen *A*-events followed by *B*-events, we anticipate future *A*-events to be followed by *B*-events, and project that anticipation into nature. » Hume, David

caustic In chemistry, descriptive of substances (normally strongly alkaline) which are destructive, particularly to biological tissue. *Caustic soda* is sodium hydroxide; *caustic potash* is potassium hydroxide. » alkali

Cavalcanti, Guido [kaval**kan**tee] (c.1255–1300) Italian poet, born in Florence. He was a friend of Dante, and wrote about 50 poems in the 'new style' of the period. A member of the papal party (the Guelphs), he married someone from the rival, imperial party (the Ghibellines), and was banished. He later returned to Florence, where he died. » Dante; Ghibellines; Guelphs; Italian literature

Cavalier poets Deriving their name from courtly associations, poets of the mid-17th-c who supported Charles I in the Civil War. The best known are Carew, Lovelace, Herrick, and Waller. Indebted to Ben Jonson, their (mostly love) poems are characterized by urbanity, elegance, and wit. » Carew; Jonson; English literature; Herrick; Lovelace; poetry; Waller

Cavaliers Those who fought for Charles I in the English Civil War. The name was used derogatorily in 1642 by supporters of Parliament to describe swaggering courtiers with long hair and swords, who reportedly welcomed the prospect of war. Similarly, the Parliamentarians were labelled 'Roundheads' by Cavaliers, dating from the riotous assemblies in Westminster during Strafford's trial in 1641, when short-haired apprentices mobbed Charles I's supporters outside the House of Lords. » English Civil War; Strafford

Cavallini, Pietro (c.1250–c.1330) Italian painter and artist in mosaic, born in Rome. A contemporary of Giotto, whom he influenced, his best-known work is the series of mosaics in the Church of Santa Maria at Trastevere, Rome. » fresco; Giotto; Italian art

Cavan (county) pop (1981) 53 855; area 1 891 sq km/730 sq ml. County in Ulster province, NC Irish Republic; bounded N by N Ireland; drained by Analee, Boyne, and Erne Rivers; capital Cavan; oats, potatoes, dairy farming. » Cavan (town); Irish Republic [i]; Ulster

Cavan (town), Gaelic **Cabháin** 54°00N 7°21W, pop (1981) 5 035. Agricultural market town and capital of Cavan county, Ulster, Irish Republic; NW of Dublin; bishopric; crystal; international song contest (Apr). » Cavan (county)

cave A natural cavity in the Earth's surface, generally hollowed out by the action of water, and most spectacularly developed in limestones (soluble in mildly acid rainwater), in which huge vaults and interconnected river systems may form. Caves are also made by the action of sea water against cliffs, as in Fingal's Cave in the Scottish Hebrides. Ice caves may form in glaciers by streams of melt water. » Altamira; Lascaux; limestone; speleology; RR13

cave art » **Palaeolithic art**

cavefish Small blind N American fish confined to limestone caves of SE states; body lacking pigment (Genera: *Amblyopsis*, *Typhlichthys*, 4 species); also two species (Genus: *Chologaster*) with small eyes and pigmented skin from coastal swamps. (Family: *Amblyopsidae*.)

Cavell, Edith [**kav**uhl] (1865–1915) British nurse, born at Swardeston, Norfolk. She became a nurse in 1895, and matron of the Berkendael Institute, Brussels, in 1907. She tended friend and foe alike in 1914–15, yet was executed by the Germans for helping Belgian and Allied fugitives to escape capture.

Cavendish, Henry (1731–1810) British physicist and chemist, born in Nice. He studied at Cambridge, but left to devote himself to science, after being bequeathed a fortune. In 1760 he studied the 'inflammable air', now known as hydrogen gas; and later ascertained that water resulted from the union of two gases. The 'Cavendish Experiment' was an ingenious means of estimating the density of the Earth. He died in London. The Cavendish Physical Laboratory at Cambridge was named after him.

Cavendish, Spencer Compton, 8th Duke of Devonshire (1833–1908) British Liberal politician, known as the **Marquis of Hartington** (1858–91), born at Lower Holker, Lancashire. Educated at Cambridge, he entered parliament in 1857, and between 1863 and 1874 was a Lord of the Admiralty, Under-Secretary for War, War Secretary, Postmaster-General, and Chief Secretary for Ireland. In 1875 he became Leader of the Liberal Opposition during Gladstone's temporary abdication, later serving under him as Secretary of State for India (1880–2) and as War Secretary (1882–5). He disapproved of Irish Home Rule, and, having led the breakaway from the Liberal Party, became head of the Liberal Unionists from 1886, serving in the Unionist government as Lord President of the Council (1895–1903). He died at Cannes, France. His younger brother, **Lord Frederick Cavendish** (1836–82), was also a Liberal MP (1865–82). He was appointed Chief Secretary for Ireland, but immediately after his arrival in Dublin was murdered by 'Irish Invincibles' in Phoenix Park. » Gladstone; Liberal Party (UK)

Cavendish, William, Duke of Newcastle (1592–1676) English soldier and patron of the arts. Educated at Cambridge, he was created Knight of the Bath in 1610, Viscount Mansfield in 1620, and Earl (1628), Marquess (1643), and Duke (1665) of Newcastle. He gave strong support to Charles I in the Civil War, and was general of all forces N of the Trent. After Marston Moor (1644) he lived on the Continent, at times in great poverty, until the Restoration. A noted patron of poets and dramatists, he was himself the author of several plays, and of two works on horsemanship. He died at Welbeck, Nottinghamshire. » English Civil War

caviar The prepared roe (eggs) of the female sturgeon, beluga, sevruga, and starlet. These fish are caught in the winter months in the rivers flowing into the Baltic Sea and the Danube. Sturgeon roe is black, and is considered superior. » sturgeon

cavitation A form of localized boiling in a liquid, caused by sudden dramatic reductions in pressure, giving rise to pockets of gas. Examples include the trailing edge of ship propellers, and powerful sound waves in a liquid. » boiling point; fluid mechanics

Cavour, Camillo Benso, Conte di ('Count of') (1810–61) Piedmontese statesman who brought about the unification of Italy (1861), born and died in Turin. As Premier (1852–9), he greatly improved economic conditions, and brought the Italian question before the Congress of Paris. He resigned over the Peace of Villafranca (which left Venetia Austrian), but returned in 1860, and secretly encouraged the expedition of Garibaldi, which gained Sicily and S Italy. » Garibaldi; Italy [i]

cavy A rodent native to S America; includes *guinea pigs* (Genus: *Cavia*), and a wide range of *cavy-like rodents*. The *domestic guinea pig* (*Caviidae porcellus*) was bred as food by the Incas, and is still eaten in S America. (Family: *Caviidae*, 15 species.) » acouchi; agouti; cane rat; capybara; chinchilla; coypu; hutia; mole rat; paca; porcupine; rodent; viscacha

Caxton, William (c.1422–c.1491) The first English printer, born in the Weald of Kent. He was trained in London as a cloth merchant, and lived in Bruges (1441–70). In Cologne (1471–2) he probably learned the art of printing, and soon after printed the first book in English, the *Recuyell of the Historyes of Troye* (1475). About the end of 1476 he set up his wooden press at Westminster, and produced the *Dictes or Sayengis of the Philosophres* (1477), the first book printed in England. Of about 100 books printed by him, including the *Canterbury Tales*, over a third survive only in unique copies or fragments. He died in London. » book; printing [i]

cayenne » **pepper 1**

Cayenne [**kay**en] 4°55N 52°18W, pop (1982) 38 135. Federal and district capital of French Guiana, NE South America; major port on Cayenne I at mouth of R Cayenne, on the Atlantic coast; founded, 1643; used as penal settlement, 1854–1938; airport; source of Cayenne pepper; timber, sugar cane, rum, pineapples; Jesuit-built residence (1890) of the prefect. » French Guiana

Cayley, Arthur (1821–95) British mathematician, born at Richmond, Surrey. Educated at London and Cambridge, he was called to the Bar in 1849. In 1863 he became professor of pure mathematics at Cambridge. He originated the theory of invariants and covariants, and worked on the theories of matrices and analytical geometry, and on theoretical astronomy. He died at Cambridge. » algebra; matrix

Cayley, Sir George (1771–1857) British pioneer of aviation, born and died at Scarborough, Yorkshire. In 1808 he constructed and flew a glider, probably the first heavier-than-air machine, and in 1853 made the first successful man-carrying glider. He also interested himself in railway engineering, allotment agriculture, and land reclamation methods, and invented a new type of telescope, artificial limbs, the caterpillar tractor, and the tension wheel. He helped to found the Regent Street Polytechnic, London (1839). » aircraft [i]; glider

cayman » **caiman**

Cayman Islands [**kay**man] pop (1989) 25 355; area 260 sq km/ 100 sq ml. British dependency in the W Caribbean, comprising the islands of Grand Cayman, Cayman Brac, and Little Cayman, c.240 km/150 ml S of Cuba; capital, George Town; other main town, West Bay; timezone GMT −5; population mainly of mixed descent (c.60%); official language, English; chief religion, Christianity; unit of currency, the Cayman Is dollar of 100 cents; low-lying, rising to 42 m/138 ft on Cayman Brac plateau; ringed by coral reefs; tropical climate, average annual rainfall 1 420 mm/56 in; hurricane season (Jul–Nov); average temperatures, 24–32°C (May–Oct), 16°–24°C (Nov–Apr); visited by Columbus, 1503; ceded to Britain, 1670; colonized by British settlers from Jamaica; British Crown Colony, 1962; a governor represents the British sovereign, and presides over a 15-member Legislative Assembly; economic activities mainly tourism, international finance, property development; marked increase in cruise ship traffic; over 450 banks and trust companies established on the islands; oil transshipment, crafts, jewellery, cattle, poultry, vegetables, tropical fish, turtle products. » George Town

CBE » **British Empire, Order of the**

CBI » **Confederation of British Industry**

CDROM [seedee**rom**] An acronym of **Compact Disc Read Only Memory**, a computer storage medium based on the use of the standard five-inch compact disc, licensed by Sony and Philips, and usually used for digital audio. One CDROM disc can store more than 600 Megabytes of computer information, which is considerably more than a comparable size of hard magnetic disk. It is however a read-only device, and data is installed during manufacture; unlike the hard disk, the data on a CDROM cannot be altered. The main applications have been in providing access to large volumes of information such as encyclopedias and databases. » byte; compact disc; magnetic disk; ROM

ceanothus » **Californian lilac**

Ceaușescu, Nicolae [chow**shes**koo] (1918–1989) Romanian statesman and President, born at Scornicești. Educated at Bucharest, he joined the Communist Party at 15, and held several junior political posts before becoming President of the State Council in 1967 and General Secretary of the Romanian Communist Party in 1969. Under his leadership, Romania became increasingly independent of the USSR, and for many years Romania was the only Warsaw Pact country to have cordial relations with China. He became the first President of the Republic in 1974, and established a strong personality cult. His policy of replacing traditional villages by collectives of concrete apartments caused much controversy in the late 1980s. In 1989 he was deposed when the army joined a popular revolt against his repressive government. Following a trial by military tribunal, he and his wife, Elena, were shot. » Romania [i]

Cebu or **Cebu City** [**say**boo] 10°17N 123°56E, pop (1980) 490 281. Seaport in Cebu province, E coast of Cebu I, Philippines; founded, 1565 (first Spanish settlement in the Philippines); airfield; four universities (1595, 1919, 1946, 1949); commerce, tobacco, copra, food processing, textiles; Spanish fort, Santo Niño Church; Santo Niño de Cebu festival (Jan). » Philippines [i]; Visayan Islands

Cecil, Robert (Arthur Talbot Gascoyne), 3rd Marquis of Salisbury (1830–1903) British Conservative statesman and Prime Minister (1885–6, 1886–92, 1895–1902), born at Hatfield, Hertfordshire. Educated at Eton and Oxford, he became an MP in 1853. In 1865 he was made Viscount Cranborne, and in 1868 Marquis of Salisbury. He was twice Indian Secretary (1866 and 1874), became Foreign Secretary (1878), and on Disraeli's death (1881) Leader of the Opposition. He was Prime Minister on three occasions, much of the time serving as his own Foreign Secretary. He resigned as Foreign Secretary in 1900, but remained as head of government during the Boer War (1899–1902). He retired in 1902, and died at Hatfield. » Boer Wars; Disraeli

Cecil, William, 1st Baron Burghley or **Burghleigh** (1520–98) One of England's greatest statesmen, born at Bourn, Lincolnshire. He was educated at Stamford, Grantham, and Cambridge, and at Gray's Inn studied law, history, genealogy, and theology. He served under Somerset and Northumberland, was made Secretary of State (1550) and knighted (1551). During Mary I's reign he conformed to Catholicism. In 1558 Elizabeth appointed him chief Secretary of State, and for the next 40 years he was the chief architect of Elizabethan greatness, influencing her pro-Protestant foreign policy, securing the execution of Mary, Queen of Scots, and preparing for the Spanish Armada. He used an army of spies to ensure security at home. In 1571 he was created Baron Burghley, and in 1572 became Lord High Treasurer – an office he held until his death, in London. » Elizabeth I; Mary I; Mary, Queen of Scots

Cecilia, St (2nd-c or 3rd-c), feast day 22 November. Patroness of music, especially church music. She was a convert to Christianity, and is said to have suffered martyrdom at Rome. » Christianity

Cecrops or **Kekrops** [**ke**krops] In Greek mythology, the ancestor and first king of the Athenians. He was born from the earth, and formed with snakelike appendages instead of legs. During his reign Athena and Poseidon fought for the possession of Athens. He was buried in the Erechtheum. » Athena; Erechtheum; Poseidon

cedar An evergreen conifer with a massive trunk and flat, wide-spreading crown, native to the mountains of N Africa, the

Himalayas, and the E Mediterranean; needles sometimes bluish, in tufts; timber fragrant and oily. It should not be confused with the 'cedar' of commerce, which is obtained from other conifers. (Genus: *Cedrus*, 4 species. Family: *Pinaceae*.) » arbor vitae; conifer; evergreen plants

Ceefax [seefaks] A UK teletext system operated by the British Broadcasting Corporation since 1974. The name derives from 'see facts'. » teletext

celandine » **lesser celandine**

Celebes » **Sulawesi**

Celebes Sea [seluhbeez], Indonesian **Laut Sulawesi** area 280 000 sq km/110 000 sq ml. Sea of SE Asia, bounded by islands of Indonesia (W and S), Malaysia (NW), and the Philippines (NE); maximum depth 5 090 m/16 700 ft; fishing, local trade.

celeriac A variety of celery, also called **turnip-rooted celery**, with a tuberous base to the stems, cooked as a vegetable or used in salads. (*Apium graveolens*, variety *rapaceum*. Family: *Umbelliferae*.) » celery; tuber

celery A strong-smelling biennial herb, growing to 1 m/3.3 ft, native to Europe, SW Asia, and N Africa; stems deeply grooved; leaves shiny, divided into triangular or diamond-shaped segments; flowers minute, greenish-white, borne in umbels 3–5cm/1¼–2 in across. Forms with swollen leaf stalks (variety *dulce*) are widely cultivated as a vegetable. (*Apium graveolens*. Family: *Umbelliferae*.) » biennial; celeriac; herb; vegetable

celesta A musical instrument resembling a small upright piano, but with metal plates instead of strings and a shorter (five-octave) compass. It was invented in 1886 by French instrument maker Auguste Mustel (1842–1919) and used a few years later by Tchaikovsky in his ballet *The Nutcracker* ('Dance of the Sugar Plum Fairy'). » keyboard instrument; percussion [i]; Tchaikovsky; transposing instrument

celestial equator The great circle in which the plane of the Earth's Equator cuts the celestial sphere. This is the primary circle for the co-ordinates right ascension and declination. » ascension; celestial sphere; declination: Equator; obliquity of the ecliptic

celestial mechanics The study of the motions of celestial objects in gravitational fields. Founded by Isaac Newton, it deals with satellite and planetary motion within the Solar System, using Newtonian gravitational theory. » gravity [i]; Newton, Isaac; Solar System

celestial sphere An imaginary sphere surrounding the Earth, used as a reference frame to specify the positions of celestial objects on the sky. Its N and S poles lie over those of Earth, and its equator is the projection of the terrestrial Equator. » celestial equator; nadir

Céline, Louis-Ferdinand [sayleen], pseudonym of **Louis-Ferdinand Destouches** (1894–1961) French novelist, born in Paris. He was invalided out of the army early in World War 1, travelled widely during the war years, then practised medicine. His reputation is based on the two autobiographical novels he wrote during the 1930s: *Voyage au bout de la nuit* (1932, Journey to the End of the Night) and *Mort à crédit* (1936, Death by Instalments). During World War 2 he collaborated with the Vichy government, and fled to Germany and Denmark in 1944. He later returned to Paris, and died at Mendon. » French literature; novel; Vichy

cell The basic unit of plant and animal bodies; it comprises, at least, a nucleus or nuclear material and cytoplasm enclosed within a cell membrane. Some cells, such as the mature red blood corpuscles of mammals, lack a nucleus, but possessed one at an earlier stage of development. Many cells are more complex, and contain other specialized structures (*organelles*), such as mitochondria, chloroplasts, Golgi bodies, and flagella. Many simple organisms comprise a single cell, and may lack a membrane separating nuclear material from cytoplasm. Advanced organisms consist of a variety of co-operating cells, often specialized to perform particular functions and organized into tissues and organs. Plant cells are typically surrounded by an outer cell wall containing cellulose. Cell division may occur by splitting into two parts (*fission*), by mitosis, and (in the case of reproductive cells) by meiosis. All nucleated cells contain within their nuclei the entire inherited genetic information of that individual, but in specialized cells, such as a liver or brain cell, only a minute fraction of their genetic database is operational. » cellulose; chloroplast; cytoplasm; fission; flagellum; genetics [i]; Golgi body; meiosis [i]; mitochondrion; mitosis; nucleus (biology)

Cellini, Benvenuto [cheleenee] (1500–71) Italian goldsmith, sculptor, engraver, and author, born in Florence, and particularly known for his autobiography (1558–62). By his own account, it seems he had no scruple in murdering or maiming his rivals; and at the siege of Rome (1527), he killed the Constable Bourbon. He was several times imprisoned. His best work includes the gold saltcellar made for Francis I of France, and his bronze 'Perseus'. He lived at times in Rome, Mantua, Naples, and Florence, where he died. » Bourbon, Charles; Italian art

cello or **violoncello** The bass instrument of the violin family, with four strings tuned to an octave below the viola's. Until the 19th-c it was usually gripped between the player's knees; the modern instrument is fitted with an adjustable endpin which rests on the floor. » continuo; string instrument **1** [i]; string quartet

cellulite According to certain beauty experts, the dimpled fat around the thigh and buttocks, which is said to resist dieting. However, all available evidence in food science shows that when an individual diets, fat is lost from all fat deposits in the body. » diet

cellulitis The bacterial infection of connective tissue, spreading between layers of tissue and adjacent organs. It may arise following wounds and after surgical operations. It is potentially dangerous, as the infection may enter the blood stream, and is best treated by an appropriate antibiotic. » connective tissue

celluloid The earliest commercial plastic (c.1865–9), consisting of cellulose nitrate plasticized with camphor. It had the great virtue of dimensional stability, which kept it in vogue for photographic film in spite of its dangerous inflammability, long after other plastics had been contrived. It was eventually superseded as a film base by dimensionally stable forms of cellulose acetate. » film; nitrocellulose

cellulose $(C_6H_{10}O_5)_n$. A structural polysaccharide found mainly in the cell walls of woody and fibrous plant material, such as cotton. It is the main raw material for paper. Many important derivatives are formed by esterifying some of the hydroxyl groups; these include rayon (*cellulose acetate*) and guncotton (*cellulose nitrate* or *nitrocellulose*). » carbohydrate; ester [i]; nitrocellulose; polysaccharide

celostat » **coelostat**

Celsius, Anders (1701–44) Swedish astronomer, born and died at Uppsala. In 1730 he became professor of astronomy at Uppsala, and in 1742 devised the centigrade thermometer and the temperature scale named after him. » thermometer

Celsius temperature A scale that takes the triple point of water to be 0.01°C, which corresponds roughly to taking the freezing point of water as 0°C and the boiling point as 100°C; named after Swedish astronomer Anders Celsius; a change in temperature of one degree Celsius is equal to a change in temperature of one Kelvin; a temperature in degrees Celsius is still often called by the old name degrees *Centigrade*. » Celsius; phases of matter [i]; temperature [i]; units (scientific); RR79

Celtiberia [keltibeeria] The territory in NC Spain inhabited by the Celtiberians, a warlike people of mixed Celtic and Iberian ancestry. Staunch opponents of the Romans, they were pacified in 133 BC after decades of intermittent but fierce resistance. » Roman history [i]

Celtic art The art which emerged in 5th-c BC in S Germany and E France, spread throughout Europe for 500 years, and affected much subsequent mediaeval art, especially decorative gold and bronze-work. Greek motifs such as rosettes and lyre-shapes were combined with arabesques and strongly stylized human and animal forms traceable to the art of nomadic tribes on the E Steppes. Ceremonial metal vessels took their shapes from Etruscan and S Italian models. » arabesque [i]; art; Celts

Celtic languages The languages of the Celts, the first Indo-

European peoples to spread throughout Europe. The dialects spoken on the continent are known as **Continental Celtic**; traces remain in several inscriptions and place-names in *Gaulish* (from the tribal name *Galli* or *Gaul*), and in *Celtiberian* (from *Celtiberi*, the name given to the Celtic tribes of Spain). **Insular Celtic** is the name given to the Celtic languages of the British Is and Brittany. There are two branches: *Goidelic* comprises the Gaelic spoken in Ireland (*Irish* or *Erse*), which spread to the Isle of Man (*Manx*) and Scotland (*Gaelic*); *Welsh*, *Cornish*, and *Breton* comprise the *Brythonic* (also called the *Brittonic* or *British*) branch. The two branches of Insular Celtic are labelled *Q-Celtic* (Goidelic) and *P-Celtic* (Brythonic), because of a distinctive divergence in the development of the Indo-European sound system: the consonant sequence *kw* became *q* or *c* in Goidelic, and *p* in Brythonic, as is evidenced in the final consonant of the surnames *Mac* (Gaelic) and *Ap* (Welsh). » Breton; Celtic literature; Celts; Cornish; Gaelic; Irish; Welsh

Celtic literature The indigenous literatures of Ireland, Scotland, and Wales, as well as some Cornish texts from the 15th-c (including the three biblical plays comprising the *Ordinalia*). There is also an extensive literature in the Breton language, consisting of saints' lives, plays, comic pieces, folk tales, and ballads. This comes mainly from the Middle Breton (12th–17th-c) and Modern Breton periods, the latter dating from 1659 with the regularization of Breton spelling by Julien Maunoir. Despite official neglect and even opposition, in the 20th-c there has been a revival of interest in the Celtic languages and literatures. » Celts; Irish/Scottish/Welsh literature

Celtic Sea [**kel**tik] Part of the Atlantic Ocean S of Ireland; separated from the Irish Sea by St George's Channel; main inlet, Bristol Channel; average depths of 100–200 m/330–650 ft. » Atlantic Ocean

Celts Different groups of prehistoric peoples who all spoke Celtic languages and lived in most parts of Europe from the Balkan regions to Ireland. Most powerful during the 4th-c BC, they probably originated in present-day France, S Germany, and adjacent territories during the Bronze Age. Celtic-speaking societies developed in the later first millennium BC, expanding through armed raids into the Iberian Peninsula, British Is, C Europe, Italy, Greece, Anatolia, Egypt, Bulgaria, Romania, Thrace, and Macedonia. They were finally repulsed by the Romans and Germanic tribes, and in Europe withdrew into Gaul in the 1st-c BC. Celtic tradition survived most, and for longest in Ireland and Britain. They were famous for their burial sites and hill forts, and their bronze and iron art and jewellery. » Celtic art/languages/literature

cement In general, any substance used to adhere to each of two materials which cannot themselves adhere, and therefore to effect a join. More usually, it refers to *Portland Cement*, an artificial mineral substance used in building and engineering construction. This is made by heating clay and limestone in retorts to form a clinker which is then finely ground. The addition of water produces a soft manageable substance which sets hard, through the formation of hydrated silicates. It is commonly mixed with other mineral substances (sand, stone) to form various grades of concrete, or used as a mortar for joining brickwork. » clay; limestone

cementation The modification of the surface layer of a metal by heating it in a packing of some substance which will diffuse into it. This was the oldest method of making steel: heating iron packed in charcoal. » case hardening; metal

Cenozoic era [seenoh**zoh**ik] or **Cainozoic** [kaynuh**zoh**ik] The most recent of the four eras of geological time, beginning c. 65 million years ago and extending to the present day; subdivided into the *Tertiary* and *Quaternary* periods. It was characterized by widespread changes in the fauna, with the dominance of mammals and flowering plants, and the development of present-day geographical features. » geological time scale; Quaternary period; Tertiary period; RR16

censors In Republican Rome (5th-c–1st-c BC), two officials (usually ex-consuls) elected every five years to compile a register of citizens and their property for military, legislative, electoral, and fiscal purposes. Though prestigious, the office was not part of the *cursus honorum*. » consul **1**; cursus honorum

censorship The controlling of access to and dissemination of material, especially on political and moral grounds. In its extreme form, it involves the wholesale banning of information, including works of fiction, enforced by the imposition of penalties against offenders. As such it is a characteristic of authoritarian states, which seek to regulate the flow of information, opinion, and expression. This is usually justified by reference to state security, the public interest, and good taste. In contemporary democracies, the term usually has wholly negative connotations. Such societies pride themselves on the freedoms enjoyed by their people, including the right of free expression, often enshrined in law (eg the First Amendment to the US Constitution). But censorship plays a part in even the most enlightened and progressive of societies, its legitimacy deriving from an assumed consensus on what is and is not acceptable at a particular time. Organizations of all kinds have certain secrets which need to be protected for reasons of security, confidentiality, and personal privacy. Such information will be 'classified' to some degree, and be restricted to those authorized to receive it. Problems arise when the censoring of information is believed to be against the wider public interest, insofar as it is used to conceal incompetence, corruption, and crime.

Art in all its forms has always been prone to censorship, often due to the desire of artists to extend the boundaries of taste and to challenge authority. For example, in the British theatre it was not until 1968 that managements ceased having to submit manuscripts of plays for approval by the official censor, the Lord Chamberlain. Formal pre-censorship of this kind is uncommon today in the West. One major exception is film and video recordings, which are usually previewed by a board of censors, before being released for public consumption, with cuts if required. Since 1972 the monthly periodical Index on Censorship has campaigned against abuses of the fundamental right of free expression throughout the world. » broadcasting; journalism; samizdat

census A count of the population resident in an area at a given time, together with the collection of social and economic data, made at regular intervals. In many countries census data form the basis for the planning of service provisions, and a census is taken every 10 years. The USA conducted its first national census in 1790, and France and the UK began to collect census data in 1801. The United Nations has tried to ensure some comparability between the questions asked in different countries, and has been partially successful. » demography; population [i]

centaur [**sen**taw] In Greek mythology, a creature combining the upper half of a man and the rear legs of a horse (as shown on vases); later and more popularly imagined as having the entire body of a horse. Centaurs came from Thessaly, and most were beastly and wild, fighting with the Lapiths and with Heracles. » Chiron

Centaurus [sen**taw**ruhs] (Lat 'centaur') A large and rich S constellation. Its brightest star, Alpha Centauri, is actually three stars, the faintest of which, Proxima Centauri, is the closest star to the Sun, 1.31 parsecs away from Earth. **Centaurus A** is a huge radio galaxy (600 kiloparsecs across) and one of the nearest (4 megaparsecs away). It is a strong source of X-rays and infrared radiation, and is thought to include a supermassive black hole in its nucleus. It has been extensively studied at S-hemisphere observatories. » Alpha Centauri; black hole; constellation; galaxy; parsec

Centigrade temperature » **Celsius temperature**

centimetre » **metre** (physics)

centipede A carnivorous, terrestrial arthropod, commonly found in soil, leaf litter, and rotting wood; body up to 300 mm/12 in long, divided into head (bearing feelers and mouthparts) and many-segmented trunk; each trunk segment has one pair of legs; c.2 500 species, some venomous. (Class: *Chilopoda*.) » arthropod

CENTO » **Central Treaty Organization**

Central (Scotland) pop (1981) 273 391; area 2 631 sq km/1 016 sq ml. Region in C Scotland, divided into three districts; N part in the Highlands, including the Trossachs (W); S part encloses the Forth river valley; drained by the Forth, Carron, and Devon

□ international airport

Rivers; contains several lochs, including Katrine, Lubnaig, Venachar (W) and part of Earn (NE); capital, Stirling; major towns include Falkirk, Alloa, Grangemouth (all in SE, region's industrial area); brewing and distilling, engineering, agriculture; Stirling castle, Loch Lomond, Bannockburn battle site. » Scotland [i]; Stirling

Central African Republic, Fr **République Centrafricaine** pop (1990e) 2 875 000; area 626 780 sq km/241 937 sq ml. Republic in C Africa, divided into 15 prefectures; bounded N by Chad, NE by Sudan, S by Zaire and Congo, and W by Cameroon; capital, Bangui; other chief towns, Berbérati, Bouar, Bossangoa; timezone GMT +1; c.80 ethnic groups, including Baya (34%), Banda (28%), and Sara (10%); religion, mainly Christianity (50%), with local and Muslim beliefs; official language, French, with Sangho widely spoken; unit of currency, the franc CFA; on plateau forming watershed between Chad and Congo river basins; mean elevation, 600 m/2 000 ft; most N rivers drain towards L Chad, S rivers towards R Ubangi; highest ground in the NE (Massif des Bongos) and NW; single rainy season in N (May–Sep), average annual rainfall 875–1 000 mm/35–40 in; more equatorial climate in S, rainfall 1 500–2 000 mm/60–80 in; part of French Equatorial Africa (Ubangi Shari); autonomous republic within the French community, 1958; independence, 1960; 1965 coup led to 1976 monarchy known as Central African Empire, under Bokassa I; Bokassa forced to flee, 1979 (returned in 1986 for trial; found guilty, 1987); military coup established 23-member committee for National Recovery, 1981; 52-member National Assembly established, 1987; c.85% of working population engaged in subsistence agriculture, growing cassava, groundnuts, cotton, maize, coffee, millet, sorghum, tobacco, rice, sesame seed, plantain, bananas, yams; timber, diamonds, uranium; sawmilling, brewing, diamond splitting, leather and tobacco processing. » Bangui; Bokassa; RR24 national holidays; RR45 political leaders

Central America A geographical region that encompasses the independent states to the S of Mexico and to the N of S America; includes Guatemala, El Salvador, Belize, Honduras, Nicaragua, Costa Rica, and Panama; the area gained independence from Spain in 1821. » Central American Common Market/Federation; Middle America

Central American Common Market (CACM) An economic association initiated in 1960 between Guatemala, Honduras, El Salvador, Nicaragua, and (from 1963) Costa Rica. Its early apparent success was offset by growing political crisis in the late 1970s. » European Economic Community

Central American Federation A federation formed in 1823, following independence from Spain, by Costa Rica, Nicaragua, Honduras, El Salvador, and Guatemala. Despite vigorous leadership by Francisco Morazán (1792–1842) of Honduras, internal tensions brought about the collapse of the federation by 1838. » federation

Central Committee Under Soviet party rules, the highest decision-making authority in the former USSR, apart from Congress, which elected it. Except in rare circumstances, however, it exercised little influence, partly because of its unwieldy size and partly because of the concentration of power in the Politburo. » Politburo

Central Criminal Court » **Old Bailey**

Central Intelligence Agency (CIA) The official US intelligence analysis organization responsible for external security, established under the National Security Act (1947). Often involved in subversive activities, and suspected of internal subversive activities from time to time, it suffered a loss of credibility following the investigation into the Watergate affair in the mid-1970s. » Watergate

central nervous system (CNS) A collection of nerve cells connected in an intricate and complex manner, involved in the control of movement and the analysis of sensation, and in humans also subserving the higher-order functions of thought, language, and emotion. In vertebrates it consists of the brain and spinal cord, being isolated from the rest of the body within the skull and vertebral column, and enclosed within the meninges. » ataxia; brain [i]; nervous system; neurone [i]; Parkinson's disease; spinal cord

Central Powers Initially, the members of the Triple Alliance (Germany, Austria-Hungary, Italy) created by Bismarck in 1882. As Italy remained neutral in 1914, the term was later used to describe Germany, Austria-Hungary, their ally Turkey, and later Bulgaria in World War 1. » Bismarck; World War 1

central processing unit (CPU) The section of a digital computer which controls and co-ordinates all the main functions of the computer; also referred to as the **processor**. The CPU contains an arithmetic and logic unit which performs the arithmetic and logical functions on data. A microprocessor is an entire CPU in the form of a single integrated circuit. » digital computer

Central Treaty Organization (CENTO) A political-military alliance signed in 1955 between Iran (which withdrew after the fall of the Shah), Turkey, Pakistan, Iraq (which withdrew in 1958), and the UK, as a defence against the Soviet Union.

Central Valley or **Great Central Valley** Valley in California, USA, between the Sierra Nevada (E) and the Coast Range (W); the Sacramento and San Joaquin Rivers feed the Central Valley Project, a series of dams and reservoirs for flood-control, irrigation and hydroelectricity. » California

centre, the The centre ground in political opinion and action which avoids the extremism and idealism of right and left, and advocates compromise solutions to societal problems. It is often characterized by pragmatic responses – more concerned with 'getting things done' than with 'fruitless' searching for the means of achieving ideal objectives. » consensus politics; left wing; right wing

Centre 42 A plan for a performing arts centre supported by trade-union money, as agreed at the 1960 Trades Union Congress. The Round House, London, was acquired with this aim, but the original plan for free performances never materialized. » trade union

Centre Beaubourg [sãtruh **boh**boorg] The popular name for the Centre National d'Art et de Culture, or **Pompidou Centre**, situated on the Plateau Beaubourg in Paris. Designed by Renzo Piano and Richard Rogers, and opened in 1977, the 6-storey building houses a modern art gallery and a centre for industrial design. Display space has been maximized by placing all services – conduits, elevators, etc – on the outside of the transparent exterior walls. » Paris; Pompidou

centre of gravity In mechanics, the point in some object upon which the action of gravity is equivalent to the sum of the action of gravity on the object's component parts. The centre of gravity of the object is identical to its centre of mass. » centre of mass; gravitation; mechanics

centre of mass In mechanics, a point whose motion represents that of an entire object or group of objects. The product of the velocity of this point with the total mass of the system equals the sum of the momentum contributions of the individual parts. For example, the centre of mass of the fragments of an exploding bomb is the position that the bomb would have had if it had not exploded. Should a force act on the system, the centre of mass undergoes an acceleration as though the entire mass were concentrated at that point. » centre of gravity; mass; mechanics; velocity

centrifuge A device for separating the components of a mixture (solid-in-liquid or liquid-in-liquid) by applying rapid rotation and consequent centrifugal force. It may be equipped for the technical separation of materials (eg cream) or for scientific observation (eg the *ultracentrifuge*, which separates particles of macro-molecular size). » particle physics

centripetal force An inward-directed radial force required to keep an object on a circular path; gravity, for example, provides a centripetal force, causing the Moon to orbit the Earth. The term *centrifugal force*, denoting an outward-acting force, is common in everyday use, but is best avoided. It is a fictitious force; such a force balancing the centripetal force is applicable only to rotating observers, for whom the object appears at rest. » Coriolis force [i]

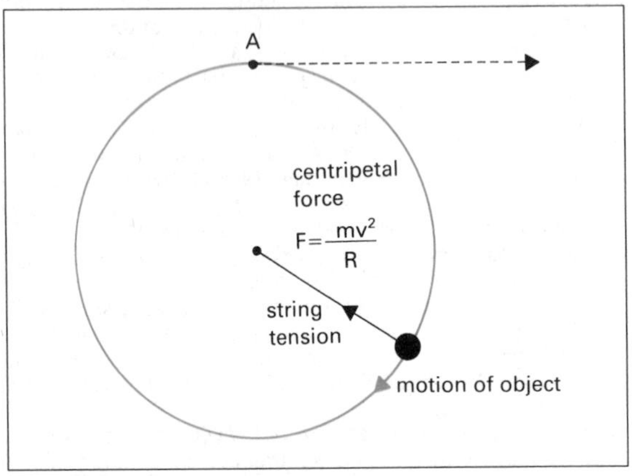

An object on which no forces act is motionless or continues to move at constant velocity in a straight line. A circular path, as described by an object twirled on a string, means that a force must be acting toward the circle's centre. For an object twirled on a string this force is provided by string tension; should the string snap at point A the object will continue on the straight line path shown as dotted line.

centrography In geography, the study of descriptive statistics for the determination and mapping of measures of central tendency. For example, the mean centre of population distribution can be mapped to show the main focus of a country's population distribution. » statistics

centromere The point on a chromosome, usually a constriction, by which it is attached to the spindle during the division of the cell nucleus. It orchestrates the division of the chromosome into its two daughter chromosomes. » cell; chromosome [i]

centuary An annual, sometimes perennial, found almost everywhere; opposite entire leaves; flowers pink, tubular with 4–5 spreading lobes, borne in dense heads. (Genus: *Centaurium*, c.50 species. Family: *Gentianaceae*.) » annual; perennial

century The smallest unit in a Roman legion. Probably consisting originally of 100, under the Empire there were 80 soldiers in a century. » legion

century plant A species of agave, so-called from the length of time thought to pass between germination and flowering – up to 100 years. In Mexico the great flow of sap during the final burst of flowering – up to 1 000 litres per plant – is collected, and is one of the sources of the national drink, pulque, as well as a spirit, mescal. (*Agave americana*. Family: *Agavaceae*.) » agave

ceorl [**chay**awl] An ordinary freeman of Anglo-Saxon England, who normally held between one and five hides of land. By the 10th-c, wealthy ceorls could become thegns; but after the Norman Conquest many ceorls lost personal freedom. The Middle English derivative *churl* has the sense of serf or ill-bred person. » serfdom; thegn; villein

cephalic index A skull's breadth as a percentage of its length. Skulls of different relative breadths are termed *brachycephalic* (broad), *mesaticephalic* (intermediate), and *dolichocephalic* (long). » skull

Cephalonia [kefa**loh**nia], Gr **Kefallinía** pop (1981) 27 649; area 781 sq km/301 sq ml. Largest of the Ionian Is, Greece, in the Ionian Sea, off the W coast of Greece; length 48 km/30 ml; hilly island, rising to 1 628 m/5 341 ft; capital, Argostolion; devastated by earthquakes in 1953; olives, grapes. » Ionian Islands

Cephalopoda [sefa**lo**puhda] A class of carnivorous, marine molluscs characterized by the specialization of the head-foot into a ring of tentacles, typically armed with hooks or suckers, and by their method of swimming using jets of water squirted out of a funnel; mouth typically with a powerful beak; eyes usually well developed; includes octopus, squid, cuttlefish, and nautilus, as well as large fossil groups such as ammonites and belemnites. » cuttlefish; fossil; mollusc; nautilus; octopus; squid

Cephas [**see**fas] » **Peter, St**

Cepheid variable [**see**feeid] A class of variable star with a period of 1–50 days, characterized by precise regularity. There is a precise correlation between the period and luminosity (the longer the period, the more luminous the star). The observed period of a Cepheid indicates its distance from Earth, and is consequently of great importance in determining the distance scale of the universe. » Cepheus; pulsating star; variable star; universe

Cepheus [**see**fiuhs] A N constellation which inclues the famous star **delta Cephei**, the prototype of regular variables used for calibrating the distance scale of the universe. » Cepheid variable; constellation; universe; RR8

ceramics The products of the baking of clay, giving hard, strong, non-conducting, brittle, heat-resistant substances. They are useful for technical purposes (eg abrasives, cutting tools, refractory linings) and for decoration. The initial value of clay arises from its plasticity, so that ceramics can be made in an unlimited variety of forms, by moulding, casting, spinning, or pressing. Clays of many kinds are used, from the coarse clay used for bricks to the fine white clay used for porcelain. Ceramics may be made in stages, such as the many ways of producing a *glaze*, a coating of a second clay or glass-like substance, which confers impermeability (as in making pipes) or decorative colours. » crystals; decorative arts; ferrites; glaze; porcelain; synroc

Cerberus [**ser**berus] In Greek mythology, the dog which guards the entrance to the Underworld, originally fifty-headed, later with three heads. Any living souls visiting Hell gave 'a sop to Cerberus', ie a honey-cake, to quieten him. Heracles carried him off as one of his labours. » Hades; Heracles

cereals Grain-bearing grasses which provide staple foods for most of the world's population. The grains are much larger than those of other grass species, including wild cereal ancestors, and are rich in protein and carbohydrates. There are eight major cereals: rice, wheat, oats, barley, rye, sorghums, millets, and maize. A number of minor types grow where conditions will not support major crops, and these assume local importance, especially in the Third World. All cereals derive from wild species, and their domestication in early times (c.8000 BC in the case of wheat and barley) marks a turning point in human history. The replacement of *ramassage* (the gathering of wild grains) by a more dependable crop allowed the development of a more settled lifestyle, and all of the great early civilizations were based on the cultivation of one or more major cereals. With domestication came selection for desirable characteristics, such as larger grains. The development of modern cereals is very sophisticated, with strains tailored for specific purposes and conditions, such as rapid ripening for areas with short growing seasons, or high disease-resistance. (Family: *Gramineae*.) » barley; buckwheat; carbohydrate; grass [i]; inflorescence [i]; maize; millet; oats; protein; rice; rye; sorghum; wheat

cerebellum [seruh**bel**uhm] A mass of neural tissue that occupies

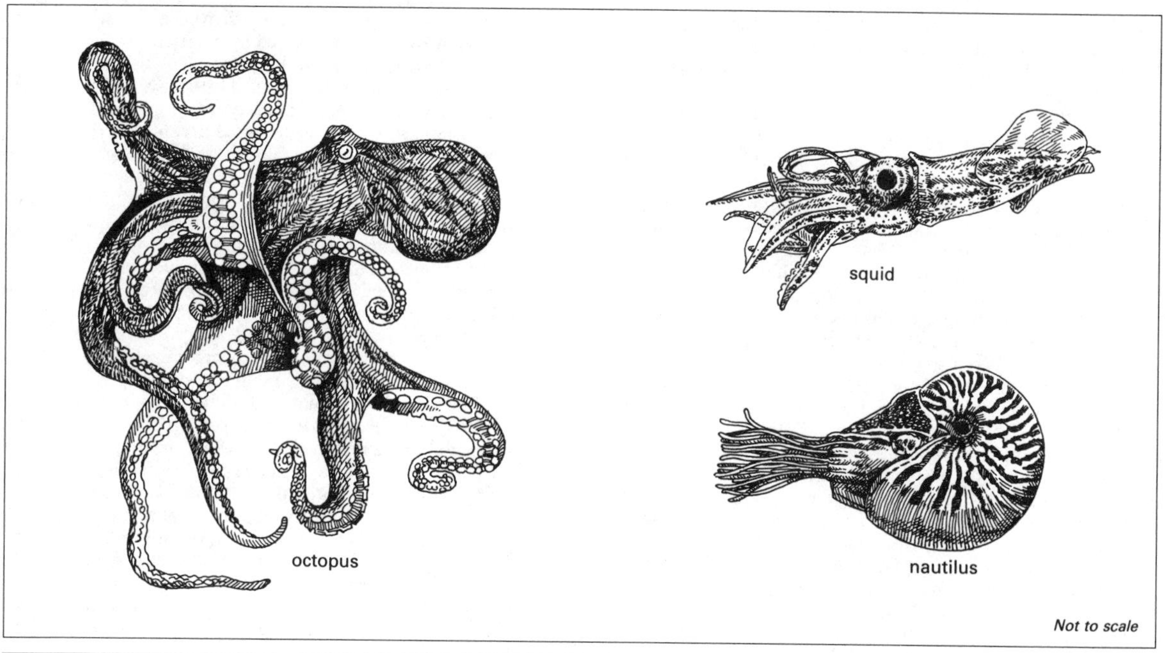

Cephalopoda

the lower back part of the cranial cavity within the skull, consisting of two hemispheres united in the midline by the *vermis*. It is connected to the brainstem by three pairs of structures called *peduncles*, and forms part of the wall of the fourth ventricle. Its principal function is the control of posture, repetitive movements, and the geometric accuracy of voluntary movements; it also appears to have an important role in learning. Damage to the cerebellum in both animals and humans results in *ataxia* (inco-ordination of movement). » brain [i]; brainstem; ventricles

cerebral haemorrhage/hemorrhage An episode of acute bleeding within the substance of the brain. It tends to occur when the blood pressure is high, or when the wall of the cerebral blood vessel is weakened by degenerative change (eg atheroma) or is the site of a localized distension (*aneurysm*). The neurological disability that follows depends on the severity of the haemorrhage and the site of the bleeding. » brain [i]; stroke

cerebral palsy A non-progressive disorder of the brain occurring in infancy or early childhood which causes weakness, paralysis, and inco-ordination of movement; the muscular spasms involved have led to the use of the term **spastic** for these children. A high proportion of infants also suffer from epilepsy and are retarded mentally. Several types of brain injury are responsible, including injury to the brain during birth, maternal diseases, and virus infections, but the cause is unknown in many cases. » brain [i]; epilepsy

cerebrospinal fluid (CSF) A clear, colourless, protein-free fluid circulating through the cerebral ventricles of the brain, the central canal of the spinal cord, and the sub-arachnoid space in vertebrates, which provides the brain with mechanical support and nutrients. In humans, CSF is sometimes collected (by *lumbar puncture*) and analysed for diagnostic purposes: an excess of CSF around the brain in the foetus and young child (through overproduction or blockage within the circulating system) leads to hydrocephalus, unless it is drained off. » brain [i]; hydrocephalus; lumbar puncture; spinal cord; ventricles

cerebrum [**ser**ibruhm] A large mass of neural and supporting tissue which occupies most of the cranial cavity within the skull. It is separated into right and left halves (the right and left **cerebral hemispheres**), connected by a body of nerve fibres known as the *corpus callosum*. Each hemisphere can be divided into four *lobes* which are named according to the skull bone that they are most closely related to (ie *frontal*, *parietal*, *temporal*, and *occipital*). The surface of each hemisphere is formed by a layer of *grey matter* known as the *cerebral cortex*, containing the cell bodies of the neurones responsible for the functions of the cerebrum. Within the cortex the hemispheres are formed by a large mass of *white matter* consisting largely of the axons of the neurones in the cerebral cortex.

The surface of the cerebrum is thrown into a series of folds (*gyri*) separated by troughs (*sulci*): the *lateral sulcus* separates the temporal lobe from the frontal and parietal lobes; the *central sulcus* separates the frontal and parietal lobes; and the *parieto-occipital sulcus* separates the parietal and occipital lobes. Immediately in front of the central sulcus is the *motor cortex*, in which the opposite half of the body is represented upside down: the face lies lowest, then the hand (a very large area), then the arm, trunk, and leg. Stimulation here results in contraction of the appropriate voluntary muscles on the opposite side of the body. Below the area of the brain representing the face, on the left side, lies the speech area (*Broca's area*). Immediately behind the central sulcus is the *sensory cortex*, which receives sensory information from the opposite side of the body via the brainstem and thalamus.

The occipital lobe is involved with vision. The parietal lobe is in general responsible for sensory functions such as the perception of touch, pressure, and body position, as well as three-dimensional perception, the analysis of visual images, language, geometry, and calculations. The frontal lobe subserves motor functions, and also governs the expression of the intellect and personality. The upper part of the temporal lobe is involved in the perception of sound, with the remainder being concerned with memory and various emotional functions. » brain [i]; neurone [i]; neurophysiology

Čerenkov radiation [che**ren**kof] Electromagnetic radiation produced by charged particles passing through some material at a velocity greater than the velocity of light in that material; discovered in 1930 by Soviet physicist Pavel Čerenkov (1904–). It is a type of electromagnetic shock wave, analogous to a sonic boom, and is used to measure particle velocities in particle physics experiments. » electromagnetic radiation [i]; particle physics; velocity

Ceres (astronomy) [**seer**eez] The first asteroid to be found, discovered on the first night of the 19th-c. Much the largest asteroid, its diameter is 1 000 km (one-quarter of the Moon's).

Ceres (mythology) [**seer**eez] The ancient Italian corn-goddess, an early cult at Rome, taking over characteristics and stories associated with Demeter. » Demeter; Persephone

CERN » **Organisation Européene pour la Recherche Nucléaire**

certificate of deposit A certificate representing a fixed-term, interest-bearing deposit in large denominations, which can be bought and sold. First introduced by Citibank in New York in 1961, sterling certificates were introduced in 1968. » interest

Cervantes (Saavedra), Miguel de [thervantays] (1547–1616) Spanish author of *Don Quixote*, born at Alcalá de Henares. His first major work was the *Galatea*, a pastoral romance (1585), and he wrote many plays, only two of which have survived. In 1594 he became a tax collector in Granada; but was imprisoned for failing to make up the sum due to the treasury. Tradition maintains that he wrote *Don Quixote* in prison at Argamasilla in La Mancha. When the book came out (1605), it was hugely popular. He wrote the second part in 1615, after several years writing plays and short novels. He died in Madrid. » Spanish literature

cervical cancer A malignant tumour arising from the lining of the cervical canal. It occurs at all ages, but young women are being increasingly affected, and it is second only to breast cancer as a cause of death from tumours in women. Its occurrence is related to frequent sexual intercourse with several partners, which has led to the view that it is possibly due to a virus, perhaps related to the genital herpes virus. Treatment is effective if diagnosis (by the Papincolaou or 'smear' test) is made early. » cancer; cervix; herpes simplex; virus

cervix The lower tapering third of the uterus (womb). Its lower, blunt part projects into the vagina; its upper part communicates with the body of the uterus through a slight constriction (the *isthmus*). The vaginal part is firm in the non-pregnant uterus, and relatively soft in the pregnant uterus. A small opening at the lower end of the cervix allows communication between the uterine cavity and the vagina. » cervical cancer; gynaecology; uterus [i]; vagina

Césaire, Aimé [sayzair] (1913–) West Indian poet, novelist, and politician, born in Martinique, and educated there and in Paris. The influential *Cahier d'un retour au pays natal* (1947, Notebook of a Return to my Native Land) records his conscious adoption of an African identity. This theme is returned to in later poems and plays, such as *Une saison au Congo* (1967, A Season in the Congo), and an African version of Shakespeare's *The Tempest* (1969). He has represented the progressive element in the politics of Martinique since 1945. » Caribbean literature

cesarian section » **caesarian section**

Cestoda [sestuhda] » **tapeworm**

Cetacea [seetayshia] » **whale** [i]

cetane number An index defining the ignition quality of fuel for diesel internal combustion engines. The number is the cetane percentage in a mixture of cetane and alpha-methyl napthalene, adjusted to match the characteristics of the fuel under test. » naphthalene [i]; octane number

Cetewayo or **Cetshwayo** (c.1826–84) Ruler of Zululand from 1873, born near Eshowe, Zululand. In 1879 he defeated the British at Isandhlwana, but was himself defeated at Ulundi. He presented his case in London, and in 1883 was restored to part of his kingdom, but soon after was driven out by his subjects, and died at Ekowe. » Zulu

Cetus [seetuhs] ('whale') The fourth largest constellation, lying above the Equator, but inconspicuous because it has few bright stars. » constellation; Mira Ceti Mira; RR8

Ceuta [thayoota] 35°52N 5°18W, pop(1981) 65 264. Freeport and military station, at E end of the Strait of Gibraltar, on the N African coast of Morocco; administered by Cádiz province, Spain; car ferries to Algeciras; became Spanish in 1580; trade in tobacco, oil products; old fortress at Monte Hacho, cathedral (15th-c), Church of Our Lady of Africa (18th-c). » Spain [i]

Cévennes [sayven], ancient **Cebenna** Chief mountain range in the S of France, on the SE edge of the Massif Central; general direction NE–SW; highest peak, Mt Mézenc (1 754 m/5 754 ft); varied landscape, including forest, barren grassland, and deep gorges, such as Gorges du Tarn near Les Vignes. » France [i]

Cézanne, Paul [sayzan] (1839–1906) French Postimpressionist painter, born and died at Aix-en-Provence. He studied law at Aix, then in 1862 was persuaded by his friend Emile Zola to go to Paris, where he began to paint. He was influenced by Pissarro, with whom he worked at Auvers and Pontoise (1872–3). He abandoned his early sombre expressionism for the study of nature, and began to use his characteristic glowing colours. In his later period (after 1886), he emphasized the underlying forms of nature – 'the cylinder, the sphere, the cone' – by constructing his pictures from a rhythmic series of coloured planes, thus becoming the forerunner of Cubism. He obtained recognition only in the last years of his life. Among his best-known paintings are 'L'Estaque' (c.1888, Louvre), 'The Card Players' (1890–2, Louvre), and 'The Gardener' (1906, Tate, London). » Cubism; French art; Pissarro; Post-impressionism; Zola

CFCs The acronym for **chlorofluorocarbons**, also called **Freons**; derivatives of methane and ethane containing both chlorine and fluorine. Important examples are CCl_2F_2 and $CClF_2$–$CClF_2$. They are inert, volatile compounds, used as refrigerants and aerosol sprays. Their decomposition in the atmosphere is thought to damage the Earth's ozone layer. » chlorine; ethane [i]; fluorine; methane [i]; ozone layer

Chabrier, (Alexis) Emmanuel [shabreeyay] (1841–94) French composer, born at Ambert. He studied law in Paris, and devoted himself to music in 1879 after hearing Wagner's *Tristan und Isolde*. He wrote operas, piano works, and songs, but his best-known pieces were inspired by the folk music of Spain, notably his orchestral rhapsody *España* (1883). He died in Paris.

Chabrol, Claude (1930–) French film critic and director, born in Paris. He financed his own first production *Le Beau Serge* (1958, Handsome Serge), and with *Les Cousins* (1959) became identified with the French Nouvelle Vague, a style which had become more publicly acceptable when he produced *Les Biches* (1968, The Does). His most widely-known films are dramas of abnormality in the provincial bourgeoisie, notably *Le Boucher* (1970, The Butcher), *Les Noces rouges* (1973, Red Wedding), and *Inspector Lavardin* (1986). » Nouvelle Vague

chacma baboon A baboon native to S Africa; large but slender body; dark brown with dark face; inhabits grassland and rocky regions; troops contain up to 100 individuals. (*Papio ursinus*.) » baboon

Chaco Canyon A remote desert canyon in New Mexico, 160 km/100 ml NW of Albuquerque, the hub in AD c.950–1300 of the Anasazi Indian culture of the American SW; now a world heritage site. A National Monument since 1907, its 650 km/400 ml road network links c.125 D-shaped pueblos or planned villages. The best-known is Pueblo Bonito, a compact five-storey settlement covering 1 ha/2.5 acres, with c.600 rooms housing 1 000 people. » Anasazi; Pueblo

Chaco War (1932–5) A territorial struggle between Bolivia and Paraguay in the disputed Northern Chaco area. Owing to the brilliant tactics of Col José Félix Estigarribia (1888–1940), Paraguay won most of the area, and a peace treaty was signed in 1938. Around 50 000 Bolivians and 35 000 Paraguayans died in the war. » Bolivia [i]; Gran Chaco; Paraguay [i]

chaconne A dance of Latin American origin. The harmonies and basses traditionally associated with it were widely used as material for arias and instrument variations in the 17th–18th-c. » aria; passacaglia

Chad, Fr **Tchad**, official name **Republic of Chad**, Fr **République du Tchad** pop (1990e) 5 678 000; area 1 284 640 sq km/495 871 sq ml. Republic in NC Africa, divided into 14 prefectures; bounded N by Libya, E by Sudan, S by Central African Republic, and W by Cameroon, Niger, and Nigeria; capital, N'Djamena; chief towns include Moundou, Sarh, and Abéché; timezone GMT +1; c.200 ethnic groups; official language, French, with many local languages also spoken; chief religion, Muslim (over half), with local religions and Christianity; unit of currency, the franc CFA; landlocked and mostly arid, semi-desert plateau at edge of Sahara Desert; average altitude of 200–500 m/650–1 650 ft; Logone and Chari Rivers drain into L Chad (SW); isolated massifs along Sudan frontier rise to 1 500 m/4 921 ft; Tibesti Mts (N) rise to 3415 m/11 204 ft at Emi Koussi; vegetation generally desert scrub or steppe; most

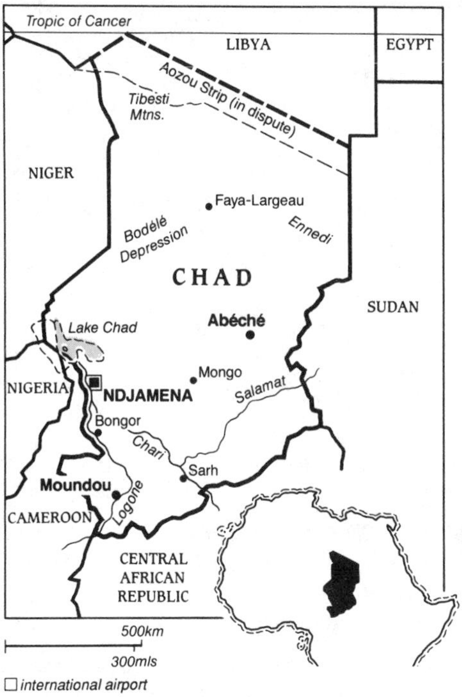

people live in tropical S; moderately wet in S (May–Oct), but dry in rest of year; N'Djamena, average annual rainfall 744 mm/29 in; hot and arid N almost rainless; C plain hot and dry, with brief rainy season (Jun–Sep); part of French Equatorial Africa in 19th-c; colonial status, 1920; independence, 1960; governed by a president with a 20-member Council of Ministers; rebel forces took capital, forming new government, 1982; fighting continued between Libyan-supported rebels and French-supported government until cease-fire agreed in 1987; new constitution established a National Assembly of 123 elected members, 1989; economy severely damaged in recent years by drought, locusts, and civil war; export of cotton, kaolin, animal products; agriculture mainly cassava, groundnuts, millet, sorghum, rice, yams, sweet potatoes, dates; livestock, fishing; oil exploration, with refining facilities; uranium, gold, bauxite in N; salt mined around L Chad. » Chad, Lake; N'Djamena; Tibesti Mountains; RR25 national holidays; RR45 political leaders

Chad, Lake, Fr **Tchad** Shallow freshwater lake in NC Africa at meeting point of Chad, Nigeria, Cameroon, and Niger; remnant of former inland sea; area 10 400 sq km/4 000 sq ml (low water), 20 700 sq km/8 000 sq ml (high water); no visible outlets; chain of inhabited islands along E coast; fishing, mineral extraction (natron); first reached by Europeans in 1823; Douguia Wildlife Reserve nearby; oil discovered nearby in Niger. » Chad [i]; Chari, River

Chadic A group of 100 languages, spoken by over 25 million people in parts of Ghana and the Central African Republic. It is assigned to the Afro-Asiatic family, though its position there is unclear. » Afro-Asiatic languages; Hausa

Chadwick, Sir James (1891–1974) British physicist, born in Manchester. He studied at Manchester, Berlin, and Cambridge, worked on radioactivity, and discovered the neutron, for which he received the Nobel Prize for Physics in 1935. He led the UK's work on the atomic bomb in World War 2. Knighted in 1945, he died in Cambridge. » atomic bomb; neutron

Chadwick, Lynn (1914–) British sculptor, born in London. He studied architecture, but after war service (c.1946) he began making mobiles, then rough-finished solid metal sculptures. In 1956 he won the International Sculpture Prize at the Venice Biennale. » Biennale; mobile

Chaetognatha [kee**tog**natha] » **arrow worm**

chafer A large, nocturnal beetle; adults feed on leaves; larvae fleshy, C-shaped, burrow in soil eating roots, often taking 3–4 years to develop. Chafers are diverse, and some are pests. The family includes the cockchafer. (Order: *Coleoptera*. Family: *Scarabaeidae*.) » beetle; cockchafer; larva

chaffinch Either of two species of bird, genus *Fringilla*. *Fringilla coelebs* is native to Europe, N Africa, the Azores, and SW Asia; inhabits forest and human habitation; colour varies over range; N populations move S for winter. The **blue chaffinch** (*Fringilla teydea*) is from the Canary Is. (Family: *Fringillidae*.) » finch

Chagall, Marc [sha**gal**] (1889–1985) Russian artist, born at Vitebsk. He studied at St Petersburg and Paris, left Russia in 1922, and settled near Paris. During World War 2 he moved to the USA, where he began to design ballet sets and costumes. He illustrated several books, but is best known for his fanciful painting of animals, objects, and people from his life, dreams and Russian folklore.The word 'Surrealist' is said to have been coined by Apollinaire to describe the work of Chagall. He died at St-Paul, France. » Russian art; Surrealism

Chaikin, Joseph [**chiy**kin] (1935–) US actor and theatre director, born in New York City. His early work as an actor was with the Living Theater, notably in *The Connection* (1960) and *Man is Man* (1962). In 1963 he founded The Open Theater, which for a decade produced some of the most original work in the US theatre, such as *America Hurrah* (1965), *Terminal* (1969), and *Nightwalk* (1973). » Living Theater; Open Theater; theatre

Chain, Sir Ernst Boris (1906–79) Anglo-Russian biochemist, born in Berlin. Educated at Berlin, he fled to Britain in 1933, where he worked at Cambridge and Oxford. He shared the Nobel Prize for Physiology or Medicine in 1945 for the development of penicillin, and also worked on snake venoms and insulin. He later held posts in Rome (1948–61) and London (1961–73). He was knighted in 1970, and died in Ireland. » insulin; penicillin

chain reaction A nuclear reaction in which nuclear fission induced by a neutron releases further neutrons that in turn may cause further fission through some material. For a large enough block of material, enough neutrons will undergo collisions, rather than escaping from the material, to sustain the reaction. Nuclear power and atomic bombs rely on chain reactions in uranium or plutonium. » atomic bomb; critical mass; neutron; nuclear fission

Chalcedon, Council of [kal**see**duhn] (451) A Council of the Church which agreed that Jesus Christ is truly God and truly man, two natures in one person (the 'Chalcedonian definition'). The definition is generally accepted by the Churches, though from the beginning there was uneasiness about its interpretation, and recently it has come under sustained criticism. » Christianity; Christology; Council of the Church

chalcedony [kal**sed**onee] A group name for the compact varieties of mineral silica (SiO_2) composed of very fine-grained crystals of quartz. It occurs in massive form with a wax-like lustre, often filling cavities in volcanic rocks. Banded varieties are agate and onyx, and coloured varieties include carnelian, jasper, bloodstone, and chrysoprase. » agate; gemstones; quartz; silica

Chalcis [**kal**sis], Gr **Khalkis**, ancient **Evripos** 38°27N 23°42E, pop (1981) 44 867. Capital of Euboea, Greece; railway; local ferries; commerce, tourism; Aristotle died here. » Aristotle; Euboea

Chalcolithic » **Three Age System**

chalcopyrite A copper iron sulphide mineral ($CuFeS_2$) found in veins associated with igneous rocks; brass-coloured and metallic. It is the main ore of copper.

Chaldaeans [kal**dee**anz] **1** Originally the name of a Semitic people (Kaldu) from Arabia who settled in the region of Ur in Lower Mesopotamia. **2** In the 7th-c and 6th-c BC, a generic term for Babylonians. **3** In Roman times, practitioners of the Babylonian science of astrology. » Babylonia; Semites; Ur

chalk A fine-grained limestone rock, mainly of calcite, formed from the shells of minute marine organisms. Often pure white in colour, it is characteristically seen in rocks of the Upper Cretaceous period of W Europe, its most famous exposures being on either side of the English Channel. Blackboard chalk is calcium sulphate. » calcite; Cretaceous period; limestone

Challoner, Richard (1691–1781) English Roman Catholic churchman and author, born at Lewes, Sussex. He studied at Douai (1704) and was ordained in 1716, remaining there as a professor until 1730. He then served as a missionary priest in London, becoming Bishop of Debra (1741) and Vicar Apostolic of the London district (1758). His best-known works are the prayer book, *The Garden of the Soul* (1740), and his revision of the Douai version of the Bible (5 vols, 1750). He died in London. » Douai Bible; missions, Christian

Chalmers, Thomas (1780–1847) British theologian and reformer, born at Anstruther, Scotland. Educated at St Andrews, he was ordained in 1803, and became a minister in Glasgow (1815), where his magnificent oratory took the city by storm. He became professor of moral philosophy at St Andrews (1823), and of theology at Edinburgh (1827). In the Disruption of 1843 he led 470 ministers out of the Established Church of Scotland to found the Free Church of Scotland. He died in Edinburgh. » Church of Scotland; Reformation; theology

chalone [**ka**lohn] A small to medium-sized protein that inhibits mitosis in cells when adrenalin is present. When injury occurs, the loss of chalones from damaged cells stimulates and directs wound healing. » adrenalin; mitosis; protein

Chamaeleon [ka**mee**liuhn] A faint S constellation, designated in 1603. » constellation; RR8

chamber music Music for two or more players intended for performance in a room rather than a concert hall, with only one player to a part. The term is a translation of the Italian 'musica da camera' and, by convention, applies only to instrumental music, and therefore mainly to music since c.1600. Until c.1750 the main type of chamber music was the trio sonata (typically for two violins and continuo). Since then the string quartet has been looked upon as the chamber ensemble *par excellence*, but any wind, string, or keyboard instrument might participate in chamber music. » sonata; string quartet; trio

chamber of commerce An association of business enterprises in a district, whose aims are to promote the area and its members' businesses. The Chambers of Commerce of the USA (established 1912) represent, through member organizations, some 5 million business firms and individuals. The International Chamber of Commerce (ICC), based in Paris, was set up in 1920, and has the affiliation of over 40 national institutions.

chamber opera Opera which employs a small cast and (especially) a small orchestra. Many 18th-c operas and intermezzos fit this description, but the term is applied particularly to 20th-c works such as Britten's *The Turn of the Screw*. » Britten; opera

chambered tomb In European prehistory, megalithic monuments usually constructed of uprights (*orthostats*) and capstones beneath a cairn or mound of earth, the burial chamber sometimes being provided with a corbelled vault; also known as a **dolmen**. Originating in the Neolithic period, they were often used for collective burial over generations. » corbelling; Maes Howe; megalith; Neolithic; New Grange

Chamberlain, Lord In the UK, the chief official of the royal household, overseeing all aspects of its management, and bearing responsibility for matters ranging from the care of works of art to the appointment of royal tradesmen. The office should be distinguished from the **Lord Great Chamberlain**, whose duties are largely ceremonial; in particular, at coronations, he presents the sovereign to the people.

Chamberlain, Sir (Joseph) Austen (1863–1937) British Conservative statesman, eldest son of Joseph Chamberlain, born in Birmingham. Educated at Cambridge, he was elected a Liberal Unionist MP in 1892, and sat as a Conservative MP until his death in 1937. He was Chancellor of the Exchequer (1903–6, 1919–21), Secretary for India (1915–17), Unionist leader (1921–2), Foreign Secretary (1924–9), and First Lord of the Admiralty (1931). He received the 1925 Nobel Peace Prize for negotiating the Locarno Pact. He died in London. » Conservative Party; Locarno Pact

Chamberlain, Joseph (1836–1914) British statesman, born and died in London. He entered the family business at 16, and became Mayor of Birmingham (1873–5), and a Liberal MP (1876). In 1880 he became President of the Board of Trade, but in 1886 resigned over Gladstone's Home Rule Bill, which split the Liberal Party. From 1889 he was leader of the Liberal Unionists, and in the Coalition Government of 1895 took office as Secretary for the Colonies. In 1903 he resigned office to be free to advocate his ideas on tariff reform, and in 1906 withdrew from public life after a stroke. » Chamberlain, Austen/Neville; Gladstone; Liberal Party (UK); radicalism

Chamberlain (Arthur) Neville (1869–1940) British statesman and Conservative Prime Minister (1937–40), born in Birmingham, the son of Joseph Chamberlain by his second marriage. Educated at Rugby and Birmingham, he was Mayor of Birmingham (1915–16), an MP from 1918, Chancellor of the Exchequer (1923–4, 1931–7), and three times Minister for Health (1923, 1924–9, 1931). He played a leading part in the formation of the National Government (1931). As Prime Minister, he advocated 'appeasement' of Italy and Germany, returning from Munich with his claim to have found 'peace in our time' (1938). Criticism of his war leadership and initial military reverses led to his resignation as Prime Minister (1940), and his appointment as Lord President of the Council. He died soon after at Heckfield, Hampshire. » Chamberlain, Joseph; Conservative Party; World War 2

Chamberlain, Wilt, properly **Wilton Norman**, byname **Wilt the Stilt** (1936–) US basketball player, born in Philadelphia. A graduate from Kansas University, height 7 ft 1 in/1.85 m, he played for the Philadelphia 76ers against the New York Knickerbockers in March 1962, and scored 100 points in a game, the only man to do so in a major league game in the USA. He scored a record 4029 points that season, and was seven times the National Basketball Association leading scorer (1960–6). During his career (1960–73) he scored 31419 points at an average of 30.1 per game. He had a brief spell playing for the Harlem Globetrotters. » basketball

Chambers, Ephraim (c.1680–1740) British encyclopedist, born at Kendal, Westmoreland. While apprentice to a globemaker in London, he conceived the idea of a cyclopaedia (2 folio vols, 1728). A French translation gave rise to the great French *Encyclopédie*. He died in London.

Chambers, Robert (1802–71) British publisher and author, born at Peebles, Borders, Scotland. He began as a bookseller in Edinburgh (1818), and gave his leisure to literary composition, writing many books on Scottish history, people, and institutions, and contributing regularly to *Chambers's Edinburgh Journal*. He died at St Andrews. His son **Robert** (1832–88) became head of the firm in 1883, and conducted the *Journal* till his death.

Chambers, William (1800–83) British publisher and author, born at Peebles, Borders, Scotland. In 1814 he was apprenticed to a bookseller in Edinburgh, and in 1819 went into business for himself. In 1832 he started *Chambers's Edinburgh Journal*, and soon after united with his brother Robert in founding the printing and publishing firm of W & R Chambers. As Lord Provost of Edinburgh (1865–9), he promoted a successful scheme for improving the older part of the city. Shortly before his death he received the offer of a baronetcy.

Chambord [shã**baw**] 47°37N 1°31E, pop(1982) 159. A village 18 km/11 ml E of Blois, France, noted for its chateau and estate; a world heritage site. Once a hunting lodge of the counts of Blois, the chateau was reconstructed (1519–33) by Francis I and Henry II as a royal residence. » Francis I; Henry II (of France)

chameleon [ka**mee**liuhn] A lizard native to Africa, the Middle East, S Spain, India, and Sri Lanka; body flattened from side to side; can change colour rapidly (controlled by nerves in skin); tail clasping, cannot be shed; eyes move independently of one another; tongue longer than head and body, with sticky tip that shoots out to hit insect prey; usually lives in trees. (Family: *Chamaeleontidae*, 85 species.) » lizard [i]

chamois [**sham**wah] A goat-antelope from S Europe (introduced in New Zealand); brown with pale patches on face or neck; horns short, vertical, with backward hooked tips; inhabits rugged mountains; skin formerly used to make 'shammy leather' (this now obtained from goats and sheep). (*Rupicapra rupicapra*.) » antelope; goral

chamomile A perennial growing to 30 cm/12 in, native to W Europe and N Africa; leaves oblong in outline, divided into narrow, fine-pointed segments; flower heads up to 2.5 cm/1 in across, solitary; outer, ray florets spreading; white, inner, disc florets yellow; also called **camomile**. It is widely used to make chamomile tea, and is a popular additive to shampoos, hair washes, etc. Chamomile lawns were formerly very popular, especially in England during Elizabethan times, giving off a pleasant aromatic smell when walked on. (*Chamaemelum nobile*. Family: *Compositae*.) » floret; perennial

champagne A sparkling wine produced in the Champagne region of NE France, using either a mixture of black and white grapes, or white grapes only. The effervescent nature of champagne is due to the fact that some of the fermentation takes place in the bottle. Sweet (*sec*), slightly sweet (*demi-sec*), and dry (*brut*) varieties are made. » fermentation

Champagne-Ardenne pop (1982) 1 345 935; area 25 606 sq km/9 884 sq ml. Region of NE France comprising the departments of Ardennes, Aube, Marne, and Haute-Marne; a long-standing scene of conflict between France and Germany; noted for the production of champagne wine; 120 km/75 ml-long 'Route du Champagne' through the vine-growing areas, starting at Rheims. » Rheims; wine

Champlain, Samuel de [**shã**plĩ] (1567–1635) French Governor of Canada, born at Brouage, France. In a series of voyages he travelled to Canada (1603), exploring the E coast (1604–7), and founding Quebec (1608). He was appointed Lieutenant of Canada (1612), and established alliances with several Indian nations. When Quebec fell briefly to the British, he was taken prisoner (1629–32). From 1633 he was Governor of Quebec, where he died. L Champlain is named after him. » Canada [i]

champlevé [**shom**luhvay] A technique of enamelling on metal, which involves engraving the image out of the metal surface, and filling it with vitreous pastes of different colours, which are then fired. Popular throughout the Middle Ages, it was produced on an almost industrial scale at Limoges in France. » enamelling

Champollion, Jean François [shãpolyõ] (1790–1832) French founder of Egyptology, born at Figeac. Educated at Grenoble, in 1807 he went to Paris, subsequently becoming professor of history at Grenoble (1809–16). Best known for his use of the Rosetta Stone to decipher Egyptian hieroglyphics (1822–4), he was the first to place the study of early Egyptian history and culture on a firm footing. In 1831 a chair of Egyptology was founded for him in the Collège de France. He died in Paris. » hieroglyphics [i]; Rosetta Stone

Ch'an [chan] A general term for meditation in Chinese Buddhism, referring to a school which dates from perhaps the 6th-c. It combines Mahayana Buddhist teachings with those of Taoism to form an outlook emphasizing meditative experience as opposed to an intellectual approach. » Buddhism; Mahayana; Taoism; Zen Buddhism

Chan Chan An ancient Chimu capital in the Moche Valley, Peru, occupied from c.1000 to the Inca conquest c.1470; a world heritage site. Its residential area covered 19 sq km/7¼ sq ml, with a population of c.30 000. The monumental centre 6 sq km/2¼ sq ml in area is notable for its ten huge rectangular enclosures, administrative centres of the kingdom during successive reigns. » Chimu; Incas

chancel The E end of a church, containing the altar, choir, and clergy; more generally, the body of the church to the E of the nave. The name is derived from the Latin *cancellus*, the screen separating the chancel from the rest of the church. » choir (architecture); church [i]; nave; transept

Chancellor, Lord (High) In the UK, a high officer of state whose office is a combination of the judicial, executive, and legislative functions of government. He is head of the judiciary, advises the Crown on senior appointments, and appoints magistrates. He is also a government minister, with his own responsibilities, and Speaker of the House of Lords. » peerage

Chancellor of the Exchequer The senior minister in charge of the UK Treasury, and a senior minister in the cabinet. The Chancellor takes responsibility for the preparation of the budget, and (unlike in most other countries) is economic as well as finance minister. » cabinet; treasury

Chancery Division A division of the High Court of England and Wales created by the Judicature Acts (1873–5). Its workload includes trusts and probate matters. Historically, the Court of Chancery was the court of equity presided over by the Lord Chancellor. In the USA, most courts of general jurisdiction combine law and equity. » equity; High Court of Justice; Lord Chancellor; probate; trust

chancroid A sexually-transmitted disease common in Egypt and the Middle East, resulting from infection with a *Haemophilus* organism. It causes ulceration of the genital organs. » ulcer; venereal disease

Chandigarh [**chan**deegah] pop (1981) 450 061; area 114 sq km/44 sq ml. City and union territory (1966) in NW India; serves as the joint state capital of the Punjab and Haryana; airfield; railway; university (1947); city designed by Le Corbusier, includes an 8 km/5 ml green belt; Asia's largest rose garden. » India [i]; Le Corbusier; Punjab

Chandler, Raymond (Thornton) (1888–1959) US writer, born in Chicago. He was educated in England, France, and Germany, then worked as a freelance writer in London. In World War 1 he served in the Canadian army in France and in the RAF. During the Depression he began to write short stories and novelettes for the detective-story pulp magazines of the day, later turning to 'private eye' novels, such as *The Big Sleep* (1939) and *Farewell, My Lovely* (1940), several of which were filmed. He is the creator of the cynical but honest detective antihero, Philip Marlowe. He died at La Jolla, California. » detective story

Chandragupta II [chandrah**gup**tah], also known as **Vikramaditya** ('Sun of Valour') (4th-c) Indian Emperor (reigned c.380–c.415), the third of the imperial Guptas of N India. He extended control over his neighbours by both military and peaceful means. A devout Hindu, he tolerated Buddhism and Jainism, and patronized learning. During his reign, art, architecture, and sculpture flourished, and the cultural development of ancient India reached its climax. » Buddhism; Jainism

Chanel, Gabrielle [sha**nel**], known as **Coco** (?1883–1971) French couturier, born at Saumur. She worked as a milliner until 1912, and after World War 1 opened a couture house in Paris. She revolutionized women's fashions during the 1920s, her designs including the 'chemise' dress and the collarless cardigan jacket. Many of the features she introduced, such as the vogue for costume jewellery and the evening scarf, still retain their popularity. She retired in 1938, but made a surprisingly successful come-back in 1954. She died in Paris.

Chaney, Lon [**chay**nee], originally **Alonso** (1883–1930) US film actor, born at Colorado Springs, Colorado. He was famous for spine-chilling deformed villains and other horrific parts, as in *The Hunchback of Notre Dame* and *The Phantom of the Opera*, and came to be called the 'man of a thousand faces'. He died in Los Angeles, California.

Changan (China) » **Xi'an**

Changchun or **Ch'angch'un** 43°50N 125°20E, pop (1984e) 1 809 200. Capital of Jilin province, NE China; on the Yitong R in C of China's NE plain; developed during Japanese military occupation (1933–45) as capital of Manchukuo; airfield; railway; university (1958); electric furnaces, vehicles, light engineering, textiles, food processing, chemicals; Changchun film studio. » China [i]; Manchukuo

change ringing A British form of bell ringing devised by 17th-c Cambridge printer Fabian Stedman. A set of differently tuned bells, usually those in a church tower, are rung in various permutations so that no sequence (or 'change') is sounded more than once. A full diatonic scale of eight bells allows 40 320 changes. A 'peal' of about 5 000 changes takes about three hours to ring. Change ringers belong to Guilds, the oldest being the Ancient Society of College Youths, founded in 1637. » bell; bell-ringing

Changsha or **Ch'angsha** 28°10N 113°00E, pop (1984e) 1 123 900. River port and capital of Hunan province, SE China; on the lower Xiang R, in intensively cultivated lowlands; founded before 1000 BC; early craft, industrial, and educational centre; foreign trade port, 1904; airfield; railway; university (1959);

textiles, food-processing, chemicals, light engineering, electronics; Hunan provincial museum; Yuelushan Park, containing Lushan Temple (founded, 268); Kaifu Temple (896). » China [i]

Chania [khanya] or **Cania** 35°31N 24°01E, pop (1981) 61 976. Capital town of Chania department, Crete; on N shore of Crete I; founded, 13th-c; capital of Crete until 1971; airport; fruit, olives, leather, crafts, tourism; dance festival to commemorate the battle for Crete (May). » Crete

Channel Islands, Fr **Iles Normandes** area 194 sq km/75 sq ml. Island group of the British Isles in the English Channel, W of the Cotentin Peninsula of Normandy; chief islands, Guernsey, Jersey, Alderney, Sark; other islands include Herm, Jethou, Brechou, the Caskets, the Minquiers, and the Chauseys; languages, English and Norman-French; granted to the Dukes of Normandy, 10th-c; occupied by Germany in World War 2; a dependent territory of the British Crown, with individual legislative assemblies and legal system; divided into the Bailiwick of Guernsey and the Bailiwick of Jersey; Bailiff presides over the Royal Court and the Representative Assembly (the States); tourism, fruit, vegetables, flowers, dairy produce, Jersey and Guernsey cattle; used as a tax haven. » Alderney; Guernsey; Jersey; Sark

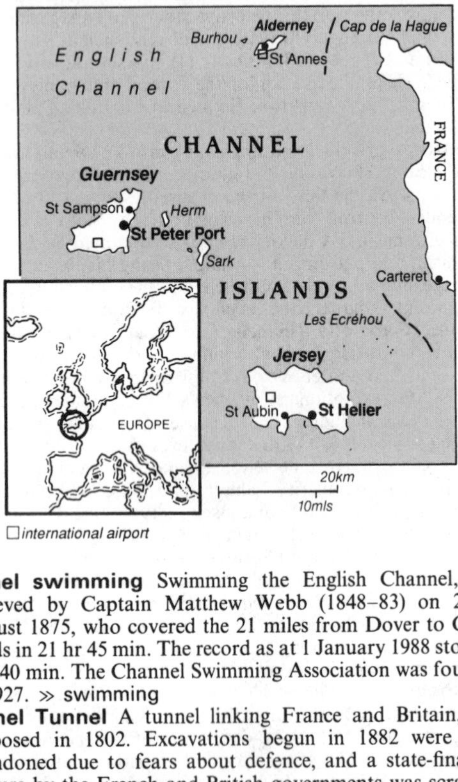

channel swimming Swimming the English Channel, first achieved by Captain Matthew Webb (1848–83) on 24–25 August 1875, who covered the 21 miles from Dover to Calais Sands in 21 hr 45 min. The record as at 1 January 1988 stood at 7 hr 40 min. The Channel Swimming Association was founded in 1927. » swimming

Channel Tunnel A tunnel linking France and Britain, first proposed in 1802. Excavations begun in 1882 were soon abandoned due to fears about defence, and a state-financed venture by the French and British governments was scrapped in the 1970s. In 1985 Eurotunnel, an Anglo-French consortium, was set up to finance the tunnel and operate it once it opened. The tunnel is to be built by the Anglo-French Transmanche Link, and will consist of twin rail tunnels between Cheriton near Folkestone and Fréthun near Calais. It will be 50 km/31 ml long (38 km/23 ml of this will be under the sea) and is due for completion in 1993.

chanoyu [**chah**nohyoo] A Japanese tea ceremony, popular among priests and warriors in the Middle Ages as a means of concentration. The tea uses a strong green powder, and is drunk in small quantities. The bowls and utensils are prized as art objects. The rigid etiquette is learnt by girls before marriage. Teachers must have a recognized licence. » samurai

chansons de geste [shãsõ duh **zhest**] (Fr 'poems of action') French poems from the 12th–13th-c, celebrating historical figures and events on an epic scale. Different cycles centre on Charlemagne (including the *Chanson de Roland*) and the Crusades. The poems provide interesting insights into feudal society. » Charlemagne; French literature; troubadours

chant A monotone or a melody, usually restricted in range, mainly stepwise in interval and free in rhythm, to which a text (especially a liturgical one) is declaimed. *Plainchant*, originally sung in unison and without accompaniment, was used for the services of the mediaeval Roman Catholic Church and later incorporated into polyphonic music. The repertory was defined and standardized in the 6th-c, reputedly by Pope Gregory the Great, but the corpus of what came to be known as 'Gregorian chant' was later enriched by new melodies. *Anglican chant* is a type of harmonized melody to which the psalms and canticles are sung in Church of England services. Its rigid metrical scheme is made to accommodate an irregular number of syllables by having as many of them as is necessary freely sung (or 'chanted') to a 'reciting chord' at the beginning of each half-verse. » African music; antiphon; Gregorian chant; Japanese music; liturgy; organum; plainchant; Psalms, Book of; sequence (music)

chanterelle [shantuh**rel**] The bright yellow, edible fruiting body of fungus *Cantharellus cibarius*; funnel-shaped, diameter up to 10 cm/4 in; gill-like ridges present on lower surface; common on ground, especially under trees, in Europe and N America. (Order: *Agaricales*.) » fungus

Chanukah » **Hanukkah**

chaos A state of disorder and irregularity whose evolution in time, though governed by simple exact laws, is highly sensitive to starting conditions: a small variation in these conditions will produce wildly different results. Long-term behaviour of chaotic systems cannot be predicted. Chaos is an intermediate stage between highly-ordered motion and fully-random motion. For example, in fluid flow, a slowly-moving fluid exhibits perfectly regular flow; as the fluid velocity increases, the flow becomes chaotic; and as the velocity increases still further, the flow becomes fully turbulent (random). In a chaotic system, the values of some quantity at two points maintain their relationship as time passes, even though the exact value of each cannot be predicted in the future. In truly random motion, there exist no such relationships. Chaos is present in most real systems, such as in weather patterns and the motion of planets about the Sun; the stable classical motion widely accepted as the norm in physics is now known to be the exception rather than the rule. The underlying structure of chaos exhibits universal features, regardless of the system in question. The modern theory of chaos is based on the work of US meteorologist Edward Lorenz (1917–) in 1963, arising from the study of convection in the atmosphere. Some degree of non-linearity is necessary for chaotic behaviour. Fractals feature in a comprehensive description of chaos. » fractals; many body theory; non-linear physics; turbulence

Chaos [**kay**os] In Greek mythology, the primaeval state of emptiness (according to Hesiod), but in later Greek philosophy a universe of muddled forms and elements which separated out into our world. It can be personified, as in Milton's 'reign of Chaos and old Night'. » Hesiod

Chapala, Lake (Span **Lago de**) [cha**pah**la] area 3 366 sq km/1 299 sq ml. Lake in SW Mexico; 77 km/48 ml long E–W; c.16 km/10 ml wide; largest lake in Mexico, on the C plateau, 48 km/30 ml S of Guadalajara; resort town of Chapala on the N shore. » Mexico [i]

chaparral [shapuh**ral**] (Span *chaparro* 'scrub oak') The evergreen scrub vegetation of semi-arid areas with a Mediterranean-type climate in SW USA and NW Mexico. It is a plant community adapted to frequent fires. Without fire every few years the chaparral would degrade. Typical vegetation species includes evergreen scrub oak, laurel sumac, and ceanothus. » evergreen plants; maquis

chapati [cha**pah**tee] A thin, flat, unleavened bread, made from a mixture of water and wheat flour containing c.95% of the original wheat. It is a traditional accompaniment to many Asian dishes, especially those of India, Pakistan, and Bangladesh. » bread

chapel Originally, a place to house sacred relics; now generally a church. In England and Wales, the term is used of Nonconformist places of worship; in N Ireland and Scotland, of Roman Catholic churches. It may also be a place of worship belonging to a college or institution, and may further denote the chancel of a church or cathedral, or part of a cathedral containing a separate altar. » church [i]; Nonconformists; Roman Catholicism

Chaplin, Charlie, byname of **Sir Charles Spencer Chaplin** (1889–1977) British film actor and director, born in London. His skill in comedy developed under Fred Karno, with whom he went to Hollywood in 1914. In his early comedies he adopted the bowler hat, out-turned feet, moustache and walking cane which became his hallmark, as in *The Kid*, *The Gold Rush*, and many others. His art was essentially suited to the silent film, and when sound arrived he experimented with new forms, as in *City Lights* (1931), with music only, and *Modern Times* (1936), part speech and part mime. His first sound film was *The Great Dictator* (1940). In *Limelight* (1952) he acted, directed, and composed the music and dances. His left-wing sympathies caused him to leave the USA for Switzerland in 1952. He was married four times, was awarded an Oscar in 1973, and was knighted in 1975. He died at Corsier-sur-Vevey, Switzerland.

Chapman, George (c.1559–1634) English poet and dramatist, born near Hitchin, Hertfordshire. He studied at Oxford, then worked in London. He is best known for his translations of Homer's *Iliad* (1598–1611) and *Odyssey* (1616), followed (about 1624) by the minor works. He joined Jonson and Marston in the composition of *Eastward Ho* (1605), and in 1607 appeared *Bussy d'Ambois*, which had a sequel in 1613. He died in London. » English literature; Homer; Jonson; Marston

Chapman horse » **Cleveland bay**

Chappaquiddick [chapa**kwi**dik] (Algonquian 'separated-island-at') Island to the E of Martha's Vineyard I, USA; in the Nantucket Sound, off the SE coast of Massachusetts. » Kennedy, Edward M; Martha's Vineyard

characin [**ka**rasin] Any of a large family of colourful carp-like freshwater fishes common in S and C America and Africa; mostly carnivorous; important as a food fish and in the aquarium trade; 40 genera, including piranhas, tigerfish, headstanders, tetras, and penguinfish. (*Characidae*.) » carp; piranha; tetra; tigerfish

character recognition The technology associated with the ability of computer-based systems to recognize specific patterns; sometimes referred to as **pattern recognition**. In particular, the ability to read printed characters from ordinary printed material is known as *optical character recognition (OCR)*. Another common type is *magnetic ink character recognition (MICR)*, used worldwide to read automatically such things as account numbers and serial numbers on cheques. » pattern recognition

Charadriiformes [karadreeuh**faw**meez] An order of essentially water-loving birds (18 families). It includes gulls, terns, skuas, auks, and many waders. » auk; gull; skua; tern

charcoal An impure form of carbon made by heating animal or vegetable substances in the absence of air to drive off the volatile constituents. It is porous and hence used as an adsorbent and filter. It burns without flame or smoke. Coke is a variety formed from coal. Animal charcoal is known as *bone-black*. » bone-black; carbon; coke

Charcot, Jean Martin [**shah**koh] (1825–93) French pathologist, one of the founders of neurology, born in Paris. He worked at the Salpêtrière, and had Freud among his pupils. He contributed much to our knowledge of chronic and nervous diseases, and made hypnotism a scientific study. The way joints deteriorate in some types of nervous disease was named after him (**Charcot's joint**). He died at Morvan, France. » hypnosis; neurology

chard A type of cultivated beet lacking a swollen root but with swollen midribs and leaf-stalks. (*Beta vulgaris*, variety *cicla*. Family: *Cheopodiaceae*.) » beet; root (botany)

Chargaff, Erwin (1905–) Czech-US biochemist, born at Czernowitz. He studied at Vienna, Yale, Berlin, and Paris, and worked at Columbia University, New York, from 1935. His pioneer work on nucleic acids showed that the DNA of an organism has a composition characteristic of the organism; and his work on the ratio of bases present in DNA (the **Chargaff rules**) provided a fundamental contribution to the double helix structure for DNA advanced in 1953. » DNA [i]; molecular biology

charge A quantity of electricity (*electrical charge*), the source of an electric field; symbol Q, units C (*coulombs*). The elementary unit of charge $e = 1.602 \times 10^{-19}$C, equal in size but opposite in sign to the electron's charge, cannot be subdivided and is a fundamental constant. Charge occurs only in multiples of e, a simple additive quantity which is always conserved. Two types of charge are possible: *positive* and *negative*. Like-sign charges repel, opposite-sign charges attract; the force between charges is expressed by Coulomb's law. Moving charges constitute a *current*. The study of stationary charges and the forces between them is called **electrostatics**. The Coulomb force between charged electrons and protons holds atoms together. The charge on an object refers to the excess of one type of charge over the other. The charge of an elementary particle is always the same for a given particle, and is one of its fundamental properties. » capacitance; Coulomb's law; current (electricity); electricity; electron

charge card » **credit card**

charge-coupled device (generally abbreviated **CCD**) An image sensor which in a video camera comprises a mosaic of minute photo-conductive diodes corresponding to the pixels and lines of a television system. Charges produced in each element by incident light are stored until read off in the required scanning sequence. » camera

Charge of the Light Brigade An incident during the Battle of Balaclava (1854), when the Light Brigade, under the command of Lord Cardigan, charged the main Russian artillery. The charge involved massive loss of life. It resulted from the misunderstanding of an order given by the commanding officer, Lord Raglan, to stop guns captured by the Russians being carried away during their retreat. » Balaclava, Battle of; Cardigan, Earl of; Raglan

Chari, River [shah**ree**] River in SW Chad, NC Africa; flows 800 km/500 ml NW to join R Logone at N'Djamena, where it forms the border between Chad and Cameroon before entering L Chad; length including main headstream (R Bamingui), 1 060 km/660 ml. » Chad, Lake

Charing Cross An area in C London, UK. It takes its name from a cross erected to mark the site of the resting-place of the body of Queen Eleanor, who died in 1290. Traditionally Charing Cross is viewed as the centre of London, when measuring distances to and from the city. » Eleanor of Castile; London [i]

charismatic movement [kariz**ma**tik] A movement of spiritual renewal, which takes a variety of forms in Roman Catholic, Protestant, and Eastern Orthodox Churches. It emphasizes the present reality and work of the Holy Spirit in the life of the Church and the individual. It is sometimes accompanied by speaking in tongues. » glossolalia; Holy Spirit; Pentecostalism

Charlemagne or **Charles the Great** (742–814) King of the Franks (771–814) and Emperor of the West (800–14), the eldest son of Pepin the Short. He defeated the Saxons (772–804), as well as the Lombards (773–4), fought the Arabs in Spain, and took control of most of Christian W Europe. In 800 he was crowned Emperor by Pope Leo III. In his later years he consolidated his vast empire, building palaces and churches, and promoting Christianity, education, agriculture, the arts, manufacture, and commerce, so much so that the period has become known as the **Carolingian Renaissance**. He died at Aachen. » Renaissance

Charleroi [shahl**rwa**] 50°25N 4°27E, pop (1982) 219 579. Town in Hainaut province, SW Belgium, on the R Sambre; formerly a fortress; location of World War 1 German attack against the French (Aug 1914); centre of coal-mining area; iron, wire and cables, cutlery. » Belgium [i]

Charles I (of Austria-Hungary) (1887–1922) Emperor of Austria (Karl I) and King of Hungary (Károly IV), born at Persenbeug Castle, Austria, who succeeded his granduncle, Francis Joseph, in 1916. He became heir presumptive on the assassination at Sarajevo (1914) of his uncle, Archduke Franz Ferdinand. In 1918 he was compelled to abdicate. Two attempts at restoration in Hungary (1921) failed, and he died in exile in Madeira.

Charles I (of England) (1600–49) King of England and Ireland (1625–49), born at Dunfermline, Scotland. He failed in his bid to marry the Infanta Maria of Spain (1623), marrying instead the French princess, **Henrietta Maria** (1609–69), and thus disturbing the nation, for the marriage articles permitted her the free exercise of the Catholic religion. Three parliaments were summoned and dissolved in the first four years of his reign; then for 11 years he ruled without one, using instead judges and prerogative courts. He warred with France (1627–9), and in 1630 made peace with Spain, but his continuing need for money led to unpopular economic policies. His attempt to anglicize the Scottish Church brought active resistance (1639), and he then called a parliament (1640). In 1642, having alienated much of the realm, Charles entered into the Civil War, which saw the annihilation of his cause at Naseby (14 Jun 1645), and he surrendered to the Scots at Newark (1646). After many negotiations, during which his attempts at duplicity exasperated opponents, and a second Civil War (1646–8), he came to trial at Westminster, where his dignified refusal to plead was interpreted as a confession of guilt. He was beheaded at Whitehall (30 Jan 1649). » English Civil War; Long Parliament

Charles II (of England) (1630–85) King of England and Ireland (1660–85), born and died in London, the son of Charles I. As Prince of Wales, he sided with his father in the Civil War, and was then forced into exile. On his father's execution (1649), he assumed the title of King, and was crowned at Scone (1651). Leading poorly organized forces into England, he met disastrous defeat at Worcester (1651). The next nine years were spent in exile until an impoverished England, in dread of a revival of military despotism, summoned him back as King (1660). In 1662 he married the Portuguese Princess Catherine of Braganza. It was a childless marriage, though Charles was the father of many illegitimate children. His war with Holland (1665–7) was unpopular, and led to the dismissal of his adviser, Lord Clarendon (1667), who was replaced by a group of ministers (the Cabal). He negotiated skilfully between conflicting political and religious pressures, including the trumped-up 'Popish Plot', and refused to deny the succession of his brother James. For the last four years of his life, he ruled without parliament. » Cabal; Clarendon; Dutch Wars; English Civil War; Popish Plot

Charles II (of Spain) (1661–1700) King of Spain (1665–1700), the last ruler of the Spanish Habsburg dynasty, born and died in Madrid, the son of Philip IV. He went to war against France in the Grand Alliance, and precipitated the War of the Spanish Succession by naming in his will Philip of Anjou as his successor. His reign saw the end of Spanish power in Europe. » Spanish Succession, War of the

Charles IV (of Spain) (1788–1819) King of Spain (1738–1808), born at Portici, Naples, the son of Charles III. His government was largely in the hands of his wife, **Maria Luisa** (1751–1819) and her favourite, Manuel de Godoy. Nelson destroyed his fleet at Trafalgar, and in 1808 he abdicated under pressure from Napoleon. He spent the rest of his life in exile, and died in Rome. » Napoleon I

Charles V (Emperor) (1500–58) Holy Roman Emperor (1519–56), born at Ghent. The son of Philip of Burgundy and Joanna of Spain, in 1517 he was made joint ruler of Spain with his mother, and in 1519 was elected to the Holy Roman Empire. His rivalry with Francis I of France dominated W European affairs, and there was almost constant warfare between them. In 1525 the defeat of Francis led to the formation of the Holy League against Charles by Pope Clement VII, Henry VIII, Francis, and the Venetians. In 1527 Rome was sacked and the Pope imprisoned, and although Charles disclaimed any part of it, the Peace of Cambrai (1529) left him master of Italy. At the Diet of Augsburg (1530) he confirmed the 1521 Edict of Worms, which had condemned Luther, and the Protestants formed the League of Schmalkald. After further battles, in 1538 the Pope, Francis, and Charles agreed at Nice to a ten years' truce. Charles's league with the Pope drove the Protestants to rebellion. They were crushed at Mühlberg (1547); but in 1552 Charles was defeated by Maurice of Saxony, and Protestantism received legal recognition. In 1555 he divided the Empire between his son (Philip II of Spain) and his brother (Ferdinand I), retiring to the monastery of Yuste in Spain, where he died. » Francis I; Holy League; Protestantism; Reformation

Charles V (of France), byname **the Wise** (1337–80) King of France, born at Vincennes. He came to the throne in 1364, and in a series of victories regained most of the territory lost to the English in the Hundred Years' War. He died at Nogent-sur-Marne. » Guesclin; Hundred Years' War

Charles VI (of France), byname **the Foolish** (1368–1422) King of France, born and died in Paris, who came to the throne as a young boy in 1380. He was defeated by Henry V at the Battle of Agincourt (1415). From 1392, he suffered from fits of madness. » Agincourt, Battle of

Charles VII (of France), byname **the Victorious** (1403–61) King of France (1422–61), born in Paris. At his accession, the N of the country was in English hands, with Henry VI proclaimed King of France. But after Joan of Arc roused the fervour of both nobles and people, the siege of Orleans was raised (1429), and the English gradually lost nearly all they had gained in France. Under his rule France recovered in some measure from her terrible calamities. He died at Mehun-sur-Yèvre. » Hundred Years' War; Joan of Arc

Charles IX (of France) (1550–74) King of France (1560–74), born at St Germain-en-Laye. The second son of Henry II and Catherine de' Medici, he succeeded his brother, Francis II. His reign coincided with the Wars of Religion. He was completely subject to his mother, whose counsels drove him to authorize the massacre of Huguenots on St Bartholomew's Day, 1572. Haunted by the memory of this event, he died at Vincennes. » Catherine de' Medici; Huguenots; Religion, Wars of

Charles X (of France) (1757–1836) The last Bourbon King of France (1824–30), born at Versailles. The grandson of Louis XV, he received the title of Comte d'Artois, and in 1773 married Maria Theresa of Savoy. He lived in England during the French Revolution, returning to France in 1814 as Lieutenant-General of the kingdom. He succeeded his brother Louis XVIII, but his repressive rule led to revolution, and his eventual abdication and exile. He died at Görz. » Bourbons; French Revolution [i]; Louis XVIII

Charles XII (of Sweden) (1682–1718) King of Sweden (1697–1718), born in Stockholm, the son of Charles XI. Following an alliance against him by Denmark, Poland and Russia, he attacked Denmark (1699), and compelled the Danes to sue for peace. He then defeated the Russians at Narva (1700), and dethroned Augustus II of Poland (1704). He invaded Russia again in 1707, and was at first victorious, but when Cossack help failed to arrive, he was defeated at Poltava (1709). He escaped to Turkey, where he stayed until 1714. He then formed another army and attacked Norway, but was killed at the siege of Halden. After his death, Sweden, exhausted by his wars, ceased to be numbered among the great powers.

Charles XIV (of Sweden), originally **Jean Baptiste Jules Bernadotte** (1763–1844) King of Sweden (1818–44), born a lawyer's son at Pau, France. He joined the French army in 1780, and fought his way up to become marshal in 1804. In 1799 he was Minister of War, and for his conduct at Austerlitz was named in 1805 Prince of Pontecorvo. He fought in several Napoleonic campaigns (1805–9), then in 1810 was elected heir to the throne of Sweden, turning Protestant, and changing his name to Charles John. He refused to comply with Napoleon's demands, and was soon involved in war with him, taking part in the final struggle at Leipzig (1813). In 1814 he was rewarded with the Kingdom of Norway, recreating the union of the two countries. Thereafter he had a peaceful reign, though his conservative rule led to opposition at home in the 1830s. He died in Stockholm. » Napoleon I

Charles (Philip Arthur George), Prince of Wales (1948–) Eldest son of HM Queen Elizabeth II and HRH Prince Philip, Duke of Edinburgh, and heir apparent to the throne of Great Britain, born in London (at Buckingham Palace). Duke of

Cornwall as the eldest son of the monarch, he was given the title of Prince of Wales in 1958, and invested at Caernarfon (1968). Educated at Cheam and Gordonstoun, he entered Trinity College, Cambridge in 1967. He served in the RAF and the Royal Navy (1971–6), and in 1981 married **Lady Diana Frances**, younger daughter of the 8th Earl Spencer. They have two sons: **Prince William Arthur Philip Louis** (1982–) and **Prince Henry Charles Albert David** (1984–). » Elizabeth II

Charles, Jacques Alexandre César [shahl] (1746–1823) French physicist, born at Beaugency. A clerk with an interest in science which led eventually to a chair in physics, he became famous by making the first ascent by hydrogen balloon, reaching 3 000 m/9 800 ft in 1783. His name is now linked with **Charles's law**, which relates the pressure of a gas to its temperature. He died in Paris. » balloon; gas 1

Charles, Ray, originally **Robinson, Ray Charles** (1930–) US singer and pianist, born at Albany, Georgia. Blind from the age of five, and orphaned at 15, he left home for Seattle and, after writing arrangements for several pop groups, was contracted to Atlantic Records in 1952. With *I've got a Woman* (1955) he established a new style of rhythm and blues which introduced elements of gospel music, and proved to be widely influential. » rhythm and blues

Charles Edward » **Stuart, Charles Edward**

Charles' Heart The star alpha Canum Venaticorum, a reference to King Charles I of England, who was beheaded; also known as **Cor Caroli**. This star is said to have shone unusually brightly in 1660, on the arrival of Charles II in England. » Charles I (of England); star

Charles's Law A law named after French physicist Jacques Charles, but first published by French physical chemist Joseph Gay-Lussac, and therefore also called **Gay-Lussac's law**: at constant pressure, the volume of a given mass of an ideal gas is directly proportional to a constant plus its temperature measure on any scale. The value of this constant fixes the zero of the absolute scale of temperature. » Charles, Jacques; gas laws; Gay-Lussac; ideal gas

Charles Martel (c.688–741) Mayor of the palace for the last Merovingian kings of the Franks, the illegitimate son of Pepin of Herstal, and the undisputed head of the Carolingian family by 723. He conducted many campaigns against the Frisians and Saxons, and in Aquitaine, Bavaria, and Burgundy. He halted Muslim expansion in W Europe at the Battle of Poitiers (732). Established as effective ruler of much of Gaul, but never crowned king, he left the kingdom to his sons, Carolman and Pepin, and in 751 was anointed as the first Carolingian King of the Franks. » Carolingians; Franks; Gaul; Merovingians

Charleston A jazz dance of Black origin popularized in the 1920s. It was, however, first seen at Charleston, South Carolina, USA in 1903, and was named after the city. It can be danced either solo, with a partner, or in a group. Music is in 4/4 time and with syncopated rhythms. » ballroom dance

Charleston (South Carolina) 32°46N 79°56W, pop (1980) 69 510. Seat of Charleston County, SE South Carolina, USA; a port on the Atlantic Ocean, at the mouths of Ashley and Cooper Rivers; the oldest city in the state, founded in 1670; survived attacks by a British fleet in 1776 and 1779; finally captured and held by the British, 1780–2; the Confederate attack on nearby Fort Sumter (12–13 Apr 1861) began the Civil War; evacuated by Confederate forces in 1865 after a 2-year siege; devastated by an earthquake in 1886; badly damaged by hurricane Hugo in 1989; airfield; railway; fertilizers, chemicals, steel, asbestos, cigars, paper products, textiles; site of a US naval and air force base; tourist centre; Charleston Museum, Old Slave Mart Museum and Gallery, Gibbes Art Gallery, several old colonial buildings. » American Civil War; South Carolina

Charleston (West Virginia) 38°21N 81°38W, pop (1980) 63 968. Capital of state in Kanawha County, W West Virginia, USA, at the confluence of Elk and Kanawha Rivers; developed around Fort Lee in the 1780s; city status, 1870; capital of West Virginia, 1870–5 and from 1885; largest city in the state; airfield; railway; an important transportation and trading centre; chemicals, glass, primary metals; various other products based on the salt, coal, natural gas, clay, sand, timber, and oil found in the region; Sternwheel Regatta (Aug). » West Virginia

Charleston, Battles of (11 Feb–12 May 1780) During the US War of Independence, the victorious British siege of Charleston, S Carolina, which marked the beginning of the Southern phase of British strategy. At a small cost, the troops of Sir Henry Clinton (c.1738–95) captured a 5 400-strong American garrison and a squadron of four ships. » American Revolution

Charlestown 17°08N 62°37W, pop (1980) 1 771. Capital and port of Nevis I, St Kitts-Nevis, N Leeward Is, E Caribbean; formerly famous for its thermal springs; tourism, garments. » St Kitts-Nevis

charlock A roughly hairy annual, 30–80 cm/12–30 in, found in most temperate regions; leaves toothed and lobed; flowers yellow, cross-shaped, capsule cylindrical, long-beaked. Related to mustard, and once grown as a leaf vegetable, it is nowadays a pernicious weed of arable land. (*Sinapis arvensis*. Family: *Cruciferae*.) » annual; mustard

Charlotte 35°13N 80°51W, pop (1980) 314 447. Seat of Mecklenburg County, S North Carolina, USA; settled c.1750; the Mecklenburg Declaration of Independence was signed here, 1775; largest city in the state; airfield; railway; two universities (1867, 1946); textiles, chemicals, machinery, food, printed materials; birthplace of President Polk. » American Revolution; Polk

Charlotte Amalie, formerly **St Thomas** (1921–36) [**shah**luht a**mal**yuh] 18°22N 64°56W, pop (1980) 11 756. Port and capital city of the US Virgin Is, Lesser Antilles, Caribbean, on S coast of St Thomas I; founded by the Danes, 1672; important cruise ship port; tourism. » Virgin Islands, United States

Charlottenburg Palace A palace in present-day W Berlin built (1695–1796) by Elector Frederick for his wife, Sophie Charlotte. The building houses a museum. » Berlin, West; Frederick I (Prussia)

Charlottesville 38°02N 78°30W, pop (1980) 39 916. Independent city and seat of Albemarle County, C Virginia, USA, on the Rivanna R; settled in the 1730s; named after the wife of King George III; railway; university (1819); electronics, navigational systems, communications equipment; Ash Lawn (home of James Monroe); Monticello (home of Thomas Jefferson) and University of Virginia are world heritage sites. » Jefferson, Thomas; Monroe, James; Virginia

Charlottetown 46°14N 63°09W, pop (1981) 15 282. Provincial capital of Prince Edward Island, NE Canada; on Hillsborough Bay; founded by the French in the 1720s; capital since 1765; university (1969); fishing, trades in textiles, potatoes, dairy products, timber. » Prince Edward Island

Charlottetown Conference A meeting of colonial representatives from New Brunswick, Nova Scotia, and Prince Edward Island (1864) to discuss Maritime Union. A delegation from the province of Canada (present-day Ontario and Quebec) successfully promoted the idea of a larger federation with the rest of mainland British North America. It was followed by the Quebec Conference, and led to Confederation in 1867. » British North America Act

Charlton, Bobby, properly **Robert** (1937–) British footballer, born at Ashington, Northumberland. He spent most of his playing career with Manchester United, making his debut in 1956. He survived the Munich air disaster (1958), which killed eight team-mates, won two League championship medals, a Football Association Cup winners' medal, and captained Manchester United to victory in the 1968 European Cup. A member of the successful England World Cup winning team in 1966 (along with his brother, Jack), he played for England 106 times, and scored a record 49 goals. He joined Preston North End as manager in 1973, and played 38 games for them before retiring in 1975. He is now a director of Manchester United. » football [i]

charm In particle physics, an internal additive quantum number conserved in strong and electromagnetic interactions, but not in weak interactions; symbol C. Charmed quarks are those having $C = +1$; charmed particles contain at least one charmed quark. It was postulated in 1974 to account for the J/ψ particle discovered that year. » particle physics; quantum numbers; quark

Charminar [chahminah] A famous city landmark at Hyderabad, Andhra Pradesh, India. The imposing archway, surmounted by four minarets 56 m/182 ft high, was built under Mohammed Quli Qutab Shah in 1591. » Hyderabad (India)

Charon (astronomy) [kairon] Pluto's only known satellite, discovered photographically in 1978; distance from the planet 20 million km/12½ million ml; diameter 1 000 km/620 ml. It is unusually large, relative to its planet, and has a surface of mainly water ice.

Charon (mythology) [kairon] The ferryman of the Underworld, who carried the shades or souls of the dead across the R Styx. Sometimes other rivers are substituted in literature, such as Acheron and Lethe. The Greeks placed a small coin in the mouth of a corpse as Charon's fee. » Acheron; Lethe; Styx

Charpentier, Gustave [shahpãtyay] (1860–1956) French composer, born at Dieuze, Lorraine. He composed both the music and libretto of his operas *Louise* (1900) and *Julien* (1913), and succeeded his teacher, Massenet, in the Académie des Beaux Arts. He died in Paris. » Massenet

charr Freshwater or anadromous (ascending rivers to breed) fish with circumpolar distribution in lakes and rivers of N hemisphere; length up to 1 m/3.3 ft; valuable food fish; popular with anglers as sport fish; includes the **Arctic charr** (*Salvelinus alpinus*) and **brook charr** or brook trout (*Salvelinus fontinalis*). (Family: *Salmonidae*.)

chartering Hiring a vessel (boat, ship, or aeroplane) and crew for a commercial activity between particular locations (a *voyage charter*) or over a particular period (a *time charter*). Most business charters are negotiated on the Baltic Exchange in London. » Baltic Exchange

Charteris, Leslie, originally **Leslie Charles Bowyer Yin** [chahterz] (1907–) British crime-story writer, born in Singapore. He was educated at Cambridge, then worked in a wide variety of jobs, changed his name in 1928, and settled in the USA (1932), becoming a Hollywood screenwriter. He is known as the creator of Simon Templar, 'the Saint'. » detective story

Chartier, Alain [shartyay] (c.1385–c.1435) French author, born at Bayeux. His preoccupation with the plight of France in the Hundred Years' War formed the background to his two best works, the *Livre des quatre dames* (1415–16, Book of the Four Ladies) and the *Quadrilogue invectif* (1422), a four-part debate on the ills of France. He also wrote the allegorical poem, *La Belle Dame sans merci* (1424). He died at Avignon. » French literature; Hundred Years' War

Chartism A largely working-class radical movement which achieved substantial but intermittent support in Britain between the late 1830s and the early 1850s. Its objective was democratic rights for all men, and it took its name from 'The People's Charter', first published in 1838. Its six points were: universal manhood suffrage; the abolition of property qualifications for MPs; parliamentary constituencies of equal size; a secret ballot; payment for MPs; and annual general elections. Chartist petitions were presented to parliament in 1839 and 1842 and on both occasions were rejected by huge majorities. Despite its immediate failure, Chartism had long-term influence on the direction of working-class political and economic organizations later in the 19th-c. » radicalism

Chartres [shahtruh], ancient **Autricum, Civitas Carnutum** 48°29N 1°30E, pop (1982) 39 243. Capital city of Eure-et-Loire department, NC France, on left bank of R Eure, 100 km/62 ml SW of Paris; railway; bishopric; agricultural centre and wheat market; abbey church of St Pierre-en-Vallée (11th–13th-c); Gothic Cathedral of Notre-Dame (1195–1220), a world heritage site; students' pilgrimage (Apr–May). » Chartres Cathedral; Gothic architecture

Chartres Cathedral [shahtruh] The cathedral of Notre Dame, built at Chartres, France, in the 13th-c and widely recognized as a masterpiece of Gothic architecture. It is now a world heritage site. » cathedral; Chartres; Gothic architecture

Chartreuse, La Grande [la grãd chahtrerz] The principal monastery of the Carthusian order, founded in 1084 by St Bruno in the Dauphin Alps of SE France. The monastery has been destroyed and rebuilt several times, and the present structure (which is now a museum) dates from the 17th-c. Chartreuse liqueur was first distilled here in 1607. » Bruno, St; Carthusians

Charybdis [karibdis] In Greek mythology, a whirlpool which swallowed ships whole; encountered by Odysseus on his wanderings, and sometimes placed in the Straits of Messina – incorrectly, since there is no whirlpool there. » Odysseus; Scylla

Chase, James Hadley, pseudonym of **René Raymond** (1906–85) British novelist, born in London. He started the vogue for tough realism in gangster stories with his *No Orchids for Miss Blandish* (1939), the first of a number in similar vein. He died at Corseaux-sur-Vevey, Switzerland.

chat The name given to numerous birds: 51 species of thrush (family: *Turdidae*), 5 species of New World warblers (Family: *Parulidae*), and 5 species of Australian chats (Family: *Ephthianuridae*). » babbler; thrush (bird); warbler

chateau Originally, a mediaeval fortified residence in France, acting as the focus of the feudal community in the same way as the contemporaneous English castle. By the 15th-c these had become private seignoral residences, while the 16th-c saw the emergence of the less fortified *chateau de plaisance*, of which Ambois, Chambord, Chenonceaux, and Azay-le-Rideau are the most notable examples. » Fontainebleau; Versailles

Château Gaillard [giyyah] A massive castle at Les Andelys, Normandy, France, sited on a promontory overlooking the R Seine, and controlling the approach to Rouen. Built 1196–8 by Richard I, King of England (1157–99) and Duke of Normandy, it was inspired by the Crusader castles of Syria and Palestine. Physically impregnable, it was captured by the French king, Philip Augustus, only after a long siege in 1203–4. » Crusades [i]; Richard 1

Chateaubriand, François Auguste René, Viscount of [shatohbreeã] (1768–1848) French writer and politician, born at St Malo. *Atala* (1801) established his literary reputation; and *Le Génie du christianisme* (1802, The Genius of Christianity) made him prominent among men of letters. He held various political and diplomatic posts after the Restoration, but was disappointed in his hope of becoming Prime Minister. In his later years, he wrote his celebrated autobiography, *Mémoires d'outre-tombe* (Memoirs from Beyond the Tomb), not published as a whole until 1902. He died in Paris. » French literature

Chatham » **Pitt, William, 1st Earl of Chatham**

Chatham Islands [chatm] pop (1983e) 770; area 963 sq km/372 sq ml. Islands of New Zealand in the SW Pacific Ocean; 850 km/528 ml E of South Island; comprises Chatham I (Whairikauri) and Pitt I (Rangihaute), and some rocky islets; visited in 1791 by the British brig *Chatham*; chief settlement, Waitangi; sheep-rearing, sealing, fishing. » New Zealand [i]

Chatila [shateela] pop (1986e) 3 200. Palestinian refugee camp on the outskirts of Beirut, Lebanon; created following the evacuation of Palestinians from the city after Israeli attacks on Palestinians and Syrians in June 1982; scene of a massacre by Christian Phalangists (Sep 1983). » Beirut; Lebanon [i]

Chatsworth One of the great English country houses, built (1687–1707) for the 1st Duke of Devonshire near Edensor village, Derbyshire, UK. The original design by William Talman (1650–1719) was altered and extended by successive architects. The gardens, laid out in 1688 by George London (?–1714), were re-landscaped by Capability Brown and Sir Joseph Paxton. » Brown, Lancelot; Paxton, Joseph

Chattanooga Campaign (Sep–Nov 1863) A series of battles in Tennessee, during the American Civil War, leading to Southern victory at Chickamauga, and Northern victories at Lookout Mountain and Missionary Ridge. It was of military importance, because it placed Northern troops in a position to bisect the Confederacy on an E–W axis. » American Civil War

chattels » **property**

Chatterton, Thomas (1752–70) British poet, born in Bristol. In 1768 he hoaxed the whole city with a description, 'from an old manuscript', of the opening of Bristol Bridge in 1248. His poems, purporting to be by Thomas Rowley, a 15th-c monk, were sent to Walpole, but (though Walpole was taken in) were soon denounced as forgeries. He then went to London, where he wrote many successful stories, essays, and other works. When his patron, Lord Mayor Beckford, died, his publishers ceased to support him. Starving and penniless, he took poison.

The debate over the authenticity of the Rowley poems waged for 80 years. ≫ English literature; Walpole, Robert

Chau [chow] A traditional theatre of E India with three regional styles: *Mayurbhanj*, dance-drama without masks, *Seraikala*, dance with masks, and *Purulia*, dance-drama with masks. ≫ Indian theatre

Chaucer, Geoffrey (c.1345–1400) English poet, born (probably) in London, the son of a tavern keeper, perhaps the John Chaucer who was deputy to the king's butler. He may have gone to Oxford or Cambridge. In 1357 and 1358 he was a page to the wife of Lionel, Duke of Clarence, and then transferred to the king's household. In 1359 he served in France, and was taken prisoner, but ransomed with the king's help. In 1367 the king granted him a pension. In 1368 a Philippa Chaucer appears amongst the ladies of the queen's bedchamber, very probably his wife, and she seems to have had two sons and a daughter. In 1369 Chaucer wrote his *Book of the Duchess*, on the death of John of Gaunt's wife. Travelling extensively abroad on the king's service, he also held royal posts at home, including that of Comptroller of the Petty Customs (1382). In 1386 he was elected a knight of the shire for Kent. During this time he wrote *Troilus and Criseyde*, and several other major works. His early writings followed French trends, but were greatly influenced by Italian authors, notably Boccaccio. Losing his offices in 1386, he fell upon hard times, though in 1399 he was awarded a pension. He died in London and was buried in Westminster Abbey. It was during this last period that he wrote his most famous work, the unfinished *Canterbury Tales*, which is unique for its variety, humour, grace, and realism. Chaucer was the first great poet of the English nation; and in the Middle Ages he stands supreme. ≫ Boccaccio; Canterbury Tales; English literature; poetry

Chautauqua movement A late 19th-c and early 20th-c US adult education movement, organized under Methodist auspices by Lewis Miller (1829–99) and Bishop John H Vincent (1832–1920), with home reading programmes and summer gatherings. At its peak it attracted up to 60 000 participants annually to regional centres in the USA and elsewhere. The original centre at L Chautauqua, New York, continues its activities. ≫ further education

Chavín de Huantar [sha**veen** duh hwan**tah**] A prehistoric ceremonial centre at 3 200 m/10 000 ft in the Mosna Valley of the E Andes, the focus c.400–200 BC of an expansive religious cult embracing all C and N Peru; a world heritage site. Its buildings cover 50 ha/125 acres, the 6 ha/15 acre civic centre being notable for its carved stone deities and the 75 m/225 ft square, 13 m/42 ft high New Temple, internally a maze of galleries, ramps, and stairways.

check ≫ **cheque**

checkers ≫ **draughts**

Cheddar 5°17N 2°46W, pop (1981) 3 900. Market town in Sedgemoor district, Somerset, SW England; 16 km/10 ml ESE of Weston-super-Mare; famous for the limestone features of the Cheddar Gorge and for the Cheddar cheese originally made here. ≫ Somerset

cheese A dairy foodstuff made from milk, originally used as a means of preserving food from periods of plenty during leaner times. Milk proteins are soluble in water at a neutral pH, but when the pH falls to a critically low level of about 4.6, the proteins no longer remain soluble. They precipitate out to form the curd of sour milk, which is the basis of cheese manufacture. The most basic cheese is known as cottage cheese, where skimmed milk (ie milk with all the fat removed) is allowed to coagulate. The wide variety of cheeses is achieved by allowing particular strains of bacteria to cause the fall in pH by fermenting lactose. The curd is then processed into cheese by a variety of methods, some of which require quite lengthy maturation in the presence of moulds. Others are matured in a smoky atmosphere, and others mixed with cream to form very creamy cheeses. The hardness of a cheese is determined by both its water content and its fat content.

Many regions of Europe have produced cheeses for which they are famous. France alone has more than 400 varieties, including Brie, Camembert, and Roquefort. Other well-known cheeses include Swiss Gruyère and Emmenthal; English Cheddar, Cheshire, and Stilton; Italian Parmesan and Gorgonzola; and Dutch Gouda and Edam. Versions of these cheeses are now made in many other countries. ≫ casein; fermentation; milk

cheetah A member of the cat family, native to Africa and SW Asia; fastest land animal (can reach 110 kph/70 mph); only cat unable to retract its claws completely; pale with solid dark spots; lean with long legs and tail; inhabits dry grassland and scrub; eats birds, hares, and antelopes; easily tamed. (*Acinonyx jubatus*.) ≫ Felidae

Cheka An acronym from Russian letters **che** + **ka**, for the All-Russian Extraordinary Commission for Combating Counter-Revolution and Sabotage, established in 1917. It was in effect a political police force whose duties were to investigate and punish anti-Bolshevik activities. During the Civil War it was responsible for executing thousands of political opponents in what came to be called the 'Red Terror'. ≫ Bolsheviks; communism

Chekhov, Anton (Pavlovitch) [**che**kof] (1860–1904) Russian dramatist and master of the short story, born in Taganrog. He studied medicine at Moscow, and began to write while a student. His first book of stories (1886) was successful, and gradually he adopted writing as a profession. His early full-length plays were failures, but when *Chayka* (1896, The Seagull) was revived in 1898 by Stanislavsky at the Moscow Art Theatre, it was a great success. He then wrote his masterpieces: *Dyadya Vanya* (1900, Uncle Vanya), *Tri sestry* (1901, The Three Sisters), and *Vishnyovy sad* (1904, The Cherry Orchard). Meanwhile he continued to write many short stories, the best of which have continued to be highly acclaimed. In 1897 he fell ill with tuberculosis and lived thereafter either abroad or in the Crimea. In 1901 he married the actress Olga Knipper, who remained for many years the admired exponent of female parts in his plays. He died at Badenweiler, Germany. ≫ drama; Russian literature; short story

chelate [**kee**layt] A complex of two or more components in which one is joined to another by two or more points of attachment. In co-ordination compounds, a chelating ligand, such as diamino-ethane, complexes metal ions more completely than do similar ligands such as ammonia with only one point of attachment to the metal. ≫ co-ordination compounds; EDTA [i]; ligand

Chelmsford 51°44N 0°28E, pop (1981) 92 479. County town in Chelmsford district, Essex, SE England; on the R Chelmer, 48 km/30 ml NE of London; railway; electronics, furniture; 15th-c cathedral. ≫ Essex

Chelonia [ke**loh**nia] An order of reptiles (244 species); body encased in a domed shell of bones covered by large horny scales

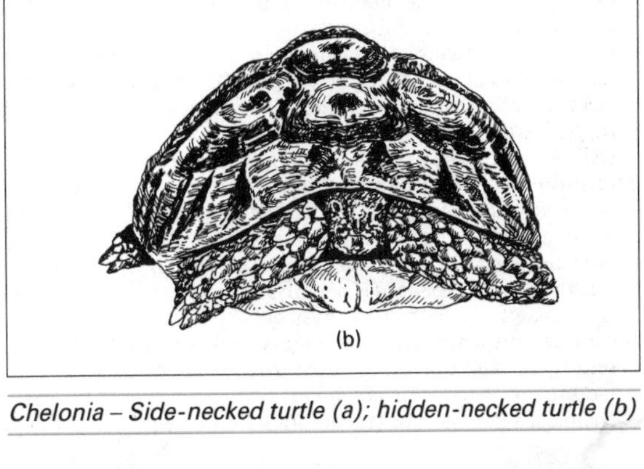

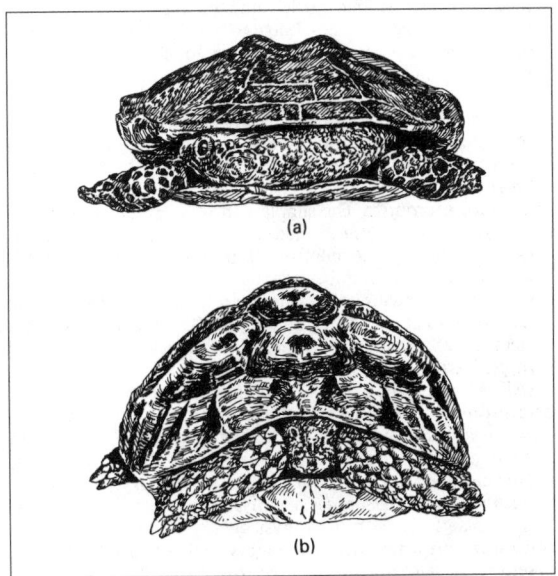

Chelonia – Side-necked turtle (a); hidden-necked turtle (b)

(*scutes*); no teeth; jaws form a hard *beak*; most withdraw head and legs into the shell for protection; head may be pulled backwards into the shell (species of suborder *Cryptodira* or **hidden-necked turtles**), or bent sideways (suborder: *Pleurodira* or **side-necked turtles**). In the USA, all species are called **turtles** (with **tortoise** used for a terrestrial **turtle** and marine forms called **sea turtles**); in the UK there is no single common name for all species, and only marine forms are called **turtles**. » reptile; terrapin; tortoise; turtle (biology)

Chelsea » **Kensington and Chelsea**

Chelsea pensioners Occupants of the hospital for old and disabled soldiers in Chelsea, London. Founded by Charles II in 1682, the Royal Hospital takes in about 420 men, usually aged over 65. Chelsea pensioners wear distinctive uniforms, navy blue in winter and scarlet in summer. » pension

Chelsea porcelain A London porcelain factory which flourished 1743–85, and was almost certainly the first to make true porcelain in the British Is. It was founded by a silversmith from Liège, Nicholas Sprimont (1716–71), and a jeweller, Charles Gouyn (died 1781). Like Bow, it produced both figures and finely-painted service wares. In 1770 the factory was bought by William Duesbury (1725–86) of Derby. » porcelain

Cheltenham [**chel**tuhnuhm] 51°54N 2°04W, pop (1981) 84 373. Residential town in Cheltenham district, Gloucestershire, SWC England; on W edge of Cotswold Hills, 12 km/7 ml NE of Gloucester; famous spa in 18th-c; railway; schools (Cheltenham College, Cheltenham Ladies' College); Cheltenham Gold Cup horse-race (Mar); National Hunt steeplechases in Prestbury Park; festival of contemporary music (Jul). » Gloucestershire

Chelyabinsk, also **Tchelyabinsk** [chil**ya**binsk] 55°12N 61°25E, pop (1989) 1 143 000. Industrial capital city of Chelyabinskaya oblast, W Siberian Russia; on E slopes of the S Ural Mts; founded in 1736 as a frontier outpost; airport; road and rail junction; iron and steel, machines, foodstuffs, chemicals. » Russia

chemical analysis The determination of the composition of a material. It may be qualitative or quantitative, and may refer to the relative amounts of different elements present, or the extent to which particular properties, such as acidity or oxidizing power, are present. » analytical chemistry

chemical bond The electric forces linking atoms in molecules and non-molecular solid phases. Three types of bond may be identified: (1) *ionic*, as in sodium chloride (NaCl), in which electrons are lost and gained so that the structure is held together by the mutual attraction of Na^+ and Cl^- ions; (2) *covalent*, as in chlorine (Cl_2), where some electrons are associated with two atomic nuclei; and (3) *metallic*, as in sodium (Na), where the valence electrons are delocalized and associated with many nuclei, giving rise to electric conductivity. Covalent bonds involving 2, 4, and 6 electrons are called *single*, *double*, and *triple*, and are represented by –, =, and ≡, respectively. The energy required to break a chemical bond (eg to convert a chlorine molecule to two chlorine atoms) is called the **bond energy**. » atom; chemical energy; hydrogen bond; valence

chemical elements The simplest substances into which matter can be broken without nuclear reactions. Each element is characterized by the number of protons in the nuclei of its atoms, the atomic number of the element, and is identified by a one- or two-letter symbol. There are about 90 elements which have been found in nature, and about 105 when artificially-made elements are included. The most common elements in the crust of the Earth are: oxygen (O), 49%; silicon (Si), 26%; aluminium (Al), 8%; iron (Fe), 5%. » atom; chemical formula; RR90

chemical energy Energy potentially or actually liberated by a chemical reaction, also called **heat of reaction**. This energy may be converted to or from electrical energy, heat, or light. Normally, energy *absorbed* in chemical change is considered positive, energy *released* is negative. It is generally expressed on the molar scale. » mole (physics)

chemical engineering The theory and practice of designing, setting up, and operating apparatus for the large-scale manufacture of the products of chemical reactions. The earliest chemical manufacture (to the mid-19th-c) was based on personal skills and on tradition. From then on, the application of mathematics and physics to chemical problems, and an increased demand for chemical products, led to the study of the ways in which known chemical and physical principles applied to large quantities, the demands for heat supply, and the control of the movement of chemicals in bulk through large systems. The various problems in manufacturing a wide variety of substances are studied in the light of common principles that apply to unit processes. University departments, professional training, and professional institutions devoted to chemical engineering have developed in all industrialized countries since 1900. » chemistry; engineering

chemical equation The quantitative expression of a chemical reaction. It must balance, in terms of both the numbers of atoms of all elements involved, and the electric charge. The example given below is the reaction of manganate(VII) (permanganate) ions with iron(II) to give manganese(II) and iron(III). The reaction also consumes acid (H+) and produces water: $MnO_4^- + 5Fe^{2+} + 8H^+ \rightarrow Mn^{2+} + 5Fe^{3+} + 4H_2O$. » chemical reaction

chemical finishing A general term used for the treatment of fabrics by chemical processing, such as bleaching, mercerizing, resin treatment, or waterproofing. It is carried out to 'finish' the fabric after weaving, knitting, etc has taken place. » bleaching; mercerizing

chemical formula The representation of a substance in terms of the symbols of its elements. Molecular compounds are given as the full molecule; thus benzene is C_6H_6 and acetylene is C_2H_2. Non-molecular compounds are given as the simplest ratio of elements, also called the *empirical formula*; thus calcium fluoride is CaF_2, and diamond is C. » chemical elements; compound

chemical laser A laser in which a chemical reaction provides the energy for laser action. For example, in a laser containing carbon dioxide with hydrogen and fluorine, the laser action would take place in the carbon dioxide, powered by the reaction of hydrogen and fluorine to give hydrogen fluoride. Chemical lasers with powers in excess of 10^6 W are possible. » chemical reaction; laser [i]

chemical reaction A process in which one or more compounds are converted into others, usually with the gain or loss of energy by the system, by the breaking and forming of chemical bonds. » addition/elimination/substitution reaction; catalysis; chemical equation; condensation (chemistry)

chemical warfare The use of deadly or disabling gases in warfare. It was forbidden by a declaration of the Hague Conference in 1899, but one of the signatories, Germany, was the first to use such weapons, the first attack being made against British troops at Ypres in April 1915. Since 1918 chemical weapons have been used in many conflicts, but not on European battlefields, although the Germans manufactured large quantities of deadly nerve gases during World War 2. Such weapons are not forbidden by treaty, and large quantities were stockpiled by the USA and the former Soviet Union. Other agents of chemical warfare include non-lethal harassing and incapacitating agents, hallucinogenic substances, and herbicides. » Agent Orange; mustard gas; nerve gas; poison gas

chemiluminescence » **bioluminescence**

chemin de fer A casino card game, often referred to as 'chemmy'. A variant of baccarat banque, it is played by up to 12 players. The object is to obtain a total as near as possible to 9 with two or three cards. If the total is a double figure then the first figure is ignored, eg 16 would count as 6. The ace counts as 1, face cards their value, and picture cards 10. » baccarat; casino; playing cards

chemisorption » **adsorption**

chemistry The study of the composition of substances and the changes that they undergo. Its origins lie partly in ancient technology (eg metallurgy and soap manufacture), partly in mediaeval speculation on methods of obtaining gold (*alchemy*), and partly in early attempts to improve medicines (*iatrochemistry*). Antoine Lavoisier is usually considered the father of modern chemistry, with his distinction between *elements* and *compounds* formed from elements, and his insistence that chemical reactions are quantitative in nature. With the development of the atomic theory of John Dalton, chemistry evolved rapidly in the 19th-c. **Organic chemistry** originated from the isolation of medicinal compounds from animals and plants, and **inorganic chemistry** from the study of minerals. They developed mainly into the synthesis and study of molecular compounds and of ionic compounds respectively, but are now often indistinguishable. **Physical chemistry** (studying the relationship of physical properties to chemical composition, structure, and reactivity) and **analytical chemistry** (studying the composition of material) also developed in parallel, particularly with 20th-c developments in spectroscopic and electrochemical methods. Modern chemistry has also been advanced by the elucidation of the nature of chemical bonding. Chemistry today is the basis of a worldwide industry concerned with almost every aspect of life, including food, fuel, clothing, building materials, and medicines. While the growth of this industry has had some undeniably bad environmental effects, chemistry provides the key to the improvement of the environment. » analytical/inorganic/organic/physical/synthetic chemistry; assaying; chemical analysis/bond/elements/energy/equation/formula/reaction; chemotherapy; Dalton, John; electrochemistry; geochemistry; histochemistry; Lavoisier; radiochemistry; stereochemistry; thermochemistry

chemoreception The perception of chemical stimuli by living organisms; usually performed by specialized receptor cells or organs. Chemoreception includes both olfaction (the perception of smells) and gustation (the perception of taste).

chemotaxis The process by which cells or organisms move in response to a chemical stimulus towards the most appropriate region of their environment. Examples include the movement of leucocytes towards the sites of inflammation, infection, or tissue damage; and the movement of bacteria towards areas that are nutritionally rich. » bacteria [i]; leucocytes

chemotherapy The drug treatment of infectious diseases (using antibiotics), parasitic diseases, and cancer. Cancer chemotherapy usually involves the administration of a cocktail of cytotoxic drugs (ie which kill or damage cells). Although designed to attack preferentially the rapidly growing cells of a tumour, they also attack normal cells (especially bone marrow) causing reduced resistance to infection, loss of hair, and sterility. Supportive therapy can now help with these problems. They also cause severe nausea and vomiting, which can prevent completion of a course of treatment, so drugs are included in the cocktail to combat this. Examples of cytotoxic drugs include alkylating agents (eg cisplatin), antimetabolites (eg methotrexate), and Vinca alkaloids. Hormones are also used to suppress the growth of some tumours. » antibiotics; cancer; drug resistance; tumour

Chenab, River [**chay**nab] River in Kashmir and Pakistan; one of the five rivers of the Punjab; rises in the Himalayas and flows NW into Kashmir, then S into Pakistan; joined by the R Sutlej E of Bahawalpur to form the R Panjnad, which then joins the R Indus to the NE of Chachran; length 1 087 km/675 ml. » Kashmir; Pakistan [i]

Cheng-hsien » **Zhengzhou**

Cheng-tu » **Chengdu**

Chengchow » **Zhengzhou**

Chengdu or **Cheng-tu** 30°37N 104°06E, pop (1984e) 2 539 600. Capital of Sichuan province, SWC China; founded 200 BC as Zhou dynastic capital; regional industrial base since 1949; airfield; railway; university (1931); rice, wheat, sweet potatoes, tea, medicinal herbs, tobacco, silk, handicrafts, coal, metallurgy, electronics; home of Sichuan opera; home of Tang poet, Du Fu (712–70); Dujiang Yan Dam (250 BC), 40 km/25 ml NW; Ching Yang Gong Temple; flower festival (Feb–Mar). » China [i]

Cheops, Ship of » **Ship of Cheops**

cheque (UK) or **check** (US) An order in writing to a bank to pay the person or institution named the sum of money specified. Cheques are commonly printed by banks for the use of their customers, but may be written on anything; examples include a tablecloth and (in legal fiction) a cow. If a bank refuses to accept a cheque, it will be marked 'R.D.', signifying 'Refer to Drawer'. » cheque card

cheque card A flexible plastic card (c.54 × 85 mm/2.1 × 3.3 in) issued by banks to customers who have a cheque book. It shows the customer's name and account number, and guarantees that the bank will honour a cheque (up to a specified sum) where the name and number correspond. Some may also be used in bank cash-dispensing machines. » cheque; credit card

chequerberry » **service tree**

Chequers The official country residence of British prime ministers, donated to the nation by Viscount Lee of Fareham in 1921. The estate is located in the Chiltern Hills, Buckinghamshire. It is mentioned in the Domesday Book.

Cherbourg [**sher**boorg], Fr [shair**boor**], ancient **Carusbur** 49°38N 1°37W, pop (1982) 40 500. Fortified seaport and naval base in Manche department, NW France; at head of the Cotentin peninsula; harbour protected by a long breakwater, 1853; France's third largest naval base; shipbuilding and dockyards; used by transatlantic shipping; ferry services to Southampton, Weymouth, Rosslare.

Cherenkov, Pavel (Alekseyevich) (1904–) Russian physicist, born at Novaya Chigla. Educated at Voronezh, he worked at the Academy of Sciences. In 1934 he noted the emission of blue light from water and other transparent media when atomic particles, moving at a speed greater than light in that medium, are passed through it. Subsequent researches by Tamm and Frank led to a definite explanation of the **Cherenkov effect**, for which all three shared the Nobel Prize for Physics in 1958. » particle physics

Chernenko, Konstantin Ustinovich (1911–85) Soviet politician and President (1984–5), born at Bolshaya Tes, Siberia. He joined the Communist Party in 1931, and held several local posts. An associate of Brezhnev for many years, he became a member of the Politburo in 1978, and the Party's chief ideologist after the death of Suslov. Regarded as a conservative, Chernenko was a rival of Andropov in the Party leadership contest of 1982, and became Party General Secretary and Head of State after Andropov's death in 1984. He suffered from ill health, and died soon after in Moscow, to be succeeded by Gorbachev. » Andropov, Yuri; Brezhnev; Gorbachev; Suslov

Chernobyl [cher**no**bil] 51°16N 30°15E. City in Ukraine; near the junction of the Pripyat and Ushk Rivers, N of Kiev; scene of the world's largest known nuclear disaster in 1986. » Ukraine

chernozem A dark, rich and fertile soil found in cool, low-humidity regions. It is typical of the Russian steppes. » soil

Cherokee [**che**ruhkee] N American Indian people, originally from the Great Lakes, who migrated to the SE after their defeat by the Iroquois and Delaware. Evicted from their land when gold was discovered on it, 15 000 were force-marched W by 7 000 US troops (the 'trail of tears', 1838–9). The survivors were settled in Oklahoma with Creeks and other SE tribes moved there by the US government in the 1830s. An estimated 66 000 still live in E Oklahoma, some on tribal landholdings. » American Indians

cherry A deciduous, mostly N temperate tree closely related to the plum, peach, and blackthorn; often a distinctive shiny reddish-brown banded bark; oval, finely toothed leaves; clusters of white flowers and bright red or purplish fruits which are sour or sweet, depending on the species. The well-known orchard fruits are mostly the **sour** or **morello cherry** (*Prunus cerasus*), a species of unknown origin, with white flowers and bright red, acid fruit; and the **sweet cherry**, probably a hybrid between gean and sour cherry with sweet, red or purplish fruits. Various other species and hybrids, especially pink-flowered Japanese ones, are popular ornamentals. (Genus: *Prunus*, subgenus: *Cerasus*. Family: *Rosaceae*.) » deciduous plants; gean; prunus

cherry laurel An evergreen shrub or small tree, native to the Balkans but cultivated since the 16th-c, and widely naturalized; leaves oblong, leathery; flowers white, fragrant, c.30 in a spike; berries red or green, turning black when ripe, poisonous. (*Prunus laurocerasus*. Family: *Rosaceae*.) » evergreen plants; prunus; shrub; tree [i]

cherry plum A deciduous, occasionally spiny, shrub or small tree, growing to 8 m/26 ft, probably one of the parents of plum; flowers white, appearing with or before ovoid, toothed leaves;

fruit globular, 2–3.5 cm/0.8–1.5 in, red or yellow; native to the Balkans, and cultivated elsewhere; also called **myrobalan**. (*Prunus cerasifera*. Family: *Rosaceae*.) » deciduous plants; plum; prunus; shrub; tree [i]

chert A very fine-grained form of silica (SiO_2), in which the quartz crystals are too small to be observed by optical microscopy. It is characteristically formed on the ocean bed by the accumulation and subsequent recrystallization of the silica shells of diatoms and radiolaria. It also occurs as concretions in limestones. » flint; quartz; silica

cherubim [**cher**uhbim], singular **cherub** In the Hebrew Bible/Old Testament, winged celestial creatures or beasts of various descriptions. Their roles include guarding the tree of life in the Garden of Eden (*Gen* 3.24), being stationed on the cover of the Ark of the Covenant (*Ex* 25.18–22), adorning Solomon's temple (1 *Kings* 6.23ff), and accompanying the throne chariot of God (*Ezek* 1, 10). » angel; Ark of the Covenant; Eden, Garden of; seraphim

Cherubini, (Maria) Luigi (Carlo Zenobi Salvatore) [keroo**bee**nee] (1760–1842) Italian composer, born at Florence. He studied at Bologna and Milan, and wrote a succession of operas, at first in Neapolitan, later (having moved to Paris) in French style. His best opera was *Les Deux Journées* (1880, The Two Days, or The Water-Carrier). His later work was mainly ecclesiastical. In 1822 he became director of the Conservatoire at Paris, where he died.

chervil A hollow-stemmed annual, growing to 70 cm/27 in, native to Europe and Asia, and often introduced elsewhere; leaves divided, the lobes dissected into narrow oblong segments; flowers small, white, borne in umbels up to 5 cm/2 in across; fruits oblong, smooth. It is often grown for its aromatic leaves, used as a flavouring. (*Anthriscus cerefolium*. Family: *Umbelliferae*.) » annual; umbel

Cherwell, Frederick Alexander Lindemann, 1st Viscount [**chah**wel] (1886–1957) British scientist, born at Baden-Baden, Germany. He was brought up in England, but went to university at Berlin and the Sorbonne. In 1914 he became director of the Experimental Physics Station at Farnborough, where he evolved the mathematical theory of aircraft spin, and tested it in a daring flight. In 1919 he became professor of experimental philosophy at Oxford, and later director of the Clarendon laboratory. A close friend of Winston Churchill, he became his scientific adviser in 1940. He was created a baron in 1941 and was paymaster-general on two occasions (1942–5, 1951–3).

Chesapeake Bay [**che**sapeek] An inlet of the Atlantic Ocean in Virginia (S) and Maryland (N) states, USA; over 300 km/185 ml long; at the mouth of the Susquehanna, Patuxent, Potomac, Chester, Choptank, Nanticoke, Rappahannock, and James Rivers; part of the Intracoastal Waterway; an early area of US settlement (explored 1607); wide range of seafood; increasing pollution. » Intracoastal Waterway; United States of America [i]

Cheshire, (Geoffrey) Leonard (1917–) British bomber pilot and philanthropist, educated at Oxford. An outstanding pilot and leader, he was repeatedly decorated (including the VC, 1944) for his many bombing missions on heavily defended German targets. He was one of the official British observers of the destruction caused by the atomic bomb over Nagasaki (1945). This experience, together with his new-found faith in Catholicism, made him decide to devote the rest of his life to tending the incurably sick, by founding 'Cheshire Homes' (220, in 45 countries). In 1959 he married Sue Ryder. » atomic bomb

Cheshire pop (1987e) 951 900; area 2 328 sq km/899 sq ml. County of NWC England, divided into eight districts, bounded W by Wales; drained by the Mersey, Weaver, Dee, Gowy, and Wheelock Rivers; Delamere Forest between Chester and Northwich; county town, Chester; chief towns include Crewe, Warrington, Widnes, Runcorn, Macclesfield; dairy farming, petrochemicals, motor vehicles. » Chester; England [i]

chess A game for two players played on a board containing 64 squares alternately black and white. Each player has 16 pieces, either black or white, consisting of 8 pawns, 2 rooks (also known as castles), 2 knights, 2 bishops, a queen, and a king. The game is one of strategy, the object being to capture the opponent's king. All pieces have set moves, and the most versatile is the queen. The game was first played in ancient India and was known as *chaturanga*. The earliest reference to chess is from c.600 AD; the current pieces have existed in standard form for more than 500 years. » draughts; shogi; RR94, 107

Chessman, Caryl (Whittier) (1922–60) US convict-author, born at St Joseph, Michigan. He was sentenced to death in 1948 on 17 charges of kidnapping, robbery and sexual assault, but was granted eight stays of execution, amounting to a record period of 12 years under sentence of death without a reprieve. During this period he conducted a brilliant legal battle from prison, learnt four languages, and wrote the best-selling books against capital punishment *Cell 2455 Death Row* (1956), *Trial by Ordeal* (1956), and *The Face of Justice* (1958). His execution, at San Quentin, California, provoked worldwide criticism of American judicial methods.

chest » thorax

Chester, Lat **Deva**, **Devana Castra**, Welsh **Caerleon**, Anglo-Saxon **Legaceaster** 53°12N 2°54W, pop (1981) 82 363. County town of Cheshire, NWC England; on the R Dee, 305 km/189 ml NW of London; important Roman port and military centre; railway; commercial centre, light engineering, tourism, car components; 13th–15th-c cathedral, city walls, two-tiered shopping arcades, 11th-c St John's Church; town hall (1869). » Cheshire

Chesterfield, Philip Dormer Stanhope, 4th Earl of (1694–1773) English statesman, orator, and man of letters, born and died in London. He studied at Cambridge, made the Grand Tour, became an MP (1715), and in 1726 succeeded his father as Earl. A bitter antagonist of Walpole, he joined the Pelham ministry (1744), became Irish Lord-Lieutenant (1745), and one of the principal Secretaries of State (1746–8). Intimate with Swift, Pope, and other contemporary authors, his own best-known work was his guide to manners and success, *Letters to his Son* (1774). » Pelham, Thomas; Walpole, Robert

Chesterton, G(ilbert) K(eith) (1874–1936) British critic, novelist and poet, born in London. Educated at St Paul's, he studied art at the Slade School. Much of his best work took the form of articles for periodicals, including his own *G.K.'s Weekly*. He wrote a great deal of poetry, as well as literary critical studies and works of social criticism. The amiable detective-priest who brought him popularity with a wider public first appeared in *The Innocence of Father Brown* (1911). Chesterton became a Catholic in 1922, and thereafter wrote mainly on religious topics, including lives of Francis of Assisi and Thomas Aquinas. He died at Beaconsfield, Buckinghamshire. » English literature; literary criticism

Chetniks (Serbo-Croatian *četnici*) Yugoslav, mainly Serbian, guerrillas during World War 2. Under the leadership of Drazha Mihailovic, they fought Tito's communist Partisans rather than the Axis occupiers. Abandoned by the Allies in 1944, they were defeated by the Partisans, and Mihailovic was tried and executed in 1945. » Mihailovic; Tito

Chevalier, Maurice [shuh**val**yay] (1888–1972) French film and vaudeville actor, born and died in Paris. He began as a child singer and dancer in small cafes, and then danced at the Folies Bergères (1909–13). His first Hollywood film was *The Innocents of Paris* (1929), and 30 years later his individual, straw-hatted, *bon-viveur* personality, with his distinctive French accent, was still much acclaimed, as in the musical *Gigi*. He won a special Academy Award in 1958.

chevet [**she**vay] The circular or polygonal E end of a church. It is surrounded by an aisle, normally called an *ambulatory*. There are usually chapels radiating outwards. » church [i]

Cheviot Hills [**chee**viuht] Hill range on the border between Scotland and England; extends 56 km/35 ml SW along the frontier between Borders region and Northumberland; rises to 816 m/2 677 ft at The Cheviot; gives its name to a famous breed of sheep. » England [i]; Scotland [i]

chevrotain [**shev**ruhtin] A ruminant artiodactyl mammal, native to tropical forest in Africa, India, Sri Lanka and SE Asia; small with stocky bodies and short slender legs; no horns or antlers; male with long protruding canine teeth; also known as **mouse**

deer or **deerlet**. (Family: *Tragulidae*, 4 species.) » antlers [i]; artiodactyl; deer; ruminant [i]

Chewa [**chay**wa] A Bantu-speaking agricultural people of Malawi, Zambia, and Zimbabwe, who speak Chinyanja, the lingua franca of Zambia and Malawi. They belong to a cluster of Bantu-speaking peoples known as the Maravi. Like many other groups in the area, descent and succession is matrilineal. Population c.2 million. » Bantu-speaking peoples; matrilineal descent

chewing gum A sugared and flavoured product made from the concentrated juice of latex of the sapodilla tree, especially popular in the USA. It is chewed for its flavour, but not swallowed. » chicle

Cheyenne (Indians) [shiy**en**, shiy**an**] N American Plains Indians, divided since the 1830s into N and S groups. Buffalo hunters on horseback, they were pushed W by various groups (such as the Ojibwa and Sioux), and their population was reduced by fighting and disease. They were involved in conflict with European prospectors and settlers (1857–9), and in the 1870s participated in the uprisings of other Plains tribes against the Whites. Population c.7 000, in Montana and Oklahoma. » American Indians; Ojibwa; Plains Indians; Sioux

Cheyenne (Wyoming) [shiy**an**] 41°08N 104°49W, pop (1980) 47 283. State capital in Laramie County, SE Wyoming, USA; founded at a railway junction, 1867; territorial capital, 1869; prospered with gold mining in the Black Hills in the 1870s; railway; livestock market and shipping centre; Frontier Days Museum; Frontier Days (Jul). » Wyoming

Chi-lung » **Jilong**

Chi-nan » **Jinan**

chi-square test [kiy] A statistical test to measure how well the values 'expected' from a model agree with the 'observed' values. If e_i is an 'expected' value and o_i the corresponding 'observed' value, the statistic $\chi^2 = \sum(o_i - e_i)^2/e_i$ » statistics

Chiang Ch'ing » **Jiang Qing**

Chiang Kai-shek [**chang** kiy **shek**] » **Jiang Jieshi**

Chiang Mai [jee-eng **miy**] 18°48N 98°59E, pop (1982) 104 910. City in NW Thailand, 700 km/435 ml N of Bangkok; N Thailand's principal city since 1296, when it was founded as the capital of Lan Na Thai kingdom; airfield; railway; university; tea, rice, groundnuts, corn, teak; flower festival (Feb), Songkran water-throwing festival (Thai New Year), Loy Krathong (Nov). » Thailand [i]

chiaroscuro [keearos**koo**roh] (Ital 'light-dark') In painting, the use of strong light and shadow to define forms in space. The technique was developed in Italy by Leonardo da Vinci and Caravaggio, and perfected by Rembrandt in 17th-c Holland. » Baroque (art and architecture); Caravaggio; Leonardo da Vinci; Rembrandt; tenebrism

Chiba [**chee**ba] 35°38N 140°07E, pop (1980) 746 430. Capital of Chiba prefecture, Kanto region, E Honshu, Japan; commuter town 40 km/25 ml E of Tokyo, on Tokyo Bay; railway; university (1949); steel, textiles, paper; Buddhist temple (8th-c). » Honshu

Chicago [shi**kah**goh] 41°53N 87°38W, pop (1980) 3 005 072. Third largest city in the USA; seat of Cook County, NE Illinois, on L Michigan; built on the site of Fort Dearborn; settled in the 1830s; city status, 1837; developed as a result of its strategic position linking the Great Lakes with the Mississippi R after the Illinois and Michigan Canal was completed (1848), and after the railway to the E was opened (1853); much of the city destroyed by fire, 1871; notorious gangster activity in the Prohibition years (1920s), notably by Al Capone; now the major industrial, commercial, financial and cultural centre for the US interior; electrical machinery, metal products, steel (one-quarter of the nation's steel produced in and around the city), textiles, chemicals, food products, printing and publishing; commerce and finance centred upon 'The Loop' area; transport centre of the USA, with one of the busiest airports in the world; major rail network and inland port; seven universities; Sears Tower (1974), the world's tallest building (443 m/1 454 ft); major league teams, Cubs, White Sox (baseball), Bulls (basketball), Bears (football); Lyric Opera, Art Institute, Museum of Science and Industry, Shedd Aquarium, Planetarium; Chicago Film Festival (Nov). » Illinois; Michigan, Lake; Prohibition; Sears Tower

Chicago School (architecture) The name given to a group of Chicago architects and office buildings in the late 19th-c. The buildings are the forerunners of 20th-c skyscrapers, and are characterized by the pioneering use of steel frame construction, clothed in masonry and with large expanses of windows, often to a great height. A prime example is the Reliance Building (1894–5), architects Burnham & Root. » curtain wall

Chicago School (economics) A group of economists at Chicago University, led by Milton Friedman from 1948 to 1979. They hold the view that competition and market forces should be allowed to act freely, and with minimal government interference, for the best results. » Friedman

Chichén Itzá [chee**chen** eet**za**] Toltec/Maya capital of the Yucatan peninsula, Mexico, c.AD 1000–1200, reputedly established by the Toltec ruler Topílitzin after his expulsion from Tula c.987. Its monumental centre (area 3 km/1¾ ml by 2 km/1¼ ml) contains temple pyramids, the largest known Meso-American ballcourt, and a *tzompantli* (skull platform). From the Great Plaza, a 275 m/900 ft causeway leads N to the Cenote (Well) of Sacrifice, a massive water-filled pit sacred to the Rain God into which votive offerings and human sacrifices were cast. » Mayas; Meso-American ballgame; Toltecs; Tula (Mexico)

Chichester, Sir Francis (Charles) (1901–72) British yachtsman, born at Barnstaple, Devonshire. Educated at Marlborough, he emigrated to New Zealand in 1919, where he made a fortune as a land agent. He became interested in flying, and made several pioneer flights, but was badly injured by a crash in Japan (1931). In 1953 he took up yacht racing, winning the first solo transatlantic yacht race (1960) in 'Gipsy Moth III', sailing from Plymouth to New York in 40 days; he repeated the success in 1962 in 33 days. He made a successful solo circumnavigation of the world (1966–7) in 'Gipsy Moth IV', sailing from Plymouth to Sydney in 107 days and from there back to Plymouth, via Cape Horn, in 119 days. He was knighted in 1967, and died at Plymouth. » sailing; yacht [i]

Chichester 50°50N 0°48W, pop (1981) 27 241. County town of West Sussex, S England; 26 km/16 ml E of Portsmouth; founded by the Romans; later taken by the Saxons and named after their leader, Cissa; railway; engineering, furniture, agricultural trade, tourism; 11th–12th-c cathedral, 12th-c bishop's palace, 13th-c St Mary's hospital, 15th-c market cross, theatre (1962), remains of Roman villa at Fishbourne (3 km/1¾ ml W); Chichester Festival Theatre season (Aug–Sep). » Sussex, West

chick-pea A branching annual, growing to 50 cm/20 in or more; leaves pinnate with 7–17 oval, toothed, glandular-hairy leaflets; pea-flowers white or bluish, solitary on long stalks; pods inflated, usually 2-seeded; also called **garbanzos**. Probably native to Asia, it has been cultivated since ancient times as a fodder plant and for its large, wrinkled, edible seeds. (*Cicer arietinum*. Family: *Leguminosae*.) » annual; pinnate

chickadee A name used in the USA for certain small birds of the tit family. (Family: *Paridae*, 7 species.) » tit

chickaree » **red squirrel**

chicken » **domestic fowl**

chickenpox A highly infectious and usually benign disease of childhood, caused by the same virus that is responsible for shingles. It has a characteristic blister-like (vesicular) eruption in the skin, which may become infected by bacteria. » shingles

chickweed A slender, spreading, often pale-green annual; a very common weed, often flowering throughout the year; leaves oval, opposite; flowers tiny, white, five petals, shorter than sepals, deeply cleft into two parts. (*Stellaria media*. Family: *Caryophyllaceae*.) » annual

chicle An evergreen tree growing to 18 m/60 ft, native to C America, cultivated elsewhere; leaves elliptical; flowers tiny, greenish-white, 6-petalled; fruit 5–10 cm/2–4 in, greyish to reddish brown with yellow flesh. The copious white latex, collected as for rubber, provides the elastic base for chewing gum; the edible fruit is called **sapodilla plum**. (*Achras zapota*.

Family: *Sapotaceae*.) » evergreen plants; latex; rubber; tree [i]

chicory A perennial growing to 120 cm/5 ft, with a long stout tap root, native to Europe, W Asia, and N Africa, and widely introduced elsewhere; leaves spear-shaped, lobed or toothed, the upper clasping the stem; flower heads nearly stalkless, 2.5–4 cm/1–1½ in across, bright blue, rarely pink or white. It is locally grown as a vegetable and as a medicinal plant. Dried and ground roots are used as a coffee substitute. (*Cichorium intybus*. Family: *Compositae*.) » coffee; perennial

chiffchaff A bird belonging to a group of Old World warblers; native to Europe, N Africa, and Asia; inhabits forest edges with thick undergrowth; eats insects; N birds move S in winter. (*Phylloscopus collybita*. Family: *Silviidae*.)

Chifley, Joseph Benedict (1885–1951) Australian statesman and Labor Prime Minister (1945–9), born at Bathurst, New South Wales. In early life an engine driver, he entered parliament in 1928, and became Defence Minister in 1929. As Prime Minister, he expanded social services and reformed the banking system. He continued as leader of the Labor Party until his death, in Canberra. » Australian Labor Party

chigger » **harvestmite**

chihuahua [chi**wah**wa] The smallest domestic breed of dog, developed in Mexico; tiny body; head disproportionately large with bulbous forehead, large widely-spaced eyes, and large ears; two forms: the *long-coat chihuahua* and *smooth-coat chihuahua*. » dog

Chihuahua [chi**wah**wa] 28°40N 106°06W, pop (1980) 406 830. Capital of Chihuahua state, N Mexico; altitude 1 428 m/4 685 ft; centre of Pancho Villa's revolutionary activities; railway; university (1954); mining, cattle raising, smelting; cathedral (18th-c); famous for its hairless small dog, which has a constant body temperature of 40°C. » Mexico [i]; Villa, Francisco

chilblains Bluish and slightly swollen areas of the skin of fingers and toes, caused by exposure to excessive cold. The lesions become red and itchy on warming. » foot; hand

childbirth » **labour**

Childe, (Vere) Gordon (1892–1957) Australian archaeologist, born in Sydney. Educated at Sydney University and Oxford, his early books, notably *The Dawn of European Civilisation* (1925), and *The Most Ancient Near East* (1928), established him as the most influential archaeological theorist of his generation. He was professor of archaeology at Edinburgh (1927–46) and director of the University of London Institute of Archaeology (1946–56). He returned to Australia on retirement, where he committed suicide. » archaeology

Childers, (Robert) Erskine (1870–1922) Irish nationalist and writer, born in London and educated at Cambridge. He fought in the South African and First World Wars, and wrote a popular spy story, *The Riddle of the Sands* (1903), and several works of nonfiction. After the establishment of the Irish Free State, he joined the Irish Republican Army, and was active in the Civil War. He was captured and executed at Dublin. His son, **Erskine Childers** (1905–74) was President of Ireland in 1973–4. » IRA; nationalism

Children's Crusade A movement in 1212 of thousands of children (some as young as six) from Germany and France, aiming to reach the Holy Land and recapture Jerusalem from the Turks. Some reached Genoa, Italy, but did not embark; some reached Marseilles, France, whence they were shipped to N Africa and sold into slavery. » Crusades [i]

Chile [chilee], official name **República de Chile** (Republic of Chile) pop (1990e) 13 173 000; area 756 626 sq km/292 058 sq ml (excluding territory claimed in Antarctica). Republic of SW South America, divided into 12 regions; bounded W by the Pacific Ocean, E by Argentina, NE by Bolivia, and NW by Peru; capital, Santiago; chief towns Valparaíso, Concepción, Talcahuano, Antofagasta, Viña del Mar; timezone GMT −4; official language, Spanish; mainly mixed Spanish and Indian descent; unit of currency, the peso of 100 centavos.

Physical description. Narrow coastal belt, backed by Andean mountain ridges rising in the N to 6 723 m/22 057 ft at Llullaillaco; mountains lower in the C and S; fertile C Andean valley,

40–60 km/25–40 ml wide at 1 200 m/4 000 ft; Atacama Desert in far NW.

Climate. Highly varied (spans 37° of latitude, with altitudes from Andean peaks to coastal plain); extreme aridity in N Atacama Desert; cold, wet, and windy in far S at Tierra del Fuego; Mediterranean climate in C Chile, with warm, wet winters and dry summers; average temperature at Valparaíso on coast varies from below 12°C (Jul) to nearly 18°C (Jan), with average annual rainfall of 505 mm/20 in; at Santiago (higher altitude), below 375 mm/14.8 in; at Antofagasta (N), just over 12 mm/0.5 in.

History and government. Originally occupied by South American Indians; arrival of Spanish in 16th-c; part of Viceroyalty of Peru; independence from Spain declared, 1810, resulting in war until Spanish defeat in 1818; first president, General Bernardo O'Higgins; border disputes with Bolivia, Peru, and Argentina brought Chilean victory in War of the Pacific (1879–84); economic unrest in late 1920s led to military dictatorship under Ibañez until 1931; Marxist coalition government of Salvador Allende ousted (1973), and replaced by military junta under Augusto Pinochet, banning all political activity, and resulting in considerable political opposition, both at home and abroad; constitution providing for eventual return to democracy came into effect in 1981; plebiscite held in 1988 resulted in a defeat for Pinochet's candicacy as president beyond 1990; followed by limited political reforms, with a schedule for further elections; National Congress restored, 1990.

Economy. Based on agriculture and mining; wheat, corn, potatoes, sugar beet, fruit, livestock; fishing in N, timber in S; copper, iron ore, nitrates, silver, gold, coal, molybdenum; oil and gas discovered in far S (1945); steel, wood pulp, cellulose, mineral processing. » Atacama Desert; Easter Island; Magallanes-La Antártica Chilena; Santiago [i]; RR25 national holidays; RR45 political leaders

Chile pine » **monkey-puzzle**

chili » **pepper 1**

Chilopoda [keelopoda] » **centipede**

Chiltern Hills Low chalk hill range in SE England; extends 88 km/55 ml NE from S Oxfordshire, through Buckinghamshire, Hertfordshire, and Bedfordshire; continued SW as the Berkshire Downs and NE as the East Anglian Ridge; rises to 260 m/853 ft at Coombe Hill. » Chiltern Hundreds; England [i]

Chiltern Hundreds In the UK, a legally fictitious office of profit under the Crown: Steward or Bailiff of Her Majesty's Chiltern Hundreds of Stoke, Desborough, and Burnham. To accept this office disqualifies an MP from the House of Commons. As an MP cannot resign, application to the Chiltern Hundreds is the conventional manner of leaving the Commons. » Commons, House of

chimaera (botany) [**kimee**ra] A mosaic organism, usually a plant, composed of tissues of two genetically different types, or a tissue composed of cells of genetically different types. It is formed either by a mutation that affects cell type, or by the artificial grafting together of parts of different individuals. » cell; genetics [i]; mutation; plant

chimaera (zoology) [**kimee**ra] Cartilaginous fish with robust body, large pelvic fins, and long tapering tail; teeth fused into plates; common in deeper waters (100–500 m/300–1 600 ft) of N Atlantic and Mediterranean; length up to 1.5 m/5 ft; cream with brown patches and metallic sheen; also called **ratfish** or **rabbitfish**. (*Chimaera monstrosa*. Family: *Chimaeridae*.) » cartilaginous fish

Chimaera » **Chimera**

Chimborazo [cheembohr**ra**soh] 1°28S 78°48W. Inactive Andean volcano in C Ecuador; height 6 310 m/20 702 ft; highest peak in Ecuadorean Andes; cone partly covered by glaciers. » Andes; Ecuador [i]

Chimbote [cheem**boh**tay] 8°59S 78°38W, pop (1981) 216 406. Port in Ancash department, N Peru; one of the few natural harbours on the W coast and Peru's largest fishing port; a new port has been built to serve national steel industry; exports fishmeal. » Peru [i]

Chimera also **Chimaera** [kiy**mee**ra, kimeera] In Greek mythology, a fabulous monster with the head of a lion, the body of a goat (the name means 'she-goat'), and the tail of a serpent, which breathed fire. » Bellerophon

chimpanzee An ape native to equatorial Africa, believed to be the closest living relative to humans; height, 1–1.7 m/3 ¼–5 ½ ft; black coat; hair on head parted or directed backwards; face and ears naked; skin pale or dark; spends most time on the ground; eats fruit and some insects, but may kill small vertebrates; uses twigs, etc as tools to obtain food; two species: **chimpanzee** (*Pan troglodytes*) and the smaller, black-faced **pygmy chimpanzee** or **bonobo** (*Pan paniscus*). » ape

Chimu A S American Indian people of Peru, the most important political and cultural group before the Incas in the 14th-c, with a highly stratified social system. They built cities with huge buildings, pyramids, and streets, and developed sophisticated irrigation systems. They were conquered by the Incas (1465–70), who absorbed many aspects of their culture. » Chan Chan; Incas; Peru [i]

China, official name **The People's Republic of China**, Chinese **Zhonghua Renmin Gonghe Guo** pop (1990) 1 133 682 501; area 9 597 000 sq km/3 704 000 sq ml; also claims island of Taiwan. Socialist state in C and E Asia, comprising 21 provinces, three municipalities (Shanghai, Beijing, Tianjin) and five autonomous regions (Ningxia, Xinjiang, Guangxi, Xizang, Nei Mongol (Inner Mongolia)); bordered N by Russia and Mongolia, E by N Korea, Bo Hai Gulf, Yellow Sea, and E China Sea (Hong Kong and Macao as SE enclaves), S by South China Sea, Gulf of Tongking, Vietnam, Laos, Burma, India, Bhutan and Nepal, and W by India, Pakistan, Afghanistan, Kazakhstan, Kirghizia, and Tadzhikistan; capital, Beijing (Peking); timezone GMT +8; 93% Han Chinese, with over 50 minorities; languages, standard Chinese (Putonghua) or Mandarin, also Yue (Cantonese), Wu, Minbei, Minnan, Xiang, Gan, Hakka, and minority languages; official romanized form of writing (*pinyin*); officially atheist, but widespread Confucianism, Taoism, Buddhism, and ancestor-worship; unit of currency (*renminbi*), the

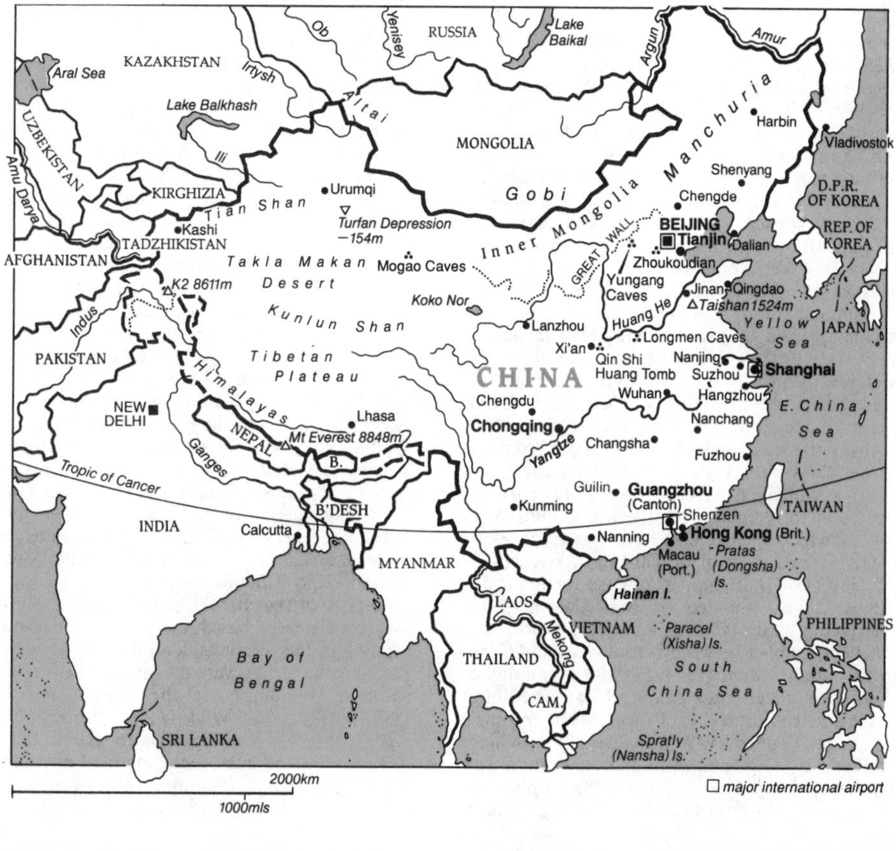

yuan or kuai of 100 fen (10 fen = 1 jiao); overseas visitors use foreign exchange certificates.

Physical description. Over two-thirds upland hill, mountain, and plateau; highest mountains in the W, where the Tibetan plateau rises to average altitude of 4 000 m/13 000 ft ('the roof of the world'); land descends to desert/semi-desert of Sinkiang and Inner Mongolia (NE); broad and fertile plains of Manchuria (NE), separated from N Korea by densely forested Changpai Shan uplands; further E and S, prosperous Sichuan basin, drained by Yangtze R; heavily populated S plains and E coast, with rich, fertile soils.

Climate. Varied, with seven zones: (1) NE China, cold winters, with strong N winds, warm and humid summers, unreliable rainfall; in Manchuria, rivers frozen 4–6 months each year, and snow lies 100–150 days; Beijing, in SW, temperatures −10–1°C (Jan), rainfall average minimum 4 mm/0.16 in (Jan), maximum 243 mm/9.6 in (Jul); (2) C China, warm and humid summers, sometimes typhoons or tropical cyclones on coast; Shanghai on E coast, temperatures 1–8°C (Jan–Feb) and 23–32°C (Jul–Aug), rainfall average minimum 36 mm/1.4 in (Dec), 180 mm/7 in (Jun); (3) S China, partly within tropics, wettest area in summer; frequent typhoons (especially during Jul–Oct); Hong Kong, hot and humid summers, temperatures 13–17°C (Feb), 26–31°C (Jul–Aug), coastal rainfall 31 mm/1.2 in (Dec) and 394 mm/15.5 in (Jul); (4) SW China, summer temperatures moderated by altitude, winters mild with little rain; summers wet on mountains; Mengzi, Yunnan, temperature 8–20°C (Dec–Jan) and 19–29°C (Jul), rainfall average 8 mm/0.3 in (Jan), 198 mm/7.8 in (Aug); (5) Xizang autonomous region, high plateau surrounded by mountains, winters severe with frequent light snow and hard frost, summers warm, but cold nights; Lhasa, temperatures −10–7°C (Jan), 9–24°C (Jul), rainfall 0 mm (Dec–Jan), 122 mm/4.8 in (Jul); (6) Xinjiang and W interior, arid desert climate, cold winters, rainfall well distributed throughout year; Kashi, temperatures −11–1°C (Jan), 20–33°C (Jul), rainfall minimum 3 mm/0.1 in (Sep–Oct), maximum 15 mm/0.6 in (Jan); (7) Inner Mongolia, extreme continental-type climate; cold winters, warm summers; winter temperatures similar to (1), strong winds in winter and spring, summer temperatures 14–28°C (Jul); little rainfall, minimum 8 mm/0.3 in (Feb), maximum 43 mm/1.7 in (Oct).

History and government. Chinese civilization believed to date from the Xia dynasty (2200–1700 BC); Western Zhou dynasty ruled over prosperous feudal agricultural society (c.1066–771 BC); Eastern Zhou dynasty (770–256 BC), era of Confucius and Lao Zi (Lao-tzu); Qin dynasty (221–206 BC) unified warring states and provided system of centralized control; expansion W during Western and Eastern Han dynasties (206 BC–AD 220), and Buddhism introduced from India; split into Three Kingdoms (Wei, Shu, Wu, 220–65); from 4th-c, series of N dynasties set up by invaders, with several dynasties in S; gradually reunited during the Sui (581–618) and Tang (618–907) dynasties; period of partition into Five Dynasties (907–60); Song dynasty (960–1279), remembered for literature, philosophy, and inventions (eg movable type, gunpowder); Genghis Khan established Mongol Yuan dynasty (1279–1368); visits by Europeans, such as Marco Polo, 13th–14th-c; Ming dynasty (1368–1644) increased contacts with West; overthrown by Manchus, who ruled until 1911, and enlarged empire to include Manchuria, Mongolia, Tibet, Taiwan, and parts of Turkestan; opposition to foreign imports led to Opium Wars (1839–42, 1858–60), which opened ports to foreign trade; Sino-Japanese War (1895) gave control of Taiwan and Korea to Japan; Boxer Rising (1900), attempt to oppose foreign influence; Republic of China, founded by Sun Yatsen, 1912; unification under Jiang Jieshi (Chiang Kai-shek), who made Nanjing capital, 1928; conflict between Nationalists and Communists led to the Long March (1934–5), with Communists moving to NW China under Mao Zedong (Mao Tse-tung); Nationalist defeat and withdrawal to Taiwan, 1950; People's Republic of China proclaimed 1949, with capital at Beijing; first Five-Year Plan (1953–7), period of nationalization and collectivization; Great Leap Forward (1958–9) emphasized local authority and establishment of rural communes; Cultural Revolution initiated by Mao Zedong, 1966; many policies reversed after Mao's death (1976), and drive towards rapid industrialization and wider trade relations with West; governed by elected National People's Congress of 2 978 deputies; State Council of over 45 ministers, led by a prime minister.

Economy. Since 1949, largely based on heavy industry, producing iron and steel, coal, machinery, armaments, textiles, petroleum; more recently, light industries (eg household goods, consumables); special economic zones set up to attract foreign investment; rich mineral deposits, especially coal, tungsten, iron, tin, phosphate, aluminium, copper, lead, zinc, antimony, manganese, sulphur, bauxite, salt, asbestos; largest oil-producing country in Far East; major subsistence crops include rice, grain, beans, potatoes, tea, sugar, cotton, oil-seed. » Beijing; Boxer Rising; Chinese; Chinese architecture/art/literature/music; Confucius; Cultural Revolution; Genghis Khan; Grand Canal; Great Leap Forward; Great Wall of China; Guomindang; Han; Jiang Jieshi; Lao-Zi; Long March; Manchu; Mao Zedong; Ming/Qin/Qing/Song/Tang/Yuan/Zhou dynasty; Opium Wars; Polo, Marco; Sino-Japanese Wars; Sun Yatsen; Taiwan [i]; Tiananmen Square; RR25 national holidays; RR46 political leaders

china clay » **kaolin**

chinch bug A small, short-winged bug that feeds by sucking juices from grasses; an important corn and grain pest in America; overwinters as hibernating adult; reproduces rapidly, with two generations each year. (Order: *Heteroptera*. Family: *Lygaeidae*.) » bug (entomology)

chinchilla S American cavy-like rodent; small (length, 350 mm/14 in); thick soft grey coat, bushy tail, large round ears. It is widely farmed for its fur, which is the most expensive in the world. (Genus: *Chinchilla*, 2 species. Family: *Chinchillidae*.) » cavy; rodent

chinchilla cat A breed of domestic cat, of the long-haired type; round head with short face; very dense white coat; each hair tipped with black (one colour form, the *blue chinchilla*, has the hairs tipped with blue-grey); also known as **silver Persian** or **silver**. » cat

chinchilla rabbit A breed of domestic rabbit with thick soft grey fur resembling that of a chinchilla. » chinchilla; rabbit

Chindits Members of the 3rd Indian Division, raised in 1942 by Brigadier Orde Wingate for long-range guerrilla operations, supported by air-supplied bases, in Japanese-occupied Burma. High casualties were sustained on the two deep penetrations of the Burmese jungle in 1943 and 1944, and their military value has been questioned. » Wingate; World War 2

Chinese The Sinitic branch of the Sino-Tibetan group of languages, comprising eight major varieties, commonly called 'dialects'. This classification is an artifact of the writing system of Chinese, which is used by all varieties. Although the orthography transfers from one variety to another, the varieties themselves are, in some cases, not mutually intelligible, and on linguistic criteria would be classed as different languages. The two best-known varieties are *Cantonese*, spoken in the S, and *Mandarin*, spoken in the N, C, and W, the Beijing (Peking) form being the basis of the modern standard language. There have been numerous attempts to romanize the Chinese writing system, and in 1958 the *pinyin* 'phonetic spelling' system of 58 symbols was officially adopted, with the further aim of popularizing the grammar, vocabulary, and pronunciation of the codified standard Mandarin, now known as *putonghua* ('common language'). Chinese has the largest number of mother-tongue speakers of all the world's languages, at over 1 000 million. » China [i]; Chinese literature; ideography; romanization; Sino-Tibetan languages

Chinese architecture Until the 20th-c, Chinese architecture was consistently based on the column, with walls used as screens rather than as load-bearing structures; apart from pagodas, buildings were mostly made from wood. The earliest surviving buildings are the Tang dynasty pagodas (618–907), such as the Wild Goose pagoda, Ch'ang-an, Shensi (701–5). Most buildings date from the Ming dynasty (1368–1644) and later, including the Imperial City and Forbidden City of Beijing (Peking), with complex symmetrical plans, colourful pavilions, and curved roofs. European styles and multi-storey structures have been increasingly used since the 1911 revolution, particularly the International Style in recent decades. » China [i]; column; International Style; Japanese architecture; Ming dynasty; Tang dynasty

Chinese art The art associated with ancient China, dating from 4000 BC, which influenced all Far Eastern countries, and even reached Europe in the 18th-c, not finally dwindling until the 19th-c. It is characterized by technical innovation (silk, porcelain, paper, printing) and great stylistic refinement. Decorated bronze vessels and jade carvings date from 1000 BC; the interconnected traditions of painting and calligraphy were established during the Han period (206 BC–AD 220). Landscape painting emerged centuries before it did in the West, but the nude figure never did. Chinese art was always deeply conservative; artists were not expected to be 'original' in the modern Western sense, but to emulate the achievements of the past. » art; calligraphy; China [i]; chinoiserie; Han; Japanese art

Chinese block » **wood block**

Chinese exclusion (1882–1943) A US immigration policy, growing out of strong anti-Chinese sentiment on the West Coast, following the importation of large numbers of Chinese as labourers.

Chinese gooseberry » **kiwi fruit**

Chinese lantern A perennial native to SE Europe and Asia; rhizomatous; flowers white with dark spots in centre; persistent bladdery calyces 5 cm/2 in long, becoming papery and bright red in fruit – the 'lanterns' often seen in dried floral displays – enclosing an edible red berry. (*Physalis alkakengi*. Family: *Solanaceae*.) » perennial; physalis; rhizome; sepal

Chinese literature The literature of China, which goes back 3 000 years. The earliest works under the Zhou dynasty (1028–256 BC) were the Nine Classics, an admixture of history, poetry, ethics, and commentary on ritual and divination, used by Confucius in his teachings. Closely associated are the 20 books of Confucius's own *Analects*, and the *Mencius* by a disciple. Late in the Zhou Dynasty we have the 'Hundred Schools of Thought', and the poetry of Ch'u Yuan, whose lyrical and allegorical *Li Sao* influenced poets in the Han dynasty (206 BC–AD 220). The introduction of Buddhism into China at this time enhanced the popularity of personal poetry, exemplified by the work of the Ts'ao family; and the political instability of the Six Dynasties that followed (221–581) further encouraged an 'escapist' or idealist literature. The following Tang dynasty (618–907) is known as the Golden Age of Chinese Poetry, providing 2 000 poets from all ranks of society, the best known being the Taoist Li Po (701–62), his friend the Confucian Tu Fu (712–70), Li Ho ('the Chinese Keats', 790–816), and the populist Po-Chu-i (772–846). At the same time, Han-Yu (768–824) replaced the elaborate 'parallel prose' of earlier dynasties with a more flexible medium. The poetry of the Song dynasty (960–1216) was likewise more versatile than Tang; Su-Shi and others experimenting with irregular metres. This period also produced a good deal of historical writing. The Yuan dynasty (1279–1368) was celebrated for its musical drama, a form favoured by the Mughal ruling class, with Ma Chih-yuan's *Autumn in the Han Palace* typical of their plots from legend and romance.

There were developments in drama in the Ming dynasty (1368–1644), with plays of historical and political significance; but this was primarily the age of the Chinese novel. Developing out of the *hua-pen* or short story, the earlier novels often dealt with historical and heroic subjects; famous examples are *Romance of the Three Kingdoms*, and *Water Margin*. The personalized novel arrived with the last, Qing dynasty (1644–1912), new ground being broken by Ts'ao Hsueh-ch'in's partly autobiographical *Dream of the Red Chamber*. This was followed by satirical works (often directed at the abuses of bureaucracy) and fine examples of the ever-popular ghost story. After 1911, Western influence completely transformed Chinese literature, which experienced its own force-fed modernist movement before Mao Zedong imposed a new discipline and encouraged folk art. The 'cultural revolution' of 1966–8 was hostile to outside influences, but there are now signs that Chinese literature is in creative dialogue with the rest of the world. » Chinese; Confucius; Li Po; Mao Zedong; novel; poetry

Chinese music The music of China, both ancient and varied, with a correspondingly rich instrumentation. The *qin*, a type of zither, the *dizi*, a bamboo flute, and the *pipa*, a pear-shaped lute, are among the oldest and most highly regarded of Chinese instruments. Until the end of the Qing dynasty (1911) most types of Chinese music were transmitted orally, although notation systems had existed for centuries. Historical writings and contemporary accounts yield much information about music among the people, at the courts, and, above all, in the theatre, where a kind of opera developed before the earliest Western operas were staged in Florence c.1600. The Beijing (Peking) opera has been of central importance in Chinese music and culture for two centuries, and since 1949 a vital mouthpiece for socialist propaganda. The Cultural Revolution of the late 1960s halted performances of traditional opera, as well as the scholarly study of ancient Chinese music that had begun in the Qing dynasty. Since the fall of Mao Zedong's wife in 1976, many traditional features have returned, and performances of Western music have also increased. » China [i]; Cultural Revolution; ethnomusicology; Jiang Qing; pipa; Qing dynasty

Chinese water deer » **water deer**

Ching-tao » **Qingdao**

chinoiserie [sheen**wa**zuhree] Silks, porcelain, and lacquer from China, which were very much admired in Europe from the time they were first imported in the late Middle Ages, and consequently much imitated. From the work of the 17th-c japanners and the productions of the early European porcelain makers, which directly copied Oriental art, a separate Western style evolved, using Chinese and Japanese motifs in an original manner in a completely Western decorative context. It reached its height in the 18th-c, being used throughout the decorative arts, as well as in such fields as book illustration, furniture, and gardening. » Chinese art; japanning; lacquer; porcelain

Chinook A N American Indian people of Washington and Oregon, one of the NW Indian groups with an artistic tradition. They were successful middlemen in the trade between coastal Indians and interior Plateau Indians; fished salmon; and traded in dried fish, slaves, canoes, and shells. White contact, dating back to 1805, eventually eroded their culture; most Chinook were moved to reservations. Population c.600. » American Indians; Northwest Coast Indians; Plateau Indians

chinook wind » **Föhn wind**

Chios [**kee**os], Gr **Khíos**, Ital **Scio** pop (1981) 48 700; area 842 sq km/325 sq ml; length 48 km/30 ml. Greek island in the Aegean Sea, off the W coast of Turkey; fifth largest of the Greek islands; crossed N–S by hills rising to 1 298 m/4 258 ft; fertile plain in SE; chief town, Chios, pop (1981) 29 742; ferry to mainland and islands; noted for its wine and figs; tanning, wine, boatbuilding, tourism; Navy Week (Jun–Jul). » Aegean Sea; Greece [i]

chip A commonly used name for an integrated circuit. Strictly the term refers to the small 'chip' of silicon on which the electronic circuits reside, rather than the encapsulated package. » integrated circuit; silicon

chipmunk A type of squirrel, all species native to N America except *Eutamias sibiricus* from W Asia; back with alternating pale and dark longitudinal stripes; cheeks with internal pouches for carrying seeds. (Genus: *Tamias*, 1 species; *Eutamias*, 22 species.) » squirrel

Chippendale, Thomas (1718–79) English cabinet-maker, born at Otley, Yorkshire. He set up a workshop in St Martin's Lane in 1753, and soon became famous for his graceful Neoclassical furniture, especially chairs, which he made mostly from mahogany. His *Gentleman and Cabinet-maker's Director* (1754) was the first comprehensive trade catalogue of its kind. He died in London, and his son **Thomas** (c.1749–1822) carried on the business. » Neoclassicism (art and architecture)

Chippewa » **Ojibwa**

Chirac, Jacques (René) [**shi**rak] (1932–) French Gaullist politician, and Prime Minister (1974–6). First elected to the

National Assembly in 1967, he gained extensive governmental experience before being appointed Prime Minister by Giscard d'Estaing. He resigned over differences with Giscard and broke away to lead the Gaullist Party. Mayor of Paris since 1977, he was an unsuccessful candidate in the 1981 and 1988 presidential elections. » de Gaulle; Giscard d'Estaing

chirality [kiyr**al**itee] Asymmetry resulting in an object not being superimposable upon its mirror image. Chemical chirality is usually associated with a carbon atom having four different substituents. Two isomers which are mirror images of one another are called *enantiomers*; the enantiomers of lactic acid are shown in the illustration.

Towards symmetrical environments, enantiomers behave identically, but towards other chiral molecules they are different. Thus they will have identical melting points, but may have different tastes and smells. » carbon; isomers; optical activity

Chirico, Giorgio de [**ki**reeko] (1888–1978) Italian artist, born at Volo, Greece. He studied at Athens and Munich, working later in Paris, and with Carrà in Italy. About 1910 he began to produce a series of dreamlike pictures of deserted squares, which had considerable influence on the Surrealists. His whole style after 1915 is often called 'metaphysical painting', including semi-abstract geometric figures and stylized horses. In the 1930s he reverted to an academic style. » abstract art; Italian art; metaphysical painting; Surrealism

chirography The various forms and styles of handwriting, which differ between the writing systems of the major language families. Early Western styles included *majuscule*, as seen in the chiselled capital letters of early Greek and Roman inscriptions from c.300 BC; *minuscule*, the use of small letters found in Greek from the 8th-c AD; *uncial* writing, large rounded letters found in Latin and Greek manuscripts from the 4th-c AD; *cursive*, used from c.4th-c BC, in which the letters are joined together in rounded strokes to promote speed; and *italic*, developed in Italy in the 14th-c, a forerunner of italic letters in printing. » black letter writing; graphology; majuscule; palaeography

Chiron [**kiy**ron] In Greek mythology, a good and wise centaur, the son of Kronos and Philyra the Oceanid, who kept a school for princes in Thessaly. He educated Asclepius in the art of medicine and music, Jason the Argonaut, and Achilles. He was wounded with a poisoned arrow of Heracles, and gladly gave up his immortality to be rid of pain. » Heracles

chiropody The study of the structure and function of the foot in health, and of its disorders and deformities. It is also known as **podiatry**. » foot

chiropractic [**kiy**ruhpraktik] The study of the alignment of the bones of the skeleton and of the anatomical relations of the nerves and muscles of the body to them. It is mainly concerned with the bones of the spine and with the pain or discomfort held to be the result of malposition, bony pressure, or muscle spasm in the neck and back. Chiropractors treat these disorders by manipulation without the use of drugs or surgery. » alternative medicine; osteopathy

Chiroptera [kiy**rop**tuhra] » **bat**

Chirripó Grande [cheeree**poh gran**day] 9°50N 83°25W. Highest peak of Costa Rica and S Central America; in the Cordillera de Talamanca; height 3 819 m/12 529 ft; Chirripó National Park, area of 437 sq km/169 sq ml. » Costa Rica [i]

chiru [**chi**roo] A goat-antelope native to the high plateau of Tibet and China; pale pinkish brown; nose swollen at tip; male with black face and long slender vertical horns growing apart towards tips; female without horns; also known as **Tibetan antelope**. (*Pantholops hodgsoni.*) » antelope

chisel-tooth lizard » **agamid**

Chisholm Trail A cattle trail from Texas, across Oklahoma, to the railheads at Abilene, Kansas. It is named after Jesse Chisholm, who pioneered the route in 1866. The trail fell into disuse with the spread of enclosure and the growth of a rail network.

chital [**chee**tl] A true deer, native to India and Sri Lanka (introduced in Australia); pale brown with white spots; antlers long, lyre-shaped; inhabits woodland; often gather under trees occupied by langur monkeys, feeding on leaves the monkeys drop; also known as **axis deer** or **spotted deer** (*Axis axis.*) » antlers [i]; deer; langur

chitarrone [keeta**roh**nay] A long-necked lute or theorbo, used in the 16th–17th-c to accompany singing. There were usually six pairs of gut or metal strings running over a fretted keyboard, and eight longer bass strings which were not stopped (ie each produced one note only). The instrument might be as long as 1 m 90 cm/6 ft 3 in. » lute; string instrument 2 [i]; theorbo

chitin [**kiy**tin] A long chain-like molecule (a linear homopolysaccharide of N-acetyl-D-glucosamine) found as a major constituent of the hormy covering (cuticle) of insects and cell walls of fungi. When cross-linked, these chains produce a lightweight but strong material. » molecule; polysaccharides

chiton [**kiy**tuhn] A marine mollusc characterized by a dorsal shell consisting of eight overlapping calcareous plates; muscular foot used for attachment to, and movement over, a substrate; several pairs of gills present in a groove around the foot; most species in shallow water; also known as **coat-of-mail shell**. (Class: *Polyplacophora.*) » calcium; mollusc; shell

Chittagong [**chit**agong] 22°20N 91°48E, pop (1984e) 1 600 000. Seaport capital of Chittagong district, SE Bangladesh; principal port of Bangladesh on the R Karnafuli, flowing into the Bay of Bengal; conquered by Nawab of Bengal, 1666; ceded to British East India Company, 1760; damaged during 1971 Indo-Pakistani War; many Hindu and Buddhist temples; university (1966); trade in tea, jute, skins, hides; cotton, iron, steel, fruit canning, matches, shipbuilding, oil refining; offshore oil installations in the 1960s. » Bangladesh [i]

Chittagong Hill Tracts pop (1981) 580 000; area 8 680 sq km/3 350 sq ml. Region in SE Bangladesh, bounded E by Burma; hilly area enclosed by rivers; reaches heights of 500–1 000 m/1 500–3 000 ft in the SE; divided into four fertile valleys, covered with thick planted forest; L Kaptia (686 sq km/265 sq ml) formed when Karnafuli hydroelectric dam built at Kaptia; capital, Rangamati. » Bangladesh [i]

Chitwin or **Royal Chitwin** area 932 sq km/360 sq ml. National park in SC Nepal; between the Sumesar Range (E) and the R Gandak (W); established in 1973; a world heritage site. » Nepal [i]

chives A perennial growing to 40 cm/15 in; tufts of narrow, tubular leaves; dense umbels of pink or purple flowers; native to the N hemisphere. It is cultivated for its leaves, which are used as flavouring. (*Allium schoenoprasum.* Family: *Liliaceae.*) » allium; perennial; umbel

chlamydia [kla**mid**ia] A spherical, non-motile bacterium that multiplies only within the cytoplasm of true nucleated (*eukaryotic*) cells. Virulent strains can cause eye, mouth, genital, and other diseases of humans and other animals. (Kingdom: *Monera.* Family: *Chlamydiaceae.*) » bacteria [i]; cytoplasm

chloracne [klaw**rak**nee] Acne-like lesions on the skin with pimple-like (papular) formations which may become infected (pustular). Its occurrence is linked to industrial exposure to chlorinated hydrocarbons. » acne

chloral CCl_3CHO, IUPAC **2,2,2-trichloroethanal**, boiling point 97°. Chloral hydrate is a sedative. » IUPAC

chlorates Salts of an oxyacid of chlorine, usually a chlorate(V), containing the ion ClO_3^-, including the weed-killer *sodium chlorate* ($NaClO_3$). Chlorate(I) or *hypochlorite* is ClO^-; chlorate(VII) or *perchlorate* is ClO_4^-. » chlorine

chlordiazepoxide » **benzodiazepines**

Chlorella [kluh**rel**a] A non-motile, single-celled green alga containing a cup-shaped chloroplast; very common in a variety of freshwater habitats. » algae; chloroplast

chlorides Compounds containing chlorine, especially those containing the ion Cl^-. Common salt is *sodium chloride* (Na^+Cl^-). » chlorine; sodium

chlorine [**kloh**reen] Cl, element 17, boiling point −35°C. A greenish-yellow gas, containing diatomic molecules (Cl_2). A very reactive substance, it does not occur free in nature, but is recovered from deposits of NaCl or KCl by electrolysis. It may also be recovered from sea water, which contains about 2% chlorine as dissolved Cl^-. The gas has an intense odour and is very poisonous. Industrially, chlorine is mainly used in reactions with organic compounds to form propellants, cleaning fluids, and monomers for rubber production. It is also widely used as a powerful disinfectant, for example in swimming pools. » chemical elements; electrolysis [i]; gas **1**; RR90

chlorofluorocarbons » **CFCs**

chloroform $CHCl_3$, IUPAC **trichloromethane**, boiling point 62°C. A dense liquid, used as a solvent and as an anaesthetic. » IUPAC

Chlorophyceae [klorohfiysee-ee] » **green algae**

chlorophyll [**klo**ruhfil] The green pigment (a magnesium-porphyrin derivative) found in plants, which absorbs radiant energy from sunlight, mainly in blue (wavelength 435–438 nm) and red (wavelength 670–680 nm) regions of the spectrum. Several variants occur, the principal ones being chlorophylls *a* and *b* in land plants, and *c* and *d* in seaweeds. » photosynthesis; spectrum

Chlorophyta [**klorofi**ta] The green algae that form zoospores or gametes having cup-shaped grass-green chloroplasts and at least two anterior flagella; classified as a phylum of the kingdom *Protoctista*. » chloroplast; flagellum; gamete; green algae; systematics

chloroplast [**klo**rohplast] A specialized structure found within plant cells. It is typically biconvex in shape, and comprises stacks of membraneous discs bearing photosynthetic pigments embedded in a matrix. It contains some genetic material (DNA), and partly controls the synthesis of its own proteins. » cell; chlorophyll; DNA [i]; photosynthesis; plant; protein

chlorpromazine » **phenothiazines**

chocolate and **cocoa** A foodstuff derived from the cacao bean, cultivated mainly in W Africa; it was introduced to Europe by the Spanish, who discovered its use during their conquest of Mexico. *Cocoa butter* is rich in fat, and *cocoa powder* contains a mixture of protein (25%), fat (30%), and carbohydrate (45%). Drinking chocolate is a blend of cocoa powder, sugar, and dried milk powder. Milk chocolate is produced by mixing finely ground cocoa powder with some cocoa butter, sugar, and dried milk. » cacao

choir (architecture) The part of a church for the singers; usually part of the chancel and separated from the nave by a screen or a rail. » chancel; church [i]; nave; transept

Choiseul-Amboise, Etienne François, Duc de ('Duke of') [shwa**zerl** om**bwahz**] (1719–85) French statesman, minister of Louis XV, born in Lorraine. He served with credit in the Austrian Wars of Succession, and became Duc de Choiseul and Foreign Minister in 1758. He arranged in 1756 the alliance between France and Austria against Frederick the Great, and obtained good terms for France at the end of the Seven Years' War (1763). He improved the army and navy, and developed trade and industry. Madame du Barry alienated Louis from his able minister, who retired in 1770. He died in Paris. » Louis XV; Seven Years' War

cholecystitis [kohluhsis**tiy**tis] Acute inflammation of the gall bladder, often induced by a blockage or partial blockage of the flow of bile, and stone formation. It causes severe upper right-sided abdominal pain and vomiting. » bile; gall bladder

cholera An acute infection of the gastro-intestinal tract by *Vibrio cholerae*, acquired by drinking contaminated water. It is associated with sudden profuse watery diarrhoea, which so depletes the body of water and electrolytes as to induce shock and death within 24–48 hours. If adequate treatment involving the replacement of body fluids is given, death should be uncommon and recovery complete. » alimentary canal; diarrhoea; vibrio

cholesterol [kuh**les**tuhrol] The most abundant steroid in animals, an essential component of plasma membranes, and the precursor of bile salts, and of the adreno-cortical and sex hormones. It is ingested in the diet as a constituent of egg-yolk, meats (particularly offal), and some shellfish; transported in the blood and synthesized in the liver, gastro-intestinal tract, and other tissues. It is implicated as a cause of atherosclerosis. » atherosclerosis; coronary heart disease; fatty acids; gallstones; hormones; plasma (physiology); steroid [i]

choline [**koh**leen] The most common form of the variable part of phospholipids, which play a key role in the structure of biological membranes. It is an essential component of the diet of some species, and is therefore often linked with vitamins; but it is not an essential dietary component for humans. Phospholipids containing choline are also known as *lecithin*, commonly sold in health food shops to reduce cholesterol absorption, a feat which it does not achieve. » cholesterol; phospholipid

Chomsky, (Avram) Noam (1928–) US linguist and political activist, born at Philadelphia, Pennsylvania. Educated at Pennsylvania and Harvard Universities, he became professor of linguistics at the Massachusetts Institute of Technology, where he wrote *Syntactic Structures* (1957), introducing a new theory of language called transformational generative grammar. His opposition to the Vietnam War involved him in the radical movement, and in 1969 he published *American Power and the New Mandarins*, attacking politically liberal intellectuals who force their ideology on other nations. He has since continued to publish major works in both linguistics and politics. » linguistics; transformational grammar

Chongqing or **Chungking** [chung**king**], also **Pahsien** 31°08N 104°23E, pop (1984e) 2 733 700. City in Sichuan province, SWC China; at confluence of Jialing Jiang and Yangtze Rivers; founded 12th-c; treaty port, 1891; capital of China, 1937–46; most important industrial city in SW; airfield; railway; river transport; steel, machinery, chemicals, textiles, light industry; hot springs nearby; US–Chiang Kai-shek Criminal Acts Exhibition Hall; Sichuan Fine Arts Academy; Chongqing Museum. » China [i]

Chopin, Frédéric (François) [**shoh**pî] (1810–49) Polish composer and pianist, born at Zelazowa Wola, near Warsaw, where his French father had settled. He played in public at the age of eight, and published his first work at 15. He studied at the Warsaw Conservatory under Elsner (1826–9), then visited Vienna and Paris, becoming the idol of the *Salons*. He lived with the novelist George Sand (Madame Dudevant) between 1838 and 1847, when they became estranged. Chopin wrote mainly for the piano, including 50 mazurkas, 27 études, 25 preludes, 19 nocturnes, 13 waltzes, 12 polonaises, 4 ballades, 3 impromptus, 3 sonatas, 2 piano concertos, and a funeral march. Long enfeebled by consumption, he died in Paris. » piano; Salon; Sand

chopsticks A pair of slender sticks used in oriental countries for eating food. Chinese chopsticks are generally round and are not pointed. Most Japanese chopsticks (*hashi*) have square sides, and when lacquered, are usually pointed. In Japan, lacquered chopsticks are normally used at home. Visitors, as in restaurants, are given plain wooden chopsticks in a paper wrapper, which are thrown away afterwards. Knives, forks, and spoons are used for Western food. » shikki

chorale 1 A hymn of the Lutheran church. The qualities most associated with its music – harmonic strength and a firm, regular metre – are those of Bach's harmonizations; he wrote few original hymn melodies himself. Like most other hymns, chorales are strophic, ie the same music is used for each stanza. » Bach, Johann Sebastian; hymn; Lutheranism **2** The term *chorale* is also used for a choir, especially in the USA.

chord In music, two or more notes sounded simultaneously. In tonal music of the period c.1600–1920 a chord functions as a unit in a harmonic progression related to (or diverging from) a particular key centre. Before then, chord progressions (though not the chords themselves) were largely determined by the direction of the individual melodic lines. In post-tonal music, chords have been formed on serial or other principles, without reference to a key centre. » chromaticism; diatonicism; note-cluster; tonality

Chordata [kaw**dah**ta] or **chordates** A phylum of animals having bilateral symmetry, a stiffening rod (*notochord*) running along the back, a hollow dorsal nerve cord, a tail extending backwards beyond the anus, and gill slits. Some of these characters may be present only in the embryo. There are three subphyla: *Cephalochordata* (*lancelets*), *Tunicata* (*sea squirts* and *salps*), and *Vertebrata* (*vertebrates*). Vertebrates are chordates in which the dorsal nerve cord is surrounded by *vertebrae* made from cartilage or bone (includes fish, amphibians, reptiles, mammals, birds). » amphibian; bird [i]; lancelet; mammal [i]; notochord; phylum; reptile; tunicate

chordophone Any musical instrument in which the sound is produced by the vibrations of one or more strings. Chordophones form one of the main categories of instruments in the standard classification of Hornbostel and Sachs (1914). They are divided into (i) those without resonators, or with resonators that can be detached while leaving the strings in place (*simple* chordophones: piano, zither, etc), and (ii) those in which an integral resonator serves to keep the strings in place (*composite* chordophones: violin, lute, etc). Each type may be further subdivided, eg according to whether the strings are bowed, plucked, or struck; but in the perception of most people the main divisions are between those with keyboards, those with bows, and those with neither. However, some keyboard instruments (such as the organ) and some bowed instruments (such as the musical saw) are not chordophones. » keyboard/musical/string instrument [i]

chorea [kuh**ree**a] A manifestation of rheumatic fever related to recent streptococcal infection; also known as **Saint Vitus' dance**. Symptoms range from periods of restlessness to exaggerated, jerky, puppet-like movement of the hands, arms, and body. » Huntington's chorea; rheumatic fever; streptococcus; Sydenham's chorea

choreography Originally, as 'chorégraphie', the writing of dances in notation; in its current general use, the making of dances by the selection of movements for a particular dance purpose, linked together to form a whole. The maker of the dance, the **choreographer**, was barely mentioned by name before the 19th-c, the dance being simply an adjunct to the musical and dramatic act. The choreographic structure is often derived from music but can also be independent of it, based directly on the rhythm of movement. Sometimes the dance is written down in dance notation, but it is frequently passed from one generation to the next orally and by demonstration. » Ashton, Frederick; Balanchine; ballet; country dance; dance notation [i]; Fokine; MacMillan, Kenneth; modern dance; Nijinsky; Petipa; postmodern dance

chorionic villus sampling (CVS) A technique for obtaining samples of placental tissue, ideally at 8–11 weeks gestation. A needle introduced through the mother's abdominal and uterine walls is advanced to the edge of the placenta, a small piece of which is removed. The tissue can be used for chromosome analysis, enzyme assay, and DNA analysis, thereby identifying the presence of Down's syndrome and such genetically-determined disorders as cystic fibrosis. » amniocentesis; DNA [i]; placenta (anatomy)

chorus The collective or impersonal voice in a drama (as distinct from the individual characters), which serves to introduce and comment on the action. It was an essential feature in classical drama, but less common later (where another character often assumes this role, as with Enobarbus in Shakespeare's *Antony and Cleopatra*); however, the chorus is used by Shakespeare in *Henry V*, and by Eliot in *Murder in the Cathedral*. » drama; Eliot, T S; English/Greek literature; Shakespeare [i]

Chou En-lai » **Zhou Enlai**

Chouans [**shoo**ã] Peasant guerrilla bands from the W provinces of France, who rose against the Republican government in Paris (1793), opposing attempts to enforce conscription and subdue the clergy. Their name comes from the Breton word for 'screech-owl', allegedly the nickname of their leader, Jean Cottereau. » French Revolution [i]

chough [chuhf] A crow-like bird (Family: *Corvidae*, 3 species), especially the **red-billed** or **Cornish chough** (*Pyrrhocorax pyrrhocorax*), native to Europe and Asia. The name is also used for the Australian **white-winged chough** (*Corcorax melanorhamphos*). (Family: *Corcoracidae*.) » crow

chow chow or **chow** A breed of dog, developed in China before 1000 BC; heavy body with thick coat and lion-like mane; blue tongue; tail curled over back; kept in temples, and bred with stern expressions to frighten away evil spirits; introduced to Europe in the 18th-c. » dog

Chrétien de Troyes [**kray**tyĩ duh **trwah**] (?–c.1183) The greatest of mediaeval French poets, born at Troyes. He enjoyed the patronage of Marie de Champagne, daughter of Louis VII. His best-known works are the great metrical Arthurian romances, such as *Lancelot* and *Perceval*, which introduce all the fantastic ingredients of Celtic legend, and add the theme of the Holy Grail. *Erec et Enide* (c.1160) is the earliest known Arthurian romance. » Arthur; French literature

Christ » **Jesus Christ**

Christ's Hospital A boarding school, founded in London (1552), but since 1902 at Horsham, Sussex. It was known as the 'blue coat' school, because of the blue cloak which was part of the pupils' uniform. » public school

Christadelphians [krista**del**fianz] A Christian sect, founded by John Thomas (1805–71) in the USA, which teaches a return to primitive Christianity and that Christ will soon come again to establish a theocracy lasting for a millennium. Christadelphians are congregational in organization, and there are no ordained ministers. The name means 'Brethren of Christ'. » millenarianism

Christchurch 43°33S 172°40E, pop (1988e) 300 700. City in Canterbury, South Island, New Zealand; on the R Avon, on the E coast, NW of its port, Lyttelton Harbour; founded, 1850; airport; railway; university (1873); corn and sheep trade from the Canterbury Plains; food processing, wool, chemicals, fertilizers, furniture; Canterbury Museum, Ferrymead Historic Park, McDougall Art Gallery; scene of 1974 Commonwealth Games. » New Zealand [i]

Christian X King of Denmark (1912–47), born at Charlottenlund. During his reign, Denmark's link with Iceland was severed (1918, 1944), but N Sleswig was recovered from Germany (1920). During the German occupation (1940–5), he attracted great acclaim by remaining in Denmark, seeking with some success to save Denmark from the harshest effects of occupation without undue collaboration. He died in Copenhagen. » Denmark [i]; World War 2

Christian, Fletcher (18th-c) British seaman, the ringleader in the mutiny on the *Bounty*, which sailed to Tahiti 1787–8. In 1808 his descendants were found on Pitcairn I. » Bligh

Christian Aid A large UK-based charity supported by most Churches in Britain. It pays for development projects in the poorest countries of the world, particularly in agriculture, water supply, and health, using its own experts as advisors. » developing countries; Third World

Christian art The art associated with the development of Christianity, emerging c.300 in Italy, using the formal style of late Roman art for new spiritual purposes; technically mediocre, but with a new iconography. Frescoes in the Roman catacombs, relief-sculptured panels on sarcophagi, and ivory carvings already in the 4th-c show basic motifs, such as the Good Shepherd, Jonah and the Whale, and scenes from Christ's Passion. The Crucifixion does not appear until the 5th-c. Christian manuscript illustration combined clasical naturalism and oriental abstraction. The earliest panel paintings date from the 7th-c, representing the Virgin and Saints. » art; Byzantine art; Christianity; iconography; Italian art; mosaic; nimbus

Christian Democratic Union » **Christian Democrats**

Christian Democrats Members of Christian Democratic political parties, most of which were formed in W Europe after 1945, and which have since become a major political force. The Christian Democratic philosophy is based upon strong links with the Catholic Church and its notions of social and economic justice. It emphasizes the traditional conservative values of the family and church, but also more progressive, liberal values such as state intervention in the economy and significant social welfare provision. Christian Democrat parties emerged to fill the vacuum created by the general disillusionment with parties of the right and left after World War 2, a major exception being the UK, which has no such party. Electorally, the most successful example is the W German Christian Democratic Union (CDU), which polled nearly 50% of the votes in 1983. » Bundestag; Roman Catholicism

Christian Science A movement, founded by Mary Baker Eddy, which seeks to reinstate the original Christian message of salvation from all evil, including sickness and disease as well as sin. The first Church of Christ, Scientist, was established in 1879 in Boston, USA, followed in 1892 by the present worldwide organization, with its headquarters at Boston. Eddy's *Science and Health with Key to the Scriptures* (1875) and the Bible are the principal texts of the movement. They believe that God is Spirit and the good creator; accordingly, sin, sickness, death, and matter itself only seem real to mistaken human belief. Health is restored, not by recourse to medical treatment, which they decline, but by applying to all aspects of life practices in keeping with the principle of divine harmony. The internationally known newspaper, *The Christian Science Monitor*, is published by the society. » Christianity; Eddy

Christian Social Union » **Christian Democrats**

Christian Socialism A range of movements aiming to combine Christian and socialist, or collectivist, ethical principles. They attempt to promote socialism through enlisting Christ's help, and though undoctrinal in nature are most commonly found in the Protestant church. Originating in 19th-c Britain, they have since spread to Scandinavia, Switzerland, France, Germany, and the USA. » Christianity; collectivism; socialism

Christianity (Gk **christos** 'anointed') A world religion centred on the life and work of Jesus of Nazareth in Israel, and developing out of Judaism. The earliest followers were Jews who, after the death and resurrection of Jesus, believed him to be the Messiah or Christ, promised by the prophets in the Old Testament, and in unique relation to God, whose Son or 'Word' (*Logos*) he was declared to be. During his life he chose twelve men as *disciples*, who formed the nucleus of the Church as a society or communion of believers, called together to worship God through Jesus Christ, Lord of history, who would come again to inaugurate the 'Kingdom of God'. The Gospel ('Good News') of Jesus was proclaimed first by word-of-mouth, but by the end of the 1st-c it was reduced to writing and accepted as authoritative as scriptures of the New Testament, understood as the fulfilment of the Jewish scriptures, or Old Testament. Through the witness of the twelve earliest leaders (*Apostles*) and their successors, the Christian faith or 'Way', despite sporadic persecution, quickly spread through the Greek and Roman world, and in 315 was declared by Emperor Constantine to be the official religion of the Roman Empire. It survived the break-up of the Empire and the 'Dark Ages' through the life and witness of groups of monks in monasteries, and formed the basis of civilization in the Middle Ages in Europe.

Major divisions, separated as a result of differences in doctrine and practice, are the *Eastern* or *Orthodox Churches*, the *Roman Catholic Church*, acknowledging the Bishop of Rome as head (the *Pope*), and the *Protestant Churches* stemming from the split with the Roman Church in the 16th-c Reformation. All Christians recognize the authority of the Bible, read at public worship, which takes place at least every Sunday, the first day of the week, to celebrate the resurrection of Jesus Christ. Most Churches recognize at least two sacraments (Baptism, and the Eucharist, Mass, or Lord's Supper) as essential. The impetus to spread Christianity to the non-Christian world in missionary movements, especially in the 19th-c and 20th-c, resulted in the creation of numerically very strong Churches in the developing countries of Asia, Africa, and S America. A powerful ecumenical movement in the 20th-c, promoted by, among others, the World Council of Churches, has sought to recover unity among divided Christians. » Bible; Christian art; Christology; ecumenism; Jesus Christ; Judaism; Reformation; sacrament; World Council of Churches; Adventists; African Methodist Episcopal Church; Anabaptists; Anglo-Catholicism; Assemblies of God; Baptists; Brethren (in Christ); Calvinism; Christadelphians; Christian Science; Christians of St Thomas; Church of Scotland; Confessing Church; Congregationalism; Coptic Church; Dutch Reformed Church; Episcopal Church; evangelicalism; Friends, Society of; Greek Orthodox Church; Lutheranism; Methodism; millenarianism; Mormons; Nonconformists; North India, Church of; Orthodox Church; Pentecostalism; Presbyterianism; Protestantism; Reformed Churches; Roman Catholicism; Russian Orthodox Church; Salvation Army; secular Christianity; South India, Church of; United Church of Christ; Waldenses

Christians of St Thomas A group of Indian Christians living on the Malabar coast. They take their name from the apostle Thomas, who is said to have brought Christianity to India, though they were founded by Nestorians in the 5th-c. They are now part of the Syrian Church, and have their own patriarch. » Nestorians; Orthodox Church; Thomas, St

Christie, Dame Agatha (Mary Clarissa), *née* **Miller** (1891–1976) British author, born at Torquay, Devon. Under the surname of her first husband (Colonel Christie, divorced 1928), she wrote more than 70 detective novels featuring the Belgian detective, Hercule Poirot, or the inquiring village lady, Miss Marple. In 1930 she married **Max E L Mallowan** (1904–78; knighted in 1968), professor of archaeology at London University (1947–78), with whom she travelled on several expeditions. Her play *The Mousetrap* opened in 1952 and holds the record for the longest unbroken run in a London theatre. Several of her stories have become popular films, such as *Murder on the Orient Express* (1974) and *Death on the Nile* (1978). She was made a Dame in 1971, and died at Wallingford, Oxfordshire. » detective story

Christie, John Reginald Halliday (1898–1953) British murderer, born in Yorkshire. He was hanged at London for the murder of his wife, and confessed to the murder of six other women, including the wife of **Timothy John Evans**, who lived in the same house. Evans had been convicted and hanged for the murder of his infant daughter in 1950, and also charged with his wife's murder. After a special inquiry, Evans was granted a free pardon in 1966. The trial of Christie thus played an important part in altering British legislation affecting the death penalty.

Christmas The Christian festival commemorating the birth of Jesus, observed by most branches of the church on 25 December but by some denominations in January. The practice of celebrating Christmas on 25 December began in the Western Church early in the 4th-c; it was a Christian substitute for the pagan festival held on that date to celebrate the birth of the unconquered Sun. Many Christmas customs are of non-Christian origin; for example, Christmas trees (introduced into Britain from Germany) and holly and mistletoe decorations are of N European pagan origin. The first Christmas cards were produced in the 1840s. » Jesus Christ

Christmas cactus A hybrid cactus (an epiphyte) with spineless, arching stems made up of flattened, jointed segments and magenta flowers. It appears in winter. (*Schlumbergera × buckleyi*. Family: *Cactaceae*.) » cactus; epiphyte

Christmas Island (Kiribati) » **Kiritimati**

Christmas Island (Indian Ocean) 10°25S 105°39E, pop (1983e) 3 000; area 155 sq km/60 sq ml. Island in the Indian Ocean 360 km/225 ml S of Java Head and 1 310 km/815 ml from Singapore; administered by Australia as an external territory; annexed by the UK, 1888; sovereignty passed to Australia, 1958; population includes Europeans, Chinese, and Malays; wet season Nov–Apr; annual rainfall c.2 040 mm/80 in; main source of income (recently threatened by reduced demand) the export of rock phosphate and phosphate dust; technical school; airport. » Indian Ocean

Christmas rose A species of hellebore, with white flowers blooming in winter. (*Helleborus niger*. Family: *Ranunculaceae*.) » hellebore

Christmas tree » **Norway spruce**

Christology The orderly study of the significance of Jesus Christ for Christian faith. Traditionally, the term was restricted to the study of the person of Christ, and in particular to the way in which he is both human and divine. Latterly, an emphasis on the inseparability of Christ's person and work has meant that Christology often encompasses enquiry into his saving significance (*soteriology*) as well. » Christianity

Christophe, Henri (1767–1829) Haitian revolutionary, born a slave on the island of Grenada. He joined the Black insurgents on Haiti against the French (1790), and became one of their leaders, under Toussaint L'Ouverture. He was appointed President in 1807, and despite civil war was proclaimed King in the

N part of the island as Henri I in 1811. He ruled with vigour, but his avarice and cruelty led to an insurrection, and he shot himself. » Toussaint L'Ouverture

Christopher, St (3rd-c), feast day 25 July. Syrian saint, said to have been 12 ft/3.6 m tall, and to have suffered martyrdom under the Emperor Decius (249–51). His name is from the Greek, 'Christ-bearer', from the legend of his carrying the Christ child across a river. » Jesus Christ

chromakey An image-combination process in video production where an area of strong colour in one scene is replaced ('keyed') by the picture from another source; also termed **Colour Separation Overlay (CSO)**. A typical application is a blue-backing shot. » blue-backing shot

chromaticism An attribute of music which uses notes, intervals, and chords outside the prevailing key; a note which does not belong to the diatonic scale is called a **chromatic note**. It was the move towards extremes of chromaticism in the 19th-c (eg by Wagner) that eventually led to the abandoning of tonality in the music of Schoenberg and others. » diatonicism; Schoenberg; tonality

chromatids The two longitudinal halves into which each chromosome appears to split at cell division, which separate to become daughter chromosomes. Studying the exchange of segments between the chromatids (*sister chromatid exchange*) is useful, for example, in diagnosing some human hereditary diseases. » centromere; chromosome [i]

chromatin The network of substance in a cell nucleus that takes up stain, and which thus can be made visible under the microscope during the process of cell division. It is organized into distinct bodies (the chromosomes). Distinctive parts of each chromosome that stain very darkly consist of *heterochromatin*; those that stain lightly, of *euchromatin*. » cell; chromosome [i]

chromatography The separation of components of a mixture (the *mobile phase*) by passing it through another phase (the *stationary phase*), making use of the different extents to which the various components are adsorbed by the stationary phase. Many systems have been developed. One is **paper chromatography**, illustrated by the separation of the constituent dyes of an ink when it is spilled on a paper tissue. Another is **gas-liquid chromatography (GLC)**, used to separate mixtures of gases. » adsorption

chromatophore [krohmatuhfaw] A pigment-bearing cell, or structure within a cell. In many animals, chromatophores are cells containing pigment granules. By dispersing or contracting these granules, the animal is able to change colour. » cell

chrominance The component of a video signal which determines the hue and saturation of a reproduced colour. The term is sometimes abbreviated to 'chroma'. » colour television [i]; luminance (photography)

chromium Cr, element 24, density 7.2 g cm^{-3}, melting point 1 857°C. A hard, lustrous metal, found combined with oxygen, especially in chromite (Cr_2FeO_4), and generally prepared as a metal by reduction of the ore with aluminium. It reacts readily with atmospheric oxygen, but, like aluminium, forms a tough oxide coat, preventing further reaction. Its principal uses are as a plating and as a component of steels, to which it gives corrosion resistance. Its compounds mainly show oxidation states +3 (salts containing Cr^{3+} ions, usually coloured green or violet) or +6 (chromate or dichromate salts containing CrO_4^{2-} or $Cr_2O_7^{2-}$ ions, and coloured yellow or orange). » aluminium; chemical elements; metal; RR90

chromophore That part of a molecule giving rise to colour. Most chromophores in dyestuffs involve double bonds, especially conjugated ones. These lower the energy of radiation absorbed, so that visible radiation as well as ultraviolet radiation is absorbed by the compound. » colour; conjugation (chemistry); dyestuff

chromosome The threads within the nucleus of a cell which become visible during cell division. The chromosomes were postulated to be the carriers of inherited information in 1903, after a study of the close correspondence between their behaviour and Mendelian factors. Chromosomes occur in pairs – one member of maternal and one of paternal origin. They are

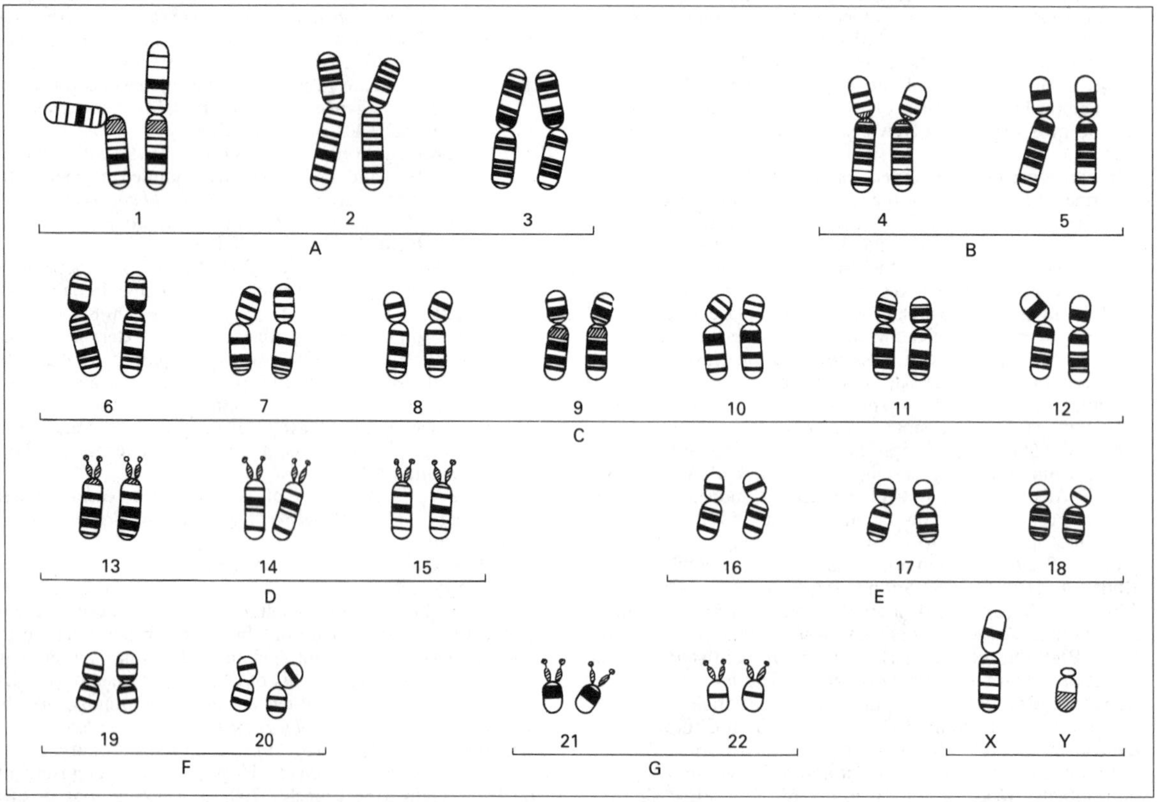

The 46 human chromosomes, showing the banding patterns characteristic of each.

regarded today as the major carriers of genetic material, consisting of DNA and various types of protein (histones). The position of a particular gene on a chromosome is called its *locus*. The number of chromosomes differs from species to species. A normal human body cell has 46 chromosomes: 22 pairs of autosomes together with (in females) one matching pair of X chromosomes and (in males) one non-matching pair, the X and Y sex chromosomes. » cell; DNA [i]; Mendel's laws; nucleus (biology); sex chromosome

chromosphere Part of the outer gaseous layers of the Sun, temperature 45 000 K. It is visible as a thin crescent of pinkish light during a total eclipse of the Sun. » corona (astronomy); eclipse; solar prominence; Sun

chronicle plays Plays (from any period) based upon historical events, often using the written record as both source and structure. Marlowe and Shakespeare used Holinshed's chronicles for their plays from English history; and Hardy wrote *The Dynasts* (1904–8) after extensive research on the Napoleonic wars. Epic theatre (after Brecht) has revived this mode of drama. » Brecht; drama; epic; Hardy, Thomas; Marlowe; Shakespeare [i]

Chronicles or **Paralipomenon, Books of** Two books of the Hebrew Bible/Old Testament, originally a single work, perhaps also linked with the books of Ezra and Nehemiah, thereby presenting a history of Judah from its beginnings to its restoration under Ezra and Nehemiah. It has many parallels with the Books of Samuel and Kings, but the Chronicler's interests are mainly in the Temple and its cult. » Ezra/Kings/Nehemiah/Samuel, Books of; Old Testament; Temple, Jerusalem

chronogram The practice of hiding a date within a series of words, by using the letters for Roman numerals (C = 100, V = 5, etc); often used on tombstones and foundation stones to mark the date of the event being commemorated. The numeral letters are usually written in capitals, eg *DoMVs* 'domus' ('house'). » RR77

chrysalis » **pupa**

chrysanthemum A name applied in a broad sense to various members of the family *Compositae*. The well-known large-flowered 'chrysanthemums' of gardens (Genus: *Dendranthema*) have a long history of cultivation, especially in China and Japan, and modern plants are derived from complex hybrids whose exact parentage is uncertain. Numerous cultivars have been developed, varying in flower colour, shape, and size, popularly grown as cut flowers and also as pot plants, often chemically treated to produce bushy, short-stemmed plants. (Family: *Compositae*.) » cultivar

chrysoprase [**kri**suhprayz] The apple-green form of chalcedony. » chalcedony

Chrysostom, St John (c.347–407), feast day 27 January. Church Father, born at Antioch. His name comes from the Greek, 'golden-mouthed', on account of his eloquence. He spent six years as a monk in the mountains, but returned in 381 to Antioch, where he was ordained, and gained a reputation as the greatest orator of the Church. In 398 he was made Archbishop of Constantinople, where he carried out many reforms, but his reproof of vices moved the Empress Eudoxia to have him deposed and banished (403). Moving from one place of exile to another, he died at Comana, in Pontus. His body was brought to Constantinople and reburied with honour in 438. » Christianity; Fathers of the Church

chrysotile [**kri**suhtiyl] The fibrous form of serpentine. It is a member of the asbestos group of minerals. » asbestos; serpentine

Chu-kiang » **Zhu Jiang**

Chu Teh » **Zhu De**

chub Fish of European streams and rivers, also found in lakes and in the Baltic Sea; body elongate, rather cylindrical, length up to 60 cm/2 ft; greenish grey above, sides silver, underside white; popular as fine sport fish; a relative of orfe and dace. (*Leuciscus cephalus*. Family: *Cyprinidae*.) » dace; orfe

Chubb Crater A meteorite crater c.410 m/1 350 ft deep in Quebec, Canada; occupied by Crater Lake, 260 m/850 ft deep; discovered in 1949 by a prospector, F W Chubb; also known as **Ungava-Quebec Crater**.

chuckwalla An iguana from N America, found in rocky deserts; dark body with thick blunt yellow tail; no crest along back; eats plants; rests in rock crevices; if disturbed, may wedge itself in the crevice by inflating its lungs. (*Sauromalus obesus*.) » iguana

Chukchi or **Chuckchee** A people of NE Siberia in the Chukchi Autonomous Okrug of the Russian SFSR. They have lived on collective farms since the Russian Revolution (1917), and are divided into *maritime* Chukchi, who are hunters and fishers of the Arctic and Bering Sea, and the previously nomadic *reindeer* Chukchi, who live inland and herd reindeer. Population c.14 000. » Siberia

Chukchi Peninsula [**chuk**chee], Russ **Chukotskiy Poluostrov** NE extremity of Asia, in Russia; bounded N by the Chukchi Sea, E by the Bering Strait, and S by the Anadyrskiy Zaliv gulf of the Bering Sea; rises to heights above 1 000 m/3 300 ft; its E point is Cape Dezhnev. » Russia

Chungking » **Chongqing**

church In architecture, a building used for public religious worship, especially Christian. First adapted by the early Christians from the Roman basilicas and martyrias, it was later developed in the Romanesque architecture of the 11th-c and 12th-c into the now more usual Latin cross plan, typically consisting of nave with side aisles, transepts, chancel, and apse, such as Pisa Cathedral (mainly 1063–1118) and the Panthéon (Sainte Geneviève), Paris (1757–90), architect J G Soufflot. The centrally-planned circular or Greek cross plan was briefly favoured in Renaissance Italy, such as Santa Maria della Consolazione, Todi (1508–1604). In the 20th-c, church design has become increasingly eclectic, most famously the Chapel of Notre Dame, Ronchamp, France (1950–5), architect Le Corbusier; the Roman Catholic Cathedral, Liverpool (1960–7), architect Frederick Gibberd; and also in numerous smaller, usually urban churches. » apse; baptistery; basilica; cathedral; chancel; chevet; choir (architecture); hall church; Romanesque architecture; nave; transept

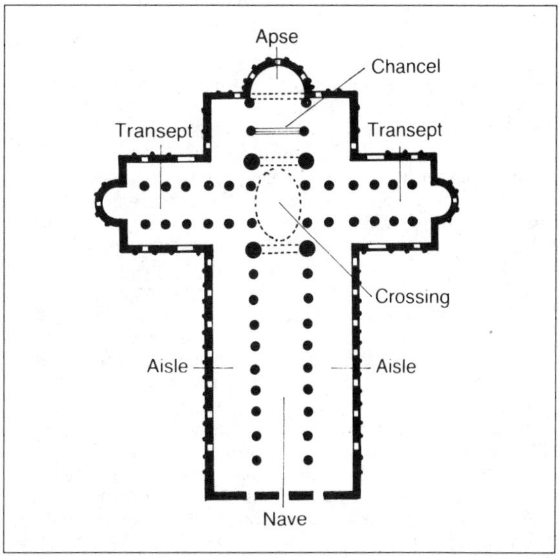

Latin cross church plan: Pisa Cathedral (1063–1118)

Church Army An Anglican organization of volunteer lay workers, founded in 1882. Its aims are evangelical, but it concentrates on social welfare and rehabilitation work, mainly in cities. » Anglicanism; Church of England; evangelist

Church of England The official state Church of England, a national Church having both Protestant and Catholic features, based on episcopal authority, and with the monarch of England formally as its head. It originated when Henry VIII broke ties with the Roman Catholic Church (c.1532–4) and was declared by Parliament to be 'the supreme head on earth of the English Church'. The Church remained largely Catholic in character, however, until reforms of doctrine and liturgy under Edward VI, when the new Book of Common Prayer appeared (1549, 1552), the later edition being significantly more Protestant in its features. Under Elizabeth I the moderately Protestant set of doctrinal statements, known as the 39 Articles, emerged. She and James I resisted efforts towards both a Catholic revival and Puritan attempts to take a more Calvinist stance, but under Charles I a presbyterian form of government was temporarily established until the episcopacy and Prayer Book were restored under Charles II. While a general attitude of toleration now exists, the tension of Catholic and Protestant inclinations tends to persist in the Church of England, as well as the tensions introduced by the newer influences of evangelicalism and liberalism.

The Church of England today consists of some 44 dioceses in the two provinces of Canterbury and York, with over 16000 churches and other places of worship. Local parishes are arranged into rural deaneries and dioceses, with each diocese led by a bishop and sometimes assisted by a suffragan or assistant bishop. The parish structure is fundamental to the organization of the church, but increasingly team ministries, priests-in-charge, and non-stipendiary priests have found a place in addition to parish priests and curates. The Church also supports its own missionary organizations and societies. The largest societies are the Mothers' Union and the Church Army, the latter being engaged in social welfare work.

In 1970 the General Synod was established for the purpose of reaching decisions and expressing views on issues of interest to the Church. It also appoints several committees, boards, and councils to advise it. There are over 500 members, divided between the three houses: the Houses of Clergy, of Bishops, and of Laity. It meets three times a year and is presided over by the Archbishops of Canterbury and York. In addition, there are synods of clergy and laity at diocesan level.

The Church of England has especially close relations in Britain with the Church in Wales and the Scottish Episcopal Church. The spread of Anglicanism more widely through the world, especially in Commonwealth countries, however, has given the Church of England a prominent role in the Anglican Communion at large. » Anglican Communion; Book of Common Prayer; episcopacy; Henry VIII; Lambeth Conferences; Protestantism; Reformation; Thirty-Nine Articles

Church of Scotland The national Church in Scotland, founded at the Reformation of 1560 under the leadership of John Knox. It comprises a larger proportion of the population than most Protestant Churches in the English-speaking world, with a strong missionary tradition, especially in Africa and India. It maintains links with and supports many Churches in developing countries. Presbyterian in its governing organization and discipline, laymen or *elders* (ordained) play a leading part with ministers in church courts at local, congregational level (in Kirk Session), district level (*presbyteries*, overseeing congregations in a given area), provincial synods, and the General Assembly. Ministers (women and men), who are ordained by presbytery, are alone authorized to administer the sacraments of baptism (of infants as well as adults) and the Lord's Supper (*communion*). Historically renowned for scholarship in Reformed theology, it has occupied a position in the world Reformed community out of proportion to its size. » Knox, John; Presbyterianism; Protestantism; Reformed Churches; sacrament

Church Slavonic » Slavic languages

Churches of Christ A religious movement whose origins lie in the work of Thomas and Alexander Campbell and Barton Stone in the 19th-c in the USA. It preaches a restoration of New Testament Christianity, and rejects all creeds and confessions. Later there was a split which led to the Disciples of Christ being distinguished from the Churches of Christ. » Christianity

Churchill, Lord Randolph (Henry Spencer) (1849–95) British Conservative statesman, born at Blenheim Palace, Oxfordshire, the third son of the 7th Duke of Marlborough, and the father of Winston Churchill. Educated at Eton and Oxford, he entered parliament in 1874, and became conspicuous in 1880 as the leader of a guerrilla band of Conservatives known as the 'Fourth Party'. He was Secretary for India (1885–6), and for a short while Chancellor of the Exchequer and Leader of the House of Commons. He resigned after his first budget proved unacceptable, and thereafter devoted little time to politics. He died in London. » Conservative Party

Churchill, Sir Winston (Leonard Spencer) (1874–1965) British statesman, Prime Minister (1940–5, 1951–5), and author, born at Blenheim Palace, Oxfordshire, the eldest son of Randolph Churchill. Educated at Harrow and Sandhurst, he was gazetted to the 4th Hussars in 1895, and his army career included fighting at Omdurman (1898) with the Nile Expeditionary Force. During the second Boer War he acted as a London newspaper correspondent. Initially a Conservative MP (1900), he joined the Liberals in 1904, and was Colonial Under-Secretary (1905), President of the Board of Trade (1908), Home Secretary (1910), and First Lord of the Admiralty (1911). In 1915 he was made the scapegoat for the Dardanelles disaster, but in 1917 became Minister of Munitions. After World War 1 he was Secretary of State for War and Air (1919–21), and – as a 'Constitutionalist' supporter of the Conservatives – Chancellor of the Exchequer (1924–9). In 1929 he returned to the Conservative fold, but remained out of step with the leadership until World War 2, when he returned to the Admiralty; then, on Chamberlain's defeat (May 1940) formed a coalition government, and, holding both the premiership and the defence portfolio, led Britain alone through the war against Germany and Italy with steely resolution. Defeated in the July 1945 election, he became a pugnacious Leader of the Opposition. In 1951 he was Prime Minister again, and after 1955 remained a venerated backbencher. In his last years, he was often described as 'the greatest living Englishman'. He achieved a world reputation not only as a great strategist and inspiring war leader, but as the last of the classic orators with a supreme command of English; as a talented painter; and as a writer with an Augustan style, a great breadth of mind, and a profound sense of history. He was knighted in 1953, and won the Nobel Prize for Literature the same year. He died in London. He left a widow, **Clementine Ogilvy Hozier**, whom he had married in 1908, and who was made a life peer in 1965 for her indefatigable charitable work (**Baroness Spencer-Churchill of Chartwell**). » Boer Wars; Chamberlain, Neville; Conservative Party; Liberal Party (UK); World War 2

Ci Xi or **Tz'u Hsi** [tsee **shee**], personal name **Yehenala** (1835–1908) Chinese Consort of the Xianfeng Emperor (1851–62), who rose to dominate China by manipulating the succession to the throne. She bore the Xianfeng Emperor his only son, who succeeded at the age of five as the T'ung Chih Emperor, but kept control even after his majority in 1873. After his death (1875), she flouted the succession laws of the Imperial clan to ensure the succession of another minor, aged three, as the Guang Xu (Kuang Hsu) Emperor, and continued to assert control even when the new Emperor reached maturity. In 1900 she took China into war against the combined treaty powers in support of the Boxer movement. Only after her death in Beijing (Peking) was it possible to begin reforms. » Boxer Rising; Hundred Days of Reform; Qing dynasty; Zai Tian

CIA » Central Intelligence Agency

Ciano, Galeazzo, Conte di ('Count of') **Cortellazzo** [**chah**-noh] (1903–44) Italian politician, son-in-law of Mussolini and leading fascist, born at Livorno. As Minister of Propaganda (1935) and of Foreign Affairs (1936–43), he supported his father-in-law's expansionist and war policy; he was nevertheless unenthusiastic about Mussolini's alliance with Germany, and from 1942 openly opposed it. Having participated in Mussolini's deposition (Jul 1943), in 1945 he was put on trial by Mussolini's supporters, and shot, at Verona. » fascism; Mussolini

Cibber, Colley [**si**ber] (1671–1757) English actor and dramatist, born and died in London. He spent most of his career at the Theatre Royal in Drury Lane. In 1696, his first comedy, *Love's Last Shift*, established his fame both as dramatist and actor. As manager and playwright, he greatly improved the decency of the theatre. From 1730 he was poet laureate. » English literature; theatre

cicada [si**kah**da] A large, typically tropical insect that spends most of its long life cycle as a nymph burrowing underground, feeding on sap from roots; adults live in trees; males typically have well-developed sound-producing organs. (Order: *Homoptera*. Family: *Cicadidae*.) » insect [i]; nymph (entomology)

Cicero, Marcus Tullius (106–43 BC) Roman orator, statesman, and man of letters, born at Arpinum in Latium. At Rome he studied law, oratory, philosophy, and literature, and embarked upon a political career, attaining the consulship in 63 BC. Though he foiled Cataline's revolutionary plot, he broke the law by executing Roman citizens without a trial, and when charges were pressed, fled to Thessalonica (58 BC) in exile. In 57 BC he was recalled by the people, but lost the esteem of both Caesar's and Pompey's factions by vacillating between the two. Living in retirement (46–44 BC), he wrote most of his chief works on rhetoric and philosophy. In 43 BC he delivered his famous speeches against Antony, the so-called 'Philippics'. He was murdered near Caieta by Antony's soldiers as he tried to escape. » Antonius; Augustus; Caesar; Pompey; triumvirate

cichlid [**sik**lid] Any of a large family of freshwater fishes found in S and C America, Africa, and India; many species in African Great Lakes; body usually perch-like; feeding and breeding habits extremely diverse; important as a food fish and in the aquarium trade. (20 genera, including *Haplochromis*, *Tilapia*. Family: *Cichlidae*.)

Cid, El (c.1043–99) Spanish hero, born at Burgos. His real name was **Rodrigo** or **Ruy Díaz de Bivar**, but he soon became known as the *Cid* (from the Moorish *Sidi*, 'lord'); *Campeador* ('warrior') is often added. A soldier of fortune and great patriot, he was constantly fighting from 1065; his great achievement was the capture of Valencia (1094), where later he died.

cider An alcoholic drink produced from the fermentation of apples, traditionally made in SW England and Normandy, France. Its alcoholic content varies widely, from 3% to 9% ethanol. Most modern ciders are artificially carbonated. In the USA, ciders are either 'sweet' (non-alcoholic) or 'hard' (containing alcohol). » fermentation

Cienfuegos [syen**fway**gohs] 22°10N 80°27W, pop(1983e) 106478. Port and capital of Cienfuegos province, WC Cuba; on S coast, 337 km/209 ml SE of Havana; founded, 1819; important industrial centre; tobacco, citrus, cattle products; naval base; botanical garden, Castillo de Jagua museum (1738–45). » Cuba [i]

ciliate [**sil**iuht] A microscopic, single-celled organism typically possessing short hair-like appendages (*cilia*) on its surface; contains two types of nucleus (macronucleus and micronucleus); commonly also with a specialized mouth region (*cytostome*); found free-living in all kinds of aquatic and terrestrial habitats, and as parasites. (Phylum: *Ciliophora*.) » cell; nucleus (biology); parasitology

Cilicia [siy**li**seea] The ancient name for the S coastal part of Turkey around the Taurus Mts. It was famous for its timber and its pirates.

Cimabué [cheema**boo**ay], properly **Cenni di Peppi** (c.1240–c.1302) Italian painter, born in Florence. He at first adopted traditional Byzantine forms, but soon turned to nature, and led the way to the naturalism of his great pupil Giotto. He executed several important frescoes in the Church of St Francis at Assisi. » fresco; Giotto; Italian art

Cimarosa, Domenico [cheema**roh**sa] (1749–1801) Italian composer of operas, born at Aversa. He studied music at Naples, and produced his first opera there in 1772. He was court musician at St Petersburg (1787) and Vienna (1791), where his comic opera, *Il Matrimonio segreto* (The Secret Marriage) was a great success, then in 1793 returned to Naples. He wrote many other works, including church and chamber music, and died at Venice. » opera

cimbalom [**sim**balom] A kind of dulcimer, native to Hungary but found also in other E European countries. The smaller types are portable, carried on a strap round the player's shoulders. The concert cimbalom has been used as an orchestral instrument by Liszt, Kodály, Bartók, and others. » chordophone; dulcimer

Cimbri [**kim**bree] A Germanic people from N Europe who migrated S towards the end of the 2nd-c BC in search of new lands. They were defeated and destroyed by the Romans (101 BC) in the Po valley.

Cimmerians [ki**mair**ianz] A nomadic people of S Russia who were driven out by the Scythians in the 8th-c BC. They migrated through the Caucasus Mts to Assyria and Asia Minor, where they caused widespread havoc and destruction. » Assyria; Scythians

Cimon (?–449 BC) Athenian commander, the son of Miltiades, particularly prominent in the 470s and 460s BC. Active in the mopping-up operations in the Aegean after the Persian Wars, his greatest exploit was the defeat, on the same day, of the Persian land and naval forces at the R Eurymedon (c.469 BC). In politics, he was less successful. His opposition to democracy at home and support for Sparta abroad brought him into conflict with Pericles, and he was ostracized in 461 BC. » Marathon, Battle of; Miltiades; ostracism; Pericles; Persian Wars

Cincinnati [sinsi**na**tee] 39°06N 84°01W, pop(1980) 385457. Seat of Hamilton County, SW Ohio, USA, on Ohio R; Fort Washington built here, 1789; city status, 1819; large numbers of German immigrants in the 1840s; airport; railway; two universities (1819, 1831); aircraft engines, vehicles, chemicals, machinery, food, metal products; several centres for culture, music, and the arts; major league teams, Reds (baseball), Bengals (football); birthplace of William Howard Taft; Taft Museum, Contemporary Arts Centre, Kings Island Park; Oktoberfest (Sep). » Ohio; Taft

Cincinnatus, Lucius Quinctius (5th-c BC) Roman statesman, farmer and folk hero. Called from the plough and given absolute power to rescue the Roman army of the consul Minucius, which had been trapped by the Aequi (458 BC), he voluntarily gave up this power and returned to his farm, as soon as the crisis was over. » Roman history [i]

cinema At the first shows of 1895 audiences were satisfied to see single short scenes of real life in movement, but these were soon supplemented by music hall turns, fantastic trick films, and stories told in continuous action, including historical reconstruction. By 1900 cross-cutting between scenes was used as well as close shots to establish detail. A practical syntax of film drama evolved rapidly, and by 1912 productions lasting longer than a single reel of film (12–15 min) were acceptable – the Italian *Quo Vadis* of 1913 ran for two hours. The star system of publicized named artistes was developed soon after, and by the 1920s the silent cinema was recognized as an established international medium for entertainment, instruction, and propaganda, with contributions to its art from many sources (eg in the dynamics of editing by Eisenstein in the USSR). Sound was added to motion pictures in 1927, and although the static staging of some of the first talkies was a retrograde step, technical limitations on movement were soon overcome, and directors were quick to realise the vast additional scope offered by dialogue, sound effects, and background music. Colour was available from the 1930s, but did not become universal until the late 1950s. Also in the 1950s, various forms of wide-screen presentation were introduced, and this format is now general. Despite competition, feature films made for the cinema still form a major source of popular entertainment, in the motion picture theatre, on broadcast television, and on video-cassettes in the home. » cinematography [i]; film production; silent film

cinéma vérité A style of film production stressing realistic documentary treatment even for fictional drama. The approach prefers non-professional actors and minimal script and rehearsal, using the mobile viewpoint of a hand-held camera and natural sound. » film production

CinemaScope A system of wide-screen cinematography, based on Henri Chrétien's invention of 1927 and adopted by 20th Century Fox in 1953. An anamorphic lens on the camera produces a laterally compressed image on 35 mm film, which is expanded on projection by a similar optical system. A squeeze factor of 2:1 horizontally is used, resulting in a screened picture of aspect ratio (width:height) 2.35:1. » lens; wide-screen cinema [i]

cinematheque A library of motion picture films, especially one presenting cinema classics and international, archival, and cultural productions to a public or specialized audience. » cinema

cinematographer » **cameraman**

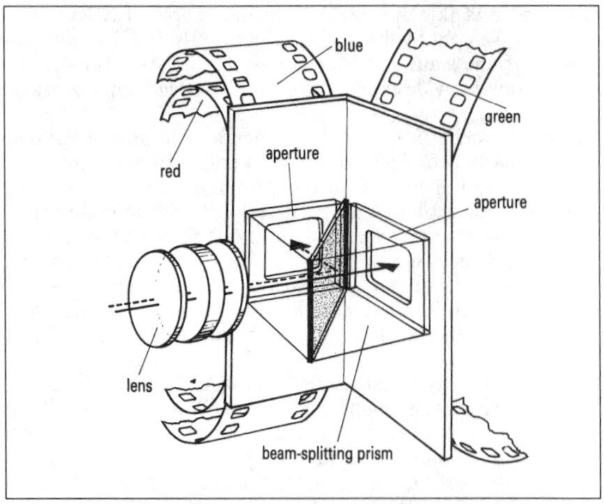

Technicolor camera – The beam-splitting prism divides the light at the two apertures. The blue, red and green components of lightwave are recorded by three separate film strips.

cinematography The presentation of moving pictures as a series of photographic images recorded and reproduced in rapid succession, the eye's persistence of vision giving the impression of continuous movement. Film in continuous strips provided the material for Edison's pioneer Kinetoscope camera of 1891, but projecting the image on a screen for a large audience originated with the Lumière brothers in 1895, establishing the film production and cinema industries. Pictures were exposed in the camera at a rate of 16 per second, the film being held stationary for each exposure and then advanced one frame at a time while a shutter obscured the lens. After developing this film as a negative, a positive print was made for projection, again with an intermittent mechanism and shutter. In the late 1920s synchronized sound was added to the picture presentation, at first from separate disc records but after 1927 from a sound track on the film itself, the frame rate being increased to 24 pictures per second. Colour cinematography developed in the 1930s but did not become general for another twenty years, when various forms of wide-screen presentation in the cinema were extensively adopted. » cinema; colour cinematography; composite cinematography; projector [i]; sound film

Cinerama One of the first systems of wide-screen cinema presentation in 1952, using three synchronized projectors to cover a very large curved screen in three blended panels. Its cost and complexity limited its use to showing travelogues in specially adapted theatres, and it ceased after 1962. » wide-screen cinema [i]

cineraria A dwarf shrub growing to 60 cm/2 ft or more, native to Africa and Madagascar; stem much-branched from the base; leaves rounded, shallowly lobed, thickly white-haired beneath; flower heads numerous, daisy-like, in dense flat-topped clusters, red to deep blue-violet. The popular garden cinerarias are derived from a related species, *Pericallis hybrida*, native to the Canary Is. (Genus: *Cineraria*, c.50 species. Family: *Compositae*.) » shrub

Cinna, Lucius Cornelius (?–84 BC) Prominent Roman politician of the turbulent 80s BC. Driven from Rome and illegally deposed while consul in 87 BC, he recaptured the city with the help of Marius amid much bloodshed, and was all-powerful there until his murder in 84 BC. » Marius; Roman history [i]; Sulla

cinnabar (entomology) [**sin**abah] A medium-sized, nocturnal tiger moth; forewings dark grey with carmine patches, hindwings carmine with black margins; caterpillar yellow and black, feeding on cabbage family plants; overwinters as pupa. (Order: *Lepidoptera*. Family: *Arctiidae*.) » caterpillar; pupa; tiger moth

cinnabar (metallurgy) A mineral of mercury sulphide (HgS), the chief ore of mercury. It consists of small, red, soft crystals formed in hydrothermal veins and volcanic deposits, and is used in the mineral pigment vermilion. » mercury

cinnamon A small evergreen tree growing to 6 m/20 ft, native to SE Asia; leaves ovoid to oblong; flowers greenish; berries black. The spice is obtained from the bark of young trees. (*Cinnamomum zeylanicum*. Family: *Lauraceae*). » evergreen plants; spice; tree [i]

Cinque Ports Originally, the five S English coast ports of Dover, Hastings, Hythe, Romney, and Sandwich, associated by royal authority (under Edward the Confessor) to provide ships for naval defence; Rye and Winchelsea were added later. They received royal privileges, including (from 1265) the right to send barons to Parliament, and charters, the first dating from 1278; they were governed by a Lord Warden who was also Constable of Dover castle. Their role declined with the growth of the navy under the Tudors and Stuarts, and the status was abolished in 1835. » Edward the Confessor

cinquefoil [**singk**foyl] The name of various species of *Potentilla*, with 5-petalled, white, yellow, or purple flowers. (Genus: *Potentilla*. Family: *Rosaceae*.) » potentilla

CIO » **American Federation of Labor – Congress of Industrial Organizations**

cipher A secret way of writing; also, anything written in such a manner. The letters comprising a message in ciphers are normally either replaced by others (*substitution*) or re-ordered (*transposition*) according to a frequently changing scheme. In either case the appropriate key is needed to decipher and understand the message. » cryptanalysis; cryptography

circadian rhythm [ser**kay**dian] (Lat *circa* 'about' + *dies* 'day') A biological rhythm that has a periodicity of about one day. This periodicity can be seen, for example, in the sleep cycle in animals and the growth cycles of plants. » biological rhythm

Circassians A people from the Caucasus, speaking a NW Caucasian language, who are divided into Adyghians (Lower Circassians) and Kabardians (Upper Circassians). Most live in Russia, but there are also Circassian communities in Syria and Turkey, and small groups in Iraq, Jordan, and Israel. They are Sunni Muslims; most are farmers and pastoralists, hierarchically organized, with princes, nobles, and (until recently) also slaves. Population c.500 000. » Caucasus Mountains; Sunnis

Circe [**ser**see] In the *Odyssey*, an enchantress who detained Odysseus and his followers on the island of Aeaea. Her house was full of wild beasts. She transformed Odysseus' men into swine with a magic drink, but he was able to defeat her charms through the protection of the herb *moly*. » Odysseus

Circinus (Lat 'compasses') [**ser**suhnuhs] A small obscure S constellation. » constellation; RR8

circle The locus of a point that is a constant distance from a fixed point. The constant distance is called the *radius*, and the fixed point the *centre*. From this definition are obtained all the properties of the circle. Thus if A and B are two points on a circle centre O, triangle OAB is isosceles, and so the perpendicular bisector of any chord of a circle passes through the centre of the circle. By the use of two isosceles triangles, it can be proved that the angle subtended by an arc of a circle at the centre of a circle is twice the angle subtended by that arc at a point on the circumference of the circle. The area of a circle radius r is πr^2; the circumference is $2\pi r$. Archimedes c.240 BC showed that $223/71 < \pi < 22/7$. » circumference; geometry; pi [i]; triangle (mathematics)

circotherm oven An oven with a fan to circulate internal hot air. It is designed to achieve uniformity of heating and to economize in heating or cooking time.

circuit An administrative division of the judicial system of England and Wales. Each circuit has a circuit administrator and two presiding judges, one senior, one junior. In the USA, federal and state judicial systems have similar administrative divisions, also known as circuits. » judge

circuit riders Early itinerant Methodist preachers on horseback who regularly covered a circuit of churches and also carried their messages to new settlements. They were instrumental in the rapid expansion of early Methodism. » Methodism

circulation In physiology, the vertebrate system in which blood is pumped intermittently from the heart and flows continuously around the body (*systemic circulation*) or to the lungs (*pulmonary circulation*) and back to the heart by a network of blood vessels. By means of the systemic circulation, tissues are provided with oxygen (taken up in the lungs), nutrients (absorbed from the alimentary canal), hormones, and enzymes for controlling metabolic processes and eliminating waste products (eg carbon dioxide carried to the lungs, urea to the kidneys). The pulmonary circulation is concerned with the exchange of oxygen and carbon dioxide with the environment. In mammals and birds, the circulatory system also functions in body temperature regulation. » blood vessels [i]; heart [i]; lungs [i]; Plate XIII

circumcision The widespread practice of removing all or part of the foreskin of the penis. The age of circumcision varies; male Jewish babies, for example, are circumcised eight days after birth, while other groups circumcise just before or at puberty as part of an initiation ceremony which marks the changing status from childhood to adulthood. In female circumcision, also widely practised, some or all external genitalia are removed. Circumcision may also be carried out for health reasons.

Circumcision, Feast of the A Christian festival (1 Jan) in honour of the circumcision of Jesus eight days after his birth (*Luke* 1). » Jesus Christ

circumference The boundary, or length of the boundary, of a closed curve, usually a circle. The circumference of a circle is $2\pi r$, where r is the radius of the circle. The circumference of an ellipse can be expressed only in terms of an integral. » circle [i]; ellipse [i]; integral calculus [i]; pi [i]

circumpolar star A star which never sets when viewed from a particular location. In Europe and N America the stars of Ursa Minor and Ursa Major are always visible. In Australia, Crux is a circumpolar constellation. » Crux; star; Ursa Major/Minor

circus Historically, games in ancient Rome involving horse and chariot races, gladiatorial combat, and wild animals; in modern times, a travelling show featuring animals and feats of human endurance and skill. Acts of bareback horse riding and lion taming formed the basis of early circuses, but other animals, such as chimpanzees, dogs, seals and elephants, are now popular features. Human feats such as sword swallowing, fire eating, trapeze, and juggling are also common. Most have a comedy routine carried out by clowns. The modern-day circus was initiated in 1768 by trick horseback rider Philip Astley (1742–1814), who built his own 'arena' in which to display his skills. Charles Hughes built his famous *Royal Circus* in 1782, and this was the first modern-day use of the word *circus*. The most famous 19th-c circuses were Barnum and Bailey's, Astley's and Spengler's. In recent times the shows of Bertram Mills, Billy Smart, and David Chipperfield have been popular.

cire perdue [seer per**doo**] or **'lost wax' process** A technique for casting metals, mainly for sculpture. The desired shape is formed (eg in clay), and a mould is made, the inside of which is then coated in wax. The inside of the wax is coated with further heat-resisting material, giving a gap filled with wax. The wax is then melted out, leaving a hollow into which molten metal can be poured. There are variants of this process; for example, the wax shape can be perfected by the sculptor before the two moulds are re-assembled for pouring. » casting [i]; sculpture; wax

Cirencester [**siy**ruhnsester, **si**sister], ancient **Corinium Dobunorum** 51°44N 1°59W, pop (1981) 13 783. Market town in Cotswold district, Gloucestershire, SWC England; in the Cotswolds, on the R Churn, 22 km/14 ml NW of Swindon; second largest town in Roman Britain during 2nd-c AD; electrical goods, engineering; Royal Agricultural College; 14th-c Church of St John the Baptist, Corinium museum. » Britain, Roman; Gloucestershire

cirque [serk] A bowl-shaped, steep-sided hollow formed at the head of a mountain valley by the erosion of ice in glaciated regions; termed **corrie** or **cwm** in Scotland and Wales respectively. Two cirques cutting back into a ridge forms an *arete*, while three or more result in pyramidal peaks such as the Matterhorn in the Alps.

cirrhosis [si**roh**sis] A chronic diffuse disorder of the liver, in which liver cells are destroyed and progressively replaced by scar tissue (*fibrosis*). The most common cause is long-continued excessive consumption of alcohol. Other causes include genetic disorders and obstruction of the common bile duct. In severe cirrhosis, it is common to find jaundice, bleeding, accumulation of fluid in the peritoneal cavity within the abdomen, and psychotic mental changes. » alcoholism; liver

Cirripedia [siri**pee**dia] » **barnacle**

cirrocumulus clouds High-level clouds above c.5 000 m/16 000 ft, composed of ice crystals. They are white in thin sheets or layers, but have the rounded appearance of cumulus clouds. Their similarity to fish markings in appearance has given them the name 'mackerel sky'. Cloud symbol: Cc. » cloud [i]; cumulus clouds

cirrostratus clouds High-level stratus or layered clouds, in which there is a transition from supercooled water droplets to ice crystals. Found at altitudes above c.5 000 m/16 000 ft, they are sheet-like and white/grey in colour. Their arrival precedes the warm front of a depression. Ice and water droplets in the clouds may refract light to produce a halo or ring of light. Cloud symbol: Cs. » cloud [i]; depression (meteorology) [i]; stratus clouds

cirrus clouds High-level clouds above c.5 000 m/16 000 ft, composed of ice crystals. They are white and wispy in appearance, producing 'mares' tails', a hooked shape, as the wisps are elongated by strong winds in the upper atmosphere. They are an indication of the leading edge of a warm front at altitude. Cloud symbol: Ci. » cloud [i]

cis-butenedioic acid » **maleic acid** [i]

Cisalpine Gaul [siz**al**piyn gawl] » **Gaul**

Cisalpine Republic N Italian state created by Napoleon I at the Peace of Campoformio (1797), comprising Milan and Lombardy, the Valtellina, the Romagna, the Venetian territories of Brescia and Bergamo, and the Duchy of Massa Carrara. By the Treaty of Lunéville (1802), it became the Italian Republic, with Bonaparte as President. » Napoleon I

Ciscaucasia The N Caucasus territory of Kuban, Stavropol, Terek, and the Black Sea, formed in 1924. It existed until 1934, when it was split into the Asov Black Sea, Ordzhonikidze, and Stavropol Territories. » Caucasus Mountains

Ciskei [**sis**kiy] pop (1987e) 1 140 000; area 7 700 sq km/2 972 sq ml. Independent Black homeland in NE Cape province, South Africa; bounded SW by the Indian Ocean; fourth homeland to gain independence from South Africa (not recognized internationally), 1981; most of the population are Xhosa, dependent on subsistence agriculture; over 105 000 people are commuters or migrant workers in South Africa; capital, Bisho; farming, wood, leather, textiles. » apartheid; South Africa [i]; Xhosa

Cistercians [sister**shuhnz**] A religious order formed by Benedictine monks by St Robert of Molesme in Citeaux, France, in 1098, under a strict rule, with an emphasis on solitude, poverty, and simplicity. The order was prominent in the Middle Ages, with leaders including Bernard of Clairvaux. By the 13th-c it had over 500 houses in Europe, but thereafter declined. In the 17th-c it was divided into communities of **Common Observance** (now abbreviated **SOCist**) and of **Strict Observance** (in full, the **Order of the Reformed Cistercians of the Strict Observance**, abbreviated **OCSO**). The latter were revived in France after the Revolution by *Trappists* (former members of the monastery of La Trappe). Common Observance is now prominent in the USA and parts of W Europe, with an abbot-general in Rome; Strict Observance, with a mother-house in Citeaux and an abbot in Rome, is active in France, Switzerland, England, and Poland. » Benedictines; Bernard of Clairvaux, St; monasticism; Trappists

citation analysis The quantitative analysis of the use of bibliographical citations in academic publications. The number of times a research study or a journal is cited by others can be interpreted as a valid indicator of its productivity and/or importance. » index

cithara » **kithara** [i]

Citizen's Advice Bureaux (CAB) In the UK, a national network of information offices, set up in 1939 to inform the public about the emergency wartime regulations. It has remained in operation since the end of the war to provide free and confidential information, particularly concerning the social services, housing, legal aid, consumer services, and family matters. Its 900 offices are staffed by 13 500 trained counsellors, 90% of whom are volunteers, and each office is funded by the local authority.

citizens' band (CB) radio A short-range two-way radio communication system for use by members of the public, typically consisting of a transceiver (a combined transmitter-receiver) and aerial. CB originated in the USA in the 1940s, and is particularly associated with long-distance truck drivers, who evolved a special language of codes and jargon to keep their messages from being understood by the police and public, such as *10–1* 'poor reception', *10–4* 'message understood', *smokey* 'policeman'. Many CB clubs were formed, especially in the 1970s. In the UK, the use of CB was illegal until 1981, when a special channel was authorized. » radio

Citlaltépetl [seetlal**tay**petl] or **Pico de Orizaba** 19°02N 97°02W. Highest peak in Mexico, rising to 5 699 m/18 697 ft in E Mexico; a dormant volcano, inactive since 1687; in the Pico de Orizaba National Park, area 197 sq km/76 sq ml, established in 1936. » Mexico [i]; volcano

citric acid cycle » **Krebs cycle**

citron A citrus fruit, 10–25 cm/4–10 in in diameter; ovoid, with thick, rough, yellowish-orange rind, and green or yellow flesh. (*Citrus medica*. Family: *Rutaceae*.) » citrus

citrus A group of plants bearing distinctive juicy, acid-tasting fruits of great economic importance. The majority belong to the genus *Citrus*, but a few come from close relatives. All species are spiny evergreen shrubs or trees; ovoid, dark green, glossy leaves with an articulated joint at the junction of blade and stalk; the stalk often winged, sometimes to the extent of appearing as a second blade attached end to end to the first. The leaves of side shoots become modified to form spines. Flowers and fruits are borne on the tree at the same time; the fragrant flowers solitary or in small clusters in the axils of the leaves, with 4–5 sepals and 4–8 white fleshy petals. The fruit is a type of berry, in which the carpels (the familiar segments containing the seeds or pips buried in a pulpy flesh composed of specialized hair-cells) are enclosed in a thick, leathery rind. Both the foliage and rind of the fruit have numerous glands containing aromatic essential oils.

Most *Citrus* species are cultivated, along with numerous cultivars. They include well-known species such as orange, lemon, lime, grapefruit, as well as more local fruits, such as the shaddock. Citrus fruits originated in China and SE Asia, but have been cultivated in many areas since early times, and a number are of obscure parentage. They are now grown in the tropics and warm temperate regions throughout the world, mainly the Mediterranean, S USA, S Africa, and Australia, and have become a major export crop for several countries. Breeding experiments to produce improved varieties and new and exotic hybrids are common. Although many citrus fruits are grown for eating, either as fresh fruit or in marmalade and preserves, some (eg bergamot orange) are grown for their essential oils, important in the perfume industry. (Genus: *Citrus*, 12 species. Family: *Rutaceae*.) » carpel; citron; cultivar; evergreen plants; grapefruit; lemon; lime; mandarin; orange; shaddock; shrub; tangerine; tree [i]

cittern A plucked string instrument of great antiquity, particularly popular in the 16th–17th-c. It resembled a lute, but with a smaller, pear-shaped body, a flat (or slightly convex) back, and usually four, five, or six courses of strings played with a plectrum. » chordophone; plectrum

city A settlement larger than a town or village, the definition of which varies according to national conventions. In Britain the term is used of cathedral towns (eg Ely) and certain other towns upon which the title has been conferred by royal authority (eg Birmingham, 1889); in the USA it is used of those urban centres which have a particular local government structure. » cathedral; suburbia

City, the A square mile of C London housing some of the world's major financial institutions, including the Stock Exchange, money markets, commercial and merchant banks, the insurance institutions, and commodity exchanges. An important source of overseas investment and earnings, its major rival is Wall Street in the USA. » London [i]

city-state » **polis**

Ciudad Guayana [syoo**dad** gwayana], also **San Félix de Guayana** 8°22N 62°37W, pop (1981) 314 497. New city in Bolívar state, E Venezuela, on the Orinoco and Caroní Rivers; founded in 1961 to link the towns of San Félix, Puerto Ordaz, Palúa, and Matanzas; population of 1 million is planned; airfield; railway; commercial port at San Félix; iron-ore loading at Puerto Ordaz; iron-ore terminal at Palúa; hydroelectric power nearby. » Venezuela [i]

Ciudad Juárez [syoo**dad hwa**res] 31°42N 106°29W, pop (1980) 567 365. Town in Chihuahua state, N Mexico; on US border, opposite El Paso, Texas, on the Río Grande; altitude 1 133 m/3 717 ft; headquarters of Benito Juárez in 1865; railway; university (1973); cotton trade. » Juárez, Benito; Mexico [i]

civet A carnivorous mammal, found in 17 species (mostly Asian); grouped as *oriental civets*, *palm civets*, *otter civet*, *African civet*, and *Malagasay civet*; also known as **civet cat** or **bush dog**, but the name *civet* is often used for any member of this family. A musky extract from the glandular secretions of some species (*civettone* or *civet*) is added to perfumes to prolong their scent. (Family: *Viverridae*.) » carnivore [i]; genet; Viverridae [i]

Civic Trust A charitable organization which exists to promote conservation and improvement of the environment in town and country, through encouraging high standards in architecture, planning, and the preservation of buildings of historic and architectural interest. Its concerns include urban wasteland, industrial dereliction, damage from heavy lorries, and town improvement schemes. There are separate Civic Trusts for England, Scotland, and Wales. » conservation (earth sciences); environmentalism

civil aviation » **aviation**

civil defence (CD) The organization of civilian defences, able to limit damage and keep communications and production moving. It became a vital part of a nation's defences during the bombing campaigns of World War 2. In the age of nuclear weapons, however, faced with the prospect of massive casualties, Britain has largely disbanded its Civil Defence operations. Countries which maintain active organizations include Switzerland, Sweden, and the USA, where Civil Defense copes with natural disasters. » Home Guard; Territorial Army

civil disobedience A political strategy adopted by M K Gandhi and his followers in India in 1930, in opposition to Britain's imperial rule: a non-violent, mass, illegal protest, intended to discredit the authority of the state. The movement was banned, and many were arrested, including Gandhi; but a pact was reached in 1931, and Congress then participated in the second Round Table Conference. The strategy was later used by Martin Luther King Jr to good effect, and is a path sometimes advocated by opponents of nuclear weapons. » Gandhi; King, Martin Luther

civil engineering A branch of engineering which deals with the design and construction of public works: buildings, bridges, tunnels, waterways, canals, streets, sewerage systems, railways, and airports. The subject includes structural, sanitary, and hydraulic engineering. Civil engineers must be familiar with the materials used in structures and with construction equipment. They also study soils and rocks, so that they can design suitable foundations, and manufactured products such as cars, aeroplanes, and missiles. The name was first used in 1750 by an English engineer, John Smeaton (1724–94).

civil law 1 A branch of law regulating relationships between private citizens. An aggrieved person must generally initiate proceedings personally in order to obtain a remedy. » criminal law; law 2 The term also refers to civil law systems such as those of continental Europe and Japan, where law is codified. The *Code Napoléon* is an influential example. The contrast is with *common law* systems, where the emphasis is on the development of law through individual cases under a system of precedent. » common law 3 Domestic law, in contrast to international law. » international law

civil liberties Individual freedoms that are thought to be essential to the operation of liberal democratic societies. These include freedom of speech, association, religion, conscience and movement, freedom before the law, and the right to a fair trial. In some political systems (eg the USA) the freedoms are constitutionally guaranteed in a bill of rights, while in others (eg the UK) they form part of the ordinary law. » civil rights

civil list In the UK, since 1760, a payment made from public funds for the maintenance of the royal household and family (except the Prince of Wales). It covers the salaries of the household staff, travel, entertaining, and public engagements at home and abroad. A sum payable from the Treasury is fixed by Act of Parliament at the beginning of each reign; in exchange, the new sovereign surrenders to the Exchequer the revenues from the Crown Estate. During the reign of Queen Elizabeth II (1952–), the original sum has had to be reviewed upwards several times because of inflation. For 1989–90 the civil list was fixed at £6 195 300, of which £4 658 000 was intended for the Queen. » Crown Estate

civil list pension Pensions originally paid from the sovereign's civil list, but now granted separately. They are awarded by the monarch on advice from the Prime Minister to persons who have given service to the Crown or public. » pension

civil rights The rights guaranteed by the state to its citizens. It incorporates the notion that governments should not arbitrarily act to infringe these rights, and that individuals and groups, through political action, have a legitimate role in determining and influencing what constitutes them. In common usage, the term is taken to mean the rights of groups, particularly ethnic and racial minorities, as opposed to the rights of the individual, although there is a clear element of overlap. Thus, the term has become closely asssociated with movements in the USA, especially 1954–68, which aimed to secure the legal enforcement of the guarantees of racial equality contained in the 13th, 14th, and 15th Amendments to the US Constitution. Beginning as an attack on specific forms of racial segregation in the Southern states, it broadened into a massive challenge to all forms of racial subordination, and achieved considerable success, especially at the level of legal and juridical reform. It was less successful in allaying Black/White economic disparity, which was the central problem outside the Southern states.

If the movement had any definite beginning, it was in the law school of the Black-oriented Howard University (Washington, DC) and in the councils of the National Association for the Advancement of Colored People (NAACP). At Howard a generation of Black lawyers received the training that would be vital during a long, well-planned assault against the legal structure of segregation. Among the most important was Thurgood Marshall (1908–), who presented the argument against school segregation in the epochal Supreme Court case of Brown vs. Board of Education of Topeka, Kansas (1954). Marshall would eventually become the first Black justice on the court. The NAACP, founded early in the 20th-c, provided the funding and organizational support for the many cases in which the courts tested the constitutional validity of segregation statutes. Throughout the movement's history, the justices of the Supreme Court proved important allies.

The movement began at the level of law, but developed into a popular confrontation with the segregationist political and social order. The first major event (1955) was a boycott of the bus system of Montgomery, Alabama. It arose from a driver's victimization of Mrs Rosa Parks after she refused to yield her seat to a White, as the law required. The boycott saw the emergence to leadership of Martin Luther King Jr, who was to be the foremost Black spokesman until his assassination in 1968. During his career King was denounced in the strongest terms by enemies of the movement. Now his birthday is a national holiday in many states.

King had a major hand in establishing the Southern Christian Leadership Conference (SCLC). This joined in coalition with the NAACP and such other organizations as the Urban League, the Congress of Racial Equality (CORE) and the Student Non-Violent Co-ordinating Committee (SNCC). Strongly influenced by the teachings of Mahatma Gandhi, King led a campaign aimed at the desegregation of all public facilities, including schools, restaurants, stores, and transport services, and at winning the rights to vote and hold public office. Major instances included: the struggle to desegregate the schools of Little Rock, Arkansas (1957); the 'Freedom Rides' of 1961 aimed at ending discrimination in long-distance bus transport; specific campaigns in many S cities, especially Albany, Georgia (1961–2), Birmingham, Alabama (1963), and Selma, Alabama (1965); and the Mississippi 'Freedom Summer' of 1964. On many occasions participants in the movement were arrested and/or injured. Some lost their lives.

The movement did benefit from growing White support, made manifest in the Freedom Rides, at the national March on Washington (1963), and in Selma and Mississippi. Whites likewise suffered arrest, injury, and death. But at all levels the driving force was the energy and anger of Black Americans, whether it was expressed in legal briefs, in strategic planning, or in direct protest. By 1965 the original goals seemed won. Court decisions, major legislation, and the actions of Presidents Eisenhower, Kennedy, and especially Johnson put the power of the federal government on the Black side. The result can be seen in the fact that Southern communities which were once bastions of segregation now have Black mayors and other officials. But even as the civil rights legislation of the mid-1960s was being passed, issues were arising that proved too great to be resolved.

The new problem was the quality of life in the ghettos of the N cities, where during 1964–7 there was massive rioting in Black neighbourhoods. Sometimes it was directed against the local police, and sometimes against the whole ghetto situation of poverty and permanent unemployment. The most articulate exponent of the situation was Malcolm X (1925–65, born Malcolm Little), who entered the Nation of Islam (Black Muslims) while in prison for youthful crimes. Malcolm X began his public career with wholly separatist ideas, but by the time of his assassination his position was changing. Neither he, nor King, who turned his attention northward during the last three years of his life, nor anyone else succeeded in working out a strategy comparable to the winning one that had been developed in the South.

Nonetheless, considerable gains were made. Philadelphia, Chicago, and Los Angeles, are three cities which have all elected Black mayors and other public officials. The powerful candidature of the Rev Jesse Jackson for the Democratic presidential nomination in 1988 demonstrated that a Black American could become a serious figure in national politics. No Black American need now endure the legal discrimination that was commonplace a generation ago. It may fairly be said that the Civil Rights Movement ranks with the American Revolution and the era of the Civil War as one of the major formative epochs in American public life. » King, Martin Luther; Jackson, Jesse; Johnson, L B; slavery

civil service Civilian personnel or officials employed on behalf of the state to administer central governmental policies, as distinct from the wider generality of public officials employed in such areas as local government, public corporations, and education, or as civilian staff of the armed forces. Most civil servants are permanent, in that they remain in post upon a change in government, though in some countries such as the USA and Germany a significant number of top positions do change hands. Civil services are hierachically organized, operate according to established rules of procedure, and are accountable through ministers to the Crown or the state. » Crown; state (politics)

cladistics A method of classifying organisms employing evolutionary hypotheses as the basis for classification. It uses recency of common ancestry as the criterion for grouping species together, rather than data on apparent similarity between species. » evolution; systematics

Cladocera [kla**do**suhra] » **water flea**

Clair, René, pseudonym of **René Chomette** (1898–1981) French film producer, born in Paris. He was a soldier, journalist, critic, and actor, before he wrote and directed his first film, in 1923. He produced both silent and talking films, in France and the USA, which were noted for his light touch and whimsical irony. His major works include *Sous les toits de Paris* (1930,

Under the Roofs of Paris), *The Ghost Goes West* (1935), and *It Happened Tomorrow* (1944). He returned to France in 1946, and continued to make films for nearly 20 years. He died at Neuilly-sur-Seine.

Clairvaux [klairvoh] A Cistercian abbey founded in 1115 by St Bernard near Ville-sous-la-Ferté, Champagne, France. The site is now occupied by a prison. » abbey; Bernard of Clairvaux, St

clairvoyance The gaining of information about an object or a contemporaneous external physical event by alleged paranormal means. The term *precognitive clairvoyance* is used to refer to the supposed paranormal gaining of information about an external physical source which will come into existence at some time in the future. Together with telepathy and precognition, clairvoyance makes up one of the three main categories of extrasensory perception, and as such is a major topic of current parapsychological research. » extrasensory perception; paranormal; parapsychology

clam The common name for a variety of bivalved molluscs; includes the giant clams, soft-shelled clams, and venus clams. (Class: *Pelecypoda.*) » bivalve; giant clam; mollusc

Clapham Sect A movement for evangelical reform of the Church of England, active in the 1780s and 1790s; also known as **The Saints**. Its members were all Anglicans, the name deriving from the estate at Battersea Rise, Clapham, owned by English economist Henry Thornton (1760–1815), where he and his cousin William Wilberforce lived. John Venn (1759–1813), Vicar of Clapham, was also a prominent evangelical. » Church of England; evangelicalism; Wilberforce

clapper board In motion picture production, a board or 'slate' with subject details, photographed at the beginning of each scene for identification. A hinged arm is 'clapped' to mark a synchronization point in the separate picture and sound records. » editing; film production

Clare, St (1194–1253), feast day 12 August. Italian abbess, born of a noble family at Assisi. In 1212, she gave up her possessions and joined a Benedictine convent, and in 1215 founded with St Francis the order of Franciscan nuns, known as the Poor Clares. She died at Assisi, and was canonized in 1255. In 1958 she was designated patron saint of television, on the ground that at Christmas 1252, while in her cell in the Convent of San Damiano, she both saw and heard the Mass in the Church of St Francis at Assisi. » Franciscans; monasticism

Clare, John (1793–1864) British poet, born at Helpston, Cambridgeshire. Though almost without schooling, he began to cultivate verse writing, and his *Poems Descriptive of Rural Life* (1820) had a good reception. Despite some patronage, he was forced to live in poverty, and spent the last 23 years of his life in an asylum at Northampton, where he wrote some of his best poetry. » English literature; poetry

Clare, Gaelic **An Chláir** pop (1981) 87 567, area 3 188 sq km/ 1 231 sq ml. County in Munster province, W Irish Republic; bounded W by Atlantic Ocean and E by Slieve Aughty Mts; Cliffs of Moher on Atlantic coast; limestone outcrops at Burren; capital, Ennis; cattle, dairy farming, fishing; 3-day folk festival at spa town of Lisdoonvarna (Jul). » Irish Republic [i]; Munster

Clarendon, Edward Hyde, 1st Earl of (1609–74) English statesman and historian, born near Salisbury, Wiltshire. He trained as a lawyer, and in 1640 became a member of the Short Parliament. At first he supported the popular party, but in 1641 became a close adviser of Charles, and headed the Royalist opposition in the Commons until 1642. He was knighted in 1643, and made Chancellor of the Exchequer, became High Chancellor in 1658, and at the Restoration (1660) was created Baron Hyde and (1661) Earl of Clarendon. In 1660 his daughter Anne (1638–71) secretly married the King's brother, James (later James II). Unpopular as a statesman, Clarendon irritated Cavaliers and Puritans alike, and in 1667 he fell victim to a court cabal. Impeached for high treason, he left the country for France, where he died at Rouen. His major work is the *History of the Rebellion in England* (3 vols, 1704–7). » English Civil War; Restoration

Clarendon Code A series of British Acts passed between 1661 and 1665 which re-asserted the supremacy of the Church of England after the collapse of the 'Puritan Revolution' in 1660. The most important were the Corporation Act (1661) and the Act of Uniformity (1662). Nonconformity was recognized as lawful, but many restrictions were placed on the activities of Nonconformists. » Corporation Act; Nonconformists; Puritanism

Clarendon, Constitutions of (1164) A written declaration of rights claimed by Henry II of England in ecclesiastical affairs, with the purpose of restoring royal control over the English Church. Promulgated at Clarendon, near Salisbury, the Constitutions – especially Clause 3, which jeopardized benefit of clergy and threatened clerical criminals with secular penalties – brought Thomas Becket and Henry II into open conflict. » Becket; Henry II (of England)

claret » wine

clarinet A woodwind instrument, with a cylindrical bore and a single reed. It evolved from the chalumeau, a somewhat coarse-toned instrument with a single reed, two keys, and seven finger-holes, developed at the end of the 17th-c; the term *chalumeau* is still used for the clarinet's lowest register. The clarinet came into regular use as a solo and orchestral instrument in the late 18th-c, since when the major development has been the addition of the Boehm key-mechanism. It is a transposing instrument, the most common models being pitched in A or B♭. The larger **bass clarinet** (in B♭) sounds one octave lower than the standard instrument. » reed/transposing/woodwind instrument [i]

Clark, Jim, properly **James** (1936–68) British motor racing driver, born at Kilmany, Fife, Scotland. He won his first race in 1956, becoming Scottish National Speed Champion (1958–9). After joining the Lotus Team in 1960, he went on to become World Champion Racing Driver (1963, 1965). He won in all 25 Grands Prix. He was killed during a formula two race at Hockenheim, Germany. » motor racing

Clark, Joe, properly **(Charles) Joseph** (1939–) Canadian statesman and Prime Minister (1979–80), born at High River, Alberta. At first a journalist and then professor of political science, he was elected to the Federal Parliament in 1972, becoming leader of the Progressive Conservative Party (1976) and of the Opposition. In 1979 he became Canada's youngest-ever Prime Minister. His minority government lost the general election the following year, and he was deposed as party leader in 1983. Since 1984 he has been Canada's Secretary of State for External Affairs. » Canada [i]

Clark, Sir Kenneth (Mackenzie), Baron (1903–83) British art historian, born in London. Educated at Winchester and Oxford, he became keeper of the Department of Fine Art in the Ashmolean Museum (1931–3), director of the National Gallery (1934–45), and Slade professor of fine art at Oxford (1946–50). He was also chairman of the Independent Television Authority (1954–7). He wrote many popular books on his subject, and became widely known through his television series *Civilisation* (1969). He was given a life peerage in 1969, and died at Hythe, Kent.

Clark, William (1770–1838) US explorer, born in Caroline Co, Virginia. He joined the army in 1789, and became joint leader with Meriwether Lewis of the successful transcontinental expedition to the Pacific coast and back (1804–6). He later became superintendent of Indian affairs in Louisiana Territory, and then Governor of Missouri Territory. He died at St Louis. » Lewis, Meriwether

Clarke, Jeremiah (c.1674–1707) English composer, born probably in London. He studied under Blow at the Chapel Royal, and became organist of Winchester College (1692) and vicar-choral of St Paul's, London (1695), following his master at the Chapel Royal in 1704. The real composer of the *Trumpet Voluntary* long attributed to Purcell, Clarke wrote theatre music, religious and secular choral works, and music for the harpsichord. He committed suicide in London after an unhappy love affair. » Blow

Clarke, Marcus (Andrew Hislop) (1846–81) Australian novelist, born in London. The son of a London barrister, he emigrated to Australia at the age of 18, where he became a journalist. His best-known work is a story of the convict settlements, *For the Term of his Natural Life* (1874). » Australian literature; novel

clarkia An annual native to western N America and Chile; leaves narrow to oblong; flowers in spikes, 4-petalled, white, pink, or violet; cultivated as ornamentals. (Genus: *Clarkia*, 36 species. Family: *Onagraceae*.) » annual

class A set or group of people sharing the same socio-economic position. A **class society** is a system of social inequality based on the unequal distribution of income and wealth between different classes. The term is used in two ways: it can be merely a convenient category used to organize people into a group (eg via occupation); or it can be seen as a real entity describing a group with specific inherent properties, such as the Marxist notions of the 'bourgeoisie' (middle class) and the 'proletariat' (working class) in capitalism. » Marxism

classical architecture » **Greek architecture; Neoclassicism** (art and architecture); **orders of architecture** [i]; **Renaissance architecture; Roman architecture**

classical art » **Greek art; Roman art**

classical literature » **Greek literature; Latin literature**

classical music Music which is part of a long written tradition, which lends itself to sophisticated study and analysis in conservatories and universities, and which is heard in concert halls, opera houses, and churches (rather than in dance halls, public houses, and discotheques). The term *classical* (with a small *c*) is a popular but vague description; *Classical* (usually with a capital *C*) is best reserved for the historical period c.1770–1830, which embraces the mature works of Haydn, Mozart, Beethoven, and Schubert. These days, the distinction between classical music on the one hand and folk music, light music, jazz, pop, etc on the other is felt to be largely unnecessary, and even injurious. » ars antiqua; ars nova; Baroque (music); Impressionism (music); Neoclassicism (music); Romanticism (music); Bach, Johann Sebastian; Beethoven; Brahms; Haydn; Mozart; Schubert

classical revival A recurrent phenomenon in Western art. The major revivals occurred in the Carolingian period (8th-c), 13th-c France, 15th-c Italy, 17th-c France, and 18th-c Rome, spreading to the rest of Europe and America. This latter is known as the Neoclassical movement. These revivals are usually characterized by a return to the classical orders in architecture, a re-affirmation of the human figure, nude or draped, as a central motif, with proportions based on Roman sculpture, and an interest in themes from classical literature. » Carolingian art; classicism; Neoclassicism (art)

classicism An adherence, in any period, to the standards of Greek and Roman art, traditionally understood in terms of 'correct' proportions of the figure, dignified poses and gestures (as in Raphael, Poussin), but also powerful expression of feeling (as in Donatello, David). The French Academy in the 17th-c laid down elaborate rules, and in the mid-18th-c Winckelmann stressed the importance of 'noble simplicity and calm grandeur'. In Western art the pendulum seems to swing between 'classical' and 'non-classical' (eg Gothic, Mannerist, Baroque, Romantic), although in certain periods a tension between the two is maintained. In literature, classicism is associated especially with Latin poets such as Horace and Virgil. It implies the skilful imitation and adaptation of permanent forms and themes, rather than new departures and 'originality'. » classical revival; Greek art; Latin literature; Mannerism; Neoclassicism (art and architecture); Roman art; David, Jacques Louis; Donatello; Horace; Poussin; Raphael; Virgil; Winckelmann

Classics The name given to horse racing's leading races in several countries. There are five Classics in England. The *One Thousand Guineas* is traditionally the first, run over 1 ml (1.6 km) at Newmarket; first run in 1814, it is open to fillies only. The *Two Thousand Guineas* is also early in the season, run over 1 ml (1.6 km) at Newmarket; first run in 1809, it is open to colts and fillies. *The Derby* or *Derby Stakes*, named after the 12th Earl of Derby, is run over 1½ ml (2.4 km) at Epsom Downs; first run in 1780, it is open to 3-year-old colts and fillies. The *Oaks*, named after the Epsom home of the 12th Earl of Derby, is run three days after the Derby over 1½ ml (2.4 km) at Epsom; first run in 1779, it is open to fillies only. The *St Leger* is the last Classic of the season, run over 1 ml 6 furlongs 127 yd (2 km 932 m) at Doncaster; first held in 1776, it is open to both colts and fillies. » horse racing; RR112

clathrate [**klath**rayt] A substance in which one type of molecule (the *guest*) is held in clefts in a matrix of the other (the *host*) without specific chemical bonding. The noble gases and some hydrocarbons form clathrates with water, occupying cavities in an open ice structure. » chemical bond; ice

Claude Lorraine [klohd], properly **Claude Gellée** (1600–82) French landscape painter, born at Chamagne, Lorraine. He studied with various Italian painters, then settled in Rome (1627). He painted about 400 landscapes, including several with biblical or classical themes, such as 'The Sermon on the Mount' (1656, New York). His compositions, if rather formal, are always graceful and well considered, and his colour is singularly mellow and harmonious. He also produced many drawings and etchings. He died in Rome. » French art; landscape painting

Claudel, Paul [kloh**del**] (1868–1955) French Catholic poet, essayist, and dramatist, born at Ville-neuve-sur-Fère. A convert at the age of 18, he joined the diplomatic service and held posts in many parts of the world. His plays, such as *L'Annonce faite à Marie* (1912, The Annunciation to Mary) and his poetry, such as *Cinq Grandes Odes* (1910, Five Great Odes), are alike remarkable for their spiritual intensity. » French literature

Claudianus, Claudius (340–410) The last of the great Latin poets, born in Alexandria, Egypt. He went to Rome in AD 395, and obtained patrician dignity by favour of Stilicho. He wrote first in Greek, then in Latin. Several of his works have survived, notably his epic poem *De Raptu Proserpinae* (The Rape of Proserpine), the work for which he was famed in the Middle Ages. He died in Rome. » epic; Latin literature; panegyric

Claudius, properly **Tiberius Claudius Nero Germanicus** (10 BC–AD 54) Roman emperor (41–54), grandson of the Empress Livia, brother of Germanicus, and nephew of the Emperor Tiberius. Kept in the background because of his physical disabilities, he devoted himself to historical studies, and thus survived the vicious in-fighting of the imperial house. Becoming emperor largely by accident in the chaos after Caligula's murder, he proved to be an able and progressive ruler, despite his gross and sometimes ridiculous indulgence of his wives and freedmen. Through his lavish public works and administrative reforms, he made a lasting contribution to the government of Rome and the empire, and through the annexation of Britain, Mauretania, and Thrace, a significant extension of its size. He died in 54, poisoned, it was widely believed, by his fourth wife Agrippina. » Agrippina the Younger; Caligula; Germanicus; Roman history [i]

Clausewitz, Karl (Philip Gottlieb) von [**klow**zevits] (1780–1831) Prussian general, born at Burg. He served with distinction in the Prussian and Russian armies, and ultimately became director of the Prussian army school, and Gneisenau's chief of staff. His posthumously published *Vom Kriege* ('On War'), advocating a policy of total war, revolutionized military theory, and was extremely influential in Germany and beyond. He died of cholera at Breslau. » Gneisenau; Prussia

Clausius, Rudolf (Julius Emanuel) (1822–88) German physicist, born at Köslin. He studied at Berlin, and in 1869 became professor of natural philosophy at Bonn. He worked on optics and electricity, formulated the second law of thermodynamics, and was influential in establishing thermodynamics as a science. He died in Bonn. » thermodynamics

clavichord A keyboard instrument in use from the 15th-c to the late 18th-c and revived in recent times, mainly for performing early music. The keys, when depressed, cause metal tangents to strike the strings, which run at right angles to the keys and are tuned in pairs. They are dampened at one end by means of cloth or felt. In early 'fretted' clavichords, one pair of strings served to produce several different notes depending on where the tangent struck them; in later 'unfretted' models, each key sounded only one pair of strings. The tone was slight but variable, and within its dynamic range capable of great sensitivity and nuance. » keyboard instrument

clavicle The curved bone, also known as the **collar bone**, lying almost horizontally at the base of the neck between the breastbone (*sternum*) and the shoulder blade (*scapula*); part of the pectoral girdle. It acts as a strut preventing the shoulder falling inwards and downwards – hence the position of the shoulder and upper limb when the clavicle is broken. >> scapula; sternum; Plate XIII

clawed toad An African or S American frog; claws on three hind toes; aquatic, seldom found on land; no tongue; may catch prey with its hands; most lack moveable eyelids; also known as **clawed frog**. (Genus: *Xenopus*, *Hymenochirus*, or *Pseudhymenochirus*. Family: *Pipidae*.) >> frog

clay A fine-grained sedimentary deposit composed mainly of clay minerals with some quartz, feldspar, and gypsum. >> clay minerals

Clay, Cassius >> **Ali, Muhammad**

Clay, Henry (1777–1852) US statesman and orator, born in Hanover Co, Virginia. The son of a Baptist preacher, he became a lawyer (1797), entered the lower house of congress in 1811, and was chosen its speaker, a post he held for many years. He was active in bringing on the war of 1812–15 with Britain, and was one of the commissioners who arranged the treaty of Ghent which ended it. He made several attempts to hold the Union together in the face of the issue of slavery, for which he earned the title of 'the great pacificator'. In 1824, 1831 and 1844 he was an unsuccessful candidate for the presidency. He died in Washington, DC. >> War of 1812

clay minerals Hydrous sheet silicates which form fine, flaky crystals, and which can absorb water, giving clay its characteristic plasticity when wet. They are formed as the product of the weathering of rocks, and are often deposited by rivers. Kaolinite, montmorillonite, and illite are important clay mineral groups. They are used extensively to make bricks and pottery, and as a filler for paper, rubber, and paint. >> kaolin; silicate minerals; vermiculite

clay pigeon shooting A pastime and sport in which clay targets are released into the air using an automatic machine. The 'clays' simulate the flight of birds, and are fired at with shotguns. It is also known as **trap shooting**. >> shooting (recreation)

clay tokens Small clay artefacts of several distinctive shapes, used in the Middle East since at least the 9th millennium BC as a system of accounting. Some of the symbols used on the earliest known writing tablets from the same area (c.3500 BC) show a striking resemblance in shape to those of the clay tokens. >> graphology

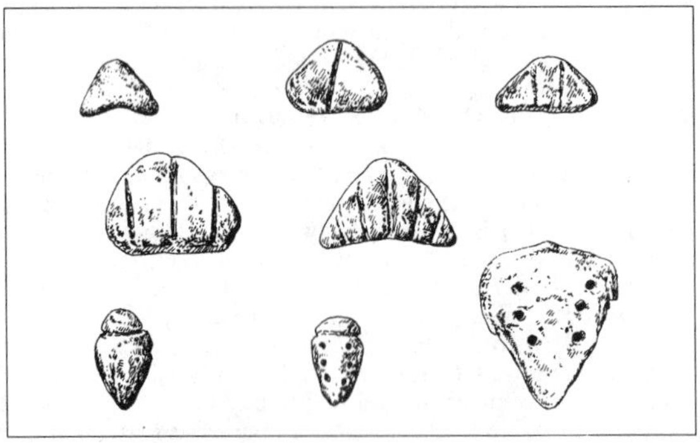

Clay tokens

Clayton-Bulwer Treaty (1850) A US/British agreement on the terms for building a canal across C America; it remained in effect until 1901. The major provision was to forbid either party to exercise exclusive control or to build fortifications. The parties involved were US secretary of state John M Clayton and British minister to Washington, Sir Henry Lytton Bulwer.

Clear Grits The name given to a Radical political reform group in Upper Canada (Canada West/Ontario) in the 1850s and 1860s. The term derived from the group's attitude of uncompromising determination. It promoted major constitutional reform, including direct election to executive posts, and secularization of Clergy Reserves. After 1867 it formed the core of the Canadian Liberal Party. >> Clergy Reserves

clearing house In economics any institution whose function is to co-ordinate and settle the debts owed by its various members; in particular, a place where cheques from different banks are sorted, and the amounts owed by and to each bank are calculated. Since 1984, the process has been mainly automated in the UK through the Clearing House Associated Payments System (CHAPS). Several million cheques and credit transfers are handled every day. In the USA, the equivalent organization is the Clearing House Interbank Payments System (CHIPS). Similar systems exist in many other countries.

clearwing moth A small moth in which scales are absent over much of the wings, leaving clear, transparent areas; mimics of bees and wasps; daytime fliers, flight rapid; larvae often tunnel into plant stems. (Order: *Lepidoptera*. Family: *Sesiidae*.) >> larva; moth

cleavage The process by which a fertilized egg cell (*zygote*) divides to give rise to all the cells of an organism. In animals, cleavage results in the formation of a blastula. The animal kingdom can be divided into two major groups on the basis of cleavage pattern: the *deuterostomes*, which include vertebrates and echinoderms, with radial cleavage, and the *protostomes*, which include molluscs and arthropods, with spiral cleavage. >> arthropod; blastula; cell; Chordata; echinoderm [i]; mollusc

cleavers >> **goosegrass**

cleft lip and palate An abnormality of development of the lips and palate, occurring in about 1 in 1 000 live births, and sometimes accompanied by other congenital abnormalities. It consists of a fissure or cleft on one or both sides of the upper lip occurring either alone or associated with a cleft in the palate. Cleft lip alone seldom causes feeding difficulties, but cleft palate usually causes the breathing in of milk or food. The use of a special palatal teat which covers the defect during feeding is useful until surgical repair can be carried out. >> congenital abnormality; mouth; palate

Cleisthenes [**kliys**thuhneez] (6th-c BC) Prominent Athenian politician of the Alcmaeonid family, and founder of Athenian democracy. His constitutional reforms (c.508 BC) paved the way for the radical democracy established by Ephialtes and Pericles (c.461 BC). >> Alcmaeonids; Pericles

Cleland, John [**klay**land] (1709–89) British novelist, educated at Westminster, London. After working and travelling abroad, he published in 1750 *Fanny Hill, or the Memoirs of a Woman of Pleasure*. A best-seller in its time, it achieved a second *succès de scandale* on its revival and prosecution under the Obscene Publications Act in 1963. Cleland also practised journalism and playwriting, excelling at neither, and dabbled in Celtic philology. He died in London. >> English literature

clematis Woody climbers native throughout temperate regions; stems sometimes thick and liane-like; leaves pinnate, the stalk sensitive on the lower side, acting as a tendril and bending around supports on contact; flowers with four petaloid perianth-segments, styles long and feathery, aiding wind dispersal of the seeds, and giving seed-heads a white, hoary appearance. Many garden forms have brightly-coloured flowers. (Genus: *Clematis*, 250 species. Family: *Ranunculaceae*.) >> climbing plant; liane; perianth; style (botany)

Clemenceau, Georges [**klem**ãsoh] (1841–1929) French statesman and Prime Minister (1906–9, 1917–20), born at Mouilleron-en-Pareds. He trained as a doctor, worked as a teacher in the USA (1865–9), then returned to France, where he became a member of the National Assembly, and (1876) a leader of the extreme left in the Chamber of Deputies. The destroyer of many ministries, he was himself twice Premier. Known as 'the tiger', he presided at the Peace Conference in 1919, showing an intransigent hatred of Germany. A brilliant journalist, he founded *L'Aurore*, and other papers. He died in Paris. >> France [i]; Versailles, Treaty of

Clement I, St, known as **Clemens Romanus** (late 1st-c), feast day 23 November. One of the apostolic Fathers, reckoned variously as the second or third successor of St Peter at Rome, possibly 88–97 or 92–101. He may have been a freedman of Jewish parentage belonging to Caesar's household. The first of two epistles attributed to him is generally accepted as his (written c.96); it is written to the Corinthian Church, and treats of social dissensions, the nature of early Christian ministry, and the resurrection. He was probably martyred. Later, several spurious works were circulated in his name, such as the Clementine *Homilies*. » Christianity; Fathers of the Church

Clement V (c.1260–1314) French bishop and Pope (1305–14), born in Bordelais. He became Archbishop of Bordeaux in 1299. As Pope, he suppressed the Templars, and removed the seat of the papacy to Avignon (1309), a movement disastrous to Italy. He died at Roquemaure, Provence. » Knights Templars; pope

Clement VII, originally **Giulio de' Medici** (1478–1534) Italian Pope (1523–34), born in Florence, who became a patron of artists and scholars. He allied himself with Francis I of France against the Holy Roman Emperor Charles V, was besieged by the Constable Bourbon, and for a while became his prisoner. His indecisiveness, along with his refusal to sanction Henry VIII's divorce from Catherine of Aragon, hastened the Reformation. He died in Rome. » Bourbon, Charles; Henry VIII; pope; Reformation

Clement of Alexandria (Lat **Clemens Alexandrinus**) (c.150–c.215) Greek theologian and Father of the early Church, born (probably) in Athens. He first studied philosophy, then became head of the celebrated Catechetical school at Alexandria, where he related Greek philosophical thought to Christian belief. In 203 the persecution under Severus compelled him to flee to Palestine. His most distinguished pupil was Origen. » Fathers of the Church; Origen

Clementi, Muzio (1752–1832) Italian composer and pianist, born in Rome. In 1766 he was brought to England, where he conducted the Italian Opera in London (1777–80), toured as a virtuoso pianist (1781), and went into the piano-manufacturing business. In 1817–26 he wrote the *Gradus ad Parnassum*, on which subsequent piano methods have been based. A composer of mainly piano and chamber music, he died at Evesham, Worcestershire. » piano

Cleon (?–422 BC) The first Athenian of rich, bourgeois stock to play a prominent role in 5th-c BC politics. Routinely dismissed as an upstart, demagogue, and warmonger, it was his capture of the Spartans on the island of Sphacteria (425 BC) that gave Athens her trump card in the peace negotiations of the late 420s BC. » Peloponnesian War

Cleopatra VII (69–30 BC) Queen of Egypt (51–48 BC, 47–30 BC), the daughter of Ptolemy Auletes. A woman of great intelligence, she made the most of her undoubted physical charms to strengthen her own position within Egypt, and to save the country from annexation by Rome. Thus, Julius Caesar, to whom she bore a son Caesarion, supported her claim to the throne against her brother (47 BC), while Antony, by whom she had three children, restored to her several portions of the old Ptolemaic Empire, and even gave to their joint offspring substantial areas of the Roman East (34 BC). Defeated along with Antony at Actium (31 BC), she preferred suicide to being captured and exhibited at Rome in Octavian's victory parade. The asp, which she used to cause her death, was an Egyptian symbol of royalty. » Actium, Battle of; Antonius; Caesar

clerestory or **clear-storey** [**kleer**stawree] The upper part of a wall in a building with windows above adjacent roofs. The term is usually applied to windows in a church above the aisle roofs. The name is derived from French *clair*, 'light'.

clergy » **abbey; archbishop; archdeacon; bishop; cardinal** (religion); **canon** (religion) **3; curate; deacon; dean; priest; rector; vicar**

Clergy Reserves A seventh of the public land in Upper and Lower Canada (Ontario and Quebec), set aside for the future use of Protestant clergy; established under the Constitutional Act (1791). In practice the Reserves became bastions of wealth and power for the predominantly Anglican elite in Upper Canada, drawing fierce criticism from Methodists and disestablishmentarians. They were secularized in 1854.

Clerk Maxwell, James » **Maxwell, James Clerk**

Clermont-Ferrand [**klair**mõ ferã] 45°46N 3°04E, pop (1982) 151 092. Capital of Puy-de-Dôme department, C France; capital of Auvergne, 16th-c; Clermont merged with Montferrand, 1630; railway; bishopric; university (1896); geographical and economic centre of the Massif Central; Michelin tyres, chemicals, textiles, foodstuffs; major source of mineral water; Gothic Cathedral of Notre-Dame (begun 1248), basilica of Notre-Dame-du-Port (11th–12th-c); birthplace of Pascal. » Gothic architecture; Massif Central; Pascal

Cleveland (UK) [**kleev**land] pop (1987e) 554 500; area 583 sq km/225 sq ml. County of NE England, divided into four districts; created in 1974 from parts of Yorkshire and Durham; bounded E by the North Sea; includes Teesside urban area with port facilities on the R Tees estuary; county town, Middlesbrough; chief towns include Stockton-on-Tees, Hartlepool; iron, steel, chemicals, fertilizers, oil, petrochemicals; North Yorkshire Moors National Park. » Middlesbrough

Cleveland (USA) 41°30N 81°42W, pop (1980) 573 822. Seat of Cuyahoga County, NE Ohio, USA; port on L Erie at the mouth of the Cuyahoga R; developed with the opening of the Ohio and Erie Canal, 1827; city status, 1836; largest city in Ohio; airfield; railway; three universities (1826, 1886, 1923); machinery, metals and metal products, electronics, transportation equipment; medical research centre; major league teams, Indians (baseball), Cavaliers (basketball), Browns (football); Play House, Holden Arboretum, Museum of Art. » Erie, Lake; Ohio

Cleveland, (Stephen) Grover (1837–1908) US statesman and the 22nd and 24th President (1885–9, 1893–7), born at Caldwell, New Jersey. The son of a Presbyterian minister, he became a lawyer, Mayor of Buffalo, and in 1882 Governor of New York. In his first term as President, he strongly advised a readjustment of the tariff on various imports. In 1895 he evoked intense excitement throughout the world by applying the Monroe Doctrine to Britain's dispute with Venezuela over the frontier question. He died at Princeton, New Jersey. » Monroe Doctrine

Cleveland bay One of the oldest English breeds of horse; height, 15–16 hands/1.5–1.6 m/5–5¼ ft; reddish-brown with long body, shortish legs, muscular hindquarters; also known as the **Chapman horse**. Crossing with thoroughbreds in the 18th-c produced the rare *Yorkshire coach horse*. » thoroughbred

Cleveland Way Long-distance footpath in North Yorkshire, England; length c.150 km/90 ml; stretches from Helmsley to near Filey. » Yorkshire, North

click beetle An elongate, usually dark-coloured beetle; an adult lying on its back can right itself with a jack-knifing movement that produces a loud click; long, cylindrical larvae live in soil, feeding on roots; can be serious crop pests, known as **wireworms**. (Order: *Coleoptera*. Family: *Elateridae*.) » beetle

click language A language in which 'click' sounds are a systematic part of the consonant system, as in such African languages as Zulu and Xhosa. Clicks are produced by an airstream which begins at the back of the mouth, and typically involve the kind of sounds made when 'tut-tutting', or in 'gee-upping' a horse. » articulation

client-centred therapy An approach developed by US psychologist Carl Rogers (1902–), sometimes referred to as **person-centred therapy**. It is based on the belief that a human being is an innately good, rational, and socialized person who continually strives to realize his/her potential (known as *self-actualization*). Psychological maladjustment is thought to occur when individuals experience events or situations in a way which conflicts with their self-concept. Therapy is 'non-directive', in that the therapist does not tell the client what to do, say, think, or feel. The therapist's role is to be warm, empathic, and genuine in dealing with the client, thus providing a climate of psychological safety within which clients can attempt to change their self-concept. » clinical psychology; personality

cliff dwellings Houses of the Pueblo Indians in SW USA from the Pueblo III cultural period (c.1100–1300 AD). Made with stone blocks and adobe mortar, some were several storeys high, and built in arched recesses of cliff walls. They were deserted by 1300 AD, when people moved further S and established pueblo villages, where they still live. Some cliff dwellings are preserved, such as Cliff Palace at Mesa Verde, Colorado. » Pueblo

climacteric » **menopause**

climate The long-term prevailing weather conditions in a region or place. There are a number of different schemes for dividing the Earth into climatic regions, the majority of which are based on a combination of indices of mean annual temperature, mean monthly temperature, annual precipitation totals, and seasonality. The climate of a place is influenced by several factors. Latitude determines the amount of solar radiation received, with the greatest in equatorial regions and the least in polar regions. Elevation affects both temperature and precipitation; mountainous areas are generally cooler and wetter. Location close to the sea or large bodies of water moderates temperature; continental areas are generally more arid and affected by greater extremes of temperature. Aspect is of local importance; in the N hemisphere, S- and W-facing slopes are warmer than N- and E-facing slopes. The scientific study of climate, describing and attempting to explain climatic differences from place to place, is known as **climatology**. » general circulation model; palaeoclimatology; precipitation; temperature [i]; weather

climax vegetation A botanical term for the final stage of plant succession which has developed without disturbance. Where climate is the major factor in determining vegetation, a climatic climax results. In most regions of the Earth, the climatic climax is dominated by trees: tropical rainforest in the humid tropics; deciduous woodland at temperate latitudes. Acceptance of the concept is not universal, and factors other than climate (eg soil type) may be important.

climbing perch Asiatic freshwater fish common in rivers, canals, and lakes; body length up to 25 cm/10 in; possesses special respiratory organ above gills for air breathing; able to move overland by jerky thrusts of tail fin; good food fish. (3 genera, including *Ariabas*. Family: *Anabantidae*.)

climbing plant A plant which reaches towards the light by clinging to neighbouring plants, walls, or other supports, sometimes referred to by the general term *vine*. Various means are used, including twining stems and leaf-stalks, tendrils, and aerial roots. *Ramblers* merely grow against and lean on their supports, but often have thorny hooks to help grip. *Lianes* have long, woody stems which reach high into the forest canopy, and are found especially in the tropics. » liane

clingfish Small marine fish found worldwide in rocky inshore habitats of tropical to temperate seas; head triangular; body smooth, flattened on underside with large sucking disc formed from pelvic fins and used for clinging to rocks; includes *Lepadogaster lepadogaster*, the Cornish sucker. (Family: *Gobiesocidae*; 9 genera.)

clinical linguistics The application of linguistics to the analysis of disorders of spoken, written, or signed language. It emerged in the 1970s as an ancillary subject to speech pathology, and has since developed into a separate academic field, investigating the nature of the problems of pronunciation, grammar, vocabulary, and language use in adults and children. » linguistics; speech pathology

clinical psychology The application of psychological knowledge to the assessment, prevention, and treatment of a variety of psychological disorders, involving behavioural, emotional, or cognitive disturbances. » behaviour/client-centred/cognitive/Gestalt therapy; psychology

clinometer A hand-held surveying instrument, also known as an **Abney level**. It is used to measure the angles of a slope by bringing a level-bubble on a graduated circle into co-incidence with a wire in a sighting tube. » surveying

Clinton, De Witt (1769–1828) US politician, born at Little Britain, New York. He became a lawyer in 1788, sat in the New York state legislature (1797) and Senate (1798–1802), was appointed Mayor of New York (1802), but defeated by Madison in the presidential contest of 1812. He planned the Erie Canal scheme ('Clinton's Ditch'), which he opened in 1825. He died at Albany, New York.

Clio [**kli**yoh] In Greek mythology, the Muse of history, and of lyre-playing. » Muses

clipper ship A mid-19th-c revolutionary US design of sailing ship. Its principal features were finer bow and stern lines, greater rake to the masts, and greater beam than in traditional vessels, resulting in faster ships with improved windward performance. » ship [i]

clitellum [kli**tel**uhm] The saddle or swollen glandular part of the skin of earthworms and leeches. It functions during reproduction, and is responsible for the formation of the cocoon containing the eggs. » earthworm; leech; reproduction

clitoris [**kli**tuhris] Part of the female external genitalia, composed of erectile tissue partly surrounded by muscle. It is the equivalent of the male penis (though it does not convey the urethra), and enlarges upon tactile stimulation. In seals and some other animals it contains a small bone (the *os clitoridis*). » penis [i]

Clive (of Plassey), Robert, Baron (1725–74) British soldier and adminstrator in India, born at Styche, Shropshire. In 1743 he joined the East India Company, and took part in the campaigns against the French. In 1755 he was called to avenge the so-called Black Hole of Calcutta, and at Plassey (1757) defeated a large Indian-French force. For three years he was sole ruler in all but name of Bengal. In 1760, he returned to England, entered parliament, and was made a baron (1762). In 1765 he returned to Calcutta, effectively reformed the civil service, and re-established military discipline. His measures were seen as drastic, and he became the subject of a select committee enquiry upon his return to England in 1767. He committed suicide in London. » Black Hole of Calcutta; East India Company, British

cloaca [kloh**ay**ka] The terminal region of the gut into which the alimentary canal, urinary system, and reproductive system all open and discharge their products via a single common aperture. » alimentary canal; reproduction; urinary system

clock A mechanism for measuring and indicating the passage of time, and for recording the duration of intervals. Its essential elements are a source of energy to drive the mechanism, and a device to maintain a regular (usually stepwise) rate of motion. (In the earliest mechanical clocks, the striking of bells was a primary function.) In mediaeval and many later clocks, the drive was a falling weight; from the 16th-c, it was the coiled mainspring; and from the late 19th-c, it was electric current from batteries or mains. Steady rate was provided first (very inadequately) by a verge escapement (projections on a freely oscillating arm engaging intermittently in the teeth of a crown wheel); then during the 17th-c by a pendulum, the accuracy of which was increased by successive refinements and corrections (eg for temperature change). From c.1670 a balance wheel was used for small clocks and watches. In modern times, clocks are powered by electric synchronous motors maintained by the mains frequency, by a maintained tuning fork, or by the oscillation of a quartz crystal. Observatory clocks use one of two methods: (i) the constancy of the difference in energy levels of different states of the cesium atom, a beam of the atoms divided by a magnetic field forming part of an electric circuit with self-correcting feedback; (ii) the natural frequency of inversion of the pyramidal ammonia molecule, the excitation

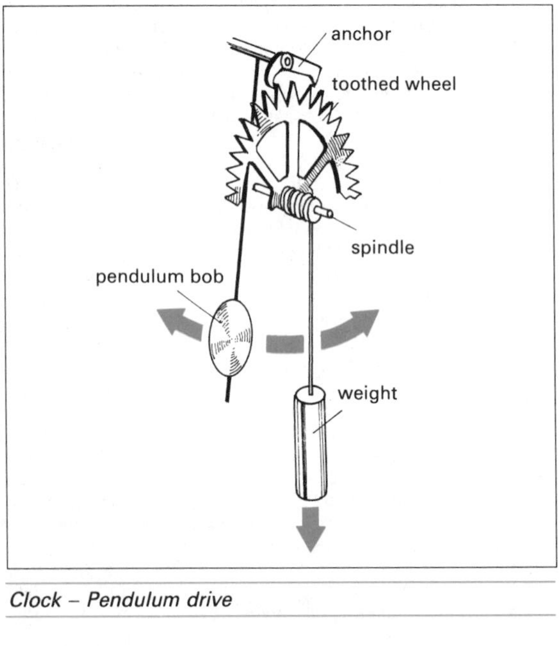

Clock – Pendulum drive

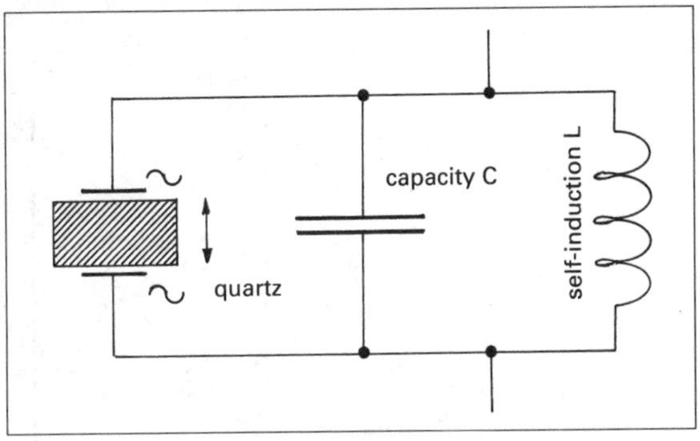

Quatz clock – Electric oscillatory circuit

radiation of the correct frequency being locked in by a feedback circuit. » ammonia; time

clock paradox A phenomenon resulting from an experiment involving two identical clocks, initially together and showing the same time, one of which is carried off on a round-trip journey. Upon returning, the clock which moved will have lost time relative to the motionless clock by an amount prescribed by special relativity. Such effects have been observed using a pair of atomic clocks, one of which is flown around the world. However, a principle of relativity which claims that all observers are equal appears violated. The apparent paradox is resolved within special relativity by noticing that any clock undergoing a round-trip journey must be accelerated at some stage. The clock paradox was first discussed by Einstein (1905). It is sometimes expressed in terms of identical twin brothers, one of whom undertakes a journey and finds himself younger than his brother upon returning (the 'twin paradox'). » Einstein; special relativity [i]; time

Clodion, properly **Claude Michel** (1738–1814) French sculptor, born at Nancy. He was trained in Paris and Rome, where he stayed from 1762 to 1771. One of the most brilliant Rococo sculptors, he specialized in small terracottas and low reliefs of dancing nymphs and satyrs, unmistakably erotic. He died in Paris. » relief sculpture; Rococo; terracotta

cloisonné [klwazon**ay**] A method of enamelling on metal, and occasionally ceramic, in which the different fields of colour are separated by metal wires soldered to the surface to be decorated. Principally an Oriental technique, it was much used in Byzantine and Mediaeval art. » enamelling

cloisters Covered walkways around an open space or court, with a colonnade or arcaded inner side and a solid outer wall. Cloisters are normally used in a monastery or convent to connect the church to other parts of the building. They are usually placed S of the nave and W of the transept. » colonnade; nave; transept

Cloisters, the A complex in Fort Tryon Park, New York City, incorporating several mediaeval structures. The Cloisters were opened as a branch of the Metropolitan Museum of Art in 1938, and house George Grey Barnard's notable collection of mediaeval art. » Metropolitan Museum of Art; New York City

clone (computing) Hardware or software products manufactured by one company which completely mimic the behaviour of products originally devised by another manufacturer. It is usually cleverly designed to avoid patent and licence restrictions.

cloning (genetics) The process of asexual reproduction observed in bacteria and other uni-cellular micro-organisms which divide by simple fission, so that the daughter cells are genetically identical to each other and to the parent, except where mutation occurs. In higher organisms, genetically identical individuals may be produced by cloning. A body (*somatic*) cell is taken from an embryo in an early stage of development, the nucleus transferred to an unfertilized ovum from which the nucleus has been removed, and the product grown in culture; daughter cells from the earliest divisions are removed, and grown in cell culture or implanted into host mothers to give genetically identical offspring. This is a very difficult procedure which has so far been achieved mainly in amphibia. There is considerable potential application in animal rearing, but its application to humans is extremely unlikely (except in some very rare instances of *in vitro* fertilization). It is also currently used in recombinant DNA technology. » cell; recombinant DNA; reproduction

Clonmel, Gaelic **Cluain Meala** 52°21N 7°42W, pop (1981) 14 808. Capital of Tipperary county, South Riding, Munster, S Irish Republic; on R Suir; centre of Irish greyhound racing and salmon fishing; railway; agricultural trade, food processing, tourism, footwear, cider, prams. » Irish Republic [i]; Tipperary

clonorchiasis [klonuh**ki**yasis] A disease caused by the infiltration of *clonorchis sinensis*, a fluke which lies in the bodies of freshwater fish in the Far East. Affected individuals may show no symptoms, but some develop cirrhosis of the liver. » cirrhosis; fluke

closed circuit television (CCTV) Any system of image presentation in which a video camera and its display screen are directly linked, even at a considerable distance, rather than by broadcast transmission or intermediate recording. Applications include surveillance, surgical and scientific demonstration, and industrial remote examination. » interactive video; surveillance TV; television

closed shop A company or works where the work force is required to be a member of one (or more) officially recognized trade unions; the opposite situation is known as an **open shop**. The advantages of the closed shop system are that negotiations between a company and its workforce are simplified and less time-consuming. Union negotiators have more authority. However, problems arise for the company if negotiations break down, as the unions can close down operations more easily where all the workforce are members. An additional drawback is that recruitment of staff may be more difficult if union membership is a prerequisite.

closer settlement The name given to Australian colonial and state government laws (1894–1906) designed to settle individuals or groups of unemployed persons on small farm blocks. Based on New Zealand's example (1892), the laws provided for the re-purchase of land by the government, either by arrangement or compulsorily at a fair price, and its sale in small blocks to settlers on easy terms. The principles of closer settlement and goverment assistance for land settlement were also applied to soldier settlement schemes after both world wars.

clostridium A rod-shaped bacterium that is typically motile by means of flagella, and produces spores (*endospores*). It is widespread in the soil and in the intestinal tract of humans and other animals. It includes the causative agents of botulism, gas gangrene, and tetanus. (Kingdom: *Monera*. Family: *Bacillaceae*.) » bacteria [i]; intestine; spore

clothes moth A small drab moth; larvae feed on dried organic matter, including woollen materials and fur; can be household pests. (Order: *Lepidoptera*. Family: *Tineidae*.) » larva; moth; tineid moth

Clotho » **Moerae**

Clotilde, St (474–545), feast day 3 June. Queen consort of Clovis I, King of the Franks, and daughter of Chilperic, King of Burgundy. She married in 493, and after Clovis's death, lived a life of austerity and good works at the abbey of St Martin at Tours, where she died. » Clovis I; Franks; monasticism

cloud A visible collection of particles of ice and water held in suspension above the ground. Clouds form when air becomes saturated and water vapour condenses around nuclei of dust, smoke particles, and salt. Four main categories of clouds are recognized: *nimbus* clouds, which produce rain; *stratus* clouds, which resemble layers; *cumulus* clouds, which resemble heaps; and *cirrus* clouds, which resemble strands or filaments of hair. These names are further modified by an indication of cloud height: *strato* – low level clouds; *alto* – middle level clouds; *cirro* – high level clouds. Fog can be considered as cloud close to ground level. » altocumulus/altostratus/cirrus/cirrocumulus/cirrostratus/cumulonimbus/cumulus/nimbostratus/nimbus/noctilucent/stratocumulus/stratus clouds; condensation

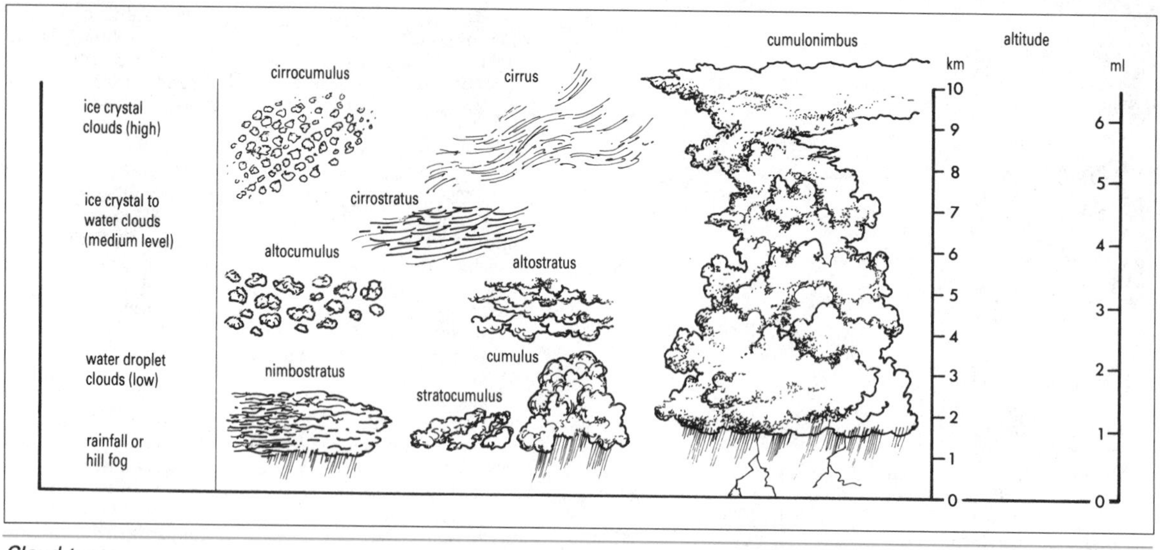

Cloud types

(physics); dewpoint temperature; fog; nephanalysis; precipitation; thunderstorm

cloud chamber A device for detecting sub-atomic particles; invented by British physicist Charles Wilson in 1912. It comprises a chamber containing vapour prone to condensing to liquid. The passage of particles forms ions, which act as centres for condensation, and the particle paths become visible as trails of mist. The cloud chamber was important in the early days of radioactivity, but has been superseded by other particle detectors. » bubble chamber; ion; particle detectors; Wilson, Charles

clouded leopard A member of the cat family, native to SE Asia; has the longest canine teeth of any living cat; coat with large brown blotches separated by thin yellow lines; inhabits forest; may leap on prey from trees; eats birds, monkeys, pigs, and grazing animals. (*Neofelis nubulosa*.) » Felidae

clouded tiger » **tortoiseshell cat**

Clough, Arthur Hugh (1819–61) British poet, born in Liverpool. Educated at Rugby and Oxford, he travelled in Europe and espoused progressive social views. Experimental techniques in his long poem *The Bothie* (1848) and the ironic narrative *Amours de Voyage* (1849) have influenced modern poets. He died in Florence. » English literature; poetry

clove tree An evergreen tree growing to 12 m/40 ft, native to Indonesia but cultivated elsewhere; leaves lance-shaped; flowers yellow, 4-petalled, in terminal clusters. The flower buds are dried to form the spice cloves. (*Syzygium aromaticum*. Family: *Myrtaceae*.) » evergreen plants; spice; tree [i]

clover A low-growing annual and perennial, occurring in both temperate and subtropical regions, but mainly in the N hemisphere; leaves with three toothed leaflets; small pea-flowers white, pink, or red, clustered into often dense, rounded heads; pods small, remaining enclosed by the calyx. The flowers are visited by hive bees, providing an important source of nectar for bee-keepers. Several species are extensively grown as fodder for cattle, and they are also valuable pasture plants, often grown with grasses, enriching the soil through the presence of nitrogen-fixing bacteria in small nodules on the root system. Yellow-flowered species are generally called **trefoils**. (Genus: *Trifolium*, 250 species. Family: *Leguminosae*.) » alsike; annual; perennial; root nodule; shamrock; trefoil

Clovis The earliest identifiable Indian culture of N America; hunter-gatherers exploiting the mammoth herds of the plains towards the end of the last glaciation, c.10000–9000 BC. It is characterized archaeologically by bifacially-flaked spear points found across the USA, notably near Clovis, New Mexico, in 1963. » Folsom; hunter-gatherers

Clovis I (Ger **Chlodwig** or **Chlodovech**) (c.465–511) Merovingian king, who succeeded his father, Childeric (481), as King of the Franks. He overthrew the Gallo-Romans, and took possession of the whole country between the Somme and the Loire by 496. In 493 he married (St) Clotilda, and was converted to Christianity along with several thousand warriors after routing the Alemanni. In 507, he defeated the Visigoth, Alaric II, captured Bordeaux and Toulouse, but was checked at Arles by the Ostrogoth, Theodoric. He then took up residence in Paris, where he died. » Gaul; Ostrogoths; Visigoths

cloze testing A test widely used in foreign language teaching to establish a learner's comprehension of a reading passage. The passage is presented with words omitted at regular intervals: the reader must try to supply the missing words, or plausible substitutes.

club An establishment where people associate to pursue social, political, or sporting activities. In the US, country clubs and women's clubs are well-established. In London, clubs for men developed in the 17th-c from the taverns and coffee houses where men met to do business. These clubs (Whites, founded 1693, Boodles 1767, Brooks's 1764, Portland 1816, Athenaeum 1824, Garrick 1831, Carlton 1832, Reform 1836, Savages 1857, Press Club 1882, Royal Automobile 1897) were used by members of the aristocratic and professional classes, and excluded women. Some have relaxed their rules; most continue to provide meals, library facilities, and overnight accommodation. » service club; Working Men's Clubs and Institutes Union

club foot A congenital deformity of one or both feet, in which the child cannot stand on the sole of the affected foot. The foot is pulled downward, and the heel turned inwards. The deformity is readily seen at birth, and cannot be manipulated, but improvement may be achieved by the application of a series of graded splints, or in severe cases by surgical operation. » congenital abnormality; foot

clubmoss A spore-bearing plant related to ferns and horsetails; stem long, regularly branched, clothed with numerous small leaves; sporangia in leaf-axils, often arranged in a terminal, cone-like strobilus. It is found almost everywhere, many in heathland or similar habitats. Clubmoss, selaginella, and quillwort form the only living members of an ancient group, the *Lycopsida*. Formerly much more diverse, especially during the Carboniferous period, its fossils include giant tree-forms. (Genus: *Lycopodium*, 450 species. Family: *Lycopodiaceae*.) » Carboniferous period; fern; horsetail; quillwort; selaginella; sporangium; spore; strobilus

clubroot A disease of cabbage-family plants (the *Brassicaceae*) that causes gall-like swellings of roots and discoloration of leaves; caused by the parasitic slime mould *Plasmodiophora brassicae*. » cabbage; parasitology; slime mould

Cluj-Napoca [kloozh **na**poka] or **Cluj**, Ger **Klausenburg** 46°47N

23°37E, pop (1983) 304 244. Capital of Cluj county, NEC Romania, on the R Someş; founded on the site of a former Roman colony, 12th-c; a former capital of Transylvania; ceded from Hungary, 1920; chief cultural and religious centre of Transylvania since the 16th-c; airfield; railway; university (1872), technical university (1948); electrical equipment, metallurgy, chemicals, machinery, textiles, footwear; St Michael Church, Austrian fort, Franciscan monastery, botanical gardens; winter sports facilities nearby. » Romania [i]; Transylvania

Clurman, Harold [**kler**man] (1901–80) US theatre director and critic, born in New York City. He was playreader for the Theater Guild (1929–31), co-founder of the Group Theater (1931–40), and one of its directors. His book *The Fervent Years* (1946) is a history of the Group. He later worked as a director in Hollywood and on Broadway. An influential drama critic, his writings include *Lies Like Truths* (1958), and *The Divine Pastime* (1974). » Group Theater; theatre

clustered wax flower » **stephanotis; wax plant**

clutch A mechanical device that allows an engine to be connected and disconnected from its load whilst the engine is running. A clutch is necessary when the power characteristics of an engine's output do not match naturally the power characteristics of the load. In such cases a gearbox has to be interposed between engine and load, together with a clutch, to allow the engine to be disconnected and a new gear to be substituted. The most common application of a clutch is in the motor car, where normally a plate covered with high friction material is sandwiched and held in place between a disc attached to the engine's flywheel and a disc fixed to the gearbox. » engine; transmission

Clutha, River [**kloo**tha] Longest river of South Island, New Zealand; rises in L Wanaka, W South Island, and flows SE to enter the Pacific near Kaitangata; length from its source, the Makarora R, c.320 km/200 ml; major hydroelectric schemes near Alexandra. » New Zealand [i]

cluttering A disorder of speech fluency, in which the main symptom is excessive rapidity while speaking. Clutterers seem unable to control their speech rate, and as a result introduce disturbances of rhythm and articulation into their speech, with sounds becoming displaced, mispronounced, or omitted, and syllables telescoping into each other. The cause is unknown, though a physical explanation in terms of the brain's motor control of speech has been suggested. » speech pathology; stuttering

Clwyd [**kloo**id] pop (1987e) 402 800; area 2 426 sq km/936 sq ml. County in NE Wales, UK, divided into six districts; created in 1974; chief town, Mold; other towns, Wrexham, Prestatyn, Rhyl, Flint, Colwyn Bay; coal, steel, engineering, chemicals, plastics, clothing, paper, microprocessors; major tourist area along N Wales coast; castle remains at Chirk, Flint, Rhuddlan, Denbigh; Ffestiniog Railway (steam), Llechwedd slate caverns. » Mold; Offa's Dyke; Wales [i]

Clyde, Lord » **Campbell, Sir Colin**

Clyde, River River in S Scotland; main headstream, Daer Water, rises in S Strathclyde, and flows generally N and NW; waterfalls near Lanark (Falls of Clyde); passes through Scotland's most important industrial area, including Glasgow, then expands into the Firth of Clyde estuary (2–30 km/1¼–20 ml wide, increasing to c.60 km/40 ml at mouth), leading to the Atlantic Ocean; length 170 km/100 ml; Glasgow head of navigation for ocean-going vessels; hydroelectricity; linked to R Forth by canal; Clyde valley noted for breeding of Clydesdale horses. » Scotland [i]

Clydesdale A breed of horse, produced in Scotland by crossing local mares with large Flemish stallions; a heavy horse, developed in the 18th-c for hauling coal; height c.16¼ hands/1.7 m/5½ ft; brown with white face and legs. » horse [i]

Clydeside pop (1981) 1 718 423. Urban area in W Strathclyde, WC Scotland; comprises the 11 districts of Bearsden and Milngavie, Clydebank, Cumbernauld and Kilsyth, East Kilbride, Eastwood, Glasgow City, Hamilton, Monklands, Motherwell, Renfrew, and Strathkelvin; airport; railway; major industrial area of Scotland. » Glasgow; Scotland [i]

Clytemnestra [kliytem**nes**tra] or **Clytemestra** In Greek legend, the twin sister of Helen and the wife of Agamemnon. She murdered him on his return from Troy, assisted by her lover, Aegisthus. She was killed in revenge by her son, Orestes. » Aegisthus; Agamemnon; Cassandra; Erinyes; Orestes

CND An acronym of the **Campaign for Nuclear Disarmament**, a mass organization founded in the UK in 1958 to mobilize public opinion against the nuclear-weapons programme and for unilateral disarmament. It organized peaceful mass marches between London and Aldermaston, where the Atomic Weapons Research Establishment was based, and was successful in securing acceptance of a resolution at the 1960 Labour Party Conference for Britain's unilateral disarmament. Partly because of a split over non-violent direct action favoured by the Committee of 100, and the course of other events such as the Cuban missile crisis (1962), the signing of the Test-Ban Treaty (1963) and detente, its appeal and activities declined. During the 1980s, however, it underwent a revival, and membership rose again as concern over the proliferation of nuclear weapons grew. » detente

Cnidaria [ni**da**ria] » **coelenterate**

CNS » **central nervous system**

Cnut » **Canute**

coal A black or brown sedimentary rock found in beds or seams, and formed by heat and pressure over millions of years on vegetation accumulated in shallow swamps. Successive stages in the formation of coal involve an increase in carbon content or 'rank': peat is the first stage, followed by lignite or brown coal (60–70% carbon), bituminous coal (more than 80% carbon), and anthracite (more than 90% carbon). » anthracite; coal tar; coke; sedimentary rock

coal gas A largely methane gas, resulting from the distillation of coal as part of the process of conversion to coke. » coal; coke; distillation

coal mining Extracting coal from beneath the ground. In **opencast mining**, the coal is near the surface: the overburden is stripped away, the coal removed, and the overburden restored for environmental conservation. In **drift mining**, the coal lies within a slope: a horizontal tunnel is driven into the side of the slope, and the coal removed on level railways or conveyors. **Deep mining** relies on vertical shafts with horizontal approaches to the seams. Coal is dug (mainly now by mechanical means) and removed by conveyors to the shaft bottom for haulage to the surface. Coal mining presents special hazards: explosion may occur from gas or fine coal dust, so ventilation must be constant and efficient; shafts and tunnels must be protected against collapse. World production in the 1980s varied at around 3 000 million tonnes per annum. Reserves are estimated at around 8 million million tonnes. » coal; firedamp

Coal Sack The finest visual example of an obscuring cloud of dust in space, 170 parsecs away. It is in the constellation Crux, where it causes a gaping hole in the Milky Way. » Milky Way

coal tar A volatile by-product of heating coal in the absence of air to form coke; a black viscous liquid consisting of a complex mixture of organic compounds. Further distillation of coal tar produces a large number of chemicals which form the basis of explosives, dyes, and drugs. » acridine; anthracene [i]; coal; coke; distillation

coal tit A small bird native to Europe, Asia, and Africa; head and throat black, cheeks and back of neck white; inhabits woodland, especially coniferous, and gardens; eats seeds, and often takes insects from tree bark. (*Parus ater*. Family: *Paridae*.) » tit

coalfish » **saithe**

coalition An inter-party arrangement established to pursue a common goal, most obviously government. Coalition governments are relatively common in electoral systems using proportional representation and/or in multi-party systems. The nature of coalition is defined by those parties with seats in the cabinet.

Coast Mountains Mountain range in W British Columbia and Alaska, extending about 1 600 km/1 000 ml NW–SE; rises to 4 042 m/13 261 ft in Mt Waddington, British Columbia; rugged terrain with several glaciers. » Alaska; British Columbia

Coast Range Mountain belt in W N America, extending along the coast of the Pacific Ocean from Alaska through British Columbia, Washington, Oregon, California, and Baja California (Mexico); includes the Kenai, Chugach, St Elias, Olympic, and Klamath Mts; highest point Mt Logan (5 950 m/19 521 ft); the Central Valley lies to the E in California. » Canada [i]; United States of America [i]

coast redwood A massive evergreen conifer, the tallest tree in the world at over 100 m/325 ft high and 8 m/26 ft thick; bark almost 1 m/3¼ ft thick, reddish, fibrous, spongy. Formerly widespread, with fossils in Greenland and China, it is now confined to the misty bottomlands of coastal California and SW Oregon. (*Sequoia sempervirens*. Family: *Taxodiaceae*.) » conifer; evergreen plants

Coastal Command A separate functional Command within the British Royal Air Force (1936–69). Moves to transfer it to the Royal Navy caused a political storm in 1958–9. During World War 2, the Command destroyed 184 German U-boats and 470 000 tonnes of enemy shipping, and played a decisive role in winning the Battle of the Atlantic. » Atlantic, Battle of the; World War 2

coastguard An institution whose duty is to keep watch on the coastline and organize rescue and lifeboat services to help those in trouble. The nature of these services varies widely; some nations use their naval forces, whereas others operate through voluntary organizations. The largest service is the US Coastguard, responsible for search and rescue, lighthouses and lightships, pilotage, fishery protection, security at ports, enforcement of maritime legislation, and oceanography. It uses 550 craft, 100 helicopters, and over 30 long-range aircraft to cover a 16 000 km/10 000 ml coastline. The Canadian Coastguard operates similarly, but also has 20 icebreakers, and mounts ice rescue missions and ice warning patrols. The UK Coastguard was formed in 1822 to combat smuggling, and was so successful that it adopted a new role as a naval reserve in addition to revenue protection; in 1925 it was taken over by the Board of Trade. The service enjoyed a major rejuvenation in 1972 due to increased yachting activity. Australia operates a similar service, while the New Zealand service carries out additional rescue operations in mountain and bush areas. » navy

coat of arms » **heraldry** [i]

coat-of-mail shell » **chiton**

coated fabrics Fabrics made by combining traditional textile fabric with a strongly adhering layer (coat) of plastic or other material. They are commonly used in protective clothing, such as rainwear.

Coates, Eric (1886–1957) British composer, born at Hucknall, Nottinghamshire. He studied in Nottingham and at the Royal Academy of Music, London, working as a violinist. Sir Henry Wood performed several of his early works at Promenade Concerts. Success as a composer of attractive light music enabled him to devote himself to composition after 1918. Among his best-known compositions are the *London Suite* (1933), *The Three Elizabeths* (1944), and a number of popular waltzes and marches. He died at Chichester.

coati [**koh**ahtee] A raccoon-like mammal, found from S USA to S America; reddish-brown; long banded tail; long narrow muzzle with overhanging tip; inhabits woodland; eats fruit and small animals; solitary males called *coatimundis* (or *koatimundis*). The name is also used for the Andean **mountain coati** (*Nasuella olivacea*). (Genus: *Nasua*, 2 species. Family: *Procyonidae*.) » raccoon

cob A type of horse, often produced when crossing a heavy cart-horse with a racing horse; height, 14½–15½ hands/1.5–1.6 m/4¾–5¼ ft; short deep body; calm natured; lacks speed; also known as **rouncy** or **roncey**. The name is also used specifically for the *Irish cob*, *Norman cob*, *Welsh cob*, and extinct *Powys cob*. » horse [i]; Welsh pony

cobalt Co, element 27, density 9 g cm^{-3}, melting point 1 495°C. A hard metal, which occurs in ores as its sulphide (CoS), along with copper and nickel. It is mainly used as a metal in steel alloys, especially for permanent magnets. Most of its compounds show +2 oxidation state. Hydrated salts are usually light red, but many anhydrous ones are bright blue, and are used as pigments. » alloy; chemical elements; metal; RR90

Cobb, Ty, properly **Tyrus (Raymond)**, byname **The Georgia Peach** (1886–1961) US baseball player, born at Narrows, Georgia. An outstanding base runner and batter, in a 23-year career with Detroit and Philadelphia he hit over 4 000 base hits, a record which survived 57 years until broken in 1985. His career batting average was an all-time record at 0.367, and he led the American League 12 times in batting. He died in Atlanta, Georgia. » baseball [i]

Cobb and Co An Australian company which operated the largest coach service in E Australia (1853–1924). Famous for the reliability of its service, it was based in Victoria to 1862, and then in Bathurst, New South Wales. By 1890, Cobb and Co had 6 400 km/4 000 ml of coach routes, but from then on found itself less able to compete with the railways. It continues today as a motor transport company.

Cobbett, William (1763–1835) British journalist and reformer, born at Farnham, Surrey. The son of a farmer, he moved on impulse to London (1783), spent a year reading widely, and joined the army, serving in New Brunswick (1785–91). In 1792 he married and went to the USA, where he wrote fierce pieces against the native Democrats under the name 'Peter Porcupine'. Returning to England in 1800, he was welcomed by the Tories, and started his famous *Weekly Political Register* (1802), which continued until his death, changing in 1804 from its original Toryism to an uncompromising Radicalism. In 1810 he was imprisoned for two years for criticizing the flogging of militiamen by German mercenaries, and in 1817 he went again to the USA, fearing a second imprisonment. Returning in 1819 he travelled widely in Britain, and finally became an MP (1832). His works include a *History of the Protestant Reformation* (1824–7) and *Rural Rides* (1830). He died near Guildford, Surrey. » Democratic Party; radicalism; Tories

Cobden, Richard (1804–65) British economist and politician, 'the Apostle of Free Trade', born at Heyshott, Sussex. He worked as a clerk and commercial traveller in London, then went into the calico business, settling in Manchester. In 1835 he visited the USA, and in 1836–7 the Levant, after which he published two pamphlets preaching free trade, nonintervention, and speaking against 'Russophobia'. In 1838 he helped to found the Anti-Corn-Law League, becoming its most prominent member. He became an MP in 1841. His lectures and parliamentary speeches focused opinion on the Corn Laws, which were repealed in 1846. He died in London. » Anti-Corn-Law League

Coblenz, Ger **Koblenz**, ancient **Confluentes** 50°21N 7°36E, pop (1983) 112 200. Capital of Koblenz district, Germany; at confluence of Mosel and Rhine Rivers, 80 km/50 ml SSE of Cologne; seat of Frankish kings (6th-c); badly bombed in World War 2; largest garrison town in former West Germany; railway; major centre of Rhine wine trade; hygienic tissues, furniture, pianos, clothing; birthplace of Metternich; St Castor's church (836), fortress of Ehrenbreitstein. » Franks; Germany [i]; Metternich

COBOL [**koh**bol] An acronym of **COmmon Business Orientated Language**, a high-level computer language widely used in the business community. It uses statements written in English which are relatively easy to understand; for example, the statement ADD VAT TO NET-PRICE could be used in a COBOL program. » programming language

cobra A venomous snake, native to S Asia and Africa; neck has loose folds of skin which can be spread as a 'hood' when alarmed; fangs short; venom (more poisonous than that of vipers) attacks the nervous system; usually inhabits forests, but also open country. Some species (**spitting cobras**) can squirt venom up to 3 m/10 ft into the eyes of threatening animals, and may leave them permanently blinded. The **king cobra** is the largest venomous snake. Cobras are the snakes of Indian 'snake charmers'. (Family: *Elapidae*, many species, most in genus *Naja*.) » king cobra; viper [i]

cocaine $C_{17}H_{21}NO_4$, melting point 98°C. A white alkaloid extracted from the leaves of the S American shrub *coca*, and used for its stimulant properties, similar to those of amphetamine. Freud used it 'to boost the flagging human spirit' of his patients, and his physician colleague Carl Koller (1857–1944) discovered its local anaesthetic actions. It is still used as a topical local anaesthetic, mainly in ophthalmology. It is widely abused; the powder is sniffed and the purified form can be smoked (*freebasing*). It causes addiction, particularly when freebased. Street names include 'Snow White', 'Charlie', and 'charge'. » alkaloids; crack; drug addiction; Freud, Sigmund

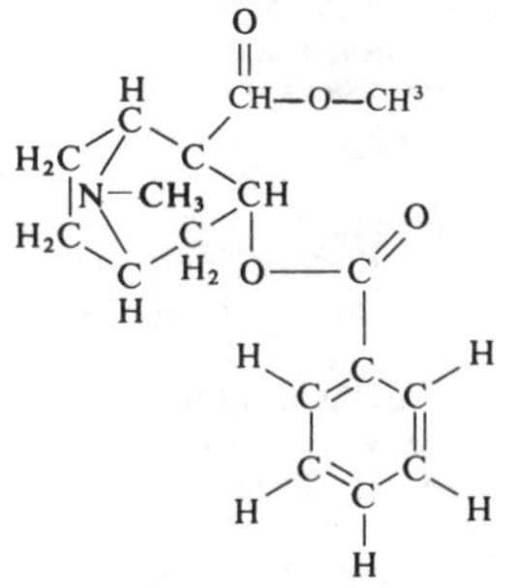

coccus Any spherical bacterium. It varies in size, and may occur in chains, clusters, or other groupings. » bacteria [i]; pneumococcus; staphylococcus; streptococcus

coccyx [**kok**siks] The lowest part of the vertebral column, forming the tail in many animals. In humans it is small and triangular, comprising three to five rudimentary vertebrae, and is situated in the groove between the buttocks. » vertebral column; Plate XIII

Cochabamba [kocha**bam**ba] 17°26S 66°10W, pop (1982) 281 962. Capital of Cochabamba department, C Bolivia; altitude 2 500 m/8 200 ft; country's third largest city, founded 1542; airfield; railway; university (1832); important agricultural centre; oil refining, furniture, footwear; Palacio de Cultura, Los Portales museum, monument to War of Independence, markets; thermal baths nearby; golf club at L Alalay; Carnival (before Lent). » Bolivia [i]

Cochin [**ko**chin] 9°55N 76°22E, pop (1983) 686 000. Naval base and seaport in Kerala, SW India; on the Malabar coast of the Arabian Sea, 1 080 km/671 ml SSE of Bombay; Portuguese trading station, 1502; Fort Cochin, first European settlement in India; shipbuilding, trade in fruit and cattle; tomb of Vasco da Gama. » Kerala; Gama, Vasco da

cochineal A dye (*carminic acid*) obtained from the dried bodies of a female bug, *Dactylopus coccus*. The bug feeds on cacti, and is native to Peru and Mexico. (Order: *Homoptera*. Family: *Coccidae*.) » bug (entomology); dyestuff

cochlea [**kok**leea] The spiral cavity in the internal ear, which is concerned with hearing. It consists of a bony part with a central pillar (the *modiolus*) and a spiral duct (part of the *membranous labyrinth*). The space between the bony and membranous parts is filled with *perilymph* (a fluid similar to cerebrospinal fluid). A thin spiral shelf projects from the modiolus, on which lies the *basilar membrane*. Sound waves in the air are transmitted from the middle ear to the cochlea through the *oval window*, making the basilar membrane vibrate. The basal part of the basilar membrane responds with nerve impulses to both high and low frequencies, while the apical part responds to low frequencies only. Vibrations of the membrane stimulate a set of hair cells, which trigger impulses in the vestibular nerve. These signals are then transmitted to the auditory areas of the brain for interpretation. » deafness; ear [i]; tinnitus; vestibular apparatus

cock of the rock A bird native to tropical S America; male with brilliant red or orange plumage and large crest on head; male poses on ground to attract females. (Genus: *Rupicola*, 2 species. Family: *Cotingidae*, sometimes placed in a separate family, *Rupicolidae*.) » cotinga

cock's comb An annual, native to tropical Asia, related to amaranth; the peculiar inflorescence, a thick fleshy crest resembling a cock's comb, is the result of mutation-induced fasciation; the normal form has a plume-like inflorescence. Both forms are grown as pot plants. (*Celosia cristata*. Family: *Amaranthaceae*.) » amaranth; annual; fasciation; inflorescence [i]

cockatiel [kokuh**teel**] An Australian parrot of the cockatoo family; long tapering crest on head; male with colourful facial markings; inhabits open country; eats grass seeds or fruit. (*Nymphicus hollandicus*. Family: *Cacatuidae*.) » parrot; cockatoo

cockatoo An Australasian parrot, separated from other parrots mainly by features of its skull, and in having an erectile crest of feathers on the head. (Family: *Cacatuidae*, 18 species.) » cockatiel; parrot

cockatrice » **basilisk** (mythology)

cockchafer A large, dark-coloured chafer; adults nocturnal, feeding on leaves; fleshy, C-shaped larvae burrow in ground for 3–4 years, feeding on roots before emerging as flying adults, typically in May, hence alternative name of **maybug**. (Order: *Coleoptera*. Family: *Scarabeidae*.) » chafer; larva

Cockcroft, Sir John Douglas (1897–1967) British nuclear physicist, born at Todmorden, Yorkshire. He was educated at Manchester and Cambridge, where he became Jacksonian professor of physics (1939–46). He and E T S Walton (1903–) succeeded in disintegrating lithium by proton bombardment (the first artificial transmutation) in 1932, pioneering the use of particle accelerators, and shared the Nobel Prize for Physics (1951). During World War 2 he was director of Air Defence Research (1941–4). He became the first director of Britain's Atomic Energy Establishment at Harwell in 1946. He was knighted in 1948, and in 1959 appointed the first master of Churchill College, Cambridge, where he died. » particle physics

cocker spaniel A breed of dog, developed in the USA from the **English cocker spaniel**; recognized as a separate breed in 1941; smaller than ancestral stock; longer coat; white with black and brown; popular as pets. » dog; English cocker spaniel

Cockerell, Sir Christopher (Sydney) (1910–) British engineer, born at Cambridge. He first worked on radio and radar, before turning to hydrodynamics, and in the early 1950s invented the amphibious hovercraft. He was knighted in 1969. » hovercraft [i]

cockfighting A blood sport in which gamecocks, aged 1–2 years, wearing steel spurs on their legs, were set against each other. Betting took place on the performance of the birds. It probably originated in Asia 3 000 years ago, and was a popular sport in England until 1849, when it was banned. » blood sports

cockle A marine bivalve mollusc whose shell comprises two more or less equal valves closed by two adductor muscles; an active burrower in inter-tidal sediments; fished extensively for human consumption. (Class: *Pelecypoda*. Order: *Veneroida*.) » adduction; bivalve; mollusc

cockroach An active, typically nocturnal insect; body depressed; legs long and adapted for running; forewings hard and leathery; hindwings membranous, sometimes lost; eggs laid in crevices, litter, caves, and other habitats; will eat almost any organic matter. (Order: *Blattaria*, c.3 700 species.) » insect [i]

Cockscomb Basin area 14.6 sq km/5.6 sq ml. Region of the Maya mountains, Belize; a forest reserve, part of which was designated the world's first jaguar reserve in 1986. » Belize [i]

cocktail party effect The technique of selective listening, whereby people surrounded by a number of different conversations cut off attention from all but one. It is often triggered by someone in the nearby conversation uttering a word which has some special significance to the listener, such as the listener's name, or the town he/she comes from. » auditory perception

coco de mer A species of palm endemic to the Seychelles. The fruit is one of largest known, up to 20 kg/45 lb, taking 10 years to ripen; buoyant and often washed ashore, it was well-known before the tree itself was discovered. The palm is sometimes called the **double coconut**, because the nut as fruit resembles two coconuts fused side by side. (*Lodoicea maldavica*. Family: *Palmae*.) » coconut palm; Seychelles

coconut crab » **robber crab**

coconut A tree with a characteristic curved trunk, growing to 30 m/100 ft, with feathery leaves up to 6 m/20 ft long; the large, single-seeded fruits (coconuts) have a fibrous outer husk and a hard inner shell enclosing a layer of white flesh and a central cavity filled with milky fluid; at the base of the fruit are three round marks which correspond to the three chambers of the ovary, and under one of which lies the embryo. The coconut palm is probably native to Polynesia. It flourishes near the sea, and the buoyant fruit is capable of floating long distances in sea water without harm, so it is a characteristic tree of oceanic islands. It has long been cultivated throughout the tropics. Like many other palms it provides a remarkable range of products. The trunk provides timber. The leaves are woven into mats and baskets and are used for thatching; the leaf-stalks are sufficiently stout to provide poles for fencing and other uses. The bud at the top of the stem is eaten as a vegetable, and the young inflorescence can be tapped to provide a sugary liquid which can be fermented and distilled into alcoholic drinks and vinegar. The coconuts themselves form the basis of many tropical island economies. They are rarely seen in natural form outside the regions where the trees grow, as the outer husk is removed before the nuts are exported to make coir, a tough fibre used for matting. Coconut milk is a refreshing drink, and the white flesh is eaten raw or cooked, sold as desiccated coconut, or dried to form copra, the world's principal source of vegetable fat. The oil obtained from pressed copra is used in margarine, and the residual cake is a valuable animal food. (*Cocos nucifera*. Family: *Palmae*.) » copra; oil (botany); palm

cocoon » **pupa**

Cocos Islands or **Keeling Islands** [**koh**kohs] 12°05S 96°53E, pop(1983) 579, total land area 14.2 sq km/5½ sq ml. Two separate groups of atolls in the Indian Ocean, 3 685 km/ 2 290 ml W of Darwin, Australia; an Australian external territory comprising 27 small, flat, palm-covered coral islands, notably **West I** (pop 216), 10 km/6 ml long, airport, mostly occupied by Europeans, and **Home I** (pop 363) occupied by the Cocos Malay community; discovered 1609 by Captain William Keeling of the East India Company; first settled 1826, and developed by the Clunies-Ross family; annexed to the British Crown (1857); granted by Queen Victoria to George Clunies-Ross (1886); incorporated with the Settlement of Singapore (1903); placed under Australian administration (1955) as the Territory of Cocos (Keeling) Islands; Australia purchased Clunies-Ross interests in the islands (1978), and the inhabitants voted to be part of Northern Territory (1984); islands council advises the administrator on all issues; copra plantation; meteorological station. » Australia [i]

Cocteau, Jean [kok**toh**] (1889–1963) French poet, playwright, and film director, born at Maisons-Lafitte, near Paris. He had early success with his poems, which he fully exploited, and figured as the sponsor of Picasso, Stravinsky, Giorgio di Chirico and the musical group known as *Les Six*. He was an actor, director, scenario writer, novelist, critic, and artist, all of his work being marked by vivacity and a pyrotechnic brilliance. His best-known works include his novel *Les Enfants terribles* (1929, Children of the Game), his play *Orphée* (1926, Orpheus), and his films *Le Sang du poète* (1932, The Blood of the Poet) and *La Belle et la bête* (1945, Beauty and the Beast). He died near Paris. » French literature; *Six, Les*

cod Any of the family *Gadidae* (15 genera; 100 species) of marine fishes, found mainly in cool temperate shelf waters of N hemisphere; body with 2–3 dorsal and 1–2 anal fins; includes the **common cod** (*Gadus morhua*); length up to 120 cm/4 ft; greenish to reddish, freckled, with a pale lateral line; adults feed mainly on crustaceans and small fishes; support very important trawl and net (seine) fisheries. » burbot; Gadidae

cod liver oil An oil obtained from the fresh liver of the cod and refined. It provides a rich source of vitamins A and D. It is now believed to be protective in heart disease because of its high content of unsaturated fatty acids. » cod; vitamins [i]

coda The final section of a piece of music (eg a sonata-form movement or a fugue), not strictly integral to the structure, but required for a satisfactory peroration. » fugue

Code Napoléon The French Civil Code, introduced (though not devised) by Napoleon Bonaparte as First Consul in 1804, to fill the void left by the abolition of the legal and social customs of pre-revolutionary France. It established the principles of equality between people, liberty of person and contract, and the inviolability of private property. From 1804 the Code was introduced into those areas of Europe under direct French control. The Civil Code of the newly-united Italian state (1865) bore close affinity to it, and it was widely emulated in S America. It is still substantially extant in France, Belgium, Luxembourg, and Monaco today. » law; Napoleon I

codeine A pain killer related to morphine that is used for treating mild types of pain (eg headache); it is rarely addictive. It does cause constipation and can be used to treat diarrhoea. It is also used in some cough mixtures, since it inactivates the cough reflex. » morphine

Codex Alimentarius A code of practice intended to set world-wide standards for food production and processing. It was established in 1963 by the Food and Agricultural Organization (FAO) of the United Nations and the World Health Organization.

Codex Juris Canonici [**koh**deks **joo**ris ka**non**ikiy] (Lat 'code of canon law') A code of canon or church law regulating the Roman Catholic Church. The codification, authorized by Pope Pius X in 1904, was completed in 1917, with revisions recommended by a commission set up in 1963. » canon law; Roman Catholicism

codling moth A small, drab-coloured moth that lays eggs on apples and other fruit. The caterpillars feed inside the fruit, before emerging to pupate in a silken cocoon. They can be a serious pest of cultivated apples. (Order: *Lepidoptera*. Family: *Tortricidae*.) » caterpillar; moth; pupa

codon [**koh**don] The sequence of three nucleotides in DNA or RNA which determine (or 'code for') the particular amino acid to be inserted into a polypeptide chain. » amino acid [i]; nucleotide; peptide

Cody, William F(rederick) (1846–1917) US showman, born in Scott Co, Iowa. He was known as 'Buffalo Bill' after killing nearly 5 000 buffalo in eight months for a contract to supply workers on the Kansas Pacific Railway with meat. He served as a scout in the Sioux wars, but from 1883 toured with his Wild West Show. The town of Cody in Wyoming stands on part of his former ranch. He died in Denver, Colorado.

Coe, Sebastian (1956–) British athlete, born in London, the world's most outstanding middle-distance runner of the 1980s. Educated at Loughborough College, he won the bronze medal in the 800 m at the 1978 European Championships, and the following year broke his first world records (800 m and 1 ml). Altogether he broke eight world records including the mile three times. At the 1980 Olympics he won the gold medal in the 1 500 m and the silver in the 800 m, repeating the achievement four years later. Fitness problems followed, and he was omitted from the British team that went to the 1988 Olympics. He retired from running after the 1990 Commonwealth Games, to pursue a career in politics » athletics

coeducation The education of boys and girls in the same school or college. In some countries, for religious or cultural reasons, schools are predominantly for children of the same sex; but in others coeducation is the norm. In many European countries, the 20th-c trend has been away from single-sex education. At the same time, there has been a sustained debate about whether girls in particular are disadvantaged by coeducation. » education

coelacanth » **crossopterygii**

coelenterate [see**len**tuhruht] A simple, multicellular animal with a body plan comprising two primary layers separated by a layer of gelatinous material (*mesoglea*); few found in freshwater; most are marine, and all are carnivorous; most exhibit radial symmetry, and possess stinging cells (*nematocysts*) for prey capture and defence; life cycle typically involves two phases: an attached polyp, which may be solitary, and a disc-shaped medusa; includes the corals, sea anemones, and jellyfish. (Phylum: *Cnidaria*.) » coral; jellyfish [i]; medusa; polyp (marine biology); sea anemone

coeliac/celiac disease [**see**liak] A disorder of the small intestine, occurring especially in children, and characterized by reduced absorption of fat and other nutrients taken in the food. It gives rise to diarrhoea, the passage of pale bulky motions, and features of nutritional deficiency including failure to grow, rickets, and anaemia. It results from damage in sensitive individuals to the lining of the gut by gluten, a protein found in wheat, barley, and rye. » intestine; malabsorption

coelom [**see**luhm] The principal body cavity in multicellular animals, arising during embryological development, and typically forming the cavity around the gut in annelid worms, echinoderms, and vertebrates. The coelom is present, but reduced in size, in molluscs and arthropods. » annelid; arthropod; echinoderm [i]; embryology; mollusc

coelostat/celostat [seeluhstat] A flat mirror driven by a clock mechanism in such a way as to project the same part of the heavens into a fixed telescope. This is particularly used for solar telescopes, which in any case do not need to survey the whole sky, as a means of controlling costs. » telescope [i]

Coelurus [seelooruhs] A lightly built, flesh-eating dinosaur; slender neck and long tail; skull long, with large orbits; two-legged; forelimbs short with three digits, one facing the other two; known from the Upper Jurassic period of Wyoming; formerly known as *Ornitholestes*. (Order: *Saurischia*.) » dinosaur [i]; Jurassic period; Saurischia

co-enzyme An organic, non-protein molecule that associates with an enzyme in catalysing a biochemical reaction. It usually acts by accepting or donating certain chemical groups. » catalysis; enzyme

coffee An evergreen shrub, leaves oval, in opposite pairs; flowers white, fragrant, 5-petalled, in axils of leaves; cherry-like fruits red, fleshy, containing two seeds (the coffee beans) rich in caffeine. **Arabian coffee** (*Coffea arabica*) is native to Ethiopia, and was introduced first to Arabia, later the E Indies, W Indies, S America, and Africa. The major world producer is now Brazil. **Robusta coffee** (*Coffea canephora*) and **Liberian coffee** (*Coffea liberica*) are inferior species grown mainly in Africa and Asia. Commercial names (eg 'Kenya') often indicate the origin of different types. (Genus: *Coffea*, 40 species. Family: *Rubiaceae*.) » caffeine; evergreen plants; shrub

cofferdam A temporary structure designed to keep water or soft ground from flowing into a site when building foundations. A cofferdam usually consists of a dam or sheet piling. More elaborate structures may consist of two rows of sheet piling with an earth fill or of walls made of steel 'cells'. » caisson; dam

Coggan, Baron (Frederick) Donald (1909–) British prelate, born in London. Educated at Merchant Taylors and Cambridge, he was a lecturer in Semitic languages at Manchester (1931–4), professor of the New Testament at Wycliffe College, Toronto (1937–44), principal of London College of Divinity (1944–56), Bishop of Bradford (1956–61), Archbishop of York (1961–74), and finally Archbishop of Canterbury (1974–80), when he was made a life peer. He is the author of several theological works. » Church of England

cognates Languages or language forms which derive from the same historical source. For example, Welsh, Breton, and Cornish are all derived from Brythonic, a branch of the Celtic language family. » Celtic languages; comparative linguistics

cognitive anthropology The branch of anthropology which studies cultural differences in perception, reasoning, and the construction of knowledge. The best-known project of cognitive anthropology has been *ethnoscience*, the study of the bodies of knowledge and theory developed by non-Western societies in such fields as botany or human physiology. » anthropology; ethnoscience

cognitive psychology A branch of psychology which studies the higher mental processes (memory, attention, language, reasoning, etc). In contrast to behaviourists, cognitive psychologists are more ready to posit mechanisms and processes that are not directly observable, such as memory stores and switches of attention. Many cognitive psychologists subscribe to the 'computer metaphor', in which the brain and the computer are seen as having the same essential characteristics. » attention; Bartlett, Frederic; bottom-up/top-down processing; cognitive science; consciousness; information processing; memory

cognitive science The formal study of mind, in which models and theories originating in artificial intelligence (AI) and in the human sciences (particularly cognitive psychology, linguistics, and philosophy) are subject to interdisciplinary development. For example, a grammar written by a linguist might be implemented on a computer by an AI scientist, and its predictions tested by a psychologist observing human subjects. The dominant partner in this enterprise is often the AI scientist, since the major criterion for success is usually whether a program can be written and successfully implemented on a computer. » artificial intelligence; cognitive psychology; linguistics; mind

cognitive therapy A form of behaviour therapy based on the supposition that the manner in which individuals cognitively perceive themselves and the world about them determines their feelings and emotions, and that restructuring of the former can lead to changes in the latter. This form of treatment was described by US psychotherapist Aaron T Beck (1921–), and has been championed in Europe by British clinical psychologist Ivy Marie Blackburn (1939–). » Beck, Aaron T; behaviour therapy

Cohan, Robert [kohhan] (1925–) US dancer, choreographer, teacher, and director, born in New York City. He trained with Martha Graham and danced with her company, becoming co-director in 1966. He came to London as artistic director of the new London Contemporary Dance Theatre in 1967, choreographing works with a wide range of subject matter. He then started the London Contemporary Dance School, and developed a British version of Graham's expressive dance technique, before retiring in 1988. » Graham, Martha; London Contemporary Dance Theatre; modern dance

coherence A relationship between waves. Two waves of the same frequency are described as coherent if their relative displacements are constant in time, ie if one wave lags behind the other at one moment, and at some later time lags by the same amount. Such waves have a constant phase difference; they are 'in step'. Light from lasers is coherent, but from ordinary bulbs it is incoherent. » phase; wave (physics)

coherence theory **1** Of truth, a theory which maintains that a proposition is true if it fits into a network of propositions; often held by idealists. **2** Of justification, a theory which claims that a necessary condition for a belief's being justified is that it should fit with the believer's other beliefs; some claim that the condition is sufficient. » correspondence theory of truth; idealism; necessary and sufficient conditions

cohort A term used especially in demographic studies to describe a group of people living at the same time whose life histories overlap, and who can be traced through the birth, death, marital, educational, and other experiences they have. » demography

Coimbatore [kohimbataw] 11°00N 76°57E, pop (1981) 917 000. City in Tamil Nadu, S India, 425 km/264 ml SW of Madras; stronghold of successive Tamil kingdoms, 9th–17th-c; ceded to Britain, 1799; airfield; railway; university (1971); agricultural centre; tea, cotton, hides, teak; glass, electrical goods, fertilizer. » Tamil Nadu

Coimbra [kwẽẽbra], ancient **Conimbriga** 40°15N 8°27W, pop (1981) 71 800. Capital of Coimbra district, C Portugal; on R Mondego, 173 km/107 ml NNE of Lisbon; former capital of Portugal, 12th–13th-c; oldest university in Portugal (founded at Lisbon in 1290, transferred here in 1537); bishopric; paper, tanning, pottery, biscuits, food processing, fabrics, wine; two cathedrals, São Sebastiano aqueduct, Monastery of the Holy Cross, national museum, Conimbriga Roman site and Children's Portugal village nearby; Queima das Fitas student festival (May). » Portugal [i]

coke A form of charcoal made by heating coal to over 1 000°C in the absence of air to remove the volatile constituents. It is a brittle, porous substance consisting mainly of carbon, and used mainly in steelmaking for fuelling blast furnaces. » charcoal; coal tar

Coke, Sir Edward [kook] (1552–1634) English jurist, born at Mileham, Norfolk. Educated at Norwich and Cambridge, he was called to the Bar in 1578, and rose to become Speaker of the House of Commons (1593), Attorney-General (1594), chief justice of the Common Pleas (1606), chief justice of the King's Bench (1613), and privy councillor. He brutally prosecuted Essex, Raleigh, and the Gunpowder conspirators, but after 1606 stands forth as a vindicator of national liberties against the royal prerogative. He was dismissed in 1617, and from 1620 led the popular party in parliament, serving nine months in prison. The Petition of Right (1628) was largely his doing. Most of his epoch-making Law Reports were published during his lifetime (1600–15). He died at Stoke Poges, Buckinghamshire. » Gunpowder Plot; Petition of Right

Coke (of Holkham), Thomas William, Earl of Leicester (1754–1842) British agriculturalist, the 'father of experimental farms', born in London, and educated at Eton. People visited his estate from all over the world, and special meetings were held at sheep clipping time – called 'Coke's Clippings', the last of which took place in 1821, lasting three days and attracting 7000 visitors. He became MP for Norfolk at 21, holding the seat for 57 years, and was the one who brought forward the motion to recognize the independence of the American Colonies. He died at Longford Hall, Derbyshire. » agriculture; American Revolution

cola » **kola**

Cola [**cho**lah] An ancient Tamil dynasty, which ruled much of S India between the 8th-c and 13th-c. The height of power was under Rajaraja (985–1014) and Rajendra (1014–44), who extended the kingdom to include Ceylon. It introduced highly-developed revenue administration, village self-organization, and irrigation systems. Tamil architecture and literature flourished. » Tamil

Colbert, Claudette, originally **Lily Claudette Chauchoin** (1903–) US film actress, born in Paris. She went to the USA as a child, and started in films with spirited comedy roles, becoming a star with *It Happened One Night* (1934), which won her an Oscar. This was followed by 10 years of romantic comedy successes, including *Tovarich* (1937), and *The Palm Beach Story* (1942), and varied character parts up to the 1960s, such as in *Parrish* (1960). On the stage her career has continued into the 1980s.

Colbert, Jean Baptiste [**kol**bair] (1619–83) French statesman, born at Rheims. In 1651 he entered the service of Mazarin, and in 1661 became the chief financial minister of Louis XIV. He found the finances in a ruinous condition, and introduced a series of successful reforms, doubling the revenue in 10 years. He reorganized the colonies, provided a strong fleet, improved the civil code, and introduced a marine code. The Academies of Inscriptions, Science, and Architecture were founded by him, and he became a patron of industry, commerce, art, science, and literature. However, his successes were undone by wars and court extravagance, and he died in Paris, bitterly disappointed. » Louis XIV

Colchester, Lat **Camulodunum**, Anglo-Saxon **Colneceaster** 51°54N 0°54E, pop (1981) 88847. Town in Colchester district, Essex, SE England; S of the R Colne, 82 km/51 ml NE of London; University of Essex (1961); claimed to be the oldest town in England, founded by Cunobelinus c.10 AD; railway; light industry, printing, oysters, rose growing; city walls, 12th-c castle; oyster festival (Oct). » Essex

colchicine [**kol**chiseen] A drug effective against gout, extracted from the corm and seeds of the meadow saffron, *Colchicum autumnale* ('autumn crocus'), so called because it grows in Colchis in Asia Minor. The plants were first used in Europe to treat gout; pure colchicine was first prepared in 1820. It is still widely used. » gout

cold An infection characterized by watering of the nose and eyes, sneezing, and nasal obstruction; also known as the 'common cold' or **coryza**. It is caused by several different viruses, most often a rhinovirus. After a few days invasion by bacteria, there is discharge of mucus or pus from the nose. The condition commonly lasts for more than a week, but in severe cases infection may spread to the pharynx and sinuses, giving sore throat and headache. » cold sore; virus

cold-bloodedness » **poikilothermy**

cold front A meteorological term for the leading edge of a parcel of cold or polar air. In a depression, the passage of a cold front is often preceded by heavy rainfall, and as it passes there is a sharp fall in temperature together with a veering of the wind followed by cold unstable air. » depression (meteorology) [i]; front; squall-line

cold fusion Nuclear fusion occurring at room temperature. In March 1989, US chemist Stanley Pons and British chemist Martin Fleischmann claimed to have observed fusion in an electrolytic cell comprising platinum and titanium electrodes in heavy water. They detected more heat from the cell than could be expected from mere chemical processes, and claimed a fusion process to be its source. The expectation is that the deuterium atoms pack together so tightly in the palladium electrode that their nuclei are forced close enough to one another to fuse. Following the announcement, some scientists claimed to have observed fusion in versions of the Pons-Fleischmann experiment, but others claimed to see nothing. Even experiments to detect the nuclear particles which might be expected to be emitted in such a process seemed to give conflicting results. By the end of 1989, the scientific consensus was that the effects discovered could not be attributed to room-temperature fusion. Theoretically it is possible, but unlikely, that a fusion process could occur in such a way. A cold fusion process which emitted the quantity of heat claimed by Pons and Fleischmann would rate technologically and economically as the most important discovery this century, since it would allow the production of very cheap electricity. » deuterium; electrolysis [i]; nuclear fusion

Cold Harbor, Battles of (1–3 Jun 1864) Battles of the American Civil War, fought in Virginia, as part of General Grant's strategy of unrelenting pressure on the South. Grant lost 12000 men in one day's fighting. » American Civil War

cold sore (*herpes labialis*) A localized blister-like rash affecting the lips and adjoining skin around the mouth, the lining of the mouth, and tongue. The lesions are due to a virus that is widespread throughout the population, and which usually lies dormant, but which is activated by intermittent illness or debility. » cold; mouth; virus

cold storage Storage for perishable foodstuffs at a temperature just above freezing point. This process minimizes deterioration from chemical or biological action, but does not subject the food to damage by ice crystal formation on freezing. It is carried on in large buildings with cold air or brine circulated from a central refrigeration plant, and is often associated with manufacturing or packing plant, or large central markets. It is sometimes installed in ships, trucks, or aircraft. » food preservation

Cold War A state of tension or hostility between states that is expressed in economic and political terms, and stops short of a 'hot' or shooting war. The policies adopted are those which attempt to strengthen one side and weaken the opposition, particularly those relating to military and weapon superiority. Thus the term is often used to describe the relationship between the USSR and the major Western non-communist powers – especially the USA – between 1945 and the mid- to late 1960s when the nuclear 'arms race' intensified. The process of detente, begun in the late 1960s, led to a 'thaw' in relations between the major powers. » detente; glasnost

Coleoptera [kolee**op**tuhra] » **beetle**

Coleridge, Samuel Taylor (1772–1834) British poet, born at Ottery St Mary, Devon. Educated at Christ's Hospital and Cambridge, he imbibed revolutionary ideas and left to enlist. His plans with Southey to found a communist society in the USA came to nothing, and he turned instead to teaching and journalism in Bristol. Marrying Sara Fricker (Southey's sister-in-law), he went with her to Nether Stowey, where they made close friends with William and Dorothy Wordsworth. From this connection a new poetry emerged, in reaction against Neoclassic artificiality. *Lyrical Ballads* (1798) opens with his magical 'Ancient Mariner'. After visiting Germany (1798–9), he developed an interest in German philosophy. In 1800 he went to the Lake District, but his career prospects were blighted by his moral collapse, partly due to opium. He rejected Wordsworth's animistic views of nature, and relations between them became strained. He began a weekly paper, *The Friend* (1809), and settled in London, writing and lecturing. In 1816 he published 'Christabel' and the fragment, 'Kubla Khan', both written in his earlier period of inspiration. His small output of poetry proves his gift, but he is known also for his critical writing, and for his theological and politico-sociological works. He died in London. » English literature; Lake poets; poetry; Romanticism (literature); Wordsworth, William

Colet, John (c.1467–1519) English theologian and Tudor humanist, born in London. He studied at Oxford, travelled in Italy, then returned to England where he became a priest.

While lecturing at Oxford, he worked with Thomas More and Erasmus. In 1505 he became dean of St Paul's, where he continued to deliver controversial lectures on the interpretation of Scripture, and founded St Paul's School (1509–12). He died at Sheen, Surrey. » Erasmus; humanism; More, Thomas; theology

Colette, (Sidonie Gabrielle) (1873–1954) French novelist, born at Saint-Sauveur-en-Puisaye. Her early books were written in collaboration with her first husband, Henri Gauthier-Villars (pen name Willy); after their divorce in 1906 she appeared in music halls in dance and mime, then settled as a writer. Her novels include the *Claudine* series (1900–3), *Chéri* (1920), and *Gigi* (1945). In 1912 she married Henry de Jouvenel, and in 1935 Maurice Goudeket. She won many awards for her work, and died a legendary figure in Paris. » French literature; novel

coleus A perennial native to Java; stems square; leaves oval, toothed, in opposite pairs; small flowers pale blue or white, in whorls forming slender spikes. A very popular pot plant, it is grown for its foliage, which is variegated in a range of bright colours. (*Coleus blumei*. Family: *Labiatae*.) » perennial

coley » **saithe**

colic Excessive contraction and spasm of smooth (involuntary) muscle, tending to occur in waves, and giving rise to severe short-lived but recurring bouts of pain. It particularly affects the smooth muscle of the gut (*intestinal colic*), the common bile duct (*biliary colic*), and the renal pelvis and ureters (*renal colic*). Calculi in the ducts are the common causes of colic. Babies are prone to develop intestinal colic as a result of swallowing air during feeding, or of other feeding difficulty. » calculi; muscle [i]

Coligny, Gaspard II de, Seigneur de ('Lord of') **Châtillon** [**kol**eenyee] (1519–72) French Huguenot leader, born at Châtillon-sur-Loing. He fought in the wars of Francis I and Henry II, and in 1552 was made Admiral of France. In 1557 he became a Protestant, and commanded the Huguenots during the second and third Wars of Religion. Catherine de' Medici made him one of the first victims in the St Bartholomew's Day massacre in Paris (1572). » Huguenots; Religion, Wars of

colitis Inflammation of the large bowel (*colon*) by micro-organisms or by immunological mechanisms; associated with lower abdominal pain and diarrhoea. *Ulcerative colitis* is the most common, affecting young adults, in which the lining of the colon and rectum ulcerate and cause blood loss. *Ischaemic/ischemic colitis* refers to colonic spasm and damage caused by an inadequate blood supply, usually in elderly people. » inflammation; intestine

collage [kol**ahzh**] A technique of picture-making introduced by the Cubists c.1912 in which pieces of paper, fabrics, or other materials are glued to the surface of the canvas. It was much used by the Surrealists in the 1920s. » Cubism; Surrealism

collagens A family of fibrous proteins found in all multicellular animals, constituting 25% of the total protein in mammals. They have a stiff, triple-stranded structure, and play an essential role in providing tissue strength. Several major types (depending on the sequence of amino acids) are known, notably Type I, found in skin, tendon, bone, ligaments, the cornea, and internal organs, which accounts for 90% of total body collagens. » cell; epithelium; polymerization; protein

collar bone » **clavicle**

collateral A valuable item used as security for a loan – often land, shares, or an insurance policy. If the borrower fails to repay the debt, the collateral can be sold and the debt (along with any costs) deducted from the proceeds.

collective bargaining Trade union negotiations on behalf of a group of workers in relation to pay and conditions of employment. If the negotiations break down, the dispute may result in industrial action (such as a strike), or the matter may be referred to arbitration by another body. » ACAS

collective farm A large co-operative farm, commonly found in socialist countries, where many small peasant holdings have been pooled to create a single unit capable of exploiting the economies of scale associated with mechanized agriculture. Technically the ownership of the land may still be retained by the peasants, but their income inside the collective is proportional to their labour services supplied and to their needs. In addition, a high proportion of the families are allocated small private plots where they can keep livestock and grow fruit and vegetables for market. In E Europe, collectives often encompass several villages, thousands of hectares, and a population of hundreds or even thousands. They were first introduced on a large scale in the USSR during Stalin's campaign for the enforced collectivization of the Russian peasantry (1928–33). The peasants initially resisted the new policies, which resulted in millions of deaths from famine, armed resistance, or execution. » economies of scale; farmer co-operative; socialism; Stalin

collective security The concept of maintaining security and territorial integrity by the collective actions of nation states, especially through international organizations such as the League of Nations, where the principle is embodied in its Covenant, and the United Nations, in its Charter. Individual member states must be prepared to accept collective decisions and implement them, if necessary, through military action. Because of the difficulty of obtaining such agreements, collective security has never been fully established. » League of Nations; United Nations

collectivism A set of doctrines asserting the interests of the community over the individual, and the preference for central planning over market systems. It advocates that economic and political systems should be based upon co-operation, a significant amount of state intervention to deal with social injustice, and central planning, decision-making, and administration to ensure uniformity of treatment. Although often treated as synonymous with socialism, collectivism is a broader term which encompasses other doctrines that justify state intervention and state or collective control, such as co-operativism, workers control, and corporatism. » corporatism; socialism

college » **university**

College of Arms » **heraldry** [i]

college of education A college specializing in the initial and in-service training of teachers. In the UK, such colleges were formerly called *training colleges*, and since the 1970s many have diversified into different fields, or merged with other colleges and become known as *colleges of higher education*. Such colleges may offer BA as well as BEd degrees. Other colleges merged with universities or polytechnics during the 1970s and 1980s, when the numbers of pupils in British schools fell, and the demand for teachers dropped accordingly. » polytechnic; university

collie or **colly** A medium-sized domestic dog; several breeds developed in Scotland as sheepdogs; **collie**, usually brown and white, with a long pointed muzzle (two forms: the long-haired *rough collie* and the rarer *smooth collie*); black and white **Border collie** similar, but not recognized as a true breed); **bearded collie** (or **Highland collie**), with a long shaggy coat, resembles a small untidy Old English sheepdog with a tail). » dog; lurcher; Old English sheepdog

colligative properties [kol**ig**ativ] Properties of a solution which vary directly with the concentration of a solute. They include depression of the vapour pressure, elevation of the boiling point, depression of the freezing point, and osmotic pressure. » cryoscopic; osmotic pressure; solution

collimator 1 An optical device for changing a divergent beam of light (from a point source) into a parallel beam, which is required for control of the optical behaviour of the beam (as in a spectroscope). Generally, light passes through a converging lens, then through a slit. The collimator in X-radiography uses slits only, in order to give a beam which will cast a sharp shadow. » lens; light **2** A small telescope fixed to a large one, to help in preliminary alignment. » telescope [i]

Collingwood, Cuthbert, Baron (1750–1810) British admiral, born in Newcastle upon Tyne. He joined the navy at 11, and from 1778 his career was closely connected with that of Nelson. He fought at Brest (1794), Cape St Vincent (1797), and Trafalgar (1805), where he succeeded Nelson as commander. He was created baron after Trafalgar, died at sea, and is buried beside Nelson in St Paul's. » Nelson, Horatio; Trafalgar, Battle of

Collins, Michael (astronaut) (1930–) US astronaut, born in

Rome. Educated at Washington and West Point, he became a test pilot, and joined the space programme in 1963. He was one of the members of the Gemini 10 project, and remained in the command module during the successful Apollo 11 Moon-landing expedition. He became undersecretary of the Smithsonian Institution in 1978. » Apollo programme

Collins, Michael (politician) (1890–1922) Irish politician and Sinn Féin leader, born near Clonakilty. He became an MP (1918–22), and with Arthur Griffith was largely responsible for the negotiation of the treaty with Great Britain in 1921. He was killed in an ambush between Bandon and Macroom. » Griffith, Arthur; Sinn Féin

Collins, (William) Wilkie (1824–89) British novelist, born in London. He spent four years in business, and then entered Lincoln's Inn, but gradually took to literature, becoming a master of the mystery story. His best-known work is *The Woman in White* (1860). He died in London.

colloid [**kol**oyd] A state midway between a suspension and a true solution. It is classified in various ways, particularly into *sols* (eg milk), in which liquid properties predominate, and *gels* (eg gelatine), which are more like solids. » solution; suspension

colobus [**kol**uhbuhs] An Old World monkey, native to tropical Africa; slender with long tail; thumbs absent; three groups: *black and white colobus* (with very long silky hair), *red colobus*, and *olive colobus*; inhabits forest; eats leaves; also known as **guereza**. (Genus: *Colobus*, c.6 species.) » Old World monkey

Cologne [kuh**lohn**], Ger **Köln** 50°56N 6°58E, pop (1983) 953 300. Manufacturing and commercial river port in Cologne district, Germany, on W bank of R Rhine; capital of N Roman Empire (3rd-c); influential centre in Middle Ages; badly bombed in World War 2; major traffic junction and commercial centre, noted for its trade fairs; archbishopric; railway; university (1388); oil refining, chemicals, wine, foodstuffs, vehicles, machinery, cosmetics, perfumes, medicaments, tools; Gothic cathedral (begun 1248); Rhineland Carnival (Feb). » Germany [i]; Gothic architecture

Colombia, official name **Republic of Colombia**, Sp **República de Colombia** [kol**om**bia] pop (1990e) 32 978 000; area 1 140 105 sq km/440 080 sq ml. Republic of NW South America; bounded N by Panama and the Caribbean, W by the Pacific Ocean, E by Venezuela, SE by Brazil, and S by Ecuador and Peru; capital, Bogotá; chief cities include Medellín, Cali, Barranquilla; timezone GMT −5; 90% of the people live in temperate Andean valleys; ethnic groups include many of mixed Spanish and Indian descent; official language, Spanish; religion, mainly Roman Catholic; unit of currency, the peso of 100 centavos.

Physical description. Coastline on both Caribbean and Pacific, with several island possessions; on mainland, Andes run N–S, branching into three ranges dividing narrow coastal plains from forested lowlands of Amazon basin; Cordillera Central, separated from Cordillera Occidental (W) by R Cauca, rises to above 5 000 m/16 000 ft, highest peak Huila at 5 750 m/18 865 ft; Cordillera Oriental (E) surrounds large areas of plateau; rivers flow to the Pacific, Caribbean, and Amazon.

Climate. Hot and humid coastal plains (NW and W), annual rainfall over 2 500 mm/100 in; drier period on Caribbean coast (Dec–Apr); Andes annual rainfall, 1 000–2 500 mm/40–100 in, falling evenly throughout year; hot and humid tropical lowlands (E), annual rainfall 2 000–2 500 mm/80–100 in.

History and government. Spanish occupation from early 16th-c, displacing Amerindian peoples; governed by Spain within Viceroyalty of Peru, later Viceroyalty of New Granada; independence in 1819, after campaigns of Simón Bolívar; union with Ecuador, Venezuela, and Panama as Gran Colombia; union ended with secession of Venezuela (1829), Ecuador (1830), and Panama (1903); civil war in 1950s; considerable political unrest in 1980s; new constitution, 1991; governed by bicameral Congress (100-member Senate, and Chamber of Representatives with 160 members elected for four years); a president, elected for 4-year term, appoints a cabinet, and is advised by a Council of State.

Economy. Virtually self-sufficient in food; major crops include coffee, bananas, cotton, sugar, maize, rice, beans, wheat, potatoes, cut flowers; textiles, leather, chemicals, consumer

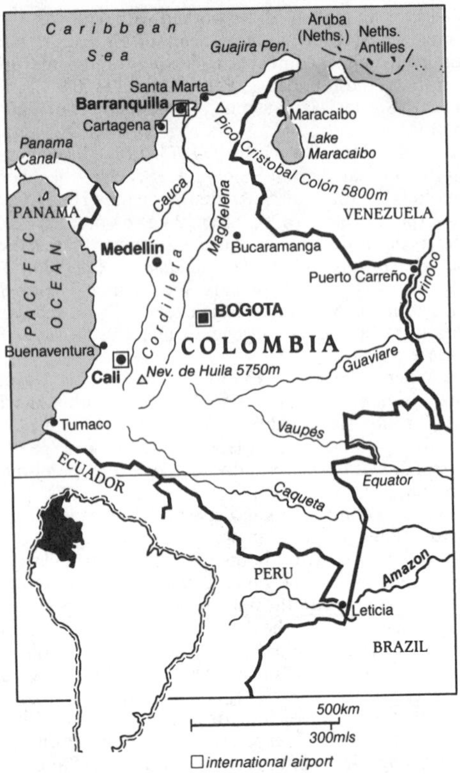

goods; gold, silver, platinum, emeralds, nickel, coal, oil, natural gas; development of interior hampered by lack of good communications; widespread illegal cocaine trafficking, which the government has been attempting to eradicate with help from the USA since mid-1989. » Andes; Bogotá; Bolívar; Gran Colombia; RR25 national holidays; RR46 political leaders

Colombo [kuh**lom**boh], originally **Kalan-Totta** 6°55N 79°52E, pop (1981) 587 647. Chief city and seaport of Sri Lanka; on the W coast, S of the R Kelani; outer suburb of Sri-Jayawardenapura the official capital since 1983; settled by the Portuguese in 1517 and by the Dutch in 1656; under British control, 1796; large artificial harbour; British defence base, 1942–5; location of the 1950 Commonwealth Conference which established the Colombo Plan; road and rail centre; university (1972); oil refining, iron and steel, trade in tea, rubber, cocoa, spices; national museum, Independence Hall, many Hindu shrines and Moorish mosques. » Colombo Plan; Sri Lanka [i]

Colombo Plan A plan drawn up by British Commonwealth foreign ministers in Colombo, Ceylon (Jan 1950), whose purpose was the co-operative development of the countries of S and SE Asia. Colombo also houses the headquarters of the Council for Technical Co-operation, which assists with planning agriculture and industry, health services, scientific research and the training and equipping of personnel. Significant contributions to the aid programme are made by the USA, along with the assisted countries themselves, other Commonwealth countries, Japan, and the International Bank. » Commonwealth, (British)

colon » intestine

Colón [**kol**on], formerly **Aspinwall** 9°21N 79°54W, pop (1980) 59 840. Port and capital city of Colón prov, N Panama, at the Caribbean end of the Panama Canal; second largest city in Panama; founded, 1850; originally named after William Aspinwall, railway builder; railway; commerce, oil refining. » Panama [i]

Colonial and Imperial Conferences A series of conferences at which representatives of the British colonies and dominions discussed matters of common imperial concern; usually held in

London. The first Colonial Conference was held in 1887, and this was followed by others in 1894, 1897, 1902 and 1907. They were particularly concerned with defence, although they also dealt with issues of trade and communications. The first Imperial Conference was held in 1911, the change of name implying a new status for the colonies, and was followed by others in 1921, 1923, 1926, 1930, and 1937, mainly concerned with constitutional changes and economic matters. After World War 2 they were replaced by the Conferences of Commonwealth Prime Ministers. » British Empire; Commonwealth (British)

colonnade A series of columns in or outside a building, usually supporting an entablature, roof, or arches. The most famous example is the enormous 284-column colonnade that forms the Piazza of St Peter's, Rome (1655–67), architect Bernini. » arch [i]; Bernini, Giovanni; cloisters; column; entablature

Colonsay or **St Columba's Isle** Island in Strathclyde region, W Scotland; N of Islay and W of Jura; separated from Oronsay by a low channel which is dry at low water; rises to 134 m/440 ft at Carn Mor; islet of Eilean nan Ron (SW) is a nature reserve with a breeding colony of grey seals; Augustinian priory. » Columba, St; Scotland [i]; Strathclyde

colony An area of land or a country held and governed by another country, usually for the purpose of economic or other forms of exploitation. It is only in the 20th-c that colonialism has become generally regarded as illegitimate, capable of justification only where it was deemed by the international community to be in the longer-term interests of the colonial territory, which usually meant preparation for independence. The present British Commonwealth comprises the former colonies and the **Crown Colonies** (those still directly administered by Britain), which made up the British Empire. » associated state; Commonwealth, (British); imperialism

colophony » **rosin**

color (entries) » **colour** (entries)

Colorado pop (1987e) 3 296 000; area 269 585 sq km/104 091 sq ml. State in WC USA, divided into 63 counties; the 'Centennial State'; E part included in the Louisiana Purchase, 1803; W part gained from Mexico by the Treaty of Guadalupe Hidalgo, 1848; settlement expanded after the gold strike of 1858; became a territory, 1861; joined the Union as the 38th state, 1876; contains the Ute Indian reservation (SW); capital, Denver; chief cities Colorado Springs, Aurora, Lakewood, Pueblo; rivers include the Colorado, Arkansas, Rio Grande, S Platte; Rocky Mts run N–S through the centre, divided into several ranges (Front Range, Sangre de Cristo Mts, Park Range, Sawatch Mts, San Juan Mts); over 50 peaks above 4 000 m/13 000 ft; highest point Mt Elbert (4 399 m/14 432 ft); forms part of the High Plains in the E, the centre of cattle and sheep ranching; the Colorado Plateau (W) has many canyons cut by the Colorado and Gunnison Rivers; several notable national parks and monuments (Rocky Mountain National Park, Dinosaur National Monument, Great Sand Dunes National Monument); wheat, hay, corn, sugar-beet, livestock; food processing, printing and publishing, electrical and transportation equipment, defence industries, fabricated metals, chemicals; lumber, stone, clay, and glass products; oil, coal, uranium; world's largest deposits of molybdenum; growing tourist industry. » Denver; Garden of the Gods; Louisiana Purchase; United States of America [i]; RR38

Colorado River River in SW USA; rises in the Continental Divide, N Colorado; flows through Utah and Arizona (via Marble Canyon and the Grand Canyon), and forms part of the Nevada–Arizona, California–Arizona and Arizona–Mexico borders; empties into the Golfo de California; length c.2 350 km/1 450 ml; major tributaries the Gunnison, Green, San Juan, Little Colorado, Gila, Virgin; used extensively for irrigation, flood-control, and hydroelectric power (Hoover, Davis, Parker and Imperial Dams). » Grand Canyon; United States of America [i]

Colorado beetle A small, leaf beetle; yellow back with 10 longitudinal black stripes on wing cases; females lay eggs on potato plants; larvae fat, reddish yellow with black side spots; pupates in ground; causes great damage to potato crops. (Order: *Coleoptera*. Family: *Chrysomelidae*.) » beetle; potato; pupa

Colorado Desert Depressed arid region in SE California and N Baja California, USA; part of the Great Basin; area 5 000–8 000 sq km/2 000–3 000 sq ml; contains the Salton Sea, a shallow saline lake, situated 71 m/233 ft below sea-level. » California; Great Basin

Colorado Springs 38°50N 104°49W, pop (1980) 215 150. Seat of El Paso County, C Colorado, USA; a residential and all-year resort city at the foot of Pikes Peak; established, 1872; city status, 1886; railway; university; electronic and aerospace equipment; the nearby mineral springs make it a popular health resort; also nearby is the US Air Force Academy; Easter Sunrise Service. » Colorado

coloratura Florid ornamentation, or 'colouring', of a melody, especially in vocal music. A *coloratura soprano* is one with a high voice who specializes in such music.

colorization The addition of colour by electronic means to the videotape transfer of a motion picture originally photographed in black-and-white. The intention is to make the picture more attractive to a modern television audience, but sometimes the former picture quality is sacrificed, and the technique has therefore proved to be controversial. » colour photography

Colossians, Letter to the [kuhl**o**sianz] New Testament writing attributed to Paul while he was in prison. It bears many similarities to the Letter to the Ephesians, but there is much current debate about whether the work is genuinely from Paul. It was apparently written to counter false teachers at Colossae who claimed a higher spiritual knowledge associated with an ascetic and ritualistic way of life and with the worship of angels (*Col* 2.8–23). » Ephesians, Letter to the; New Testament; Paul, St; Pauline Letters

Colossus of Rhodes A huge, bronze statue of the Sun-god Apollo which stood at the harbour entrance of the seaport of Rhodes. It was built c.280 BC. » Seven Wonders of the Ancient World

colour/color » **light; quark; spectrum**

colour/color blindness » **colour/color vision**

colour/color cinematography Regular black-and-white films were hand-tinted or chemically toned even before 1900, but true motion-picture photography in colour was slow to develop. Kinemacolor (1906) had some success as a novelty, taking and projecting successive black-and-white frames through red and blue-green filters, relying on the eye's persistence of vision to provide an additive two-colour mixture. Additive systems with three separation images on one frame, optically superimposed in colour on projection, had limited use (Francita, Opticolor 1930–7), as did the Dufay mosaic (1931–40), but were inconvenient and inefficient in the cinema. From 1928 Technicolor made two-colour subtractive prints by dye-transfer, which readily produced multiple copies for cinema release, and in 1932 introduced a three-colour camera exposing three black-and-white separation colour negatives, with prints in three-colour dye-transfer. By the end of the 1930s this process was firmly established as the dominant medium for professional colour cinematography. It was not until Kodak produced their masked Eastmancolor negative that Technicolor's process was challenged. By 1955 the three-strip camera was obsolete, but dye-transfer printing continued into the 1970s. Eastmancolor negative/positive films opened the way to a vast expansion of colour cinematography, and similar materials are now manufactured worldwide. » colour photography; Technicolor

colour/color filter A transparent material which transmits light from only a selected portion of the visible spectrum, partially or completely absorbing the remainder. Colour filters are used to provide light of a required spectral composition, or to give an overall colour balance to a colour photograph. In black-and-white photography, their use can change the tonal values of coloured objects, such as emphasizing the depth of a blue sky. » colour photography; Plate X

colour/color photography The photographic reproduction of colour from negatives recording separately the red, green, and blue light components of a scene. A positive picture is formed by the superimposition of three corresponding images, either projected in the light of the same hues (*additive*) or printed in the complementary colours, cyan, magenta, and yellow (*subtractive*). Cameras exposing three plates simultaneously through colour filters and beam-splitting prisms or mirrors were made from the 1880s onwards, with subtractive prints by the carbro process or by dye-transfer. A major advance was the integral *tripack*, recording in three separate photographic layers on a common base and developed with colour couplers. The first was Kodachrome (1935), the film exposed in the camera being reversal-processed to a subtractive colour positive transparency. In 1939 Agfa introduced a multilayer colour negative from which positives could be printed on a corresponding tripack, either as transparencies on film or on paper. Integral masking in the negative emulsions (Ektacolor 1949) greatly improved the colour quality of the resultant prints and is now incorporated by all manufacturers. Modern tripack films embody two or more separate coatings in each of the three colour-sensitive layers, and provide high sensitivity combined with high resolution and low grain. » carbro process; masking; integral tripack; photography; reversal process

Colour/Color Separation Overlay » **chromakey**

colour/color television When television broadcasting in colour was introduced in the 1950s, it was essential that a compatible picture should be obtained on existing monochrome sets, and all current systems were established on that basis. The image formed by the lens of a camera is divided into its components of red, green, and blue light, either by a beam-splitting prism with colour filters and three separate sensors, or by a filter with fine stripes of the three colours and a single sensor. Scanning the image provides separate red, green, and blue signals (RGB) and these are combined in the proportions of 30% R, 59% G, and 11% B to form the *luminance* signal, Y, which represents the picture in neutral tones from white to black. The colour information, *chrominance*, is handled as two colour-difference signals, B–Y and R–Y, which are coded in phase relationship and added to the luminance signal for transmission, in what is termed the *composite mode*. The colour coding details vary in different systems – NTSC in America and Japan, and PAL or SECAM in Europe and elsewhere. In the late 1980s, the alternative *component* mode was developed, in which the chrominance signals are kept separate from the luminance, but compressed in time to occupy the same period. This provides improved picture quality, and is widely used in the latest generation of videotape recorders. It will also be employed for high-definition TV broadcasting, as in the MAC (multiple analogue component) system.

In the receiver, scanning controlled by the luminance signal alone provides a black-and-white image on the screen of a monochrome cathode ray tube, but in a colour set both chrominance and luminance are decoded to give separate RGB signals controlling the three electron guns of a shadow-mask tube. As these beams are scanned across the screen they stimulate groups of minute phosphor dots which glow in the corresponding colour, red, green and blue, to form the elements of the complete picture by additive colour mixture. » colour photography; NTSC; PAL; scanning [i]; SECAM

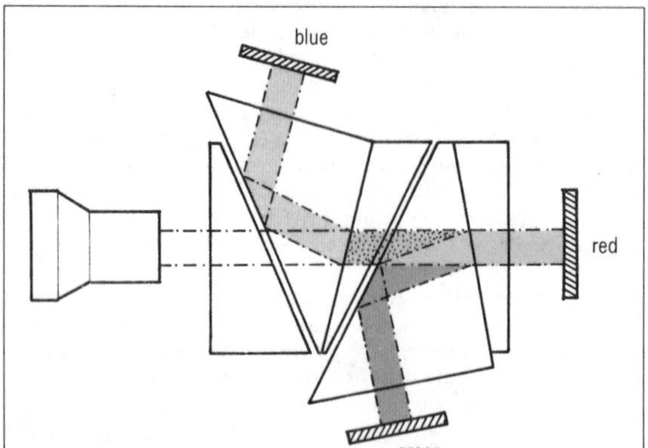

Colour Television Camera – Light through the camera lens is divided by a beam-splitting prism system to separate red, green and blue sensors.

colour/color vision The ability to detect differences between light of various wavelengths reaching the retina by converting them into colours. It is dependent on the presence of light-sensitive pigments in the cones (*retinal photoreceptors*), each being sensitive to light of a specific wavelength. The cones send coded information to the brain (via certain retinal neurones and the optic nerve) for processing and colour appreciation. In humans, the cones contain pigments most sensitive to red, green, or blue light. Absence of one or more of these pigments results in **colour blindness**: red-blindness (*protanopia*) affects the ability to distinguish red and green; blue-blindness (*deuteranopia*) affects blue and yellow; and green-blindness (*tritanopia*) affects the green range of the spectrum. Colour blindness is a sex-linked characteristic, about 20 times more common in males; women cannot suffer from the defect unless both parents have the same defect. » eye [i]; light; retina; rods and cones

Coloured » **Cape Coloured**

colouring/coloring agents Dyes used for colouring food which are either natural, nature identical, or synthetic (artificial or synthetic). Tartrazine is an example of a synthetic colouring agent, while carotine is a natural colourant. Hypersensitivity to colours has been reported. The incidence of perceived hypersensitivity (c.7%) is far higher than the true incidence (0.1%). » carotene; E-number; tartrazine

colourization » **colorization**

colourpoint/colorpoint » **Himalayan cat**

Colt, Samuel (1814–62) US inventor, born and died at Hartford, Connecticut. He ran away to sea in 1827, and about 1832 travelled over the USA, lecturing on chemistry. In 1835 he took out his first patent for a revolver, which after the Mexican war was adopted by the US army, founding the fortunes of his company, Colt's Patent Fire-Arms. » revolver

coltsfoot A perennial with long whitish rhizomes, native to Europe, W and N Asia, and N Africa; leaves all basal, up to 30 cm/12 in across, rounded to shallowly lobed, white-felted beneath; flower heads bright yellow, solitary on stems to 15 cm/6 in, appearing before the leaves. It is an old herbal medicine for chest complaints. (*Tussilago farfara*. Family: *Compositae*.) » perennial; rhizome

colugo [kuh**loo**goh] A nocturnal mammal, native to SE Asia; face lemur-like; large gliding membrane along each side of body, extending to tips of fingers, toes, and long tail; lives in trees; eats plant material; closely related to insectivores; only member of the order *Dermoptera*; also known as **flying lemur**. (Family: *Cynocephalidae*, 2 species.) » insectivore; lemur

Colum, Padraic (1881–1972) Irish poet and playwright, born at Longford. Educated at Trinity College, Dublin, he was a leader of the Irish literary revival. He wrote several plays for the Abbey Theatre, and helped to found *The Irish Review* (1911). From 1914 he lived in the USA, and published two studies on Hawaiian folklore (1924, 1926). He wrote several volumes of poetry, and also children's stories. He died at Enfield, Connecticut. » Abbey Theatre; drama; Irish literature

Columba ('dove') A small S constellation, accepted since 1679. » constellation; RR00

Columba, St, also **Columcille** or **Colm** (521–97), feast day 9 June. Irish missionary and abbot, born at Gartan, Donegal. He founded monasteries at Derry (546) and Durrow (553), and then at Iona, in the Inner Hebrides (c.563), from where he and his followers brought Christianity to Scotland. In his system, bishops were subordinate to abbots, and Easter was kept on a different day from the Roman churches. He is said to have written 300 books with his own hand. He died at Iona. » Christianity; monasticism

Columbae » **Columbiformes**

Columban or **Columbanus, St** (c.543–615), feast day 23 November. Irish missionary and abbot, 'the younger Columba', born in Leinster. About 585 he went to Gaul and founded the monasteries of Anegray, Luxeuil, and Fontaine in the Vosges. His adherence to the Celtic Easter involved him in controversy;

and the courage with which he rebuked the vices of the Burgundian court led to his expulsion. He later went to Lombardy, and in 612 founded the monastery of Bobbio, in the Appenines, where he died. » Easter; monasticism

Columbia 34°00N 81°03W, pop (1980) 101 208. State capital in Richland County, C South Carolina, USA; at the confluence of the Broad and Saluda Rivers, which join to form the Congaree R; settled, early 1700s; state capital, 1786; city status, 1854; burned by General Sherman, 1865; airfield; railway; two universities (1801, 1870); commercial and trading centre in a rich farming area; printing; textiles, plastics, electrical equipment, machinery. » Sherman; South Carolina

Columbia River River in NW USA and SW Canada; rises in the Rocky Mts in E British Columbia, flows into Washington state, USA, and enters the Pacific at Cape Disappointment, SW of Tacoma, Oregon; length 1 953 km/1 214 ml; many rapids and falls; major gorge through the Cascade range; source of irrigation and hydroelectric power. » Cascade Range; Rocky Mountains

Columbia University » Ivy League [i]

Columbiformes [koluhmbi**fawmeez**] An order of birds encompassing the pigeons, sandgrouse, and the extinct dodo and dodo-like solitaires; also known as **Columbae**. » dodo; pigeon; sandgrouse

columbine A perennial native to Europe, N Africa, and Asia; leaves divided into three segments, each again divided into three; flowers blue, rarely white, each of the five petals with a curved backward-pointing spur containing nectar. The popular garden forms, often called **aquilegia**, include hybrids with long straight spurs and more colourful flowers. (*Aquilegia vulgaris*. Family: *Ranunculaceae*.) » perennial

Columbus, Christopher, Ital **Cristoforo Colombo**, Span **Cristóbal Colón** (1451–1506) Discoverer of the New World, born at Genoa. He went to sea at 14, and after being shipwrecked off Portugal, settled there about 1470. His plans to reach India by sailing W were rejected by John II of Portugal, but finally supported by Ferdinand and Isabella of Spain. He set sail from Saltes (3 Aug 1492) in the *Santa Maria*, with 50 men, and attended by the *Pinta* and the *Niña*. He reached the Bahamas (12 Oct), and then visited Cuba and Hispaniola (Haiti), where he left a small colony. He returned (15 Mar 1493) to be received with the highest honours by the court. His second voyage (1493–6) led to the discovery of several Caribbean islands. On his third voyage (1498–1500) he discovered the S American mainland, but after a revolt against his command, was sent home in irons by a newly appointed royal governor. Restored to favour in Spain, he went on his last great voyage (1502–4) along the S side of the Gulf of Mexico. He died at Valladolid, in Spain, but in 1536 his remains and those of his son Diego were removed to Santo Domingo, in Hispaniola. They were returned to Spain in 1899, and deposited in Seville Cathedral. » Columbus Day; Ferdinand (of Castile)

Columbus 39°58N 83°00W, pop (1980) 564 871. Capital of state in Franklin County, C Ohio, USA, at the confluence of the Olentangy and Scioto Rivers; laid out opposite the earlier settlement of Franklinton, 1812; state capital, 1824; city status, 1834; railway; three universities (1850, 1870, 1902); air force base; electronics, machinery, fabricated metals, aircraft and automobile parts; centre for research in science and information technology; Centre of Science and Industry, Ohio Historical Centre, Ohio Railway Museum, Ballet Metropolitan. » Ohio

Columbus Day A national holiday in the USA, held in most states on the second Monday in October in commemoration of Christopher Columbus's discovery of America (12 Oct 1492). It is also celebrated in several countries of Central and South America. » Columbus, Christopher

column A vertical support in a building, usually made up of base, circular shaft, and spreading capital, and designed to carry a load bearing down from above, such as an entablature. It is also used as an aesthetic device to add ornament or to divide a space. Occasionally it is built in total isolation as a free-standing object. » capital; entablature; orders of architecture [i]

coly [**koh**lee] A bird native to Africa S of the Sahara, also known as **mousebird**; small, greyish; head crest, short curved bill, long tail; outer toe reversible; lives in groups. It is placed in a separate order (*Coliiformes*). (Genus: *Colius*, 6 species. Family: *Coliidae*.)

coma A state of unconsciousness from which individuals cannot be roused. Brain functions are progressively depressed, but the vital activities of respiration and constriction of the heart continue. The causes include trauma to the brain, meningitis, alcohol and drug overdosage, and metabolic disorders such as severe kidney and liver failure and complications of diabetes. » metabolism

coma (physics) » aberrations 1 [i]

Coma Berenices [**koh**muh beruh**niy**seez] (Lat 'Berenice's hair') A faint constellation established in 1602 by Tycho Brahe. It includes the huge Come cluster of galaxies, located 150 megaparsecs away. » Brahe; constellation; RR8

COMAL An acronym of **COMmon ALgorithmic language**. An enhanced version of the BASIC computer language which combines aspects of both BASIC and PASCAL. It was developed by Danish computer scientist Borge Christiansen in 1974. » algorithm; BASIC; PASCAL

Comanche [kuh**man**chee] Shoshonean-speaking N American Plains Indians who migrated S from Wyoming and became a powerful group, raiding and displacing others (eg the Apache), and terrorizing White settlers. They were one of the first to acquire horses from the Spanish, and hunted buffalo. The S Comanche were settled on reservations in the mid-19th-c, but the N Comanche held out against the White settlers, finally agreeing to settle on a reservation in Oklahoma in 1867. Population c.4 250. » American Indians; Plains Indians; Shoshoni

Comaneci, Nadia [koma**nech**] (1961–) Romanian gymnast, born at Onesti, Moldavia. She was the star of the 1976 Olympic Games, when at the age of 14 (coached by Bela Karolyi) she won gold medals in the beam, vault, and floor disciplines. She retained the beam and floor exercise gold medals in 1980. In 1976 she became the first gymnast to obtain a perfect score of 10.00 for her performance on the parallel bars and beam. Later she became an international judge, and coach to the Romanian national team. In 1989 she defected to the USA via Hungary, amid much publicity. » gymnastics

comb jelly » ctenophore

combassou » whydah

Combination Acts British legislation passed in 1799 and 1800 which prohibited the coming together ('combination') of workers in trade unions. The Acts were part of anti-reformist legislation passed by the Pitt government during the French wars, though combinations in many trades were already illegal. The Acts were repealed in 1824–5, and trade unions, though under severe restrictions, legalized. » Pitt (the Younger); trade union

combine harvester A machine which cuts, threshes, and cleans all types of cereals, oilseeds, and legumes. Most com-

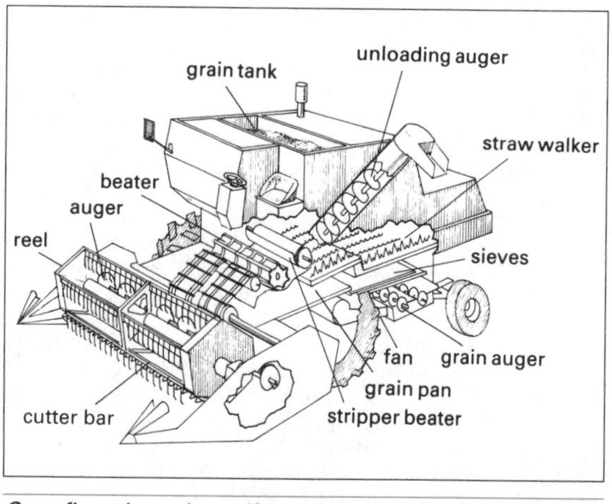

Crop flow through a self-propelled combine harvester

bines are now self-propelled, and are equipped for handling grain and seed in bulk. » cereals; legume; oil (botany)

Combined Operations Command A British force established in 1940 when Churchill appointed Admiral of the Fleet Lord Keyes to co-ordinate British commando raids against German-occupied Europe. Keyes' successor Lord Mountbatten (1941–3) directed larger operations involving all three Services, and prepared for the eventual Allied invasion of France, in which Combined Operations techniques were to play a crucial role. » Churchill, Winston; D-Day; Mountbatten, Earl; World War 2

combing In spinning, a post-carding process which removes unwanted short fibres, termed *noil*, and straightens and aligns the remaining fibres (*sliver*). The sliver may then be spun into fine smooth yarns. » carding; yarn

combustion A burning, usually in a supply of oxygen to form oxides. The complete combustion of a hydrocarbon yields carbon dioxide and water. The energy associated with the combustion of a mole of a substance is called its **heat of combustion**. » mole (physics); oxide

COMECON » **Council for Mutual Economic Assistance**

Comédie-Française, La [**ko**maydee frãsez] The oldest surviving theatre company in France, dating officially from 1680. Having been formed seven years after the death of Molière by a combination of troupes which included his former company, it was soon referred to as *La Maison de Molière*. Despite various vicissitudes it has continued to the present to be the guardian of the French classical tradition. It is organized as a co-operative society, with its longest serving actor as the Doyen or head of the company. All full members of the society, as share-holders, are eligible for a pension on retirement. » Molière; theatre

comedy The term may be used of a poem or a novel, but most usually a play with a happy ending, marked by clarification, reconciliation, and marriage. Comedy derives from fertility rituals, which had a positive and celebratory function involving the whole community; hence despite proliferating forms in all cultures its general commitment is to the continuity and self-regulation of human society – to which (by contrast with tragedy) the individual interest is always subservient. The Old Comedy of Aristophanes and Menander exposed the weakness and wickedness of individuals and cliques against the social sanity of the chorus; the more tolerant if mechanical New Comedy of Plautus and Terence added a love interest to the stock comic deviations from the norm. The mediaeval miracle and morality plays had a crude, corrective, comic aspect. Ben Jonson recreated the best of classical comedy in Jacobean England, with intellectual but festive satires such as *The Alchemist* (1610); while the contemporary comedies of Shakespeare, such as *Twelfth Night* (1600) and *Measure for Measure* (1604), are formally and ethically more complex, at once profound and problematical. The succeeding Restoration comedies of Wycherley (1670s) and Congreve (1690s) were coarse in comparison, and the later 'sentimental' comedies of Goldsmith and Sheridan (1770s) superficial. Meanwhile the prolific Lope de Vega and his successor in Madrid, Calderón, delineated the contradictions of the Spanish character, and Molière brought the comedy of manners to perfection at the court of Louis XIV in France. The rationalist 18th-c and idealizing Romantic age were not productive of comedy, but the dark dramas of Ibsen and the ambiguities of Chekhov introduce the modern 'problem' comedy of relativistic values. In the 20th-c the comedy of ideas (Shaw), the theatre of the absurd (Ionesco, Beckett, Pinter), and black comedy (Orton, Albee) have taken the form in new directions. » Albee; Aristophanes; Beckett; black comedy; Calderón de la Barca; Chekhov; Congreve; drama; Goldsmith; Ibsen; Ionesco; Jonson; Lope de Vega; Menander; Molière; Orton; Pinter; Plautus; Shakespeare [i]; Shaw, George Bernard; Sheridan, Richard; Terence; tragedy; Wycherley

Comenius, John Amos, Czech **Komenský, Jan Ámos** (1592–1670) Czech educational reformer, born in Moravia. He studied at Herborn and Heidelberg, and became rector of the Moravian school of Prerau (1614–16) and minister at Fulnek, but fled to Poland at the beginning of the Thirty Years' War. Settling at Lissa (1628), he worked out his new theory of education, and was chosen bishop of the Moravian Brethren in 1632. He visited England and Sweden, and in 1650 went to Hungary, where he composed his *Orbis Sensualium Pictus* (1658, The Visible World in Pictures), the first picture book for children. He then settled in Amsterdam, and died at Naarden. » Moravian Brethren

comet A small Solar System body made of ice and dust. Comets are asteroidal in appearance at distances of many astronomical units from the Sun (when they consist of a bare, inactive nucleus) and are often spectacularly active when nearer to the Sun. The characteristic bright head (*coma*) and streaming tails (both dust and ion) are created by solar heating, which causes sublimation of the ices (and entrainment of the dust) with subsequent solar-induced emission of light from gas molecules and scattered light from the dust. The source of comets is believed to be a spherical halo cloud about the Sun called the *Oort Cloud* – representing a region to which cometary planetesimals scattered gravitationally after their formation 4.6 billion years ago. Oort Cloud comets are loosely bound in a solar orbit at distances of c.50 000 astronomical units.

Observable comets are occasionally scattered into the inner Solar System by the gravitational fields of nearby stars and giant molecular clouds. Most can be observed only once because of their long period of about a million years; some (eg Halley's comet) are captured into relatively short period orbits as a result of gravitational interactions with giant planets. There are about 50 known periodic comets in the 'Jupiter' family whose aphelion distance is near Jupiter's. These are potential targets for spacecraft missions, and represent the most primitive material, dating back to the origin of the Solar System. International Cometary Explorer encountered Comet Giacobini-Zinner in 1985, and a small 'armada' of spacecraft (Sakigake and Suisei, VEGA 1 and 2, Giotto) encountered Halley's comet in 1986.

From spacecraft and telescopic measurements it is now known that the comet nucleus is a few km in size, irregularly shaped and very dark; dust in the coma contains carbon and silica; there is evidence of polymerized organic molecules; the gases of the coma include water, carbon monoxide, carbon dioxide, ammonia, methane, and hydrocarbons; the 'dirty snowball' hypothesis of astronomer Fred Whipple (1906–) is basically confirmed. Cometary impacts on Earth over geologic time may have been an important source of volatile material and organics contributing to the pre-biotic environment. Cometary and asteroidal impacts may also have contributed to periodic extinctions of species in the past. » asteroids; cosmic dust; Giotto/International Cometary Explorer/Sakigake and Suisei/VEGA project; meteorite; periapsis; Solar System; sublimation (chemistry)

comfrey A bristly perennial, native to Europe and the Mediterranean region; leaves grow to 30 cm/12 in, narrowly oval, rough, the upper with stalks forming wings on the stem; inflorescence coiled; flowers drooping, tubular, or funnel-shaped, white, yellow, or pink in bud, and opening blue. (Genus: *Symphytum*, 25 species. Family: *Boraginaceae*.) » inflorescence [i]; perennial

comic opera A light, amusing opera, particularly one which (like those of Gilbert and Sullivan) alternates songs and ensembles with spoken dialogue. The modern equivalent is the musical. » musical; opera; Sullivan, Arthur

Cominform An abbreviation for the USSR's **Communist Information Bureau**, and a successor to the Comintern. It was established upon Stalin's orders at a meeting in Poland (Sep 1947), its purpose being the co-ordination of the 'voice' and activities of the communist parties of Bulgaria, Czechoslovakia, France, Hungary, Italy, Poland, Romania, the USSR, and Yugoslavia. Its headquarters were moved from Belgrade to Bucharest following the break between Stalin and Tito which culminated in Yugoslavia's expulsion in 1948. Cominform reflected a new hard line, expressing hostility towards the capitalist camp of the world, and was used by Stalin as an instrument for Soviet domination of E Europe.

After the rapprochement of the USSR and Yugoslavia in 1956, the Cominform was dissolved. » Comintern; communism; Stalin

Comino [ko**mee**noh] 36°00N 14°20E; area 2.7 sq km/1.04 sq ml. Smallest of the three main islands of the Maltese group, midway between Malta and Gozo; highest point, 247 m/810 ft; harbour for pirates until the 1700s; 20-minute boat trip from the main island; no cars allowed; Blue Lagoon. » Malta [i]

Comintern An abbreviation for the **Communist International**, founded in Moscow (Mar 1919) at the behest of the Russian Communist Party, its purpose being the rallying of left-wing socialists and communists. It adopted Leninist principles in its policies, rejecting reformism in favour of revolutionary action, which it encouraged against capitalist governments. It was disbanded in May 1943. » Cominform; Marxism-Leninism

Commagene [koma**jee**nee] An area in N Syria, ruled in Seleucid and Roman times by a Hellenized dynasty of Persian (Achaemenid) origin. The Romans suppressed the dynasty in AD 72 because of its pro-Parthian leanings, and made Commagene part of the Syrian province. » Hellenization; Parthians; Roman history [i]

command economy » **market economy**

commedia dell'arte [ko**may**deea del**ah**tay] (Ital 'comedy of the profession') A distinctive form of theatre which originated in Italy about the middle of the 16th-c. Its performance was the prerogative of professional troupes, unlike that of the literary comedies, which was open to learned amateurs. The skills of the form were performance skills passed on from player to player. The dialogue and comic business was not written down, but the storyline, its division into acts, and the entrances and exits of the characters were. The comedy relied on stock characters, many represented by masks. The popularity of *commedia* spread throughout Europe, and many of these masks developed an independent stage history. » Harlequin; Pierrot; Punch and Judy; theatre

commensalism A type of interaction between two different species in which one species (the *commensal*) derives benefit from a common food supply, while the other species (the *host*) is not adversely affected. » biology; parasitology; species; symbiosis

commercial bill » **bill of exchange**

commercial paper A short-term negotiable instrument for payment of money, such as a bill of exchange. In the USA the term is used to describe a short-term note (between four and twelve months) issued by a company with a very high credit-rating. » bill of exchange

Committees of Correspondence In the American Revolution, an informal network linking communities and provinces for the purpose of sharing political information. Committees began to appear in 1772, and during the independence crisis (1775–6) they assumed full power in many places. » American Revolution

commodity market A market where buyers and sellers of commodities – mainly agricultural crops and metals – trade (*commodity trading*). Often prices are fixed on a bargain-by-bargain basis. The dealers who negotiate on behalf of clients are known as *commodity brokers*.

Common Agricultural Policy (CAP) The most important of the common policies of the European Community, costing in 1988 £19 000 million and absorbing 65% of the total Community budget. The basic principles behind the CAP are free trade for agricultural commodities within the Community, Community preference for domestic production, control of imports from the rest of the world, and common financing. The objectives of the CAP were stated in the Treaty of Rome to be increased agricultural productivity, a fair standard of living for farmers, reasonable consumer prices, stability of markets, and secure food supplies. Most of these objectives have been met, through the use of high price-support measures, which in turn have generated surpluses in most major commodities (eg the 'butter mountain' and 'wine lake'). An important additional objective for the CAP is now to contain these surpluses and limit the huge cost associated with their disposal. » agricultural controls; European Economic Community

common law A source of English law, the first source common to the entire kingdom. The system of common law replaced over a period of centuries local courts and customs. Henry II was particularly influential in developing the common law in, for example, sending out royal representatives on circuit. The common law tradition is one which emphasizes the development of law through individual cases rather than prescriptive codes. » civil law **2**; Henry II (of England)

Common Market » **European Economic Community**

common seal A true seal native to N Pacific and N Atlantic Oceans; usually grey with dark blotches; may dive deeper than 90 m/300 ft; eats fish, squid, and crabs; also known as **harbour seal** or **hair seal**. (*Phoca vitulina*.) » seal (biology)

Commons, House of The lower, and effectively the ruling, chamber of the bicameral legislature of the UK. It contains 650 members, elected by universal adult suffrage, each representing a single constituency. The Commons is elected for a maximum period of five years, though the prime minister may call an election at any time within that period, and the government is drawn from the party that wins the majority of seats. The ascendancy of the House of Commons over the House of Lords began during the 16th-c, and was completed with the passage of the Parliament Acts of 1911 and 1949. The Commons is dominated by a disciplined party system, which means that governments are generally assured of a majority in the passage of legislation. In this sense the Commons serves a legitimizing rather than a legislating function. » bicameral system; Lords, House of

Commonwealth, (British) A free association of independent nations formerly subject to British imperial government, and maintaining friendly and practical links with the UK. In 1931 the Statute of Westminster established the British Commonwealth of Nations; the adjective 'British' was deleted after World War 2. Most of the states granted independence, beginning with India in 1947, chose to be members of the Commonwealth. There are annual meetings between finance ministers, and biannual meetings between Commonwealth heads of government, as well as various committees concerned with education, agriculture, and science. Ireland resigned from the association in 1948, South Africa in 1961, Pakistan in 1972, and Fiji in 1987. » British Empire; Commonwealth Conference/Day/Development Corporation/Games

Commonwealth (English history) English republican regime, established in 1649, lasting until the Instrument of Government created a Protectorate in 1653. It failed to achieve political settlement at home, but its armies pacified Scotland and Ireland. The Navigation Acts (1650, 1651) and war with the Dutch (1652–4) fostered overseas trade and colonies. » Dutch Wars; English Civil War; Protectorate

Commonwealth Conference An annual meeting of prime ministers of the independent nations that evolved from the former British Empire and now comprise the Commonwealth. Its role is somewhat elusive, but it acts as a forum for maintaining political and economic links between the member countries. » Commonwealth, (British)

Commonwealth Day The second Monday in March, celebrated with receptions, educational events, etc throughout the British Commonwealth; originally instituted as **Empire Day** (by which name it was known until 1960) and held on 24 May, the anniversary of Queen Victoria's birthday; from 1967, celebrated on the Queen's official birthday in June; changed to its present date in 1977. » Commonwealth, (British)

Commonwealth Development Corporation An organization established by the British government under the 1948 Overseas Resources Development Act, until 1963 known as the Colonial Development Corporation. Its functions were to develop trade and defence in former British colonial territories and countries through a loans programme, which lasted until the early 1970s. » Commonwealth, (British)

Commonwealth Games A multi-sport gathering every four years by representatives of the nations of the Commonwealth. The first Games were at Hamilton, Canada in 1930. Edinburgh is the only city to have staged two Games. » Commonwealth, (British); RR102

Commonwealth Institute An organization founded in 1959 to replace the Imperial Institute, itself founded in 1886 to promote commerce and industry between the countries of the British Empire. Based in London and Edinburgh, its main activity is the promotion of the heritage and culture of its member nations. » Commonwealth, (British)

Commonwealth of Independent States A body comprising 11 of the republics of the former Soviet Union, established after the dissolution of the Soviet state in December 1991. Georgia did not join the Commonwealth (*Sodruzhestvo*) because of continuing civil unrest. » Armenia; Azerbaijan; Byelorussia; Georgia (republic); Kazakhstan; Kirghizia; Moldova; Russia; Tadzhikistan; Turkmenia; Ukraine; Uzbekistan

Commonwealth Scientific and Industrial Research Organization (CSIRO) Australia's leading government science organization, formed in 1920; its present name dates from 1949.

commune A settlement of people at village or household level, usually based on the common ownership of material goods. Communes often have a tradition of self-government. The Paris Commune in 1871 challenged the authority of the national government of France. » Commune of Paris

Commune of Paris An uprising by Parisian Republicans (18 Mar–28 May 1871) following France's humiliating defeat in the Franco-Prussian War. The insurgents rose against the Versailles government, personified by the veteran Thiers and a conservative Assembly. The climax came amid vicious fighting and destruction: the Communard rump was cornered and shot, leaving an unprecedented legacy of bitterness. » commune; Franco-Prussian War; Thiers

communicable disease A disease caused by a micro-organism which can be transmitted from infected animals or humans to non-infected individuals. The infection may be by direct contact (eg venereal diseases), via the air (eg meningitis), by ingestion (eg dysentery), or by insect transmission (eg malaria). » infection

communication theory The application of information theory to human communication in general. Communication is seen to involve an information source encoding a message which is transmitted via a channel to a receiver, where it is decoded and has an effect. Efficient, error-free transmission is assumed to be the primary goal, especially in engineering contexts. Attempts to apply this model more generally have been criticized for neglecting the importance of other factors, such as feedback, social context, and the active role played by human receivers in the production of meaning. » feedback; information theory; semiotics

communicative competence The ability to communicate with another person about the whole range of everyday situations and events. In foreign language teaching, this emphasis led to courses being based principally on contemporary spoken and written language about topics such as shopping, travel, leisure, and family life. In examinations, it produced marking schemes where more of the marks were given for oral and written fluency. » competence

Communion, Holy » Eucharist

communism A political ideology which has as its central principle the communal ownership of all property, and thereby the abolition of private property. Although examples of early social and religious groupings based upon communal sharing of property have been cited, modern communism is specifically associated with the theories of Karl Marx. Marx saw the emergence of a communist society as being the final stage in a historical process that was rooted in human material needs, preceded by feudalism, capitalism, and (a transitional stage) socialism. Communism, according to Marx, would abolish class distinctions and end the exploitation of the masses inherent in the capitalist system. The working class, or proletariat, would be the instrument of a revolution that would overthrow the capitalist system and liberate human potential. A fully developed communist system would operate according to the principle of 'from each according to his ability, to each according to his need', and as there would be no need for the state to regulate society, it would 'wither away'.

Marx's writings have provided a powerful ideological basis for communist and many socialist parties and governments, which have legitimized the implementation of their policies by reference to Marxism or some variant of it. The Communist Party of the Soviet Union (CPSU), first of all under Lenin's leadership and followed by Stalin, re-interpreted Marxist ideology as Marxism-Leninism-Stalinism, the major feature of which is democratic centralism. Unlike the spontaneous, decentralized organization envisaged by Marx, the CPSU is a highly centralized, monolithic, and secretive organization. Under Stalin's leadership it became an instrument in the development of a totalitarian dictatorship.

The CPSU provided the ideological lead for European communist parties; indeed, at the creation of the *Third International* in 1919, it was clear that only those socialist parties which accepted the discipline, leadership, and organizational structure of the (then) Russian Communist party would be allowed to join. During the latter part of the 20th-c, however, the compulsory leadership of the CPSU has been questioned and challenged, partly because of the economic difficulties resulting from the rigidities of democratic centralism in industrial states, where decentralization and flexibility are required. Nonetheless, Yugoslavia had been the only country to challenge Soviet dominance successfully (1952), other countries such as Hungary, Czechoslovakia, and Poland being prevented by military force from breaking away from the Soviet model. In 1989, the establishment of a non-communist Government in Poland, popular uprisings in Eastern Europe and the decision by the Soviet Union not to intervene to maintain communist supremacy, saw the dominant position of the Communist Party eroded. The popular uprisings were political, rather than economic, with demands for greater democracy and the ending of repression. Whether communism can adapt to non-authoritarian, pluralistic politics remains to be seen.

Following the assumption of leadership by Gorbachev, democratic reform emerged in the CPSU through the process of perestroika. The challenge also arose because of the difficulties encountered by opposition communist parties in liberal democracies, which found themselves increasingly isolated from their working-class supporters. Italy was the most successful here, and, as a consequence of its condemnation of Soviet aggression abroad and of oppression at home, managed for a time to retain a significant measure of popularity with the Italian electorate. The main challenge from outside the Eurocommunist parties has been the development of Chinese communist ideology in the form of Maoism. Other socialist and social democratic parties have, however, rejected the revolutionary path to socialism, advocating instead a gradual, reformist strategy which operates within constitutional frameworks. Such was the hallmark of the Socialist International, with the major split between the two socialist strands occurring after the formation of the *Third International* (Comintern) in 1919. » Agitprop; capitalism; Comintern; Communist Party of the Soviet Union; Eurocommunism; International; Maoism; Marxism; Marxism- Leninism; perestroika; totalitarianism

Communism Peak, Russ **Pik Kommunizma**, formerly **Mt Garmo** (to 1933), **Mt Stalin** (1933–62) 39°00N 72°02E. Highest peak in the former USSR, in the Pamir range, N Tadzhikistan; height, 7 495 m/24 590 ft; first climbed in 1933. » Tadzhikistan

Communist Party of the Soviet Union (CPSU) The party which controlled political, economic, and social life in the USSR. It was the only party with the right to put forward candidates in elections, and most of the country's important jobs were controlled by the party. Many posts were confined to party members, who comprised only c.10% of the population. » apparat; communism

community charge A flat-rate charge on every adult resident in a particular area to contribute towards the provision of local government services. As the **poll tax**, it was first levied on each adult or 'head' (Middle English, *polle*) in 1377, and periodically reimposed (eg in 1513, 1641, and during the reign of Charles II). Most tax systems have abandoned the poll tax, but in the UK it has been revived as a way of overcoming weaknesses in the domestic rating system, applying to all adults who use the services in a district, not just to those who own property. Exemptions can be made for poor families, and certain other categories (eg religious orders). The charge came into operation in Scotland in 1989, and was scheduled to apply in England and Wales from 1990. Its introduction has been controversial, with claims that it is unjust in its impact on the poorer members of society. » Peasants' Revolt; rates; taxation

community dance The widespread participation in dance in community, arts, and dance centres. It started in Britain in the 1970s based on the French notion of the cultural 'animateur', initiated and funded jointly by charitable trusts, regional arts associations, local authorities, and the Arts Council of Great Britain. The dance styles range from tap to Indian and Egyptian, and people both participate and learn to appreciate. All ages are catered for. » traditional dance

community medicine A branch of medicine in which the health needs of communities, as distinct from individuals, are studied and assessed; also known as **social medicine**. It includes epidemiology, preventive medicine, the planning and delivery of health care, occupational medicine, the study of industrial disease, and public hygiene. » epidemiology; industrial disease; National Health Service; occupational diseases; preventive medicine

community politics An emphasis by candidates in general and parliamentary elections upon local, rather than national, issues and policies, the suggestion being that national parties pay insufficient attention to local concerns. The term became popular in the UK following the successful adoption of such tactics by the Liberal Party in the Sutton and Cheam by-election (Dec 1972), and the general election of 1974. » political science

community school/college A school or college which is open to the whole community, not just to those of school age. It may therefore be open seven days a week, during evenings as well as through the day, and in some cases children and adults may study in the same class or take part in the same recreational activities. » adult education

community service order A sentence of the criminal courts whereby a convicted defendant can be required to undertake constructive unpaid work in the community, rather than being detained or paying a fine. » sentence

commutative operation In mathematics, an operation where the order of combination does not affect the result. Thus addition is commutative, because $a+b=b+a$ for all values of a and b; but subtraction is not commutative, because $a-b\neq b-a$ for all a,b. » associative operation; distributive operation

Como 45°49N 9°06E, pop (1981) 95 571. Capital town of Como province, Lombardy, NW Italy, at SW end of L Como; railway; silk, motor cycles, glass, furniture, tourism; marble cathedral (1396), 11th-c twin-towered church of Sant'Abbondio (11th-c), old town largely encircled by mediaeval wall; some Roman remains. » Como, Lake; Lombardy

Como, Lake (Ital **Lago di**) or **Lario**, ancient **Larius Lacus** area 146 sq km/56 sq ml. Narrow lake in Como province, Lombardy, N Italy, at the foot of the Bernese Alps; length 50 km/31 ml; 4 km/2½ ml wide at its half-way point; maximum depth 410 m/1 345 ft, the deepest of the N Italian lakes; promontory of Bellagio divides it into two branches, with Como at the S end of the SW branch; lake resorts include Tremezzo and Menaggio. » Como; Italy [i]

Comodoro Rivadavia [kohmoh**doh**roh reeva**da**via] 45°50S 67°30W, pop (1980) 96 865. Seaport and largest city in Chubut province, Patagonia, S Argentina; on the Golfo San Jorge, on the Atlantic coast; university (1961); railway; airfield; natural gas pipeline linked to Buenos Aires; oil, petrochemicals. » Argentina [i]

Comoé [ko**moh**ay] National park, largely in Bouna department, NE Côte d'Ivoire; crossed by R Comoé; area 11 500 sq km/4 450 sq ml; established in 1968; a world heritage site. » Côte d'Ivoire [i]

Comoros [kom**o**ros], official name **Federal and Islamic Republic of the Comoros, République Fédérale Islamique des Comores** pop (1990e) 463 000; area 1 862 sq km/719 sq ml. Group of three volcanic islands (Grand Comore, Anjouan, Mohéli) at the N end of the Mozambique Channel, between Mozambique and Madagascar; capital, Moroni; timezone GMT +3; chief language, Kiswahili; chief religion, Islam (over 85%); unit of currency, the franc CFA of 100 cents; tropical climate; dry season (May–Oct), hot humid season (Nov–Apr); average temperatures, 20°C (Jul), 28°C (Nov); under French control, 1843–1912; French overseas territory, 1947; internal political autonomy, 1961; unilateral independence declared, 1975; Mayotte decided to remain under French administration; established as a Federal Islamic Republic, 1978; a one-party state, governed by a president (elected for a 6-year term) who is head of government as well as head of state, a Council of Ministers, and a 42-member unicameral Federal Assembly elected every five years; largely agricultural economy; vanilla, copra, cacao, sisal, coffee, cloves, vegetable oils, perfume. » Grande Comore; Islam; Mayotte; Moroni; RR46 political leaders

compact camera » **miniature camera**

compact disc A plastic disc of 120 mm/4.7 in diameter, holding on a single side up to an hour of digitally encoded sound recording, stored as a succession of pits and plateaux in tracks 1.6 μ wide. The disc is coated in a reflective material (usually aluminium), which either scatters or reflects back into a photoelectric detector a laser beam used to read (play) the encoded sound when the disc is rotated at high constant linear speed. Launched in 1982–3 by Philips and Sony jointly, digital compact discs are free of stylus wear, are essentially immune to surface blemishes, and thus appear near to perfection in sound recording. » digital recording; laser [i]; sound recording

Companions of Honour, Order of the (CH) In the UK, an award instituted in 1917, made to members of either sex for outstanding service to the nation. It now consists of the sovereign and a maximum of 65 members. The ribbon is carmine with gold edges.

company An association existing for a commercial or business purpose, considered to be a legal entity independent of its members. It may be formed by Act of Parliament, by Royal Charter, or by registration under company law (referred to as a *limited liability* or *joint-stock* company). The main regulating law in England is the Companies (Consolidated) Act (1985). A company registered under this Act has limited liability: its owners (the shareholders) have no financial liability in the event of winding up the affairs of the company, but they might lose the money already invested in it. *Ltd* after the company's name signifies *limited*, and *PLC* (*public limited company*) indicates that its shares are widely held. In the USA, companies are registered in a particular state – Delaware being especially favoured – and become *Incorporated* (*Inc*). » corporation tax; dividend; holding company; horizontal integration

comparative history A form of historical enquiry reacting against an excessive concentration on accounts of national development. Comparative historians usually study the development of different societies within a similar period. Their techniques can be used, for example, to help explain why Britain industrialized in the late 18th-c and early 19th-c, when European competitors did not. More recently, some comparative studies have looked at similar phenomena across very different periods. For example, attempts have been made to identify the similarities between European peasant societies in the later Middle Ages, and underdeveloped agrarian societies in Africa and India in the 20th-c. It is characteristic of comparative history that it tends to concentrate on specific themes or problems, rather than attempting to provide narrative accounts of the societies studied. » history

comparative linguistics The comparison of the features of different languages or dialects, or the different historical states of a language. In the 19th-c, the concern was exclusively historical, as linguists explored the similarities and differences between languages, and tried to set up common antecedents on the basis of the correspondences they observed to exist between their sounds. In this way, Greek, Latin, and the Germanic languages were all shown to belong to the Indo-European language family. This field of study was known as **comparative philology**, and the process of deducing the characteristics of the antecedent or parent language as *internal reconstruction*. » linguistics; sound law

comparative literature The study of literature across national and linguistic boundaries. This developed during the 19th-c in the spirit of Schlegel's *Universalpoesie* and Goethe's *Weltliteratur*, and studies by Mme de Staël. Abel François Villemain

(1790–1870) introduced the term *littérature comparée* in 1829; it was taken up by Sainte-Beuve, and there are clear influences on Matthew Arnold in his pursuit of 'the best that is known and thought in the world'. During the 20th-c, comparative literature has been cultivated especially in Europe and the USA, its admixture of historical and synthetic methods producing some fine works of scholarship and interpretation. Notable contributions have been made by Rene Wellek (1903–), Leo Spitzer (1887–1960), Erich Auerbach (1892–1957), and George Steiner (1929–). There are several journals devoted to the discipline. » Arnold, Matthew; Goethe; literary criticism; literature; Sainte-Beuve; Schlegel; Staël

comparative method In anthropology, initially an attempt to locate individual human societies within the framework of an evolutionary history of mankind. The aim was to classify societies into types, corresponding to a particular evolutionary level. The term may now apply to any method for comparing different cultures or social institutions. » anthropology

comparative philology » **comparative linguistics**

comparative psychology Studies of the differences among animal (including human) species in behaviour and psychological capacities. It is traditionally concerned with attempts to rank groups of vertebrates in terms of 'intelligence', and to relate intelligence to relative brain size and other characteristics. However, it is now accepted that different species cannot be ordered on a single scale of intelligence, but that each species' capacities partly reflect specialized adaptations to particular environmental conditions. » ethology; intelligence

comparative religion The objective investigation of the religions of the world by scientific and historical methods. Its approach is descriptive and comparative, and is not concerned with questions of the truth or falsity of the beliefs it examines. Friedrich Max Müller (1823–1917), often called 'the father of comparative religion', did much to bring a knowledge of the world's religions to the notice of the English-speaking world. The discipline has contributed greatly to our knowledge of religions by identifying recurring patterns of belief and practice among religions widely separated by culture and geography, as well as by indicating what is distinctive in each religion. » religion

compass A device for determining a horizontal geographical direction or bearing. The **magnetic compass** depends on a magnet, free to rotate in a horizontal plane locating itself in line with the Earth's magnetic field. It is subject to the irregularity and to the short- and long-period variation of the Earth's field. » gyrocompass [i]; magnetic field [i]

compensatory education A form of enrichment for learners thought in some way to be deprived. It was specially popular during the 1960s in US programmes such as Project Head Start, or British initiatives such as the establishment of educational or social priority areas. The emphasis was often on the development of language and communication skills which would help children benefit more from their lessons. The notion was sometimes criticized for not sufficiently respecting the cultural values of the groups at whom it was aimed. » education; Head Start

competence In linguistics, an idealized conception of language, representing the system of grammatical rules which any speaker of a language subconsciously knows. It is contrasted with **performance**, the way in which sentences actually appear, containing 'imperfections' such as hesitations, false starts, and grammatical errors. » communicative competence; linguistics

compiler A computer program which translates (*compiles*) the source code of a high-level computer language program, such as BASIC, into a set of machine-code instructions which can be understood by the central processing unit. Compilers are very large programs, and contain error-checking and other facilities. » program, computer

complementary colour/color Colours located opposite to each other, if the hues of the spectrum are arranged in a circle in their natural order, eg red-green, blue-orange, yellow-violet. » spectrum

complementation (genetics) The process by which two recessive mutant genes at different loci in a chromosome can supply each other's deficiency. An individual carrying both genes (a double heterozygote) appears phenotypically normal. » chromosome [i]; genotype

complex A psychiatric term coined by Jung to indicate a set of feelings or ideas which influence (usually unconsciously) our behaviour and attitudes. The term also refers to a series of childhood fantasies underlying a neurotic process. » inferiority complex; Jung; mental disorders; neurosis; Oedipus complex

complex ion » **co-ordination compounds**

complex number A number that is partly real and partly imaginary (ie contains i, representing the square root of -1). The real part may be zero, and if the imaginary part is also allowed to be zero, real numbers are a subset of the set of complex numbers, so that numbers of the form $2+3i$, $4+5i$ are all considered as complex numbers. In the same way that real numbers are represented on a number-line, complex numbers are represented in a plane, the diagram used being called an *Argand diagram*, after the Swiss mathematician Jean Robert Argand (1768–1822). The complex number $x+iy$ is represented by a point, co-ordinates (x,y). » numbers

component (chemistry) A substance present in a system, regardless of its state of matter. Water will be a single component, whether it is present as a solid, liquid, gas, or some combination of these.

componential analysis In semantics, an approach which analyses words in terms of a series of identifying features or 'components' of meaning. For example, *boy* could be analysed with reference to the components 'male', 'young', and 'human'. » semantics

composite cinematography Motion picture photography involving the combination of images from two or more different sources, typically live actors and miniature or painted settings, or back- and front-projection.

Composite order The most decorative of the five main orders of classical architecture, characterized by the combination of the Ionic volute with the acanthus capital of the Corinthian order. It may have a plain or fluted shaft. » acanthus; capital (architecture); Greek/Roman architecture; orders of architecture [i]

compound In chemistry, an entity with a definite composition, containing atoms of two or more elements. » chemical bond; chemical elements; mixture

comprehensive school A school catering for the whole of the ability range; opposed to a **selective school**, which takes only a section of the population. In countries such as Sweden and the USA, these schools have been commonplace for most of the 20th-c. In other places, such as the UK, the non-selective school did not become widespread until the 1960s. Some countries have no comprehensive schools at all, and others operate both comprehensive and selective schools in different places. According to some definitions, a school would be truly comprehensive only if it really did take all pupils, losing none to private, selective, or special schools. » education; grammar school

compressibility » **bulk modulus**

Compromise of 1850 A US attempt to resolve conflict over the expansion of slavery by legislation. Its major terms were the admission of California as a free state, and the passage of a strong Fugitive Slave Law to placate the South. » American Civil War; slave trade

Compton, Arthur (Holly) (1892–1962) US physicist, born at Wooster, Ohio. Educated at Princeton, he became professor of physics at Chicago (1923), and a leading authority on nuclear energy, X-rays, and quantity production of plutonium. The **Compton effect**, explaining the change in the wavelength of X-rays when they collide with electrons, is named after him. He shared the Nobel Prize for Physics in 1927. He became chancellor of Washington University in 1945, and also professor of natural history there (1953–61). He died at Berkeley, California. » plutonium; X-rays

Compton, Denis (Charles Scott) (1918–) British cricketer, born in London. He played cricket for England 78 times, and scored 5 807 runs at an average of 50.06. His county team was Middlesex. In the 1947 season he scored a record 3 816 runs, including a record 18 centuries. During his career (1936–57) he made 38 942 runs and took 622 wickets. A winger at soccer, he won an England cap during the war years. His career was spent with Arsenal, and along with his brother, Leslie, he won a Football Association Cup winner's medal in 1950. His later career was as a journalist and broadcaster. » cricket (sport) [i]

Compton, Fay (1894–1978) British actress, born in London, daughter of the actor Edward Compton, and sister of Sir Compton Mackenzie. She first appeared on the stage in 1911, and won acclaim in London in *Peter Pan* (1918). She later played many famous parts, especially in plays by Barrie. » Barrie, J M

Compton-Burnett, Ivy (1892–1969) British novelist, born at Pinner, Middlesex. She graduated in classics at London, and became a prolific writer. Her rather stylized novels have many features in common, being set in upper-class Victorian or Edwardian society; the characters usually belong to a large family, spanning several generations. Her first novel was *Pastors and Masters* (1925), later works including *Brothers and Sisters* (1929), and *Mother and Son*. She died in London. » English literature; novel

computational linguistics The application and development of statistical and computational techniques as part of the study of language. Areas of interest include analysing the frequency of occurrence of particular words to investigate the authorship of a text, the use of computers in speech analysis and synthesis, the study of techniques of automatic ('machine') translation, and the development of computational models of linguistic structure and interaction as part of research into artificial intelligence. » artificial intelligence; computer; linguistics; statistics

computer The modern electronic digital computer is the result of a long series of developments, which started some 5 000 years ago with the abacus. The first mechanical adding device was developed in 1642 by the French scientist-philosopher, Pascal. His 'arithmetic machine', was followed by the 'stepped reckoner' invented by Leibnitz in 1671, which was capable of also doing multiplication, division, and the evaluation of square roots by a series of stepped additions, not unlike the methods used in modern digital computers. In 1835, Charles Babbage formulated his concept of an 'analytical machine' which combined arithmetic processes with decisions based on the results of the computations. This was really the forerunner of the modern digital computer, in that it combined the principles of sequential control, branching, looping, and storage units.

In the later 19th-c, George Boole developed the symbolic binary logic which led to Boolean algebra and the binary switching methodology used in modern computers. Herman Hollerith, a US statistician, developed punched card techniques, mainly to aid with the US census at the turn of the century; this advanced the concept of automatic processing, but major developments awaited the availability of suitable electronic devices. J Presper Eckert and John W Manchly produced the first all-electronic digital computer, ENIAC (Electronic Numerical Integrator and Calculator), at the University of Pennsylvania in 1946, which was 1 000 times faster than the mechanical computers. Their development of ENIAC led to one of the first commercial computers, UNIVAC I, in the early 1950s, which was able to handle both numerical and alphabetical information. Very significant contributions were made around this time by Johann von Neumann, who converted the ENIAC principles to give the EDVAC computer (Electronic Discrete Variable Automatic Computer) which could modify its own programs in much the same way as suggested by Babbage.

Advances followed rapidly from the 1950s, and were further accelerated from the mid-1960s by the successful development of miniaturization techniques in the electronics industry. The first microprocessor, which might be regarded as a computer on a chip, appeared in 1971, and nowadays the power of even the most modest personal computer can equal or outstrip the early electronic computers of the 1940s. » analog computer; Babbage; Boole; computer science; digital computer; electronics; hacker; Leibniz; mainframe computer; memory, computer; Neumann, Johann von; Pascal; program, computer

computer-aided design (CAD) The use of computers in various design activities, such as designing the interconnections on printed circuit boards and optimizing the aerodynamic shapes of aeroplanes. CAD makes great use of computer graphics, and generally requires relatively fast computers. » computer; computer graphics

computer-aided instruction (CAI) The use of computers as teaching aids or substitute teachers. Through the use of suitable programs the computer can provide information, ask questions, react appropriately to the student's response, and score multiple-choice tests. It is also known as **computer-assisted learning** (CAL). » computer; Skinner

computer-aided manufacture (CAM) The use of computers in controlling and supervising various manufacturing activities, usually involving robotics, such as the assembly of complex mechanical units and the welding or spraying of motor cars. CAM forms the basis of the fully automatic production line. » computer

computer art An art style begun after 1945 when wartime analogue computers were adapted to make abstract drawings; for example, the work of English artist and philosopher, Desmond Paul Henry (1921–), included in the 'Cybernetic Serendipity' exhibition, London, 1968. However, since the mid-1960s, modern digital computers have been used to produce drawings, paintings, and even sculpture (eg Charles Csuri, Robert Mallory). Typically, the artist designs programmes, which may include some randomizing element, and the results are printed out by machine; but it is possible to incorporate light and sound input, and frequently the artist intervenes during the production of the image. » abstract art; art; computer

computer generations Different eras of technical development of digital computers, defined as different 'generations'. **First-generation** computers were the early devices in the 1940s and 1950s, built using thermionic valves. **Second-generation** computers replaced these valves by discrete transistors. **Third-generation** computers replaced transistors by integrated circuits. **Fourth-generation** computers were built with very large integrated circuits (VLSI). **Fifth-generation** computers are those showing artificial intelligence with which we can communicate in natural language. » artificial intelligence; integrated circuit; thermionic valve; transistor

computer graphics The use of computers to display information in graphical or pictorial form, usually on a visual display unit (VDU), a printer, or a plotter. Computer graphics are now used in an increasing number of applications, ranging from the manipulation of highly detailed engineering drawings to computer games, from high definition views in aircraft simulators to automatic production of animated film, even indeed as an art form in its own right. Computer graphics can make very heavy demands on computing power, and many of the faster computers have been designed with graphics very much in mind. » computer; graphics tablet; X-Y plotter; Plate XVI

computer memory » **memory, computer**

computer music The use of computers to compose, arrange, modify, or synthesize musical sounds. The advent of digital computers has greatly extended the potential of electronic music, both in popular and classical fields. » computer; electronic music

computer peripheral Any device which can be connected to a computer. Examples include printers, magnetic disks, visual display units, and plotters. The peripheral may be an input device or an output device. » computer; input-output device

computer program » **program, computer**

computer science The whole area of knowledge associated with the use and study of computers and computer-based processes. It encompasses computer design and programming, and inter-computer communication, and intersects with a number of other established disciplines such as mathematics, information theory, and electronic engineering. » computer; information theory

computer virus A term applied to computer programs which can spread from computer to computer, usually via shared software, and damage other programs stored on the computers. The 'virus' program is often attached, by the human perpetrator, to a genuine program and is not readily detectable. » program, computer

computerized axial tomography (CAT) A medical X-ray scanning technique which makes a series of pictures that are then reconstructed by computer programs to represent a 'slice' through the patient. The X-ray tube rotates round the patient and produces images in sequence on a number of detectors. The system has been developed since the 1970s and nowadays it is possible to produce multicoloured images showing great detail. The data stored in the computer can be further analysed in many different ways to produce information about a variety of tissues. These machines are now widely available, and have a special use in setting up radiotherapy treatment for precise action on small target areas in the patient. » computer; radiotherapy; X-rays

Comte, Auguste (1798–1857) French philosopher and sociologist, the founder of Positivism, born at Montpellier. He studied for a while at Paris, and was for some years a disciple of Saint-Simon. He published his lectures on positivist philosophy in six volumes (1830–42). He taught mathematics privately, and in his later years was supported by his friends. His *Système de politique positive* (1851–4, System of Positive Polity, 4 vols), shows the influence of his brief relationship with Clothilde de Vaux. In his philosophy, all sciences are regarded as having passed through a theological and then a metaphysical stage into a positive or experiential stage; the sociological development is from militarism to industrialism. In positive religion, the object of reverence is humanity, and the aim the well-being and progress of the race. He died in Paris. » Saint-Simon, Comte de

Conakry [**ko**nakree] 9°30N 13°43W, pop (1980) 763 000. Seaport capital of Guinea, W Africa; on Tumbo island, 710 km/441 ml SE of Dakar (Senegal); linked to the mainland by a causeway; established in 1889; airport; railway terminus; technical college (1963); textiles, trade in fruit, iron ore, alumina. » Guinea [i]

Conan Doyle, Arthur » **Doyle, Arthur Conan**

concentration In chemistry, the number of atoms, molecules, or ions of a substance present in a given volume. It is generally measured in moles per litre or per cubic metre. » mole (physics)

concentration camp A detention centre for political prisoners; known primarily from the camps established in Germany soon after the Nazi seizure of power, which were administered with extreme cruelty. The coming of war swelled the camp population with millions of Jews, Gypsies, slave workers, Soviet prisoners-of-war, and other 'enemies of the state'. Following the Wannsee Conference of 1942, which plotted the destruction of European Jewry, the concentration camps established in Poland, such as Auschwitz and Treblinka, became purpose-made extermination centres in which over 6 million Jews died. » Nazi Party

Concepción [konsep**syohn**] 36°49S 73°03W, pop (1982) 206 107. Industrial capital of Concepción province, C Chile; 15 km/9 ml up the R Bío-Bío; third largest city in Chile; founded, 1550; often damaged by earthquakes; airfield; railway; university (1919); coal, steel, textiles, paper, oil refining, ship repairing; Cerro Caracol (SE), with major views at Mirador Chileno and Mirador Alemán; craft fair (Feb). » Chile [i]

Conceptual Art A movement, dating from the 1960s, where the artist, instead of producing a physical object (eg a painted canvas) presents ideas, often in the form of a written text, a map, or a sound cassette. For example, Claes Oldenburg (1929–) had a hole dug in Central Park, New York, then had it filled in again. Others have buried themselves, the event being recorded by photographs taken at various stages. » art; earthworks; happening

conceptualism In philosophy, any theory about universals which maintains that they are concepts, existing only in the mind; acquired, in the case of empirical properties and relations, by abstraction from sense experience. Conceptualists claim, for example, that although there are many red things in nature, there is no redness independent of minds.

concertina A portable reed organ similar in principle to the accordion, but hexagonal in vertical cross-section, smaller, and without a keyboard. The English type, fully chromatic, was patented in 1844: it was largely superseded by the fully developed piano accordion early in the 20th-c. » accordion; reed organ

concertino [konsher**tee**noh] **1** A musical work for soloist(s) and orchestra, shorter than a concerto and usually with a lighter accompaniment. » concerto **2** The solo group in a concerto grosso. » concerto grosso

concerto A musical work for one or more solo instruments and orchestra. The earliest examples, such as those written by Corelli in the 1680s, were of the concerto grosso type, contrasting two instrumental groups of unequal size. The early concerto with a single soloist is associated above all with Vivaldi, whose three-movement form (fast–slow–fast) was adopted by J S Bach, and remained standard in the concertos of Mozart, Beethoven, and most later composers. The cult of virtuosity in the 19th-c placed most Romantic concertos (such as those for piano or violin by Liszt, Brahms, Tchaikovsky, and Rachmaninov) beyond the capabilities of all but the most brilliant technicians, but some 20th-c composers (such as Bloch and Stravinsky) have treated the soloist more as 'first among equals' in the Baroque manner, while others (such as Bartók and Kodály) have written 'concertos for orchestra' in which the orchestral instruments are treated as soloists in turn. » Baroque (music); cadenza; concertino; concerto grosso; movement; Bach, Johann Sebastian; Beethoven; Corelli, Arcangelo; Mozart; Vivaldi

concerto grosso A musical work in which a small group of instruments (*concertino*: typically two violins and cello) is contrasted with the full string orchestra (*ripieno*). The Baroque concerto grosso, in four or more movements, was cultivated with particular distinction by Corelli and Handel. It later declined in favour of the solo concerto, but the title of 'concerto grosso' has been used by some 20th-c composers (such as Bloch) for works based in some measure on Baroque models. » Baroque (music); concerto; Corelli, Arcangelo; Handel

conch A large marine snail found in shallow seas around coral reefs; the queen conch, *Strombus gigas*, is abundant in the Caribbean, and is gathered for food and the curio trade. (Class: *Gastropoda*. Order: *Mesogastropoda*.) » snail

conchoid In geometry, a curve used in early investigations of the problems of trisecting an angle and duplicating a cube. If O is a fixed point and l a fixed straight line, through any point P on l draw the line OP produced beyond P. On this line mark points Q, Q' each a distance b from P. As P moves on l, Q and Q' describe a conchoid. If instead of a straight line l, we use a circle through O, we obtain a different curve (a *limaçon*) $r = b + a \cos \theta$. » angle; geometry

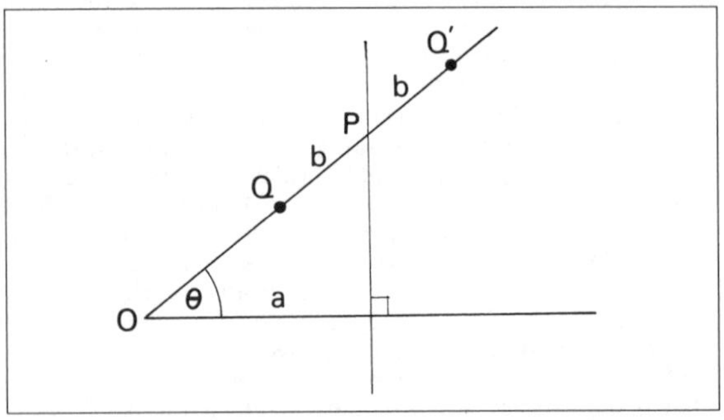

A conchoid: QP = PQ'

conciliarism The theory that the General Council (consisting of all bishops) has supreme authority in the Church. It gained prominence in disputes concerning the authority of the papacy in the W Church in the Middle Ages, but declined after 1460 when Pope Pius II forbade appeals from a pope to a General Council. Interest revived with the recognition of corporate or collegial authority of bishops at the Second Vatican Council (1962–6). » bishop; Council of the Church; papacy; Vatican Councils

conclave (Lat **cum clave**, 'with a key') A meeting of cardinals of the Roman Catholic Church. Its original purpose was to elect a pope; by a tradition dating from 1271, the cardinals are locked into an apartment to hasten election. » cardinal (religion); pope

Concord (Massachusetts) 42°28N 71°21W, pop (1980) 16293. Town in Middlesex county, E Massachusetts, USA; on the Concord R, 8 km/5 ml WNW of Boston; railway; in April 1775 British soldiers attempted to seize military stores in Concord but were resisted by minutemen; battles at Concord (19 Apr) and Lexington marked the start of the American War of Independence; home of Alcott, Emerson, Hawthorne, and Thoreau. » Alcott; American Revolution; Emerson, Ralph Waldo; Hawthorne; Thoreau

Concord (New Hampshire) 43°12N 71°32W, pop (1980) 30400. Capital of New Hampshire state, USA; in Merrimack County, S New Hampshire, on the Merrimack R; established, 1727; city status, 1853; state capital, 1808; railway; New Hampshire Technical Institute (1964); electrical goods; home of Mary Baker Eddy. » Eddy; New Hampshire

Concorde The world's first (and only remaining) supersonic airliner, built jointly by the British Aircraft Corporation and the French company, Aerospatiale. It entered full-time operational service in January 1976. Its maximum speed is 2.2 times the speed of sound, though normal cruising speed is reduced to twice the speed of sound, ie c.2000 kph/1300 mph. The maximum range is c.6400 km/4000 ml, and the time taken to cross the Atlantic is 3½ hours. » aircraft [i]

concrete art Defined by the Dutch artist Theo van Doesburg (1883–1931) in 1930 as a totally abstract art 'constructed entirely from purely plastic elements, that is to say planes and colours'. After van Doesburg's death, the term was used by Max Bill (1908–) and Jean Arp (1887–1966), Bill staging several exhibitions, such as in Zurich in 1964. » abstract art; art; Constructivism

concrete music » **musique concrète**

concrete poetry Poetry which emphasizes the visual presentation of the poem on the page. Classical inscriptions provide a model, and 17th-c emblem poems are simple examples; Lewis Carroll's 'Mouse' in Alice is more playful. The French poets Mallarmé (*Un Coup de dès*, 1897), and Apollinaire (*Calligrammes*, 1918) considerably extended visual techniques. Later experiments (notably in S America) have been very various, including the use of different typefaces, colour, collage, and more recently computer graphics. » Apollinaire; computer graphics; French/Latin-American literature; Mallarmé; poetry

concussion A state of reversible unconsciousness which may immediately follow a severe blow to the head, but which outlasts the trauma. On regaining consciousness there is no memory of the accident or of immediately preceding events (*retrograde amnesia*). There is no gross damage to the brain, but microscopic examination reveals some reversible neuronal damage.

Condé [kõday] The junior branch of the French royal line, the House of Bourbon, which played a prominent role in French dynastic politics, particularly in the 16th–17th-c. Ten generations bore the title of *Prince de Condé*, the most eminent being Louis II de Bourbon (1621–86), better known as the *Great Condé*. » Bourbons; Condé, Louis I/II

Condé, Louis I de Bourbon, Prince de ('Prince of') (1530–69) Leader of the Huguenots during the French Wars of Religion, born at Vendôme, the younger brother of Antony of Bourbon, King of Navarre. He fought in the wars between Henry II and Spain (1551–7), and joined the Huguenots on the accession of Francis II (1559). He was defeated at Dreux during the first civil war (1562); and in the second war (1567–9), was defeated at Jarnac, taken prisoner, and shot. » Condé; Huguenots; Religion, Wars of

Condé, Louis II de Bourbon, Prince de ('Prince of') (1621–86) French military leader, known as 'the Great Condé', born in Paris. During the Thirty Years' War he defeated the Spaniards (1643, 1648) and Bavarians (1645–6). The court party came to terms with the Fronde by his help; but his arrogance led to his imprisonment, and when he was released he joined the rebels. Defeated at the Battle of the Dunes, near Dunkirk (1658), he was then pardoned, and became one of Louis XIV's greatest generals, defeating the Spanish in Franche-Comté (1668) and William of Orange at Seneffe (1674). Ill health led to his retirement to Chantilly, where he died. » Condé; Frondes, the; Louis XIV; Thirty Years' War

condensation (chemistry) The combination of two or more substances to form a product, with the elimination of a relatively small side-product. *Condensation polymerization* usually involves the elimination of water, and is important in the production of synthetic fabrics of the polyester and polyamide varieties. » polyamides; polyesters

condensation (physics) The process by which water changes from a gaseous state (*water vapour*) to a liquid state. It occurs either when a parcel of air becomes saturated, or is cooled to below its dew point temperature. Cooling can result from uplift of air, radiation cooling on a calm cloudless night, or when warm moist air comes into contact with a cooler surface. In such situations, vapour condenses around condensation nuclei, such as salt, dust, and smoke particles in the air. When condensation occurs at altitude, clouds form; close to the ground, it results in fog or dew. » atmospheric physics; cloud [i]; cloud chamber; dew; dew point temperature; fog; precipitation

condensed matter physics » **solid-state physics**

Condillac, Etienne Bonnot de [kõdeeyak] (1715–80) French philosopher, born at Grenoble. He was ordained a Catholic priest in 1740, and became a tutor to the Duke of Parma, and Abbé de Mureaux. He based all knowledge on the senses, his works including *Essai sur l'origine des connaissances humaines* (1746, Essay on the Origin of Human Knowledge) and *Traité des sensations* (1754, Treatise on Sensations). He died at Flux.

condition In law, a relatively important term in a contract. Breach of condition gives the innocent party the right to treat the contract as at an end. A less important term in a contract is a **warranty**. Breach of a warranty does not give the innocent party the right to end the contract, though a claim for damages may be possible. In US contract law, a condition usually specifies some uncertain future event which, if it occurs, will trigger, terminate, or modify the contractual obligations. » contract; damages

conditioning Two types of elementary associative learning process, seen in many invertebrates and all vertebrates. **1** In **Pavlovian**, **classical**, or **respondent conditioning**, a stimulus which reliably precedes another stimulus of biological significance (eg food, pain, a potential mate) comes to evoke a new pattern of reaction (a *conditioned response*) similar to that evoked by the biologically significant (*unconditioned*) stimulus. For example, salivation, normally evoked by the taste of food, comes to be evoked by the sight of food or the sound of a dinner gong. **2** In **instrumental** or **operant conditioning**, an individual's action reliably causes a change in stimulation of biological significance, and this alters the way the individual performs the action. If the consequence is an increase in a 'positive' stimulus, such as food, or a decrease in a 'negative' stimulus, such as pain, the action is performed more frequently than before; if the consequences are of the opposite kind, the action will be performed less frequently. An example would be waiting for a pigeon to select a particularly coloured object from a group of objects, and then rewarding (eg with food) this random event; in due course, if repeated, the pigeon will selectively pick out only objects of the colour rewarded. » aversion therapy; learning; Pavlov; Skinner

condominium In government, the joint rule, tenancy, or co-ownership of a territory by two or more countries, often suggested as appropriate where ownership of a territory is disputed. For example, the former New Hebrides (now the republic of Vanuatu) was, until 1980, jointly administered by Britain and France.

condor Either of two species of New World vulture; the **Californian condor** (*Gymnogyps californianus*) and the **Andean condor** (*Vultur gryphus*). The Andean condor, which inhabits the mountains, has the largest wingspan of any living bird (up to 3 m/10 ft). The Californian condor is in danger of extinction. (Family: *Cathartidae*.) >> bird of prey; vulture

Condorcet, Marie Jean Antoine Nicolas de Caritat, Marquis de [kõdorsay] (1743–94) French statesman, philosopher, and mathematician, born at Ribemont. He studied at Paris, and his work in mathematics became highly regarded in the 1760s. At the Revolution he made eloquent speeches and wrote famous pamphlets on the popular side, was sent to the Legislative Assembly (1791), and became its president, siding usually with the Girondists. Accused and condemned by the extreme party, he was captured, and found dead in prison, at Bourg-la-Reine. In his philosophy, he proclaimed the ideal of progress, and the indefinite perfectibility of the human race. >> French Revolution [i]; Girondins

condottiere [kondot**tyay**ray] A leader of mercenary soldiers in 14th–15th-c Italy; from Italian *condotta* 'contract'. Hired by city-states and the papacy, they were often of foreign origin (eg Englishman Sir John Hawkwood or Giovanni Acuto), but they also included Italian noblemen (eg the d'Este dukes of Ferrara, Gonzaga marquises of Mantua, and Sforza dukes of Milan).

conductance >> **resistance**

conduction >> **electrical conduction; thermal conduction**

conductivity >> **resistivity**

condyloma [kondi**loh**ma] A localized cauliflower-like lesion or overgrowth of the epidermis in moist parts of the body, such as the vulva and around the anus. Condylomata result from infection with the virus that causes warts in drier regions of the body. >> virus; wart

cone In gymnosperms, a spike-like structure formed of woody, overlapping scales bearing seeds. Clubmosses and horsetails have similar structures bearing spores. The term is also used for the cone-like fruits of some flowering plants. >> clubmoss; gymnosperms; horsetail; seed; spore

cone shell A typically predatory marine snail; length up to 30 cm/12 in; its shell has a pronounced canal for a front-placed organ (siphon) for drawing in fluid; over 400 species, many producing poison to paralyse prey; occasionally causes human fatalities. (Class: *Gastropoda*. Order: *Neogastropoda*.) >> gastropod; snail

coneflower >> **rudbeckia**

cones >> **rods and cones**

coney >> **pika; rabbit**

Coney Island [**koh**nee] (Dutch 'rabbit'), 40°35N 73°59W. Resort on the S coast of Long Island in Brooklyn borough, New York State, USA; S of New York City, near the mouth of the Hudson R; developed as a pleasure resort since the 1840s; New York Aquarium. >> Long Island; New York

Confederacy >> **Confederate States of America**

Confederate States of America The official name of the states that seceded in 1860–1, precipitating the American Civil War: Virginia, N Carolina, S Carolina, Georgia, Florida, Tennessee, Alabama, Mississippi, Louisiana, Texas, and Arkansas. The Confederacy's constitution was modelled on the US Constitution, and its only president was Jefferson Davis of Mississippi. It never won foreign recognition, and collapsed in 1865. The other four slave states (Delaware, Maryland, Kentucky, and Missouri) did not secede, and neither did the NW counties of Virginia, which became West Virginia. >> American Civil War; Davis, Jefferson; slave trade

Confederation, Articles of >> **Articles of Confederation**

Confederation of British Industry (CBI) A federation of UK employers, founded in 1965, with a membership of some 250 000 companies. Its role is to ensure that the needs, intentions, and problems of business organizations are generally understood. It carries out surveys and research into matters affecting business, and expresses opinions to government on matters that affect its members.

Confederation of the Rhine (1806–14) A union of all the German states except Prussia and Austria, established by Napoleon I on the dissolution of the Holy Roman Empire in 1806. The 18 states were placed under French control to assist the French war effort, although the long-term effect was to stimulate the movement for German unification. >> Napoleonic Wars

Confessing Church A Church formed in Germany by Evangelical Christians opposed to Nazism and the Nazi-supported 'German Christian Church Movement'. Its Synod of Barmen published the *Barmen Declaration* (1934), which became influential in Germany and beyond as a basis for resistance to oppressive civil authorities. It was succeeded in 1948 by the 'Evangelical Church in Germany'. >> Barth, Karl; Christianity; evangelicalism; Nazi Party

confession 1 A declaration or profession of faith, originally by an individual martyr, later by a group or church. Such a document became common after the Reformation. >> Augsburg Confession; Westminster Confession of Faith; martyr; Reformation 2 An acknowledgment of sin, made either corporately in the course of public worship or privately and individually as *auricular* confession, 'into the ear' of a priest. >> priest; sin;

confessional poetry Poetry which takes as its subject the intimate details of the poet's own life, often disparaged by critics for this reason. Generally considered a recent phenomenon, it has been encouraged by US poets such as Robert Lowell and Sylvia Plath; but the songs of Sappho (6th-c BC) and the sonnets of Shakespeare (1598) indicate that lyric poetry at all times has included confessional elements. >> Lowell, Robert; Plath; poetry; Sappho; Shakespeare [i]

confinement In particle physics, the postulate that quarks and gluons interact in such a way that they are always constrained to remain inside sub-atomic particles, and so may never be observed directly. It was proposed to account for the continuing failure to observe quarks directly. Understanding the nature of confinement continues to present difficulties. >> gluon; particle physics; quark

confirmation (logic) In inductive inferences, a premiss tends to confirm the conclusion if the truth of the premiss would make the conclusion more probable. Confirmation has degrees: 'All elephants in Asia and Africa are grey' is stronger than 'All elephants in Asia are grey' for confirming 'All elephants are grey'. >> induction; inference

confirmation (religion) The Christian sacrament of initiation, the nature and theology of which have been understood in varying ways in Christian history. In early usage, it was difficult to distinguish baptism from confirmation as acts of initiation into Christian belief, but by the Middle Ages there was a tendency in the West to separate the two, so that confirmation was performed only by the laying on of hands (or by anointing with oil, or both) by a bishop. Children are not usually confirmed before reaching 7 years of age, and many Churches prefer them to reach adolescence. In Anglicanism it is often seen as the young person assuming personal responsibility for earlier baptismal vows. The Second Vatican Council ordered that the rite should be revised so as to emphasize more clearly its character of initiation. >> baptism; Christianity; sacrament

conformation In chemistry, the arrangement of atoms of a molecule relative to other atoms to which they are not bonded. For example, the structure of ethane (shown at **ethane**) illustrates its most stable conformation, in which the hydrogen atoms interact as little as possible. >> ethane [i]; molecule

conforming In film and video production, the final assembly of original material to match the approved continuity resulting from editing. With films this is done by the physical cutting and joining of the picture negative, while in video it involves the transfer of selected portions of the original videotapes in sequence to form the master record. >> editing

Confucianism The oldest school of Chinese thought, Confucianism has two ethical strands. One, associated with Confucius and Hsün Tzu (c.298–238 BC), is conventionalistic; we ought to follow traditional codes of behaviour for their own sake. The other, associated with Mencius and the mediaeval Neo-Confucians, is intuitionistic; we ought to do as our moral natures dictate. >> Confucius; Mencius

Confucius, Latin for **K'ung Fu-tse**, 'the Master K'ung' (551–479 BC) Chinese philosopher, born and died in the state of Lu (modern Shantung). Largely self-educated, he married at 19, became a local administrator, and in 531 BC began his career as a teacher. In 501 he was appointed Governor of Chung-tu, then Minister of Works, and later Minister of Justice. His ideas for social reform made him the idol of the people; but his enemies caused him to leave Lu, and he travelled widely, followed by many disciples. He later edited the ancient writings, and the *Confucian Analects*, memorabilia compiled soon after his death, are a collection of his sayings and doings. His moral teaching stressed the importance of the traditional relations of filial piety and brotherly respect. » Confucianism

conga An Afro-Cuban dance usually performed (often with singing) in a long line, using simple and repetitive steps. It was popular in Western ballrooms in the mid-20th-c.

congenital abnormality An anatomical abnormality or malformation found at birth or within a few weeks of birth. It may be so severe as to be incompatible with life, such as failure of the brain to grow (*anencephaly*). Some disorders result from chromosome abnormalities or genetic defects. Others arise from environmental factors, such as infections (eg rubella), drugs given to the mother (eg thalidomide), or sporadic faults in development: these include the failure of testicles to descend, malformation of the heart, and short or rudimentary arms or legs. » achondroplasia; cleft lip and palate; club foot; genetically determined disease; spina bifida

conger eel Predatory marine fish found in shallow coastal waters of N Europe and Mediterranean, usually within cover of rocks, jetties, or wrecks; body cylindrical, length up to 2.7 m/8¾ ft; jaws powerful, teeth conical and close set; feeds mainly on fishes, crustaceans, and cephalopods; may be dangerous to divers. (*Conger conger*. Family: *Congridae*.)

conglomerate (mineralogy) Sedimentary rock composed of rounded pebbles of pre-existing rocks and embedded in a fine matrix of sand and silt. It is commonly formed along beaches or on river beds.

conglomerate (economics) A company owning a variety of different business activities which have little or nothing in common. The advantage is that the risk can be shared, so that even if one business is faring badly, another activity, which is doing well, helps the firm to survive. The disadvantage of such companies is that they often do not produce outstanding results for their shareholders.

Congo [**kong**goh], official name **Republic of the Congo**, Fr **République du Congo** pop (1990e) 2 326 000; area 341 945 sq km/ 132 000 sq ml. WC African republic, divided into nine provinces; bounded W by Gabon, NW by Cameroon, N by Central African Republic, E and S by Zaire, and SW by the Atlantic Ocean; encloses Angolan province of Cabinda (apart from its coast); capital, Brazzaville; chief towns, Pointe-Noire (port), Loubomo, N'Kayi; timezone GMT +1; c.15 main ethnic groups, notably the Kongo (48%), Sangha (20%), M'Bochi (12%), and Téké (17%); main religions, Christian (40.5% Roman Catholic, 9.5% Protestant) and local beliefs (47%); official language, French; unit of currency, the franc CFA.

Physical description and climate. Short Atlantic coastline fringing a broad mangrove plain; rises inland to a ridge of mountains reaching 900 m/2 950 ft, deeply cut by R Congo flowing SW to coast; beyond this ridge, Niari valley rises up through terraced hills to reach 1 040 m/3 412 ft at Mont de la Lékéti on Gabon frontier; mainly covered by dense grassland, mangrove, and forest; several rivers flow E and S to meet the Oubangui and Congo Rivers, which form E and S borders; hot, humid equatorial climate; annual rainfall 1 250–1 750 mm/50–70 in, decreasing near Atlantic coast and in S; temperatures vary little, Brazzaville average daily maximum 28–33°C; dry season (Jun–Sep).

History and government. Visited by Portuguese, 14th-c; French established colonial presence, 19th-c; part of French Equatorial Africa, known as 'Middle Congo', 1908–58; independence as Republic of Congo, 1960; military coup created first Marxist state in Africa, renamed People's Republic of the Congo, 1968; 1979 constitution provided for an executive president elected for a 5-year term, assisted by a Council of Ministers, 60-member Central Committee, and 133-member National Assembly.

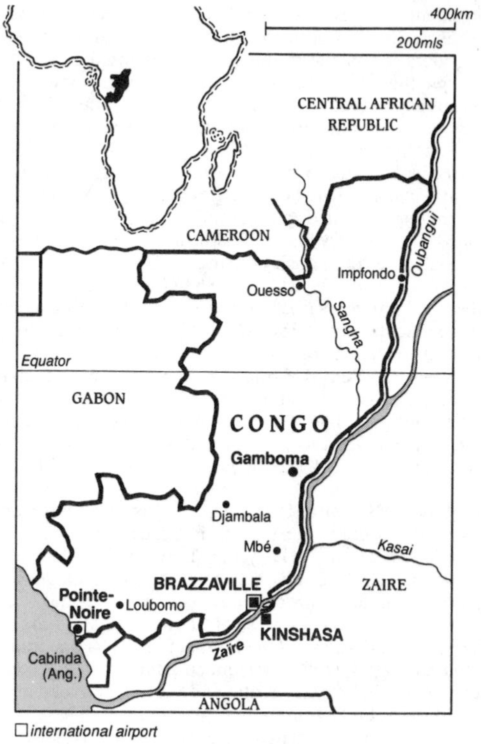

Economy. Based on agriculture and forestry; main cash crops, sugar cane, coffee, cocoa, palm oil, tobacco, groundnuts; main subsistence crops, manioc, rice, yams, potatoes, maize, bananas; oil, timber, diamonds, lead, zinc, gold, potash, cement; oil refining, timber processing, brewing, sugar refining, soap. » Brazzaville; RR25 national holidays; RR46 political leaders

Congo, River » Zaire, River

Congonhas [kon**goh**nyas] 23°38S 46°38W, pop (1980) 22 623. A town in the Brazilian highlands, noted for its 18th-c Sanctuary of Bom ('good') Jesus, an imposing church with chapels and gardens; a world heritage site. The sanctuary, which contains Antonio Francisco Lisboa's (1738–1814) sculptures of the 12 Apostles, is a major centre of pilgrimage. » Brazil [i]

Congregationalism A movement which sees the Christian Church as essentially a gathered community of believers, covenanting with God, keeping God's law, and living under the Lordship of Christ. It derived from the Separatists of the 16th-c Reformation in England, of whom Robert Browne was an early leader. Persecution drove the Congregationalists to Holland and the USA (the Pilgrim Fathers, 1620). Church affairs, including calling a minister and appointing deacons to assist, are regulated by members at a 'Church Meeting'. As a world denomination, it has a strong missionary tradition. One denomination formed the International Congregational Council in 1949, which merged with Presbyterians as the World Alliance of Reformed Churches in 1970. With a strong tradition of tolerance and freedom of belief, its major contribution to ecumenism has been its insistence on the importance of the local church in the event of union with other denominations. » Browne, Robert; Christianity; ecumenism; missions, Christian; Pilgrim Fathers; Presbyterianism; Reformation

Congress The national, or federal, legislature of the USA, consisting of two elected chambers: the Senate and the House of Representatives. Unusually powerful for a modern legislature, Congress can initiate legislation, and significantly amend or reject presidential legislative proposals. The constitution endows it with the 'power of the purse', as all revenue bills must originate in the House. For a bill to become law it must be passed in identical form by both chambers and signed by the president. A presidential veto may be overturned by a two-thirds majority in both chambers. Legislation receives detailed consideration in the powerful Congressional committees. Although the chambers are organized along party lines, party discipline is weak. The majority party leader of the House occupies the influential position of Speaker. » House of Representatives; Senate

Congress Kingdom of Poland The name of that part of Poland given to Russia at the Congress of Vienna (1815). Tsar Alexander I granted a constitution (Nov 1815) which established the country as a constitutional monarchy united to Russia. After the Polish uprising of 1830 the constitution was suspended, and after that of 1863 Congress Poland was fully absorbed into the Russian Empire and subjected to a campaign of russification. » Poland, Partitions of; Russian history; Vienna, Congress of

Congress of Racial Equality A prominent US civil rights organization which campaigns for the rights of Blacks, and which was particularly involved in the attack on discrimination and racism in the 1960s. It still exists, and is regarded as one of the more militant Black rights organizations. » Black power; civil rights

Congreve, William (1670–1729) English dramatist and poet, born at Bardsey, Yorkshire. Educated at Trinity College, Dublin, he became a lawyer in London, but then took up a career in literature. His first comedy, *The Old Bachelor*, was produced under Dryden's auspices in 1693, and was highly successful, as were *The Double Dealer* (1693), *Love for Love* (1695), and *The Way of the World* (1700). His one tragedy, *The Mourning Bride* (1697), was much admired by his contemporaries. He largely ceased writing after 1700, and died in London. » Dryden; English literature

congruence In mathematics, a type of equivalence between expressions. Numbers b and c are said to be congruent relative to a number a if a divides the difference of b and c: a is called the *modulus* (mod) of the congruence. We write $b \equiv c \bmod a$, eg $12 \equiv 2 \bmod 5$. The algebra of congruences was devised by Gauss. » algebra; congruent triangles; Gauss

congruent triangles Triangles such that one could be superimposed on the other. Two triangles are congruent if either (1) each side of one triangle is equal to a side of the other; or (2) each of two sides of one triangle is equal to the corresponding side of the other, and the angles between the two sides are equal; or (3) one side of one triangle is equal to a side of the other triangle, and two angles of one are equal to two angles of the other; or (4) each triangle contains a right angle, the hypotenuses are equal, and one other side of one triangle is equal to the corresponding side of the other. » angle; geometry; triangle (mathematics)

conic sections The figure in which a plane cuts a right circular double cone. Several cases arise: (1) If the plane passes through the vertex V of the cone, it may cut the cone in a single point V (*a*), or in two straight lines (*b*) through V, generators of the cone. (2) If the plane is at right angles perpendicular to the axis of the cone, and not through V, it cuts the cone in a circle (*e*). (3) If the plane is parallel to a generator of the cone, it cuts the cone in a parabola (*d*); otherwise it cuts the cone in an ellipse (*f*) or a hyperbola (*c*).

conifer A cone-bearing tree; strictly, any member of the gymnosperm order *Coniferales*, which includes pines, cypresses, and monkey-puzzles, but sometimes loosely used to include all gymnosperms except cycads. » cycad; cypress; gymnosperms; monkey-puzzle; pine

Coniston Water [**kon**istn] Lake in the Lake District of Cumbria, NW England; W of L Windermere and Grizedale Forest; length 9 km/6 ml; village of Coniston on NW shore; on E shore is Brantwood, former home of John Ruskin; Old Man of Coniston rises to 802 m/2 631 ft in the W; scene of world water speed record by Malcolm Campbell in 1939; Donald Campbell killed here in 1967 trying to break this record. » Campbell, Malcolm; Lake District; Ruskin

conjugation (biology) A process of sexual reproduction during which individuals of the same species but different mating types (*strains*) pair and exchange limited amounts of genetic material. It is found in unicellular micro-organisms, such as bacteria and protozoans. Conjugation is also used to describe related processes, such as the union of similarly-sized gametes in some green algae (eg *Spirogyra*) and some fungi. » bacteria [i]; gamete; Protozoa; reproduction

conjugation (chemistry) The real or apparent alternation of single and double bonds in a compound. » benzene [i]; butadiene; chemical bond

conjugation (linguistics) The scheme of inflections which mark contrasts of tense, person, and number in verbs. Latin and Greek had complex conjugational systems; English has very few verbal inflections (eg *-ing*, *-ed*, *-en*); by comparison, French and German are intermediate in complexity. » derivation; grammar

conjunctivitis An infection of the membrane covering the inner surface of the eyelids and the front surface of the eye (the *conjunctiva*). It causes a feeling of grittiness of the eyes, and is associated with stickiness of the eyelids and a discharge. The whites of the eyes are red and infected. » eye [i]; ophthalmia

Connacht or **Connaught** [**kon**ot] pop (1981) 424 410; area 17 121 sq km/6 609 sq ml. Province in W Irish Republic, comprising counties of Sligo, Leitrim, Mayo, Roscommon,

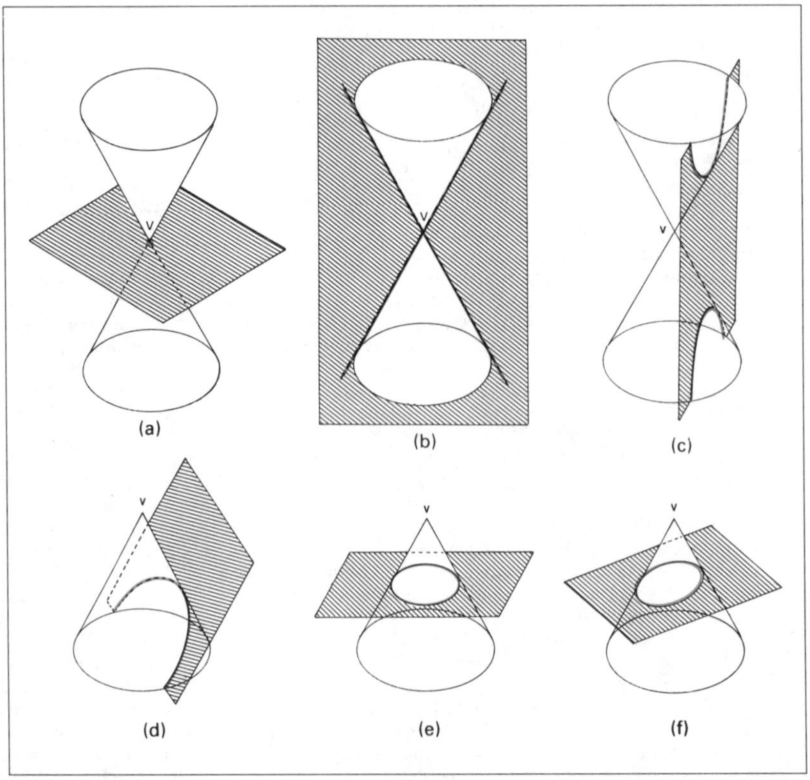

Cone (sometimes double) cut by a plane in (a) a single point (b) a pair of straight lines (c) a hyperbola (d) a parabola (e) a circle (f) an ellipse

Galway; chief towns include Sligo, Galway, Castlebar; agriculture, livestock. » Irish Republic [i]

Connaught » **Connacht**

Connecticut [kuh**net**ikuht] pop (1987e) 3 211 000, area 12 996 sq km/5 018 sq ml. A New England state in NE USA, divided into eight counties; the 'Constitution State' or 'Nutmeg State'; densely populated; explored by Adriaen Block, 1614; one of the original states of the Union, fifth to ratify the Federal Constitution; capital, Hartford; other major cities Bridgeport, New Haven, Waterbury, Stamford; the Thames, Connecticut, and Housatonic Rivers flow S through the state to empty into Long Island Sound; highest point, Mt Frissell (725 m/2 379 ft); coast largely urbanized, with many industries; interior mainly woodland and forest, with some cropland producing dairy produce, poultry, and tobacco; machinery, transport equipment, electrical goods, firearms, metal products. » Hartford; United States of America [i]; RR38

connectionism A form of computer modelling in which information-processing is carried out by a network of interconnected units. It is sometimes called **parallel distributed processing**, because information is processed in many parts of the network simultaneously, and specific information is not localized at a particular point in the network. » artificial intelligence; information processing

connective tissue Tissue which binds together and is the ground substance of various parts and organs of the body. The character of the tissue depends on the organization of its constituent cells and fibres (eg the amount of collagen it contains). In the embryo, it forms a loose cellular network known as *mesenchyme*, from which develop such specialized connective tissues as bone, cartilage, blood cells, and fat. » cellulitis; collagens; embryology; Marfan's syndrome; tissue

Connemara [koni**mah**ra] Mountainous region in W Galway county, Irish Republic; W of L Corrib; rocky coastline with mountains rising to 765 m/2 510 ft at Croagh Patrick in the Twelve Bens; peat bogs; numerous lakes. » Irish Republic [i]

Connolly, Maureen (Catherine), byname **Little Mo** (1934–69) US lawn tennis player, born in San Diego, California, the first woman to win all four major titles in one year (1953). She won the US championship in 1951 at the age of 16, and thereafter lost only four matches in her career, twice to Doris Hart and once each to Shirley Fry and Beverley Fleitz. She won the Wimbledon singles in 1952–4, the US title in 1951–3, the French Open in 1953–4, and the Australian title in 1953. She married Norman Brinker in 1954, broke her leg in a riding accident the same year, and was forced to retire. She died of cancer in Dallas, Texas. » tennis, lawn [i]

Connors, Jimmy, properly **James Scott** (1952–) US lawn tennis player, born in Belleville, Illinois. The All-American and National Intercollegiate champion from the University of California in 1971, he went on to become Wimbledon champion in 1974 (against Ken Rosewall) and 1982 (against John McEnroe). He won the US Open in 1974, 1976, 1978, and 1982–3. A left-handed player, he was one of the first to use the double-fisted backhand. » tennis, lawn [i]; McEnroe

connotation In linguistics, the emotional associations connected with the meanings of words; for example *green* carries implications of 'youth' and 'inexperience'. It is contrasted with **denotation**, the objective reference a word has to an object ouside language, such as the physical properties of a colour. » semantics

conquistador [kon**kee**stador] Literally, 'conqueror'; the standard term for the leaders of the Spanish expeditions of the early 16th-c that undertook the invasion and conquest of America. » Cortés; Spain [i]

Conrad, Joseph, originally **Józef Teodor Konrad Korzeniowski** (1857–1924) British novelist, born of Polish parents in Berdichev, by then Russian. He joined the British merchant navy, and became a British national in 1886. He sailed to many parts of the world, married in 1896, and settled at Ashford, Kent. His first novel was *Almayer's Folly* (1894). His best-known works are *The Nigger of the Narcissus* (1897), *Lord Jim* (1900), *Nostromo* (1904), *The Secret Agent* (1907), *Under Western Eyes* (1911), and *Chance* (1914). He also wrote many short stories; and the short novel *Heart of Darkness* (1902) anticipates many 20th-c themes and effects. He died in Canterbury, Kent. » English literature; novel

Conran, Jasper (1959–) British fashion designer, born in London. He trained at Parsons School of Art and Design in New York City, leaving in 1977 to work as a designer. He produced his first collection of easy-to-wear, quality clothes in London in 1978. » fashion

Conran, Sir Terence (Orby) (1931–) British designer and businessman, born at Esher, Surrey. He founded and ran the Habitat Company, based on his own success as a furniture designer and the virtues of good design and marketing. He has since been involved in the management of several related businesses and has won many design awards. He was knighted in 1983.

conscientious objection A refusal to accept a particular policy, plan, or course of action, because to do so would go against one's conscience. It is often invoked by pacifists or others objecting to military service, though the State may not always recognize conscientious objection as a citizen's 'right'. » pacifism

consciousness The psychological state of being aware. Several different meanings can be distinguished, including the state of being awake (in contrast to *unconscious*) and the state in which mental experiences are directly accessible and reportable (in contrast to *subconscious* or *preconscious*). William James stressed the continuity of consciousness (the 'stream of thought'). Cognitive psychologists have emphasized that consciousness may be restricted to certain levels of processing; for example, we may be conscious at a high level of what someone has said, but not be aware (nor be capable of being aware) of the low-level processing details of the acoustic signal that conveyed the message. » cognitive psychology; James, William; subliminal perception

conscription The practice, dating from the Napoleonic era, of compelling young men of eligible age and fitness to serve by statute in the armed forces of a nation. To meet the huge manpower needs of World War 1, conscription was introduced in Great Britain in early 1916 and then in the USA under the Selective Service Act (May 1917). Conscription was again enforced in Britain from 1939–45, continuing in peacetime as *National Service*, which was finally abolished in 1962. Women are also required to perform military service in certain countries, such as Israel. In popular US usage, conscription is often referred to as the **draft**. » women's services

consensus politics An emphasis, usually contained in the prescriptions of centrist political parties, upon the need to formulate policies that avoid or resolve conflict, and build consensus in society. Consensus refers to the sharing by individuals of a set of norms, values, and beliefs. A policy's correctness tends to be judged less by whether it conforms to some ideal aim, and more by whether it is capable of furthering consensus and thereby social cohesion. » centre, the

Consentes Dii or **Di** [kon**sen**teez **dee**-ee, **dee**] The Roman name for the twelve major gods, whose statues, grouped in male/female pairs, stood in the Forum. They were probably Jupiter/Juno, Neptune/Minerva, Mars/Venus, Apollo/Diana, Volcanus/Vesta, and Mercury/Ceres. » Roman religion

consequence In philosophy, any proposition which follows validly from a set of propositions. The set consisting of 'Either London is small or polluted' and 'London is not small' has, as some of its consequences, 'London is polluted', 'London is not small', and 'It is not the case that London is not polluted.' » logic; validity

consequentialism » **teleological ethics**

conservation (earth sciences) The protection and preservation of the Earth's resources (eg plants, animals, land, energy, minerals) or of historical artefacts (eg books, paintings, monuments) for the future. The term is most widely used with reference to the environment, where several reasons are given for conservation. The World Conservation Strategy (1980) concluded that conservation of living resources was needed to preserve genetic diversity, to maintain essential ecological processes, and to ensure the sustainable use of species and ecosystems. This would maintain viable stocks of all animal and plant species, pure air and water, and fertile soil for future use, and allow animals, plants, and land to be there indefinitely. In this way conservation ensures that both present and future generations will be able to make maximum sustainable use of available resources. This definition is essentially economic. Some non-economic, though not necessarily non-utilitarian, reasons for conservation include the enjoyment and spiritual nature of wildlife and the land, the continued use of the land for recreation, and the moral responsibility to future generations to conserve the Earth and its resources. » ecology; endangered species; environment; environmentalism; Nature Conservancy Council; Nature Reserve; recycling

conservation (psychology) The hallmark of the concrete operations stage in Piagetian psychology. It is the ability to understand the invariance of such properties as number or volume, despite a change in appearance, eg that a row of counters which is lengthened by increasing the space between them retains the same number. » Piaget

conservation laws Sets of rules describing quantities which are the same before and after some physical process. The identification of these laws is central to physics; all physical laws express conservation principles. A conservation law is related to a symmetry of the system. The most important such law is the **conservation of energy**, which is related to the symmetry of physical systems under translation in time. **Conservation of momentum** results from symmetry under translation in space. In particle physics, these complex interactions are expressed in terms of conserved but unfamiliar quantum numbers. » physics; quantum numbers; symmetry

conservatism A set of political ideas, attitudes, and beliefs which stress adherence to what is known and established in the political and social orders, as opposed to the innovative and untested. Generally associated with right-wing political parties, conservatives view humanity as inherently imperfect, emphasizing the need for law and order and the value of tradition. Society is often viewed as an organic whole, and as it is only imperfectly understood, change should rarely, or only gradually, be attempted. It implies the acceptance of inequality in society and limited state intervention. Conservatives reject the notion that conservatism is an ideology, and indeed in some cases it can become highly reactionary. Burke's conception of conservatism was developed as an attack upon revolutionary action. » Burke, Edmund; New Right; right-wing; Thatcher, Margaret

Conservative Party One of the two main political parties in the UK, its full name being the **Conservative and Unionist Party**. It has been the most successful party electorally this century. In common with other conservative parties it is on the right of the political spectrum, though in the 1980s it fused conservative with radical neo-liberal ideas. » conservatism; liberalism; New Right

conservatory (music) An institution dedicated to the training of musicians. Conservatories originated as charitable foundations for the care of poor or orphaned children. In the 17th-c the *conservatorii* for boys at Naples and the *ospedali* for girls at Venice found that a concentration on musical training could be educationally and financially profitable. Later they began to attract fee-paying pupils, and the idea of the modern conservatory, as exemplified by the Paris Conservatoire (1795) began to take shape. » Royal Academy of Music; Royal College of Music

consols Loan-stock issued by the British government, first introduced in 1751; its name derives from *consolidated fund*. It is a form of gilt-edged stock, but 'undated' – no redemption date is given for the return of the capital. » gilt-edged securities; stocks

consonant A sound made with a closure or narrowing of the vocal tract, so that the airflow is either momentarily impeded or restricted. For example the lips close to produce a [p], and the tongue contacts the palate in producing an [s]. Consonants occur at the beginning or end of a syllable, eg *cup*. The notion is also used with reference to the written language: in English, for example, all letters apart from A, E, I, O, and U, and in some circumstances W and Y, are classed as consonants. » articulation; vowel

Constable, John (1776–1837) British landscape painter, born at East Bergholt, Suffolk. Son of a miller, he trained at the Royal Academy (1799). In 1816 he married Maria Bicknell; and in 1828 received an inheritance which enabled him to continue as a painter. Among his best-received works were 'Haywain' (1821, National Gallery, London) and 'White Horse' (1825, New York), which both gained gold medals. His work was especially popular in France, though he exhibited regularly at the Royal Academy, becoming a member in 1829. His later years were saddened by the death of his wife, and by ill health. He died in London. » English art; landscape painting

Constance, Ger **Konstanz**, ancient **Constantia** 47°39N 9°10E, pop (1983) 69 100. Lake port in Tübingen district, Germany, on L Constance, close to the Swiss border; former episcopal see and imperial city; railway; university (1966); tourism, commerce, wine, computers, metals, pharmaceuticals, textiles; council hall (1388), cathedral (15th-c). » Constance, Lake; Germany [i]

Constance, Lake, Ger **Bodensee**, ancient **Lacus Brigantinus** area 541 sq km/209 sq ml. Lake on the N side of the Swiss Alps, forming a meeting point of Switzerland, Austria, and W Germany; length, 64 km/40 ml; part of the course of the R Rhine; contains islands of Mainau and Reichenau; NW arm known as the *Überlingersee*; chief towns on the shore, Konstanz, Friedrichshafen, Lindau, Bregenz. » Alps

constancy In the study of perception, the tendency to perceive the intrinsic properties of objects correctly, despite dramatic changes in, for example, the size (as a function of distance), the shape (as a function of viewpoint), or the brightness (as a function of illumination) of their image on the retina. » vision

Constant (de Rebeque), (Henri) Benjamin (1767–1830) French novelist and politician, born at Lausanne, Switzerland. Educated at Oxford, Erlangen, and Edinburgh, he settled in Paris (1795) as a publicist. He supported the Revolution, but was banished in 1802 for his opposition to Napoleon. He returned in 1814, and became leader of the liberal opposition. His best-known work is the novel *Adolphe* (1816), based on his relationship with Mme de Staël. He died in Paris. » French literature; Staël, Madame de; French Revolution [i]

Constanța, Eng **Constantza**, ancient **Tomis** or **Constantiniana** 44°10N 28°40E, pop (1983) 315 662. Major port and capital of Constanța county, SE Romania, on the W shores of the Black Sea; third largest city in Romania; established as a Greek colony, 7th-c BC; under Roman rule from 72 BC; Ovid lived in exile here; named after Constantine I (4th-c AD); ceded to Romania, 1878; airport; railway; naval shipyards, tourism, textiles, foodstuffs, metal products, soap, oil refining. » Constantine I (Emperor); Ovid; Romania [i]

Constantine I (Emperor), byname **the Great**, properly **Flavius Valerius Constantinus** (c.274–337) Roman emperor, the eldest son of Constantius Chlorus. Though proclaimed Emperor by the army at York on his father's death in 306, it was not until his defeat of Maxentius at the Milvian Bridge in Rome (312) that he became Emperor of the West; and only with his victory over Licinius, the Emperor of the East, that he became sole Emperor (324). Believing that his victory in 312 was the work of the Christian God, he became the first emperor to promote Christianity, whence his title 'Great'. His edict of Milan (313), issued jointly with Licinius, brought toleration to Christians throughout the empire, and his new capital at Constantinople, founded on the strategically important site of Byzantium (324), was from the outset a Christian city. » Byzantine Empire; Roman history [i]

Constantine I (of Greece) King of Greece (1913–17, 1920–22), born in Athens. He played a leading part in Greece's victories in the Balkan Wars (1912–13), and succeeded his father, George I, as King. During World War 1, his policy of neutrality led to bitter conflict with interventionist forces led by liberal politician Venizelos, culminating (1916–17) in virtual civil war, Anglo-French intervention, and his abdication. Restored after the war, he abdicated once again (1922) following Greece's defeat by Turkey and an internal military revolt. He died at Palermo, Sicily. » Greece [i]; Venizelos; World War 1

Constantine II (1940–) King of Greece (1964–7), born near Athens, who succeeded his father, Paul I. In 1964 he married

Princess Anne-Marie of Denmark (1946–) and has two sons and a daughter. He fled to Rome (Dec 1967) after an abortive coup against the military government which had seized power, and was deposed in 1973. The monarchy was abolished by a national referendum in 1974. » Greece [i]

Constantine [**kon**stanteen], ancient **Ciria**, **Qacentina** 36°22N 6°40E, pop (1980e) 384 000. Chief town of Constantine department, NE Algeria, N Africa; 320 km/200 ml ESE of Algiers; oldest city in Algeria, important since the 3rd–4th-c BC; Roman provincial capital of Numidia; destroyed in 311 AD during a civil war, rebuilt by Constantine I; seat of successive Muslim dynasties in Middle Ages; prospered under Turks in the 18th-c; French occupation in 1837; university (1969); airport; railway; tourism, handicrafts; Old Town. » Algeria [i]; Constantine I (Emperor)

Constantinople, Latin Empire of A 13th-c empire based at Constantinople (ancient Byzantium, modern Istanbul), the capital of the mediaeval (Eastern) Roman or Byzantine Empire. During the Fourth Crusade, diverted from Palestine, Constantinople was taken (1204) and a Latin Empire created, with Baldwin count of Flanders as the first emperor. It succumbed in 1261 after a precarious existence. » Baldwin I; Dandolo

constellation From ancient times, a group of prominent stars apparently near to each other as perceived in our sky, so that they form a geometrical shape or picture. Some constellations are genuine groupings of stars, but generally they are arrangements of stars which are actually at greatly different distances from the Solar System. Different cultures have their own ways of delineating the constellations. The system in use by astronomers today has its origins in ancient Mesopotamia, and still includes many names from Greek mythology. Until the 20th-c, the traditional mythological figures were still used to illustrate even professional star atlases.

The boundaries of the constellations were at first drawn using arbitrary curves. This led to great confusion until half of them were agreed in 1875, with the remainder being adopted by the International Astronomical Union in 1930. The whole patchwork quilt now includes 88 constellations, which vary enormously in size and shape: the largest, Hydra, is 20 times bigger than the smallest, Crux. The Egyptian systematic astronomer Claudius Ptolemy listed 48 constellations in *Syntaxis* c.AD 140; the modern ones were mostly invented in the 16th–18th-c. The brightest stars are named from the constellation in which they are found, using the Greek alphabet and the Latin genitive or possessive form for the constellation: *alpha Ursae Majoris* is thus the brightest star in Ursa Major. Most professional astronomers today could point out very few of the constellations if challenged to do so. This ancient way of mapping the sky has been replaced for all practical purposes by numerical co-ordinates that computers can readily interpret. » astronomy; star; RR8

constipation A condition in which there is infrequent and difficult emptying of the bowel. The interval between bowel movements varies widely in healthy individuals. However, a period of more than three days, especially if followed by difficult defaecation, suggests constipation. It results from the delayed transit of faeces through the colon, or its retention in the rectum, and often arises in the course of illness or following surgical operations. In healthy individuals, it may be due to insufficient vegetable fibre in the diet. » defaecation

constituency A territorial division that in many countries serves as a unit in the election of one or more political representatives to national assemblies. Population usually serves as the main criterion in determining the size of each constituency, but variations exist across political systems. For example, in the USA 435 people are elected to the House of Representatives from constituencies with roughly equivalent populations, while two senators are elected from each state, regardless of population size. The UK contains 650 single-member constituencies, most with electorates of c.65 000. » House of Representatives

constituent analysis In linguistics, the analysis of linguistic forms into the components ('constituents') from which they are made. Sentences can be analysed into subjects and predicates (eg *John slept*) and words into stems and affixes (eg *de/nation/al/ize*). In more complicated sentences, several 'layers' of grammatical analysis can be shown:

CONSTITUTENT ANALYSIS

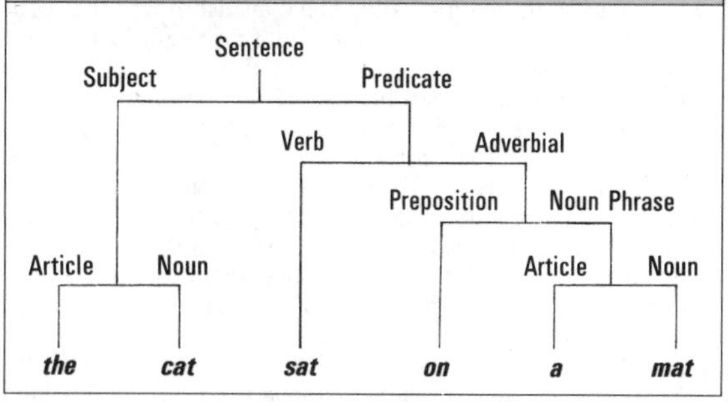

constitution Usually a written document which forms the rules determining the way that a country may be governed in terms of the sources, purpose, use, and limits upon the exercise of political power. The UK is one of a few exceptions in having an unwritten constitution, although in all countries the identification of constitutional principles must make reference to statute law, judicial interpretation, tradition, and other constitutional practices. Written constitutions normally include: a preamble; a description of governmental institutions and their powers, including the processes for amending the constitution and reviewing decisions that are claimed to infringe the constitution; a bill of rights; and amendatory articles. » bill of rights; Constitution of the United States

Constitution of the United States Founded upon the principles of the Declaration of Independence, the US constitution is based upon the concepts of limited and responsible government, and federalism. Power is divided amongst three independent branches of government: legislative; executive; judicial. The constitutional document comprises a short preamble followed by seven articles which include: the organization, powers and procedures of the legislative branch (Congress); the powers of the president and executive; the powers of the judiciary, including the Supreme Court; the rights of the states; and procedures for amending the constitution. The articles are then followed by 26 amendments, the first ten of which are known as the *bill of rights* (although later amendments also deal with civil rights issues), while the others cover such matters as the election, death or removal of the president, and eligibility to stand for election to Congress. » bill of rights; civil rights; Congress; constitution; Declaration of Independence; federalism; Supreme Court

Constitutional Convention (1787) A gathering at Philadelphia during the American Revolution that produced the present US Constitution; 12 of the original 13 states were represented. The term, by extension, is also used for any political meeting empowered to write a state or national constitution. » American Revolution

Constitutions of Clarendon » **Clarendon, Constitutions of**

constrictor A snake which wraps its body tightly around its prey and, by squeezing, induces suffocation; teeth carry no venom; lips often have heat-sensitive pits. » boa; python; snake

Constructivism An imprecise term usually applied to a form of abstract art that began in Russia in 1917, using machine-age materials such as steel, glass, and plastic. Leading practitioners were Vladimir Tatlin (1885–1953), who projected the gigantic spiral monument to the Third International, and the brothers Antoine Pevsner and Naum Gabo. In Russia this impetus was soon channelled into industrial design (*Soviet Constructivism*), and Pevsner and Gabo left Russia in the early 1920s. Their ideas subsequently exerted a deep influence on abstract artists in the West (*International Constructivism*). » abstract art; art; Concrete Art; Gabo; Pevsner, Nikolaus

consubstantiation A theory attributed to Luther, describing the presence of Christ in the Eucharist 'under or with the elements of bread and wine'. It is to be contrasted with the Roman Catholic doctrine of transubstantiation. » Eucharist; Luther; transubstantiation

consul 1 In Republican Rome (5th-c–1st-c BC), a chief executive officer of state, with military and judicial functions. Two consuls were elected annually. The consulship was the highest office in the *cursus honorum* and could not be held before the age of 36. Under the Empire, it became mainly honorific. » cursus honorum; Roman history [i] 2 » ambassador

consumer protection Activities devised to protect buyers of goods and services against inferior or dangerous products and misleading advertising. These may be statutory (eg the USA Food and Drug Administration) or by means of a voluntary code within an industry. They may also be introduced through consumer organizations, as in the movement led by US lawyer Ralph Nader (1934–) in the early 1960s, criticizing the dangers in certain cars.

consumer society The advanced stage of (Western) industrial society where a high availability and consumption of consumer goods and services obtains. The extension of banking and retail credit in the late 20th-c has allowed widespread increase in consumption – as well as indebtedness. The term is associated with the notion of *consumer sovereignty*, ie goods are produced to meet consumer needs or demands, and consumption is increased through production of 'convenience' and disposable goods. » consumerism

consumerism The promotion of policies aimed at regulating the standards of manufacturers and sellers in the interests of buyers. The stimulus may come from a government, through legislation, from an industry itself, through setting up codes of practice, or from consumer pressure groups. » consumer protection/society

contact potential An electromotive force (emf) produced across the junction between two dissimilar metals at the same temperature. Contact emf is proportional to the difference between workfunctions of the two metals, and is caused by the migration of electrons from one metal to the other, until the resulting emf means that to remove an electron from either metal in the junction is equally difficult. It is also observed in the junction of two identical metals at different temperatures. The effect is exploited in thermocouples. » electromotive force; thermocouple; thermoelectric effects; workfunction

Contadora, Isla [eelya kontadohra] 8°40N 79°02W. Island of Panama, in the Pearl Is, Gulf of Panama; meeting place of the foreign ministers of Colombia, Mexico, Panama, and Venezuela (the Contadora Group) in 1983 to discuss the problems of C America; their proposed solutions became known as the **Contadora process**. » Panama [i]

contagious abortion » **brucellosis**

container ship A cellular ship, designed to carry 6 m/20 ft or 12 m/40 ft boxes in pre-determined positions, thus largely dispensing with the lashing or stowage problems associated with traditional cargo. The first purpose-built ships were commissioned in 1966 by a British company. » ship [i]

containment The policy adopted by the USA and thereafter her Western allies aimed at containing, by political, economic, and diplomatic means, the 'expansionist tendencies' of the USSR. The policy, first advocated in 1947, also involved the provision of technical and economic aid to non-communist countries.

containment building A steel or concrete structure enclosing a nuclear reactor, designed to withstand high pressure and high temperature and, in an emergency, to contain the escape of radiation. Such a building must also withstand external hazards, such as high winds and heavy snow. » nuclear reactor [i]

conté crayon [kõntay] A type of synthetic chalk named after its French inventor, Nicolas Jacques Conté (1755–1805). It is used by artists, and is available in black, white, red, and brown.

contempt of court A wide-ranging term which includes failure to comply with an order of the court, and conduct which obstructs the process of the courts (eg by intimidating witnesses or causing a disturbance in court). A person in contempt may be committed to prison or fined. » court of law; subpoena

continent A term applied to the seven large land masses on the Earth's surface: Asia, Africa, N America, S America, Antarctica, Europe, and Australia, in decreasing order of size. The continents (including the submerged continental shelves) make up about 35% of the Earth's crust, the rest being made up of the oceanic plates. The thickness of the crust below the continents is 30–40 km/15–25 ml, and is composed of lower density rocks enriched in silica and aluminium compared to the oceanic crust. » continental drift; continental margin; plate tectonics [i]

Continental Congress (1774–8) The gathering that declared and led the struggle for American independence. Each of the 13 colonies (states after 1776) had one vote. The First Congress met for six weeks in 1774. The Second (convened Apr 1775) did not formally dissolve until replaced by the government under the present Constitution, adopted in 1788. » American Revolution; Articles of Confederation; Declaration of Independence; Ordinance of 1787

Continental Divide or **Great Divide** A line of mountain peaks in N America extending SSE from NW Canada down the W USA into Mexico, C America, and S America where it meets the N end of the Andes; a major watershed; includes the Rocky Mts in Canada and the USA and the Sierra Madre ranges in Mexico. » Andes; Rocky Mountains

continental drift A theory which proposes that the present positions of the continents and oceans results from the breaking up of a single large land mass or 'supercontinent', termed *Pangaea*, c.200 million years ago. The idea is generally ascribed to Alfred Wegener (1910) but gained little support until the 1960s, when the theory of plate tectonics was established. » continent; Pangaea; plate tectonics [i]; Wegener

continental margin The boundary province between the deep ocean basins and continents, which makes up about 20% of the ocean area. Though continental margins vary considerably, there are two main groups: the *passive* (or *aseismic*) and the *active* (or *seismic*). Atlantic Ocean margins are dominantly of the passive type, sometimes referred to as *Atlantic-type margins*. Active margins are typical of the Pacific Ocean and are sometimes called *Pacific-type margins*. The margins of the Indian Ocean are of the Atlantic type, except in the NE, where the boundary is an active margin.

Passive continental margins consist typically of three parts: a shelf, slope, and rise. The **continental shelf** is a seaward extension of the continent, usually with low relief and a gentle gradient, averaging less than 1:1000. At the edge of the shelf (the *shelf break*), there is a marked increase in steepness. The depth of the break is 20–500 m/65–1 600 ft, averaging 130 m/ 425 ft in most areas. The width of the shelf ranges from a few km to more than 400 km/250 ml, averaging just over 75 km/ 45 ml. The **continental slope** lies seaward of the continental shelf, and extends to 1 500–3 500 m/5 000–11 000 ft), with a much steeper gradient, averaging 1:40. It is a relatively narrow zone, usually 20–100 km/12–60 ml in width. The continental shelf and slope together form the **continental terrace**. In many areas of the ocean, this is cut by submarine canyons, which serve to carry sediment from the continent to the continental rise and the deep ocean. The **continental rise** lies between the slope and the ocean basin. It has a gentle gradient between 1:100 and 1:700, and a width of 100–1 000 km/60–600 ml, averaging about 600 km/375 ml. The rise is formed by sediment eroded from the continents accumulating at the base of the slope. It too may be cut by submarine canyons which allow the transport of sediment beyond the rise to the ocean basin. A **continental borderland** is a continental terrace consisting of a series of basins and ridges. The true shelf is a few km wide only, but the adjacent zone of basins, banks, and islands may extend up to 200 km/125 ml in width. An example is the continental margin off S California. » continent; earthquake; neritic zone; Pacific Ocean; submarine canyon

continental shelf » **continental margin**

Continental System The process of economic warfare introduced by Napoleon to destroy British commercial power, after Trafalgar put paid to his invasion plans. The Decrees of Berlin (1806) and Milan (1807) established a blockade of European and neutral trade with Britain and her colonies. » Napoleonic Wars

continuing education ≫ **adult education**

continuo The practice, common to most Baroque music, of filling out the harmonic texture by reference to a specially notated bass line (a 'figured bass'). The continuo is usually supplied by a harmony instrument (harpsichord, organ, lute, etc) reinforced by a melodic bass instrument (cello, double bass, bassoon, etc). ≫ Baroque (music); theorbo

continuous assessment The appraisal of students' work on a regular basis rather than exclusively by final examination. Essays, practical work, projects, and assignments done during the course might form all or part of the final assessment, which can be based on marks, grades, or a profile.

continuous representation In art, the practice of including several consecutive stages of a story in one picture. For example, in a Nativity, the shepherds who adore the Child in the foreground may also be shown in the distance watching their flocks. ≫ Jesus Christ

contrabassoon ≫ **bassoon**

contraception The prevention of pregnancy following sexual intercourse; also known as **birth control** or **family planning**. For centuries its practice was opposed by the Church and the medical profession, but it has come to be widely advocated in order to control populations, protect against venereal disease, and regulate the size of families.

The earliest methods adopted did not involve chemical or mechanical devices. Cleaning the vagina with water (*douching*), although widely practised, has never been effective. The use of a 'safe period' or **rhythm method** is based on the fact that both spermatozoa and ova survive for only a day or two after release. Attractive to the Roman Catholic Church, it is fallible because of the difficulty in timing ovulation, and because of the variability of the duration of the menstrual cycle. The most fertile period is between 10–17 days of a regular 28-day menstrual cycle, but in practice for most women this period and the need to avoid it is considerably longer, as few follow a sufficiently regular pattern. Thus, other than for religious or moral grounds, the rhythm method is best avoided in couples for whom an unwanted pregnancy would be a disaster, but it can be acceptable to those for whom an unplanned pregnancy would merely be an inconvenience. *Coitus interruptus* involves withdrawal of the penis from the vagina just prior to ejaculation. Formerly popular, its efficacy clearly depends on self-control on the part of the male in all circumstances, and often leads to anxiety on the part of both partners.

The use of a condom was first described in the 16th-c as a protection against syphilis; it consisted of a linen sheath. The modern condom is made of siliconed latex with an expanded part or teat on the end. It is appropriately and widely advocated because its mechanical protection guards not only against pregnancy but also against AIDS. It is probably the most widely used contraceptive method in the Western world. Other mechanical devices include shields, diaphragms, or caps inserted into the vagina over the cervix. These require proper insertion some time before coitus, and should be retained for 6–8 hours afterwards. Their efficacy can be improved by the use of spermicidal agents. **Intra-uterine devices** (IUD) are empirically designed spring-like foreign bodies that are inserted by a trained person into the uterus. Made of inert plastic or metal, they do not prevent ovulation and are not spermicidal, but appear to act by preventing the products of conception becoming embedded in the wall of the uterus. They have found great use in the control of population in some developing countries. They should not be used in women who suffer from pelvic infection; their use may indeed lead to this complication, and result later in permanent infertility.

The most important development in contraception has been the introduction of the **contraceptive pill**. This contains synthetic steroids similar to the female sex hormones oestrogen and progesterone, either together or progesterone alone. Their use is based on the action of inhibiting ovulation. Combined oestrogen and progesterone pills are the most effective, and are taken for 21 days followed by a 7-day interval during which menstrual bleeding occurs. The use of combined oestrogen/progesterone pills carries a small risk of blood clotting and embolic episodes, especially in women over 35 years. The single progesterone pill (the 'minipill') taken daily without a break has a higher failure rate, but is safer in older individuals; it is believed to act by thickening the secretions of the cervix and Fallopian tubes, thereby preventing the sperm from reaching the egg. Post-coital contraceptives (the 'morning-after pill') contain the synthetic oestrogen stilboestrol. When taken after intercourse, stilboestrol prevents implantation of any fertilized egg. It is insufficiently safe to be used as an ordinary contraceptive device, and is reserved for emergencies (such as following rape).

An alternative approach to the avoidance of pregnancy is sterilization. ≫ DES; oestrogen; pregnancy [i]; sterilization

contract A legally enforceable agreement. A contract has certain essential features. It arises from an offer which has been accepted in identical terms. Unless there is (in the terminology of English law) a promise under seal (ie a covenant), there must be *consideration* – that is, the promisee must confer some benefit or suffer some detriment in return for the promise made. There must be an intention to create *legal relations* (ie to enter into a legally enforceable agreement), and the parties must have *legal capacity* (ie be legally able to enter into the agreement – for example, by being old enough). There is no general rule that a contract must be in writing – buying something in a shop is a contractual agreement – but there are exceptions (eg by statute, a contract to buy land must be evidenced in writing). ≫ condition; covenant **1**; exemption clause; injunction

contract bridge ≫ **bridge** (recreation)

contrapposto [kontrah**pos**toh] In art, a pose in which the top half of the body is turned in a different direction from the lower. It occurs in classical sculpture, and was much used in 16th-c Italy, for example by Michelangelo and the Mannerists. ≫ Mannerism

Contras ≫ **Nicaragua** [i]

contrast In the visual medium, the relation between the light and dark areas of a scene or their reproduction by photographic or electronic means. It is expressed numerically as the *brightness range* of the subject or the *gamma value* of a process. ≫ light

contre-jour Describes a scene taken with the camera pointing in the direction of the main source of light. This tends to show foreground objects in silhouette, often with a bright halo effect at their edges. ≫ cinematography [i]

control ≫ **seance**

control character A non-printing character or code which, when sent to a computer peripheral, causes a specific operation to take place. Examples are carriage return and line feed characters which make the printer operate in a particular way.

control engineering The branch of engineering concerned with the control and adjustment of systems. A human operator need not be involved. Control is achieved by using closed loop systems: when an error is detected, the information is returned to the input and used to correct the error – a system known as *feedback*. Control engineering uses servo-mechanisms as automatically-operating control devices, such as are found in measuring instruments, detectors, amplifiers, and power units. ≫ automation; servo system

control group A group of subjects in an experiment, similar in all relevant respects to the experimental group, and submitting to the same conditions and changes except those specifically under investigation. The effect of the experimental treatment is assessed by taking the difference after treatment between experimental and control group on whatever measure is being used. ≫ experimenter effect

convection The flow of heat by the actual movement of a gas or liquid. For example, air warmed by a fire expands, becomes less dense, and so rises, creating a **convection current** as fresh cool air is drawn in to replace the warmed air. Convection currents spread heat round a room. **Forced convection** takes place when heated fluid is forced to move, as in hot water heating systems. ≫ diffusion (science); heat; thermal conduction

convective rain A type of rain commonly associated with equatorial climates, and with the cold front of unstable polar air masses; also known as **convectional rain**. When a parcel of air is heated from below, it expands and rises; as it cools, condensation occurs to form cumulonimbus clouds from which heavy rainfall is produced. » condensation (physics); cumulonimbus clouds; hail; rainfall; thunderstorm

conventionalism In philosophy, a doctrine which maintains that scientific theories (or parts thereof) are not confirmed by evidence, but are the product of linguistic stipulation. A conventionalist might claim that in Newtonian physics, for example, no evidence counts for or against the proposition that force is the product of mass and acceleration; 'force' is simply defined that way. » instrumentalism

convergence (biology) The independent evolution of a structural or functional similarity, not based on an inherited similarity of genetic material, in two or more unrelated organisms as an adaptation to a particular way of life. For example, the similarities between a bird and a bat that are related to their ability to fly are the result of convergent evolution. » evolution

convergence (linguistics) The process whereby variant forms of a language become more alike, as in the 'levelling' of dialect differences under the influence of a standard language. When varieties come increasingly to differ in structure, the process is known as **divergence**. » dialectology; standard language

conversation analysis » **discourse analysis**

conversation piece A type of small group portrait which flourished in 18th-c England, representing a family and/or friends grouped informally either indoors or in a landscape or garden setting. Hogarth, Philippe Mercier (c.1689–1760), and Francis Hayman (1708–76) were masters of this genre. » Hogarth, William

conversion (law) Dealing with goods so as to deny the owner's rights; or claiming rights inconsistent with those of the owner. Conversion is classed as a tort. The term is not recognized in all jurisdictions (eg in Scotland). » tort

conversion (linguistics) The potential for words to alternate between different grammatical categories without any change in their form. For example, *smell* can be both noun (*there's a smell*) and verb (*I can smell something*). English coins many new words in this way, eg *an impact→to impact*; *round→a round* (of drinks). » word class

conversion (psychiatry) A loss or alteration of physical functioning which gives the impression of a physical disorder, but which is in fact the result of psychological mechanisms. For example, a patient might describe a sensation of back pain and paralysis of the legs when there is no organic disease and following an argument with his wife who has asked him to leave home. » mental disorders

conversion (religion) A change in affiliation from one religion to another, or the transition from non-involvement to belief in a religion. It also designates a change involving a transformation and reorientation affecting every aspect of a person's life, which can occur suddenly or gradually. » religion

conveyance A legal document which when signed, sealed, and delivered transfers a legal estate in land (specified in the document) from one party to another. On the sale of a house, a conveyance is drawn up so as to transfer ownership of the property effectively. In England and Wales, in the case of land which has been registered, the procedure is modified: a completed form transferring the land must be lodged at the district land registry in order to transfer the legal estate. The Solicitors Act (1974) preserved the monopoly of solicitors with regard to preparing a conveyance of land for a fee. As a modification of this privilege, the Administration of Justice Act (1985) permits licensed conveyancing to be carried on for payment by a class of persons who are not solicitors. These **licensed conveyancers** are subject to the professional controls of the Council for Licensed Conveyancers. » land registration; solicitor

Convocation A gathering of Church of England clergy, originally in the provinces of Canterbury and York, to regulate affairs of the Church. The *Upper House* consists of the archbishop and bishops; the *Lower House* of representatives of the lower clergy. Since the early 20th-c, the two convocations meet together, all now forming the Church Assembly, which meets two or three times a year, with powers regulated by Parliament. » Church of England

convolvulus » **bindweed**

Conwy, English **Conway** 53°17N 3°50W, pop(1981) 12950. Historic market town and resort in Aberconwy district, Gwynedd, NW Wales, UK; at head of R Conwy (Conway); engineering, market town, tourism; 13th-c castle, with walls around the town; road tunnel beneath river, completion in 1991. » Gwynedd

cony » **hyrax; pika; rabbit**

Cook, James (1728–79) British navigator, born at Marton, Yorkshire. He spent several years as a seaman in North Sea vessels, then joined the navy in 1755, becoming master in 1759. He surveyed the area around the St Lawrence R, Quebec, then in the *Endeavour* carried the Royal Society expedition to Tahiti to observe the transit of Venus across the Sun (1768–71). He circumnavigated New Zealand and charted parts of Australia. In his second voyage he sailed round Antarctica (1772–5), and discovered several Pacific island groups. Thanks to his dietary precautions, there was only one death among the crew. His third voyage (1776–9) aimed to discover a passage round the N coast of America from the Pacific; but he was forced to turn back, and on his return voyage was killed by natives on Hawaii. » Australia [i]

Cook, Thomas (1808–92) British railway excursion and tourist pioneer, born at Melbourne, Derbyshire. He worked at several jobs before becoming a Baptist missionary in 1828. He organized his first railway excursion in 1841, from Leicester to Loughborough. He died at Leicester. His travel agency is now a worldwide organization.

Cook Islands pop(1981) 17754; area 238 sq km/92 sq ml. Widely scattered group of 15 volcanic and coral islands, c.3200 km/2000 ml NE of New Zealand, S Pacific Ocean; self-governing country in free association with New Zealand; capital, Avarua (on Rarotonga); timezone GMT −10; mainly Polynesian population; main religion, Christianity; official language, English, with local languages widely spoken; unit of currency, New Zealand dollar; airport at Avarua; highest island, Rarotonga, rises to 650 m/2132 ft; climate damp and tropical, with rainfall heavy on forested volcanic slopes of S islands; hurricane season (Nov–Apr); placed under British protection, 1888–1901; New Zealand dependency, 1901; internally self-governing, 1965; elected 24-member Legislative Assembly, with a premier as head of state; a high commissioner represents British sovereign and New Zealand interests; economy mainly agriculture and fishing, especially copra, citrus fruits, pineapples, tomatoes, bananas; fruit processing, tourism (especially in Rarotonga and Aitutaki). » New Zealand [i]; Pacific Ocean; Polynesia

Cook, Mount 43°37S 170°08E. Mountain in W South Island, New Zealand, in the Southern Alps; height, 3764 m/12349 ft; highest peak in New Zealand; in Mount Cook National Park, area 944 sq km/364 sq ml, established in 1953, a world heritage site; park contains 22 of the 27 peaks in the country over 3000 m/10000 ft; Tasman Glacier. » New Zealand [i]; Southern Alps

Cook Strait Channel of the Pacific Ocean separating North Island from South Island, New Zealand; 23–130 km/14–80 ml wide; visited by Captain Cook in 1770. » New Zealand [i]

cooking fats Solid fats derived from vegetable oils, used in cooking; often referred to as **shortening**. Vegetable oils with the exception of coconut or palm oil tend to be unsaturated and liquid at room temperature. They are treated with hydrogen to produce the solid fat used in cooking. » polyunsaturated fatty acids

Cookson, Catherine (Ann) (1906–) British novelist, born at East Jarrow, Tyneside. She did not begin to write until in her 40s, publishing her first novel, *Kate Hannigan*, in 1950. Most of her novels are set in the NE of England, several of them belonging to a series tracing the features of a single character or family, such as *Tilly Trotter* (1981). Other novels include *Rooney* (1957), *The Round Tower* (1968), and *The Moth* (1986). A national survey showed that in 1988 a third of all fiction borrowed from public libraries in the UK was by this author. » English literature; novel

cool jazz A jazz movement (originating in the 1940s in opposition to 'hot jazz') in which emphasis was placed on light, unforced playing. It is exemplified in the music of Miles Davis

(1926–), Gerry Mulligan (1927–), and John Lewis (1920–). » jazz

Coolidge, (John) Calvin (1872–1933) US statesman and 30th President (1923–9), born at Plymouth, Vermont. He became a lawyer, was Governor of Massachusetts (1919–20), Vice-President 1921–3, then President on Harding's death. A strong supporter of US business interests, he was triumphantly re-elected by the Republicans in 1924, but refused renomination in 1928, and died at Northampton, Massachusetts.

Cooper, Gary (Frank) (1901–61) US film actor, born at Helena, Montana, of British immigrant parents. A newspaper cartoonist in Los Angeles before working as an extra in silent films, his first leading role came in *The Winning of Barbara Worth* (1926). With the coming of sound, he continued as a star for more than 30 years, not only as the archetypal hero of Westerns (notably in *High Noon* (1952) and in the Hemingway epics *A Farewell to Arms* (1932) and *For Whom the Bell Tolls* (1943), but also representing the best of American small-town virtues in *Mr Deeds Goes to Town* (1936) and *Meet John Doe* (1941). In addition to two Oscars for Best Actor he received a Special Academy Award in 1960 for his many memorable performances. He died in Los Angeles.

Cooper, Henry (1934–) British boxer, born at Bellingham, Kent, the only man to win the Lonsdale Belt outright on three occasions. He beat Brian London to win his first British heavyweight title in 1959, and won his first Lonsdale Belt in 1961 when he beat Joe Erskine. After flooring Cassius Clay at Wembley in 1963, he had his only world title fight at Highbury Stadium in 1966, when a bad cut against Muhammad Ali (formerly Cassius Clay) forced his early retirement. He lost his British heavyweight title in a disputed contest against Joe Bugner in 1971, and announced his retirement. He carries out a lot of charity work, and is a popular television personality. » Ali, Muhammad; boxing [i]

Cooper, James Fenimore (1789–1851) US novelist, born at Burlington, New Jersey. Expelled from Yale, he joined the navy in 1806, but in 1811 resigned his commission, married, and began to write novels. He is best known for his frontier adventures such as *The Last of the Mohicans* (1826) and *The Pathfinder* (1840). He also wrote novels and historical studies about the sea. After visiting England and France, he was US consul at Lyons (1826–9). His later years were much disturbed by literary and newspaper controversies and actions for libel. He died at Cooperstown, New York. » American literature; novel

Cooper, Leon Neil (1930–) US physicist, born in New York City, and educated there at Columbia University. His theory of the behaviour of electron pairs (**Cooper pairs**) in certain materials at low temperatures was a major contribution to the theory of superconductivity, which he helped to develop. » Bardeen; superconductivity

Cooper pairs » **BCS theory**

co-operative » **collective farm; farmer co-operative**

Co-operative Party A British political party which grew out of the ideas of voluntary mutual economic assistance developed in the 19th-c by Robert Owen. Established in 1917, one candidate, who joined with the Parliamentary Labour Party, was elected to the House of Commons in 1918. Thereafter it became closely integrated with the Labour Party. » Labour Party; Owen, Robert

co-operative society A business venture owned by its members, who may be customers (in the case of a retail co-operative) or the employees (in a manufacturing company). The profits are distributed among members only. The first society was set up in 1844 in Rochdale by a group of textile workers (the Rochdale Society of Equitable Pioneers, or 'Rochdale Pioneers'); it bought food at wholesale prices, sold it at retail prices, and distributed any profits to its members in proportion to the value of their purchases. Soon each town had a 'co-op' store. In 1862, the retail co-operative societies set up the **Co-operative Wholesale Society (CWS)**, which manufactures and distributes goods to its members, its profits being ploughed back or distributed to member societies. In recent years, competition from the supermarket chains has eroded the market share of the retail co-operatives, and many small branches have closed down. Even so, together they command considerable buying power. Independent co-operative business enterprises also exist; many have sprung up since the mid-1970s, often in inner city areas and regions with high unemployment. By no means all have been successful.

co-ordinate geometry » **analytic geometry**

co-ordination compounds Compounds containing metal atoms to which other atoms, molecules, or ions are bonded by means of the donation of lone pairs of electrons; also called **complex ions**. Most common for the transition metals, they are very widespread. Examples range from simple ions such as the brilliant blue salt tetra-amminecopper(II) sulphate, $[Cu(NH_3)_4]^{2+}SO_4^{2-}$, to enzymes including haemoglobin (iron) and chlorophyll (magnesium). » enzyme; transition elements

coot A bird of the rail family, inhabiting freshwater; front of head with horny shield; sides of toes lobed, to assist swimming; pelvis and legs modified for diving. The name is sometimes misapplied to related birds. (Widespread genus: *Fulica*, 9 species.) » moorhen; rail

copal » **kauri gum**

Copán [ko**pahn**] 14°52N 89°10W. An ancient Mayan city in the Motagua Basin of W Honduras, noted for its three-dimensional stone carving; flourished in the 8th-c AD; area 39 sq km/15 sq ml; now a world heritage site; town of Copán (or Santa Rosa de Copán) nearby, pop (1983e) 19 055. In 1839 the US explorer John Lloyd Stephens (1805–52) and artist Frederick Gatherwood (1799–1856) bought the site for $50 from the local inhabitants so they could uncover and record the monuments uninterrupted. » Honduras [i]; Mayas

Copenhagen, Danish **København**, ancient **Hafnia** 55°43N 12°34E, pop (1981) 493 771. Capital city of Denmark, on E coast of Zealand and N part of Amager I; developed around 12th-c fortifications; charter, 1254; capital, 1443; airport (Kastrup); railway; university (1479); technical university of Denmark (1829); shipping and commercial centre; engineering, foodstuffs, brewing; old citadel of Frederikshavn; Tivoli amusement park (May–Sep); Amalienborg Palace (residence of Danish monarch since 1794); Christiansborg Palace; town hall (1894–1905); national (Thorwaldsen) museum; cathedral; Little Mermaid sculpture; 17th-c Trinitatiskirke; Rosenborg Castle (1610–24), now a museum. » Denmark [i]

Copenhagen Interpretation In quantum mechanics, the view expressed by Danish physicist Neils Bohr and others that any quantum system must be considered in conjunction with relevant measuring equipment, since the act of making a measurement is part of the system. A definite quantum state does not exist until some measurement is performed. This is the current orthodox interpretation of quantum measurement. » quantum mechanics

copepod [**koh**puhpod] A small aquatic arthropod; free-living forms extremely abundant in most marine and freshwater habitats, forming a vital link in the food chain by feeding on minute plant plankton; contains c.9 000 species, many being commensals or parasites of other animal groups. (Subphylum: *Crustacea*. Subclass: *Copepoda*.) » arthropod; commensalism; cyclops; food chain; parasitology; plankton

Copernican system A model of the Solar System in which the Sun is at the centre, with the Earth and other planets moving in perfectly circular orbits around it (a *heliocentric* system). Prior to the publication of this theory in 1543, it was held that the Earth lay at the centre of the universe. To reproduce the observed planetary motions in that system, a complex arrangement of circular orbits is needed. By adopting the simpler heliocentric viewpoint, Copernicus was able to sweep away the mediaeval cosmic clockwork of wheels within wheels, and thus give the first modern view of our place in the universe. It fell to Kepler to demonstrate that elliptical orbits were superior to perfect circles, and to Newton to explain the orbits through gravitational theory. » Copernicus; Kepler; Newton; Ptolemaic system; Solar System; Sun

Copernicus, Nicolas, Polish **Mikołaj Kopernik** (1473–1543) The founder of modern astronomy, born at Toruń, Poland. He studied mathematics and optics at Kraków, then canon law at Bologna, before becoming canon of Frombork. His 400-page treatise, *De revolutionibus orbium coelestium* (On the Revolutions of the Celestial Spheres, completed 1530) had a hostile reception when it was published (1543), as it challenged the ancient teaching. He died at Frombork. » astronomy; Copernican system

Copland, Aaron [**kohp**land] (1900–90) US composer, born in New York City. He studied under Rubin Goldmark, and in France under Nadia Boulanger, returning to the USA in 1924. A series of early works influenced by Stravinsky, neoclassical in outlook and employing jazz idioms, was followed by compositions in which he tapped a deeper vein of US tradition and folk music, as in the ballets *Billy the Kid* (1938) and *Appalachian Spring* (1944). He has also composed film scores, two operas, and three symphonies.

Copleston, Frederick (Charles) (1907–) British Jesuit philosopher, born near Taunton. Educated at Marlborough and Oxford, he was ordained in 1937, and became professor of the history of philosophy at Heythrop College (1939) and of metaphysics at the Gregorian University, Rome (1952). He wrote several books on individual philosophers and movements, as well as an 8-volume *History of Philosophy* (1946–66).

copper Cu, element 29, density 9 g cm^{-3}, melting point 1 080°. The only brown metal, known from ancient times; its name derives from Cyprus, the main source in Roman times. It occurs free in nature, but more commonly as CuS and $CuCO_3$. It corrodes slowly, conducts electricity well, and is used mainly in electrical apparatus. Compounds show oxidation states +1 and, more commonly, +2. Copper(II) sulphate ($CuSO_4.5H_2O$) is used as an antiseptic and pesticide. » brass; bronze; chemical elements; metal; RR90

Copper Age » **Three Age System**

Copperbelt pop (1980) 1 248 888; area 31 328 sq km/12 093 sq ml. Province in C Zambia; economic centre of the country because of its vast copper and cobalt reserves, the world's largest known deposits; capital, Ndola; chief mines at Mufulira, Nkana, and Chibuluma; mining area extends into the N of the country and into S Zaire. » copper; Zambia [i]

Copperhead A term for members of the US Democratic Party who opposed the Civil War, derived from the name of a poisonous snake. In the election of 1864, Copperheads included a peace plank in their party platform, but this was repudiated by the presidential candidate, George McClellan. » American Civil War

copperhead A pit viper native to SE USA; top of head reddish-brown; bites more people in N America than any other venomous snake, but venom is weak and deaths are rare. (*Agkistrodon contortrix*.) The name is also used for the SE Australian *Austrelaps superbus* of family *Elapidae*. The Asian pit viper *Agkistrodon acutus* is called the **Chinese copperhead**. » pit viper [i]

coppice Woodland in which the trees are periodically cut to near ground-level to encourage new growth. The cutting is usually done in rotation, and the regular opening up of the canopy encourages woodland flowers. The practice was widespread in the management of woods in the UK until the 19th-c.

Coppola, Francis Ford (1939–) US film director and screenwriter, born in Detroit. He studied the theatre in New York, and film-making in Los Angeles. His first feature as director was *Dementia 13* (1963), and this was followed by the musical, *Finian's Rainbow* (1967). Among his outstanding productions were *The Godfather* (1972; *Part II*, 1974) and his controversial study of the Vietnam War *Apocalypse Now* (1979). Later films include *The Cotton Club* (1984), *Peggy Sue Got Married* (1987), and *Tucker, the Man and the Dream* (1988).

copra The dried kernel of the coconut. In the 1860s, to supplement supplies of animal fats, manufacturers of soap, margarine, and lubricants turned to tropical vegetable oils, especially coconut oil. At first traders bought oil from local people, but later plantations were set up to produce copra, from which the oil is extracted by crushing. The Philippines, Indonesia, Sri Lanka (Ceylon), Malaysia, and the Pacific islands have been the largest producers. » coconut palm

co-processor An additional processor used in some computers or microcomputers to carry out specialized tasks such as fast arithmetical calculations or computer graphics displays. The co-processor is often designed to do this task more efficiently than the main processor, and its presence results in a substantial increase in the overall speed of the computer. » computer graphics

coprolalia The uncontrolled verbalization of obscenities. It occurs rarely in a variety of psychiatric disorders. » psychiatry

Coptic art A style of art which flourished in Egypt, 5th–8th-c. The Copts were Christians, and their wall-paintings, woven textiles, and stone carvings reflected late-Roman, Syrian, and Byzantine influences. After the 9th-c Islamic influence predominated. » art; Byzantine art; Egyptian art

Coptic Church (Gk **aigyptos** 'Egyptian') The Christian Church in Egypt of ancient origin, claiming St Mark as founder, and scholars and bishops of Alexandria in the early centuries of Christianity as fathers (eg Clement, Athanasius). With the condemnation of Patriarch Dioscuros and the Monophysite doctrine by the Council of Chalcedon (451), the Copts split from the rest of the Church, and by the 6th-c included almost all Egypt. This Church was gradually weakened by religious strife, invasions by Arabs in the 7th-c and 11th-c, and Turks in the 16th-c, accompanied by mass conversions to Islam. It preserves the Coptic (ancient Egyptian) language, and observes the liturgy and sacraments of the ancient Alexandrian rite. It maintains a monastic tradition and structure, its head (called a 'pope') being elected by a religious tribunal and confirmed by the Egyptian government. » Athanasius; Chalcedon, Council of; Clement of Alexandria; Islam; Mark, St; Monophysites

copyright Ownership of and right of control over all possible ways of reproducing a 'work', ie the product of an original creative act by one or more people, in a form which makes it possible to be copied. In particular, copyright protection is given to literary, dramatic, and artistic works (paintings, drawings, photographs, etc), sound recordings, films, television and sound broadcasts, and various productions of the new technology. All major countries (except for China) and most minor ones have copyright laws, and international protection is given via two major conventions. The laws of each country differ, but there are important characteristics common to most. Copyright is a property owned by the creator (unless working under a contract of employment), but it is transferable: the creator can either assign full copyright to another party or, retaining copyright, lease out (directly or through a publisher or agent) any of the separate rights (eg to translate) which make up the copyright. It extends to all 'works': the hurried private letter receives as much protection as the great novel. It is finite: at some time or other (commonly, 50 years after the creator's death) the work falls into public ownership and can be copied without permission. It is divisible: copyright in a novel, for example, will include the right to publish in translation, to turn into a film, to anthologize, etc. It is independent of the work as a physical object: ownership of a manuscript or painting does not in itself constitute ownership of the copyright. » publishing

cor anglais ('English horn') A woodwind instrument with a slightly conical bore, a double reed, and a distinctive bulb-shaped bell. Neither English nor a horn, it is in effect a tenor oboe, a transposing instrument (in F) sounding a 5th below the written pitch. » reed instrument; woodwind instrument [i]

coracle A small circular craft first constructed from reeds in basket form by ancient Britons. Watertightness was achieved originally with hides, but latterly with pitch. It was light enough to be carried on a man's back. The tradition mainly survives in Wales, where coracles are still used by salmon fishermen.

CORAL An acronym of **Computer On-line Real-time Application Language**, a high-level computing language often used in military applications for real-time programming. » programming language; real-time computing

coral A typically massive hydroid, found in colonies in warm shallow seas; many produce a calcareous external skeleton forming coral reefs; polyp phase of life cycle dominant, with many specialized types of individuals; medusa often small and transparent. (Phylum: *Cnidaria*. Class: *Hydrozoa*.) » calcium; coelenterate; Hydrozoa; medusa; polyp (marine biology)

Coral Sea or **Solomon Sea** Arm of the Pacific Ocean, bounded

W by NE Australia, N by Papua New Guinea and the Solomon Is, and E by Vanuatu and New Caledonia; many coral islands; maximum depth in New Hebrides Trench, 9 175 m/30 101 ft; Great Barrier Reef along W edge; scene of US victory over Japanese (1942). >> Great Barrier Reef; Pacific Ocean

Coral Sea Islands, Territory of the Uninhabited territory in the Coral Sea off the NE coast of Australia, administered by the Australian government since 1969; comprises scattered reefs and islands (including the Great Barrier Reef) over a sea area of about 1 million sq km; manned meteorological station on Willis I. >> Australia [i]

coral snake A venomous snake native to the New World (genera: *Micrurus* and *Micruroides*) and E Asia (genus: *Calliophis*); usually with bold alternating bands of black, yellow, and red; strong venom, but not aggressive; short fangs do not inject venom easily, and snake either grips prey in mouth after strike, or bites several times. (Family: *Elapidae*.) >> snake

coral tree A tropical tree and shrub armed with spines; leaves with three leaflets; pea-flowers red or orange, often waxy-looking, showy, in dense clusters, borne when the tree is bare of leaves. The flowers are an important source of nectar and water for birds and animals during the dry season, and also attract ants, which guard the tree. Coral trees are grown as ornamentals in warmer countries, and provide shade in crop plantations. (Genus: *Erythrina*, 100 species. Family: *Leguminosae*.) >> shrub; tree [i]

corbelling A prehistoric method of constructing a vault, using courses of dry stone stepped successively inwards until they come close enough together to span with a single slab or capstone. The chambered tombs of Maes Howe and New Grange afford notable early examples in N Europe. In the Aegean, the so-called Treasury of Atreus of c.1300 BC at Mycenae is the widest single-span chamber known ever to have been built before Hadrian's Pantheon, its corbelled dome measuring 14.5 m/48 ft in diameter, and standing 13 m/43 ft high. >> chambered tomb; Maes Howe; New Grange

Corbières [kaw**byair**] Sparsely populated upland district in Aude department, S France, lying between the Massif Central and the Pyrenees; highest point, Pic de Bugarach (1 231 m/4 039 ft); lower-lying area known for its red wine; chief locality, Quillan. >> Massif Central; Pyrenees

Corbusier, Le [kaw**bü**zyay] pseudonym of **Charles Edouard Jeanneret** (1887–1965) Swiss architect and city planner, born at La Chaux-de-Fonds. He worked in Paris with Auguste Perret, and then with Peter Behrens in Germany (1910–11). In 1919 he published, with Amédée Ozenfant, the Purist manifesto, and developed a theory of the interrelation between modern machine forms and architectural techniques. His first building, based on the technique of the Modulor (a system using units whose proportions were those of the human figure), was the *Unité d'habitation*, Marseilles (1945–50). Some of his buildings are raised on stilts or *piloti*, an innovation he first used in the Swiss Pavilion at the Cité Universitaire at Paris. His city planning designs include those used in Algiers (1938–42), Buenos Aires (1938), and Chandigarh (1951). He wrote several books, and has had a worldwide influence on town planning and building design. He died at Cap Martin, France. >> architecture

cord grass A perennial marine grass, native to coasts in temperate regions, mainly N America. *Spartina* x *townsendii*, a fertile hybrid between a British and an American species, is often planted as a mud-binder, and is spreading rapidly in the wild in Britain. (*Genus: Spartina*, 16 species. Family: *Gramineae*.) >> grass [i]; perennial

Corday (d'Armont), (Marie) Charlotte (1768–93) French noblewoman, born at St Saturnin, who murdered the revolutionary leader Jean Paul Marat. She sympathized with the aims of the Revolution, but was horrified by the acts of the Jacobins. She managed to obtain an audience with Marat, while he was in his bath, and stabbed him. She was guillotined four days later. >> French Revolution [i]; Jacobins (French history); Marat

Cordeliers, Club of the [kawdel**yay**] An extreme revolutionary club founded in Paris (1790) by Danton and Marat; also called the **Society of the Friends of the Rights of Man and Citizen**. Under Hébert's leadership its programme became increasingly radical (1792–4), contributing to the downfall of the Girondins (1793). >> Danton; French Revolution [i]; Girondins; Hébert; Marat

Córdoba (Argentina) [**kaw**dohba], Span [**kor**thoba] 31°25S 64°11W, pop (1980) 968 664. Capital of Córdoba province, C Argentina; on the R Primero, near the foothills of the Sierra de Córdoba; founded by Cabrera in 1573; renowned as a Jesuit mission centre; 3 universities (including Argentina's first, 1613); airport; railway; vehicles, textiles, cement, glass; cathedral (1758). >> Argentina [i]; Cabrera; Jesuits

Córdoba (Spain) [**kaw**dohba], Span [**kor**thoba] 37°50N 4°50W, pop (1981) 284 737. Capital of Córdoba province, Andalusia, S Spain; on R Guadalquivir, 400 km/250 ml SSW of Madrid; capital of Moorish Spain, 8th-c; bishopric; airport; railway; tourism, brewing, wine, olives, textiles, paper, tools, copper; cathedral, old Jewish quarter, Moorish Alcazar; Great Mosque is a world heritage site; Festival of los Patios Cordobeses (May), fair of Our Lady of la Salud (May), autumn fiestas (Sep). >> Andalusia; Córdoba Cathedral; Spain [i]

Córdoba Cathedral Originally a mosque built (785–6) by Abd-er-Rahman I (731–88) in Córdoba, Spain, and extended in the 9th-c and 10th-c. It has been used as a Christian cathedral since 1238, when the Moors lost control of the area. It is now a world heritage site. >> cathedral; Córdoba (Spain)

core curriculum A basic central provision for all pupils, as opposed to a set of options taken only by some. It usually contains subjects like mathematics, science, and the pupil's native language, though in some schools and in some countries the core may be larger.

core electrons Electrons closer to the nucleus than the valence electrons. They usually play no part in chemical reactions. >> valence

Corelli, Arcangelo (1653–1713) Italian composer, born at Fusignano. From c.1675 he lived in Rome, where he was in great demand as a violinist, spending the last 22 years of his life in the service of Cardinal Ottoboni. His concerti grossi, and his solo and trio sonatas for violin, mark an epoch in chamber music, and greatly influenced a whole generation of composers. He died in Rome. >> concerto grosso

Corelli, Marie, pseudonym of **Mary Mackay** (1855–1924) British novelist, born in London. She trained for a musical career, but then became a writer of romantic melodramas, which proved to be extremely popular, such as *A Romance of Two Worlds* (1886), *Barabbas* (1893), and *The Sorrows of Satan* (1895). She died at Stratford-upon-Avon, Warwickshire. >> English literature; novel

Corfu, Gr **Kérkira** pop (1981) 96 533; area 592 sq km/228 sq ml. Northernmost and second largest of the Ionian Is, Greece, off NW coast of Greece; seventh largest Greek island; length 64 km/40 ml; semi-mountainous terrain (highest point 907 m/2 976 ft), dense vegetation; chief town, Corfu, pop (1981) 33 561; airport; local ferries to mainland Greece and to Italy, Yugoslavia, Turkey; textiles, fishing, tourism, olive oil, fruit; Church of St Spyridon, old fortress (1386); Navy Week (Jun–Jul). >> Greece [i]; Ionian Islands

corgi The only British spitz breed of dog; small with long body, very short legs, pointed muzzle, large erect ears; two varieties: short-tailed *Pembroke* and long-tailed *Cardigan*; also known as **Welsh corgi**. >> dog; spitz

coriander An annual, growing to 50 cm/20 in, native to N Africa and W Asia; leaves with narrow linear lobes; flowers white or pink, petals unequal, in umbels 1–3 cm/0.4–1.2 in across; fruit 3–4 mm/0.12–0.16 in, globular. It is cultivated for the leaves, which are used in Chinese, Indian, and Mexican cooking, and for the fruits, used as a spice in sausages, curries, confectionery, and liqueurs. (*Coriandrum sativum*. Family: *Umbelliferae*.) >> annual; spice; umbel

Corinth, Gr **Kórinthos** 37°56N 22°55E, pop (1981) 22 658. Capital town of Corinth department, Greece; on an isthmus separating the Adriatic Sea from the Aegean; founded before 3000 BC; influential Greek city-state of Dorian origins, often at odds with Ionian Athens; famous in antiquity for its commercial and colonizing activities; ancient Kórinthos, 7 km/4 ml SW; transferred to new site in 1858, after a severe earthquake;

railway; ferry to Italy; wine trade, tourism; extensive remains, including Archaic Temple of Apollo and several basilicas; Navy Week (Jun–Jul). » Dorians; Greece [i]; Greek history; Ionians; Peloponnesian War

Corinth Canal An artificial waterway bisecting the Isthmus of Corinth in Greece; built 1881–93, although excavation of a canal through the Isthmus was begun as early as AD 67; length 6.5 km/4 ml.

Corinthian order One of the five main orders of classical architecture, characterized by a fluted shaft and a decorative acanthus capital. It was first invented in Athens in the 5th-c BC, later developed by the Romans, and used extensively in the Renaissance period. » acanthus; capital; column; Greek/Renaissance/Roman architecture; orders of architecture [i]

Corinthians, Letters to the Two New Testament writings, widely accepted as genuinely from the apostle Paul to the church that he founded in Corinth. The first describes his efforts to deal with a variety of ethical and doctrinal problems dividing the church at Corinth; the second is his response to later developments in this church, to the efforts to collect funds for the Jerusalem church, and to charges against him by opponents. » New Testament; Paul, St; Pauline Letters

Corinto [kohreentoh], formerly **Punta Icacos** 12°29N 87°14W, pop (1980e) 12 000. Port in Chinandega department, Nicaragua; chief Pacific port of Nicaragua; founded, 1840; railway; trade in sugar, coffee, hides, timber. » Nicaragua [i]

Coriolanus, Gaius or **Gnaeus Marcius** (5th-c BC) Roman folk hero, so named from his capture of the Volscian town of Corioli. Banished by the Romans for tyrannical behaviour (491 BC), he took refuge with the Volscians, and proceeded to lead them against his native city. After entreaties from his mother and wife, he spared Rome, and was executed by the Volscians. » Roman history [i]

Coriolis force An apparent force acting on objects moving across the Earth's surface; named after French mathematician Gustave Gaspard Coriolis (1792–1843). It results from the Earth's rotation, and is distinct from centripetal force. In the N hemisphere, the path of an object appears deflected to the right, in the S hemisphere to the left. It is responsible for wind and ocean current patterns, and is applicable to rotating systems generally. » centripetal force [i]

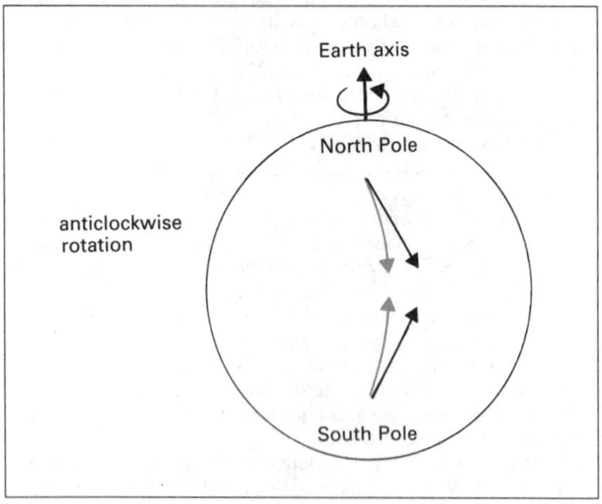

Deflections (red lines) from expected paths (black lines) resulting from the Coriolis force. They are observed in the flight of missiles and artillery shells.

cork A spongy, protective layer just beneath the outer bark in trees, made up of thin-walled cells impregnated with a waxy substance (*suberin*). The cork layer may be built up over several years, becoming very thick. » bark; cork oak

Cork (county), Gaelic **Chorcaigh** pop (1981) 402 465; area 7 459 sq km/2 879 sq ml. County and county borough, Munster, S Irish Republic; prosperous agricultural and industrial county bounded S by Atlantic Ocean and watered by the Lee, Bandon and Blackwater Rivers; the Boggeragh and Nagles Mts rise to the NW and N; capital, Cork; fishing, agriculture; natural gas and oil off Kinsale Head, with terminal facilities at Whiddy I; Blarney Castle. » Blarney; Cork (city); Irish Republic [i]; Munster

Cork (city), Gaelic **Chorcaigh** 51°54N 8°28W, pop (1981) 149 792. Commercial seaport, county borough, and capital of Cork county, Munster, S Irish Republic; on R Lee near its mouth on Lough Mahon; third largest city in Ireland; airport; docks and ferry terminal; railway; university (1845); shipbuilding, brewing, tanning, food processing; St Finbarr's Cathedral, St Mary's Cathedral; cattle shows (Feb); international folk dance and choral festival. » Cork (county); Irish Republic [i]

cork oak An evergreen tree growing to 20 m/65 ft, native to the Mediterranean region; leaves holly-like, glossy, with spiny margins; bark produces very thick cork layer which can be removed in cylindrical sheets from the trunk without harming the tree. It is cultivated as a commercial source of cork. (*Quercus suber*. Family: *Fagaceae*.) » cork; evergreen plants; oak; tree [i]

corm A short underground shoot containing food reserves. Early growth of foliage and flowers totally depletes the reserves, and a new corm is formed on top of the old one at the end of each year before the plant dies back. » bulb

Cormack, Allan Macleod (1924–) South African physicist, born in Johannesburg, where he worked at the Groote Shuur Hospital after graduating in physics at Cape Town. There he developed a technique for computer-assisted X-ray imaging (*CAT scanning*) which has proved valuable in diagnostic medicine. He shared the Nobel Prize for Physiology or Medicine in 1979. » computerized axial tomography; Hounsfield; X-rays

cormorant A large gregarious seabird, found worldwide; dark plumage, often with bright naked facial skin; flies fast, usually close to water surface; swims underwater using feet; eats fish. Some species are called **shags**. Cormorants are important guano producers in the S hemisphere. (Family: *Phalacrocoracidae*, 31 species.) » guano

corn belt The major agricultural region of the US Midwest. It is centred on the states of Iowa and Illinois, and includes parts of S Dakota, Minnesota, Nebraska, Kansas, Missouri, Ohio, and Indiana. Its main products are corn (maize) and other feed-grain. Livestock raising is also common. » maize; Middle West

corn borer A small, dull-coloured moth with long snout-like mouthparts; caterpillars feed on plants, especially maize, burrowing into stalks, leaves, and ears; an important pest of maize worldwide. (Order: *Lepidoptera*. Family: *Pyralidae*.) » maize; moth

Corn Laws British legislation regulating the trade in corn. This was common in the 18th-c, but the most famous Corn Law was that enacted by Lord Liverpool's government in 1815. Passed at a time when market prices were dropping rapidly, it imposed prohibitively high duties on the import of foreign corn when the domestic price was lower than 80 shillings (£4) a quarter. Widely criticized by radical politicians as legislation designed to protect the landed interest at the expense of the ordinary consumer, the Corn Law was amended in 1828, with the introduction of a sliding scale, and duties were further reduced by Peel in 1842. The Laws were repealed in 1846. » Anti-Corn-Law League; Liverpool, Earl of; Peel

corn marigold An annual native to Europe and W Asia; leaves toothed or divided, somewhat fleshy, the upper clasping the stem; flower-heads golden yellow. Once a troublesome cornfield weed, it is still found on arable land. (*Chrysanthemum segetum*. Family: *Compositae*.) » annual; marigold

corn poppy An erect annual, growing to 60 cm/2 ft, producing white latex, native to Europe and Asia, and introduced elsewhere; leaves divided, bristly; flowers round, four petals, bright scarlet, with or without dark basal patch; capsule pepper-pot shaped with a ring of pores around the rim. It was formerly a widespread weed, with seeds lying dormant in the soil for many years, rapidly reappearing when soil is freshly turned, as in arable or disturbed land; now declining because of improved farming techniques. It is a poignant symbol of World War 1, when fields bloomed with poppies after the churning by battle.

(*Papaver rhoeas*. Family: *Papaveraceae*.) » annual; latex; poppy

corn spurrey A slender annual, 7–40 cm/2¾–15 in; leaves very narrow, fleshy, in clusters; flowers 4–7 mm/⅛–¼ in in diameter, white, five petals; seeds 1.2–1.5 mm/0.047–0.059 in, black. It is a cosmopolitan weed, but was a crop plant grown for its seeds from pre-Roman to mediaeval times, and is occasionally used today for fodder. (*Spergula arvensis*. Family: *Caryophyllaceae*.) » annual

corncockle An annual with a little-branched stem, 30–100 cm/12–40 in, clothed in white hairs; flowers 3–5 cm across with stalks and calyx-tube woolly, petals reddish-purple, slightly notched. Once a common weed of cornfields everywhere, it is now decreasing, and is rare in places. The seeds are thought to be poisonous; when numerous, they reduce the quality of flour. (*Agrostemma githago*. Family: *Caryophyllaceae*.) » annual; cereals; sepal

corncrake A bird of the rail family, native to Europe and W Asia, also known as the **landrail**; migrates to tropical Africa in winter, otherwise seldom seen flying or in groups; inhabits grassland and cultivation; eats seeds and insects. (*Crex crex*.) » crake; rail

cornea The transparent front part of the outer protective fibrous coat of the eyeball. The degree of its curvature varies from person to person, and also with age (greater in youth than in old age). A large inequality in its vertical and horizontal curvatures is known as *astigmatism* (an inability to focus vertical and horizontal lines at the same point). The cornea is largely responsible for the refraction of light entering the eye, focusing it approximately on the retina, so that the lens can make the final fine adjustment. It is devoid of blood vessels in the adult (except at its margins), which presumably explains why corneal grafts escape rejection. » eye [i]; refraction [i]; retina; transplantation

Corneille, Pierre (1606–84) French dramatist, born at Rouen. He trained as a lawyer, but in 1629 went to Paris, where his comedy *Mélite* was highly successful, and he became a favourite of Cardinal Richelieu. Other comedies followed, then in 1636 *Le Cid*, a classical tragedy, took Paris by storm. Other major tragedies were *Horace* (1639), *Cinna* (1639), and *Polyeucte* (1640). *Le Menteur* (1642, The Liar) entitles him to be called the father of French comedy as well as of French tragedy. A master of the alexandrine verse form, he wrote many other plays, and in 1671 joined Molière and Quinault in writing the opera *Psyché*. After his marriage in 1640 he lived in Rouen until 1662, then settled in Paris, where he died. » alexandrine; comedy; drama; French literature

cornelian cherry A deciduous shrub or tree, growing to 8 m/26 ft, native to Europe and W Asia; leaves oval, opposite; flowers appearing before leaves in small clusters 2 cm/¾ in in diameter, 4-petalled, yellow; berries bright red, acid but edible. (*Cornus mas*. Family: *Cornaceae*.) » deciduous plants; shrub; tree [i]

Cornelius, Peter von (1783–1867) German painter, born at Düsseldorf, who influenced the revival of fresco painting in 19th-c Germany. In 1811 he joined a group of painters (the Nazarenes) in Rome, and helped in the decoration of the Casa Bartoldi. He went to Munich in 1819, where he executed the large frescoes of Greek mythology in the Glyptothek and the New Testament frescoes in the Ludwigskirche. In 1841 he became director of the Academy in Berlin, where he died. » fresco; German art; Nazarenes

cornet A musical instrument made of brass. The modern cornet, resembling a small trumpet with three valves, is used above all in brass bands. It is sometimes used in symphony orchestras, especially in France. » brass instrument [i]; flugelhorn

cornetfish Colourful tropical marine fish found around reefs and sea-grass beds; head and body very slender, length up to 1.8 m/6 ft; scaleless, tail bearing a whip-like process; predatory, feeding on other small fishes; also called **flutemouth**. (Family: *Fistulariidae*.)

cornett A musical instrument in use from the 15th-c to the mid-18th-c, made from two pieces of hollowed wood, glued together and covered with leather to form a tube, usually curved, with a conical bore. This was provided with finger-holes and a cup-shaped mouthpiece like that of a brass instrument. The cornett has been revived in modern times for performing older music, including Bach's cantatas, in which it often doubles the highest voice part. » Bach, Johann Sebastian; brass instrument [i]; woodwind instrument [i]

cornflour The flour of the maize seed, favoured by cooks as a thickening agent in sauces and soups.

cornflower A branched annual growing to 80 cm/30 in, native to SE Europe; leaves narrowly lance-shaped, with grey cottony hairs, the lower lobed; flower heads 1.5–3 cm/½–1½ in across, solitary, long-stalked; outer florets bright blue, spreading, larger than the inner red-purple florets; also called **bluebottle**. It was once widely introduced as a cornfield weed, but is now rare because of the improved cleaning of seed grain. Its petals were used to produce a blue pigment used by artists. (*Centaurea cyanus*. Family: *Compositae*.) » annual; floret

cornice [**kaw**nis] In classical or Renaissance architecture, the crowning, projecting part of an entablature. In a general sense, it may refer to any crowning ornamental projection along the top of a building or wall. » entablature

Cornish The Celtic language once spoken to the W of the R Tamar in Cornwall. It shares some features with dialects of S Welsh, with which it was originally geographically contiguous. There is some religious literature, mainly translations from English, from the 15th–16th-c, showing vast lexical borrowing from English. The last speakers died in c.1800, and there is some interest in a modern revival of the language. » Celtic languages

cornucopia A classical motif of a ram's horn overflowing with fruit and flowers, symbolizing abundance and plenty. It was much used in Renaissance and later decorative schemes to do with eating and drinking. » Renaissance

Cornwall, Celtic **Kernow** pop (1987e) 453 100; area 3 564 sq km/1 376 sq ml. County in SW England, divided into eight districts and the Isles of Scilly; bounded S by the English Channel, and W by the Atlantic Ocean; county town, Truro; tin mining, dairy farming, market gardening, fishing, tourism; Cornish nationalist movement revived the Stannary (Tinners' Parliament) in 1974, and there is renewed interest in the Cornish language. » Cornish; England [i]; Stannaries; Truro

Cornwallis, Charles, 1st Marquis (1738–1805) British general and statesman, born in London. Educated at Eton and the Military Academy of Turin, he served in the Seven Years' War. Though personally opposed to taxing the American colonists, he accepted a command in the war, defeated Gates at Camden (1780), but was forced to surrender at Yorktown (1781). In 1786 he became Governor-General of India, where he defeated Tippoo Sahib, and introduced the series of reforms known as the **Cornwallis Code**. He returned in 1793, to be made marquis. He was Lord-Lieutenant of Ireland (1798–1801), and negotiated the Peace of Amiens (1802). Reappointed Governor-General of India (1804), he died at Ghazipur. » American Revolution; Tippoo Sahib

corolla » flower [i]; petal

Coromandel Coast The E coast of India, extending more than 650 km/400 ml from Point Calimere in the S to the mouth of the Krishna R in the N.

coromandel screen A screen made of wood, lacquered and incised with coloured decoration. Such screens were imported in large numbers for the European luxury trade in the later 17th-c from the Far East. » lacquer

corona (astronomy) The outermost layers of the Sun's atmosphere, visible as a pinkish halo of light during a total eclipse, temperature 500 000 K. It is a source of strong X-rays. » chromosphere; solar wind; Sun; X-rays

corona (botany) An extension of the corolla (petals) of a flower, such as the central trumpet of a daffodil. » flower [i]

Corona Australis (Lat 'southern crown') [kuh**roh**na aw**stra**lis] A small but prominent S constellation on the fringes of the Milky Way. » constellation; Milky Way; RR8

Corona Borealis (Lat 'northern crown') [kuh**roh**na bohree**a**lis] A small N constellation, the stars forming a striking semicircle. » constellation; RR8

corona discharge An electrical discharge accompanied by the emission of blue light that sometimes occurs in the air surrounding the sources of an intense electric field. Electrons and ions in the air are accelerated by the field, giving rise to further ions; light is produced by the recombination of ions with electrons. » electron; ion

coronagraph An optical instrument for producing an artificial eclipse inside a telescope. Real eclipses last only a few minutes, and most take place far from any observatory. With a coronagraph, it is possible to study the outer layers of the solar atmosphere without waiting for the next eclipse. » eclipse; telescope [i]

coronary heart disease Atherosclerosis of the coronary arteries, the most important cause of death over 40 in developed countries in the West, and the commonest cause of angina pectoris and myocardial infarction; also known as **ischaemic/ischemic** heart disease. Although coronary artery disease may cause sudden death, this likelihood may vary greatly in areas where coronary atheroma is similar in prevalence. Smoking also contributes to sudden death, and is especially liable to do so in the presence of atherosclerosis. There are large differences in the prevalence of coronary artery disease between countries, and it appears to be a disorder of affluence, unbalanced diet, stress, and obesity. The prevalence also changes if individuals alter their socio-economic status; for example, there is a rise in incidence in Bantu who migrate to South Africa, or in Irish who migrate to the USA.

There is a positive relationship between coronary artery disease and the level of blood cholesterol, but this level is on the whole little influenced by changes in the dietary intake of cholesterol (apart from a few cases where blood cholesterol is extremely high). Increasing evidence points to an important role in the diet of polyunsaturated fats, which possibly have a protective influence on the development of atheroma. In communities (eg Eskimos) with a high intake of these fats, the incidence of coronary artery disease is low. » angina; atherosclerosis; cholesterol; heart disease; myocardial infarction; polyunsaturated fatty acids

coroner A public officer who investigates the cause of a death, especially one where there is reason to suspect that it was not due to natural causes, in some cases holding an official inquiry, or *inquest*. Inquests into treasure trove are also held in the coroner's court. Coroners are appointed by the Crown, and must be qualified as a medical doctor or a lawyer.

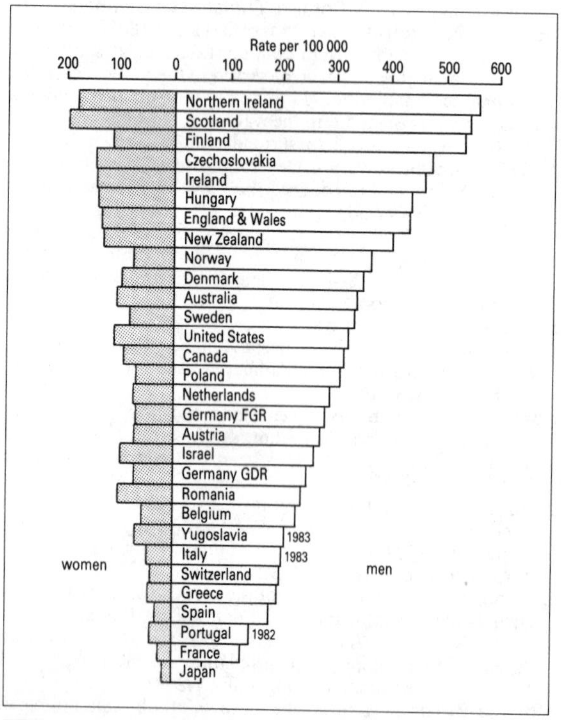

Coronary heart disease – The chart shows age–standardized rates of mortality for men and women aged 40 to 49 in 1985

Corot, (Jean Baptiste) Camille [koroh] (1796–1875) French landscape painter, born and died in Paris. Educated at Rouen, he took up art in 1822, and after visiting Italy, settled in Paris (1827). His main sketching ground was at Barbizon, in the Forest of Fontainebleau; but he made two other visits to Italy in 1835 and 1843. Several of his masterpieces, such as 'La Danse des nymphes' (1850) are in the Louvre. » Barbizon School; French art; landscape painting

corporate state » **corporatism**

Corporation Act A British Act passed by the Cavalier Parliament in 1661, soon after the Restoration of Charles II. Office in municipal corporations was restricted to those who took the sacrament according to the usage of the Church of England. Part of the re-assertion of Anglican supremacy represented by the Clarendon Code, the Act remained on the statute book until 1828. » Church of England; Clarendon Code; Restoration

corporation tax A tax levied on company profits by the UK government, created in 1966; its predecessor was the *profits tax*. The tax rate payable has been changed over the years, and small firms pay the tax at a lower rate. » company; taxation

corporatism Arrangements where the authority to decide and implement economic and social policies is either shared with or delegated to groups of producers who are expected to abide by principles laid down by the state. Failure to do so may lead to a withdrawal of decision-making and representational rights. It produces a quasi-private system of government. Corporatism (often termed **corporativism** in the 1920s and 1930s) is found in authoritarian countries, which are sometimes referred to as **corporate states**, where the freedom of producers' associations is severely curtailed, and they act largely as agents of the state. Less formalized, but often widespread corporatist arrangements are also found in many liberal democracies which operate by negotiation; the term **neo-corporatism** is usually applied, and such developments have become increasingly prominent in recent years (eg in Japan and parts of W Europe).

Corpus Christi, Feast of [kawpus kristee] A festival of the Roman Catholic Church in honour of the Eucharist, instituted by Pope Urban IV in 1264 and observed on the Thursday after Trinity Sunday. » Eucharist

Corpus Juris Canonici [korpus jooris kanonikiy] (Lat 'body of canon law') The chief collection of church or canon law of the Roman Catholic Church and, to an extent, of the Anglican Churches. It includes the decrees of popes and canons, and rules formulated by the Councils, eg the Decretals of Gregory IX. Canon law exercised considerable influence on the development of civil and international law. The 'Corpus' was succeeded in the Roman Catholic Church by the **Codex Juris Canonici** (1918). » canon law; Codex Juris Canonici

Corpus Juris Civilis » **Justinian Code**

corpus luteum [cawpuhs lootiuhm] The mass of yellowish tissue remaining after ovulation, when a mature Graafian follicle ruptures from the ovary of a mammal. If fertilization does not occur after ovulation, the corpus luteum rapidly breaks down. » fertilization; Graafian follicle

Correggio, originally **Antonio Allegri** (c.1494–1534) Italian Renaissance painter, born at Correggio. In 1518 he began his great series of mythological frescoes for the convent of San Paolo at Parma, and 1521–4 was engaged upon 'The Ascension' in the cupola of San Giovanni. The decoration of the cathedral of Parma was commissioned in 1522. He also painted many easel pictures on religious themes, such as 'The Nativity', known as 'The Night' (Dresden). He returned to Correggio in 1530, where he died. » fresco; Italian art; Renaissance

correlation In mathematics, a measure of the extent to which there is a linear relation between two variables. Given a set of data (x_i, y_i), standard deviation of x and y s_x and s_y, and covariance s_{xy}, a **correlation coefficient** r is defined by $s_{xy}/s_x s_y$. If r is close to 1, there is said to be good positive correlation: y increases as x increases. If r is close to -1, there is good negative correlation: y decreases as x increases. **Rank correla-**

tion compares orders, not numerical values, using different statistics. » statistics

Correns, Karl Erich (1864–1933) German botanist, born in Munich. He taught at Tübingen (1892–1902), Leipzig (1902–9), and Münster (1909–14), and from 1914 was director of the Kaiser Wilhelm Biological Institute at Berlin. He rediscovered the neglected results reported in Mendel's paper on the principles of heredity, and confirmed them by his research on the garden pea. He died in Berlin. » genetics [i]; Mendel

correspondence principle (physics) The requirement that the quantum theory of sub-microscopic systems, when applied to macroscopic systems, gives results consistent with those of classical mechanics. The principle ensures that classical and quantum mechanics are compatible. » mechanics; quantum mechanics

correspondence theory of truth A theory which maintains that a proposition's truth consists in its corresponding to a fact, independent of beliefs. It contrasts with *coherence* theories, which maintain that a proposition's truth consists in its 'fit' with other beliefs, and *pragmatic* theories, which maintain that truth consists in the effectiveness of one's beliefs. » coherence theory; pragmatism

corrie » **cirque**

Corrigan, Mairead (1944–) One of the two Roman Catholic women who founded the movement for peace in Northern Ireland, known as the 'Peace People' (1976). Along with **Betty Williams** (1943–), she won the Nobel Peace Prize in 1977. » Northern Ireland [i]

corroboree [kuh**rob**uhree] A term used by 19th-c settlers in New South Wales, Australia, for any Aboriginal ceremonial or festive gathering which included singing and dancing. Later it came into common use among non-Aborigines, but it fails to mark the distinction between religious ceremonies and non-religious performance practised by Aboriginal peoples. » Aborigines

corrosion Destructive oxidation, usually by air in the presence of water; most marked for metals, especially iron. It is an electrochemical process, occurring most rapidly when two different metals are in contact with one another and with air and water, the more reactive metal being oxidized while the other provides a surface for the reduction of O_2. Corrosion prevention is best carried out by isolating the reactive metal surface from air and water. Some metals, including aluminium and zinc (*passive* metals) form adherent oxide coatings which serve this purpose. » aluminium; metal; oxidation; rust; tin; zinc

corsairs Dutch, English, and French privateers licensed by governments to prey upon enemy shipping in the Channel and Atlantic during the Wars of the Grand Alliance (1689–97) and the Spanish Succession (1702–13). The most famous were Captain Kidd, who turned to piracy, and Frenchman Jean Barth, who was enobled. » buccaneers; Kidd

Corsica, Fr **Corse** pop (1982) 240 178; area 8 680 sq km/3 350 sq ml. Mountainous island and region of France in the Mediterranean Sea, comprising the departments of Corse-du-Sud and Haute-Corse; length 183 km/114 ml; width up to 84 km/52 ml; separated from Sardinia (S) by the Strait of Bonifacio; part of France since 1768; France's largest island; mountainous interior, rising to 2 710 m/8 891 ft at Mont Cinto; fertile alluvial plains (E), edged with lagoons and swamps; airport; car ferries from Nice, Toulon, Marseilles; capital, Ajaccio; chief towns Bastia, Calvi, Corte, Bonifacio; corks, asbestos, vines, olives, fruit, sheep, goats; major scenic area, with a wide range of tourist activities; the 'Calanches' (above Gulf of Porto), granite pinnacles worn into bizarre forms resembling fabulous animals; Parc de la Corse regional nature park, area 1 483 sq km/572 sq ml. » France [i]; maquis; Sardinia

Cort, Henry (1740–1800) British ironmaster, born at Lancaster, Lancashire. He became a navy agent in London, then in 1775 bought an ironworks near Plymouth, inventing the 'puddling' process for converting pig iron into wrought iron, as well as a system of grooved rollers for the production of iron bars. Ruined by a prosecution for debt, he was ultimately pensioned, and died in London. » iron

Cortés or **Cortéz, Hernán** [kawtez] (1485–1547) The Spanish conqueror of Mexico, born at Medellín. He studied at Salamanca, then accompanied Velázquez in his expedition to Cuba (1511). In 1519 he commanded an expedition against Mexico, fighting his first battle at Tabasco. He founded Vera Cruz, marched to Tlascala, and made allies of the natives. He then marched on the Aztec capital, capturing the king, Montezuma; but the Mexicans rose, and Cortés was forced to flee. He then launched a successful siege of the capital, which fell in 1521. He was formally appointed Governor and Captain-General of New Spain in 1522, but his authority was later superseded. He spent the years 1530–40 in Mexico, then returned to Spain. He died near Seville. » Aztecs; New Spain

Cortes [**kaw**tez] The representative assembly in Spain, which became the Spanish parliament after the fall of the monarchy in 1931. It continued to exist under Franco, but with little or no powers. In 1977 it became a two-chamber parliament, elected upon universal suffrage, and its powers were extended in 1978 after a national referendum. » Franco; parliament

cortex An outer layer of an organism or biological system. For example, the adrenal cortex is the outer layer of the adrenal gland. In the brain of vertebrates, the cerebral cortex is a layer of grey matter lying above each cerebral hemisphere. In plants, the cortex is the tissue lying just below the epidermis. » adrenal glands; brain [i]; cerebrum; epidermis

corticosteroids Steroid hormones produced and secreted by the adrenal glands, including hydrocortisone, corticosterone, and aldosterone. They have numerous effects in the body, influencing metabolism, salt and water balance, and the function of many organs. Preparations of natural and synthetic corticosteroids (eg cortisol, prednisolone) are used to treat a wide range of diseases, such as arthritis and cancer. » adrenal glands; aldosterone; cortisol; hormones; steroid [i]

corticotrophin » **adrenocorticotrophic hormone**

cortisol A steroid hormone found in the adrenal cortex of vertebrates; also known as **hydrocortisone**. In some mammals (eg humans, dogs), it is the major glucocorticoid hormone. It promotes the conversion of protein and fat into glucose, and has an important role in the body's resistance to physical and psychological stress, especially after trauma. Its synthesis and release are primarily controlled by adrenocorticotrophic hormone. » adrenal glands; biological rhythm; corticosteroids; glucocorticoids; steroid [i]

corundum A mineral formed from aluminium oxide (Al_2O_3); extremely hard and used as an abrasive. Gemstone varieties are ruby and sapphire. » emery; gemstones; ruby; sapphire

Corunna [ko**ruh**na], Span **La Coruña**, ancient **Caronium** 43°20N 8°25W, pop (1981) 232 356. Seaport and capital of La Coruña province, Galicia, NW Spain; on the Atlantic coast, 609 km/378 ml NW of Madrid; base of the Spanish Armada, 1588; city sacked by Drake, 1589; scene of British victory during the Peninsular War, and the death of Sir John Moore; airport; railway; car ferries to the Canary Is; watersports; oil, iron and steel, shipbuilding, clothes, food canning, fishing; Hercules Tower, Church of Santiago; Fiesta of the Virgen del Carmen (Jul), Fiesta of Maria Pita (Aug), Galician Pilgrimage (Sep). » Drake, Francis; Galicia; Moore, John; Spanish Armada

corvette [kaw**vet**] A small single-screw warship designed for convoy escort duties in World War 2. In former times, it was a single gun-decked, three-masted, square-rigged sailing vessel, originally of French design and adopted by the British. » warships [i]

Corvus (Lat 'crow') [**kaw**vuhs] A small N constellation, named in ancient times. » constellation; RR8

Corybantes [koree**ban**tayz] The attendants and eunuch priests of the Phrygian nature goddess, the Cybele, whose orgiastic cult was officially introduced into Rome towards the end of the Punic Wars. » Phrygia

coryphaena [kori**fee**na] » **dolphinfish**

coryza [kuh**riy**za] » **cold**

Cos, Gr **Kós**, Ital **Coo** area 290 sq km/112 sq ml. Island of the Dodecanese, E Greece, in the Aegean Sea, off the SW coast of Turkey; length 43 km/27 ml; width 2–11 km/1¼–7 ml; hilly E region, rising to 846 m/2 776 ft at Mt Dikaios; severely damaged by earthquakes in 1933; capital, Cos, pop (1981) 11 851; cereals, olive oil, wine, fruit, tourism; famous in antiquity for its wine, amphorae, and 'Coan garments', and for the cult of Asclepius and its doctors, notably Hippocrates; sanctuary of Asclepios, 15th-c Castle of the Knights of St John; Plane Tree of Hippocrates; Navy Week (Jun–Jul). » Asclepius; Dodecanese; Greece [i]; Hippocrates

Cosgrave, William Thomas (1880–1965) Irish statesman and first President of the Irish Free State (1922–32), born and died in Dublin. He joined the Sinn Féin movement at an early age, and took part in the Easter Rising (1916). He was elected a Sinn Féin MP (1918–22), and after his years as President became Leader of the Opposition (1932–44). His son, **Liam** (1920–) was Leader of the Fine Gael Party (1965–7) and Prime Minister (1973–7). » Fine Gael; Sinn Féin

Cosmas and **Damian, Saints** (?–c.303), feast day 27 September (W), 27 October (E). Arabian twin brothers, said to have been physicians at Aegaea, Cilicia, who were cast into the sea as Christians, but rescued by an angel. Thereafter, burning and stoning having proved ineffectual, they were beheaded by Diocletian. They are the patron saints of physicians. » Christianity; Diocletian

cosmetics Preparations for artifically beautifying the human hair and complexion, used at various historical periods by both men and women. Fashionable women in W Europe have painted their faces since the Greek and Roman periods, to conform to a sequence of youthful ideals. The effects were formalized and unnatural in the later mediaeval period and during the 16th-c; in the 17th-c and 18th-c, black 'patches' representing moles or beauty spots were popular, to contrast with the flawless effect of the rest of the complexion: for most of the 19th-c, detectable 'make-up' was considered the mark of the fast or theatrical rather than the respectable woman. Many of the preparations used until recent times were dangerous to the health, or even potentially fatal (eg white lead).

cosmic dust Microscopic grains of dust of extraterrestrial origin. It enters Earth's atmosphere at high velocity, and is slowed down by friction in the uppermost atmosphere. It spends months floating in the stratosphere, and can be collected by high-flying research aircraft or in space at space stations. The particles are a few microns in size, often with porous structure. Some are believed to be dust from comets; also called **Brownlee particles**, after the original collector. » comet; meteorite; meteor; space station

cosmic rays High energy electrons and ions moving through space, thought to be produced by exploding stars. When the particles strike the Earth's atmosphere, secondary rays comprising mostly pions and muons are produced. Cosmic rays are a useful source of high-energy particles for experiments. They also contribute to natural background radiation. » background radiation; muon; pion; particle physics

cosmic string Hypothetical massive filaments of matter (10^{19} kg/cm) predicted in supersymmetry theory as an important component of the very early universe. » supersymmetry; universe

cosmogony » **cosmology**

cosmological argument An argument for the existence of God as the first cause of all things, championed especially by Aquinas. The argument appeals to the intuitions that the existence of the universe cannot be explained by things *in* the universe, and that there should be only one first cause. » Aquinas; God

cosmological constant A constant introduced by Einstein into equations of general relativity to give a static model of the universe, later claimed by him to be a mistake; symbol Λ; sign unknown; size uncertain, but less than 10^{-25} kg/m^3; often assumed to be zero. In cosmology, the value and sign are related to the expansion or contraction of the universe. » cosmology; Einstein; general relativity

cosmology The study of the universe on the largest scales of length and time, particularly the propounding of theories concerning the origin, nature, structure, and evolution of the universe. A cosmology is any model said to represent the observed universe. Western cosmology is entirely scientific in its approach, and has produced two famous models in modern times: the Big Bang and the steady state hypotheses. The study of the origin and mode of formation of various celestial objects is known as **cosmogony**. » astronomy: Big Bang; steady state theory; universe

cosmonaut The Russian term for a spacecraft crew member. Over 60 crewed flights, involving over 125 personnel, including two women, were carried out in the Soviet space programme to the end of 1987. The longest flight duration by an individual was that of Yuri Romanenko who spent 326 days in the space station Mir in 1987. Four cosmonauts have lost their lives as a direct result of spaceflight-related accidents. » astronaut; Soviet space programme; space physiology and medicine; space station

Cossacks Originally, members of semi-independent communities of fugitive peasants and military adventurers inhabiting the steppelands of S Russia and the Ukraine. Attempts to limit Cossack freedom led to several large-scale rebellions against the Russian government in the 17th–18th-c. In the 18th–19th-c they were formed into military organizations (*hosts*), and earned a reputation for ferocious fighting and skilled horsemanship. » Russian history

cost-accounting A branch of accountancy which seeks to calculate the cost of a product, operation, department, or activity, both historically and as planned, thereby establishing a current standard or norm. The actual cost can be compared against the standard to determine whether costs are getting out of line with expectations. » accountancy

cost-benefit analysis An attempt to quantify in money terms the benefits which will come from a capital expenditure scheme by a government department, where no direct savings are apparent, as in the case of a new motorway. The decision to proceed depends on the benefits being greater than the costs incurred.

cost of living (index) » **retail price index**

Costa Blanca [**kos**ta **blang**ka] The coastal resort regions of Murcia, Alicante, and part of Almería provinces, E Spain; on the Mediterranean coast extending S from Cabo San Antonio to the Punto Almerimar; summer and winter tourism; the name means 'white coast'. » Spain [i]

Costa Brava [**kos**ta **brah**va] The Mediterranean coastal resort region of Catalonia, E Spain, between Barcelona and the French border; the name means 'wild coast'. » Spain [i]

Costa de la Luz [**kos**ta t͟hay la **loos**] Resort region on the Atlantic coastline of Huelva and Cádiz provinces, S Spain; from the Portuguese border to the most S tip of Spain at Tarifa on the Strait of Gibraltar; the name means 'coast of light'. » Spain [i]

Costa del Azahar [**kos**ta t͟hayl aza**khahr**] Mediterranean coastal resort region of Castellón de la Plana and Valencia provinces, E Spain; between the Costa Dorada (N) and Costa Blanca (S); longest stretch of coast in Spain; the name means 'orange-blossom coast'. » Spain [i]

Costa del Sol [**kos**ta t͟hayl **sol**] Mediterranean coastal resort region, Andalusia, S Spain, extending from Punto Almerimar to the most S point in Spain at Tarifa; the name means 'coast of the sun'. » Spain [i]

Costa Dorada [**kos**ta duh**rah**da] Mediterranean coastal resort region S of the Costa Brava, Barcelona, and Tarragona provinces, E Spain; the name means 'golden coast'. » Costa Brava; Spain [i]

Costa Dourada [**kos**ta **do**rada] Atlantic coastline of W Portugal between the Ponta da Arrifana and the mouth of the R Sado; chief resorts, Aljezur, Vila Nova de Milfontes, Porto Covo; the name means 'golden coast'. » Portugal [i]

Costa Rica, official name **Republic of Costa Rica**, Span **República de Costa Rica** [**kos**ta **ree**ka] pop (1990e) 3 015 000; area 51 022 sq km/19 694 sq ml. Second smallest republic in C America, divided into seven provinces; bounded W by the Pacific Ocean, N by Nicaragua, E by the Caribbean, and SE by Panama; capital, San José; chief towns, Cartago, Heredia, Liberia, Puntarenas, Limón; timezone GMT −6; mainly Spanish descent; main religion, Roman Catholicism; official language, Spanish; unit of currency, the colón of 100 centavos; crossed by Inter-American Highway; airport at San José; formed by a series of volcanic ridges; highest peak, Chirripó

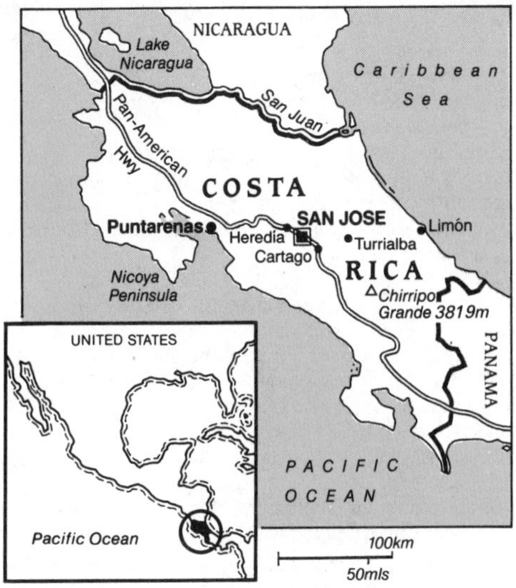

□ international airport

Grande (3 819 m/12 529 ft) in the Cordillera de Talamanca; central plateau, Meseta Central, area 5 200 sq km/2 000 sq ml, altitude 800–1 400 m/2 600–4 600 ft; drained W by R Grande into the Pacific, NE by R Reventazón into the Caribbean; much swampy land near coast, with tropical forest as land rises; tropical climate, with small temperature range and abundant rainfall; more temperate in C uplands; dry season (Dec–May); average annual rainfall, 3 300 mm/130 in, with much local variation; average annual temperature, 26–28°C; visited by Columbus, 1402; named Costa Rica ('rich coast') in the belief that vast gold treasures existed; independence from Spain, 1821; member of Federation of Central America, 1824–39; democratic republic governed by an executive president and Legislative Assembly of 57 deputies (elected for four years), and a 20-member cabinet; economy primarily agriculture, mainly coffee (especially in Meseta Central), bananas, sugar, cattle; timber, fishing, gold, silver, bauxite; oil exploration in collaboration with Mexico; food processing, textiles, fertilizers, plastics, pharmaceuticals, electrical equipment. » Pan-American Highway; San José (Costa Rica); RR25 national holidays; RR46 political leaders

costmary A sweetly aromatic perennial growing to 90 cm/3 ft, native to W Asia; leaves elliptical, minutely toothed; flower heads numerous, in flat-topped clusters; spreading outer florets white, inner disc florets yellow; also called **alecost**. Its strong-smelling foliage was formerly used for flavouring ales. (*Balsamita major*. Family: *Compositae*.) » floret; perennial

Cosway, Richard (1742–1821) British miniaturist, born at Tiverton, Devon. He studied with Thomas Hudson in London, and became a fashionable painter of portraits, patronized by the Prince of Wales. The use of watercolour on ivory is a notable feature of his work. In 1781 he married the artist **Maria Hadfield** (1759–1838), also a miniaturist. He died at Edgware, Middlesex. » English art; miniature painting; watercolour

cot death » **sudden infant death syndrome**

Côte d'Ivoire [koht deev**wah**], official name **Republic of Côte d'Ivoire** (Eng **Ivory Coast**), Fr **République de Côte d'Ivoire** pop (1990e) 12 657 000; area 320 633 sq km/123 764 sq ml. Republic of W Africa, divided into 26 departments; bounded SW by Liberia, NW by Guinea, N by Mali and Burkina, E by Ghana, and S by Gulf of Guinea; capital, Yamoussoukro; chief towns Abidjan, Bouaké, Daloa, Man, Korhogo, Gagnoa; timezone GMT; wide range of ethnic groups, including the Agni, Baoule, Krou, Senoufou, and Mandingo; chief religions, local beliefs (63%), with Muslim (25%) and Christian (12%); official language, French, with many local languages; unit of currency, the franc CFA; sandy beaches and lagoons backed by broad forest-covered coastal plain; land rises towards savannah at 300–350 m/1 000–1 150 ft; Mt Nimba massif in NW at 1 752 m/5 748 ft; rivers generally flow N–S; tropical climate, varying with distance from coast; rainfall decreases N; average annual rainfall at Abidjan, 2 100 mm/83 in; average temperatures 25–27°C; explored by Portuguese, 15th-c; French influence from 1842; declared French protectorate, 1889; colony, 1893; territory within French West Africa, 1904; independence, 1960; governed by a 175-member National Assembly and executive president (both elected for 5-year terms), with a Council of Ministers; economy largely based on agriculture, which employs c.82% of the population; world's largest cocoa producer, third largest coffee producer; bananas, rice, pineapples, cotton, coconuts, palm oil, sugar, cassava, corn; livestock, fishing, food processing, timber, textiles, clothing, vehicle assembly, small shipyards, fertilizers, battery production, oil refining, cement. » Abidjan; Yamoussoukro; RR25 national holidays; RR46 political leaders

cotinga [kuh**ting**gga] A bird native to the New World tropics; inhabits woodland. Most species eat fruit; some catch insects in flight. (Family: *Cotingidae*, 65 species.) » cock of the rock; umbrella bird

Cotman, John Sell (1782–1842) British watercolourist, born at Norwich, Norfolk. He studied art in London, and in 1806 returned to Norwich, where he became a leading member of the Norwich School. At Yarmouth (1811–23), he executed some fine oil paintings and etchings; but lack of success made him sell his pictures and possessions and return to London (1834), where he became drawing master of King's College. His best work shows a masterly arrangement of masses of light and shade, with a minimum of modelling, as in 'Greta Bridge' (c.1805). His two sons were also landscape painters. He died in London. » English art; landscape painting; Norwich School; watercolour

cotoneaster [kuhtohnee**as**tuh] A deciduous or evergreen shrub or small tree, native to N temperate regions; variable in size and shape, branches arching, spreading or erect; leaves oval to rounded, often with bright autumn colours; flowers usually in clusters, 5-petalled, white or pink; berries yellow, red, or black. They are widely used as ornamental and amenity plants. (Genus: *Cotoneaster*, 50 species. Family: *Rosaceae*.) » deciduous plants; evergreen plants; shrub; tree [i]

Cotonou [kohton**oo**] 6°24N 2°31E, pop (1982e) 487 020. Port in Ouémé province, S Benin, W Africa; on a sandspit between the Bight of Benin and L Nokoué; largest city in Benin, and its

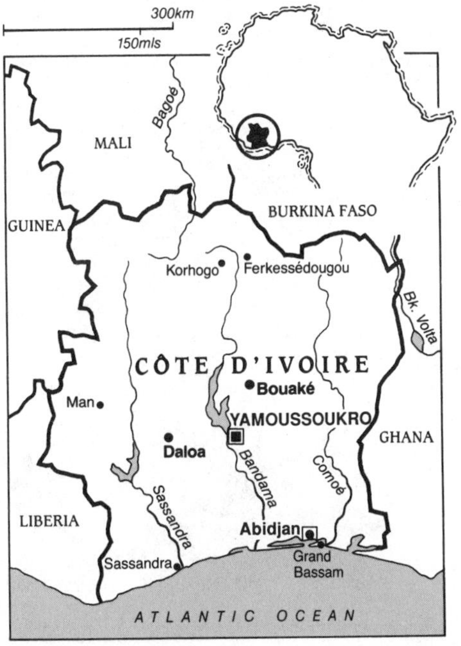

□ international airport

political and economic centre, though not the official capital; seat of the Presidency, most ministries, the National Assembly, and all embassies; centre for most commercial activities; airport; railway; university (1970); vegetable oils, soap, brewing, textiles, power plant. » Benin [i]; Porto Novo

Cotopaxi [kohtoh**pak**see] 0°40S 78°26W. Active Andean volcano in NC Ecuador; 48 km/30 ml S of Quito; height 5 896 m/19 344 ft; highest active volcano in the world; national park, area 340 sq km/131 sq ml, established in 1975; llama breeding station and NASA satellite tracking station nearby. » Andes; Ecuador [i]; NASA

co-trimoxazole [kohtriy**moks**azohl] An antibiotic containing the two drugs trimethoprim and sulfamethoxozole, each of which kills infecting bacteria by a different mechanism. The combination is therefore more effective, and resistance is less likely to occur. It is used for kidney and bladder infections. » antibiotics; drug resistance

Cotswold Hills or **Cotswolds** [**kotz**wohld] Hill range mainly in Gloucestershire, SE England; extends 80 km/50 ml NE from Bath to Chipping Camden, separating the lower R Severn from the source of the R Thames; rises to 333 m/1 092 ft at Cleeve Cloud, near Cheltenham; gives its name to a breed of sheep; district noted for its mellow-coloured limestone, used in many picturesque villages. » England [i]

Cottian Alps, Fr **Alpes Cottiennes** Division of the W Alps in SE France along the French–Italian frontier, from the Alpes Maritimes at Maddalena Pass to the Alpes Graian at Mont Cenis; highest peak, Monte Viso (3 851 m/12 634 ft). » Alps

cotton The name of both a plant and the fibre it produces. Cotton is related to mallows, hollyhocks, and hibiscus, all members of the mallow family (*Malvaceae*). They include annuals and perennials, many shrubby and growing up to 6 m/20 ft high, though usually much less in cultivation. The leaves are palmately lobed; the funnel-shaped flowers, up to 5 cm/2 in diameter, with creamy-white, yellow or reddish petals, are visited by bees and hummingbirds. The ovoid seed pods (*bolls*) burst when ripe to reveal tightly-packed seeds covered with creamy-white fibres which contain 87–90% cellulose.

Cotton is graded according to the length (*staple*) and appearance of the fibres. The highest quality are **long staple**, such as Sea island cotton (*Gossypium barbadense*), with lustrous fibres 2.5–6.5 cm/1–2½ in long, used for yarns and fine fabrics. **Medium staple**, such as American upland cotton (*Gossypium hirsutum*) has fibres 1.3–3.3 cm/½–1¼ in long, used for a variety of fabrics. **Short staple** cottons have coarse fibres 1–2 cm/0.4–0.8 in long, used for cheap fabrics, blankets, and carpets. The bolls are picked when ripe, either by hand or by machine after the plants have been chemically defoliated, causing all the bolls to open simultaneously. Four processes then follow: removal of the seeds (*ginning*), cleaning and separating (*carding*), stretching (*drawing*), and finally *spinning* into yarn. One of the most useful natural fibres, cotton is a crop of worldwide importance; major producing countries include the USA, Russia, China, India, Egypt, and Turkey. (Genus: *Gossypium*, c.20 species. Family: *Malvaceae*.) » annual; cellulose; cotton gin; mallow; mercerizing; palmate; perennial

cotton gin A machine, invented in 1793 by Eli Whitney in the USA, which separated the seeds from the cotton boll quickly and efficiently. It greatly increased productivity, meant that the short staple cotton grown in the USA could be used, and provided a large, cheap supply of raw cotton for the world. » cotton [i]; Whitney, Eli

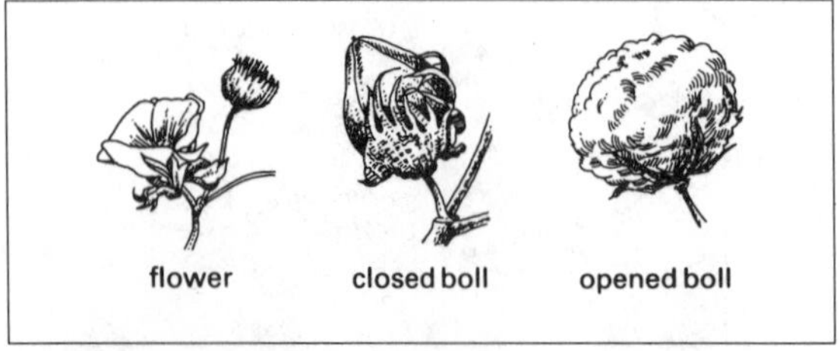

Cotton flower and boll

cotton stainer A plant-feeding bug that feeds by sucking sap; its habit of piercing the bolls of cotton plants transmits a fungus that stains the cotton fibres. (Order: *Heteroptera*. Family: *Pyrrhocoridae*.) » bug (entomology); cotton [i]

cotton tree » **kapok tree**

cottongrass A grass-like perennial, native to cool and arctic parts of N temperate regions; stem leafy; flower spikes brownish, perianth consisting of numerous white hairs which elongate in fruit, forming a conspicuous cottony head. (Genus: *Eriophorum*, 21 species. Family: *Cyperaceae*.) » grass [i]; perennial; perianth

cottonmouth A pit viper native to SE USA; inside of mouth white; lives near water; mainly nocturnal; eats vertebrates (especially fish and frogs); one of the few snakes to eat carrion; venom very dangerous, coagulates the blood (collected for this purpose in medicine); also known as **water moccasin**. (*Agkistrodon piscivorus*.) » pit viper [i]

cottontail A type of rabbit, native to the New World; inhabits open country or woodland clearings; only one species digs burrows; remainder shelter in burrows of other animals or under vegetation. (Genus: *Sylvilagus*, 13 species.) » myxomatosis; rabbit

cottonwood » **poplar**

cottony cushion scale A small scale insect that lives on stems and leaves of citrus trees; adult females immobile, covered by protective scale; eggs laid in mass of waxy fibres resembling cotton wool; a serious pest of citrus orchards. (Order: *Homoptera*. Family: *Margarodidae*.) » citrus; scale insect

cotyledons [kotil**ee**dnz] Embryo leaves present in a seed. Usually very different in appearance to the true leaves, they are either fleshy and remain underground as a food store, or are thin and raised above ground to act as the first leaves of the seedling. » dicotyledons; germination; leaf [i]; monocotyledons

couch grass [kooch, kowch] A dull-green perennial grass with numerous creeping rhizomes, native to temperate regions; spikelets set edge-on to stem in a stiff, erect spike; a tenacious weed, difficult to eradicate; also called **twitch grass**. (*Elymus repens*. Family: *Gramineae*.) » grass [i]; perennial; rhizome

cougar A member of the cat family, found from Canada to S America; grey or reddish brown; solitary; territorial; lives in diverse habitats; eats mainly deer; also known as **puma**, **mountain lion**, **catamount**, **panther**, **painter**. (*Felis concolor*.) » Felidae

Coulomb, Charles (Augustin de) [koolõ] (1736–1806) French physicist, born at Angoulême. He experimented on friction, and invented the torsion balance for measuring the force of magnetic and electrical attraction. He died in Paris. » coulomb; Coulomb's law; electricity

coulomb [**coo**lom] SI unit of electric charge; symbol C; named after French physicist Charles Coulomb; defined as the quantity of electricity transported by a current of one ampere in one second. » Coulomb; electricity; units (scientific); RR70

Coulomb's law In physics, a law expressing the force F between two electrical charges p and q separated by a distance d as $F=\frac{pq}{4\pi\varepsilon_0 d^2}$, where ε_0 is the permittivity of free space, $8.854\times10^{-12}C^2/(N.m^2)$; stated by French physicist Charles Coulomb in 1785. The direction of force along the line joining the charges is repulsive for like charges, and attractive for opposite charges. » Coulomb; electrostatics; permittivity

council A political body appointed or elected to perform specific functions or provide services, whose powers may be advisory or executive. It may be locally, nationally, or internationally based; at local level, county and district councils exist in England and Wales, regional and district councils in Scotland. » county/district/parish council; local government

Council for Mutual Economic Assistance (COMECON) A body founded in 1949 by Stalin, and dominated by the Soviet Union; its purpose was ostensibly the economic integration of the Eastern bloc as a means of counteracting the economic power of the EEC and EFTA. The 10 member states were the USSR, Bulgaria, Cuba, Czechoslovakia, Hungary, Poland, Romania, East Germany, Mongolia, and Vietnam. It was disbanded in 1991, and replaced by the Organization for

International Economic Co-operation. » European Economic Community; European Free Trade Association

Council for the Protection of Rural England A pressure group founded in 1926 as the Council for the Preservation of Rural England. With 42 county branches, it aims to promote the protection and improvement of the countryside and rural amenities. Subjects of recent campaigns include afforestation, new towns, motorways, and energy policy. The Council for the Protection of Rural Wales is a similar organization. » conservation (earth sciences)

Council of Europe An association of European states, established in 1949, whose representatives include the UK, France, Germany, Italy, Netherlands, and Eire. It has a Committee of Foreign Ministers and a representative Consultative Assembly which meets at Strasbourg to discuss matters of common concern, but which may only offer recommendations to ministers. A European Court of Human Rights was later added to this structure. There were 25 members in 1991.

Council of Ministers The body which allows the expression of national interest within the European Community, the minister involved depending on the subject under consideration. There are around 20 different types of council meetings; agriculture and foreign affairs have the most regular meetings. » European Community; European Council

Council of the Church In the Orthodox and Roman Catholic Churches, a meeting of bishops of the whole Church to regulate doctrine and discipline. The last Ecumenical Council (of the undivided Church) is generally held to be the Second Council of Nicaea (787). The Roman Catholic Church recognizes a Council if called by a pope, and its decisions, if approved by the pope, as infallible, with guaranteed assistance of the Holy Spirit, and binding on the whole Church. Non-Roman Catholic Churches recognize the World Council of Churches (formed in 1948), but infallibility is not claimed. » Basle/Chalcedon/Lateran/Nicaea/Vatican, Councils of; bishop; conciliarism; infallibility; Orthodox Church; pope; Roman Catholicism

count (textiles) In spinning, a numerical system indicating the fineness of yarn. The *tex* unit (from *textile*), is the weight mass in grams of one kilometer of yarn, and is gradually replacing older systems such as 'cotton count' and 'denier'. » yarn

count and **countess** The English translation of various foreign titles, such as Fr *comte/comtesse*, Ger *Graf/Gräfin*, and Span *conde/condesa*). It is not part of the UK peerage. However, the title is used for the wife of an earl. » earl

counter-intelligence » **military intelligence**

Counter-Reformation A general movement of reform and missionary activity in the Roman Catholic Church from the mid 16th-c, stimulated in part by the Protestant Reformation. It included the revival of the monastic movement (eg Capuchins, 1528; Oratorians, 1575), especially the creation of the Jesuit Order. It provided for the enforcement of disciplinary measures by the Roman Inquisition; its doctrinal formulations were made by the Council of Trent; and liturgical and moral reforms were introduced throughout the Church. There was a strong influence from mystics (eg John of the Cross, Teresa of Avila) and devotional teachers (eg Francis of Sales). In a secular sense, the term also refers to the success of Roman Catholic powers in Europe in the late 16th-c and early 17th-c. » Capuchins; Francis of Sales, St; Francis Xavier, St; Inquisition; Jesuits; John of the Cross, St; liturgy; monasticism; Reformation; Roman Catholicism; Teresa of Avila, St

counterfeiting Imitating some object (chiefly, currency notes and coin) in order to pass off the imitation as genuine. It is a criminal offence to counterfeit coin currently in circulation. Alterations to coins are also covered by statute. » forgery

counterpoint In music, the simultaneous combination of two or more melodic strands; distinct from 'harmony', which implies (in general terms) a chordal texture accompanying one or more melodic lines. In **invertible counterpoint**, any of the melodic strands can form a satisfactory bass line for the others. » canon (music); descant; fugue; harmony

countertenor The falsetto voice of the adult male, trained and developed to sing alto parts, especially in sacred polyphony. The revival of interest in the countertenor as a solo voice has been largely due to the artistry of Alfred Deller. » Deller

country and western A type of popular US music stemming from the hillbilly tradition of the years between the two World Wars. The country music of that time was identified with White communities in the rural areas of the Southern states; it was played at barn dances, fairs, and similar gatherings, typically on a violin, banjo, and guitar. 'Country and western', a post-war fusion of the hillbilly tradition with the more jazz-orientated country music of the SW, has developed a more urbanized, pan-American style, popularized by such performers as Merle Haggard (1937–), Johnny Cash (1932–), and Charley Pride (1938–). The influence of rock has also been felt, as in the music of Kris Kristofferson (1937–). » gospel music; pop music

country dance Historic social dances based on John Playford's *The English Dancing Master* (1651). They spread across Europe, taught by travelling dancing masters, adding 19th-c forms such as the waltz, quadrille, and polka. The emphasis was on spatial design, with couples in long or circular sets, using simple walking steps. Their decline is associated with the Industrial Revolution and the growth of towns. » traditional dance

Country Party (Australia) » **National Party** (Australia)

Country Women's Association (CWA) Australia's largest and oldest women's organization. Based on Canadian (1890s) and British examples (1913), the CWA began in New South Wales and spread to the other States. Non-sectarian and non-political, its aims are to improve welfare of rural women and children. Its many achievements include rest rooms and baby health centres in country towns. The CWA is represented at three-yearly conferences of the Associated Country Women of the World.

Countryside Commission for England and Wales A UK government amenity agency set up in 1968 to replace the National Parks Commission. It advises the government on matters of countryside interest, and formulates policy for National Parks. It provides grants for nature reserves, wardens, footpaths, and for public access to open countryside. The Countryside Commission for Scotland has similar functions, but there are no National Parks in Scotland. » National Park

county council The body elected to carry out such responsibilities as may be statutorily determined, within a defined geographical boundary. In the UK, it is normally the first in a two-tier local government system whose powers are delegated by parliament. Actions beyond these powers may be declared by the courts to be *ultra vires* (outside its authority). » council; local government

county court A court system of England and Wales, concerned with civil disputes, established in 1846. The county courts deal with cases of contract and tort, where the amount claimed does not exceed £5 000; landlord and tenant disputes, and matrimonial cases (including divorce) also come within its jurisdiction, as does the relatively informal small-claims procedure, where the sum in dispute generally does not exceed £500. The county court ranks lower in the hierarchy of courts than the High Court. » contract; High Court of Justice; tort

Couperin, François [**koo**puhrĩ] (1668–1733) French composer, born and died in Paris. He was taught by his father, whom he eventually followed as organist of St Gervais (1685). In 1693 he also became organist to Louis XIV, and in 1717 composer-in-ordinary of chamber music to the King. Known mainly as a harpsichord composer (whose influence on Bach was profound), he also composed chamber concertos and church music. » harpsichord

couple In physics, two forces equal in magnitude, acting in opposite directions, whose lines of action are not coincident, causing a turning motion. The magnetic forces on a compass needle illustrate a couple. » moment [i]; torque [i]

couplers In photographic processing, chemicals which combine with the oxidized developer to form coloured compounds adjacent to the silver image. They can form part of the developing solution, but are normally incorporated in the photographic emulsion layers. » colour photography

courante A Baroque dance in triple metre; it became a standard movement of the instrumental suite. » Baroque (music); suite

Courbet, Gustave [**koor**bay] (1819–77) French painter, born at

Ornans. He was sent to Paris to study law, but turned to painting. The founder of Realism, in 1844 he began exhibiting pictures in which everyday scenes were portrayed with complete sincerity and absence of idealism, such as 'Burial at Ornans' (1849, Louvre). His best-known work is the large 'Studio of the Painter: an Allegory of Realism' (1855, Louvre). Republican in sympathies, he joined the Commune in 1871, and on its suppression was imprisoned. Released in 1873, he fled to Switzerland, where he died, at Vevey. » French art; Realism

coureurs de bois [koorer duh **bwah**] French fur traders or voyageurs who ranged throughout the interior of America from the 1660s. They played a significant role in the exploration of NW Canada. » Métis

courgette (UK) or **zucchini** (US) A variety of marrow with small, yellow fruits. (*Cucurbita pepo*. Family: *Cucurbitaceae*.) » marrow (botany)

Courrèges, André [koo**rezh**] (1923–) French fashion designer, born at Pau. He studied civil engineering, but later turned to fashion in Paris, where he was trained by Balenciaga, and opened his own house in 1961. Famous for stark, futuristic, 'Space Age' designs, he has featured trouser (pants) suits, white boots, and short skirts. He produces ready-to-wear as well as couture clothes. » Balenciaga; fashion

courser A long-legged, short-winged running bird, native to Africa and SW Asia; inhabits deserts; dull-coloured plumage; long curved bill; three forward-pointing toes only on each foot; seldom flies; nests on ground. (Family: *Glareolidae*; subfamily: *Cursoriinae*, 7 species.) » pratincole

coursing A blood sport involving greyhounds who seek out their prey by sight and not scent. The dogs pursue in pairs, as opposed to being in packs, and the performance of one dog against another is judged. The most popular coursing event is the Waterloo Cup at Altcar, near Formby, Merseyside. First held in 1836, it takes its name from the nearby Waterloo Hotel. » blood sports

Court, Margaret (Jean), *née* **Margaret Smith** (1942–) Australian lawn tennis player, born at Albury, New South Wales. She was the winner of more Grand Slam events (66) than any other player: 10 Wimbledon titles (including the singles in 1963, 1965, 1970), 22 US titles, 13 French, and 21 Australian. In 1970 she became the second woman (after Maureen Connolly) to win all four major titles in one year. She retired in 1977. » Connolly, Maureen; tennis, lawn [i]

court martial A court which tries offences against naval, military (ie army), and air force law. The court is composed of 3–5 serving officers advised on the law by a judge advocate, a barrister. » barrister

Court of Appeal An English court, with civil and criminal divisions, which hears appeals from other courts. The civil division hears appeals from the High Court and the county court; its head is the Master of the Rolls. The criminal division hears appeals from the Crown Court; its head is the Lord Chief Justice. Appeal on a point of law may be allowed from the Court of Appeal to the House of Lords. » county court; High Court of Justice; House of Lords

Court of Justice of the European Communities The European Court which sits at Luxembourg, an institution of the European Communities, with its judges being appointed by the member states. Its functions involve the interpretation of Community treaties and legislation, and it can decide whether the conduct of any member state breaches Community law. The court also gives rulings on relevant points of law referred to it by domestic courts of member states. » European Economic Community

court of law A forum for settling legal disputes. There are two broad categories of courts as traditionally distinguished: **civil courts**, dealing with disputes between private persons; and **criminal courts**, dealing with offences against society generally. » Admiralty/Assize/Divisional Court; Court of Appeal/Justice of the European Communities/Session; arbitration; civil law; criminal law; tribunal

Court of Session A Scottish court, sitting in Edinburgh, which deals with civil matters. It has an Outer House and a more senior Inner House, analogous to the High Court and Court of Appeal respectively. » Court of Appeal; High Court of Justice

courtly love The conception of an ideal and exalted relation between the sexes, which developed in mediaeval times from sources as various as Plato's *Phaedrus*, Ovid's *Ars Amatoria*, and the cult of the Virgin Mary. Mediaeval love poetry was deeply infused by the idea, which also influenced Renaissance sonneteers, although by this time the convention was treated with some irony. » literature; Ovid; poetry; Renaissance

Cousin, Jean, known as **the Elder** [**koozī**] (c.1490–c.1560) French engraver, glass-stainer, and painter, born at Soucy. He was probably responsible for two stained-glass windows in Sens Cathedral, and a picture of a nude woman ('Eva Prima Pandora') in the Louvre. He died in Paris. His son, **Jean (the Younger**, c.1522–c.94), was also a versatile artist, who continued many aspects of his father's work. » engraving; French art

Cousin, Victor (1792–1867) French philosopher, born in Paris. After the 1830 revolution, he became a member of the Council of Public Instruction, and in 1832 a peer of France and director of the Ecole Normale. In 1848 he aided the government of Cavaignac, but after 1849 left public life. His eclectic philosophy can be seen in his *Fragments philosophiques* (1826) and *Du vrai, du beau, et du bien* (1854, On the True, the Beautiful, and the Good). He died at Cannes.

Cousins, Frank (1904–86) British trade union leader, born at Bulwell, Nottingham. A miner's son, he worked in the pits at 14, turned lorry driver, and by 1938 was a full-time union organizer. In 1955 he became General Secretary of the Transport and General Worker's Union. He was Minister of Technology (1964–6) until he resigned over the prices and incomes policy, and MP for Nuneaton (1965–6), and Chairman of the Community Relations Commission (1968–70). He died at Chesterfield, Derbyshire. » nuclear disarmament; prices and incomes policy; trade union

Cousteau, Jacques (Yves) [koos**toh**] (1910–) French naval officer and underwater explorer, born at Saint-André. He invented the Aqualung diving apparatus (1943) and a process of underwater television. In 1945 he founded the French Navy's Undersea Research Group, and commanded the research ship *Calypso* in 1950. He became director of the Oceanographic Museum of Monaco in 1957. He has written widely on his subject, and his films include the Oscar-winning *The Golden Fish* (1960). » oceanography

covalent » **chemical bond**

covariance A term describing mathematical equations whose form is identical in different co-ordinate systems; also called **form invariance**. It is an essential property of the equations of theories of gravitation and nuclear forces. » equations; gravitation; nuclear physics; variance

covenant **1** A term used in certain legal systems (eg in England and Wales, but not in Scotland) for a written document under seal; also known as a **deed**. It contains a promise to act in a certain way, which is signed, sealed, and takes effect on delivery (in the USA, the requirement of seal is now largely abolished). A transfer of property may be made by deed. In some cases there may be a tax advantage: the term is often used in the UK for members of charities to covenant their membership subscriptions (it being assumed that the subscription is paid after tax has been deducted). The charity claims back from the tax authorities a sum equal to the tax paid by the member. » contract; restrictive covenant; taxation **2** In the Hebrew Scriptures, the agreement between God and his chosen people which was the basis of Jewish religion; especially identified with the giving of the law to Moses on Mt Sinai, but preceded by a covenant with Abraham. Some New Testament writers portray the death of Jesus as a 'new covenant'. » Abraham; Moses; Ten Commandments

Covenanters Originally, signatories (and their successors) of the National Covenant (1638) and the Solemn League and Covenant (1643) in Scotland, who resisted the theory of 'Divine Right of Kings' and the imposition of an episcopal system on the Presbyterian Church of Scotland. When declared rebels, they resorted to open-air preaching. Until Presbyterianism was restored in 1690, they were savagely persecuted, with imprisonment, execution without trial, and banishment (eg to Holland or the USA). » Church of Scotland; episcopacy; Presbyterianism

Covent Garden A square in C London, known for the fruit and vegetable market that operated there for nearly three centuries; it also gives its name to the Royal Opera House close by. Once the garden of a convent in Westminster, the site was developed in the 17th-c. It was initially a fashionable area, but with the growth of the market wealthy families moved away, and cheap coffee houses and lodging houses sprang up. The market was relocated in 1974, and the buildings restored by the Greater London Council. » London [i]; Royal Opera House

Coventry [**kov**ntree], ancient **Couentrey** 52°25N 1°30W, pop (1987e) 308 900. Modern industrial city in West Midlands, C England; 150 km/93 ml NW of London; Benedictine priory founded in 1043, around which the town grew; important centre of clothing manufacture from 17th-c; University of Warwick (1965); railway; vehicles, machine tools, agricultural machinery, telecommunications equipment, artificial fibres; old cathedral (1433) destroyed during World War 2; new cathedral designed by Sir Basil Spence (consecrated 1962); 15th–16th-c Church of Holy Trinity; St Mary's Hall (1343), built for the merchants' guild; museum of British road transport. » West Midlands

cover crop A crop which protects the crop planted beneath it. Cereals are often used as a cover crop for newly sown grass and clover seeds. The term may also refer to crops, such as kale, which provide cover for game birds. » cereals

Coverdale, Miles (1488–1568) English Bible scholar, born at York. He studied at Cambridge, was ordained priest in 1514, and joined the Augustinian Friars at Cambridge, but was converted to Protestantism. His own translation of the Bible (the first complete one in English) appeared in 1535, and he then superintended the work which led to the 'Great Bible' (1539). He also edited the work known as 'Cranmer's Bible' (1540). Forced to live abroad for several years, he returned to England in 1548 and became Bishop of Exeter in 1551. On Queen Mary's accession he went abroad again, but returned in 1559, to live in London, where he died. » Bible; Protestantism; Reformation

covered wagon » **prairie schooner**

cow » **bull**

cow parsley A biennial or perennial, growing to 1.5 m/5 ft, native to Europe, temperate Asia, and N Africa; stems hollow, grooved; leaves divided, leaflets with toothed oval segments; flowers small, white, in umbels 2–6 cm/¾–2½ in across; fruit 7–10 mm/0.28–0.39 in, smooth; also called **Queen Anne's lace** and **keck**. It is often the most common and early flowering of the umbellifers. (*Anthriscus sylvestris*. Family: *Umbelliferae*.) » biennial; parsley; perennial; umbel

cow parsnip » **hogweed**

cow pea A sprawling annual, growing to 2 m/6½ ft, native to Africa; leaves with three leaflets; pea-flowers white or yellow, pinkish at the base; pods to 30 cm/12 in long. Numerous varieties cultivated in warmer countries for the edible seeds and young pods, eaten like French beans; also commonly grown for pasturage. (*Vigna unguiculata*. Family: *Leguminosae*.) » annual; bean; pea [i]

cow pox A virus disease of cattle characterized by small blisters (*pocks*) on the teats; also known as **kine pox**. The contents of these blisters were used by Edward Jenner in 1798 to vaccinate humans against the related *smallpox*. » cattle; Jenner; smallpox; virus

Coward, Sir Noel (Peirce) (1899–1973) British actor, playwright, and composer, born at Teddington, Middlesex. An actor from the age of 12, his first play, written with Esme Wynne, was produced in 1917. Among his many successes were *The Vortex* (1924), *Hay Fever* (1925), *Private Lives* (1930), and *Blithe Spirit* (1941). He wrote the music as well as the lyrics for most of his works, and was an accomplished singer. Knighted in 1970, he died at St Mary, Jamaica. » drama; theatre

cowberry A small evergreen shrub growing to 30 cm/12 in, native to N temperate regions; leaves oval, often notched at tip; flowers in terminal clusters, drooping, bell-shaped, pinkish-white; berry red, edible but acid; also called **red whortleberry**. (*Vaccinium vitis-idaea*. Family: *Ericaceae*.) » bilberry; evergreen plants; shrub

cowbird A strong-billed bird, native to the Americas; eats seeds and insects; may seek food by using bill to lift stones or cow dung. Few species build nests; most lay eggs in the nests of unrelated birds. (Family: *Icteridae*, 7 species.)

Cowell, Henry (Dixon) (1897–1965) US composer, born at Menlo Park, California. He studied in New York City and Berlin, and earned his living as a pianist, lecturer, and writer. As a composer he was noted for his experimental techniques, including note-clusters produced on the piano by using the fist or forearm. He founded *The New Musical Quarterly* in 1927. His works include two ballets, an unfinished opera, and 20 symphonies. He died at Shady, New York.

Cowes [kowz] 50°45N 1°18W, pop (1981) 16 278. Town in Medina district, I of Wight, S England; on R Medina estuary; a notable yachting centre; ferries and hydrofoil to Southampton; boat and hydrofoil building, radar, tourism; Osborne House (East Cowes), summer residence of Queen Victoria and Prince Albert; Cowes Castle, built by Henry VIII (1543), home of the Royal Yacht Squadron; Cowes Week (Aug). » Wight, Isle of

Cowley, Abraham (1618–67) English poet, born in London. Educated at Westminster School and Cambridge, he was publishing poetry at the age of 15. During the Civil War he went with the queen to Paris, was sent on Royalist missions, and carried on her correspondence in cipher with the king. After the Restoration (1660), he retired to Chertsey, where he died. His main works were the influential *Pindarique Odes* (1656), and his unfinished epic on King David, *Davideis* (1656). » English Civil War; English literature; poetry

Cowpens, Battle of (1781) During the US War of Independence, an engagement in S Carolina in which a small American army under Daniel Morgan (1736–1802) defeated a British force under Banastre Tarleton (1754–1833). » American Revolution

Cowper, William [**koo**puh] (1731–1800) British poet, born at Berkhamsted, Hertfordshire. Educated at Westminster School, he was called to the Bar in 1754. He suffered frequently from mental instability, and attempted suicide several times. While living at Olney, he collaborated with the clergyman John Newton to write the *Olney Hymns* (1779). His ballad of John Gilpin (1783) was highly successful, as was his long poem about rural ease, *The Task* (1785). He died at East Dereham, Norfolk. » English literature; poetry; Wordsworth, William

cowrie A marine snail with a glossy, smooth, and often highly patterned shell, largely covered by lobes of mantle; used as decorations and even as currency on Pacific Islands; mostly tropical in distribution, living on coral reefs. (Class: *Gastropoda*. Order: *Mesogastropoda*.) » coral; gastropod; shell; snail

cowslip A perennial with rosette of oblong, slightly crinkled leaves, native to Europe and Asia; flowers 1–30 at the tip of a common stalk, drooping, calyx tubular, petals yellow with orange spots at base. (*Primula veris*. Family: *Primulaceae*.) » perennial; polyanthus

coyote [kuh**yoh**tee] A member of the dog family, native to N and C America; inhabits grassland and open woodland; eats hares, rodents, other animals, berries; also known as **prairie wolf, barking wolf, little wolf**, or (in fur trade) **cased wolf**. (*Canis latrans*.) » Canidae

coypu [**koy**poo] A cavy-like rodent, native to S America (introduced elsewhere); large (length over 1 m/3¼ ft); rat-like with broad blunt muzzle; inhabits wetlands; burrows may damage dykes, etc; farmed for soft underfur; also known as **nutria**. (*Myocastor coypus*. Family: *Myocastoridae*.) » cavy; rodent

Cozzens, James Gould [**kuz**nz] (1903–78) US novelist, born in Chicago. He published his first novel, *Confusion*, at the age of 19. He fought in the US Air Force in World War 2, and then wrote *Guard of Honour* (1948, Pulitzer Prize). His most popular success was *By Love Possessed* (1958). He died at Stuart, Florida. » American literature; novel

CP/M An acronym of **Control Program Monitor**, a widely used operating system for microcomputers which use the Z80 microprocessor. » operating system

CP violation The violation of a fundamental symmetry

principle, observed in 1964 by US physicists James Watson Cronin (1931–) and Val Logsdon Fitch (1923–), using subatomic particles called kaons (a type of meson). C stands for *charge conjugation* (in quantum mechanics, the operation of turning a particle into its antiparticle) and P for parity (the operation of changing left- to right-hand co-ordinates). CP violation allows an absolute definition of right- and left-handedness in the universe; but its mechanism and role is not understood. » meson; parity (physics); symmetry; weak interaction

CPU » **central processing unit**

crab A typically marine crustacean with a front pair of legs specialized as pincers (*chelipeds*) and used for food capture, signalling, and fighting; usually walks sideways, using four pairs of walking legs; also capable of swimming; body broad, flattened, with a hard outer covering (carapace); abdomen permanently tucked up beneath body; eyes usually movable on stalks; some species terrestrial, some found in freshwater; eggs carried by females, usually hatching into a planktonic larval stage (*zoea*); many species exploited commercially for food. (Class: *Malacostraca*. Order: *Decapoda*.) » crustacean; Decapoda [i]; fiddler/hermit/horseshoe/land/pea/robber/spider crab; larva; plankton

Crab nebula The remnant of a star seen by Oriental astronomers to explode spectacularly on 4 July 1054. The nebula itself was named in 1848 by the 3rd Earl of Rosse. Photographs show a tangled web of filaments threading a luminous nebula. The explosion which triggered the nebula was a supernova, which expelled its outer layers and left a dense neutron star at the centre, now observed as a pulsar rotating 30 times a second. » nebula; neutron star; pulsar; supernova

crab-plover » **plover**

Crabbe, George (1754–1832) English poet, born at Aldeburgh, Suffolk. He trained as a surgeon, but turned to literature. He was ordained in 1782, and held livings in Suffolk and Wiltshire. His best-known work from this early period is *The Village* (1783), a realistic portrait of rural life. He then wrote nothing for over 20 years. His later narrative poems include *The Parish Register* (1807), *The Borough* (1810), and other volumes of *Tales*. He died at Trowbridge, Wiltshire. » Burke, Edmund; English literature; poetry

crabeater seal A true seal native to the Antarctic and sub-Antarctic; teeth with deeply notched margins, forming a sieve when mouth is shut; eats krill (despite its name); fastest true seal on land (up to 25 kph/15 mph); one of the world's most numerous large mammals (may be 15 000 000 individuals). (*Lobodon carcinophagus*.) » krill; seal (biology)

crack A blend of cocaine, baking powder, and water. The cocaine hardens to white cinder chunks which can be smoked in a small pipe. The effect is immediate. This form of cocaine is held to be extremely addictive. » cocaine [i]; drug addiction

Cracow » **Kraków**

Craig, Edward (Henry) Gordon (1872–1966) British stage designer, actor, director, and theorist, born at Stevenage, Hertfordshire. He worked for nine years as an actor in Irving's company, but left the Lyceum in 1897 to be both a director and a designer. He settled in Italy in 1906, where he published the theatre journal, *The Mask* (1908–29), which together with his scene designs and his books, *On the Art of the Theatre* (1911) and *The Theatre Advancing* (1921), had a profound influence on modern theatre practice. He died in poverty at Vence, France. » Irving, Henry; theatre

Craig, Roger (1960–) US footballer, born at Preston, Mississippi. A running back with the San Francisco 49ers, in the 1985 Super Bowl he scored 18 points and three touchdowns, both records. Also in 1985 he became the first player in National Football League history to rush for 1 000 yards and receive passes for 1 000 yards. » football [i]

Craigie, Sir William Alexander (1867–1957) British scholar, born at Dundee, Tayside, Scotland. Educated at St Andrews, he was professor of Anglo-Saxon at Oxford (1916–25), and of English at Chicago (1925–35). He was joint editor of the *New English Dictionary* (1901–33), and also editor of dictionaries on Scots and on American English. He died at Watlington, Oxfordshire. » dialectology; dictionary

crake The name often given to any smallish rail with a short, chicken-like bill (45 species). » corncrake; rail

Cram, Steve, properly **Stephen** (1960–) British athlete, born at Gateshead, Durham. The European junior champion at 3 000 m in 1979, he won senior titles at 1 500 m in 1982 and 1986. He won the World Championship gold medal at 1 500 m in 1983, and the Commonwealth Games gold medals at 1 500 m (1982, 1986) and 800 m (1986). In 1985 he set three world records in 20 days at 1 500 m, 1 ml, and 2 000 m. His time for the mile was 3 min 46.32 sec. » athletics

cramp The involuntary spasm of a muscle, or a group of skeletal muscles, which causes pain. Cramp tends to occur in the elderly and in pregnancy. The calf muscles are particularly affected. » muscle [i]

Cranach, Lucas ('the Elder') (1472–1553) German painter, so named from Kronach, near Bamberg, where he was born. In 1504 he became court painter at Wittenberg to the Elector Frederick. His paintings include sacred and a few classical subjects, hunting scenes, and portraits. He was closely associated with the German Reformers, many of whom (including Luther and Melanchthon) were portrayed by himself and his pupils. A 'Crucifixion' in the Stadkirche, Weimar, is his masterpiece. He died at Weimar. Of three sons, all painters, the second, **Lucas**, 'the Younger' (1515–86), painted so like his father that their works are difficult to distinguish. » German art; Reformation

cranberry A dwarf, creeping, evergreen shrub, native to N temperate regions on boggy, acid soils; stems very slender, rooting; leaves 4–8 mm/0.15–0.3 in, oblong-oval, pointed, bluish beneath, margins inrolled; flowers on long, slender stalks, 5–6 mm/0.2–0.24 in, pink, four petals, curling backwards; berry round or pear-shaped, red- or brown-spotted, edible. (*Vaccinium oxycoccos*. Family: *Ericaceae*.) » evergreen plants; shrub

crane A long-legged, long-necked bird, height 0.6–1.5 m/2–5 ft; worldwide except S America, New Zealand, and the Pacific; adult usually with head partly naked; inhabits flat wetlands and wet plains; eats small animals, grain, and other plant material. (Family: *Gruidae*, 14 species.) » demoiselle; whooping crane

Crane, (Harold) Hart (1899–1932) US poet, born at Garrettsville, Ohio. After an unhappy childhood, he settled in New York as a writer in 1923. His most important work is contained in *The White Buildings* (1926), a collection on New York life, and *The Bridge* (1930), an epic using Brooklyn Bridge as its focal point. He drowned himself while returning from a visit to Mexico. » American literature; poetry

Crane, Stephen (1871–1900) US writer and war correspondent, born at Newark, New Jersey. He began as a journalist in New York, and became known as a novelist through *Maggie: a Girl of the Streets* (1893) and *The Red Badge of Courage* (1895), a vivid story of the Civil War. He also wrote poems and short stories, and worked as a war correspondent in Greece and Cuba. He died at Badenweiler, Germany. » American literature; novel

cranefly A long-legged, true fly; adult body slender, legs fragile, readily discarded if trapped; female egg-laying tube prominent; larvae known as **leatherjackets**, typically ground-dwelling, feeding on roots, rarely predaceous; adults also known as **daddy longlegs**; c.13 500 species. (Order: *Diptera*. Family: *Tipulidae*.) » fly; larva

cranesbill An annual or perennial of the genus *Geranium*, native to temperate regions; leaves with lobes radiating from central point; flowers usually white to purple or blue, 5-petalled; fruit with long beak resembling a bird's bill, exploding when ripe, the beak of each seed rolling up and flicking seed away; many of the so-called geraniums of horticulture belong to the genus *Pelargonium*. (Genus: *Geranium*, 400 species. Family: *Geraniaceae*.) » annual; geranium; herb Robert; pelargonium; perennial

Cranko, John (1927–73) British dancer, choreographer, and director, born in Dublin, Ireland. He studied in South Africa at the Cape Town University ballet school and at Sadler's Wells School in London. He choreographed for both Sadler's Wells and the Royal Ballet companies, and in 1961 became ballet director of the Stuttgart Ballet. He is known chiefly for his full-length dramatic works, such as *Romeo and Juliet* (1962) and *Onegin* (1965). » ballet; choreography

Cranmer, Thomas (1489–1556) Archbishop of Canterbury, born at Aslacton, Nottinghamshire. Educated at Cambridge, he took orders in 1523, and became a divinity tutor. His suggestion that Henry VIII appeal for his divorce to the universities of Christendom won him the King's favour, and he was appointed a royal chaplain. He was made Archbishop of Canterbury in 1533, making allegiance to the Pope 'for form's sake'. He later annulled Henry's marriages to Catherine of Aragon and to Anne Boleyn (1536), and divorced him from Anne of Cleves (1540). He was largely responsible for the Book of Common Prayer (1549, 1552). On Henry's death, Cranmer rushed Protestant changes through. He had little to do with affairs of state, but agreed to the plan to divert the succession from Mary to Lady Jane Grey (1553), for which he was later arraigned for treason. Sentenced to death, he retracted the seven recantations he had been forced to sign, before being burned alive. » Book of Common Prayer; Church of England; Henry VIII; Protestantism; Reformation

craps A casino dice game of American origin, adapted from the game 'hazard' by Bernard de Mandeville in New Orleans in 1813. Using two dice, a player loses throwing 2, 3, and 12, but wins with 7 or 11. » casino

craquelure [krakuh**lür**] The distinctive pattern of fine cracks on the surface of a painting or glazed pottery. Normally the result of aging, craquelure can be faked.

Crashaw, Richard (c.1613–49) English religious poet, born in London. Educated at Charterhouse and Cambridge, he went to Paris, became a Catholic (1644), and in 1649 was given a church post at Loretto in Italy, where he died. He is best-known for his volume of Latin poems, *Epigrammatum Sacrorum Liber* (1634, A Book of Sacred Epigrams) and *Steps to the Temple* (1646). » English literature; poetry

Crassus, Marcus Licinius, byname **Dives** ('wealthy') (c.115–53 BC) Roman politician. As praetor he defeated Spartacus at the Battle of Lucania (71 BC), and in 70 BC was made consul with Pompey. The richest of Roman citizens, he became a friend of Caesar, and formed the first triumvirate with him and Pompey (60 BC). In 53 BC, as Governor of Syria, he attacked the Parthians, but was routed and killed at the Battle of Carrhae. » Caesar; Pompey; Roman history [i]; Spartacus

crater A circular depression on the surface of a planetary body. Those on Mercury, the Moon, and most of the natural satellites of planets have been formed by impacts with meteorites in the remote past. The Moon, Mars, and Io (one of Jupiter's satellites) also have volcanic craters. Craters on Earth have been caused by meteorites (eg Meteor Crater, Arizona) and by volcanic explosions (eg Crater Lake, Oregon). » meteorite; volcano

Crater (Lat 'cup') An ancient constellation in the N sky. » constellation; RR8

Crater Lake (USA) Circular crater lake in SW Oregon, USA, in the Cascade Range; 9.5 km/6 ml across; area 52 sq km/20 sq ml; 604 m/1 982 ft deep; altitude 1 879 m/6 165 ft; in a large pit formed by the destruction of the summit of a prehistoric volcano (now called Mt Mazama); no inlet or outlet, but remains at a near-constant level from rainfall and melting snow; Small Wizard I near the W shore rises 237 m/778 ft above the surface, and has a crater at the top; located in Crater Lake National Park. » caldera; Oregon

Crater Lake (Canada) » **Chubb Crater**

crawfish » **spiny lobster**

Crawford, Joan, originally **Lucille Fay Le Sueur** (1904–77) US film actress, born at San Antonio, Texas. At first a nightclub dancer, she started in silent films in 1925, taking the lead in *Our Dancing Daughters* (1928). She became an established star in the 1930s and 1940s, winning an Oscar for *Mildred Pearce* (1945); her last great role was in *Whatever Happened to Baby Jane?* (1962), in which she co-starred with her long-standing rival, Bette Davis. After her death in New York City, a very critical biography, *Mommie Dearest*, by her adopted daughter Christine, was filmed in 1981.

Craxi, Bettino (1934–) Italian statesman and Prime Minister (1983–7), born in Milan. He was active in the Socialist Youth Movement, and joined the Central Committee of the Italian Socialist Party in 1957. A member of the National Executive in 1965, he became Deputy Secretary (1970–6), General Secretary (1976), and Italy's first Socialist Prime Minister. » Italy [i]; socialism

crayfish A typically freshwater, lobster-like crustacean with a well-developed abdomen and front pair of legs modified as powerful pincers (*chelipeds*); many species exploited commercially for food. (Class: *Malacostraca*. Order: *Decapoda*.) » crustacean; Decapoda [i]; lobster

Crazy Horse, Indian name **Ta-Sunko-Witko** (c.1849–77) Oglala Sioux Chief, born in South Dakota, regarded as the foremost Sioux military leader. He defeated General Custer at the Battle of Little Big Horn (1876), leading a combined force of Sioux and Cheyennes. He and his followers surrendered the following year, and he died in custody at Fort Robinson, Nebraska. » Custer

cream of tartar » **tartaric acid** [i]

creamware A hard durable type of earthenware which became popular in Staffordshire by the middle of the 18th-c. A much-refined version of it was perfected by Josiah Wedgwood. In 1765 he sold a service of creamware to Queen Charlotte, who was so satisfied with it that she permitted Wedgwood to market it as *Queensware*. High quality creamware was also produced in Leeds. » pottery; Wedgwood, Josiah

creationism Originally, the belief that God creates a soul for each human individual at conception or birth. It is now commonly applied to the belief that the Genesis account of creation in the Bible accurately describes the origins of the world and humanity. It is opposed to the theory of evolution, and some evangelical conservative Christians claim there is scientific evidence to support creationism, though this has not been supported by other scientists. » Christianity; evangelicalism; evolution; evolutionism

Crécy, Battle of [**kray**see] (1346) A battle between France and England in the Hundred Years' War. Using tactics perfected against the Scots, Edward III routed a larger French army, mainly cavalry, near Abbeville (Somme). It was a classic demonstration of the superiority over mounted knights of a co-ordinated force of dismounted men-at-arms, and archers providing offensive fire-power. English longbows, effective up to c.180 m/600 ft, could dispatch ten flights a minute. » Edward III; Hundred Years' War

credibility An element in strategic defence strategies, in particular deterrence, originating in the USA. It is designed to demonstrate to the East that the West has a sufficient number of accurate and dependable weapons which it would be prepared to use in the event of a first strike by the other side. » deterrence

credit card A plastic card which is used instead of cash or cheque to pay for goods or services. Card holders present their card when making a payment. The credit-card company sends a statement of account monthly to each account holder, listing their purchases and showing the sum of money owed. If the statement is settled in full by a specified date, no interest is payable. The best-known companies in the UK are *Visa* and *Access*. Credit cards differ from **charge cards**, in that there is a specified credit limit. Charge cards have no limit, but full repayment is to be made each month. » cheque card

credit insurance An insurance taken out where a business sells on credit terms (ie asks for payment at a later date). In this way the insurer provides a safeguard against the possibility of a customer not paying, thus creating a 'bad debt'.

credit rating A system used to assess the ability of a company (or individual) to pay for goods and services, or the ability to borrow and repay. Some rating firms suggest a maximum amount of credit to be allowed. Popular rating systems in the USA are *Moody's* and *Standard and Poor's*. All companies are assigned a rating code: the highest is AAA, next is AA, and so on.

credit union A co-operative venture where members save together and lend to each other, mainly short-term consumer loans. The system is popular in N America, where there are some 50 000 credit unions.

credits The recognition given to someone who has successfully completed a part of a modular course. American education is firmly based on the notion of accumulated credits, whereas in some countries the principle does not exist at all. The advantages are that students know from the beginning how many credits they must acquire in order to obtain the qualification they seek, and that the transfer of credit for partially-completed courses is useful for someone who wishes to study at more than one institution. » Open University

Cree Algonkian-speaking N American Indian group from the Canadian Subarctic region, originally hunters and fishermen. With guns acquired from French fur traders in the 17th-c, they began to expand: one group, the Plains Cree, moved W, adopting the culture of the Plains Indian, while the Woodland Cree remained in forested areas and continued to hunt. Population c.2 000. » American Indians

Creek N American Indian people, originally from Georgia and Alabama. The Spanish invaded their territory in the 16th-c. They were defeated in the Creek War (1813–14) against US troops, and forced to cede much of their land. Finally they were forcibly moved to Oklahoma in 1837, where they became one of the Five Civilized Tribes. Population c.17 000, living in Oklahoma. » American Indians; Five Civilized Tribes; Seminole

Creeley, Robert (1926–) US poet and novelist, born at Arlington, Massachusetts, and educated at Harvard. Influenced by Charles Olson's Black Mountain school, he developed a spare, minimalist style evident in *For Love: Poems 1950–60* (1960). His manner becomes even more fragmentary in later volumes, *Words* (1965), *Pieces* (1969), and *Hello: A Journal* (1978). » American literature; Black Mountain poetry; poetry

creep The gradual deformation of a solid subjected to continual stress, such as the lengthening of a wire under load. In crystalline materials such as metals, creep is caused by the movement of dislocations through the material. » crystal defects [i]; mechanical properties of matter

cremation Burning the remains of a dead person. The practice was recorded in ancient Greece for soldiers killed in battle, and was later adopted by the Romans. Discouraged in the past by Christians because of its pagan associations, it is the regular form of disposal by Hindus. Today cremation is becoming more common in many countries, because of lack of space in cemeteries.

creodont An extinct flesh-eating mammal; known from the early Tertiary period around the world except Australia and S America; distinguished from true carnivores by their shorter limbs, unfused wrist bones, cleft claw bone, and shearing teeth (*carnassials*) formed from molars. (Order: *Creodonta*.) » carnivore [i]; mammal [i]; Tertiary period; RR16

creole A pidgin language which has become the mother-tongue of a speech community, as has happened with Jamaican creole. A creole develops a wider range of words, grammatical structures, and styles than is found in a pidgin. » pidgin

Creon or **Kreon** [**kree**on] A name (meaning 'ruler') given to several legendary Greek kings, but especially to the brother of Jocasta, regent of Thebes, who awarded the throne to Oedipus. Later, after the siege of the city by the seven Champions, he commanded that Polynices should not be buried, and condemned Antigone for disobedience. » Antigone; Jocasta; Oedipus; Polynices

creosote [**kree**uhsoht] A fraction of coal tar, boiling point c.250°C, containing a variety of toxic aromatic compounds giving it strong antiseptic and preservative properties. » coal tar

cresol [**kree**sol] $(CH_3)C_6H_4(OH)$, three isomeric compounds, 2-, 3-, and 4-hydroxytoluene, oils with boiling point c.200°. They are ingredients of coal tar, and are important raw materials for plastics. » coal tar; isomers

cress The name given to several different members of the cabbage family, often small weeds, some cultivated as salad plants. (Family: *Cruciferae*.) » cabbage; garden cress; watercress

Cressida [**kres**ida] In mediaeval accounts of the Trojan War, the daughter of Calchas, a Trojan priest; probably the story was a misunderstanding of Calchas and Chryseis in the *Iliad*. Beloved by Troilus, a Trojan prince, she deserted him for Diomedes when transferred to the Greek camp. » Diomedes; Pandarus; Troilus

crested tit A small bird native to Europe and E to the Urals; inhabits coniferous and mixed woodlands; often found with coal tits. (*Parus cristatus*. Family: *Paridae*.) » coal tit; conifer; tit

Cretaceous period [kre**tay**shuhs] The last geological period of the Mesozoic era, lasting from 144 million to 65 million years ago, characterized by the emergence of flowering plants and the dominance and extinction of dinosaurs. It was also a period of marine transgressions and the deposition of widespread chalk deposits in NW Europe. » dinosaur [i]; geological time scale; Mesozoic era; RR16

Cretan and Mycenaean/Mycenean architecture [**kree**tan, miysuh**nee**an] A form of architecture prevalent in the Aegean c.3000–1100 BC. It mainly uses post-and-lintel masonry construction without mortar; characterized by thick walls covered with stucco, and asymmetrically planned. The most famous example is the Palace of Knossos, with a labyrinthian series of rooms, courtyards, and passages, which was destroyed by an earthquake in 1400 BC. » column; Greek architecture; post and lintel [i]; stucco

Crete, Gr **Kríti**, Ital **Candia**, Lat **Creta** pop (1981) 502 165; area 8 336 sq km/3 218 sq ml. Island region of Greece, in the Mediterranean Sea, S of the Cyclades island group; length 256 km/159 ml; width 14–60 km/9–37 ml; largest of the Greek islands and fifth largest in the Mediterranean; White Mts (W) rise to 2 452 m/8 044 ft; Idhi Oros (C) rise to the highest point of the island, Psiloritis (2 456 m/8 058 ft); N coastline deeply indented; evidence of settlement from c.6000 BC; important Minoan civilization, c.2000 BC; ruled at various times by Greeks, Romans, Turks, and Arabs; passed to Greece in 1913; German occupation in World War 2, after airborne invasion (1941); capital, Heraklion; other chief towns, Chania, Agios Nikolaos; fruit, olive oil, wine, sheep, goats, tourism; ancient sites at Knossos, Gortys, Lato, Phaistos. » Greece [i]; Heraklion; Knossos; Minoan civilization

cretinism A condition affecting the newly-born child who suffers from the inadequate production of thyroid hormones (*thyroxine*). The thyroid gland is enlarged in some forms only. There is a failure of normal growth and development, with puffiness of the skin, notably of the face. The tongue enlarges. Hair on the head may be excessive at birth, then fall out. » dwarfism; thyroid hormone

Creus, Cape (Span **Cabo**) [kray**oos**], Gr **Aphrodisium** 42°19N 3°19E. The most E point on the Iberian peninsula; picturesque fishing village of Cadaques nearby, preserved by local artists. » Spain [i]

cribbage A card game popular in public houses in the UK, played by two, three, or four people with a standard pack of 52 cards and a holed board known as the peg board. The number of cards dealt to each player varies according to the number of players, but will be five, six, or seven. Cards are discarded into a dummy hand, which each player has in turn. Points are scored according to cards dropped (ie for playing a card that makes a pair, a run of three or more, etc). Cards are discarded in each round until a total of 31 is reached. Play continues until the players have each discarded all their cards. The value of the hand is then calculated. All scores are marked on the peg board. » playing cards

Crick, Francis (Harry Compton) (1916–) British biophysicist, born at Northampton. Educated at Mill Hill, London and Cambridge, from 1949 he carried on research in molecular biology at the Cavendish Laboratory. With J D Watson in 1953 he constructed a molecular model of the complex genetic material DNA; and in 1958 proposed that the DNA determines the sequence of amino acids in a polypeptide. He shared the Nobel Prize for Physiology or Medicine in 1962. » DNA [i]; peptide; Watson, James

cricket (entomology) A large, grasshopper-like insect; forewings box-like and bent down round sides of body; female egg-laying tube (*ovipositor*) cylindrical; many species have a well-developed sound-producing mechanism for auditory communication; c.2 000 species, including some pests. (Order: *Orthop-*

tera. Family: *Gryllidae*.) » bush/mole cricket; grasshopper; insect [i]

cricket (sport) A bat-and-ball team game of 11-a-side. A wicket consisting of three stumps surmounted by a pair of bails is placed at each end of a grassy pitch 22 yd (20.1 m) in length. Each team takes it in turn to bat and bowl. The aim of the batting team is to defend the two wickets while trying to score as many runs as possible before being dismissed. Each member of the team must bat, and two batsmen are on the field at any one time, one in front of each wicket. The attacking team consists of a bowler, a wicket-keeper (who stands behind the wicket which the bowler is attacking), and nine fielders, who are placed at strategic positions around the field. A bowler delivers an 'over' of (usually) six balls to one wicket, before a different bowler attacks the other wicket.

If the batsman hits a ball (and in certain other circumstances), he may decide it is safe to run between the two wickets, exchanging places with the other batsman, in which case he scores a 'run'. Several runs may be scored following a single hit, but if the ball reaches the boundary of the field, four runs are scored automatically, and six if it has not bounced on the way. A batsman can be got out by being 'bowled' (the ball from the bowler knocks his wicket down), 'caught' (the batsman hits the ball so that it is caught by a fielder), 'stumped' (the wicket-keeper knocks the wicket down with the ball while the defending batsman is standing outside his 'safe ground' or 'crease'), 'run out' (the wicket towards which one of the batsmen is running is knocked down before the batsman reaches the safe ground), and 'leg before wicket', or 'lbw' (the lower part of the batsman's leg prevents the ball from the bowler from reaching the wicket). Once ten batsmen have been dismissed, the innings comes to a close, but a team can stop its innings ('declare') at any time before that, if it thinks it has made enough runs. Each team has two innings, and the one with the greater number of runs at the end of the match is the winner.

A similar game was played in the mid-16th-c, but the first known county match was in 1719. The earliest known laws of cricket were drawn up in 1744, and the Marylebone Cricket Club (MCC) was founded in 1787. The first test match was played at Melbourne in March 1877. Principal domestic competitions in the UK consist of the County Championship, NatWest Bank Trophy, Benson and Hedges Cup, and Refuge Assurance League. The Sheffield Shield is the principal competition in Australia. Test matches are normally over five days, county championship matches over three or four days. Limited-over competitions are normally concluded in one day, and last for a specific number of overs per side. » Ashes, the; MCC; Sheffield Shield; RR108

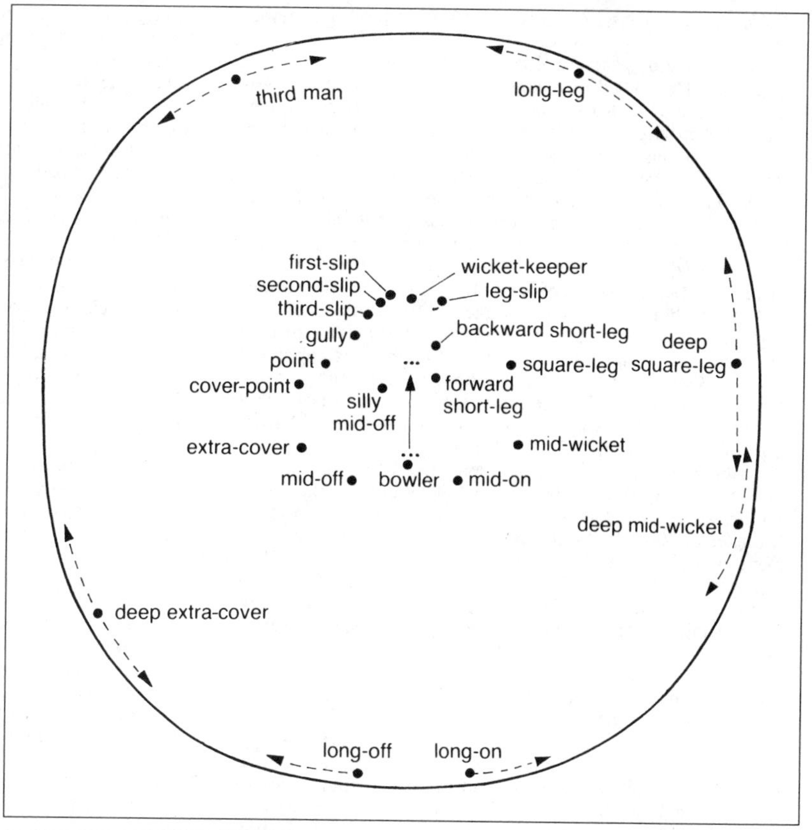

Cricket field positions

Crimea [kri*mee*a], Russ **Krym** area 25 900 sq km/9 997 sq ml. Peninsula in S Ukraine; bounded S and W by the Black Sea, and E by the Sea of Azov; separated from the mainland (N) by the narrow Perekop Isthmus, and from the Taman Peninsula (E) by the Kersh Strait; length, 320 km/200 ml; Greek colonization, 7th-c BC; invaded by Goths (AD 250), Huns (373), Khazars (8th-c), Byzantine Greeks (1016), Kipchaks (1050), Tatars (13th-c), Ottomans (late 15th-c), and Russians, 1736; scene of the Crimean War, 1854–6; an autonomous Soviet republic, 1921; an oblast of the Russian SFSR, 1946; transferred to the Ukraine SSR, 1954; rich in minerals (iron, gypsum, limestone); chief cities include Simferopol, Sevastopol, Kerch; subtropical Black Sea coast is a major tourist attraction, notably at Yalta. » Black Sea; Crimean War; Ukraine

Crimean War (1854–6) A war fought in the Crimean peninsula by Britain and France against Russia, whose origins lay in Russian successes against the Turks in the Black Sea area, and the British and French desire to prevent further westward expansion by the Russians, which threatened the Mediterranean and overland routes to India. Major battles were fought in 1854 at the R Alma (20 Sep), Balaclava (25 Oct), and Inkerman (5 Nov). The fall of the Russian fortress at Sebastopol (Sep 1855) led to peace negotiations, finally agreed at Paris (Mar 1856). Russia ceded S Bessarabia to neighbouring Moldavia. The war was notable both for the nursing exploits of Florence Nightingale at Scutari and the pioneer war reports of W H Russell in *The Times*. » Balaclava, Battle of; Crimea; Nightingale

criminal law A branch of law which deals with offences against society generally. Investigation of breaches of the criminal law is generally the responsibility of the police. The responsibility for prosecution varies between jurisdictions: for example, in England and Wales, it belongs to the Crown Prosecution Service; in Scotland, to the Procurator Fiscal. Private prosecutions are possible but uncommon. » civil law; law

crimp The waviness which occurs naturally in wool fibres, imparting a soft bulkiness to yarns. Crimping of synthetic fibres extends their range of uses into knitting and carpet yarns, and the manufacture of softer woven fabrics. » bulked yarn

crinoid [kri*y*noyd] A primitive marine invertebrate (echinoderm), typically attached to the sea bed by a long stalk; occasionally base-attached (sessile) or free-swimming; mouth and arms on upper surface; most feed on suspended particles transported to the mouth via food grooves on arms; long fossil record; c.650 living species found from shallow waters to deep sea; also known as **sea lilies** and **feather stars**. (Phylum:

Echinodermata. Class: *Crinoidea*.) » echinoderm [i]; feather star

Crippen, Hawley Harvey (1862–1910) US murderer, born in Michigan. He studied medicine and dentistry, eventually settling in London (1896) with his second wife, **Cora Turner**. Having transferred his affections to his secretary, **Ethel le Neve**, he poisoned his wife, dissected the body, and interred the remains in the cellar. He and his mistress attempted to escape to the USA on board an Atlantic liner as Mr and Master Robinson. The suspicious captain contacted Scotland Yard by radiotelegraphy (the first use of radio for a murder case). They were arrested, and Crippen was hanged in London.

Cripps, Sir (Richard) Stafford (1889–1952) British Labour statesman, born in London. Educated at Winchester and London, he was called to the Bar in 1913, and made a fortune in patent and compensation cases. In 1930 he was appointed Solicitor-General in the second Labour government, and became an MP in 1931. During the 1930s he was associated with several extreme left-wing movements, and was expelled from the Labour Party in 1939 for his 'popular front' opposing Chamberlain's policy of appeasement. He sat as an independent MP during World War 2, was Ambassador to the Soviet Union (1940–2), and in 1942 became Lord Privy Seal, and later Minister of Aircraft Production. In the 1945 Labour government, he was readmitted to the Party and appointed President of the Board of Trade (1942–5). In 1947 he became Minister of Economic Affairs and then Chancellor of the Exchequer, introducing a successful austerity policy. He resigned due to illness in 1950. » Chamberlain, Neville; Labour Party; left wing

crisis apparition » **apparition**

crisis management A term first employed by Robert McNamara shortly after the 1962 Cuban missile crisis. It implies, given the limited information about other actors, and their unpredictability, that long-term strategic planning cannot provide the basis for action. Crises between states can be resolved only by managing them as they arise. » Cuban Missile Crisis; McNamara, Robert S

crisis theology A type of Protestant theology initiated after World War 1 under the inspiration of Karl Barth (1886–1968), and very influential during the 1920s and 1930s. The term 'crisis' essentially applied to the judgment (Gr *krisis*) of God upon all merely human social, moral, and religious endeavours. The approach exercised a decisive influence on the Declaration of Barmen (1934) which, in opposition to the readiness of the so-called 'German Christians' to integrate the racialist ideology of the German National Socialists into Christian doctrine, affirmed Jesus Christ as God's sole and sufficient revelation and denied any revelations in nature, history, or race apart from him. » Barth, Karl; Christianity; Christology; revelation

Cristóbal Colón, Pico [**pee**koh kreest**oh**bal kohl**on**] Snow-capped Andean peak in N Colombia; rises to 5 800 m/19 029 ft, 113 km/70 ml E of Barranquilla; highest peak in Sierra Nevada de Santa Marta and in Colombia. » Andes

Cristofori, Bartolommeo [kristoforee] (1655–1731) Italian harpsichord-maker, born in Padua. He is usually credited with the invention of the pianoforte in about 1710. He died in Florence. » harpsichord; piano

criterion-referenced test A test which requires the candidate to meet a set of criteria, as opposed to a *norm-referenced test* which simply ranks students alongside others. Thus a criterion-referenced test in mathematics might list for each grade what a student must do to obtain that grade, eg be able to convert a fraction to a decimal, or multiply two three-digit numbers. » norm-referenced test; objective test

critical mass The smallest mass of material of a given type and formed into a given shape able to sustain a nuclear-fission chain reaction. For a mass of material greater than the critical mass, large amounts of energy are released via the fission-chain reaction in a small fraction of a second. For a sphere of uranium-235, the critical mass is 52 kg/114.6 lb, corresponding to a radius of 8.7 cm/3.4 in. » atomic bomb; chain reaction

critical phenomena The physical properties of systems at their critical points, ie at the temperature where the distinction between two phases vanishes. They are typified by dramatic changes in the parameters used to describe the system; for example, the spontaneous magnetization of iron is reduced to zero when its temperature is raised beyond the critical temperature (the *Curie point*). Critical phenomena are observed in many systems, such as the superfluid, superconducting, ferroelectric, and ferromagnetic transitions. Certain aspects are nevertheless common to all. » Curie temperature; ferroelectrics; ferromagnetism; phases of matter [i]; superconductivity; superfluidity

critical point (physics) » **critical phenomena**

critical theory » **Frankfurt School**

Crittenden Compromise (1860) In the months preceding the American Civil War, an attempt by Senator John J Crittenden of Kentucky to resolve the crisis between North and South by formally recognizing slavery in territories S of 36°30. This proved unacceptable to Abraham Lincoln, whose election as President was causing secession by the slave-holding South. » American Civil War; slave trade

Cro-Magnon Man [kroh**man**yon] A prehistoric form of fully modern man named after the 1868 discovery of fossil skeletons at Cro-Magnon in SW France. Cro-Magnons were cave-dwelling big-game hunters who lived in the steppes and tundra of late Ice Age Europe. They created figurines and fine cave paintings. » *Homo* [i]

croaker » **drumfish**

Croatia [kroh**ay**sha], Serbo-Croatian **Hrvatska** pop (1981) 4 601 469; area 56 538 sq km/21 824 sq ml. Constituent republic of Yugoslavia; bounded W by the Adriatic Sea, N by Slovenia and Romania; formed a joint crownland with Slavonia, 1888; proclaimed an independent state during occupation by the Axis Powers, 1941–5; declaration of independence (1991), followed by confrontation with the National Army and civil war; capital, Zagreb; chief towns include Rijeka, Čakovec, Split, Zadar; chiefly an agricultural region. » Yugoslavia [i]; Zagreb

Croce, Benedetto [**kroh**chay] (1866–1952) Italian philosopher, historian, and critic, born at Pescasseroli. He studied at Rome, and in Naples devoted himself at first to literature and antiquarian studies, founding the review, *La Critica*, in 1903, and making major contributions to idealistic aesthetics in his *Estetica* (1902, Aesthetic) and *La Poesia* (1936, Poetry). In 1910 he became Senator, and was Minister of Education (1920–1) when, with the rise of Mussolini, he had to resign his professorship at Naples. He was opposed to totalitarianism, and with the fall of Mussolini (1943) helped to resurrect Liberal institutions in Italy. He died in Naples. » idealism; totalitarianism

crocket [**kro**kit] In Gothic architecture, a decorative leaf-shaped carving, projecting from the raking lines of spires, pinnacles, canopies, etc. It is particularly common in English Decorated style churches, such as Wells Cathedral (1290–c.1340). » Gothic architecture

Crockett, Davy (David) (1786–1836) US backwoodsman, born in Tennessee. He distinguished himself against the Creek Indians in Jackson's campaign of 1814, and was elected to the Tennessee state legislature (1821) and to the congress (1826). He died fighting for Texas at the battle of the Alamo. Highly embellished stories of his exploits have assumed mythological proportions. » Alamo

Crockford, William (1775–1844) British founder of a famous gaming club in London (1827). He was previously a fish-monger, but his successes at gambling led to a change in his fortunes. He is reputed to have won over a million pounds at the game of hazard.

crocodile A reptile native to tropical rivers and estuaries worldwide (estuarine species sometimes cross open sea); length, up to 7.5 m/25 ft; fourth tooth from the front on each side of the lower jaw is visible when the jaws are closed (unlike the alligator); snout long and slender, or short and broad; eats a range of vertebrate prey; eggs have hard shells (like birds' eggs). Crocodilians (crocodiles, alligators, and the gharial) are the descendants of an ancient reptile group, the *archosaurs* (which included the extinct dinosaurs and pterodactyls) and have changed little in appearance during the last 65 million years. (Order: *Crocodylia*. Family: *Crocodylidae*, 14 species.) » alligator [i]; dinosaur [i]; gharial; mugger; reptile

crocodile-bird The name used for birds reported to feed on parasites and food residue found in the mouths of basking crocodiles. It is not certain that such feeding occurs, but the name is sometimes used for any birds frequently found associating with crocodiles, such as certain plovers or the **common sandpiper** (*Actitis hypoleucos*). » crocodile; plover; sandpiper

crocus A perennial producing corms, native to Europe and Asia; leaves grass-like with distinctive silvery stripe down centre; stalkless flowers, goblet-shaped with long, slender tube, mainly white, yellow, or purple, closing up at night; many cultivated for ornament. The autumn-flowering species produce flowers before leaves appear in the spring. They are often attacked by birds, which prefer the yellow flowers, reason unknown. (Genus: *Crocus*, 75 species. Family: *Iridaceae*.) » corm; perennial

Croesus [**kree**suhs] (?–c.546 BC) The last king of Lydia (c.560–546 BC), who succeeded his father, Alyattes. He made the Greeks of Asia Minor his tributaries, and extended his kingdom eastward from the Aegean to the Halys. His conquests and mines made his wealth proverbial. Cyrus II defeated and imprisoned him (546 BC), but his death is a mystery. » Cyrus II; Ionia; Lydia

crofting A form of small-scale subsistence farming characteristic of the Highlands and Islands of Scotland. A croft usually comprises a house, a few hectares of arable land, and grazing rights on the hill. It is often combined with other part-time or full-time jobs, such as fishing and tourism. » subsistence agriculture

Crohn's disease A persisting but fluctuating inflammation of any part of the alimentary canal, but especially of the small intestine. Colicky pain, diarrhoea, and fever are common. It is named after US physician Burrill Crohn (1884–1983). » alimentary canal; inflammation

Crome, John, byname **Old Crome** (1768–1821) British landscape painter, the chief of the Norwich School, born and died in Norwich, Norfolk. He was apprenticed to a housepainter (1783), then became a drawing master, and founded (1803) the Norwich Society of Artists. He visited Paris in 1814. His subjects derived from the scenery of Norfolk, such as 'Poringland Oak' and 'Mousehold Heath' (Tate, London). » English art; landscape painting; Norwich School

cromlech » **megalith**

cromoglycate [krohmoh**gliy**sayt] An anti-allergy drug used in the prevention of asthma, also known as **cromolyn** or **Intal**. It is administered using a special inhaler which dispenses very fine powder into the inspired air. Chromoglycate is also used in other allergic conditions, such as hay fever and allergic rhinitis. » allergy; asthma

Crompton, Richmal, pseudonym of **Richmal Samuel Lamburn** (1890–1969) British writer of children's books, born at Bury, Lancashire. Educated at London, she taught Classics at Bromley High School until she contracted poliomyelitis in 1923. She wrote the first of the 'William' books (*Just William*) in 1922, and had written 40 of them before her death.

Crompton, Samuel (1753–1827) British inventor of the spinning-mule, born at Firwood, near Bolton, Lancashire. In 1779 he devised a machine which produced yarn of such astonishing fineness that the house was beset by persons eager to know the secret. He had no funds to obtain a patent, so he was forced to sell his idea to a Bolton manufacturer for very little return. The mule was such a great success that he was awarded a national grant of £5 000 in 1812. His later ventures, in bleaching and cotton, were failures. He died at Bolton. » cotton [i]; spinning; yarn

Cromwell, Oliver (1599–1658) English soldier and statesman, born at Huntingdon, Cambridgeshire. Educated at Huntingdon and Cambridge, he studied law in London. A convinced Puritan, he sat in both the Short and the Long Parliaments (1640), and when war broke out (1642) fought for the parliament at Edgehill. He formed his unconquerable Ironsides, combining rigid discipline with strict morality, and it was his cavalry that secured the victory at Marston Moor (1644), while under Fairfax he led the New Model Army to decisive success at Naseby (1645). He quelled insurrection in Wales in support of Charles I, and defeated the invading army of Hamilton. He then brought the King to trial, and was one of the signatories of his death warrant (1649). Having established the Commonwealth, Cromwell suppressed the Levellers, Ireland (1649–50), and the Scots (under Charles II) at Dunbar (1650) and Worcester (1651). He dissolved the Rump of the Long Parliament (1653), and after the failure of his Barebones Parliament, established a Protectorate (1653). He refused the offer of the crown in 1657. At home he reorganized the national Church, upheld toleration, and gave Scotland and Ireland parliamentary representation. Under him the Commonwealth became the head and champion of Protestant Europe. He died in London, and was succeeded by his son **Richard** (1626–1712), who was forced into French exile in 1659. » Barebones Parliament; Charles I (of England); English Civil War; Levellers; Protectorate; Long Parliament

Cromwell, Thomas, Earl of Essex (c.1485–1540) English statesman, born in London, known as *malleus monachorum*, 'the hammer of the monks'. He served as a soldier on the Continent (1504–12), then entered Wolsey's service in 1514, and became his agent and secretary. He arranged Henry VIII's divorce with Catherine of Aragon, and put into effect the Act of Supremacy (1534) and the dissolution of the monasteries (1536–9). He became Privy Councillor (1531), Chancellor of the Exchequer (1533), Secretary of State and Master of the Rolls (1534), Vicar-General (1535), Lord Privy Seal and Baron Cromwell of Oakham (1536), Knight of the Garter and Dean of Wells (1537), Lord Great Chamberlain (1539), and finally Earl of Essex (1540). In each of his offices, he proved himself a highly efficient administrator and adviser to the King; but Henry's aversion to Anne of Cleves, consort of Cromwell's choosing, led to his ruin. He was sent to the Tower and beheaded. » Henry VIII; Reformation

Cronin, A(rchibald) J(oseph) (1896–1981) British novelist, born at Cardross, Dunbartonshire, Scotland. He studied medicine at Glasgow (1919), but in 1930 took up literature and at once was successful with *Hatter's Castle* (1931). Subsequent works include *The Citadel* (1937) and *The Keys of the Kingdom* (1942). Several of his books were filmed, and the television series *Dr Finlay's Casebook* was based on his stories. He died at Montreux, Switzerland. » novel; Scottish literature

Cronin, James Watson (1931–) US physicist, born and educated in Chicago, where he was appointed to a chair in 1971. He helped to demonstrate the non-conservation of parity and charge conjugation in certain atomic particle reactions. This surprising result is of fundamental interest in particle physics, and he shared the Nobel Prize for Physics in 1980. » particle physics

Cronje, Piet [**kron**jay] (1835–1911) Boer general, born at Colesberg, South Africa. He was a leader in the Boer Wars (1881, 1899–1900), defeated Methuen at Magersfontein, but surrendered to Lord Roberts at Paardeberg (1900). He died at Potchefstroom, Transvaal. » Boer Wars

Cronus [**kro**nuhs] or **Kronos** In Greek mythology, the second ruler of the Universe, a Titan, the youngest son of Uranus, who rebelled against his father. During his rule people lived in the Golden Age. Probably a pre-Greek deity, he is incorrectly, but popularly, confused with *chronos* 'time', because he devoured his children. » Rhea (mythology); Saturn (mythology); Zeus

Crookes, Sir William (1832–1919) British chemist and physicist, born in London. He studied at London, then superintended the meteorological department of the Radcliffe Observatory, Oxford, and from 1855 lectured on chemistry at Chester. In 1859 he founded the *Chemical News*, and edited it until 1906. He was an authority on sanitation; discovered the metal thallium (1861); improved vacuum tubes and promoted electric lighting; and invented the radiometer (1873–6). He was knighted in 1897, and died in London.

crop rotation A system of farming which involves growing crops in sequence. The aim is to control pests and weeds, and to maintain fertility. Modern sprays and chemical fertilizers now make it possible to farm successfully with intermittent or even no rotations, but soil structure may suffer. Most farmers still practise some form of rotation, but it is not usually as rigid as the famous 18th-c Norfolk four-course rotation of roots, barley, clover, wheat, and then back to roots. » arable farming; monoculture

croquet A ball-and-mallet game for 2–4 players, played on a lawn about 35 yd (32 m) long and 28 yd (25 m) wide, on which have been arranged six hoops and a central peg. The four balls are coloured blue, red, black, and yellow. The object is to strike your own ball through the hoops in a prescribed order before finally hitting the central peg. » RR108

Crosby, Bing, originally **Harry Lillis Crosby** (1904–77) US singer and film star, born at Tacoma, Washington. He began his career playing the drums in the evenings while still at school, and later became one of the trio known as Paul Whiteman's Rhythm Boys. He began to make films, specializing in light comedy roles, and his distinctive style of crooning made him one of the best-known names in the entertainment world. His recordings of 'White Christmas' and 'Silent Night' were the hits of the century. He starred in many films, notably the *Road* films with Bob Hope and Dorothy Lamour. A keen sportsman, he died on a golf course near Madrid.

Crosland, Tony, properly **(Charles) Anthony (Raven)** (1918–77) British Labour politician, born at St Leonards-on-Sea, Sussex, and educated at Oxford, where he also taught after serving in World War 2. He was elected an MP in 1950 and became Secretary for Education and Science (1965–7), President of the Board of Trade (1967–9), Secretary for Local Government and Regional Planning (1969–70), Environment Secretary (1974–6), and Foreign Secretary (1976–7). A strong supporter of Hugh Gaitskell, he was a key member of the revisionist wing of the Labour Party, and wrote one of its seminal texts, *The Future of Socialism* (1956). He died at Oxford. » Gaitskell; socialism

cross The instrument of execution of criminals in ancient times, closely associated with the display of corpses or the heads of enemies impaled on sticks; also a widespread religious symbol, even in pre-Christian times. In Christianity, the symbol refers to Jesus' execution by crucifixion. The earliest design was a single vertical post, but crossbeams were present at least in ancient Roman times, and there have been many variations. » crucifixion; Jesus Christ; RR93

cross-country running An athletic running event using a predetermined course over natural terrain. The length of race varies, but world championships are over 12 km/7.5 ml for men and 5 km/3.1 ml for women. The first recorded international race was in May 1898, and covered a 14.5 km/9 ml course at Ville D'Avray near Paris.

Cross Fell Highest peak of the Pennine Chain in Cumbria, NW England; rises to 893 m/2 930 ft, 32 km/20 ml SE of Carlisle. » Pennines

cross-hatching » **hatching**

cross-section In the scattering experiments of atomic, nuclear, and particle physics, the area presented by a target to an oncoming beam of particles. Its value depends on the particle energy and the type of interaction; symbol σ; units m^2; sometimes expressed in barns, $1 \text{ barn} = 10^{-28} m^2$. » scattering

crossbill A finch native to the N hemisphere, especially N regions; inhabits coniferous forests. The tips of its bill cross over, an adaptation for extracting seeds from pine cones. (Genus: *Loxia*, 4 species. Family: *Fringillidae*.) » conifer; finch

crossbow A form of bow mounted in a stock, with a crank to wind back and tension the bow itself, and a trigger to discharge the arrow, or 'bolt'. Crossbows were fired more slowly than longbows, but were especially useful in sieges. They were much used in the Crusades and by troops of mercenary expert bowmen. » longbow

Crossman, Richard (Howard Stafford) (1907–74) British Labour politician. He was educated at Winchester and Oxford, where he became a philosophy tutor, and leader of the Labour group on Oxford City Council (1934–40). In 1938 he joined the staff of the *New Statesman*. In 1945 he became an MP, and under Wilson was Minister of Housing and Local Government (1964–6), then Secretary of State for Social Services and head of the Department of Health (1968–70). He was editor of the *New Statesman* (1970–2). His best-known work is his series of political diaries, begun in 1952, keeping a detailed record of the day-to-day workings of government. They were published in four volumes (1975–81), despite attempts to suppress them. » Labour Party; Wilson, Harold

crossopterygii [krosoptuh**rij**eeiy] A subclass of bony fishes comprising the tassel-finned (or lobe-finned) fishes, having an extensive fossil record from the Devonian to Cretaceous periods. The only living representative is the coelacanth, *Latimeria*. » bony fish; Cretaceous/Devonian period

croup A hollow crowing noise during respiration and on coughing which results from infection affecting the larynx and trachea. It is caused by several viruses that cause swelling and narrowing of the respiratory passages. » larynx; trachea; virus

crow A bird of the worldwide family *Corvidae*. It can be a common name for the whole family, or just for the 40 species of the genus *Corvus* (other genera being jays, magpies, choughs, nutcrackers, and the piapiac), or just for some species of *Corvus* (others being ravens, rooks, and jackdaws). The name is also sometimes misapplied to birds not belonging to *Corvidae*. » carrion crow; chough; jackdaw; jay; magpie; nutcracker; piapiac; raven; roller; rook

Crow N American Sioux-speaking Plains Indians. They separated from the Hidatsa in the 18th-c, and lived between the Missouri and Yellowstone Rivers, becoming nomadic buffalo hunters on horseback, and traders. They allied with Whites in the Indian wars of the 1860s and 1870s; and in 1868 were settled on reservations in Montana, where most Crow still live. Population c.4 000. » American Indians; Hidatsa; nomadism; Plains Indians; Sioux

crowberry A spreading, evergreen, heather-like shrub, native to arctic and N temperate moors; leaves 4–6 mm/⅛–¼ in; alternate, separate male and female flowers, three sepals, three petals; berry 5 mm/0.2 in diameter, black. (*Empetrum nigrum*. Family: *Empetraceae*.) » evergreen plants; sepal; shrub

Crowley, Aleister, originally **Edward Alexander Crowley** (1875–1947) British writer and 'magician'. He became interested in the occult while an undergraduate at Cambridge, and later founded the order known as the Silver Star. He travelled widely, settling for some years in Sicily with a group of disciples at the Abbey of Thelema, near Cefalù. Rumours of drugs, orgies, and magical ceremonies led to his expulsion from Italy. He liked to be known as 'the great beast' and 'the wickedest man alive' – and certainly many who associated with him died tragically.

Crown In the UK, and many former colonial countries, an alternative legal definition to that of the state, which represents the organs of government. It reflects the former power of the monarchy, and although now a legal fiction, in that such powers are largely exercised by the government of the day, they are carried out in the name of the Crown. » royal prerogative

Crown Agents (for Overseas Governments and Administrations) A UK agency which provides professional, financial, and commercial services to governments and other public authorities in developing countries and to international agencies. It also acts on behalf of the World Bank. » International Bank for Reconstruction and Development

Crown Colony » **colony**

Crown Court A court in England and Wales, established by the Courts Act (1971), which abolished the Assizes and Quarter Sessions. Crown Courts have power to deal with indictable offences, and also hear most appeals from magistrates' courts. In addition to the criminal jurisdiction, a High Court judge may hear civil cases in this court. » Assize Court; Central Criminal Court; indictment; recorder (law); summary trial

Crown Estate Property belonging by heredity to the British sovereign, comprising some 109 260 ha/270 650 acres in England, Scotland, and Wales. Most of Britain's foreshore is included, together with the sea bed within territorial waters. Revenue from the Crown Estate is made over to the government at the beginning of each reign. » New Forest

crown jewels Regalia and jewellery belonging to a sovereign. The British crown jewels have been displayed at various sites in the Tower of London for 300 years, since 1967 in the Jewel House. After the abolition of the monarchy in 1649, much of the regalia was sold or broken up, with the exception of the gold anointing spoon (12th-c) and eagle-headed ampulla

(14th-c). Most of the crown jewels date from the Restoration (1660). They include St Edward's Crown, used in most coronations since that of Charles II; the Imperial State Crown; the gold spurs made for Charles II's coronation; the armills (gold-enamelled bracelets); the King's Orb; the King's Sceptre with the Cross (since 1909 containing the largest cut diamond in the world at 530 carats); the King's sceptre with the Dove; the jewelled Sword of State and four other ceremonial swords; the Imperial Crown of India; and Queen Elizabeth the Queen Mother's crown, which is set with the Koh-i-Noor ('mountain of light') diamond. » Tower of London

crown of thorns A large starfish up to 60 cm/2 ft in diameter, with 9–23 arms; body and arms with long spikes on upper surface; found in shallow waters on coral reef areas in tropical Indo-West Pacific; feeds on live coral polyps; when abundant, can cause massive damage to reefs. (Phylum: *Echinodermata*. Subclass: *Asteroidea*.) » coral; starfish

Crown Proceedings Act A UK act (1947) which permits ordinary civil actions against the Crown. It had been possible before this date for someone to take certain proceedings against the Crown by personal petition (*petition of right*), as in breach of contract cases. The significance of the 1947 Act is that it permitted action in tort in respect of conduct by Crown servants. The Crown had enjoyed a special status by virtue of the doctrine that the monarch could do no wrong. The extension of the activities of the state in the 20th-c necessitated a revision of this immunity. However, the monarch remains personally immune from civil or criminal liability. The analogous act in the USA is the Federal Tort Claims Act (1946). » contract; tort

crucifixion A common form of capital punishment in the Roman world, in which a person was nailed or bound to a wooden cross by the wrists and feet, and left to die. The method, probably borrowed from the Carthaginians, was inflicted only upon slaves and people of low social status (*humiliores*). It was regularly preceded by flagellation, as happened in the case of Christ himself. » cross; Jesus Christ

Cruden, Alexander (1701–70) British scholar and bookseller, born in Aberdeen. He worked as a tutor then started as a bookseller in London. In 1737 appeared his *Concordance of the Holy Scriptures*. He suffered from bouts of insanity and, assuming the title of 'Alexander the Corrector', from 1755 went through the country reproving Sabbath-breaking and profanity. He died in London. » Bible

Cruelty, Theatre of A term created by Antoine Artaud to describe his vision of a metaphysical theatre in which both actors and audience could experience, without any avoidance or illusion, existential realities. » Artaud; theatre

Cruft, Charles (1852–1939) British showman, who organized the first dog show in London in 1886. He was for many years the general manager of James Spratt. The annual shows have since become world famous, and have helped to improve standards of dog breeding. » dog

Cruikshank, George [**krook**shank] (1792–1878) British caricaturist and illustrator, born and died in London. He contributed often to topical magazines, and illustrated several children's books. His best-known work includes Grimm's *German Popular Stories* (1824–6) and Dickens's *Oliver Twist*. In his later years he used his etchings and oil paintings in a vigorous protest against drunkenness, as in the series for 'The Bottle' (1847). » caricature; English art

cruise missile A type of missile which flies continuously on wings, and is propelled continuously by an engine using air from the atmosphere as its oxidant to mix with the fuel it carries. The German V-1 of 1944 was a cruise missile, but the weapon came to prominence again 30 years later when it was revived by US weapon scientists to provide a comparatively cheap means of delivering a nuclear or conventional warhead over a long distance, using onboard computer power to provide pinpoint accuracy. The US armed forces have deployed a range of cruise missile systems including *ground-launched* (GLCMs), *sea-launched* (SLCMs, capable of being launched from small warships and submarines), and *air-launched* weapons (ALCMs). » missile, guided; V-1

cruiser A medium-sized warship designed to protect trade routes and to act as a scout for a battle fleet. Size, speed, and armament varied enormously with the passing years, depending upon the strength of enemy cruisers. » warships [i]

crumhorn A musical instrument made from wood with a small cylindrical bore, and curved at the end like a hockey stick. It had a double reed and a wind-cap (so that the player's lips did not touch the reed), and was made in various sizes. There were seven finger-holes and a thumb-hole, and the larger instruments had metal keys. It was widely used in Europe in the 16th–17th-c, and revived in the 20th-c for performing early music. » reed instrument

Crusades Holy Wars authorized by the Pope in defence of Christendom and the Church. They were fought against the infidels in the East, Germany, and Spain, against heretics and schismatics who threatened Catholic unity, and against Christian lay powers who opposed the papacy. Crusaders committed themselves with solemn vows, and by the 13th-c were granted the full Indulgence, ie remission of all punishment due for sin and an assurance of direct entry into heaven. Papal authorizations of war against Islam continued to be made until the 18th-c. » Hospitallers; Livonian Knights; Templars; Teutonic Knights; *see panel p 322*

crustacean [kruhs**tay**shuhn] A typically aquatic arthropod possessing a pair of jaws (*mandibles*) and two pairs of antennae situated in front of the mouth in adults; contains c.40 000 species, mostly marine, but also in freshwater and terrestrial habitats; great diversity of forms; life cycle commonly involves a larval stage with three pairs of limbs (the *nauplius*). (Subphylum: *Crustacea*.) » arthropod; barnacle; copepod; crab; fish louse; krill; larva; lobster; sand hopper; shrimp; water flea; woodlouse

Crux (Lat 'cross') The smallest constellation in the sky, and one of the most distinctive. Also known as **crux Australis**, or **Southern Cross**, it features on the national flags of Australia and New Zealand. Originally part of Centaurus, it received a separate identity in the 16th-c. » Centaurus; constellation; RR8

Cruyff, Johann [kriyf] (1947–) Dutch footballer, born in Amsterdam. He joined his first club, Ajax, at the age of 10, and at 19 made his debut in the Dutch League. He won 11 Dutch League and Cup medals with Ajax, and helped them to three consecutive (1971–3) European Cup successes. In 1973 he joined Barcelona (Spain) and won Spanish League and Cup medals with them. He captained Holland in the 1974 World Cup final (beaten by West Germany). He returned to Holland as a player in 1983, joining Feyenoord in 1984, but returned to Barcelona as manager in 1988. » football [i]

crwth [krooth] A Celtic (especially Welsh) lyre, played with a bow or plucked. The earliest types, known from the 12th-c onwards, had three strings, but by the 18th-c, when it became obsolete, the crwth had acquired a further three, tuned in unison with the others or at the octave. » lyre; string instrument **1** [i]

cryogenics The study of physical systems at temperatures less than c.90 K (−183°C). Many processes are more easily understood and measured at low temperatures, where unwanted thermal effects are reduced. Some processes can be observed only at low temperatures, either because of masking by thermal effects or because the phenomena (eg superconductivity, superfluidity) exist only at low temperature. » Joule-Thompson effect; magnetic cooling; superconductivity; superfluidity

cryolite A mineral composed of sodium, aluminium, and fluorine (Na_3AlF_6), used in the smelting of aluminium ores. It occurs in important quantities in Russia and Greenland. » aluminium

cryoscopic [kriyoh**skop**ik] In chemistry, to do with melting point; especially the determination of molecular weight of a solute by the depression of the freezing point of a solvent. » solution

crypt Part of a building below the main floor and usually underground. In particular, it refers to the part of a church containing graves and relics. » church [i]

cryptanalysis The deciphering or codebreaking of messages intended for others. The use of codes and ciphers to protect sensitive information from falling into the hands of enemies or

THE MAIN CRUSADES TO THE EAST

	BACKGROUND	LEADER(S)	OUTCOME
First Crusade (1096–9)	Proclaimed by Urban II to aid the Greeks against the Seljuk Turks in Asia Minor, liberate Jerusalem and the Holy Land from Seljuk domination, and safeguard pilgrim routes to the Holy Sepulchre.	Bohemond I Godfrey of Bouillon Raymond, Count of Toulouse Robert, Count of Flanders Robert Curthose, Duke of Normandy Stephen, Count of Blois	Capture of Nicaea in Anatolia (Jun 1097); Turks vanquished at Battle of Dorylaeum (Jul 1097); cauture of Antioch in Syria (Jun 1098), Jerusalem (Jul 1099). Godfrey of Bouillon became ruler of the new Latin kingdom of Jerusalem, and defeated the Fatimids of Egypt near Ascalon in Palestine (Aug 1099). Three other crusader states were founded: Antioch, Edessa, Tripoli.
Second Crusade (1147–8)	Proclaimed by Eugenius III to aid the crusader states after the Muslim reconquest of Edessa (1144).	Conrad III of Germany Louis VII of France	German army heavily defeated by Turks near Dorylaeum (Oct 1147), and the French at Laodicea (Jan 1148); Damascus in Syria invested, but siege abandoned after four days (Jul 1148). The crusaders' military reputation was destroyed, and the Syrian Muslims united against the Latins.
Third Crusade (1189–92)	Proclaimed by Gregory VIII after Saladin's defeat of the Latins at the Battle of Hattin (Jul 1187) and his conquest of Jerusalem (Oct 1187). (By 1189 all that remained of the kingdom of Jerusalem was the port of Tyre.)	Frederick I Barbarossa Philip II Augustus of France Richard I of England	Cyprus conquered from Greeks (May 1191), and established as new crusader kingdom (survived until 1489); capture of Acre in Palestine (Jul 1191); Saladin defeated near Arsuf (Sep 1191); three-year truce guaranteeing safe-conduct of Christian pilgrims to Jerusalem. Most cities and castles of the Holy Land remained in Muslim hands.
Fourth Crusade (1202–4)	Proclaimed by Innocent III to recover the Holy Places.	Boniface of Montferrat	Despite papal objections, crusade diverted from Egypt or Palestine (1) to Zara, a Christian town in Dalmatia, conquered for Venetians (Nov 1202); (2) to Byzantium, where embroilment in dynastic struggles led to sack of Constantinople (Apr 1204) and foundation of Latin Empire of Constantinople (survived until 1261). The crusading movement was discredited; the Latins in Palestine and Syria were hardly helped at all; the Byzantine empire never fully recovered; and the opportunity was lost of a united front between the Latins and Greeks against the Muslims.
Fifth Crusade (1217–21)	Proclaimed by Innocent III when a six-year truce between the kingdom of Jerusalem and Egypt expired.	Andrew II of Hungary John of Brienne, King of Jerusalem Leopold, Duke of Austria	Three indecisive expeditions against Muslims in Palestine (1217); capture of Damietta in Egypt after protracted siege (May 1218–Nov 1219); further conquests attempted, but crusaders forced to relinquish Damietta (Aug 1221) and withdraw.
Sixth Crusade (1228–9)	Emperor Frederick II, who first took the Cross in 1215, married the heiress to the kingdom of Jerusalem in 1225. Excommunicated by Gregory IX for delaying his departure, he finally arrived at Acre in Sep 1228.	Frederick II	Negotiations with Egyptians secured Jerusalem and other places, including Bethlehem and Nazareth (Feb 1229); Frederick crowned King of Jerusalem in church of Holy Sepulchre (Mar 1229). Jerusalem was held until recaptured by the Khorezmian Turks in 1244.
Seventh Crusade (1248–54)	Proclaimed by Innocent IV after the fall of Jerusalem and defeat of the Latin army near Gaza by the Egyptians and Khorezmians (1244).	Louis IX of France	Capture of Damietta (June 1249); defeat at Mansurah (Feb 1250); surrender of crusaders during attempted withdrawal; Damietta relinquished and large ransoms paid (May 1250). Louis spent four years in Palestine, refortifying Acre, Caesarea, Joppa and Sidon, and fruitlessly attempting to regain Jerusalem by alliances with the Mameluks and Mongols.
Eighth Crusade (1270–2)	Proclaimed after the Mameluk conquest of Arsuf, Caesarea, Haifa (1265), Antioch and Joppa (1268).	Charles of Anjou, King of Naples-Sicily Edward of England (later Edward I) Louis IX of France	Attacked Tunisia in N Africa (Jul 1270); Louis died in Aug; Charles concluded treaty with Tunis and withdrew; Edward negotiated 11-years' truce with Mameluks in Palestine. By 1291 the Latins had been driven from the Holy Land.

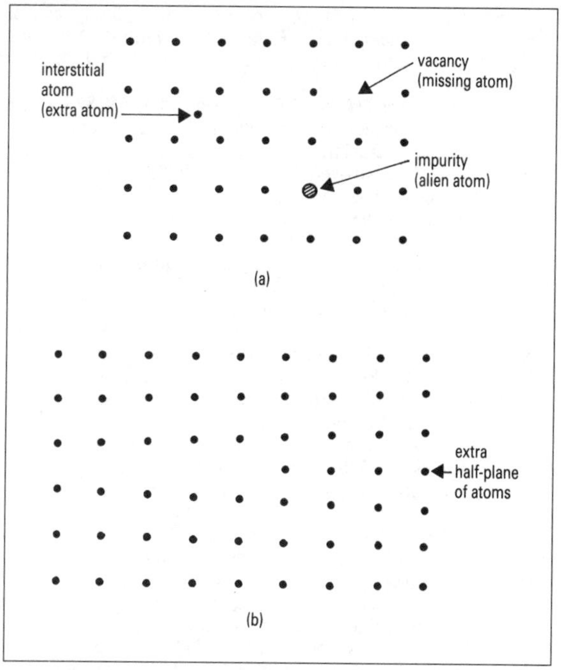

Crystal defects – Possible defects in a crystal (a); a dislocation in a crystal, corresponding to an extra half-plane of atoms (b).

rivals creates a reciprocal demand for cryptanalysis. This involves firstly intercepting a message, then analysing it to reveal its contents. Since languages can be distinguished by the different frequencies with which the letters of the alphabet occur, the prime task is to search for such enciphered patterns. The use of computers has greatly facilitated this process, but even they have major problems with the more arbitrary nature of highly sophisticated modern codes. » cipher; cryptography

cryptography The alteration of the form of a message by codes and ciphers to conceal its meaning. Codewords, normally from a code book, stand for one or more words of the *plaintext* (the original message). With ciphers, the letters of the plaintext are individually substituted or transposed (re-ordered), according to a secret key. » cipher; cryptanalysis

cryptomeria » **Japanese cedar**

cryptomonad » **cryptophyte**

cryptophyte [**krip**tohfiyt] A single-celled alga with two ribbon-like flagella located in a front oral groove; typically with various pigments (phycobilins) in addition to chlorophylls *a* and *c*; also called **cryptomonad**. (Class: *Cryptophyceae*.) » algae; flagellum

crystal defects Irregularities in otherwise perfectly regular crystals. Some, such as cracks and dislocations, strongly influence crystal mechanical properties, typically causing weakness. Others, such as impurities, affect electrical properties (eg the semiconductor crystals used in electronics) or give colour to crystals (eg chromium in red ruby). The illustration gives a 2-dimensional representation of certain 3-dimensional defects. » crystals; semiconductor

crystal growth The formation of crystals when a saturated solution of a suitable substance is either cooled or some solvent removed by evaporation. The growth usually starts on small introduced 'seed' crystals. The shape of the final crystals reflects the underlying crystal structure of the substance. » crystals

Crystal Palace An iron-framed, prefabricated, glass building designed by Sir Joseph Paxton to house the Great Exhibition of 1851. The structure, dubbed the 'Crystal Palace' by *Punch* magazine, was erected in London's Hyde Park. It was re-erected in S London, but destroyed by fire in 1936. » Great Exhibition; Paxton, Joseph

crystallography The study of crystals, both of their external form and their internal structure. The symmetries shown by natural crystals strongly suggested an atomic theory, and the application of the diffraction of X-rays by crystals acting as optical gratings has given a great deal of information about the arrangements and bonding of atoms in crystals, and, by analogy, in other environments. » crystals; X-rays

crystals True solids, made up of regularly repeating groups of atoms, ions, or molecules. In contrast with liquids and other amorphous materials, the properties of crystals vary with the direction in which they are measured. A complete crystal structure is defined by giving both a lattice of points, of which only 14 types are possible, and the group of atoms associated with each lattice point. » crystal defects [i]; crystal growth; crystallography; liquid crystals; quasi-crystals

CS gas US military designation for a chlorinated compound, 1-o-chlorophenyl-2,2-dicyanoethylene, $Cl–C_6H_4–CH=C(C\equiv N)_2$. It causes irritation and watering of the eyes, and is widely used in riot control. » chlorine

ctenophore [**ten**uhfaw] A marine animal with a transparent, jelly-like (gelatinous) body, which swims using eight comb-like rows of plates (*ctenes*); carnivorous, using paired tentacles armed with stinging cells to catch prey; c.80 species, found mostly in open sea; known as **comb jellies** or **sea gooseberries**. (Phylum: *Ctenophora*.)

cu lan » **loris**

Cuauhtémoc [kwow**tay**mok] (c.1495–1525) The last Aztec ruler, successor to Montezuma, who resisted the Spaniards under Cortés at the siege of Tenochtitlán (now Mexico City) in 1521. He was later executed while on an expedition with Cortés to Honduras. » Aztecs; Cortés

Cuba, official name **Republic of Cuba**, Span **República de Cuba** pop (1990e) 10 603 000; area 110 860 sq km/42 792 sq ml. Island republic in the Caribbean Sea, divided into 14 provinces and city of Havana; W of Haiti, N of Jamaica, and S of Florida; capital, Havana; chief towns, Santiago de Cuba, Camagüey, Holguín, Santa Clara; timezone GMT −5; people mainly Spanish and African descent; official language, Spanish; before 1959, 85% Roman Catholic; Castro regime discourages religious practices; unit of currency, the peso of 100 centavos; Central Highway crosses the island for 1 216 km/756 ml; airport at Havana.

Physical description and climate. An archipelago, comprising the island of Cuba, Isla de la Juventud, and c.1 600 islets and cays; main island 1 250 km/777 ml long, varying in width from 191 km/119 ml (E) to 31 km/19 ml (W); heavily indented coastline; S coast generally low and marshy, N coast steep and rocky, with some fine harbours; main ranges, Sierra del Escambray (C), Sierra de los Organos (W), and Sierra Maestra (E); highest peak, Pico Turquino (2 005 m/6 578 ft); mostly flat, with wide, fertile valleys and plains; subtropical climate, warm and humid; average annual temperature 25°C; dry season

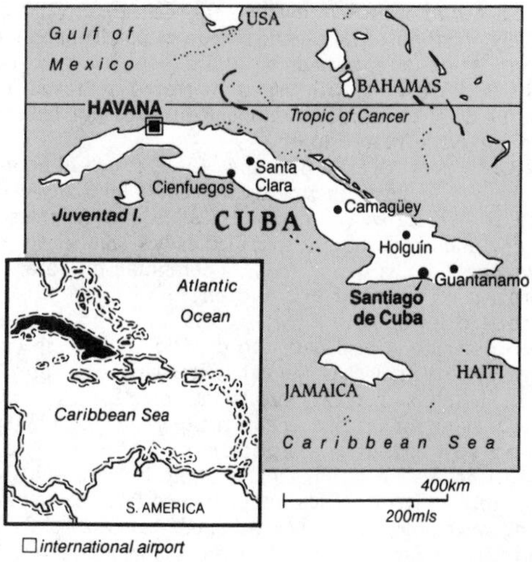

(Nov–Apr); mean annual rainfall, 1 375 mm/54 in; hurricanes (Jun–Nov).

History and government. Visited by Columbus, 1492; Spanish colony until 1898, following revolution under José Martí, with support of USA; independence, 1902, with USA retaining naval bases, and reserving right of intervention in domestic affairs; struggle against dictatorship of General Batista led by Castro, unsuccessful in 1953, finally successful in 1959, and Communist state established; invasion of Cuban exiles with US support, defeated at Bay of Pigs, 1961; US naval blockade, after Soviet installation of missile bases, 1962; governed by a 31-member State Council, appointed by a National Assembly of People's Power (510 deputies) following the proposal of the head of state.

Economy. After 1959, plantation estates nationalized, and land plots distributed to peasants; world's second largest sugar producer (accounting for 75% of export earnings); tobacco, rice, maize, coffee, citrus, dairy cattle; fishing, tourism, sugar milling, oil refining, food and tobacco processing, textiles, paper and wood products, metals, cement; world's fifth largest producer of nickel; before Castro, over half of Cuba's trade was with the USA; later, with the USSR. » Batista; Bay of Pigs; Castro; Havana; RR25 national holidays; RR47 political leaders

Cuban Missile Crisis A period of acute international tension and potential military confrontation between the USA and USSR in October 1962, following the USA's discovery of Soviet nuclear missile sites in Cuba. President Kennedy demanded the dismantling of the base and the return of the missiles, and threw a naval blockade around the island. The crisis ended on 28 October, when Soviet leader Khrushchev agreed to Kennedy's demands. » Cuba; Kennedy, John F; Khruschev

Cubism The most influential of all modern art movements, from which grew most of the early forms of abstraction. About 1907 Picasso and Braque rejected Renaissance perspective and Impressionist attention to light and atmosphere. Objects, painted in sombre shades of brown and grey, were analysed into geometrical planes with several views depicted simultaneously (*analytic cubism*). After c.1912 a flatter, more colourful and decorative hard-edged style emerged (*synthetic cubism*), using collage and painted relief constructs. » abstract art; art; Braque; collage; Futurism; modern art; Picasso

Cubitt, Thomas (1788–1855) British builder, born at Buxton, Derbyshire. He revolutionized trade practices in the building industry, and with his brother **Lewis** (1799–1883) was responsible for many large London projects, including Belgravia, and the E front of Buckingham Palace. Another brother, **William** (1785–1861) became Lord Mayor of London.

Cuchulain [koo**hoo**lin] (Irish **Cu Chulainn**) The hero of many Irish legends, the chief warrior of Ulster, who obtained his name (meaning 'the hound of Culaan') after killing a huge dog. He took its place in guarding the property of its owner.

cuckoo A bird of the worldwide family *Culculidae* (130 species), mostly inhabiting woodland; some (eg roadrunners) inhabit desert. About 50 species do not build nests, but lay eggs in the nests of other birds, with the young reared by 'foster' parents. The name is sometimes misapplied to birds not belonging to this family. » roadrunner

cuckoo flower An erect perennial, 15–60 cm/6–24 in, native to temperate N hemisphere; rosette leaves pinnate with oval leaflets, stem leaves with narrower leaflets, flowers cross-shaped lilac, sometimes white; also called **lady's smock**. (*Cardamine pratensis*. Family: *Cruciferae*.) » perennial; pinnate

cuckoo-pint » lords-and-ladies

cuckoo-roller » roller

cuckoo shrike A bird native to the Old World, especially the tropics; also known as the **caterpillar bird**; dull, greyish plumage; inhabits trees; eats insects and some fruit. It is neither a true cuckoo nor a shrike. (Family: *Campephagidae*, 70 species.)

cuckoo-spit insect » froghopper

cucumber A vine, trailing or climbing by means of tendrils, probably native to Africa but cultivated from early times as a salad vegetable; leaves heart-shaped, palmately lobed; male and female flowers 2.5 cm/1 in in diameter, yellow, funnel-shaped; fruit up to 45 cm/18 in or more, green, fleshy, cylindrical or oval. (*Cucumis sativa*. Family: *Cucurbitaceae*.) » climbing plant; gherkin; gourd; palmate; squash (botany); squirting cucumber

Cúcuta [**koo**koota] 7°55N 72°31W, pop (1985) 440 823. Capital of Norte de Santander department, NE Colombia; 16 km/10 ml from Venezuelan frontier; within a Tax Free Zone; founded, 1733; destroyed by earthquake, 1875, then rebuilt; gateway to Venezuela, and a focal point in Colombia's fight for independence; airfield; railway; university (1962); coffee, tobacco, cattle trade. » Colombia [i]

Cudworth, Ralph (1617–88) English philosopher and theologian, born at Aller, Somerset. He was educated at Cambridge, where he became a tutor, and leader of the 'Cambridge Platonists'. He was professor of Hebrew (1645), rector of North Cadbury, Somerset (1650), and master of Christ's College (1654). His best-known work, *The True Intellectual System of the Universe* (1678), aimed to establish the reality of a supreme divine Intelligence against materialism. He died at Cambridge. » Cambridge Platonists; materialism

Cuenca [**kwen**ka] 2°54S 79°00W, pop (1982) 152 406. Capital of Azuay province, SC Ecuador; third largest city in Ecuador; founded by Spanish, 1557; airfield; railway; two universities (1868, 1970); tobacco, dairy products, meat packing, fruit canning, textiles, leatherworks, motor vehicles, agricultural machinery, chemicals; La Concepción convent (1599), now religious art museum; cathedral, modern art museum, folk museum; sulphur baths nearby. » Ecuador [i]

Cukor, George D(ewey) (1899–1983) US film director, born in New York City. He worked first on Broadway, but went to Hollywood in 1929, starting a career of 50 years directing with *Girls About Town* (1931) and *Little Women* (1933). He was particularly successful with the great actresses of the star system – Garbo, Crawford, Hepburn – but his range was wide, including *Gaslight* (1944), *A Star is Born* (1954), and *My Fair Lady* (1964), for which he was awarded a long-awaited Oscar. His last film was *Rich and Famous* (1981). He died in Los Angeles.

Culicidae [kyoo**li**suhdee] A family containing c.3 000 species of true flies, including mosquitoes and gnats. Many species are of primary medical and veterinary importance as carriers of diseases such as malaria, yellow fever, dengue, and elephantiasis. (Order: *Diptera*.) » fly; gnat; mosquito

Cullinan diamond The largest gem diamond ever found, weight 3 255 carats (650 grams/22.9 avoirdupois ounces). It was found in Premier Diamond Mine, Transvaal in 1905 and named after Sir Thomas Cullinan, who had discovered the mine. It was cut into 9 large and 96 small stones, the largest of which (Star of Africa) is in the Royal Sceptre of the British Crown Jewels. » crown jewels; diamond

Culloden Moor, Battle of (1746) A battle fought near Inverness, the last major battle on British soil, which marked the end of the Jacobite rebellion of 1745 led by Charles Edward Stuart. His force, mainly of Scottish highlanders, was crushed by a superior force of English and lowland Scots under the Duke of Cumberland. » Forty-five Rebellion; Stuart, Charles Edward

Culpeper, Nicholas (1616–54) British astrologer, born in London. He studied at Cambridge, and in 1660 began to practise astrology in Spitalfields. In 1649 he published an English translation of the College of Physicians' Pharmacopoeia, *A Physical Directory*, and in 1653 appeared *The English Physician Enlarged, or the Herbal*. Both books had an enormous sale. » astrology

Culpeper's Rebellion (1677–80) An attempt by settlers in North Carolina to establish a government in opposition to 'proprietors' who claimed control of the province on effectively feudal terms. It was named for John Culpeper, the settlers' chief spokesman, who was subsequently acquitted on a charge of treason, and who died, as he was born, in obscurity.

cult Any set of beliefs and practices associated with a particular god or group of gods, forming a distinctive part of a larger religious body. The focus of the worship or devotion of a cult is usually a god or gods, spirit or spirits, associated with particular objects and places. The focus of devotion may be an animal (eg the whale cult in Eskimo religions), a particular deity (eg the Hindu cult devoted to Shiva), or even a deified human being (eg the emperor cult in ancient Rome). » cargo cult; religion; sect

cultivar A contraction of **cultivated variety**; in names further abbreviated to **cv**. It refers to any distinct type of plant produced in cultivation, but not growing in the wild. Many cultivars do not breed true, and are propagated vegetatively. » vegetative reproduction

cultivator An agricultural implement carrying rows of prongs (*tines*); some versions carry blades. It is used for breaking up soil and creating a seed-bed before planting, and is also used in the control of weeds. » soil

cultural anthropology » **anthropology**

cultural evolution (anthropology) A theory popular among Victorian anthropologists that human cultures could be ranked on an evolutionary scale, and even that every community was fated to pass through a fixed series of stages of cultural evolution. This view is now discredited, but the term is still used to describe the cultural adaptation of a particular community to its human and natural environment. » anthropology; culture (anthropology)

cultural history An approach to the study of history, dating from the work of Hegel, who argued that all epochs are characterized by a certain 'spirit', culture, or *Zeitgeist*. The most notable practitioner of this brand of history was Burckhardt, who was influenced by Hegelian historical thought and whose influential book *Die Kultur der Renaissance in Italien* (The Civilization of the Renaissance in Italy) appeared in 1860. In later generations the Burckhardt approach fragmented into the more limited fields of the history of art, intellectual history, and the history of science; but more recently there has been a return to cultural history, including the history of popular culture. » Burckhardt; culture (anthropology); Hegel; Renaissance

cultural pluralism » **plural society**

Cultural Revolution An abbreviation for the Great Proletarian Cultural Revolution, a radical Maoist mass movement initiated as a rectification campaign in 1966, which ended only with the death of Mao Zedong (Mao Tse-tung) and the arrest of the Gang of Four in the autumn of 1976. To prevent the Chinese revolution from stagnating and to avoid 'revisionism', Mao aimed at replacing the old guard, including Liu Shaoqi (died in prison in 1969), Peng Zhen, and Deng Xiaoping (both disgraced in 1966), with a new generation of fervent revolutionaries. He appealed directly to the masses, in particular to young students, the Red Guards, who with the support of the People's Liberation Army overthrew not only party leaders but all so-called 'bourgeois reactionaries' and 'capitalist-roaders' in authority in schools, universities, factories, and the administration. The ten years of social and political turmoil saw the closure of schools and universities, factories at a standstill, and millions of people sent to undertake manual labour in the countryside as re-education. » Gang of Four; Mao Zedong; People's Liberation Army; Red Guards

culture (anthropology) The way of life of a group of people, consisting of learned patterns of behaviour and thought passed on from one generation to the next. The notion includes the group's beliefs, values, language, political organization, and economic activity, as well as its equipment, techniques and art forms (referred to as *material culture*). » anthropology; cultural evolution/history; sociology

culture (microbiology) An artifically maintained population of micro-organisms, or of dissociated cells of a tissue, grown in a nutrient medium and reproducing by asexual division. The process is used in experimental microbiological research and also in medical applications, chiefly as part of the task of diagnosis. » micro-organism; reproduction

Cumae [kyoomee] The oldest Greek colony in Italy, founded c.750 BC near present-day Naples. It was famous in Roman times as the home of the oracular prophetess, the Sibyl.

Cumberland, William Augustus, Duke of (1721–65) British general, the second son of George II, born in London. He adopted a military career, and in the War of the Austrian Succession (1740–8) was wounded at Dettingen (1743) and defeated at Fontenoy (1745). He crushed the Young Pretender's rebellion at Culloden (1746), and by his harsh policies afterwards earned the lasting title of 'Butcher'. In the Seven Years' War (1756–63), he surrendered to the French (1757), and thereafter retired. He died in London. » Austrian Succession, War of the; Culloden Moor, Battle of; Seven Years' War

Cumberland A former county of NW England; part of Cumbria since 1974. » Cumbria

Cumbria pop (1987e) 486 900; area 6 810 sq km/2 629 sq ml. County in NW England, divided into six districts; bounded W by the Irish Sea, NW by the Solway Firth, N by Scotland; Pennines in the E; 40% of the county within the Lake District and Yorkshire Dales national parks; created in 1974 from the former counties of Westmorland and Cumberland; county town, Carlisle; chief towns include Penrith, Kendal, Barrow-in-Furness; agriculture, tourism, shipbuilding, marine engineering, chemicals; atomic energy at Windscale and Calder Hall. » Carlisle; England [i]; Lake District

cumin A slender annual growing to 50 cm/20 in, native to N Africa and SW Asia; leaves divided into narrow thread-like lobes; flowers white or pink, petals notched; fruit oblong with slender ridges. It is cultivated for the aromatic fruits used for spice, is an ingredient of curry powder, and is much used in Mexican cooking. (*Cuminum cyminum*. Family: *Umbelliferae*.) » annual; curry; spice

cummings, e e, properly **E(dward) E(stlin) Cummings** (1894–1962) US writer and painter, born at Cambridge, Massachusetts. He was educated at Harvard, and studied art at Paris, but his writings attracted more interest than his paintings. His several successful collections of poetry, starting with *Tulips and Chimneys* (1923), are striking for their unorthodox typography and linguistic style. He died at North Conway, New Hampshire. » American literature; poetry

cumquat » **kumquat**

cumulonimbus clouds Clouds of the cumulus family which rise to great heights (up to 10 km/6 ml). They are often dark and threatening when seen from below, and are associated with thunderstorms and the arrival of a cold front during the passage of a depression. At the top, the cloud may form an 'anvil' shape. Cloud symbol: Cb. » cloud [i]; cold front; cumulus clouds; depression (meteorology) [i]; nimbus clouds; thunderstorm

cumulus clouds A family of clouds with a predominantly vertical extent but relatively horizontal base. They range from small, white fluffy clouds typical of summer afternoons, to black and threatening storm or cumulonimbus clouds. Convection is responsible for their vertical extent, and the cloud base occurs c.450–2 000 m/1 500–6 500 ft. Cloud symbol: Cu. » altocumulus/cirrocumulus/cumulonimbus/stratocumulus clouds; cloud [i]

cuneiform A form of writing used throughout the Middle East for over 3 000 years until about the 1st-c BC. Originally derived from pictograms, the symbols were later used to represent words, syllables, and phonetic elements. The earliest examples were written from top to bottom, but later the symbols were turned on their sides and written from left to right. At first, the

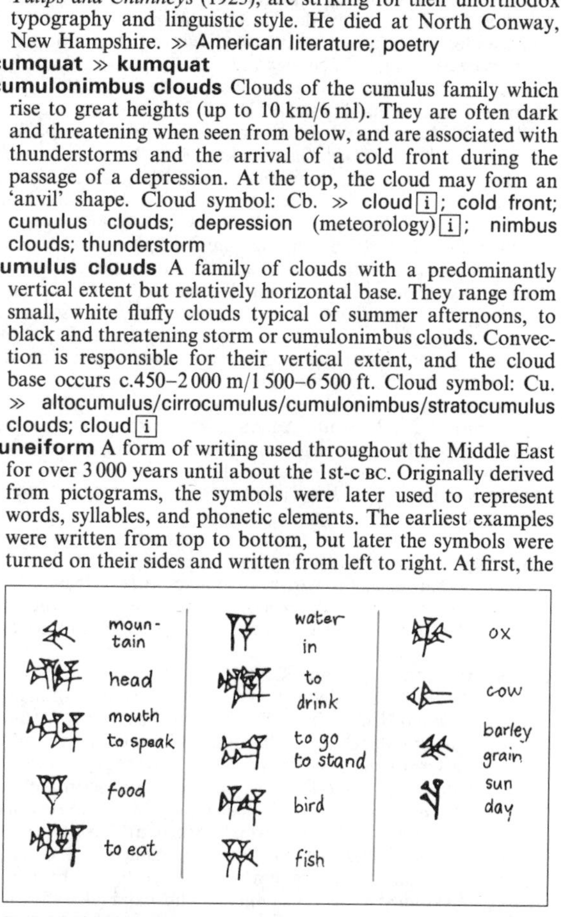

Symbols from the later period of cuneiform script, 1st millennium BC

symbols took the form of impressions made on soft clay with a stylus, but subsequently a harder writing surface was used. Cuneiform writing was not deciphered until the 19th-c. » alphabet [i]; writing systems

Cunningham, Merce (1919–) US dancer, choreographer, teacher, and director, born at Centralia, Washington. He experienced a range of dance forms before attending the Bennington School of Dance to study modern dance. He danced with the Martha Graham company (1939–45), and started his own company in 1952. He is one of the major figures in the development of a concern with form and abstraction in modern dance. Among his many works are *Summerspace* (1958), *Scramble* (1967), *Rain Forest* (1968) and *Duets* (1980). » Graham, Martha; modern dance; postmodern dance

Cunobelinus » **Cymbeline**

Cuomo, Mario (1932–) US politician, born in New York City. Educated at St John's University, New York, he became Governor of New York State, and was strongly boosted for the presidency in 1984 and 1988.

cup fungus A fungus producing a cup-shaped fruiting body that opens at maturity to expose the fertile layer; most grow on decaying organic matter, some are parasitic. (Subdivision: *Ascomycetes*. Class: *Discomycetes*.) » Ascomycetes; fungus

Cupid The Roman god of Love, son of Venus, depicted as a naked winged boy with bow and arrows. Apuleius tells the story of *Cupid and Psyche*. He is equivalent to Greek Eros. » Eros (mythology); Psyche

cupola [kyoo**po**hla] A small dome over a circular, square, or polygonal part of a building, usually above a roof or turret; more loosely, a dome of any size. A good example is the Royal Pavilion, Brighton, UK (1815–23), architect John Nash, where cupolas of near- and far-eastern origin are used in abundance.

cuprite A red copper oxide (Cu_2O) mineral, which is widely distributed. It is an important source of copper. » copper

cupronickel An alloy of copper and nickel, silver in colour. It is used extensively for coinage. » alloy; copper; nickel

Curaçao [koora**sah**oh] pop (1981) 147 388; area 444 sq km/171 sq ml. Largest and most populous island of the Netherlands Antilles, E Caribbean, 60 km/37 ml N of Venezuela; composed of coralline limestone; generally flat, but rises to 373 m/1 224 ft in the NW; length 58 km/36 ml; width 13 km/8 ml; visited by Europeans, 1499; Dutch colony, 1634; capital, Willemstad; airport; tourism, oil refining, phosphate mining, ship repairing, liqueur. » Netherlands Antilles [i]

curare [kyoo**rah**ree] An extract of the S American plants *Chondrodendron tomentosum* or *Strychnos toxifera*, used as an arrow poison for hunting by S American Indians. The active principle, tubocurarine, is widely used to induce muscle paralysis during surgery. » strychnine

curassow [**kyoo**rasoh] A large, tree-dwelling, turkey-like bird, native to C and N South America; head with a conspicuous crest of curved feathers; legs long, strong; eats buds, leaves, and small animals. (Family: *Cracidae*, 13 species.)

curate Strictly, a Christian clergyman admitted to the 'cure of souls' and having the 'cure' or charge of a parish. Popularly, the term is used of an assistant or unbeneficed clergyman, helping or temporarily replacing the priest, rector, vicar, or other incumbent of the parish. » priest; rector; vicar

curia In ancient Rome, the Senate house. It stood on the NW side of the forum, adjacent to the comitium. » forum; Senate, Roman

Curia Romana » **Roman Curia**

curie In radioactivity, defined as 3.7×10^{10} disintegrations per second; symbol Ci; 1 Ci = 3.7×10^{10} Bq (becquerel, SI unit); original definition related to the activity of radioactive radon; named after French physicists Pierre and Marie Curie. » becquerel; Curie; radioactivity units [i]; units (scientific)

Curie, Marie, *née* **Manya Skłodowska** (1867–1934) Polish physicist, born in Warsaw, who worked at Paris with her French husband **Pierre** (1859–1906) on magnetism and radioactivity, and discovered radium. She emigrated to France in 1891, and studied at the Sorbonne. Her husband, also educated at the Sorbonne, became professor of physics there in 1901. Pierre and his brother, Jacques, discovered piezo-electricity. Pierre and Marie Curie shared the 1903 Nobel Prize for Physics with Becquerel for the discovery of radioactivity. After her husband's death in a road accident, Mme Curie succeeded to his chair, isolated polonium and radium in 1910, and won the Nobel Prize for Chemistry in 1911. She died near Sallanches, France. » Becquerel; curie; Curie's law; Curie temperature; piezo-electric effect; radioactivity; radium

Curie point » **Curie temperature**

Curie's law A law for paramagnetic materials which states that the magnetization is proportional to B/T, where B is magnetic flux density and T is temperature in kelvin; stated by French physicist Pierre Curie in 1895. Physically, increasing B serves to align individual atomic magnetic moments; increasing T gives more thermal agitation, which upsets alignment. » Curie; magnetic moment; paramagnetism

Curie temperature In ferromagnetism, the material-dependent temperature above which a ferromagnetic material becomes merely paramagnetic; symbol T_c, units K; introduced by French physicist Pierre Curie in 1895; also called **Curie point**. It results from the increased thermal agitation of atoms, which overcomes the aligning force between neighbouring atoms. For iron, $T_c = 1043$ K. » Curie; ferromagnetism; paramagnetism

Curitiba [kooree**chee**ba] 25°24S 49°16W, pop (1980) 842 818. Commercial and industrial capital of Paraná state, S Brazil; SW of São Paulo, altitude 900 m/2 950 ft; two universities (1912, 1959); railway; airfield; commercial centre; tobacco, furniture, paper, textiles, cars, maté, cattle; cathedral (1894), Palácio Iguaçu, Paranaense Museum, Passeio Público park, temple in Egyptian style on L Bacacheri to the N. » Brazil [i]

curlew A long-legged sandpiper; breeds in the N hemisphere, but flies S (some as far as Australia) during the N winter; has long, down-curved bill; probes for food in sediments. (Genus: *Numenius*, 8 species.) » sandpiper; whimbrel

curling A game played usually by teams of four on an ice rink, using special stones fitted with handles. The object is similar to that of bowls, to deliver the stones nearest to a target object, known as the *tee*. Sweeping the ice with a broom in front of the running stone can help it to travel a great deal further. It is popular in Scotland, Canada, and the Nordic countries. » bowls; RR109

currant A deciduous shrub, native to N temperate regions and the Andes; leaves palmately lobed; flowers borne in clusters on short lateral shoots, 4–5 sepals and petals, petals slightly shorter and rounded; berries juicy; cultivated for ornament and as soft fruit. The currants used for 'fruit' cakes are dried grapes. (Genus: *Ribes*, 150 species. Family: *Grossulariaceae*.) » blackcurrant; deciduous plants; grapevine; palmate; redcurrant; sepal; shrub

currency The money of a country. **Convertible currency** is that proportion of a country's money which can be exchanged for the money of another country. A nation's currency *depreciates* when the rate of exchange between it and another currency falls. For example, if £1 can be exchanged for $2, but subsequently the rate falls to £1 for $1.50, the pound has depreciated against the dollar; the dollar, by comparison, has *appreciated*. » devaluation; dollar; European Monetary System; exchange controls/rates; petrocurrency; pound; purchasing power parity; sovereign; sterling; RR32

current (oceanography) Flowing water in the ocean. The surface currents depicted on the Atlases of the Seas are long-term averages of the direction of water motion at the sea surface, driven primarily by the winds. Because most do not extend deeper than 300–500 m/1 000–1 600 ft, they can be conveniently separated from the circulation of intermediate and deep waters, driven by varying densities of sea water caused by differences in temperature and salinity. (The situation is more complex, in fact, because the Antarctic Circumpolar Current and even parts of the Gulf Stream system do extend all the way to the sea floor.)

The surface circulation has certain similarities in each of the major ocean basins. The strong, persistent Trade Winds, blowing out of the NE in the N hemisphere and out of the SE in the S hemisphere, produce major W-flowing equatorial currents. These currents flow along bands of latitude until, deflected by continents, they form boundary currents flowing N or S. In the Atlantic and Pacific Oceans these equatorial and boundary currents are parts of semi-enclosed circulation cells called *gyres*. The gyres are oval-shaped, elongated E–W, and centred in the subtropics (30°N and S). Their centres are displaced towards the W side of ocean basins because of the rotation of the Earth, which results in an intensifying of boundary currents on the W side and a weakening of E boundary currents.

In general, a subtropical gyre has four components. (1) An equatorial current travelling W in response to the Trade Winds. (2) A W boundary current flowing toward the Poles; these currents are important in transporting heat from lower to higher latitudes; they are narrow, swift, and deep. (3) An E-flowing current pushed along by the bands of W winds at temperate latitudes. (4) An E boundary current flowing towards the Equator; these currents transport cool water from higher to lower latitudes, and are broad, shallow, and weak. Smaller subpolar gyres, turning in the opposite direction to the subtropical gyres, are present especially in the N hemisphere where continents deflect current flow.

The W-flowing N and S equatorial currents of the N and S subtropical gyres are separated by an E-flowing equatorial counter-current. Counter-currents are developed at the inter-tropical convergence (ITC), the area of weak and variable winds known as the *doldrums*. The ITC is not found at the geographic equator, but is shifted to c.5°N in the Atlantic and Pacific and to c.7°S in the Indian Ocean. The shift of this 'climatic equator' away from the geographic equator is the result of the unequal distribution of land and sea between the N and S hemispheres. » Equator; thermohaline circulation; wind [i]

current (electricity) The flow of electric charge, symbol i or I, units A (amp). A current of one amp means that a charge of one coulomb flows every second. Current flows positive to negative by convention. **Current density**, symbol j or J, is the total current divided by the cross-sectional area of the conductor. » alternating current; charge; coulomb; direct current; electrical power; skin effect

curry A spiced dish of fish, meat, poultry, or vegetables, originating in the East. Among the spices used in curries are coriander, cumin, chilli, cinnamon, cardamom, cloves, fenugreek, ginger, and turmeric. It is often thought that spices serve to act as a preservative in the cuisine of hot climates. Other common ingredients are garlic, yogurt, and coconut milk. » herbs and spices

cursus honorum [**koor**sus o**naw**rum] Literally, 'the course of honours'; the ordered career structure which was obligatory for any man in ancient Rome who wished to hold high public office. Under the cursus, the major offices of state – such as the quaestorship, praetorship, and consulship – had to be held in a strict order, and not before a certain age. » consul **1**; praetors; quaestors; tribunes

curtain wall A non-loadbearing wall used as a protective screen over the structural frame of a building. The materials used are varied: they include aluminium, steel, and especially glass. In mediaeval military architecture, the term referred to the defensive outer wall of a castle.

Curtin, John (Joseph) (1885–1945) Australian statesman and Labor Prime Minister (1941–5), born at Creswick, Victoria. He was active in trade union work, and edited a Perth newspaper. In 1928 he entered parliament, became leader of the Labor Party (1934), and Prime Minister. He organized national mobilization during the Japanese war, and died in office, at Canberra. » Australian Labor Party

Curtis, Glenn Hammond (1878–1930) US engineer and aeronaut, born at Hammondsport, New York. In 1904 he designed and built an engine for the dirigible *California Arrow*. In 1908 he won the *Scientific American* trophy for the first public flight of 1 km in the USA, and in 1911 he demonstrated the practicality of the seaplane. He died at Buffalo, New York. » dirigible; seaplane

curvature of space-time An expression of the effect of mass and energy on space and time. This is zero for Newtonian mechanics and special relativity, corresponding to flat space-time. It is known from observation of the bending of star light by the Sun that space-time is not flat. In the general relativity theory of gravitation, space-time curvature is due to the presence of mass. Regions of infinite curvature are predicted (black holes). At a large distance from massive bodies, space-time is almost flat, corresponding to weak gravity. » general relativity; Minkowski space

Curwen, John (1816–80) British music educationist, born at Heckmondwike, Yorshire. He became a Nonconformist minister in 1838, but devoted himself to promoting the tonic sol-fa musical system. His method came to be widely used, and in 1864 he left his ministry, having established a publishing house for music. He died at Heaton Mersey, Lancashire. » tonic sol-fa

Curzon (of Kedleston), George Nathaniel, Marquis (1859–1925) British statesman, born at Kedleston Hall, Derbyshire. Educated at Eton and Oxford, he became an MP in 1886, and travelled widely in Eastern countries. He became Under-Secretary for India (1891–2), and for Foreign Affairs (1895), and in 1898 was made Viceroy of India and given an Irish barony. He introduced many social and political reforms, established the NW Frontier Province, and partitioned Bengal. He resigned after a disagreement with Lord Kitchener (1905), returning to politics in 1915 as Lord Privy Seal. He became Foreign Secretary (1919–24), and was created a marquis (1921). He died in London. » Curzon Line; Kitchener

Curzon, Sir Clifford (1907–82) British pianist, born and died in London. He studied at the Royal Academy in London, and in Berlin (1928–30). He taught for some years at the Royal Academy, but resigned in 1932 and devoted himself to concert work, specializing in Mozart and other Viennese classics. He was knighted in 1971. » Mozart

Curzon Line A line of territorial demarcation between Russia and Poland proposed in 1920 by the British Foreign Secretary, Lord Curzon. Poland rejected the proposal, subsequently gaining larger territories. In September 1939 a boundary similar to the Curzon Line became the border between German- and Soviet-occupied Poland, and in 1945 was recognized as the frontier between Poland and the USSR. » Curzon (of Kedleston); Poland [i]; Yalta Conference

cuscus [**kus**kus] » **phalanger**

Cush The name used by the pharaohs for Nubia – the land stretching S from the First Cataract to the Sudan. Its capital was first Napata and then Meroe. Relations between Egypt and Cush were of a see-saw nature, Cush being tributary to Egypt in the second millennium, yet ruling it in the first. Egypt's XXVth dynasty (751–668 BC) came from Cush. » Meroe; Napata

Cushing, Harvey Williams (1869–1939) US neurosurgeon and physiologist, born in Cleveland, Ohio. He was educated at Johns Hopkins, Yale, and Harvard, graduating in medicine in 1895, then taught at Harvard (1912–32) and Yale (from 1933), his main research field being the brain and the pituitary gland. He died at New Haven, Connecticut. » brain [i]; Cushing's disease; pituitary gland

Cushing's disease A disorder resulting from excessive production of the hormones secreted by the cortex of the adrenal glands. It causes profound metabolic and sexual effects, including excessive hair growth, obesity, amenorrhoea, high blood pressure, and osteoporosis. » adrenal glands; amenorrhoea; Cushing; osteoporosis

Cushites A group of peoples in NE Africa, including the Somali and Galla. Their economies are primarily pastoral. It may be that in the early part of the Christian era they inhabited a wider area of E Africa. On the Red Sea coast they fused with Semitic colonists to found the kingdom of Axum. » African history; Axum; Ethiopia [i]

cusp In Gothic architecture, a projecting point formed by the intersection of two or more curves in the tracery; hence, usually carved in stone. » Gothic architecture; tracery [i]

custard apple A deciduous tree growing to 6 m/20 ft, native to tropical America; leaves lance-shaped; flowers with six greenish-yellow petals; fruit 10 cm/4 in, roughly heart-shaped, greenish, with an appearance rather like a tortoise's shell, containing numerous seeds buried in a sweet pulp; also called **sweet sop**. It is widely cultivated for the edible fruit. (*Annona squamosa*. Family: *Annonaceae*.) » deciduous plants; tree [i]

Custer, George Armstrong (1839–76) US soldier, born at New Rumley, Ohio. He graduated at West Point (1861), and after a brilliant career as a cavalry commander in the Civil War served in the campaigns against the Indian tribes of the Great Plains. His actions were controversial, but his gift for self-publicity made him a symbol of the cavalry. His defeat by a combined Sioux-Cheyenne force at Little Big Horn, Montana (25 Jun 1876), shocked the nation, but did no lasting good to the Indians' cause. » Indian Wars

customs and excise The government department charged with collecting taxes due on specified goods and services, and controlling imports into a country where there are tariffs or quota restrictions, or where the imports are illegal. It is most visible at airports and ports checking goods imported, and charging tax (*duty*) as appropriate. It also ensures that goods in bonded warehouses (ie where dutiable products are held before tax is paid) are properly managed. The department also handles value-added tax. » taxation; VAT

customs union An economic agreement where nations adopt common excise duties, thereby eliminating the need for customs checks along their common frontier. They thus create a free trade area. A good example is the Benelux countries' agreement, set up in 1948, which subsequently formed part of the EEC, itself a customs union. » Benelux; customs and excise; European Economic Community

Cuthbert, St (c.635–87), feast day 20 March. English missionary, born in Ireland or Northumbria. He became a monk (651), prior of Melrose (661) and of Lindisfarne (664). In 676 he left to become a hermit, but in 684 was persuaded to take the bishopric of Hexham, then of Lindisfarne. After two years he returned to his cell, on the island of Farne, where he died. His body was moved to many places, and finally buried at Durham in 999. » Christianity; monasticism

Cutner, Solomon » **Solomon** (music)

cutter A single-masted, fore- and aft-rigged sailing vessel with more than one headsail, usually requiring a bowsprit. Although sailing cutters are fairly uncommon today, the term is still in use, especially in compounds (eg *revenue cutter*). It is also applied to a ship's boat which is rigged for sailing and rowing, and in the USA it applies to vessels which would elsewhere be called *sloops*. » ship [i]; sloop

cutting A portion of a plant, usually a side shoot but also a leaf or root which, when removed from the parent, will grow to form a new individual. It is commonly used by gardeners as a means of propagation. » vegetative reproduction

cuttlefish A squid-like marine mollusc with eight arms and two tentacles, used to capture prey; internal calcareous shell (cuttlebone) may be straight or curved; found on or near the sea bed in shallow water; capable of complex behaviour and rapid colour changes. (Class: *Cephalopoda*.) » calcium; Cephalopoda [i]; mollusc; squid

cutworm The caterpillar larva of moths of the family *Noctuidae*. It can cause serious damage to crops by feeding on the stems and foliage of seedlings. (Order: *Lepidoptera*.) » caterpillar; larva; moth

Cuyp or **Cuijp, Albert** [kiyp] (1620–91) Dutch painter, born at Dordrecht. He excelled in the painting of landscapes, often suffused with golden sunlight, and containing cattle and other figures, such as 'Herdsmen with Cows by a River' (National Gallery, London). He died at Dordrecht. His father **Jacob Gerritsz** (1594–1651) was primarily a portrait painter. » Dutch art; landscape painting

Cuzco [**koos**koh] 13°32S 71°57W, pop (1981) 181 604. Capital of Cuzco department, S Peru; altitude 3 500 m/11 500 ft; ancient capital of the Inca empire, serving as both ceremonial capital and hub of the 40 000 km/25 000 ml Inca road network; oldest continuously occupied city in the Americas; a world heritage site; airfield; railway; university (1969); trade centre of an agricultural region; noted for its colonial churches, monasteries, convents, and extensive Inca ruins; cathedral (17th-c), Church of La Compañía de Jesús (17th-c), Church of Santo Domingo (17th-c). » Incas; Peru [i]

cwm » **cirque**

cyanide A compound containing the group $-C{\equiv}N$ in a molecule, or salts of hydrocyanic acid containing the ion CN^-. It is a very rapidly acting poison, which can kill within minutes. Cyanide gas has been used in gas chambers, and was used for more than 900 religious 'suicide-murders' in Guyana in 1978. It acts by preventing oxygen from being used by cells. Amyl nitrite (by inhalation) can treat cyanide poisoning if administered in time. » amyl nitrite; hydrocyanic acid

cyanide process A process for extracting gold and silver from ores. The finely divided ore is treated with a dilute solution of sodium or potassium cyanide. The gold or silver forms a soluble complex, from which it is regenerated by treatment with zinc dust. » cyanide; gold; silver

cyanocobalamin The chemical name for vitamin B_{12}. This vitamin is involved in cell division and in the manufacture of the sheath surrounding nerve cells. It is found only in animal-derived food, so that a true deficiency rarely occurs except among vegans, who eat no animal food. A secondary deficiency can occur if there is a deficiency of the intrinsic factor, a substance in the gut which aids B_{12} absorption. In individuals where the intrinsic factor is low or absent, pernicious anaemia develops. » anaemia; vegetarianism; vitamins [i]

cyanogen [siy**an**ohjen] $N{\equiv}C{-}C{\equiv}N$, boiling point −21°C. A colourless, inflammable, poisonous gas, with a bitter almond smell. It bears the same relation to cyanide ion (CN^-) as chlorine (Cl_2) does to chloride ion (Cl^-). » chlorine; gas **1**

Cyanophycota [siyanohf**iy**kuhta] » **blue-green bacteria**

Cybele [**si**belee] In Greek mythology, a mother-goddess, especially of wild nature, whose cult originated in Phrygia, and was taken over by the Greeks. She was depicted with a turreted mural crown, and was attended by lions. » Attis

cybernetics The study of control systems that exhibit characteristics similar to those of animal and human behaviour. The term was coined by Norbert Wiener in the 1940s, based on a Greek word meaning 'steersman'. Although the term has tended to fall into disuse with the expansion of the computer field, cybernetics is essentially a broad-based discipline which includes information, message, and noise theories, and can reconcile the work of neurophysiologists, psychologists, and computer engineers. » computer science; feedback; Wiener

cycad [**siy**kad] A tropical and sub-tropical gymnosperm, palm-like in appearance, trunk usually unbranched, armoured with old leaf bases or scar-like remains, with a crown of tough, feathery leaves; flowers borne in separate male and female cones, the female very large. Cycads are considered to be the most primitive living seed-plants, appearing in the late Palaeozoic era, and thought to be related to seed-ferns, a fossil group dominant during the Triassic period. The slow-growing trunks have a large, starchy central pith which in some species yields sago. (Family: *Cycadaceae*, 100 species.) » gymnosperms; Palaeozoic era; sago palm; seed fern

Cyclades [**sik**ladeez], Gr **Kikládhes** pop (1981) 88 458; area 2 572 sq km/993 sq ml. Island group in the Aegean Sea, Greece, between the Peloponnese (W) and the Dodecanese (E); chief islands are Tinos, Andros, Mikonos, Milos, Naxos, Paros, Kithnos, Serifos, lying in a circle around Siros; capital, Siros; several now popular holiday resorts. » Aegean Sea; Greece [i]

cyclamate [**sik**lamayt] A derivative of cyclohexylsulphamic acid, shown in the illustration. It has c.30 times the sweetening

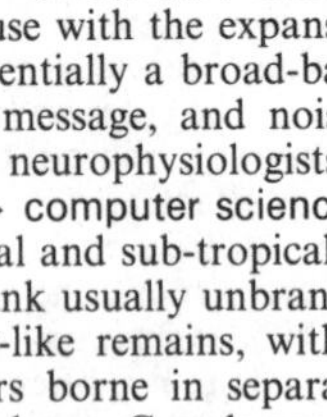

power of sucrose, and was previously used widely in sweetening 'diet foods'. It is less used now because of possible health risks. » sucrose [i]

cyclamen [**sik**lamuhn] A perennial with leaves growing direct from fleshy corm, native to Europe and Asia; flowers nodding, white, pink, or purple, corolla lobes bent back; after flowering, stalk coils to bring ripening fruit to the soil. Pot plants are derived mainly from *Cyclamen persicum*. (Genus: *Cyclamen*, 15 species. Family: *Primulaceae*.) » corolla; perennial

cycling The riding of a bicycle for fitness, pleasure, or as a sport. The first cycle race was in Paris in 1868, and won by James Moore of England. There are several popular forms of cycling as a sport. In *time trials* cyclists race against the clock. *Cyclo-cross* is a mixture of cycling and cross-country running, with the bike on the shoulder. *Track racing* takes place on purpose-built concrete or wooden velodromes. *Criteriums* are races around town or city centres. *Road races* are normally in excess of 150 km/100 ml in length, and take place either from one point to another, or involve several circuits around a predetermined road course. *Stage races* involve many days' racing, each consisting of 100 miles or more. The most famous cycle race is the Tour de France. » bicycle; Tour de France; RR109

cycloid The path traced out by a point on the circumference of a circle as the circle rolls along a straight line. Using the angle θ through which the circle has turned as parameter, the equation of the cycloid is $x=a(\theta-\sin\theta)$, $y=a(1-\cos\theta)$. » circle; circumference

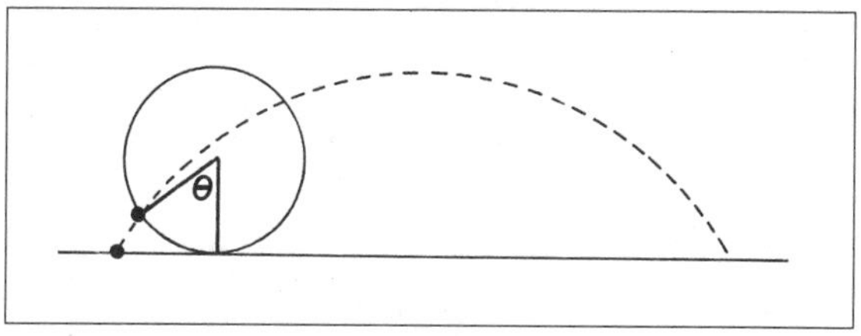

A cycloid

cyclone » **depression** (meteorology) [i]; hurricane

cyclops [**siy**klops] A freshwater copepod named after its conspicuous single eyespot; abundant in lake plankton, but also found on mud and in damp semiterrestrial habitats; feeds on fine particulate matter, or as a carnivore on insect larvae and other invertebrates. (Subphylum: *Crustacea*. Class: *Copepoda*.) » copepod; plankton

Cyclops [**siy**klops], plural **Cyclopes** In Greek mythology, a race of one-eyed giants who worked as smiths and were associated with volcanic activity. In the *Odyssey*, the Cyclops Polyphemus is outwitted and blinded by Odysseus, and hurls rocks into the sea at the departing ship. The Greeks called any pre-Greek structures incorporating huge stones 'Cyclopean'. » Galatea; Polyphemus

cyclostome [**siy**kluhstohm] Any of a group of jawless fishes with a large sucking mouth. » hagfish [i]; lamprey

cyclothymia In psychiatry, a persistent instability of affect, with repeated periods of mild elation and mild depresion. This may be a feature of an individual's personality or a forerunner of manic-depressive illness. It usually commences in adolescence or early adulthood and runs a chronic course. » manic depressive psychosis

cyclotron A machine for accelerating charged particles, typically protons; developed by US physicist Ernest Lawrence and others in 1931, and now largely superseded by the synchrotron. Acceleration is provided by an oscillating electric field. A large constant magnetic field guides particles in a spiral path, having a radius that increases as particle velocity increases. » Lawrence, Ernest; particle accelerators; proton

Cygnus (Lat 'swan') [**sig**nuhs] A large N constellation, imagined by the ancients as a swan flying along the Milky Way. Its brightest star is Deneb, a supergiant, distance 500 parsec. Of all the stars visible to the naked eye, this is the most luminous, 50 000 times the Sun's light. **Cygnus A**, a strong radio source, is identified with a distant peculiar galaxy that is also an X-ray source. It is one of the most powerful radio galaxies known. » constellation; galaxy; Milky Way; radio galaxy; supergiant; X-rays; RR8

cymbals Musical instruments of great antiquity. Modern orchestral cymbals are made in pairs, from an alloy of copper and tin, with a diameter of about 40–50 cm/16–20 in. They are clashed together, or suspended from a stand and played with a drumstick. They are of no definite pitch, but the small 'antique cymbals' or *crotales*, are tuned to precise pitches. » hi-hat cymbals; percussion [i]

Cymbeline (?–c.43) Pro-Roman king of the Catuvellauni, who from his capital at Camulodunum (Colchester) ruled most of SE Britain. Shakespeare's character was based on Holinshed's half-historical Cunobelinus. » Britain, Roman; Camulodunum; Caractacus; Cassivellaunus

cymbidium Orchids (epiphytes) native to tropical forests from Asia to Australia. They are widely cultivated for the spikes of large, showy flowers much used in floristry and the cut-flower trade. (Genus: *Cymbidium*, 40 species. Family: *Orchidaceae*.) » epiphyte; orchid [i]

cyme [siym], **cymose** » **inflorescence** [i]

Cynewulf [**kin**ewulf] (8th-c) Anglo-Saxon poet, identified by some with Cynewulf, bishop of Lindisfarne (737–80). Four poems, *Juliana*, *Christ*, *Elene*, and *The Fates of the Apostles*, have his name worked into the text in runes. » Anglo-Saxons; poetry; runes [i]

Cynics (literally, the 'dogs') In philosophy, a discontinuous group of philosophers, early members of which included Antisthenes and Diogenes of Sinope, influential in Greece and Rome 4th-c BC–6th-c AD. They taught by their example an ascetic life in conformity with nature, avoiding all societal conventions and artificially-induced desires. Their thought was influential on Stoicism. » Antisthenes; Diogenes; Stoicism

cypress An evergreen conifer, native to the temperate N hemisphere; leaves small, scale-like; cones like the head of a mace, with 4–12 woody scales joined at their margins, sometimes remaining on the branches for years. The timber is insect-repellant. It is susceptible to extreme cold, and is most common in warm climates. (Genus: *Cupressus*, 15–20 species. Family: *Cupressaceae*.) » evergreen plants; false/leyland/summer/swamp cypress

Cyprian, St (Thascius Caecilius Cyprianus) (c.200–58), feast day 16 September. One of the great Fathers of the Church, born (probably) at Carthage. He became a Christian in c.245, and was made Bishop of Carthage in 248, when his zealous efforts to restore strict discipline brought him a host of enemies. He was forced to flee from Roman persecution, and eventually suffered martyrdom under Valerian (reigned 253–60). At a synod in Carthage in 256 he argued for a notion of Church unity as expressed through the consensus of bishops. His writings remained influential. » Christianity; Fathers of the Church

Cyprus [**siy**pruhs], Gr **Kypros**, Turkish **Kibris**; official name **Republic of Cyprus**, Gr **Kypriaki Dimokratia**, Turkish **Kibris Cumhuriyeti** pop (1990e) 568 000; area 9 251 sq km/3 571 sq ml. Island republic in NE Mediterranean Sea, c.80 km/50 ml S of Turkey; capital, Nicosia; chief towns, Famagusta, Larnaca, Limassol, Kyrenia; airports at Larnaca, Paphos; chief ports, Limassol, Larnaca; Famagusta (chief port prior to 1974 Turkish invasion) now under Turkish occupation, and declared closed by Cyprus government; timezone GMT +3; c.77% Greek-speaking Orthodox Christians and 18% Turkish-speaking Muslims; almost all Turks now live in N sector (37% of island); official languages, Greek and Turkish, with English widely spoken; unit of currency, Cyprus pound of 100 cents.

Physical description. Third largest island in Mediterranean; Kyrenia Mts extend 150 km/90 ml along N coast, rising to 1 024 m/3 360 ft at Mt Kyparissovouno; forest-covered Troödos Mts in SW, rising to 1 951 m/6 401 ft at Mt Olympus; fertile Mesaoria plain extends across island centre; indented coastline, with several long, sandy beaches.

Climate. Typical Mediterranean climate with hot, dry summers and warm, wet winters; mean annual rainfall, 500 mm/20 in, with great local variation; mean daily temperature (Jul–Aug) from 22°C on Troödos Mts to 29°C on C plain; mild winters, with mean temperature of 4°C (Jan) in higher parts of mountains, and 10°C on plain; snow on higher land in winter.

History and government. Recorded history of 4 000 years, rulers including Greeks, Ptolemies, Persians, Romans, Byzantines, Arabs, Franks, Venetians, Turks (1571–1878), and British; British Crown Colony, 1925; Greek Cypriot demands for union with Greece (*enosis*) led to guerrilla warfare, under

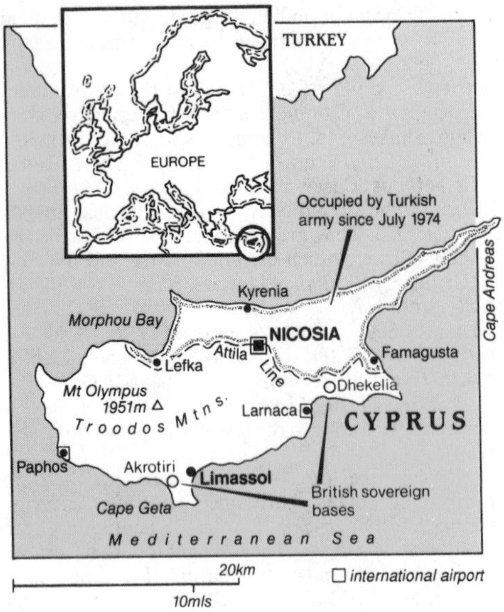

Grivas and Makarios, and 4-year state of emergency (1955–9); independence, 1960, with Britain retaining sovereignty over bases at Akrotiri and Dhekelia; Greek–Turkish fighting throughout 1960s, with UN peacekeeping force sent in 1964; further terrorist campaign in 1971; Turkish invasion (1974) led to occupation of over a third of the island, with displacement of over 160 000 Greek Cypriots; island divided into two parts by the Attila Line, from NW coast above Pomos to Famagusta in the E, cutting through Nicosia (where it is called the Green Line); governed by a president (head of state), elected for a 5-year term by the Greek community, and a House of Representatives of 80 elected members; Turkish members ceased to attend in 1983, when the Turkish community declared itself independent (as 'Turkish Republic of Northern Cyprus', recognized only by Turkey).

Economy. Greek Cypriot area now largely recovered from the 1974 invasion, with light manufacturing a main growth sector; paper, paperboard products, chemicals, food and wine, clothing, footwear, cigarettes; petroleum refining, cement production, electricity generation; mineral exports of asbestos, clay, chrome, umber; tourism recovering after 1974, now accounting for c.15% of national income; Turkish Cypriot economy heavily dependent on agriculture; tourism from Turkey, potatoes, citrus fruit, grapes, cereals, carobs, vegetables, olives, almonds; irrigation schemes aiming to increase area under cultivation. » enosis; EOKA; Greece [i]; Grivas; Makarios; Nicosia; Turkey [i]; RR25 national holidays; RR47 political leaders

Cyrano de Bergerac, Savinien [sira**h**noh duh **ber**zhuhrak] (1619–55) French satirist and dramatist, born in Paris. In his youth he fought more than a thousand duels, mostly on account of his extremely large nose. His works include satirical accounts of visits to the Moon and Sun, published posthumously, *Histoire comique des états et empires de la lune* and *...du soleil*, which suggested 'Gulliver' to Swift. » French literature; satire; Swift

Cyrenaics [siruh**nay**iks] A school of 4th-c and 3rd-c BC Greek philosophers, whose founder was Aristippus of Cyrene. They believed that the immediate sensation of pleasure is the only good, that all such sensations are equal in worth, and that past and future pleasures have no present value. » Aristippus

Cyrene [siy**ree**nee] 32°49N 21°52E. A prosperous Greek city-state in N Africa, famous in antiquity for the export of silphium, a plant used in ancient medicine. Ruled over by the Ptolemies, it became part of the Roman province of Cyrene in 74 BC. It is now a world heritage site, and the location of the village of Shahhat, E Libya. » Ptolemy I Soter

Cyril and Methodius, Saints (c.827–69; c.825–85), feast day 7 July. Greek brothers, born in Thessalonica, who became missionaries to the Slavs. Cyril first worked among the Tartar Khazars, and Methodius among the Bulgarians of Thrace and Moesia. Together they went to Moravia, where they prepared a Slavonic translation of the Scriptures and chief liturgical books. Cyril died in Rome, leaving Methodius to complete the evangelization of the Slavs as Bishop of Moravia. Called to Rome in 879 to justify his celebration of the Mass in the native tongue, he gained the approval of Pope John VIII. He may have died at Hradiště. The Cyrillic alphabet, modified out of the Greek by Cyril, superseded a more ancient Slavonic alphabet. » Bible; Cyrillic alphabet; missions, Christian

Cyril of Alexandria, St (376–444), feast day 9 June (E) or 27 June (W). Eminent theologian, and one of the Fathers of the Church, born at Alexandria. He became Patriarch of Alexandria in 412, and vigorously implemented orthodox Christian teaching. He expelled the Jews from the city (415), and relentlessly persecuted Nestorius, whose doctrine was condemned at the Council of Ephesus (431). » Fathers of the Church; Nestorians; theology

Cyril of Jerusalem, St (c.315–86), feast day 18 March. Theologian and Bishop of Jerusalem, who took a leading part in the doctrinal controversies concerning Arianism. Twice expelled from his see, he regained it and spoke for the Orthodox churchmen at the Council of Constantinople (381). He died in Jerusalem. » Arius

Cyrillic alphabet An alphabet attributed to St Cyril, and used for Slavonic languages, such as Russian and Bulgarian. It is used for many non-Slavonic languages in the republics of the former USSR. » alphabet [i]; Cyril and Methodius, Saints

Cyrus II, byname **the Great** (?–529 BC) The founder of the Achaemenid Persian Empire, the son of Cambyses I. He defeated the Medes (549 BC), became King of Persia (548 BC), and took Lydia (c.546 BC) and Babylon (539 BC). His empire eventually ran from the Mediterranean to the Hindu Kush. He had a policy of religious conciliation: the nations who had been carried into captivity in Babylon along with the Jews were restored to their native countries, and allowed to take their gods with them. » Achaemenids; Croesus; Lydia

Cyrus the Younger (424–401 BC) The second son of Darius II of Persia. He was accused of conspiring against his brother, Artaxerxes II, and sentenced to death (404 BC), but was afterwards pardoned and restored as satrap of Asia Minor. In 401 BC he led an army of Greek mercenaries, against his brother, but was killed at Cunaxa. » Xenophon

cyst (biology) Any relatively thick-walled resting cell formed by an organism as a means of dispersal or as a way of surviving a period of adverse conditions. Eggs and spores are often protected in cysts, but whole organisms may also encyst, to re-emerge when favourable conditions return. » biology

cyst (medicine) A benign (non-malignant) swelling within a tissue, very often containing fluid. It is sometimes caused by the blockage of a duct (eg a sweat gland cyst in the skin), by abnormal embryological development (eg a renal cyst), or by infection (eg an amoebic or hydatid cyst). » ganglion **2**; hydatid disease

cystic fibrosis A widespread genetically-determined disorder affecting mucous secretions in many parts of the body, which become thickened and viscid. The consequent blockage of mucus-secreting small ducts causes small cystic swellings behind the sites of the blockage. It results in damage to the lungs, liver, and pancreas, and obstruction in the alimentary tract. » cyst (medicine)

cystitis An infection of the wall of the urinary bladder. It induces frequency of urination, with a burning sensation on passing urine. » bladder

cytochrome [**siy**tuhkrohm] An iron-containing protein (*haemoprotein*) found in virtually all aerobic organisms. It functions as an electron-carrier in a variety of oxidation-reduction reactions that take place within living cells during normal metabolism. » aerobe; oxidation; protein

cytokinin [siytuh**kiy**nin] A hormone found in plants which acts in combination with other hormones (*auxins*) to promote cell division. » cell; hormone

cytology [siytoluhjee] The study of the structure and function of cells. Microscopic studies of cells, using a variety of staining techniques to identify cell types, are important in the diagnosis of some diseases, especially cancer. The use of the electron microscope enables detailed study of the fine structures within cells. » cell; electron microscope [i]; karyology

cytoplasm That part of an animal or plant cell enclosed by the cell membrane (*plasma membrane*) but excluding the nucleus. The cytoplasm contains a range of organelles, such as mitochondria, ribosomes, and golgi bodies, each with a specialized function. » cell

cytosine [siytuhseen] $C_4H_5N_3O$. A base derived from pyrimidine, one of the four found in nucleic acids, where it is generally paired with guanine. » DNA [i]

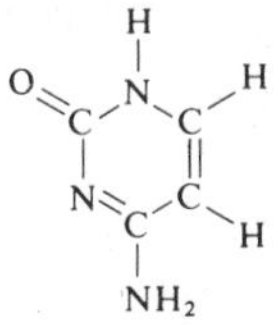

cytotoxic drugs » chemotherapy

Czech Republic, Czech **České Zeme** pop (1984) 10 328 221; area 78 864 sq km/30 441 sq ml. Republic in W Czechoslovakia, divided into seven regions; united with Slovak Republic in 1918 to form Czechoslovakia; comprises former provinces of Bohemia, Silesia, Moravia; capital, Prague. » Czechoslovakia [i]

Czechoslovak literature Modern Czechoslovakia brings together two distinct literary and linguistic traditions, Czech and Slovak. From its chronicle beginnings in the 11th-c, Czech literature has always looked to the West, and the late 13th-c *Alexandreida* also signals an endemic political awareness – evident in the Chaucerian *Groom and Student*, and the *New Council of Animals* by Flaška z Pardubic (died 1403). The verse legend, courtly romance, and love lyric also flourished from the 14th-c, alongside the publication of the first Czech dictionary and the foundation of Prague University (1348). The early Renaissance brought many translations and travelogues, while the Reformation stimulated the vigorous prose writings of the martyr John Huss (1372–1415), and the philosophy of Petr Chelčický (1390–1460), who influenced Tolstoy.

The publication of the Kraliká Bible (1579–93, 6 vols) helped create the modern Czech language, and it was the Czech National Revival, heralded by the scholar Josef Dobrovský (1753–1829) which laid the foundation for modern Czech literature. Prominent writers were the historical novelist Josef Linda (1789–1834), the poet Jan Kollár (1793–1852), who promoted the Pan-Slav idea at this time; and Karel Mácha (1810–36), who is regarded as the greatest of Czech poets. The influential almanacs *May* (1858–), *Ruch* (1868–), and *Lumír* (c.1875) directed a predominantly patriotic taste, publishing writers such as Jan Neruda (1834–91), Svatopluk Čech (1846–1908), Julius Zeyer (1841–1901), and Jaroslav Vrchlický (1853–1912); and the 'Czech Walter Scott', Alois Jirásek (1851–1930). World War 1 produced Hašek's satirical masterpiece *The Good Soldier Sweik* (1921–3); Karel Čapek, who invented the word for 'robot', foresaw the dangers of advanced technology. Czech literature veered left with Vladislav Vančura (1891–1942), Vitězslav Nezval (1900–58), and the poet Jaroslav Seifert (1901–) before succumbing to stagnation under communist rule. In these conditions, writers such as the poet Miroslav Holub (1923–), the novelists Bohumil Hrabal (1914–) and Milan Kundera (1929–), and the dramatist Vaclav Havel (1936–) have maintained a courageous witness.

Slovak literature existed only in oral tradition before the 19th-c. The 'National Awakening' produced the poets L'udovit Štúr (1815–56) and Janko Král' (1822–76), and Ján Botto's lyrical epic *The Death of Jánošík* (1862); also novels by Ján Kalinčiak (1822–71) and Jonáš Záborský (1812–76). More sophistication is apparent in the works of the poet Hviezdoslav (pseudonym of Pavol Országh, 1849–1921), the novelist Martin Kukučín (1860–1928), and the later Symbolist Ivan Krasko (1876–1958). Since the war, Slovak literature has endured the same trials as Czech; but the work of several fine lyrical poets, among them Vojtech Mihálik (1926–), Ivan Kupec (1922–), L'ubomir Feldek (1936–), and Miroslav Pius (1942–), attest to an unquenched spirit. » Čapek; Hašek; Havel; Kundera; Polish literature; Seifert

Czechoslovakia [chekuhsluh**vah**kia], Czech **Československo**, official name **Czech and Slovak Federative Republic**, Czech **Česka a Slovenska Federadivini Republika** pop (1990e) 15 664 000; area 127 899 sq km/49 369 sq ml. Land-locked federal state consisting of the Czech Republic (W) and the Slovak Republic (E), divided into ten regions (*kraj*); bounded N by Poland, E by Ukraine, S by Hungary and Austria, SW by W Germany, and NW by E Germany; capital Prague; chief towns include Bratislava, Brno, Ostrava, Košice, Plzeň, Olomouc; timezone GMT +1; official languages, Czech and Slovak, with Hungarian widely spoken; population, 65% Czech, 30% Slovak, several minorities; unit of currency, the koruna or crown of 100 haler.

Physical description and climate. Bohemia and W Moravia separated by R Morava valley from E Moravia and Slovakia; W range of the Carpathians in the E, sloping S to R Danube and Hungarian plains; major rivers, the Elbe, Oder, Danube; richly wooded (35%), chiefly with mixed and coniferous forests; continental climate, with warm, humid summers and cold, dry winters; winter snow lies 40–100 days; fog in low-lying areas; little E–W climatic variation.

History and government. Formerly ruled by Austrian Habsburgs; Czech lands united with Slovakia to form separate state, 1918; Mazaryk elected first President of parliamentary democracy; Germans occupied Sudetenland region, 1938, and then the whole country; government in exile in London during World War 2; independence with loss of some territory to USSR, 1946; communist rule following 1948 coup; attempt at liberalization by Dubček terminated by intervention of Warsaw Pact troops, 1968; continued strong dissident protest movement; each republic governed by a National Council (200 deputies in Czech and 150 in Slovak Republic); overall power vested in the Federal Assembly, which elects a President, and comprises the Chamber of Nations (75 Czech and 75 Slovak delegates) and Chamber of the People (200 elected deputies). Continued strong protest movement culminated in the fall from power of the Communist Party in 1989.

Economy. Based on concept of central planning with 5-year economic plans; iron, steel, chemicals, machinery, glass, vehicles, cement, armaments, wood, paper, beer; steel production around Ostrava coalfields; oil and gas refineries near Bratislava, supplied by pipeline from Ukraine; mainly collectives and state farms, producing sugar beet, potatoes, wheat, barley, maize; large dams and reservoirs on Vltava and Váh Rivers for energy and water conservation; over 22 000 lakes; over 1 500 mineral springs, with development of many health spas. » Bohemia; Czech Republic; Dubček; Havel; Moravia; Prague; Slovak Republic; RR25 national holidays; RR47 political leaders

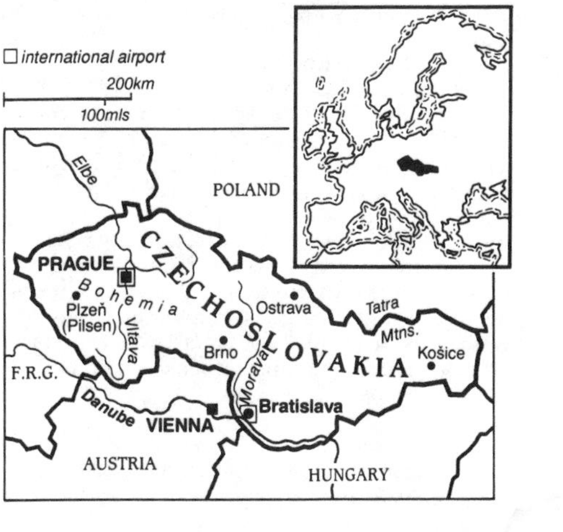

D and C » **dilatation and curettage**

D'Annunzio, Gabriele (1863–1938) Italian author, born at Prescara, and educated at Rome. During the 1890s he wrote several novels, influenced by the philosophy of Nietzsche, notably *Il trionfo della morte* (1894, The Triumph of Death). His best-known poetic work is *Laudi del cielo del mare della terra e degli eroi* (1899, In Praise of Sky, Sea, Earth, and Heroes), and his major plays include *La figlia di Iorio* (1904, The Daughter of Jorio) and the tragedy *La Gioconda* (1899), which he wrote for the actress Eleonor Duse. Their tempestuous relationship was exposed in his erotic novel, *Il fuoco* (1900, The Flame of Life). He died at Gardone Riviera. » Italian literature; Nietsche

d'Arc » **Joan of Arc**

D-Day (6 Jun 1944) The day when the Allies launched the greatest amphibious operation in history (code-named 'Overlord'), and invaded German-occupied Europe. By the end of D-Day, 130 000 troops had been landed on five beach-heads along an 80 km/50 ml stretch of the coast of Normandy, at a cost of 10 000 casualties. » Normandy campaign: World War 2

d'Indy, (Paul Marie Théodore) Vincent [**dã**dee] (1851–1931) French composer, born and died in Paris. He studied law there from a sense of family duty, but at the same time developed an interest in musical composition under the guidance of César Franck. He helped to found the Schola Cantorum in 1894, and taught there and at the Conservatoire until his death. His works include several operas and orchestral pieces, notably *Symphonie sur un chant montagnard français* (1886, Symphony on a French Mountaineer's Song). » Franck, César

D'Oyly Carte » **Carte, Richard D'Oyly**

D1 and D2 formats Videotape recording systems using digital rather than analogue techniques. The D1 format was introduced by Sony in 1987, using separate component tracks for luminance and chrominance on ¾ in (19 mm) tape at a speed of 28.69 cm/sec. In contrast, the D2 system, developed by Ampex in 1988, records a composite signal on ¾ in metal particle tape at a more economical speed of 13.17 cm/sec; three sizes of cassette are available, giving playing time of 32, 94, and 208 minutes. » videotape recorder

Da Nang [dah **nang**], formerly **Tourane** 16°04N 108°13E, pop (1972e) 500 000. Seaport in Quang Nam-Danang prov, C Vietnam; on the South China Sea; site of an important US military base during the Vietnam War; textiles. » Vietnam [i]; Vietnam War

Da Vinci » **Leonardo Da Vinci**

dab European flatfish abundant on sandy bottoms in inshore waters to 150 m/500 ft depth; feeds on crustaceans and other invertebrates; both eyes on right side of head; scales rough; body length up to 40 cm/16 in; valuable food fish, exploited commercially using trawls and nets (seines). (*Limanda limanda*. Family: *Pleuronectidae*.) » flatfish

dabbling duck A duck of the tribe *Anatini*; obtains food from water surface, or turns vertically 'tail up' to feed on vegetation on shallow lake beds, rivers, etc. One species, the **mallard**, has given rise to various domestic forms. (Sub-family: *Anatinae*.) » diving duck; duck; mallard; pintail; shoveller; teal; wigeon

dabchick The common name for some smaller birds of the grebe family. » grebe

Dacca » **Dhaka**

dace Freshwater fish widespread in rivers of Europe and Russia; length up to 30 cm/1 ft, body slim; olive green above, underside silvery white; feeds on aquatic invertebrates and plants, including flying insects at surface; close relative of chub and orfe. (*Leuciscus leuciscus*. Family: *Cyprinidae*.) » chub; orfe

dachshund A breed of dog, developed from small terriers in Germany; small, with extremely short legs; long muzzle, pendulous ears; used for hunting (sent into burrows); several sizes: *standard*, *miniature*, and *rabbit*, each with *smooth-haired*, *wire-haired*, and *long-haired* varieties; also known as **sausage dog**. » dog; terrier

Dacia [**day**sha] In antiquity, the name given to the area N of the Danube roughly corresponding to modern Romania. Conquered by the Romans in the early 2nd-c AD, its rich deposits of silver, iron, and gold were actively exploited by them. » Roman history [i]

dactylology A means of communication in which the fingers are used to sign the different letters of the alphabet; also known as **finger-spelling**. The system has been documented from the 17th-c, and is widely used among the adult deaf population. Both two-handed and one-handed manual alphabets have been devised. » deafness; sign language; RR82

Dada or **Dadaism** (French 'rocking horse') A modern art movement founded in Zürich in 1916 which, against the background of disillusionment with World War 1, attacked traditional artistic values. The name was chosen at random from a dictionary. The founders included poets such as Tristan Tzara (1896–1963) as well as artists such as Hans Arp. Important contributors included Duchamp (whose *Fountain*, 1917 – a porcelain urinal – is perhaps the best-known 'work' of Dada), Ernst, Picabia, and Ray. The Dadaists influenced the Surrealists, and their deliberate shock-tactics were revived by some artists in the 1960s. » art; collage; modern art; readymade; Surrealism; Arp; Duchamp; Ernst; Picabia; Ray, Man

daddy longlegs » **cranefly**

Daedalus [**dee**daluhs] A legendary Athenian inventor, who worked for King Minos in Crete and constructed the labyrinth. Later he escaped to Sicily with wings he had made for himself and Icarus; there he made the golden honeycomb kept at Mt Eryx. Any archaic work of skill was ascribed to him, and he was a patron saint of craftsmen in Ancient Greece. » Icarus (mythology); Minos; Minotaur; Pasiphae (mythology)

daffodil A species of narcissus, yellow, with a central trumpet up to 2.5 cm/1 in long, and darker than the six surrounding perianth-segments; native to Europe, the widely-grown garden plants are mainly large-flowered hybrids. (*Narcissus pseudonarcissus*. Family: *Amaryllidaceae*.) » narcissus; perianth

Dafydd ap Gwilym [**da**vit͟h ap **gwil**im] (c.1320–c.1380) Welsh poet, who wrote love songs, satirical poems, and nature poems in the complex *cywydd* metre which he perfected, much extending the range of such poetry. His work may be compared with that of the Troubadours. He is buried at Strata Florida, Dyfed, Wales. » poetry; troubadours; Welsh literature

Dagda, the [**dag**da] Irish protective deity, noted for his enormous club on wheels which both kills and restores to life, and for his cauldron which inspires and rejuvenates. Oengus and Brigit were his children. » Brigit

Daguerre, Louis Jacques Mandé [dagair] (1789–1851) French photographic pioneer, born at Cormeilles. He had been a scene painter in Paris, when, from 1826 onwards, and partly in conjunction with Joseph Niepce, he perfected the photographic process named after him. He died at Bry-sur-Marne, France. » daguerreotype

daguerreotype [dageruhtiyp] An early system of photography established by Louis Daguerre in France in 1839. A silver-plated sheet was sensitized by iodine vapour, and after a long exposure in the camera the image was developed over heated mercury and fixed in a solution of common salt. It became obsolete in the 1850s. » Daguerre; photography

Dahl, Roald (1916–90) British writer, born at Llandaff, S Wales, of Norwegian parents. Educated at Repton School, he worked for the Shell Oil Company in London and Africa, then served as a fighter pilot in the RAF during World War 2. He specialized in writing short stories of unexpected horror and macabre surprise, such as in *Someone Like You* (1953) and *Kiss, Kiss* (1960). His children's books display a similar taste for the grotesque, such as *James and the Giant Peach* (1961) and *Charlie and the Chocolate Factory* (1964). » short story

dahlia A tuberous perennial up to 8 m/26 ft high, sometimes an epiphyte, native to mountains from Mexico to Colombia. Several species with large, showy, chrysanthemum-like flower-heads were introduced into cultivation, originally for the tubers, which were eaten as a vegetable; but they are now commonly grown as garden ornamentals. Extensive hybridization has resulted in a great variety of flower colour and form. (Genus: *Dahlia*, 28 species. Family: *Compositae*.) » chrysanthemum; epiphyte; perennial; tuber

Dahomey W African kingdom based on its capital at Abomey, which in the late 17th-c and early 18th-c extended its authority from the coast to the interior, to the W of the Yoruba states. In the 1720s the cavalry of the Oyo kingdom of the Yoruba devastated Dahomey, but when the Oyo Empire collapsed in the early 19th-c, Dahomey regained its power. The state was annexed by the French in 1883, and regained its independence (later renaming itself Benin) in 1960. » African history; Benin [i]

Daibutsu [diy**but**soo] A Japanese statue of Buddha, the finest example in Japan being the bronze figure cast in 1252 at Kamakura, 11.5 m/37 ft high. » Buddha

Dáil Éireann [**doyl air**an] The lower house of the parliament of the Irish Republic. Unlike the upper house, the Senate (*Seanad Éireann*), which is appointed, the Dáil is elected by universal suffrage by proportional representation for a period of five years. It nominates the prime minister for appointment by the president. There are 144 members, who are called *Teatcha Dala*.

Daimler, Gottlieb (Wilhelm) (1834–1900) German engineer, born at Schorndorf. He worked from 1872 on improving the gas engine, and in 1885 designed one of the earliest roadworthy motor cars. In 1890, he founded the Daimler Automobile Company at Cannstatt, where he died. » car [i]; engine

daimyo [**diy**myoh] A Japanese feudal lord, equivalent to a mediaeval baron in Europe. Powerful under the Tokugawa Shoguns (1603–1868), *daimyo* lost power at the Meiji Restoration. They had responsibility for keeping the peace. The amount of rice their domains produced showed their prestige. » Meiji Restoration; samurai

dairy farming A farming system specializing in the production of milk – usually from cows, but in some regions from sheep, goats, yaks, buffaloes, or reindeer. Specialist dairy-cow breeds include Friesians, Ayrshires, and Jerseys. Dairy farming is most common in the wetter, temperate parts of the world, where grass grows well, and where cows can graze outside for all or part of the year. In hotter climates dairy cows tend to be confined all year round, and fodder is harvested and carried to them. Farmers specializing in dairy husbandry sell their milk to dairy manufacturers, from which is made butter, cheese, cream, yogurt, and skimmed milk. These foods are **dairy products**. » animal husbandry; cow

daisy A perennial native to Europe and W Asia, with a basal rosette of oval or spoon-shaped leaves; leafless flowering stems up to 20 cm/8 in, each bearing a solitary flower head; outer ray florets white often tinged red, inner disc florets yellow. It grows in short grassland and garden lawns where regular mowing prevents it from being smothered by taller vegetation. It spreads by short rhizomes, often becoming a pernicious weed. Forms with double flowers are grown for ornament. (*Bellis perennis*. Family: *Compositae*.) » capitulum; floret; immortelle; perennial; rhizome

daisy-wheel printer A type of impact printer, used in computer systems and in typewriters, in which the individual print characters are carried on separate 'petals' of a segmented disc called the *daisy-wheel*. The daisy-wheel is rotated to bring the relevant character in front of a striking hammer. Daisy-wheel printers are relatively slow, but are capable of producing high quality typescript. » printer, computer

Dakar [da**kah**] 14°38N 17°27W, pop (1979) 978 553. Seaport capital of Senegal, at the S extremity of the Cape Verde peninsula; W Africa's second largest port, serving Senegal and Mauritania; founded, 1857; capital of French West Africa, 1902; part of Dakar and Dependencies, 1924–46; held by Vichy forces during World War 2; capital of Senegal, 1958; airport; railway terminus; university (1957); commerce, soap, sugar, leather products, pharmaceuticals, textiles, metal products, plastics, food processing; Great Mosque, cathedral (consecrated, 1936), ethnographical museum, notable markets. » Senegal [i]; Vichy

Daladier, Edouard [da**la**dyay] (1884–1970) French statesman and Prime Minister (1933, 1934, 1938–40), born at Carpentras. In 1927 he became leader of the Radical Socialists, and in 1933 Minister of War and Prime Minister of a short-lived government, a pattern which was repeated in 1934. In 1936 he was Minister of War in the Popular Front Cabinet, and as Premier (1938) supported appeasement policies and signed the Munich Pact. In 1940 he resigned, became successively War and Foreign Minister, and on the fall of France was arrested and interned until 1945. After the war he continued in politics until 1958. He died in Paris. » appeasement; France [i]

Dalai Lama (Mongolian, 'ocean-like guru') [**da**liy **lah**ma] The traditional religious and temporal head of Tibet, regarded as an incarnation of the Bodhisattva Avalokiteshavara. Tensin Gyatsho (1935–), held to be the 14th incarnation, ruled in Tibet from 1940 to 1959. After temporarily fleeing Tibet (1950–1) during the Chinese invasion of the country, he escaped to India during a local uprising in 1959. Tibetans still regard him as their spiritual leader. He won the Nobel Peace Prize in 1989. » bodhisattva; guru; Lamaism; Panchen Lama

Dales pony A breed of horse, developed in N England; height, 14–14½ hands/1.4–1.5 m/4.6–4.8 ft; black or brown; sturdy with short legs; strong; formerly used for farm work and carrying loads; now popular for pony trekking. » horse [i]

Dalhousie, James Andrew Broun Ramsay, 1st Marquis of (1812–60) British Governor-General of India (1847–56), born and died at Dalhousie Castle, Midlothian, Scotland. Educated at Harrow and Oxford, he became an MP (1837), Earl of Dalhousie (1838), and President of the Board of Trade (1845). In India (1847), he encouraged the development of railways and irrigation works. He annexed Satara (1847) and Punjab (1849), but the annexation of Oudh (1856) caused resentment which fuelled the 1857 Rebellion. He was made a marquis in 1849, and retired through ill health in 1856. » Indian Mutiny

Dali, Salvador (Felipe Jacinto) [**dah**lee], Span **Dalí** [dah**lee**] (1904–89) Spanish artist, born at Figueras. After studying at the Academy of Fine Arts, Madrid, he moved to Paris and joined the Surrealists (1928), becoming one of the principal figures of the movement. His study of abnormal psychology and dream symbolism led him to represent 'paranoiac' objects in landscapes remembered from his Spanish boyhood. In 1940 he settled in the USA, became a Catholic, and devoted his art to symbolic religious paintings. He wrote *The Secret Life of Salvador Dali* (1942), and collaborated with Luis Buñuel in the surrealist films *Un Chien andalou* (1928, An Andalusian Dog) and *L'Age d'or* (1930, The Golden Age). One of his best-known paintings is 'The Persistence of Memory' (known as the 'Limp Watches', 1931, New York). He died at Figueras. » Spanish art; Surrealism

Dalian, also **Luda**, **Lu-ta**, **Dairen**, **Dalien** 38°53N 121°37E, pop (1984e) 1 587 800. Port city in Liaoning province, NE China; port built (1899–1930) by Japanese; Soviet occupation (1945–54); deep natural harbour, silt-free and ice-free; resort beaches nearby; airfield; railway; designated a special economic zone; diesel engines, shipbuilding, machine tools, chemicals, textiles, glass, fishing (especially shellfish); centre of fruit-growing area (well-known apples). » China [i]

Dallapiccola, Luigi (1904–75) Italian composer, born at

Pisino, Istria. He studied at Florence, becoming a pianist and music teacher. After World War 2 he taught composition in the USA for several years. His compositions make wide use of twelve-note technique, and include songs, a piano concerto, three operas, a ballet, and choral works such as *Canti di prigionia* (1938–41, Songs of Prison). He died in Florence. » serialism; twelve-tone music

Dallas 32°47N 96°49W, pop(1980) 904078. Seat of Dallas County, NE Texas, USA, on the Trinity R; seventh largest city in the USA; commercial and financial centre of the SW; founded, 1841; city status, 1871; President Kennedy assassinated here (22 Nov 1963); airport (Dallas–Fort Worth); railway; two universities (1910, 1956); electronic and transportation equipment, machinery, textiles, clothing, leather goods, oil refining; cultural, educational and artistic centre; tourism; scene of the television series 'Dallas'; major league teams, Mavericks (basketball), Cowboys (football). » Kennedy, John F; Texas

Dalmatia [dal**may**sha] A name applied since early times to the strip of territory bordering the Adriatic Sea in W Yugoslavia; from the S end of Pag I to Cavtat, S of Dubrovnik; largely mountainous and barren, with few lines of communication to the interior; formerly part of the Greek province of Illyria, settled 6th-c BC; occupied by Slavs, 7th-c AD; harbours at Zadar, Split, Dubrovnik; wine, tourism. » Adriatic Sea; Yugoslavia [i]

dalmatian A breed of dog, officially from Yugoslavia, but probably developed in India many centuries ago; large, lightly-built, with long legs, tail, and muzzle; ears short, pendulous; coat short, white with black or brown spots. » dog

Dalton, (Edward) Hugh (John Neale), Baron (1887–1962) British Labour politician, born at Neath, S Wales, and educated at Eton and Cambridge. First elected as a Labour MP in 1924, he held the posts of Minister of Economic Warfare (1940–2) and President of the Board of Trade (1942–5). In the postwar Labour government he was Chancellor of the Exchequer (1945–7), Chancellor of the Duchy of Lancaster (1948–50), Minister of Town and Country Planning (1950–1), and, briefly, Minister of Local Government (1951). Elevated to the peerage in 1960, he died in London. » Crosland; Labour Party; revisionism

Dalton, John (1766–1844) British chemist, born at Eaglesfield, Cumberland. He early developed an interest in mathematics and physics, and taught these subjects at Manchester. From 1787 until his death he kept a diary of detailed meteorological observations. In 1794 he first described colour blindness ('Daltonism'), exemplified in his own case and that of his brother. His chief physical researches were on mixed gases, the force of steam, the elasticity of vapours, and the expansion of gases by heat. His development of the atomic theory of matter elevated chemistry to a quantitative science. He died in Manchester. » chemistry; Dalton's law of partial pressures

Dalton's law of partial pressures A law in chemistry, formulated by John Dalton: in a mixture of gases, each gas exerts the same pressure as it would if it were the only gas present in the given volume. For example, as the atmosphere contains roughly 80% nitrogen, the pressure exerted by nitrogen is 80% of the total pressure. » Dalton, John; gas **1**; nitrogen; vapour pressure

dam A barrier constructed to control the flow of water, thus forming a reservoir. Dams are built to allow storage of water, giving a controlled supply for domestic or industrial consumption, for irrigation, to generate hydro-electric power, or to prevent flooding. Large dams are built of earth, rock, concrete or of some combination of these materials (eg earth and rockfill). They are built either as *gravity* dams, where the strength is due entirely to the great weight of material; as *arch* dams, where abutments at either side support the structure; or as *arch gravity* dams, a combination of the two. » Afsluitdijk/Aswan High/Bratsk/Grand Coulee/Hoover/Itaipu/Kariba/Tarbela dam

damages A remedy providing money compensation for a civil wrong. In breach of contract cases, the compensation aims to put the innocent party in the same position he or she would have been in had the contract been performed as agreed. In tort, the aim is to compensate the plaintiff for the loss actually suffered. » contract; plaintiff; tort

daman » hyrax

Damascus, Arabic **Dimashq** 33°30N 36°19E, pop(1981) 1112214. Capital city of Syria, on the R Barada; claimed to be the world's oldest continuously inhabited city; a world heritage site; in ancient times a great trade and commercial centre; satellite city Dimashq ad-Jadideh; airport; railway; university (1923); famous for its crystallized fruits, brass and copper ware, silks, woodwork; mediaeval citadel (1219), Great Mosque (8th-c, burned 1893, then restored); ancient Via Recta, runs E–W for 1500 m/5000 ft with Roman gateways at either end; international fair (Aug). » Syria [i]; Ummayyad Mosque

Damavand, Mount [dama**vand**] 35°56N 52°08E. Volcanic cone in the Elburz Mts, N Iran; height 5670 m/18602 ft; highest peak in Iran, with a permanent snowcap; Damavand resort at its S foot. » Iran [i]

Damocles [**dam**ohkleez] (4th-c BC) A legendary courtier of the elder Dionysius, tyrant of Syracuse (405–367 BC). He extolled the happiness of royalty, but the tyrant showed him the precarious nature of fortune in a singular manner. While seated at a richly-spread table, Damocles looked up to see a keen-edged sword suspended over his head by a single horsehair. » Dionysius the Elder

Damon and Pythias, or **Phintias** (4th-c BC) Two Pythagoreans of Syracuse, remembered as the models of faithful friendship. Condemned to death by the elder Dionysius, tyrant of Syracuse, Pythias begged to be allowed to go home to arrange his affairs, and Damon pledged his own life for his friend's. Pythias returned just in time to save Damon from death. Struck by so noble an example, the tyrant pardoned Pythias, and desired to be admitted into their sacred fellowship. » Dionysius the Elder

Dampier, William (1652–1715) English navigator and buccaneer, born near Yeovil. He journeyed to Newfoundland and the West Indies, then (1679) joined a band of buccaneers along the Pacific coast of S America. In 1683 he sailed across the Pacific, visiting the Philippines, China, and Australia. On his return to England, he published his *New Voyage round the World* (1697). He then led a voyage of discovery to the South Seas (1699), exploring the NW coast of Australia, and giving his name to the Dampier Archipelago and Strait, and made further journeys there in 1703 and 1708. He died in London.

damping Reduction of the size of oscillations by the removal of energy. For example, the indicator needles of gauges are often immersed in oil to give frictional damping; and resistive circuit components reduce electrical oscillations. » oscillation

damselfish Any of the family *Pomacentridae*; small brightly-coloured marine fishes widespread in tropical and temperate seas around reefs and rocky shores; body length 10–25 cm/4–10 in; includes anemonefish, which lives in close association with sea anemones. (7 genera, including *Chromis* and *Pomacentrus*.) » anemone

damselfly A large, long-bodied insect with two pairs of slender wings typically held together over the abdomen at rest. Damselflies are powerful predators, both as aquatic larvae and as flying adults. (Order; *Odonata*. Suborder: *Zygoptera*, c.3000 species.)

damson A type of plum in which the ovoid fruit is purplish with a waxy bloom; thought to be a cultivated form of bullace. (*Prunus domestica*, subspecies *institia*. Family: *Rosaceae*.) » bullace; plum

Dan, tribe of One of the twelve tribes of ancient Israel, said to be descended from the fifth son of Jacob, Dan's mother having been Bilhah, Rachel's maid. Its territory was vaguely defined, but was initially a coastal plain surrounded by the territories of Ephraim, Benjamin, and Judah; later they were forced to migrate N near the sources of the Jordan R. » Israel, tribes of [i]

Danae [**dan**ayee] In Greek mythology, the daughter of King Acrisius of Argos. When an oracle prophesied that her son would kill his grandfather, Acrisius imprisoned her in a bronze tower, where Zeus visited her in the form of a golden shower. She gave birth to a son, Perseus, who accidentally killed Acrisius with a discus. » Perseus (mythology)

Danakil Depression [danakil] Desert area in NE Ethiopia, occupying parts of Eritrea (SE), Tigray (E), Welo (NE), and Harerge (N) regions; low-lying region bounded by Red Sea (N, E) and Rift Valley (S, W); mountainous in parts, rising to 1 000 m/3 000 ft; land also dips to 116 m/381 ft below sea-level; extremely hot area, temperatures close to 60°C; major salt reserves; inhabited by the Afar; crossed by Djibouti–Addis Ababa railway. » Ethiopia [i]

dance » **African/Black/British Ballroom/Caribbean/community/country/disco/European court/Indian/jazz/maypole/modern/Morris/National Youth/post-modern/Oriental/step/street/sword/traditional dance; allemande; ballet; conga; courante; dance notation [i]; fandango; farandole; flamenco; gavotte; gigue; hornpipe; jig; London Contemporary Dance Theatre; mazurka; minuet; pavane; polka; polonaise; quadrille; Rambert Dance Company; rumba; samba; sarabande; tarantella; waltz**

Dance, George, known as **the Elder** (1695–1768) English architect, born in London, who designed the Mansion House (1739) and many other London buildings, and was surveyor to the City of London (1735–68), where he died. His son, **George (the Younger**, 1741–1825), was also an architect, and succeeded his father as surveyor. An exponent of Neoclassicism, deriving from his studies in Italy, his best-known building was Newgate Prison (1770–83). He was one of the original Royal Academicians. » Neoclassicism (art and architecture)

dance notation The recording of dance movement through symbols. More than 100 systems have been created, using letter abbreviations (15th-c), track drawings (18th-c), stick figure and music note systems (19th-c), and abstract symbol systems. Three are in current use; Benesh, Eshkol, and Labanotation. They are used in dance education, choreography, movement behaviour in work and therapy, and anthropology. Recently, systems have been developed to computerize notation. » choreography

dance of death A common theme in late mediaeval art: the allegorical representation of a dance or procession in which the living and the dead take part. Holbein the Younger designed a famous set of woodcuts on this theme (published 1538). » Holbein; woodcut

dandelion A perennial, leaves in a basal rosette, entire or variably lobed and toothed; flower heads solitary, borne on leafless hollow stems, florets yellow; fruits with a parachute of white hairs attached by a long stalk, the whole fruiting head forming the familiar 'clock'. Many dandelions reproduce from fruits formed without fertilization having taken place, resulting in many distinct populations or microspecies, with over a thousand described from Europe alone. The best-known species, *Taraxacum officinale*, is a cosmopolitan weed, its young leaves eaten as a salad vegetable, tap roots ground into a coffee substitute, and flower heads used for wine-making. (Genus: *Taraxacum*, c.60 species. Family: *Compositae*.) » floret; perennial

dandie dinmont A breed of dog, developed in Britain in the 19th-c from wire-haired hunting terriers; small terrier with short legs; long soft hair, especially on the head; ears pendulous; tail long. » dog; terrier

Dandolo, Enrico (c.1110–1205) Italian statesman, born in Venice. In 1173 he was Ambassador to Constantinople, and in 1192 became Doge of Venice. In 1202 he marched at the head of the Fourth Crusade, subduing Trieste and Zara, the coasts of Albania, the Ionian Is, and (1205) Constantinople, where he established the Empire of the Latins, and where he died. » Crusades [i]

dandruff Fine dry scales which fall from an eruption of the skin of the scalp, usually noticed when the scales fall on to clothing around the shoulders. It possibly results from infection with the fungus *Pityrosporum*. » skin [i]

Dane, Clemence, pseudonym of **Winifred Ashton** (c.1891–1965) British novelist and playwright, born in London. Her novels include *Regiment of Women* (1917), *Legend* (1919), and *The Flower Girls* (1954). Many of her plays have achieved long runs, notably *A Bill of Divorcement* (1921), and the ingenious reconstruction of the poet's life in *Will Shakespeare* (1921). » English literature

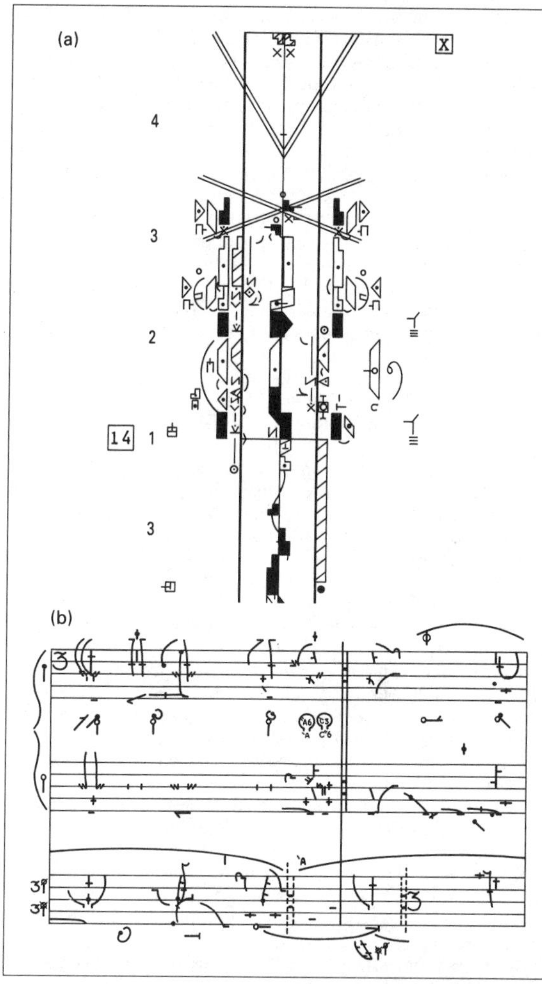

Two major 20th-c dance and movement notation systems. (a) An extract from Doris Humphrey's Water Study (1928) written in Labanotation, a system which dates from the 1920s in C Europe. It is read from the bottom to the top of the page. The central vertical line discriminates between left and right. The two central columns indicate steps or gestures of the left and right leg. The outer columns describe movement in the upper part of the body. The symbols are part of an abstract conceptualization of movement based on Rudolf Laban's analysis. » Laban
(b) An excerpt from Glen Tetley's Voluntaries (1973), written in Benesh Movement Notation, a system which was developed by Rudolf and Joan Benesh in England in the 1950s. It is read from left to right like a music score. It is an abstracted pictorial representation of the human body. The top stave shows the movement of the female dancer, and the second stave shows the male. The movements for an accompanying group of six dancers are shown together in the lower stave.

Danelaw That part of England where Danish conquest and colonization in the late 9th-c left an imprint on not only legal and administrative practices, but on place-names, language, and culture. Danish-derived customs survived even the Norman Conquest, and in the 12th-c all E England from the Thames to the Tees was so designated. » Vikings; Wessex

Dangerfield, Thomas (1650–85) English conspirator, born at Waltham, Essex. A thief, vagabond, and soldier, in 1679 he accused the Presbyterians of plotting to destroy the government. Imprisoned when this was shown to be a lie, he claimed he had been deceived by Catholics plotting against the life of

Charles II. Convicted of libel, he was whipped and pilloried, and on returning from Tyburn was killed by a blow from a bystander. » Charles II (of England)

Daniel, Book of A book of the Hebrew Bible/Old Testament named after Daniel, its main character. It falls into two parts: chapters 1–6 contain narrative accounts about Daniel and his three companions, ostensibly set during the Babylonian Exile in the 6th-c BC; chapters 7–12 describe apocalyptic revelations of Daniel recorded as first-person visions. Although some date the work in the 6th-c BC, many prefer a later date of the 3rd–2nd-c BC, with several stages of compilation. The **Additions** are three works found joined to the Book of Daniel in some ancient Greek versions and in the modern Catholic Bible, but part of the Protestant Apocrypha. » Azariah, Prayer of; Bel and the Dragon; Old Testament; Song of the Three Young Men; Susanna, Story of

Daniel, Glyn (Edmund) (1914–86) British archaeologist, born at Barry, S Wales. He was educated at Cardiff and at Cambridge, where he lectured (1945–74) and became professor of archaeology (1974–81). His career was devoted less to excavation and research than to stimulating popular interest in archaeology through writing, editing, and broadcasting. He was a pioneer historian of archaeology and an energetic editor, both of the journal *Antiquity* (1958–86) and of the book series 'Ancient Peoples and Places' published from 1955. On British television he achieved particular popularity in the 1950s as the genial chairman of the archaeological panel game *Animal, Vegetable, Mineral*. He died in Cambridge. » archaeology

Danilova, Alexandra (Dionysievna) [da**nil**ohva] (1903–) Russian-US dancer and teacher, born at Peterhof, Russia. She studied at the Imperial and State Ballet Schools in St Petersburg, and in 1924 toured Europe, joining Diaghilev until his death. She danced as prima ballerina with the Ballet Russe de Monte Carlo (1938–52), and created leading parts in Balanchine and Massine's works. She continues to teach at the School of American Ballet. » Balanchine; ballet; Diaghilev; Massine

danio [**day**neeoh] Colourful freshwater fish from India and Sri Lanka, extremely popular amongst aquarists; body with blue and golden side stripes, length up to c.13 cm/5 in. (*Danio malabaricus*. Family: *Cyprinidae*.)

Danish » **Danish literature; Germanic languages; Scandinavian languages**

Danish literature The important *Gesta Danorum* (Deeds of the Danes) was written in Latin by Saxo Grammaticus in the 12th-c. There was an oral tradition of epic balladry (13th–15th-c) but Danish literature begins with the translation of the Bible in 1550. Classical imitations marked the 17th-c, and the influence of English and French literature was strongly felt in the 18th-c, while the Norwegian-born dramatist Ludwig Holberg (1684–1754) was the first significant Danish writer. The 19th-c brought radicals and Romantics, including the poets Adam Oehlenschlager (1779–1850), Steensen Blicher (1782–1848), and Henrik Hertz (1798–1870). The early existentialist Søren Kierkegaard wrote at this time, as did Hans Christian Andersen, whose fairy tales appeared from 1835. The critic Georg Brandes (1842–1927) led the 'modern breakthrough' of the 1870s, when Jens Peter Jacobsen (1847–85) introduced naturalist fiction (*Niels Lyhne*, 1880), and Holger Drachmann (1846–1908) became Denmark's finest poet. The 20th-c has seen a peasant movement, Expressionism, and inter-war restlessness, notably the fantasies of Karen Blixen (1885–1962, eg *Six Gothic Tales* 1934), and the novels and plays of Hans Christian Branner (1903–66) and Martin Hansen (1909–55), which are much concerned with World War 2. » Andersen; epic; existentialism; Expressionism; Holberg; Kierkegaard; Norwegian literature; Romanticism (literature)

Dante (Alighieri) (1265–1321) The greatest Italian poet, born in Florence. A lawyer's son, he was baptized Durante, later contracted into Dante. In 1274, when he was nine, a meeting with **Beatrice** (c.1265–90), possibly the daughter of the Florentine aristocrat Folco Portinari, influenced the rest of his life. His platonic devotion to her continued despite her marriage, and despite his own marriage (after her death) to Gemma Donati, daughter of a powerful Guelph family. In 1300, he became one of the six priors of Florence. His sympathy for the moderate 'White Guelphs' led to his exile in 1302, when the Black faction became dominant. His travelling after this date is unclear, but he never returned to his native city. He may have visited Paris and Oxford. Some believe he was recalled to Italy when Henry of Luxembourg became emperor, but when Henry died (1313), he took refuge in Ravenna, where he stayed until his death. Dante had six sons and one daughter. The dates and sequence of his various works are not known. The *Vita Nuova*, which tells of his boyish passion for Beatrice, is probably the earliest. By far the most celebrated is the *Divina Commedia* (Divine Comedy), a vision of hell, purgatory, and heaven which gives an encyclopaedic view of the highest culture and knowledge of his age. He also wrote several shorter poems, as well as treatises on government and language. » Guelphs; Italian literature; poetry

Danton, Georges (Jacques) [dãtõ] (1759–94) French revolutionary politician, born at Arcis-sur-Aube. He became a lawyer, and was practising in Paris at the outbreak of the Revolution. In 1790 he formed the Cordeliers' Club, a rallying point for revolutionary extremists, and in 1792 became Minister of Justice. He voted for the death of the King (1793), and was one of the original members of the Committee of Public Safety. He tried to abate the pitiless severity of his own Revolutionary Tribunal, but lost the leadership to Robespierre. He was arrested, and brought before the Tribunal, charged with conspiracy. Despite a heroic and eloquent defence, he was guillotined. » French Revolution [i]

Danu In Celtic religion, a mother-goddess who is associated with hills and the earth. » Tuatha De Danann

Danube, River, Ger **Donau**, Bulgarian **Dunav**, Russian **Dunai**, Romanian **Dunarea** River in C and SE Europe, rising in the Black Forest, SW Germany; flows generally E and S through Austria, Czechoslovakia, and Hungary, forming most of the Romania–Bulgaria border; enters the Black Sea through a wide, swampy delta; second longest river in Europe (2 850 km/1 770 ml); important commercial route, linked by canals to other major rivers (part of the Trans-Europe Waterway); flows through Vienna, Budapest, and Belgrade.

Danube School Pioneers of imaginative landscape painting who worked in the Danube region in the early 16th-c. Their members included Altdorfer and Cranach. » German art; landscape painting; school (art); Altdorfer; Cranach

Danzig » **Gdańsk**

Daphne In Greek mythology, the daughter of a river-god, Ladon (or, in another story, Peneios). Pursued by the god Apollo, she was saved by being turned into a laurel, which became Apollo's sacred tree. » Apollo

Daphnia [**daf**nia] A common type of water flea, found in freshwater bodies. (Class: *Branchiopoda*. Order: *Cladocera*.) » water flea

Daphnis In Greek mythology, a Sicilian shepherd, half-brother of Pan, who was loved by a nymph. He did not return her love, so she blinded him. He became the inventor of pastoral poetry. In another story he would love nobody; when he died, all the beings of the island mourned him. » Pan

Dar es Salaam [**dahr** es sa**lahm**] 6°51S 39°18E, pop (1978) 757 346. Seaport and capital of Dar es Salaam region, E Tanzania; on the Indian Ocean, 45 km/28 ml S of Zanzibar; founded, 1882; occupied by German East Africa Company, 1887; capital of German East Africa, 1891; occupied by the British in World War 1; capital of Tanganyika, 1916–64; capital of Tanzania until 1974; chief port and industrial, commercial, and financial centre; airport; university (1970); food processing, glass, crafts, car parts, printing, oil products, chemicals, aluminium, steel, polystyrene, textiles, timber, machinery; national museum (contains the Olduvai Gorge fossils), Tanzanian State House; Saba Saba festival (Jul). » Dodoma; Olduvai Gorge; Tanzania [i]

Dardanelles or **Hellespont** [dahda**nelz**], Turkish **Çanakkale Boğazi**, ancient **Hellespontus** Narrow strait in NW Turkey, connecting the Aegean Sea (W) and the Sea of Marmara (E), and separating the Gallipoli peninsula of European Turkey from Anatolia; length 65 km/40 ml; width varies from

1.6–6.4 km/1–4 ml; scene of an unsuccessful Allied campaign in World War 1. » Gallipoli; Marmara, Sea of; Turkey [i]

Darién [daryen] pop (1980) 26 524; area 16 803 sq km/6 486 sq ml. Province of E Panama, bounded SE by Colombia and W by the Gulf of Panama; capital, La Palma; chief towns, Yaviza and El Real; attempted settlement by the Scots in the 1690s (the Darién Scheme) is still remembered in local placenames such as Punta de Escoces and Caledonia Bay. » Panama [i]

Darío, Rubén, pen name of **Félix Rubén García Sarmiento** (1867–1916) Nicaraguan poet, born at Metapa. He lived a wandering life of journalism, amours, and diplomatic appointments. His *Azul* (1896, Blue) and *Prosas profanas* (1896, Profane Hymns) gave new vitality to Spanish poetic modernism. After 1898 he worked mainly in Europe, where he wrote *Cantos de vida y esperanza* (1905, Songs of Life and Hope). He died soon after his return to Nicaragua, at Léon. » Latin-American literature; poetry

Darius I, byname **the Great** (548–486 BC) King of Persia (521–486 BC), one of the greatest of the Achaemenids. He is noteworthy for his administrative reforms, military conquests, and religious toleration. His division of the empire into provinces called *satrapies* outlasted the Achaemenids. His conquests, especially in the East and Europe (Thrace and Macedonia) consolidated the frontiers of the empire. Patriotic Greek writers made much of the failure of his two punitive expeditions against Athens, the first miscarrying through the wreck of his fleet off Mt Athos (492 BC), the second coming to grief at Marathon (490 BC); but in Persian eyes they were probably not very important. Although a worshipper himself of Ahura Mazda, who turned Zoroastrianism into a state religion, he showed an unusual respect for the religions of his subjects. » Achaemenids; Greek-Persian Wars [i]; Marathon, Battle of; satrapy; Zoroastrianism

Darjeeling or **Darjiling** [dahjeeling] 27°02N 88°20E, pop (1981) 57 603. Hill station in West Bengal, NE India, in Himalayan foothills, near the Sikkim state frontier; population mainly Bhutanese and Nepalese; centre of a tea-growing region; tourism; former summer residence of the Bengal government. » West Bengal

Dark Ages A term occasionally applied to the period of European history from c.500 to c.1000, but misleading because of its negative implications. It underestimates very real achievements, notably in religion, learning, and government, and how far the period can be studied and understood. Historians usually describe the whole period c.500–c.1500 as the *Middle Ages*. » Middle Ages

darkling beetle A small to medium-sized ground beetle; most species brown or black; many flightless with vestigial wings; well-adapted for living in dry conditions; feeds mostly on plant material, including stored products such as flour. (Order: *Coleoptera*. Family: *Tenebrionidae*, c.25 000 species.) » beetle; vestigial organ

Darling Range Mountain range in Western Australia, near Perth; extends 320 km/200 ml S along the SW coast, and rises to 582 m/1 909 ft at Mt Cooke. » Western Australia

Darling River Longest tributary of the Murray R; formed by the Dumaresq and Macintyre Rivers at the New South Wales–Queensland border; flows generally SW to join the Murray R; length 3 070 km/1 908 ml; major tributaries the Gwydir, Namoi, Castlereagh, Macquarie, Bogan, and Warrego Rivers; used for irrigation in New South Wales. » Australia [i]; Murray River

Darnley, Henry Stewart, Lord (1545–67) English nobleman, the second husband of Mary, Queen of Scots and father of James I of England, born at Temple Newsom, Yorkshire. He married Mary (his cousin) in 1565, and was made Earl of Ross and Duke of Albany. His debauchery and arrogance made him unpopular, and his part in the murder (1566) of the Queen's secretary, David Rizzio, caused his downfall. He became estranged from the Queen, and during an illness was killed at Edinburgh, when Kirk O'Field, the house in which he was sleeping, was destroyed by gunpowder – the result of a plot probably organized by the Earl of Bothwell, perhaps with Mary's knowledge. » Bothwell, Earl of; Mary, Queen of Scots

Darrow, Clarence (Seward) (1857–1938) US lawyer, born at Kinsman, Ohio. He was admitted to the Bar in 1878, and practised in Ohio and Illinois. When 37, he became counsel for Chicago and North Western Railways, but left this post when a strike of the American Railway Union occurred, and defended Eugene Debs who had called it. He took on further labour cases, and after World War 1, was involved in several notable defences, including the murder case against Nathan Leopold and Richard Loeb (1924), and the trial of John T Scopes (1925) for the teaching of Darwinian evolution in school. Noted for his liberal views on segregation, he died in Chicago. » evolution; industrial action

Dart, Raymond (Arthur) (1893–1988) South African palaeoanthropologist, born in Brisbane, Australia. Educated at the Universities of Queensland and Sydney, he taught at University College, London (1919–22), before becoming professor of anatomy at Johannesburg (1923–58). His discovery (1924) in a quarry at Taung, near the Kalahari Desert, of *Australopithecus africanus* substantiated Darwin's view of Africa as the cradle of the human species. » anthropology; Australopithecus; Darwin, Charles; Johanson

Dart, Thurston (1921–71) British keyboard player, conductor, and musical scholar, born and died in London. Educated at the Royal College of Music and London University, he became professor of music at Cambridge (1962) and at London (1964). He was also director of the Philomusica of London (1955–9). A specialist in early music, he edited several editions of 16th-c and 17th-c English works.

darter A slender bird native to warm regions world-wide; spears fish underwater with long pointed bill; swims with only head and long neck out of water; inhabits still water; called **anhinga** in the New World, **darter** in the Old World; also known as **snake bird** and **water turkey**. (Genus: *Anhinga*, 1 or 2 species, experts disagree. Family: *Anhingidae*.)

Dartmoor National park in Devon, S England; area 913 sq km/567 sq ml; established in 1951; noted for its granite tors and hanging oak woods; highest point, High Willhays, 621 m/2 039 ft; several Bronze and Iron Age settlements; popular area for walking and riding. » Devon; Three Age System

Dartmoor pony A small pony, developed on Dartmoor, England; tough and sure-footed; calm natured; height, up to 12½ hands/1.3 m/4¼ ft; usually brown or black; slim legs, long bushy tail and mane, short erect ears. » Dartmoor; horse [i]

Dartmouth College » **Ivy League** [i]

darts An indoor game played by throwing three darts (or 'arrows') at a circular board. The throwing distance is normally 8 ft (2.4 m), and the height from the floor to the centre of the board (known as the *bull*) is 5 ft 8 in (1.7 m). The standard dartboard is divided into 20 segments, numbered 1–20, but not in numerical order. Within each segment are progressively smaller segments which either double or treble that number's score if hit. The centre ring (*the bull*) is worth 50 points, and the

Darter

area around it (*the outer*) is worth 25 points. The most popular game is 501, in which players start at that figure and deduct all scores from it; the final shot must consist of a double. The modern game is credited to a Lancashire carpenter Brian Gamlin (1852–1903) who devised the present-day board and scoring system. » RR109

Darwin, Charles (Robert) (1809–82) British naturalist, the discoverer of natural selection, born at Shrewsbury. He studied medicine at Edinburgh (1825), then biology at Cambridge (1828). In 1831 he became the naturalist on HMS Beagle, which was to make a scientific survey of S American waters, and returned in 1836, having travelled extensively throughout the S Pacific. By 1846 he had published several works on his geological and zoological discoveries, and become one of the leading scientists of his day. In 1839 he married his cousin, Emma Wedgwood (1808–96). From 1842 he spent his time at Downe, Kent, working in his garden and breeding pigeons and fowls, and here he devoted himself to his major work, *The Origin of Species by Means of Natural Selection* (1859). An epoch-making work, it was given a mixed reaction throughout Europe, but in the end received widespread recognition. He then worked on a series of supplemental treatises, including *The Descent of Man* (1871), which postulated the descent of the human race from the anthropoid group. He wrote many other works on plants and animals, but is remembered primarily as the leader in the field of evolutionary biology. He died at Downe, Kent, and was buried in Westminster Abbey. » biology; Darwinism

Darwin, Erasmus (1731–1802) British physician, grandfather of Charles Darwin, born at Elton, Nottinghamshire. He studied at Cambridge and Edinburgh, and at Lichfield became a popular physician and prominent figure, known for his freethinking opinions, poetry, large botanical garden, mechanical inventions, and position in the Lunar Society. Many of his ideas on evolution anticipated later theories. His chief prose work is *Zoonomia, or the Laws of Organic Life* (1794–6). After his second marriage (1781), he settled in Derby, where he died. » evolution

Darwin (Australia), formerly **Palmerston** (to 1911), **Port Darwin** 12°23S 130°44E, pop(1981) 56 482. Seaport capital of Northern Territory, Australia, on the Beagle Gulf, Clarence Strait; an important communications centre serving Arnhem Land (E) and the surrounding mining districts; first European settlement (1869) destroyed by hurricane in 1879; attacked by the Japanese, 1942; destroyed by cyclone Tracy, 1974; airport; railway; university college; Government House (1869); Overland Telegraph Memorial; Stuart Memorial (John McDouall Stuart crossed Australia from Adelaide to Darwin 1861–2); Ross and Keith Smith memorial (first flight from England, Dec 1919); cathedral (1902); Fannie Bay Gaol Museum; S of Darwin is Australia's first commercial crocodile farm; Darwin Beer Can Regatta for craft made almost entirely of beer cans (Jun); Darwin Royal Show Day (Jul). » Northern Territory; Stuart, John McDouall

Darwin (Falkland Is) 51°48S 58°59W. Settlement on East Falkland, Falkland Is; at the head of Choiseul Sound, on the narrow isthmus that joins the N half of East Falkland to Lafonia in the S; c.70 km/43 ml from Stanley. » Falkland Islands [i]

Darwin's finches A closely related group of birds, native to the Galapagos Is (off Ecuador); also known as **Galapagos finches**. Thought to have evolved from one ancestral species, 14 species are now recognized, differing in diet (and related bill shapes), habitat preferences, and distribution. The classification of the group is currently uncertain; they may be put in the family *Fringillidae* (**finches**) or the family *Emberizidae* (**buntings** and their allies). Charles Darwin's observations on this group were important to his ideas about natural selection. » bunting; finch

Darwinism The theory of evolution proposed jointly by Charles Darwin and Alfred Wallace, and later expanded upon by Darwin in *On the Origin of Species by Means of Natural Selection*. Individuals of a species show variation. On average, more offspring are produced than are needed to replace the parents, but population size remains more or less stable in nature. There must therefore be competition for survival, and it is the best adapted (the fittest) variants which survive and reproduce. Evolution occurs by means of natural selection acting on individual variation, resulting in the survival of the fittest. The discovery of the genetic mechanism causing variation has resulted in a modified version of the theory, known as **neo-Darwinism**. » Darwin, Charles; evolution; natural selection; Wallace, Alfred Russel

dasheen » **taro**

dassie » **hyrax**

dasyure [**das**yoor] A marsupial native to Australia and New Guinea; most superficially resembles the mouse, but some are larger; comprises most Australian carnivorous marsupials; includes quolls, dunnarts, and the Tasmanian devil. (Family: *Dasyuridae*, 51 species.) » carnivore [i]; marsupial [i]; Tasmanian devil

data bus The system of wires or connections within a digital computer which is used to communicate data between the various parts of the computer, such as between the central processing unit and the memory. The data is usually transferred along 8 or 16 separate channels in microcomputers, and 32 or more in mainframe computers. » address bus; input-output bus

data processing (DP) A general term used to describe various uses of computers in business. These include clerical functions (eg scheduling and stock control), financial functions (eg salaries and budget management), and many other aspects of business management and planning. » computer

data protection The techniques of maintaining the privacy and the integrity of computer-based information. The UK Data Protection Act (1987) requires formal registration of all computer users who store information on individuals, and gives certain rights to the individual if they wish to obtain access to this information.

database A file of computer data structured in such a way that it can be of general use and is independent of any specific application. This information can be managed by a **database management system (DBMS)**, a software system or program which allows data to be modified, deleted, added to, and retrieved from one or more databases. » computer

Date Line An imaginary line, based by international agreement on the meridian of 180° (with deviations to keep certain islands in the same zone as their respective mainlands); the date is altered to compensate for the gain or loss of time (1 hour per 15°) which occurs when circumnavigating the globe. » RR17

date palm A tree reaching 30 m/100 ft; thick trunk covered with old, spiny leaf bases; leaves feathery; inflorescence large; native to Near East, and widely cultivated since 6000 BC. A single tree produces up to 250 kg/550 lb of deep orange, sugary dates each year for up to 100 years or more. (*Phoenix dactylifera*. Family: *Palmae*.) » inflorescence [i]; palm

date plum » **persimmon**

Datong or **Ta-t'ung** [dahtung] 40°12N 113°12E, pop(1984e) 981 000. City in Shanxi province, NEC China, W of Beijing (Peking); founded in the 4th-c as capital of N Wei dynasty; railway; livestock, fur, coal mining, cement, locomotives, soda; Jiulong Bi (Nine Dragon Screen), Yungang Caves, 16 km/10 ml W (earliest Buddhist stone-carving in China, 460–94 AD). » China [i]

Daubigny, Charles François [**doh**beenyee] (1817–78) French artist, born and died in Paris. He studied for a while in Italy (1835–6), but worked mainly in Paris. He was a member of the Barbizon School, painting landscapes, especially moonlight and river scenes, such as 'The Banks of the Oise' (1872, Reims). » Barbizon School; French art

Daudet, Alphonse [**doh**day] (1840–97) French writer, born at Nîmes. He moved to Paris in 1857, where he devoted himself to literature. He wrote a book of poems and several theatrical pieces, including *L'Arlésienne*, for which Bizet composed incidental music. Some of his best work appears in the journals, notably his sketches of Provençal subjects, collected as *Lettres de mon moulin* (1869, Letters from my Mill), and the extravaganza *Tartarin de Tarascon* (1872), with its two sequels. He died in Paris. » Bizet; French literature

Daughters of the American Revolution A patriotic society

designed to supply Hong Kong and Guangdong province with power in 1993. » China [i]

Dayak or **Dyak** The Malayo-Polynesian-speaking indigenous inhabitants of Borneo and Sarawak, including the Bahau, Ngaju, Land Dayak, and Iban, or Sea Dayak. They mostly live along rivers in small village communities in longhouses, cultivating rice, hunting, and fishing. Population c.2 million. » Borneo; Sarawak

Dayan, Moshe (1915–81) Israeli general and statesman, born at Deganya, Palestine. During the 1930s he joined the illegal Jewish defence organization, Haganah, and was imprisoned by the British (1939–41), then released to fight with the Allies in World War 2 (when he lost his left eye, thereafter wearing his distinctive black eye patch). He became Chief-of-Staff (1953–8), joined the Knesset as a Labour member in 1959, but left the Labour Party in 1966 to set up the Rafi Party with Ben Gurion. He won international acclaim as Defence Minister in 1967 when his heavily-outnumbered forces triumphed over Egypt, Jordan, and Syria in the so-called 'Six Day War', and he himself became a symbol of Israeli dash and courage. As Foreign Minister, he helped to secure the historic peace treaty with Egypt (1977). He resigned from the Begin government in 1979, and launched a new centre party in 1981, but died the same year, at Tel Aviv. » Israel [i]; Six Day War

Daylight Saving Time A means of making fuller use of the hours of daylight over the summer months, usually by putting clocks forward one hour so that daylight continues longer into the evening. First proposed by Benjamin Franklin, and later by William Willett, an English builder. Adopted during World War 1 by Germany in 1917, it was retained after the war by the UK, where it is known as (British) **Summer Time**; it was not finally adopted by the USA until 1966. Many countries now have some form of daylight saving time. » Franklin, Benjamin; time

Dazu [dazoo] 29°47N 106°30E. Town in Sichuan province, SWC China; 160 km/100 ml NW of Chongqing; important Buddhist archaeological site, containing over 50 000 stone carvings (9th–13th-c); Bei Shan (North Hill) nearby, site of first Buddhist shrine in China (892), with over 10 000 figures; 15 km/9 ml NE, Baoding Shan, with 10 000 figures sculpted between 1179 and 1249, including the Sleeping Buddha (over 30 m/100 ft) and the Yuan Jue (Total Awakening) Grotto. » Buddhism; China [i]

DDT A chemical mixture, largely consisting of *d*ichloro*d*iphenyl*t*richloroethane, shown in the illustration. One of the earliest successful insecticides, it has now been largely abandoned both because new strains of insects have developed immunity to it

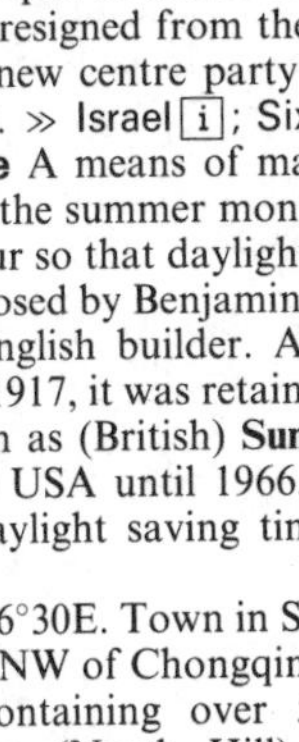

and because its decomposition products are harmful to other organisms, and are not readily decomposed to harmless materials in nature. » Carson, Rachel; insecticide

de Beauvoir, Simone [**boh**vwah] (1908–86) French existentialist writer and novelist, born in Paris. She studied philosophy with Sartre at the Sorbonne, where she became professor (1941–3). Closely associated with his literary activities after World War 2, she remained his companion until his death (1980). Her own works provide existentialism with an essentially feminine sensibility, notably *Le Deuxième sexe* (1949, The Second Sex) and her masterpiece *Les Mandarins* (1954), which won the 1954 Prix Goncourt. With Sartre she founded *Les Temps modernes* in 1945. She died in Paris. » existentialism; French literature; novel; Sartre

de Broglie, Louis » **Broglie, Louis, Duc de**

de Duve, Christian (René) [duh **düv**] (1917–) Belgian biochemist, born at Thames Ditton, Surrey, UK. He graduated in medicine in Louvain in 1941, and held a chair of biochemistry there from 1951 and a similar post concurrently at Rockefeller University, New York, from 1962. He had a major part in discovering the lysosomes which contain the enzymes within animal and plant cells, and afterwards in studying their activity and the diseases linked with their disfunction. He shared the Nobel Prize for Physiology or Medicine in 1974. » cell; lysosome

de Forest, Lee (1873–1961) US inventor, born at Council Bluffs, Iowa. Educated at Yale and Chicago, he became a pioneer of radio, introducing the grid into the thermionic valve, and inventing the Audion and the four-electrode valve. He also did much early work on sound reproduction for films. He was widely honoured as the 'father of radio' and the 'grandfather of television'. He died at Hollywood, California. » radio; valve

de Gasperi, Alcide » **Gasperi, Alcide de**

de Gaulle, Charles (André Joseph Marie) [duh **gohl**] (1890–1970) French general and first President of the Fifth Republic, born at Lille. He fought in World War 1, and became a strong advocate of mechanized warfare, but his efforts to modernize the French Army made little progress. With the fall of France (Jun 1940), he fled to England to raise the standard of the 'Free French', and entered Paris at the head of one of the earliest liberation forces (Aug 1944). He became head of the provisional government, then withdrew to the political sidelines. Following the troubles in N Africa he became Prime Minister (1958), and emerged as the one man able to inspire confidence after the postwar procession of indecisive leaders. In late 1958 he became President, and practised a high-handed yet extremely successful foreign policy, repeatedly surviving political crises by the lavish use of the referendum. Independence was granted to all French African colonies (1959–60), and Algeria became independent (1962). He developed an independent French nuclear deterrent, signed a historic reconciliation treaty with West Germany, and blocked Britain's entry into the Common Market. He had an overwhelming victory in the 1968 election, after the 'student revolution', but in 1969 resigned after the defeat of his referendum proposals for senate and regional reforms. He then retired to Colombey-les-Deux-Eglises, where he died. » France [i]; referendum; World War 2

de Havilland, Sir Geoffrey (1882–1965) British aircraft designer, born at Haslemere, Surrey. He built his first plane in 1908 and became director of the firm bearing his name, producing many types of aircraft during and between the two world wars, including the Tiger Moth, the Mosquito, and the Vampire jet. He established a height record for light aircraft in 1928, won the King's Cup air race at the age of 51, and was knighted in 1944. He died at Watford, Hertfordshire. » aircraft [i]

de Kooning, Willem or **William** (1904–) US painter, born in Rotterdam, The Netherlands. He studied at Rotterdam, and emigrated to the USA in 1926. By the 1950s he had emerged as a leader of the abstract Expressionist movement, especially as seen in action painting. Among his best-known works is his controversial series 'Woman I–VI' (1952–3, New York), with its violent, aggressive images. In his later years, he worked increasingly with clay sculptures. » action painting

de La Mare, Walter (John) (1873–1956) British writer, born at Charlton, Kent. Educated at London, he worked for an oil company (1890–1908), then devoted himself to writing. His first work, *Songs of Childhood* (1902), was under the pseudonym of **Walter Ramal**. He wrote several volumes of poetry, novels, and short stories, including the prose romance *Henry Brocken* (1904), the poetic collection *The Listeners* (1912), and his fantastic novel *Memoirs of a Midget* (1921). He died at Twickenham, Middlesex. » English literature

de la Renta, Oscar (1932–) US fashion designer, born in Santo

Domingo, Dominican Republic. After studying art in Santo Domingo and Madrid, he worked at Balenciaga's couture house in Madrid. He joined the house of Lanvin-Castille in Paris in 1961, but after two years went to Elizabeth Arden, New York City. In 1965 he started his own company. He has a reputation for opulent, ornately trimmed clothes, particularly evening dresses, but he also designs day wear and accessories. » Balenciaga; fashion

de La Roche, Mazo (1885–1961) Canadian novelist, born at Newmarket, Ontario. In 1927 she wrote *Jalna* (1927), the first of a series of novels about the Whiteoak family. *Whiteoaks* (1929) was dramatized with considerable success. She also wrote children's stories and travel books. She died in Toronto. » Canadian literature

de la Tour, Georges [la **toor**] (1593–1652) French artist, born at Vic-sur-Seille. He was identified about 1915, some of his works having been previously attributed to others. Only 14 of his paintings have been found, the best-known being candle-lit religious scenes, such as *St Jerome* and *St Joseph* (Louvre). He died at Lunéville. » French art

de Lorris, Guillaume [duh **lo**ris] (c.1200–?) French poet, born at Lorris-en-Gatinais, who wrote the first 4 000 lines of the *Roman de la Rose* (Romance of the Rose) c.1235; it was continued by Jean de Meun. This allegory, which presents love as a garden, the lady as the rose, and the knight as in quest of her favour, was widely influential throughout mediaeval Europe. » allegory; French literature; Jean de Meun

de Man, Paul [duh **man**] (1919–83) Cultural theorist, born and educated in Belgium. Controversy has surrounded his writings for collaborationist journals during World War 2. After the war he emigrated to the USA, and taught at several universities, including Yale, where he became a leading exponent of the critical method known as *deconstruction*. His most important essays were published in *Blindness and Insight* (1971) and *Allegories of Reading* (1979). » deconstruction; Derrida; literary criticism

de Mille, Cecil B(lount) (1881–1959) US film producer and director, born at Ashfield, Massachusetts. He was an actor and writer before making the first American feature film in Hollywood, *The Squaw Man* (1913). He made a reputation for box-office spectacles with such films as *The Ten Commandments* (1923, re-made in CinemaScope, 1957), *The Plainsman* (1937), and *The Greatest Show on Earth* (1952). He also organized the first commercial passenger airline service in the USA (1917). He died at Hollywood, California.

de Morgan, Augustus (1806–71) British mathematician, born at Madura, India. Educated at Cambridge, in 1828 he became the first professor of mathematics at University College, London. He helped to develop the notion of different kinds of algebra, and collaborated with Boole in the development of symbolic logic. He died in London. » algebra; Boole; logic

de Quincey, Thomas (1785–1859) British writer, born in Manchester. Educated at Manchester Grammar School, he ran away, and wandered in Wales and London. He then spent a short time at Oxford, where he became addicted to opium. On a visit to Bath, he met Coleridge, and through him Southey and Wordsworth; and in 1809 went to live near them in Grasmere. There he set up as an author, largely writing magazine articles. His *Confessions of an Opium-eater* appeared as a serial in 1821, and brought him instant fame. In 1828 he moved to Edinburgh, and for 20 years wrote for various magazines. He died in Edinburgh. » Coleridge; English literature; Southey; Wordsworth, William

de Sica, Vittorio (1901–74) Italian actor and film director, born in Sera and educated in Naples and Rome. He established himself as a romantic star of Italian stage and screen in the 1930s, and became a director in 1940, achieving international success in the neo-realist style with *Sciuscià* (1946, Shoeshine), *Ladri di biciclette* (1948, Bicycle Thieves), and *Miracolo a Milano* (1951, Miracle in Milan). His subsequent work was more smoothly sophisticated, but *Il giardino dei Finzi-Continis* (1970, The Garden of the Finzi-Continis) provided a late triumph. He died in Paris.

de Soto, Fernando (c.1496–1542) Spanish explorer, born at Jerez de los Caballeros. In 1539 he entered Florida, and crossed the Mississippi (1541), but died of a fever on its banks.

De Stijl [duh **shteel**] A group of Dutch artists and architects formed in 1917, strongly influenced by Cubism, Dutch Calvinism, and theosophy. Its members included Theo van Doesburg, J J P Oud, Piet Mondrian, and Gerrit Rietveld. The group advocated a new, wholly abstract aesthetic style composed solely of straight lines, primary colours, and black and white, typified by the paintings of Mondrian. The group formally ended in 1931, but has had a great and lasting influence on 20th-c art, architecture, and design. » abstract art; Bauhaus; Cubism; International Style; Mondrian; Neoplasticism; theosophy

de Valera, Eamon [deva**lay**ra] (1882–1975) Irish statesman, Prime Minister (1932–48, 1951–4, 1957–9), and President (1959–73), born in New York City. Brought up on a farm in Co Limerick, he became a teacher in Dublin, and was active in various Republican movements. A commandant in the 1916 rising, he was arrested and narrowly escaped the firing squad. He became an MP in 1917, and Leader of Sinn Féin (1917–26). He was elected President of Dáil Eireann, and in 1926 became Leader of Fianna Fáil, his newly-formed Republican opposition party, which won the 1932 elections. In spite of his colourful early career, his leadership was moderate, and he opposed extremism and religious intolerance. He died in Dublin. » Fianna Fáil; Sinn Féin

de Vries, Hugo (Marie) [duh **vrees**] (1848–1935) Dutch botanist, born at Haarlem. He was professor at Amsterdam (1878–1918), where he carried out research into the nature of mutation in plant-breeding. His conclusions paralleled those of Mendel, whose work he discovered in 1900. He died near Amsterdam. » genetics [i]

de Vries, Peter [duh **vrees**] (1910–) US novelist and short-story writer, born in Chicago, Illinois, and educated at Calvin College and Northwestern University. He became a regular staff contributor to the *New Yorker* in 1943, where he developed the comic manner which was later displayed in such novels as *The Tunnel of Love* (1954) and *The Mackerel Plaza* (1958). His upbringing in the Dutch Reformed Calvinist faith provided the background of his later, serious novel about a child's terminal illness, *The Blood of the Lamb* (1961). » American literature; Calvinism; novel

de Wet, Christian (Rudolf) [duh **vet**] (1854–1922) Afrikaner statesman and general, born in Smithfield district, Orange Free State. He became conspicuous in the Transvaal war of 1880–1; and in the war of 1899–1902 was the most audacious of all the Boer commanders. In 1907 he became Minister of Agriculture of the Orange River Colony, and in 1914 joined the South African insurrection, but was captured. Sentenced to six years' imprisonment, he was released in 1915. He died in Dewetsdorp district, South Africa. » Boer Wars

de Witt, Jan [duh **vit**] (1625–72) Dutch statesman, the Grand Pensionary (chief minister) of the United Provinces of the Netherlands (1653–72), born at Dort. As leader of the Republican Party, he sought to abolish the office of Stadholder, and to limit the power of the House of Orange. However, when France invaded the Netherlands in 1672, William of Orange was made Stadholder and Commander of the Dutch forces. De Witt's brother, Cornelius, was accused of conspiracy and imprisoned. De Witt went to see him in prison at The Hague, where they were killed by an infuriated mob. » Dutch Wars; William of Orange

deacon (Gr *diakonos*, 'servant') An official of the Christian Church appointed to assist the minister or priest in administrative, pastoral, and financial affairs. The office developed into a third order of ministry after bishops and priests. In the late 20th-c, ecumenical factors revived interest in an order of deacons (the **diaconate**). In many churches, deaconesses are a separate order of parish assistants. » clergy; ecumenism

dead man's fingers A soft coral that forms erect, branching colonies up to 20 cm/8 in high; polyps embedded in a body packed with calcareous slender spikes (spicules); with polyps retracted, branches of the colony can resemble human fingers. (Phylum: *Cnidaria*. Order: *Alcyonacea*.) » calcium; coral; polyp

dead-nettle An annual or perennial, found almost everywhere, except in the tropics; stem square, leaves wrinkled, in opposite pairs; flowers 2-lipped, the upper hooded, in whorls at the nodes; mainly pollinated by bees. Several large-flowered or variegated species are cultivated for ornament; others are common weeds, including the **white dead-nettle** (*Lamium album*), a white flowered perennial, and **purple dead-nettle** (*Lamium purpureum*), a pinkish-purple flowered annual. When not in flower, some species, especially white dead-nettle, resemble true nettles, but lack stinging hairs, hence the name. (Genus: *Lamium*, c. 50 species. Family: *Labiatae*.) » annual; perennial; stinging nettle

dead room » **anechoic chamber**

Dead Sea, ancient **Lacus Asphaltites**, Hebrew **Bahrat Lut** (Sea of Lot), Old Testament **Salt Sea, Sea of the Plain, East Sea** Inland lake in the Great Rift Valley on the Jordan–Israel border; lowest point on Earth, 394 m/1 293 ft below sea-level; fed by Jordan R (N), but no outlet; one of the most saline lakes in the world, containing magnesium, sodium, potassium, and calcium salts; potash and magnesium bromide exploited since 1921; sea level falling because water from the R Jordan used for irrigation and home supply; there are plans for a direct link with the Mediterranean to stabilize sea levels; tourism. » Great Rift Valley; Jordan, River

Dead Sea Scrolls Parchment scrolls in Hebrew and Aramaic, many representing books of the Old Testament, a thousand years older than previously known copies, found accidentally in 1947 and 1952–5 concealed in pottery jars in 11 caves near Qumran on the Dead Sea. They are thought to represent the library of an ascetic Jewish sect, the Essenes, concealed when their settlement was overrun by the Roman army in AD 68. » Essenes; Old Testament; Qumran

deadly nightshade A stout, large-leaved perennial up to 1.5 m/5 ft high, native to limestone and chalk areas of Europe, W Asia, and N Africa; dull flowers 2.5–3 cm/1¼–1½ in, solitary in leaf-axils; tubular, 5-lobed corolla, brownish-violet; berry 1.5–2 cm/0.6–0.8 in diameter, shiny black and cupped by the green sepals. All parts of the plant are narcotic and highly poisonous because of the presence of the alkaloids atropine, hyoscyamine, and solanine. (*Atropa belladonna*. Family: *Solanaceae*.) » alkaloids; corolla; perennial

deafness Inability or reduced capacity to hear external sounds. **Conductive deafness** is caused by blockage of the entry of sound to the external canal of the ear (eg through wax in ear), or by abnormalities of the tympanic membrane or of the ossicles in the middle ear (eg through middle-ear infection). All sounds irrespective of their pitch are heard with difficulty, and if they are sufficiently loud or amplified they may become clearly heard. **Sensorineural deafness** results from a disturbance of the cochlea, auditory nerve, or neuronal pathways in the brain. Loss of hearing tends to be patchy, affecting only certain frequencies, and amplified or loud sounds are distorted. Causes include certain drugs and lengthy exposure to industrial noise, and it may also develop as a normal part of ageing. » ear [i]; Ménière's disease

Deák, Francis [day**ak**] (1803–76) Hungarian statesman, born at Zala into the gentry class. He practised as an advocate, and entered the national Diet in 1832, playing a moderate liberal role. In 1848 he became Minister of Justice, dissociating himself from Kossuth's more extreme Magyar nationalism. In the restored Diet of 1861, he emerged as leader of moderate liberalism; his efforts helped Hungary to recover her constitution (1867), and on her behalf he negotiated the *Ausgleich* of 1867, establishing the Dual Monarchy of Austria-Hungary. » Ausgleich; Hungary [i]; Kossuth

Deakin, Alfred (1857–1919) Australian statesman and Prime Minister (1903–4, 1905–8, 1909–10), born and died in Melbourne. He entered the Victorian Legislative Assembly in 1880, became Minister of Public Works and Water Supply, Solicitor-General of Victoria, and then Commonwealth Attorney-General. He helped to draft Australia's constitution, and as Prime Minister helped to form many of the new country's policies, notably the 'White Australia' policy. » Australia [i]; White Australia Policy

dean (Ital *decem*, 'ten') Originally, in a monastery, a monk in charge of ten novices. Later, the term denoted a senior clergyman (after the bishop) in a cathedral chapter or diocese. In lay terms, it is used of a head of a university college or faculty. » cathedral; clergy; monasticism

Dean, Christopher » **Torvill, Jayne**

Dean, James (Byron) (1931–55) US film star, born at Marion, Indiana. He started acting at university, joined the Actors' Studio, and after small parts in theatre, films, and television gained overnight success in the film *East of Eden* (1955). He made only two more films, *Rebel Without a Cause* (1955) and *Giant* (released 1956), before he was killed in a car crash at Paso Robles, California; but in just over a year he became the personification of contemporary American youth, a cult figure, for many years after his death remaining a symbol of youthful rebellion and self-assertion.

death The cessation of all cellular activity in an organism. The age, distribution, and causes of death in a society closely reflect the level of community health. Infant and maternal mortality rates vary directly with standards of sanitation and hygiene, and are affected by standards of nutrition and health care. The commonest cause of death in young adults in developed countries is road traffic and other accidents, while in developing countries infections such as tuberculosis are more common. In older age groups in several countries, heart diseases, cancer, and cerebrovascular disorders are dominant. More males die at all ages throughout life, so widows are more common than widowers. » brain death

death cap A deadly poisonous, mushroom-like fungus; cap pale greenish or white, with white gills on underside; common on the ground in broad-leaved woodland in late summer and autumn. (Order: *Agaricales*. Family: *Amanitaceae*.) » fungus; mushroom

'death of God' theology A style of theology popular especially in the USA in the 1960s. It sought to assert the rationality of the Christian faith and belief in the uniqueness of Christ, without belief in a transcendent God. It is associated with such theologians as William Hamilton (1924–), Paul van Buren (1924–), Gabriel Vahanian (1927–), and Thomas J J Altizer (1927–), who claimed Hegel, Nietzsche, and Bonhoeffer as intellectual forerunners. » Bonhoeffer; Christianity; Hegel; Nietzsche; theology

death's head moth A large, nocturnal hawk moth; wingspan up to 120 mm/4¾ in; forewings dark with yellow markings; hindwings ochre-yellow with black bands; black thorax with yellow skull-like marking; feeds on honey and sap exuding from trees; caterpillar feeds on plants, pupates in the ground. (Order: *Lepidoptera*. Family: *Sphingidae*.) » caterpillar; hawk moth; pupa

Death Valley SE California, USA; ancient rift valley lake bed beside the Nevada border; a deep and arid desert basin; one of the hottest places in the world; contains the lowest point in N America (the Badwater River, altitude −86 m/−282 ft); 225 km/140 ml long; 6–26 km/3¾–16 ml wide; set in a National Monument, area 8 400 sq km/3 250 sq ml; highest point Telescope Peak (3 367 m/11 046 ft); less than 50 mm/2 in rainfall per year; summer temperatures reach 74°C (ground) and 57°C (air); numerous salt and alkali flats, colourful rock formations, desert plants, small animal life, and footprints of prehistoric animals; named in 1849 by a party of gold prospectors, some of whom died while trying to cross it; major source of borax in 19th-c; Scott's Castle, built by the American adventurer Walter Scott. » California; desert

deathwatch beetle A small, brownish beetle, 5–9 mm/0.2–0.35 in long; lives in decaying trees, but now found mostly in house timbers; larvae, fleshy with tiny legs, bore into wood; adults tap on wood at mating time (Apr–May); leave large holes in timber when they emerge. (Order: *Coleoptera*. Family: *Anobiidae*.) » beetle; larva

debenture A loan raised by a company, usually with a fixed rate of interest and repayable at a specified date. It is sometimes secured against a firm's assets. » company

Debrecen [**deb**retsen] 47°33N 21°42E, pop (1984e) 205 000. Capital of Hajdú-Bihar county, E Hungary; economic and cultural centre of the Great Plain; third largest city in Hungary; Kossuth proclaimed independence in the great church, 1849; railway; three universities (1868, 1912, 1951); commercial

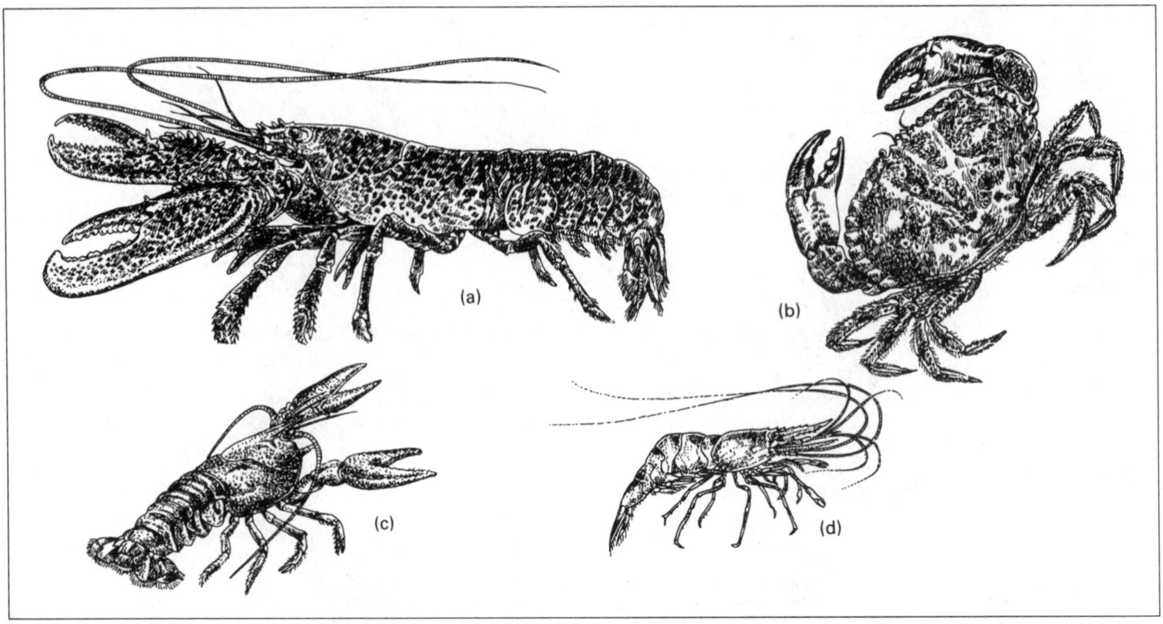

Decapoda – Lobster (a); crab (b); crayfish (c); prawn (d)

centre for agricultural region; tobacco, pharmaceuticals, agricultural machinery. » Alföld; Hungary [i]; Kossuth

Debrett's Peerage A reference guide to the titled aristocracy of Great Britain, named after John Debrett (c.1752–1822). Peers and baronets are listed separately. Debrett's also offers information on forms of address, precedence, the wearing of decorations, and etiquette. » peerage

Debreu, Gerard [duh**brer**] (1921–) US economist, born in Calais, France, and educated in Paris. He went to the USA in 1950, and held chairs at Yale (1955–61) and California (1962–). His work on the equilibrium between prices, production, and consumer demand in a free-market economy led to his Nobel Prize for Economics in 1983.

Debs, Eugene V(ictor) (1855–1926) US politician, born at Terre Haute, Indiana. He worked as a locomotive fireman, and in 1893 became president of the American Railroad Union, in 1894 leading a successful national strike for higher wages. He helped to establish the Socialist Party of America, was imprisoned for labour agitation, and between 1900 and 1920 stood five times as socialist candidate for president. His pacifism brought him imprisonment (1918–21). He died at Elmhurst, Illinois. » socialism

debt Money borrowed by an individual, company, or government on which interest is payable. Companies that overborrow are 'highly-geared', and are considered financially more risky. Many poorer countries have had difficulties repaying their debt, especially to Western banks, which have been forced to write off several such loans against their profits in recent years. » bankruptcy; capital; factoring

debugging » **bug** (computing)

Deburau, Jean-Gaspard, originally **Jan Kaspar Dvorak** [debü**roh**] (1796–1846) French mime artist, born at Kolín, Bohemia, into a family of acrobats. He joined the Théâtre des Funambules in Paris (1816), and developed the character of Pierrot, to the delight of audiences, into a pale-faced hero. He died in Paris. » harlequinade; Pierrot

Debussy, Claude (Achille) (1862–1918) French composer, born at St Germain-en-Laye. Educated at the Paris Conservatoire (1873–84), he studied piano under Marmontel, and in 1884 won the Prix de Rome. His early successes were the *Prélude à l'après-midi d'un faune* (1894), and his piano pieces, *Images* and *Préludes*, in which he experimented with novel techniques and effects, producing the pictures in sound which led to his work being described as 'musical Impressionism'. He extended this new idiom to orchestral music in *La Mer* (1905) and other pieces. He died in Paris. » Impressionism (music)

decadence A period of cultural decline – often in reaction to the rule of morality and order – where intellectual and moral licence is reflected in artistic sophistication and excess. Themes are morbid and perverse; treatment is sensational and self-indulgent. The 1890s in England and France provide an example. » Decadents; English/French literature

Decadents Specifically, a group of French writers in the late 1880s whose journal *La Décadent* appeared briefly at that time: the poets Baudelaire, Verlaine, Rimbaud, and Mallarmé, and the novelist Huysmans. More generally, any writers exhibiting decadent tendencies, such as Poe in the USA in the 1840s; the poet Swinburne, the playwright Oscar Wilde, and the artist Aubrey Beardsley in England in the 1890s; and D'Annunzio in Italy, also during the 1890s. » Baudelaire; decadence; English/French literature; Huysmans; Mallarmé; Rimbaud; Verlaine

Decalogue » **Ten Commandments**

Decameron (Gr 'ten days') A series of narratives written by the Italian poet Boccaccio in the period 1349–51. The 'frame' story relates how ten Florentines, taking refuge from the plague, relate one tale each for ten days. This device and the stories themselves (many of which were traditional) were widely influential in late mediaeval Europe, for example on Chaucer's *Canterbury Tales*. » Boccaccio; Chaucer; Italian literature

Decapoda [duh**kap**uhda] A large order of mostly marine crustaceans characterized by three pairs of thoracic legs modified as pincers (*maxillipeds*) for feeding, and five pairs of walking legs; horny covering (*carapace*) fused along back to form gill chamber above leg bases; contains c.10 000 living species, including crabs, lobsters, and shrimps. (Class: *Malacostraca*.) » crab; crustacean; lobster; shrimp

decathlon A multi-event track-and-field discipline consisting of ten events, held over two days. The events, in order, are: 100 metres, long jump, shot, high jump, 400 m, 110 m hurdles, discus, pole vault, javelin, and 1 500 m. Points are awarded in each event based on individual performance. » athletics; discus throw; high jump; javelin throw; long jump; pole vault; shot put; RR104

Decatur, Stephen [duh**kay**tuh] (1779–1820) US naval commander, born at Sinepuxent, Maryland, of French descent. He served against the French, and gained great distinction in the war with Tripoli (1801–5), burning the captured *Philadelphia*, and escaping under the fire of 141 guns. Promoted captain in

1804 and commodore in 1810, in the war with England in 1812 he captured the frigate *Macedonian*, but in 1814 surrendered to the British. He was killed in a duel at Bladensburg, Maryland. » War of 1812

decay rate » **mean life**

Deccan [**de**kan], Sanskrit **Dakshin** Eastward sloping plateau occupying most of CS India, S of the Vindhya Mts; bounded by the Eastern Ghats and the Western Ghats; average altitude 600 m/2 000 ft; includes most of Karnataka, S Andhra Pradesh, SE Maharashtra and NW Tamil Nadu states; major towns include Hyderabad and Bangalore; noted for cotton; Carnatic plains area was the arena for the British struggle against the French for control of India during the 18th-c. » Ghats; India [i]

Decembrists A group of progressive-minded Russian army officers who attempted a coup against the autocratic government (12 Dec 1825). The rebellion was suppressed, five of its leaders hanged, and over 100 conspirators exiled to Siberia. They were later regarded as martyrs and founders of the 19th-c Russian revolutionary movement. » Romanovs; Russian history

decibel Unit of sound level intensity; symbol db; named after Scottish inventor Alexander Graham Bell; defined as $10\log_{10}(I/I_0)$, where I is the sound level intensity in question and I_0 is defined as $10^{-12}W/m^2$; roughly equal to the faintest audible sound; a tenth of a **bel**. » Bell, Alexander Graham; sound; units (scientific)

deciduous plants Plants which shed their leaves before the onset of harsh seasons, during which they remain dormant. Leaf fall prevents excessive water loss during drought, or when water is locked up as ice, and minimizes frost damage. » evergreen plants; leaf [i]; transpiration

decimal system The number system in common use, in which the place values of the digits in a number correspond to multiples of powers of 10. Thus the number 'two hundred and thirty four' is $2\times10^2+3\times10^1+4$, so is written 234. Decimal fractions are fractions whose denominators are powers of 10, such as $^{23}/_{100}$, usually written 0.23. » base (mathematics); numbers

Declaration of Independence (1776) Following the American Revolution, the document adopted by the Continental Congress to proclaim the separation of the 13 colonies from Britain. Written mainly by Thomas Jefferson, it announced the right of revolution and detailed the Americans' reasons for the break. » Continental Congress; Jefferson, Thomas

Declaration of Rights (1689) A British statute which ended the brief interregnum after James II quit the throne in December 1688, establishing William III and Mary II as joint monarchs. The Bill effectively ensured that monarchs must operate with the consent of parliament, and must not suspend or dispense with laws passed by that body. » bill of rights; James II (of England); William III

Declaration of the Rights of Man and Citizen A declaration made by the French National Assembly (27 Aug 1789), proclaiming liberty of conscience, of property, and of the press, and freedom from arbitrary imprisonment. It finally ended the privileged system of the *ancien régime*. » *ancien régime*; French Revolution [i]

declension In linguistics, the scheme of inflections for case contrasts in the noun, seen in a well-developed form in inflected languages, such as Greek or Latin. A language may have several declensions classified according to the particular vowels or consonants which figure in the case forms; for example, in Latin there are many nouns where the *a* vowel is the main feature, as can be seen in *puella* ('girl'), where the cases in the singular are *puella* (nominative, vocative, ablative), *puellam* (accusative), and *puellae* (genitive, dative). » case; derivation

declination A co-ordinate which together with right ascension specifies the location of celestial objects on the sky, or celestial sphere. Analogous to latitude, it is measured in degrees, positive to the N of the celestial equator and negative to the S. » celestial equator; latitude and longitude [i]; right ascension

decomposition The breaking down of the complex organic molecules of dead plant and animal matter into simple organic and inorganic molecules which may be recycled as nutrients for primary producers. In natural systems, most decomposition is carried out by bacteria and fungi. » bacteria [i]; fungus

decompression sickness An occupational disease of individuals who work under higher than atmospheric pressure, such as in underwater exploration; also known as **caisson disease**. Gases of the air inhaled into the lungs go into solution in the body fluids. If these workers return to normal atmospheric pressures too quickly, nitrogen is released as tiny bubbles which lodge in small blood vessels throughout the body. This deprives the tissues of their normal blood supply. Permanent damage to the brain or death can follow. In less severe cases, dizziness and cramp-like pain in the muscles and joints (the *bends*) occur. Treatment of an established case is to return the victim to high atmospheric pressure, and then expose them very slowly to normal atmospheric pressure. » deep sea diving; occupational diseases

deconstruction An approach to literary criticism, also known as **post-structuralism**, which takes the insights of structuralism to their logical conclusion (or point of a-logical inconclusiveness) by emphasizing not only the arbitrariness but also the radical instability existing between sign and referent, and therefore the impossibility of 'meaning' in any simple sense. The French philosopher Jaques Derrida has demonstrated in several books how language must fail in its attempt to relate by reference to a world 'out there' beyond our discourse, and how that discourse itself may/must be broken open (or 'deconstructed') in order to expose the self-protecting fallacies of our 'logocentric' or word-centred conception of reality. » Derrida; De Man; language; literary criticism; structuralism

Decorated Style The form of English Gothic architecture prevalent in the late 13th-c and 14th-c, characterized by a maximum of surface decoration, usually in the form of stylized leaves and the double-S curve known as an *ogee*. Good examples are Wells Cathedral (1290–c.1340) and the Lady Chapel and Octagon at Ely (1321–53), UK. » arch [i]; Early English Style; Gothic architecture; Perpendicular Style; vault [i]

decoration A badge of honour bestowed to reward civil and military achievements. In the UK, many decorative orders are of feudal origin; in some other European countries the abolition of the monarchy has meant the lapse of their chivalric orders also. Newer states, such as Africa, have created orders modelled after the European ones. » Albert Medal; Distinguished Flying Cross; Distinguished Service Order; George Cross; George Medal; honours list; Iron Cross; Legion d'Honneur; medal [i]; Medal of Honour; orders; Presidential Medal of Freedom; Purple Heart; Victoria Cross

Decoration Day » **Memorial Day**

decorative arts The design and ornamentation of objects, usually with some practical use and outside the field of 'fine art' (painting, sculpture, and architecture); nowadays more exactly called the **applied arts**. Metalwork, ceramics, glass, textiles, and woodwork have all been wrought and decorated to a degree which transcends their functional purpose, and gives them an important role in the development of mainstream artistic styles. The distinction with fine art is often almost non-existent, as in the case of ceramic sculpture and tapestry hangings. » art; ceramics

Decroux, Etienne-Marcel [duh**kroo**] (1898–) French actor responsible for the renaissance of mime in the 20th-c, by developing and teaching a system of physical expression he termed *mime corporel*. In 1940 he opened a school in Paris, and from 1941 onwards toured extensively both teaching and performing. » mime; theatre

Dedication, Feast of » **Hanukkah**

deduction In logic, any inference whose conclusion follows validly and necessarily from its premisses. The premisses may or may not be true: 'London and Chicago are planets; therefore London is a planet' is valid, whereas 'Either London or Mars is a planet; therefore Mars is a planet' is invalid. » logic; premiss; validity

Dee, John (1527–1608) English alchemist, geographer, and mathematician, born in London. Educated at Cambridge, he travelled widely in Europe, brought back many astronomical instruments, and earned the reputation of a sorcerer. For most of his life he was concerned with the search for the Northwest Passage to the Far East. He died at Mortlake, Surrey.

deed » covenant 1

deep-freezing Freezing to −20°C or below in either a chest freezer or cabinet freezer. The level of ability of a freezer cabinet to maintain a sufficiently low temperature for prolonged food preservation is shown on the cabinet by a series of stars; deep-freezers will allow three months storage, a level which is symbolized by four stars. Some foods, such as raw beef, fresh vegetables, and fruit, may be stored for up to one year. » food preservation

deep scattering layer A layer in the sea which reflects sound signals. During World War 2 it was discovered that sonar signals were scattered by a mysterious layer which moved up and down in the water. This was later found to be caused by organisms in the water column. Much of the phenomenon is produced by the air bladders of fishes, but animals as small as microscopic zooplankton may also contribute to it. The layer has been observed to move down towards greater depths during the day and towards the surface at night – a movement known as *vertical migration*. » plankton; sound

deep sea diving The descent to the sea bed by divers, usually for long periods to carry out exploration, salvage, or construction work. The airtight diving suit was invented by Augustus Siebe in 1837. Modern diving suits have fibreglass helmets with viewports, and weighted boots for stability. Air, or an oxygen/helium mixture, is pumped to the diver. Communication between the diver and people on the surface is vital. » decompression sickness

Deep Space Network (DSN) A NASA tracking and telecommunications system used to operate interplanetary spacecraft. Stations are located at three widely spaced locations around the world (Goldstone, California; Canberra, Australia; Madrid, Spain) to provide a continuous communications capability in all parts of the Solar System. Each station operates one 70 m/230 ft diameter radio antenna and two 34 m/112 ft antennas, capable of two-way communications with spacecraft to beyond Neptune's orbit. It is operated by NASA's Jet Propulsion Laboratory. » NASA; Solar System; space exploration

deep structure In grammatical theory, the abstract grammatical relationships which underlie the structure of sentences, and which people use to interpret what is said. At this level of analysis, it is possible to identify the correspondences between such pairs of sentences as statement and question, or negative and positive, or active and passive – for example, the identity of meaning between active voice *the dogs chased the cat* and passive voice *the cat was chased by the dogs*. Deep structure is contrasted with **surface structure**, which is a level of grammatical analysis corresponding closely to the structure of the sentences people speak and hear – the particular order of words and affixes in the above sentences *the+dog+s...* This distinction was introduced into linguistics by US linguist Noam Chomsky in the 1960s, and has since been developed in a sophisticated form as part of generative grammar. » Chomsky; generative grammar; grammar

Deeping, (George) Warwick (1877–1950) British novelist, born at Southend, Essex. He trained as a doctor, but after a year gave up his practice to devote himself to writing. His early novels were mainly historical, and it was not until after World War 1 that he gained recognition with his bestseller, *Sorrell and Son* (1925). » English literature; novel

deer A type of hoofed mammal of families *Cervidae* (**true deer**, 36 species), *Moschidae* (**musk deer**), and *Tragulidae* (**mouse deer**; an artiodactyl; only true deer have antlers; male musk deer and mouse deer have long prominent canine teeth; true deer found worldwide except Africa and Australasia; usually found in or near woodland; male called a *stag* or *buck*, female a *hind* or *doe*, young a *fawn* or *kid* (names depend on species). » antlers [i]; artiodactyl; chevrotain; chital; elk; mammal [i]; muntjac; ungulate; fallow/musk/Père David's/red/roe/water deer

deer mouse A mouse native to N America; grey or brown with white underparts; ears large; used widely in science laboratories; also known as **white-footed mouse** or **deer-footed mouse**. Its agility reminded early observers of a deer. (Genus: *Peromyscus*, 49 species.) » mouse (biology)

deerhound A breed of dog, developed in Scotland from Mediterranean ancestors; tall, slim; very long legs, long tail; shaggy grey coat; head small with short soft ears; also known as the **Scottish deerhound**, **staghound**, or **buckhound**. » dog

deerlet » chevrotain

deësis [dayeesis] In art, the representation of Christ enthroned in majesty flanked by the Virgin and St John. It is the central motif of certain Byzantine altarpieces. » Byzantine art; Jesus Christ; John, St; Mary (mother of Jesus)

defaecation/defecation The expulsion of faeces from the bowel. Distension of the rectum by faeces leads to the reflex contraction of its musculature, and the relaxation of the involuntary internal anal sphincter, accompanied by the desire to defaecate. This is accomplished voluntarily by contraction of the abdominal muscles (straining) and relaxation of the external anal sphincter. » anus; constipation; rectum

defamation The publication of a statement which tends to lower a person in the view of right-thinking members of society generally. In England and Wales, it takes the form of either libel or slander (neither of these terms is used in Scottish law, which recognizes only defamation). Both are actionable at civil law, though libel exists as a criminal offence. » libel; slander; tort

defecation » defaecation

defence/defense mechanism A pattern of feeling and thinking which controls sensations of guilt, anxiety, and internal conflict, and which inhibits unacceptable impulses. Examples include repression and denial. It is a normal process which usually occurs unconsciously, but if excessive in any particular form has been considered pathological. » regression; repression

Defence of the Realm Act A British Act introduced in 1914 at the beginning of World War 1 to give the government greater controls over the activities of its citizens. The most important control related to restrictions on press reporting and other forms of censorship. The restrictions were increased as the war progressed. » World War 1

defendant In law, the person who is called on to answer proceedings brought against him or her by some other person, called the **plaintiff**. In criminal cases the defendant is the accused; in civil cases, the person who is sued. The term *defender* is used in Scotland. » court of law

Defender of the Faith (Lat *fidei defensor*) A title conferred on Henry VIII of England by Pope Leo X as a reward for the king's written opposition to the teachings of Martin Luther. After the Reformation, the title was confirmed by parliament, and is still used by British sovereigns. » Henry VIII; Luther; Reformation

deficit financing A government policy to stimulate the economy by planning a budget deficit, where expenditure will exceed the revenues from taxes. Money is thus pumped into the economy to stimulate demand. » budget

deflation A government economic policy designed to reduce inflationary pressures. Steps taken include higher interest and tax rates, and a tighter money supply. » inflation

Defoe, Daniel (1660–1731) English author, born and died in London. The son of a butcher, he was educated at a dissenting academy, travelled widely in Europe, and set up in the hosiery trade. In 1688 he joined William III's army, and until 1704 strenuously supported the King's party. In 1702 his satire *The Shortest Way with the Dissenters* raised Queen Anne's anger, and he was imprisoned at Newgate, where he continued his pamphleteering. On his release in 1704 he started *The Review*, writing it single-handed, three times a week, until 1713. During this time, his political conduct became highly equivocal: he supported, rejected, then supported again the Tory minister, Harley. After the accession of George I (1714) he returned to the writing of fiction, and achieved lasting fame with *Robinson Crusoe* (1719–20). His other major works include *A Journal of the Plague Year*, *Moll Flanders* (both 1722), and *Roxana* (1724). » English literature; novel; satire

defoliant Any preparation which removes or kills the leaves of a plant. » Agent Orange

deforestation The removal of forest areas, either to make use of the wood or to clear the land for agricultural, industrial, or urban purposes. In W Europe the first major phase occurred about 5 000 years ago with the spread of agriculture in the Neolithic period. Today, large scale deforestation is occurring in areas of tropical rain forest. » afforestation; rain forest; Three Age System

Degas, (Hilaire Germain) Edgar [duh**gah**] (1834–1917) French artist, born and died in Paris. After studying at the Ecole des Beaux-Arts, he went to Italy, where he was influenced by the Renaissance painters. On his return to Paris he associated with the Impressionists and took part in most of their exhibitions from 1874 to 1886. He was also influenced by Japanese woodcuts and by photography. Among his best-known works are 'Dancer Lacing her Shoe' (c.1878, Paris) and 'Jockeys in the Rain' (1879, Glasgow). Latterly, because of failing sight, he concentrated on sculpture. » French art; Impressionism (art)

degaussing [dee**gow**sing] The neutralizing of an object's magnetic field using current-carrying coils to produce an opposing magnetic field of equal strength. The process is applied to ships, to protect them from magnetically-activated mines. » magnetism

degree (education) The award given at the conclusion of a course in higher education. Most countries use the terms *Bachelor* to denote a first degree, *Master* to signify a higher degree at postgraduate level, and *Doctor* for those who have successfully undertaken a significant piece of original research. The doctorate was originally intended as the licence to teach in higher education. » university

degree (mathematics) One 360th part of a complete revolution, usually symbolized by °. $90° = 1$ right angle. $180° = \pi$ rad; $90° = 100$ grad. » angle

dehydration Literally, 'loss of water'; but in medicine, the process of salt depletion as well as water loss. This usage is unfortunate, as depletion of water and salt can occur in different relative proportions and affect the body in different ways. Water loss occurs in those who do not or cannot drink water, and also because of the normal continuous loss of water from the surface of the body and in the breath. It causes great thirst and, when severe, mental confusion. Excessive loss of salt-containing fluids, such as occurs after severe vomiting, diarrhoea, or excessive urination (as in untreated diabetes mellitus), particularly affects the circulation, with a rise in pulse rate and falling blood pressure. Circulatory collapse and shock then ensue. » blood; diabetes mellitus

Deimos [**diy**mos] One of the two natural satellites of Mars, discovered in 1877; distance from the planet 2 346 000 km/ 1 458 000 ml; diameter c.15 km/9 ml; orbital period 30 hr 17 min. It is in synchronous rotation with Phobos, and similar to it in structure, with a dark, irregularly cratered surface. » Mars (astronomy); Phobos; RR4

deism [**day**izm] Originally, belief in the existence of a god or gods; today, belief in the existence of a supreme being who is the ground and source of reality but who does not intervene or take an active interest in the natural and historical order. It also designates a largely British 17th-c and 18th-c movement of religious thought emphasizing natural religion as opposed to revealed religion, and seeking to establish reasonable grounds for belief in the existence of God; represented by, among others, Lord Herbert of Cherbury (1583–1648), Matthew Tindal (1657–1733), and Anthony Collins (1676–1729). » theism

Dekker, Thomas (c.1570–c.1641) English dramatist, born in London. He was a prolific writer, but only a few of his plays were printed. His best-known works are the comedy *The Shoemaker's Holiday* (1600) and *The Honest Whore* (1604; part II, 1630). He wrote several plays in collaboration with other Elizabethan dramatists, and was also well known as a writer of prose pamphlets giving a lively account of London life. During the 1630s he dropped out of notice, and nothing is known of his last years. » drama; English literature

Delacroix, (Ferdinand Victor) Eugène [duhla**krwah**] (1798–1863) French painter, born at Charenton. He exhibited his 'Dante and Vergil in Hell' at the Paris Institute in 1822, following this with 'The Massacre at Chios' (1823, Louvre). These pictures, with their loose drawing and vivid colouring, aroused a storm of criticism. In his later work he moved even further away from traditional treatment in his canvases of historical and dramatic scenes, often violent or macabre in subject, such as 'Liberty Guiding the People' (1831, Louvre). He died in Paris. » French art

Delaroche, (Hippolyte) Paul (1797–1856) French painter, born and died in Paris. He studied under Gros, from whom he absorbed the technique of the large historical subject painting, as seen in his 'Death of Queen Elizabeth' (1828), and 'Execution of Lady Jane Grey' (1834). His major work was the series of murals for the Ecole des Beaux-Arts, where he became professor of painting (1833). » French art; Gros

Delaunay, Robert [duhloh**nay**] (1885–1941) French artist, born in Paris. At first a stage designer, he turned to painting in 1905. He was associated with the Blaue Reiter (1911–2), but is principally known as the founder of Orphism. He painted many pictures of Paris (particularly the 'Eiffel Tower'), and his research into colour orchestration as applied to abstract art was influential. He died at Montpellier. » Blaue Reiter, der; French art; Orphism

Delaware pop (1987e) 644 000; area 5 296 sq km/2 045 sq ml. State in E USA, divided into three counties; the 'First State' or 'Diamond State'; the original Swedish settlers were supplanted (1655) by the Dutch, who were in turn supplanted by the British (1664); part of Pennsylvania until 1776; one of the original states and first to ratify the Federal Constitution, 1787; capital, Dover; other chief cities, Wilmington and Newark; bounded E by Delaware Bay and the Atlantic Ocean; the Delaware R forms part of the border with New Jersey; highest point Ebright Road (135 m/443 ft); the second smallest state; poultry, soybeans, corn, dairy products; mainly an industrial state, centred around Wilmington; chemicals, transportation equipment, processed food, plastics, metals; several large corporations based in Wilmington, taking advantage of the state's taxation laws. » Dover (USA); United States of America [i]; RR38

Delaware River River in E USA; rises in the Catskill Mts, New York, and empties into Delaware Bay; length 450 km/280 ml; marks the state frontiers of Pennsylvania, New York, and New Jersey; navigable to Trenton. » United States of America [i]

Delbrück, Max (1906–81) German-US biophysicist, born in Berlin. He studied physics in Germany, and worked with Bohr at Copenhagen before turning to chemistry and, from 1937 (at the California Institute of Technology), to biology. He did much to create bacterial and bacteriophage genetics, and to inspire early work in biophysics and molecular biology. He shared the Nobel Prize for Physiology or Medicine in 1969. » bacteria [i]; biophysics; Bohr; molecular biology

delegated legislation Provisions in an act of parliament whereby government ministers, local authorities, or other designated persons may supplement the legal rules in the parent act. The person to whom powers are delegated must operate within the powers conferred by the act; action which goes beyond this may be challenged in the courts. Delegated legislation has the advantage of permitting details to be added to the broad principles of legislation without the need for a new act of parliament. While there is some parliamentary scrutiny of certain delegated legislation, there is no doubt that the growth of this form of legislation reflects the relative strength of the executive branch of government. » judicial review; legislature

Delescluze, (Louis) Charles [duhlay**kluz**] (1809–71) French radical Republican and journalist, born at Dreux. His revolutionary politics drove him from France to journalism in Belgium (1835), but the February Revolution (1848) brought him back to Paris. His writing made him popular, but brought him imprisonment (1849–53), and he was transported until 1859. He played a prominent part in the Paris Commune, and died on the last barricade. » radicalism; Revolutions of 1848

Delft 52°01N 4°22E, pop (1984e) 86 733. Ancient city and municipality in W South Holland province, W Netherlands, on the R Schie; famous for linen-weaving (14th-c), pottery and porcelain (16th-c); William the Silent assassinated here, 1584; railway; technical university (1863); vehicles, machines, pharmaceuticals, yeast, alcohol, consumer products, electrical engineering, building materials, paper, cardboard, porcelain (delftware); birthplace of Vermeer; Nieuwe Kerk (1396–1496), Italian Renaissance town hall, Prisenhof. » Delftware; Netherlands, The [i]; Vermeer; William I (of the Netherlands)

Delftware The Dutch and English version of faience, named after the town of Delft where it was made in large quantities in the 17th-c. Usually blue and white, its decoration is generally copied from Chinese porcelain. » Delft; faience; porcelain

Delhi, Hindi **Dilli**, formerly **Shahjahanabad** 28°38N 77°17E, pop (1991) 8 380 000. Capital of India and administrative centre of Delhi union territory, NC India, 1 190 km/739 ml NNE of Bombay; **Old Delhi**, enclosed within the walls built by Shah Jahan in 1638, on R Yamuna; Mughal architecture and thronged bazaars contrast with formal architecture and wide boulevards of **New Delhi** to the S, largely designed by Lutyens; New Delhi the administrative centre of India since 1912; largest commercial centre in India; airport (Palam); railway junction; university (1922); chemicals, machine tools, clothing, footwear, drinks, food processing, plastics, bicycles, radios, televisions; traditional crafts include jewellery, papier mâché, textiles, ivory carving; Red Fort, containing imperial palace of Shah Jahan (17th-c); Jama Masijid, largest mosque in India (1644–58); Rajghat, where Gandhi was cremated (1948). » Gandhi; India [i]; Lutyens; Qutb Minar; Shah Jahan

Delhi Sultanate The principal N Indian Muslim kingdom between the 13th-c and 16th-c, in which Sultan Iltutmish (1211–36) made his permanent capital at Delhi. It became an imperial power under the Khalji dynasty (1290–1320), but its power was much reduced under the Saiyid and Lodi dynasties, and the Sultanate was destroyed by Babur at Panipat in 1526. » Delhi; Mughal Empire

Delian League [**dee**leean] The association of Greek city-states under Athenian leadership that was formed after the Persian Wars (478–477 BC) for the continuing defence of the Aegean area against the Persians. It was so called because the treasury of the League was initially on the island of Delos. » Greek history; Persian Wars

Delian problem » **duplication of the cube**

Delibes, (Clément Philibert) Léo [duh**leeb**] (1836–91) French composer, born at St Germain du Val. He became second director at the Opéra, Paris (1864) and a Conservatoire professor (1881). He wrote light operas, of which *Lakmé* had the greatest success, but is chiefly remembered for the ballet *Coppélia* (1870). He died in Paris.

Delilah Biblical character, who at the instigation of the Philistines enticed Samson to reveal the secret of his great strength – his uncut hair, according to his Nazirite vow. She contrived to cut his hair to weaken him (*Judges* 16). » Judges, Book of; Samson

deliquescent In chemistry, taking up water from the atmosphere. Some salts, such as calcium chloride, will absorb enough water from a damp atmosphere to dissolve in the water absorbed. The term is essentially equivalent to **hygroscopic**.

delirium An acute and reversible alteration of attention and consciousness associated with impaired memory and impaired orientation, usually the result of organic causes. It may incorporate hallucinatory and delusional experiences, as well as restlessness and irritability. In earlier usage, it was a general term referring to madness of any form. » delirium tremens; hallucination; memory

delirium tremens A form of delirium which occurs following withdrawal of alcohol from alcoholics. Hallucinations often take the form of a sensation of insects crawling on the skin, and of Lilliputian individuals or objects. It is usually associated with other features of alcoholic brain damage, notably tremor of the hands and arms. » alcoholism; delirium

Delius, Frederick [**dee**liuhs] (1862–1934) British composer, of German-Scandinavian descent, born at Bradford, Yorkshire. He followed a commercial career until he was 20, when he went to Florida as an orange planter, studying music in his spare time. He entered the Leipzig Conservatory in 1886, and became a friend of Grieg. After 1890 he lived almost entirely in France, composing prolifically. He wrote six operas, including *A Village Romeo and Juliet* (1901), and a variety of choral and orchestral works, such as *Appalachia* (1902) and *On Hearing the First Cuckoo in Spring* (1912). In 1924 he became paralysed and blind, but with the assistance of Eric Fenby (1906–), his amanuensis from 1928, he continued to compose. He died at Grez-sur-Loing, France.

Deller, Alfred (George) (1912–79) British countertenor, born at Margate, Kent. A church chorister from the age of 11, he began a full-time musical career in 1947. He made many recordings of early English songs, notably those of Dowland and Purcell, and in 1950 formed the Deller Consort, devoted to the authentic performance of early music. In 1963 he founded the Stour Music Festival. » countertenor

Delphi, Gr **Dhelfoí**, formerly **Pytho** 38°29N 22°30E. Village and ancient site in Fokis department, Greece, on the slopes of Mt Parnassos, 176 km/109 ml from Athens; altitude 520–620 m/ 1 706–2 034 ft; renowned throughout the ancient Greek world as the sanctuary of Apollo and the seat of his oracle; remains of the temple and precincts were excavated in the 19th-c. » Apollo; Delphi, Oracle of; Greece [i]

Delphi, Oracle of [**del**fee] The oracular shrine of Apollo at Delphi in C Greece. It was the most prestigious oracle in the Graeco-Roman world, for centuries being consulted by states about public policy and by individuals about private matters. On the payment of a fee, enquirers put their questions to Apollo's medium, a priestess called the Pythia. Her ecstatic responses (oracles) were notorious for their ambiguity. » Delphi; Pythian Games

Delphi technique A forecasting technique used in business planning. Experts are invited to give their opinion on the likelihood of occurrence of a specific event on or by a specific date. The consensus view is taken as a forecast. » Delphi, oracle of

delphinium A tall perennial native to the N hemisphere; leaves palmately lobed or finely divided; flowers blue, rarely pink or white, each with a conical spur and borne in long showy spikes. A popular garden ornamental, it contains poisonous alkaloids including delphinin. (Genus: *Delphinium*, 250 species. Family: *Ranunculaceae*.) » alkaloids; palmate; perennial

Delphinus (Lat 'dolphin') [del**fiy**nuhs] A small N constellation. » constellation; RR8

delta A fan-shaped body of alluvium enclosed within the bifurcating channels at the mouth of a river. It is formed when a river deposits sediment as its speed decreases, and the coastal processes of erosion are not sufficiently strong to carry the material away. Deltas may take many forms, depending on the environmental factors at the river mouth, but in all cases the coarse sediment is deposited first, with progressively finer material carried further out from the shore. Deltas may form large fertile plains, but are subject to frequent flooding. » alluvium; sedimentation

Deluge » **Flood, the**

Delvaux, Paul [del**voh**] (1897–) Belgian Surrealist painter, born at Antheit. He lived mainly in Brussels, where he studied. Influenced by Chirico and Magritte, he produced a series of paintings depicting nude and seminude girls in dreamlike settings, such as 'The Call of the Night'. He was professor of painting at Brussels (1950–62). » Chirico; Divisionism; Magritte; Surrealism

demand In economics, the quantity of goods (products) or services demanded at a particular price (*market demand*). This quantity will vary at different price levels: usually the higher the price, the lower the demand, and vice-versa. » elasticity (economics); supply and demand

dementia A decline in intellectual capacity as a result of an alteration of brain functioning which leads to impaired social or occupational abilities. It is commonly due to cerebrovascular disease and the ageing process, in which brain cells are destroyed and brain size is markedly reduced. Features include loss of memory, alteration of personality, impaired judgment, and poor impulse control. There is disorientation in time and place, and a failure to recognize friends and relatives. The term is one of many used previously as synonymous with madness. » Alzheimer's disease; brain [i]; echolalia; mental disorders

Demeter [dee**mee**ter] The Greek goddess of agriculture, especially corn, so that a basket or an ear of corn is her symbol. She is the mother of Persephone, for whom she searched through the world, and is also connected with the Mysteries at Eleusis. » Ceres (mythology); Persephone

democracy From Greek *demos* ('people') and *kratia* ('authority'), hence 'rule by the people'; contrasted with rule by the few (*oligarchy*) or by one (*monarchy* or *tyranny*); also known as a **liberal democracy**. Since the Greeks first introduced *demokratia* in many city states in the 5th-c BC, there has been disagreement about what constitutes the essential elements of democracy. One debate concerns who should compose 'the people', and only in the 20th-c has this notion been viewed as covering the total adult citizenship. Another relates to how the people should rule, particularly in relation to the increasing size of states, which has resulted in a shift from direct democracy to systems of representation. Today it is widely accepted that because the people are too numerous and scattered to come together in assemblies, decision-making has to be handed over to a small group of representatives. Elections, including the right to choose among different groups of representatives offering different doctrines and party programmes, have therefore become seen as essential to democracy. Further necessary conditions are the legal equality of citizens, and the free flow of information to ensure that citizens are in an equal and informed position to choose and hold accountable their rulers. Some radicals argue that economic equality is also necessary, but moves towards economic democracy have been limited. » monarchy; pluralism (politics); polyarchy

Democratic Labor Party (DLP) An Australian political party, formed in 1957 from anti-communist groups which had formerly been part of the Australian Labor Party (ALP). The DLP was largely centred in Victoria, and drew most of its support from parts of the Catholic section of Australian society. At its height, in the late 1950s and through the 1960s, its importance lay in its ability to prevent the ALP from winning national government. Its policies were strongly anti-communist and pro-defence, and incorporated elements of Catholic teaching on social matters. No DLP representative has been elected to the national parliament since 1974. » Australian Labor Party

Democratic Party One of the two major parties in contemporary US politics. It was originally composed in the late 18th-c of those opposed to the adoption of the US Constitution. The first successful presidential candidate was Thomas Jefferson; and in the early 1800s it dominated its opponent, the Federalist Party. The party was split over slavery and secession during the Civil War (1861–5), its dominant position being taken over by the Republican Party. After the war the party became conservative, based in the South and West, achieving only intermittent success. It returned to a majority position in 1932, when Roosevelt introduced his 'New Deal', and added large urban areas and ethnic, racial, and religious support to its conservative Southern base. It also became associated with a more liberal stance of social reform and minority rights, especially in the 1960s. It retains the preference of the majority of Americans, but since the early 1960s it has had great difficulty winning the presidency. There remain divisions between its liberal and conservative wings. » Barnburners; Copperhead; Federalist Party; Jefferson, Thomas; Republican Party; Roosevelt, Franklin D; Whig Party

Democritus [duh**mo**krituhs] (c.460–370 BC) Greek philosopher, born at Abdera in Thrace. He travelled in the East, and was by far the most learned thinker of his time. He wrote many physical, mathematical, ethical, and musical works, but only fragments survive. His *atomic system* assumes an infinite multitude of everlasting atoms, from whose random combinations springs an infinite number of successive world-orders in which there is law but not design. His system, derived from Leucippus (about whom little is known), was developed by Epicurus and Lucretius. » atomism; Epicurus; Lucretius

demography A branch of sociology which studies the population patterns of the past, present, and future. Demography has been very important in estimating future trends in population growth in order to calculate the pressures on global resources. » cohort; population density; sociology

demoiselle [duhmwa**zel**] A crane native to S Europe, Asia, and N Africa (migrates further S in winter); mainly white with dark chest and throat; ornamental feathers on head. (*Anthropoides virgo*. Family: *Gruidae*.) » crane

Demosthenes [duh**mos**thuhneez] (c.383–322 BC) The greatest of the Greek orators, the son of a rich Athenian arms manufacturer. After studying rhetoric and legal procedure, he took up the law as a profession, becoming first a speechwriter, then an assistant to prosecutors in public (state) trials. In c.354 BC he entered politics, but did not gain prominence until 351 BC, when he delivered the first of a long series of passionate speeches (the 'First Philippic') advocating all-out resistance to Philip of Macedon. Swayed by his oratory, the Athenians did eventually go to war (340 BC), only to be thoroughly defeated at Chaeronea (338 BC). Put on trial by the peace party of Aeschines, he fully vindicated himself in his oratorical masterpiece, *On the Crown*. It was the high point of his career. Exile for embezzlement followed in 325 BC, and enforced suicide in 322 BC, after the failure of the Athenian revolt from Macedon in the aftermath of Alexander's death. » Aeschines; Greek history; Lamian War; Philip II (of Macedon)

demotic script An ancient Egyptian form of writing, derived from hieroglyphic script, and used for everyday purposes. The term is also applied to any 'common' style of speech or writing, as opposed to the official or formal system used by a community. » hieroglyphics [i]

demythologizing A programme of interpretation of the Bible, systematized by Rudolf Bultmann. He attempted to understand the so-called 'mythical' language of Biblical times, which presupposed a pre-scientific world-view, by interpreting it 'existentially' (ie in categories of the existentialist philosopher, Heidegger) making it meaningful to the modern scientifically-minded world. » Bible; Bultmann; Heidegger; hermeneutics 1; mythology

dendrite » **neurone** [i]

dendrochronology The construction of archaeological chronologies from annual tree-ring sequences. Rings vary in width and structure from year to year, depending on the prevailing climatic conditions; overlapping patterns observed in preserved timbers can therefore be matched and linked to form an accurate and absolute chronology extending back unbroken from the present day. Notable sequences derived from the long-lived Californian Bristlecone Pine (*Pinus aristata*, to c.7000 BC) and Irish bog oaks (to c.4000 BC) have proved a crucial check on radiocarbon dates. » archaeology; Novgorod; radiocarbon dating

Deneb » **Cygnus**

Deng Xiaoping or **Teng Hsiao-p'ing** [deng syow**ping**] (1902–) Leader of the Chinese Communist Party, since 1978 the dominant figure in Chinese politics, born in Sichuan province. Educated in France, where he joined the Communist Party, and in the Soviet Union, he became associated with Mao Zedong (Mao Tse-tung) during the period of the Jiangxi Soviet (1928–34). In 1954 he became Secretary-General of the Chinese Communist Party, but reacted strongly against the excesses of the Great Leap Forward (1958–9). When Mao launched the Cultural Revolution (1966), Deng was criticized and purged along with Liu Shaoqi, but retained the confidence of Premier Zhou Enlai and was restored to power in 1974. Again dismissed in 1976, after the death of Mao he was restored once more to power, and since 1978 has taken China through a rapid course of pragmatic reforms. » communism; Cultural Revolution; Great Leap Forward; Liu Shaoqi; Mao Zedong; Zhou Enlai

dengue [**deng**gee] A short-lived acute feverish illness common in tropical countries, caused by a virus transmitted by mosquitoes. Characterized by headache, a brief skin rash, and enlarged lymph nodes, it usually resolves within one to two weeks. » mosquito; virus

Denham, Sir John (1615–69) English poet, born in Dublin, Ireland. Educated in London and Oxford, he succeeded to his father's estate, and at the outbreak of the Civil War was high sheriff of Surrey. His best-known works were the tragedy, *The Sophy* (1641), and his descriptive poem, *Cooper's Hill* (1642). At the Restoration he was appointed surveyor-general of works, and in 1661 created a Knight of the Bath. He died in London. » English Civil War; English literature; poetry

denim A popular clothing fabric made originally by filling indigo-dyed warp yarns with undyed cotton weft to give a twill structure. The indigo slowly leaches out of the fabric, causing a characteristic lightening of the blue colour. The fabric is hard-wearing, and was used for working clothes, but from the 1950s acquired a fashionable cult status. » indigo; twill

Denis or **Denys, St** (3rd-c), feast day 9 October. Traditional apostle of France and first Bishop of Paris, who was sent from Rome about 250 to preach the Gospel to the Gauls. He was martyred at Paris under the Roman Emperor Valerian (reigned 253–60). » apostle; Gaul; missions, Christian

Denis, Maurice [duh**nee**] (1870–1943) French artist and art theorist, born at Grandville. One of the original group of Symbolist painters, Les Nabis, he wrote several influential critical works, and in 1919 helped to found the Studios of Sacred Art, devoted to the revival of religious painting. Perhaps his most famous painting is 'Hommage à Cézanne' (1900, Paris). He died in Paris. » French art; Nabis; Symbolists

Denmark, Danish **Danmark**, official name **Kingdom of Denmark**, Danish **Kongeriget Danmark** pop (1990e) 5 139 000; area (excluding Greenland and Faroes) 43 076 sq km/16 627 sq ml. Kingdom of N Europe, divided into 14 counties (*amt*); consists of most of the Jutland peninsula, several islands in the Baltic Sea (largest, Sjaelland (Zealand), Fyn (Finen), Lolland, Falster, Bornholm), and some of the N Frisian Is in the North Sea; bounded by the Skagerrak (N), Kattegat, Øresund, and Baltic Sea (E), Germany (S), and North Sea (W); coastline 3 400 km/2 100 ml; capital, Copenhagen; chief towns, Århus, Odense, Ålborg, Esbjerg, Randers, Kolding; timezone GMT + 1; language, Danish; chief religion, Lutheranism (97%); unit of currency, krone of 100 øre.

Physical description and climate. Uniformly low-lying, highest point (Ejer Bavnehöj in E Jylland) less than 200 m/650 ft; no large rivers and few lakes; shoreline indented by many lagoons and fjords, largest Lim Fjord (which cut off N extremity of Denmark in 1825); climate much modified by Gulf Stream, giving cold and cloudy winters, warm and sunny summers; annual rainfall usually below 675 mm/25 in.

History and government. Part of Viking kingdoms, 8th–10th-c; Danish Empire under Canute (11th-c); joined with Sweden and Norway under one ruler, 1389; Sweden separated from the union (16th-c), as did Norway (1814); Schleswig-Holstein lost to Germany, 1864; N Schleswig returned after plebiscite, 1920; occupied by Germany, World War 2; Iceland independent, 1944; Greenland and Faroe Is remain dependencies; constitutional monarchy since 1849; unicameral system adopted, 1953; legislative power lies with the monarch and the 179-member Diet (*Folketing*) jointly.

Economy. Lack of raw materials, resulting in development of processing industries, such as foodstuffs, brewing, machinery, hardware, shipping, furniture, glass, porcelain, chemicals, pharmaceuticals; windmill production; intensive agriculture, with corn, horticulture, vegetables; pigs, cattle, poultry; forestry; wide range of food processing; joined European Economic Community, 1973. » Canute; Copenhagen; Faroe Islands; Greenland [i]; Iceland [i]; Kalmar Union; Vikings; RR25 national holidays; RR47 political leaders

□ international airport

Denning (of Whitchurch), Baron Alfred Thompson (1899–) British judge, educated at Oxford. He was called to the Bar in 1923, became a KC in 1938, and a judge of the High Court of Justice in 1944. In 1963 he led the enquiry into the circumstances of John Profumo's resignation as Secretary of State for War. As Master of the Rolls (1962–82) he was responsible for many often controversial decisions. He was knighted in 1944 and made a life peer in 1957. Among his many books are *The Road to Justice* (1955) and *What Next in the Law* (1982). » Profumo

denotation » **connotation**

density (physics) The mass of a substance divided by its volume; symbol ρ, units kg/m^3. The density of water is 1 000 kg/m^3. An object placed in a liquid more dense than itself will float, whereas an object more dense than the liquid will sink. Density is measured using a hydrometer. » Archimedes; relative density

dentistry The treatment and prevention of diseases of the mouth and teeth; with medicine and nursing, one of the major health professions. Dentistry was first practised by barber surgeons. Surgeon dentists first formed a separate guild in France in the reign of Louis XIV, and were required to pass a prescribed examination. In the UK, dental hospitals were built to serve the poor, but formal dental schools were not founded until 1840 in the USA and 1860 in the UK. They were originally privately funded and staffed. Today the practice of dentistry is well-controlled, and its practitioners are licensed under a number of authorities in different countries following specifically dental-oriented training. In Russia, dentists are first trained as physicians and then in operative dentistry, and are called *stomatologists*. In the UK, the right to practise is granted by a General Dental Council, which controls professional and ethical standards. The great majority of dentists in the USA and Europe (but not Russia) are in private dental practice, and in the UK hold contracts with the state, which funds some of the costs. In some countries, **dental hygienists** provide services such as X-rays, scaling of teeth, and dental health education. In the UK, dental assistants and auxiliaries work closely with the dentist, assisting in clinical work, as well as discharging secretarial and receptionist duties.

The trend in dental practice has moved from the repair of individual teeth, or their wholesale removal for the relief of pain, to that of conservation and the prevention of disease. Hospital dental care for larger and specialist procedures is available in the UK as part of the National Health Service. Apart from general dentistry, several special branches of the subject have developed. **Periodontics** is concerned with the prevention, diagnosis, and treatment of disorders of tissue that surround and support the teeth. The most common disorder is infection of the gums, causing *pyorrhea*, which when severe may lead to loss of teeth. It is believed that bacteria cause the deposition of plaque, a hard material that adheres to teeth and promotes gum damage. Scaling of teeth and hygiene tends to prevent these complications. **Orthodontics** is concerned with correcting the malposition of teeth, usually arising from faults in dental development; it includes repair of difficulties in chewing, dento-facial deformities, and the treatment of dental caries. The provision of artificial **prosthesis** attempts to restore oral function after the loss of teeth or of tissue; it includes the use of fixed and removable prostheses. **Oral surgery** is concerned with the repair of injury to the jaws by disease or by trauma; it includes the diagnosis and treatment of infections, tumours and cysts, and congenital defects such as cleft palate. The diagnosis of the nature of such conditions is a branch of pathology. » caries; fluoridation of water; teeth [i]

denudation The process of removing the surface of the land by the agents of weathering and erosion, ultimately to form a stable flat landscape. While tectonic processes within the Earth form fold mountains and volcanoes, surface processes continuously remove material and carry it down to the seas and oceans. » erosion

Denver 39°44N 104°59W, pop (1980) 492 365. State capital in Denver County, NC Colorado, USA; largest city in the state and a port on the S Platte R; the gold-mining settlement of Auraria was united with two other villages to form Denver, 1860; airport; railway; university (1864); processing, shipping, and distributing centre for a large agricultural area; stockyards and meat packing plants; electronic and aerospace equipment, rubber goods, luggage; tourism (several national parks in the area); major league teams, Nuggets (basketball), Broncos (football); Fornery Transport Museum, art museum, US Mint; National Stock Show (Jan). » Colorado

Deodoro da Fonseca, Manuel [dayo**doo**roo da fon**say**ka] (1827–92) Brazilian general and President (1889–91), born in Alagoas province. He served in the War of the Triple Alliance, headed the revolt that overthrew Emperor Pedro II (Nov 1889), and instituted the republic. Forced out of office in 1891, he died in Rio de Janeiro. » Brazil [i]

deontological ethics Any normative ethical theory which emphasizes principles of rightness and wrongness independent of good and bad consequences, in contrast to teleological or consequentialist theories. Thus a deontological theory might imply that slavery is unjust even if it might maximize a particular society's welfare on balance, or that one ought to keep a promise made to a dying person even though no one would benefit thereby. Deontologists typically try to ground moral judgments in such notions as natural rights, personal dignity, or (in theological versions) God's commands. » teleological ethics

deoxyribonucleic acid » DNA [i]

deoxyribose [deeoksi**riy**bohs] $C_5H_{10}O_4$. A 5-carbon sugar, particularly important for its role in the genetic material DNA. The atoms

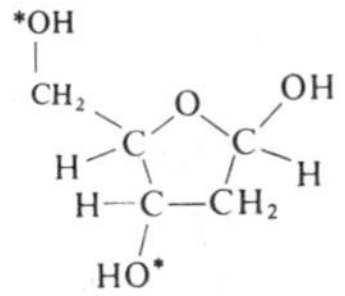

marked * in the illustration are connected to phosphate groups in DNA. » DNA [i]; ribose [i]; sugars

depaato [de**pah**toh] A Japanese department store. Tokyo's first such store, Mitsukoshi ('the Harrods of Japan'), opened in 1904, and now has 14 branches in major cities. A visit to a *depaato* by a Japanese family is more than a shopping trip, taking on the character of a day out or social occasion, especially popular at weekends. The stores present high standards of service, contain roof gardens and restaurants, and lay on cultural exhibitions and other attractions.

depersonalization A sensation in which the individual feels unreal and not in the living world. It includes feelings of part of the body changing in size or not belonging to the self, or a sense of looking at oneself from the outside. It can be a normal phenomenon, as when associated with extreme fatigue, and appears frequently as a symptom in a variety of psychiatric disorders. » mental disorders

depilatory A chemical used to remove unwanted hair on the skin, including alkalis, metallic sulphides, and mercaptans. They act by disrupting the chemical structure of the hair protein. » hair

depreciation An accountancy term measuring the loss of value of an asset due to age, wear and tear, and obsolescence. *Straight-line* depreciation assumes that the asset loses value evenly over its life, by the same amount each year. A *reducing balance* depreciation assumes a higher loss of value in early years. » accountancy; amortization

depression (economics) An economic situation where demand is slack, order-books are low, firms dispense with staff, and profits are poor or absent. The Great Depression of the early 1930s (often referred to as the *slump*) saw many bankruptcies and many millions of people out of work. A less severe form is a *recession*. » Great Depression; recession; trade cycle

depression (meteorology) A meteorological term for a low pressure system at high and mid-latitudes; also known as a **cyclone** at low latitudes. The system generally passes through a number of well-defined stages, each of which is accompanied by characteristic weather patterns, although not all depressions follow the idealized cycle. A depression is initiated when a wave develops on a *front* (a boundary between cold and warm air masses). Pressure falls at the crest of the wave. A *warm front* is the leading edge of the depression, followed by the *cold front*, with a warm sector between the two fronts. As the cold front travels faster than the warm front, it catches up, to produce an *occluded front*. When this happens, pressure rises and the depression loses velocity. Surface winds travel anticlockwise

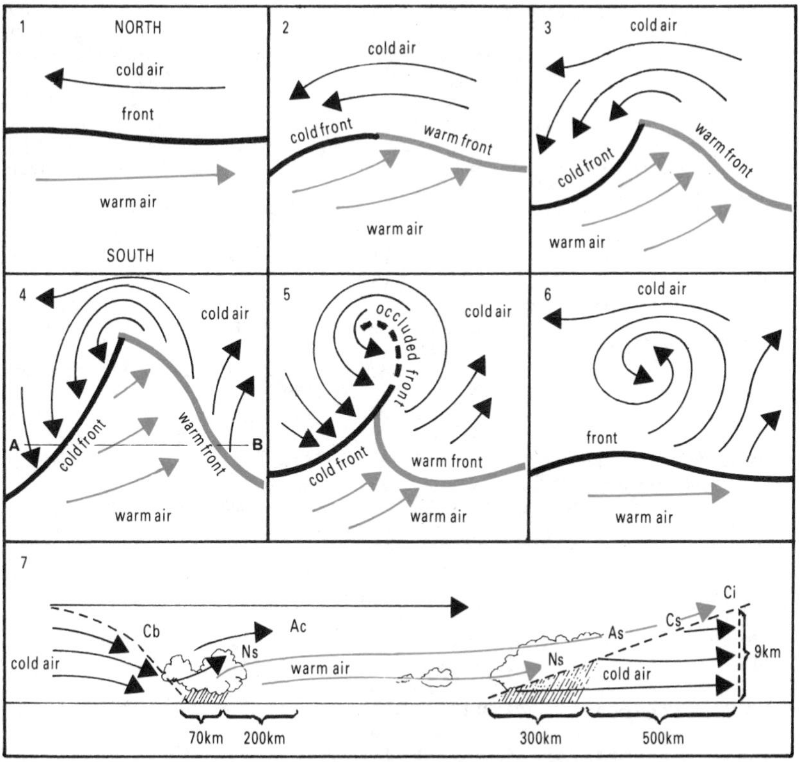

Depression – Plan view of the six idealized stages in the development and final occlusion of a depression along the polar front in the Northern Hemisphere. Stage 4 shows a well developed depression system and stage 5 shows the occlusion. The cross-section is taken along the line AB in stage 4. The cloud types are: Cb – cumulonimbus; As – altostratus; Ac – altocumulus; Cs – cirrostratus; Ns – nimbostratus; Ci – cirrus

around a depression in the N hemisphere, and clockwise in the S hemisphere. Depressions are typically 1 000–2 000 km/ 600–1 250 ml across, but are temporary features with an average lifespan of 4–7 days. They form regularly in a number of regions (eg along the Polar Front of the N Pacific and N Atlantic Oceans, and in the Mediterranean). The most intense depressions usually form in winter. Their formation is associated with Rossby waves. » anticyclone; atmospheric pressure; cold front; general circulation model; hurricane; Polar Front; Rossby waves [i]

depression (psychiatry) A mental condition or state in which there are feelings of low mood, despondence, self-criticism, and low esteem. It may be associated with a change (up or down) in appetite for sleep, food, or sex. The term has been used in a variety of ways: in lay use, it may mean little more than common sadness; in psychiatric use, it may refer to specific conditions, such as melancholia or manic-depressive illness, or be a factor in a wide range of disorders. It can be measured by a variety of rating scales, and there are certain biological markers thought to distinguish between depressed and non-depressed individuals. There is a wide variety of treatments that can be used for this condition, including behavioural and psychoanalytic forms of psychotherapy, pharmacological treatments and, in certain situations, electroconvulsive therapy. » electroconvulsive therapy; manic depressive psychosis; mental disorders; psychotherapy; seasonal affective disorder

Depression, the » **Great Depression**

depth charge A munition used by surface warships as a means of destroying submarines, typically an explosive-packed container dropped over the stern of a warship, armed by a fuse primed to detonate when it senses the water-pressure at a predetermined depth. From the middle of World War 2 the depth charge was supplanted by weapons which threw the explosive munition ahead of the anti-submarine warship. From the late 1950s, nuclear depth charges with explosive radii greater than one kilometre have been in service with nuclear-equipped navies. These require a device such as a missile or pilotless aircraft to take them a safe distance away from the launching warship. » submarine

depth psychology A group of psychological treatments which emphasize unconscious mental processes as the cause of neurotic illnesses; opposed to behavioural forms of psychology. In psychoanalytic forms of depth psychology, Freudian concepts of id, ego, and superego would be considered, whereas in analytical psychology described by Jung, the collective unconsciousness is considered paramount. » behaviour therapy; ego; Freud, Sigmund; Jung; psychoanalysis

Derain, André [duh**ri**] (1880–1954) French artist, born at Chatou. He is most famous for his Fauvist pictures (1904–8), when he was associated with Vlaminck and Matisse. Later landscape pictures show a romantic realism influenced by Cézanne. He also designed for the theatre (notably the Diaghilev ballet) and illustrated several books. He died at Garches. » Cézanne; Diaghilev: Fauvism; French art; Matisse; Vlaminck

Derby, Edward Geoffrey Smith Stanley, 14th Earl (1799–1869) British statesman and Conservative Prime Minister (1852, 1858–9, 1866–8), born at Knowsley Hall, Lancashire. Educated at Eton and Oxford, he entered parliament as a Whig in 1828, and became Chief-Secretary for Ireland (1830) and Colonial Secretary (1833), when he carried the Act for the emancipation of West Indian slaves. In 1834, he withdrew from the Party and soon after joined the Conservatives (subsequently party leader, 1846–68). In 1844 he entered the House of Lords as a baronet. He retired from the Cabinet in 1845, when Peel decided to repeal the Corn Laws, and in 1846 headed the Protectionists in the Lords. In 1851 he succeeded his father as Earl of Derby. Premier on three occasions, his third administration passed the Reform Bill (1867). He died in London. » Conservative Party; Corn Laws; slave trade; Tories; Whigs

Derby [**dah**bee] 52°55N 1°30W, pop(1987e) 215 800. City in Derbyshire, C England; on the R Derwent, 56 km/35 ml NE of Birmingham; chartered in 1637; railway; first silk mill (1719); porcelain centre in 18th-c (Derby ware); aero engines, railway engineering; lawnmowers, sugar refining, textiles, chemicals, plastics, china; Cathedral of All Saints (1525), old silk mill industrial museum. » Derbyshire; porcelain

Derby, the » **Classics**

Derby china A variety of porcelain china, which seems to have been made in Derby, England, as early as the 1750s. However, the history of the factory only becomes clear in 1770, when its owner William Duesbury (1725–86) bought the Chelsea Porcelain works, and transferred its moulds, patterns, and even some of the workmen to the North. The Derby factory specialized in fine Neoclassical figures and wares, and should not be confused with the quite separate Crown Derby Porcelain Company, established in 1877. » Chelsea porcelain; Neoclassicism (art and architecture); porcelain

Derbyshire [**dah**bisheer] pop(1987e) 918 700; area 2 631 sq km/ 1 015 sq ml. County of C England, divided into nine districts; rises to The Peak at 636 m/2 086 ft; drained by Derwent, Dove, Wye, and Trent Rivers; county town, Matlock; chief towns include Derby, Chesterfield, Glossop; sheep and dairy farming, coal, textiles, iron smelting, engineering. » Derby; England [i]; Matlock

Dere Street » **Roman roads** [i]

Dergue [derg] The regime which has ruled Ethiopia since the revolution in 1974, under the leadership of Haile Mariam Mengistu. The word means 'Committee', from the Committee of the Armed Forces which overthrew the Emperor Haile Selassie. » Ethiopia [i]; Haile Selassie; Mengistu

derivation One of the two main processes of word formation, the other being **inflection**. In derivational modifications, new words are formed which often belong to a different word class from the base form, as with *truth* (noun), *truth-ful* (adjective), *false* (adjective), *false-hood* (noun). In inflectional modifications, the word class of the form is never altered, but its grammatical status is changed (eg singular to plural, present tense to past tense), as in *girl/girls*, *talk/talked*. » conversion (linguistics); fusional language; word class

Dermaptera [der**map**tuhra] » **earwig**

dermatitis The commonest single skin disorder; also known as **eczema**. Causes include chemical and physical irritants, hypersensitivity reactions from contact with chemicals (eg detergents, watch straps), bacteria, and ingested food and drugs. The initial reaction in the skin is an increase in blood supply, which causes redness of the affected part (*erythema*). This is followed by vesicles and blisters which rupture, giving rise to the 'weeping' phase of the disorder. Repair then takes place with the overgrowth of keratin, which causes thickening of the superficial layers of the skin, and which may become chronic. » skin [i]

dermatology The scientific study of the structure and function of the skin and of its diseases. It is a specialized branch of medical practice. » dermatitis; skin [i]

Derrida, Jacques [**de**rida] (1930–) French philosopher, born in Algeria and educated in Paris, where he teaches at the Ecole Normale Supérieure. His critique of the referentiality of language and the objectivity of structures founded the school of criticism called *deconstruction*. Among his highly influential works are *De la Grammatologie* (1967, Of Grammatology), *L'écriture et la différence* (1967, Writing and Difference), and *La dissémination* (1972, Dissemination). » De Man; deconstruction; literary criticism; structuralism

Derry (county) or **Londonderry**, Gaelic **Doire** pop(1981) 186 751; area 2 067 sq km/798 sq ml. County in N Northern Ireland, divided into four districts; bounded N by Lough Foyle and the Atlantic Ocean, SE by Lough Neagh, and NW by the Republic of Ireland; hilly, with part of the Sperrin Mts rising in the S; county town, Derry; other chief towns, Coleraine, Portstewart; seed potatoes, flax, dairy produce, fishing, textiles, light engineering. » Derry (town); Northern Ireland [i]

Derry (town) or **Londonderry** (to 1984) 55°00N 7°19W, pop(1981) 62 697. County town of Derry, NW Northern Ireland; on a hill above the R Foyle, 8 km/5 ml above its mouth into Lough Foyle; monastery founded by St Columba, c.546; James I proclaimed the city to be part of the Corporation of London, 1613; renamed London-Derry, and settled by a Protestant colony; resisted a siege by James II for 105 days, 1689; railway; textiles, chemicals, engineering, ceramics; old town walls and gates, St Columba's Cathedral (Protestant, 1628–33), St Columba's Church (Catholic, 1873), Guildhall (1912). » Columba, St; Derry (county); James II (of England); Protestantism

dervish A member of the *Sufi*, mystical sects which emerged throughout the Islamic world in the 12th-c. Dervishes were known for their ecstatic prayer rituals, in which they often engaged in whirling dances. There are various orders, each with its own rule and ritual. » Sufism

DES An abbreviation of **diethylstilboestrol** or **diethylstilbestrol** – a synthetic oestrogen for the treatment of menopausal symptoms and prostate cancer. When first introduced, it was used to prevent spontaneous abortion – a use found to cause genital cancer during puberty in daughters born from these pregnancies. Paradoxically, it is now used as the 'morning-after' pill. It has also been used to promote the growth of domestic animals, but residues can remain in animals after slaughter, and their use is banned in some countries. » contraception; menopause; oestrogen; prostate gland

Des Moines [di**moyn**] 41°35N 93°37W, pop(1980) 191 003. Capital of state in Polk County, C Iowa, USA; at the junction of the Racoon and Des Moines Rivers; developed around a fort established in 1843; city and state capital, 1900; largest city in the state; airport; railway; university (1881); important industrial, commercial, and transportation centre in the heart of Iowa's Corn Belt; agricultural processing, machinery, printing and publishing; the Capitol, Des Moines Art Centre, Centre of Science and Industry. » Iowa

Desai, Morarji (Ranchhodji) [day**siy**] (1896–) Indian politician and Prime Minister (1977–9), born in Gujarat. Educated at Bombay University, he became a civil servant, entering politics in 1930. After various ministerial posts, he became a candidate for the premiership in 1964 and 1966, but was defeated by Indira Gandhi. He became Deputy Prime Minister in 1969 to lead the Opposition Congress Party. Detained during the state of emergency (1975–7), he was then appointed leader of the newly-formed Janata Party, and elected Premier. The Janata government was, however, characterized by internal strife, and he was forced to resign in 1979. » Gandhi, Indira

desalination The removal of salt from sea-water or brine to produce potable or industrially usable water, or water for ships' boilers. Distillation is the oldest process and, in revised efficient forms, still one of the most widely used. Membrane processes are useful with weak brackish water, the brine being forced under pressure against a membrane to produce a reverse osmosis, fresh water passing through to leave increasingly salt water behind. Electrodialysis and the freezing out of ice are also sometimes useful. About half of the world's desalinated water is produced in the Middle East, the rest in Africa, Asia, Australia, and the USA. » osmotic pressure

descant A melody sung or played above another well-known one, such as a hymn tune. The term (often as **discant**) is also used for a type of mediaeval polyphony, and to distinguish the highest-pitched member of a family of instruments (eg the descant recorder). » counterpoint; polyphony

Descartes, René, Lat **Renatius Cartesius** [day**kaht**] (1596–1650) French rationalist philosopher and mathematician, 'the father of modern philosophy', born at La Haye, near Tours. Trained at the Jesuit College at La Flèche, he remained a Catholic throughout his life, but soon became dissatisfied with scholasticism. While serving in the Bavarian army in 1619, he conceived it to be his task to refound human knowledge on a basis secure from scepticism. He expounded the major features of his project in his most famous work, the *Meditationes de Prima Philosophia* (1641, Meditations on First Philosophy). He began his enquiry by claiming that one can doubt all one's sense experiences, even the deliverances of reason, but that one cannot doubt one's own existence as a thinking being: *cogito ergo sum* ('I think, therefore I am'). From this basis he argued that God must exist and cannot be a deceiver; therefore, his beliefs based on ordinary sense experience are correct. He also argued that mind and body are distinct substances, believing that this dualism made possible human freedom and immortality. His *Discours de la méthode pour bien conduire sa raison, et chercher la vérité dans les sciences* (1637, Discourse on the Method for Rightly Conducting One's Reason and Searching for Truth in the Sciences) contained appendices in which he virtually founded co-ordinate or analytic geometry, and made major contributions to optics. In 1649 he moved to Stockholm to begin teaching Queen Christina of Sweden, but died of pneumonia the next year. » dualism; rationalism (philosophy); scepticism; scholasticism

descent In anthropology, the tracing of an individual's ancestry in the male line only (*patrilineally*), in the female line only (*matrilineally*), or through both males and females. Descent may be traced for various purposes, most commonly in order to regulate inheritance, or succession to office, or to define rights to the membership of groups. Some social groups may be defined by common descent. Anthropologists call such groups *lineages* or *clans*.

deschooling The notion proposed by Ivan Illich in his book *Deschooling Society* (1973) that formal schooling should be abolished. Children and adults should learn from each other outside the structure of an institutionalized education system. » education; Illich

desensitization Small repeated subcutaneous injections of the antigen believed to be responsible for allergic reactions in a hypersensitive individual. The basis of the treatment is that the antibody produced in response to the injections coats tissue cells, and blocks the access of a later dose of the offending antigen to which the individual was sensitive. » allergy

desert An arid and empty region of the Earth, characterized by little or no vegetation, and meagre and intermittent rainfall, high evaporation rates, and low humidity and cloud cover. Low-latitude deserts such as the Sahara are hot and dry, caused by high pressure air masses which prevent precipitation. Mid-latitude deserts such as the Gobi are cold and dry, and are related to mountain barriers which seal off moist maritime winds. Polar deserts of the Arctic and Antarctic are permanently covered by snow and ice. Approximately one third of the Earth's land surface is desert. » Antarctica [i]; Arctic; Gobi Desert; Sahara Desert; RR13

desert fox » **fennec fox**

desert rat » **jerboa**

Desert Rats Members of the 7th British Armoured Division, which in 1940 took as its badge the jerboa or desert rat, noted for remarkable leaps. The media applied the name generally to all British servicemen in the North Africa campaign, and it was readily adopted by those not entitled to wear the jerboa shoulder-flash. » North African Campaign; World War 2

desertification The environmental degradation of arid and semi-arid areas through overcultivation, overgrazing, deforestation, and bad irrigation practices. Changing climatic patterns are also implicated. The land loses its fertility, and is no longer able to support its population. The problem is worsened in many regions by climatic instability (particularly drought), by rapidly-growing populations, and by cash cropping, which reduces the area available for the production of food crops for the local population. In the 1970s and 1980s, desertification occurred at one time or another in most of the Sahel. » drought; Dust Bowl; nomadism; pastoralism; sahel

Desiderio da Settignano [dezi**de**ryoh da setin**yah**noh] (c.1428–61) Italian sculptor, born at Settignano, near Florence. He worked in the early Renaissance style, influenced by Donatello and Della Robbia, producing many notable portrait busts of women and children. He died in Florence. » Donatello; Florentine School; Italian art; Renaissance

design, argument from An argument, especially popular in the 18th-c and 19th-c, that the existence of complex organisms can be explained only by the existence of a supremely wise, powerful, beneficent God. The argument lost its appeal with the development of evolutionary theory. » evolution; God

designer drugs Synthetic drugs, often narcotics, which are not controlled by law in the USA; they are so called because they are specifically designed by chemists to be slightly different structurally to drugs that are controlled by law (which are 'named', and thus illegal), yet still chemically so close to them that they have similar biological effects. These 'legal' drugs are produced covertly and sold on the streets to illicit drug users. The normal dangers of drug abuse are increased by the possibility of contamination. In the early 1980s, such contamination (1-methyl-4-Phenyl-1,2,3,6-tetrahydropyridine, or *MPTP*) was found to induce permanent symptoms of Parkinson's disease in young users. » ecstasy; narcotics; Parkinson's disease

desk-top publishing The preparation of typeset output using a microcomputer with appropriate software for the line-by-line composition and editing of text, the creation of illustrations, the compilation and editing of structured pages, and the typographical articulation. The image of typeset text and illustrations can then be output on paper through a compatible dot-matrix printer, laser printer, or phototypesetter. 'Publishing' in this now familiar turn of phrase is a misnomer: 'typesetting' or 'text composition' would be more appropriate. » publishing

desman (biology) An insectivore of the mole family (2 species), native to the Pyrenees and W Asia; red-brown; long mobile snout; webbed hind feet; long tail flattened from side to side; lives in streams and pools; eats aquatic animals. » insectivore; mole (biology)

Desmond, Gerald Fitzgerald, 15th Earl of (c.1538–83) Irish Catholic nobleman, who (1579–80) rebelled against Queen Elizabeth, sacked Youghal by night, and was proclaimed a traitor. He was eventually killed in a cabin in the Kerry Mts. » Elizabeth I

Desmoulins, (Lucie Simplice) Camille (Benoist) [daymoo**li**] (1760–94) French revolutionary and journalist, born at Guise. He studied law in Paris, but owing to a stutter never practised. He nonetheless was an effective crowd orator, and played a dramatic part in the storming of the Bastille. He was also an influential pamphleteer. A member of the Cordeliers' Club from its foundation, he was elected to the National Convention, and voted for the death of the King. He actively attacked the Girondists, but by the end of 1793 argued for moderation, thus incurring the hostility of Robespierre. He was arrested and guillotined. » French Revolution [i]

Desprez, Josquin » Josquin Desprez

Dessalines, Jean Jacques [desa**li**] (c.1758–1806) Emperor of Haiti, born a slave probably at Grande Rivière du Nord, Saint Domingue (Haiti). In the slave insurrection of 1791 he was second only to Toussaint L'Ouverture. After compelling the French to leave Haiti (1803), he was created Governor and crowned Emperor as Jacques I. But his cruelty and debauchery alienated his adherents, and he was assassinated near Port-au-Prince. » Haiti [i]; Toussaint L'Ouverture

destroyer A small fast warship designed in the late 19th-c to destroy enemy torpedo boats. It has undergone much development and adopted many other roles: submarine hunting, evacuation, invasion, assault support, and convoy escort, as well as providing a battleship screen in both world wars. Modern destroyers are usually guided-missile carriers and pack immense fire power compared to their ancestors. They are more akin to World War 2 cruisers in size. » cruiser; warships [i]

detached retina » retina

detective story A story turning on the commission of a crime (usually a murder) and the discovery by a detective of the culprit. It is this element of mystery which makes it distinct from the crime novel. Although Voltaire's *Zadig* (1747) and Godwin's *Caleb Williams* (1794) contain precursive elements, the first true detective stories were Poe's *Murders in the Rue Morgue* (1841) and *The Purloined Letter* (1845), featuring the detective Dupin. These were followed by Emile Gaboriau's full-length detective novels, and then Wilkie Collins's *The Moonstone* (1866). The popularity of the genre was assured after the introduction of Sherlock Holmes by Conan Doyle (in *A Study in Scarlet*, 1887), and the next 50 years were a golden age, with authors such as Austin Freeman, A E W Mason, E C Bentley (*Trent's Last Case*, 1913), and G K Chesterton (*The Father Brown Stories*, 1929). Maurice Leblanc created a French rival to Holmes in Arsène Lupin. Between the wars, Agatha Christie (Poirot), Dorothy L Sayers (Peter Wimsey), and Georges Simenon (Maigret) wrote to the same classic formula, which still survives in such writers as Dick Francis and P D James, though more cynical crime and spy fiction is now in fashion. » Christie, Agatha; Doyle; Poe; spy story

detente An attempt to lower the tension between states as a means of reducing the possibility of war and of achieving peaceful coexistence between different social and political systems. A prominent feature of relations between the USA and USSR in the 1970s, it led to several agreements over arms (SALT) and security and cooperation (Helsinki). In the early 1980s, there was a cooling towards detente on the part of the USA, on the grounds that too many concessions had been made and that the USSR did not adhere to the spirit of such agreements; but there was a considerable improvement in relations in the later part of the decade. » Cold War; Helsinki Conference; SALT

detention centre A British institution to which male offenders aged not less than 14 and not more than 21 years of age may be sentenced. Detention periods range from 21 days to 4 months. » sentence; youth custody centre

detergent A material which lowers the surface tension of water, and makes it mix better with oils and fats. Most detergents contain molecules or ions with a combination of polar (water-seeking) and non-polar (oil-seeking) parts, which serve to bind oil and water together. » oil (earth sciences); water

determinant In mathematics, a number determined by the elements of a square matrix. For a 2×2 matrix $\begin{pmatrix} a & b \\ c & d \end{pmatrix}$, the determinant $\begin{vmatrix} a & b \\ c & d \end{vmatrix}$ is defined as $ad-bc$. If the matrix is represented by $\mathbf{A}$, the determinant of $\mathbf{A}$ is written det $\mathbf{A}$ or $|\mathbf{A}|$. The determinant of a 3×3 matrix $\begin{vmatrix} a & b & c \\ d & e & f \\ g & h & j \end{vmatrix}$

is defined as $a\begin{vmatrix} e & f \\ h & j \end{vmatrix} - b\begin{vmatrix} d & f \\ g & j \end{vmatrix} + c\begin{vmatrix} d & e \\ g & h \end{vmatrix}$

The determinant of an $n \times n$ matrix can be similarly defined in terms of determinants of $(n-1) \times (n-1)$ matrices. Alternative definitions have been developed for $n \times n$ determinants. » matrix

determinism *Causal* determinism is the thesis that every event has a cause, and that, given the laws of nature and the relevant previous history of the world, the event could not have failed to occur. Philosophers have disagreed about whether causal determinism is compatible with human freedom. *Logical* determinism is the stronger thesis, attributed to the Stoics, that the laws of logic alone necessitate every event; it is contradictory to conceive of anything having been different from what it is. *Theological* determinism, held by Calvin and others, maintains that the decrees of God necessitate everything in creation. » Calvin, John; free will; Stoicism

deterrence The concept that has developed in strategic military thinking since the 1930s, following the emergence of long-range weapons of mass destruction. It is based on the threat of effective military or economic counter-action as a means of discouraging acts of aggression. The deterrence can also be extended to protect a state's allies. **Graduated deterrence** refers to a strategy of having a range of counter-actions demonstrating a state's abilities to respond to a number of hostile actions, depending on their severity. It is argued by some that this can lead to an escalation of conflict, while others suggest that it is less likely to inflame the situation. **Mutual deterrence**, most commonly associated with the nuclear weapons of the two superpowers, is a situation in which each side is deterred from attacking the other because of the unacceptably high destruction that would result. There is considerable uncertainty about the effectiveness of deterrence in different circumstances. » arms race; credibility

detonator A sensitive explosive (eg mercuric fulminate, lead azide) used in a small quantity to initiate the function of larger quantities of principal explosive. By extension, the term is used for any device containing a detonating explosive actuated by heat, percussion, friction, or electricity. » explosives

Detroit [dee**troyt**] 42°20N 83°03W, pop (1980) 1 203 339. Seat of Wayne County, SE Michigan, USA; port on the Detroit R, W of L St Clair; sixth largest city in the USA; founded by the French as a fur-trading outpost, 1701; became the trading and political centre for the Great Lakes region; surrendered to the British during the Seven Years War, 1760; handed over to the USA, 1796; much of the city rebuilt after a fire in 1805; capital of state, 1837–47; airport; railway; two universities (1877, 1933); the nation's leading manufacturer of cars and trucks (one-third of the country's cars assembled in and around the city); aeroplanes, machinery, metal products, chemicals, food products, printing and publishing; in the early 1980s recession caused high unemployment and a fall in population; major league teams, Tigers (baseball), Pistons (basketball), Red Wings (ice hockey), Lions (football); Science Centre, Historical Museum, Institute of Arts, Motown Museum, Belle Isle; Freedom Festival (Jul). » Michigan

Deucalion [dyoo**kay**liuhn] In Greek mythology, a son of Prometheus. When Zeus flooded the world, Deucalion and his wife Pyrrha built an 'ark' which grounded on the top of Parnassus. As the only survivors, they asked how the human race was to be restored; an oracle told them 'to throw their mother's bones over their shoulders'. They correctly interpreted this oracle, and threw stones which turned into human beings. » Zeus

deus ex machina [**day**us eks **ma**kina] (Lat 'god from the machine') A device used mainly by classical dramatists to resolve by supernatural intervention all the problems which have arisen during the course of a play. The returning Duke may be said to function as a *deus ex machina* in the last scene of Shakespeare's *Measure for Measure*. » Latin literature; Plautus; Shakespeare; Terence

deuterium A heavy isotope of hydrogen, in which the nucleus comprises a proton and a neutron rather than a proton alone (as for common hydrogen); symbol D or ^{2}H. It forms 0.015% of naturally occurring hydrogen. Water made with deuterium is called *heavy water*, with a density of 1.1 g cm^{-3}, and is used in some nuclear reactors. Deuterium is also important in nuclear fusion. » heavy water; hydrogen; isotopes; nuclear fusion; tritium

Deuteronomistic History The theory that the Biblical narratives from Deuteronomy to 2 Kings were essentially the work of a historian or historians in the mid 6th-c BC, though scholars differ about the date and the nature of the activity, with some accepting only a Deuteronomistic 'revision' of earlier narratives during the exilic period. It portrayed Israel's fate in terms of her leaders' compliance or disregard for Israel's Law and the true prophets. » Deuteronomy/Joshua/Judges/Kings/Samuel, Book of; Old Testament

Deuteronomy, Book of The fifth and last book of the Pentateuch, in the Hebrew Bible/Old Testament. Its title means 'a repetition of the law' (from the Septuagint's mistaken rendering into Greek of *Deut* 17.18, where the Hebrew means 'a copy of the law'). It was traditionally attributed to Moses, but many date it much later, c.7th-c BC. It surveys Israel's wilderness experiences, and presents an extensive code of religious laws and duties. » Deuteronomistic History; Old Testament; Pentateuch; Septuagint

devaluation A fall in the rate of exchange from one currency to another. For example, if £1 = $2 and the pound falls to $1.80, then the pound 'falls against' the dollar; it has been devalued. Until the early 1970s, currencies had fixed exchange rates, and devaluations were resisted. Nowadays currencies 'float', and market forces alter exchange rates continually. The EEC is moving towards a unified currency system where all currencies move within a specified range. Devaluation makes a country's exports cheaper and its imports dearer, thus helping its currency reserves. » currency; European Economic Community; European Monetary System

Devanagari [duhvana**gah**ri] A range of alphabets used for Indian languages, consisting of a set of consonantal letter-symbols. Vowels are represented by a system of diacritics which can occur above, below, preceding, and following the consonant-letters. » alphabet [i]

developing countries A label which includes most of the countries of Africa, Asia, and Latin America. Many are predominantly agricultural economies, though Brazil, India, and Pakistan have a well-developed industrial base, and others have rich mineral wealth. They are characterized by very low income per capita (by Western standards), and therefore low savings. Development has often been held back by rapid population growth, crop failure, drought, war, and insufficient demand (at a reasonable price) for their commodities, crops, and goods. In addition to many bilateral aid agreements, there are the aid programmes of the international agencies, such as the United Nations, Commonwealth Development Corporation, Alliance for Progress, and USAid. There are also many privately-funded charities with aid programmes. Western banks have lent large sums to the developing nations, and overdue debt servicing has proved to be a problem. » Alliance for Progress; Christian Aid; debt; development economics; Three Worlds theory

development The photographic process by which the latent image formed by exposure to light is made visible. It generally involves reducing the exposed silver compounds in the sensitive material to black metallic silver. In colour photography, couplers may be used to form a coloured dye image at the same time. » photography; processing

development economics Economic theories concerned with solving the problems of relatively underdeveloped nations; in particular, how to reach a level of national income where savings and investment can occur. » developing countries; national accounts

developmental psychology A branch of psychology which examines the biological, social, and intellectual development of people from before birth throughout the life-course. Most attention has been paid to young children, in whom shifts in understanding appear more obvious. While some psychologists study individual patterns of development, most focus upon the *developmental function* – the changes which are common to all people at various 'stages' of life. » attachment; educational psychology; Piagetian psychology; psychology

deviance Any behaviour which is regarded as contrary to 'normal' or expected standards of social behaviour, which may or may not be contrary to the law. Within criminology, **deviance theory** claims that what is deviant is 'in the eye of the beholder' because no act is in itself inherently or obviously criminal. Behaviour is judged according to the context in which it occurs; the same action regarded as deviant in one situation may be acceptable in another. Conceptions of deviance therefore vary from one culture to another. » labelling theory; sociology

deviationism A tendency within communist parties to move away or deviate from the official party position. It can be a move to either the left or the right (*adventurism*). Deviation is regarded as a political offence because it undermines the principle of democratic centralism, and it can therefore occur even in cases where those so charged hold to an orthodox Marxist position. It is often used as a term of abuse and denunciation. » communism

Devil When referring to a specific character, the chief of the evil spirits or fallen angels; also known as **Satan**. It is a rare term in the Hebrew Scriptures (where *Satan* is more common), but more frequent in the New Testament, where the Devil is sometimes represented as a serpent (*Rev* 12.9) or as a tempter (*Matt* 4.1), and in later Christian literature. » angels; Beelzebub; Bible; Gog and Magog; hell

devil ray Any of the giant rays widespread in surface waters of tropical and warm temperate seas; pectoral fins forming large triangular wings; body width up to 6 m/20 ft; sides of head prolonged as fleshy 'horns'; tail whip-like; young are born live; feed on plankton and small fishes. (Genera: *Mobula, Manta*. Family: *Mobulidae*.) » manta ray; ray

devil's coach horse A large, black rove beetle; body slender, 20–30 mm/¾–1¼ in long; wing cases short, hindwings present; produces acrid-smelling chemical when threatened; commonly found in woods; predaceous on insects, snails, and worms. (Order: *Coleoptera*. Family: *Staphylinidae*.) » rove beetle

Devil's Island » Salut, Iles du

Devil's Tower The first US national monument, in NE Wyoming, USA; a natural tower of volcanic rock with a flat top, 263 m/863 ft high; used as the setting for the film *Close Encounters of the Third Kind.* » Wyoming

Devine, George (Alexander Cassidy) (1910–65) British actor and theatre director, born at Hendon, Greater London. With Michel Saint-Denis and others he founded the London Theatre Studio (1936–9) in an attempt to reform British theatre training. After the War, he continued this work at the Old Vic Centre (1947–52), and directed the Young Vic touring company. In 1956 he became artistic director of the newly formed English Stage Company at the Royal Court Theatre, and for the rest of his career was instrumental in the development and success of this 'writer's theatre'. He died in London. » English Stage Company; theatre

devise » **property**

Devlin, Bernadette » **McAliskey, Bernadette**

devolution The delegation of authority from a country's legislature or government to a subordinate elected institution on a more limited geographical basis. Devolution is distinguished from federalism, where the powers of the central government and the federal bodies are set out in the constitution. Under devolution, the subordinate body receives its power from the government, which retains some right of oversight. The idea is to provide for more self-government and to bring decision-making closer to the people, but such democratic arguments are countered by the view that allowing for differences in decisions within the state poses a threat to the state's unity. » federalism; home rule

Devolution, War of (1667–8) A conflict prompted by Louis XIV of France in pursuit of his wife's legal claims to the Spanish Netherlands. According to the laws of devolution of the provinces of Brabant and Hainault, females of a first marriage took precedence over males of a second with regard to property inheritance. To uphold the claims of Queen Maria Theresa, the elder daughter of Philip IV of Spain, Louis' armies overran Flanders, prompting the Dutch, England, and Sweden to negotiate the Triple Alliance (1668); to this France responded with the invasion of Franche-Comté. The war ended with a secret treaty of compromise between Louis and the Emperor Leopold (1668). » Leopold I (Emperor); Louis XIV

Devon pop (1987e) 1 010 000; area 6 711 sq km/2 590 sq ml. County of SW England, divided into ten districts; bounded NW by the Bristol Channel and Atlantic and S by the English Channel; rises to Dartmoor in SW and Exmoor in NE; drained by the Exe, Dart, Torridge, and Tow Rivers; county town, Exeter; chief towns include Plymouth, Torquay, Barnstaple; tourism, especially on coast; livestock, dairy products (notable for clotted cream), cider; naval base at Plymouth. » Dartmoor; England [i]; Exeter; Exmoor

Devonian period A geological period of the Pleistocene epoch extending from 408 million to 360 million years ago. It contains the oldest widespread continental deposits in Europe (Old Red Sandstone) as well as extensive marine sediments containing fossils of armoured fish, corals, ammonites, and molluscs. » geological time scale; Pleistocene epoch; RR16

dew The deposit of moisture on vegetation and ground surfaces. It occurs at night when terrestrial radiation cools the Earth's surface, and the layer of air closest to the ground, to below the dew point temperature, resulting in condensation. » condensation (physics); dew point temperature; precipitation

dew point temperature The temperature at which a parcel of air would become saturated with water vapour if it were cooled without a change in pressure of moisture content. When moist air is cooled to below this temperature, condensation in the form of dew or hoar frost occurs. » condensation (physics); dew; humidity

Dewar, Sir James (1842–1923) British chemist and physicist, born at Kincardine, Fife, Scotland. He studied chemistry at Edinburgh, and in 1875 became professor at Cambridge. Two years later he also became professor at the Royal Institution, London, where he lived, lectured, and pursued a wide range of experimental research; he visited Cambridge rarely. In the 1870s he invented the **Dewar flask** (or *thermos flask*), using it in his studies of low temperatures and gas liquefaction. With Abel he invented cordite, for long the British standard military propellent. He died in London. » cryogenics; Dewar flask [i]

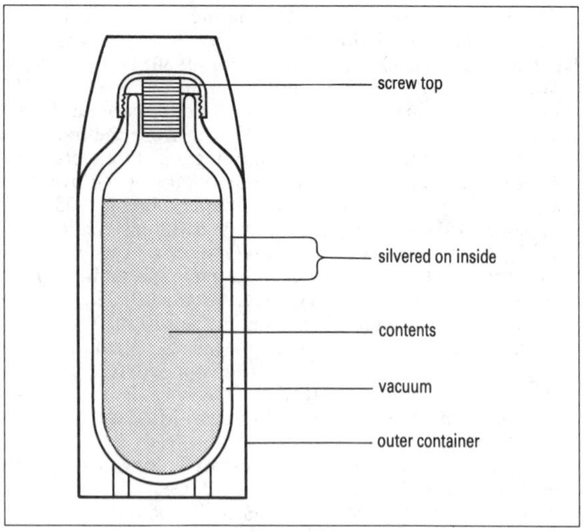

Dewar flask

Dewar flask An insulated vessel with double walls, the inner space being made into a vacuum and silvered; heat losses by convection and radiation are thus reduced to a minimum. It was devised by British chemist James Dewar to hold gases liquefied at very low temperatures. First used for liquefied gases in 1892, it later developed for industrial and domestic use for maintaining liquids at constant high or low temperatures. Everyday names include **vacuum flask** and the trade name **Thermos flask**. » Dewar; insulation; vacuum

Dewey, John (1859–1952) US philosopher and educator, born at Burlington, Vermont. He studied at Vermont and Johns Hopkins universities, taught at Michigan (1884) and Chicago (1894), finally becoming professor of philosophy at Columbia University (New York) in 1904. He was a leading exponent of pragmatism. Dewey's philosophy of education, which stressed development of the person, understanding of the environment, and learning through experience, was extremely influential. His writings include (on philosophy) *The Quest for Certainty* (1929), and (on education) *The Child and the Curriculum* (1902). He died in New York City. » education; pragmatism

Dewey decimal system A library classification system in widespread international use, devised in 1873 by US librarian Melvil Dewey (1851–1931). It recognizes ten main classes of subject-matter, each class containing 100 numbers, with decimal sub-divisions for unlimited supplementary classes. For example, class 600 is Applied Sciences, Medicine, Technology; 612 is Physiology, Human and Comparative, and 612.1 is Blood and Circulation. The system is regularly revised. » library science; RR95

dextrin A complex sugar, a mixture of glucose polymers, obtained from starch which has been broken down enzymatically or by gentle heat. Dextrins are used as thickening agents in foods, as well as adhesives and glazes in paper and textiles. However, their main use is to improve the palatability of starchy foods, and to reduce the osmotic load on the stomach in convalescent drinks. » enzyme; glucose [i]; osmotic pressure; polymerization

dextrorotatory » **optical activity**

dextrose » **glucose** [i]

Dezhnev, Cape [**dyezh**nif] 66°08N 169°40W. Northeasternmost point of Asia, NE Siberian Russia; at E end of the Chukchi Peninsula, projecting into the Bering Sea; named after the Russian navigator who discovered it in 1648. » Asia; Russia

Dhaka, former spelling **Dacca** 23°42N 90°22E, pop (1981)

3 458 602. Capital city of Bangladesh, in Dhaka region, W of the R Meghna, on a channel of the R Dhaleswari; former French, Dutch, and English trading post; capital of Mughal province of East Bengal (1608–1704); capital of British province of East Bengal and Assam (1905–12); small university town before 1947; major expansion since becoming capital of East Pakistan (1947), with large-scale immigration and growth of industry; centre of the world's greatest jute-growing region; university of Dhaka (1921), Bangladesh University of Engineering and Technology (1961); airport; railway; trade in jute, rice, oilseed, sugar, tea; textiles, chemicals, matches, soap, glass, shoes, printing, engineering, boatbuilding; Suhrawardy Uddyan (city park), Central Shahid Minar monument; known as the 'city of mosques' (over 1 000); Sadarghat market; Langalband 12 km/7 ml SE, a sacred Hindu site. » Bangladesh [i]

dharma [**dah**ma] In Hinduism, a Sanskrit word with various levels of meaning. Basically, it is the universal law that applies to the universe, human society, and the individual. As the moral law, it is both a general code of ethics applicable to all, and a moral law specific to an individual's station in life. » Buddha; Buddhism; Hinduism

dhole [dohl] A member of the dog family, native to S and SE Asia; red-brown, with white underneath; black tip to tail; inhabits woodland or open country; hunts large mammals in packs; runs prey to exhaustion; also known as **Asiatic wild dog** or **Indian wild dog**. (*Cuon alpinus*.) » Canidae

diabetes insipidus [diya**bee**teez in**sip**idus] An uncommon disorder in which a large volume of dilute urine is produced daily, independently of the volume of fluid ingested. It is caused by the absence or inadequate production of the anti-diuretic hormone by the hypothalamus, or by conditions (eg potassium depletion), which reduce the sensitivity of the kidneys to its action. » hypothalamus; urine

diabetes mellitus [diya**bee**teez **mel**itus] A common metabolic disorder in which there is failure of the pancreas to produce insulin in amounts needed to control sugar metabolism. As a result, the blood sugar rises above normal values and spills over into the urine, causing large volumes to be produced (*polyuria*). In some cases the lack of insulin is primary, and results from auto-immune damage to the pancreatic islets. In others, reduced tissue responsiveness, and glucagon, adrenocortical hormones, and some pituitary hormones oppose the action of insulin, and the ensuing diabetes is a secondary consequence. » hormones; insulin; pancreas

diablotin [diya**bl**uhtin] » **oilbird**

diachrony The historical dimension of language development, studying the structural changes in sounds, grammar, and meaning that occur in languages over periods of time. It contrasts with **synchrony**, the study of a language as it is at a given time, without reference to its historical development. This distinction, introduced by Saussure, formed one of the most important conceptual developments in 20th-c linguistics. » linguistics; Saussure

diagenesis The physical and chemical processes whereby an unconsolidated sediment is changed to a solid rock. It includes compaction and partial dewatering, followed by cementation and low temperature re-equilibration to a more stable chemical and textural state. It excludes metamorphism.

Diaghilev, Sergei (Pavlovich) [dee**ag**ilef] (1872–1929) Russian ballet impresario, born at Novgorod. He obtained a law degree, but was preoccupied with the arts. In 1898 he became editor of *Mir Iskousstva* (World of Art) and during the next few years arranged exhibitions and concerts of Russian art and music. His permanent company was founded in 1911, and remained perilously in existence for 20 years, triumphantly touring Europe. All the great dancers, composers, and painters of his period contributed to the success of his Ballets Russes. He also encouraged several major choreographers (eg Fokine, Nijinsky, Balanchine), and gave them opportunities for artistic collaboration. He died in Venice. » Balanchine; ballet; Ballets Russes; Fokine; Massine; Nijinska; Nijinsky

dialect » **dialectology**

dialectic The study of the logic involved in conversational argument, emphasizing the techniques involved in putting forth hypotheses, counter-hypotheses, criticisms, refutations, and modifications of one's original views. As used by Hegel and Marx, dialectic is an analogous process that occurs in nature. » dialectical materialism; logic; Marxism

dialectical materialism A central doctrine of Marxism. Its claims are that quantitative changes in matter yield qualitative changes (for example, the emergence of mind); that nature is a unity of contradictory opposites; and that the result of one opposite (thesis) clashing with another (antithesis) is a synthesis that preserves and transcends the opposites. » dialectic; Marxism

dialectical psychology Psychological theory and/or research informed by Hegelian or Marxist notions of tension, co-action, and change. It was promoted principally by Soviet psychologists, following Vygotsky, and places particular emphasis on the influence exerted by social processes on the individual's development. » Hegel; Marxism; Vygotsky

dialectology The study of varieties of a language (*dialects*) which are regionally or socially distinctive. They are marked by having distinctive words, grammatical structures, and pronunciations. Dialects are studied by wide-ranging questionnaires which gather information about the same linguistic features over the whole geographical area of a language. The result is a *dialect atlas*, which shows dialect areas and boundaries. Dialects which are socially distinctive identify social groups within a community, with reference to such factors as age, sex, occupation, and ethnic background. » accent 1

dialysis A process of separating dissolved substances (solutes) of different molecular weights by using the differences in their rates of diffusion across thin layers of certain materials (eg cellulose, peritoneal membranes). Artificial kidney machines (dialysers) perform **haemodialysis**, whereby waste products (such as urea or excess salts) are removed from the patient's blood, while blood cells and protein are retained. The system can also be used to provide the patient with nutrients (eg glucose). It causes anaemia, but this can be treated with erythropoietin. » erythropoietin; kidney failure; kidneys

diamagnetism A magnetic effect, measurable in many materials (eg water, copper), in which individual atomic magnetic moments induced within the material align in opposition to an applied magnetic field. The material is repelled by the source of the magnetic field. The effect is characterized by negative magnetic susceptibility. » magnetic moment; magnetism; permeability

diaminoethanetetra-acetic acid » **EDTA**

diamond A naturally occurring form of crystalline carbon formed at high pressures and temperatures deep in the Earth's crust; the hardest natural substance known. It is the most precious of gemstones; major mines are near Kimberley, South Africa. Poor quality or *black diamonds* are used for industrial purposes. » carbon; Cullinan diamond; gemstones; Koh-i-noor

diamondback N American rattlesnake with bold diamond-shaped markings along back; also known as **diamondback rattlesnake**; two species: the **Eastern diamondback rattlesnake** (*Crotalus adamanteus*), the most venomous snake in N America (bite can kill in one hour); and the **Western diamondback rattlesnake** (*Crotalus atrox*). » rattlesnake

diamondbird A small woodland bird native to Australia, also known as **pardalote**; short tail and bill; eats insects; nests in holes. Some migrate within Australia, moving N for the winter. They are placed in the **flowerpecker** family, but their affinity is uncertain. (Genus: *Pardalotus*, 5 or 8 species, experts disagree. Family: *Dicaeidae*.) » flowerpecker

diamorphine » **heroin**

Diana [diy**a**na] Roman goddess, associated with the Moon, virginity, and hunting. She was considered to be equivalent to the Greek Artemis, whose cult was primarily at Ephesus; hence the cult of 'Diana of the Ephesians', who was a fertility-goddess. » Artemis

diaphragm (anatomy) A sheet of muscle and tendons separating the thoracic and abdominal cavities. The convex thoracic surface is lined by the *pleura*; the abdominal surface by the *peritoneum*. There are major openings for the passage of structures between the two cavities. The diaphragm is the principle muscle of respiration, and is also an important muscle used in expulsive acts: coughing, vomiting, micturition, defaecation, and childbirth. » abdomen; defaecation; hernia; micturition; peritoneum; respiration; thorax

diaphragm (photography) A circular opening, generally adjustable in diameter, controlling the amount of light passing through a lens into an optical system, such as a camera. » camera

diarrhoea/diarrhea The frequent passage of semi-formed or liquid motions. Acute diarrhoea usually results from inflammation of the bowel, chemical irritants in food, or infection by micro-organisms (eg dysentery). Chronic or recurring diarrhoea occurs in several chronic diseases of the small or large intestine (eg colitis). Important consequences are loss of body water, salt, and nutrients. » dysentery

Diaspora [diy**as**puhra] (Gr 'scattering', Heb *golah* or *galut* 'exile') The Jews scattered in the world outside the land of Israel, from either voluntary or compulsory resettlements, such as the Assyrian and Babylonian deportations in the 8th-c and 6th-c BC, or later dispersions in the Graeco-Roman period; also known as the **Dispersion**. The Babylonian Talmud and the Septuagint were important literary products of those Jews that had settled 'abroad'. » Judaism; Talmud

diastole [diy**as**tuhlee] The interval between successive contractions of the heart. During this period, the heart chambers fill with blood flowing from the veins into the atria, and continuing into the ventricles. » heart [i]; systole

diastrophism The deformation of large masses of the Earth's crust to form mountain ranges, ocean basins, and continents. » orogeny; plate tectonics [i]

diathermy The application of heat to muscles or joints for the relief of pain. The heat is produced by means of high frequency electric current, or by high-frequency electromagnetic short-wave radiation.

diatom [**diy**atuhm] A microscopic, single-celled green alga common in marine and freshwater habitats; possesses an often ornate, external shell (*frustule*) containing silica, and consisting of two separate valves; commonly reproduces by splitting in two (binary fission); green colour derived from chlorophyll pigments. (Class: *Bacillarophyceae*.) » chlorophyll; green algae; shell; silica

diatonicism An attribute of a piece or section of music built, exclusively or predominantly, from notes belonging to a particular major or minor scale (*diatonic* notes). For example, the note F♯ is diatonic in the key (scale) of D major, but chromatic in the key of C major. » chromaticism; scale; tonality

Diaz or **Dias, Bartolomeu** (c.1450–1500) Portuguese navigator and explorer. In 1487 King John II gave him two vessels to follow up the discoveries already made on the W coast of Africa. Driven by a violent storm, he sailed round the Cape of Good Hope, and discovered Algoa Bay. The discontent of his crew compelled him to return (1488). He also travelled with Vasco da Gama in 1497, and with Cabral in 1500, during whose expedition he was lost in a storm. » Cabral, Pedro Alvarez; Gama, Vasco da

Díaz, (José de la Cruz) Porfirio (1830–1915) President of Mexico (1876–80, 1884–1911), born at Oaxaca. He fought against the French occupation of Mexico (1862–7). Defeated in the presidential election of 1875, he seized power, and served as President for 30 years, until the revolution of Francisco Madero (1873–1913) forced him to resign (1911) and flee into exile. He died in Paris. His regime did much to stimulate material progress in Mexico. » Mexico [i]

diazepam » **benzodiazepines**

diazo process » **photocopying**

Dibdin, Charles (1745–1814) British composer, author, and theatre manager, born in Southampton. He early attracted notice by his singing, and began a stage career in 1762. In 1789 he started his popular series of one-man musical entertainments. He wrote over 1000 songs (such as 'Poor Jack' and 'Tom Bowling') and many stage works, musical pieces, and novels. He died in London.

dice A six-sided cube, each side generally numbered between 1 and 6, with opposing faces totalling 7. It is used in games of chance and in many children's games, such as snakes-and-ladders. Other forms of dice include **poker dice**, which contain the pictures of the six highest value cards (9 to Ace); poker hands have to be formed as a result of a random throw. A popular form of dice as a casino game is craps. » casino; craps; poker

dichotic listening An experimental technique used in psychology and psycholinguistics to determine which side of the brain is dominant in its ability to process particular kinds of sound. It can be tested by feeding different stimuli into both ears at the same time, and identifying the brain's involvement by the accuracy with which the input to the ear is reported by the subject. Generally, people have a right-ear advantage for linguistic signals, and a left-ear one for others, such as music. » psycholinguistics

Dickens, Charles (John Huffam) (1812–70) British novelist, born at Landport, near Portsmouth, the son of a clerk in the navy pay office. In 1814 he moved to London, then to Chatham, where he received some schooling. He found a menial post with a solicitor, then took up journalism, becoming a reporter at Doctors' Commons, and at 22 joining a London newspaper. He published various papers in the *Monthly Magazine*, following this up with sketches and papers for the *Evening Chronicle*. In 1836 his *Sketches by Boz* and *Pickwick Papers* were published; and that year he married Catherine, the daughter of his friend George Hogarth. They had 10 children, but were separated in 1858. Dickens worked relentlessly, producing several successful novels, which first appeared in monthly instalments, notably *Oliver Twist* (1837–9), *Nicholas Nickleby* (1838–9) and *The Old Curiosity Shop* (1840–1). Thereafter a great part of his life was spent abroad. His later novels include *David Copperfield* (1849–50), *Bleak House* (1852–3), *A Tale of Two Cities* (1859), *Great Expectations* (1860–1), and the unfinished *The Mystery of Edwin Drood* (1870). In addition, he gave talks and readings, and wrote many pamphlets, plays, and letters. He died at Gadshill, Kent. » English literature; novel

Dickey, James (1926–) US poet and novelist, born in Atlanta, Georgia. Early volumes *Into the Stone* (1960), *Drowning With Others* (1962), and *Helmets* (1964) contain brightly-coloured poems concerned with outdoor life and vigorous physical activity. The aggressively-entitled *The Eye-Beaters, Blood, Victory, Madness, Buckhead, and Mercy* (1970) deals with more extreme situations, as does his novel *Deliverance* (1970). » American literature; novel; poetry

Dickinson, Emily (Elizabeth) (1830–86) US poet, born at Amherst, Massachusetts. At the age of 23 she withdrew from all social contacts, and lived a secluded life at Amherst, writing in secret over 1000 poems. Hardly any of her work was published until after her death, when her sister Lavinia brought out three volumes (1891–6). Her writing, intensely personal and often spiritual, shows great originality both in thought and in form, and has had considerable influence on modern poetry. » American literature; poetry

dicotyledons [diykoti**lee**dnz] One of the two major divisions of the flowering plants, often referred to simply as **dicots**; contrasted with *monocotyledons*. The seed embryo has two cotyledons, and the primary root of the seedling persists, forming a taproot. Dicots usually have broad leaves with reticulate veination and floral parts in fours, fives, or multiples thereof. The vascular bundles form a ring within the stem, and a cambium layer is present, capable of producing secondary vascular tissue and thus woody stems. About 250 different families of dicots are currently recognized. (Subclass: *Dicotyledonae*.) » cambium; cotyledons; flowering plants; monocotyledons; seed; vascular tissue

Dictation Test A method used by Australian governments (1902–58) to exclude certain classes of intending immigrants. Based on the example of Natal (1897), immigrants received a test in a European language, usually one with which they were unfamiliar. Non-Europeans were the main target, but it was also used with those considered politically undesirable; the most celebrated case was the anti-fascist, Egon Kisch

(1885–1948), who was tested in Gaelic (1934). ≫ White Australia Policy

dictator In strict terms, a single ruler who is not elected but enjoys authority by virtue of some personal characteristic, ie an autocrat. In practice, a dictatorship often refers to rule by several people, who are nonetheless unelected and authoritarian in character, such as a military dictatorship. Personal dictatorships are now very rare. Not all involve arbitrary rule or despotism, and some dictators take account of popular wishes ('benevolent dictatorships').

dictionary A work of reference, traditionally in the form of a book, and now often available as a computational data base, giving linguistic information about the words of a language, arranged in alphabetical order under headwords (or *catchwords*). Dictionaries may be *bilingual* or *multilingual*, giving only lists of word correspondences between the languages, or they may provide information about the senses, pronunciation, and grammatical status of the headwords, and illustrate the idiomatic usages into which they can enter. *Monolingual* dictionaries generally present these facts in varying degrees of detail (depending on the size of the dictionary), expanding on the range of meanings and uses of a word. Some dictionaries (especially those falling within the US and European – particularly French and German – traditions) add encyclopedic data, in the form of pictures, tables, and facts about people and places, or provide special features, such as notes on usage or closely-related words (*synonym essays*). *Etymological* dictionaries give information on the historical derivation of the headwords, and on the changes in meaning which they have undergone over time. The process of compiling dictionaries, and the study of the issues involved, is known as **lexicography**. ≫ bilingualism; Johnson, Samuel; semantics; Webster, Noah

Dicynodon [diy**siy**nuhduhn] A plant-eating fossil reptile known from the late Permian period; skull mammal-like, with single opening behind orbit for insertion of jaw muscles; jaws with horny plates for cutting and crushing vegetation; upper canine tusks prominent. (Order: *Therapsida*.) ≫ fossil; reptile; Therapsida

Didache [**did**akhay] (Gr 'teaching') The short title for 'The Teaching of the Lord through the Twelve Apostles', dated near the beginning of the 2nd-c AD. It consists of a short manual of Christian moral teaching and church order, overlapping somewhat with the canonical Gospels, but also important for its description of early Christian ministry and sacramental practices. ≫ apostle; Christianity; Gospels, canonical

Diderot, Denis [**dee**deroh] (1713–84) French writer and philosopher, born at Langres, the chief editor of the *Encyclopédie*, a major work of the age of the Enlightenment. Trained by the Jesuits, he became a tutor and bookseller's hack (1733–44), before beginning as a writer. Always controversial, his *Pensées philosophiques* (1746, Philosophical Thoughts) was burned by the Parliament of Paris for its anti-Christian ideas, and he was imprisoned for his *Lettre sur les aveugles* (1749, Essay on Blindness). For 20 years he worked tirelessly as editor of an expanded version of Chambers's *Cyclopaedia* (1751–76). A prolific and versatile writer, he published novels, plays, satires, essays, and letters. He died in Paris. ≫ Chambers, Ephraim; Enlightenment; French literature

didgeridoo, didjeridoo or **didjeridu** A primitive trumpet of the Australian aborigines, made from a hollow eucalyptus branch about 120–150 cm/4–5 ft long. It is used, with a wide variety of playing techniques, to accompany singing and dancing. ≫ Aborigines; aerophone

Dido [**diy**doh] In the *Aeneid*, the daughter of the King of Tyre, who founded Carthage. Aeneas was diverted to Africa by storms, and told her his story. They fell in love, but when Aeneas deserted her she committed suicide by throwing herself upon a pyre. ≫ Aeneas

Diefenbaker, John G(eorge) [**dee**fuhnbayker] (1895–1979) Canadian Conservative statesman and Prime Minister (1957–63), born at Neustadt, Ontario. Educated at Saskatoon, Saskatchewan, he was called to the Bar in 1919. In 1940 he entered the Canadian Federal House of Commons, becoming leader of the Progressive Conservatives (1956) and Prime Minister (1957) after 22 years of Liberal rule. His government introduced important agricultural reforms, and extended the federal franchise to Canada's Amerindian peoples. He remained active in national politics until his death in Ottawa.

dieffenbachia ≫ **dumb cane**

dielectric A non-conducting material whose molecules align or polarize under the influence of applied electric fields. The degree is indicated by the *dielectric constant*: the ratio of a charge stored by a capacitor with dielectric material between the plates to that stored by a capacitor having a vacuum between the plates. Dielectrics are an essential constituent of capacitors. ≫ capacitance; electric dipole moment; permittivity

dielectric constant ≫ **permittivity**

Diemen, Antony Van ≫ **Tasman, Abel Janszoon**

diencephalon [diyin**se**falon] The part of the forebrain which lies deep within the cerebral hemispheres, consisting of several component parts (the thalamus, metathalamus, epithalamus, and hypothalamus). The *thalamus* is the largest part, whose diverse functions include various motor, sensory, and emotional responses. Each *metathalamus* consists of two major parts concerned with certain auditory and visual processes. The *epithalamus* is a strip of tissue connecting the two thalami; projecting from it is the pineal gland. ≫ brain [i]; hypothalamus; pineal gland

Dieppe [dee-**ep**] 49°55N 1°05E, pop (1982) 26 000. Seaport in Seine-Maritime department, NW France; below high chalk cliffs on the R Arques, where it meets the English Channel, N of Rouen; scene of heavy fighting in World War 2; ferry links with Newhaven.

Diesel, Rudolph (Christian Carl) [**dee**zl] (1858–1913) German engineer, born in Paris. He studied at the Munich Polytechnic, then, subsidized by Krupps, constructed a 'rational heat motor', demonstrating the first compression-ignition engine in 1897. He spent most of his life at his factory at Augsburg. He was drowned while crossing the English Channel. ≫ diesel engine; engine

diesel engine An internal combustion engine, working upon the diesel cycle, which ignites its fuel/air mixture by heating it to combustion point through compression. Because of this, the diesel engine is classed as a *compression ignition engine*. ≫ Carnot cycle; Diesel; engine

diet The combination of foods which provide the necessary nutrients for the body. Diets may be rated in quality depending on the balance of nutrients consumed, and not primarily on the type of food eaten. Often a 'diet' is used to imply a restriction of calories for slimming: strictly speaking this is a 'low-calorie' diet, just as there are low-fat diets, low-salt diets, or high-fibre diets. ≫ dietetics; macrobiotics; nutrients

Diet, Imperial The *Reichstag* or assembly of the Holy Roman Empire, mediaeval in origin, representing the separate estates of electors, princes, and free cities, and consisting of three bodies (curias), summoned at the will of the Emperor. Although its powers and procedures had expanded considerably by the late 15th-c, its authority was undermined by the religious divisions of the Reformation and the separate ambitions of the German princes after Westphalia (1648). Failing to develop as a supreme legislature, it became increasingly little more than a permanent congress of ambassadors during the last century and a half of its existence (1663–1806). ≫ Holy Roman Empire; Reformation

dietetics The clinical management of a patient through dietary intervention, as practised professionally by **dietitians**. The two diseases most commonly treated by dietitians are obesity and diabetes. ≫ diabetes mellitus; diet; obesity

diethylstilboestrol ≫ **DES**

Dietrich, Marlene, originally **Maria Magdalene von Losch** [**dee**trikh] (1904–) German film actress, born in Berlin. She became famous in a German film *Der blaue Engel* (1930, The Blue Angel), and developed a glamorous and sensual film personality in such Hollywood films as *Morocco* (1930) and *Blond Venus* (1932). During World War 2, she often appeared in shows for Allied troops, and continued to make films after the War, such as *Judgment at Nuremberg* (1961). She also became an international cabaret star.

differential calculus A system of mathematical rules which considers small increments of a variable x, and the corresponding changes in $f(x)$, to find the rate at which $f(x)$ is changing. The early development of calculus was associated with Isaac Newton, whose *Method of fluxions* was written in 1671, although not published until 1736. » function [i]; integral calculus [i]; Newton, Isaac

diffraction An interference effect, a property of waves, responsible for the spreading of waves issuing from a small aperture (eg sound waves from a public address loudspeaker). Diffraction causes the waves to 'bend round' objects, which in light produces shadows surrounded by tiny light and dark bands (**diffraction fringes**). Atoms in crystals cause the diffraction of incident X-rays, electrons, or neutrons to give patterns which allow the determination of crystal structure. A **diffraction grating** corresponds to many hundreds of slits per centimetre, and provides a useful way of dividing a light beam into component colours. Diffraction represents the ultimate limit of the resolving power of optical instruments. Haloes round the Sun on misty days are caused by diffraction. » electron diffraction; interference [i]; neutron diffraction; X-ray diffraction

diffusion (anthropology) The spread of one or several cultural traits from one group to another. Diffusionism, which dominated 19th-c German anthropology, is the notion that cultural similarities are a result of diffusion, and in its extreme form, that all cultures have a common origin. » culture (anthropology)

diffusion (photography) The scattering of light by a translucent medium; in studio lighting, a sheet of metal gauze, tracing paper, or etched plastic placed in front of a lamp to give softer and less directional illumination. Diffusion discs or nets of very fine fabric can also be placed in front of a camera lens to reduce the sharpness of the image.

diffusion (science) In physics and chemistry, the movement of atoms or particles through bulk material via their random collisions. For example, ions diffuse through solids, and atoms of a gas introduced into a volume of still air will become evenly distributed through it by diffusion. Molecules diffuse at rates inversely proportional to their molecular weights. » Brownian motion; convection; ion; kinetic theory of gases; molecule

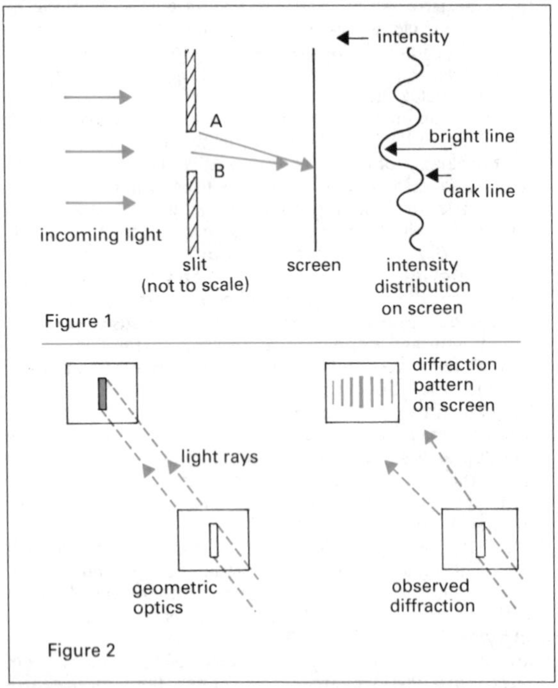

Diffraction – Light falling on the narrow (1/10 mm) slit in Figure 1 gives an interference pattern of light and dark lines on the screen. Dark lines obtain when distance A to the screen differs from distance B to the screen by $\frac{1}{2}$, $\frac{3}{2}$, $\frac{5}{2}$ ... wavelengths. Geometrical optics, by contrast, predicts a single line for a single slit, as shown in Figure 2.

Digby, Sir Kenelm (1603–65) English diplomat, scientist, and writer, born at Gayhurst, Buckinghamshire. He was brought up a Catholic, studied at Oxford, but left to travel abroad. In Madrid he met Prince Charles (1623), and on returning to England was knighted and entered his service. During the Civil War he was imprisoned by the parliament (1642–3), and had his estate confiscated. After the Restoration, he was until 1664 Chancellor to Queen Henrietta Maria. He died in London. » English Civil War; Restoration

digestion A physiological process of animals in which complex foodstuffs are broken down by enzymes into simpler components (monosaccharides, amino acids, fatty acids, and other substances) which can be used by body cells. In certain animals (eg protozoa, porifera), digestion is entirely intracellular: food is taken up and digested, simple molecules are formed, and waste products eliminated all by a single cell. Many animals (eg vertebrates, arthropods) depend entirely on extracellular digestion, in which enzyme-rich fluids are secreted into the cavity of the alimentary canal, where digestion takes place. In some animals (eg coelenterates, lamellibranchs), digestion occurs both within and outside the cell. » alimentary canal; cell; indigestion

digger wasp A hunting wasp that stings and paralyses prey for use in provisioning its nest. In the primitive family *Ampulicidae*, females typically catch the prey before preparing a nest in a shallow scrape in soil. In the family *Sphecidae*, they dig nests in soil or wood, place the prey in a cell, and lay eggs in each cell. Adults feed on nectar or honeydew. (Order: *Hymenoptera*.)

Diggers A radical group in England formed during the Commonwealth, led by Gerrard Winstanley (1609–72), preaching and practising agrarian communism on common and waste land. From April 1649 they established the Digger community at St George's Hill, Surrey, followed by colonies in nine other S and Midland counties. The movement was suppressed and its communities dispersed by local landowners. » Commonwealth (English history)

digital computer A programmable machine which operates using binary digital data. The basic operations carried out in a digital computer are simple arithmetic or logical operations, but in combination and when carried out at high speed these provide a very powerful facility. Digital computers, both large and small, contain (i) a *central processing unit* which controls and co-ordinates all the functions of the computer, and performs the arithmetic and logical operations; (ii) a *memory*, which holds data and program instructions; and (iii) various *input/output devices*, which allow communication to and from the outside world. These units are interconnected by various complex sets of interconnections, called *busses*, which carry data, and control information and memory addresses. Although the basic structure is common to almost all digital computers, they vary in size from small hand-held computers to mainframe computer systems occupying very large rooms. » central processing unit; computer; input-output device; memory, computer

digital recording A technique of sound recording, developed in the 1970s, in which a series of coded pulses replaces the waveform analogues of earlier methods. The advantages of digital recording are that tape noise, pitch fluctuations, and distortion are virtually eliminated. Digitally-recorded master tapes have been widely used in the production of conventional long-playing discs, but the full advantages of the technique can be realized only when the signal is fed directly from a decoder into an amplifier, as happens in the case of the compact disc and digital audio tape. » compact disc; sound recording

digital techniques In audio and video transmission and recording, the conversion of a continuously varying analogue signal, for example representing acoustic sound waves or image brightness, into a series of coded numerical values. The original signal is sampled at regular intervals, sufficiently frequent to represent its detailed variation, and the instantaneous value at each interval allocated to one of a series of discrete numerical quantities. These are conveniently expressed in binary terms and processed in groups ('words') of simple on/off signals ('bits'), which are much less liable to distortion and loss in handling than the continuous analogue. At the receiver the digital signal is converted to analogue for final presentation as picture or sound. For the fine detail of scanned television images a very high sampling rate is necessary, 13.5 million times a second (13.5 MHz), with words of 8 bits providing 256 levels of brightness; with sound, a lower sampling rate of 48 KHz can be used, but a much extended intensity scale of 20-bit words (1 048 576 levels) is required. » digital-to-analog conversion; electronics

digital-to-analog conversion The process of converting digital numbers produced by a computer into an electrical signal such as a corresponding voltage or current; usually carried out by electronic circuits or discrete integrated circuits called **digital-to-analog (D-A) converters**. In many applications the electrical signal is fed into a transducer, which converts the electrical signal into another form of energy such as heat or sound. D-A converters and A-D converters are common in computer-controlled machinery. » transducer

digitalis [dijitahlis] An extract of *Digitalis purpurea* (the foxglove) which has been used for the treatment of heart failure and oedema ('dropsy') for at least 800 years. The extract contains cardiac glycosides as active ingredients. Purified cardiac glycosides (eg digoxin) are today's first-line treatment for heart failure. All are toxic at doses only slightly higher than therapeutic doses. » foxglove; glucose [i]; heart disease; oedema

diglossia A situation in which a language community uses distinct varieties for specific social functions. The varieties are generally distinguished as *high* (used for education, religion, and other public functions, and the one accorded highest prestige) and *low* (used for family interaction, talk with servants, joke-telling, and other everyday functions). Arabic, Modern Greek, and Swiss German are examples of diglossic languages. » sociolinguistics

dihydroxybutanedioic acid » **tartaric acid** [i]

Dijon [deezhõ], ancient **Dibio** 47°20N 5°00E, pop (1982) 145 569. Industrial and commercial city and capital of Côte d'Or department, E France; at confluence of rivers Ouche and Ruzon; railway; bishopric; university (1722); historic capital of Burgundy; famous for its restaurants and its mustard; cars, foundries, foodstuffs, centre of wine trade; Palais des Ducs de Bourgogne, Gothic Church of Notre-Dame, Church of St Michel, Palais de Justice (16th–17th-c), Cathedral of St-Benigne, remains of 14th-c Chartreuse de Champmol (now a hospital). » Burgundy; Gothic architecture

dik-dik A dwarf antelope, native to Africa; small (height, up to 400 mm/16 in); large ears, elongate nose; male with short straight horns and pronounced secretory gland in front of eye. (Genus: *Madoqua*, 3 species.) » antelope

dikkop [dikuhp] » **thick-knee**

dilatation and curettage (D and C) A minor gynaecological operation to investigate the cause of menstrual disorders and possible carcinoma of the uterus. A special type of scoop (*curette*) is passed through the dilated cervix into the uterine cavity, the inner surface of which is scraped. Tissue lining the cavity is removed and examined microscopically. » menstruation; uterus [i]

dill An aromatic annual, growing to 60 cm/2 ft, native to India and SW Asia; leaves feathery, finely divided into narrow linear lobes; flowers yellow, in umbels up to 15 cm/6 in across; fruit ellipsoid, strongly compressed, dark brown with a paler wing. It is cultivated as a herb; the leaves and the seeds are used as flavouring. (*Anethum graveolens*. Family: *Umbelliferae*.) » annual; herb; umbel

Dillinger, John (Herbert) (1903–34) US gangster, born at Indianapolis, Indiana. He specialized in armed bank robberies, terrorizing Indiana and neighbouring states (1933–4). After escaping from Crown Point county jail, where he was held on a murder charge, he was shot dead by FBI agents in Chicago.

Dilthey, Wilhelm [diltiy] (1833–1911) German philosopher, born at Biebrich. He studied at Heidelberg and Berlin, then taught at Basle, Kiel, Breslau, and finally Berlin (1882), where he was professor of philosophy. Using some of Hegel's writings as a point of departure, he argued that human knowledge can only be understood as involving the knower's life lived in a historically conditioned culture. His ideas exerted considerable influence on Heidegger. He died at Seis-am-Schlern, S Tirol. » Hegel; Heidegger; hermeneutics 1

Dilwara Temples A group of five Jain temples near Mt Abu, Rajasthan, India. Built during the 11th–13th-c, they are renowned for the profusion and delicacy of their sculpture. » Jainism

DiMaggio, Joe, properly **Joseph (Paul)**, byname **The Yankee Clipper** (1914–) US baseball player, born at Martinez, California. He spent his entire career with the New York Yankees (1936–54). An outstanding fielder, he also holds the record for hitting safely in 56 consecutive games (1941). His second wife was the film star, Marilyn Monroe. » baseball [i]

Dimbleby, Richard (Frederick) (1913–65) British broadcaster, born at Richmond on Thames, and educated at Mill Hill School, near London. He worked on the editorial staff of various newpapers before joining the BBC in 1931. He became the Corporation's first foreign correspondent, its first war correspondent, and was the first radio man to go into Berlin and Belsen at the end of World War 2. In the postwar era, he established himself as a magisterial TV anchorman on *Panorama*, and a commentator on major events, especially royal occasions and the funerals of Kennedy and Churchill. He died in London. » BBC; broadcasting

dim-dip The control of motor car headlights enabling the light's beam to be altered in direction to avoid dazzling an oncoming driver. The effect is achieved by using a single reflector and a single lamp fitted with two filaments, each so arranged that when it is lit the beam is of the required strength and direction. The filament in use is controlled by means of a switch operated by the driver. » car

dimensional analysis The analysis of mathematical expressions representing physical theorems in terms of dimensions, using M for mass, L for length, T for time. For example, velocity has dimensions $[v]=LT^{-1}$, force $[F]=MLT^{-2}$, where square brackets denote dimensions. Both sides of an equation must have the same dimensions, as must all terms separated by addition and subtraction signs. It is a powerful technique for deriving new relations between quantities and for checking results. » mathematics; physics; theorem

dimer [diymer] A compound composed of two units (*monomers*), which may react either by addition or by condensation. » chemical reaction; disaccharide; monomer

dimethylpropane » **pentane**

dimethylsulphoxide [diymeethiylsuhlfoksiyd] CH_3SOCH_3, known as **DMSO**, melting point 18°C, boiling point 189°C. A colourless substance, an important solvent for many compounds, but not alkanes. » alkanes; solution

diminishing returns, law of A prediction in economics that, as more capital and labour is put into a factory, the resulting increases in output will eventually start to get smaller. Ultimately the average output per unit of labour or capital will also fall. » marginal productivity

Dinaric Alps [dinarik], Serbo-Croatian **Dinara Planina**, Ital **Alpi Dinariche** Mountain range following the Adriatic coast of Yugoslavia and NW Albania; linked to the main Alpine system via the Julian Alps; rises to 2 522 m/8 274 ft at Durmitor; limestone ranges in the Karst region (NW). » Alps; Karst

Dinesen, Isak » **Blixen, Karen**

dingo An Australian subspecies of domestic dog, descended from dogs introduced thousands of years ago with aboriginal settlers; tawny yellow; cannot bark; eats kangaroos (and now rabbits and sheep); persecuted as a pest. (*Canis familiaris dingo*.) » Canidae; dog

Dinka E Sudanic-speaking transhumant cattle herders of the Upper Nile in the Sudan Republic, occupying a vast area of low-lying and often swampy country. Lacking centralized political authority, they comprise many subgroups recognizing

Dinosaurs

only the authority of religious chiefs. Population c.2 million. » Nilotes; Sudan [i]; transhumance

dinoflagellate [diynoh**flaj**uhluht] A microscopic, single-celled organism classified either as an alga (Class: *Dinophyceae*) or as a flagellate protozoan (Phylum: *Mastigophora*); sometimes containing chlorophyll pigment for photosynthesis; characterized by two whip-like organelles (*flagella*), one lying in a groove around the cell; most species enclosed in a rigid shell (*test*) encrusted with silica. » algae; flagellum; Protozoa; shell; silica; systematics

dinosaur A member of a group of reptiles (Subclass: *Archosauria*) that dominated life on land for 140 million years from the late Triassic period until their extinction at the end of the Cretaceous period, 64 million years ago. Dinosaurs are distinguished from other reptiles by the way they stood with their limbs held vertically beneath the body, rather than sticking out sideways. This posture allowed them a much more efficient locomotion than the sprawling gait of a typical reptile. There are over 800 species of dinosaurs, all sharing the specialized kind of hip joint that allowed this upright posture. They fall into two contrasting groups: the **reptile-hipped** dinosaurs (Order: *Saurischia*), and the **bird-hipped** dinosaurs (Order: *Ornithischia*). The saurischian dinosaurs include the more primitive **theropod** groups, which comprised the carnivores such as *Tyrannosaurus*, which were exclusively two-legged, and the enormous **sauropods** such as *Apatosaurus* and *Diplodocus*, which were four-legged and predominantly plant-eating. The ornithischians included ankylosaurs, ceratopsians, hadrosaurs, stegosaurs, and *Iguanodon*.

Many dinosaurs attained great size. *Diplodocus* reached a length of 28 m/90 ft but weighed only 10 tonnes, whereas *Apatosaurus* was shorter at 25 m/80 ft, but weighed 30 tonnes. Even larger dinosaurs, up to 30 m/100 ft long, are being discovered. These giants were slow-moving (3–4 kph/2–2.5 mph) and probably lived in herds. Heavily built flesh-eaters, such as *Allosaurus*, could walk at 8 kph/5 mph. The largest flesh-eater, *Tyrannosaurus*, was a relatively slow-moving scavenger capable of moving at little more than 4 kph/2.5 mph. These large dinosaurs were probably warm-blooded. Dinosaurs laid eggs, often on a nest mound of mud, and there is evidence that hadrosaurs showed parental care, protecting their young in a nursery based around the nest.

Dinosaurs all became extinct suddenly, at the end of the Cretaceous period. The reason for the extinction is unknown, but a combination of climatic changes and competition from mammals in the changing conditions seems most probable. The modern descendants of dinosaurs, the birds, continue to flourish. » Ornithischia; reptile; Saurischia

Dinosaur Provincial Park A provincial park in Alberta, SW Canada; a world heritage site. The park is noted as a region of severe erosion and fossil deposits; in the early 20th-c the fossil remains of some 60 different species of dinosaur were discovered here. » dinosaur [i]

Diocletian, properly **Gaius Aurelius Valerius Diocletianus** (245–316) Roman emperor (284–305), a Dalmatian of humble birth, born **Diocles**. He rose through the ranks of the army to become the greatest of the soldier emperors of the 3rd-c. He saw the answer to the Empire's problems in a division of power at the top and re-organization of the provincial structure below. In 286 the Empire was split in two, with Diocletian retaining the East, and Maximian, a loyal friend, taking the West. Further refinement followed in 293 when, under the famous tetrarchy, the Empire was divided into four. Diocletian abdicated in 305. » Galerius; Nicomedia; Roman history [i]

diode An electronic valve having two electrodes (an anode and a cathode); invented in 1904 by British physicist John Ambrose Fleming. It permits current flow in only one direction, and is thus widely used as a rectifier, changing alternating current

(AC) into direct current (DC). » Fleming, John Ambrose; light-emitting/semiconductor/tunnel/zener diode; rectifier; triode

Diogenes of Sinope [diyojuhneez] (412–323 BC) Cynic philosopher, born at Sinope, Pontus. He came to Athens, was fascinated by the teaching of Antisthenes, and became an austere ascetic. His unconventional behaviour, which became legendary in antiquity (eg looking with a lantern in daylight for an honest man), was intended to portray the ideal of a life lived according to nature. » Antisthenes; Cynics

Diogenes Läertius (3rd-c) Greek author, born at Läerte, Cilicia. He is remembered for his *Lives, Teachings and Sayings of the Great Philosophers*, in 10 books, a compilation of excerpts. » Greek literature

Diomedes [diyohmeedeez] or **Diomede** A Greek hero who fought in the Trojan War, even taking on the gods in battle; also a wise counsellor, the partner of Odysseus in various schemes. In the mediaeval version of the story, he became the lover of Cressida. » Cressida; Philoctetes; Troilus

Dio(n) Cassius or **Cassius Dio Cocceianus** (c.150–c.235) Roman senator and prominent man of affairs, from Bithynia in Asia Minor, who wrote a comprehensive history of Rome in Greek, extending from the foundation of the city down to his own day (229). Large parts still survive, either in full or an abbreviated form, and are an invaluable source, particularly for historians of the early Roman Empire. » Bithynia

Dion Chrysostom or **Dio Chrysostomus** (c.40–c.112) Greek rhetorician and philosopher, born at Prusa, Bithynia. He went to Rome under Vespasian, but was banished by Domitian. He then visited, in the disguise of a beggar, Thrace, Mysia, and Scythia. On Nerva's accession (96) he returned to Rome, and lived in great honour under him and Trajan. About 80 orations or treatises on politics and philosophy are extant. » rhetoric

Dione [diyohnee] The fourth natural satellite of Saturn, discovered in 1684; distance from the planet 377 000 km/234 000 ml; diameter 1 120 km/700 ml; orbital period 2.737 days; heavily cratered. Another tiny moon, **Dione B**, is also associated with it. » Saturn (astronomy); RR4

Dionne, Cécile, Yvonne, Annette, Emilie, and **Marie** [deeon] (1934–) Girl quintuplets successfully delivered to their French-Canadian parents, Oliva and Elzire Dionne in N Ontario, Canada. As the first documented quintuplets to survive, they soon became international celebrities, appearing in advertising and films. Emilie died in 1954, and Marie in 1970.

Dionysia [diyonizeea] Festivals in honour of Dionysus, the Greek god of fertility, ecstasy, inspiration, drama, and wine. At Athens, the Great Dionysia was the main occasion for dramatic contests. » Bacchanalia

Dionysius of Halicarnassus (1st-c BC) Influential Greek critic, historian and rhetorician, from Halicarnassus in Asia Minor, who lived and worked in Rome at the time of Augustus. Much of his writing survives, including about half of his masterpiece, his *Early Roman History*. Extending from earliest times to the outbreak of the First Punic War (264 BC), it is a mine of information about early Roman society. » Halicarnassus; Roman history [i]

Dionysius the Areopagite [diyohniysiuhs] (1st-c) Greek Church leader, one of the few Athenians converted by the apostle Paul (*Acts* 17.34). Tradition makes him the first Bishop of Athens and a martyr. The Greek writings bearing his name were probably written by an Alexandrian. They are first mentioned in 533, from which time they were generally accepted as genuine, and had a great influence on the development of theology. » Christianity; Paul, St; theology

Dionysius the Elder [diyohniysiuhs] (c.431–367 BC) Tyrant of Syracuse (405–367 BC) and ruler of half of Sicily, whose influence extended over most of S Italy. His reign was dominated by intermittent warfare with the Carthaginians, his chief rivals for power in Sicily. A patron of the arts, he invited Plato to his court, and even won a prize himself for tragedy at one of the great Athenian dramatic festivals.

Dionysius the Younger [diyohniysiuhs] (c.397–? BC) Tyrant of Syracuse (367–357/6 BC, 347/6–344 BC), the son and successor of Dionysius the Elder. Groomed by Plato as a potential philosopher-king, he turned out to be a rake and an oppressor. Twice overthrown, he ended his days in exile at Corinth.

Dionysius Thrax [diyohniysiuhs **thrayks**] (1st–2nd-c) Greek grammarian, born at Alexandria, who taught at Rhodes and at Rome. His *Technē Grammatikē* is the basis of all European works on grammar. » grammar

Dionysus [diyohniysuhs] In Greek mythology, the god of wild and uncontrolled ecstasy; later, more specifically, the god of wine, associated with music and dramatic festivals. He was the son of Zeus and Semele; his foreign cult came to Greece from Thrace. He was accompanied by a procession of maenads and satyrs, which was said to have reached India. » maenads; satyr; Semele; Sileni

Diophantine equations Equations that are indeterminate themselves, but have solutions in the set of integers. Thus $3x+4y=11$ has solutions of the form $x=1-4\lambda$, $y=2+3\lambda$, where λ is an integer. » Diophantus; equations; numbers

Diophantus (c.200–299) Greek mathematician, who lived at Alexandria c.275. Of his three known works, only six books of *Arithmetica*, the earliest extant treatise on algebra, have survived. His name was later given to that part of algebra which treats of the finding of particular rational values for general expressions under a surd form (**Diophantine analysis**). » algebra; Diophantine equations

dioptre/diopter [diyoptuh] In optics, the power of a lens; symbol dpt; defined as 1 divided by focal length, when the focal length is measured in metres; used mostly in optometry. » lens; optometry; units (scientific)

Dior, Christian [deeaw] (1905–57) French couturier, born at Granville, Normandy. He was the founder of the international fashion house of that name, and first began to design clothes in 1935. After working for Piguet and Lelong in Paris, he founded his own Paris house in 1945, and in 1947 achieved worldwide fame with his long-skirted 'New Look'. His later designs included the 'H' line and the 'A' line. He died at Montecatini, Italy. » fashion

diorite A coarse-grained intermediate igneous rock composed mainly of plagioclase feldspar and ferromagnesian minerals, with up to 10% quartz. » feldspar; igneous rock; quartz

dioxan(e) [diyoksan, diyoksayn] $C_4H_8O_2$, 1,4-dioxacyclohexane, boiling point 101°C. A colourless liquid, used as a solvent for fats and waxes.

dioxin (tetrachlorodibenzo-p-dioxin, or TCDD) A highly toxic contaminant of the chlorphenoxy group of herbicides whose level is currently regulated at 0.1 parts per million or less. It causes a severe form of skin eruption (*chloracne*), and in laboratory animals causes cancer and damages the foetuses of mothers exposed to it. Dioxin seems to be less toxic in humans than in animals. The jungle defoliant Agent Orange used in Vietnam contained high levels of dioxin as a contaminant. Many violent explosions have occurred during the manufacture of chlorophenoxy herbicides, causing the release of dioxin, including the Monsanto plant in W Virginia, USA (1949) and in Seveso, Italy (1976). » Agent Orange; herbicide

dip and strike Geological terms to describe the disposition of rock layers. *Dip* is the angle at which a bed of rock is inclined to the horizontal plane, measured in the direction where the slope is the greatest. It is perpendicular to the *strike*, which is the direction of the intersection of the horizontal with the inclined plane.

diphtheria A specific infection by *Cornybacterium diphtheriae*, which usually lodge in the throat but occasionally in wounds on the skin. Formerly common, immunization has resulted in a dramatic fall in incidence. The illness is severe and potentially lethal. Infection of the throat and larynx, attended by considerable swelling of the tissues, may cause obstruction to the respiratory airways. Toxin secreted by the bacteria may seriously damage the heart leading to heart failure. Nerve damage also results in muscle paralysis and double vision. » infection; Schick test

diphthong A vowel in which there is a change in auditory quality during a single syllable, as in *my*, *how*. The term is also used for a sequence of two written vowels within the same syllable, eg *fear*, *weight*. » vowel

Diplodocus [diplodohkuhs] A semi-aquatic, long necked dinosaur; body length up to 28 m/92 ft, including an extremely long, whip-like tail; plant-eating, feeding around swamps and lakes; four-legged, limbs pillar-like, hindlimbs longer than forelimbs; known from the Upper Jurassic period of N America and Europe. (Order: *Saurischia*.) » dinosaur [i]; Jurassic period; Saurischia

diplomatic service The body of public servants who are official representatives of their country in another country; or who provide support to them. In many countries the diplomatic service has more prestige than the home civil service. » civil service

diplomatics The study of legal and administrative documents, to determine their authenticity. The evidence is gathered by an analysis of the writing styles of scribes at different periods in history, the linguistic features characteristic of a period or of an individual scribe, and the nature of the writing materials used.

Diplopoda [di**plo**puhda] » **millipede**

dipnoi [**dip**noy] A subclass of bony fishes, comprising the lungfishes. » bony fish; lungfish

dipole A separation of charge. Diatomic molecules have dipoles when the atoms have different electronegativities, the more electronegative atom having a partial negative charge. In polyatomic molecules, dipoles add as vectors, so the bent molecule H_2O has a dipole, but the linear CO_2 ($O=C=O$) does not. » electric dipole moment; electronegativity; magnetic moment; molecule; polarity

dipper A starling-like bird, native to mountains of Eurasia and the W New World; inhabits fast-flowing streams; not obviously modified for aquatic lifestyle, but swims underwater using wings; eats small aquatic animals. (Genus: *Cinclus*, 4 species. Family: *Cinclidae*.) » ouzel; starling

Diprotodon [diy**proh**tuhduhn] A heavily-built, fossil marsupial known from the Pleistocene epoch of Australia; large, up to 2 m/6.5 ft tall at the shoulder; front legs short; walked with entire sole of foot in contact with ground; plant-eating, with one pair of forward-pointing lower incisors. (Order: *Diprotodonta*.) » fossil; marsupial [i]; Pleistocene epoch

Diptera [**dip**tuhra] » **fly**

diptych A picture consisting of two panels, hinged like the pages of a book. Small portable devotional pictures and altarpieces sometimes took this form in the late Middle Ages. » altarpiece

Dirac, P(aul) A(drien) M(aurice) (1902–84) British physicist, born in Bristol. He studied engineering at Bristol and physics at Cambridge, where he became professor of mathematics (1932–69). His main research was in the field of quantum mechanics, in which he applied relativity theory, and developed the theory of the spinning electron. He received the Nobel Prize for Physics in 1933. He moved to the USA in 1968, and in 1971 became professor of physics at Florida State University, Tallahassee, where he died. » Dirac equation; quantum mechanics

Dirac equation The basic equation of relativistic quantum mechanics; stated by British physicist Paul Dirac in 1928. It expresses the behaviour of electron waves in a way consistent with special relativity, requiring that electrons have spin ½, and predicting the existence of an antiparticle partner to the electron (the positron). » Dirac; electron; positron; relativistic quantum mechanics

direct current » **alternating current**

direct injection engine An engine working on the diesel cycle where fuel is injected directly into the combustion chamber formed in the cylinder between the top of the piston and the bottom of the cylinder head. This single *undivided* combustion chamber volume contrasts with a *divided* chamber combustion system, where the initial mixing of fuel and air takes place in one chamber, and combustion in a smaller connected chamber. » Carnot cycle; diesel engine; engine

directed energy weapons A technology under investigation for military purposes, using energy sources such as laser beams, particle beams, plasma beams, and microwave beams, all of which travel at the speed of light. Such weapons, potentially capable of shooting down missiles in space, are regarded as a vital component of the US Strategic Defense Initiative. » laser [i]; particle beam weapons; plasma (physics); radiation; SDI

direction finder A device which determines the direction of an incoming radio signal, and which thus can be used as a navigation aid (eg the radiocompass used in ships and planes). A loop antenna is rotated until the maximum strength signal is received, giving the line of transmission of that signal. This operation is then repeated from a different position, thus enabling a navigator to pinpoint the position of the transmitting station. A receiving position can also be determined, by taking measurements from two transmitters. » radio beacon

Directoire Style A French style of furniture, and women's clothes, strictly belonging to the years 1795–9, but generally used to describe the furniture fashionable between the outbreak of the French Revolution and the introduction of the Empire Style. It was a restrained Neoclassical style strongly influenced by antique Greek art. » Directory; Empire Style; Neoclassicism (art and architecture)

director In films, the person who has the primary responsibility for a motion picture, initially approving the script and choice of production team and artists. The director's visualization is the basis for the designer, and guides the lighting cameraman. Directors rehearse and direct the actors' performances, and when shooting is complete it is their concept that the editor must realize in assembling picture and sound. In television they have similar responsibilities, but often work during shooting from the studio control suite, giving direct instructions to the floor manager and camera operators in the studio. » auteur theory; film production

Directory The government of the First Republic of France (1795–99), established in the Thermidorian reaction to the Reign of Terror, with five executive Directors. Its limited franchise and narrow social base added to the difficulties of rampant inflation. After political conspiracies from Left and Right, it was overthrown by the *coup* of 18 Brumaire (9–10 Nov), bringing Napoleon to power. » French Revolution [i]; Napoleon I

dirigible A cigar-shaped, steerable, rigid-framed, fabric-covered airship. It is fitted with horizontal engines driving propellers which provide the forward thrust. » airship; propeller

disaccharide [diy**sak**ariyd] A carbohydrate consisting of two simple sugars joined together, condensed with the elimination of water. The most abundant in nature are *sucrose* (table sugar) which combines one glucose and one fructose molecule, and *lactose*, the sugar of milk, which is a combination of glucose and galactose. Fructose, glucose, and galactose are single-unit sugars, classed as **monosaccharides**. » carbohydrate; lactose; maltose; sucrose [i]

disarmament Arms control which seeks to promote international security by a reduction in armed forces and/or weapons. The levels are set by agreement, and then opened up for inspection and enforcement by the other side or an independent inspectorate. General (ie applies to all countries) and comprehensive (ie applies to all categories of forces and weapons) disarmament was first attempted in 1927 and 1934 by the League of Nations, and by the United Nations in the 1950s, but such moves have not been successful. Disarmament is therefore limited to agreements between two or a few countries, and restricted to particular classes of weapons and troop levels. Problems arise in determining equivalences between different types of weapons held by different countries, and in verifying arms reduction treaties, especially in respect of nuclear weapons, largely because weapons can be re-assembled. There is also the possibility of nuclear disarmament involving no agreement with other countries, used as a means of encouraging others to follow. Such *unilateral* action may also be taken for moral reasons and as a means of diminishing the chances of being attacked, particularly as regards nuclear and chemical weapons. » arms control; chemical warfare; nuclear weapons

discant » **descant**

Disciples of Christ » **Churches of Christ**

disco dance A popular form of dance mainly for young people, originating in the late 1960s; the main feature of the accompanying music, which is played very loudly, is a heavy, rhythmic beat. There are definite fashions such as the new romantic style, soul, punk, break dancing, robotics, and gothic style. It takes account of Black music, particularly rapping, and heavy rock. » street dance

Discomycetes [diskohmiyseeteez] » **cup fungus**

discount houses UK financial institutions which buy short-dated government stock (Treasury Bills) with money borrowed from commercial banks for very short periods. The difference between the borrowing rate and the lending rate provides the discount house with its profit. » stocks

discounted cash flow (DCF) A notion used in business to assess if a capital expenditure proposal will generate an adequate return on the investment (ie sufficient profit). It is useful where projects are expected to last several years, recognizing the 'time value' of money – £100 received next year is better than £100 received in three year's time. Cash flowing in is discounted back to its present-day value, giving a percentage discount rate. This is the effective rate of interest in the project. » investment

discourse analysis The systematic study of stretches of language, whether in speech or writing, to discover the regularities which govern them. An example is the use of grammatical criteria to link certain sequences of text, creating cohesion, as in the use of pronouns *he* and *it* in the sequence *John went to the play last night. He didn't think much of it.* This approach is usually distinguished from **conversation analysis**, the study of the sequential structure of real-life conversations, to understand the strategies used to link different strands and themes, and the ways in which people interact. » grammar; linguistics

discriminant A mathematical expression which shows whether a quadratic equation has real distinct roots, equal roots, or no real roots. The discriminant of the quadratic equation $ax^2+bx+c=0$ is b^2-4ac. If $b^2-4ac>0$, the quadratic has real distinct roots; if $b^2-4ax=0$, it has equal roots; and if $b^2-4ac<0$, it has no real roots. The roots are then expressed in terms of complex numbers. » complex number; equations

discus throw An athletics field event using a circular disc of wood with metal plates, weighing 2 kg/4.4 lb for men and 1 kg/2.2 lb for women. The competitor throws the discus with one hand from within the confines of a circle 2.5 m/8.2 ft in diameter, with the aim of achieving a greater distance than anyone else. In competition, six throws are allowed. The current world record for men is 74.08 m/243 ft, achieved by Jürgen Schult (East Germany, born 11 May 1960) on 6 June 1986 at Neubrandenburg, Germany; for women it is 74.56 m/244 ft 7 in, achieved by Zdenka Silhava (*née* Bartonova) (Czechoslovakia, born 15 Jun 1954) on 26 August 1984 at Nitra, Czechoslovakia. » athletics

dish In telecommunications using microwaves, an antenna having a concave reflecting surface which acts as a secondary radiator to concentrate the signal on the main pick-up element. In television broadcasting by satellite, the main transmission dish is 2–3 m/6–10 ft in diameter, but for domestic reception 30 cm/12 in may be sufficient. » electromagnetic radiation [i]

disinfectant A material toxic to bacteria. Phenol (carbolic acid) was one of the earliest used, but is also toxic and corrosive to humans. Phenol derivatives are, however, used in chemical toilets. » alcohols; chlorine; phenol

disk » **magnetic disk**

disk operating system » **DOS**

dislocation (medicine) The displacement of a bone from its joint with another bone. Ligaments within or around the affected joint (*capsule*) binding adjacent bones together are torn or otherwise damaged. The result is pain, swelling, and deformity over the joints. Most dislocations can be restored manually. » bone; joint

dislocation (physics) » **crystal defects** [i]

Disney, Walt(er Elias) (1901–66) US artist and film producer, born in Chicago. After World War 1, he worked as a commercial artist before setting up a small studio in which he produced animated cartoons, his most famous character being Mickey Mouse (1928). Among his early successes were the *Silly Symphonies* (from 1929) and the first full-length coloured cartoon film, *Snow White and the Seven Dwarfs* (1937). This was followed by *Pinocchio* (1940), *Dumbo* (1941), and *Fantasia* (1940), the first successful attempt to realize music in images. In 1948 he began his series of coloured nature films, including *The Living Desert* (1953). He also directed several swashbuckling colour films for young people, such as *Treasure Island* (1959) and *Robin Hood* (1952), and family films such as *Mary Poppins* (1964). He opened **Disneyland**, the first of several family amusement parks, in California in 1955. He died in Los Angeles.

disorientation Confusion about time, place, or person. People who are disoriented may not know the date and time, where they are, or how to get from one point to another. They may forget their own name or other personal details.

dispersion The spreading out of some quantity. Examples include the spread by diffusion and convection of ink introduced into water, or the separation of light into component colours upon passing through a prism. » spectrum

Dispersion » **Diaspora**

displacement activity In biology, the performance of a particular behaviour pattern out of its normal context, as a result of the inability of an animal to respond instinctively to a stimulus. For example, a bird in an aggressive situation, in which there are simultaneous tendencies to attack and to flee, may preen its feathers as a displacement activity. » biology

display A behaviour pattern or signal given by an animal, conveying a particular kind of information. It is often a stereotyped and genetically controlled pattern associated with courtship, in which physical characters (eg antlers, plumage) are used as a means of attracting a mate. » ethology; Plate IX

Disraeli, Benjamin, 1st Earl of Beaconsfield [dizraylee] (1804–81) British statesman and twice Prime Minister (1868, 1874–80). He was born in London, the eldest son of an Anglicized Jew, baptized in 1817, and educated at a private Unitarian school. He made his early reputation as a novelist, publishing his first novel, *Vivian Grey*, in 1826. He is better known for his two political novels, *Coningsby* (1844) and *Sybil* (1846), which date from his period as a Romantic Tory, critical of industrial developments. He became leader of the 'Young England' movement which espoused these values, and came to prominence as a critic of Peel's free trade policies, especially the repeal of the Corn Laws (1845–6). He became leader in the Commons of the Conservatives, after the Peelites left the Party, and was Chancellor of the Exchequer in Derby's minority governments of 1852 and 1858–9. While Chancellor in the government of 1866–8, he piloted the 1867 Reform Bill through the Commons. He became Prime Minister on Derby's resignation in 1868, but was defeated soon afterwards in the general election. His second administration was notable both for diplomacy and social reform, though much of the latter only consolidated legislation begun under Gladstone. During his administration, Britain became half-owner of the Suez Canal (1875), and the Queen assumed the title Empress of India (1876). His skilful diplomacy at the Congress of Berlin (1878) contributed to the preservation of European peace after conflict between the Russians and the Turks in the Balkans. Defeated in 1880 by Gladstone and the Liberals, he then effectively retired, dying in London the following year. » Berlin, Congress of; Corn Laws; Derby, Earl; Gladstone; Peel; Suez Canal [i]; Tories; Victoria

Dissenters Christians who separate themselves from the established Church or general religious belief of a country. In a wider sense, it is applied to those who dissent from the very principle of an established or national Church. » Christianity; Nonconformists

dissidents People who oppose the particular regime under which they live, often through peaceful means, and who as a result suffer discrimination and harassment from the authorities. Dissidents may, for example, lose their jobs or be banished to certain areas of the country. They tend to take a moral rather than an overtly political stance in their opposition. » Sakharov; Solzhenitsyn

dissociation In chemistry, separation into two or more parts; used especially of acids to describe their ionization in water. Stronger acids dissociate more completely than weak acids. **Association** is the combination of two or more particles; often used of interactions in solution. » acid; ion

dissolve A transition effect in motion pictures or video in which the whole image of a scene gradually disappears as it is replaced by the following scene. It is also termed a **lap dissolve**, as the pictures are overlapped, or a **mix**.

dissonance A psycho-acoustic phenomenon explicable on several levels. In terms of pure sound, two or more notes whose soundwaves peak out of phase (producing a discernible rapid 'beat') may be described as *dissonant*. The phenomenon may also be viewed as a conjunction of two or more notes producing a 'painful', 'harsh', or merely 'unpleasant' effect, or as a chord requiring resolution. This view is more subjective, and the degree of acceptable dissonance has varied at different periods of music history. The concept is nevertheless basic to the harmonic theory of most Western music up to the 20th-c, and many would argue that it is rooted in immutable laws about the nature of sound. » harmony; tonality

distance education Teaching people, usually at home or in their place of work, by means of correspondence units, radio, cassettes, telephone, television, or microcomputer, rather than through face-to-face contact. Often, though not always, a tutor may be involved to give advice or mark written work, either at a distance or through occasional meetings. Distance education has been particularly popular in sparsely populated areas, or for people not able to attend courses in schools and colleges. Institutions such as the British Open University and Open College have made extensive use of it. » adult education; Open University

distemper A viral disease of the dog (*canine distemper*) and ferret families, characterized by attacks of catarrh. Canine distemper may also spread to the seal family. » dog; ferret; virus

distillation (chemistry) The chemical procedure of evaporating a liquid from one container and recondensing it into another container. In the purification of water, dissolved gases will vaporize and not recondense, while solids will not evaporate. Liquids of varying volatility can be separated. In particular, distillation of a mixture of water and ethanol will produce a vapour rich in ethanol (which is recondensed), and leave a residue rich in water and dissolved solids. » condensation (chemistry); ethanol; evaporation

Distinguished Flying Cross (DFC) In the UK, a decoration instituted in 1918, awarded to officers and warrant officers in the RAF for acts of gallantry performed on active service. The ribbon is blue and grey (equal diagonal stripes). » decoration; Royal Air Force

Distinguished Service Order (DSO) A military award in the UK, founded in 1886, to recognize special service by officers of the army and navy. The ribbon is red edged with blue. » decoration

distortion (lens) » **aberrations 1** [i]

distribution coefficient In chemistry, the ratio of the solubility of a solute in one solvent to that in another solvent not mixable with the first; also known as the **partition coefficient**. Thus, a solute can be essentially removed from one solvent by several extractions with a second. » chromatography; solution

distributive operation In mathematics, an operation whose properties can be illustrated by the relation between multiplication and addition. Multiplication is said to be distributive over addition in the set of real numbers, for $a\times(b+c)=(a\times b)+(a\times c)$; but addition is not distributive over multiplication in the set of real numbers, for $a+(b\times c)\neq(a+b)\times(a+c)$. In general, an operation * is distributive over another operation # for all elements in a set S if $a*(b\#c)=a*b\#a*c$, for all a,b,c in S. » associative operation; commutative operation

district council In the UK, the second tier of local government below that of a county or region. There is a notable imprecision in the use of the term, both across countries and over time, with considerable variation in the area and population covered by a district. » borough; council

District of Columbia pop (1986e) 626 000; area 174 sq km/67 sq ml. Federal district in E USA, co-extensive with the city of Washington; established 1790–1 from land taken from Maryland and Virginia. » Washington (DC)

dittany An aromatic herb, native to Europe; leaves pinnate with 9–13 leaflets; flowers 4-petalled, purple or white. It gives off a highly inflammable volatile oil, which in hot conditions can ignite and burn without harming the plant; hence its alternative name, **burning bush**. (*Dictamnus albus*. Family: *Rutaceae*.) » herb; pinnate

diuretics [diyuretiks] Drugs which increase the production of urine, used in the treatment of fluid retention, heart failure, and high blood pressure. » urine

diurnal tide A tidal cycle with one high and one low tide per lunar day (12 h and 50 min). Also known as **daily tides**, they are common in the Gulf of Mexico and along parts of the coast of China. » tide

diver A large diving bird native to N waters of the N hemisphere; eats mainly fish; only comes ashore to breed; plumage with fine contrasting patterns, usually black and white; also known in the USA as the **loon**. (Genus: *Gavia*, 5 species. Family: *Gaviidae*.)

divergence (linguistics) » **convergence** (linguistics)

diverticulitis A disorder of the large bowel that affects older people. Small pouches form in the lining of the bowel that penetrate the muscle coat of the gut at points of weakness. Many patients suffer no symptoms, but complications include bleeding, infection, and narrowing of the colonic canal leading to obstruction. » intestine

divertimento A light musical composition. Mozart and his contemporaries wrote divertimentos in five or more movements for an ensemble of soloists. » Mozart

dividend An allocation of the profits of an enterprise to its shareholders. Companies may pay out all profits as dividends, retain a proportion, or pay out nothing. There is no legal obligation to pay; the distribution depends on the level of profits and the company's financial needs. The dividend is stated in pence (in the UK) or cents (in the USA) per share, and is usually paid half-yearly. **Dividend cover** is the profit per share divided by the dividend per share; this shows the proportion of profit distributed. **Dividend yield** is the dividend per share divided by the current share price; this equates with the interest payable on other savings. » company; shares

divination A term applied to several traditional methods of attempting to acquire information by alleged paranormal means. The information to be interpreted is conveyed by some physical source, such as dowsing or palm reading. Divinatory practices are found in many cultures, both past and present. » dowsing; paranormal

Divine Right of Kings The concept of the divinely-ordained authority of monarchs, widely held in the mediaeval and early modern periods, and often associated with the absolutism of Louis XIV of France and the assertions of the Stuarts. » absolutism; Louis XIV; Stuarts

diving Any method of descending under water. The most common form at competitive level is by jumping from an elevated board into a swimming pool. The board can be rigid or sprung, and competitors perform a variety of twists and somersaults. Marks are gained for style, and for successfully completing the dive, based on the level of difficulty of each attempt. Springboard events take place from a board 3 m (9 ft 10 in) above the water; platform diving is from a rigid board 10 m (30 ft 5 in) above the water. » scuba diving; skin diving; RR119

diving beetle A large, shiny beetle found in aquatic habitats as adults and larvae; adult up to 38 mm/1½ in long; traps air beneath wing cases for breathing under water; hindlegs paddle-like; predator of insect larvae, molluscs, and small fishes. (Order: *Coleoptera*. Family: *Dytiscidae*.) » beetle; larva

diving duck A duck which obtains food by diving beneath the water surface. There are two groups: the inland species favours shallow lakes, and eats vegetation; the marine species (**sea ducks**) dives deeper, and eats fish and invertebrates. The name is sometimes restricted to ducks of genera *Aythya* and *Netta*. » dabbling duck; duck; eider; goldeneye; goosander; merganser; pochard; stifftail

Divisional Court A court in England and Wales presided over by at least two judges from a division of the High Court. One of its functions is to hear certain appeals; another is to exercise supervisory jurisdiction over inferior bodies. » appeal; High Court of Justice; judicial review

Divisionism In painting, a technique (sometimes called **Pointillism**) whereby small patches or spots of pure colour are placed close together so that they mix not on the palette or canvas, but in the eye of the beholder. It was developed systematically by some of the French Post-Impressionists, notably Seurat, and designated **Neoimpressionism** by the French critic Félix Fénéon (1861–1944). » Postimpressionism; Seurat

divorce The termination by court order of a valid marriage, the criteria for which vary greatly between countries and jurisdictions. English courts now recognize only one ground for divorce; the irretrievable breakdown of marriage. This must be supported by one of five 'facts'. The person applying for the divorce (the *petitioner*) must show that the other party (the respondent) has (1) committed adultery; (2) displayed unreasonable behaviour; (3) deserted the petitioner for two years prior to the divorce petition; (4) lived apart from the petitioner for two years, and consents to the divorce; and (5) lived apart for five years. Custody of any children, and financial arrangements, may be agreed between the parties or be decided by the court. The number of divorces has increased steadily since the 1960s. » annulment; maintenance; marriage

Diwali [dee**wah**lee] The Hindu festival of lights, held in October or November (Asvina K 15) in honour of Rama, an incarnation of the god Vishnu, and Lakshmi, goddess of wealth and luck; lamps are lit and gifts exchanged. Sikhs celebrate Diwali in memory of the sixth Guru's release from prison. Diwali is also a Jain religious festival. » Hinduism; Jainism; Sikhism; RR23

Dix, Dorothea (Lynde) (1802–87) US humanitarian, born at Hampden, Maine. She was largely responsible for the emergence of the concept of mental illness in the USA, and for the establishment of mental hospitals there. She died at Trenton, New Jersey.

Dixieland A style of jazz associated with the 'classic' New Orleans school, and especially with white musicians who based their music on that of the Original Dixieland Jazz Band in the early 1920s. » jazz

Djakarta » **Jakarta**

Djem, El [el **jem**] The world's most intact example of a Roman amphitheatre, situated in the present-day village of El Djem in W Tunisia; a world heritage monument. It is one of the few surviving relics of the ancient city of Thysdrus, and had a capacity for 35 000 people. » amphitheatre

Djemila [**je**mila] The former Roman garrison of Cuicul in N Algeria; a world heritage site. Founded in the late 1st-c AD, the settlement spread and flourished in the 3rd–4th-c, but had declined by the 6th-c. The ruins include temples, forums, thermal baths, and Christian basilicas. » Roman history [i]

Djibouti (country), official name **Republic of Djibouti**, Arabic **Jumhouriya Djibouti** [ji**boo**tee] pop (1990e) 530 000; area 23 310 sq km/8 998 sq ml. NE African republic, divided into five districts; bounded NW, W, and S by Ethiopia, SE by Somalia, and N by the Gulf of Aden; capital, Djibouti; chief towns, Tadjoura, Dikhil, Obock, Ali-Sabieh; timezone GMT +3; chief ethnic group, Somali (60%); chief religion, Islam (94%); official language, Arabic; unit of currency, Djibouti franc; series of plateaux dropping down from mountains to flat, low-lying, rocky desert; 350 km/220 ml fertile coastal strip around the Gulf of Tadjoura, which juts deep into the country; highest point, Moussa Ali, rising to 2 020 m/6 627 ft in the N; semi-arid climate, with hot season (May–Sep); very high temperatures on coastal plain all year round, maximum average daily temperature dropping below 30°C for only three months (Dec–Feb); slightly lower humidity and temperatures in interior highlands (over 600 m/2 000 ft); sparse rainfall, annual average of 130 mm/5 in at Djibouti; French colonial interest in mid-19th-c, setting up French Somaliland, 1896; French Overseas Territory, following World War 2; French Territory of the Afars and the Issas, 1967; independence, 1977; governed by a president (elected for six years), a legislative chamber of 65 deputies (elected for five years), an executive prime minister, and a council; crop-based agriculture possible only with irrigation; date palms, fruit, vegetables; livestock raising among nomadic population; some fishing on coast; economy based on port of Djibouti, well situated to handle ships using Suez Canal and Red Sea; badly affected by local wars, and by closure of Suez Canal (1967–75); small industrial sector, especially for construction materials and bottling of mineral water; some tourism. » Djibouti (city); Suez Canal [i]; RR25 national holidays; RR47 political leaders

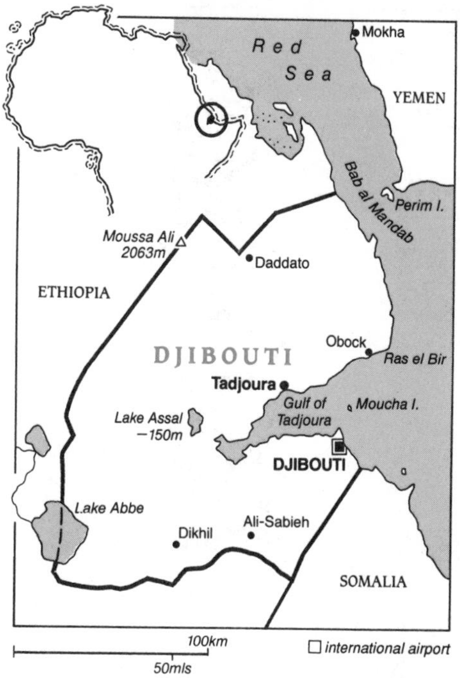

Djibouti (city) [ji**boo**tee] 11°36N 43°08E, pop (1984e) 180 000. Free-port capital of Djibouti, NE Africa; on a coral peninsula 565 km/351 ml NE of Addis Ababa (Ethiopia); NE terminus of railway from Addis Ababa; built 1886–1900 in Arab style; official port of Ethiopia, 1897 (trade declining in recent years); airport; commercial port trade, fishing, tourism. » Addis Ababa; Djibouti (country) [i]

Djilas, Milovan [**jee**las] (1911–) Yugoslav politician and writer, born in Montenegro. A lifelong friend of Tito, he rose in the government as a result of his wartime exploits as a partisan. He was discredited and imprisoned as a result of outspoken criticism of the communist system as practised in Yugoslavia, but was released from prison under amnesty at the end of 1966. His books include *The New Class* (1957) and *Conversations with Stalin* (1962) » communism; Stalin; Tito

DNA or **deoxyribonucleic acid** The nucleic acid which occurs in combination with protein in the chromosomes, and which contains the genetic instructions. It consists of four primary nitrogenous bases (adenine, guanine, thymine, cytosine), a sugar (2-deoxy-D-ribose), and phosphoric acid, arranged in a regular structure. The skeleton of the DNA consists of two chains of alternate sugar and phosphate groups twisted round each other in the form of a double spiral, or double helix; to each sugar is attached a base; and the two chains are held together by hydrogen bonding between the bases. The sequence of bases provides in code the genetic information, which is transcribed, edited, and acted on by the RNA. Each human cell nucleus contains approximately 6×10^9 base pairs of DNA, totalling in length about 2 m/6.6 ft, but coiled upon itself and coiled again and again, so that it fits inside the cell nucleus of less than 10 μm in diameter. DNA replicates itself accurately during cell growth and duplication, and its structure is stable, so that heritable changes (mutations) are very infrequent. The structure of DNA was discovered by geneticists James Watson

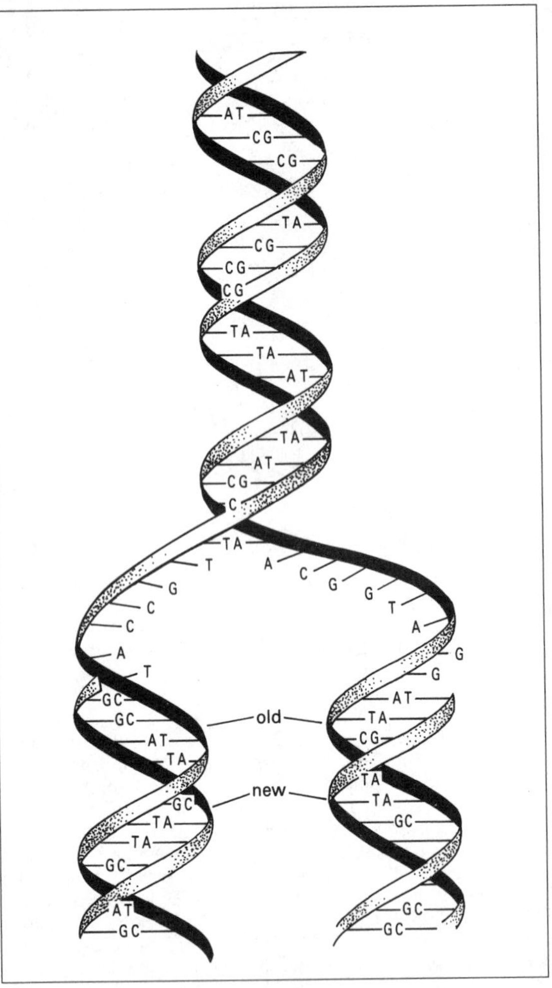

DNA replication, following Watson and Crick. The two strands of the double helix separate, and a daughter strand is laid down alongside each with a constitution determined by the base sequence of its parent strand.

and Francis Crick in 1953. » cell; chromosome [i]; Crick; genetic code [i]; RNA; Watson, James; Plate XVI

Dnepropetrovsk, formerly **Ekaterinoslav** (to 1926) [duh**nye**-pruhpyetrofsk] 48°29N 35°00E, pop (1989) 1 179 000. Port capital of Dnepropetrovskaya oblast, Ukraine, on R Dnieper; founded in 1783 on the site of a Cossack village; airport; railway; university (1918); iron and steel, machines, chemicals, foodstuffs; cathedral (1830–5). » Ukraine

Dnestr, River » **Dniester, River**

Dnieper, River [**nee**per], Russ **Dnepr**, ancient **Borysthenes** River in W Russia; rises in the S Valdayskaya Vozvyshennost range, flows S and W past Smolensk, then makes a wide bend through the Ukraine to enter the Black Sea at Kherson; length, c.2 200 km/1 400 ml; third longest river in Europe; water from the Kakhovka reservoir irrigates large areas of the lower Dnieper basin and the plain of N Crimea. » Russia

Dniester, River, also **Dnestr**, Pol **Dniestr** [**nee**ster] River in Ukraine and Moldavia, rising in the Carpathian Mts; flows generally SE to enter the Dnestrovskiy Liman, a N inlet of the Black Sea, SW of Odessa; length, 1 400 km/870 ml; freezes over (Dec–Mar); formed the USSR–Romanian border, 1918–40. » Moldavia; Ukraine

Doberman(n) pinscher [**doh**berman **pin**sher] A breed of dog, developed c.1900 by a German dog-catcher, Herr Dobermann, who cross-bred stray dogs, intending to produce the meanest, most vicious dog possible; subsequently cross-bred with greyhounds and terriers, and now less vicious; popular guard dogs; large, lean; short brown or black and tan coat; long neck and muzzle; pendulous ears. » dog; greyhound; terrier

dobsonfly A large, soft-bodied insect; adult wingspan up to 160 mm/6¼ in, but flight clumsy and fluttering; found near streams; larvae voracious predators, found in streams and under stones. (Order: *Megaloptera*. Family: *Corydalidae*, c.200 species.) » insect [i]; larva

Docetism [**do**sitizm] The belief, arising in early Christianity, that the natural body of Jesus Christ was only apparent (Gr *dokeo*, 'appear, seem') and not real, thereby stressing the divinity of Christ and denying any real physical suffering on his part. It was especially prevalent amongst 2nd-c gnostics, but was also perhaps a problem encountered in 2 *John* 7. » Christology; Gnosticism

dock (botany) A perennial N temperate herb with strong roots; leaves large, oval, oblong or spear-shaped; flowers tiny, in long, loose, branched inflorescences, three sepals, three petals; fruit a three-sided nut enclosed in papery often reddish valves. Some species are persistent weeds. (Genus: *Rumex*, c.200 species. Family: *Polygonaceae*.) » herb; inflorescence [i]; perennial; sorrel

dock (shipping) A basin in which ships may load cargo, take stores, or be repaired, with or without gates depending on the tidal range. Exceptionally the term has been applied to a straight length of quay side, such as the New Docks (1934) at Southampton, UK. A **dry dock** (or **graving dock**) is one in which the ship can be placed on blocks as the water is pumped out, so that work can be performed on the underwater part of the hull.

Doctor Barnardo's Homes » **Barnardo, Thomas John**

dodder A parasitic annual reduced to a reddish, thread-like stem bearing clusters of tiny white or pink flowers; native to temperate and tropical regions. The germinating seed produces a short-lived root and a twining stem which moves in search of a host. When contact is made, the root atrophies, further contact with the soil being unnecessary. The parasite stem produces haustoria which penetrate that of the host, drawing off water and nutrients. A wide variety of host plants are attacked, including crop plants such as hops and flax, which can be severely damaged. (Genus: *Cuscuta*, 170 species. Family: *Convolvulaceae*.) » annual; haustorium; parasitic plant; tropism

Dodecanese [dohdekan**eez**], Gr **Dhodhekanisos** area 2 682 sq km/1 035 sq ml. Group of 12 main islands and several islets in the SE Aegean Sea, Greece, off SW coast of Turkey; part of Greece since 1947; chief islands include Cos, Patmos, and Rhodes, the largest island; ancient sites include the Asklepieion on Cos, the Acropolis of Rhodes, and the Acropolis of Lindos; several major tourist centres. » Cos; Patmos; Rhodes; Samos

Dodgson, Charles Lutwidge » **Carroll, Lewis**

dodo An extinct bird related to pigeons; native to high forests in Mascarene I, E of Madagascar; turkey-like with large bill and rudimentary wings. The probable dates of extinction were: the **common dodo** (*Raphus cucullatus* = *Didus ineptus*) from Mauritius, 1665–70; the **Rodriguez solitaire** (*Pezophaps solitaria*), c.1761; and the **Réunion solitaire** (*Ornithaptera solitaria*), 1715–20. The **white dodo** (*Victoriornis imperialis*), supposedly from Réunion I, is not generally accepted as a valid species. (Family: *Raphidae*, 3 species.) » pigeon; solitaire

Dodoma [doh**doh**ma] 6°10S 35°40E, pop (1984e) 180 000. Capital of Tanzania, E Africa; altitude 1 120 m/3 674 ft; replaced Dar es Salaam as capital in 1974, after a 10-year transfer plan; administration, trade in live and stuffed birds. » Tanzania [i]

dog A carnivorous mammal, probably evolved from the wolf; first animal to be domesticated; c.400 modern domestic breeds, sometimes classed as *working*, *sporting*, *hound*, *terrier*, *non-sporting*, and *toy*. The name is also used for some mammals of other families (eg the *prairie dog*). The male of several mammal species is called a *dog*, the female a *bitch*, and the young a *puppy*. (*Canis familiaris*. Family: *Canidae*, 1 species.) » affenpinscher; African hunting dog; bush dog; carnivore [i]; Canidae; chihuahua; chow chow; civet; collie; dachsund; dalmatian; dhole; dingo; Doberman(n) pinscher; German shepherd; Great Dane; hound; Lhasa apso; lurcher; mastiff; Newfoundland (zoology); non-sporting dog; papillon; prairie dog; pug; puli; Pyrenean mountain dog; rottweiler; St Bernard; schipperke; Shih Tzu; spitz; sporting dog; terrier; whippet; wolf; working dog

dog daisy » **ox-eye daisy**

dog's mercury A perennial, native to Europe and Asia, 15–40 cm/6–15 in, with creeping rhizomes; leaves opposite, elliptical, toothed; flowers tiny, greenish, with three sepals, males forming long drooping spikes, female in clusters; very early-flowering herb, often dominating woodland floors. (*Mercurialis perennis.* Family: *Euphorbiaceae.*) » herb; perennial; rhizome; sepal

dog's tooth violet A perennial, 10–15 cm/4–6 in, producing corms, native to woods in Europe and Asia; leaves oval, bluish, marbled with brownish-purple; flowers 5 cm/2 in diameter, red-purple or white, solitary, drooping, six perianth-segments curled back to form a Turk's cap. (*Erythronium dens-canis.* Family: *Liliaceae.*) » corm; perennial; perianth

Dog Star » **Sirius**

dog violet A species of violet with short, non-creeping stems and bluish-violet flowers, native to Europe; in contrast to the related *sweet violet*, it is devoid of scent. (*Viola riviniana.* Family: *Violaceae.*) » violet

Doge's Palace The residence of the former Doges of Venice. Although parts of the structure date from the 12th-c, the loggias and marble facade of the present-day building are renaissance additions. It is the repository of many art treasures. » Bridge of Sighs; Venice

dogfish Small bottom-living shark found from Norway to the Mediterranean, and common around British coasts; length to 75 cm/30 in, skin very rough; sold in shops as rock eel or rock salmon. The name is also used for several other small species of sharks. » shark

Dogger Bank A large sandbank forming the shallowest part of the North Sea, c.17–37 m/ 55–120 ft deep. It is approximately 200 km/125 ml E of the Cleveland coast and 250 km/155 ml N of the Norfolk coast, England. It is an important breeding ground for North Sea fish. » North Sea

dogwood A deciduous shrub, growing to 4 m/13 ft, native to Europe and SW Asia; leaves oval, in opposite pairs, turning purple in autumn, veins prominent; flowers small, numerous, in flat-topped clusters, 4-petalled; berries black. Related ornamental species from China and N America have crimson young stems. (*Cornus sanguinea.* Family: *Cornaceae.*) » deciduous plants; shrub

Doha [**doh**ha], Arabic **Ad Dawhah** 25°25N 51°32E, pop (1985e) 150 000. Seaport capital of Qatar, on the E coast of the Qatar Peninsula, in the Arabian Gulf; reclamation of West Bay has created New Doha; chief commercial and communications centre; airport; university; oil refining, shipping, engineering, foodstuffs, refrigeration plant, construction materials; old Turkish fort (1850). » Qatar [i]

Dohnányi, Ernst von, Hung **Ernő** [doh**nan**yee] (1877–1960) Hungarian composer and pianist, born at Pressburg. He studied at Budapest, travelled widely as a pianist, and taught at Berlin (1908–15). He had some success with his opera *The Tower of Voivod* (1922), but is best known for his piano compositions, especially *Variations on a Nursery Song*, for piano and orchestra. He was musical director of Hungarian radio (1931), and in 1948 left Hungary as an exile, living in Argentina and (from 1949) the USA, where he was composer in residence at Florida State University. He died in New York City.

Dolby system The first effective and still the most widely used noise reduction system, devised originally for professional tape recording (Dolby A) by Dr Ray Dolby (1933–) in the mid-1960s. He adapted the circuitry to a simpler form (Dolby B) widely incorporated in cassette tape players. Dolby C followed in the 1980s, giving noise reduction of up to 20 dB and over a wider frequency range. The removal of background hiss, which originated in the granular nature of the tape coating, is achieved by artificially raising the quiet signals most affected and restoring them to their original levels on replay, simultaneously reducing hiss by c.10 dB. » decibel; magnetic tape **1**; sound recording

Dolci, Danilo [**doh**lchee] (1925–) Italian social worker, 'the Gandhi of Sicily', born at Trieste. He qualified as an architect, but decided to fight poverty in Sicily, building schools and community centres in the poorest areas, helped by social workers from many European countries. Opposition to his work led to his imprisonment on two occasions. Although not a communist, he was awarded the Lenin Peace Prize in 1956.

Doldrums Traditionally a zone of cloudy, calm conditions, with light westerly winds associated with the low atmospheric pressure of the intertropical convergence zone in oceanic areas. The region is bounded to the N by the NE trade winds, and to the S by the SE trade winds; however, satellite observations have shown that the region is one of easterly winds, and that it is discontinuous. Formerly, sailing ships would often get becalmed in the Doldrums. » current (oceanography); general circulation model; intertropical convergence zone

Dole, Elizabeth (1936–) US public official, born at Salisbury, N Carolina. Educated at Duke, Harvard, and Oxford, she became a lawyer in Washington and served in appointive offices under Presidents Johnson, Nixon, Ford, and Carter. She became Secretary of Transportation in the Reagan administration in 1983, and was named Secretary of Labor under President Bush, but resigned in 1990. » Dole, Robert

Dole, Robert (1923–) US politician, born at Russell, Kansas. Educated at the University of Kansas, he served in the Kansas state legislature and the House of Representatives before winning a Senate seat in 1968. He has been chair of the Republican national committee, and unsuccessful Republican nominee for the vice-presidency (1976), and he sought the Republican nomination for the presidency in 1988. He is married to Elizabeth Dole. » Dole, Elizabeth

dolerite A medium-grained basic igneous rock, dark-green in colour and composed mainly of plagioclase feldspar and pyroxene crystals. It is the common rock of dykes and sills throughout the world. » dyke (geology); feldspar; pyroxenes; sill

dollar ($) A unit of currency in the USA, Canada, Australia, New Zealand, and certain other countries. The US dollar is the world's most important currency. Much international trade is conducted in it, and prices of goods and commodities are often quoted in it (notably, the price of oil). Also, over half the official reserves of countries are held in dollars. US domestic economic policy affects the value of the dollar which, in turn, affects the economies of other nations. » currency; Eurodollar; exchange rates; sterling

Dollfuss, Engelbert (1892–1934) Austrian statesman and Chancellor (1932–4), born at Texing. He studied at Vienna and Berlin, and became leader of the Christian Socialist Party. As Chancellor, he suspended parliamentary government, drove the socialists into revolt and militarily crushed them (Feb 1934). In July 1934, an attempted Nazi putsch in Vienna culminated in his assassination. » Nazi Party; socialism

dolly A mobile platform for a film or video camera and its operator, allowing forward and sideways movement of the point of view during the action of the scene in addition to the pan and tilt of the camera itself. A **dolly shot** is a scene planned to make use of such camera movement. » camera operator; film production

dolmen » **chambered tomb**

Dolmetsch, (Eugène) Arnold (1858–1940) British musician of Swiss origin, born at Le Mans, France, and naturalized in 1931. He is known for the revival of interest in early music and musical instruments. He established workshops at his home in Haslemere, Surrey, and promoted festivals on early music. His son **Carl** (1911–) is also known as an expert in early instruments and as a recorder virtuoso. He and other members of the family have kept the tradition alive, and the Haslemere Festival is now an established event in the musical world. » musical instruments

dolomite A mineral formed from calcium magnesium carbonate $(Ca,Mg)CO_3$. The term is also applied to sedimentary carbonate rocks with more than 50% dolomite. It is usually formed by the alteration of calcite $(CaCO_3)$. » calcite

Dolomites [**dol**uhmiyts], Ital **Alpi Dolomitiche** Alpine mountain range in NE Italy; limestone formation of jagged outlines and isolated peaks, rising to 3 342 m/10 964 ft at Marmolada; major area for walking, climbing, winter sports, and health resorts; centres include Cortina d'Ampezzo and San Martino di Castrozza. » Alps; Italy [i]

dolphin A small toothed whale. The name is usually used for species with a long slender snout (or 'beak') and streamlined body (though in some dolphins the beak is almost absent). Species with less streamlined bodies and blunt snouts are usually called **porpoises** (especially in genera *Phocoena*, *Phocoenoides*, and *Neophocoena*). The name is also used for **fresh water** (or **river**) **dolphins** (family: *Platanistidae*, 6 species from S Asia and S America), which have a very long beak used for probing in mud for food. (Worldwide Family: *Delphinidae*, c.28 species.) » grampus; whale [i]

dolphinarium » **aquarium**

dolphinfish Large predatory marine fish widespread in tropical and temperate seas; feeds at surface on fish and crustaceans; length up to 1.5 m/5 ft, greenish blue above, underside silver; prized as sport fish and also exploited commercially in some areas. (Genus: *Coryphaena*. Family: *Coryphaenidae*.)

Dom 46°06N 7°52E. Highest mountain entirely in Switzerland, rising to 4 545 m/14 911 ft NE of Zermatt in the Pennine Alps. » Alps

Dome of the Rock A masterpiece of Islamic architecture completed in AD 691 on Mt Moriah, Jerusalem. The shrine, which is built on an octagonal plan and surmounted by a gilded wooden cupola, encloses the holy rock where, according to tradition, Mohammed ascended to heaven and Abraham prepared to sacrifice Isaac. » Islam; Jerusalem

Domenichino, originally **Domenico Zampieri** (1581–1641) Italian painter, born in Bologna. He trained under Ludovico Carracci, and joined the Bolognese artists in Rome. His masterpiece is the 'Last Communion of St Jerome' (1614) in the Vatican. He died in Naples. » Carracci; Italian art

Domesday Book The great survey of England S of the Ribble and Tees rivers (London and Winchester excepted), compiled in 1086 on orders of William the Conqueror; sometimes spelled **Doomsday Book**. Information is arranged by county and, within each county, according to tenure by major landholders; each manor is described according to value and resources. Domesday is one of the greatest administrative achievements of the Middle Ages, yet its central purpose remains unclear. Most probably, it was to assist the royal exploitation of crown lands and feudal rights, and to provide the new nobility with a formal record and confirmation of their lands, thus putting a final seal on the Norman occupation. » manor; Norman Conquest; William I (of England)

domestic fowl A bird kept worldwide for its meat or eggs, also known as the **chicken** or **hen**; descended from one or more species of wild jungle fowl, probably the **red jungle fowl** (*Gallus gallus*); domesticated over 5 000 years ago. Modern breeds are grouped as **Mediterranean** or **Asian**. » jungle fowl [i]

dominance (genetics) A term applied by Mendel in 1866 to describe the genetic situation in which one allele manifests its effect and obscures that of the other. For example, a mother who is of blood group A and has a blood group O child must be carrying both A and O blood group genes. The presence of her O gene is impossible to detect by testing, since the A gene is dominant. » allele; blood types; Mendel

Domingo, Placido (1941–) Spanish tenor, born in Madrid. He moved to Mexico with his family and attended the National Conservatory of Music, Mexico City, studying piano and conducting. In 1959 he made his debut as a baritone, took his first tenor role in 1960, and became a member of the Israeli National Opera (1962–5). He first sang in New York in 1966, at La Scala in 1969, and at Covent Garden in 1971. His vocal technique and acting ability have made him one of the world's leading lyric-dramatic tenors, notably in works by Puccini and Verdi. He has made numerous recordings and film versions of operas.

Dominic, St (c.1170–1221), feast day 4 August. Spanish founder of the Order of Friars Preachers, born at Calaruega, Old Castile. He studied at Palencia, where he acquired such a name for piety and learning that he was made a canon in 1193. He led a life of rigorous asceticism, and devoted himself to missionary work, notably among the Albigenses of S France. His preaching order was approved by Pope Honorius III in 1216. By the time of his death, at Bologna, his order occupied 60 houses, and had spread as far as England, where from their dress the monks were called Black Friars. He was canonized in 1234 by Gregory IX. » Albigenses; Dominicans; friar; missions, Christian

Dominica, Fr **Dominique**, official name **Commonwealth of Dominica** [domineeka] pop (1990e) 82 200; area 751 sq km/290 sq ml. Island in the Windward group of the West Indies, E Caribbean Sea, divided into ten parishes; situated between Guadeloupe (N) and Martinique (S); capital, Roseau; chief towns, Portsmouth, Grand Bay; timezone GMT −4; mainly African or mixed African–European descent; main religion, Roman Catholicism; official language, English, with French widely spoken; units of currency, E Caribbean dollar, pound sterling, and French franc; airport; roughly rectangular in shape, with deeply-indented coastline; c.50 km/30 ml long and 26 km/16 ml wide, rising to 1 447 m/4 747 ft at Morne Diablotin; volcanic origin, with many fumaroles and sulphur springs; central ridge, with lateral spurs and deep valleys, with several rivers; 67% of land area forested; climate warm and humid; average monthly temperatures 25.6–32.2°C; average annual rainfall 1 750 mm/70 in (coast), 6 250 mm/250 in (mountains); visited by Columbus, 1493; colonization attempts by French and British in 18th-c; British Crown Colony, 1805; part of Federation of the West Indies, 1958–62; independence, 1978; independent republic within the Commonwealth, governed by a House of Assembly of 30 members (21 elected for a 5-year term); a cabinet is presided over by a prime minister; an elected president is head of state; agricultural processing, tourism, coconut-based products, cigars; citrus fruits (notably limes), bananas, coconuts, cocoa; lime juice, lime oil, bay oil, copra, rum; pumice, water bottling. » Caribbean Sea; Roseau; RR25 national holidays; RR47 political leaders

Dominican Republic, Span **República Dominicana** pop (1990e) 7 170 000; area 48 442 sq km/18 699 sq ml. Republic of the West Indies, divided into 27 provinces; comprises E two-thirds of the island of Hispaniola, bordering W on Haiti; capital, Santo Domingo; chief towns, Santiago, La Vega, San Juan, San Francisco de Macorís; timezone GMT −4; people mainly Spanish or mixed Spanish and Indian descent; state religion, Roman Catholicism; official language, Spanish; unit of currency, peso oro of 100 centavos; three airports; crossed NW–SE by Cordillera Central, heavily-wooded range with many peaks over 3 000 m/10 000 ft; Pico Duarte (3 175 m/10 416 ft), highest peak in the Caribbean; L Enriquillo (SW)

in broad valley cutting E–W; wide coastal plain (E); tropical maritime climate with rainy season (May–Nov); Santo Domingo, average temperature (Jan) 23.9°C, (Jul) 27.2°C, annual rainfall 1400 mm/55 in; hurricanes (Jun–Nov); visited by Columbus, 1492; Spanish colony, 16th–17th-c; E province of Santo Domingo remained Spanish after partition of Hispaniola, 1697; taken over by Haiti on several occasions; independence in 1844, under modern name; reoccupied by Spain, 1861–5; governed by National Congress (30-member Senate, 120-member Chamber of Deputies); all members and president elected for 4-year terms; economy mainly agriculture, especially sugar, cocoa; coffee, rice, cotton, tobacco, bananas, mangoes, tomatoes, oranges; sugar processing, bauxite, iron, nickel, gold, textiles, cement; tourism expanding, with new resort complexes on N coast. » Santo Domingo; RR25 national holidays; RR47 political leaders

Dominicans A religious order, officially *Ordo Praedicatorum* (Lat 'Order of Preachers'), abbreviated **OP**; also known as the **Friars Preachers**, **Black Friars**, or **Jacobins**. It was founded by St Dominic in 1216 in Italy to provide defenders of the Roman Catholic Faith. The order exercises individual and corporate poverty, but is devoted mainly to preaching and teaching. It has a fine record of learning (eg Thomas Aquinas, Albertus Magnus), and also of missionary activity, with houses in every part of the Christian world. There is also a second order (of nuns), and a third or tertiary order (of members not enclosed). » Albertus Magnus, St; Aquinas; Dominic, St; monasticism; Roman Catholicism

Dominion Day » **Canada Day**

domino theory A political theory first used by President Eisenhower in 1954, reflecting the view that, as neighbouring states are so interdependent, the collapse of one will spread to the others. The theory particularly relates to military collapse, but also covers insurgence, and is used to justify intervention in a country not immediately threatened, but whose neighbour is. It was an important element in the US policy of intervention in SE Asia in the 1960s and 1970s, and in C America in the 1980s. » Eisenhower

dominoes An indoor game, popular in public houses in the UK, which can be played in various forms by any number of players from two upwards (ideally, four). The dominoes are either wooden or plastic rectangular blocks, with the face of each block divided into two halves, each half containing a number of spots. No two dominoes have the same markings on them. In a double-six set of dominoes, every combination between 6–6 and 0–0 is marked on the 27 dominoes. The object of the basic game is to lay out a sequence (or 'line') of dominoes, each player in turn having to put down a domino of the same value as the one left at either end of the line by a previous player.

Domitian, properly **Titus Flavius Domitianus** (51–96) Roman emperor (81–96), the younger son of Vespasian, and the last of the Flavian emperors. An able but autocratic ruler, he thoroughly alienated the ruling class by his rapacity and tyrannical ways. Becoming paranoid about opposition after the armed revolt of Saturninus, the Governor of Upper Germany (89), he unleashed a reign of terror in Rome which lasted until his own assassination. » Agricola, Gnaeus Julius; Roman history [i]

Don, River River in SW European Russia, rising SE of Tula; flows generally S then sweeps round in a wide bend to enter the Sea of Azov; length, 1958 km/1217 ml; linked to the R Volga (E) by canal; accessible to seagoing vessels as far as Rostov-na-Donu; notable fisheries, especially on the lower course. » Russia

Donat, Robert (1905–58) British actor, born in Manchester. He worked on the stage in the 1920s, and had many leading film roles over the next decade, including *The Thirty-nine Steps* (1935), *Good-bye, Mr Chips* (1939), for which he won an Oscar, *The Young Mr Pitt* (1942), and *The Winslow Boy* (1948). Ill health limited his later career, and his final appearance was in *The Inn of the Sixth Happiness* (1958), shortly before his death in London.

Donatello, properly **Donato di Betto Bardi** (c.1386–1466) The greatest of the early Tuscan sculptors, born and died in Florence. He may be regarded as the founder of modern sculpture, as the first producer since classical times of statues complete and independent in themselves, and not mere adjuncts of their architectural surroundings. Among his works are the marble statues of Saints Mark and George for the exterior of Or San Michele; and the tomb of Pope John XXIII in the Baptistery. » Italian art; sculpture

Donatists African Christian schismatics named after Donatus (4th-c), elected as rival to the Bishop of Carthage. The movement was rigorist and puritan, supported rebaptism, and declared invalid the sacraments celebrated by priests suspected of collaboration in times of persecution. It flourished in Africa in the 4th-c and 5th-c, and despite condemnation by Augustine, the Roman emperor, and the Catholic Church (411), continued until the 7th–8th-c. » Augustine, St (of Hippo); heresy

Donatus, Aelius (c.300–c.399) Latin grammarian and rhetorician, who taught at Rome c.AD 360. His treatises on Latin grammar were in the Middle Ages the only textbooks used in schools, so that 'Donat' in W Europe came to mean a grammar book. He also wrote commentaries on Terence and Virgil. » grammar; rhetoric; Terence; Virgil

Donau, River » **Danube, River**

Doncaster, ancient **Danum** 53°32N 1°07W, pop (1981) 76042, urban area 133178. Town in Doncaster borough, South Yorkshire, N England; on R Don, 27 km/17 ml NE of Sheffield; founded as a castle 1st-c AD, later an important Roman station on road from Lincoln to York; railway; coal, nylon, rope, machinery, railway engineering; South Yorkshire industrial museum; St Leger Stakes, the oldest horse-race in England (Sep). » Britain, Roman; horse racing; Yorkshire, South

Donegal [donigawl, donigol], Gaelic **Dún na nGall** pop (1981) 125112; area 4830 sq km/1864 sq ml. Scenic county in Ulster province, N Irish Republic; bounded W and N by the Atlantic Ocean and E by N Ireland; watered by Finn and Foyle Rivers; Blue Stack Mts (W), Derry Eagh (NW), and Slieve Snaght (N) rising to 752 m/2467 ft at Errigal; capital, Lifford; tweed manufacture, agriculture, livestock; deposits of uranium; Station I on L Derg an important place of pilgrimage, associated with St Patrick. » Irish Republic [i]; Ulster

Donetsk, formerly **Stalino** (to 1961), **Yuzovka** (to 1924) 48°00N 37°50E, pop (1989) 1110000. Industrial capital city of Donetskaya oblast, Ukraine; on the R Kalmius, in the Donbas coal basin; founded, 1870; airport; railway; university (1965); coal, metallurgy, engineering, machines, chemicals, foodstuffs; natural gas piped from Stavropol. » Ukraine

Dönitz, Karl [doernits] (1891–1980) German naval commander, born at Grünau, near Berlin. He entered the submarine service of the German Navy in 1916, and became a staunch advocate of U-boat warfare. He planned Hitler's U-boat fleet, was made its commander in 1936, and in 1943 became Commander-in-Chief of the German Navy. Becoming Führer on the death of Hitler, he was responsible for the final surrender to the Allies, and in 1946 was sentenced to 10 years' imprisonment for war crimes. He died at Aumühle, Germany. » submarine; World War 2

Donizetti, (Domenico) Gaetano (Maria) (1797–1848) Italian composer, born at Bergamo. He studied music at Bergamo and Bologna, and produced his first opera in 1818 at Venice. The work which carried his fame beyond Italy was *Anna Bolena* (1830), and he had several other successes, notably *Lucia di Lammermoor* (1835). Stricken by paralysis, he became mentally ill, and died at Bergamo.

donkey » **ass; mule** (zoology)

Donleavy, J(ames) P(atrick) (1926–) Irish-US author, born in New York City, of Irish parents. He served in the US Navy during World War 2, then studied microbiology at Dublin, and became a friend of Brendan Behan. His first novel, *The Ginger Man* (1955) was hailed as a comic masterpiece. Among his other works are *A Singular Man* (1963), *The Beastly Beatitudes of Balthazar B* (1968), *The Onion Eaters* (1971), and *Leila* (1983). He has been an Irish citizen since 1967. » Irish literature; novel

Donne, John (?1572–1631) English poet, born and died in London. Educated at Oxford and Cambridge, he studied law in London, and in 1598 became secretary to Thomas Egerton, Keeper of the Great Seal. His career prospects were excellent, but his secret marriage to the Lord Keeper's niece had him dismissed and cast into prison. Originally a Catholic, he then joined the established Church, eventually taking Orders. He was made Dean of St Paul's, where his sermons were extremely popular. His creative years fall into three periods. The first (1590–1601) was a time of passion and cynicism, as seen in his *Elegies* and *Songs and Sonnets*. The second, from his marriage to his ordination, was a period of anguished meditation and flattery of the great, as seen in his *Anniversaries* and funeral poems. His third period includes sonnets and hymns, and shows that in transferring his allegiance from the world to God he retained his earlier passion. » English literature; metaphysical poetry

Donoghue, Stephen (Steve) (1884–1945) British jockey, born at Warrington. He won the Derby six times, including a record three consecutive wins (1921–3). Champion jockey in 10 successive years (1914–23), he won a total of 14 classics. » Classics; horse racing

Doolittle, Hilda, byname **H D** (1886–1961) US poet, born at Bethlehem, Pennsylvania. She lived in London from 1911, and became an exponent of Imagism. She wrote several books of poetry, beginning with *Sea Garden* (1916) and *Hymen* (1921), and also several prose works and translations. In 1913 she married Richard Aldington, and after their divorce (1937) settled near L Geneva. She died in Zürich. » American literature; Imagism; poetry

Doomsday Book » **Domesday Book**

dopa [**do**pa] $C_9H_{11}NO_4$, dihydroxyphenylalanine. A catechol derivative from plants, which can form strong complexes with

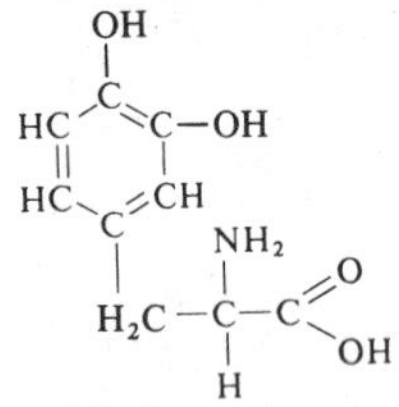

many metals. It is used in the treatment of Parkinson's disease. » catechol [i]; Parkinson's disease

dopamine [**do**pameen] A chemical compound (*catecholamine*) widely distributed in the brain and peripheral nervous system, a precursor of noradrenaline and adrenaline, and a central nervous system transmitter. It is a hormone which inhibits the secretion of prolactin, and promotes the release of growth hormone from the front lobe of the pituitary gland. The degeneration of certain dopamine-containing brain cells results in Parkinsonism, and is probably also implicated in schizophrenia. » catecholamine; Parkinson's disease; releasing hormone; schizophrenia

doping In chemistry, adding a controlled amount of an impurity, which can radically change the properties of a substance. For example, the addition of minute quantities of aluminium or phosphorus to silicon will increase its semiconducting properties greatly. » electrical conduction; semiconductor; silicon

Doppler, Christian (1803–53) Austrian physicist, born in Salzburg. He was educated at Vienna, where he became professor of physics (1851), and is best known for his explanation of perceived frequency variation under certain conditions (the 'Doppler effect'). He died in Venice. » Doppler effect

Doppler effect The change in wavelength observed when the separation between a wave source and an observer is changing; named after Austrian physicist Christian Doppler. The wavelength increases as the source and observer move apart, and decreases as they come closer. The increasing separation of the Earth and the stars is demonstated by the Doppler redshift of star light. The changing tone of passing motor vehicles represents the Doppler shift in sound waves. » Doppler; redshift; wavelength

dor beetle A large, blackish beetle; adult length up to 24 mm/1 in; wing cases furrowed; antennae clubbed; lays eggs in tunnels beneath cattle and horse dung; larvae white and fleshy, feed on dung. » beetle; larva

Dorado (Lat 'swordfish') [duh**rah**doh] A small and inconspicuous S constellation, which includes the Large Magellanic Cloud. » constellation; Magellanic Clouds; RR8

dorcas gazelle A gazelle native to N Africa and S Asia; light brown with white underparts; dark smudge along flank and along side of face; short backward-curving horns ringed with ridges; also known as **jebeer**. (*Gazella dorcas*.) » antelope

Dorchester, ancient **Durnovaria** 50°43N 2°26W, pop (1981) 14 225. County town in West Dorset district, Dorset, S England; on the R Frome, 12 km/7 ml N of Weymouth; the Roman ramparts became known as 'The Walks' in the 18th-c; mint established here by King Athelstan; Judge Jeffreys' Bloody Assizes held here (1685); model for Casterbridge in Hardy's novels; railway; brewing; Dorset county museum, Dorset military museum, Maiden Castle prehistoric fort (3 km/1¾ ml S); Thomas Hardy festival (Aug). » Athelstan; Dorset; Hardy, Thomas; Jeffreys; Maiden Castle

Dordogne, River Eng [daw**doyn**], Fr [dor**dony**], ancient **Duranius** River in SW France, rising in the Auvergne hills; formed by confluence of Dor and Dogne Rivers; flows SW and W to meet R Garonne at Bec d'Ambes, where it forms the Gironde estuary; length 472 km/293 ml; vineyards along valley slopes; source of hydroelectricity. » France [i]

Dordrecht [**daw**drekht], also **Dordt** or **Dort** 51°48N 4°39E, pop (1984e) 199 156. River port and industrial city in S South Holland province, W Netherlands, 19 km/12 ml ESE of Rotterdam; founded, 1008; Synod of Dort (meeting of the Reformed churches), 1618–19; railway; shipbuilding, engineering, chemicals; Grote Kerk (14th–16th-c). » Netherlands, The [i]

Doré, (Paul) Gustave [do**ray**] (1833–83) French painter and book illustrator, born in Strasbourg. He first made his mark by his illustrations to books by Rabelais (1854) and Balzac, notably the latter's *Contes drolatiques* (1865). These were followed by illustrated editions of Dante, the Bible, Milton, and other works. He died in Paris. » Balzac; French art; Rabelais

Dorians A sub-group of Hellenic peoples, thought to have migrated into Greece around 1100 BC. Dorian settlements there included Argos, Corinth, and Sparta; later Dorian foundations include Halicarnassus and Syracuse. » Corinth; Greek history; Halicarnassus; Sparta (Greek history)

Doric order The earliest of the five main orders of classical architecture, characterized by a fluted shaft and plain capital. It is sub-divided into **Greek Doric** and **Roman Doric**, the former having no base, as used for the Parthenon, Athens (447–438 BC). » capital (architecture); column; entablature; Greek architecture; orders of architecture [i]; Roman architecture

dormancy In biology, a state of relative metabolic inactivity in a plant or animal, such as is seen both in winter (*hibernation*) and summer (*aestivation*). The notion is particularly used for the state in which viable seeds and buds fail to germinate even under favourable conditions. » germination; hibernation; metabolism

dormouse A mouse-like rodent of family *Gliridae* (10 species); native to Africa, Europe and C Asia; intermediate between squirrels and true mice; most resemble mice, with long bushy tails. The name is also used for the **desert dormouse** of family *Seleviniidae*, and for **oriental dormice** of family *Muridae* (subfamily: *Platacanthomyinae*, 2 species). » mouse (zoology); rodent; squirrel

Dornier, Claude [**dawn**yuh] (1884–1969) German aircraft engineer, born at Kempten. In 1911 he designed the first all-metal plane. He founded the Dornier works at Friedrichshafen and Altenrhein, where he made seaplanes and flying boats, including the famous twelve-engined Do X (1929). The Dornier twin-engined bomber was a standard Luftwaffe type in World War 2. He died at Zug, Switzerland. » aircraft [i]

Dorset pop (1987e) 648 600; area 2 654 sq km/1 024 sq ml. County of S England, divided into eight districts; bounded S by the English Channel; extensive heathlands and chalk down, drained by the Frome and Stour Rivers; county town, Dorchester; chief towns include Bournemouth, Weymouth, Poole; tourism, livestock, quarrying; setting for many of Hardy's novels. » Dorchester; England [i]; Hardy, Thomas

Dortmund [**dawt**munt] 51°32N 7°28E, pop (1983) 595 200.

Industrial, mining, and commercial city in Arnsberg district, Germany; river port in the Ruhr valley, connected to the North Sea by the Dortmund-Ems Canal (272 km/169 ml); one of Germany's largest inland harbours; railway; university (1966); iron and steel, engineering, machinery, non-alcoholic drinks, textiles, brewing; sporting centre. » Germany [i]

DOS An acronym of **Disk Operating System**, referring to the computer program – part of the operating system – which oversees the communication of data between the computer processor and its magnetic disks, as well as the management of files and programs on the disks. » computer program; operating system

Dos Passos, John (Roderigo) (1896–1970) US novelist and war correspondent, born in Chicago, Illinois. Educated at Harvard, he was an ambulance driver in the later years of World War 1, out of which came his antiwar novel *Three Soldiers* (1921). He then worked in Europe and elsewhere as a newspaper correspondent. His best-known work is the trilogy on US life, *U.S.A.* (1930–6). He died in Baltimore. » American literature; novel

dose equivalent » **radioactivity units** [i]

Dostoevsky or **Dostoyevsky, Fyodor (Mikhailovich)** [dostuh-**yef**skee] (1821–81) Russian novelist, born in Moscow, the son of a surgeon. He became a military engineer, but turned to literature, publishing *Bednye lyudi* (Poor Folk) in 1846. Joining revolutionary circles in St Petersburg, he was condemned to death (1849), reprieved at the last moment, and sent to hard labour in Siberia. In 1859 he returned to St Petersburg, where he wrote his masterpiece, *Prestupleniye i nakazaniye* (1866, Crime and Punishment), one of the most powerful realistic works of fiction. Other important books are *Idiot* (1868–9, The Idiot) and *Bratya Karamazovy* (1879–80, The Brothers Karamazov). Domestic trials, financial troubles (caused by gambling debts), and ill health (epilepsy) clouded his late life. He lived for a time in W Europe (1867–71), then returned to work as a journalist in St Petersburg, where he died. » novel; Russian literature

dot-matrix printer A type of impact printer, where characters are formed by the selection of sets of dots from a rectangular matrix. It is widely used with microcomputer systems, being relatively fast and inexpensive, but it can be noisy. » printer, computer

dotterel A species of plover, native to mountainous areas of Europe and Asia. The name is also used for two species of plover from S America, and six species of plover from Australia and New Zealand. (*Eudromias morinellus*. Family: *Charadriidae*.) » plover

Dou, [doh] or **Douw, Gerard** (1613–75) Dutch painter, born at Leyden. He studied under Rembrandt (1628–31) and at first mainly occupied himself with portraiture. His 200 works include his own portrait, 'The Poulterer's Shop' (National Gallery, London) and his celebrated 'Dropsical Woman' (Louvre). He died at Leyden. » Dutch art; Rembrandt

Douai Bible [**doo**ay] An early English translation of the Bible by Roman Catholic scholars. The New Testament was first published at Rheims in 1582; the Old Testament in 1609. It is sometimes called the Rheims-Douai translation (the English college at Douai having moved to Rheims in 1578). » Bible; Roman Catholicism

Douala or **Duala** [doo**a**la] 4°04N 9°43E, pop (1984) 784 000. Seaport capital of Littoral province, Cameroon, W Africa; on R Wouri estuary, 25 km/15 ml from Gulf of Guinea coast; capital of German Cameroon, as Kamerunstadt, 1885–1901; present name, 1907; capital of French Cameroon, 1940–6; airport; railway; many import-export companies; trade in minerals, agricultural products, foodstuffs; centre for petroleum exploration; aluminium smelting, paper, pulp, textiles, flour milling, metal work, chemicals, brewing, food processing; Pagoda of King Manga Bell. » Cameroon [i]

double bass The largest and lowest in pitch of the orchestral string instruments. There are two basic types: the first, belonging to the viol family, has sloping shoulders and a flat back; the other, belonging to the violin family, has squarer shoulders and a slightly rounded (sometimes also flat) back. Both types have four strings, tuned in 4ths: sometimes a fifth, lower string is added. There are similarly two types of bow: the German (or viol) type, held underhand, and the French type, held like a cello bow. The strings are often plucked, almost invariably so in jazz and dance music. » bow (music); string instrument 1 [i]

double coconut » **coco de mer**

double exposure The intentional combination of two or more images separately exposed on a single photographic record, either in the camera or by subsequent printing. The images may be superimposed so that one is seen through the other, or appear without overlapping by the use of masks or mattes to reserve specific areas. It is widely used for artistic effects and in trick photography. » special effects

double glazing Two layers of glass separated by an air space to give improved thermal or acoustic insulation. The two layers are either permanently sealed with a partial vacuum inside, or openable for occasional ventilation. The former provides significantly better insulation. » insulation; triple glazing

double jeopardy The legal doctrine that no person can be convicted twice for the same crime, or for different crimes arising from the same set of facts unless the crimes involve substantially different wrongs. Also, no person having been acquitted of an offence can be subjected to a second trial for the same offence.

double refraction » **birefringence**

double star A pair of stars that appear close together in our sky when viewed through a telescope. Some pairs are stars at very different distances that merely coincide from our vantage point. If the stars are close enough to be linked through their gravitational attractions, they constitute a binary star. » binary star

double vision A weakness or paralysis of one or more of the muscles which move one or other of the eyes, resulting in a failure of the eyes to move together in parallel. As a result, light from a single object does not fall on comparable parts of the two retinae, and the object appears as two images. » eye [i]

Doublespeak Awards Mock awards made annually by the National Council of Teachers of English in the USA to those public figures who have used language that is distorted, unfactual, deceptive, evasive, or euphemistic, usually in an attempt to conceal the real implications of policies advocated. An example is 'collateral damage', referring to civilians killed in war.

Douglas, Gawain or **Gavin** (c.1474–1522) Scottish poet and bishop, born at Tantallon Castle. Educated at St Andrews for the priesthood, he became dean of St Giles, Edinburgh (1501) and Bishop of Dunkeld (1515). His works include *The Palice of Honour* (c.1501) and a translation of the *Aeneid* (finished c.1513), the first version of a Latin poet published in English. After the death of James IV of Scotland at Flodden, he became involved in political intrigues, and in 1521 was forced to flee to London, where he died.

Douglas 54°09N 4°29W, pop (1981) 19 944. Seaport capital of the Isle of Man; on the E coast, 80 km/50 ml W of Barrow-in-Furness; railway; tourism, brewing, light engineering; House of Keys, Manx National Museum, Castle Mona (1804), Tower of Refuge on Conister rock (1832), casino, steam railway. » Man, Isle of

Douglas-Home, Sir Alexander Frederick » **Home of the Hirsel**

Douglass, Frederick (c.1817–95) US abolitionist and journalist, born in slavery at Tuckahoe, Maryland. He escaped in 1838, and in 1841 emerged as a major anti-slavery force. He also supported the cause of women's rights, and became US Minister to Haiti. He died in Washington, DC. » slave trade

Doukhobors or **Dukhabors** [**doo**kuhbaws] A religious sect originating in Russia c.1740. It teaches that God is manifested in the human soul, which is eternal, and which at death passes into another body (*metempsychosis*). Frequently in conflict with the authorities, especially for refusing military service, the adherents were persecuted until 1898, when they were allowed to emigrate. Most settled in Canada. » sect; soul (religion)

Doulton An English firm which began making chimney-pots and large architectural ornaments in their Lambeth factory in

London in the first half of the 19th-c. They became leading art potters at around the period of their expansion to Burslem in 1854, and were renowned for tiles, figures, and decorative panels in faience, while still manufacturing large quantities of sanitary ware. » faience; pottery

Dounreay [doon**ray**] Nuclear research station, Caithness, Highland region, N Scotland; on the coast of the Pentland Firth, 13 km/8 ml W of Thurso; site of world's first experimental fast-breeder nuclear reactor. » nuclear reactor [i]

Douro, River [**daw**ooroo], Eng [**doo**roh], Span **Río Duero** [**dway**roh], ancient **Durius** River of Spain and Portugal; rises in NC Spain, and flows 609 km/378 ml W to the Portuguese border, which it follows for 107 km/66 ml; turns W across N Portugal, emptying into the Atlantic near Oporto; used extensively for irrigation and hydroelectric power; five dams are operated jointly by Spain and Portugal; length 895 km/556 ml; navigable 200 km/124 ml to Barca de Alva; vineyards in the upper Douro valley produce port and Mateus Rosé. » Portugal [i]

douroucouli [doorook**oo**lee] A nocturnal New World monkey; long tail, large eyes, spherical head; cannot see in colour; moves silently; the only nocturnal monkey; may be kept as a pet to control mice and insects; also known as **night monkey**, **night ape**, or **owl monkey**. (*Aotus trivirgatus*.) » New World monkey

dove (ornithology) A bird of the pigeon family. Usually the large-bodied species with rounded tails are called *pigeons*; the smaller-bodied with longer slender tails are called *doves*. However, this distinction is not applied consistently. » mourning dove; pigeon; quail; turtle dove

dove (politics) In US foreign policy, someone who prefers to use diplomacy instead of reliance on military power to settle international problems. The term was first used in the period of the Kennedy and Johnson presidencies. Today it is probably used to describe anyone who takes a relatively soft line in foreign policy matters. A **hawk** represents the opposite position, favouring a tougher line. Doves are seen as being left-leaning, while hawks are right-wing.

dove tree » **handkerchief tree**

Dover (UK), Fr **Douvres**, Lat **Dubris Portus** 51°08N 1°19E, pop (1981) 34 304. Seaport in Dover district, Kent, SE England; principal cross-Channel port, the shortest link with France (35 km/21¾ ml); the largest of the Cinque Ports; railway; 13th–14th-c Dover Castle; 13th-c St Edmund's Chapel, the smallest chapel in England; Roman painted house (2nd-c AD). » Cinque Ports; Kent

Dover (USA) 39°10N 75°32W, pop (1980) 23 512. Capital of state in Kent County, C Delaware, USA; founded, 1683; state capital, 1777; city status, 1929; railway; university; trade in fruit and vegetables; air force base; Old Dover Days (May). » Delaware

Dow Jones Index A statistic showing the state of the New York stock market, computed on working days by Dow Jones and Co. It enables a measurement to be made of changes in the price of shares of 30 leading US corporations, and is the primary indicator of share price movements in the USA. » stock market

Dowding, Hugh (Caswell Tremenheere), 1st Baron (1882–1970) British air chief marshal of World War 2, born at Moffat, Dumfriesshire, Scotland. He served in the Royal Artillery and the Royal Flying Corps in World War 1. As Commander-in-Chief of Fighter Command (1936–40), he organized the air defence of Britain, which resulted in the victorious Battle of Britain (1940). He retired in 1942 and was created a peer in 1943. He died at Tunbridge Wells, Kent. » Britain, Battle of; World War 2

Dowell, Anthony (1943–) British dancer and director, born in London. He studied at the Sadler's Wells and Royal Ballet Schools, and joined the Royal Ballet company in 1961, becoming one of the premier male ballet dancers of the period, noted for his lightness and elegance in classical roles. He was principal dancer of the American Ballet Theatre (1978–80), and became artistic director of the Royal Ballet in 1986. » ballet; Royal Ballet

Dowland, John (1563–1626) English lutenist songwriter, born possibly at Westminster, and educated at Oxford. Having failed to become a court musician to Queen Elizabeth, he entered the service of the Duke of Brunswick (1594), and subsequently went to Italy. He returned to England in 1596, where he wrote his first book of 'ayres'. In 1598 he became lutenist to Christian IV of Denmark, producing further collections of music. In London in 1605 he composed *Lachrimae*, which contains some of the finest instrumental consort music of the period. He died in London. » lute

Down, Gaelic **An Dun** pop (1981) 339 229; area 2 448 sq km/945 sq ml. County in SE Northern Ireland, divided into six districts; bounded N by Belfast Lough, S by Carlingford Lough, and E by the Irish Sea; coastline indented (N–S) by Strangford Lough, Dundrum Bay, and Carlingford Lough; Mourne Mts in the S; rises to 852 m/2 795 ft at Slieve Donard; county town, Downpatrick; other chief towns, Newry, Bangor, Newtownards; oats, potatoes, vegetables, stock-rearing, linen. » Downpatrick; Northern Ireland [i]

Down's syndrome A common congenital abnormality especially liable to affect babies born to mothers over 40 years. The head of the child is small with high cheek bones and flattened nose; the eyes are slanted with a prominent fold over the inner part of either eye; the hands are short and broad, and there are varying degrees of mental handicap. The defect stems from a failure of one chromosome of a germ cell to split in the normal way to form a healthy ovum with 23 chromosomes; an ovum with 24 chromosomes is produced, and if this ovum is fertilized, the developing embryo possesses an extra chromosome. The condition is named after English physician J L H Down (1828–96), and is sometimes referred to as *mongolism*. » genetically determined disease

Downing Street A street off Whitehall in C London. Of the original terraced houses only numbers 10 (since 1735 the Prime Minister's official residence), 11 (used by the Chancellor of the Exchequer), and 12 (used by the Party Whip) remain. One side of the street has been replaced by the Foreign Office building. » Whitehall

Downpatrick, Gaelic **Dun Padraig** 54°20N 5°43W, pop (1981) 8 245. County town in Down, SE Northern Ireland, near the S end of Strangford Lough; a major centre of pilgrimage; St Patrick is said to have landed here in 432 and to have founded a church c.440; reputed burial place of Saints Patrick, Columbus, and Bridget of Kildare; textiles, agricultural trade; St Patrick's Cathedral (1798–1812), remains of Inch Abbey (c.1187) nearby. » Down; Patrick, St

Downs Low-lying chalk hill ranges rising in Dorset and Hampshire and extending into Surrey, Kent, and East and West Sussex, S England; North Downs extend from the chalk cliffs of Dover in the E, through Kent and into Surrey; separated from the South Downs by the Weald; South Downs stretch W to Beachy Head, running parallel to the S coast; North Downs rise to 294 m/964 ft at Leith Hill, South Downs to 264 m/866 ft at Butser Hill. » England [i]; Weald, the

dowsing A traditional method of trying to locate hidden subterranean features, such as water, by observing the movement of a device such as a forked twig or pendulum held in the dowser's hands, as he or she passes over the relevant area. Despite its widespread use, formal studies examining its effectiveness remain inconclusive. » divination

Doyle, Sir Arthur Conan (1859–1930) British writer, the creator of Sherlock Holmes, born in Edinburgh, Scotland. Educated at Stonyhurst and in Germany, he studied medicine at Edinburgh, but poverty made him turn to writing. His first book, *A Study in Scarlet* (1887), introduced the super-observant, deductive Holmes, his good-natured question-raising friend, Dr Watson, and the whole apparatus of detection mythology associated with Baker Street, Holmes' fictitious home. After *The Adventures of Sherlock Holmes* was serialized in the *Strand Magazine* (1891–3), the author tired of his popular creation, and tried to kill off his hero, but was compelled in 1903 to revive him. Conan Doyle himself set greater stock by his historical romances, such as *The White Company* (1890). He served as a physician in the Boer War (1899–1902), and his pamphlet, *The War in South Africa* (1902), earned him a knighthood (1902). He also wrote on spiritualism, to which he became a convert in later life. He died at Crowborough, Sussex. » detective story; English/Scottish literature

Dr Barnardo's Homes » **Barnardo, Thomas John**

Drabble, Margaret (1939–) British novelist, born in Sheffield, and educated at York and Cambridge. Her novels, which describe some of the emotional and moral problems experienced by women during the postwar years, include *The Millstone* (1965), *The Needle's Eye* (1972), and *The Radiant Way* (1987). » English literature; novel

draco » **flying lizard**

Draco (astronomy) (Lat 'dragon') [**dray**koh] The eighth largest constellation, a sinuous zone of the N sky. » constellation; RR8

Draco [**dray**koh] (ancient Greece) (7th-c BC) Athenian legislator whose harsh codification of the law in 621 BC has given us the word 'draconian'. With death the penalty of almost every offence, the code was so unpopular that it was largely abolished by Solon (594 BC). Only his ruling on homicide remained. » Solon

draft » **conscription**

drag A force which impedes the motion of an object through a fluid. It results from both the friction between the object and the fluid flowing over it (**viscous** or **frictional drag**), and the pressure differences caused by the flow around the object (**form** or **profile drag**). Drag experienced by an object in an air stream is called *air resistance*. » aerodynamics [i]; fluid mechanics; Stokes' law

drag racing A specialized form of motor racing which is a test of acceleration. Large-engined 'vehicles' with big rear wheels and small front ones race normally two at a time on a 400 m/440 yd straight track, from a standing start. Parachutes are fitted to the machines to help with braking. The sport developed in California in the 1930s, and is now very popular in the USA. Speeds of over 400 kph/250 mph are not uncommon. » motor racing

dragger A framework attached to a ship, made in an emergency from anything that will float, to stop the ship from drifting down wind too rapidly. More commonly known as a *sea anchor*, it is made fast to a hawser and paid out over the bow. » anchor [i]

dragonet Any of a small family of fishes, widespread in coastal waters of tropical to warm temperate seas; includes European *Callionymus lyra* found from Norway to the Mediterranean, living on or in sand and shingle sediments; length up to 30 cm/1 ft, body rather flattened, pelvic fins broad, dorsal fin striped blue and yellow in male; gill openings small on top of head, eyes prominent. (Family: *Callionymidae*.)

dragon-fish Deep-water fish with slender snake-like body; length up to 40 cm/16 in; short head and very long mouth, bearing fang-like jaw teeth; light organs present in rows along underside of body, behind eye, and on long chin barbel that serves as lure to attract prey. (Family: *Stomiatidae*.)

dragonfly A large, long-bodied insect with two pairs of slender wings held horizontally at rest; large compound eyes enable adults to catch insects in flight; larvae aquatic, broad-bodied, predatory. (Order: *Odonata*. Suborder: *Anisoptera*.) » insect [i]; larva

dragon-tree An evergreen tree native to the Canary Is and Madeira; short, thick branches, bearing clusters of greyish or bluish sword-shaped leaves at the tips; flowers small, greenish-white; berries orange. Red resin exuded by the trunk is known as **dragon's blood**, used in varnish. (*Dracaena draco*. Family: *Agavaceae*.) » evergreen plants; resin; tree [i]

Drake, Sir Francis (c.1540–96) Greatest of the Elizabethan seamen, born at Crowndale, Devon. In 1567 he commanded the *Judith* in his kinsman John Hawkins's ill-fated expedition to the West Indies, and returned there several times to recover the losses sustained from the Spaniards, his exploits gaining him great popularity in England. In 1577 he set out with five ships for the Pacific, through the Straits of Magellan, but after his fleet was battered by storm and fire, he alone continued in the *Golden Hind*. He then struck out across the Pacific, reached the Pelew Is, and returned to England via the Cape of Good Hope in 1580. The following year, the Queen visited his ship and knighted him. In 1585 he sailed with 25 ships against the Spanish Indies, bringing home tobacco, potatoes, and the dispirited Virginian colonists. In the battle against the Spanish Armada (1588), which raged for a week in the Channel, his seamanship and courage brought him further distinction. In 1595 he sailed again to the West Indies, but died of dysentery off Porto Bello. » Elizabeth I; Spanish Armada

Drakensberg Mountains, Zulu **Kwathlamba** or **Quathlamba** Mountain range in South Africa, extending NE–SW through Transvaal, Natal, and Cape provinces; highest peak, near Natal–Lesotho frontier, Thaban Ntlenyana (3 482 m/11 424 ft). » South Africa [i]

drama (Gr 'action') A representation of human action by actors impersonating characters on stage. One of the oldest literary forms, developing in different directions out of religious ritual, its origins are reflected in the frequent use of music, dance, and chorus. Drama was divided by Aristotle into tragedy and comedy, a distinction valid for classical times, with the strict separation of styles. But with the development of drama in the mediaeval and modern world, these categories have proved inadequate. Dr Johnson said Shakespeare's own plays were 'neither comedies nor tragedies, but compositions of a distinct kind', and defended the hybrid tragi-comedy against purist critics because it 'exhibits the true state of sublunary nature'. The drama has indeed served as a forum for the testing of old and new feelings and ideas, and competing perceptions of truth; with sentimentality, heroism, and high ideals cast against cynicism, self-indulgence, and practicality. This century, Brecht has advocated an epic drama which stands outside Aristotelian categories and assumptions. Meanwhile, film and television have allowed unprecedented developments in the drama, at formal, technical, and ideological levels. » Aristotle; Brecht; chronicle plays; comedy; literature; Shakespeare [i]; tragedy

dramatherapy The use of drama as a creative medium to help in clarifying and alleviating personal and social problems. As a practice it fuses both artistic and therapeutic skills. » educational drama; psychodrama

draughts A popular board game played on a standard chess board containing 64 squares of alternate colours (normally black and white); known as **checkers** in the USA. Played by two players, each has 12 small flat round counters (known as *pieces*), one set normally being black, the other white. The pieces are lined on alternate squares on the first three rows at either side of the board. The object is to remove your opponent's pieces from the board by jumping over them onto a vacant diagonal square. Only forward moves are allowed until the back line of the opposing 'territory' is reached, when that piece becomes a *king* and can move forward or backward. Pieces cannot be moved between squares of different colour. Draughts is believed to have been played in ancient Egypt; the first book about the game was published in Spain in 1547. » chess; RR110

Dravidian languages A group of more than 20 languages, spoken mainly in S India. The principal ones are Telugu, Tamil, Kannada, and Malayalam, which together have some 150 million speakers within the S states. The origin of this group of languages is obscure, but there is general agreement that they were once spoken throughout India, and were displaced from the N by the advance of the Indo-Aryan branch of Indo-European. » Indo-Aryan languages

Drayton, Michael (1563–1631) English poet, born at Hartshill, Warwickshire. His earliest work was *The Harmony of the Church*, a metrical rendering of scriptural passages, which gave offence to the authorities, and was condemned to be destroyed. His best-known works were *England's Heroical Epistles* (1597) and *Polyolbion* (1613–22), an ambitious description of the English countryside. He died in London. » English literature; poetry

dreaming » **sleep**

Dreamtime or **The Dreaming** In the mythology of the Australian Aborigines, one of the names for the time of the Ancestors, who created the world and are still alive in the sacred places. This time continues to exist, and it may be possible to find it through dreams. » Aborigines

dredger A vessel designed to remove spoil from the sea bed in order to maintain or increase the depth in a harbour or approaches. Dredgers are also used to obtain sand and gravel from the sea bed for constructional purposes. » ship [i]

Dreiser, Theodore (1871–1945) US writer, born at Terre Haute, Indiana. He became a journalist in Chicago, St Louis, and New York. His first novel *Sister Carrie* (1900), starkly realistic, was criticized for obscenity, and he did not write another until 1911, when *Jennie Gerhardt* won acclaim. *An American Tragedy* (1925), based on a famous murder case, brought him success. In 1939 he moved to Hollywood, where he died. » American literature; novel

Dresden [**drez**dn] 51°02N 13°45E, pop (1982) 521 011. Capital of Dresden county, SE Germany; on R Elbe, ESE of Berlin, close to the Czechoslovak frontier; former capital of Saxony; almost totally destroyed by bombing in 1945, now rebuilt; airport; railway; technical university (1828); Dresden china now manufactured in Meissen; motor vehicles, electronics, pharmaceuticals, food processing, optical instruments, market gardening. » Germany [i]; Saxony

dressage An equestrian discipline which is a test of the horse's obedience skills, consisting of a series of movements at the walk, trot, and canter. Dressage can have its own competition or form part of a three day event. » equestrianism

Dreyer, John (Louis Emil) [**dray**er] (1852–1926) Danish astronomer, born in Copenhagen. He worked at Birr Castle, Ireland, then became director of Armagh Observatory. He produced the standard catalogue on star clusters, nebulas, and galaxies, the *New General Catalogue* (NGC), which is still in use today. He died at Oxford. » galaxy; nebula; star

Dreyfus, Alfred (c.1859–1935) French Jewish army officer, born at Mülhausen, Alsace. An artillery captain on the General Staff, in 1893–4 he was falsely charged with delivering defence secrets to the Germans. He was court-martialled and transported to Devil's I, French Guiana. The efforts of his wife and friends to prove him innocent provoked a vigorous response from militarists and anti-Semites, and deeply divided the French intellectual and political world. After the case was tried again (1899), he was found guilty but pardoned, and in 1906 the verdict was reversed. Proof of his innocence came when German military documents were uncovered in 1930. He died in Paris. » Zola

Driesch, Hans (Adolf Eduard) [dreesh] (1867–1941) German zoologist and philosopher, born at Bad Kreuznach, Prussia. He studied at Jena and other universities, becoming professor of philosophy at Heidelberg (1912), Cologne (1919), and Leipzig (1921). He did valuable work in embryology and parapsychology, and became an exponent of vitalism. Forced to retire early by the Nazis, he died at Leipzig. » embryology; parapsychology; vitalism

drift A geological term for glacial or glaciofluvial sedimentary deposits, generally unsorted and unstratified, with a wide range of particle sizes from boulders to clay. » continental drift; till

drift chamber » **proportional counter**

drill A baboon native to W African forests; resembles the mandrill, but smaller, with a black face. Drills live to the N of the Sanaga R in Cameroun; mandrills live to the S. (*Mandrillus leucophaeus*.) » baboon; mandrill

Drinkwater, John (1882–1937) British poet, dramatist, and critic, born at Leytonstone, Essex. He was an insurance clerk who achieved an immediate success with his play *Abraham Lincoln* (1918), following this with *Mary Stuart* (1921) and other historical dramas. His first volume of poems appeared in 1923, and he also wrote several critical studies. He was one of the founders of the Pilgrim Players, and became manager of the Birmingham Repertory Theatre. He died in London. » English literature; theatre

driver ant A tropical ant; colonies large, with millions of individuals and a single, permanently wingless queen; workers forage in groups; colony nomadic, changing nest site frequently; living workers form walls of bivouac nest to protect queen and brood. (Order: *Hymenoptera*. Family; *Formicidae*.) » ant

Drogheda [**drou**hduh], Gaelic **Droichead Atha** 53°43N 6°21W, pop (1981) 23 615. Industrial seaport town in Louth county, NE Leinster, E Irish Republic; on R Boyne, N of Dublin; Irish parliaments met here until 1494; railway; brewing, textiles, chemicals; Neolithic passage graves, 7 km/4 ml W; remains of 5th-c monastery at Monasterboice, 8 km/5 ml N; Battle of the Boyne field (1690) 6 km/3¾ ml SW. » Boyne, Battle of the; Irish Republic [i]; Louth; New Grange

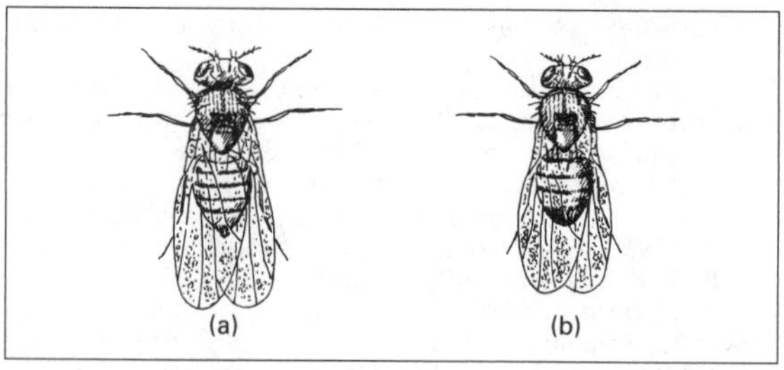

Drosophila – Female (a); male (b)

dromedary A camel formerly wild in Arabia, now known only in domestication; comprises 90% of the world's camels; found in hot deserts from N Africa to SW Asia (introduced elsewhere); also known as the **Arabian camel** or **one-humped camel**. Originally it was a fast light Arabian camel bred for riding and racing, but the name is now used for all single-humped camels. (*Camelus dromedarius*.) » camel

drone The male of colonial ants, bees, and wasps, whose only function is to mate with fertile females. It plays no part in brood maintenance. (Order: *Hymenoptera*.) » ant; bee; wasp

drongo A bird native to the Old World tropics; plumage usually glossy black; long forked tail; inhabits woodland; eats mainly insects; fearless in chasing other birds, including hawks. (Family: *Dicruridae*, 20 species.)

Dronning Maud Land » **Queen Maud Land**

dropwort An erect perennial, growing to 80 cm/30 in, native to Europe, W Asia, and N Africa; roots tuberous; leaves pinnate, with pairs of small leaflets lying between 8–20 pairs of large leaflets; flowers 6-petalled, sepals reflexed, cream tinged with purple, forming an irregular terminal mass; carpels straight. (*Filipendula vulgaris*. Family; *Rosaceae*.) » carpel; perennial; pinnate; sepal; tuber

Drosophila [drosofila] A genus of brownish-yellow fruit flies with typically red eyes. They lay eggs near fermenting fruit, on which the larvae feed. There are c.2 600 species, some of which are economically important pests of fruit. The chromosome structure and genetics of *Drosophila* species have been studied extensively. (Order: *Diptera*. Family: *Drosophilidae*.) » fruit fly; genetics [i]; larva

Droste-Hülshoff, Annette Elisabeth, Baroness von [**dros**tuh **hüls**hohf] (1797–1848) German poet, born near Münster, Westphalia. Commonly regarded as Germany's greatest woman writer, she led a retired life on her family estate. Her poetry is mainly on religious themes and on the Westphalian countryside. She also wrote a novella, *Die Judenbuche* (1842, The Jew's Beech). She died at Meersburg, Baden, and her works were published posthumously in 1851. » German literature; poetry

drought An extended period of dry weather, generally associated with a blocking anticyclone in which evapotranspiration exceeds precipitation, causing soil moisture deficits. Some regions, especially arid and semi-arid areas, are particularly prone to droughts, which can result in food shortages and human suffering. In the Sahel region on the S edge of the Sahara Desert, rainfall 1968–1972 was only 50% of the 1931–60 average, and was accompanied by major famine. In the UK an official drought occurs when there is a period of 15 consecutive days on each of which there is no more than 0.25 mm/0.1 in of rain. » anticyclone; arid zone; desertification; Dust Bowl; evapotranspiration; sahel

drug addiction or **drug dependence** A state whereby an addict habitually takes a drug, the compulsion being fuelled by a continuous need to experience the psychic effect of the particular drug or to avoid the pain and discomfort of its absence. Frequently, long-term addicts need to increase the dose of the drug they are taking to feel the same effect (*drug tolerance*) and often develop anti-social habits, such as theft, to pay for their addiction (if it is to an illegal drug). Addictive drugs include narcotics (eg heroin, cocaine), many types of sedative and tranquillizer, and nicotine. » barbiturates; benzodiazepines; narcotics; nicotine

drug resistance A state in which a patient does not respond to a therapeutic drug. Bacteria may acquire resistance through gene mutation to a particular antibiotic by its overuse or misuse; for example, the first class of antibiotics, the sulphonamides, fell out of use when many common strains of bacteria became resistant. Cancer cells may also acquire resistance to drugs which had previously been effective, requiring a change in the course of treatment. Resistance to malarial drugs is a major problem in tropical countries, where malaria causes a million deaths per year. Similarly, insects and other pests acquire resistance to agents which previously controlled them. » antibiotics; bacteria [i]; cancer; malaria; sulphonamides

drum A musical instrument consisting of a membrane of skin or plastic (rarely of other materials) stretched over a hollow resonator or frame, usually of wood or metal. Drums are normally played by striking the membrane with a stick or with the hands, and may be classified according to their shape (eg conical, cylindrical, 'hourglass', kettledrums) and whether they have a single membrane or are double-headed. The kettledrum is one of the few that can be tuned to a definite pitch. » bongos; membranophone; percussion [i]; side drum; tambourine; timpani; tom-tom

drumfish Any of a large family of marine and estuarine fishes that have the ability to produce sounds by resonating the swimbladder; many species live in muddy estuarine habitats, and thus have a well-developed sensory apparatus; also known as **croakers**. (Family: *Sciaenidae*.)

drumlins Small, streamlined, ice-moulded hills made of till, produced by the pressure of moving ice over glacial deposits. They often occur in groups producing a 'basket of eggs' topography. The shape indicates ice flow direction, with their long axis parallel to the ice flow, and their blunter ends pointing towards the ice source. » glaciation; till

Drummond, William, of Hawthornden (1585–1649) Scottish poet, born and died at Hawthornden, near Edinburgh. He studied law at Bourges and Paris, then became laird of Hawthornden, where he devoted his life to poetry and mechanical experiments. He was the first Scottish poet to write in a form of English not from Scotland. His chief collection, *Poems*, appeared in 1616. His prose works include several royalist pamphlets. » poetry; Scottish literature

drupe A fleshy fruit in which each of the one or more seeds is enclosed by a stony layer. » fruit; prunus; seed

Druze A religious faith which originated during the closing years of the Fatimid caliph al-Hakim (996–1021 AD), who some extremist Ismailis regarded as a manifestation of the Divinity. The Druze, who survive in parts of Jordan, Lebanon, and Syria, deviate considerably in belief and practice from the main Muslim body. They await the return from divine concealment of both al-Hakim and his disciple, Hamza ibn Ali. They assemble on Thursdays, instead of the usual Fridays, reject many of the prescriptions of the Shariʿa, affirm monogamous marriage, and believe in the transmigration of souls. They number c.500 000. » Ismailis; Jumblat; Shariʿa

dry cleaning The cleaning of textiles using organic solvents rather than water. Soil (solid dirt) is held on to fabrics by oil and grease, which are removed by detergents during washing. In dry cleaning, the oil/grease is dissolved by the solvent, and the solid dirt falls away easily. » felt

dry dock » **dock** (shipping)

dry ice » **carbon; sublimation** (chemistry)

dry rot A serious type of timber decay caused by the fungus *Serpula lacrymans*; infected wood shows a surface growth of white filaments (mycelium); fruiting bodies leathery, bearing rust-coloured spores; common on structural timbers of buildings in damp, poorly ventilated conditions. (Subdivision: *Basidiomycetes*.) » fungus

dryad [**dri**yad] In Greek mythology, a being originally connected with oak-trees, but more usually referring to a wood-nymph, living in or among the trees. Dryads were usually friendly, but could frighten travellers. » Aristaeus

Dryden, John (1631–1700) English poet, born at Aldwinkle, Northamptonshire. Educated at Westminster and Cambridge, he went to London in 1657, where he wrote several plays and satires for the court. His first successful play, written in heroic couplets, was *The Indian Emperor* (1665). After 1676, he began to write in blank verse, producing his best play, *All for Love* (1678). In 1668 he became poet laureate and in 1670 historiographer royal. Called to defend the King's party, he wrote a series of satires, notably *Absalom and Achitophel* (1681), which did much to turn the tide against the Whigs. To this era also belong the didactic poem *Religio Laici* (1682), which argues the case for Anglicanism, and *The Hind and the Panther* (1687), marking his conversion to Catholicism. His political reward was a place in the customs; but he lost his laureateship on the accession of William III (1688). He died in London. » English literature; heroic couplet; satire

Dryopithecus [driyoh**pith**uhkuhs] A fossil ape abundant in Africa and the Mediterranean region during the Miocene epoch; about the size of a rhesus monkey; walked on all fours; brain gibbon-like; jaw projecting moderately; canine teeth prominent; includes *Proconsul*. (Superfamily: *Hominoidea*. Family: *Pongidae*.) » ape; fossil; Miocene epoch

drypoint A method of intaglio printing whereby the metal plate is incised by direct pressure using a steel point. The greatest master was Rembrandt, who often combined drypoint with straightforward etching. » engraving; etching; intaglio **1**; Rembrandt

Drysdale, Russell (1912–81) Australian painter, born at Bognor Regis, England. He studied at the George Bell Art School, Melbourne, in London, and in Paris, where he was influenced by Surrealism. His powerful scenes of the outback were a major contribution to modern art in Australia. He was knighted in 1969, and became a Companion of the Order of Australia in 1980. » Australian art; Surrealism

DTP » **desk-top publishing**

du Barry, Marie Jeanne Gomard de Vaubernier, Comtesse ('Countess') (c.1743–93) The favourite mistress of Louis XV, born at Vaucouleurs. Brought up in a Paris convent, she won the notice of Louis XV (1768), and married Comte Guillaume du Barry before becoming official royal mistress. Her influence reigned supreme until the death of Louis in 1774, when she was dismissed from court. She was tried before the Revolutionary Tribunal, and guillotined. » French Revolution [i]; Louis XV

du Bois, W(illiam) E(dward) B(urghardt) [doo **boyz**] (1868–1963) US historian, sociologist, and equal rights campaigner, born into a small Black community at Great Barrington, Massachusetts. He studied at Fisk, Harvard, and Berlin, and in his writings explored the history and lives of Black Americans. In politics he campaigned for full equality, opposing the tactics of Booker T Washington. He helped found the National Association for the Advancement of Colored People, and in his old age lived in Ghana, where he died. » Black consciousness; Washington, Booker T

du Maurier, Dame Daphne (1907–89) British novelist, born in London, the granddaughter of George du Maurier. She wrote several successful period romances and adventure stories, including *Jamaica Inn* (1936), *Rebecca* (1938), and *The Flight of the Falcon* (1965). She has also published plays, short stories, and literary reminiscences. She was made a Dame in 1969, and died at Par, Cornwall. » English literature; novel

du Maurier, George (Louis Palmella Busson) [dü **moh**ryay] (1834–96) British artist and illustrator, born in Paris. He studied chemistry in London (1851), but on returning to Paris adopted art as a profession. In 1860 he went back to London, where he gained a reputation as a designer and book illustrator. Finally he joined the staff of *Punch*, and became widely known as a gentle, graceful satirist of fashionable life. He wrote and illustrated three novels, notably *Trilby* (1894). He died in London. » English art; satire

du Mont, Allen B(alcom) [doo**mont**] (1901–65) US electronics engineer, born in New York City. Early work in manufacturing radio valves gave him the opportunity to supervise the production of more than 30 000 valves each day by 1931, when he developed cathode-ray tubes for use in oscilloscopes and television. He also invented the radio set's 'magic eye' tuning indicator. He died in New Jersey. » cathode-ray tube; thermionic valve

du Pré, Jacqueline [doo **pray**] (1945–87) British cellist, born at Oxford. In 1967 she married the pianist Daniel Barenboim, with whom she gave many recitals. Her career as a player ended in 1973, when she developed multiple sclerosis, but thereafter she continued as a teacher. She died in London. » cello

Duala » **Douala**

dualism In philosophy, any theory which asserts the existence of two different kinds of thing; for example, Plato's distinction between temporal things and timeless forms. The most familiar dualism, held by Plato, Descartes, and many others, is between mind and matter. Descartes claimed that matter is a substance, whose essence is spatial extension, and that the mind or soul is a non-spatial substance, whose essence is thinking; a person, then, is a dualistic compound of these substances. Some dualists claim, not that the mind is a substance, but that there are mental properties of persons that are in no way reducible to physical properties. » Descartes; monism; Plato

Duarte, Pico [**dwah**tee], formerly **Monte Trujillo** Mountain in the Cordillera Central of the Dominican Republic, West Indies; height 3 175 m/10 416 ft; highest peak in the Caribbean. » Dominican Republic [i]

Dubai or **Dubayy** [doo**biy**] pop (1980) 278 000; area 3 900 sq km/1 505 sq ml. Second largest of the United Arab Emirates, NE of Abu Dhabi; capital, Dubai, pop (1980) 265 702; chief town, Mina Jebel Ali, a free trade zone; oil discovered in 1966; natural gas, petrochemicals, desalination, cables, aluminium smelting, steel. » United Arab Emirates [i]

dubbing The combination of several separate sound recordings into the final composite sound track for a motion picture or video production; sometimes known as **mixing**. The term also refers to the operation of replacing spoken dialogue of a completed sound track by its equivalent in another language, producing a *dubbed* version. » film production

Dubček, Alexander [**dub**chek] (1921–) Czechoslovakian statesman, born at Uhrovek, Slovakia. He joined the Communist Party in 1939, fought as a Slovak patriot against the Nazis (1944–5), and rose to become First Secretary in the Party (1968). He introduced a series of far-reaching economic and political reforms, including abolition of censorship and increased freedom of speech. His liberalization policy led to the occupation of Czechoslovakia by Soviet forces (Aug 1968), and in 1969 he was replaced by Husak. He became President of the Federal Assembly, but was then expelled from the Presidium, and deprived of party membership in 1970. In 1989, following a popular uprising, and the resignation of the communist government, he was elected Chairman of the Czechoslovak parliament. » communism; Czechoslovakia [i]

Dublin (county), Gaelic **Baile Átha Cliath** pop (1981) 1 003 164; area 922 sq km/356 sq ml. County in Leinster province, E Irish Republic; bisected W–E by R Liffey and the Grand Canal; Wicklow Mts to the S, and Irish Sea to the W; capital, Dublin; agriculture, livestock, Dublin trade and industries. » Dublin (city); Irish Republic [i]

Dublin (city), Gaelic **Baile Átha Cliath**, ancient **Eblana** 53°20N 6°15W, pop (1981) 860 619. County borough and capital of the Irish Republic; at mouth of R Liffey where it meets the Irish Sea; on site of Viking settlement; first Sinn Féin parliament met here, 1919; airport; railway; ferries to Liverpool and Holyhead (from Dublin and Dun Laoghaire); two universities (1591, 1908); trading port, brewing, distilling, textiles, chemicals, food processing; natural gas pipeline from Kinsale; King's Inns, national museum, national gallery, Leinster House, Dublin Castle, Abbey Theatre; literary associations with Oscar Wilde, W B Yeats, George Bernard Shaw, Jonathan Swift, and James Joyce. » Dublin (county); Irish Republic [i]; Sinn Féin

Dubrovnik [doo**brov**nik], Ital **Ragusa** 42°40N 18°07E, pop (1981) 66 131. Port on the Dalmatia coast of Croatia republic, W Yugoslavia; capital of Dalmatia; earthquake damage, 1979; badly damaged during siege by the Federal Army in the civil war, 1991; airport; car ferries to Italy and Greece; silk, leather, dairy products, liqueurs, tourism; mediaeval town walls surrounding the old town, a world heritage site; cathedral, Rector's palace; Dubrovnik Summer Festival (Jul–Aug). » Croatia; Yugoslavia [i]

Dubuffet, Jean [dü**bü**fay] (1901–85) French artist, born at Le Havre, and studied at the Académie Julian in Paris. He invented the concept of Art Brut, pioneering the use of rubbish (eg discarded newspapers, broken glass, rough plaster daubed and scratched like an old wall) to create 'pictures'. He is regarded as a forerunner of the Pop Art and Dada-like fashions of the 1960s. He died in Paris. » Art Brut; Dada; Pop Art

Du Cange, Charles Du Fresne, Seigneur ('Lord') [dü **kãzh**] (1610–88) French scholar, born at Amiens. He became a parliamentary advocate, and a prolific writer and editor. He is best known for his glossaries of the Middle Ages, published in 1678 and 1688. He died in Paris.

Duccio di Buoninsegna [**doo**cheeoh dee bwoninsaynya] (c.1260–c.1320) Italian painter, founder of the Sienese School, born at Siena. In his work the Gothic tradition in Italian art is seen in its most highly-developed state. His masterpiece is the 'Maestà' for the altar of Siena cathedral (1311), from which come the 'Annunciation' and 'Transfiguration' in the National Gallery, London. » Gothic art; Italian art; Sienese School

Duchamp, Marcel [düshã] (1887–1968) French painter, born at Blainville. He was associated with several modern movements, including Cubism and Futurism, and shocked his generation with such works as 'Nude descending a staircase' (1912, Philadelphia). He was one of the pioneers of Dadaism. In 1915 he left Paris for New York, where he laboured eight years on his best-known work, 'The Bride Stripped Bare by Her Bachelors, Even' (1915–23, Philadelphia). He died at Neuilly. » Cubism; Dada; French art; Futurism

Duchy of Cornwall The oldest of English duchies, instituted by Edward III in 1337 to provide support for his eldest son, Edward, the Black Prince. Since 1503 the eldest son of the sovereign has inherited the dukedom; it consists of lands (totalling c.52 000 ha/130 000 acres) in Cornwall, Devon, Somerset, and S London, including the Oval cricket ground. The present Prince of Wales pays one quarter of the (tax-free) revenue into the Treasury. » Oval, the; Prince of Wales; Stannaries

Duchy of Lancaster A duchy created in 1267 by Henry III of England for his son Edmund. It was attached to the Crown in 1399 when the last Duke of Lancaster became Henry IV. The duchy lands consist of some 21 000 ha/52 000 acres of farmland and moorland, mostly in Yorkshire; the (untaxed) revenue is paid direct into the Monarch's private allowance (the Privy Purse), so the duchy functions as a department of state. It is controlled by the Chancellor of the Duchy of Lancaster, a political appointment generally held by a member of the Cabinet.

duck A smallish bird (the larger species are called **geese** or **swans**), primarily aquatic, with full webbing between the three front toes; relatively long necks; blunt flattened bills; male has penis (rare in birds). (Family: *Anatidae*.) » dabbling/diving/harlequin/muscovy/perching/whistling duck; eider; gadwall; garganey; goosander; goose; merganser; shelduck; stifftail; swan; teal; water-fowl

duck-billed platypus A mammal native to E Australia; length, up to 750 mm/30 in; thick brown fur, soft duck-like bill, short legs with webbed feet, short flattened tail which stores fat; pouch inside each cheek where food is 'chewed' by horny ridges; male with venomous 'spur' on hind leg; inhabits muddy freshwater; eats aquatic invertebrates (especially insect larvae); also known as **platypus** or **duck-bill**. (*Ornithorhynchus anatinus*. Family: *Ornithorhynchidae*.) » monotreme

duck hawk » **peregrine falcon**

duckweed Tiny floating or submerged herbs found in freshwater everywhere. It consists of a flat or convex green thallus a few millimetres across, with a groove concealing the flowers on the margin, and roots on the underside. (Genus: *Lemna*, 15 species. Family: *Lemnaceae*.) » herb; thallus; wolfia

ductile material » **plastic deformation**

ductless glands » **endocrine glands**

due process A legal principle, deriving from the 39th clause of Magna Carta (1215) which provides that 'no freeman shall be arrested or imprisoned or deprived of his freehold or outlawed or banished or in any way ruined, nor will we (ie the monarch) take or order action against him, except by the lawful judgment of his equals and according to the law of the land'. The notion of due process is also embodied in the 5th and 14th amendments of the US Constitution. » jury

Dufay, Guillaume [düfay] (c.1400–74) French composer, born (probably) in Cambrai and died there. By 1420 he was in Italy and sang in the papal choir (1428–33, 1435–7). He was later a canon at Cambrai (1439–50, 1458–74), and was also employed for lengthy periods at the courts of Ferrara and Savoy. During a year spent in Florence he wrote one of his most famous motets *Nuper rosarum flores*, for the dedication of the dome of Florence Cathedral (1436). He also wrote masses and a large number of secular songs. » motet

Dufourspitze [doo**foor**shpitsuh], Ital **Punta Dufour** 45°57N 7°53E. Mountain peak in Switzerland; highest peak of the Monte Rosa group of the Pennine Alps, on the Italian–Swiss border; second highest Alpine peak; height 4 634 m/15 203 ft. » Alps

Dufy, Raoul [**dü**fee] (1877–1953) French artist and designer, born at Le Havre. He studied at the Ecole des Beaux-Arts, and was much influenced by Fauvism, which he later abandoned. From 1907 to 1918 he produced many fabric designs and engraved book illustrations, and in 1919 went to the Riviera, where he began a long series of swift calligraphic sketches of seascapes, regattas, and racecourse scenes. He died at Forcalquier. » Fauvism; French art

dugong [**doo**gong] A marine mammal, native to tropical coasts of the Old World; streamlined, with a short broad head; male with short tusks hidden beneath fleshy cheeks; front legs are flippers; hind legs absent; tail with pointed horizontal blades (like the tail of a whale); inhabits shallow waters; eats underwater plants. (*Dugong dugon*. Family: *Dugongidae*. Order: *Sirenia*.) » mammal [i]

Duhamel, Georges (1884–1966) French novelist, poet, and man of letters, born in Paris. He studied medicine and became an army surgeon, which provided the background for such works as *Civilisation* (1918, awarded the Prix Goncourt). His best-known works are his novel cycles *Salavin* (1920–32) and *Chronique des Pasquier* (1933–44, The Pasquier Chronicles). He died near Paris. » French literature

duiker [**diy**kuh] A small African antelope; both sexes with arched back and short horns separated by a tuft of long hairs; two types: the **common (grey, savanna**, or **bush) duiker** (*Sylvicapra grimmia*), and the **forest duiker** (genus: *Cephalophus*, 16 species). The name is Afrikaans for 'diver', because they dive into undergrowth when disturbed. » antelope

Duisburg [**düs**boorkh] 51°27N 6°42E, pop (1983) 541 800. Industrial and commercial city in Düsseldorf district, Germany; river port on W edge of R Ruhr, at confluence of Ruhr and Rhine; largest inland port in Europe; badly bombed in World War 2; railway; university (1972); steel, copper, zinc, heavy equipment, plastics, oil refining, brewing, river craft; home of Gerhard Mercator; international rowing regattas at Wedau sports park. » Germany [i]; Mercator

Dukakis, Michael S(tanley) [doo**kah**kis] (1933–) US politician, born in Boston. Educated at Swarthmore and Harvard, he entered Massachusetts politics and became Governor of the state (1975–9, 1983–). In 1988 he was Democratic nominee for the presidency. » Bush, George; Democratic Party

Dukas, Paul (Abraham) [dü**kah**] (1865–1935) French composer, born in Paris. Some of his music is classical in approach, but he tended mainly towards impressionism. His best-known work is the symphonic poem *L'Apprenti sorcier* (1897, The Sorcerer's Apprentice). He also wrote several orchestral and piano pieces, and was professor of composition at the Paris Conservatoire from 1927 until his death, in Paris.

duke In the UK, a nobleman of the highest order. A royal duke is a son of the sovereign who has been given a dukedom, such as Queen Elizabeth's son Andrew, Duke of York. Philip, Duke of Edinburgh is a royal duke, but not a duke of the blood royal, since he is not a descendant of a British sovereign in the male line. » peerage

Dukeries, the Area of NW Nottinghamshire, C England; includes Sherwood Forest and the parks of former ducal seats at Clumber, Thoresby, Welbeck, and Worksop. » Nottinghamshire

Dukhabors » **Doukhobors**

dulcimer A type of zither, consisting of a wooden soundbox, usually trapeziform, strung with a variable number of metal strings which pass over (or through) one or more bridges held in place by the pressure of the strings themselves. It is played with hammers of various types, and has been widespread in different forms throughout the world since the 15th-c or even longer. » chordophone; cimbalom; psaltery; zither

Dulles, John Foster (1888–1959) US Republican politician, born in Washington, DC. Educated at Princeton and the Sorbonne, he became a lawyer. During World War 2 he advocated a world governmental organization, and in 1945 advised at the Charter Conference of the United Nations, thereafter becoming US delegate to the General Assembly. In 1953 he became US Secretary of State, opening a vigorous diplomacy of personal conferences with statesmen in other countries. He resigned in 1959, and was awarded the Medal of Freedom shortly before his death, in Washington, DC. » United Nations

Dulong, Pierre Louis (1785–1838) French chemist, born at Rouen. He trained in medicine and science at Paris, and later became director of its Ecole Polytechnique. His name is now most linked with **Dulong and Petit's law** (1819), devised in association with Alexis Thérèse Petit (1791–1820), which relates the specific heat capacity of a solid element to its relative atomic mass, and which for over a century was a valuable route for finding approximate atomic weights. He died in Paris. » relative atomic mass

Duluth [duh**looth**] 46°47N 92°07W, pop (1980) 92 811. Seat of St Louis County, NE Minnesota, USA, at the W end of L Superior; established in the 1850s; airfield; railway; major lake port handling grain and iron ore; steel, cement, metal products, electrical equipment; Aerial Lift Bridge and Leif Erikson Park; Grandma's Marathon (Jun). » Minnesota; Superior, Lake

duma A political assembly in pre-revolutionary Russia, such as the mediaeval 'Boyars' Council'. Municipal dumas (town councils) similar to the rural *zemstvos* were introduced as part of local government reforms in 1870. After the 1905 revolution the State Duma, a quasi-parliamentary body, was established with limited constitutional powers. Four State Dumas were elected between 1906 and the 1917 revolution, when the institution was abolished. » boyars; Revolution of 1905; Russian history; Russian Revolution; zemstvo

Dumas, Alexandre [dü**mah**] (1802–70) French novelist and playwright, born at Villers-Cotterêts, Aisne. He moved to Paris in 1823, where he obtained a clerkship, and began to write. At 27 he became famous with his play *Henri III* (1829). After several other plays, some in collaboration, he turned to travelogues and historical novels. He gained enduring success as a storyteller, his purpose being to put the history of France into novels. Among his best-known works are *Le Comte de Monte Cristo* (1844–5, The Count of Monte Cristo), *Les Trois Mousquetaires* (1845, The Three Musketeers), and *La Tulipe noire* (1850, The Black Tulip). He spent two years in exile in Brussels (1855–7), and helped Garibaldi in Italy (1860–4). He died in Dieppe. His son, **Alexandre** (1824–95), often known as 'Dumas *fils*', was also a writer, whose best-known work was *La Dame aux camélias* (1848). » French literature; novel

dumb cane An evergreen perennial, native to tropical America; leaves large, narrowly oval with long stalks, often yellow or white variegated; flowers in a spadix surrounded by a large spathe. If eaten, the bitter sap causes swelling of the tongue and throat, hence the name. (Genus: *Dieffenbachia*, 30 species. Family: *Araceae*.) » evergreen plants; perennial; spadix; spathe

Dumbarton 55°57N 4°34W, pop (1981) 23 430. Capital of Dumbarton district, Strathclyde, W Scotland; at confluence of Leven and Clyde Rivers, 22 km/14 ml NW of Glasgow; railway; distilling, electronics; Dumbarton castle. » Scotland [i]; Strathclyde

Dumfries [dum**frees**] 55°04N 3°37W, pop (1981) 32 100. Market town and capital of Nithsdale district, and of Dumfries and Galloway region, SW Scotland; on R Nith, 97 km/60 ml SE of

Glasgow; railway; light engineering, textiles; Burns's House and Mausoleum, Old Bridge House (1662), Devorgilla's Bridge; Dumfries and Galloway arts festival (May). » Burns; Dumfries and Galloway

Dumfries and Galloway pop (1981) 145 139; area 6 370 sq km/2 459 sq ml. Region in SW Scotland, divided into four districts; bounded SE by England, S by the Solway Firth, Wigtown Bay, and Luce Bay; Rinns of Galloway peninsula (W); drained by the Cree, Dee, Nith, and Annan Rivers; capital, Dumfries; major towns include Kirkcudbright, Stranraer; sheep and cattle, agriculture, forestry, tourism; Stranraer linked by ferry to Larne in N Ireland; Ruthwell Cross, Glen Trool National Park, Galloway Hills. » Dumfries; Scotland [i]

Dumont D'Urville, Jules Sébastien César [dümõ dürveey] (1790–1842) French navigator, born at Condé-sur-Noireau, Calvados. He entered the navy in 1807, and commanded expeditions to survey the S Pacific (1826–9) and the Antarctic (1837–40), discovering Joinville I and Adélie Land. He was killed in a railway accident near Versailles. A French Antarctic station is named after him. » Antarctica [i]

Dumouriez, Charles François (du Périer) [dümooryay] (1739–1823) French general, born at Cambrai. In 1792 he defeated the Prussians at Valmy and the Austrians at Jemappes, but in 1793 lost to the Austrians at Neerwinden. His leanings towards the monarchy caused him to be denounced by the revolutionaries, and to save his head he went over to the Austrians. He later settled in England, and died near Henley-upon-Thames, Oxfordshire. » French Revolutionary Wars

dumping An economic process where goods made (often with government subsidy) in one country are exported to another country and sold cheaply, flooding that market, and damaging domestic industry as a result. In economics, dumping occurs when the goods are sold in a foreign market at less than marginal cost. In the mid-1980s, for example, it was asserted that there had been dumping of Japanese compact disc players on the European market. Assertions of this kind are not always possible to prove. » marginal cost

Dun Laoghaire [doonlaee], Eng **Dunleary** [duhnleeree], formerly **Kingstown** 53°17N 6°08W, pop (1981) 54 496. Borough in Dublin county, Leinster, E Irish Republic; on Irish Sea, S of Dublin; fishing port, resort town, yachting centre, dormitory town for Dublin; named Kingstown when George IV landed here in 1821; railway; ferries to Holyhead. » Dublin (county); Holyhead; Irish Republic [i]

Dunant, (Jean) Henri [dünã] (1828–1910) Swiss philanthropist, born in Geneva. He inspired the foundation of the International Red Cross after seeing the plight of the wounded on the battlefield of Solferino. His efforts brought about the conference at Geneva (1863) from which came the Geneva Convention (1864), and in 1901 he shared the first Nobel Peace Prize. He died at Heiden, Switzerland. » Red Cross

Dunbar, William (c.1460–c.1520) Scottish poet, born (probably) in East Lothian. Educated at St Andrews, he became a Franciscan novice, and travelled widely, before leaving the order and entering the diplomatic service. He was a courtier of James IV, who gave him a pension in 1500. His poems include *The Thrissill and the Rois* and *Lament for the Makaris*, and several satires, such as *The Dance of the Sevin Deadly Synnis*. His name disappears from the records after 1513. » poetry; satire; Scottish literature

Duncan I » **Macbeth**

Duncan, Andrew (1744–1828) British physician, born near St Andrews, Scotland. He studied medicine at Edinburgh, and in 1773 started the publication 'Medical and philosophical commentaries', which was the only journal of its kind in Britain at that time. In 1792 he prompted the Royal College of Physicians in Edinburgh to establish a lunatic asylum, which came to fruition in 1807. » psychiatry

Duncan, Isadora, originally **Angela Duncan** (1877–1927) US dancer and choreographer, born in San Francisco. She travelled widely in Europe, performing her own choreography, and founding schools in several cities, such as Berlin, Salzburg, and Vienna. She was one of the pioneers of modern dance, basing her work on Greek-derived notions of beauty and harmony, but using everyday movements of running, skipping, and walking. Her unconventional views on marriage and women's liberation gave rise to scandal. She was killed in a car accident in Nice. » ballet; modern dance

Dundalk, Gaelic **Dun Dealgan** [duhndolk] 54°01N 6°25W, pop (1981) 29 135. Capital of Louth county, Leinster, NE Irish Republic; on R Castletown near its mouth on Dundalk Bay; railway; brewing, cigarettes, food processing, textiles, printing, chemicals, livestock trade; Dun Dealgan mound 3 km/1¾ ml W (birthplace of Cuchulain); Maytime theatre festival. » Cuchulain; Irish Republic [i]; Louth

Dundee, John Graham of Claverhouse, 1st Viscount (c.1649–89) Scottish soldier, born of a noble family. In 1672 he entered the Prince of Orange's horse-guards, and at the Battle of Seneff saved William's life. He returned to Scotland in 1677, and defeated the Covenanters at Bothwell Brig (1679). He was made a Privy Councillor in 1683, and became Viscount Dundee (1688). Joined by the Jacobite clans, he raised the standard for James against William and Mary, but died from a musket wound after his successful battle against Mackay at the Pass of Killiecrankie. He was variously known as 'Bloody Claverse' and 'Bonnie Dundee'. » Covenanters; Jacobites; James II (of England); William III

Dundee 56°28N 3°00W, pop (1981) 174 345. Port capital of Tayside region, E Scotland; on N side of the Firth of Tay, 29 km/18 ml E of Perth; royal burgh since 12th-c; airfield; railway; university (1881); jute, textiles, paper, confectionery, oil-related industries, electronics; Barrack Street natural history museum, Caird Hall (1914–23), Broughty Castle Museum, Claypotts Castle (1569–88). » Scotland [i]; Tayside

Dunedin [duhneedin] 45°52S 170°30E, pop (1988e) 106 600. City in Otago, SE South Island, New Zealand; on the E coast at the S end of Otago peninsula; seaport at Port Chalmers, 13 km/8 ml NE; founded by Scottish settlers, 1848; airfield; railway; university (1869); wool, footwear, clothing, agricultural machinery, trade in wool, meat, fruit, and dairy produce; Scottish influence in buildings, parks, and statues; two cathedrals, Octagon, Burns statue, municipal chambers (1878–80), Fortune Theatre (1869), Knox Church (1876), Early Settlers' Museum, Hocken Library. » New Zealand [i]

Dunfermline [dunfermlin] 56°04N 3°29W, pop (1981) 52 227. Capital of Dunfermline district, Fife, E Scotland; 27 km/17 ml NW of Edinburgh; royal burgh since 1588; ancient residence of Scottish kings and the burial place of several, including Robert the Bruce; birthplace of Charles I and Andrew Carnegie; railway; textiles, clothing, metal products, electronics; Dunfermline Abbey and Palace (11th-c foundation). » Bruce, Robert; Carnegie, Andrew; Charles I (of England); Fife; Scotland [i]

dung beetle A shiny, dark coloured beetle; lives under dung, on fungi, and in other rotting materials; digs vertical holes beneath dung, placing a single egg on a plug of dung. The adults and larvae produce sound by vibration (*stridulation*). (Order: *Coleoptera*. Family: *Geotrupidae*.) » beetle; larva; sacred scarab beetle

Dungannon [duhnganuhn], Gaelic **Dun Geanainn** 54°31N 6°46W, pop (1981) 8 295. Market town in Tyrone, SC Northern Ireland, 56 km/35 ml WSW of Belfast; former stronghold of the Earls of Tyrone; textiles (linen), engineering, food processing; High Cross of Arboe (9th-c) nearby; prehistoric stone circles with grave mounds (c.1800 BC) at Beaghmore. » Tyrone

Dung beetles rolling a ball of dung

Dungeness Head [duhnjnes] 5°55N 0°58E. Point on the S coast of Kent, S England, projecting into the English Channel SE of Lydd; nearby is Dungeness nuclear power station, with gas-cooled, graphite-moderated reactors (operational 1965), and an advanced gas-cooled reactor (1983). » Kent; nuclear reactor [i]

Dunkirk [duhnkerk], Fr **Dunkerque**, Flemish **Duinekerke** 51°02N 2°23E, pop (1982) 73 618. Seaport in Nord department, NW France, at the entrance to the Straits of Dover; third largest port of France, with extensive docks and quays; ferry connections to Dover and Harwich; during World War 2, the retreating British Expeditionary Force was rescued from the beaches near the town; railway; shipbuilding, oil refining, fishing equipment, cotton spinning. » British Expeditionary Force; World War 2

dunlin A small wading bird, native to the N hemisphere; mottled brown plumage with pale undersides; slender probing bill; inhabits shoreline or open areas near water; forms large flocks. (*Calidris alpina*. Family: *Scolopacidae*.) » sandpiper

Dunlop, Joey, properly **(William) Joseph** (1952–) British motorcyclist, an outstanding rider at Isle of Man TT races, born at Ballymoney, Northern Ireland. Between 1977 and 1988 he won 13 races (one short of the all-time record of Mike Hailwood), including the Senior Tourist Trophy (TT) in 1985 and 1987–8. He won the Formula One TT for the sixth successive season in 1988, and was Formula One world champion 1982–6. » Hailwood; motorcycle racing

Dunlop, John Boyd (1840–1921) British inventor, born at Dreghorn, Ayrshire, Scotland. He was a flourishing veterinary surgeon near Belfast, when (c.1887) he invented the pneumatic tyre, at first for bicycles. His company, formed in 1889, became known as the Dunlop Rubber Company in 1900. » tyre

Dunmow flitch A side of bacon offered as a prize to any man who could in honesty swear that for a year and a day he had not quarrelled with his wife, nor wished himself unmarried. Instituted at Little Dunmow, Essex, in the 13th-c or earlier, the custom continued into the 18th-c, and has been revived in modern times.

Dunn, Douglas (1942–) British poet, born in Renfrewshire, Scotland. Educated at the Scottish School of Librarianship and at Hull, he worked for some years as a librarian in the USA and at Hull, and now lives as a freelance writer in Scotland. His early work, including *Terry Street* (1969) and *Love or Nothing* (1974), was noted for its registration of urban experience. Later volumes, such as *Barbarians* (1979) and *Elegies* (1985), have more emotional and more intellectual appeal. » poetry; Scottish literature

Dunne, Finley Peter (1867–1936) US journalist and humorist, born in Chicago. As 'Mr Dooley', he became widely known from 1900 as the exponent of American-Irish humorous satire on current personages and events. Many of his essays were republished in book form, such as *Mr Dooley in Peace and War* (1898). He died in New York City. » satire

Dunnet Head 58°41N 3°22W. Cape in NE Highland region, NE Scotland; at W end of Pentland Firth, 13 km/8 ml NE of Thurso; northernmost point of the British mainland. » Highland; Scotland [i]

dunnock A small, grey-brown, ground-feeding bird with short slender bill; native to Europe and W Asia (N Africa in winter); inhabits woodland, scrubland, and gardens; eats invertebrates; also known as **(European) hedge sparrow** or **hedge accentor**. (*Prunella modularis*. Family: *Prunellidae*.) » accentor

Dunois, Jean d'Orléans, Comte ('Count'), byname **The Bastard of Orléans** [dünwah] (1403–68) French general in the Hundred Years' War, born in Paris, the natural son of Louis, Duke of Orleans. He defeated the English at Montargis (1427), defended Orleans with a small force until its relief by Joan of Arc (1429), then inflicted further defeats on the English, forcing them out of Paris, and by 1453 from Normandy and Guyenne. » Hundred Years' War; Joan of Arc

Duns Scotus, Johannes (c.1265–1308) Mediaeval philosopher and theologian, born (probably) at Maxton, Roxburghshire. He became a Franciscan, studied at Oxford, and lectured there. His works are chiefly commentaries on the Bible, Aristotle, and the *Sentences* of Peter Lombard. A critic of preceding scholasticism, his dialectical skill gained him the title of 'Doctor Subtilis' (the Subtle Doctor); but his defence of the papacy led to his ideas being ridiculed at the Reformation (hence the word 'dunce'). He died at Cologne. » Aquinas; Aristotle; Bible; Franciscans; Lombards; scholasticism; theology

Dunstable, John (?–1453) The most important English composer of the 15th-c, whose influence on his continental contemporaries was considerable. He wrote motets, masses and secular songs including the three-part *O Rosa bella*. He was also skilled in mathematics and astronomy. He died in London. » counterpoint

Dunstable, Lat **Durocobrivae** 51°53N 0°32W, pop (1981) 48 629. Town in S Bedfordshire district, Bedfordshire, SC England; at N end of the Chiltern hills, 7 km/4 ml W of Luton; at the junction of the Roman Watling Street and the earlier Icknield Way; engineering, paper; Whipsnade Zoo nearby; London Gliding Club headquarters on Dunstable Downs. » Bedfordshire; Britain, Roman

Dunstan, St (c.909–88), feast day 19 May. English abbot, born near Glastonbury. Educated at the abbey of Glastonbury, he became a monk there, and was appointed abbot in 945. He began a great work of reformation, making the abbey a centre of religious teaching. An adviser to King Edmund, he later became Bishop of Worcester (957) and of London (959), then (under King Edgar) Archbishop of Canterbury (960). He died at Canterbury. » Christianity; Edgar

duodenal ulcer An acute or persisting localized area of ulceration of the first part of the duodenum. The cause is unknown, but may be related to acid secretions of the stomach impinging on the duodenal wall. It is a common cause of indigestion. » duodenum; indigestion; ulcer

duodenum [dyoouhdeenuhm] A region of the alimentary canal in vertebrates, important in digestion. In humans it is the C-shaped first part of the small intestine, continuous with the stomach at the pylorus, and continuing as the jejunum. It receives secretions from the liver (bile) and the pancreas (digestive enzymes) via ducts which pierce its wall, and itself secretes important enzymes and hormones concerned with digestion. It provides a large area for the absorption of digestive products. » alimentary canal; duodenal ulcer; gall bladder; hydatid disease; intestine; peptic ulcer

Duparc, (Marie Eugène) Henri (Fouques-) (1848–1933) French composer, born in Paris. He studied under César Franck, and is remembered for his songs, which, though only 15 in number, rank among the world's greatest. His self-criticism led him to destroy much of his writing and correspondence, and he wrote little after 1890. He died at Mont-de-Marsan, France.

duplication of the cube A classical problem in mathematics, which requires one to build a cube double the volume of a given cube, using ruler and compasses only to construct the length of an edge of the cube. It is sometimes called the **Delian problem**, as it was originally set by the oracle of Delos in the 5th-c BC. The Delians were instructed that, in order to rid themselves of a plague, they must double the altar of their god – its shape being a perfect cube. The problem exercised many mathematicians, but only in the 19th-c was it proved to be impossible, using the techniques of group theory. » group (mathematics)

Dupré, Marcel (1886–1971) French organist, born at Rouen. He won the Prix de Rome for composition in 1914, and became renowned throughout Europe for his organ recitals. The composer of many chorales and an organ concerto, he also wrote on improvisation, and directed the Conservatoires at Fontainebleau (1947–54) and Paris (1954–6). He died in Paris.

Dura-Europos [doora yoorohpos] In Roman times, a major caravan city on the middle Euphrates, and a flourishing frontier town until its sack by the Sassanids in AD 256. The wall paintings from its 3rd-c synagogue form an important link between Hellenistic and early Christian art. » Palmyra (Roman history); Petra; Sassanids

duralumin [dyooralyoomin] The trade name for an alloy of aluminium (over 90%) with copper (about 4%) and minor amounts of magnesium and manganese. It is used in the aircraft industry. » alloy; aluminium; copper

Durand, J(ean) N(icolas) L(ouis) [dürã] (1760–1834) French architect, theorist, and educator, born and died in Paris. He studied architecture at Paris, built little, but had a great influence on contemporary Neoclassical architecture through his teaching at the Ecole Polytechnique (1795–1830) and his *Recueil et parallèle des édifices en tout genre* (1800, Collection and Comparison of Buildings of All Types). » architecture; Neoclassicism (art and architecture)

Durango, also **Victoria de Durango** 24°01N 104°40W, pop (1980) 321 148. Capital of Durango state, NWC Mexico; 903 km/561 ml NW of Mexico City; altitude 1 889 m/6 197 ft; founded, 1563; railway; university (1957); timber, iron ore, textiles, farming; cathedral (1695); famous for its iron-water spring. » Mexico [i]

Duras, Marguerite, pseudonym of **Marguerite Donnadieu** [düra] (1914–) French novelist, born and educated in French Indochina, who went to France in 1932. Her reputation was made by the novels she wrote in the 1950s, such as *Un Barrage contre le Pacifique* (1950, The Sea War), *Le Marin de Gibraltar* (1952, The Sailor from Gibraltar), and *Le Square* (1955, The Square). She achieved a wider celebrity with the screenplay for Alain Resnais' film *Hiroshima mon amour* (1959, Hiroshima, My Love). » French literature; novel; Resnais

Durban or **Port Natal** 29°53S 31°00E, pop (1985) 634 301. Seaport in Natal province, South Africa; on Indian Ocean coast, 485 km/300 ml SE of Johannesburg; population includes many Indians, descendants of those brought to South African sugar plantations in the 1860s; South Africa's third largest city; mission settlement founded here, 1834; airport; railway; university (1960); shipbuilding, oil refining, chemicals, fertilizers, food processing, textiles, tourism; museum and art gallery, oldest Hindu temple in South Africa. » Natal (South Africa); South Africa [i]

Dürer, Albrecht (1471–1528) German painter and engraver, born and died at Nuremberg. He studied under Wolgemut, travelled widely (1490–4), and in 1497 set up his own studio, producing many paintings. In 1498 he published his first great series of designs on wood, the illustrations of the Apocalypse. He was much employed by Emperor Maximilian I, in whose honour he drew the 'Triumphal Car' and (with others) the 'Triumphal Arch', the largest known woodcut (100 sq ft/ 9 sq m). » etching; German art; woodcut

duress Violence or threats of violence against a person for the purpose of causing that person to act in a particular way, such as to commit a crime. The developing area of **economic duress** refers to a situation where a contract may be entered into or, more usually, altered as a result of improper pressure. Such contracts may be set aside in appropriate cases; more than ordinary commercial pressure must be involved. » contract

Durey, Louis (1888–1979) French composer, born in Paris. In 1916, under the influence of Erik Satie, he became one of the group of young French composers known as *Les Six*, but broke with them in 1921. He wrote large orchestral and choral works, but is chiefly known for his songs and chamber music. » Satie; *Six, Les*

Durga Puja » **Navaratri**

Durham (UK county) [**duh**ram] pop (1987e) 598 700; area 2 436 sq km/940 sq ml. County in NE England, divided into eight districts; bounded E by the North Sea, rising to the Pennines in the W; drained by the Tees, Derwent, and Wear Rivers; county town, Durham; chief towns include Darlington, Chester-le-Street, Bishop Auckland; coal, engineering, chemicals, agriculture. » Durham (UK city); England [i]

Durham (UK city) [**duh**ram] 54°47N 1°34W, pop (1981) 41 178. City and administrative centre of county Durham, NE England; on the R Wear; founded in the 10th-c by monks who had fled from Lindisfarne; university (1832); railway; textiles, clothing, coal mining, engineering, carpets; Norman cathedral (1093) and castle (11th-c) designated a world heritage site; Gulbenkian Museum, Durham Light Infantry museum; Durham Rowing Regatta (Jun); miners' gala (Jul). » Durham (UK county)

Durham Report A government report of 1837 recommending the union of Upper and Lower Canada into a single political structure; produced by Lord Durham, Governor of Canada, it called for the assimilation of French-Canadian into English-Canadian economic and linguistic culture. » Durham, John George Lambton

durian An evergreen tree native to Malaysia; pink or white flowers growing directly from trunk and main branches; fruit a large spiny capsule, with delicate-tasting but evil-smelling flesh considered to be a delicacy. (*Durio zibethinus*. Family: *Bombacaceae*.) » evergreen plants; shrub

Durkheim, Emile (1858–1917) French sociologist, born at Epinal, generally regarded as one of the founders of sociology. He studied at Paris, and became a teacher, then taught at the university of Bordeaux (1887), and at the Sorbonne. His writings include *Les Règles de la méthode sociologique* (1894, The Rules of Sociological Method) and a definitive study of suicide (1897). He is perhaps best known for his concept of 'collective representations', the social power of ideas stemming from their development through the interaction of many minds. He died in Paris. » sociology

Durmitor [**door**meetaw] Highest mountain in Montenegro republic, Yugoslavia; in the Dinaric Alps, rising to 2 522 m/8 274 ft; in a national park, which is a world heritage site. » Alps; Montenegro; Yugoslavia [i]

Durrell, Gerald (Malcolm) (1925–) British zoologist, traveller, writer, and broadcaster, brother of Lawrence Durrell. His popular animal stories and reminiscences include *My Family and Other Animals* (1956), *A Zoo in My Luggage* (1960), and *Birds, Beasts and Relatives* (1969). He founded a zoo and wildlife centre in Jersey. » Durrell, Lawrence

Durrell, Lawrence (George) (1912–90) British novelist and poet, born at Darjeeling, India. Educated at Canterbury, he eloped with his future wife to Paris, where he began to write novels. He taught English in Athens, then served in the Foreign Office in Cairo, Athens, and Belgrade, settling (1953) in Cyprus. He first made his name with *Prospero's Cell* (1945), followed by the cosmopolitan multi-love story comprising the 'Alexandria Quartet' (1957–60): *Justine*, *Balthazar*, *Mountolive* and *Clea*. A series of five novels commenced in 1974 with *Monsieur*, followed by *Livia* (1978), *Constance* (1982), *Sebastian* (1983), and *Quinx* (1985). He also wrote several books of poems, short stories, and travel books. He died at Sommières, France. » English literature; novel; poetry

Dürrenmatt or **Duerrenmatt, Friedrich** (1921–90) Swiss author, born at Konolfingen, Berne. Educated at Berne and Zürich, he turned from painting to writing. His plays include *Die Ehe des Herrn Mississippi* (1952, The Marriage of Mr Mississippi), which established his international reputation, *Die Physiker* (1962, The Physicists), and *Die Frist* (1977, The Appointed Time). He has also written novels, short stories, critical essays, and works for radio. » German literature

Durrës [**door**uhs], formerly **Durazzo**, Turkish **Draj** 41°18N 19°28E, pop (1980) 65 900. Seaport and capital of Durrës district, W Albania; on the Adriatic Sea, 30 km/19 ml W of Tiranë; Albania's principal port; railway; founded as Epidamnos (627 BC) and renamed Dyrrhachium (229 BC); occupied by Italians and Austrians in World War 1, when capital of Albania (1912–21); population largely of Muslim origin; shipbuilding, metalworking, foodstuffs, tobacco, leatherwork, rubber, fishing, tourism; a seaside health resort; former royal villa and the remains of Byzantine-Venetian fortifications. » Albania [i]

durum A wheat (*Triticum durum*) with a high protein content, whose flour is used to make pasta. The flour is harder than that produced by other varieties of wheat, used in bread-making. » pasta; semolina; wheat

Dushanbe, formerly **Diushambe** (to 1929), **Stalinabad** (1929–61) 38°38N 68°51E, pop (1989) 595 000. Capital city of Tadzhikistan, on the R Dushanbe; airfield; railway; university (1948); electrical engineering, metalworking, machines, textiles, silk, foodstuffs. » Tadzhikistan

Duse, Eleonora [**doo**zay] (1859–1924) Italian actress, born near Venice. She rose to fame in Italy, then triumphed (1892–3) throughout the European capitals, mainly acting in plays by contemporary French dramatists, Ibsen, and the works of her lover, Gabriele D'Annunzio. Her histrionic genius ranks 'The Duse' as one of the world's greatest actresses. She retired through ill health in 1909, but returned to the stage in 1921, and died during a US tour, at Pittsburgh.

Düsseldorf [**dü**suhldawf] 51°13N 6°47E, pop(1983) 579 800. Industrial capital of Düsseldorf district, Germany; on the lower Rhine, 34 km/21 ml NNW of Cologne; city status, 1288; railway; university (1965); administrative centre of North Rhine–Westphalia province's heavy industry; iron and steel, aluminium, machinery, oil refining, chemicals, textiles, glassware, plastics, electronics, paper; birthplace of Heinrich Heine; Schloss Benrath (18th-c), art academy (1767), opera house, theatre; fashion centre, congresses, trade fairs. » Germany [i]; Heine

Dust Bowl The semi-arid area of the US prairie states from Kansas to Texas, which suffers from dust storms. In the 1930s, after several years of good crop yield overcultivation, strong winds and dry weather resulted in major dust storms and soil erosion. » desertification; drought; Great Plains

Dutch A variety of the W Germanic family of languages, spoken by c.20 million in the Netherlands, Belgium, Suriname, and the Antilles. It is the official language of Holland, and mutually intelligible with its sister variety in Belgium, Flemish. These are designated as separate languages for political and nationalistic reasons. » Afrikaans; Germanic languages

Dutch art The art of the mainly Protestant Dutch Republic (the United Provinces), one of the glories of 17th-c European civilization. The greatest achievements were in painting (Hals, Rembrandt, Steen, Ruysdael, Vermeer) which combined the realistic vision and fine craftsmanship inherited from the early Netherlandish tradition (van Eyck, Bosch) with a new feeling for light and space derived from Renaissance Italy. By the late 16th-c, Haarlem (where Hals worked) was the main centre for painting, while Utrecht saw the latest Italian style of Caravaggio being developed by Terbrugghen and Honthorst. Amsterdam, where Rembrandt worked from 1632, was the prosperous centre of the European art market. There was little call for religious subjects, so painters specialized in genre scenes, portraits, landscapes, or still lifes. » Appel; Bosch, Hieronymus; Bouts; Campin; Cuyp; Dou; Fabritius; Hals; Hobbema; Honthorst; Hooch; Lucas van Leyden; Mondrian; Ostade; Potter, Paul; Rembrandt; Ruysdael; Snyders; Steen; Terborch; Terbrugghen; van de Velde, Willem; van Eyck; van Gogh; Vermeer; Wouwermans; genre painting; landscape painting; still life

Dutch elm disease A disease affecting all species of elm (genus: *Ulmus*) caused by the fungus *Ceratocystis ulmi*; symptoms include wilting, yellowing of foliage, and eventually death; transmitted from tree to tree by elm-bark beetle. (Order: *Eurotiales*.) » elm

Dutch New Guinea » **Irian Jaya**

Dutch Reformed Church The largest Protestant Church in Holland, stemming from the Calvinist Reformation in the 16th-c. Its leaders and scholars have been influential in Dutch life, in former Dutch colonies, and also in Reformed theology. The Dutch Reformed Church in South Africa (totally separated from the Church in Holland) is the official Church of dominant White Afrikaans-speaking nationals, condemned in 1982 by the other Reformed Churches for justifying both theologically and practically the policy of apartheid. » apartheid; Calvinism; Protestantism; Reformed Churches

Dutch Wars Three wars between England and the Dutch Republic (1652–4, 1664–7, 1672–4) concerned with issues of trade and the colonies. The first followed the Navigation Acts, in which England sought to increase its trade; the second involved the colonies in Africa and N America; and the third resulted from English support of the French in the Treaty of Dover (1670). The wars brought on the decline of Dutch power, and signalled the growing predominance of the English.

Dutch West India Company The organization of Dutch merchants responsible for the settlement of New Netherland, now New York. The Company was established in 1621, and was dissolved in 1674. It was later reorganized as a trading venture. » New York

Dutchman's breeches » **bleeding heart**

Dutchman's pipe A perennial climber with twining stems and kidney-shaped leaves native to N America; flowers shaped like a tobacco pipe with a flaring mouth. It is a carrion flower with a typical mottled colouring and scent of decay, which attracts flies to act as pollinators. (*Aristolochia macrophylla*. Family: *Aristolochiaceae*.) » carrion flower; climbing plant; perennial

Duval, Claude (1643–70) French highwayman, born at Domfront, Normandy. He came to England at the Restoration in the train of the Duke of Richmond. Taking soon to the road, he pursued a successful career, gaining a popular reputation, especially for his gallantry towards women. He was captured drunk, and hanged at Tyburn, London.

Duvalier, François, byname **Papa Doc** (1907–71) Haitian politician and President (1957–71), born at Port-au-Prince, where he was educated as a doctor. He held power from 1957 until his death, ruling in an increasingly arbitrary fashion. His regime saw the creation of the civilian militia known as the Tonton Macoute, and the exile of many people. He became President for life in 1964, and was succeeded in this post by his son, **Jean-Claude** (1951–), known as **Baby Doc**, whose regime lasted until 1986. » Haiti [i]

Dvořák, Antonín (Leopold) [**dvaw**zhak] (1841–1904) Czech composer, born near Prague. He was sent to the organ school in Prague in 1857, and began to earn his living from the viola. In 1877 Brahms introduced his music to Vienna, and was a great influence on him. His work, basically classical in structure, but with colourful Slavonic motifs, won increasing recognition, culminating in European acclaim for his *Stabat mater* (1880). By then he had written six symphonies and much chamber and piano music, and in 1891 he was offered the directorship of the New York Conservatory. In the USA he wrote his ninth symphony, the ever-popular 'From the New World'. In 1895 he returned to Prague, where he died.

dwarf buffalo » **African buffalo; anoa**

dwarf star Any star in which the source of energy is the nuclear burning of hydrogen in its core to helium, and therefore lying on the main sequence of stellar evolution. Our Sun, 109 times the diameter of Earth, is a dwarf star. » brown dwarf; helium; star; Sun

dwarfism A disorder of slowed growth in children, caused by many factors, such as malnutrition, rickets, and serious illness (eg congenital heart disease). True dwarfism occurs in achondroplasia, and in a number of disorders in which there is a deficiency of specific hormones. These include pituitary dwarfism (in which there is inadequate production of growth hormone), cretinism, and other types of hypothyroidism in which there is deficiency of thyroid hormone secretion. It also occurs rarely in conditions associated with increased secretion of the male hormone, testosterone, which causes premature closure of the growing ends of long bones, arresting their linear growth. » achondroplasia; cretinism; thyroid hormone; pituitary gland

Dyak » **Dayak**

dyarchy A system where political authority is divided; associated with constitutional reforms introduced by the British into India in 1919. Under the reforms, some departments of provincial government were under Indian control, while others including finance and security remained under British control. The reforms did not extend to central government.

dybbuk [**di**buhk] In Jewish tradition, an evil spirit, or the soul of a dead person, that enters the body of a living person and controls his or her behaviour until exorcized by a religious rite.

dye laser A laser in which the lasing medium is a liquid organic dye. It can be made to produce laser light of virtually any frequency, either by altering slightly the chemical composition of the dye, or by including a tuning device within the laser cavity that exploits the unusually broad absorption and emission spectrum of dyes. » laser [i]; resonant ionization spectroscopy

dyeing The process of permanently changing the colour of a material. This ancient art has developed into a high technology industry for the coloration of textiles, leather, and other goods. Dyes are usually applied by soaking the material in a solution, which is fixed onto the material by heating. » dyestuff

dyer's broom or **dyer's greenweed** A variable shrub growing to

2 m/6½ ft, with slender branches, native to Europe and Asia Minor; leaves oblong to lance-shaped; pea-flowers numerous, yellow, borne in long, leafy, terminal inflorescences. The leaves and flowers have been used since Roman times to produce a yellow dye, or mixed with woad to give green. (*Genista tinctoria.* Family: *Leguminosae.*) » inflorescence [i]; shrub; woad

dyer's rocket » **weld**

dyestuff Strongly coloured substances, generally complex organic molecules, which are absorbed by textile materials. Natural dyestuffs of animal and plant origins have now been largely superseded by synthetic dyes. Their uses extend beyond textiles into many areas, including cosmetics, foodstuffs, paper, wood, and bio-medical science. Indigo and cochineal are two of the best-known natural dyes, both still in use today. The synthetic 'vat' dyes produce strong, bright colours of the highest fastness, and are often used on cotton furnishing fabrics. » chromophore; dyeing; indigo

Dyfed [**duh**vid] pop (1987e) 343 200; area 5 768 sq km/ 2 226 sq ml. County in SW Wales, UK, divided into six districts; created in 1974; bounded W by Cardigan Bay and St George's Channel, S by the Bristol Channel; drained by the Ystwyth, Towy and Teifi Rivers; administrative centre, Carmarthen; other chief towns, Aberystwyth, Cardigan, Lampeter; agriculture, oil refining, dairy products, fishing, coal, tinplate, tourism; Brecon Beacons National Park; Laugharne (home of Dylan Thomas). » Carmarthen; Thomas, Dylan; Wales [i]

dyke (geography) A ditch or natural watercourse. The term is also used to describe a long ridge or embankment constructed to prevent flooding, such as those in the Netherlands made to hold back the sea. Low-lying areas of flat land such as the Fens and Broads have many dykes. » Broads, the; Fens

dyke (geology) A sheet-like igneous body cross-cutting the bedding planes of country rock, injected under pressure while molten. *Radial* dyke swarms may be associated with doming because of a large igneous intrusion, and *parallel* dyke systems occur as a result of tension at mid-ocean ridges. Usually composed of basic igneous rock (typically dolerite), they vary in thickness from centimetres to tens of metres, and up to hundreds of kilometres in length. » igneous rock; intrusive rock; sill

Dylan, Bob, originally **Robert Zimmerman** (1941–) US folk-singer and songwriter, born at Duluth, Minnesota. Taking his professional name from the poet Dylan Thomas, he rose to fame in the 1960s, following the folk tradition of Woody Guthrie but introducing a fresh social and political awareness. His lyrics made his songs the dominant influence in the popular music and culture of the period. Opposition to war, the nuclear bomb, and racial and social injustice are the themes of some of his most famous songs, such as *Blowin' in the Wind* and *The Times They are A-Changin'*. In the late 1960s he changed from specific protest to more general and personal themes, and to a more traditional Country and Western style of music, as in *Nashville Skyline* (1969). In 1979 he became a convert to Christianity, which led to religious albums such as *Saved*.

dynamics In mechanics, the study of the properties of the motion of objects, and the relation of this motion to the forces causing it. It is more general than kinematics, which is the study of the motion of objects without attention to forces. » electrodynamics; mechanics

dynamite Once a specific name, now a general term for industrial high explosives consisting of nitroglycerine absorbed on some porous or granular non-explosive substance (such as the *kieselguhr* porous earth of Nobel's first invention) to minimize its vulnerability to shock. » explosives; Nobel, Alfred

dyne » **force**; RR70

dysarthria A speech disorder caused by a weakness or paralysis of the vocal organs, resulting in a poor or indistinct articulation or voice quality. The effects can range from mild to severe – from a slight slurring to total unintelligibility. In its more severe forms, it is sometimes referred to as **anarthria**. » speech pathology

dysentery The name given to two different intestinal infections associated with diarrhoea and the passage of blood and mucus in the stool. Both are world-wide in distribution, and occur wherever standards of sanitation and hygiene are inadequate. **Bacillary dysentery** results from bacteria of the genus *Shigella*; the disease is usually mild and short-lived. **Amoebic/amebic dysentery** results from infection with the protozoa *Entamoeba hystolytica*, and is more serious, with more severe and persistent diarrhoea. The liver is also commonly affected in amoebic dysentery, and amoebic abscesses may form within its substance. » diarrhoea; intestine; Protozoa

dysgraphia A disorder affecting a person's ability to write and spell; also called **agraphia**. In adults, it is often associated with damage to the language areas of the brain, for example following a stroke or tumour. The writing may contain badly formed lines and letter shapes, and letters may be misplaced, omitted, or repeated. In particular, several types of spelling disability have been noted, and many patients have related problems of reading. » dyslexia

dyslexia Reading disability, in people with apparently adequate intellectual and perceptual abilities and adequate educational opportunities; sometimes called **alexia**. **Developmental dyslexia** is the term applied to people who have never learned to read. **Acquired dyslexia** describes those who could once read, but who have lost this ability as a result of brain damage. Further distinctions can be drawn. **Deep** or **phonological** dyslexics can read real words, but have great difficulty with unfamiliar words or nonsense. **Surface dyslexics** can read words showing a regular correspondence between letters and sounds (eg *cat*), but not words where this correspondence is irregular (eg *yacht*). There is no single theory which explains dyslexia, and the nature of the problem has been a source of some dispute. Nevertheless it is common for several members of a family to exhibit similar difficulties with reading and writing, and various educational programmes have been developed for helping sufferers to cope. » illiteracy; neuropsychology

dysmenorrhoea/dysmenorrhea [dismenuh**ree**a] Discomfort or pain in the lower abdomen associated with menstruation. It is a common, usually mild (but sometimes very painful) complaint, which lasts 12–24 hours from the start of bleeding. It is not usually caused by any underlying disease, but when it occurs in older women it may be due to pelvic infection or to abnormalities of the uterus (*endometriosis*). » menstruation

dyspareunia [dispa**roo**nia] Discomfort or pain experienced by women during sexual intercourse. The most frequent cause is insufficient vaginal lubrication, often as a result of insufficient foreplay prior to sexual intercourse. It may also result from spasm of the vaginal muscle, vulvar infections, or more deeply-sited pelvic disorders. » vagina; vaginismus

dyspepsia » **indigestion**

dysphasia » **aphasia**

dysphonia [dis**foh**nia] A speech disorder in which the voice has an abnormal quality; also known as **aphonia**, especially when referring to some of the more severe syndromes. Voice pitch, loudness, and timbre may be so inefficient that speech can be largely unintelligible; but even when the speech can be understood, the voice quality interferes with communication by drawing attention to itself (eg by being noticeably hoarse or nasal) The condition may arise from physical or psychological causes. » speech pathology

dyspraxia » **apraxia**

Dzaoudzi 12°47S 45°12E; pop (1978) 4 147; area 6.7 sq km/ 2.6 sq ml. Capital and second largest commune of Mayotte, on La Petite Terre I; airport; fishing, agricultural trade. » Mayotte

Dzerzhinsk [jer**zhinsk**], formerly **Chernorech** (to 1919), **Rastiapino** (1919–29) 56°15N 43°30E, pop (1983) 269 000. City in Gorkovskaya oblast, W European Russia; on R Oka, 32 km/20 ml W of Nizhni Novgorod; railway; chemicals, construction materials, furniture, textiles, foodstuffs. » Russia

dzo » **yak**

E layer » **Heaviside layer**

E-number A code number on food labels, used by food manufacturers in member states of the EEC, which identifies all materials added to the food. Among food additives, four categories (preservatives, colourants, anti-oxidants, and emulsifiers) each have code numbers. For example, E102 is the colourant tartrazine, E210 the preservative benzoic acid, and E420 is the emulsifier guar gum. » additives; antioxidants; colouring agents; European Economic Community; emulsifiers; food preservation

eagle A large-bodied bird of prey that kills its own food (smaller birds of prey – buzzards, falcons, hawks, harriers, or kites). **True** or **booted** eagles have fully feathered, not partly bare, legs. (Family: *Accipitridae*, 30 species.) » bald/golden/harpy/sea eagle; bird of prey; buzzard; falcon; harrier (ornithology); hawk; kite

eagle owl An owl native to the Old World; the genus includes the largest of all owls (0.7 m/2.3 ft). It has eyelashes, which are an unusual feature in owls. (Genus: *Bubo*, 11 species. Family: *Strigidae*.) » owl

Eakins, Thomas (1844–1916) US painter, born in Philadelphia. He studied in Paris under Gérôme, and became known for his portraits and genre pictures, especially of sporting scenes. His best-known work is his realistic depiction of a surgical operation, 'The Gross Clinic', which was controversially received on account of its detail. He spent most of his life in Philadelphia, where he died.

ear A compound organ concerned with hearing and balance, situated on the side or (in some animals) the top of the head. The **external ear** consists of the *auricle* (commonly referred to as 'the ear') and the *external auditory canal*, a tube leading down to the ear drum (*tympanic membrane*). In many animals (eg dogs, horses), the auricle can be moved to scan the environment to locate sounds. The **middle ear** is an air-filled space, separated from the external ear by the tympanic membrane, and from the internal ear by the oval window and round window. It is continuous with the nasopharynx via the auditory (Eustachian) tube, and contains the auditory *ossicles* (the *malleus*, *incus*, and *stapes*) and two small muscles which act to damp down sound vibrations. The **internal ear** consists of a number of parts, but can be divided into that concerned with hearing (the *cochlea*) and that concerned with assessing head position and its movements (the *vestibular apparatus*). The round window is filled with a fibrous membrane which allows movement of the fluid (*perilymph*) within the cochlea, when compressed by the stapes.

Sound waves directed down the external auditory canal cause the tympanic membrane to vibrate; movements of the malleus are conveyed to the oval window (via the incus and stapes), where the vibrations are transmitted to the basilar membrane of the cochlea. The *vestibulocochlear nerve* (the VIIIth cranial nerve) conveys information from both parts of the internal ear to the brain. Blockage of the Eustachian tube leads to the loss of pressure in the middle ear (due to the absorption of air), increased concavity of the tympanic membrane, and progressive deafness. When the blockage is associated with infection of the middle ear, the accumulation of fluid causes the tympanic membrane to bulge towards the external auditory canal, again leading to increasing deafness. » audiology; cochlea; deafness; Eustachian tube; Ménière's disease; sound; tinnitus; vestibular apparatus

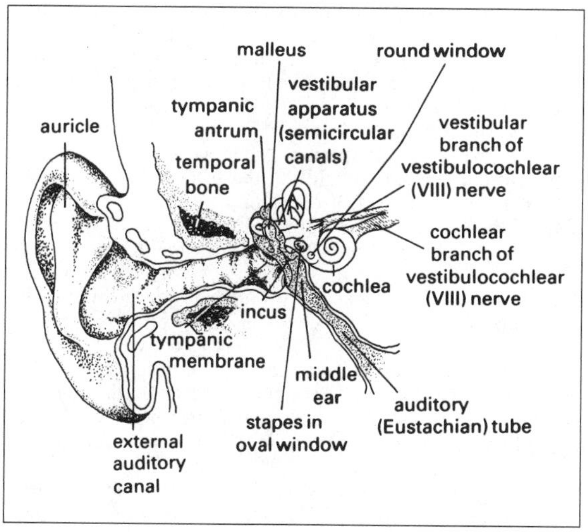

Structure of the auditory apparatus seen in a frontal section through the right side of the skull

Earhart, Amelia [ayrhaht] (1897–1937) US aviator, born at Atchison, Kansas. She was the first woman to fly the Atlantic, as a passenger, and followed this by a solo flight in 1932. In 1935 she flew solo from Hawaii to California. In 1937 she set out to fly round the world, but her plane was lost over the Pacific. » aircraft [i]

earl In the UK, a member of the third most senior order of noblemen, and the most ancient title, dating from before the Norman Conquest (Danish *jarl*). The wife of an earl is a countess. » peerage

Earl Marshal In the UK, the hereditary post held by the Howard Dukes of Norfolk. One of the great officers of state, the Earl Marshal is head of the College of Arms and is also responsible for organizing state ceremonies. » heraldry [i]

Early Christian art » **Christian art**

Early English Style The form of English Gothic architecture prevalent during the 13th-c, characterized by pointed arches, rib vaults, and a greater stress on the horizontals than is found in French Gothic architecture. Good examples are the chancel of Lincoln cathedral (c.1192) and Salisbury cathedral (c.1220–70), UK. » arch [i]; Decorated Style; Gothic architecture; Perpendicular Style; vault [i]

EAROM An acronym of **Electrically Alterable Read-Only Memory**, a type of integrated circuit read-only memory, where the data can be altered electronically while the EAROM remains in circuit. It generally requires rather complicated circuitry, and is not widely used. » EPROM; PROM

Earth The third planet from the Sun, having the following characteristics: mass 5.97×10^{27}g; orbital period 365.26 days; radius (equatorial) 6 378 km/3 963 ml; obliquity 23°27′; mean density 5.52 g/cm^3; orbital eccentricity 0.017; equatorial gravity 978 cm/s^2; mean distance from the Sun 149.6×10^6 km; rotational period 23 hr 56 min 4 sec. It has one large natural satellite, the Moon. There is an oxygen/ nitrogen-rich atmosphere, liquid water oceans filling lowland regions between continents, and permanent water ice caps at each pole. It is unique in the Solar System in being able to support life, for which there is fossil evidence in rocks dating from 3.5 thousand million years ago. The interior of the planet is differentiated into zones: an iron/nickel-rich molten *core* (radius c.3 500 km/2 175 ml) an iron-magnesium silicate *mantle* (c.85%

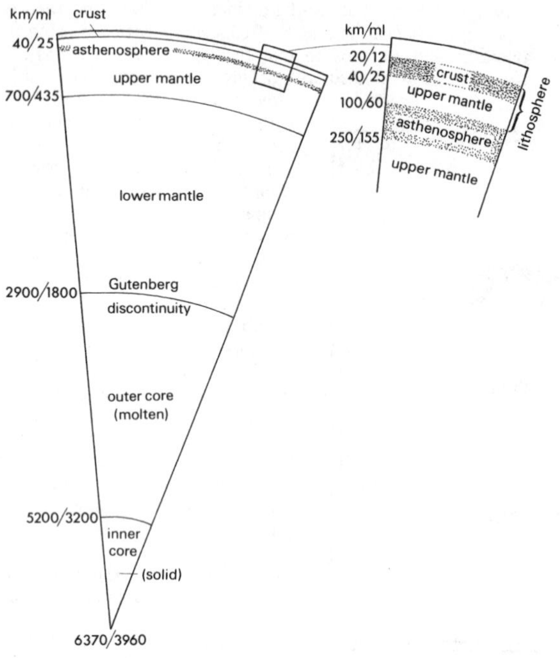

The structure of the Earth

by volume of the Earth); and a *crust* of lighter metal silicates (relatively thin, c.6 km/3½ ml thick under the oceans to c.50 km/30 ml under the continents). The boundary between core and mantle is called the *Gutenberg discontinuity*; that between mantle and crust is the *Mohorovicic* (or *Moho*) *discontinuity*.

The interior is hot as a result of energy released through the continuing decay of a small proportion of long-lived radioactive isotopes of potassium, thorium, and uranium. Temperatures in the upper mantle cause partial melting at depths of c.100 km/60 ml. Large sections (*plates*) of the uppermost mantle and crust (the *lithosphere*) move slowly and horizontally relative to one another over the more fluid and partially molten zone (the *asthenosphere*), which extends to a depth of c.250 km. The evolution of the Earth's crust is dominated by such motions (*plate tectonics*): the spreading, subduction, and collision of lithospheric plates creates most of the major planetary scale features that have shaped Earth as a planet – volcanism, rifting, mountain building, and continental wandering. The effects of asteroidal impacts are erased/disguised by the rapid rate at which the Earth's surface is reshaped and eroded. Such impacts would have been a dominant process in the earliest evolution of the Earth, and still occur periodically. A complex atmospheric circulation is driven primarily by the non-uniform solar heating of the planet and by its rapid rotation; and there is evidence of repeated climatic changes throughout the geological record. » greenhouse effect; magnetosphere; planet; plate tectonics [i]; seismology; Solar System; RR12

Earth art » **Earthworks**

earth pig » **aardvark**

earth sciences A general term for the study of the Earth and its atmosphere, encompassing geology and its subdisciplines as well as oceanography, glaciology, meteorology, and the origin of the Earth and the Solar System. » geology

earthnut A slender perennial growing to 60 cm/2 ft, native to Europe; irregular-shaped tubers up to 3.5 cm/1½ in across, which supposedly resemble nuts; leaves deeply divided into narrow linear segments, soon withering; flowers white or pinkish, in flat-topped umbels 3–6 cm/1¼–2½ in across; also called **pignut**. The dark brown tubers are edible, cooked or raw. (*Conopodium majus*. Family: *Umbelliferae*.) » perennial; nut; tuber; umbel

earthquake A series of shock waves generated at a point (*focus*) within the Earth, and caused by the movement of rocks on a fault plane releasing stored strain energy. The point on the surface of the Earth above the focus is the *epicentre*. Major earthquakes are associated with the edges of plates that make up the Earth's crust, and along mid-oceanic ridges where new crust is forming. The greatest concentration of earthquakes is in a belt around the Pacific Ocean (the 'ring of fire'), and along a zone from the Mediterranean E to the Himalayas and China. The magnitude of an earthquake is measured on the Richter scale. Major earthquakes, such as in San Francisco in 1906 and Japan in 1923, can cause much damage to property and loss of life. » plate tectonics; Richter scale; seismology; RR14

earthshine A phenomenon observable close to new moon, when the entire disc of the Moon is often bathed in a faint light. The cause is sunlight reflected from the Earth. » Moon

earthstar A ground-living fungus with a globular fruiting body; when ripe, outer layer splits into rays, and peels back into a star-shaped structure. (Order: *Lycoperdales*. Genus: *Geastrum*.) » fungus

Earthworks or **Land Art** A modern art movement which started in the late 1960s, in which holes are dug, stones arranged in patterns, etc.; the results are often photographed. Thus in 1968 the US artist Walter de Maria (1935–) chalked two parallel white lines in the Nevada desert and exhibited photographs of them, entitled 'Mile Long Drawing'. » art; Conceptual/Minimal/modern art

earthworm A terrestrial segmented worm found in soil, feeding mainly on decomposing organic matter; head simple, without sensory appendages; body cylindrical, length up to 4 m/13 ft; hermaphrodite; when breeding, develops a saddle (*clitellum*) which secretes material for use during mating and in production of egg cocoon. (Phylum: *Annelida*. Class: *Oligochaeta*.) » annelid; hermaphrodite; worm

earwig A slender insect with large pincers at rear end of body, used for courtship, defence, grooming, or predation; forewings small and hard; hindwings membraneous; c.1 500 species, most abundant in tropics. (Order: *Dermaptera*.) » insect [i]

easement A right exercised by one landowner over the land of another. The easement must benefit the land of its owner; and will be extinguished if both properties (the *dominant* and *servient tenements*) are subsequently owned and occupied by one person. A private right of way may exist as an easement, though a person may instead have permission to cross land by virtue of a licence. Easements may be expressly or impliedly granted. They may also be acquired through long use (*prescription*). Further examples include easement of light, the support of buildings, and the taking of water. Certain matters may not be the subject of an easement, such as an unspoilt view, though in this particular case a restrictive covenant against building may achieve the desired effect. » property; restrictive covenant

East Bank Region in Jordan, E of the R Jordan; comprises the governorates of Amman, Al Balqa, Irbid, Al Karak, and Maan; corresponds roughly to the former Amirate of Trans-jordan. » Jordan [i]; West Bank

East End An area of London situated N of the R Thames and E of Shoreditch and Tower Bridge. With the increasing importance of London as a port in the 19th-c it became a densely-populated industrial area. Although it was heavily bombed during World War 2 and has since been hit by recession, the Dockland Development scheme has recently sought to bring industry and finance into the area. » London [i]

East India Company, British A British trading monopoly, established in India in 1600, which later became involved in politics. Its first 'factory' (trading station) was at Surat (1612), with others at Madras (1639), Bombay (1688) and Calcutta (1690). A rival company was chartered in 1698, but the two companies merged in 1708. During the 18th-c it received competition from other European countries, in particular France. The company benefited territorially from local Indian disputes and Mughal weakness, gaining control of Bengal

(1757), and receiving the right to collect revenue from the Mughal emperor (1765). Financial indiscipline among company servants led to the 1773 Regulating Act and Pitt's 1784 India Act, which established a Board of Control responsible to Parliament. Thereafter it gradually lost independence. Its monopoly was broken in 1813, and its powers handed over to the British Crown in 1858. It ceased to exist as a legal entity in 1873. » India [i]

East India Company, Dutch The *Vereenigde Oostindische Compagnie*, a trading company founded in 1602 to protect trade in the Indian Ocean and assist in the war against Spain. It established 'factories' (trading stations) on the Indian peninsula, but made little political/cultural contact there, though it did exercise political control in Ceylon. It was at the height of its prosperity during the 17th-c and was dissolved in 1799.

East India Company, French The *Compagnie des Indes Orientales*, a commercial/political organization founded in 1664 which directed French colonial activities in India. It established major trading stations at Chandernagore, Pondicherry, and Mahé, and competed for power with the British during the 18th-c. Its governer, Dupleix, captured Madras (1746), but was defeated during the Seven Years' War (1756–63). The Company lost government support and ceased to exist during the French Revolution. » East India Company, British

East Sussex » **Sussex, East**

Easter The chief festival of the Christian Church, commemorating the resurrection of Christ after his crucifixion. Observed in the Western Churches on a Sunday between 22 March and 25 April inclusive, depending on the date of the first full moon after the spring equinox; the Orthodox Church has a different method of calculating the date. The name Easter perhaps derives from Eostre, the name of an Anglo-Saxon goddess. Easter customs such as egg-rolling are probably of pagan origin. » Christianity

Easter Island, Span **Isla de Pascua** [**pas**kwa] 109°20W 27°05S; pop (1985e) 2 000; area 166 sq km/64 sq ml; maximum length 24 km/15 ml; maximum width 12 km/7 ml. Chilean island just S of the Tropic of Capricorn and 3 790 km/2 355 ml W of Chile; triangular, with an extinct volcano at each corner; rises to 652 m/2 139 ft at Terevaka; undulating grass and tree-covered hills with numerous caves and rocky outcrops; a third covered by Rapa-Nui National Park, established in 1968; rainy season (Feb–Aug); first European discovery by Dutch admiral Jacob Roggeveen on Easter Sunday 1722; islanders largely of Polynesian origin; capital Hanga Roa; airport; famous for its *moai* stone statues depicting the human head and trunk of local ancestors; nearly 1 000 carved from the slopes of Rano Raraku, where the largest (19 m/62 ft) still lies; remains of the ceremonial city of Orongo on Rano Kau. » Chile [i]; Polynesia

Easter Rising (24–29 Apr 1916) A rebellion of Irish nationalists in Dublin, organized by two revolutionary groups, the Irish Republican Brotherhood led by Patrick Pearse (1879–1916), and Sinn Féin under James Connolly (1870–1916). The focal point of the rebellion was the seizing of the General Post Office. The rising was put down and several leaders were executed. The extent of the reprisals increased support for the nationalist cause in Ireland. » nationalism; Pearse; Sinn Féin

Eastern Orthodox Church » **Orthodox Church**

Eastern Woodlands Indians N American Indian group living in the forested region along the Atlantic seaboard from Canada to S Carolina, and stretching W just beyond the Mississippi R. Algonkin-, Iroquoian- and Siouan-speaking, they lived by hunting, fishing, and gathering, with some farming of maize, squash, and beans in those areas with a long enough growing season (towards the S). They were gradually pushed W and N towards the Great Plains and Canada; others were placed on reservations, some of which still exist in upstate New York and New England. » American Indians

Eastman, George (1854–1932) US inventor and philanthropist, born at Waterville, New York. He turned from banking to photography, producing a successful roll film on paper (1884) and the 'Kodak' camera (1888). In 1889 he manufactured the transparent celluloid film used by Edison and others in experiments which made possible the moving-picture industry. He committed suicide at Rochester, New York. » cinematography [i]

Eastwood, Clint (1930–) US film actor and director, born in San Francisco. He began acting in television Westerns, especially the *Rawhide* series (1959–65), and became an international star with three Italian-made 'spaghetti' Westerns, beginning with *A Fistful of Dollars* (1964). In the USA his box-office status was confirmed with several violent crime thrillers, such as *Dirty Harry* (1971), and from that time he began to combine acting performances with directing, beginning with *Play Misty for Me* (1971) and continuing with *Bronco Billy* (1980), *Heartbreak Ridge* (1986), and *Bird* (1987), among many others.

eau de Cologne mint » **mint**

Ebbinghaus, Hermann (1850–1909) German psychologist, born at Barmen, near Bonn. He is best remembered for *Über das Gedächtnis* (1885, Memory), which first applied experimental methods to memory research, and which introduced the nonsense syllable as a standard stimulus for such work. He taught at Berlin, and became professor at Breslau (1894–1905), then at Halle, where he died. » memory

EBCDIC code An acronym of **Extended Binary Coded Decimal Interchange Code**, a binary code used by IBM for information exchange: 256 different characters are defined using an 8-bit code. The characters include all the alphanumeric, punctuation, and non-printing control characters, as well as a considerable number of special characters. » alphanumeric characters; ASCII code

Ebionites [**eb**iuhniyts] Literally, 'poor men'; a Judaeo-Christian sect of the early Christian era, opposed by Irenaeus in the late 2nd-c AD. They were apparently ascetic, and continued to observe rigorously the Jewish Law. They also believed that Jesus was the Messiah, a virtuous man anointed by the Spirit, but not truly 'divine'. » Christology; Irenaeus, St

Ebla An important Syrian city-state of the third millennium BC, lying S of Carchemish. It traded with Anatolia, Assyria, and Sumeria, and exacted tribute from such places as Mari. » Assyria; Carchemish; Mari; Sumer

ebonite » **vulcanite**

ebony An evergreen or deciduous tree, native to tropical and subtropical regions, but mainly concentrated in lowland rainforest; leaves alternate, entire, often forming flattened sprays; flowers unisexual, solitary or in small clusters in leaf axils, urn-shaped with 3–5 spreading lobes, white, yellow, or reddish; fruit a berry seated on a persistent calyx. In most species the white outer wood is soft, but the black heartwood, the ebony of commerce, is very hard. Several species are cultivated, both for their superior timber and for the edible fruits (*persimmons*). (Genus: *Diospyros*, 500 species.) » deciduous plants; evergreen plants; persimmon; sepal

Ebro, River (Span **Río**) [**eb**roh], ancient **Iberius** Longest river flowing entirely in Spain; rises in the Cordillera Cantabrica and flows SE to enter the Mediterranean at Cape Tortosa; three major reservoirs on its course; used for hydroelectricity and irrigation; length, 910 km/565 ml. » Spain [i]

Eccles, Sir John Carew (1903–) Australian physiologist, born in Melbourne. Educated at Melbourne and Oxford, he became director of the Kanematsu Institute of Pathology at Sydney (1937), professor of physiology at Otago (1944–51), then at Canberra (1951–66). In 1968 he moved to the State University of New York at Buffalo. A specialist in neurophysiology, he was knighted in 1958, and shared the 1963 Nobel Prize for Physiology or Medicine for his work on the functioning of nervous impulses. » Huxley, Andrew Fielding; nervous system

Ecclesiastes, Book of [ekleezee**as**teez] A Biblical work, specifically attributed to 'The Preacher, the son of David, King of Jerusalem', who has traditionally been identified as Solomon, although the work is more usually now dated in the post-exilic period of Israel's history. It is largely philosophical in its reflections on the meaning of life, often declaring that 'all is vanity'. The title is derived from the Greek rendering of the Hebrew Koheleth: 'the preacher, one who speaks or teaches in an assembly'. » Old Testament; Solomon (religion) [i]

Ecclesiasticus, Book of [ekleezeeastikuhs] (Lat 'The Church (Book)') Part of the Old Testament Apocrypha or Catholic deuterocanonical writings, originally attributed to a Jewish scribe c.180 BC, but later translated into Greek by his grandson; also called *The Wisdom of Jesus, the Son of Sirach*, or just *Sirach* or *Ben Sira*. It consists largely of collections of proverbs and exhortations; praises wisdom, attempting to link it with a Torah-centred way of life; and ends with a historical survey in praise of Israel's famous leaders. » Apocrypha, Old Testament; Jesus Christ; Torah

ecclesiology [ikleezeeoluhjee] The theological study of the nature of the Christian Church. The term can also signify the science of church construction and decoration. » Christianity

Ecevit, Bülent [echevit] (1925–) Turkish statesman and Prime Minister (1974, 1977, 1978–9), born in Istanbul. After working as a government official and a journalist, he became an MP for the centre-left Republican People's Party in 1957. He was Minister of Labour, then in 1966 became Secretary-General of his Party and subsequently (1972) Chairman. He headed a coalition government in 1974, during whch he ordered the invasion of Cyprus. In 1978 he imposed martial law on Turkey. After the military coup of 1980, he was imprisoned twice for criticizing the military regime. » Cyprus [i]; Turkey [i]

ECG » **electrocardiography**

echidna [ekidna] An Australasian mammal; coat with spines; minute tail; long claws used for digging; long narrow snout and sticky tongue; eats ants and termites, or larger insects and earthworms; young develop in pouch. (Family: *Tachyglossidae*, 2 species.) » monotreme

Echidna [ekidna] In Greek mythology, a fabulous creature, half-woman and half-snake, who was the mother of various monsters. » Cerberus; Hydra (mythology); sphinx

echinoderm [ekiynohderm] A spiny-skinned, marine invertebrate characterized by its typically 5-radial (*pentamerous*) symmetry; body enclosed by a variety of calcareous plates, ossicles, and spines; water vascular system operates numerous tubular feet used in feeding, locomotion, and respiration; includes starfishes, brittle stars, sea lilies, sea urchins, and sea cucumbers, as well as a diverse range of fossils. (Phylum: *Echinodermata*.) » brittle star; calcium; crinoid; sea cucumber; sea urchin; starfish

Echinoidea [ekinoydia] » **sea urchin**

Echiura [ekiyoora] » **spoonworm**

Echo In Greek mythology, a nymph of whom several stories are told. Either she was beloved by Pan, and was torn to pieces, only her voice surviving; or she was punished by Hera so that she could only repeat the last words of another speaker. She loved Narcissus, who rejected her, so that she wasted away to a voice. » Hera; Narcissus; Pan

echo-sounding Bouncing sound waves off the seafloor to determine the depth of water in the oceans. Echo-sounding is based on the simple principle of measuring the time an acoustic signal takes to travel to the sea floor, be reflected as an echo, and travel back to the sea surface. If the speed of sound in sea water is known, the depth to the sea floor can be calculated. In practice, a device known as a *precision depth recorder* (PDR) is used to print a visual trace of the water depth and provide a picture of the sea floor topography. » bathymetry; echolocation; sound

echolalia The automatic repetition of the last words or phrases uttered by someone else. The effect is most commonly seen in dementia, but is also found in childhood psychiatric disorders and in schizophrenia. » dementia; schizophrenia

echolocation The perception of objects by means of reflected sound waves, typically high frequency sounds. The process is used by some animals, such as bats and whales, for orientation and prey location. » echo-sounding; sound

Eck, Johann Mayer von (1486–1543) German Roman Catho-

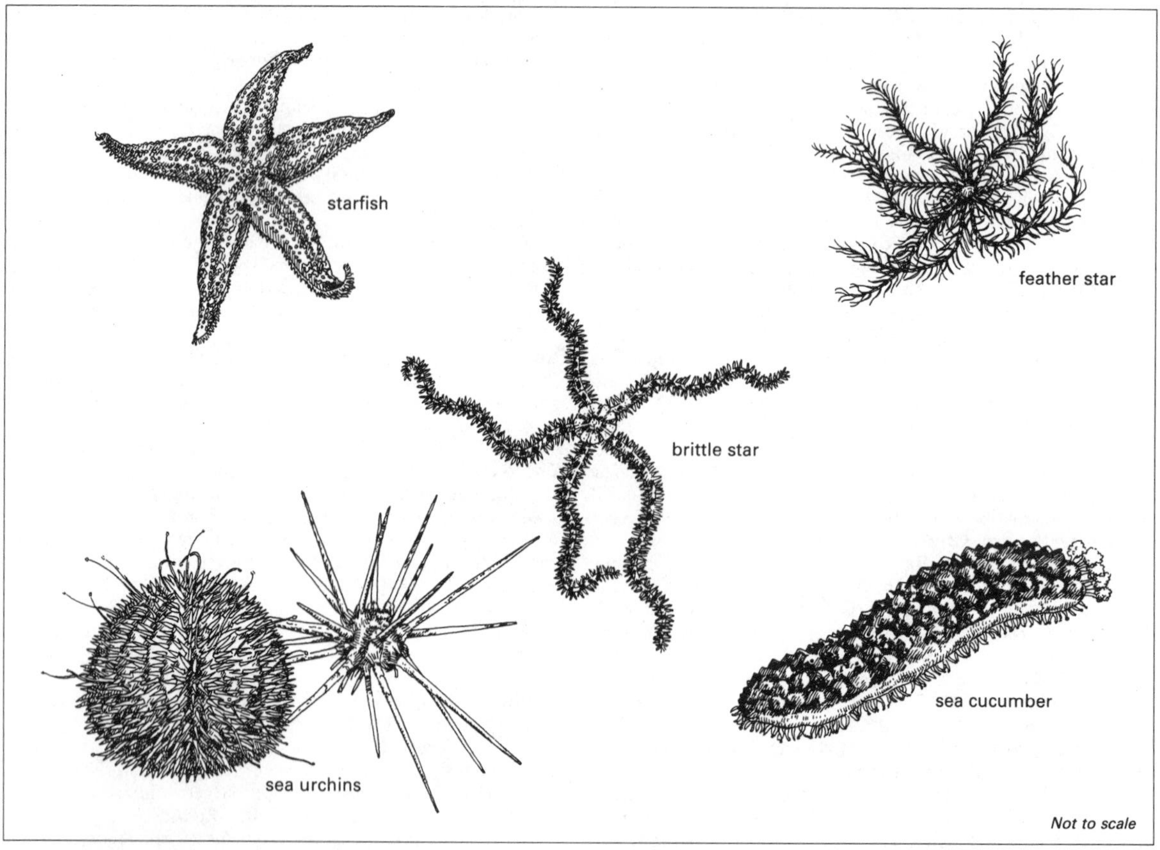

Echinoderms

lic theologian, born at Egg, Swabia. He became professor of theology at Ingolstadt (1510), and was the ruling spirit of that university until his death. After his Leipzig disputation with Luther, he wrote on papal authority, and went to Rome in 1520, to return with the bull which declared Luther a heretic. » bull (religion); Luther; Roman Catholicism; theology

Eckhart, Johannes, known as **Meister Eckhart** (c.1260–c.1327) German theologian and mystic, born at Hochheim, near Gotha. He entered the Dominican order, studied and taught in Paris, and became Dominican provincial in Saxony (1303–11). From 1312 he preached at Strasbourg, Frankfurt, and Cologne. His teaching is a mystic pantheism, influential on later religious mysticism and speculative philosophy. In 1325 he was arraigned for heresy by the Archbishop of Cologne, and two years after his death his writings were condemned by Pope John XXII. He died at Avignon, France. » Dominicans; pantheism; theology

eclampsia A rare disorder of pregnancy which is dangerous to both the mother and foetus; also known as **toxaemia of pregnancy**. It may occur in the second half of pregnancy, and is characterized by very high blood pressure and convulsions. » pre-eclampsia; pregnancy [i]

eclipse 1 The passage of a planet or satellite through the shadow cast by another body, so that it is unable to shine as it normally does by reflected sunlight. In the case of our Sun, a **solar eclipse** can occur only at new Moon, when the Moon is directly between the Earth and the Sun. Although the Moon is much nearer the Earth than the Sun, a coincidence of nature makes both appear nearly the same size in our sky. A **total eclipse**, when the whole disc is obscured, lasts a maximum of 7.5 minutes, often less; during such an eclipse, the chromosphere and corona may briefly be seen. A **partial eclipse** of much longer duration occurs before, after, and to each side of the path of totality. Sometimes the apparent size of the lunar disc is just too small for a total eclipse, and an **annular eclipse** results, in which a bright ring of sunlight surrounds the Moon. A **lunar eclipse** occurs when the Moon passes into the shadow of the Earth, which can happen only at full moon. Then the Moon is a dim coppery hue. Moons and satellites of other bodies in the Solar System are eclipsed when they pass through the shadow of their primary bodies. » chromosphere; corona; Moon; Sun **2** The total or partial disappearance from view of an astronomical object when it passes directly behind another object. In binary star systems it is also possible for one star to eclipse another (an *eclipsing binary star*). » binary star; RR5

ecliptic That great circle which is the projection of the Earth's orbit onto the celestial sphere, and therefore is the apparent path of the Sun across our sky. Positions of the planets as viewed from Earth are generally very close to the ecliptic. » celestial sphere; great circle

eclogue [**ek**log] A short dramatic poem, originally with a pastoral setting and theme. Of classical derivation (notably in Theocritus and Virgil), the form was popular in the 16th–17th-c (as Spenser's *Shepheardes Calendar*, 1579), satirized in the 18th-c (eg Gay, Swift), and has been adapted to more general purposes by some 20th-c poets (eg Auden, MacNeice). » classicism; Greek/Latin literature; Neoclassicism (art and architecture); poetry; Theocritus; Virgil

Eco, Umberto [**ay**koh] (1929–) Italian novelist and critic, born in Allesandra and educated in Turin. He has taught semiotics at the University of Bologna for many years, and published several important works on the subject. His novel *Il nome della rosa* (1981, The Name of the Rose), an intellectual detective story, achieved instant fame, and attracted much critical attention; it was filmed in 1986. *Foucault's Pendulum* appeared in 1989. » Italian literature; novel; semiotics

ecology The study of the interaction of living organisms with their physical, biological, and chemical environment. Because of the complexity of ecosystems, ecological studies of individual ecosystems or parts of ecosytems are often made, from which links between different systems can be established. In this way, ecologists attempt to explain the workings of larger ecosystems. Important ecological concepts have had considerable influence in conservation; an example is *carrying capacity*, which relates the available resources of an area to the number of users that can be sustained by these resources. Some ecologists question the role of people in the environment: is humanity dependent on, or independent of, nature? The ecological movement of the 1960s onwards has argued that people must live within the limitations of the Earth's finite supply of resources, and that humanity is very much dependent on its environment. Ecology is therefore seen as a social as well as a scientific subject, providing a link between physical and human environments. » conservation (earth sciences); ecosystem; environmental studies

econometrics A branch of economics which uses mathematical and statistical models of the economy in order to make economic forecasts and to assess the likely results of different actions by the government. » economics

Economic and Social Council » **United Nations**

Economic Community of West African States (ECOWAS) An organization formed in May 1975 by 15 W African signatories to the Treaty of Lagos: Benin, Gambia, Ghana, Guinea, Guinea-Bissau, Ivory Coast (Côte d'Ivoire), Liberia, Mali, Mauritania, Niger, Nigeria, Senegal, Sierra Leone, Togo, and Upper Volta (now Burkina Faso); Cape Verde joined in 1977. Its principal objectives are the ending of restrictions on trade, the establishment of a common customs tariff, the harmonization of economic and industrial policies, and the elimination of differences in the level of development of member states.

economic history The study of the economies and forms of wealth-creation in past societies. Such work tended to appear as subordinate parts of predominantly political accounts, especially in Britain, until the early 20th-c, but departments of economic history began to appear in universities in the inter-war period. Most of the subject was empirically based, but after c.1950 more attention was paid to prevalent economic theory, especially in the wake of Keynesian analyses, as a means of directing historical enquiry. Sub-specialisms include agricultural history and business history. » economics; history; Keynesian

economics The study of the allocation of scarce resources among competing ends, the creation and distribution of wealth, and national income. The first major economist was Adam Smith, and the economic theory of the classical school (equilibrium) dominated thinking until the 1930s. The main change in thinking at that time was the result of work by Keynes, whose economic theories attempted to solve the problems of depression and economic stagnation. After 1945, the main aim of economic policy was to maintain high employment levels. Inflationary pressures were a test of Keynesian economics: monetarist theories were popular in the 1970s as an attempt to reduce inflation, but these are now believed to have contributed to the high levels of unemployment seen in the early 1980s. Two main aspects are often recognized. **Microeconomics** is the study of the economic problems of firms and individuals, and the way individual elements in an economy behave (such as specific products, commodities, or consumers). **Macroeconomics** is the study of the country as a whole, including such matters as trade, monetary policy, prices, national income, output, exchange rates, growth, and forecasting (*econometrics*). Particular concerns are how to manage an economy to achieve high growth, low inflation, and high employment; and, for individual firms, to predict those economic factors which will affect them in the future, thus enabling them to improve their own planning. » economic history; equilibrium; Keynes; monetarism; Smith, Adam; social science

economies of scale The economic theory that, the larger the enterprise, the more profitable will be its operations because there will be higher productivity, stronger buying power (therefore materials will be bought cheaper), and better plant utilization. However, there are also *dis-economies of scale*: control becomes more difficult, and bureaucratic systems increase costs. The theory is often used to support an argument for merging two companies; but it does not always work out in practice.

ecosocialism A branch of socialism of relatively recent origin which wishes to see socialist practice linked with concern for environmental and ecological matters. In particular, it represents the view that resources other than labour should be used in a socially useful manner, and reacts against increases in economic growth and high technology production. » ecology; socialism

ecosystem An ecological concept which helps to explain the relationships and interactions between one or more living organisms and their physical, biological, and chemical environment (eg a pond and its associated plants, fish, insects, birds, and mammals). The concept is helpful in describing interactions at any level, from the individual plant in its community to planet Earth. The study of ecosystems is commonly based on transfers of energy along a food chain by examining four elements: *abiotic* or inorganic and dead organic substances (eg inorganic compounds in soil and water); green plants or *producers*, which fix energy from the Sun by photosynthesis and use inorganic material from the soil or atmosphere to manufacture complex organic substances; *consumers* (eg birds, insects, mammals) which use the energy fixed by plants; and *decomposers* (eg bacteria, fungi), which break down dead organisms, releasing nutrients back to the environment for use by the producers. In most natural ecosystems, several food-chains interact to form complex food or energy webs. An ecosystem is a convenient model which does not, however, convey the complexity of the interactions which actually take place. » ecology; environment; food-chain; photosynthesis

ecstasy A designer drug which is supposedly mildly hallucinogenic; also called *MDMA* (methylenedioxymethamphetamine) or 'Adam'. It is reported to heighten the tactile senses of touch and skin sensations, and thereby act as an aphrodisiac. Its street name is 'E'. » designer drugs; hallucinogens

ectopic pregnancy The implantation of the fertilized ovum in some site other than within the uterus. The most common abnormal site is within the Fallopian tube, where the pregnancy can end only in tubal abortion or tubal rupture. » Fallopian tubes

ectoplasm A substance said to exude from the body of a medium during a seance, and from which materializations sometimes supposedly form. This alleged phenomenon was primarily produced by mediums in the late Victorian era. It is the subject of much controversy, as some mediums were discovered to simulate such effects fraudulently, by such means as regurgitation of a previously swallowed substance (such as a piece of cloth). » medium (parapsychology); seance

ECU » **European Monetary System**

Ecuador [ekwadaw], official name **Republic of Ecuador**, Span **República del Ecuador** pop (1990e) 10 780 000; area 270 699 sq km/104 490 sq ml. Republic in NW S America straddling the Equator; bounded N by Colombia, S and E by Peru, and W by the Pacific Ocean; includes the Galápagos Is 970 km/600 ml W; capital, Quito; chief towns, Guayaquil, Cuenca, Riobamba, Esmeraldas; timezone GMT −5; population 25% Indian, 55% Mestizo, 10% Spanish, 10% African; official language, Spanish, with Quechua also spoken; main religion, Roman Catholicism; unit of currency, the sucre of 100 centavos.

Physical description and climate. Coastal plain (*Costa*) in the W, descending from rolling hills (N) to broad lowland basin averaging 100 km/60 ml in width before opening out into the Gulf of Guayaquil; Andean uplands (*Sierra*) in C, three main ranges rising to snow-capped peaks which include Cotopaxi (5 896 m/19 343 ft); forested alluvial plains of the *Oriente* (E), dissected by rivers flowing from the Andes towards the Amazon; frequent serious earthquakes; Galápagos Is comprise six main volcanic islands, land area c.7 812 sq km/3 015 sq ml; hot and humid coast, rain throughout year (especially Dec–Apr); varies from 2 000 mm/80 in (N) to 200 mm/8 in (S); C Andes temperatures much reduced by altitude; Quito, warm days and chilly nights, with frequent heavy rain in afternoon; hot and wet equatorial climate (E).

History and government. Formerly part of Inca Empire; taken by Spanish, 1527; within Viceroyalty of New Granada; independent, 1822; joined with Panama, Colombia, and Venezuela to form Gran Colombia; left union, to become indepen-

dent republic, 1830; highly unstable political history (22 presidents 1925–48, none completing a term in office); unicameral National Congress consisting of 71-member House of Deputies and four permanent committees of 28 members elected every four years; a president is elected for a 4-year term.

Economy. Agriculture employs c.50% of workforce; beans, cereals, potatoes, livestock in the *Sierra*; bananas, coffee, cocoa, cane sugar, rice, cotton, vegetable oil in the *Costa*; fishing (especially shrimps), balsawood, food processing, textiles, petrochemicals, steel, cement, pharmaceuticals; oil piped from the *Oriente* to refineries at Esmeraldas. » Andes; Galápagos Islands; Gran Colombia; Incas; Quito; RR25 national holidays; RR47 political leaders

ecumenism [ekyoomuhnizm] (Gr *oikoumene*, 'the inhabited world') A movement seeking visible unity of divided churches and denominations within Christianity. The 4th-c and 5th-c 'Ecumenical Councils' had claimed to represent the Church in the whole world. A dramatic increase of interest in ecumenism and the reuniting of Churches followed the Edinburgh Missionary Conference (1910), and led to the formation in 1948 of the World Council of Churches. Assemblies are held every seven years, the decisions of which guide but do not bind member Churches. The movement encourages dialogue between Churches of different denominations, unions where possible (as in the Churches of N and S India), joint acts of worship, and joint service in the community. » Council of the Church; World Council of Churches

eczema » **dermatitis**

edaphology The study of soil as a medium for growth of living organisms. The word is from Greek *edaphos* 'ground, soil'. » soil; soil science

Edda (Old Norse 'great-grandmother') The name of two separate collections of Old Norse literature. The **Elder Edda**, dating from the 9th-c, consist of heroic and mythological poems; the later Edda were written (mainly in prose) in the early 13th-c by the Icelandic poet Snorri Sturluson. » Icelandic/Norwegian literature; saga; Snorri Sturluson

Eddington, Sir Arthur Stanley (1882–1944) British astronomer, born at Kendal, Cumbria. He was educated at Manchester and Cambridge, where he became professor of astronomy (1913) and director of the Cambridge Observatories, working mainly on the internal structure of stars. In 1919 his observations of star positions during a total solar eclipse gave the first direct confirmation of Einstein's general theory of relativity. He became a renowned popularizer of science, notably in *The Expanding Universe* (1933). Knighted in 1930, he died at Cambridge. » astrophysics; general relativity; stellar evolution

Eddy, Mary Baker (Glover) (1821–1910) US founder of the Christian Scientists, born at Bow, New Hampshire. Brought up a Congregationalist, she had little formal education, because of ill health. In 1866 she received severe injuries after a fall, but read about the palsied man in Matthew's Gospel, and claimed to have risen from her bed similarly healed. Thereafter she devoted herself to developing her spiritual discovery, in 1876 founded the Christian Science Association, and in 1879 organized at Boston the Church of Christ, Scientist. She died at Chestnut Hill, Massachusetts. » Christian Science; Congregationalism

eddy currents Circulating electrical currents induced in bulk conducting material, rather than circuits, by changing magnetic fields or by the motion of the material in a magnetic field. They are a consequence of electromagnetic induction. The heating effect due to eddy currents in the core material of transformers and motors is a source of power wastage. » electromagnetic induction

Ede, James Chuter, Baron Chuter-Ede of Epsom (1882–1965) British Labour politician, born at Epsom, Surrey. He was educated at Cambridge, and became a teacher (1905–14) and local councillor (1920–27), before entering parliament briefly in 1923. He became Home Secretary in the 1945 Labour government, and Leader of the House of Commons in 1951. A humanitarian reformer, he was responsible for the Criminal Justice Act of 1948. He became a life peer in 1964. » Labour Party

Edelman, Gerald (Maurice) (1929–) US biochemist, born in New York City. He was educated at Pennsylvania and Rockefeller universities, and became professor of biochemistry in the latter in 1966. His special interest was in the chemical structure and mode of action of the antibodies which form a major part of a vertebrate animal's defence against infection. He shared the Nobel Prize for Physiology or Medicine in 1972. » antibodies

edelweiss [**ay**dlviys] A perennial growing to 20 cm/8 in, native to the mountains of SE Europe; leaves narrowly lance- or spoon-shaped, with a dense covering of white woolly hairs pressed flat against the surface; flower heads yellowish-white, arranged in a flat-topped cluster surrounded by pointed, spreading and star-like, woolly bracts. It is a well-known alpine plant with romantic associations, protected by law in many districts. (*Leontopodium alpinum*. Family: *Compositae*.) » alpine; bract; perennial

edema » **oedema**

Eden (of Avon), Sir (Robert) Anthony, 1st Earl (1897–1977) British statesman and Conservative Prime Minister (1955–7), born at Windlestone, Durham. Educated at Eton and Oxford, he became an MP in 1923, and was Foreign Under-Secretary (1931), Lord Privy Seal (1933), and Foreign Secretary (1935), resigning in 1938 over differences with Chamberlain. In World War 2 he was first Dominions Secretary, then Secretary of State for War, and Foreign Secretary (1940–5). Again Foreign Secretary (1951–5), he was involved with the negotiations in Korea and Indo-China, and the 1954 Geneva Summit Conference. He succeeded Churchill as Prime Minister, and in 1956 ordered British forces (in collaboration with the French and Israelis) to occupy the Suez Canal Zone. His action was condemned by the United Nations and caused a bitter controversy in Britain which did not subside when he ordered a withdrawal. In failing health, he abruptly resigned in 1957. He was created an earl in 1961, and died at Alvedision, Wiltshire. » Churchill, Winston; Conservative Party; Suez Crisis

Eden, Garden of Biblical place associated with 'Paradise', where Adam and Eve lived prior to their sin and expulsion (*Gen* 2, 3). 'Eden' may mean 'delight' (Heb) or simply and more probably 'a plain' (Sumerian). It is also used in Ezekiel as a symbol for the future restitution of Israel after the exile. » Adam and Eve; Ezekiel, Book of

Edentata [eeduhn**tah**ta] (Lat 'with no teeth') An order of mammals characterized by having extra contacts between some of the bones in the spine, and by having no front teeth; comprises anteaters, sloths, and armadillos; anteaters have no teeth; sloths and armadillos have simple molar teeth. » anteater; armadillo; sloth

Edgar (943–75) King of Mercia and Northumbria (957) and (from 959) King of all England, the younger son of Edmund I. He encouraged the reform of the English Church as a means of enhancing his prestige and power, though his lavish support for the monasteries caused bitterness among an important section of the nobility. In c.973 he introduced a uniform currency based on new silver pennies. » Anglo-Saxons; Edmund I

Edgar the Atheling [**ath**uhling] (c.1050–1125) Anglo-Saxon prince, the grandson of Edmund Ironside. Though chosen as King by some influential Englishmen after the Battle of Hastings, he was never crowned. He submitted to William the Conqueror (by Dec 1066), but then rebelled and fled to Scotland (1068), where his sister Margaret married Malcolm Canmore. He was finally reconciled with King William in 1074. He was taken prisoner at the Battle of Tinchebrai (1106), fighting for Duke Robert of Normandy against Henry I of England, and lived in obscurity after his release. » Anglo-Saxons; Edmund Ironside; William I (of England)

Edgeworth, Maria (1767–1849) Anglo-Irish writer, born at Blackbourton, Oxfordshire. She is best-known for her children's stories, and her novels of Irish life, such as *Castle Rackrent* (1800) and *The Absentee* (1812). Her work influenced Walter Scott, whom she visited on several occasions. She died at her family home, at Edgeworthstown, Ireland. » Irish literature; Scott, Walter

Edinburgh, Duke of, Prince Philip (1921–) The husband of Queen Elizabeth II of the United Kingdom, the son of Prince Andrew of Greece and Princess Alice of Battenberg, born at Corfu. Educated at Cheam, Gordonstoun, and Dartmouth, he entered the Royal Navy in 1939 as Lieutenant Philip Mountbatten. He became a naturalized British subject in 1947, when he was married to the Princess Elizabeth (20 Nov). Seriously interested in science and the technology of industry, as well as in youth adventure training and awards, he is also a keen sportsman, yachtsman, and qualified airman. In 1956 he began the **Duke of Edinburgh Award Scheme** to foster the leisure activities of young people. » Elizabeth II

Edinburgh [**ed**inbuhruh] 55°57N 3°13W, pop(1981) 420 169. Capital of Lothian region and of Scotland; in EC Scotland, between Pentland Hills and S shore of Firth of Forth; port facilities at Leith; castle built by Malcolm Canmore (11th-c); charter granted by Robert Bruce, 1392; capital of Scotland, 1482; in the 1760s, New Town area designed by James Craig (1744–95), but the business centre remained in the Old Town; Nor' Loch separating old and new towns was drained and laid out as gardens (Princes Street Gardens); airport; railway; Edinburgh University (1583); Heriot-Watt University (1966); commercial, business, legal, and cultural centre; brewing, distilling, finance, tourism, printing, publishing, trade in grain; Edinburgh Castle (oldest part, St Margaret's Chapel, 12th-c); Royal Mile from castle to Palace of Holyroodhouse, official residence of the Queen in Scotland; Holyrood Park, containing Arthur's Seat, extinct volcano; Scott Monument (1844), 61 m/200 ft high; observatory on Calton Hill, with unfinished reproduction of the Parthenon; Royal Observatory on Blackford Hill; Gladstone's Land (6-storey tenement, 1620), house of John Knox (15th-c), St Giles Cathedral (15th-c), National Gallery of Scotland, Scottish National Gallery of Modern Art, Scottish National Portrait Gallery, Royal Museum of Scotland, Museum of Childhood, Wax Museum, Royal Botanic Garden, zoo, Meadowbank Stadium sports complex, artificial ski slope; folk festival (Mar), Royal Highland Agricultural Show (Jun), Military Tattoo (Aug); International, Fringe, Jazz, and Film Festivals, and Highland Games (Aug–Sep). » Bruce, Robert; Edinburgh Festival; Holyrood House; Knox, John; Lothian; Malcolm III; Scotland [i]; Scott, Walter

Edinburgh Festival An international festival of the arts, particularly music and drama, that takes place in the last three weeks of August every year in Edinburgh, Scotland. Established in 1947, it was run by Rudolf Bing until 1950; the present artistic director is Frank Dunlop. As well as the Festival proper, the 'Fringe' offers a lively and ever-growing selection of 'alternative' events. » Edinburgh

Edison, Thomas (Alva) (1847–1931) US inventor, born at Milan, Ohio. He began as a railroad newsboy, and purchasing some old type he published the *Grand Trunk Herald*, the first newspaper printed in a train. A stationmaster taught him telegraphy, and he invented an automatic repeater, by which messages could be sent from one wire to another without the intervention of the operator. In 1871 he invented the printing-telegraph for quotations. He was the author of over 1000 inventions, including the phonograph (1877), the electric light bulb (1879), and motion picture equipment. He died at West Orange, New Jersey. » phonograph; telegraphy

editing (cinema) The physical cutting and joining of the first prints of a motion picture film negative ('rush prints'), each scene and take having been identified and synchronized with the corresponding magnetic sound by the clapper board at the head end. Material is studied on an editing table, with separate paths for picture and sound, the picture being shown on a small screen. Selected frames are marked with grease pencil, and the cut sections joined with transparent adhesive tape to build up the work print. When this is finally approved by the director, it acts as the guide for assembling the corresponding original picture negative. In videotape editing, the original is not cut. Scenes are assembled by re-recording selected sections on to another tape, a standard time-code giving precise identification of the chosen points. Time-codes are now increasingly used in film editing also. » clapper board; conforming; film production; videotape

Edmonton 53°34N 113°25W, pop (1984) 560085. Capital of Alberta province, W Canada, on banks of N Saskatchewan R; most northerly large town in N America; Fort Edmonton built by Hudson's Bay Company, 40 km/25 ml below present site, 1795; destroyed by Indians, 1807, and rebuilt on new site, 1819; reached by railway, 1891; chosen as capital, 1905; rapid growth after discovery of oil nearby, 1947; University of Alberta (1906) and Athabasca University (1972); airport; airfield; petrochemicals, retail and trade centre; ice hockey team, Edmonton Oilers; Legislative Building, George McDougall Memorial Shrine and Museum (1871); Klondike Days display, including the Sourdough Raft Race (Jul). » Alberta; Hudson's Bay Company

Edmund I (921–46) King of the English (from 939), the half-brother of Athelstan. On Edmund's accession, Scandinavian forces from Northumbria, reinforced by levies from Ireland, quickly overran the E Midlands. He re-established his control over the S Danelaw (942) and Northumbria (944), and for the remainder of his life ruled a reunited England. He was killed by an outlaw at Pucklechurch, Gloucestershire. » Anglo-Saxons; Athelstan; Danelaw

Edmund II, byname **Edmund Ironside** (c.980–1016) King of the English, the son of Ethelred the Unready. He was chosen King by the Londoners on his father's death (Apr 1016), while Canute was elected at Southampton by the Witan. Edmund hastily levied an army, defeated Canute, and attempted to raise the siege of London, but was routed at Ashingdon or possibly Ashdon, Essex (Oct 1016). He agreed to a partition of the country, but died a few weeks later, leaving Canute as sole ruler. » Canute

Edmund, St, originally **Edmund Rich** (1170–1240), feast day 16 November. English churchman and Archbishop of Canterbury, born at Abingdon, Oxfordshire. He studied and taught at Oxford and Paris, became famous as a preacher, and was commissioned by the Pope to preach the sixth crusade throughout England (c.1227). As archbishop (1234), he became the spokesman of the national party against Henry III, defending Church rights. He died on a journey to Rome, at Pontigny, France. » Christianity; Crusades [i]; Henry III (of England)

Edomites [eeduhmiyts] According to the Bible (*Gen* 36), the descendants of Esau who settled in the mountainous area S of the Dead Sea to the Gulf of Aqabah; in Greek, **Idumeans**. They often appear as enemies of Israel, having been conquered by David, but retaking parts of Judah and becoming a kingdom in the 8th-c BC. They participated in the overthrow of Judah in 587 BC by the Babylonians, but were eventually conquered by John Hyrcanus in the late 2nd-c BC, forcing their integration into the Jewish people. Herod I (the Great) was of Edomite descent. » Babylonia; Bible; David; Esau; Herod the Great; Hyrcanus I, John; Judah, Kingdom of

EDTA $C_{10}H_{16}N_2O_8$, *diaminoethanetetra-acetic acid* (the acronym is from an older form of the name). One of the most versatile of the complexing agents; up to 6 of its O and N atoms can co-ordinate to a metal ion at one time. It is used to remove

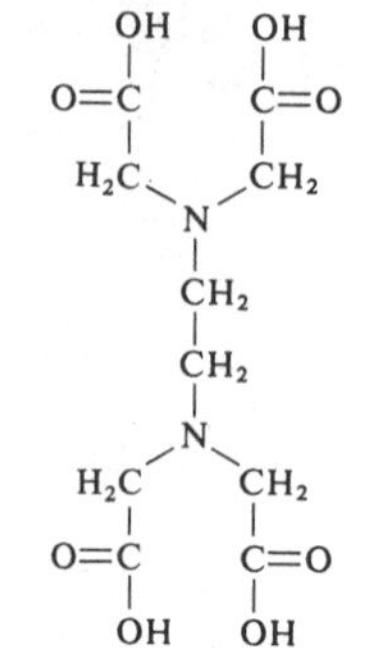

small traces of metal ions from solutions. » chelate; co-ordination compounds

education What takes place when human beings learn something, often from others but sometimes for themselves. It may happen during the day in specially constructed buildings with qualified teachers following structured, approved courses based on books, equipment, or activities, or more informally away from institutions in homes, streets, or meeting places. It is not confined to traditional school subjects such as mathematics or history, though these will usually constitute an important part of it, nor is it offered only by paid teachers, for parents and elder brothers and sisters may well play a central part in it.

Increasingly, education is seen as something which should develop the whole person, not just as a narrow academic training. Thus in a vast variety of locations around the world, from lavishly equipped buildings with the latest laboratory equipment to simple huts in poorer countries, children and adults are learning the basic skills of reading, writing, and arithmetic, developing qualities which will be valuable in adult life whether at home or work, and in many cases taking retraining courses because the job for which they originally prepared has been transformed.

There is considerable variety in educational provision. In some countries the curriculum is prescribed from the centre, with content, books, and even teaching styles laid down in the capital city; in others, with a less centralized curriculum, such decisions are delegated to regional or even individual school level. Most countries operate a primary phase for children up to 11 or 12, a secondary stage for those up to 15, 16, 17, or 18, and then further and higher education for anyone wishing to study beyond the minimum school-leaving age. » adult/compensatory/distance/further/multicultural/preschool/tertiary/vocational education; coeducation; college of education; educational drama/psychology; local education authority; mainstreaming; polytechnic; university

educational psychology A branch of psychology developed earlier this century to apply the findings of psychology to the understanding of learning. It was greatly influenced by the psychometric movement, which resulted in the traditional role of the educational psychologist often being limited to one of testing children and placing 'backward' ones into special education. With the decline in popularity of IQ tests and of segregated education, the profession has turned its attention increasingly to the task of assisting teachers in programmes designed to help individual children, and in advising schools about their function as organizations. » education; intelligence; learning; psychology; psychometrics

Edward I (1239–1307) King of England (1272–1307), the elder son of Henry III and Eleanor of Provence, born at Westminster. He married Eleanor of Castile (1254) and later Margaret of France, the sister of Philip IV (1299). In the Barons' War (1264–7), he at first supported Simon de Montfort, but rejoined his father, and defeated de Montfort at Evesham (1265). He then won renown as a crusader to the Holy Land, and did not return to England until 1274, two years after his father's death. In two devasting campaigns (1276–7, 1282–3), he annexed N and W Wales, and ensured the permanence of his conquests by building magnificent castles. He reasserted English claims to the overlordship of Scotland when the line of succession failed, and decided in favour of John Balliol as King (1292). But Edward's insistence on full rights of suzerainty provoked the Scottish magnates to force Balliol to repudiate Edward and ally with France (1295), thus beginning the Scottish Wars of Independence. Despite prolonged campaigning and victories such as Falkirk (1298), he could not subdue Scotland as he had done Wales. He died at Burgh-by-Sands, near Carlisle, while leading his army against Robert Bruce. » Barons' War; Bruce, Robert; Crusades [i]; Llywelyn; Montfort, Simon de; Wallace, William; Westminster, Statutes of

Edward II (1284–1327) King of England (1307–27), the fourth son of Edward I and Eleanor of Castile, born at Caernarfon, Wales. In 1301 he was created Prince of Wales, the first English heir apparent to bear the title, and in 1308 married Isabella of France, the daughter of Philip IV. Throughout his reign, Edward mismanaged the barons, who sought to rid the country of royal favourites and restore their rightful place in government. The Ordinances of 1311 restricted the royal prerogative in matters such as appointments to the King's household, and demanded the banishment of Piers Gaveston, who was ultimately captured and executed (1312). Edward was humiliated by reverses in Scotland, where he was decisively defeated by Robert Bruce at the Battle of Bannockburn (1314). The Ordinances were formally annulled (1322), but the King's new favourites, the Despensers, were acquisitive and unpopular, and earned the particular enmity of Queen Isabella. With her lover Roger Mortimer, she toppled the Despensers (1326) and imprisoned Edward in Kenilworth Castle. He renounced the throne in favour of his eldest son (1327), who succeeded as Edward III, and was then murdered in Berkeley Castle, near Gloucester. » Bannockburn, Battle of; Bruce; Edward I/III; Gaveston; Isabella of France

Edward III (1312–77) King of England (1327–77), the elder son of Edward II and Isabella of France, born at Windsor, Berkshire. He married Philippa of Hainault in 1328, and their eldest child Edward, later called the Black Prince, was born in 1330. By banishing Queen Isabella from court and executing her lover, Roger Mortimer, he assumed full control of the government (1330), and began to restore the monarchy's authority and prestige. He supported Edward Balliol's attempts to wrest the Scots throne from David II, and his victory at Halidon Hill (1333) forced David to seek refuge in France until 1341. In 1337, after Philip VI had declared Guyenne forfeit, he revived his hereditary claim to the French crown through Isabella, the daughter of Philip IV, thus beginning the Hundred Years' War. He destroyed the French navy at the Battle of Sluys (1340), and won another major victory at Crécy (1346). David II was captured two months later at the Battle of Neville's Cross, near Durham, and remained a prisoner until 1357. Renowned for his valour and military skill, Edward died at Sheen (now Richmond), Surrey. » David II; Edward II; Hundred Years' War; William of Wykeham

Edward IV (1442–83) King of England (1461–70, 1471–83), the eldest son of Richard, Duke of York, born at Rouen, France. His father claimed the throne as the lineal descendant of Edward III's third and fifth sons (respectively Lionel, Duke of Clarence, and Edmund, Duke of York), against the Lancastrian King Henry VI (the lineal descendant of Edward III's fourth son, John of Gaunt.) Richard was killed at the Battle of Wakefield (1460), but Edward entered London in 1461, was recognized as King on Henry VI's deposition, and with the support of his cousin Richard Neville, Earl of Warwick, decisively defeated the Lancastrians at Towton. He threw off his dependence on Warwick, and secretly married Elizabeth Woodville (1464). Warwick forced him into exile in Holland (Oct 1470), and Henry VI regained the throne. Edward returned to England (Mar 1471), was restored to kingship (11 Apr), then defeated and killed Warwick at the Battle of Barnet (14 Apr), and destroyed the remaining Lancastrian forces at Tewkesbury (4 May). Henry VI was murdered soon afterwards, and Edward remained secure for the rest of his reign. He died at Westminster. » Edward III; Henry VI; Roses, Wars of the; Warwick, Earl of

Edward V (1470–83) King of England (Apr–Jun 1483), born at Westminster, the son of Edward IV and Elizabeth Woodville. Shortly after his accession, he and his younger brother Richard, Duke of York, were imprisoned in the Tower by their uncle Richard, Duke of Gloucester, who usurped the throne as Richard III. The two Princes were never heard of again, and were most likely murdered (Aug 1483) on their uncle's orders. In 1674 a wooden chest containing the bones of two children was discovered in the Tower, and these were interred in Westminster Abbey as their presumed remains. » Edward IV; Richard III; Roses, Wars of the

Edward VI (1537–53) King of England (1547–53), born in London, the son of Henry VIII by his third queen, Jane Seymour. During his reign, power was first in the hands of his uncle, the Duke of Somerset, and after his execution in 1552, of John Dudley, Duke of Northumberland. Edward became a devout Protestant, and under the Protectors the English Reformation flourished. He died of tuberculosis in London, having agreed to the succession of Lady Jane Grey (overthrown after 9 days by Mary I). » Grey, Jane; Reformation

Edward VII (1841–1910) King of the United Kingdom (1901–10), born and died in London, the eldest son of Queen Victoria. Educated privately, and at Edinburgh, Oxford, and Cambridge, in 1863 he married **Alexandra** (1844–1925), the eldest daughter of Christian IX of Denmark. They had three sons and three daughters: **Albert Victor** (1864–92), Duke of Clarence; **George** (1865–1936); **Louise** (1867–1931), Princess Royal; **Victoria** (1868–1935); **Maud** (1869–1938), who married Haakon VII of Norway; and **Alexander** (born and died 1871). As Prince of Wales, his behaviour led him into several social scandals, and the Queen excluded him from affairs of state. As King, he carried out several visits to Continental capitals which strove to allay international animosities. » Victoria

Edward VIII (1894–1972) King of the United Kingdom (Jan–Dec 1936), born at Richmond, Surrey, the eldest son of George V. Educated at Osborne, Dartmouth, and Oxford, he joined the navy and (in World War 1) the army, travelled much, and achieved considerable popularity. He succeeded his father in 1936, but abdicated (11 Dec) in the face of opposition to his proposed marriage to Mrs Ernest Simpson, a commoner who had been twice divorced. He was then given the title of Duke of Windsor, and the marriage took place in France in 1937. They lived in Paris, apart from a period in the Bahamas (1940–5), where Edward was Governor. He died in Paris. His wife, the **Duchess of Windsor** (1896–1986) was born Bessie Wallis Warfield at Blue Ridge Summit, Pennsylvania. She married (1916–27) Lieutenant E W Spencer of the US Navy, then (1927–36) Ernest Simpson, a US-born Englishman. Well known in London Society, she met the Prince of Wales at a country house party. After her husband's death, she lived in seclusion, and was in ill health for many years before she died, in Paris. She was buried beside her husband at Windsor Castle.

Edward the Confessor (c.1003–66), feast day 13 October. King of England (1042–66), the elder son of Ethelred the Unready and Emma of Normandy, and the last king of the Old English royal line. After living in exile in Normandy, he joined the household of his half-brother Hardicanute in 1041, and then succeeded him on the throne. Until 1052 he maintained his position against the ambitious Godwin family by building up Norman favourites, and in 1051 he very probably recognized Duke William of Normandy (later William I) as his heir. But the Godwins regained their ascendancy, and on his deathbed in London, Edward, who remained childless, nominated Harold Godwin (Harold II) to succeed, the Norman Conquest following soon after. Edward's repuation for holiness began in his lifetime, and he rebuilt Westminster Abbey, where he was buried, in the Romanesque style. His cult grew in popularity, and he was canonized in 1161. » Ethelred (the Unready); Hardicanute; Harold II; Norman Conquest

Edward the Elder (c.870–924) King of Wessex (899–924), the elder son of Alfred the Great. He built on his father's successes and established himself as the strongest ruler in Britain. By one of the most decisive military campaigns of the whole Anglo-Saxon period, he conquered and annexed to Wessex the S Danelaw (910–18). He also assumed control of Mercia (918), and although he exercised no direct power in the N, all the chief rulers beyond the Humber, including the King of Scots, formally recognized his overlordship in 920. He died at Farndon, Cheshire. » Alfred; Anglo-Saxons; Danelaw; Wessex

Edward the Martyr (c.962–78), feast day 12 October. King of England (975–8), son of Edgar. During his reign there was a reaction against the policies in support of monasticism espoused by his father. He was murdered at Corfe, Dorset, by supporters of his stepmother, Elfrida, and canonized in 1001. » Edgar

Edward the Black Prince (1330–76) Eldest son of Edward III, born at Woodstock, Oxfordshire. He was created Earl of Chester (1333), Duke of Cornwall (1337), and Prince of Wales (1343). In 1346, though still a boy, he fought at Crécy, and is said to have won his popular title (first cited in a 16th-c work) from his black armour. He won several victories in the Hundred Years' War, including Poitiers (1356). He had two sons: Edward (1365–70) and the future Richard II. In 1362 he was created Prince of Aquitaine, and lived there until 1371, until a revolt forced him to return to England. A great soldier, he was a failure as an administrator. He died at Westminster, London. » Edward III; Hundred Years' War

Edward, Lake, Zaire **Lake Rutanzige** area 4 000 sq km/1 500 sq ml. Lake in EC Africa, in the W Rift Valley on the frontier between Zaire and Uganda; length, c.80 km/50 ml; width, 50 km/30 ml; altitude, 912 m/2 992 ft; receives the Rutshuru R; Semliki R flows N into L Albert; European discovery by Henry Stanley in 1889; named after the Prince of Wales (later Edward VII). » Africa; Rift Valley; Stanley, Henry Morton

Edwards, Jonathan (1703–58) US theologian and metaphysician, born at East Windsor, Connecticut. Educated at Yale, he was ordained in 1727, and ministered at the Congregational church in Northampton, Massachusetts. He was successful for many years, but his extreme Calvinistic orthodoxy led to controversy, and he was dismissed in 1750. He then worked as a missionary with the Housatonnuck Indians until 1758, when he became president of Princeton College, but died soon after his installation. His works, which include *Freedom of the Will* (1754), led to the religious revival known as the 'Great Awakening'. » Calvinism; Great Awakening; missions, Christian

Edwin, St (584–633), feast day 12 October. King of Northumbria (616–33), brought up in N Wales. Under him, Northumbria became united. He pushed his power W as far as Anglesey and Man, obtained the overlordship of East Anglia, and (by a victory over the West Saxons) that of all England, save Kent. He was converted to Christianity, and baptized with his nobles in 627. He fell in battle with Mercians and Welsh at Hatfield Chase, and was afterwards canonized. » Anglo-Saxons; Christianity

EEC » **European Economic Community**

EEG » **electroencephalography**

eel Any of numerous marine and freshwater fishes with an elongate cylindrical body form; median fins continuous, pelvics absent, and pectorals present or absent; adults live in fresh water, returning to sea to spawn; common European eel (*Anguilla anguilla*. Family: *Anguillidae*) an important food fish; larval stage called a *leptocephalus*. The name is also used for c.20 families of shallow water and deep-sea fishes that have similar long narrow bodies.

eel grass A grass-like marine plant found in shallow waters around all but tropical coasts; adapted to withstand salt water, it grows completely submerged. It is a major source of food for migrating brent geese. (Genus: *Zostera*, 12 species. Family: *Zosteraceae*.) » brent goose; grass [i]

eelpout Slender-bodied fish with broad head, long dorsal and anal fins, well-developed pectorals, abundant in European coastal waters; length up to 50 cm/20 in; young born fully-formed. The name is also used generally for members of the family *Zoarcidae*, and as an alternative name for the burbot, *Lota lota*. (*Zoarces viviparous*. Family: *Zoarcidae*.)

eelworm » **nematode**

Efate [efatee], Fr **Vaté**, Eng **Sandwich Island** 17°40S 168°23E; pop (1979) 18 000; area 985 sq km/380 sq ml. Volcanic island, Vanuatu, SW Pacific; length, 42 km/26 ml; width, 23 km/14 ml; capital, Vila. » Vanuatu

EFTA » **European Free Trade Association**

egalitarianism A political philosophy which places a high value on equality among members of society, and advocates the removal of barriers to it. It is based on the view that all people are fundamentally equal, and that certain social and political institutions produce inequalities, such as in wealth and income, education, legal rights, and political power. Egalitarianism was one of the tenets of the French Revolution, and is associated with radical and socialist politics. » radicalism; socialism

Egbert (?–839) King of Wessex (from 802). After his victory in 825 over the Mercians at Ellendun (now Wroughton) in Wiltshire, Essex, Kent, Surrey, and Sussex submitted to him; but his conquest of Mercia itself (829) was soon reversed. He extended his control over Cornwall, defeating an alliance between the Vikings and Britons at Hingston Down (838). These successes gave him mastery over S England from Kent to Land's End, and established Wessex as the strongest Anglo-Saxon kingdom. » Anglo-Saxons; Vikings; Wessex

egg The mature female reproductive cell (*ovum*) in animals and plants; also the fertilized ovum in egg-laying animals, such as birds and insects, after it has been laid. This type of egg is covered by egg membranes, including the hard shell, which prevent it from drying out or being damaged. The eggs produced by domestic poultry (especially hens) are widely used as a food. The hen's egg contains all the nutrients needed for a single cell to develop into a day-old chick; it is thus a highly nutritious food – except for vitamin C, which the chick does not need, and minerals such as calcium, which are present in the shell. The yolk is rich in cholesterol, which has led some people for health reasons to restrict their egg intake. In 1987, an increase in food poisoning cases due to salmonella bacteria led to government investigations in both the UK and USA, and advice that eggs should be thoroughly cooked before being eaten. In the UK, the consequences of a statement on the matter by the junior Health Minister, Edwina Curry, in 1988 led to public controversy over the extent of the problem, and her eventual resignation. » cholesterol; hen; reproduction; salmonella

egg-plant » **aubergine**

eggs and bacon » **birdsfoot-trefoil**

eglantine A species of rose with aromatic, sweet-smelling foliage; also called **sweet briar**. (*Rosa eglanteria*. Family: *Rosaceae*.) » rose

Egmont, Mount, Maori **Taranaki** 39°18S 174°05E. Symmetrical volcanic peak, W North Island, New Zealand, S of New Plymouth; height, 2 518 m/8 261 ft; in a national park, area 335 sq km/129 sq ml, established in 1900. » New Zealand [i]

ego In psychiatry, that aspect of the personality which deals with the practical aspects of the external world. This was one component of Freud's description of the psychic structure which comprises the *id*, the *ego*, and the *superego*. The id represents the most primitive aspect of the personality: basic biological drives (eg hunger, sex, anger, and elimination) and instincts striving for pleasure. The superego represents the conscience and values an individual acquires from parents and society. The ego represents a middle ground in which a compromise between forces maximizing pleasure and those minimizing displeasure are reconciled. » Freud, Sigmund

egocentrism In Piagetian psychology, the apparent inability to understand another's viewpoint. Piaget argued that young children are egocentric, acting as if others see the world from the same perspective and share their interests and feelings. However, recent research shows that young children are not wholly egocentric.

egoism 1 A psychological thesis which maintains that people always *do* promote their own self-interest; espoused by Machiavelli and Hobbes. 2 A normative ethical theory which claims that people always *should* promote their own self-interest. Ethical egoists who argue for their position by appeal solely to the psychological thesis are accused of committing the naturalistic fallacy. » altruism; Hobbes; Machiavelli; naturalistic fallacy

egret The name used for a number of heron species. It is not applied consistently, and some species are called *egret* by some observers, and *heron* by others. » heron

Egypt, official name **Arab Republic of Egypt**, Arabic **Jumhuriyat Misr Al-Arabiya** pop (1990e) 53 170 000; area 1 001 449 sq km/ 386 559 sq ml. NE African republic, divided into 25 governorates; bounded W by Libya, S by Sudan, E by the Red Sea, NE by Israel, and N by the Mediterranean Sea; capital, Cairo; chief towns include Alexandria, Port Said, Aswan; timezone GMT +2; population mainly of E Hamitic origin (90%); religion, mainly Sunni Muslim, minority largely Coptic Christian; official language, Arabic; unit of currency, the gold Egyptian pound.

Physical description. R Nile flows N from Sudan, dammed S of Aswan, creating L Nasser; huge delta N of Cairo, 250 km/150 ml across and 160 km/100 ml N–S; narrow Eastern Desert, sparsely inhabited, between Nile and Red Sea; broad Western Desert, covering over two-thirds of the country, and containing seven major depressions, largest and lowest the Qattara Depression (133 m/436 ft below sea-level); Sinai Peninsula (S), desert region with mountains rising to 2 637 m/8 651 ft at Gebel Katherîna, Egypt's highest point; 90% of population lives on Nile floodplain (c.3% of country's area).

Climate. Mainly desert, except for 80 km/50 ml-wide Mediterranean coastal fringe, where annual rainfall is 100–200 mm/4–8 in; very hot on coast when dust-laden *khamsin* wind blows N from Sahara (Mar–Jun); Alexandria, annual average rainfall 180 mm/7.1 in, average maximum daily temperatures 18–30°C; elsewhere, rainfall less than 50 mm/2 in.

History and government. Neolithic cultures on R Nile from c.6000 BC; Pharaoh dynasties from c.3100 BC; pyramids at El Giza constructed during the 4th dynasty; Egyptian power greatest during the New Empire period (1567–1085 BC); became Persian province, 6th-c BC; conquered by Alexander the Great, 4th-c BC; Ptolemaic Pharaohs ruled Egypt until 30 BC; conquered by Arabs, AD 672; occupied by France under Napoleon, 1798–1801; Suez Canal constructed, 1869; revolt in 1879 put down by British, 1882; British protectorate, 1914; declared independent, 1922; used as base for Allied forces during World War 2; King Farouk deposed by Nasser, 1952; Egypt declared a republic, 1953; attack on Israel followed by Israeli invasion in 1967, resulting in loss of Sinai Peninsula and control over part of Suez Canal (regained following negotiations by Sadat in 1970s); governed by a People's Assembly of 454 members (including 10 presidential appointments) which elects a president every six years; president appoints a prime minister and Council; there is also a 210-member Consultative Council.

Economy. Agriculture on floodplain of R Nile accounts for about a third of national income; building of Aswan High Dam extended irrigated cultivation; cotton, rice, fruit, vegetables; food processing, textiles, construction, light manufacturing, military equipment; oil, iron ore, aluminium, cement, gypsum, phosphates, manganese, tin, nitrates; a major tourist area. » Arab–Israeli Wars; Aswan High Dam; Cairo; Egyptian architecture/art/religion; Egyptian history, Ancient [i]; Farouk I; Nasser; pharaoh; pyramid; Sadat; Suez Canal; RR25 national holidays; RR48 political leaders

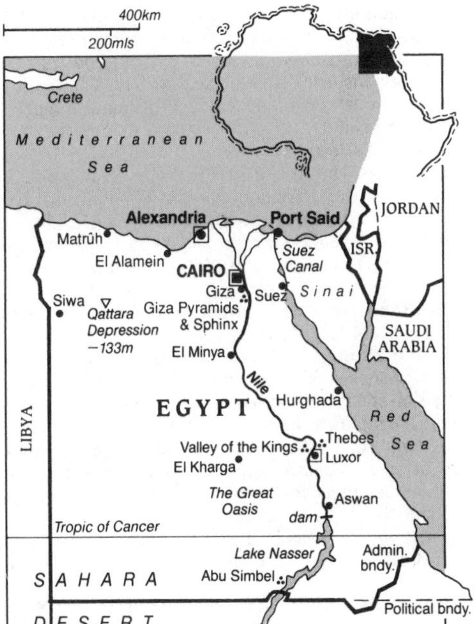

□ international airport

Egyptian An extinct Semitic language, which survives in inscriptions and papyrus manuscripts. In the 2nd-c AD, it evolved into **Coptic**, which is still used as a language of devotion by the Monophysite Christians in Egypt. » Afro-Asiatic languages; Coptic Church; hieroglyphics [i]

Egyptian architecture The style of architecture of ancient Egypt, characterized by the use of stone on a massive scale and most commonly associated with funereal pyramids, the earliest large example of which is the stepped 68 m/200 ft-high monument at Saqqara (2650–2600 BC). Regular pyramids came later, including those at Giza (2600–2400 BC). Egyptian temples, such as that of Amon at Karnak (c.1570–1085 BC), are equally monumental, using natural rock formations, battered walls, pillared halls, colonnades, and ramps. Other unique Egyptian features are the obelisk, a monolithic tapering shaft of stone, and the pylon, a truncated pyramidical tower. Domestic architecture, by contrast, was intended to be more temporary, and was built of clay and even papyrus. » colonnade; Egypt [i]; obelisk; pyramid

Egyptian art The art which flourished under the Pharaohs from c.3000 BC until the conquest of Egypt by Alexander the Great (332 BC). Largely funerary in character, it reflected a rigidly conservative society and religion, and style remained static. Tombs were decorated with wall paintings and reliefs, and contained portrait statues of the dead, together with household utensils, including fine work in metal, ivory, terracotta, etc for use in the next world. Human figures were invariably painted with profile head, single large front-view eye, frontal shoulders, and side-view legs. Statues such as the sphinxes similarly combined profile and front view in a way reflecting the shape of the original block. Mummy-cases were often richly decorated. » art; Coptic art; Egypt [i]

Egyptian cobra » asp

Egyptian history, Ancient The history of ancient Egypt stretches roughly from 3100 BC, when a unified kingdom embracing lower and upper Egypt was first created, to 332 BC, when Alexander the Great brought the rule of the pharaohs to an end. In the intervening millennia, Egypt experienced alternate phases of strong, centralized government and periods of near anarchy, when competing dynasties and warlords fought for power. The periods marked by strong government at home and expansionist policies abroad are called the Old, Middle and New Kingdoms. The chaotic phases go by the name of Intermediate Periods (I–III). In the so-called Late Period, the centuries immediately before Alexander's conquest, Egypt lacked central authority, and the country was easy prey for the great expansionist powers of the Middle East – Assyria conquered her in 671 and Persia in 525 BC. » Cush; Egypt [i];

DYNASTIES OF RULERS: ANCIENT EGYPT

DYNASTY	PERIOD	DATE BC
I	Early Dynastic Period	c.3100–2890
II		c.2890–2686
III	Old Kingdom	c.2686–2613
IV		c.2613–2494
V		c.2494–2345
VI		c.2345–2181
VII	First Intermediate Period	c.2181–2173
VIII		c.2173–2160
IX		c.2160–2130
X		c.2130–2040
XI		c.2133–1991
XII	Middle Kingdom	1991–1786
XIII		1786–1633
XIV	Second Intermediate Period	1786–c.1603
XV		1674–1567
XVI		c.1684–1567
XVII		c.1660–1567
XVIII	New Kingdom	1567–1320
XIX		1320–1200
XX		1200–1085
XXI	Third Intermediate Period	1085–945
XXII		945–730
XXIII		817?–730
XXIV		720–715
XXV		751–668
XXVI	Late Period	664–525
XXVII		525–404
XXVIII		404–399
XXIX		399–380
XXX		380–343
XXXI		343–332

Hyksos; Memphis; Punt, land of; pharaoh; Ptolemy I Soter; Saqqarah; Thebes **1**

Egyptian mongoose » **ichneumon** (mammal)

Egyptian religion The religion of ancient Egypt, covering the period from c.3100–30 BC. It emerged from the worship of tribal deities represented as totemic animals. These developed into animal-headed local and state gods, many of which represented forces in the natural world which needed to be entreated through worship and sacrifice. For example, the hawk was sacred to the Sun-god Re and the sky-god Horus; the Ibis to the Moon-god Toth; and the ram to Khnum. In the 14th-c, Akhenaton made an unsuccessful attempt to establish Aten, the Sun's disk, as the sole national deity. Immortality was secured through the rite of mummification. » Egyptian history, Ancient [i]; religion

Ehrenburg, Ilya (Grigoryevich) (1891–1967) Russian writer, born and died in Moscow. He worked for many years in Paris as a journalist, returning at intervals to the USSR. He wrote poetry, short stories, travel books, essays, and several novels, notably *Padeniye Parizha* (1941, The Fall of Paris) and *Burya* (1948, The Storm), both of which won Stalin Prizes. » Russian literature

Ehrlich, Paul [**ayr**leekh] (1854–1915) German bacteriologist, born at Strehlen, Silesia. After studying at Leipzig, he carried out research at Berlin, becoming a pioneer in haematology, immunology, and chemotherapy. He discovered a cure for syphilis (Salvarsan), and propounded the side-chain theory in immunology. He shared the Nobel Prize for Physiology or Medicine in 1908, and died at Bad Homburg, Germany. » haematology; immunology

Eichmann, (Karl) Adolf [**iykh**mahn] (1906–62) Austrian Nazi war criminal, born at Solingen, Germany. He became a member of the SS in 1932, and organizer of anti-Semitic activities. Captured by US forces in 1945, he escaped from prison some months later, having kept his identity hidden, and in 1950 reached Argentina. He was traced by Israeli agents, taken to Israel in 1960, condemned, and executed. » Nazi Party

Eid-ul-Adha; **Eid-ul-Fitr** » **Id-ul-Adha**; **Id-ul-Fitr**

eider [**iy**duh] Any of four species of sea duck native to the northern N hemisphere; also known as **eider duck**. The female lines her nest with the soft downy feathers from her breast; these are collected commercially as *eiderdown*. (Subfamily: *Anatinae*, tribe: *Somateriini*.) » diving duck; duck

eidophor A large-screen projection television system in which a scanning electron beam modulated by the video signal distorts the surface of an oil layer in a vacuum tube to refract the beam of light from a xenon lamp. Colour requires a triple-tube unit with the light divided by dichroic filters and recombined in projection. » projection television

Eiffel, (Alexandre) Gustave [**efel**] (1832–1923) French engineer, born at Dijon. He designed several notable bridges and viaducts, before working on his most famous project, the Eiffel Tower. He also designed the framework of the Statue of Liberty, New York, and built the first aerodynamic laboratory, near Paris. In 1893 he was imprisoned for two years and fined for breach of trust in connection with the Panama Canal. He died in Paris. » Eiffel Tower

Eiffel Tower [**iy**fuhl] A famous city landmark in Paris, designed by Gustave Eiffel and erected (1887–9) in the Champs-de-Mars for the Paris Exhibition of 1889. The tower consists of an open-lattice framework supporting three tiered platforms. At 300 m/984 ft high, it was the tallest building in the world until 1930. » Eiffel, Gustave; Paris

Eiger [**iy**ger] 46°34N 8°01E. Mountain peak with three ridges in the Bernese Alps, SC Switzerland; its N face is one of the most formidable climbs in the Alps; height, 3 970 m/13 025 ft; first ascent by Barrington in 1858; N face first climbed in 1938. » Alps

Eigg [eg] Island in Highland region, W Scotland; S of Skye, 11 km/7 ml from mainland (E); area 67 sq km/26 sq ml; reserve managed by Scottish Wildlife Trust; rises to 397 m/1 302 ft at Sgurr of Eigg; historically associated with the Clan Macdonald; ferry connections to Mallaig; cattle, crofting, fishing. » Highland; Scotland [i]

Eight, the » **Ashcan School**

Eightfold Path The fourth of Buddha's Four Noble Truths, prescribing the way to enlightenment. The Path involves right understanding, right aspiration, right speech, right conduct, right means of livelihood, right endeavour, right mindfulness, and right contemplation. » Buddha; Buddhism; Four Noble Truths

Eighth Route Army The Chinese 'Red Army', formed by the communists in 1927. It was given this name in 1937 when it entered into an uneasy alliance with the Nationalist Army of Chiang Kai-shek against the Japanese invaders of China. » Chiang Kai-shek; communism

Eijkman, Christiaan [**iykh**man] (1858–1930) Dutch physician, born at Nijkerk, Netherlands. He was the first to produce a dietary deficiency disease experimentally, and to propose the concept of essential food factors, later called vitamins. He shared the Nobel Prize for Physiology or Medicine in 1929. After working in Java, he became (1898–1928) professor of public health and forensic medicine at Utrecht, where he died. » vitamins [i]

Eilat or **Elat** [ay**lat**] 29°33N 34°57E, pop (1982e) 19 500. Seaport in Southern district, S Israel, on N shore of the Gulf of Aqaba; founded in 1949; airfield; terminus of oil pipeline from Ashkelon; nature reserve with underwater observatory. » Israel [i]

Eindhoven [**iyn**thohvn] 51°26N 5°30E, pop(1984e) 374 109. Modern industrial city in SE North Brabant province, S Netherlands; on the R Dommel, 88 km/55 ml SE of Rotterdam; airport; railway; technical university (1956); electronics, engineering, trucks, tractors, engines, military vehicles, glassware, synthetic fibres, paper, textiles, tobacco; Philips Evoluon museum of modern technology, Centre of Micro-Electronics. » **Netherlands, The** [i]

Einstein, Albert (1879–1955) German mathematical physicist, born at Ulm, Bavaria. He was educated at Munich, Aarau, and the Zürich Polytechnic. Taking Swiss nationality in 1901, he was appointed examiner at the Swiss Patent Office (1902–5), where he began to publish original papers on theoretical physics. He became world famous by his special (1905) and general (1916) theories of relativity. He was professor at Zürich (1909), Prague (1911), and again at Zürich (1912), then director of the Kaiser Wilhelm Physical Institute in Berlin (1914–33). He was awarded the Nobel Physics Prize for 1921. After Hitler's rise to power, he left Germany, lectured at Oxford and Cambridge, and worked from 1934 at Princeton, USA. In 1940 he became a US citizen and professor at Princeton, and spent the remainder of his life attempting by means of his unified field theory (1950) to establish a merger between quantum theory and his general theory of relativity. After the war, he urged international control of atomic weapons. He died at Princeton, New Jersey. » **general relativity; mass-energy relation; Planck; special relativity** [i]

Einstein shift » **gravitational red shift**

Einthoven, Willem [**ayn**thohfen] (1860–1927) Dutch physiologist, born at Semarang, Java. Educated at Utrecht, he became professor of physiology at Leyden in 1886. He invented the string galvanometer for measuring the electrical rhythms of the heart, and introduced the term 'electrocardiogram'. He was awarded the Nobel Prize for Physiology or Medicine in 1924, and died at Leyden. » **electrocardiography**

Eisenhower, Dwight D(avid), byname **Ike** (1890–1969) US general and 34th US President (1953–61), born at Denison, Texas, of German immigrant stock. He graduated from the West Point Military Academy in 1915, and by 1939 had become chief military assistant to General MacArthur in the Philippines. In 1942 he commanded Allied forces for the amphibious descent on French N Africa. His greatest contribution to the war effort was his talent for smooth co-ordination of the Allied staff, and this led to his selection as Supreme Commander for the 1944 cross-channel invasion of the continental mainland. In 1950 he was made Supreme Commander of the Combined Land Forces in NATO, and in 1952 the popularity which he had gained in Europe swept him to victory in the presidential elections, standing as a Republican, and he was re-elected in 1956. During his presidency the US government was preoccupied with foreign policy and pursued a campaign against communism. He died in Washington, DC. » **MacArthur; Republican Party; World War 2**

Eisenstein, Sergei (Mikhailovich) [**iy**zenstiyn] (1898–1948) Russian film director, born in Riga. He launched into films from theatrical scene painting, and became a major influence on the development of the cinema. His films are notable for the substitution of the group or crowd for the traditional hero, and for his skilful cutting and recutting to achieve mounting impressionistic effects, as in the Odessa steps sequence of *Potemkin* (1925). Later films included *Alexander Nevski* (1938) and *Ivan the Terrible* (1944). He died in Moscow.

eisteddfod [iy**stetħ**vod] A Welsh gathering of 12th-c origin for competitions in music and literature, the earlier *eisteddfodau* [iystetħ**vod**iy] being concerned with the testing of bards in their art. At the annual National Eisteddfod, held in August (entirely in Welsh) alternately in N and S Wales, the central event is the award of a Chair for a poem in strict bardic verse-form. » **bard; Gorsedd; Mod; Oireachtas; poetry**

ekistics (Gr *ekos* 'habitat') The science which analyses the nature, origin, and evolution of human settlements. It can be divided into ekistic geography, ekistic economics, and social ekistics.

El Alamein or **Al-Alamain, Battle of** (23 Oct–4 Nov 1942) World War 2 battle, named after a village on Egypt's Mediterranean coast, which ended in the victory of the British Eighth Army commanded by Montgomery over Rommel's Afrika Corps. It proved to be a turning point in the war in Africa. » **North African Campaign**

El Cid » **Cid, El**

El Dorado [el do**rah**doh] Literally, 'the gilded one'; a powerful early colonial Spanish-American legend of a ruler coated in gold, believed to exist in New Granada (now Colombia); by extension, a land of fabulous wealth. Raleigh organized two expeditions (1595 and 1617) in search of El Dorado. » **Incas; New Granada; Raleigh, Walter**

El Greco » **Greco, El**

El Niño An anomalous weather condition which results in major changes in ocean circulation and biological productivity along the coast of Peru. Under normal conditions, upwelling along the coast brings up nutrient-enriched deeper waters which result in high biological productivity. During El Niño, wind patterns along the Peruvian coast change, the upwelling is interrupted, and warm water invades the coast. This is thought to be the result of the reduction in trade-wind intensity following periods of extremely strong winds which would cause warm tropical waters to pile up along the coast of S America and then spread S. Failure of the upwelling produces massive mortality of marine organisms and the collapse of the important Peruvian anchovy fishery. The phenomenon usually occurs around Christmas, hence the name, which is Spanish for 'the child'. » **current (oceanography); Peru** [i]

El Paso [el **pa**soh] 31°45N 106°29W, pop(1980) 425 259. Seat of El Paso County, W Texas, USA; port on the Rio Grande opposite Ciudad Juarez, Mexico; founded, 1827; airfield; railway; university (1913); cattle, cotton, vegetables; refined petroleum, copper, foods, clothing, machinery; tourism; part transferred to Mexico in 1963, after the settlement of the Chamizal border dispute. » **Texas**

El Salvador, official name **Republic of El Salvador**, Span **República de El Salvador** pop(1990e) 5 220 000; area 21 476 sq km/8 290 sq ml. Smallest of the C American republics; divided into 14 departments; bounded N and E by Honduras, W by Guatemala, and S by the Pacific Ocean; capital, San Salvador; chief towns include Santa Ana, San Miguel, Mejicanos, Delgado; population mainly Spanish–Indian (89%); official language, Spanish; chief religion, Roman Catholicism; unit of currency, the colón of 100 centavos; two volcanic ranges run E–W; narrow coastal belt (S) rises through upland valleys and plateaux (average height, 600 m/2 000 ft) to mountains (N), highest point, Santa Ana (2 381 m/7 812 ft); R Lempa, dammed for hydroelectricity, flows S to the Pacific; many volcanic lakes; earthquakes common; climate varies greatly with altitude; hot tropical on coastal lowlands; single rainy season (May–Oct); temperate uplands; average annual temperature at San Salva-

dor, 23°C; average annual rainfall, 1 775 mm/70 in; originally part of the Aztec kingdom; conquest by Spanish, 1526; independence from Spain, 1821; member of the Central American Federation until its dissolution in 1839; independent republic, 1841; war with Honduras, 1965, 1969; considerable political unrest in 1970s and 1980s; assassination of Archbishop of San Salvador, Oscar Romero, 1980; peace plan agreed, 1991; governed by a president elected for five years, and a 60-member elected National Assembly; economy largely based on agriculture; main crops coffee and cotton; sugar, maize, balsam (world's main source), food processing, textiles, shoes, furniture, chemicals, fertilizers, pharmaceuticals, cement, rubber goods, oil products. » Aztecs; Central American Federation; San Salvador; RR25 national holidays; RR48 political leaders

El Tajín [el **ta**heen] An ancient Meso-American city near Papantla, N Veracruz, Mexico, flourishing in c.600–900 but abandoned after 1100. About 9.5 sq km/3¾ sq ml in area, it has a 60 ha/150 acre ceremonial centre with 12 ballcourts – more than any other site. The 18 m/60 ft high Pyramid of the Niches (c.600) has 365 external niches, each reputed to have contained an idol for one day of the year. » Meso-America; Meso-American ballgame

Elam [**ee**lam] The name given in antiquity to what is now SW Iran. Its main city was Susa, and at its zenith in the 13th-c BC it ruled an empire stretching from Babylonia in the W to Persepolis in the E. » Babylonia; Persepolis; Susa

eland [**ee**land] An African spiral-horned antelope; cattle-like, with narrow face and straight horns; the largest antelope (shoulder height, up to 1.8 m/6 ft); easily tamed; two species: the **common** (or **Cape**) **eland** (*Taurotragus oryx*) and the **giant** (or **derby**) **eland** (*Taurotragus derbianus*). » antelope; cattle

Elara [**ee**lara] The seventh natural satellite of Jupiter, discovered in 1905; distance from the planet 11 740 000 km/7 295 000 ml; diameter 80 km/50 ml. » Jupiter (astronomy); RR4

elastic hysteresis [histuh**ree**sis] A property of some materials (eg rubber), where the strain due to a given stress is larger when the stress is decreasing than when it is increasing. A graph of stress versus strain, while stress is gradually applied then removed, produces a loop with the area proportional to the energy dissipated in the material. A large loop area means the substance makes a good shock absorber. » strain; stress (physics)

elastic modulus » **Young's modulus**

elastic rebound theory » **isostasy**

elasticity (economics) The extent to which the quantity supplied or demanded of a product is affected by a change in the price. The volume demanded or supplied is *inelastic* if it remains unchanged when the price rises or falls (eg cigarettes). It is *elastic* when a change in price alters the demand or supply (eg caviare). *Cross-elasticity* is the sensitivity of price changes in one product to changes in the supply or demand in another; for example, if the price of fuel rises, the demand for cars might fall. *Income elasticity* is the extent to which a change in demand is affected by individuals' income. » demand

elasticity (physics) In solids, the property that a stressed material will return to its original size and shape when the stress is removed. It usually corresponds to a direct proportionality between stress and strain. In a metal bar, for example, up to a strain of about 1%, doubling the tension along the bar's length causes double the extension. » plastic deformation; strain; stress (physics); Young's modulus

elastomers [ee**las**tohmerz] Materials, usually synthetic, having elastic properties (ie capable of recovery from severe deformation). Examples include natural rubber and polyisoprene. » isoprene [i]; rubber

Elat » **Eilat**

Elba, Gr **Aithalia**, Lat **Ilva** area 223 sq km/86 sq ml. Island in the Tyrrhenian Sea, between the N Italian coast and Corsica, separated from the mainland by the 10 km/6 ml-wide Strait of Piombino; length 27 km/17 ml; width 18.5 km/11½ ml; chief town, Portoferraio; iron working, fisheries, fruit, wine, tourism; Napoleon lived here after his abdication (1814–15). » Italy [i]; Napoleon I

Elbe, River [**el**buh], Czech **Labe**, ancient **Albis** River in Czechoslovakia and Germany; rises on S slopes of the Riesengebirge, Czechoslovakia; flows N and NW to enter the North Sea at Cuxhaven, Germany; length 1 158 km/720 ml; connected by canals with R Oder and Baltic Sea; navigable to beyond Czech border.

Elbert, Mount 39°05N 106°27W. Mountain in Lake County, C Colorado, USA; the highest peak in the Rocky Mts (4 399 m/14 432 ft). » Colorado; Rocky Mountains

elbow The region of the upper limb between the arm and forearm; specifically, the joint between the humerus and the radius/ulna. It enables shortening of the upper limb, so allowing the hand to reach the mouth (as in eating and drinking). Banging the medial side of the elbow (the 'funny bone') against a solid object may give rise to a dull aching and tingling sensation over the hand; when this happens, the ulnar nerve has been compressed between the object and the humerus. » radius; tennis elbow; ulna

Elbrus, Mount [**el**bruhs] 43°21N 42°29E. Highest peak of the Caucasus range, S European Russia; height 5 642 m/18 510 ft; highest peak in Europe; formed by two extinct volcanic cones; its glaciers give rise to the Kuban, Malka, and Baksan Rivers. » Caucasus Mountains

elder (botany) A deciduous shrub, growing to 10 m/30 ft, very widespread; bark furrowed, corky; leaves opposite, pinnate, leaflets toothed; flowers creamy, in large, flat-topped clusters 10–20 cm/4–8 in across; berries purplish-black. The flowers and berries are used in wines and preserves, but all other parts of the plant are poisonous. (*Sambucus nigra*. Family: *Caprifoliaceae*.) » deciduous plants; pinnate; shrub

elder (religion) One who by reason of age or distinction is entrusted with shared authority and leadership in a community. **1** In the ancient Biblical world, the elders of Israel exercised both religious and civil influence from the tribal period onwards; and city elders were active at a local level. Jewish synagogues were also governed by elders, but the title is reserved for scholars in the Mishnaic period. In the New Testament, elders were church officials (Gr *presbuteroi*, 'presbyters') with a collective authority for general oversight of a congregation, and are sometimes even called 'bishops' (Gr *episkopoi*; *Acts* 20.28, *Titus* 1.5–7) but not yet in the monarchical sense. » bishop; Judaism; synagogue **2** In Reformed Churches, an officer ordained to 'rule' along with the minister (a 'teaching' elder). Elders exercise discipline, and oversee the life of a congregation and its individual members. » Presbyterianism; Reformed Churches

Eleanor of Aquitaine (c.1122–1204) Queen consort of Louis VII of France (1137–52) and, after the annulment of this marriage, of the future Henry II of England (1154–89). She was imprisoned (1174–89) for supporting the rebellion of her sons, two of whom became kings as Richard I (in 1189) and John (in 1199). She died at Fontevrault, France. » Henry II (of England)

Eleanor of Castile (?–1290) Queen consort of Edward I of England (1254–90), the daughter of Ferdinand III. She accompanied him to the Crusades, and is said to have saved his life by sucking the poison from a wound. She died at Harby, Nottinghamshire, and the 'Eleanor Crosses' at Northampton, Geddington, and Waltham Cross are survivors of the 12 erected by Edward at the halting places of her cortège. The last stopping place was Charing Cross, where a replica now stands. » Crusades [i]; Edward I

Eleatics A trio of 5th-c BC philosophers – Parmenides, Melissus, and Zeno – from Elea, Italy, who argued that reality is unbegotten, imperishable, atemporal, indivisible, motionless, and utterly changeless; the world as it appears is a misrepresentation. The arguments profoundly influenced subsequent Greek philosophy. » Parmenides; Zeno of Elea

elective mutism An emotionally determined selectivity in speaking, which in severe cases results in no speech at all. It is often associated with anxiety or withdrawal.

electoral college A body made up of people who are responsible for electing a person to some office. These people can hold a particular office themselves (as in the case of the College of Cardinals who elect the Pope) or be elected from a wider electorate. The most famous electoral college is the one that elects the president of the USA. It is made up of electors from each state pledged to cast their vote for the particular candidate for whom the wider electorate in their state has voted (though they are not legally bound to do so when the time for electing arrives).

electors Members of the electoral college that chose Holy Roman Emperors. By the 13th-c, membership was limited to seven – the Duke of Saxony, King of Bohemia, Count Palatine of the Rhine, Margrave of Brandenburg, and Archbishops of Cologne, Mainz, and Trier. The Golden Bull (1356) of Emperor Charles IV permanently granted the right of election to the seven. » Holy Roman Empire

Electra [elektra] In Greek tragedies, but not in Homer, the daughter of Agamemnon and Clytemnestra, who assisted her brother Orestes when he came to Argos to avenge his father, and who later married his friend Pylades. Her personality is developed in different ways by the playwrights. » Agamemnon; Clytemnestra; Oedipus complex; Orestes

Electra complex » **Oedipus complex**

electric-arc furnace An electric furnace used particularly in steel making, where a very high temperature is generated in the 'arc' or discharge between two electrodes, the current passing through material evaporated from the electrodes. In the original process devised in 1870 by Siemens, the arc was struck beneath the crucible, heating the metal indirectly. Later, in the type invented by French metallurgist Paul Heroult (1863–1914) the arc was struck between electrodes and the metal itself. In the type devised in 1898 by Italian metallurgist Enrico Stassano, the arc is struck between electrodes above the metal, heating being by radiation. » Siemens, Ernst; steel

electric car A motor car designed to be propelled by an electric motor. Although electric traction has been used extensively in delivery vehicles such as milk floats (UK) and in golf carts (USA), it has not been possible for the electric car to compete with the traditionally driven internal-combustion-engined car because of the size and weight of batteries needed. Although much research has gone into the improvement of batteries and alternative battery technology, the electric car is still not competitive with the internal combustion engine for power, weight, and size. » car [i]; internal combustion engine

electric charge » **charge**

electric conductance » **resistance**

electric dipole moment Symbol p, units C.m (coulomb.-metre), a vector quantity; for charges +q and −q separated by distance l (a *dipole*), the electric dipole moment is p=ql. A dipole placed in an electric field experiences a twisting force, proportional to p, which attempts to line up the dipole with field direction. Some molecules may have electric dipole moments if the centre of negative charge is displaced from that of positive charge. This displacement may be brought about by the applied field to give an induced dipole moment, or may be present permanently due to the structure of the molecule, in which case the molecule is described as *polar*. Water molecules are polar; for water, $p=10^{-29}$ C.m approximately. » dielectric; moment [i]; permeability; van der Waals' interaction; vector

electric eel Large freshwater fish found in shallow streams of the Orinoco and Amazon basins of S America; body cylindrical at front, becoming compressed posteriorly, length up to 2.4 m/8 ft; long anal fin; dorsal, tail, and pelvic fins absent; produces powerful electric shocks to stun prey, as defence, and for navigation in turbid waters. (*Electrophorus electricus*. Family: *Electrophoridae*.)

electric field The region of electric influence surrounding positive or negative electric charges; symbol *E*, units V/m (volt per metre); a vector quantity, with field direction specified as the direction of motion of a positive charge placed in the field. For a force *F* on a test charge of *q* coulombs, the field is given as $E=F/q$, ie the electric field is the electric force per unit charge. It may be represented using field lines. » Coulomb's law; electricity; Gauss's law; potential; vector (mathematics)

electric ray Any of sluggish bottom-living marine rays, widespread in tropical to temperate seas; body disc rounded, skin smooth, tail robust; well-developed electric organs produce strong shocks to stun prey; also called **torpedo rays**; includes large N Atlantic species, *Torpedo nobiliana*; length up to 1.8 m/6 ft. (Family: *Torpedinidae*.) » ray

electric resistance » **resistance**

electrical and magnetic properties of solids Electrical and magnetic effects exhibited by matter, because the atoms of which it is composed contain charged components, and the binding forces between atoms are electrical. Magnetic effects arise because of the motion of electrical charges. Light is affected as it passes through matter because of its electromagnetic nature. » diamagnetism; dielectric; electrical conduction; Faraday effect; ferroelectrics; ferromagnetism; liquid crystals; magnetostriction; magnon [i]; paramagnetism; piezo-electric effect; pyroelectrics; solid-state physics; thermoelectric effects; Zeeman effect

electrical conduction The transport of electrical charge through some substance. Only metals conduct electricity well; conduction is by means of the free electrons in the electron gas characteristic of metal structure. Ionic and covalently bound solids are insulators; but ionic solids such as salt (sodium chloride) conduct when dissolved in water, as the electrically charged ions become free to move. In *semiconductors*, the low electrical conductivity is due to a small number of electrons acquiring sufficient energy to become released into the body of the material in a way similar to conduction electrons in metals. The spaces vacated by the electrons (*holes*) behave as positively charged particles, and also contribute to conduction. Conduction in semi-conductors may be altered by 'doping' – the introduction of impurities to provide more holes and electrons. » electrolysis [i]; electron; electronic structure of solids; Hall effect; photoconductivity; resistivity; semiconductor; superconductivity

electrical engineering A branch of engineering which studies the practical applications of electricity and electronics. Until the 1940s electrical engineering was a small part of the general field of engineering, confined to communications, lighting, and the generation and transmission of electrical power. As progress was made in the area of electrical and electronic communications, it developed into a separate field, now dealing with the production, distribution, control, and use of electricity in all its forms. Production aspects include the design of generators run by water power (hydroelectricity), coal, oil, and nuclear fuels. Distribution and control concern the delivery of electricity to the consumer: transmission systems need to be designed which are safe and efficient. Any devices which use electricity fall within the field, such as radio, radar, lighting, motors, power generators, and transmission systems. **Electronic engineering** developed as a subdivision of electrical engineering, and is now primarily concerned with automation, missile control systems, satellites, spacecraft, and communication systems. » electricity; electronics; engineering; technology

electrical power The rate of transfer of energy in electrical circuits; symbol *P*, units W (watt) An example is the rate of heat lost from a circuit due to resistive heating ($P=I^2R$ for current *I* and resistance *R*). An electric light of power 60 W running for 1 hour consumes as much energy as a 30 W light running for 2 hours. » electricity; energy; power

electricity Phenomena associated with electrical charges and currents, and the study of such phenomena. Between collections of positive and negative charges there exists a potential difference. If a conducting path exists between the two charge groups, charges will flow from one to the other, constituting an electric current. Electric charge which builds up on an insulator and is thus unable to flow is termed **static electricity**. » anode; cathode; charge; Coulomb's law; current (physics); electric dipole moment; electric field; electrical and magnetic properties of solids; electrodynamics; electromagnetism; electromotive force; electrostatics; Gauss's law; permittivity; potential difference; resistance; screening

electrocardiography The investigation of the electrical activity of the heart. The electric voltages produced by heartbeats can be recorded from the surface of the skin in the form of an electrocardiogram (**ECG**). Electrodes are attached to the skin of the limbs and chest, and the voltages between various pairs of electrodes are recorded on sensitive portable electronic machines. The interpretation of the printout requires skill, but electrocardiography is one of the commonest medical investigations, providing diagnostic information in diseases of the ductless glands and lungs as well as in all aspects of heart disease. » electricity; heart [i]

electrochemistry The study of chemical change in a solution, resulting from the uptake of electrons from an external circuit or their supply to a circuit. Storage batteries (*accumulators*) illustrate this process, as they charge and discharge respectively. In all cases, changes in the oxidation states of elements occur, and energy is converted between chemical and electrical forms. » chemistry; electrolysis [i]

electroconvulsive therapy (ECT) A highly successful treatment for patients with severe psychiatric disorders in which an electric current is passed through the brain of an anaesthetized patient. The technique is often used in depression and schizophrenia. » depression (psychiatry); schizophrenia; shock therapy

electrocution Death from contact with high-voltage electric current. Electric shock induces spasm of the skeletal muscles and rapid irregular contractions (*fibrillation*) of the ventricle of the heart. Lesser voltages and electricity arising outside the body but near to it induce burns due to high temperatures. » burn; heart [i]

electrodynamics The study of the motion of electric charges caused by electric and magnetic fields. » dynamics; electromagnetism; electrostatics; quantum electrodynamics

electroencephalography [ilectrohensefa**lo**grafee] The investigation of the electrical activity of the brain, using electrodes applied to the scalp, and usually recorded as a tracing on paper (an electroencephalogram, or **EEG**). The EEG changes with the mental activity of the subject, and characteristic patterns of electrical activity (eg for sleep, coma, epileptic seizure) can be recognized. The *alpha rhythm* (c.10 Hz) appears with relaxation and eye closure. The *delta rhythm* (1–4 Hz) appears in deep sleep. » brain [i]; electricity; sleep

electrolaryngography A technique for recording the vibrations of the vocal cords electronically. Electrodes are attached to the neck on each side of the thyroid cartilage, and the vocal cord activity is displayed as traces on a screen. The rises and falls of the fundamental frequency of the vibrations (corresponding largely to the intonation of the voice) can be clearly seen. The technique was developed in the 1970s, and is now widely used in speech science, in relation to both normal and abnormal use of the voice. » intonation; larynx; vocal cords

electrolysis The splitting of a compound into simpler forms by the input of electrical energy. When water is electrolysed between inert electrodes, the following two half-reactions take place:

	cathode (reduction)	anode (oxidation)
	$2e^- + 2H_2O \rightarrow H_2 + 2OH^-$	$H_2O \rightarrow \frac{1}{2}O_2 + 2H^+ + 2e^-$

» electricity

electrolyte A system, usually a solution, in which electrochemical reactions occur. It must be sufficiently conducting to allow current to pass – an effect which is often achieved by using a high concentration of electrochemically inert ions. » electrochemistry; solution

electromagnet » **magnet**

electromagnetic induction The production of electromotive force (emf) – loosely, a voltage – in a conductor, either by moving the conductor in a magnetic field or by changing the field around the conductor. The emf induced in a circuit equals the rate of change of magnetic flux through it, multiplied by −1 (Faraday's law, 1831). Induction is crucial to the operation of transformers, generators, and motors. » eddy currents; electromagnetic pump; electromagnetism; electromotive force; Faraday; Fleming's rules [i]; inductance; Lenz's law; magnetic flux; Maxwell, James Clerk

electromagnetic pump A device for pumping conducting fluids. Current is applied to the fluid at right angles to the flow direction. A magnetic field is applied at right angles to both flow direction and electric current. Electromagnetic force acts on the fluid, in the same way that a current-carrying wire placed in a magnetic field experiences a force. The device is used to pump liquid metals. » electromagnetism; magnetohydrodynamics

THE ELECTROMAGNETIC SPECTRUM

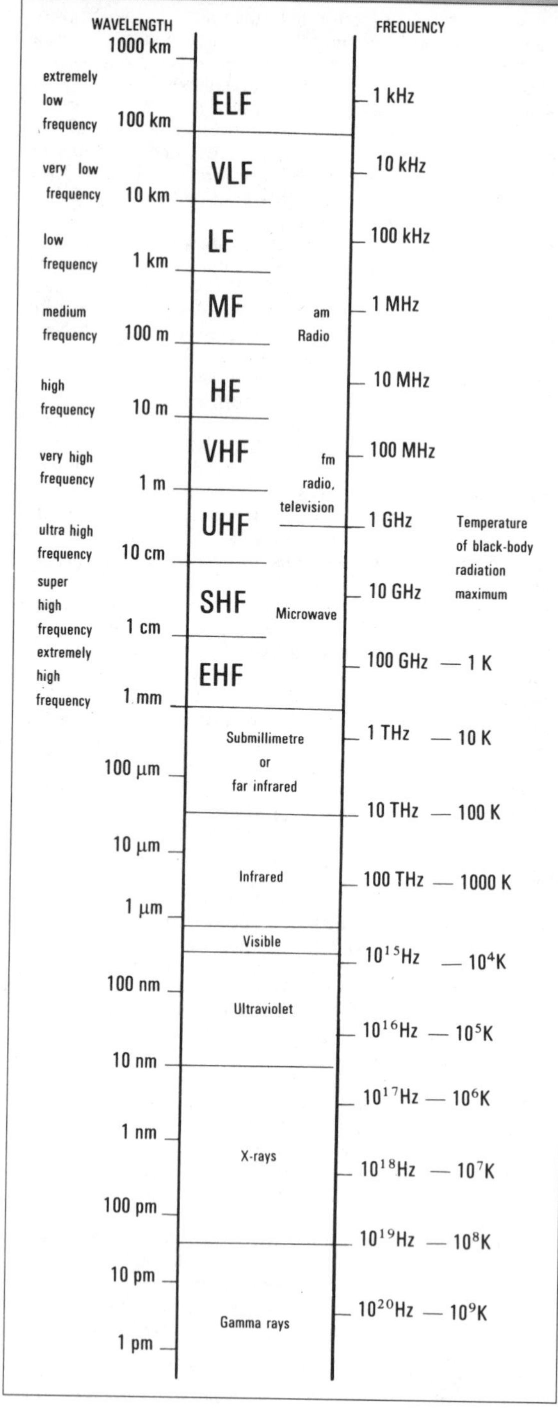

electromagnetic radiation Oscillating electric and magnetic fields which propagate together through empty space as a radiated wave; velocity c, the velocity of light. They include radio waves, light, and X-rays. No ether is required for the propagation of electromagnetic waves, which exhibit particle-like properties, more noticeable for higher frequencies, consistent with quantum theory. » blackbody radiation; electromagnetism; ether; gamma rays; infrared radiation; light; microwaves; radiometry; radio waves; ultraviolet radiation; wave (physics) [i]; X-rays

electromagnetism Phenomena involving both electric and magnetic fields, and the study of such phenomena. The first indication of a link between electricity and magnetism was shown by Danish physicist Hans Christian Oersted, who demonstrated that an electrical current caused the deflection of a compass needle (1819). This established that magnetic effects are produced by a moving electrical charge. Oersted's observation was interpreted by British scientist Michael Faraday in terms of lines of magnetic influence circulating around the wire. Ampère deduced an expression for the magnetic force between two current-carrying wires to give the original form of what is now called Ampère's law (1827). Faraday demonstrated that switching off a current in a circuit produced a momentary current in a nearby circuit, and that moving a magnet close to a circuit also produced momentary currents (1831). This established that electrical charge can be made to flow by changing magnetic fields, the basis of electromagnetic induction (expressed as Faraday's law). Similar work was performed by US physicist Joseph Henry (1830). The first generator was built by Faraday in 1831.

The unification of electricity and magnetism into a single theory of electromagnetism is due to British physicist James Clerk Maxwell, who first expressed the laws of Faraday and Ampère in their modern form as two of the four Maxwell's equations. Using his equations of electromagnetism, Maxwell postulated that light is electromagnetic disturbance with velocity $c = \frac{1}{\sqrt{\varepsilon_0 u_0}}$, where ε_o and μ_o are the permittivity and permeability of empty space, respectively (1864). German physicist Heinrich Hertz used oscillating electrical circuits to produce radio waves which travelled at the velocity of light (1887), thereby providing experimental support for Maxwell's work. The expression of the velocity of light in terms of fundamental constants suggested to Einstein that it should always be the same for all observers. This conclusion is central to his theory of special relativity (1905), which in turn explains more fully the relationship between electric and magnetic effects. While an observer stationary with respect to an electric charge will see it as a source of electric field only, a second observer moving relative to the first will see the same charge as a source of both electric and magnetic fields in a way dictated by special relativity. » Ampère; Einstein; electricity; electromagnetic induction; electromagnetic radiation [i]; Faraday; Fleming's rules [i]; Henry, Joseph; Hertz; Lorentz; magnetic field [i]; magnetic moment; magnetism; Maxwell, James Clerk; Oersted; special relativity [i]

electromotive force The work done by some source in separating electrical charges to produce a potential difference capable of driving current round a circuit; often abbreviated **emf**. The term 'force' is a misnomer; generally, emf is a property of the source, whereas potential difference depends on both source and current flow. A source of emf transfers energy to the circuit by doing work in raising potential. For example, a battery is a source of emf in which chemical energy moves charges to the terminals, making one positive, the other negative. The emf is work done on the charges to bring about this separation: an emf of one volt means that the battery expends one joule of energy to bring about the separation of one coulomb of charge. » contact potential; electricity; electromagnetic induction; photovoltaic effect; potential difference

electromyography The study of the muscular contractions which take place during speech. Muscles produce tiny amounts of electrical activity when they contract. The activity is recorded by applying electrodes to the individual muscles of the vocal tract, and displaying the signals on a screen or on paper. » muscle [i]

electron A fundamental particle, denoted e^-, where the minus sign indicates that the charge is negative; charge of -1.602×10^{-19}C; mass 9.110×10^{-31}kg or 0.511 MeV, approximately $1/_{1836}$ that of the proton; spin ½ fermion; stable against decay; no known size, assumed point-like; no known substructure; a carrier of negative charge in matter, including electrical currents in conductors. Electrons together with the positively-charged nucleus form atoms. They were discovered by British physicist Joseph Thomson in 1897 through studying cathode rays (now called electron beams) in electric and magnetic fields. The charge was determined by US physicist Robert Millikan in 1913. Wave-like properties are exhibited in electron diffraction. The electron is associated with weak nuclear force, as in radioactive beta decay, where the beta particle is the electron. » atomic physics; charge; electron diffraction/gun/microscope [i]; fundamental particles; magnetic moment; Millikan; photoelectric effect; positron; spin; thermionics; Thomson, Joseph

electron capture A radioactive decay in which an atomic electron combines with a proton in the nucleus to form a neutron (which remains in the nucleus) and a neutrino. Nucleon number remains unchanged; proton number is reduced by one. For example, the decay of fluorine to oxygen, $_9F^{17} + e^-$ gives $_8O^{17} + \nu$. » electron; neutron; neutrino; proton; radioactivity

electron diffraction An interference effect involving electrons scattered from different layers of atoms in a solid, giving distinctive intensity patterns which can be used to determine its structure. It is especially useful for surface studies, since electrons (being charged) do not penetrate far into the material. The original observation of electron diffraction was made in 1927 by US physicists Clinton Davisson (1881–1958) and Lester Germer (1896–1971), and has been crucial in establishing the dual wave-particle nature of electrons. » diffraction [i]; electron; solid

electron gas » **electronic structure of solids**

electron gun A device for producing electron beams. A heated cathode produces electrons by thermionic emission. These are attracted away by a nearby positively-charged grid, which regulates the number of electrons and hence beam brightness. Electric fields then accelerate and focus the beam. It is an essential component of television tubes, electron microscopes, and cathode ray tubes. » cathode; electron; electron microscope [i]; thermionics

electron microscope A microscope using a beam of electrons instead of light, and magnetic or electrostatic fields as lenses. If considered as a wave system, the electron beam has a much higher frequency than visible light, and so provides a much higher resolution. There are two main types. In the *transmission* electron microscope, the direct passage of the beam through the specimen produces an image on a fluorescent screen. The specimen must be very thin, but the resolution is high: c.0.2–0.5 nm. In the *scanning* electron microscope, the specimen is scanned by the beam, which produces secondary electron emission. The consequent current produced can be amplified and the signal fed to a cathode ray screen to give the image. The specimen can be thicker, and an image of some depth

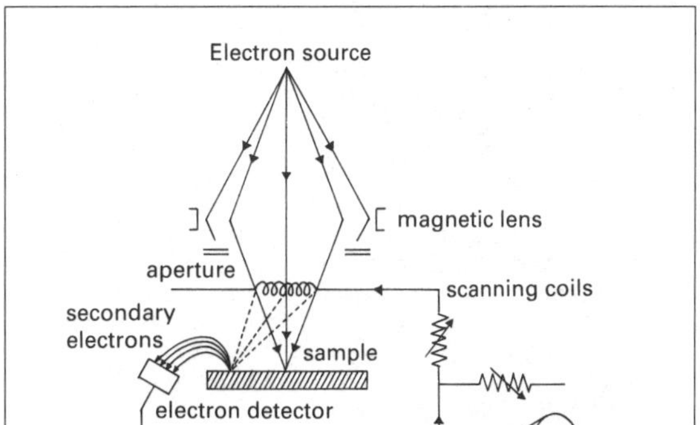

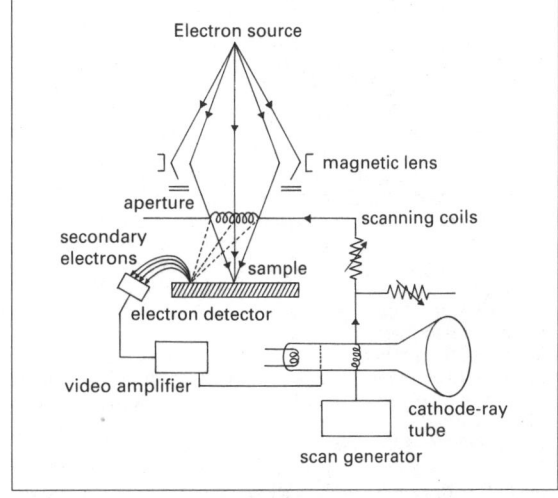

Scanning electron microscope

produced, but resolution is limited to c.10–20 nm. » electron; electron gun; microscope

electron spin resonance » **paramagnetic resonance**

electron volt A unit of energy common in atomic, nuclear, and particle physics; symbol eV; equals the change in energy of an electron moving through a potential difference of 1 volt; 1 eV = 1.602×10^{-19} J (joule, SI unit); commonly used as keV (10^3 eV), MeV (10^6 eV), and GeV (10^9 eV). » electron; joule; physics; units (scientific); RR70

electronegativity A qualitative measure of the tendency to hold electrons, or to form the negative end of a dipole in a bond to other atoms. It is roughly proportional to the sum of the ionization energy and the electron affinity for an atom. A rough scale of values is: F, 4; O, 3.5; Cl, 3.2; N,Br, 3; S,I, 2.7; C, 2.5; other non-metals 2–2.2; metals 1.0–1.8. » dipole; ionization energy

electronic cinematography The production of entertainment programmes for the cinema by video methods, from initial shooting up to final editing and conforming. Only the completed master videotape is transferred to film for release printing. » cinematography [i]

electronic games Games programmed and controlled by a small microprocessor. Most electronic games are connected to a visual display unit and are known as *video games*. Multi-coloured visual effects and varying sounds are incorporated. Many games are based on war themes or ideas related to 'Star Wars'. Most sports are simulated in various forms, and many popular board games (eg Monopoly, Scrabble, Trivial Pursuit) are available in electronic form. Games are operated either by using a computer keyboard or a joystick plugged into the home computer. Larger versions of games are produced for use in purpose-built amusement arcades and other places of public enjoyment. The first video game appeared in the USA in the early 1970s; it was called *Pong*, and was a simple form of table tennis. » visual display unit; Plate XVI

electronic mail The use of computer systems to transfer messages between users. Messages are usually stored centrally until acknowledged by the recipient. Electronic mail facilities are provided by most large computer systems for their users, and are also available on a national and international basis.

electronic music Music in which the sound is generated by electronic instruments (especially synthesizers), processed by means of tape recorders heard through loudspeakers. The electronic music studios at Cologne (West German Radio), Brussels (Studio de Musique Électronique), and Paris (Institut de Recherche et de Coordination Acoustique/Musique) have been among the most influential. » bruitisme; electrophone; musique concrète; synthesizer; Berio; Boulez; Stockhausen

electronic photography Exposure of a single picture in a special video camera (an *electronic stills camera*, or *ESC*), which records the image digitally on a rotating 50 mm floppy magnetic disk. This has the capacity for up to 25 individual shots, which are available for immediate display on a video screen or as a paper printout within 90 seconds. The definition of the image is much below that of a photograph, but the instant replay and the capacity for electronic manipulation, including transmission by telephone landline, are important in special applications. » photography; video

electronic publishing The issuing to identified users of selected, edited textual and illustrative material taken from an electronic database. The data may be communicated on-line to the customer's computer, or transferred to a portable medium such as magnetic tape or disk or CD-ROM disk. The term is used generally to cover all publishing except print on paper (though some electronic journals are issued also in conventional printed form). » database

electronic structure of solids Atoms in a solid bound in one of three ways. In *ionic solids*, such as salt (sodium chloride), an exchange of electrons gives an ionic bond between charged ions. In *covalent solids*, such as carbon and silicon, covalent bonds form between neighbouring atoms by electron sharing. In both these types, electrons are localized and the solid is an insulator. In *metals*, atoms each donate one or more electrons to a sea of nearly free electrons (the *free electron gas*) in which the array of positively-charged metal ions is immersed. Free electron gas results in good electrical and thermal conductivity. The type of bonding in solids is reflected in all physical and mechanical properties. » chemical bond; covalent bond; electrical conductance; electron; Hall effect; luminescence; metal; quantum mechanics; semiconductor; thermal conduction; van der Waals' interaction

electronics The scientific study and application of the movement of electrons. The field developed out of 19th-c experiments with electricity, which resulted in the invention of thermionic valves and their subsequent replacement by transistors, introduced at Bell Laboratories in 1948. Transistors facilitated the miniaturization of electronic components, as did the silicon chip and the integrated circuit. The social impact of electronics is far-reaching, including the development of television, computerized office systems, video games, personal computers, pacemakers, and spacecraft. » computer; electrical engineering; electron; electronic cinematography / games / mail / music / photography / publishing; integrated circuit; microelectronics; optoelectronics; silicon chip; thermionic valve; transistor

electro-optic effects Optical effects induced by electric fields applied to a substance through which light passes. Transparent materials (eg water, benzene) become birefringent when placed in an electric field (the *Kerr effect*, discovered in 1875 by British physicist John Kerr (1824–1907)). This is exploited in the Kerr cell, which is used as a high frequency shutter (up to 10^{10} Hz) in laser switching. The *Pockels effect* (discovered by Friedrich Pockels (1865–1913) in 1893) is a birefringence also caused by electric fields, but distinct from the Kerr effect, being present only in certain crystals with particular symmetry properties. It is exploited in the Pockels cell for high speed shutters and beam modulators. » birefringence; electric field; liquid crystals; modulation

electropalatography The study of the way the tongue makes contact with the palate during speech. An artificial palate containing electrodes is inserted in the subject's mouth. When the tongue makes contact with the electrodes, impulses are transmitted to a monitoring device. As the subject speaks, the changing pattern of contacts can be displayed as lights on a screen or as printed dots on computer paper. » palate

electrophone Any musical instrument in which the sound is generated by mechanical or electronic oscillators (eg a synthesizer) or in which acoustically-generated vibrations require electrical amplification before they can be heard (eg the electric guitar). Electrophones form a fifth main category of instruments, additional to the four included in the standard classification of Hornbostel and Sachs (1914). » electronic music; guitar; musical instruments; ondes Martenot; organ; synthesizer

electrophoresis [ilektrohfuhreesis] The migration of charged particles under the influence of an electrical field, usually in solution. Cations will move towards the negative pole, and anions towards the positive. It is possible to separate amino acids this way by adjusting the pH of the solution so that some are cations and others anions. » anion; cation; pH; solution

electroplating The depositing of a metal on another metal by electrolysis. The object to be plated is made the cathode; the metal to be deposited is derived from the anode. The plating may be intended for decoration, or to provide resistance to corrosion. » electrolysis; metal

electroscope A device for detecting the presence of an electric charge and estimating its amount. The simplest form consists of two thin gold leaves which repel each other when charged, the degree of divergence indicating the amount of the charge. It is used indirectly for the measurement of ionizing radiation, indicating the rate of leakage of the charge produced by the passage of radiation around the leaves. » electricity

electrosleep » **shock therapy**

electrostatic generator A device for producing a large electric charge, usually by the repetition of an induction process and the successive accumulation of the charge produced. An important 19th-c type was the Wimshurst machine (1878), devised by British engineer James Wimshurst (1832–1903). Modern very high voltage machines were initiated by the van de Graaff belt-operated generator (1929). »

electricity; electromagnetic induction; van de Graaff generator

electrostatic separation The separation of fine particles from each other or from a gaseous medium, by subjecting them to an electric field. The process is used for separating the components of a mixture (eg the valuable content of an ore from unwanted mineral substances), or for removing the solid content of an effluent gas (*electrostatic precipitation*). » electricity

electrostatics The study of fields and potentials due to stationary electric charges. Electrostatic forces bind electrons to the nucleus in atoms. » Coulomb's law; electricity; electrodynamics; Gauss's law; static electricity

elegy In classical times, any poem in elegaic metre (a couplet consisting of one hexameter and one pentameter), such as those written (in Greek) by Archilochus (7th-c BC), and (in Latin) by Propertius. In modern literatures, it is a poem of mourning or lament, such as Milton's *Lycidas* (1637) or Shelley's *Adonais* (1821), often incorporating serious general reflections on life, as in Grey's *Elegy in a Country Churchyard* (1751). » Greek/Latin literature; metre (literature); poetry

elementary particle physics » **particle physics**

elements (chemistry) » **chemical elements**

elephant A large mammal of family *Elephantidae*; the only living members of order *Proboscidea* (many extinct forms); almost naked grey skin; massive forehead; small eyes; upper incisor teeth form 'tusks'; snout elongated as a muscular grasping 'trunk'; ears large and moveable (used to radiate heat). There are two living species. The **African elephant** is the largest living land animal (height up to 3.8 m/12½ ft), with three subspecies: the **savanna** (or **bush**) **elephant**, **Cape elephant**, and **forest elephant** (*Loxodonta africana*). The **Asian elephant** has four subspecies: **Indian elephant**, **Ceylon elephant**, **Sumatran elephant**, and **Malaysian elephant** (*Elephas maximus*). The African is larger, with larger ears, a triangular lip on the top and bottom of the trunk tip (not just on the top), and obvious tusks in the female. » pachyderm

elephant bird An enormous bird, known from the Pleistocene and Holocene epochs; fossil remains found on Madagascar; flightless, stood up to 3 m/10 ft tall, and laid eggs more than 30 cm/1 ft long. (Family: *Aepyornithidae*.) » bird [i]; Pleistocene epoch

elephant's-ear » **begonia**

elephant seal A huge true seal; adult male up to 6 m/20 ft long, weight 3 700 kg/8 150 lb; swollen pendulous snout (more pronounced during breeding season); two species: the **sea elephant** or **southern elephant seal** from the sub-Antarctic (*Mirounga leonina*), and the **northern elephant seal**) from the NE Pacific (*Mirounga angustirostris*.) » seal (marine biology)

Elephanta Caves A group of Hindu cave-temples located on Elephanta I off the W coast of Maharashtra, India; a world heritage site. The temples, which were excavated in the 8th–9th-c, are noted for their sculptures, in particular the 'Trimurti', an enormous bust of Shiva, Vishnu, and Brahma. » Hinduism; Trimurti

elephantiasis [elifan**tiy**uhsis] A gross swelling of one or both legs, scrotum, and occasionally arms as a result of blockage of the lymphatic channels by filariasis. The condition is found only in the tropics. » filariasis

Eleusinian Mysteries [elyoo**si**nian] The secret initiation ceremonies connected with the worship of the corn-goddess Demeter and her daughter Persephone, held annually at Eleusis near Athens in ancient times. In origin agricultural fertility rites, they later came to have a moral dimension. Initiation, preceded by ritual purification, was believed to secure happiness in the after-life for those who had led a blameless life. » mystery religions

eleven-plus examination A test taken by pupils towards the end of their primary education, in areas where there are selective secondary schools, to determine which school they shall attend. In much of Britain the eleven-plus declined, though did not disappear, with the spread of comprehensive schools in the 1960s and 1970s. » comprehensive school; grammar school

Elgar, Sir Edward (1857–1934) British composer, born at Broadheath, Worcestershire. He was largely self-taught, and in his youth worked as a violinist before becoming conductor of the Worcester Glee Club and the County Asylum Band, and organist of St George's Church, Worcester. After his marriage (1889) he went to London, but in 1891 settled in Malvern, devoting himself to composition. The *Enigma Variations* (1899) and the oratorio *The Dream of Gerontius* (1900) made him the leading figure in English music. After the Elgar Festival (London, 1904) he was knighted. His further works included oratorios, symphonies, concertos, and incidental music. From 1924 he was Master of the King's Musick. He died at Worcester.

Elgin Marbles Marble sculptures of the mid-5th-c BC from the Parthenon of Athens. Acquired in 1801–3 by Thomas Bruce, 7th Earl of Elgin (1766–1841), in circumstances of doubtful legality while Greece was under Turkish rule, they were shipped to England and in 1816 purchased by the government for the British Museum. In the 1980s in particular, the question of their return to Greece became a heated political issue there, led by the Greek Minister of Culture, Melina Mercouri (1925–). » Acropolis; frieze; Parthenon; pediment (architecture)

Elijah [e**liy**ja] (9th-c BC) Hebrew prophet, whose activities are portrayed in four stories in 1 *Kings* 17–19, 21; 2 *Kings* 1–2. He was prominent in opposing the worship of Baal in Israel under King Ahab and Jezebel, and by virtue of his loyalty to God was depicted as ascending directly into heaven. » Ahab; Baal; Kings, Book of; prophet

elimination reaction A chemical reaction characterized by the removal of part of a molecule to leave a smaller one. In the following example, bromine is eliminated from dibromoethane to give ethylene: $CH_2Br{-}CH_2Br + Zn \rightarrow CH_2{=}CH_2 + ZnBr_2$. » chemical reaction

Elint The practice of '*el*ectronic *int*elligence' gathering, in which one finds out the performance factors of hostile weapons systems by interpreting their electronic emissions. » electronics; military intelligence

Eliot, George, pen name of **Mary Ann** or **Marian Evans** (1819–80) British novelist, born near Nuneaton, Warwickshire. She took charge of the family household when her mother died (1836), and was taught at home. After the death of her father (1849) she travelled abroad, then settled in London, and began to write for the *Westminster Review*. She became assistant editor, and the centre of a literary circle, one of whose members was G H Lewes, with whom she lived until his death. Her first story appeared in 1857. Her major novels were *Adam Bede* (1859), *The Mill on the Floss* (1860), *Silas Marner* (1861), and *Middlemarch* (1871–2). After Lewes' death (1878), she married an old friend, John Cross, in 1880, but died soon after, in London. » English literature; novel

Eliot, T(homas) S(tearns) (1888–1965) British poet, critic, and dramatist, born at St Louis, Missouri. He studied at Harvard and Paris, then obtained a travelling scholarship to Oxford, and was persuaded to stay in England by Ezra Pound, to whom he had shown his poems. He worked as a teacher and in a bank before becoming a director of Faber publishers. The enthusiastic support of Pound led to his first book of poetry, *Prufrock and Other Observations* (1917), and he was introduced by Bertrand Russell into the Bloomsbury Circle. He then published *The Waste Land* (1922) and *The Hollow Men* (1925), and edited the quarterly review, *The Criterion* from its beginning to its demise (1922–39). In 1927, he became a British subject, and was baptized and confirmed, adhering to the Anglo-Catholic movement within the Church of England. There followed several other works, including his major poetic achievement, *Four Quartets* (1944), and a series of plays, notably *Murder in the Cathedral* (1935) and *The Cocktail Party* (1950). He also wrote much literary and social criticism, dealing with individual authors as well as general themes, wherein he could be highly provocative. In 1948 he was awarded the Nobel Prize for Literature. He died in London. » Bloomsbury Group; English literature; poetry

Elisabethville » **Lubumbashi**

Elisha [e**liy**sha] (second half of 9th-c BC) Hebrew prophet in succession to Elijah; his activities are portrayed in 1 *Kings* 19 and 2 *Kings* 2–9,13. He was active in Israel under several kings from Ahab to Jehoash, was credited with miraculous signs, counselled kings, and attempted to guide the nation against her external enemies, especially the Syrians. » Ahab; Elijah; Kings, Books of; prophet

Elizabeth I (1533–1603) Queen of England (1558–1603), the daughter of Henry VIII by his second wife, Anne Boleyn, born at Greenwich, near London. On the death of Edward VI (1553) she sided with her half-sister Mary against Lady Jane Grey and the Duke of Northumberland, but her identification with Protestantism made Mary suspicious, and she was imprisoned for her alleged part in the rebellion of Wyatt (1554). Ascending the throne on Mary's death, she saw that her role in Europe must be as a Protestant sovereign, and it is from this time that the Anglican Church was formally established. She made peace with France and Scotland, and strengthened her position by secretly helping Protestants in these countries. Mary, Queen of Scots, was thrown into her power (1568) and imprisoned, causing endless conspiracies among English Catholics. After the most sinister plot was discovered (1586), Elizabeth was reluctantly persuaded to execute Mary (1587), and subsequently persecuted Catholics. Infuriated by this, and by Elizabeth's part in inciting the Netherlands against him, Philip of Spain attacked England with his 'invincible armada' (1588), but England managed to repel the attack. She died at Richmond, Surrey. Of all her relationships, only one touched her deeply, that with Robert Dudley, Earl of Leicester, whom she would probably have married had it not been for her adviser Cecil's remonstrances. A strong, cruel, and capricious woman, the 'Virgin Queen' was nevertheless popular with her subjects, becoming later known as 'Good Queen Bess'; and her reign is seen as the period when England assumed the position of a world power. » Church of England; Mary, Queen of Scots; Spanish Armada

Elizabeth II (1926–) Queen of the United Kingdom (1952–) and Head of the Commonwealth, born in London, the daughter of George VI. Formerly **Princess Elizabeth Alexandra Mary**, she was proclaimed queen on 6 February 1952, and crowned on 2 June 1953. Her husband was created Duke of Edinburgh on the eve of their wedding (20 Nov 1947), and styled Prince Philip in 1957. They have three sons, **Prince Charles Philip Arthur George** (14 Nov 1948), **Prince Andrew Albert Christian Edward** (19 Feb 1960–), and **Prince Edward Anthony Richard Louis** (10 Mar 1964), and a daughter, **Princess Anne Elizabeth Alice Louise** (15 Aug 1950). » Anne, Princess; Charles, Prince; Edinburgh, Duke of; *see illustration p 487*

Elizabeth, Queen Consort » **George VI**

Elizabeth Petrovna (1709–62) Empress of Russia (1741–62), the daughter of Peter the Great and Catherine I, born near Moscow. She was passed over for the succession in 1727, 1730, and 1740, but finally became Empress on the deposition of Ivan VI. She was guided by favourites throughout her reign. A war with Sweden was brought to a successful conclusion, and her animosity towards Frederick the Great led her to take part in the War of the Austrian Succession and in the Seven Years' War. She died in St Petersburg. » Austrian Succession, War of the; Peter the Great; Seven Years' War

Elizabethan Style A form of early English Renaissance architecture of the period 1558–1603, characterized by symmetrical facades combined with Netherland decoration and over-sized windows. Plans are often E- or H-shaped; a good example is Longleat, UK (c.1568 onwards). » Elizabeth I; Jacobean Style; Renaissance architecture

elk The largest of the true deer (shoulder height, 2.4 m/8 ft); widespread in temperate N hemisphere; usually solitary; long snout, with broad overhanging top lip; throat with loose flap of skin (called the 'bell'); antlers broad, dish-like, with marginal projections; also known in N America as **moose**. (*Alces alces*.) » antlers [i]; bull; deer; elkhound; red deer

elkhound A spitz breed of dog, used in Scandinavia (especially Norway) to hunt elk; medium-sized, broad, solid body with thick grey coat; also known as **Norwegian elkhound** or **elk**. » elk; spitz

Ellesmere Island [elezmeer] Arctic island in Northwest Territories, Canada; separated from Greenland by the Nares Strait; area 196 236 sq km/75 747 sq ml; barren and mountainous,

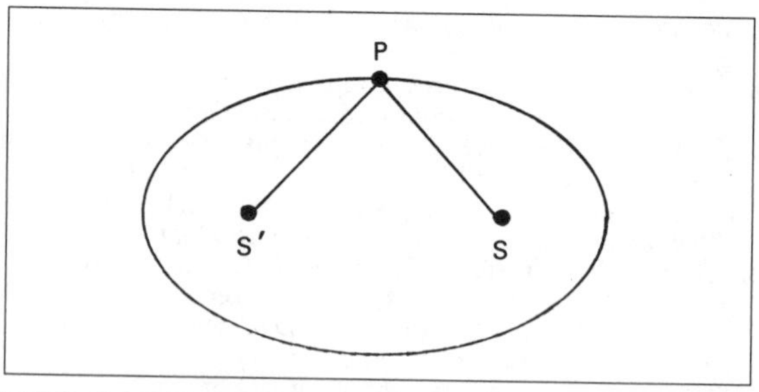

Ellipse, foci S, S'. PS + PS' is constant

large ice-cap (SE), fjord coastline; several small settlements; Cape Columbia, northernmost point in Canada. » Northwest Territories

Ellice Islands » **Tuvalu**

Ellington, Edward Kennedy, byname **Duke** (1899–1974) US composer, arranger, bandleader, and pianist, born in Washington, DC. He was an itinerant piano player in dance bands in Washington and New York until 1924, when he became leader of the house band at the Kentucky Club and then (1927–32) at the Cotton Club. He developed a unique sound for his musicians by blending instruments ingeniously into startling harmonies. Among his early successes were 'Black and Tan Fantasy' (1927), 'Creole Love Call' (1927), and 'Mood Indigo' (1930). After a European tour in 1933, he worked on extended concert pieces, beginning with 'Reminiscing in Tempo' (1935), and initiated a series of annual concerts at Carnegie Hall (1943–50). His creative peak is generally said to be 1939–42, with such recordings as 'Warm Valley', 'Cotton Tail', and 'Take the A Train'. Later works included suites such as 'Such Sweet Thunder' (1957) and 'Gutelas Suite' (1971), film scores, ballets, and a series of 'sacred concerts' (1968–74) performed in cathedrals around the world. He died in New York City. » jazz

ellipse In mathematics, the locus of a point which moves so that the sum of its distances from two fixed points (or *foci*) is constant. It can also be defined as a section of a double cone, or as the locus of a point which moves so that the distance from the focus is proportional to its distance from a fixed line (the *directrix*), the constant of proportion being less than 1. The Cartesian equation of an ellipse can be put in the form $x^2/a^2 + y^2/b^2 = 1$. The polar equation of an ellipse with the focus as pole and the major axis as base line is $r = l/(1 + e \cos \theta)$. The planets move around the Sun in ellipses, and the shape is much used in art and architecture. » conic sections [i]; hyperbola

elliptic geometry » **geometries, non-Euclidean**

Ellis, (Henry) Havelock (1859–1939) British physician and writer on sex, born at Croydon, Greater London. He travelled widely in Australia and S America before studying medicine in London. His interest in human biology and his personal experiences led him to compile the 7-volume *Studies in the Psychology of Sex* (1897–1928), the first detached treatment of the subject, which was highly controversial at the time.

Ellison, Ralph (Waldo) (1914–) US Black writer, born in Oklahoma City, and educated as a musician at the Tuskegee Institute, Alabama. His major work is the novel, *Invisible Man* (1952), a semi-autobiographical account of a young Black intellectual's search for identity and authentic consciousness, set mainly in the slums of New York. » American literature; novel

Ellora Caves » **Kailasa Temple**

elm A deciduous N temperate tree; leaves ovoid, doubly toothed, asymmetric at base; flowers tiny, appearing before leaves; seed oval, with broad papery wing. In recent years the European and N American elm populations have been largely destroyed by **Dutch elm disease**, first identified in Holland in 1967. The disease spread rapidly in the UK, killing millions of trees, mainly **English elms** (*Ulmus procera*), which often reproduce by suckers, giving genetically similar populations. **Wytch elm** (*Ulmus glabra*) reproduces only by seed, and has some resistance. (Genus: *Ulmus*, 45 species. Family: *Ulmaceae*.) » deciduous plants; Dutch elm disease; fungus; slippery elm; tree [i]

elm bark beetle A small brown beetle with pitted wing cases; adults excavate a vertical, shaft-like egg chamber beneath the bark of the elm tree; larvae tunnel away from the chamber, horizontally at first. It carries the fungus that causes Dutch elm disease. (Order: *Coleoptera*. Family: *Scolytidae*.) » beetle; Dutch elm disease; elm

elocution The study and practice of excellence in the manner and style of vocal delivery. Dating from classical Greek and Roman times, it includes far more than training in effective pronunciation: grammatical structure, choice of vocabulary, and stylistic construction must all be taken into account in order to achieve the greatest effect in using the voice. » oratory; rhetoric

Elohim [elohheem] (Heb 'gods') A divine name for the God of Israel, the plural form here being purged of its polytheistic meaning, and used as a plural of majesty. There are over 2 500 occurrences in the Hebrew Bible, making it one of the most common divine names therein, but it could still be applied to other gods, angels, or even figures such as Moses. » God; Yahweh

elongation The angular distance between the Sun and a planet as viewed from Earth. The two inner planets, Mercury and Venus, have elongations of 28° and 48° respectively. The small value for Mercury means that it is never far from the Sun, and is thus a most elusive object to spot. » planet; Sun

Elsinore, Danish **Helsingor** 56°03N 12°38E; pop (1983) 56 246. Seaport on The Sound, NE Zealand, Denmark, opposite Helsingborg, Sweden; railway; shipbuilding, engineering; site of Kronborg Castle, famous as the scene of Shakespeare's *Hamlet*. » Denmark [i]

Eluard, Paul, pseudonym of **Eugène Grindal** (1895–1952) French poet, born at Saint-Denis. He was one of the founders of the Surrealist movement in literature. His first collection of poetry was *Capitale de la douleur* (1926, Capital of Sorrow). Many of his works reflect the major events of the century, such as the Wars, the Resistance, and the aspirations of the Communist Party, which he joined in 1942. He died at Charenton-le-Pont, France. » French literature; poetry; Surrealism

Elvström, Paul [elvstrerm] (1928–) Danish yachtsman. He is the only yachtsman to win four individual Olympic gold medals: in the Firefly class in 1948 and the Finn class in 1952, 1956, and 1960. He was also the first to win the same event at four consecutive Olympics. He came fourth in the Tornado class at the 1984 Olympics, his seventh Games, with his daughter, Trine. » sailing

Ely [eelee] 52°24N 0°16E, pop (1981) 9 122. Small city in East Cambridgeshire district, Cambridgeshire, EC England; in fertile, wheat-growing fens, on R Ouse, 23 km/14 ml NNE of Cambridge; railway; paper, agriculture, engineering, plastics, tourism; 12th-c cathedral (octagonal tower), King's School (1543); Isle of Ely (higher ground surrounded by fens) the location of Hereward the Wake's defence against the Normans. » Cambridgeshire; Hereward

Elyot, Sir Thomas (c.1490–1546) English writer and diplomat, born in Wiltshire. In 1523 he became clerk of the king's council, and was ambassador to Emperor Charles V in 1531–2. His chief work, *The Boke Named the Gouernour* (1531), is the earliest English treatise on moral philosophy. He was a strong supporter of the use of English (as opposed to Latin) in scholarly work. MP for Cambridge in 1542, he died at Carlton, Cambridgeshire. » English literature

Elysée, Palais de l' [palay duh layleezay] Since 1873 the official residence of the French president, situated on the Rue du Faubourg Sainte-Honoré in Paris. It was built in 1718 for the Compte d'Evreux and, although it was used as a dance-hall for a period during the Revolution, it later became the home of Napoleon I and III. » Paris

Elysium [eliziuhm] or **Elysian fields** In Greek and Roman mythology, the happy fields, often located on the borders of the Underworld, where the good remain after death in perfect happiness. It is sometimes confused with the pre-Greek Islands of the Blessed, where heroes are said to live immortally. » Hades

ema » **rhea**

Emancipation Proclamation (1 Jan 1863) A document issued by President Lincoln during the American Civil War, declaring the freedom of all slaves in areas then in arms against the US government; it did not free slaves in areas not in rebellion. He had issued a preliminary proclamation on 22 September 1862. » American Civil War; Lincoln, Abraham; slavery

Emanuel or **Manuel I**, bynames **the Great** or **the Fortunate** (1469–1521) King of Portugal (1495–1521), born at Alcochete. He consolidated royal power, and his reign, marred only by persecution of the Jews, was the golden age of Portugal. He prepared the code of laws which bears his name, and made his court a centre of chivalry, art, and science. He sponsored the voyages of Vasco da Gama, Cabral, and others, which helped to make Portugal the first naval power of Europe and a world centre of commerce. He died in Lisbon. » Cabral; Gama

embargo An order obstructing or impeding the movement of ships of a foreign power, which can entail preventing them from either leaving or entering a port. In the past, embargoes were associated with anticipating the outbreak of war, but their use is limited today. The term is also employed to describe any attempt to suspend trading with another country.

Ember Days In the Christian Church, the Wednesday, Friday and Saturday of the weeks (Ember Weeks) following the first Sunday in Lent, Whitsunday, Holy Cross Day (14 Sep) and St Lucia's Day (13 Dec); formerly observed as special times of fasting and abstinence. » Christianity

embezzlement The dishonest taking of money or other property entrusted to an employee on behalf of his or her employer. It is a form of theft, the separate offence of embezzlement having been abolished in England and Wales by the Theft Act (1968). Many US penal codes, likewise, subsume this offence under theft. However, in Scottish law, it is distinguished from both theft and fraud. » theft

emblematic staging A style of theatre which uses single scenic images, often three-dimensional and free-standing, to symbolize or indicate an idea or location relevant to the action. A raised throne under a golden canopy might represent Heaven, while a dragon's head with gaping jaws would locate Hell. A number of such images can be portrayed simultaneously, and the acting area close to each image is determined by it, while the rest of the stage conveys no specific scenic connotations. » stage; theatre

embolism An obstruction of a blood vessel by the accumulation and adhesion of any undissolved material (such as a blood clot) carried to the site in the blood stream. It is usually identified according to the vessel involved (cerebral, coronary, pulmonary) or the undissolved material (air, fat). Air embolisms may occur in the course of surgery, following an injury, or during intravenous infusions undertaken without satisfactory precautions. » blood vessels [i]; pulmonary embolism; stroke

embrasure A recess in a building for a window. It also refers to the splayed opening between any two upstanding parts of a parapet or crenellated wall.

embroidery The ornamentation of fabrics with decorative stitching – an art which dates from very early times (as shown in Egyptian tomb paintings), when the designs were sewn on to a base fabric by hand. It was highly developed in the Middle and Far East, and in India, for rich garments and furnishings. In Europe, church vestments provided consistently sumptuous examples. Embroidery skills were part of the needleworking ability required by most women, and applied to the making of clothes, linens, and soft furnishings; one of the most famous examples is the 11th-c Bayeux tapestry. Whilst hand-embroidery survives as a craft, many of today's goods are embroidered using computer-controlled sewing machines, capable of reproducing complex multi-coloured patterns.

embryo [embreeoh] In flowering plants, the young plant developed from an ovum and contained within the seed. In animals, the developing young animal, typically derived from a sexually fertilized ovum, contained either within the egg membranes or inside the maternal body. The embryonic phase commences with the division of the fertilized egg (*zygote*), and ends with the hatching or birth of the young animal. » embryology; foetus; plant; reproduction

embryology The study of the development of animals from the first division of the fertilized egg, through the differentiation and formation of the organ systems, to the ultimate hatching or birth of the young animal. » biology; embryo; pregnancy [i]

emerald A gem variety of beryl, coloured green by minor amounts of chromium oxide. The finest crystals are from Columbia. » beryl; gemstones; Plate V

Emerson, Ralph Waldo (1803–82) US poet and essayist, born at Boston, Massachusetts. Educated at Harvard, he became a teacher, and then (1829) pastor of a Unitarian church in Boston, but his controversial views caused his resignation. In 1833 he came to Europe, and visited Thomas Carlyle, thereafter corresponding with him for 38 years. In 1834 he moved to Concord, Massachusetts, where he wrote his prose rhapsody, *Nature* (1836), and many poems and essays, notably *The Conduct of Life* (1860). A transcendentalist in philosophy, a rationalist in religion, and a bold advocate of spiritual individualism, he died at Concord. » American literature; Carlyle; poetry; transcendentalism; Unitarians

emery A natural mixture of crystalline corundum with iron oxides, occurring as dark granules. Very hard, it is used as an abrasive. » corundum

emigration » **migration**

Emmet, Robert (1778–1803) Irish patriot, born in Dublin. He left Trinity College to join the United Irishmen, and travelled on the Continent for the Irish cause, at one point meeting Napoleon. In 1803, he plotted an insurrection against the English, but it proved a failure. He was captured and hanged in Dublin.

Empedocles [em**pe**duhkleez] (c.490–c.430 BC) Greek philosopher and poet, born at Acragas, Sicily. In *On Nature* he agreed with Parmenides that there could be no absolute coming to exist or ceasing to exist; all change in the world is the result of two contrary cosmic forces, Love and Strife, mixing and separating four everlasting elements, Earth, Water, Air, and Fire. The doctrine of four elements became central to Western thought for 2 000 years through its adoption by Aristotle. » Aristotle; Parmenides; Pythagoras

emperor moth A large, broad-winged moth; wings grey or grey brown with conspicuous eye-spots on forewings and hindwings; caterpillar green, with hairy warts on each segment, found from May to August; hibernates as pupa in a brown cocoon. (Order: *Lepidoptera*. Family: *Saturniidae*.) » caterpillar; hercules emperor moth; moth; pupa

emperor penguin The largest of penguins (1.2 m/4 ft tall); never comes to true land; inhabits seas around Antarctica; may dive to depths of 268 m/879 ft; breeds on pack ice at beginning of winter; single egg incubated on the male's feet for 64 days during bitter polar blizzards. (*Aptenodytes forsteri*.) » penguin

emphysema [emfi**see**ma] A disorder of the lungs in which there is destruction of the elastic fibres that normally cause lung tissue to recoil during expiration. As a result, the lungs become progressively more distended and overfilled with air. The small air tubes (*bronchioles*) become dilated, and large areas of alveoli are destroyed and replaced by air-filled cavities (*bullae*). The chest slowly becomes barrel-shaped, and shortness of breath can become severe. The condition is common in heavy cigarette smokers in whom inhaled cigarette products activate enzymes that digest the elastic tissue. The destruction of tissues also promotes secondary infection. » bronchi; lungs

Empire Day » **Commonwealth Day**

Empire State Building An office block in Manhattan, New York City, designed by the firm of Shreve, Lamb & Harman, built 1930–1. At 449 m/1 472 ft high (including a 68 m/222 ft high television mast added in 1951) it was the tallest building in the world until 1954. » New York City

Empire Style The style of decoration associated with Napoleon I's court after he became Emperor in 1804. It is massive, and heavily ornamented with classicizing motifs, particularly Egyptian sphinxes, winged lions, and caryatids. These are cast in ormulu, and gilded or elaborately carved on the furniture (eg the chaise-longue). The style was also seen in costume (eg high-waisted 'Grecian' dresses for women). The equivalent style in Britain was *Regency*. » caryatid; classicism; French art; ormulu

empirical formula » **chemical formula**

empiricism A philosophical tradition which maintains that all or most significant knowledge is based on sense experience; it is usually contrasted with rationalism. Mathematical knowledge and language-competence provide difficult cases for empiricism. Some empiricists, such as Locke, claim that all concepts but not all propositions are empirical; the senses give the concept of twoness, and reason dictates that 2+2=4. Some claim that mathematical truths are not 'significant'; others that they are just highly confirmed generalizations (Mill). Many allow that some patterns of reasoning are independent of experience. Some allow that there might be innate structures in the mind necessary to explain various human capacities, such as language-learning, but insist that the structures provide no evidence for rationalism. » Locke, John; logical positivism; Mill, John Stuart; rationalism (philosophy)

employers' association or **trade association** A society of companies in the same line of business, whose purpose is to discuss matters of common interest, carry out research, make representations to government on industrial matters, and negotiate with trade unions for industry-wide standards and wages. The companies must not collude on prices in ways contrary to the Restrictive Trade Practices and Competition Acts in the UK and the Anti-Trust Laws in the USA. » cartel

employment exchange A UK government-run agency to help out-of-work people find a job; originally called a *labour exchange*, and more recently known as a *job centre*. Employers seeking workers send particulars to the local job centre; these are matched with the skills and qualifications of the persons registered.

Empson, Sir William (1906–84) British poet and critic, born at Howden, Yorkshire. Educated at Cambridge, he became professor of English literature at Tokyo (1931–4) and Peking (1937–9, 1947–53), working in the interim with the BBC's Far Eastern Service. In 1953 he became professor of English literature at Sheffield University. He wrote several major critical works, notably *Seven Types of Ambiguity* (1930), and his *Collected Poems* were published in 1955. He was knighted in 1979, and died in London. » literary criticism; poetry

empyema [empi**yee**ma] An infection occurring between the two layers of the membranes which cover the lung (the *pleura*). This frequently leads to the accumulation of large amounts of infected fluid in this cavity. » lungs

Ems, River, Dutch **Eems**, ancient **Amisia** German river, rises N of Paderborn; meanders 400 km/250 ml W and N to the North Sea, forming a 32 km/20 ml-long estuary; length 328 km/204 ml; navigable length 238 km/148 ml; linked to the Ruhr via the Dortmund-Ems Canal. » Germany [i]

Ems telegram A despatch (13 Jul 1870) describing the refusal of William (Wilhelm) I of Prussia to accept French conditions over the disputed candidature to the Spanish throne. Altered and published by Bismarck, it helped achieve his aim of provoking Napoleon III of France into declaring war on Prussia. » Bismarck; Franco-Prussian War; William I (Emperor)

emu A flightless bird native to Australia; the second largest living bird (after the ostrich), 1.9 m/6¼ ft tall; inhabits dry plains and woodland; eats fruit, shoots, flowers, and insects; runs at nearly 50 kph/30 mph; swims well; related to the cassowary. (Family: *Dromaiidae*, *Dromaius novaehollandiae*.) » cassowary

emu wren A small, brightly-coloured bird native to Australia, also known as the **Australian wren** or **wren-warbler**; tail often long and held erect (resembling true wrens); forages on ground or lower branches of vegetation; inhabits scrub or dense grass; eats insects. (Genus: *Stipiturus*, 3 species. Family: *Maluridae*.) » wren

emulsifiers Chemical substances which help liquids to mix with each other, forming an emulsion. For example, oil and water, which do not normally mix, can be combined into a single phase using an emulsifier, as in margarine and mayonnaise. Emulsifiers also allow gas to be trapped in liquids, as when cream is beaten. Emulsifying agents include algin, agar, and lecithin. » E-number; emulsion

emulsion A suspension of one liquid in another, particularly of an oil in water. All emulsions eventually separate, 'stable' emulsions merely separating more slowly than 'unstable' ones. » colloid; detergent

enamel A decorative medium for producing a highly glazed surface on metal. The common base is a soft glass flux, which is painted over the metal. Colours (which are generally inorganic or mineral materials, such as metal oxides) are added, in desired patterns or pictorially. The whole is then fired in a furnace. Similar techniques are carried out industrially to produce enamelled containers or body work for machinery (eg bowls, ovens, refrigerators). » dentistry; enamelling; flux; teeth [i]

enamelling The use of brightly coloured substances similar to glass which are fired on to metalwork or ceramics as decoration. The techniques used on metalwork are champlevé, cloisonné, basse taille, and painting. Painted enamels of the highest quality on copper were produced in Limoges in the 16th-c, and the same technique was widely used in Europe in the 18th-c for snuff boxes and other small items. Enamel decoration on ceramics is applied during a second or subsequent firing at a lower temperature on top of the main body and glaze. » basse taille enamel; champlevé; cloisonné; enamel

enantiomer [e**nan**tiuhmuh] » **chirality** [i]

Enceladus [en**sel**aduhs] The second natural satellite of Saturn, discovered in 1789; distance from the planet 238 000 km/148 000 ml; diameter 500 km/310 ml; orbital period 1.370 days. » Saturn (astronomy); RR4

encephalitis [ensefuh**liy**tis] A diffuse infection of the brain, caused mainly by viruses, but syphilis, malignant malaria, and some helminths (eg cystercerosis) may also be responsible. Bacterial encephalitis is rare. The features are those of infection, plus drowsiness and a clouding of consciousness. » brain [i]; helminthology; virus

Encke's comet [**eng**kuh] A comet discovered in 1787 and studied by German astronomer Johann Franz Encke (1791–1865) in 1819, which has the shortest period of any known comet, just 3.3 years. It has been recorded at more than 50 apparitions. Encke's name became attached to this comet because he investigated non-gravitational forces which make it orbit 2.5 hours faster than expected. » comet

enclosure The fencing-off of land previously either waste or part of large open fields farmed in strips. Enclosure generally permitted more intensive and profitable cultivation. Attention is generally paid to enclosure by private Acts of Parliament in Britain passed between c.1760 and 1820, but much land was enclosed by agreement from the 16th-c onwards. » agriculture

encopresis » **enuresis**

encounter group A form of group therapy in which the leader facilitates the acquisition of insight and sensitivity to others, using such techniques as bodily contact and the sharing of emotional experiences. Also known as *T-* ('training') *groups*, sessions vary greatly in length and type, and can have both positive and negative effects on members. » group therapy

encyclical, papal [en**sik**likl] Originally, a letter sent to all the churches in a particular area. The term is now restricted to official letters of instruction, usually doctrinal or pastoral in nature, issued by a pope to the whole Roman Catholic Church. » pope; Roman Catholicism

Encyclopaedists/Encyclopedists A collective term for the distinguished editors (Diderot and d'Alembert) and contributors (notably Voltaire, Montesquieu, Condorcet, Helvetius, and Rousseau) to the *Encyclopédie*, a major work of social and political reference published in France (1751–76), associated with the French Enlightenment. » Alembert; Diderot; Enlightenment; Philosophes

encyclopedia/encyclopaedia A comprehensive reference work containing entries on a single subject, a set of related subjects, or all branches of knowledge. Such works may be single or multi-volume publications, with or without illustrations. The entries may be grouped thematically or alphabetically, and involve the use of such editorial aids as cross-references, and pronunciation guides. Encyclopedic treatments date from classical Greek and Roman times, but the most notable developments took place in 18th-c Britain and France, with Ephraim Chambers' *Cyclopaedia* (1728), the 35-volume *Encyclopédie* of Diderot and his associates (1751–76), and the first edition of the *Encyclopaedia Britannica* (1768–71). » Chambers, Ephraim; dictionary; Diderot, Denis

endangered species Plant and animal species which are in danger of becoming extinct. Their classification as endangered species is made by the International Union for the Conservation of Nature and Natural Resources. The danger of extinction generally comes from habitat loss and disturbance caused by human activity, overexploitation, and in many cases pollution. For example, disturbance threatens the pupping beaches of the endangered Hawaiian Monk Seal (*Monachus schauinslandi*), causing increased juvenile mortality. The category also includes species which are possibly now extinct, but which have definitely been seen in the wild within the past 50 years. » conservation (earth sciences); habitat loss; International Union for the Conservation of Nature and Natural Resources; Nature Reserve; wildlife refuge

Ender, Kornelia (1958–) East German swimmer, born at Bitterfeld. She won three Olympic silver medals in 1972, aged 13, and between 1973 and 1976 broke 23 world records (the most by a woman under modern conditions). At the 1973 and 1975 World Championships she won 10 medals, including a record eight golds. In 1976 she became the first woman to win four gold medals at one Olympic Games: the 100 m and 200 m freestyle, the 100 m butterfly, and the 4 × 100 m medley relay. » swimming

endive An annual or biennial growing to 120 cm/4 ft, native to S Europe; basal leaves lobed, upper leaves lance-shaped, clasping the stem at their base; flower heads blue, in clusters of 2–5. Closely related to chicory, it is widely grown as a salad plant, cultivated varieties having many different, often crisped leaf forms. (*Cichorium endivia*. Family: *Compositae*.) » annual; biennial; chicory

endocrine glands Ductless glands, present in some invertebrates (certain molluscs, arthropods) and all vertebrates, which synthesize and secrete chemical messengers (hormones) into the blood stream, or lymph for transport to target cells. In vertebrates they collectively form a major communication system (the **endocrine system**) which with the nervous system regulates and co-ordinates body functions. This system classically comprises the pituitary, thyroid, parathyroid, and adrenal (suprarenal) glands, the pancreas (the islets of Langerhans), and the gonads; however, other regions (the hypothalamus, kidneys, gastro-intestinal tract, thymus, and pineal gland) have endocrine function. Disorders of the endocrine glands are numerous, and may result in disturbances of growth and development, metabolism, and reproduction. The study of the structure, function, and disorders of the endocrine glands is **endocrinology**. » adrenal/parathyroid/pineal/pituitary/thyroid glands; gland; gonad; pancreas

endogamy and exogamy The broad social rules that define who are to be regarded as legitimate marriage partners in society. Endogamy allows marriage between members of one's own group or lineage; exogamy allows marriage between members of different groups only, to encourage transfer of members and their resources (eg via dowries) between lineages. » marriage

endogenous opioids » **opioid peptides**

endorphins [en**daw**finz] Natural substances present throughout the body which have similar (but more controlled) effects to morphine and other narcotics. Since narcotics have such potent effects, it was long suspected that natural counterparts might exist in the body. British neuroscientist John Hughes (1942–) and British pharmacologist Hans Walter Kosterlitz (1903–) succeeded in isolating and purifying endorphins in 1975. The substances are believed to act as neurotransmitters. » narcotics; neurotransmitter; opioid peptides

endoscopy The introduction of an instrument into a body aperture or duct for direct visual inspection and biopsy. It is mainly carried out today with a flexible glass fibre **endoscope**, which can much more readily pass narrow channels and bends than can the rigid instruments used formerly. Examples include *bronchoscopy* (bronchi), *gastroscopy* (stomach), *colonoscopy* (colon), *cystoscopy* (bladder), *jejunoscopy*) (jejunum), and *peritoneoscopy* (peritoneum). Powerful light sources and fibre optics make modern endoscopes very efficient, and some incorporate extra devices (eg laser beams) intended to carry out actual operations deep inside the body. » biopsy; optical fibres [i]

endothelium » epithelium

Endymion [en**dim**iuhn] In Greek mythology, a handsome shepherd of Mt Latmos, who was loved by the Moon-goddess Selene. Zeus put him to sleep, while Selene looked after his flocks, and visited him every night. He was also said, as King of Elis, to have founded the Olympic Games. » Selene

energy An abstract calculable quantity associated with all physical processes and objects, whose total value is found always to be conserved; symbol E, units J; one of the most important concepts in physics. It is an additive, scalar quantity, which may be transferred but never destroyed, and so provides a useful book-keeping device for the analysis of processes. It is sometimes called the capacity for doing work. Although many terms are used to describe energy (eg thermal energy, kinetic energy), they refer to the same energy, but indicate its different manifestations. For example, a battery driving a propeller immersed in water converts chemical energy to electrical energy, which is converted to mechanical energy in the propeller, and finally to heat energy as the water temperature is increased.

The main sources of energy are fossil fuels (petroleum, coal, and natural gas), water power, and nuclear power. Solar power, wind power, and coal provide c.75% of world energy needs; natural gas c.20%; water power (hydroelectricity) c.2%; and nuclear energy c.1%. The search for new sources of energy is a continuing one, since that provided by the fossil fuels will eventually run out. » energy levels; heat; kinetic energy; mass-energy relation; perpetual motion; potential energy; power; thermodynamics; work

energy levels The fixed values of the energy of quantum systems. By contrast, ordinary mechanical systems have energies that can vary continuously, without discrete levels. The state of lowest energy in quantum systems is called the *ground state*. For example, electrons in atoms exist only in well-defined energy levels; an atom in the ground state has electrons only in its lowest energy levels. If such an atom absorbs energy, one of its electrons will be raised to a higher level, and the atom is then said to be in an *excited state*. » atomic spectra [i]; luminescence; quantum mechanics

Engels, Friedrich (1820–95) German socialist philosopher, collaborator with Marx, and founder of 'scientific socialism', born at Barmen. From 1842 he lived mostly in England. He first met Marx at Brussels in 1844 and collaborated with him on the *Communist Manifesto* (1848). He died in London, after spending his later years editing and translating Marx's writings. » Marx; socialism

engine A mechanical device that transforms some of the energy of its fuel into a convenient and controllable form (usually rotational motion), for use by other devices. There is no recognized standard classification of engine types, although the majority convert the motion of an oscillating piston in a cylinder to rotary motion by means of a crank linkage mechanism. The piston is made to oscillate by means of gases expanding and contracting. These gases may be created internally within the cylinder (as in spark ignition and diesel engines) or externally (as in steam engines). Other types of engine use the hot gases to create rotary motion direct (gas turbine and Wankel engines), whist others eject their gases direct to the environment to create thrust (jet engines). Particularly important landmarks in the development of the engine are the application of the separate condenser to the steam engine by James Watt in 1765, the invention of the diesel engine by Otto Diesel in 1892, and the simultaneous invention of the turbo-jet in Germany and Britain during World War 2. » diesel/direct injection/gas/heat/internal combustion/ion/jet/spark ignition/steam/Wankel engine; antifreeze; camshaft; car [i]; carburettor; Carnot cycle; clutch; Diesel; four-stroke engine [i]; gear; knocking; propellor; transmission; two-stroke engine; Watt

engineering The branch of technology which makes power and materials work for people. Engineers study ways of harnessing power sources, such as the use of gasoline and other fuels to power cars, aeroplanes, ships, trains, and space vehicles, and the conversion of water power into hydroelectricity. They also analyse and use many types of materials, depending on the problem to be solved; for example, the properties of steel and concrete make them ideal for constructing buildings, bridges, roads, and dams; metal, glass, and plastic have different properties widely used in the manufacturing industry. To make the best use of what is available, the engineer has to keep constantly up to date with advances in materials and their properties, and often needs to create new materials or sources of power to solve a particular engineering problem. The field as a whole was traditionally subdivided into five main branches: *civil, mechanical, mining and metallurgical, chemical*, and *electrical engineering*. The modern field has expanded, and the boundaries are not now so clearly defined. Also, as each branch of engineering has become more specialized, new fields have developed, such as aeronautical, aerospace, computer, control, marine, nuclear, and systems engineering. » civil/control/electrical/mechanical engineering; Industrial Revolution

England, Lat **Anglia** pop (1981) 46 229 955; area 130 357 sq km/50 318 sq ml. Largest area within the United Kingdom, forming the S part of the island of Great Britain, since 1974 divided into 46 counties; bounded N by Scotland, S by the English Channel, E by the North Sea, and W by Wales, the Atlantic Ocean, and the Irish Sea; includes the Isles of Scilly, Lundy, and the Isle of Wight; largely undulating lowland, rising (S) to the Mendips, Cotswolds, Chilterns, and North Downs, (N) to the N–S ridge of the Pennines, and (NW) to the Cumbria Mts; drained E by the Tyne, Tees, Humber, Ouse, and Thames Rivers and W by the Eden, Ribble, Mersey, and Severn Rivers; Lake District (NW) includes Derwent Water, Ullswater, Windermere, and Bassenthwaite; capital, London; chief cities include Birmingham, Bristol, Leeds, Liverpool, Manchester, Newcastle upon Tyne, Plymouth, Sheffield; chief ports at Felixstowe, Grimsby, Immingham, Portsmouth, Southampton, Tilbury; linked to Europe by ferry and hovercraft from Folkestone, Dover, Newhaven, Ramsgate, Portsmouth, Southampton, Weymouth, Plymouth, Harwich, and Hull; minerals include coal, tin, china clay, salt, potash, lead ore, iron ore, North Sea oil and gas; vehicles, heavy engineering, petrochemicals, pharmaceuticals, textiles, food processing, electronics, telecommunications, publishing, brewing, fishing, livestock, agriculture, horticulture, pottery, tourism. » English; English

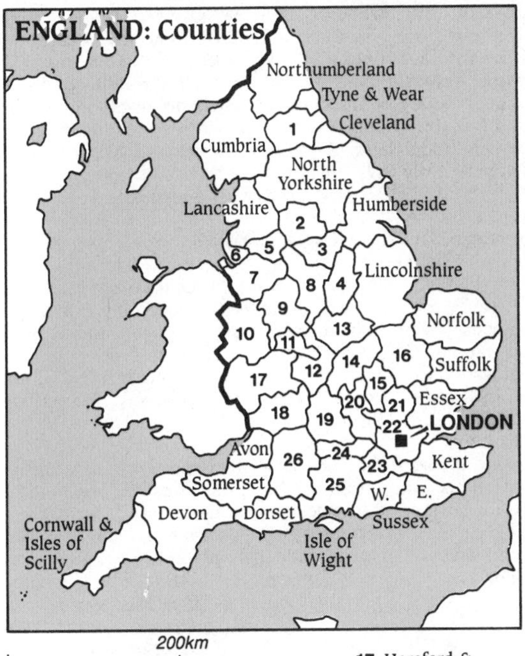

1 Durham
2 West Yorkshire
3 South Yorkshire
4 Nottinghamshire
5 Gtr. Manchester
6 Merseyside
7 Cheshire
8 Derbyshire
9 Staffordshire
10 Shropshire
11 West Midlands
12 Warwickshire
13 Leicestershire
14 Northamptonshire
15 Bedfordshire
16 Cambridgeshire
17 Hereford & Worcester
18 Gloucestershire
19 Oxfordshire
20 Buckinghamshire
21 Hertfordshire
22 Greater London
23 Surrey
24 Berkshire
25 Hampshire
26 Wiltshire

art / Channel / Heritage / history / literature; Lake District; London [i]; Pennines; United Kingdom [i]; RR40 counties; RR25 national holidays

Engler, (Gustav Heinrich) Adolf (1844–1930) German botanist, born at Sagan. Educated at Breslau, he worked at Munich, Kiel, and Breslau, before becoming professor and director of the botanical gardens at Berlin (1889–1921). He proposed a major system of plant classification that is still widely used. He died in Berlin. » botany

English A language belonging to the Germanic branch of the Indo-European family. Its unbroken literary heritage goes back to the inflecting language, Anglo-Saxon, notably in the 8th-c epic poem *Beowulf*. Standard English prose evolved from the Chancery (law-court) English of the 14th-c, and has been codified continuously – its grammatical structure in such early works as Lindley Murray's *English Grammar* (1794), and its lexicon in Dr Johnson's *Dictionary of the English Language* (1755), which laid the foundations for a long tradition of scholarship into the nature of English usage.

English was one of the principal languages of W colonialism, and has been established as the official and majority language in such major political contexts as the USA and Australia, and in several African countries, where it is seen as neutral to the linguistic rivalries provoked by competing indigenous languages. It is jointly the official language alongside other colonial languages (eg in South Africa, where it shares official language status with Afrikaans), and also alongside indigenous languages (eg in India, where it has the advantage of neutrality to the local ethnic and political self-interest of speakers of Hindi in the N, and of the Dravidian languages in the S). English is now used by over 60 countries as an official or semi-official language. It is the main world language of book and newspaper publication, of science and technology, of advertising and pop music, and of computer information storage. There are over 300 million people who speak English as a mother-tongue, and another 300 million or so who use it in countries where it has been given special status (as a 'second' language); at least a further 100 million use it fluently as a foreign language. It is also the medium for auxiliary (restricted) languages, such as those used by international airline pilots and seafarers for intercommunication. The worldwide role of English has resulted in its having an extremely wide range of accents and dialects. In vocabulary, for example, there are thousands of dialect differences, eg UK *lift* alongside US *elevator*, Australian *cobber* alongside UK *mate*. US English has gone some way towards simplifying the complexity which history has endowed on the spelling system, eg replacing *-our* by *-or* in such words as *color*. It has also introduced new grammatical usages, such as the past tense form of the verb (eg *I just ate*) instead of the present perfect form (eg *I've just eaten*). And the variation which arises from the influence of indigenous languages in situations like that of India introduces a new and dramatic dimension into English language dialectology which is largely unmeasured as yet. » Anglo-Saxon; auxiliary language; dialectology; English literature; Germanic languages; Indo-European languages; inflecting language; Johnson, Samuel; Seaspeak

English art The art associated with England, since prehistoric times influenced by the commercial and cultural links with both the Mediterranean and N Europe. Thus the classical style was introduced by the Roman occupation, but Anglo-Saxon invaders in the 5th-c reaffirmed the priority of abstract pattern-making and animal ornament. The Norman conquest in the 11th-c ushered in one of the greatest periods of English art, attested by cathedrals such as Durham and Ely. The glories of mediaeval art ended at the Reformation (c.1530). A new wave of classical Italian influence in architecture and decoration, as well as the Baroque style of van Dyck in painting, set the standard for the Georgian period and the 'Rule of Taste' (17th–18th-c). The 19th-c saw the major achievements of Turner and Constable in romantic landscape painting. Perhaps the outstanding 20th-c figure is the sculptor Henry Moore. » art; Arts and Crafts movement; Camden Town Group; Constable; Euston Road School; London Group; Moore, Henry; New English Art Club; Norwich School; Pre-Raphaelite Brotherhood; Royal Academy of Arts; Turner, J M W

English Channel, Fr **La Manche**, Lat **Mare Britannicum** Arm of the Atlantic Ocean, bounded N by England and S by France; formed with the rise in sea level after the last glacial period; connected to North Sea by Straits of Dover (E), 34 km/21 ml wide; 565 km/350 ml long by 240 km/150 ml wide at its widest point (Lyme Bay–Golfe de St-Malo); crossings by ferry and hovercraft, linking Dover to Dunkerque and Boulogne, Folkestone to Calais and Boulogne, Plymouth to Roscoff, and Portsmouth to Le Havre, Cherbourg, and St-Malo via Channel Is; one of world's busiest shipping lanes; tunnel undergoing construction; first aeroplane crossing by Bleriot, 1909; first swim by Matthew Webb, 1875; main islands, I of Wight, Channel Is. » Channel Islands; Channel Tunnel; Wight, Isle of

English Civil War (1642–8) The country's greatest internal conflict, between supporters of Parliament and supporters of Charles I, caused by parliamentary opposition to royal policies. Although the King left London in March 1642, open hostilities between Royalists and Parliamentarians did not immediately break out. The prospect of compromise was bleak, but both sides, fearing the consequences of civil strife, moved slowly towards the use of armed force. Charles finally issued commissions of array (Jun 1642), and raised his standard two months later at Nottingham. The first major engagement took place at Edgehill in October. It was a draw, but Royalist forces then threatened London, the key parliamentary stronghold. Royalist strategy in 1643 centred upon taking the capital by a three-pronged attack from armies in the N, the SW and the Thames valley. By autumn the N and the W (apart from a garrison in Gloucester) were in their hands, although Parliament held back the tide in the (drawn) first Battle of Newbury. The crucial event of 1643 was Parliament's alliance with the Scots in the Solemn League and Covenant, which strengthened its hand militarily and threatened the King's forces on a new front.

In 1644 Parliament, assisted by the Scots, became a formidable foe. This was clear in July when its forces, aided by Scottish invaders, inflicted a serious defeat upon the Royalists at Marston Moor. The King's forces in the W, however, were another matter. In 1643 they were victorious over the Earl of Essex in the Battle of Lostwithiel, and in the second Battle of Newbury they were successful against the combined forces of Essex, the Earl of Manchester, and Sir William Waller. But 1645 saw Parliament's cause advance in the Midlands and the W, with important victories at Naseby and Langport. The next year brought to an end the first civil war. Charles surrendered to the Scots at Newark in May, and his stronghold of Oxford fell in June. He was taken into parliamentary custody (Jan 1647) when the Scots left for home, and in June was seized by the army.

From June 1646 to April 1648 there was an uneasy peace and attempts at compromise. Negotiations between the King and Parliament had begun as early as 1645, but they achieved little. The main sticking points were religion, particularly Parliament's disestablishment of the Church, and the King's prerogative rights, many of which had been abolished by Parliament. The climax came (Aug 1647) when the army presented the King with the Heads of Proposals, calling for religious toleration, and parliamentary control of the armed forces. Charles made a secret alliance with the Scots, promising to establish Presbyterianism in England (which Parliament had failed to do); they invaded England (Apr 1648), and were repulsed only after the Battle of Preston (Aug). Bitterly fought, the second war earned Charles the epithet 'that man of blood' and, ultimately, his execution (30 Jan 1649). Possibly 100 000 died in the two wars – 1 in 10 of adult males. » Cavaliers; Charles I (of England); Commonwealth (English history); Covenanters; Cromwell, Oliver; New Model Army

English cocker spaniel A small, active, friendly spaniel; shoulder height, 450 mm/18 in; long ears set low on head; tail docked short when young; gave rise to the American *cocker spaniel*. » spaniel

English foxhound » **foxhound**

English Heritage In the UK, a body directly responsible for over 350 buildings and monuments formerly in the care of the Department of the Environment, and for protecting and preserving England's collection of 12 500 designated monuments and over 300 000 'listed' buildings. The Historic Buildings and Monuments Board for Scotland, and *Cadw* (Welsh 'heritage'), have similar functions. » Europa Nostra; National Trust

English history The study of England's past. Many accounts of English history exist, from the Venerable Bede's 7th-c account of the Christianization of England onwards. The systematic, professional study of English history, however, dates from the second half of the 19th-c. With notable exceptions, early studies were predominantly political and constitutional, tracing the development of forms of government in England and the rise of the country to imperial greatness. Much of this writing was heavily coloured by a concern to emphasize those aspects of England's past which seemed to presage later achievements. It was also concerned with the story of England's development *per se*; the histories of Ireland, Scotland, and Wales tended to be casually incorporated. Much 'British' history was overwhelmingly 'English'.

With professionalization came specialization. It became normal to divide English history into recognizable periods for detailed research. These were generally associated with dynasties or major political events. The traditional divisions, often used also for university and school examinations, were Anglo-Saxon (vaguely and misleadingly running from the collapse of Roman rule in the 5th-c to the Norman Conquest in 1066); Norman (1066–1154); Plantagenet (1154–1485); Tudor (1485–1603); Stuart (1603–1714); Hanoverian (1714–1815, although the dynasty proper continued until the death of Queen Victoria in 1901); and Nineteenth Century (1815–1914). In the 20th-c, studies of English history have paid greater attention to non-political themes, with consequential fracturing and elision of traditional chronologies. In the inter-war period, the study of the creation, increase, and distribution of resources developed into a distinct discipline called *economic history*. Much work since the late 1950s has been directed towards the primary study of social groups, their organization and movements, rather than national leaders. Some of this work drew heavily upon the methodology and insights of social science. More recently still, attempts have been made to fuse social and political history to produce more rounded explanations of the forces making for change. Much has been done by gifted amateurs and those for whom the study of English history, while undeniably a skilled craft, was more a means of relaxation than of livelihood. Winston Churchill's much-read *History of the English Speaking Peoples* is a prime example in this latter category, while folk history studies and much-used modern techniques, such as oral history, have been developed by non-professionals. » Anglo-Saxons; economic history; Hanover, House of; Lancaster, House of; Normans; Plantaganets; social history; Stuarts; Tudors; Windsor, House of; York, House of

English literature The earliest texts written in English are chronicles dating from the 7th-c, but literature begins with the heroic poems and fragments of the next century, written in Old English; the most famous is *Beowulf*. After the Norman conquest, the language and culture underwent fundamental changes, and Middle English (11th–14th-c) offers a range of lyrical, courtly, realistic, and satirical poems, the most celebrated by Chaucer (notably *The Canterbury Tales*, c.1400) as well as significant prose works (eg Malory's *Morte d'Arthur*, 1470). Poets such as Wyatt and Surrey brought the Renaissance to England, and the late 16th-c produced important works such as Sidney's *Arcadia* (1590) and Spenser's *Faerie Queene* (1590–6). The sonnet sequence was also popular; but the theatre attracted the most adventurous talents of this time, and the plays of Marlowe, Ben Jonson, Webster and others proved immensely popular. The dramatic works of Shakespeare, unprecedented in their variety, profundity, originality, and poetic power, make this one of the most remarkable ages of English, and indeed of world literature. The 'metaphysical' poets Donne, Herbert, and Marvell also broke new ground; and the way was prepared for Milton, whose *Paradise Lost* (1667) is the greatest English epic poem.

The Restoration period (1660–) provided a brief resurgence of a distinctive if decadent drama; but by now prose was beginning to assert itself as the dominant medium, and Bunyan's *Pilgrim's Progress* (1678) became the most popular book in English after the Bible. Dryden, the first poet laureate, wrote great topical satires as well as plays and criticism: he was matched by Pope, master of the heroic couplet (*The Dunciad* 1728–42), and with Swift, whose *Gulliver's Travels* (1726) and other prose satires created public delight and consternation. These typify the English Augustan age. The immense erudition and labour of Dr Johnson (*Dictionary*, 1755) helped to ratify these classical writers; but by the end of the 18th-c the new mood of Romanticism is established (Wordsworth and Coleridge's *Lyrical Ballads*, 1798). The lyrics of Keats, Shelley, and Clare, the visionary works of Blake, and the immensely popular poems of Byron represent another period of great achievement, to be built on by Browning and popular laureate Tennyson, whose poems incorporate much dramatic and novelistic material.

The novel asserted itself in the 18th-c, with writers such as Defoe, Richardson, Fielding, Smollett, and Sterne. By the 19th-c it is clearly the dominant literary form – Scott made his fortune after switching from verse narrative to novels. Dickens, Thackeray, and Hardy wrote for the nation; and novelists such as Jane Austen, Emily and Charlotte Bronte, Mrs Gaskell, and George Eliot claimed a new territory for the woman writer. In the present century, the novel has been the vehicle of much literary experiment (Joyce *Ulysses*, 1921; Virginia Woolf *Mrs Dalloway*, 1927; Beckett's Trilogy, 1951–3) whilst still surviving in its traditional form as the 'one bright book of life' (D H Lawrence). English poetry in the 20th-c has likewise been profoundly marked by new techniques and attitudes associated with modernism, brought from Europe by Americans (T S

Eliot, Ezra Pound); but the native lyric has persisted from Hardy through to Philip Larkin, and the poems of Ted Hughes and the Irishman Seamus Heaney offer a new and powerful synthesis of traditional materials. Much important work has also been produced this century by people writing in English from other cultures. » African / American / Australian / Caribbean / Indian / Irish / Scottish / Welsh literature; Austen; Blake, William; Bloomsbury group; Brontë, Charlotte/Emily; Browning, Robert; Bunyan, John; Byron; Chaucer; Clare, John; Coleridge; Defoe; Dickens; Donne; Dryden; Eliot, George; Eliot, T S; Fielding; Gaskell; Hardy, Thomas; Heaney; Herbert, George; Johnson, Samuel; Jonson; Keats; Larkin; Marlowe; Marvell; Milton; Pope, Alexander; Pound; Richardson, Samuel; Scott, Walter; Shakespeare; Shelley, Percy Bysshe; Smollett; Sterne; Swift; Tennyson; Thackeray; Webster, John; Wordsworth, William; Wyatt, Thomas

English pointer A breed of dog, developed in England; large, taller at shoulder than at rear end; muzzle long, deep and concave on top; tail tapering, carried almost horizontally; coat short; also known as **pointer**. » dog; pointer

English setter A large breed of dog, developed in England; taller at shoulder than at rear end; muzzle deep; coat long, white with dark markings. » setter

English sheepdog » **Old English sheepdog**

English sparrow » **house sparrow**

English-Speaking Union A charity founded by Sir Evelyn Wrench (1882–1966) in 1918 with the purpose of 'improving understanding about people, international issues, and culture through the bond the English language provides'. Based in London, the Union also has branches in the USA, the Commonwealth, Europe, and other countries; its membership numbered over 45 000 in 1986.

English springer spaniel » **springer spaniel**

English Stage Company An organization established under George Devine in 1956 to encourage new playwrights. It had a lasting effect on post-war British theatre through its insistence on the value and importance of the contemporary writer. Its base was the Royal Court Theatre in London. » theatre

engraving A process of printmaking by the intaglio method; also the resulting print. The term is often used less precisely to mean any process whereby a design is printed on paper. *Reproductive* engraving simply reproduces an already existing work of art and has been superseded by photography; an *original* engraving is a work of art in its own right. » burin; drypoint; etching; intaglio; line-engraving; mezzotint; steel engraving; wood engraving

enhanced radiation weapon » **neutron bomb**

enkephalins » **opioid peptides**

enlightened despots European rulers of the 18th-c, influenced by the French and German Enlightenment. They aimed at increasing the ruler's power within a more efficient state-system at the expense of the Church, nobility, and estates. Some, such as Joseph II of Austria, instituted social reforms to improve the general welfare of the population. » Enlightenment; Joseph II

Enlightenment A European philosophical movement of the 18th-c, rooted in the 17th-c Scientific Revolution and the ideas of Locke and Newton. Its basic belief was the superiority of reason as a guide to all knowledge and human concerns; from this flowed the idea of progress and a challenging of traditional Christianity. » Encyclopaedists; enlightened despots; Hume, David; Locke, John; Newton, Isaac; Philosophes

Enlil The Mesopotamian god of the wind, son of Anu the sky-god, king of the gods before the creation of Marduk. » Marduk; Mesopotamia

Enniskillen [iniskilin], also **Inniskilling**, Gaelic **Inis Ceithleann** 54°21N 7°38W, pop (1981) 10 429. County town in Fermanagh, SW Northern Ireland, on an island in the R Erne; English families were settled here after Tyrone's rebellion; scene of a victory of William III over James II, 1689; became an important Protestant stronghold; scene of an IRA bombing at the Remembrance Day service in 1987, killing 11 people; airfield; tourism, watersports, engineering, food processing; castle ruins (15th–16th-c), cathedral (Protestant, 17th–18th-c). » Fermanagh; Protestantism; William III

Ennius, Quintus (c.239–169 BC) Latin epic poet and dramatist, born at Rudiae, Calabria, Italy. He is said to have served in the Punic Wars, and returned to Rome with Cato the Elder, where he taught Greek, and attained the rank of Roman citizen. He introduced the hexameter into Latin; but only fragments of his many writings survive. » epic; Latin literature; metre

Enoch [eenok] Biblical character, son of Jared, father of Methuselah. He was depicted as extraordinarily devout, and therefore as translated directly into heaven without dying (*Gen* 5.24). In the Graeco-Roman era his name became attached to Jewish apocalyptic writings allegedly describing his visions and journeys through the heavens (1, 2, and 3 Enoch). » apocalypse; Genesis, Book of; Methuselah; Pseudepigrapha

enosis A political movement in Cyprus for union with Greece, reflecting the demands of Cypriots opposed to foreign rule, and closely associated with the leadership of the Greek Orthodox Church. There was an enosis rising in 1931, and since then there has been serious conflict, at times amounting to civil war, between the Greek and Turkish populations. Now independent, Cyprus has never achieved union with Greece because of Turkish opposition. » Cyprus [i]; EOKA; Grivas

Enright, D(ennis) J(oseph) (1920–) British writer, born at Leamington, Warwickshire, and educated at Cambridge and at Alexandria, Egypt. Many years teaching in universities abroad are recalled in *Memoirs of a Mendicant Professor* (1969). He has written four novels and much criticism, but is best known for his poetry. Eleven volumes since 1953, including *Some Men Are Brothers* (1960), *Unlawful Assembly* (1968), and *A Faust Book* (1979) are represented in his *Collected Poems* (1981). » English literature; poetry

Ensor, James (Sydney), Baron (1860–1949) Belgian painter, born at Ostend. He became known for his bizarre and fantastic images, using masks, skeletons, and other ghostly effects as symbols of the evils of society. His paintings aroused much controversy when they were first shown, as in his best-known work, 'Entry of Christ into Brussels' (1888, Brussels). Made a baron in 1929, he died at Ostend.

entablature The upper part in any of the five main orders of classical architecture. It consists of an architrave, frieze, and cornice, and is supported by a colonnade. » orders of architecture [i]

Entebbe [entebay] 0°05N 32°29E, pop (1983e) 20 472. Town in S Uganda, E Africa; on N shore of L Victoria, 25 km/15 ml SW of Kampala; founded, 1893; former capital of Uganda, 1894–1962; airport; railway; scene in 1976 of a dramatic rescue by Israeli forces of Israelis whose plane had been hijacked by a group of Palestinian terrorists. » Uganda [i]

entellus [enteluhs] A langur native to S Asia, and traditionally sacred in India; sandy brown, with a black face; long tail; inhabits diverse regions; also known as **entellus langur** or **hanuman monkey**. (*Presbytis entellus*.) » langur

Entente Cordiale A term first used in the 1840s to describe a close relationship between the UK and France; then given to a series of agreements in 1904 between the two countries, dealing with a range of issues, in particular establishing the predominant role of the UK in Egypt, and France's interests in Morocco.

enteric fever » **typhoid fever**

enterprise zones In the UK, parts of the country designated by the government as areas where business start-up schemes will get favourable financial help; for example, no rates might be payable for ten years. They are usually located in inner-city areas with high unemployment levels. Over 20 such zones exist in the USA, and a similar number in the UK. Schemes of this kind are in operation in many W European countries.

enthalpy An energy quantity appearing frequently in thermodynamics; symbol H, unit J (joule); defined as $H=U+pV$, where U is internal energy, p is pressure, and V is volume. For example, for a gas at constant pressure, the total heat that must be added to raise the temperature of the gas is the sum of the increase in internal energy of the gas plus the work done in expanding against surrounding pressure, so the total heat equals the increase in H. There is no absolute zero of enthalpy, so only changes in enthalpy can be measured. » energy; heat; thermodynamics

entomology The branch of biology dealing with all aspects of the study of insects. Insects are the most diverse group of organisms on Earth, and their importance has led to the development of several specialized areas of entomology. Many insects are beneficial to humans, such as those responsible for the pollination of crop plants, but others are harmful, by feeding on the crops or their stored products, or by transmitting fungal, bacterial, and viral diseases to the plants. They can cause enormous economic losses. The development of insecticides and alternative techniques for controlling pest insects forms the basis of *applied economic entomology*. *Medical entomology* is a specialized field dealing with the study of insect carriers of numerous diseases (eg typhus, malaria, sleeping sickness) and with the methods of controlling them. Insects have also been used as tools in scientific studies, and many significant discoveries have been made, for example in genetic research using the fruit fly *Drosophila*. » biology; Drosophila [i]; genetics [i]; insecticide

entresol » **mezzanine**

entropy A thermodynamic quantity which always increases for irreversible processes, giving a direction in time for processes which might otherwise appear reversible from energy considerations alone; symbol S, units J/K (joule per kelvin). An increase in entropy is equal to the quantity of heat added to a system divided by the temperature in kelvin, at a constant temperature. An increase in entropy of 1 kg of ice melting to water at 273 K (0°C) is 1223 J/K. Freezing water to ice decreases the entropy of the water, but at the expense of increasing the entropy of the total system, such as the refrigerator and the room containing it. Entropy may be understood as a measure of disorder at a microscopic level, caused by the addition of heat to collections of atoms. The second law of thermodynamics states that for all processes entropy either is constant or increases. » heat; thermodynamics

enuresis A condition typified by involuntary voiding of urine. The behaviour is abnormal in relation to the individual's mental age, and is not due to organic causes. The involuntary passage of faeces, also not a result of organic illness, is known as **encopresis**.

Enver Pasha (1881–1922) Turkish soldier and politician, born in Constantinople. A leader in the revolution of Young Turks in 1908, he later became Minister of War (1914). He fled to Russia in 1918 after the Turkish surrender, and was killed in an insurrection in Turkestan. » Young Turks

environment The conditions and influences of the place in which an organism lives. The large number of different types of environment (eg urban environment, tropical rainforest environment) makes it impossible to formulate a single definition. In general, the *physical* environment describes the characteristics of a landscape (eg climate, geology) which have not been markedly changed by human impact, whereas the *geographical* environment includes the physical environment together with any human modifications (eg agricultural systems, industrialization, urbanization). The relationship between living organisms and their environment forms part of the subject of *ecology*. Concern that large parts of the physical environment are suffering from misuse and overexploitation is central to conservation, and the environmental movement which promotes conservation has gained considerable momentum in recent decades as new threats (eg acid rain, soil erosion, ozone depletion) are widely recognized. » conservation (earth sciences); ecology; ecosystem; environmental archaeology/studies; environmentalism

environmental archaeology The study of past environments and ecological interaction over time between human and contemporary animal and plant communities. The basic raw materials consist of animal bones and teeth; preserved pollen and plants; snails, fish, and insect remains; and soils and sediments. » archaeology; ecology; environment; palynology

Environmental Protection Agency A US government agency established in 1970. Its job is to determine, regulate, and enforce environmental pollution controls, such as legislation governing the use of pesticides. » environment; pollution

environmental studies Those aspects of biology, ecology, and geography which are related to an understanding of the environment: its physical and human components. It is sometimes used synonymously with *ecology*, though environmental studies are more wide-ranging. » biology; ecology; environment; geography

environmentalism A term which has several meanings according to the perspective of the user. Its broadest meaning is a concern with all environmental matters: a recognition of increasing environmental degradation brought about by mismanagement of the Earth's resources (eg the burning of fossil fuels), and therefore the need for conservation. More narrowly, its use can be applied to the ideology which rejects the 'technocentric' view of the environment, that all environmental problems can be solved through the use of technology and without a reduction in economic growth. Environmentalism adopts an 'ecocentric' approach. This advocates that environmental problems cannot be solved without a shift away from policies of economic growth at any price; therefore economic growth is not seen as a central social issue. There is the recognition that the Earth's resources are finite, and that higher priority should be given to non-material values. Little confidence is placed in the ability of science to solve environmental problems. » conservation (earth sciences); environment; Friends of the Earth; Greenpeace

Environmentally Sensitive Areas (ESAs) A European Community scheme introduced in 1985 to protect areas of ecological and landscape importance from drainage and loss caused by agricultural change. Payments can be made for farming in ways which help to conserve landscape and wildlife habitats, and so resist pressures to intensify production. Examples include the Broads and the Breckland in E Anglia, UK. » Breckland; Broads, the; ecology; Less Favoured Areas

enzyme A specialized protein molecule produced by a living cell, which acts as a biological catalyst for biochemical reactions. Each enzyme is specific to a particular reaction or group of similar reactions. The molecule undergoing a reaction (the *substrate*) binds on to an active site on the enzyme to form a short-lived compound molecule, thereby greatly increasing the rate of the reaction. Enzyme activity is strongly influenced by substrate concentration, acidity (pH), temperature, and the presence of other substances (*co-factors*). The names of enzymes typically end in *-ase*, and their names are derived from the substrates on which they act; for example, lipase is an enzyme that breaks down lipid (fat). » amylases; catalysis; co-enzyme; lipase; protein

Eocene epoch [eeohseen] The second of the five geological epochs of the Tertiary period, lasting from 55 million to 38 million years ago. It was characterized by a warmer climate and the appearance of modern flora and fauna. » geological time scale; Tertiary period; RR16

Eohippus [eeoh**hip**uhs] » **Hyracotherium**

EOKA The acronym for **Ethniki Organosis Kipriakou Agonos** (National Organization of Cypriot Struggle), a Greek Cypriot underground movement seeking to end British rule and achieve *enosis*, the union of Cyprus with Greece. Founded in 1955 by a Greek army officer, Colonel George Grivas, with the support of Archbishop Makarios III, it pursued a campaign of anti-British violence which climaxed in 1956–7. EOKA declined and was later disbanded following Makarios's acceptance of Cypriot independence rather than *enosis* (1958). In 1971–4 it was unsuccessfully resurrected as EOKA B. » Cyprus [i]; enosis; Grivas; Makarios III; nationalism

Eos [eeohs] In Greek mythology, the goddess of the dawn, daughter of Helios, mother of Memnon. She abducted various mortals. When she took Tithonus, Zeus granted her request that he should be made immortal, but she forgot to ask for perpetual youth, so he grew older and older, finally shrinking to no more than a voice or, possibly, the cicada. » Memnon

Epaminondas (c.418–362 BC) Theban general and statesman, whose victory at Leuctra (371 BC) broke the military power of Sparta and made Thebes the most powerful state in Greece. His death at the Battle of Mantinea abruptly brought this supremacy to an end. » Sparta (Greek history); Thebes

ephedrine [efidrin, efidreen] A drug with similar actions to adrenaline, used as a nasal decongestant. Earlier, it was also used in the treatment of asthma and low blood pressure. » adrenaline; asthma

ephemeral An annual plant with a very short life-cycle, usually producing several generations in a single season. Many weed species are ephemeral, as are desert plants which experience very short favourable seasons. » annual

ephemeris [efe**m**uhris] (plural **ephemerides** [efuh**me**rideez]) A numerical description of the orbit of a celestial object, particularly a comet or planet. It includes the orbit period, inclination, eccentricity, and positional direction of the object at the moment when the orbit crosses the equatorial plane of the primary body. The name is also used for a book, published annually, which lists all predictable astronomical phenomena for the coming year, such as planetary, lunar, and eclipse data. » astronomy; Solar System

ephemeris time [efe**m**uhris] A fundamental measure of time used between 1958 and 1972, defined by reference to the position of the Sun in 1900, and the length of the tropical year. It was used as an invariable measure of time until replaced by international atomic time in 1972. » time

Ephemeroptera [uhfemuh**rop**tuhra] » **mayfly**

Ephesians, Letter to the [e**fee**zhans] New Testament writing attributed to Paul, but of disputed authorship, and with no specific addressees in the best manuscripts (which lack the words 'in Ephesus' in *Eph* 1.1); many similarities can be detected with the Letter to the Colossians. It sets out God's purposes in establishing the Church and uniting both Jews and Gentiles in it, and concludes with exhortations directed at the Church. » Colossians, Letter to the; New Testament; Paul, St; Pauline Letters

Ephesus [**ef**uhsuhs], Turkish **Efes** 37°55N 27°19E. Ancient city of Lydia and important Greek city-state on the W coast of Asia Minor; at the mouth of R Bayindir, near the Aegean coast; centre of the cult of Cybele (an Anatolian fertility goddess) and worship of Artemis/Diana, whose temple was one of the Seven Wonders of the Ancient World; in Roman times, principal city of the province of Asia, and seat of the Roman governor; visited by St Paul; ruins excavated, 19th–20th-c; resort village of Kuşadasi 12 km/7 ml SSW on the Aegean coast; museum at Selçuk; camel wrestling festival (Jan); 7 km/4 ml from Selçuk is the Mereymana chapel where the Virgin Mary is believed to have spent the last days of her life. » Artemis; Mary (mother of Jesus); Paul, St; Seven Wonders of the Ancient World

Ephraim, tribe of [**ee**frayim] One of the twelve tribes of ancient Israel, said to be descended from Joseph's younger son, who was adopted and blessed by Jacob. It was apparently a powerful tribe in ancient Israel, whose territory included the C hill country of Palestine, stretching to Bethel in the S and almost to Shechem in the N. » Israel, tribes of [i]; Joseph/Manasseh, tribe of

epic A heroic poem; a narrative of wars and adventures where larger-than-life characters perform deeds of great public and national significance. The earlier epic poems, in the oral tradition, reached back into myth and legend, where men and gods moved on the same scene; among these are the Sumerian epic *Gilgamesh* (c.3000 BC), the Homeric epics *Iliad* and *Odyssey* (c.1000 BC), and the Indian *Mahabharata* and *Ramayana* (c.500 BC): also the N European epics such as the Old English *Beowulf* (8th-c), the Norse sagas, and even the 13th-c German *Nibelungenlied.* The term 'secondary epic' refers to works written in conscious imitation of these primary epic models, such as Virgil's *Aeneid* (30–19 BC), Tasso's *Gerusalemme Liberata* (1575), and Milton's *Paradise Lost* (1667). The novel has been presented as an 'epic poem in prose', and some works of significant scale such as Melville's *Moby Dick* (1851) and Tolstoy's *War and Peace* (1863–9) may be so described. Brecht also proposed an 'epic theatre'. Although some films have achieved truly epic status, the form and the term have generally been travestied in the cinema. » Brecht; Homer; literature; Milton; novel; poetry; Tolstoy; Virgil

epicalyx An additional whorl of flower parts attached outside of the sepals or calyx, which they resemble in both form and function. It is characteristic of some plants, such as members of the *Rosaceae*. » flower [i]; sepal

epicentre » **earthquake**

Epictetus [epik**tay**tuhs] (c.50–c.130) Stoic philosopher, born at Hierapolis. At first a Roman slave, on being freed he devoted himself to philosophy. He was banished by the Emperor Domitian, and settled at Nikopolis in Epirus, where he died. He wrote no works; the *Enchiridion* is a collection of maxims dictated to a disciple. » Stoicism

Epicureanism A philosophical school founded by Epicurus in the 4th-c BC, surviving into the 3rd-c AD. It based its moral theory of hedonism on atomism, asserting that the gods and death are not to be feared, and that pleasure is easy to obtain, since the best pleasures are simple, and do not require extravagance. » atomism; Epicurus; hedonism

Epicurus (c.341–270 BC) Greek philosopher, born at Samos. He visited Athens when he was 18, then opened a school at Mitylene (310 BC), and taught there and at Lampsacus. In 305 BC he returned to Athens, where he established a successful school of philosophy, leading a life of great temperance and simplicity. He is said to have written 300 volumes on many subjects, but only a few letters and other fragments have survived. He held that pleasure is the chief good, by which he meant freedom from pain and anxiety, not (as the term 'epicurean' has since come to mean) one who indulges sensual pleasures without stint. He died in Athens. » Epicureanism

Epidaurus [epee**dow**ruhs] A Greek city-state situated in the E Peloponnese. It was famous in antiquity for its sanctuary to Asclepius, the god of healing, and for its magnificent open theatre, which is still used today. » polis

epidemiology The study of the distribution and causes of disease in populations. In the 19th-c, the major causes of death were infections. Study of the occurrence of outbreaks in relation to the social conditions prevailing at the time led to effective measures in their control. For example, epidemics of cholera were traced to polluted water, and of puerperal fever to the contaminated hands of medical attendants. In this century the emphasis has changed with the changing pattern of disease and the increased sophistication of epidemiological methods. Thus, the link between cancer of the lung and smoking has been established, and information about the relative occurrence of coronary heart disease in different countries and of cancers of different types obtained. It is likely that advances in this field of activity will assist in the prevention of these and many other complaints. » infant mortality rate; medicine; screening tests

epidermis The outermost layer of a plant or animal. In plants and many invertebrates, the epidermis is a single cell thick. In vertebrates it is many cells thick, and in terrestrial vertebrates it is formed from dead, hardened cells. » skin [i]

epididymis [epi**di**dimis] » **testis**

epidural anaesthesia The injection of a local anaesthetic into the epidural space located within the vertebral canal outside the dura (a membrane covering the spinal cord). The anaesthetic blocks the nerve roots emerging from the spinal cord on their way to organs, muscle, and skin. It is often used in surgical procedures on the lower half of the body, and in normal or abnormal childbirth. » anaesthetics, local; vertebral column

epiglottis A pear-shaped sheet of elastic fibrocartilage, broad above (where it lies immediately behind the tongue) and narrow below (where it attaches to the back of the thyroid cartilage), and covered on both surfaces by mucous membrane. The back surface contains taste buds and mucous glands. It moves on swallowing, and partly covers the opening into the larynx. In some mammals it extends above the soft palate into the nasopharynx, making this directly continuous with the larynx. » larynx; mucous membrane

Epigoni [e**pi**gonee] In Greek mythology, the 'next generation' of heroes. After the failure of the Seven Champions to take Thebes, their sons made another expedition and succeeded; this was shortly before the Trojan War. » Alcmaeon (mythology); Diomedes; Seven against Thebes

epigram Originally, an inscription; hence, any short, pithy poem. The Latin poet Martial wrote over a thousand. Coleridge's definition is also an example: 'What is an epigram? A dwarfish whole,/Its body brevity, and wit its soul'. » Martial; poetry

epigraphy The study of ancient inscriptions, variously inscribed on memorial stones, clay pots and tablets, marble, wood, wax, and other hard surfaces, and using a wide variety of techniques (eg carving, embossing, painting). The field provides insights into the early development of writing systems, as seen in the carvings on the Egyptian pyramids, and the memorial inscriptions on Ogam stones in the Celtic-speaking parts of the British Is. » hieroglyphics [i]; Ogam

epilepsy A transient seizure or fit usually associated with a short-lived disturbance of consciousness. It stems from a synchronous high-voltage electrical discharge from groups of neurones in the brain. The disorder takes several forms, which include loss of consciousness with generalized convulsions (**grand mal**), short periods of loss of consciousness in which patients simply stop what they are doing and look blank ('absence' or 'drop attacks', or **petit mal**), seizures with involuntary movements of only part of the body, such as a limb (**Jacksonian epilepsy**), and short-lived sensations of smell and smacking of the lips (**temporal lobe epilepsy**). The majority of cases do not have an obvious cause, but in some individuals seizures follow organic damage resulting from trauma or tumour. » brain [i]; EEG

Epimetheus [epi**mee**thiuhs] The eleventh natural satellite of Saturn, discovered in 1980; distance from the planet 151 000 km/94 000 ml; diameter 140 km/90 ml. » Saturn (astronomy); RR4

epinephrine » **adrenaline**

epipelagic environments The shallowest pelagic zone in the ocean, usually defined as extending from the surface to a depth of about 200 m/750 ft. It includes the *euphotic* (or *photic*) zone, the surface layer with light penetration sufficient to support photosynthesis by marine plants. The clearer the water, the greater the depth of this zone: in the clearest waters, it may extend to the base of the epipelagic zone; in the neritic realm, it is usually shallower, around 50 m/150 ft, because of the increased turbidity of the water. » neritic zone; pelagic environments

Epiphany A Christian festival (6 Jan) which commemorates the showing of the infant Jesus to the Magi (*Matthew* 2), the manifestation of Jesus' divinity at his baptism (*Matthew* 3), and his first miracle at Cana (*John* 2). Its eve is Twelfth Night. In some countries, gifts are exchanged at Epiphany rather than at Christmas. » Jesus Christ; Magi

epiphenomenalism A theory which maintains that mental phenomena are distinct from and caused by physical phenomena, but that mental phenomena themselves exert no causal influence on the physical world, everything in the physical world being explicable entirely in physical terms. The theory was espoused by Thomas Huxley, Santayana, and others. » Huxley, Thomas Henry; Santayana

epiphyte A plant not rooted in the soil, but growing above ground level, usually on other plants. It uses such hosts for support only, and should not be confused with *parasites*, which also obtain food from their hosts. Epiphytes have aerial roots which help to attach them to their supports, and to trap organic debris, providing nutrients. They also absorb water, either as rain or directly from the air, and may be green and capable of photosynthesis. In some, the leaves may form a water reservoir in the centre of the rosette. Epiphytes are especially common in tropical rain forests, where the adoption of this lifestyle allows them to grow in the light, which is otherwise shut out by the dense canopy. Orchids and bromeliads are particularly prominent here; elsewhere, mosses and lichens are the most frequent epiphytes. » bromeliad; lichen; moss; orchid [i]; parasitic plant; photosynthesis

episcopacy [**epis**kuhpuhsee] (Gr *episkopos*, 'bishop', 'superintendent') A hierarchical (as opposed to consistorial) system of Church government, with bishops occupying the dominant role and authority. In the Roman Catholic, Orthodox, and Anglican communions, those consecrated bishops are the chief ecclesiastical officers of a diocese, normally with a cathedral as the mother church, and have the power to ordain priests and confirm baptized members of the Church. They are responsible for the general oversight of the clergy and the spiritual life of a diocese. They are often claimed to be the direct successors of the first twelve Apostles, but not in the Lutheran and other Reformation Churches which recognize the office of bishop. » Anglican Communion; apostolic succession; bishop; Lutheranism; Orthodox Church; Roman Catholicism

Episcopal Church, Protestant The Anglican Church in the USA, formally established in 1784 after the War of Independence when Samuel Seabury (1729–86) was consecrated the first Bishop of Connecticut (by the bishops of the Episcopal Church of Scotland). It is an active missionary Church, especially in the Far East and S America. Traditionally, it has allowed more lay participation in the government of the Church than has the Church of England, and some bishops allow ordination of women as priests. » Anglican Communion; episcopacy; Protestantism

epistemology The philosophical theory of knowledge: What is it? Can we have any? Are there different kinds? How are they justified? These are often taken to be the central questions of philosophy. Most philosophers think that knowledge involves beliefs that are true and justified; many claim in addition that the beliefs must be produced in the right way. *Sceptics* argue either that we can have no knowledge at all or considerably less than might be thought, usually citing lack of justification. *Foundationalists* require that if a belief is justified it must be directly immune from scepticism, or derived from such beliefs by immune inferential processes. *Coherence* theorists claim instead that beliefs need only 'hang together' to be justified. *Empiricists* claim that all non-trivial knowledge is *a posteriori*, derived from experience. *Rationalists* disagree, claiming that some if not all significant knowledge is *a priori*, independent of experience. » coherence theory; empiricism; foundationalism; rationalism (philosophy); scepticism

epistolary novel A novel in letters – one whose narrative is conducted by an exchange of letters between the characters. Richardson's *Clarissa* (1748) popularized the form, and influenced Laclos' *Les Liaisons dangereuses* (1782, Dangerous Liaisons). Interesting possibilities and complications arise due to the shifting point of view, and the absence of an omniscient narrator. » English/French literature; Laclos; novel; Richardson, Samuel

epithelium A layer of cells lining all internal surfaces (organs, tubes, ducts) and covering the external surface of the body; the internal lining is also known as **endothelium**. Its function varies in different regions of the body (eg protection, secretion, absorption). Several types have been identified according to the shape of the individual cells (*columnar*, *cuboidal*, *squamous*), their arrangement (*stratified*, *pseudostratified*), or the presence of hairlike processes on their free surface (*ciliated*). *Transitional epithelium* is a type characteristically found lining hollow organs subject to large mechanical changes arising from contraction and distension (such as the bladder). In closed body cavities (eg pericardial, peritoneal, pleural) the epithelium provides a smooth, moist surface which facilitates movement. » cell

epoch In geology, an arbitrary unit of time used as a subdivision of a *period*. » geological time scale; RR16

epoxy resin [i**pok**see **re**zin] A polymer formed by the condensation of the two compounds shown in the illustration. Polymerization occurs with little shrinkage, and the resulting hard

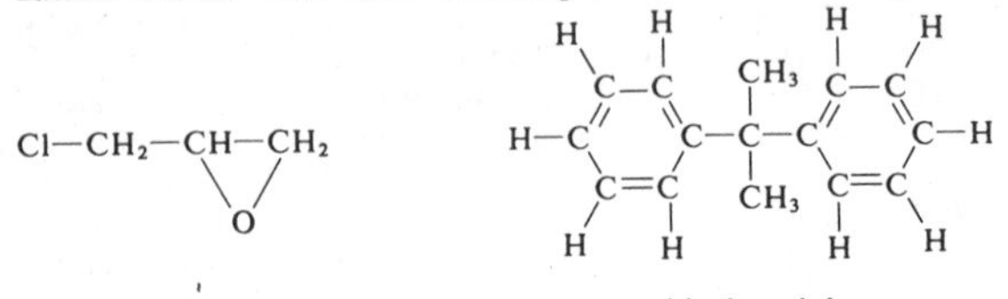

epichlorohydrin bisphenol-A

material is useful as an adhesive, a coating, and an embedding material for electrical components. » condensation (chemistry); polymerization; thermoset

EPROM An acronym of **electrically programmable read-only memory**, a type of integrated circuit read-only memory which can be reused by removing the chip from the computer, erasing its contents, electrically writing new data into it, and replacing it in the computer. EPROMs are more widely used than the related EAROMs. » EAROM; PROM

Epsom salts » magnesium

Epstein, Sir Jacob [epstiyn] (1880–1959) British sculptor, born a Russian-Polish Jew in New York City. He studied at the Ecole des Beaux-Arts in Paris, moving to London in 1905, and becoming a British subject. Several of his symbolic sculptures, such as 'Ecce Homo' (1934), resulted in accusations of indecency and blasphemy. He was an outstanding modeller of bronze portrait heads of celebrities and children. In the 1950s, his last two large works, 'Christ in Majesty' (in aluminium; Llandaff Cathedral) and 'St Michael and the Devil' (in bronze; Coventry Cathedral), won more immediate acclaim. He was knighted in 1954, and died in London. » English art; sculpture; Symbolism

equal area map projection A map projection in which all areas are portrayed at the same scale, eg Lambert's cylindrical equal area projection. This is only possible through a distortion of shape at high latitudes. Consequently this projection is rarely used for areas polewards of 40° N and S of the Equator. » map projection

equations The statement that one mathematical expression is equal to another. An equation may always be true (eg $2+2=4$; $x+y=y+x$, $(x-1)(x+1)=x^2-1$), when it is called an *identity*, usually written $\equiv$, or it may be true only for some values of the unknowns. Equations may contain more than one unknown quantity. Those containing only one unknown are classified by the *degree* of that unknown. Equations of degree one, called **linear equations**, are of the form $ax=b$, and have the solution $x=b/a$, given $a\neq0$. Equations of degree two, **quadratic equations**, are of the form $ax^2+bx+c=0$, and have solutions $x=[-b\pm\sqrt{(b^2-4ac)}]/2a$; these solutions are in the set of real numbers if the discriminant of the equation (b^2-4ac) is greater than or equal to zero. A method for solving general equations of degree three, **cubic equations**, was given in the 16th-c by the Italian mathematician Nicola of Brescia (nicknamed Tartaglia), and his pupil Ferrari later gave a method for solving the general equation of degree four. For centuries, mathematicians tried to find a general solution to equations of degree five, but in 1824 N H Abel proved that no such solution could be found.

A **polynomial** equation contains the sum of multiples of powers of a variable, say x; for example $a_0x^n+a_1x^{n-1}+a_2x^{n-2}\ldots=0$, where n, the highest power of the unknown, is called the degree of the polynomial. Equations are also used in analytical geometry to describe curves. For example, the equation $x^2+y^2=1$ describes the circle, centre the origin, radius 1. In recent years the development of computers has stimulated the discovery of methods of finding successive approximations to the solutions of equations, especially non-algebraic equations, such as $x=e^{-kx}$. » algebra; Diophantine equations; simultaneous equations

Equator The great circle on the Earth's surface, halfway between the Poles, dividing the Earth into the N and S hemispheres; known as the **terrestrial equator**. Its own latitude is 0°, and from here latitude is measured in degrees N and degrees S. The **celestial equator** is the great circle in the sky in the same plane as the terrestrial equator. When the Sun is on it, day and night are everywhere equal (hence it is also called the *equinoctial line* or *circle*). » Earth; great circle

Equatorial Guinea, official name **Republic of Equatorial Guinea, República de Guinea Ecuatorial** pop (1990e) 350 000; mainland area 26 016 sq km/10 042 sq ml; total area 28 051 sq km/10 828 sq ml. Republic in WC Africa comprising a mainland area (Río Muni), bounded N by Cameroon and E and S by Gabon, and several islands (notably Bioko and Annabón) in the Gulf of Guinea; divided into seven provinces; capital, Malabo; chief towns, Bata and Evinayoung on mainland, Luba and Riaba on Bioko; timezone GMT +1; mainland population mainly Fang; chief religion, Roman Catholicism (80%); official language, Spanish; unit of currency, the ekuele; mainland rises sharply from a narrow coast of mangrove swamps towards the heavily-forested African plateau; deeply cut by several rivers; hot and humid equatorial climate; average annual rainfall c.2 000 mm/80 in; average maximum daily temperature, 29–32°C; first visited by Europeans in 15th-c; island of Fernando Póo claimed by Portugal, 1494–1788; occupied by Britain, 1781–1843; rights to the area acquired by Spain, 1844;

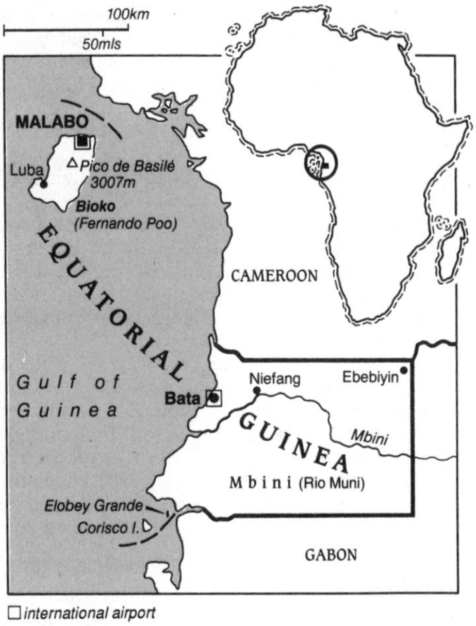

independence, 1968; military coup, 1975; governed by a military council headed by a president; 1982 provision for a new constitution to establish an elected House of Representatives and a smaller State Council; economy largely based on agriculture; cocoa, coffee, timber, bananas, cassava, palm oil, sweet potatoes. » Bioko; Malabo; RR25 national holidays; RR48 political leaders

equestrianism The skill of horsemanship. As a sport it can fall into one of four categories; *show jumping*, *dressage*, *three day eventing* (also known as *horse trials*), and *carriage driving*. The governing body is the International Equestrian Federation. » dressage; horse trials; Pony Club; show jumping; Spanish Riding School; RR110

equilibrium (economics) A point where the price and volume that suppliers are willing to supply matches the price and volume levels that customers demand. It is one of the basic tenets of the classical school of economics that the economy will always move to equilibrium. » economics

equilibrium (mechanics) A state of balance. In mechanics, if several forces act simultaneously on an object such that it suffers no net force, these forces are said to be in equilibrium. An object or system in equilibrium is unchanging until acted upon by some outside force. » mechanics; thermal equilibrium

equinox 1 Either of the two points on the celestial sphere where the ecliptic intersects the celestial equator. Physically these are the points at which the Sun, in its annual motion, crosses the celestial equator – the **vernal equinox** as it crosses from S to N, and the **autumnal equinox** as it crosses from N to S. The vernal equinox is the zero point in celestial co-ordinate systems. **2** Either of the two instants of time at which the Sun crosses the celestial equator, being about March 21 (vernal) and September 23 (autumnal). » celestial equator/sphere

equisetum » horsetail

equity (economics) The capital of a company, belonging to the shareholders (who are legally the owners). It consists of issued share capital (the money received from the sale of shares); the profits retained (traditionally known as *reserves*); share premiums (excess receipts from the sale of shares over their nominal value); and the revaluation reserve (sums resulting from the increase in the value of assets since their purchase). In the event of winding-up the company, this sum is divided among the shareholders. The shares themselves are called **equities**. » capital (economics); company; shares

equity (law) A source of English and Scottish law, originally developed by the Lord Chancellor and later by the Court of

Chancery. It arose from the right of litigants to petition the monarch. In time these petitions were handled by the Lord Chancellor. Originally flexible, equity developed into a fixed set of rules, its court being notorious for delay. While the Court of Chancery was abolished under the Judicature Acts (1873–5), much equitable work falls within the current jurisdiction of the Chancery Division. Trust law and equitable remedies (such as the injunction) are examples. » Chancery Division; injunction; trust

equivalence In logic, two sentences are equivalent if and only if they are either both true or both false; the commonest English signal for equivalence is 'if and only if'; in formal languages, either ≡ or ○ is typically used. In set theory, two sets are equivalent if there is a one-to-one correspondence between their members. » logic; set

equivalence principle A principle arising from the observation that gravitational and inertial mass have the same value, expanded by Einstein to the principle that, locally, effects of gravitation are equivalent to acceleration. The (strong) equivalence principle states that physical laws in any local free-falling inertial reference frame are the same as in special relativity. The principle is of central importance to the general relativity theory of gravity. » Einstein; general relativity; mass; thought experiment

Equuleus (Lat 'little horse') [ikwooliuhs] The second smallest constellation in the N sky. » constellation; RR8

era The second largest of the time divisions used in geology, each being divided into a number of periods. » geological time scale; RR16

Erasistratus [erasistratuhs] (3rd-c BC) Greek founder of a school of medicine, born in Ceos. He settled in Alexandria, where he studied the nature of the nervous system, and came near to discovering the circulation of the blood. He died at Samos. » circulation

Erasmus, Desiderius, originally **Gerrit Gerritszoon** (1466–1536) Dutch humanist, born in Rotterdam. After six years in an Augustinian monastery, he became private secretary to the Bishop of Cambrai, and a priest (1492). He went to Paris, where he lived as a teacher, moving to England in 1498, eventually becoming professor of divinity and of Greek at Cambridge. Here he wrote his satire, *Encomium Moriae* (1509, The Praise of Folly). After 1514 he lived alternately in Basle and England, and at Louvain (1517–21). In 1519 appeared his masterpiece, *Colloquia*, an audacious handling of church abuses. He also made the first translation of the Greek New Testament (1516), and edited the works of St Jerome (1519). In 1521 he left Louvain, and lived mainly in Basle, where he was engaged in continual controversy, and edited a long succession of writers. He died in Basle, having done more than any other person to advance the Revival of Learning. » humanism; Jerome, St; Luther; New Testament; Reformation; Renaissance; satire

Erastianism An understanding of the Christian Church which gives the state the right to intervene in and control Church affairs. This tendency is associated with Thomas Erastus (1524–83), who, in 16th-c Heidelberg, had argued against Calvinists for the rights of the state in Church affairs, and against the Church's practice of excommunication. It is also evident in the teaching of the Anglican, Richard Hooker; and in the rights of the British Crown in electing bishops in the Church of England. » Calvinism; Church of England; Hooker, Richard

Erato [eratoh] In Greek mythology, the Muse responsible for lyric poetry and hymns. » Muses

Eratosthenes [eratosthuhneez] (c.276–c.194 BC) Greek astronomer and scholar, born at Cyrene. He became chief librarian at Alexandria, and is remembered for the first scientific calculation of the Earth's circumference, which he got correct to 80 km/50 ml. He died at Alexandria. » Earth [i]

Erechtheum [erekthayuhm] The latest building on the Athenian Acropolis, named (by Pausanias in the 2nd-c AD) after the legendary king Erechtheus of Athens. It is a symmetrical, two-part Ionic marble temple dedicated to Athena and Poseidon-Erechtheus, and built during the Peloponnesian War (c.420–407 BC). The six caryatids of the porch (one now amongst the Elgin marbles) are particularly noteworthy. » caryatid; Elgin marbles; Ionic order; Parthenon; Peloponnesian War

Erechtheus [erekthiuhs] In Greek mythology, an early king of Athens, born from the Earth and nurtured by Athena. He sacrificed his daughter Chthonia to secure victory over the Eleusinians, but was killed by Poseidon. The Erechtheum, a temple on the Acropolis, is probably on the site of his palace. » Acropolis; Athena; Poseidon

Eretria [eretreea] In antiquity, a Greek city-state situated on the island of Euboea off the coast of Attica. It was sacked in the first Persian War for the help it had given to the Ionian cities of Asia Minor in their revolt (499 BC) against Persia. » Attica; Ionians; Persian Wars

erg » **energy; heat; work;** RR70

ergonomics The study of work, including the design of the work situation, the analysis and training of work skills, the effects of physical and psychological environments, work-stress, errors, and accidents. **Human engineering** and **human factors** are equivalent terms. Ergonomic investigations commonly involve collaboration between anatomists, physiologists, psychologists, and engineers. Large amounts of data are collected on the capabilities of the human body in terms of strength and size. The systematic study of work developed from the early 20th-c introduction of mass production, and the use of time and motion study for job analysis and improvement. The subject has applications in such areas as factory design, power station layouts, and the design of vehicle instruments. Recommendations are made about noise and pollution limits, operating times, and lighting conditions. With increasing automation, the requirements for work skills have shifted from eye-hand co-ordination towards information-monitoring and decision-making. Whereas much of pre-1970 ergonomics was concerned with 'man-machine interaction' (MMI), contemporary ergonomics is more concerned with 'human-computer interaction' (HCI). » occupational psychology

ergot [erguht] A fungal disease of grasses caused by *Claviceps purpurea*; forms hard black fruiting bodies (*sclerotia*) in flower heads of infected grasses, including cereal crops; sclerotia contain chemicals (alkaloids) which can cause severe poisoning if ingested. (Class: *Pyrenomycetes*.) » ergotism; fungus

ergotism A condition which results from eating bread made from rye heavily infected with the fungus *Claviceps purpurea*, which contains ergot alkaloids. These substances constrict blood vessels, so that victims develop burning sensations in the limbs, gangrene, and convulsions. It also induces abortion in pregnant women. Ergotism is now rare, but epidemics occurred well into the 19th-c. Outbreaks caused great fear, and were referred to as *St Anthony's fire*, in the belief that a visit to the tomb of this saint would bring a cure. » alkaloids; ergot; rye

Erhard, Ludwig (1897–1977) German economist, statesman, and Christian Democratic Chancellor (1963–6), born at Furth. Professor of economics at Munich, in 1949 he was elected to the Federal Parliament at Bonn and made Chancellor of the Exchequer in the Adenauer administration. He was the pioneer of the West German 'economic miracle' of recovery from wartime devastation. He succeeded Adenauer as Chancellor, but economic difficulties forced his resignation. He died in Bonn. » Adenauer; Christian Democrats

Eric the Red, byname of **Erik Thorvaldson** (10th-c) Norwegian sailor who explored the Greenland coast and founded the Norse colonies there (985). His son Leif Eriksson landed in 'Vinland', often identified as America (1000). Both men are the subject of Icelandic sagas. » saga

erica » **heath**

Ericsson, John (1803–89) Swedish inventor, born at Långbanshyttan. He was a Swedish army engineer before he moved to England (1826) where he invented the first successful screw-propeller (1836). In 1839 he went to the USA, where he designed the warship *Princeton*, the first steamer with engines and boilers entirely below the water-line, and in 1861, during the Civil War, built the ironclad *Monitor* and other vessels. His inventions revolutionized the construction of warships. He died in New York City. » warships [i]

Eridanus (name of a river) [**iri**danuhs] An inconspicuous S constellation, but the sixth largest. Its brightest star is Achernar, which is the ninth brightest in our sky. Distance: 35 parsec. » constellation; RR8

Eridu The oldest of the Sumerian city-states, lying SW of Ur. Excavations of the site have revealed a continuous series of temples starting in the sixth millenium BC and ending in the third with the great ziggurat. » Sumer; Ur; ziggurat [i]

Erie Canal An artificial waterway extending 580 km/360 ml between Albany and Buffalo, New York State. Constructed 1817–25, it greatly accelerated the development of the mid-West and of New York by providing a water route from the Hudson R to L Erie. Although improved rail transport in the late 19th-c spelled its decline, it is still a significant element in the New York State Barge Canal System. » canal; Erie, Lake; New York

Erie, Lake [eeree] Fourth largest of the Great Lakes, N America, on frontier between Canada and USA; 388 km/241 ml long, 48–92 km/30–57 ml wide; area 25 667 sq km/9 907 sq ml; Detroit R inlet from L Huron (W), via L St Clair; Niagara R (E) outlet to L Ontario; Welland Ship Canal bypasses Niagara Falls; generally closed by ice during winter months (Dec–Mar); major (US) ports include Buffalo, Cleveland, Detroit; islands include Bass, Kelleys, Pelee; British defeated at Battle of Lake Erie, 1813. » Erie Canal; Great Lakes

Erinyes [**ereen**ieez] In Greek mythology, spirits of vengeance, depicted as carrying torches and covered with snakes. They are best thought of as personified curses, avengers of crime 'within the kindred' (outsiders could be pursued by the blood-feud). Their names are Alecto 'never-ceasing', Megaira 'grudger', and Tisiphone 'avenger of blood'. » Alcmaeon (mythology); Eumenides; Orestes

Eris [eris] In Greek mythology, the daughter of Night and the sister of Ares. A late story tells how she was present at the wedding of Peleus and Thetis and threw a golden apple 'for the fairest'; this brought Hera, Athene, and Aphrodite into contention, and was the first cause of the Trojan War. The name means 'strife' in Greek. » Paris

Eritrea [eri**tree**a], Amharic **Ertra** pop (1984e) 2 614 700; area 117 600 sq km/45 394 sq ml. Coastal region in N Ethiopia, NE Africa, on the Red Sea; capital, Asmara; taken by Italy, 1882; colony declared, 1890; used as base for Italian invasion of Abyssinia, 1935; part of Italian East Africa, 1936; taken by British, 1941; federated as part of Ethiopia, 1952; made province of Ethiopia, 1962, which led to political unrest; civil war in 1970s, with separatists making major gains; Soviet- and Cuban-backed government forces regained most areas after 1978 offensive; continuing conflict in the region. » Ethiopia [i]

ERM » European Monetary System

ermine » **stoat**

Ermine Street » **Roman roads** [i]

Ernst, Max (1891–1976) German painter, born at Brühl, near Cologne. After studying philosophy at Bonn, he turned to painting, and in 1919 founded at Cologne the German Dada group. He later participated in the Surrealist movement in Paris. He settled in the USA in 1941, but returned to France in 1953. He died in Paris. » Dada; frottage; German art; Surrealism

Eros (astronomy) [eeros] An asteroid that passed within 23 million km/14 million ml of Earth in 1975. » asteroids

Eros (mythology) [erohs], commonly [**ee**ros] Originally, in Homer, simply an abstract force of 'erotic desire'; but in Greek mythology, the son of Aphrodite and Ares. He is first depicted on vases as a handsome athlete, then as a boy with wings and arrows, and finally, in the Hellenistic period, as a chubby baby. » Cupid

erosion In geology, the alteration of landforms through the removal and transport of material by water, wind, glacial movement, gravity, or living organisms. Rivers are the most effective agents of erosion, forming the pattern of hills and valleys, while wave action forms the coastlines. Erosion can have serious economic effects by removing the topsoil. » soil

Erse » **Irish**

Ershad, Hussain Muhammad (1929–) Bangladesh soldier, chief martial law administrator, and President (1983–90). Appointed army Chief-of-Staff by President Ziaur Rahman in 1978, he repeatedly demanded that the armed forces should be involved in the country's administration. In 1982 he led a bloodless military coup, becoming President the following year. » Bangladesh [i]; Ziaur Rahman

erysipelas [eri**si**puhluhs] A severe illness resulting from infection of the skin with *haemolytic Streptococcus*. The bacterium enters through a small break in the skin, and a red rash advances rapidly from the site. Usually associated with a high fever, it is easily cured with penicillin. » skin [i]; streptococcus

erythrocytes [**erith**ruhsiyts] Haemoglobin-containing blood cells present in most vertebrates, whose primary function is the transport of oxygen and carbon dioxide in the blood; also known as **red blood cells**. They are manufactured in bone marrow, usually as large, round, bi-concave, nucleated cells. With maturation of the cells their diameter decreases, haemoglobin is accumulated, and (in mammals) the nucleus is lost before the cells enter the circulation. » blood; bone marrow; erythropoietin; haemoglobin

erythropoietin [erithroh**poy**itin] A type of hormone (a polypeptide) present in vertebrates, secreted mainly by the kidneys, but also by other organs (eg the liver). It stimulates the proliferation and maturation of red blood cells (*erythrocytes*) in red bone marrow. The enhanced secretion of erythropoietin follows oxygen deficiency in some (as yet unknown) kidney cells, which results in compensatory increases in circulating erythrocytes and blood oxygen. » blood; dialysis; erythrocytes; hormones; peptide

ESA » **European Space Agency**

Esaki, Leo (1925–) Japanese physicist, born in Osaka. He studied physics at Tokyo, and in 1957, working for the Sony Corporation, developed the **Esaki diode**, a semiconductor device with widespread electronic uses in computers and microwave systems. In 1960 he moved to the IBM Research Center in New York, and shared the Nobel Prize for Physics in 1973. » electronics; semiconductor

Esarhaddon (?–669 BC) King of Assyria (680–669 BC), son of Sennacherib and father of Assurbanipal. He is best-known for his conquest of Egypt (671 BC). » Assurbanipal; Assyria

Esau [**ee**saw] Biblical character, the elder son of Isaac. He was depicted as his father's favourite son, but was deprived of Isaac's blessing and his birthright by his cunning brother Jacob (*Gen* 27). The story was used to explain why Esau's descendants, the Edomites, were thereafter hostile to Jacob's descendants, the Israelites. » Bible; Edomites; Isaac; Jacob

Esbjerg [aysbyer] 55°28N 8°28E, pop (1983) 80 317. Seaport on W coast of Ribe county, SW Jutland, Denmark; railway; ferry link with UK and Faroe Is; base for North Sea oil and gas exploration; fishing, trade in agricultural produce; the most important Danish North Sea port. » Denmark [i]

escalator A moving staircase, used to transport people or goods from one level to another, found mainly in large department stores and in railway stations and airports; introduced in the USA in the 1890s. The steps are mounted on an endless belt, lying flat at the top and bottom to enable people to get on and off, and there is a moving handrail. Modern escalators are usually inclined at an angle of 30°, and travel at a rate of up to 35 m/120 ft per minute. The treads pass through a metal comb at the top and bottom of the escalator, which helps to remove objects. A moving ramp, which transports people or goods horizontally, or at a slight incline, is known as a **travelator**.

escape velocity Spacecraft velocity at which the energy of a craft is sufficient to overcome the gravitational attraction of the parent body, and will thus not return to that body. Earth escape velocity is c.11 km/7 ml per sec (root 2 × circular orbit velocity); Sun escape velocity is about 42 km/26 ml per sec, reached by Voyagers 1 and 2 after Jupiter flyby, when velocity was increased by gravity assist. » acceleration due to gravity; geosynchronous Earth orbit; gravity assist; low Earth orbit

Escaut, River » **Schelde, River**

eschatology [eska**tol**uhjee] The Christian doctrine concerning the 'last things' – the final consummation of God's purposes in creation, and the final destiny of individual souls or spirits and of humanity in general. The expected imminent return of Christ to establish the Kingdom of God was not realized, in early Christianity, which led to alternative, often symbolic, representations of the 'last things'. The notion is sometimes represented as a present spiritual condition rather than as a future cosmic event. Others believe that the Kingdom of God has been inaugurated by the coming of Christ, and then give varying accounts of its future fulfilment. Some continue to adhere to the early belief in the literal 'second-coming' of Christ. » Adventists; Christianity; Messiah; Messianism; millenarianism; parousia

escherichia [eshuhrikia] A rod-shaped bacterium that occurs in the intestinal tract of animals, including humans, and is common in soil and aquatic habitats. It can cause bacterial dysentery. The only species, *Escherichia coli*, has been intensively studied by microbiologists. (Kingdom: *Monera*. Family: *Enterobacteriaceae*.) » bacteria [i]; dysentery

Escoffier, (Georges) Auguste [eskofyay] (c.1847–1935) French chef, born at Villeneuve-Loubet. He became *chef de cuisine* to the general staff of the Rhine army in the Franco-Prussian War (1871) and of the Grand Hotel, Monte Carlo, before coming to the Savoy, London, and finally to the Carlton. The inventor of *Pêche melba* and other dishes, he wrote several books on culinary art. He died at Monte Carlo.

Escorial, El [eskoreeal] A palace-monastery built (1563–84) for Philip II in New Castile, Spain; a world heritage site. The granite edifice, constructed by Juan Bautista de Toledo and his successor Juan de Herrara, is renowned for its austere grandeur. It houses a substantial library (founded by Philip II) and an art gallery which includes works by El Greco, Velazquez, and Titian. » monasticism; Philip II (of Spain)

Esdras, Books of [ezdras] **1** The **First Book of Esdras**, known also as **3 Esdras** (in the Vulgate), part of the Old Testament Apocrypha; an appendix to the Catholic Bible. It reproduces much of 2 *Chron* 35–6, Ezra, and *Nehem* 7–8, covering two centuries from the reign of Josiah to Ezra's reforms after the exile, with an additional story about three young men of Darius' bodyguard. » Apocrypha, Old Testament; Ezra; Josiah **2** The **Second Book of Esdras**, known also as **4 Esdras** (in the Vulgate) or **4 Ezra**, sometimes considered part of the Old Testament Apocrypha; also an appendix to the Catholic Bible. It depicts seven apocalyptic visions, ostensibly to Ezra (also called Salathiel), which address the problem of why God has permitted Israel's sufferings and the destruction facing the world. Dated probably late 1st-c AD; chapters 1–2 and 15–16 may be two later Christian additions, today sometimes called 5 Ezra and 6 Ezra, respectively. » Apocrypha, Old Testament; apocalypse; Ezra; Pseudepigrapha

Esfahan [esfahahn], ancient **Isfahan, Aspadana** 32°40N 51°38E, pop (1983) 926 601. Capital city of Esfahan district, WC Iran; on R Zaindeh, 336 km/209 ml S of Teheran; third largest city in Iran; airport; railway; university (1950); steel, carpets, handprinted textiles, metalwork; Lutfullah mosque, 17th-c royal mosque, Ali Kapu gate, Chihil Satun, Jolfa cathedral. » Iran [i]

esker A long, narrow hill of gravel and sand which may wind for long distances along a valley floor, probably formed by water flowing in tunnels underneath glaciers. » drumlins; glaciation

Eskimo or (in Canada) **Inuit** Eskimo-Aleut-speaking peoples of N America, Russia, and Greenland, living along the N edge of the continent, from Alaskan and E Asian shores in the W to Greenland and Labrador in the E, mostly S of the Arctic Circle. They are closely related to the Aleut. Their ancestors came from Asia, crossing over the Bering Straits when Alaska and Siberia were connected by a strip of land, 10–15 000 years ago, and gradually expanded across the continent. Despite geographical separation, the way of life in different Eskimo groups was very similar, determined largely by climatic considerations – living on the coast during the winter months, and moving inland for the brief summers to hunt land and sea game, and to fish.

As a consequence of later contact with Europeans in the 18th-c, the Eskimos' way of life was radically altered, from hunting for food to hunting for furs, which they exchanged for European manufactured goods. By the late 20th-c, many had settled in villages, and while some continued to hunt and fish, most had at least seasonal employment in the wage economies of the countries where they lived, mainly as labourers in the mining and oil industries. In Russia, Eskimos have been organized into hunting collectives. The combined populations of Eskimos and Aleuts in Russia is c.1 300, with 33 000 in Alaska, 24 000 in Canada, and 43 000 in Greenland. » Aleut; Greenland [i]

eskimo dog » **husky**

esophagus » **oesophagus**

ESP » **extrasensory perception**

esparto A tufted perennial grass, native to N Africa, and naturalized elsewhere, consisting of spikelets with long, feathery bristles in narrow panicles. The leaves are used to make paper. (*Stipa tenacissima*. Family: *Gramineae*.) » grass [i]; panicle; perennial; spikelet

Esperanto The best-known of the world's auxiliary languages, invented by Ludwig Lazarus Zamenhof in 1887, designed to overcome problems of international communication. It has 5 vowels and 23 consonants, a mainly W European lexicon, and with Slavonic influence on syntax and spelling. Precise estimates of numbers and levels of speaker fluency are difficult to obtain: there are anywhere between 1 and 15 million speakers. Newspapers and journals are published in Esperanto, together with the Bible and the Koran. It is used for broadcasting, and is taught as a school subject in many countries. » auxiliary language; Zamenhof

Essen 51°28N 6°59E, pop (1983) 635 200. Industrial city in Düsseldorf district, Germany; 29 km/18 ml NNE of Düsseldorf, between Emscher and Ruhr Rivers; badly bombed in World War 2; bishopric; railway; headquarters of many large industrial corporations; important centre of retail trade; mining, iron and steel, engineering, locomotives, electronics, glass, chemicals, plastics, brewing, machine tools, shipbuilding, textiles; Minster (9th–14th-c), Werden Abbey church; Baldeney Festival (summer). » Germany [i]; Ruhr, River

Essenes [eseenz] A Jewish sect renowned in antiquity for its asceticism, communistic life-style, and skill in predicting the future. The famous Dead Sea Scrolls are believed to have belonged to a local Essene community. » Dead Sea Scrolls; Qumran, Community of

essential amino acids » **amino acid** [i]

essential fatty acids » **carboxylic acids**

essential oil A natural volatile oil produced by plants, giving a distinctive aromatic scent to the foliage. Mostly terpenoids, they help to reduce water loss by evaporating and forming a barrier around the leaf surface; the oil glands can often be seen as shining coloured dots scattered over the foliage or flowers. Common in plants from hot dry habitats, both the quality and quantity of oil is to some extent dependent on the amount of sunshine received. » attar; mint; oil (botany); patchouli; terpene

essentialism A doctrine, articulated by Aristotle and many subsequent philosophers, which claims that everything has a nature or essence – a cluster of properties such that if the thing were to lose any one of them, it would cease to be. Being a mammal is an essential property of a cow; in contrast, being brown is an *accidental* property, something a cow could lose without ceasing to be. Some philosophers have claimed that each individual thing has its own non-repeatable individual essence, or *haecceity*. Leibniz claimed that *every* property is essential to its possessor. Other philosophers, including the Pragmatists, have attacked the doctrine of essentialism. » Aristotle; Leibniz; pragmatism

Essequibo, River [esuhkeeboh] Largest river in Guyana, South America, draining over half the country; rises in the Guiana Highlands on the Brazilian border; flows c.970 km/600 ml N to meet the Atlantic at a 32 km/20 ml-wide delta, WNW of Georgetown; navigable for large vessels up to Bartica (c.80 km/50 ml); course interrupted by many rapids and falls. » Guyana [i]

Essex, Robert Devereux, 2nd Earl of (1566–1601) English soldier and courtier to Elizabeth I, born at Netherwood, Herefordshire. He served in the Netherlands (1585–6), and distinguished himself at Zutphen. At court, he quickly rose in the favour of Elizabeth, despite his clandestine marriage in

1590 with Sir Philip Sidney's widow. In 1591 he commanded the forces sent to help Henry IV of France, and took part in the sacking of Cadiz (1595). He became a Privy Councillor (1593) and Earl Marshal (1597). He alienated the Queen's advisers, and there were constant quarrels with Elizabeth (notably the occasion when he turned his back on her, and she boxed his ears). His six months' lord-lieutenancy of Ireland (1599) proved a failure; he was imprisoned and deprived of his dignities. He attempted to raise the City of London, was found guilty of high treason, and beheaded in the Tower. » Elizabeth I

Essex pop (1987e) 1 521 800; area 3 672 sq km/1 417 sq ml. County of SE England, divided into 14 districts; NE of London; bounded E by the North Sea and S by the Thames estuary; county town, Chelmsford; major towns include Harwich (ferry port), Colchester, Southend-on-Sea; agriculture (especially grain), oysters, electronics, motor vehicles, tourism. » Chelmsford; England [i]

Estado Novo [est**ah**doo **noh**voo] Literally, 'new state'; the name given by President Getúlio Vargas to his authoritarian regime in Brazil (1937–45). The term was copied from the Estado Novo established in Portugal by Dr Salazar. » Vargas; Salazar

estate duty A tax formerly payable in the UK by the family or descendants of a deceased person, based on the value of that person's estate – the sum of all assets of value held (including furniture, property, and investments). Small estates were exempt. The amount payable was varied by the government from time to time, and has now been replaced by the inheritance tax. » inheritance tax; taxation

ester A compound obtained by the condensation of an alcohol with an acid, as in the following example:

$$(CH_3CH_2OH) + (CH_3COOH) \rightarrow (CH_3COOCH_2CH_3) + (H_2O)$$

ethanol	acetic acid	ethyl acetate	water
(*alcohol*)	(*acid*)	(*ester*)	

Esters are named as if they were salts, the first part being derived from the alcohol, and the second part from the acid. Most simple esters have characteristic fruity odours: ethyl acetate has the odour of pears, and is also an important solvent. Vegetable and animal fats and oils are mainly esters of glycerol. » acid; alcohols; condensation (chemistry)

Esther, Book of A book of the Hebrew Bible/Old Testament, telling the popular story of how Esther, a cousin and foster daughter of the Jew, Mordecai, became the wife of the Persian king Ahasuerus (Xerxes I) and prevented the extermination of Jews by the order of Haman, a king's officer. The event is said to be the source of the Jewish feast of Purim. The **Additions to the Book of Esther** are several enhancements found in the Septuagint but not in the Hebrew Bible. They are part of the Old Testament Apocrypha, and appear as *Esther* 11–16 in the Catholic Bible. These chapters consist of Mordecai's dream and its interpretation, the prayers of Mordecai and Esther, and edicts issued by the king. They may supply a specifically religious perspective which the Book of Esther lacks. » Mordecai; Old Testament; Purim; Septuagint; Xerxes I

Esthetic Movement » **Aesthetic Movement**

Estigarribia, José Félix [esteegar**ee**beea] (1888–1940) Paraguayan general and war hero, born at Caraguatay, Paraguay. He won fame as a brilliant commander in the Chaco War, on the strength of which he became President (1939–40). He died in a plane crash near Asunción. » Chaco War; Paraguay [i]

Estonia, Est **Eesti**, Russ **Estonskaya** pop (1990e) 1 600 000; area 45 100 sq km/17 409 sq ml. Republic in E Europe, bounded W and N by the Baltic Sea; many islands on the coast, notably Saaremaa, Hiiumaa, Muhu; over 1 500 lakes; 36% forested; ceded to Russia, 1721; independence, 1918; proclaimed a Soviet Socialist Republic, 1940; occupied by Germany in World War 2; resurgence of nationalist movement in the 1980s; declared independence, 1991; capital, Tallinn; chief towns, Tartu, Narva, Kohtla-Järve; shale oil, machines, metalworking, chemicals, food processing, cotton fabrics, timber, dairy farming, pigs, fishing. » Baltic Sea; Soviet Union [i]; Tallinn

Estremadura (Portugal) [eeshtrema**doo**ra], Lat **Extrema Durii** ('farthest land on the Douro') area 3 249 sq km/1 254 sq ml. Province and former region of WC Portugal; chief town, Lisbon; vines, fruit, olives, wheat, maize, vegetables; sheep and goats in upland areas (N); thermal springs; the political and cultural centre of Portugal, as well as a popular tourist region. » Extremadura; Portugal [i]

estrildid finch » **finch**

estrogens » **oestrogens**

estuary A partly enclosed coastal water body connected with the open ocean and filled with sea water significantly diluted by fresh water run-off from land. Estuaries are among the most biologically productive areas on Earth. The addition of nutrient material from land via surface run-off is trapped by estuarine circulation patterns and continuously recycled by organisms.

Esztergom [ester**gom**], Ger **Gran**, ancient **Strigonium** 47°47N 18°44E, pop (1984e) 31 000. River-port town in Komárom county, N Hungary; on R Danube, NW of Budapest; fortress in Roman times; capital, 10th-c; seat of primate, 1198; railway; school of forestry; coal, lignite, wine, machinery; birthplace of St Stephen, Hungary's first king; 19th-c Basilica (largest church in Hungary); thermal springs nearby. » Hungary [i]

etching A form of intaglio printing invented in the early 16th-c, whereby the design on a copper plate is bitten with acid, rather than cut directly with the engraving tool (*burin*). The greatest master of the technique was Rembrandt. » aquatint; burin; drypoint; intaglio; Rembrandt

Eteocles [et**ee**okleez] In Greek legend, the elder of Oedipus' two sons, whom he both cursed. Eteocles became king of Thebes after his father's death, and refused to share power with his brother Polynices. Seven Champions attacked the city, and Eteocles was killed by Polynices. » Antigone; Creon; Polynices; Seven against Thebes

ethanal » **acetaldehyde**

ethane [eethayn, ethayn] C_2H_6, boiling point −89°C. The second member of the alkane series; the three-dimensional structure of its molecule is shown in the illustration. It is an odourless gas, used for refrigeration, which forms explosive mixtures with air. The molecular shape, two joined tetrahedra, is characteristic of the whole alkane series. The structure shown is the most stable conformation for the molecule. » alkanes

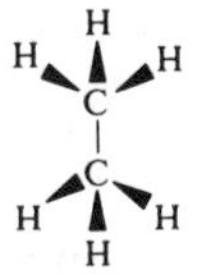

ethanedioic acid » **oxalic acid**

ethanoic acid [ethan**oh**ik] » **acetic acid**

ethanol CH_3CH_2OH, boiling point 78°, also called **ethyl alcohol, grain alcohol**, and simply **alcohol**. It is a colourless liquid with characteristic odour, mainly prepared by the fermentation of sugars. An important solvent, disinfectant, and preservative, it is mainly known for its intoxicating properties in beverages. » alcohols; sugars

ethanoyl » **acetyl**

Ethelbert (c.552–616) King of Kent (560–616). In his reign Kent achieved (c.590) control over England S of the Humber, and Christianity was introduced by St Augustine (597). To him we owe the first written English laws. » Anglo-Saxons; Augustine, St (of Canterbury)

Etheldreda, St (c.630–79), feast day 23 June. Daughter of the King of East Anglia, she was twice married, but withdrew first to the monastery founded by her aunt on St Abb's Head, and then to the Isle of Ely, where in 673 she founded a nunnery. Her name was corrupted into St Audrey. » Christianity; monasticism

Ethelred or **Aethelred I** (c.830–71) King of Wessex (865–71), the elder brother of Alfred the Great. During his reign the Danes launched their main invasion of England. He died soon after his victory over the invaders at Ashdown, Berkshire. » Alfred

Ethelred or **Aethelred**, byname **the Unready** (c.968–1016) King of England (from 978), the son of Edgar. He was aged about 10 when the murder of his half-brother, Edward the Martyr, placed him on the throne. In 1002 he confirmed an alliance with Normandy by marrying as his second wife Duke Richard's daughter Emma – the first dynastic link between the two countries. Renewed attacks by the Vikings on England began as raids in the 980s, and in 1013 Sweyn Forkbeard secured mastery over the whole country, and forced Ethelred into exile in Normandy. After Sweyn's death (1014), he returned to oppose Canute, but the unity of English resistance was broken when his son, Edmund Ironside, rebelled. He died in London. 'Unready' is a mistranslation of *Unraed*, not recorded as his nickname until after the Norman Conquest, which means 'ill advised' and is a pun on his given name, Aethelred (literally, 'good counsel'). » Canute; Edmund Ironside; Sweyn; Vikings

Ethelred of Rievaulx » **Ailred of Rievaulx**

ethene » **ethylene**

ether [eether] **1** An organic compound containing an oxygen atom bonded to two alkyl groups. Ethers are relatively unreactive compounds. The best known is *ethyl ether* (CH_3CH_2–O–CH_2CH_3), a volatile liquid, boiling point 35°C, used as an anaesthetic. » alkyl; oxygen **2** A substance once believed to pervade all space, thought necessary as the medium of the propagation of light; also spelled **aether**. The Michelson-Morley experiment was important in demonstrating the absence of ether, which is no longer required by the modern theory of light. » light; Michelson

Etherege, Sir George (1635–92) English Restoration dramatist, born (probably) at Maidenhead, Berkshire. His three plays, *The Comical Revenge; or, Love in a Tub* (1664); *She Would if She Could* (1668); and *The Man of Mode; or, Sir Fopling Flutter* (1676), were highly popular in their day, and introduced the comedy of manners to English theatre. He died in Paris. » drama; English literature; Restoration

ethics In philosophy, the theoretical study of human values and conduct. Its two main branches are normative ethics and metaethics. **Normative ethics** attempts to address such topics as what sort of life we should live, and what sorts of things have ultimate value. **Metaethics** seeks to determine whether the pronouncements of normative ethics are objective, to clarify the meanings of normative concepts, and to investigate what kinds of justification normative judgments might have. Ethical theory is distinct from the results of empirical research done on different cultures and societies by anthropologists and sociologists. Thus an *objectivist* claims that there are some ultimate principles of rightness and wrongness which should govern the behaviour of all societies, independent of what societies might happen to believe. A *relativist* claims that nothing is absolutely right or wrong, even if all cultures believe the contrary. *Subjectivists* argue that because many moral disputes appear to be irresoluble, there is no objective justification in ethics. Several distinct theoretical approaches have been taken up by philosophers within these general positions. » Categorical Imperative; deontological ethics; egoism; intuitionism; naturalism; relativism; teleological ethics; utilitarianism

Ethiopia [eetheeohpia], formerly **Abyssinia**, official name **Socialist Ethiopia**, Amharic **Hebretesebawit Ityopia** pop (1990e) 50 340 000; area 1 221 918 sq km/471 660 sq ml. State of NE Africa, divided into 15 regions; bounded W and SW by Sudan, S by Kenya, E and NE by Somalia, and N by Djibouti and the Red Sea; capital, Addis Ababa; chief towns Asmara, Jimma, Dire Dawa; timezone GMT +3; ethnic groups include Galla (40%), Amhara and Tigray (32%); chief religions, Islam (40–45%), Ethiopian Orthodox (35–40%); official language, Amharic; unit of currency, the Ethiopian birr of 100 cents.

Physical description. Dominated by mountainous C plateau, mean elevation 1 800–2 400 m/6 000–8 000 ft; split diagonally by the Great Rift Valley; highest point, Ras Dashan Mt (4 620 m/15 157 ft); crossed E–W by Blue Nile, source in L Tana; N and E relatively low-lying; Danakil Depression (NE) dips to 116 m/381 ft below sea-level.

Climate. Tropical, moderated by higher altitudes; distinct wet season (Apr–Sep); temperatures warm, but rarely hot all year round; annual rainfall generally over 1 000 mm/40 in; Addis Ababa, 1 236 mm/48.7 in, average maximum daily temperatures 21–25°C; hot, semi-arid NE and SE lowlands receive less than 500 mm/20 in annually; severe droughts in 1980s caused widespread famine, deaths, and resettlement, with massive amounts of foreign aid.

History and government. Oldest independent country in sub-

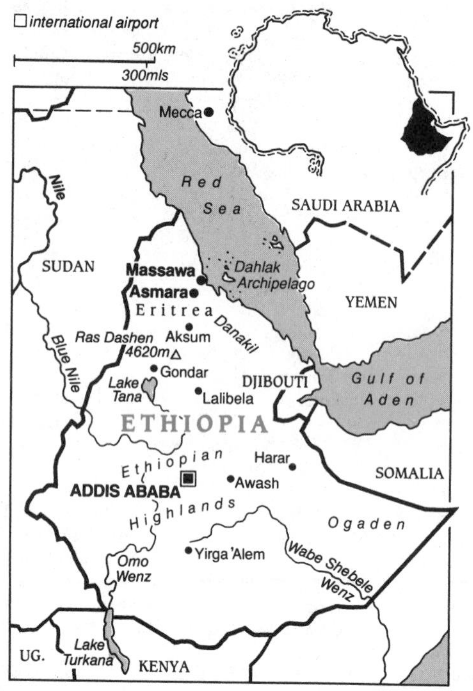

Saharan Africa; first Christian country in Africa; Eritrea occupied by Italy, 1882; Abyssinian independence recognized by League of Nations, 1923; Italian invasion, 1935; annexation as Italian East Africa, 1936–41; Haile Selassie returned from exile, 1941; military coup, with formation of Provisional Military Administrative Council (PMAC), 1974; opposition by left-wing civilian groups countered by mass arrests and executions, 1977–8; ongoing conflict with Somalia over Ogaden region; internal conflict with regional separatist Eritrean and Tigrean forces; government offensive successful in 1978, but received setbacks in early 1980s; PMAC dissolved, 1987, with transfer of power to People's Democratic Republic; plans for provisional government in Eritrea; 87-member Council of Representatives.

Economy. One of the world's poorest countries; over 80% of population employed in agriculture, especially subsistence farming; exports mainly coffee, also sugar, cotton, pulses, oil seeds; production severely affected by drought; small amounts of oil, gold, cement, salt; food processing, tobacco, textiles; distribution of foreign aid hindered by internal conflicts and poor local organization. » Addis Ababa; Dergue; Eritrea; Haile Selassie; Mengistu; Ogaden; Tigray; RR25 national holidays; RR48 political leaders

Ethiopian Churches Separatist African churches which have broken away from parent missionary bodies, and which seek to select those aspects of Christianity deemed appropriate to African cultural and social needs. They take their inspiration from the Donatist and Coptic churches, and have appeared in W, C, and S Africa. Some have been apolitical, but many have become a focus for political discontent. » Coptic Church; Donatists; Ethiopia [i]

Ethiopianism A form of nationalist movement founded among US and W Indian Blacks which looks towards Africa (Ethiopia being used as a synonym for Africa) as their place of origin. It is connected with messianism and the independent Black Churches that broke away from established Christianity. A major example was the Universal Negro Improvement Association founded by Marcus Garvey in 1914, which preached a form of African nationalism and self-development, as well as proposing a return to Africa. » Black Zionism; messianism

ethnic group A segment of a population within a society who share common descent (actual or putative), attitudes and behaviour, and cultural and physical characteristics, and who perceive themselves as a distinct group. » ethnic relations; ethnicity

ethnic relations The interactions between different ethnic groups within a society. The main forms are *assimilation*, where ethnic groups adopt common cultural patterns, and eventually merge; *domination*, where one ethnic group controls the other(s), establishing its culture as the main one; and *consociationalism*, as in Switzerland, where groups retain distinct cultures and identity, but are more or less equal. » ethnicity

ethnicity A term which may be confused with 'race', but which refers to a shared cultural identity that has a range of distinctive behavioural and possibly linguistic features, passed on through socialization from one generation to another. There are never clear boundaries, cultural or geographic, that mark the limits of ethnic groups, even though many regard ethnicity as though it were naturally determined. Ethnic differences have been a source of political unrest, often associated with religious or clan difference. » ethnic group/relations; ethnocentrism; race

ethnocentrism A limited or parochial perspective which evaluates other societies and their cultures according to one's own cultural expectations. It implies a very restricted understanding of foreign cultures, and a notion that one's own is not only different, but 'better'. Ethnocentric comments are often heard emanating from disdainful but narrow-minded tourists. » ethnicity

ethnography A detailed description of the culture of a particular society, based on fieldwork by ethnographers or anthropologists, using the method of participant observation. In Europe, the subject is often referred to as **ethnology**. » anthropology; ethnography of communication; ethnomethodology

ethnography of communication The study of the correlations between language and ethnic types and behaviour. It includes a wide range of cultural activities, such as speech-making, conventions of greeting and leave-taking, religious rituals, and marriage ceremonies. More generally, it includes the study of the social variables which lead to culturally-based misunderstandings between the participants in a discourse. » ethnography; sociolinguistics

ethnohistory A historical discipline which emerged from anthropology, principally concerned with the reconstruction of the histories of non-literate peoples using oral techniques. It has enjoyed some remarkable successes, in that the past of peoples formerly thought not to have a history in the conventional sense have offered insights for the history of the human race as a whole. The term is now unfashionable, implying a distinction no longer accepted by many historians. » African history; history

ethnolinguistics The study of the relationship between language and culture. It is concerned with all aspects of language, including its structure and usage, which have any connection with culture and society. » culture; ethnography; linguistics

ethnomethodology The sociological theory developed out of the work of the US sociologist Harold Garfinkel (1917–) and others in the 1960s. It studies the methods people use to accomplish successful social interaction, and is derived from earlier phenomenological and symbolic interactionist theories. » ethnography; phenomenology; sociology; symbolic interactionism

ethnomusicology The scientific study of folk and national music, especially that of non-Western countries, in its anthropological, cultural, and social contexts. Studies of some remote or exotic musical cultures were made in the 18th–19th-c, but because ethnomusicology deals with oral traditions, it was not until sound recording became easily available that the discipline could establish itself widely and on a scientific basis. » African/Chinese/folk/Japanese/Javanese music; musicology

ethnoscience A branch of social/cultural anthropology which investigates folk beliefs or ideologies that correspond to such fields of Western science as medicine, astronomy, and zoology. » anthropology; ethnography; sociology

ethology [eet**hol**uhjee] The study of animal behaviour from the viewpoint of zoology and ecology. It considers the fine details of individual species behaviour in relation to properties of the natural environment to which the species has adapted (its *ecological niche*). The data are derived from direct observation and monitoring (eg by radio-tracking) of animals under natural or quasi-natural conditions. It assumes that most aspects of feeding, prey-predator interaction, and reproductive, competitive, and social behaviour are explicable in terms of (1) the past evolutionary selection pressures influencing the species' genetic endowment, and (2) the physiological or environmental conditions typically present during the natural development of species members. » ecology; Lorenz; Tinbergen; zoology

ethyl [**ee**thiyl, **e**thil] C_2H_5–. A functional group derived from ethane. Adding it to a name usually indicates its substitution for hydrogen in that compound. » ethane

ethyl alcohol » **ethanol**

ethylene [**e**thileen] $CH_2=CH_2$, IUPAC **ethene**, boiling point −104°C. A colourless gas, the first member of the alkene series. It is a very important industrial chemical, which polymerizes to *polyethylene*. Small traces hasten the ripening of fruit. » alkenes; IUPAC

ethyne [**ee**thiyn] » **acetylene**

Etna, Mount [**et**na], in Sicily **Mongibello** 37°45N 15°00E. Isolated volcanic mountain in Catania province, E Sicily, Italy, 29 km/18 ml NNW of Catania; height 3 323 m/10 902 ft; Europe's largest active volcano; recent major eruptions, 1949, 1971; over 200 subsidiary cones, notably Monti Rossi (948 m/3 110 ft); fertile lower slopes, growing oranges, lemons, olives, vines; forest and maquis higher up, and a desert zone of lava and ashes; snow-covered nine months of the year; solar power station *Eurhelios* on S slope, average annual sunshine 3 000 hours. » maquis; Sicily; volcano; RR14

Eton » **Windsor** (UK)

Etruria [et**roo**ria] The heartland of the Etruscan people, roughly corresponding to modern Tuscany. In antiquity, it was defined as the area between the Arno, Tiber, Apennines, and Tyrrhenian Sea. » Etruscans

Etruscan art The art which flourished 7th–2nd-c BC in what is now Tuscany, containing a mixture of native Italian, Greek, and oriental elements. It can be seen in many lively and colourful wall-paintings in tombs, sculptured sarcophagi, pottery, and decorative metalwork. » art; Etruscans; Italian art

Etruscans A people of obscure origin who sprang to prominence in WC Italy in the 8th-c BC. At the height of their power their influence extended from the Po valley to Campania, taking in Rome itself. Although they succumbed to the Romans politically in the 3rd-c BC, culturally their influence remained strong. In religion, civil engineering, and urban planning the Romans owed much to them. Their lavishly equipped tombs show that they were particularly skilled in metal work, and heavily engaged in trade with the Greek world. » Etruria; Etruscan art

Etty, William (1787–1849) British painter, born and died in York. He studied at the Royal Academy Schools, then with Lawrence, and in 1822–3 went to Italy, where he was deeply influenced by the Venetian masters. He depicted Classical and historical subjects, and became renowned for his nudes. » English art; Lawrence, Thomas; Venetian School

etymology The study of the origins of the form and meaning of words and their history; a branch of historical linguistics. The 'parent' of a later word form is known as its *etymon*. Words can be mistakenly analysed in relation to some similarity of form or meaning with other words, to give a **folk etymology**, as when asparagus is referred to as 'sparrow-grass'. The **etymological fallacy** maintains that the 'real' meaning of a word is an earlier or 'original' one, eg that *villain* really means 'farm labourer', because it had this meaning several hundred years ago. » linguistics; semantics

Euboea [yoo**bee**a], Gr **Évvoia**, Ital **Negropon** pop (1981) 185 626; area 3 655 sq km/1 411 sq ml. Second largest Greek island, in the Aegean Sea, separated from the mainland by a narrow channel; length 144 km/89 ml; rises to 1 744 m/5 722 ft; capital, Chalcis; chief towns Istiaia, Kimi, and Karistos; olives, grapes, cereals, sheep, goats; several tourist resorts on coast. » Aegean Sea; Chalcis; Greece [i]

eucalyptus » **gum tree**

eucaryote or **eukaryote** [yookarioht] An organism in which cells have an organized nucleus, surrounded by a nuclear envelope, with paired chromosomes containing DNA that are recognizable during mitosis and meiosis. It includes all animals, plants, fungi, and many micro-organisms. » cell; DNA [i]; meiosis [i]; mitosis; nucleus (biology); procaryote

Eucharist (Gr *eucharistia*, 'thanksgiving') For most Christian denominations, a sacrament and the central act of worship, sometimes called the *Mass* (Roman Catholic), *Holy Communion*, or *Lord's Supper* (Protestant). It is based on the example of Jesus at the Last Supper, when he identified the bread which he broke and the wine which he poured with his body and blood (1 *Cor* 11.23–5; *Matt* 26.26–8; *Mark* 14.22–4; *Luke* 22.17–20), and generally consists of the consecration of bread and wine by the priest or minister and distribution among the worshippers (*communion*). Theological interpretations vary from the literal transformation of the elements into the body and blood of Christ, re-enacting his sacrifice on the Cross, through different interpretations such as transubstantiation and consubstantiation, to symbolism representing the real presence of Christ and a simple memorial meal. » Christianity; communion; consubstantiation; Jesus Christ; real presence; sacrament; transubstantiation

euchromatin [yookrohmatin] » **heterochromatin**

Euclid, Gr **Eucleides** (4th–3rd-c BC) Greek mathematician who taught in Alexandria about 300 BC, and was probably the founder of its mathematical school. His chief extant work is the 13-volume *Elements*, which became the most widely known mathematical book of classical antiquity, and is still much used in geometry. The approach which obeys his axioms became known as **Euclidean geometry**. » geometries, non-Euclidean; geometry

Eudoxos of Cnidus (c.408 BC–c.353 BC) Greek geometer and astronomer, born and died at Cnidus, Asia Minor. In geometry, he established principles that laid the foundation for Euclid, then applied the subject to the study of the Moon and planets. He introduced an ingenious system of 27 nested spheres in an attempt to explain planetary motion. » astronomy; Euclid; geometry

Eugene [yoojeen] 44°05N 123°04W, pop (1980) 105 624. Capital of Lane County, W Oregon, USA, on the Willamette R; founded, 1851; airfield; railway; university (1872); timber, food processing, tourism. » Oregon

Eugene of Savoy, Prince, properly **François Eugène de Savoie Carignan** (1663–1736) Austrian general, born in Paris. He was refused a commission by Louis XIV of France, and entered the service of the Emperor Leopold against the Turks. Made field marshal in 1693, he defeated the Turks on several occasions, putting an end to their power in Hungary (1699–1718). He fought against France in two wars between 1689 and 1714, and while in command of the imperial army he helped Marlborough at Blenheim (1704), Oudenarde (1708), and Malplaquet (1709). Crippled by the withdrawal of Holland and England, he was defeated by Villars (1712). He later won several further victories against the Turks, capturing Belgrade in 1718. He died in Vienna. » Grand Alliance, War of the; Marlborough, Duke of; Spanish Succession, War of the

eugenics [yoojeniks] The science that deals with the effects on the individual of biological and social factors. The term was coined in 1883 by Francis Galton as 'the science which deals with all influences that improve the inborn qualities'. The responsible study of eugenics was made difficult in the earlier years of this century by the propagation (eg in Germany and the USA) of political doctrines, in the name of eugenics, which are now seen as non-scientific, illiberal, or inhumane. Today the science has evolved to a position where biologists, clinicians, demographers, sociologists, and other professionals can work together with the aim of increasing understanding of the human species and improving the quality of life. » Eugenics Society

Eugenics Society A society founded in London in 1907 as the Eugenics Education Society, adopting its present name in 1926. Its American counterpart changed its name in 1971 to the Society for the Study of Social Biology, to meet the changing orientation of the subject. With the arrival of modern genetic knowledge, and particularly of clinical genetics, much of the Society's earlier activity (eg in family planning, genetic advisory work, monitoring changes in the population) has been incorporated into the National Health Service and other government departments. Today the Society sponsors lectures, symposia, and publications, and promotes research into the biological, genetic, social, and cultural factors relating to human reproduction, development, and health. » eugenics

Eugénie, Empress » **Napoleon III**

Euglena [yoogleena] A freshwater, single-celled micro-organism with a whip-like flagellum at its front end used for swimming; usually contains chlorophyll in chloroplasts, and classified as a green alga (class: *Chlorophyceae*); sometimes lacks chlorophyll, and classified as a protozoan flagellate (phylum: *Mastigophora*); feeds by ingestion of organic material. » chlorophyll; chloroplast; flagellum; green algae; Protozoa; systematics

Eulenspiegel, Till [oylenshpeegl] A legendary 14th-c peasant prankster of Brunswick, Germany, who through his jokes, which consisted largely in taking figuratively-expressed commands literally, revenged himself on a narrow-minded bourgeoisie. He is celebrated in an epic poem by Gerhard Hauptmann (1928) and musically in a tone poem by Richard Strauss (1894).

Euler, Leonhard [oyler] (1707–83) Swiss mathematician, born at Basle. He studied at Basle, then in 1727 moved to St Petersburg, where he became professor of physics (1730) and mathematics (1733). In 1741 he went to Berlin, returning to St Petersburg in 1766. A highly prolific scholar, his many works dealt with number theory, geometry, calculus, and several applications in astronomy and technology. His *Lettres à une princesse d'Allemagne* (1768–72, Letters to a German Princess) expounded the most important facts in physics. He died, totally blind, in St Petersburg. Several important notions in mathematics are named after him. **Euler's constant** (usually denoted by γ) is the limit, as $n \to \infty$, of $1 + \frac{1}{2} + \frac{1}{3} + \frac{1}{4}\, n \to \infty \ldots 1/n - \log_e n$, approximately 0.577. **Euler's function** (denoted by $\phi(n)$) refers to the number of integers in the set $1,2,3,\ldots n-1$ which are prime to n; thus $\phi(9)=6$, since 6 of the integers $1,2,3,\ldots 8$ are prime to 9. **Euler's formula for polyhedra** states that if a polyhedron has v vertices, f faces, and e edges, $v+f-e=2$ for all polyhedra; thus a cube has 8 vertices, 12 edges, and 6 faces, and $8+6-12=2$. A **Euler line** can be shown for any triangle, where the centre O of the circumcircle, the orthocentre H, and the centroid G lie on a straight line, and $OG{:}GH=1{:}2$. » polyhedron

Euler-Lagrange equations A set of equations relating the velocity, time, and space dependence of a Lagrangian; also known as **Lagrange's equations**; named after Swiss mathematician Leonhard Euler and French mathematician Joseph-Louis

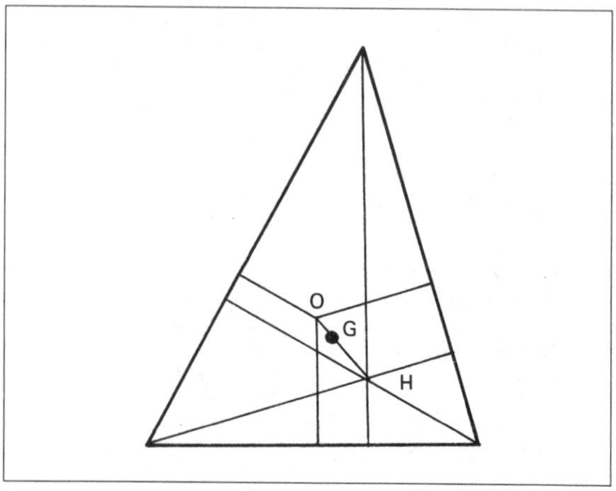

Euler line – OG:GH = 1:2

Lagrange. Given the Lagrangian for some mechanical system, then the Euler–Lagrange equations give the equations of motion for that system. They are central to advanced mechanics. » action; Euler; Lagrangian; least-action principle

Eumenides [yoo**men**ideez] A euphemistic name given to the Furies after being domesticated at Athens in Aeschylus' play of the same name. The name means 'the kindly ones'. » Aeschylus; Erinyes

Eumycota [yoo**mi**ysuhta] » **fungus**

Eupen [**uh**puhn] 50°38N 6°02E, pop (1982) 16 788. Town in E Liège province, Belgium; principal town in German-speaking Belgium; popular health resort (Kneipp water-cure) and holiday centre; largest artificial lake in Belgium; railway; textiles, artificial fibres, tourism, cables and wires; St Nicholas Church (1727); carnival (Nov). » Belgium [i]

euphonium A musical instrument of the tuba family, much used in brass bands and occasionally in orchestral music. » brass instrument [i]; tuba

euphorbia » **spurge**

euphotic zone » **epipelagic environments**

Euphrates, River [yoo**fray**teez], Arabic **Al Furat**, Turkish **Firat** Longest river in W Asia; length 2 735 km/1 700 ml; formed in EC Turkey by the confluence of the Kara (W Euphrates) and Murat; flows generally S to the Syrian border, then SE into Iraq; unites with the Tigris NW of Basra to form the Shatt al-Arab, which flows for 192 km/119 ml to enter the Arabian Gulf; upper course flows swiftly through deep canyons; used extensively for irrigation in Syria; canals link with R Tigris; remains of several ancient cities (eg Babylon, Erech, Larsa, Borsippa) along present or former banks. » Iraq [i]

EURATOM An acronym for the **European Atomic Energy Commission**, one of the bodies set up during the general movement towards Europeanization in the 1950s. It was originally established as an independent body by the Treaty of Rome (1957), but was brought into the EEC with the European Iron and Steel Community in 1962. Its objectives are the promotion of peaceful uses of atomic energy. » European Economic Community; nuclear reactor [i]

Eureka In Australian history, an armed clash between gold-miners and a combined police and military force at the Eureka Stockade, Ballarat, Victoria, (1854), which cost the lives of 30 miners and 5 soldiers, with many others wounded. The miners had objected to the expensive mining licence imposed by the government. Public opinion swung behind the miners, reforms to the goldfields were carried out, and the government was forced to back down. » Australian gold rush

eurhythmics [yoo**rith**miks] A system of musical training devised by Jaques-Dalcroze, designed to develop a quick response to changing rhythms by fitting bodily movements to pieces of music. » Jaques-Dalcroze

Euripides [yoo**rip**ideez] (c.480–406 BC) Greek tragic dramatist, born in Athens. He abandoned painting for literature, writing about 80 dramas, of which 19 survive, such as *Alcestis*, *Medea*, *Orestes*, and *Electra*. The *Bacchae* and *Ipigenia in Aulis* were put on the Athenian stage only after the author's death, when his work became very popular. He died at the court of Archelaus, King of Macedonia. » drama; Greek literature; tragedy

Eurocommunism An attempt by W European communist parties to fashion a programme and organization more appropriate to liberal democracies and market economies. The Italian communist party was at the forefront, and achieved the most in reform. Such refashioning of Marxism-Leninism has not led to a resurgence of communism, however, and did not receive support from the Soviet communist party. » communism; Marxism-Leninism

Eurocurrency » **Euromoney**

Eurodollar US dollars held in banks in W Europe. Considerable sums are involved, resulting from such major concerns as the oil industry, where trade is conducted in dollars. They may be borrowed by companies, as Eurodollar loans, and are particularly useful when international trade is planned. » dollar; Euromoney

Eurofighter The name given to the standardized air-to-air and ground-attack aircraft which will equip the air forces of Great Britain, Germany, Spain, and the Netherlands by the mid-1990s. A major multi-national collaborative development programme is involved. » air force

Euromoney or **Eurocurrency** Convertible currencies such as pounds sterling, French and Swiss francs, Deutschmarks, and US dollars held in banks in W Europe, but outside the country of origin. They can be borrowed by commercial undertakings for trade. » currency; Eurodollar

Europa (astronomy) The second natural satellite of Jupiter, discovered by Galileo in 1610; distance from the planet 671 000 km/417 000 ml; diameter 3 400 km/1 925 ml; orbital period 3.551 days. It has a crust of ice/water 75–100 km/50–60 ml thick. It was seen only distantly by Voyager as a bright globe criss-crossed by dark curvilinear markings (typically 20–40 km/15–25 ml wide and thousands of km long), which may be of tectonic origin. » Galilean moons; Jupiter (astronomy); Voyager project [i]; RR4

Europa (mythology) [yoo**roh**pa] or **Europe** [yoo**roh**pee] In Greek mythology, the daughter of Agenor, king of Tyre, who was abducted by Zeus in the shape of a bull, and swam with her on his back to Crete. Her children were Minos and Rhadamanthus. » Cadmus; Zeus

Europa Nostra (Ital 'our Europe') An international federation established in 1963 for the preservation of historic sites, buildings, and monuments. It represents more than 200 organizations from 20 countries. » English Heritage

Europe Second smallest continent, forming an extensive peninsula of the Eurasian land-mass, occupying c.7% of the Earth's surface; bounded N and NE by the Arctic Ocean, NW and W by the Atlantic Ocean, S by the Mediterranean Sea, and E by Asia beyond the Ural Mts; supports over 25% of the world's population; major rivers include the Danube, Rhine, Rhône, Loire, and Tagus; major mountain systems include the Alps, rising to 4 807 m/15 771 ft at Mont Blanc, and the Pyrenees, rising to 3 404 m/11 168 ft at Pico de Aneto. » European Commission / Community / Council / Economic Community / Parliament; RR12

European Atomic Energy Commission » **EURATOM**

European Atomic Energy Community » **European Community**

European Coal and Steel Community (ECSC) The first European economic institution, set up in 1952. It has worked to remove customs duties and quota restrictions in coal, iron ore, and scrap, and aims to ensure that competition in these commodities is fair. » European Economic Community

European Commission The administrative bureaucracy of the European Community, conducting both political and administrative tasks. Its functions are to uphold the European ideal, propose new policy initiatives, and ensure that existing policies are implemented. In a narrow sense it comprises 17 commissioners directly nominated by the member states; the UK, France, Germany, Italy, and Spain each nominate two commissioners, the rest one each. They serve a 4-year term, are each responsible for a specific area of work, and are supported by a bureaucracy employing c.15 000 people. The Commission decides by majority vote, and is collectively responsible to the European Parliament, which can remove it on a censure motion carried by a two-thirds majority. The Commission was originally intended, as a true supranational institution, to be the main source of direction and decision-making within the Community, but in practice this role has fallen to the Council of Ministers. » European Community/Council/Parliament

European Community (EC) A community of twelve states in W Europe created for the purpose of achieving economic and political integration. It comprises three communities. The first of these was the *European Coal and Steel Community*, established in 1952 under the Treaty of Paris by France, West Germany, Italy, Belgium, the Netherlands, and Luxembourg. It created common institutions for regulating the coal and steel industries under a common framework of law and institutions, thereby producing the first breach in the principle of national sovereignty. In the early 1950s, unsuccessful attempts were made to establish a European Defence Community and a European Political Community. In 1958, under the Treaty of Rome, the six states established the *European Economic Com-*

munity and the *European Atomic Energy Community*, which provided for collaboration in the civilian sector of nuclear power. Six members have been added to the original six: Denmark, Ireland, and the UK (1973); Greece (1981); and Portugal and Spain (1986). Turkey is seeking to become a member. To develop and oversee the policies of economic and political integration there are a number of supranational community institutions: the Commission, the Council, the European Parliament, and the European Court of Justice. While the Community has grown in the 1970s and 1980s and continues to progress towards economic integration, a political union seems still a distant possibility. » Council of Ministers; Court of Justice of the European Community; EURATOM; European Commission/Council/Defence Community/Economic Community/Monetary System/Parliament

European Council The body which brings together the heads of state and/or government of the member states of the European Community. Since the mid-1960s, when President de Gaulle demanded the right of veto over any decision taken by the Council (formalized in the Luxembourg Accord), it has tended to take decisions on the basis of unanimity rather than majority voting. The need for agreement among 12 states has resulted in severe difficulties in achieving reform, particularly in the area of agriculture. » Council of Ministers; de Gaulle; European Community

European court dance A dance tradition based on 16th-c and 17th-c dances such as the pavane, galliard, and courante. Later the minuet, gigue, gavotte, bourrée, sarabande, and hornpipe were popular. These dance forms were the forerunners of the quadrille and lancers. The 19th-c saw the introduction of the waltz and the polka. » traditional dance

European Court of Justice » **Court of Justice of the European Communities**

European Currency Unit (ECU) » **European Monetary System**

European Defence Community A supranational community which was to ensure the security of its members against aggression, and produce a more coherent grouping than the North Atlantic Treaty Organization. A treaty was signed in May 1952 by the six members of the European Steel and Coal Community (other W European countries could join) but was never ratified by the French parliament, and the project was abandoned. » European Community; NATO; Western European Union

European Economic Community (EEC) An association within the European Community, established in 1958 after the Treaties of Rome (1957), often referred to as the **Common Market**. It is essentially a customs union, with a common external tariff and a common market with the removal of barriers to trade among the members. In addition it has a number of common policies, the most important of which is the Common Agricultural Policy, providing for external tariffs to protect domestic agriculture and mechanisms for price support. The cost of support to agriculture takes up about 70% of the European Community's budget and has shown an alarming propensity to grow. Reform of agricultural policy has been on the agenda for a number of years, but many member governments are reluctant to entertain the wrath of the farming vote which remains sizable in their countries. There are common policies for fisheries, regional development, industrial intervention, and economic and social affairs. There is also a European Monetary System, which regulates exchange rate movements among the member states' currencies in an attempt to achieve monetary stability. In 1986 the Single European Act was passed, allowing for the completion of the process of creating a common market within the Community by 1992. This will generate further competition among the industries of member states. » Common Agricultural Policy; customs union; European Community / Council / Commission / Monetary System/Parliament

European Free Trade Association (EFTA) An association originally of seven W European states who were not members of the European Economic Community (EEC), intended as a counter to the EEC; it was established in 1959 under the Stockholm Convention. The members (Austria, Denmark, Norway, Portugal, Sweden, Switzerland, and the UK) agreed to eliminate over a period of time trade restrictions between them, without having to bring into line individual tariffs and trade policies with other countries. Agriculture was excluded from the agreement, although individual arrangements were permitted. Both the UK (1973) and Portugal (1986) left to join the EEC, but there has been a free trade agreement between the remaining EFTA countries and the European Community, and considerable trade between the two groupings. Finland joined in 1985. » European Economic Community

European Monetary System (EMS) A financial system set up in 1979 by members of the EEC with the aim of stabilizing and harmonizing currencies. Member-states use a special currency – the **European Currency Unit (ECU)**. A percentage of members' foreign exchange reserves is deposited with the European Monetary Co-operation Fund, and ECUs are received in exchange. Members join an **exchange rate mechanism (ERM)** which regulates currency exchange fluctuations. (Exchange rates are allowed to float within narrow bands only, except for the Spanish peseta.) This mechanism is sometimes called the 'snake', though this term strictly refers to the international currency agreement of 1971 (the Smithsonian Agreement), originally termed 'the snake in the tunnel', because an individual currency was not allowed to fluctuate by more than ± 2.25 per cent. The present system has a similar margin, except for the Spanish peseta (± 6 per cent). Sterling joined the ERM in 1990. » currency; European Economic Community

European Parliament The representative assembly of the European Community. Despite its name, it has no legislative powers, but it does have the right to be consulted by the Council, to dismiss the Commission (a right never so far used), and to reject or amend the Community budget (exercised in 1979, 1984, 1985, and 1986). The more forceful role played by the Parliament in recent years reflects the fact that it has been directly elected since 1979. European-wide elections are held every five years, with seats divided as follows: UK, France, Germany, and Italy (81); Spain (60); the Netherlands (25); Belgium, Greece, and Portugal (24); Denmark (16); Ireland (15); and Luxembourg (6). The administration of the Parliament lies in Luxembourg; its plenary sessions are held in Strasbourg; and its committees are in Brussels, where the Commission is based and the Councils meet. » European Community

European Recovery Program » **Marshall Plan**

European Southern Observatory (ESO) An agency of eight member states founded in 1962 to operate a European astronomical observatory in the S hemisphere. It is a world-class observatory with a number of optical telescopes, the largest of which is the 3.6 m aperture at La Silla, Chile (2 430 m/7 972 ft), and a share in a sub-millimetre telescope. Construction has begun of an array of four 8 m aperture telescopes (ESO VLT), which can be combined to form an effective 16 m telescope. The European headquarters is at Garching, Munich, Germany; this also houses the Space Telescope European Co-ordinating Facility. » observatory [i]; telescope [i]

European Space Agency (ESA) A consortium space agency of 13 European countries (Belgium, Denmark, Germany, France, Ireland, Italy, the Netherlands, Spain, Sweden, Switzerland, UK (founding nations) together with Austria and Norway, and associate member Finland) to promote space research, technology, and applications for exclusively peaceful purposes; Canada also participates in some programmes. It was created in 1975 as an amalgamation of two predecessors – the European Space Research Organization (ESRO) and the European Launcher Development Organization (ELDO). Its headquarters is in Paris, where programme plans originate. Projects are managed from the European Space Research and Technology Centre (ESTEC) in Noordwijk, Netherlands, which is also the centre for space technology development. Orbital spacecraft operations are managed by the European Space Operations Centre (ESOC) in Darmstadt, Germany. Launches use the Ariane family of vehicles from a launch centre in Kourou, French Guiana. » Giotto project; launch vehicles [i]; space exploration; Spacelab; Ulysses project

European Steel and Coal Community » European Community

Europort » Rotterdam

Eurovision Song Contest An annual contest organized by television companies throughout Europe to choose a winning pop song from among those entered by the participating countries. The first was held at Lugano, Switzerland, in 1956; since then it has been customary for the winning country to host the following year's contest. » pop music

Eurydice [yoo**ri**disee] In Greek mythology, a dryad, the wife of Orpheus. After her death, Orpheus went down to the Underworld and persuaded Hades to let her go by the power of his music. The condition was that she should follow him, and that he should not look at her until they reached the light. Not hearing her footsteps, he looked back, and she disappeared. » Aristaeus; dryad; Orpheus

eurypterid [joo**rip**tuhrid] An extinct, aquatic water scorpion; large, up to 3 m/10 ft in length; resembling a scorpion with a stout body bearing fangs anteriorly and a long, slender tail; known from the Ordovician period to the end of the Palaeozoic era. (Phylum: *Arthropoda*. Class: *Eurypterida*.) » arthropod; Ordovician period; Palaeozoic era; scorpion

Eusebio [yoo**say**bioh], properly **Eusebio Ferreira da Silva**, byname **The Black Pearl** (1942–) Portuguese footballer, born in Lourenço Marques, Mozambique. He was largely responsible for Portugal's rise in international football in the 1960s. He made his international debut in 1961, and played for his country 77 times. At club level he played for Benfica, winning 15 Portuguese League and Cup winner's medals. He appeared in four European Cup finals, winning just once, in 1962. He retired in 1978 after a brief spell playing in the USA, and was later appointed coach to Benfica. » football [i]

Eusebius of Caesarea [yoo**see**beeus] (c.264–340) Historian of the early Church, born (probably) in Palestine. He became Bishop of Caesarea c.313, and in the Council of Nicaea held a moderate position between the views of Arius and Athanasius. His great work, the *Ecclesiastical History*, is a record of the chief events in the Christian Church until 324. » Arius; Athanasius, St; Christianity

Eustachian tube [joo**stay**shuhn] A tube connecting the middle ear to the nasopharynx, made partly of bone and cartilage, and lined with mucous membrane; named after Italian physician Bartolommeo Eustachio (1520–74). It enables air to enter or leave the middle ear, so balancing the pressure on either side of the eardrum, thus allowing it to vibrate freely. In aeroplanes, failure to equalize pressure during take-off and landing leads to popping sounds (and occasional pain) in the ear; chewing helps to keep the Eustachian tube open and so reduce this tendency. In the young child (up to age 7) the tube is more horizontal than in the adult, leading to a greater incidence of ear infections. » ear [i]; mucous membrane

eustasy [**yoo**stuhsee] Worldwide changes in sea-level caused by the advance or recession of the polar ice caps. This has caused a gradual rise in the sea-level over the last century. Eustatic changes are distinct from localized variations in sea-level due to Earth movements, such as are seen in the Aegean Sea. » Poles

Euston Road School A group of English painters working 1937–9 in London, including William Coldstream (1908–87), Victor Pasmore (1908–), Graham Bell (1910–43), and Claude Rogers (1909–79). They rejected abstraction and surrealism, and practised a quiet naturalism concentrating on domestic subjects. » English art; Pasmore; school (art)

Euterpe [yoo**ter**pee] In Greek mythology, one of the Muses, usually associated with flute-playing. » Muses

euthanasia The painless ending of life, usually as an act of mercy to relieve chronic pain or suffering. It has been advocated by pressure groups such as *Exit*, and by some physicians as a dignified death for the very poorly elderly who have lost the will or desire to live. However, no country officially sanctions the practice. » hospice

eutrophication The enrichment of lake waters through the discharge of run-off carrying excessive fertilizers from agricultural land, and human waste from settlements. The inflow of phosphate and nitrogen-rich waters can result in the loss of lake flora and fauna, as once-clear waters become turbid with microscopic algae. These are better able to live in the enriched conditions, and cause oxygen depletion for other flora and fauna. » Broads, the; fertilizer

Evangelical Alliance A religious movement, founded in 1846 – the formal expression of an international evangelical community embracing a variety of conservative evangelical churches and independent agencies. They are united by the common purpose of winning the world for Christ. » evangelicalism; Jesus Christ

Evangelical United Brethren Church A Christian denomination established in the USA in 1946 through the merger of the Church of the United Brethren in Christ and the Evangelical Church. Both Churches were similar in belief and practice, emphasizing the authority of scripture, justification, and regeneration. In 1968 it merged with the Methodist Church to form the United Methodist Church. » Christianity; evangelicalism; Methodism

evangelicalism Since the Reformation, a term which has been applied to the Protestant Churches because of their principles of justification through faith alone and the supreme authority accorded to scripture. Subsequently, it has been applied more narrowly to Protestant Churches emphasizing intense personal conversion ('born-again Christianity') and commitment in their experience of justification and biblical authority. » Christianity; Lutheranism; Protestantism; Reformation

evangelist (Gr *evangel*, 'good news') One who preaches the gospel of Jesus Christ. The New Testament suggests that some Christians have special gifts of evangelizing. Although evangelizing is now understood to be the task of the whole Church, the term has been more recently applied to popular preachers at missionary rallies. » Graham, Billy; John, St; missions, Christian

Evans, Sir Arthur (John) (1851–1941) British archaeologist, born at Nash Mills, Hertfordshire. He was curator of the Ashmolean Museum, Oxford (1884–1908), where he developed an interest in the ancient coins and seals of Crete. Between 1899 and 1935 he excavated the city of Knossos, discovering the remains of the civilization which in 1904 he named 'Minoan', after Minos, the Cretan king of Greek legend. He was knighted in 1911, and died at Youlbury, Oxfordshire. » archaeology; Knossos

Evans, Dame Edith (Mary) (1888–1976) British actress, born in London. She earned a great reputation for her versatility, with many notable appearances in the plays of Shakespeare and Shaw. Her most famous role was as Lady Bracknell in Wilde's *Importance of Being Earnest*. During World War 2 she entertained the troops at home and abroad, and in 1946 was created a Dame. In 1948, she made her first film appearance in *The Queen of Spades*, and she continued to be active on both stage and screen into her eighties. She died at Cranbrook, Kent. » theatre

Evans, Sir Geraint (Llewellyn) (1922–) British baritone, born at Pontypridd, Wales. He studied in London and on the Continent, making his operatic debut at Covent Garden (1948). He soon earned international fame, particularly in comic roles such as Mozart's Leporello, Verdi's Falstaff, and Wagner's Beckmesser. He was knighted in 1971, and retired from the operatic stage in 1984. » opera

Evans, Timothy John » Christie, John

Evans, Oliver (1755–1819) US inventor, born at Newport, Delaware. He improved flour mills, introducing an automated production line (1784), and invented the first high-pressure steam engine (1790). His steam dredging machine (1804) is considered the first American steam land carriage. He died in New York City. » steam engine

evaporation The passing from a liquid phase to a gas phase; in particular, the process by which water is lost from the Earth's surface to the atmosphere as water vapour. It is an important part of the exchange of energy within the Earth-atmosphere system which produces atmospheric motions, and therefore climate (the *global energy cascade*). Rates of evaporation depend on such factors as solar radiation, the temperature difference between the evaporating surface and the overlying air, humidity, and wind. » evapotranspiration; humidity; radiation

evaporite deposits Mineral deposits formed by the precipitation of dissolved salts (most commonly rock salt, NaCl and gypsum, $CaSO_4.2H_2O$) from water. » salt

evapotranspiration The combined processes of evaporation and transpiration, and therefore the transfer of water vapour to the atmosphere from ground surfaces and vegetation. Rates of evapotranspiration are determined by factors such as wind velocity, water availability, vapour pressure gradient, and energy availability. *Actual* evapotranspiration is the observed rate, and differs from *potential* evapotranspiration, which is what would occur if there were no limiting factors such as supply of moisture. » evaporation; transpiration

Eve » **Adam and Eve**

Evelyn, John (1620–1706) English diarist and author, born and died at Wotton, Surrey. Educated at Oxford and London, he travelled abroad during the Civil War. He was much at court after the Restoration, acted on public committees, and became one of the Commissioners of the Privy Seal (1685–7) and treasurer of Greenwich Hospital (1695–1703). His main literary work is his *Diary*, a detailed sourcebook on life in 17th-c England. » Restoration

even functions In mathematics, functions such that $f(x)=f(-x)$. The graph of an even function is symmetrical about the y-axis, eg $y=x^2$, $y=\cos x$. By contrast, an **odd function** has the property $f(x)=-f(-x)$, eg $y=x^3$, $y=\sin x$. » function [i]

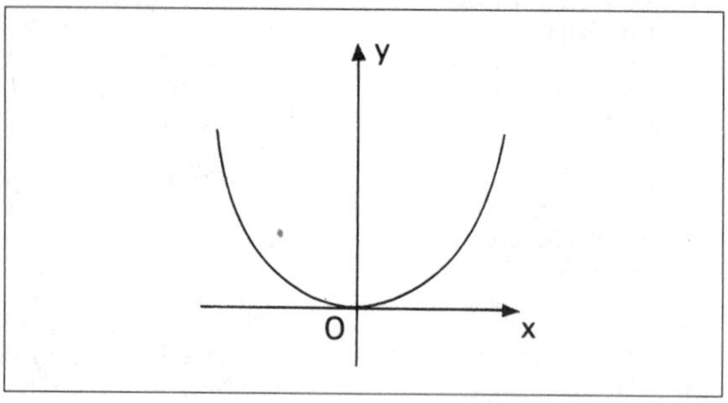

Even functions

evening primrose The name given to several very similar species of erect, robust biennials, native to N America, but cultivated and naturalized in many other countries; leaves lance-shaped to oval; flowers large, several cm diameter, broadly funnel-shaped with four narrow sepals and four overlapping yellow (sometimes red or white) petals, usually fragrant and opening at night. The oil from *Oenothera biennis* and *Oenothera lamarkiana* is claimed to be beneficial in several disorders, including multiple sclerosis, premenstrual tension, heart disease, and skin disorders. These claims have not yet been proven. (Genus: *Oenothera*, 80 species. Family: *Onagraceae*.) » biennial; sepal

Evenki [evenkee] » **Altaic**

event horizon » **black hole**

Everest, Mount, Nepali **Sagarmatha**, Chinese **Qomolangma Feng** 27°59N 95°26W. Mountain peak in the Himalayas of C Asia, on the border between Nepal and the Tibet region of China; height 8 848 m/29 028 ft; highest mountain in the world; named after Sir George Everest (1790–1866), surveyor-general of India; following attempts in 1921 and 1922, Mallory and Irvine, members of the 1924 British Expedition, climbed beyond 8 534 m/27 998 ft but failed to return; summit first reached via the Southeast Ridge on 29 May 1953 by Sir Edmund Hillary and Sherpa Tenzing Norgay of Nepal in a British expedition under Col John Hunt; the summit was reached via the West Ridge by a US team in 1963, the Southwest face by a British team in 1975, and the North Wall by a Japanese team in 1980; claimed by China, in 1952 the Chinese banned the name Everest in favour of Qomolangma Feng ('sacred mother of waters'). » Hillary; Himalayas; Hunt, John

everglade kite » **snail kite**

Everglades S Florida, USA; swampy, subtropical region, length c.160 km/100 ml, width 80–120 km/50–75 ml, area c.12 950 sq km/5 000 sq ml; covers most of the Florida peninsula S of L Okeechobee; consists of saw grass savannahs and water dotted by clumps of reeds; in an area of heavy rainfall only a few metres above sea-level; drainage and reclamation schemes have made a large amount of land productive, mostly in citrus fruits and sugar; originally occupied by Seminole Indians, driven out in the 1830s; Everglades National Park (area 5 668 sq km/2 188 sq ml) in the S includes much of Florida Bay, with its many keys; a world heritage site. » Florida; Florida Keys; mangrove; savannah

evergreen plants Plants which retain their leaves throughout the year. They either grow in climates which have no adverse seasons or have leaves adapted to withstand cold and drought. The leaves are shed and replaced gradually, so that the plant always bears foliage. » deciduous plants; leaf [i]

Evert (Lloyd), Chris(tine Marie) (1954–) US lawn tennis player, born at Fort Lauderdale, Florida. She won her first Wimbledon title in 1974 at age 19, and later won in 1976 and 1981. She also won the US singles title in 1975–80 and 1982, the French Open in 1974–5, 1979–80, and 1984, and the Australian Open in 1982 and 1984. She married British tennis player John Lloyd (marriage dissolved in 1987). She retired from professional tennis in 1989. » tennis, lawn [i]

Evesham [eevsham] 52°06N 1°56W, pop (1981) 15 280. Town in Wychavon district, Hereford and Worcester, WC England; in the Vale of Evesham in a fruit- and vegetable-growing area; railway; foodstuffs, engineering. » Hereford and Worcester

evolution Any gradual directional change; now most commonly used to refer to the cumulative changes in the characteristics of populations of organisms from generation to generation. Evolution occurs by the fixation of changes (*mutations*) in the structure of the genetic material, and the passing on of these changes from ancestor to descendant. It is well demonstrated over geological time by the sequence of organisms preserved in the fossil record. There are two opposing schools of thought regarding the pattern and tempo of evolution. The **gradualist** school is based on a model of evolution in which species change gradually through time by slow directional change within a lineage, producing a long graded series of differing forms. The **punctuated equilibria** school is based on a model in which species are relatively stable and long-lived in geological time, and that new species appear during outbursts of rapid speciation, followed by the differential success of certain of the newly formed species. » convergence (biology); Darwinism; fossil; genetics [i]; mutation

evolutionary humanism A form of humanism which holds that modern science and knowledge have emancipated people from bondage to supernaturalistic and dogmatic religion. In this view, the universe has no special human meaning or purpose. Humankind is part of an evolutionary process, and the application of science and human reason are its only resources in creating a more human world. » evolution; freethought; humanism

evolutionism A widely held 19th-c belief that organisms – individuals, races, and even societies – were intrinsically bound to improve themselves, that changes were progressive, and that acquired characters could be transmitted genetically. » evolution

Evora [ayvoora], Lat **Ebora** or **Liberalitas Julia** 38°33N 7°57W, pop (1981) 34 100. Ancient walled market town and capital of Évora district, S Portugal, 112 km/70 ml ESE of Lisbon; a world heritage site; airfield; railway; agricultural trade, carpets, wool, cork; cathedral (1186), archbishop's palace, Roman Temple of Diana, Church of the Loios (15th-c), old university (1551); São João fair (Jun). » Portugal [i]

Evreux [ayvrer] 49°00N 1°08E, pop (1982) 48 653. Capital of Eure department, NW France, in fertile Iton valley; railway; textiles, rubber goods, chemicals; Cathedral of Notre Dame (begun 11th-c), Bishop's Palace (15th-c), former Benedictine abbey church of St-Taurin.

Ewald, Johannes [ivahl] (1743–81) Danish poet and dramatist, born and died in Copenhagen. After serving as a soldier, he devoted himself to poetry. He is best known for his prose tragedy, *Rolf Krage* (1770) and his mythological play *Balders Död* (1773, The Death of Baldur). The national song of Denmark comes from his operetta, *Fiskerne* (1779, The Fishermen). » Danish literature; poetry; tragedy

ewe » **sheep**

Ewe [**ay**way] A cluster of Kwa-speaking agricultural peoples of Togo, Ghana, and Benin; the coastal people also fish. They share common traditions of origin – from Oyo, in W Nigeria – and formed alliances in times of war, but they never constituted a centralized state. Population c.2 million. » Benin [i]; Ghana [i]; Togo [i]

Excalibur [eks**ka**liber] In Arthurian legend, the name of King Arthur's sword, which was given to him by the Lady of the Lake. As he lay dying he instructed Sir Bedivere to throw it back into the lake, where a hand drew it under. » Arthur

excess profits tax A tax levied on a company's profits above a specified level. It was used in both World Wars to curb excessive profits by firms producing goods for the war effort, and has also been used at other times to control 'profiteering'. » taxation

exchange controls Government measures aimed at restricting the movement of currency between countries. They are frequently used by developing nations, but also from time to time by Western nations when their reserves are low. Restrictions on the export of currency were lifted in the UK in 1979, after years of gradual easement of controls. » currency

exchange rates The price at which a currency may be bought in terms of a unit of another currency. Until the mid-1970s, rates were fixed from time to time; today, most are floating (ie the rate is determined by the ongoing supply and demand for the currency). » devaluation; European Monetary System

excise tax A tax levied on many goods and services by governments as a way of raising revenues; often called 'duty'. Best-known are the duties on tobacco, alcoholic drinks, and fuel, Value Added Tax in the UK, and Sales Tax in the USA. » taxation

excited state » **energy levels**

exciton In insulating and semiconductor crystals, a quantized ripple in electron energy that moves about the crystal transferring energy but not charge. A type of quasi-particle, it is important in understanding optical reflection and transmission properties. » crystal; quasi-particles

exclusion principle » **Pauli exclusion principle**

exemption clause A term in a contract whereby one party seeks to exclude or (in the case of a **limitation clause**) limit liability in respect of obligations arising under the contract. The Unfair Contract Terms Act (1977) renders certain such clauses invalid in the UK. » contract

Exeter, ancient **Isca Damnoniorum** 50°43N 3°31W, pop (1981) 91 938. County town in Exeter district, Devon, SW England; on the R Exe, 70 km/43 ml NE of Plymouth; founded by the Romans 1st-c AD; stone wall erected in 3rd-c against Saxons and (later) Danes; port status partially restored by the construction of England's first ship canal (1560); W headquarters of Royalist forces during Civil War; university (1955); railway; airfield; agricultural trade, textiles, leather goods, metal products, pharmaceuticals, wood products, tourism; 12th-c cathedral (damaged by bombing in World War 2), 12th-c Guildhall, maritime museum. » Britain, Roman; Devon; English Civil War

existentialism A philosophical movement, closely associated with Kierkegaard, Sartre, and Heidegger. Its most salient theses are that there is no ultimate purpose to the world; that persons find themselves in a world which is vaguely hostile; that persons choose and cannot avoid choosing their characters, goals, and perspectives; that not to choose is to choose not to choose; and that truths about the world and our situation are revealed most clearly in moments of unfocused psychological anxiety or dread. These themes have influenced literature (eg Dostoevsky and Camus), psychoanalysis (eg Binswanger and Rollo May), and theology (eg Tillich and Bultmann). » Heidegger; Kierkegaard; Sartre

Exmoor National park in Somerset and Devon, England; area 686 sq km/265 sq ml; established in 1954; occupies coastline between Minehead and Combe Martin Bay; highest point, Dunkery Beacon, 520 m/1 707 ft; Brendon Hills (E); known for its ponies; major tourist area. » Devon; Somerset

Exmoor pony The oldest British breed of horse; a small pony developed on Exmoor, England; height, 11½–12¾ hands/ 1.2–1.3 m/3¾–4¼ ft; very hardy; broad chest, deep body, stiff springy coat; brown with cream muzzle; broad nostrils, eyes slightly protruding. » Exmoor; horse [i]

Exmouth [**eks**muhth] 50°37N 3°25W, pop (1981) 28 661. Resort town in Teignbridge district, Devon, SW England; on the R Exe, 15 km/9 ml SE of Exeter; centre for recreational sailing; railway; engineering. » Devon

exobiology The study of extraterrestrial life; also known as **astrobiology**. Techniques include the monitoring of radio waves emitted by other star systems, and the use of space probe experiments designed to detect life forms, or the presence of the molecules required for life to develop. » biology; space exploration

Exodus, Book of The second book of the Pentateuch in the Hebrew Bible/Old Testament. It narrates stories about the deliverance of the Jews from slavery in Egypt under the leadership of Moses, and about the giving of the Law to Israel through a revelation to Moses on Mt Sinai. It also provides instructions for building the wilderness tabernacle. » Moses; Pentateuch; Sinai, Mount; Tabernacle; Ten Commandments

exogamy » **marriage**

exosphere The outer shell in the atmosphere (at c.400 km/250 ml) from which light gases can escape. » atmosphere [i]

expanded town A British solution to the problems of city growth. Following the designation of *new towns*, a number of towns were chosen for expansion under the 1953 Expanded Towns Act. Cities with surplus population could negotiate with these towns to take the 'overspill' population. For example, the market towns of Haverhill, Suffolk, and Huntingdon and St Neots, Cambridgeshire, expanded to take the overspill from Greater London. Financial aid was available from central government for the provision of amenities, such as waterways and mains sewerage, in the expanding towns. » garden city; new town

expanding universe » **Big Bang**

experimental psychology The name given to a branch of psychology whose meaning has altered along with the growth of the present-day subject. First used to indicate the emergence of a distinct scientific discipline of psychology at the end of the 19th-c, it came to refer to the study of mental phenomena by experimental methods in contrast to sheer speculation ('armchair psychology'). It is now used for an approach which relies principally on laboratory experiments. » psychology

experimenter effect An effect on a subject's performance wrongly attributed to the manipulation of an experimental condition (*variable*) which can be shown to be due to the influence of the experimenter. A well-known example is the *Hawthorne effect*. Improvement in the performance of workers at the Hawthorne factory of the Western Electric Company in the USA was assumed to be an effect of specific changes made in working conditions (eg in the level of illumination), whereas it was eventually established that the workers were responding to the interest shown towards them by the investigators. » control group; experimental psychology; placebo

expert system A computer system which can perform at least some of the functions of the relevant human expert. Expert systems have been developed for use in areas such as medical diagnosis and geological prospecting, which require a large amount of organized knowledge plus deductive skills. » artificial intelligence; knowledge-based system

Explorer 1 The first US space satellite (launched 31 Jan 1958); a joint effort of the US Army's Ballistic Missile Agency, later to become NASA's George C Marshall Space Flight Center, and the California Institute of Technology's Jet Propulsion Laboratory, later to become NASA's leading centre for planetary exploration. The simple 14 kg/31 lb spacecraft was launched on a Redstone (Jupiter C) rocket vehicle from Cape Canaveral, and instrumented with basic radiation counters built at the University of Iowa. It discovered belts of energetic charged particles trapped in the Earth's magnetic field, which were named after Iowa's James van Allen. 'Explorer' later became the generic name of a series of relatively simple Earth orbital space physics and astronomy missions carried out by NASA. » magnetosphere; NASA; solar wind; van Allen radiation belts; RR10

explosives Substances capable of undergoing a rapid chemical change to produce hot gases which occupy a much greater volume, and therefore exert a sudden very high pressure. Many types of reaction may proceed explosively, but most military and industrial explosives consist largely of nitrated carbon compounds. (The chief exception is the oldest explosive, gunpowder.) They are distinguished as *propellants* and *high explosives*. Propellants burn rapidly but smoothly, so as to exert a great but steady pressure on a projectile in the barrel of a gun. High explosives change so fast as to produce a violent and disruptive shock in adjacent material. Industrial explosives generally contain some inert moderator to provide control (eg dynamite). » amatol; detonator; gelignite; gunpowder; nitroglycerine; propellant

exponent In mathematics, the index or power to which a number has been raised. For example, in the expression x^4, 4 is the exponent.

exponential function In mathematics, a function in which the variable is in the exponent, eg 2^x. The most important exponential function is $y=e^x$, which has the property that $dy/dx=y$ for all values of x. In its more general form $y=Ae^{kx}$, this function models many physical situations, such as laws of growth and decay, and the discharge of condensors. The **exponential series** is $e^x=1+\frac{x}{1!}+\frac{x^2}{2!}+\frac{x^3}{3!}+\frac{x^4}{4!}\cdots$. The trigonometric functions can also be defined in terms of exponentials,

$\sin x=\frac{1}{2i}(e^{ix}-e^{-ix})$, $\cos x=\frac{1}{2}(e^{ix}+e^{-ix})$ and Euler established the remarkable result: $e^{i\pi}+1=0$. » calculus; Euler; function [i]; logarithm; trigonometry

exposure (photography) The controlled presentation of a photo-sensitive surface to light in order to record an image. For a given sensitivity, exposure level is determined by the intensity of the light and the time of exposure, and must be correctly set to ensure satisfactory reproduction of tone and colour. In still cameras this is done by a suitable combination of lens aperture and shutter speed, but in motion picture and video cameras the exposure time is normally fixed, and level is set by the lens aperture. An **exposure meter** is an instrument for measuring light, either incident on the subject or reflected from it, giving a scale reading from which lens aperture and shutter setting may be determined for a given photographic material. Modern still cameras embody a meter for reflected light, coupled for automatic exposure setting; while in video cameras a signal from the electronically scanned image automatically controls lens aperture. » aperture; camera

exposure (physics) A measure of exposure to ionizing radiation, based on the amount of ionization produced in dry air by X-rays or gamma rays; symbol X, unit R (röntgen). The modern notions of *absorbed dose* and *dose equivalent* are generally more useful. » radioactivity units [i]; X-rays

Expressionism A movement in art, architecture, and literature which aims to communicate the internal emotional realities of a situation, rather than its external 'realistic' aspect; the term was first used in Germany in 1911, but the roots of the movement can be traced to van Gogh and Gauguin in the 1880s. Their influence was felt by the Norwegian Edvard Munch, and the Belgian James Ensor, but the full flowering of Expressionism occurred in Germany from c.1905 until suppressed by Hitler. In this approach, traditional ideas of beauty and proportion are disregarded, so that artists can express their feelings more strongly by means of distortion, jarring colours, and exaggerated linear rhythms. The movement was also influential in literature, especially in German theatre after World War 1. The use of dislocation and distortion in fiction and poetry (eg in the writing of Kafka and Joyce) has also been described as Expressionist. » Blaue Reiter, der; Brücke, die; Ensor; Fauvism; Gauguin; German art; Joyce, James; Kafka; modern art; Munch; Neue Sachlichkeit; organic architecture; van Gogh

expressivity The degree of manifestation of a gene in those individuals in whom its presence is detectable. The gene for tuberose sclerosis, for example, in one individual may cause epilepsy, mental retardation, and a skin rash, but in another only the skin condition. Such cases are said to be of variable expressivity. » gene

extended family » **family**

extensive farming Farming with relatively low input levels, especially of fertilizers, sprays, and pharamaceuticals. Lower yields per hectare may be compensated for by larger areas per farm and per farmer; so acceptable income levels may still be achieved. » intensive farming

extinction The disappearance of a species from a particular habitat (*local* extinction), or the total elimination of a species worldwide. Animal species are categorized as extinct if they have not been definitely located in the wild for the past 50 years. » species

extracellular fluid (ECF) The fluid which surrounds the cells of the body. In humans, the adult volume is c.14 1/25 UK pt/30 US pt, and consists of blood plasma, the interstitial fluid of tissues, and transcellular fluids. Its principal components (apart from water) are sodium, chloride and bicarbonate ions, and proteins. The concept that the body's cells are protected from a continuously changing and often hostile external environment by their own internal environment, a fluid of constant volume and composition, was introduced by French physiologist, Claude Bernard. Although the basic concept still holds, extracellular fluid is no longer considered to be constant, but to vary within very narrow limits. » homeostasis; plasma (physiology); transcellular fluid

extradition The removal of a person by a state in which that person is currently located to the territory of another state where the person has been convicted of a crime, or is said to have committed a crime. The process is normally conducted through extradition treaties, which specify the cases and the procedures under which extradition will take place. Treaties are normally restricted to more important crimes, but exclude political crimes.

extrapolation » **interpolation**

extrasensory perception (ESP) One of the two major categories of allegedly paranormal phenomena of interest to parapsychologists (the other being *psychokinesis*). Extrasensory perception is defined as the apparent gaining of information about an object or event (mental or physical; past, present, or future) by means other than those currently understood by the physical sciences. Clairvoyance, telepathy, and precognition are specific types of extrasensory perception. » clairvoyance; parapsychology; psi; psychokinesis

extraversion » **introversion/extraversion**

Extremadura [ekstraymad**oo**ra] or **Estremadura** [aystrayma**doo**ra] pop (1981) 1 064 968; area 41 602 sq km/16 058 sq ml. Autonomous region of W Spain on the Portuguese frontier; crossed by the Tagus and Guadiana Rivers, bounded (N) by the Sierra de Gata and Sierra de Gredos (rising to 2 592 m/8 504 ft); merino sheep, pigs, vines, figs, olives, almonds; considerable industrial development since the 1970s through the use of hydroelectricity and irrigation channels. » Estremadura (Portugal); Spain [i]

extreme unction » **anointing the sick**

extrusive rock Igneous rocks which have formed from molten magma, or volcanic fragments ejected onto the Earth's surface; also termed **volcanic rock**. They are most commonly basalt or pyroclasts. » igneous rock; magma; pyroclastic rock

eye A specialized receptor organ responding to light stimuli. Various forms exist, such as the stigmata of certain protozoa, the ocelli of annelids, and the compound eye of insects. In land-based vertebrates, such as humans, the eyeball is composed of two parts: the transparent *corneal* part at the front, and the opaque *scleral* part at the back. Three concentric coats form the wall of the eyeball: an outer *fibrous* coat, consisting of the cornea and sclera; a middle *vascular* coat, consisting of the choroid, ciliary body, and iris; and an inner *nervous* coat (the *retina*). The coats surround and partly divide the contents of

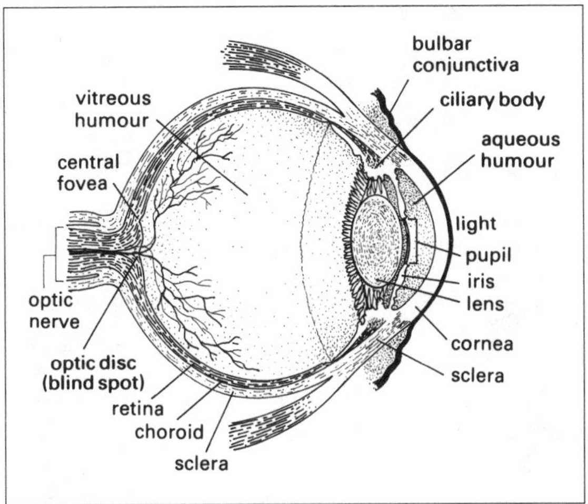

The structure of the eye

the eyeball. The *vitreous body* (a jelly-like substance containing a meshwork of fine fibres) lies between the lens and the retina. The space between the lens and the cornea contains a watery fluid (the *aqueous humour*), and is further partly divided by the iris into front and rear chambers. The *lens* is transparent and biconvex, lying between the iris and the vitreous body; changes in its convexity alter its focal length (the greater the convexity, the shorter the focal length), and are brought about by the action of the ciliary muscles. The lens is soft and elastic in the foetus, but becomes hardened and flatter with increasing age, making focusing on close objects more difficult (*presbyopia*); it may also become opaque in the elderly (*cataract*).

Light entering the eye is refracted by the cornea, and passes through the lens, which focuses it to form an inverted image on the retina. This image is coded by the retina and sent to the visual areas of the cerebral cortex for interpretation, thus enabling the original pattern of light stimuli to be 'seen'. The amount of light entering the eye is determined by the size of the pupil, which in turn is determined by the degree of contraction of the iris. If the image from distant objects is focused in front of the retina, the condition is known as *myopia*, with vision being better for near objects ('short-sightedness'). If the image is focused beyond the retina, the condition is known as *hypermetropia*, with vision being better for distant objects ('long-sightedness'). Glasses using concave lenses are used to correct short sight; a convex lens is used for long sight. » blindness; cataract; conjunctivitis; cornea; double vision; glaucoma; intra-ocular lens implantation; iris (anatomy); light; nightblindness; ophthalmia; ophthalmology; optometry; retina; river blindness; rods and cones; spectacles; stye; trachoma; vision

eyebright A small annual or perennial, native to most temperate regions; all hemiparasitic, mainly on grasses; leaves opposite or alternate, toothed or lobed; flowers usually white with yellow or violet markings, 2-lipped, upper lip erect, 2-lobed, lower with three notched, spreading lobes. (Genus: *Euphrasia*, 200 species. Family: *Scrophulariaceae*.) » annual; parasitic plant; perennial

Eyre Lakes [ayr] Dry salt lakes in NE South Australia; includes L Eyre North (145 km/90 ml long, 65 km/40 ml wide, area 7 692 sq km/2 969 sq ml) and L Eyre South (61 km/38 ml long, 26 km/16 ml wide, area 1 191 sq km/460 sq ml); L Eyre North is the largest lake in Australia, normally a shallow pan of glistening white salt; has filled with water only three times since European discovery; 15 m/50 ft below mean sea-level; fed by a series of intermittently flowing rivers, including the Finke, Diamantina, and Cooper Creek; site of Donald Campbell's world land speed record (1964). » Campbell, Malcolm; South Australia

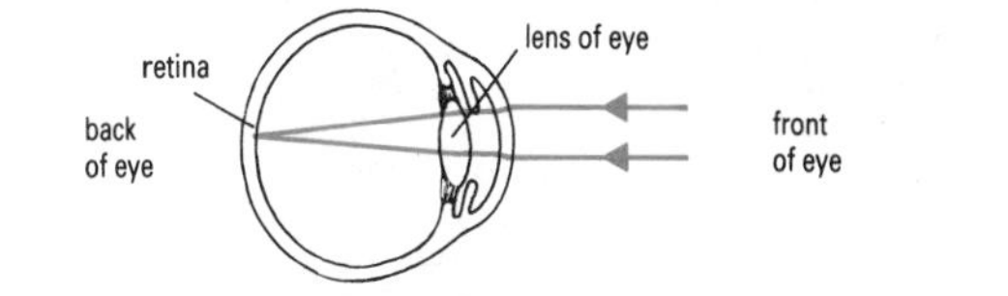

Normal eye. The image is in focus on the retina without a correcting lens in front.

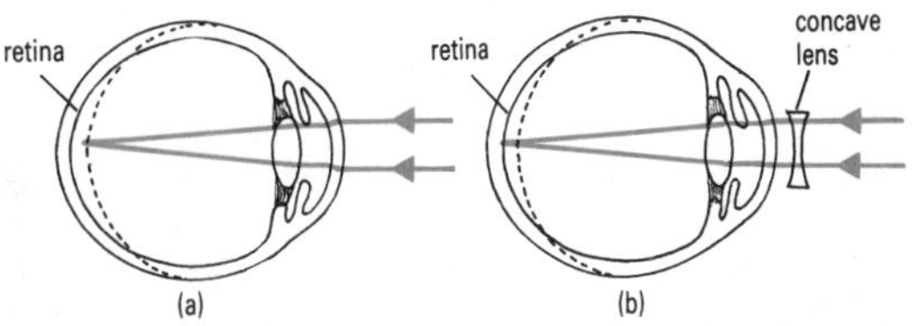

Short-sighted eye. (a) The eye is too long and the image is not in focus on the retina. (b) The use of a concave lens brings the image into focus.

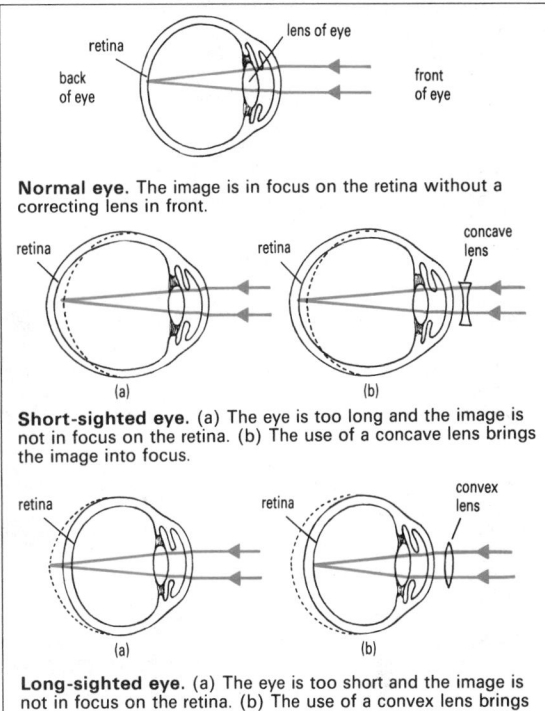

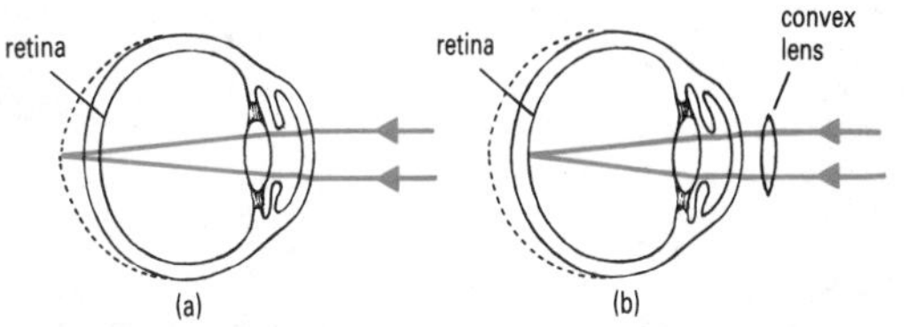

Long-sighted eye. (a) The eye is too short and the image is not in focus on the retina. (b) The use of a convex lens brings the image into focus.

The human eye – Normal, short-sighted and long-sighted

Ezekiel or **Ezechiel, Book of** [eezeekeey-el] A major prophetic work in the Hebrew Bible/Old Testament, attributed to Ezekiel, a 6th-c BC priest amongst the Jews exiled in Babylonian territories after 597 BC. The prophecies in Chapters 1–24 warn of the impending destruction of Jerusalem (587 BC); Chapters 25–32 present oracles condemning foreign nations; and Chapters 33–48 promise hope for a restoration of Israel. The collection of these prophecies may have been the work of a later editor. » Old Testament; prophet

Ezra [ezra] (5th–4th-c BC) Religious leader who lived in Babylon during the reign of King Artaxerxes (I or II), who reorganized the Jewish community in Jerusalem, and who renovated its religious cult. He may have brought part of the Mosaic law (the Pentateuch) with him; an Old Testament book bears his name, as well as the apocryphal works of 1 and 2 Esdras (the Greek equivalent of 'Ezra'). » Apocrypha, Old Testament; Ezra/Esdras, Book of; Pentateuch

Ezra, Book of [ezra] Part of the Hebrew Bible/Old Testament, and originally probably part of a historical work including Chronicles and Nehemiah. It describes stages in the return to Palestine of exiled Jews from 538 BC onwards, the attempts to rebuild the Temple and city of Jerusalem, and the story of Ezra's mission under Artaxerxes I or II to restore adherence to the Jewish law amongst Palestinian Jews. » Chronicles/Esdras/Nehemiah, Book of; Ezra; Old Testament

F layer » Appleton layer

Fabergé, Peter Carl, originally **Karl Gustavovich Fabergé** [**fa**berzhay] (1846–1920) Russian goldsmith and jeweller of Huguenot descent, born at St Petersburg. Educated in several countries, in 1870 he inherited his father's establishment in St Petersburg, moving from the design and manufacture of conventional jewellery to the creation of more elaborate and fantastic objects, most famous of which are probably the celebrated imperial Easter eggs, first commisioned by Alexander III for his tsarina in 1884. He died in exile at Lausanne after his business had been destroyed by the events of the Russian revolution. » Russian Revolution

Fabian Society A socialist group established in 1884 which took its name from the Roman general Fabius Cunctator, noted for his cautious military tactics. It adopts a gradualist approach to social reform, and sometimes 'Fabian' is applied to people who are not members of the Society but who believe in reformist socialism. The Society has remained a small select group, but has a close association with the British Labour Party, and has been a source of socialist ideas and arguments. » Labour Party; Shaw, George Bernard; Webb, Sidney and Beatrice; Wells, H G

Fabius Maximus, Quintus, byname **Cunctator** ('the Delayer') (c.260–203 BC) Roman general, statesman, and hero of the Second Punic War, whose refusal to engage Hannibal in set battle earned him his nickname. Originally a term of abuse, it became an honorific title after 216 BC, when Rome's massive and unnecessary defeat at the Battle of Cannae proved that his cautious tactics had been right. » Punic Wars

fable (Lat *fabula* 'story') A story about animals which may be interpreted as referring to human behaviour. The mode has been popular at all times; famous examples include Aesop's *Fables* (6th-c BC), the *Fables* of La Fontaine (late 17th-c), and George Orwell's *Animal Farm* (1945). » Aesop; allegory; La Fontaine; novel; Orwell

fabliau [**fab**leeoh] A short narrative poem popular in 12th–14th-c France, and also appearing in English (eg Chaucer's *Miller's Tale*). The subjects were usually bawdy, misogynist, and anticlerical. » Chaucer; English/French literature; poetry; Realism

Fabriano, Gentile da [fabree**ah**noh] (c.1370–c.1427) Italian painter, born at Fabriano. He worked chiefly in Venice and Brescia until 1419, and thereafter in Rome, Florence, and Siena. He painted religious subjects, notably 'The Adoration of the Magi' (1423, Florence), but few of his paintings have survived. He died in Rome. » Italian art

Fabricius, Hieronymus [fa**bree**tsiuhs] or **Girolamo Fabrici** (1537–1619) Italian anatomist, born at Acquapendente. He studied under Fallopius at Padua, becoming his successor as professor of anatomy (1562). He made the first detailed description of the valves of the veins, the placenta, and the larynx. William Harvey was one of his pupils. He died at Padua. » Fallopius; Harvey; vein

fabrics » **batik; coated fabrics; denim; felt; non-woven fabrics; square cloth; tweed; twill**

Fabritius, Carel [fa**bree**tsiuhs] (c.1624–54) Dutch painter, born at Beemster. He studied under Rembrandt, and from about 1650 lived mainly at Delft, where he was killed in an explosion. Vermeer was much influenced by Fabritius' sensitive experiments in composition and the painting of light, as in the tiny 'View of Delft' (1652, National Gallery, London). » Dutch art; Rembrandt; Vermeer

facade [fa**sahd**] The exterior face or elevation of a building. Every building has a facade, simply by virtue of having an outside; but the term is particularly associated with consciously designed, overtly formal, aesthetic qualities, such as those incorporated into the Palais de Versailles (1661–1756), principal architects Louis Le Vau, Jules Hardouin Mansart, and J A Gabriel. The term derives from Italian *facciata*, for the front of a building. » axonometric [i]; section [i]

factor analysis A set of techniques popular in psychometric research to reduce data to manageable form. Given a set of correlations between various measures (eg responses to items on a questionnaire), factor analysis identifies a small number of factors (weighted combinations of the observed measures) which best account for the correlations. Such factors are statistical: giving them a psychological interpretation is sometimes difficult and contentious. » intelligence; psychometrics; statistics

factor VIII One of a series of enzymes present in the blood which controls the clotting process. Sufferers from classical haemophilia lack this factor, and their blood therefore lacks the capacity to clot. They are treated by intravenous administration of factor VIII that has been separated from fresh blood. This process carries the risk of transferring infections from the blood donor, such as AIDS; in the future, factor VIII may be produced using genetic engineering which will eliminate this risk. A rarer form of haemophilia results from the absence of factor IX (the Christmas factor, named after the first patient studied in detail with this deficiency), which can similarly be replaced. » AIDS; blood; enzyme; genetic engineering; haemophilia

factoring or **debt factoring** The selling of a company's list of debtors (ie customers who owe the firm money) to an agent (*factor*) at a discount. The factor then retrieves the sums due. Factored goods are goods bought and resold without any further processing. The firm acts as an agent for the manufacturer. » debt

Factory Acts Legislation passed in Britain from 1802 onwards to regulate employment in factories. The early Acts were generally concerned to limit the hours of work of women and children. The 1833 Factory Act prohibited children under nine from working in textile mills, and was the first to appoint factory inspectors. A maximum 10-hour working day for women and older children was agreed in 1847.

factory farming An intensive form of livestock production, usually carried out indoors with strict control over the environment and over feeding regimes; also known as **battery farming**. Currently the predominant production technique for eggs, poultry meat, and pig meat, it is opposed by many environmentalists. » environmentalism

Fadeyev, Aleksandr Aleksandrovich (1901–56) Russian novelist, born at Kimry, near Kalinin. He became a communist in 1918, and fought in Siberia. Deeply influenced by Tolstoy, his works include *Molodaya gvardiya* (1946, The Young Guard). As general secretary of the Soviet Writers' Union (1946–55) he mercilessly exposed any literary 'deviationism' from the party line, but after becoming a target himself, he committed suicide in Moscow. » novel; Russian literature; Tolstoy

faeces/feces Material discharged from the alimentary canal, consisting mainly of the undigested remains of ingested matter, bacteria, and water. In humans the colour is due to pigment formed in the intestine by bacterial decomposition of bilirubins. The odour is the result of the formation of certain amines by intestinal bacteria. » alimentary canal; anus; cloaca

Faeroe or **Faroe Islands** [**fair**oh], Danish **Faerøerne** 62°00N 7°00W; pop (1989e) 47 800; area 1 400 sq km/540 sq ml. Group of 22 sparsely vegetated volcanic islands in the N Atlantic between Iceland and the Shetland Is; 17 inhabited; settled by Norse, 8th-c; part of Norway, 11th-c; passed to Denmark, 1380; self-governing region of Denmark since 1948; parliament (*Lagting*), restored in 1852, consists of 34 members; capital, Tórshavn; largest islands, Strømø, Østerø; inhabitants speak a Germanic language, Faroese; fish, crafts, sheep, potatoes. » Denmark [i]; Tórshavn

Fahd ibn Abd al-Aziz (1923–) Ruler of Saudi Arabia (1982–), born at Riyadh. As effective ruler since the assassination of his older half-brother Faisal in 1975, he became king on the death of his other half-brother, Khaled. » Saudi Arabia [i]

Fahrenheit, Gabriel Daniel (1686–1736) German physicist, born in Danzig. He invented the alcohol thermometer in 1709, following this with a mercury thermometer in 1714. He spent most of his life in the Netherlands, and died in The Hague. » Fahrenheit temperature; thermometer; RR79

Fahrenheit temperature A scale which takes the freezing point of water as 32°F and the boiling point as 212°F; symbol °F; introduced by German physicist Gabriel Fahrenheit, based originally on the freezing point of salt solution and human body temperature. » Fahrenheit; temperature [i]; units (scientific); RR79

faience Earthenware decorated with an opaque glaze containing oxide of tin. The name derives from the Italian town of Faenza, but is usually applied to wares from France and Germany. English and Dutch Delftware and Italian maiolica employ exactly the same technique. » Delftware; maiolica

fainting A brief episode of loss of consciousness, usually sudden in onset; also known as **syncope**. It is caused either by the reduction of blood supply to the brain or by changes in its electrical activity. Less commonly, low blood sugar may be responsible. Reduced cerebral blood flow may occur from the pooling of blood in the lower limbs as a result of overactivity of the vagus nerve which also slows the heart beat (a *vasovagal attack*) and from prolonged standing. Myocardial infarction, severe valvular disease, and disturbances in rhythm which reduce the output of blood may also be responsible. » Adam Stokes attacks; epilepsy

Fair Deal The name adopted by US President Truman (in office 1945–53) for his liberal and pro-labour domestic policies. » New Deal; Truman, Harry S

Fairbanks, Douglas, originally **Douglas Elton Ulman** (1883–1939) US film actor, born in Denver, Colorado. He first appeared in stage plays (1901), but in 1915 went into films and made a speciality of swashbuckling hero parts, as in the *Three Musketeers* (1921) and *Robin Hood* (1922). His son **Douglas Fairbanks Jr** (1909–), followed in his footsteps, starring in such films as *The Prisoner of Zenda* (1937), and becoming a television producer. He also made a name for himself as a diplomat, and won distinction in World War 2.

Fairbanks 64°50N 147°50W, pop (1980) 22 645. City in North Star Borough, C Alaska; terminus of the Alaska railway and highway; founded in 1902 after the discovery of gold; university (1922); mining, oilfield services. » Alaska

Fairfax (of Cameron), Thomas, 3rd Baron (1612–71) English Parliamentary general, born at Denton, Yorkshire. In the Civil War, he distinguished himself at Marston Moor (1644), and in 1645 was given command of the New Model Army, defeating Charles I at Naseby. He was replaced by Cromwell in 1650 for refusing to march against the Scots, who had proclaimed Charles II King, and withdrew into private life. In 1660 he was head of the commission sent to The Hague to arrange for the King's return. He died at Nunappleton, Yorkshire. » Charles II (of England); English Civil War

fairies Supernatural beings that appear in folklore under many names and in a variety of (more or less human-derived) shapes, with multifarious characteristics and tendencies. The brownies of English tradition are almost wholly benevolent; pixies and elves are tiny and mischievous; goblins ugly and malicious. Some fairies, such as gnomes, Irish leprechauns and Scandinavian trolls, traditionally guard treasure. Others, such as the vindictive Arabic jinn, inhabit stones and trees and other natural objects. » banshee; dryad; folklore; jinni; leprechaun; nymph (mythology); peri; Robin Goodfellow; troll

fairy bluebird A bird native to SE Asia (India to Philippines); shiny blue and black plumage; inhabits high forest canopy; eats mainly fruit, especially figs; sheds feathers easily when handled. (Genus: *Irena*, 2 species. Family: *Irenidae*.)

fairy penguin The smallest of all penguins (height 40 cm/15 in); inhabits shallow waters around S Australia and New Zealand; also known as **little blue penguin**; nests in a burrow. (Family: *Spheniscidae*, *Eudyptula minor*.) » penguin

fairy shrimp A slender and delicate aquatic crustacean that typically swims on its back, beating its leaf-like legs; contains c.180 species, found in ephemeral freshwater pools and inland saline lakes all over the world. (Class: *Branchiopoda*. Order: *Anostraca*.) » brine shrimp; crustacean

fairy wren » wren

Faisal I, also **Faysal** [**fiy**sl] (1885–1933) King of Iraq (1921–33), born at Ta'if, son of Hussein-bin-Ali, king of the Hejaz. He played a major role in the Arab revolt of 1916, and was for a short while King of Syria after World War 1. Installed as King of Iraq by the British, he became a leader of Arab nationalism. He died in Berne, Switzerland. » Iraq [i]

Faisal II, also **Faysal** [**fiy**sl] (1935–58) King of Iraq (1939–58), born at Baghdad, great-grandson of Hussein-bin-Ali. He succeeded his father, King Ghazi, who was killed in an accident, and after an education at Harrow was installed as king. In February 1958 he concluded with his cousin King Hussein of Jordan a federation of the two countries in opposition to the United Arab Republic of Egypt and Syria. In July that year, he and his entire household were assassinated during a military coup, and Iraq became a republic. » Iraq [i]

Faisal ibn Abd al-Aziz, also **Faysal** [**fiy**sl] (1904–75) King of Saudi Arabia (1964–75), born at Riyadh. Appointed Viceroy of Hejaz in 1926, he became Minister for Foreign Affairs in 1930, Crown Prince in 1953, and succeeded his half-brother Saud as King. He was assassinated in the royal palace in Riyadh by his nephew Faisal ibn Musaid. » Saudi Arabia [i]

Faisalabad [**fiy**salabad], formerly **Lyallpur** (to 1979) 31°25N 73°09E, pop (1981) 1 092 000. City in Punjab province, Pakistan; W of Lahore, in an important cotton and wheat-growing region; railway; grain, textiles, flour, soap, chemicals, textile machinery. » Pakistan [i]

faith healing The alleviation of physical and mental ailments by the prayer of a healer relying on a higher source (usually, the power of God) working in response to faith. Known in several religions, the practice is now a major feature of Christian pentecostal and charismatic movements, often accompanied by the laying on of the healer's hands, usually in the context of worship. Critics assert that, even when apparently effective, it is difficult to ascribe healing to the action of the higher source, because so little is currently understood by medical science about the effects of psychological attitudes upon the body's biochemistry. » Pentacostalism; placebo; prayer

Fajans, Kasimir [**fah**yans] (1887–1975) Polish-US physical chemist, born in Warsaw. He studied at Heidelberg and Munich, and moved to the USA in 1936, teaching at Michigan thereafter. His early work was on radioactive elements, but he is now best known for **Fajans' rules**, dealing with the types of bond between atoms in compounds. » chemical bonding; radioactivity

falabella The smallest breed of horse in the world; height, 7 hands/0.7 m/2¼ ft; developed by the Falabella family in Argentina; descended from a small thoroughbred and Shetland ponies; now kept mainly as a pet. » Shetland pony; thoroughbred

Falange [fa**lãzh**] Span [fa**lan**khay] A Spanish fascist movement, founded in 1933 by José Antonio Primo de Rivera (1903–36). It merged in 1934 with the *Juntas de Ofensiva Nacional-Sindicalista* (JONS) to form the *Falange Española de las JONS*, and participated in the right-wing rising of July 1936 and the subsequent Civil War. It was fused by Franco in 1937 with other rightist forces to form the single party of Nationalist Spain. » fascism; Spanish Civil War

falcon Any bird of prey of the family *Falconidae* (c.60 species); worldwide; includes the carrion-feeding **caracara**, the **forest falcon** (large eyes, acute hearing, hunts in near-darkness), and the **true falcon** (a fast-flying predator which usually kills its prey in flight). True falcons include kestrels, hobbies and the merlin. » bird of prey; caracara; falconry; gyrfalcon; harrier (bird); hobby; kestrel; lanner falcon; merlin; peregrine falcon; sparrowhawk

falconry A sport in which birds of prey are trained to hunt animals and other birds; also known as **hawking**. Two kinds of falcon are used. *Long-winged* birds, such as the peregrine, are used in open country, swooping on their prey from a great height and with devastating speed. The *short-winged* birds, or accipiters, perch on the falconer's gloved fist or tree branch until they see their prey, and then rely on speed. The birds are hooded until such time as they are ready to 'work'.

Falkenlust » **Augustusburg**

Falkland Islands, Span **Islas Malvinas** pop (1986) 1 919; area c.12 200 sq km/4 700 sq ml. British Crown Colony in the S Atlantic, c.650 km/400 ml NE of the Magellan Strait; consists of East Falkland and West Falkland, separated by the Falkland Sound, with over 200 small islands; timezone GMT −4; **Falkland Islands Dependencies** (c.8 million sq km/3 million sq ml) stretch c.2 400 km/1 500 ml through the S Atlantic, and include South Georgia, South Sandwich Islands, Shag Rocks, and Clerke Rocks; population mainly of British descent; no permanent population in the Dependencies; airport at Mt Pleasant near Stanley with a new runway built since the Falklands War; deeply indented coastline; hilly terrain, rising to 705 m/2 313 ft at Mt Usborne (East Falkland) and 700 m/2 297 ft at Mt Adam (West Falkland); strong winds; narrow temperature range, 19°C (Jan), 2°C (Jul); low annual rainfall (635 mm/25 in); seen by several early navigators, including Capt John Strong in 1689–90, who named the islands; French settlement, 1764; British base established, 1765; French yielded their settlement to the Spanish, 1767; occupied in the name of the Republic of Buenos Aires, 1820; Britain asserted possession, 1833; formal annexation, 1908 and 1917; the whole area claimed since independence by Argentina; invasion by Argentine military forces, April 1982; dispatch of British Task Force led to the return of the islands to British rule, June 1982; external affairs and defence are the responsibility of the British government, which appoints civil and military commissioners; internal affairs are governed by executive and legislative councils; chiefly agricultural economy; oats, sheep, service industries to the continuing military presence in the islands. » Falklands War; South Georgia; South Sandwich Islands; Stanley

Falklands War (Apr–Jun 1982) A war between Britain and Argentina, precipitated by the Argentine invasion of the Falkland Is, known to Argentinians as the **Malvinas**. Britain had ruled the islands continuously since 1833, but Argentina claimed them by inheritance from the Spanish Empire and through their proximity to her shores. The British had been conducting talks with Argentina on sovereignty over the Falklands, involving either a leaseback arrangement or a joint administration. When these talks broke down, the Argentinian government of General Galtieri issued a warning to the British. The British government announced the withdrawal of HMS *Endurance* from the S Atlantic, and on 19 March scrap merchants landed on South Georgia, ostensibly to demolish a whaling station, but they also raised the Argentine flag.

On the night of 1–2 April the full-scale invasion of the Falklands began. The 70 Royal Marines on the islands were overwhelmed, and the Governor, Mr Rex Hunt, was deported to Uruguay. The British immediately began to fit out a task force to retake the islands, and the Foreign Office team of Lord Carrington, Humphrey Atkins, and Richard Luce resigned. The task force, under the command of Rear Admiral John Woodward, consisted of almost 70 ships; 40 of them were requisitioned merchantmen, including well-known passenger vessels such as the *Canberra* and *Queen Elizabeth 2*. A 200-mile maritime exclusion zone was declared around the Falklands, and on 2 May the Argentine cruiser *General Belgrano* was sunk by the nuclear submarine *Conqueror*. This brought to an end peace initiatives conducted by the US Secretary of State Alexander Haig and the Peruvian Government. South Georgia was retaken on 25 April; the destroyer HMS *Sheffield* was sunk by an Exocet missile on 4 May; 5 000 British troops were landed at Port San Carlos on 21 May; and more troops were landed at Bluff Cove on 6–8 June, an operation attended by much loss of life when the Argentine air force attacked the *Sir Tristram* and *Sir Galahad*. The British forces, under the command of Major General Jeremy Moore, took Darwin and Goose Green on 28 May, and after the recapture of the capital, Port Stanley, the Argentinians surrendered on 14 June. The war cost the British £700 million; 254 British and 750 Argentine lives were lost; and some political commentators claim that it did much to save the declining fortunes of the government of Margaret Thatcher. » Argentina [i]; Falkland Islands [i]; Haig, Alexander; Thatcher, Margaret

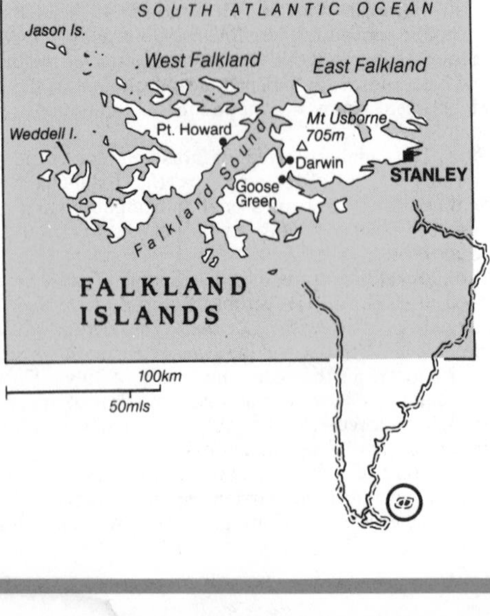

Falla, Manuel de [**fal**ya] (1876–1946) Spanish composer, born at Cadiz. He won prizes in 1905 as a pianist and for his first opera, then moved to Paris (1907–14), where he published his first piano compositions. On returning to Madrid, his works became known for their colourful national Spanish idiom. He is best known for his ballet, *The Three-Cornered Hat* (1919). With the outbreak of the Spanish Civil War, he settled in Argentina, where he died, at Alta Gracia.

fallacy A mistaken inference, often thought to be correct. 'All cats are mammals, Fido is a mammal; therefore Fido is a cat' is a deductive fallacy easily confused with the valid 'All cats are mammals, Fido is a cat; therefore Fido is a mammal'. 'Everything the Bible says is so; the Bible says that God exists; therefore God exists' is an example of a valid inference, but it commits the fallacy of *begging the question* if one accepts the first premiss only because one accepts the conclusion. Fallacies in inductive inferences typically arise from selecting an unrepresentative sample or from inferring causal connections solely from positive correlations. » deduction; induction; inference

Fallopian tubes A pair of long ducts passing outwards from the upper part of the uterus towards the ovary, also known as the **uterine tubes**. Each tube has a funnel-shaped lateral end (the *infundibulum*) with projecting finger-like processes (one of which is connected to the ovary), an expanded region, and a narrow part (the *isthmus*). The infundibulum collects the ovum released from the ovary and conveys it towards the uterus. Fertilization occurs within the Fallopian tube. » ectopic pregnancy; Fallopius; Graafian follicle; gynaecology; infertility; pregnancy [i]; sterilization; test-tube baby; uterus [i]

Fallopius, Gabriele, Ital **Gabriello Fallopio** (1523–62) Italian anatomist, born at Modena. He studied at Ferrara, then became professor of anatomy at Pisa (1548) and Padua (1551). He made several discoveries relating to bones and to the organs of reproduction. The **Fallopian tube** connecting the ovaries with the uterus is named after him. He died at Padua. » Fallopian tubes

fallout » **radioactive fallout**

fallow deer A true deer native to Mediterranean countries (introduced elsewhere); in summer, pale brown with white spots; in winter, grey without spots; antlers long, usually flattened with marginal projections; young male developing antlers for the first time called a 'pricket'. (*Dama dama.*) » antlers [i]; deer

false acacia A deciduous tree growing to 25 m/80 ft, native to E and C N America; leaves pinnate with 3–10 pairs of oval leaflets, silvery-haired when young; pea-flowers fragrant, white tinged with yellow, in many-flowered pendulous clusters up to 20 cm/8 in long; also called **locust tree**. Often planted as an ornamental, both in N America and Europe, it provides hard and very durable timber. (*Robinia pseudacacia*. Family: *Leguminosae.*) » carob; deciduous plants; pinnate

false bulrush » **reedmace**

false cypress An evergreen conifer, native to N America, Japan, and Formosa; similar to cypress, but with foliage in flattened sprays. As well as producing timber, most species have numerous ornamental forms. (Genus: *Chamaecyparis*, 6 species. Family: *Cupressaceae.*) » conifer; cypress; evergreen plants; Lawson/leyland cypress

Falwell, Jerry L (1933–) US religious leader, born at Lynchburg, Virginia. After studying at Baptist Bible College, Missouri, he was ordained a Baptist minister. In 1956, he founded Thomas Road Baptist Church, Lynchburg, Virginia, which became the basis of an extensive evangelical campaign. He was also responsible for founding the Moral Majority, Inc, and Liberty University. He has published widely, and broadcasts regularly to large audiences. » Baptists; evangelicalism

Famagusta [famagoosta], Gr **Ammokhostos**, Turkish **Magusa** 35°07N 33°57E, pop (1973) 38 960. Capital town of Famagusta district, E Cyprus, on Famagusta Bay; occupies site of ancient Arsinoë (3rd-c BC); strongly fortified by Venetians (15th–16th-c); chief port of Cyprus until 1974 Turkish invasion; now under Turkish occupation; declared by Cyprus government closed to shipping and an illegal port of entry; old town wall; 14th-c citadel; ruins of Church of St George of the Latins (late 13th-c); cathedral of St Nicholas (early 14th-c French Gothic). » Cyprus [i]

family An ambiguous term, referring to both the group formed by a co-resident husband, wife, and children (which sociologists term the *nuclear* family) or to a wider category of relatives, including non-resident grandparents, uncles, aunts, cousins, etc (the *extended* family). The nuclear family was once regarded as the key domestic institution of modern societies, but marriage has become somewhat less common, and the divorce rate has greatly increased, so that in societies such as contemporary England the majority of the population no longer lives within a nuclear family group. According to some estimates, only c.20% of all households are made up of nuclear families, the rest being constituted by single parents, foster, childless, or extended families, or simply individuals living alone. For different reasons, the same may have been true in many European peasant communities and in the early industrial cities. In many parts of the world, and in Europe in the pre-industrial period, the nuclear family was commonly part of a larger domestic group including some other relatives, and also employees, apprentices, etc. Anthropologists have been particularly interested in the circle of kin beyond the nuclear family, and have demonstrated that kinship groupings wider than the nuclear family may have crucial social functions. » family reconstitution/therapy; foster care; marriage

family of languages A set of 'daughter' languages which derive from the same 'parent' language, and which are thus genetically related. They can be represented by a *family tree*, as with the Indo-European languages, in which Celtic, Germanic, and Romance languages are all inter-related. They will show systematic correspondences in pronunciation. For example, words with *p* in Latin are often *f* in English, as in *pater/father*, *piscis/fish*. » comparative linguistics; Indo-European languages; *see panel p 434*

family planning » **contraception**

family reconstitution A technique developed by historical demographers since the 1960s, which uses parish registers and civil register entries of births, marriages, and deaths to reconstruct a family's fertility, nuptiality, and mortality patterns. These micro-studies of families and local communities permit wider estimates of changes in age-specific fertility and mortality to be made. » family; historical demography

family therapy A type of psychiatric treatment in which the family is the therapeutic unit, and an attempt is made to change the structure and functioning of the unit as well as to improve relationships within it. The main development of this technique took place in the 1960s as a form of psychotherapy. It has subsequently had a number of different schools with distinctive styles of treatment. » family; psychotherapy

fan palm A dwarf palm, native to dry places in the Mediterranean, often planted as an ornamental; trunk fibre-covered, sometimes extremely short, suckering and forming clumps; leaves fan-shaped. It is the only widespread native palm in Europe. (*Chamaerops humilis*. Family: *Palmae.*) » palm

Fan Si Pan [fan see **pan**] 22°19N 103°46E. Highest mountain in Vietnam, rising to 3 143 m/10 311 ft SW of Lao Cai, N Vietnam. » Vietnam [i]

fandango A Spanish dance in triple time, usually accompanied by guitars and castanets. It was known from c.1700 as a popular dance at roadside inns, and later became fashionable in aristocratic ballrooms.

Fanfani, Amintore [fan**fah**nee] (1908–) Italian statesman and Prime Minister, born at Pieve Santo Stefano. A former professor of political economics, he was Prime Minister on five occasions – in 1954, 1958–9, 1960–3 (twice), and 1982–3. Nominated a life Senator in 1972, he became President of the Italian Senate in 1968–73 and 1976–82. He is a member (and former Secretary and Chairman) of the Christian Democratic Party. » Christian Democrats; Italy [i]

Fangio, Juan Manuel [**fan**joh] (1911–) Argentine racing motorist, born at Balcarce, of Italian descent. He served his apprenticeship to road racing first as a mechanic and then (with a car he built himself) in S American events. He first took part in European Grand Prix racing in 1949, and by 1957 had won the World Championship a record five times (1951, 1954–7). He won 24 Grands Prix. After his retirement (1958) he joined Mercedes-Benz in Argentina. He was once held hostage by Castro's revolutionaries in Cuba. » Castro; motor racing

fantail The name used for a group of birds of uncertain affinity, native to SE Asia (India to the Philippines, Australia); inhabits forests; eats insects. Some authors classify fantails with flycatchers in the family *Muscicapidae*; others make a separate family, *Rhipiduridae*. (Genus: *Rhipidura* contains most of the c.42 species.) » flycatcher; wagtail

fantasia An instrumental piece in which the composer's imagination is allowed free rein in one direction or another. An element of improvisation is often suggested, but some fantasias (such as Purcell's for strings) are carefully structured. » improvisation; Purcell, Henry

Fantin-Latour, (Ignace) Henri (Jean Théodore) (1836–1904) French painter, pastellist, and lithographer, born at Grenoble. He studied at Paris, and stayed for a while in England. He is best known for his flower studies and portrait groups, such as 'Hommage à Delacroix' (Louvre). In his later years he specialized in lithography. He died at Buré. » French art; lithography

fanworm A sedentary marine worm that lives within a tube which it constructs; possesses a crown of tentacles or gills (*branchiae*) around its mouth, used for catching suspended food particles and for respiration; c.800 species, most from shallow seas. (Class: *Polychaeta*. Order: *Sabellida.*) » worm

farad SI unit of capacitance; symbol F; named after British chemist Michael Faraday; defined as the capacitance of a capacitor comprising two parallel plates between which is a potential difference of one volt when the capacitor is charged with one coulomb of electricity; commonly used as μF (**microfarad**, 10^{-6} F) and pF (**picofarad, 10^{-12}** F). » capacitance; electricity; units (scientific); RR70

faraday The electrical charge on a mole (6.02×10^{23}) of electrons, 9.65×10^{4} coulombs. This amount of charge is required, for example, to reduce one mole (108 g) of silver ions by the reaction: $Ag^{+}+e^{-}\rightarrow Ag$. » Avogadro's number; coulomb; Faraday; mole (physics)

Faraday, Michael (1791–1867) British chemist, experimental physicist, and natural philosopher, born at Newington Butts,

FAMILY OF LANGUAGES

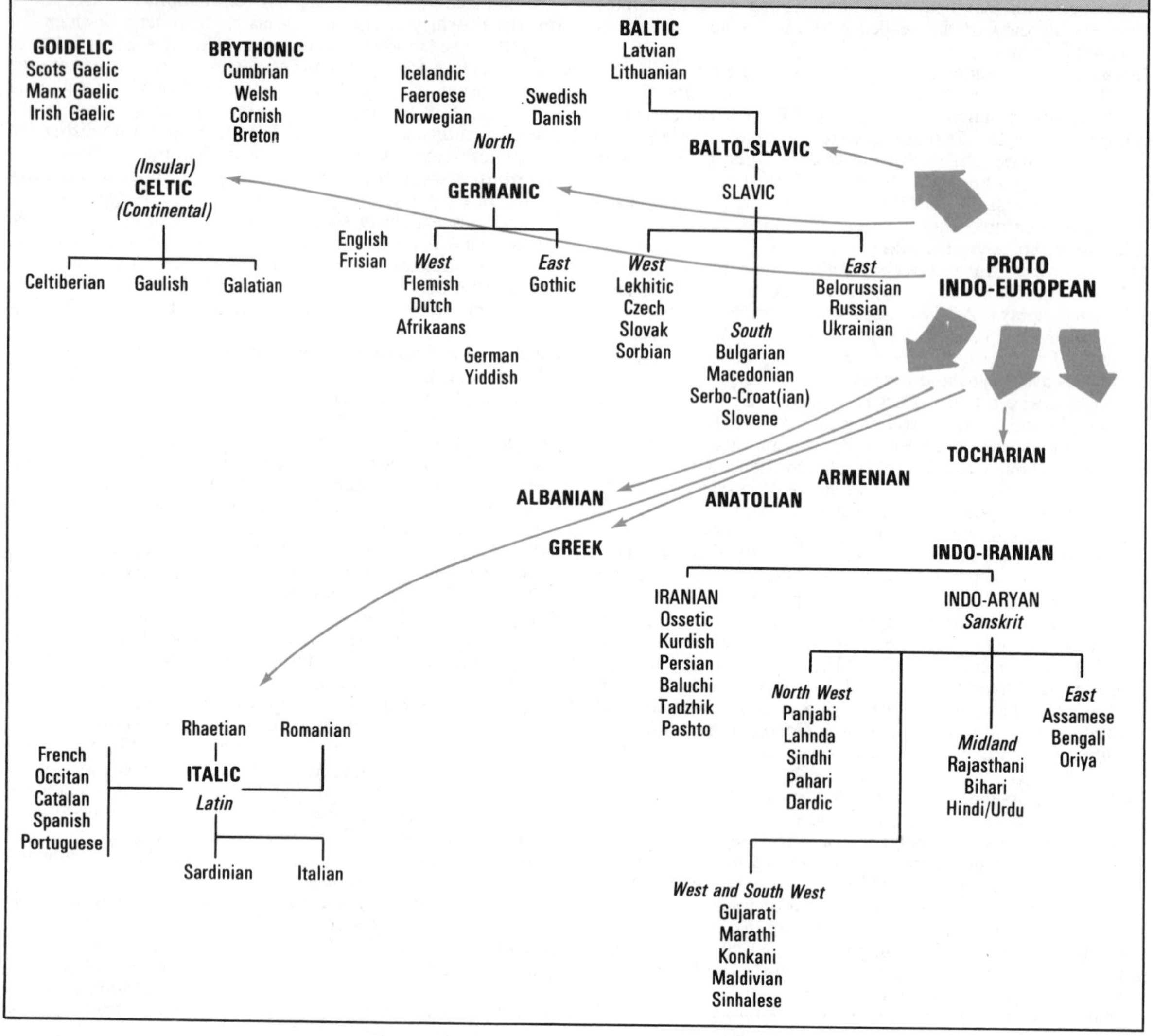

Surrey. Apprenticed to a bookbinder, he devoted his leisure to science. In 1813 he was engaged by Davy as his assistant at the Royal Institution, and in 1827 he succeeded to Davy's chair of chemistry. His research contributed to an extremely broad area of physical science, such as the condensation of gases, the conservation of force, and studies on benzene and steel. His major work is the series of *Experimental Researches on Electricity* (1839–55), in which he reports a wide range of discoveries about the nature of electricity, notably electrolysis, and the relationship between electricity and magnetism. He died at Hampton Court, Surrey. » Davy; electrolysis [i]; electromagnetic induction; Faraday effect

Faraday cage » **screening**

Faraday effect The rotation of polarization plane for linearly polarized light passing through some substance in the presence of a strong magnetic field; described by British physicist Michael Faraday in 1845, and historically important as a means of demonstrating the link between light and magnetism. It is a type of magneto-optical effect, caused by anisotropy induced by the applied field. It is distinct from optical activity: rotation due to optical activity vanishes if the ray retraces its original path, whereas for the Faraday effect the rotation would be doubled. » Faraday; isotropic; optical activity; polarimetry; Zeeman effect

Faraday's law » **electromagnetic induction**

farandole [faran**dol**] A folkdance from Provence performed to music in a moderate tempo; usually played on a flute and a drum. » Provence

Farel, Guillaume (1489–1565) Swiss Protestant reformer, born at Gap, France. He studied at Paris, where he became a convert to Protestantism, and was forced to flee to Switzerland (1524). After being twice compelled to leave Geneva, he returned there in 1534, the town council soon after proclaiming the Reformation. He was responsible for making Calvin stay in Geneva, but the severity of the ecclesiastical discipline which Calvin imposed caused their expulsion from the city (1538). He later returned with Calvin to Geneva, and then went to Neuchâtel (1543), where he died. » Calvinism; Reformation

Farm Credit Administration (FCA) A system set up in the USA in the 1920s and 1930s to revive agriculture by providing adequate finance, especially mortgages. It was made independent in 1953, and is still in existence.

farmer co-operative A form of organization which enables farmers to work together for mutual benefit. It may involve co-operative production, processing, marketing, or the provision of requisites. It usually enables farmers to exploit economies of scale without losing financial control over the operation. Control of co-operatives is typically based on one-man one-vote, and returns are strictly in proportion to patronage. » collective farm; economies of scale

farming » **arable/dairy/extensive/factory/intensive/livestock/organic farming**

Farnaby, Giles (c.1560–1640) English composer, born (probably) at Truro, Cornwall. He was a joiner by trade, but graduated in music at Oxford, and lived for a time near Lincoln. By 1614 he seems to have moved to London, where he died. His works include madrigals and settings of the psalms, but he is best remembered for his keyboard music. » madrigal

Farne Islands or **The Staples** A group of basaltic islets in the North Sea, 3 km/1¾ ml NE of the mainland, Northumberland, NE England; sanctuary for birds and Atlantic seals; St Cuthbert lived and died here; scene of heroic rescue in 1838 by Grace Darling (1815–42) and her father, **William** (1795–1860), the lighthouse keeper, of survivors of the *Forfarshire*. » North Sea

Farnese, Alessandro [fahn**ay**zay] (1545–92) Italian general, born in Rome. He fought in the service of Philip II of Spain, who was his uncle, and distinguished himself against the Turks at Lepanto (1571). As Governor-General of the Spanish Netherlands (1578–92), he captured Antwerp (1585), and compelled Henry IV of France to raise the siege of Paris (1590). He died at Arras, France. » Henry IV (of France); Philip II (of Spain)

Faro [f**a**roo] 37°02N 7°55W, pop (1981) 28 200. Industrial seaport and capital of Faro district, S Portugal; on S coast, 219 km/136 ml SSE of Lisbon; airport; railway; trade in wine, cork, fish, fruit; focal point of Algarve tourism; cathedral, Churches of the Carmo and of Santo Antonio do Alto (1754); Senhora do Carmo fair (Jul), Santa Iria fair (Aug). » Portugal [i]

Faroe Islands » **Faeroe Islands**

Faroese » **Germanic languages; Scandinavian languages**

Farouk I [far**oo**k] (1920–65) Last King of Egypt (1936–52), born in Cairo. He was educated in England, and studied at the Royal Military Academy, Woolwich. After World War 2 he turned increasingly to a life of pleasure. The defeat of Egypt by Israel (1948) and continuing British occupation led to increasing unrest, and General Neguib's coup (1952) forced his abdication and exile. In 1959 he became a citizen of Monaco, and died in Rome. » Egypt [i]

Farquhar, George [f**ah**ker] (c.1677–1707) Irish playwright, born at Londonderry. Educated at Dublin, he became an actor in a Dublin theatre, but soon left the stage and joined the army. His first comedy, *Love and a Bottle* (1698), proved a success, as were several other plays, notably *The Recruiting Officer* (1706). His best work, *The Beaux' Stratagem* (1707), was written during his last illness. He died in London. » drama; Irish literature

Farrell, James T(homas) (1904–79) US writer of starkly realist novels of American life, born in Chicago. His best-known book is the *Studs Lonigan* trilogy (1932–5), set in the slums of Chicago. He died in New York City. » American literature; novel

Farsi » **Iranian languages**

farthing A small British coin, a quarter of an old (pre-decimalization) penny, its value therefore being $\frac{1}{960}$th of one pound. It was withdrawn from circulation in 1960.

Fasching [f**a**shing] The period of merrymaking in Munich, S Germany, between Epiphany (6 Jan) and Lent. » Munich

fasciation The abnormal, flattened growth of a single shoot, which resembles several stems fused together and often bears several inflorescences. Its causes include mechanical damage to meristems, infections by the bacterium *Phytomonas*, and mutation. It is common in such plants as dandelions and plantains. Cock's comb is a mutant which breeds true. » bacteria [i]; cock's comb; gall; inflorescence [i]; meristem

Fasciola [fas**ee**uhla] » **liver fluke**

fascism A term applied to a variety of vehemently nationalistic and authoritarian movements that reached the peak of their influence in 1930–45. The original fascist movement was founded by Mussolini in Italy (1921), and during the 1930s several such movements grew up in Europe, the most important being the German Nazi Party. The central ideas of fascism are a belief in the supremacy of the chosen national group over other races, and the need to subordinate society to the leadership of a dictator who can pursue national aggrandisement without taking account of different interests. Fascism advocates the abolition of all institutions of democracy, the suppression of sources of opposition such as trade unions, and to varying degrees the mobilization of society under fascist leadership. Fascism is also strongly associated with militaristic and belligerent foreign policy stances. Since World War 2 its appeal has declined, although in some Latin American countries fascist-type governments have held office. » authoritarianism; neofascism

fashion A prevailing style in dress adopted by large numbers of the population. This is a Western phenomenon; in other cultures, styles have altered little over the centuries, until very recent times when 'Westernization' has occurred in some cases. Although many think of 'fashion' as relating only to women's clothing, from the Middle Ages until the 19th-c, it involved men equally. In the latter third of the 20th-c many designers have made collections for men as well as women. Until this century, clothes for the wealthy were made-to-measure, fashions changing quite slowly; the influence was from the top (the court) downwards. However, during the 19th-c a new influence, that of the fashion designer or couturier, began to make itself felt. Charles Worth (1825–95), in Paris and London, not only made clothes for those wealthy clients who could afford his services, he also sold designs to manufacturers who could produce cheaper copies. With the invention around the same time (1860s) of the sewing machine and the paper pattern, followed much later by the development of mass production and artificial fibres, ready-to-wear clothing has gradually become the main source of fashion as we understand it. The French influence, supreme throughout the first half of this century, is now tempered by the work of designers in London, Milan, Rome, and New York.

Fashoda [fash**oh**da] A settlement (now called Kodok) on the upper White Nile, which was the scene of a major Anglo-French crisis in 1898. French forces under Captain Jean Baptiste Marchand (1863–1934) had reached the Nile after an 18-month journey from Brazzaville. The British, who were in the process of retaking the Sudan, issued an ultimatum, but France was unprepared to go to war, and Marchand was ordered to withdraw. The incident destroyed French ambitions for a trans-continental African empire, and confirmed British mastery of the Nile region. » Africa, Partition of; Kitchener, Earl

Fasil Ghebbi [f**a**sil g**e**bee] The royal complex of Emperor Fassilides (1632–67) in Gondar, NW Ethiopia; a world heritage site. Gondar was the permanent capital of Ethiopia in the 17th–18th-c, and today efforts are being made to preserve the castles and monuments of this period. » Ethiopia [i]

Fassbinder, Rainer Werner [f**a**sbinder] (1946–82) West German film director, born at Bad Wöshofen. He began his career as an actor in fringe theatre in Munich, founding his own 'anti-theatre' company. His work in cinema began in 1969, and was much influenced by Jean-Luc Godard. He completed over 40 full-length films, largely politically committed criticisms of contemporary Germany, notably *Die bitteren Tränen der Petra von Kant* (1972, The Bitter Tears of Petra von Kant) and *Die Ehe der Maria Braun* (1979, The Marriage of Maria Braun), which won 1st prize at the 1979 Berlin Film Festival. The most prolific writer-director-actor of the New German Cinema of the 1970s, he died in Munich at 36, as a result of alcohol and drugs.

fast reactor » **nuclear reactor** [i]

fat 1 A complex mixture of many different triglycerides, each formed when three molecules of fatty acids combine with one of glycerol. It is the major storage fuel of plants and animals. » fatty acids; triglyceride **2** A white or yellowish animal tissue (*adipose tissue*) in which individual cells are swollen with the accumulation of fat forming a single globule within the cytoplasm. The stored triglycerides are an energy source for the organism. In hibernating animals in particular, the fat forms a large number of fine globules in the cytoplasm, giving the cells a foamy appearance (*brown fat*). Fat acts as a packing and insulating material in many animals (eg subcutaneous tissues in humans), but it can also act as a shock absorber (eg under the heel, the palm of the hand). Human excess accumulation of body fat (*obesity*) arises when energy intake (diet) exceeds energy output (physical activity). » cytoplasm; obesity; saturated; triglyceride

fat hen An annual found in most temperate regions; the whole plant with mealy white covering, flowers minute. Once used as a spinach-like vegetable, the seeds providing flour, nowadays it remains as a common weed of cultivated and waste ground. (*Chenopodium album*. Family: *Chenopodiaceae*.) » annual; beet

Fatah, (al-) [**fa**ta] The Palestine National Liberation Movement (PNLM), created in 1957 and headed by Yasser Arafat. Fatah is the single biggest Palestinian movement, and operates under the umbrella of the PLO. The name *fatah* means 'victory'. » Arafat; PLO

fatalism A philosophical doctrine, attributed to the Stoics and others, which maintains that the future is as unalterable as the past; that what will be will be, no matter what a person may do to avert its happening. Fatalists are determinists, but not all versions of determinism entail fatalism. » determinism; Stoicism

Fateh Singh, Sant [**fate sing**] (1911–72) Sikh religious leader and campaigner for Sikh rights, born in the Punjab. He was involved in religious and educational activity in Rajasthan, founding many schools and colleges there. In 1942 he joined the Quit India Movement, and was imprisoned for his political activities. During the 1950s he agitated for a Punjabi-speaking autonomous state, which was achieved with the creation of the Indian state of Punjab in 1966. He died at Amritsar, Punjab. » Punjab (India); Sikhism

Fatehpur Sikri or **Fathpur Sikri** [fatuh**poor sik**ree] A legendary ghost city and architectural masterpiece of the Mughals in Uttar Pradesh, India. Founded as the Imperial capital of Emperor Akbar in 1569, the city was abandoned within two decades because of water shortages. » Akbar the Great

Fates » Parcae

Father's Day In some countries, a day on which fathers are honoured. In the USA and the UK, it is held on the third Sunday in June; in Australia, the first Sunday in September.

Fathers of the Church A title usually applied to the leaders of the early Christian Church, recognized as teachers of truths of the faith. They were characterized by orthodoxy of doctrine and personal holiness, and were usually beatified. The study of their writings and thought is known as **patristics**. » Christianity; saint

Fatima (c.605–33) The youngest daughter of Mohammed, and wife of the fourth Muslim caliph, Ali. From them descended the Fatimids, a radical Shiite movement, who ruled over Egypt and N Africa (909–1171), and later over Syria and Palestine. » Mohammed; Shiites

Fatima (Portugal), also **Fátima** [**fa**tima] 39°37N 8°38W, pop (1981) 6 500. Pilgrimage town, Santarém district, C Portugal, where three peasant children claimed to have seen the 'Virgin of the Rosary' in 1917; Basilica (begun 1928, consecrated 1953). » Portugal [i]

fatty acids » carboxylic acids

Faulkner or **Falkner, William (Harrison)** (1897–1962) US author, born at New Albany, Mississippi. He served with the RAF in World War 1, and began his literary career with *Soldier's Pay* (1926), a novel on the aftermath of war. With *The Sound and the Fury* (1929) he began to experiment in literary form and style. *Sartoris* (1929) was the first in a series dealing with the social and racial problems of an imaginary Southern county, Yoknapatawpha. Other major novels include *As I lay Dying* (1930), *Absalom, Absalom!* (1936) and *The Reivers* (1962). He was awarded the Nobel Prize for Literature in 1949, and died near Oxford, Mississippi. » American literature; novel

fault In geology, a fracture in rock along which displacement has occurred due to stresses in the Earth. Where relative movement is vertical or nearly so, *normal faults* are caused by compression, which in extreme cases may lead to the overthrusting of one body of rock over another, and *reverse faults* are caused by crustal extension. *Tear faults* release compressional stress by sideways displacement, the best known example being the San Andreas Fault in California. Major faults can create significant features of landscape, such as block mountains and rift valleys. » horst; rift valley [i]

Faure, Edgar (Jean) [fohr] (1908–) French statesman and Prime Minister (1952, 1955–6), born at Béziers. He trained as a lawyer in Paris, entering politics as a radical-socialist. He was Minister of Finance and Economic Affairs several times in the 1950s, becoming Premier for two short periods. He was later Minister of Agriculture (1966), Education (1968), and Social Affairs (1969), and President of the National Assembly (1973–8). He has been a member of the European Parliament since 1979. He has also written several detective novels under the pseudonym of **Edgar Sanday**. » France [i]

Fauré, Gabriel (Urbain) [**foh**ray] (1845–1924) French composer, born at Pamiers. He became organist (1896) at La Madeleine, Paris, and director of the Conservatoire (1905–20). Though chiefly remembered for his songs, including the evergreen *Après un rêve* (c.1865), he also wrote operas and orchestral pieces, such as *Masques et bergamasques* (1919), and a much-performed *Requiem* (1887–90). He died in Paris.

Faust or **Faustus** [fowst, **fow**stus, **faw**stus] A legendary German scholar of the early 16th-c (derived from a historical magician of that name), who sold his soul to the devil in exchange for knowledge, magical power, and prolonged youth. His story inspired Marlowe's *Dr Faustus* (1592), literary works by Lessing (1784), Goethe (1808, 1832) and Thomas Mann (1947), and musical works including Gounod's opera *Faust* (1859).

Fauvism [**foh**vizm] (Fr *les fauves* 'the wild beasts') A name given in 1905 to a group of modern painters including Matisse, Derain, and Vlaminck by a hostile critic. Their work was inspired by van Gogh, Gauguin, and Cézanne. » Expressionism; French art; Derain; Matisse; Vlaminck

favism A type of anaemia caused by a genetic defect involving a key enzyme in maintaining the integrity of red blood cells. The disease can be exacerbated by certain drugs or by broad beans, and is more likely to be found where broad beans are a common part of the diet. » anaemia; enzyme

Fawcett, Dame Millicent, *née* **Garrett** (1847–1929) British women's rights campaigner, born at Aldeburgh, Suffolk. Keenly interested in the higher education of women and the extension of the franchise to her sex, she was made President of the National Union of Women's Suffrage Societies (1897–1919). She died in London. » women's liberation movement

Fawkes, Guy (1570–1606) English conspirator, born at York of Protestant parentage. He became a Catholic at an early age, and served in the Spanish army in the Netherlands (1593–1604). He crossed to England at Catesby's invitation, and became a member of the Gunpowder Plot. Caught red-handed, he was tried and hanged. » Catesby; Gunpowder Plot

fax The facsimile transmission of documents, diagrams, and photographs over a telephone network, widely available for international communication since 1986. The original is scanned by laser beam and digitally coded for transmission to the receiver, where it is printed out line by line on thermo-sensitive paper. Reading time is approximately 15 seconds for an A4 sheet of typescript or line diagram; somewhat slower for half-tone illustrations. » laser

FBI » Federal Bureau of Investigation

feather A structure formed from the skin of birds. It may be less than 0.5 mm/0.2 in long, or more than 1.5 m/5 ft. Birds evolved from reptiles, and feathers are modified scales. The naked region of the central shaft, near the skin of the bird, is called the *calamus*. Beyond this is the *rachis*, bearing many side branches (*barbs*). Each barb also has small side branches (*barbules*). The barbules of adjacent barbs interlock, creating the familiar flattened structure. This flat blade is called the *vane*, or *vexillum*, and the region bearing it is the *pennaceous* part of the feather. At the base of the vane, by the calamus, there may be some wispy barbs. This downy region is the *plumulaceous* part of the feather. The relative proportions of the pennaceous and plumulaceous regions vary between feathers from different parts of the body. Some feathers have no barbs, and the naked shafts resemble simple bristles. 'Down' feathers have flexible

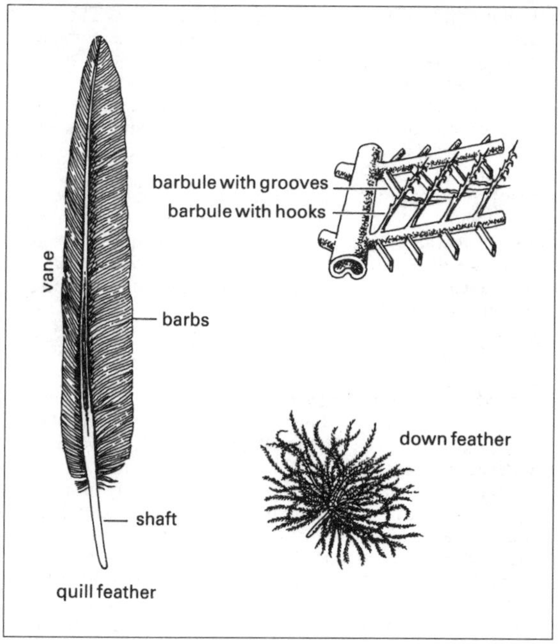

Feathers – Flight feather with closeup of structure, and down feather

and sometimes branched barbs, and the barbules hold the barbs in a three-dimensional shape. This creates a fluffy ball rather than a vane. Down feathers provide insulation; vaned feathers provide smooth aerodynamic surfaces. In many species feathers are important in display, and may be modified in shape and colour. » bird [i]; reptile

feather star An unattached sea lily, lacking a stalk in the adult; often brightly coloured, with 40 or more arms; abundant on coral reefs, but also found in deep waters. (Phylum: *Echinodermata.* Class: *Crinoidea.*) » coral; crinoid

February Revolution (France) (1848) The revolution in France (22–24 Feb 1848) which resulted in the abdication of King Louis Philippe, the proclamation of a Republic, and the establishment of a provisional government. Although not the first of the European revolutions of 1848, it inspired subsequent revolutionary activity in Germany and Austria. » Louis Philippe; Revolutions of 1848

February Revolution (Russia) (1917) Popular demonstrations, strikes, and military mutinies in Petrograd, Russia (Feb–Mar 1917), which led to the abdication of Nicholas II and the collapse of the tsarist government. The regime was succeeded by a series of provisional governments composed of liberal and moderate socialist ministers, and by the establishment of the Soviet ('council') of Workers' and Soldiers' Deputies, a situation known as 'dual power'. » April Theses; Bolsheviks; July Days; Mensheviks; Nicholas II; October Revolution; Russian history

feces » **faeces**

Fechner, Gustav (Theodor) [**fekh**ner] (1801–87) German physicist, philosopher, anthropologist, and psychologist, born at Gross Särchen. His interest in mind-body relationships led to his book *Elemente der Psychophysik* (1860, Elements of Psychophysics), in which he developed the ideas of Ernst Heinrich Weber on the measurement of sensory thresholds, and laid the foundations for psychophysics. He was also the founder of experimental aesthetics, and his methods were influential in the development of experimental psychology. » experimental psychology; psychology; psychophysics; Weber

Fedayeen [feda**yeen**] A label commonly used to describe commandos operating under the umbrella of the Palestine Liberation Organization. The name is from the Arabic *fidai*, 'one who sacrifices oneself' (for a cause or country). » PLO

Federal Bureau of Investigation (FBI) The US organization primarily concerned with internal security or counter-intelligence operations, although it also has responsibility for investigating violations of federal law not remitted by the federal government to any other organization. The FBI is a branch of the Department of Justice.

Federal Constitutional Convention » **Constitutional Convention**

Federal Reserve System (FRS) The USA Central Bank, known as 'The Fed', set up in 1913. It divides the USA into twelve districts, each with its own Federal Reserve Bank, carries out the normal duties of a central bank, and also manages cheque clearance on behalf of member banks. Less than half of the 14 000 banks in the USA are members of the Fed.

federalism A form of territorial political organization which aims to maintain national unity while allowing for regional diversity. This is achieved by distributing different constitutional powers to national and regional governments. Power is not hierarchically distributed, but allocated among independent yet interacting centres; the national government is thus not in a position to dictate to regional governments, as could happen under a system of local government. The key features of federalism usually are: (at least) two tiers of government enjoying their own right of existence under the constitution; separate legislative and executive powers; separate sources of revenue; an umpire (normally the supreme court) to decide upon disputes between the different levels; and a bicameral parliament which provides for representation in regional or state government. Beyond that, federalism can and does take a variety of forms: examples include the USA, Canada, Australia, and Germany. » devolution

Federalist Party One of the two political parties that took shape in the USA in the 1790s. The issues behind its formation included President Washington's foreign policy and the domestic policies of Secretary of the Treasury Alexander Hamilton. Washington (in office 1789–97) and John Adams (in office 1797–1801) were Federalist presidents, but after Jefferson's victory in the 1800 election the Federalists never held the presidency, and the Party slowly faded. » Adams, John; Hamilton, Alexander; Hartford Convention; Washington, George

feedback The process by which information is conveyed to the source of the original output; also, the information itself. The term comes from cybernetics, and is applied both to machines and to animal and human communication, whereby it enables the sender of a message to monitor its reception and make any necessary modification. » biofeedback; cybernetics

Feininger, Lyonel (Charles Adrian) [**fiy**ninger] (1871–1956) US painter of German origin, born and died in New York City. He worked as a political cartoonist, then devoted himself to painting (1907). After World War 1 he taught at the Bauhaus in Weimar and Dessau, and adopted a style reminiscent of Cubism. After the Nazi rise, he returned to the USA where he helped to found the New Bauhaus in Chicago. » Bauhaus; Cubism

feldspar or **felspar** An important group of minerals constituting about half of the rocks of the Earth's crust. All are aluminosilicates containing various proportions of potassium, sodium, and calcium (and, rarely, barium). Important minerals of the group are *orthoclase* and *microcline* (both $KAlSi_3O_8$), *albite* ($NaAlSi_3O_8$) and *anorthite* ($CaAl_2Si_2O_8$). Na,Ca feldspars are termed *plagioclase*. » orthoclase; silicate minerals

Felidae The cat family (37 species); a family of muscular carnivores with camouflaged coloration; round head with powerful jaws, long canine teeth; sharp claws (usually retractable); cannot chew food; eats meat almost exclusively; usually catches own prey; hunts by stalking followed by a pounce or short sprint; species of genus *Panthera* called *big cats.* » caracal; carnivore [i]; cat; cheetah; clouded leopard; cougar; fossa; golden cat; jaguar; jaguarundi; leopard; leopard cat; liger; lion; lynx; margay; ocelot; Pallas's cat; panther; serval; snow leopard; tiger; wild cat

Fellini, Federico (1920–) Italian film director, born at Rimini. Educated at Bologna, he was a cartoonist, journalist, and scriptwriter before becoming an assistant film director in 1942. His highly individual films, always from his own scripts, include *La Strada* (1954, The Road; foreign film Oscar winner, 1957), *Fellini's Roma* (1972), *Amarcord* (1974, I Remember), and, his most famous and controversial work, *La Dolce Vita* (1960, The Sweet Life; Cannes Festival prize winner), a *succès de scandale* for its cynical evocation of modern Roman high life. In 1943 he married the actress Giulietta Masina, star of several of his films. Among his later productions are *Citta della Donna* (1980, City of Women) and *Ginger and Fred* (1986).

felspar » **feldspar**

felt A non-woven cloth consisting of loose 'webs' of natural or synthetic fibre, formed by fabrics or the action of moisture, heat, and repeated pressure; the fibres become locked together by entanglement. Felts are important industrial and domestic materials.

feminism A socio-political movement whose objective is equality of rights, status, and power for men and women. It has its roots in early 20th-c struggles for women's political emancipation (the suffragettes), but has been broadened in its political scope by the influence of radical left-wing beliefs, especially Marxism, which has led feminists to challenge both sexism and the capitalist system which is said to encourage patriarchy. Feminists are not necessarily 'anti-men', but against any social system which produces female subordination. » feminist criticism/theology; gender; sexism; suffragettes; women's liberation movement

feminist criticism Literary criticism written from a feminist standpoint. The main objectives are to re-assess the established 'canon', exposing sexist attitudes in works themselves and their selection; and also to promote the works of neglected women writers. Early influences were Virginia Woolf (eg *A Room of One's Own*, 1929) and Simone de Beauvoir's *Le Deuxième Sexe* (1949, The Second Sex). The field is now large, active, and various. » American/English/French literature; de Beauvoir; feminism; literary criticism

feminist theology The theological critique of a religious tradition, especially Christianity, which is regarded as being predominantly male-oriented and presented in non-inclusive language. In its reconstruction of traditional theology, emphasis is placed on symbols, models, and images which express the religious, social, and psychological experience of women. » Christianity; feminism; theology

femur [**fee**muh] The long bone of the thigh, having a rounded head, neck, and shaft, and an expanded lower end. It articulates by the head with the pelvis (via the hip joint), the patella, and the tibia (via the knee joint). It is the largest and longest bone in the body, and gives attachment to powerful muscle groups which move the thigh with respect to the trunk, and also the calf with respect to the thigh. » pelvis; tibia; Plate XIII

fencing The art of fighting with a sword, one of the oldest sports, which can be traced back to the ancient Egyptians c.1300 BC. Fencing was popular in the Middle Ages, and the rapier was developed by the end of the 16th-c. Modern weapons consist of the sabre, foil, and épée. In competitive fencing, different target areas exist for each weapon, and contestants wear electronically wired clothing to indicate successful hits. Because of its dangers, competitors also wear protective masks. » RR110

Fénelon, François de Salignac de la Mothe [**fay**nuhlõ] (1651–1715) French Roman Catholic theologian, born at Fénelon, Périgord. Ordained in 1675, in 1689 Louis XIV made him tutor to his grandson, and in this position he wrote several works, notably *Les Aventures de Télémaque* (1699, The Adventures of Telemachus), which received the King's censure for its political undertones. He became Archbishop of Cambrai in 1695. In 1697 he wrote *Explication des maximes des saints sur la vie intérieure* (1697, Explanation of the Sayings of the Saints on the Interior Life). The book was condemned by the Pope, a decision which Fénelon accepted. He retired to Cambrai, where he died. » Louis XIV; Roman Catholicism; theology

Fenians The short title of the Irish Republican Brotherhood, a nationalist organization founded in New York in 1857. The movement quickly espoused violence as a means of achieving its objective, and is best known for attacks in Manchester and London in 1867 to rescue imprisoned supporters. The fatalities which occurred caused these to be called 'The Fenian Outrages'. » nationalism; Sinn Féin

fennec fox A small nocturnal fox native to deserts in N Africa and Kuwait; smallest member of the dog family; thick pale coat, enormous ears; digs long burrows in sand; eats rodents, birds, lizards, insects; also known as **desert fox**. (*Vulpes zerda.*) » Canidae; dog; fox

fennel A strong-smelling, bluish-green biennial or perennial, growing to 2.5 m/8 ft, native to the Mediterranean region; leaves feathery, much divided into thread-like segments; flowers yellow, in umbels to 8 cm/3 in across; fruit ovoid, ribbed. Cultivated since classical times, the leaves are used as a flavouring. Cultivated forms with swollen bases to the leaf stalks are eaten raw in salads or cooked as a vegetable. (*Foeniculum vulgare*. Family: *Umbelliferae*.) » biennial; perennial; umbel

Fens, the or **Fen Country** Flat marshy land surrounding the Wash, in Lincolnshire, Norfolk, Suffolk, and Cambridgeshire, E England; extends 112 km/70 ml N–S and 6 km/4 ml E–W; watered by the Witham, Welland, Nene, and Ouse Rivers; remnant of a silted-up North Sea bay; artificially drained since Roman times; major reclamation in 17th-c under 5th Earl of Bedford and his Dutch engineer, Cornelius Vermuyden; in mediaeval times, monasteries built on 'islands' of dry land; market gardening, fruit, vegetables, grazing. » Bedford Level; England [i]; Wash, the

fenugreek An annual growing to 50 cm/20 in, a native of SW Asia; leaves have three shallowly toothed leaflets; pea-flowers yellowish-white, solitary or in pairs, stalkless in the upper leaf axils; pod up to 10 cm/4 in long. Grown for fodder, its seeds are edible (used in curries), and it is also employed medicinally. (*Trigonella foenum-graecum*. Family: *Leguminosae*.) » annual

fer-de-lance [fair duh **lahns**] (Fr 'spearhead') A New World pit viper; powerful venom; two species: *Bothrops atrox* (**southern fer-de-lance**) and *Bothrops asper* (**Central American fer-de-lance**), two of the species most responsible for human death by snakebite; also known as **lancehead viper**. Other pit vipers may also be referred to as lanceheads. » pit viper [i]

Ferdinand (of Castile), byname **the Catholic** (1452–1516) King of Castile, as Ferdinand V (from 1474), of Aragon and Sicily, as Ferdinand II (from 1479), and of Naples, as Ferdinand III (from 1503), born at Sos, Aragon. In 1469 he married Isabella, sister of Henry IV of Castile, and ruled jointly with her until her death. He introduced the Inquisition (1478–80), and in 1492, after the defeat of the Moors, expelled the Jews. Under him, Spain gained supremacy following the discovery of America, and in 1503 he took Naples from the French, with the help of the Holy League. After Isabella's death (1504) he was Regent of Castile for his insane daughter Juana, and in 1512 gained Navarre, thus becoming monarch of all Spain. To him and Isabella, Spain owed her unity and greatness as a nation and the foundation of her imperial influence. He died at Madrigalejo, Spain. » Holy League; Inquisition; Isabella of Castile

Ferdinand I (of the Two Sicilies) (1751–1825) King of Naples, as Ferdinand IV (1759–99, 1799–1806) and of the Two Sicilies (1816–25), born and died at Naples. He joined England and Austria against France in 1793, and suppressed the French-supported Roman Republic (1799), but in 1801 was forced to make a treaty with Napoleon. In 1806 he took refuge in Sicily, under English protection, being reinstated by the Congress of Vienna (1815). In 1816 he united his two states into the Kingdom of the Two Sicilies, and despite demands for constitutional government, retained a harsh absolutism. » French Revolutionary Wars; Napoleonic Wars; Vienna, Congress of

Ferdusi » **Firdausi**

Fermanagh [fer**mana**], Gaelic **Fear Manach** pop (1981) 51 008; area 1 676 sq km/647 sq ml. County in SW Northern Ireland; bounded NW, W, S and SE by the Republic of Ireland; hilly in the NE and SW, rising to 667 m/2 188 ft at Cuilcagh; Upper and Lower Lough Erne run SE–NW through the centre; county town, Enniskillen; potatoes, livestock, textiles. » Enniskillen; Northern Ireland [i]

Fermat, Pierre de [fer**mah**] (1601–65) French mathematician, born at Beaumont-de-Lomagne. He became a lawyer, and then turned to mathematics, making many discoveries in the properties of numbers, probabilities, and geometry. With Descartes, he was one of the two leading mathematicians in the early 17th-c. He died at Castres. » Fermat's last theorem; Fermat's principle [i]

Fermat's last theorem A mathematical theorem proposed by Pierre Fermat, which states that there are no positive integers *x*, *y*, *z*, and *n* (where *n* is greater than 2), such that $x^n + y^n = z^n$ (compare $x^2 + y^2 = z^2$, where there is an infinite number of integers satisfying this relation.) Fermat wrote in the margin of a book 'I have found an admirable proof of this theorem, but the margin is too narrow to contain it'. The theorem has been proved for all *n* less than about 30 000, using computers, but a general proof has not yet been found. Many have claimed to have found a proof, but all claims have so far been shown to be fallacious. » Fermat

Fermat's principle A principle in physics: light rays travel between two points in such a way that the time taken is a

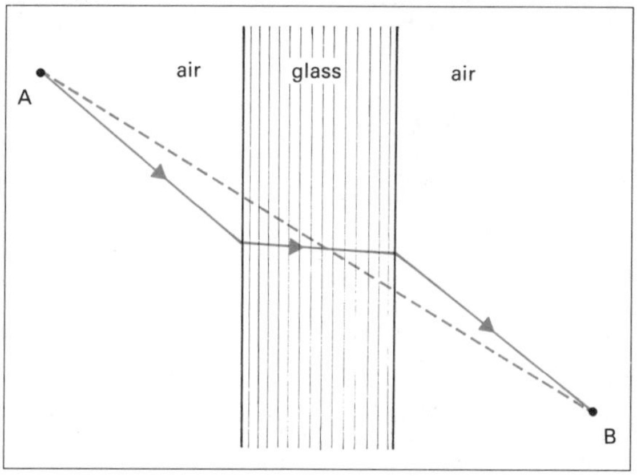

Fermat's Principle – The dotted line shows the shortest path between A and B. A light beam follows the solid line, consistent with the laws of refraction, because the velocity of light in the glass is less than in air. The solid line is the path of least time.

minimum; stated by French mathematician Pierre de Fermat in 1657. It is a special case of the least-action principle. » Fermat; least-action principle

fermentation A chemical reaction in which an organic compound is broken down through the action of an enzyme. This process is typically carried out using bacteria or yeast to metabolize carbohydrates in the absence of oxygen. The two most common end products of fermentation are lactic acid and ethanol, but the exact end product depends on the type of bacteria and the nature of the material used. » anaerobe; bacteria [i]; enzyme; ethanol; lactic acid; wine; yeast; yogurt

Fermi, Enrico (1901–54) Italian nuclear physicist, born in Rome. He studied at Pisa, Göttingen, and Leyden, and became professor of theoretical physics at Rome in 1927. In 1934 he and his colleagues split a number of nuclei by bombardment with neutrons, for which he was awarded the 1938 Nobel Prize for Physics. He did not return to Italy from his Nobel Prize presentation in Stockholm because the Italian anti-Semitic Laws affected his Jewish wife, but became professor at Columbia University (1939). He played a prominent part in developing atomic energy, and constructed the first US nuclear reactor (1942). He died in Chicago. » Fermi-Dirac statistics; fermions; nuclear physics

fermi [**fer**mee] » RR70

Fermi-Dirac statistics [**fer**mee di**rak**] In quantum statistical mechanics, the description of collections of many non-interacting fermions. The Fermi-Dirac distribution expresses the partition of energy amongst fermions, used for example in the study of the free electron gas in metals. » Bose-Einstein statistics; Dirac; electronic structure of solids; Fermi; fermions; statistical mechanics

fermions Sub-atomic particles having half integer spin, the particles of matter; named after Italian physicist Enrico Fermi. The Pauli exclusion principle states that no two fermions may occupy the same state. Electrons, protons, and quarks are all fermions. » baryon; boson; Fermi; Fermi-Dirac statistics; lepton; Pauli exclusion principle; muon; particle physics; spin

fern A large group of spore-bearing, vascular plants related to clubmosses and horsetails, and containing some 10 000 species which comprise the class *Filicopsida* or *Filicinae*. Like their relatives, they have a long fossil record containing many extinct forms. Ferns appear as early as the Devonian period, but they were especially abundant and diverse during the Carboniferous. The visible plant is the diploid sporophyte, the dominant generation in ferns. It typically has one or more large, often much-divided fronds which are characteristically coiled in a crozier shape when young, unfurling as they grow. The undersides of fertile fronds bear sporangia, which may be grouped into sori forming distinctive patterns; the position, shape, and covering (*indusium*) of each sorus is diagnostically important. When released from the sporangia, the spores germinate to form haploid *prothalli*, the gametophyte generation. In ferns these are very small, often heart-shaped and short-lived; this is the more vulnerable generation, requiring damp habitats and being easily killed by harsh conditions.

Ferns embrace a large number of forms. A few are annuals, but most are perennials with tough rhizomes. The fronds typically form a rosette, but may be produced singly or at intervals along the rhizome. Several species are climbers; some have stout, erect, trunk-like rhizomes; and a few are genuinely arborescent – tree forms with tall, rigid trunks bearing a crown of fronds. A small number of species are aquatic. In these the fronds are very reduced, and have non-wettable hairs to ensure they float. Although more or less cosmopolitan, the majority of species is concentrated in the tropics and in the warmer, more humid parts of the world. (Class: *Filicinae*.) » annual; clubmoss; Carboniferous/Devonian periods; fossil; horsetail; perennial; rhizome; sorus; sporangium; sporophyte; vascular tissue

Fernandel, stage name of **Fernand Joseph Désiré Contandin** (1903–71) French film comedian, born in Marseilles. He worked in a bank and a soap factory before his debut on the stage in 1922, and from 1930 appeared in over 100 films. He established himself internationally as the country priest of *Le Petit Monde de Don Camillo* (1953, The Little World of Don Camillo). He was renowned for his wide grin and his remarkable facial mobility. He died in Paris.

Fernando Póo » **Bioko**

Ferrar, Nicholas (1592–1637) English Anglican clergyman and spiritual mystic, born in London. After studying medicine, and a brief period in politics, he became a deacon in the Church of England (1626). At Little Gidding in Huntingdonshire he founded a small religious community which engaged in constant services and perpetual prayer, while carrying out a range of crafts, such as bookbinding. It was broken up by the Puritans in 1647. He died at Little Gidding. » Church of England; Puritanism

Ferrara [fay**rah**ra] 44°50N 11°38E, pop (1981) 149 453. Ancient town and capital of Ferrara province, Emilia-Romagna region, N Italy; seat of the Council of Ferrara (1438) and of the 15th-c Renaissance court; ceded to France (1797–1815); part of Kingdom of Sardinia, 1859; archbishopric; railway; university (1391); sugar, chemicals, trade in fruit and wine; birthplace of Savonarola; Castello Estense (14th–16th-c), Cathedral of San Giorgio (1135). » Italy [i]; Savonarola

ferrate A compound containing iron as part of an anion. » anion; iron

ferret A domesticated form of the *European polecat* (*Mustela putorius*); yellowish-white with pink eyes; domesticated over 2 000 years ago; sent down burrows to chase out rabbits; bred white so it is not mistaken for a rabbit. The name **black-footed ferret** is used for the N American polecat *Mustela nigripes*. » badger; polecat

ferricyanide $Fe(CN)_6^{3-}$, IUPAC **hexacyanoferrate(III)** (red) and **hexacyanoferrate(II)** (yellow); $Fe(CN)_6^{4-}$ is called *ferrocyanide*. Both react with more iron ions to form an intense blue precipitate called *Prussian blue*. » ion; IUPAC; precipitate

Ferrier, Kathleen (1912–53) British contralto singer, born at Higher Walton, Lancashire. A singing prize at a local music festival led her to undertake serious studies in 1940, and she rapidly won a great reputation. One of her greatest successes was in Mahler's *Das Lied von der Erde* (The Song of the Earth) at the first Edinburgh Festival (1947). She died in London.

ferrimagnetism The magnetic property of materials for which neighbouring atomic magnetic moments are of different strengths and are aligned antiparallel. It is related to ferromagnetism, but exhibiting much weaker gross magnetic properties. It is observed in ferrites and certain other materials. » ferrites; ferromagnetism

ferrites A class of ceramic materials composed of oxides of iron and some other metal such as copper, nickel, or manganese. Of low electrical conductivity, and ferrimagnetic, they are used as core material in high-frequency electrical coils, loudspeaker magnets, and video/audio tape-recorder heads. Ferrous ferrite ($Fe^{2+}Fe^{3+}{}_2O_4$), or *magnetite*, is the lodestone of antiquity. » ceramics; ferrimagnetism; oxide

ferro-alloys Combinations of elements added to molten steel to impart various properties, such as greater corrosion resistance or strength. » alloy; steel

ferroelectrics Crystalline materials (eg barium titanate, $BaTiO_3$) having an overall electric dipole moment, even without an external field present, that can be reversed by the application of an external electric field. The effect is due to displacement between the atoms in the entire lattice, such that the centres of positive and negative charge no longer coincide. Above a certain material-dependent temperature, thermal motion disrupts the lattice ordering, and the ferroelectric property is lost. » crystals; electric field; electrical and magnetic properties of solids; pyroelectrics

ferromagnetism A property of ferromagnetic substances (eg iron, nickel, cobalt, gadolinium, dysprosium, and many alloys) arising from large-scale alignment between atomic magnetic moments. An applied magnetic field intensity H, supplied by a surrounding electric coil, causes a disproportionately large magnetic flux density B to appear in the bulk material. A field may remain in the material even when the external field has been removed, resulting in permanent magnets. The atoms of many elements have unpaired electrons, giving rise to magnetic moments which typically cause paramagnetism in the bulk material. Ferromagnetism is like paramagnetism, with an extra ingredient causing alignment. » Curie temperature; ferrimagnetism; magnetic domain; magnetic hysteresis; magnetic moment; magnetism; magnetostriction; paramagnetism; permeability

fertility drugs Drugs which treat infertility in women – usually successfully if it is due to a failure to ovulate. Early fertility drugs caused multiple pregnancies, but newer drugs such as clomiphene are not so extreme, though the incidence of twins is 10% of all successful pregnancies. Infertility in males is more difficult to treat. » pregnancy [i]

fertilization The union of two gametes to form a zygote, as occurs during sexual reproduction. The gametes are typically male (a sperm) and female (an egg), and both are haploid (possess a single chromosome set). Fertilization involves the fusion of the two haploid nuclei to form a diploid zygote that develops into a new individual. The process is external in some aquatic animals, such as echinoderms, with both sperm and eggs being released into the water. Most terrestrial organisms, including the higher vertebrates, have internal fertilization, in which union of the gametes occurs inside the female. » alternation of generations; cleavage; echinoderm [i]; gamete; reproduction; zygote

fertilizer A substance which provides plant nutrients when added to soil. The term normally refers to inorganic chemicals containing one or more of the basic plant nutrients: nitrogen, phosphorus, or potash. However it may also refer to compounds containing trace elements such as boron, cobalt, copper, iron, manganese, molybdenum, and zinc; to lime, which is used to correct acidity; or to a concentrated organic substance such as dried blood and bonemeal. Fertilizers are added to the soil in granular, crystalline, powder, or liquid forms and may be injected directly into the ground or broadcast on the surface. High levels of fertilizer application, especially of nitrogenous compounds, can cause pollution of watercourses and drinking water supplies. In some countries, legal limitations are imposed on the total quantity of fertilizer which may be added to the land during each season. » organic farming; trace elements

Fès » **Fez**

fescue A tufted grass with inrolled, bristle-like leaves, found almost everywhere; important as pasture grass. Upland species are often viviparous, ie the seeds germinate to form plantlets before being shed from the inflorescence. (Genus: *Festuca*, c.80 species. Family: *Gramineae*.) » germination; grass [i]; vegetative reproduction

Festival of Britain An event organized in 1951 to mark the centenary of the Great Exhibition held in London in 1851, intended to demonstrate 'the British contribution to civilization, past, present and future, in the arts, in science and technology and in industrial design'. The Royal Festival Hall was built for the occasion.

fetch » **wave** (oceanography)

feudalism A modern construct from Lat *feudum* ('fief'), originally coined in 1839, referring to phenomena associated more or less closely with the Middle Ages. In a narrow sense, the word is used to describe the mediaeval military and political order based on reciprocal ties between lords and vassals, in which the main elements were the giving of homage and the tenure of fiefs. Though normally associated with political fragmentation, feudalism as here defined could serve as the ally of royal power. Polemicists apply it to whatever appears backward or reactionary in the modern world. » Middle Ages; vassal

Feuerbach, Ludwig (Andreas) (1804–72) German philosopher, born at Landshut, Bavaria. He studied theology at Heidelberg and Berlin, then philosophy at Erlangen. His most famous work, *Das Wesen des Christentums* (1841, The Essence of Christianity), claims that religion rises from one's alienation from oneself, and the projection of ideal human qualities onto a fictitious supreme 'other'. He died at Nuremberg, his thought later influencing Marx. » idealism; Marx; rationalism (philosophy)

Feuillants, Club of the [feryã] An association of moderate deputies and former members of the Jacobin Club, led by the Marquis de Lafayette (1757–1834), Antoine Barnave (1761–93), and Jean Bailly (1736–93), who aimed at establishing a constitutional monarchy in France during the first stage of the Revolution (1791). » Barnave; French Revolution [i]; Jacobins (French history); Lafayette

fever A clinical condition when the temperature of the body rises above the upper limit of normal, namely 37.7°C taken in the mouth; also known as **pyrexia**. Individuals with a higher temperature are said to be *febrile*. Taking the temperature of a patient has been routine in sickness for over 100 years. Most fevers are due to infections, and virtually all infectious diseases cause fever. Body temperature depends upon a balance between heat production and heat loss, and is regulated by the hypothalamus. Many micro-organisms liberate substances (*pyrogens*) which alter the level of this control mechanism to produce a fever. Pyrogenic substances are also liberated from damaged or dead tissues, so fever occurs in some non-infectious diseases where this happens; examples are myocardial infarction (dead heart tissue) and in many cancers. » hypothalamus; infection; temperature [i]

feverfew An aromatic perennial growing to 60 cm/2 ft, probably native to SE Europe and parts of Asia, and widely introduced elsewhere; leaves yellowish-green, with lobed or toothed leaflets; flower heads up to 2 cm/¾ in across, long-stalked in loose, flat-topped clusters; spreading outer florets white, inner disc florets yellow. It is grown for ornament and as a medicinal herb, reputed to provide relief from migraines. (*Tanacetum parthenium*. Family: *Compositae*.) » herb; migraine; perennial

Feynman, Richard (Phillips) (1918–88) US physicist, born in

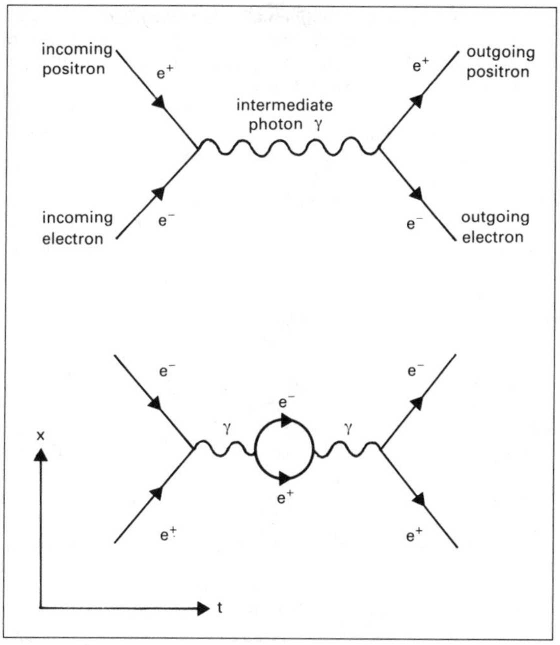

Two of the many Feynman diagrams used when calculating the scattering of electrons (e^-) with positrons (e^+), expressed $e^+e^- \rightarrow e^+e^-$; γ represents a photon.

New York City. He worked on the US atomic bomb in World War 2, then became a professor of theoretical physics at Cornell (1945) and the California Institute of Technology (1951). He shared the Nobel Prize for Physics in 1965 for his work on quantum electrodynamics, and is also known for his visual representation of the behaviour of interacting particles, known as **Feynman diagrams**. » electrodynamics; Feynman diagrams [i]; particle physics

Feynman diagrams Diagrams representing specific terms in calculations in quantum field theory; developed by US physicist Richard Feynman in the 1940s. Each line and junction between lines has a precise mathematical equivalent. Such diagrams are extensively used in particle physics calculations, and also in solid-state physics. Any physical process corresponds to an infinite number of diagrams, whilst actual calculations incorporate only the simplest. The branch of mathematics involved is called *perturbation theory*. » Feynman; quantum field theory; perturbation theory

Fez or **Fès** [fez] 34°05N 5°00W, pop (1982) 448 823. City in Centre-Nord province, NC Morocco, 240 km/150 ml ENE of Casablanca; oldest of Morocco's four imperial cities; Old Fez, a world heritage site, founded in 808 by Moulay Idriss II; New Fez founded in 1276 by the Merinade dynasty, includes the Sultan's palace (Dar el Makhzen); modern Fez (Ville Nouvelle) S of the railway; name given to a type of red felt hat worn by many Islamic followers; railway; textiles, carpets, leather, soap, fruit, crafts; major centre of Islamic learning; Karaouine mosque (first built, 9th-c) became famous as a Muslim university. » Morocco [i]

Fianna Fáil [feeana **foyl**] An Irish political party founded in 1926 by those opposed to the 1921 Anglo-Irish Treaty. It first came to power under De Valera in 1932, and has been the governing party for most of the period since. In the 1930s it emphasized separation from the British, and has consistently supported the unification of Ireland. In domestic issues its approach is more pragmatic than ideological. » de Valera

Fibonacci, Leonardo [fibuh**nah**chee], also known as **Leonardo Pisano** (c.1170–c.1250) Italian mathematician, born at Pisa, arguably the most outstanding mathematician of the Middle Ages. He popularized the modern decimal system of numerals, and in his greatest work, the *Liber quadratorum* (1225, The Book of Square Numbers), made an advanced contribution to number theory. He also discovered the 'Fibonacci sequence' of integers in which each number is equal to the sum of the preceding two (0,1,1,2,3,5,8...). » number theory

fibre That part of plant carbohydrates which cannot be digested by the normal carbohydrate-digesting enzymes in the small intestine. Fibre is largely contained in the structural part of plants, ie the roots, stem, seed coat, or husk. The most abundant fibre in nature, cellulose, is made up of repeating glucose units in long single strands, making it ideal for conversion into the fabric cotton. Other fibre fractions are hemicellulose and pectin. Some fibres are fermented by bacteria in the large bowel, which leads to an increase in stool weight through an increase in faecal bacteria. Other fibres are more resistant to bacterial fermentation, but increase stool weight through their water-binding capacity. » bran; carbohydrate; cellulose; intestine

fibre-glass A composite material for the construction of light, generally complex-curved structures, made of glass fibres embedded in a polyester or epoxy resin which can be moulded before setting; more fully described as *glass fibre reinforced plastic*. It is much used for such structures as hulls of boats, tanks for liquids, and occasionally for car bodies. » epoxy resin [i]; polyesters

fibre optics » **optical fibres** [i]

fibres The fundamental units from which textiles are made. Natural fibres occur naturally in fibrous form, and include wool, cotton, linen, jute, cashmere, and silk. Synthetic fibres are made from polymers using oil as the raw material; examples include nylons, polyesters, and acrylics. » carbon fibre; cashmere; cotton [i]; nylon; polyesters; silk; yarn

fibrositis An imprecise lay term referring to aching in the muscles, which may be locally tender. It is usually felt in the neck, shoulders, or back. The underlying nature of the disorder is unknown in the majority of cases. » muscle [i]

fibula A long slender bone in the calf, which articulates with the foot (via the ankle joint) and the tibia. It has a head, neck, shaft, and an expanded lower end. It is thought to have no weight-bearing function, but gives attachment to many of the muscles of the calf. Compression on or fracture of the neck of the fibula may lead to nerve damage (the common peroneal nerve) leading to foot drop. » foot; tibia; Plate XIII

Fichte, Johann Gottlieb (1762–1814) German philosopher, born at Rammenau, Saxony. He studied theology and then philosophy at Jena, becoming an ardent disciple of Kant. As professor of philosophy at Jena (1794) he modified the Kantian system by substituting for the 'thing-in-itself' as the absolute reality, the more subjective *Ego*, the primitive act of consciousness. In 1805 he became professor at Erlangen, where he published the more popular versions of his philosophy. His historical importance is as the author of *Reden an die deutsche Nation* (1807–8, Addresses to the German Nation), in which he invoked a metaphysical German nationalism to resistance against Napoleon. In 1810 the University of Berlin was opened and Fichte, who had drawn up its constitution, became its first rector. He died in Berlin. » Kant

Fichtelberg [**fikh**telberk] Mountain in the Erzgebirge range, S of Karl Marx Stadt, on the frontier between Germany and Czechoslovakia; height 1 214 m/3 983 ft; highest mountain in former East Germany; heavily forested.

Fichtelgebirge [**fikh**telguhbeerguh], Czech **Smrčiny** Horseshoe-shaped mountain range in Bavaria, Germany; highest peak Schneeberg (1 051 m/3 448 ft); source of rivers Main, Saale, Eger, Naab; largely covered with fir forests; some minerals; links the Erzgebirge and the Bohemian Forest. » Bavaria; Bohemian Forest; Germany [i]

fiddler crab A marine crab commonly found on inter-tidal mud flats in tropical and subtropical regions; adults make burrows in mud, emerging to feed on surface when tide is out; males have a large claw used for signalling during courtship. (Class: *Malacostraca*. Order: *Decapoda*.) » crab

Fidei Defensor » **Defender of the Faith**

fideism Any view which maintains that the principles of some area of inquiry cannot be established by reason, but must be accepted on faith. Fideism in religion may claim either that the basic tenets of religious belief go beyond what reason can establish or, more radically, that they contradict reason. » religion

field (photography) In television, one complete top-to-bottom traverse of the scanned picture. With interlaced scanning, two such fields of alternate lines are required to build up the complete image or frame. » scanning [i]; television

Field, Cyrus W(est) (1819–92) US financier, born at Stockbridge, Massachusetts. After a career as a paper manufacturer, he helped to finance the first telegraph cable across the Atlantic, achieved after several attempts in 1866. He also organized the New York, Newfoundland, and London Telegraph Company (1854), and the Atlantic Telegraph Company (1856), but suffered heavy financial losses. He died in New York City. » telegraphy

Field, John (1782–1837) Irish composer and pianist, born in Dublin. An infant prodigy, he was apprenticed to Clementi, who used him to demonstrate the capabilities of his pianos. In 1804 he settled in Russia as a music teacher, in 1821 moving to Moscow, where he died. He wrote mainly for the piano (including seven concertos), and is credited with originating the nocturne. His music influenced Chopin. » Chopin; Clementi; nocturne; piano

field emission The emission of electrons from a metal surface caused by the application of an intense electric field. Field emission microscopes guide electrons emitted from a sharp metal point to a screen, forming a highly magnified image of the metal's structure. » electron; field ion microscope; photoelectric effect; secondary emission; thermionics

field ion microscope A sharply pointed metal electrode maintained at a high positive potential relative to a screen. Gas ions form from gas atoms close to the tip, due to the extreme electric field (a form of field emission), and are guided to the screen producing an image of the tip structure. Magnifications of 1.5 million may be achieved, allowing individual atoms to be resolved. » field emission; microscope

Field of the Cloth of Gold A meeting between Henry VIII and Francis I near Calais in 1520, in which England sought to mediate in the Habsburg-Valois wars; named for the lavish pavilions of golden cloth erected by the French. The English built a two-storey palace, 320 ft/97 m square, of glass and wood, in which they were housed. » Francis I (of France); Henry VIII

fieldfare A thrush native to Europe and Asia; found in S Greenland since 1937; brown back, mottled breast, grey head; inhabits woodland and farmland; eats fruit, insects, worms, and slugs. (*Turdus pilaris*.) » redwing; thrush (bird)

Fielding, Henry (1707–54) English playwright and novelist, born at Sharpham Park, Glastonbury. Educated at Eton and Leyden, he began to write theatrical comedies, becoming author/manager of the Little Theatre in the Haymarket (1736). However, the sharpness of his burlesques led to the Licensing Act (1737), which closed his theatre. In search of an alternative career, he was called to the Bar (1740), but his interests lay in journalism and fiction. On Richardson's publication of *Pamela* (1740), he wrote his famous parody, *Joseph Andrews* (1742). Several other works followed, notably *Tom Jones, A Foundling* (1749), which established his reputation as a founder of the English novel. As a reward for his government journalism, he was made justice of the peace to Westminster, where he helped to form the Bow Street Runners within the police force. He died in Lisbon. » English literature; novel; Richardson, Samuel; theatre

fieldmouse A mouse of genus *Apodemus* (*Old World field mice* or *wood mice*, 13 species) or of genus *Akodon* (*South American field mice* or *grass mice*, 41 species). Old World fieldmice often jump (they may leap 1 m/3¼ ft vertically); South American fieldmice have short legs, and are less athletic. » mouse (zoology)

Fields, Dame Gracie, stage name of **Grace Stansfield** (1898–1979) British singer and variety star, born in Rochdale, Lancashire. She first appeared on stage at the age of 10, made her London debut in 1915, and by 1928 was firmly established in variety. With her sentimental songs and broad Lancashire humour, she won a unique place in the affections of British audiences. Her theme tune, 'Sally', she first sang in 1931. Created a Dame in 1978, she died in Capri, Italy.

Fields, W C byname of **William Claude Dukenfield** (1879–1946) US actor, born in Philadelphia. He ran away from home and became a vaudeville actor and juggler in the early 1900s. He appeared in the Ziegfeld Follies, but established his comic persona in silent films such as *Sally of the Sawdust* (1925). His characteristic gravelly voice found its full scope with the coming of sound in the cinema, and he was in regular demand during the 1930s. He died at Pasadena, California.

FIFA The abbreviation of **Fédération Internationale de Football Association**, the world governing body of association football, founded in Paris in 1904 with seven members. There are now 150 member countries affiliated. FIFA stages its World Cup tournament every four years. » football [i]

fife A small, high-pitched, transverse flute, with six finger-holes and (in modern and some older instruments) metal keys. Fifes have been mainly military instruments, used (like the bugle) for calls and signals, and also, in 'drum and fife' bands, for marching. » flute; woodwind instrument [i]

Fife, also **Kingdom of Fife** pop (1981) 327 362; area 1 307 sq km/504 sq ml. Region in E Scotland, divided into three districts; bounded by the Firth of Tay (N), North Sea (E), and the Firth of Forth (S); low-lying region, drained by Eden and Leven Rivers; Lomond Hills in the W; many small fishing ports; oil, gas, and chemical developments in the W at Mossmorran; coal mining (open cast, and the only working deep mine in Scotland, the Longannet complex); interior mainly farmland; capital, Glenrothes; major towns include Dunfermline, Cowdenbeath, Cupar, St Andrews (notable golf course). » Glenrothes; Scotland [i]

Fifteen Rebellion The name given to the first of the Jacobite rebellions against Hanoverian monarchy to restore the Catholic Stuart Kings to the British throne. The rising began at Braemar (Sep 1715) by the Earl of Mar, proclaiming James Edward Stuart (the 'Old Pretender') as King. Jacobite forces were defeated at Preston in November, and the rebellion collapsed early in 1716. » Jacobites; Stuart, James

fifth column A popular expression from the early days of World War 2 to describe enemy sympathizers who might provide active help to an invader. The name originally described the rebel sympathizers in Madrid in 1936 during the Spanish Civil War, when four rebel columns were advancing on the city. » Spanish Civil War

fifth force A new force postulated by US physicist Ephraim Fischbach (1942–) and others in 1986, in addition to the four recognized fundamental forces. It is weaker than gravity, and of intermediate range. It is claimed that, due to the fifth force, the apparent gravitational force between objects separated by distances of a few hundred metres depends on the material from which they are made, and varies only approximately as r^{-2}. However, the experimental results are ambiguous, and the theory is speculative. » forces of nature [i]

fifth-generation computers » **computer generations**

fifty-four forty or fight A slogan used in the 1840s to advocate US seizure of British Columbia, whose N boundary is at 54°40N. The issue was resolved in 1846 by a treaty establishing the present US/Canadian border, at 49°N.

fig A large genus of trees, shrubs, and climbers, mostly native to the tropics; characteristic inflorescence consists of tiny flowers borne on the inner surface of a hollow, fleshy receptacle which forms the fig after fertilization, symbiotic gall-wasps acting as pollinators. Many species are large evergreen trees, such as the indiarubber tree and the banyan. The **common fig** (*Ficus carica*) is a small deciduous tree with greenish-purple, edible fruits. **Strangler figs** begin as epiphytes, eventually enclosing and strangling the host in a network of aerial roots. (Genus: *Ficus*, 800 species. Family: *Moraceae*.) » banyan; climbing plant; deciduous plants; epiphyte; evergreen plants; indiarubber tree; inflorescence [i]; peepul; shrub; symbiosis; tree [i]

fighting fish Small freshwater fish, native to Thailand; feeds on aquatic insects, especially mosquito larvae; length up to 6 cm/2½ in; eggs laid in bubble nest at surface; renowned for its aggressive behaviour; commonly held in captivity for staged fights. Captive breeding has produced an immense variety of colour and form. (*Betta splendens*. Family: *Belontidae*.)

figurative art Any form of visual art in which recognizable aspects of the world, especially the human figure, are represented, in however simplified, stylized, or distorted a form, in contrast to abstract or *non-figurative art*. » abstract art; art

figurative language Language used in such a way that 'simple' meaning is elaborated and complicated by various rhetorical means. Although 'plain style' was recommended to the Royal Society in 1667, and has always been the implicit objective of scientists and philosophers, non-figurative (and therefore, supposedly, unambiguous) language is actually difficult to sustain. Language has been described as a 'graveyard of dead metaphors', and all forms of emphasis and parallelism, as well as imagery, may be considered 'figurative'. » hyperbole; imagery; metaphor; metonymy; poetry; rhetoric

figwort A perennial, native to Europe and Asia; stems square, robust, erect; leaves opposite, toothed; inflorescence tall, branched; flowers with greenish, almost globose tube and five small lobes, the upper two forming a reddish-brown lip, pollinated by wasps. There are many very similar species from temperate regions. (*Scrophularia nodosa*. Family: *Scrophulariaceae*.) » inflorescence [i]; perennial

Fiji, official name **Republic of Fiji [feejee]** pop (1990e) 740 000; land area 18 333 sq km/7 076 sq ml. Melanesian island group of 844 islands and islets in the SW Pacific Ocean (c.100 permanently inhabited), divided into four divisions; 1 770 km/ 1 100 ml N of Auckland, New Zealand; capital, Suva; chief towns, Lautoka, Ba, Labasa, Nadi, Nausori; timezone GMT + 11; two main islands of Viti Levu and Vanua Levu, containing c.90% of population; chief ethnic groups, indigenous Fijians (44%) and Indian (51%); native Fijians mainly Christian (c.85% Methodist, 12% Roman Catholic); Indo-Fijians mainly Hindu (c.70%) and Muslim (25%); official language, English; unit of currency, the Fijian dollar; main archipelago located 15–22°S and 174–177°E; larger islands generally mountainous and rugged; extensive areas of flat land in river deltas; fertile plains around coastline; highest peak, Tomaniivi (Mt Victoria) on Vita Levu (1 324 m/4 344 ft); hot springs in isolated places; most smaller islands consist of limestone, with little vegetation; extensive coral reef (Great Sea Reef) stretching for 500 km/300 ml along W fringe; dense tropical forest on wet, windward side (SE); mainly treeless on dry, leeward side; winds variable in wet season (Nov–Apr), with tropical cyclonic storms likely; temperatures 23–27°C; annual rainfall, 1 900–3 050 mm/75–120 in, higher in E and SE; humidity on windward slopes averages 74%; visited by Tasman in 1643, and by Cook in 1774; British colony, 1874; independence within the Commonwealth, 1970; 1987 election brought to power an Indian-dominated coalition, which led to military coups (May and Sep), and proclamation of a republic outside the Commonwealth; civilian government restored (Dec); bicameral parliament of a nominated Senate of 34 members and an elected House of Representatives of 70 members; new constitution upholding ethnic Melanesian political power, 1990; economy primarily agrarian, with sugar cane accounting for over two-thirds of export earnings; copra, ginger, vegetables, fruit, livestock, tuna, timber; sugar-milling, processing of coconut-oil, gold-mining, light industry; major tourist area; important air staging post between N America and Oceania. » Suva; Vanua Levu; Viti Levu; RR25 national holidays; RR49 political leaders

filariasis [filariyasis] A disease caused by the nematode worms *Wuchereria bancrofti* and *Brugia malayi* of genus *Filaria*. Larvae are transmitted to uninfected human beings by mosquitoes. Adult forms develop within the body, and settle in lymph nodes, very often in the groin. The lymph nodes enlarge and interfere with the flow of lymph, causing gross oedema of the limbs. » elephantiasis; nematode

filbert A species of hazel, native to the Balkans, and cultivated elsewhere for its edible nuts, which are completely enclosed in a leafy cup, constricted above the nut to form a neck. (*Corylus maxima*. Family: *Corylaceae*.) » hazel; nut

filefish Deep-bodied fish common in shallow tropical and warm temperate waters; body strongly compressed, length up to 25 cm/10 in; dorsal fin spiny; scales finely toothed and rough to touch; valuable food fish in some areas; also called **porky**. (Genus: *Stephanolepis*. Family: *Balistidae*.)

filibuster To hold up the passage of a bill in the US Senate, by organizing a continuous succession of long speeches in opposition. If more than a third of the senators in a vote on the issue are opposed to closure of the debate, the filibuster cannot be prevented, and the bill is 'talked out'. The term is also more generally applied to any attempt to delay a decision or vote by exercising the right to talk on an issue. Many legislatures have procedures for curtailing such obstructionism. » Senate

Filioque [fileeohkwee] (Lat 'and from the Son') A dogmatic formula expressing the belief that in the operations of God, the Holy Trinity, the Holy Spirit 'proceeds' from the Son as well as from the Father. The term does not appear in the original Nicene-Constantinopolitan Creed, but was inserted by the Western Church, and insistence on its retention was a major source of tension and eventual breach between the Western (Roman Catholic) and Eastern (Orthodox) Churches in 1054. In the late 20th-c, attempts are being made by the World Council of Churches to reinterpret this doctrine in a sense acceptable to the Orthodox. » God; Holy Spirit; Nicene Creed; Orthodox Church; Roman Catholicism; Trinity

Fillmore, Millard (1800–74) US statesman and 13th President (1850–3), born at Summer Hill, New York. He educated himself, and became a lawyer. A member of the state assembly in 1829, he was elected to Congress in 1833, and comptroller of New York State in 1847. He was Vice-President to Zachary Taylor in 1848, becoming President on his death. On the slavery question he was a supporter of 'compromise'. He died in Buffalo, New York. » slavery

film A light-sensitive photographic emulsion on a thin flexible transparent support, originally celluloid (cellulose nitrate), but later the less inflammable cellulose triacetate. Film for still cameras is supplied in cut sheets and film packs, but more generally as short rolls in various standard widths. Motion picture film is used in long rolls, up to 300 m, in widths 16, 35 and 70 mm, with accurately spaced perforations along the edge for transport and location in the camera and other mechanisms. The amateur movie gauges of 8 mm, Super-8 and 9.5 mm are obsolescent. » camera; cinema

film production There are four stages:

(1) **Preparation.** The producer organizes finance and resources; the director, production team and artistes are chosen; and sets are designed and constructed in the studio.

(2) **Shooting.** Once photography starts on the studio stage or on location, the director is primarily concerned with the actors and their performance. The visual realization of the director's ideas on film is in the hands of the cameraman, who decides the character and distribution of lighting and selects the camera viewpoints and movement by the camera operator, aided by a focus-puller and grips. A clapper-loader assistant is responsible for the film magazines and shot identification. Sound recording is supervised by the floor mixer, with an assistant and engineer, while the boom operator positions the microphone during shooting. The negative exposed each day is developed at the laboratory, and rush prints returned to the studio for viewing by the director and his team. An assistant editor then assembles the chosen material in script order.

(3) **Post-production.** The period of editing, music recording, etc. after photography is complete, up to the premiere.

(4) **Distribution.** The general release to cinemas, with foreign versions dubbed in other languages, television broadcasts, and video-cassette sale and hire in the domestic market. » cameraman; director; grip; post-production; producer

filmy fern A small fern with creeping rhizomes, commonly found as an epiphyte; fronds pinnate or bi-pinnate, only one cell thick, and translucent except for the veins. These ferns are vulnerable to drying out, and are found only in moist areas outside the tropics. (Genus: *Hymenophyllum*, 25 species. Family: *Hymenophyllaceae*.) » epiphyte; fern; pinnate; rhizome

filofax The trade name of a 'personal organizer', or portable information and filing system. Paperback-size, loose-leaf, with a flexible binder, filofaxes typically contain a diary, address book, note-book, and information sections (hence 'file of facts'). Their prominence increased through association with the yuppies of the 1980s.

filter 1 A device for removing fine solid particles from a mixture.

It usually consists of some woven or felted material (eg paper, textile), and is thus distinct from a *sieve*, which removes coarse particles with a wire mesh or perforated metal. By analogy, the term is also used for any device which separates the components of a wave system (eg sound, light, radio frequency currents). **2** In photography, a transparent material which modifies the light passing in a specified manner. It is used in front of light sources to alter colour temperature, reduce intensity, or scatter light by diffusion. On camera lenses it changes colour balance or tonal rendering. Other camera filters introduce soft focus, fog effects, or star patterns around bright points. » diffusion (photography); photography

fin The external membranous process of an aquatic animal, such as a fish or cetacean, used for locomotion and manoeuvring; may be variously modified as suckers and claspers. The median fins are called *dorsal*, *anal*, and *caudal* (tail); the paired lateral fins are *pectorals* and *pelvics*. » Cetacea; fish [i]

finch Any bird of the family *Fringillidae*; commonly kept as song-birds; bill internally modified to crush seeds. The name is also applied loosely to any small seed-eating bird with a stout conical bill, such as **estrildid finches** (family: *Estrildidae*). » brambling; bullfinch; canary; chaffinch; crossbill; Darwin's finches; Fringillidae; goldfinch; greenfinch; hawfinch; linnet; quail; redpoll; waxbill; weaverbird; weaver-finch; whydah

Fine Gael [feen **gayl**] An Irish political party created out of the pro-Anglo-Irish Treaty (1921) wing of Sinn Féin. It was known as *Cummann na nGaedheal* from 1923 until it changed its name in 1933. The first government of the Irish Free State, it has largely been in opposition since the 1930s, and has never held power on its own. It supports an Irish confederation, and is largely pragmatic in domestic matters. » Sinn Féin

finfoot A water bird, native to C America, S Africa, and S Asia; slender, with long pointed bill; toes with side lobes; inhabits fresh or brackish water margins; eats small animals and some plant material; angle of wing bears a claw; also called **sungrabe**. (Family: *Heliornithidae*, 3 species.)

Fingal's Cave A cave situated on the coast of Staffa in the Inner Hebrides, Scotland. The cavern, which is renowned for its natural beauty, is celebrated in Mendelssohn's *Hebrides* overture. It is 69 m/227 ft deep and of volcanic origin, being formed from huge hexagonal pillars of basalt. The name derives from the legendary Irish figure, Finn MacCool. » basalt; Finn MacCool; Hebrides; Mendelssohn, Felix

Finger Lakes A group of long, narrow, finger-like lakes in W New York State, USA; includes (W–E) Canandaigua, Keuka, Seneca, Cayuga, Owasco, and Skaneateles lakes. » New York

finger-spelling » **dactylology**

Finisterre, Cape (Span **Cabo**) [finis**tair**] 42°50N 9°16W. Cape at La Coruña, NW Spain; the most W point on the Spanish mainland; scene of a British naval victory against the French in 1747. » Spain [i]

Finland, Finnish **Suomi**, official name **Republic of Finland**, Finnish **Suomen Tasavalta**, Swedish **Republiken Finland** pop (1990e) 4 978 000; area 338 145 sq km/130 524 sq ml. A republic of N Europe divided into 12 provinces (*laani*); bounded E by Russia, S by the Gulf of Finland, W by the Gulf of Bothnia and Sweden, and N by Norway; capital, Helsinki; chief towns, Tampere, Turku, Espoo, Vantaa; timezone GMT +2; slow population growth since 1950, with large numbers emigrating to Sweden; first languages, Finnish (94%), Swedish (6%); mainly Finns, with Swedish, Lapp, and Russian minorities; chief religion, Lutheran Christianity; unit of currency, the markka of 100 penni.

Physical description. A low-lying glaciated plateau, average height 150 m/500 ft; highest peak, Haltiatunturi (1 328 m/4 357 ft) on NW border; over 60 000 shallow lakes in SE, providing a system of inland navigation; land still rising from the sea, area increasing by 7 sq km/2.7 sq ml each year; over a third of the country N of the Arctic Circle; chief rivers, Tornio, Kemi, Oulu; archipelago of Saaristomeri (SW), with over 17 000 islands and skerries; Ahvenanmaa (Åland) islands (SW); forest land covers 65% of the country, water 10%.

Climate. N location ameliorated by the Baltic Sea; W winds bring warm air currents in summer; Eurasian winds bring cold spells in winter and heatwaves in summer; annual precipitation

(S) 600–700 mm/24–28 in, (N) 500–600 mm/20–24 in with half falling as snow; Sun does not go down beyond the horizon for over 70 days during summer.

History and government. Ruled by Sweden from 1157 until ceded to Russia in 1809; autonomous Grand Duchy of the Russian Czar, 19th-c, with development of nationalist movement; independent republic, 1917; parliamentary system created, 1928; invaded by Soviets in 1939 and 1940, and lost territory to USSR after 1944; governed by a single-chamber House of Representatives (*Eduskunta*) of 200 elected members, serving a 4-year term, and a president elected for 6 years, assisted by a Council of State.

Economy. Traditional focus on forestry and farming, with rapid economic growth since 1950s, and diversification of exports; metals, engineering, clothing, chemicals, food processing; copper, iron ore mining; wide use of hydroelectric power; hay, barley, oats, spring and autumn wheat, rye, sugar beet, potatoes, spring oil-yielding plants; forestry, mainly pine, spruce, and birch; timber products, especially paper; tourism. » Ahvenanmaa; Helsinki; Lapland; Saimaa; RR25 national holidays; RR49 political leaders

Finland, Gulf of Arm of the Baltic Sea (E), bounded N by Finland, S and E by Russia; c.4 600 km/2 900 ml long, 16–120 km/10–75 ml wide; shallowness and low salinity result in ice cover (Dec–Mar); main ports, Helsinki, Kotka, Vyborg, St Petersburg, Tallinn. » Baltic Sea

Finn MacCool A legendary Irish hero, the son of Cumhall, and father of Ossian (Oisin). He became leader of the Fenians, and was famous for his generosity.

fiord » **fjord**

Fiordland area 10 232 sq km/3 949 sq ml. National park, SW South Island, New Zealand; largest of New Zealand's national parks, with mountains, lakes and a coastline indented by fjords; established in 1904; a world heritage site. » New Zealand [i]

fir » **silver fir**

Firdausi [fir**dow**zee] or **Ferd(a)usi**, pen name of **Abú Al-Qásim Mansúr** (940–c.1020) The greatest of Persian poets, born near Tús, Khorassan. His major work was the epic poem, *Shah Náma* (1010, The Book of Kings), based on actual events from the annals of Persia. He also wrote a number of shorter pieces. He died at Tús. » Persian literature; poetry

Fire of London A devastating fire which started in a baker's shop in Pudding Lane (2 Sep 1666) and lasted several days. It engulfed c.160 ha/400 acres – four-fifths of the city – destroying 13 000 houses, 89 parish churches, and most public buildings; but casualties were low (no more than 20 died). The capital was rebuilt with safer materials, new churches including Wren's St Paul's. » Wren, Christopher

fire salamander A salamander native to Europe, NW Africa, and SW Asia; black with yellow stripes or spots; broad head; short tail; inhabits damp upland deciduous forest; only adult female enters water (to give birth to live tadpoles). (Family: *Salamandridae. Salamandra salamandra.*) » salamander [i]

firearms A generic description for small arms, from pistols to rifles. The development of such portable weapons began with the first gunpowder-primed, hand-held cannon of the 14th-c, which had to be touched off by a second operator using a flame. The arquebus and later wheel-lock automated and simplified the process of touching off the priming, but still required a flame. The flintlock principle perfected in the 18th-c, which used a spring-loaded lever holding a flint to strike a spark and thus ignite the propellant charge, made pistols and muskets much more wieldy in combat. The percussion lock, using a hammer to set off a self-contained charge in the barrel of the gun, dates from the early 19th-c. » arquebus; ballistics; blunderbuss; musket; percussion cap; pistol; rifle

firebrat A widely-distributed bristletail. It is found as a pest in human dwellings, favouring warm places such as kitchens. (Order: *Thysanura.* Family: *Lepismatidae.*) » bristletail

fireclay Clay with high alumina content that can withstand high temperatures without excessive deformation. It is used for making firebricks and other refractory materials. » clay; kaolin

firecrest A small bird native to Europe, N Africa, and Madeira; head with orange stripe and white 'eyebrows'; inhabits woodland or scrubland; eats insects; Europe's smallest breeding bird. (*Regulus ignicapillus.* Family: *Regulidae*, sometimes placed in *Silviidae.*)

firedamp Methane found in coal mines. A mixture of methane and air is inflammable or explosive in certain proportions, and has been the cause of many pit disasters. The reduction of the hazard is a major consideration in coal mine operation. One of the best methods of firedamp detection remains the Davy safety lamp. » coal mining; methane [i]; safety lamp

firefly A small, mostly nocturnal beetle; males with soft wing cases, females larva-like, often wingless; jaws hollow, used to inject digestive juices into prey; larvae found in soil and leaf litter; all stages luminous, but most pronounced in adults; luminous organs near tip of abdomen used to produce mating signals; also known as **glowworms** and **lightning bugs**. (Order: *Coleoptera.* Family: *Lampyridae*, c.2 000 species.) » beetle; larva

firethorn A thorny, evergreen shrub growing to c.1.5 m/5 ft, occasionally a small tree, native to S Europe; leaves oval, toothed; flowers numerous, 5-petalled, white, in small clusters; berries bright red. An orange fruited form is commonly cultivated for ornament. (*Pyracantha coccinea.* Family: *Rosaceae.*) » evergreen plants; shrub; tree [i]

fireweed » **rosebay willow-herb**

fireworks Artificial devices, normally used for display purposes, which when ignited produce an array of coloured lights, sparks, and explosions. They contain flammable and explosive materials (eg charcoal, sulphur) which react with oxygen-yielding substances (eg nitre, chlorate of potash). Government control is very strict on their manufacture and sale to children. The majority of fireworks in the UK are displayed on 5 November to celebrate Guy Fawkes night, commemorating his attempt to blow up the Houses of Parliament in 1605. Spectacular displays are very popular in the Far East, and also on major public occasions such as US Independence Day. The making of fireworks is called *pyrotechny.* » Guy Fawkes Night

firmware A concept intermediate between software and hardware, used to describe devices which combine elements of each. A computer program stored in an unalterable form in an integrated circuit such as a read-only memory could be described as *firmware*, while the same program written on paper or stored on a floppy disk, both of which can be altered, could be described as *software.* » hardware; software

first aid The treatment and management of a victim at the site of an accident or collapse. In conscious individuals, important steps include the arrest of bleeding by the application of pressure (dressing, plastic bags, or paper) and by laying the victim flat. Injured parts must be handled gently. Unskilled extrication of victims who have suffered neck injury can cause serious damage. Otherwise the individual should be lifted on a flat board or by hands in such a way as to maintain the normal curvature of the spine, which should never be flexed. A simple splint to a leg is obtained by bandaging the injured leg to the uninjured one, or an arm to the trunk. Tea, alcohol, or other fluids should not be given. Passing traffic should be controlled, and an ambulance called. In unconscious individuals, all of these points should be carried out, but cardiac and respiratory resuscitation should also be given to those whose breathing or heart has stopped. » artificial respiration [i]; cardiac resuscitation [i]; Heimlich manoeuvre [i]

first cause » **cosmological argument**

first fleet In Australian history, the name given to the 11 ships which left Portsmouth, England (1787) carrying the first European settlers to E Australia. The fleet carried officials, 212 marines and their families, and 579 convicts plus provisions. Unusual for the time, all who embarked arrived safely in Australia. The fleet's captain, Arthur Phillip, decided that Botany Bay was unsuitable and proceeded north to Sydney Cove, Port Jackson, where he hoisted the British flag (26 Jan 1788). » Australia Day; Botany Bay

first-footing » **Hogmanay**

first-generation computers » **computer generations**

First Point of Aries The zero point of the celestial co-ordinate system, defined as the intersection of the Equator and ecliptic, or vernal equinox. When Hipparchos used this term, it lay in Aries, but precession of the equinoxes has moved it to the adjacent constellation Pisces. » celestial equator; Hipparchos; precession of the equinoxes

first-strike capability » **strategic capability**

First World » **Three Worlds theory**

First World War » **World War 1**

fiscal drag The effect of inflation on tax revenues. If tax allowances are not kept in line with inflation, individuals pay relatively higher amounts of tax, thus dragging down post-tax incomes; consequently the demand for goods and services falls. » inflation; taxation

fiscal policy The use by government of tax and its own rate of spending to influence demand in the economy. When a government decides to lower taxes or raise public expenditure, the effect is to stimulate economic activity by increasing the demand for goods and services. There is a risk that this may lead to increasing inflation, or an increase in imports, resulting in a trade deficit. In contrast, a tightening of fiscal policy is where taxes are raised or public expenditure is reduced, in order to reduce aggregate demand. » balance of payments; demand; inflation; stabilizers (economics)

Fischer, Bobby, properly **Robert (James)** (1943–) US chess player, born in Chicago. He was world champion from 1972–5, taking the title from Boris Spassky (USSR) in a much-publicized match. He has a ranking of 2 785 (on the Elo grading system), the highest ever, making him the greatest of all Grand Masters. He resigned his title shortly before a defence against Anatoly Karpov in 1975, and has not competed at a major international level since. » chess

Fischer-Dieskau, Dietrich [**dees**kow] (1925–) German baritone, born in Berlin. He studied under Georg Walter and Hermann Weissenborn, making his professional debut at Freiburg in 1947. He joined the Berlin Municipal Opera as a principal baritone, but he soon became one of the foremost interpreters of German Lieder, particularly the song-cycles of Schubert. » Lied

Fischer-Tropsch process A method of obtaining hydrocarbons by passing hydrogen and carbon monoxide over a

Fish

catalyst, either cobalt or iron, at high temperature and pressure. It is named after German chemists Franz Fischer (1877–1948) and Hans Tropsch (1889–1935). » catalysis; hydrocarbons

Fischer von Erlach, Johann Bernard (1656–1723) Austrian architect, born at Graz. He studied in Rome under Bernini, then moved to Vienna, where he became the court architect (1687), and a leading exponent of the Baroque style. He designed many churches and palaces, notably the Karlskirche at Vienna, and the University church at Salzburg. He also wrote a major work on architectural history (1721). He died at Vienna. » Baroque (art and architecture)

fish Any cold-blooded aquatic vertebrate without legs, but typically possessing paired lateral fins as well as median fins. There is a 2-chambered heart, a series of respiratory gills present throughout life in the sides of the pharynx, and a body usually bearing scales and terminating in a caudal (tail) fin. As a subgroup of the Vertebrata, the fishes are sometimes referred to collectively as *Pisces*. The primitive jawless fishes, the hagfishes and lampreys, are the only living members of a formerly large group, the *Agnatha*, which have an abundant fossil record. Members of another major group, the *Chondrichthyes* (800 living species), containing the sharks, rays, and ratfishes, are characterized by a cartilaginous skeleton, and are commonly referred to as the **cartilaginous fishes**. By far the largest extant group are the **bony fishes** (*Osteichthyes*; 20 000 living species), exhibiting a rich diversity and found in all aquatic habitats – freshwater, estuarine, and marine, from the tropics to polar latitudes, and from high altitude streams to the ocean abyss.

Although many fish have the familiar elongate shape, body form shows great variety – strongly compressed from side to side or (in bottom-living species) from top to bottom, asymmetrical with both eyes on the same side (as in the true flatfishes), extremely slender or heavily robust, armoured, spinose, or with reduced tails and huge heads (as in some of the bizarre deep-sea species). Body length ranges from as small as a few centimetres to over 18 m/60 ft in the massive whale shark. Many species have bright coloration, others well-developed camouflage patterns. Light organs are common in those forms living in the darkness of deep oceanic waters. Several species that inhabit turbid shallow waters have well-developed electric organs used for navigation, as defence against predators or for stunning prey. Some fish that live in shallow waters low in oxygen have evolved a capacity for air-breathing, using lungs or other accessory respiratory organs. A few, such as the mudhopper, are well-adapted to living out of water on coastal mud flats. Fish are of immense importance as a source of food, and to the angler and aquarist in pursuit of leisure. » angling; bony fish; cartilaginous fish; fin

fish eagle » **osprey; sea eagle**

fish hawk » **osprey**

fish louse A flattened parasitic crustacean found externally on fishes and occasionally amphibians, mainly in freshwater; usually attaches to host by means of suckers; feeds on blood and mucus by means of a tubular sucking mouth. (Class: *Branchiura*, c.150 species.) » crustacean; parasitology

fish owl A typical owl, adapted to live near water; found in Asia (Genus: *Ketupa*, 4 species) and Africa (Genus: *Scotopelia*, 3 species); plucks fish from water in flight using talons; also eats crayfish, frogs, insects, small mammals; noisier flight than other owls. » owl

Fishbourne Roman palace near Chichester (*Noviomagus Regnorum*), Sussex, S England, discovered in 1960. Probably erected in the AD 60s for the British client-king Cogidubnus, a noted Roman collaborator, it continued in use into the 4th-c. Major features are the formal courtyard garden, the monumental entrance and audience hall, the mosaics of the four colonnaded wings, and the site museum. » Britain, Roman

Fisher, Geoffrey, Baron Fisher of Lambeth (1887–1972) Archbishop of Canterbury (1945–61), born at Higham-on-the-Hill, Warwickshire. He was educated at Marlborough and Oxford, ordained in 1912, and became headmaster of Repton School (1914–32). He was 45 when he took up his first ecclesiastical appointment as Bishop of Chester (1932). In 1939 he became Bishop of London, and as Archbishop crowned Queen Elizabeth II in Westminister Abbey (1953). He was created a life peer in 1961. » Church of England

Fisher, St John (1469–1535), feast day 22 June. English prelate and humanist, born at Beverley, Yorkshire. He was educated at Cambridge, where he became professor of divinity (1503). He zealously promoted the New Learning, and resisted the Lutheran schism. In 1527 he pronounced against the divorce of Henry VIII, refused the oath of succession, and was sent with More to the Tower. In 1535 he was made a cardinal, and soon after was tried and beheaded on Tower Hill. He was canonized in 1935. » Henry VIII; humanism; Lutheranism; More, Thomas

fisher A mammal, related to the marten, native to N America; length, up to 1 m/3¼ ft; thick brown-black coat; inhabits dense forest; eats small mammals, birds, carrion; also known as **pekan**. (*Martes pennanti*. Family: *Mustelidae*.) » marten; Mustelidae

fishing » **angling**

fission A method of asexual reproduction by splitting into two (**binary fission**) or more (**multiple fission**) parts, each of which develops into an independent organism. The process is common amongst single-celled micro-organisms. » reproduction

fitchet » **polecat**

Fitt, Gerry, properly **Gerard, Baron** (1926–) Northern Ireland politician, born and educated in Belfast. He was a merchant seaman before entering local politics (1958–81), becoming a Republican Labour MP (1966). He founded and led the Social Democratic and Labour Party (1970–9), until he resigned the leadership to sit as an Independent Socialist. He lost his Westminster seat in 1983 when he received his peerage. He had earlier been a member of the Northern Ireland Executive (1973–5), and was its Deputy Chief Executive in 1974. » Northern Ireland [i]

Fitzgerald, Ella (1918–) US singer, born at Newport News, Virginia. Discovered in 1934 singing in an amateur contest in Harlem, she joined Chick Webb's band and recorded several hits, notably *A-tisket A-tasket* (1938). Her lucid intonation and broad range made her a top jazz singer. Her series of recordings for Verve (1955–9) in multi-volume 'songbooks' are among the treasures of US popular song. Since 1971 her concert schedule has occasionally been interrupted because of glaucoma. » jazz

Fitzgerald, F(rancis) Scott (Key) (1896–1940) US novelist, born at St Paul, Minnesota. He captured the spirit of the 1920s – 'The Jazz Age' – in *The Great Gatsby* (1925), his best-known book. In 1920 he married **Zelda Sayre** (1900–47), moving in 1924 to the French Riviera, where her subsequent mental breakdown and his alcoholism attracted wide publicity. His other novels include *The Beautiful and the Damned* (1922) and *Tender is the Night* (1934). In 1937 he returned to Hollywood, where he died. » American literature; novel

Fitzgerald, Dr Garrett (Michael) (1926–) Irish statesman and Prime Minister (1981–2, 1982–7), born in Dublin. He was educated at Dublin, where he became a barrister and a lecturer in political economy (1959–73). In 1969 he was elected Fine Gael member of the Irish parliament for Dublin SE, and became Minister for Foreign Affairs (1973–7), and Leader of the Fine Gael Party (1977–87). » Fine Gael

Fitzgerald, George Francis (1851–1901) Irish physicist, born and died in Dublin. He was professor of natural philosophy at Dublin (1881–1901). Independently of Lorentz, he concluded that a body becomes shorter as its velocity increases (the **Lorentz–Fitzgerald contraction**), a notion used by Einstein as part of his theory of special relativity. » electrolysis [i]; electromagnetism; Lorentz; special relativity [i]

Fitzsimmons, Bob, properly **Robert** (1863–1917) British boxer, born at Helston, Cornwall. He was brought up in New Zealand, and moved to the USA in 1890, where he won the world middleweight (1891), heavyweight (1897), and light heavyweight championships (1903). He is the only English-born holder of the world heavyweight crown. He continued fighting until he was over 50, and died in Chicago. » boxing [i]

Fiume » **Rijeka**

Five, the A group of 19th-c Russian composers, also known as 'The Mighty Handful', who came together to promote nationalist ideals and styles in music. They were led by Balakirev. » Balakirev; Borodin; Moussorgsky; Rimsky-Korsakov

Five Civilized Tribes The Muskogean-speaking nations of Indians (Chickasaws, Creeks, Choctaws, Cherokees, Seminoles) who originally inhabited the present SE USA. The Cherokees, in particular, adopted White ways, establishing a republic, and acquiring literacy in their own language and English. Nonetheless, they were removed to beyond the Mississippi R in the 1830s, along the 'trail of tears'. » American Indians

Five Holy Mountains » **Wu Yue**

fives A handball game played by two or four players, derived from the French game *jeu de paume* ('palm [of hand] game'). The first recorded game was at Eton school in 1825; other variations include Rugby and Winchester fives. The origin of the name is uncertain: it may be because the game was played with the five fingers of the hand or because the original scoring system was in multiples of five. » handball

fixative (painting) A liquid preparation sprayed over charcoal drawings, chalks, or pastels to prevent smudging. It is effective with monochromatic work, but less so with pastels, because of the inevitable alteration of colour values brought about when it is applied. » paint

fixing (photography) In photographic processing, the removal of unexposed silver halides remaining in the emulsion after development, allowing safe handling in the light. A solution of ammonium or sodium thiosulphate (*hypo*) is usually employed. » photography

fixture An object which is regarded for legal purposes as having become part of the land. Both the degree and the purpose of annexation are relevant to deciding whether the object has become a fixture or remains a chattel. It may be important to define fixtures when land is transferred; for example on a sale of land it is implied, unless otherwise agreed, that fixtures are left for the purchaser. » property

fjord A long, narrow, steep-sided coastal inlet extending far inland and often reaching very great depths. Most are drowned valleys formed by glacial erosion, with subsequent sea-level rise after their retreat. The best-known fjords are in Norway and E Greenland. » glaciation

flag (botany) A species of iris with yellow flowers 7.5–10 cm/3–4 in diameter, found in wet, swampy ground in Europe, W Asia, and N Africa. (*Iris pseudacorus.* Family: *Iridaceae.*) » iris (botany)

flag (politics) A piece of cloth, usually with a design, used as an ensign, standard, or signal, or to mark a position, commonly attached at one end to a staff or halyard. Flags have been used since ancient times, and some symbols are universal; a white flag signals a truce; a yellow flag the presence of infectious disease. A nation signifies its mourning by flying its flags at halfmast. » inside front and back cover

Flag Day In the USA, the anniversary (14 Jun) of the day on which the Stars and Stripes was adopted as the national flag in 1777.

flagellate [**fla**jiluht] A microscopic, single-celled organism that possesses 1, 2, 4, or more thread-like organelles (*flagellae*), typically used for swimming; many are parasites of animal hosts; others live in aquatic or even terrestrial habitats. (Phylum: *Mastigophora.*) » cell; flagellum; parasitology

flagellum A thread-like structure found on some bacteria and on or in many eucaryotic organisms. Flagella usually function in locomotion, bacterial flagella rotating and eucaryotic flagella undulating as they beat. In eucaryotic organisms there are two main kinds of flagella: a smooth whip-like type, and a tinsel type with rows of long hairs along its length. » bacteria [i]; eucaryote

flageolet [flajoh**let**] A simple, high-pitched, end-blown flute, made of wood, with six finger-holes; later, often fitted with metal keys and an ivory mouthpiece. It was popular during the 16th–18th-c, and did not become obsolete until about the mid-19th-c. An inferior keyless variety, made of brass, is known as the 'tin whistle', or 'penny whistle'. » flute; woodwind instrument [i]

Flagstad, Kirsten (1895–1962) Norwegian soprano, born at Hamar. She studied in Stockholm and Oslo, where she made her operatic debut in 1913. She excelled in Wagnerian roles, and was acclaimed in most of the world's major opera houses. In 1958 she was made director of the Norwegian State Opera. She died in Oslo. » opera; Wagner

Flaherty, Robert (Joseph) (1884–1951) US pioneer documentary film-maker, born at Iron Mountain, Michigan. Trained as a mining prospector, he took a movie camera on his expeditions to Hudson Bay in 1913, returning many times to make the silent *Nanook of the North* (1922). He then made further productions in the South Seas: *Moana* (1924) and *Tabu* (1930). For the commercial cinema his films included *Elephant Boy* (1937) and *The Louisiana Story* (1948). He died at Dummerston, Vermont.

Flamboyant The style of French late Gothic architecture prevalent in the 15th-c, characterized by long wavy flame-like bars of stonework in the tracery. It was especially common in Normandy. » Gothic architecture; tracery [i]

flamboyant tree A showy deciduous tree growing to 15 m/50 ft, native to Madagascar and widely cultivated for ornament in the tropics and subtropics; leaves large, to 60 cm/2 ft, finely divided, each with up to 1 000 individual leaflets; flowers bright scarlet, often appearing before the leaves, with five long stalked petals, one suffused with yellow; pods reddish-brown, up to 60 cm/2 ft long; also called **flame tree**. (*Delonix regia.* Family: *Leguminosae.*) » deciduous plants

flame tree » **flamboyant tree**

flamenco A type of Spanish song, dance, and guitar music of uncertain origin, associated particularly with Andalusia and probably influenced by Arab songs from N Africa. It involves highly stylistic dance movements and gestures, the use of castanets by the dancers, and an animated and highly specialized technique of guitar playing. » folk music; guitar

flamingo A large wading bird, native to S America, Africa, S Europe, and W Asia; plumage white or pink (pink colour deriving from pigments in food); inhabits shallow soda or brine lakes; filters minute organisms from water with stout, downwardly angled bill; swims well; forms immense flocks. (Family: *Phoenicopteridae*, 5 species.)

flamingo flower An evergreen perennial native to Costa Rica; leaves oblong to lance-shaped, leathery; flowers in a slender spadix 5–10 cm/2–4 in long, with a bright scarlet spathe. (*Anthurium scherzerianum.* Family: *Araceae.*) » evergreen plants; perennial; spadix; spathe

Flaminian Way The second of Rome's major trunk roads, constructed in •220 BC. It ran NE from Rome across the Apennines to Rimini on the Adriatic coast. » Roman roads [i]

Flaminius, Gaius (?–217) Roman general and statesman at the time of the Second Punic War, whose name lived on in his two most popular projects: the Flaminian Way and the Circus Flaminius (the biggest arena for chariot-racing in Republican times). He died at the Battle of L Trasimene after falling into Hannibal's ambush. » Flaminian Way; Hannibal; Punic Wars

Flamsteed, John (1646–1719) The first astronomer royal of England (1675–1719), born at Denby, Derbyshire. Educated at Cambridge, in 1676 he instituted reliable observations at Greenwich, near London, providing data from which Newton was later able to verify the gravitational theory. He died at Greenwich. » Newton, Isaac

Flanders, Flemish **Vlaanderen**, Fr **Flandre** Historical region of NW Belgium; autonomous in early Middle Ages; densely populated industrial area; chief towns Bruges, Ghent, Sint-Niklaas, Aalst, Ronse; traditional textile industry, with linen, silk, cotton processing; intensive farming, especially wheat, sugar-beet, oats, barley, potatoes; scene of heavy fighting in both World Wars. » Belgium [i]; Bruges; Ghent

flat foot A condition affecting the normal arches of the foot, which distribute weight of the body over the heel and sole of the forefoot. Loss of the arches strains the ligaments and muscles of the foot, and leads to discomfort on standing. However, many people with flat feet suffer no discomfort. » foot

flat racing » **horse racing**

flatfish Any of the bottom-dwelling mainly shallow-water fishes in which the adult body is strongly compressed laterally and asymmetrical, with both eyes on the same side of the head; nine families (sole, tongue-sole, plaice, halibut, dab, flounder, turbot, brill, topknot); excellent food fishes, very important commercially. » brill; dab; flounder; halibut; plaice; turbot

flathead Bottom-living fish of the Indo-Pacific and tropical Atlantic oceans; body slender, length up to 1 m/3¼ ft, flattened anteriorly with prominent spinose fins; important food fish in some areas. (Genera: *Platycephalus*, *Thysanophrys.* Family: *Platycephalidae.*)

Flathead A Salish-speaking Indian group living on L Flathead, Montana, the most easterly-based of Plateau Indian groups. They traded in furs with Europeans during the early 19th-c, and under their influence many converted to Christianity. Population c.3 700. » American Indians

flatworm A flattened, worm-like animal with a definite head but without a true body cavity (*coelom*); digestive system usually lacks an anus; free living flatworms typically feed on small invertebrates; parasitic forms include tapeworms and flukes. (Phylum: *Platyhelminthes.*) » blood fluke; fluke; tapeworm; worm

Flaubert, Gustave [**floh**bair] (1821–80) French novelist, born at Rouen. He studied law at Paris, then turned to writing. His masterpiece was *Madame Bovary* (1857), which was condemned as immoral and its author (unsuccessfully) prosecuted. His other works include *Salammbô* (1862) and *La Tentation de St Antoine* (1874, The Temptation of St Anthony). *Trois contes* (1877, Three Tales) reveals his mastery of the short story. » French literature; novel

flavouring agent Any compound when added to a food to alter its taste, the most widely used being salt and sugar. Monosodium glutamate is an example of a flavour enhancer, bringing out a 'meaty flavour'. Artificial flavours which mimic natural flavours are also commonplace. » monosodium glutamate; salt; sugars

flax A slender erect annual, growing to 60 cm/2 ft; leaves narrow; flowers numerous, blue, c.3 cm/1½ in diameter, with five spreading petals; fruit a capsule with numerous seeds. Its origin is unknown, but it is cultivated throughout temperate and subtropical regions for flax fibre obtained from the stems, and for linseed oil from the seeds. (*Linum usitatissimum*. Family: *Linaceae*.) » annual

Flaxman, John (1755–1826) British sculptor and illustrator, born at York. He studied at the Royal Academy, and thereafter was constantly engaged upon sculpture; but his chief source of income was the Wedgwood house, which he furnished with renowned pottery designs. He also studied at Rome (1787–94), where he began his illustrations to the *Iliad* and *Odyssey* (1793), and other works. In 1810 he became professor of sculpture to the Royal Academy. He died in London. » English art; Neoclassicism (art and architecture); sculpture; Wedgwood, Josiah

flea A small, wingless insect that as an adult is a blood-feeding external parasite of warm-blooded animals (mostly mammals, but including some birds); body flattened from side to side, usually hairy; mouthparts specialized for piercing and sucking; hindlegs adapted for jumping; larvae maggot-like, feeding on organic refuse around domicile of host; c.1 750 species, many of medical and veterinary importance as carriers of disease. (Order: *Siphonaptera*.) » insect [i]; larva

fleabane A leafy perennial growing to 60 cm/2 ft, native to marshes and wet places in Europe, N Africa, and Asia Minor; leaves lance-shaped, clasping the stem at the base, wavy-margined, softly hairy; flower heads up to 3 cm/1.2 in across, golden yellow, daisy-like; fruit with a parachute of hairs. Its dried leaves were formerly burnt to repel insects. (*Pulicaria dysenterica*. Family: *Compositae*.) » perennial

fleawort The name applied to certain species of the genus *Senecio*. **Marsh fleawort** (*Senecio congestus*) is a biennial or perennial with stout hairy stems growing to 2 m/6½ ft; leaves numerous, lance-shaped, wavy-margined; flower heads numerous, up to 3 cm/1.2 in across, in dense clusters, with c.21 pale yellow outer ray florets; native to C Europe. **Field fleawort** (*Senecio integrifolius*) is a variable perennial growing to 70 cm/27 in; smaller clusters of flower heads with c.13 bright yellow outer ray florets; native to much of Europe. (Family: *Compositae*.) » biennial; floret; perennial

Flecker, James Elroy (1884–1915) British poet, born in London. He studied Oriental languages at Cambridge, and entered the consular service. His best-known works are the verse drama *Hassan* (staged, 1923) and *The Golden Journey to Samarkand* (1913). He died in Switzerland. » English literature; poetry

Flémalle, Master of » **Campin, Robert**

Fleming, Sir Alexander (1881–1955) British bacteriologist, born at Lochfield, Ayrshire, Scotland. He was the first to use antityphoid vaccines on human beings, pioneered the use of salvarsan against syphilis, and discovered the antiseptic powers of lysozyme. In 1928 he discovered penicillin, for which he shared the Nobel Prize for Physiology or Medicine in 1945. He became professor of bacteriology at London in 1938, and was knighted in 1944. He died in London. » arsenicals; lysozyme; penicillin

Fleming, Ian (Lancaster) (1908–64) British author and journalist, born in London. He was educated at Eton and Sandhurst, studied languages at Munich and Geneva, worked with Reuters in Moscow (1929–33), then became a banker and stockbroker (1933–9). He served with British Naval Intelligence during World War 2, and was foreign manager of the *Sunday Times* (1945–59). He achieved worldwide fame and fortune as the creator of a series of spy novels, starting with *Casino Royale* (1953), built round the exploits of his amoral hero James Bond. He died at Canterbury, Kent. » spy story

Fleming, Sir John Ambrose (1849–1945) British physicist, born at Lancaster, Lancashire. He studied at London and Cambridge, and became professor of electrical engineering at University College, London (1885–1926). He invented the

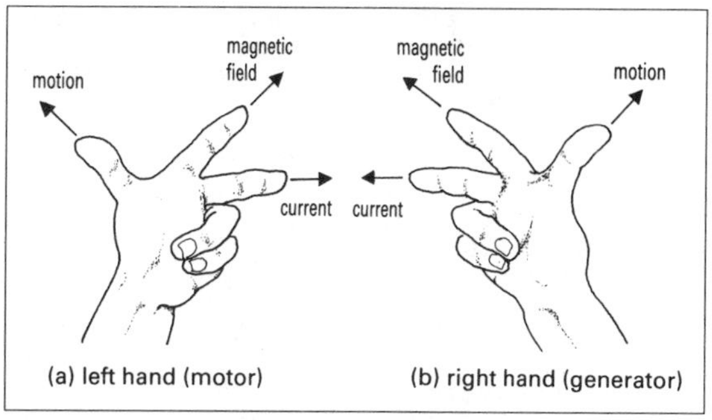

Fleming's rules – Left hand (a) A current-carrying wire in a magnetic field undergoes motion in the direction indicated; right hand (b) A moving wire in a magnetic field produces a current flowing in the direction indicated

thermionic valve, and was a pioneer in the application of electricity to lighting and heating on a large scale. He was knighted in 1929, and died at Sidmouth, Devon. » thermionic valve

Fleming and Walloon The two main linguistic and cultural groups of present-day Belgium. Flemings (5.5 million) are based in the N and W, and speak Dutch (Vlaams). The French-speaking Walloons (3 million) live in the S and E. Both groups are predominantly Catholic. Linguistic disputes between the two groups have been a major feature of Belgian politics since the creation of the Kingdom in 1830, but especially since World War 2. » Belgium [i]; Flanders; Wallonia

Fleming's rules A set of rules which link the direction of magnetic field, motion, and current using the thumb, first finger, and second finger, held at right angles; named after British physicist John Ambrose Fleming (1849–1945). The left hand/right hand correspond to motor/generator respectively. » electromagnetism

Flemish art The art of the predominently Catholic S Netherlands, roughly modern Belgium and Luxembourg. Its major achievements were in painting, especially 14th-c manuscript illumination and 15th-c altarpieces and portraits on panel (Campin, van Eyck, van der Weyden, Bouts, Memlinc). The tradition continued in the 16th-c with Bosch and Breughel, one of the greatest landscape painters, and the Baroque masters Rubens, van Dyck, and Jordaens in the 17th-c. Wars and religious iconoclasm have destroyed much, yet what survives attests to one of the greatest traditions of Western art. Flemish art, unlike Dutch, was always courtly and ecclesiastical in character, yet was largely independent of Italy. In the 20th-c Magritte and Delvaux have made a distinct contribution to Surrealism. » art; altarpiece; iconoclasm; Romanist; Bosch, Hieronymus; Bouts; Breughel; Campin; Delvaux; Jordaens; Magritte; Memlinc; Rubens; van Dyck; van Eyck; Weyden

Flemming, Walther (1843–1905) German biologist, born at Sachsenberg. He studied medicine at five German universities, and in 1876 became professor of anatomy at Kiel. In 1882 he gave the first modern account of cytology, including the process of cell division, which he named *mitosis*. He died at Kiel. » cytology; mitosis

Fletcher, John (1579–1625) English dramatist, born at Rye, Sussex. He came of a literary family, and studied at Cambridge, but little else is known about him apart from his theatrical work. It is difficult to disentangle his own plays from those in which he collaborated with Beaumont, Massinger, Rowley, and Shakespeare. He is best known for his collaboration with Beaumont in such works as *Philaster* (1610), *A King and No King* (1611), and *The Maid's Tragedy* (1611). Collaboration with Shakespeare probably resulted in *Two Noble Kinsmen* and *Henry VIII*. He died of the plague in London. » Beaumont, Francis; drama; English literature; Shakespeare [i]

Fleury, André-Hercule de [**fler**ree] (1653–1743) French prelate and statesman, born at Lodève. As a young priest he entered court service (1679), became almoner to Louis XIV (1683), Bishop of Fréjus (1698), and in 1715 tutor to the future

Louis XV. Replacing the Duke de Bourbon as Chief Minister (1726), he was made cardinal, and effectively controlled the government of Louis XV until 1743. Through skilful diplomacy he limited French involvement in the War of the Polish Succession (1733–8), restoring the country's prestige as a mediator. His moderation gave France the tranquility her tangled finances demanded, and he carried out legal and economic reforms which stimulated trade. He died in Paris. » Louis XIV/XV; Polish Succession, War of the

Flinders, Matthew (1774–1814) British explorer, born at Donington, Lincolnshire. He joined the navy in 1789, and became a navigator. In 1795 he sailed to Australia, where he explored the SE coast, and later (1801–3) circumnavigated the country. On his way home he was wrecked off the Great Barrier Reef, and later kept prisoner by the French Governor of Mauritius until 1810. He died in London. The Flinders R in Queensland, and the Flinders range in South Australia are named after him. » Australia [i]

Flinders Ranges » Lofty-Flinders Ranges, Mount

flint A type of chert, occurring as grey, rounded nodules in chalk or other limestone. It breaks into sharp-edged flakes and hence was used as a Stone Age tool. » chert; Three Age System

flint glass Heavy crystal glass, containing lead, highly suitable for cutting and engraving. It was first introduced c.1675, and so called because early examples were made with powdered flint instead of the more usual sand. » glass **2** [i]

FLN The acronym for the **Front de Libération Nationale**, an organization founded in the early 1950s, which campaigned and fought for Algerian independence from France, under the leadership of Mohammed Ben Bella (1918–). The war with the FLN led to the collapse of the Fourth French Republic in 1958, and the return to power of de Gaulle. France's inability to defeat the FLN led to the Evian conference in 1962, and complete Algerian independence. » Algeria [i]; de Gaulle; OAS

floating rate » exchange rates

Flodden, Battle of (1513) A victory of the English over the Scots, fought in the Borders. James IV, allied with France, invaded England in August, but was defeated by English forces under Thomas Howard, Earl of Surrey. The Scottish dead included James, 13 earls, and three bishops; the battle ended the Scottish threat for a generation. » James IV

Flood, the In the Bible, the story that in Noah's time God caused a widespread deluge to destroy all people because of their sin (except Noah and his family), this purge providing a new start for mankind (*Gen* 6–8) and the animal world. Similar legends are found also in other ancient near-eastern sources, such as the Babylonian Gilgamesh Epic. » Genesis, Book of; Gilgamesh Epic; Noah

Flood, Henry (1723–91) Irish statesman, educated at Dublin and Oxford. He became leader of the popular party in the Irish parliament after his election in 1759. In 1775 he became Vice-Treasurer of Ireland, but was removed in 1781 as a strong Nationalist. In 1783 he was returned for Winchester, and in 1785 for Seaford, but he failed to make a great mark at Westminster. He died at Farmley, Kilkenny. » Irish Republic [i]; nationalism

floods (lighting) » **luminaires**

floppy disk or **floppy** A flexible plastic disk coated with magnetic material, used as a storage medium for microcomputers. The disks are housed in cardboard jackets and generally have diameters of either 5.25 in (13.3 cm) or 8 in (20.3 cm), although the latter are becoming less common. In use, the disks are rotated at some 300 revolutions per minute and are written to, or read from, by movable magnetic heads. The data is stored on a number of concentric tracks (usually 40 or 80); 5.25 in disks, for example, can store up to 1 Megabyte or more of information, the exact amount depending on the particular system. » byte; hard disk; minidisk; Winchester disk

Flora An ancient Roman goddess of flowers and flowering plants, who appears with the Spring. She was given a temple in 238 BC, and her games were celebrated on 28 April.

Florence, Ital **Firenze** 43°47N 11°15E, pop (1981) 448 331. Ancient city and capital of Florence province, Tuscany, Italy, on R Arno; ancient Etruscan town; major trading centre by 12th-c; cultural and intellectual centre of Italy from the Middle Ages; provisional capital of new Kingdom of Italy, 1865–71; badly damaged by floods, 1966; archbishopric; airport; railway; university (1321); European University Institute (1972); seat of the Accademia della Crusca; iron and steel, copper products, cosmetics, medicinal products, tourism; city centre a world heritage site; famed for its many religious buildings and palaces, notably the Baptistery of San Giovanni (c.1000), the Duomo (1296); Churches of Santa Croce (begun 1295), Santa Maria Novella (1278–1350), Santa Maria del Carmine (largely rebuilt, 1782), San Lorenzo (393, rebuilt 1425), San Marco (13th-c, since rebuilt), Santissima Annunziata (1250), Or San Michele, (13th–14th-c); Palazzo Vecchio (1298–1314), Palazzo degli Uffizi (1560–74), Palazzo Medici-Riccardi (1444–52), Palazzo Pitti (15th-c and later), Ponte Vecchio (rebuilt 1345); religious festivals throughout the year, particularly at Easter; music festival (May). » Florentine School; Ghibellines; Guelphs; Medici; Pitti Palace; Ponte Vecchio; Tuscany; Uffizi

Florentine School One of the major centres of European art during the Renaissance period, whose leading figures were chronicled by their fellow-citizen Vasari, in his great *Lives of the most excellent Painters, Sculptors and Architects* (1550, enlarged 1568), written partly to glorify Florentine achievements over those of other schools such as the Venetian. The classical revival of the 15th-c began in Florence, as did the rediscovery of perspective; and the first academy of art was founded there in 1563. After c.1500 the leadership in Italian art shifted to Rome and Venice. » classical revival; Florence; Italian art; Mannerism; perspective; Renaissance art; school (art); Angelico; Brunelleschi; Donatello; Ghirlandaio; Giotto; Leonardo da Vinci; Masaccio; Michelangelo; Vasari; Verrocchio

floret A very small or reduced flower, usually one of many aggregated together in a head which may itself resemble a single flower, as in members of the daisy family. » daisy; flower [i]; inflorescence [i]

Florey, Sir Howard Walter, Baron Florey of Adelaide (1898–1968) Australian pathologist, born in Adelaide. He studied medicine at Adelaide and Oxford, taught at Cambridge and Sheffield, then became professor of pathology at Oxford (1935–62), where he worked with Chain on penicillin, and shared the Nobel Prize for Physiology or Medicine (1945). He was appointed provost of Queen's College, Oxford (1962) and chancellor of the Australian National University, Canberra (1965). Knighted in 1944, he became a life peer in 1965. He died at Oxford. » Chain; penicillin

Florida pop (1987e) 12 023 000; area 151 934 sq km/58 664 sq ml. State in SE USA, divided into 67 counties; the 'Sunshine State'; discovered and settled by the Spanish in the 16th-c; ceded to Britain in 1763, and divided into East and West Florida; given back to Spain after the War of Independence, 1783; West Florida gained by the US in the Louisiana Purchase, 1803; East Florida purchased by the US, 1819; admitted as the 27th state of the Union, 1845; seceded, 1861; slavery abolished, 1865; re-admitted to the Union, 1868; capital, Tallahassee; other major cities Jacksonville, Miami, Tampa, St Petersburg, Fort Lauderdale; a long peninsula bounded W by the Gulf of Mexico and E by the Atlantic Ocean; rivers include the St Johns, Caloosahatchee, Apalachicola, Perdido, St Marys; C state has many lakes, notably L Okeechobee (fourth largest lake wholly within the USA); highest point in Walton County (105 m/345 ft); the Florida Keys Islands stretch in a line SW from the S tip of the state, all linked by a series of causeways; the NW is a gently rolling panhandle area, cut by deep swamps along the coast; the S is almost entirely covered by the Everglades; the SE coast is protected from the Atlantic by sandbars and islands, creating shallow lagoons and sandy beaches; a warm sunny climate; many famous resorts (Palm Beach, Miami Beach); one of the fastest-growing metropolitan areas in the country; the Everglades National Park, Walt Disney World entertainment park, John F Kennedy Space Center at Cape Canaveral; the nation's greatest producer of citrus fruits; second largest producer of vegetables; sugar cane, tobacco, cattle and dairy products; processed foods, chemicals, electrical equipment, transportation equipment, wood products; phosphate and other minerals; large Hispanic population (especially from Cuba). » Canaveral, Cape; Disney; Everglades; Florida Keys; Louisiana Purchase; Tallahassee; United States of America [i]; RR38

Florida Keys S Florida, USA; series of small islands curving approx 240 km/150 ml SW around the tip of the Florida peninsula, about 160 km/100 ml NNE of Havana; include (NE to SW) Key Largo, Long Key, Key Vaca, Big Pine Key, Sugarloaf Key and Key West; tropical products (limes, pineapples, etc) in the S; tarpon fishing; tourism; Overseas Highway (1938) runs from the mainland to Key West, 198 km/123 ml long. » Florida

florin The name of a coin in British currency, the predecimalization two-shilling piece (now the 10p piece). The name was also used for a gold coin at the time of Edward III.

flotation process The process of separating useful parts of minerals from waste (*gangue*), through the selective attachment of particles of the desired material to bubbles in a froth. The material to be treated is immersed in water and air is blown through. Bubble formation may be promoted by a surface-active or foam-promoting agent.

Flotow, Baron Friedrich von [**floh**toh] (1812–83) German composer, born at Teutendorf, Mecklenburg. He studied music at Paris, and made his reputation with several operas, notably *Martha* (1847). He was director of the theatre at Schwerin (1855–63). He died at Darmstadt, Germany.

flotsam, jetsam and lagan [**lay**gan] Three terms used in describing goods or wreckage found in the sea. *Flotsam* refers to anything found floating. *Jetsam* includes anything deliberately jettisoned from a ship, usually for the purposes of lightening it or because it would otherwise be dangerous to the ship. *Lagan* refers to goods on the bottom of the sea, either alone or within the hull of a wrecked vessel.

flounder Common European flatfish found in shallow inshore waters from Norway to the Mediterranean, also penetrating into fresh water in N areas; upper body surface grey brown with dark patches and orange spots, underside white; length up to 50 cm/20 in; locally important as a food fish. (*Platichthys flesus*. Family: *Pleuronectidae*.) » flatfish

flour The finely ground product of a cereal seed, especially wheat, primarily used to make bread. A wheat seed consists of an outer coat (husk), a germinal centre (germ), and a starchy centre (endosperm). When the seed is ground, it forms a wholemeal flour suitable for baking; if the flour is refined to increase the proportion of endosperm, white flour is produced. Wholemeal flour is richer in fibre, and an important constituent of high-fibre diets, which aid the process of defaecation. » cereals; fibre

flowchart A diagrammatic representation of a sequence of events. In the computing context, a **data flowchart** describes the overall operations in a complete data-processing system, such as an accounting system, without giving specific details of the individual computer programs; a **program flowchart** describes the sequence of operations within the program. There are recognized symbols to indicate the various types of operation. » data processing; program, computer

flower The reproductive organ of a flowering plant (*angiosperm*) derived from a leafy shoot of limited growth in which the leaves are modified for specific roles. It typically consists of four distinct *whorls* of parts attached to a receptacle: the sepals (*calyx*), the petals (*corolla*), the stamens (*androecium*), and the carpels or ovary (*gynoecium*). The parts of any whorl may be fused or otherwise highly modified or absent. Structurally, flowers can be divided into two types: **actinomorphic** or radially-symmetrical, and **zygomorphic** or bilaterally-symmetrical. Both the colour and structure of the flower are closely linked to the method of pollination: brightly-coloured petals, along with any scent or nectar produced by the flower are used to attract pollinators. The colour may be quite specific, so that red is typically a bird-colour, blue and yellow are bee-colours, and dull-purplish flowers are often wasp-pollinated. Flowers which are one colour in the visible spectrum may be another colour in the ultraviolet, visible to many insects. The structure, especially in zygomorphic flowers, may also be geared to particular visitors: flat, open blossoms are visited by a wide range of

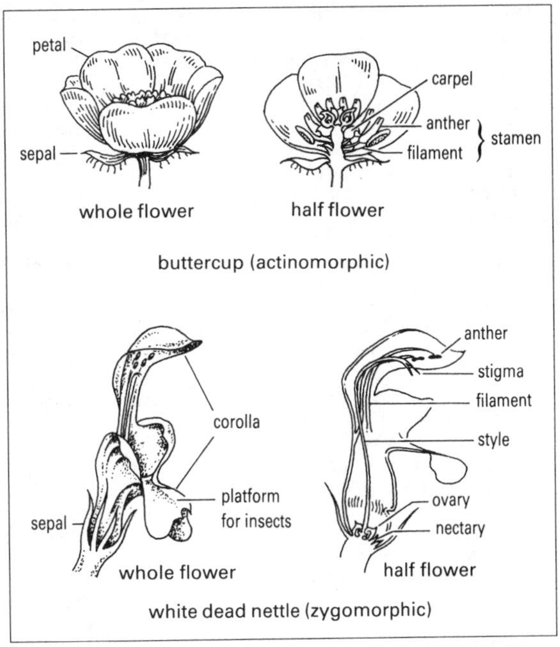

Parts of a flower

pollinators, including flies and beetles; more complex blooms may have nectar concealed in long, gullet-like corolla tubes or behind closed lips accessible only to long-tongued bees, moths, or humming-birds. In wind-pollinated flowers, attractive petals are superfluous, and are usually much-reduced or absent. Double or multiple-petalled flowers such as garden roses are rare in nature, being mostly the product of horticultural breeding. » carpel; epicalyx; floret; flowering plants; inflorescence [i]; ovary; perianth; petal; pollen; receptacle; sepal; stamen

flowering plants One of the two divisions of seed plants, sometimes referred to as the **angiosperms**, the other division being the *gymnosperms*. They are characterized by having the seed enclosed in an ovary which has a specialized extension (the *stigma*) for receiving pollen. The male gametes produced by the pollen undergo double fertilization of the ovum, forming a zygote and a special seed storage tissue (the *endosperm*). Secondary vascular tissue develops from *cambial layers*, and contains cells unique to flowering plants: vessels in the *xylem*, companion cells in the *phloem*. The group includes all plants in which the reproductive organ is a flower, hence the commonly used name. The flowering plants are divided into *monocotyledons* and *dicotyledons* on the basis of cotyledon number, and further subdivided into various major groups such as orders and families, the exact divisions varying with the system in use. Flowering plants are the most advanced vascular plants, and the most common in terms of both numbers and distribution, with an estimated 250 000 species occurring in all parts of the globe. (Class: *Angiospermae*.) » cotyledons; Cretaceous period; dicotyledons; flower [i]; fossil; gamete; gymnosperms; monocotyledons; ovary; stigma; vascular tissue; zygote

flowering quince » **japonica**

flowering rush A perennial native to Europe and temperate Asia, growing in or beside water; stems to 1.5 m/5 ft; rhizomatous; leaves grass-like, triangular in cross-section; flowers c.2.5–3 cm/1–1¼ in diameter, pink, 3-petalled, in a terminal umbel. (*Butomus umbellatus*. Family: *Butomaceae*.) » perennial; rhizome; umbel

flowerpecker A name applied loosely to many small woodland birds of the family *Dicaeidae*; more precisely, the 41 species of the genera *Prionochilus* and *Dicaeum*; found from India to Australia; tongue tube-like; eats nectar and berries, especially mistletoe. » diamondbird

flugelhorn [**floo**glhawn] A musical instrument made of brass, somewhat like a cornet and with a similar compass, but with a slightly larger bell. It is a standard instrument in British brass bands, and is used in jazz, but is rarely found in orchestras. » brass instrument [i]; cornet

fluid A substance which flows and is able to fill its container: a liquid, gas, or plasma. Stationary fluids cannot sustain transverse or twisting forces. Their mechanical properties are governed by the laws of fluid mechanics. » fluid mechanics; fluidics; gas **1**; liquid; plasma (physics)

fluid mechanics The study of the mechanics of fluids. **Fluid statics** is concerned with the properties of fluids at rest. **Fluid dynamics** considers the properties peculiar to moving fluids. **Hydrostatics** and **hydrodynamics** are the study of stationary and moving incompressible fluids (usually liquids), respectively. **Aerodynamics** is concerned with the flow of gases, especially air. The properties of fluids include *density*, the mass per unit volume, and *compressibility*, which is high for gases but essentially zero for liquids. A fluid also exerts a *pressure* on an object immersed in it, which is the same in all directions. In the absence of gravity, the pressure applied by a fluid is the same on all parts of its container. Objects immersed in fluid experience an upward *buoyancy* force. *Viscosity* measures a fluid's reluctance to flow, more properly its internal friction. The theory of fluids sometimes uses ideal fluids having zero viscosity and compressibility.

The early understanding of fluid pressure (especially atmospheric pressure) was due to Italian physicist Evangelista Torricelli. Pressure applied to a stationary fluid is transmitted undiminished throughout the fluid, and to the walls of the container independent of container shape. This is *Pascal's principle* (after French mathematician Blaise Pascal, 1653), and forms the basis of hydraulics. The *flow* of fluid is the movement of fluid from one place to another, measured by *flow rate*, which is the mass of fluid passing some point every second. The principal of continuity states that for an incompressible fluid the amount of fluid flowing into some pipe network equals the amount flowing out. Early studies of fluid flow were due to Swiss mathematician Daniel Bernoulli, who in particular noted the pressure variation in a fluid flowing along a pipe of varying cross section (*Bernoulli's principle*). Modern mathematical theory of fluid flow is based on an approach introduced by Swiss mathematician Leonard Euler, who treated a fluid as a continuous substance rather than discrete particles. The theory of viscous fluid flow was developed by British physicist George Stokes (1819–1903). » aerodynamics [i]; atmospheric physics; Bernoulli; Bernoulli's principle; bow wave; buoyancy; capillarity; cavitation; density (physics); drag; Euler; fluid; fluidics; hydraulics; magnetohydrodynamics; Pascal; porosity; pressure; rheology; shock wave; siphon; supersonic; surface tension [i]; Torricelli; turbulence; Venturi tube; viscosity

fluidics The study of control and detection systems based on fluid movement. Available devices include fluid amplifiers (in which a small flow modifies a large flow), logic circuits, and switches. Fluidic devices contain no moving parts, are robust, and constitute no electrical hazard. An example is the fluidic vortex valve, which uses a controlling stream to alter the principal flow by creating a vortex, and is used in pumping systems in the nuclear industry for radioactive waste, and in mining for abrasive slurries. » fluid mechanics; hydraulics

fluke Either of two groups of parasitic flatworm; **digenetic** flukes, typically parasites of vertebrates as adults, with complex life cycles involving at least two hosts; **monogenetic** flukes, usually external parasites of fishes with single host life cycles. (Phylum: *Platyhelminthes*. Class: *Trematoda*.) » blood fluke; flatworm; parasitology

fluorescein [floouhreseen] $C_{20}H_{12}O_5$. An anthraquinone dye, red with an intense green fluorescence. Very dilute solutions are used to detect leaks in water systems, and to trace water flow patterns. » anthracene [i]; dyestuff

fluorescence Light produced by an object excited by means other than heating, where light emission ceases as soon as the energy source is removed. It is a type of luminescence, exploited in dyes and in the coating of fluorescent light tubes. » fluorescent brighteners/lamp; luminescence

fluorescent brighteners Colourless substances which are easily absorbed by textiles, and which emit blue or blue/green light when exposed to ultraviolet light. The effect is to counteract the natural yellowness of textiles to maintain clean bright colours. They are an essential component of most detergents. » fluorescence

fluorescent lamp A lamp consisting of a tube, coated inside with fluorescent material (phosphor), filled with mercury vapour, and with an electrode at each end. Light is generated by passing a current between the electrodes through the vapour, producing ultraviolet light that is converted to visible light by phosphor fluorescence. Such lamps are more efficient than filament lamps. » fluorescence; light; luminescence

fluoridation of water Water containing small amounts of fluorine (1 part/million), whose regular consumption greatly reduces the incidence of caries of the teeth. Water supplies in many regions contain fluorine naturally in sufficient concentrations to increase the resistance of teeth to attack. This has led the authorities to recommend the addition of fluorine to reservoirs deficient in the element. While this is done in many instances, a vociferous minority of the population who object to adding 'chemicals' to water have succeeded in preventing it from becoming universal. » caries; fluorine; teeth [i]

fluoride A compound containing fluorine, especially one containing F^- ions. *Sodium fluoride* (NaF) is commonly added in small amounts to drinking water or dentifrice to supply fluoride ions necessary for strong dental enamel. » CFCs; fluorine; fluorocarbons

fluorine Element 9, composed of molecules F_2, boiling point −187°C. A yellow gas, the first of the halogens, the most electronegative element, oxidation state −1 in nearly all its compounds. It reacts with nearly all substances, including some of the noble gases, and is very corrosive and toxic. It occurs mainly in the mineral *fluorite* (CaF_2), obtained by the electrolysis of a mixture of hydrogen and potassium fluorides. » chemical elements; electronegativity; halogens; noble gases; RR90

fluorite or **fluorspar** A common mineral of calcium fluoride (CaF_2), typically blue or purple in colour, and the main source of fluorine. It is found in veins and pockets associated with igneous rocks, and fluoresces in ultraviolet light. It is used as a flux in steel production. » fluorine; igneous rock; Plate IV

fluorocarbons Compounds of carbon and fluorine, the simplest being CF_4, tetrafluoromethane. The C−F bond is very stable, and saturated fluorocarbons are very unreactive. Tetrafluoroethylene ($CF_2{=}CF_2$) forms the very stable polymer PTFE (*teflon*) by addition polymerization. » carbon; CFCs; fluorine; ozone layer; polymerization

fluorspar » **fluorite**

Flushing, Dutch **Vlissingen**, Fr **Flessingue** 51°27N 3°35E, pop(1984e) 46 150. Seaport in Zeeland province, W Netherlands, on Walcheren I at the mouth of the Schelde river estuary; scene of Allied landing, 1944; railway; site of a nuclear power station; shipbuilding, machinery, vehicles, leather, fish processing, aluminium, chemicals; 14th-c Grote Kerk. » Netherlands, The [i]

flute Broadly speaking, a musical instrument in which a column of air is activated by the player blowing across a mouth-hole or (as in the recorder) against a sharp edge (or 'fipple') towards which the breath may be directed through a duct. Flutes may therefore be divided into two categories: cross-blown (or transverse) and end-blown. The unqualified term 'flute' generally refers to the transverse concert type, known in Britain until c.1900 as the 'German flute'. This is made of wood or (more often now) of metal in three jointed sections, with 13 toneholes, and an elaborate system of keys which allow a fully chromatic compass of three octaves from middle C upwards. The smaller piccolo sounds one octave higher. » fife; flageolet; ocarina; piccolo; recorder (music); woodwind instrument [i]

flutemouth » **cornetfish**

fluting or **flutes** Shallow vertical channelling on a building, usually on the shaft of a column or pilaster. It is common in the Doric, Ionic, Corinthian, and Composite orders, but not in the Tuscan. » column; orders of architecture [i]; pilaster

flux (physics) A term indicating flow, such as a flux of particles flowing past a point, or the flux of some fluid moving from high to low pressure. For electric and magnetic fields, flux indicates the total amount of field flowing from a source through some region. » electric field; Gauss's law; magnetic flux

flux (technology) Any substance used in metallurgical processes to promote the flow of molten metal and waste (*slag*) and to segregate unwanted impurities. Limestone fulfils this purpose in iron smelting. In soldering, rosin is often used. » smelting; solder

fluxoid » **BCS theory**

fly The common name of many small flying insects. True flies have a single pair of membraneous flying wings only; hind-wings modified as club-shaped, balancing organs (*halteres*); mouthparts forming a proboscis adapted for sucking, occasionally for piercing; feed on nectar, plant and animal secretions, blood, and decomposing matter; larvae maggot-like, lacking true legs, varied in feeding habits; c.150 000 species, many of great medical and veterinary importance as carriers of disease. (Order: *Diptera*.) » black/bot/caddis/fruit/gad/horse/robber/sand/scorpion/tsetse/warble fly; bluebottle; cranefly; Culicidae; housefly; hoverfly; insect [i]; larva; mayfly; midge; mosquito; sandfly; screwworm; sheep ked

fly agaric [agarik] A toadstool that forms a bright red fruiting body, typically with white patches on cap; common on ground under trees such as birch and pine during autumn; produces hallucinogenic poisons that can be fatal to humans if eaten. (*Amantia muscaria*. Order: *Agaricales*.) » hallucinogens; muscarine; toadstool

flycatcher A name applied to birds of three distinct groups: **New World** or **tyrant flycatchers** (Family: *Tyrannidae*, 375 species); **Old World flycatchers** (Family: *Muscicapidae*, 150 species); and **silky-flycatchers** (Family: *Ptilogonatidae*, 4 species). All usually eat insects caught in flight. The name is also used for several birds of other families. » fantail; thrush (bird); wagtail

flying buttress » **buttress**

flying doctor service The provision of medical services to isolated communities spread over wide areas, based on the use of Air Ambulances. It is particularly well-known in the Australian interior.

Flying Dutchman A ghost ship of disastrous portent, haunting the seas around the Cape of Good Hope; its captain had sworn a blasphemous oath when he failed to round the Cape in a storm, and was condemned to sail those waters forever. The story inspired Wagner's opera *Der Fliegende Holländer* (1843). » Wagner

flying fish Small surface-living fish with greatly enlarged pelvic and pectoral fins, and the ability to jump and glide above the water surface; *Exocoetus volitans* (length up to 30 cm/1 ft), is widespread in tropical and warm temperate seas. (Family: *Exocoetidae*.)

flying fox » **bat**

flying lemur » **colugo**

flying lizard A SE Asian agamid lizard; able to glide between trees using a semicircular membrane on each side of the body; membrane supported by moveable ribs; can be folded back when not in use; also known as **flying dragon**. (Genus: *Draco*, several species.) » agamid

flying phalanger A nocturnal squirrel-like marsupial, native to Australia and New Guinea; gliding membrane between front and hind limbs; can glide up to 114 m/374 ft; inhabits woodland; eats plant material and animals. (Family: *Petauridae*, 4 species.) » marsupial [i]; squirrel

flying snake A snake from SE Asia; glides between trees; launches itself into the air, then flattens the body and forms several S-shaped curves; several regions of the body are then broadside to the direction of travel and act like wings; may glide 20 m/65 ft or more. (Genus: *Chrysopelea*, 2 species. Family: *Colubridae*.) » snake

flying spot scanner A device for reproducing a slide transparency or motion picture film on television by scanning the picture area with a spot of light, usually generated on the screen of a cathode-ray tube. The transmitted light is collected by a photocell or sensor tube to produce the video signal. » scanning [i]; telecine; television

flying squirrel A squirrel with a large flap of skin between its front and hind legs; glides between trees (up to 450 m/1 475 ft in one leap); active at dawn and dusk; 33 species in Asia (one reaches E Europe, most in SE Asia), and two species in N America. » scaly-tailed squirrel; squirrel

Flynn, Errol (Leslie Thomson) (1909–59) Australian film star, born in Hobart, Tasmania. He came to England to gain acting experience, joined the Northampton Repertory Company, and after a part in a film was offered a Hollywood contract. His first American film, *Captain Blood* (1935), established him as a hero of historical adventure films, and his good looks and athleticism confirmed him as the greatest Hollywood swashbuckler, in such films as *The Adventures of Robin Hood* (1938) and *The Sea Hawk* (1940). During the 1940s his off-screen reputation for drinking, drug-taking, and womanizing became legendary and eventually affected his career. He died of a heart attack, in Vancouver, Canada.

flywheel A wheel attached to the shaft of an engine, whose distribution of weight enables it to act as a smoothing device for the engine's power output. » engine

Fo, Dario (1926–) Italian dramatist, designer, and actor, born at San Giano, Lombardy. After working in radio and TV he founded, along with his wife, Franca Rame, a radical theatre company in 1959. His populist plays use the comic traditions of farce and slapstick, as well as surreal effects; best known are *Morte accidentale di un anarchico* (1970, Accidental Death of an Anarchist), *Non si paga, non si paga* (1974, Can't Pay, Won't Pay), and *Female Parts* (1981), one-woman plays written with his wife. » Italian literature; theatre

foam A suspension of gas in liquid or of liquid in gas, also called **froth**. It is stabilized by the addition of detergents to the liquid phase. Foams are controlled by adding agents to raise the surface tension of the liquid. They are useful, especially in mineral extraction, as differences in the surface properties of components of an ore can be used to float off part in a foam. They are also used in fire-fighting. » colloid; detergent

Foch, Ferdinand [fosh] (1851–1929) French marshal, born at Tarbes. He taught at the Ecole de Guerre, proved himself a great strategist at the Marne (1914), Ypres, and other World War 1 battles, and commanded the Allied armies in 1918. He died in Paris. » World War 1

focus The point of convergence for rays of light passing through a lens at which the sharpest image is formed. The position of a camera lens must be adjusted ('focused') so that this image coincides with the photosensitive surface. » camera

foetus/fetus The embryo of a mammal, especially a human, at a stage of development when all the main features of the adult form are recognizable. In humans, the embryo from 8 weeks to birth is called a foetus. » embryo

fog A cloud which occurs at ground level, resulting in low visibility. It forms when two air masses with differing temperatures and moisture contents mix together. **Radiation fog** develops on cold, clear nights when terrestrial radiation cools the ground surface, and lowers the temperature of the air close to the ground to below the dew point temperature, causing condensation. **Advective fog** forms when warm, moist air blows over a cold ground surface, is cooled, and condensation results. Fog may also be associated with frontal activity when warm rain falls through cold but saturated air. » cloud [i]; condensation (physics); dew point temperature; front; precipitation; temperature inversion

Föhn/Foehn wind [fern] A warm dry wind descending on the leeward side of a mountain. As moist air rises on the windward side, it cools and loses moisture before descending and warming. It may cause a sudden rise in temperature, such as 10°C in a few hours. It is found in the European Alps and other mountainous areas. In the Rockies, N America, it is known as a *chinook* wind, in New Zealand as a *Nor-Wester*, and in Argentina as a *zonda*. » katabatic wind; wind [i]

Fokine, Michel, originally **Mikhail Mikhaylovich Fokine** [fokeen] (1880–1942) Russian-US dancer and choreographer, born in St Petersburg. He worked with Diaghilev's Ballets Russes in Paris from 1909, and in 1923 went to New York, where he

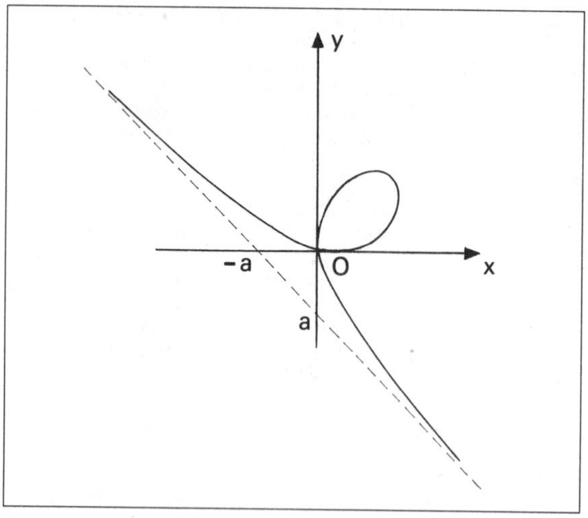

Folium of Descartes

became a US citizen (1932). He is credited with the creation of modern ballet from the artificial, stylized mode prevalent at the turn of the century. His works include *Les Sylphides* (1907) and *Petrouchka* (1911). He died in New York City. » Ballets Russes; choreography

Fokker, Anthony Herman Gerard (1890–1939) Dutch aircraft engineer, born at Kediri, Java. He built his first plane in 1911, and in 1913 founded the Fokker aircraft factory at Schwerin, Germany, which made warplanes for the German air force in World War 1. After the war he set up a factory in the Netherlands and later operated also in Britain and the USA, where he became a US citizen. He died in New York City. » aircraft [i]

fold In geology, a bend or flexure in a stratified rock resulting from compressional or gravitational forces. It may exist on many different scales from centimetres to many kilometres. Upward folds are termed *antiforms*; downward folds are *synforms*. » anticline; syncline

folic acid A B-vitamin found in liver and most green vegetables, required for the synthesis and functioning of red cells. A deficiency, which is rare in developed countries, leads to anaemia. Folic acid is often given in association with iron for the routine prevention of anaemia, as in pregnancy. » anaemia; pregnancy [i]

Folies-Bergère [**fo**lee bair**zhair**] A music hall in Paris, opened in 1869. By the end of the 19th-c its stage was dominated by circus acts and semi-nude female performers. It remains famous for its lavish displays. » music hall

folium of Descartes One of the simplest curves (and one of the first to be found) with a node, ie a point at which the curve crosses itself. It is represented by the Cartesian equation $x^3+y^3=3axy$.

folk music Music which is transmitted orally, usually with modifications from generation to generation and from place to place, so that its original form and composer are forgotten. Much folk music exhibits melodic inflections, rhythmic characteristics, or performing styles which link it to a particular country or locality, but it is not unknown for folktunes to cross boundaries, and even seas. Sound recording has greatly facilitated the collecting and transcribing of folk music in the 20th-c. » ethnomusicology; flamenco; gospel music; monody

folklore The traditional songs, tales, legends, superstitions and proverbs of a people. The term was suggested in 1846 by William John Thoms (1803–85), founder of the folklore journal *Notes and Queries*. Nowadays it also embraces material culture (utensils, arts and crafts) and social culture (festivals, dances and rituals). A scientific study of folklore was first undertaken by Jacob Grimm. » Grimm; legend; mythology

follicle stimulating hormone (FSH) A chemical substance (a glycoprotein gonadotrophin) secreted by the front lobe of the pituitary gland in vertebrates. It has an important role in reproduction: in mammals it stimulates the early maturation of ovarian follicles (in females) and the production of sperm (in males). » gonadotrophin; Graafian follicle; luteinizing hormone; pituitary gland; releasing hormone;

Folsom A prehistoric 'kill site' in New Mexico, USA, excavated in 1926: 19 fluted spear points of 9000–8000 BC, found with the skeletons of 23 extinct long-horned bison (*Bison antiquus*), established for the first time the co-existence of humans with Ice Age mammals in the New World and the antiquity of the native American population. Still earlier occupation, c.20 000–5 000 BC, is now attested. » Clovis; Ice Age

Fomalhaut [**fo**malhoht] A bright S hemisphere star. Distance: 7 parsecs.

Fonda, Henry (Jaynes) (1905–82) US actor, born at Grand Island, Nebraska, and educated at the University of Minnesota. After some success on the Broadway stage, he went to Hollywood in 1935. His performances in the *Young Mr Lincoln* (1939), *The Grapes of Wrath* (1940), and *The Ox-bow Incident* (1943) established him in the role of the American folk hero, the common man of integrity, and he played many such parts over the next 30 years. His last major appearance was in *On Golden Pond* (1981), for which he was awarded an Oscar, and he died not long after in Los Angeles.

Fonda, Jane (1937–) US actress, daughter of Henry Fonda, born in New York City. After appearances on Broadway and in films in the early 1960s, she married director Roger Vadim (1965–73), with whom she made *La Ronde* (1964) and *Barbarella* (1968). Later roles widened her dramatic scope: *Klute* (1971), for which she won her first Oscar, *The China Syndrome* (1978), *On Golden Pond* (1981), and *The Morning After* (1986). She is politically active in anti-nuclear and feminist peace movements, often reflected in her films, and in the 1980s she became involved with womens' health and fitness activities. » Fonda, Henry; Vadim

Fontainebleau [**fõ**tenbloh] A magnificent 16th-c chateau built by Italian craftsmen for Francis I on the site of an earlier royal chateau-fortress at Fontainebleau in France; a world heritage site. It was used by Napoleon as his imperial palace. » chateau; Francis I (of France); Napoleon I

Fontainebleau School [**fõ**tenbloh] A group of artists including Italian Mannerists such as Giovanni Battista Rosso (1495–1540), Niccolo dell' Abbate (c.1512–71) and Francisco Primaticcio (1504–c.70), working for Francis I of France c.1530–60. The main centre was at the royal palace of Fontainebleau. » Francis I (of France); French art; Mannerism; Renaissance art; school (art)

Fontana, Domenico (1543–1607) Swiss architect, born at Melide, near Lugano. He was papal architect in Rome, employed on the Lateran Palace, the Vatican Library, and St Peter's Dome. He was afterwards royal architect in Naples, where he died.

Fontenay Abbey A Cistercian abbey, founded in 1119 by Bernard of Clairvaux at Fontenay in NE France; a world heritage monument. It was abandoned by the order in the 18th-c, but the abbey remains were restored after 1906. » Clairvaux

Fonteyn, Margot, stage name of **Dame Margot Fonteyn de Arias,** *née* **Margaret Hookham** (1919–91) British ballerina, born at Reigate, Surrey. She joined the Sadler's Wells Ballet (later the Royal Ballet) in 1934, where she made her first solo appearance in *The Haunted Ballroom*, and became one of the greatest ballerinas of the 20th-c, in classic roles and in creating new roles for Ashton. A new partnership with Nureyev in the 1960s extended her performing career. She married Roberto Emilio Arias (1918–), then Panamanian Ambassador to the Court of St James, in 1955, and was created a Dame in 1956. » Ashton, Frederick; ballet; Nureyev; Royal Ballet

Foochow » **Fuzhou**

food Any plant or animal material which is primarily eaten for nutritional purposes. Anything eaten specifically for its therapeutic purposes, real or otherwise, is strictly speaking not a food, even though it may have some nutritive properties. Thus vitamin C supplements, taken to prevent a cold, are being used pharmacologically and not nutritionally. » additives; food fortification / labelling / poisoning / preservation; nutrition; vitamins [i]

food chain The sequence of organisms on successive feeding (*trophic*) levels within an ecological community, through which energy is transferred by feeding. Energy enters the food chain mainly during photosynthesis by green plants (*primary producers*), and passes to the herbivores (*primary consumers*) when they eat plants, and then to the carnivores (*secondary and tertiary consumers*) when they prey on herbivores. Food chains are interconnected, forming a complex food web. » carnivore [i]; ecology; herbivore; photosynthesis

food fortification Food to which a nutrient has been added. Many breakfast cereals are fortified with iron by the choice of the manufacturer. Margarine manufacturers are obliged to add vitamins A and D to their product. Food fortification is used by governments to ensure that the intakes of certain nutrients are increased. Thus 'iodized' salt ensures that goitre, an iodine deficiency, is rare. » food; goitre; vitamins [i]

food labelling The provision of identifying labels on food, which must not only declare the product and manufacturer but also provide data on the product weight, the additives which have been incorporated, and nowadays a brief outline of key nutritional data. Food labelling is suitable only for packaged foods, and is not applicable to fresh food such as meat, fish, fruit, and vegetables. » additives; nutrition

food poisoning An illness that arises from eating contaminated food or liquid. Most cases result from food contaminated with different species of *Salmonella*. The illness is then acute, and associated with vomiting and diarrhoea. Other organisms may be responsible. Sometimes, even when adequately heated food is eaten, pre-formed toxins produce a similar illness. The exotoxin of *Staphylococcus aureus* is well-known in this respect, as is the rare and potentially lethal botulism, in which the toxin is secreted by *Clostridium* bacteria. Non-bacterial food poisoning may be due to eating poisonous mushrooms and shellfish. » botulism; salmonella; toxin

food preservation The treatment of food to maintain its quality and prevent deterioration. Food tends to become available during specific seasons, leading to a glut at harvest. How to preserve perishable food to make it available over a longer period has been an essential component of the technological conquest of nature. Drying removes the water necessary for the growth of spoilage organisms, while bacterial growth can be prevented by acidifying (pickling), salting, heating, canning, freezing, and now by irradiation. » canning; cold storage; deep-freezing; food; freeze drying; lyophilization; nitrates/nitrites; sorbic acid; vinegar

fool's gold » pyrite

foot The terminal part of the lower limb which makes contact with the ground or other substrate; an instrument of support when standing, and of propulsion and restraint when walking or running. It consists of a number of bony elements (the *tarsal*, *metatarsal*, and *phalangeal* bones), whose size, number, and arrangement differs between species, bound together by ligaments, and supported by tendons and muscles. The tarsal bones articulate with the metatarsals, which in turn articulate with the phalanges. In humans there are seven tarsal bones, five metatarsals, two phalanges in the big toe, and three in the other toes. Many animals use only the toes to make contact with the environment, unlike humans and primates, who use the whole foot. The structural arrangement of the foot (in terms of the bones, muscles, and nerves) is similar to that of the hand. Consequently individuals who have no hands or upper limbs (as in thalidomide defects) can develop the use of the feet to such an extent that they can use them to paint, write, and drive. » bunion; chilblains; chiropody; club foot; flat foot; hand; mycetoma; nails; thalidomide; Plate XIII

Foot, Michael (Mackintosh) (1913–) British Labour politician, born at Plymouth, Devon. Educated at Oxford, he joined the staff of the *Tribune* in 1937, becoming editor (1948–52, 1955–60). He was also acting editor of the *Evening Standard* (1942–4) and a political columnist on the *Daily Herald* (1944–64). He became an MP in 1945, and was Secretary of State for Employment (1974–6), Deputy Leader (1976–80) then Leader (1980–3) of the Labour Party, resigning after his Party's heavy defeat in the general election. A pacifist, he has long been a supporter of the Campaign for Nuclear Disarmament. A prolific writer, his best-known work is his biography of Aneurin Bevan. » Bevan, Aneurin; CND; Labour Party

foot-and-mouth disease A contagious feverish disease of artiodactyls characterized by blistering inside the mouth and in the cleft of the hooves; also known as **hoof-and-mouth disease**. It can be caught by humans. In domestic stock, diagnosis would lead to the immediate destruction of the affected herd. » artiodactyl

football A field team game using an inflated ball, which has developed several different forms.

1 Association football (also known as **soccer**) An 11-a-side team game played on a grass or synthetic pitch measuring 90–120 m/100–130 yd in length, and 45–90 m/50–100 yd wide. At each end of the pitch is a goal net measuring 8 yd (7.3 m) wide by 8 ft (2.4 m) high. The object is to move the ball around the field, with the feet or head, until a player is in a position to put the ball into the net and score a goal. The goalkeeper defends the goal, and he is the only person allowed to touch the ball with his hands while it is in play, provided he touches it within his specifically defined area. The ancient Greeks, Chinese, Egyptians and Romans all played a form of football. In the early 19th-c it became an organized game in Britain, and was played in most universities and public schools. Standard rules were drawn up at Cambridge University in 1848, and in 1863 the Football Association was formed. The first FA Cup final was played in 1872. Professionalism increased amongst northern clubs, and the game was legalized in 1885. The Football League was formed in 1888. The world governing body, the Fédération Internationale de Football Association (FIFA), was formed in Paris in 1904. The first World Cup was organized in Uruguay in 1930. The European governing body, the Union of European Football Associations (UEFA), was formed in 1954, and they control the major European club competitions. *See illustration p 456*

2 American football The national winter sport in the USA, played between October and January. It resembles rugby, but forward passing of the ball is permitted. It is played on a rectangular field 300 ft (91m) by 160 ft (49 m), divided into 5 yd (4.6 m) segments which give the pitch a gridiron effect. The object is to score touchdowns, similar to tries in rugby, but progress has to be made upfield by a series of 'plays', and a team must make 10 yds (9.1 m) of ground within four plays, otherwise they lose possession of the ball. Six points are awarded for a touchdown and one point for a 'point after', for kicking the ball between the posts and over the crossbar – the equivalent of a conversion in rugby. A goal kicked from anywhere on the field (a 'field goal') is worth three points. Teams consist of more than 40 squad members, but only 11 are allowed on to the field at any one time. Special units come on for specific roles. When a team is attacking, the 11 players will be different to those on the field when they are on the defence. The game was first played in US colleges in the mid-19th-c, and the first rules were drawn up at Princeton College in 1867. The professional game in the USA comes under the auspices of the National Football League, which is divided into two 'leagues': the American Football Conference (AFC) and National Football Conference (NFC). The winners of the two conferences play-off each January for the Superbowl tournament (instituted 1966–7). *See illustration p 456*

3 Australian Rules football A handling and kicking game which is a cross between association football and rugby. Surprisingly, it has few rules. It is played with 18 players per side on an oval pitch measuring c.165 m/180 yd long by c.137 m/150 yd wide. The object is to score goals by kicking the ball between the opponent's goal posts for 6 points. Smaller posts are positioned either side of the main goal, and if the ball is kicked through that area then 1 point is scored. The first recorded game was played between Scotch College and Melbourne Grammar School in 1858. *See illustration p 456*

4 Gaelic football A mixture of rugby, soccer, and Australian Rules football. The first game resembling Gaelic football took place at Slane, Ireland, in 1712, between Meath and Louth. Originally played with 21 players per side, it was reduced to 15 in 1913. It is played on a rectangular pitch 84–100 yd

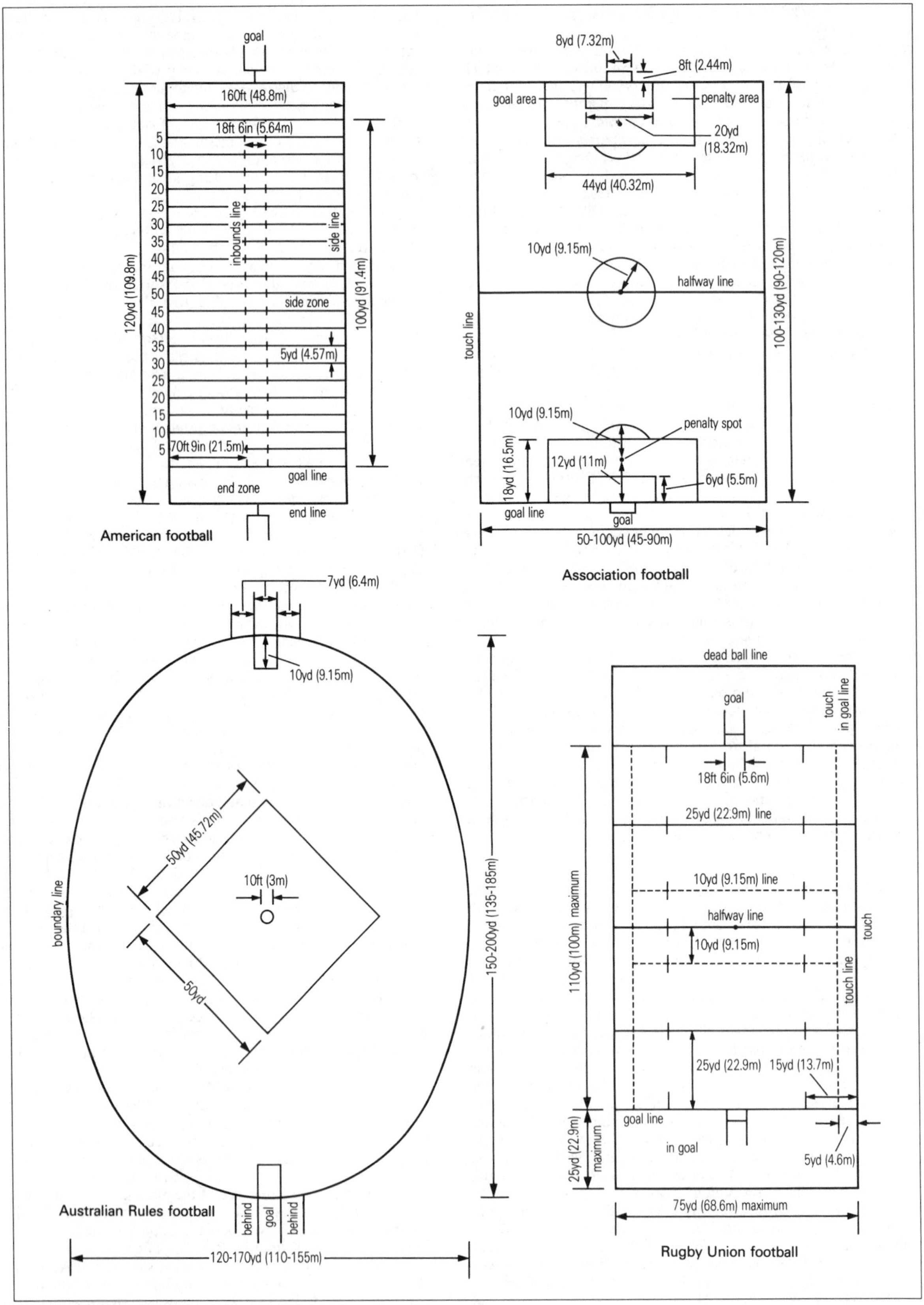

Football fields – Dimensions

(77–91 m) wide and 140–160 yd (128–146 m) long. At each end is a goal which resembles a set of rugby posts with a soccer-style net attached. The object is to score points by either putting the ball into the goal net, worth 3 points, or over the crossbar and between the uprights, worth 1 point. » FIFA; Football League; UEFA; rugby football; RR103

football hooliganism Hooliganism at football matches, regarded as a recent social problem, but found since the turn of the century. The Scottish Cup was withheld in 1909 after the fans of Glasgow Celtic and Rangers were engaged in a battle which resulted in pay boxes being burned down. A new wave of hooliganism started in the 1960s, and became particularly severe in the mid-1980s, when English 'fans' were involved in several serious incidents at European games, notably, the 1985 riots at the Heysel stadium in Brussels, in which 39 people were killed. After that event, English clubs were banned from playing matches in Europe. Modern hooligans work in organized gangs, and often do not attend 'home' matches but only those involving their club when playing away from home, in an effort to cause aggravation in other towns or countries. More sophisticated methods of policing and crowd control are the main measures being used to combat the problem. » football 1 [i]

Football League The oldest association football league in the world, formed after a formal meeting at the Royal Hotel, Manchester on 17 April 1888. Twelve clubs became founder members, and Scotsman William McGregor (1847–1911), a Birmingham shop owner, was its first president. » football 1 [i]

Football War (1969) A lightning war fought over several days in July 1969 between Honduras and El Salvador, rapidly halted by international pressure. It was so named because recriminations between the two C American states had come to a head during the qualifying matches for the 1970 World Cup. » El Salvador [i]; Honduras [i]

foraminiferan [forami**nif**uhran] An amoeba-like protozoan that secretes an external shell (*test*), typically calcareous and chambered; feeds and moves by means of protoplasmic processes (*pseudopodia*) extruded through shell openings; largely marine; remains can form a sediment on the sea bed known as *foraminiferal ooze*; includes many fossils. (Order: *Foraminifera*.) » amoeba; calcium; protoplasm; Protozoa; shell

Forbidden City The Imperial Palace in Beijing (Peking), the residence of the imperial rulers of China from its construction by 200 000 workmen in 1420 until the fall of the Qing dynasty in 1911. The walled and moated palace complex covers 74 ha/183 acres, and is the best preserved example of mediaeval Chinese architecture. » Beijing; Qing dynasty

force An influence applied to an unrestrained object which results in a change in its motion, causing it to accelerate in some way; symbol F, units N (newton); a vector quantity. Force equals mass of object multiplied by acceleration (Newton's second law). » acceleration; buoyancy; forces of nature [i]; mechanics; Newton's laws; pressure; torque [i]; torsion; vector (mathematics); weight; work

forces of nature In physics, taken to mean gravitation, electromagnetism, strong nuclear force, and weak nuclear forces. Their properties are summarized in the panel. » electromagnetism; fifth force; grand unified theories; gravitation; physics; strong interaction; weak interaction

FORCES OF NATURE

	GRAVITY	ELECTRO-MAGNETISM	WEAK NUCLEAR FORCE	STRONG NUCLEAR FORCE
Range m	infinite	infinite	10^{-18} (sub-atomic)	10^{-15} (sub-atomic)
Relative strength	6×10^{-39}	1/137	10^{-5}	1
Examples of application	orbit of Earth around Sun	force between electrical charges	radio-active β-decay	binds atomic nucleus together

Ford, Ford Madox, originally **Ford Hermann Hueffer** (1873–1939) British writer, born at Merton, Surrey. He collaborated with Conrad in *The Inheritors* (1901) and *Romance* (1903), wrote *The Good Soldier* (1915) and several other works, and founded the *English Review* (1908). After World War 1, he changed his name to Ford, and exiled himself to France and the USA, where he edited *The Transatlantic Review* (1924), wrote poetry, a series of war novels, and the tetralogy *Parade's End* (1920s). He died at Deauville, France. » English literature

Ford, Gerald R(udolph) (1913–) US statesman and 38th President (1974–6), born at Omaha, Nebraska. Educated at the University of Michigan and Yale, he served in the US Navy during World War 2. He became a Republican member of the House of Representatives (1949–73), and on the resignation of Spiro Agnew in 1973 was appointed Vice-President. He became President in 1974 when Nixon resigned because of the Watergate scandal. The full pardon he granted to Nixon the same year made him unpopular, and he was defeated in the 1976 presidential election by Jimmy Carter. » Nixon, Richard M; Watergate

Ford, Henry (1863–1947) US automobile engineer and manufacturer, born at Dearborn, Michigan. He produced his first petrol-driven motor car in 1893, and in 1899 founded a company in Detroit, designing his own cars. In 1903 he started the Ford Motor Company, pioneering the modern 'assembly line' mass-production techniques for his famous T-model (1908–9), 15 million of which were produced up to 1928. He also branched out into aircraft and tractor manufacture. In 1919 he was succeeded by his son **Edsel** (1893–1943), and in 1945 by his grandson **Henry** (1917–87). He died at Dearborn, Michigan. » car [i]

Ford, John (c.1586–c.1640) English dramatist, born at Ilsington, Devon. He studied for a while at Oxford and entered the Middle Temple in 1602. He often collaborated with Dekker, Rowley, and Webster. His own plays were much influenced by Richard Burton's *Anatomy of Melancholy* (1621), which led him into the stage presentation of the melancholic, the unnatural, and the horrible in such works as *The Lover's Melancholy* (1629) and *'Tis Pity She's a Whore* (1633). » Burton, Richard; Chatterton, Thomas; Dekker; drama; English literature; Webster, John

Ford, John, originally **Sean Aloysius O'Fearna** (1895–1973) US film director, born at Cape Elizabeth, Maine. He went to Hollywood in 1913, where he worked as stunt man, actor, and assistant director. His skilful portrayal of US pioneering history reached a peak with *Stagecoach* (1935), *The Grapes of Wrath* (1940). After World War 2 his films included *My Darling Clementine* (1946), and *The Quiet Man* (1952), which gained him his fourth Oscar. He died at Palm Springs, California.

Ford Foundation A philanthropic foundation set up in 1936 by Henry Ford and his son, Edsel, as an international charity mainly concerned with food shortages and population control in developing nations. It has also been involved in the arts and humanities, and in public television in the USA. » Ford, Henry; foundation, philanthropic

foreign aid The help given by one nation to another, usually poorer, by means of grants, gifts, special trading deals, cheap loans or credit terms, expertise, or goods. It may be bilateral, or multilateral. » multilateralism

foreign exchange The amount of currency of foreign origin held in a country. It is derived from exporting and from overseas investment. » reserves

Foreign Legion The elite formation of the French Army, recruited from non-French nationals. 'La Légion Étrangère' was first raised in 1831, and has seen action almost wherever French arms have been engaged. Always the subject of romance and adventure, the legion retains its reputation for toughness. » army

forensic medicine The discipline which relates the practice of medicine to the law. The provision of medicines, the supply of drugs of addiction and of human tissues for surgical transplantation, the control of experiments on living animals, the mental health acts, and abortion are all authorized in the UK by Acts of Parliament. Forensic medicine concerns itself with the interpretation of these laws, and with their application by individual doctors. In addition, **forensic pathology** includes the study of wounds self-inflicted or caused by others, and with death in which other factors than natural causes might have played a part. It involves the identification of individuals (such as following a mass disaster), the detection of death from poisoning, and analysing sequences of DNA in body cells in possible criminal cases. » DNA [i]; medicine

forensic psychiatry A branch of psychiatry concerned with legal matters, including the soundness of mind of an accused, laws concerning guardianship, the mental health of prisoners, and the protection of society from the criminally insane. » forensic science; psychiatry

foreshortening In art, the representation of forms, especially the human figure, in perspective; for example, a hand stretched out towards the beholder will appear large in proportion to the arm, which will appear short, or even barely visible. It was a common device in Mannerist and Baroque painting, and the principle behind the famous World War 1 poster 'Your Country Needs You'. » Baroque (art and architecture); Mannerism; perspective

forest buffalo » **African buffalo**

forest falcon » **falcon**

Forester, C(ecil) S(cott) (1899–1966) British writer, born in Cairo, Egypt. Chiefly a novelist, he also wrote biographical and travel books. He is known especially for his creation of Captain Horatio Hornblower. He won the James Tait Black Memorial Prize for Literature in 1938 with *Ship of the Line*, and several of his works have been filmed, notably *The African Queen* (1935). He died at Fullerton, California. » English literature; novel

forestry The business of growing, harvesting, and marketing trees and of managing the associated wildlife and recreational resources. Over 31% of the world's land area is covered by forest and woodland. The former USSR had the largest area (943 million ha/2 330 million acres), followed by Brazil (560 million ha/1 384 million acres), Canada (352 million ha/870 million acres), and the USA (265 million ha/655 million acres). The UK has about 2 million ha/5 million acres of forest and woodland. Total world production of forest products reached 4.6 billion cubic m/6 billion cubic yd in 1984. » tree [i]

forgery The act of falsely making, reproducing, altering, or signing a document with the intention of defrauding others. It is essential to the criminal offence of forgery that the false document is to be used as if it were genuine, as in the cases of wills and bank-notes. » counterfeiting; criminal law

forget-me-not An annual or perennial, native to temperate regions; inflorescence coiled, straightening as it elongates; flowers tubular with five spreading lobes, often pink in bud, opening blue, sometimes with a yellow or white eye as a honey guide, or wholly these colours. (Genus: *Myosotis*, 50 species. Family: *Boraginaceae*.) » annual; inflorescence [i]; perennial

forging The shaping of metal from a single piece by hammering into a desired shape or into intimate contact with a shaped die. In **drop forging**, the hammer or die is dropped onto the heated metal to be shaped. In **impact forging**, two dies forcibly approach each other from opposite sides of the metal to be forged. In **roll forging**, a strip is run between cylindrical dies with countersunk depressions. » metal

formaldehyde [fawmalduhhiyd] HCHO, IUPAC **methanal**, boiling point −21°C. The simplest aldehyde, a gas with a characteristic odour, which polymerizes readily and reversibly to *paraformaldehyde* $(CH_2O)_n$. An aqueous solution, called *formalin*, is used as a disinfectant and preservative. Manufactured by the incomplete oxidation of methanol, it is an ingredient in plastic manufacture of the phenol–formaldehyde type. » aldehyde; IUPAC; methanol

Formalists A school of critics in early 20th-c Russia who believed that formal properties were of primary importance in a work of art. Viktor Shklovsky (1893–) and Evgeny Zamyatin (1884–1939) were original members; Roman Jakobson (1896–1982) later exported their ideas, which had considerable influence on the New Criticism. » Jakobson; literary criticism; New Criticism

Forman, Miloš (1932–) Czech-US film director, born at Caslav, Czechoslovakia. Two feature films, *Lásky jedné plavovlásky* (1965, A Blonde in Love) and *Hoří, má panenko!* (1967, The Firemen's Ball), made in Prague, brought him international recognition. Being abroad at the time of the 1968 Russian repression, he went to the USA, where he became a US citizen. His tragi-comedy of insanity, *One Flew Over the Cuckoo's Nest* (1975), won five Oscar awards, including Best Director, and was successfully followed by his interpretations of stage presentations, *Hair* (1979), *Ragtime* (1980), and *Amadeus* (1983), which won him another Oscar.

formants The dominant acoustic components which determine the sound quality of particular vowels. They are formed by the air flowing through the vocal tract, and vibrating at different bands of frequencies as it responds to changes in the tract's shape. » phonetics; vowel

Formentera [formentayra] 38°43N 1°26E; pop(1981) 3 500; area 100 sq km/39 sq ml. Island in the Balearic Is, Spain, S of Ibiza; capital, San Francisco; largely formed by two high pine-clad capes (La Mola and Berberia) with a C depression edged by white-sand beaches; tourism; patronal festival (Jul). » Balearic Islands

formic acid HCOOH, IUPAC **methanoic acid**, boiling point 101°C. A liquid with a pungent odour, the simplest carboxylic acid. It is a moderately strong acid; partially neutralized solutions have a pH of about 4. Formic acid is secreted by some insects, especially red ants, in the sting. It is used in textile and leather manufacture, and as an industrial solvent. » carboxylic acids; IUPAC; pH

formication A sensation of small insects crawling on or under the skin. It is often seen in drug-induced states, after overdoses, and during withdrawal of (for example) cocaine or alcohol.

Fornax (Lat 'furnace') A faint S constellation. » constellation; RR8

Forrest, Edwin (1806–72) US actor, born and died in Philadelphia, where he made his debut in 1820. He had successful seasons in London (1836–7), but in 1845 his Macbeth was hissed by the audience; and a resentment which prompted him to hiss Macready in Edinburgh destroyed his reputation in Britain. The hissing of Macready's Macbeth by Forrest's sympathizers in New York in 1849 led to a riot which cost 22 lives. » Macready; theatre

Forster, E(dward) M(organ) (1879–1970) British novelist, born in London, and educated at Tonbridge School and Cambridge. His works include *Where Angels Fear to Tread* (1905), *The Longest Journey* (1907), *A Room with a View* (1908), *Howards End* (1910), and his masterpiece, *A Passage to India* (1924). He also wrote several volumes of essays and short stories. In 1951 he collaborated with E Crozier in the libretto of Britten's opera, *Billy Budd*. His novel *Maurice* (written 1913–14), on the theme of homosexuality, was published in 1971 after his death, at Coventry, Warwickshire. » English literature; novel

Forsyth, Bill (1948–) British film-maker, born in Scotland. He entered the film industry in 1963, making his own documentaries, and was one of the original intake at the National Film School in 1971. *That Sinking Feeling* – a comedy using actors from the Glasgow Youth Theatre – was warmly received at the 1979 Edinburgh Festival. He has since made two very successful comedies, *Gregory's Girl* (1981) and *Local Hero* (1983), as well as productions for television. He moved to Hollywood in the mid-1980s, directing *Housekeeping* (1987).

forsythia A deciduous shrub, suckering and rooting from the tips of arching branches, native to SE Europe and E Asia; leaves oval, toothed, opposite; flowers yellow, with four spreading petals, in clusters appearing before leaves on last season's wood. It is named after Scottish gardener William Forsyth (1737–1804). The commonly planted ornamental is hybrid *Forsythia × intermedia*. (Genus: *Forsythia*, 7 species. Family: *Oleaceae*.) » deciduous plants; shrub

Fort-de-France [fawduhfrãs], formerly **Fort Royal** 14°36N 61°05W, pop (1982) 99 844. Capital town of Martinique, Lesser Antilles, E Caribbean; airport; naval base; chief commercial and shipping centre, tourism; cathedral (1895). » Martinique

Fort Knox A US army post established in Kentucky in 1917, and noted as the site, since 1937, of the US Bullion Depository.

Fort William 56°49N 5°07W, pop (1981) 11 061. Capital of Lochaber district, Highland region, W Scotland; on E side of Loch Linnhe; airfield; railway; aluminium, distilling; Inverlochy castle; Neptune's Staircase (N), eight locks (1805–22) raising the Caledonian Canal by 19.5 m/64 ft; Ben Nevis (ESE). » Ben Nevis; Caledonian Canal; Highland; Scotland [i]

Fort Worth 32°45N 97°18W, pop (1980) 385 164. Seat of Tarrant County, NE Texas, USA, on the Trinity R; established as an army post, 1847; cattle town, and still an important livestock market centre; airport at Dallas–Fort Worth; airfield; railway; university (1873); aircraft and aerospace industries, oil refining, pharmaceuticals, textiles, leather goods; Fort Worth Art Center, Amon Carter Museum of Western Art, Greer Island Nature Center; Southwestern Exposition (Jan). » Texas

Fortaleza [fawta**lay**za] 3°45S 38°35W, pop (1980) 647 917. Port capital of Ceará state, NE Brazil, on the Atlantic coast; airfield; railway; commercial and industrial centre, especially for agriculture; centre for coastal and overseas trade; two universities (1955, 1973); new tourist centre in old waterfront prison; cathedral; local festival with raft (*jangada*) races (Jul). » Brazil [i]

FORTH A compact computer programming language originally written for astronomers in the USA, which has advantages for use in control applications using small computer systems. The name is derived from *fourth*, as in 'fourth generation language'. » computer generations; programming language

Forth, River River in SEC Scotland; formed at Aberfoyle, W Central region, by the confluence of headstreams rising on Ben Lomond; flows generally E, widening into the Firth of Forth estuary (82 km/51 ml from Alloa to the North Sea, width 2.5 km/1½ ml–28 km/17 ml); crossed by road bridge at Kincardine, and by Forth road and rail bridges at Queensferry; length 186 km/116 ml; connected to the Clyde via the Forth and Clyde Canal. » Scotland [i]

FORTRAN An acronym of **FORmula TRANslation**, a widely used high-level computer programming language developed in the USA during the 1960s for mathematical, engineering, and scientific use. » programming language

Fortress America A view held by many US people before World War 2 and during the cold war that the USA should stay out of international politics outside the Western hemisphere. This isolationism from international developments, especially those in Europe, was held to be sustainable because of the relative physical isolation of the American continents. There was, however, support for a high level of armaments to deter attacks on mainland America, hence the 'fortress' label. » isolationism

Fortuna [faw**too**na] The ancient Roman goddess of Fortune, introduced by King Servius Tullius (578–534 BC). In the Middle Ages she was highly revered as a divine and moral figure, redressing human pride. Her wheel is frequently referred to and depicted, as at St Etienne in Beauvais, where figures can be seen climbing and falling off.

Forty-five Rebellion The Jacobite rebellion of 1745–6 to restore the Catholic Stuart kings to the British throne and displace the Hanoverians. It began in July 1745 when Charles Edward Stuart (the 'Young Pretender') arrived in Scotland and proclaimed his father King James III. Support came mainly from the Scottish Highland Clans, and there were some early successes. The Jacobite forces reached as far south as Derby, but the rebellion lost support, and was crushingly defeated at Culloden in 1746. » Culloden Moor, Battle of; Jacobites; Stuart, Charles Edward

forty-niners Adventurers who swarmed to California in 1849, after the discovery of gold there the previous year. Their number may have been as high as 100 000. » gold rush

forum The Roman equivalent of the Greek *agora*; originally the market-place of a town, later its civic centre. Besides shops and stalls, it contained the principal municipal buildings, such as the Council chamber and law courts. » curia

Foscolo, Ugo (1778–1827) Italian author, born at Zante. Educated at Spalato and Venice, his disappointment when Napoleon ceded Venice to Austria found vent in the *Ultime lettere di Jacopo Ortis* (1802, Last Letters of Jacopo Ortis). After a period in the French army, he returned to Milan, and published his best poem, *Dei Sepolcri* (1807, Of the Sepulchres). After 1814 he sought refuge in London, where he supported himself by teaching and writing. His last years embittered by poverty and neglect, he died in London. » Italian literature

Foss, Lukas, originally **Fuchs** (1922–) US composer, born in Berlin. He studied in Berlin and Paris, and moved to the USA in 1937. He first attracted attention with his cantata, *The Prairie* (1941), and has since written two symphonies, concertos, chamber music, and operas. He was appointed professor of music at the University of California in 1953, and in 1981 became director of the Milwaukee Symphony Orchestra.

fossa A carnivore, native to Madagascar; superficially cat-like with short, thick reddish-brown (occasionally black) coat; long thin tail; inhabits woodland; an efficient predator; eats lemurs, smaller vertebrates, and insects. (*Cryptoprocta ferox*. Family: *Viverridae*.) » carnivore [i]; Felidae; Viverridae [i]

Fosse Way » **Roman roads** [i]

fossil The remains of a once-living organism, usually restricted to organisms that lived prior to the last Ice Age. Fossils typically comprise the bodies or part of the organisms themselves, but also include a variety of trace fossils such as burrows, tracks, impressions, and faeces. Fossils are usually mineralized and found in sedimentary rocks. » Ice Age; palaeontology; sedimentary rock

fossil fuel Fuels derived from the fossilized remains of plants and animals, such as peat, coal, and crude oil. » coal; fuel; oil (earth sciences); peat

Foster, Stephen (Collins) (1826–64) US songwriter, born in Pittsburgh. His first songs, such as 'Open the Lattice, Love' (1844), were conventional concert songs of the day. When he began writing 'minstrel songs' influenced by itinerant Black singers, his melodies and rhythms brightened. Songs such as 'Oh! Susanna' (1848), 'Old Folks at Home' (1851), and 'Beautiful Dreamer' (1864) sold thousands of song-sheets, and became seminal works of the American songwriting tradition.

foster care A form of child care in which children who have been separated (by death, custodial, or other reasons) from their biological parents live with a 'foster family' for varying lengths of time, often many years. Foster parents usually receive some state aid to help support the children. The system was developed in the UK during the late 1940s when many children had become orphaned through World War 2. Fostering is a form of 'social parenting', as is adoption. » adoption; family

Foucault, Jean Bernard Léon [**foo**koh] (1819–68) French physicist, born and died in Paris. He began by studying medicine, but turned to physics. He determined the velocity of light, and showed that light travels more slowly in water than in air (1850), invented the gyroscope (1852), and improved the mirrors of reflecting telescopes (1858). » Foucault pendulum; gyroscope; light

Foucault, Michel [**foo**koh] (1926–84) French philosopher, born at Poitiers. At Paris he studied philosophy, psychology, and psychopathology, then taught at Uppsala, Clermont-Ferrand, and Paris, becoming professor of the history of systems of thought at the Collège de France (1970). He sought consistently to test cultural assumptions in given historical contexts. His most important writings include *Histoire de la Folie* (1961, Madness and Civilization), *Les Mots et les Choses* (1966, The Order of Things), and the unfinished *Histoire de la Sexualité* (1976–84, The History of Sexuality). He died in Paris.

Foucault pendulum A pendulum that is free to swing in any direction, such that the plane of swing gradually rotates as the Earth turns under it; devised by French physicist Jean Foucault in 1851. At the North and South Poles, the pendulum would complete one cycle every 24 hours, but would take longer at other latitudes, with no rotation at the Equator – a consequence of the Coriolis force. The pendulum was used by Foucault as proof that the Earth spins. » Coriolis force [i]; Foucault, Jean Bernard Léon

Fouché, Joseph, Duc d'Otrante ('Duke of Otranto') [**foo**shay] (1763–1829) French statesman, born at Nantes. He was elected to the National Convention in 1792 as a Jacobin, and in 1799 became Minister of Police, a post which he held successfully until 1815. A consummate intriguer, he was banished after the Bourbon restoration, and died in exile at Trieste. » French Revolution [i]; Jacobins (French history)

foul marten » **polecat**

foumart [**foo**maht] » **polecat**

foundation, philanthropic An organization for distributing private wealth for public benefit. Such endowments have existed since ancient times, and typically supported schools, hospitals, or almshouses. Since the 19th-c huge foundations have been endowed by successful businessmen or corporations: Carnegie's bequests founded a number of such organizations. The Ford Foundation, established in 1936, is the biggest philanthropic trust; others include the Rockefeller Foundation (1913), and the John A Hartford Foundation (1942). Money from these bodies funds education, international activities, health, the arts, social welfare, and religious groups. » Carnegie, Andrew; Ford Foundation; Smithsonian Institution

foundationalism A strategy in epistemology which in its purest form classifies all justified beliefs as foundational – about which the believer cannot be mistaken – or as derived from foundational beliefs by indubitable inferences. Foundationalists can be empiricists (Hume) or rationalists (Descartes); some, despairing of success, have been led to scepticism. » Descartes; empiricism; epistemology; Hume, David; rationalism; scepticism

founding Casting molten metal in a mould made to a high degree of precision. Mould materials are compounded of sand and clay, packed over a pattern to which the eventual casting is to conform. Pattern making is consequently a highly skilled craft, but much founding is now automatized. » casting; metal

Fountains Abbey A Cistercian monastery founded in 1132 near Ripon in Yorkshire, UK; a world heritage site. The ground plan of what was once the wealthiest Cistercian house in England can be clearly discerned today. The abbey ruins stand in the magnificent water gardens of Studley Royal, which were laid out in the early 18th-c. » abbey; Cistercians; monasticism

Fouqué, Friedrich Heinrich Karl, Baron de la Motte [**foo**kay] (1777–1843) German Romantic author, born at Brandenburg. He served as a Prussian cavalry officer, devoting himself between campaigns to literary pursuits. He published a long series of romances based on Norse Legend and old French poetry, his masterpiece being *Undine* (1811). He died in Berlin. » German literature; Romanticism (literature)

Fouquet, Jean [**foo**kay] (c.1420–c.1480) French painter, born and died at Tours. He opened a prosperous workshop at Tours, and in 1475 received the official title of king's painter. His most notable illuminations are found in the *Antiquities of the Jews* of Josephus and the *Hours of Etienne Chevalier* at Chantilly. » French art

Fouquet, Nicolas [**foo**kay] (1615–80) French statesman, born in Paris. Mazarin made him *Procureur-Général* to the parliament of Paris (1650) and Superintendent of Finance (1653). He became extremely rich, and was ambitious to succeed Mazarin, but Louis XIV himself took up the reins of power on Mazarin's death, and Fouquet was arrested for embezzlement (1661). He was sentenced to life imprisonment in the fortress of Pignerol, where he died. » Louis XIV; Mazarin

four-colour process Techniques for the replications of all the colours in the spectrum by printing in only four colours of ink. The 'original' – colour transparency or photographic print, painting, or other image – is photographed, either by a camera using colour-filters, or by an electronic scanner. Single pieces of film are produced, each corresponding to one of the colours of ink to be used: magenta, yellow, cyan, and black (the usual order of printing). » printing [i]; spectrum

four-colour theorem A mathematical proposition which states that every map on a plane surface can be coloured using at most four colours. Clearly three colours are not sufficient to distinguish between regions with a common boundary, as shown in the figure. The difficulty is to prove that all maps, whatever the shape of the regions, can be coloured using at most four colours. First conjectured by Francis Guthrie in 1852, the problem has fascinated many distinguished mathematicians, but the theorem was not proved until 1976, when US mathematicians Kenneth Appel and Wolfgang Haken used computers to carry out the massive reductions required.

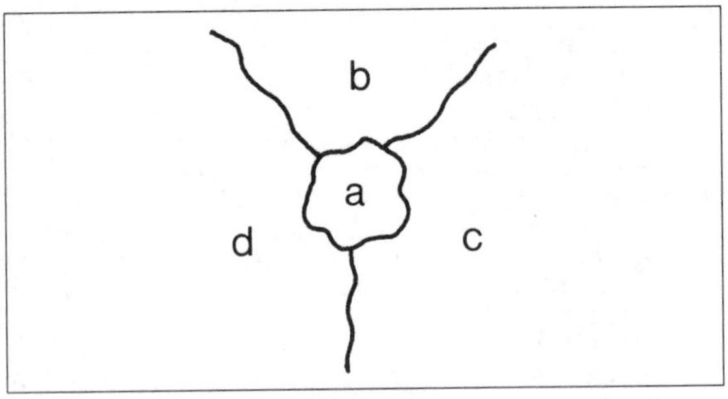

Four colours are needed to colour a map

Four Corners 37°00N 109°00W. The only place in the USA where the boundaries of four states come together: Colorado, Utah, New Mexico, and Arizona. » United States of America [i]

four-eyed fish Slender-bodied fish found in turbid shallow coastal waters, estuaries, and freshwater lakes of S and C America; length up to 30 cm/1 ft; eyes prominent on top of head, divided into distinct upper and lower parts providing simultaneous vision in air and water while swimming along the surface.

Four Freedoms (1941) Four basic human rights proclaimed in an annual message to Congress by President Roosevelt as basic human rights. They included freedom of speech and worship, and freedom from want and fear. » Roosevelt, Franklin D

Four Horsemen of the Apocalypse Symbolic Biblical characters described in *Rev* 6 (also *Zech* 6.1–7), where they signal the beginning of the messianic age. Each comes on a steed of different colour, symbolizing devastations associated with the world's end (black = famine; red = bloodshed, war; pale = pestilence, death), except for the white horse, which has a 'crown' and is sent 'to conquer'. » Revelation, Book of

Four Noble Truths The summary of the central teachings of Buddha. **1** All life involves suffering, and is inevitably sorrowful. **2** The cause of suffering and sorrow is craving or desire arising from ignorance. **3** There is escape from suffering, because craving and desire can end. **4** There is an Eightfold Path leading to the end of suffering and sorrow. » Buddha; Buddhism; Eightfold Path

four-stroke engine An engine that works on a practical cycle with one in every four strokes of the piston being the power stroke. This is the type of engine normally used to drive motor cars. » Carnot cycle; engine; two-stroke engine

Fourier, (Jean Baptiste) Joseph, Baron (1768–1830)

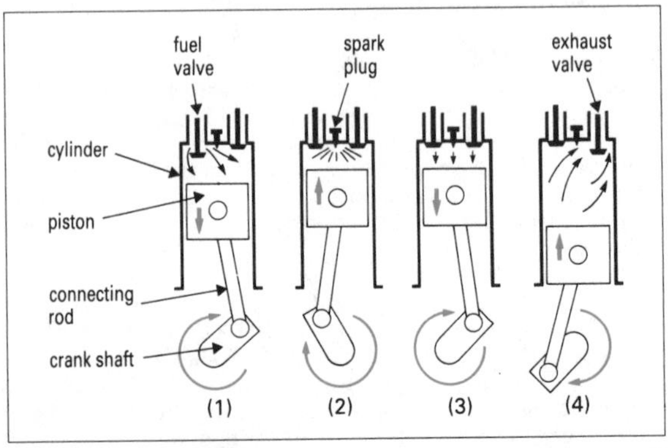

Four-stroke engine cycle. (1) Fuel and air drawn into cylinder. (2) Fuel/air mixture compressed and ignited by spark. (3) Power stroke. (4) Exhaust gases expelled.

French mathematician, born at Auxerre. He accompanied Napoleon to Egypt (1798), and on his return (1802) was made prefect of the department of Grenoble, and created baron (1808). He then took up his first interest, mathematics, and while working on the flow of heat discovered the theorem which bears his name, that any function of a variable can be expanded in a series of sines of multiples of the variable (the **Fourier series**). He died in Paris.

Fourier analysis » **wave** (physics) [i]

Fourneyron, Benoît [foornayrõ] (1802–67) French hydraulic engineer, born at St Etienne. In 1832 he patented the general design of his hydraulic turbine installations, and eventually built more than 100 of these in different parts of the world. He died in Paris. » hydraulics; turbine

Fourteen Points A peace programme outlined by US President Wilson to Congress in 1918. The Germans subsequently asked Wilson for an armistice agreement based on their acceptance of these points, which, with two reservations, were accepted by the Allied powers as the basis for a peace settlement. » Atlantic Charter; Wilson, Woodrow; World War 1

fourth-generation computers » **computer generations**

Fourth of July or **July Fourth** A public holiday in the USA, commemorating the adoption of the Declaration of Independence (4 Jul 1776).

fowl pest The name applied to two diseases of birds, **fowl plague** and **Newcastle disease**; several strains, caused by viruses; usually noticed in poultry, but most birds are vulnerable; attacks nervous, digestive, and respiratory systems; often fatal.

Fowler, H(enry) W(atson) (1858–1933) British lexicographer, born at Tonbridge, Kent. He was educated at Rugby and Oxford, became a schoolmaster at Sedbergh (1882–99), then went to London as a freelance journalist. In 1903 he joined his tomato-growing brother, **F(rank) G(eorge)** (1871–1918), in Guernsey, and their literary partnership began. Their joint reputation rests on *The King's English* (1906) and *The Concise Oxford Dictionary* (1911). Henry later wrote the *Dictionary of Modern English Usage* (1926), a household work for all who attempt to write good English, even though it is sometimes as mannered as the mannerisms he set out to eradicate. He died at Hinton St George, Somerset. » dictionary; English

Fowler, William A(lfred) (1911–) US astrophysicist, born in Pittsburgh, and educated at Ohio State University and the California Institute of Technology. He established a research group working on the application of nuclear physics to all aspects of astronomy, and is considered the founder of the theory of nucleosynthesis. » Hoyle, Fred; nucleosynthesis; stellar evolution

Fowles, John (Robert) (1926–) British novelist, born in London, and educated at Bedford School and at Oxford. His writings combine a topographical interest in Devon, a respect for the Victorian novel of social life and personal relationships, and an interest in contemporary developments in the French novel. His major works include *The French Lieutenant's Woman* (1969) and *A Maggot* (1985). » English literature; novel

fox A small member of the dog family (21 species), worldwide except SE Asia; usually thin muzzle, large pointed ears, long bushy tail; hunts alone; renowned for its cunning; often nocturnal; lives in a den (burrow or rock crevice). » Arctic/fennec/red fox; Canidae

Fox An Algonkin-speaking N American Indian group originally from N Wisconsin. They were mainly sedentary agriculturalists, but they also hunted and fished. Affected by Iroquois expansionism and White settlers, they settled permanently in Iowa in 1842 and are still there, retaining many traditional organizational features. » Algonkin; American Indians

Fox, Charles James (1749–1806) British statesman and Foreign Secretary (1782, 1783, 1806), born in London. Educated at Eton and Oxford, he became an MP at 19, and two years later was a junior Lord of the Admiralty. He supported Lord North, but in 1772 resigned over American policy. He became Secretary of State after North's downfall, and in 1783 formed a coalition with him, which held office for a short period in 1783. He supported the French Revolution, and strongly opposed the war with France. After Pitt's death (1806) he was recalled to office, but died soon afterwards, at Chiswick, Devon. » French Revolution [i]; North, Frederick; Pitt (the Younger)

Fox, George (1624–91) Founder of the Quakers, born at Fenny Drayton, Leicestershire. Apprenticed to a Nottingham shoemaker, he felt at 19 a divine call to leave his friends, and Bible in hand he wandered about the country, on a small income. The 'inner light' was the central idea of his teaching, and he argued against sacerdotalism, formalism, and all social conventions. His life is a record of insults, persecutions, imprisonments, and missionary travel to several parts of the world. He died in London. As a writer he is remembered by his *Journal* (posthumously published), which records the birth of the Quaker movement. » Bible; Christianity; Friends, Society of

fox-grape » **grapevine**

fox terrier An active British terrier with a deep chest, pointed muzzle, and soft, folded ears held high; tail docked short when young; usually white with black and brown markings; two forms: *wire-haired* and *smooth-haired*. » dog; terrier

foxglove A softly hairy biennial growing to 150 cm/5 ft, native to Europe; rosette leaves up to 30 cm/1 ft, narrowly oval, toothed; tall flower-spike produced in second year; flowers all on one side of the stem, bell-shaped with five very short lobes, drooping, pink to purple, rarely white, usually with dark spots forming honey guide within tube. It is the original source of the heart drug digitalin. (*Digitalis purpurea*. Family: *Scrophulariaceae*.) » perennial

foxglove tree A deciduous tree growing to 12 m/40 ft or more, native to China; leaves heart-shaped or with a single large tooth on each side; flowers resembling a foxglove, 6 cm/20 in, tubular with five spreading lobes, purple, yellowish within the tube, in erect clusters. It is a popular ornamental and street tree in Europe. (*Paulownia tomentosa*. Family: *Bignoniaceae*.) » deciduous plants; foxglove; tree [i]

foxhound A domestic dog bred for hunting foxes; large with brown, black, and white coat; soft ears; two breeds: the **English foxhound**, and its larger descendant, the **American foxhound**. » fox; hound

foxhunting A blood sport, which developed in the UK in the late 17th-c, and which since the early 19th-c has been regarded as the pastime of the aristocracy and the wealthy. The foxhunting season lasts from November to April. Famous hunts include the Quorn, Cottesmore and Belvoir, all in the Shire counties in the E Midlands. Each hunt is controlled by a Master of Hounds, and the hounds are controlled by the Huntsman. Foxhounds are similar in shape and colour to the beagle, but slightly larger. In recent years, animal rights saboteurs have attempted to thwart hunts, and since 1949 (when an anti-foxhunting bill went before parliament) there has been a movement to try to get the sport banned in the UK. » blood sports

foxtail millet » **millet**

Foyle, Lough Inlet of the Atlantic, on the N coast of Ireland, bounded W by Donegal (Republic of Ireland) and E by Co Derry (Northern Ireland); mouth 1.5 km/0.9 ml wide; length, 24 km/15 ml; width, 16 km/10 ml; fed by the R Foyle. » Ireland [i]

fractals Geometrical entities characterized by basic patterns that are repeated at ever decreasing sizes. For example, trees describe an approximate fractal pattern, as the trunk divides into branches which further subdivide into smaller branches which ultimately subdivide into twigs; at each stage of division the pattern is a smaller version of the original. Fractals are not able to fill spaces, and hence are described as having fractional dimensions. They were devised in 1967 by French mathematician Benoît Mandelbrot (1924–), during a study of the length of the coastline of Britain. They are relevant to any system involving self-similarity repeated on diminishing scales, such as in the study of chaos, fork lightning, or the movement of oil through porous rock. They are also used in computer graphics. » chaos; geometry; Plate XVI

fractionation The separation of the components of a mixture from one another. It is usually carried out chemically by (1) *fractional crystallization*, making use of varying solubilities of the different substances, or (2) *fractional distillation*, making use of differing boiling points.

fractions ≫ **numbers**

fracture (medicine) A physical break in the continuity of a bone. Most commonly the result of external force, it occurs occasionally as a consequence of disease, as when cancer affects bone substance (a *pathological* fracture). The break in the bone takes a number of forms, from a simple transverse fracture to one in which the bone is shattered into a number of small pieces (*comminuted*). Bones possess a considerable ability to reunite their fragments, and the extent to which the broken pieces remain or can be placed in alignment with the original bone influences the outcome and the treatment. Well-aligned fragments may unite while being kept in place by a simple splint. Comminuted fractures may need manipulation and the insertion of metal pins to hold the pieces together. ≫ bone

fracture (physics) The breaking of a material subject to excessive stress. The atomic layers are pulled away from one another. Prior to the fracture, most materials undergo elastic then plastic deformation. The fracture occurs when the applied stress exceeds the tensile strength of the material. ≫ elasticity (physics); plastic deformation; tensile strength

Frampton, Sir George James (1860–1928) British sculptor, born in London. He studied in London and Paris. Among his works are Peter Pan in Kensington Gardens, and the Lions at the British Museum. He was knighted in 1908, and died in London. ≫ English art; sculpture

franc The currency unit of many countries, notably France, Belgium, and Switzerland. The name derives from the words on a 14th-c gold coin, *Francorum rex* ('King of the Franks'). ≫ RR32

France, Anatole, pseudonym of **Jacques Anatole François Thibault** (1844–1924) French writer, born in Paris. He worked as a publisher's reader, and in 1879 published his first volume of stories. He wrote several graceful, lively novels, which contrast with his later satirical, sceptical works. The Dreyfus case (1896) stirred him into politics as a champion of internationalism. Among his later novels are *L'Ile des pingouins* (1908, Penguin Island) and *Les Dieux ont soif* (1912, The Gods are Athirst). He was awarded the Nobel Prize for Literature in 1921. ≫ Dreyfus; French literature

France, ancient **Gallia**, official name **Republic of France, République Française** pop (1990e) 56 647 000, area 551 000 sq km/ 212 686 sq ml; overseas departments pop (1982) 1 251 843, area 97 014 sq km/37 447 sq ml. Republic of W Europe, divided into 22 regions and 96 departments; bounded N and NE by Belgium, Luxembourg, and W Germany, E by Switzerland, Italy, and Monaco, and S by Spain and Andorra; includes island of Corsica in the Mediterranean, and overseas departments of Guadeloupe, Martinique, Guiana, Réunion, St Pierre et Miquelon, and Mayotte; also administers overseas territories of New Caledonia, French Polynesia, Wallis and Futuna, and the Southern and Antarctic Territories; capital, Paris; chief towns, Marseille, Lyon, Toulouse, Nice, Strasbourg; timezone GMT +1; population largely of Celtic and Latin origin, with several minorities; chief religion, Roman Catholicism (90%); official language, French (also widely used as international language); unit of currency, the French franc of 100 centimes.

Physical description and climate. A country of low and medium-sized hills and plateaux deeply cut by rivers; bounded S and E by large mountain ranges, notably (interior) the Armorican massif, Massif Central, Cévennes, Vosges, and Ardennes, (E) the Jura and Alps (rising to 4 807 m/15 771 ft at Mont Blanc), and (S) the Pyrenees; chief rivers include the Loire, Rhône, Seine, and Garonne; Mediterranean climate in S, with warm, moist winters and hot dry summers; maritime type in NW, annual rainfall average 573 mm/22.6 in, average temperature 3°C (winter), 18°C (summer); E has continental climate with annual average rainfall of 786 mm/31 in.

History and government. Prehistoric settlement seen in Palaeolithic carvings and rock paintings (eg at Lascaux) and Neolithic megaliths (eg at Carnac); Celtic-speaking Gauls dominant by 5th-c BC; part of Roman Empire, 125 BC to 5th-c AD; invaded by several Germanic tribes, 3rd–5th-c; Franks inaugurated the Merovingian epoch, 5th-c; Carolingian peak of development, 8th-c; feudal monarchy founded by Hugh Capet, 987; Plantagenets of England acquired several territories,

□ international airport

12th-c; lands gradually recovered in Hundred Years' War (1337–1453), apart from Calais (regained, 1558); Capetian dynasty followed by the Valois (from 1328) and the Bourbons (from 1589); 16th-c struggle between Francis I and Emperor Charles V; Wars of Religion (1562–95); 17th-c kings (with ministers Sully, Richelieu, and Mazarin) restored power of the monarchy, at its peak under Louis XIV; French Revolution, 1789; First Republic declared, 1792; First Empire, ruled by Napoleon, 1804–14; monarchy restored, 1814–48; Second Republic, 1848–52, and Second Empire, 1852–70, ruled by Louis Napoleon; Third Republic, 1870–1940; great political instability between World Wars, with several governments holding office for short periods; occupied by Germany 1940–4, with pro-German government at Vichy and Free French in London under de Gaulle; Fourth Republic, 1946; war with Indo-China, 1946–54; conflict in Algeria, 1954–62; Fifth

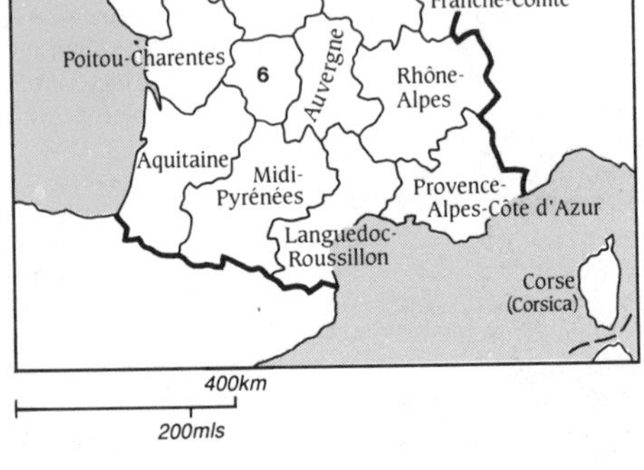

Republic, 1958; governed by a president, elected every seven years, who appoints a prime minister and presides over a Council of Ministers; bicameral legislature consists of a National Assembly of 577 deputies elected every five years, and a 319-member Senate indirectly elected by an electoral college, triennially (a third at a time), for 9-year terms.

Economy. W Europe's foremost producer of agricultural products, chiefly cereals, beef, sugar beet, potatoes, wine, grapes, dairy products; coalfields in N France, Lorraine, and the Massif Central; hydroelectric power from the Alps; several nuclear power sites; metal and chemical industries, based on reserves of iron ore, bauxite, potash, salt, sulphur; heavy industry (steel, machinery, textiles, clothing, chemicals, vehicles) based around N coalfields; food processing, armaments, electronics, tourism, fishing. » Bourbons; Capetians; Carolingians; Celts; de Gaulle; Franks; French art/history/literature/Revolution [i] /Revolutionary Wars; Gaul; Hundred Years' War; Louis XIV; Merovingians; Napoleon I/III; Paris [i]; Plantagenets; Roman history [i]; Valois; Religion, Wars of; RR25 national holidays; RR49 political leaders

Francesca da Rimini [fran**chay**ska da **ree**meenee] (?–1285) Daughter of Guido da Polenta, Lord of Ravenna, whose tragic love story has often been recounted in literary and artistic works. She was married to Gianciotto the Lame, son of Malatesta, Lord of Rimini; but she already loved Paolo, Gianciotto's brother. Gianciotto, surprising the lovers together, killed them both. The story is woven into Dante's Inferno. » Dante

franchise (economics) A licence to carry out some business activity, using the name, products, and know-how of the franchisor; for example, in fast-food restaurants. The franchisee pays a licence fee and a percentage of the business done to the franchisor, and undertakes to conform to pre-set standards.

franchise (politics) The right to vote. It is only during the 19th-c and 20th-c that the franchise has been extended to all citizens in most democratic countries. Various qualifications and rules determine who may be eligible and how the vote may be exercised: in the UK, people over the age of 18 who are registered may vote, providing they are not peers or peeresses in their own right, felons, or lunatics, and have not been convicted of electoral malpractice in the preceding five years. » proportional representation; suffragettes

Francis I (of France) (1494–1547) King of France (1515–47), born at Cognac. He was Count of Angoulême and Duke of Valois before succeeding Louis XII as King and marrying his daughter, Claude. He combined many of the attributes of mediaeval chivalry and the Renaissance prince, the dominant feature of his reign being his rivalry with the Emperor Charles V, which led to a series of wars (1521–6, 1528–9, 1536–8, 1542–4). After establishing his military reputation against the Swiss at Marignano (1515) in his first Italian campaign, he later suffered a number of reverses, including his capture at Pavia (1525) and imprisonment in Madrid. Though he avoided religious fanaticism, he became increasingly hostile to Protestantism after 1534. He died at Rambouillet. » Charles V (Emperor)

Francis II (Emperor) and **Francis I** (of Austria) (1768–1835) Last Holy Roman Emperor (1792–1806), the first Emperor of Austria (1804–35), and King of Hungary (1792–30) and Bohemia (1792–1836), born in Florence. Defeated on several occasions by Napoleon (1797, 1801, 1805, 1809), he made a short-lived alliance with him, sealed by the marriage of his daughter, Marie Louise, to the French Emperor. Later he joined with Russia and Prussia to win the Battle of Leipzig (1813). By the Treaty of Vienna (1815), thanks to Metternich, he recovered several territories (eg Lombardy-Venetia). He died in Vienna. » Metternich; Napoleonic Wars

Francis Joseph, properly **Franz Josef I** (1830–1916) Emperor of Austria (1848–1916) and King of Hungary (1867–1916), the grandson of Emperor Francis I, born near Vienna. During his reign the aspirations of the various nationalities of the Empire were rigorously suppressed. He was defeated by the Prussians in 1866, and established the Dual Monarchy of Austria-Hungary in 1867. His annexation of Bosnia-Herzegovina in 1908 agitated Europe; and his attack on Serbia in 1914 precipitated the World War 1. He died near Vienna. » Austria-Hungary, Dual Monarchy of

Francis of Assisi, St, originally Giovanni Bernardone (?1181–1226), feast day 4 October. Italian founder of the Franciscan Order, born at Assisi. In 1205 he left his worldly life, devoting himself to the care of the poor and the sick, and living as a hermit. By 1210 he had a brotherhood of 11 for which he drew up a rule which became the Franciscan way of life, in which all property is repudiated. By 1219 the order had 5 000 members. He preached widely in Europe and the Holy Land, and on returning to Italy he is said to have received on his body the marks (*stigmata*) of the wounds of the Redeemer (1224). He died at Assisi, and was canonized in 1228. He is often represented in art among animals and birds, which he called his sisters and brothers. » Franciscans; missions, Christian; stigmata

Francis of Sales, St (1567–1622), feast day 24 January. French Roman Catholic bishop and writer, born at Sales, Savoy. Educated at Paris and Padua, he became a distinguished preacher, successfully converting the Calvinistic population of Chablais. He became Bishop of Nicopolis (1599) and Bishop of Geneva (1602), where he helped to found a congregation of nuns of the Visitation. He died at Lyons, and was canonized in 1665. » Calvinism; monasticism

Francis Xavier, St [zay**veeuh**], Span **San Francisco Javier** [hav**eeayr**] (1506–52), feast day 3 December. Roman Catholic missionary who brought Christianity to India and the Far East, born at Navarre. He studied in Paris, where he became one of the first seven members of the Jesuit order (1534). He began his missionary work in Goa, India (1542), later travelling to the Malay Is (1545) and Japan (1549). He died of a fever while trying to enter China. Known as the 'Apostle of the Indies', he was canonized in 1622 and named patron saint of all missionary work in 1927. » Jesuits; missions, Christian

Franciscans Religious orders founded by St Francis of Assisi in the early 13th-c. The first order, of **Friars Minor**, is now divided into three groups: the **Observants** (**OFM**), the **Conventuals** (**OFMConv**), and the **Capuchins** (**OFMCap**). These lead active lives preaching to the poor and needy. The second order is made up of nuns, known as the **Poor Clares** (**PC**). The third order is a lay fraternity. Together, they constitute the largest religious order in the Roman Catholic Church, notable for missionary and social work. » Capuchins; Clare, St; Francis of Assisi, St; friar; Roman Catholicism

Francistown 21°11S 27°32E, pop (1981) 31 065. Independent township in Central district, Botswana, S Africa; altitude 990 m/3 248 ft; area 79 sq km/49 sq ml; industrial and commercial centre of Botswana; originally a gold-mining settlement; airfield; railway; textiles, light industry, trade, services. » Botswana [i]

Franck, César (Auguste) (1822–90) French composer, born at Liège, Belgium. He studied at the Liège Conservatoire and at Paris, where he acquired French nationality, and settled as a teacher and organist, composing in his leisure hours. His reputation rests on a few masterpieces all written after the age of 50, the best known being a string quartet, a symphony, and the *Variations symphoniques* for piano and orchestra. He died after a street accident in Paris.

Franco (Bahamonde), Francisco (1892–1975) Spanish general and dictator (1936–75), born at El Ferrol, Galicia. He graduated from Toledo military academy in 1910, acquired extensive combat experience in Morocco, and by 1926 was Spain's youngest general. He led the repression of the Asturias miners' revolt (1934), and during 1935 served as Chief-of-Staff. In 1936 he belatedly joined the conspiracy against the Popular Front government (elected Feb 1936) which on 17–18 July launched the rebellion from which the Spanish Civil War (1936–9) resulted. Franco's leadership of the vital Army of Africa, and his close relations with the rebels' Italian and German allies, led to his becoming (Sep 1936) *generalissimo* of the rebel forces and chief of the Nationalist state. Between October 1936 and April 1939 he led the Nationalists to victory, and presided over the construction of an authoritarian regime that endured until his death. During World War 2, he initially stood close to Germany and Italy, opting (1940) for nonbelligerency rather than neutrality. He nevertheless kept Spain out of the war, and from 1943 shrewdly distanced himself from the Axis. During the 1950s, his anti-communism made possible a rapprochement with the Western powers. In 1969 he announced that upon his death the monarchy would return in the person of Juan Carlos, grandson of Spain's last ruling king. Franco died in Madrid, and within two years almost every vestige of his dictatorship had disappeared. » Axis Powers; Juan Carlos I; Spain [i]; Spanish Civil War

Franco-German Treaty of Co-operation A treaty signed (Jan 1963) by President de Gaulle and Chancellor Adenauer signalling a rapprochement and the ending of centuries of conflict. It made provisions for regular summit meetings, and co-operation and consultation in foreign, economic, and cultural affairs. A symbol of the new, post-war order in Europe, the treaty also underpinned the European Economic Community. » Adenauer; de Gaulle; European Community

Franco-Prussian War (1870–1) A conflict occasioned by the Hohenzollern candidature for the Spanish throne and the Ems telegram, and caused by the changing balance of power in Europe. It resulted in crushing defeats for France at Sedan and Metz by Moltke's reformed Prussian army, the siege of Paris, and the humiliating treaty of Frankfurt. » Ems telegram; Hohenzollerns; Moltke; Prussia

francolin A partridge native to Africa and S Asia; large bird with patches of bare skin on head and neck; inhabits forest or scrubland. (Genus: *Francolinus*, 40 species.) » partridge; redwing

Francome, John [**frank**uhm] (1952–) British jockey and trainer, born at Swindon, Wiltshire. In 1970–85 he rode a record 1 138 winners over fences. He won the 1978 Cheltenham Gold Cup, the 1981 Champion Hurdle, and twice won the King George VI Chase (1982, 1984). Only the second man to surpass 1 000 winners, he was seven times National Hunt champion jockey (1976, 1979, 1981–5). He retired in 1985, and became a trainer and novelist. » horse racing

Franconia A European duchy which, as its name denotes, was once part of the lands of the Franks. These lands were divided in 843 into three broad divisions, including E Francia (later the kingdom of Germany), with Franconia, between Upper Lotharingia and Thuringia, as one of its constituent duchies. » Franks; Lotharingia

Franconian Forest, Ger **Frankenwald** Mountain range in Bavaria, Germany; extends 36 km/22 ml between R Rodach (NW) and the Fichtelgebirge (SE); highest peak, the Döbraberg (795 m/2 608 ft). » Bavaria; Germany [i]

frangipani [franji**pah**nee] A shrub or small tree growing to c.6 m/20 ft, native to tropical America; leaves oval; flowers in large clusters, very fragrant, five petals, white, yellow, or pink. It is widely cultivated in the tropics for the scented flowers which are often placed in Buddhist temples. (*Plumeria rubra.*) » shrub; tree [i]

Frank, Anne (1929–45) Jewish concentration camp victim, born at Frankfurt am Main. She fled from the Nazis to Holland in 1933, and after the Nazi occupation hid with her family and four others in a sealed-off office backroom in Amsterdam from 1942 until they were betrayed in 1944. She died in Belsen concentration camp. The lively, moving diary she kept during her concealment was published in 1947, dramatized, and filmed, and she became a symbol of past suffering under the Nazis. » Holocaust; Nazi Party

Frankfort 38°12N 84°52W, pop (1980) 25 973. Capital of state in Franklin County, NC Kentucky, USA, on the Kentucky R; founded by Daniel Boone, 1770; state capital, 1792; railway; university; trade and shipping centre for tobacco, livestock and limestone; whisky, automobile parts, shoes, metal items; graves of Daniel and Rebecca Boone; Capital Expo (Jun). » Boone; Kentucky

Frankfurt (am Main) [**frangk**foort am **miyn**] 50°07N 8°40E, pop (1983) 614 700. Manufacturing and commercial city in Darmstadt district, Germany; port on R Main, 27 km/17 ml N of Darmstadt; most of the German Emperors crowned here; meeting place of first German National Assembly (1848–9); international junction for rail, road, and air traffic; university (1914); headquarters of the leading German stock exchange; banking, river craft, precision engineering, chemicals, pharmaceuticals, brewing, metals, machinery, packaging, publishing, oil products, domestic appliances, office machines, telecommunications; birthplace of Goethe; Gothic cathedral (13th–15th-c), the Römer (ancient town hall), Goethe House (rebuilt, 1949); International Frankfurt Fair (Aug), and many other trade fairs; some of Germany's finest health resorts nearby. » Germany [i]; Goethe; Gothic architecture

Frankfurt (an der Oder) 52°50N 14°31E, pop (1981) 81 009. Capital of region in Frankfurt district, E Germany; 80 km/50 ml E of Berlin, on R Oder, where it follows the frontier with Poland; badly bombed in World War 2; railway; textiles, machinery, furniture, semiconductors. » Germany [i]; Oder, River

Frankfurt Parliament An elected assembly convened following the German revolutions of March 1848 to draft a liberal constitution for all of Germany. It represented every state in the German Confederation, but proved to be disunited and powerless. After its offer of the imperial crown to the King of Prussia was repudiated by Austria and rejected by the King himself, the parliament disintegrated. » Frankfurt (am Main); German Confederation; Revolutions of 1848

Frankfurt School The group of philosophers, sociologists, and psychologists who belonged to the Frankfurt Institute for Social Research (1923–69); leading figures included Max Horkheimer (1895–1973), Theodore Adorno (1903–69), Herbert Marcuse (1898–1979), and more recently Jürgen Habermas (1929–). The School developed **critical theory**, an ethical, politically prescriptive critique of society which draws its inspiration from the works of Marx and Freud. » Frankfurt (am Main); Freud, Sigmund; Habermas; Marcuse; Marx

frankincense An evergreen tree or shrub growing to 6 m/20 ft, native to Somaliland; leaves pinnate with oval leaflets, crowded towards the ends of the twigs; flowers white, 5-petalled. Aromatic resin is obtained from cuts in the bark. (*Boswellia carteri*. Family: *Burseraceae*.) » evergreen plants; pinnate; resin; shrub; tree [i]

Franklin, Benjamin (1706–90) US statesman, author, and scientist, born in Boston, Massachusetts. He set up a printing house in Philadelphia, bought the *Pennsylvania Gazette* (1729), and built a reputation as a journalist. In 1736 he became clerk of the Assembly, in 1737 postmaster of Philadelphia, and in 1754 deputy postmaster-general for the colonies, and was sent on various diplomatic missions to England. In 1746 he began his research into electricity, proving that lightning and electricity are identical, and suggesting that buildings be protected by lightning conductors. In 1775 he was actively involved in framing the Declaration of Independence. A skilled negotiator, he successfully won Britain's recognition of US independence (1783). He was US Minister in Paris until 1785, then three times president of the State of Pennsylvania. In 1788 he retired from public life and died in Philadelphia. » Declaration of Independence; electricity

Franklin, Sir John (1786–1847) British Arctic explorer, born at Spilsby, Lincolnshire. He joined the navy at 14, and was present at the Battles of Copenhagen (1801) and Trafalgar (1805). Knighted in 1829, he became Governor of Van Diemen's Land (Tasmania) 1834–45. He then commanded an expedition to discover the Northwest Passage, but his ships were beleaguered by thick ice in the Victoria Strait, and he and his crew died. Their remains, and a record of the expedition, were found several years later. He is credited with the discovery of the Passage, because his ships came within a few miles of known American waters. » Northwest Passage

Franks Germanic peoples, originally from the lower Rhine region. Clovis led the Salian and Ripuarian Franks and founded a kingdom embracing much of Gaul; Charlemagne, their greatest ruler, attempted to revive the Roman Empire in the West. They gave their name to Francia, which by the 13th-c stood for what is now France, but earlier had diverse territorial connotations, reflecting the vicissitudes of Frankish royal power. » Carolingians; Charlemagne; Clovis I; Franconia; Merovingians; Salic Law

Franz Josef Land, Russ **Zemlya Frantsa-Iosifa** area 20 700 sq km/8 000 sq ml. Archipelago in the Arctic Ocean, N of Novaya Zemlya, NW Russia; over 160 islands of volcanic origin; declared Soviet territory in 1926; most northerly land of the E hemisphere; uninhabited save for a meteorological station on Ostrov Gukera (Hooker I). » Russia

Fraser, Dawn (1937–) Australian swimmer, born at Balmain, near Sydney. She is the only swimmer to take the same individual title at three consecutive Olympics, winning the 100 m freestyle in 1956, 1960, and 1964. She also won a gold medal in the 4 x 100 m freestyle relay in 1956. She took six Commonwealth Games gold medals, and set 27 world records. In 1962 she became the first woman to break the 1-minute barrier for the 100 m. In 1964 she was banned by the Australian association for 10 years (later reduced to 4) following an over-exuberent party in Tokyo after winning her third Olympic title in 1964. » swimming

Fraser, (John) Malcolm (1930–) Australian statesman and Liberal Prime Minister (1975–83), born in Melbourne. Educated at Melbourne and Oxford, in 1955 he became the youngest MP in the House of Representatives. He was Minister for the Army (1966–8), Defence (1969–71), and Education and Science (1968–9, 1971–2). He became leader of the Liberal Party in 1975, and Prime Minister in a Liberal–National Country coalition. His government was defeated in the 1983 elections, and soon after he resigned his parliamentary seat. He is a farmer, owning a large estate at Nareen, W Victoria. » Australia; Liberal Party (Australia)

Fraser River River in SW Canada, rises in the Rocky Mts, flows NW, S, and W to enter the Strait of Georgie and the Pacific Ocean 16 km/10 ml S of Vancouver; length 1 368 km/850 ml; navigable below Yale; Fraser R canyon above Yale; 1858 gold rush along upper reaches led to independent colonial status for the mainland, and the beginnings of permanent non-native settlement; river course followed by major railroads. » Canada [i]

fraternity and sorority In the USA, associations at universities, for men and women respectively, named usually with two or three letters of the Greek alphabet. They are formed mainly for social purposes; membership is by invitation, and is in some cases discriminatory. The oldest association is *Phi Beta Kappa*, founded in 1776 at the College of William and Mary, Williamsburg, Virginia.

fraud A false statement made knowingly or without belief in its truth; the fact that there may have been no intention to cheat anyone is irrelevant. Any person injured by fraud may bring an action to recover damages in the tort of deceit. Any contract induced by fraud is voidable at the instance of the innocent party. Fraud is an element in a number of criminal offences, such as obtaining a pecuniary advantage by deception. In the USA, a tort action for fraud requires not only misrepresentation, but also the intent to deprive the other of some right or to do some other legal injury. » tort

Fraunhofer, Joseph von [**frown**hohfer] (1787–1826) German physicist, born at Straubing, Bavaria. In 1807 he founded an optical institute at Munich, where he improved prisms and telescopes, enabling him to discover the dark lines in the Sun's spectrum, since named after him. In 1823 he became professor and academician at Munich, where he died. » Fraunhofer lines; prism; telescope [i]

Fraunhofer lines Sharp, narrow, absorption lines in the spectrum of the Sun, 25 000 of which are now identified. The most prominent lines are due to the presence of calcium, hydrogen, sodium, and magnesium. Most of the absorption occurs in cool layers of the atmosphere, immediately above the incandescent photosphere. » Fraunhofer; photosphere; spectrum; Sun

Fray Bentos [friy **ben**tohs] 33°10S 58°20W, pop (1985) 20 091. River-port capital of Río Negro department, W Uruguay, on R Uruguay; airfield; railway; ferry; meat packing and canning (especially of corned beef); international toll bridge across the R Uruguay to Puerto Unzué (Argentina). » Uruguay [i]

Frazer, Sir James George (1854–1941) British social anthropologist, classicist, and folklorist, born in Glasgow, Scotland. He studied at Glasgow and at Cambridge, where he spent most of his adult life as a fellow of Trinity College. His major work was *The Golden Bough* (1890; rewritten in 12 vols, 1911–15). He became professor of social anthropology at Liverpool in 1907, and was knighted in 1914. He died at Cambridge. » anthropology

Frederick I (Emperor), byname **Barbarossa** ('Redbeard') (c.1123–90) Born of the Hohenstaufen family, he succeeded his uncle Conrad III in 1152. His reign was a continuous struggle against unruly vassals at home, the city-republics of Lombardy, and the papacy. He went on several campaigns in Italy, and though severely defeated at Legnano (1176), he quelled Henry the Lion of Bavaria, and asserted his feudal superiority over Poland, Hungary, Denmark, and Burgundy. He led the Third Crusade against Saladin (1189), and was victorious at Philomelium and Iconium. He died in Cilicia. » Crusades [i]; Hohenstaufen; Lombard League

Frederick I (of Prussia) (1657–1713) Born at Königsberg, he succeeded to the electorate of Brandenburg in 1688 (as Frederick III) and was made the first King of Prussia in 1701 for his loyalty to the Emperor Leopold against the French. He maintained a large court, established a standing army, and was a great patron of the arts and learning. He died in Berlin. » Frederick William; Prussia

Frederick II (Emperor) (1194–1250) Born at Jesi, near Ancona, the grandson of Frederick I, he succeeded Henry VI in 1220, and was the last Emperor of the Hohenstaufen line. He was also King of Sicily (1198) and of Germany (1212). He keenly desired to consolidate Imperial power in Italy at the expense of the papacy, and devoted himself to organizing his Italian territories, but his plans were frustrated by the Lombard cities and by the popes. Embarking on the Sixth Crusade in 1228, he took possession of Jersusalem, and crowned himself King there (1229). Returning to Italy, he continued his struggles with the papacy until his death, at Fiorentino. » Crusades [i]; Lombard League

Frederick II (of Prussia), byname **the Great** (1712–86) Born at Berlin, the son of Frederick-William I, he became King of Prussia in 1740. His childhood was spent in rigorous military training and education. In 1733 he married, and lived at Rheinsberg, where he studied music and French literature, and himself wrote and composed. As King, he fought to oppose Austrian ambitions, and earned a great reputation as a military commander in the War of the Austrian Succession (1740–8). He seized Silesia, and defeated the Austrians at Mollwitz (1741) and Chotusitz (1742). The second Silesian War (1744–5) left him with further territories which, by good luck and great effort, he retained after fighting the Seven Years' War (1756–63). In 1772 he shared in the first partition of Poland. Under him, Prussia became a leading European power. He died at Potsdam, having doubled the area of his country, and given it a strong economic foundation. » Austrian Succession, War of the; Prussia; Seven Years' War

Frederick IX (of Denmark) (1899–1972) King of Denmark (1947–72), born near Copenhagen, the son of Christian X. He married in 1935 Ingrid, daughter of King Gustav VI Adolf of Sweden, and they had three daughters, Margrethe (later Queen Margrethe II), Benedikte, and Anne-Marie, who married the former King Constantine II of Greece. During World War 2, he encouraged the Danish resistance movement, and was imprisoned by the Germans (1943–5). He died in Copenhagen.

Frederick William, byname **The Great Elector** (1620–88) Elector of Brandenburg (1640–88), born near Berlin. On his accession, he found the state exhausted by the Thirty Years' War. He therefore made a treaty of neutrality with the Swedes, regulated the finances, sought to re-people the deserted towns, and reorganized the army and administrative system of the Hohenzollern state. He recovered some territory and gained East Pomerania by the Treaty of Westphalia (1648), retrieving the sovereignty of Prussia from Poland (1657). He died at Potsdam, his reforms laying the foundation of future Prussian greatness. » Hohenzollerns; Thirty Years' War

Frederick William III (of Prussia) (1770–1840) King of Prussia (1797–1840), the son of Frederick William II, born at Potsdam. At first cautiously neutral towards Napoleon's conquests, he eventually declared war (1806) and was severely defeated at Jena and Auerstadt, with the loss of all territory W of the Elbe. To further Prussia's recovery, he sanctioned the reforms of

Hardenburg and Stein and the military reorganization of Scharnhorst and Gneisenau, sharing in the decisive victory of Leipzig with Alexander I (1813). By the Treaty of Vienna (1815) he recovered his possessions, and thereafter tended to support the forces of conservatism. He died in Berlin. » Gneisenau; Napoleonic Wars; Prussia; Scharnhorst; Stein, Baron von

Fredericksburg, Battle of (1862) In the American Civil War, a fruitless attempt by the Northern army of 113 000 to capture the town of Fredericksburg, Virginia, defended by a Southern army of 75 000. » American Civil War

Fredericton 45°57N 66°40W, pop (1981) 43 723. Capital of New Brunswick province, E Canada, on the St John R; originally settled by Acadians, 1731, as St Anne's Point; renamed 1785 for Prince Frederick, second son of George III; capital, 1787; airfield; railway; university (1783); timber products, plastics, tourism; York-Sunbury Historical Museum, Beaverbrook Art Gallery, Provincial Legislature (1880), Christ Church Cathedral (1853), Old Government House (1828), now headquarters of Royal Canadian Mounted Police. » Acadia; New Brunswick (Canada)

Fredrikshamn [**fray**dreeks-hamuhn] » **Hamina**

Fredriksson, Gert (1919–) Swedish canoeist. In 1948–60 he won eight Olympic medals, including six golds, and 13 world titles, all at either kayak singles or pairs. His winning margin of 6.7 seconds in the 1948 Olympic singles final was the biggest for any kayak race other than the 10 000 m. When he won his last Olympic gold in 1960, he was aged 40 yr 292 days – the oldest canoeing gold medallist. » canoeing; kayak

free electron gas » **electronic structure of solids**

free electron laser A device which produces laser light using a beam of electrons rather than a collection of excited atoms. First demonstrated in 1976, it provides a good source of variable wavelength light. It works by passing a beam of high-speed electrons between a set of magnets with alternating north-south poles. Side-to-side oscillations cause electromagnetic radiation to be emitted, which is produced in a forward direction due to high electron velocity. Such lasers could have a military application, with an ability to pierce armour plating. » electromagnetic radiation [i]; electron; laser [i]

free enterprise An economic system where commercial and business activity is free of government control, particularly where supply and demand determine the allocation of resources without regulation. It is sometimes referred to as *free-market economy*.

free fall The motion of objects allowed to fall under the influence of gravity, in which air resistance and variations in gravity with altitude are ignored. The rate of free fall is the same for all objects, regardless of mass or substance, a result deriving from Galileo. » acceleration due to gravity; ballistics; Galileo; terminal velocity

Free French Frenchmen who answered General de Gaulle's appeal, broadcast from London (18 Jun 1940) to reject the impending armistice between France and Germany, and join him in fighting on. He became leader of the Free French forces, and the 2nd French Armoured Division helped liberate Paris (25 Aug 1944). » de Gaulle; World War 2

free port An area near a port or airport where business enterprises may import materials and components free of tax or import duties, as long as the resulting finished articles are exported. It is a means of avoiding problems created by import tariffs and other restrictions, such as high raw material costs, or shortages of key components. An example is Shannon Airport, Ireland (established 1961). The term is also used for a port where goods may be imported without local taxes, as long as they are re-exported. The world's largest ports in this category are Hong Kong and Singapore. The UK set up six free ports in 1984, including Liverpool and Southampton. » customs and excise

free selection In Australian history, the colonial governments' laws passed between 1861 and 1872 to force pastoral occupiers to give way to freehold farming. Anyone could 'select' any land up to 130 ha/320 acres that had not been sold, granted, or dedicated by the Crown. The first law to embody this idea was passed in New South Wales (1861). Although the laws achieved some success, they often failed because of the tactics used by the occupiers ('squatters'), the unsuitability of the land for farming, or the selectors' lack of capital. » peacocking

free trade An economic doctrine that trade between countries should not be controlled in any way; there should be no tariffs or other barriers. The problems which result from tariffs were identified by Adam Smith in 1776, and the cause of free trade, taken up by Sir Robert Peel, led to the repeal of the Corn Laws in 1846. Since the 19th-c, tariff barriers have become universal, but groups of countries may agree to lower or remove them, forming a *free-trade area*, as in the case of the EEC. » Corn Laws; laissez-faire; Manchester School; Smith, Adam; tariff

free verse Verse which, while being rhythmical, observes no strict or recurrent metrical pattern. Much if not most 20th-c verse is written in free verse. Many poets (such as T S Eliot) have maintained it is more difficult to write well than formal verse. » Eliot, T S; metre (literature); poetry

free will Philosophers have offered two major competing accounts of this faculty or condition. According to one, an action is free if the agent had the power to do it and the power to refrain from doing it, undetermined by the previous causal history of the world. According to the other, an action is free if it conforms to the agent's desires. The latter account, unlike the former, can be held consistently with causal determinism, the thesis that every event is caused. On both accounts, free will is a necessary precondition for a person's being morally responsible. » determinism

freefalling » **skydiving**

freehold Land or property held by a registered owner for free use. The notion is opposed to **leasehold**, where the estate is rented to others for their use, on payment of rent, for a specified period of time (eg 99 years).

freemasonry A movement claiming great antiquity, whose members are joined together in an association based on brotherly love, faith, and charity. The one essential qualification for membership is a belief in a supreme being. Non-political, open to men of any religion, freemasonry is known for its rituals and signs of recognition that date back to ancient religions and to the practices of the mediaeval craft guild of the stonemasons (in England). During the 17th-c the masons' clubs, or *lodges*, began to be attended by gentlemen who had no connection with the trade. The Grand Lodge of England was founded in 1717, that of Ireland in 1725, and Scotland in 1736; freemasonry spread to the USA, the British colonies, and European countries. Freemasons are now mainly drawn from the professional middle classes. The organization regularly comes under attack for the secrecy with which it carries out its activities.

freesia A perennial growing to 75 cm/30 in, producing corms, native to S Africa; leaves sword-shaped, forming flat fans; flowers up to 5 cm/2 in long, goblet-shaped, creamy white, fragrant, in one-sided sprays. Cultivars may have orange-to-crimson or blue-to-mauve flowers. (*Freesia refracta*. Family: *Iridaceae*.) » corm; cultivar; perennial

freethought A post-Reformation movement which rejected the control of any religious authority over reason in the examination of religious issues. The term was used by the 17th–18th-c deists, such as Anthony Collins (1676–1729). It is represented in the 19th-c by the National Secularist Society (1866) and in the 20th-c by the Secular Society. » deism; humanism

Freetown 8°30N 13°17W, pop (1985) 469 776. Seaport capital of Sierra Leone; visited by the Portuguese, 15th-c; founded in the 1790s as a foundation for freed slaves; capital of British West Africa, 1808–74; W Africa's oldest university, Fourah Bay, founded as a college in 1827; capital of Sierra Leone, 1961; airport; oil refining, plastics, sugar, cement, footwear, soap, fish processing; trade in platinum, diamonds, gold, chromite, palm kernels, ginger, kola nuts; fort at Bunce I. » Sierra Leone [i]

freeze drying » **lyophilization**

freezing » **deep-freezing**

Frege, (Friedrich Ludwig) Gottlob [**fray**guh] (1848–1925) German mathematician and logician, born at Wismar. Educated at Jena and Göttingen, he became professor of mathematics at Jena (1896). His *Begriffsschrift* ('Concept-script',

1879) outlined the first complete system of symbolic logic. The technical difficulties involved gave rise to his distinctive philosophical doctrines, forcefully set out in his *Grundlagen der Arithmetik* (1884, The Foundations of Arithmetic). His *Grundgesetze der Arithmetik* (1893–1903, Basic Laws of Arithmetic) contained a postscript acknowledging that Russell had spotted a contradiction in his thinking. Depressed by the poor reception of his ideas, he wrote little after 1903, and died at Bad Kleinen, Germany. » arithmetic; Russell, Bertrand; logic

Frei (Montalva), Eduardo [fray] (1911–82) Chilean statesman and President (1964–70), born, educated, and died in Santiago. He became one of the leaders of the Social-Christian Falange Party in the late 1930s, and of the new Christian Democratic Party after 1957. His presidency saw an ambitious programme of social reform. » Chile [i]

Fremantle [**free**mantl] 32°07S 115°44E, pop (1981) 22 484. Seaport city in Western Australia state, Australia, at the mouth of the Swan R, part of Perth metropolitan area; known locally as 'Freo'; founded as a penal colony, 1829; railway terminus; shipbuilding, trade in petroleum, iron and steel products, grain, wool, fruit; the Round House (1830), a former jail; maritime museum; a notable sailing club; centre for the 1986–7 America's Cup yacht race. » Perth (Australia); Western Australia

French, John (Denton Pinkstone), Earl of Ypres (1852–1925) British field marshal (1913), born at Ripple, Kent. He joined the navy (1866), then the army (1874), and distinguished himself in the Sudan (1884–5) and South Africa (1899–1901). Chief of Imperial General Staff (1911–14), he held supreme command of the British Expeditionary Force in France (1914–15), but was criticized for indecision, and resigned. He was made a viscount (1915) and earl (1921), and was Lord-Lieutenant of Ireland (1918–21). He died at Deal, Kent. » British Expeditionary Force; World War 1

French » **Romance languages**

French and Indian War (1756–63) The last of the 18th-c wars between France and Britain for the control of N America. France accepted final defeat at the Treaty of Paris (1763) » Seven Years' War

French art The art associated with France can be traced back to remote prehistoric times. It absorbed Greek and Celtic influences from the 6th-c BC onwards, and flourished under Roman rule (the Gallo-Roman period, 120 BC–AD 3rd-c). The glories of mediaeval art include architecture, sculpture, and stained-glass at churches and cathedrals, such as Moissac, Vézelay, Souilhac, Saint-Denis, Chartres, Reims, and Notre-Dame in Paris. Italian Renaissance ideas are reflected in 16th-c chateaux of the Loire and the royal residences at Fontainebleau and the Louvre. French classicism flowered under Louis XIV, especially in the paintings of Claude Lorraine and Poussin, and in the architecture of Jacques Lemercier (1585–1654), Mansard, and Louis le Vau (1612–70). In the 18th-c the Rococo style of Watteau and Boucher was superseded by the Neoclassicism of David. Major 19th-c artists include Ingres, Courbet, Manet, and the Impressionists. From the early 19th-c down to c.1940, Paris was the centre of European art, especially painting. » art; Art Deco; atelier; Barbizon School; Beaux-Arts, Ecole des; Carolingian art; Empire Style; Fauvism; Fontainebleau School; Impressionism (art); Intimisme; *maisons de la culture*; Nabis; Neoclassicism (art and architecture); Post-impressionism; Rubénisme; Salon; Boucher, François; Claude Lorraine; Courbet; David, Jacques Louis; Ingres; Manet; Mansard; Poussin; Watteau

French bean » **haricot bean**

French bulldog A breed of dog, developed in France by crossing British bulldogs with local breeds; narrower and taller than the British breed, with smaller head and straighter legs. » bulldog

French Community A grouping of some former French colonies which under the Constitution of the Fifth Republic (1958) opted to stay closely associated with France. The member states had full internal autonomy, but many matters, including currency, defence, and foreign affairs remained the responsibility of the Community, which in effect meant France. Some twelve overseas territories opted to join. Pressures for full independence continued to build up, and in 1960 it became possible to be fully independent within the Community, thus rendering it of no practical relevance. » French Union

French Guiana [gee**ah**na], Fr **La Guyane Française** pop (1989e) 95 000; area 90 909 sq km/35 091 sq ml. Overseas department of France in S America, bordering the Atlantic, divided into two districts; bounded W by Suriname, E and S by Brazil; capital Cayenne; timezone GMT −3½; mixed Creole, European, and Amerindian population; official language, French; chief religion, Roman Catholicism; unit of currency, the franc; low-lying near the coast; rises S towards the Serra de Tumucumaque, reaching 635 m/2 083 ft at Mont Saint Marcel; many rocky islets along the coast, notably Devil's Island; hot and humid tropical climate; rainy season (Dec–Jun); average daily temperatures at Cayenne, 23–33°C; monthly rainfall 551 mm/21.7 in (May), 31 mm/1.2 in (Sep); area settled by Europeans, 17th-c; territory of France, 1817; used as penal colony 1798–1935; overseas department of France, 1946; elects two members to the French National Assembly; timber the main export, from forests covering c.80 000 sq km/ 30 000 sq ml; minerals little exploited; some bauxite, kaolin, gold; shrimps, rum, essence of rosewood; only 104 sq km/ 40 sq ml under cultivation; rice, maize, manioc, bananas, sugar cane, fruit, vegetables, spices; some cattle, pigs, poultry. » Cayenne; France [i]; Salut, Iles du

French history Traditionally divided into chronological periods reflecting the development of the French nation-state after the Gallo-Roman, Merovingian, and Carolingian periods. The accepted divisions coincide with dynasties and constitutions: the Capetians (987–1328); the Valois (1328–1589); the Bourbons (1589–1793); the Revolution and First Empire (1789–1814/15); the Restoration and July Monarchy (1815–48); the Second Republic (1848–52); the Second Empire (1852–70); the Third Republic (1870–1940); the Fourth Republic (1945–58); and the Fifth Republic (1958–). Within this framework certain episodes have evoked considerable controversy, such as the 1789 Revolution, and wartime France and the Vichy regime (1940–4). Political history fell somewhat out of favour with the pre-eminence of the *Annales* school and the present emphasis on social history through local studies, as in the work of French scholar, Emmanuel Le Roy Ladurie (1929–). » Bourbons; Capetians; Carolingians; French Revolution [i]; Merovingians; Valois

French horn » **horn**

French literature A literature emerging in the 12th-c from late Latin, which continued to exercise a powerful influence. The earliest vernacular works were the *chansons de geste*, soon followed by courtly romances dealing with both classical and Celtic subjects (Chrétien de Troyes' *Lancelot*, late 12th-c), and the allegorical romance, of which the *Roman de la Rose* (mid-13th-c) is the finest example, its two parts contrasting romance and early realism. François Villon (1431–?) was the most remarkable lyric poet in mediaeval France, to be matched by Ronsard of La Pléiade, while the greatest French writer of the 16th-c was Rabelais, with his inexhaustible masterpieces *Gargantua* and *Pantagruel* (1532–52). The 17th-c was a golden age in French literature, the milieu of court and salon producing not only the three great dramatists Corneille, Racine, and Molière, but the classicists Malherbe and Boileau, the philosopher Descartes, Pascal (*Pensées*, 1660), La Rochefoucauld (*Maximes*, 1665–78), and La Fontaine. It also saw the creation of the Académie Française by Richelieu in 1634. The 18th-c is best characterized by the rationalist satire of Voltaire and the vast *Encyclopédie* (1751–65) written under Diderot. Rousseau heralded the Romantic movement (*Confessions* 1764–70), which was powerfully represented in France by Chateaubriand and Lamartine, Musset, and Vigny, and by the dominating figure of Victor Hugo in verse and prose (*Les Misérables*, 1862). The Realist/Naturalist novel took centre stage in the mid-19th-c, with Balzac, Flaubert (*Madame Bovary*, 1857), and Zola; but the Symbolist poets claimed their due, in Baudelaire, Verlaine, Rimbaud, and Mallarmé.

In the 20th-c, French literature has been very diverse,

EVENTS OF THE FRENCH REVOLUTION, 1789–1799

1789

Mar–May	Election of deputies to the Estates General.
5 May	Opening of the Estates General.
17 Jun	Title of National Assembly adopted by the Third Estate.
Jul	The 'Great Fear'.
14 Jul	Seizing of the Bastille in Paris.
4 Aug	Abolition of the feudal regime.
26 Aug	Declaration of the Rights of Man and Citizen.
Oct	Foundation of the Club des Jacobins.
5–6 Oct	Louis XVI brought to Paris from Versailles.
19 Oct	National Assembly installed in Paris.

1790

19–23 Jun	Abolition of hereditary nobility and titles.
July	Foundation of the Club des Cordeliers.

1791

20–21 Jun	Flight of the King to Varennes.
16 Jul	Foundation of the Club des Feuillants.
13 Sep	Acceptance of the Constitution by the King.
Oct	Formation of the Legislative Assembly.

1792

9–10 Aug	Attack on the Tuileries. Functions of the King suspended.
12 Aug	King and royal family imprisoned in the Temple.
2–6 Sep	Massacre of nobles and clergy in prisons.
21 Sep	Abolition of the monarchy.
22 Sep	Proclamation of the Republic.

1793

17 Jan	National Convention votes for the death of the King.
21 Jan	Execution of the King.
1 Feb	Declaration of war against England and Holland.
Mar	Tribunal created in Paris (later called the Revolutionary Tribunal).
6 Apr	Creation of the Committee of Public Safety.
27 Jul	Robespierre elected to the Committee of Public Safety.
5 Sep–27 Jul 1794	Reign of Terror.
11 Sep	Creation of the Revolutionary Army of Paris.
16 Oct	Trial and execution of Marie Antoinette.
24–31 Oct	Trial and execution of the Girondins.

1794

5 Apr	Execution of the Cordeliers, including Danton.
24 Mar	Execution of the Hébertists.
8 Jun	Inaugural Feast of the Supreme Being and of Nature.
27 Jul (9 Thermidor)	Fall of Robespierre.
19 Nov	Closure of the Club des Jacobins.

1795

21 Feb	Separation of Church and State.
31 May	Suppression of the Revolutionary Tribunal.
8 Jun	Death of Louis XVII in the Temple.
5 Oct (13 Vendémiaire)	Royalists crushed by Bonaparte.
27 Oct–4 Nov	Institution of the Directory.

1799

9 Nov (18 Brumaire)	Abolition of the Directory.

ranging from the intense self-exploration of Proust and Genet and the experiments with the *nouveau roman* of Nathalie Sarraute and Robbe-Grillet to the Catholic revival with Claudel and Maritain and the political *engagement* of Aragon and Sartre. In addition, there is the existentialist fiction of Camus and the absurdist theatre of Ionescu and Beckett. Meanwhile, Surrealism in all its forms has remained a pervasive influence. » chansons de geste; classicism; fabliau; Latin literature; Naturalism (art); Neoclassicism (art and architecture); Realism (art and literature); romance; Romanticism (literature); Surrealism; Symbolism; Aragon; Balzac; Baudelaire; Beckett; Boileau; Camus; Chateaubriand; Claudel; Corneille; Diderot; Flaubert; Genet; Hugo; Ionesco; La Fontaine; La Rochefoucauld; Lamartine; Malherbe; Mallarmé; Maritain; Molière; Musset; Proust, Marcel; Rabelais; Racine; Rimbaud; Ronsard; Rousseau, Jean Jacques; Sarraute; Sartre; Verlaine; Vigny; Villon; Voltaire; Zola

French marigold » **African marigold**

French Polynesia, official name **Territory of French Polynesia**, formerly **French Settlements in Oceania** pop (1989e) 192 000; area 3 941 sq km/1 521 sq ml. Island territory comprising five scattered archipelagoes in the SE Pacific Ocean, between the Cook Is (W) and the Pitcairn Is (E); capital, Papeete; timezone GMT −6; chief ethnic group, Polynesian; chief religion, Christianity (87%); official language, French, with local languages widely spoken; island groups include the Society Is (including Tahiti and Bora-Bora), Tuamotu Archipelago, Gambier Is, Marquesas Is, and Tubuai Is; mainly volcanic, mountainous, and ringed with coral reefs; some low-lying coral atolls; hot and humid climate (Nov–Apr); tropical storms less frequent than in the W Pacific; French missionary activity, 19th-c; French protectorates introduced from 1842; 'French Oceania' became an Overseas Territory, 1958; administered by a high commissioner and 10-member Council of Ministers, elected by a 30-member Territorial Assembly; economy based on agricultural smallholdings (vegetables, fruit) and plantations (coconut oil, copra); cultured pearls, vanilla, citrus fruits, tourism; maintenance of the French nuclear test base. » Marquesas Islands; Mururoa; Papeete; Society Islands; Tuamotu Archipelago; Tahiti; Tubuai Islands

French Republican calendar A calendar introduced during the French Revolution by the National Convention to herald the beginning of a new epoch for France and for humanity in general, and to further the anti-clerical campaign for dechristianization. The structure and nomenclature were devised by a committee under the deputy, Fabre d'Eglantine, Year 1 dating from the abolition of the monarchy and the declaration of the Republic (22 Sep 1792). Twelve 30-day months were introduced and divided into three 10-day weeks of *decadi*, eliminating Sundays. They were given names derived from nature, notably from the seasons: Vendémiaire, Brumaire, Frimaire, Nivôse, Pluviôse, Ventôse, Germinal, Floréal, Prairial, Messidor, Thermidor, and Fructidor. The system was abolished under Napoleon (1805). » calendar; French Revolution [i]; Thermidor

French Revolution (1789) A complex upheaval, profoundly affecting every aspect of government and society, and therefore considered a significant turning point in French history. Although its causes have been subject to conflicting interpretation, conventionally the start was the summoning of the States General (spring 1789). Subsequently the National Assembly and its successor, the Constituent Assembly, responded to public pressure, such as the storming of the Bastille (14 Jul 1789), with wide-sweeping political, social, and economic measures (1789–91). These included the abolition of feudal, aristocratic, and clerical privileges, a Declaration of the Rights of Man, the establishment of a constitutional government, the confiscation of church estates, and a reorganization of Church-state relations in the Civil Constitution of the Clergy (1790). Thus the *ancien régime* was effectively dismantled in the name of liberty, equality, and fraternity.

Meanwhile the royal family had been removed from Versailles to Paris (Oct 1789, but after their flight to Varennes (Jun 1791) their fate was sealed. A Legislative Assembly was elected, and France was declared a republic (1792). Louis XVI and his queen, Marie Antoinette, were executed (1793). The Revolution then entered more dramatic phases, marked by political extremism and bitter rivalry between Girondins and Jacobins (the latter led by Robespierre). Though the Jacobins seized control of the Committee of Public Safety (Jul 1793) and instituted the dictatorship of the Terror, Robespierre's short-lived triumph ended with his execution (1794). The Convention suppressed the sans-culottes with military force before establishing the government of the Directory (1795), which was in turn overthrown by Napoleon Bonaparte in the Brumaire coup (1799). Under the Consulate (1799–1804) and the First Empire (1804–15), many of the ideas of the Revolution, such as popular sovereignty and civil equality, were disseminated in those areas of Europe subjected to French rule. » *ancien régime*; Bastille; Chouans; Directory; French Republican calendar; French Revolutionary Wars; Girondins; Jacobins (French history); Mountain, the; Plain, the; Public Safety, Committee of; Reign of Terror; sans-culottes; Babeuf; Barère; Barnave; Barras; Beauharnais; Blanqui; Brissot de Warville; Carnot, Lazare; Condorcet; Corday; Danton; Desmoulins; Fouché; Hébert; Louis XVI; Marat; Marie Antoinette; Mirabeau; Napoleon I; Orléans, Duke of; Paine; Robespierre; Rousseau, Jean Jacques; Saint-Just; Sieyès; Talleyrand; Tallien

French Revolutionary Wars (1792–9) A series of campaigns between France and neighbouring European states hostile to the Revolution and to French hegemony, merging ultimately into the Napoleonic Wars (1799–1815). Starting with France's declaration of war on Emperor Francis II, Prussia, and Sardinia, which precipitated the War of the First Coalition (1792–7), French forces attacked the Rhine, the Netherlands, and Savoy, after checking an initial Austro-Prussian advance at Valmy (1792). France later extended hostilities to Britain, Holland, and Spain (1793); after successfully invading the Netherlands (1794), the French broke the Coalition (1795–6), isolating Britain (1797). A Second Coalition (1798) expelled French forces from Italy and the Rhinelands, before suffering defeat by Napoleon (1799–1800). » Dumouriez; French Revolution [i]; Mortier; Murat; Napoleonic Wars

French Southern and Antarctic Territories, Fr **Terres Australes et Antarctiques Françaises** French overseas territory, comprising Adélie Land in Antarctica and the islands of Kerguélen, Crozet, Amsterdam, and St Paul in the S Indian Ocean; established, 1955; governed by an administrator and 7-member consultative council which meets twice-yearly in Paris. » Adélie Land; Antarctica [i]

French Union A term for the French Empire introduced by the constitution of the Fourth Republic in 1946. Former colonies were reclassified as departments of France or overseas territories; trust territories became overseas territories; and former protectorates became associated states. The latter had all become independent when the Union was replaced by the Community in 1958. » colony; French Community; protectorate; Trust Territory

Freon » **CFCs**

frequency The number of complete cycles per second for a vibrating system or other repetitive motion; symbol f or v; measured in Hertz, Hz. For wave motion, it corresponds to the number of complete waves per second. The frequency of tuning C on the piano is 523.25 Hz; the frequency of yellow light 5×10^{14}Hz. » frequency modulation; wave (physics) [i]

frequency modulation (FM) In wave motion, the altering of frequency in a systematic way, leaving amplitude unchanged. In FM radio, an electrical signal modulates the frequency of a broadcast carrier radio wave by an amount proportional to the signal amplitude. Demodulation takes place in the radio receiver to give a copy of the original signal. » amplitude; frequency; modulation; radio waves; superheterodyne; wave (physics) [i]

fresco An ancient technique for painting on walls, perfected in the 14th–16th-c in Italy; it is difficult, and is nowadays uncommon. The wall is prepared with layers of plaster, sometimes as many as four, the penultimate (*arricciato*) being marked out with the artist's design (underdrawing or *sinopia*). The final layer of lime-plaster (*intonaco*) is then laid, and, while it is still wet (*fresco* means 'fresh' in Italian), the artist works on this with a water-based paint. Just enough intonaco is laid for one day's work (*giornata*). The colours bond into the plaster by chemical action and are therefore very permanent, but they dry lighter, a factor the artist must bear in mind. » cartoon (art); Correggio; Giotto; Masaccio; Michelangelo; Piero della Francesca; Raphael; sinopia

Fresno 36°44N 119°47W, pop (1980) 218 202. Capital of Fresno County, C California, USA; founded, 1872; city status, 1889; airfield; railway; university; centre of a wine-producing region; grapes, grain, cotton, cattle, agricultural machinery, food processing. » California

Freud, Anna [froyd] (1895–1982) Viennese-born British psychoanalyst, the daughter of Sigmund Freud. She chaired the Vienna Psychoanalytic Society, and emigrated with her father to London in 1938, where she organized (1940–5) a residential war nursery for homeless children. A founder of child psychoanalysis, she died in London. » psychoanalysis

Freud, Sigmund [froyd] (1856–1939) Austrian founder of psychoanalysis, born at Freiburg, Moravia, of Jewish parentage. He studied medicine at Vienna, then specialized in neurology, and later in psychopathology. Finding hypnosis inadequate, he substituted the method of 'free association', allowing the patient to express thoughts in a state of relaxed consciousness, and interpreting the data of childhood and dream recollections. He became convinced, despite his own puritan sensibilities, of the fact of infantile sexuality, a theory which isolated him from the medical profession. In 1900 he published his major work, *Die Traumdeutung* (The Interpretation of Dreams), arguing that dreams are disguised manifestations of repressed sexual wishes (in contrast with the widely-held modern view that dreams are simply a biological manifestation of the random firing of brain neurones during a particular state of consciousness). In 1902, he was appointed to a professorship in Vienna, despite previous academic anti-semitism, and began to gather disciples. Out of this grew the Vienna Psychoanalytical Society (1908) and the International Psychoanalytic Association (1910), which included Adler and Jung. It was not until 1930, when he was awarded the Goethe prize, that his work ceased to arouse active opposition from public bodies. In 1933 Hitler banned psychoanalysis, and after Austria had been overrun, Freud and his family were extricated from the hands of the Gestapo and allowed to emigrate. He settled in Hampstead, London, where he died. » ego; Freud, Anna; Freudian criticism; Neo-Freudian; psychoanalysis

Freudian criticism Literary criticism which uses the insights of psychoanalysis, as in Freud's own reading of *Hamlet* in terms of the Oedipus complex (1900); also known as **psychoanalytical criticism**. Such criticism may be 'reductive', although Freud himself cautioned against offering simple psychoanalytic explanations for complex works of art. The early tendency to psychoanalyse characters or, more doubtfully, their creators, has been replaced or at least supplemented by a recognition of the fluidity of the self and a more sophisticated awareness of how language transgresses the boundary of conscious/unconscious. Analysis therefore involves the whole critical discourse, including author, text, and reader. » Freud, Sigmund; literary criticism; Oedipus complex; psychoanalysis

Frey » **Freya**

Freya or **Freyja** [**fray**a] In Northern mythology, the goddess of love and beauty, especially first love. She and her brother **Frey**, the male fertility god, were the children of Niord and Skadi. To obtain the Brising necklace she betrayed her husband, Odur, and had to wander through the world looking for him. » Germanic religion

friar A member of one of the mendicant ('begging') Christian religious orders founded in the Middle Ages. Unlike monks, they are not confined to a single monastery or abbey. » Augustinians; Carmelites; Dominicans; Franciscans

friarbird A bird of the honeyeater family, native to N Australia and the adjacent islands of SE Asia, also known as the **leatherhead**; songbird with head partly or totally naked (hence

Friarbird

its common names); eats fruit, insects, and nectar. (Genus: *Philemon*, 17 species. Family: *Meliphagidae*.) » honeyeater

Friars balsam A resin from the stem of *Styrax benzoin* and *S. paralleloneurus* containing aromatic acids (benzoic and cinnamic acids), prepared in an alcoholic solution. It is used as an inhalation in the treatment of chronic bronchitis, and can also be used undiluted as an antiseptic. » bronchitis; resin

Fribourg [**free**boorg], Ger **Freiburg** [**friy**boork] 46°49N 7°09E, pop(1980) 37 400. Mediaeval town and capital of Fribourg canton, W Switzerland; on a peninsula in the R Sarine, 27 km/17 ml SW of Bern; founded, 1178; persisted as a Catholic stronghold in the Reformation; bishopric; railway junction; university (1889); foodstuffs, beer, engineering; Cathedral of St Nicholas (13th–15th-c), Church of the Woodcutters (13th-c), town hall (16th-c). » Switzerland [i]

Fricker, Peter (Racine) (1920–90) British composer, born in London. Educated at St Paul's School and the Royal College of Music, he became musical director of Morley College, London (1952–64), professor of music at California (1964–5), and then resident composer there. Influenced by Bartók and Schoenberg, he has written several symphonies, an oratorio, *The Vision of Judgment* (1957–8), and other chamber, choral, and keyboard works. He died in Los Angeles.

friction A force acting against the direction of motion for two objects in contact sliding across one another. Friction may be sufficient to prevent actual relative motion. It is caused by surface roughness, and by the attraction of the atoms of one surface for those of the other. The **coefficient of friction**, μ, expressed as a number, has only two possible values for a given pair of surfaces, depending on whether the surfaces are moving relative to one another (the *kinetic coefficient of friction*) or are stationary (the *static coefficient of friction*, which is larger). A small coefficient of friction means that the two surfaces slide easily across one another. » rheology; surface physics; tribology; viscosity

Friedan, Betty (Naomi), *née* **Goldstein** (1921–) US feminist leader and author, born at Peoria, Illinois. She studied at Smith College, and emerged to fame in 1963 with the publication of her book *The Feminine Mystique*. She was the founder and first president of the National Association for Women in 1966. In *The Second Stage* (1981), she emphasised the importance of both the new and the traditional female roles. » feminism

Friedman, Milton [**freed**man] (1912–) US economist, born in New York City. Educated at Rutgers and Columbia, he was in US government service before becoming professor of economics at Chicago (1948–83). A leading monetarist, his work includes the permanent income theory of consumption, and the role of money in determining events, particularly the US Great Depression. His ideas have been influential with a number of right-wing governments. He was awarded the Nobel Prize for Economics in 1976. » Great Depression; monetarism

friendly society A voluntary mutual-aid organization in the UK which provides financial assistance to members in times of sickness, unemployment, or retirement. The register of Friendly Societies includes some that are several hundred years old. Their operations are governed by the Friendly Society Acts (1974–1984). » insurance

Friends of the Earth An international federation of environmental pressure groups with autonomous organizations in member countries. It conducts campaigns on topics such as safe energy, the recycling of waste, acid rain, tropical rainforest destruction, the preservation of endangered species, and transport. » environmentalism

Friends, Society of A Christian sect founded by George Fox and others in mid-17th-c England, and formally organized in 1667; members are popularly known as **Quakers**, possibly because of Fox's injunction 'to quake at the word of the Lord'. Persecution led William Penn to establish a Quaker colony (Pennsylvania) in 1682. Belief in the 'inner light', a living contact with the divine Spirit, is the basis of its meetings for worship, where Friends gather in silence until moved by the Spirit to speak. They emphasize simplicity in all things, and are active reformers promoting tolerance, justice, and peace. Today most meetings have programmed orders of worship, though meetings based on silence (unprogrammed) still prevail in the UK and parts of the USA. » Christianity; Fox, George

Friese-Greene, William, originally **William Edward Green** (1855–1921) British photographer and inventor, born in Bristol. In the 1880s he designed a camera to expose a sequence of photographs for projection by lantern slides as a moving image, and is thus claimed by some as the English inventor of cinematography; but he did not in fact propose perforated strips of film for either photography or projection. He died in poverty in London. » cinematography

Friesland [**frees**lant], ancient **Frisia** pop(1984e) 597 200; land area 3 352 sq km/1 294 sq ml. Province in N Netherlands; includes most of the West Frisian Is; capital, Leeuwarden; chief towns, Harlingen, Sneek; major livestock farming area, specializing in butter and Frisian cattle; extensive land reclamation along North Sea coast. » Frisian Islands; Netherlands, The [i]

frieze The middle part of an entablature on a classical building, usually decorated. It may also be the decorative band running along the upper part of an internal wall and below the cornice. » cornice; entablature; Greek/Roman architecture

frigate A small warship in World War 2, superior in speed and armament to a corvette, but less powerful and smaller than a destroyer. Its present role is mainly anti-submarine and general purpose. In days of sail, frigates were used as scouts for the main fleet, being smaller, faster, and less heavily armed than ships of the line. » corvette; destroyer; warships [i]

frigate bird A large bird, native to tropical seas; male with coloured inflatable pouch on throat; steals fish from other birds; unable to take off from level ground, but a good flier, covering long distances. (Genus: *Fregata*, 5 species. Family: *Fregatidae*.) » Plate IX

Frigg or **Frigga** In Norse mythology, the wife of Odin, and goddess of married love (often confused with Freya). » Germanic religion; Odin

frigidity A condition in which the female's participation in the sexual act is not accompanied by physiological or psychological arousal, and there is loss of sexual desire. It is sometimes associated with dyspareunia. » dyspareunia

frilled lizard An agamid lizard native to New Guinea and N Australia; slim body; neck with large cape-like frill of brightly coloured skin; frill usually folded, but can be expanded in courtship and to deter predators; inhabits dry woodland; may climb tree or run upright on hind legs when alarmed. (*Chlamydosaurus kingi*.) » agamid

Friml, (Charles) Rudolf (1879–1972) Czech composer, born in Prague. He studied at the Prague Conservatory, and in 1906 settled in the USA, where he made a name as a composer of light operas, including *Rose Marie* (1924) and *The Vagabond King* (1925.) He became a US citizen in 1925, and died in Hollywood. » opera

Fringe, the Cultural events, particularly theatrical performances, presented around a Festival but not central to it. The term has thus come to be applied to theatre groups working on the margins of the establishment, or to any style of theatre not part of orthodoxy.

Fringillidae [frin**jil**uhdee] A family of small seed-eating birds (approximately 125 species); native to the Americas, Eurasia, and Africa, and introduced in Australasia; also known as **finches**; 9 large primary feathers in wing, 12 large feathers in tail; female builds nest and incubates eggs. » finch

fringing reef » atoll

Frisbee A plastic disc approximately the size of a dinner plate, thrown through the air. Most are used as a leisure pursuit, but competitions exist. The Frisbee was introduced in the USA in the late 1950s by the Wham-O Manufacturing Company. The name is said to have derived from the defunct Frisbie Baking Company which produced the Mother Frisbie's Pies.

Frisch, Max (Rudolf) (1911–91) Swiss playwright and novelist, born in Zürich. He became a newspaper correspondent and a student of architecture, while developing his literary career. His novels include *Stiller* (1954), a satire on the Swiss way of life, *Homo Faber* (1957), and *Bluebeard* (1983). His plays, modern morality pieces, include *Nun singen sie wieder* (1945, Now They Sing Again), *Andorra* (1962), and *Triptych* (1981). » drama; novel

Frisch, Otto Robert (1904–79) Austrian physicist, born in Vienna. He studied at Vienna, and in 1939 became head of the nuclear physics division at Harwell. He and Meitner (his aunt) first described 'nuclear fission' in 1939 to explain Hahn's results with uranium and neutrons. During World War 2 he was involved in atomic research at Los Alamos, USA. In 1947 he became professor of natural philosophy at Cambridge, and directed the nuclear physics department of the Cavendish Laboratory. He died at Cambridge. » Hahn; Meitner; nuclear physics

Frisch, Ragnar (Anton Kittil) (1895–1973) Norwegian economist, born in Oslo. A pioneer of econometrics, he created national economic planning decision models, and advised developing countries. In 1969 he shared the first Nobel Prize for Economics. » econometrics; economics; Tinbergen, Jan

Frisian » Germanic languages

Frisian Islands Island chain in the North Sea, extending along the coasts of the Netherlands, Germany, and Denmark, and politically divided between these countries; includes the **North Frisian Is** (Ger **Nordfriesische Inseln**), notably (German) Sylt, Föhr, Nordstrand, Pellworm, Amrum, and (Danish) Rømø, Fanø, Mandø; the German **East Frisian Is** (Ger **Ostfriesische Inseln**), notably Borkum, Juist, Norderney, Langeoog, Spiekeroog, Wangerooge; and the Dutch **West Frisian Is** (Dutch **Friese Eilanden**), notably Texel, Vlieland, Terschelling, Ameland, Schiermonnikoog; tourism, fishing, sheep, cattle, potatoes, oats; several areas of reclaimed land. » North Sea

fritillary (botany) [fri**til**uhree] A perennial with a small scaly bulb, native to Europe; stem growing to 50 cm/20 in; leaves grass-like, bluish; flower a broad bell 3–5 cm/1½–2 in, drooping, dull purple rarely white, with a distinctive chequered pattern; cultivated for ornament. It is also called **snake's head** and **Guinea flower** from its colour and the drooping habit of the flower. (*Fritillaria meleagris*. Family: *Liliaceae*.) » bulb; perennial

fritillary (entomology) [fri**til**uhree] A colourful, day-flying butterfly; wings typically yellow-brown with black markings; forelegs reduced, non-functional; eggs ribbed; caterpillars with spines. (Order: *Lepidoptera*. Family: *Nymphalidae*.) » butterfly; caterpillar

Frobisher, Sir Martin (c.1535–94) English navigator, born at Altofts, Yorkshire. He made several attempts to find a North-west Passage to Cathay (1576–8), reaching Labrador and Hudson Bay. In 1585 he commanded a vessel in Drake's expedition to the West Indies. Knighted for his services against the Armada, he died at Plymouth, Devon. » Drake, Francis; Spanish Armada

Fröding, Gustaf [**frer**ding] (1860–1911) Swedish poet, born near Karlstad. He studied at Uppsala, became a schoolmaster and journalist, and suffered several periods of mental illness. Perhaps the greatest Swedish lyric poet, he is often compared with Burns. His use of dialect and folksong rhythm in the portrayal of local characters can be seen in his first collection, *Guitarr och dragharmonika* (1891, Guitar and Concertina). He died in Stockholm. » poetry; Swedish literature

Froebel, Friedrich (Wilhelm August) [**frer**bl] (1782–1852) German educationist, born at Oberweissbach. He studied at Jena, Göttingen, and Berlin, and in 1805 began teaching at Frankfurt-am-Main. In 1816 he put into practice his educational system whose aim, to help the child's mind grow naturally and spontaneously, he expounded in *Die Menschenerziehung* (1826, The Education of Man). In 1836 he opened his first kindergarten school at Blankenburg, and spent the rest of his life organizing other such schools, as well as providing educational materials (eg geometrical shapes) for young children, to encourage learning through play. He died at Marienthal, Thuringia. » education

frog An amphibian of order *Anura* (3 500 species), found worldwide except in the Arctic and Antarctic; short body with less than 10 vertebrae in the spine; inhabits diverse environments. The smooth wet-skinned species are called **frogs**; the rough dry-skinned species (adapted to drier habitats) are called **toads**. This distinction reflects the different life styles of the species; there is no technical difference between the two (and the name *frog* is sometimes used for all species). Anurans of the family *Ranidae* are sometimes called **true frogs**, those of the family *Bufonidae* **true toads**. » amphibian; Anura; arrow-poison / goliath / hairy / tree frog; clawed / horned / midwife / spadefoot toad; bullfrog; natterjack

frogbit A free-floating aquatic plant producing stolons with leaves and roots at nodes, native to Europe and Asia; leaves 3 cm/1¼ in diameter, kidney-shaped; flowers unisexual, c.2 cm/¾ in diameter, white, 3-petalled. It produces winter buds which sink and remain dormant, floating to the surface in the spring. (*Hydrocharis morsus-ranae*. Family: *Hydrocharitaceae*.) » stolon

frogfish Bizarre bottom-dwelling fish found amongst rocks and marine growths of warm seas; length up to 20 cm/8 in; body with strong cryptic coloration, skin loose and warty, pectoral fins used for crawling across bottom; filament on front of head acts as lure to attract prey; includes *Antennarius hispidus*, also known as **toadfish**. (Genus: *Antennarius*. Family: *Antennariidae*.)

froghopper A small, hopping insect that feeds by sucking the sap of plants; also known as **cuckoo-spit insect** and **spittlebug**. The eggs are laid on the plants, and hatch into sedentary larvae which surround themselves with mucus-like cuckoo spit that protects them against drying out and predation. (Order: *Homoptera*. Family: *Cercopidae*, c.2 500 species.) » insect [i]; larva

frogmouth A large, nocturnal, nightjar-like bird native to Australasia (except New Zealand) and SE Asia; short but very broad bill (hence the name); inhabits forests; eats mainly small animals foraged from ground. (Family: *Podargidae*, 12 species.) » nightjar

Fröhlich, Alfred » Babinski, Joseph

Froissart, Jean [**frw**asah] (c.1333–c.1404) French historian and poet, born at Valenciennes, Hainault. He served Philippa of Hainault, wife of Edward III of England (1361–9), and also travelled widely in Scotland, France, and Italy. Returning to Hainault, he began to compile his *Chronicles*, wrote poems for noble patrons, and became private chaplain to Guy of Châtillon. His *Chronicles*, covering European history from 1325 to 1400, deal in particular with the Hundred Years' War, and were heavily influenced by his devotion to chivalric principles. » Hundred Years' War

Frome [froom] 51°14N 2°20W, pop (1981) 19 817. Town in Mendip district, Somerset, SW England; on the R Frome, 17 km/10 ml S of Bath; a town of Anglo-Saxon origin with narrow alleys and old stone houses; railway; textiles, plastics, printing, engineering, perry making; Longleat House (1568), 8 km/5 ml NE. » Somerset

Fromm, Erich (1900–80) German-US psychoanalyst, born in Frankfurt. Educated at Frankfurt, Heidelberg, Munich, and the Berlin Institute of Psychoanalysis, he held various university appointments before becoming professor of psychiatry at New York in 1962. A neo-Freudian, he is known for his investigations into motivation. His works include *Escape from Freedom* (1941) and *The Sane Society* (1955). He died at Muralto, Switzerland. » Freud, Sigmund; neo-Freudian

Frondes, the [frõd] A series of civil revolts in France during the

Regency of Anne of Austria, caused by economic grievances and the excessive opportunism of central government, directed by Cardinal Mazarin. The disturbances, named after a contemporary street urchins' game, developed into two phases: the Parlementaire Fronde (1648–9), and that of the Princes (1650–3). After the declaration of Louis XIV's majority (1651), the princes' opposition was slowly undermined; royal forces under Turenne recovered Paris (1652) and the provinces (1652–3), ending the most serious threat to the central government during the *ancien régime*. » Anne of Austria; Louis XIV; Mazarin; Turenne

front A meteorological term for the sharp boundary between two parcels of air of different origin and characteristics, along which a steep horizontal temperature gradient exists. A *warm front* is the leading boundary of tropical or warm air, and a *cold front* is the leading boundary of polar or cold air. Each front is associated with its characteristic weather. In a depression, the meeting of the cold front with the warm front results in an *occluded front*. » cold front; depression (meteorology) [i]; jet stream; occluded front; Polar front

Front de Libération Nationale » **FLN**

front projection The projection of an image on to an opaque screen to be viewed from the same side as the projector, the normal practice for cinema and audio-visual presentation. In a form of composite cinematography, a highly directional reflective screen is used to show a moving background scene against which actors in the foreground are photographed. » back projection; cinematography [i]; reflex projection; screen

Frontenac, Louis de Buade, Count of [frõtuhnak] (1620–98) French-Canadian statesman, born at St Germain-en-Laye, France. He served in the army, and in 1672 was appointed Governor of the French possessions in N America. He was recalled for misgovernment in 1682, but was sent out again in 1689. He extended the boundaries of New France down the Mississippi, launched attacks on New England villages, repulsed the British siege of Quebec, and broke the power of the Iroquois. He died in Quebec. » Iroquois

frost A meteorological condition which occurs when the air temperature is at or below the freezing point of water, causing condensation. It may cause considerable damage to plants, especially if ground frost is accompanied by air frost. » cloud [i]; condensation (physics)

Frost, Robert (Lee) (1874–1963) US poet, born in San Francisco. He studied at Harvard, and became a teacher, cobbler, and New Hampshire farmer before going to Britain (1912–15), where he published *A Boy's World* (1913) and *North of Boston* (1914), which gave him an international reputation. Back in the USA, he taught at Amherst and Michigan. *New Hampshire* (1923) won the Pulitzer Prize, as did his first *Collected Poems* in 1930 and *A Further Range* (1936). A last collection *In the Clearing* appeared in 1962. At the time of his death, in Boston, he was regarded as the unofficial laureate of the USA. » American literature; poetry

frostbite The damage of exposed parts of the body by the direct effect of extreme cold. The fingers, nose, or feet are especially vulnerable, and the part may die and become gangrenous. » gangrene

frottage A technique used by some modern artists, notably Max Ernst, whereby paper is placed over a textured surface, such as a plank of wood, and rubbed with a pencil or crayon producing an impression. It is often combined with collage. » collage; Ernst

Froude, James Anthony [frood] (1818–94) British writer and historian, born at Dartington, Devon. He was educated at Westminster and Oxford, where he became part of the Oxford Movement. His early novels were controversial, notably *The Nemesis of Faith* (1848), and he was forced to resign his post. He then worked as an essayist and editor, and wrote his *History of England* (12 vols 1856–69). He became rector of St Andrews in 1869, and professor of modern history at Oxford in 1892. He died at Kingsbridge, Devon. » Oxford Movement

fructose $C_6H_{12}O_6$. A simple sugar (a monosaccharide) found mainly in fruits in combination with glucose to produce the disaccharide, sucrose (table sugar). Fructose is twice as sweet as glucose, and has been used as a sweetening agent. Fructose consumption does not cause a rise in blood glucose, and so it can be tolerated by diabetics. Fructose intolerance is a very rare hereditary disease. » diabetes mellitus; disaccharide; glucose [i]; sucrose

fruit Strictly, the ripened ovary and seeds of a plant, but more generally used to include any structures closely associated with these, such as a swollen receptacle. A *simple* or *true* fruit develops from a flower with one or several fused carpels; an *aggregate* fruit from a flower with several free carpels; and a *multiple* fruit from several flowers. When structures or tissues other than those of the gynoecium are involved, the result is an *accessory* or *false* fruit. Fruits can be divided into two main groups: **dry** and **fleshy**; in the latter, the middle layer of the ovary wall becomes succulent. Further classification is based mainly on carpel or seed number, dehiscence (ie whether the fruit splits to release the seeds), and to a lesser extent on derivation of tissues. Dry fruits can be dehiscent or not; fleshy fruits are always indehiscent. Common names such as 'nut' and 'berry' are often wildly inaccurate in describing the actual type of fruit to which they are applied.

The role played in seed dispersal greatly influences the structure of the fruit, which may itself be dispersed as a single unit. Shape may be important for scattering the seeds, as with winged fruits, and in the use of bristles for attaching the fruit to passing animals or for anchoring it in the soil. Corky fruits provide buoyancy in water, while fleshy fruits may attract animals. Some plants produce different types of fruits to take advantage of more than one dispersal agent. A few plants are able to produce fruits without prior pollination and thus fertilization of the flowers, giving seedless fruits, eg banana, cucumber, and some citrus fruits. This trait, called *natural parthenocarpy*, can be commercially desirable, and fruit growers can imitate it by the use of hormones (*induced parthenocarpy*) to produce crops such as seedless tomotoes. » auxins; carpel; gibberellins; hormones; ovary; receptacle; seed

fruit bat » **bat**

fruit fly A common name for flies of the families *Drosophilidae* and *Tephritidae*; mostly tropical. The latter contains c.4 000 species of colourful flies, feeding on sap and fruit. Some are pests of economically important crops such as fruit, cucumber, and celery. (Order: *Diptera*.) » Drosophila [i]; fly

fruit sugar » **fructose**

Frunze [**frun**zye], formerly **Pishpek** (to 1925), now Bishkek (1991) 42°54N 74°46E, pop (1989) 616 000. Capital city of Kirghizia; in the Chu valley, at the foot of the Kirgizskiy Khrebet; altitude, 750–900 m/2 500–3 000 ft; founded, 1825; airport; railway; university (1951); major transportation, industrial, and cultural centre; agricultural machinery, textiles, foodstuffs, tobacco products. » Kirghizia

Fry, Christopher, originally **Christopher Harris** (1907–) British dramatist, born in Bristol. Educated at Bedford, he was a teacher and actor before becoming director of Tunbridge Wells Repertory Players (1932–6) and of the Playhouse at Oxford (1940). After service in World War 2 he began a series of major plays in free verse, often with undertones of religion and mysticism, including *A Phoenix too Frequent* (1946) and *The Lady's not for Burning* (1949). His later works include *Curtmantle* (1962) and *A Yard of Sun* (1970). » drama; English literature

Fry, Elizabeth (1780–1845) British Quaker prison reformer, born at Norwich, Norfolk. In 1810 she became a preacher in the Society of Friends, and after seeing the terrible conditions for women in Newgate prison, she devoted her life to prison reform at home and abroad. She also founded hostels for the homeless and charitable societies. She died at Ramsgate, Kent.

Fry, Roger (Eliot) (1866–1934) British art critic, aesthetic philosopher, and painter, born in London. Educated at Cambridge, he is mainly remembered for his support of the Postimpressionist movement in England. He propounded an extreme formal theory of aesthetics, seeing the aesthetic quality of a work of art solely in terms of its formal characteristics. He became Slade professor of fine art at Cambridge in 1933, and died in London. » aesthetics; Postimpressionism

FT-SE Index (Financial Times-Stock Exchange Index),

byname **Footsie** A UK share index which records changes in the prices of shares of 100 leading British companies. It has been in operation since 1982, when it started with a notional value of 1 000. » Dow Jones Index; index number

FT30 Index (Financial Times Index) A UK share index which records changes in the prices of shares of 30 leading British companies. It started in 1935 with a notional value of 100. » FT-SE Index; index number

Fu-chou » **Fuzhou**

Fuad I [**foo**ahd] (1868–1936) King of Egypt (1922–36), born in Cairo, the son of Khedive Ismail Pasha. He was sultan of Egypt from 1917, and became king when the British protectorate was ended. In an attempt to control the ultranationalist Wafd party, he suspended the constitution in 1931, but was forced to restore it in 1935. He was succeeded by his son, Farouk I. » Wafd

Fuchs, Klaus (Emil Julius) [fookhs] (1912–88) Former British atom spy, born at Rüsselsheim, Germany. Educated at Kiel and Leipzig, he escaped from Nazi persecution to Britain in 1933. Interned on the outbreak of World War 2, he was released and naturalized in 1942. From 1943 he worked in the USA on the atom bomb, and in 1946 became head of the theoretical physics division at Harwell, UK. In 1950 he was sentenced to 14 years' imprisonment for disclosing nuclear secrets to the Russians. On his release in 1959 he worked at East Germany's nuclear research centre until his retirement in 1979. » atomic bomb

Fuchs, Sir Vivien Ernest [fookhs] (1908–) British Antarctic explorer and scientist, born in Kent. Educated at Brighton College and Cambridge, he went on expeditions to E Africa (1929–38), served in World War 2, then became leader of the Falkland Islands Dependencies Survey (1947–50) and director (1950–5). As leader of the British Commonwealth Trans-Antarctic Expedition (1956–8), he made an overland crossing from Shackleton Base via the S Pole to Scott Base (3 500 km/2 200 ml). Knighted in 1958, he became director of the British Antarctic Survey (1958–73). » Antarctica [i]

fuchsia [**fyoo**shuh] An evergreen or deciduous shrub, native to C and S America and New Zealand; leaves lance-shaped to oval, paired or in whorls; flowers pendulous with a long, red 4-lobed tube surrounding a purple bell with projecting stamens and style; numerous cultivars show a wide range of flower colours. It was named in honour of the German physician and herbalist, Leonhard Fuchs (1501–66). (Genus: *Fuchsia*, 100 species. Family: *Onagraceae*.) » cultivar; deciduous plants; evergreen plants; shrub; stamen; style

Fucus [**fyoo**kuhs] Genus of brown seaweed, found in great abundance in inter-tidal zones of shores in the N hemisphere; some species have cavities in the blades for buoyancy; commonly known as **wrack**. (Class: *Phaeophyceae*. Order: *Fucales*.) » seaweed

fuel A substance capable of releasing thermal energy in chemical, electrochemical, or nuclear processes. The oldest are combustible natural fuels (such as wood and cow dung). The chief solid *fossil fuels* are fossil vegetable matter in various degrees of carbonization, such as coal, lignite, and peat. *Liquid fuels* include some vegetable oils, but are mainly petroleum products. *Gaseous fuels* mainly comprise manufactured and natural gas. Some use is made of gaseous products arising from the degradation of biological waste. *Fuel cells* operate on an electrochemical reaction which takes place between hydrogen and oxygen. *Nuclear fuels* consist of radioactive isotopes, emitting energy spontaneously by nuclear change. *Rocket fuels* operate by reaction against high speed gases emitted on combustion. Fuels may be used to provide heat for steam generation, for direct combustion or explosion within a machine, for promoting chemical or metallurgical processes, or for environmental heating. » coal; gas; nuclear reactor [i]; petroleum

fuel injection **1** In a diesel engine, the system that injects the fuel at high pressure directly into the combustion chamber. » diesel engine **2** In a petrol engine, a system that uses a special fuel/mixture control unit, as an alternative to a carburettor, to produce improved running and transient performance. In this system, the petrol is usually injected into the port immediately preceding the inlet valve rather than directly into the cylinder. » carburettor; engine

Fugard, Athol (Harold Lanigan) (1932–) South African dramatist and theatre director, born at Middleburg, Cape Province. Educated at Port Elizabeth Technical College and Cape Town University, he became director of the Serpent Players in Port Elizabeth (1965), and co-founded the Space Experimental Theatre, Cape Town (1972). His plays, set in contemporary South Africa, have met with official opposition, notably *Blood Knot* (1960) and *Boesman and Lena* (1969). He has also written film scripts and a novel, *Tsotsi* (1980). » African literature; drama; theatre

fugu [**fu**goo] A Japanese globe fish or puffer fish, eaten at special restaurants, cooked or in small slices, raw. Parts of this white fish are poisonous and cause instant death. Only restaurant staff who have passed the official examination and have a special licence are allowed to prepare it. It is nonetheless considered a delicacy. » sashimi

fugue A musical composition (or part of one) in which a single theme announced by each 'voice' in turn, serves to generate the whole, and usually reappears in different keys and sometimes in different guises (inverted, in shorter or longer note-values, etc). » counterpoint

Fujairah, Al [al foo**jiy**ra] pop (1980) 32 200; area 1 150 sq km/444 sq ml. Member state of the United Arab Emirates, bounded E by the Gulf of Oman; partly mountainous, with a fertile coastal plain and no desert; capital, Al Fujairah; people live mostly in scattered villages, depending on agriculture. » United Arab Emirates [i]

Fuji, Mount or **Fujiyama**, Jap **Fuji-san** [**foo**jee san] 35°23N 138°42E. Highest peak in Japan, in Chubu region, C Honshu; 88 km/55 ml WSW of Tokyo; dormant volcano rising to 3 776 m/12 388 ft; an isolated peak with an almost perfect cone; crater diameter c.600 m/2 000 ft; last eruption, 1707; snow-capped (Oct–May); sacred since ancient times; until the Meiji Restoration of 1868, no woman was allowed to climb it. » Honshu; Japan [i]; Meiji Restoration

Fujiwara style A style of art which flourished in Japan during the late Heian period (9th–12th-c). The aristocratic Fujiwara clan built temples and pagodas, decorated in a delicate, refined manner. » Japanese art

Fukuoka [fookuh**wo**ka], formerly **Najime** 33°39N 130°21E, pop (1980) 1 088 588. Port capital of Fukuoka prefecture, NE Kyushu, Japan; 145 km/90 ml NNE of Nagasaki; airport; railway; university (1911); institute of technology (1909); chemicals, textiles, paper, metal goods, shipbuilding; Dazaifu Temman gu nearby (10th-c shrine, restored 1950). » Kyushu

Fulani [ful**ah**nee], also called **Fulbe** or **Peul** Fula-speaking peoples dispersed across the Sahel zone of W Africa from Senegal to Cameroon. Originally pastoralists, they are today socially very diverse, and in many places are assimilated into the local culture. Predominantly Muslim, in the 19th-c they initiated several holy wars, and in some areas they established kingdoms. In the early 20th-c they became one of the prototypes of the indirect rule system. Population c.8 million. » indirect rule; Islam; sahel; pastoralism

Fulbe » **Fulani**

Fulbright, J(ames) William (1905–) US politician, lawyer, and author, born at Sumner, Missouri. Educated at the University of Arkansas, Oxford, and George Washington University Law School, he taught law in Washington and Arkansas, entered the House of Representatives as a Democrat in 1943, and the Senate in 1945. As chairman of the Senate Committee on Foreign Relations, he became a major critic of the Vietnam War. He lost his Senate seat in 1974. » Democratic Party; Vietnam War

Fuller, (Richard) Buckminster (1895–1983) US inventor, designer, and philosopher, born at Milton, Massachusetts. Educated at Harvard, he served in the US Navy (1917–19). He developed the Dymaxion ('dynamic and maximum efficiency') House in 1927, and the Dymaxion streamlined, omnidirectional car in 1932. He also developed the geodesic dome. An enthusiastic educationalist, he held a chair at S Illinois University (1959–75), and in 1962 became Norton professor of poetry at Harvard. His many books include *Nine Chains to the Moon*

(1938) and *Critical Path* (1981). He died in Los Angeles. » geodesic dome

Fuller, J(ohn) F(rederick) C(harles) (1878–1966) British general and military thinker, born at Chichester, Sussex. He served in South Africa, and in World War 1 as a staff officer with the Tank Corps. He planned the breakthrough tank battle of Cambrai in 1917, and proposed the unfulfilled 'Plan 1919', advocating an all-mechanized army. His ideas were discounted, and he retired in 1933 to continue his prophetic if controversial military writings. He died at Falmouth, Cornwall. » World War 1

Fuller, (Sarah) Margaret (1810–50) US writer, feminist, and revolutionary, born at Cambridgeport, Massachusetts. She entered the Transcendentalist circle that centred on Emerson, and despite a lack of higher education became known as one of its brightest stars. Her *Woman in the Nineteenth Century* (1845) is the earliest major piece of US feminist writing. She died in a shipwreck after taking part in the abortive Italian revolution of 1848. » Emerson, Ralph Waldo; feminism; transcendentalism

Fuller, Roy (Broadbent) (1912–91) British poet and novelist, born at Oldham, Lancashire. He trained as a solicitor, and served in the Royal Navy during World War 2. His first collection, *Poems*, appeared in 1939, and his war-time experiences prompted *The Middle of a War* (1942) and *A Lost Season* (1944). His later poetic works include *Brutus's Orchard* (1957) and *Retreads* (1979). His novels include *Second Curtain* (1953) and *Image of a Society* (1956). He was professor of poetry at Oxford (1968–73). *New and Collected Poems, 1934–84* were published in 1985. » English literature; novel; poetry

Fuller's earth Fine earthy material containing montmorillonite clay; formerly used for cleansing oil and grease from wool (*fullering*), and now used for clarifying vegetable oils by absorbing impurities. » clay

fuller's teasel » **teasel**

fulmar A marine tubenosed bird, native to N oceans (*Fulmarus glacialis*) or S oceans (2 species); comes to land only to breed; can eject oily and foul-smelling vomit to deter predators. (Family: *Procellariidae*.) » petrel; tubenose

fulminate A salt containing the ion CNO^-, also called **isocyanate**. As its name suggests (Lat 'thunder'), it is an explosive; $Hg(CNO)_2$ is used as a detonator. » explosives

Fulton, Robert (1765–1815) US engineer, born in Lancaster Co, Pennsylvania. He became a painter of miniature portraits and landscapes, then went to London (1786) and studied mechanical engineering. His inventions included a machine for spinning flax, a dredging machine, and the torpedo, but he is best known for his development of the steamboat, which he made a commercial success in the USA. He died in New York City. » engineering; steam engine

fumaric acid [fyoo**mar**ik] $C_2H_2(COOH)_2$, IUPAC **trans-butenedioic acid**, melting point 300°C (in a sealed tube). An unsaturated dicarboxylic acid, used in the manufacture of polyester resins. The salts are called *fumarates*, and are often used in preparations of drugs. It is a geometrical isomer of maleic acid. » carboxylic acids; isomers; maleic acid [i]; polyesters

fumitory A brittle-stemmed annual, sometimes scrambling or climbing, native to the N hemisphere and S Africa; leaves finely divided, bluish; flowers strongly zygomorphic, 2-lipped, with rounded spur. The name is sometimes claimed to mean 'ground smoke', referring to the foliage colour. There are two genera: *Corydalis*, petals lacking dark tips, capsules many-seeded; *Fumaria*, petals dark-tipped, nutlets 1-seeded. (Family: *Fumariaceae*.) » annual; capsule **1**; zygomorphic flower

Funafuti [foona**foo**tee] 8°30S 179°12E, pop (1983e) 2620. Port and capital town of Tuvalu, SW Pacific, on the E side of Funafuti atoll; airfield; US military base; copra. » Tuvalu

Funchal [**fun**shal] 32°40N 16°55W, pop (1981) 119 481. Capital of Madeira, on S coast of Ilha da Madeira; third largest Portuguese city; bishopric; exports Madeira wine, embroidery, fruit, fish, dairy produce, wickerwork; sugar milling, distilling, tobacco products, soap, canning; important port and tourist resort on the transatlantic route; cathedral (1485), forts (17th-c), Chapel of Santa Catarina (15th-c), São Lourenço Palace (16th-c), Jardim de São Francisco; Senhora do Monte festival (Aug). » Portugal [i]

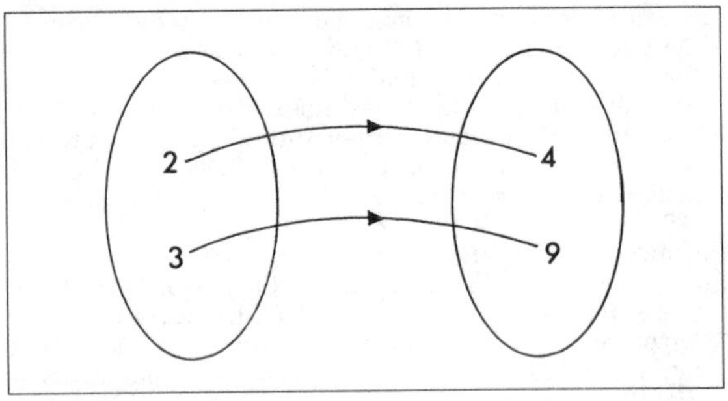

A function

function (mathematics) In mathematics, a relation which associates any one element in one set (the *domain*) with one and only one element in another set (the *range*). For example, the square function $f:x \to x^2$ maps 2 into 4, 3 into 9, and is shown by the graph in the illustration. » even functions [i]; set

functional group A part of a molecule with characteristic reactions. Important examples include the hydroxyl group, $-OH$, characteristic of alcohols, and the amino group, $-NH_2$, characteristic of amines. » aldehyde; carbonyl; carboxylic acids; ketone

functionalism (art and architecture) The theory, rooted in Greek philosophy, that beauty should be identified with functional efficiency. Occasionally discussed in the 18th-c and 19th-c, it became fashionable in the 1920s and 1930s, especially under Bauhaus influence. In architecture, the form of a building was to be determined by the function it was meant to fulfil – as in the famous definition of a house as a machine for living in. » Bauhaus; Corbusier, Le; Fuller, Buckminster; Gropius; International Style; rationalism (architecture)

functionalism (sociology) A theory widely accepted in social anthropology and sociology in the mid-20th-c, according to which particular social institutions, customs, and beliefs all have a part to play in maintaining a social system. The central notion is that a community or society has an enduring structure, its parts fitting together to form a single integrated system. In social theory, the approach was dominated by the work of two US sociologists: Talcott Parsons (1902–79) and Robert Merton (1910–). It is now generally thought that functionalism offers too static a view of social organization, and understates the conflicts which are likely to be present in the life of any community. The strength of functionalist theory was that it directed attention to the interrelationships between the institutions in a community. » anthropology; sociology; structuralism

fundamental constants A set of numerical quantities having the same fixed value for all observers. Values of these constants control all physical processes. Planck's constant, the velocity of light, the gravitational constant, Avogadro's number, the electron charge, the molar gas constant, permittivity, permeability, and certain particle masses are all regarded as fundamental constants. » Avogadro's number; gravitational constant; permeability; permittivity; velocity of light

fundamental forces » **forces of nature** [i]

Fundamental Orders (1639) In US colonial history, an agreement for self-government adopted by the Connecticut towns of Hartford, Windsor, and Wethersfield, and extended to other towns. It was replaced by a royal charter in 1662.

fundamental particles Those sub-atomic particles that are thought to be indivisible into smaller particles. They are the *matter* particles (quarks, neutrinos, electrons, muons, and taus) and the *force* particles (gluons, photons, W and Z bosons, and gravitons). » particle physics; sub-atomic particles

fundamentalism A theological tendency seeking to preserve what are thought to be the essential doctrines ('fundamentals') of the Christian faith. The term was originally used of the conservative US Protestant movement in the 1920s, characterized by a literal interpretation of the Bible, and revived with conservative Christian movements in the late 20th-c. Generally, it is any theological position opposed to liberalism. » Bible

Fundy, Bay of A bay separating the provinces of New Brunswick and Nova Scotia, E Canada. The world's greatest tidal height (16.2 m/53 ft) is used to generate electricity. » Canada [i]

Fünen » **Fyn**

fungicide Any chemical (eg sulphur or sulphur compounds) used to kill fungi that are harmful to plants, animals, or foodstuffs. It is particularly important in controlling rusts in cereals, blight in potatoes, and mildew in fruit. » fungus; sulphur

fungus A primitive plant that obtains its nourishment either *saprophytically*, by secreting enzymes to dissolve insoluble organic food externally before absorption, or *parasitically*, by absorbing food from a host. The body form may be single-celled, but usually consists of a network (*mycelium*) of thread-like strands (*hyphae*) which may produce a compact, fruiting body bearing the reproductive tissues. Cell walls are usually made of chitin, occasionally of cellulose. The true fungi belong to the division *Eumycota* of the kingdom *Plantae*, containing all fungi except the slime moulds and their allies. Fungi are sometimes classified as a separate kingdom characterized by their lack of flagella at all stages of the life cycle; those with flagellae are transferred to the kingdom *Protista*. Fungi fulfil a vital ecological role in recycling nutrients. Many are pests of crops or are human pathogens; some are edible or produce useful by-products. » Ascomycetes; Basidiomycetes; bread mould; cell; cellulose; chanterelle; chitin; cup/honey/rust/smut fungus; death cap; dry rot; earthstar; ergot; flagellum; fungicide; inkcap; morel; mushroom; mycology; potato blight; slime mould; truffle; wet rot; yeast

funnel-web spider A predatory spider that constructs a funnel-shaped web to trap its prey. Some species are venomous. The bite of the Australian funnel-web spider causes severe pain, blindness, and paralysis of the respiratory muscles. (Class: *Arachnida*. Order: *Araneae*.) » spider

fur A covering of hairs found today only in mammals, though there is some evidence that extinct flying reptiles had fur. It presumably evolved as a means of controlling heat loss from the body (most modern mammals maintain a constant body temperature). » hair; mammal [i]; reptile

Furies » **Erinyes**

furniture beetle A small, brown beetle; larvae, known as **woodworm**, are C-shaped, white and fleshy with tiny legs, which bore into dead wood as they feed; adults emerge leaving typical woodworm holes. (Order: *Coleoptera*. Family: *Anobiidae*.) » beetle; larva

Fürstenbund [**für**shtenbunt] A league of German Princes founded at Frederick the Great's instigation in the last phase of his conflict with the Austrian Habsburgs. The leading German states (eg Prussia, Saxony, Hanover, Baden, Saxe-Weimar, Palatinate-Zweibrucken) signed an agreement in Berlin (1785) to preserve the status quo, countering the ambitions of Emperor Joseph II. » Frederick II (of Prussia); Habsburgs; Joseph II

further education A level of educational provision offered in many countries, often distinguished from *higher education*. Further education is post-school education leading, usually, to qualifications at sub-degree level, though it may not lead to any award at all but simply be taken for its own sake. A great deal is of a vocational nature, and involves study and practical work related to someone's job; but it can also be non-vocational, and take place in informal settings like the home. Higher education, by contrast, takes place in institutions where most or all of the work is at degree level or above. » education; vocational education

Furtwängler, (Gustav Heinrich Ernst Martin) Wilhelm [**foort**vengluh] (1886–1954) German conductor, born in Berlin. He studied in Munich, and in 1922 became conductor of the Gewandhaus concerts in Leipzig and of the Berlin Philharmonic. International tours established his reputation, though his highly subjective interpretations of the German masters aroused controversy. His ambivalent attitude to the Hitler regime cost him some popularity outside Germany, but after the war he quickly re-established himself. He died near Baden-Baden, Germany.

furze » **gorse**

fusel oil [**fyoo**zl] Organic material obtained along with ethanol in fermentation, mostly alcohols of higher molecular weight, with 3, 4, or 5 carbon atoms. The presence of a very small proportion of the alcohols contributes to the characteristic flavour of fermented beverages, pleasant or otherwise; larger quantities tend to cause thirst and headaches. » ethanol; fermentation

Fuseli, Henry, originally **Johann Heinrich Füssli** (1741–1825) British painter and art critic, born in Zürich, Switzerland. He went to England in 1763, where he worked as a translator, then studied painting in Italy (1770–8). His 200 paintings include 'The Nightmare' (1781) and two series to illustrate Shakespeare's and Milton's works, by which he is chiefly known. He became professor of painting at the Royal Academy in 1799, and died in London. » English art

fusional language A type of language in which words contain several features of meaning that cannot be identified in a one-to-one way with the sequence of forms which make up the words; also known as **inflecting** languages. For example, in the Latin *dominus* ('lord'), the suffix *-us* 'fuses' the meanings of 'masculine', 'nominative', and 'singular'. » derivation

futhark [**fuhth**ahk] » **runes** [i]

futon [fu**ton**] A Japanese quilt, equivalent to Western eiderdowns or duvets, traditionally filled with (heavy) cotton padding (now polyester or feathers). Most Japanese sleep on a *futon* on the thick *tatami* matting, with another on top in winter. All bedding is kept in a cupboard during the day, leaving the room free for use. » tatami

futures In economics, a *futures market* (or *terminal market*) is where commodities are bought and sold for delivery at some future date. Speculators may buy futures in the hope that the price will rise, and thus be able to make a profit by selling on. A *futures contract* enables sellers to guard against the risk that the price will fall, and protects buyers from the risk that the price will rise (*hedging*). There is also a market in financial futures: *LIFFE* [liyf], the *London International Financial Futures Exchange*, which deals with foreign exchange, interest rates, and equities. » equity (economics); foreign exchange; interest

Futurism A modern art movement founded by the poet Marinetti in Milan in 1909. Futurism glorified machinery, war, speed, and the modern world generally; artists included Boccioni, Carrà, Balla, and Severini, working in a style derived from Cubism. It had petered out by c.1918. » Cubism; modern art; Vorticism; Balla; Boccioni; Carrà; Marinetti; Severini

futurology A controversial area of study which aims to discern the shape of future developments on the basis of analysing the present and the past. A distinction is made between *projections*, based on collected data and existing trends, and *conjectures*, which are mostly speculative. » history

Fuzhou [foo**joh**], **Fu-chou**, or **Foochow** 26°09N 119°17E, pop (1984e) 1 164 800. Provincial capital of Fujian province, SE China; on N bank of Min Jiang R, founded 202 BC; capital of autonomous state, 10th-c; open port, 1842; airfield; railway; steel, fishing, food processing; trade in rice, sugar cane, tea, oranges, fruit; West Lake Park (imperial garden), Twin Pagodas, White Pagoda (904, rebuilt 1548), Ebony Pagoda (941), several temples on Yushan and Wushan hills; 10 km/6 ml outside city is Yongquan Si (Bubbling Spring Temple), containing a tooth of Buddha. » Buddha; China [i]; Opium Wars

Fyn [foon] or **Funen**, Ger **Fünen** pop (1981e) 453 626; area 3 486 sq km/1 346 sq ml. Danish island between S Jutland and Zealand, bounded by the Little Belt (W) and the Great Belt (E); capital, Odense; other towns include Svendborg and Nyborg; second largest island in Denmark; agriculture ('the garden of Denmark'); Viking remains; train ferry from Nyborg to Korsør. » Denmark [i]

g-factor In atomic, nuclear, and particle physics, a factor which relates a point-like particle's magnetic moment to its spin; also known as the **Landé g-factor**, after US physicist Alfred Landé (1888–). For electrons, the *g*-factor is the gyromagnetic ratio in units of μ_B, the Bohr magnetron. From relativistic quantum mechanics, a point-like electron should have $g=2$; experiments yield a value about 0.1% larger. Corrections are calculated using quantum electrodynamics, which considers the electron as a bare particle surrounded by a cloud of (virtual) photons that alter the *g* value. The corrected calculated value agrees with the experiment to better than eight decimal places. It is an important test of quantum electrodynamics, sometimes called the most precise theory in physics, because of the *g*-factor agreement. » Bohr magnetron; gyromagnetic ratio; magnetic moment; quantum electrodynamics; spin

gabbro A coarse-grained basic (low in silica) igneous rock composed of calcic plagioclase feldspar, pyroxene, and sometimes olivine. » igneous rock; silica

Gabin, Jean [gabĩ], originally **Jean-Alexis Moncorge** (1904–76) French actor, born in Paris. He started his stage career as a music-hall singer and dancer, and played light juvenile leads in films from 1930, but a series of dramatic roles brought him greater depth and international recognition, especially in *Pépé Le Moko* (1936), *Quai des Brumes* (1938, Port of Shadows) and *Le Jour se Lève* (1939, Daybreak). After the War he continued to appear frequently in tough character roles until shortly before his death in Paris.

Gable, (William) Clark (1901–60) US actor, born at Cadiz, Ohio. He had various industrial jobs before joining a small theatrical stock company. His first leading film role was in *The Painted Desert* (1931). Growing popularity in tough but sympathetic parts soon labelled him the 'King of Hollywood', reaching its peak with his portrayal of Rhett Butler in *Gone With the Wind* (1939). In 1942, after the death of his third wife (Carole Lombard) in an air crash, he joined the US 8th Air Force and was decorated for bomber combat missions. He died at Reno, Nevada, immediately after completing his role in *The Misfits* (1961).

Gabo, Naum, originally **Naum Neemia Pevsner** (1890–1977) US Constructivist sculptor, born at Bryansk, Russia. In 1920 he helped to form the group of Russian Constructivists, who had considerable influence on 20th-c architecture and design. Forced into exile, he lived in Berlin, Paris, and England, moving to the USA in 1946. He died at Waterbury, Connecticut. » Constructivism

Gabon [gabohn] official name **Gabonese Republic**, Fr **République Gabonaise** pop (1990e) 1 170 000; area 267 667 sq km/103 319 sq ml. Republic of W equatorial Africa, divided into nine provinces; bounded S, E, and NE by the Congo, N by Cameroon, NW by Equatorial Guinea, and W by the Atlantic Ocean; capital, Libreville; chief towns include Lambaréné and Franceville; timezone GMT +1; population comprises c.40 Bantu tribes (notably, Fang), and c.10% expatriate Africans and Europeans; chief religion, Christianity; official language, French; unit of currency, the franc CFA.

Physical description and climate. On the Equator for 880 km/550 ml W–E; lagoons and estuaries on coast; land rises towards the African central plateau, cut by several rivers, notably the Ogooué; typical equatorial climate, hot, wet, and humid; annual average rainfall, 1 250–2 000 mm/50–80 in inland; Libreville rainfall, 2 510 mm/99 in, average maximum daily temperature, 33–37°C.

History and government. Visited by Portuguese, 15th-c; under French control from mid-19th-c; 1849, slave ship captured by the French, the liberated slaves forming the settlement of Libreville; occupied by France, 1885; one of four territories of French West Africa, 1910; independence, 1960; governed by a president elected for a 7-year term, an appointed Council of Ministers, and a legislative National Assembly of 111 elected and 9 appointed members serving a 5-year term.

Economy. Small area of land under cultivation, but employing 65% of population; corn, coffee, cocoa, bananas, rice, yams, cassava; major industry, timber extraction, notably of okoumé (world's largest producer); rapid economic growth since independence, largely because of offshore oil, natural gas, and minerals; manganese, gold, uranium; timber and mineral processing, food processing, oil refining; completion of a road-building programme and the Trans-Gabon railway system have been a stimulus to the economy. » Libreville; RR25 national holidays; RR50 political leaders

Gaboon viper or **Gabon viper** One of the largest vipers (length, up to 2 m/6½ ft), with the longest fangs of any viper (50 mm/2 in); broad flat head shaped like an arrow-head, with two small 'horns' between nostrils; inhabits African forest; body with bold markings resembling leaves on forest floor; nocturnal; moves little; eats small vertebrates. » viper [i]

Gabor, Dennis (1900–79) Hungarian-British physicist, born in Budapest. He studied at Berlin, and became a research engineer. Leaving Germany in 1933, he worked for a British company before joining the staff of Imperial College, London (1948), where he became professor of applied electron physics (1958–67). In 1971 he received the Nobel Prize for Physics for his invention of holography. He died in London. » holography

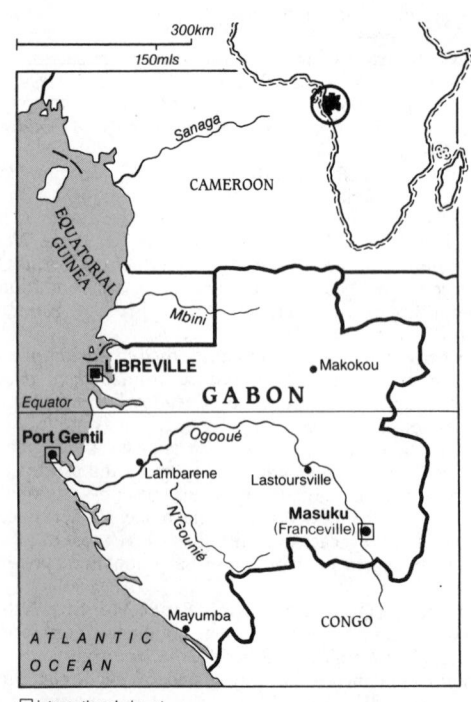

□ international airport

Gaborone [gabuh**roh**nay] 24°45S 25°55E, pop(1981) 59 657. Independent township and capital of Botswana, S Africa; altitude 1 000 m/3 300 ft; area 97 sq km/37 sq ml; WNW of Pretoria (South Africa); capital moved there from Mafeking, 1965; airport; a campus of University of Botswana and Swaziland; light industry, textiles, trade, services. » Botswana [i]

Gabriel An angel named in both the Old and New Testaments, the only other named angel in the Bible being the archangel Michael (although seven archangels are named in the Jewish apocalyptic work 1 *Enoch*). Gabriel is said to have helped Daniel interpret visions (*Dan* 8, 9). He is also recorded as foretelling the births of John the Baptist and of Jesus (*Luke* 1). » angel; Annunciation; apocalypse; Bible; Daniel, Book of; Michael (angel)

Gabrieli, Andrea (c.1533–85) Italian composer, born and died in Venice. He studied under Lassus, and became organist of St Mark's Church, writing madrigals, masses, and other choral works. Several of his organ pieces foreshadow the fugue. » fugue; Lassus

Gad One of the twelve tribes of ancient Israel, said to be descended from Jacob's seventh son (the first by Zilpah, Leah's maid). Its territory originally included the valley to the E of the Jordan River, bordered by the tribe of Manasseh in the N. » Israel, tribes of [i]

gad fly A robust, biting fly; eyes usually large, often iridescent; females suck blood of cattle and horses, inflicting painful bites; eggs laid in damp or marshy soil; larvae are predators of other insects; c.2 000 species, some of medical and veterinary importance. (Order: *Diptera*. Family: *Tabanidae*.) » fly; larva

Gadamer, Hans-Georg [**ga**duhmuh] (1900–) German philosopher, born in Marburg. Educated at Munich and Marburg, he taught at Marburg (1937), Leipzig (1939), and Frankfurt (1947), and was appointed to a chair at Heidelberg (1949), where he is professor emeritus. Influenced by Heidegger, he has made major contributions to the study of hermeneutics, notably in *Wahrheit und Methode* (1960, Truth and Method). » Heidegger; hermeneutics **1**

Gaddafi or **Qaddafi, Colonel Muammar** [ga**da**fee] (1942–) Libyan political and military leader, born into a nomadic family. Abandoning university studies, he attended military academy in 1963, and formed the Free Officers Movement which overthrew King Idris in 1969. He became Chairman of the Revolutionary Command Council, promoted himself to colonel (the highest rank in the revolutionary army) and became Commander-in-Chief of the Libyan Armed Forces. As *de facto* head of state, he set about eradicating colonialism by expelling foreigners and closing down British and US bases. He also encouraged a religious revival and return to the fundamental principles of Islam. A somewhat unpredictable figure, Gaddafi has openly supported violent revolutionaries in other parts of the world while ruthlessly pursuing Libyan dissidents both at home and abroad. He has waged a war in Chad, threatened other neighbours, and in the 1980s saw his territory bombed and aircraft shot down by the Americans. » Islam; Libya [i]

Gaddi, Taddeo (c.1300–66) Florentine painter, the godson and best pupil of Giotto. His finest work is seen in the frescoes of the 'Life of the Virgin' in the Baroncelli chapel of San Croce. His style deviated from that of his master, whom he does not match in figure painting, but whom he excels in architectural perspective. He died in Florence. » Florentine School; Giotto; Italian art

Gadidae [**gay**diday] The cod family of fishes, a large group comprising about 15 genera and 100 species of marine fish found primarily in continental shelf waters of the cool temperate N hemisphere; only the burbot is freshwater; many are extremely important commercially as food fish, including cod, burbot, haddock, ling, pollack, saithe, torsk, and whiting. » cod

Gadsden Purchase (1853) An area in S Arizona and New Mexico bought from Mexico for $10 000 000 as a route for a transcontinental railroad. The purchase defined the present-day US/Mexican border.

gadwall A duck native to the N hemisphere S of 60°; male grey with black rear end; female brown; feeds at surface; eats weeds and small animals. (*Anas strepera*. Family: *Anatidae*.) » duck

Gaea, Gaia, or **Ge** [**gee**a, **gi**ya, **gee**] In Greek mythology, 'the Earth' personified, and then the goddess of the whole Earth (not a particular piece of land). She came into being after Chaos, and was the wife of Uranus, producing numerous children. Her Roman equivalent was **Tellus** [**tel**uhs]. » Chaos; Deucalion; Gigantes

Gaelic The Celtic language spoken in the Scottish highlands and the Western Is. In steady decline, its speakers now number only about 80 000. » Irish; Irish literature

Gaelic football » **football 4** [i]

gaffer The chief electrician in a film or television production crew, working closely with the lighting director. The charge-hand electrician working directly under the gaffer is known as the **best boy**. » film production

Gagarin, Yuri (Alekseyevich) [ga**gah**rin] (1934–68) Russian cosmonaut, born near Gzhatsk, Russia. He joined the Soviet Air Force in 1957, and in 1961 became the first man to travel in space, completing a circuit of the Earth in the *Vostok* spaceship satellite. A Hero of the Soviet Union, he shared the Galabert Astronautical Prize with Glenn in 1963. He was killed in a plane accident while training near Moscow. After his death, Gzhatsk was renamed Gagarin. » RR10

Gage, Thomas (1721–87) British general, born at Firle, Sussex. In 1760 he became Military Governor of Montreal, in 1763 Commander-in-Chief of the British forces in America, and in 1774 Governor of Massachusetts. In 1775 (18 Apr) he sent a force to seize a quantity of arms at Concord; and next day the skirmish of Lexington took place which began the Revolution. After the battle of Bunker Hill (Jun 1775) he resigned, and returned to England, where he died. » American Revolution

gaillardia [gay**lah**dia] An annual or perennial, mostly native to N America, several species being grown in gardens for their cut flowers and long flowering period. Two species are the parents of many garden hybrids: *Gaillardia pulchella*, an annual growing to 30–60 cm/1–2 ft with coarsely toothed, lance-shaped leaves, yellow outer ray florets coloured crimson at the base; and *Gaillardia aristata*, a perennial growing to 70 cm/27 in with yellow and red ray florets. (Genus: *Gaillardia*, 28 species. Family: *Compositae*.) » annual; floret; perennial

Gainsborough, Thomas (1727–88) British landscape and portrait painter, born at Sudbury, Suffolk. In his youth he copied Dutch landscapes and at 14 was sent to London where he learnt the art of Rococo decoration. He moved to Bath in 1759, where he established himself with his portrait of Earl Nugent (1760). His great landscapes include 'The Harvest Wagon' (1767, Birmingham) and 'The Watering Place' (1777, Tate). He moved to London in 1774, painting further portraits and landscapes, notably 'George III' and 'Queen Charlotte' (1781, Windsor) and 'Cottage Door' (1780, Pasadena). He died in London. » English art; landscape painting; Rococo

Gaiseric or **Genseric** [**giy**suhrik] (c.390–477) King of the Vandals and Alans (428–77), who led the Vandals in their invasion of Gaul. He crossed from Spain to Numidia (429), captured and sacked Hippo (430), seized Carthage (439), and made it the capital of his new dominions. He built up a large maritime power, and his fleets carried the terror of his name as far as the Peloponnese. He sacked Rome in 455, and defeated fleets sent against him. The greatest of the Vandal kings, he was succeeded by his son Huneric.

Gaitskell, Hugh (Todd Naylor) (1906–63) British Labour politician, born in London. Educated at Winchester and Oxford, he became a socialist during the 1926 General Strike. An MP in 1945, he was Minister of Fuel and Power (1947) and of Economic Affairs (1950), and Chancellor of the Exchequer (1950–1). In 1955 he was elected Leader of the Opposition by a large majority over Bevan. He bitterly opposed Eden's Suez action (1956), and refused to accept a narrow conference vote for unilateral disarmament (1960). This caused a crisis of leadership in which he was challenged by Harold Wilson (1960) and Arthur Greenwood (1961), but he retained the loyalty of most Labour MPs. He died in London. » Bevan, Aneurin; Butskellism; Eden; Labour Party; left wing; nuclear disarmament; Suez Crisis; Wilson, Harold

galactic cluster » **open cluster**

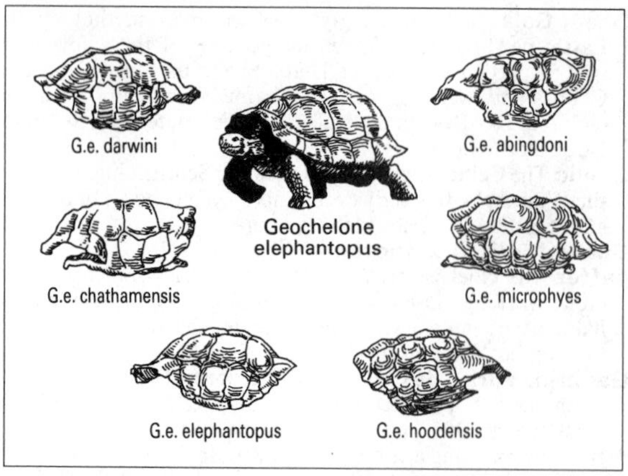

Galapagos giant tortoise

galactose A simple sugar (monosaccharide), found in the sugar of milk along with glucose; otherwise, it is rare in nature. Galactosemia, a genetic defect leading to an inability to metabolize galactose, is very uncommon and requires dietary management. » glucose [i]; lactose

galago » **bushbaby**

Galahad, Sir One of King Arthur's knights, son of Lancelot and Elaine. Distinguished for his purity, he alone was able to succeed in the adventures of the Siege Perilous and the Holy Grail. » Arthur; Grail, Holy; Lancelot, Sir

Galápagos finches » **Darwin's finches**

Galápagos giant tortoise The largest known tortoise; length of shell, up to 1.2 m/4 ft; native to the Galapagos Is; each island has its own subspecies differing in shell shape. (*Geochelone elephantopus*. Family: *Testudinidae*.) » Galápagos Islands; tortoise

Galápagos Islands [galapagohs], Span **Archipiélago de Colón** pop (1982) 6 119; area 7 812 sq km/3 015 sq ml. Ecuadorian island group on the Equator, 970 km/600 ml W of S American mainland; six main islands of San Cristóbal, Santa Cruz, Isabela, Floreana, Santiago, and Fernandina, and over 50 smaller islands; highest peak, Volcán Wolf (1 707 m/5 600 ft) on Isabela I; visited by Spanish, 1535, but no colony established; Ecuador took possession, 1832; became well-known after visit of Charles Darwin, 1835; volcanic origin, almost entirely composed of basaltic lava flows with shallow, cratered cones, some active; diverse vegetation and landforms, from lava deserts to tropical forests; many unique species of flora and fauna evolved independent of mainland; marine iguanas on Isla Fernandina; giant tortoises, especially on Isabela and Santa Cruz; Charles Darwin Biological Research Station (1959) on Santa Cruz; serious fire on Isabela destroyed much wildlife in 1985; Galápagos National Park established in 1934; area 6 912 sq km/2 668 sq ml; a world heritage site. » Darwin, Charles; Ecuador [i]

Galatea [galateea] In Greek mythology, a sea-nymph, wooed by Polyphemus the Cyclops with uncouth love-songs. In some versions Polyphemus destroys his rival Acis with a rock; in other versions he happily marrries Galatea. It is probably a Sicilian story. » Cyclops; Polyphemus

Galatians, Letter of Paul to the [galayshanz] New Testament writing, widely accepted as genuinely from the apostle Paul to the churches in some part of Galatia in C Asia Minor. It is a strongly-worded letter arguing that non-Jewish converts to Christianity were no longer subject to Jewish practices and laws, and defending Paul's own mission on this basis. » New Testament; Paul, St; Pauline Letters

galaxy A huge family of stars held together by the mutual gravitational attractions of one star for another. Galaxies exist in a great variety of forms, ellipticals predominating, but spirals featuring prominently in popular books on account of their notable shapes. Masses range from a few million suns to ten million million times as much. The nearest galaxies to the Milky Way are the Magellanic Clouds, some 55 000 parsecs away. The furthest seen to date could be 2 000 megaparsecs or more. Galaxies are the fundamental building blocks of the universe, and are consequently of immense importance in cosmology. There are numerous special types. About one galaxy in a million is a **radio galaxy**, an intense source of cosmic radio waves. A **Seyfert galaxy** has a brilliant nucleus and inconspicuous spiral arms; it is a strong emitter of infrared radiation, and is also detectable as a radio and X-ray source. A **Markarian galaxy** is one with excessive ultraviolet emission, discovered by Russian astronomer B E Markarian at Byurakan Observatory in the 1970s. Quasars could be a type of extremely luminous galaxy. A galaxy which is either unusually energetic or varies in luminosity is known as an **active galaxy**. » electromagnetic radiation [i]; Galaxy; Magellanic Clouds; quasar; star

Galaxy The huge star family to which our Sun belongs, seen as the Milky Way. In shape it is basically a bulging flat disc, diameter 15 kiloparsecs, thickness 3 000 parsecs at the centre, and 300 parsecs elsewhere. The Sun is 8 000 parsecs from the nucleus. Within this disc there are star clusters and interstellar matter. A pair of spiral arms merges from the nucleus and is superimposed on the general distributions of stars. The Galaxy as a whole rotates, faster at the centre than further out. The Sun takes 250 million years for one circuit. There are around 100 000 000 000 stars in all, and the Galaxy is 13–20 thousand million years old. » Local Group; Milky Way; star cluster; Sun

Galbraith, J(ohn) Kenneth (1908–) Canadian economist and diplomat, born at Iona Station, Ontario. Educated at the Universities of Toronto, California, and Cambridge, he became professor of economics at Harvard (1949–75), where he spent his career except for a short period at Princeton, wartime service in Washington, and two years (1961–3) as US Ambassador to India. He was an advisor to Presidents Kennedy and Johnson, and is one of the major intellectual forces in American liberalism. » Johnson, Lyndon B; Kennedy, John F; liberalism

Galdós, Benito Pérez (1843–1920) Spanish writer, born in Las Palmas, Canary Islands. Brought up in Madrid, he came to be regarded as Spain's greatest novelist after Cervantes. His series of 46 short novels, *Episodios nacionales* (1873–1912), gives a vivid picture of 19th-c Spain from the viewpoint of the people. He also wrote many longer novels, including *Fortunata y Jacinta* (1886–7), and several plays, which also achieved success. He died in Madrid. » Cervantes; novel; Spanish literature

Galen, byname of Lat **Claudius Galenus [gayluhn]** (c.130–201) Greek physician, born at Pergamum, Mysia. He studied medicine at Pergamum, Smyrna, Corinth, and Alexandria, and later lived in Rome. He was a voluminous writer on medical and philosophical subjects, and gathered up all the medical knowledge of his time, thus becoming the authority used by subsequent Greek and Roman medical writers. He is thought to have died in Sicily. » anatomy

galena [galeena] A lead sulphide (PbS) mineral, with very dense, dark-grey crystals. It is an important source of lead. » lead

Galerius, properly **Gaius Galerius Valerius Maximus** (c.250–311) Roman emperor (305–11), a Roman soldier of humble extraction who rose from the ranks to become deputy ruler of the E half of the empire under Diocletian (293), and chief ruler after Diocletian's abdication in 305. He was a notorious persecutor of the Christians (303–11) until near the end of his reign, when after an illness he granted them some toleration. » Diocletian

Galicia [galeesha] pop (1981) 2 811 912; area 29 434 sq km/ 11 361 sq ml. Autonomous region of Spain in the NW corner of the Iberian peninsula extending S to the Portuguese border; crossed by several rivers, reaching the sea in deep fjord-like inlets; a mediaeval kingdom within Castile, 11th-c; ports include Corunna and Vigo; maize, wine, fishing, wolfram, tin; a distinctive cultural and linguistic region; there is a separatist political movement. » Castile; Spain [i]

Galilean moons The principal natural satellites of Jupiter, discovered by Galileo in 1610; Io (the innermost), Europa, Ganymede, and Callisto. They are distinct worlds in their own right, in the same size range as the Moon. They lack sensible atmospheres and lie in near circular orbits in Jupiter's equatorial plane. Io and Europa are mainly 'rocky' silicate bodies while Ganymede and Callisto contain an equal component of ice. It is conjectured that the four moons were formed by accretion from the material that collapsed to form Jupiter. » Galileo project; Jupiter (astronomy); Voyager project [i]

Galilee [**ga**lilee], Hebrew **Galil** N region of former Palestine and now of Israel, bounded W by the Mediterranean Sea, N by Lebanon, E by Syria, L Tiberias, and the Jordan valley, and S by the Jezreel plain; chiefly associated in Biblical times with the ministry of Jesus; main centre of Judaism in Palestine after the destruction of Jerusalem (AD 70); scene of fierce fighting during the Arab invasion of Israel, 1948. » Arab–Israeli Wars; Israel [i]; Jesus Christ; Judaism

Galilee, Sea of » **Tiberias, Lake**

Galileo, properly **Galileo Galilei** [gali**lay**oh] (1564–1642) Italian astronomer and mathematician, born at Pisa, where he entered the university as a medical student in 1581. He became professor of mathematics at Padua (1592–1610), where he improved the refracting telescope (1610), and was the first to use it for astronomy. His realization that the ancient Aristotelian teachings were unacceptable brought severe ecclesiastical censure, and he was forced to retract before the Inquisition. By 1637 he had become totally blind, and he died in Florence. » astronomy; Copernican system

Galileo project A scientifically ambitious orbiter/atmospheric probe mission developed by NASA to explore the Jovian atmosphere, moons, rings, and magnetosphere. Originally planned for launch in 1982, it was finally launched by a space shuttle in October 1989. » Jupiter (astronomy); NASA; Voyager project [i]

gall An abnormal outgrowth of tissue which can appear on any part of a plant, caused by insects, bacteria, fungi, nematodes, or mites. The precise infecting agent is often, but not always, identifiable from the type of gall. Common examples are oak-apples and the pincushion galls of roses. » bacteria [i]; fasciation; fungus; mite; nematode

Gall, Franz Joseph (1758–1828) German anatomist, born at Tiefenbrunn, Baden. As a physician in Vienna (1785), he evolved a theory in which a person's talents and qualities were traced to particular areas of the brain. His lectures on phrenology were popular, but suppressed in 1802 as being subversive of religion. He died near Paris. » phrenology

gall bladder A small muscular sac found near or in the liver of many vertebrates, which acts as a reservoir for the storage and concentration of bile. During digestion, food (especially fat) directly stimulates the duodenal mucosa to release cholecystokinin-pancreozymin (CCK). This induces the gall bladder to contract, and expel bile into the intestine via the biliary duct system. » biliary system; cholecystitis; duodenum; gallstones; liver

gall midge A minute, delicate fly; eggs and hatching larvae often cause gall-like swellings on host plants; c.4 000 species, including pests of important crops such as wheat and peas. (Order: *Diptera*. Family: *Cecidomyiidae*.) » midge; larva

gall wasp A very small wasp, each species causing a characteristic gall on its host plant, typically the oak; one or more larvae develops inside each gall. The life cycle is complex, often involving an alternation between sexual and asexual generations. (Order: *Hymenoptera*. Family: *Cynipidae*, c.2 000 species.) » gall; larva; reproduction; wasp

Galla or **Oromo** A cluster of Cushitic-speaking peoples of Ethiopia and N Kenya; the largest group in Ethiopia. Traditionally pastoralists, the groups in N Ethiopia are farmers, while the S Galla are still cattle herders. The S Galla have preserved much of their traditional social organization and religion; the N Galla have mostly become Christian or Muslim. Population c.10 million. » Amhara; Ethiopia [i]; pastoralism

Gallaudet College A college of higher education for the deaf, in Washington, DC. It was founded by Edward Miner Gallaudet (1837–1917) in 1857, and is financed both privately and publicly. » university

Galle, Johann Gottfried (1812–1910) German astronomer, born at Pabsthaus, near Wittenberg. In 1846, at Berlin Observatory, he discovered the planet Neptune, whose existence had been postulated in the calculations of Leverrier. He died at Potsdam. » Adams, John Couch; Leverrier; Neptune (astronomy)

galleon An elaborate, four-masted, heavily-armed 16th-c warship, with a pronounced beak reminiscent of the ram on a galley, hence 'galleon'. The forecastle was relatively small, but the poop was high and ornate. » ship [i]; trireme [i]

galliard » **pavane**

Gallic Wars The name traditionally given to Julius Caesar's brutal campaigns (58–51 BC) against the Celtic tribes of Gaul (ancient France). They were also the occasion of his two unsuccessful invasions of Britain. » Britain, Roman; Roman history [i]

Gallicanism A French religious doctrine, emphasizing royal or episcopal authority over matters pertaining to the French church at the expense of papal sovereignty. It emerged during Philip the Fair's struggle with Boniface VIII (1297–1303), and remained a traditional, though controversial force in France, invoked to defend established liberties against ultramontanism and papal interference. » Philip IV; pope; Ultramontanism

Galliformes [gali**faw**meez] A world-wide order of medium-sized, mainly ground-feeding birds; includes the megapodes, curassows, the hoatzin, and the 'game birds' (pheasants, turkeys, domestic fowl); also known as **gallinaceous birds**. » curassow; domestic fowl; hoatzin; megapode; pheasant; turkey

gallinaceous birds » **Galliformes**

gallinule [**ga**linyool] A water bird of the rail family (c.12 species); native to the Old World and much of S America; toes often very long for walking on floating vegetation. Renowned oceanic wanderers, the birds may appear thousands of miles from their usual species' location. » moorhen; rail

Gallipoli, Turkish **Gelibolu** [ga**lip**uhlee] Narrow peninsula extending SW from the coast of Istanbul province, NW Turkey; between the Dardanelles (SE) and the Aegean Sea (W); length c.100 km/60 ml; the scene of fierce fighting in 1915–16. » Gallipoli campaign; Turkey [i]; World War 1

Gallipoli campaign A major campaign of World War 1 (1915–16). With stalemate on the Western Front, the British War Council advocated operations against the Turks to secure the Dardanelles and aid Russia. The land campaign began with amphibious assaults on the Gallipoli Peninsula (Apr 1915). Australian and New Zealand forces were heavily involved: the beach where they landed is still known as Anzac Cove. Allied casualties were 250 000 out of 480 000 engaged. It was abandoned as a costly failure, with successful evacuations of all remaining troops (Jan 1916). » Dardanelles; World War 1

gallium Ga, element 31. A metal with a remarkable liquid range (melting point 28°C, boiling point 2 400°C), relatively rare and found mainly as an impurity in ores of other elements. In virtually all its compounds, it shows oxidation state +3. It is mainly important as gallium arsenide (GaAs), a compound converting electrical energy into visible light, and used in light-emitting diodes. » chemical elements; diode; metal; RR90

gallon » RR70

Galloway » **Dumfries and Galloway**

gallstones Small stones in the gall bladder and its associated ducts. They are found in about 20% of individuals, but give rise to symptoms in only a small proportion of these. Most stones are composed of cholesterol with a little admixture of calcium. Cholesterol stones tend to occur in individuals over 50 years old, and are often attended by infection of the gall bladder (*cholecystitis*); if they obstruct the common bile duct, they cause jaundice. In younger people, small bile pigment stones sometimes form in conditions associated with the breakdown of red blood cells, which liberate haemoglobin (*haemolytic anaemia*). When gallstones cause significant discomfort or jaundice, they are best usually removed surgically. In a minority of cases, small stones may be dissolved by giving a derivative of bile salts by mouth. » biliary system; cholecystitis; cholesterol; gall bladder; jaundice

Gallup, George (Horace) (1901–84) US public opinion expert, born at Jefferson, Iowa. He was professor of journalism at Drake and Northwestern Universities until 1932, and after a period directing research for an advertising agency, became professor at the Pulitzer School of Journalism, Columbia University. In 1935 he founded the American Institute of Public Opinion, and evolved the **Gallup Polls** for testing the state of public opinion. He died at Tschingel, Switzerland.

Galsworthy, John (1867–1933) British novelist and playwright, born at Combe, Surrey. Educated at Harrow and Oxford, he was called to the Bar, but elected to travel and set up as a writer. From the start he was a moralist and humanitarian, but his novels were also to be documentaries of their time. His great sequence, *The Forsyte Saga* (1906–28), recording the life of the affluent British middle class before 1914, began a new vogue in novel writing. His plays, such as *Strife* (1909), illustrate his reforming zeal, and his interest in social and ethical problems. He won the Nobel Prize for Literature in 1932, and died in London. » drama; English literature; novel

Galton, Sir Francis (1822–1911) British scientist and explorer, born in Birmingham. He studied at Birmingham, London, and Cambridge, but left the study of medicine to travel in N and S Africa. He is best known for his studies of heredity and intelligence, such as *Hereditary Genius* (1869), which led to the field he called *eugenics*. Several of his ideas are referred to in the work of his cousin, Charles Darwin. Galton was knighted in 1909, and died at Haslemere, Surrey. » Darwin, Charles; eugenics

Galuppi, Baldassare [ga**loo**pee] (1706–85) Italian light operatic composer, born near Venice. He was educated in Venice, where he lived most of his life, apart from visits to London (1741–3) and St Petersburg (1765–8). His comic operas were extremely popular, and he also composed sacred and instrumental music. He died in Venice.

Galvani, Luigi [gal**vah**nee] (1737–98) Italian physiologist, born at Bologna. He was educated at Bologna, where in 1762 he became professor of anatomy, and investigated the role of electrical impulses in animal tissue. In his most famous experiment he connected the leg muscle of a frog to its corresponding nerve, and observed the twitching which took place (which he attributed to 'animal electricity'). He died at Bologna. The galvanometer is named after him. » galvanometer

galvanizing The application of a zinc coating to iron or steel to protect against atmospheric corrosion. In *hot galvanizing*, the cleaned metal is passed through a flux, then through a bath of molten zinc. The zinc may also be applied electrolytically. Although the term 'galvanizing' derives from Galvani, the process was not devised by him, but by Henry William Crawford in 1837. » corrosion; Galvani; zinc

galvanometer An instrument for measuring small electrical currents. The moving coil galvanometer consists of an indicating needle or mirror attached to a coiled wire suspended in a magnetic field. The coil rotates when a current passes through it. The angle through which it rotates (indicated by the deflection of the needle or by a beam of light reflected from the mirror) is used to measure the current. Other models are ballistic galvanometers and moving-magnet instruments. » current (electricity)

Galway, James (1939–) British flautist, born in Belfast. He studied in London and Paris, and played in various orchestras in London and in the Berlin Philharmonic (1969–75). He has since followed a highly successful solo career, playing on a solid gold flute of astonishing tonal range. » flute

Gama, Vasco da (c.1469–1525) Portuguese navigator, born at Sines in Alentejo. He led the expedition which discovered the route to India round the Cape of Good Hope (1497–9), and in 1502–3 led a squadron of ships to Calicut to avenge the murder of a group of Portuguese explorers left there by Cabral. In 1524 he was sent as viceroy to India, but he soon fell ill, and died at Cochin. His body was brought home to Portugal. » Cabral, Pedro

Gambetta, Leon (Michel) (1838–82) French Republican statesman, born at Cahors. He was called to the Bar in 1859, and was elected Deputy in 1869. After the surrender of Napoleon III he helped to proclaim the Republic (1870), became Minister of the Interior in the Government of National Defence, made a spectacular escape from the siege of Paris in a balloon, and for five months was dictator of France. He led the resistance to MacMahon (1877), became President of the Chamber (1879) and briefly Prime Minister (1881–2), but fell from office before implementing a programme of radical reform. He died near Paris. » France [i]; MacMahon; Napoleon III

Gambia, River, Fr **Gambie** River in W Africa, rising in the Fouta Djallon massif in Guinea; flows c.800 km/500 ml W to the Atlantic Ocean; runs along the length of The Gambia for the last 470 km/292 ml of its course; navigable by ocean-going ships for 200 km/125 ml. » Gambia, The [i]

Gambia, The, official name **The Republic of the Gambia** pop (1990e) 860 000; area 10 402 sq km/4 015 sq ml. W African republic, divided into eight local government areas; bounded on all sides by Senegal except for Atlantic Ocean coastline; capital, Banjul; chief towns, Serrekunda, Brikama, Bakau; timezone GMT; ethnic groups include Madinka, Fula, Wolof; chief religion, Islam (85%); official language, English; unit of currency, the dalasi of 100 butut; strip of land 322 km/200 ml E–W along the R Gambia; flat country, not rising above 90 m/295 ft; tropical climate; rainy season (Jun–Sep), rainfall decreasing inland; high humidity in wet season, with high night temperatures; average annual rainfall at Banjul, 1 295 mm/51 in, average temperatures 22.8°C (Jan), 26.7°C (Jul), rising inland to over 40°C; visited by Portuguese, 1455; settled by English in 17th-c; independent British Crown Colony, 1843; independent member of Commonwealth, 1965; republic, 1970; The Gambia and Senegal joined to form the Confederation of Senegambia, 1982–9; governed by a 50-member House of Representatives, elected for a 5-year term, and a president (also elected for five years) and cabinet; economy chiefly agriculture, especially groundnuts; cotton, rice millet, sorghum, fruit, vegetables, livestock; groundnut processing, brewing, soft drinks, agricultural machinery assembly, metal working, clothing, tourism. » Banjul; Senegal [i]; RR25 national holidays; RR50 political leaders

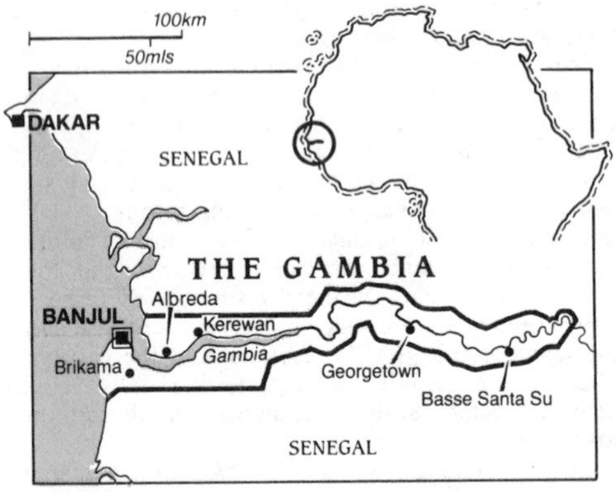

□ international airport

games, theory The branch of mathematics that analyses a range of problems involving decision-making. Although often illustrated by games of chance, there are important applications to military strategy, economics, ecology and other applied sciences. Game theory was developed in this century, principally by French mathematician Émile Borel (1871–1956) and US mathematician Johann von Neumann (1903–57). Games involving one, two, or more players are distinguished, as in patience, chess, and roulette respectively. Game theory analyses the strategies each player uses to maximize the chance of winning, and attempts to predict outcomes. » Neumann, Johann von

gamete [**gam**eet] A specialized reproductive cell which fuses with another gamete of the opposite sex or mating type, during fertilization, to form a zygote. Gametes are typically *haploid* (possessing a single chromosome set), and the zygote is *diploid* (possessing a double set, one derived from each gamete). Gametes are usually differentiated into male and female: male gametes (sperm) are typically motile and have reduced cytoplasm; female gametes (eggs, ova) are typically non-motile and have large amounts of cytoplasm, containing mitochondria. » cell; chromosome [i]; cytoplasm; fertilization; mitochondrion; zygote

gamete intrafallopian transfer A procedure undertaken to remedy infertility. Eggs are collected from the surface of the ovaries after stimulation with gonadotrophin or drugs with a similar action. These are then introduced into the uterus together with spermatozoa, permitting natural fertilization to occur. » pregnancy [i]; test-tube baby

gametophyte The sexual (ie gamete-producing or *haploid*) generation in the life of a plant. It is the dominant part of the life cycle in algae and bryophytes; it is the free-living but minor generation in ferns; while in flowering plants it is represented only by the pollen tube and embryo-sac. Free-living gametophytes are relatively unspecialized, are prone to dehydration, and are generally confined to damp habitats. » algae; alternation of generations; bryophyte; fern; flower [i]; sporophyte

gamma globulins The most abundant fraction of the antibodies in blood serum, produced by the plasma cells of B lymphocytes (derived from bone marrow); also known as **immunoglobulin G (IgG)**. Gamma globulins combine with antigens such as viruses and parasites to kill them by a number of different mechanisms, including enhancement of the inflammatory processes. Newborn infants are protected against infection in early life by gamma globulins received from the mother via the placenta. » antibodies; serum

gamma-ray astronomy The study of radiation from celestial sources at wavelengths shorter than 0.01 nm. Gamma-rays have been detected from the gamma-ray background, from a few energetic galaxies and quasars, and from certain highly evolved stars. » astronomy; gamma rays

gamma rays Electromagnetic radiation of very short wavelength, less than 3×10^{-11}m; no electric charge; highly penetrating. Emitted in natural radioactivity, it is the result of transitions from high-energy excited states to lower-energy states in atomic nuclei. Cobalt-60 is a common gamma source, with a half-life of 5.26 years. » electromagnetic radiation [i]; gamma-ray astronomy; half-life; Mössbauer effect; radioactivity

Gamow, George [**ga**mov] (1904–68) Russian-US physicist, born in Odessa. He graduated at Leningrad, becoming professor of physics there (1931–4), and also in the USA at George Washington (1934–55) and Colorado (1956–68) universities. In 1948 he helped to develop the 'big bang' theory of the origin of the universe. When the double helix model of DNA was announced (1953), he deduced that its informational mode probably resided in the bases within the helix, forming groups of three bases (*codons*) which direct protein formation. Also a highly successful popular science writer, he died at Boulder, Colorado. » Alpher; Big Bang; codon; cosmology; DNA [i]; molecular biology

Gand [gã] » **Ghent**

Ganda A Bantu-speaking people of S Uganda, the largest traditional kingdom in the area, founded about the 12th-c. The king, the *kabaka*, was assisted by bureaucratic chiefs. In the 19th-c, most Ganda became Christian, although there is a significant Muslim minority. The kingship was abolished by the Uganda government in 1967. Population c.2 million. » Bantu-speaking peoples; Uganda [i]

Gandhi, Indira (Priyadarshini) [**gan**dee] (1917–84) Indian politician and Prime Minister (1966–77, 1980–4), daughter of Jawaharlal Nehru, born at Allahabad. Educated at Visva-Bharati University (Bengal) and Oxford, in 1942 she married Feroze Gandhi (died 1960). She became President of the Indian Congress Party (1959–60), Minister of Information (1964), and Prime Minister in 1966 after the death of Shastri. After her conviction for election malpractices, she declared a state of emergency (1975–7), and was Premier again in 1980. She achieved a considerable reputation through her work as a leader of the developing nations, but was unable to stem sectarian violence at home. She was assassinated in New Delhi by Sikh extremists who were members of her bodyguard. She was succeeded by her elder son, **Rajiv** (1944–91), who was Prime Minister until 1989, and was himself assassinated while campaigning for re-election. Her other son, **Sanjay** (1946–80), was killed in an air crash. » Indian National Congress; Shastri

Gandhi, (Mohandas Karamchand) [**gan**dee], byname **the Mahatma** ('of great soul') (1869–1948) Indian nationalist leader, born at Poorbandar, Kathiawar. He studied law in London, but in 1893 went to South Africa, where he spent 21 years opposing discriminatory legislation against Indians. In 1914 he returned to India, where he supported the Home Rule movement, and became leader of the Indian National Congress, advocating a policy of non-violent non-co-operation to achieve independence. Following his civil disobedience campaign (1919–22), he was jailed for conspiracy (1922–4). In 1930 he led a 200-mile march to the sea to collect salt in symbolic defiance of the government monopoly. On his release from prison (1931), he attended the London Round Table Conference on Indian constitutional reform. In 1946 he negotiated with the Cabinet Mission which recommended the new constitutional structure. After independence (1947), he tried to stop the Hindu/Muslim conflict in Bengal, a policy which led to his assassination in Delhi by Nathuram Godse, a Hindu fanatic. » Indian National Congress; Non-Co-operation Movement

Gang of Four 1 A description given by Mao Zedong (Mao Tse-Tung) to the Shanghai-based hard-core radicals of the Cultural Revolution: Zhang Chunqiao, Yao Wenyuan, Wang Hongwen, and Jiang Qing. Zhang and Yao were veterans of the Shanghai party machine. Wang emerged as a workers' leader in the Shanghai 'January Revolution' of 1967. Jiang, Mao's wife, enjoyed his trust and was the acknowledged leader of the Gang. All were members of the politburo when they were arrested and disgraced in 1976. » Cultural Revolution; Jiang Qing **2** In British politics, the name given to the four politicians who broke away from the Labour Party to found the Social Democratic Party in 1981: Roy Jenkins, William Rodgers, David Owen, and Shirley Williams. » Social Democratic Party

Gangdisê Shan [**gung**dise] or **Kailas Range** Mountain range in Tibet, SW China, N of the Himalayas; rises to 6 714 m/22 027 ft at Kangrinboqê Feng peak; a watershed between the inland and Indian Ocean drainage systems. » China [i]; Himalayas

Ganges, River [**gan**jeez], Hindi **Ganga** River in N India, formed in the E Himalayas; flows W through the Silwalik Range onto the Ganges Plain; continues SE to Allahabad, then E to Benares; turns E through Bihar, then SE into West Bengal, where it follows the frontier with Bangladesh; joined by the R Brahmaputra NNW of Faridpur; as the R Padma it continues SE through Bangladesh, branches into many tributaries, and forms the vast Ganges–Brahmaputra delta in the Bay of Bengal; length 2 510 km/1 560 ml; important trade artery and irrigation source; the most sacred Hindu river. » Hinduism; India [i]

ganglion 1 In anatomy, an aggregation of grey (non-myelinated) nervous tissue within the nervous system, constituting the bulk of many invertebrate central nervous systems. In vertebrates, there are some ganglia within the central nervous system (eg the basal ganglia), but the majority occur in the peripheral nervous system, as collections of cell bodies of neurones (eg the spinal ganglia). They are often the site of communication between nerve cells. » myelin; nervous system **2** In clinical medicine, a cyst which forms in relation to a tendon sheath, producing a painless, harmless swelling. It is commonly found over the wrist or back of the hands. » cyst

gangrene A form of death (*necrosis*) of tissue, variably associated with bacterial infection. **Dry gangrene** refers to the death of a part of the body deprived of its blood supply, such as a toe, foot, or leg in which the supply of blood is insufficient to maintain its life. Infection is usually slight, at least in the early stages, and the part becomes black and shrivelled. **Wet gangrene** affects internal tissues, such as the gut when deprived of its blood supply; in these cases, bacterial infection is prominent. » gas gangrene

ganja » **cannabis**

gannet A large marine bird closely related to the booby; native to the N Atlantic, S Africa, Australia, and New Zealand; long blue bill with no external nostrils; bare patches of blackish skin on face; similar habits to boobies. (Family: *Sulidae*, 3 species.) » booby

Gansu Corridor » **Hexi Corridor**

Ganymede [**gan**imeed] In Greek mythology, a beautiful boy, the son of Tros, a Trojan prince. Zeus sent a storm-wind, or (later and more usually) an eagle, who carried Ganymede up to Olympus, where he became the cup-bearer. In return his father was given a stud of exceptional horses. » Zeus

Ganymede The third natural satellite of Jupiter, discovered by Galileo in 1610; distance from the planet 1 070 000 km/ 665 000 ml; diameter 5 260 km/3 270 ml; orbital period 7.155 days. It is the largest moon in the Solar System, and larger than Mercury. The brightest of the Galilean satellites, it seems to have a large rocky core surrounded by a mantle of water and a thick crust of ice. It has many impact craters. » Galilean moons; Jupiter (astronomy); RR4

ganzfeld A type of partial sensory deprivation, in which a person is exposed to unpatterned visual and auditory stimulation. As used in parapsychological research, the ganzfeld technique typically consists of fixing translucent hemispheres over the eyes of a reclining person while a red light is shone upon the face, and masking noises, such as the sound of waves or white noise, are presented via headphones. The ganzfeld is often used in extrasensory perception studies to encourage internally-produced imagery and thoughts. » extrasensory perception; parapsychology

Gao Gang or **Kao Kang** [gow **gang**] (c.1902–55) One of the leaders of the Chinese Communist Party, born in Shensi province. In the mid-1930s he was in charge of a small independent communist area at Baoan, Shaanxi, where the Long March led by Mao Zedong (Mao Tse-tung) ended. Mao and Kao Kang became close political allies, and he later became chief Party Secretary of Manchuria (1949). He set the national pace in economic development, but in 1955 was accused of attempting to set up a 'separate kingdom'. He apparently committed suicide. » communism; Long March; Mao Zedong

Gaoxiong [gow**shyung**] or **Kao-hsiung**, Jap **Takao** 22°36N 120°17E, pop (1982e) 1 250 000. Special municipality and seaport in SW Taiwan; on the SW coast, facing the Taiwan Strait; largest seaport and industrial city in Taiwan; world's largest shipbreaking centre, and second largest dry dock; occupied by the Japanese, 1895–1945; airport; railway; oil refining, fishing, foodstuffs; Cheng Ching Lake resort, Kenting National Park, Fo Kuang Shan (Buddha Torch Mountain), with 25 m/ 82 ft-tall statue of Buddha on a 12 m/39 ft-high pedestal. » Buddha; Taiwan [i]

gar Primitive slender-bodied fish confined to fresh and brackish rivers and lakes of N America; length up to 3 m/10 ft, scales rhomboidal, jaws prolonged to form a narrow snout; feeds voraciously on other fishes and crustaceans, caught by rapid striking movements; also called **garpikes**. (Genus: *Lepisosteus*. Family: *Lepisosteidae*.)

Garamba National park established in 1938 in N Zaire, on the Sudanese border; area 4 480 sq km/1 730 sq ml; noted for its unique population of heavy-jawed 'white' rhinoceroses; a world heritage site. » Zaire [i]

garbanzos » **chick-pea**

Garbo, Greta, professional name of **Greta Lovisa Gustafsson** (1905–90) Swedish film actress, born in Stockholm. She went to the Royal Theatre Dramatic School, Stockholm, and starred in Mauritz Stiller's *Gösta Berling's Saga* (1924, The Story of Gösta Berling). She moved to the USA in 1925, where she starred in such successes as *Anna Karenina* (1935) and *Ninotchka* (1939). She retired from films in 1941, and became a US citizen in 1951, living in seclusion in New York City.

García Lorca » **Lorca, Federico García**

García Márquez, Gabriel [**mah**kez] (1928–) Colombian novelist, born at Aracataca, and educated in Bogotá. He began writing while working as a journalist in Europe, publishing his first novel, *La Hojarasca* (Leaf Storm) in 1955. His masterpiece is *Cien años de soledad* (1967, One Hundred Years of Solitude). *El amor en los tiempos del cólera* (Love in a Time of Cholera) appeared in 1985. He won the Nobel Prize for Literature in 1982. » Latin-American literature; novel

Gard, Pont du An aqueduct built by the Romans early in the 1st-c AD to carry the water supply of the city of Nîmes in S France. It is c.275 m/900 ft long and towers 55 m/180 ft above the R Gard. Regarded as the finest surviving example of Roman engineering, it is a world heritage site. » aqueduct; Nîmes; Roman history [i]

Garda, Lake (Ital **Lago di**), ancient **Lacus Benacus** Area 370 sq km/143 sq ml. Largest Italian lake, between Lombardy and Venetia; length 52 km/32 ml; width 5–16.5 km/3–10 ml; maximum depth 346 m/1 135 ft; N part narrow and fjord-like; fertile Riviera Bresciana on W side; resort towns include Desenzano, Garda, Sirmione. » Italy [i]

Gardel, Carlos [gar**del**] (1890–1935) The most popular Latin American singer of the 20th-c, born in Toulouse, France, and brought up in Buenos Aires. He made his name as a tango singer and later as a film star. He died in an aircraft accident in Medellín, Colombia.

garden bunting » **ortolan**

garden city In the UK, a planned settlement designed to provide a spacious, high-quality, living and working environment. The concept is based on 19th-c ideas of utopian communities, and was developed by Ebenezer Howard in 1898. Each garden city was planned to a concentric land use pattern, with c.32 000 people and a residential density of 75 per ha/30 per acre. The design featured wide streets and public parks inside the city, with farmland and green belt beyond. The first was built at Letchworth, Hertfordshire, in 1903, followed by Welwyn in 1919. The ideas were developed further in the British 'new towns' of the 1950s, and were also influential in Europe and the USA. » green belt; Howard, Ebenezer; new town

garden cress A slender annual, single stem 20–40 cm/8–15 in, with lobed basal leaves and pinnate stem leaves; flowers small, white, cross-shaped; possibly native to W Asia. Long cultivated as a salad plant, it is the cress of mustard-and-cress. (*Lepidium sativum*. Family: *Cruciferae*.) » annual; pinnate

garden myrrh » **sweet cicely**

Garden of the Gods A park of 312 ha/770 acres situated in C Colorado. Its name derives from the fantastic groups of white and red sandstone rocks and outcrops that are scattered across the area. » Colorado

gardenia An evergreen shrub or small tree, native mostly to the Old World tropics, China, and Japan; leaves elliptical, glossy; flowers white, fragrant, petals forming a tube with spreading lobes. It is named after the 18th-c physician and botanist Alexander Garden (1730–91). (Genus: *Gardenia*, 250 species. Family: *Rubiaceae*.) » Cape jasmin; evergreen plants; shrub; tree [i]

Gardiner, Stephen (c.1483–1555) English prelate, born at Bury St Edmunds, Suffolk. He studied at Cambridge, became Wolsey's secretary (1525), Bishop of Winchester (1531), and was sent to Rome to further Henry VIII's divorce (1527–33). He supported the royal supremacy, but opposed doctrinal reformation, and for this was imprisoned and deprived of his bishopric on Edward VI's accession. Released and restored by Mary in 1553, he became an arch-persecutor of Protestants. He died in London. » Edward VI; Henry VIII; Mary I; Reformation; Wolsey

Garfield, James A(bram) (1831–81) The 20th President of the USA (Mar–Sep 1881), born at Orange, Ohio. He was a farmworker, teacher, lay preacher, and lawyer before being elected to the Ohio State Senate in 1859. He fought in the Civil War until 1863, when he entered congress, and became leader of the Republican Party. After his election as President, he identified himself with the cause of civil service reform, thereby irritating many in his own party. He was shot at Elberon, New Jersey, by a disappointed office-seeker, Charles Guiteau, and died two months later.

garfish » **needlefish**

garganey [**gah**guhnee] A small, slender duck, native to S Eurasia, W and NE Africa, and Indonesia; male brown with white stripe from eye to back of neck; migrates to tropics for winter; the most numerous duck wintering in Africa. (*Anas querquedula*. Family: *Anatidae*.) » duck

Garibaldi, Giuseppe (1807–82) Italian patriot, born in Nice. In 1834 he joined Mazzini's 'Young Italy' movement, and was condemned to death for participating in the attempt to seize

Genoa, but escaped to S America. Returning to Europe, in 1849 he joined the revolutionary government of Rome, but was again forced to leave Italy. After working in New York, he returned to Italy in 1854 and took up the life of a farmer on the island of Caprera. With the outbreak in 1859 of Italy's war of liberation he returned to action; with his 'thousand' volunteers he sailed from Genoa (May 1860) and arrived in Sicily where he assisted Mazzinian rebels to free Sicily from Neapolitan control. Crossing with his army to the mainland, he swiftly overran much of S Italy, and drove King Francis of Naples from his capital (Sep 1860). Thereafter he allowed the conquest of S Italy to be completed by the Sardinians under Victor Emmanuel II. With the Kingdom of Italy a reality, and refusing all personal reward, he retired into private life on Caprera, where he died. » Italy [i]; Mazzini; Risorgimento; Thousand, Expedition of the

Garland, Judy, originally **Frances Gumm** (1922–69) US actress and singer, born at Great Rapids, Minnesota. She made her first stage appearances with her vaudeville parents, and became a juvenile film star in *Broadway Melody of 1938*, followed by *The Wizard of Oz* (1939) and *Meet Me in St Louis* (1944), directed by Vincente Minelli, whom she later married. A demanding series of musical leads coupled with drug problems exhausted her by 1950, and she spent the next four years in variety performances, returning to films with the 1954 remake of *A Star is Born*. Concerts and occasional films continued with public success, but her private life was full of overwhelming difficulties, and she died in London, apparently from an overdose of sleeping pills.

garlic A perennial bulb up to 60 cm/2 ft; narrow, flat leaves; greenish-to-purple star-shaped flowers mixed with bulbils. Native to Asia, it has been cultivated in the Mediterranean region since ancient times for the strongly flavoured bulbs. Wild relatives are sometimes used as poor substitutes. (*Allium sativum*. Family: *Liliaceae*.) » allium; bulb; bulbil; perennial

garlic mustard A biennial 20–120 cm/8 in–4 ft high, native to Europe and Asia; bright pale-green, heart-shaped leaves; heads of small, white, cross-shaped flowers; The whole plant smells of garlic, especially when crushed. Commonly found along hedgerows, it is sometimes called **hedge garlic**. (*Alliaria petiolata*. Family: *Cruciferae*.) » biennial; garlic

garnet A group of silicate minerals occurring mainly in metamorphic rocks, but also found in pegmatites. It displays a wide range of composition and colour. Important members and their primary constituents are *pyrope* (Mg,Al), *almandine* (Fe,Al), *grossularite* (Ca,Al), and *andradite* (Ca,Fe). Some varieties are important as gemstones. » gemstones; silicate minerals; Plates IV, V

Garonne, River [garon], ancient **Garumna** Chief river of SW France, rising in the Val d'Aran, 42 km/26 ml inside the Spanish border; flows from the C Pyrenees NE and NW to the Bec d'Ambes, 32 km/20 ml below Bordeaux, where it meets the R Dordogne to form the Gironde estuary; length 575 km/357 ml; linked to the Mediterranean Sea at Toulouse by the Canal du Midi. » France [i]

garpike » gar

Garrick, David (1717–79) British actor, theatre manager, and playwright, born in Hereford. His first play was performed at Drury Lane in 1740, and the following year he won acting fame as Richard III. For 30 years he dominated the English stage, in a wide range of parts. As joint manager of Drury Lane (1747–76) he encouraged innovations in scenery and lighting design. He died in London, and was buried in Westminster Abbey. » Johnson, Samuel; theatre

garrigue [gareeg] Evergreen scrubland vegetation found in areas with thin soils and a Mediterranean-type climate; also known as **garigue** or **garriga**. Low thorny shrubs and stunted oak are characteristic. In places it may result from the degradation of maquis vegetation through mismanagement of the land. » evergreen plants; maquis

Garrison, William Lloyd (1805–79) US abolitionist, born at Newburyport, Massachusetts. Educated informally, he emerged in 1830 as the foremost anti-slavery voice in the USA. His newspaper *The Liberator* argued the case for immediate abolition, and his American Anti-Slavery Society mobilized the energies of thousands of people in the cause. He died in New York City. » slave trade

Garter, the Most Noble Order of the The most ancient order of chivalry in Europe, founded by Edward III of England between 1344 and 1351. The emblem of the order is a gold-edged blue garter, inscribed in gold with *Honi soit qui mal y pense* (Fr. 'Shamed be he who thinks evil of it'), traditionally the words spoken by Edward after he picked up the Countess of Salisbury's dropped garter. There are usually 25 Companions of the Order, in addition to the sovereign. » decoration

gas 1 A state of matter in which atoms are disordered and highly mobile, moving in a random way with little interaction. Gases are characterized by low densities (typically $^1/_{1000}$ of a solid), an ability to flow and to fill a container, and high compressibility. All substances will pass into the gas or vapour phase if heated to a high enough temperature. All gases which do not react with one another are completely mixable in all proportions. » gas laws; ideal gas; phases of matter [i]; sublimation (chemistry); vapour pressure **2** A fuel which includes both **manufactured gas**, derived from solid or liquid fossil fuels, and **natural gas**, drawn from existing gaseous subterranean accumulations. Manufactured (or *town gas*) was made from the early 19th-c by the distillation of coal. The economics of the coal-gas industry depended to a great extent on its non-gaseous by-products. In the 20th-c, town gas has also been made by the chemical conversion of surplus naphtha from the petroleum industry or natural solid fuels other than coal. Natural gas occurs on its own or in association with oil deposits in many locations throughout the world. The main constituent of town gas is hydrogen; that of natural gas is methane. The calorific value of natural gas is about double that of town gas. » fuel; hydrogen; methane [i]; natural gas

gas constant The constant, usually given as *R*, which relates the volume, pressure, and temperature of a mass of gas. It has a value of about 8.3 joules per mole. » gas laws; ideal gas; joule; mole (physics)

gas-cooled reactor » **nuclear reactor** [i]

gas engine A specially adapted or designed internal combustion engine which uses gas as its fuel. In the 19th-c such engines were run off the gas mains, but modern practice stores the gas (usually methane) in pressurized tanks as a liquid. » gas **2** [i]; internal combustion engine; methane [i]

gas gangrene An infection of muscle and soft tissue by *Clostridium welchii*. The bacteria secrete a toxin that digests tissues, and causes gangrene with bubbles of gas from fermentation. » gangrene

gas laws Boyle's and Charles' Laws together, interrelating pressure, volume, and temperature for a given mass of an ideal gas. These laws may be summarized in a single equation: $pV = nRT$, where p is the pressure exerted by n moles of a gas contained in a volume V at an absolute temperature T. » Boyle; Charles' Law; gas **1**; gas constant; ideal gas

gas oil A liquid fuel, the heavier fraction of petroleum distillation. It is used as a heating fuel and in diesel engines. » fuel; petroleum

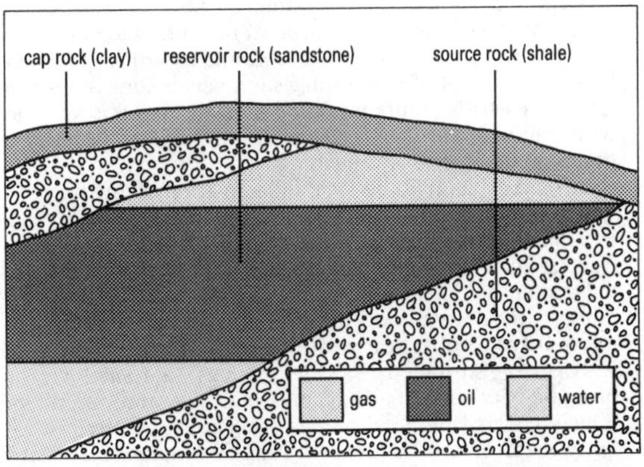

Gas – Reservoir formation

gas turbine An engine that passes the products of the combustion of its fuel/air mixture over the blades of a turbine. The turbine drives an air compressor, which in turn provides the air for the combustion process. The energy of the combustion products not taken up by the compressor can be used to provide a jet of exhaust gases, or drive another turbine. » engine; jet engine [i]; turbine

gas warfare » **chemical warfare**

Gascony [**gas**kuhnee], Fr **Gascogne**, Lat **Vasconia** Former province in Aquitaine region, SW France, now occupying the departments of Landes, Gers, Hautes-Pyrénées, and some adjacent areas; bounded S by the Pyrenees and W by the Bay of Biscay; part of the Roman Empire; conquered by the Visigoths, later by the Franks, who made it a duchy; joined to Guienne, 1052; in English hands, 1154–1453. » Aquitaine; Franks

Gaskell, Mrs Elizabeth (Cleghorn), *née* **Stevenson** (1810–65) British novelist, born in London. In 1832 she married William Gaskell (1805–84), a Unitarian minister in Manchester. She did not begin to write until middle age, when she published *Mary Barton* (1848). Her other works include *Cranford* (1853), *Ruth* (1853), *North and South* (1854–5), *Wives and Daughters* (1865), and a biography of Charlotte Bronte. She died near Alton, Hampshire. » English literature; novel

gasohol A mixture of gasoline with 5/15 % ethanol (ethyl alcohol which must be water-free), useful as a high-octane rating fuel in internal combustion engines. It is economically important in countries with a cheap supply of ethyl alcohol. » ethanol; fuel; octane number

gasoline » **petrol**

Gasperi, Alcide de [gas**pay**ree] (1881–1954) Italian statesman and Prime Minister (1945–53), born in Trentino. He studied at Innsbruck and Vienna, entered parliament in 1911, and was imprisoned by Mussolini as an anti-fascist (1927). From 1929 he worked in the Vatican library until he became Prime Minister of the new republic, heading a succession of coalition cabinets. He died at Sella di Valsugana. » Christian Democrats; Mussolini

gastric juice A mixture of substances secreted by cells and glands within the stomach, consisting of hydrochloric acid (from parietal cells), pepsinogen (from chief cells), mucus, and intrinsic factor (from mucous cells). Excessive secretion of acid and pepsinogen may lead to the formation of ulcers. Inability to produce intrinsic factor results in pernicious anaemia. » anaemia; gastrin; pepsin; ulcer

gastric ulcer Acute or chronic damage to the lining of the stomach, which leads to ulcer formation. It is a common cause of indigestion. » indigestion; stomach; ulcer

gastrin A type of hormone (a peptide) secreted in the stomach in response to both the presence of protein in the pylorus and increased discharge of the vagus nerve. It stimulates the parietal cells of the stomach to secrete hydrochloric acid, through the mediation of histamine released from cells (*histaminocytes*) close by. It is also present in the duodenum, pituitary gland, and the brain (where it may function as a neurotransmitter). » hormones; peptide; stomach; vagus

gastritis Inflammation of the stomach lining. **Acute gastritis** occurs as a result of several mucosal irritants, such as alcohol, strongly acid or alkaline substances, and aspirins. These cause local patch areas of acute congestion which sometimes bleed. **Chronic gastritis** occurs in older age groups, and is associated with thinning (*atrophy*) of the lining of the stomach. » mucous membrane; stomach

gastro-enteritis Irritation and inflammation of any part of the gastro-intestinal tract, characterized by abdominal pain, vomiting, diarrhoea, and severe prostration in some cases. As infants have smaller reserves of water and salt, they are especially vulnerable to losses of body fluids. » alimentary canal; cholera; dysentery; food poisoning; typhoid fever

gastro-intestinal tract » **alimentary canal**

gastropod [**gas**truhpod] The snails, slugs, and snail-like molluscs; body consists of a head, muscular foot, and visceral mass largely covered by a calcareous shell, usually spirally coiled; body characterized by torsion during development, so that the anus opens above the head; typically feeds on plant material using a band-like set of rasping teeth (the *radula*); many advanced forms are carnivorous, some are parasitic; includes land and freshwater snails and slugs, as well as a great diversity of marine snails such as the conches, cowries, limpets, sea slugs, whelks, and winkles. (Phylum: *Mollusca*. Class: *Gastropoda*.) » calcium; conch; cowrie; limpet; mollusc; sea slug; shell; slug; snail; whelk

gastrotrich [**gas**truhtrik] A minute, worm-like animal found in or on bottom sediments and in association with other aquatic organisms in various habitats; body covered in a horny layer (cuticle), and may have bristles. (Phylum: *Gastrotricha*, c.150 species.) » worm

gastrula [**gas**troola] The stage following the blastula in the embryonic development of animals. During this phase (*gastrulation*), cells of the embryo move into their correct position for development into the various organ systems of the adult. » blastula; embryology

Gates, Horatio (1728–1806) US general, born at Maldon, Essex. He joined the British army, served in America in the Seven Years' War (1756–63), and then settled there. In the War of Independence he sided with his adoptive country, and in 1777 took command of the Northern department, and compelled the surrender of the British army at Saratoga. In 1780 he commanded the army of the South, but was routed by Cornwallis near Camden, and was superseded. He retired to Virginia until 1790, emancipated his slaves, and settled in New York City, where he died. » American Revolution

Gatling, Richard Jordan (1818–1903) US inventor, born at Maney's Neck, North Carolina. He invented several agricultural machines, but is remembered for his invention of the **Gatling gun** (1861–2), a revolving battery gun, with 10 parallel barrels, firing 1 200 shots a minute. He died in New York City.

gaucho [**gow**choh] A nomadic, fiercely independent mestizo horseman of the Argentine pampa, first appearing in the 17th-c. With the advent of ranches, railways, and settled government in the 19th-c, the gaucho vanished, though gaucho skills live on among the rural population of Argentina and Uruguay. An inhabitant of the S states of Brazil is known by a similar name. » Argentina [i]; pampas

Gaudí (I Cornet), Antonio [gow**dee**] (1852–1929) Spanish architect, born at Riudoms, Catalonia. Educated at the Escuela Superior de Arquitectura, Barcelona, he was the most famous exponent of Catalan 'modernisme', one of the branches of the Art Nouveau movement. He is best known for the extravagant and ornate church of the Sagrada Familia in Barcelona, which occupied him from 1884 until his death, at Barcelona. » Art Nouveau

Gaudier-Brzeska, Henri [**gohd**yay **bres**ka] (1891–1915) French sculptor, born at St Jean de Braye, near Orleans. He lived in London from 1911, and exhibited with the London Group in 1914 before joining the French army. He was killed in action at Neuville-Saint-Vaast. A pioneering modernist who drew upon African tribal art, he rapidly developed a highly personal abstract style exemplified in both carvings and drawings. » abstract art; London Group

gauge theory A type of theory in mechanics in which interactions correspond to special symmetry transformations of the basic equations of the theory. Quantum gauge theories, in which interactions between sub-atomic particles are related to the preservation of symmetry properties at each point in space and time, are essential to nuclear and particle physics. Quantum electrodynamics, quantum chromodynamics, and the Glashow-Weinberg-Salam theory are all gauge theories. In quantum electrodynamics, the requirement of conservation of electric charge at each point of space and time corresponds to the observed interaction of photons with charged particles. » electrodynamics; Glashow-Weinberg-Salam theory; quantum chromodynamics; quantum field theory; symmetry

Gauguin, (Eugène Henri) Paul [**goh**gĩ] (1848–1903) French Postimpressionist painter, born in Paris. He went to sea at 17, settled in Paris in 1871, married, and became a successful stockbroker who painted as a hobby. By 1876 he had begun to exhibit his own work. He left his family, visited Martinique (1887), and became the leader of a group of painters at Pont Aven, Brittany (1888). From 1891 he lived mainly in Tahiti and the Marquesas Is, using local people as his subjects. He gradually evolved his own style, *synthétisme*, reflecting his hatred of civilization and the inspiration he found in primitive peoples. Among his best-known works are 'The Vision after the Sermon' (1888, Edinburgh), and the major allegorical work, 'D'où venons-nous? Que sommes-nous? Où allons-nous?' (1897–8, Where Do We Come From? What Are We? Where Are We Going?; Boston) He also excelled in woodcarvings of pagan idols. He died in the Marquesas Is. » French art; Postimpressionism; Plate XI

Gaul (Lat *Gallia*) In ancient geography normally used for **Transalpine Gaul**, bounded by the Alps, the Rhine, and the Pyrenees. Julius Caesar completed the Roman conquest in 58–51 BC, the impact of Romanization being felt most in the S, where Roman law remained in use until 1789. With the gradual Roman withdrawal in the 5th-c, Germanic colonies became independent kingdoms. Unity was superficially achieved under Clovis and Charlemagne; later, after many vicissitudes, Gaul – its easternmost territories excluded – developed into the mediaeval kingdom of France. **Cisalpine Gaul** lay S of the Alps and N of the Apennines. Conquered by the Romans in 201–191 BC, it was incorporated into Italy in 42 BC. » Charlemagne; Clovis I; Franks; Roman history [i]; Visigoths

Gaulish » **Celtic languages**

Gaullists Members of the French political party, the *Rassemblement pour la République* (RPR) whose programmes are based on the doctrine developed by President de Gaulle in 1958–69. Nationalistic in character, Gaullists emphasize the need for strong government, especially in relations with the EEC and foreign powers such as the USA. » de Gaulle; European Economic Community

Gaumont, Léon Ernest [gohmõ] (1864–1946) French cinema inventor, manufacturer, and producer, born in Paris. He synchronized a projected film with a phonograph in 1901, and was responsible for the first talking pictures, demonstrated at Paris in 1910. He also introduced an early form of coloured cinematography in 1912. » cinematography [i]

Gaunt, John of » **John of Gaunt**

gaur [gowuh] A rare wild ox native to hill forests of India and SE Asia; largest of wild cattle (shoulder height, 2 m/6½ ft); dark brown with white 'stockings'; bony ridge along back behind neck; high, strongly curved horns; also known as **Indian bison** or **seladang**; domesticated form called a **gayal** (or **mithan**). (*Bos gaurus*.) » ox

Gauss, (Johann) Carl Friedrich [gows] (1777–1855) German mathematician, born at Brunswick. A mental prodigy, he pioneered the application of mathematics to such areas as gravitation, magnetism, and electricity. In 1807 he became professor of mathematics and director of the observatory at Göttingen, and in 1821 was appointed to conduct the trigonometrical survey of Hanover, for which he invented a heliograph. He died at Göttingen. The unit of magnetic induction has been named after him. » Gauss's law; magnetism; number theory; RR70

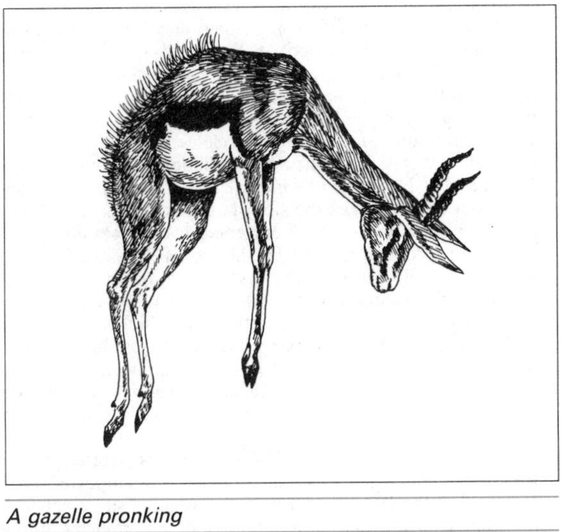

A gazelle pronking

Gauss's law In electrostatics: the total electric flux through some closed surface is proportional to the total charge enclosed by that surface; stated by German mathematician Carl Gauss. The constant of proportionality is $1/\varepsilon$, where ε is permittivity. The law is the expression of charge as a source of electric field. » charge; electrostatics; flux (physics); Gauss; Maxwell's equations; permittivity

Gautier, Théophile (1811–72) French author and critic, born at Tarbes. From painting he turned to literature, and became an extreme Romantic. In 1830 he published his first long poem, *Albertus*, and in 1835 appeared his celebrated novel, *Mademoiselle de Maupin*. His most important collection was *Emaux et camées* (1852, Enamels and Cameos). He died at Neuilly. » French literature; Romanticism (literature)

Gavaskar, Sunil (Manohar) (1949–) Indian cricketer, born in Bombay. He played 125 Test Matches, scoring a record 10 122 runs, and between 1974–5 and 1986–7 played in a record 106 consecutive Test Matches. He scored 25 834 runs in first-class cricket at an average of 51.46 per innings. His highest innings was 236 not out against the West Indies at Madras in 1983–4, the highest score by an Indian batsman in Test cricket. » cricket (sport) [i]

gavial » **gharial**

gavotte A French folk dance, popular also as a court dance during the 17th–18th-c, and often included in instrumental and orchestral suites of the period. It was in a moderately quick duple or quadruple metre. » suite

Gawain or **Gawayne** [gawayn] One of King Arthur's knights, the son of King Lot of Orkney, whose character varies in different accounts. In the mediaeval *Sir Gawayn and the Grene Knight*, he is a noble hero undergoing a test of faith. In other stories he is a jeering attacker of reputations, especially that of Lancelot. » Arthur; Lancelot, Sir

Gay, John (1685–1732) English poet and dramatist, born at Barnstaple, Devon. He was apprenticed to a London silk mercer, but turned to literature, writing poems, pamphlets, and in 1727 the first series of his popular satirical *Fables*. His greatest success was *The Beggar's Opera* (1728), which achieved an unprecedented theatrical run of 62 performances. A friend of Pope and Swift, he died in London, and was buried in Westminster Abbey. » drama; English literature; poetry; Pope, Alexander; Swift

Gay-Lussac, Joseph Louis (1778–1850) French chemist and physicist, born at St Léonard, Haute Vienne. Educated in Paris, he began a series of investigations into gases, temperature, and the behaviour of vapours. He made balloon ascents to study the laws of terrestrial magnetism, and to collect samples of air for analysis, which led to his major discovery, the law of volumes named after him (1808). In 1809 he became professor of chemistry at the Polytechnic in Paris, and from 1832 at the Jardin des Plantes. He died in Paris. » Charles' Law

gayal [gayal] » **gaur**

Gaza Strip area 202 sq km/78 sq ml. Israeli-occupied district under military administration since 1967, bounded NW by the Mediterranean Sea; length, 50 km/30 ml; chief town, Gaza; formerly part of Egyptian Sinai, after Arab–Israeli War of 1948–9; contains many Palestinian refugee camps; considerable tension in the area since the beginning of the uprising (*intifada*) in 1988. » Arab–Israeli Wars; Israel [i]; West Bank

Gazankulu [gazang**koo**loo] pop (1985) 497 213. National state or non-independent Black homeland in Transvaal province, NE South Africa; achieved self-governing status in 1973. » apartheid; South Africa [i]

gazelle An elegant athletic antelope, native to Africa and S Asia; usually pale brown above with white underparts; some species with thick black line along side; face often with weak stripes; when alarmed, moves by 'pronking' (or 'stotting') – a vertical leap using all four legs simultaneously. (Tribe: *Antilopini*, 18 species.) » antelope; blackbuck; dorcas gazelle; gerenuk; springbok

gazelle hound » **saluki**

GCSE An acronym for the **General Certificate of Secondary**

Education, introduced in England and Wales for the first time in 1988, which merged what had previously been two separate examinations for pupils aged about 16 or older. These earlier examinations were the *General Certificate of Education* (GCE), which was originally aimed at about the top 20% of the ability range, and the *Certificate of Secondary Education* (CSE), which was meant for the next 40%. In practice the situation had become much more complex, with about 90% of pupils taking one or other of the exams, and some schools entering the same pupils for both. A similar examination reform, the *Standard Grade*, had been introduced in Scotland two years earlier.

Gdańsk, formerly Ger **Danzig** 54°22N 18°38E, pop (1983) 464 600. Industrial port and capital of Gdańsk voivodship, N Poland; at the mouth of the Martwa Wisła; held by Prussia, 1793–1919; free city within the Polish tariff area, 1919; annexation by Germany in 1939, precipitating World War 2; Lenin shipyard the scene of much labour unrest in 1980s, in support of Solidarity; part of the *Tri-city* with Sopot and Gdynia; airport; railway; two universities (1945, 1970); maritime research institutes; largest shipyard in Poland; textiles, televisions, fertilizer, oil refining, food processing, cold storage; High Gate, Golden Gate, Bakers' Gate, St George Fraternity Mansion (1487–94), Artus Court, Swan Tower, Royal Granary (1620), national museum, archaeological museum; Churches of the Virgin Mary, St John, St Elizabeth, St Catherine, Holy Trinity; Gdańsk Festival (Aug), Polish film festival (Sep). » Poland [i]; Solidarity

GDP » **gross domestic product**

gean [jeen] A species of cherry native to Europe and Asia, forming a tall tree with white flowers and dark, purplish-red, sweet or sour fruit; also called **wild** or **bird cherry**. It is a parent of the sweet cherry of orchards. (**Prunus avium**. Family: *Rosaceae*,) » cherry; tree [i]

gear A device used to transform one rotary motion into another, in terms of speed and direction. The fundamental type of gear is the toothed gear wheel, which can be used in a wide variety of combinations and configurations to produce the desired ratio of output rotation to input rotation. » clutch; engine; transmission

gecko A lizard native to warm regions worldwide; body usually flattened top-to-bottom; skin soft; eyes large, without moveable eyelids; tongue short, often used to lick eyes; many species with flattened toes for walking on vertical surfaces; eats mainly insects; most individuals nocturnal; males are the only lizards with loud calls. (Family: *Gekkonidae*, 800 species.) » lizard [i]; tokay gecko

gedankenexperiment » **thought experiment**

Geelong [jee**long**] 38°10S 144°26E, pop (1986) 148 300. Port in S Victoria, Australia, on the W side of Corio Bay, part of Port Phillip Bay; Deakin University (1974); railway; aluminium and oil refining, motor vehicles, trade in wheat, wool; many 19th-c villas with beautiful gardens; customs house the oldest wooden building in Victoria. » Victoria (Australia)

gegenschein [**gay**guhnshiyn] » **zodiacal light**

Gehenna [guh**hen**na] (Gr form of the Heb *Gehinnom* 'Valley of Hinnom', a ravine SW of Jerusalem) In c.7th-c BC, the site of cultic sacrifices of children to Baal by fire, condemned by Jeremiah (*Jer* 19.4–6); later considered an entrance to the underworld. The name is metaphorically used in both Judaism and the New Testament as a place where the wicked would be tormented (usually by fire) after death (eg *Mark* 9.43). » Baal; hell; Jeremiah, Book of

Gehrig, Lou, properly (Henry) Louis byname **Iron Horse** (1903–41) US baseball player, born and died in New York City. He played 2 130 consecutive games for the New York Yankees between 1925 and 1939. An outstanding first-base fielder, he ended his career with a batting average of 0.340 and scored 493 home runs. » baseball [i]

Geiger, Hans [**giy**guh] (1882–1945) German physicist, born at Neustadt-an-der-Haardt. Educated at Erlangen, he moved to Manchester, working under Rutherford (1906–12). He investigated beta-ray radioactivity, and helped to devise a counter to measure it, which now bears his name. He was professor at Kiel (1925) and at Tübingen (1929), and later worked at Berlin. He died at Potsdam. » Geiger counter [i]; Rutherford, Ernest

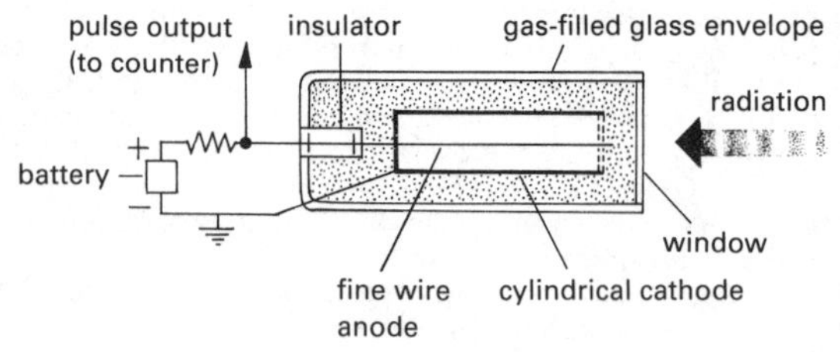

Geiger counter tube

Geiger counter A device for counting atomic particles, named after German physicist Hans Geiger. Gas between electrodes is ionized by the passage of a particle, and so transmits a pulse to a counter. » Geiger

Geisel, Ernesto [**giy**zel] (1908–) Brazilian general and President (1974–9), born at Rio Grande do Sul. His military presidency was notable for its policy of 'decompression', which led to the restoration of democracy in 1985. » Brazil [i]

gel [jel] A colloidal suspension of a solid in a liquid, in which the properties of the solid predominate. An example is gelatine. » colloid;

gelada baboon [**je**lada] A baboon native to the mountains of Ethiopia; brown coat (long and thick over head and shoulders); long pale 'whiskers' surround face; top of muzzle ridged; cheeks sunken; tail long; chest with areas of naked scarlet skin. (*Theropithecus gelada.*) » baboon

gelatin(e) [**je**latin] A protein formed when collagen (a fibrous protein found in animal bones, skin, and hair) is boiled in water. Its dilute suspension in water sets to a firm colloid. It is used in foods, adhesives, and photographic emulsions. » collagens; colloid; protein

Geldof, Bob (1954–) Irish rock musician and philanthropist, born in Dublin. Educated at Black Rock College, he worked in Canada as a pop journalist, then returned home in 1975 to form the successful rock group, the Boomtown Rats (1975–86). Moved by television pictures of widespread suffering in famine-stricken Ethiopia, he established the pop charity 'Bandaid' trust in 1984, which raised £8 million for African famine relief through the release of the record 'Do they know it's Christmas?'. In 1985, simultaneous 'Live Aid' charity concerts were held in London and Philadelphia which, transmitted by satellite throughout the world, raised a further £48 million. He was awarded an honorary knighthood in 1986.

gelignite A group of industrial explosives consisting of a gelatinized mixture of nitroglycerine and nitrocellulose. Inert non-explosive material (*extenders*) promote safety in handling. » explosives

Gell-Mann, Murray (1929–) US theoretical physicist, born in New York City. Educated at Yale and the Massachusetts Institute of Technology, he became professor of theoretical physics at the California Institute of Technology in 1956. At 24 he made a major contribution by introducing the concept of *strangeness* into the theory of elementary particles. This allowed new classifications and predictions, outlined by Gell-Mann and Y Ne'man in their book *The Eightfold Way* (1964). He also helped to devise the idea of quarks as constituents of all nuclei, and the idea of weak currents for understanding a type of nuclear interaction. He won the Nobel Prize for Physics in 1969. » atomic/particle physics; quark; strangeness

Gemara [guh**mah**ra] (Aramaic 'completion') A commentary on the Jewish Mishnah, which together with the Mishnah constitutes the Talmud. It consists largely of scholarly rabbinic discussions that interpret and extend the applications of legal teachings in Rabbi Judah's Mishnah. Distinct versions were produced in Palestine and Babylon. » Judaism; Mishnah; Talmud

Gemayel, Amin [gemiy**el**] (1942–) Lebanese statesman and President (1982–?). Trained as a lawyer, he supported Bashir Gemayel in the 1975–6 civil war, and was his successor to the presidency. Politically more moderate, his policies initially proved no more successful in determining a peaceful settlement of the problems of Lebanese government. » Gemayel, Bashir

Gemayel, Bashir [gemiyel] (1947–82) Lebanese army officer and statesman. He joined the militia of his father's Phalangist party, and came to be the party's political director in the Ashrefieh sector of E Beirut, where he was an active leader of the Christian militia in the civil war of 1975–6. By the systematic elimination of rivals he came to command the military forces of E Beirut. He distanced his party from Israeli support, and aimed to expel all foreign influence from Lebanese affairs. Having twice escaped assassination, he was killed in a bomb explosion while still president-elect.

Gemayel, Sheikh Pierre [gemiyel] (1905–) Lebanese politician, a member of the Maronite Christian community of Lebanon. Educated at Beirut and Paris, he trained as a pharmacist. In 1936 he founded the Kataeb or Phalangist party, modelled on the Spanish and German fascist organizations, and in 1937 became its leader. He was twice imprisoned (1937, 1943), held various ministerial posts (1960–7), and led the Phalangist Militia in the 1975–6 civil war.

Gemini (Lat 'twins') [jemuhniy] A conspicuous N constellation with a bright pair of stars **Castor** and **Pollux**. It is a spring sign of the zodiac, lying between Taurus and Cancer. Castor is a double star, easy to see in a small telescope. Pollux is a bright orange star, the nearest giant star to Earth. Distance: 11 parsec. » constellation; double star; star; RR8

Gemini programme A second-generation US-crewed spacecraft programme, following Mercury and preceding Apollo, using a 2-member crew. It was used to demonstrate the new capabilities of extra-vehicular activity, and extended astronaut endurance to a degree needed to accomplish lunar landing missions. It also perfected the orbital rendezvous and docking technique. There were 10 successful missions between March 1965 and November 1966. » Apollo programme; Mercury programme; space physiology and medicine; RR10

gemma A multicellular unit, usually disc-shaped or filamentous, formed in special structures called *gemmae cups* produced by bryophytes as a means of vegetative reproduction. When dispersed, the gemmae grow into new plants. » bryophyte; vegetative reproduction

gemsbok » **oryx**

gemstones A general term for precious or semi-precious stones or minerals valued for their rarity, beauty, and durability; usually cut and polished as jewels. The most highly valued are hard and transparent crystals such as diamond, ruby, emerald, and sapphire. » beryl; chalcedony; corundum; diamond; emerald; garnet; jade; opal; pegmatite; quartz; ruby; rutile; sapphire; spinel; topaz; tourmaline; turquoise; zircon; Plate V

gender The social expression of the basic physiological differences between men and women – social behaviour which is deemed to be appropriate to 'masculine' or 'feminine' roles and which is learned through primary and secondary socialization. Thus, while sex is biological, gender is socially determined. » role; sexism

gene A unit of heredity; a segment of the DNA which contains the instructions for the development of a particular inherited characteristic. When first coined by Johannsen (1909) it still referred to a hypothetical entity, and it is only recently with the intensive study of DNA that the structure, length, and location of genes is being established. A gene in the nuclear DNA coding for a particular protein (or part of a protein) exists in several pieces, interrupted by intervening non-coding DNA sequences. The non-coding sequences are then cut and spliced in transcribing the DNA information into the RNA message to be acted upon in the cytoplasm. » DNA [i]; gene probe/therapy; Johannsen; protein; RNA

gene probe A fragment of single-stranded DNA, labelled with the radioisotope ^{32}P, capable of finding and hybridizing with the DNA fragments that carry the complementary sequence. Such probes are in increasing use, in families where an inherited disorder occurs, to detect carriers of the gene responsible. » DNA [i]; gene; radioisotope

gene therapy The notion that a particular gene might be inserted into the body cells of individuals who are born with a defective or absent gene. The most likely body cells would be those in the bone marrow, which can be temporarily withdrawn and returned to replicate. Technical difficulties have so far restricted this idea to laboratories and a few animals. » bone marrow; gene

genealogy The study of family history. It originated as an oral tradition, the ancestry of important members of society (especially sovereigns) being memorized by a priest or bard. Later

PART OF THE FAMILY TREE OF THE BRITISH ROYAL FAMILY

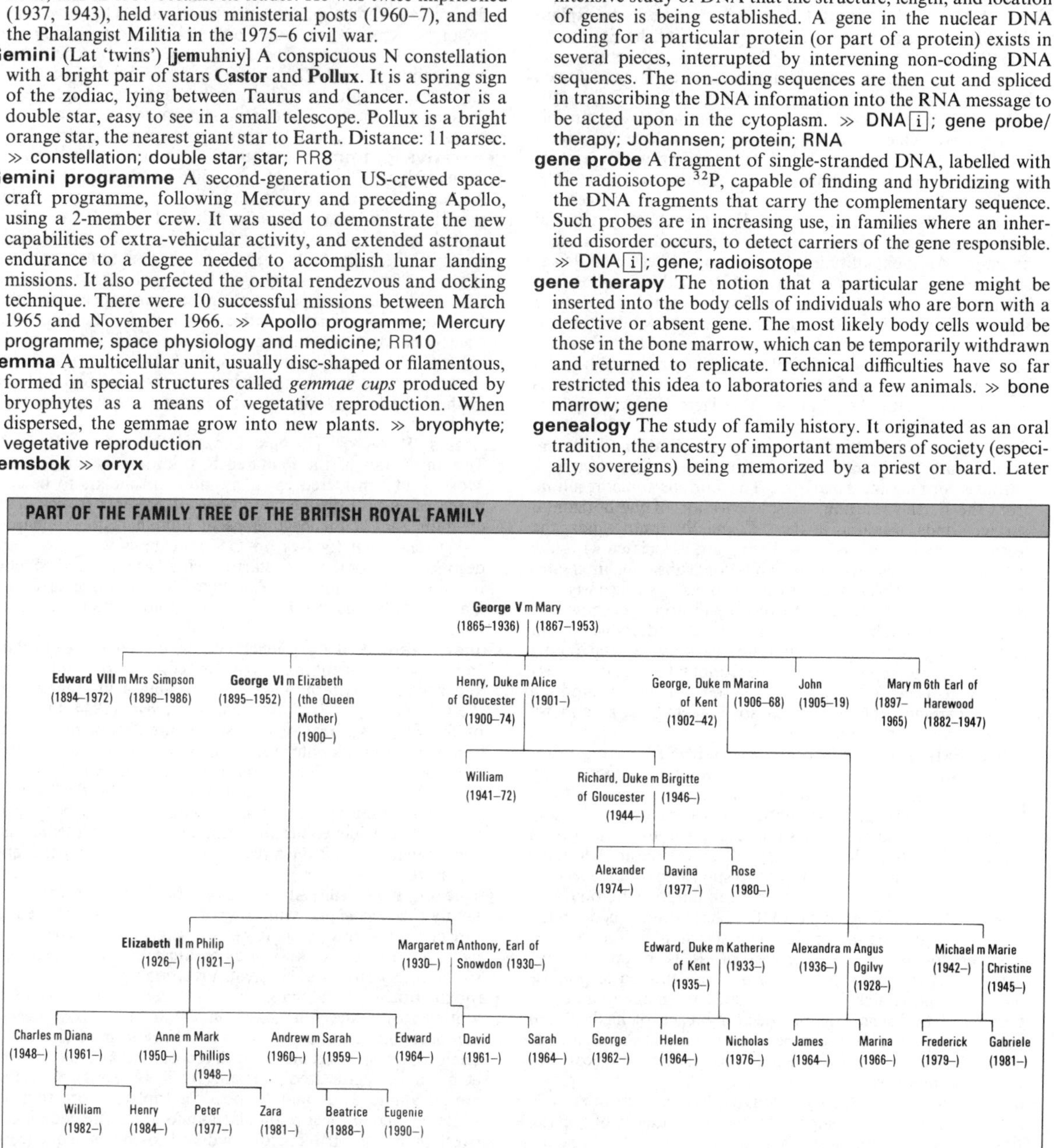

these lists of ancestors were written down, as in the Bible. Since the 16th-c, records of family descent have been strictly kept in many countries, so that most people in W Europe could trace their ancestry if they wished. A chart showing genealogical descent is a *pedigree*: this may be crucial in establishing a matter of inheritance. In countries where wealth and position were commonly inherited, such as the UK, genealogy has been very important; but even in countries where the legal and social reasons for interest in genealogy are fewer, such as the USA and Australia, many individuals attempt to trace their 'family tree'. *See illustration p 487*

General Assembly (politics) » **United Nations**

General Assembly (religion) The highest court, in Churches of Presbyterian order. It normally meets annually and comprises equal numbers of ministers and elders, elected by presbyteries in proportion to their size. It is presided over by a moderator, elected annually. » elder (religion); moderator; Presbyterianism; presbytery **3**

general circulation model A model which seeks to explain the atmospheric circulation or wind patterns of the Earth, and also the redistribution of energy and moisture between the tropical and polar regions. Atmospheric circulation is driven by temperature differences between tropical and polar latitudes, and several models have been proposed to explain this phenomenon. One of the simplest recognizes three circulation cells in each hemisphere, based on observations of surface pressure, wind, temperature, and precipitation data. The *Hadley Cell* accounts for the circulation pattern between the Equator and subtropical regions. Heating of the equatorial surface by solar radiation results in rising air and low surface pressure. At high altitudes (upper troposphere and lower stratosphere), this air is carried away from the Equator to a latitude of about 30°, the region of subtropical high pressure systems, where it descends and warms. Surface winds blow out of this high pressure area as trade winds towards the Equator. Mid-latitude surface westerlies also originate in the subtropical high pressure areas and blow towards the low pressure areas centred on a latitude of about 50°. Here the warm air is vertically displaced by cold polar air. Some of the rising air flows back at high altitudes to the subtropical high pressure areas forming the *Ferrel Cell*, and some flows polewards at high altitudes forming the *Polar Cell*. The Coriolis force, resulting from the Earth's rotation, causes deflection of the horizontal surface winds, resulting in the NE and SE trade winds, the westerlies, and polar easterlies. Rising air, associated with low pressure, creates clouds and precipitation; subsiding air creates dry conditions. This model fits observations of surface weather conditions. It is, however, an oversimplification, as shown by satellite observations of upper atmosphere winds, which are in fact westerly (jet streams) and not easterly, as the model predicts. » atmospheric pressure; Coriolis force [i]; depression (meteorology) [i]; Doldrums; intertropical convergence zone; jet stream; Polar Front; Rossby waves [i]; stratosphere; trade winds; troposphere; wind [i]

General Extrasensory Perception (GESP) In parapsychology, a situation in which there is information potentially available to the subject from the thoughts or experiences of another (as in telepathy), from the physical environment (as in clairvoyance), and/or from some event yet to occur (as in precognition). In such situations it is impossible to determine theoretically which of these three is responsible for an effect. » clairvoyance; extrasensory perception; parapsychology

General Medical Council (GMC) The statutory body in the UK which controls the professional standing and conduct of members of the medical profession. It is responsible for maintaining the Medical Register of those entitled to practise medicine, and retains the power to erase the name of a doctor because of negligence, malpractice, or breach of medical and professional ethics. It also supervises and maintains standards of undergraduate and immediately postgraduate medical education. » medicine

general relativity A theory of gravity deriving almost entirely from Einstein (1915). It supersedes Newton's theory of gravitation, which is reproduced as a weak gravity, low velocity special case, and replaces the Newtonian notion of instantaneous action at a distance via the gravitational field with a distortion of space-time due to the presence of mass. For example, the Earth moves round the Sun because of the distortion of space-time by the Sun's greater mass. An analogy represents space-time as a rubber sheet distorted by a heavy ball representing the Sun; a smaller ball rolling by, representing a planet, will tend to fall into this depression, apparently attracted. General relativity is supported by experiments which measure the bending of star light due to the presence of the Sun's mass, and also the precession of Mercury's orbit. Other predictions include black holes and the expansion of the universe. » black hole; cosmological constant; cosmology; covariance; curvature of space-time; Einstein field equations; equivalence principle; geodesic; gravitational collapse/redshift/waves; Hawking radiation; Kaluza-Klein theory; Mach's principle; metric; quantum gravity

General Strike (4–12 May 1926) A national strike in Britain, organized by the Trades Union Congress (TUC) in support of the miners' campaign to resist wage cuts. The government organized special constables and volunteers to counter the most serious effects of the strike, and issued an anti-strike propaganda journal, *The British Gazette*. The TUC called off the strike, though the miners' strike continued fruitlessly for three more months. » industrial action; trade union

generation, computer » **computer generations**

generative grammar A type of grammar, devised by US linguist Noam Chomsky in the 1950s, which explicitly defines the set of grammatical sentences in a language, rather than providing an informal characterization of them. It comprises a formal set of rules which predict the grammatical set from amongst the potentially infinite number of sentences which might occur in any language. Each is assigned a unique structural description, representing the grammatical knowledge (or *competence*) which a native speaker uses. Best-known is **transformational grammar**, in which one set of rules assigns a structure to a basal set of sentences, and another 'transforms' those structures into the forms in which they will actually occur in the language. » Chomsky; competence; deep structure; grammar

Genesis, Book of The first book of the Hebrew Bible/Old Testament and of the Pentateuch; traditionally attributed to Moses, but considered by many modern scholars to be composed of several distinct traditions. It presents stories of the creation and of the beginnings of human history (Chapters 1–11), and then focuses on God's dealings with the people destined to become Israel, starting with Abraham and concluding with Jacob's sons. » Abraham; Adam and Eve; Enoch; Isaac; Jacob; Joseph; Moses; Noah; Old Testament; Pentateuch

Genet, Jean (1910–86) French author, born and died in Paris. In his youth he spent many years in reformatories and prisons, and began to write in 1942 while serving a life sentence for theft. His first novel, *Notre-Dame des Fleurs* (1944, Our Lady of the Flowers) created a sensation for its portrayal of the criminal world. He later turned from novels to plays, such as *Les Bonnes* (1947, The Maids) and *Les Paravents* (1961, The Screens). In 1948 he was granted a pardon by the President after a petition by French intellectuals. Sartre's book *Saint Genet* (1952) widened his fame among the French intelligentsia. He wrote little in his later years. » absurdism; drama; French literature

genet or **genette** [**jen**it] An African or European carnivore of the family *Viverridae*; pale with rows of dark spots and banded tail; rare chestnut-brown **aquatic genet** or **Congo water civet** (*Osbornictis piscivora*); also known as **bush cat**. (Genus: *Genetta*, 10 species.) » carnivore [i]; civet; Viverridae [i]

genetic code The alphabet in which genetic instructions are written, using the four bases in DNA and RNA: *adenine*, *cytosine*, *guanine*, and *thymine* (for DNA) or *uracil* (for RNA). Each triplet of bases indicates that a particular kind of amino acid is to be synthesized (see panel for RNA bases). Since there are 20 amino acids and 64 possible triplets, more than one triplet can code for a particular amino acid. The code is non-overlapping; the triplets are read end-to-end in sequence (eg UUU = Phenylalanine, UUA = Leucine, CCU = Proline); and

GENETIC CODE IN RNA TRIPLETS

1st Base	2nd Base U	C	A	G	3rd Base
U	Phenylalanine	Serine	Tyrosine	Cysteine	U
	Phenylalanine	Serine	Tyrosine	Cysteine	C
	Leucine	Serine	—*	—*	A
	Leucine	Serine	—*	Tryptophan	G
C	Leucine	Proline	Histidine	Arginine	U
	Leucine	Proline	Histidine	Arginine	C
	Leucine	Proline	Glutamine	Arginine	A
	Leucine	Proline	Glutamine	Arginine	G
A	Isoleucine	Threonine	Asparagine	Serine	U
	Isoleucine	Threonine	Asparagine	Serine	C
	Isoleucine	Threonine	Lysine	Arginine	A
	Methionine	Threonine	Lysine	Arginine	G
G	Valine	Alanine	Aspartic acid	Glycine	U
	Valine	Alanine	Aspartic acid	Glycine	C
	Valine	Alanine	Glutamic acid	Glycine	A
	Valine	Alanine	Glutamic acid	Glycine	G

*Chain termination

there are three triplets not translated into amino acid, indicating chain termination. The code is universal, in that it applies to all species. » amino acid [i]; DNA [i]; RNA

genetic counselling/counseling The giving of advice to prospective parents concerned at the risk that their future child may suffer from a genetic disease, a worry usually due to their having already produced an affected child or to the existence elsewhere in the family of an affected relative. In the UK there are specialist genetic clinics in the National Health Service in almost all regions; clinics are also widely available in the USA and W Europe, but are not yet common in other countries. The procedure consists of confirmation of the diagnosis in the affected individual; calculation of the risk of occurrence of the disease from the family history and relevant clinical investigations; advising on the risk; discussing the implications if the child should be affected; and advising on procedures by which the birth of an affected child can be avoided. » genetics [i]; medicine

genetic engineering The formation of new combinations of heritable material. Nucleic acid molecules, produced artificially or biologically outside the cell (eg by recombinant DNA technology), are inserted into a carrier (such as a virus or bacterial plasmid) so as to allow their incorporation into a host organism in which they do not naturally occur, but in which they are capable of continued propagation. Genetic engineering has many uses. Particular DNA sequences from an organism can be produced in large amounts, and with very great purity, so that the structure of specific DNA regions can be analysed. Biological compounds can be produced industrially (eg human insulin, blood clotting factor, interferon, vaccines, growth hormone). New synthetic capabilities can be incorporated into plants (eg for nitrogen fixation). Ultimately it will be possible to excise genes responsible for hereditary disease and replace them with normal DNA sequences.

The implications of genetic engineering have led to considerable public debate, and in most countries there is government control over work using recombinant DNA techniques. There is also some public fear that the presence of foreign genetic elements may adversely affect the normal functions of cells. To counter this, physical and biological safety measures are used to minimize the risk of spread of a host organism with foreign genetic elements inserted. Physical containment makes use of refined micro-biological techniques and equipment designed to prevent the escape of the host organism. Biological containment minimizes the chance of a host organism surviving outside the laboratory, usually by using host cells carrying deleterious mutations which permit their growth only under restricted artificial laboratory conditions. » DNA [i]; gene

genetically determined disease Disorders which stem directly from abnormalities in chromosomes, each one of which carries many genes, or defects in or absence of single genes. Chromosome abnormalities stem from defects in cell division in which the expected complement of 46 normal chromosomes is not achieved in body cells. Some of these produce recognizable abnormalities, such as Down's syndrome. Defects of a single gene arise from a primary error or mutation in the DNA code, and are inherited in a simple fashion following Mendelian Laws. If the gene is located on one of the sex chromosomes, the disorder will be sex-linked; if it is located on a chromosome not concerned with sex determination, it will not be sex-linked and is said to be *autosomal*. Haemophilia is the best known sex-linked disorder, occurring in males and transmitted by females. Achondroplasia, cystic fibrosis, and Marfan's syndrome are among the more common autosomal disorders. At present there is no way in which these disorders can be treated by direct replacement of the gene. » achondroplasia; cystic fibrosis; Down's syndrome; genetic counselling; genetics [i]; haemophilia; Marfan's syndrome; prenatal diagnosis

genetics The modern science of heredity. It originated with the discovery by Austrian biologist Gregor Mendel that observable hereditary characteristics are determined by factors transmitted without change and in predictable fashion from one generation to the next. The term was coined by British biologist William Bateson in 1907. Initially slow to develop, its pace increased rapidly during this century, and today it is one of the most vigorous areas of science. Genetics occupies a unique position, for its principles and mechanisms extend throughout almost all biology, it ties together all branches that deal with individual and population variation, and gives a unifying core at all levels – the molecular structure of cells and tissues, the development of individuals, and the evolution of populations. Today the mechanisms of genetics are being applied to make, in the laboratory, substances formerly obtainable only from organisms (eg vaccines, hormones), and the time may not be far distant when genetic errors responsible for disease may be correctable by such procedures. » Bateson; biology; gene; genetic code [i]; genetic counselling/engineering; genetically determined disease; Mendel's laws; population genetics

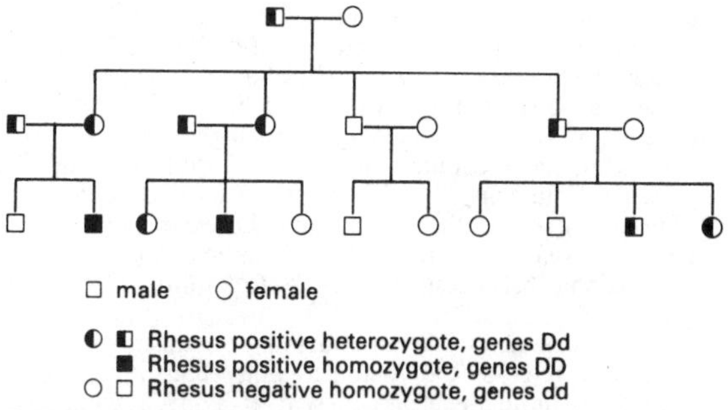

A pedigree diagram showing the inheritance of Rhesus positive and negative blood groups. » rhesus factor

genette » genet

Geneva [juhneeva], Fr **Genève**, Ger **Genf**, Ital **Ginevra** 46°13N 6°09E, pop (1980) 156 505. Capital city of Geneva canton, W Switzerland; on R Rhône at W end of L Geneva; built on the site of a Roman town; free city until end of 13th-c; independent republic until becoming a Swiss canton in 1814; centre of the Reformation under Calvin; former seat of the League of Nations (1920–46); capital of French-speaking Switzerland; airport (Coitrin); railway; university (1559); banking, commerce, administration, precision instruments, chemicals; world capital of high-class watchmaking and jewellery; Old Town on left bank of the Rhône; headquarters of over 200 international organizations (eg International Red Cross, World Health

Organization); renowned for its numerous quays and its fountain, Jet d'Eau, which reaches 745 m/2 500 ft; St Peter's Cathedral (12th-c); International Automobile Show (annual). » Calvin, John; League of Nations; Reformation; Switzerland [i]

Geneva Bible An English translation of the Bible, prepared and published in Geneva by Protestant exiles from England; first appeared complete in 1560. It was notable for its small size and legible Roman type, for its notes, and for its verse divisions. It was especially popular in Scotland, and also in England until the Authorized Version. » Authorized Version of the Bible; Bible; Breeches Bible

Geneva Convention An international agreement on the conduct of warfare first framed in 1864 and ratified in 1906. It is chiefly concerned with the protection of wounded and the sanctity of the Red Cross, while prohibiting methods of war (such as the use of 'dumdum' bullets, which expand on impact) that might cause unnecessary suffering. The terms were extended in 1950 and again in 1978 to confirm the prohibition of attacks on non-defended civilians, reprisals against civilians, and the prisoner-of-war rights of guerrilla fighters. » international law; POW; Red Cross

Geneva, Lake, Fr **Lac Léman**, Ger **Genfersee**, ancient **Lacus Lemanus** area 581 sq km/224 sq ml. Crescent-shaped lake in SW Switzerland and SE France; largest of the Alpine lakes; height, 371 m/1 217 ft; maximum depth, 310 m/1 017 ft; maximum width, 14 km/9 ml; on the course of the R Rhône; wine-growing area; chief towns include Morges, Rolle, Lausanne, Vevey; steamer services. » Alps

Genghis Khan [**jen**gis **kahn**] (1162–1227) Mongol conqueror, born at Deligun Bulduk on the R Onon. He succeeded his father at 13, and struggled for many years against hostile tribes, subjugating the Naimans, conquering Tangut, and receiving the submission of the Turkish Uigurs. In 1206 he changed his name Temujin to Ghengis (Jingis or Chingis) Khan, 'Very Mighty Ruler'. From 1211, in several campaigns, he overran the empire of N China, the Kara-Chitai empire, the empire of Kharezm, and other territories, so that by his death the Mongol empire stretched from the Black Sea to the Pacific. » Mongols

genie » **jinni**

Genoa, Ital **Genova** 44°24N 8°56E, pop (1981) 762 895. Seaport and capital of Genoa province, Liguria, NW Italy, on the Gulf of Genoa; larger conurbation extends 35 km/22 ml along the coast; founded as a Roman trading centre; leading Mediterranean port by 13th-c; rebuilt after World War 2, becoming a major Mediterranean port; archbishopric; airport; railway; ferries; university (1471); Academy of Fine Arts (1751); Verdi Institute of Music; shipbuilding, oil refining, chemicals, paper, textiles, animal feedstuffs, detergents, motorbikes, sugar; birthplace of Columbus; Doge's Palace (13th-c), Church of San Matteo (1278), Cathedral of San Lorenzo (12th–14th-c), Palazzo Reale (begun 1650), Palazzo Rosso (17th-c); international ballet festival (Jul). » Columbus, Christopher; Italy [i]

genotype The genes that an individual organism carries. The term may refer to the total hereditary constitution of the individual, or to the genes present at a given point in the chromosomes. The interaction of genes in the genotype, with each other, and with the environment in which the organism develops, gives rise to the **phenotype** – the characteristics that are observed. » gene

genre painting Realistic scenes from everyday life, typically on a small scale, as produced by Dutch 17th-c masters such as Steen and Vermeer; the term may be applied, however, to any period. The genre flourished in 19th-c Britain, largely due to the popularity of the anecdotal scenes of Scottish village life by Wilkie. » bodégon; painting; Steen; Vermeer; Wilkie

Genscher, Hans-Dietrich (1927–) German politician, born at Reideburg, Germany. He trained as a lawyer, studying at Leipzig before coming to the West in 1952. He became Secretary-General of the Free Democratic Party (FDP) in 1959, and was Minister of the Interior for five years before becoming in 1974 Vice-Chancellor and Foreign Minister in Schmidt's coalition government. In the same year, he became Chairman of the FDP, a post to which he was re-elected in 1982. He retained his Cabinet post after 1982 in the coalition between the FDP and the Christian Democrats. » Germany [i]; Schmidt

Genseric » **Gaiseric**

Gent » **Ghent**

gentian Any of several species, mostly perennials, found almost everywhere, except for Africa; many are low-growing alpines; leaves opposite, entire; flowers usually several cm long, funnel- or bell-shaped, with often long tubes and five spreading lobes, usually deep blue, but also white, yellow, or red. (Genus: *Gentiana*, 400 species. Family: *Gentianaceae*.) » alpine; leaf [i]; perennial

Gentile, Giovanni [jen**tee**lay] (1875–1944) Italian philosopher, born at Castelvetrano. He was professor of philosophy at Palmero, Pisa, and Rome, and became with Croce the leading exponent of 20th-c Italian idealism. He quarrelled with Croce's complex distinctions between the theoretical and practical categories of mind, arguing that nothing is real except the pure act of thought. He became a philosophical mouthpiece for Mussolini, and was Minister of Education (1922–4). He was assassinated by an anti-fascist in Florence in 1944. » Croce; fascism; idealism

Gentile da Fabriano » **Fabriano**

Gentlemen at Arms, Honourable Corps of In the UK, noncombatant troops in attendance upon the sovereign. They provide an escort at coronations, state openings of parliament, receptions, royal garden parties, and during state visits; because of their close proximity to the sovereign, they are known as the 'nearest guard'. Originated as the 'Gentlemen Spears' by Henry VIII in 1509, today the 27 members are chosen from officers in either the Army or the Royal Marines who have received decorations. » decoration

genus [**jee**nuhs] A category in biological classification consisting of one or more closely related and morphologically similar species. The name of the genus (eg *Panthera*) and the species (eg *leo*) together form the scientific name of an organism (eg the lion, *Panthera leo*). » systematics; taxonomy

geochemistry A branch of geology concerned with the abundances of elements and their isotopes in the Earth, and the processes that affect their distribution. It also subsumes the study of chemical processes in the evolution of the Earth and the Solar System. Commercial applications include geochemical prospecting, in which the chemical analysis of soils, sediments, and stream waters is used to detect concealed ore deposits. » Earth [i]; geology

geochronology The science of dating rocks or geological events in absolute terms (ie in years), usually by radiometric dating. For more recent rocks, varve counting may be applicable to Pleistocene sediments, or tree-ring dating can measure ages back to about 7 000 years before the present. » radiometric dating; varve dating

geodesic The extension of the concept of a straight line to curved space, representing the shortest distance between two points. Special cases include straight lines in planes, and great circles on spheres. In general relativity, freely falling bodies move along geodesics in curved space-time. » curvature of space-time; general relativity

geodesic dome A structurally stable dome constructed of a grid of straight members connected to each other to form a continuous surface of small triangles. It was invented by Buckminster Fuller in the 1950s. An example is the Climatron in St Louis, Missouri, built in 1960. » Fuller, Buckminster

geodesy [jee**od**uhsee] A branch of science concerned with the size and shape of the Earth, its gravitational field, and the location of fixed points. Geodesic surveying, unlike plane surveying, takes into account the Earth's curvature. The shape of the Earth (the *geoid*) is defined as the figure which is perpendicular to the direction of gravity at all points, and approximates to an oblate spheroid, first postulated by Newton on the basis of accurate astronomical observations. » Newton, Isaac; surveying

Geoffrey of Monmouth (c.1100–54) Welsh chronicler, consecrated Bishop of St Asaph in 1152. His *Historia Regum Britanniae* (History of the Kings of Britain), composed before

1147, profoundly influenced English literature, introducing the stories of King Lear and Cymbeline, the prophecies of Merlin, and the legend of Arthur in the form we know. The stories have little basis in historical fact. » Arthur; English/Welsh literature

geography The study of the nature of the physical and human environments. It is often divided broadly into **physical geography**, which concerns the Earth's physical environment (the atmosphere, biosphere, hydrosphere, and lithosphere), and **human geography**, the study of people and their activities. In both there is emphasis on *spatial analysis*, the study of location and patterns; on *ecological analysis*, the interaction between the human and physical environments; and on *scale*, as in regional and local studies. Geography encompasses both the physical and social sciences, using and contributing to their methodologies and content. It can be divided into a number of specialist disciplines: for example, **geomorphology**, the scientific study of the origin and development of landforms; **population geography**, concerned with the composition, distribution, growth, and migration of populations; and **resource geography**, the study of the location and exploitation of natural resources. Geography became a separate academic subject in the late 19th-c. The nature of the subject has changed considerably since then, away from an essentially descriptive and regional study towards a more quantitative and scientific approach. » biogeography; demography; ecology; geology; geomorphology; locational analysis; palaeogeography; phytogeography; zoogeography

geological time scale Divisions and subdivisions of geological time, based on the relative ages of rocks determined using the methods of stratigraphy. Correlations between rocks of the same age are made from a study of the sedimentary sequences and the characteristic fossils they contain. The major divisions are termed *eons* (or *aeons*) which are further subdivided into *eras*, *periods*, and *epochs*. With the advent of radiometric dating, absolute ages have been assigned to the time scale. Although the current estimate of the age of the Earth is 4 600 million years, evidence of geological events only becomes abundant about 1 000 million years later, and the time scale lacks detail until the beginning of the Cambrian period c.590 million years ago. » geochronology; stratigraphy; RR16

geology The science of the Earth as a whole: its origin, structure, composition, processes, and history. » earth sciences; geochemistry; geological time scale; geomorphology; geophysics; mineralogy; palaeontology; petrology; stratigraphy; tectonics

geomagnetic field The magnetic field of the Earth which arises from the metallic core, and which may be regarded as produced by a magnetic dipole pointing towards the geomagnetic N and S Poles. The positions of the Poles have varied considerably during geological time, and can be studied by analysing the direction of the residual magnetism present in rocks. Local variations or anomalies in the magnetic field are due to variations in the nature and structure of the rocks in the crust – a property which may be used to prospect for oil and mineral deposits. » magnetic declination/dip/poles; palaeomagnetism

geometric mean » **mean**

geometric sequence A sequence in which the ratio of any one term to the next is constant; sometimes called a **geometric progression**. The terms 1,2,4,8 form a geometric sequence; 1+2+4+8 is a **geometric series**. If the first term of a geometric sequence is a and the common ratio is r, the nth term is ar^{n-1} and the sum of the terms in the sequence is $a\dfrac{r^n-1}{r-1}$. If $r<1$, this approaches $\dfrac{a}{1-r}$ as n becomes large. » arithmetic sequence

geometrid moth A moth, small to medium-sized, often with large and cryptically coloured wings; caterpillars often resemble twigs, known as **loopers**, because of their looping mode of progression; c.20 000 species, including many serious pests, such as cankerworm, inch worm, and winter moth. (Order: *Lepidoptera*. Family: *Geometridae*.) » caterpillar; looper; moth

geometries, non-Euclidean Geometries developed by varying Euclid's fifth axiom, as stated by the British mathematician John Playfair (1748–1819), 'Through any one point there can be drawn one and only one straight line parallel to a given straight line'. Variations on this took either the form 'Through any one point can be drawn more than one straight line parallel to a given straight line' or 'Through any one point can be drawn no straight line parallel to a given straight line'. The first form was called *hyperbolic geometry*, the second *elliptic geometry*. Mathematicians associated with hyperbolic geometry include Gauss and Lobachevski. Early work on elliptic geometry was carried out by Riemann. There are other non-Euclidean geometries. » Euclid; Gauss; geometry; Lobachevski; Riemann

geometry The branch of mathematics which studies the properties of shapes and space, originally (as its name suggests) of the Earth. About 2000 BC, the Babylonians were familiar with rules for the area of rectangles, right-angled triangles, and isosceles triangles. They took the circumference C of a circle, diameter d, as $3d$, and the area as $\dfrac{1}{12}C^2$; they subdivided the circumference of a circle into 360 equal parts; and developed a considerable body of geometrical knowledge. The Egyptians had a similar body of knowledge, but the story that they knew of special cases of Pythagoras' theorem has been disputed. The Greeks from c.300 BC developed geometry on a logical basis, many of the early results being collected in Euclid's *Elements*. Although some of the proofs were probably due to Euclid, the great merit of this work was its skilful selection and arrangement into a logical sequence, showing a statement as a necessary logical consequence of a previous statement, the chain starting with some propositions or axioms. In the past 200 years, abstract geometries have been developed, notably by Gauss and Lobachevski. » analytic geometry; arc [i]; axiom; ellipse [i]; Euclid; Gauss; geometries, non-Euclidean; hyperbola [i]; Lobachevski; parabola [i]; Pythagoras' theorem [i]; triangle (mathematics)

geomorphology A branch of geology (or geography) which studies and interprets landforms and the processes of erosion and deposition which form the surface of the Earth and other planets. » erosion; geography; geology

geophagy » **pica**

geophysics A broad branch of geology which deals with the physical properties of Earth materials and the physical processes that determine the structure of the Earth as a whole. Major subjects include seismology, geomagnetism, and meteorology, as well as the study of large-scale processes of heat and mass transfer in the Earth and variations in the Earth's gravitational field. Geophysical surveys measure local variations in magnetic and gravitational field to determine variations in the structure and composition of rocks, and to prospect for oil and mineral reserves. » geology; geomagnetic field; meteorology; palaeomagnetism; seismology

geopolitics The study of the way geographical factors help to explain the basis of the power of nation states; a combination of political geography and political science. Important characteristics include territory, resources, climate, population, social and political culture, and economic activity. Prior to World War 2 it was associated with German nationalism and the Nazi regime. » nationalism; political science

George I (1660–1727) King of Great Britain and Ireland (1714–27), born at Osnabrück, Hanover, the great-grandson of James I of England, and proclaimed King on the death of Queen Anne. Elector of Hanover since 1698, he had commanded the Imperial forces in the Marlborough wars. He divorced his wife and cousin, the Princess Dorothea of Zell, imprisoning her in the castle of Ahlde, where she died (1726). He took relatively little part in the government of the country. His affections remained with Hanover, and he lived there as much as possible. He died at Osnabrück. » Jacobites; Walpole, Robert

George II (of Great Britain) (1683–1760) Son of George I, King of Great Britain and Ireland (1727–60), and Elector of Hanover, born at Herrenhausen, Hanover. In 1705 he married

Caroline of Anspach (1683–1737). Though he involved himself more in the government of the country than his father had, the policy pursued during the first half of the reign was that of Walpole. In the War of the Austrian Succession, he was present at the Battle of Dettingen (1743), the last occasion on which a British sovereign commanded an army in the field. His reign also saw the crushing of Jacobite hopes at the Battle of Culloden (1746), the foundation of British India after the Battle of Plassey (1757), the beginning of the Seven Years' War, and the capture of Quebec (1759). He died in London. » Austrian Succession, War of the; Culloden Moor, Battle of; Seven Years' War; Stuart, Charles; Walpole, Robert

George II (of Greece) (1890–1947) King of Greece (1922–24, 1935–47), born near Athens, who first came to the throne after the second deposition of his father, Constantine I. He was himself driven out in 1924, but was restored in late 1935 after a plebiscite. When Greece was overrun by the Germans, he withdrew to Crete, then to Egypt and Britain. After a plebiscite in 1946 in favour of the monarchy, he re-ascended the Greek throne, and died in Athens. » Greece [i]

George III (1738–1820) King of Great Britain and Ireland (1760–1820), Elector (1760–1815) and King (from 1815) of Hanover, born in London, the eldest son of Frederick Louis, Prince of Wales (1707–51). His father predeceased him, and he thus succeeded his grandfather, George II. Eager to govern as well as reign, he caused considerable friction. With Lord North he shared in the blame for the loss of the American colonies, and popular feeling ran high against him for a time in the 1770s. In 1783 he called Pitt (the Younger) to office, which brought an end to the supremacy of the old Whig families. In 1810 he suffered a recurrence of a mental derangement, and the Prince of Wales was made Regent. He died at Windsor, Berkshire, insane and blind. » American Revolution; North, Frederick; Pitt (the Younger)

George IV (1762–1830) King of the United Kingdom and of Hanover (1820–30), the eldest son of George III, born in London. He became Prince Regent in 1810, because of his father's insanity. Rebelling against a strict upbringing, he went through a marriage ceremony with Mrs Fitzherbert, a Roman Catholic, thus forfeiting his title to the crown. The marriage was later declared invalid, and in 1795 he married Princess Caroline of Brunswick, whom he tried to divorce when he was King. Her death in 1821 ended a scandal in which the people sympathized with the Queen. He died at Windsor, Berkshire. » Caroline of Brunswick

George V (1865–1936) King of the United Kingdom (1910–36), born in London, the second son of Edward VII. He served in the navy, travelled in many parts of the Empire, and was created Prince of Wales in 1901. His reign saw the Union of South Africa (1910), World War 1, the Irish Free State settlement (1922), and the General Strike (1926). He died at Sandringham, Norfolk. His consort, **Mary**, formerly Princess Victoria Mary Augusta Louise Olga Pauline Claudine Agnes of Teck (1867–1953), was born in London, and married Prince George in 1893. She organized women's war work (1914–18), and continued with many public and philanthropic activities after the death of her husband. They had five sons and one daughter.

George VI (1895–1952) King of the United Kingdom (1936–52), born and died at Sandringham, Norfolk, the second son of George V. Educated at Dartmouth Naval College and at Cambridge, he served in the Grand Fleet at the Battle of Jutland (1916). In 1920 he was created Duke of York, and was married in 1923. He played at Wimbledon in the All-England tennis championships in 1926. After ascending the throne (on the abdication of his elder brother, Edward VIII), during World War 2 he continued to reside in bomb-damaged Buckingham Palace, visited all theatres of war, and delivered many broadcasts, for which he mastered a speech impediment. His wife, **Elizabeth** (1900–), was born Elizabeth Angela Marguerite Bowes-Lyon at Waldenbury, Hertfordshire. They had two children: Princess Elizabeth (later Queen Elizabeth II) and Princess Margaret. During the War she paid many visits to hospitals, civil defence centres, and women's organizations. In her later years, she has continued to undertake a heavy programme of royal engagements at home and overseas. » Elizabeth II; Margaret, Princess; *see illustration p 487*

George, St (early 4th-c), feast day 23 April. Patron of chivalry, and guardian saint of England and Portugal. He may have been tortured and put to death by Diocletian at Nicomedia, or he may have suffered (c.250) at Lydda in Palestine, where his alleged tomb is exhibited. His name was early obscured by fable, such as the story of his fight with a dragon to rescue a maiden. » Christianity; Diocletian

George, David Lloyd » **Lloyd George, David**

George, Stefan [gayorguh] (1868–1933) German poet, born at Büdeshein. He studied in Paris, Munich, and Berlin, and travelled widely. In Germany he founded a literary group, and edited its journal. His poems show the influence of the French Symbolists, dispensing with punctuation and capitals, and conveying an impression rather than a simple meaning. In *Das neue Reich* (1928, The New Reich) he advocated a new German culture, not in accord with that of the Nazis. He exiled himself in 1933, and died near Locarno, Switzerland. » German literature; poetry; Reich; Symbolism

George-Brown, Baron, originally **George (Alfred) Brown** (1914–85) British Labour politician, born in London. He was an official of the Transport and General Workers Union before becoming an MP in 1945 and Minister of Works (1951). As opposition spokesman on defence (1958–61), he supported Gaitskell in opposing unilateral disarmament. Vice-Chairman and Deputy Leader of the Labour Party (1960–70), he unsuccessfully contested Wilson for party leadership in 1963. As Secretary of State for Economic Affairs (1964–6), he instigated a prices and incomes policy, and later became Foreign Secretary (1966–8). Having lost his seat in the 1970 election, he was created a life peer. » Gaitskell; Labour Party; prices and incomes policy; Wilson, Harold

George Cross (GC) In the UK, a decoration bestowed on civilians for acts of great heroism or conspicuous bravery, or on members of the armed forces for actions in which purely military honours are not normally granted. (The island of Malta was a recipient in 1942.) Instituted in 1940 and named after George VI, the award, inscribed 'For Gallantry', with a blue ribbon, ranks second after the Victoria Cross. » decoration

George Medal (GM) In the UK, the second highest award which may be bestowed on civilians for acts of bravery; instituted in 1940 by George VI. The ribbon is scarlet with five narrow blue stripes. » decoration

George Town (Cayman Is) 19°20N 81°23W, pop (1979) 7 617. Seaport and capital of the Cayman Is, W Caribbean, on Grand Cayman I; financial and administrative centre; airport nearby. » Cayman Islands

George Town (Malaysia), also **Penang** or **Pinang** 5°26N 100°16E, pop (1980) 248 241. Capital of Penang state, W Peninsular Malaysia, on NE coast; named after King George III of Great Britain; Malaysia's chief port; railway; ferry to Butterworth on the mainland; large Chinese population; electronics, textiles, silk, toys; trade in tin, rubber; Fort Cornwallis, St George's Church (oldest Anglican Church in SE Asia). » Malaysia [i]; Penang

Georgetown 6°46N 58°10W, pop (1983e) 188 000. Federal and district capital and major port, N Guyana; at mouth of R Demerara; tidal port, protected by sea wall and dykes; founded, 1781; airport; airfield; railway; university (1963); food processing, shrimp fishing, sugar, rice, bauxite; city hall (1887), St George's Cathedral (1892), Guyana House (1852), Law Courts (1878), Botanic Gardens. » Guyana [i]

Georgia (republic), Russ **Gruzinskaya** pop (1989) 5 443 000; area 69 700 sq km/26 900 sq ml. Republic in C and W Transcaucasia, bounded SW by Turkey and W by the Black Sea; contains the Greater Caucasus (N) and Lesser Caucasus (S); highest point in the republic, Mt Shkhara (5 203 m/17 070 ft); chief rivers, the Kura and Rioni; c.39% forested; proclaimed a Soviet Socialist Republic, 1921; made a constituent republic, 1936; declaration of independence, 1991; capital, Tbilisi; chief towns, Kutaisi, Rustavi, Batumi, Sukhumi, Poti; manganese, coal, iron and steel, oil refining, chemicals, machines, textiles, food processing, tea, fruit; Kakhetia region famed for its orchards and wines. » Caucasus Mountains; Soviet Union [i]; Transcaucasia

Georgia (USA) pop(1987e) 6 222 000; area 152 571 sq km/ 58 910 sq ml. State in SE USA, divided into 159 counties; the 'Empire State of the South' or the 'Peach State'; discovered by the Spanish; settled as a British colony, 1733; named after George II; the last of the original 13 colonies to be founded; the fourth of the original 13 states (first Southern state) to ratify the Constitution, 1788; seceded from the Union, 1861; suffered much damage in the Civil War (especially during General Sherman's March to the Sea, 1864); slavery abolished 1865; last state to be re-admitted, 1870; capital, Atlanta; other major cities Columbus, Savannah, Macon; part of the E border is the Atlantic Ocean; rivers include the Savannah (SE border), the Chattahoochee (part of the W border) and Flint, which join to form the Apalachicola, and the Oconee and Ocmulgee, which join to form the Altamaha; highest point Mt Brasstown Bald (1 457 m/4 780 ft); a low coastal plain in the S, heavily forested; the fertile Piedmont plateau, the Appalachian plateau, and Blue Ridge Mts in the N; many local paper mills in the S; leads the nation in production of pulp; major cotton textile producer; transportation equipment, food products, chemicals; grows nearly half US crop of peanuts; cotton, tobacco, corn, poultry, livestock, soybeans; popular tourist resorts, such as the Golden Isles (off the Atlantic coast) and Okefenokee Swamp. » American Civil War; Atlanta; Stone Mountain Memorial; United States of America [i]; RR38

Georgian poetry English poetry published by British literary critic Edward Marsh (1872–1953) in five anthologies of Georgian Poetry (1912–22), during the reign of George V. It was more traditional than the work of the early Modernists. » Housman; Graves; Lawrence, D H; Modernism; Owen, Wilfred; poetry; Thomas, Edward

Georgian Style English architecture of the period 1714–1830. The name is derived from the kings George I, II, and III of that period. The style is characterized by a restrained use of classical elements in low relief on the exterior, and more elaborately decorated interiors, such as those by Robert Adam. » classical architecture

geostrophic wind A wind which blows parallel to isobars, representing the balanced motion between the equal but opposing pressure gradient force and Coriolis force. It is found only in the upper atmosphere, where the frictional force of the Earth's surface is absent. » atmospheric pressure; Coriolis force [i]; isobar; jet stream; wind [i]

geosynchronous Earth orbit A spacecraft orbit about the Earth's Equator, where the period of the orbit matches the Earth's day and causes the spacecraft to appear stationary at the longitude in question; orbit altitude is 36 000 km/ 22 500 ml. The orbit is ideally suited for communications satellites, as it permits spacecraft to be in continuous communication with specific ground stations. It is also ideal for meteorological satellites, as it permits spacecraft to have broad coverage of the surface and atmosphere. » launch vehicle [i]; low Earth orbit

geothermal energy Energy extracted in the form of heat from the Earth's crust, arising from a combination of the slow cooling of the Earth since its formation, and heat released from natural radioactive decay. Geologically active regions such as plate margins have higher heat flow values and result in hot springs and geysers. Geothermal energy is commercially exploited for generating electricity in Lardorello in Italy, Warakai in New Zealand, and California, USA. » energy; geyser; hot spring

geranium The name used for two related plant genera: the **cranesbills** (Genus: *Geranium*) and the geraniums of horticulture, the **pelargoniums** (Genus: *Pelargonium*). » cranesbill; horticulture; pelargonium

Gérard, François (Pascal Simon), Baron [zhay**rahr**] (1770–1837) French painter, born in Rome. He was brought up in Paris, and became a member of the Revolutionary Tribunal in 1793. His portrait of Isabey the miniaturist (1796) and his 'Cupid and Psyche' (1798), both in the Louvre, established his reputation. He later painted several historical subjects, such as the 'Battle of Austerlitz' (1808, Versailles). He was made court painter and baron by Louis XVIII, and died in Paris. » French art; Louis XVIII

gerbil A type of mouse, native to Africa, Middle East, and C Asia; long hind legs and long furry tail; lives in social groups; inhabits dry open country; digs burrows; eats seeds, roots, etc (some species eat other animals, including reptiles and rodents); one species, the *Mongolian gerbil* (*Meriones unguiculatus*) is a popular pet; also known as **jird**. (Subfamily: *Gerbillinae*, 81 species.) » mouse (zoology)

gerenuk [**ge**ruhnuk] An E African gazelle; pale brown; slender, with long neck and small head; male with thick horns (usually curling forwards at tips); browses from bushes by standing vertically on hind legs; inhabits dry regions; seldom drinks; also known as **giraffe antelope**. (*Litocranius walleri*.) » gazelle [i]

geriatrics The study of the health needs of the aged and their provision. The numbers of elderly persons have increased in recent years in most Western societies, and continue to do so, making increasing demands on the specialized health and social services. There are few diseases specific to old age, but the elderly often suffer from several chronic disorders at the same time. These lead to a number of disabilities which curtail their ability to care for themselves in their own homes, and has given rise to the need for such services as district nurses, home helps, meals on wheels, and health visitors. For those who become unable to live independently in their own homes, institutional accommodation often becomes necessary. » medicine

Géricault, (Jean Louis André) Théodore [**zhay**reekoh] (1791–1824) French painter, born in Rouen. A pupil of Guérin, he was a great admirer of the 17th-c Flemish schools. He painted many unorthodox and realistic scenes, notably 'The Raft of the Medusa' (1819, Louvre), based on a shipwreck which had caused a sensation in France. It was harshly criticized and he withdrew to England, where he painted racing scenes and landscapes. He died in Paris. » French art; Romanticism (art)

Gerlachovsky [**ger**lakofskee], or **Gerlachovsky Štit** formerly **Franz Josef-Spitze**, **Stalin Peak** Highest peak of the Carpathian range and of Czechoslovakia in the Vysoké Tatry (High Tatra), rising to 2 655 m/8 710 ft. » Carpathian Mountains

germ-line therapy An attempt to insert a gene into sex cells. In contrast to somatic cell gene therapy, success in this task would alter the inheritance of genetically derived disorders in offspring. As in the case of gene therapy, the procedure remains experimental. » gene therapy

German » **German literature; Germanic languages**

German, Sir Edward, originally **Edward German Jones** (1862–1936) British composer, born at Whitchurch, Shropshire. He studied at the Royal Academy of Music, and in 1888 became musical director of the Globe Theatre, London. In 1901 he emerged as a light opera composer, completing Sullivan's *The Emerald Isle* after the composer's death, and writing *Merrie England* (1902). He also wrote two symphonies, orchestral suites, chamber music, and songs. He was knighted in 1928, and died in London.

German art A term used loosely to cover art in C and E Europe, more narrowly for the region that became Germany in 1871. The tradition began under the Ottonian emperors, 10th–11th-c; great Romanesque basilicas followed at Mainz, Worms, and Speyer; Hildesheim was a centre for bronze sculpture, and manuscript illumination flourished at Reichenau. The Gothic style arrived from France in the 13th-c; 15th-c painting developed partly under Flemish influence; woodcut and line engraving was strong, culminating in the greatest German master, Dürer. The N was affected by the Reformation, but S Germany and Austria saw a flowering of Baroque architecture and decoration in the late 17th-c. Late 18th-c and early 19th-c Germany fully exploited Neoclassicism and Romanticism, as in the landscapes by Caspar David Friedrich (1774–1840). Major 20th-c contributions have included Expressionism and the Bauhaus. » Bauhaus; Biedermeierstil; Blaue Reiter, der; Brücke, die; Danube School; Dürer; Expressionism; Neue

Künstlervereinigung; Neue Sachlichkeit; Ottonian art; Sezession

German Confederation A C European state system created at the Congress of Vienna (1815) to fill the void left by Napoleon I's destruction (1806) of the Holy Roman Empire. Dominated until after 1848 by Austria, it was rendered unstable by the subsequent rising power of Prussia, and was dissolved in 1866 following the Austro-Prussian War. » Austro-Prussian War; North German Confederation; Prussia

German Democratic Republic » **Germany, East** [i]

German literature The Old Saxon poem *Heliand* and the Old High German *Hildebrandslied* date from the 9th-c, but it was not until the 12th-c Minnesingers (troubadours) that the vernacular became established as a medium over Latin. Court epics such as *Tristan und Isolde* and *Parzifal* also appeared at this time. The prose works *Tyll Eulenspiegel* and *Dr Faust* appeared in the 15th-c, to be followed by the Meistersingers ('master singers'), Hans Sachs of Nuremberg being the most celebrated. Luther's German Bible (1522–34) provided an opportunity which was lost to German literature because of the Thirty Years' War (1618–48) – reflected in Grimmelshausen's *Simplicismus* (1669) – and foreign influence; and it was not until the mid-18th-c that it found a new direction. The classicist Lessing and the nationalist Herder provided inspiration for the *Sturm und Drang* ('Storm and Stress') school, characteristic of German Romanticism. The Schlegel brothers contributed an important element (Wilhelm's translation of Shakespeare appeared 1797–1810), as did the poet Hölderlin, the novelist J-P Richter and the dramatist Schiller; but the greatest writer of the age was Goethe, whose imaginative range transcends any movement or national boundary.

There have been distinguished contributors to the German novel, including Thomas Mann, Herman Hesse, and two Austrians: Herman Broch and Franz Kafka, the latter with his unique haunted fictions. Günter Grass's novel *Die Blechtrommel* (1959, The Tin Drum) is the best-known German work since the war. German drama has been very active, from the Expressionist plays of Wedekind and Schnitzler to the epic theatre of Brecht; while poetry produced in Rilke one of its greatest figures. » epic; Expressionism; literature; Sturm und Drang; Brecht; Broch; Goethe; Grass; Herder; Hesse; Hölderlin; Kafka; Lessing, Gotthold; Mann; Richter, Johann Paul; Rilke; Schiller; Schlegel; Schnitzler; Wedekind

German measles (rubella) A highly infectious disease of virological origin that affects older children and young adults. Although a trivial short-lived illness, its importance lies in the fact that a woman who develops the infection in the first 18 weeks of pregnancy is likely to have a child with a congenital abnormality. A vaccine to prevent the disease is now available, and is given to schoolgirls. » measles; vaccination; virus

German shepherd A breed of large dog developed in Germany in the late 19th-c by crossing spitz breeds with local sheepdogs; thick coat; long pointed muzzle and ears; trains well; popular with police and military worldwide; also known as an **alsatian**. » dog; sheepdog; spitz

German wirehaired pointer A pointer developed in Germany by crossing many other breeds of sporting dog; coat rough, thicker on the eyebrows and ears, and also on the jaws, giving it a short beard. » pointer

germander An annual or perennial, sometimes shrubby, found almost everywhere, most abundant in the Mediterranean region; stems square; leaves in opposite pairs; flowers greenish, pink, or purple with spreading 5-lobed lower lip, upper lip absent. (Genus: *Teucrium*, 300 species. Family: *Labiatae*.) » annual; perennial; shrub

Germanic languages A branch of Indo-European comprising the **North Germanic** Scandinavian languages in N Europe, and the **West Germanic** languages English, Frisian, German, and Dutch (with its colonial variant Afrikaans in South Africa) in the W. Scandinavian inscriptions in the runic alphabet date from the 3rd-c AD. Anglo-Saxon and Old High German, precursors of modern English and German, are evidenced from the 8th-c, and the Scandinavian languages from the 12th-c. **East Germanic** languages are extinct, though there are manuscript remains of Gothic. Germanic languages are spoken by over 500 million people as a first language, mainly because of the wide dissemination of English, with c.350 million mother-tongue speakers. There are some 100 million speakers of German, mainly in E and W Germany, but also in Austria, Switzerland, parts of E Europe, the Americas, and S Africa. » Afrikaans; Anglo-Saxon; Dutch; English; English/German literature; family of languages [i]; Indo-European/Scandinavian languages

Germanic religion The pre-Christian religion of the people bounded by the Rhine, Vistula, and Danube rivers. What little is known of these peoples comes largely from Roman accounts of varying reliability, missionaries, and archaeological finds. There was a pantheon of deities represented in human form, of whom four were particularly important during the Viking Age (9th–11th-c). Odin (Germanic *Wotan*), father of the gods and ruler of Valhalla, was the god of poetry, wisdom and the dead. Thor (Germanic *Donar*), a sky-god, was the god of law and order. Frigg and Freyja were fertility deities. The powers of nature were held to be magical, and were represented as sprites, elves, and trolls. » Freya; Frigg; Hel; Loki; Odin; Thor; Valhalla; Vikings

Germanicus, properly **Gaius Germanicus Caesar** (15 BC–AD 19) The son, father, and brother of Roman emperors (Tiberius, Caligula, and Claudius respectively), and heir apparent himself from AD 14. A man of great charm but mediocre ability, his sudden and suspicious death in Antioch marked a turning point in Tiberius' reign. It crystallized the growing disenchantment with the emperor, and sent his reign on its downward spiral. » Agrippina the Elder; Caligula; Claudius; Tiberius

germanium [jer**mayn**iuhm] Ge, element 32, melting point 937°C. A metalloid found in composite ores, especially with silver and zinc. It is extracted from other metals as $GeCl_4$, which boils at c.80°. Ultrapure germanium is used as a semiconductor, and as its properties are markedly changed by doping with arsenic or gallium, its main use is in transistor manufacture. » antimony; chemical elements; doping; metalloids; transistor; RR90

Germany, Ger **Deutschland**, official name **Federal Republic of Germany**, Ger **Bundesrepublik Deutschland** pop (1990) 79 112 831; area 357 868 sq km/138 136 sq ml. C European state formed by the political unification of West and East Germany (3 Oct 1990); capital, Berlin; most populous state in W Europe; timezone GMT + 1; population mainly Germanic, with several minorities; chief religion, Christianity, 55% Protestant, 38% Roman Catholic; unit of currency, the deutschmark of 100 pfennig; new public holiday, Day of German Unity (3 Oct); the five former East German provinces (*Länder*), abolished after World War 2, re-established (Brandenburg, Mecklenburg-West Pomerania, Saxony, Saxony-Anhalt, Thuringia), with unified Berlin formed a sixth *Land*; West German electoral system adopted in East Germany; 144 delegated members of the East German *Volkskammer* sat as interim observers in the West German *Bundestag* until the first national elections (Dec 1990); West German *Bundesrat* reconstituted on the basis of a new system of allocating seats to each *Land* according to population (minimum three, maximum eight); the new parliament would decide the final location of the seat of government; new regulations in force governing ownership of land and buildings in East Germany; files of the East German State Security Police ('Stasi') to remain in East Germany, for the time being; existing East German laws on abortion to continue for two years, until a fresh law is passed by the new parliament; first merger of an East and West German political party (the Liberals), Aug 1990, with new elections for party office in 1991; following unification, a major socio-economic division emerged between West and East, leading to demonstrations in the E provinces in 1991. » Berlin; Bonn; Brandenburg; Bundestag; Kohl; Pomerania; Saxony; Thuringia

Germany, East, official name **German Democratic Republic**, Ger **Deutsche Demokratische Republik** pop (1990) 16 433 796; area 108 333 sq km/41 816 sq ml. Former Socialist republic of NC Europe, divided into 15 counties; bounded N by the Baltic Sea, E by Poland, W and SW by West Germany, and S by Czechoslovakia; in the centre of the country was West Berlin (480 sq km/185 sq ml); capital, East Berlin; chief towns in-

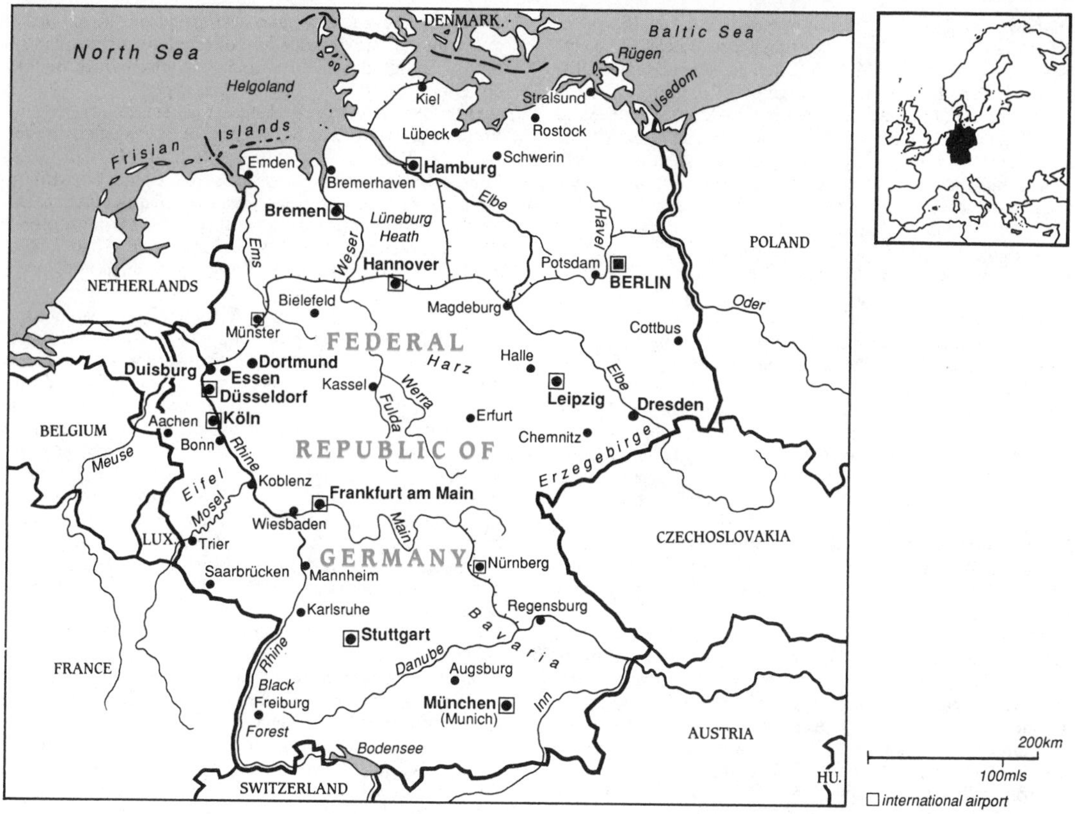

cluded Leipzig, Dresden, Karl Marx Stadt, Magdeburg, Halle, Rostock, Erfurt; timezone GMT + 1; chief religion, Christianity; unit of currency to July 1990, the Mark (DDR) of 100 pfennigs.

Physical description and climate. Baltic coastline of 250 km/155 ml, dunes and lagoons, backed by a fertile low-lying plain, pine-clad low hills, and many glacial lakes; land rises (S) in several ranges, notably the Harz Mts of the Thuringian Forest; major rivers include the Elbe and Oder; Hohenzollern canal links the Oder and Elbe; Mittelland canal links the Elbe and Ruhr; temperate climate, with relatively mild winters and cool summers; mean annual temperature, 10°C; often, long spells of cold weather in winter, with the freezing of canals; low summer rainfall (C), average monthly maximum of 73 mm/2.9 in (Jul); wetter and colder at higher altitudes (S).

Constitution and government. Administered by USSR after 1945 partition of Germany, and Soviet model of government established, 1949; anti-Soviet demonstrations put down, 1953; recognized by USSR as an independent republic, 1954, with E border following the Oder and Neisse Rivers; flow of refugees to West Germany continued until 1961, largely stopped by building of the Berlin Wall; governed by the People's Chamber, a single-chamber parliament (*Volkskammer*) of 500 deputies, which elected a 29-member Council of State (*Staatsrat*), a Council of Ministers (*Ministerrat*), and a National Defence Council; movement for democratic reform culminated (Nov 1989) in the opening of the Wall and other border crossings to the West, and a more open government policy; free elections (Mar 1990) paved the way for a currency union with West Germany (Jul) and full political unification (Oct).

Economy. Since World War 2, a centrally-planned Socialist economy, with the creation of state and co-operative farms, and movement of industry to the formerly rural N and E; few mineral resources apart from potash and coal; precision tools, optical instruments, semiconductors, shipbuilding, chemicals, textiles, motor vehicles, food processing. » Berlin, East; Berlin, West; German art/literature; Germany, West [i]; RR25 national holidays; RR50 political leaders

Germany, West, Ger **Deutschland** or **Deutsches Reich**, official name **Federal Republic of Germany**, Ger **Bundesrepublik Deutschland** pop (1990) 62 679 035; area 249 535 sq km/96 320 sq ml, including West Berlin. Former C European state, divided into 10 provinces (*Länder*); bounded E by East Germany and Czechoslovakia, SE by Austria, SW by Switzerland, W by France, Luxembourg, Belgium, and the Netherlands, and N by Denmark, the North Sea, and the Baltic Sea; includes the N and E Frisian Is, Heligoland, and the Sanddüne Is in the North Sea, and the Fehmarn Is in the Baltic Sea; federal capital, Bonn; largest city, West Berlin; chief towns include Hamburg, Munich, Cologne, Essen, Frankfurt am Main, Dortmund; population almost entirely Germanic; chief religion, Christianity, c.44% Protestant (mainly Lutherans), 45% Roman Catholic; currency, the Deutschmark of 100 pfennig.

Physical description. N lowland plains rise through C uplands and Alpine foothills to the Bavarian Alps (S); highest peak, the Zugspitze (2 962 m/9 718 ft); C uplands include the Rhenish Slate Mts, rising to 879 m/2 884 ft, the Black Forest, part of the Harz Mts, and the Odenwald and Spessart; most rivers drain into the North Sea, including the Ems, Weser, and Elbe; the Rhine crosses the country S–N; complex canal system links chief rivers.

Climate. Oceanic influences strongest in NW, where winters are mild but stormy; elsewhere, a continental climate; lower winter temperatures in E and S, with considerable snowfall; average winter temperature (N) 1.6°C, (S) −2.7°C; summer temperatures average (N) 16°C, slightly higher in S; average annual rainfall on the plains, 600–700 mm/23–27 in, increasing in parts of the Alps to 2 000 mm/80 in.

History and government. Ancient Germanic tribes united in 8th-c within the Frankish Empire of Charlemagne; elective monarchy after 918 under Otto I, with Holy Roman Empire divided into several hundred states; after Congress of Vienna (1814–15), a confederation of 39 states under Austria; under Bismarck, Prussia succeeded Austria as the leading German power; union of Germany and foundation of the Second Reich, 1871, with King of Prussia as hereditary German Emperor; aggressive foreign policy, eventually leading to World War 1; after German defeat, Second Reich replaced by democratic

Weimar Republic; political power passed to the Nazi Party in 1920s; Hitler dictator of the totalitarian Third Reich, 1933; acts of aggression led to World War 2 and a second defeat for Germany, with collapse of the German political regime; area of Germany reduced, and occupied by the UK, USA, France, and USSR; Western occupation ended with the creation of the Federal Republic of Germany, 1948; federal system of government was built around 10 States (*Länder*) with considerable powers; two-chamber legislature consisted of a 519-member Federal Diet (*Bundestag*) and a 45-member Federal Council (*Bundesrat*); federal president elected for five years by members of the *Bundesrat* and *Land* parliaments; chancellor elected by the *Bundestag* from the majority party; political unification with East Germany, October 1990.

Economy. A leading industrial nation, following major reconstruction after World War 2; substantial heavy industry in N and C, especially iron and steel, coal mining, cement, metal products, chemicals, textiles, machinery, electrical goods, food processing, precision and optical equipment, vehicles; coal, iron ore, zinc, lead, potash; arable and livestock farming, fruit, wheat, barley, potatoes, sugar beet, forestry; major wine industry in Rhine and Moselle valleys; increasing tourism, especially in the S. » Bismarck; Charlemagne; German art / Confederation / literature; Germany, East; Hitler; Holy Roman Empire; Mittelland Canals; Nazi Party; Otto I; Prussia; Reich; Weimar Republic; World War 1/2; RR25 national holidays; RR50 political leaders

germination The onset of growth of a seed or spore. It only begins when sufficient warmth, water, and oxygen are available, and any preconditions for breaking dormancy are fulfilled. The young root (*radicle*) emerges first, followed by the young shoot (*plumule*). In **hypogeal** germination the cotyledons remain underground; in **epigeal** germination they are raised above soil level. » cotyledons; gibberellins; seed

Geronimo, Indian name **Goyathlay** (1829–1909) Chiricahua Apache Indian, born in Mexico. The best known of all Apaches, he forcibly resisted the internment of his people on a reservation, escaping from White control on several occasions. In his old age, he became a Christian and a figure in public spectacles, including President Theodore Roosevelt's inauguration parade. He died at Fort Sill, Oklahoma. » Indian Wars

gerrymander A term describing the reorganization of electoral areas so as to give unfair advantage to one or more political parties in forthcoming elections. It was first coined in the USA in 1812 by conflating the name of Elbridge Gerry, Governor of Massachussetts, with *salamander*, the shape of which a new electoral district was said to resemble.

Gershwin, George (1898–1937) US composer, born in New York City. He published his first song in 1914, and had his first hit, 'Swanee', in 1919. In 1924 he began collaborating with his brother **Ira** (1896–1983) as lyricist, producing numerous classic songs, such as 'Lady Be Good' (1924) and 'I Got Rhythm' (1930). He also composed extended concert works including 'Rhapsody in Blue' (1924), 'American in Paris' (1928), and the opera *Porgy and Bess* (1935), importing jazz, blues, and pop-song devices into European classical contexts. » blues; jazz

Gerson, Jean (Charlier) de [**zhayrsõ**] (1363–1429) French theologian and mystic, born at Gerson. He was educated at Paris, where in 1397 he became Chancellor. He supported the proposal for putting an end to schism between Rome and Avignon by the resignation of both the contending pontiffs, and participated in the Councils of Pisa (1409) and Constance (1414). He died at Lyons. » Council of the Church; pope

Gesamtkunstwerk [guh**zamt**koonstverk] (Ger 'total work of art') A term sometimes applied to Wagnerian opera, in which music is combined with costume and visual effects to create a total unified work. The idea has roots in early 19th-c German Romanticism. » Wagner

Gesner, Conrad von (1516–65) Swiss naturalist and bibliographer, born in Zürich. In 1537 he became professor of Greek at Lausanne, and in 1541 of physics and natural history at Zürich. His *Bibliotheca universalis* (1545–49) contained the titles of all the books then known in Hebrew, Greek, and Latin, with criticisms and summaries of each. His *Historia animalium* (1551–8) aimed at bringing together all that was known of cribed by the ancients, and was preparing a major work on every animal. In botany he collected over 500 plants undes-botany at his death, in Zürich. He also wrote on medicine, mineralogy, and philology. » botany

Gestalt psychology [guh**shtalt**] A school of psychological thought characterized by the phrase 'the whole is greater than the sum of its parts' – hence, 'wholistic'. It is probably most famous for the Gestalt 'laws' of perception, which attempted to describe which properties of visual elements make them appear to 'belong together' as an entity. It was developed by the German psychologists Max Wertheimer (1880–1943), Kurt Koffka (1886–1941), and Wolfgang Kohler (1887–1967). » Gestalt therapy; vision

Gestalt therapy [guh**shtalt**] A humanistic-existential therapy derived from Gestalt psychology, which aims to make individuals 'whole' by increasing their awareness of aspects of their personality which have been denied or disowned. Its most important proponent was German-born US psychiatrist Frederick Perls (1893–1970). It is usually conducted in groups and concentrated over a short period of time. Clients are allowed to speak only in the present tense, and non-verbal behaviour (eg movements, hesitations) is considered as important as verbal. Conflicts are acted out in therapy, as are the thoughts and feelings given to images in dreams. Generally clients are encouraged to be more expressive, spontaneous, and responsive to their own needs. » Gestalt psychology; personality

Gestapo [guh**stah**poh] An abbreviation of *Geheime Staatspolizei*, the political police of the German Third Reich, founded in 1933 by Göring on the basis of the Prussian political police. It soon extended throughout Germany, and from 1936 came under the control of Himmler, as head of the SS. » Goering; Himmler; SS

gestation period The interval of time from conception to birth in a viviparous animal, during which development of the embryo within the uterus takes place. It is usually relatively constant for any particular species. » embryo; viviparity

Gethsemane [geth**sem**anee] A place outside Jerusalem near the Mt of Olives where Jesus and his disciples went to pray immediately before his betrayal and arrest (*Mark* 14.32ff); described as a 'garden' in *John* 18.1. It is the scene of Jesus' agony over whether to accept martyrdom. » Jesus Christ; Olives, Mount of

Getty, J(ean) Paul (1892–1976) US oil executive, multi-millionaire, and art collector, born in Minneapolis. After studying at Berkeley and Oxford, he entered the oil business and made a quarter of a million dollars in his first two years. His father (also an oil man) died in 1930, leaving him $15 million. He merged his father's interests with his own, went on to control more than 100 companies, and became one of the richest men in the world. He was married and divorced five times, and was known for his eccentricity. He founded the J Paul Getty Museum at Malibu, California, in 1954. In his later years he settled at Sutton Place, Surrey, UK, where he died.

Gettysburg Address (19 Nov 1863) During the American Civil War, a speech given by President Lincoln at the dedication of a war cemetery in Pennsylvania on the site of the Battle of Gettysburg. Ill-regarded at the time, it is now thought of as one of the masterpieces of American oratory. » American Civil War; Gettysburg, Battle of; Lincoln, Abraham

Gettysburg, Battle of (Jun–Jul 1863) A major series of engagements in the American Civil War between the army of N Virginia (Confederate) and the army of the Potomac (Union), after Robert E Lee, the Southern commander, decided to take the war into the N. Union victory ended any prospect of foreign recognition for the Confederacy. » American Civil War; Lee, Robert E

Geulincx or **Geulingx, Arnold** [**ger**links] (1625–69) Belgian philosopher, born in Antwerp. He was educated at Louvain, where he lectured (1646–58), but was deposed for his anti-scholasticism. After turning Calvinist, he lived in great distress at Leyden, where in 1665 he became professor of philosophy. A leading exponent of Descartes, he defended the doctrine of occasionalism. » Descartes; dualism; occasionalism

geyser A natural spring which erupts intermittently, throwing up fountains of superheated water and steam from a crack deep in the Earth's crust. Geysers occur in volcanically active areas in New Zealand, Iceland, and the USA. » geothermal energy; hot spring

Geysir [geeser] 64°19N 20°19W. Location in Suðurland, W Iceland, 30 km/19 ml NE of Laugarvatn, E of Reykjavík; water columns of 40–60 m/130–200 ft; gave its name to the word 'geyser'. » geyser; Iceland [i]

Gezhouba Dam [gezhooba] Dam on the R Yangtze, C China, near Yichang; at mouth of Yangtze gorges; largest water control project in the world. » Yangtze, River

Ggantija Temples A Copper Age temple complex on Gozo, NW Malta; a world heritage site. The two temples, built 3600–3300 BC, were excavated in 1827, and are in a remarkable state of preservation. » Gozo; Three Age System

Ghana, official name **Republic of Ghana** [**gah**na] pop (1990e) 15 020 000; area 238 686 sq km/92 133 sq ml. Republic of W Africa, divided into nine administrative regions; bounded W by Côte d'Ivoire, N by Burkina Faso, and E by Togo; capital, Accra; chief towns include Sekondi-Takoradi, Kumasi, Tamale; timezone GMT; c.75 tribal groups, including Akan (44%), Mole-Dagbani (16%), Ewe (13%), and Ga (8%); official language, English, with several African languages spoken; chief religions, Christianity (43%), local beliefs (38%), Islam (12%); unit of currency, the cedi of 100 pesewas; coastline of sand bars and lagoons; low-lying plains inland, leading to the Ashanti plateau (W) and R Volta basin (E), dammed to form L Volta; mountains rise (E) to 885 m/2 903 ft at Afadjado; tropical climate, including a warm dry coastal belt (SE), a hot humid SW corner, and a hot dry savannah (N); Kumasi, average annual rainfall 1 400 mm/55 in; visited by Europeans in 15th-c; centre of slave trade, 18th-c; modern state created by union of two former British territories, British Gold Coast (Crown Colony, 1874) and British Togoland, 1957; independent republic within the Commonwealth, 1960; first British colony in Africa to achieve independence; constitution provides for 140-member parliament elected every five years, and an executive president elected every four years, with a 20-member cabinet and Council of State; series of military coups (1966, 1972, 1979, 1982), with the creation of a Provisional National Defence Council, which rules by decree; mainly agricultural; commercial reserves of oil, diamonds, gold, manganese, bauxite, wood; cocoa (world's leading producer) provides two-thirds of export revenue; tobacco, rubber, cotton, peppers, pineapples, avocados, ginger; mining, lumbering, light manufacturing, fishing, aluminium; 40 forts and castles built along the coast from the late 15th-c onwards have been designated world heritage monuments. » Accra; Volta, River; RR25 national holidays; RR50 political leaders

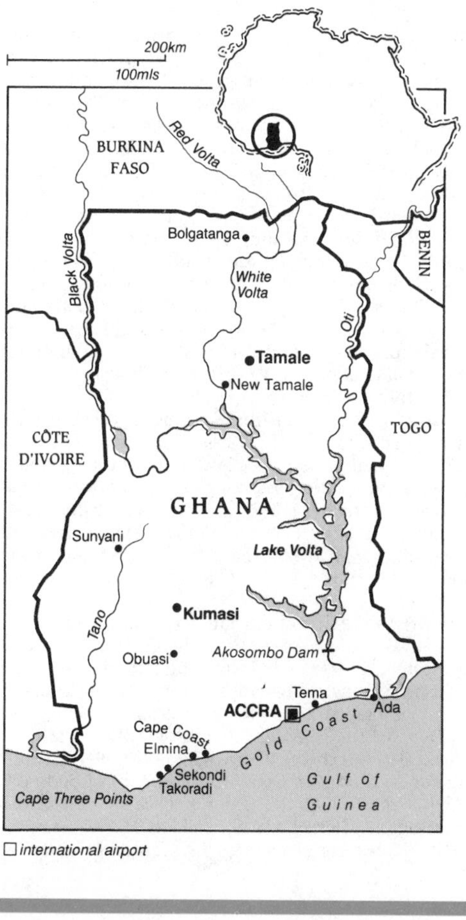

□ *international airport*

gharial [**gair**ial] or **gavial** A rare S Asian crocodile-like reptile of family *Gavialidae* (*Gavialis gangeticus*); length, up to 6.6 m/21½ ft; very narrow snout; nostrils of male swollen as a bulbous 'pot'; inhabits rivers; eats fish and frogs. The name is also used for the **false gharial** of the family *Crocodylidae. Gavial* was a slip of the pen during early accounts of the gharial. » alligator [i]; crocodile; reptile

Ghats [gahts] Two mountain ranges in India; **Western Ghats** runs parallel to the Bay of Bengal, forming the E edge of the Deccan Plateau; series of disconnected hill ranges, including the Velikonda, Nallamala, Seshachalam, Palkonda, Melagiri, and Nilgiri Hills; Doda Betta in the Nilgiri Hills reaches 2 636 m/8 648 ft; **Eastern Ghats** runs parallel to the Arabian Sea, forming the W boundary of the Deccan plateau; length c.1 600 km/1 000 ml; joined to the Eastern Ghats in the Nilgiri Hills; chief watershed of peninsular India; highest point, Anai Mudi Peak (2 695 m/8 842 ft) in the Cardamon Hills; subject to heavy rainfall during the SW monsoon; dense tropical forest. » Deccan; India [i]

ghee An edible fat derived from butter by removing all or most of the water. It is popular in hot climates, where the absence of water improves the keeping quality of the butter-fat. » butter

Ghent [gent], Flemish **Gent**, Fr **Gand** 51°02N 3°42E, pop (1982) 237 687. River port and capital city of East Flanders province, NW Belgium, at the confluence of the Scheldt and Leie Rivers; third largest urban region in Belgium, and second largest port; harbour connected by canal to the North Sea; focus of Flemish nationality; university (1816); railway; spinning and weaving (Flemish linen), chemicals, steel, cars, electrical engineering, publishing, banking; Cathedral of St Bavon (begun 10th-c), town hall (15th–17th-c), House of Free Boatmen (1531), Abbey of St Bavon (642), castle of Gravensteen (1180–1200). » Belgium [i]

gherkin A variety of cucumber with very small fruits. (*Cucumis sativa.* Family: *Cucurbitaceae.*) » cucumber

Ghibellines [**zhi**buhleenz] The pro-imperial party in Italian cities of the 13th–14th-c, favouring the involvement of the Holy Roman Emperor in Italian politics, even after the decline of the Hohenstaufen state from 1266. They supported the invasion of Emperor Henry VII (c.1270–1313) in 1308, although the power and status of the Empire had much diminished by that date. » Guelphs; Holy Roman Empire

Ghiberti, Lorenzo [gee**bair**tee] (1378–1455) Italian goldsmith, bronze-caster, and sculptor, born and died in Florence. In 1401 he won the competition to make a pair of bronze gates for the baptistery in Florence Cathedral. When these were completed (1424), he worked on a further pair of gates, which were finished in 1452. » Italian art

Ghirlandaio, Domenico [geerlan**dah**yoh], originally **Domenico di Tommaso Bigordi** (1449–94) Italian painter, born and died in Florence. He was apprenticed to a goldsmith, a metal garland-maker or 'Ghirlandaio'. His main works were frescoes, in his native city, notably a series illustrating the lives of the Virgin and the Baptist in the choir of Santa Maria Novella (1490). » Florentine School; fresco; Italian art

Giacometti, Alberto [jahko**met**tee] (1901–66) Swiss sculptor and painter, born at Stampa. He studied at Geneva and worked mainly in Paris, at first under Bourdelle. He joined the Surrealists in 1930, producing many abstract constructions of a symbolic kind, arriving finally at the characteristic 'thin man' bronzes, long spidery statuettes, such as 'Pointing Man' (1947, Tate). He died at Chur. » Surrealism

giant clam The largest living bivalve mollusc; length up to

135 cm/2½ ft; weight over 250 kg/550 lb; found in Indo-Pacific seas in shallow water; its mantle tissues contain many microscopic algae, which it digests. (*Tridacna gigas*. Class: *Pelecypoda*. Family: *Tridacnidae*.) » algae; bivalve; clam; mollusc

giant redwood » **mammoth tree**

Giant's Causeway Volcanic basalt formation on the N coast of Co Antrim, Northern Ireland, 11 km/7 ml NE of Portrush; a world heritage site; a natural 'pavement' of columnar basalt projecting into the North Channel, formed by the tops of thousands of small basaltic columns (usually hexagonal, diameter 38–50 cm/15–20 in), which resulted from the cooling of a volcanic flow; according to legend, the causeway was built for giants to travel across to Scotland. » basalt; Northern Ireland [i]

giant star A huge star in a late stage of stellar evolution. Hydrogen in the central core is exhausted, and that remaining in the outer layers burns in shells. As a consequence the star balloons outwards. This will be the fate of the Sun, about five thousand million years in the future. » star

gibberellins [jibuh**re**linz] A group of plant hormones involved in many processes, often in conjunction with auxins. They are concerned with controlling cell-elongation during growth, but can also promote fruit and seed formation, delay ageing in leaves, and are believed to be involved in sexual expression in male and female flowers. They are used commercially to produce male flowers in naturally female hybrids (such as some cucumbers), to induce parthenocarpy, and to stimulate seed germination. » auxins; fruit; germination; hormones; plant

gibbon An ape native to rain-forests of SE Asia; acrobatic; slender with small head; thumb small; fingers long; arms as long as body and legs together; arms folded above head when walking; also known as **lesser ape**. (Genus: *Hylobates*, 6 species.) » ape; siamang

Gibbon, Edward (1737–94) British historian, born at Putney, Surrey. He was educated at Westminster and Oxford, became a Catholic at 16, and was sent to Lausanne, where he boarded with a Calvinist pastor who wooed him back to Protestantism. After a visit to Rome in 1764 he began to plan for his major work, *The History of the Decline and Fall of the Roman Empire* (5 vols, 1776–88). Left money by his father, he settled in London for the task (1772), in 1774 entering parliament, and becoming Commissioner of Trade and Plantations. After completing his *History*, he spent much of the rest of his life with Lord Sheffield, who published his *Miscellaneous Works* (1796). He died in London.

Gibbon, Lewis Grassic, pseudonym of **James Leslie Mitchell** (1901–35) British novelist, born at Auchterless, Aberdeenshire, Scotland. Educated at Stonehaven Academy, he worked as a journalist in Aberdeen, and served in the RAF until 1929. He published the historical novels *Three Go Back* (1932) and *Spartacus* (1933) under his own name, but adopted his pseudonym for the three novels *Sunset Song* (1932), *Cloud Howe* (1933), and *Grey Granite* (1934), which form the trilogy *A Scots Quair*. He died in Welwyn Garden City, Hertfordshire. » novel; Scottish literature

Gibbons, Grinling (1648–1721) English sculptor and woodcarver, born in Rotterdam, the Netherlands. He moved to England, where he was appointed by Charles II to the Board of Works, and employed in the chapel at Windsor, and in St Paul's, London. At Chatsworth, Burghley, and other mansions he executed an immense quantity of carved fruit and flowers, cherubs' heads, and other typical Baroque embellishment. He died in London. » Baroque (art and architecture); English art; sculpture

Gibbons, Orlando (1583–1625) English composer, born at Oxford. He studied at Cambridge, and c.1615 was appointed organist of the Chapel Royal, London, and in 1623 of Westminster Abbey. His compositions include services, anthems, and madrigals (notably *The Silver Swan*), and also hymns, fantasies for viols, and music for virginals. He died at Canterbury, Kent.

Gibbons, Stella (Dorothea) (1902–89) British writer, born and died in London. She worked as a journalist, and later began a series of successful novels, as well as writing poetry and short stories. Her *Cold Comfort Farm* (1933), a light-hearted satire on melodramatic rural novels, has established itself as a classic of parody. » English literature; parody

Gibbs, J(osiah) Willard (1839–1903) US mathematician and physicist, born at New Haven, Connecticut. He was educated at Yale, where he became professor of mathematical physics (1871–1903). The field of chemical thermodynamics developed largely from his work, and he was a founder of physical chemistry. He died at New Haven. » thermodynamics

Gibraltar [jib**rawl**ter], Span [kheevral**tahr**] Arabic **Jebel Tariq**, 36°09N 5°21W; pop (1988) 30 127; area 5.9 sq km/2.3 sq ml. Narrow rocky peninsula rising steeply from the low-lying coast of SW Spain at the E end of the Strait of Gibraltar; gateway between the Atlantic Ocean and the Mediterranean Sea; important strategic point of control for the W Mediterranean; British Crown Colony, playing a key role in Allied naval operations during both World Wars; military base; 8 km/5 ml from Algeciras; length, c.5 km/3 ml; width 1.2 km/¾ ml, narrowing to the S; official language, English, with Spanish widely spoken; British currency and local banknotes used; timezone GMT +1; airport; car ferries to Tangier; limestone massif, 'The Rock', height 426 m/1 398 ft, connected to the Spanish mainland by a sandy plain; extensive limestone caves; home of the Barbary apes, the only native monkeys in Europe; settled by Moors, 711; taken by Spain, 1462; ceded to Britain, 1713; Crown Colony, 1830; British monarch represented by a governor; 18-member House of Assembly; economy largely dependent on the presence of British forces; Royal Naval Dockyard converted to a commercial yard in 1985; transshipment trade, fuel supplies to shipping, tourism; Moorish castle; proposal to end British rule defeated by referendum, 1967; Spanish closure of frontier, 1969–85; Spain continues to claim sovereignty. » Gibraltar, Strait of; Mediterranean Sea; Spain [i]

Gibraltar, Strait of, Arabic **Bab al Zakak**, Lat **Fretum Herculeum** Channel connecting the Mediterranean Sea to the Atlantic Ocean; length, 60 km/37 ml; width between the Rock of Gibraltar and Cape Ceuta (the Pillars of Hercules), 24 km/15 ml; widest point, 40 km/25 ml; narrowest point, 15 km/9 ml. » Gibraltar

Gibson, Guy (Penrose) (1918–44) British wing commander in the RAF, who led the famous 'Dambusters' raid on the Möhne and Eder Dams in 1943, an exploit for which he received the VC. He was killed on a later operation. » World War 2

Gibson, Mike, properly **(Cameron) Michael (Henderson)** (1942–) British rugby player, born in Belfast, Northern Ireland. He played as centre and outside half with the North of Ireland, Cambridge University, and the British Lions, appearing a world record 69 times for his country (the most for any International Board nation). He toured with the British Lions in 1966, 1968, and 1971, and made 12 international appearances. He is now a Belfast solicitor. » rugby football

Gibson Desert Central belt of the Western Australian Desert; area c.220 000 sq km/85 000 sq ml; consists of sand dunes, scrub, and salt marshes; includes the salt lakes L Disappointment and L Auld; contains Rudall R national park. » Western Australia

Gide, André (Paul Guillaume) [zheed] (1869–1951) French writer, born and died in Paris. He was author of over 50 volumes of fiction, poetry, plays, criticism, biography, belles-lettres, and translations. Among his best-known works are *Les Nourritures terrestres* (1897, Fruits of the Earth) and *Les Faux Monnayeurs* (1926, The Counterfeiters), his translations of *Oedipus* and *Hamlet*, and his *Journal*. He received the Nobel Prize for Literature in 1947, and died in Paris. » French literature

Gideons International An international organization, which began in Wisconsin in 1898, with the aim of spreading the Christian faith by the free distribution of copies of the Bible to public places, including hotel rooms, hospitals, and military bases. It is named after the Biblical judge 'Gideon', who led Israel against the Midianites. » Bible; Midianites

Gielgud, Sir (Arthur) John [**gil**good] (1904–) British actor and producer, born in London. Educated in London, he made his debut in 1921 at the Old Vic Theatre, and established a reputation as Hamlet (1929) and in *The Good Companions* (1931). He became a leading Shakespearian actor, directing many of the Shakespeare Memorial Theatre productions. His film appearances include Disraeli in *The Prime Minister* (1940) and in *Arthur* (1970), for which he received an Academy Award. He was knighted in 1953. » Shakespeare [i]; theatre

gift tax A tax formerly levied in the UK on gifts having a substantial value. Capital transfer tax was in part a gift tax, the aim being to stop the practice of transferring property during a person's lifetime, thus avoiding death duties. In the USA, the tax is levied on the value of the property given away (payable by the donor). » capital transfer tax

Gigantes [jiyganteez, giganteez] In Greek mythology, the sons of Earth and Tartaros, with snake-like legs; their name means 'the giants'. They made war on the Olympian gods, were defeated, and are buried under various volcanic islands. The Gigantomachy ('war of the giants') was the subject of large-scale sculpture, as at Pergamum. A sub-group, the Aloadi, piled Mt Pelion upon Mt Ossa. » Cyclops; Titan (mythology); Typhon

Gigli, Beniamino [zheelyee] (1890–1957) Italian tenor, born at Recanati. He won a scholarship to the Liceo Musicale, Rome, and made his operatic debut in Ponchielli's *La Gioconda* in 1914. By 1929 he had won a worldwide reputation as a lyric-dramatic tenor of great vitality, at his best in the works of Verdi and Puccini. His last concert was in 1956, and he died in Rome. » opera

gigue [zheeg] A lively dance, probably of British origin, popular during the 17th–18th-c. It became a standard movement in instrumental suites of the period. » jig; suite

gila monster [heela] An American lizard of family *Helodermatidae*; the only venomous lizard (venom is a nerve poison, but the bite is seldom fatal); length, up to 600 mm/24 in; dark with yellow mottling; bead-like scales; blunt head; fat tail; eats eggs and small vertebrates; two species: **gila monster** (*Heloderma suspectum*) and **Mexican beaded lizard** (*Heloderma horridum*). » lizard [i]

Gilbert, William (1544–1603) English physician and physicist, born at Colchester, Essex. After a period at Cambridge, he settled in London (1573), becoming physician to Queen Elizabeth. He established the magnetic nature of the Earth, and conjectured that terrestrial magnetism and electricity were two allied emanations of a single force. He was the first to use the terms 'electricity', 'electric force' and 'electric attraction'. His book, *De magnete* (1600, On the Magnet) is the first major English book in science. He died in London or Colchester. The *gilbert*, unit of magnetomotive power, is named after him. » electricity; magnetism

Gilbert, Sir W(illiam) S(chwenck) (1836–1911) British parodist and librettist of the 'Gilbert and Sullivan' light operas, born in London. He studied at London, became a clerk in the privy-council office (1857–62), and was called to the Bar (1864). Failing to attract lucrative briefs, he subsisted on magazine contributions to *Fun*, for which he wrote much humorous verse under his boyhood nickname 'Bab', collected in 1869 as the *Bab Ballads*. He also wrote fairy comedies and serious plays in blank verse. He is remembered for his partnership with Sir Arthur Sullivan, begun in 1871, with whom he wrote 14 popular operas, from *Trial by Jury* (1875) to *The Gondoliers* (1889). The partnership was broken by a quarrel, and on its resolution they wrote little more before Sullivan's death in 1900. He was knighted in 1907, and died at Harrow Weald, Middlesex. » Sullivan, Arthur

Gilbert of Sempringham, St (c.1083–1189), feast day 4 or 16 February. English priest, born at Sempringham, Lincolnshire. He studied in Paris, and was ordained in 1123. In 1131 he founded the Order of Gilbertines for monks and nuns, the only mediaeval order to originate in England. He died at Sempringham, and was canonized in 1202. The order was dissolved by Henry VIII. » Henry VIII; monasticism

Gilbert Islands pop (1985) 61 014; area 264 sq km/102 sq ml. Island group of Kiribati, C Pacific Ocean; chain of 17 coral atolls spread over c.680 km/420 ml; mainly 200–300 m/700–1 000 ft wide, but 15–100 km/10–60 ml long; most have central lagoons; part of the British colony of Gilbert and Ellice Is until 1977; capital, Tarawa; fishing, farming, copra, phosphate. » Kiribati

gilding The ancient craft of sticking gold (or other metallic) leaf on to a surface, usually wood. Gilding flourished in the Middle Ages in manuscript illumination and panel painting, and later for picture-frames and furniture.

Giles, Carl (1916–) British cartoonist. He trained as an animator and worked for the film-maker Alexander Korda in 1935. Since 1937 he has produced his distinctive and popular humorous drawings, first for *Reynolds News*, then (from 1943) for the *Express* newspapers, celebrating the down-to-earth reactions of ordinary British people to great events. » cartoon (art); Korda

Gilgamesh Epic [gilgamesh] A Babylonian epic poem, partially preserved in different versions, named after its hero, the Sumerian King Gilgamesh (3rd millennium BC). It describes Gilgamesh's legendary adventures, and narrates a story of the Flood that has striking parallels with the Biblical account. » Babylonia; epic; Flood, the

Gill, (Arthur) Eric (Rowton) (1882–1940) British carver, engraver, and typographer, born at Brighton. He trained as an architect, but then took up letter-cutting, masonry, and engraving. After his first exhibition (1911) he maintained a steady output of carvings in stone and wood, engravings, and type designs. Among his main works is 'Prospero and Ariel' (1931) at Broadcasting House, London. He died at Uxbridge, Middlesex. » engraving; typography

Gillespie, Dizzy, byname of **John Birks Gillespie** (1917–) US jazz trumpeter and composer, born at Cheraw, South Carolina. He worked in prominent swing bands (1937–44), and as a leader, often with Charlie Parker on saxophone, he developed the music called 'bebop', with dissonant harmonies and polyrhythms, a reaction to swing. His own raucous big band (1946–50) was his masterpiece, affording him scope as both soloist and showman. His memoirs, *To Be or Not to Bop* (with Al Fraser) appeared in 1979. » bebop; Parker, Charlie

Gillette, King C(amp) [jilet] (1855–1932) US inventor of the safety razor, born at Fond du Lac, Wisconsin. Brought up in Chicago, he became a travelling salesman for a hardware company. He founded his razor blade company in 1901. Later he wrote a series of books on industrial welfare and social reform. He died in Los Angeles, California.

gilliflower » **stock**

Gillray, James (1757–1815) British caricaturist, born and died in London. A letter engraver by training, from about 1779 he turned to caricature. He issued about 1500 caricatures of political and social subjects, notably of Napoleon, George III, and leading politicians. » caricature; English art

Gilman, Charlotte Anna Perkins *née* **Perkins** (1860–1935) US feminist and writer, born at Hartford, Connecticut, into the same family as Catharine Beecher and Harriet Beecher Stowe. She had limited schooling, an unhappy marriage, and severe mental distress, then began a career as a writer, arguing in many books that women's equality required major social change. Her most notable books are *Women and Economics* (1898), *The Home* (1903), and *Man-Made World* (1911). She died at Pasadena, California. » Beecher, Catharine; feminism; Stowe

gilt-edged securities The name given to UK government loan stock, considered to be a safe investment. The name derives from the book in which transactions were originally recorded, which was edged in gold. » consols; stocks

gin A spirit distilled from grain or malt, and flavoured with juniper berries; the name derives from Dutch *jenever* 'juniper'. Gin was once the true drink of the masses, often referred to as 'mothers' ruin' and associated with 'gin palaces', but its image has changed considerably in the present century. Dutch gin is drunk neat with beer, while London or dry gin is usually mixed with tonic.

gin rummy » **rummy**

Ginckell or **Ginkel, Godert de** (1630–1703) Dutch general, born at Utrecht. He accompanied William III to England in 1688, and fought at the Battle of the Boyne (1690). As Commander-in-Chief in Ireland, he defeated the remaining rebels, and was created Earl of Athlone (1692). He later led the Dutch troops under Marlborough. » Boyne, Battle of the; Marlborough, Duke of; William III

ginger A perennial native to SE Asia; stem to 1 m/3¼ ft;

rhizomatous; leaves with sheathing stalks, in two rows; yellow and purple flowers, complex, sterile, resembling those of orchids, in long dense spikes with overlapping yellow and green bracts. An important spice since ancient times, it reached Europe by the 1st-c, and England by the 11th-c. The aromatic rhizome contains the essential oil *zingiberene*, used in perfumes as well as food and drink (such as ginger-ale). Because the flowers are sterile, propagation is vegetative. (*Zingiber officinale*. Family: *Zingiberaceae*.) » bract; perennial; orchid [i]; rhizome; spice; vegetative reproduction

Ginger Meggs A famous Australian cartoon character, created in 1921 by J C Bancks in Sydney. Ginger is a boy about 10 years old, living in the suburbs, who stands up against a bully and stupid parents. Syndicated nationally and overseas, he has appeared in book, pantomime, and play form, as well as in a film (1982).

ginger mint » **mint**

gingivitis [jinjiviytis] Infection of the gums by bacteria in the mouth. It causes redness and bleeding, and the gums retract from the teeth rendering them unstable. Untreated gingivitis leads ultimately to loss of teeth. » bacteria [i]; dentistry

ginkgo A deciduous gymnosperm originally from SW China, but probably no longer existing in the wild; leaves fan-shaped; seed with a fleshy aril covering the edible kernel; also called **maidenhair tree**. It is the sole living survivor of a formerly large and widespread family. (*Ginkgo biloba*. Family: *Ginkgoaceae*.) » aril; deciduous plants; gymnosperms

Ginsberg, Allen (1926–) US poet, born at Newark, New Jersey. He studied at Columbia, then worked in a number of jobs before publishing his first book, *Howl* (1957), the prototype poetry of the Beat school. In the 1960s he travelled widely, and wrote several other volumes, such as *Empty Mirror* (1961) and *Angkor Wat* (1968). His prose works include *Allen Verbatim* (1974) and *Journals* (1977). His *Collected Poems* were published in 1987. » beat generation

ginseng Two species of thick-rooted perennials, native to N America and Asia; rhizomatous; palmate leaves; 5-petalled, yellowish-green flowers; round, red fruits. The powdered roots are said to have aphrodisiac as well as medicinal and rejuvenative properties. (*Panax pseudoginseng*, *Panax quinquefolium*. Family: *Araliaceae*.) » palmate; perennial; rhizome

Giordano, Luca (1634–1705) Italian painter, born and died in Naples. He was able to work with extreme rapidity (hence his nickname, Fa Presto, 'Make haste'), and to imitate the great masters. In 1692 he went to Madrid, at the request of Charles II of Spain, to embellish the Escorial. » fresco; Italian art; oil painting

Giorgione, originally **Giorgio da Castelfranco** (c.1478–1510) Italian painter, born at Castelfranco. He studied under Giovanni Bellini in Venice, where he painted frescoes, though few have survived. A great innovator, he created the small, intimate easel picture with a new treatment of figures in landscape. Among the paintings reliably attributed to him are 'The Tempest' (c.1505, Venice) and 'The Sleeping Venus' (c.1510, Dresden). He died in Venice. » Bellini

Giotto (di Bondone) [jottoh] (1267–1337) Italian painter and architect, born near Vespignano, the founder of the Florentine School of painting. His major work was the fresco cycle, 'The Lives of Christ and the Virgin', in the Arena Chapel, Padua (1305–8). In 1330–3 he was employed by King Robert in Naples, and in 1334 was appointed Master of Works of the cathedral and city of Florence, designing the campanile. He died in Florence. » Florentine School; fresco; Italian art

Giotto project The first European interplanetary spacecraft launched (2 Jul 1985) from Kourou, French Guiana, to intercept Halley's Comet. It encountered the comet successfully (13 Mar 1986) at a distance of 500 km/300 m from the active nucleus, protected by a dust shield, and obtained TV images of the nucleus, and measurements of gases and dust; it survived the encounter, with potential for flyby of another comet. The final targeting was assisted by optical navigation data provided by the Soviet VEGA project and NASA's Deep Space Network, in a notable example of international space co-operation. It was managed by the European Space Agency's Space Research and Technology Centre. » comet; European Space Agency; NASA; VEGA project

Gippsland District of SE Victoria, Australia; mountains in the N drop down to fertile plains in the S; lignite, dairy products, cereals, hops. » Victoria (Australia)

Gipsy » **Gypsy**

giraffe An African ruminant mammal, the tallest land animal (height, 5.5 m/18 ft); extremely long legs and neck; an artiodactyl; head with 2–5 blunt 'horns'; inhabits savannah and woodland; eats leaves from thorn trees; usually silent; usually pale with large angular brown blotches; nine geographical races with different patterning (*Angolan*, *Kordofan*, *Masai*, *Nubian*, *Reticulated*, *Rothschild*, *Thornicroft*, *South African* (or *Cape*), and *West African*); also known as **camel(e)opard**. (*Giraffa camelopardalis*. Family: *Giraffidae*.) » artiodactyl; okapi; ruminant [i]

giraffe antelope » **gerenuk**

Giralda [heeralda] A bell tower adjacent to Seville Cathedral, in Spain. Built (1163–84) as an Islamic minaret, it was converted in the 16th-c after the mosque it served had been displaced by the present cathedral. The tower is 93 m/305 ft high, and takes its name from the *giraldillo* or weathervane which surmounts it. » Seville

Giraldus Cambrensis or **Gerald de Barri** (c.1147–1223) Norman-Welsh historian and churchman, born at Manorbier Castle, Pembrokeshire. He was elected Bishop of St David's in 1176, but when Henry II refused to confirm his election, he withdrew to lecture at Paris. Later appointed a royal chaplain, in 1185 he accompanied Prince John to Ireland. He wrote an account of Ireland's natural history and inhabitants, following this with *Expugnatio Hibernica* (c.1189, History of the Conquest of Ireland). In 1188 he travelled through Wales to recruit soldiers for the Third Crusade, and wrote up his observations in the *Itinerarium Cambriae* (1191, Itinerary of Wales). He died at St David's. » Crusades [i]; Henry II (of England)

Giraudoux, (Hippolyte) Jean [zheerohdoo] (1882–1944) French writer and diplomat, born at Bellac, Limousin. He joined the diplomatic service and was for a time head of the French Ministry of Information during World War 2. He is chiefly remembered for his plays, mainly fantasies based on Greek myths and biblical lore, satirically treated as commentary on modern life. They include *La Guerre de Troie n'aura pas lieu* (1935, trans *Tiger at the Gates*, 1955), *Ondine* (1939), and *La Folle de Chaillot* (1945, The Mad Woman of Chaillot). He died in Paris. » French literature

Girl Guides » **scouting**

giro A state-operated low-cost banking system which commenced in the UK in 1968. Now called *Girobank PLC*, it is operated by the Post Office Corporation through its 20 000 post offices, carrying out the normal range of banking services. Similar systems have been operated by post offices in many European countries. Commercial banks have operated a giro system in the UK since 1961, referred to as a *credit-transfer* system.

Girondins [jirondinz] A group of deputies in the Legislative Assembly (1791–2) and French Convention (1792–5), led by Jean Roland (1734–93), Charles Dumouriez (1739–1823), and Jacques Brissot (1754–93). Sympathetic to the provinces rather than to Paris (their name derived from the Gironde region of SW France), they aroused the hostility of Robespierre and the 'Mountain' in the Convention, many being executed during the Reign of Terror (1793). » Brissot de Warville; Dumouriez; French Revolution [i]; Mountain, the; Plain, the; Robespierre

Girtin, Thomas (1775–1802) British landscape painter, born in London. His landscapes included many on subjects in the N of England and also in France, which he visited in 1802. His works were among the first to exploit watercolour as a true medium, as distinct from a tint for colouring drawings. He died in London. » English art; landscape painting; watercolour

Gisborne [gizbern] 38°41S 178°02E, pop (1988e) 32 000. Port and resort town in East Coast, North Island, New Zealand, at the head of Poverty Bay; site of Captain Cook's landing, 1769; airfield; railway; trade in wine, market gardening, farm produce, timber. » Cook, James; New Zealand [i]

Giscard d'Estaing, Valéry [zheeskah daystĩ] (1926–) French statesman and President (1974–81), born at Koblenz, Germany. He was educated in Paris, and worked for the Resistance during World War 2, after which he entered the Ministry of Finance as a civil servant. In 1955 he became an Assistant Director of the Cabinet, Finance Minister (1962–6), and launched his own Party (National Federation of Independent Republicans). He returned to the Finance Ministry in 1969, defeated Mitterand to become President in 1974, and was then beaten by Mitterand in 1981. » France [i]; Mitterand

Gish, Lilian, originally **Lillian de Guiche** (1896–) US actress, born at Springfield, Ohio. She started in silent films as an extra under D W Griffith in 1912, and became the girl heroine in all his classics from *The Birth of a Nation* (1915) and *Intolerance* (1916) to *Orphans of the Storm* (1922). After the coming of sound films she lost interest in the cinema, but continued on the stage, occasionally returning to film and television in character roles, even in the 1970s.

Gissing, George (Robert) (1857–1903) British novelist, born at Wakefield, Yorkshire, and educated in Manchester. Expelled from the university, he travelled to the USA, returning to work as a tutor in London. *Workers in the Dawn* (1880) was the first of over 20 novels largely presenting realistic portraits of poverty and misery, such as *Born in Exile* (1892) and *The Odd Women* (1893). His best-known novel is *New Grub Street* (1891), a bitter study of the venality of the literary world. He died at Saint-Jean de Lux, France. » English literature; novel

gittern A mediaeval musical instrument resembling a lute, but with a shorter neck which curved smoothly into the body of the instrument. It usually had three or four courses of strings played with a plectrum. » lute; plectrum; string instrument 2 [i]

Giulio Romano, originally **Giulio Pippi de' Giannuzzi** [**joo**lyoh ro**mah**noh] (c.1499–1546) Italian painter and architect, born in Rome. He assisted Raphael in the execution of several of his later works, and in 1524 went to Mantua, where he drained the marshes and protected the city from floods. He also restored and adorned the Palazzo del Te, the cathedral, and a ducal palace. He died at Mantua. » Italian art; Mannerism; Raphael

Giza [**gee**za], **El-Giza, Gizeh**, or **Al-Jizah** 30°36N 32°15E, pop (1976) 1 246 713. Capital of El Giza governorate, N Egypt; on W bank of R Nile, 5 km/3 ml SW of Cairo; railway; cotton, footwear, brewing, cinema industry; Sphynx, and pyramids of Cheops, Khafra, and Mankara, 8 km/5 ml SW. » Egypt [i]; pyramid; Seven Wonders of the Ancient World; sphinx

Glaciares, Los [lohs glas**yar**ays] Andean national park in SW Santa Cruz province, Patagonia, Argentina; area 4 459 sq km/ 1 721 sq ml; established in 1937; includes the E parts of L Viedma and L Argentino; borders Chile in the W; a world heritage site. » Argentina [i]

glaciation The coverage of the surface of the Earth by glaciers, as well as the erosive action produced by the movement of ice over the land surface. The most extensive period of recent glaciation was in the Pleistocene epoch, when polar ice caps repeatedly advanced and retreated, covering up to 30% of the Earth's surface. Glaciation produces erosional landforms resulting from abrasion and deposition. *Periglacial* processes result from frost and snow activity marginal to the ice sheet. » cirque; drumlins; fjord; glacier; Ice Age; moraine; Pleistocene epoch; till

glacier A body of ice originating from recrystallized snow in cirques in mountain areas and flowing slowly downslope by creep under its own weight (*alpine glaciers*). Huge glaciers on continental plateaux are termed *ice sheets*. Glaciers flow until the rate of ice loss at the snout equals the rate of accumulation at the source. » cirque; glaciation

glaciology The scientific study of ice in all its forms, including its crystal structure and physical properties, as well as glaciers and ice sheets in a geological and meteorological context. » glacier

gladiators In ancient Rome, heavily armed fighting men who fought duels, often to the death, in public. An import from Etruria, originally their contests were connected with funerary rites. Under the empire, they performed for public entertainment only. They were usually slaves, prisoners of war, or condemned criminals. » Etruria

gladiolus A perennial with a large fibrous corm, native to Europe, Asia, and Africa; leaves sword-shaped, in flat fans; flower slightly zygomorphic with a short tube and six spreading or hooded perianth-segments in a variety of colours, in one-sided spikes. There are numerous large-flowered cultivars. (Genus: *Gladiolus*, 300 species. Family: *Iridaceae*.) » corm; perennial; perianth; zygomorphic flower

Gladstone, W(illiam) E(wart) (1809–98) British Liberal statesman and Prime Minister (1868–74, 1880–5, 1886, 1892–4), born in Liverpool. Educated at Eton and Oxford, he entered parliament in 1832 as a conservative, working closely with Peel. From 1834 he held various junior posts, becoming President of the Board of Trade (1843–5). He was Chancellor of the Exchequer in Aberdeen's coalition (1852–5) and again under Palmerston (1859–66). In 1867 he became leader of the Liberal Party, and soon after served his first term as Premier. He disestablished and disendowed the Irish Church, established a system of national education (1870). Frequently in office until his resignation in 1894, he succeeded in carrying out a scheme of parliamentary reform which went a long way towards universal male suffrage. In his last two ministries he introduced bills for Irish Home Rule, but both were defeated. He died at Hawarden, Flintshire, and was buried in Westminster Abbey. » Conservative Party; Liberal Party (UK); Palmerston, Viscount; Peel

Glåma, Glommen, or **Glomma** [**glo**ma] River in E Norway, rising in Dovrefjell plateau at L Rien; flows S through Øyeren L to Oslo Fjord at Fredrikstad; length 598 km/372 ml; longest river in Norway; brings logs to the sawmills and paper-mills further downstream. » Norway [i]

Glamorgan » **Mid Glamorgan; South Glamorgan; West Glamorgan**

gland A single cell or group of cells secreting specific substances (eg hormones) for use elsewhere in the body. In mammals, most glands are *exocrine*: their secretions are discharged via duct systems into the cavity of a hollow organ (eg the salivary glands), or open directly onto an outer epidermal surface (eg the sweat glands of mammals). Vertebrates and some invertebrates also possess *endocrine* glands (eg the pituitary glands in vertebrates, the thoracic glands in insects), whose secretions are released directly into the blood stream. » adrenal/endocrine/ parathyroid / pituitary / prostate / salivary glands; glandular fever; liver; pancreas; sweat

glanders or **the glanders** A malignant disease of horses, characterized by a swelling of the glands (especially beneath the jaw) and a mucous discharge from the nostrils; fatal and contagious; may be caught by humans. » gland; horse [i]

glandular fever A benign but generalized and sometimes prolonged acute infectious disease due to Epstein Barr (EB) virus, which tends to affect young people. The blood contains characteristic mononuclear cells, and the condition is technically known as **infectious mononucleosis**. The symptoms include headache, sore throat, and tiredness; the lymph nodes are usually easily felt, and the condition may be followed by severe debility lasting several months. There is no specific antiviral remedy. » blood; gland; lymph; ME syndrome; virus

glare » **Polaroid 1**

Glaser, Donald A(rthur) (1926–) US physicist, born in Cleveland, Ohio. While working at the University of Michigan (1949–60), he developed the 'bubble chamber' for observing the paths of atomic particles, for which he won the Nobel Prize for Physics in 1960. He became professor of physics and molecular biology at Berkeley, California, in 1964. » bubble chamber

Glasgow 55°53N 4°15W, pop (1981) 765 030. Capital of Strathclyde region, W Scotland; on R Clyde, 66 km/41 ml W of Edinburgh; largest city in Scotland; expansion in 17th-c, with trade from the Americas; airport; railway; metro; University of Glasgow (1451); Strathclyde University (1964); shipyards, engineering, commerce, whisky blending and bottling, chemicals, textiles, carpets; Kelvin art gallery and museum, Hunterian art gallery and museum, Royal Scottish Academy of Music (1847), Museum of Transport, ruins of 15th-c Cathcart castle, St Mungo's cathedral (12th-c), Provand's Lordship (1471), 15th-c Crookston castle, Haggs castle (1585); Mitchell Library (1874);

People's Palace (1898); Victorian tenement museum; Mayfest. » Gorbals; Scotland [i]; Strathclyde

Glashow-Weinberg-Salam theory A modern relativistic quantum theory of weak interactions, in which weak nuclear force and electromagnetic force are unified; formulated in 1968 by US physicists Sheldon Glashow (1932–) and Steven Weinberg (1933–), and Pakistani physicist Abdus Salam (1926–). Radioactive decays are viewed as mediated by the W particle. The theory predicts the correct mass for W and Z particles using spontaneous symmetry breaking. » gauge theory; quantum field theory; spontaneous symmetry breaking; weak interaction; W particle; Z particle

glasnost (Russ 'speaking aloud') A term describing the changes in attitude on the part of leaders of the Soviet Union since 1985 under Gorbachev, which brought about a greater degree of openness both within Soviet society and in its relations with foreign powers. » Gorbachev; perestroika

glass 1 Any non-crystalline solid; one in which there is no orderly pattern, or arrangement of atoms. It is usually formed by the rapid cooling of a viscous liquid, such that the atoms have insufficient time to align into a crystal structure. Glass is sometimes termed a liquid having a viscosity greater than 10^{13} poise. It is not in thermodynamic equilibrium, and may gradually change into crystal form over days or years. » amorphous solid; crystals; metallic glass; poise; viscosity 2 The transparent or translucent product of the fusion of lime (calcium oxide), soda (sodium carbonate), and silica (silicon(IV) dioxide). There may be other constituents, yielding a great variety of properties. Boron gives the *borosilicate glass* ('Pyrex') which is stronger and more heat-resistant than common soda glass. *Flint glass* contains lead, and is particularly suitable for decoration by cutting and engraving. Having no sharp melting point, glass can be formed by many techniques while hot, most being variants on blowing or moulding. Flat glass used to be made by spinning a flat circle and cutting to size, or by blowing a large cylinder and slitting it. It is now made by drawing a sheet continuously out of a bath of molten glass. The best flat glass is today made by the 'float' process: molten glass flows continuously over a bed of molten tin. » boron; flint glass; lime; silica

glass harmonica » **musical glasses**

glass snake A lizard native to N America, Europe, and Asia; snake-like, with no limbs; length, up to 1.3 m/4¼ ft; scales hard and bony; stiff body with groove along each side; tail can be shed to confuse predators, and may break into several pieces (like breaking glass, hence the name); also known as **glass lizard**. (Genus: *Ophisaurus*, several species. Family: *Anguidae*.) » lizard [i]

glassfish 1 Small fish widespread in fresh and brackish waters of the Indo-Pacific region; length up to 10 cm/4 in; popular amongst aquarists for its iridescent colours and glass-like transparency. (Genus: *Chanda*. Family: *Centropomidae*.) 2 Small slender transparent fish of the NW Pacific; important locally as a food fish. (*Salangichthys microdon*. Family: *Salangidae*.)

glasswort An annual herb growing along coasts and in salt marshes more or less everywhere; fleshy, leafless jointed stems resemble spineless miniature cacti with flowers sunk into stems; also called **marsh samphire**. It was burnt to provide soda for early glass-making, and was (to a limited extent still is) pickled and eaten as a vegetable. (Genus: *Salicornia*, 35 species. Family: *Chenopodiaceae*.) » annual; herb

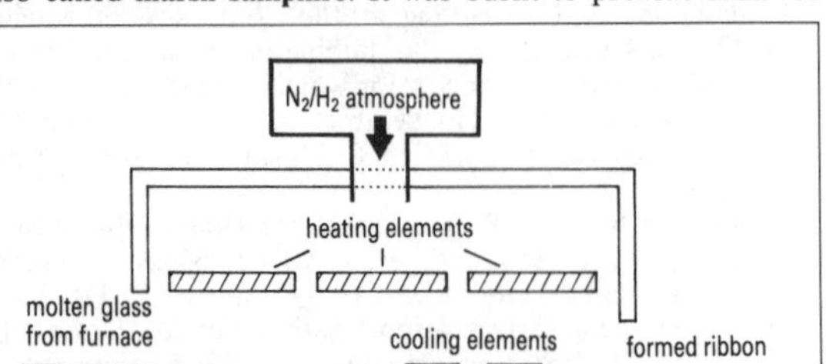

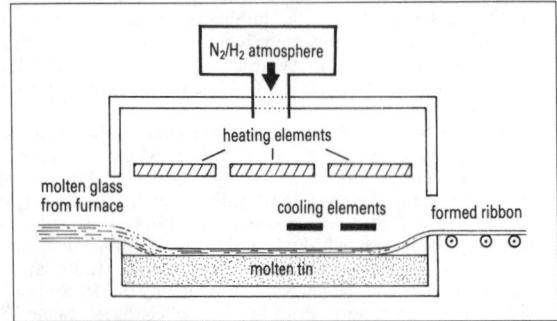

Glass – The float glass process

Glastonbury lake village A marshland settlement of the 3rd–1st-c BC near Glastonbury, Somerset, UK, renowned for its exceptional preservation of timber, wooden utensils, and basketry. Excavations (1892–1907) revealed an artificial island of felled trees, its wooden palisade enclosing c.80 reed-roofed circular huts 5.5–8.5 m/18–28 ft in diameter, their floors made of boards on clay. » Swiss lake dwellings

Glauber's salt Hydrated sodium sulphate, $Na_2SO_4.10H_2O$. It is named after German chemist, Johann Rudolph Glauber (1604–70), a follower of Paracelsus. » hydration

glaucoma [glow**kow**ma] A rise in the pressure of the aqueous fluid within the eye. Acute glaucoma arises when drainage of this fluid is blocked because of infection or cataract rupture. There is sudden pain in the affected eye, variable interference with vision, and blindness may develop. In other patients the onset is insidious; visual loss is slower in its development, and may not be noted until irreversible damage to the retina has occurred. Pressure within the eye can now be measured in most hospitals with a tonometer. Screening for increased pressure is important in the prevention of blindness. » eye [i]

glaze In oil painting, a transparent layer of paint sometimes mixed with varnish laid over dry underpainting. In pottery it is a thin vitreous coating fused to the surface of a pot by firing. » oil painting

Glazunov, Aleksandr (Konstantinovich) (1865–1936) Russian composer, born in St Petersburg. He studied under Rimsky-Korsakov, and became director of the Conservatory at St Petersburg (1906–17), when he was given the title of People's Artist of the Republic. Among his compositions are eight symphonies and works in every branch of music except opera. In 1928 he emigrated to Paris, where he died. » Rimsky-Korsakov

Glendower, Owen or **Glyndwr, Owain** (c.1354–1416) Welsh chief, born in Montgomeryshire. He studied law at Westminster, and became esquire to the Earl of Arundel. In 1401 he rebelled against Henry IV, proclaimed himself Prince of Wales, established an independent Welsh parliament, and joined the coalition with Harry Percy Hotspur, who was defeated at the Battle of Shrewsbury (1403). He continued to fight for Welsh independence until his death. » Henry IV (of England); Percy

Glenn, John H(erschel) (1921–) US astronaut, the first American to orbit the Earth, born at Cambridge, Ohio. Educated at the University of Maryland, he joined the US Marine Corps in 1943, and served in the Pacific during World War 2, and later in Korea. In 1957 he completed a record-breaking supersonic flight from Los Angeles to New York. He became an astronaut in 1959, and in 1962 made a three-orbit flight in the 'Friendship 7' space capsule. He resigned from the Marine Corps in 1965, has been a Senator from Ohio since 1975, and sought the Democratic nomination for the presidency in 1984. » space exploration; RR10

Glenrothes [glen**roth**is] 56°12N 3°11W, pop(1981) 32 971. Town in Kirkcaldy district; capital of Fife region, E Scotland; designated a new town in 1948; airfield; centre for electronic research; timber, plastics, electronics, machinery, paper, food processing. » Fife; Scotland [i]

gliadin A simple protein occurring mainly in wheat. An adverse reaction to this protein is a feature of coeliac disease. » coeliac disease; gluten; protein; wheat

glider An aircraft that flies without the aid of mechanical propulsion. The wings may be fixed or flexible, and if the latter, the machine is known as a **hang glider**. Gliders usually remain aloft by finding rising currents of hot air (*thermals*), and remaining in them. The first piloted glider was designed in 1853 by aviator and inventor Sir George Cayley (1773–1857). » aircraft [i]; hang glider [i]

Glinka, Mikhail (Ivanovich) (1804–57) Russian composer, born at Novopasskoi, Smolensk. He was a civil servant, but after a visit to Italy began to study music in Berlin. His opera *A Life for the Tsar* (1836, known earlier as *Ivan Susanin*) was followed by *Russlan and Ludmilla* (1842), which pioneered the style of the Russian national school of composers. He left

Russia in 1844, and lived in Spain and France, returning home in 1854. He died during a visit to Berlin.

Glittertind or **Glittertinden** [**gli**tuhtin] 61°40N 8°32E. Highest mountain in Norway, a peak in the Jotunheimen range, SC Norway; height 2 470 m/8 104 ft. » Jotunheimen; Norway [i]

Global Maritime Distress and Safety System » **Morse code**

globe artichoke A robust perennial growing to 2 m/6½ ft; leaves up to 80 cm/30 in, deeply divided; flower heads blue, very large, surrounded by distinctive leathery, oval bracts. It is unknown in the wild, but has a long history of cultivation, especially in S Europe. The soft receptacle of the young flower heads and the fleshy bases to the bracts are eaten as a vegetable, and it is also grown as an ornamental. (*Cynara scolymus*. Family: *Compositae*.) » bract; perennial; receptacle; vegetable

Globe Theatre A theatre built in 1598 on Bankside in London. In 1613 it was burnt down and, although subsequently rebuilt, was demolished by the Puritans in 1644. Nearly all of Shakespeare's greatest works were performed here. A project to build a working replica of the theatre on the original site was initiated in 1987 under the direction of US actor and film producer Sam Wanamaker (1919–). » Puritanism; Shakespeare [i]; theatre

globeflower A perennial growing to 60 cm/2 ft, native to Europe and arctic N America; long-stalked basal leaves palmately 3–5-lobed, stem leaves 3-lobed, all deeply toothed; flowers 2–3 cm/¾–1¼ in diameter, globular, with c.10 incurved, yellow, petaloid sepals. (*Trollius europaeus*. Family: *Ranunculaceae*.) » palmate; perennial; sepal

globigerina [globijuh**ri**yna] A type of amoeba-like microscopic organism commonly found in marine plankton; secretes a delicate external shell (*test*), often ornate with spines; dead tests sink, forming a calcareous sediment (*globigerina ooze*), covering large areas of sea floor. » amoeba; calcium; foraminiferan; plankton; shell

globular cluster A densely packed family of stars arranged characteristically as a compact sphere of stars. It contains tens of thousands to millions of stars, formed at the same time. Over 100 are known in our Galaxy. » Galaxy; star

globulin [**glob**yoolin] A simple protein folded into a globular 3-dimensional shape. It is insoluble or only sparingly soluble in water, but soluble in dilute salt solutions. It is found in many animal tissues and in plant seeds, serving a variety of functions. » gamma globulins; protein

glockenspiel [**glok**uhnshpeel] A musical instrument consisting of tuned metal bars arranged in two rows like a piano keyboard, and played with small hammers held in each hand (in some models an actual keyboard is fitted). Most have a compass of 2½ octaves. » keyboard instrument; percussion [i]; transposing instrument

glomerulonephritis [glomuhroolohnuh**fri**ytis] An inflammation of the glomeruli (part of the kidneys responsible for the initial blood-filtering process) caused by foreign antigens invading the body, and stimulating the production of antibodies; the antigens combine with the antibodies to form protein complexes which circulate in the blood stream and settle in tissues. Those complexes trapped by the capillaries of the glomeruli set up an allergic reaction. Damage to the glomeruli impairs the filter, and leads to proteins and blood cells escaping into the urine. The illness is often preceded by recognizable infections (eg sore throats), but subsequently leads to oedema and elevation of blood pressure. In young people it usually resolves in two to three weeks, but in adults may lead to persisting kidney failure. » kidneys; oedema

Glommen or **Glomma** » **Glåma**

Glorious First of June, Battle of the (1794) A naval battle fought off the Isle d'Ouessant (near Brest) between British and French navies. The victory for Admiral Richard Howe resulted in the capture of a third of the French ships, and confirmation of British naval supremacy. » Howe, Richard; French Revolutionary Wars

Glorious Revolution The name given to the events (Dec 1688–Feb 1689) during which James II fled from England, effectively abdicating the throne, and William III and Mary II were established by parliament as joint monarchs. The title, coined by Whigs who in the long term benefited most from it, celebrates the bloodlessness of the event, and the assertion of the constitutional importance of parliament. » James II (of England); parliament; Whigs; William III

glory pea » **parrot's bill**

glossolalia The practice of 'speaking in tongues' – uttering sounds whose meaning is unknown to the speaker, who is undergoing a religious experience. The phenomenon is closely related to **xenoglossia**, using a language that the speaker has never known or heard, a power ascribed to the Apostles during the first days of Christianity, as recounted in the Acts of the Apostles. No scientifically attested case of xenoglossia has come to light, but speaking in tongues is nonetheless widely practised by several Christian groups, such as Pentecostalists or charismatic Catholics, and interpreted among its practitioners as a supernatural sign of religious sincerity or conversion. » apostle; Pentecostalism; Roman Catholicism

glottis The narrow part of the larynx at the level of the vocal cords (or vocal folds), which is most directly concerned with the production of sound. » larynx

Gloucester, Humphrey, Duke of (1391–1447) Youngest son of Henry IV, and protector during the minority of Henry VI (1422–9). He greatly increased the difficulties of his brother, Bedford, by his greed, irresponsibility, and factious quarrels with their uncle, Cardinal Beaufort. In 1447 he was arrested for high treason at Bury St Edmunds and five days later was found dead in bed (apparently from natural causes). His patronage of literature led to his nickname 'the Good Duke Humphrey'. » Henry VI

Gloucester, Prince Richard (Alexander Walter George) of (1944–) English prince, the younger son of Henry, Duke of Gloucester (the third son of George V). In 1972 he married Birgitte van Deurs; they have one son, **Alexander, Earl of Ulster** (1974–) and two daughters, **Lady Davina Windsor** (1977–) and **Lady Rose Windsor** (1980–).

Gloucester [**glos**ter], Lat **Glevum**, Anglo-Saxon **Caer Glou** 51°53N 2°14W, pop (1987e) 90 500. County town of Gloucestershire, SWC England; NE of Bristol; connected to R Severn by canal; founded by Romans 1st-c AD; railway; airfield; boatbuilding, trade in timber and grain, engineering; 13th-c cathedral, Bishop Hooper's Lodging; Three Choirs Festival in rotation with Hereford and Worcester (Sep). » Britain, Roman; Gloucestershire

Gloucestershire [**glos**tersheer] pop (1987e) 522 200; area 2 643 sq km/1 020 sq ml. County in SWC England, divided into six districts; bounded W by Gwent in Wales; features include the Cotswold Hills, Forest of Dean; drained by the R Severn; county town, Gloucester; chief towns include Cheltenham, Cirencester; agriculture, fruit, dairy farming, light engineering. » Cotswold Hills; England [i]; Gloucester; Severn, River

glowworm » **firefly**

gloxinia A Brazilian genus of plants with large, showy, funnel-shaped flowers in a variety of colours; related to the African violet, and similarly popular as house plants. They are sometimes called **slipper** or **florist's gloxinia** to distinguish them from the genus *Gloxinia*. (Genus: *Siningia*, 20 species. Family: *Gesneriaceae*.) » African violet

Glubb, Sir John Bagot, byname **Glubb Pasha** (1897–1986) British soldier, born at Preston, Lancashire. Educated at Cheltenham and the Royal Military Academy, Woolwich, he served in World War 1, and became the first organizer of the native police force in the new state of Iraq (1920). In 1930 he was transferred to British-mandated Transjordan, organizing the Arab Legion's Desert Patrol, and becoming Legion Commandant (1939). He had immense prestige among the Bedouin, but was dismissed from his post in 1956 following Arab criticism. Knighted in 1956, he then became a writer and lecturer. He died at Mayfield, Sussex. » Bedouin

glucagon [**gloo**kaguhn] A type of hormone (a polypeptide) found in vertebrates, synthesized in the pancreas by A-cells of the islets of Langerhans. It is secreted in response to low blood glucose concentrations. Its main action is to raise blood glucose levels by promoting the conversion of liver glycogen into glucose. It also stimulates the secretion of insulin, pancreatic somatostatin, and growth hormone. » glucose [i]; hormones; pancreas; peptide

Gluck, Christoph (Willibald) [glook] (1714–87) Austro-German composer, born at Erasbach, Bavaria. He taught music at Prague, then studied in Vienna and Milan. In 1741 he began to write operas, and after collaborating with the librettist Ranieri Calzabigi he produced such works as *Orfeo ed Euridice* (1762) and *Alceste* (1767). In the late 1770s, Paris was divided into those who supported Gluck's French opera style and those supporting the Italian style of Niccolo Piccinni (1728–1800) – the Gluckists and Piccinnists. Gluck finally conquered with his *Iphigénie en Tauride* (1779), and retired from Paris full of honour. He died in Vienna.

glucocorticoids [glookoh**kaw**tikoydz] Steroid hormones synthesized and released from the adrenal cortex of vertebrates, important in carbohydrate metabolism and the resistance of the body to stress. In humans, they include *cortisol* (*hydrocortisone*), *corticosterone*, and *cortisone*. They are used therapeutically in replacement therapy (eg Addison's disease, a result of glucocorticoid deficiency), and in the suppression of inflammatory and allergic disorders. » Addison's disease; adrenocorticotrophic hormone; cortisol; hormones; mineralocorticoids; steroid [i]

glucose $C_6H_{12}O_6$, also called **dextrose**. By far the most common of the six carbon sugars, its most stable structure is the ring form shown in the illustration. It is the primary product of plant photosynthesis. Starch and cellulose are both condensation polymers of glucose. Maltose, lactose, and sucrose contain at least one glucose residue, and glucose may be obtained from them by acid or enzymatic hydrolysis. » carbon; condensation (chemistry); diabetes mellitus; hydrolysis; hyperglycaemia; insulin; polymerization; photosynthesis; sugars

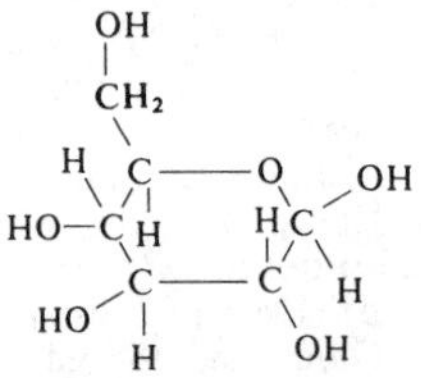

glue » **adhesives**

gluon A fundamental particle that carries the strong force between quarks, and binds them together into other sub-atomic particles; symbol g; mass 0, charge 0, spin 1. There are eight species of gluon distinguished by the colour combinations they carry. Gluons interact with one another; they are never observed directly. » confinement; fundamental particles; quantum chromodynamics; quark

gluten The main protein of wheat, subdivided into two other proteins, *gliadin* and *glutenin*. When mixed with water and kneaded, these proteins become aligned along one plane, imparting an elastic property to the dough. Gas bubbles of carbon dioxide produced by yeast fermentation allow the dough to rise because of entrapment of the gas by gluten. Maize, barley, and oats do not contain gluten and so cannot be used for baking. They tend to be used for flat cereal products such as cookies, biscuits, and tortillas. The small intestine in some people is abnormally sensitive to gliadin, a condition known as coeliac disease. » cereals; coeliac disease; fermentation; gliadin

glutton » **wolverine**

glycerides [**gli**seriydz] Esters of glycerol. Glycerol forms three series of ester: mono-, di- and tri-glycerides. Fats are examples of triglycerides. » ester [i]; fats; glycerol

glycerine » **glycerol**

glycerol [**gli**serol] $OHCH_2–CH(OH)–CH_2OH$, IUPAC **1,2,3-trihydroxypropane**, also known as **glycerine**, boiling point 290°C. A colourless, viscous, and sweet-tasting liquid, obtained from all vegetable and animal fats and oils by hydrolysis, and thus a by-product of soap manufacture. It reacts with nitric acid to form nitroglycerine. » hydrolysis; nitric acid

glycine [**gli**yseen] $NH_2–CH_2–COOH$, IUPAC **aminoethanoic acid**, melting point 260°C. A colourless solid, freely soluble in water. It is the simplest of the amino acids, found in almost all proteins, and obtainable from them by acid hydrolysis. It exists in solution as a zwitterion: ^+NH » amino acid [i]; hydrolysis; zwitterion

glycogen [**gli**ykohjen] $(C_6H_{10}O_5)_n$. A polysaccharide found in both plant and animal tissue (eg the liver) as an energy store. It is essentially a condensation polymer of glucose, and very similar to starch. » condensation (chemistry); glucose [i]; polysaccharides

glyptodon [**glip**tuhduhn] An armadillo-like, fossil mammal that grazed the pampas of S America during the Plio-Pleistocene epochs; large, up to 2.5 m/8 ft tall and 3.3 m/11 ft in length; whole body, except underside, enclosed in armoured shell formed of bony plates. (Order: *Xenarthra*.) » fossil; mammal [i]; Pleistocene/Pliocene epoch

gnat **1** An alternative name for mosquitoes. » Culicidae. **2** A swarming gnat; a type of small, delicate fly. The males fly in dancing swarms low over water or in woodland clearings. Most are predatory, feeding on other insects. (Order: *Diptera*. Family: *Epididae*.) » Culicidae; fly; mosquito

gnatcatcher A name used for many small birds often classified with Old World warblers; native to the New World from Argentina to New England; inhabits broken woodland; eats insects and spiders; builds nests using cobwebs. (Family: *Polioptilidae*, 10 species.) » warbler

Gneisenau, August (Wilhelm Anton), Graf Neithardt von ('Count Neithardt of') [**gni**yzuhnow] (1760–1831) Prussian general, born at Schildau, Prussian Saxony. In 1786 he joined the Prussian army, fought at Saalfeld and Jena (1806), helped to reorganize the army after its defeat by Napoleon (1807), and in the war of liberation gave distinguished service at Leipzig (1813). In the Waterloo campaign as chief of Blücher's staff he directed the strategy of the Prussian army. He died at Posen. » Blücher; Napoleonic Wars; Prussia; Waterloo, Battle of

gneiss [niys] A coarse, high-grade metamorphic rock with a banded appearance due to the segregation of light- and dark-coloured minerals. » metamorphic rock; schist

Gnosticism [**nos**tisizm] (Gr *gnosis*, 'knowledge') A system of belief which became prominent within 2nd-c Christianity, but which may have had earlier, non-Christian roots. It emphasized salvation through acquiring secret revealed knowledge about cosmic origins and the true destiny of the spirit within people; in later forms, this knowledge was imparted by a heavenly redeemer figure. Gnosticism was considered a heresy by the early Church Fathers, particularly for its appeal to secret traditions, its deprecatory view of the Creator God, and its docetic view of Christ. » Christianity; Docetism; Nag Hammadi texts

GNP (Gross National Product) » **Gross Domestic Product**

gnu [noo] » **wildebeest**

go The national game of Japan, first played in China c.1500 BC. It is a tactical game, played on a board divided into 324 squares (18 × 18). Each player has a supply of rounded counters or stones (like draughts pieces); one player has black, the other white. They take it in turn to fill up the board with the intention of surrounding the opponents pieces (army) and capturing them. It is a far more complex game than chess, and a handicapping system exists to enable players of different levels to compete on an equal basis. » chess

go-away bird » **turaco**

Goa, Daman, and Diu [**go**ha, da**mahn**, **dee**oo] pop (1981) 1 082 117; area 3 813 sq km/1 472 sq ml. Union territory in W India; capital, Panaji; governed by a Legislative Assembly of 30 members; Goa conquered by Muslims, 1312; taken by Portugal, 1510; island of Diu taken, 1534; Daman area N of Bombay ceded to Portugal, 1539; Old Goa a prosperous port city in the 16th-c; occupied by India, 1961; manganese, iron ore, fishing, rice, wheat, ragi, pulses, fruit; burial place of St Francis Xavier; colonial churches and convents are world heritage monuments, notably the Sé Cathedral (1652) and the Bom Jesus Basilica (1604). » Francis Xavier, St; India [i]; Portugal [i]

goat A mammal of family *Bovidae*; may be classified as an antelope; tail with naked undersurface; both sexes with horns; males with beard; inhabits dry rugged country; browses coarse vegetation; male called a *billy*, female a *nanny*, young a *kid*; six species in genus *Capra*: **wild goat** or **bezoar** (*Capra aegagrus*, the ancestor of the domestic goat, probably domesticated in SW Asia 8–9 000 years ago), **ibex**, **Spanish ibex** (also called **Pyrenean ibex**, **Spanish goat**, or **iz(z)ard**), **East Caucasian tur**, **West Caucasian tur**, and **markhor**. The name is also used for the N American *Rocky Mountain goat* (*Oreamnos americanus*). » Angora goat; antelope; Bovidae; markhor; Rocky Mountain goat

goat antelope » **antelope; Rocky Mountain goat**

goat moth A large, nocturnal moth; wings brownish-grey with dark markings; caterpillar smells like a goat; bores ascending tunnels in stems and branches of trees, especially willow; pupates after 3–4 years. (Order: *Lepidoptera*. Family: *Cossidae*.) » caterpillar; moth; pupa

goatfish » **red mullet**

goatsbeard 1 A variable annual to perennial, native to Europe and parts of Asia, growing to 80 cm/30 in; also called **Jack-go-to-bed-at-noon** because of the flower heads' habit of closing up about mid-day; leaves, grass-like; flower-heads yellow, surrounded by eight or more narrow bracts; fruits with a parachute of feathery interwoven hairs, the fruiting head being similar to a very large dandelion 'clock'. (*Tragopogon pratensis*. Family: *Compositae*.) **2** A perennial growing to 1 m/3¼ ft or more; native to the temperate N hemisphere; leaves feathery, much divided; flowers tiny, white, 5-petalled, in plume-like inflorescences. » annual; bract; inflorescence [i]; perennial

goatsucker The name used in the USA for nightjars with long bristles around the mouth (Subfamily: *Caprimulginae*). Nightjars without bristles are called **nighthawks** (Subfamily: *Chordeilinae*.) » nightjar; whip-poor-will

Gobbi, Tito (1915–84) Italian baritone, born at Bassano del Grappa. He studied law at Padua, and then took up singing in Rome, making his operatic debut in 1935 at Gubbio. He appeared regularly with the Rome Opera from 1938, and soon made an international reputation, especially in Verdian roles such as Falstaff and Don Carlos. He died in Rome. » Verdi

Gobelins, Manufacture nationale des [**goh**buhlĩ] A factory on the Left Bank of the R Seine at Paris. It was established in 1440 by Jean Gobelin as a dye works, and in the 17th-c a number of tapestry workshops were brought together here. The quality of the work produced is such that the term *Gobelins* has become synonymous with the art of tapestry making. » Paris [i]

Gobi Desert [**goh**bee] Desert in C Asia; area c.1 295 000 sq km/ 500 000 sq ml, extends c.1 600 km/1 000 ml E–W across SE Mongolia and N China; on a plateau, altitude 900–1 500 m/3 000–5 000 ft; series of shallow, alkaline basins; completely sandy in W; some nomadic Mongolian tribes on grassy margins; many fossil finds, including dinosaur eggs, and prehistoric implements. » desert; China [i]; Mongolia [i]

goblin shark Strange-looking shark with a long shovel-like process on front of head, and protruding teeth; body length up to c.3.5 m/11½ ft; known from Atlantic, Pacific and Indian Oceans, primarily from deep water. (*Mitsukurina owstoni*. Family: *Mitsukurinidae*.) » shark

goby [**goh**bee] Any of a large family of mostly small, elongate fishes with stout head, fleshy lips, and large eyes, abundant in coastal waters of tropical to temperate seas; length up to 25 cm/10 in, many less than 5 cm/2 in; pelvic fins joined to form single sucker-like fin; 19 genera, including European **black goby** (*Gobius niger*) and **painted goby** (*Pomatoschistus pictus*). (Family: *Gobiidae*.)

God A supernatural being or power, the object of worship. In some world religions (eg Christianity, Judaism, Islam) there is one God only (**monotheism**), who is transcendent, all-powerful, and related to the cosmos as creator. In other religions (eg Hinduism, Classical Greek and Roman religions, and primitive religions) many gods may be recognized (**polytheism**), with individual gods having particular properties and powers. In the Judaeo-Christian tradition, God, though transcendent and invisible, is believed to have revealed himself in history through the life and response of the people Israel, and, in the Christian tradition, supremely and finally in the life, death, and resurrection of Jesus of Nazareth, the Christ, all as testified to in the scriptures of the Old and New Testaments. The conviction that Jesus stood in a unique relation to God led to the development in Christian thought of the Trinitarian understanding, whereby the one God is confessed as three persons (Father, Son, and Holy Spirit) of one substance.

In the mainstream Western tradition, influenced by Classical Greek philosophy as well as Christianity, God is conceived as 'being itself' or 'pure actuality' (St Thomas Aquinas), in whom there is no unactualized potentiality or becoming; as absolute, infinite, eternal, immutable, incomprehensible (ie unable to be comprehended by human thought), all-powerful (omnipotent), all-wise (omniscient), all-good (omni-benevolent), and everywhere present (omni-present). He is also said to be impassible, or incapable of suffering. The fact that the New Testament sums up its understanding of God as 'Love' (1 *John* 4.8), coupled with the apparent fact of evil in the world, has led to various modifications of this traditional Western conception. Thus God is sometimes understood as all-good but finite (and therefore unable to prevent evil); or as di-polar, ie in one aspect absolute and infinite but in another aspect, in so far as he relates to the cosmos, relative and finite (*panentheism* or *process theology*); or as comprising the whole of nature (*pantheism*). Corresponding to particular concepts of God are particular understandings of God's power in relation to human beings and the world of nature. These vary from absolute transcendence, such that God is reponsible for initiating the world process and laying down its laws, thereafter letting it run its course (*deism*) to total immanence, whereby God is understood as a power or spirit within the world motivating human beings. Orthodox Christianity seeks to preserve both the transcendence and immanence of God.

From the time of the ancient Greeks, philosophers have tried to prove the existence of God by reason alone (ie not by divine revelation), and of these attempts the 'ontological' arguments of St Anselm and Descartes, the 'Five Ways' of St Thomas Aquinas, and Kant's moral argument are among the more famous and abiding. While the general philosophical consensus seems now to be that none of these arguments is coercive, discusssion in the 20th-c of various aspects of individual arguments has continued unabated. Attempts to disprove the existence of God or to show concepts of God to be incoherent have been likewise generally unpersuasive. » Anselm, St; Aquinas, St Thomas; Bible; Christianity; deism; Descartes; Hinduism; Islam; Jesus Christ; Judaism; Kant; monotheism; pantheism; polytheism; religion; Trinity

God Save the King/Queen The British national anthem, written anonymously in the 18th-c. It is the oldest of all national anthems, and the music has often been used for those of other countries: it is still used for the national anthem of Liechtenstein.

Godard, Jean-Luc [**goh**dah] (1930–) French film director, born in Paris. Educated in Paris, he was a journalist and film critic before turning director. His first major film *A Bout de souffle* (1960, *Breathless*) established him as one of the leaders of *Nouvelle Vague* cinema. He wrote his own filmscripts on contemporary and controversial themes, his prolific output including *Vivre sa vie* (1962, My Life to Live) and *Weekend* (1968). He then collaborated with other film-makers in the making of politically radical films, but returned to feature films with *Sauve qui peut* (1980, Slow Motion), *Detective* (1984), and *Je vous salue, Marie* (1985). » Nouvelle Vague

Goddard, Robert H(utchings) (1882–1945) US physicist and rocketry pioneer, born at Worcester, Massachusetts, and educated there and at Princeton. Professor of physics at Clark University (1919–43), he elaborated the theory of rocketry, developing the first successful liquid-fuelled rocket, launched in 1926. In 1929 he launched the first instrumented rocket, and later conducted research for US Navy applications. He died in Baltimore, Maryland. NASA's Goddard Space Flight Center is named in his honour. » rocket; Tsiolkovsky

Gödel or **Goedel, Kurt** [**ger**del] (1906–78) Austrian logician, born at Brünn, Austria-Hungary. He taught at Vienna, then emigrated to the USA (1940), where he became a US citizen (1948) and professor at the Institute of Advanced Study, Princeton,

New Jersey. He showed in 1931 that any formal logical system adequate for number theory must contain propositions not provable in that system (**Gödel's proof**). He died at Princeton. » logic; number theory

Godfrey of Bouillon [**boo**eeyõ] (c.1061–1100) Duke of Lower Lorraine (1089–95), and leader of the First Crusade, born at Baisy in Belgian Brabant. He served under Emperor Henry IV against Rudolph of Swabia and in 1084 in the expedition against Rome. He was elected one of the principal commanders of the First Crusade, and later became its chief leader. After the capture of Jerusalem (1099) he was proclaimed king, but he refused the crown, accepting only the title Defender of the Holy Sepulchre. He died at Jerusalem. » Crusades [i]

Godiva, Lady [go**diy**va] (?–c.1080) An English lady and religious benefactress, who, according to tradition, rode naked through the market place at Coventry, in order to obtain the remission of a heavy tax imposed by her husband, Leofric, upon the townsfolk (1040). The story occurs in Roger of Wendover (1235).

Godolphin, Sidney Godolphin, 1st Earl of (1645–1712) English statesman, born near Helston, Cornwall. He entered parliament (1668), visited Holland (1678), and was made head of the Treasury and a baron (1684). He stood by James when William of Orange landed (1688), and voted for a Regency; yet in 1689 William reinstated him as First Commissioner of the Treasury. He was ousted in 1696, but made Lord High Treasurer by Queen Anne (1702) and created earl (1706). His able management of the finances helped Marlborough in the War of the Spanish Succession (1701–13); but court intrigues led to his dismissal in 1710. He died at St Albans, Hertfordshire. » Anne; Spanish Succession, War of the; William III

Godoy, Manuel de (1767–1851) Spanish court favourite and chief minister (1792–1808) under Charles IV. An obscure guards officer, he achieved dictatorial power at the age of 25 through the favour of the Queen, Maria Luisa, whose lover he was. In 1795 he assumed the title 'Prince of the Peace', following Spain's defeat by Revolutionary France; in 1796 he allied with France against England – a disastrous move which turned Spain into a virtual French satellite, and contributed massively to her losing her American Empire. In 1808 he was overthrown, spending the rest of his life exiled in Rome and in Paris, where he died. » enlightened despots; French Revolutionary Wars

Godthåb or **Godthaab** [**got**hop] Eskimo **Nûk** or **Nuuk** 64°11N 51°44W, pop (1983e) 9 848. Capital and largest town of Greenland; on SW coast, on Davis Strait; founded, 1721; ruins of 10th-c Norse settlement nearby; fishing and fish processing, scientific installations, oil and liquid gas storage, reindeer, sheep. » Greenland [i]

Godunov, Boris Fyodorovich (1552–1605) Tsar of Russia (1598–1605), previously Regent (from 1584) for Fyodor, the imbecilic elder son of Ivan IV (the Terrible). Ivan's younger son Dimitry had been banished to the upper Volga, where he died in 1591 – murdered, it was said, at Boris's command. A pretender, claiming to be Dimitry, later started a revolt, overcame Boris's troops, and after the sudden death of Boris in Moscow, was crowned in 1605. » Ivan IV; Moussorgsky; Pushkin; Time of Troubles

Godwin (?–1053) Earl of Wessex, probably son of the South Saxon Wulfnoth. He became powerful under King Canute, and in 1042 helped to raise Edward the Confessor to the throne, marrying him to his daughter Edith. He led the struggle against the King's foreign favourites, which Edward revenged by confining Edith in a monastery, and banishing Godwin and his sons (1051). In 1052 Godwin landed in England, received the support of the people, and was reinstated. He died at Winchester, his son Harold for a few months being Edward's successor. » Anglo-Saxons; Edward the Confessor; Wessex

Godwin, Mary » **Wollstonecraft, Mary**

Godwin, William (1756–1836) British political writer and novelist, born at Wisbech, Cambridgeshire. His major work of social philosophy was *An Enquiry Concerning Political Justice* (1793), which greatly impressed the English Romantics. His masterpiece was the novel, *The Adventures of Caleb Williams* (1794). He married Mary Wollstonecraft in 1797. A bookselling business long involved him in difficulties, and in 1833 he was glad to accept the sinecure post of yeoman usher of the Exchequer. He died in London. » English literature; novel; Romantics; Wollstonecraft

Godwin-Austen, Mount » **K2**

godwit A large sandpiper, native to the N hemisphere but may winter in the S; bill long, very slightly up-curved; probes into sediments for small animals. (Genus: *Limosa*, 4 species.) » sandpiper

Goebbels, (Paul) Joseph (1897–1945) German Nazi politician, born at Rheydt. A deformed foot absolved him from military service, and he attended several universities. He became Hitler's enthusiastic supporter, and was appointed head of the Ministry of Public Enlightenment and Propaganda (1933). A bitter anti-Semite, his gift of mob oratory made him a powerful exponent of the more radical aspects of Nazi philosophy. Wartime conditions greatly expanded his responsibilities and power, and by 1943, while Hitler was running the war, Goebbels was virtually running the country. He retained Hitler's confidence to the last, and in the Berlin bunker he and his wife committed suicide, after taking the lives of their six children. » Hitler; Nazi Party; World War 2

Goeppert-Mayer, Maria [**ger**pert **may**er] (1906–72) German-US physicist, born at Kattowicz, Poland. She studied physics at Göttingen, and married the US chemist Joseph Mayer in 1930. They then worked at Johns Hopkins and Columbia Universities, where she continued her work in theoretical physics. In World War 2 she was involved in the atom bomb project, and afterwards worked in Chicago on the theory of atomic nuclei. In 1948 she discovered the 'magic numbers' of subnuclear particles, and from 1950 devised a complete shell theory of nuclear structure. She shared the Nobel Prize for Physics in 1963, and died in San Diego, California. » atomic bomb; atomic/particle physics

Goering or **Göring, Hermann (Wilhelm)** (1893–1946) German politico-military leader, born at Rosenheim, Bavaria. In the 1914–18 war he fought on the Western Front, then transferred to the Air Force, and commanded the famous 'Death Squadron'. In 1922 he joined the Nazi Party and was given command of the Hitler storm troopers. He became President of the Reichstag in 1932, and joined the Nazi government in 1933. He founded the Gestapo, and set up the concentration camps for political, racial, and religious suspects. In 1940 he became economic dictator of Germany, and was made Marshal of the Reich, the first and only holder of the rank. As the war went against Germany, his prestige waned. In 1944 he attempted a palace revolution, was condemned to death, but escaped, to be captured by US troops. In 1946 he was sentenced to death at the Nuremberg War Crimes Trial, but before his execution could take place he committed suicide. » Hitler; Nazi Party; World War 2

Goes, Hugo van der » **van der Goes, Hugo**

Goethe, Johann Wolfgang von [**ger**tuh] (1749–1832) German poet, dramatist, and scientist, born in Frankfurt-am-Main. He studied law at Leipzig and Strasbourg, came under the influence of Herder, and became interested in alchemy, anatomy, and the antiquities. He returned to Frankfurt as a newspaper critic, and captured the spirit of German nationalism with his drama, *Götz von Berlichingen* (1773), following this with his novel *Leiden des jungen Werther* (1774, The Sorrows of Young Werther). In 1776 he accepted a post in the court of the Duke of Weimar, where he studied a variety of scientific subjects. He wrote much lyric poetry at this time, inspired by his love for Charlotte von Stein. Visits to Italy (1786–8, 1790) contributed to a greater preoccupation with poetical form, seen in such plays as *Iphigenie auf Tauris* (1789) and *Torquato Tasso* (1790). His love for classical Italy, coupled with his passion for Christiane Vulpius, whom he married in 1806, was expressed in the poems *Römische Elegien* (1795, Roman Elegies). In his later years he wrote *Wilhelm Meisters Lehrjahre* (1796, Wilhelm Meister's Apprentice Years), continued as *Wilhelm Meisters Wanderjahre* (1821–9, Wilhelm Meister's Journeyman Years). His masterpiece is his version of *Faust*, on which he worked for most of his life, published in two parts (1808, 1832). He died at

Weimar. » drama; German literature; Herder; poetry; Romanticism (literature)

Gog and Magog [gog, **may**gog] Biblical names, applied in different ways to depict future foes of the people of God. *Ezek* 38.2–6 predicted that a ruler (Gog) of the land or people from 'the north' (Magog) would battle against Israel in the days before her restoration. *Rev* 20.8 and rabbinic literature treat Gog and Magog as paired figures representing Satan in the final conflict against God's people. In British folklore, the names are given to the survivors of a race of giants annihilated by Brutus, the founder of Britain. Their statues in the Guildhall, London, replace a pair destroyed by World War 2 bombing. » Bible; Devil; folklore; rabbi

goggle-eye » **thick-knee**

Gogol, Nikolai (Vasilievich) [**goh**guhl] (1809–52) Russian novelist and dramatist, born at Sorochinstsi, Poltava. In 1829 he settled in St Petersburg, and became famous through two masterpieces: *Revizor* (1836, The Inspector General), a satire exposing the corruption and vanity of provincial officials, and a novel, *Myortvye dushi* (1842, Dead Souls). He also wrote several short stories. He lived abroad for many years, mostly in Rome (1836–46), then returned to Russia, and died in Moscow. » drama; novel; Russian literature

Goiânia [goh**yan**ia] 16°43S 49°18W, pop (1980) 702 858. Capital of Goiás state, WC Brazil, SW of Brasília; founded, 1933; replaced old capital, 1937; railway; two universities (1959, 1960); rice, cattle raising, nickel; Parque Mutirama (with an Educational Park), racecourse, motor racetrack. » Brazil [i]

Goidelic [goy**del**ik] » **Celtic languages**

goitre/goiter Enlargement of the thyroid gland. When associated with hyperthyroidism, it is called a *toxic* goitre; otherwise, it is *non-toxic*. » hyperthyroidism; thyroid gland

Gokstad ship [**gok**shtat] A Viking oak-built sailing ship found in 1881 beneath a burial mound at Gokstad, 80 km/50 ml SE of Oslo, Norway. Spectacularly preserved by the surrounding clay, and complete with mast, spars, ropes, blocks, gangplank, and 16 pairs of oars, it measured 23.3 m/76 ft 6 in long, with a 5.2 m/17 ft beam, and was probably 50 years old when buried in the late 9th-c AD. A replica successfully crossed the Atlantic in 1893. » Sutton Hoo ship burial; Vikings

Golan or **Golan Heights** [**goh**lan], Arabic **Al Jawlan** pop (1983) 19 727; area 1 176 sq km/454 sq ml. Israeli-occupied area of Syria administered as part of Northern district, N Israel, E of the Sea of Galilee; of great strategic importance; occupied by Israel in 1967, and annexed in 1981; several Jewish settlements founded; rises to 1 204 m/3 950 ft at Mt Avital. » Arab–Israeli Wars; Israel [i]; Syria [i]

gold Au, element 79, melting point 1 064°C. A soft yellow metal of high density (19 g cm^{-3}), known from ancient times. It is rare and found uncombined in nature. Much of its value is due to its lack of reactivity, its main uses being for decoration and for monetary reserves. It is also used sparingly for electrical contacts. It will react with very strong oxidizing agents, giving compounds showing oxidation states +1 and +3. » chemical elements; metal; RR90; Plate V

Gold Coast (Australia) 27°59S 153°22E, pop (1986) 219 300. Urban area in Queensland, Australia, S of Brisbane, partly overlapping New South Wales; airfield; railway; university (1987); largest resort region in Australia, with restaurants and beaches stretching for 32 km/20 ml; includes Southport, Surfers' Paradise, Broadbeach, Mermaid Beach, Burleigh Heads, Coolangatta; Dreamworld, Sea World, bird sanctuary, air museum. » Queensland

gold rush A burst of enthusiasm for mining, following the discovery of gold deposits. Major rushes in the USA included California (1849), Colorado (1858–9), Idaho (1861–4), Montana (1863), South Dakota (1875), and Alaska (1896). » Australian/Fraser River/Klondike gold rush; Mother Lode

Goldbach's conjecture A mathematical proposition which states that every even integer greater than 2 can be expressed as the sum of two prime numbers; for example, 14 = 3 + 11. This conjecture was first made by Christian Goldbach (1690–1764) in a letter to Euler in 1742. » Euler; numbers

goldcrest A small woodland bird, native to Europe and Asia; head with orange or yellow stripe; eats insects; also known as the **golden-crested wren**. Many die during hard winters. (*Regulus regulus*. Family: *Regulidae*, sometimes placed in family *Silviidae*.) » wren

Golden Bull Any document whose importance was stressed by authentication with a golden seal (Lat *bulla*). Specifically, the term is used for the edict promulgated by Emperor Charles IV in 1356 to define the German constitution. It formally affirmed that election of an emperor was by a college of seven princes, and recognized them as virtually independent rulers.

golden calf An idolatrous image of worship, fashioned by Aaron and the Israelites at Sinai (*Ex* 32), and destroyed by Moses. Two such figures were apparently set up later under Jeroboam I, first king of the N kingdom of Israel, in competition with the worship of God in Jerusalem (1 *Kings* 12). » Aaron; Moses; Sinai, Mount

golden cat A member of the cat family; found mainly in forests; eats deer, domestic animals, and birds; two species: **African golden cat** (*Felis aurata*) from C Africa, solitary, digs a den; **Asian golden cat** (*Felis temmincki*) from SE Asia, hunts in pairs. » Felidae

golden chain » **laburnum**

golden-crested wren » **goldcrest**

golden eagle A large eagle, native to the N hemisphere, probably the most numerous large eagle in the world; inhabits mountains and moorland; eats mainly rabbits, hares, and carrion; catches prey on ground, but attacks from the air; kills with talons; lays two eggs; the first chick to hatch usually kills the second. (*Aquila chrysaetos*. Family: *Accipitridae*.) » eagle

Golden Fleece In Greek mythology, the object of the voyage of the *Argo*. Hermes saved Phrixus from sacrifice by placing him upon a golden ram, which bore him through the air to Colchis, where a dragon guarded the Fleece in a sacred grove. Jason obtained the fleece with Medea's help. The legend may be based on the gold of Colchis. » Argonauts; Jason; Medea

Golden Gate Bridge A major steel suspension bridge across the Golden Gate, a channel connecting San Francisco Bay with the Pacific; completed in 1937; length of main span 1 280 m/4 200 ft. » bridge (engineering) [i]; San Francisco

golden hamster » **hamster**

Golden Horde A feudal state organized in the 13th-c as part of the Mongol Empire, occupying most of C and S Russia and W Siberia. Its capital was at Sarai on the R Volga. The Russian princes were vassals of the Khan of the Golden Horde, and paid regular tribute. It was finally overthrown by the Grand Princes of Moscow in the early 16th-c. » Mongols; Russian history

golden mole An African insectivore, resembling the golden hamster, but with eyes and ears hidden under shiny fur; nose with leathery pad; front feet with claws for digging; digs burrows or, in desert areas, 'swims' through sand just beneath the surface, leaving a visible ridge. (Family: *Chrysochloridae*, 18 species.) » hamster; insectivore

Golden Pavilion » **Kinkakuji**

golden pheasant A pheasant native to W China and introduced in Britain; male with a crest of golden feathers; female brown and black; inhabits low vegetation on rocky hillsides (introduced in woodland); eats seeds, shoots, and insects. (*Chrysolophus pictus*. Family: *Phasianidae*.) » pheasant

golden potto » **angwantibo**

golden ratio In mathematics, a proportion obtained if a point *P* divides a straight line *AB* in such manner that *AP*:*PB* = *AB*:*AP*; also known as the **golden section**. It is often denoted by τ. It

$$\frac{\tau}{1} = \frac{\tau - 1}{\tau}$$

was applied to architecture by Vitruvius, and much discussed during the Renaissance. Pietro della Francesca's 'Baptism of Christ' (National Gallery, London) is just one example of a composition set up according to this proportion. » Vitruvius

golden retriever A breed of dog, developed in Britain in the late 19th-c; large with long golden or cream coat; solid body, strong legs, long muzzle; calm temperament; popular choice as a guide-dog for blind people. » dog; retriever

golden rod The name applied to several species of *Solidago*. The plant commonly grown in gardens is **Canadian golden rod** (*Solidago canadensis*), a late-flowering perennial growing to 1.5 m/5 ft, a native of N America; leaves lance-shaped, long pointed; flower heads numerous, tiny, golden-yellow, arranged on more or less horizontally spreading branches in a dense pyramidal panicle. **European golden rod** (*Solidago virgaurea*) is a smaller perennial, growing to 1 m/3¼ ft, with larger flower heads up to 1 cm/0.4 in across, borne in leafy clusters. (Genus: *Solidago*. Family: *Compositae*.) » panicle; perennial

Golden Rule The name given today to the saying of Jesus about one's duty to others: 'Whatever things you wish that people would do to you, do also yourselves similarly to them' (*Matt* 7.12; *Luke* 6.31). Similar sayings can be traced in earlier Jewish and Greek ethical teaching. » Jesus Christ; Sermon on the Mount/Plain

Golden Temple » Harimandir

goldeneye Either of two species of diving duck, native to the N hemisphere: the **goldeneye** (*Bucephala clangula*) and **Barrow's goldeneye** (*Bucephala islandica*). They inhabit coastal waters, but breed inland. (Family: *Anatidae*.) » diving duck; duck

goldenrain tree » laburnum; pride of India

goldfinch A bird native to the N hemisphere; one species in the Old World, *Carduelis carduelis*, three in the Americas; inhabits forest, scrubland, or cultivated areas; closely related to the siskin. (Genus: *Carduelis*, 4 species. Family: *Fringillidae*.) » finch; siskin

goldfish Colourful carp-like freshwater fish, native to weedy rivers and lakes of Eurasia, but now very widely distributed as popular ornamental fish; body length up to 30 cm/1 ft, young fish brownish, becoming golden as they mature; mouth lacking barbels; immense variety of forms have been produced through captive breeding. (*Carassius auratus*. Family: *Cyprinidae*.) » carp

Golding, William (Gerald) (1911–) British novelist, born near Newquay, Cornwall. Educated at Marlborough School and Oxford, he became a teacher, served in the navy in World War 2, then returned to teaching until 1960. His first novel was *Lord of the Flies* (1954), and this was followed by *The Inheritors* (1955), *Pincher Martin* (1956), *Free Fall* (1959), and *The Spire* (1964). Later novels include *Rites of Passage* (1980), which won the Booker Prize, and *The Paper Men* (1984). He was awarded the Nobel Prize for Literature in 1983. » English literature; novel

Goldman, Emma (1869–1940) US anarchist, feminist, and birth control advocate, born at Kaunas, Lithuania. Her family left Russia to avoid anti-Jewish persecution, moving to Germany. In 1885 she migrated to the USA, where she began her anarchist career. She was imprisoned during World War 1 for opposing government policy, then deported to the Soviet Union, eventually settling in France. She died in Toronto, Canada. » anarchism

Goldsmith, Oliver (1728–74) Anglo-Irish playwright, novelist, and poet, born at Kilkenny West, Ireland. He studied erratically at Dublin, tried law at London, then medicine at Edinburgh, drifted to Leyden, and returned penniless in 1756. He practised as a physician in London, held several temporary posts, and took up writing and translating. *The Vicar of Wakefield* (1766) secured his reputation as a novelist, *The Deserted Village* (1770) as a poet, and *She Stoops to Conquer* (1773) as a dramatist. He died in London. » drama; English literature; novel; poetry

Goldwater, Barry M(orris) (1909–) US politician and author, born at Phoenix, Arizona. Educated at the University of Arizona, he became a US Senator for that state in 1952. In 1964 he gave up his Senate seat to become Republican nominee for the presidency, but was overwhelmingly defeated by Lyndon Johnson. He returned to the Senate in 1969, serving until 1987, and was one of the architects of the conservative revival within the Republican Party. *The Conscience of a Conservative* (1960) is his most notable book. » Johnson, Lyndon B; Republican Party

Goldwyn, Samuel, originally **Samuel Goldfish** (1882–1974) US film producer, born in Warsaw. He emigrated to London and the USA as a child, and helped to found a film company, producing *The Squaw Man* in 1913. In 1917 he founded the Goldwyn Pictures Corporation, in 1919 the Eminent Authors Pictures and finally in 1925 the Metro-Goldwyn-Mayer Company, allying himself with the United Artists from 1926. His 'film-of-the-book' policy included such films as *Bulldog Drummond* (1929) and *All Quiet on the Western Front*. He died in Los Angeles.

golem [**goh**lem] A Hebrew word meaning something unformed or embryonic, used in Jewish folklore to refer to an image or automaton endowed with life, typically the servant and protector of a rabbi.

golf A popular pastime and competitive sport, played on a course usually consisting of 18 holes, although some have only 9, 12, or 15. A standard course is usually between 5 000 and 7 000 yards (c.4 500–6 500 m). A *hole* consists of three areas: the flat starting point where the player hits the ball (the *tee*), a long stretch of mown grass (the *fairway*), and a putting green of smooth grass where the hole itself (4.25 in/10.8 cm) is situated. Obstacles are placed at various points, such as areas of sand (*bunkers*) and trees. The object is to hit a small, rubber-cored ball from a starting point into the hole, which is generally between 100–500 yd (90–450 m) away. The winner is the player who completes a round with the lowest number of strokes. The expected number of strokes a good player would be expected to play for any given hole is referred to as the *par* for that hole. If the player holes the ball in one stroke below par, this is called a *birdie*; two strokes below is an *eagle*; an occasional possibility is a *hole in one*. Players may carry up to 14 clubs in their golf bag, each of which is designed for a specific purpose and shot.

The ruling body of the game in Britain and most countries is the Royal and Ancient Club at St Andrews, Scotland. Major tournaments include the British Open, the US Open, the US Professional Golfers' Association (PGA), and the US Masters. The origins of the game are uncertain, but it is believed that the Dutch first played a similar game with a stick and ball c.1300, known as *kolf* or *colf*. *Gouf* (as it was called) was definitely played in Scotland in the 15th-c, and the world's first club, the Gentlemen Golfers of Edinburgh (later the Honourable Company of Edinburgh Golfers) was formed in 1744. » British Open Golf Championship; Masters; Royal and Ancient Golf Club of St Andrews; Ryder Cup; RR111

golf-ball printer A high quality impact printer with a spherical print head used mainly in typewriters. The printhead is removable, allowing different typesets to be used. » printer, computer

Golgi, Camillo (1843–1926) Italian cell biologist, born at Corteno, Lombardy. As professor of pathology at Pavia, he discovered the bodies in animal cells which, through their affinity for metallic salts, become readily visible under the microscope. His work opened up a new field of research into the central nervous system. He shared the Nobel Prize for Physiology or Medicine in 1906, and died at Pavia. » cytology; Golgi body

Golgi body [**gol**jee] A system of flattened, membraneous sacs (vesicles, or *cisternae*) arranged in parallel stacks about 20–30 nm apart and surrounded by numerous smaller vesicles. Found within almost all eucaryotic cells, Golgi bodies possibly function to package some of the products of cell metabolism. » cell; eucaryote; Golgi

Golgotha » Calvary

goliards Wandering scholars and clerks of the 12th–13th-c, who wrote reckless celebrations of women and wine, and satirical verses against the Church. The name may derive from the giant Goliath, a figure of evil and excess. » French literature; satire

Goliath [guh**li**yath] Biblical character described (1 *Sam* 17) as a giant from Gath in the Philistine army who entered into single combat with the young David and was slain by a stone from David's sling, resulting in Israel's victory. Some confusion exists over a similar name in 2 *Sam* 21.19 (also 1 *Chron* 20.5). » David; Samuel, Books of

goliath beetle A very large, brightly-coloured beetle, up to 150 mm/6 in long; adults active in daytime; feeds mostly on fruit and flowers; larvae found in decaying plants. (Order: *Coleoptera*. Family: *Scarabeidae*.) » beetle; larva

goliath frog A West African frog, the largest frog in the world (length, up to 360 mm/14 in, not including the legs); lives in deep pools in rivers. Local tradition claims the thigh bones have magical properties and bring good luck. (*Conraua goliath*. Family: *Ranidae*.) » frog

Gollancz, Sir Victor [go**langks**] (1893–1967) British publisher, author, and philanthropist, born in London. Educated at St Paul's School and Oxford, he became a teacher, then entered publishing, founding his own firm in 1928. In 1936 he founded the Left Book Club, which had a great influence on the growth of the Labour Party, and after World War 2 founded the Jewish Society for Human Service, and War on Want (1951). He was knighted in 1965, and died in London.

Gomateswara, statue of The tallest monolith statue in the world, sculpted in AD 983 at Sravanabelagola, Karnataka, India. The statue, which is 17 m/56 ft high, represents Gomateswara, a Jain holy man, and is the focus of a major Jain festival every 12 years. » Jainism; Karnataka

Gomułka, Władysław [go**mool**ka] (1905–82) Polish communist leader, born at Krosno, SE Poland. A professional trade unionist, in 1943 he became Secretary of the outlawed Communist Party. He was Vice-President of the first postwar Polish government (1945–8), but his criticism of the Soviet Union led to his arrest (1951–4). He returned to power as Party First Secretary in 1956. In 1971, following a political crisis, he resigned office, and spent his remaining years largely in retirement. He died in Warsaw. » communism; Poland [i]

gomuti palm » sugar palm

gonad The organ responsible for the production of reproductive cells (*gametes*): in males the gonads (*testes*) produce spermatozoa, in females the gonads (*ovaries*) produce ova. In vertebrates the gonads also synthesize and secrete sex hormones (androgens, oestrogens, and progestogens): androgens are most abundant in males; oestrogens and progestogens in females. » embryology; intersexuality; sex hormones; testes; uterus [i]

gonadotrophin [gonadoh**troh**fin] A substance having a stimulating effect on the gonads. In vertebrates it includes certain pituitary hormones (follicle-stimulating hormone, luteinizing hormone) and additionally in mammals a placental hormone (chorionic gonadotrophin). It is responsible for the production of sex hormones, and the onset of sexual maturity, and it influences breeding cycles by promoting the maturation of ova and sperm in ovaries and testes respectively. In humans, pregnancy diagnosis depends on the detection of chorionic gonadotrophin in the urine or plasma. » gonad; superovulation syndrome

Goncourt, Edmond and **Jules de** [gõkoor] (1822–96 and 1830–70) French novelists, born respectively at Nancy and Paris. Artists primarily, in 1849 they travelled across France for watercolour sketches. They then collaborated in studies of history and art, and took to writing novels, notably *Germinie Lacerteux* (1865) and *Madame Gervaisais* (1869). They are also remembered for their *Journal*, begun in 1851, a detailed record of French social and literary life which Edmond continued for over 40 years. Edmond also founded in his will the Goncourt Academy to foster fiction. Jules died at Auteuil; Edmond at Champrosay. » French literature; novel; watercolour

Gondar » Fasil Ghebbi

Gondwanaland [gond**wah**naland] The name given to the postulated S 'supercontinent' which began to break away from the single land mass Pangaea about 200 million years ago. It included Australia, Africa, Antarctica, India, and S America; the N supercontinent was Laurasia. » continental drift; Laurasia

gong A percussion instrument: a circular bronze plaque, usually with a turned-down rim, commonly suspended from a frame or bar and struck with a soft beater. The orchestral gong (or **tam-tam**) is of indefinite pitch; other, usually smaller, gongs are tuned to precise pitches. » gong chime; percussion [i]

gong chime A set of tuned bossed gongs, arranged horizontally in rows or in a circle, and played with sticks by one or more players. They appear in the gamelan of Java and Bali and in other ensembles of SE Asia. » gong; idiophone

Góngora y Argote, Luis de [**gon**gora ee ah**goh**tay] (1561–1627) Spanish lyric poet, born at Córdoba. He studied law, but in 1606 took orders and became a prebendary of Córdoba, and eventually chaplain to Philip III. His earlier writings were sonnets, romances, and satirical verses, but his reputation largely rests on his later, longer poems, such as *Solidades* and *Polifemo* (both 1613), executed in an obscure and elaborate style which came to be called 'gongorism'. He died at Córdoba. » poetry; Spanish literature

gonorrhoea/gonorrhea An acute infection of the genital tract acquired by sexual intercourse with a partner infected with *Neisseria gonorrhoea*. Males suffer from a discharge from the penis, with pain on urination. The disorder sometimes leads to narrowing of the urethra from scarring. Local symptoms are less obvious in females in whom vaginal discharge is usually due to other causes. It may later lead to inflammation of the Fallopian tubes and also to conjunctivitis in the newborn (*ophthalmia neonatorum*). » urinary system; venereal disease

Gonzaga, Luigi, known as **St Aloysius** (1568–91), feast day 21 June. Italian Jesuit, born near Brescia. He renounced his marquisate, and joined the Jesuits in 1585. In a plague at Rome he devoted himself to the care of the sick, but was himself infected and died. He was canonized in 1726, and is the Italian patron saint of youth. » Jesuits

González, Felipe (1942–) Spanish statesman and Prime Minister (1982–), born in Seville. He practised as a lawyer, and in 1962 joined the Spanish Socialist Workers' Party (PSOE), then an illegal organization. The Party regained legal status in 1977, three years after he became Secretary-General. He persuaded the PSOE to adopt a more moderate policy, and in the 1982 elections they won a substantial majority, becoming the first left-wing administration since 1936.

Good Friday In the Christian Church, the Friday before Easter, commemorating the crucifixion of Jesus Christ; in many Christian denominations, a day of mourning and penance. » Easter; Jesus Christ

Goodman, Benny, properly **Benjamin (David)** (1909–86) US clarinettist and bandleader, born in Chicago, who reigned as the King of Swing in the big-band era. At 16, he joined the Ben Pollack orchestra, and at 20 began freelancing in New York City. In 1934, he formed a big band and made live network broadcasts; when the band toured the USA, it unexpectedly created a sensation in Los Angeles at the Palomar Ballroom – an event said to mark the beginning of the Swing Era. Among the band's hit recordings at that time were 'Let's Dance', 'Stompin' at the Savoy', and 'One O'Clock Jump'. He also featured trios and quartets in his performances, with Lionel Hampton and other Black jazz musicians. In 1938 he began performing classical music, and in 1949 relearned the clarinet in a conservatory regimen. He died in New York City. » jazz

Goodyear, Charles (1800–60) US inventor, born at New Haven, Connecticut. In 1834 he began research into the properties of rubber. Amid poverty and ridicule he pursued the experiments which led to the invention (1844) of vulcanized rubber, and ultimately a major industry. He died in New York City. » vulcanization

Goons, The Four comedians who came together after the War to create the Goon Show, which revolutionized British radio comedy. **Spike Milligan** (1918–) born in India, **Peter Sellers** (1925–80) born in Southsea, **Sir Harry Secombe** (1921–) born in Swansea, and **Michael Bentine** (1922–) born in Watford, first performed on radio together in 1951. The show, called *Crazy People*, soon became *The Goon Show*, running for nine years and winning a worldwide band of devotees. The Goons prefigured much of British comedy since the fifties, especially in their imaginative use of sound effects, their mixture of surrealism and slapstick, and their anarchic humour. The members of the group later each developed individual careers in the world of entertainment. Milligan has also become known as a comic author, especially of children's poetry, and Secombe as a professional singer and media personality. Secombe was knighted in 1981. Sellers went on to act in many successful films, such as *The Millionairess* (1961), the *Pink Panther* series (1963–77), and *Being There* (1980). He died in London.

goosander A sea duck native to N areas of the N hemisphere, also known in the USA as the **common merganser**; both sexes with dark head and long red bill; male with dark back; inhabits freshwater. (*Mergus merganser*. Family: *Anatidae*.) » diving duck; duck

goose A term not applied precisely, but used for large birds with more terrestrial habits than the 'swans' or 'ducks' comprising the rest of the family. The 14 N hemisphere species comprising the **grey geese** (Genus: *Anser*) and **black geese** (Genus: *Branta*) are sometimes called **true geese**. (Family: *Anatidae*.) » barnacle / brent / Canada / greylag / Hawaiian / snow goose; duck; magpie; perching duck; sheldgoose; swan; water-fowl

Goose Green 51°52S 59°00W, pop (1980) 100. Settlement on East Falkland, Falkland Is; at the head of Choiseul Sound, on the narrow isthmus that joins the N half of East Falkland to Lafonia in the S; second largest settlement in the Falkland Is. » Falkland Islands [i]; Falklands War

gooseberry A deciduous shrub growing to c.1 m/3¼ ft, native to Europe and N Africa; stems and branches spiny; leaves 3–5-lobed; flowers greenish, tinged purple, in ones or twos on drooping axillary stalks; berry oval, up to 4 cm/1½ in long, green or reddish, bristly or smooth. It is cultivated for its fruit. (*Ribes uva-crispa*. Family: *Grossulariaceae*.) » deciduous plants; shrub; stem (botany)

goosefish » **anglerfish**

goosegrass An annual, sometimes overwintering; a common weed native to Europe and Asia; 4-angled stems weak and straggling, climbing by means of small reflexed hooks; 6–8 leaves in whorls, margins with hooks; flowers tiny, white, 4-petalled; fruit a burr with two more or less equal globular halves covered in whitish bristles, dispersed by clinging or cleaving to animals; hence the alternative name **cleavers**. (*Galium aparine*. Family: *Rubiaceae*.) » annual

Goossens, Sir Eugene (1893–1962) British composer and conductor, born in London. He studied in Bruges and London, became associate conductor to Sir Thomas Beecham, then worked in the USA (1923–45) as conductor of orchestras in Rochester (New York) and Cincinnati. As conductor of the Sydney Symphony Orchestra and director of the New South Wales Conservatory (1947–56), he became a major influence on Australian music. His compositions include two operas, a ballet, an oratorio, and two symphonies. He was knighted in 1955, and died at Hillingdon, Middlesex.

Goossens, Léon (1897–1988) British oboist, born in Liverpool. He studied at the Royal College of Music, London, and held leading posts in most of the major London orchestras, before devoting himself to solo playing and teaching. He died at Tunbridge Wells, Kent. He was the brother of the conductor **Eugene**; his sisters **Marie** (1894–1991) and **Sidonie** (1899–) became well-known harpists. » Goossens, Eugene

gopher A name used in N America for many animals which burrow (eg *pocket gophers*, some sousliks, a burrowing tortoise, a burrowing snake, and some salamanders); said to be from the French word *gaufre*, 'honeycomb' – a reference to the burrows. » pocket gopher; souslik

goral A small goat antelope, native to the high mountains of E Asia; thick yellow-grey coat, pale throat; both sexes with short horns; also known as the **common goral**, **red goral**, or **Himalayan chamois**. (*Nemorhaedus goral*.) » antelope

Gorbachev, Mikhail (Sergeyevich) [**gaw**bachof] (1931–) Soviet politician, General Secretary of the Communist Party of the Soviet Union (1985–91) and President of the Supreme Soviet of the USSR (1988–91), born at Privolnoye, and educated at Moscow State University and Stavropol Agricultural Institute. He began work as a machine operator (1946), and joined the Communist Party in 1952. He held a variety of senior posts in the Stavropol city and district Party organization (1956–70), and was elected a deputy to the USSR Supreme Soviet (1970) and a member of the Party Central Committee (1971). He became Central Committee Secretary for Agriculture (1979–85); candidate member (1979–80) and full member (1980) of the Politburo of the Central Committee; and, on the death of Chernenko, General Secretary of the Central Committee (1985–91). In 1988 he also became Chairman of the Presidium of the Supreme Soviet, ie head of state, and in 1990, the first executive President of the USSR. On becoming Party General Secretary he launched a radical programme of reform and restructuring (*perestroika*) of the Soviet economic and political system. A greater degree of civil liberty, public debate, journalistic and cultural freedom, and a reappraisal of Soviet history was allowed under the policy of *glasnost* (openness of information). In foreign and defence affairs he reduced military expenditure, pursued a policy of detente and nuclear disarmament with the West, and ended the Soviet military occupation of Afghanistan (1989). He survived a coup in August 1991, but was forced to resign following the dissolution of the Soviet Union in December 1991. » Chernenko; communism; glasnost; perestroika; Soviet Union [i]

Gorbals A district of Glasgow, Scotland. Originally a village on the S bank of the R Clyde, it developed into a fashionable suburb, but by the end of the 19th-c had become infamous as an area of overcrowding and deprivation. Redevelopment, involving the rehousing of the community in high-rise flats or in new towns, started in the late 1950s. » Glasgow

Gorboduc [**gaw**boduk] A legendary King of Britain, first heard about in Geoffrey of Monmouth's *History*. He was the subject of an early Elizabethan tragedy in the Senecan style, written by Norton and Sackville (1561). » Geoffrey of Monmouth

Gordian knot In Phrygia, a complicated knot with which the legendary King Gordius had tied up his wagon. An oracle said that whoever succeeded in untying it would rule Asia. Alexander the Great cut it with his sword. » Alexander the Great; Phrygia

Gordimer, Nadine (1923–) South African novelist, born at Springs, Transvaal. She has lived in Johannesburg since 1948, and taught in the USA during the early 1970s. In novels such as *A Guest of Honour* (1970), *The Conservationist* (1974), *Burger's Daughter* (1979), and *A Sport of Nature* (1987), she adopts a liberal approach to problems of race and repression, both in her native country and in other African states. » African literature; novel

Gordon, Charles George (1833–85) British general, born at Woolwich, near London. Educated at Woolwich Academy, he joined the Royal Engineers in 1852, and 1855–6 fought in the Crimean War. In 1860 he went to China, where he crushed the Taiping Rebellion, for which he became known as 'Chinese Gordon'. In 1877 he was appointed Governor of the Sudan. He resigned in poor health in 1880, but returned in 1884 to relieve Egyptian garrisons which lay in rebel territory. He was besieged at Khartoum for 10 months by the Mahdi's troops, and was killed there two days before a relief force arrived. » Mohammed Ahmed; Taiping Rebellion

Gordon Riots Anti-Catholic riots in London which caused a breakdown of law and order in parts of the capital for several days in early June 1780. They occurred after Lord George Gordon (1751–93), leader of the Protestant Association, had failed in his attempt to have clauses in the 1778 Catholic Relief Act (removing restrictions on the activities of priests) repealed. » Catholic Emancipation

Gordon setter A breed of dog developed in Britain, slightly larger than the English setter; coat black with small brown patches on underside. » English setter; setter

Gorée Island [**go**ray] A small island off the Cape Verde peninsula, Senegal. Throughout the 18th-c and early 19th-c, when Gorée was first a French, and then a British colony, it was a major centre of slave storage before shipping to the Americas. Today it is a museum of slave trade history, and a world heritage site. » Senegal [i]; slave trade

Göreme [**ge**reme] Valley in Cappadocia, C Turkey; noted for its cave dwellings; a world heritage site. » Turkey [i]

Gorgias [**gaw**jeeas] (c.485–c.380 BC) Greek sophist, sceptical philosopher, and rhetorician, born at Leontini, Sicily. He went to Athens as ambassador in 427 BC, and, settling in Greece, won wealth and fame as a teacher of eloquence. In his work *On Nature* he argued that nothing exists; even if something did exist, it could not be known; and even if it could be known, it could not be communicated. Plato's dialogue *Gorgias* is written against him. » Plato; scepticism

Gorgon A terrible monster of Greek mythology. There were three Gorgons, who had snakes in their hair, ugly faces, and huge wings; their staring eyes could turn people to stone. Perseus killed Medusa (the only mortal one), and cut off her head; this was used to rescue Andromeda, and eventually found a place on Athena's aegis. It is the detached head which is frightening; this occurs in art before the Gorgons were invented to explain it. » aegis; Andromeda; Perseus (mythology)

gorilla An ape native to the rain forests of WC Africa; the largest primate (height, up to 1.8 m/6 ft); massive muscular body; usually walks on all fours (resting on the knuckles of its hands); ears small; adult male with marked crest; black, except in old males (*silverbacks*), which have a silvery-grey torso; two races: the **lowland gorilla** and the shaggier **mountain gorilla**. (*Gorilla gorilla.*) » ape; primate (biology)

Göring, Hermann » **Goering, Hermann**

Gorky, Arshile, originally **Vosdanig Manoog Adoian** (1905–48) US painter, born at Khorkom Vari, Turkish Armenia. He emigrated in 1920, and studied at the Rhode Island School of Design and in Boston. He combined ideas and images derived from Surrealism and Biomorphic art, and played a key role in the emergence of the New York school of Action painters in the 1940s. He died at Sherman, Connecticut. » action painting; biomorphic art; Surrealism

Gorky, Maxim, pseudonym of **Aleksei Maksimovich Peshkov** (1868–1936) Russian novelist, born at Nizhni Novgorod (now Gorky). He held a variety of menial posts before becoming a writer, producing several Romantic short stories, then social novels and plays, notably the drama *Na dne* (1902, The Lower Depths). An autobiographical trilogy (1915–23) contains his best writing. Involved in strikes and imprisoned in 1905, he was an exile in Italy until 1914, and then engaged in revolutionary propaganda for the new regime. He was the first president of the Soviet Writers Union, and a supporter of Stalinism. He died in mysterious circumstances, and may have been the victim of an anti-Soviet plot. » novel; Russian literature

Gorky, formerly (pre-1932) and from 1990 **Nizhny Novgorod** 56°20N 44°00E, pop (1989) 1 438 000. River port and industrial capital of Gorkovskaya oblast, E European Russia; at the confluence of the Volga and Oka Rivers; founded as a frontier post, 1221; famous for its annual trade fairs (1817–1930); renamed in honour of Maxim Gorky; airport; railway; university (1918); machines, chemicals, woodworking, foodstuffs. » Russia

gorse A spiny shrub growing to 2 m/6½ ft, from Europe and NW Africa; green-stemmed; leaves reduced to rigid needle-like spines, or small scales in mature plants; pea-flowers yellow, fragrant; pod 2-valved, exploding to release the seeds; also called **furze**. (*Ulex europaeus.* Family: *Leguminosae.*) » shrub

Gorsedd [gawse<u>th</u>] A society of Welsh bards founded in 1792 by Iolo Morganwg, that takes a major part in the organization of the National Eisteddfod, in particular the bardic ceremony. » eisteddfod

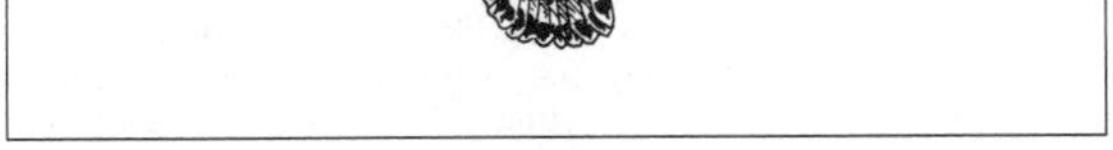

Goshawk

goshawk [goshawk] A smallish hawk with short rounded wings and a long tail (20 species). The **northern goshawk** (*Accipiter gentilis*) is found in much of the N hemisphere; other species are native to Africa, S and SE Asia, and Australia; inhabits woodland; eats vertebrates or insects. (Family: *Accipitridae.*) » bird of prey; hawk

gospel music A religious type of popular US music originating in the revivalist movement of the late 19th-c with the *Gospel Hymns* (1875–94) of US evangelists Philip Paul Bliss (1838–76) and Ira David Sankey (1840–1908). Since then it has absorbed elements from popular secular music, especially from 'soul' and 'country' music. » country and western; soul (music)

Gospels, apocryphal Several writings from the early Christian era which are often somewhat similar to the canonical gospels in title, form, or content, but which have not been widely accepted as canonical themselves. They include popular infancy stories about Jesus (eg *Infancy Gospel of Thomas*, *Protoevangelium of James*), apocryphal accounts of Jesus' final suffering (*Gospel of Peter*, *Gospel of Nicodemus*), gnostic collections of sayings and stories (*Gospel of Thomas*, *Gospel of Philip*), and Judaeo-Christian works (*Gospel of the Hebrews*). Many are known from citations in the early Church fathers or from recent Nag Hammadi discoveries. » Apocrypha, New Testament; Christianity; Gnosticism; Gospels, canonical; Nag Hammadi texts

Gospels, canonical Four books of the New Testament, known as the Gospels according to Matthew, Mark, Luke, and John; called 'gospels' by the 2nd-c Church (Gr *euangelion* 'good news'), but not itself a recognized genre in earlier Greek literature. Each portrays a perspective on the ministry and teaching of Jesus of Nazareth, concluding with the account of his arrest, crucifixion, and resurrection. Three of the four (Matthew, Mark, Luke) are sufficiently close in wording and order to suggest a close literary interrelationship, but the precise solution to this relationship is much debated (the *synoptic* problem). John's Gospel is different in character, and raises questions about whether its author knew the other Gospels at all, even though it is frequently dated as the latest because of the extent of theological reflection. None of the writings actually states its author's name. » Gospels, apocryphal; Jesus Christ; John/Luke/Mark/Matthew, Gospel according to; synoptic gospels

Gosplan The name of the State Planning Commission in the USSR. Established in 1921, it supervised various aspects of planning, translating the general economic objectives of the state into specific plans. Its responsibilities varied over the years, as the focus of state policy changed.

Gossaert, Jan [gosaht], also called **Jan Mabuse** (c.1478–1532) Flemish painter, born (possibly) at Maubeuge, Hainault. He registered as a master in the Antwerp guild in 1503, and went to Rome c.1508–9. After this he introduced Italianate details such as classical architecture, putti, and nude figures into his otherwise traditional early Netherlandish pictures. The National Gallery in London has an elaborate 'Adoration of the Kings' in his pre-Italian manner, while 'Hercules' in Birmingham (Barber Institute) adequately demonstrates his later 'Romanist' style. » Flemish art; Renaissance

Gothenburg [gothuhnberg] Swed **Göteborg** 57°45N 12°00E, pop (1982) 425 696. Seaport and capital city of Göteborg och Bohus county, SW Sweden; at the mouth of the R Göta älv on the Kattegat; second largest city in Sweden; founded, 1619; free port, 1921; railway; ferry services to England, Denmark, Germany; university (1891), technical university (1829); linked to the Baltic by the Göta Canal; shipbuilding, vehicles, chemicals, ball-bearings; cathedral (1633, restored 1956–7), town hall (1750). » Sweden [i]

Gothic » **black letter writing; Germanic languages**

Gothic architecture A form of architecture, usually religious, prevalent in W Europe from the 12th-c to the late 15th-c AD. It is characterized by a structural system comprising the pointed arch, rib vault, flying buttress, and a propensity for lofty interiors and maximum window area. Various styles were developed. » arch [i]; buttress [i]; Decorated Style; Early English Style; Flamboyant; Gothic Revival; Norman architecture; Perpendicular Style; Romanesque architecture; vault [i]

Gothic art A term first used by Renaissance artists to mean 'barbaric', referring to the non-classical styles of the Middle Ages. Since the 19th-c, it has been in standard use to mean European art roughly of the period 12th–15th-c. » Gothic architecture; International Gothic

Gothic novel A type of fiction, written in reaction to 18th-c rationalism, which reclaims mystery and licenses extreme emotions. Some (eg Mrs Radcliffe's novels) are actually quite innocent; others (eg Lewis's *The Monk*, 1797) make confident forays into the unconscious, exploring sexual fears and impulses. It was parodied by Jane Austen in *Northanger Abbey*

(1818). » Austen; Lewis, Matthew; novel; Radcliffe; rationalism (philosophy)

Gothic Revival The movement to revive Gothic architecture, prevalent during the late 18th-c and 19th-c, popular in England, France, Germany, and N America. It often displayed ideological associations with the spiritual and social conditions of the Middle Ages, particularly in the writings of Pugin and Ruskin. The style was considered to be especially suitable for churches, such as St Denys-de-l'Estrée (1864–7), architect Viollet-le-Duc. It was also extensively applied to a multitude of different building types, including railway stations, hotels, town halls, memorial buildings, and the parliament buildings at London and Ottawa. » Arts and Crafts Movement; Gothic architecture; Pugin; Queen Anne Style; Ruskin

Goths Germanic peoples who moved S, possibly from the Baltic area (Gotland), to the lower Vistula valley. They had expanded into the Black Sea region by the 3rd-c, and divided into two confederations, Ostrogoths and Visigoths. Displaced by the Huns, they created two kingdoms in the 5th-c out of the ruins of the Roman Empire in the W. » Huns; Ostrogoths; Roman history [i]; Visigoths

Gotland, Gottland, or **Gothland** pop (1983) 55 895; land area 3 140 sq km/1 212 sq ml. Island county of Sweden, in the Baltic Sea off the SE coast; includes Gotland (the largest island), Fårö, and Karlsö; colonized by Germans, 12th-c; taken by Sweden in 1280, by Denmark in 1361, and again by Sweden in 1645; capital, Visby; cattle, sheep, tourism. » Sweden [i]

gouache [gooahsh] A type of opaque watercolour paint, also known as 'body colour', used by artists since the Middle Ages, especially on the Continent. It is sometimes combined with pencil, watercolour, and ink. » watercolour

Goujon, Jean [goozhõ] (c.1510–c.68) The foremost French sculptor of the 16th-c, born (probably) in Normandy. His finest work is a set of reliefs for the Fountain of the Innocents (1547–9, Louvre). He worked for a while at the Louvre in Paris, but his later career is obscure. He was a Huguenot, but seems to have died before the St Bartholomew massacre (1572). » French art; Huguenots

Gould, Glenn (Herbert) (1932–82) Canadian pianist and composer, born in Toronto. He studied at the Royal Conservatory of Music, Toronto, before making his debut as a soloist with the Toronto Symphony Orchestra. He then toured extensively in the USA and Europe, and especially after 1964 made many recordings, particularly of works by Bach and Beethoven. He died in Toronto.

Gounod, Charles (François) [goonoh] (1818–93) French composer, born in Paris. He studied at the Paris Conservatoire and in Rome, then became organist of the Church of the Missions Etrangères, Paris, where his earliest compositions, chiefly polyphonic in style, were performed. His major works include the comic opera, *Le Médecin malgré lui* (1858, The Mock Doctor), and his masterpiece, *Faust* (1859). He also published masses, hymns and anthems, and was popular as a songwriter. He died near Paris.

gourami [gooramee] Deep-bodied freshwater fish native to rivers and swamps of SE Asia, but now more widespread from India to China through aquaculture; length up to 60 cm/2 ft, with large median fins and very long pelvic fin ray; valuable food fish that survives well out of water. (*Osphronemus goramy*. Family: *Osphronemidae*.)

gourd Any of several members of the cucumber family, with hard, woody-rinded fruits of various shapes and colours. All are trailing or climbing vines with tendrils, palmately-lobed leaves, funnel-shaped flowers, and round pear- or bottle-shaped fruits. The best-known are **ornamental gourds** (*Cucurbita pepo*, variety *ovifera*), flowers yellow, native to America, and **bottle-gourd** or *calabash*. (Family: *Cucurbitaceae*.) » calabash; calabash tree; cucumber; palmate

gout A disease associated with a raised concentration of uric acid in the blood, which is deposited in the soft tissues. It predominantly affects males who suffer from acute attacks of arthritis, and in whom accumulations of uric acid form on the fingers and the ear lobes. » arthritis; uric acid

goutweed » **ground elder**

Gower, John (c.1325–1408) English mediaeval poet, a friend of Chaucer. His works include many French ballads, written in his youth, and *Vox Clamantis*, in Latin elegiacs (1382–4), describing the rising under Wat Tyler. His best-known work is the long English poem, *Confessio Amantis* (c.1383), comprising over 100 stories from various sources on the theme of Christian and courtly love. He became blind a few years before he died, probably in London. » Chaucer; English literature; poetry; Tyler, Wat

Gowers, Sir Ernest (Arthur) (1880–1966) British civil servant, and author of an influential work on English usage. Educated at Rugby and Cambridge, he was called to the Bar in 1906. After a distinguished career in the civil service, he wrote *Plain Words* (1948) and *ABC of Plain Words* (1951) in an attempt to maintain standards of clear English, especially in official prose. » English

Goya (y Lucientes), Francisco (José) de [gohya] (1746–1828) Spanish artist, born at Fuendetodos. After travelling in Italy, he returned to Spain to design for the Royal Tapestry factory. In 1798 he produced a series of frescoes, incorporating scenes from contemporary life, in the Church of San Antonio de la Florida, Madrid, and over 80 satirical etchings, 'Los caprichos' (1799, The Caprices). He became famous for his portraits, and in 1799 was made court painter to Charles IV, which led to the 'Family of Charles IV' (1800, Prado) and other works. He settled in France in 1824, and died at Bordeaux. » etching; fresco; Spanish art

Goyen, Jan van (1596–1656) Dutch painter, born at Leyden. He moved to The Hague c.1632, and became a pioneer of realistic 'tonal' landscape, emphasizing the movement of light and shadow across wide plains and rivers under huge cloudy skies. Church towers, castles, and windmills punctuate his small, carefully painted scenes, based on pen-and-ink drawings made while travelling. He died at The Hague. » landscape painting

Gozo [gohzoh], Maltese **Ghaudex**, ancient **Gaulus** 36°00N 14°13E; pop (1983e) 23 644 (with Comino); area 67 sq km/26 sq ml. Island in the Maltese group, often called the 'Isle of Calypso'; 6 km/4 ml NW of the main island of Malta; coastline, 43 km/27 ml; chief town, Victoria; largely given over to agriculture; prehistoric temples, Ta' Pinu church a centre of pilgrimage to the Virgin Mary. » Malta [i]

Gozzi, Count Carlo [gotzee] (1720–1806) Italian dramatist, born in Venice. After a period in the army, he took up writing in Venice. Among his works are several satirical poems and plays, defending the traditions of the *commedia dell' arte* against the innovations of Goldoni and others. His best-known works include the comedy, *Fiaba dell' amore delle tre melarance* (1761, The Love of the Three Oranges) and *Turandot* (1762). He died in Venice. His brother, **Gasparo** (1713–86) was a journal editor and press censor, who also became known for his verse satires. » *commedia dell' arte*; drama; Italian literature; satire

Graafian follicle A structure within the mammalian ovary, part of which may develop into a mature ovum to be released at ovulation; named after the Dutch physiologist, Reijaier de Graaf (1641–73). Each follicle consists of a primordial germ cell (*ovum*), surrounded by epithelial cells. At birth the human female may have as many as 400 000 follicles contained within the ovaries (of which only 300–400 come to maturity); at this stage they are known as primary follicles. During the early years of life, the primary follicles remain quiescent, but with the onset of puberty and menstruation several follicles each month begin to develop further, resulting in usually just one follicle discharging its ovum from the ovary into the abdominal cavity (*ovulation*). The stimulus to further development of the follicles is due to the ovaries coming into full function in response to the secretion of follicle-stimulating hormone (FSH) and luteinizing hormone (LH).

During the first half of the menstrual cycle, stimulation of the ovary by FSH causes the development and maturation of the follicle and increased oestrogen secretion. In many mammals, secretion of oestrogen at this time causes the female to be 'on heat' (*in oestrus*), being the only time she is receptive to the male. In humans, ovulation is about halfway through the menstrual cycle. When oestrogen secretion reaches its peak in the human female, secretion of LH causes the follicle to enlarge quickly and rupture into the abdominal cavity, where it is collected by the Fallopian tube. If fertilization occurs, it does so inside the Fallopian tube, usually within 24 hours of release of the ovum. LH secretion also causes the remains of the follicle to develop into the *corpus luteum*, which secretes progesterone and some oestrogen. Unless pregnancy occurs, the *corpus luteum* does not last for more than 12 days (progesterone is therefore not continuously secreted in the non-pregnant female). The secretion of progesterone prepares the lining of the uterus (*endometrium*) for implantation. If implantation does not result, the cessation of progesterone secretion (which occurs with regression of the corpus luteum) causes the endometrium to disintegrate and bleed (menstruation). » Fallopian tubes; gynaecology; menstruation; oestrogens; ovary; pregnancy [i]; progesterone

graben [**grah**bn] A rift valley, usually of great size, formed when a narrow block of the Earth's crust drops down between two normal faults. » fault; horst; rift valley [i]

Gracchi (the brothers) [**gra**kee], in full **Tiberius Sempronius Gracchus** (c.168–133 BC) and **Gaius Sempronius Gracchus** (c.159–121 BC) Roman politicians of aristocratic lineage who attempted to solve the major social and economic problems of their day – the growing landlessness of the Roman peasantry and the consequent decline in army recruitment – by forcing through sweeping reforms while tribunes of the plebs (133 BC, 123–122 BC). The ruthlessness of their methods provoked such a backlash that on each occasion rioting broke out on the streets of Rome. Tiberius was lynched, and a decade later Gaius was forced to commit suicide. » Roman history [i]; Scipio Aemilianus

grace In Christianity, the free and unmerited assistance or favour or energy or saving presence of God in his dealings with humankind through Jesus Christ. The term has been understood in various ways, eg as *prevenient* (leading to sanctification), or *actual* (prompting good actions). Sacraments are recognized as a 'means of grace', but the manner of their operation and the extent to which humans co-operate has been a subject of controversy. » Jesus Christ; Reformation; sacrament; Trent, Council of

Grace, W(illiam) G(ilbert) (1848–1915) British cricketer, born at Downend, near Bristol. By 1864 he was playing cricket for Gloucester County, and was chosen for the Gentlemen v. the Players at 16. He practised medicine in Bristol, but his main career was cricket. He toured Canada, the USA, and Australia, twice captaining the English team. His career in first-class cricket (1865–1908) as batsman and bowler brought 126 centuries, 54 896 runs, and 2 876 wickets. He died at Eltham, Kent. » cricket (sport) [i]

Graces, the (Gr *Charites*) In Greek mythology, three daughters of Zeus and Hera, embodying beauty and social accomplishments. They are sometimes called Aglaia, Euphrosyne, and Thalia.

grackle A bird of the New World, any of 11 species of the family *Icteridae* (American blackbirds and orioles). The name is also used for several starlings from SE Asia and Indonesia (family: *Sturnidae*). » blackbird; oriole; starling

Grade, Baron Lew, originally **Louis Winogradsky** (1906–) British theatrical impresario, born near Odessa, Russia, the eldest of three brothers who were to dominate British show-business for over 40 years. He arrived in Britain in 1912, accompanied by his parents and younger brother Boris, who became **Bernard Delfont** (1909–). The brothers became dancers, then theatrical agents, along with the youngest brother **Leslie**. Bernard entered theatrical management in 1941, and acquired many properties, notably the London Hippodrome. His many companies embraced theatre, film, television, music, and property interests. From 1958 to 1978 he presented the annual Royal Variety Performance. He was knighted in 1974 and made a Life Peer (**Baron Delfont of Stepney**) in 1976. Lew was an early entrant to the world of commercial television, and became managing director of ATV in 1962. He has headed several large film entertainment and communications companies. Knighted in 1969, he became a Life Peer (**Baron Grade of Elstree**) in 1976. » theatre

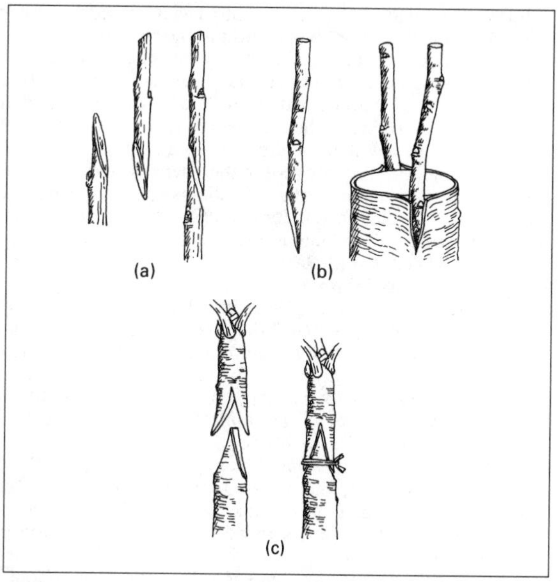

Grafts – Splice (a); crown (b); saddle(c)

gradient A measure of the inclination of a straight line to a fixed straight line. In mathematical terms, the gradient of a straight line, in a rectangular co-ordinate system, is the tangent of the angle made by the straight line and the positive x-axis. The gradient of a curve at a point P is the gradient of the tangent to the curve at the point P. » straight line; tangent

Graf, Steffi (1969–) West German lawn tennis player, born at Bruehl. In 1982 she became the youngest person to receive a World Tennis Association ranking, aged 13, and reached the semifinal of the US Open in 1985. She won the French Open in 1987, and took all four major titles in 1988, as well as the Wimbledon doubles. She beat Natalya Zvereva 6-0 6-0 to win the Australian title, the first such scoreline in a major final since 1911, and retained the Wimbledon title in 1989. » tennis, lawn [i]

graffito » **sgraffito**

graft (botany) The portion of a woody plant inserted into a slot cut in the stem or rootstock of another plant, so that the vascular tissues combine and growth continues. Successful only between closely-related species, grafting is widely used in horticulture to combine desirable but weak-growing varieties with vigorous or disease-resistant ones. Sometimes the rootstock donor breaks out, producing suckers bearing their own flowers among those of the other donor. » horticulture; vascular tissue

graft (medicine) The surgical transplantation of tissues from one part of the body to another (eg a skin graft), or from one person to another (eg a kidney graft). It also refers to the insertion of a synthetic device surgically implanted into the body, such as an aortic graft, in which a synthetic tube is used to replace a diseased aorta.

Graham, Billy, byname of **William Franklin Graham** (1918–) US evangelist, born at Charlotte, North Carolina. The son of a dairy farmer, he attended Florida Bible Institute, was ordained a Southern Baptist minister in 1939, and quickly gained a reputation as a preacher. During the 1950s he conducted a series of highly organized revivalist campaigns in the USA and UK, and later in S America, the USSR, and W Europe. He visited the UK frequently during the 1980s. » Baptists; evangelicalism

Graham, Martha (1894–1991) US dancer, teacher, and choreographer, born in Pittsburgh. She first appeared in vaudeville and revue, and started the Martha Graham School of Contemporary Dance in 1927. She was the most famous exponent of expressionist modern dance in the USA. Her works dealt with frontier life, as in *Appalachian Spring* (1944), Greek myths, as in *Clytemnestra* (1958), and psychological drama. Her method of dance training has been widely adopted in professional schools. » choreography; modern dance

Graham, Thomas (1805–69) British chemist and physicist, born in Glasgow, Scotland. He was professor of chemistry at Glasgow (1830–7) and London (1837–55), and master of the Mint (1855–69). One of the founders of physical chemistry, he formulated the law that the diffusion rate of gases is inversely proportional to the square root of their density (**Graham's law**). He also studied the properties of colloids and their separation by dialysis. He died in London. » chemistry; colloid

Graham Land Mountainous Antarctic peninsula; rises to c.3 600 m/11 800 ft at Mt Jackson; Weddell Sea lies to the E. » British Antarctic Territory

Grahame, Kenneth (1859–1932) British author, born in Edinburgh, Scotland. He entered the Bank of England in 1879, became its secretary in 1898, and retired for health reasons in 1908. He wrote several stories for children, the best known being *The Wind in the Willows* (1908), which was dramatized in 1930 by A A Milne as *Toad of Toad Hall.* He died at Pangbourne, Berkshire. » Milne

Graiae [**gri**yee] In Greek mythology, three sisters with the characteristics of extreme old age, who had one eye and one tooth between them. Perseus took the eye and made them tell the route to the Gorgons, who were their sisters. » Gorgon; Perseus (mythology)

Graian Alps [**gri**yan], Fr **Alpes Graian**, Ital **Alpi Graie** N division of the W Alps in SE France and NW Italy, on French–Italian border; extending in an arc from the Alpes Cottiennes at Mont Cenis to the St Bernard Pass and Dora Baltea valley; highest peak, Gran Paradiso/Grand Paradis (4 061 m/13 323 ft). » Alps

Grail, Holy or **Sangreal** In the Arthurian legends, the dish used by Christ at the Last Supper. Joseph of Arimathea brought it to Glastonbury. It appeared at Pentecost at King Arthur's table, and the knights set out to find it; this diversion of energy into unworldly matters may have led to the break-up of the Round Table. The grail may have features of Celtic magic cauldrons, but the cult of relics is a better clue to its origins. » Arthur; Jesus Christ

grain (agriculture) A single cereal seed or a growing cereal crop. The grain harvest refers to the total bulk of cereals harvested, and includes seed grain for planting the following year, feed grain destined for animal rations, grain used for human consumption in the form of flour products or breakfast cereals, and grain used in the production of alcohol. » cereals

grain (photography) The clumping of the black metallic silver particles which form a developed photographic image. Their size and distribution can be measured with a micro-densitometer and expressed as a numerical factor termed *granularity.* **Graininess**, the degree to which grain is visible in a picture, is a subjective concept affected by both the image structure and the conditions of viewing. » photography

Grainger, Percy (Aldridge) (1882–1961) Australian composer and pianist, born in Melbourne. He studied in Melbourne and Frankfurt, then in 1914 settled in the USA. He championed the revival of folk music, in such works as *Molly on the Shore* and *Shepherd's Hey* (1911), which make skilful use of traditional dance themes. He often returned to Australia, and in 1935 founded the Grainger Museum at Melbourne. He died at White Plains, New York.

gram » **kilogram**

Gram's stain An important staining procedure used in the identification of bacteria. The bacteria are stained with basic dyes, such as crystal violet, and then exposed to organic solvents. Some (*Gram-negative* bacteria) lose their colour readily with exposure to organic solvents, whereas others (*Gram-positive* bacteria) retain the dye. The procedure is named after Danish bacteriologist Hans Christian Joachim Gram (1853–1938). » bacteria [i]

grammar The study of the structure of words (also known as *morphology*), phrases, clauses, and sentences (also known as *syntax*). At word level, the grammarian is concerned with the changes in form that signal such features as case and number (eg */mouse/mice/*, */cat/cats/*); at phrase level, with the structure of such units as *the very tall building* ('noun phrases') and *may have been running* ('verb phrases'); at clause and sentence level, with the order of such constituents as subject, verb, and object (*the bear/ate/an apple*) and the relationship between constructions, such as statement and question. Several types of grammar exist. A **prescriptive grammar** lays down conventions of usage regarded by some sections of society as being 'correct', such as 'Never end a sentence with a preposition'. By contrast, a **descriptive** grammar describes actual usage patterns, without making value judgments about their social standing. A **comparative** grammar compares the grammatical features of languages that are genetically related, and a **universal** grammar investigates those grammatical features shared by the structure of all languages. » constituent analysis [i]; generative grammar; linguistics; morphology; prescriptivism; word class

grammar school In the UK, a selective school choosing usually the most able 15–25% of 11-year-olds on the basis of the eleven-plus examination. The oldest schools date back to mediaeval times, and were originally established to teach Latin. During the 1960s and 1970s many were reorganized, along with local secondary modern schools, and became comprehensive schools. In the USA, the term was used for schools which educated children between the elementary and high-school phase. » comprehensive school; secondary modern school

gramophone An acoustic device for reproducing sounds, stored as acoustically-generated laterally-cut grooves in the flat surface of a disc rotated on a turntable beneath a stylus. First demonstrated in 1888 by US inventor Emile Berliner (1851–1929), it progressively displaced the phonograph, as discs could be multiply produced with relative ease, and played longer than most cylinders. » phonograph; record player; sound recording

Grampian pop (1981) 471 942; area 8 704 sq km/3 360 sq ml. Region in NE Scotland, divided into five districts; bounded N and E by the North Sea; part of the Cairngorms and the Grampian Mts in the SW; drained by the Spey, Dee, Don, Ythan, and Deveron Rivers; capital, Aberdeen; major towns include Peterhead, Stonehaven, Fraserburgh, Elgin; fishing, farming, oil-related industries, whisky; Balmoral castle, Braemar Highland Games. » Aberdeen; Scotland [i]

Grampians (Australia) Mountain range in SWC Victoria, Australia, SW spur of the Great Dividing Range; rises to 1 167 m/3 829 ft at Mt William. » Great Dividing Range

Grampians (Scotland) or **Grampian Mountains** Mountain system extending SW–NE across Scotland; gentle slopes in the S, steep slopes in the N; rises to 1 344 m/4 409 ft at Ben Nevis; includes several smaller chains of mountains, such as the Cairngorms; source of the Dee, Don, Spey, Findhorn, Esk, Tay, and Forth Rivers. » Ben Macdhui; Ben Nevis; Cairngorms; Scotland [i]

grampus A toothed whale; correctly the **grey grampus** or **Risso's dolphin** (*Grampus griseus*), a widespread temperate and tropical deep-water species of short-nosed dolphin which eats squid. The name was formerly used for other species, especially the killer whale. (Family: *Delphinidae.*) » dolphin; killer whale; whale [i]

Gran Canaria [gran ca**nar**ya], Eng **Grand Canary** 28°00N 15°35W; area 1 532 sq km/591 sq ml. Volcanic Atlantic island in the Canary Is; highest point, Pozo de las Nieves (1 980 m/6 496 ft); steep cliffs in N and W; wide beaches in S, with tourist facilities; chief town, Las Palmas de Gran Canaria; sugar cane, distilling, tobacco, chemicals, light engineering; airport on the E coast. » Canary Islands

Gran Chaco [gran **cha**koh] Lowland plain covering part of N Argentina, W Paraguay, and S Bolivia; consists of Chaco Boreal in the N (250 000 sq km/100 000 sq ml), Chaco Central (130 000 sq km/50 000 sq ml), and Chaco Austral in the S (250 000 sq km/100 000 sq ml); drained by R Paraná and R Paraguay; scrub forest and grassland, with a tropical savannah climate and sparse population; cattle raising; disputed area in the Chaco War between Paraguay and Bolivia (1932–5). » Argentina [i]; Chaco War

Gran Colombia [grankol**om**biah] Literally, 'Greater Colombia'; the name given by historians to the union of Venezuela, New Granada, and Quito (Ecuador) formed in 1819 by Simón Bolívar and known by him as Colombia. The union dissolved in 1830; the name Colombia was later adopted by New Granada. » Bolívar; Colombia [i]

Granada 37°10N 3°35W, pop (1981) 262 182. Capital of Granada province, Andalusia, S Spain; on R Genil, 434 km/270 ml S of Madrid; average altitude 720 m/2 360 ft; founded by the Moors, 8th-c; capital of the Kingdom of Granada, 1238; last Moorish stronghold in Spain, captured in 1492; archbishopric; airport; railway; university (1531); textiles, paper, soap, tourism; cathedral (16th-c), with tombs of Ferdinand and Isabella; Generalife Palace and the Alhambra, a world heritage site; Conquest Day (Jan), Fiesta of Las Cruces de Mayo (May), international festival of music and dance (Jun–Jul), international sports week (winter), Costa del Sol Rally (Dec). » Alhambra; Andalusia; Ferdinand (of Castile); Isabella of Castile; Spain [i]

granadilla Any of several species of passion flower which produce edible fruits. **Purple granadilla** (*Passiflora edulis*) has purple fruits, 5–7.5 cm/2–3 in long. The **giant granadilla** (*Passiflora quadrangularis*) has greenish-yellow fruits, up to 10 cm/4 in long. (Family: *Passifloraceae*.) » passion flower [i]

Granby, John Manners, Marquis of (1721–70) British army officer, the eldest son of the Duke of Rutland. His reputation was made in the Seven Years' War (1756–63), when he led the British cavalry in a major victory over the French at Warburg (1760). He became a popular hero, and in 1763 was appointed Master-General of the Ordnance. He died at Scarborough, Yorkshire. » Seven Years' War

Grand Alliance, War of the (1805–7) A phase in the Napoleonic Wars. A Third Coalition of states (Britain, Austria, Russia, Sweden, and Prussia) was formed to attack France by land and sea. Despite Britain's success at Trafalgar (1805), the coalition was undermined by spectacular French victories at Ulm, Austerlitz (1805), and Jena (1806). The Treaties of Pressburg (1805) and Tilsit (1807) ended hostilities. » Napoleonic Wars

Grand Army of the Republic (GAR) An organization of veterans of the Union side in the Civil War. Established in 1866, the GAR became an important force in postwar politics. » American Civil War

Grand Bahama pop (1980) 33 102; area 1 372 sq km/530 sq ml. Island in the NW Bahamas; fourth largest island in the group; length 120 km/75 ml; chief town Freeport-Lucaya; popular tourist resort; home of the Underwater Explorers' Club; International Bazaar; oil transshipment at South Riding Point. » Bahamas [i]

Grand Banks A major fishing ground in the N Atlantic Ocean, off the coast of Newfoundland, Canada, formed by an extensive submarine plateau on the continental shelf. The plankton-rich shallow waters are an important breeding area for fish. » Atlantic Ocean; fog; plankton

Grand Canal, Chin **Da Yunhe** Canal in E China, length 1 794 km/1 115 ml, average width, 30 m/100 ft; longest artificial waterway in the world; from Beijing (Peking) municipality to Hangzhou in Zhejiang province; begun 5th-c BC to carry tribute rice from the Yangtze Plain to the imperial government in Beijing; opened in AD 610; major transport artery between N and S China, 13th–19th-c; its use declined with silting and the coming of railways. » canal; China [i]

Grand Canyon Enormous gorge in NW Arizona, USA; 349 km/217 ml long; 8–25 km/5–15 ml wide from rim to rim; maximum depth c.1 900 m/6 250 ft; the result of large-scale erosion by the Colorado R, exposing 1 500 million years of geological formations; parts of the side walls have formed isolated towers ('temples') due to stream erosion (best known are Vishnu Temple, Shiva Temple, Wotan's Throne); located in Grand Canyon National Park (4 931 sq km/1 903 sq ml); one of the main US tourist attractions. » Arizona; Colorado River

Grand Canyon of the Snake » **Hell's Canyon**

Grand Coulee [**koo**lee] Valley in Douglas County, NE Washington, USA; the **Grand Coulee Dam** is a major gravity dam on the Columbia R, impounding L Franklin D Roosevelt; built 1933–42; height 168 m/550 ft; length 1 272 m/4 173 ft; can generate 6 180 megawatts of hydroelectricity. » Colorado River; dam

Grand Guignol Short sensational shows, in vogue in Paris in the late 19th-c, which depict violent crimes in a style designed to shock and titillate. Guignol was originally a puppet in the French marionette theatre. » theatre

grand mal » **epilepsy**

Grand National The most famous steeplechase in the world, first held at Maghull near Liverpool in 1836. The race moved to its present course at Aintree in 1839. Raced over 4 ml 855 yd (7.2 km) the competitors have to negotiate 31 severe fences, including the hazardous Becher's Brook. There is also a greyhound Grand National. » steeplechase **1**

Grand Remonstrance The statement of Charles I of England's abuses, and of reforms made by the Long Parliament in 1640–1; passed by 11 votes in the House of Commons (22 Nov 1641), and thereafter published as an appeal for support. The close vote reflected the formation of roughly equal parties of 'royalists' and 'parliamentarians'. » Charles I (of England); Long Parliament

Grand St Bernard 45°53N 7°11E. Alpine mountain pass between Martigny, Switzerland, and Aosta, Italy, on the Italian–Swiss border; in the SW Pennine Alps, E of the Mont Blanc group; usually open only from June until October; construction of the St Bernard Tunnel (5 828 m/19 120 ft long) in 1959–63 made the route passable throughout the year; height, 2 469 m/8 100 ft; hospice run by monks nearby. » Alps

grand unified theories (GUTs) A class of speculative theories which seek to express strong nuclear, weak nuclear, and electromagnetic forces in a single theory by combining quantum chromodynamics and the Glashow-Weinberg-Salam theory. The earliest attempts to construct such theories were made in 1974 by US physicists Howard Georgi (1947–) and Sheldon Glashow (1932–), predicting super-heavy particles denoted X and Y of mass approximately 10^{15} that of a proton, the slow decay of protons, and the existence of heavy magnetic monopoles. None of these predictions have been observed. » anthropic principle; forces of nature [i]; Glashow-Weinberg-Salam theory; Kaluza-Klein theory; quantum chromodynamics; quantum gravity; supergravity; superstrings

Grande Comore [kuh**maw**], also **Njazidja** 11°45S 43°15E; pop (1980) 189 000; area 1 148 sq km/443 sq ml. Largest island of the Comoros group in the Mozambique Channel; chief town, Moroni; steep mountains rise to the peak of Kartala, an active volcano (2 361 m/7 746 ft); timber. » Comoros

Grande-Terre [grãn **tair**] pop (1982) 157 696; area 585 sq km/226 sq ml. One of the two main islands of the Overseas Department of Guadeloupe, Lesser Antilles, E Caribbean; chief town, Pointe-à-Pitre; of coral formation, rising to only 150 m/500 ft; tourism. » Basse-Terre; Guadeloupe

Granger movement A US organization of farmers, officially known as the **Patrons of Husbandry**, founded in 1867, which adopted a radical stance towards farmers' problems and big business. The name stems from the title *grange* (or farm) adopted by local units. The organization still exists. » Populist Party

granite A coarse-grained, acid (high in silica) igneous rock containing orthoclase feldspar, quartz, and mica (and/or hornblende); pale pink or grey in colour, its durability makes it an important building stone. » feldspar; igneous rock; micas; quartz

Grant, Cary, originally **Archibald Leach** (1904–86) British-US actor, born in Bristol. He went to Hollywood in 1928, played opposite Marlene Dietrich and Mae West, and from the late 1930s developed in leading comedy roles, especially under the direction of Howard Hawks, such as *Bringing Up Baby* (1938) and *His Girl Friday* (1940). He also provided several memorable performances for Hitchcock in *Suspicion* (1941), *Notorious* (1946), *To Catch a Thief* (1955), and *North by North-West* (1959), but during the 1960s his appearances were fewer. He died at Davenport, Iowa. » Hawks; Hitchcock

Grant, Duncan (James Corrow) (1885–1978) British painter, born at Rothiemurchus, Inverness, Scotland. He studied at the Westminster and Slade Schools, in Italy, and in Paris, and was associated with Fry's Omega Workshops (1913–19), and then with the London Group. His works were mainly landscapes, portraits, and still life, and he also designed textiles, pottery, and stage scenery. He died at Aldermaston, Berkshire. » English art; Fry, Roger

Grant, Ulysses S(impson) (1822–85) US general and 18th US President (1869–77), born at Point Pleasant, Ohio. After education at West Point, he fought in the Mexican War (1846–8), then settled as a farmer in Missouri. On the outbreak of the Civil War (1861), he rejoined the army and rose rapidly, leading Union forces to victory, first in the Mississippi Valley, then in the final campaigns in Virginia. He accepted the Confederate surrender at Appomatox Court House (1865), and was made a full general in 1866. Elected President in 1868 and 1872, he presided over the reconstruction of the South, but his administration was marred by scandal. He died at Mount McGregor, New York. » American Civil War

Granth Sahib » **Adi Granth**

granulation (astronomy) » **photosphere**

Granville, Earl » **Carteret, John**

Granville-Barker, Harley (1877–1946) British actor, playwright, and producer, born in London. After a career in acting, he entered theatre management at the Court Theatre (1904) and the Savoy (1907). He wrote several plays himself, such as *The Voysey Inheritance* (1905), collaborated in translations, and wrote a famous series of prefaces to Shakespeare's plays (1927–45). He died in Paris. » Shakespeare [i]; theatre

grape » **grapevine**

grape hyacinth A bulb native to Europe and the Mediterranean region; leaves grass-like, semi-cylindrical; flowers in a dense spike-like inflorescence, drooping, urn-shaped with six small lobes; the blue upper flowers often sterile, brighter-coloured, acting as an extra attractant. It is cultivated for ornament. (Genus: *Muscari*, 60 species. Family: *Liliaceae*.) » bulb; inflorescence [i]

grapefruit A citrus fruit 10–15 cm/4–6 in diameter, globose with thick, pale, yellow rind. (*Citrus paradisi*. Family: *Rutaceae*.) » citrus

Grapelli, Stephane (1908–) French jazz violinist, born in Paris. He and Django Reinhardt were the principal soloists in the Quintet of the Hot Club of France (1934–9), the first European jazz band to exert an influence in the USA. Grapelli's suave, piercing violin lines made a perfect foil for Reinhardt's busy guitar. Their partnership ended when Grapelli escaped to England in the Occupation. He returned to Paris in 1948, since when he has made many international appearances. » jazz; Reinhardt, Django; violin

grapevine A deciduous woody climber, entering cracks and swelling to form a sticky mass which provides support; leaves palmately 3–5-lobed, toothed; flowers numerous, in drooping inflorescences, tiny, green; ripe fruits sweet, yellowish or purple, often with a waxy, white bloom; tendrils negatively phototropic. Probably native to E Asia, it is now cultivated in most temperate regions, especially those with a Mediterranean climate, and is of considerable economic importance as the source of wine. N American species resistant to the insect pest *Phylloxera*, such as **summer-grape** (*Vitis aestivalis*) and **fox-grape** (*Vitis labrusca*), are used as root-stocks for European vines. Dried grapes are sold as currants, raisins, and sultanas. (*Vitis vinifera*. Family: *Vitidaceae*.) » climbing plant; currant; deciduous plants; inflorescence [i]; palmate; tendril; tropism; wine

graph A diagram illustrating the relationship between two sets of numbers, such as the relationship between the height of a plant in centimetres and the time in days since germination. The sets of numbers may be purely algebraic; for example, described by the equation $y=x-1$. Although the scales on the axes are usually constant, that is not necessary. Logarithmic graph paper is so calibrated that a logarithmic graph appears as a straight line. Many other kinds of graph paper can be obtained. » Cartesian co-ordinates; equations; logarithm

graphic design A set of skills and techniques employed in the design of all printed matter. The major skills include typography, photography, illustration, and printmaking. These disciplines, formerly taught and practised more or less in isolation, have been successfully brought together through the dominance of offset lithography as the most popular printing method and the development of allied photographic techniques. » offset lithography [i]; typography

graphics tablet A device by which the movements of a pen over a special surface can be translated into digital input for a computer. This provides a means of converting two-dimensional information, such as maps and drawings, into computer-readable form. It is very widely used in engineering and design applications. » computer graphics

graphite A mineral form of carbon, found in metamorphic rocks; black, soft, and greasy to the touch. It is a very good electrical conductor and dry lubricant. Mixed with clay, it is used in pencil 'leads'. » carbon

graphology 1 The analysis of handwriting as a guide to the character and personality of the writer. It was introduced during the late 19th-c by the French abbot, Jean Hippolyte Michon (1806–81). Graphologists study such factors as the size, angle and connection of letters, line direction, shading of strokes, and layout, and interpret these with reference to a wide range of psychological and physiological states. Scientific evidence of the validity of these techniques is lacking, but they are quite widely practised, and have sometimes proved to be of value (eg in forensic investigations). » chirography **2** In linguistics, the study of the writing system of a language; also the writing system itself. The system is analysed into a set of graphemes, most of which have a more-or-less systematic relationship with its sounds (as with those in *dog*). Other types of grapheme include those which indicate punctuation conventions (?, ', !, etc) and those which refer to whole words (eg &, +, $\sum$). » alphabet [i]; logography; phonology; punctuation; romanization; writing systems

graptolite An extinct marine animal (a hemichordate), mostly found in surface plankton, living in colonies; known from the Cambrian to the Carboniferous periods; individual polyps of colony lived in chitinous tubes arranged in single or double rows along the main axes. (Class: *Graptolithina*.) » Cambrian/Carboniferous period; chitin; hemichordate; plankton; polyp

Grasmere 54°28N 3°02W, pop (1981) 1 100. Scenic resort village in Cumbria, NW England; by L Grasmere, 23 km/14 ml N of Kendal; home (Dove Cottage) and burial place of Wordsworth; Church of St Oswald. » Cumbria; Wordsworth, William

grass One of the largest flowering plant families, with over 9000 species distributed worldwide, including the Arctic and the Antarctic, where they are the only flowering plants to survive. They are monocotyledons, ranging from tiny annuals to perennials over 30 m/100 ft high. Most are herbaceous; a few are woody shrub or tree-like in form; but all show great uniformity of structure. A typical grass has fibrous roots and hollow, cylindrical stems which branch at the base to form a tuft, and may also produce rhizomes or stolons, forming a turf. Long, narrow leaves grow singly from the nodes of the stem and have an upper part (the *blade*), and a lower part (the *sheath*), which fits around the stem like a sleeve. The junction of blade and sheath often bears a flap or ring of hairs (the *ligule*), which is diagnostically important. Unlike most other plants which have meristems at the tip of the shoot, those of grasses are at the base of the stem, at or even below ground level. This, together with the basal branching of the stems, is important, allowing the plant to withstand damage to the aerial parts by cutting, grazing, or trampling, with little adverse effect on further growth. Grasses are wind-pollinated, and have specialized and very reduced flowers. The stamens and ovary are enclosed in a series of small bracts or scales, together forming a spikelet. The spikelets are arranged in inflorescences ranging from dense, cylindrical spikes to loose, spreading panicles.

Grasses occur in every type of habitat, terrestrial and aquatic, including the sea, and especially in the vast, open prairies, savannah, and steppe, where their ability to survive grazing allows them to dominate other vegetation. They are the most important economic plant group. As well as providing forage for wild and domesticated animals in the form of grazing, hay, and silage, they include grain-bearing species (the *cereals*), which are staple foods for most of the world's

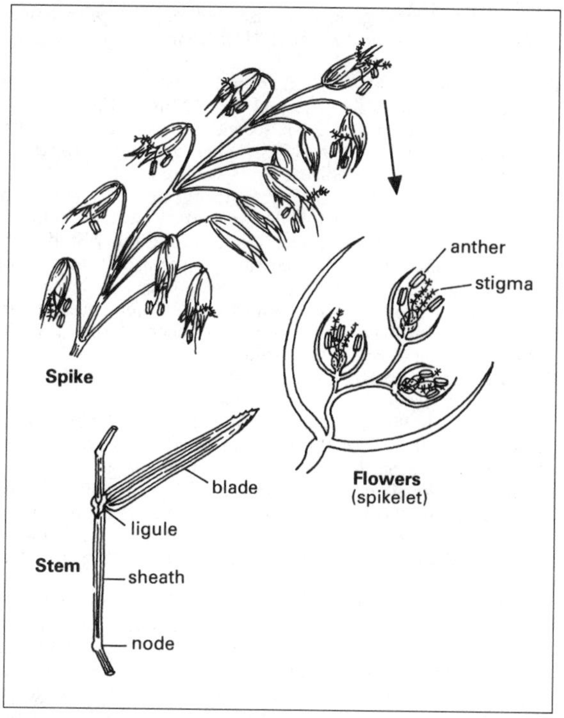

Grass – Flower, stem, spike

population. They also provide sugar, materials for thatching, paper, mats and even light timber. Minor products include aromatic oils and beads. They have an important role as soil stabilizers, and are used for lawns and verges. A few are ornamentals but, conversely, a number are tenacious weeds. (Family: *Gramineae*.) » annual; cereals; herbaceous plant; inflorescence[i]; meristem; monocotyledons; perennial; rhizome; spikelet; stolon

Grass, Günter (Wilhelm) (1927–) German writer and political activist, born in Danzig. He moved to Paris in 1956, and achieved a European reputation with his first novel, *Die Blechtrommel* (1959, The Tin Drum). This was followed by other political novels, including *Hundejahre* (1963, Dog Years) and *Die Ratten* (1987, The Rats). He worked as a ghost-writer for the leader of the Social Democrats, Willy Brandt, and has published a collection of speeches and essays, *Der Bürger und seine Stimme* (1974, The Citizen and his Vote). » Brandt, Willy; German literature; novel

grass monkey » **vervet monkey**

grass mouse » **fieldmouse**

grass owl An owl native to Africa, India, and Australasia; resembles barn owls but legs naked; inhabits grassland; eats small mammals; nests on ground. (Genus: *Tyto*, 3 species. Family: *Tytonidae*.) » barn owl; owl

grass snake A harmless snake native to the Old World from Europe to SE Asia, and in N America; lives near water; swims well; eats mainly frogs; anal gland emits foul-smelling secretion when alarmed; often called **water snake** in the USA – a name also used for snakes of other groups. (Genus: *Natrix*, many species. Family: *Colubridae*.) » snake; wart snake

grass tree A perennial with a woody trunk up to 4.5 m/15 ft, crowned with a tuft of narrow, arching leaves over 1 m/3.3 ft long, and a cylindrical spike of small white flowers; native to Australia, and characteristic of vegetation there; also called **blackboy**, from the scorching of the fire-resistant stems by bush-fires. As with several Australian trees, flowering is stimulated by fire. (*Xanthorrhoea hastilis*. Family: *Xanthorrhoeaceae*.) » perennial

grassfinch A bird found mainly in Australia; usually inhabits open grasslands near water; eats seeds and insects. (Family: *Estrildidae*, 15 species.)

grasshopper A medium to large, terrestrial insect with hindlimbs adapted for jumping; forewings leathery; hindwings forming membraneous fan, or reduced; feeds mostly on plants; many produce sound by rubbing together forewings, or hindlimbs, or rubbing forewings against hindlimbs; antennae may be long (as in the family *Tettigoniidae*) or short (as in the family *Acrididae*). (Order: *Orthoptera*.) » insect[i]; locust

grasswren » **wren**

Grattan, Henry (1746–1820) Irish statesman, born in Dublin. In 1772 he was called to the Irish Bar, and in 1775 entered the Irish parliament, where his oratory made him the leading spokesman for the patriotic party. He secured Irish free trade in 1779, and legislative independence in 1782. He was returned for Dublin in 1790, and in 1805 was elected to the House of Commons, where he fought for Catholic emancipation. He died in London. » Flood, Henry

gravel Unconsolidated deposits of rock in the form of pebbles (2–60 mm/0.08–2.5 in in size) laid down by rivers or along seashores. It may be mined for alluvial mineral deposits, but is most commonly used as an aggregate in concrete. » concrete

Gravenhage, 's- [**skhrah**vuhnhahguh] » **Hague, The**

graver » **burin**

Graves, Robert (Ranke) (1895–1985) British poet and novelist, born in London. He was educated at Charterhouse and Oxford, became professor of English at Cairo, and after 1929 lived mainly in Majorca. His best-known novels are *I, Claudius* and its sequel, *Claudius the God* (both 1934), which were adapted for television in 1976. He wrote several autobiographical works, notably *Goodbye to All That* (1929) and *Occupation Writer* (1950), published critical essays, carried out Greek and Latin translations, and was professor of poetry at Oxford (1961–6). His *Collected Poems* (1975) draws on more than 20 volumes. He died at Deyá, Majorca. » English literature; novel; poetry

Graves' disease » **hyperthyroidism**

Gravettian [grav**e**tiuhn] A European archaeological culture of the Upper Palaeolithic Age, c.26 000–18 000 BC (sometimes referred to as the **Later Aurignacian/Later Perigordian**). It is named after the cave at La Gravette, Dordogne, SW France, notable for its associations with carved Venus figurines. » Three Age System; Willendorf

gravitation The mutually attractive force between two objects due to their masses; expressed by Newton's law of gravitation $F=Gm_1m_2/r^2$, where F is the force between objects of mass m_1 and m_2 separated by distance r, and G is the gravitational constant. The direction of force is along a line joining the two bodies. It is the weakest of all forces, important only on a large scale. The form of Newton's law was verified experimentally by determining the force between heavy spheres placed close together, as in the experiment to measure G by British scientist Henry Cavendish (1798). Newtonian theory is adequate for predictions of planetary motion to high accuracy. The improved theory is general relativity, in which gravitation is viewed as a distortion of space-time. Attempts to produce a gravitation theory consistent with quantum theory have been unsuccessful. **Gravity** refers to the intensity of gravitation at the surface of the Earth or some other celestial body. » acceleration due to gravity; Cavendish, Henry; Einstein; escape velocity; general relativity; gravitational constant; mass; Newton, Isaac; potential; quantum gravity

gravitational collapse A phenomenon which occurs when the supply of nuclear energy in the core of a star runs out, and the star cools and contracts; a prediction of general relativity. This disturbs the precise balance inside the star between the inward pull of gravity and the star's gas pressure. Once the star radius is less than a critical value (Schwarzschild radius, $R=2MG/c^2$, value 3 km for the Sun), the collapse cannot be reversed by any force now known to physics. Implosion to a black hole seems inevitable. » black hole; general relativity; gravitation; star; stellar evolution

gravitational constant A fundamental constant, symbol G, value $6.673\times10^{-11}\,Nm^2/kg^2$, which measures the strength of gravitation. It is a constant of proportionality in Newton's law of gravity, and also appears in equations of general relativity. » gravitation

gravitational lens A phenomenon resulting from Einstein's general theory of relativity. The theory showed that light follows a curved path when it passes close to massive objects, and thus presented the possibility that galaxies can focus the light of more distant objects along the same line of sight. This lensing effect has been observed for a handful of quasars. » general relativity; light; quasar

gravitational radiation Very weak gravity waves produced when a massive body is disturbed or accelerated. The phenomenon is predicted by the general theory of relativity, but not yet observed with certainty. » general relativity; gravitation; gravitational waves

gravitational red shift A prediction of general relativity that time will appear to run more slowly in regions of higher gravitational field; also called the **Einstein shift**. It means that light travelling away from a massive body appears at a lower frequency (red-shifted) than expected. Observation in the Earth's field using the Mössbauer effect has been important in promoting acceptance of general relativity. » Einstein; general relativity; Mössbauer effect

gravitational waves A prediction of general relativity that changes in some large mass (eg the collapse of a star into a black hole) will produce space-time 'ripples' spreading radially from the source at the speed of light. Such waves will cause distortions in any large object through which they pass. Attempts to detect gravitational waves by monitoring such distortions have so far been unsuccessful. » general relativity

graviton A hypothetical quantum of gravitation whose role is the mediation of gravitational force between masses; mass 0, spin 2, charge 0. Gravitons are the quanta of gravitational waves, as photons are the quanta of electromagnetic waves; but, unlike photons, gravitons will interact with one another, one reason why quantum gravity is hard to formulate. » quantum gravity

gravity » **gravitation**

gravity assist The additional increment of velocity acquired by a spacecraft on passing a planet. Through accurate targeting, it can be used to speed up a spacecraft to achieve a trajectory not possible using present launch capabilities. The technique made possible the Mariner 10 mission to Mercury, the Pioneer 11 mission to Saturn, the Voyager mission beyond Jupiter, and the VEGA mission to Halley's Comet; in future it may be used to slow down spacecraft at Mercury to allow chemical rocket orbit insertion. » gravitation; Mariner programme; Pioneer programme; VEGA project; Voyager project [i]

gravure A form of printing in which the image to be communicated is engraved or etched into the surface of a metal cylinder; after inking, surplus ink is removed from the surface of the cylinder, and the ink retained in the engraved cells is transferred to paper when that is brought into contact with the cylinder. Gravure is the principal process used in the printing of popular illustrated magazines. » printing [i]

gray In radioactivity, the unit of absorbed dose, ie the energy deposited in an object by radiation, divided by the mass of the object; SI unit; symbol Gy; 1 Gy defined as 1 J/kg. » radioactivity units [i]; units (scientific); RR70

Gray, Asa (1810–88) US botanist, born in Paris. He trained in medicine, but then took up botany, becoming professor of natural history at Harvard (1842–73), and a strong Darwinian. His main works were the *Flora of North America* (1838–42), which he compiled with John Torrey, and the *Manual of the Botany of the Northern United States* (1848), often known simply as 'Gray's Manual'. He died at Cambridge, Massachusetts.

Gray, Thomas (1716–71) British poet, born in London, and educated at Eton and Cambridge. In 1742 he wrote his 'Ode on a Distant Prospect of Eton College', and began his masterpiece, 'An Elegy in a Country Churchyard' (1751), set at Stoke Poges, Buckinghamshire. He then settled in Cambridge, where he wrote his *Pindaric Odes* (1757). In 1768 he became professor of history and modern languages at Cambridge, where he died. » English literature; poetry

Gray's Inn » **Inns of Court**

grayling Freshwater fish widespread in clean swift rivers of N Europe; length up to 50 cm/20 in; body silvery with longitudinal violet stripes; good food fish and popular with anglers. (*Thymallus thymallus*. Family: *Thymallidae*; sometimes placed in *Salmonidae*.)

Graz [grahts] 47°05N 15°22E, pop (1981) 243 166. Capital of Steiermark state, SE Austria; on the R Mur, at the foot of the Schlossberg (473 m/1 552 ft); second largest city in Austria; airport; two universities (1585, 1811); airport; railway; outskirts heavily industrialized; iron, steel, coal, paper, textiles, chemicals; opera house, Renaissance Landhaus (1557–65), Landeszeughaus (Provincial Arsenal), Gothic cathedral (15th-c); 28 m/92 ft-high clock tower (1561); Piber Stud Farm, where Lippizaner horses bred for the Spanish Riding School in Vienna, 3.5 km/2 ml NE; Austrian open air museum at Stübing, 15 km/9 ml N; Southeast Fair (engineering and production display, end Sep); Steirischer Herbst ('Styrian Autumn', Oct–Nov). » Austria [i]

Great Australian Bight Area of the Southern Ocean off the S coast of Australia between Cape Pasley (W) and Port Lincoln (E) (1 450 km/900 ml); depth 70 m/230 ft over the continental shelf to c.5 600 m/18 400 ft over the Great Bight abyssal plain. » abyssal plains; Antarctic Ocean; Australia [i]

Great Awakening A widespread 18th-c Christian revival movement in the USA, which reached its high point in the 1740s in New England. Jonathan Edwards and George Whitefield were among its leaders. » Christianity; Edwards, Jonathan; Whitefield, George

Great Barrier Reef Coral reef in the Coral Sea off the NE coast of Australia, part of the Coral Sea Islands Territory; 50–150 km/30–90 ml offshore and 2 000 km/1 200 ml long; the largest accumulation of coral known, yielding trepang, pearlshell, and sponges to divers; the surf is violent and dangerous, but the intervening channel, clustered with atolls, forms a safe, shallow passage connected by several navigable channels with the deeps of the Coral Sea; a major tourist area. » atoll; Australia [i]

Great Basin Vast interior region in W USA, between (W) the Sierra Nevada and the Cascade Range and (E) the Wasatch Range and Colorado Plateau; covers parts of Oregon and Idaho, most of Nevada, W Utah, and part of SE California; rugged N–S mountain ranges; semi-arid climate; the few streams (largest are the Humboldt and Carson Rivers) drain into saline lakes or sinks; biggest lakes are the Great Salt, Utah, Sevier, Pyramid, and Walker, remnants of the enormous prehistoric lakes, Bonneville and Lahontan; also several deserts (Great Salt Lake, Mojave, Colorado, Black Rock, Smoke Creek, Death Valley, Carson Sink); agriculture possible only with irrigation; some minerals and grazing land. » United States of America [i]

Great Bear Lake Lake in Northwest Territories, NW Canada, on the Arctic Circle; 320 km/200 ml long; 40–177 km/25–110 ml wide; maximum depth 413 m/1 356 ft; area 31 153 sq km/12 025 sq ml; drained SW by the Great Bear R; navigable for only four months each year because of ice. » Northwest Territories

Great Bitter Lake, Arabic **Buheiret Murrat El Kubra** Lake on Suez Canal between Ismailiya (N) and Suez (S); Little Bitter Lake lies SE. » Egypt [i]; Suez Canal [i]

Great Britain » **United Kingdom** [i]

great burnet » **burnet**

great circle A circle described on the surface of a sphere with its plane passing through the centre of the sphere. The shortest distance between any two points on a sphere lies along a great circle. On the Earth, lines of longitude lie on great circles. » latitude and longitude [i]

great crested grebe A large water bird native to Europe, Asia, Africa S of the Sahara, Australia, and New Zealand; long slender neck and long sharp bill; both sexes with head crest; catches fish by diving from surface. (*Podiceps cristatus*. Family: *Podicipedidae*.) » grebe

Great Dane One of the largest breeds of dog (height, 0.75 m/2½ ft), perfected in Germany from a mastiff-like ancestor; used for hunting; long powerful legs; square head with deep muzzle and pendulous ears; coat short, pale brown with dark flecks. » dog; mastiff

Great Depression The worldwide slump in output and prices, and the greatly increased levels of unemployment, which developed between 1929 and 1934. It was precipitated by the collapse of the US stock market (the Wall Street crash) in October 1929. This ended American loans to Europe and greatly reduced business confidence worldwide. A major Austrian bank also collapsed, producing destabilization in much of C and E Europe. » Jarrow March; stock market

Great Divide » **Continental Divide**

Great Dividing Range Mountain range in Queensland, New South Wales, and Victoria, Australia; extends 3 600 km/2 200 ml from Cape York Peninsula to the Victoria–South Australia border; includes the McPherson and New England Ranges, the Australian Alps, the Blue Mts and the Grampians; rises to 2 228 m/7 310 ft at Mt Kosciusko. » Australia [i]

Great Exhibition An exhibition held in Hyde Park, London (May–Oct 1851). Intended as a celebration of 'the Works of Industry of all Nations', in reality it symbolized the industrial supremacy of Britain in the mid-19th-c. Prince Albert helped to organize the Exhibition, for which the Crystal Palace was constructed. » Albert, Prince; Industrial Revolution; Paxton

Great Indian Desert » **Thar Desert**

Great Lakes The largest group of freshwater lakes in the world, in C N America, on the Canada–USA border; drained by the St Lawrence R; consists of Lakes Superior, Michigan (the only one entirely in the USA), Huron, Erie, Ontario; sometimes L St Clair is included; water surface c.245 300 sq km/94 700 sq ml, c.87 270 sq km/33 700 sq ml in Canada; connected by navigable straits and canals (St Mary's R and the Soo Canals, Strait of Mackinac, St Clair R and Lake, Detroit R, Niagara R, Welland Canal and the St Lawrence R and Seaway); used (May–Dec) for an enormous volume of coal, ore, grain, and other products; water pollution a recent problem. » Canada [i]; Erie/Huron/Michigan/Ontario/Superior, Lake; United States of America [i]

Great Leap Forward A movement in China, initiated in 1958, which aimed at accelerating both industrial and agricultural progress, 'walking on two legs'. Abandoning Russian models, it planned the creation of 'communes' in a true collective system. It failed miserably. » collective farm

Great Malvern » **Malvern**

Great Northern War (1700–21) A war between Russia and Sweden for the mastery of the Baltic coastal region. Charles XII of Sweden defeated Peter I of Russia's army at Narva in 1700, but failed to pursue his advantage. Peter introduced military reforms, and later defeated Sweden at the battle of Poltava (1709). The war was finally concluded by the Treaty of Nystadt. » Charles XII; Peter I

Great Plains Region of C N America; a sloping plateau, generally 650 km/400 ml wide, bordering the E base of the Rocky Mts from Alberta (Canada) to the Llano Estacado in New Mexico and Texas; includes parts of Alberta and Saskatchewan, the E parts of Montana, Wyoming, Colorado, and New Mexico, and the W parts of North Dakota, South Dakota, Nebraska, Kansas, Oklahoma, and Texas; limited rainfall, short grass; large level tracts, with some highlands (Black Hills, South Dakota), badlands (South Dakota), sand hills (Nebraska), and lowlands; drained by the headwaters of the Missouri and by the Platte, Republican, Arkansas, Kansas, and Canadian Rivers; used chiefly for stock grazing and grain growing; mineral resources of oil, natural gas, coal, and lignite; dry farming on unsuitable land and overpasturing led to the dust storms of the drought years of the mid-1930s, creating the **Dust Bowl**, semi-arid regions where wind storms carry off large quantities of topsoil. » United States of America [i]

Great Red Spot The largest, best-known, and probably longest-lived 'storm' feature of Jupiter's atmosphere; a reddish oval feature in the S hemisphere, about 30 000 km/19 000 ml across, first noted 300 years ago. It was observed in detail by Voyager spacecraft cameras for many days, and determined to be a region high in atmosphere exhibiting a counter-clockwise rotation lasting about 6 days. Similar but smaller (10 000 km/6 000 ml) features were discovered by Voyager at other latitudes – 'white ovals'. Jupiter's clouds are basically white condensates, so the red colour of the Spot and of other jovian clouds is ascribed to chemicals (eg sulphur) in the atmosphere. » Jupiter (astronomy); Voyager project [i]

Great Rift Valley » **Rift Valley**

Great Salt Lake Large inland salt lake in NW Utah, USA, NW of Salt Lake City; length 120 km/75 ml; width 80 km/50 ml; maximum depth 11 m/36 ft; average depth 4 m/13 ft; fed by the Jordan, Weber, and Bear Rivers; has no outlet and fluctuates greatly in size; includes Antelope I and Fremont I; its water is 20–27% saline; commercial salt extraction; crossed by a railway (completed 1903); a remnant of the enormous prehistoric L Bonneville. » Utah

Great Salt Lake Desert Arid region in NW Utah, USA, to the W of the Great Salt L; extends 177 km/110 ml S from the Goose Creek Mts; Bonneville Salt Flats near the Nevada border, where world speed car records were established in the 1930s. » Great Salt Lake; Utah

Great Sandy Desert (Australia) N belt of the Western Australian Desert; consists mostly of sand dune, scrub and salt marsh; area c.450 000 sq km/175 000 sq ml; extends W as far as the Indian Ocean. » Australia [i]

Great Sandy Desert (USA) Arid region in S Oregon, USA; length 240 km/150 ml; width 48–80 km/30–50 ml; largely volcanic area, on a foundation of porous mantle rock into which surface waters disappear. » Oregon

Great Slave Lake Lake in W Northwest Territories, C Canada; 483 km/300 ml long; 48–225 km/30–140 ml wide; maximum depth over 600 m/2 000 ft; area 28 570 sq km/11 028 sq ml; contains numerous islands; drained W by the Mackenzie R; town of Yellowknife on N shore. » Northwest Territories; Yellowknife

Great Smoky Mountains Mountain range, part of the Appalachians, on the Tennessee–North Carolina state frontier, USA; a national park, protecting the largest tract of red spruce and hardwood in the USA; rises to 2 025 m/6 644 ft at Clingmans Dome. » Appalachian Mountains; hardwood; spruce

great tit A typical tit, native to Europe, NW Africa, S Asia, and Indonesia, also known as **tomtit** (a name additionally used for the bluetit); plumage blue and yellow with black cap and breast; eats seeds, fruit, buds, and small animals; usually lives in large groups. (*Parus major*. Family: *Paridae*.) » tit

Great Trek The movement of parties of Boers (*Voortrekkers*) which made them the masters of large tracts of the interior of S Africa. They began to leave Cape Colony in 1836 in separate trekking groups. Two parties were wiped out by African resistance and malaria, when they headed for Delagoa Bay in Mozambique. Some settled in the Transvaal, where they were threatened by the Ndebele. A party in Natal was massacred by the Zulu, an event avenged by the Battle of Blood River in 1838. When the British annexed Natal in 1843, the majority of the Boers returned to the interior. The British made several unsuccessful attempts to resolve the divisions in the area, but when the region was reunited it was largely under Boer control. » Afrikaners; Boer Wars; nationalism; Zulu

Great Victoria Desert or **Victoria Desert** S belt of the Western Australian Desert, N of the Nullarbor Plain; consists of sand dunes and salt marsh; area c.325 000 sq km/125 000 sq ml; contains three national parks. » Australia [i]; Nullarbor Plain

Great Wall of China (Chin *chang cheng*, 'long wall') The defensive and symbolic frontier stretching 4 100 km/2 150 ml across N China from the Yellow Sea to the C Asian desert; a world heritage site. Under Qin Shihuangdi, using 300 000 troops, the earliest connected wall was built from 221 BC to repel attacks from the Jung and Ti nomads to the N. It was improved during later dynasties, notably during the Han (202 BC–AD 220), by extension to Yumen in the W and the addition of 25 000 turrets. Considerably later is the conserved stretch of stone-faced wall now seen by visitors at Badeling Pass, N of Beijing (Peking), which dates to the Ming dynasty (AD 1368–1644). The wall is c.7.6 m/25 ft high and 3.7 m/12 ft broad, made of earth and stone with a facing of bricks. » China [i]; Ming dynasty; Mount Li

Great Zimbabwe A group of drystone enclosures near Fort Victoria, SE Zimbabwe, capital of a powerful African chiefdom in the 14th–15th-c, its prosperity based on cattle-herding, gold production, and trade; a world heritage site. The largest valley enclosure, internally subdivided, is 244 m/800 ft long, up to 5 m/16 ft thick and 10 m/33 ft high; it contains c.5 150 cu m/ 6 750 cu yd of stonework, and incorporates a 9 m/29 ft drystone tower. The population of the city was c.10–18 000. » African history; Zimbabwe [i]

Greater Manchester » Manchester, Greater

grebe An aquatic bird, native to temperate regions or high tropical lakes world-wide; swims underwater using feet; toes lobed and slightly webbed; inhabits fresh or shallow coastal waters. Some species are small and eat invertebrates; others are large and eat fish; fish eaters eat large numbers of their own feathers. (Family: *Podicipedidae*, 22 species.) » dabchick; great crested grebe

Greco, El, byname of **Domenikos Theotokopoulos** (1541–1614) Spanish painter, born at Candia, Crete. He studied in Italy, probably as a pupil of Titian, and is known to have settled in Toledo about 1577. He became a portrait painter whose reputation fluctuated because of the suspicion which greeted his characteristic distortions, such as his elongated, flamelike figures. His most famous painting is probably the 'Burial of Count Orgaz' (1586) in the Church of San Tomé, Toledo. He died at Toledo. » Spanish art; Titian

Greece, ancient **Hellas**, Gr **Ellás**, official name **The Hellenic Republic**, Gr **Elliniki Dimokratia** pop (1990e) 10 038 000; area 131 957 sq km/50 935 sq ml. Republic of SE Europe, occupying the S part of the Balkan peninsula and numerous islands in the Aegean and Ionian seas, divided into 10 geographical regions, subdivided into departments (*nomoi*); bounded N by Albania, Yugoslavia, and Bulgaria, E by Turkey and the Aegean Sea, S by the Mediterranean, and W by the Ionian Sea; capital, Athens; chief towns, Thessaloniki, Patras, Heraklion, Volos, Larisa; timezone GMT +2; population mainly Greek (98%); chief religion, Greek Orthodox (98%); official language, Greek; unit of currency, the drachma of 100 lepta.

Physical description and climate. Mainland includes the Peloponnese (S), connected via the narrow Isthmus of Corinth; over 1 400 islands, notably Crete, Euboea, Lesbos, Rhodes, Chios, Cephalonia, Corfu, Lemnos, Samos, Naxos; nearly 80% of Greece is mountainous or hilly; ranges include the Pindhos Mts (N), Rhodope Mts (NE), and E coast range, which includes Olympus (2 917 m/9 570 ft), highest point in Greece; several rivers and small lakes; Mediterranean climate for coast and islands, with mild, rainy winters and hot, dry summers;

☐ *international airport*

rainfall almost entirely in winter; average annual rainfall at Athens, 414 mm/16 in.

History and government. Prehistoric civilization culminated in the Minoan–Mycenean culture of Crete; Dorians invaded from the N, 12th-c BC; Greek colonies established along N and S Mediterranean and on the Black Sea; many city-states on mainland, notably Sparta and Athens; Persian invasions, 5th-c BC, repelled at Marathon, Salamis, Plataea, Mycale; Greek literature and art flourished, 5th-c BC; conflict between Sparta and Athens (Peloponnesian War) weakened the country, which was taken by the Thebans and Macedonians (4th-c BC); under Alexander the Great military expeditions penetrated Asia and Africa; Macedonian power broken by the Romans, 197 BC; part of the Eastern Byzantine Empire of Rome; ruled by Turks from 15th-c until 19th-c; national reawakening led to independence, 1830; republic established, 1924; restored monarchy, 1935; German occupation in World War 2, followed by civil war 1944–9; military coup, 1967; abolition of monarchy, 1969; democracy restored, 1974; governed by a prime minister, cabinet, and unicameral parliament of 300 deputies, elected for four years; a president (head of state) elected by parliament for five years; Mount Athos in Macedonia is a self-governing community of 20 monasteries.

Economy. Strong service sector accounts for c.55% of national income; agriculture based on cereals, cotton, tobacco, fruit, figs, raisins, wine, olive oil, vegetables; iron, magnesite, bauxite, lignite, coal, oil; processed foods, textiles, metals, chemicals, electrical equipment, cement, glass, transport equipment, petroleum products; major tourist area, especially on islands; member of the EEC, 1981. » Athens; Crete; Cyclades; Dodecanese; enosis; EOKA; Greek architecture/art/history/literature/Orthodox Church/religion [i]; Ionian Islands; Macedonia (Greece); Mount Athos; Olympia (Greece); Peloponnese; Persian Wars; RR25 national holidays; RR50 political leaders

Greek architecture The architecture evolved by the Greek city states during the classical period, 7th–4th-c BC, and further developed in the Hellenistic kingdoms 4th–2nd-c BC. It is characterized by the use of stone or marble in post-and-lintel construction that imitated the principles and form of earlier timber buildings. The basic elements are the column, entablature, and pitched roof, with details refined over time to produce a bold yet simple unity of design. Decoration is used to enhance rather than hide structure, and is controlled according to one of four architectural orders: Tuscan, Doric, Ionic, and Corinthian (the Composite was not used by the Greeks). The apogee is the Parthenon, Athens (447–438 BC). Greek architecture has had a profound influence upon much of Western architecture for over 2 000 years. » column; Corinthian/Doric/Ionic/Tuscan order; entablature; Greece [i]; post and lintel [i]

Greek art The art associated with classical Greece, which can usefully be divided into four periods: *Geometric* (11th–8th-c BC), known mainly through painted pottery; *Archaic* (late 8th-c–480 BC), when oriental influences were absorbed, and the human figure emerged as a central theme; *Classical* (480–323 BC), the zenith of ancient civilization, when architecture, sculpture, and painting achieved an ideal beauty and sense of proportion that set standards for figurative art for nearly 2 500 years; and *Hellenistic* (323–27 BC), which saw technically skilful and dramatic works in a variety of styles, from realism to Baroque. The tradition was prolonged by the Romans. » classicism; figurative art; Greece [i]; Hellenistic Age; Roman art

Greek history Throughout antiquity, Greece was poor and over-populated; this helped to make the Greeks one of the most restless and mobile peoples of the ancient world. In the Dark Ages (c.1000–800 BC) they migrated en masse to the shores of Asia Minor. In the Archaic period (c.800–600 BC) they colonized the entire Mediterranean and Black Sea areas, and from 600 BC they served by the thousand as mercenaries overseas. Competition for resources made them quarrelsome at home. *Stasis* – chronic, economically based feuding – was endemic to the Greek city-state (*polis*), and inter-state warfare was the norm rather than the exception. Rarely did they unite to face a common enemy – hence the ease with which they were undermined, first by Philip of Macedon (330s BC), then by Rome (2nd-c BC); Greek history is not the history of a single, unified state; it is the history of individual sub-groups (Dorians, Ionians, Aeolians) and individual city-states (such as Athens, Sparta, Corinth). » Aeolians; Corinth; Cumae; Dorians; Ephesus; Greece [i]; Halicarnassus; Magna Graecia; Miletus; polis; Sparta (Greek history)

Greek Independence, War of (1820–8) The struggle of the Greeks against Turkish rule. Until 1825 Greece fought unaided; thereafter her cause was seconded by Britain, Russia, and later France. In 1830, following Turkey's naval defeat at Navarino (1827) and the Treaty of Adrianople (1829), Greek independence was guaranteed by her allies. » Greece [i]

Greek literature The earliest works belong to the oral tradition; the *Iliad* and *Odyssey* of Homer come down from 1000 BC. Lyric poetry was written from the 6th-c BC (elegiac by Archilochus, erotic by Sappho), and reached perfection with Pindar. The great moment of Greek drama came in the 5th-c BC, with the tragedies of Aeschylus, Sophocles, and Euripides, and the comedies of Aristophanes. Most of these plays are now lost. Simultaneous with these were the historical writings of Herodotus, to be followed within half a century by those of Xenophon; and then the flowering of Greek philosophy with the teachings of Socrates, and the comprehensive works of Plato and Aristotle. During the Hellenistic period (327–37 BC) prose writing continued to flourish, comedy persisted with Menander, while the Ptolemaic court at Alexandria, where Theocritus introduced pastoral poetry, also revived epic and didactic verse. Greek literature survived the Roman dominance into the 2nd-c AD with such writers as Plutarch, Longinus, and Lucian. » Aeschylus; Archilochus of Paros; Aristophanes; Aristotle; comedy; Euripides; Greece [i]; Herodotus; Homer; Longinus; Lucian; Menander; Pindar; Plato; Plutarch; Sappho; Socrates; Sophocles; Theocritus; tragedy; Xenophon

Greek Orthodox Church The self-governing ('autocephalous') Orthodox Church of Greece. After the schism of 1054, the Orthodox Church in Greece remained under the patriarch of Constantinople, but was declared independent in 1833. The governing body is the Holy Synod, which comprises 67 metropolitan bishops, presided over by the archbishop of all Greece in the head see of Athens. In doctrine, it shares the beliefs of Orthdox Churches, and in worship uses the Byzantine liturgy. There is a strong monastic movement, still maintained in 150 monasteries. » Christianity; liturgy; monasticism; Orthodox Church; patriarch

Greek-Persian Wars » **Persian Wars**

Greek religion The religion of the Ancient Greeks was polytheistic, as were earlier systems of belief in the Near East. The gods each had a sphere of influence (eg Poseidon over the sea) or an attachment to a locality (eg Athena at Athens); often both. Though mythologists try to systematize the relationships between the gods, it is unwise to take their tidying up too seriously. It is doubtful whether the average Greek knew more than is contained in Homer. Besides the twelve major Olympian gods, there were later introductions of 'Oriental' deities, especially female, such as Cybele and Isis, who acquired great influence. The Homeric gods are very human in their passions and spiteful jealousies; the main difference is that they do not eat human food, and they do not die. They shade into a lower group of demi-gods and heroes, special people whose cults centred round their tombs. In the cults, ritual and sacrifice were important duties, in return for which the suppliant expected benefits. The system had to be seen to work, as in the case of the oracle at Delphi. In the 5th-c the whole basis of religion was challenged by the Sophists, and the weakening of supernatural belief reinforced Greek humanism. Yet, at the same time, the Eleusinian and Orphic mystery cults began to grow; though highly secret, they were concerned with personal survival after death. Finally, after Alexander the Great had himself proclaimed as a god, the way was open to the ruler-cults of the Roman Empire. » Delphi, Oracle of; Eleusinian Mysteries; Greece [i]; Homer; Roman religion [i]; Sophists

Green, Lucinda, *née* **Prior-Palmer** (1953–) British equestrian rider, born in London. An outstanding three-day eventer, she is the only person to win the Badminton Horse Trials six times (1973, 1976–7, 1979, 1983–4), and the Badminton and Burghley Horse Trials in the same year, on *George* in 1977. She was individual European champion in 1975 and 1977, and the 1982 world champion on *Regal Realm*, when she also won a team gold medal. She married Australian eventer David Green in 1981. » equestrianism

Green (politics) » **Greens**

green algae A large and diverse group of alga-like plants characterized by the photosynthetic pigments, chlorophylls *a* and *b*, which give them their green colour; typically storing food as starch in chloroplasts; found predominantly in freshwater; many have motile stages (*zoospores*) that swim using flagella. (Class: *Chlorophyceae*.) » algae; Chlorophyta; chloroplast; flagellum; photosynthesis

green belt A planning measure in which areas are designated free from development to prevent urban sprawl encroaching into the countryside, and the merging of neighbouring towns. It surrounds existing major urban areas, not necessarily continuously. It provides open land for recreation, and protects agricultural land. The concept is incorporated into garden cities and new towns. » garden city; new town

Green Line The dividing line between Muslim W Beirut and Christian E Beirut, Lebanon, during the 1975–6 civil war. It continues to be recognized. » Beirut

green monkey » **vervet monkey**

green monkey disease A rare but serious virus infection with widespread tissue and organ involvement and high mortality; also known as **Marburg disease**. It occurs in scattered out-

PRINCIPAL GREEK GODS

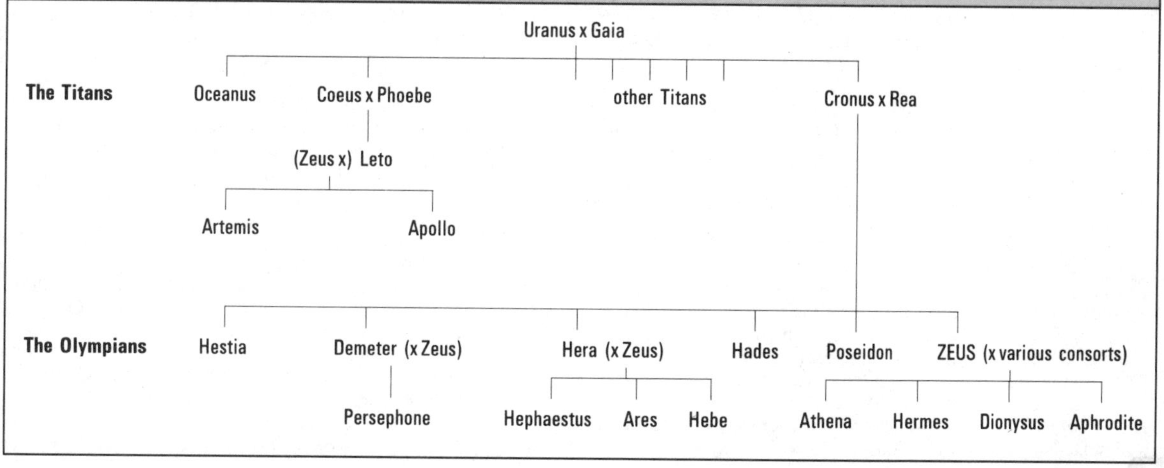

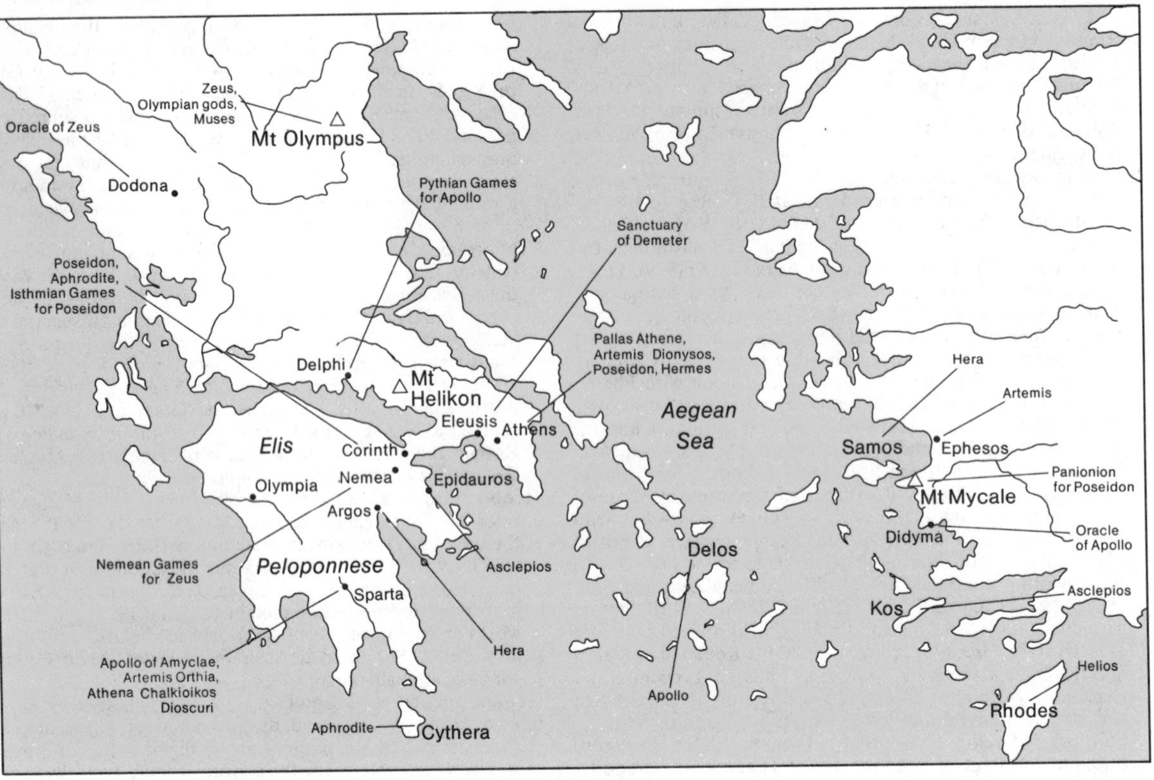

The locations of the Greek gods

breaks in Africa. The natural animal reservoir of the disease is unknown. » virus

Green Mountain Boys A movement in the American Revolution that created the state of Vermont, from territory disputed between New York and New Hampshire. Of many rural insurrections in early America, the Green Mountain Boys was the only one that succeeded. They helped capture the British fort at Ticonderoga, on L Champlain (1775). The cannon taken were important in the successful American siege of occupied Boston. » American Revolution

green paper In the UK, a document published by the government for discussion by interested parties, usually prior to formulating or changing policy. The practice first began in the late 1960s in response to calls for more consultation and open government. » white paper

green pound The special agricultural exchange rate in the EEC, which ensures that currency movements are not reflected in national farm prices. The aim is that the price of each agricultural product should be the same throughout the EEC. If ordinary exchange rates were used, prices would be changing continuously as exchange rates vary. Different 'green currency' exchange rates are therefore fixed for different products, and special adjustments are made from time to time to offset the gap between the green exchange rate and the national exchange rate. This is the *Monetary Compensation Amount* (*MCA*). » European Economic Community

Green Revolution A description for the phenomenal increase in cereal output which occurred in some developing countries during the 1960s and 70s. This was made possible by Borlaug's plant breeding research in Mexico, which produced high-yielding dwarf wheat varieties, and by work at the International Rice Research Institute in the Philippines, which did the same for rice varieties. Success with these new varieties depended on an integrated production system, with high fertilizer applications, adequate water supplies, and efficient weed and pest controls. » Borlaug; cereals

green turtle The only vegetarian sea turtle; worldwide in warm seas; slender head with saw-like jaws; eats mainly sea-grass and sea weeds; turtle soup made from this species; endangered due to overhunting. (*Chelonia mydas*. Family: *Chelonidae*.) » turtle (biology)

Greenaway, Kate (1846–1901) British artist and book illustrator, born in London. She became well known in the 1880s for her coloured portrayals of child life, in such works as *The Birthday Book* (1880). The Greenaway Medal is awarded annually for the best British children's book artist. » English art

Greene, Graham (1904–91) British novelist, born at Berkhamsted, Hertfordshire. Educated at Oxford, he converted from Anglicanism to Catholicism, and moved to London, where he became a journalist, and then a freelance writer. His early novels, beginning with *The Man Within* (1929), and 'entertainments', such as *Stamboul Train* (1932), use the melodramatic technique of the thriller. In his major novels, central religious issues emerge, first apparent in *Brighton Rock* (1938), and more explicit in *The Power and the Glory* (1940), *The End of the Affair* (1951), and *A Burnt-Out Case* (1961). He also wrote several plays, film scripts (notably, *The Third Man*, 1950), short stories, and essays, as well as three volumes of autobiography. His later works include *Dr Fischer of Geneva* (1980), *Monsignor Quixote* (1982), and *The Tenth Man* (1985). He lived in Antibes, France, for many years, and died at Vevey, Switzerland. » English literature; novel

Greene, Nathanael (1742–86) US general, born at Warwick, Rhode Island. In the American Revolution, he fought (1775–6) at Boston, Trenton, Brandywine, and Germanton, and in 1780 took command of the Southern army, which had just been defeated by Cornwallis. By great activity he got his army into better condition, and though Cornwallis defeated him at Guilford Courthouse, the victory was so costly that Greene was able to recover S Carolina and Georgia, paving the way to American victory in the South. A general second perhaps only to Washington, he died at Mulberry Grove, Georgia. » American Revolution

Greene, Robert (1558–92) English dramatist, born at Norwich, Norfolk. Educated at Oxford and Cambridge, he moved to London, where he began to write a stream of plays and romances, his most popular work being the comedy *Friar Bacon and Friar Bungay* (c.1591). He helped to lay the foundations of English drama, and his *Pandosto* (1588) was a source for Shakespeare's *The Winter's Tale*. In his final years, his work grew more serious, and after his death appeared his *Groat's Worth of Wit bought with a Million of Repentance* (1592), in which he lays bare the wickedness of his former life. He died in London. » drama; English literature; Shakespeare [i]

greenfinch A bird of the finch genus, *Carduelis* (4 species), native to S Europe and S Asia; inhabits forest and cultivated areas; eats seeds and insects; closely related to goldfinches. (Family: *Fringillidae*.) » finch; goldfinch

greenfly A soft-bodied aphid that feeds by sucking plant sap; wingless female has plump, greenish body, winged male darker; secretes honeydew, and may be tended by ants. It has a complex life cycle, with up to 10 generations each year produced asexually. It can be a serious pest when present in large numbers. » aphid; life cycle

Greenham Common The site of a US military base in Berkshire, England, subjected to continuous picketing during most of the 1980s by the Women's Peace movement, opposed in particular to the siting of Cruise missiles in Britain, and in general to nuclear weaponry. » Cruise missile; nuclear weapons

greenheart An evergreen tree growing to 18 m/60 ft, native to subtropical S America; leaves alternate, oval, leathery; flowers greenish, bell-shaped, 6-petalled; berries black. (*Nectandra rodiaei*. Family: *Lauraceae*.) » evergreen plants; laurel; tree [i]

greenhouse effect A planetary atmosphere warming phenomenon, resulting from the absorption of infrared radiation by atmospheric constituents. Radiant energy arrives at the planetary surface mainly as visible light from the Sun, which is then re-emitted by the surface at infrared wavelengths as heat. Carbon dioxide and water vapour in the atmosphere absorb this infrared radiation and behave as a blanket, with the net effect that atmospheric temperatures rise. On Earth, the burning of fossil fuels and large-scale deforestation enhance the effect, so that there is likely to be a gradual increase in mean air temperature of several degrees, with the consequent melting of polar ice and a rise in mean sea level. Experimental models predict global temperature increases of between 1°C and 5°C by 2050, but there are many uncertainties about possible effects. It is also likely that global rainfall patterns will shift away from the sub-tropical areas towards higher latitudes, so disrupting present agricultural patterns. The energy balance between incoming solar radiation and outgoing radiation (both heat and reflected sunlight) takes place at the top of the atmosphere. For Earth, the warming effect is about 35°C at the surface; for Venus, in spite of reflective cloud cover, surface temperatures of over 400°C are reached. It is postulated that early Venus had oceans that were warmed by a carbon dioxide greenhouse effect, leading to the evaporation of water which, in turn, amplified warming and produced a 'runaway' greenhouse effect and the total loss of surface liquid water (later lost to space). (The term 'greenhouse' is misleading, since the mechanism by which glasshouses provide warming is mainly due to the inhibition of convection.) » acid rain; atmosphere [i]; Earth [i]; fluorocarbons; fossil fuel; ozone; planet; radiation; Venus (astronomy)

Greenland, Danish **Grønland**, Eskimo **Kalâtdlit-Nunât** pop (1990e) 55 900; area 2 175 600 sq km/839 781 sq ml. Second largest island in the world (after Australia), NE of N America in the N Atlantic and Arctic Oceans; capital, Nuuk (Godthåb); timezone GMT 0, −1, −4; population largely Inuit (Eskimo), with Danish admixtures; languages, Danish, Eskimo; main religions, Lutheran Christianity, Shamanism; largely covered by an ice-cap (up to 4 300 m/14 000 ft thick); deeply indented coastline; coastal mountains rise to 3 702 m/12 145 ft at Gunnbjørn Fjeld (SE); natural vegetation includes mosses, lichens, grasses, sedges; dwarf trees on SW coast; major animal species include polar bear, musk ox, polar wolf, Arctic hare, lemming, reindeer; less than 5% inhabitable; settled by seal-hunting Eskimos from N America c.2500 BC; Norse settlers in SW, 12th–15th-c; explored by Frobisher and Davis, 16th-c; Danish colony, 1721; self-governing province of Denmark, 1979; elected Provincial Council sends two members to the Danish Parliament; economy largely dependent on inshore and deep-water fishing from ice-free SW ports; some sheep farming in SW; hunting for seal and fox furs in N and E; cryolite mined at Iviglut; reserves of lead, zinc, molybdenum, uranium, coal. » Davis, John; Denmark [i]; Eskimo; Frobisher; Godthåb; Inuit; Peary Land

Greenland Sea Gulf connecting the Atlantic and Arctic Oceans; bounded W by Greenland, E by Svalbard; cold surface current from the Arctic brings icebergs and fog; depths range from c.180 m/590 ft on the continental shelf to 3 535 m/11 598 ft in the abyssal plain. » abyssal plains; Arctic Ocean

Greenland shark Very large shark widespread in the N Atlantic and Arctic Oceans; length up to 6.5 m/21 ft; weight 1 400 kg/3 000 lb; greyish brown; feeds on fish, seals, seabirds, and squid; in the past was fished commercially around Greenland. (*Somniosus microcephalus*. Family: *Dalatiidae*.) » shark

Greenpeace An international environmental pressure group which began in Canada and the USA in 1971, and was set up in the UK in 1976. It campaigns by direct action (non-violent passive resistance) against commercial whaling and seal culling, the dumping of toxic and radioactive waste at sea, and the testing of nuclear weapons. » environmentalism; hazardous substances; nuclear weapons; radioactive waste; waste disposal; whaling

Greens A generic label applied to members of political parties or movements which oppose many of the ecological and environmental effects resulting from modern technological and economic policies, and base their demands on a set of post-materialist values. They emerged in the West in the 1970s, when they had only limited electoral success. However, they made considerable political gains in the 1989 European elections. » conservation; ecology; environment

greenshank A wading bird, native to N Europe and N Asia; migrates to Africa, S Asia, Australia, and New Zealand for winter; long pale green legs; long bill slightly up-turned; inhabits freshwater, estuaries, and upland moors. (*Tringa nebularia*. Family: *Scolopacidae*)

Greenwich [grenich], Anglo-Saxon **Grenawic** 51°28N 0°00, pop(1987e) 216600. Borough of EC Greater London, England; S of R Thames; site of the original Royal Greenwich Observatory; meridians of longitude reckoned from this point; also the source of world time standard, Greenwich Mean Time (GMT); birthplace of Henry VIII, Elizabeth I, and Mary I; railway; Greenwich Hospital (1694), Royal Naval College, National Maritime Museum, including Inigo Jones' Queen's House (1637); clipper *Cutty Sark* and Francis Chichester's *Gypsy Moth IV* at Greenwich Pier. » Chichester, Francis; Greenwich Mean Time; Jones, Inigo; London [i]; Royal Greenwich Observatory

Greenwich Mean Time The basis for world time zones, set by the local time at Greenwich, near London. This is located on the Greenwich Meridian, longitude 0°, from which other time zones are calculated. It was originally established within the UK to regularize railway timetables nationally, and later adopted internationally. » meridian; Royal Greenwich Observatory; standard time

Greenwich Village A district of Manhattan, New York City, which became famous during the 20th-c as the quarter of writers, intellectuals, and bohemians. It has recently developed into a more fashionable residential area. » New York City

Greenwood, Walter (1903–74) British writer, born at Salford, Lancashire. His best-known novel is *Love on the Dole* (1933), inspired by his experiences of unemployment and depression in the early 1930s. It made a considerable impact as a document of the times and was subsequently dramatized. » English literature; novel

Greer, Germaine (1939–) Australian feminist, author, and lecturer, born in Melbourne. Educated at Melbourne, Sydney, and Cambridge, she became a lecturer in English at Warwick University (1968–73). Her controversial and highly successful book *The Female Eunuch* (1970) portrayed marriage as a legalized form of slavery for women, and attacked the misrepresentation of female sexuality by male-dominated society. She was (1979–82) director of the Tulsa Center for the Study of Women's Literature. » feminism; women's liberation movement

Gregorian calendar A calendar instituted in 1582 by Pope Gregory XIII, and now used in most of the world. Its distinguishing feature is that a century year is a leap year if and only if divisible by 400. This gives a year of 365.2425 days when averaged over 400 years, very close to the actual value 365.2422 days. When introduced, a discrepancy of 10 days had built up, which was eliminated by jumping straight from the 4th to the 15th of October in Catholic countries. Britain switched in 1752, and also moved New Year's Day from 25 March back to 1 January. » calendar

Gregorian chant The monophonic and (in its purest form) unaccompanied chant of the Roman Catholic liturgy. The earliest musical sources date from the late 9th-c and 10th-c, but the compilation of the repertory has been credited to Pope Gregory the Great. Its rhythmic interpretation has been the subject of much controversy, since the sources do not indicate note lengths. » chant; Gregory I; monody

Gregory I, St (the Great) (c.540–604), feast day 12 March. Pope (590–604), a Father of the Church, born in Rome. Appointed praetor of Rome, he left this office (c.575), distributed his wealth among the poor, and withdrew into a monastery at Rome. It was here that he saw some Anglo-Saxon youths in the slave market, and was seized with a longing to convert their country to Christianity. As Pope, he was a great administrator, reforming all public services and ritual, and systematizing the sacred chants. In his writings the whole dogmatic system of the modern Church is fully developed. He died in Rome, and was canonized on his death. » Anglo-Saxons; Arius; Augustine, St (of Canterbury); Gregorian chant; missions, Christian

Gregory VII, St, originally **Hildebrand** (c.1020–85), feast day 25 May. Italian Pope (1073–85), the great representative of the temporal claims of the mediaeval papacy, born near Soana, Tuscany. He became a cardinal in 1049. As Pope, he worked to change the secularized condition of the Church, which led to conflict with the German Emperor Henry IV, who declared Gregory deposed in a diet at Worms (1076), but then yielded to him after excommunication. In 1080 Henry resumed hostilities, appointing an antipope (Clement III), and after a siege took possession of Rome (1084). Gregory was freed by Norman troops, but was forced to withdraw to Salerno, where he died. He was canonized in 1606. » antipope; pope; Roman Catholicism; simony

Gregory XIII, originally **Ugo Buoncompagni** (1502–85) Italian Pope (1572–85), born at Bolgona. He was professor of law at Bologna for several years, settled at Rome in 1539, was one of the theologians of the Council of Trent, and became a cardinal in 1565. As Pope, he displayed great zeal for the promotion of education; many of the colleges in Rome were wholly or in part endowed by him. He also corrected the errors of the Julian calendar, and in 1582 introduced the calendar named after him. He died in Rome. » Gregorian calendar; Julian calendar; Trent, Council of

Gregory of Tours, St, originally **Georgius Florentinus** (c.538–c.594), feast day 17 November. Frankish historian, born at Arverna (now Clermont). His recovery from sickness, through a pilgrimage to the grave of St Martin of Tours, led Gregory to devote himself to the Church, and he was elected Bishop of Tours in 573. His *Historia Francorum* is the chief authority for the history of Gaul in the 6th-c. He died at Tours. » Franks; Gaul; Martin, St

Gregory of Nazianzus, St (c.329–90), feast day 2 January (W), 25 or 30 January (E). Bishop and theologian, born in Cappadocia, Asia Minor. Educated at Caesarea, Alexandria, and Athens, he became a close friend of Basil the Great, and was made Bishop of Sasima, but withdrew to a life of religious study at Nazianzus. » Arius; Basil, St; Christianity; theology

Gregory of Nyssa (c.331–95), feast day 9 March. Christian theologian, born at Caesarea, Asia Minor. He was consecrated Bishop of Nyssa in Cappadocia by his brother Basil the Great (c.371). Deposed in 376 by the Arian Emperor Valens, he regained office in 378 after Valens' death. An outstanding scholarly defender of orthodoxy, he wrote several theological works, sermons, and epistles. » Basil, St; Christianity; theology

Grenada [gruhnayda] pop(1990e) 101000; area 344 sq km/133 sq ml. Most southerly of the Windward Is, E Caribbean, c.240 km/150 ml SW of Barbados; divided into six parishes; capital, St George's; chief towns, Gouyave, Victoria, Grenville; timezone GMT −4; population mainly of Black African descent; chief religion, Roman Catholicism; official language, English; unit of currency, the Eastern Caribbean dollar of 100 cents; comprises the main island of Grenada (34 km/21 ml long, 19 km/12 ml wide) and the S Grenadines, an arc of small islands extending from Grenada N to St Vincent; Grenada volcanic in origin, with a ridge of mountains along its entire length; highest point, Mt St Catherine, rising to 843 m/2766 ft; subtropical climate; average annual temperature 23°C; annual rainfall varies from 1270 mm/50 in (coast) to 5000 mm/200 in (interior); visited by Columbus, 1498, and named Concepción; settled by French, mid-17th-c; ceded to Britain, 1763; retaken by France, 1779; ceded again to Britain, 1783; British Crown Colony, 1877; independence, 1974; popular people's revolution, 1979; Prime Minister Maurice Bishop killed during further uprising, 1983; a group of Caribbean countries requested US involvement, and troops invaded the island (Oct 1983) to restore stable government; bicameral legislature comprises an appointed 13-member Senate and an elected 15-member House of Representatives; a prime minister heads a cabinet of 15 ministers; economy based on agriculture, notably fruit, vegetables, cocoa, nutmegs, bananas, mace; diversification policy, introducing guavas, citrus fruits, avocados, plums, mangoes, cashew nuts; processing of agricultural products and their derivatives (sugar, rum, coconut oil, lime juice, honey). » St George's; RR25 national holidays; RR51 political leaders

grenade A munition, typically an explosive-packed container with a simple ring-pull fuse, designed for use in close-quarters fighting. It may be either thrown by hand or projected from a launcher.

grenadier (biology) » rat-tail

Grenadines, The [grenadeenz] Group of 600 small islands and islets in the Windward Is, E Caribbean; administered by St Vincent (N Grenadines) and Grenada (S Grenadines); includes Carriacou, Union, Mustique, Bequia, Canouan, Mayreau; airfield (Cariacou); some agriculture, tourism. » St Vincent; Windward Islands (Caribbean)

Grenoble [gruhnobl], ancient **Cularo, Gratianopolis** 45°12N 5°42E, pop (1982) 159 503. Ancient fortified city and capital of Isère department, E France; at confluence of rivers Isère and Drac, in a striking Alpine setting; Mont Blanc to the NE; prospered during French colonial period; railway; bishopric; university (1339); electro-metallurgy, chemicals, plastic products, electrical engineering, nuclear research, glove manufacturing, walnuts; important sports and tourist centre; skiing facilities to the E and SW; World Trade Centre, Industrial Science Park (the Zirst); 12th–13th-c Cathedral of Notre-Dame, 13th-c brick church of St André, Palais de Justice (part 15th-c); scene of 1964 Olympic skating championships and 1968 Winter Olympics. » Blanc, Mont; Olympic Games

Grenville, Sir Richard (1542–91) British naval commander, a cousin of Sir Walter Raleigh. He fought in Hungary and Ireland (1566–9), was knighted c.1577, and in 1585 commanded the seven ships carrying Raleigh's first colony to Virginia. In 1591, as commander of the *Revenge*, he fought alone against a large Spanish fleet off the Azores, dying of wounds on board a Spanish ship. » Raleigh, Walter

Grenville, William Wyndham, 1st Baron (1759–1834) British statesman, the son of Prime Minister George Grenville (1712–1770). He studied at Eton and Oxford, entered parliament in 1782, and became Paymaster-General (1783), Home Secretary (1790), and Foreign Secretary (1791). He resigned with Pitt in 1801 on the refusal of George III to agree to Catholic emancipation. In 1806–7 he formed the coalition government of 'All the Talents', which abolished the slave trade. He died at Dropmore, Buckinghamshire. » Pitt (the Younger); slave trade

Gresham, Sir Thomas (1519–79) British financier, born and died in London. Educated at Cambridge, he passed into the Mercers' Company, and in 1551 was employed as 'king's merchant' at Antwerp. He was knighted in 1559, and was for a time ambassador at Brussels. An observation in economics is attributed to him (**Gresham's Law**): if there are two coins of equal legal exchange value, and one is suspected to be of lower intrinsic value, the 'bad coin' will tend to drive the other out of circulation, as people will begin to hoard it. He built the Royal Exchange (1566–8), and founded Gresham College.

Gretzky, Wayne, byname **The Kid** (1961–) Canadian ice hockey player, born at Brantford, Ontario. He scored a record 92 goals in the National Hockey League (NHL) in 1981–2, and a record 215 points in 1985–6. In 1988–9 he surpassed Gordie Howe's record of 1 890 points in a career. He won the NHL Most Valuable Player Award for the ninth consecutive year in 1988. A member of four Stanley Cup winning teams with Edmonton, in 1988 he was transferred to Los Angeles Kings for a record $15 million. » ice hockey

Greville, Sir Fulke, 1st Baron Brooke (1554–1628) English poet, born at Beauchamp Court, Warwickshire. Educated at Shrewsbury and Cambridge, he travelled abroad on several diplomatic missions. He wrote several didactic poems, over 100 sonnets, and two tragedies. His life of Sir Philip Sidney appeared in 1652. Knighted in 1597, he was Chancellor of the Exchequer (1614–22), and created baron in 1620. He died at Warwick. » English literature; poetry; Sidney, Philip

Grey, Charles Grey, 2nd Earl (1764–1845) British statesman and Prime Minister (1830–4), born at Fallodon, Northumberland. Educated at Eton and Cambridge, he became a Whig MP in 1786, and was a leading supporter of parliamentary reform in the 1790s. In 1806 he became First Lord of the Admiralty, Foreign Secretary, and Leader of the House of Commons. In 1807 he succeeded his father as second Earl Grey. In 1830 he formed a government promising peace, retrenchment, and reform, and after considerable difficulties secured the passage of the 1832 Reform Bill. In the new parliament he carried the Act for the abolition of slavery in the colonies, but was forced to resign following disagreement over the Irish question. He died at Alnwick. » Reform Acts; slave trade; Whigs

Grey, Lady Jane (1537–54) Queen of England for nine days in 1553, born at Broadgate, Leicestershire, the eldest daughter of Henry Grey, Marquis of Dorset, and great-granddaughter of Henry VII. In 1553 the Duke of Northumberland, foreseeing the death of Edward VI, aimed to secure the succession by marrying Jane (against her wish) to his fourth son, Lord Guildford Dudley. Three days after Edward's death (9 Jul), she was named as his successor, but was forced to abdicate in favour of Mary, who had popular support. She was imprisoned, and beheaded on Tower Hill. » Edward VI

Grey, Zane, originally **Pearl Grey** (1875–1939) US novelist, born at Zanesville, Ohio. He first worked as a dentist, but after a trip out west in 1904 began to write Westerns. Best known of his 54 books was *Riders of the Purple Sage* (1912), which sold nearly 2 million copies. He also wrote on big-game fishing and other outdoor pursuits. He died at Altadena, California. » Western

grey mullet Any of a large family of fish, widespread in tropical and warm temperate seas; body elongate, robust; dorsal profile rather flat; feeds on detritus and small algae from sea bottom; blue grey above, sides silvery; valuable food fish in some areas; includes the common European thick-lipped mullet (*Chelon labrosus*). (Family: *Mugilidae*, 4 genera.)

greyhound A breed of dog, now raced for sport, but used thousands of years ago for hunting hares, foxes, and deer; thin with short coat; long legs, tail, and muzzle; the *Italian greyhound* is a miniature breed developed in Italy. Greyhound racing takes place on an enclosed circular or oval track, round which dogs are lured to run by a mechanical hare. The first regular track was at Emeryville, California, in 1919. Betting takes place at greyhound race meetings. » dog; hound; lurcher; Pharaoh hound; saluki; RR111

greylag goose A goose native to Europe and Asia, where it is the most numerous and widespread goose species; plumage mainly grey; inhabits estuaries and flood plains; eats vegetation in water or on land. It is the ancestor of the domestic goose. (*Anser anser*. Family: *Anatidae*.) » goose

greywacke [graywakuh] A type of impure sandstone, composed of angular grains in a matrix of clay. It is deposited in areas of rapid fluid flow, specifically turbidity currents formed in tectonically active, mountain-building regions. » turbidity current

gribble A small wood-boring crustacean that burrows into boat hulls and other submerged timber, causing extensive damage. (Class: *Malacostraca*. Order: *Isopoda*.) » crustacean

grid reference A unique set of numbers locating any place on a map onto which a grid of numbered squares has been imposed. References in the UK are based on the National Grid. The distance eastwards (*easting*) is always given before the distance northwards (*northing*) when giving a National Grid reference. » National Grid reference system

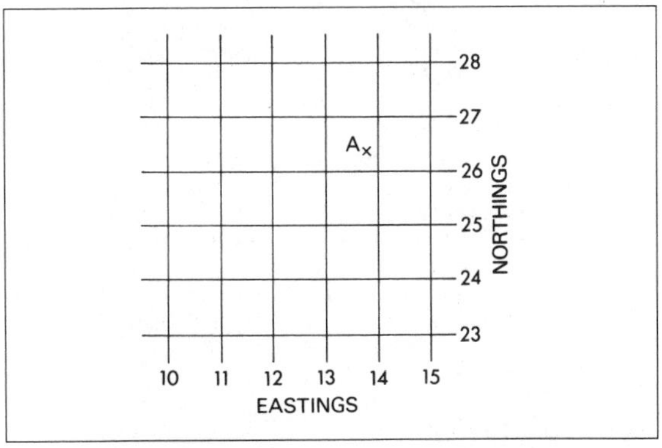

The grid reference for position A is 138264 within grid square 1326

Grieg, Edvard (Hagerup) (1843–1907) Norwegian composer, born at Bergen. He studied at Leipzig, where he was much influenced by Schumann's music, then worked in Copenhagen (1863–7), and developed into a strongly national Norwegian composer. After some years teaching and conducting in Christiania, the success of his incidental music for Ibsen's *Peer Gynt* (1876), and a state pension, enabled him to settle near Bergen, where he died. His other major works include the A minor Piano Concerto, orchestral suites, violin sonatas, and numerous songs and piano pieces.

Grierson, John (1898–1972) British producer of documentary films, born at Kilmadock, Stirlingshire. Educated at Glasgow, he studied film art in the USA, made his name with *Drifters* (1929), and is regarded as the founder of the British documentary movement. He moved to the GPO Film Unit in 1933 for his most creative period, and in 1938 was invited to set up the Canadian Film Board, with which he remained until 1945. He died at Bath, Somerset.

grievous bodily harm » **bodily harm**

griffin or **gryphon** A fabulous beast, originating in Greek tales of the Arimaspians, who hunted the creature for its gold. It had a lion's body, and an eagle's head, wings, and claws. It collected fragments of gold to build its nest, and, instead of an egg, laid an agate.

Griffin, Bernard (1899–1956) British cardinal, born in Birmingham. Educated at the English and Beda Colleges, Rome, he became Archbishop of Westminster in 1943 and Cardinal in 1946. He toured postwar Europe and the USA, and in 1950 was Papal Legate for the centenary celebrations of the reconstitution of the English hierarchy. » Roman Catholicism

Griffith, Arthur (1872–1922) Irish nationalist politician, born and died in Dublin. He worked as a compositor, then as a miner and journalist in South Africa (1896–8), before editing *The United Irishman*. In 1905 he founded *Sinn Féin*, editing it until 1915, was twice imprisoned, became an MP (1918–22), signed the peace treaty with Great Britain, and was a moderate President of Dáil Éireann (1922). » nationalism; Sinn Féin

Griffith, D(avid) W(ark) (1875–1948) US pioneer film director, born at Floydsfork, Kentucky. He began with literary ambitions, then turned to film-making, where he experimented with new techniques in photography and production, and brought out two masterpieces, *The Birth of a Nation* (1915) and *Intolerance* (1916). He continued to make films until 1931, but his studio failed during the recession. He died in Hollywood.

griffon (mammal) A domestic dog, found in two unrelated breeds: **Brussels griffon**, developed to catch rats; small with short muzzle, jutting jaw, small beard; the **wire-haired pointing griffon**, a French pointer and retriever; muscular body, long legs, soft ears; last two-thirds of tail docked. » pointer; retriever

griffon (bird) An Old World vulture, native to S Europe, Africa, and S Asia; head and neck lacks long feathers; inhabits open country; eats carcasses of large mammals; usually numerous when present. It can eat a quarter of its own body weight at one meal. (Genus: *Gyps*, 7 species.) » vulture

Grignard, (François Auguste) Victor [**green**yahd] (1871–1935) French organic chemist, born at Cherbourg. He studied chemistry at Lyons, and became professor there in 1919. He introduced the use of organo-magnesium compounds (**Grignard reagents**), which form the basis of the most valuable class of organic synthetic reactions, for which he shared the Nobel Prize for Chemistry in 1912. He died in Lyons. » magnesium; radical

Grimaldi, Joseph (1779–1837) Comic actor, singer, and acrobat, born in London. From 1800 until his retirement through ill-health in 1828, he dominated the stage of Sadler's Wells as the figure of Clown in the English harlequinade. Many of his innovations became distinctive characteristics of the pantomime clown, or 'Joey'. He died in London, and his memoirs were edited by Charles Dickens. » harlequinade; pantomime

Grimes Graves Prehistoric flint mines on the Norfolk Breckland, E England, in use c.3000–2500 BC. Spread over 14 ha/35 acres are 300–400 shafts up to 15 m/50 ft deep and 5 m/16 ft wide, with radial shafts at the bottom following the flint seams. Though two-thirds of the site remains unexcavated, ancient production is estimated at 14 000 tonnes – enough to make 28 million flint axes. » flint

Grimké, Sarah Moore (1792–1873) and **Angelina Emily** (1805–79) US abolitionists and feminists, born to a major slaveholding family in Charleston, South Carolina. The sisters rejected their family's way of life, and joined the Quakers, who were officially anti-slavery. They moved to Philadelphia and lived quietly until in 1835 Angelina published a letter in the anti-slavery newspaper, *The Liberator*. They became public figures, and Angelina undertook an unprecedented speaking tour. She resisted efforts to silence her, but gave up public life after her marriage to the abolitionist Theodore Weld (1803–95). Sarah lived with the couple thereafter, and the two remained committed to social change. They both died at Hyde Park, Massachusetts. » feminism; Garrison; slave trade

Grimm (1785–1863) Two German brothers, **Jacob Ludwig Carl** (1785–1863) and **Wilhelm Carl** (1786–1859), folklorists and philologists, both born at Hanau, Hesse-Kassel. After studying at Marburg, Jacob became a clerk in the war office at Kassel, and in 1808 librarian to Jerome Bonaparte, King of Westphalia. Wilhelm, in poorer health, remained in Kassel, where he became secretary of the Elector's library. He was joined there by Jacob in 1816. Between 1812 and 1822 they published the three volumes known as *Grimm's Fairy Tales* (*Kinder-und Hausmärchen*). Jacob's *Deutsche Grammatik* (1819, Germanic Grammar, revised 1822–40) is perhaps the greatest philological work of the age; he also formulated **Grimm's Law** of sound changes. In 1829 the two removed to Göttingen, where Jacob became professor and librarian, and Wilhelm under-librarian (professor 1835). In 1841 they both received professorships at Berlin, and in 1854 began work on their historical dictionary, *Deutsches Wörterbuch*. They both died in Berlin. » comparative linguistics; folklore

Grimmelshausen, Hans Jacob Christoph von (c.1622–76) German novelist, born at Gelnhausen. He served on the imperial side in the Thirty Years' War, led a wandering life, then settled at Renchen, near Kehl. In later life he wrote a series of novels, the best of them on the model of the Spanish picaresque romances, such as the *Simplicissimus* series (1669–72). He died at Renchen. » German literature; novel: picaresque novel

Grimond, Jo(seph), Baron [**grim**uhnd] (1913–) British Liberal politician, born at St Andrews, Fife, Scotland. Educated at Eton and Oxford, he was called to the Bar in 1937, served in World War 2, and entered parliament in 1950. Elected leader of the Liberal Party (1956–67), he was largely responsible for the modernizing of both the Party and Liberalism, and called for a 'realignment of the left' of British politics. He served again as Party leader for a short period following the resignation of Jeremy Thorpe (1976), retiring from the House of Commons in 1983 when he was created a life peer. » liberalism; Thorpe

Grimsby, formerly **Great Grimsby** 53°35N 0°05W, pop (1981) 92 596. Port town in Great Grimsby district, Humberside, NE England; on the S side of the R Humber estuary; railway; largest fishing port in England; fertilizers, chemicals, engineering; trade in fish, coal, grain, timber. » Humberside

grip The member of a camera crew in film or TV production who moves equipment and mountings. A **key grip** may also take part in associated set construction. » film production

Griqua [**greek**wa] People of mixed race who spoke Dutch and established stock-raising, hunting, and trading communities under patriarchal leadership on the frontier of Cape Colony in the late 18th-c and early 19th-c. Their peoples are now integrated into the Cape Coloured community. » African history; Cape Coloured; Griqualand

Griqualand [**greek**waland] Region of Cape province, South Africa, mostly in the homeland of Transkei; bounded N by Lesotho; **East Griqualand** joined to Cape Colony in 1879; **West Griqualand**, including the diamond fields of Kimberley, joined in 1880; chief towns include Kokstad and Kimberley. » South Africa [i]; Transkei

grisaille [**gree**ziy] A painting executed entirely in shades of grey. This may be made for its own sake, to look like sculpture as part of a decorative scheme. A reduced grisaille copy of a painting was often made for an engraver to work from. Many Renaissance painters began their pictures with a grisaille underpainting. >> engraving; underpainting

grison [**griy**sn, grizn] A mammal native to S America; resembles a large weasel, with a coarse coat and colour pattern of a badger; formerly domesticated and used to chase chinchillas out of their holes. (Genus: *Galictis*, 2 species. Family: *Mustelidae*.) >> badger; chinchilla; Mustelidae; weasel

Grivas, Georgeios (Theodoros) [**gree**vas] (1898–1974) Leader of EOKA, born at Trikomo, Cyprus. He commanded a Greek Army division in the Albanian campaign of 1940–1, and led a secret organization called 'X' during the German occupation of Greece. In 1955 he became head of the underground campaign against British rule in Cyprus, calling himself 'Dighenis' after a legendary Greek hero. In 1959, after the Cyprus settlement, he left Cyprus and was promoted general in the Greek army. In 1971 he returned secretely to Cyprus and, as leader of EOKA-B, directed a terrorist campaign for *enosis* (union with Greece) until his death, at Limassol. >> Cyprus [i]; EOKA

grivet monkey >> **vervet monkey**

grizzly bear >> **brown bear**

Gromyko, Andrei Andreevich [gruh**mee**koh] (1909–89) Soviet statesman and President (1985–8), born near Minsk. He studied agriculture and economics, and became a research scientist at the Soviet Academy of Sciences. In 1939 he joined the staff of the Russian embassy in Washington, becoming Ambassador in 1943, and after World War 2 was permanent delegate to the UN Security Council (1946–9). As longest-serving Foreign Minister (1957–85), he was responsible for conducting Soviet relations with the West during the Cold War, presenting an austere and humourless demeanour for which he became notorious in diplomatic circles. He became President in 1985, but retired from office following the 19th Party Conference (1988) and was replaced by Gorbachev. He died in Moscow. >> Gorbachev

Groningen [**khron**ingn] 53°13N 6°35E, pop (1984e) 206 611. Capital of Groningen province, N Netherlands; at the confluence of the Drentse Aa (Hoornse Diep) and Winschoter Diep; bishopric; most important city in N Netherlands; connected to its outer port, Delfzijl, by the Eems Canal; airport; railway; university (1614); large market, dealing in cattle, vegetables, fruit, and flowers; headquarters of the Dutch Grain Exchange; shipbuilding, chemicals, electrical equipment, textiles, paper, tobacco, cigarettes, furniture; Martinkerk (13th-c), town hall (1777–1810). >> Netherlands, The [i]

Gropius, Walter (Adolph) (1883–1969) German architect, born in Berlin. He studied at Munich, and after serving in World War 1 was appointed director of the Grand Ducal group of schools of art in Weimar, which he reorganized to form the Bauhaus, aiming at a new functional interpretation of the applied arts. His revolutionary architectural methods and bold use of unusual building materials were condemned in Weimar, and the Bauhaus was transferred to Dessau in 1925. When Hitler came to power, he moved to London (1934–7), designing factories and housing estates, and then to the USA, where he was professor of architecture at Harvard (1937–52). He died in Boston. >> Bauhaus

Gros Morne [groh **mawn**] National park on the W coast of Newfoundland, Canada, established in 1970; area 2 000 sq km/ 775 sq ml; noted for its landscape of forests and fjords, and for its wildlife, which includes caribou, moose, arctic hares, pine martins, seals, and whales; a world heritage site. >> Newfoundland (Canada)

grosbeak [**grohs**beek] A name applied to birds of several unrelated groups, all with a large, stout bill: the finch family *Fringillidae* (12–32 species); the weaver family *Ploceidae* (1 species); and the **cardinal grosbeaks** of the family *Emberizidae* (14 species). >> finch; weaverbird

Gross, Michael, byname **The Albatross** [grohs] (1964–) West German swimmer, born in Frankfurt. An outstanding butterfly and freestyle swimmer, he uses his great height (6ft 7in/201 cm) and long arm span to advantage. In 1981–7 he won a record 13 gold medals at the European Championships. He was the world 200 m freestyle and 200 m butterfly champion in 1982 and 1986, and has won three Olympic gold medals: the 100 m butterfly and 200 m freestyle in 1984, and the 200 m butterfly in 1988. >> swimming

gross domestic product (GDP) A measure of wealth of a nation, calculated in any of three ways. The *output method* is the total of selling prices less the cost of bought-in materials. The *income method* is the total of wages, rents, dividends, interest, and profits. The *expenditure method* is the national expenditure on goods and services (known as 'GDP at factor cost'). The last method is the one most used by economists in forecasting economic growth. The **gross national product (GNP)** is similarly calculated, but includes residents' income from economic activity overseas.

Grosseteste, Robert (c.1175–1253) English scholar, bishop, and Church reformer, born at Stradbroke, Suffolk. Educated at Lincoln, Oxford, and Paris, he taught theology at Oxford, then became Bishop of Lincoln in 1235. He undertook the reformation of abuses in the Church, which brought him into conflict both locally and with the papacy. He died at Buckden, Buckinghamshire. >> Christianity; pope

Grossglockner [**grohs**glokner] 47°05N 12°44E. Mountain in the Hohe Tauern range, SC Austria; height 3 797 m/12 457 ft; highest peak in Austria; first climbed in 1800; feeds the Pasterze glacier; at 2 505 m/8 218 ft the Grossglocknerstrasse is Austria's highest pass. >> Alps; Austria [i]

Grossmith, George (1847–1912) British comedian and entertainer, born in London. From 1877 to 1889 he took leading parts in Gilbert and Sullivan's operas, and with his brother, **Weedon** (1853–1919), he wrote *Diary of a Nobody* in *Punch* (1892). He died at Folkestone, Kent. His son **George** (1874–1935) was a well-known musical-comedy actor, songwriter, and manager of the Gaiety Theatre, London. >> English literature; theatre

Grosz, George [grohs] (1893–1959) US artist, born in Berlin. He studied at Dresden and Berlin, and was associated with the Berlin Dadaists (1917–18). While in Germany he produced a series of bitter, ironical drawings attacking German militarism and the middle classes. He fled to the USA in 1932, was naturalized in 1938, and subsequently produced many oil paintings of a symbolic nature. He returned to Berlin in 1959, where he died. >> Dada; Neue Sachlichkeit

grotesque In art, a form of decoration derived from antiquity and revived during the Renaissance. Human and animal forms are mixed fancifully with plants and abstract shapes to create a bizarre kind of decorative pattern.

Grotius, Hugo, or **Huig de Groot** [**groh**shius] (1583–1645) Dutch jurist and theologian, born at Delft. He studied at Leyden, practised in the Hague, and in 1613 was appointed pensionary of Rotterdam. In 1618 religious and political conflicts led to his imprisonment, but he escaped to Paris, where Louis XIII for a time gave him a pension. In 1625 he published his great work on international law, *De Jure Belli et Pacis* (On the Law of War and Peace). He retired in 1645, and died at Rostock, Mecklenburg.

Grotowski, Jerzy [gro**tof**skee] (1933–) Polish theatre director, teacher, and drama theorist, born at Rzeszów, whose work had a major impact on experimental theatre and actor training in the West during the 1960s and 1970s. After studying in Cracow and Moscow, he founded the Theatre of 13 Rows in Opole (1956–64), which moved to Wrocław as the Laboratory Theatre (1965–84). Since 1982 he has lived in the USA. >> theatre

ground beetle An active, terrestrial beetle; adults mostly predatory, found in litter or vegetation; larvae external parasites or predatory, feeding on predigested prey; c.30 000 species. (Order: *Coleoptera*. Family: *Carabidae*.) >> beetle; mealworm

ground elder A perennial native to Europe and temperate Asia, and introduced into N America; long creeping underground stems give rise to numerous leafy shoots and stems to 1 m/1¼ ft; leaves divided into toothed oval segments up to 8 cm/3 in long; flowers white, in umbels 2–6 cm/¾–2½ in across. It is a persistent weed of gardens. The young leaves are sometimes eaten like spinach. It is an old remedy for gout, hence its alternative name, **goutweed**. (*Aegopodium podagraria*. Family: *Umbelliferae*.) >> gout; perennial; umbel

ground ivy A creeping perennial, native to Europe and Asia; stems square; leaves rounded, bluntly toothed, in opposite pairs; flowers in pairs in leaf axils, all facing the same way, 2-lipped, with long tube, violet-blue. It was used for brewing ale before the advent of hops. (*Glechoma hederacea.* Family: *Labiatae.*) » hops; perennial

ground-roller » **roller**

ground squirrel » **souslik**

ground state » **energy levels**

groundhog » **woodchuck**

Groundhog Day A day (2 Feb) recognized in US popular tradition when the groundhog (or woodchuck), an American marmot, is supposed to appear from hibernation; it is said that if the groundhog sees its shadow, it goes back into hibernation for six more weeks, thereby indicating six weeks of winter weather to come.

groundnut » **peanut**

groundsel A very variable annual growing to 45 cm/18 in, native to Europe, Asia, and N Africa, and widely introduced elsewhere; leaves slightly succulent, oblong with irregular toothed lobes; flower heads numerous, cylindrical, surrounded by narrow black-tipped bracts; florets yellow; fruit with a parachute of hairs. Flowering all year round, it is a common and often problematic weed of cultivated ground and waste places. (*Senecio vulgaris.* Family: *Compositae.*) » annual; bract; floret

groundwater Water which is present in porous rocks such as sandstones and limestones. It may originate from percolated surface waters (*meteoric water*), from water present when the sedimentary rock was originally deposited (*connate water*), or from igneous intrusions (*juvenile water*). The water table is the level below which the rocks are saturated, and springs develop where this reaches the Earth's surface. » limestone; sandstone

group (chemistry) **1** a column in the periodic table, the elements being related by having the same configuration of valence electrons. » periodic table **2** » functional group

group (mathematics) In mathematics, a set of elements S under an operation $*$, if (1) S is closed under $*$; (2) the operation $*$ is associative over S, ie $a*(b*c)=(a*b)*c$ for all a,b,c in S; (3) there is an identity element e in S, ie an element e such that $a*e=e*a$ for all a in S; and (4) every element a in S has an inverse, a^{-1} in S, where $a*a^{-1}=a^{-1}*a=e$. If in addition the operation $*$ is commutative, the group is called an **Abelian group**. Examples of groups are the integers under addition; the numbers $1, i, -1, -i$ under multiplication; and the rotations about a common point through 60°, where $*$ is 'first one rotation then another rotation'. The properties of groups is studied by **group theory**. » associative/commutative operation; set

Group Theater A New York theatre company founded in 1931, whose importance extends beyond the 23 plays it produced during its nine years of existence. The company was dedicated to the principles of group work and to the social importance of a theatre independent of commercialism. Among the names of those involved in the venture (Clurman, Strasberg, Kazan, Odets, Carnovsky) are many who came to be associated with the best of US theatre for more than a generation. » theatre

group therapy The interaction of several individuals on a cognitive and emotional level, as part of a therapeutic programme. It incorporates the sharing of personal experiences and feelings, with the purpose of increasing self-understanding and the treatment of psychological problems. This form of treatment is attributed to US physician Joseph Hersey Pratt (1872–1942). » encounter group; psychodrama

grouper Large heavy-bodied fish with mottled cryptic coloration, common around reefs, rocks, and wrecks but also found in open water; prized as a sport fish and food fish; Indo-Pacific grouper *Epinephelus lanceolatus*, may reach 3.7 m/12 ft, weight 270 kg/600 lb. (Family: *Serranidae.*)

grouse A plump, ground-dwelling bird of the family *Tetraonidae* (19 species); inhabits high latitudes of the N hemisphere; camouflaged coloration; short curved bill; nostrils covered by feathers; legs feathered; eats vegetation and insects. Many (possibly millions) are killed annually by hunters. The name is also used for the **sandgrouse** of the family *Pteroclidae.* » black/red [i] /sage grouse; capercaillie; prairie chicken; ptarmigan; sandgrouse; Plate IX

Grove, Sir George (1820–1900) British musicologist, born in London. He practised as a civil engineer, then became secretary to the Society of Arts (1849), and secretary and director of the Crystal Palace Company (1852). His major work was as editor of the *Dictionary of Music and Musicians* (1878–89), and he also edited *Macmillan's Magazine* (1868–83) and contributed to biblical study. He was knighted in 1883 on the opening of the Royal College of Music, of which he was director till 1895. He died in London. » musicology

Grove, Sir William Robert (1811–96) British lawyer and physicist, born in Swansea, Wales. He graduated at Oxford in 1835, and became a barrister, then turned to electrochemistry, and taught physics. He returned to the law to improve his income, becoming a judge in 1871. In 1842 he made the first fuel cell, generating electric current from a chemical reaction using gases, and the first filament lamp (1845). He also published early ideas on energy conservation. He died in London. » electricity

Groves, Sir Charles (1915–) British conductor, born in London, where he studied at the Royal College of Music. He trained the BBC Chorus (1938–42), conducted the BBC Northern Orchestra (1944–51), the Bournemouth Symphony Orchestra (1951–61), and the Royal Liverpool Philharmonic (1963–77), and was also musical director of the Welsh and English National Operas (1961–3 and 1978–9 respectively). He was knighted in 1973.

growth factor Small peptide factors that are produced by certain cells which, when released, have a growth-promoting effect on other specific types of cell. Their action is similar to that of oncogenes, and they may play a role in some cancers. Examples include *epidermal growth factor* (EGF) and *platelet-derived growth factor* (PDGF). Insulin can also act as a growth factor. » carcinogen; insulin; oncogene; peptide

growth hormone (GH) A type of hormone (a polypeptide), which is secreted by the front lobe of the pituitary gland in vertebrates with jaws and which stimulates body growth through its effects on protein, carbohydrate, and lipid metabolism; also known as *somatotrophin* or *somatotrophic hormone*. It is species-specific in its actions. Its abnormal secretion may result in dwarfism, gigantism, or acromegaly (the abnormal enlargement of the facial features, hands, and feet). » acromegaly; hormones; peptide; releasing hormone; somatomedins; somatostatin

growth ring » **annual ring**

Groznyi [**groz**nee] 43°21N 45°42E, pop (1983) 387 000. Capital city of Checheno-Ingushskaya, SE European Russia; on a tributary of the R Terek, in the N foothills of the Greater Caucasus; founded as a fortress, 1818; airfield; railway; university (1972); oil refining, chemicals, foodstuffs. » Russia

Grünewald, Matthias, originally **Mathis Gothardt** (?1470–1528) German artist, architect, and engineer, born (probably) at Würzburg. Very little is known of his life, but he was court painter at Mainz (1508–14) and Brandenburg (1515–25), and in 1516 completed the great Isenheim altarpiece (Colmar Museum). He died at Halle. » German art

grunion Slender-bodied fish confined to inshore waters of the Californian coast; length up to 18 cm/7 in; body with silvery side-stripe. Communal spawning occurs inter-tidally on the spring tide, the eggs being buried in moist sand near the high-water mark. (*Leuresthes tenuis.* Family: *Atherinidae.*)

grunt Any of the family *Haemulidae* (formerly *Pomadasyidae*, 5 genera) of mainly tropical fishes common in shallow coastal waters and around coral reefs. They are so called because they produce audible sounds by grinding their pharyngeal teeth.

Grus (Lat 'crane') [groos] A S constellation, introduced in 1603. » constellation; RR8

Grylloblattaria [grilohblat**aire**ea] » **rock crawler**

gryphon » **griffin**

guacharo » **oilbird**

Guadalajara [gwat͟halak**hah**ra] 20°30N 103°20W, pop (1980) 2 244 715. Capital of Jalisco state, WC Mexico, 535 km/332 ml WNW of Mexico City; altitude 1 567 m/5 141 ft; founded,

1530; second largest city in Mexico; airport; railway; two universities (1792, 1935); textiles, clothing, tanning, soap, glass, pottery, food processing; many colonial buildings, cathedral (1561–1618), government palace (1643), Jalisco state museum, Santa Mónica Church (1718), San Francisco Church (1550), Museo Taller José Clemente Orozco; fiesta (Oct), fiesta of the Virgin of Guadalupe (Oct–Dec). » Mexico [i]

Guadalcanal [gwadalka**nal**] pop (1984) 63 335; area 5 302 sq km/2 047 sq ml. Largest of the Solomon Is, SW Pacific; length, 144 km/89 ml; maximum width, 56 km/35 ml; rises to 2 477 m/8 126 ft at Mt Makarakomburu; capital, Honiara; airport; copra, rubber, rice, oil palms, gold; scene of the first World War 2 Allied Pacific invasion northward (1942). » Solomon Islands

Guadalquivir, River (Span **Río**) [gwadalkee**veer**], ancient **Baetis**, Arabic **Vad-el-kebir** River rising in the Sierra de Cazorla, Andalusia, S Spain; flows W then SW to enter the Atlantic at Sanlúcar de Barrameda; length, 657 km/408 ml; navigable to Seville; reservoirs for irrigation and hydroelectric power. » Spain [i]

Guadalupe Hidalgo, Treaty of (1848) The agreement that settled the Mexican War, with Mexico yielding all of Texas, Arizona, Nevada, California, and Utah, and parts of New Mexico, Colorado, and Wyoming. The US paid $15 000 000, and assumed Mexican debts worth $3 250 000. » Mexican War

Guadeloupe [gwad**loop**] pop (1989e) 341 000; area 1 779 sq km/687 sq ml. Overseas department of France, a group of seven islands in the C Lesser Antilles, E Caribbean; capital, Basse-Terre; largest town, Pointe-à-Pitre; timezone GMT −4; 90% Black or mulatto population, with several minorities; chief religion, Roman Catholicism; official language, French; unit of currency, the French franc; main islands of Grand-Terre and Basse-Terre make up 80% of total land area and accommodate over 90% of the population; warm and humid climate; average annual temperature, 28°C; visited by Columbus, 1493; occupied by France, 1635; later held by Britain and Sweden; returned to France, 1816; departmental status, 1946; administrative region, 1973; two senators and three deputies sent to the National Assembly in Paris; Commissioner advised by a 36-member General Council and a 41-member elected Regional Council; economy mainly agricultural processing, especially sugar refining and rum distilling; chief crops, sugar cane, bananas, aubergines, sweet potatoes. » Basse-Terre; Grande-Terre; Pointe-à-Pitre

Guam [gwahm] 13°N 144°E; pop (1990e) 138 000; area 541 sq km/209 sq ml. Largest and southernmost island of the Mariana Is, W Pacific Ocean, 2 400 km/1 500 ml E of Manila; capital, Agaña; timezone GMT +10; chief ethnic groups, Chamorros (42%), Caucasians (24%), Filipinos (21%); official languages, Chamorro, English; chief religion, Roman Catholicism; volcanic island, fringed by a coral reef; length, c.48 km/30 ml long; rises to 406 m/1 332 ft at Mt Lamlam; tropical maritime climate; temperatures 24–30°C; average annual rainfall, 2 125 mm/84 in, mainly in the wet season (Jul–Dec); occupied by Japan, 1941–4; unincorporated territory of the USA; elected Governor and a unicameral legislature of 21 members; economy highly dependent on government activities; military installations cover 35% of the island; diversifying industrial and commercial projects; oil refining, dairy products, garments, printing, furniture, watches, copra, palm oil, processed fish; rapidly growing tourist industry. » Agaña

Guan Di or **Kuan Ti** [**kwahn dee**] In Chinese mythology, the god of war, based on a historical person who died in the 3rd-c AD. He was made a god in 1594, and greatly revered.

guan yin or **kuan yin** [gwan yin] The goddess of mercy and protector of women and children in popular Chinese Buddhism. She is the equivalent of Avalokiteshvara, the Bodhisattva of compassion in Mahayana Buddhism, who is represented as a male in India. » bodhisattva; Buddhism; Mahayana

guanaco [gwa**nah**koh] A wild member of the camel family, native to the Andean foothills and surrounding plains; brown with white underparts and grey head; inhabits dry open country; eats mainly grass; can survive without liquid water; possibly ancestor of llama and alpaca. (*Lama guanicoe*.) » alpaca; Camelidae; llama

Guangzhou [kwang**joh**], **Canton**, or **Kwang-chow** 23°08N 113°20E, pop (1984e) 3 221 600. Capital of Guangdong province, S China, on Pearl R delta; founded in 200 BC; opened to foreign trade following Opium War of 1839–42; occupied by Japan (1938–45); airport; railway; university (1958); medical college (1953); designated a special economic zone; industrial and foreign trade centre in S China; engineering, textiles, shipbuilding, chemicals, clothes; Yuexiu public park, containing Guangdong historical museum and Five Goats Statue; Huaisheng Mosque (627), National Peasant Movement Institute (1924), mausoleum of the 72 martyrs, Sun Yatsen memorial hall; bi-annual Chinese Export Commodities Fair. » China [i]; Opium Wars; Sun Yatsen

guanine [**gwa**neen] $C_5H_5N_5O$. One of the purine bases in DNA, normally paired with cytosine. » DNA [i]; purines

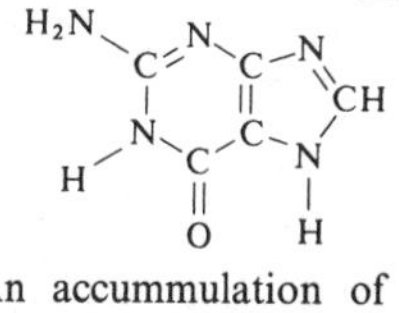

guano [**gwah**noh] An accummulation of animal droppings, typically of birds but also of mammals such as bats. Guano deposits build up beneath breeding colonies, and are a rich source of phosphates and nitrates. They are often used as a fertilizer. » fertilizer; nitrate; phosphate

guarana A woody liana with coiled tendrils, fern-like leaves and clusters of small, 5-petalled flowers; native to tropical America, cultivated in Brazil. The seeds are rich in caffeine, and it is used like cacao to produce a drink called guarana. (*Paullinia cupana*. Family: *Sapindaceae*.) » caffeine; liana

Guaraní [gwara**nee**] A Tupian-speaking S American Indian group, who lived in Brazil, Paraguay, and Argentina, practising slash-and-burn agriculture, hunting, and fishing. A few scattered groups still live in the forests of Paraguay and Brazil. About a million speak Guaraní, the only Indian language to achieve the status of becoming a country's majority language. » American Indians; Paraguay [i]

Guaranis, Jesuit Missions of the [gwara**nee**] Religious settlements established in the 17th–18th-c by Spanish Jesuit missionaries to convert the Guarani Indians of Latin America to Christianity. Five of these missions, São Miguel das Missões in Brazil, and San Ignacio Mini, Santa Ana, Nuestra Señora de Loreto, and Santa Maria la Mayour in Argentina, are world heritage sites. » Guarani; Jesuits

Guardi, Francesco [**gwah**di] (1712–93) Italian painter, born and died in Venice. A pupil of Canaletto, he was noted for his views of Venice, full of sparkling colour, with an impressionist's eye for effects of light, as in the 'View of the Church and Piazza of San Marco' (National Gallery, London). » Canaletto; Italian art

guardian A person who takes care of the interests of, and has parental rights and duties in respect of, a minor. In the normal case, the parents of a child are its guardians. They may arrange for the appointment of another guardian in the event of their death. The High Court has powers to appoint a guardian if there is none. In the USA, guardians may also be appointed for incompetents other than minors. » High Court of Justice

guardian angel An angel believed to have been appointed by God to watch over a new-born soul. Although never an official doctrine of the Church, such belief enjoyed a certain popularity, especially in primitive communities. » angel

Guareschi, Giovanni [gwah**res**kee] (1908–68) Italian writer and journalist, born at Parma. He became editor of the Milan magazine *Bertoldo*, and after World War 2 he continued in journalism. He achieved fame with his stories of the village priest, beginning with *The Little World of Don Camillo* (1950). The books were illustrated with his own drawings. » Italian literature

Guarini, (Giovanni) Battista [gwah**ree**nee] (1538–1612) Italian poet, born at Ferrara. He was entrusted by Duke Alfonso II with diplomatic missions to the Pope, the Emperor, Venice, and Poland. His chief work was the pastoral play, *Il pastor fido*

(1585, The Faithful Shepherd), which helped to establish the genre of pastoral drama. He died in Venice. » drama; Italian literature

Guarneri or **Guarnieri** [gwahn**nay**ree] A celebrated Italian family of violin-makers of Cremona, of whom the most important were **Andrea** (c.1626–98), his sons **Giuseppe** (1666–c.1740) and **Pietro** (1655–1720), and Giuseppe's son **Giuseppe** (1698–1744). The last-named became especially famous, and was commonly known as 'Giuseppe del Gesù', because he signed his violins with 'I H S' (derived from 'Jesus') after his name. » violin

Guatemala, official name **Republic of Guatemala**, Span **República de Guatemala** [gwatuh**mah**la] pop (1990e) 9 197 000; area 108 889 sq km/42 031 sq ml. Northernmost of the C American republics, divided into 22 departments; bounded N and W by Mexico, SW by the Pacific Ocean, E by Belize and the Caribbean Sea, and SE by Honduras and El Salvador; capital, Guatemala City; chief towns, Quezaltenango, Escuintla, Antigua, Mazatenango; timezone GMT −6; chief ethnic groups, Indian (41%) and mestizo; chief religion, Roman Catholicism; official language, Spanish, but several Indian languages spoken; unit of currency, the quetzal of 100 centavos.

Physical description and climate. Over two-thirds mountainous, with large forested areas; narrow Pacific coastal plain, rising steeply to highlands of 2 500–3 000 m/8 000–10 000 ft; many volcanoes on S edge of highlands; rivers flow to both Pacific and Caribbean; low undulating tableland of El Petén to the N; humid tropical climate on lowlands and coast; rainy season (May–Oct); Guatemala City average temperatures, 17.2°C (Jan), 20.6°C (Jul), mean annual rainfall 1 316 mm/51.8 in; much higher rainfall on exposed slopes; area subject to hurricanes and earthquakes, which have caused great damage (eg 1976).

History and government. Mayan and Aztec civilizations before Spanish conquest, 1523–4; independence as part of the Federation of Central America, 1821; Federation dissolved, 1840; thereafter, a series of dictatorships broken by short periods of representative government; 1985 constitution provides for the election of a president (who appoints a cabinet), and a National Assembly of 100 deputies elected for 5-year terms; a claim is still made over the territory of Belize to the E.

Economy. Agricultural products account for c.65% of exports, chiefly coffee, bananas, cotton, sugar; on higher ground, wheat, maize, beans; cotton, sugar cane, rice, beans on the Pacific coastal plain; cattle raising and beef production; forestry; foodstuffs, chemicals, textiles, construction materials, tyres, pharmaceuticals; newer industries, electrical goods, plastic sheet, metal furniture; reserves of nickel, lead, silver, oil. » Aztecs; Guatemala City; Mayas; RR25 national holidays; RR51 political leaders

□ international airport

Guatemala City or **Guatemala** [gwatuh**mah**la] 14°38N 90°22W, pop (1983e) 1 300 000. Capital city of Guatemala, on a plateau in the Sierra Madre mountain range; founded to serve as capital, 1776, after Antigua destroyed by earthquake; itself almost totally destroyed by earthquakes in 1917–18, and since rebuilt; altitude 1 500 m/4 920 ft; airport; railway; University of San Carlos (1680) and four other universities; foodstuffs, textiles, footwear, tyres, cement; cathedral (1782–1815); Churches of Santo Domingo and San Francisco; Mayan ruins of Kaminal Juyú to the W. » Antigua; Guatemala [i]

Guayaquil [gwiya**keel**] 2°13S 79°54W, pop (1982) 1 199 344. Capital of Guayas province, W Ecuador; major seaport and commercial city, on W bank of R Guayas; founded, 1537; airport; railway; four universities (1867, 1958, 1962, 1966); banana trade (world's chief exporter), mining (sand, clay), food processing, textiles, engineering, pharmaceuticals, iron and steel, oil refining, chemicals; racecourse; golf, tennis, and yachting clubs; location of world's first submarine trial; municipal and government palaces, museum, House of Culture, San Francisco Church (1603, rebuilt 1968), Santo Domingo Church (1548). » Ecuador [i]

gudgeon Small bottom-dwelling freshwater fish widespread in clean gravelly rivers and lakes of Europe; body elongate, cylindrical, length up to 20 cm/8 in; head large, mouth with pair of barbels; greenish brown with darker patches on back, sides yellowish, underside silver. (*Gobio gobio.* Family: *Cyprinidae.*)

Gudrun [**gud**run] In Norse mythology, the wife of Sigurd the Volsung. After his death she married Atli (the legendary Attila) who put her brothers to death; in revenge she served up his sons in a dish, and then destroyed him by fire. In the similar German story she is known as Kriemhild. » Nibelungen; Sigurd

guelder rose [**gel**duh] A deciduous shrub or small spreading tree, growing to 4 m/13 ft, native to Europe and W Asia; leaves with 3–5 irregularly-toothed lobes; flowers 5-petalled, white, in a cluster 4–10 cm/1½–4 in across, the outer flowers sterile and much larger than the inner; fruits berry-like, red, often persisting after the leaves have fallen. A mutant form with only sterile flowers in globular clusters first appeared in Guelderland province, Holland, in the 14th-c. It is much grown as an ornamental under the name **snowball tree**. (*Viburnum opulus.* Family: *Caprifoliaceae.*) » deciduous plants; shrub; tree [i]

Guelph [gwelf] 43°34N 80°16W, pop (1981) 71 207. Town in SE Ontario, S Canada, on the Speed R; 43 km/27 ml NW of Hamilton; founded, 1827; railway; university (1964); agricultural centre; iron, steel, textiles, rubber, chemicals; Church of Our Lady, modelled on Cologne cathedral; waterfowl park, electric railway museum. » Ontario

Guelphs The pro-papal, anti-imperial party in Italian cities in the 13th–14th-c, opposed to the power of the Holy Roman Emperors, and successful in resisting the authority of the Hohenstaufen family, whose power was eclipsed after 1266. Allied with the papacy, the Guelphs resisted the claims of potential successors, and dominated Florentine politics. » Ghibellines; Holy Roman Empire

guenon [guh**non**] An Old World monkey native to Africa S of the Sahara; round head with beard, and 'whiskers' at side of face; slender, with long hind legs and tail; some species with colourful coats. The name *red guenon* is used for the *patas monkey*; **pygmy guenon** for the *talapoin*. (Genus: *Cercopithecus*, c.17 species.) » mona/Old World/patas/vervet monkey; talapoin

Guercino, Il [eel gwer**chee**noh], byname of **Giovanni Francesco Barbieri** (1591–1666) Italian painter of the Bolognese School, born at Cento. His major work is the ceiling fresco, the 'Aurora' at the Villa Ludovisi for Pope Gregory XV. After 1642 he became the leading painter of Bologna, where he died.

His nickname means 'the squint-eyed'. » Baroque (art and architecture); fresco; Italian art

guereza » **colobus**

Guericke, Otto von [**gay**rikuh] (1602–86) German physicist, born in Magdeburg. An engineer in the Swedish army, he later defended his home town in the Thirty Years' War, resulting in his election as one of its four burgomasters in 1646. He improved a water pump so that it would exhaust air from a container, and was able with this air pump to give dramatic demonstrations of pressure reduction (the **Magdeburg hemisphere**); he also made the first recorded electrostatic machine. He died in Hamburg. » electrostatics

Guernica [**gair**neeka] Span [gair**nee**ka] 43°19N 2°40W, pop (1981) 17 836. Basque town in Vizcaya province, NE Spain; 25 km/15 ml ENE of Bilbao, on an inlet of the Bay of Biscay; German planes bombed the town in 1937, during the Spanish Civil War, an event recalled in a famous painting by Picasso (now in Madrid); armaments, metal products, furniture, foodstuffs. » Picasso; Spain [i]; Spanish Civil War

Guernsey [**gern**zee] pop (1981) 53 313; area 63 sq km/24 sq ml. Second largest of the Channel Is, NW of Jersey and W of Normandy; rises to c.90 m/300 ft; airport; ferries to the UK and France; forms the Bailiwick of Guernsey with Alderney, Sark, and some smaller islands; chief town, St Peter Port; horticulture, dairy farming (Guernsey cattle), tourism. » Channel Islands

Guesclin, Bertrand du [**gay**klĩ] (c.1320–80) French knight and military leader during the Hundred Years' War, born at La Motte-Broons, Brittany. He entered royal service on the eve of Charles V's accession, and on becoming Constable of France (1370) assumed command of the French armies, reconquering Brittany and most of SW France. He died while besieging Châteauneuf-de-Randon in the Auvergne. » Charles V (of France); Hundred Years' War

Guevara, Che, byname of **Ernesto Guevara (de la Serna)** [gay**vah**ra] (1928–67) Argentine revolutionary leader, born in Rosario. He trained as a doctor (1953), and played an important part in the Cuban revolution (1956–9), after which he held government posts under Castro. He left Cuba in 1965 to become a guerrilla leader in S America, and was captured and executed in Bolivia. » Castro

Guiana Highlands [gee**ah**na] Mountainous tableland mainly in S and SE Venezuela, and extending into Brazil and Guyana, South America; forested plateau, covering half of Venezuela; rises to 2 875 m/9 432 ft at Mt Roraima; vast plateaux separated by deep valleys with major waterfalls; Angel Falls considered to be the highest waterfall in the world. » Roraima, Mount; Venezuela [i]

guide dog A dog trained to assist the blind in finding their way, notably in urban traffic and crowded areas. The dogs are selectively bred, and include labradors, often crossed with golden retrievers, and German shepherds. » blindness

Guido d'Arezzo [**gwee**doh da**ret**zoh], or **Guido Aretino** (c.990–c.1050) Italian Benedictine monk and musical theorist, probably born at Arezzo. He was a monk at Pomposa, and is supposed to have died prior of the Camaldolite monastery of Avellana. He contributed much to musical science: the invention of the staff is ascribed to him, and he introduced the system of naming the notes of a scale with syllables. » scale; solmization

Guienne » **Guyenne**

Guildford [**gil**fuhd] 51°14N 0°35W, pop (1981) 63 086. Town in Guildford district, Surrey, SE England; on the R Wey, 45 km/28 ml SW of London; originally a ford over the R Wey; University of Surrey (1966); burial place of Lewis Carroll; railway; vehicles, engineering, plastics, pharmaceuticals; Royal King Edward VI Grammar School (1557), cathedral (completed in 1964), Archbishop Abbot's Hospital, Women's Royal Army Corps museum. » Carroll, Lewis; Surrey

guilds Religious and trade organizations, mediaeval in origin, but lasting into early-modern times. First formed for devotional and charitable purposes, their functions increasingly split from c.1300 into the economic and the spiritual. Trading and craft guilds controlled economic life in mediaeval towns; religious guilds flourished in cities and villages. » Merchant Adventurers

Guilin or **Kweilin** [gway**lin**] 25°21N 110°11E, pop (1984e) 446 900. Town in Guangxi autonomous region, S China, on W bank of Li R; contains majority of China's Muslim population; badly damaged while US air base in World War 2; airfield; railway; grain, fishing, cotton, spun silk, rubber, medicines, machinery, tourism; Reed Flute Cave, with Shuiqinggong (Crystal Palace) Grotto; Zengpiyan Cave (Stone Age village); Seven Star Park, with Forest of Tablets (stelae from the Tang and Ming dynasties); river boat trips. » China [i]

Guillaume de Machaut [gee**yohm** duh ma**shoh**] (c.1300–77) French poet and musician, born possibly at Rheims. He worked successively under the patronage of John of Luxemburg and John II of France. One of the creators of the harmonic art, he wrote a mass, motets, songs, and ballads. His poetry greatly influenced Chaucer. He died (probably) at Rheims. » ars nova; Chaucer

Guillemin, Roger C(harles) L(ouis) (1924–) US physiologist, born at Dijon, France. Educated at Dijon, Lyons, and Montreal, he joined Baylor University, Texas, in 1953, where he became professor and director of neuroendocrinology (1963–70). Since 1970 he has been at the Salk Institute for Biological Studies. He shared the 1977 Nobel Prize for Physiology or Medicine prize for his work on the isolation of peptide hormones of the hypothalamus. » hormones; hypothalamus; peptide

guillemot [**gil**imot] An auk with a long pointed bill, also known as **tystie** or (in USA) **murre**; eats larger fish than other auks; nests colonially on cliffs. (Genera: *Uria*, 2 species, or *Cepphus*, 4 species. Family: *Alcidae*.) » auk; pigeon; razorbill

Guillotin, Joseph Ignace [gee**yoh**tĩ] (1738–1814) French physician and revolutionary, born at Saintes. He proposed to the Constituent Assembly, of which he was a deputy, the use of a decapitating instrument as a means of execution. This was adopted in 1791 and named after him, though a similar apparatus had been used earlier in Scotland, Germany, and Italy.

Guimarães [geema**rĩ**ysh] 41°26N 8°19W, pop (1981) 22 100. Fortified city in Braga district, N Portugal, 21 km/13 ml SE of Braga; first capital of Portugal; textiles, cutlery; birthplace of Alfonso I; castle (10th-c), ducal palace, Chapel of São Miguel (1105); Cruzes festival (May), International Folk Festival (Jul). » Portugal [i]

Guinea [**gin**ee], Fr **Guinée**, formerly **French Guinea**, official name **The Republic of Guinea**, Fr **République de Guinée** pop (1990e) 6 876 000; area 246 048 sq km/94 974 sq ml. W African republic, divided into four administrative regions; bounded NW by Guinea-Bissau, N by Senegal and Mali, E by the Côte d'Ivoire,

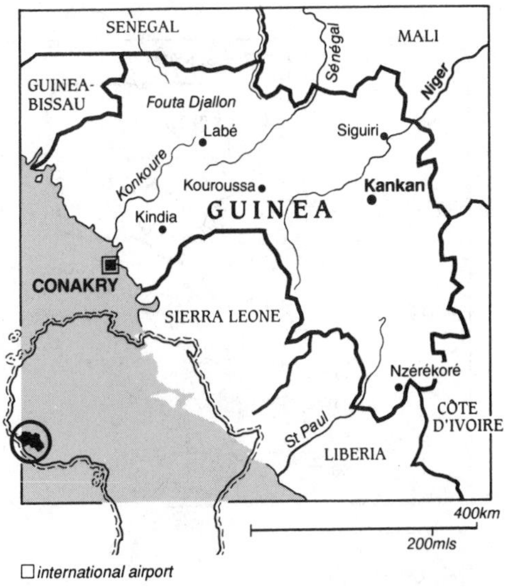

S by Sierra Leone and Liberia, and SW by the Atlantic Ocean; capital, Conakry; chief towns include Kankan, Kindia, Labé; timezone GMT; ethnic groups include Fulani (40%), Malinké (25%), Susu (11%); chief religions, Islam (75%) and local beliefs (24%); official language, French, with several local languages widely spoken; unit of currency, the syli of 100 couris; coast characterized by mangrove forests, rising to a forested and widely cultivated narrow coastal plain; Fouta Djallon massif beyond (c.900 m/3 000 ft); higher peaks near Senegal frontier include Mt Tangue (1 537 m/5 043 ft); savannah plains (E) cut by rivers flowing towards the upper basin of the R Niger; forested Guinea Highlands (S) generally rise above 1 000 m/3 200 ft; tropical climate (wet season May–Oct); average temperature in dry season on coast is 32°C, dropping to 23°C in the wet season; cooler inland; average annual rainfall at Conakry, 4 923 mm/194 in; part of Mali empire, 16th-c; French protectorate, 1849; governed with Senegal as Rivières du Sud; separate colony, 1893; constituent territory within French West Africa, 1904; overseas territory, 1946; independent republic, 1958; coup in 1984 established a Military Committee for National Recovery; governed by a president and a 10-member Council of Ministers; largely agricultural country, growing rice, maize, yams, cassava, sugar cane, groundnuts, coffee, bananas, palm kernels, pineapples, timber; rich in minerals, with a third of the world's bauxite reserves; iron ore, diamonds, gold, uranium; independence brought a fall in production and a deterioration in infrastructure as a result of withdrawal of French expertise and investment. » Conakry; Mali [i]; Senegal [i]; RR25 national holidays; RR51 political leaders

Guinea-Bissau [ginee bisow], formerly **Portuguese Guinea** (to 1974), official name **Republic of Guinea-Bissau**, Port **Republica da Guiné-Bissau** pop (1990e) 973 000; area 36 260 sq km/ 13 996 sq ml. Republic of W Africa, divided into eight administrative regions and the capital; bounded SE by Guinea, N by Senegal, and SW by the Atlantic Ocean; capital, Bissau; chief towns, Bafatá, Bolama, Gabù, Mansôa, Catió, Farim; timezone GMT; chief ethnic groups, Balanta (30%), Fula (20%), Manjaca (14%), Mandingo (13%); chief religions, local beliefs (65%), Islam (35%); official language, Portuguese, with many African languages also spoken; unit of currency, the peso of 100 centavos; an indented coast typified by islands and mangrove-lined estuaries, backed by forested coastal plains; chief rivers the Cacheu, Geba, Corubal; low-lying with savannah-covered plateaux (S, E), rising to 310 m/1 017 ft on the Guinea border; includes the heavily-forested Bijagos archipelago; tropical climate with a wet season (Jun–Oct); average annual rainfall at Bissau, 1 950 mm/76.8 in; temperature range, 24.4–26.7°C; visited by Portuguese, 1446; Portuguese colony, 1879; overseas territory of Portugal, 1952; independence, 1973; military coup, 1980; governed by a president and Council of Ministers; new constitution in 1984, with members elected to a 150-seat National People's Assembly; economy based on agriculture, especially rice, maize, sorghum, cassava, beans, yams, peanuts, coconuts, palm oil, groundnuts, timber; cattle, sheep, shrimps, fish; construction, food processing, brewing, soft drinks; reserves of petroleum, bauxite, phosphate. » Bissau; RR25 national holidays; RR51 political leaders

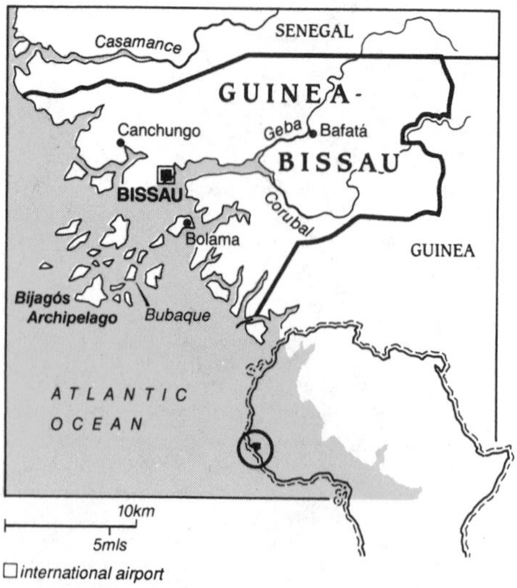

guinea corn » sorghum

Guinea flower » fritillary (botany)

guinea fowl A sturdy, ground-dwelling bird native to Africa; plumage speckled grey; head and neck virtually naked, often with coloured or rough, folded skin; top of head may bear crest of feathers or horny projection (*casque*). (Family: *Numididae*, 7 species.)

Guinea, Gulf of Arm of the Atlantic Ocean, lying in the great bend of the W African coast; bounded (N) by Côte d'Ivoire, Ghana, Togo, Benin and (E) by Nigeria, Cameroon, Equatorial Guinea, Gabon; the Equator lies to the S. » Atlantic Ocean

guinea pig » cavy

guineaworm A thread-like parasitic worm, a serious human parasite in Africa and India; larvae found in copepod crustaceans are swallowed in untreated drinking water; adult worm develops in musculature of lower limbs, causing ulceration and incapacitation. (Phylum: *Nematoda*.) » copepod; nematode; parasitology; worm

Guinevere [gwiniveer] King Arthur's queen; originally **Guanhamara** in Geoffrey of Monmouth's *History*, and there are other spellings. In later romances, much is made of her affair with Sir Lancelot (an example of courtly love). In Malory's epic poem she survives Arthur's death and enters a nunnery. » Arthur; courtly love; Lancelot, Sir

Guinness, Sir Alec (1914–) British actor, born in London. He began acting in 1934, and joined the Old Vic company in 1936, rejoining it in 1946 after serving in the Royal Navy. His famous stage performances include Hamlet (1938) and Macbeth (1966). Among his notable films are *Kind Hearts and Coronets* (1949) and *The Lavender Hill Mob* (1951). In 1958 he received an Academy Award for his part in the film *The Bridge on the River Kwai*. Later roles include Ben Kenobi in the *Star Wars* series, and Smiley in the television versions of John Le Carré's novels (1979, 1982). He was knighted in 1959. » theatre

Guiscard, Robert [geeskah] (c.1015–85) Norman adventurer, the son of Tancred de Hauteville, who campaigned with his brothers against the Byzantine Greeks, and created a duchy comprising S Italy and Sicily. In 1059 the papacy recognized him as Duke of Apulia, Calabria, and Sicily. He ousted the Byzantines from Calabria by 1060, then conquered Bari (1071) and captured Salerno (1076). In 1081 he crossed the Adriatic, seized Corfu, and defeated the Byzantine Emperor, Alexius Comnenus, at Durazzo. He died at Cephalonia, while advancing on Constantinople. » Alexius Comnenus; Normans

Guise [geez] French ducal house of Lorraine, named after the town of Guise, whose members were prominent as staunch leaders of the Catholic Party during the 16th-c civil wars, through their relationship with the Stuart and Valois royal houses. The first duke was Claude de Lorraine (1496–1550), who served under Francis I in Italy and was given the ducal title in 1528. Henry, the third duke, instigated the murder of Coligny in the Massacre of St Bartholomew (1572). On the death of the seventh duke, Francis Joseph (1675) the estates reverted to Mary of Lorraine, on whose death the line became extinct. » Coligny; Religion, Wars of

guitar In its modern form, a musical instrument with a wooden, 'waisted' body, flat back, fretted neck, and six strings which are plucked (usually by fingers or fingernails) or strummed. Before the late 18th-c, most guitars had four or five courses (a 'course' being one or more strings tuned to a single pitch). Since its earliest days the guitar has been associated with folk and popular music, especially Spanish flamenco, but the 19th-c six-course instrument also attracted an extensive printed repertory from guitarist-composers such as Mauro Giuliani (1781–1829) and Fernando Sor (1778–1839). The elevation of the classical

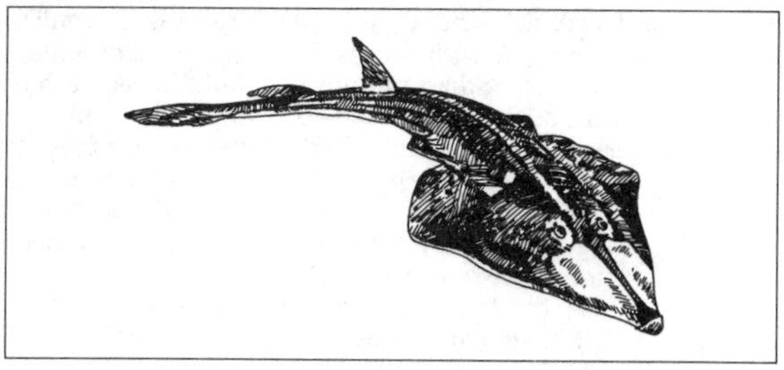

Guitar fish

guitar to the status of a recital and concerto instrument owes much to the example and influence of Segovia.

The electric guitar, the sound of which is amplified and fed through a loudspeaker, exists in two types: the semi-acoustic, with a hollow body, and the more common type with a solid body acting as an anchor for the strings, and a panel to which the electronic pickups and tone and volume controls are attached. The standard instrument has six strings, played with plectrum or fingers; the **bass guitar** has four strings, tuned one octave below the four lowest strings of the standard instrument. Both are used widely in modern popular music. » chordophone; flamenco; Hawaiian guitar; Segovia

guitar fish Bottom-dwelling ray-like fish of families *Rhinobatidae* or *Rhynchobatidae*, the flattened head, broad pectoral fins, and slender body resembling a guitar or violin; includes *Rhinobatus rhinobatus*, widespread in NE Atlantic and Mediterranean; length up to 1 m/3¼ ft. » ray

Guitry, Sacha, originally Alexandre Georges Guitry [**gee**tree] (1885–1957) French actor and dramatist, born in St Petersburg. He wrote nearly 100 plays, mostly light comedies, many performed in English. He first appeared on stage in Russia, and later acted in Paris (1902) and London (1920). He also wrote and directed several films, including *Le Roman d'un tricheur* (The Cheat). He died in Paris.

Guiyang or **Kuei-yang** [kway**yang**] 26°35N 106°40E, pop (1984e) 1 352 700. Capital of Guizhou province, S China; airfield; railway; steel, machinery, aluminium. » China [i]

Guizot, François (Pierre Guillaume) [**gee**zoh] (1787–1874) French historian and statesman, born at Nîmes. He studied law in Paris, but in 1812 he became professor of modern history at the Sorbonne. A member of the Doctrinaires under Louis XVIII, he became Minister of the Interior (1830), and of Public Instruction (1832). As the King's chief adviser (1840), he relapsed into reactionary methods of government, and escaped to London with Louis Philippe in 1848. He died at Val-Richer. » Louis Philippe

Gujarat [gooja**raht**] pop (1981) 33 960 905; area 195 984 sq km/ 75 650 sq ml. State in W India, bounded N by Pakistan, SW, S and SE by the Arabian Sea; independent sultanate, 1401; part of Mongol Empire, 1572; retained its own princely rulers under British control; part of Bombay state, 1947; created in 1960 from the N and W Gujarati-speaking areas of Bombay state; capital, Gandhinagar; governed by a 182-member Legislative Assembly; airfield; six universities; highly industrialized; textiles, electrical engineering, petrochemicals, machine tools, cement, oil refining, fertilizers; cotton, rice, groundnuts; reserves of crude oil and gas; scene of flood disaster in 1983, after bursting of the Fodana Dam. » Gujarati; India [i]

Gujranwala [guj**rahn**vala] 32°06N 74°11E, pop (1981) 654 000. City in NE Punjab province, Pakistan, 67 km/42 ml NW of Lahore; Sikh ruler Ranjit Singh born there, 1780; former Sikh capital; railway; copper and brass handicrafts, grain trade, textiles, ceramics. » Pakistan [i]; Sikhism

Gujrat [guj**raht**] 32°35N 74°06E, pop (1981) 154 000. City in Punjab province, E Pakistan; 109 km/68 ml N of Lahore, between the Jhelum and Chenab Rivers; founded, 16th-c; railway; gold and silver crafts, trade in wheat, millet, cotton, rice. » Pakistan [i]

Gujarati [guja**rah**tee] » **Indo-Aryan languages**

gulag An acronym of **Glavnoye Upravleniye Ispravitelno-Trudovykh Lagerey** (Main Administration of Corrective Labour Camps), the Soviet Unions' secret police department which administered the system of forced labour for those found guilty of crimes against the state. Forced labour was the 'punishment' of many Soviet dissidents.

Gulbenkian, Calouste (Sarkis) (1869–1955) British financier, industrialist, and diplomat, born at Scutari, of Ottoman-Turkish nationality. He entered his father's oil business in 1888, and became a naturalized British subject in 1902. He left $70 000 000 and vast art collections to finance an international Gulbenkian Foundation.

Gulf » **Arabian Gulf**

Gulf Co-operation Council (GCC) An organization providing co-operation between the states of the Arabian Gulf. It was established in 1981 by Bahrain, Kuwait, Oman, Qatar, Saudi Arabia, and the United Arab Emirates. » Arabian Gulf

Gulf Intracoastal Waterway » **Intracoastal Waterway**

Gulf Stream Ocean current named for the Gulf of Mexico; flows past Florida and up the E coast of the USA until deflected near Newfoundland NE across the Atlantic Ocean (the N Atlantic Drift); its warm water moderates the climate of NW Europe. » Mexico, Gulf of

Gulf War 1 (1980–88) A war between Iran and Iraq. Although the 1975 peace agreement with Iran ended Iraq's Kurdish revolt, Iraq still wanted a readjustment of its borders with Iran. After the Islamic Revolution in Iran, the Iranians accused Baghdad of fomenting demands for autonomy by the Arabs of Iran's Khuzestan province. In addition, Iraq feared Iranian provocation of its own 60% Shiite population. After some border fighting in 1980, Iraqi forces advanced into Iran (22 Sep). By the time a peace was agreed (1988), the war had cost about half a million lives on both sides, and represented a serious threat to shipping in the Gulf. Iraq accepted Iran's terms in August 1990. » Arabian Gulf; Iran [i]; Iraq [i]; Kurds; Shiites **2** (Jan-Feb 1991) A war caused by the invasion of Kuwait by Iraq (Aug 1990). Iraq failed to comply with a UN resolution calling withdrawal, which resulted in the formation of a 29-member coalition, led by the USA, launching an attack against Iraq (Operation Desert Storm) on 16 January, followed by a ground war on 24 February. Kuwait was liberated two days later, and hostilities were suspended on 28 February (a total of 43 days fighting). Iraq then accepted the UN resolutions. Among notable events of the conflict were the Scud missile attacks on Israel and the defence provided by US Patriot missiles; Iraq's pumping of Kuwaiti oil into the Gulf; and the burning of Kuwaiti oil wells (all capped by November 1991). Arabian Gulf; Hussein, Saddam; Iraq [i]; Kuwait [i]

gull A medium or large bird, found world-wide, usually near water; feet webbed; plumage white, grey, and black; wings long and slender; bill long, stout; omnivorous, often scavenging; related to terns and skuas. (Family: *Laridae*, 44 species.) » herring gull; kittiwake; peewit; skua; tern

gullet » **oesophagus**

gum arabic A resin which exudes from the branches of several species of *Acacia*, particularly *Acacia senegal*, a shrub or small tree native to dry areas of Africa, from Senegal to Nigeria. The gum arabic of commerce is harvested in dry season, and used as an adhesive, and in ink and confectionary manufacture. (Family: *Leguminosae*.) » resin; wattle [i]

gum tree A genus of evergreen trees, native to and typical of Australia. The leaves are often of two kinds: the *juvenile* are fused in pairs to form discs with the stem passing through the centre; the *adult* are alternate, oval or lance-shaped. The flowers are modified to form woody cups with lids which fall to release numerous, showy stamens. Groups are recognized by characteristic bark: smooth gum trees, scaly blood-woods, fibrous stringy-barks, and hard iron-barks. They are a major or sole food for various animals, such as koalas. Rapid growing, the tallest reach 97 m/318 ft. They provide eucalyptus oil, and are grown the world over for timber, ornament, and soil stabilization. (Genus: *Eucalyptus*, 500 species. Family: *Myrtaceae*.) » evergreen plants; oil (botany); stamen

gums Dense fibrous connective tissue surrounding the base of the teeth, firmly attached to the underlying bone (the alveolar bone of the jaws). They are covered by a smooth vascular mucous membrane continuous with the lining of the lips and cheeks. » gingivitis; teeth [i]

gun-cotton » **nitrocellulose**

gun-metal A form of bronze once favoured for the making of weapons. Modern gun-metal, with a composition of c.88% copper, 10% tin, and some zinc, has good anti-corrosion properties within the conditions encountered in valves and other steam fittings. » bronze; corrosion

Gundelach, Finn Olav (1925–81) Danish diplomat and European Commissioner, born at Vejle. Educated at Aarhus, he joined the Danish Diplomatic Service, and became Ambassador to the European Economic Community (EEC) in 1967, directing the negotiations for Denmark's entry into the Community (1973), and becoming his country's first European Commissioner. In 1977 he was made Vice-President of the new European Commission, and was given charge of the EEC's Common Agricultural Policy. » European Economic Community

gundog » **sporting dog**

Gunn, Thom(son) William (1929–) British poet, born at Gravesend, Kent. Educated at Cambridge, he went to California (1954), where he taught English at Stanford and Berkeley. His often erotic poems are written in an intriguing variety of regular and free forms. Volumes include *Fighting Terms* (1955), *My Sad Captains* (1961), *Jack Straw's Castle* (1976) and *The Passages of Joy* (1982). » English literature; poetry

Gunnbjørn Fjeld [**goon**byawn] 68°50N 29°45W. Highest mountain in Greenland, rising to 3 702 m/12 145 ft near the SE coast. » Greenland [i]

gunnel Small slender-bodied fish found in inshore and intertidal habitats of the N Atlantic and Pacific Oceans; length up to 30 cm/1 ft; pelvic fins reduced or absent; includes the Atlantic butterfish (*Pholis gunnellus*), common among rocks and kelp. (Family: *Pholidae*.)

gunpowder The oldest known explosive, a mixture of sulphur, charcoal and saltpetre (nitre, potassium nitrate). Known to the Chinese at least as early as the 10th-c, it was in use in Europe by the 14th-c. Gunpowder mixtures have a range of properties depending on formulation and granulation . It was the principal military explosive until late in the 19th-c, and is still valuable in primers, fuses, and pyrotechnics. » explosives

Gunpowder Plot A conspiracy by Catholic gentry, led by Robert Catesby, to blow up the English Houses of Parliament. It failed when Guy Fawkes, who placed the explosives, was arrested (5 Nov 1605). The plot failed because one conspirator, Francis Tresham, warned his brother-in-law, Lord Monteagle, not to attend; and Monteagle reported the matter to the government. The scheme reflected Catholic desperation after the failure of previous plots to remove James I in 1603; peace with Spain in 1604, which ended the prospect of foreign support; and new sanctions against recusant Catholics, resulting in 5000 convictions in the spring of 1605. » Catesby; Fawkes; James I (of England)

Guomindang or **Kuomintang (KMT)** The Chinese Nationalist Party, founded by Sun Yatsen in 1919 and later led by Jiang Jieshi (Chiang Kai-shek). It ruled China from Nanjing (Nanking) 1927–37 and 1945–9, and from Chonqing during the war with Japan 1937–45. It retreated to Taiwan in 1949. » Jiang Jieshi; Sun Yatsen; Taiwan [i]

guppy Small freshwater fish native to S and C America but now widespread through the aquarium trade; feeds on invertebrates and algae; length up to 3 cm/1.2 in; males with metallic blue-green coloration. Captive breeding has produced a considerable variety of forms and colours. (*Poecilia reticulata*. Family; *Poecilidae*.)

Gupta Empire [**gup**tah] (320–540) A decentralized state system covering most of N India, with provinces (*desa*) and districts (*pradesa*). It was materially prosperous, especially in urban areas, and is known as India's 'Classical' or 'Golden' Age, when norms of Indian literature, art, architecture, and philosophy were established, and Hinduism underwent revival.

Gur Amir or **Gur Emir** [goor am**eer**] The mausoleum of Tamerlane, Ulugh Beg, and others of the house of Timur, built in Samarkand (in present-day Uzbekistan) in the 15th-c. The interior of the mausoleum is decorated with turquoise and gold designs, while the exterior is dominated by a splendid ribbed dome. The Gur Amir was restored in 1967. » Samarkand; Timur

gurdwara (Sanskrit, 'guru's door') [**gurd**wara] A Sikh temple, or any place where the scripture is installed. In addition to a worship area housing the scripture, it should include a hostel and a place for serving meals. » Adi Granth; Sikhism

Gurkhas [**ger**kuhz] **1** The name of the Nepalese ruling dynasty since 1768. **2** An elite infantry unit of the British army recruited from the hill tribes of Nepal. Their characteristic weapon, the Kukri fighting knife with its curved blade, has contributed to their fame, in battles from the North West Frontier of India in the 19th-c, via the Western Front in World War 1, to the Burma and Italian campaigns of World War 2. Gurkha infantry also took part in the Falklands War of 1982. » army; Nepal [i]

gurnard [**ger**nuhd] Any of the bottom-living marine fishes of the family *Triglidae*, widespread in inshore waters of tropical to temperate seas; also called **sea robins**; length up to 75 cm/30 in; head armoured with bony plates; pectoral fin rays used as feelers or as stilts; many produce audible sounds; includes European **grey gurnard** (*Eutrigla gurnardus*).

Gurney, Edmund (1847–88) British psychical researcher, born at Hersham, Surrey, and educated at Cambridge. One of the founding members of the Society for Psychical Research, he conducted important experimental studies of hypnosis and telepathy, and a statistical survey of hallucinations. His investigation of apparitions, telepathy, and other such phenomena culminated in his classic *Phantasms of the Living* (with F W H Myers and F Podmore, 1886). He died at Brighton. » parapsychology

Gurney, Ivor (1890–1937) British composer and poet, born in Gloucester, and educated at the Royal College of Music in London. Gassed and shell-shocked in 1917, he published two volumes of poems from hospital: *Severn and Somme* (1917) and *War's Embers* (1919), and later *Five Elizabethan Songs* (1920). From 1922 he was confined in an asylum, and died in London. Some 300 songs and 900 poems survive, whose quality is increasingly recognized. » English literature; poetry

guru [**goo**roo] In Hinduism, a spiritual teacher or guide who gives instruction to a disciple or pupil, who in return is required to render reverence and obedience. In Sikhism, it is identified with the inner voice of God, of which the ten Gurus were the human vehicles. » Hinduism; Sikhism

Gush Emmunim [goosh emoo**neem**] An Israeli pressure group set up after the 1973 elections, dedicated to an active settlement policy in territories such as the West Bank, occupied by the Israelis after the 1967 war. The name is Hebrew, meaning 'Group of those who keep the faith'. » Arab-Israeli Wars

Gustavus I or **Gustav Vasa** (1496–1560) King of Sweden (1523–60), founder of the Vasa dynasty, born into a gentry family at Lindholmen, Upland. In 1518 he was carried off to Denmark as a hostage, but escaped to lead a peasant rising against the occupying Danes, capturing Stockholm (1523) and driving the enemy from Sweden. He was elected King by the Diet and, despite several rebellions, his 40-year rule left Sweden a peaceful realm. He died in Stockholm. » Lutheranism; Sweden [i]

Gustavus II or **Gustavus Adolphus** (1594–1632) King of Sweden (1611–32), born in Stockholm, the son of Charles IX. On ascending the throne, he reorganized the government with the assistance of Chancellor Oxenstierna, raised men and money, and recovered his Baltic provinces from Denmark. He ended wars with Russia (1617) and Poland (1629), and carried out major military and economic reforms at home. In 1630 he entered the Thirty Years' War, leading the German Protestants against the Imperialist forces under Wallenstein, and won several victories, notably at Breitenfeld (1631). He was killed during the Swedish victory at Lützen, near Leipzig. » Oxenstjerna; Thirty Years' War; Wallenstein

gut » **alimentary canal**

Gutenberg, Johannes (Gensfleisch) [**goo**tnberg] (1400–68) German printer, regarded as the inventor of printing from movable type, born at Mainz. Between 1430 and 1444 he was in Strasbourg, probably working as a goldsmith, and here he may have begun printing, In Mainz again by 1448 he entered into partnership with Johann Fust (c.1400–66), who financed a printing press. This partnership ended in 1455, when Fust sued

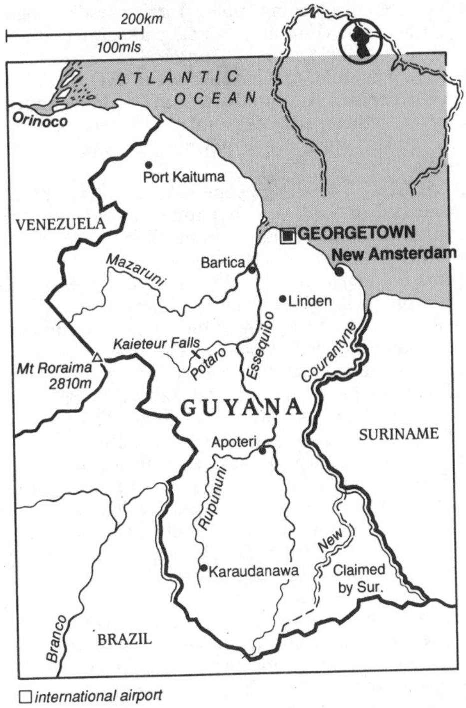

him for repayment of the loan, and forced him to give up his machinery, leaving him ruined. Aided by Konrad Humery, he was able to set up another press, but little is known of his work thereafter. His best-known book is the 42-line Bible, often called 'Gutenberg's Bible' (c.1455). He died at Mainz. » printing [i]

Guthrie, Sir (William) Tyrone (1900–71) British theatrical producer, born at Tunbridge Wells, Kent. Educated at Wellington College and Oxford, he became director of The Scottish National Players (1926–8) and the Cambridge Festival Theatre (1929–30). He was responsible for many fine productions of Shakespeare at the Old Vic during the 1930s, and became administrator of the Old Vic and Sadler's Wells (1939–45), and director of the Old Vic (1950–1). He often worked abroad, and founded the Tyrone Guthrie Theatre in Minneapolis in 1963. He was knighted in 1961, and died at Newbliss, Ireland. » Shakespeare [i]; theatre

Guthrie, Woody, byname of **Woodrow Wilson Guthrie** (1912–67) US folksinger and songwriter, born at Okemah, Oklahoma. He took to the road during the Great Depression, singing for his meals, and wrote hundreds of songs, many as topical as headlines, lauding migrant workers, pacifists, and underdogs of all kinds. His best-known songs are 'So Long, It's Been Good to Know You' and 'This Land Is Your Land'. He helped to form the Almanac Singers, a group that advocated public power at workers' rallies. In 1952, he was hospitalized with Huntington's chorea, and died of it after 15 years, in New York City, by which time a new generation, including Joan Baez and Bob Dylan, had learned his songs and adopted his causes. » Baez; Depression, Great; Dylan

Gutland, also **Pays Gaumais [gootlant]** Geographical region of S Luxembourg, occupying nearly 70% of the country, part of the fertile uplands of Lorraine; includes important wine-producing area along the R Moselle; city of Luxembourg in C of region. » Luxembourg [i]

gutta percha A grey-black substance similar to rubber, but non-elastic, obtained from the latex of *Palaquium*, a genus of tropical trees related to chicle. It has been widely used in dental fillings, electrical insulation, and (especially) golf balls. » chicle; latex; rubber

Guy, Thomas [giy] (c.1644–1724) British philanthropist, born and died in London. He began business in 1668 as a bookseller, and then became a printer of Bibles, amassing a fortune of nearly half a million pounds. In 1707 he built and furnished three wards of St Thomas's Hospital, and in 1722 founded the hospital in Southwark which bears his name.

Guy Fawkes Night The evening of 5 November, the anniversary in the UK of the Gunpowder Plot, celebrated with fireworks and bonfires, on which are often burned effigies of Guy Fawkes known as *guys*. » Fawkes; Gunpowder Plot

Guyana, official name **Co-operative Republic of Guyana**, formerly (to 1966) **British Guiana** pop (1990e) 756 000; area 214 969 sq km/82 978 sq ml. Republic on N coast of South America, on the Atlantic, divided into nine districts; bounded E by Suriname, W by Venezuela, and S by Brazil; capital, Georgetown; timezone GMT −3½; population mainly East Indian (51%), mixed Afro-Indian (43%); official language, English; chief religions, Christianity (57%), Hindu (33%); unit of currency, the Guyana dollar of 100 cents; inland forest covers c.85% of land area; grass-covered savannah in the hinterland; coastal plain, below sea-level at high tide, protected by sea defences, dams, and canals; main rivers, the Essequibo, Demerara, and Berbice, with many rapids and waterfalls in upper courses; highest peak, Mt Roraima, rising to 2 875 m/9 432 ft in the Pakaraima Mts (W); equatorial climate in the lowlands, hot, wet, with constant high humidity; Georgetown, minimum temperatures 23°C, maximum 34°C, two seasons of high rainfall (May–Jul, Nov–Jan); lower temperatures and less rainfall on high plateau inland; sighted by Columbus, 1498; settled by the Dutch, late 16th-c; several areas ceded to Britain, 1815; consolidated as British Guiana, 1831; racial disturbances between East Indians and Blacks, 1962; independence, 1966; republic, 1970; governed by a president and a unicameral 65-member National Assembly, elected every five years; high unemployment, influenced by labour unrest, low productivity, and high foreign debt; International Monetary Fund made Guyana ineligible for further credits due to lack of repayment, 1985; economy largely based on sugar, rice, bauxite; shrimps, livestock, cotton, molasses, timber, rum. » Georgetown; RR25 national holidays; RR51 political leaders

Guyenne or **Guienne** [güyen], Lat **Acquitania** A mediaeval duchy, including Gascony, in SW France, bounded W by the Bay of Biscay. The rump of Aquitaine, it remained a possession of the English crown after Normandy and other French territories were lost in 1204–5. The claim of the kings of England to be independent rulers of Guyenne was one of the causes of the Hundred Years' War. It was finally conquered by the French in 1453. The area is now occupied by the departments of Gironde, Dordogne, Lot, Aveyron, Tarn-et-Garonne, and Lot-et-Garonne. » Angevins; Hundred Years' War

Guzmán Blanco, Antonio [goos**mahn**] (1829–99) Venezuelen dictator, born in Carácas. He was Vice-President from 1863 to 1868. Driven from office (1868), he headed a revolution which restored him to power (1870), and became dictator, holding the presidency on three occasions (1873–7, 1879–84, 1886–8). He then retired to Paris, where he died. » Venezuela [i]

Gwalior 26°12N 78°09E, pop (1981) 556 000. City and former princely state in Madhya Pradesh, C India; founded, 8th-c; famous cultural centre, 15th-c; Mughal city, 15th–16th-c; taken by the British, 1780; railway; commercial centre; fort on Gwalior Rock, with several palaces, temples, and shrines. » Madhya Pradesh

Gwent pop (1987e) 443 100; area 1 376 sq km/531 sq ml. County in SE Wales, UK, divided into five districts; created in 1974; bounded E by England and S by the Bristol Channel; capital, Cwmbran; other chief towns, Abergavenny, Newport, Tredegar; drained by the Usk and Wye Rivers; coal mining, chemicals, aluminium, tinplate, market gardening, food processing, dairy farming, tourism; Wye Valley, Tintern Abbey, castles at Chepstow and Raglan, Roman remains at Caerleon. » Wales [i]

Gweru [**gway**roo], formerly **Gwelo** 19°25S 29°50E, pop (1982) 79 000. Capital of Midlands province, Zimbabwe, 155 km/96 ml NE of Bulawayo; airfield; railway; important communications and administrative centre; shoes, glassware, metal alloys, dairy products, batteries. » Zimbabwe [i]

Gwyn or **Gwynne, Nell**, originally **Eleanor Gwyn** (c.1650–87)

Mistress of Charles II of England, possibly born in London. Of humble parentage, she lived precariously as an orange girl before going on the boards at Drury Lane, where she established herself as a comedienne. She had at least one son by the King – Charles Beauclerk, Duke of St Albans – and James Beauclerk is often held to have been a second. She died in London. >> Charles II (of England)

Gwynedd [**gwineth**] pop (1987e) 236 300; area 3 869 sq km/ 1 493 sq ml. County in NW Wales, UK, bounded N, W, and SW by the Irish Sea; created in 1974, divided into five districts, including the island of Anglesey (Ynys Môn), separated by the Menai Straits; rises to 1 085 m/3 560 ft at Snowdon in Snowdonia National Park; drained by the R Conwy; bilingual language policy; administrative centre, Caernarfon; other chief towns, Bangor, Pwllheli, Barmouth, Holyhead; livestock, slate quarrying, textiles, electronics, light engineering, tourism; Holyhead linked by ferry to Dun Laoghaire, Ireland; castles at Caernarfon, Beaumaris, Conwy, Criccieth, Harlech; Llyn Tegid (Bala), largest Welsh lake. >> Caernarfon; Wales [i]

gymkhana A mixed sports meeting in a public place, especially one involving a range of horse riding skills for young riders. Gymkhanas originated in India in 1860, where horse and pony races were introduced for British soldiers' entertainment. Over the years athletic events and other competitions (eg model aeroplane flying) have been introduced. In the USA, the term is often used for an obstacle competition for automobiles.

gymnastics A series of physical exercises now used primarily for sporting contests. The ancient Greeks and Romans performed such exercises for health purposes. Modern techniques were developed in Germany towards the end of the 18th-c. At competitive level, gymnasts perform exercises which are subsequently marked out of a score of 10 by a series of judges. Men compete on the parallel bars, pommel horse, horizontal bar, rings, horse vault, and floor exercise. Women compete on the asymmetrical bars, beam, horse vault, and floor exercise. >> RR111

gymnosperms The commonly used name for one of the two divisions of seed plants, the other being the *flowering plants* (*angiosperms*). They are characterized by having naked seeds (ie not enclosed in an ovary), but the members differ widely from each other, and are now regarded as deriving from several entirely separated ancestral lines. It contains both living (eg conifers) and entirely fossil groups. Early gymnosperms were abundant during the Carboniferous period, forming many of the coal deposits, and becoming the dominant vegetation during the Jurassic and Cretaceous periods, after which many became extinct. Living genera again became widespread, particularly during the last glaciations, and are still found from cold temperate to subtropical regions, and even in the tropics on high mountains; but many genera are now confined to small geographical areas. (Class: *Gymnospermae*.) >> Carboniferous/Cretaceous/Jurassic period; flowering plants; fossil; seed

gymnure [**jim**nyoor] >> **moonrat**

gynaecology/gynecology [giyni**kol**uhjee] The study of the functions and disorders of the female organs of reproduction. Disorders of menstruation and of fertility constitute a major part of the discipline. In addition, it includes the investigation and treatment of infections of the reproductive organs, as well as benign and malignant tumours of the cervix, uterus, and ovaries. Liberalization of the laws relating to abortion has increased the need for specialized gynaecological care. >> cervix; Fallopian tubes; Graafian follicles; uterus [i]

gynaecomastia/gynecomastia [giynikoh**mas**tia] Enlargement of the male breast due to overgrowth of its cells. It occurs naturally and transiently in many male adolescents, and also develops if female sex hormones are given to men, and as a consequence of certain drugs. >> breast

gynoecium >> **flower** [i]; **ovary**

Györ [dyür], Ger **Raab**, Lat **Arrabona** 47°41N 17°40E, pop (1981) 125 000. Industrial city and capital of Györ-Sopron county, NW Hungary; at the junction of the Rába and Repce Rivers and the R Danube; linked to L Fertö by canal; railway; bishopric; vehicles, steel, machinery, foodstuffs, textiles, distilling, horse breeding; noted for its modern ballet company; Carmelite convent (18th-c), cathedral (12th-c, rebuilt 18th-c), city hall (18th-c). >> Hungary [i]

gypsum A mineral of calcium sulphate ($CaSO_4.2H_2O$) found in evaporite deposits as crystals (*selenite*) or fine-grained masses (*alabaster*). When partly dehydrated, it forms *Plaster of Paris*, a fine, quick-setting, white powder. >> alabaster; evaporite deposits

Gypsy or **Gipsy** Travelling people whose origins are unknown, concentrated in S Europe, but found throughout the world. They call themselves *Rom*, from their language Romany, possibly derived from Sanskrit (which is why they are thought to come originally from the Indian subcontinent), and which varies from country to country. Many speak the national language of the country where they live, or a combination of Romany and the local language. They have also adopted the religion of the country where they live, but have their own baptismal, marriage, and burial practices. Because of the negative connotations of the word Gypsy, 'Traveller' is generally the preferred term in Britain. There are an estimated 2–3 million Gypsies today, worldwide. >> Romany

gypsy moth A medium-sized tussock moth; rare in Britain but a pest of fruit trees in N America; wings whitish with dark zigzag markings; caterpillar greyish with tufts of brown hair; pupates in a loose cocoon. (Order: *Lepidoptera*. Family: *Lymantridae*.) >> caterpillar; pupa; tussock moth

gyre A large semi-enclosed ocean circulation cell made up of surface currents. As these circulate around the oceans, the currents which make up their limbs receive, store, and give up heat to the atmosphere and adjacent ocean currents, resulting in temperature changes in the surface water. In many cases the heat transported by gyres strongly influences the weather and climate of surrounding land areas. >> current

gyrfalcon [**jer**fawlkn] The largest of all falcons (length 50–60 cm/20–24 in); native to Arctic regions; inhabits mountains and tundra; plumage white, grey, or dark; hunts close to ground; eats mainly ground-dwelling birds. (*Falco rusticolus*.) >> bird of prey; falcon

gyrocompass A form of gyroscope which is set to maintain a N-seeking orientation as an aid to navigation. >> compass; gyroscope

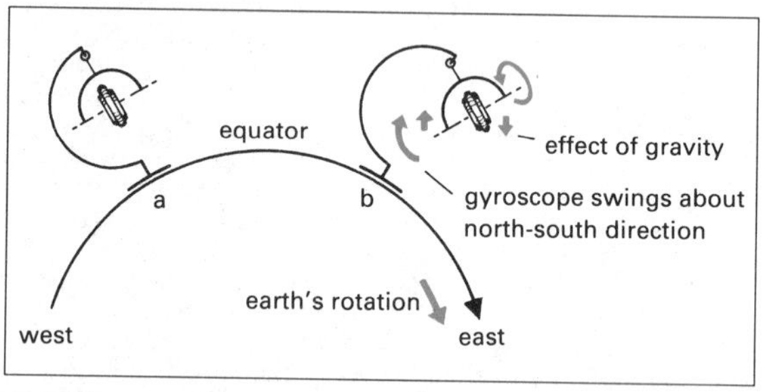

Principle of the gyrocompass – A gyroscope at the equator will move from a to b as a result of the Earth's rotation

gyromagnetic ratio For spinning particles, the ratio of magnetic moment to particle spin; symbol γ, units $T^{-1}s^{-1}$ (per tesla per second) For protons, $\gamma = 2.675 \times 10^8$ $T^{-1}s^{-1}$. >> g-factor; magnetic moment; spin

gyroscope An instrument consisting of a rapidly spinning wheel so mounted as to utilize the tendency of such a wheel to maintain a fixed position in space, and to resist any force which tries to change it. The way it will move if a twisting force is applied depends on the extent and orientation of the force and the way the gyroscope is mounted. A free vertically spinning gyroscope (in *gimbals*, two semicircular mountings at right angles, such that the mounted object can turn in any direction) remains vertical as the carrying vehicle tilts, so providing an artificial horizon. A horizontal gyroscope will maintain a certain bearing, and therefore indicate a vessel's heading as it turns. >> gyrocompass [i]

H

H-bomb » hydrogen bomb [i]

Haakon VII (1872–1957) King of Norway (1905–57), born at Charlottenlund. He became King when Norway voted herself independent of Sweden in 1905, dispensed with regal pomp, and emerged as the 'people's king'. During World War 2, he carried on Norwegian resistance to Nazi occupation from England. He died in Oslo. » Norway [i]

Haarlem, Eng **Harlem** [**hah**luhm] 52°23N 4°38E, pop (1984e) 217 191. Capital city of North Holland province, W Netherlands; 7 km/4 ml from the North Sea coast, on the R Spaarne; part of the Randstad conurbation; founded, 10th-c; charter, 1245; sacked by the Spaniards (1573); railway; centre for tulip, hyacinth, and crocus bulbs; chemicals, publishing and printing, shipyards, railway works, machines, food processing; town hall (13th–17th-c), Grote Kerk (1472), Frans Hals museum. » Netherlands, The [i] Ranstad

Habakkuk or **Habacuc, Book of** [**ha**bakuhk] One of the twelve so-called 'minor' prophetic books of the Hebrew Bible/Old Testament, attributed to the otherwise unknown prophet Habakkuk, possibly of the late 7th-c BC. It consists of two dialogues about why God allows the godless to 'surround' the righteous (Israel), with the response that 'the just shall live by his faith' (*Hab* 2.4; *Rom* 1.17; *Gal* 3.11). The final prayer celebrates God's coming in victory over his enemies. » Old Testament; prophet

habeas corpus A writ requiring a person who detains another to appear in court and justify that detention. If there is no good reason for the detention, release is ordered. The writ can be obtained whether the detainee is held by the state or privately. In England and Wales it is issued by the Divisional Court of the Queens Bench Division (or, in the vacation, by a High Court judge). The expression is not used in Scottish law. » Divisional Court; High Court of Justice

Haber, Fritz [**hah**buh] (1868–1934) German chemist, born at Breslau. Professor of chemistry at Karlsruhe and Berlin, he became known for his invention of the process for making ammonia from the nitrogen in the air. He was awarded the Nobel Prize for Chemistry in 1918, and died in Basle, Switzerland. » Born-Haber cycle; Haber-Bosch process

Haber-Bosch process [**hah**buh **bosh**] A chemical process developed in the early 20th-c for making ammonia from the nitrogen of the atmosphere. It is one of the most important chemical processes ever devised, because it makes possible the fixation of atmospheric nitrogen and therefore, by conversion of the ammonia to nitric acid, the production of nitrates needed for fertilizers (and explosives). Fritz Haber showed theoretically and experimentally how to maintain the reaction between nitrogen from air and hydrogen from water at suitable temperature and pressure, and with effective catalysts. Carl Bosch showed how to operate the process on an industrial scale. The overall reaction is $3H_2 + N_2 \rightarrow 2NH_3$. » ammonia; Bosch; fertilizers; Haber; nitrogen

Habermas, Jürgen [**ha**bermas] (1929–) German philosopher and social theorist, born in Düsseldorf. Educated at Göttingen and Bonn, he taught at Heidelberg (1962) and Frankfurt (1964), and became director of the Max Planck Institute (1971). His books include *Erkenntnis und Interesse* (1968, Knowledge and Human Interests) and *Theorie des kommunikatives Handelns* (1982, Theory of Communicative Action).

Habima A theatre company formed in Moscow, after the Revolution, to stage plays in Hebrew. It became one of the studios of the Moscow Art Theatre and toured extensively. The company moved to Palestine in 1931, and in 1953 became Israel's National Theatre. » Moscow Art Theatre

habitat loss The loss of distinctive areas which provide breeding and range territories for plants and wildlife. Destruction and disturbance by human activity is a major threat to wild species. Many areas of wilderness have been modified into artificial landscapes of settlement, agriculture, and industry. There is increased intrusion into remote areas for exploitation of timber, oil, and mineral resources. » conservation (earth sciences); endangered species

habituation The weakening or disappearance of an individual's initial spontaneous reaction to a stimulus (eg alertness, defence, attack) as a result of the stimulus occurring repeatedly without any interesting consequences. Changes in the form or consequences of the stimulus may cause the habituated response to reappear. » learning

Habsburgs One of the principal dynasties of modern Europe, pre-eminent in Germany from the mediaeval period as sovereign rulers of Austria, from which the family extended its territories and influence to secure the title of Holy Roman Emperor (1452–1806). The zenith of Habsburg power was reached under Charles V (1500–58), who presided over an empire stretching from the Danube to the Caribbean. After Charles's retirement (1556) his inheritance was divided between his son and brother, thus creating the *Spanish* Habsburg line, rulers of Spain until 1700, and the *Austrian* Habsburgs, whose descendants retained the imperial title and ruled the Habsburg possessions in C Europe until 1918. » Charles V (Emperor); Holy Roman Empire; Pragmatic Sanction

hacker A computer user who communicates with other remote computers usually via the telephone network. In recent years, the term has acquired a pejorative sense, referring to those who access remote computers without permission, often obtaining access to confidential information of a personal or business nature. The position of the hacker in law is unclear. » computer

hackney horse An English breed of horse; height, 14¾–16 hands/1.5–1.6 m/5–5¼ ft; graceful and spirited, with an emphasized strutting step; black or brown with tail held high. There is also a **hackney pony** (**bantam hackney** in USA), bred to pull carriages. » horse [i]

haddock Bottom-living fish widespread in cold N waters of the Atlantic; length up to c.80 cm/32 in; body dark greenish brown on back, sides silvery grey with dark patch above pectoral fins, underside white, lateral line black; feeds mainly on molluscs, worms, and echinoderms; exploited commercially throughout the N Atlantic. Exceptionally high stock in the 1960s and 1970s was followed by a decrease in the 1980s, which led to quotas being imposed for catches under the Common Fisheries Policy in 1983. (*Melanogrammus aeglefinus*. Family: *Gadidae*.)

Hades [**hay**deez] In Greek mythology, the king of the Underworld, terrible but just; he was responsible for the seizure of Persephone. To the Greeks, Hades was always a person, never a place, but by transference the Underworld – 'the house of Hades' – became known by that name (which means 'the unseen'). It is located below the Earth or in the far West; there the shades or feeble spirits of the dead continue to exist. » Persephone; Pluto (mythology)

Hadith [ha**deeth**] Islamic tradition on a variety of subjects, traced to the prophet Mohammed or one of his companions. It provides guidance for Muslims on all aspects of life, and is second in authority to the Koran. The teachings are prefaced by a chain of authorities through whom the tradition is said to have been transmitted and validated. » Islam; Koran

Hadlee, Sir Richard (John) (1948–) New Zealand cricketer, born at Christchurch, his country's best all-round cricketer. He scored more then 2 800 Test runs since making his debut in 1973. He started his first-class career with Canterbury in 1971–72, and has also played for Nottinghamshire and Tasmania. In 1988 he surpassed Ian Botham's record of 373 Test wickets. A right-arm fast bowler, he bats left-handed. He was knighted in 1990. » Botham; cricket (sport) [i]

Hadrian IV (Pope) » **Adrian IV**

Hadrian, properly **Publius Aelius Hadrianus** (76–138) Roman emperor (117–38), ward, protégé, and successor of the Emperor Trajan, a fellow Spaniard and relation by marriage. Coming to power in ambiguous circumstances, Hadrian was always unpopular at Rome, and even the object of a serious conspiracy there (118). He spent little of his reign at Rome, but tirelessly toured the empire, consolidating the frontiers (as in Britain, where he initiated the building of the wall named after him), visiting the provinces, and promoting urban life. » Britain, Roman; Hadrian's Wall; Trajan

Hadrian's Wall The principal N frontier of the Roman province of Britain. Built AD 122–8 on the orders of the Emperor Hadrian (117–138) and possibly inspired by travellers' accounts of the Great Wall of China, it runs 117 km/73 ml from Solway Firth to the R Tyne, the wall itself 4.5 m/15 ft high (probably with a 2 m/6 ft timber parapet), its forward defensive ditch c.8.5 m/28 ft wide and 3 m/10 ft deep. Sixteen forts (the best preserved at Housesteads and Chesters) were supplemented by 80 milecastles and numerous signal turrets. Overrun by Picts and N tribes in AD 139 and again in 367, the Wall was finally abandoned c.400–410. It is now a world heritage site. » Antonine Wall; Britain, Roman; Great Wall of China; Hadrian; Picts

hadron In particle physics, a collective term for all particles which experience strong interactions. All baryons and mesons are hadrons (eg protons and pions). » baryon; meson

hadrosaur [**had**rohsaw] A duck-billed dinosaur; front of snout flattened and expanded to form duck-like bill; dentition specialized, with several rows of teeth; fed on tough plant material; widely distributed during the Cretaceous period; probably organized into social groups, with nurseries for nest protection. (Order: *Ornithischia*.) » Cretaceous period; dinosaur [i]; Ornithischia

Haeckel, Ernst (Heinrich Philipp August) [**hay**kuhl] (1834–1919) German naturalist, born at Potsdam. Educated at Würzburg, Berlin, and Vienna, he became professor of zoology at Jena (1862–1909). One of the first to sketch the genealogical tree of animals, he strongly supported Darwin's theories of evolution. He died at Jena. » Darwin, Charles

haematemesis/hematemesis [heematuh**mee**sis] Vomiting of blood or of blood-stained vomitus. It indicates bleeding in the oesophagus, stomach, or upper gastro-intestinal tract, and usually results from ulceration of the lining of the gastro-intestinal tract or tumour growth. » alimentary canal

haematite/hematite A mineral iron oxide (Fe_2O_3), the most important ore of iron. It often occurs as dark-brown nodules (*kidney ore*). Powdered haematite is used as a pigment (red ochre). » iron

haematology/hemotology [heemuh**tol**uhjee] The study of the formation and function of the cells which circulate in the blood stream and reside in the bone marrow and lymph nodes, and of the abnormalities that cause diseases. » blood; medicine

haematuria/hematuria [heema**tyoo**ria] Passage of blood in the urine. Severe haematuria gives rise to obviously red urine; lesser degrees may be detected only by chemical tests of the urine or by its examination by microscope. It indicates disease somewhere in the urinary tract, including the kidneys. » urine

haemodialysis » **dialysis**

haemoglobin/hemoglobin A widely occurring red-coloured protein, found for example in some protozoa, many invertebrates, vertebrates, certain yeasts, and plants of the *Leguminosae* family. In vertebrates it is the oxygen-carrying pigment present in red blood cells (*erythrocytes*). When bound to oxygen it appears scarlet, while in the absence of oxygen it is dark-blue. Haemoglobin shows species differences in its structure, molecular weight, and affinity for oxygen. It consists of an iron-containing element (the *haem*) which combines reversibly with oxygen, and polypeptide (*globin*) chains. Variations in the position or type of amino acids in the polypeptide chains give different forms of haemoglobin, which may have different affinities for oxygen (eg human foetal haemoglobin). » erythrocytes; peptide; sickle cell disease; thalassaemia

haemophilia/hemophilia [heemuh**fil**ia] An inherited disorder of blood coagulation, resulting from a deficiency in one of the proteins responsible for normal blood clotting. This is the antihaemophilic factor (AHF, or factor VIII), which is normally produced by the liver and circulates in the blood. The gene responsible is X-linked, so the condition is transmitted by the mother and reveals itself in the sons. There is a 50% chance of a mother carrying the disease transmitting it to her sons, and a 50% chance of her daughter becoming a carrier. It causes recurrent bleeding after minor trauma, mainly into joints. Damaged joints result in deformity and crippling. Bleeding can be ameliorated by giving fresh plasma which contains Factor VIII, or by giving a concentrate of the factor prepared from freshly donated blood. » AIDS; blood; blood products; genetically determined disease

haemoptysis/hemoptysis [hi**mop**tisis] Coughing up blood or blood-stained sputum. It usually indicates underlying lung disease, such as tuberculosis or cancer, but also occcurs in embolism and some forms of heart disease. » cancer; heart disease; tuberculosis

haemorrhage/hemorrhage Loss of blood externally or internally from any size of blood vessel. It is caused by injury to a blood vessel, or by a defect in normal blood clotting, as in haemophilia. Damage to the blood vessel may be the result of trauma, infection, or disease. Arterial bleeding is pulsatile and appears in spurts; it is usually the most severe, as the arterial blood pressure is higher than that within veins or capillaries, and excessive loss of blood may lead to shock or death. Venous and capillary bleeding often induces a slower ooze of blood from the skin or between planes of tissues. » blood vessels [i]; haemophilia

haemorrhoids/hemorrhoids A cluster of distended veins at the junction of the rectum and the anal canal, 2–3 cm/¾–⅞ in above the opening of the anus; also known as **piles**. Usually there is no detectable cause, but they may occur as a result of blockage to the passage of blood draining the intestines, as in cirrhosis of the liver. They are also associated with constipation, and sometimes develop during pregnancy, when the uterus slows the passage of blood draining the pelvic organs. Anaemia may develop from slow but persistent loss of blood. Haemorrhoids can be removed surgically when large and giving discomfort; otherwise they may be treated by injections of a sclerosing solution. » rectum

haemostasis/hemostasis [heemoh**stay**sis] The spontaneous arrest of bleeding from a damaged vessel, involving a series of interrelated events. The vessel constricts to reduce blood flow and loss. A platelet plug forms to seal the vessel wall and to release *vasoconstrictor* substances, which further reduce blood flow and initiate coagulation. The blood coagulates (soluble plasma protein fibrinogen is converted to insoluble fibrin) by a series of enzymatic reactions involving several factors present in blood and tissues. The resulting meshwork traps blood cells to form a clot, which strengthens the platelet plug formed earlier. Deficiencies or defects in any of these factors can lead to bleeding disorders (eg haemophilia). » blood; haemophilia; platelets

Haerbin or **Haerhpin** » **Harbin**

Hafiz or **Hafez**, pseudonym of **Shams ed-Din Mohammad** (c.1326–c.1390) Persian lyrical poet, born at Shiraz. He worked as a religious teacher and wrote commentaries on sacred texts. A member of the mystical sect of Sufi philosophers, his short poems (*ghazals*), all on sensuous subjects, such as love, wine, and flowers, contain an esoteric signification to the initiated. He died at Shiraz. » Persian literature; poetry; Sufism

Haganah [haga**hna**] The Jewish underground militia in Palestine, founded during the period of the British Mandate in the 1920s. After the declaration of the State of Israel in 1948, the Haganah became the official Israeli army, fielding some 100 000 troops during the war of that year. » Israel [i]

Hagar [**hay**gah] Biblical character, the maid of Sarah (the wife of

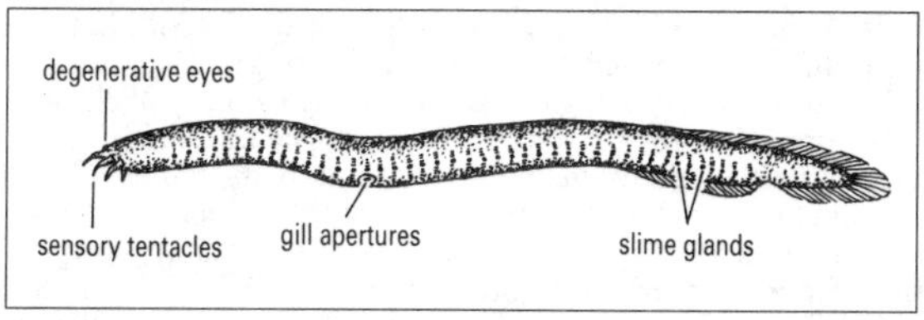

Hagfish

Abraham). Due to Sarah's barrenness, Abraham had a son Ishmael by Hagar (*Gen* 16), but Hagar and her son were later expelled into the wilderness by Abraham after Isaac's birth (*Gen* 21). » Abraham; Bible; Isaac; Ishmael; Sarah

Hagen [**hah**gn] 51°22N 7°27E, pop (1983) 212 500. Industrial city in Freiburg district, Germany; 48 km/30 ml ENE of Düsseldorf; at junction of important traffic routes; railway; household goods, ironworking, accumulators, foodstuffs, textiles, paper; Westphalian Open-Air Museum of Technology. » Germany [i]

Hagen, Walter (Charles) [**hay**guhn], byname **The Haig** (1892–1969) US golfer, born at Rochester, New York. The first US-born winner of the British Open, he won the title four times (1922, 1924, 1928–9), the US Open twice (1914, 1919), the US Professional Golfers' Association Championship a record five times (1921, 1924–7), and captained the first six US Ryder Cup teams (1927–37). He died at Traverse City, Michigan. » golf

hagfish Primitive marine fish lacking true jaws, vertebrae, paired fins, and scales; includes *Myxine glutinosa*, widespread in the N Atlantic and Arctic; body eel-like, covered in copius slime, length up to 60 cm/2 ft; mouth slit-like surrounded by stout barbels; burrows in soft mud, feeding off invertebrates and fish. (Family: *Myxinidae*, 3 genera.)

Haggai, Book of [**hag**iy] One of the twelve so-called 'minor' prophetic books of the Hebrew Bible/Old Testament, attributed to the prophet Haggai, a contemporary of Zechariah, both of whom supported the rebuilding of the Temple in Jerusalem in c.520 BC after the return from exile. It consists of exhortations to the governor and high priest in Judea to pursue the rebuilding of the Temple, and to purify the Temple cult as preparations for God's new kingdom. » Old Testament; Temple, Jerusalem; Zechariah, Book of

Haggard, Sir H(enry) Rider (1856–1925) British novelist, born at Bradenham Hall, Norfolk. Educated at Ipswich, he travelled widely in government service in South Africa, before taking up a literary life in England in 1881. *King Solomon's Mines* (1885) made his work known, and was followed by *She* (1887) and several other stories. He was knighted in 1912. » English literature; novel

haggis A traditional Scottish dish comprising the minced heart, liver, and lungs of a sheep, as well as suet, oatmeal, and various seasonings. The ingredients are cooked in a bag made from the rumen or forestomach of a sheep.

Hagia Sophia [**hah**ja soh**fee**a] or **Santa Sophia** A masterpiece of Byzantine architecture built (532–7) at Constantinople (now Istanbul). The lavishly-decorated, domed basilica was commissioned by Emperor Justinian I and designed by Anthemius of Tralles and Isidore of Miletus. The Ottoman Turks, who took Constantinople in 1453, converted it into a mosque. Since 1935 it has been a museum. » Istanbul; Justinian; museum

Hague, The, Dutch **'s-Gravenhage** or **Den Haag** 52°05N 4°16E, pop (1984e) 672 127. Capital city of South Holland province, W Netherlands, and seat of the Dutch government; 3 km/1¾ ml from the North Sea; third largest city in the Netherlands, part of the Randstad conurbation; meeting-place of the States-General, 1527; centre of European diplomacy from 17th-c; Hague Convention (1907) formulated much of the law governing international warfare; a cultural, administrative, and political city; ministries, embassies, and headquarters of several international organizations, including the International Court of Justice and the Permanent Court of Arbitration; railway; noted for its furniture, pottery, and silverware; textiles, electronic equipment, hardware, furniture, printing, rubber, pharmaceuticals, cigarettes, car parts, food processing; home of many Dutch painters; 13th-c Gothic Hall of the Knights, Palace of Peace (1913), Nieuwe Kerk (1641), royal residence 'House in the Wood' (1647), town hall (16th-c); seaside resort of Scheveningen nearby. » International Court of Justice; Netherlands, The [i]; Randstad

Hague Agreement A convention of 1899 for the Pacific Settlement of International Disputes. It established a Permanent Court of Arbitration – the forerunner of the World Court. » International Court of Justice

Hague Peace Conferences Two conferences at The Hague, Netherlands, in 1899 and 1907. The first met to discuss the limitation of armaments, but the 26 countries represented made little progress. A permanent court of arbitration was set up for states in dispute wishing to use its services. The second produced a series of conventions to try to limit the horrors of war.

Hahn, Otto (1879–1968) German physical chemist, born in Frankfurt. He lectured in Berlin from 1907, becoming director of the Kaiser-Wilhelm Institute there in 1927. With Meitner he discovered the radioactive protactinium (1917), and in 1938 bombarded uranium with neutrons to find the first chemical evidence of nuclear fission products. He was awarded the Nobel Prize for Chemistry in 1944, and died in Göttingen. » Meitner; nuclear fission

Hahnemann, (Christian Friedrich) Samuel (1755–1843) German physician and founder of homeopathy, born at Meissen. He studied at Leipzig, and for ten years practised medicine. He experimented on the curative power of bark, concluding that medicine produces a similar condition in healthy persons to that which it relieves in the sick. His methods caused him to be prosecuted wherever he tried to settle. He taught again in Leipzig (1810–21), but was driven out, retired to Köthen, and in 1835 moved to Paris, where he pursued a very lucrative practice, and where he died. » homeopathy

Haida [**hiy**duh] A Pacific Northwest Coast American Indian group in Queen Charlotte I, British Columbia, famous for their wood carvings, totem poles, and canoes. They traditionally lived by fishing and hunting, and held potlatch ceremonies, distributing ceremonial goods. Population (including the Tlingit) c.7 500. » American/Northwest Coast Indians; potlatch; Tlingit

Haidar Ali or **Hyder Ali** [**hiy**der **ah**lee] (1722–82) Indian Muslim ruler of Mysore, born at Budikote, Mysore. Having conquered Calicut and fought the Marathas, he waged two wars against the British, in the first of which (1767–9) he won several gains. In 1779 he and his son, Tippoo, again attacked the British, initially with great success; but in 1781–2 he was defeated. He died at Chittoor. » Tippoo Sahib

Haifa or **Hefa** [**hiy**fa] 32°49N 34°59E, pop (1982) 226 100. Industrial centre and seaport in Haifa dist, NW Israel; third largest city in Israel; airfield; railway; university (1963); oil, agricultural produce, steel, shipbuilding, chemicals, textiles; Bahai Shrine, Persian Gardens. » Israel [i]

Haig, Alexander (Meigs) (1924–) US army officer and statesman, born in Philadelphia. Educated at West Point and Georgetown, he held a number of staff and field positions, serving in the Vietnam War. A full general by 1973, he then retired from the army to become White House Chief of Staff during the last days of the Nixon presidency. Returning to active duty, he became supreme NATO commander before returning again to civilian life, as president of United Technologies Corporation. He served President Reagan as Secretary of State in 1981–2, and sought the Republican nomination for the presidency in 1988. » Nixon, Richard M; Reagan, Ronald; Republican Party

Haig, Douglas, 1st Earl Haig of Bemersyde (1861–1928) British field marshal, born in Edinburgh, Scotland. Educated at Clifton, Oxford, and Sandhurst, he obtained a commission in the 7th Hussars, and served in Egypt, South Africa, and India. In 1914 he led the 1st Army Corps in France, and in 1915 became Commander of the British Expeditionary Force. He waged a costly and exhausting war of attrition, for which he was much criticized, but led the final successful offensive (Aug 1918). In postwar years he devoted himself to the care of ex-servicemen, organizing the Royal British Legion. His earldom was awarded in 1919, and he died in London. » British Expeditionary Force; World War 1

haiku [**hiy**koo] A Japanese poetic miniature, consisting of three lines of 5, 7, and 5 syllables. (The classic *tanka* has two further lines of 7 syllables.) This highly concentrated form has proved very popular outside Japan, and influenced among others the Imagists. » Imagism; Japanese literature; metre (literature); poetry

hail A form of precipitation comprising small balls or pieces of ice, which may reach up to 50 mm/2 in in diameter. It is generally associated with rapidly rising convection currents in low latitudes, or the passage of a cold front in temperate latitudes. Hail storms can cause considerable damage to crops and property. » cold front; convective rain; precipitation

Hail Mary (Lat *Ave Maria*) A prayer to the Virgin Mary, also known as the **Angelic Salutation**, used devotionally since the 11th-c in the Roman Catholic Church, and finally officially recognized in 1568. The first two parts are quotations from scripture (*Luke* 1.28, 42), the third part being added later. In its Latin form, it is often sung in Roman Catholic ceremonies, and has received many famous musical settings. » Mary (mother of Jesus); liturgy; rosary

Haile Selassie I, [**hiy**li silasee] originally **Prince Ras Tafari Makonnen** (1891–1975) Emperor of Ethiopia (1930–6, 1941–74), born near Harer, Ethiopia. He led the revolution in 1916 against Lij Yasu, and became Regent and heir to the throne, westernizing the institutions of his country. He settled in England after the Italian conquest of Abyssinia (1935–6), but in 1941 was restored after British liberation. In the early 1960s he helped to establish the Organization of African Unity. The disastrous famine of 1973 led to economic chaos, industrial strikes, and mutiny among the armed forces, and he was deposed (1974) in favour of the Crown Prince. Accusations of corruption levelled at him and his family have not destroyed the reverence in which he is held by certain groups, notably the Rastafarians. » Ethiopia [i]; Organization of African Unity; Rastafarianism

Hailsham, Quintin (McGarel) Hogg, 2nd Viscount (1907–) British Conservative politician, born in London. Educated at Eton and Oxford, he was called to the Bar (1932), and became an MP (1938). He succeeded to his title in 1950, and was First Lord of the Admiralty (1956–7), Minister of Education (1957), Lord President of the Council (1957–9, 1960–4), Chairman of the Conservative Party (1957–9), Minister for Science and Technology (1959–64), and Secretary of State for Education and Science (1964). In 1963 he renounced his peerage and re-entered the House of Commons in an unsuccessful bid to become Leader of the Conservative Party. In 1970 he was created a life peer (Baron Hailsham of Saint Marylebone) and became Lord Chancellor (1970–4), a post he held again from 1979 until his retirement in 1987. » Conservative Party

Hailwood, Mike, properly **(Stanley) Michael (Bailey)** (1940–81) British motorcyclist, born at Oxford. He took nine world titles: the 250 cc in 1961 and 1966–7, the 350 cc in 1966–7, and the 500 cc in 1962–5, all using Honda or MV Agusta machines. In addition, he won a record 14 Isle of Man Tourist Trophy races between 1961 and 1979, and during the 1960s he also had a career in motor racing. His awards included the George Medal. He was killed in a car accident near his Birmingham home. » motor racing; motorcycle racing

Hainan Island [**hiy**nan] area 34 000 sq km/13 000 sq ml. Island off S coast of China, a prefecture of Guangdong province, separated from mainland by Hainan Strait; rises to 1 879 m/6 165 ft at Wuzhi Shan; airport at Haikou; opened to tourism and foreign trade in 1982; rubber, coconut, sugar, coffee, cocoa, betel nut, pineapple, fishing; reserves of many minerals, including limestone, marble, quartz, china clay, iron ore; principal cities Haikou, Dongfang, and resort port of Yulin. » China [i]

Haiphong [hiy**fong**] 20°50N 106°41E, pop (1979e) 1 279 667. Seaport in N Vietnam; in the Red R delta, 88 km/55 ml SE of Hanoi; founded, 1874; badly bombed in Vietnam War; third largest city in Vietnam; rail link to Kunming, China; plastics, textiles, phosphates, rice. » Vietnam [i]

hair A thread-like structure consisting of dead keratinized cells produced by the epidermis in mammalian skin. The root of the hair below the skin surface is contained in a hair follicle, which is responsible for producing the hair. The covering of hair in mammals helps to maintain constant body temperature by insulating the body. Some hairs, such as whiskers, have a specialized sensory function. » baldness; keratin; skin [i]

hair fibres Animal fibre other than that derived from sheep. Often such fibres are identified with the animal from which they are obtained, eg mohair from the Angora goat. » fibres

hair seal » **common seal**

hairstreak An inconspicuous butterfly; wings typically blackish-brown, often with coloured patches; wingspan up to 40 mm/1½ in. The name is applied to several different species of the family *Lycaenidae*. (Order: *Lepidoptera*.) » butterfly

hairy frog An African frog of the family *Hyperoliidae*; lives almost entirely in water. During the breeding season the male has hair-like projections from the skin on the sides of the body and tops of the legs. (*Trichobatrachus robustus*.) » frog

Haiti [**hay**tee], official name **Republic of Haiti**, Fr **République d'Haiti** pop (1990e) 5 862 000; area 27 750 sq km/10 712 sq ml. Republic in the West Indies, occupying the W third of the island of Hispaniola, 80 km/50 ml E of Cuba; divided into five departments; capital, Port-au-Prince; chief towns, Port-de-Paix, Cap-Haïtien, Gonaïves, Les Cayes; timezone GMT −5; population mainly of African descent (95%); chief religions, Roman Catholicism, voodoo; official language, French, with Creole French widely spoken; unit of currency, the gourde of 100 centimes; consists of two mountainous peninsulas (Massif du Nord (N) and Massif de la Hotte (S)), separated by a deep structural depression, the Plaine du Cul-de-Sac; to the E, Massif de la Selle, with Haiti's highest peak, La Selle (2 680 m/8 793 ft); includes islands of Gonâve (W) and Tortue (N); tropical maritime climate; mean monthly temperatures range from 24°C to 29°C; annual average rainfall for N coast and mountains, 1 475–1 950 mm/58–77 in, but only 500 mm/20 in on W side; wet season (May–Sep); hurricanes common; Hispaniola visited by Columbus, 1492; Haiti created when W third of island ceded to France (1697); slave rebellion followed by independence, 1804; united with Santo Domingo (Dominican Republic), 1822–44; under US occupation, 1915–34; Duvalier family had absolute power, 1957–86; after 1986 coup, new constitution provided for a bicameral assembly of a 27-member Senate and 77-member Chamber of Deputies elected for 5-year terms, led by a president and prime minister; economy based on agriculture; large plantations grow coffee,

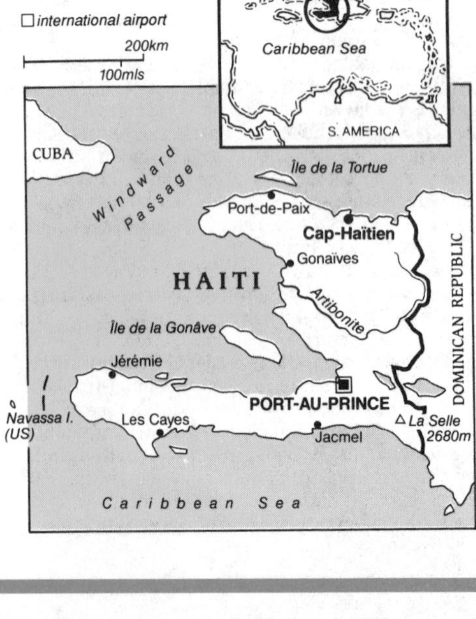

sugar, sisal; rice, bananas, corn, sorghum, cocoa; sugar refining, textiles, flour milling, cement, bauxite, tourism, light assembly industries. » Duvalier; Hispaniola; Port-au-Prince; Toussaint L'Ouverture; RR25 national holidays; RR51 political leaders

Haitink, Bernard [**hiy**tingk] (1929–) Dutch conductor, born in Amsterdam. He studied at the Amsterdam Conservatory, and was an orchestral violinist before becoming second conductor of the Netherlands Radio Union (1955). He was later conductor of the Amsterdam Concertgebouw Orchestra (from 1961) and of the London Philharmonic (1967–79), and was appointed musical director at Glyndebourne in 1977 (the year he was granted an honorary knighthood) and at Covent Garden in 1987.

Hajj [haj] A formal pilgrimage to the holy city of Mecca during the Islamic month of Dhu-ul-Hijja. It is one of the Five Pillars of Islam. » Islam; Mecca

hake Commercially important cod-like fish widely distributed in offshore continental shelf waters of temperate seas; includes the European *Merluccius merluccius*, length up to c.1 m/3¼ ft, head and jaws large, teeth strong; blue-grey on back, underside silvery white; feeds mainly on fish and squid. (Genus: *Merluccius*. Family: *Merlucciidae*.) » cod

Hakka A people from N China who settled in S China in the 12th–13th-c and remained unassimilated. During the 18th–19th-c they were involved in feuds over land, and many eventually migrated to other areas, including Taiwan, Hongkong, Indonesia, Malaysia, and Singapore. » China [i]; Han

Hakluyt, Richard [**hak**loot] (c.1552–1616) English geographer, born in Hertfordshire. He was educated at Westminster and Oxford, where he lectured in geography, and was ordained some time before 1580. He wrote widely on exploration and navigation, notably his *Principal Navigations, Voyages, and Discoveries of the English Nation* (1598–1600). He also introduced the use of globes into English schools. Made a prebendary of Westminster in 1602, he is buried in Westminster Abbey. The *Hakluyt Society* was instituted in 1846.

Hal Saflieni Hypogeum [hal saf**lye**nee hiypuh**jee**uhm] A vast prehistoric rock-cut catacomb for multiple burial in Paola, SE Malta; a world heritage site. The excavation, which was in use throughout the Copper Age, consists of three layers of tomb-chambers dug into a mound of soft limestone and linked by halls and corridors. It was discovered in 1902. » Malta [i]; Three Age System

Halakhah [**ha**lakah] The subject matter contained in the Talmudic and Rabbinic literature of Judaism dealing with the laws governing religious or civil practice in the community. It is distinguished from the **Haggadah**, which is not concerned with religious law, and includes such material as parables, fables, sagas, and prayers. » Judaism; midrash; Talmud

halation The spread of the photographic image of a bright object, caused by light scattered in the emulsion and reflected from the rear surface of the base. In some films, this surface is coated with a thin black 'anti-halation' layer to reduce the effect. » photography

Halcyone or **Alcyone** [hal**siy**onee] In Greek mythology, **1** A daughter of Aeolus, who married Ceyx, son of the Morning Star. Either for impiety, or because she mourned his death at sea, both were changed into sea-birds – halcyons, or kingfishers – who are fabled to calm the sea. **2** One of the Pleiades. » Pleiades (mythology)

Haldane, J(ohn) B(urdon) S(anderson) (1892–1964) British biologist and geneticist, born at Oxford, the son of John Scott Haldane. Educated at Eton and Oxford, he became reader in biochemistry at Cambridge (1922–32), and professor of genetics (1933–57) and of biometry (1937–57) at London. He then emigrated to India, adopting Indian nationality, and worked at Calcutta and Orissa. He wrote widely on his subject, and was well known for his popularizations. He was also chairman of the editorial board of the *Daily Worker* (1940–9), but left the British Communist Party in 1956. He died at Bhubaneswar, India. » Haldane, John Scott

Haldane, John Scott (1860–1936) British physiologist, born in Edinburgh, Scotland. A fellow of New College, Oxford, he made a study of the effects of industrial occupations upon human physiology, especially respiration, and served as director of a mining research laboratory at Birmingham. He died at Oxford. » Haldane, J B S; physiology

Hale, George Ellery (1868–1938) US astronomer, born in Chicago, who discovered magnetic fields within sunspots. He was director of Yerkes Observatory (1897–1905) until he moved to Mount Wilson, where he initiated the construction of some of the world's largest telescopes. He was also responsible for the 5 m Palomar telescope. He died at Pasadena, California.

Haleakala Crater [halayaka**la**] or **Kolekole** 20°42N 156°16W. Dormant volcano in E Maui I, Hawaii, USA; rises to 3 055 m/10 023 ft; contains the largest inactive crater in the world: area 49 sq km/19 sq ml; depth 600 m/2000 ft, length 12 km/7½ ml, width 3.8 km/2.4 ml, circumference 32 km/20 ml; in Haleakala National Park. » Hawaii (state); volcano

Halévy, (Jacques François) Fromental (Elie) (1799–1862) French composer, born in Paris. He studied in Paris, and won the Prix de Rome in 1819. His first successful opera was *Clari* (1828), but he is best known for *La Juive* (1835), which established his reputation. Bizet and Gounod studied under him. He died in Nice.

Haley, Bill, properly **William** (1927–1981) US popular singer and musician, who with his group *The Comets* popularized rock-and-roll in the 1950s. His most famous song, 'Rock Around the Clock', was used in the film *Blackboard Jungle* (1955). » rock music

half-life In radioactivity, the time taken for a group of atoms to decay to half their original number; symbol $T_{1/2}$, units s (second), also minutes and years. It varies from seconds to thousands of years. The half-life of plutonium-239 is 24 000 years; for helium-6 it is 0.8 seconds. The term also applies to the decay of excited atoms by the emission of light. » atom; mean life; radioactivity

half-marathon » marathon

halibut Largest of the Atlantic flatfishes, found on sandy and stony bottoms (100–1 500 m/300–5 000 ft) in cold N waters; length up to 2.5 m/8 ft; eyes on right side, mouth and teeth large; brown to greenish brown with white underside; commercially important and prized by sea anglers. (*Hippoglossus hippoglossus*; family: *Pleuronectidae*.) » flatfish

Halicarnassus [haleekah**nas**us] A Greek city-state founded by the Dorians on the coast of SW Asia Minor; modern Bodrum, Turkey. It was the birth-place of Herodotus, and the site of the Tomb of Mausolus. » Dorians; Herodotus; Mausolus, Tomb of; polis

Halifax, Charles Montagu, 1st Earl of (1661–1715) English Whig statesman, born at Horton, Northamptonshire. Educated at Westminster and Cambridge, he became MP for Maldon (1688) and a Lord of the Treasury (1692), establishing the National Debt and the Bank of England (1694). As Chancellor of the Exchequer (1694–5), he introduced a new coinage. In 1697 he was First Lord of the Treasury and Leader of the House of Commons, but resigned when the Tories came to power in 1699, and became Baron Halifax. On Queen Anne's death he was made a member of the Council of Regency, and on George I's arrival (1714) became an earl and Prime Minister. He was also a patron of letters, and a poet. He died in London. » Bank of England; Tories; Whigs

Halifax, George Savile, 1st Marquis of (1633–95) English statesman, born at Thornhill, Yorkshire. He was created viscount (1668) for his share in the Restoration, and in 1672 was made a marquis and Lord Privy Seal. On the accession of James II (1685) he became President of the Council, but was dismissed soon after. He was one of the three Commissioners appointed to treat with William of Orange after he landed in England (1688). He gave allegiance to William and resumed the office of Lord Privy Seal; but, joining the Opposition, resigned his post in 1689. He died in London. » James II (of England); William III

Halifax 44°38N 63°35W, pop (1981) 114 594. Seaport capital of Nova Scotia province, SE Canada; major transatlantic port and rail terminus; joined to Dartmouth by two suspension bridges; founded in 1749 as a British military and naval base, used in the American Revolution and the War of 1812; naval base and convoy terminal in both World Wars; scene of harbour disasters, 1917, 1945; victims of the *Titanic* disaster buried here, 1912; airport; four universities (1789, 1802, 1818, 1925); shipbuilding, clothing, furniture, food processing, trade in fish and timber; Historic Properties area, including Privateers' Warehouse; Citadel Hill (height 82 m/269 ft), a National Historic Park, cannon fired daily at noon; Maritime Museum of the Atlantic. » Nova Scotia

halite [**hal**iyt] The mineral form of sodium chloride (NaCl); also known as *rock salt*.

Hall, Sir Peter (Reginald Frederick) (1930–) British theatre, opera, and film director, born at Bury St Edmunds, Suffolk. He was educated at the Perse School and Cambridge, where he produced and acted in more than 20 plays. After working in repertory and for the Arts Council, he became artistic director of the Elizabethan Theatre Company (1953), director (1955–6) of the London Arts Theatre, and formed his own company, The International Playwrights' Theatre (1957). After several productions at Stratford, he became director of the Royal Shakespeare Company, and remained as managing director of the company's theatres in Stratford and London until 1968. He was also director of the Covent Garden Opera (1969–71), and became successor to Olivier as director of the National Theatre (1973–88). He was knighted in 1977. » Olivier; theatre

hall church A form of church with nave and aisles of approximately equal height, and without transepts or a distinct chancel. It first developed in 11th-c Germany. » chancel; church [i]; nave; transept

Hall effect The deflection of the carriers of charge in a conductor, caused by an externally applied magnetic field; described in 1879 by US physicist Edwin Hall (1855–1938). A potential difference forms at right angles to both current and field. It may be used to demonstrate the difference in the nature of the charge carriers in metals and semiconductors. » electrical conduction; magnetic field [i]; quantum Hall effect

Hallé, Sir Charles [**hal**ay] (1819–95) British pianist and conductor, born at Hagen, Westphalia. He studied at Darmstadt and Paris, where his reputation was established by his concerts of classical music. The 1848 revolution drove him to England, and he ultimately settled in Manchester, where in 1858 he founded his famous orchestra. He was knighted in 1888, and died in Manchester.

Halle or **Halle an der Saale** [**hal**uh] 51°29N 12°00E, pop (1982) 233 437. Capital of Halle county, SE Germany; NW of Leipzig, on R Saale; railway; university (1694); Academy of Agricultural Science; birthplace of Handel; mechanical engineering, rolling stock, chemicals, sugar refining. » Germany [i]; Handel

Haller, Albrecht von (1708–77) Swiss anatomist, botanist, physiologist, and poet, born and died at Berne. He began in medical practice in 1729, but in 1736 was called to a chair at Göttingen. There he organized a botanical garden, an anatomical theatre, and an obstetrical school, helped to found the Academy of Sciences, and took an active part in the literary movement. In 1753 he resigned and returned to Berne, where he became a magistrate.

Halles, Les [layz **al**] The former wholesale food-markets and, by association, the district in C Paris in which they were situated for over 700 years. In 1969 the markets were moved to the suburbs, and a multilevel shopping complex (**Forum des Halles**) was constructed on the site.

Halley, Edmond [**haw**lee] (1656–1742) English astronomer and mathematician, born in London. Educated at Oxford, from 1676 he investigated orbits in the Solar System, discovering that some comets pursue elliptical orbits. From this he successfully predicted the return of the comet named after him. He is the father of modern geophysics, on account of his work on trade winds, terrestrial magnetism, and monsoons. He was Astronomer Royal (1720–42), and died at Greenwich, near London. » Halley's comet

Halley's comet [**ha**lee] The most famous of all comets, first recorded in 239 BC, a spectacular periodic comet orbiting the Sun in a retrograde direction with a period of 76 years. It is named for Edmund Halley, who applied to comets Newton's theory of planetary motions and correctly predicted the return of the bright comet of 1531, 1607, and 1682 in the year 1758, sixteen years after his death. Its present-day spectacular appearance is due to the relatively long period and subsequent slow rate at which the volatile content of the nucleus is lost on its relatively close passage (0.59 Astronomical Units) by the Sun. During its 1986 apparition, it was the subject of an intense study by an 'armada' of spacecraft, and by a ground-based International Halley Watch. The spacecraft encounters were at high speed (c.75 km/sec), because of the comet's retrograde motion. The images revealed a nucleus of irregular shape, about 16 × 8km/10 × 5ml. The very dark surface of the nucleus, and the presence of carbon in the comet dust indicate that there are significant quantities of organic molecules in the nucleus: water, carbon monoxide, carbon dioxide, methane, and ammonia ices have been inferred from measurements of the emitted gases. » comet; Giotto project; Halley; Newton, Isaac; Sakigake and Suisei project; VEGA project

hallmarks The official marks struck on all modern and much old English, Scottish, and Irish silver and gold, and since 1975 on platinum. The metal is tested (*assayed*) for standard or quality. Hallmarks date from 1300, when a decree was made that no silver or gold items should leave the smith until they had been assayed and marked with a leopard's head. Each assay office had its own mark.

Hallowe'en The evening of 31 October, when spirits of the dead are supposed to return to their former homes, and witches and demons are thought to be abroad at night. This was the last day of the Celtic and Anglo-Saxon year, and many Hallowe'en customs have their origin in pagan ceremonies. On Hallowe'en, children in some parts of the UK dress up, especially as witches or ghosts, and go from door to door offering short entertainments in return for presents; similarly, in the USA, children go around demanding 'trick or treat' – if no 'treat' or present is forthcoming, a trick or practical joke will be played on the householder. » All Saints' Day

Hallstatt [**hal**shtat] 47°34N 13°39E, pop (1981) 1 500. Small market town in the Salzkammergut of Oberösterreich state, N Austria; on the SW shore of Hallstätter See, 50 km/30 ml SE of Salzburg; known for the **Hallstatt period**, the first phase of the European Iron Age (8th–4th-c BC), characterized by goods from burial tombs nearby; salt mines; lake procession at Corpus Christi. » Austria [i]; Three Age System

hallucination A sensory perception occurring without any stimulation of the sense organ. In its true form the individual is fully awake and the perception is located out of the body. Hallucinations indicate a loss of contact with reality, but they can be a normal phenomenon, such as during grief. This term was introduced in its current form by the French physician Jean Etienne Esquirol (1772–1840).

hallucinogens or **psychotomimetic drugs** Drugs that produce hallucinations, also called **psychedelic drugs**. Many naturally occurring hallucinogens have been used in ancient medicine and in religious ceremonies. Some are widely used (illegally) for

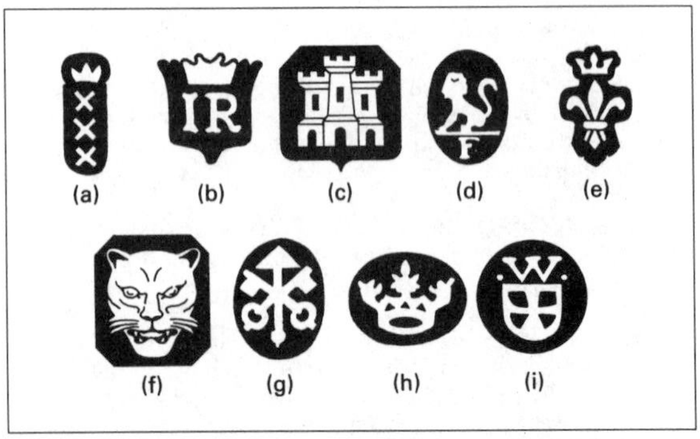

Selection of silver hallmarks – Amsterdam 18th-c (a); Jonathon Reid, Boston USA 1725–1740 (b); Edinburgh (c); Florence 17th–18th-c (d); Lille 1750 (e); London (f); Rome late 17th-c (g); Stockholm 1500–1600 (h); Vienna 1570–1674 (i)

recreational purposes. Their use was particularly prevalent in the 1960s and early 1970s. » angel dust; LSD; magic mushrooms; mescaline

Halmahera [halma**he**ra], formerly **Djailolo** area 17 936 sq km/ 6 923 sq ml, pop (1980) 93 895. Largest island in the Moluccas, Indonesia, on the Equator SW of the Philippines; forested mountain chains, including active volcanoes; taken by the Dutch in 1683; independence, 1949; hunting, fishing, rice, coconuts. » Moluccas

halogens [**hal**uhjnz] The group of the periodic table with seven valence electrons. It comprises fluorine, chlorine, bromine, iodine, and the artificial element astatine. All are characterized by salts in which they appear as ions with a charge of −1. » chemical elements; RR90

Hals, Frans (c.1580–1666) Dutch portrait and genre painter, born probably at Antwerp. Among his best-known works are 'The Laughing Cavalier' (1624, Wallace Collection, London) and 'Gypsy Girl' (c.1628–30, Louvre), and several portraits of militia groups, notable for their lively facial expressions, and bold use of colour. After 1640, his mood became more contemplative and sombre, as in 'Man in a Slouch Hat' (c.1660–6, Kassel). For most of his life, he lived at Haarlem, where he died. » Dutch art; genre painting

Hälsingborg » **Helsingborg**

Ham Biblical character, one of Noah's three sons, the brother of Shem and Japheth, and father of Canaan. He is described as helping Noah to build the ark, but after the Flood his son Canaan is cursed by God for Ham's apparent sin of having seen 'the nakedness of his father' Noah (*Gen* 9.22). This curse may be an attempt to explain the later subjugation of the Canaanites to Israel as resulting from Canaanite sexual perversion. » Bible; Canaan; Flood, the; Noah

hamadryad (mythology) [hama**dri**yad] In Greek mythology, a tree-nymph. The hamadryad was offended or died when the tree containing her was harmed. » dryad

hamadryad (biology) [hama**dri**yad] » **king cobra**

hamadryas baboon [hama**dri**yas] A baboon native to NE Africa and SW Arabia; silver-brown fur (long and thick over male's head and shoulders); naked face; long tail; inhabits rocky hillsides; sacred to ancient Egyptians; also known as **sacred baboon**. (*Papio hamadryas*.) » baboon

Hamburg [**ham**boork] 53°33N 10°00E, pop (1983) 1 617 800. Industrial port, cultural city, and province of Germany; on the R Elbe, 109 km/68 ml from its mouth; area 755 sq km/ 291 sq ml (including islands of Neuwerk and Scharhörn); largest German port; second largest city of Germany; founded by Charlemagne in the 9th-c; formed alliance with Lübeck in the 12th-c, which led to the Hanseatic League; badly bombed in World War 2; railway; university (1919); commerce, shipbuilding, oil, metalworking, electronics, engineering, aircraft, vehicles, packaging, rubber, cosmetics, chemicals, foodstuffs, brewing, cigarettes; birthplace of Brahms and Mendelssohn; town hall (1886–97), St Michael's Church (1750–62), art gallery, opera house; Hamburger Dom (Nov–Dec), international boat show. » Brahms; Charlemagne; Germany [i]; Hanseatic League; Mendelssohn

Hamersley Range Mountain range in NW Western Australia, S of the Fortescue R; extends for 257 km/160 ml; rises to 1 244 m/4 081 ft at Mt Meharry; the great iron-bearing area of Western Australia; contains a national park (6 176 sq km/ 2 384 sq ml). » Western Australia

Hamilcar, byname **Barca** ('Lightning') (c.270–228 BC) Carthaginian statesman and general at the time of the First Punic War, the father of Hannibal. Following Carthage's defeat in 241 BC, and the loss of her Empire in Sicily and Sardinia to Rome, he set about founding a new Carthaginian Empire in Spain. Between 237 BC and his death, he conquered most of the S and E of the peninsula. » Hannibal; Punic Wars

Hamilton, Alexander (1757–1804) US statesman, born in the West Indian island of Nevis. Educated at King's (now Columbia) College, New York, he fought in the American Revolution, becoming Washington's aide-de-camp (1777–81). After the war, he studied law, and in 1782 was returned to Congress. He was instrumental in the movement to establish the USA in its present political form. As Secretary of the Treasury (1789–95), he restored the country's finances to a firm footing, and was leader of the Federalist Party until his death. His successful effort to thwart the ambition of his rival, Aaron Burr, led to a duel in New Jersey, in which Hamilton was killed. » American Revolution; Federalist Party; Washington, George

Hamilton, Emma, Lady, originally **Emily Lyon** (c.1765–1815) Lord Nelson's mistress, born (probably) at Ness, Cheshire. In 1782 she accepted the protection of Charles Greville, to exchange it in 1786 for that of his uncle, Sir William Hamilton (1730–1803), whom she married in 1791. She first met Nelson in 1793, and bore him a daughter, Horatia (1801–81). After the death of her husband and Nelson, she became bankrupt, and in 1813 was arrested for debt. The next year she fled to Calais, where she died. » Nelson, Horatio

Hamilton, James, 1st Duke of (1606–49) Scottish Royalist commander during the English Civil War. He fought during the Thirty Years' War, leading an army in support of Gustavus Adolphus (1631–2), and later played a conspicuous part in the contest between Charles I and the Covenanters. Created duke in 1643, he led a Scottish army into England (1643), but was defeated by Cromwell at Preston, and beheaded. » Covenanters; English Civil War; Thirty Years' War

Hamilton (Bermuda) 32°18N 64°48W, pop (1980) 1 617. Port, resort, and capital of Bermuda, on Great Bermuda; deep harbour approached by a long intricate channel through Two Rock Passage; modern berthing and container facilities; founded 1612; capital since 1815; tourism; cathedral, Bermuda College. » Bermuda [i]

Hamilton (Canada) 43°15N 79°50W, pop (1981) 306 434. Town in SE Ontario, SE Canada, at head (W) of L Ontario, 58 km/36 km SW of Toronto; founded, 1813; site of Battle of Stoney Creek (1813); railway; McMaster University (1887); industrial and commercial centre; textiles, iron and steel, vehicles, agricultural machinery, electrical equipment. » Ontario

Hamilton (New Zealand) 37°46S 175°18E, pop (1988e) 103 500. City on North Island, New Zealand, on R Waikato; New Zealand's largest inland city; airfield; railway; university (1964); noted for horse breeding and agricultural research; dairy farming, market gardening, forest products; Waikato Art Museum; regatta at Turangawaewae Marae (home of the Maori Queen) to the N (Mar). » New Zealand [i]

Hamiltonian The total energy of a mechanical system; symbol H, units J (joule); after Irish mathematician William Hamilton (1805–65). It is equal to the sum of kinetic energy K and potential energy V; $H = K + V$. Mechanics can be formulated using H in a way complimentary to that based on Lagrangians. » energy; Lagrangian; mechanics

Hammarskjöld, Dag (Hjalmar Agne Carl) [**ham**uhshohld] (1905–61) Swedish statesman, who became Secretary-General of the United Nations (1953–61), born at Jönköping. After teaching at Stockholm University, he was secretary (1935) then chairman (1941–8) of the Bank of Sweden, and Swedish Foreign Minister (1951–3). At the UN, he helped to set up the Emergency Force in Sinai and Gaza (1956), and worked for conciliation in the Middle East (1957–8). He was awarded the 1961 Nobel Peace Prize after his death in an air crash near Ndola, Zambia, while engaged in negotiations over the Congo crisis. » United Nations

hammer throw An athletics field event in which the contestant throws with both hands a hammer weighing 16 lb (7.6 kg), from within the confines of a 7 ft (2.13m) circle. In competition, six throws are allowed, the object being to attain a greater distance than anyone else. Because of the dangers, the throwing circle is protected by a wire cage. The current world record is 86.74 m/284 ft 7 in, achieved by Yuriy Sedykh (USSR, born 11 Jun 1955) on 30 August 1986 at Stuttgart, West Germany. » athletics; RR104

hammerhead » **hammerkop**

hammerhead shark Large active shark of inshore tropical and temperate waters, characterized by a flattened head with broad lateral lobes which are thought to aid manoeuvrability; eyes and nostrils widely spaced; includes the **great hammerhead** of tropical Atlantic waters (*Sphyrna mokarran*), length up to 6 m/20 ft. (Genus: *Sphyrna*. Family: *Sphyrnidae*.) » shark

hammerkop A large brown bird, native to tropical Africa and SW Arabia, also known as **hamerkop, hammerhead, hammer-headed stork**, or **anvilhead**; feathers on head give a hammer-like profile; lives near water; eats mainly fish, frogs, and tadpoles; common in fishing villages; builds huge unkempt nest of twigs in tree. (*Scopus umbretta*. Family: *Scopidae*.)

Hammerstein (II), Oscar [**ham**uhstiyn] (1895–1960) US librettist, born in New York City. He wrote the book and lyrics for many operettas and musical comedies. With composer Jerome Kern, he wrote *Show Boat* (1928), a landmark of musical theatre, with such songs as 'Ol' Man River' and 'Only Make Believe'. Later, with composer Richard Rodgers (1902–79), he wrote some of the greatest musicals, including *Oklahoma!* (1943), *South Pacific* (1949), *The King and I* (1951), and *The Sound of Music* (1959). He died at Doylestown, Pennsylvania. » Kern; musical

Hammett, (Samuel) Dashiell (1894–1961) US writer, born in St Mary's Co, Maryland. His early career was spent with the Pinkerton Detective Agency in New York, after which he became the first US author of authentic 'private eye' crime stories. His best-known books are *The Maltese Falcon* (1930) and *The Thin Man* (1934). He died in New York City. » detective story

Hammond, Dame Joan (1912–) New Zealand soprano, born at Christchurch. She studied at the Sydney Conservatory, and played violin in the Philharmonic Orchestra there, making her operatic debut in 1929. She toured widely, and became noted particularly for her Puccini roles. She was made a Dame in 1974. » opera; Puccini

Hammurabi [hamoo**rah**bee] (18th-c BC) Amorite king of Babylon (c.1792–1750 BC), best-known for his Code of Laws. He is also famous for his military conquests that made Babylon the greatest power in Mesopotamia. » Amorites; Babylonia

Hamnett, Katharine (1948–) British fashion designer, born at Gravesend, Kent. She studied fashion at art school in London, then worked as a free-lance designer, setting up her own business in 1979. She draws inspiration for designs from workwear, and from social movements, such as the peace movement, which she supports. » fashion

Hampden, John (1594–1643) English parliamentarian and patriot, born in London. Educated at Oxford, he became a lawyer, and in 1621 an MP. His opposition to Charles I's financial measures led to his imprisonment (1627–8), and in 1634 he became famous for refusing to pay Charles' imposed levy for outfitting the navy ('ship money'). A member of both the Short and the Long Parliaments, he was one of the five members whose attempted seizure by Charles (1642) precipitated the Civil War. He fought for the Parliamentary army at Edgehill and Reading, but was killed at Thame. » English Civil War; Long Parliament; ship money

Hampi The site of the former Hindu capital of Vijayanagar, near the SW Indian village of Hampi. The city was founded in the 14th-c, and remained the centre of a vast and powerful Hindu empire until 1565, when it was sacked. It remains an important religious and tourist centre, and is a world heritage site. » Hinduism

Hampshire pop (1987e) 1 537 000; area 3 777 sq km/1 458 sq ml. County of S England, divided into 13 districts; bounded S by the English Channel; crossed by the North Downs in the NW and W; drained by Test and Itchen Rivers; W of Southampton is the New Forest; county town, Winchester; chief towns, Portsmouth, Southampton; agriculture, livestock, shipbuilding, oil refining, chemicals, pharmaceuticals, electronics, tourism; naval bases at Portsmouth and Gosport. » England [i]; New Forest; Winchester

Hampton Court The royal residence situated by the R Thames near London, built by Cardinal Wolsey, who occupied it until 1529. Thereafter it became the favourite residence of British monarchs for over two centuries. Queen Victoria declared it open to the public in 1851, and its gardens and maze are a major tourist attraction. » Wolsey, Thomas

Hampton Institute A privately-funded, co-educational college established in 1869 by Samuel Chapman (1839–93) in Hampton, Virginia, to provide vocational training for black slaves freed after the American Civil War. The foundation received a charter in 1870 and achieved college status in 1929. It is an important centre for studies in Black American history. » American Civil War; university

hamster A small rodent of the subfamily *Cricetinae* (24 species); short tail, large ears; food can be stored in internal cheek pouches; lives in burrows; communicates using very high frequency sound. One species, the **golden hamster** (*Mesocricetus auratus*), is a popular pet. It is thought that all domestic golden hamsters are descended from a family of 13 (mother plus 12 young), dug from their burrow in 1930 at Aleppo, Syria. » mouse (zoology); rodent

Hamsun, Knut [**ham**soon], pseudonym of **Knut Pederson** (1859–1952) Norwegian writer, born at Lom in the Gudbrandsdal. He had no formal education, and sprang to fame with his novel *Sult* (1888, Hunger). His best-known book is *Markens Grøde* (1917, The Growth of the Soil). He received the Nobel Prize for Literature in 1920, and lived largely as a recluse in his later years. He died near Grimstad, Norway. » Norwegian literature; novel

Han The name of several early Chinese dynasties, now used to distinguish those of native Chinese stock from the national minorities. The Western Han ('Former Han', 206 BC–AD 24), founded by Liu Bang, a leader of the rebellion that overthrew the Qin dynasty, was characterized by expansion of the Chinese empire into Korea and C Asia, incessant campaigns against the Huns (Chinese *Xiongnu*), the triumph of Confucianism as state orthodoxy, and great achievements in literature and learning. Its capital was at Changan (present-day Xi'an). After an interregnum (AD 8–23), during which the reformist Wang Mang usurped the throne, the Eastern Han ruled China from Luoyang (AD 25–220). During this period Buddhism was introduced to China, and trade links developed with Europe via the Middle East. » Confucianism; Qin dynasty

Han-kou; Han-kow » **Wuhan**

hand The terminal part of the upper limb, used to manipulate (motor function) or assess (sensory function) the environment. It is a highly mobile organ, capable of fine discriminative function and manipulation, both of which require a copious blood supply. It is richly endowed with sensory nerve endings, and consists of a number of bony elements (the *metacarpals* and *phalanges*) whose size and arrangement differs between species, bound together by ligaments and supported by tendons and muscles. In humans the bony elements are the five metacarpals, the three phalanges in each finger, and the two phalanges in the thumb. In primates (including humans) the thumb is set almost at right angles to the fingers, and is capable of being brought into contact with each finger in turn (*opposition*). Opposition is important in precision grips (eg holding needle and thread when threading a needle). In power grips, the thumb is used as a buttress to support the object and prevent it from slipping out of the hand (eg holding a power tool). In hook grips, only the fingers are used (eg carrying a shopping bag). The fine sensory discriminative ability of the fingers enables the blind to read braille. » arm; braille; chilblains; nails; Plate XIII

handball An indoor and outdoor game first played in Germany c.1890, resembling Association football, but played with the hands. The indoor game is played with 7 on each side. The outdoor game (known as *field handball*) is played on a field with 11 on each side. » fives; football 1 [i]; RR112

Handel, George Frideric (1685–1759) German-English composer, born at Halle. He was organist of Halle Cathedral at the age of 17, while also studying law, and worked as a violinist and keyboard player in the Hamburg opera orchestra (1703–6). In Italy (1706–10) he established a great reputation as a keyboard virtuoso and had considerable success as an operatic composer. He was appointed in 1710 to the court of the Elector of Hanover (later George I). In 1720 he worked at the King's Theatre, London, where he produced a stream of operas, and then developed a new form, the English oratorio, which proved to be highly popular. After a stroke in 1737, he rallied, and afterwards wrote some of his most memorable work, such as *Saul* (1739), *Israel in Egypt* (1739), and *Messiah*

(1742). His vast output included over 40 operas, about 20 oratorios, cantatas, sacred music, and orchestral, instrumental, and vocal works. He died in London, and was buried in Poet's Corner, Westminister Abbey. » oratorio

handkerchief tree A deciduous tree growing to 18 m/60 ft, often much smaller in cultivation, native to China; leaves ovoid, toothed; flower clusters tiny, protected by two large, white, pendulous bracts, which give the tree its name; also called **dove tree**. It is named after the French missionary Père David (1826–1900), who introduced it to Europe. (*Davidia involucrata*. Family: *Nyssaceae*.) » bract; deciduous plants; tree [i]

Handley, Tommy, properly **Thomas (Reginald)** (1892–1949) British comedian, born in Liverpool. He served in World War 1, then worked in variety, and in the infancy of radio became known as a regular broadcaster. In 1939 he achieved nationwide fame through his weekly programme ITMA (It's That Man Again), whose wit and satire helped to boost wartime morale. The programme continued to be a prime favourite until his death. » broadcasting

handloom A weaving machine operated by hand. In industrial societies, such looms are now almost exclusively restricted to craft weavers and designers, but in less developed nations (such as several countries of C and S America), hand-looom weaving is often of great economic importance. » weaving

handwriting » **chirography**

Handy, W(illiam) C(hristopher) (1873–1958) US Black composer, born in Florence, Alabama. He joined a minstrel show as a cornet player, and in 1903 formed his own band in Memphis, subsequently moving to Chicago and New York, where he formed his own publishing company. He was the first to introduce the 'blues' style to printed music, his most famous work being the *Saint Louis Blues* (1914). He died in New York City. » blues

hang glider A person-carrying glider using a delta-shaped flexible wing, developed for NASA in the late 1950s as a gliding parachute. The pilot is suspended by a harness from the light frame holding the wing, and controls the movement of the craft by body movement. Providing the angle of attack is maintained, lift is generated. Later, engines were fitted, wing spans increased, the delta wing configuration was dropped for reasons of efficiency, and the type developed into a form of ultra-light aircraft called a **microlight**. A typical microlight has a span of 10 m/33 ft and a speed of 90 kph/55 mph. Although popularized in the mid-1970s, hang gliding was pioneered in the 1890s by Otto Lilienthal in Germany. » aircraft [i]; glider; Lilienthal

Hangchow » **Hangzhou**

hangul » **red deer**

Hangzhou or **Hangchow** [hang**joh**] 30°18N 120°07E, pop (1984e) 1 222 900. Capital of Zhejiang province, E China; on Qiantang R at S end of Grand Canal; founded, 2200 BC; grew rapidly as trade and administration centre, from 6th-c; capital of several kingdoms and dynasties, 8th–12th-c; airfield; railway; technical university (1927); university (1959); iron and steel, refining, engineering, hydroelectricity, silk; trade in bamboo, wheat, barley, rice, cotton, sweet potatoes, tea; Spirits' Retreat (Buddhist temple founded in 326). » China [i]; Grand Canal

Hanif Mohammad (1934–) Pakistani cricketer, born at Junagadh, India. One of five Test-playing brothers, he made his first-class debut for Karachi at the age of 16. Noted for his dour play, he took 970 minutes to amass 337 runs against Australia in 1957–8, and established a world record score of 499 against Bahawalpur in 1959. He made his Test debut at the age of 17, and played in 55 Tests, scoring 3 915 runs. He captained Pakistan 11 times between 1964 and 1967. » cricket (sport) [i]

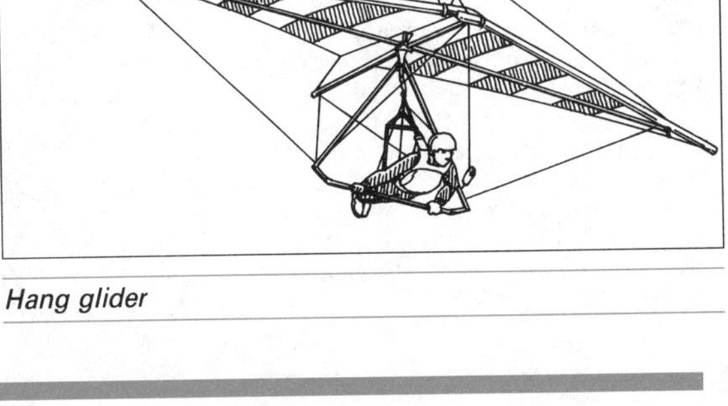

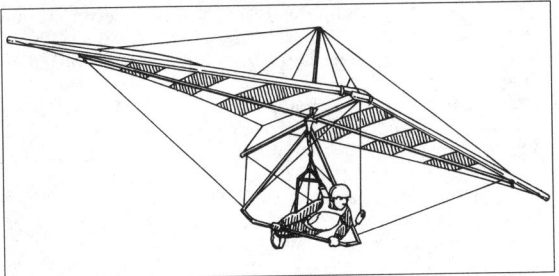

Hang glider

haniwa » **Kofun**

Hannibal (247–182 BC) Carthaginian general and statesman, the son of Hamilcar Barca. As a child, his father made him swear eternal enmity to Rome. He served in Spain under Hamilcar and Hasdrubal, and as general reduced most of S Spain (221–219 BC). In the Second Punic War, he left New Carthage on his famous journey (218 BC), defeated the Gauls, and crossed the Alps in fifteen days, in the face of almost insuperable obstacles. He marched on Rome, and defeated the Romans at L Trasimene (217 BC) and at Cannae (216 BC). Denied support by his countrymen, he fought on for several years, until recalled to Africa in 203 BC. He was defeated by Scipio at Zama (202 BC), leaving Carthage at the mercy of Rome. After making peace, Hannibal turned to political reform, but raised such opposition that he voluntarily exiled himself, first to Syria, then Crete and finally Bithynia, where he committed suicide to avoid Roman capture. » Fabius Maximus; Hamilcar; Punic Wars; Scipio Africanus Major

Hannover » **Hanover**

Hanoi [ha**noy**] 21°01N 105°52E, pop (1979e) 2 570 905. Capital of Vietnam; on Red R, 88 km/55 ml NW of Haiphong; former capital of Vietnamese Empire, 11th–17th-c; capital of French Indo-China, 1887–1946; occupied by the Japanese in World War 2; severely damaged by bombing in Vietnam War; university (1956); centre of industry and transport; textiles, tanning, brewing, engineering, rice milling, coal, food processing, tapioca, sesame, millet, wood products, resins, footwear; many historical sites destroyed by war; surviving sites include Co Loa citadel (3rd-c BC), Temple of Literature (11th-c), Mot Cot Pagoda (11th-c), several museums. » Vietnam [i]

Hanover, Ger **Hannover** 52°23N 9°44E, pop (1983) 524 300. Commercial and industrial capital city of Lower Saxony province, Germany; on R Leine, 56 km/35 ml WNW of Brunswick; chartered, 1241; home of the dukes of Brunswick-Lüneburg (later electors of Hanover) in the early 17th-c; Elector George Louis became George I of Great Britain, 1714; badly bombed in World War 2; railway; on the Mittelland Canal; three universities (1831, 1913, 1961); commerce, electronics, vehicles, tyres, metals, cement, pharmaceuticals, brewing, engineering, rubber, foodstuffs; Neoclassical opera house (1845–52), Leine Palace, Gothic Old Town Hall (15th-c); Hanover Trade Fair (Apr), International Aviation Trade Fair (every 2 years). » George I; Germany [i]

Hanover, House of A dynasty of British monarchs, encompassing George I (1714–27), George II (1727–60), George III (1760–1820), George IV (1820–30), William IV (1830–7), and Victoria (1837–1901), though only the Georges and William are usually referred to as 'Hanoverians'. The dynasty secured the Protestant succession after the death of Queen Anne, and was descended through the female line from Princess Elizabeth, the sister of Charles I. » Anne; English history

Hanoverian One of the oldest German breeds of horse; developed in the 17th-c from *Hanoverian creams* (also known as *Isabellas*); height, 15¾–17 hands/1.6–1.7 m/5¼–5½ ft); powerful body, with shortish muscular legs; popular for show-jumping. » horse [i]

Hansard, Luke (1752–1828) British printer, who went from Norwich to London, and entered the office of Hughes, printer to the House of Commons, becoming acting manager in 1774, and in 1798 succeeding as sole proprietor of the business. He and his descendants printed the parliamentary reports from 1774 to 1889.

Hanseatic League A late mediaeval association of 150 N German towns, including Bremen, Hamburg, and Lübeck. It dominated trade from the Atlantic to the Baltic, and fought successful wars against neighbours between 1350 and 1450. The **Hansa**, as it was also known, declined because of internal divisions, English and Dutch competition, and the growth of princely power.

Hansen, Martin (Jens) Alfred (1909–55) Danish novelist, born at Stroby. He worked on the land and as a teacher, but after 1945 devoted himself to writing. His early novels deal with social problems in the 1930s, and he later developed a more profound style, notably in his psychological novel *Løgneren* (1950, The Liar) and the metaphysical *Orm og Tyr* (1952, The Serpent and the Bull). He died in Copenhagen. » Danish literature; novel

Hansen's disease » **leprosy**

Hanukkah or **Chanukah** [**ha**nuka] An annual Jewish festival held in December (begins 25 Kislev), commemorating the rededication of the Temple at Jerusalem after the victory of Judas Maccabaeus over the Syrians in 165 BC (1st Book of Maccabees); also known as the **Feast of Dedication** or **Feast of Lights** (candles being lit on each of the eight days of the festival). » Maccabees; RR23

Hanuman The monkey-god of the Ramayana epic, who is the courageous and loyal supporter of Rama. A popular Hindu deity, he is represented as half-human and half-monkey. » Hinduism

hanuman monkey » **entellus**

happening A modern art 'event', or performance; often planned but sometimes 'spontaneous'. Happenings (so-called since c.1960) need not take place in a gallery but may occur in the street, or anywhere, and usually involve spectator participation. The event itself, rather than any finished, saleable product, is regarded as the work of art. » auto-destructive art; Body art; Conceptual art

Harappa [ha**ra**pa] A prehistoric city on the dried-up course of the R Ravi in the Pakistani Punjab, c.800 km/500 ml S of Islamabad, occupied c.2300–1750 BC. Its 20 m/65 ft high mound with a circuit of 5 km/3 ml was discovered in 1826, and excavated from 1921. To the W is a massive, walled citadel of moulded mudbrick; to the E a residential lower city with a rectangular street grid. Its houses were provided with drains, washrooms, and latrines. Its ancient population numbered c.25 000. » Indus Valley civilization; Mohenjo-daro

Harare [hara**h**ray], formerly **Salisbury** (to 1982) 17°43S 31°05E, pop (1982) 656 000. Capital and largest city of Zimbabwe, 370 km/230 ml NE of Bulawayo; altitude, 1 473 m/4 833 ft; founded in 1890, and named after Lord Salisbury; airport; railway; university (1970); administration, commerce, packaging, polythene, paints, adhesives, timber, textiles, tobacco; international conference centre; horse-racing and trotting tracks; motor-racing circuit; Queen Victoria Museum, national gallery, national archives, national botanical garden, two cathedrals. » Cecil, Robert; Zimbabwe

Harbin, Haerhpin, or **Haerbin**, formerly **Pinkiang** 45°54N 126°41E, pop (1983e) 2 560 000. Capital of Heilongjiang province, NE China; industrial centre on Songhua R; founded, 12th-c; developed as major rail junction; c.500 000 White Russians fled here in 1917; airfield; food processing, machinery, linen, sugar refining, paper; Stalin Park, Harbin Zoo (1954); Harbin Summer Music Festival (Jul). » China [i]; Russian Revolution

harbour seal » **common seal**

hard copy Computer output which is, for example, printed on paper and can therefore be directly read and understood by the user. The contrast is with **soft copy**, which refers to information stored in ways which can be understood only by a machine, such as on a floppy disk or in a computer memory. » floppy disk; memory, computer

hard disk A rigid magnetic storage disk for computer data, such as the Winchester disk. It is generally capable of storing much more data than a similar-sized floppy disk. On larger computers, stacks of removable hard disks are often used, and give very large data storage potential. » floppy/magnetic/Winchester disk

Hardanger Plateau [hah**dang**er] or **The Vidda**, Norwegian **Hardangervidda** Extensive mountain plateau in SW Norway, extending 160 km/100 ml between the head of Hardanger Fjord and the Hallingdal valley; average elevation of 1 000 m/3 500 ft, rising to 1 862 m/6 109 ft at Hardangerjøkulen; winter sports and tourist area. » Norway [i]

Hardicanute or **Harthacnut** (c.1018–42) King of Denmark (1035–42), and the last Danish King of England (1040–2), the only son of Canute and Emma of Normandy. Canute had intended that Hardicanute should succeed him in both Denmark and England simultaneously, but he was unable to secure his English inheritance until his stepbrother, Harold I, died in 1040. Hardicanute's death without children led to the restoration of the Old English royal line in the person of Edward the Confessor, the only surviving son of Emma and Ethelred the Unready. » Canute; Edward the Confessor; Harold I

Hardie, (James) Keir (1856–1915) British Labour Party politician, born near Holytown, Lanarkshire, Scotland. He worked in the mines between the ages of 7 and 24, and was victimized as the miners' champion. He became a journalist and the first Labour candidate, entering parliament in 1892. He founded and edited *The Labour Leader*, and was Chairman of the Independent Labour Party (founded 1893). Instrumental in the establishment of the Labour Representation Committee, he served as Chairman of the Labour Party (1906–8). His strong pacifism led to his becoming isolated within the Party, particularly once World War 1 had broken out. He died in Glasgow. » Labour Party

Harding, Warren G(amaliel) (1865–1923) US politician and 29th President (1921–3), born at Blooming Grove, Ohio, and educated at Ohio Central College. He became a successful journalist, gained a seat in the Ohio State Senate (1899) and the lieutenant-governorship (1902), after which he returned to journalism until 1914, when he was elected to the US Senate. Emerging as a power in the Republican Party, he won its nomination and the presidency in 1920, campaigning against US membership of the League of Nations. He died in San Francisco. » League of Nations; Prohibition; Republican Party; women's liberation movement

hardness A measure of a material's resistance to denting, scratching, and abrasion, related to the yield stress and tensile strength of the material. It is determined using indentation tests, which measure the size of a hole formed by a hard indenter driven into the material, as in the Vickers and Brinell tests. It is sometimes classified using the Mohs test of mineral hardness (devised by German mineralogist Friedrich Mohs in 1812), which rates talc as hardness 1 and diamond as hardness 10. » Brinell hardness test; mechanical properties of matter

hardware In computing, a term used, in contrast to *software*, to include all the physical units which make up an electronic or computer system, such as keyboards, magnetic disks, circuits, and visual display units. » firmware; software

Hardy, Oliver » **Laurel, Stan**

Hardy, Thomas (1840–1928) British novelist and poet, born at Upper Bockhampton, Dorset. After schooling in Dorchester, he studied as an architect, and at 22 moved to London, where he began to write poems expressing his love of rural life. Unable to publish his poetry, he turned to the novel, and found success with *Far from the Madding Crowd* (1874). He then took up writing as a profession, and produced a series of novels, notably *The Return of the Native* (1878), *The Mayor of Casterbridge* (1886), *Tess of the D'Urbervilles* (1891), and *Jude the Obscure* (1896). His main works were all tragedies, increasingly pessimistic in tone, and after *Tess* he was dubbed an atheist. He then took up poetry again, writing several volumes of sardonic lyrics, and the epic drama, *The Dynasts* (1903–8). He died at Dorchester, Dorset. » English literature; novel; poetry; tragedy

hardy plants Plants which are able to withstand frost damage. All perennials and some annuals from cold and cool temperate regions are hardy; most (though not all) tropical and some warm temperate plants are not.

hare A mammal of the genus *Lepus* (11 species); also known as **jackrabbit**. There are several differences from the closely-related rabbit: hares give birth to young (*leverets*) with fur, are larger, have black tips to the ears, are more solitary, and do not burrow. (Family: *Leporidae*. Order: *Lagomorpha*.) » lagomorph; pika; rabbit

Hare, David (1947–) British dramatist and director, born in London. Educated at Lancing and Cambridge, he went on to be resident dramatist at the Royal Court (1969–71) and elsewhere. His politically engaged plays include *Slag* (1970), *Plenty* (1978), and *Pravda* (1985), this last written in collaboration with Howard Brenton. He has also written several plays for TV, including *Licking Hitler* (1978) and *Dreams of Leaving* (1980), and the film *Wetherby* (1985). » drama; theatre

Hare, William » **Burke, William**

Hare Krishna movement [haree **krish**nah] A religious movement founded in the USA in 1965 by His Divine Grace A C Bhaktivedanta, Swami Prabhupada as The International Society for Krishna Consciousness. The movement promotes human well-being by promoting God consciousness based on the ancient Vedic texts of India. It is one of the best known of the new religious movements coming from the East, largely as a result of saffron-robed young people gathered in town centres chanting the Maha mantra, from which their popular name is derived. In their pursuit of spiritual advancement devotees practise vegetarianism, do not use intoxicants, do not gamble, and are celibate apart from procreation within marriage. » Bhagavadgita; Krishna

hare lip » **cleft lip and palate**

harebell A slender perennial with creeping underground stolons, native to N temperate regions; stems horizontal at base, becoming erect, growing to 40 cm/15 in; lowest leaves heart-shaped, toothed, becoming narrower and entire up the stem; flowers 5-lobed bells c.1.5 cm/0.6 in, blue, rarely white, 1–several, drooping on slender stalks. In Scotland it is known as the **bluebell**. (*Campanula rotundifolia*. Family: *Campanulaceae*.) » bell-flower; bluebell; perennial; stolon

Harewood, George Henry Hubert Lascelles, 7th Earl of, [**hah**wud] (1923–) Elder son of Princess Mary, and cousin of Queen Elizabeth II, born at Harewood, near Leeds. Educated at Eton and Cambridge, he served as captain in the Grenadier Guards in World War 2, and was a prisoner of war. Since the 1950s he has been much involved in the direction of operatic and arts institutions, such as at Covent Garden, Edinburgh, and Leeds. » George V; opera

Hargreaves, James (?–1778) British inventor, born (probably) at Blackburn, Lancashire. An illiterate weaver and carpenter, c.1764 he invented the spinning jenny (named after his daughter); but his fellow spinners broke into his house and destroyed his frame (1768). He moved to Nottingham, where he erected a spinning mill, and continued to manufacture yarn until his death. » spinning

haricot bean An annual growing to 3 m/10 ft, sometimes climbing, a native of S America; leaves with three broadly oval leaflets; pea-flowers white, yellow, or bluish, in small shortly stalked clusters in the leaf axils; pods up to 20 cm/8 in long, containing ellipsoid or kidney-shaped seeds; also called **kidney bean** and **French bean**. Numerous varieties are cultivated as a vegetable, both the young pods and the mature beans being eaten. The whole plants provide fodder for livestock. (*Phaseolus vulgaris*. Family: *Leguminosae*.) » annual; climbing plant; vegetable

Harimandir or **Golden Temple** The centre of the Sikh religion at Amritsar, Punjab, India. The temple dates from 1766 and stands in a sacred lake. It is faced with copper-gilt plates bearing inscriptions from the Granth Sahib, the holy book of the Sikhs, which is housed within. » Sikhism

Harlem Globetrotters An American professional touring basketball team, formed in 1927 by London-born immigrant Abraham Saperstein (1903–66). They developed a comedy routine to add to their skills, and now tour worldwide, giving exhibitions. Their signature tune is *Sweet Georgia Brown*. » basketball

Harlequin An acrobatic clown-like servant, with a costume of multi-coloured diamond-shaped patches, whose cunning and ingenuousness has had a long and varied theatrical history. He originated as one of the stock masks of the *commedia dell' arte*. » *commedia dell' arte*; harlequinade

harlequin duck A small duck, native to N areas of N hemisphere; dark with white stripes and spots; inhabits fast-flowing streams in summer, rough coasts in winter; dives for small animals which it pulls from rocks. (*Histrionicus histrionicus*. Family: *Anatidae*.) » duck

harlequinade An English theatrical entertainment developed in the 18th-c by the actor John Rich, who specialized in the acrobatic and pantomimic portrayal of Harlequin. Scenes of this character's comic courtship of Columbine interspersed the performance of a serious play, which they served to satirize. By the beginning of the 19th-c, these largely silent harlequinades had become a separate form, with spectacular scenic transformations and magical fairy-tale locations, and as such were the immediate precursors of the English pantomime. » Harlequin; pantomime; Pierrot

Harley, Robert, 1st Earl of Oxford (1661–1724) British statesman, born in London. He became a lawyer, and a Whig MP in 1689. In 1701 he was elected speaker, and in 1704 became Secretary of State. Shortly after, he became sympathetic to the Tories, and from 1708 worked to undermine the power of the Whigs. In 1710 Godolphin was dismissed, and Harley made Chancellor of the Exchequer, head of the government, and (1711) Earl of Oxford and Lord High Treasurer. The principal act of his administration was the Treaty of Utrecht (1713). In 1714 he was dismissed, and after the Hanoverian succession spent two years in prison. He then retired from politics, and died in London. » Godolphin; Hanover, House of; Tories; Whigs

Harlow, Jean, originally **Harlean Carpentier** (1911–37) US film actress, born in Kansas City. After a broken childhood she started in short films in 1928, and starred in *Hell's Angels* (1930). From film performances such as *Platinum Blonde* (1931) and *Bombshell* (1933), and the scandals of her private life, she became known as the 'Blonde Bombshell', and portrayed the sex symbol of the 1930s until her early death in Hollywood during the shooting of *Saratoga*.

Harmattan [hahma**tan**] A hot, dry wind which blows from the Sahara desert in W Africa. Dust carried by the Harmattan may be blown across to the Caribbean. » wind [i]

harmonic A pitch sounded by a string or column of air vibrating at a half, a third, a quarter, etc of its length. The timbre of a voice or instrument depends on the prominence or otherwise of these harmonics (or *upper partials*) when the fundamental note is sounded. Harmonics may be sounded independently of the fundamental note, on brass instruments by means of the player's embouchure (tightening or slackening of the lips), and on the harp and instruments of the violin family by lightly touching the vibrating string at an appropriate node. » harmonic series [i]; timbre

harmonic motion » **simple harmonic motion**

harmonic series The complex of musical pitches produced when a string or column of air is made to vibrate. The first 16 partials of the note *C* are shown below; the black notes are 'out of tune', ie their pitches cannot be adequately represented on a staff designed to accommodate the notes of the tempered scale. » brass instrument [i]; harmonic; scale; temperament (music)

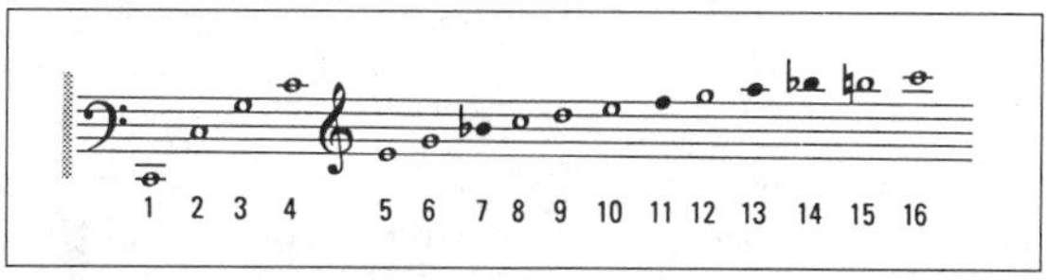

Harmonic series

harmonica A musical instrument, popularly known as the **mouth organ**, in which metal 'reeds' arranged in a row are made to vibrate by the inhalation and exhalation of the player's breath. The standard diatonic model is tuned to a 'gapped' scale (ie one with some notes missing) and is suitable only for simple, unsophisticated melodies. In the chromatic model a slide mechanism brings into play a second set of reeds tuned a semitone higher; virtuosi such as Larry Adler (1914–) and Tommy Reilly (1919–) inspired many serious composers to write for it. » reed instrument; scale

harmonium A type of reed organ patented in 1842 by French instrument maker A F Debain (1809–77). The name has been widely used for reed organs in general. » reed organ

harmony The combining of musical notes into chords, and then into sequences of chords, with emphasis on the 'vertical' component of the music rather than on the 'horizontal' fitting together of melodic strands (counterpoint). Harmony is thus generally thought of as accompanying, or 'clothing', one or more lines of melody. It may be *diatonic* (using wholly or mainly the notes of a particular key), *chromatic* (employing many notes foreign to the key), or *atonal* (independent of any reference to a key centre). In a looser sense, the term *harmonious* is often used to mean 'pleasant-sounding', in contrast to *discordant*, but in reality discord has been an essential part of the harmonic theory of all periods of music history. » atonality; chromaticism; counterpoint; diatonicism; dissonance; music; tonality

Harmsworth, Alfred (Charles William), 1st Viscount Northcliffe (1865–1922) British journalist and newspaper magnate, one of the pioneers of mass circulation journalism, born near Dublin. Brought up in London, he became editor of *Youth* and with his brother founded *Comic Cuts* (1890), the basis for the Amalgamated Press. In 1894 he absorbed the *London Evening News*, published a number of Sunday magazine papers, and in 1896 revolutionized Fleet Street with his *Daily Mail*, introducing popular journalism to the UK. In 1908, he became proprietor of *The Times*. A baronet in 1904, he was created baron in 1906 and viscount in 1917. He died in London. » newspaper

Harmsworth, Harold (Sydney), 1st Viscount Rothermere (1868–1940) British newspaper magnate, born in London. Closely associated with his brother, he also founded the Glasgow *Daily Record* and in 1915 the *Sunday Pictorial*. He became Air Minister (1917–18), and after his brother's death acquired control of the *Daily Mail* and *Sunday Dispatch*. A baronet in 1910, he was created baron in 1914 and viscount in 1919. He died in Bermuda. » newspaper

Harnack, Adolf (Karl Gustav) von (1851–1930) German Protestant Church historian and theologian, born at Dorpat. He was professor at Leipzig (1876), Giessen (1879), Marburg (1886), and Berlin (1889), where he also became keeper of the Royal (later State) Library (1905–21). His major writings include works on the history of dogma, on early Gospel traditions, and on a reconstruction of the essence of Jesus' teachings. He died in Berlin. » Apostles' Creed; Jesus Christ; Protestantism; theology

harness racing A horse race in which the rider is seated in a small two-wheeled cart, known as the *sulky*. The horses either trot or pace. Races are run on an oval dirt track measuring between 400–1500 m/½–1 ml in circumference. It was first introduced in Holland in 1554, but popularized in the USA in the mid-19th-c. » horse racing

Harold I, byname **Harefoot** (c.1016–40) King of England (1037–40), the younger son of Canute and Aelfgifu of Northampton. Canute had intended that Hardicanute, his only son by Emma of Normandy, should succeed him in both Denmark and England. But in view of Hardicanute's absence in Denmark, Harold was accepted in England, first as Regent (1035–6), and from 1037 as King. He died at Oxford. » Canute; Hardicanute

Harold II (c.1022–66) Last Anglo-Saxon King of England (1066), the second son of Earl Godwin. By 1045 he was Earl of East Anglia, and in 1053 succeeded to his father's earldom of Wessex, becoming the right hand of Edward the Confessor. After Edward's death (Jan 1066), Harold, his nominee, was crowned as King. He defeated his brother Tostig and Harold Hardrada, King of Norway, at Stamford Bridge (Sep 1066), but Duke William of Normandy then invaded England, and defeated him near Hastings (14 Oct 1066), where he died, shot through the eye with an arrow. » Edward the Confessor; Harold III; William I

Harold III, byname **Hardrada** ('the Ruthless') (1015–66) King of Norway (1047–66). Until 1045 he served in Constantinople as captain of the Scandinavian bodyguard of the Greek emperors, and defeated the Saracens in Sicily and Italy. Returning to Norway, he divided the kingdom with his nephew Magnus, becoming sole ruler in 1047. He waged war against Denmark until 1064. In 1066 he landed in England to aid Tostig against the English King Harold II, but fell at Stamford Bridge. » Harold II

harp A musical instrument of great antiquity existing in a wide variety of forms and sizes, its distinguishing characteristic being that its strings run in a plane perpendicular to the resonator. Early types had a single row of strings tuned diatonically; later, one or (as in the Welsh triple harp of the 17th-c) two further rows were added, enabling chromatic notes to be played. The modern concert harp, designed in 1810 by French pianoforte maker Sébastien Érard (1752–1831), has a single row of 46 or 47 strings tuned to the major scale of C♭, and seven pedals by means of which any pitch may be raised by a semitone or a tone. » string instrument 2 [i]

Harpers Ferry Raid (1859) An attack on the Federal arsenal in Virginia, led by abolitionist John Brown, intending to launch a slave insurrection. The raiders were captured, and Brown was executed amidst great publicity. » Brown, John; slavery

Harpies [**hah**peez] In Greek mythology, fabulous monsters with women's features and birds' wings and claws. They were originally rapacious ghosts or the storm-winds. They plagued Phineus, until chased away by the Argonauts. The name means 'snatchers'. » Argonauts

Harpocrates » **Horus**

harpsichord A keyboard instrument in use from the 15th-c to the early 19th-c and revived in recent times, mainly for performing early music. The keys, when depressed, cause wooden 'jacks', fitted with plectrums of leather or quill (or, in some modern instruments, plastic), to pluck the strings, which extend away from the keyboard and are dampened when the jacks fall into place again. » continuo; keyboard instrument

harpy eagle The world's largest eagle (90 cm/3 ft); inhabits lowland rainforest from C America to Argentina; rare; black, white, and grey; feet large; eats tree-dwelling mammals (monkeys, sloths, etc), and some birds. (*Harpia harpyja*. Family: *Accipitridae*.) » eagle

harrier (bird) A medium-sized hawk of world-wide genus *Circus* (10 species); wings and tail long; inhabits marsh, moors, and grassland; eats mainly small mammals and birds; hunts by flying low, following regular search pattern; most nest on ground. The name **brown harrier eagle** is used for the hawk *Circaetus cinereus*; **harrier hawk** is used for two hawks of the genus *Polyboroides* and several falcons of the genus *Micrastur*. (Family: *Accipitridae*.) » falcon; hawk; marsh harrier

harrier (mammal) A hound used for hunting hares; slightly smaller than a foxhound, with a keen sense of smell. » foxhound; hound

Harriman, W(illiam) Averell (1891–1986) US statesman and diplomat, born in New York City. Educated at Yale, he became Ambassador to the USSR (1943) and to Britain (1946), Secretary of Commerce (1946–8), and special assistant to President Truman (1950–1), helping to organize NATO. He was Director of Foreign Aid (1951–3), Governor of New York (1955–8), ambassador-at-large (1961, 1965–9), and US representative at the Vietnam peace talks in Paris (1968). He negotiated the partial nuclear test-ban treaty between the USA and USSR in 1963, and continued to visit the USSR on behalf of the government, making his last visit there at the age of 91. He died at Yorktown Heights, New York. » NATO; Truman; Vietnam War

Harris, Sir Arthur Travers, byname **Bomber Harris** (1892–1984) British airman, born at Cheltenham, Gloucestershire. He served in the Royal Flying Corps in World War 1, and as Commander-in-Chief of Bomber Command in World War 2 (1942–5) organized mass bomber raids on industrial Germany. Knighted in 1942, and created a baronet in 1953, he died at Goring-on-Thames, Oxfordshire. » Royal Air Force

Harris, Joel Chandler (1848–1908) US author, born at Eatonton, Georgia. He was in turn printer, lawyer, and journalist, and became known for his stories of *Uncle Remus* (1880), and several other children's books. He died at Atlanta, Georgia.

Harris, Paul » **service club**

Harris, Roy, byname of **LeRoy Ellsworth Harris** (1898–1979) US composer, born in Lincoln Co, Oklahoma. Brought up in

California, he worked as a truck driver before studying music in Los Angeles, and then in Paris under Nadia Boulanger. His works are ruggedly American in character and include 13 symphonies, as well as much instrumental, choral, and chamber music. He died at Santa Monica, California.

Harris S part of the Lewis with Harris island district in the Western Isles of Scotland; area c.500 sq km/200 sq ml; ferry links between Tarbert and Uig (Skye) and Lochmaddy (N Uist); tweed manufacture. » Lewis with Harris; Western Isles

Harrisburg 40°16N 76°53W, pop (1980) 53 264. Capital of state in Dauphin County, S Pennsylvania, USA, on the Susquehanna R; scene of many important conventions, especially the Harrisburg Convention (1788); site of Camp Curtin, the first Union camp in the Civil War; scene of nuclear power station accident on Three Mile Island (1979); railway; former steel industry giving way to a more diversified economy based on textiles, paper, machinery, food processing, bricks. » American Civil War; Pennsylvania

Harrison, Benjamin (1833–1901) US Republican statesman and 23rd President (1889–93), born at North Bend, Ohio. In 1854 he became a lawyer in Indianapolis, and during the Civil War fought in Sherman's Atlanta campaign. He was elected US Senator for Indiana in 1880. In 1888 he defeated Cleveland on the free trade issue, but failed to gain re-election in 1892. He returned to his law practice in Indianapolis, Indiana, where he died. » American Civil War; Cleveland, Grover

Harrison, George » **Beatles, The**

Harrison, Rex, originally **Reginald Carey Harrison** (1908–90) British actor, born at Houghton, Lancashire. He reached the London stage by 1930, and had his first leading film role in *Storm in a Teacup* (1937). His charming, somewhat blasé style attracted many star comedy parts, such as in *Blithe Spirit* (1945), *The Constant Husband* (1958), and *My Fair Lady* (1964), for which he won an Oscar. He died in New York.

Harrison, Tony, properly **Anthony** (1937–) British poet, born and educated in Leeds. After teaching in Nigeria and Prague, he became known with *The Loiners* (1970) and *Palladas* (1975). His combination of classical technique and colloquial language has produced powerful effects in the open sequences *The School of Eloquence* (1978) and *Continuous* (1981), also evident in his vigorous adaptations from French, Greek, and mediaeval drama. » English literature; poetry

Harrison, William Henry (1773–1841) US soldier, statesman, and ninth President (1841), born in Charles City Co, Virginia. He fought against the Indians, and when Indiana Territory was formed (1800) he was appointed Governor. He tried to avoid further Indian wars, but was compelled to quell Tecumseh's outbreak, which ended in the Battle of Tippecanoe (1811). In the war of 1812–14 he defeated the British in the Battle of the Thames (1813). In 1816 he was elected to Congress, became a Senator in 1824, and President in 1841, but died at Washington a month after his inauguration. His grandson was Benjamin Harrison. » Harrison, Benjamin; Tecumseh

Harte, (Francis) Bret(t) (1836–1902) US author, born at Albany, New York. He became a compositor in San Francisco, and then secretary of the US Mint there (1864–70). During this period he wrote some of his most famous poems, such as 'John Burns of Gettysburg'. In 1868 he founded and edited the *Overland Monthly*, to which he contributed several short stories, notably those later collected in *The Luck of Roaring Camp* (1870). He was US consul at Krefeld (1878–80) and at Glasgow (1880–5), and then lived in London until his death. » American literature; poetry

hartebeest [**hah**tibeest] An ox-antelope closely related to the topi; pale brown; two species: the **hartebeest** or **kongoni** (*Alcelaphus buselaphus*, 12 subspecies), and **Lichtenstein's hartebeest** (*Alcelaphus lichtensteini*). » antelope; topi

Hartford 41°46N 72°41W, pop (1980) 136 392. Capital of Connecticut, USA; in Hartford County on the Connecticut R; founded by Dutch settlers, 1633; city status, 1784; railway; university; aeroplane parts, motor vehicles, electrical equipment, machinery, metal products; world's largest concentration of insurance companies; major league team, Whalers (ice hockey); Old State House, Wadsworth Atheneum, Museum of Connecticut History. » Connecticut

Hartford Convention (1814–15) A gathering at Hartford, Connecticut, of delegates from the New England states to oppose the War of 1812 and to propose changes in the US Constitution. The Treaty of Ghent, ending the war, and US victory at New Orleans discredited both the Convention and the Federalist Party, with which it was associated. » Federalist Party; War of 1812

Hartington, Lord » **Cavendish, Spencer Compton**

Hartley, L(eslie) P(oles) (1895–1972) British writer, born near Peterborough. His early short stories, such as *Night Fears* (1924), established his reputation as a master of the macabre. Later, he turned to psychological relationships and made a new success with such novels as *The Shrimp and the Anemone* (1944), *The Boat* (1950), and *The Go-Between* (1953). He died in London. » English literature; novel; short story

Hartnell, Sir Norman (1901–78) British couturier and court dressmaker. Educated at Cambridge, he started his own business in 1923, receiving the Royal Warrant in 1940. He was president of the Incorporated Society of London Fashion designers (1946–56). His work included costumes for leading actresses, wartime 'utility' dresses, the WRAC uniform, and Princess Elizabeth's wedding and coronation gowns. He was knighted in 1977.

Hartono, Rudy properly **Rudy Hartono Kurniawan** [hah**toh**noh] (1948–) Indonesian badminton player. The winner of a record eight All-England titles (1968–74, 1976), he was also a member of Indonesia's Thomas Cup winning teams in 1970, 1973, 1976, and 1979. He was world champion in 1980. » badminton

haruspices [ha**rus**pikayz] In ancient Rome, the practitioners of the Etruscan system of divination, of which inspection of the entrails of sacrificial animals was the main part. Though less prestigious than augurs, haruspices were widely employed, and their art survived well into the Christian era. » augury; Etruscans

Harvard University » **Ivy League** [i]

harvest moon The full moon closest to the autumnal equinox. It rises at almost the same time on successive evenings, seemingly to help the farmers of old get in the harvest. » equinox; Moon

harvest mouse A mouse of the genus *Reithrodontomys* (**American harvest mouse**, 19 species) from C and N America; also, **Old World harvest mouse** (*Micromys minutus*) from Europe and Asia, the smallest living rodent (may weigh as little as 5 grams/0.2 oz); build spherical nests of dry grass attached to tall grass stems. » mouse (zoology)

Harvester judgment A landmark decision for the Australian industrial relations system, which introduced the concept of the 'basic wage' that remained a central feature of the national system until 1967, and of the State system until 1967–70. The case was brought by a manufacturer of agricultural harvesters in 1907.

harvestman An extremely long-legged arthropod; typically a predator of small insects, molluscs, or worms; some are scavengers; body compact, carried on four pairs of long legs; female with long egg-laying tube. (Class: *Arachnida*. Order: *Opiliones*, c.4 500 species.) » arthropod

harvestmite A small, predatory mite; tiny, red-coloured, 6-legged larvae often occur in large numbers in damp fields in autumn; feed by sucking blood of small mammals and humans, causing severe itching and rash; larvae known as **chiggers**. (Order: *Acari*. Family: *Thrombidiidae*.) » larva; mite

Harvey, William (1578–1657) British physician, who discovered the circulation of the blood, born at Folkestone, Kent. Educated at Canterbury, Cambridge, and Padua, he settled in London as a physician, holding appointments at St Bartholomew's Hospital (1609–43) and from 1615 at the College of Physicians. His celebrated treatise, *De Motu Cordis et Sanguinis in Animalibus* (On the Motion of the Heart and Blood in Animals) was published in 1628. He was physician to James I and Charles I, and in 1646 returned to London, where he died. » blood; Fabricius

Harwich [**ha**rich] 51°57N 1°17E, pop (1981) 17 329. Port in Tendring district, Essex, SE England; on the North Sea coast, 26 km/16 ml E of Colchester; railway; container freight terminal; ferries to Denmark, Germany, Holland; engineering. » Essex

Hasdrubal The name of several Carthaginian leaders, notably **1** Hamilcar Barca's son-in-law and successor in Spain (died 221 BC), and **2** Hannibal's younger brother, who died in battle with the Romans at the R Metaurus (207 BC). » Hamilcar; Hannibal; Punic Wars

Hašek, Jaroslav [**ha**shek] (1883–1923) Czech novelist and short-story writer, born in Prague. An accomplished practical joker who despised pomposity, he is best known for his novel *The Good Soldier Švejk* (1920–3), a satire on military life and bureaucracy, four volumes of which were completed by his death, at Lipuice, Czechoslovakia. » Czechoslovak literature; novel; short story

Haselrig or **Heselrige, Sir Arthur** (?–1661) English parliamentarian who in 1640 sat in the Long and Short Parliaments for his native county, Leicestershire, and who was one of the five members whose attempted seizure by Charles I in 1642 precipitated the Civil War. He commanded a parliamentary regiment, and in 1647 became Governor of Newcastle. After the Restoration, he died a prisoner in the Tower. » Charles I (of England); English Civil War

hashish » **cannabis**

Hashman, Judy, properly **Judith**, *née* **Devlin** (1935–) US badminton player, born at Winnipeg, Canada. The winner of the singles title at the All-England Championships a record ten times (1954, 1957–8, 1960–4, 1966–7), she also won seven doubles titles (six with her sister, Susan Peard (1940–)). She was a member of the United States Uber Cup winning teams in 1957, 1960, and 1963. Her Irish-born father, **Frank Devlin** (1899–), won 18 All-England titles. » badminton

Hasidim or **Chasidim** [**has**ideem], also **Hasideans** (Heb 'faithful ones') Originally, those Jews in the 2nd-c BC who resisted Greek and pagan influences on Israel's religion and sought strict adherence to the Jewish law; probably ancestors of the Pharisees. They supported the early Maccabean revolt, but refused to fight for national independence once the legitimate high priesthood had been restored. » Hasidism; Judaism; Maccabees; Pharisees

Hasidism [**has**idizm] A popular movement of Jewish mysticism, usually traced to a persecuted sect in the latter half of the 18th-c in Poland, characterized by an ascetic pattern of life, strict observance of the commandments, and loud ecstatic forms of worship and prayer. It was originally opposed to rabbinic authority and traditional Jewish practices, stressing prayer rather than study of the Torah as the means of communicating with God, but as it spread through the Ukraine, E Europe, and eventually W Europe and America, it was finally accepted as a part of Orthodox Judaism. » Judaism; Kabbalah; Torah

Hasmoneans » **Maccabees**

Hastings, Warren (1732–1818) British colonial administrator in India, born at Churchill, Oxfordshire. Educated at Westminster, he joined the East India Company in 1750, and by 1774 was Governor-General of Bengal. Carrying out several reforms, he made the Company's power paramount in many parts of India. However, wars (1778–84) interfered with trade, and damaged his reputation, and on his return to England in 1884 he was charged with corruption. After a seven-year trial, he was acquitted. The Company made provision for his declining years, which he spent as a country gentleman at Daylesford, Worcestershire. » East India Company, British

Hastings, Battle of (14 Oct 1066) The most decisive battle fought on English soil, which led to the successful Norman Conquest of England. Norman cavalry overcame the resolute defence of the Anglo-Saxon army fighting on foot, and Harold II's death in battle cleared the way for Duke William of Normandy's coronation. Not until 1092 (the capture of Carlisle) were the Normans masters of all England. » Harold II; Norman Conquest; William I (of England)

hatchetfish Small strongly compressed fish, with a deep body resembling a hatchet; two different groups, the deep-sea *Sternoptychidae* (2 genera), and the S and C American freshwater flying hatchetfishes, *Gasteropelecidae*, which achieve true flight by rapid beats of large pectoral fins.

hatching In art, the technique of shading a drawing with close-set parallel lines. When this is crossed at right angles by another series of lines, the technique is called **cross-hatching**. » modelling 1

Hathaway, Anne » **Shakespeare, William** [i]

Hathor [**hah**thaw] The ancient Egyptian goddess of love, together with joyful music and dancing. She is represented by a cow, or has cow-like features, and is often associated with the papyrus plant. She was identified by the Greeks with Aphrodite. » Aphrodite

Hatra [**hat**ra] An ancient Parthian fortress city located between the Tigris and Euphrates rivers in N Iraq; a world heritage site. Founded in the 1st-c BC, it flourished as a trading and religious centre for four centuries before being razed by the Persian Sassanids. » Parthians; Sassanids

Hatshepsut [hat**shep**soot] (c.1540–c.1481 BC) A queen of Egypt of the XVIIIth dynasty, the daughter of Thothmes I. She was married to Thothmes II, on whose accession (1516 BC) she became the real ruler. On his death (1503 BC) she acted as Regent for his son, Thothmes III, then had herself crowned as Pharaoh. Maintaining the fiction that she was male, she was represented with the regular pharaonic attributes, including a beard. » pharaoh; Punt, land of; Thutmose III

Hattersley, Roy (Sydney George) (1932–) British Labour politician, educated at Hull. He was a journalist and local authority politician before becoming a Labour MP in 1964. A supporter of Britain's membership of the EEC, he was a Minister at the Foreign Office (1974–6), then Secretary of State for Prices and Consumer Protection in the Callaghan government (1976–9). He has since been Opposition spokesman on the environment and on home affairs, Shadow Chancellor, and he was elected Deputy Leader of the Labour Party in 1983. He is a regular contributor to newspapers and periodicals. » Callaghan, James; Labour Party

Hattusas or **Hattusha** The ancient capital of the Hittites, now Bogazkoy in C Turkey, 160 km/100 ml E of Ankara. Originally an Assyrian trading colony, the settlement was taken by the Hittites in the 17th-c BC. It was destroyed in 1200 BC by marauders known as the Sea Peoples. The ruins were discovered in 1834, and are now a world heritage site. » Assyria; Hittites; Sea Peoples

Haughey, Charles (James) (1925–) Irish politician and Prime Minister (1979–81, 1982, 1987–92), born at Castlebar, Co Mayo. Educated at Dublin, he was called to the Bar in 1949, and became a Fianna Fáil MP in 1957. From 1961 he held posts in justice, agriculture, and finance, but was dismissed in 1970 after a quarrel with the Prime Minister, Jack Lynch. He was subsequently tried and acquitted on a charge of conspiracy to import arms illegally. After two years as Minister of Health and Social Welfare, he succeeded Lynch as Premier in 1979, was in power again for a 9-month period in 1982, and defeated Garrett Fitzgerald in the 1987 elections. He resigned after a phone-tapping scandal. » Fianna Fáil; Fitzgerald, Garrett; Lynch

Hauptmann, Gerhart (Johann Robert) [**howpt**man] (1862–1946) German author, born at Obersalzbrunn, Silesia. He studied sculpture in Breslau and Rome before settling in Berlin (1885), where he established a reputation with his first play, *Von Sonnenaufgang* (1889, Before Dawn). He followed this with several other social dramas, such as *Die Weber* (1892, The Weavers). He also wrote several novels, as well as poetry, and was awarded the Nobel Prize for Literature in 1912. He died at Agnetendorf. » drama; German literature

Hausa [**how**suh] A Chadic (Afro-Asiatic)-speaking, predominantly Muslim people of Nigeria and Niger; the largest ethnic group in the area. They are intensive farmers, and Hausa traders are found throughout W Africa; they are also famed for their crafts. Most Hausa were conquered by the Fulani in the early 19th-c, and today form the populations of the Muslim emirates of Nigeria. The Hausa language which has c.25 million mother-tongue speakers, is used as a lingua franca throughout N Nigeria and adjacent territories. It is the only Chadic language to be written, now in a Roman alphabet which has displaced an Arabic one used from the 16th-c. Population c.12 million. » Chadic; Fulani; lingua franca; Niger [i]; Nigeria [i]

Hauser, Kaspar [**how**suh] (?1812–33) German foundling, a 'wild boy', found in the marketplace of Nuremberg in May 1828. Though apparently 16 years old, his mind was a blank, and his behaviour that of a little child. He later gave some account of himself, as having lived in a hole, looked after by a man who had brought him to the place where he was found. In 1833 he was discovered with a wound in his side, from which he died. Many have regarded him as an imposter who committed suicide: others, as a person of noble birth who was the victim of a crime.

Haussmann, Georges Eugène, Baron [**hows**man] (1809–91) French financier and town planner, born in Paris. He entered public service, and under Napoleon III became prefect of the Seine (1853), improving Paris by widening streets, laying out boulevards and parks, and building bridges. He was made baron and senator; but the heavy burden laid upon the citizens led to his dismissal (1870). Elected to the Chamber of Deputies in 1881, he died in Paris. » Paris [i]

haustorium A sucker-like organ inserted by a parasite into the cells of the host, through which food is withdrawn. It is found in fungi and parasitic flowering plants, such as dodder. » dodder; fungus; parasitic plant

hautbois strawberry » **strawberry**

Havana, Span **La Habana** [havana] 23°07N 82°25W, pop (1983e) 1 972 363. Capital city and province of Cuba, on N coast; founded on this site, 1519; airport; railway; country's chief port on fine natural harbour; university (1721); trade in sugar, cotton, tobacco; cathedral (1704), presidential palace (1920); several old fortresses including La Fuerza (1538), oldest building in Cuba; old city centre a world heritage site; castles of El Morro (1589–1630) and La Punta (late 16th-c); International Conference Centre; carnival in July. » Cuba [i]

Havana cat A breed of domestic cat, developed in the UK from Siamese cats; green eyes and plain brown coat; a *foreign short-haired* cat, also known as **Havana brown** or **Chestnut brown (foreign) short-hair**. » cat; Siamese cat

Havel, Vaclav [**hav**uhl] (1936–) Czech dramatist and President (1988–), born in Prague, and educated there at the Academy of Dramatic Art. He began work in the theatre as a stagehand, then became resident writer for the Prague 'Theatre on the Balustrade' (1960–9). His work was then judged subversive, and he was imprisoned in 1979 for four years, his plays only being performed abroad. These include *Zahradni slavnost* (1963, The Garden Party), *Spiklenci* (1970, The Conspirators), and *Temptation* (1987). He was imprisoned again in 1989, but was elected president by direct popular vote (Dec 1989) following the resignation of the hardline Communist Party leadership. » Czechoslovak literature; drama

Haw-Haw, Lord » **Joyce, William**

Hawaii (island) [haw**ah**ee] pop (1980) 92 053; area 10 488 sq km/ 4 048 sq ml. Largest island and county of the US state of Hawaii; the 'orchid isle'; chief town, Hilo; Volcanoes National Park; tourism; Hula Festival (Apr). » Hawaii (state)

Hawaii (state) [haw**ah**ee] pop (1987e) 1 083 000; area 16 759 sq km/ 6 471 sq ml. Pacific state of the US, a group of eight major islands (Hawaii, Kahoolawe, Kauai, Lanai, Maui, Molokai, Niihau, Oahu) and numerous islets in the C Pacific Ocean; the 'Aloha State', divided into five counties; reached by the Polynesians over 1 000 years ago; discovered by Captain Cook in 1778, and named the Sandwich Is; King Kamehameha I united the islands in 1810, and encouraged trade with the USA; arrival of Christian missionaries, 1820; monarchy overthrown, 1893; a request for annexation to the USA rejected by President Cleveland, then accepted by President McKinley, 1898; became a territory, 1900; surprise attack by Japanese planes on the US naval base at Pearl Harbor, Oahu I (7 Dec 1941) brought the USA into World War 2; remained the chief US Pacific base throughout the war; under martial law until March 1943; admitted to the Union as the 50th state, 1959; capital, Honolulu; islands of volcanic origin, with offshore coral reefs; highest point Mauna Kea, a dormant volcano on Hawaii I (4 201 m/13 783 ft), a major astronomical site; Mauna Loa (4 169 m/13 678 ft) an active volcano; generally fertile and highly vegetated, although Kahoolawe is arid; food processing, pineapples, sugar cane; coffee, cattle, dairy produce, macadamia nuts; fishing (especially tuna); defence installations at Pearl Harbor; major tourist area; Haleakala and Hawaii Volcanoes National Parks; diverse ethnic population, a large proportion of Japanese descent. » Cook, James; Honolulu; Mauna Kea/Loa; United States of America [i]; World War 2; RR38

Hawaiian goose A rare goose, native to the uplands of Hawaii; wings short; feet with reduced webbing; eats fruit and herbs; also known as **nene**. There were less than 50 individuals in 1950, but captive breeding has increased this number to more than 2 000. (*Branta sandvicensis*. Family: *Anatidae*.) » goose

Hawaiian guitar A guitar with a straight body placed across the player's knees. It has metal strings which are stopped with a steel bar, instead of the fingers of the left hand, to produce the characteristic scooping (glissando) sound. It was developed in Hawaii during the second half of the 19th-c. Electric Hawaiian (or 'steel') guitars, sometimes free-standing, have been manufactured since the 1930s. » guitar; string instrument **2** [i]

hawfinch A stout finch native to Europe, Asia, and N Africa; golden brown with black face; bill huge, strong, used for cracking tree fruits; shy, inhabits treetops in mature woodland. The name is also used for some birds of the genus *Eophona*. (*Coccothraustes coccothraustes*. Family: *Fringillidae*.) » finch

hawk A bird of prey of the family *Accipitridae*, the name being used especially for smaller members of the family (but not for Old World vultures, which also belong to this family). It includes sparrowhawks, harriers, kites, and buzzards. Larger members are called eagles. In the USA, the name is also used for some falcons (Family: *Falconidae*). » bateleur; bird of prey; buzzard; eagle; falcon; harrier (bird); kite; marsh harrier; sparrowhawk; vulture

hawk (politics) » **dove** (politics)

hawk moth A medium to large moth, typically with long, triangular wings and an elongate body; fast fliers, capable of hovering flight; proboscis often long, used to suck nectar; c.1 000 species, most abundant in tropics. (Order: *Lepidoptera*. Family: *Sphingidae*.) » death's head moth; moth

hawk owl A typical owl, native to N areas of the N hemisphere; short pointed wings; long tail; resembles the hawk when flying and perching; inhabits forests; eats mammals and birds; hunts in daylight. (*Surnia ulula*. Family: *Strigidae*.) » owl

Hawke (of Towton), Edward Hawke, 1st Baron (1705–81) British admiral, born in London. As a young commander, he fought against the French and Spanish, for which he was knighted (1747). His major victory was against the French at Quiberon Bay (1759), which caused the collapse of their invasion plans. He also became an MP (1747), First Lord of the Admiralty (1766–71), and a baron (1776). He died at Shepperton, Middlesex.

Hawke, Robert (James Lee) (1929–) Australian statesman and Labor Prime Minister (1983–), born at Bordertown, S Australia. Educated at the University of Western Australia and Oxford, he worked for the Australian Council of Trade Unions for over 20 years, before becoming an MP in 1980. His Labor Party defeated the Liberals in the 1983 election only one month after adopting him as leader. Frequently described as a colourful figure, he is a skilled negotiator who has won praise for his handling and settling of industrial disputes. In 1987 he became the first Labor Prime Minister to win a third term in office. » Australian Labor Party

Hawking, Stephen (William) (1942–) British theoretical physicist, born in Oxford, where he graduated. He has spent his career in Cambridge, holding a chair there from 1977. His work has been concerned with cosmology in a variety of aspects, dealing with black holes, singularities, and the Big Bang theory of the origin of the universe. His popular writing is also notable, especially *A Brief History of Time* (1988). The achievement is all the more noteworthy because since the 1960s he has suffered from a neuromotor disease causing extreme physical disability. He was made a Companion of Honour in 1989. » Big Bang; cosmology; Hawking radiation

Hawking radiation A type of radiation predicted by British physicist Stephen Hawking (1974) to emerge continuously from black holes. Of pairs of particles produced by quantum effects in space near a black hole, one is absorbed by the black hole whilst the other is radiated. The theory predicts that black holes slowly evaporate into photons and other particles, finally expiring in a huge burst of gamma rays. » black hole; Hawking; quantum field theory

Hawkins, Coleman (1901–69; he claimed 1904 as his birth year) Jazz tenor saxophonist, born at St Joseph, Missouri. He joined Fletcher Henderson's jazz orchestra in 1923. The performances on romping swing tunes such as 'The Stampede' (1926) and on slow ballads such as 'One Hour' (1929) altered forever the way the tenor saxophone was played. He played widely in Europe (1934–9), and on returning to New York recorded 'Body and Soul', a jazz landmark. He died in New York City. » bebop; jazz; saxophone

Hawkins, Sir John » **Hawkyns, Sir John**

Hawks, Howard (1896–1977) US film director, born in Indiana. He was educated at Cornell, working as a prop man in Hollywood on vacations. He wrote and directed his first feature, *The Road to Glory* (1926), and was always closely involved with the scripts in his later productions. With the coming of sound films, he had many successes over some 40 years, in such varied genres as airforce dramas (eg *The Dawn Patrol*, 1930), detection and crime (eg *The Big Sleep*, 1946), Westerns (eg *Rio Lobo*, 1970), and comedy (eg *Man's Favorite Sport?*, 1962). He died at Palm Springs, California.

hawksbill turtle A sea turtle, native to tropical oceans; narrow head with hooked 'beak'; back with saw-tooth outline due to overlapping plates of shell; produces the finest quality tortoiseshell; endangered due to overhunting. (*Eretmochelys imbricata*. Family: *Chelonidae*.) » turtle (biology)

Hawksmoor, Nicholas (1661–1736) English architect, born at East Drayton, Nottinghamshire. His most individual contributions are the London churches, St Mary Woolnoth, St George's (Bloomsbury), and Christ Church (Spitalfields), as well as parts of Queen's College and All Souls, Oxford. He died in London.

hawkweed A widely distributed perennial, mostly occurring in the N hemisphere; leaves entire to deeply toothed, arranged spirally around the stem or often in a basal rosette; flower heads solitary or in loose clusters, florets usually yellow. Many hawkweeds reproduce from fruits formed without fertilization having occurred, resulting in vast numbers of distinct populations or microspecies, perhaps as many as 20 000. (Genus: *Hieracium*, c.250 species. Family: *Compositae*.) » floret; perennial

Hawkyns, Sir John (1532–95) British sailor, born at Plymouth. He was the first Englishman to traffic in slaves (1562) between W Africa and the West Indies, but on his third expedition his fleet was destroyed by the Spanish (1567). He became navy treasurer (1573), and was knighted for his services against the Armada in 1588. In 1595, with his kinsman Drake, he commanded an expedition to the Spanish Main, but died at Puerto Rico. » Drake, Francis; Spanish Armada

hawthorn A spiny, deciduous shrub or tree, growing to 18 m/60 ft, native to Europe; leaves oval to rhomboidal, deeply 3–7-lobed; flowers white, in clusters; berries (*haws*) red to maroon, flesh thin over a large stone; also called **quickthorn** and **may**. It is very common and much planted, forming dense stock-proof hedges and attractive park or street trees. (*Crataegus monogyna*. Family: *Rosaceae*.) » shrub; tree [i]

Hawthorne, Nathaniel (1804–64) US novelist and short-story writer, born at Salem, Massachusetts. He started his first novel while at college, and lived in seclusion for 12 years. His first success was a collection of short stories, *Twice-told Tales* (1837), which was acclaimed in London, but his best-known works are his novels, notably *The Scarlet Letter* (1850) and *The House of the Seven Gables* (1851). He settled at Concord in 1852, apart from a period as consul in Liverpool (1853–7), continuing to write articles and stories. He died at Plymouth, New Hampshire, and was only belatedly recognized in his own country. » American literature; novel; short story

Hawthorne effect » **experimenter effect**

Hay, John (Milton) (1838–1905) US statesman and writer, born at Salem, Indiana. Educated at Brown University, he became a lawyer, and private secretary to President Lincoln. After Lincoln's death (1865), he served as a diplomat in Paris, Vienna, and Madrid. He returned to the USA and to journalism in 1870, and went on to write poetry, fiction, and a multivolume biography of Lincoln. He became Assistant Secretary of State (1878), Ambassador to Britain (1897), and Secretary of State (1898), serving under Presidents McKinley and Roosevelt. » Lincoln, Abraham; McKinley; Roosevelt, Theodore

hay fever A type of physical reaction affecting the eyes and nasal passages on contact with a foreign protein. It involves watering of the eyes and nose, nasal congestion, and sneezing. The name is derived from the common cause of exposure to the pollen of grasses in the air, which in the UK are present in highest concentrations in May and June, but the reaction is not confined to any season or to a single stimulus. Other allergens are house dust, spores of fungi, and dander from animals. Symptoms may be ameliorated by antihistamine drugs. » allergy; anaphylaxis

Haydn, (Franz) Joseph [**hiy**dn] (1732–1809) Austrian composer, born at Rohrau, Lower Austria. Educated at the Cathedral Choir School of St Stephen's, Vienna, he earned his living initially by playing in street orchestras and teaching. He became musical director (1759–60) for Count von Morzin's court musicians, for whom he wrote his earliest symphonies. He entered the service of the Esterházy family as musical director in 1761, staying with them until 1790. He was given great scope for composition, and among his innovations were the four-movement string quartet and the 'classical' symphony. His output was vast, and he earned a major international reputation. His works include 104 symphonies, about 50 concertos, 84 string quartets, 24 stage works, 12 Masses, orchestral divertimenti, keyboard sonatas, and diverse chamber, choral, instrumental, and vocal pieces. He died in Vienna.

Hayes, Rutherford B(irchard) (1822–93) US Republican statesman and 19th President (1877–81), born in Delaware, Ohio. He practised as a lawyer in Cincinnati (1849–61), served in the Civil War, entered congress (1865–7), and became Governor of Ohio (1868–76). Under his presidency, the country recovered commercial prosperity. His policy included reform of the civil service and the conciliation of the Southern states. He died at Fremont, Ohio. » Republican Party

haymaker » **pika**

Haywood, William D(udley), byname **Big Bill** (1869–1928) US labour leader, born at Salt Lake City, Utah. After working as a miner, homesteader, and cowboy, he joined the Western Federation of Miners in 1896, and quickly achieved prominence. In 1905 he helped to found the Industrial Workers of the World, which was committed to revolutionary labour politics and to the organization of all workers in one big union. An active socialist, he was convicted of sedition in 1917 for his opposition to World War 1. He fled from the USA in 1921, and took refuge in the Soviet Union, dying in Moscow. » socialism; trade union

Hayworth, Rita, originally **Margarita Carmen Cansino** (1918–87) US film actress, born in New York City. She started as a Spanish night-club dancer and appeared in short films, then partnered both Fred Astaire and Gene Kelly in musicals of the 1940s, and found her best-known lead in *Gilda* (1946). A scandal involving her romance with Aly Khan (1949–51), whom she later married, effectively closed her Hollywood career, and during the 1960s she appeared in character parts, often in Europe, including *The Money Trap* (1966) and *The Wrath of God* (1972). She died in New York City.

hazard A card game for four players in pairs. It is similar to solo, but all cards with a face value of 2 to 8 are discarded, and the joker is added, to make 25 cards. » playing cards; solo

hazardous substances Generally human-made substances, potentially damaging to health, which when incorrectly disposed of result in contamination and pollution of the environment. They include toxic substances, heavy metal pollutants (eg lead, mercury), and radioactive waste produced in the generation of nuclear power. The disposal of hazardous substances is a source of environmental concern in many countries. » pollution; radioactive waste; waste disposal

hazel A deciduous shrub or small tree, native to Europe and Asia Minor; leaves broadly oval, toothed; male catkins long, pendulous; females short, bud-like with prominent red stigmas;

edible nut partially enclosed in a ragged green leafy cup. It is cultivated on a small scale, but is common in hedgerows, and is often coppiced. (*Corylus avellana.* Family: *Corylaceae.*) » coppice; deciduous plants; shrub; tree [i]

Hazlitt, William (1778–1830) British essayist, born at Maidstone, Kent. The son of a Unitarian minister, he took up painting, but was encouraged by Coleridge to write *Principles of Human Action* (1805), and further essays followed. In 1812 he found employment in London as a journalist, and also contributed to the *Edinburgh Review* (1814–20), proving himself to be a deadly controversialist, and a master of epigram, invective, and irony. His best-known essay collections are *Table Talk* (1821) and *The Spirit of the Age* (1825). He died in London. » Coleridge; English literature

Head-Smashed-In Bison Jump An important archaeological site in the Porcupine Hills of SW Alberta, Canada. From c.4000 BC until the early 19th-c, indigenous peoples slaughtered vast herds of bison here by stampeding them over the edge of the 'jump', a 10 m/33 ft high cliff. It is now a world heritage site. » bison

Head Start A project begun in the USA in the early 1960s to help pre-school children from a disadvantaged background prepare for schooling. The main emphasis was on language and social development, but attention was also paid to health care and parent education. » compensatory education

headache An aching sensation over the vault of the skull, temples, or back of the head, usually diffuse and poorly localized. In the majority of instances, the complaint is trivial and responds to simple analgesics, such as aspirin. Occasionally, headaches herald serious intracranial disease such as tumour. The brain itself is insensitive to touch, and headaches arise from the stretching or distortion of its covering membranes, from tension arising from the muscles overlying the skull, or from vascular dilatation with increased blood supply, as occurs in generalized fevers or over-indulgence in alcohol. » migraine

Healey, Denis (Winston) (1917–) British politician, born at Eltham, Kent. Educated at Oxford, he served in N Africa and Italy (1940–45), then became Secretary of the Labour Party's international department, and an MP (1952). He was Secretary of State for Defence in the Wilson governments of 1964–70, and Chancellor of the Exchequer (1974–9). Unsuccessful in the Labour leadership contests of 1976 and 1980, he became Deputy Leader (1980–3), narrowly fighting off a challenge from Tony Benn in 1981, and in 1983 was appointed Shadow Foreign Minister. » Benn, Tony; Labour Party; Wilson, Harold

health foods An umbrella term for so-called 'whole food', additive-free food, and diet supplements such as minerals, vitamins, trace elements, essential fatty acids, and other nutrients. Many of these are sold simply as a supplement to diet, but others make specific therapeutic claims that a particular mix of nutrients will have a specific therapeutic effect, eg that vitamin B6 in megadoses will cure pre-menstrual tension. Most health food shops are now actively promoting what is popularly called alternative medicine. » alternative medicine; carboxylic acids; diet; nutrients; vitamins [i]

health insurance A way of offsetting the cost of medical treatment. The individual pays an annual fee (premium) to a health insurance company, and when treatment is needed the company pays the bills. This is common practice in the USA, and in the UK before 1948, when the National Health Service was introduced. Today, private health insurance is re-emerging as a major factor in British health care. » insurance; National Health Service

Heaney, Seamus (1939–) Irish poet, born on a farm in Londonderry, Northern Ireland. He was educated in Belfast, and moved to Dublin in 1976. He now commutes between there and an appointment at Harvard. Early works such as *Death of a Naturalist* (1966) and *Door into the Dark* (1969) established a deep bond between language and the land. Later volumes (*North*, 1975; *Field Work*, 1979; *Station Island*, 1984) have extended this to reveal a problematic political dimension, and to confirm him as one of the most significant of contemporary English-language poets. » Irish literature; poetry

Heard and McDonald Islands area 412 sq km/159 sq ml. Island group in S Indian Ocean, about 4 000 km/2 500 ml SW of Fremantle, Australia; an Australian external territory comprising Heard I, Shag I, and the McDonald Is; transferred from UK to Australian control in 1947; Heard I (rises to over 2 000 m/6 500 ft) is actively volcanic and has a weather station. » Australia [i]; Indian Ocean

hearing » **auditory perception; cochlea; ear** [i]

hearing aid A device for amplifying sound, used by persons with defective hearing. The earliest type was the ear-trumpet – a conical apparatus collecting sound at the wide end and delivering it to the ear-drum at the small end. Modern aids are electronic, consisting of a microphone, amplifier, and earphone, usually compressed into a very small container to fit directly on to the ear. Transmission may be to the ear-drum or by bone conduction. » ear [i]

Hearns, Thomas, bynames **Hit Man** and **Motor City Cobra** (1958–) US boxer, born at Memphis, Tennessee. In 1988 he became the first man to win world titles at four different weights, and in 1988 the first to win titles at five different weights: he defeated Pipino Cuevas for the welterweight title (WBA, 1980), Wilfred Benitez for the super-welterweight (WBC, 1982), Roberto Duran for the world junior-middleweight (WBC, 1984), Dennis Andries for the light-heavyweight (WBC, 1987), Juan Roldan for the middleweight (WBC, 1987), and James Kinchen for the super-middleweight (WBC, 1988). At the end of 1988 he had won 46 of his 49 contests. » boxing

Hearst, William Randolph (1863–1951) US newspaper owner, born in San Francisco. After studying at Harvard, he took over the San Francisco *Examiner* from his father (1887), and revolutionized journalism by the introduction of banner headlines, lavish illustrations, and other sensational methods. He then took over the New York *Journal* (1895), and made himself the head of a chain of newspapers and periodicals. He died at Beverly Hills, California. His career inspired the film *Citizen Kane.* » newspaper

heart A hollow muscular organ, divided into chambers (right and left *atria*, right and left *ventricles*) and enclosed within a fibrous sac (the *pericardium*) found within the thorax. It lies directly under the sternum, being protected by it and the adjacent ribs. It is the first organ to develop in the embryo (in humans by three weeks). In mammals it is separated into right and left halves concerned with pulmonary and systemic circulation respectively. It consists mainly of cardiac muscle (the *myocardium*) enclosed between two sheets of fibrous and elastic tissue, the *epicardium* and the *endocardium.* The myocardium forms a network of sheets and strands which have a characteristic arrangement in different parts of the heart. The heart also possesses a fibrous skeleton which strengthens many of its openings.

In humans, the ventricles have a capacity of between 90 and 120 ml. The right atrium receives deoxygenated blood from the

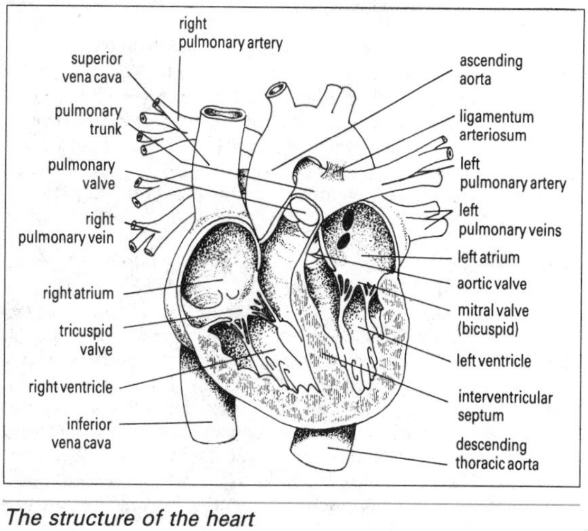

The structure of the heart

body (via the superior and inferior *venae cavae*) and from the heart itself (via the *coronary sinus*) during diastole, and conveys it to the right ventricle via the right atrioventricular opening (guarded by the *tricuspid valve*). The right ventricle expels blood into the pulmonary trunk (guarded by the *pulmonary valve*) and thence to the lungs. The left atrium receives blood from the lungs and conveys it to the left ventricle via the left atrioventricular opening (guarded by the *mitral valve*). The left ventricle forcibly expels blood into the aorta (guarded by the *aortic valve*) and thence to the rest of the body.

In the foetus, blood bypasses the non-functioning lungs in two ways. Freshly oxygenated blood returning from the placenta enters the right atrium and passes directly into the left atrium through an opening in the inter-atrial wall, to be distributed to body tissues via the left ventricle. Deoxygenated blood returning to the right atrium passes into the right ventricle and pulmonary trunk and then into the descending aorta by a communicating channel (the *ductus arteriosus*). After birth, the interatrial opening closes (failure to do so leads to a 'hole in the heart', with the mixing of pulmonary and systemic blood), and the ductus arteriosus becomes obliterated.

The conducting system of the mammalian heart consists of a 'pacemaker' (the *sinuatrial node*), a 'relay station' (the *atrioventricular node*), and the *atrioventricular bundle* within the *interventricular septum*. Both nodes are situated in the right atrium. Damage to the atrioventricular bundle (by disease or experimentally) causes the ventricles to contract independently and at a slower rate than the atria (known as 'heart block'). The rate of contraction is under autonomic control. The walls of the heart are supplied by the coronary arteries, and drained by the cardiac veins and by *venae cordae minimae* (small veins draining the deeper layers of myocardium). A **heart attack** (*myocardial infarction*) occurs when part of the coronary arterial supply becomes blocked by a blood clot (*thrombus*), leading to the cessation of blood flow and death of the myocardium. » Adam Stokes attacks; angina; blood; cardiac resuscitation [i]; coronary heart disease [i]; diastole; heart disease; lungs; myocardial infarction; pacemaker; pulmonary embolism; pulse (physiology); Q fever; rheumatic fever; systole; transplantation; Plates XII, XIII

heart disease Disease of the heart and the associated blood vessels; a major cause of death in all countries, though the pattern of individual disorders varies in different parts of the world and in different age groups. For example, coronary heart disease is common in the UK and the West as a whole, but less common in Japan or Hong Kong. Rheumatic heart disease is now rare in the UK, but common in many parts of the world, notably India and the Middle East. As the heart is essentially a pump, interference with its function whatever the cause gives rise to the cardinal symptoms of shortness of breath, fluid retention (*oedema*), palpitations, chest pain, and fainting. » angina; cardiac resuscitation [i]; coronary heart disease [i]; heart [i]; hypertension; myocardial infarction; rheumatic fever

heart-lung machine An apparatus which takes over the pumping action of the heart, together with the breathing action of the lungs, so that the heart can be stopped and operated upon. Roller-pumps are used to move the blood through special plastic tubing. Oxygen is put into the blood and carbon dioxide released in a bubble oxygenator. The blood is filtered and kept at a suitable temperature during its passage through the machine – if necessary, for several hours. » blood; heart [i]; lungs

heart urchin A bilaterally symmetrical sea urchin which burrows into soft sediment, maintaining breathing passages to the surface by means of its tube feet; mouth displaced to a front position. (Class: *Echinoidea*. Order: *Spatangoida*.) » sea urchin

heartburn A burning sensation usually felt intermittently within the chest over the lower part of the breast bone. It results from regurgitation of the contents of the stomach into the lower part of the oesophagus, inducing a spasm. » oesophagus; sternum

heartsease A species of violet, also called **wild pansy**, native to Europe. The flowers are blue, yellow, white, or a combination of these colours. (*Viola tricolor*. Family: *Violaceae*.) » pansy; violet

heat The transfer of energy from one object to another, due solely to their difference in temperatures; symbol Q, units J (joule). The quantity of heat sometimes ascribed to an object or process is the total amount of energy transferred in this way. » adiabatic process; calorimetry; convection; energy; enthalpy; heat capacity; heat engine; internal energy; isothermal process; latent heat; radiometry [i]; thermal conduction/equilibrium/expansion/insulation; thermodynamics

heat capacity The quantity of heat needed to produce a temperature rise of one kelvin (or 1°C) in some material. Loosely, it measures the ability of a substance to get hot whilst absorbing energy. Specific heat capacity c (also called *specific heat*), units J/(kg.K), is the heat capacity per kilogram of material. For water, $c = 418$ J/(kg.K). » calorie [i]; heat; ratio of specific heats

heat engine The name given to a device that transforms disordered heat energy into ordered, useful, mechanical work. This is achieved by taking a working fluid at high temperature and high heat energy, and subjecting it to a thermodynamic cycle involving compression and expansion, during which time heat is expelled at a lower temperature. The differences in heat energy of the working fluid between input and output appear as work. For physical and theoretical understanding, the thermodynamic cycle is usually idealized, and does not take into account such factors as frictional losses. A large number of idealized thermodynamic cycles exist, of which the Carnot, Diesel, Otto and Stirling cycles are particular examples. » Carnot cycle; engine; thermodynamics

heat of reaction » **chemical energy**

heat stroke A condition which occurs in unacclimatized individuals exposed to high environmental temperatures, in whom body temperature rises to 42–43°C/107–108°F or more. It is attended by rapid loss of consciousness, absence of sweating, and acute kidney and liver failure. Treatment is by urgent cooling of the body. The condition is also known as **sunstroke**, though it may occur with or without exposure to direct sunlight. » temperature [i]

heat treatment Subjecting a metal component to a cycle of heating and cooling so as to modify its internal crystalline structure and therefore promote desirable physical and mechanical properties. The form and rate of the cycle is important: for example, the rapid quenching of a heated alloy may preserve at the low temperature the crystalline structure or chemical composition characteristic of the high temperature. » alloy; annealing; heat

heath A low evergreen shrub or small tree, native to Europe, Asia, N Africa, and especially S Africa; leaves small, narrow to needle-shaped with inrolled margins, in whorls of three or more; flowers often numerous, bell- or urn-shaped, pink, purple, or white. It is often dominant on poor, acid soils of moors and heathland, but some grow on alkaline soils. Many species are grown for ornament. They are also called **ericas**, and are widely known as **heathers**, which is a source of possible confusion with true heather, from which they are easily distinguished by the latter's different leaves and four green sepals. (*Genus Erica*, c.500 species. Family: *Ericaceae*.) » evergreen plants; heather; mycorrhiza; shrub; soil; tree [i]

Heath, Edward (Richard George), byname **Ted** (1916–) British conservative politician and Prime Minister (1970–4), born at Broadstairs, Kent. Educated at Oxford, he served in World War 2, and became an MP in 1950. Following a career in the Whip's office (1951–9), he was Minister of Labour (1959–60), then Lord Privy Seal (1960–3) and the chief negotiator for Britain's entry into the European Common Market. Elected Leader of the Conservative Party in 1965, he was Leader of the Opposition until his 1970 victory. After a confrontation with the miners' union in 1973, he narrowly lost the two elections of 1974, and in 1975 was replaced as leader by Mrs Thatcher. He has continued to play an active part in politics, and is also known for his interests in yachting and music. » Conservative Party; Home of the Hirsel; Thatcher, Margaret

heather 1 A small, bushy, evergreen shrub, native to Europe, especially N and W; leaves in pairs, 1–2 mm/0.04–0.08 in, scale-like with backward projecting basal lobes; flowers tiny, in loose spikes, four sepals, four petals, all purple; also called **ling**. Often the dominant plant on acid soils, especially heathland and moors, in Scotland it forms the major food source of endemic red grouse. A rare form with white flowers is considered lucky. (*Calluna vulgaris*. Family: *Ericaceae*.) » evergreen plants; sepal; shrub **2** » heath

heaven Generally, the dwelling-place of God and the angels, and in traditional Christianity the ultimate eternal destiny of the redeemed, there to reign with Christ in glory. In the Bible, it is usually conceived as high above the Earth. In modern theology, the emphasis is more on the quality, transformation, or fulfilment of life, the fully-revealed presence of God, and the perfection of the divine-human relationship, than on a place. » angel; eschatology; God

Heavenly Twins » **Gemini**

Heaviside, Oliver (1850–1925) British physicist, born in London. He worked as a telegrapher until 1870, when deafness caused him to retire, and he took up the study of electricity. He made important advances in the study of electrical communications, and suggested the existence of an ionized gaseous layer capable of reflecting radio waves. He died at Torquay, Devon. » Heaviside layer

Heaviside layer A region of the ionosphere between c.90–120 km/55–75 ml responsible for the reflection of radio waves back to Earth; also known as the **E layer**. It was discovered in 1902 independently by Oliver Heaviside in England and Arthur E Kennelly in the USA (where it is also known as the **Kennelly layer**). » Appleton layer; Heaviside; ionosphere; Kennelly; radio waves

heavy water » **deuterium**

Hebb, Donald Olding (1904–85) Canadian psychologist, born at Chester, Nova Scotia. He spent most of his academic career at McGill University, Montreal, where he became an influential theorist concerned with the relation between brain and behaviour. His most important book, *The Organization of Behavior* (1949), was influential in the development of connectionism. » connectionism; cortex

Hebe [**hee**bee] In Greek mythology, the goddess of youth and youthful beauty, daughter of Zeus and Hera. She became cupbearer to the Olympians, and was married to Heracles after he was deified. » Heracles

Hébert, Jacques René [ay**bair**] (1757–94) French revolutionary extremist who represented the aspirations of the sansculottes, born at Alençon. He became a popular political journalist, assumed the psuedonym 'Le père Duchesne' after launching a satirical newspaper of that name (1790), and joined both the Cordelier and Jacobin Clubs. He became a member of the Revolutionary Council, playing a major part in the September Massacres and the overthrow of the monarchy. After denouncing the Committee of Public Safety for its failure to help the poor, he tried to incite a popular uprising, but having incurred the suspicion of Danton and Robespierre, he and 17 of his followers ('Hébertists') were guillotined. » Danton; French Revolution [i]; Girondins; Jacobins (French history); Robespierre; sans-culottes

Hebrew A Semitic language which dates from around the 2nd millennium BC. Classical Hebrew is the written language of Judaism, and its modern variety is the official language of the state of Israel. It is spoken by c.4 million people around the world. » Afro-Asiatic languages; Hebrew literature

Hebrew literature The classical period was from the 10th-c to the 4th-c BC, the time of the composition of the Pentateuch (the five books of Moses) and much more of the Bible, though some of the later books are in Aramaic. The Hebrew Mishna and the Aramaic Gemara form the Talmud, the basis of Jewish law and scholarship. Despite frequent persecution, Hebrew literature survived through the Middle Ages, when many fine *piyytim* or liturgical poems were composed. European (especially Spanish) Judaism produced several important Hebrew writers, such as the poet Judas Ha-Levi (c.1080–1141) and Moses Maimonides (1135–1204). Hebrew literature contributed to the 18th-c enlightenment with Moses Mendelssohn (1729–86), and to the 19th-c novel with Abraham Mapu's *Ahavat Zion* (1853, The Love of Zion). The 20th-c has seen a revival of Hebrew literature with Zionism and the State of Israel, though writers such as I L Peretz (1851–1915), Shmuel Agnon (1888–1970), and Amos Oz (1939–) also write in Yiddish. » Agnon; Aramaic; Bible; Hebrew; Maimonides; Mendelssohn; Mishnah; Talmud; Yiddish

Hebrews, Letter to the New Testament writing of unknown authorship and recipients, sometimes attributed to Paul, but this attribution widely doubted even from early times. It emphasizes how Jesus as Son of God is superior to the prophets, the angels, and Moses, and how Jesus acts as the perfect heavenly high priest in the heavenly sanctuary. Whether warning Jewish Christians not to return to Judaism, or challenging proto-gnostic heresies or Gentile cultic practices, the main instructions are against spiritual lethargy and falling back into sin. » Jesus Christ; New Testament; Paul, St; Pauline Letters

Hebrides [**heb**rideez] Over 500 islands off the W coast of Scotland; divided into the **Inner Hebrides** (notably Skye, Eigg, Coll, Mull, Iona, Staffa, Islay, Jura) and **Outer Hebrides** (notably Lewis with Harris, the Uists), separated by the Minch; farming, fishing, Harris tweed, tourism. » Eigg; Fingal's Cave; Iona; Lewis with Harris; Scotland [i]; Skye; Western Isles

Hebron, Arabic **El Khalil**, Hebrew **Hevron** 31°32N 35°06E, pop (1984e) 75 000. Capital city of Hebron governorate (Jordan), Israeli-occupied West Bank, W Jordan; 29 km/18 ml SSW of Jerusalem; one of the oldest cities in the world, built 1730 BC; a religious centre of Islam; the home of Abraham; shrine of Haram El-Khalil over the Cave of Machpelah. » Abraham; Israel [i]; Jordan [i]

Hecate [**hek**atee, **hek**at] In Greek mythology, the goddess associated with witchcraft, spooks, and magic. Not in Homer, she appears in Hesiod, and seems to represent the powerful mother-goddess of Asia Minor. She is worshipped with offerings at places where three roads cross, and so given three bodies in sculpture. » Hesiod

Hector [**hek**taw] According to Greek legend, the bravest Trojan, who led out their army to battle; the son of Priam, and married to Andromache. Achilles killed him and dragged his body behind his chariot; Priam ransomed it at the end of the *Iliad*. » Achilles; Andromache; Trojan War

Hecuba [**hek**yooba] or **Hecabe** [**hek**abee] In Greek legend, the wife of Priam, King of Troy, and mother of 18 children, including Hector and Cassandra. After the Greeks took Troy, she saw her sons and her husband killed, and was sent into slavery. » Trojan War

hedge garlic » **garlic mustard**

hedge sparrow » **dunnock**

hedgehog A mammal (an insectivore) native to Europe, Africa, and Asia; body covered with spines; tail short; many species dig burrows; young born with spines hidden beneath the skin; adults coat spines with saliva. In heraldry, the hedgehog is called a *herisson*. (Family: *Erinaceidae*, 12 species.) » insectivore; moonrat; tenrec

hedging » **futures**

hedonism 1 An ethical doctrine, held by Cyrenaics, Epicureans, and most utilitarians, which maintains that the only intrinsic good is pleasure; the only intrinsic evil is pain. **2** A psychological thesis, often enlisted in aid of ethical hedonism, which claims that people are always motivated to seek pleasure and avoid pain. » Cyrenaics; Epicureanism; utilitarianism

Heenan, John Carmel (1905–75) Roman Catholic Archbishop of Westminster (1963–75), born at Ilford, Essex. Educated at Ushaw and the English College, Rome, he was ordained in 1930, became a parish priest in E London, and during World War 2 worked with the BBC, when he was known as the 'Radio Priest'. He was Bishop of Leeds (1951), and Archbishop of Liverpool (1957) and of Westminster (1963). A convinced ecumenist, he was created a cardinal in 1975. » ecumenism; Roman Catholicism

Hegel, Georg Wilhelm Friedrich [**hay**guhl] (1770–1831) With Kant, whose system he modified, the greatest of the German idealist philosophers, born in Stuttgart. He studied theology at Tübingen, and in 1801 edited with Schelling the *Kritische Journal der Philosophie* (1802–3), in which he outlined his system with its emphasis on reason rather than the romantic intuitionism of Schelling, which he attacked in his first major work, *Phänomenologie des Geistes* (1807, The Phenomenology of the Mind). He was editor of a Bamberg newspaper, then headmaster of a Nuremberg school (1808–16), during which time he wrote his *Wissenschaft der Logik* (1812–16, Science of Logic). He then published his *Enzyklopädie der philosophischen Wissenschaften* (1817, Encyclopedia of the Philosophical Sciences), in which he set out his tripartite system of logic, philosophy of nature, and mind. He became professor in Heidelberg (1816) and Berlin (1818), and to his death was virtually dictator of German philosophical thinking. His approach rejects the reality of finite and separate objects and minds in space and time, and establishes an underlying, all-embracing unity, the Absolute. The quest for greater unity and truth is achieved by the famous dialectic, positing something (*thesis*), denying it (*antithesis*), and combining the two half-truths in a *synthesis* which contains a greater portion of truth in its complexity. His works exerted considerable influence on subsequent European and American philosophy. He died of cholera in Berlin. » Hegelianism; idealism; Kant; Schelling

Hegelianism A philosophical movement begun in the 1820s, inspired by Hegel; it soon split into the Hegelian Right and the Hegelian Left. The Right adhered to Hegel's rationalism and idealism. The left (including Marx) adopted Hegel's dialectic to attack his commitment to idealism, Christianity, monarchy, and bourgeois ideals. » Hegel; Marxism

hegira [hi**ji**ra] The migration of the Prophet Mohammed from Mecca to Medina in 622. The departure marks the beginning of the Muslim era. » Islam; Mohammed; RR22

Heidegger, Martin [**hiy**deguh] (1889–1976) German philosopher, born at Messkirch, Baden. He became professor of philosophy at Marburg (1923–8) and Freiburg (1929–45), when he was retired for his connections with the Nazi regime. In his uncompleted main work *Sein und Zeit* (1927, Being and Time), he presents an exhaustive ontological classification of 'Being', through the synthesis of the modes of human existence. He disclaimed the title of existentialist, since he was not only concerned with personal existence and ethical choices but primarily with the ontological problem in general. Nevertheless, he was a key influence in Sartre's existentialism. He died at Messkirch. » existentialism; ontology; Sartre

Heidelberg [**hiy**dlberk] 49°23N 8°41E, pop(1983) 133 600. Industrial city in Karlsruhe district, Germany; 18 km/11 ml ESE of Mannheim; centre of German Calvinism during the 16th-c; railway; oldest university in Germany (1386); printing presses, pens, machinery, adhesives, scientific apparatus, cement, plaster, publishing, tourism; castle (1583–1610), Holy Ghost Church (15th-c), town hall (18th-c). » Calvinism; Germany [i]

Heidelberg jaw [**hiy**dlberg] A massive, chinless human jaw perhaps 500 000 years old, found in 1907 at Mauer near Heidelberg, W Germany. It probably represents a European form of *Homo erectus*. » *Homo* [i]

Heifetz, Jascha [**hiy**fets] (1901–87) US violinist, born in Vilna, Lithuania. In 1910 he studied at St Petersburg Conservatory, touring Russia, Germany, and Scandinavia at the age of twelve. After the Revolution he settled in the USA, becoming a US citizen in 1925. He died in Los Angeles.

Heilong Jiang » **Amur River**

Heimlich manoeuvre [**hiym**likh] A first-aid life-saving procedure used to dislodge food or other obstruction from the upper respiratory passage; also known as an **abdominal thrust**. A forceful upward thrust is applied to the upper abdomen above the umbilicus by the clenched fist, and repeated until the difficulty in breathing is relieved. It is often applied by clasping the victim around the waist from the back. It is named after US physician Henry J Heimlich. » trachea

Heine, (Christian Johann) Heinrich [**hiy**nuh] (1797–1856) German poet and essayist, born at Düsseldorf of Jewish parentage. He studied banking and law, and in 1821 began to publish poetry, establishing his reputation with his 4-volume *Reisebilder* (1826–7, 1830–1, Pictures of Travel) and *Das Buch der Lieder* (1827, The Book of Songs). In 1825 he became a Christian to secure rights of German citizenship, but this alienated his own people, and his revolutionary opinions made him unemployable in Germany. Going into voluntary exile in Paris after the 1830 revolution, he turned from poetry to politics, and became leader of the cosmopolitan democratic movement, writing widely on French and German culture. He died in Paris. » German literature; poetry

Heinz, H(enry) J(ohn) [hiynts] (1844–1919) US food manufacturer and packer, born of German parents at Pittsburgh, Pennsylvania. In 1876 he became co-founder, with his brother and cousin, of F & J Heinz. The business was reorganized as the H J Heinz Company in 1888, and he was its president 1905–19. He invented the slogan '57 varieties' in 1896, promoted the pure food movement in the USA, and was a pioneer in staff welfare work.

Heisenberg, Werner (Karl) [**hiy**zenberg] (1901–76) German theoretical physicist, born at Würzburg. Educated at Munich and Göttingen, he became professor of physics at Leipzig (1927–41), director of the Kaiser Wilhelm Institute in Berlin (1941–5), and director of the Max Planck Institute in Göttingen (1945–58) and Munich (from 1958). With Max Born he developed quantum mechanics, and formulated the revolutionary principle of indeterminacy in nuclear physics (1927). He won the Nobel Prize for Physics in 1932, and died in Munich. » Born; Heisenberg uncertainty principle; quantum mechanics

Heisenberg uncertainty principle In quantum theory, a fundamental limit on the precision of simultaneous measurements, irrespective of the quality of the measuring equipment used; stated by German physicist Werner Heisenberg in 1927. The product of uncertainty in position with uncertainty in momentum exceeds $h/2\pi$, where h is Planck's constant. Hence, the precise measurement of a sub-atomic particle's position means that the uncertainty in its momentum will be large, and vice versa. A consequence of the wave description of matter, the principle may be interpreted as a result of disturbance to a system due to the act of measuring it. It is sometimes expressed as the product of uncertainty in energy with uncertainty in time exceeding $h/2\pi$. » Heisenberg; quantum field theory; virtual particle

Hel or **Hela** In Norse mythology, the youngest child of Loki; half her body was living human flesh, the other half decayed. She was assigned by Odin to rule Helheim (the Underworld) and to receive the spirits of the dead who do not die in battle. » Germanic religion; Loki; Valhalla

Helen In Greek legend, the wife of Menelaus of Sparta, famous for her beauty; her abduction by Paris the Trojan caused the Trojan War. She was the daughter of Zeus and Leda, in mythical accounts. According to Stesichoros, however, Helen stayed in Egypt, while a phantom accompanied Paris to Troy.

Heimlich manoeuvre

» Leda (mythology); Menelaus; Paris (mythology); Trojan War

Helena, St (c.255–c.330), feast day 18 August (W), 21 May (E). Mother of the Roman Emperor Constantine (the Great), born in Bithynia, Asia Minor. The wife of Emperor Constantius Chlorus, she early became a Christian, and when Constantine became Emperor he made her Empress Dowager. In 326, according to tradition, she visited Jerusalem, and founded the basilicas on the Mount of Olives and at Bethlehem. She died in Nicomedia. » Christianity; Constantine I (Emperor)

helical scan A system of magnetic tape recording in which the tape is wrapped in a partial helix around a drum carrying two or more rotating heads which trace a series of tracks diagonally across its width. The relative head-to-tape velocity, the 'writing speed', is much higher than the rate at which the tape itself advances, so that very high frequencies can be recorded economically. The technique was originally developed for video recording, but later applied to produce compact high quality audio tracks. » tape recorder; videotape recorder

Helicon [**hel**ikon] The largest mountain in Boeotia. In Greek mythology, it was the sacred hill of the Muses, whose temple was to be found there, together with the fountains of Aganippe and Hippocrene. » Boeotia; Muses; Pegasus (mythology)

helicopter A vertical take-off and landing aircraft whose lift is provided by means of a horizontal, large-diameter set of powered blades which force the air downwards and by reaction create a lifting force upwards. Forward flight is achieved by tilting the plane of the blades in the direction of flight, varying their angle to the horizontal as they rotate. » aircraft [i]

Heligoland, Ger **Helgoland** 54°09N 7°52E, pop (1983e) 2011. Rocky North Sea island of the North Frisian Is, in Heligoland Bay, Schleswig-Holstein, Germany, 64 km/40 ml NW of Cuxhaven; area 2.1 sq km/0.8 sq ml; captured from Denmark by the UK, 1807; ceded to Germany in exchange for Zanzibar, 1890; German naval base in both World Wars; tourism; centre for the study of birds. » Frisian Islands

heliocentric system Any theory of our planetary system that has the Sun at the centre. It was proposed by Aristarchus in the 3rd-c BC, and revived with great success by Copernicus in 1543. » Aristarchus of Samos; Copernican system; Solar System

Helios [**heel**eeos] In Greek mythology, the Sun-god, represented as a charioteer with four horses. In early times Helios was not worshipped, except at Rhodes; in the late classical period, there was an Imperial cult of the Sun, Sol Invictus. » Phaethon

Helios project A joint space mission of West Germany and the USA, designed to study the interplanetary medium to as close as 0.3 astronomical units (AU) from the Sun, ie to the inside of Mercury's orbit. Two spacecraft were built by West Germany and launched on Titan III–Centaur vehicles (Dec 1974, Jan 1976). They operated successfully for over 10 years, tracked by West German ground stations and by NASA's Deep Space Network. » Space Organizations Worldwide

heliotrope A small evergreen shrub 0.5–2 m/1½–6½ ft, a native of Peru; leaves lance-shaped to oblong, hairy, puckered; flowers small, tubular, with spreading lobes, white to lilac or violet, in terminal clusters. It is cultivated for its fragrant flowers. (*Heliotropium peruvianum*. Family: *Boraginaceae*.) » evergreen plants; shrub

helium He, element 2, the most inert of the chemical elements, forming no stable compounds; the lightest of the 'noble' or 'inert' gases. It condenses to a liquid only at −269°C (4K). Formed by radioactive decay of the heaviest elements, it is obtained mainly as a small fraction of natural gas. Because of its inertness and low density (less than 15% of the density of air), it is used to fill balloons. Liquid helium is used as the ultimate coolant, and was important in the discovery and development of superconductivity. » chemical elements; noble gases; superfluidity; RR90

hell In traditional Christian thought, the eternal abode and place of torment of the damned. It developed out of Hebrew *sheol* and Greek *hades* as the place of the dead. Much contemporary Christian thought rejects the idea of vindictive punishment as incompatible with belief in a loving God. The emphasis acccordingly shifts from hell as a place of retribution to a state of being without God. » Devil; eschatology; God

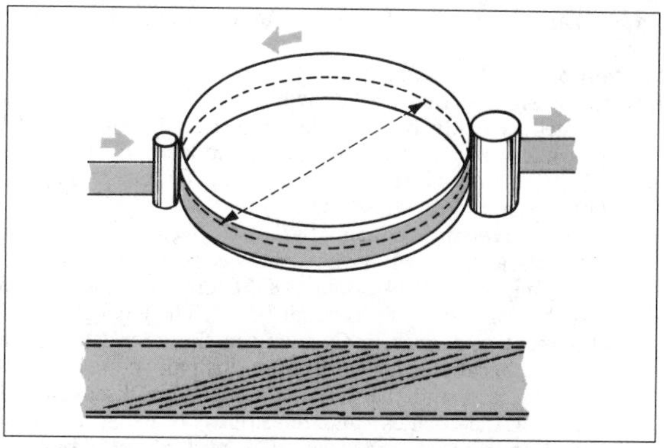

Helical scan – A continuously moving magnetic tape is wrapped around a rapidly rotating drum. The drum carries the recording heads, which trace a series of diagonal tracks.

Hell's Canyon or **Grand Canyon of the Snake** Gorge on the Snake R where it follows the Oregon–Idaho state frontier, USA; with a depth of c.2450 m/8030 ft, it is one of the deepest gorges in the world; length 65 km/40 ml. » Snake River

hellbender A nocturnal salamander, native to E and C USA; length, up to 750 mm/30 in; small eyes, broad head, deep narrow tail, loose skin along sides of body; inhabits streams and rivers; eats invertebrates and fish. (*Cryptobranchus alleganiensis*. Family: *Cryptobranchidae*.) » salamander [i]

hellebore [**hel**ibaw] A perennial with glossy divided leaves and large flowers, native to Europe and W Asia; flowers with five green, white, or pinkish-purple petaloid sepals, and up to 20 prominent 2-lipped nectar-secreting glands; highly poisonous, with a burning taste because of the presence of alkaloids. (Genus: *Helleborus*, 20 species. Family: *Ranunculaceae*.) » alkaloids; Christmas rose; perennial; sepal

helleborine [**hel**ibuhrin] Either of two closely related genera of orchids. *Epipactis* (24 species), from N temperate regions and parts of the tropics, has stalked flowers in which the lower lip (*labellum*) forms a nectar-containing cup with a tongue-like extension. *Cephalanthera* (12 species), from N temperate regions, has stalkless flowers which never fully open. (Family: *Orchidaceae*.) » orchid [i]

Hellen [**hel**en, **hel**een] In ancient Greek genealogies, the eldest son of Deucalion, and father of Doros, Xuthos, and Aiolos, who were the progenitors of the Dorian, Ionian, and Aeolic branches of the Greek race. The Greeks (or *Hellenes*) were named after him. » Deucalion

Hellenistic Age The period from the death of Alexander the Great (323 BC) to the beginning of the Roman Empire (31 BC), during which a number of Greek or Hellenized dynasties, many descended from Alexander's generals (such as the Ptolemies and Seleucids), ruled the entire area from Greece to the N of India. » Attalids; Bithynia; Hellenization; Ptolemy I Soter; Seleucids

Hellenists [**hel**uhnists] A group referred to in the Book of Acts (6.1, 9.29), contrasted with the 'Hebrews', and usually interpreted as Greek-speaking Jewish Christians who were critical of the Temple worship and who prepared for the Christian mission to non-Jews. Stephen may have been one of them. Other interpretations of this group consider them Jews (not Christians) whose mother-tongue was Greek, or even non-Jews (Greeks). » Acts of the Apostles; Christianity; Stephen, St

Hellenization In the ancient world, the process by which Greek language and culture were disseminated among non-Greek (usually oriental) peoples. Initially a spontaneous development, from the time of Alexander the Great, it became a deliberate policy: he and his successors planted Greek city-states all over their dominions to produce cultural unification. » polis

Heller, Joseph (1923–) US novelist, born in New York City. He served with the US Air Force in World War 2, and his wartime experience forms the background for his first novel, *Catch-22* (1961), which was an immediate success. He has written four more novels, including *Something Happened*

(1964) and *Picture This* (1988). » American literature; Catch-22; novel

Hellespont » **Dardanelles**

helmet shell A marine snail known mostly from warm tropical seas; shell typically has a series of external flange-like ribs (*varices*), and is much sought after by collectors; used as raw material for cameos. (Class: *Gastropoda*. Order: *Mesogastropoda*.) » gastropod; shell; snail

Helmholtz, Hermann von (1821–94) German physiologist and physicist, born at Potsdam. He was professor of physiology at Königsberg (1849), Bonn (1855), and Heidelberg (1858), and in 1871 professor of physics at Berlin. The key figure in the development of science in Germany in the later 19th-c, with over 200 publications, his works are principally connected with the eye, the ear, and the nervous system. He discovered the function of the cochlea, and developed a theory of colour vision. Ennobled in 1883, he died at Charlottenburg. » cochlea; vision

helminthology The study of parasitic worms (*helminths*), including roundworms, flatworms, and their larval stages. » flatworm; nematode; parasitology; worm

Helmont, Jan Baptista van (1579–1644) Flemish chemist, born in Brussels. He studied medicine, mysticism, and chemistry under the influence of Paracelsus, devoting much study to gases, and invented the term *gas*. He was the first to take the melting-point of ice and the boiling-point of water as standards for temperature. Through his experiments he bridged the gap between alchemy and chemistry. He died at Vilvoorde, Belgium. » chemistry; Paracelsus

Héloïse » **Abelard, Peter**

Helpmann, Sir Robert (Murray) (1909–86) Australian dancer, actor, and choreographer, born at Mount Gambier. He made his debut in Adelaide in 1923, studied with Pavlova's touring company in 1929, and in 1931 came to Britain to study under Ninette de Valois. He was first dancer of the newly founded Sadler's Wells Ballet (1933–50), and became known for his dramatic roles in de Valois' works. His ballets include *Hamlet* (1942) and *Miracle in the Gorbals* (1944), and he also appeared in many films. Joint artistic director of Australian ballet in 1965, he was knighted in 1968, and died in Sydney. » ballet; Pavlova; Royal Ballet; Valois, Ninette de

Helsingborg, Swed **Hälsingborg** 56°03N 12°43E, pop (1982) 102 951. Seaport and commercial town on W coast of Malmöhus county, SW Sweden; on The Sound opposite Helsingør, Denmark; railway; ferry services to Denmark; shipbuilding, textiles, machinery, copper refining, fertilizers, trade in chemicals, timber, paper; town hall (1897), St Mary's Church (13th-c). » Sweden [i]

Helsingfors [**hel**singfawz] » **Helsinki**

Helsingør » **Elsinore**

Helsinki [hel**sing**kee], Swedish **Helsingfors** 60°08N 25°00E, pop (1982) 483 400. Seaport, capital of Finland and Uudenmaa province, S Finland; on the Gulf of Finland, on a peninsula surrounded by islands; founded by Gustavus Vasa in 1550; capital, 1812; heavily bombed in World War 2; airport; railway; university (transferred from Turku, 1828); technical university (1908); shipbuilding, textiles, engineering, porcelain, metals, paper, export trade; cathedral (completed 1852), Olympic Stadium, Rock Church (Tempeliaukio), Ateneum Museum, National Museum, open-air museum of country life on nearby island of Seurasaari. » Finland [i]; Gustavus I

Helsinki Conference (1975) A conference on security and co-operation in Europe, attended by the heads of 35 states, including the USA and USSR, with the objective of forwarding the process of detente through agreements on economic and technological co-operation, security, and disarmament. These were set out in the Final Act within the principles of sovereignity and self-determination. » detente

Helvellyn [hel**vel**in] 54°32N 3°02W. Mountain in the Lake District of Cumbria, NW England; rises to 950 m/3 117 ft between Ullswater and Thirlmere; Striding Edge descends to the E. » Lake District

Helvetii [hel**way**tiee] Celtic people forced S by Germanic tribesmen in the 2nd-c BC into modern Switzerland. In 58 BC, when renewed Germanic pressure prompted Helvetian migration into Gaul, Julius Caesar drove them back to their Swiss lands. They became allies then subjects of Rome, until c.400. The official names for Switzerland derive from this source: *Helvetia* and *Confederatio Helvetica*. » Caesar; Celts; Gaul

hem- » also under **haem-**

hemichordate A bottom-living, marine invertebrate with gill slits in its pharynx similar to those of primitive vertebrates; includes the acornworms and graptolites. (Phylum: *Hemichordata*.) » acornworm; graptolite

Hemingway, Ernest (Miller) (1899–1961) US author, born at Oak Park, Illinois. He became a journalist, saw action at the end of World War 1 as an ambulance driver, then moved to France as a foreign correspondent. His first short stories appeared in 1925, and his first novels in 1926. His major novels include *A Farewell to Arms* (1929), *For Whom the Bell Tolls* (1940), and *The Old Man and the Sea* (1952), which won him a Pulitzer Prize in 1953. In 1954 he was awarded the Nobel Prize for Literature. He was a war correspondent in World War 2, and took part in the D-Day landings (1944). After the Spanish Civil War he went to live in Cuba, staying there until the 1960 revolution, when he moved to the USA. Subject to depression, and fearing ill health, he shot himself, at Ketchum, Idaho. » American literature; novel; short story

hemione » **ass**

hemiplegia » **paralysis**

hemipode » **button quail; plains wanderer**

Hemiptera [he**mip**tuhra] A group of insects comprising two orders, the *Homoptera* and the *Heteroptera*. » Heteroptera; Homoptera

hemispheric specialization » **laterality**

hemlock 1 An evergreen conifer native to N America and E Asia; branches drooping; leaves short, narrow, in two ranks; cones ripe after one year, but do not shed seeds until the second year. It yields timber, Canada pitch, and tanning bark. (Genus: *Tsuga*, 15 species. Family: *Pinaceae*.) » conifer; evergreen plants **2** A biennial growing to 2.5 m/8 ft, native to Europe and temperate Asia, and widely introduced; stem hollow, furrowed, spotted with purple; leaves divided with oblong toothed segments; flowers white, lacking sepals, in umbels 2–5 cm/¾–2 in across; fruit ovoid; a fetid smell. All parts are very poisonous because of the presence of the alkaloid *coniine*, used as a poison since classical times, and reputedly the poison given to Socrates by the Athenian leaders. (*Conium maculatum*. Family: *Umbelliferae*.) » alkaloids; biennial; sepal; Socrates; umbel

hemo- » **haemo-**

hemp » **abaca; cannabis**

hen » **domestic fowl**

henbane An annual or biennial, sticky-haired and fetid, native to Europe, W Asia, and N Africa; leaves large, soft, coarsely toothed; flowers 2–3 cm/¾–1¼ in across, borne in a curved inflorescence; calyx tubular; corolla 5-lobed, lurid yellow and purple. It is poisonous, containing various aklaloids, principally hyoscyamnine and scopalomine. Its extracts are still used in modern medicine, mainly as sedatives. (*Hyoscyamus niger*. Family: *Solanaceae*.) » alkaloids; annual; biennial; corolla; inflorescence [i]; sepal

Henbury Crater A meteorite crater at Henbury, Northern Territory, Australia; c.100 km/60 ml SW of Alice Springs. » meteorite

Hendrix, Jimi (1942–70) US rock guitarist, singer, and songwriter, born in Seattle, Washington. He learned basic blues licks as a sideman for Little Richard and the Isley Brothers. After his 1965 discharge from the army, he explored electronic tricks on his guitar at ear-splitting amplitude, to which he added stage gimmicks, playing behind his back or with his teeth. His raucous blues style influenced heavy metal bands. He died in London, after taking barbiturates and alcohol. » blues; guitar; rock music

Hengduan Shan Mountain range in SW China; series of parallel ranges running N–S; average height, 3–4 000 m/10–13 000 ft; rises to 7 556 m/24 790 ft at Gongga Shan peak. » China [i]

Hengist and Horsa Two brothers, leaders of the first Anglo-Saxon settlers in Britain, said by Bede to have been invited over by Vortigern, the British king, to fight the Picts in about AD 450. According to the *Anglo-Saxon Chronicle*, Horsa was killed in 455 and Hengist ruled in Kent until his death in 488. » Anglo-Saxons; Bede

Henie, Sonja [henee] (1912–69) Norwegian figure skater, born in Oslo. The winner of three Olympic gold medals (1928, 1932, 1936), she also won a record 10 individual world titles (1927–36). She retired from competitive skating in 1936 after winning 1 473 cups, medals, and trophies, and then appeared in films. She became a US citizen in 1941, and died in an aeroplane ambulance while flying to Oslo. » ice skating

Henley Royal Regatta Rowing races which take place annually on the R Thames, Henley-on-Thames, UK, inaugurated in 1839. The Diamond Sculls and the Grand Challenge Cup are the most coveted events. The course has varied over the years, but is now approximately 2 km 112 m/1 ml 550 yd. It is as much a social occasion for the public as a sporting one. » rowing

henna An evergreen shrub growing to 3 m/10 ft, native to the Old World tropics; leaves opposite, oval to lance-shaped; flowers 4-petalled, white, pink, or red; fruit a 3-chambered capsule. The powdered leaves produce a red dye, used as a cosmetic for skin and hair since ancient times. (*Lawsonia inermis*. Family: *Lythraceae*.) » dyestuff; evergreen plants; shrub

Henrietta Maria (1609–69) Queen of Charles I of England, born at the Louvre, the youngest child of Henry IV of France. She married Charles in 1625, but her French attendants and Roman Catholic beliefs made her unpopular. In 1642, under the threat of impeachment, she fled to Holland and raised funds for the Royalist cause. A year later she landed at Bridlington, and met Charles near Edgehill. At Exeter she gave birth to Henrietta Anne, and a fortnight later she was compelled to flee to France (1644). She paid two visits to England after the Restoration (1660–1, 1662–5), and died near Paris. » English Civil War

henry SI unit of inductance; symbol H; named after US physicist Joseph Henry; defined as the inductance of a closed circuit in which a current changing at the rate of one ampere per second produces an electromotive force (emf) of one volt. » Henry, Joseph; inductance; units (scientific); RR70

Henry I (of England) (1068–1135) King (1100–35) and Duke of Normandy (1106–35), the youngest son of William the Conqueror. Under Henry, the Norman Empire attained the height of its power. He conquered Normandy from his brother, Robert Curthose, at the Battle of Tinchebrai (1106), maintained his position on the Continent, and exercised varying degrees of authority over the King of Scots, the Welsh princes, the Duke of Brittany, and the Counts of Flanders, Boulogne, and Ponthieu. His government of England and Normandy became increasingly centralized and interventionist, with the overriding aim of financing warfare and alliances, and consolidating the unity of the two countries as a single cross-Channel state. His only legitimate son, William Adelin, was drowned in 1120, and in 1127 he nominated his daughter Empress Matilda, widow of Emperor Henry V of Germany, as his heir for both England and Normandy. But Matilda and her second husband, Geoffrey of Anjou, proved unacceptable to the King's leading subjects. After Henry's death at Lyons-la-Forêt, near Rouen, the crown was seized by Stephen, son of his sister, Adela. » Angevins; Stephen; William I (of England)

Henry II (of England) (1133–89) King (1154–89), the son of Empress Matilda, Henry I's daughter and acknowledged heir, by her second husband Geoffrey of Anjou, born at Le Mans, Maine-et-Loire. Already established as Duke of Normandy (1150) and Count of Anjou (1151), and as Duke of Aquitaine by marriage to Eleanor of Aquitaine (1152), he invaded England in 1153, and was recognized as the lawful successor of the usurper, Stephen. He founded the Angevin or Plantagenet dynasty of English kings, and ruled England as part of a wider Angevin Empire. He restored and transformed English governance after the disorders of Stephen's reign. His efforts to restrict clerical independence caused conflict with his former Chancellor Thomas Becket, Archbishop of Canterbury, which was ended only with Becket's murder (1170). He led a major expedition to Ireland (1171), which resulted in its annexation. The most serious challenge to his power came in 1173–4 when his son the young Henry, encouraged by Queen Eleanor, rebelled in alliance with Louis VII of France, William I of Scotland, and Count Philip of Flanders. All parts of the King's dominions were threatened, but his enemies were defeated. In 1189 he faced further disloyalty from his family when his sons, John and Richard, allied with Philip II of France, who overran Maine and Touraine. Henry agreed a peace which recognized Richard as his sole heir for the Angevin Empire, and he died shortly afterwards at Chinon. » Angevins; Becket; Clarendon, Constitutions of; Stephen; William I (of Scotland)

Henry II (of France) (1519–59) King (1547–69), born near Paris, the second son of Francis I, who became heir to the throne in 1536. In 1533 he married Catherine de' Medici. Soon after his accession, he began to oppress his Protestant subjects. Through the influence of the Guises he formed an alliance with Scotland, and declared war against England, which ended in 1558 with the taking of Calais. He continued the long-standing war against the Emperor Charles V, gaining Toul, Metz, and Verdun, but suffered reverses in Italy and the Low Countries, which led to the Treaty of Cateau-Cambrésis (1559). Soon after he was accidentally wounded in a tournament, and died in Paris. » Catherine de' Medici; Charles V (Emperor); Guise

Henry III (of England) (1207–72) King (1216–72), the elder son and successor, at the age of nine, of John. He declared an end to his minority in 1227, and in 1232 stripped the justiciar, Hubert de Burgh, of power. His arbitrary assertion of royal rights conflicted with the principles of Magna Carta, and antagonized many nobles. Although he failed to recover Poitou (N Aquitaine) in 1242, he accepted the Kingdom of Sicily (1254). This forced him to seek the support of the barons, who under the leadership of the King's brother-in-law, Simon de Montfort, imposed far-reaching reforms by the Provisions of Oxford (1258), which gave them a definite say in government. When Henry sought to restore royal power, the barons rebelled and captured the King at Lewes (1264), but were defeated at Evesham (1265). The Dictum of Kenilworth (1266), though favourable to Henry, urged him to observe Magna Carta. Organized resistance ended in 1267, and the rest of the reign was stable. Henry died in London, and was succeeded by his elder son, Edward I. » Barons' Wars; Edward I; John; Magna Carta; Montfort, Simon de; Oxford, Provisions of

Henry III (of France) (1551–89) King (1574–89), born at Fontainebleau, the third son of Henry II. In 1569 he gained victories over the Huguenots, and took an active share in the massacre of St Bartholomew (1572). In 1573 he was elected to the crown of Poland, but two years later succeeded his brother, Charles IX, on the French throne. His reign was a period of almost incessant civil war between Huguenots and Catholics. In 1588 he engineered the assassination of the Duke of Guise, enraging the Catholic League. He joined forces with the Huguenot Henry of Navarre, and while marching on Paris was assassinated by a fanatical priest. The last of the Valois line, he named Henry of Navarre as his successor. » Charles IX; Huguenots; Religion, Wars of; Valois

Henry IV (of England) (1366–1413) King (1399–1413), the first King of the House of Lancaster, the son of John of Gaunt, who was the fourth son of Edward III. He was surnamed Bolingbroke, from his birthplace in Lincolnshire. In 1397 he supported Richard II against the Duke of Gloucester, and was created Duke of Hereford, but was banished in 1398. After landing at Ravenspur, Yorkshire, Henry induced Richard, now deserted, to abdicate in his favour. During his reign, rebellion and lawlessness were rife, and he was constantly hampered by lack of money. Under Owen Glendower the Welsh maintained their independence, and Henry's attack on Scotland in 1400 ended in his defeat. Henry Percy (Hotspur) and his house then joined with the Scots and the Welsh against him, but they were defeated at Shrewsbury (1403). A chronic invalid in later years, he died at Westminster, London. » Glendower; Percy; Richard II

Henry IV (of France) (1553–1610) The first Bourbon King of France (1589–1610), born at Pau, the third son of Antoine de Bourbon. Brought up a Calvinist, he led the Huguenot army at the battle of Jarnac (1569), and became leader of the Protestant Party. He married Margaret of Valois in 1572. After the massacre of St Bartholomew (1572), he was spared by professing himself a Catholic, and spent three years virtually a prisoner at the French court. In 1576 he escaped, revoked his conversion, and resumed command of the army in continuing opposition to the Guises and the Catholic League. After the murder of Henry III, he succeeded to the throne. In 1593 he became a Catholic, thereby unifying the country, and by the Edict of Nantes Protestants were granted liberty of conscience. His economic policies, implemented by his minister, Sully, gradually brought new wealth to the country. He was assassinated in Paris by a religious fanatic. » Bourbons; Huguenots; Nantes, Edict of; Sully; Religion, Wars of

Henry V (of England) (1387–1422) King (1413–22), born at Monmouth, the eldest son of Henry IV. He fought against Glendower and the Welsh rebels (1402–8), and became constable of Dover (1409) and captain of Calais (1410). To this time belong the exaggerated stories of his wild youth. The main effort of his reign was his claim, through his great-grandfather Edward III, to the French crown. In 1415 he invaded France, and won the Battle of Agincourt against great odds. By 1419 Normandy was again under English control, and in 1420 was concluded the 'perpetual peace' of Troyes, under which Henry was recognized as heir to the French throne and Regent of France, and married Charles VI's daughter, Catharine of Valois. He died at Vincennes. » Agincourt, Battle of; Hundred Years' War

Henry VI (of England) (1421–71) King (1422–61, 1470–1), the only child of Henry V and Catherine of Valois, born at Windsor, Berkshire. During Henry's minority, his uncle John, Duke of Bedford, was Regent in France, and another uncle Humphrey, Duke of Gloucester, was Lord Protector of England. Henry was crowned King of France at Paris in 1431, two years after his coronation in England. But once the Burgundians had made a separate peace with Charles VII (1435), Henry V's French conquests were progressively eroded, and by 1453 the English retained only Calais. Henry had few kingly qualities, and from 1453 suffered from periodic bouts of insanity. Richard, Duke of York, seized power as Lord Protector in 1454, and defeated the King's army at St Albans (1455), the first battle of the Wars of the Roses. Fighting resumed in 1459, and although York himself was killed at Wakefield (1460), his heir was proclaimed King as Edward IV after Henry's deposition (1461). In 1464 Henry returned from exile in Scotland to lead the Lancastrian cause, but was captured and imprisoned (1465–70). Richard Neville, Earl of Warwick, restored him to the throne (Oct 1470), his nominal rule ending when Edward IV returned to London (Apr 1471). After the Yorkist victory at Tewkesbury (May 1471), where his only son was killed, Henry was murdered in the Tower. » Charles VII; Edward IV; Henry V (of England); Hundred Years' War; Roses, Wars of the; Warwick, Earl of

Henry VII (of England) (1457–1509) King (1485–1509), born at Pembroke Castle, the grandson of Owen Tudor, who married Queen Catherine, the widow of Henry V; the founder of the Tudor dynasty. After the Lancastrian defeat at Tewkesbury (1471), Henry was taken to Brittany, where several Yorkist attempts on his life and liberty were frustrated. In 1485 he landed unopposed at Milford Haven, and defeated Richard III at Bosworth. As King, his policy was to restore peace and prosperity to the country, and this was helped by his marriage of reconciliation with Elizabeth of York. He was also noted for the efficiency of his financial and administrative policies. He firmly dealt with Yorkist plots, such as that led by Perkin Warbeck. Peace was concluded with France, and the marriage of his heir to Catherine of Aragon cemented an alliance with Spain. He died at Richmond, Surrey, and was succeeded by his son, as Henry VIII. » Bosworth Field, Battle of; Richard III; Tudors; Warbeck

Henry VIII (of England) (1491–1547) King (1509–47), born at Greenwich, near London, the second son of Henry VII. Soon after his accession he married Catherine of Aragon, his brother Arthur's widow. As a member of the Holy League, he invaded France (1512), winning the Battle of Spurs (1513); and while abroad, the Scots were defeated at Flodden. In 1521 he published a book on the Sacraments in reply to Luther, receiving from the Pope the title 'Defender of the Faith'. From 1527 he determined to divorce Catherine, whose children, except for Mary, had died in infancy. He tried to put pressure on the Pope by humbling the clergy, and in defiance of Rome was privately married to Anne Boleyn (1533). In 1534 it was enacted that his marriage to Catherine was invalid, and that the King was the sole head of the Church of England. The policy of suppressing the monasteries then began. In 1536 Catherine died, and Anne Boleyn was executed for infidelity. Henry then married Jane Seymour (c.1509–37), who died leaving a son, afterwards Edward VI. In 1540 Anne of Cleves became his fourth wife, in the hope of attaching the Protestant interest of Germany; but dislike of her appearance caused him to divorce her speedily. He then married Catherine Howard (1540), who two years later was executed on grounds of infidelity (1542). In 1543 his last marriage was to Catherine Parr, who survived him. His later years saw further war with France and Scotland, before peace was concluded with France in 1546. He died in London, and was succeeded by his son as Edward VI. » Anne of Cleves; Boleyn; Catherine of Aragon; Church of England; Cromwell, Thomas; Fisher, St John; Howard, Catherine; More, Thomas; Parr, Catherine; Seymour, Jane; Reformation; Wolsey, Thomas

Henry, Joseph (1797–1878) US physicist, born at Albany, New York. In 1832 he became professor of natural philosophy at Princeton, and in 1846 first secretary of the Smithsonian Institution. He discovered electrical induction independently of Faraday, constructed the first electromagnetic motor (1829), demonstrated the oscillatory nature of electric discharges (1842), and introduced a system of weather forecasting. The unit of inductance is named after him. He died in Washington, DC. » electricity; Faraday; henry

Henry, O, pseudonym of **William Sydney Porter** (1862–1910) US writer, master of the short story, born at Greenboro, North Carolina. Brought up during the depression in the South, he began to write short stories while in jail for embezzlement. In 1902 he moved to New York City, and produced the first of many volumes, *Cabbages and Kings*, in 1904. His stories provide a romantic and humorous treatment of everyday life, and are noted for their use of coincidence and trick endings. He died in New York City. » American literature; short story

Henry, Patrick (1736–99) American revolutionary and statesman, born in Hanover Co, Virginia. After training as a lawyer, he entered the colonial Virginia House of Burgesses, where his oratorical skills won him fame. He was outspoken in his opposition to British policy towards the colonies, particularly on the subject of the Stamp Act (1765), and he made the first speech in the Continental Congress (1774). In 1776 he became Governor of independent Virginia, and was four times re-elected. He died near Brookneal, Virginia. » American Revolution; Continental Congress

Henry, William (1774–1836) British chemist, born and died in Manchester, the son of a prosperous chemical manufacturer. He qualified in medicine, but his work was mainly in chemistry. An expert on gas analysis, his name was given to **Henry's law**. A childhood injury led to continuing pain, and he committed suicide. » gas **1**; Henry's law

Henry the Lion (1129–95) Duke of Saxony (1142–80) and Bavaria (1156–80), the head of the Guelphs. His ambitious designs roused against him a league of princes in 1166, but he retained power through an alliance with Emperor Frederick I Barbarossa. After breaking with Frederick in 1176, he was deprived of most of his lands, and exiled. Ultimately he was reconciled to Frederick's successor, Henry VI. He encouraged commerce, and founded the city of Munich. He died at Brunswick, Saxony. » Frederick I (Emperor); Guelphs

Henry the Navigator (1394–1460) Portuguese prince, the third son of John I, King of Portugal, and Philippa, daughter of John of Gaunt, Duke of Lancaster. He set up court at Sagres, Algarve, and erected an observatory and school of scientific navigation. He sponsored many exploratory expeditions along the W African coast, and the way was prepared for the discovery of the sea route to India. He died near Sagres.

Henry's law In chemistry, a law formulated by British chemist William Henry: the solubility of a gas in a liquid at any given temperature is proportional to the pressure of the gas on the liquid. This has wide application, including the production of carbonated beverages, and in 'the bends', a condition in deep-sea divers where nitrogen, having dissolved in the blood at high pressure, is released with sometimes fatal consequences when the diver returns to the low pressure of the surface. » gas **1**; Henry, William

Henryson, Robert (c.1425–1508) Scottish mediaeval poet. He is usually designated schoolmaster of Dunfermline, and was certainly a notary in 1478. His works include *Testament of Cresseid; Robene and Makyne*, the earliest Scottish specimen of pastoral poetry; and a metrical version of 13 *Morall Fabels of Esope*, often viewed as his masterpiece. » Chaucer; poetry; Scottish literature

Henslowe, Philip (c.1550–1616) English theatre manager, originally a dyer and starchmaker, who in 1584 became lessee of the Rose Theatre on the Bankside, London. From 1591 until his death he was in partnership with Edward Alleyn, who married his stepdaughter. Henslowe's business diary (1593–1609) contains invaluable information about the stage of Shakespeare's day. » Alleyn; Shakespeare [i]; theatre

Henze, Hans Werner (1926–) German composer, born at Gütersloh. He studied at Heidelberg and Paris, and was influenced by Schoenberg, exploring beyond the more conventional uses of the twelve-tone system. His more recent works, which include operas, ballets, symphonies, and chamber music, often reflect his left-wing political views. He settled in Italy in 1953, and has taken master classes in composition at the Salzburg Mozarteum since 1961.

heparin [**hep**arin] A chemical substance (a polysaccharide) found in the mast cells of the liver, lungs, and intestinal mucosa, which prevents blood clotting. Its physiological importance is controversial, but its extracted and purified form is used as an anti-coagulant drug in medicine, eg in the prevention of thrombosis. » anticoagulants; disaccharide; haemostasis; mast cells; thrombosis

hepatitis Inflammation of the liver, caused by one of several hepatic viruses. The commonest is caused by virus A (*infective hepatitis*), usually a mild febrile disorder, with loss of appetite some days before jaundice develops. Almost all patients recover completely within one to two months. Virus B infection (*serum hepatitis*) is much more serious, and carries a significant mortality; the carrier state is also more frequent and persisting, and recurring liver disease is common. Virus A infection is acquired by contact with contaminated food or water; Virus B infection by close personal contact or by the introduction of infected blood or blood products into the bloodstream. Other viruses that may cause hepatitis include those responsible for glandular fever and yellow fever. » fever; jaundice; liver; venereal disease; virus

Hepburn, Katharine (1909–) US actress, born at Hartford, Connecticut. Educated at Bryn Mawr College, she made her debut on stage at Baltimore. From 1932 she attained international fame as a film actress, notably in *Morning Glory* (1933), *Guess Who's Coming to Dinner* (1967), *The Lion in Winter* (1968), and *On Golden Pond* (1981), all of which gained her Academy Awards, and *The African Queen* (1952). In 1984 she starred in the television film, *The Ultimate Solution of Grace Quigley*.

Hephaestus [he**fees**tus] In Greek mythology, a god of fire, associated with volcanic sites; then of the smithy and metalwork. Because of his marvellous creations, such as the shield of Achilles, he was worshipped as the god of craftsmen. He was the son of Hera, who was annoyed at his lameness and threw him out of heaven; he landed on Lemnos. » Vulcan (mythology)

heptane C_7H_{16}. An alkane hydrocarbon with seven carbon atoms. There are nine structural isomers, most of which occur in the gasoline fraction of petroleum. The straight-chain compound, n-heptane, $CH_3CH_2CH_2CH_2CH_2CH_2CH_3$, boiling point 98°C, is particularly bad for causing 'knocking' in petrol engines. » alkanes; knocking; petroleum

heptathlon A multi-event track-and-field competition, contested usually by women. It consists of seven events; 100 m hurdles, shot put, high jump, 200 m, long jump, javelin, and 800 m. Held over two days, it replaced the pentathlon in 1981. » athletics; high jump; javelin throw; long jump; pentathlon; shot put

Hepworth, Dame (Jocelyn) Barbara (1903–75) British sculptor, born at Wakefield, Yorkshire. She studied at the Leeds School of Art, the Royal College of Art, and in Italy, and became one of the foremost nonfigurative sculptors of her time, notable for the strength and formal discipline of her carving, as in her 'Contrapuntal Forms' exhibited at the Festival of Britain (1951). She was married to John Skeaping, the sculptor, and to Ben Nicholson, the artist. She was made a Dame in 1965, and died at St Ives, Cornwall. » English art; sculpture

Hera [**heer**a] In Greek mythology, the daughter of Cronus and wife of Zeus, but a most independent and powerful goddess, probably illustrating the survival of pre-Hellenic cults of the mother-goddess. She was associated with Argos and hostile to Troy. The name means 'lady', and is the feminine form of Hero. » Juno (mythology)

Heracles [**her**akleez], Lat **Hercules** A Greek hero, depicted as a strong man with lion-skin and club, and often represented as a comic on stage. He undertook Twelve Labours for Eurystheus of Argos: (1) to kill the Nemean Lion, (2) to kill the Hydra of Lerna, (3) to capture the Hind of Ceryneia; (4) to capture the Boar of Erymanthus, (5) to clean the Stables of Augeas; (6) to shoot the Birds of Stymphalus, (7) to capture the Cretan Bull, (8) to capture the Horses of Diomedes, (9) to steal the Girdle of the Amazon, (10) to capture the oxen of the giant Geryon, (11) to fetch the Apples of the Hesperides; (12) to capture Cerberus, the guardian of Hades. His wife Deianira killed him by mistake with a shirt smeared with the poison of Nessus; after dying on a pyre he was received into Olympus, and became the subject of a cult. His name means 'Hera's glory'. » Cerberus; Hesperides; Hydra (mythology)

Heraclitus [herak**lii**tuhs] (?–460 BC) Greek philosopher, born at Ephesus. Although only fragments of his writings survive, he seems to have thought that all things are composed of opposites (eg hot/cold, wet/dry). Because the opposites are constantly at strife with one another, all things are in perpetual change. Yet the change is governed by *Logos*, a principle of order and intelligibility.

Heraklion [herak**lee**on], Gr **Iráklion**, Ital **Candia** 35°20N 25°08E, pop (1981) 110 958. Administrative centre and capital town of Crete region (since 1971), S Greece; on N coast of Crete I; airfield; ferries to Piraeus; commercial harbour; leather, soap, tourism, agricultural trade; Church of St Titos; Cathedral of St Minas (19th-c); old city within Venetian walls (begun 1538), archaeological museum; Navy Week (Jun–Jul). » Crete [i]

heraldry The granting and designing of pictorial devices (*arms*) originally used on the shields of knights in armour to identify them in battle. In the early 12th-c these devices became hereditary in Europe through the male line of descent, though with occasional modifications. The science of describing such devices is *blazonry*. Arms are regarded as insignia of honour,

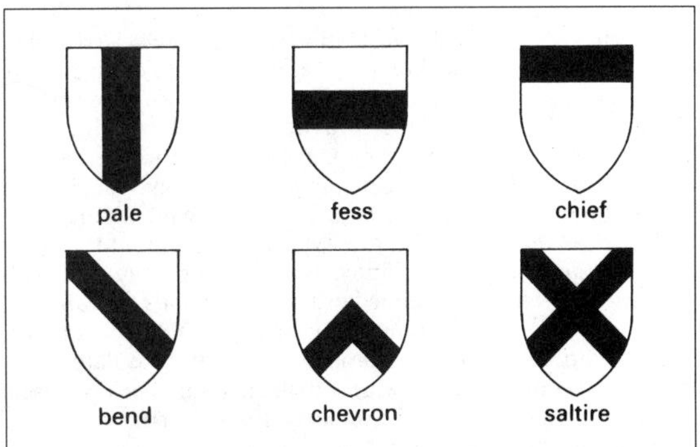

Some common heraldic devices

and their unauthorized display is subject to legal sanction in most European countries. It is regulated by the College of Arms in England and by the Court of the Lord Lyon King of Arms in Scotland (whose heraldic rules are by no means the same as England's). » blazonry

herb A plant with a distinctive smell or taste, used to enhance the flavour and aroma of food. Herbs are usually grown in temperate climates (whereas spices are usually tropical). They are often used for their medicinal properties, hence the speciality of the *herbalist*. In the USA the word is usually pronounced [erb], to distinguish it from herb [herb] referring to non-woody plants in general. » angelica; basil; borage; campion; carrot; catchfly; celery; dill; dittany; dock (botany); feverfew; herbaceous plant; horsetail; mint; rosemary; rue; sage; salvia; spice; sweet bay; trefoil; woundwort; yarrow

herb Bennet » **avens**

herb Paris A perennial growing to 40 cm/15 in, native to woodland in Europe and Asia; rhizomatous; four or more leaves in a single whorl near top of stem; flower 2.5–3.5 cm/1–1½ in, green, solitary, terminal, four sepals, four thread-like petals; berry black. (*Paris quadrifolia*. Family: *Liliaceae*.) » perennial; rhizome; sepal

herb Robert An annual or biennial species of cranesbill, growing to 50 cm/20 in; leaves with red stalks, palmately divided into deeply toothed lobes; flowers c.1 cm/0.4 in diameter, pink; fruit beaked; native to temperate Europe, Asia, and N Africa, and introduced elsewhere. (*Geranium robertianum*. Family: *Geraniaceae*.) » annual; biennial; cranesbill; palmate

herbaceous plant Any non-woody plant which dies at the end of the growing season; often referred to simply as **herb**. Herbaceous perennials die back to ground level, but survive as underground organs such as bulbs or tubers, sending up new growth in the spring. » annual; bulb; herb; perennial; tuber

Herbert (of Cherbury), Edward, 1st Baron (1583–1648) English soldier, statesman, and philosopher, brother of George Herbert, born at Eyton, Shropshire. Educated at Oxford, he was knighted at James I's coronation, became a member of the privy council, and ambassador to France (1619). He is regarded as the founder of English deism. His main works are *De Veritate* (1624, On Truth), *De Religione Gentilium* (published 1663, On the Religion of the Gentiles), and his *Autobiography* (published 1764). He died in London. » deism

Herbert, George (1593–1633) English clergyman and poet, born at Montgomery Castle, Wales. Educated at Westminster and Cambridge, he was public orator at Cambridge (1619) and an MP before entering the church (1630), to become parish priest of Bemerton, Wiltshire. His verse is collected in *The Temple* (1633), and his chief prose work, *A Priest in the Temple*, was published in *Remains* (1652). He died at Bemerton. » English literature; poetry

Herbert, Zbigniew [**hair**bairt] (1924–) Polish poet, born at Lvov. His first collection was *Struna Swiatla* (1956, Chords of Light). Later volumes include *Studium przedmiotu* (1961, Study of the Object), *Pan Cogito* (1974, Mr Cogito) and *Raport z oblezonego miasta* (1983, Report from a Besieged City). He has also written plays which have been broadcast in Poland and abroad. » poetry; Polish literature

herbicide A chemical which kills weeds. **Non-selective** herbicides may be used to kill all vegetation before cultivation and planting begins. Once the crop has emerged, **selective herbicides** are used. These target the troublesome weeds and leave other weeds and the growing crop unharmed. » agriculture

herbivore [**herb**ivaw] An animal that feeds on vegetation – a label used especially of the large plant-eating mammals, such as the ungulates. Its teeth are typically adapted for grinding plants, and its gut is adapted for digesting cellulose. Unlike *Carnivora*, which is a defined order of mammals, *Herbivora* is a descriptive term, encompassing many unrelated forms. » carnivore [i]; cellulose; mammal [i]; plant; ungulate

herbs and spices Plants with a distinctive smell or taste used to enhance the flavour and aroma of food. Herbs are generally grown in temperate climates, and spices are usually grown in tropical climates. Examples of herbs include basil, mint, parsley, and thyme; spices include ginger, clove, chilli, and pepper. Herbs are also used for their medicinal properties, hence the speciality of the *herbalist*.

Herculaneum [herkyoo**lay**niuhm] In Roman times, a prosperous town situated near Mt Vesuvius in SW Italy. It was destroyed completely in the volcanic eruption of AD 79. » Pompeii

Hercules (astronomy) The fifth largest constellation in the N sky, but hard to recognize because its stars are faint. » constellation; RR8

Hercules (mythology) » **Heracles**

hercules beetle A dark, shiny beetle, one of the largest in the world; males up to 170 mm/7 in long, females smaller; adults nocturnal. It belongs to the rhinoceros beetle group, in which the males have a slender, recurved horn on their heads. (Order: *Coleoptera*. Family: *Scarabeidae*.) » beetle

hercules emperor moth One of the largest known insects, with a wingspan up to 270 mm/10½ in; found in New Guinea and N Australia. » emperor moth

Herder, Johann Gottfried von (1744–1803) German critic and poet, born at Mohrungen, E Prussia. He studied at Königsberg, becoming court preacher at Bückeburg (1770) and Weimar (1776). He wrote on folksongs, poetry, and mythology, developing a historical method best seen in his masterpiece, *Ideen zur Geschichte der Menschheit* (1784–91, Outlines of a Philosophy on the History of Man), in which he anticipated evolutionary theories. A major influence on Goethe and German Romanticism, he was ennobled in 1802, and died at Weimar. » German literature; Goethe; Romanticism (literature)

hereditary diseases » **genetically determined diseases**

Hereford [**he**ruhfuhd] 52°04N 2°43W, pop (1981) 47 804. Town in Hereford district, Hereford and Worcester, WC England; on the R Wye at the centre of a rich farming region; railway; foodstuffs, engineering, cattle (Herefords), hops, cider; 11th-c Cathedral of St Mary and St Ethelbert, with the largest chained library in the world and the *Mappa Mundi*, a mediaeval map of the world; Three Choirs Festival in rotation with Gloucester and Worcester (Sep). » Hereford and Worcester

Hereford and Worcester [**he**ruhfuhd, **wus**ter] pop (1987e) 665 100; area 3 926 sq km/1 515 sq ml. County of WC England, divided into nine districts; created 1974 from former counties of Herefordshire and Worcestershire; bounded W and SW by Wales; drained by the Severn, Wye, and Teme Rivers; Malvern Hills rise SW of Worcester; county town, Worcester; chief towns include Hereford, Kidderminster, Malvern, Evesham; horticulture (hops, soft fruit, vegetables), especially in Vale of Evesham; cattle (Herefords), high technology, food processing. » England [i]; Worcester

heresy False doctrine, or the formal denial of doctrine defined as part of the Catholic or universal faith. If consciously adhered to, heresy entails excommunication, and in certain countries has been punishable as a crime. Total heresy or the rejection of all faith is termed **apostasy**. » Albigenses; Arius; Arminius; Donatists; Inquisition; Monophysites; Nestorians; Pelagius

Hereward, byname **the Wake** (?–c.1080) Anglo-Saxon thegn who returned from exile to lead the last organized English resistance against the Norman invaders. He held the Isle of Ely against William the Conqueror for nearly a year (1070–1), then disappeared from history, and entered mediaeval outlaw legend as a celebrated opponent of the forces of injustice. » Norman Conquest; thegn

herm » **term**

Hermandszoon, Jakob » **Arminius, Jacobus**

hermaphrodite An animal or plant having both male and female reproductive organs. The male organs may mature before the female (*protandrous*), after the female (*protogynous*), or simultaneously (*synchronous*). Species in which both sets of organs mature simultaneously often have mechanisms that prevent self-fertilization. » reproduction

Hermaphroditus [hermafruh**diy**tuhs] In Greek mythology, a minor god with bisexual characteristics, the son of Hermes and Aphrodite. The nymph Salmacis, unloved by him, prayed to be united with him; this was granted by combining them in one body. » Aphrodite; Hermes (mythology)

hermeneutics [hermuh**nyoo**tiks] **1** The theory of the interpretation and understanding of texts. Though its origins lie in ancient Greek philosophy, hermeneutics received fresh impetus in 18th-c discussions of the problems of biblical interpretation posed by the development of historical-critical method. Schleiermacher shifted attention from the formulation of rules of interpretation to the question of how is is possible to understand the written discourse of different cultures and ages. The discussion was carried further by Dilthey and, in this century, by Heidegger and especially Gadamer. During this time the discussion expanded to embrace all aspects of the understanding of texts and entered many fields, including literary theory, the social sciences, social philosophy, and aesthetics. » biblical criticism; Dilthey; Gadamer; Heidegger; Schleiermacher **2** In psychology, the term has been applied to psychological methods which go beyond mere experimentation in an attempt to understand the reason behind human actions. » experimental psychology

Hermes (astronomy) An asteroid which came within 760 000 km/475 000 ml of Earth in 1937, closer than any other asteroid on record. It was only a few km in diameter, and was lost to view within a few days. » asteroids

Hermes (mythology) [**her**meez] In Greek mythology, the ambassador of the gods, the son of Zeus and Maia; depicted with herald's staff (the *caduceus*), and winged sandals. He is variously associated with stones, commerce, roads, cookery, and thieving; also arts such as oratory. He was the inventor of the lyre, and, as Hermes Psychopompos, the guide of souls. » Mercury (mythology)

hermetic A term used to describe obscure and difficult poetry, as of the Symbolist school. The allusion is to the mythical Hermes Trismegistus (Egyptian Thoth), the supposed author of mystic doctrines actually composed in the Neoplatonic tradition c.3rd-c AD. Hermeticism was influential in the Renaissance, after the translation of these texts by Marsilio Ficino (1433–99). » Neoplatonism; Renaissance; Symbolism

hermit crab A crab-like crustacean which uses an empty snail shell as a portable refuge covering its soft abdomen; body typically asymmetrical to fit inside spiral shells; changes shells as it grows; common in shallow coastal waters. (Class: *Malacostraca*. Order: *Decapoda*.) » crab; crustacean; shell

Hermitage A major art gallery in St Petersburg, Russia, built in the 18th–19th-c to house the art collection of the Czars, and opened to the public in 1852. The complex now includes the Winter Palace, built for Czarina Elizabeth Petrovna by Bartolomeo Rastrelli (1754–62). After the deposition of the Czar, this became the headquarters of Kerensky's provisional government, but was stormed by the Bolsheviks (Nov 1917). » Elizabeth Petrovna; Kerensky; Leningrad

hernia The protrusion of tissue from its natural site through an adjacent orifice or tissue space. Examples are *inguinal*, *femoral*, and *umbilical* herniae, in which the intestine pushes its way through weak sites in the abdominal wall; the herniae emerge as externally protruding masses in the groin, over the upper thigh, and at the navel, respectively. Umbilical herniae are common in babies, and resolve within one to two years. The blood supply of intestinal herniae may be imperilled and lead to death of part of the contents of the herniae, such as the gut; this is a dangerous complication, and demands urgent surgical attention. Internal herniation also occurs, for example, when part of the stomach enters the lower chest through an aperture in the diaphragm. This is a common defect, which gives rise to heartburn in a minority of cases. » abdomen; diaphragm; femur; intestine; umbilical cord

Hero and Leander [**heer**oh, lee**an**der] A Greek legend first found in the Roman poet, Ovid. Two lovers lived on opposite sides of the Hellespont; Hero was the priestess of Aphrodite at Sestos, and Leander, who lived at Abydos, swam across each night guided by her light. When this was extinguished in a storm, he was drowned, and Hero committed suicide by throwing herself into the sea. » Ovid

Hero of Alexandria (1st-c AD) Greek mathematician and inventor. He devised many machines, among them a fire engine, a water organ, coin-operated devices, and the 'aeolipile', the earliest known steam engine. He showed that the angle of incidence in optics is equal to the angle of reflection, and devised the formula for expressing the area of a triangle in terms of its sides. » optics [i]; steam engine; triangle (mathematics)

Herod Agrippa I (10 BC–AD 44) King of Judaea (41–4), the grandson of Herod the Great. Reared at the court of the Emperor Augustus, Agrippa's early contacts with the imperial family stood him in good stead later on. Caligula gave him two thirds of the former kingdom of Herod the Great, while Claudius added the remaining third, the Judaean heartland (41). Loved by the Jews, despite being a Roman appointee, and an active Hellenizer, he was no friend to the Christians, executing St James and imprisoning St Peter. » Caligula; Claudius; Hellenization; Herod Antipas; Herod the Great

Herod Agrippa II (c.27–c.93) King of Chalcis (49/50–53), ruler of the Ituraean principality (53–c.93), the son of Herod Agrippa I. He was not permitted by Rome to succeed to his father's Judaean kingdom in 44, but given various minor territories to the N, mostly Arab. A supporter of Rome in the Jewish War (66–70), he was rewarded for it afterwards with grants of land in Judaea and public honours in Rome. It was before him that St Paul made his defence and was found innocent. » Herod Agrippa I; Nero; Paul, St

Herod Antipas (?–AD 39) The son of Herod the Great and ruler (tetrarch) of Galilee and Peraea (4–39), after Herod's death. An able client of the Romans, he enjoyed an especially good relationship with the Emperor Tiberias, but fell foul of his successor, Caligula, largely through the machinations of his nephew, Herod Agrippa. In the Christian tradition, he looms large as the capricious murderer of John the Baptist. » Herod Agrippa I; Herod the Great; John the Baptist; Tiberius

Herod the Great (c.73–4 BC) King of Judea, the younger son of the Idumaean chieftain, Antipater. He owed his initial appointment as Governor of Galilee (47 BC) to Julius Caesar, his elevation to the kingship of Judea (40 BC) to Marcus Antonius, and his retention in that post after Actium (31 BC) to Octavian, later Augustus. Besides being a loyal and efficient Roman client king, who ruthlessly kept all his subjects in check, he was also an able and far-sighted administrator who did much to develop the economic potential of his kingdom, founding cities, and promoting agricultural projects. Life at court was marked by constant and often bloody infighting between his sister, his various wives, and their many offspring. Undoubtedly he was cruel, and this is reflected in the Gospel account of the Massacre of the Innocents. » Antipater; Antonius, Marcus; Augustus; Caesar

Herodotus [he**rod**ohtuhs] (c.485–425 BC) Greek historian, born at Halicarnassus, Asia Minor. He travelled widely in Asia Minor and the Middle East, and in 443 BC joined the colony of Thurii, from where he visited Sicily and Lower Italy. On his travels, he collected material for his great narrative history, which gave a record of the wars between the Greeks and the Persians. Cicero called him 'the father of history'. » Persian Wars

heroic couplet A pair of rhymed 10-syllable lines, usually in iambic pentameter. First found in Old French, then Chaucer, it became the staple of Augustan satiric poetry (Dryden and Pope), and is often revived on account of its pointedness and economy: 'A fop her passion, but her prize a sot;/ Alive, ridiculous, and dead, forgot' (Pope). » Augustan age; Dryden; poetry; Pope

heroin (diamorphine) A derivative of morphine developed in 1896, and originally launched as a non-addictive narcotic. It was soon found to be extremely addictive. Because of its extreme potency it is used to ease the severe pain that can accompany terminal illness, but even this medical use is banned in the USA. It is widely abused. » drug addiction; morphine; narcotics

heron A wading bird related to the bittern; worldwide (mainly tropical); flies with neck retracted, not extended; some feathers ('powder-down') break down to form a powder used in preening. There are three main groups: **day** or 'typical herons' (including egrets), **night herons**, and **tiger herons**. (Family: *Ardeidae*, 64 species.) » bittern; boatbill; egret; night heron

Herophilus [he**rof**iluhs] (c.335–c.280 BC) Greek anatomist, a founder of the medical school of Alexandria, born at Chalcedon. He was the first to dissect the human body, and to compare it with that of other animals. He described the brain, liver, spleen, sexual organs, and nervous system, dividing the latter into sensory and motor.

herpes labialis » **cold sore**

herpes simplex A viral infection which affects the lips, the mouth, or the genital region. A rash is followed by the appearance of small blisters which contain fluid; these ulcerate and may become infected. Recurrent attacks are common, between which the virus lies dormant. » virus

herpes zoster » **shingles**

herpesvirus A spheroidal virus, contained within an outer envelope c.150 nm in diameter. It stores genetic information in a double strand of deoxyribonucleic acid. Herpesviruses are associated with a variety of systemic diseases which often remain latent for long periods between outbreaks. It includes the causative agent of chickenpox. » DNA [i]; virus

Herrick, Robert (1591–1674) English poet, born in London. Educated at Cambridge, he was ordained in 1623, and worked in Devon, until deprived of his living as a royalist in 1647. His writing, both secular and religious, is mainly collected in *Hesperides* (1648), and includes such well-known lyrics as 'Cherry ripe'. He resumed his living at the Restoration, and died at Dean Prior, Devon. » English literature; poetry; Restoration

herring Surface-living marine fish abundant in the N Atlantic and Arctic, ranging S to Portugal (E) and Cape Hatteras (W); body length up to 40 cm/16 in; colour deep blue on back, underside silvery white; feeds on plankton, especially crustaceans; prey to many larger fish, seabirds, and marine mammals; supports important commercial fisheries, being sold fresh, smoked as kippers or bloaters, or preserved in salt or vinegar; first-year herring sold as whitebait; the name is also used for several other herring-like species. A combination of overfishing and natural causes led to a collapse of stock in the North Sea in 1965–77, culminating in closure of the North Sea fishery in 1978–82. This coincided with a depletion of stock throughout the N Atlantic. During the 1980s, stock recovered significantly. (*Clupea harengus*. Family: *Clupeidae*.) » whitebait

herring gull A large gull common in the N hemisphere; legs usually pink (sometimes yellow); head white; bill yellow with red spot below tip; considered a pest and controlled in some areas. (*Larus argentatus*. Family: *Laridae*.) » gull

Herschel, Sir William (Frederick) (1738–1822) British astronomer, born in Hanover, Germany. He became skilled at building the largest reflecting telescopes made at the time, and these enabled him and his sister **Caroline** (1750–1848) to advance stellar astronomy rapidly, a tradition continued by his son, **John** (1792–1871). William discovered Uranus in 1781, in the course of a systematic survey of the sky, found two satellites of Saturn, extensively observed double stars, and produced a notable star catalogue. He was knighted in 1816, and died at Slough, Buckinghamshire. His house in Bath has been restored as a museum. » double star; Saturn (astronomy); Uranus (astronomy)

Hertford [**haht**fuhd] 51°48N 0°05W, pop (1981) 21 606. County town in East Hertfordshire district, Hertfordshire, SE England; on R Lea, 32 km/20 ml N of London; railway; plastics, brewing, engineering, printing; 12th-c Hertford Castle; Waltham Abbey (20 km/12 ml SE). » Hertfordshire

Hertfordshire [**haht**fuhdsheer] pop (1987e) 986 800; area 1 634 sq km/631 sq ml. County of SE England, divided into 10 districts; N of Greater London; drained by the Colne and Lee Rivers and the Grand Union Canal; county town, Hertford; chief towns include St Albans, Harpenden, Welwyn Garden City; wheat, cattle, horticulture, brewing, paper, printing, electronics, pharmaceuticals, aerospace. » England [i]; Hertford

hertz SI unit of frequency; symbol Hz; named after German physicist Heinrich Hertz; defined as the number of complete cycles per second; applicable to all wave and periodic phenomena. » frequency; Hertz; units (scientific); RR70

Hertz, Heinrich (Rudolf) (1857–94) German physicist, born in Hamburg. He studied at Berlin under Helmholtz, and became professor of physics at Bonn in 1899. His main work was on electromagnetic waves (1887), and he discovered radio waves. He died in Bonn. The unit of frequency is named after him. » electromagnetism; Helmholtz

Hertzog, J(ames) B(arry) M(unnik) (1866–1942) South African statesman and Prime Minister (1924–39), born at Wellington, Cape Colony. He was a Boer general (1899–1902), and in 1910 became Minister of Justice in the first Union government. In 1913 he founded the Nationalist Party, advocating complete South African independence. As Premier, in coalition with Labour (1924–9), and with Smuts in a United Party (1933–9), he pursued a legislative programme which destroyed the African franchise, created reservation for Whites, and tightened land segregation. He renounced his earlier secessionism, but at the outbreak of World War 2 declared for neutrality, was defeated, and in 1940 retired. He died in Pretoria. » South Africa [i]

Hertzsprung-Russell diagram The graphical representation of the correlation between the spectrum and luminosity for a sample of stars, discovered independently in 1913 by Danish astronomer Ejnar Hertzsprung (1873–1967) and US astronomer Henry Norris Russell (1877–1957). The diagram achieves its astrophysical significance when the plotted points are restricted to a particular sample (such as all the members of a star cluster) or a particular type (such as one class of variable star). It then effectively graphs surface temperature against luminosity. In the diagram, normal stars that are burning hydrogen form a broad band known as the *main sequence*. Evolved stars clump together as red giants. Almost defunct stars are grouped as white dwarfs. The theory of stellar evolution explains the main features of the diagram. » luminosity; main sequence; Russell, H N; spectrum; star; stellar evolution

Herzl, Theodor (1860–1904) Hungarian Zionist leader, born in Budapest. He trained as a lawyer at Vienna, then became a journalist and playwright. After reporting the Dreyfus trial

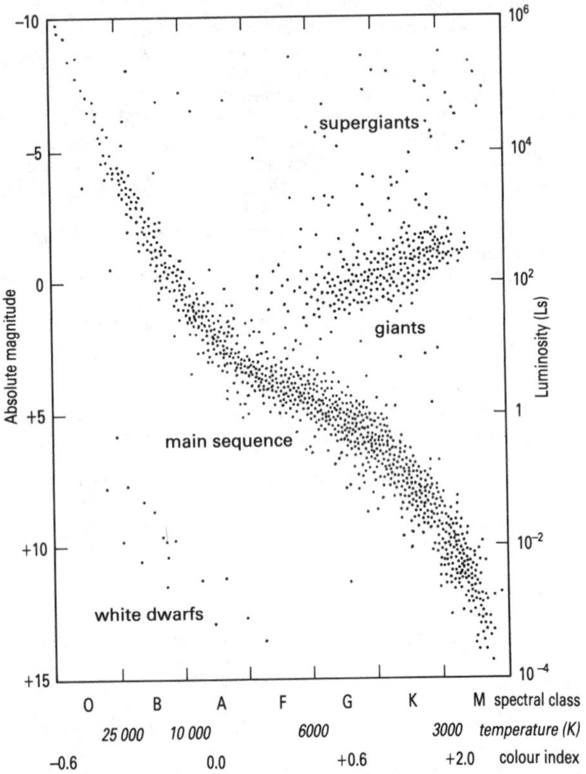

Hertzsprung-Russell diagram – Schematic colour–magnitude diagram for many stars

(1894), he was converted to Zionism, and in the pamphlet *Judenstaat* (1896, The Jewish State) he called for a world council to discuss the question of a homeland for the Jews, convened the first Zionist Congress at Basle (1897), and became the first President of the World Zionist Organization. He died at Edlach, Austria. » Dreyfus; Zionism

Herzog, Werner, originally **Werner Stipetic** (1942–) German film director, screenwriter, and producer, born in Sachrang. He made numerous shorts in the 1960s, and became recognized as a leading member of the New Cinema in Germany with his features *Aguirre, der Zorn Gottes* (1973, Aguirre, Wrath of God) and the story of Kaspar Hauser (1975). His treatment of *Nosferatu, the Vampyre* (1979) reflected the German silent film expressionists of the 1920s, but his general themes are metaphysical in character, often with remoteness in time or location, as in *Where the Green Ants Dream* (1984).

Heselrige, Arthur » **Haselrig, Arthur**

Heseltine, Michael (Ray Dibdin) [**hes**uhltiyn] (1933–) British Conservative politician, born in Swansea, S Wales. He was educated at Oxford, and built up a publishing business before becoming an MP in 1966. After holding junior posts in Transport (1970), Environment (1970–2), and Aerospace and Shipping (1972–4), he was appointed Secretary of State for the Environment (1979–83), and then Defence Secretary (1983–6). He resigned from the government in dramatic fashion by walking out of a Cabinet meeting over the issue of the takeover of Westland helicopters. He stood unsuccessfully as a candidate in the leadership contest following Mrs Thatcher's resignation (Nov 1990), then became Environment Minister. » Brittan; Conservative Party

Hesiod (8th-c BC) Greek poet, seemingly somewhat later than Homer, born at Ascra, at the foot of Mt Helicon. Little is known about his life. Two of his epics have survived: *Works and Days*, which deals with the farmer's life, and the *Theogony*, which teaches the origin of the universe and the history of the gods. His fame led to several other works being spuriously attributed to him. » Greek literature; Homer; poetry

Hesperides [hes**per**ideez] In Greek mythology, the daughters of the evening star (Hesper), who guard the Golden Apples together with the dragon, Ladon. They sing as they circle the tree, which was given by Gaia to Hera as a wedding-present. When Heracles had to fetch the apples, he either killed the dragon, or sent it to sleep, or, more usually, persuaded Atlas to get them for him while he took over Atlas' function of holding up the sky. » Atalanta; Atlas (mythology); Heracles

Hess, Dame Myra (1890–1965) British pianist, born and died in London. She studied at the Royal Academy of Music, and was an immediate success on her first public appearance in 1907. During World War 2 she organized the lunchtime concerts in the National Gallery. She was made a Dame in 1941. » piano

Hess, (Walter Richard) Rudolf (1894–1987) German politician, Hitler's deputy as Party leader, born at Alexandria, Egypt. Educated at Godesberg, he fought in World War 1, then studied at Munich. He joined the Nazi Party in 1920, and became Hitler's close friend and (in 1934) deputy. In 1941, on the eve of Germany's attack on Russia, he flew alone to Scotland to plead the cause of a negotiated Anglo-German peace. He was temporarily imprisoned in the Tower of London, then placed under psychiatric care near Aldershot. At the Nuremberg Trials (1946) he was sentenced to life imprisonment, and remained in Spandau prison, Berlin (after 1966, as the only prisoner) until his death. » Hitler; World War 2

Hesse, Hermann (1877–1962) German novelist and poet, born at Calw, Württemberg. He was a bookseller and antiquarian in Basle (1895–1902), and published his first novel in 1904. His works include *Rosshalde* (1914), *Siddhartha* (1922), *Steppenwolf* (1927), and *Das Glasperlenspiel* (1945, The Glass Bead Game). He was awarded the Nobel Prize for Literature in 1946. From 1911 he lived in Switzerland, where he died, at Montagnola. His psychological and mystical concerns made him something of a cult figure after his death. » German literature; novel

Hestia [**hes**teea] Greek goddess of the hearth, the daughter of Cronus and Rhea. She has two functions: looking after the family fire, and the public cult of the communal hearth. » Vesta (mythology)

Heston, Charlton, originally **John Charles Carter** (1923–) US actor, born at Evanston, Illinois. After service in the air force, he appeared on Broadway and on television, and was attracted to Hollywood to play the lead in *Dark City* (1950). De Mille's *The Greatest Show on Earth* (1951) and *The Ten Commandments* (1956) brought him great success, and he won an Oscar for *Ben Hur* (1959). He continued in heroic roles, his later films including *The Awakening* (1980) and *Mother Lode* (1982).

heterochromatin [hetuhroh**kroh**matin] Those parts of chromosomes showing an excessive degree of contraction and heavier staining properties during the process of nuclear division, as distinct from **euchromatin**, which shows normal condensation and staining. Heterochromatin seems to be deficient in coding genes, but contains repetitive DNA sequences and elements that control gene activity. » cell; chromatin; chromosome [i]; DNA [i]; gene

Heteroptera [hetuh**rop**tuhra] A large order of insects comprising the true bugs; body typically depressed, forewings usually leathery at base and membraneous at tip; mouthparts modified for piercing and sucking; feeding on plants, fungi, or as predators; life cycle without pupal stage; c.35 000 species, including many crop pests and disease carriers. (Class: *Insecta*.) » bug; insect [i]; pupa

heterosexism A belief which regards attraction to the opposite sex as the only legitimate form of sexual expression. That such a term has appeared indicates the strength of the debate over what is to be regarded as 'normal' or 'acceptable' sexuality. » gender; homosexuality

Heuneberg, the [**hoy**nuhberg] A prehistoric hillfort of the Halstaat Iron Age on a spur overlooking the R Danube near Binzwagen, Württemburg, S Germany. Of five building periods covering the 7th–late 5th-c BC, the second (early 6th-c) is notable for its spectacular defensive wall of unbaked clay bricks, 3–4 m/10–13 ft high with square bastions, clearly constructed under Greek influence. » Three Age System

heuristic Any set of rules whose application to a complex problem will tend to yield satisfactory if not optimal results (in contrast to an algorithm). 'Control the centre of the board' is a heuristic for playing chess. Some heuristics can be made precise enough to be programmed into computers. » algorithm

Heuss, Theodor [hoys] (1884–1963) First President of the Federal Republic of Germany (1949–59), born at Brackenheim, Württemberg. Educated at Munich and Berlin, he became editor of the political magazine *Hilfe* (1905–12), professor at the Berlin College of Political Science (1920–33), and an MP (1924–8, 1930–2). A prolific author and journalist, he wrote two books denouncing Hitler, and when the latter came to power in 1933, he was dismissed from his chair and his books publicly burnt. In 1946 he became a founder member of the Free Democratic Party, and helped to draft the new federal constitution. He died at Stuttgart. » Germany [i]

hexachlorophene [heksa**klor**uhfeen] $C_{13}H_6Cl_6O_2$. A white powder with antiseptic properties, widely used in toilet preparations. » antiseptic

hexadecanoic acid » **palmitic acid**

hexadecimal coding A number notation using the number base 16. The sixteen individual characters are 0–9, and A–F inclusive, representing decimal 10 to decimal 15 respectively. The notation is widely used in computer applications for writing binary numbers. » binary code

hexane C_6H_{14}. An alkane hydrocarbon with six carbon atoms. There are five structural isomers. The straight-chain compound, n-hexane, $CH_3CH_2CH_2CH_2CH_2CH_3$, has boiling point 69°C. » alkanes

hexanedioic acid » **adipic acid**

Hexi Corridor [**heshee**] or **Gansu Corridor** Natural corridor from C China through Gansu province to Xinjiang autonomous region; length c.1 200 km/750 ml; a major part of the ancient Silk Road; scene of numerous battles, from 3rd-c BC. » China [i]; Silk Road [i]

Heyerdahl, Thor [**hiy**uhdahl] (1914–) Norwegian anthropologist, born at Larvik. Educated at Oslo, he served with the free Norwegian forces in World War 2. In 1947 he set out to prove, by sailing a balsa raft (the *Kon-Tiki*) from Peru to Tuamotu I in the S Pacific that the Peruvian Indians could have settled in

Polynesia. His success in this venture, and his archaeological expedition to Easter I, won him popular fame and several awards. In 1970 he sailed from Morocco to the West Indies in a papyrus boat, *Ra II*, and made the journey from Iraq to Djibouti in a reed boat, the *Tigris*, in 1977–8.

Heysel stadium » football hooliganism

Heywood, Thomas (c.1574–1641) English dramatist and poet, born in Lincolnshire. Educated at Cambridge, he was writing plays by 1596, and by 1633 had shared in the composition of 220 plays, and written 24 of his own, notably his domestic tragedy, *A Woman Killed with Kindness* (1607). He also wrote many pageants, tracts, treatises, and translations. He died in London.

Hezekiah [hezekiya] Biblical character, King of Judah in the late 8th-c BC (precise dating much disputed), renowned for his religious reforms, including the re-establishment of Temple worship in Jerusalem (2 *Chron* 29–32), and for his political attempts to obtain independence from Assyrian domination (2 *Kings* 18–20; *Isa* 36–9). » Bible; Chronicles/Isaiah/Kings, Books of

hi-fi » high fidelity sound system

hi-hat cymbals A pair of cymbals mounted on a stand, and operated by a foot-pedal which brings the upper cymbal into contact with the fixed, lower one. Also known as 'Chinese cymbals', they have been used since 1927 in dance bands, and in jazz and pop groups. » cymbals; percussion [i]

Hiawatha The name of a real Red Indian of the 16th-c, used by Longfellow for his hero in *The Song of Hiawatha*, which retells Indian legends in the manner and metre of the Finnish *Kalevala*. Hiawatha is educated by his grandmother Nokomis, and marries Minnehaha. » Kalevala; Longfellow

hibernation A strategy for passing the cold winter period in a torpid or resting state, found in mammals and some other animals. Metabolism is reduced, and the animal enters a deep sleep, surviving on body food reserves stored during a favourable summer period. The similar strategy for surviving a hot, dry summer is known as *aestivation*. » dormancy; metabolism

hibiscus An annual, perennial, or shrub native to warm regions; flowers often very large and showy, 5-petalled, the stamens united into a central column. It is best-known as a decorative plant with many species grown as ornamentals, but some also provide useful fibres and edible fruits. (Genus: *Hibiscus*, species 300. Family: *Malvaceae*.) » annual; perennial; shrub; stamen

hiccup/hiccough An involuntary contraction of the diaphragm causing an intake of air which is halted by spasm (closure) of the glottis, thereby producing a sharp, characteristic inspiratory sound. Its cause is unknown, but there are many folk-remedies, such as drinking vinegar, or drinking from the 'wrong side of the glass'. The standard medical treatment is the administration of chlorpromazine. » diaphragm; glottis; phenothiazines

hickory A tall deciduous tree, sometimes with shaggy bark, native to E Asia and eastern N America; leaves pinnately divided into finely toothed leaflets; flowers small, green, lacking petals; males in catkins, females in clusters; nut 4-valved, edible. (Genus: *Carya*, 25 species. Family: *Juglandaceae*.) » deciduous plants; pinnate; tree [i]

Hidatsa [hidatsuh] American Plains Indians living in villages along the Missouri R in the 18th-c; an offshoot group were the Siouan Crow. They later joined with the Mandan and Arikara (the 'Three Affiliated Tribes') to defend themselves against the Dakota. In 1868 they were settled by the US government on Fort Berthold Reservation in N Dakota. Population (including Mandan) c.1 700. » American Indians; Plains Indians

hidden curriculum A term developed by sociologists of education to describe the unwritten, informal code of conduct to which children are expected to conform in the classroom. Children are said to be rewarded not only for learning their subject curriculum but appearing to do so with enthusiasm, alertness, and deference to and respect for authority. In this way education imparts not only formal knowledge but an understanding of how to act 'properly' in wider society. » education

Hideyoshi, Toyotomi [hidayoshee] (1536–98) The second of the three great historical unifiers of Japan, between Nobunaga and Ieyasu Tokugawa, sometimes called 'the Napoleon of Japan'. Unusually, he was an ordinary soldier who rose to become Nobunaga's foremost general. His law forbade all except samurai to carry swords (1588), and he banned Christianity for political reasons (1597). His armies invaded Korea (1592–8), but withdrew after his death at Fushimi Castle, Kyoto. » Nobunaga; samurai; Tokugawa

EGYPTIAN HIEROGLYPHIC

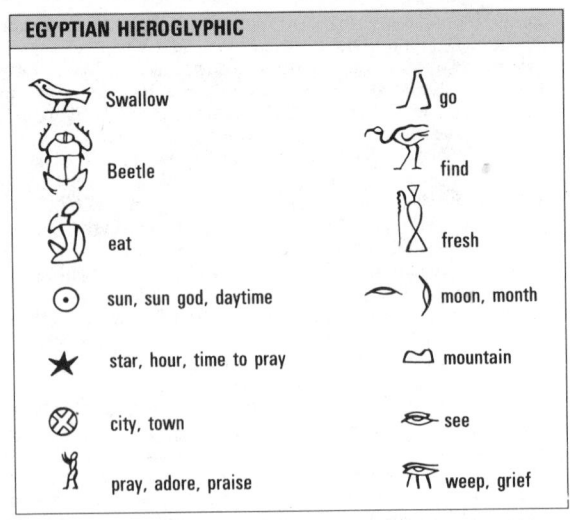

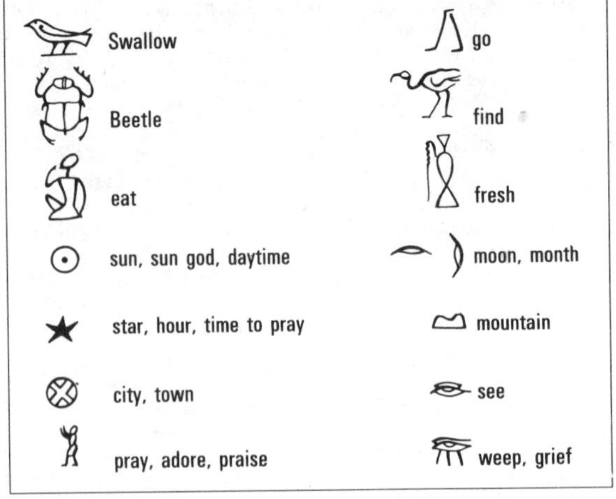

hieroglyphics The study of the symbols of ancient Egyptian writing. The characters were originally pictograms, and were named *hieroglyphs* (from the Greek 'sacred carving') because of their frequent use in religious contexts, such as temple and tomb inscriptions. The symbols are usually written from right to left, and were developed to represent three kinds of information: some are ideograms, representing objects or concepts in the real world; others stand for a consonant or consonant sequence; and a third type has no phonetic value, but serves to disambiguate a hieroglyph with more than one meaning. » ideography; pictography [i]

Higgins, Alex, properly **Alexander (Gordon)**, byname **The Hurricane** (1949–) British snooker player, born in Belfast, Northern Ireland. He has had a tempestuous career since becoming the youngest world champion in 1972, at age 23. A former trainee jockey, he became a professional snooker player in 1971, and won the world title at the first attempt. He won the title for a second time in 1982, and though less successful thereafter he has remained a favourite with snooker fans despite (or because of) his confrontations with the authorities. » snooker

High Commissioner A person carrying out the same duties and possessing the same rank as an ambassador, representing one Commonwealth country in another Commonwealth country. The High Commission is the Commissioner's residence and houses the administrative organization. » ambassador

High Court of Justice A court established for England and Wales by the Judicature Acts (1873–5), principally a trial court for civil cases. It hears appeals on points of law from magistrates' courts in both civil and criminal cases, and also undertakes judicial review. The court has three divisions: Queens Bench Division, Chancery Division, and Family Division. » Chancery Division; judicial review; justice of the peace

high-definition television (HDTV) Any television system using substantially more scanning lines than the 500–600 of established broadcast standards, with improved picture quality in a wide-screen format. In the 1980s, the Japanese NHK proposed a completely new system, Hi-Vision, as a worldwide standard, using 1125 lines at 60 fields per second (60 Hz). However, the need to provide transmissions having some compatibility with existing receivers led to alternative approaches, such as the Eureka project in Europe (related to PAL, using 1250 lines/50 Hz) and several proposals in the USA (with NTSC compatibility, such as Advanced Compatible TV, using 1050 lines/60 Hz). » NTSC; PAL; scanning [i]; television

high energy physics » **particle physics**

high fidelity sound system An assembly of sound reproduction components capable of regenerating an original musical performance to the highest attainable quality across the whole range of audible frequencies (20–20 000 Hz) and amplitudes; also known as **hi-fi**. It was a concept which emerged after World War 2, made possible by a combination of several factors. A new record material (vinylite) facilitated the introduction of the long-playing record at the end of the 1940s; stereophonic recording was patented in 1931, though not marketed significantly until 1958; and transistors after 1948 gradually replaced thermionic valve circuitry. Digital recording, noise reduction, and the compact disc were later embellishments. » sound recording; transistor

high jump An athletics field event in which competitors attempt to clear a bar without any aids. The height of the bar is gradually increased, and competitors are allowed three attempts to clear each new height; they are eliminated if they fail. The person clearing the greatest height, or (if more than one) the person with the least failures is the winner. The current world record for men is 2.42 m/7 ft 1¼ in, achieved by Jan Sjöberg (Sweden, born 5 Jan 1965) on 30 June 1987 at Stockholm, Sweden; for women, it is 2.09 m/6 ft 10¼ in, achieved by Stefka Kostadinova (Bulgaria, born 25 Mar 1965) on 30 August 1987 at Rome, Italy. » athletics

high-level language A computer language in which every instruction or statement is equivalent to several machine-code instructions (ie those instructions which can be directly understood by the computer). High-level languages, such as BASIC, FORTRAN, and PASCAL, are written using notations which are relatively easy for the user to understand. Programs written in high-level languages can be run on different computers with different processors. » low-level language; machine code

high pressure physics The study of the effects of increased pressure on matter. Most properties of matter are affected by pressure. For example, some semiconductors become metallic conductors, iron loses its strong magnetic properties, and typically gases turn to liquid. Pressures of 500 000 times atmospheric pressure can be achieved. » electrical and magnetic properties of solids; mechanical properties of matter; physics; pressure

high school The common form of secondary school in the USA for 15–19-year-olds, following the **junior high school** phase for 11–15-year-olds. The schools are non-selective, and the successful completion of this phase of education results in graduation, with the award of the high-school diploma. » secondary education

high-speed anti-radiation missile (HARM) A guided missile developed initially by the US Navy following experience in the air combat over Vietnam. HARMs are equipped with a 'homing head' designed to pick up, lock onto, and cause the missile to fly towards enemy ground-based radar transmitters. The missile's high speed means that the hostile radar should not have time to switch off before the HARM arrives and destroys it. » missile, guided

high-speed photography The photographic recording of transient phenomena with very short periods of exposure. Electronic flash can be as brief as one-millionth of a second, and non-mechanical shutters (such as the polarizing Kerr cell) can operate 200 times faster. In an indirect system, an instantaneous video image is stored on the screen of a cathode ray tube for photography over a longer period. In cinematography the limit for mechanical intermittent film movement is about 600 pictures per second, but rotating prism optics and continuously moving film can expose at a rate of 10 000 frames a second for a very short burst. » photography

higher education » **further education**

Highland pop (1981) 200 150; area 25 391 sq km/9 801 sq ml. Region in N Scotland, divided into eight districts; bounded N and E by the North Sea, W by the Minch and Little Minch; includes Inner Hebrides; sparsely inhabited region of great scenic beauty; Grampian, Monadhliath, and Cairngorm Mts; crossed by numerous rivers, mountain ranges and lochs (notably Linnhe, Lochy, Oich, Ness); route of the Caledonian Canal; rises to 1 344 m/4 409 ft in Ben Nevis (SW); capital, Inverness; major towns include Wick, Dingwall, Thurso, Nairn; forestry, livestock, oil, winter skiing, fishing, fish farming, game hunting; Eas Coul Aulin (NW), highest waterfall in UK (drop of 200 m/650 ft); John o' Groats (extreme NE); Glencoe in SE, site of 1692 battle. » Ben Nevis; Cairngorms; Caledonian Canal; Grampians; Hebrides; Inverness; Scotland [i]

Highland Games Athletic meetings held in the highlands of Scotland; the first Games were organized by the St Fillans (Perthshire) Highland Society in 1819. A range of athletic events takes place, in addition to specifically Scottish events, such as tossing the caber. There may also be highland dancing and bagpipe-playing competitions. The most famous is the Braemar gathering. » athletics; caber tossing

Highland pony A Scottish breed of horse; two types: *Western Isles* (two divisions: height 12½–13½ hands/1.2–1.3 m/4–4¼ ft, and height 13½–14½ hands/1.3–1.4 m/4¼–4½ ft), and the more powerful **garron** or **Mainland** (height, 14½ hands/1.5 m/4¾ ft); formerly used for stalking deer. The garron has Arab blood, and is the largest of British pony breeds. » Arab horse; horse [i]

Highsmith, Patricia (1921–) US novelist, born at Fort Worth, Texas, and educated at Barnard College and Columbia University, New York. Her first novel, *Strangers on a Train* (1949), became famous as a source of Hitchcock's 1957 film of that name, but her best novels are generally held to be those describing the criminal adventures of her psychotic hero Tom Ripley, beginning with *The Talented Mr Ripley* (1956). » American literature; Hitchcock; novel

hijra [**hij**ra] » **hegira**

Hilary (of Poitiers), St (c.315–c.368), feast day 13 January. French churchman and Doctor of the Church, born of pagan parents at Limonum (Poitiers). He became a Christian quite late in life, and c.350 was elected Bishop of Poitiers. A leading opponent of Arianism, his principal work is on the Trinity. His feast day marks the beginning of a term at Oxford and Durham Universities, and English law sittings, to which his name is consequently applied. » Arius; Christianity; Trinity

Hilbert, David (1862–1943) German mathematician, born at Königsberg, where he studied and became professor (1893). He moved to Göttingen in 1895, where he critically examined the foundations of geometry. He also made important contributions to the theory of numbers, the theory of invariants, and the application of integral equations to physical problems. He died at Göttingen. » geometry; number theory

Hildebrand » **Gregory VII**

Hildesheim [**hil**duhshiym] 52°09N 9°55E, pop (1983) 101 900. Port in Hanover district, Germany; 29 km/18 ml SSE of Hanover; founded, 1300; railway; linked to the Mittelland Canal; iron, machinery, hardware, carpets, electronics; St Michael's Church (11th-c) and Romanesque cathedral (1054–79), world heritage sites. » Germany [i] canal

Hill, Geoffrey (1932–) British poet, born at Bromsgrove, Worcestershire, and educated at Oxford. He has taught at the Universities of Leeds and Cambridge. His first volume *For the Unfallen* (1959) introduced a serious and astringent voice, which has commanded increasing authority with *King Log* (1968), *Mercian Hymns* (1971), and *Tenebrae* (1978). Hill's religious preoccupation is fully revealed in *The Mystery of the Charity of Charles Peguy* (1983). » English literature; poetry

Hill, (Norman) Graham (1929–75) British motor racing driver, born in London. He won 14 races from a record 176 starts (since surpassed) between 1958 and 1975, and was world champion in 1962 (in a BRM) and in 1968 (Lotus). He won the Monaco Grand Prix five times (1963–5, 1968–9). In 1975 he started his own racing team, Embassy Racing, but was killed when the plane he was piloting crashed near Hendon, N London. » motor racing

Hill, Octavia (1838–1912) British housing reformer and founder of the National Trust, born and died in London. She worked among the London poor, and in 1864, supported by Ruskin, commenced her project to improve the homes of working men in the slums – methods which were imitated in Europe and the USA. » Ruskin

Hill, Sir Rowland (1795–1879) British originator of penny postage, born at Kidderminster, Worcestershire. He became a teacher, and helped to found the Society for the Diffusion of Useful Knowledge (1826). In his *Post-office Reform* (1837), he advocated a low and uniform rate of postage, to be prepaid by stamps, and in 1840 a uniform penny rate was introduced. In 1854 he became secretary to the Post Office. He was knighted in 1860, and died in London.

hill mynah A bird of the starling family, native to India and SE Asia; inhabits forest; eats fruit, insects, nectar, and occasionally lizards; black with yellow wattles on head; lives in small groups; nests in hole in tree trunk. It is a common cage bird because it mimics the human voice; in the wild it does not mimic sounds. (*Gracula religiosa*.) » mynah; starling

Hillary, Sir Edmund (Percival) (1919–) New Zealand mountaineer and explorer, more recently author and lecturer, born at Auckland. As a member of Hunt's Everest expedition he reached, with Sherpa Tenzing, the summit of Mt Everest in 1953, for which he was knighted. With a New Zealand party, under Fuchs, he reached the S Pole in 1958. He was appointed New Zealand High Commissioner to India in 1984. » Everest, Mount; Fuchs, Vivien Ernest; Hunt, John

Hillel I [**hil**ayl] or **Hillel the Elder**, surnamed **Hababli** ('the Babylonian') or **Hazaken** (1st-c BC–1st-c AD) One of the most respected Jewish teachers of his time, born (probably) in Babylonia, who immigrated to Palestine at about age 40. He founded a 'school' of followers bearing his name which was frequently in debate with (and often presented more tolerant attitudes than) the contemporary followers of Shammai. Noted for his use of seven rules in expounding Scripture, his views were influential for later rabbinic Judaism. » Judaism; Shammai

Hillery, Patrick (John) (1923–) Irish politician and President of the Irish Republic (1976–), born in Co Clare, and educated at Dublin. Following his election as an MP (1951), he held ministerial posts in Education (1959–65), Industry and Commerce (1965–6), and Labour (1966–9), then became Foreign Minister (1969–72). Before becoming President, he served as the EEC Commissioner for Social Affairs (1973–6). » European Economic Community; Ireland [i]

Hilliard, Nicholas (1547–1619) English court goldsmith and miniaturist, born at Exeter. He served Elizabeth I and James I, and founded the English school of miniature painting. He died in London. » English art

Hillsborough Football stadium in Sheffield, England, the scene of the worst disaster in British sporting history, when 95 Liverpool fans died and 400 people were injured at the FA Cup semi-final match between Liverpool and Nottingham Forest (15 Apr 1989). The tragedy occurred when police opened a main gate into the terraced area to relieve pressures caused by a build-up of people at the entrance allocated to Liverpool fans. This caused a flood into the packed terraces, and people were crushed at the perimeter fences. » football [i]

Hilton, James (1900–54) British novelist, born at Leigh, Lancashire. Educated at Cambridge, he quickly established himself as a writer, his first novel, *Catherine Herself* being published in 1920. His success was dual, for many of his novels were filmed, notably *Lost Horizon* (1933), awarded the Hawthornden Prize in 1934, and *Goodbye Mr Chips* (1934). He settled in the USA in 1935, and died at Long Beach, California. » English literature; novel

Hilversum 52°14N 5°10E, pop(1984e) 105 570. City in SE North Holland province, W Netherlands; famous for its radio and television stations; fashionable residential and commuter district of Amsterdam; railway; textiles, leatherwork, printing, electrical engineering, pharmaceuticals. » Amsterdam; Netherlands, The [i]

Himalayan cat A domestic cat, known as **Himalayan** in the USA and **colourpoint** in the UK; a *long-haired* cat, with a pale coat, and dark face, legs, and tail; breeds named after the dark colour (eg *blue point Himalayan* or *blue colourpoint*). » cat; Siamese cat

Himalayan chamois » **goral**

Himalayas [hi**mahl**yaz, hima**lay**az] Gigantic wall of mountains in C Asia, N of the Indus and Brahmaputra Rivers; a series of parallel ranges, generally rising towards the N; length over 2 400 km/1 500 ml, from the Pamirs (NW) to the borders of Assam and China (E); three main ranges, the Outer, Middle, and Inner Himalayas, which become five ranges in Kashmir – the Lesser and the Great Himalayas, the Zāskār Range, the Ladākh Range, and the Karakorams; Mt Everest rises to 8 848 m/29 028 ft on the Nepal–Tibet border; other major peaks include K2 in the Karakorams (8 611 m/28 251 ft), Kangchenjunga (8 586 m/28 169 ft), Makalu (8 475 m/27 805 ft), Dhaulagiri (8 167 m/26 794 ft), Nanga Parbat (8 126 m/26 660 ft), and Annapurna (8 091 m/26 545 ft); in Hindu mythology the mountains are highly revered. » Annapurna, Mount; Asia; Everest, Mount; Kangchenjunga, Mount

Himalia [hi**mah**lia] The sixth natural satellite of Jupiter, discovered in 1904; distance from the planet 11 480 000 km/7 134 000 ml; diameter c.180 km/110 ml. » Jupiter (astronomy); RR4

Himmler, Heinrich (1900–45) German Nazi leader and chief of police, born in Munich. He joined the Nazi Party in 1925, and in 1929 was made head of the SS (*Schutzstaffel*, protective force), which he developed from Hitler's personal bodyguard into a powerful party weapon. He also directed the secret police (*Gestapo*), and initiated the systematic liquidation of Jews. In 1943 he became Minister of the Interior, and in 1944 Commander-in-Chief of the home forces. He was captured by the Allies, and committed suicide at Lüneburg. » Gestapo; Hitler; Holocaust; SS; World War 2

Hinault, Bernard [**hee**noh] (1954–) French cyclist, born at Yffignac, Brittany. In 1985 he joined Eddy Merckx and Jacques Anquetil as a five-times winner of the Tour de France. He was French pursuit champion in 1974, and turned professional in 1977. In 1982 he won the Tours of Italy and France, and overcame knee surgery in 1983 to win his fifth Tour de France. He has also won the Tour of Italy three times and the Tour of Spain twice. » Anquetil; cycling; Merckx

Hindemith, Paul [**hin**duhmit] (1895–1963) German composer, born at Hanau, near Frankfurt. He studied at Frankfurt, and then played violin in the Rebner Quartet and the Opera Orchestra (1915–23), which he often conducted. His works include operas, concertos, and a wide range of instrumental pieces. He also pioneered *Gebrauchsmusik*, pieces written with specific aims, such as for newsreels and community singing. His music was banned by the Nazis in 1934, and he moved to Turkey, the UK, and the USA. In 1941 he was appointed professor at Yale and in 1953 at Zürich. He died in Frankfurt.

Hindenburg A famous airship, of rigid-frame construction, built by the German government in 1936, capable of carrying 72 passengers in a style matching the ocean liners of the day. After 63 successful flights, most of which were across the Atlantic, the Hindenburg caught fire in May 1937 whilst coming in to moor at New Jersey. The fire was probably due to hydrogen leaks being ignited by atmospheric electricity. » airship

Hindenburg, Paul (Ludwig Hans Anton von Beneckendorff und) von (1847–1934) German general and President (1925–34), born at Posen, Prussia. Educated at Wahlstatt and Berlin, he fought in the Franco-Prussian War (1870–1), rose to the rank of general (1903), and retired in 1911. Recalled at the outbreak of World War 1, he won victories over the Russians (1914–15), but was forced to direct the German retreat on the Western Front (to the **Hindenburg line**). A national hero, he became the second President of the German Republic in 1925. He was re-elected in 1932, and in 1933 appointed Hitler as Chancellor. He died at Neudeck. » Hitler; World War 1

Hindi » **Indo-Aryan languages**

Hindu Kush [**hin**doo **kush**], ancient **Paropamisus** Mountain range in C Asia, an extension of the Himalayan system, covering c.800 km/500 ml; world's second highest range; runs WSW, rising to 7 690 m/25 229 ft in Tirich Mir; four subsidiary ridges; peaks permanently snow-covered, little vegetation; crossed by several passes; the Salang Tunnel allows Kabul to be linked to the N area and Tadzhikistan; Alexander the Great and Tamerlane followed these passes in their invasions of India. » Afghanistan [i]; Alexander the Great; Timur

Hinduism [**hin**dooizm] The Western term for a religious tradition developed over several thousand years and intertwined with the history and social system of India. Hinduism does not trace its origins to a particular founder, has no prophets, no set creed, and no particular institutional structure. It emphasizes the right way of living (*dharma*) rather than a set of doctrines, and thus embraces diverse religious beliefs and practices. There are significant variations between different regions of India, and even from village to village. There are differences in the deities worshipped, the scriptures used, and the festivals observed. Hindus may be theists or non-theists, revere one or more gods or goddesses, or no god at all, and represent the ultimate in personal (eg Brahma) or impersonal (eg Brahman) terms.

Common to most forms of Hinduism is the idea of reincarnation or transmigration. The term *samsara* refers to the process of birth and rebirth continuing for life after life. The particular form and condition (pleasant or unpleasant) of rebirth are the result of *karma*, the law by which the consequences of actions within one life are carried over into the next and influence its character. The ultimate spiritual goal of Hindus is *mohsha*, or release from the cycle of samsara.

There is a rich and varied religious literature, and no specific text is regarded as uniquely authoritative. The earliest extant writings come from the Vedic period (c.1200–500 BC), and are known collectively as the Veda. Later (c.500 BC–AD 500) came the religious law books (*dharma sutras* and *dharma shastras*) which codified the classes of society (*varna*) and the four stages of life (*ashrama*), and were the bases of the Indian caste system. To this was added the great epics, the Ramayana and the Mahabharata. The latter includes one of the most influential Hindu scriptures, the Bhagavadgita.

There have been many developments in Hindu religious thought. In particular, Shankara (9th-c AD) formulated the *Advaita* (non-dual) position that the human soul and God are of the same substance. Ramanuja (12th-c AD) established the system of *Vishishtadvaita* (differentiated non-duality) which, while accepting that the human soul and God are of the same essence, holds that the soul retains its self-consciousness and, therefore, remains in an eternal relationship with God. This provided the impetus for the later theistic schools of Hindu thought.

Brahma, Vishnu, and Shiva are the chief gods of Hinduism, and together form a triad (the *Trimurti*). There are numerous lesser deities, including the goddesses Maya and Lakshmi. Hinduism is concerned with the realization of religious values in every part of life, yet there is a great emphasis upon the performance of complex and demanding rituals under the supervision of Brahman priests and teachers. There are three categories of worship: temple, domestic, and congregational. Pilgrimage to local and regional sites is common, and there is an annual cycle of local, regional and all-Indian festivals. There are over 500 million Hindus. » Advaita; Arya Samaj; ashrama; atman; Avatar; Bhagavadgita; bhakti; Brahma; Brahmo Samaj; dharma; karma; Krishna; Lakshmi; lingam; mandala; mantra; Nataraja; Shiva; tantra; Trimurti; Veda; Vishnu; RR22

Hines, Earl, byname **Fatha** ('Father') (1905–83) US jazz pianist and bandleader, born at Duquesne, Pennsylvania. Part of the jazz immigration to Chicago in the 1920s, his first recordings with Louis Armstrong in 1928, including 'Weather Bird' and 'West End Blues', revolutionized jazz piano. He improvised single-note lines in the treble clef and punctuated them with internal rhythms in the bass, a style that became known as 'trumpet piano'. As the Swing Era ended, he faded into obscurity. In 1965, he took part in a New York concert and was rediscovered, making many recordings and playing all over the world. He died at Oakland, California. » Armstrong, Louis; jazz; piano

hinny » **mule** (zoology)

Hinshelwood, Sir Cyril Norman (1897–1967) British chemist, born in London. He was educated at Oxford, where he became professor of chemistry (1937–64). In the interwar years he investigated chemical reaction kinetics, for which he shared the Nobel Prize for Chemistry in 1956. A considerable linguist and classical scholar, he had the unique distinction of being president of both the Royal Society and the Classical Association. He was knighted in 1948, and died in London.

Hinton, Christopher, Baron Hinton of Bankside (1901–83) British nuclear engineer, born at Tisbury, Wiltshire. Educated at Cambridge, he became an engineer at ICI (1931–40). From 1946 he constructed the world's first large-scale commercial atomic power station at Calder Hall, opened in 1956, and from 1954 was managing director of the industrial group of the UK Atomic Energy Authority. He was knighted in 1951, and created a life peer in 1965. He died in London. » nuclear reactor [i]

hip The outer rounded region at the side of the thigh. The circumference of the trunk at the level of the hip is an important measurement in the fitting of clothes. In anatomical terms, it is the joint between the head of the femur and the pelvis, being the point of articulation of the lower limb with the trunk. It possesses great strength and stability, at the expense of limitation of movement. » femur; pelvis; Plate XIII

Hipparchos [hi**pah**kos] (c.190 BC–125 BC) Greek astronomer, born at Nicaea, Bithynia. Probably the greatest observer in antiquity, he is most noted for his catalogue of the positions of 1 080 stars. He discovered precession of the equinoxes, estimated the relative distances of the Sun and Moon from the Earth, and found the length of the solar year (correct to seven minutes). He may have died at Rhodes. » precession of the equinoxes

Hipparion A fossil horse that originated in N America about 15 million years ago, and spread extensively over grasslands of the Old World; became extinct in the Pleistocene epoch; cheek teeth with complex enamel patterns; lateral toes very reduced. (Family: *Equidae*.) » fossil; horse [i]; Pleistocene epoch

hippeastrum [hipee**as**truhm] » **amaryllis**

Hippocrates [hi**po**krateez] (c.460–c.377 BC) The most celebrated physician in antiquity, born in the Greek island of Cos. He practised in Cos, where he gathered together all that was sound in the previous history of medicine. Over 70 works have been ascribed to him, and he is traditionally regarded as 'the father of medicine'. He died at Larissa, Thessaly. » Hippocratic oath

Hippocratic oath An ethical code attributed to Hippocrates. Parts of it are still used in medical schools throughout the world to encourage young graduates to aspire to conduct that befits those who care for sick people. An extract is as follows: 'Whatsoever house I enter, there will I go for the benefit of the sick, refraining from all wrongdoing... Whatsoever things I see or hear in my attendance on the sick which ought not to be voiced abroad, I will keep silence thereon.' » Hippocrates; medicine

Hippolytus [hi**po**lituhs] A Greek hero, son of Theseus and Hippolyta. Theseus' new wife, Phaedra, made advances to Hippolytus, which were refused; so she falsely accused Hippolytus of rape. Theseus invoked a curse, Poseidon sent a frightening sea-monster, and Hippolytus was thrown from his chariot and killed. » Asclepius; Phaedra

hippopotamus ('river horse') A mammal of family *Hippopotamidae*; an artiodactyl, found in two species: **hippopotamus** (*Hippopotamus amphibius*) of tropical African rivers; body large, barrel-shaped; naked skin dehydrates easily; spends day in water, emerges at night; skin exudes red droplets which protect from sunburn (and possibly infection); large oblong head; nostrils, ears, and eyes level with water surface when swimming; four webbed toes on each foot; can submerge for five minutes; also, the **pygmy hippopotamus** (*Choeropsis liberiensis*) from W Africa; inhabits swamps and forests; shoulder height, 750 mm/30 in; less aquatic than *Hippopotamus amphibius*; also known as **hippo**. » artiodactyl

hippotigris » **zebra**

hire purchase (UK)/**installment credit** (US) A legal agreement to buy an article by means of small regular payments, meanwhile having use of the article. The item is not owned by the buyer until the final payment has been made. Each payment includes an element of interest as well as part of the cost of the article. » interest

Hirohito [hirohheetoh] (1901–89) Emperor of Japan (1926–89), the 124th in direct lineage, born in Tokyo. His reign was marked by rapid militarization and the aggressive wars against China (1931–2, 1937–45) and Britain and the USA (1941–5), which ended with the atomic bombs on Hiroshima and Nagasaki. Under American occupation, Hirohito in 1946 renounced his mythical divinity and most of his powers, and became a democratic constitutional monarch. » Akihito; Japan [i]; World War 2

Hiroshige, Ando [hirohsheegay] (1797–1858) Japanese painter, born at Edo (modern Tokyo). He is celebrated for his impressive landscape colour prints. His 'Fifty-three Stages of the Tokaido' had a great influence on Western Impressionist painters, but heralded the decline of *ukiyo-e* (wood block print design) art. He died at Edo. » Japanese art; ukiyo-e

Hiroshima [hirohsheema, hiroshima] 34°23N 132°27E, pop (1980) 899 399. Capital of Hiroshima prefecture, S Honshu I, Japan; on the S coast, on R Ota delta; founded as a castle, 1594; military headquarters in the Sino-Japanese War (1894–5) and the Russo-Japanese War (1904–5); atomic bomb dropped here (6 Aug 1945), c.150 000 killed or wounded, 75% of the buildings destroyed or severely damaged; town rapidly rebuilt; airport; railway; university (1949); shipping services, naval shipyards, cars, chemicals, textiles, food processing; Peace Memorial Park, containing the Cenotaph, Eternal Flame, Fountain of Prayer, Peace Memorial Museum, shell of the Industrial Exhibition Hall (only major building to survive the holocaust, now known as the Atom Dome); Ri jô Castle (rebuilt, 1958); Peace Festival (6 Aug). » atomic bomb; Honshu; Peace Memorial Museum

Hispanic American Any person resident in the USA who comes from, or whose parents came from, Spanish-speaking countries in C and S America, including the Caribbean. They are now thought to number c.11.5 million, but the figures are highly inaccurate because there are many illegal immigrants – possibly as many as 12 million. Hispanic Americans are Roman Catholics, and the second-largest (after the Black Americans), poorest, and fastest-growing ethnic group in the country. The main groups are Mexican Americans, Puerto Ricans, and Cubans. There are (officially) about 7 million Mexican Americans, concentrated in California, Texas, and other parts of the SW. Called *Chicanos*, they migrated to the USA to find work, and the majority hold poorly-paid unskilled jobs. They are racially *mestizo*, descended from Europeans and Indians. The Puerto Ricans (1.6 million), of mixed European, Indian, and Black ancestry, are the poorest of the Hispanic ethnic groups, with many unemployed; they live mostly in New York City (where they are the largest ethnic minority) and the NE. By contrast, most of the 600 000 Cubans are well-off middle-class White political refugees who have fled from Castro's Cuba, and now live in Miami, Florida, which is today a predominantly Spanish-speaking city. » Cuba [i]; Mexico [i]; Puerto Rico [i]; United States of America [i]

Hispaniola, formerly **Santo Domingo** Second largest island of the Greater Antilles, E Caribbean; between Cuba (W) and Puerto Rico (E); W third occupied by Haiti, remainder by the Dominican Republic; predominantly mountainous, traversed NW–SE by several forested ranges, notably the Cordillera Central, where the highest peak in the West Indies rises to 3 175 m/10 416 ft at Pico Duarte; named by Columbus La Isla Española in 1492. » Antilles; Dominican Republic [i]; Haiti [i]

Hiss, Alger (1904–) US State Department official, born in Baltimore, and educated at Harvard. He reached high office as a State Departmnent official, then stood trial twice (1949, 1950) on a charge of perjury, having denied before a Congressional Un-American Activities Committee that he had passed secret state documents to Whittaker Chambers, in 1938 an agent for an international communist spy ring. The case roused great controversy, but he was convicted at his second trial, and sentenced to five years' imprisonment. He did not return to public life after his release. The justice of his conviction continues to be disputed. » communism; McCarthy, Joseph R

histamine [histameen] A local hormone derived from the amino acid *histidine*, found in virtually all mammalian tissues, and particularly abundant in the skin, lungs, and gut, in association with mast cells. It is released by antigen-antibody reactions, and after skin damage by heat, venom, or toxins. Its actions include the dilation and increased leakiness of blood vessels, and the stimulation of gastric acid secretion. » amino acid [i]; gastrin; paracrine; urticaria

histochemistry The chemistry of living biological tissue. It is particularly significant in the study of immune response, such as in organ transplant surgery. » biochemistry; immunology

histology The microscopic study of the tissues of living organisms. Particular use is made of staining techniques to differentiate between cell types and between parts of cells. » cell

histopathology The microscopic examination of diseased tissues to determine the nature of the condition. Small pieces of tissue taken at autopsy or by biopsy are placed in a fixative solution, cut into thin slices, and then subjected to a number of chemical stains which colour the cell membrane, cytoplasm, and nucleus, rendering them more easily visible. Characteristic changes are found in the presence of cell death (*necrosis*), inflammation, malignancy, scarring, ischaemia, and other disease processes. The extent to which the normal structure of the tissue is replaced and disrupted can also be seen. » biopsy; cell; histology

historical demography A recent technique for the study of population movements in the past. It involves the systematic collection of data from parish and civil registers, from which estimates of birth rates, death rates, and marriage rates can be more reliably made. Historical demographers, using the technique of family reconstitution, have advanced empirically-grounded hypotheses about the long-term factors which underlie differential rates of population growth and decline. The technique has embraced both wide-ranging hypotheses and detailed community studies. » demography; family reconstitution; history

historical materialism The perception of history informed by Marxist theories, concentrating on material factors as the primary agents of change. In most guises, such explanations stress the crucial importance of economic factors. Orthodox Marxist histories are rooted in studies of interaction, identified by Marx, between the 'economic base' and the 'political superstructure'. In recent years, uniform interpretations of this type have been in retreat, with Marxist historians offering broader interpretations of materialism which encompass cultural factors and social interaction. Critics of historical materialism argue that its emphasis on economic causation over-simplifies and distorts the complex of factors making for change. » economics; history; Marxism

history » **African/Egyptian, Ancient/English/French/Greek/Roman/Russian history; comparative history; cultural history; economic history; ethnohistory; historical demography; historical materialism; metahistory; oral history; psychohistory; social history**

Hitchcock, Sir Alfred (Joseph) (1899–1980) British film producer, born in London. He studied engineering at London, and began in films as a junior technician in 1920. He directed his first film in 1925, and rose to become an unexcelled master of suspense, internationally recognized for his intricate plots and novel camera techniques. His British films included *The Thirty-Nine Steps* (1935) and *The Lady Vanishes* (1938). His first US film, *Rebecca* (1940), won an Academy Award. Later films included *Psycho* (1960), *The Birds* (1963), and *Frenzy* (1972). He was knighted in 1980, and died in Bel Air, California.

Hitler, Adolf, byname **Der Führer** ('The Leader') (1889–1945) German dictator, born at Braunau, Upper Austria, the son of a minor customs official, originally called Schicklgrüber. Educated at Linz and Steyr, he attended an art school in Munich, but failed to pass into the Vienna Academy. He lived on his wits in Vienna (1904–13), doing a variety of menial jobs. In 1913 he emigrated to Munich, where he found employment as a draughtsman. In 1914 he served in a Bavarian regiment, became a corporal, and was wounded in the last stages of the war. In 1919 he joined a small political party which in 1920 he renamed as the National Socialist German Workers' Party. In 1923, with other extreme right-wing factions, he attempted to overthrow the Bavarian government, but was imprisoned for nine months in Landsberg jail, during which time he dictated his political testament, *Mein Kampf* (1925, My Struggle), to Rudolf Hess. He expanded his Party greatly in the late 1920s, and though he was unsuccessful in the presidential elections of 1932 against Hindenburg, he was made Chancellor in 1933. He then suspended the constitution, silenced all opposition, exploited successfully the burning of the *Reichstag* building, and brought the Nazi Party to power, having several of his opponents within his own Party murdered by his bodyguard, the SS, in the Night of the Long Knives (1934). He openly rearmed the country (1935), established the Rome-Berlin 'axis' with Mussolini (1936), created 'Greater Germany' by the Anschluss with Austria (1938), and absorbed the German-populated Sudeten region of Czechoslovakia, to which Britain and France acquiesced at Munich (1938). He then demanded from Poland the return of Danzig and free access to East Prussia, which, when Poland refused, precipitated World War 2 (3 Sep 1939). His domestic policy was one of total Nazification, enforced by the Secret State Police (*Gestapo*). He established concentration camps for political opponents and Jews, over six million of whom were murdered in the course of World War 2. With his early war successes, he increasingly ignored the advice of military experts, and the tide turned in 1942 after the defeats at El Alamein and Stalingrad. He miraculously survived the explosion of the bomb placed at his feet by Colonel Stauffenburg (Jul 1944), and purged the army of all suspects. When Germany was invaded, he retired to his *Bunker*, an air-raid shelter under the Chancellory building in Berlin. With the Russians only several hundred yards away, he went through a marriage ceremony with his mistress, Eva Braun, in the presence of the Goebbels family, who then poisoned themselves. All available evidence suggests that Hitler and his wife committed suicide and had their bodies cremated (30 Apr 1945). » Anschluss; Braun, Eva; Gestapo; Goebbels; Hess, Rudolf; Hindenburg, Paul; Night of the Long Knives; SS; Stauffenburg; World War 2

Hittites A people of uncertain origin who became prominent in C Asia Minor in the first part of the second millennium BC; they spoke an Indo-European language, known as Hittite. At their zenith (1450–1200 BC), their Empire covered most of Anatolia and parts of N Syria (eg Carchemish). It was destroyed by marauding invaders, known as the Sea Peoples, around 1200 BC. » Carchemish; Hattusas; Indo-European languages; Sea Peoples; Ugarit

HIV The acronym of **Human Immunodeficiency Virus**; a retrovirus that can cause the breakdown of the human immune system known as Acquired Immunodeficiency Syndrome. » AIDS; retrovirus

hives » **urticaria**

Hizbullah or **Hizbollah** [hizbu**lah**] The umbrella organization in S Beirut of militant Shiite Muslims with Iranian links; the name means 'Party of God'. They came to world attention after the TWA hijacking in Cairo in 1985, and the subsequent taking of hostages. » Shiites

HLA » **human leucocyte antigens**

Ho Chi-minh [hoh chee **min**], originally **Nguyen That Thanh** (1892–1969) Vietnamese statesman, Prime Minister (1954–5) and President (1954–69), born in Central Vietnam. From 1912 he visited London and the USA, and lived in France from 1918, where he was a founder member of the Communist Party. From 1922 he was often in Moscow. He led the Viet Minh independence movement in 1941, and directed the successful military operations against the French (1946–54), becoming president of North Vietnam. A leading force in the war between North and South Vietnam during the 1960s, he died in Hanoi. » Vietnam War

Ho Chi Minh City [hoh chee **min**], formerly **Saigon** (to 1976) 10°46N 106°43E, pop (1979e) 3419978. Largest city in Vietnam; on R Saigon, 54 km/34 ml from the South China Sea; former capital of French Indochina, 1887–1902; former capital of South Vietnam; occupied by the USA in Vietnam War; jointly administered with Cholon city; airport; chief industrial centre of Vietnam; shipbuilding, metalwork, textiles, rubber products, soap, brewing, food processing, bamboo, fruit, vegetables. » Vietnam [i]

Hoare–Laval Pact An agreement concluded in 1935 by the British Foreign Secretary Samuel Hoare (1880–1958) and the French Prime Minister Pierre Laval (1883–1945) aimed at the settlement of a dispute between Italy and Abyssinia. The terms included ceding large parts of Abyssinia to Italy. A public outcry in Britain against the pact led to its repudiation by Britain and to Hoare's resignation. » Abyssinia [i]; Laval

hoarhound » **horehound**

hoatzin [hoh**at**sin] An unusual S American bird, found on wooded banks of the Amazon and Orinoco; large wings and tail; small head with untidy crest; eats fruit and leaves; flies weakly; uses wings for balance on branches; juveniles have two hooked claws at the bend of each wing to assist climbing. (*Opisthocomus hoazin*. Family: *Opisthocomidae*.)

Hobart [**hoh**baht] 42°54S 147°18E, pop (1986) 180300. Seaport and state capital in SE Tasmania, Australia; on the Derwent R at the foot of Mt Wellington; fine natural harbour; founded as a penal colony, 1804; state capital, 1812; city status, 1842; airport; railway; University of Tasmania (1890); textiles, zinc, paper, food processing; Hobart Theatre Royal. » Tasmania

Hobbema, Meindert [**hob**ema] (1638–1709) Dutch landscape painter, born (probably) in Amsterdam. He studied under Jacob van Ruysdael, and eventualy became collector of the city's wine customs. His paintings mainly deal with placid woodland and watermill scenes. His masterpiece, 'The Avenue, Middelharnis' (1689, National Gallery, London) has greatly influenced modern landscape artists. He died in Amsterdam. » Dutch art; landscape painting; Ruysdael

Hobbes, Thomas (1588–1679) English political philosopher, born at Malmesbury. Educated at Oxford, he began a long tutorial association with the Cavendish family, through which he travelled widely. After being introduced to Euclidian geometry, he thought to extend its method into a comprehensive science of man and society. Obsessed by the civil disorders of his time, he wrote several works on government. In 1646 he became mathematical tutor to the Prince of Wales at the exiled English court in Paris, where he wrote his masterpiece of political philosophy, the *Leviathan* (1651). In 1652 he returned to England, submitted to Cromwell, and settled in London. At the Restoration, he was given a pension, and died at Hardwick Hall, Derbyshire.

Hobbs, Sir John Berry, byname **Jack** (1882–1963) British cricketer, born at Cambridge. He played in county cricket for Cambridgeshire (1904) and Surrey (1905–34), and for England (1908–30), when he and Sutcliffe established themselves as an unrivalled pair of opening batsmen. He made 3636 runs, including 12 centuries, in test matches against Australia, and a record number of 197 centuries and 61167 runs in first-class cricket. He was knighted in 1953, and died at Hove, Sussex. » cricket (sport) [i]

hobby A small falcon native to the Old World; usually hunts at dusk; eats insects or birds caught in flight. (Genus: *Falco*, 4 species. Family: *Falconidae*.) » falcon

Hochdorf [**hokh**dawf] An exceptional prehistoric chariot-burial of c.550–500 BC near Ludwigsburg, S Germany, intact when excavated in 1978–9. Beneath a 60 m/200 ft diameter barrow lay a timber-lined tomb 5 m/16 ft square, containing a decorated long bronze couch, a cauldron (both imports from Italy), drinking horns, dishes, textiles, weapons, gold jewellery and clothing decorations, a chariot, and horse-trappings.

Hochhuth, Rolf [**hokh**hoot] (1931–) German dramatist, born at Eschwege, and educated at Heidelberg and Munich. His play *Der Stellvertreter* (1963, The Representative), focusing on the role of the Pope in World War 2, excited controversy and introduced the fashion for 'documentary drama'. Later plays have touched on other sensitive issues: *Soldaten* (1967, Soldiers) on the war morality of the Allies, and *Juristen* (1980, The Legal Profession) on collaboration with the Nazis. » drama; German literature

hockey A stick-and-ball game played by two teams, each of 11 players. The object is to move the ball around the field with the stick until a player is in a position to strike the ball into the

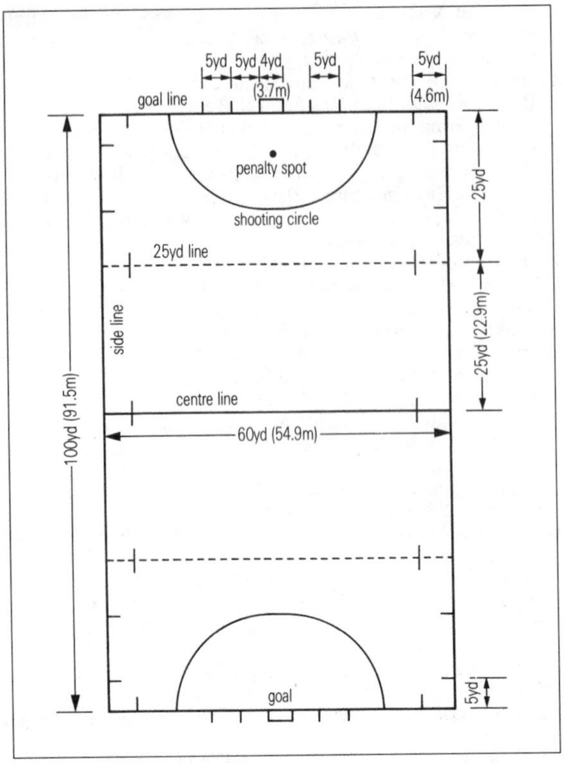

Hockey – Dimensions of the field

opposing side's goal. The playing area is 100 yd (91 m) long and 60 yd (54 m) wide. A game lasts 70 minutes, split into two 35-minute halves. A similar game to hockey was played by the ancient Greeks c.2500 BC. Modern hockey dates from 1875, when the English Hockey Association was formed in London. Indoor hockey is increasingly popular during the winter months. » ice hockey; octopush; street hockey; RR112

Hockney, David (1937–) British artist, born at Bradford, Yorkshire. He studied at Bradford and the Royal College of Art, London, and was associated with the Pop Art movement from his earliest work. He taught in the USA (1965–7), and afterwards was a frequent visitor there. He has also worked in printmaking and photography, and designed sets and costumes. » English art

Hoddinott, Alun (1929–) British composer, born at Bargoed, Glamorganshire. He studied in Cardiff, and taught at the College of Music and Drama there before joining the music staff at University College, Cardiff in 1959 (professor, 1967–87). In 1967 he was co-founder of the Cardiff Festival, of which he remains artistic director. He is a prolific composer of operas, symphonies, concertos, and a large corpus of choral and chamber works.

Hodgkin, Thomas (1798–1866) British pathologist, born at Tottenham, Middlesex. Educated at Edinburgh, he held various posts at Guy's Hospital, London, and described the glandular disease, *lymphadenoma*, named after him. He died while travelling in Palestine, and is buried at Jaffa. » Hodgkin's disease

Hodgkin's disease An uncommon disease of unknown cause in which there is progressive painless enlargement of lymphoid tissue throughout the body. The enlargement is due to multiplication of lymphoid cells, and the tissue contains specific multinucleated cells. Although attended by weakness, anaemia, fever, and sweating, no infective agent has been isolated, and the condition is generally believed to be malignant. » Hodgkin; lymphoid tissue; lymphoma

Hoff, Jacobus Henricus van't (1852–1911) Dutch chemist, a founder of physical chemistry and stereochemistry, born in Rotterdam. Educated at Leyden, he became professor of chemistry at Amsterdam (1877), Leipzig (1887), and Berlin (1895). He won the first Nobel Prize for Chemistry in 1901, and died in Berlin. » chemistry; stereochemistry

Hoffman, Dustin (1937–) US actor, born in Los Angeles. He received his stage training at the Pasadena Playhouse and in New York. His first leading film role was *The Graduate* (1967), and this was followed by a number of similar 'anti-hero' roles: *Midnight Cowboy* (1969), *Little Big Man* (1970), and *Marathon Man* (1976). He found wider scope in *All The President's Men* (1976) and *Kramer v Kramer* (1979), for which he was awarded an Oscar, and returned to comedy in *Tootsie* (1982). He received the 1989 Academy Award for best actor in *Rain Man* (1988).

Hofmannsthal, Hugo von [**hof**manztahl] (1874–1929) Austrian poet and dramatist, born in Vienna. He early attracted attention by his symbolic, neo-Romantic poems, then wrote several plays, notably *Electra* (1903), the morality play *Jedermann* (1912), and the comedy, *Der Schwierige* (1921, The Difficult Man). He also collaborated with Richard Strauss, for whom he wrote the libretti for *Der Rosenkavalier* (1911) and other works. With Strauss and Max Reinhardt, he founded the Salzburg Festival after World War 1. He died in Vienna. » drama; German literature; poetry; Strauss, Richard

Hofmeister, Wilhelm (Friedrich Benedikt) [**hohf**miystuh] (1824–77) German botanist, born at Leipzig. He was professor at Heidelberg (1863) and Tübingen (1872), carried out fundamental work on plant embryology, and pioneered the science of comparative plant morphology. He died near Leipzig. » botany

hog » **pig**

hog cholera » **swine fever**

Hogan, Ben, properly **William Benjamin** (1912–) US golfer, born at Dublin, Texas. A professional at various country clubs, he fought his way to the top despite financial difficulties. In 1948 he became the first man in 26 years to win all three US major titles, and despite a bad car accident in 1949, he returned to win three of the four 'major' golf titles in 1953. He won the US Open four times before retiring in 1970. » golf

Hogarth, William (1697–1764) English painter and engraver, born in London. By 1720 he had his own business as an engraver, and by the late 1720s as a portrait painter. Tiring of conventional art forms, he began his 'modern moral subjects', such as 'A Rake's Progress' (1733–5), and his masterpiece, the 'Marriage à la Mode' (1743–5, Tate). His crowded canvases are full of revealing details and pointed subplots. In 1743 he visited Paris, and followed this with several prints of low life, such as the 'Industry and Idleness' series (1747). He died in London. » English art; engraving

hogfish Deep-bodied bottom-living fish, *Lachnolaimus maximus*, belonging to the wrasse family, *Labridae*, found in the warmer waters of the W North Atlantic; length up to 90 cm/3 ft; excellent food fish, but now scarce in some areas. » wrasse

Hogg, James (1770–1835) British writer, known as the 'Ettrick Shepherd', born near Ettrick, Selkirkshire, Scotland. He tended sheep in his youth, and after only a spasmodic education, became a writer of ballads, which achieved some success thanks to the patronage of Walter Scott. He eventually settled in Edinburgh, and wrote several works in verse and prose, notably *Private Memoirs and Confessions of a Justified Sinner* (1824). He died at Altrive, Selkirkshire. » poetry; Scott, Walter; Scottish literature

Hogg, Quintin » **Hailsham, Viscount**

Hoggar Mountains » **Ahaggar Mountains**

Hogmanay [**hog**manay, hogma**nay**] The name in Scotland for New Year's Eve, the last day of the year. One custom associated with Hogmanay, although it does not take place until after midnight, is **first-footing**, the first-foot being the first person to enter a house on New Year's Day. Traditionally the first-foot should be dark-haired and male, and should carry gifts of food, drink, and fuel.

hogweed A very variable robust biennial (*Heracleum sphondylium*), growing to 3 m/10 ft, native to N temperate regions; leaves up to 30 cm/12 in, divided into oval or lance-shaped segments, often lobed or toothed; flowers white or pinkish in umbels 5–15 cm/2–6 in across; fruit flattened, broadly winged; also called **keck** or **cow parsnip**. The closely related **giant hogweed** (*Heracleum mantegazzianum*) is distinguished by its greater size, growing to 5 m/16 ft tall; stems red-spotted, umbels up to 50 cm/20 in across; native to SW Asia. Sometimes grown for ornament, it can cause painful skin irritations if touched in bright sunlight. (Family: *Umbelliferae*.) » biennial; umbel

Hohenstaufen [**hoh**henshtowfn] A German dynasty named after the castle of Staufen in Swabia. Dukes of Swabia from 1079, they ruled as German kings or king-emperors (1138–1254), and as kings of Sicily (1194–1266). The greatest member of the family was Emperor Frederick I Barbarossa. » Frederick I (Emperor); Frederick II (Emperor)

Hohenzollerns [**hoh**uhntzolernz] A German ruling dynasty of Brandenburg-Prussia (1415–1918) and Imperial Germany (1871–1918). Originating in Swabia in the 9th-c, one branch of the family became Burgraves of Nuremberg; a descendant, Frederick VIII, was rewarded by the Emperor with the title of Elector of Brandenburg (1415). After the Thirty Years' War, the Hohenzollerns pursued a consistent policy of state expansion and consolidation, generating a long-standing rivalry with the Habsburgs (1740–1871), from which Bismarck ensured the Hohenzollerns emerged successfully with the imperial title (1871). The First World War ruined Hohenzollern militarism, and forced the abdication of the last emperor, William II (1918). » Frederick I/II (of Prussia); Frederick III (of Germany); Frederick William (of Brandenburg); Frederick WIlliam III (of Prussia); William I/II (Emperors)

Hohokam [hoh**hoh**kam] The prehistoric inhabitants of the S Arizona desert c.300 BC–AD 1400, ancestors of the modern Pima and Papago Indians. From c.AD 500, they adopted maize cultivation, the Meso-American ballgame, and the ceremonial use of platform mounds, under Mayan influence. From c. 1000, sophisticated irrigation engineering and intensive agriculture allowed a population spread over c.26 000 sq km/10 000 sq ml, stimulating the development of an extended trade network. Hohokam jewellery of this period is notable. » Meso-american ballgame; Papago

Hokan languages [**hoh**kan] A group of about 30 N American Indian languages, spoken by small numbers, but forming a bridge between the indigenous languages of N and S America. The only language with more than 20 000 speakers is Tlapanek. » American Indians

Hokkaido [ho**kiy**doh], formerly **Yezo** or **Ezo** pop (1980) 5 576 000; area 83 513 sq km/32 236 sq ml. Northernmost and second largest island of the Japanese archipelago; bounded by the Sea of Japan (W), Pacific Ocean (E), and Sea of Okhotsk (NE); separated from Honshu I (S) by the Tsugaru-kaikyo Strait, from Sakhalin I (N) by the La Pérouse (Soya-kaikyo) Strait; 418 km/260 ml N–S, 450 km/280 ml E–W, with an irregularly shaped peninsula SW; largely mountainous, with active and inactive volcanic cones (C); numerous hot springs (SW); rises to 2 290 m/7 513 ft at Mt Asahi-dake; originally populated by the Ainu; capital, Sapporo; rice, rye, sugar beet, grazing, forestry, fishing; iron, gold, chrome, oil, natural gas; winter sports resort. » Ainu; Japan [i]; Sapporo

Hokusai, Katsushika [**hoh**koosiy] (1760–1849) Japanese artist and wood engraver, born and died in Edo (modern Tokyo). He early abandoned traditional styles of engraving for the coloured woodcut designs of the *ukiyo-e* school. His ten volumes of the 'Mangwa' (1814–19, Sketches at Random) depict most facets of Japanese life. He is best-known for his 'Hundred Views of Mount Fuji' (1835), many of which grace Western homes in reproduction today. His work greatly influenced the French Impressionists. » Expressionism; Impressionism (art); Japanese art; ukiyo-e

Holbein, Hans (the Younger) (1497–1543) German painter, born at Augsburg, the son of **Hans Holbein the Elder** (c.1460–1524), also a painter of merit. He studied under his father, worked in Zürich and Lucerne, and from about 1516 was in Basle, where he settled in 1520. Among several notable paintings and woodcuts of that period are the series 'The Dance of Death' and the 'Old Testament Cuts' (issued 1538). In 1526 he visited England, where he began a major series of portraits of eminent English people of his time. He returned to Basle in 1529, but was back in London c.1532, and in 1536 was appointed painter to Henry VIII. He died of the plague in London. » German art; woodcut

Holberg, Ludvig, Baron (1684–1754) Danish poet, playwright, and philosopher, born at Bergen, Norway. He was professor at Copenhagen of metaphysics (1717), eloquence (1720), and history (1730). His first notable works were satirical poems, among them *Peder Paars* (1719–20), the earliest classic in Danish. After 1724 he turned to history, producing a *History of Denmark*, and other works. In 1741 appeared another classic, the satirical comic romance *Nicolai Klimii Iter Subterraneum* (Niels Klim's Subterranean Journey). He became a baron in 1747, and died in Copenhagen. » Danish literature

Holden The brand name of the first mass-produced car designed and built for Australian conditions; previously, most motor vehicles had been imported. Holdens were first produced in 1948 by General Motors-Holden Ltd, which was the leading Australian car manufacturer until 1982.

Hölderlin, (Johann Christian) Friedrich [**herl**duhlin] (1770–1843) German poet, born at Lauffen on the R Neckar. He studied theology at Tübingen and philosophy at Jena, and trained as a Lutheran minister, then became a family tutor in Frankfurt. He began to publish, with the help of Schiller, notably the philosophical novel, *Hyperion* (1797–9). He became increasingly schizophrenic, spent a period in an asylum (1806–7), and lived in Tübingen until his death. » German literature; poetry; Schiller

holding company A company which effectively controls another by owning at least half of the nominal value of its ordinary share capital or controlling the composition of its board of directors. The owned company is thereby a *subsidiary* of the holding company. » company

Holi [**hoh**lee] A Hindu festival in honour of Krishna, occurring in February or March (Phalguna S 15), characterized by boisterous revelry, including the throwing of coloured water over people. Sikhs also celebrate Holi, with sports competitions. » Hinduism; Krishna; Sikhism; RR23

Holiday, Billie, originally **Eleanora Fagan** (1915–59) US singer, born in Baltimore, Maryland. Her troubled life – raped as a child, jailed for prostitution as a teenager, addicted to heroin as an adult – made sensational reading in her 1956 'autobiography' (actually written by William Dufty), *Lady Sings the Blues*. She created many memorable ballads, such as 'Easy Living' (1937), 'Yesterdays' (1939), and 'God Bless the Child' (1941). She died while under house arrest in a New York City hospital. » blues; jazz

Holinshed, Raphael (?–c.1580) English chronicler, born apparently of a Cheshire family. He went to London early in Elizabeth's reign, and became a translator. His compilation of *The Chronicles of England, Scotland, and Ireland* (1577), was a major source for many of Shakespeare's plays. » Shakespeare [i]

holism A thesis which maintains that some wholes cannot be fully understood in terms of their parts; the wholes could be biological organisms, societies, art works, or networks of scientific theories. Methodological holism claims that there are large-scale laws of societal behaviour which do not reduce to laws of individual behaviour. » individualism

holistic medicine An approach to medical treatment based on the theory that living creatures and the non-living environment function together as a single integrated whole (*holism*). Implicit in this view is that, when individual components of a system are put together to produce a larger functional unit, qualities develop which are not predictable from the behaviour of the individual components. The holistic approach to medicine insists not only on the study of individual disease but also on the study of the response of people to their disease physically, psychologically, and socially. All aspects of an illness are taken into account, such as the effect of the illness on personal relations, the family, work, and the patient's emotional well-being. » alternative medicine

Holland » **Netherlands, The** [i]

Holles (of Ifield), Denzil, 1st Baron (1599–1680) English statesman, born at Houghton, Nottinghamshire. He entered parliament in 1624, and in 1642 was one of the five members whom Charles I tried to arrest. In the Civil War, he advocated peace, was accused of treason, and fled to Normandy. In 1660 he was the spokesman of the commission delegated to recall Charles II at Breda, and in 1661 was created a baron. » Charles I (of England); English Civil War

holly An evergreen tree or shrub growing to 10 m/30 ft, native to Europe; bark silvery-grey; leaves leathery, glossy above with wavy, spiny margins; flowers 4-petalled, white, males and females on separate trees; berries scarlet. It is widely cultivated for ornament; many cultivars have variegated leaves or yellow berries. (*Ilex aquifolia*. Family: *Aquifoliaceae*.) » cultivar; evergreen plants; shrub; tree [i]

hollyhock A biennial or perennial, native to China, and a popular garden plant; stem growing to 3 m/10 ft in second year; leaves 30 cm/12 in across, rounded and shallowly-lobed; flowers 6–7 cm/2½–2¾ in diameter in a wide range of colours, forming a long spike. (*Althaea rosea*. Family: *Malvaceae*.) » biennial; perennial

Hollywood A suburb of Los Angeles, California, which after 1912 developed into the centre of film production in the USA. Its studios dominated the world motion picture market from the 1920s, and it is still a major centre for the production of visual entertainment in both film and television. » cinema; Los Angeles

HOLMES Abbreviation for **Home Office Large Major Enquiry System**, a computer system introduced in the 1980s for crime detection in the UK. It gives the police immediate access to large data-bases containing information about crimes, thus saving time and reducing the risk of human error in carrying out investigations.

Holmes, Larry, byname **The Easton Assassin** (1949–) US boxer, born at Cuthbert, Georgia. He beat Ken Norton for the World Boxing Council heavyweight title in 1978, and held it until 1985, when he lost to Michael Spinks in his 49th contest, just one short of Rocky Marciano's record. He lost the return contest with Spinks, and in 1988 challenged Mike Tyson for the title, but was defeated in four rounds. He won 48 of his 51 contests, 34 by a knockout. » boxing; Tyson

Holmes, Oliver Wendell, byname **The Great Dissenter** (1841–1935) US judge, born at Boston, son of the writer, **Oliver Wendell Holmes** (1809–94). Educated at Harvard, he became a lawyer, and served in the Union army in the Civil War. From 1867 he practised law in Boston, became editor of the *American Law Review*, and professor of law at Harvard (1882). He became chief justice (1899–1902) of the Supreme Court of Massachusetts, and associate justice of the US Supreme Court (1902–32). He died in Washington, DC.

Holocaust The attempt by Nazi Germany to systematically destroy European Jews. From the inception of the Nazi regime in 1933 Jews were deprived of civil rights, persecuted, physically attacked, imprisoned, and murdered. With the gradual conquest of Europe by Germany, the death toll increased, and a meeting at Wannsee (Jan 1942) made plans for the so-called 'final solution'. Jews were herded into concentration camps, slave labour camps, and extermination camps. By the end of the war in 1945, more than six million Jews had been murdered out of a total Jewish population of eight million in those countries occupied by the Nazis. Of these the largest number, three million, were from Poland. Other minorities (gypsies, various religious sects, homosexuals) were also subject to Nazi atrocities, but the major genocide was against the Jewish people. » Babi Yar; Judaism; Nazi Party; World War 2

Holocene epoch [**hol**uhseen] The most recent of the two geological epochs of the Quaternary period, from 10 000 years ago to the present time. » geological time scale; Quaternary period; RR16

holography A method of lensless photography which gives true 3-dimensional images; invented by Hungarian-British physicist Dennis Gabor in 1948. Modern holograms are made using laser light. The light beam is divided into two parts: one falls directly onto photographic film; the other is reflected onto the film via the object. An interference pattern forms, which is recorded on the film; there is no actual picture in the usual sense. The processed film is the hologram. The image is viewed by illuminating the hologram using laser light; it may be viewed using ordinary light, but the image is multi-coloured. Holograms are now used as a security device on credit cards. » Gabor; interference [i]; laser [i]; photography

holophrase A one-word utterance, characteristic of the usage of very young children in the process of language acquisition, eg *naughty*, *gone*. It takes the place of what would be a full sentence in older speech.

holoplankton » **plankton**

Holothuroidea [holuhthuh**roy**dia] » **sea cucumber**

Holst, Gustav (Theodore) (1874–1934) British composer, born of Swedish origin in Cheltenham, Gloucestershire. He studied at the Royal College of Music, London, but neuritis in his hand prevented him from becoming a concert pianist. From 1905 he taught music at St Paul's School, Hammersmith, and from 1907 at Morley College. He emerged as a major composer with the seven-movement suite *The Planets* (1914–16), and gave up most of his teaching in 1925. Among his other major works are *The Hymn of Jesus* (1917), his comic operas *The Perfect Fool* (1922) and *At the Boar's Head* (1924), and his orchestral tone poem, *Egdon Heath* (1927). He died in London.

Holub, Miroslav [**ho**loob] (1933–) Czechoslovak poet, born at Plzen. He studied medicine in Prague, specializing in immunology, and worked at the Max Planck Institute in Freiburg (1968–9). His collections include *Kam tece krev* (1963, Where the Blood Flows), *Udalosti* (1971, Events), and *Naopal* (1982, On the Contrary). » Czechoslovak literature; poetry

Holy Ghost » **Holy Spirit**

Holy Innocents' Day A Christian festival (28 Dec) which commemorates the killing of the male children around Bethlehem by Herod (*Matt* 2). » Herod the Great

Holy Island » **Lindisfarne**

Holy League 1 (1571) An alliance of the three Catholic powers, Venice, Spain, and the Papacy, after protracted negotiations by Pope Pius V (1570–1) to counter Turkish supremacy in the E Mediterranean. The League's fleet commanded by Don John of Austria smashed the Turks at Lepanto (1571), before disagreements divided the Allies; by 1573 Spain continued the struggle alone. » John of Austria; Lepanto, Battle of; Pius V **2** (1684) The union of the Empire, Poland, Venice, and the Papacy against Turkey, following the Imperial repossession of Vienna (1683). Pope Innocent XI planned further crusades in Hungary, Greece, and Moldavia; the latter failed (1686), but after several years' fighting (1683–99) the League recovered most of Hungary for the Habsburgs, and began the reconquest of Greece (1685–7). » Habsburgs

Holy of Holies The innermost and most sacred part of the Jewish tabernacle, and later of the Jerusalem Temple, cubic in shape, which contained the Ark of the Covenant. Only the High Priest was permitted to enter, and only once yearly on the Day of Atonement. » Ark of the Covenant; Tabernacle; Temple, Jerusalem

Holy Orders » **Orders, Holy**

Holy Roman Empire The revived mediaeval title of the Roman Empire, dating from the 9th-c, when the papacy granted the title to Charlemagne, King of the Franks. It was later bestowed upon German princely families, including the Hohenstaufen, Luxemburgs, and Habsburgs. After Charlemagne, imperial power was greatest under the Hohenstaufen in the 12th–13th-c: the full title 'Holy Roman Empire' (*sacrum Romanum imperium*) was used from the reign of Frederick I ('Barbarossa'); and Frederick II came close to uniting diverse imperial territories that covered much of C Europe and Italy. From the 14th-c, the Empire's power declined with the rise of princely power and city-states; the title was dropped in 1806. » Charlemagne; electors; Frederick I (Emperor); Frederick II (Emperor); Swabian League

Holy Shroud A relic, alleged to be the burial-sheet of Jesus Christ, known since the 14th-c, and preserved in the Cathedral at Turin since 1578. It portrays an image (clearer when shown using a photographic negative) of the front and back of a man's body, with markings that seem to correspond to the stigmata of Jesus. Controversy over its authenticity resulted in the use of independent radiocarbon-dating tests by three research centres in 1988, using a tiny piece of the fabric. The results indicated a late provenance for the shroud. The question of how the body image was produced remains open. » Jesus Christ; radiocarbon dating; relics

Holy Spirit A term used to denote the presence or power of God, often imbued with personal or quasi-personal characteristics; in Christian thought considered the third person of the Trinity, alongside the Father and the Son. Doctrinal differences exist, though, between Western churches which regard the Spirit as 'proceeding from' both the Father and the Son, and Eastern Christianity which accepts procession from the Father only. In the Bible the Spirit was often the vehicle of God's revelatory activity, inspiring the prophets, but it was also depicted as an agent in creation. In the New Testament, the Spirit is described as descending upon Jesus 'as a dove' at his baptism (*Mark* 1.10), as glorifying Jesus after his death (*John* 16.12–15), and even as 'the Spirit of Christ' in *Rom* 8.9. In Acts, the Church received the Spirit at Pentecost, from which time it continued to direct the Church's missionary activities. Paul not only considered the 'gifts of the Spirit' as empowering various ministries in the Church, but also as associated with the ecstatic practices of speaking in tongues and prophesying (1 *Cor* 12–14), which continue to feature prominently in Pentecostal churches. » Christianity; God; Trinity

Holy Week In the Christian Church, the week before Easter, beginning on Palm Sunday. It includes Maundy Thursday and Good Friday. » Easter; Palm Sunday

Holyhead [holeehed], Welsh **Caergybi** 53°19N 4°38W, pop (1981) 12 652. Port on the island of Anglesey (Ynys Môn), Gwynedd, NW Wales, UK; on N coast of Holy I; railway; ferry to Dun Laoghaire and Dublin, Ireland; aluminium, marine engineering, light industry, tourism, yachting; Holyhead Mountain (Mynydd Twr), 216 m/710 ft; breakwater (1845–73), 2.4 km/1½ ml long; St Cybi's Church (founded 6th-c) within 3rd-c Roman walls; summer Leisure Island Festival (Aug); Arts Festival (May). » Ynys Môn

Holyoake, George (Jacob) (1817–1906) British social reformer, born in Birmingham. He taught mathematics, lectured on Owen's socialist system, edited the *Reasoner*, and promoted the bill legalizing secular affirmations. He was the last person imprisoned in England on a charge of atheism (1842). He wrote histories of the co-operative movement and of secularism. » Owen, Robert; socialism

Holyrood House [holeerood] The official residence in Scotland of the reigning monarch. Built in the 16th-c at Edinburgh, the palace was reconstructed in the 1670s by the architect Sir William Bruce (?–1710). » Edinburgh

Holywell [holeewel], Welsh **Treffynnon** 53°17N 3°13W, pop (1981) 11 160. Town in Delyn district, Clwyd, NE Wales, UK; 6 km/4 ml NW of Flint; woollens, rayon, chemicals; the 'Welsh Lourdes', place of pilgrimage since the 7th-c, where St Winefride (Gwenfrewi) beheaded; 15th-c St Winefride's Chapel; pilgrimages (Jun, Nov). » Clwyd; Lourdes

Home of the Hirsel, Baron, formerly **Sir Alec Douglas-Home**, originally **Alexander Frederick Douglas-Home, 14th Earl of Home** [hyoom] (1903–) British Conservative statesman and Prime Minister (1963–4), born in London. Educated at Eton and Oxford, he became an MP in 1931 and was Chamberlain's secretary during the negotiations with Hitler and beyond (1937–40). He became Minister of State at the Scottish Office (1951–5), succeeded to the peerage as 14th Earl (1951), was Commonwealth Relations Secretary (1955–60), and Foreign Secretary (1960–3). After Macmillan's resignation, he astonished everyone by emerging as Premier. He made history by renouncing his peerage and fighting a by-election, during which, although Premier, he was technically a member of neither House. After the 1964 defeat by the Labour Party, he was Leader of the Opposition until replaced in 1965 by Edward Heath, in whose 1970–4 government he was Foreign Secretary. In 1974 he was made a life peer. » Chamberlain, Neville; Conservative Party; Heath, Edward; Macmillan, Harold

home counties Those counties which border London, and into which the city has expanded. These are Essex, Middlesex, Kent, Surrey, Buckinghamshire, Berkshire, and Hertfordshire. » London [i]

Home Guard A home defence militia, raised during the summer of 1940, when the German armies seemed poised to complete the conquest of W Europe by invading Great Britain. At first called the Local Defence Volunteers, the name was changed at Prime Minister Winston Churchill's urging to the more evocative title of 'Home Guard'. The force was finally stood down in 1945. » militia; World War 2

home rule The handing down of certain legislative powers and administrative functions, previously exercised by a higher authority, to an elected body within a geographically defined area; usually put forward as an alternative to separatism. It was illustrated by the government of Northern Ireland until 1972 when Stormont, the Northern Ireland Parliament, was abolished. Since the early 1970s in the UK, for political movements such as the Scottish National Party and Irish republicans, home rule has tended to become synonymous with separatism. » devolution; IRA; Plaid Cymru; separatism; Scottish National Party

Homelands » **apartheid; South Africa** [i]

homeopathy A practice of medicine devised by German physician Christian Hahnemann in the early 19th-c with the principles of (1) like cures like; and (2) drug activity is enhanced by dilution. Thus a drug which in large doses would induce particular symptoms in a healthy individual is used after a series of dilutions to treat a sick individual suffering such symptoms. There is no scientific evidence that the theory of homeopathy is correct. » alternative medicine; Hahnemann

homeostasis A term initially used to describe the stability or steady state of the extracellular fluid apparent in healthy individuals. Nowadays it is often used to describe the ways in which this stability is achieved, not only in humans but also in other animals. Disturbance of the volume, composition, and temperature (in warm-blooded animals) of extracellular fluid may result in ill-health and possibly death. Consequently much of physiology is concerned with the study of the mechanisms which operate to ensure that this fluid is maintained within precise limits at all times. For example, body temperature in warm-blooded mammals is maintained by active metabolic mechanisms such as shivering, if it falls too low, or panting, if it rises too high. » extracellular fluid; homoiothermy; physiology

Homer, Gr **Homēros** (c.9th-c BC) Greek poet to whom are attributed the great epics, the *Iliad*, the story of the siege of Troy, and the *Odyssey*, the tale of Ulysses's wanderings. The place of his birth is doubtful, probably a Greek colony on the coast of Asia Minor, and his date, once put as far back as 1200 BC, from the style of the poems attributed to him is now much later. Arguments have long raged over whether his works are in fact by the same hand, or have their origins in the lays of Homer and his followers (*Homeridae*), and there seems little doubt that the works were originally based on current ballads which were much modified and extended. Of the true Homer, nothing is positively known. The so-called Homeric Hymns are certainly of a later age. » Greek literature; poetry

Homer, Winslow (1836–1910) US marine and genre painter, born in Boston, Massachusetts. He was apprenticed to a lithographer, studied in New York and Paris, and during the Civil War was artist to *Harper's Weekly*. He painted rural and domestic scenes, but was at his best in his seascapes, mostly painted after 1881 while staying at Prout's Neck on the Maine Coast, where he died. » genre painting

Homestead Act (1862) A US law allowing a grant of 160 acres of public land to settlers, conditional on their staying five years, the making of improvements to the property, and the payment of fees. Homesteaders had to be US citizens or intending citizens, and either heads of families or over 21, but could be of either sex.

homicide The action of a person who kills another. The term varies in its application among different jurisdictions. In England and Wales, for example, unlawful homicide includes the crimes of murder, manslaughter, and infanticide. In certain circumstances homicide may be lawful, such as in self-defence, but the action taken has to be reasonable in the circumstances. In the USA, homicide involves causing the death of another either by an act or by an omission when there is a duty to act. Criminal homicide usually includes murder, manslaughter, and negligent homicide. » infanticide; manslaughter; murder

homing overlay device Part of a US experiment to achieve a practical ballistic missile defence using space-based systems. A 'layer' of defences would be established outside the atmosphere to intercept incoming nuclear warheads. » ballistic missile; SDI

hominid A primate of worldwide family *Hominidae*, also known as **human**; one living species, *Homo sapiens* (literally 'wise man'). The family appears to have evolved in the E African Rift Valley, and is closely related to the great apes of family *Pongidae*. The body of a great ape is adapted for swinging through trees (with long arms and short curved legs); in hominid evolution, this pattern was modified for two-legged locomotion on the ground (with a straightening of the back and legs). Long hair was lost except for a tuft on the head and around the genitals (adult males usually develop facial hair and often lose hair from the top of the head). Humans have greater reasoning ability than other species, and have developed language and a wide use of tools. Unlike most species, they no longer have an intimate biological relationship with one particular habitat, but can use their powers of reason and technology to control the environment, allowing them to occupy virtually all habitats. Worldwide population reached 5 000 000 000 in the late 1980s. » ape; chimpanzee; *Homo* [i]; primate

Homo [**hoh**moh] ('man') A genus in the family *Hominidae*, order Primates. Homo features a big braincase, high brain-body ratio, bipedal gait and posture, opposable thumb, and adaptable hands with power and precision grip. Males are larger than females. The genus probably emerged in Africa from a species of *Australopithecus*. Environmental change (grassland ousting forest) may have spurred the emergence and evolution of Homo by favouring co-operative hunting and food-gathering, food sharing at a home base, toolmaking and tool-use involving hand-eye co-ordination, communication, and an extended period of infant care and childhood learning.

There are three named species of *Homo*, two extinct. **Homo habilis** was named in 1964 from fossil finds some think australopithecine. It lived in E Africa (and possibly elsewhere) about 2 to 1.5 million years ago; height 1.2–1.5 m/4–5 ft; weight 50 kg/110 lb; brain capacity 650–800 cc. *Homo habilis* had long arms, brow ridges, projecting jaws, and flat nose, but allegedly a bigger braincase, and smaller face, jaws, and cheek teeth than its possible ancestor *Australopithecus afarensis*. It evidently made crude pebble tools, and was a plant gatherer and hunter-scavenger, perhaps with rudimentary speech.

Homo erectus had a bigger body and brain than its likely ancestor *Homo habilis*, and resembled a strongly built modern human but for a smaller brain, thicker skull, and flatter face with sloping forehead, jutting chinless jaws, and larger teeth; height 1.5–1.8 m/5–6 ft; weight 40–70 kg/88–160 lb; brain capacity 880–1100 cc. It lived about 1.6 million to 200 000 years ago, spreading (probably) from Africa to Europe and Asia. Use of fire, stone hand-axes and chopper tools, and improved hut building seemingly enabled *Homo erectus* to colonize a range of habitats and climates.

Homo sapiens, our own species, evolved from *Homo erectus* through archaic forms resembling Neanderthal man, to fully modern man, *H. sapiens sapiens*, which seemingly emerged in Africa 100 000–200 000 years ago. This subspecies has a relatively light build, large rounded braincase, high forehead, straight (not projecting) face, slight or no brow ridges, small nose, small crowded teeth, small jaws, and pronounced chin. (Reduced jaws and body size reflect increased tool use.) Early Europeans had a height of 1.69–1.77 m/5 ft 6 in–5 ft 8 in; weight c.68 kg/150 lb; brain capacity 1 400 cc. New tools, techniques, and behaviour patterns enabled this subspecies to colonize all continents except Antarctica by 10 000 years ago, and later brought explosive population growth. » Australopithecus; Cro-Magnon/Heidelberg/Java/Neanderthal/Peking Man; hominid

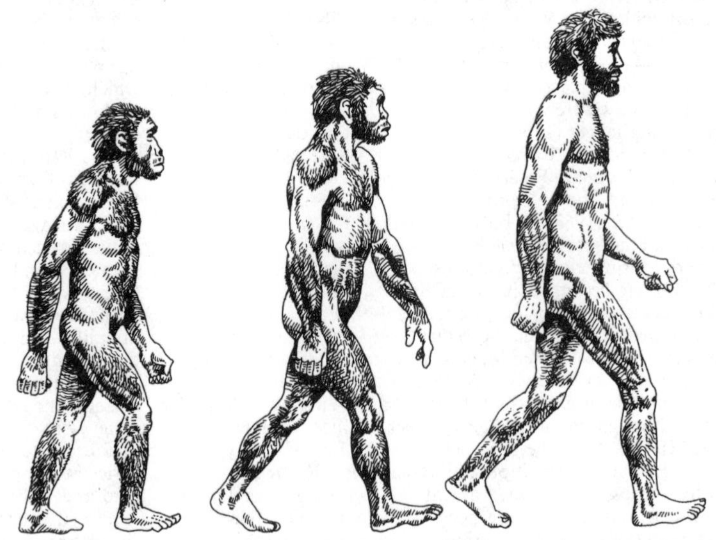

Homo

homoiothermy [huh**moy**ohthermee] The regulation of internal body temperature at a relatively constant level, independent of fluctuations in ambient temperature. Higher vertebrates, such as mammals and birds, are warm-blooded (*homoiothermic*), and typically have insulated body coverings to aid temperature regulation. » homeostasis

homology The relationship between equivalent structures and traits in living organisms, derived from the same part of the embryo but existing in different states in related organisms. The forelimb of a horse, the wing of a bird, and the human arm are all homologous structures, as they are derived from the same part of the embryo, even though they differ in appearance. » embryo

Homoptera [huh**mop**tuhra] A large order of insects comprising c.45 000 species, including the cicadas, plant hoppers, frog-hoppers, leaf hoppers, psyllids, whiteflies, aphids, scale insects, and mealybugs; hindlegs often adapted for jumping; feeding on plants, with modified mouthparts for piercing and sucking. » insect [i]

homosexuality A form of sexuality in which the sexual attraction is between members of the same sex; commonly applied to males. There are both clinical (eg Freudian psycho-medical) and sociological theories to account for homosexuality. Most sociological theories see any form of sexuality as a social construction rather than as displaying any specific, pre-given biological process. Homosexuality has been a subject of considerable political controversy in the West, especially since the formation of the Gay Liberation Movement and the onset of the AIDS virus. » AIDS; heterosexism; lesbianism

Homs or **Hims**, ancient **Emesa** 34°44N 36°43E, pop (1981) 354 548. Industrial capital city of Hims governorate, WC Syria; on R Orontes, 160 km/100 ml N of Damascus; road and rail junction; commercial centre in well-irrigated area; oil refining, sugar refining, textiles, cement, metals, silk, rayon, fertilizers, refrigeration plant; Crusader fortress. » Syria [i]

Honan » **Luoyang**

Honduras [hon**dyoo**ras], official name **Republic of Honduras**,

Span **República de Honduras** pop (1990e) 4 674 000; area 112 088 sq km/43 266 sq ml. C American republic, divided into 18 departments; bounded SW by El Salvador, W by Guatemala, E and SE by Nicaragua, N by the Caribbean Sea, and S by the Pacific Ocean; capital, Tegucigalpa; chief towns, San Pedro Sula, Choluteca, La Ceiba, El Progreso; timezone GMT −6; population mainly of Spanish–Indian origin (90%); official language, Spanish; chief religion, Roman Catholicism; unit of currency, the lempira of 100 centavos; coastal lands (S) separated from Caribbean coastlands by mountains running NW–SE; S plateau rises to 2 849 m/9 347 ft at Cerro de las Minas; also includes Bay Is in the Caribbean Sea and nearly 300 islands in the Gulf of Fonseca; Laguna Caratasca in extreme NE; tropical climate in coastal areas, temperate in C and W; two wet seasons in upland areas (May–Jul, Sep–Oct); variable temperatures in the interior, 15–24°C; coastal plains average c.30°C; centre of Mayan culture, 4th–9th-c; settled by the Spanish, early 16th-c, and became province of Guatemala; independence from Spain, 1821; joined Federation of C America; independence, 1838; several military coups in 1970s; a democratic constitutional republic, governed by a president elected for four years, and a 134-member unicameral legislature (National Congress); the least developed country in C America; dependent largely on agriculture (providing a third of national income), forestry (nearly half the land area), mining, and cattle raising; bananas, coffee, beef, cotton, tobacco, sugar; gold, silver, lead, zinc; offshore oil exploration in the Caribbean; cement, textiles, wood products, cigars, light manufacturing, fishing. » Tegucigalpa; Mayas; RR25 national holidays; RR51 political leaders

Honecker, Erich [**hon**ekuh] (1912–) East German statesman, born at Neunkirchen, Germany. Active in the Communist youth movement from an early age, he was involved in underground resistance to Hitler, and was imprisoned for 10 years. Released by Soviet forces, he became the first Chairman of the Free German Youth in the German Democratic Republic (1946–55). He first entered the Politburo in 1958 and was elected Party chief in 1971, becoming head of state from 1976 to 1989, when he was dismissed as a consequence of the anti-communist revolution. » Germany [i]

Honegger, Arthur [**hon**eguh] (1892–1955) Swiss composer, born at Le Havre. He studied in Zürich and at the Paris Conservatoire, and after World War 1 became one of the group of Parisian composers known as *Les Six*. His dramatic oratorio *King David* established his reputation in 1921, and *Pacific 231* (1923), his musical picture of a locomotive, won considerable popularity. His other works include five symphonies. He died in Paris. » *Six, Les*

honesty A roughly hairy biennial 30–100 cm/12–40 in, native to SE Europe; leaves heart-shaped; flowers cross-shaped, reddish-purple, rarely white; capsules 3–4.5 cm/1¼–1¾ in, flat, oval, with a persistent, silvery, central dividing wall (septum). It is often grown in gardens, especially for the old fruiting stems with persistent septa, and is used in dried decorations. (*Lunaria annua*. Family: *Cruciferae*.) » biennial

honey A substance prepared by bees from nectar found in blossoms. Because of its palatability and its relative rarity, honey has always been a highly prized food. Furthermore its intimate association with nature (meadows and bees, milk and honey) has imparted a curative quality to honey which is not justified. Nectar is sucrose, and this disaccharide is broken down by the bee to yield an equal quantity of the monosaccharides of glucose and fructose (*invert sugar*). The protein, mineral, and vitamin content of honey is negligible. The colour and flavour of honey varies with the flora on which bees feed. » bee; disaccharide; mead; sucrose [i]

honey ant An ant that stores honeydew in specialized workers, called **repletes**. The abdomen of the replete becomes distended, and it hangs from the ceiling of underground chambers, acting as a food store. (Order: *Hymenoptera*. Family: *Formicidae*.) » ant

honey badger » **ratel**

honey bear » **kinkajou; sun bear**

honey fungus A mushroom-shaped fungus which produces creamy white spores on gills on underside of cap; destructive parasite of trees, shrubs, and other plants. (*Armillaria mellea*. Order: *Agaricales*.) » fungus; mushroom; parasitology

honey guide Markings, usually patterns of lines or dots, on the petals of a flower which help guide pollinators to the nectar within. » flower [i]; pansy

honey locust A deciduous tree growing to 45 m/150 ft, a native of N America; trunk and branches covered with stout, often branched spines; leaves divided into oblong leaflets; flowers fragrant, greenish, and inconspicuous, arranged in catkin-like inflorescences; pods up to 4.5 cm/1¾ in long, dark brown, twisted. It is sometimes planted for hedging, and as an ornamental or street tree. (*Gleditsia triacanthos*. Family: *Leguminosae*.) » deciduous plants; inflorescence [i]; tree [i]

honey possum A marsupial, native to SW Australia; superficially shrew-like, with a long clasping tail and long narrow snout; tongue brush-like at tip; inhabits heathlands; eats nectar and pollen; also known as **honey mouse**. (*Tarsipes rostratus*. Family: *Tarsipedidae*.) » marsupial [i]

honeybee The European honeybee (*Apis mellifera*), and three other species of genus *Apis* (Order: *Hymenoptera*. Family: *Apidae*). It is a bee that forms true perennial societies, typically consisting of one queen, several hundred drones, and 50 000 to 80 000 workers. The queen daily lays up to 3 000 eggs, one per wax cell on the honeycomb. The drones fertilize new queens during nuptial flights. The workers forage, clean the hive, feed larvae, and perform all other duties. Colonies do not hibernate, but survive overwinter on stored honey and pollen. » bee; drone; larva

honeycreeper A name used for two distinct groups of birds inhabiting woodland and eating insects, fruit, and nectar: the **Hawaiian honeycreeper** (Family; *Drepanididae*, c.17 living species), and some **tanagers** (Family: *Thraupidae*, 16 species) native to C and S America. » solitaire; tanager

honeyeater An Australasian bird specialized to eat nectar; tongue long with brush-like tip; also eats fruit and insects; inhabits trees and bushes; lives in small groups; shows great variation in bill shape and life style. (Family: *Meliphagidae*, 167 species.) » friarbird [i]; tui

honeyguide A small brownish bird native to Africa and S or SE Asia; inhabits evergreen forest; eats insects (especially bees) and beeswax; some said to lead animals to bees' nests; lays eggs in nests of other birds. (Family: *Indicatoridae*, c.13 species.)

honeysuckle A large genus mainly comprising shrubs, with a few well-known species of woody climbers with twining stems, deciduous or evergreen; native to the N hemisphere, and widely grown as ornamentals; leaves opposite, members of a pair often joined around the stem; flowers tubular, 2-lipped, often fragrant, in the axils of leaves; berries red, blue, or black. The **common honeysuckle** or *woodbine* is pollinated by night-flying moths, and produces sweet scent at night. (Genus: *Lonicera*, 200 species. Family: *Caprifoliaceae*.) » climbing plant; deciduous plants; evergreen plants; shrub

Hong Kong pop (1990e) 5 841 000; area 1 066.53 sq km/411.68 sq ml. British Crown Colony off the coast of SE China, on the South China Sea, lying E of the Pearl R estuary; divided into Hong Kong Island, Kowloon, and New Territories (includes most of the colony's 235 islands); timezone GMT +8; population mainly Chinese (98%); many illegal immigrants from China and refugees from Vietnam; official languages, English, Cantonese; chief religions, Buddhism, Taoism; official currency, the Hong Kong dollar of 100 cents; subtropical climate, with hot, humid summers and cool, dry winters; average monthly temperatures, 16°C (Jan), 29°C (Jul); ceded to Britain, 1842; New Territories leased to Britain, 1898; occupied by the Japanese in World War 2; a governor represents the British Crown, advised by a 14-member Executive Council and a 56-member Legislative Council; economy based on banking, import-export trade, tourism, shipbuilding, and a diverse range of light industry; textiles, electronic goods, watches, jewellery, cameras, footwear, toys, plastic goods; imports c.80% of its food; an important freeport acting as a gateway to China for the West.

In 1997, Britain's 99-year lease of the New Territories will expire, whereupon, under the Sino-British Declaration initialled in 1984, Hong Kong will be restored to China on 1 July 1997. China has designated Hong Kong a special administrative region from 1997, and has stated it will allow regional independence in domestic affairs. Hong Kong will stay a freeport and separate customs zone, foreign markets will be retained, and the Hong Kong dollar will remain as official currency. However, anxiety about the colony's political future grew in 1989, in the aftermath of the shootings in Tiananmen Square, Beijing (Peking), followed by controversy over the UK's refusal to guarantee Hong Kong's British residents a home in Britain, should conditions prove unacceptable to them. » China [i]; Hong Kong Island; Kowloon; New Territories; Tiananmen Square

Hong Kong Island area 75 sq km/29 sq ml. Island within Hong Kong colony, bounded on all sides by the South China Sea; contains the city of Hong Kong; highest point, Victoria Peak (554 m/1 818 ft). » Hong Kong [i]

Honiara [hohneeara] 9°28S 159°57E, pop (1979) 18 346. Port and capital town of the Solomon Is, SW Pacific, on R Mataniko, NW coast of Guadalcanal I; airport; developed after World War 2 around the site of US military headquarters; coconuts, fishing, timber. » Solomon Islands

Honolulu [honuh**loo**loo] 21°19N 157°52W, pop (1980) 365 048. State capital in Honolulu County, Hawaii, USA; largest city in the state, and a port on Mamala Bay, Oahu I; a noted tourist resort, with the famous beach at Waikiki; harbour entered by William Brown, an English captain, 1794; capital of the Kingdom of Hawaii, 1845; US naval base at Pearl Harbor, attacked by the Japanese (7 Dec 1941); airport; three universities; sugar processing, fruit canning; headquarters of US Pacific Fleet; Bishop Museum, Pearl Harbor, Iolani Palace (the only royal palace in the USA), Aloha Tower, Diamond Head Crater; King Kamehameha Day (Jun), Aloha Week (Sep). » Hawaii (state)

Honorius, Flavius (384–423) Roman Emperor of the West (393–423), the younger son of Theodosius I. A young and feeble ruler, he abandoned Britain to the barbarians, and cowered in Ravenna while Alaric and the Goths besieged and sacked Rome (408–10). From 395 to 408, power was effectively in the hands of Stilicho. » Alaric I; Stilicho; Theodosius I

honours list In the UK, the military and civil awards suggested by the Prime Minister and approved by the sovereign at New Year and on the Queen's official birthday. » decoration

Honshu [**hon**shoo] pop (1980) 93 246 000; area 230 897 sq km/89 126 sq ml. Largest of the four main islands of Japan; bounded W by the Sea of Japan, E by the Pacific Ocean; separated from Hokkaido I (N) by the Tsugaru-kaikyo Strait, from Shikoku I (S) by the Seto Naikai Sea, and from Kyushu I (SW) by the Kammon-kaikyo Tunnels and Suo-nada Sea; c.1 290 km/800 ml long, 48–240 km/30–150 ml wide; broadest in the C, rising to the Japan Alps; highest peak, Mt Fuji (3 776 m/12 388 ft); Lake Biwa (W), largest lake in Japan; coastal lowlands include most of the population, and several major cities; earthquakes common; rice, tea, cotton, fruit, silk; oil, zinc, copper; wide range of industries centred on cities. » Fuji, Mount; Japan [i]; Nagoya; Osaka; Tokyo

Honthorst, Gerard van [**hon**thawst] (1590–1656) Dutch painter, born at Utrecht. He moved to Italy (c.1610), returning to Holland in 1620, and twice visited England (1620, 1628), where he painted portraits of the royal family. He was fond of painting candle-lit interiors. He died at Utrecht. His brother **William** (1604–66), historical and portrait painter, worked for the court of Berlin (1650–64). » Dutch art

Hooch, or **Hoogh, Pieter de** [hohk] (c.1629–c.1684) Dutch genre painter, born in Rotterdam. He studied at Haarlem, and by 1654 was living in Delft. His 'Interior of a Dutch House' (National Gallery, London) is one of the best-known examples of the Dutch School of the 17th-c. About 1665 he moved to Amsterdam, and died at Haarlem. » Dutch art; genre painting

Hood (of Whitley), Samuel, 1st Viscount (1724–1816) British admiral, born at Thorncombe, Dorset. He joined the navy in 1741, and fought during the American Revolution, when he defeated the French in the West Indies (1782), for which he was made a baron in the Irish peerage. In 1784 he became an MP, and in 1788 a Lord of the Admiralty. In 1793, he directed the occupation of Toulon and the operations in the Gulf of Lyons. Made viscount in 1796, he died at Bath. » American Revolution

Hood, Thomas (1799–1845) British poet and humorist, born and died in London. He achieved recognition when, with **John Hamilton Reynolds** (1794–1852), he published *Odes and Addresses to Great People* (1825). In his *Whims and Oddities* (1826) he showed his graphic talent in 'picture-puns', of which he seems to have been the inventor. In 1844 he started his own *Hood's Monthly Magazine*. » English literature; poetry

hooded crow » **carrion crow**

hooded seal A true seal, native to the N Atlantic and adjoining seas; grey with irregular black patches; adult male with enlarged nasal cavity which inflates, forming enormous bulbous 'hood' on top of head; lives around drifting ice; young called *bluebacks*. (*Cystophora cristata*.) » seal

hoof-and-mouth disease » **foot-and-mouth disease**

Hooft, Pieter (1581–1647) Dutch poet, dramatist, and historian, born in Amsterdam, and educated in Leyden. He wrote lyrical verse early in his career, then plays (*Granida*, 1605; *Baeto*, 1626), and finally turned to the writing of history with his unfinished *Nederlandsze Historien 1555–85* (1642–54), important also for the establishment of the Dutch language. He died at La Haye. » drama; Dutch

Hook of Holland, Dutch **Hoek van Holland** Cape on the SW coast of South Holland province, SW Netherlands; N of the mouth of the Nieuwe Maas R; also the name of a port 27 km/17 ml WNW of Rotterdam; ferry links with Harwich, UK. » Netherlands, The [i]

Hooke, Robert (1635–1703) English chemist and physicist, born at Freshwater, Isle of Wight. Educated at Westminster and Oxford, in 1662 he became curator of experiments to the Royal Society, and in 1677 its secretary. He formulated the law governing elasticity (**Hooke's law**), and invented the balance spring for watches. The Gregorian telescope and microscope are materially his inventions, with which he made important observations, many of which were published in his *Micrographia* (1665). He died in London. » Hooke's law; microscope; telescope [i]

Hooke's law In physics, a law expressing the proportionality of strain to the stress causing it; stated by English physicist Robert Hooke. It is valid for small stresses only. When applied to springs, a small extension x of the spring exerts a proportional restoring force, $F = -kx$, where k is a constant, a measure of the spring's stiffness. » Hooke; non-linear physics; simple harmonic motion; Young's modulus

Hooker, Richard (1554–1600) English theologian, born near Exeter. Educated at Oxford, he took orders in 1581, and became rector of a parish near Tring. After engaging in doctrinal controversy, he resolved to set forth the basis of Church government, and in 1591 accepted the living of Boscombe near Salisbury, where he began his 8-volume work *Of the Laws of Ecclesiastical Polity* (1594, 1597, 1648, 1662). It is mainly to this work that Anglican theology owes its tone and direction. He died at Bishopsbourne, Kent. » Church of England; theology

hookworm infestation An important cause of anaemia and ill health in tropical countries, resulting from the worms *Ancylstoma duodenale* and *Necator americanus*. It is so-called because the adult worm becomes hooked on to the lining of the small intestine, and sucks blood. It is acquired by larvae penetrating the skin of people working in wet land. » anaemia; worm

hoopoe A ground-dwelling bird native to Africa and S Eurasia; pink body; black and white wings and tail; large crest; long curved bill; inhabits woodland edges; eats worms and insects. (*Upupa epops*. Family: *Upupidae*.) The name is also used for **wood-hoopoes** (Family: *Phoeniculidae*) and **hoopoe larks** (Family: *Alaudidae*).

Hoover, Herbert (Clark) (1874–1964) US Republican statesman and 31st President (1929–33), born at West Branch, Iowa. Educated at Stanford, during and after World War 1 he was associated with relief of distress in Europe. In 1921 he became Secretary of Commerce. As President, his opposition to direct governmental assistance for the unemployed after the world slump of 1929 made him unpopular, and he was beaten by Roosevelt in 1932. He assisted Truman with the various American European economic relief programmes which followed World War 2. He died in New York City. » Great Depression; Hoover Dam; Roosevelt, Franklin D; Truman

Hoover Dam, formerly **Boulder Dam** (1936–47) 36°01N 114°45W. One of the world's major dams, on the Colorado R, Arizona, USA, impounding L Mead; built 1931–6; height 221 m/726 ft; length 379 m/1 244 ft; can generate 1 345 megawatts of hydroelectricity. » Colorado River (USA); dam

Hope, A(lec) D(erwent) (1907–) Australian poet and critic, born at Cooma, New South Wales. Educated at Sydney and Oxford, he became professor of literature at the Australian National University. His works include *The Wandering Islands* (1955) and *Poems* (1960). His *Collected Poems* (1972) is one of the major books of Australian verse. » Australian literature; poetry

Hope, Anthony, pseudonym of **Sir Anthony Hope Hawkins** (1863–1933) British novelist, born in London. Educated at Marlborough and Oxford, in 1887 he was called to the Bar, but after the success of his 'Ruritanian' romance *The Prisoner of Zenda* (1894) he turned entirely to writing. He was knighted in 1918, and died at Walton-on-the-Hill, Surrey. » English literature; novel

Hope, Bob, originally **Leslie Townes Hope** (1903–) US comedian, born near London, whose parents emigrated to the USA in 1907. After some years on the stage as a dancer and comedian, he made his first film appearance in *The Big Broadcast of 1938*, and from that show 'Thanks for the Memory' became his signature tune for over 50 years. In partnership with Bing Crosby and Dorothy Lamour he appeared in the six highly successful *Road to...* comedies (1940–52), and in many others until the early 1970s. During World War 2 and the Korean and Vietnam Wars he spent much time entertaining the troops in the field. For these activities and for his continued contributions to the industry he was given a Special Academy Award on five occasions.

Hopewell The native American culture of the SE USA c.100 BC–AD 400, its focus the Scioto R valley of S Ohio. Though socially and agriculturally unsophisticated, it is notable for its geometric ceremonial earthworks – at Newark, Ohio, covering 6.4 sq km/2.5 sq ml – and richly furnished burial mounds averaging 30 m/100 ft in diameter and 12 m/40 ft in height. The enclosure at Hopewell itself, excavated in the 1890s, included the largest such mound in the USA. » Woodland culture

Hopi [**hoh**pee] A Shoshonean-speaking Pueblo Indian group living in Arizona. They farmed corn and other crops and became famous for their basketry and pottery. Peaceful (Hopi means 'peaceful ones') and democratic, they lived in houses of stone and adobe. Today many work in cities, but several features of their traditional life survive. Population c.7 000. » American Indians; Pueblo (Indians); Southwest Indians

Hopkins, Sir Frederick Gowland (1861–1947) British biochemist, born at Eastbourne. Professor at Cambridge from 1914, he was a pioneer in the study of accessory food factors, now called vitamins. He was knighted in 1925, and shared the Nobel Prize for Physiology or Medicine in 1929. He died at Cambridge. » vitamins [i]

Hopkins, Gerard Manley (1844–89) British poet, born in London. Educated at Oxford, he became a Catholic in 1866, was ordained a Jesuit in 1877, and in 1884 was made professor of Greek at Dublin. None of his poems was published in his lifetime. His friend and literary executor, Robert Bridges, published an edition in 1918, which was given a very mixed reception, notably to Hopkins' experiments with 'sprung rhythm'; but a new and expanded edition in 1930 was widely acclaimed, and his work became influential. His best-known poems include 'The Wreck of the Deutschland' and 'The Windhover'. He died in Dublin. » Bridges, Robert; English literature; metre (literature); poetry

hops A perennial climber native to Europe and W Asia; stems 3–6 m/10–20 ft, twining clockwise with small hooks to aid support; male and female flowers on separate plants; males tiny, 5-petalled; females forming papery cones in fruit. It was used in brewing from the 13th-c, but not cultivated on a large scale until the 16th-c. Only the fruiting heads are used to flavour and preserve brew. (*Humulus lupulus*. Family: *Cannabidaceae*.) » beer; brewing; climbing plant; perennial

Horace, in full **Quintus Horatius Flaccus** (65–8 BC) Latin poet and satirist, born near Venusia, Italy. The son of a freed slave, he was educated in Rome and Athens. While in Athens he joined Brutus, and fought at Philippi. Back in Italy, he joined the civil service, but had to write verses to avoid poverty. His earliest works were chiefly satires and lampoons, and through the influence of Virgil he came under the patronage of Maecenas, a minister of Octavianus. Given a farm in the Sabine Hills, he devoted himself to writing, and became the unrivalled lyric poet of his time. He produced his greatest work, the three books of *Odes* in 19 BC. He died in Rome. » Latin literature; Maecenas; poetry; satire; Virgil

Horae [**haw**riy] In Greek mythology, 'the seasons', implying the right or fitting time for something to happen. They are therefore given various names either connected with fertility or (as in Hesiod) justice, being called Eunomia 'good government', Dike 'right', and Eirene 'peace'. » Hesiod

Horatii and Curiatii [hor**ah**tiee, kyoori**ah**tiee] An early Roman legend used to justify appeals. Under Tullus Hostilius there was war between Rome and Alba. Two groups of three brothers were selected from Rome (the Horatii) and Alba (the Curiatii)

to fight, the winners to decide the battle. All were killed except one Horatius. When his sister, who was betrothed to a Curiatius, abused him, he murdered her, but was acquitted after appealing to the Roman people.

Horeb, Mount >> **Sinai, Mount**

horehound or **hoarhound** A perennial occurring in two species, native to Europe, Asia, and N Africa, both related to mint; stems square; leaves wrinkled, in opposite pairs; flowers 2-lipped, in whorls. **Black horehound** (*Ballota nigra*) is a fetid plant with hooded, purple flowers. **White horehound** (*Marrubium vulgare*) is a white-hairy plant, the flowers white with a centrally clefted upper lip, used as a medicinal herb for cough remedies. (Family: *Labiatae*.) >> mint; perennial

horizontal integration A business situation where a company achieves growth by buying up, or merging with, other companies in the same line of business. This has the effect of reducing competition, but can lead to economies of scale. >> company; economies of scale

hormones Chemical messengers synthesized and secreted in small amounts by the endocrine glands of vertebrates and some invertebrates (eg certain molluscs and arthropods), which affect the functioning of the body's cells and organs. They are usually classified chemically into *amines* (eg noradrenaline, thyroxine), *peptides* (eg oxytocin), *proteins* (eg insulin), and *steroids* (eg aldosterone, testosterone). They are usually carried by the blood to bind to specific protein receptors within or on target cells some distance away. Hormone-receptor binding triggers a series of events within the cell, culminating in a cellular response (such as contraction or secretion). Some disorders (eg diabetes insipidus, insulin resistance) are due to the absence or abnormality of receptor sites. >> adrenocorticotrophic/antidiuretic/follicle stimulating/growth/luteinizing/melanocyte-stimulating/parathyroid/releasing/sex hormones; amines; peptides; protein; second messenger; steroid [i]

Hormuz, Strait of [hawr**mooz**] Passage linking the Arabian Gulf to the Arabian Sea; between the S coast of Iran and the Musandam Peninsula of Oman; 50–80 km/30–50 ml wide; a strategic route controlling ocean traffic to the oil terminals of the Gulf; Qeshm I separated from Iran by Clarence Strait; major point of international tension in the Iran–Iraq War. >> Arabian Gulf; Gulf War

horn A musical instrument made from metal (usually brass) tubing, with a conical bore, coiled and twisted several times and ending in a wide bell; the narrow end is fitted with a small, funnel-shaped mouthpiece. It was traditionally associated with hunting. Until the 19th-c the orchestral (or **French**) horn was largely restricted to the notes of the harmonic series, the fundamental pitch of which could be varied by fitting 'crooks' (pieces of tubing) to alter the instrument's overall length. Since about 1840 valves have performed the same function more easily. The tubing of the modern horn is about 3.6 m/12 ft in length; it has four valves and is a transposing instrument pitched in F. The **double horn** can be switched from F to B♭. >> brass instrument [i]; harmonic series [i]; transposing instrument

hornbeam A deciduous tree growing to 30 m/100 ft, native to Europe and Asia Minor; leaves ovoid, double-toothed; flowers tiny in pendulous male and female catkins; nutlets each with a 3-lobed wing-like bract which aids dispersal. It is often the dominant tree in coppices. (*Carpinus betulus*. Family: *Corylaceae*.) >> bract; coppice; deciduous plants; tree [i]

hornbill A large bird native to tropical Africa, S Asia, and Australasian islands; bill large, often brightly coloured, topped with large ornamental outgrowth; plumage black, brown, and white; inhabits forest or savannah; eats fruit or small animals. (Family: *Bucerotidae*, 45 species.)

hornblende A common variety of the amphibole group of ferromagnesian silicate minerals; a hydrated calcium magnesium iron aluminosilicate that is dark green or black in colour. It is widely found in granite and other igneous rocks. >> amphiboles; silicate minerals

Horne Tooke, John >> **Tooke, John Horne**

horned lizard An iguana native to N and Central America; body covered with sharp spines, especially around the neck; usually inhabits dry sandy areas; as a defence may squirt blood from its eyes; not known to shed tail; also called **horned toad** or **horny toad**. (Genus: *Phrynosoma*, 14 species.) >> iguana

horned poppy A deep-rooted perennial producing yellow latex; chiefly coastal and native to Europe, the Mediterranean region, and W Asia; leaves lobed, slightly fleshy, bluish; flowers 6–9 cm/2½–3½ in diameter, yellow, 4-petalled; fruit a long, slender capsule with 2-lobed, horn-like stigma. (*Glaucium flavum*. Family: *Papaveraceae*.) >> latex; perennial; poppy; stigma

horned toad A SE Asian frog of the family *Pelobatidae* (76 species); head often with spiky extensions of skin resembling horns; adults usually live on dry land. The name is also sometimes used for the horned lizard, and also for some S American frogs of genus *Ceratophrys* (Family *Leptodactylidae*). >> frog; horned lizard

horned viper A nocturnal viper native to N Africa and Arabia; a horn-like scale above each eye; spends day buried in sand. (*Cerastes cerastes*.) The name is also used for the European sand viper (*Vipera ammodytes*), with a small horn on its nose. >> sidewinder [i]; viper [i]

hornet The largest social wasp; a fierce predator, up to 35 mm/1.4 in long; yellow and black coloration; nests often built in old trees, containing several horizontal combs; colonies with up to 4 000 individuals. (Order: *Hymenoptera*. Family: *Vespidae*.) >> wasp

hornpipe A dance of British origin, popular in the 16th–19th-c. Although the best-known example is the 'Sailors' Hornpipe' the dance was not associated particularly with the navy.

horntail A large woodwasp; body typically long, cylindrical, without distinct waist; coloured black, banded with yellow or red; egg-laying tube large, used for wood boring; eggs laid in wood, larvae burrow deep into tree timber. (Order: *Hymenoptera*. Family: *Siricidae*.) >> larva; woodwasp

hornwort 1 A plant (a bryophyte) belonging to the class *Anthoceratae*, resembling and related to thallose liverworts, but with a long-lived, green sporophyte capable of surviving after the gametophyte dies. (Class: *Anthoceratae*.) >> bryophyte; liverwort; sporophyte **2** Submerged aquatic perennial without roots; stems growing to 1 m/3¼ ft; leaves regularly forked, in whorls, the old ones translucent, stiff and horn-like; one flower at each node, tiny, unisexual, lacking petals; fruits warty and sometimes spiny; very widespread in fresh water. (Genus: *Ceratophyllum*, 10 species. Family: *Ceratophyllaceae*.) >> bryophyte; perennial; sporophyte

horny devil >> **Moloch** (reptile)

Horologium (Lat 'clock') [horuh**loh**jiuhm] A faint S constellation contrived in the 1750s by French astronomer Nicolas Lacaille. >> constellation; Lacaille; RR8

Horowitz, Vladimir [**ho**rovits] (1904–89) Russian pianist, born in Kiev, where he studied. He made his concert debut when he was 17, and toured widely before settling in the USA and becoming a US citizen. There were long periods of retirement from concert life, but in 1986 he played again in Russia. He died in New York City. >> piano

Horrocks, Sir Brian (Gwynne) (1895–1985) British general, born at Ranikhet, India. Educated at Uppingham and Sandhurst, he joined the army in 1914, and served in France and Russia. In 1942 he commanded the 9th Armoured Division and then the 13th and 10th Corps in N Africa, where he helped to defeat Rommel. Wounded at Tunis, he headed the 30th Corps during the Allied invasion (1944). Well known as a military journalist and broadcaster, he died in West Sussex. >> North African campaign; Rommel; World War 2

Horsa >> **Hengist and Horsa**

horse A hoofed mammal with many domestic breeds. Modern breeds are thought to have developed from three wild ancestral types: the heavy **forest** type, and the lighter **steppe** and **plateau** types. Modern breeds may be classed as *coldbloods* (strong heavy horses suitable for work, supposedly descended from forest types), *hotbloods* (fast athletic horses such as the *Arab*, supposedly descended from steppe and plateau types), or *warmbloods* (produced by interbreeding the other two), but these groups are not well defined. Technically any horse up to 14½ hands/1.5 m/58 in high at the shoulder is termed a *pony*; taller than this it is a *horse* (in the strict sense). An *entire* (ie not

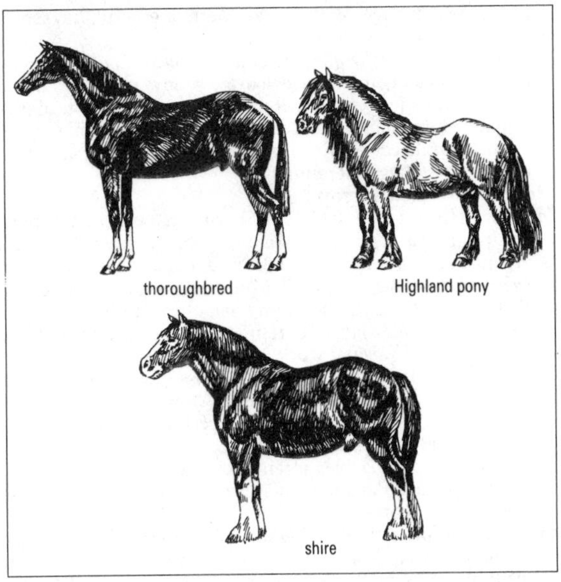

Three types of horse

castrated) male horse aged 1–4 years is called a *colt*; older than 4 years it is a *stallion*; a castrated male is a *gelding*. A female of 1–4 years is a *filly*; older than 4 years it is a *mare*. A horse less than one year old is a *foal* (*colt foal* or *filly foal*). The name *horse* is also used for any member of the family *Equidae* (including asses and zebras). (Order: *Perissodactyla*. Family: *Equidae*, 1 species: *Equus caballus*.) » albino/Andalusian/Arab / hackney / quarter / Tennessee walking horse; Appaloosa; ass; Cleveland bay; Clydesdale; cob; falabella; Hanoverian; horse racing/trials; Morgan; mustang; palomino; Percheron; perissodactyl [i]; Przewalski's horse; Schleswig; shire; Suffolk punch; tarpan; Waler; zebra

horse antelope » **antelope; roan antelope**

horse bean » **broad bean**

horse chestnut A large, spreading, deciduous tree growing to 25 m/80 ft, native to the Balkans, and a widely planted park tree; leaves palmate with 5–7 leaflets each 8–20 cm/3–8 in, widest above the middle, toothed; flowers 2 cm/¾ in, 4-petalled, white with yellow and pink spots, in pyramidal spikes; nuts (*conkers*) brown, shiny, two in a leathery, prickly capsule. The red-flowered trees commonly seen in parks are *Aesculus carnea*, a hybrid of garden origin. (*Aesculus hippocastanum*. Family: *Hippocastanaceae*.) » deciduous plants; palmate; tree [i]

horse fly A biting fly with large, often iridescent eyes; mouthparts form a piercing proboscis in females, used to suck mammalian blood, inflicting painful bites; eggs laid in damp soil; larvae are predators of other insects. (Order: *Diptera*. Family: *Tabanidae*, c.2 000 species.) » fly; larva

Horse Guards An elite regiment of the British Army, first raised in 1661, known as the Royal Horse Guards, whose nickname is 'the Blues'. Amalgamated in 1969 with the Royal Dragoon Guards, the 'Blues and Royals' form, with the Life Guards, the British Sovereign's Household Cavalry. » army

Horse Latitudes Two belts of ocean calm at 30° N and S of the Equator, where conditions of high atmospheric pressure exist almost permanently; Trade Winds constantly blow from these belts towards the Doldrums. » Doldrums; wind [i]

horse racing The racing of horses against one another, each ridden by a jockey. The ancient Egyptians took part in horse races c.1200 BC, and the sport was part of the Ancient Olympic Games. Popularized in England in the 12th-c, most monarchs have supported the sport, which has thereby become known as the 'sport of kings'. The first recorded meeting at England's oldest course, Chester, was on 9 February 1540. Racing comes in two categories: **flat racing** and **national hunt racing**. Flat racing is a straightforward race on a flat surface (grass or dirt) over a predetermined distance which can be anything between 5 furlongs (1 km) and 2½ miles (4 km). National hunt racing involves the horses negotiating fences which can be either movable hurdles or fixed fences. These races (eg the Grand National) are longer than flat races, and can be anything up to 4½ miles (6.5 km) in length. » Classics; Grand National; harness racing; horse [i]; hurdling; Jockey Club; Melbourne Cup; Phar Lap; point-to-point; Prix de l'Arc de Triomphe; steeplechase **1**; RR112

horse-radish A perennial, probably native to S Europe, but long cultivated for the pungent seasoning prepared from the roots, and widely naturalized; fleshy, cylindrical roots; coarse, oblong leaves; white, cross-shaped flowers. (*Armoracia rusticana*. Family: *Cruciferae*.) » perennial

horse trials A combined training competition comprising the three main equestrian disciplines: dressage, show jumping, and cross country. » equestrianism; horse [i]

horsehair worm An extremely elongate, unsegmented worm; feeds as an internal parasite of arthropods when juvenile, emerging into aquatic habitats as a non-feeding adult; adults are a short-lived reproductive stage. (Phylum: *Nematomorpha*.) » arthropod; parasitology; worm

Horsehead nebula A famous dark nebula in the constellation Orion. It bears a plausible resemblance to the silhouette of a horse's head. » nebula; Orion (astronomy)

horsepower Unit of power; symbol hp; equal to 745.7 W (watt, SI unit); almost obsolete, but still used in engineering to describe the power of machinery; equal to 1.0139 metric horsepower. » power; units (scientific); watt

horseshoe bat A bat of the family *Rhinolophidae* (genus: *Rhinolophus*, 68 species), worldwide except for the New World; nose shaped like a horseshoe with an upward pointing flap (*nose leaf*). *Rhinonicteris aurantius* (family: *Hipposideridae*) is called the **golden horseshoe bat**. » bat

horseshoe crab A bottom-living, marine arthropod related to the arachnids (subphylum: *Chelicerata*) not to the true crabs (subphylum: *Crustacea*); body divided into a *prosoma*, covered by a horseshoe-shaped carapace, and an *opisthosoma*, carrying six pairs of legs and five pairs of gills; also known as **king crabs**. (Class: *Merostomata*. Order: *Xiphosura*.) » Arachnida; arthropod; crab

horsetail A primitive, spore-bearing perennial related to ferns and clubmosses; creeping rhizomes; annual, distinctively jointed stem; whorl of scale-like leaves around each joint; cone-like strobilus at the tip. It is found everywhere, except for Australasia, and the only living genus of a large and formerly widespread group, the *Sphenopsida*, dominant during the Carboniferous period. All extant species are herbs, but many fossil species were arborescent. (Genus: *Equisetum*, 23 species. Family: *Equisetaceae*.) » Carboniferous period; clubmoss; fern; herb; rhizome; spore; strobilus

horst An uplifted block of the Earth's crust, usually of great size, bounded by two normal faults. It is often elongated in shape, and may form block mountains. » graben

Horthy (de Nagybánya), Miklós [**haw**tee] (1868–1957) Hungarian statesman and Regent (1920–44), born at Kenderes. He commanded the Austro-Hungarian fleet (1918), and was Minister of War in the counter-revolutionary 'white' government (1919), opposing Bela Kun's communist regime, which he suppressed (1920). He became Regent, presiding over a resolutely conservative, authoritarian regime. In World War 2 he supported the Axis Powers until Hungary was overrun by the Germans in 1944. He was imprisoned by the Germans, and released by the Allies in 1945. He then lived in Estoril, Portugal, where he died. » Axis Powers; Kun

horticulture The business of growing, harvesting, and marketing fruit, vegetables, flowers, and shrubs. It is usually associated with the intensive production of high-value crops, and often involves the use of irrigation in drier areas, and glass or polythene protection in cooler areas. Glass or polythene houses may be heated to allow all-year-round production, and polythene tunnels are becoming increasingly popular as a means of bringing on early crops. » market gardening; polyethylene

Hortobagy [**hor**tobady] area 520 sq km/201 sq ml. National park in NEC Hungary; established in 1973; noted for its wild birds, plants and stock breeding; contains a nine-arched bridge, the longest stone bridge in Hungary. » Hungary [i]

Horus [hawruhs] An ancient Egyptian sky-god in the shape of a man with a hawk's head; also depicted as the child of Isis, when he is often called **Harpocrates**. He is associated with the divinity of the Pharaoh, who is the 'living Horus' ruling Egypt. » Isis

Horyuji Temple [horeeoojee] A complex built at Nara, Japan, for Prince Shotoku in the 7th-c. The Horyuji comprises 45 buildings (of which 17 are national treasures) and houses many magnificent works of art. » Nara

Hosea or **Osee, Book of** [hohzeea] The first of the twelve so-called 'minor' prophetic writings of the Hebrew Bible/Old Testament; attributed to the prophet Hosea, who was active in the N kingdom of Israel c.750–725 BC, during a period of Assyrian military invasions. The work warns of judgment for Israel's defection to the Canaanite Baal cult, but affirms God's love in seeking to restore Israel. Many of these prophecies are presented as corresponding to Hosea's own experiences with his unfaithful wife Gomer. » Baal; Old Testament; prophet

hospice A type of hospital normally reserved for the treatment of the terminally ill, usually catering for specific age groups, typically children or the elderly. The term was originally used to describe a hostel or refuge attached to a monastery. » euthanasia

hospital An institution in which certain kinds of illness are investigated and treated. In the Middle Ages the well-to-do were all treated at home, while the sick poor were cared for in a hospital attached to the local poor house. This pattern of care persisted into the 18th-c, when voluntary hospitals were built throughout the UK, and physicians and surgeons from the locality attended to the inmates without remuneration. With the advance of scientific medicine and the development of increasingly elaborate and specialized investigative and therapeutic procedures, all sections of the population whose medical needs might benefit from admission to hospital are now treated in hospital. Most hospitals not only cater for emergencies of all types and for those whose illnesses develop acutely and unexpectedly (the *acute hospital*), but they contain specialized departments for non-emergency work and for numerous branches of medicine, such as cardiology and neurology. Other hospitals have become exclusively specialized, and cater for the needs of single categories of ill health, such as psychiatric, orthopaedic, maternity, paediatric, and geriatric hospitals. An additional important role is the provision of out-patient departments providing consultative services for the patients of general practitioners who are under care in their own home. » medicine

Hospitallers Members (priests or brother knights subject to monastic vows) of the Order of the Hospital of St John of Jerusalem, originally a purely charitable organization to care for sick pilgrims to the Holy Land. The warrior element developed and became predominant, and from the 12th-c they played a prominent role in the Crusades as an international religious-military order. After the loss of Acre in 1291, they transferred their headquarters to Limassol, Cyprus (1292), then Rhodes (1309), but were expelled by the Ottoman Turks in 1523. They moved to Malta (1530), which they held until dislodged by Napoleon I in 1798. The Sovereign Order is now based in Rome. It is known also as the Order of the Hospital of St John of Jerusalem, the Knights of Rhodes, Knights of Malta, or Knights of St John of Jerusalem. » Aubusson; Crusades [i]; knight; St John ambulance brigade

hosta A perennial native to China and Japan; striking leaves up to 45 cm/18 in long, lance-shaped to broadly oval, often variegated or bluish; flowers tubular, violet, or white, in spike-like inflorescences; also known as **plantain lily**. (Genus: *Hosta*, 10 species. Family: *Liliaceae*.) » inflorescence [i]; perennial

hot-air balloon » **balloon**

hot rock » **geothermal energy**

hot spring A spring of hot or warm groundwater which emerges at the Earth's surface and which often contains dissolved minerals and sulphurous gases. Such springs are often used as health spas, and were popular in Victorian Britain. Very hot springs emerge as geysers, and may be used as sources of geothermal energy. » Bath; geothermal energy; geyser

Hotspur, Harry » **Percy**

Hottentot fig A sprawling perennial native to S Africa; pairs of thick, succulent, three-sided leaves; yellow or pink daisy-like flowers; fruits juicy, edible. Related to the Livingstone daisy, it is planted in many countries as a coastal sandbinder, and often naturalized. (*Carpobrotus edulis*. Family: *Aizoaceae*.) » Livingstone daisy; perennial

Hottentots » **Khoisan**

Hotter, Hans (1909–) German baritone, born at Offenbach-am-Main. He studied in Munich and, after working as an organist and choirmaster, made his debut as an opera singer in 1930. In 1940 he settled in Munich, but sang frequently in Vienna and Bayreuth, becoming one of the leading Wagnerian baritones of his day. He retired from opera in 1972, but continued to do recital work. » opera; Wagner

Houdini, Harry, originally **Erich Weiss** (1874–1926) US magician, born in Budapest, Hungary. After his family emigrated to the USA, he became a trapeze performer, then gained an international reputation as an escape artist, freeing himself from handcuffs, shackles, straitjackets, and other devices, often while imprisoned in a box under water or in midair. He died in Detroit. » theatre

Houdon, Jean Antoine [oodõ] (1741–1828) French classical sculptor, born at Versailles. In 1761 he won the Prix de Rome, spent 10 years in Rome, and executed the colossal figure of St Bruno in Santa Maria degli Angeli (1767). In 1805 he was appointed professor at the Ecole des Beaux-Arts, Paris. His works as a portrait sculptor include busts of Diderot, Voltaire, and Napoleon. He died in Paris. » French art; sculpture

hound A category of domestic dog; name is applied to breeds developed for hunting, especially those which track by scent; sometimes used for any hunting dog, including those which track by sight (eg greyhounds, borzois). » Afghan/basset/otter hound; beagle; bloodhound; borzoi; deerhound; dog; foxhound; greyhound; harrier (mammal); Irish wolfhound; sporting dog

Hounsfield, Sir Godfrey (Newbold) (1919–) British physicist, born at Newark, Nottinghamshire. Educated in London, he joined Electrical and Musical Industries (EMI) in 1951. Independently of A M Cormack, he developed the method of X-ray computer-assisted tomography (CAT), the first body scanners being made by EMI in the early 1970s. He continued to work on new medical imaging methods, and shared the Nobel Prize for Physiology or Medicine in 1979. » CAT scanning; Cormack; X-rays

Houphouët-Boigny, Félix [oofway bwinyee] (1905–) African statesman, the first President of Côte d'Ivoire (1960–), born at Yamoussoukro, Côte d'Ivoire (Ivory Coast). He became a doctor, and the leading African politician of French West Africa. He was a member of the French Constituent Assembly (1945–6) and of the National Assembly (1946–59), holding several ministerial posts. He became President following the country's independence. » Côte d'Ivoire [i]

House of Commons » **Commons, House of**

House of Lords » **Lords, House of**

House of Representatives In the USA, one of the two chambers of the bicameral legislature, in which, under the constitution, all legislative power is vested. The 435 members of the House are elected from single member constituencies, although each state has at least one representative. All revenue bills must originate in the House. » bicameral system; Congress; Constitution of the United States; Senate

house sparrow A small, brown and grey, ground-feeding bird, native to Europe, Asia, and N Africa, and introduced worldwide; usually near habitation; eats almost anything; nests in holes; also known as the **English sparrow**. (*Passer domesticus*. Family: *Ploceidae*.) » sparrow

housefly A small, darkish fly; females lay masses of 100–150 eggs on decaying organic matter or dung; white, worm-like maggots mature in a few days; adults feed on decomposed matter. It is a pest and carrier of diseases. (Order: *Diptera*. Family: *Muscidae*.) » fly; maggot

houseleek A succulent, mat-forming perennial, native to the mountains of S Europe; leaves thick, fleshy, in dense rosettes to 14 cm/5½ in diameter, sometimes with a cobweb of hairs, often bluish or tinged dull red; inflorescences curved, branched, on thick stalks; flowers starry, with 6–18 narrow petals, often pink, purplish, or yellow. It was formerly planted to help keep roofs weatherproof. (Genus: *Sempervivum*, 25 species. Family: *Crassulaceae*.) » inflorescence [i]; perennial; succulent

housemaid's knee A painful inflammation of the liquid-filled pouch (*bursa*) in front of the knee joint, provoked by trauma or excessive kneeling. It is so-called because of its former frequent occurrence as an occupational hazard. » bursitis; knee

Houses of Parliament The Palace of Westminster in London. The first palace on the site was built by King Canute in the 11th-c, and this was replaced and embellished over the centuries until it was destroyed by fire in 1834. The present structure was begun in 1839, and was occupied by the Commons and Lords in 1852. » Big Ben; Commons/Lords, House of

Housman, A(lfred) E(dward) (1859–1936) British scholar and poet, born near Bromsgrove, Worcestershire. Educated at Bromsgrove and Oxford, he failed his degree, and entered the Patent Office, but his contributions to learned journals enabled him to return to academic life, and in 1892 he became professor of Latin at London, and in 1911 at Cambridge. He is best known for his own poetry, notably *A Shropshire Lad* (1896) and *Last Poems* (1922). He died at Glastonbury, Somerset. » English literature; poetry

Houston [**hyoo**stn] 29°46N 95°22W, pop (1980) 1 595 138. Seat of Harris County, SE Texas, USA; port on the Houston Ship Channel (1914), near Galveston Bay; fifth largest city and third busiest port in the USA; settled, 1836; capital of the Republic of Texas, 1837–9, 1842–5; airports (Intercontinental, Hobby); railway; five universities; industrial, commercial, financial, and cultural centre; deep-water channel enables ocean-going vessels to reach the city; major oil centre with huge refineries and the largest petrochemical complex in the world; corporate headquarters of numerous energy companies; base for several space and science research firms; at nearby Clear Lake City is NASA's Lyndon B Johnson Space Center; steel, shipbuilding, brewing, paper, rice, cotton; major league teams, Astros (baseball), Rockets (basketball), Oilers (football); National Space Hall of Fame, San Jacinto battleground, Astroworld, Sam Houston Historical Park, the battleship *Texas*. » NASA; Texas

hovercraft A revolutionary form of sea transport designed by Christopher Cockerell in 1950. Its production was delayed for 10 years whilst awaiting the development of a flexible skirt which would allow the vehicle to surmount obstacles up to five feet high. The craft is propelled by an airscrew, and rides on a cushion of air trapped between the hull and the surface of the water by the flexible skirt, which is usually made of heavy-duty neoprene. The first regular hovercraft service operated across the Dee estuary in summer 1962. » Cockerell, Christopher; hydrofoil

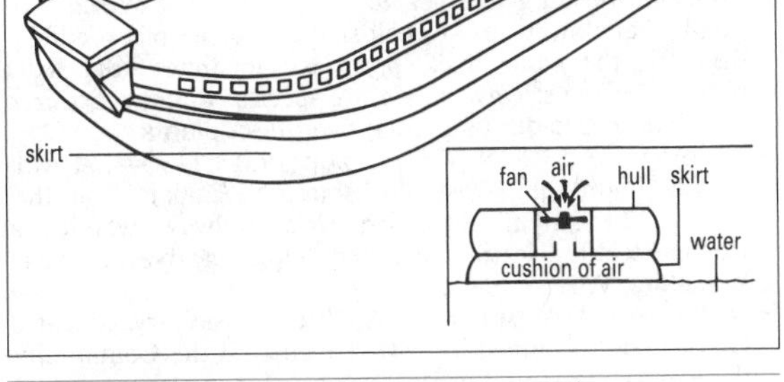

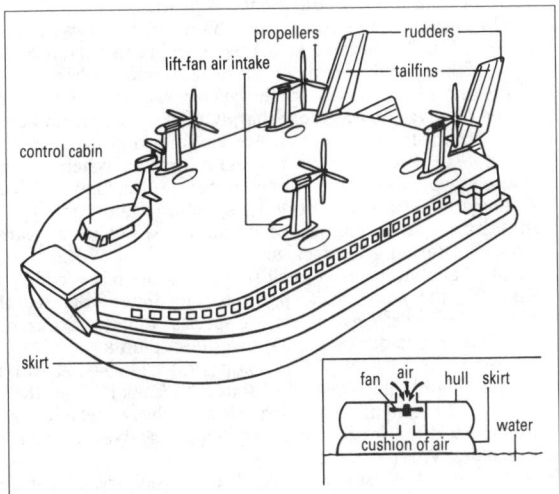

Hovercraft – Inset shows method of operation

hoverfly A medium to large-sized fly often found hovering over flowers; adults resemble wasps, feeding on pollen and nectar; larvae diverse in habits, may be plant feeders, predators of aphids and insect larvae, or scavengers. (Order: *Diptera*. Family: *Syrphidae*, over 5 000 species.) » aphid; fly; larva; wasp

Howard, Catherine (?–1542) Fifth wife of Henry VIII, a granddaughter of the 2nd Duke of Norfolk. She became Queen in the same month as Anne of Cleves was divorced (July 1540). A year later she was charged by Cranmer with intercourse before her marriage with a musician and a kinsman, and was beheaded for treason. » Henry VIII

Howard, Charles, 1st Earl of Nottingham (1536–1624) English lord high admiral, a cousin of Queen Elizabeth I, who commanded the English fleet against the Spanish Armada (1588). He succeeded to his father's title in 1573, and became lord high admiral in 1585. For his role in the Cadiz expedition (1596) he was created an earl, and in 1601 he quelled Essex's rising. He died near Croydon, Surrey.

Howard, Sir Ebenezer (1850–1928) British founder of the garden city movement, born in London. He emigrated to Nebraska in 1872, but returned to England in 1877 and became a parliamentary shorthand-writer. His *Tomorrow* (1898) envisaged self-contained communities with both rural and urban amenities and green belts, and led to the laying out of Letchworth (1903) and Welwyn Garden City (1919) in Hertfordshire, where he died. » garden city

Howard, Henry » **Surrey, Earl of**

Howard, John (1726–90) British prison reformer, born in London. While travelling in Europe he was captured by the French, and spent some time in prison at Brest. In 1773 he became high sheriff for Bedfordshire, and began a series of tours in which he investigated the condition of prisons and prisoners. As a result, two acts were passed in 1774, one providing for fixed salaries to jailers, and the other enforcing cleanliness. Whilst at Kherson, in Russia, he caught camp fever from attending a prisoner and died. » Howard League for Penal Reform; prison

Howard, Leslie, originally **Leslie Howard Stainer** (1893–1943) British actor, born in London. During the 1930s he had many leading film roles, both in Hollywood (notably in *Gone with the Wind*, 1939), and in the UK (eg *The Scarlet Pimpernel*, 1935, and *Pygmalion*, 1938, which he co-directed). He appeared in several British war-time productions, such as *The First of the Few* (1942), and is thought to have been killed when a special mission flight from Lisbon to London was shot down.

Howard, Thomas, 3rd Duke of Norfolk (1473–1554) English statesman, the brother-in-law of Henry VII, who held several high offices under Henry VIII. He was the uncle of Anne Boleyn and Catherine Howard, after whose execution (1542) he lost power. The father of the Earl of Surrey, who was executed for treason by Henry VIII, he would himself have been executed as an accessory, but for Henry's own death. He remained in prison during the reign of Edward VI, but was released by the Catholic Queen Mary. He died at Kenninghall, Norfolk. » Henry VIII; Howard, Catherine

Howard, Trevor (1916–88) British actor, born at Cliftonville. He trained in London and had a successful stage career until joining the army at the beginning of World War 2. Invalided out in 1944, he turned to films, and sprang to stardom with *Brief Encounter* (1945), followed by *The Third Man* (1949) and *Outcast of the Islands* (1951). His versatile and often eccentric characterizations were regularly in demand for both film and television, with later appearances in *Gandhi* and *The Mission-ary* (both 1982), *Dust* (1985), and *White Mischief* (1987). He died in London.

Howard League for Penal Reform A charity dedicated to the cause of penal reform, named after John Howard; formed by the amalgamation of the Howard Association with the Prison Reform League in 1921. Internationally, it urges the UN to promote the standard minimum rules for the treatment of prisoners, and campaigns for the abolition of corporal and capital punishment. » Howard, John

Howe, Elias (1819–67) US inventor, born at Spencer, Massachusetts. He worked as a mechanic at Lowell and Boston, where he constructed and patented (1846) the sewing machine. He made an unsuccessful visit to England to introduce his invention, and returning in 1847 to Boston, found his patent had been infringed. Harassed by poverty, he entered on a seven years' war of litigation to protect his rights, was ultimately successful, and amassed a fortune. He died in New York City.

Howe, Sir (Richard Edward) Geoffrey (1926–) British Conservative statesman, educated at Winchester and Cambridge. He was called to the Bar in 1952 and became an MP in 1964. Knighted in 1970, he became Solicitor-General (1970–2), Minister for Trade and Consumer Affairs (1972–4), Chancellor of the Exchequer (1979–1983), and Foreign Secretary (1983–9). In 1989 he was made Deputy Prime Minister, Lord President of the Council, and Leader of the House of Commons, but resigned from the government (Nov 1990) in opposition to Mrs Thatcher's hostility towards European Monetary Union. » Conservative Party; European Monetary System; Thatcher

Howe, Richard, 1st Earl (1726–99) British admiral, born in London. He entered the navy at 13, and distinguished himself in the Seven Years' War (1756–63). He became a Lord of the Admiralty (1763), Treasurer of the Navy (1765), First Lord of the Admiralty (1783), viscount (1782), and earl (1788). In 1778 he defended the American coast against a superior French force, and in the French Revolutionary Wars defeated the French at 'the glorious first of June' (1794). » French Revolutionary Wars; Seven Years' War

Howe, William, 5th Viscount (1729–1814) British soldier who commanded the army in N America during the American Revolution. He joined the army in 1746, and served under Wolfe at Louisburg (1758) and Quebec, where he led the famous advance to the Heights of Abraham. He became an MP in 1758. In the American War of Independence his victories included Bunker Hill (1775), Brandywine Creek (1777), and the capture of New York City (1776). He returned to England, was made a viscount in 1799, and died at Plymouth, Devon. » American Revolution; Wolfe, James

howitzer An artillery piece in which the shell is projected at a high angle of trajectory, typically at low muzzle velocity, to fall on to its target as plunging fire. » artillery

howler monkey A New World monkey; thick coarse coat and naked face; long 'beard' covers throat, which produces a very loud call; sometimes swings from branches using only its long tail. (Genus: *Alouatta*, 6 species.) » New World monkey

howling jackass » kookaburra

Hoxha or **Hodja, Enver** [hojuh] (1908–85) Albanian statesman, born at Gjirokastër. He founded and led the Albanian Communist Party (1941) in the fight for national independence. In 1946 he deposed King Zog (who had fled in 1939), and became head of state, first as Prime Minister (1946–54), then as Party Secretary (1954–85). He died at Tiranë. » Albania [i]

Hoyle, Edmond (1672–1769) English writer on card games, called the 'father of whist', who lived and died in London. His popular *Short Treatise on Whist* (1742) ran into many editions, and was ultimately incorporated with his manuals on backgammon, brag, quadrille, piquet, and chess into an omnibus volume (1748). » whist

Hoyle, Sir Fred (1915–) British astronomer, mathematician, astrophysicist, and science fiction writer, born at Bingley, Yorkshire. He was educated at Cambridge, where he taught applied mathematics, became professor of astronomy (1958–72), and founded a world-famous Institute of Theoretical Astronomy. His work on the origin of chemical elements is particularly important. He is a leading proponent of steady-state cosmology, of the notion that viruses come from outer space, and a believer in an extraterrestrial origin for life on Earth. He was knighted in 1972. » steady state theory; virus

Hradčany Castle Since 1918, the official residence of the Czechoslovak president in Prague. The Premysl dynasty founded a stronghold on the site in the late 9th-c. This was destroyed by fire in 1303, and the present citadel, which incorporates both Gothic and Renaissance architecture, was built from 1344 onwards. The complex includes St Vitus' Cathedral and the royal palace. » Prague

Hua Guofeng or **Hua Kuo-feng** [hwah gwoh**feng**] (1920–) Chinese statesman and Prime Minister (1976–80), born in Hunan province. He was Vice-Governor of Hunan (1958–67), but came under attack during the Cultural Revolution. A member of the Central Committee of the Party from 1969 and of the Politburo from 1973, he became Deputy Prime Minister and Minister of Public Security (1975–6), and in 1976 was made Prime Minister and Chairman of the Central Committee. Under him China adopted a more pragmatic domestic and foreign policy, with emphasis on industrial and educational expansion, and closer relations with Western and Third World countries. He resigned as Chairman in 1981. » Cultural Revolution; Mao Zedong

Huang He; Huang Ho » Yellow River

Huangguoshu Falls Waterfall in W Guizhou province, SC China; largest waterfall in China, 84 m/275 ft wide, 67 m/220 ft high; on Bai Shui R; at the side is Waterfall Cave, 100 m/325 ft-long cavern set in the cliff face. » China [i]

Huari [hoo**ah**ree] An ancient Andean city near Ayacucho, the capital (AD c.650–800) of a powerful pre-Inca state, controlling all Peru N of Cuzco. At its peak c.700, the 1.5 sq km/0.6 sq ml core contained 70–80 walled rectangular compounds, housing over 20 000 people. » American Indians; Incas

Huascarán [waska**ran**] area 3 400 sq km/1 312 sq ml. National park in W Peru; a world heritage site; consists of the Cordillera Blanca, part of the Andean Cordillera Occidental; established in 1975; rises to 6 768 m/22 204 ft in Nevado de Huascarán, highest peak in Peru. » Peru [i]

Hubbard, (Lafayette) Ron(ald) (1911–86) US writer and founder of the Church of Scientology, born at Tilden, Nebraska. He wrote science-fiction stories before his most famous work, *Dianetics: The Modern Science of Mental Health* (1950) became an instant best seller, and the basic text of the scientology movement. Hubbard, who claimed to have visited heaven twice, was banned (1968) from re-entering Britain amid public concern over his aims and methods. In 1984 he was accused of embezzlement, his Church's tax-exempt status was revoked, and he withdrew into seclusion. He died at San Luis Obispo, California. » scientology

Hubble, Edwin (Powell) (1889–1953) US astronomer, born at Marshfield, Missouri. Educated at Chicago and Oxford, he worked at the Mt Wilson Observatory from 1919. He studied the velocities (redshifts) of galaxies, and was able to relate these to distances from the Milky Way, using a graph known as a **Hubble diagram**. This led to the discovery of the expanding universe, by attributing the redshifts to velocities of recession. The **Hubble constant** is a measure of the rate at which the expansion of the universe varies with distance. **Hubble's law** states that the recession velocity of a distant galaxy is directly proportional to its distance from the observer. He died at San Marino, California. » Big Bang; redshift

Hubble Space Telescope An orbiting observatory, a joint project of the European Space Agency and NASA, launched in 1990 with a 2.4 m (96 in) aperture telescope for visible and ultraviolet observations. In the visible spectrum, it was expected to image objects more sharply than telescopes on Earth, and detect fainter sources. However, following the launch, a defect was discovered in the main optical system, which severely limited its operational range. » European Space Agency; NASA; observatory [i]; spectrum; telescope [i]

huckleberry An evergreen or deciduous shrub which varies from mat-forming to erect, native to the New World; leaves small, oval; flowers urn- or bell-shaped; berries black, edible. In the UK, the name huckleberry is sometimes used for the bilberry. (Genus: *Gaylussacia*, 49 species. Family: *Ericaceae*.) » bilberry; deciduous plants; evergreen plants

Huddersfield 53°39N 1°47W, pop (1981) 148 544. Town in Kirklees borough, West Yorkshire, N England; on the R Colne, 17 km/10 ml S of Bradford; railway; woollen and worsted textiles, textile machinery, clothing, dyes, carpets. » Yorkshire, West

Huddleston, Trevor (1913–) Anglican missionary, educated at Oxford, and ordained in 1937. He entered the Community of the Resurrection, and in 1943 went to Johannesburg, where he ultimately became Provincial of the Order (1949–55). After working in England (1956–60), he became Bishop of Masasi, Tanzania (1960–8), Bishop Suffragan of Stepney until 1978, then Bishop of Mauritius and Archbishop of the Indian Ocean. After his retirement, he returned to London, and became chairman of the Anti-Apartheid Movement. » apartheid; Church of England; missions, Christian

Hudson, Henry (?–1611) English navigator, who explored the NE coast of N America. Nothing is known about his early life. He sailed in search of a passage across the Pole (1607), reached Novaya Zemlya (1608), entered the river which was named after him (1609), and (1610) travelled through the strait and bay which now bear his name. He resolved to winter there; but food fell short, the men mutinied, and he and eight others were cast adrift to die. » Hudson Bay/River

Hudson Bay area c.1 230 250 sq km/475 000 sq ml. Inland sea in Northwest Territories, Canada; connected to the Arctic Ocean via the Foxe Basin and Channel, and to the Atlantic Ocean by the 800 km/500 ml-long Hudson Strait; maximum length c.1 600 km/1 000 ml, including James Bay (S); maximum width c.1 000 km/650 ml; slowly becoming shallower; generally ice-clogged (but open to navigation mid-July–Oct); rocky E shore, fringed by small islands; explored by Henry Hudson (1610) during his search for the North-West Passage. » Hudson; Hudson's Bay Company; Northwest Territories

Hudson River River rising in the Adirondack Mts, New York State, USA; flows 560 km/350 ml S past New York City to the Atlantic Ocean; navigable for large craft as far as Albany; tidal for 240 km/150 ml; explored in 1609 by Henry Hudson. » Hudson; New York [i]

Hudson River School A group of 19th-c US landscape painters, including Thomas Cole (1801–48) and Thomas Doughty (1793–1856). The Hudson R valley and Catskill Mts provided favourite subjects. » landscape painting; school (art)

Hudson's Bay Company A London-based corporation which was granted a Royal Charter to trade (principally in furs) in most of N and W Canada (Rupert's Land) in 1670. It annexed its main competitors, the North West Company, in 1821, and developed extensive sea-based trade in otter pelts along the coast of British Columbia. Rupert's Land was purchased by the Canadian Government in 1870. » Northwest Company

Hué [hway] 16°28N 107°35E, pop (1973e) 209 000. Town in Binh Tri Thien province, C Vietnam; near the mouth of R Hué, 8 km/5 ml from the South China Sea; ancient town, part of the Chinese Empire; former capital of Annam and of the Vietnamese Empire; many historical sites destroyed in Vietnam war; railway; university (1957); commerce, rice, timber, textiles. » Vietnam [i]

Hueffer, Ford Hermann » **Ford, Ford Madox**

Huelva [**wel**va], Lat **Onuba** 37°18N 6°57W, pop (1981) 127 806. Port and capital of Huelva province, Andalusia, SW Spain; in the delta of the Odiel and Tinto Rivers, 632 km/393 ml SW of Madrid; bishopric; railway; shipbuilding, fishing, canning, chemicals, oil refining, trade in ores, wine; New World fiesta (Aug), patronal fair of Our Lady La Cinta (Sep). » Andalusia; Spain [i]

Hugh Capet » **Capet, Hugh**

Hughes, Howard (Robard) (1905–76) US millionaire businessman, film producer and director, and aviator, born in Houston, Texas. He inherited his father's oil-drilling equipment company at 18, and in 1926 began to involve himself in Hollywood, producing several films. Already known as an eccentric, he left Hollywood in 1932, and began to design, build, and fly aircraft. He broke most of the world's air speed records (1935–8), then abruptly returned to film making, producing and directing *The Outlaw* (1943). After severe injuries in an air crash (1946), his eccentricity increased, and he eventually became a recluse, from 1966 living in complete seclusion. He died during a flight to Houston.

Hughes, Richard (Arthur Warren) (1900–76) British writer, born at Weybridge, Surrey, and educated at Charterhouse and Oxford. He wrote poetry and drama (including the first play for radio, *Danger*, in 1924), but is known principally as a novelist. His books take a wide-ranging view of developments in 20th-c society. *The Fox in the Attic* (1961) was the first of a projected series of novels about the rise of fascism in Germany (1933–45), but only one other book, *The Wooden Shepherdess* (1977), was completed. He also wrote several children's stories (eg *The Spider's Palace*, 1931). From 1934 he lived in Wales, and died at Talsarnau, Gwynedd. » English literature; fascism; novel

Hughes, Ted, properly **Edward (James)** (1930–) British poet, born at Mytholmroyd, Yorkshire, and educated at Cambridge. Best known for his very distinctive animal poems, his first collection was *The Hawk in the Rain* (1957). He married the US poet, Sylvia Plath, in 1954, and after her death edited her collected poems (1981). His *Selected Poems, 1957–81* appeared in 1982, and he became poet laureate in 1984. » English literature; Plath; poetry

Hughes, Thomas (1822–96) British novelist, born at Uffington, Berkshire. Educated at Rugby and Oxford, he was called to the Bar (1848) and became a county court judge (1882). He was a Liberal MP (1865–74), closely associated with the Christian Socialists, and helped to found the Working Men's College (1854), of which he became principal (1872–83). He is primarily remembered as the author of the public school classic, *Tom Brown's Schooldays* (1856), based on his school experiences at Rugby under the headmastership of Arnold. He died at Brighton, Sussex. » Arnold, Thomas; English literature; novel

Hughes, William M(orris) (1864–1952) Australian statesman and Prime Minister (1915–23), born in Llandudno, Wales. He went to Australia in 1884, entered the New South Wales and Commonwealth parliaments, and became Federal Prime Minister. He was the major proponent of conscription in World War 1, and as Nationalist Prime Minister represented Australia at the Versailles conference. A founder of the United Australian Party in the early 1930s, he served in successive cabinets until 1941, and remained an MP until his death, in Sydney. » Australia [i]

Hugo, Victor (Marie) (1802–85) French author, born at Besançon. Educated in Paris and Madrid, he wrote his first play at the age of 14, and went on to become the most prolific French writer of the 19th-c. His early works include *Odes et Ballades* (1822, 1826), and *Hernani* (1830), the first of the 'five-act lyrics' which compose his drama. The 1830s saw several plays, such as *Marion Delorme* (1831), books of poetry, notably *Les Feuilles d'automne* (1831, Autumn Leaves), and novels, of which the most popular is *Notre Dame de Paris* (1831, trans The Hunchback of Notre Dame). He was elected to the legislative assembly, and joined the democratic republicans; but in 1851, after the coup, he fled into exile in Brussels, and in 1852 moved to the Channel Is. There he wrote several major works, notably his poems *Les Châtiments* (1853, Punishments) and *Les Contemplations* (1856), and his panoramic novel of social history, *Les Misérables* (1862). He returned to Paris in 1870, was made a Senator in 1876, and upon his death was given a national funeral. » French literature; Napoleon I; novel; poetry

Huguenots [**hyoo**guhnohz] French Calvinist Protestants whose political rivalry with Catholics (eg the House of Guise) led to the French Wars of Religion (1562–98). Their leader, Henry of Navarre, succeeded to the throne (1589), granting them important concessions on his conversion to Catholicism (Edict of Nantes, 1598); these were later revoked by Louis XIV (1685), resulting in persecution and emigration. » Henry IV (of France); Louis XIV; Nantes, Edict of; Religion, Wars of; Saint Bartholomew's Day Massacre

huia [**hoo**yuh] A bird native to forests in New Zealand; probably extinct; black with long white-tipped tail; yellow wattle on each cheek; weak flier; female with long, slender, down-curved bill; male with shorter, straighter bill; ate insects and fruit. (*Heteralocha acutirostris*. Family: *Callaeidae*.) » saddleback

Huitzilopochtli [wheetzeeloh**pohch**tlee] Aztec god of the Sun and of war; there were human sacrifices before his image. He has been identified with the Toltec Quetzalcoatl, whom he replaced after the Aztec conquest. » Aztecs; Quetzalcoatl

Hull, Cordell (1871–1955) US statesman, born at Overton, Tennessee. He became Secretary of State under Roosevelt in 1933, and served for the longest term in that office until he retired in 1944, having attended most of the great wartime conferences. He was a strong advocate of maximum aid to the Allies. He helped to organize the United Nations, for which he received the Nobel Peace Prize in 1944. He died at Bethesda, Maryland. » United Nations

Hull (Canada) 45°26N 75°45W, pop (1981) 56 225. Town in S Quebec, SE Canada, on the Ottawa R, NW of Ottawa; founded in 1801 by settlers from the USA; railway; timber, paper milling, textiles, meat packing, cement. » Quebec

Hull, properly **Kingston-upon-Hull** 53°45N 0°20W, pop (1987e) 252 700. Seaport in Humberside, NE England; at the junction of the Hull and Humber Rivers, 35 km/22 ml from the North Sea and 330 km/205 ml N of London; city status granted 1897; a major UK container port; university (1954); railway; ferry service to Rotterdam, Zeebrugge; the Humber Bridge, completed 1981, the largest single span suspension bridge in the world; chemicals, paper, pharmaceuticals, iron and steel, fishing, service industries; William Wilberforce house. » Humberside; Wilberforce

human engineering » ergonomics

human immune-deficiency virus » AIDS

human leucocyte antigens (HLA) Antigens originally discovered on the surface of human white blood cells (leucocytes), and now known to be present on all nucleated cells, platelets, and human lymphocytes. Over 100 different antigens exist, with most people possessing their own individual complement. They are inherited from both parents, and only identical twins have the same HLA patterns. Their importance first lay in their influence in predicting the outcome in organ transplantation, but there are strong associations between HLA and susceptibility to certain diseases, notably auto-immune diseases. » ankylosing spondylitis; antibodies; auto-immune diseases; blood

human rights A concept deriving from the doctrine of natural rights, which holds that individuals, by virtue of their humanity, possess fundamental rights beyond those prescribed in law. First formally incorporated into the US Declaration of Independence (1776), a Declaration of the Rights of Man and the Citizen was adopted by the French National Assembly (1789). Most written constitutions contain a bill of rights. Although having no legal standing, the UN's General Assembly adopted a Universal Declaration of Human Rights in 1948, detailing individual and social rights and freedoms, followed in 1953 by the European Convention on Human Rights. The European Court of Human Rights was established within this framework. » Amnesty International; civil liberties; civil rights

humanism Historically, a movement that arose with the Italian Renaissance, in the writings of Ficino, Pico della Mirandola, and others, emphasizing the liberation of humanity from the thralldom of the mediaeval church and state; continued by such thinkers as Erasmus and More. More generally, any position which stresses the importance of persons, typically in contrast with something else, such as God, inanimate nature, or totalitarian societies. » Erasmus; More, Thomas; Pico della Mirandola

Humber Bridge The longest single-span suspension bridge in the world; built (1973–81) across the R Humber, England; length of main span 1 410 m/4 626 ft; total length 2 220 m/7 283 ft. » bridge (engineering); Humber, River

Humber, River River estuary in Humberside, NE England; estuary of Ouse and Trent Rivers; runs 64 km/40 ml E and SE; entrance dominated by Spurn Head; Hull on N shore, Immingham and Grimsby on S; Humber Bridge completed 1981, largest single-span suspension bridge in the world. » England [i]; Humber Bridge

Humberside pop (1987e) 846 500; area 3 512 sq km/1 356 sq ml. County of NE England, divided into nine districts; created in 1974 from parts of Lincolnshire and Yorkshire; bounded E by the North Sea; drained by the R Humber, and divided by the Humber estuary; county town, Beverley; major ports at Grimsby, Goole, and Immingham on the R Humber; cereals, sugar beet, livestock, fishing, iron and steel, chemicals, petrochemicals. » Beverley; England [i]; Hull

Humboldt, (Friedrich Wilhelm Heinrich) Alexander, Baron von (1769–1859) German naturalist and geographer, born in Berlin. He studied at Frankfurt, Berlin, Göttingen, and Freiberg, then in 1799 spent five years with Aimé Bonpland (1773–1858) exploring S America. He worked mainly in France until 1827, then explored Central Asia. From 1830 he was employed in political service. His major work, *Kosmos* (1845–62), endeavours to provide a comprehensive physical picture of the universe. He died in Berlin. The ocean current off the W coast of S America is named after him.

Humboldt, (Karl) Wilhelm von (1767–1835) German statesman and philologist, born at Potsdam. After travelling in Europe, he became a diplomat, and for some years devoted himself to literature. He became Prussian Minister at Rome (1801), First Minister of Public Instruction (1808), and Minister in Vienna (1810). He was the first to study Basque scientifically, and also worked on the languages of the East and of the South Sea Is. He died near Berlin. » Basques; comparative linguistics; Prussia

Hume, Cardinal (George) Basil (1923–) British Roman Catholic Benedictine monk and cardinal. Educated at Ampleforth, Oxford, and Fribourg, he was ordained in 1950. He became Magister Scholarum of the English Benedictine Congregation (1957–63), and in 1963 Abbot of Ampleforth, where he remained until created Archbishop of Westminster and a cardinal in 1976. His books include *Searching for God* (1977) and *In Praise of Benedict* (1981). » Benedictines

Hume, David (1711–76) British philosopher and historian, born and died in Edinburgh, Scotland. He studied at Edinburgh, took up law, and in 1734 went to La Flèche in Anjou, where he wrote his masterpiece, *A Treatise of Human Nature* (1739–40), consolidating and extending the empiricist legacy of Locke and Berkeley. His views became widely known only when he wrote two volumes of *Essays Moral and Political* (1741–2). He wrote the posthumously published *Dialogues concerning Natural Religion* in the 1750s. His atheism thwarted his applications for professorships at Edinburgh and Glasgow, and he became a tutor, secretary, and keeper of the Advocates' Library in Edinburgh, where he published his popular *Political Discourses* (1752), and his six-volume *History of England* (1754–62). His views inspired Kant to argue for the inadequacy of empiricism. » Berkeley, George; empiricism; Kant; Locke, John; natural law; naturalistic fallacy; social contract

Hume, Joseph (1777–1855) British radical politician, born at Montrose, Scotland. He studied medicine at Edinburgh, and in 1797 became assistant surgeon under the East India Company. After returning to England (1808), he sat in parliament (1812, 1819–55), where his arguments for reform included the legalizing of trade unions, freedom of trade with India, and the abolition of army flogging, naval impressment, and imprisonment for debt. He died in Norfolk.

humidity The amount of water vapour in a sample of air, usually expressed as relative or absolute humidity. **Absolute humidity** is the total mass of water in a given volume of air, expressed in grams per cubic centimetre. A sample of air of a given temperature and pressure can hold a certain amount of water, above which point (known as the *dew point*) saturation occurs. Warmer air is able to hold more water vapour than cold air and so, for the same pressure, has a higher absolute humidity. » condensation (physics); dew point temperature; hygrometer; vapour pressure

hummingbird A small bird restricted to the New World; possibly related to swifts; eats nectar and small insects caught in flight; fast wing-beat and modification of wing structure allows hovering; important pollinator for some flowers. (Family: *Trochilidae*, 320 species.) » swift; thornbill

humpback whale A baleen whale of the rorqual family, found worldwide; dark back and pale undersurface; wide tail and very long slender flippers; jaws and flippers with many rough knobs; have complex 'songs' unique to each population; may 'breach' (leap vertically from water). (*Megaptera novaeangliae*.) » baleen [i]; rorqual; whale [i]

humped cattle » zebu

Humperdinck, Engelbert (1854–1921) German composer, born at Siegburg, near Bonn. He studied music at Cologne, Frankfurt, Munich, and Berlin, and travelled widely as a teacher. He composed several operas, one of which, *Hänsel und*

Gretel (1893), was highly successful. He died at Neustrelitz, Germany. » opera

Humphrey, Doris (1895–1958) US dancer, choreographer, and teacher, born at Oak Park, Illinois. She studied a range of dance forms, including ballroom dancing, before joining Ruth St Denis to learn an early form of modern dance. She formed her own group with Charles Weidman (1901–75) in 1928, and toured with performances of her own choreography. Her dances were often concerned with form and based on musical structures, such as *With my Red Fires* (1935–6) and *Day on Earth* (1947). She also wrote the key text on dance composition in modern dance, *The Art of Making Dances* (1959). She died in New York City. » choreography; modern dance; St Denis, Ruth

Humphrey, Hubert H(oratio) (1911–78) US Democratic statesman, born at Wallace, South Dakota. He became Mayor of Minneapolis in 1945, and was elected Senator in 1948. He built up a strong reputation as a liberal, particularly on the civil rights issue, but, as Vice-President from 1964 under Johnson, alienated many of his supporters by defending the policy of continuing the war in Vietnam. Although he won the Democratic presidential nomination in 1968, a substantial minority of Democrats opposed him, and he narrowly lost the election to Nixon. He then returned to the Senate, and died at Waverly, Minnesota. » civil rights; Johnson, Lyndon B; Nixon, Richard M; Vietnam War

Humpty Doo 12°37S 131°14E, pop(1981) 1265. Town in Northern Territory, Australia; site of Graeme Gow's Reptile Park, a collection of Australia's most venomous snakes and reptiles; bird sanctuary. » Northern Territory

humus Decomposed organic matter, usually present in the topsoil layers. It improves soil structure, making cultivation easier, and gives the soil a characteristically dark colour. » soil

hundred An old subdivision of a shire, sometimes containing about 100 hides, which had its own court, and formed a unit of local administration in the government of England from at least the 10th-c to the 19th-c, especially for tax-collection and maintaining public order. In the Danelaw, the corresponding unit was the *wapentake*. » Danelaw

Hundred Days (Mar–Jun 1815) An interlude between Napoleon I's escape from Elba and his defeat at the Battle of Waterloo, during which he returned to Paris and tried to reconstitute the Empire. He was finally exiled to St Helena. » Napoleon I; Waterloo, Battle of

Hundred Days of Reform A reform movement in China in 1898, which lasted for just over a hundred days, during which period Kang Youwei and his supporters succeeded in securing the Guangxu emperor's approval of radical reforms affecting the constitution, administration, army, and education. All were rescinded on the intervention of the empress dowager Ci Xi. Six leading reformers were executed, and Kang fled abroad. » Qing dynasty

Hundred Flowers A campaign in China (1956–7) which encouraged freedom of expression, under the slogan 'Let a hundred flowers bloom and a hundred schools of thought contend', in art and literature as well as political debate. By June 1957 a clampdown was imposed on the violent criticism of the Communist Party, and an anti-rightist campaign was launched. » communism

Hundred Years' War A series of wars between England and France dated by convention 1337–1453. They formed part of a longer contest which began when England was linked with Normandy (1066), then with Anjou and Aquitaine (1154). In the 13th-c, the Capetians redoubled their efforts to rule all France. But when Edward III claimed the French throne, from 1340 styling himself 'king of England and France', traditional rivalries exploded into a dynastic struggle. In 1417 the English turned from raiding to territorial conquest, a task ultimately beyond their resources. Eviction from Guyenne (1453) reduced England's French territories to Calais (lost 1558) and the Channel Is, but the title of king of France was abandoned only in 1801. » Agincourt, Battle of; Angevins; Bedford, Duke of; Capetians; Dunois; Edward III; Guyenne; Philip VI

Hungarian uprising (Oct–Nov 1956) National insurgency in Budapest following the denunciation of Stalin at the 20th Soviet Communist Party Congress. Rioting students and workers overthrew Stalin's statues and demanded radical reform. When the new Prime Minister, Imre Nagy, announced plans for Hungary's withdrawal from the Warsaw Pact, Soviet troops and tanks crushed the uprising. Many were killed, thousands fled abroad, and Nagy was executed. » Nagy; Stalin; Warsaw Pact

Hungary, Hungarian **Magyarország**, official name **Hungarian People's Republic**, Hungarian **Magyar Népköztársaság** pop(1990e) 10437000; area 93036 sq km/35912 sq ml. Republic in the Danube basin, C Europe, divided into 19 counties; bounded N by Czechoslovakia, E by Ukraine and Romania, S by Yugoslavia, and W by Austria; capital, Budapest; chief towns include Miskolc, Debrecen, Szeged, Pécs, Györ; timezone GMT +1; population mainly Magyar (92%), with several minorities; official language, Magyar; chief religions, Roman Catholic (67%), Calvinist (20%); unit of currency, the forint of 100 fillér.

Physical description and climate. Drained by the R Danube (flows N–S) and its tributaries; frequent flooding, especially in the Great Plains (E); crossed (W) by a low spur of the Alps, separating the Little Hungarian Plain from the Transdanubian downlands; highest peak, Kékestetö (1014 m/3327 ft); landlocked position gives a fairly extreme continental type of climate, with a marked difference between summer and winter; wettest in spring and early summer; cold winters, with snow lying 30–40 days and R Danube sometimes frozen over for long periods; frequent fogs.

History and government. Kingdom formed under St Stephen I, 11th-c; conquered by Turks, 1526; part of Habsburg Empire, 17th-c; Austria and Hungary reconstituted as a dual monarchy, 1867; republic, 1918; communist revolt led by Béla Kun, 1919; monarchical constitution restored, 1920; new republic with communist government, 1949; uprising crushed by Soviet forces, 1956; during 1989, pressure for political change was led from within the Communist Party by Imre Pozsgay, a multiparty system being intended; governed by a unicameral legislature (National Assembly), elected every five years; this elects the executive 21-member Presidential Council and the 17-member Council of Ministers.

Economy. Large-scale nationalization as part of the centralized planning strategy of the new republic, 1946–9; greater independence to individual factories and farms, from 1968; grain, potatoes, sugar beet, fruit, wine; coal, bauxite, lignite; metallurgy, engineering, chemicals, textiles, food processing. » Austria-Hungary, Dual Monarchy of; Budapest; Habsburgs; Hungarian uprising; Kun; Stephen I; RR25 national holidays; RR52 political leaders

Huns An Asiatic people who in 375 overran the Gothic tribes of

S Russia, and precipitated the great Germanic migration into the Roman Empire. They were feared for their brutality throughout the Empire. United under Attila, they laid waste parts of Gaul and Italy (451–2), but were then forced to retreat, and Hunnic dominance was soon eclipsed. » Attila; Gaul: Goths; Vandals

Hunt, Geoff(rey) (1947–) Australian squash rackets player, born in Victoria. He was the Australian amateur champion at age 17, the world amateur champion in 1967, 1969, and 1971, and the world Open champion in 1976–7 and 1979–80. » squash rackets

Hunt, Henry, byname **Orator Hunt** (1773–1835) British radical agitator, born at Upavon, Wiltshire. He was a well-to-do farmer who in 1800 became a staunch radical, and spent the rest of his life advocating the repeal of the Corn Laws, democracy, and parliamentary reform. In 1819, on the occasion of the Peterloo massacre, he delivered a speech which cost him three years' imprisonment. He became an MP in 1831, and died at Alresford, Hampshire. » Corn Laws; Peterloo Massacre

Hunt (of Llanfair Waterdine), (Henry Cecil) John, Baron (1910–) British mountaineer, born at Marlborough, Wiltshire. A British army officer, he saw military and mountaineering service in India and Europe, and in 1953 led the first successful expedition to Mt Everest. He also led the British party in the British-Soviet Caucasian mountaineering expedition (1958). He was knighted in 1953, and made a life peer in 1966. » Everest, Mt; Hillary

Hunt, (James Henry) Leigh (1784–1859) British poet and essayist, born at Southgate, Middlesex. Educated at Christ's Hospital, from 1808 he edited with his brother *The Examiner*, which became a focus of Liberal opinion and attracted leading men of letters, including Byron, Shelley, and Lamb. After travelling with Shelley to Italy, and associating with Byron, he returned to England in 1825. His *Autobiography* (1850) is a valuable picture of the times. He died in London. » Byron; English literature; essay; Lamb, Charles; poetry; Shelley, Percy Bysshe

Hunt, William Holman (1827–1910) British painter, born and died in London. He studied at the Royal Academy, and with Millais and Rossetti inaugurated the Pre-Raphaelite Brotherhood. His works in this vein included, notably, 'The Light of the World' (1854, Keble, Oxford). » English art; Millais; Pre-Raphaelite Brotherhood; Rossetti, Dante Gabriel; Plate XI

hunter-gatherers Populations living entirely, or almost so, by hunting animals and gathering food; also called *foragers* or *band societies*, as they are typically organized in bands. In all cases, the men hunt and women forage. In 10 000 BC the entire world population were hunters and gatherers; today they are less than 0.001%, including the Pygmies, Khoisan, and Hadza in Africa, Australian Aborigines, and scattered groups in Malaysia, India, and the Philippines. Some pastoral and agricultural groups also engage in part-time hunting and gathering. » Aborigines; Khoisan; Pygmies

Hunterston 55°42N 4°51W. Port facility in Cunninghame district, Strathclyde, W Scotland; gas-cooled nuclear reactors came into commercial operation in 1964, and advanced gas-cooled reactors in 1976–7; iron ore and coal trade. » nuclear reactor [i]; Scotland [i]; Strathclyde

Huntingdon, Selina Hastings, *née* **Shirley, Countess of** (1707–91) British Methodist leader, born at Staunton Harold, Leicestershire. In 1728 she married the Earl of Huntingdon, but was widowed in 1746. Joining the Methodists in 1739, she made Whitefield her chaplain, and assumed a leadership among his followers, who became known as 'The Countess of Huntingdon's Connexion'. She built a training school for ministers, and many chapels. She died in London. » Methodism; Whitefield, George

Huntingdon 52°20N 01°12W, pop (1981) 17 603, with Godmanchester. Town in Huntingdon district, Cambridgeshire, EC England; on Great Ouse R, 24 km/15 ml NW of Cambridge; birthplace of Oliver Cromwell; railway; engineering, plastics, furniture, transport equipment; 13th-c Hinchingbrooke House, 13th-c Church of St Mary the Virgin, Cromwell Museum, Buckden Palace (8 km/5 ml SW). » Cambridgeshire

Huntingdonshire Former county of EC England; part of Cambridgeshire since 1974. » Cambridgeshire

Huntington's chorea An inherited disorder of the brain, presenting in early adult life, in which slowly developing dementia is associated with uncontrolled jerking or slow writhing movements. There is no effective treatment. It is named after US physician George Sumner Huntington (1850–1916). » chorea

Huntsville 34°44N 86°35W, pop (1980) 142 513. Seat of Madison County, N Alabama, USA; railway; university; major US space research centre; tyres, glass, agricultural equipment, electrical goods; Alabama Space and Rocket Center (NASA), world's largest space museum. » Alabama; NASA

Hunyady, János [**hoon**yodi] (c.1387–1456) Hungarian statesman and warrior, apparently a Wallach by birth, who was knighted and in 1409 presented by Emperor Sigismund with the Castle of Hunyad in Transylvania. His life was one unbroken crusade against the Turks, whom he defeated in several campaigns, notably in the storming of Belgrade (1456). During the minority of Ladislaus V he acted as Governor of the Kingdom (1446–53). He died in Belgrade. One of his sons, Matthias, became King of Hungary. » Matthias I

Hupa Athapascan-speaking Pacific Coast Indians of NW California. They lived in villages along Trinity R, and hunted, trapped, gathered, and fished. They were renowned for their basketry, but, unlike groups further N, did not make fine wood carvings. Population c.1 000. » American/Northwest Coast Indians

Hurd, Douglas (Richard) [herd] (1930–) British Conservative politician, educated at Eton and Cambridge, who followed a career in the Diplomatic Corps (1952–66) before moving to work in the Conservative Research Department (1966–70). An MP from 1974, he became Northern Ireland Secretary (1984), Home Secretary (1985), and Foreign Secretary (1989). He stood unsuccessfully as a candidate in the leadership contest following Mrs Thatcher's resignation (Nov 1990). » Conservative Party; Thatcher

hurdling **1** An athletics event which involves foot racing while clearing obstacles (*hurdles*) en route. Race distances are 100 m and 400 m for women, 110 m and 400 m for men. The height of a hurdle varies according to the type of race: 2¾ ft (84 cm) for the 100 m; 3 ft (91.4 cm) for the 400 m; and 3½ ft (106.7 cm) for the 110 m. Hurdles are also included in the steeplechase. The current world record for men (110 m) is 12.92 sec, achieved by Roger Kingdom (USA) in 1989 at Zürich, Switzerland, and (400 m) 47.02 sec, achieved by Edwin Moses (USA) in 1983 at Koblenz, Germany; for women (100 m) it is 12.21 sec, achieved by Yordanka Donkova (Bulgaria) in 1988 at Stara Zagora, Bulgaria, and (400 m) 52.94 sec, achieved by Marina Styepanova (*née* Makeyeva) (USSR) in 1986 at Tashkent, Uzbekistan. **2** A form of horse race in which the horses have to clear hurdles. It is not as severe as the steeplechase. » steeplechase; RR104

hurdy-gurdy A mechanically bowed string instrument known since mediaeval times, especially among folk musicians. The player turns a handle which causes a wooden wheel, coated with resin, to rotate and to sound a number of accompanimental drone strings. Melodies are played on a simple keyboard, operated by the other hand. » string instrument 1 [i]

hurling or **hurley** An Irish 15-a-side team field game played with curved sticks and a ball. The object is to hit the ball with the stick into your opponents' goal: under the crossbar scores 3 points; above the crossbar but between the posts scores 1 point. It has been played since 1800 BC, and was standardized in 1884 following the formation of the Gaelic Athletic Association. The All-Ireland Championships have taken place since 1887. » RR113

Huron Iroquoian-speaking N American Indians, who settled in large towns and farming villages in Quebec and Ontario in the 16th-c. They supplied furs to French traders, competing with tribes of the Iroquois League. Defeated by the Iroquois in 1648–50, many were driven to the W, and eventually settled on land in Ohio and Michigan. They were finally driven by Whites to Oklahoma. » American Indians; Iroquois

Huron, Lake [hyooron] Second largest of the Great Lakes, N America, on the US–Canadian frontier; 330 km/205 ml long; 294 km/183 ml wide; maximum depth 229 m/751 ft; area 59 570 sq km/22 994 ft, 60% in Canada; linked to L Superior (NW) via St Mary's R and Sault Ste Marie Canals, and to L Michigan (W) via the Straits of Mackinac; empties into L Erie (E) via the St Clair R, L St Clair, and the Detroit R; contains Georgian Bay (NE) and Saginaw Bay (SW); ports include Bay City, Alpena, Cheboygan, Midland; generally ice-bound in winter months (Dec–Apr); probably the first of the Great Lakes to be visited by Europeans, c.1612. » Great Lakes

Hurrians An ancient, non-Semitic, non-Indo-European people first detected in the Caucasus area in the latter part of the third millenium. From there they migrated in great numbers to N Mesopotamia, Syria, and E Anatolia, where in the next millenium they greatly influenced the Hittites. » Hittites; Nuzi

hurricane An intense, often devastating, tropical storm which occurs as a vortex spiralling around a low pressure system. Wind speeds are very high (above 34 m per sec/75 ml per hour), but the centre (*eye*) of the storm is characterized by calm weather. Hurricanes originate over tropical oceans, usually between July and October, and move in a W or NW direction (SW in the S hemisphere), losing energy as they reach land. Each year they are named in alphabetical sequence as they occur. Originally female names were used, but male names were introduced for the first time in 1978. They are also known as *typhoons* in the western N Pacific and *cyclones* in the Bay of Bengal. » Beaufort Scale; depression (meteorology) [i]; Plate III

husky A domestic dog, one of several spitz breeds traditionally used in the Arctic as a beast of burden (especially to pull sledges); powerful body with thick double-layered insulating coat; also known as **eskimo dog**. » Alaskan malamute; dog; Siberian husky; spitz

Huss or **Hus, John** (c.1369–1415) Bohemian religious reformer, born at Husinetz, from which his name derives. In 1398 he lectured on theology at Prague, where he was influenced by the writings of Wycliffe. In 1408 he continued to preach in defiance of a papal bull, and was excommunicated (1411). After writing his main work, *De Ecclesia* (1413, On the Church), he was called before a General Council at Constance, and burned after refusing to recant. The anger of his followers in Bohemia led to the Hussite Wars, which lasted until the middle of the 15th-c. » heresy; Hussites; Reformation; Wycliffe

hussar monkey » **patas monkey**

hussars Light cavalry, regiments of which were formed in many national armies from the late 18th-c onwards. They were modelled on an idealized 'Hungarian' style of horseman-warrior, with an exotic uniform typically trimmed with braid and knots, and an elaborate fur helmet.

Hussein (ibn Talal) [hoosayn] (1935–) King of Jordan since 1952, born at Amman, and educated at Alexandria, Harrow, and Sandhurst. He steered a middle course in the face of the political upheavals inside and outside his country, favouring the Western powers, particularly Britain, and pacifying Arab nationalism. After the 1967 war with Israel, the PLO made increasingly frequent raids into Israel from Jordan, their power developing to such an extent that he ordered the Jordanian army to move against them, and after a short civil war (1970), the PLO leadership fled abroad. His decision to cut links with the West Bank (1988) prompted the PLO to establish a government in exile. He has been married four times; his second wife was an Englishwoman, by whom he had an heir, **Abdullah**, in 1962. » Jordan [i]; PLO

Hussein, Saddam, also **Husain** (1937–) President of Iraq (1979–), born at Takrit. He joined the Arab Baath Socialist Party in 1957, and was sentenced to death in 1959 for the attempted execution of General Kassem, but escaped to Egypt. He played a prominent part in the 1968 revolution, and became Vice-President of the Revolutionary Command Council in 1969. On the retirement of his colleague President al-Bakr, he became sole President. His attack on Iran in 1980, to gain control of the Strait of Hormuz, led to a war of attrition which ended in 1988. » Gulf War; Iraq [i]

Husserl, Edmund (Gustav Albrecht) (1859–1938) German philosopher, founder of the school of phenomenology, born at Prossnitz, Austrian Empire. He studied mathematics at Berlin and psychology at Vienna, and taught at Halle (1887), Göttingen (1901), and Freiburg (1916). His 2-volume *Logische Untersuchungen* (1900–1, Logical Investigations) defended the view of philosophy as an *a priori* discipline, unlike psychology. He developed phenomenology while at Göttingen – an approach which was particularly influential in Germany and the USA, and gave rise to *Gestalt* psychology. He died at Freiburg, Germany. » Gestalt psychology; phenomenology

Hussites Followers of John Huss, who in the early 15th-c constituted a movement for the reform of the Church in Bohemia (Czechoslovakia). They anticipated the 16th-c Reformation by demanding the moral reform of the clergy, free preaching of the Word of God, and the availability of the Eucharist for all believers in two species or kinds (ie bread and wine). » Huss; Reformation; Wycliffe

Huston, John (1906–87) US film director, born at Nevada, Missouri. He came to Hollywood in 1930 as a script writer, and in 1941 was given the direction of *The Maltese Falcon*, following this with a series of films for the US army. After the War, several films, such as *The Asphalt Jungle* (1950) and *The African Queen* (1951), established him as a leading director of action drama, and his imaginative use of colour was given full expression in such films as *Moulin Rouge* (1952) and *Moby Dick* (1956). In 1982 he made the musical, *Annie*. He died at Newport, Rhode Island.

Hutcheson, Francis (1694–1746) Scottish philosopher, born probably at Drumalig, Co Down, Ireland. He studied for the Church at Glasgow (1710–16), but then started a successful private academy in Dublin. In 1729 he became professor of moral philosophy at Glasgow. His main work was published posthumously, *A System of Moral Philosophy* (1755), in which he argues that moral distinctions are intuited, rather than arrived at by reasoning. His view of 'the greatest happiness for the greatest number' in judging an action anticipated utilitarianism. He died in Glasgow. » utilitarianism

Hutchinson, Anne (1591–1643) American religious figure, born at Alford, Lincolnshire, England. Intensely committed to the Puritan movement, in Boston she began to organize religious discussion meetings, which rapidly took on a political tone. These meetings were suppressed in 1637, and she was expelled from the province after being convicted of heresy. She and her family migrated first to Rhode Island and then to the Dutch colony of New Netherland (New York), where she and all but one of her children died in an Indian raid in 1643. » Puritanism

hutia [hooteea] A cavy-like rodent, native to the Caribbean Is; resembles a large rat (weight, up to 7 kg/15½ lb); inhabits woodland; eats vegetation and lizards; related to the coypu. (Family: *Capromyidae*, 12 living species, and nearly 20 recently extinct.) » cavy; coypu; rodent

Hutton, James (1726–97) British geologist, born and died in Edinburgh, Scotland. He studied medicine at Edinburgh, Paris, and Leyden, in 1754 devoted himself to agriculture and chemistry, and then to mineralogy and geology. The Huttonian theory, emphasizing the igneous origin of many rocks and deprecating the assumption of other causes than those we see still at work, was expounded in *A Theory of the Earth* (1795), which forms the basis of modern geology. » geology; igneous rock

Hutton, Len, properly **Sir Leonard** (1916–90) British cricketer, born at Fulneck, Yorkshire. He was the inspiration of England after World War 2, and skipper of the team which regained the Ashes in 1953. England's first professional captain, he never captained his county, Yorkshire. Playing for England against Australia at the Oval in 1938, he scored a world record 364 runs. Between 1937 and 1955 he scored 6 971 Test runs at an average of 56.67, and during his first-class career (1934–60) scored 40 140 runs (average 55.51), including 129 centuries. He was knighted in 1954. » Ashes, the; cricket (sport)

Hutu and Tutsi Bantu-speaking peoples of the republic of Burundi and Rwanda, EC Africa. The Hutu, mostly peasant farmers, comprise more than 80% of the total population in both countries. They were subjugated by the Tutsi, warrior-pastoralists of Nilo-Hamitic stock, who migrated S in the 14th–15th-c. The Tutsi dominated Rwanda until 1961, when Belgian colonial rulers helped the Hutu to seize power and form the first independent government, and 10 000 Tutsi were killed. In Burundi, the Hutu led an unsuccessful revolt against the Tutsi in 1971, in which over 100 000 Hutu were massacred by the army, and 120 000 fled to Tanzania. Both Hutu and Tutsi speak the same language and have a common culture. » Bantu-speaking peoples; Burundi [i]; pastoralism; Rwanda [i]

Huxley, Aldous (Leonard) (1894–1963) British novelist and essayist, born at Godalming, Surrey. Educated at Eton and Oxford, he lived mainly in Italy in the 1920s, and moved to California in 1937. His early writing included poetry, short stories, and literary journalism, but his reputation was made with his satirical novels *Crome Yellow* (1921) and *Antic Hay* (1923). Later novels include *Point Counter Point* (1928) and, his best-known work, *Brave New World* (1932), where he warns of the dangers of moral anarchy in a scientific age. His later writing became more mystical in character, as in *Eyeless in Gaza* (1936) and *Time Must Have a Stop* (1944). He died in Los Angeles. » English literature; novel; satire

Huxley, Sir Andrew Fielding (1917–) British physiologist, born in London. He was educated at Cambridge, where he taught in the department of physiology (1941–60). He helped to provide a physico-chemical explanation for nerve transmission, and outlined a theory of muscular contraction. He was professor of physiology at London (1960–9) and a Royal Society Research Professor (1969–83). He shared the Nobel Prize for Physiology or Medicine in 1963, and was knighted in 1974. » action potential; Eccles; muscle [i]; neurone [i]

Huxley, Sir Julian (Sorell) (1887–1975) British biologist, born and died in London. Educated at Eton and Oxford, he became professor of zoology at London (1925–7) and at the Royal Institution (1926–9), then secretary to the Zoological Society of London (1935–42). He applied his scientific knowledge to political and social problems, formulating a pragmatic ethical theory based on the principle of natural selection. He was the first director-general of UNESCO (1946–8), and was knighted in 1958. » natural selection

Huxley, T(homas) H(enry) (1825–95) British biologist, born at Ealing, Middlesex. He studied medicine at London, worked as a naval surgeon, and developed his interest in natural history during a visit to the Australian coast. In 1854 he was appointed professor of natural history at the Royal School of Mines, and became the foremost expounder of Darwinism, to which he added an anthropological perspective, in *Man's Place in Nature* (1863). He also studied fossils, influenced the teaching of science in schools, and wrote essays on theology and philosophy from an 'agnostic' viewpoint, a term he introduced. He died at Eastbourne, Sussex. » agnosticism; Darwinism

Huygens, Christiaan [**hoy**genz] (1629–93) Dutch physicist and astronomer, born at The Hague. Educated at Leyden and Breda, in 1655 he discovered the ring and fourth satellite of Saturn, and in 1657 made the first pendulum clock. In optics he propounded the wave theory of light, and discovered polarization. He lived in Paris, a member of the Royal Academy of Sciences (1666–81), but as a Protestant felt it prudent to return to The Hague, where he died. » Huygens' principle [i]; light

Huygens' principle In wave theory, a construction technique for deducing the shape of an evolving wavefront; devised by Dutch physicist Christian Huygens in 1678. Each point of the wavefront is taken to be the source of secondary waves spreading in all directions. The new wavefront is the surface tangent to these wavelets. The principle is applicable to all waves, especially in optics. » Huygens; wave (physics) [i]

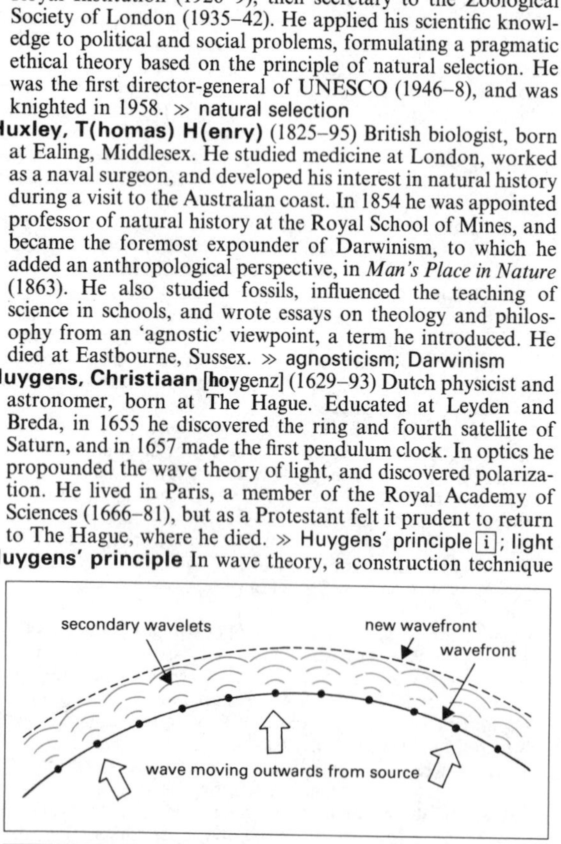

A wave construction may be used to demonstrate the laws of reflection and refraction of light, historically the importance of Huygens' principle.

Huysmans, Joris Karl [**hoys**mahnz] (1848–1907) French novelist of Dutch origin, born in Paris. His books reflect many aspects of the spiritual and intellectual life of late 19th-c France. His best-known works are *À rebours* (1884, Against the Grain), a study of aesthetic decadence (which influenced Oscar Wilde); the controversial *Là-Bas* (1891, Down There), which dealt with devil-worship; and *En Route* (1892), an account of his return to Catholicism. He died in Paris. » French literature; novel; Wilde

Hvannadalshnjúkur [hwana**dals**hunyookur] 64°02N 16°35W. Highest mountain in Iceland, rising to 2 119 m/6 952 ft in SE Iceland at S edge of Vatnajökull glacier. » Iceland [i]

hyacinth A bulb native to the Mediterranean region and Africa; leaves narrow or approximately trap-shaped; flowers bell-shaped, held horizontally or drooping in spikes. Rather variable in size and flower density, large florists' hyacinths are fragrant cultivars with a wide range of colours. (Genus: *Hyacinthus*, 30 species. Family: *Liliaceae*.) » bulb; cultivar

Hyades [**hi**yadeez] A bright open cluster of stars c.50 parsecs distance. It makes a V-shaped group for the bull's face in Taurus. » open cluster; Taurus

hyaena » **hyena**

hybrid An individual animal or plant resulting from cross-breeding between genetically dissimilar parents. It is typically used for the offspring of mating between parents of different species or subspecies, such as the mule (produced by cross-breeding an ass and a horse). Hybrids are often sterile. » genetics [i]

hybrid computer A combination of a digital and an analog computer. It was widely used in the 1960s and 1970s especially in the field of numerical control. Since then the digital computer has taken over many of the roles previously assigned to analog computers. » analog computer; digital computer; numerical control

hydatid disease [**hiy**datid] A disease acquired by ingesting eggs of the dog tapeworm (*Echinococcus*) following the handling of infected dogs or the eating of contaminated food. The eggs hatch in the duodenum, and embryos enter the blood stream, producing large cysts in many organs, notably the liver, lungs, spleen, and brain. Fluid within the cyst, if released, may cause an anaphylactic reaction. » anaphylaxis; cyst; duodenum; tapeworm infestation

Hyde, Douglas, Ir **Dubhighlas de Hide** (1860–1949) Irish author and philologist, born at Frenchpark, Co Roscommon, Ireland. Educated at Dublin, he was founder and first president (1893–1915) of the Gaelic League, professor of Irish in the National University (1909–32), wrote *A Literary History of Ireland* (1889), poems, plays, works on history and folklore, in Irish and English, and was first President (1938–45) of Eire. He died in Dublin. » comparative linguistics; Irish literature

Hyde Park A royal park covering 255 ha/630 acres in C London. It was first opened to the public during the reign of James I, and became a popular place for riding for members of fashionable society until the end of World War 1. The Albert Memorial, Speaker's Corner, and Marble Arch are situated in the park. » London [i]

Hyder Ali » **Haidar Ali**

Hyderabad (India) [**hiy**duhrabad] 17°22N 78°26E, pop (1981) 2 528 000. Capital of Andhra Pradesh, S India; on R Musi, 611 km/380 ml ESE of Bombay; founded in 1589 as capital of the Kingdom of Golconda; former capital of Hyderabad state; joined with India, 1948; Muslim stronghold in S India; airfield; railway; four universities (1918, 1964, 1972, 1974); commercial centre; vehicle parts, cigarettes, textiles, pharmaceuticals; ruins of Golconda fort, tombs of the Qutb Shahi kings, mosque modelled on the Great Mosque of Mecca, Charminar (1591). » Andhra Pradesh; Charminar; Islam

Hyderabad (Pakistan), also **Haidarabad** [**hiy**darabad] 25°23N 68°24E, pop (1981) 795 000. Second largest city in Sind province, SE Pakistan; 164 km/102 ml ENE of Karachi, on the E bank of the R Indus, c.190 km/120 ml N of its mouth; provincial capital from 1768 until captured by the British in 1843; airfield; railway; university (1947); gold and silver embroidery, enamelware, pottery, shoes, glass, furniture. » Pakistan [i]

Hydra (astronomy) (Lat 'sea serpent') [**hi**ydra] The largest and longest constellation in the S hemisphere. It contains just one bright star. » constellation; RR8

Hydra (biology) A solitary, freshwater coelenterate; stalk-like body attached at the base; apical mouth surrounded by tentacles; catches prey using stinging cells on tentacles; typical green colour derived from green algal cells contained in body; reproduces mostly by budding. (Phylum: *Cnidaria*. Class: *Hydrozoa*.) » algae; coelenterate

Hydra (mythology) [**hi**ydra] In Greek mythology, a many-headed monster, the child of Typhon and Echnida, which lived in a swamp at Lerna. As the heads grew again when struck off, Heracles could kill it only with the assistance of Iolaos, who cauterized the places where the heads grew. The name means 'water-snake'. » Heracles

Hydra (Greece) [**hi**ydra], Gr **Ídhra** pop(1971) 3 531; area 50 sq km/20 sq ml. Island in the Aegean Sea, Greece, off the E coast of the Peloponnese; linked by ferry to Piraeus; chief town, Hydra; popular resort island. » Aegean Sea; Greece [i]

hydrangea [hiy**drayn**juh] An evergreen or deciduous shrub, or a climber with aerial roots, native to Asia, and N/S America; leaves oval, in opposite pairs; flowers in heads, often composed of small fertile and large sterile flowers. Two forms of the shrub *Hydrangea macrophylla* are popular ornamentals: **lacecaps** have heads with large, sterile flowers surrounding the fertile ones; **hortensias** or **mop-heads** have heads composed entirely of large, sterile flowers. Both forms produce blue flowers on acid soils, pink on alkaline soils. (Genus: *Hydrangea*, 80 species. Family: *Hydrangaceae*.) » climber/deciduous/evergreen plants; shrub; soil

hydrate A compound containing water, usually one in which the water is present as 'water of crystallization', such as in gypsum ($CaSO_4.2H_2O$), a hydrate of calcium sulphate. However, the water may have been incorporated into a molecule, as with chloral hydrate ($CCl_3CH(OH)_2$) from chloral (CCl_3CHO). » water

hydration A reaction with water to form an adduct. For example, the hydration of ethylene ($CH_2=CH_2$) gives ethanol (CH_3–CH_2OH). Often, the product of the reaction is a hydrate. » addition reaction; hydrate

hydraulic machinery Machines operated by pressure, transmitted through a pipe, by a liquid such as water or oil. Cars have hydraulic brakes in which the braking force is transmitted from the pedal to the brakes by a liquid under pressure. The hydraulic press and hydraulic ram use the same principle. » hydraulics

hydraulics The study of systems using liquids, whether stationary or moving, for the transmission of force; often, water or oil is the transmitting fluid. Any machine which uses, controls, or conserves a liquid makes use of the principles of hydraulics. The applications include such fields as irrigation, domestic water supply, hydroelectric power, and the design of dams, canals, and pipes. Most motor vehicles have hydraulic braking systems. The hydraulic press relies on applying a small force f to a small area a, to produce a pressure $p=f/a$. By Pascal's principle this pressure is transmitted through pipes to a larger area A to give force F available to perform work, such that $F/A=p$. The produced and applied forces are in the ratio $F/f=A/a$, so the hydraulic press is a force transmitter and multiplier. » fluidics; fluid mechanics; hydraulic machinery; Pascal

hydraulis An early type of organ, devised by the Greek inventor Ctesibius in the 3rd-c BC, in which water was used to maintain a constant pressure of air to the pipes. It is considered to be an ancestor of the modern pipe organ. » organ

hydride Any compound of hydrogen. Three types are usually distinguished: (1) *covalent hydrides*, molecular compounds formed with other non-metals, such as hydrogen chloride (HCl), water (H_2O), and ammonia (NH_3); (2) *metallic hydrides*, with properties of alloys, formed with most transition elements; and (3) *saline hydrides*, ionic compounds formed with alkali and alkaline earth elements, where hydrogen is present as the hydride ion, H^-, eg sodium hydride (NaH). » alkali; alloy; hydrogen

hydrobiology The branch of biology dealing with the study of life in aquatic habitats, especially those in freshwater. Its core is formed by the study of planktonic plants and animals, and of their relationship to the major physical and chemical features of the water column. » biology; plankton

hydrocarbons Compounds containing only carbon and hydrogen. Many hundreds of such compounds are known, and most occur in coal, petroleum, or natural gas. There are two main subdivisions: *aliphatic*, of which methane (CH_4) is the simplest, and *aromatic*, based on benzene. Aliphatic compounds are further divided into alkanes, alkenes, and alkynes. » aliphatic compound; aromatic compound; carbon; hydrogen

hydrocephalus [hiydroh**se**faluhs] The abnormal accumulation of cerebrospinal fluid within the ventricular system inside the brain. It arises because of an abnormal rate of fluid formation or an obstruction to its flow out of the brain. It causes distension of the brain, and in infants enlargement of the skull. » brain [i]; cerebrospinal fluid

hydrochloric acid An aqueous solution of hydrogen chloride (HCl), a strong acid, fully dissociated into H^+ and Cl^- ions. It is the only common strong acid that is not an oxidizing agent, and is widely used as a general acid. Gastric juice in the human stomach is 2% hydrochloric acid. » acid; chlorides; hydrogen

hydrocortisone » **corticosteroids; cortisol**

hydrocyanic acid [hiydrohsiy**a**nik] Hydrogen cyanide (HCN), or its aqueous solution; also known as **prussic acid**. Pure hydrogen cyanide is an exceedingly poisonous liquid, boiling at 26°C, and having an odour of almonds. It is a very weak acid; partially neutralized solutions have pH>9, and solutions of cyanide salts have substantial concentrations of it. It is a potent fumigant, and an important reagent in organic syntheses. » acid; cyanide; hydrogen; pH

hydrodynamics » **fluid mechanics**

hydroelectric power (HEP) Electricity generated using the potential energy of water. It is a renewable energy source with considerable potential worldwide, although it accounts for only a small proportion of the world's energy needs. It is especially important in countries with scarce oil, coal, or gas reserves. A major source of energy in countries such as Norway, Switzerland, and Sweden, it is also important in developing countries. The world's largest HEP scheme, at Itaipu on the Parana R, will supply 20% of Brazil's electricity needs and a large proportion of those of Paraguay. » alternative energy; electricity; energy; Itaipu Dam; renewable resources

hydrofluoric acid Hydrogen fluoride (HF), or its aqueous solution. Although extremely corrosive, it is only a moderately strong acid, partially neutralized solutions having a pH of about 3. The acid etches glass by the reaction: $4HF+SiO_2 \rightarrow SiF_4+2H_2O$, as the silicon fluoride formed is volatile. » acid; fluoride; hydrogen; pH

hydrofoil A vessel able to reduce its effective displacement by raising itself clear of the water on attaining a certain speed. Foils are fitted at a depth greater than the draft of the hull. Successful trials were first held in Italy in 1906, but 50 years elapsed before the Italians put it to commercial use. Hydrofoils are used extensively for inland water transport in Russia, and have been used for many years in the Channel Is and Southampton Water. Speeds of around 40 knots are common in commercial service. » hovercraft [i]; jetfoil

hydrogen H, element 1, the lightest of the chemical elements, the commonest isotope having only one proton and one electron in an atom. Its stable form is a gas with diatomic molecules (H_2). Although it makes up more than 90% of the atoms in the universe, it is much less common on Earth, does not occur free, and mainly occurs combined with oxygen in water and with carbon in hydrocarbons. It is of great industrial importance, and is prepared in large quantities by various means, such as the action of steam on hot carbon. It forms compounds with most elements, generally showing oxidation numbers of ± 1. » chemical elements; hydrogenation; hydride; RR90

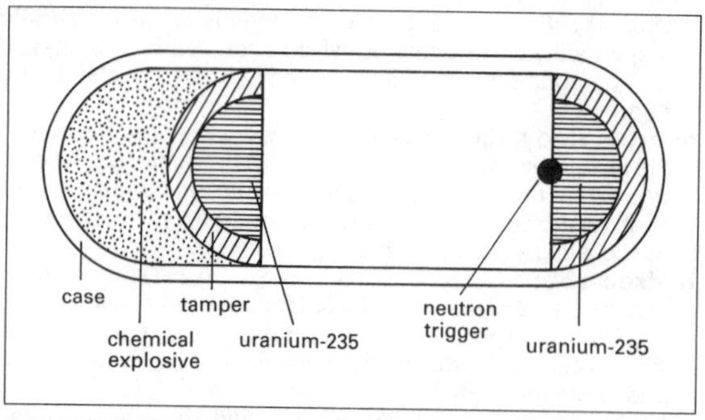

Atomic bomb, gun barrel design. Chemical explosives drive together two portions of uranium to produce a single portion of mass greater than the critical mass. Tamper reflects neutrons back into the uranium. An alternative design relies on compressing fissionable material, using a surrounding jacket of explosives.

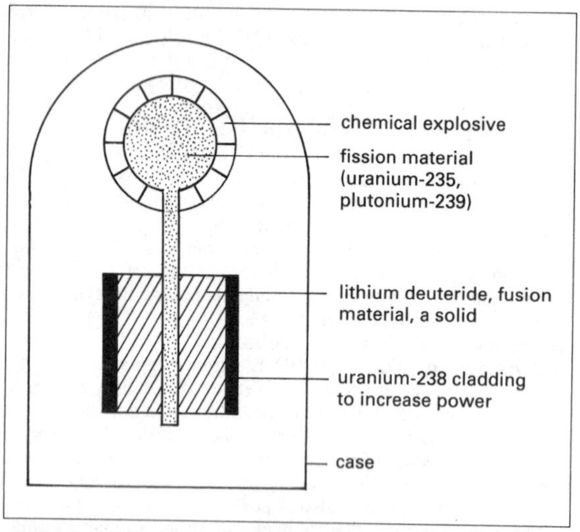

Schematic diagram of a hydrogen bomb. The top portion is a fission (atomic) bomb, used to initiate the lower fusion section.

hydrogen bomb The popular name (often shortened to **H-bomb**) for thermonuclear weapons which achieve their destructive effects through the intense release of heat and blast produced when the nuclei of hydrogen isotope materials used in the construction of the weapon are fused together in a nuclear reaction. The reaction is triggered by the detonation of an atomic bomb used as the weapon's core. Unlike atomic weapons, whose yield is limited by the critical mass of fissile material at their core being finite, the yield of thermonuclear weapons is limited only by the amount of hydrogen isotope 'fuel' the weapon contains. The biggest weapon ever tested (by the Soviets in 1961) yielded the equivalent explosive force of 60 million tons (60 megatons) of TNT chemical explosive. The hydrogen bomb was first developed in the USA, the principle theoretical work being performed by Edward Teller at Los Alamos laboratories. The first successful test was made at Eniwetok Atoll in November 1952. The USSR first tested a thermonuclear device in August 1953. » nuclear fission/fusion/weapons; Teller

hydrogen bond A very strong intermolecular attraction between the electrons of one electronegative atom and the nucleus of a hydrogen atom bonded to another. The strongest hydrogen bonds involve fluorine atoms, but those involving oxygen are much more common, and are important in explaining the properties of water and ice. Hydrogen bonds may also be formed within molecules, and are the main force giving shape to a protein molecule. » atom; chemical bond; ice; water

hydrogenation The addition of hydrogen to a compound, also often called **reduction**. One of the most important hydrogenation reactions is that at a hydrocarbon double bond, for example the conversion of ethylene to ethane: $CH_2=CH_2+H_2 \rightarrow CH_3-CH_3$. This reaction is particularly important in the saturation of fats and in petroleum refining. » hydrogen

hydrography The science of charting the water-covered areas of the Earth, including the determination of water area, coastline, and depth, as well as the flow characteristics of rivers, lakes, and seas. It also includes the location of shoals and wrecks, and the use of navigational aids.

hydrology The science concerned with the occurrence and distribution of water on or near the Earth's surface, in oceans and in the atmosphere, particularly in relation to the interaction of water with the environment and fresh water as a resource. It involves the study of the *hydrological cycle*: water from the oceans evaporates; moist air moves onto continents, condenses, and precipitates; it then eventually migrates back into the sea by run-off or groundwater movement, or back into the atmosphere by evaporation from open water or transpiration from plants. **Applied hydrology** covers topics such as irrigation schemes, dam design, drainage, flood control, hydroelectric power, and the management of all resources depending on variations in the supply and flow of water. » groundwater; river

hydrolysis [hiy**drol**isis] The splitting of a molecule by the action of water. It is applied particularly to the conversion of an ester into an alcohol and an acid (eg fats into fatty acids and glycerol), and to the reversal of condensation polymerization, converting proteins into amino acids and polysaccharides into sugars. It is also used to describe the conversion of a salt of an acid or base back into that acid or base. » condensation (chemistry); ester [i]; molecule; water

hydrophilic [hiydruh**fil**ik] In chemistry, water-seeking; a property of compounds with polar groups and most ionic compounds. It is opposed to **hydrophobic**, water-avoiding, a property of nonpolar covalent compounds, especially hydrocarbons (eg oils). » detergent

hydrophobia » **rabies**

hydroponics The growing of plants in nutrient solutions, without soil. The method is especially used in the production of high quality tomatoes and cucumbers, under glass.

hydrostatics » **fluid mechanics**

hydrothermal deposit A deposition of minerals from the hot, hydrous fluids within the Earth's crust associated with igneous activity. Many of the world's most important ore minerals form in hydrothermal vein deposits. » minerals

hydrothermal vents Sea floor hot springs found along the rift valleys of oceanic ridge systems. In some cases metal sulphides and oxides precipitate from the very hot (350°C) hydrothermal solutions as they surface at the sea floor and build edifices up to 10 m/30 ft in height, known as 'smokers'. High concentrations of hydrogen sulphide are present in the hydrothermal waters and support large populations of sulphide-oxidizing bacteria. These bacteria are the base of a diverse benthic food-chain restricted to the hydrothermal vents, and one of the few food-chains on Earth that do not depend on solar radiation as their ultimate energy source. » bacteria [i]; benthic environments; oceanic ridges

hydroxide The ion OH^- or a compound containing it. The only metal hydroxides soluble in water are those of the alkali metals and, to a lesser extent, calcium, strontium, and barium. These are strong bases, giving solutions with a high pH. » alkali; base (chemistry); pH

hydroxybenzene » **phenol**

hydroxybutanedioic acid » **malic acid**

hydroxypropanoic acid » **lactic acid**

Hydrozoa [hiydruh**zoh**a] A class of mainly marine coelenterates in which the life cycle involves alternation between attached polyp and planktonic medusa phases; polyps mostly in colonies, often with an external skeleton that may be calcified, as in the corals. (Phylum: *Cnidaria*.) » coelenterate; coral; medusa; polyp (biology)

Hydrus (Lat 'water snake') [**hiy**druhs] An inconspicuous constellation introduced to the S hemisphere in 1603 by German astronomer Johann Bayer (1572–1625) as a counterpart to Hydra. » constellation; Hydra (astronomy); RR8

hyena or **hyaena** [hiy**ee**na] A nocturnal carnivorous mammal; stocky, dog-like, with short back legs; large head with strong jaws; inhabits plains; eats carrion, insects, and fruit; also hunts mammals; related more to mongooses and cats than to dogs. (Family: *Hyaenidae*, 3 species.) » aardwolf; carnivore [i]; cat; dog; mongoose

Hyères, Iles d' or **Les Iles d'Or** [eel dyer] Island group in the Mediterranean Sea, SE France, SE of Toulon; chief islands are (E–W) Levant (occupied partly by the French Navy, partly by a nudist colony), Port-Cros (nature reserve), and the fortified island of Porquerolles. » France [i]

Hygeia [hiy**gee**a] In Greek mythology, a minor deity, the daughter of Asclepius; the name is a personification of the word for 'health'. » Asclepius

hygrometer A meteorological instrument used for measuring the relative humidity of the air. A **hygrograph** gives a continuous record of relative humidity. » humidity

hygroscopic » **deliquescent**

Hyksos [**hik**sos] The so-called 'shepherd kings' of ancient Egypt, who founded the XVth dynasty there c.1670 BC. Originally desert nomads from Palestine, the Egyptians themselves called them 'the princes from foreign parts'. » Egyptian history, Ancient [i]

Hymen [**hiy**men] In Ancient Greece and Rome, the cry of 'O Hymen Hymenaie' at weddings (later a marriage song) led to the invention of a being called Hymen or Hymenaeus, who was assumed to have been happily married, and therefore suitable for invocation as a god of Marriage. He is depicted as a youth with a torch.

Hymenoptera [hiymin**op**tuhra] A diverse order of insects containing about 130 000 species, including the sawflies, horntails, wasps, bees, and ants; adults typically with two pairs of membraneous wings; mouthparts adapted for chewing, or sucking nectar; social organization exhibited by many species; egg-laying tube (*ovipositor*) often modified for stinging. » insect [i]

hymn A song of praise to God, usually with a non-Biblical text in verses and sung congregationally with accompaniment on the organ or other instruments. In ancient times, however, hymns were sung in honour of heroic or notable people, and the Latin hymns of the early Christian church were sung without harmony or accompaniment. » chorale; liturgy; Psalms, Book of

Hypatia (c.375–415) Neoplatonist philosopher, daughter of Theon, an astronomer and mathematician of Alexandria. Her learning, wisdom, and high character made her the most influential teacher in Alexandria, her philosophy being an attempt to combine Neoplatonism with Aristotelianism. Associated by many Christians with paganism, she was murdered by a fanatical mob at Alexandria. » Neoplatonism

hyperactivity The combination of overactive, poorly-controlled behaviour with inattention and lack of concentration for a particular task. This condition is most frequently seen in children, and may have its origin in organic brain injury. It has also been observed in autistic children, anxiety states, hyperthyroidism, catatonic schizophrenic patients, and following the epidemic of encephalitis which occurred shortly after World War 1. » autism; encephalitis; hyperthyroidism; schizophrenia

hyperbola In mathematics, the locus of a point which moves so that the difference of its distances from two fixed points (*foci*) is constant. A hyperbola can also be defined as a section of a double cone or as the locus of a point which moves so that its distance from a focus is proportional to its distance from a fixed line (a *directrix*), the constant of proportion being greater than 1. Some of the comets move in hyperbolae, and the curve is much used in architecture. » asymptote [i]; conic sections [i]; ellipse [i]; geometry; parabola [i]

hyperbole Exaggeration, used often for comic or rhetorical effect, as throughout the writings of Rabelais, or in the mouth of Shakespeare's Falstaff. It is the staple of the tabloid press, and also of ordinary conversation ('I'm dying for a drink'). » figurative language

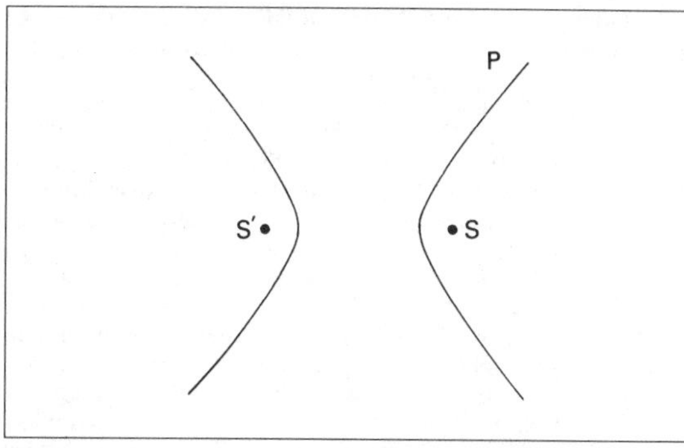

Hyperbola, foci S, S' PS' – PS is constant

hyperbolic geometry » **geometries, non-Euclidean**

Hyperboreans In Greek mythology, an unvisited people of fabled virtue and prosperity, living in the land 'beyond the North Wind'; in Herodotus they worship Apollo and still send offerings to Delos. This could refer to a lost Greek colony in what is now Romania, or even to the Swedes at the end of the trans-European amber route.

hypercube In mathematics, the four-dimensional analogue of a cube. A cube has four square faces meeting at each vertex; a hypercube has 4 cubes meeting at each vertex. It is (fairly) hard to draw a cube on paper, as this requires representing a 3-dimensional solid in 2 dimensions; to draw a hypercube requires using 2 dimensions to represent a 4-dimensional solid. The illustration shows that each cube is face to face with each of six others, and that four cubes meet at each vertex. There is one large cube, one small cube, and six others distorted by 'perspective' to look like truncated pyramids. » geometry; polytope

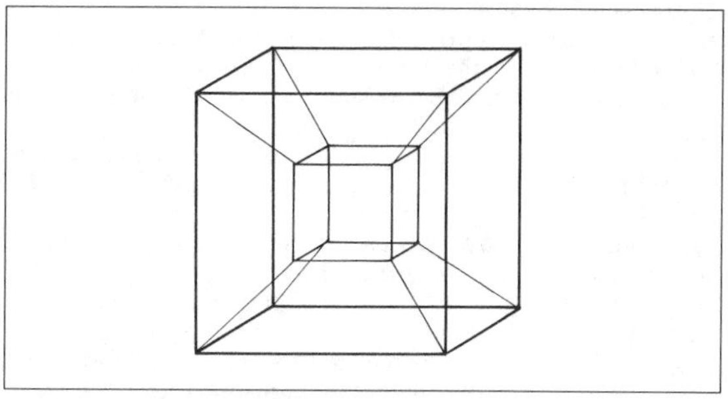

A hypercube

hyperglycaemia [hiypergliy**seem**ia] A level of blood sugar above the upper limit of the normal range (>160 mg/100 ml). » diabetes mellitus

Hyperion (astronomy) [hiy**peer**iuhn] The seventh natural satellite of Saturn, discovered in 1848; distance from the planet 1 481 000 km/920 000 ml; diameter 400 km/250 ml; orbital period 21.277 days. » Saturn (astronomy); RR4

Hyperion (mythology) [hiy**peer**iuhn] In Greek mythology, a Titan, son of Uranus and Gaia, and father of Eos (the Dawn), Helios (the Sun), and Selene (the Moon). Later, as in Shakespeare and Keats, identified with the Sun. » Helios

hypermetropia » **eye** [i]

Hyperrealism » **Photorealism**

hypersensitivity » **allergy**

hypertension A condition in which both systolic and diastolic blood pressure (BP) rise above normal levels. *Malignant* hypertension is a severe degree of high BP in which the diastolic pressure is above 130 mmHg, and an immediate threat to life. All levels of BP above normal damage blood vessels throughout the body; the greater the increase, the greater the damage. The vessels most vulnerable are those of the brain, eyes, heart, and kidneys. As a result, individuals may develop a stroke, poor vision, coronary heart disease, and renal failure. In the majority of cases the cause of the high BP is unknown. In a few cases the condition is attributable to specific hormonal disturbances or to kidney disease. » blood pressure

hyperthyroidism Oversecretion of thyroid hormones, leading to an increase in the body's metabolic rate; also known as **Graves' disease** after Irish physician Robert James Graves (1796–1853). The thyroid gland is stimulated to over-activity by an aberrant immunoglobulin which activates the gland and causes it to enlarge. Patients develop a warm skin with tremor of the hands; there is intolerance to warm weather, a voracious appetite, and weight loss; a rapid heart rate with palpitations is common, and can lead to heart failure in older individuals. A curious complication is protrusion of the eyes with weakness of some of the muscles which move them. Treatment is by drugs which block the synthesis of the thyroid hormone, or by destruction of the gland using radioactive iodine. » antibodies; goitre; thyroid hormone

hypnosis A temporary trance-like state induced by suggestion, in which a variety of phenomena (eg increased suggestibility and alterations in memory) can be induced in response to verbal or other stimuli. A hypnotic trance is not in any way related to sleep, but there is a constriction of responses by the hypnotized subject. As a treatment technique it is unreliable; spectacular achievements can be obtained in some patients, while for many total failure of benefit is recorded. It has been used as a technique for limiting addictive behaviour (eg cigarette smoking) and for relieving anxiety (eg wedding nerves). The technique was first used by Mesmer in France, and the term *hypnosis* coined by the British surgeon James Braid (1795–1860). » Mesmer

hypnotics Drugs that promote drowsiness and sleep. They include benzodiazepines (Mogadon) and barbiturates. Low doses of hypnotics are sometimes used as sedatives. » barbiturates; benzodiazepines; sedatives

hypo Popular name for sodium thiosulphate, incorrectly known as 'hyposulphite'. It is used as a fixing solution in photographic processing. » photography

hypoglycaemia/hypoglycemia [hiypohgliy**seem**ia] A level of blood sugar below the lower limit of normal (< 60 mg/100 ml), causing weakness, sweating, faintness, and ultimately mental confusion. It is often due to an overdose of insulin in diabetic patients. The features are quickly reversed by giving glucose by mouth or by intravenous injection. » diabetes mellitus; insulin

hyponym [**hiy**puhnim] » **synonym**

hypophysis » **pituitary gland**

hypothalamus A region of the vertebrate brain, situated below the thalamus, which has an important regulatory role regarding the internal environment (eg the control of food intake, water balance, body temperature in mammals, and the release of hormones from the pituitary gland). It is also involved in the control of emotions by the limbic system. » brain [i]; diabetes insipidus; diencephalon; fever; homeostasis

hypothermia The presence of a deep body temperature of 35°C or less, measured clinically by a rectal thermometer. It occurs after immersion in cold water; in old age after exposure to low environmental temperatures; and following prolonged unconsciousness due to alcohol poisoning, hypothyroidism, or immobilization after strokes or heart attacks. Infants are also liable to hypothermia. The initial response to falling body temperature is shivering. Thereafter interference with muscle function, especially cardiac muscle, causes a fall in heart output, slowing of the pulse, and cardiac arrythmias. Mental confusion, loss of memory, and ultimately loss of consciousness and death may ensue. » heart [i]; temperature [i]

hypothyroidism Reduced function of the thyroid gland, with a fall in the secretion of thyroid hormones. It occurs from a primary failure of secretion by the thyroid gland, or secondarily to pituitary disease. Body metabolism falls, and patients develop an increased dislike of cold weather; physical and mental activity slows down. » thyroid hormone

hypsometer An instrument for measuring altitude by observing the effect on boiling point of a liquid. Boiling point, being dependent on incumbent pressure, decreases with increasing altitude.

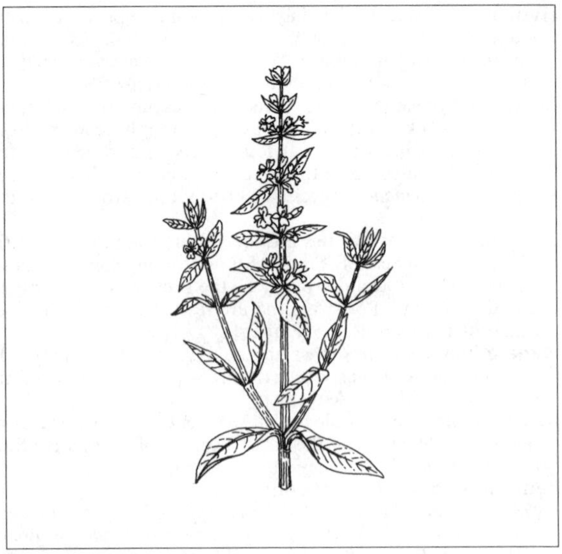

Hyssop

Hyracotherium [hiyrakoh**thee**riuhm] The first fossil horse, known from the early Eocene epoch of N America, Europe, and Asia; small, short-faced, lamb-sized mammals; four hoofed toes on forelimbs, three on hind limbs; formerly known as **Eohippus**. (Family: *Equidae*.) » Eocene epoch; fossil; horse [i]

hyrax [**hiy**raks] A mammal, native to Africa and Arabia, related to the elephant and aardvark; superficially resembles a large guinea pig, with pointed muzzle and round ears; three types: *rock*, *bush*, and *tree* hyraxes; the only members of the order *Hyracoidea*; also known as **daman**, **dassie**, **rock rabbit**, or (in Bible) **cony**. (Family: *Procaviidae*, 11 species.) » aardvark; cavy; elephant; mammal [i]

Hyrcanus I, John [hir**kay**nuhs] (2nd-c BC) High priest of Israel and perhaps also a king subject to Syrian control (c.134–104 BC); the son of the high priest Simon, and in the line of Hasmonean priestly rulers. He consolidated his own hold over Israel, destroyed the Samaritan temple on Mt Gerizim, and forced the Idumeans (residents of S Judea) to adopt Judaism. Eventually he supported the Sadduceans against the Pharisees, who opposed his combination of political and religious leadership. » Maccabees; Pharisees; Sadducees

hyssop A small, shrubby perennial growing up to 60 cm/2 ft, native to S Europe and W Asia; leaves narrow, in opposite pairs; flowers 2-lipped, violet-blue, in whorls forming long, loose 1-sided spikes. Originally cultivated as a medicinal herb, it is sometimes found naturalized. (*Hyssopus officinalis*. Family: *Labiatae*.) » herb; perennial; shrub

hysterectomy The surgical removal of the uterus. This operation is indicated in cases of malignant tumours of the uterus, in benign growths when these have become large, and in menorrhagia (excessive menstrual bleeding), when this is severe and not controlled by hormone treatment. » uterus [i]

hysteresis » **elastic hysteresis; magnetic hysteresis**

hysteria In its most general sense, a colloquial and derogatory term, used especially for histrionic female behaviour. More specifically, it is used in psychiatry to describe a personality profile or a neurotic illness. It may also describe a symptom in which there is a physical manifestation without an organic cause to account for the physiological dysfunction. Hysteria is additionally used to describe a group of states of altered consciousness – a situation where patients may suddenly wander away from what they were doing and subsequently have amnesia for that period. In psychoanalytic use, the term also applies to a psychopathological pattern in which the predominant defence mechanism is repression. » conversion (psychiatry); neurosis; personality; repression

I

i.t.a. An acronym for the **Initial Teaching Alphabet**, devised in 1959 by UK educationalist James Pitman (1901–85), to assist children in the early stages of reading. It is a lower-case system of 44 symbols in which each symbol represents a phoneme, giving a closer correlation between symbol and sound than in traditional English orthography, which it was intended not to replace, but to supplement. At its peak, i.t.a. was being used in many schools in Britain and abroad; but its popularity has declined since the 1970s. » alphabet [i]; graphology; phoneme

iamb A metrical foot consisting of one unstressed and one stressed syllable; as in the word 'release'; notated as ◡ or ⁄. It is the most common measure in English verse: 'And leaves the world to darkness, and to me' (Gray). » metre (literature); poetry

Iapetus (astronomy) [iyapituhs] The eighth natural satellite of Saturn, discovered in 1671; distance from the planet 3 560 000 km/ 2 212 000 ml; diameter 1 440 km/ 900 ml; orbital period 79.331 days. » Saturn (astronomy); RR4

Iapetus (mythology) [iyapituhs] In Greek mythology, one of the Titans, the father of Prometheus, Epimetheus, Atlas, and Menoetius; the grandfather of Deucalion. The close resemblance to Japhet may indicate borrowing from near Eastern sources. » Deucalion; Titan

iatrogenic disease [iyatrohjenik] A disorder that arises as a result of the treatment of another disease. It includes adverse and unwanted effects of drug treatment, and complications of surgical treatment which outlast the original conditions.

Ibadan [eebadan] 7°23N 3°56E, pop (1981e) 2 100 000. Capital of Oyo state, Nigeria, 113 km/70 ml NNE of Lagos; founded in the 1830s; British control, 1896; airfield; railway; regarded as the intellectual centre of the country; university (1948); metals, chemicals, brewing, vehicles, electronics, trade in cotton and cocoa; zoo. » Nigeria [i]

Ibáñez, Vicente Blasco [eevahnyeth] (1867–1928) Spanish novelist, born at Valencia. He dealt in realistic fashion with provincial life and social revolution, such as *Sangre y arena* (1909, Blood and Sand). *Los cuatro jinetes del Apocalipsis* (1916, The Four Horsemen of the Apocalypse) vividly portrays World War 1 and earned him world fame. He died at Menton, France. » novel; Spanish literature

Ibárruri (Gómez), Dolores, byname **La Pasionaria** ('The Passionflower') (1895–1989) Spanish communist orator and politician, born of a Catholic mining family at Gallarta. She became a member of the Central Committee of the Spanish Communist Party (1930), served as Spanish delegate to the Third International (1933, 1935), and was elected deputy to the Spanish Cortes (1936). With the outbreak of the Civil War (1936), she became the Republic's most emotional and effective propagandist. After the War she took refuge in the USSR, becoming President of the Spanish Communist Party in exile. In 1977 she returned to Spain as communist deputy for Asturias. » Asturias; communism; Spanish Civil War

Iberian Peninsula [iybeerian] area c.593 000 sq km/229 000 sq ml. The region of Europe SW of the Pyrenees, including Portugal and Spain; the name is probably derived from *Iberus*, the Roman name for the R Ebro; Iberia is an ancient name for Spain » Portugal [i]; Spain [i]

Iberians A group of iron-age peoples inhabiting the S and E periphery of present-day Spain (Andalusia, Valencia, Aragon, and Catalonia), and extending N into present-day France as far as the Rhône valley. » Three Age System

Ibert, Jacques (François Antoine) [eebair] (1890–1962) French composer, born in Paris. He studied in Paris, won the Prix de Rome (1919), and became director of the French Academy in Rome (1937–55) and of the Opéra-comique in Paris. His works include operas, ballets, cantatas, and chamber music, and the popular orchestral *Divertissement* (1930), based upon his incidental music for Labiche's play, *The Italian Straw Hat*. He died in Paris.

ibex A wild goat with high sweeping curved horns; horns round in cross-section and ringed with ridges; two species: **ibex** (*Capra ibex*) from the mountains of Europe, N Africa, and S Asia; **Spanish ibex** (*Capra pyrenaica*) from the Pyrenees. » goat

Ibibio A cluster of Kwa-speaking peoples of SE Nigeria, including the Efik, Oran, and Ibibio proper. Agriculturalists, they export palm oil and kernels, and are renowned for their woodcarvings. They are also well known for their secret societies (*ekpo*). Population c.3.5 million. » Nigeria [i]

ibis A wading bird native to tropical and warm temperate regions; related to spoonbills; long curved bill; face naked; eats small water creatures and insects. The **wood-ibis** (*Mycteria ibis*) of S Africa is a stork, not an ibis. (Family: *Threskiornithidae*, c.23 species.) » sacred ibis; spoonbill; stork

Ibiza [ibeetha] or **Iviza** [eeveetha], ancient **Ebusus** pop (1981) 40 000; area 572 sq km/221 sq ml. Third largest island in the Mediterranean Balearic Is, 88 km/ 55 ml SW of Majorca, surrounded by islets; a major tourist island; car ferries to Alicante, Valencia, Palma de Mallorca, Barcelona, Genoa; capital, Ibiza, pop (1981) 25 489, founded by the Carthaginians, 645 BC; almonds, figs, olives, apricots; Roman Portus Magnus, now San Antonio Abad, with its chapel-catacomb of Santa Ines, a national monument. » Balearic Islands

Iblis [iblis] The Islamic name for the archangel Lucifer, who rebelled against God and was banished from heaven to become Satan, the tempter. » Islam; Satan

Ibn Gabirol » **Avicebrón**

Ibn Saud, properly **Ibn Abd al-Rahman al-Saud** [sahood] (1880–1953) The first King of Saudi Arabia (1932–53), born at Riyadh. He followed his family into exile in 1890 and was brought up in Kuwait. In 1901 he succeeded his father, and set out to reconquer the family domains from the Rashidi rulers, an aim which he achieved with British recognition in 1927. He changed his title from Sultan of Nejd to King of Hejaz and Nejd in 1927, and in 1932 to King of Saudi Arabia. After the discovery of oil (1938) he granted substantial concessions to US oil companies. He died at at-Ta'if, Saudi Arabia. His son, **Saud** (1902–69) had been Prime Minister for three months when he succeeded his father (1953). In 1964 he was peacefully deposed by the Council of Ministers, and his brother **Faisal** (1904–75) became King, as well as remaining Prime Minister and Minister of Foreign Affairs. » Saudi Arabia [i]

Ibo » **Igbo**

Ibsen, Henrik (Johan) (1828–1906) Norwegian dramatist and poet, born at Skien. He worked at theatres in Bergen and Kristiania, and wrote several conventional dramas before his first major play, *Konsemnerne* (1857, The Pretenders). His theatre having gone bankrupt, and angry at Norway's aloofness in the struggle of Denmark with Germany, he went into voluntary exile to Rome, Dresden, and Munich (1864–92). His international reputation began with *Brand* and *Peer Gynt* (1866–7). He regarded his historical drama, *Kejser og Galilaer* (1873, Emperor and Galilean) as his masterpiece, but his fame rests more on the social plays which followed, notably *Et Dukkehjem* (1879, A Doll's House) and *Gengangere* (1881, Ghosts), which was controversially received. In his last phase he turned more to symbolism, as in *Vildanden* (1884, The Wild

Duck), *Rosmersholm* (1886), and *Bygmester Solness* (1892, The Master-Builder). The realism of *Hedda Gabler* (1890) was a solitary escape from symbolism. He suffered a stroke in 1900 which ended his literary career, and he died in Kristiania. » drama; Norwegian literature; poetry

Icaria, Gr **Ikaría** [ik**a**ria] area 255 sq km/98 sq ml. Greek island in the Aegean Sea, WSW of Samos; named after the legendary Icarus; medicinal springs at Thermai; Ayios Kyrikos is a popular resort. » Aegean Sea; Greece [i]; Icarus (mythology)

Icarus (astronomy) [**ik**aruhs] An asteroid discovered in 1949. It passes inside the orbit of Mercury, closer to the Sun than any other. » asteroids

Icarus (mythology) [**ik**aruhs, **iy**karus] In Greek mythology, the son of Daedalus. His father made him wings to escape from Crete, but he flew too near the Sun; the wax holding the wings melted; and he fell into the Aegean at a point now known as the Icarian Sea. » Daedalus

ICBM » **intercontinental ballistic missile**

ice The common solid form of water, stable below 0°C. Unlike most solids, it is less dense than its liquid, this being explained by the fact that the strong hydrogen bonds formed hold the molecules in a relatively open network. An even more open network occurs when ice forms around noble gas atoms or hydrocarbon molecules. Such clathrates may be important reservoirs of natural gas. » clathrate; water

Ice Age A period of time in the Earth's history when ice sheets and glaciers advanced from polar regions to cover areas previously of temperate climate. Several ice ages are evident in the geological record, the most recent ('the Ice Age') being from c.1 million years ago and lasting until c.10 000 years ago, when the ice retreated to its present polar extent. » glaciation

ice hockey A sport played on ice between two teams of 6 players who each wear ice skates and protective clothing. It is a fast game, played with sticks and a small circular rubber puck, on a rink 56–61 m/184–200 ft long and 26–30 m/85–98 ft wide. The aim is to hit the puck into your opponent's goal. It is thought to have been first played in Canada in the 1850s. The governing body is the International Ice Hockey Federation, founded in 1908. » hockey [i]; Stanley Cup; RR113

ice plant An annual lying flat on the ground, with broad succulent leaves and white, daisy-like flowers. The whole plant is covered with glistening papillae, resembling ice crystals. Native to S Africa, and introduced elsewhere, it was formerly a source of soda ash (commercial sodium carbonate), obtained by burning the plants. (*Mesembryanthemum crystallinum*. Family: *Aizoaceae*.) » annual; sodium; succulent

ice skating 1 Figure skating, artistic dancing on ice. Competitions are held for individual, pairs, and ice dancing. The first known skating club was formed mid-18th-c in London, and the first artifical rink was opened at Baker Street in 1876. **2 Speed skating**, in which one competitor races against another on an oval ice track over distances between 500–10 000 m (550–11 000 yds). » RR113

iceberg A floating mass of ice, detached from ice sheets or glaciers, drifting on ocean currents for up to several years and for many hundreds of kilometres before melting. With only a fraction of their mass above water level they are a danger to shipping, particularly in the N Atlantic, where they originate in Greenland. Antarctic icebergs are characteristically huge and tabular and many tens of kilometres in size. » glacier

icebreaker A vessel designed to clear waterways of ice by propelling itself onto the surface of the ice, breaking it with the weight of the fore part of its hull, which is specially shaped and strengthened for this purpose. Icebreakers are commonly employed in Russia, the Baltic, and Canada. » ship [i]

icefish Sedentary bottom-living fish found in icy antarctic waters around South Georgia; blood pale in colour, lacking haemoglobin; body length up to 60 cm/2 ft. (*Chaenocephalus aceratus*. Family: *Channichthyidae*.) » haemoglobin

Iceland, Icelandic **Ísland**; official name **Republic of Iceland**, Icelandic **Lýdhveldidh Ísland** pop (1990e) 254 000; area 103 000 sq km/40 000 sq ml. Island state lying between the N Atlantic and Arctic Oceans, SE of Greenland and 900 km/550 ml W of Norway; divided into eight regions; capital, Reykjavík; timezone GMT; official language, Icelandic;

chief religion, Lutheran Protestantism (95%); unit of currency, the krónur of 100 aurar; volcanic island, at N end of mid-Atlantic Ridge; several active volcanoes; famous for its geysers; many towns heated by subterranean hot water; geothermal power station at Krafla; heavily indented coastline with many long fjords; high ridges rise to 2 119 m/6 952 ft at Hvannadalshnjúkur (SE); several large snowfields and glaciers; changeable climate, with relatively mild winters; average daily temperatures, minimum −2°C (Jan), maximum 14°C (Jul–Aug); Reykjavík generally ice-free throughout year; summers cool and cloudy; average monthly rainfall reaches 94 mm/3.7 in (Oct); settled by the Norse, 9th-c; world's oldest parliament, the *Althing*, 10th-c; union with Norway, 1262; union with Denmark, 1380; independent kingdom in personal union with Denmark, 1918; independent republic, 1944; extension of the fishing limit around Iceland in 1958 and 1975 precipitated the 'Cod War' disputes with the UK; governed by a 63-member parliament, which includes a 21-member Upper House; a president appoints a prime minister and cabinet; economy based on inshore and deep-water fishing (three-quarters of the national income); stock farming, dairy farming, potatoes, greenhouse vegetables; aluminium, diatomite; tourism. » Látrabjarg; Reykjavík; Surtsey Island; Thingvellir; RR25 national holidays; RR52 political leaders

Iceland spar » **calcite**

Icelandic » **Germanic/Scandinavian languages; Icelandic literature**

Icelandic literature The earliest writing was the 11th-c skaldic poetry, followed in the next century by the documentary *Landnámabók* (Book of Settlements). In the 13th-c appeared the great Icelandic sagas, masterpieces of mediaeval prose; among them *Egils saga* and *Njals saga*. Humanism made its mark in the 16th–17th-c, and the Enlightenment found a voice in Eggert Olaffson (1726–68). Romantic poetry and the novel were represented in the 19th-c by Jonas Hallgrímsson (1807–45) and Jón Thoroddsen (1828–68). In the 20th-c, writers such as Einar Benediktsson (1864–1940), Gunnar Gunnarsson (1889–1975), and Halldór Laxness (Nobel Prize, 1955) have continued to make Icelandic literature known abroad. » Danish/Norwegian/Swedish literature; Enlightenment; humanism; Laxness; saga; skaldic poetry

Iceni [ik**ay**nee] An ancient British tribe occupying what is now Norfolk and NW Suffolk. They rebelled in AD 47 and again in 60, when their queen, Boadicea, led them and other tribes in a major revolt that nearly brought about the collapse of the Roman administration in Britain. » Boadicea; Britain, Roman

Ichkeul [ish**kerl**] area 108 sq km/42 sq ml. National park in Tunisia, established in 1978, now a world heritage site. » Tunisia [i]

ichneumon (insect) [ik**nyoo**muhn] A slender, parasitic wasp; females often have elongate egg-laying tube; eggs typically deposited on larvae or pupae of other insects and spiders; larvae feed on these as parasites during their development. (Order: *Hymenoptera*. Family: *Ichneumonidae*.) » larva; pupa; wasp

ichneumon (mammal) [ik**nyoo**muhn] The largest living mongoose (length, 1 m/3¼ ft), native to Africa and the Middle East (introduced in S Europe); also known as **Egyptian mongoose**, or **Pharaoh's rat**. (*Herpestes ichneumon*.) » mongoose; Viverridae [i]

ichthyosaur [**ik**thiohsaw] An aquatic reptile with streamlined body for fast swimming; tail typically large, paddle-like; eyes large, usually surrounded by bony plates; teeth small, fed mainly on cephalopods and fish; bore live young; known mainly from the Jurassic period. (Subclass: *Ichthyopterygia*.) » Jurassic period; reptile

Icknield Way [**ik**neeld] A Neolithic track linking Salisbury Plain in SE England to the E coast. The Romans gravelled it and used it as a secondary road. » Roman roads [i]; Salisbury Plain

Ickx, Jacky [iks] (1945–) Belgian racing driver, born in Brussels. He won eight races from 116 starts in Formula One. Outstanding at endurance racing, he won 34 world sports car championship races, and was world champion in 1982–3 (both Porsche). He won the Le Mans 24-hour race a record six times, in 1969 (with Oliver), 1975 (with Bell), 1976 (with van Lennep), 1977 (with Barth and Haywood), and 1981–82 (both with Bell). » motor racing

icon (computing) In computing, a small image or symbol used in graphic displays to represent a particular item, such as a program or a disk drive. Icons can be activated by using a computer mouse, and provide a means of communication with the computer other than through the keyboard. » mouse (computing)

icon (art/religion) (Gr *eikon*, 'image') A representation of Christ, the Virgin Mary, angels, saints, or even events of sacred history, used since the 5th-c for veneration and an aid to devotion, particularly in the Greek and Russian Orthodox Churches. They are typically in Byzantine style, flat, and painted in oils on wood, often with an elaborately decorated gold or silver cover. They are believed to be the channel of blessing from God. » Byzantine art; Christianity; iconoclasm; liturgy; Orthodox Church

iconoclasm [iy**kon**uhklazm] (Gk 'image breaking') The extreme rejection of the veneration of images. The practice was justified as an interpretation of the second of the Ten Commandments (*Ex* 20.4), and was supported by the pope and the Roman emperor in the 8th-c, and again by certain Reformers in the 16th-c. » icon (art/religion); Reformation; Ten Commandments

iconography The branch of art history which, faced with a picture, or any kind of image, takes as its central question: who or what is represented? Originally it was concerned with the identification of portraits; thus van Dyck's *Iconography* (1645) is a set of engraved portraits. Since the pioneer work of Mrs Anna Jameson (1794–1860) and Adolphe Didron Napoléon (1806–67) in the mid-19th-c it has been extended to cover the whole science of subject-matter and symbolism, especially under the influence of Aby Warburg (1866–1929) and his followers. » iconology

iconology A term used by the Italian writer Cesare Ripa (c.1560 –?) as the title of his collection of personifications (eg 'Deceit' with serpent's tail, 1593). Nowadays it is used for the historical study of the meaning of works of art in a broad sense – religious, social, political – following German art historian Erwin Panofsky (1892–1968), whose seminal article 'Iconography and Iconology' was published in 1939; but modern usage is often imprecise.

Ictinus (5th-c BC) Greek architect, who shares with Callicrates the glory of designing the Parthenon at Athens (438 BC). He was also architect of temples at Eleusis and near Phigalia. » Bassae; Parthenon

id » **ego**

Id-ul-Adha [eed ul **adh**a] The Muslim 'Feast of Sacrifice', celebrating the faith of Abraham who was willing to sacrifice his son at Allah's request; sheep and goats are killed as a reminder of the sheep Allah provided as a substitute for the boy, and the meat is shared with the poor. » Abraham; Allah; RR23

Id-ul-Fitr [eed ul **fee**ter] A Muslim festival, the 'Feast of Breaking Fast', occurring on the first day after Ramadan, and celebrated with festive meals, the wearing of new clothes, and giving gifts to charity. » Ramadan; RR23

Idaho [**iy**da-hoh] pop (1987e) 998 000; area 216 422 sq km/ 83 564 sq ml. State in NW USA, divided into 44 counties; the 'Gem State'; first European exploration by Lewis and Clark, 1805; held jointly by Britain and the USA until 1846; discovery of gold (1860) led to an influx of settlers; Territory of Idaho established, 1863; admitted to the Union as the 43rd state, 1890; capital, Boise; other chief cities, Pocatello and Idaho Falls; bounded N by Canada (British Columbia); rivers include the Snake (forms part of W border) and Salmon; the Bitterroot Range lies along much of the Montana border; in the C and N are the Sawtooth Mts, Salmon River Mts, and Clearwater Mts; highest point Borah Peak (3 860 m/12 664 ft); largely rugged, mountainous country, with nearly half the state (mostly N) under national forest; the Snake R Plain is one of the largest irrigated areas in the USA; river dams also generate hydroelectric power; mainly an agricultural state; cattle, wheat, potatoes, hay, sugar-beets, dairy produce; wood products, processed foods, chemicals; silver and antimony mined; contains one of the deepest gorges in the world, on the Snake R (Hell's Canyon). » Boise; Hell's Canyon; Lewis, Meriwether; United States of America [i]; RR38

ide » **orfe**

ideal gas A model gas in which atoms do not interact with one another, approximated well by noble gases such as helium and neon, and other gases at low pressures; also called **perfect gas**. More exactly, an ideal gas is one for which the equation of state is $pV = nRT$, where p is pressure, V volume, n number of moles of gas, T temperature, and R the molar gas constant having the value 8.314 $J.mol^{-1}K^{-1}$. » Charles' law; gas **1**; gas laws; kinetic theory of gases; statistical mechanics

idealism In philosophy, the metaphysical thesis that the only things which really exist are minds and their contents. Berkeley maintained that 'to be is to be perceived or a perceiver'; physical objects are collections of ideas that exist only insofar as they are perceived by finite, human minds or by the infinite mind, God. Hegel claimed that even the minds of persons are mere fragments of the Absolute, an immaterial object that is not a person. » Berkeley, George; Hegel; materialism

idée fixe [**ee**day **feeks**] A short theme associated with a particular person, object, or idea, which recurs (sometimes in altered form) in different movements or sections of a musical work. The term is used particularly with reference to the *Symphonie fantastique* and other works by Berlioz. » Berlioz; leitmotif

ideography The study of writing systems which use symbols called **ideographs** or **ideograms** – a development from primitive picture writing, found in early systems of the Far and Middle East. In an ideograph, the original pictogram has lost its direct reference to an object in the real world, and has come to represent an abstract concept to which the shape of the ideograph bears no clear relationship. For example, a representation of stars in the sky might come to represent darkness or evil, and a hand might represent friendship. Most of the symbols in fact come to represent words, and are thus more precisely referred to as *logographs*. » hieroglyphics [i]; pictography [i]

ideology A term first coined by the philosopher Destutt de Tracy (1754–1836) to refer to the study of ideas; now typically used to describe any set of beliefs that support sectional interests. The prevailing ideologies in society are likely to reflect and justify interests of the dominant (class, political, or religious) groups. The term implies that ideological beliefs are in some way exaggerations or distortions of reality. Several individual uses of the term have emerged in different political theories (eg Marxism). » class

ides [iydz] In the Roman calendar, the name given to the day in mid-month corresponding originally to the full moon. In March, May, July, and October this was the 15th, and in all other months the 13th.

idiolect [**id**eeohlekt] The total linguistic system of an individual, in a given language, at any specific time. Dialects are made up of more-or-less similar idiolects. It is unlikely that any two people have identical idiolects: different preferences in usage, grammar, vocabulary, and pronunciation will serve to keep them apart. » dialectology

idiophone Any musical instrument whose sound proceeds from the body of the instrument itself, without the action of vibrating strings, membranes, loudspeakers, or columns of air. Idiophones form one of the main categories in the standard classification of Hornbostel and Sachs (1914). » bell; carillon; castanets; gong chime; Jew's harp; maracas; musical glasses; musical instruments; percussion [i]; saw, musical; tuning fork

Idomeneus [iy**dom**enyus] According to Homer, the leader of the Cretans who assisted the Greeks at Troy; a descendant of Minos. Being caught in a storm at sea, he vowed to sacrifice the first thing he met on his safe return. This was his own son; and after carrying out the sacrifice he was driven into exile. » Homer; Trojan War

Idumeans » **Edomites**

Ieper [**ee**pruh] » **Ypres**

Ife [**ee**fay] A Yoruba ceremonial and trading centre in SW Nigeria, occupied from the 11th-c AD, from which the Yoruba dispersed to found their kingdoms. It is noted for its naturalistic figures in brass and terracotta, possibly dating from the late 14th/early 15th-c. The related Benin tradition may also derive from Ife. » African history; Benin [i]; bronze; terracotta; Yoruba

Igbo or **Ibo** [**ee**boh] A people of E Nigeria, a collection of many small and traditionally autonomous communities, with a common culture; the Igbo language is a member of the Kwa branch of the Niger-Congo family. Principally agriculturalists, with some export crops, they dominated the long-distance trade in Nigeria, and produced the earliest bronze art in the region. They established the short-lived state of Biafra (1960–70), and genocide of Igbo living in other parts of Nigeria occurred during this period. Population c.13 million. » Biafra; Niger-Congo languages; Nigeria [i]

Ignatius (of Antioch), St (c.35–c.107), feast day 1 February. One of the apostolic Fathers, reputedly a disciple of St John, the second Bishop of Antioch. According to Eusebius, he died a martyr in Rome. The *Ignatian Epistles*, whose authenticity was long controversial, were written on his way to Rome after being arrested. They provide valuable information on the nature of the early Church. » apostle; Christianity

Ignatius Loyola » **Loyola, Ignatius de**

igneous rock Rocks that have formed by crystallization of magma originating within or below the Earth's crust. Two main classifications exist. In terms of chemical composition, there are *acid* rocks, with more than 66% total silica (SiO_2); *basic* rocks with less than 55% total silica; and intermediate rocks. In terms of crystal size and mode of occurrence, *plutonic* rocks form deep in the Earth and are coarse-grained (eg granite); *volcanic* rocks form on the Earth's surface and are fine-grained (eg basalt); and *hypabyssal* rocks form at relatively shallow depths (eg dolerite). » basalt; dolerite; extrusive rock; granite; intrusive rock; magma

ignis fatuus [**ig**nis **fat**yoouhs] Flickering lights sometimes seen at night in marshy areas, and thought to be due to the spontaneous combustion of marsh gas (methane) generated by decaying vegetation. It is commonly termed *will-o'-the-wisp* or *Jack-o'-lantern*. » methane [i]

Iguaçu [igwa**soo**] National park on both sides of the border between Argentina and Brazil; area 1 950 sq km/750 sq ml; noted for its spectacular scenery, particularly the 82 m/269 ft-high Iguaçu Falls; a world heritage site.

iguana [ig**wah**na] A lizard, native to the New World, Madagascar, Fiji, and Tonga; active during the day; often has crest of tooth-like projections along back; tongue thick and fleshy, not long and forked. (Family: *Iguanidae*, 650 species.) » anole; basilisk (biology); chuckwalla; horned lizard; lizard [i]

Iguanodon [ig**wah**nuhduhn] A heavily-built two-legged dinosaur; up to 8 m/26 ft in length; plant-eating, with a cropping, horny beak present at the front of both jaws; probably lived in herds; known mainly from the Lower Cretaceous period of Europe. (Order: *Ornithischia*.) » Cretaceous period; dinosaur [i]; Ornithischia

Iguvine tablets A set of seven inscribed bronze tablets, relating to the period c.400–90 BC, discovered in 1444 near Iguvium (modern Gubbio), Italy. They contain rules for the ceremonies of a brotherhood of priests, with a wealth of information about the cults of Roman gods and goddesses, including Jupiter and Pomona. » Jupiter (mythology); Roman history [i]

Ikaría » **Icaria**

ikebana The formal Japanese style of flower arrangement, which selects a few blooms or leaves and places them in a very careful relationship to one another. It was a popular pastime in W Europe in the 1950s and 1960s.

Illampu, Nevado de [eel**yam**poo], also **Mount Sorata** 15°51S 68°30W. Highest mountain in the Andean Cordillera Oriental, in the Cordillera de la Paz; consists of two peaks, Illampu (6 485 m/21 276 ft) and Ancohuma (6 388 m/20 958 ft). » Andes

Illinois [**il**inoy] pop (1987e) 11 582 000; area 145 928 sq km/56 345 sq ml. State in NC USA, divided into 102 counties; the 'Prairie State'; 21st state admitted to the Union, 1818; explored by Jolliet and Marquette in 1673 and settled by the French, who established Fort St Louis, 1692; included in French Louisiana, it was ceded to the British in 1763 and by the British to the USA in 1783; capital, Springfield; other major cities include Chicago, Rockford, Peoria; the Mississippi R forms the W border, the Ohio R follows the Kentucky border, the Wabash R forms the lower part of the Indiana border, and the Illinois R flows SW across the state to meet the Mississippi R; highest point is Charles Mound (376 m/1 234 ft); mostly flat prairie producing maize, soybeans, wheat; grazing pigs and cattle; coal mining; diverse manufacturing centred on the Chicago area; Lincoln began his political career here. » Chicago; Lincoln, Abraham; Springfield (Illinois); United States of America [i]; RR38

illiteracy » **literacy**

illuminance In photometry, the incident luminous flux per unit area, ie the amount of visible light available to provide illumination per square metre; symbol E, units lx (lux); also called **illumination**. It decreases with the square of the distance from the source. The human eye can detect down to 10^{-9} lx. » light; photometry [i]

illumination » **illuminance**

illusion A true sensory stimulus which is misinterpreted. For example, the sound of a dripping tap may be thought to be malevolent voices, or flickering shadows in a dark room might be interpreted as ferocious animals. » vision

illusionism In art, the use of perspective, foreshortening, light and shade, and other devices to deceive the eye. Ancient Roman wall-paintings (such as at Pompeii), Renaissance stage-scenery, and Baroque ceiling-decoration are notable examples. » perspective; *trompe l'oeil*

Illyria [**il**eereea] In antiquity, the E seaboard of the Adriatic and its mountainous hinterland. It was roughly the equivalent of the W half of modern Yugoslavia and NW Albania; its inland boundaries were never precisely defined.

ilmenite A black oxide mineral, iron titanate ($FeTiO_3$), found in basic igneous rocks and beach sand deposits. It is the major ore of titanium. » titanium

Ilyushin, Sergei (Vladimirovich) [il**yoo**shin] (1894–1977) Russian aircraft designer, born at Dilialevo, Vologda province. After working as an aviation mechanic, he graduated in engineering, and in 1931 took charge of the design of both military and civil aircraft, including the Il-4 long-range bomber, which was important in World War 2. Afterwards his passenger aeroplanes became the basic Soviet carriers. He died in Moscow. » aircraft [i]

imagery Figurative language; the illustration and emphasis of an idea by analogies and parallels of different kinds, to make it more concrete and objective. Images may be explicit in the form of a simile ('As cold as any stone') or implicit in the form of a metaphor ('You blocks, you stones, you worse than senseless things'). They may be incidental, or form part of a system of imagery running through a work; organized images may also function as symbols. Imagery is often thought of as mainly visual, but this is far from being the case: images often invoke the other senses (smell, taste, touch, hearing) individually or combined (*synaesthesia*), and may even operate on an abstract, intellectual level. Imagery is a recognized grace of poetry, but also plays an important part in much prose writing. » figurative language; Imagism; metaphor; poetry; Symbolism

imaginary number » **numbers**

Imagism An early 20th-c poetic movement which sought to return (and confine) poetry to its essential ingredient, the image, which 'presents an intellectual and emotional complex in an instant of time' (Ezra Pound). Imagist poetry as such may lack interest through such reduction, but the movement has been widely influential. » imagery; poetry; Pound

imam [**imahm**] **1** A religious leader and teacher of a Sunni Muslim community, who leads worship in the Mosque. **2** A charismatic leader among Shiite Muslims, who believe that in every generation there is an imam who is an infallible source of spiritual and secular guidance. The line of imams ended in the 9th-c, and since then the ayatollahs serve as the collective caretakers of the office until the return of the expected imam. » ayatollah; Shiites; Sunnis

IMAX A large-screen cinematograph system, developed in Canada in 1968, using a frame 70 × 46 mm on 70 mm film running horizontally. This is projected on a screen typically 18–23 m/60–75 ft wide and 14–18 m/45–60 ft high, which is viewed by an audience seated comparatively close, so that the picture fills their field of vision. Sound from six magnetic tracks is reproduced from speakers around the auditorium. OMNIMAX was a further development in 1972, using wide-angle lenses for projection on a domed screen c.23 m/75 ft in diameter. » cinematography [i]

Imhotep (c.27th-c BC) Egyptian physician and adviser to King Zoser (3rd dynasty), probably the architect of the famous step-pyramid at Sakkara near Cairo. In time he came to be commemorated as a sage, and during the Saite period (500 BC) he was worshipped as the life-giving son of Ptah, god of Memphis. The Greeks identified him with Asclepius, because of his reputed knowledge of medicine. » Asclepius; Saqqarah

Immaculate Conception The belief that the Virgin Mary from the moment of her conception was free from sin. After many centuries' history, this was promulgated as a dogma of the Roman Catholic Church by Pope Pius IX in 1854. It was always rejected by Protestants as unbiblical, and, since 1854, has been rejected by the Orthodox Church. » Mary (Mother of Jesus); Roman Catholicism

Immanuel or **Emmanuel** [**iman**yooel] (Heb 'God with us') In the Hebrew Bible, a name which appears only in *Isaiah* (7.14, 8.8 (10)), where the birth of a son of this name to a young woman is a sign to King Ahaz of Judah's security against her N enemies. The text of *Isa* 7.14 is cited in *Matt* 1.23 as a prophecy of the birth of Jesus the Messiah, one to be born of a young woman (or virgin), whose name is to be called Immanuel. » Isaiah, Book of; Jesus Christ

immigration » **migration 1**

immortelle The name applied to various species of the daisy family, *Compositae*, cultivated for the papery flower-heads which retain their colour and are often used dried in flower arrangements. Commonly grown species include *Helichrysum bracteatum*, a perennial growing to 120 cm/4 ft, native to Australia, but often grown as an annual; flower heads surrounded by large shining papery bracts in yellow, orange, purple, or white. (Family: *Compositae*.) » annual; bract; daisy; perennial

immunity In medicine, the ability to resist the development of a disease-causing organism; originally used to identify those who did not contract an infection during an epidemic. Immunity is a graded phenomenon, varying from individuals who are extremely vulnerable to a specific infection to those who are resistant to it. Naturally-occurring or *innate immunity* protects individuals who have not had previous contact with a particular infection; this is influenced by genetic factors and by a person's physical well-being. Several non-infectious diseases (eg diabetes mellitus, uraemia, hypothyroidism) result in reduced natural resistance to infection. *Acquired immunity* is the second line of defence, provoked by the presence of the infecting agent in the tissue. There are two specific reactions within the body. The first is the production of antibodies which circulate in the blood; the second is called *cell-mediated immunity*, in which sensitized cells in the tissue react directly with the foreign agent and destroy it. Once these have occurred, subsequent exposure to the same infection causes an accelerated immune response which frequently conveys complete immunity. » immunization; interferons; severe combined immunodeficiency

immunity, diplomatic A provision of the Vienna Convention on Diplomatic Relations (1961), an international treaty, which states that diplomatic agents will have immunity from all criminal jurisdiction of the receiving state and immunity from certain civil jurisdiction. Technical and service staff have criminal immunity, but civil immunity is limited to their official acts. The ambassador may waive immunity. » civil law; criminal law; international law

immunization The artificial introduction into the body (*inoculation*) of antigens which are themselves harmless, derived from micro-organisms capable of causing specific disease, in order to provoke the production of protective antibodies. Infections in which immunization is widely carried out include poliomyelitis, tuberculosis, measles, mumps, and German measles. » antibodies; immunity; injection; vaccination

immunoglobulin » **antibodies**

immunology Originally the study of the biological responses of a living organism to its invasion by living bacteria, viruses, or parasites, and its defence against these. It now also includes the study of the body's reaction to foreign substances, particularly proteins, such as those in transplanted organs, and of how the body recognizes such proteins as being foreign. » autoimmune diseases; immunity; immunization; inflammation

immunosuppression The controlled suppression of the immune response of the body to the presence of foreign protein. This occurs in a number of special clinical conditions, such as organ and bone marrow transplantation, and in the treatment of certain malignant tumours (eg leukaemias, lymphomas) and auto-immune disorders. Several groups of drugs can be used, such as alkylating drugs, which are toxic to dividing cells, and antimetabolites, which reduce the power of cells of the immune system to manufacture antibodies and corticosteroids. Wide field X-irradiation is also sometimes used. Immunosuppression helps the body to accept the foreign tissue or organ; its major disadvantage is that it renders patients vulnerable to infections in general, and to micro-organisms which are not commonly the cause of disease in normal individuals (*opportunistic* infections). » immunity

impact printer Any printer which relies on the character being pressed onto the paper via an inked ribbon. Examples include daisy-wheel, golfball, and line printers. » printer, computer

impala [imp**ah**la] An African grazing antelope; golden brown, paler on underside; tuft of dark hairs on each heel; dark stripe each side of tail; male with lyre-shaped horns ringed with ridges; lives in groups at edge of open woodland. (*Aepyceros melampus*.) » antelope

impasto Oil paint applied with a heavily loaded brush so that it stands up on the surface of the picture. Traditionally, artists worked with a mixture of smooth underpainting, thinly-executed shadows, and thick (impasted) lights, plus transparent glazing. » oil painting

impatiens [imp**ay**sheeuhnz] A large genus of annuals and perennials, native to Europe, Asia, most of Africa, and N America; translucent, watery stems; leaves alternate or opposite, oval, toothed; flowers hanging horizontally from a slender stalk, showy, zygomorphic and complex, appearing to have either five flat petals and a slender curved spur, or 2-lipped with a funnel-shaped tube and spur; fruit a capsule exploding audibly and scattering seeds. Hybrids between *Impatiens holstii* and *Impatiens sultanii*, with mostly red, pink, or white flowers, are popular ornamentals known as **busy Lizzie**.

(Genus: *Impatiens*, 500–600 species. Family: *Balsaminaceae*.) » annual; balsam; perennial; zygomorphic flower

impeachment A legal process for removing undesirable persons from public office. Originating in mediaeval England, it was revived in the 17th-c during the conflict between the monarch and parliament. Normally it is the legislature that can move to impeach a public official, although there are usually simpler mechanisms (eg parliamentary votes) for removing persons from office, whatever the reason for their failure to maintain support. It is generally agreed that impeachment is a cumbersome method because of the problem of defining unacceptable behaviour and crimes. The move to impeach US President Nixon did, however, force his resignation. The previous move to impeach President Andrew Johnson in 1868 on suspect political grounds failed. » Johnson, Andrew; Nixon, Richard M

impedance In alternating current circuits, a measure of the restriction of current flow (in much the same way as resistance is used for direct current circuits); defined as voltage divided by current; symbol Z, units Ω (ohm). A complex quantity, with a real part equal to resistance, it depends on the inductance and capacitance of the circuit components. » alternating current; complex number; reactance; resistance

Imperial Conferences » **Colonial and Imperial Conferences**

Imperial War Museum The Museum of British and Commonwealth military operations since 1914, founded in London as a memorial to those who died in World War 1. It was housed in the Crystal Palace until 1924, when it was moved to the former Imperial Institute and then to the Royal Bethlehem Hospital. » Commonwealth Institute; Crystal Palace; museum

imperialism The extension of the power of the state through the acquisition, normally by force, of other territories, which are then subject to rule by the imperial power. Many suggest that the motivation behind imperialism is economic, through the exploitation of cheap labour and resources, and the opening up of new markets. Others suggest that non-economic factors are involved, including nationalism, racism and the pursuit of international power. The main era of imperialism was the 1880s to 1914, when many European powers sought to gain territories in Africa and Asia. Imperialism of the form associated with the establishment of European empires has in large measure disappeared, but the term is now often applied to any attempts by developed countries to interfere in underdeveloped countries. There is also increasing interest in the idea of *neo-colonialism*, where certain countries are subjugated by the economic power of developed countries, rather than through direct rule. » colony; indirect rule

impetigo [impuh**tiy**goh] A superficial infection of the skin common in children, usually due to *Staphylococcus aureus*. Infection affects the face, hands, and knees, and is characterized by reddened areas followed by transient blisters which break and then develop crusts. » skin [i]; staphylococcus

impotence Inability in males to engage in sexual intercourse because of failure to achieve an erection. A minority of cases of impotence are from a number of organic diseases; these include inadequate secretion of sex hormones by the pituitary gland or the testes; conditions such as diabetes, in which there is damage to the sympathetic nerve supply to the blood vessels of the penis; and in other severe debilitating diseases. More commonly a number of psychological causes are responsible. These include factors such as the strength of the sexual drive, attitudes to sex held by either of the partners, and the marital, family and social relationships. » penis [i]

Impressionism (art) A modern art movement which started in France in the 1860s; the name, coined by a hostile critic, was taken from Claude Monet's picture, *Impression: sunrise* (1872). The Impressionists, who included Pissarro, Sisley, and Renoir, rejected the dark tones of 19th-c studio painting, set up their easels out-of-doors, and tried to capture the brilliant effects of sunlight on water, trees and fields, and pretty girls. Impressionist pictures are typically bright and cheerful, avoiding the sort of social realism favoured earlier by Gustave Courbet (1819–77), and others, and have been enormously popular with 20th-c art-lovers and collectors. » French art; landscape painting; modern art; Post-Impressionism; Monet; Pissarro; Renoir, Pierre Auguste; Sisley

Impressionism (literature) A term taken from painting to signify the conveying of a subjective impression of the world rather than its objective appearance. In literature the term is rather imprecise, and to some extent overlaps with Expressionism. It relates primarily to the practice of the Symbolist poets and the psychological or stream-of-consciousness novel, drawing attention to the blurred outlines, shifting categories, and uncertain truth-values of the relativized modern world. » Expressionism; stream of consciousness; Symbolism

Impressionism (music) A style of harmony and instrumentation which, on analogy with the Impressionist school of painting, blurs the edges of tonality, shuns the primary instrumental colours of the Romantics, and generally aims for veiled suggestion and understatement. The term has been used (sometimes indiscriminately) with reference to music by Debussy and some of his French contemporaries. » Debussy; Romanticism (music)

imprinting The process whereby animals rapidly learn the appearance, sound, or smell of significant individual members of their own species (eg parent, offspring) or important subcategories (eg suitable mates, potential competitors) through being exposed to them, often during a restricted period of life. Imprinting to parent or offspring usually results in attachment/following behaviour. » ethology; learning

improvisation The performance of music without following a predetermined score; an important constituent of music for many centuries. In the Baroque period, a keyboard continuo player was expected to improvise an accompaniment from a figured base, while the reputations of singers and instrumentalists depended greatly on their ability to introduce suitable ornaments and embellishments, especially into slow pieces. In the classical concerto, the cadenza provided a major formal context for brilliant soloistic improvisation, but most of the major composers of the 18th–19th-c, including Bach, Mozart, Beethoven, and Liszt, were renowned for their abilities in improvising entire pieces. Since then the art of improvising on a given theme has survived mainly in organ lofts and in jazz, where both individual and ensemble improvisations have always played an important role. » aleatory music; blues; cadenza; continuo; jazz

***in vitro* fertilization** » **test-tube baby**

Incahuasi, Cerro [seroh eengkawasee] 27°03S 68°20W. Andean volcano on the Chile–Argentina border; 200 km/124 ml ENE of Copiapó (Chile); height 6 709 m/22 011 ft. » Andes

incandescent lamp A lamp which produces visible light from a heated source or filament. Examples include arc lamps, gas lights, and filament electric light bulbs. A filament light bulb produces light from a tungsten wire heated to over 2 000°C by an electric current. » electricity; light

Incarnation (Literally, 'the putting on of flesh') In Christianity, the union between the divine and human natures in the one Jesus Christ; the 'Word' of God becoming 'flesh' (*John* 1.14). The term is also appropriate to other religions (eg Hinduism) in which a life-spirit is given a material form. » Jesus Christ; Hinduism

Incas Originally a small group of Quechua-speaking Indians living in the Cuzco Basin of the C Andean highlands; during the 15th-c, one of the world's major civilizations, and the largest Precolumbian state in the New World, with an estimated population of 5–10 million. Inca was originally the name of their leader. In the 11th-c, they established their capital at Cuzco, the Sacred City of the Sun, where they built huge stone temples and fortresses, and covered their buildings in sheets of gold. During the 15th-c, they brought together much of the Andean area, stretching along the entire W length of S America, from near the present Ecuador-Columbia border to SC Chile, and occupied much of the Andean regions of Bolivia as well.

The Incas succeeded in creating an organizational structure that could hold a vast area together, and were able to extract from it the resources necessary to support armies of conquest and a sizeable state apparatus. They used former rulers as regional administrators (provided they were loyal) but these were denied any independence, and Inca culture, language (Quechua), and the cult of the Sun were forcibly imposed. The Inca emperor was a despotic ruler of a highly stratified society, a quasi-religious figure, and a direct descendant of the Sun-god Inti. Underneath him, a noble class ran the empire. The Incas were not innovative; they merely expanded and intensified existing practices, such as in agriculture. They had a system of more than 15 000 km of roads, and hundreds of way stations and administrative centres that provided an essential infrastructure for communication, conquest, and control. They also had impressive storage facilities, such as the food warehouses at the administrative city of Huanuco Pampa in C Peru.

In 1523, Spanish invaders under Pizarro encountered the Incas. They captured the emperor Atahualpa, whom they later murdered, and took control of the empire, and by the 1570s Indian power was totally destroyed. The present descendants of the Incas, 3 million Quechua-speaking peasants of the Andes, comprise 45% of Peru's population. » Atahualpa; Pizarro; Quechua

incendiary bomb A bomb which causes its destructive effects by burning fiercely and igniting the structures on which it lands. It was used with great effect by the Allies during World War 2 in 'firestorm' bombing raids on German and Japanese cities. » bomb; World War 2

incense A mixture of gums and spices which gives off a fragrant odour when burnt. It is widely used in many religious rites, and its smoke is often regarded as symbolic of prayer. Its use in Christianity cannot be traced before c.500. Its use in the Churches of the East is more widespread than in those of the West. » religion

incense cedar An evergreen conifer native to N America; related and similar to arbor vitae, but its foliage is not aromatic. Conical with spreading branches in the wild, cultivated forms are dwarf or, more commonly, very narrowly columnar. (*Calocedrus decurrens*. Family: *Cupressaceae*.) » arbor vitae; evergreen plants

incest Sexual relations with close kin. In Western society, it refers to sex in the nuclear family other than between man and wife, but the precise specification of when a relationship is too close to allow sexual relations varies between cultures and over time. The forbidding of sexual intercourse – and marriage – between kin who are regarded as too closely related, is known as an *incest taboo*.

inch worm » **looper**

Inch'ŏn [**in**chon], also **Jinsen** or **Chemulpo** 37°30N 126°38E, pop (1984) 1 295 107. Special city of W Korea; W of Seoul, on the coast of the Yellow Sea; scene of battle between Japanese and Russian navies, 1904; UN forces landed there during Korean War, 1950; major port for Seoul, to which it is linked by subway; university (1954); fishing; Songdo leisure resort (S). » Korea [i]; Seoul

income tax A major means for governments to raise revenue, consisting of a levy on wages and salaries, often set as a fixed percentage of income. Low incomes are usually not taxable, and higher levels of income often attract very high tax rates. The rates of income tax can vary from time to time, and are fixed by a government in its budgetary statement. Employers are usually obliged to collect the tax directly before paying wages to their staff. » budget; negative income tax; PAYE; taxation

incomes policy » **prices and incomes policy**

incubator bird » **megapode**

incubus [**in**kyubuhs] A malevolent male spirit supposed in mediaeval superstition to have intercourse with women in their sleep. Witches and demons were the offspring of such unions. » succubus

Independence Hall A building in Independence National Historical Park, Philadelphia, where the Declaration of Independence was proclaimed; a world heritage site. The Liberty Bell, rung at the proclamation, is kept here. » Declaration of Independence

Independent Labour Party A British political party formed in 1893 with the objective of sending working men to parliament. It was socialist in aim, but wished to gain the support of working people whether they were socialist or not. One of its leading figures was Kier Hardie. Many of its leaders played a major part in founding the Labour Representation Committee (1900), which became the Labour Party in 1906. It was affiliated to the Labour Party but put up its own candidates, and was disaffiliated in 1932. It continued to have a few members of parliament up to 1950. » Hardie; Labour Party

independent schools Schools in the UK which are not dependent on either the government or local authorities for their income, but derive it principally from the fees paid by parents. Many are run by independent trusts. » maintained school; public school

Independent Treasury System (1840–1) A system of handling the finances of the US government, independent of banks and private business. First set up under President van Buren (in office 1837–41), but repealed almost immediately, it was re-established in 1846, and remained in effect until the introduction of the Federal Reserve System. » van Buren

index (bibliography) » **indexing**

index/indices (mathematics) A notation which simplifies the writing of products, eg $2 \times 2 \times 2 \times 2$ is written 2^4, where 4 is the index (or *exponent*); it can be extended to give meaning to fractional, negative, and other indices. When numbers are written in index form, eg $16 = 2^4$, certain **laws of indices** exist. These are $a^m \times a^n = a^{m+n}$; $a^m \div a^n = a^{m-n}$; $(a^m)^n = a^{mn}$; $a^0 = 1$; $a^{-*1} = 1/a^n$; $a^{p/q} = (\sqrt[q]{a})^p$.

index fund An investment fund where shares are bought in all the companies listed in the main stock exchange index, then held. In this way the portfolio of shares will always equal movements in the stock market. The strategy is attractive where there is a fear of underperforming the market. It is more popular in the USA than in the UK. » Dow Jones Index; FT-SE Index; stock market

Index Librorum Prohibitorum [**in**deks lib**raw**ruhm prohhibi**taw**ruhm] (Lat 'index of forbidden books') A list of books which members of the Roman Catholic Church were forbidden to read. It originated with the Gelasian Decree (496), and was frequently revised, the last revision being published in 1948. Although the Roman Catholic Church still claims the right to prevent its members reading material harmful to their faith or morals, it was decided in 1966 to publish no further editions. » Inquisition; Roman Catholicism

index-linking Adjusting the price of goods, the interest on investments, or the level of salaries and wages, upwards or downwards in proportion to rises or falls in the retail price index. The strategy is popular in times of high inflation. » inflation; retail price index

index number A statistical device used mainly in economic and financial practice for tracking changes in some activity over time. Most start from a base of 100. » Dow Jones Index; FT-SE Index; retail price index

indexing The compiling of systematic guides to the location of words, names, and concepts in books and other publications. An index consists of a list of entries, each of which comprises a heading, together with any qualifying phrase and/or subheading(s), and at least one page reference or cross-reference ('see...'). The basic principles and mechanics of indexing, including the use of computers, have been codified and can readily be learned. However, individual judgment and sensitivity remain essential for producing an index that is effective and a pleasure to use. » library science

India, Hindi **Bharat**, official name **Republic of India** pop (1991) 843 930 861; area 3 166 829 sq km/1 222 396 sq ml. Federal republic in S Asia, divided into 22 states and nine union territories; bounded NW by Pakistan, N by China, Nepal and Bhutan, E by Myanmar and Bangladesh, SE by the Bay of Bengal, and SW by the Arabian Sea; capital, New Delhi; chief cities include Ahmadabad, Bangalore, Bombay, Calcutta, Hyderabad, Jaipur, Kanpur, Lucknow, Madras, Nagpur, Poona; timezone GMT +5½; chief ethnic groups, 72% Indo-Aryan, 25% Dravidian; official languages, Hindi, English, and 14 others; chief religion, Hinduism (83%); unit of currency, the Indian rupee of 100 paise.

Physical description. Asia's second largest state; folded mountain ridges and valleys in N, highest peaks over 7 000 m/23 000 ft in the Karakoram range and Ladakh plateau;

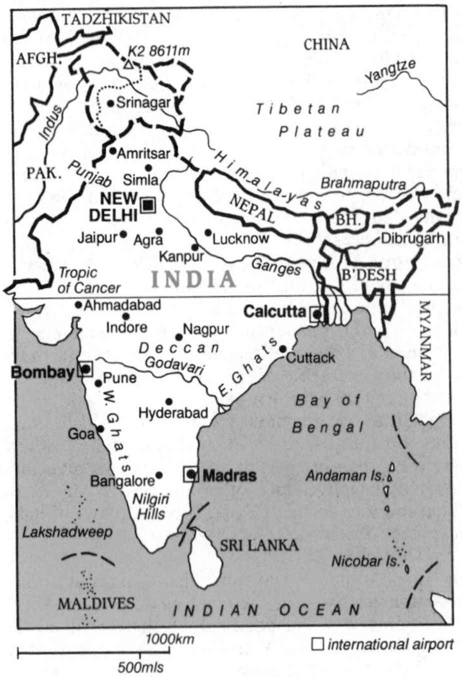

C river plains of the Ganges, Yamuna, Ghaghari, and Brahmaputra to the S; best agricultural land in the E; control measures needed to prevent flooding; Thar Desert NW of Rajasthan, bordered by semi-desert areas; Deccan Plateau in the S peninsula, with hills and wide valleys, bounded by the Western and Eastern Ghats; coastal plains, important areas of rice cultivation.

Climate. Dominated by the Asiatic monsoon; rains come from the SW (Jun–Oct); rainfall decreases (Dec–Feb) as winds blow in from the N, followed by drought until March or May; temperatures in mountains vary greatly with altitude, rainfall more widely distributed; rainfall decreases E–W on the N plains, with desert conditions in extreme W; temperatures vary with altitude on Deccan Plateau, tropical in S even in cool season; W coast subject to rain throughout year, particularly in S, with high humidity; cyclones and storms on SE coast (especially Oct–Dec), with high temperatures and humidity during monsoon season.

History and government. Indus civilization emerged c.2500 BC, destroyed in 1500 BC by the Aryans, who developed the Brahmanic caste system; Mauryan Emperor Asoka unified most of India, and established Buddhism as the state religion, 3rd-c BC; spread of Hinduism, 2nd-c BC; Muslim influences during 7th–8th-c, with sultanate established at Delhi; Delhi captured by Tamerlane, 1398; Mughal Empire established by Babur, 1526, extended by Akbar and Aurangzeb; Portuguese, French, Dutch, and British footholds in India, 18th-c; conflict between France and Britain, 1746–63; development of British interests represented by the East India Company; British power established after the Indian Mutiny crushed, 1857; movement for independence, late 19th-c; Government of India Act (1919) allowed election of Indian ministers to share power with appointed British governors; further Act (1935) allowed election of independent provincial governments; passive resistance campaigns of Gandhi from 1920s; independence granted, 1948, on condition that a Muslim state be established (Pakistan); Indian states later reorganized on a linguistic basis; Pakistan–India war over disputed territory in Kashmir and Jammu, 1948; Hindu–Muslim hostility, notably in 1978, and further India–Pakistan conflict in 1965 and 1971; separatist movements continue, especially relating to Sikh interests in the Punjab; suppression of militant Sikh movement in 1984 led to assassination of Indira Gandhi; federal democratic republic within the Commonwealth, 1950; each of the 25 states administered by a governor appointed by the president for five years; each state has an Assembly (numbers range from 30 to 425 members); each of the seven union territories is administered by the president; president elected for a 5-year term, advised by a Council of Ministers, appoints a prime minister; parliament comprises the president, an Upper House (*Rajya Sabha*) of no more than 250 members, and a 544-member House of the People (*Lok Sabha*).

Economy. Over two-thirds of the labour force employed in agriculture; tea, rice, wheat, coffee, sugar cane, cotton, jute, oilseed, maize, pulses, milk; floods and drought cause major problems; fishing, forestry; considerable increase in industrial production since independence; iron, steel, aluminium, vehicles, oil products, cement, chemicals, fertilizers, paper, jute goods, textiles, sugar; coal, iron, mica, manganese, bauxite, limestone, chromite, barites, oil, natural gas. » caste; Delhi; East India Company, British; Gandhi, Indira; Gandhi; Hinduism; Indian architecture/art/dance/literature/National Congress/theatre; Indian Mutiny; Islam; Mughal Empire; Pakistan [i]; Punjab (India); Sikhism; RR25 national holidays; RR52 political leaders

Indian architecture Architecture of the Indian sub-continent, which varies greatly according to time, location, and religion. Before the 16th-c, the earliest examples are Buddhist cave temples and stupas. Hindu temples are characterized by an elaborate use of carved decoration, and can be sub-divided into three geographical types: Northern, Chalukyan, and Dravidian. The formation of the Mughal dynasty in 1526 preceded the construction of the great Islamic monuments, such as the city of Fatehpur-Sikri (1568–75), built on a monumental scale with great attention to rich and intricate detail. The extension of the British Empire into India led to the introduction of Western architectural forms, including the idiosyncratic classicism used by Edwin Lutyens for New Delhi (1913–31). The most notable 20th-c buildings are in the new regional capital of Chandigarh, designed in the 1950s by Le Corbusier. In recent years, a more basic and suitable modern architecture for Indian conditions has been promoted by Indian architects themselves, including Charles Correa. » India [i]; Islamic architecture; Mughal Empire; Taj Mahal

Indian art The art associated with the Indian sub-continent. Visual art, especially sculpture, has flourished here since prehistoric times, but the historical tradition of Indian art really begins in the 3rd-c BC during the reign of Asoka (264–223 BC). Buddhist *stupas* (earth mounds) were adorned with relief sculpture from the 1st-c AD. Figurative sculpture at Ganhara (2nd–6th-c AD) reflected Hellenistic influence from Egypt and Syria. Richly-coloured Buddhist wall-paintings occur at Ajanta. The Gupta period (4th–5th-c AD) is considered the 'classical' period of Indian civilization especially in literature, but much of the visual art has vanished. Islamic influence increased, reaching its zenith under the Mughal emperors in the 17th-c. » Buddhism; India [i]; Indian architecture; Islam; Mughal Empire

Indian bean tree A domed deciduous tree growing to 20 m/65 ft, native to SE USA and widely planted as a street tree and ornamental; leaves opposite, 7–22 cm/2¾–8½ in, more or less heart-shaped; flowers 5 cm/2 in, bell-shaped with five spreading, frilled lobes, white with purple and yellow spots; fruit a long pendulous capsule resembling a bean pod. (*Catalpa bignioides*. Family: *Bignoniaceae*.) » deciduous plants; tree [i]

Indian corn » maize

Indian dance An ancient dance tradition based on Hindu thought, but showing Arab and Mughal influences. Shiva is the god who symbolizes eternal movement. Dance forms can be divided into classical and folk. Classical dance forms are of religious or court origin, while folk forms are social and based in village life. Indian classical dance is traditionally learned through attachment to a guru, the dances ranging in style from highly controlled forms of religious temple worship to the performance of violent legends based on mythical characters, which may last for a whole night. Religious or mythical themes rely on the poetic language of codified hand gestures (*mudras*) and facial expressions. They are accompanied by traditional instruments such as the tabla and sitar, and by voices, often in rhythmic counterpoint to the dance. » Bharata Natyam; Hinduism; India [i]; Kathak; Kathakali; Manipuri; Mohiniyattam; Odissi

Indian languages » **Devanagari; Dravidian languages; Indo-Aryan languages**

Indian literature A label which includes the literatures of numerous languages, principally Classical Sanskrit, Tamil, Hindi, Urdu, and Bengali. The oldest works are in Sanskrit. These include the texts of the Veda ('sacred love') in four collections which date back to the first millennium BC: *Rigveda, Atharvarvedra, Yagurvedra*, and *Samavedra*; and also the great Hindu epics *Mahabharata* and *Ramayana*. Later Sanskrit literature featured ritual Tantras, philosophical poems, and scholarly lyrics. A vernacular literature in Prakrit also developed in modern times. The early Tamil anthologies, *Ettutogaiad* and *Pattuppattu*, contain romantic and heroic verse from the 1st–4th-c AD; later Tamil literature was influenced by other Indian traditions, and then in the 19th–20th-c by European forms. A similar underlying pattern may be observed in Bengali literature, documented from 1400, which contains translations of Sanskrit epics, and later shows successive Muslim, Christian, and English influences. Distinguished individual writers are the 19th-c novelist Bakim Chandra Chatterji and the poet and Nobel prizewinner Rabindranath Tagore (1861–1941).

By contrast with Classical Sanskrit writings, the literatures of both Hindi and Urdu are essentially populist and reformist. Hindi has a tradition of poetry going back to the Rajasthani bards of c.1400, and includes 16th-c devotional poetry and (later) erotic literature such as the *Kesav Das*; there is also a modern vernacular. But the vernacular initiative passed in the 17th-c to Urdu, enriched by Persian models and material, and favoured by the Muslim nobility. Poets such as the satirist Saudi (died 1781), and the *ghazal* love poets Mir (died 1810) and Ghalib (died 1869), have been matched in the 20th-c by the mystical poet Mohammed Iqbal; and modern Urdu literature flourishes in all forms in Pakistan. » Bengali; epic; Hindi; India [i]; Iqbal; literature; Mahabharata; Ramayana; Sanskrit; Tagore; Tamil; Urdu; Veda

Indian Mutiny (1857–9) A serious uprising against British rule, triggered off by the belief among Indian troops in British service that new cartridges had been greased with animal fat – something which would have been abhorrent to both Hindus and Muslims. At the same time there was resentment among the old governing class over the reduction in their power, and western innovations. The mutiny at Meerut (10 May 1857) spread throughout N India; Delhi quickly fell; and Kanpur and Lucknow garrisons were beseiged. The British finally regained full control in mid-1858. The immediate result was the transfer of government from the East India Company to the British Crown (1858), but the long-term result was a legacy of bitterness on both sides. The element of national consciousness present made the episode a source of inspiration for later Indian nationalists. » East Indian Company, British

Indian National Congress A broad-based political organization, founded in 1885, which spearheaded the nationalist movement for independence from Britain under the leadership of charismatic figures such as M K Gandhi and Jawaharlal Nehru. It has been the dominant political party in India since 1947. » Gandhi; Nehru; Non-Co-operation Movement; Quit India Movement

Indian Ocean, ancient **Erythræan Sea** area 73 427 000 sq km/ 28 343 000 sq ml. Third largest ocean in the world, bounded W by Africa, N by Asia, E by Australia and the Malay archipelago, and S by the Southern Ocean; width c.6 400 km/ 4 000 ml at the Equator; maximum depth of 7 125 m/ 23 375 ft in the Java Trench; linked to the Mediterranean by the Suez Canal; floor divided into E and W sections by the Mid-Oceanic Ridge; rift valley runs along ridge axis, centre of sea-floor spreading; main island groups, Andaman, Nicobar, Chagos, Seychelles; largest islands, Madagascar and Sri Lanka.

Indian Territory Land set aside in the USA as a 'permanent' home for Indians removed from the area E of the Mississippi R between 1825 and 1840. Originally it included most of Oklahoma and parts of Kansas and Arkansas, but by the end of the 19th-c most of it had been opened to Whites. » Five Civilized Tribes

Indian theatre/theater The theatrical traditions of the Indian sub-continent, with an ancient history and diverse regional forms. A semblance of order is given by the traditional division into *Margi* ('belonging to the path'), equivalent to 'classical', illustrated in Sanskrit theatre, and *Desi* ('place' or 'region'), equivalent to 'folk', illustrated in Chau. However it is clear that many of its most distinctive styles (eg Kathakali and Yakshagana) lie between these two categories. » Chau; India [i]; Kathakali; Kutiyattam; Sanskrit theatre

Indian Wars (1622–1890) The process of invasion and conquest by which White people settled the present USA. The Europeans set out to remake the New World in the image of the old, if possible by persuasion, if necessary by force. The result was the destruction of the Indians' population, cultures, and economies.

The Whites' two greatest allies were disease and their own culture, as represented by artifacts as diverse as the bottle and the Bible. The total hemispheric drop in native population was from roughly 90 million at first contact to a low of about 9 million. Microbes to which the Indians had no natural resistance were the prime cause. Faced with such a disaster, their culture collapsed as well, and its place was taken by European ways. Most Europeans believed this was as it should be. Thus the first Puritan settlers, knowing that an epidemic had just swept through Massachusetts, took it as God's way of clearing the region for them.

The main effect of actual warfare was to remove the remaining Indians from the land and to destroy their political structures. It was not always easy. The woodland tribes of the E kept the Dutch, English, and French at bay from the early 17th-c to the late 18th-c, retreating only a few hundred miles inland before the American Revolution. But after independence they faced a powerful, single-mindedly expansionist state. Now bereft of potential allies, the Indians quickly lost whatever the Whites wanted.

The list of specific Indian wars is endless, beginning with a bloody attack by the Powhatan Confederacy on White Virginians in 1622 and ending with the massacre at Wounded Knee in 1890; but four main phases can be distinguished.

(1) In the 17th-c, the coastal tribes confronted the earliest invaders. Specific conflicts included the 'massacres' (as Whites called them) of 1622 and 1644, which brought many White deaths, the war of Bacon's Rebellion (1676) in Virginia, and the Pequot War (1636) and King Philip's War (1676) in New England.

(2) From 1689 to 1763 Indian warfare was bound up with the great struggle between France and Britain for control of the continent. King William's War (1689–97), Queen Anne's War (1702–13), the War of Jenkins' Ear (1739–42), King George's War (1740–8), and the great French and Indian War (1754–63) were the White colonists' names for specific conflicts. The English, eventually victorious, enjoyed the support of the Iroquois Confederacy of W New York, important both for their internal strength and for their control of the Mohawk Valley and Lake Ontario plain, which formed the only natural break in the Appalachian Mountains.

(3) Whichever side a tribe chose during the American Revolution, it made no difference, for the new United States implemented a policy of almost total Indian removal E of the Mississippi. Despite resistance in the Ohio Valley (Fallen Timbers in 1794 and Tippecanoe in 1811), and from the 'Five Civilised Tribes' of the South, the cause was hopeless. The Seminoles of Florida, whose number included many escaped Black slaves, were most successful, accepting final defeat only in 1842.

(4) The last phase imposed White control on the trans-Mississippi plains and on the deserts of the SW. This was the era of the most famous tribes (Cheyenne, Sioux, Apaches), Indian leaders (Black Kettle, Sitting Bull, Cochise) Indian fighters (Sheridan, Terry, Custer), and events (Sand Creek 1864, the Washita 1868, Little Big Horn 1876). By this time the few remaining Indians were facing the full might of an indus-

trial civilization. The plains wars were sometimes spectacular, but there was no question of long-term Indian victory.

Throughout the wars, the Indians fought at material and numerical disadvantage. They were disadvantaged as well by their own concept of what warfare was about, for they understood it in wholly different terms from their foes. Finally, they were handicapped by their own lack of unity. Specific Indian tribes approached each war in terms of their own friendships and enmities. That gave some, such as the Iroquois, great power to shape their own futures. But only on a very few occasions, such as King Philip's War, 'Pontiac's Rebellion' (1763), Tecumseh's War (1811), and the victory over Custer at Little Big Horn did Indians surmount tribal boundaries and act together. On even fewer occasions did they succeed. » American Indians; Bureau of Indian Affairs; Iroquois Confederacy; King Philip's War; Little Bighorn, Battle of the; Pontiac's Conspiracy; Powhatan Confederacy

Indiana pop (1987e) 5 531 000; area 93 716 sq km/36 185 sq ml. State in E USA, S of L Michigan, divided into 92 counties; the 'Hoosier State'; 19th state to join the Union, 1816; visited by La Salle in 1679 and 1681; occupied by the French, who ceded the state to the British in 1763; scene of many major Indian battles; capital, Indianapolis; chief towns include Fort Wayne, South Bend, Gary, Evansville; hilly in the S, fertile plains in the C, and flat glaciated land in the N; grain, soybeans, pigs, cattle; bituminous coal, limestone, steel and iron, chemicals, motor vehicles, electrical goods. » Indian Wars; Indianapolis; La Salle; United States of America [i]; RR38

Indianapolis [indeea**na**puhlis] 39°46N 86°09W, pop (1980) 700 807. Capital of state in Marion County, C Indiana, USA, on the White R; founded, 1820; state capital, 1825; airport; railway; university (1855); major medical centre at Indiana–Purdue Universities campus (1969); aircraft, motor vehicles, electronics, telephones, machinery, chemical and metal products; major league teams, Indiana Pacers (basketball), Colts (football); state museum, museum of art, City Market Internationale, Motor Speedway (where the world-famous 'Indianapolis 500' motor race is held). » Indiana

Indians, American » American Indians

indiarubber tree An evergreen tree with elliptical, leathery, very glossy leaves, native to India and SE Asia. It is a relative of the edible fig. A source of rubber, sometimes used as a shade tree, young specimens are sold as house plants under the name *rubber plants*. (*Ficus elastica*. Family: *Moraceae*.) » evergreen plants; fig; rubber

indictment A document specifying the particulars of an offence of which a person is accused. More than one offence may be involved; these are listed as separate 'counts' or 'charges' within the one document. **Indictable offences** are those triable before a judge and jury, such as murder. However, many indictable offences may be tried on a summary basis (ie relatively quickly, in the magistrates' court), such as theft. » Crown Court; jury; justice of the peace; murder

indigestion Upper abdominal pain or discomfort related to eating; also known as **dyspepsia**. It is an extremely common complaint that may be precipitated by overeating, or by particular foods such as spices, fried foods, or beer. The majority of sufferers have no demonstrable organic disease, but may suffer from stress or anxiety. The condition is usually relieved by taking antacids. A number of organic diseases, notably peptic ulceration, are responsible in a minority of cases. » digestion

indigo A dye obtained from a species of *Indigofera*, particularly anil (*Indigofera anil*), a tropical American shrub, and *Indigo tinctoria*, a shrubby perennial growing to 2.5 m/8 ft; leaves pinnate; pea-flowers red, in short clusters. It was formerly cultivated in India and Sumatra, but is now little grown, since the demand for natural indigo virtually ceased following the introduction of aniline dyes. At first widely used on wool, silk, and cotton, it is now mainly used to dye the warp yarns of denim. (Family: *Leguminosae*.) » anil; dyestuff; perennial; pinnate; shrub

indigo bird/finch » whydah

indirect rule A form of colonial rule especially characteristic of British rule in Africa during the inter-war years. In general terms it involved the use of existing political structures, leaders, and local organs of authority. Thus local political elites enjoyed considerable autonomy, although they still had to keep in accord with the interests of the colonial power. It was adopted on grounds of its cheapness and to allow for independent cultural development, but was increasingly criticized for its failure to introduce a modernizing role into colonial administration, and was gradually given up after 1945. » Fulani; imperialism; Lozi

individualism Any thesis which maintains that wholes of a certain type (organisms, societies) can be fully understood and explained in terms of the properties and relations of their individual parts. Methodological individualism is the thesis that the workings of societies can be explained entirely by explaining the activities of individuals. Individualists such as Popper have argued that to deny individualism is to be committed to some form of totalitarianism. » holism; Popper; totalitarianism

Indo-Aryan languages The easternmost branch of the Indo-European languages, comprising some 500 languages spoken by 500 million people in N and C India. Its subgroupings are exemplified by Panjabi (or Punjabi, c.70 million) in the NW; Gujarati (c.35 million) and Marathi (c.50 million) in the W and SW; Hindi and Urdu (together, 200 million) in the mid-N; and Bengali and Assamese (together, c.150 million) in the E. The pairs Hindi/Urdu and Bengali/Assamese are mutually intelligible, and distinguished from each other only on socio-political grounds. Romany also belongs to this family. » Indo-European languages; Romany; Sanskrit

Indo-European languages The family of languages which developed in Europe and S Asia, and which gave the modern languages of W Europe (eg the Germanic, Romance, and Celtic languages) as well as many in the Baltic states, Russia, and N India. The parent language of the family has been labelled **Proto-Indo-European** (PIE); there is no documentary evidence for it, but it is thought to have been spoken before 3000 BC. The forms of PIE have been reconstructed on the basis of correspondences of sound between the forms of the related languages. The key relationships were discovered in the 19th-c, when it was shown that the main European languages and Sanskrit (the oldest language of the Indian sub-continent) were derived from the same parent language. » Baltic/Celtic/Germanic/Indo-Aryan/Iranian/Romance/Slavic languages; comparative linguistics; family of languages [i]; reconstruction; Sanskrit

Indo-Iranian languages The E branch of the Indo-European family of languages. It comprises the Iranian and Indo-Aryan subgroups. » Indo-Aryan/Indo-European/Iranian languages

Indo-Pacific languages A group of languages, centred on Papua New Guinea, located in the middle of the geographical area of the Austronesian group, but independent of it linguistically. There seem to be fewer than three million speakers, but little is known of the languages, and many tribes have not been contacted. The isolation of some of these tribes means that they are able to maintain independent languages with in some cases as few as 100 speakers. » Austronesian languages

Indonesia, official name **Republic of Indonesia**, Bahasa Indonesian **Republik Indonesia**, formerly **Netherlands Indies, Dutch East Indies, Netherlands East Indies, United States of Indonesia** [indoh**neezha**] pop (1990e) 180 763 000; area 1 906 240 sq km/735 809 sq ml. Republic of SE Asia, comprising the world's largest island group, divided into 27 provinces; five main islands, Sumatra, Java, Kalimantan (two-thirds of Borneo I), Sulawesi, Irian Jaya (W half of New Guinea I); capital, Jakarta; timezones GMT +7 (Java, Sumatra), +8 (Kalimantan, Sulawesi, Lesser Sundas), +9 (Moluccas, Irian Jaya); chief ethnic groups, Javanese, Sundanese, Madurese, Malays; official language, Indonesian, with English, Dutch, and Javanese widely spoken; chief religion, Islam (90%); unit of currency, the rupiah; five main islands and 30 smaller archipelagos, totalling 13 677 islands and islets, of which c.6 000 are inhabited; over 100 volcanic peaks on Java, 15 active; hot and humid equatorial climate; dry season (Jun–Sep), rainy season (Dec–Mar), apart from the Moluccas (Jun–Sep); average temper-

*East Timor incorporated into Indonesia July 1976

□ international airport

ature of 27°C on island coasts, falling inland and with altitude; settled in early times by Hindus and Buddhists whose power lasted until the 14th-c; Islam introduced, 14th–15th-c; Portuguese settlers, early 16th-c; Dutch East India Company established, 1602; Japanese occupation in World War 2; independence proclaimed, 1945, under Dr Sukarno; federal system replaced by unified control, 1950; military coup, 1966; 1945 constitution established a 1000-member People's Consultative Assembly; governed by a president elected for a 5-year term, advised by a cabinet and several advisory agencies; separatist movements in Irian Jaya and East Timor; United Nations refuses to recognize Indonesian sovereignty in East Timor; mainly agrarian economy, notably rice; maize, cassava, sugar, sweet potatoes, bananas, coffee, tobacco, tea, rubber, coconuts, palm oil; fishing, timber; oil, natural gas, and petroleum products from Borneo and Sumatra account for nearly 60% of national income; tin, nickel, bauxite, copper, manganese; small manufacturing industry, based on textiles, paper, cement, chemicals, fertilizers, motorcycles, household goods. » Bali; Borneo; Irian Jaya; Jakarta; Java; Kalimantan; Komodo; Moluccas; Nias; Siberut; Sulawesi; Sumatra; Sunda Islands; Timor; RR25 national holidays; RR52 political leaders

Indonesian » **Bahasa Indonesia**

Indra In Hinduism, the Vedic king of the gods, to whom many of the prayers of the Rig Veda are addressed. » Hinduism; Veda

indri or **indris** A leaping lemur, the largest living primitive primate (body length, 700 mm/7½ in); very short tail; dark with white legs and hindquarters; fluffy round ears; has a very loud, far-reaching cry; inhabits tree tops; eats leaves. (*Indri indri.*) The name *woolly indri* is used for the **woolly lemur** or **avahi** (*Avahi laniger*). » lemur; prosimian

Indricotherium [indrikuh**thee**riuhm] The largest land mammal that ever lived; known from the Oligocene epoch of C Asia; a gigantic, hornless rhinoceros standing 5.4 m/18 ft at the shoulder; probably weighing 30 tonnes; fed by browsing on vegetation. (Order: *Perissodactyla.*) » mammal [i]; Oligocene epoch; rhinoceros

inductance A measure of a coil's ability to produce a voltage in another coil (**mutual inductance**, M) or in itself (**self inductance**, L) via changing magnetic fields; units H (henry). It is equal to the ratio of electromotive force produced to rate of change of current. » electromagnetic induction; electromotive force

induction (logic) In logic, any inference whose premisses, if true, do not entail the truth of the conclusion, but make it more likely to be true. It is always possible for the conclusion of an induction to be false even if the premisses are true: 'The Sun has always risen in the past; therefore it will rise tomorrow' illustrates the point. » confirmation; logic; premiss

induction (obstetrics) The initiation of childbirth by artificial means. A common technique is the injection of the hormone oxytocin, which causes contractions of the uterus. » hormones; labour; obstetrics

induction (physics) » **electromagnetic induction**

induction (embryology) The action of natural stimuli that cause unspecialized tissue to develop into specialized tissue. In the earliest embryonic stage immediately after the zygote starts dividing, the cells of the embryo are unspecialized, and have the potential to develop into any cell type. As development proceeds, certain cells (*inducers*) influence neighbouring cells to develop along a determined course into a particular type of cell. » cell; embryo

indulgences In Roman Catholicism, grants of remission of sin to the living, following repentance and forgiveness; also, to the dead in purgatory. They were based on the Church's treasury of merit, accumulated through the good works of Jesus Christ and the saints. Abuses in the Middle Ages, leading to the 'buying and selling' of places in heaven, finally occasioned Martin Luther's '95 Theses', which launched the Reformation. » Jesus Christ; Luther; purgatory; Reformation; Roman Catholicism; sin

Indus (astronomy) (Lat 'Indian') An inconspicuous constellation introduced to the S hemisphere in 1603 by German astronomer Johann Bayer (1572–1625). » constellation; RR8

Indus, River, Sanskrit **Sindhu** River of Asia, mostly in NW India, the longest of the Himalayan rivers (3 000 km/1 900 ml); rises in the Kalias Range in Xizang region (Tibet); flows NW through Tibet, Jammu, and Kashmir, then S into Pakistan; within Pakistan the flow is generally SSW in a broad braided channel, to enter the Arabian Sea SE of Karachi in a level, muddy delta supporting little cultivation; navigable for small vessels as far as Hyderabad; barrage at Sukkur supplies an extensive irrigation system and power project; relics of Indus civilization (flourished 4000–2000 BC) excavated at Mohenjo-daro and Harappa. » India [i]; Indus Valley civilization; Mohenjo-daro; Pakistan [i]

Indus Valley Civilization The earliest known S Asian civilization, flourishing c.2300–1750 BC across 1.1 million sq km/½ million sq ml around the R Indus in Pakistan. Over 100 sites have been identified with important urban centres at Mohenjo-daro and Harappa (Pakistan), and Kalibangan and Lothal (W India). There were uniform principles of urban planning, with streets set out in a grid pattern and public drainage systems. Weights and measures were standardized, and there was widespread trade with W Asia. A common writing system was used, which remains undeciphered. Great granaries on citadel mounts suggest the existence of priest-kings or a priestly oligarchy. There is no firm explanation for the decline of the civilization. » Harappa; Mohenjo-daro

indusium » **sorus**

industrial action The activities of a trade union, or other group of employees in a company or industry, where ordinary negotiating has proved unsuccessful. The aim is to disrupt normal output, by introducing 'work-to-rule' and 'go-slow' tactics, as well as strike action. » lockout; picketing; strike (economics)

industrial democracy A situation in companies where

employees have a say in determining corporate policies. Examples include works councils, and employee representatives on the board of directors. » company

industrial design A term used increasingly nowadays to refer to the design of anything made by machine, from Coke bottles to Volkswagens. Early industrial design included Wedgwood pottery and Sheffield plate. » Art Deco; Arts and Crafts Movement; Bauhaus; functionalism

industrial disease » **occupational diseases**

industrial espionage The discovery of information about a company's activities in order to negate its competitive advantage. Examples include the acquisition of secret formulae, designs, and plans for new products, as well as prior information about profits.

industrial relations The dealings and relationships which exist between the workforce and management of a business, particularly one where trade unions are present and collective bargaining is normal; also known as *labour* or *employee relations*. The aims are to preserve the best possible relationship, to ensure that output is maintained, and that employees are properly rewarded for their work. » industrial action

Industrial Revolution A term usually associated with the accelerated pace of economic change, the associated technical and mechanical innovations, and the emergence of mass markets for manufactured goods, beginning in Britain in the last quarter of the 18th-c with the mechanization of the cotton and woollen industries of Lancashire, C Scotland, and the W Riding of Yorkshire. After the harnessing of steam power, cotton and woollen factories were increasingly concentrated in towns, and there were hugely increased rates of urbanization. A rapid population increase, stimulated by greater economic opportunities for early marriage, is also associated with this type of economic growth. The mechanization of heavier industries (iron and steel) was slower, but sustained the Industrial Revolution in its second phase from c.1830. » engine; spinning; steel

industrial textiles Textiles used for industrial purposes, as found in the manufacture of conveyor belts, filter cloths, geotextiles, and ropes. Some 30% of all textile products are categorized as industrial.

inert » **kinetic**

inert gases » **noble gases**

inertia The reluctance of a massive object to change its motion. Inherent to mass, it is present in the absence of gravity. Newton's first law is sometimes called the law of inertia, and is equivalent to ascribing the property of inertia to objects. » Mach's principle; mass; moment of inertia; Newton's laws

inertial guidance An automatic navigation system used in guided missiles, aeroplanes, and submarines, which depends on the tendency of an object to continue in a straight line (*inertia*). Any changes in the direction and magnitude of motion of the vehicle are sensed and corrected automatically. » inertia

infallibility In the Roman Catholic Church, the claim that statements on matters of faith or morals, made by a pope speaking *ex cathedra* ('from the throne'), or by a General Council if confirmed by the pope, are guaranteed the assistance of the Holy Spirit (ie free from error). The claim is rejected by Protestants, for whom only God and the word of God are infallible. » Holy Spirit; Council of the Church; pope; Protestantism; Roman Catholicism; Vatican Councils

infant mortality rate The number of deaths of infants in the first year of life (age 0–1) in relation to the number of live births. It is a sensitive measure of community health, for when standards of hygiene, sanitation, and nutrition are low, many infants die of gastro-enteritis and respiratory infections. However because deaths during the first week of life are more influenced by pre-natal and intra-natal factors, congenital defects, prematurity, and birth injury, another statistic is also employed: the **perinatal mortality rate**. This is defined as the number of deaths, including stillbirths, occurring in the first week of life in relation to the total live and stillbirths occurring in the same year, and reflects the standards of antenatal and obstetrical care. Both statistics have fallen steadily in developed countries for over 100 years, perinatal mortality being especially affected because of advances in the care of small and premature babies. » epidemiology

infant school A UK school taking children from the age of 5 up to 7 or 8. In areas with middle schools, such schools are sometimes known as 'first schools'. » middle school; primary education

infante/infanta In Spain and Portugal, the title given to the sons and daughters of the sovereign.

infanticide In England and Wales, a term used for the crime committed where a mother causes the death of her child. The child must be under one year old, and at the time of the mother's act or omission the mother must have been disturbed in her mind as a result of the stress of the birth. The difficulty of obtaining jury convictions for murder in these situations led to the introduction of this crime in an act of 1922. In the USA, the offence is usually subsumed under the general homicide statute. » homicide

infantile paralysis » **poliomyelitis**

infection The invasion of the body by micro-organisms that are capable of multiplying there and of producing illness. Such organisms are called *pathogenic*. However, some pathogenic organisms can exist on the skin or in other parts of the body without causing illness; in these circumstances the individual is said to be a 'carrier' of the organism. An infection begins by the entry of an organism at a specific site, such as the tonsils, skin, or respiratory passage. This is followed by a short interval in which the person feels well (the *incubation period*), then by dispersion of the organism throughout the body, usually with the predominant involvement of one or more specific tissues, as in cystitis (the bladder), pneumonia (the lungs), and hepatitis (the liver). » communicable disease; isolation unit; micro-organism

inference In logic, any sequence of steps leading from a set of premisses to a conclusion. Each step is either a premiss, or it is drawn from previous premisses by the use of correct **rules of inference**. Successful deductive inferences are *valid*; successful inductive inferences *confirm* their conclusions. » confirmation; deduction; induction (logic); logic; premiss

inferiority complex A fundamental sense of inadequacy and insecurity out of proportion to real circumstances. An example may be of a short individual who has a driven need to assert himself in social situations to overcome his sensitivity about his height. » complex; narcissism

infertility The inability of a male or female to have children. Estimates of subfertility amount to c.10% of couples, with a wide range of causes affecting both partners. In the female, failure of ovulation is common, and ovaries may be stimulated to produce ova by giving gonadotrophic hormones or by drugs which simulate their action in the body. Infection of the cervix, obstruction to the Fallopian tubes, and abnormalities in the uterus are also recognized factors. In the male, factors include the absence or inadequate production of sperm, and the clumping of sperm (*agglutination*) with impaired mobility due in some individuals to sperm antibodies in the male serum. » artificial insemination; cervix; Fallopian tubes; gamete intrafallopian transfer; gonadotrophin; semen; test-tube baby; uterus [i]

infinity In mathematics, a number greater than any other number. The symbol ∞ was first used for infinity by the English mathematician John Wallis (1616–1703). Cantor and other mathematicians in the 19th-c and 20th-c showed the complexity of the concept of infinity, arising out of their work on set theory, investigating, for example, how the cardinal number of the set of all points in an infinite straight line compares with the cardinal number of the set of all points in an infinite plane. » Cantor; set

infix » **affix**

inflammation A defensive reaction of the body's tissues to invasion by pathogenic micro-organisms, or to the presence of a foreign body or other injury. Initially there is an increased blood flow to the damaged part, due to chemical substances which dilate the small blood vessels. Certain types of white blood cells (*neutrophil polymorphs*) and monocytes are attracted to the site, and these engulf and digest micro-organisms

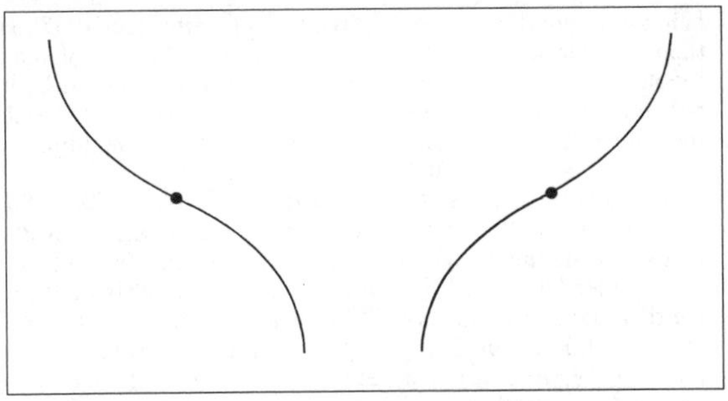

Points of inflexion

(*phagocytosis*) and tissue debris. The reaction is accompanied by local swelling and pain. If the defence is successful, resolution of the inflammation occurs. » arthritis; blood; immunity; infection

inflation An economic situation where the general level of prices is rising, as popularly measured by the retail price index. Inflation causes the real value of money to fall, and savings to lose their value. It is also believed to slow down economic growth. If inflation is too high ('galloping inflation') or very severe ('hyperinflation'), a country's currency becomes unacceptable. The most serious examples of inflation running out of control took place in Germany in the early 1920s, and in many S American countries in the 1970s and 1980s. The control of inflation is a major aim of government economic policy in many countries; but its causes and cures are subjects of much debate by economists and politicians. The major fear is that action to reduce inflation causes an increase in unemployment. » deflation; fiscal drag; stagflation

inflationary universe A theory proposed in 1980 by US physicist Alan Guth (1947–) and others which provides a mechanism for the extraordinary expansion of the early universe from a diameter of 10^{-26} m to 10 cm in 10^{-32} sec. Such expansion is thought necessary to understand the present observed universe. The theory is linked to grand unified theories in particle physics. » Big Bang; cosmology; grand unified theories; universe

inflecting language » fusional language

inflection » derivation; fusional language

inflexion, point of In mathematics, the point at which a curve changes the nature of its concavity, either from being concave upwards to concave downwards, or vice-versa. If the equation of the curve is given in Cartesian co-ordinates x and y, $d^2y/dx^2 = 0$, and (a factor often forgotten) changes sign at that point.

inflorescence The arrangement of more than one flower on the stem, together with any associated structures, such as bracts. Development is triggered by changes in light duration or temperature, and is probably controlled by hormones. The vegetative growth of the plant may cease with production of the inflorescence, or may continue afterwards; this is of significance in some crop plants where yield, ripening, and harvesting techniques are important. The type of inflorescence is often significant as a diagnostic character in recognizing plant families. Basic types are distinguished by the different branching patterns and by the positions of the oldest and youngest flowers. In **cymose** inflorescences, the meristem of the main axis differentiates into a flower with new growth coming from a lateral branch (*monochasia*) or branches (*dichasia*) which in turn are terminated by a flower. In **racemose** inflorescences, the main axis continues to grow, flowers being formed below the tip. » bract; flower [i]; hormones; meristem

influenza An infection caused by the influenza virus, tending to occur in epidemics and pandemics. It causes an acute respiratory illness associated with headache, fever, and muscle pain. There is a significant mortality, mainly affecting the elderly and the debilitated. Vaccination is difficult, because the virus develops different strains with varying antigenic properties. The name is derived from *influentia coeli*, a mediaeval name for the disease, thought to be due to the influence of the sky. » respiration; virus

information processing A psychological approach in which the performance of an organism is described in terms of the elementary operations or computations it performs on *input* information (the *stimulus*) to produce *output* information (the *response*). It is often associated with cognitive psychology. » cognitive psychology; connectionism

information retrieval The act of tracing information contained in databases. Applicable in principle to any search for information, the term has been associated since the 1960s with the online technique of scanning and interrogating large computer files for specific data. This may take the form of bibliographic references, full-length documents, or constantly updated information (eg share prices). The use of computers makes the process not only quick and relatively cheap, but also thorough and reliable. » computer; database

information technology A term commonly used to cover the range of technologies relevant to the transfer of information, in particular to computers, digital electronics, and telecommunications. Technological developments during the 1970s and 1980s, such as very large scale integration, and satellite and optical-based communication methods, have been responsible for enormous scientific and commercial growth in this area. » computer; electronics; telecommunications; very large scale integration

information theory The mathematical theory of information, deriving from the work of the US mathematicians Claude E Shannon and Warren Weaver, in particular *The Mathematical Theory of Communication* (1949), and from the theory of

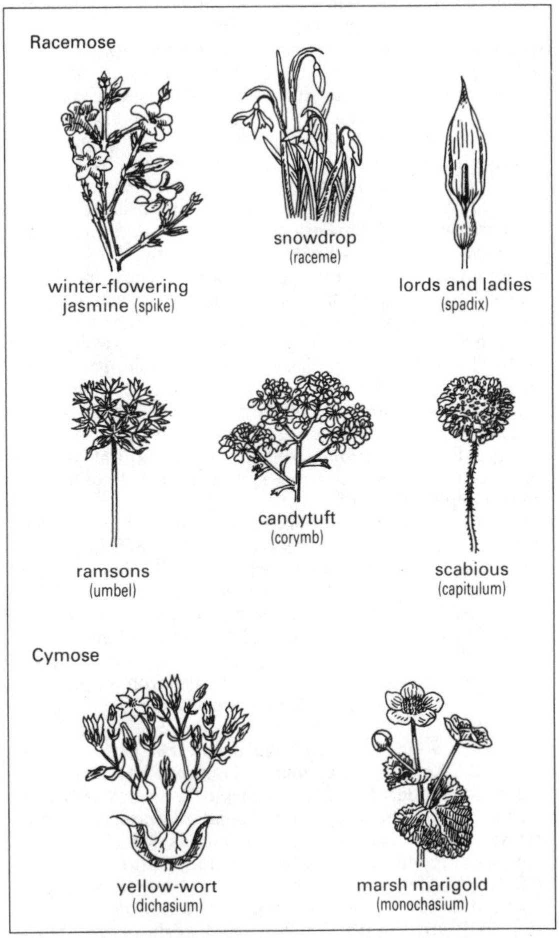

Types of inflorescence

probability. It is concerned with defining and measuring the amount of information in a message, with the encoding and decoding of information, and with the transmission capacity of a channel of communication. The basic notion is that the less predictable something is, the more information it contains. For example, the letter *z* carries a lot more information than *e* (in English, less so in German), when it occurs in a message. In contrast, the *u* after *q* carries no information at all, since it is wholly predictable, and thus technically redundant.

The theory also deals with the problem of *noise* (random interference) in the channel, which can impair the reception and decoding of a signal. To reduce the risk of errors which may arise, and thereby to increase efficiency, a signal should contain a degree of redundancy. For example, the final digit of the number identifying books (the ISBN) provides information to check that the rest of the number is valid. Information theory has been influential in generating models for understanding communication processes and in the design of codes for the transmission of information, especially by computers. It is not, however, concerned with the content, meaning, or importance of that information or any other communication. » communication theory; computer science

Infrared Astronomical Satellite (IRAS) project The first mission to survey the universe in the thermal infrared region of the electromagnetic spectrum, where the 'signature' of relatively cool materials in space can be observed. Launched in January 1983, it operated successfully for 300 days until the helium was exhausted, achieving an all-sky survey. It catalogued 250 000 IR sources, identified stars apparently in the process of forming, and discovered six comets and their long dust tails. It was a collaborative project of the UK, The Netherlands, and the USA. » comet; electromagnetic radiation [i]; infrared astronomy; star

infrared astronomy The study of celestial objects by their radiation in the wavelength range 1 000 nm–1 mm. Absorption by water vapour in our atmosphere poses severe difficulties, some of which are overcome at high altitude observatories such as Mauna Kea in Hawaii at 4 000 m/13 000 ft, or by using cryogenically-cooled telescopes on spacecraft. Many objects emit most of their radiation in the infrared waveband. This type of astronomy has increased in importance with the availability of two-dimensional (2D) detector arrays; further advances will come with the launch of the Infrared Space Observatory by the European Space Agency in 1993. » astronomy; cryogenics; infrared radiation; observatory [i]

infrared photography Photography which uses wavelengths beyond visible red light, 700–900 nm. Black-and-white film has medical and forensic application; for example, it is used for camouflage detection, since chlorophyll in green living foliage reflects infrared strongly, unlike visually matching pigments. Multi-layer colour film including an infrared sensitive emulsion gives a false colour rendering in which natural vegetation appears red or magenta; this is used in aerial surveying. » photography; Plate III

infrared radiation Electromagnetic radiation of a wavelength a little longer than light, between 10^{-3} m and 7.8×10^{-7} m; discovered by German-British astronomer William Herschel in 1800. Emitted by oscillating and rotating molecules and atoms, and invisible to the naked eye, it is perceived by us as 'radiant heat'. Infrared detectors are used in night and smoke vision systems (for fire fighting), intruder alarms, weather forecasting, and missile guidance systems. » electromagnetic radiation [i]; Herschel; infrared astronomy/photography; radiometry [i]

infrasound Sound having a frequency of less than 20 Hz. Such waves cannot be heard by humans, but may be felt. Infrasonic waves are produced by explosions and by an unsteady airflow past an object. The study of infrasound is **infrasonics**. » sound

infrastructure The network of factors which enables a country's economy or an industrial operation to function effectively. They include such matters as transport, power, communication systems, housing, and education.

Inge, William Ralph (1860–1954) British divine, born at Crayke, Yorkshire. Educated at Eton and Cambridge, he taught at Eton and was vicar of All Saints, Kensington, before being appointed professor of divinity at Cambridge (1907). He then became Dean of St Paul's (1911–34). Author of many theological and devotional works, he earned for himself by his pessimistic prognostications in sermons and newspaper articles the sobriquet of 'the Gloomy Dean'. He died at Wallingford, Berkshire. » Christianity; theology

Ingres, Jean Auguste Dominique [ĩgruh] (1780–1867) French painter, the leading exponent of the classical tradition in France in the 19th-c, born at Montauban. He studied in Paris under David in 1796, and in 1801 won the Prix de Rome. He then lived in Rome (1806–20), where he began many of his famous nudes, including 'Baigneuse' and 'La Source' (completed 1859, Louvre). He became professor at the Ecole des Beaux-Arts, Paris, and director of the French Academy in Rome. He was made a Senator in 1862, and died in Paris. » classicism; David, Jacques; French art

inheritance tax A UK tax started in 1986 which replaced capital transfer tax. It is levied on the value of a deceased person's 'estate', and includes property, land, investments, and other valuable assets. Small estates are not liable to tax. » capital transfer tax; taxation

Initial Teaching Alphabet » **i.t.a.**

initiation rites Ceremonies effecting a transition from one social condition or role to another, especially from childhood to adulthood; also known as **passage rites**. They usually involve three stages; removing individuals from their old social status (*rites of separation*), transforming them in subsequent rites (*rites of transition*), and returning them in their 'reborn' social position back into the community (*rites of aggregation*).

injection The administration by a syringe of a drug or other pharmacological preparation in solution or suspension through a needle inserted into the skin (*intradermal*), underneath the skin (*subcutaneous*), into the muscle tissue (*intramuscular*), or into a vein (*intravenous*). » immunization; vaccination

injection engine » **fuel injection**

injection moulding A process used in the manufacture of plastics. Raw plastic, usually in granular form, is heated until soft enough to squeeze through a nozzle into a mould of the shape of the desired article. With thermoplastics, the mould is cold. With thermosetting resins, the mould is kept hot to promote the setting reactions. This type of manufacture is highly automated. » plastics

injunction A court order instructing a defendant to refrain from committing some act or, less commonly, to carry out some act; the term *interdict* is used in Scottish law. It is a remedy; for example, a prohibitory injunction might be granted to stop a continuing nuisance. » nuisance

ink A substance, usually coloured, used for writing, drawing, or printing. At its simplest, it is a solution of a pigment or dye in a liquid (eg soot in water). The production of the many kinds of inks required for commercial, educational, and cultural purposes has now become a sophisticated chemical-industrial process. » quill

ink-jet printer A type of fast and relatively quiet printer which produces characters or graphics by squirting very fine jets of rapid-drying ink onto paper. » printer, computer

inkcap A mushroom-like fungus with spore masses that appear dark brown or black; gills on cap liquefy by self-digestion as the spores mature; resulting black fluid can be boiled, strained, and used as ink. (Order: *Agaricales*. Family: *Coprinaceae*.) » fungus; mushroom

INLA » **Irish National Liberation Army**

inlaying A method of decorating furniture and other wooden objects by cutting away part of the surface of the solid material, and replacing it with a thin sheet of wood in another contrasting colour. Occasionally slivers of ivory, bone or shell are used in this way.

innateness hypothesis A controversial claim that the speed and efficiency with which children acquire language can be explained only by attributing to them a genetic predisposition for this particular task. They are thought to be born with an innate knowledge of at least some of the universal features of language structure, which they are able to apply to the facts of a particular language as they are exposed to them. The hypothesis was proposed by US linguist Noam Chomsky in the

1960s, and became a tenet of generative linguistic theory. » Chomsky; linguistics

Inner Mongolia, Chinese **Nei Mongol** pop(1982) 19 274 279; area 450 000 sq km/173 700 sq ml. Autonomous region in N China, bordered N by Mongolia and Russia; part of S border formed by Great Wall of China; two-thirds grasslands, remainder desert; Greater Khingan range (NE) rises to over 1 000 m/3 000 ft; Hetao Plain, fertile area N of Yellow R; several deserts further S; capital, Hohhot; principal town, Baotou; horse breeding, cattle and sheep rearing, forestry, iron and steel, coal mining; wheat now grown in irrigated areas. » China [i]; Great Wall of China; Mongolia [i]

Inner Temple » **Inns of Court**

Innocent III, originally **Lotario de' Conti di Segni** (1160–1216) Italian Pope (1198–1216), born at Agnagni. His pontificate is regarded as the high point of the temporal and spiritual supremacy of the Roman see. He judged between rival emperors in Germany, and had Otto IV deposed. He laid England under an interdict and excommunicated King John for refusing to recognize Stephen Langton as Archbishop of Canterbury. Under him the fourth Lateran Council was held in 1215. He died in Perugia. » John; Langton; pope

Innocents' Day » **Holy Innocents' Day**

Inns of Court Voluntary unincorporated societies having the exclusive right to confer the rank of barrister in England, Wales, and Northern Ireland. For England and Wales, four Inns have existed in London since the 14th-c: the Inner Temple, the Middle Temple, Lincoln's Inn, and Gray's Inn. The Inn of Court of Northern Ireland was established in Belfast in 1926. Each Inn is governed by its Benchers (Masters of the Bench). » barrister; Temple

Innsbruck [inzbruk] 47°17N 11°25E, pop(1981) 117 287. Capital of Tirol state, W Austria; in the valley of the R Inn, surrounded by mountains; a mediaeval old town, with narrow and irregular streets and tall houses in late Gothic style; a great tourist attraction, noted for its mountaineering course and tobogganing, and a popular winter skiing centre; 1964 and 1976 Winter Olympic Games held here; Alpine zoo; university (1914–23); glass, textiles; Goldenes Dachl ('golden roof', 1494–6); cathedral (1717–22); Hofburg (15th–16th-c palace), Hofkirche (Court Church, 1553–63), Altes Landhaus (1725–8); Tirolean Summer (Jul–Aug), Festival of Old Music (Aug), Innsbruck Fair (Sep), Alpine Folk Music Competition (Oct). » Austria [i]

inoculation » **immunization**

Inönü, Ismet [inernü], adopted name of **Ismet Paza** (1884–1973) Turkish soldier, statesman, and Prime Minister (1923–37, 1961–5), born at Izmir, Asia Minor. He fought in World War 1, then became Atatürk's Chief-of-Staff in the war against the Greeks (1919–22), defeating them twice at Inönü. As the first Premier of the new republic, he introduced many political reforms, and was elected President in 1938 on Atatürk's death. From 1950 he was leader of the Opposition, and became Premier again in 1961. He resigned in 1965, and died at Ankara. » Atatürk

inorganic chemistry That branch of chemistry which deals with the structures, properties, and reactions of the elements and compounds of elements other than carbon. » chemistry; organic chemistry

inositol A component of phytic acid in cereal and other vegetable foods. Some species (eg mice) require inositol for growth; humans do not, though large amounts are present in the body, especially in the brain.

input device A computer peripheral which can accept data and present that information in a suitable form to the central processing unit. Input devices include keyboards, graphic-tablets, and lightpens. » central processing unit; computer peripheral; graphics tablet; lightpen; mouse (computing)

input-output analysis In economics, an analysis which shows how materials and goods flow between industries, and where additional value is created. It enables economists to examine how the various sectors of an economy interrelate. Much of the work in this area has been carried out by Wassily Leontief. » Leontief

input-output bus (I/O bus) A system of wires or connections within a digital computer which is used to communicate information to and from peripheral devices. » address bus; computer peripheral; data bus

inquilinism [ingkwiluhnizm] An association between two different species, in which one (the *inquiline*) lives within another (the *host*) without causing harm. The term is also used for the relationship in which a species lives inside the burrow, nest, or other domicile of a host species. » biology; species; symbiosis

Inquisition A tribunal for the prosecution of heresy, originally of the mediaeval Christian Church. Pope Gregory IX (13th-c) gave special responsiblity to papal inquisitors to counter the threat to political and religious unity from heretical groups. The activities of the inquisitors were later characterized by extremes of torture and punishment, most notoriously in the case of the Spanish Inquisition, which survived until the 19th-c. » heresy; Roman Catholicism

INRI The first letters of the Latin wording of the inscription placed on Jesus' cross at Pilate's command (*John* 19.19–20): *Iesus Nazarenus, Rex Iudaeorum* ('Jesus of Nazareth, the king of the Jews'). » crucifixion; Jesus Christ; Pilate

insect An arthropod belonging to the largest and most diverse class of living organisms, the *Insecta*; c.1 million recognized species, estimated as representing a small fraction of the total world fauna; head typically bears a pair of feelers (*antennae*) and a pair of compound eyes; each of three thoracic segments bears a pair of legs, the last two also typically bear a pair of wings each; genital openings located at rear end of abdomen; known as fossils from the Devonian period. Insects exhibit varied habits, and are of vital importance as pollinators of plants, as pests, and as carriers of diseases. » alderfly; Arachnida; arthropod; beetle; centipede; cockroach; damselfly; Devonian period; dobsonfly; dragonfly; earwig; entomology; flea; fly; Hemiptera; Heteroptera; Homoptera; Hymenoptera; Lepidoptera; mayfly; millipede; mite; Neuroptera; nymph (entomology); Orthoptera; Phasmida; Protura; pupa; rock crawler; scorpion fly; spiracle; stonefly; termite; thrip; *see illustration p 610*

insecticide A substance which kills insects. Most commonly these are synthetic organic compounds, applied as sprays by farmers, but they may also be applied in granular or powder forms. There is current concern about these substances entering the food chain and having a detrimental impact on wildlife, and perhaps on humans. DDT was one of the most widely used insecticides in the postwar period; it is now banned in many countries, because of its persistence in the food chain. » DDT [i]; food chain

insectivore The most primitive of placental mammals, native to Africa, Europe, Asia, and N America; small with narrow pointed snouts; most are solitary, nocturnal; eats insects and other invertebrates. (Order: *Insectivora*, 345 species.) » hedgehog; mammal [i]; mole (biology); shrew; tenrec

insectivorous plant » **carnivorous plant**

insider dealing (UK) or **insider trading** (US) A business situation where an individual takes advantage of information about a company before it is made public, in order to make a profit (or avoid a loss) by dealing in the company's stocks or shares. It is illegal in most countries. In the UK it has been so since 1980, but there were few prosecutions until the Financial Services Act (1986) was passed, which gave the Department of Trade and Industry power to investigate and prosecute. However, it is not always easy to prove that such activities have taken place. » shares; stocks

insolation The amount of solar radiation (both diffuse and direct) which reaches the Earth. Insolation varies with latitude and season: it is consistently high at the Equator, and high at the Poles during the polar summer, but zero in winter. The amount of solar radiation which reaches the outer limit of the Earth's atmosphere is the *solar constant*, and is only a small proportion of the Sun's energy. Of the solar constant, 53% is lost before reaching the Earth's surface by scattering, absorption, and reflectance by clouds and dust. » albedo; solar constant; radiation; troposphere

insomnia Unsatisfactory sleep, whether in quantity or in quality. It may be a component of a variety of physical or

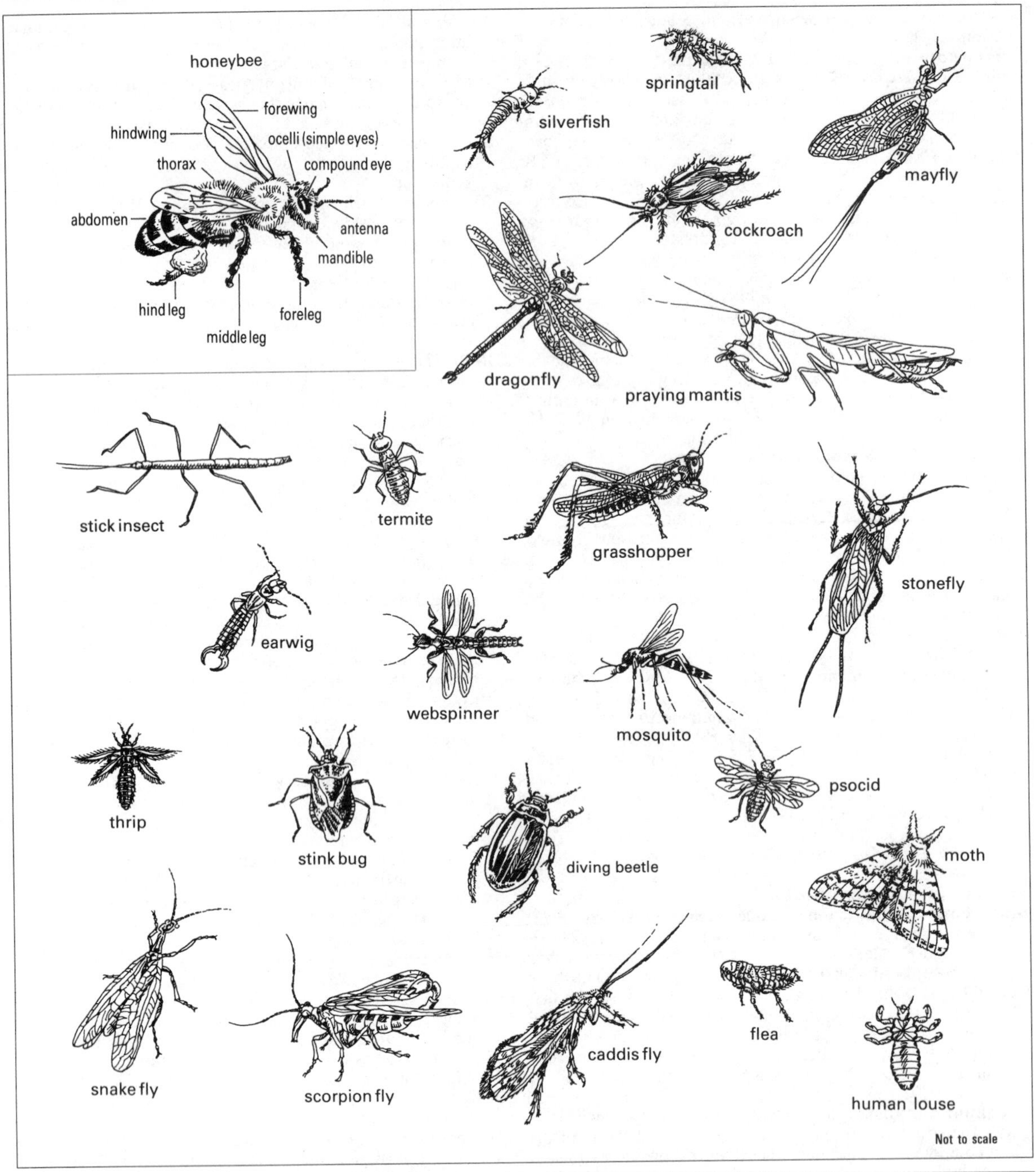

Insects – Representatives of each order, with inset of a typical insect (honeybee)

mental disorders. There may be difficulty in either initiating or maintaining sleep, a preoccupation about sleep, and interference with social and occupational functioning as a result of sleep disruption. » sleep; sleep-walking

installment credit » **hire purchase**

instinct An unlearned tendency to behave in a particular way. Instinctive behaviours are those actions or reactions to specific stimuli, shown in similar form by all normally-developed members of a species (or sex or age-group thereof), no specific life-experience being necessary for their emergence. The distinctive courtship-displays of several species are an illustration. » learning

Institute of Space and Astronautical Science (ISAS) of Japan An agency for space science research in Japan; established in 1981 by re-organizing the University of Tokyo's Institute of Space and Aeronautical Science. It is responsible for developing science spacecraft and launch vehicles (space applications programmes are the responsibility of the National Space Development Agency). Launches are made from Kagoshima Space Centre on Kyushu I at the S tip of Japan. » Sakigake and Suisei project; space exploration

instruction (computing) Usually the simplest form of command that can be recognized by a computer, ie a machine-code instruction. These perform relatively simple operations such as add, subtract, fetch, or store a value, and they must be combined to carry out more complicated operations. The complete set of machine-code instructions which a particular computer can recognize and carry out is known as an **instruction set**. » machine code

instrumental learning In psychology, an elementary learning process. An individual comes to perform a certain action more/less frequently or intensely than before, by virtue of that action having produced positive/negative consequences. » conditioning

instrumentalism A doctrine, enunciated by Dewey and others, which maintains that scientific theories are neither true nor false; they function solely as helpful explanatory tools. Scientific progress for an instrumentalist is not closer approximation to truth, but the replacement of theories by other theories more satisfactory in terms of simplicity, unification, and predictive power. » conventionalism; Dewey, John; realism

insulation » **thermal insulation**

insulator A material or covering which prevents or reduces the transmission of electricity, heat, or sound. All electrical devices are insulated for protection from the passage of electricity. Thermal insulators keep things hot, cold, or maintain an even temperature. Sound insulators act as mufflers. » thermal insulation

insulin A protein of vertebrates, secreted by B-cells of the islets of Langerhans (in the pancreas) in response to increases in blood glucose concentration (eg after a meal). It has widespread effects in the body, but its main action is to lower blood glucose concentration by accelerating its uptake by most tissues (except the brain), and promoting its conversion into glycogen and fat. Insulin-like substances are present in some invertebrates, but their significance is not known. » diabetes mellitus; glucose [i]; hypoglycaemia; pancreas

insurance A system of guarding an individual or institution against the possibility of an event occurring which will cause some harm – usually financial. The insured pays a fee (the *premium*) to an insurance company. The size of the premium (calculated by actuaries) depends on the size of the risk at stake, the number of premiums to be received, and the risk (or chance) of the event occurring. It is possible to obtain cover against most events. There are four main classes of insurance: marine, fire, life, and accident. An **insurance broker** is an agent for anyone who wishes to be insured, by finding others who are willing to underwrite the risk. Their commission is termed *brokerage*. » actuary; health/life/motor/national insurance; Lloyds

intaglio 1 A technique of printmaking. The design is incised into a metal plate, ink is forced into the cut lines and wiped off the rest of the surface; damp paper is laid on top; and both plate and paper are rolled through a press. This differs from other types of printing, in which the ink lies on the raised surface of the plate or block. » engraving; etching; relief printing; surface printing 2 A type of engraved gem in which the design is cut into the stone, instead of standing up in relief as in a *cameo*. » cameo

integers » **numbers**

integral calculus A system of mathematical rules, often defined as the inverse of differentiation, but developed on its own by Riemann and others as the limit of a sum. The region between a curve representing a function $f(x)$ and the x-axis is divided into n strips of equal width, each of which has an area less than that of one rectangle and greater than that of another rectangle. As n increases, the sums of the larger rectangles and of the smaller rectangles approach the same limit (assuming $f(x)$ is integrable), which is the *integral* over that interval. » differential calculus; Riemann

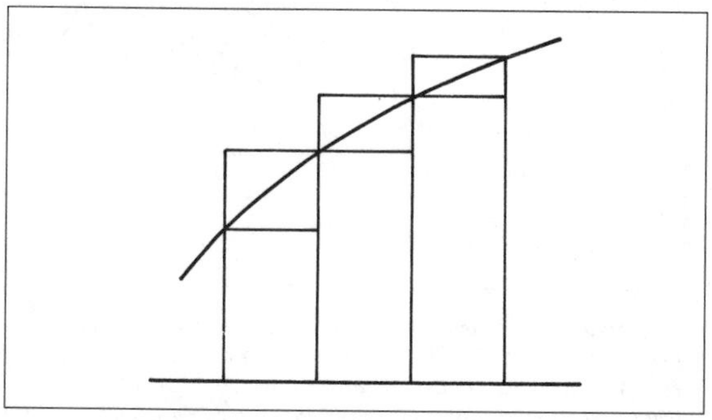

An integral as the limit of sums of areas of rectangles

integral tripack Material for colour photography with three separate emulsion coatings on one base, also termed **monopack**. In negative and reversal films the upper layer is sensitive to blue light, the middle to green, and the bottom to red. While processing after exposure, dye images are formed in each layer in colours complementary to their original sensitivity. » colour photography; tripack

integrated circuit A single chip of semiconductor, such as silicon, in which a large number of individual electronic components are assembled. Integrated circuits are smaller, lighter, and faster than conventional circuits. They use less power, are cheaper, and last longer. The circuit is usually made from pure silicon, doped with impurities – the type of impurity determining the job of that part of the chip: transistors, diodes, or resistors. When an integrated circuit fails, the whole chip is replaced, so making maintenance easier. Microelectronics using integrated circuits have made the development of sophisticated electronic watches and pocket calculators possible. » microchip; microelectronics; resistor; semiconductor; silicon; transistor

integrated optics The study of minute optical devices linked by light guides into single units containing several components. Such an integrated optical circuit might contain semiconductor lasers, modulators, and switches, all fabricated on a single chip. It may offer improved information-handling capacity, low weight, and high protection against interference, compared to conventional electronic chips. Currently experimental, its first likely applications will be in telecommunications. » optoelectronics; semiconductor laser; silicon chip

intelligence The ability to respond adaptively to novel situations. Psychologists attempt to measure this ability by constructing tests which appear related to intelligence, and extensively using these tests on a target population, so enabling them to assess the mental age of any individual. (For a given score on a particular test, mental age is the average age of those members of the tested population having this score.) **IQ (Intelligence Quotient)** equals Mental Age divided by actual (Chronological) Age. It is usual to distinguish **fluid intelligence** (mental flexibility) from **crystallized intelligence** (knowledge). Statistical techniques such as factor analysis can be used to identify various subcategories of ability, particularly **verbal** and **non-verbal intelligence**. A general intelligence factor derived by these methods is sometimes called *Spearman's g*. » cognitive psychology; comparative psychology; factor analysis; mental handicap

intelligence service A state agency which gathers information regarded as important to state security concerning foreign threats. In democratic countries it is usually kept separate from internal security agencies, whereas in such countries as the USSR the KGB was responsible both for external espionage and internal counter-intelligence. In the USA and UK, the CIA and MI5 respectively are examples of the former, while the FBI and MI6 are examples of the latter. The operations of such agencies are more or less secret in nature, but in the USA much more information is available about the work of the intelligence service than is the case in the UK, where governments do not officially recognize the existence of MI5. The extent to which the UK government is concerned to suppress all information relating to MI5 operations was apparent in the lengthy court battle in Australia and the UK to prevent publication, or reporting in the media, of the book *Spycatcher*. This was written by Peter Wright, a former intelligence officer, who alleged misconduct and 'misuse' of the law by MI5, in particular as it related to a 'plot' to destabilize the Wilson government of the 1970s. The government's claim that former members of the security forces are bound by a life-long duty of confidentiality was upheld by a House of Lords judgment in 1988, but the Lords rejected the claim that other parties receiving confidential information from a Crown servant in all circumstances were so bound. This judgment had implications for the government's attempts to reform the Official Secrets Act. » Central Intelligence Agency; Federal Bureau of Investigation; open government

intension The meaning or connotation of a singular or general term, contrasted with its extension or reference. The intensions of *the morning star* and *the evening star* are different (the terms are not synonymous) but their extension is identical – the planet Venus. » connotation

intensive care The continuous monitoring of several bodily vital functions in very seriously ill patients and in premature infants. The variables most commonly assessed (depending on the nature of the illness) are systemic arterial blood pressure, heart output, central venous blood pressure, pulmonary artery blood pressure, blood oxygen, carbon dioxide, sugar and acidity, the electrical activity of the heart, pulse and respiratory rate, and body temperature. These are usually assessed and recorded electronically. Supervision is needed to detect dangerous deviations from normal in these functions, and to supervise life support systems such as assisted respiratory machines, artificial kidneys, and pumps supplying the intravenous administration of fluids, blood, antibiotics, or anticoagulants.

intensive farming Farming with relatively high input levels, especially of fertilizers, sprays, and pharmaceuticals. It produces higher yields per hectare, which may compensate for limited farm size and allow the small farmer to make an acceptable income. » extensive farming; factory farming

intentional fallacy A term used by the US literary critic W K Wimsatt to identify the mistake of grounding meaning in what a writer intended or professed to say rather than what the work actually available to the reader *does* say, or appears to say. The idea was very influential within New Criticism. » literary criticism; New Criticism

intentionality A feature of mental phenomena which distinguishes them from physical phenomena; a position espoused by Brentano, and others. One's thought of gold is directed at gold: gold is the object or content of the thought. Unlike physical relations, psychological attitudes such as beliefs and desires can be directed towards objects which do not exist: one can search for the Fountain of Youth, but not drink from it. Brentano was among the first to emphasize the importance of intentionality, but the concept is now widely invoked not only by philosophers of mind but also (and controversially) by specialists in artificial intelligence and cognitive science. » artificial intelligence

Inter-American Development Bank An international bank set up in 1959 to finance economic development projects in S and C America. The main subscribers are the USA, Argentina, Brazil, Mexico, and Venezuela.

interactive computing A mode of computing in which the user converses with the computer and receives a fairly rapid response. Almost all microcomputers work in an interactive mode, as can most larger computers. » batch processing; PRESTEL; real-time computing

interactive video A closed-circuit recorded video system in which the display responds to the instructions of the viewer. Applications range from simple press-button or touch-screen question-and-answer interactions to complex branched learning programmes. » closed circuit television

intercellular fluid » **interstitial fluid**

intercontinental ballistic missile (ICBM) A very large, long-range nuclear-armed missile developed by the USA and Soviet Union from the late 1950s onwards. ICBMs are based in silos spread out over a wide land mass. They are capable of delivering a load of independently-targetted nuclear warheads (MIRVs) on the enemy heartland some 30 minutes after launch. » ballistic missile; MIRV

interest The amount of money charged by a person or institution that lends a sum to a borrower. The sum lent, on which interest is calculated, is known as the *principal*. The lender will be paid a small percentage of the principal as interest on the loan, the rate of interest depending on the amount of the principal, the length of time the loan is outstanding, and the risk involved. Interest rates in general vary according to the state of the economy. Economists regard interest as the price of money, the rate rising and falling as the demand for money rises and falls. The **interest rate** is the percentage payable; for example, an 8% interest rate on £100 gives the lender £8 interest at the end of a year. The **annual percentage rate** (APR) shows the actual rate of interest payable on borrowings, especially hire-purchase agreements, where interest has to be paid more often than once a year. In **simple interest**, the interest gained in a given year is paid to the lender, so that the principal available does not change from year to year. In **compound interest**, the interest gained in a given year is not paid to the lender, but is added to the principal, which thereby increases year by year. » hire purchase; money-market funding

interest group » **pressure group**

interest profiles » **selective dissemination of information**

interference In physics, the result of two or more waves of similar frequency passing through the same point simultaneously. It is usual to consider simplified interference (*superposition*), in which the net result of waves overlapping is described by the simple addition of the original waves. An interference pattern is determined by the relative phases of the constituent waves. Beats and diffraction are interference effects. Interference is a property of all types of waves, including light. However, light beams arriving at a point from two ordinary light bulbs do not appear to produce such patterns. This arises from the mixture of colours in such light, as well as from incoherence (ie if a maximum of one wave corresponds to the maximum of another at one moment, such a relationship will not exist moments later). Light waves arriving from two independent bulbs are incoherent. Although at any one instant interference occurs, no stable pattern is formed. To observe

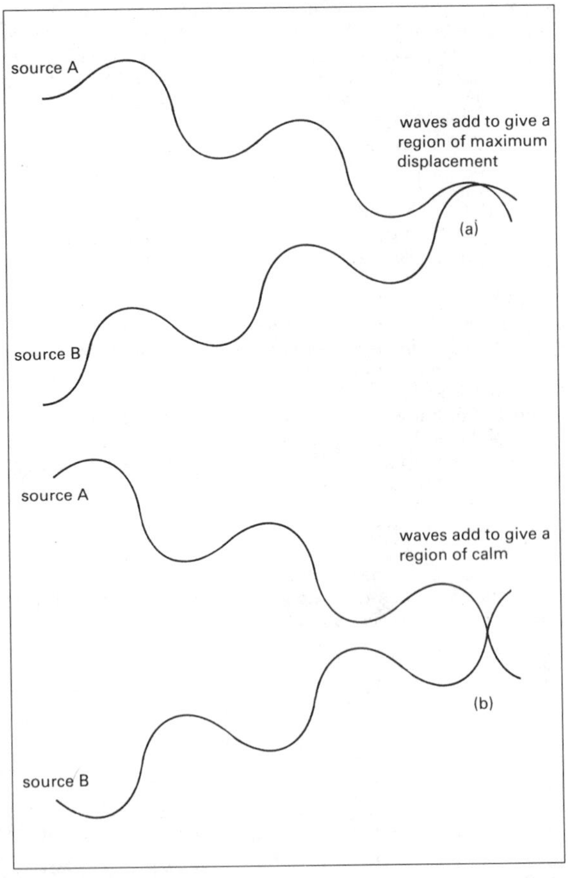

The waves are crossing one another's paths. At the crossing point, the waves will add. If the two crests are coincident (a), the maximum disturbance will be produced. Should the crest of one wave coincide with the trough of the other (b), the crossing point appears calm.

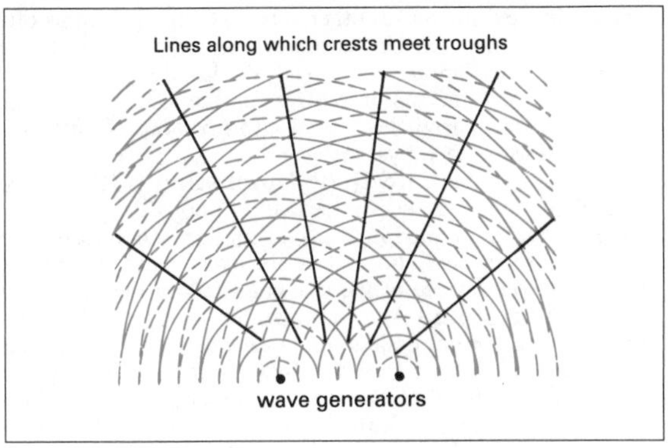

Waves produced by two synchronized mechanical wave generators. Waves from each source separately would appear as concentric circles (dotted lines). With the sources working together, the waves interfere to give a pattern of maximum disturbance (solid lines) and minimum disturbance. This is an interference pattern, *which is stationary in time even though the waves themselves are moving.*

interference in light, it is necessary to use light of a single colour from a single source, with the beam divided into two parts which are then brought together at a screen. Using such an arrangement, and passing a beam through two narrow parallel slits to divide it, British physicist Thomas Young observed such interference, and concluded that light was a wave (1804). Lasers provide an ideal light source. Interference is exploited in interferometers, including certain telescopes, compact disc players, phased-array radar, and holography. » Aharanov-Bohm effect; beats; coherence; diffraction [i]; holography; interferometer; phase; wave (physics) [i]; Young, Thomas

interferometer A device which relies on monitoring the interference pattern formed by combining two wave beams, usually light, derived from a single source. Changes to one beam, for example by passing it through some gas, produce changes in the interference pattern. The technique is used in the study of gas flow, in wind tunnels, and in plasma physics. The laser ring gyroscope is a type of interferometer. » interference [i]

interferons A class of protein molecules produced by body cells that are part of the body's defences against infection, notably by viruses. Their mode of action remains obscure. They are extremely potent substances, but cells need to be exposed to them for several hours before resistance to a virus develops. Interferons appear to inhibit the multiplication of viruses within cells, and to stimulate the immune system to combat infection. Some interferons, produced by genetic engineering technology, are currently being tested as drugs for viral infection and some cancers. Clinical trials suggest that they are beneficial in some leukaemias, myeloma, and non-Hodgkin's lymphoma, but their use in medical practice remains uncertain. » blood; cancer; cell; genetic engineering; immunity; leukaemia; lymphoma (non-Hodgkin's); myeloma; virus

intergalactic medium A general term for the material isolated in space far from any galaxy. Theoretical considerations suggest that an enormous quantity of undetected material exists, far exceeding the contribution from visible galaxies. » galaxy

Intergovernmental Maritime Consultative Organization » **United Nations**

interior design The design of the interior of a building; usually concerned with decoration, furniture, and fittings rather than the permanent fabric of the building, and carried out only after all other work has been completed. The work of the Renaissance artists such as Raphael and Michaelangelo, of the 18th-c Robert Adam, and of the 19th-c Arts and Crafts Movement might all be called interior design, but the term is usually restricted to the 20th-c profession. » Adam, Robert; Arts and Crafts Movement; Georgian Style; Renaissance architecture

Intermediate Nuclear Force Treaty A treaty signed (Dec 1987) in Washington by US President Reagan, and USSR General Secretary Gorbachev, involving the elimination of 1 286 missiles from Europe and Asia, and over 2 000 warheads. It was noted for its inclusion of the most comprehensive and stringent verification procedures ever seen in an arms control treaty, including short notice on-site verification, and was regarded as a major break in the arms race and a step forward in arms control. » guided missile; nuclear weapons

intermedin » **melanocyte-stimulating hormone**

intermezzo An instrumental piece, especially for piano, in a lyrical style and in no prescribed form. The title has been used by Brahms and other 19th–20th-c composers. Earlier it was used for short, comic interludes performed on stage between the acts of a serious opera; Pergolesi's *La serva padrona* (1733) is a famous example. » Brahms; Pergolesi

internal combustion engine An engine (such as a diesel or petrol engine) which burns its fuel/air mixture within the engine as part of its operating cycle. This cycle may be *two stroke* (one power stroke for every two strokes of the piston) or *four stroke* (one power stroke for every four strokes of the piston). » carburettor; diesel/gas/Wankel engine; motorcycle

internal energy In thermodynamics, the difference between the heat supplied to a system and the work done by that system on its surroundings; symbol U, units J (joule). In general, adding heat to a system will increase its internal energy, corresponding to an increase in the system's temperature. » enthalpy; heat; thermodynamics

International An abbreviation of **International Working Men's Association**, the name given to attempts to establish international co-operative organizations of socialist, communist, and revolutionary groups. The **First International** was created in 1848 by Marx, and inspired the Communist Manifesto. The **Second International** was formed in Paris in 1889, and still survives as a forum for reformist socialist parties. The **Third International** (Comintern) was founded by Lenin, and represented communist parties until abolished in 1943. There was a brief attempt in the 1930s by Trotsky to launch a **Fourth International**. » Comintern; communism; Lenin; Marx; Trotsky

International Amateur Athletic Federation (IAAF) The supreme governing body which controls athletics worldwide. Founded in Stockholm in July 1912 with 17 members, membership now exceeds 170. The IAAF is responsible for ratifying world records. » athletics

International Atomic Energy Agency (IAEA) An international agency which promotes research and development into the peaceful uses of nuclear energy, and oversees a system of safeguards and controls governing the misuse of nuclear materials for military purposes. Founded in 1957, and based in Vienna, in 1990 it had 113 member countries. » nuclear physics/reactor [i]

International Baccalaureate An award taken by 18-year-old school leavers, and accepted in most countries as a qualification for entry to higher education. Particularly popular in international schools or with students whose parents have to work abroad, the examination covers a spread of subjects including languages, mathematics, science, humanities, and the arts. » tertiary education

International Bank for Reconstruction and Development (IBRD) A bank, generally known as the **World Bank**, founded in 1945, to help raise standards of living in the developing countries. It is affiliated to the United Nations, and based in Washington, DC. » Bretton Woods Conference; International Development Association; United Nations

International Brigades In the Spanish Civil War (1936–9), foreign volunteer forces recruited by the Comintern and by individual communist parties to assist the Spanish Republic. Almost 60 000 volunteers, mostly workers, fought in Spain between October 1936 and the brigade's withdrawal in October 1938, playing a particularly important role in the defence of Madrid (1936–7). » Comintern; Spanish Civil War

International Bureau for American Republics » **Pan-American Union**

International Cometary Explorer (ICE) project The first space mission to encounter a comet, flying through the dust and ion tails of the periodic Comet Giacobini-Zinner (11 Sep 1985). Originally launched in 1978 as the International Sun-Earth Explorer to monitor solar wind at Earth-Sun libration point L1, it was retargeted to the comet in 1983 by means of a series of propulsive manoeuvres, multiple Earth swing-bys, and a final close lunar flyby which added the gravitational energy needed to place the spacecraft on a comet-intercept trajectory. It made the first measurements of the interaction of a comet with the solar wind, and demonstrated an ability to survive a high speed (21 km/13 ml per sec) encounter with cometary dust. It was managed by NASA's Goddard Space Flight Center. » comet; libration; Solar System; solar wind

International Confederation of Free Trade Unions (ICFTU) An association of some 114 trade union federations from 89 countries in W Europe, USA, and the British Commonwealth, located in Brussels, and founded in 1949. It was created after withdrawing from the World Federation of Trade Unions because of differences with the communist unions. Its aim is collaboration between free and democratic trade unions throughout the world. » trade union; World Federation of Trade Unions

International Court of Justice A court established by the United Nations for the purpose of hearing international law disputes; known widely as the 'World Court'. Nation states must consent to the jurisdiction of the court with regard to contentious proceedings. The court sits at The Hague, Netherlands, and is presided over by 15 judges. » Hague Agreement; international law; United Nations

International Development Association (IDA) An organization affiliated to, but distinct from, the International Bank for Reconstruction and Development, based in Washington, DC. It was set up in 1960 to provide help to the world's 50 poorest countries by giving them aid on very easy terms.

International Gothic A style of art which flourished in W Europe c.1375–c.1425, characterized by jewel-like colour, graceful shapes, and realistically-observed details. The style was seen especially in miniature paintings, drawings, and tapestries, often representing secular themes from courtly life. » Gothic art

International Labour Organization An autonomous agency associated with the League of Nations, founded in 1919, which became a specialized agency of the United Nations in 1946. A tripartite body representing governments, employers, and workers, it is concerned with industrial relations and the pay, employment, and working conditions of workers. » League of Nations; United Nations

international law The law that governs relationships between nation states. It is based principally on custom; there is no worldwide international legislature, and thus the enforcement of international law may pose problems. Although there is an International Court, it may not be able to adjudicate in a particular case. Alternative use of sanctions may well be unsatisfactory if the injured state is less powerful than the wrongdoer. The United Nations Security Council has a limited power to impose sanctions on behalf of member states. » immunity, diplomatic; International Court of Justice; law; sea, law of the; space law

International Monetary Fund (IMF) A financial agency affiliated to the United Nations, and located in Washington, DC. It was formed in 1945 to promote international monetary co-operation, the expansion of international trade, and exchange rate stability, and to give financial assistance to states in need. » Bretton Woods Conference

international monetary system A financial system which enables international trade to function effectively. Until 1914, the pound sterling was the currency in which most world trade was conducted. By 1945, the US dollar had taken over the role. The Bretton Woods Agreement established exchange rates for most major currencies which linked the dollar to the price of gold. By 1973 this system was working less well, and was abandoned in favour of the present system of floating exchange rates. The USA allows the dollar to float freely, without government intervention. The governments of most other Western countries intervene from time to time to control the exchange rates of their currencies by, for example, raising or lowering interest rates. The EEC nations are now moving towards a linked currency system. Some countries have convertible currencies, in that they can be bought and sold freely and exchanged for one another. The developing nations often restrict movement of their currency and the export of foreign exchange. The 'money markets' of London, New York, and Tokyo are the major centres for the sale and purchase of convertible currencies. » Bretton Woods Conference; European Monetary System

International Standard Book Numbering (ISBN) A system of ten-digit numbers allocated to books on publication. Internationally adopted in 1971, it simplifies identification and ordering, since each book has its own individual number printed on the reverse of the title page and on the back cover.

International Style 1 A term sometimes used by art historians to refer to the more or less homogeneous Gothic style which flourished throughout Europe c.1400. » International Gothic **2** A term first used in the USA to describe a new style of architecture developed in the 1920s, principally in Europe; also known as the **Modern Movement**. It is characterized by geometric shapes, an absence of decoration and historical references, white rendered walls, flat roofs, large expanses of glass, pilotis, and asymmetrical compositions. It was at first particularly concerned with low-income, standardized housing projects. » Bauhaus; De Stijl; functionalism (art and architecture); pilotis; Post-Modernism; prefabrication; rationalism

International Telecommunication Union (ITU) An agency of the United Nations, which since 1947 has promoted worldwide co-operation in all aspects of telecommunications, such as the regulation of radio frequencies. The ITU produces a monthly 'Telecommunication Journal' in separate English, French, and Spanish editions from its Geneva headquarters. » broadcasting; United Nations

International UN Agencies (International Atomic Energy Authority/Civil Aviation Organization/Court of Justice/Development Association/Finance Corporation/Fund for Agricultural Development/Telecommunication Union) » **United Nations**; RR37

International Union for the Conservation of Nature and Natural Resources (IUCN) An international organization which exists to promote sustainable use and conservation of natural resources. Founded in 1948, and based in Switzerland, it has 500 member organizations from 116 countries. Its Commissions consist of more than 2 000 conservation experts. It publishes Red Data books which list endangered species of plants and wildlife, and administers the Convention on International Trade in Endangered Species. » conservation (earth sciences); endangered species; World Wide Fund for Nature

International Union of Pure and Applied Chemistry » **IUPAC**

International Working Men's Association » **International**

International Youth Hostel Association In the UK and 49 other countries, an organization which provides simple, low-cost accommodation for those wishing to travel. In many youth hostels the guests cook their own meals and help with the cleaning; in some countries there is a maximum age limit for guests.

interplanetary matter Material in the Solar System other than the planets and their satellites. It includes streams of charged particles from the solar wind, dust, meteorites, and comets. » Solar System

interpolation In mathematics, estimating an intermediate value of a variable between two known values of that variable; for example, if $f(1)$ and $f(2)$ are known, estimating $f(1.1)$. **Linear interpolation** is the form used most frequently, which assumes that the function $f(x)$ is linear. Then if $x_0 < x_0 + h < x_1$, $f(x_0 + h) = h\dfrac{f(x_1) - f(x_0)}{x_1 - x_0}$. If $x_1 - x_0$ is small, this is likely to be a good approximation. **Extrapolation** is estimating a value of a variable *outside* the interval between two known values; for example, if $f(1)$ and $f(2)$ are known, estimating $f(2.1)$. This is often not justified mathematically, but may be necessary in making projections for the future.

interpreter A computer program which translates (*interprets*) the source code of a high-level computer language, line by line, into a set of machine-code instructions, which are immediately executed by the computer. It differs in this respect from a *compiler*, which checks and translates the entire source code into a set of machine-code instructions in one operation. » compiler

intersection (mathematics) » **set**

intersexuality Abnormal sexual development, either because of anomalies in the normal complement of sex chromosomes (XX in the female and XY in the male) or as a result of faults in the development of gonads in the early embryo. Thus babies may be born whose sex is in doubt, while in other cases intersex or ambiguous sexual states may be suspected only at puberty. Detailed chromosomal studies, the estimation of sex hormone secretions, and biopsy of sex glands may be needed to disentangle what is a complex but rare problem. » chromosome [i]; gonad

interstellar molecule More than 50 species of molecule are found within the gas nebulae of the interstellar medium, particularly in cold dense clouds. The most common include CO, H_2O, NH_3, HCHO, CH_4, and CH_3OH. » molecule

interstitial cell-stimulating hormone » **luteinizing hormone**

interstitial fluid That part of the extracellular fluid which lies outside the vascular system and surrounds the tissue cells of animals; also known as **tissue fluid** and **intercellular fluid**. It is similar in composition to blood plasma, except for a relatively low protein content (due to the low permeability of capillaries to plasma proteins). » extracellular fluid; plasma (physiology)

intertidal zone » **benthic environments**

intertropical convergence zone (ITCZ) A discontinuous zone of low pressure around the Equator, on which the NE and SE trade winds converge. The converging air rises, lowering the atmospheric pressure, and convective clouds form, associated with heavy precipitation. The ITCZ coincides approximately with the heat equator, and shifts N and S with the seasons, through about 5° of latitude. The zone is weakly defined over the oceans, particularly in the areas known as the Doldrums. » atmospheric pressure; Doldrums; general circulation model; monsoon climates; trade winds

interval In mathematics, all numbers between two fixed numbers *a* and *b* form an **open interval**, written (a,b). If the numbers *a* and *b* are themselves included in the interval, this is called a **closed interval** $[a,b]$. *a* and *b* are the *limits* of the interval. An open interval is represented on the number-line with the end-circles unshaded; a closed interval has shaded end-circles.

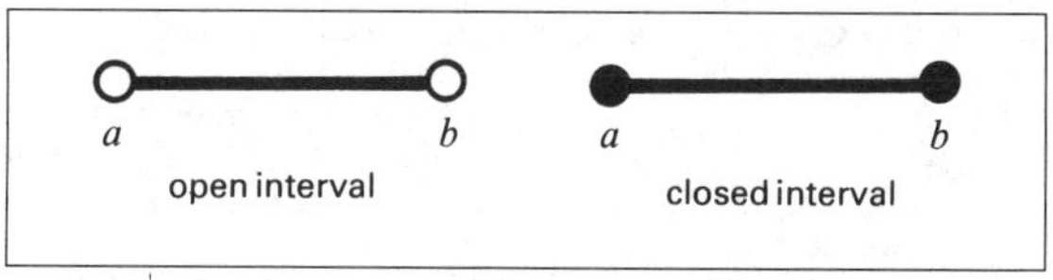

Interval

intestacy The situation where a person dies without having made a will. In the case of a *partial intestacy*, the will does not provide for the disposal of the entire estate. » property

intestine A tube of muscular membrane extending from the pyloric opening of the stomach to the anus, generally divided into the **small intestine** (*duodenum*, *jejunum*, and *ileum*), the **large intestine** (*caecum*, *appendix*, and the *ascending*, *transverse*, *descending*, and *sigmoid colon*), and the **rectum**. Most digestion and absorption of digestive products, vitamins, and fluids (both ingested and secreted from the gastro-intestinal tract) occurs in the small intestine, while the large intestine absorbs electrolytes and water from the fluid that enters it, as well as synthesizing vitamin K and some B complex vitamins, and forming the faeces ready for expulsion from the body. The rectum lies in contact with the pelvic surface of the sacrum, and pierces the pelvic diaphragm to become the anus. » abdomen; alimentary canal; coeliac disease; colic; colitis; diverticulitis; dysentery; hernia; malabsorbtion; peritoneum; rectum; Plate XII

intifada [intifa**h**da] » **West Bank**

Intimisme [inteemeezm] A modern art movement that flourished from c.1890 in France. Vuillard's quiet little paintings and lithographs of Montmartre, and Bonnard's more colourful nudes and family scenes typify the movement. » Bonnard; French art; Impressionism; Vuillard

Intolerable Acts (1774) The American name for laws passed by Parliament to punish Massachusetts for the Boston Tea Party (1773). They were the Boston Port Act, the Massachusetts Government Act, the Administration of Justice Act, and a Quartering Act. » Boston Tea Party

intonaco » **fresco**

intonation The melody of an utterance, brought about by the distinctive use of pitch patterns in sentences. It has several functions, notably the marking of grammatical structure (eg statements with a falling pitch, and questions with a rising pitch), and the expression of speaker attitudes (eg surprise, sympathy, irony). » prosody

intra-ocular lens implantation A perspex lens introduced into the front chamber of the eye following surgical removal of a cataract. The power of the lens chosen is calculated from the curvature of the cornea and the length of the eye. » eye [i]; lens

intra-uterine device » **contraception**

intracellular fluid The fluid contained within cells. In humans the total adult volume is about 28 l/49 UK pt/59 US pt. Its composition varies from tissue to tissue depending on their functions. Its principal components (apart from water) are potassium ions, organic phosphates, and proteins. » extracellular fluid; interstitial fluid

Intracoastal Waterway A shipping route extending 5 000 km/3 100 ml from Boston, Massachusetts to Key West, Florida (the **Atlantic Intracoastal Waterway**) and from Apalachee Bay, Florida, to Brownsville, Texas (the **Gulf Intracoastal Waterway**). The waterway is composed of natural water routes, such as bays and rivers, linked by canals. It is used by both commercial and pleasure craft. » canal

intravenous feeding Nutrients given to a patient through a tube which enters the bloodstream directly via a vein; also known as *parenteral nutrition*. All nutrients used are of basic structure, ie glucose and not starch; amino acids and not protein. » amino acid [i]; glucose [i]

Intrepid » **Stephenson, William**

intron A non-coding sequence of DNA that occurs within a gene, separating two parts of the coding sequence. In the translation of the genetic instructions into protein, the introns are excised and the coding portions spliced together. » DNA [i]; gene

introversion/extraversion Psychological terms formerly used as two categories of personality ('introvert', 'extravert'). The distinction is now considered to be a dimension with high levels of extraversion and introversion at the extremes. Strongly extraverted individuals are sociable, excitement-seeking, and carefree. They are often aggressive, may lose their temper quickly, and be unreliable. Strongly introverted individuals are quiet, reserved, and have few friends. They dislike excitement, are reliable, serious-minded, and like a well-ordered life. These behavioural differences are thought to have a biological basis in cortical and subcortical arousal systems. » personality

intrusive rock Igneous rock formed by the emplacement and crystallization of magma formed at depth into higher levels of the Earth's crust. Igneous intrusions form a variety of rock masses. » batholith; dyke (geology); sill

intuitionism The metaethical position, defended by the Scottish philosopher William David Ross (1877–1971), according to which the truth or falsity of moral judgments is ascertained by a special mental faculty, not by empirical means. Intuitionists, unlike naturalists, believe that the facts obtainable through sense experience are insufficient to tell us what is good and bad, right and wrong. » ethics; naturalism

Inuit » **Eskimo**

Invalides, Hôtel des [ohtel dayzăvah**leed**] A hospital for the care of old and disabled soldiers, founded in Paris by Louis XIV and built in 1671–6. The main building, which now houses fewer than 100 soldiers and is mainly given over to a museum, was designed by Libéral Bruant (c.1635–97). In the courtyard stands Hardouin-Mansart's St Louis Church, where Napoleon's tomb has rested since 1840. » Paris [i]

invar An alloy containing 65% iron with 35% nickel. It has very low thermal expansion, and hence is used in surveying rods and pendulum bars. » alloy; iron; nickel

Inverness 57°27N 4°15W, pop (1981) 40010. Capital of Highland region, NE Scotland; at mouth of R Ness, 181 km/112 ml NW of Edinburgh; airfield; railway; NE terminus of the Caledonian Canal; electronics, distilling, boatbuilding, textiles, tourism; Inverness museum and art gallery, castle (Victorian); battle site of Culloden Moor (1746), 8 km/5 ml E; Highland games (Jul). » Caledonian Canal; Culloden Moor, Battle of; Highland; Scotland [i]

inversion temperature » **Joule-Thompson effect**

invert sugar » **sucrose** [i]

invertebrate A multicellular animal that lacks a vertebral column. It includes the vast majority (over 97%) of all animal species. » vertebral column

Investiture Controversy (1075–1122) A conflict between reforming popes and lay rulers, notably the German emperor, over the leadership of Christian society. It was named after the royal practice of investing a newly appointed bishop or abbot with a ring or pastoral staff, the symbols of his spiritual office. This was condemned in 1075 by Pope Gregory VII as epitomizing secular domination of the Church.

investment In general terms, putting money into an activity, institution, or object, in the expectation of obtaining further financial benefit. Examples include buying ('investing in') antiques in the hope of having their value appreciate, or lending to a building society in order to obtain interest. In finance, the term refers specifically to the purchase of securities, such as bonds or shares in companies. In business, it refers to the purchase of physical resources, such as property, machinery, and equipment in order to carry out some business venture and gain a return after a period of time. Economists distinguish three types: investment in new plant and equipment; new residential housing; and stocks of materials or goods. » interest; investment bank/company; portfolio theory

investment bank A US bank handling new share issues, often in a syndicate with others. It may buy all the shares on offer and then resell them to the general public, in effect underwriting the issue. It is similar in function to the British merchant bank. » investment; merchant bank

investment company or **investment trust** A company which holds a portfolio of shares in a range of other companies, aimed at obtaining a reasonable dividend yield, growth, and with less risk (ie a *balanced* portfolio). Such a company is of value to investors without experience or time, who wish to invest in the stock market. » investment; open-ended investment company; unit trust

invisibles The export and import of services; opposed to goods, which are known as **visibles**. Invisible exports include tourism, shipping, air freight, banking, insurance, and other financial services. They are a major contributor to a country's balance of payments. » balance of payments

Inyangani, Mount [inyang**gah**nee] 18°18S 32°54E. Highest peak in Zimbabwe; rises to 2592 m/8504 ft near the Mozambique frontier. » Zimbabwe [i]

Io (astronomy) [**iy**oh] The first natural satellite of Jupiter, discovered by Galileo in 1610; distance from the planet 422000 km/262000 ml; diameter 3650 km/5850 ml; orbital period 1.769 days. It is the most volcanically active object in the Solar System, being in a state of continuous eruption; fountains of gases and fine particles have been observed by Voyager to reach altitudes of 280 km/175 ml. The volcanic features are found across the entire body, including hot regions that may be lava lakes. » Galilean moons; ionosphere; Jupiter (astronomy); Voyager project [i]; RR4

Io (mythology) [**iy**oh] In Greek mythology, the daughter of Inachos of Argos. She was beloved by Zeus, who turned her into a heifer to save her from Hera's jealousy. Hera kept her under the gaze of the Argus; but she escaped with Hermes's help. She was then punished with a gad-fly which drove her through the world until she arrived in Egypt. There Zeus changed her back into human shape, and she gave birth to Epaphos, ancestor of many peoples. » Argus 1

iodine I, element 53, melting point 114°C. A violet solid with a sharp odour; a halogen, not found free in nature, but as an impurity in sodium nitrate deposits, and concentrated in kelp and other seaweeds. It is an essential element in biological systems, and lack of it causes goitre in humans. Its compounds show oxidation numbers of −1, +1, +3, +5, and +7. » chemical elements; goitre; halogens; RR90

iodoform [iy**oh**duhfawm] CHI_3, triiodomethane, melting point 119°C. A yellow solid with a peculiar odour, used as a mild antiseptic.

ion An atom which has lost one or more electrons (a *positive* ion) or which has gained one or more electrons (a *negative* ion). Atoms with a net positive charge are called **cations**; those with a net negative charge, **anions**. The type and magnitude of a charge is indicated by a superscript; for example, the positively charged sodium ion is identified as Na^+, and the negatively charged chloride ion as Cl^-. The formation of ions is called **ionization**: they may be formed by firing light or electrons on to atoms, or by passing an electric spark through gas. Ions are present in all animal and plant cells, where they are involved in many important and diverse roles, including the activation of enzymes, osmotic balance, muscle contraction, and nerve impulse conduction. » action potential: atom; electrolysis [i]; electron; extracellular fluid; ion trap; proton

ion engine An engine designed to propel spacecraft or manoeuvre satellites by means of the reaction caused by the discharge of charged particles (*ions*). These particles are accelerated within the engine by means of electrostatic fields. The continuous discharge of ions produces a charge of opposite polarity in the vehicle, which must be removed. This is usually accomplished by discharging separately charged negative and positive beams and recombining them behind the vehicle. The engine has an energy source, such as a nuclear reactor, and a conversion system that converts the reactor's heat into electricity. The electricity is then used to convert a propellant (such as argon) into an ionized state, and then to accelerate it. » engine; ion

ion plating Coating a metal surface by exposing it to ions of a metal, generated by discharge or thermionically. The ions are directed to the metal by making it the cathode in a low pressure discharge circuit. Non-conductors may also be ion-plated by siting them in a shielded region of ion transfer. The special value of the process is its ability to coat intricate and convoluted surfaces uniformly and firmly. » ion; metal

ion trap A device for confining ions slowed by laser cooling to a region typically less than a centimetre across. It relies on a system of electric and magnetic fields. Ions may be trapped singly or in clusters, thus enabling the study of their properties, such as atomic energy levels, lifetimes, and reactions. » atom trap; ion; laser cooling

Iona [iy**oh**na] A remote island off Mull, W Scotland, the site of a monastery established in AD 563 by the Irish missionary St Columba and 12 companions to convert the inhabitants of N Britain to Christianity. The monastery flourished until the onset of Viking attacks (c.800), then declined until c.1200, when a Benedictine abbey was founded on the site. » Benedictines; Columba, St; Lindisfarne; Vikings

Ionesco, Eugene [yo**nes**koh] (1912–) French playwright, born at Slatina, Romania. He was educated at Bucharest and Paris, where he settled before World War 2. After the success of *La Cantatrice chauve* (1950, The Bald Soprano), he became a prolific writer of one-act plays which came to be seen as typical examples of the Theatre of the Absurd. His later, full-length plays centre around a constant, semi-autobiographical figure, Berenger. Since 1970, his writing has been mainly non-theatrical, including essays, children's stories, and a novel. » absurdism; drama; theatre

Ionia [iy**oh**neea] In antiquity, the C part of the W coast of Asia Minor, the birthplace of Greek philosophy and science. The name came from the extensive occupation of the area by Ionian Greeks around the beginning of the first millennium BC. » Ephesus; Miletus

Ionian Islands, Gr **Ioníoi Nísoi** or **Eptánisos** pop (1981) 182651;

area 2 307 sq km/890 sq ml. Region and island group of W Greece, from the Albanian frontier to the Peloponnese; a chain of about 40 islands, including Corfu, Cephalonia, and Zacynthus; under British control, 1815–64; mountainous with fertile plains and valleys; wine, olives, fruit, tourism. » Cephalonia; Corfu; Greece [i]; Zacynthus

Ionian Sea Part of the Mediterranean Sea, lying W of the Greek islands and S of Italy; separated from the Adriatic Sea by the Strait of Otranto; connected to the Aegean Sea by the Sea of Crete. » Mediterranean Sea

ionic » **chemical bond**

Ionic order [iyonik] One of the five main orders of classical architecture; lighter and more elegant than the Doric, with slim, usually fluted shafts and spiral scrolls known as *volutes* on the capitals. It originated in Asia Minor in the 6th-c BC. » capital; column; Greek architecture; orders of architecture [i]; Roman architecture

ionization » **ion**

ionization energy The energy required to remove an electron from an atom in the gas phase. This is characteristic of an atom, and is relatively low for alkali metals (eg 500 kJ/mol^1 for sodium) and relatively high for halogens (eg 1 680 kJ/mol^1 for fluorine). » atom

ionosphere The region of the Earth's upper atmosphere from c.50–500 km/30–300 ml in height where short-wave radiation from the Sun is absorbed and partly ionizes the gas molecules or atoms, removing their outer electrons and leaving them positively charged. The ionized layers reflect short-wavelength radio waves, and so make long-distance radio communication possible. The ionosphere is layered according to the concentration of free electrons: the lowest layers, termed D and E (also called the *Heaviside* or *Kennelly layer*) result from molecular ionization, and the upper layer F (the *Appleton layer*) from atomic ionization. The thicknesses of the layers vary with latitude, season, time of day, and solar activity. » atmosphere [i]; aurora; ion; radio waves; thermosphere

Ios [eeos] 36°43N 25°17E; area 108 sq km/42 sq ml. Island of the Cyclades, Greece, in the Aegean Sea, SSW of Naxos; linked by boat to Piraeus, Paros, and Santorini; Homer is said to have died here; port of Ormos Iou on the W coast. » Cyclades

Iowa [iyohwa] pop (1987e) 2 834 000; area 145 747 sq km/56 275 sq ml. State in NC USA, divided into 99 counties; the 'Hawkeye State'; 29th state admitted to the Union, 1846; became part of USA with the Louisiana Purchase, 1803; became a state, 1846; capital moved from Iowa City to Des Moines, 1857; other major cities are Cedar Rapids, Davenport, Sioux City; Mississippi R follows the E border; Des Moines R flows SE before emptying into the Mississippi; Big Sioux R forms the border with South Dakota, emptying into the Missouri R, which then follows the Nebraska state border; highest point is Ocheyedan Mound (511 m/1 677 ft); almost entirely prairie-land (95%) with rich soil; chief crops corn and soybeans; over half the corn grown used for feeding pigs and cattle; leads the nation in corn and pig production; industry dominated by food processing and machinery manufacture; also chemicals, electrical equipment. » Des Moines; Louisiana Purchase; United States of America [i]; RR38

Iowa City 41°40N 91°32W, pop (1980) 50 508. Seat of Johnson County, E Iowa, USA, on the Iowa R; founded, 1838; capital of Iowa Territory, 1839–57; railway; university (1847); major medical research and treatment centre. » Iowa

Ipatieff, Vladimir (Nikolayevich) [eepatyef] (1867–1952) Russian chemist, born in Moscow. He served in the Russian army, then became professor of chemistry at St Petersburg (1898–1906). He discovered the structure of isoprene in 1897. Throughout World War 1 he largely controlled the Russian chemical industry. Doubtful of his safety under the Soviets, he emigrated to the USA in 1931, where he made contributions of great value to the oil industry. He died in Chicago. » isoprene [i]

ipecacuanha [ipikakyooahna] A perennial with roots thickened to resemble a string of beads, native to Brazil; stems sprawling; leaves oval; flowers small, white, in heads. The roots provide the drug ipecacuanha, used to induce vomiting and to treat dysentery. (*Cephaelis ipecacuanha*. Family: *Rubiaceae*.) » dysentery; perennial; root (botany)

Iphigeneia [iyfijeniya] According to Greek legend, the daughter of Agamemnon and Clytemnestra. She was about to be sacrificed at Aulis as the fleet could not sail to Troy, because the winds were against it. At the last moment she was saved by Artemis, who made her a priestess in the country of the Tauri (the Crimea). Finally her brother Orestes saved her. » Agamemnon; Clytemnestra; Orestes; Trojan War

Ipswich, Anglo-Saxon **Gipeswic** 52°04N 1°10E, pop (1981) 129 908. Port and county town in Suffolk, E England; at the head of the R Orwell estuary, 106 km/66 ml NE of London; a major wool port in the 16th-c; birthplace of Cardinal Wolsey; home of Thomas Gainsborough; railway; engineering, brewing, food processing, agricultural machinery, electrical equipment, textiles, tobacco products, fertilizers, plastics; Churches of St Mary-le-Tower and St Margaret, Ipswich museum; music festival at Aldeburgh (32 km/20 ml NE). » Gainsborough; Suffolk; Wolsey

IQ » **intelligence**

Iqbal, Sir Mohammed (1875–1938) Indian poet and philosopher, born at Sialkot (now in Pakistan). He was educated at Lahore, Cambridge (where he read law and philosophy), and Munich. On his return to India, he achieved fame through his poetry, whose compelling mysticism and nationalism caused him to be regarded almost as a prophet by Muslims. His efforts to establish a separate Muslim state eventually led to the formation of Pakistan. He was knighted in 1923, and died at Lahore, Punjab. » Indian literature; Islam; Pakistan [i]; poetry

Iquique [eekeekay] 20°13S 70°09W, pop (1982) 109 033. Port capital of Iquique province, N Chile; free port, S of Arica; founded in 16th-c; partly destroyed by earthquake, 1877; scene of naval battle in War of the Pacific (1879); airfield; railway; trade in fishmeal, fish oil, tinned fish, salt, nitrates; naval museum, Palacio Astoreca (1903); La Fiesta de Tirana (religious festival) at nearby village (Jul). » Chile [i]

Iquitos [eekeetohs] 3°51S 73°13W, pop (1981) 173 629. Capital of Loreto department, NE Peru; fast-developing city on the W bank of the Amazon, 3 700 km/2 300 ml from its mouth; limit of navigation for ocean vessels; access only by air and river; university (1962); chief town of Peru's jungle region; rubber, nuts, timber; centre for oil exploration in Peruvian Amazonia. » Peru [i]

IRA An acronym of **Irish Republican Army**, an anti-British paramilitary guerrilla force established in 1919 by Irish nationalists to combat British forces in Ireland. It opposed the Anglo-Irish Treaty of 1921 because Ireland was a dominion and the six counties of the North of Ireland were part of the UK, but it was suppressed by the Irish government in the 1922 rising, and remained largely inactive until the late 1960s. In 1969, a major split in its ranks led to the formation of the **Provisional IRA** alongside the **Official IRA**, and a serious schism between the two sides in the early 1970s. The Official IRA has been virtually inactive since 1972, and generally supports political action to achieve Irish unity. The Provisionals have become the dominant republican force, responsible for shootings and bombings in the N of Ireland, Britain, and W Europe. Targets have mainly been security and military personnel and establishments, although there have been many sectarian killings. Its total membership is reputed to be presently c.500. » Sinn Féin

IRAM The acronym of **Institute Radio Astronomie Millimetrique**, an observatory for millimetre wave astronomy funded jointly by France and Germany. It has facilities in Bonn (Germany), Grenoble and Plateau de Burne (France), and Pico Valeta (Spain). » observatory [i]

Iran [iran], formerly **Persia** (to 1935), official name **Islamic Republic of Iran**, Persian **Jomhori-e-Islami-e-Iran** pop (1990e) 56 293 000; area 1 648 000 sq km/636 128 sq ml. Republic in SW Asia, divided into 24 provinces; bounded N by Armenia, Azerbaijan, Turkmenistan, and the Caspian Sea, E by Afghanistan and Pakistan, S by the Gulf of Oman and the Persian Gulf, SW by Iraq, and NW by Turkey; capital, Teheran; chief cities, Mashhad, Esfahan, Tabriz, Shiraz; timezone

GMT + 3½; chief ethnic groups, Persian (63%), Turkic (18%); official language, Farsi, with several minority languages; chief religion, Islam (93% Shiite, 5% Sunni); unit of currency, the rial.

Physical description and climate. Largely composed of a vast arid C plateau, average elevation 1 200 m/4 000 ft, with many salt and sand basins; rimmed by mountain ranges that drop down to narrow coastal lowlands; bounded N by the Elburz Mts, rising to 5 670 m/18 602 ft at Mt Damavand; Zagros Mts in W and S, rising to 3 000–4 600 m/10 000–15 000 ft; mainly a desert climate, with annual rainfall below 300 mm/12 in; average temperatures at Teheran, 2.2°C (Jan), 29.4°C (Jul), average annual rainfall 246 mm/9.7 in; Caspian coastal strip much wetter (800–2 000 mm/30–80 in); hot and humid on Arabian Gulf; frequent earthquakes.

History and government. An early centre of civilization, dynasties including the Achaemenids and Sassanids; ruled by Arabs, Turks, and Mongols until the Sasavid dynasty (16th–18th-c) and the Qajar dynasty (19th–20th-c); military coup (1921) led to independence under Reza Shah Pahlavi, 1925; protests against Shah's regime in 1970s led to revolution, 1978; exile of Shah and proclamation of Islamic Republic under Ayatollah Khomeini, 1979; occupation of US embassy in Teheran, 1979–81; Gulf War following invasion of Iraq, 1980–8; governed by a president, elected for a 4-year term, who appoints a prime minister and other ministers; the Ayatollah is the appointed religious leader with authority to protect the constitution; there is a 270-member National Consultative Assembly; since the death of Khomeini (1989), there has been a political struggle for power.

Economy. World's fourth largest oil producer, but production severely disrupted by the 1978 revolution and Gulf War; natural gas, iron ore, copper, manganese, chromite, coal, salt; textiles, sugar refining, food processing, petrochemicals, iron and steel, cement, fertilizers, machinery, traditional handicrafts (especially carpets); a third of the population involved in agriculture and forestry; wheat, rice, tobacco, barley, sugar beet, cotton, dates, raisins, tea; sheep, goats, silkworms. » Achaemenids; Gulf War; Irangate; Iranian Revolution; Islam; Khomeini; Pahlavi; Persian architecture/art/Empire/literature; Sassanids; Teheran; RR25 national holidays; RR53 political leaders

Irangate The popular nickname for a political scandal in 1986 that grew out of the Reagan administration's efforts to obtain the release of US captives held in the Middle East by the covert supply of arms to the hostile government of Iran. In an additional complication, officials (notably, Colonel Oliver North) tried to use the proceeds of arms sales to Iran as a means of financing support for the anti-government *Contra* rebels in Nicaragua, despite official prohibition by Congress, and without the knowledge of the President. In addition to questions surrounding violations of the law, the affair raised issues concerning executive incompetence, which a Congressional Committee reported on in 1988. » Iran [i]; Reagan; Watergate

Iranian languages A branch of the E Indo-European language family, spoken in the region of present-day Iran and Afghanistan. Old Persian, and Avestan, in which the sacred texts of the Zoroastrians was written, are recorded from the 6th-c BC. Modern Iranian languages, of which Persian (Farsi) is one of the major examples, are spoken by over 60 million people. » Indo-Iranian languages; Zoroastrianism

Iranian Revolution The 1979 revolution in Iran which deposed the Shah (15 Jan) and led to the triumphant return (1 Feb) from his French exile of the Ayatollah Khomeini. Khomeini appointed Dr Mehdi Bazargan as Prime Minister (1979–80), although real power was to remain with Khomeini's 15-man Islamic Revolutionary Council. Revolutionary forces took control of the country, and Khomeini announced the establishment of the Islamic Republic. » Iran [i]; Khomeini

Iraq [irak], official name **Republic of Iraq**, Arabic **Al Jumhouriya al Iraquia** pop (1990e) 17 754 000; area 434 925 sq km/167 881 sq ml. Republic in SW Asia, divided into 18 governorates; bounded E by Iran, N by Turkey, NW by Syria, W by Jordan, SW and S by Saudi Arabia, and SE by Kuwait and the Arabian Gulf; capital, Baghdad; chief towns, Basra, Kirkuk, Mosul; timezone GMT + 3; population 79% Arab, 16% Kurd (largely in NE); chief religion, Islam; official language, Arabic; unit of currency, the dinar.

Physical description. Largely comprises the vast alluvial tract of the Tigris–Euphrates lowland (ancient Mesopotamia), separated in upper courses by the plain of Al Jazirah, rising to 1 547 m/5 075 ft; rivers join to form the navigable Shatt al-Arab; lowland swamp vegetation; mountains (NE) rise to over

3 000 m/9 800 ft; desert in other areas; mainly arid climate; summers very hot and dry; winters often cold; temperatures at Baghdad, 10°C (Jan), 35°C (Jul), average annual rainfall, 140 mm/5.5 in; rainfall highest in NE, average 400–600 mm/15–24 in.

History and government. Part of the Ottoman Empire from 16th-c until World War 1; captured by British forces, 1916; British-mandated territory, 1921; independence under Hashemite dynasty, 1932; monarchy replaced by military rule, 1958; since 1960s, Kurdish nationalists in NE fighting to establish a separate state; invasion of Iran (1980) led to the Gulf War, lasting until 1988; invasion of Kuwait (1990) led to UN sanctions, the 1991 Gulf War, and Iraqi withdrawal; a democratic socialist republic, governed by 9-member Revolutionary Command Council, which elects a president; 250-member National Assembly is elected for four years; Kurdish regional assembly has limited powers of legislation.

Economy. World's second largest producer of oil, but production severely disrupted during both Gulf Wars, with several oil installations destroyed; natural gas, oil refining, petrochemicals, cement, textiles; several new industrial plants being developed with Soviet assistance; dates, cotton, rice, winter wheat, barley, lentils, sheep, cattle; major irrigation schemes under way; rich archaeological remains, especially along the Euphrates valley. » Baghdad; Euphrates, River; Gulf War; Islam; Kurds; Mesopotamia; RR25 national holidays; RR53 political leaders

Ireland, John (Nicholson) (1879–1962) British composer, born at Bowdon, Cheshire. He studied at the Royal College of Music, London. He established his reputation with his Second Violin Sonata (1917), and between the wars was a prominent member of the English musical renaissance. His later work includes a piano concerto, choral works, and settings of poems by Shakespeare, Hardy, and others.

Ireland, Lat **Hibernia** Island on W fringe of Europe, separated from Great Britain by the Irish Sea; maximum length 486 km/302 ml, maximum width 275 km/171 ml; since 1921, divided politically into the independent 26 counties of the **Irish Republic** (area 70 282 sq km/27 129 sq ml; pop (1981) 3 440 427), and **Northern Ireland**, part of the UK, containing six of the nine counties of the ancient province of Ulster (area 14 120 sq km/5 450 sq ml; pop (1981) 1 547 000); known poetically as *Erin*, derived from Strabo's name for the island, *Ierne*; 6th–13th-c, often known as *Scotia*; the name is also in widespread use for the Irish Republic. » Irish Republic [i]; Northern Ireland [i]

Irenaeus, St [iruh**nay**uhs] (c.130–c.200), feast day 28 June (W), 23 August (E). One of the Christian Fathers of the Greek Church, born (probably) near Smyrna. A priest of the Graeco-Gaulish church of Lyons, he became bishop there in 177. A successful missionary bishop, he is chiefly known for his opposition to Gnosticism, his theological writing, and his attempts to prevent a rupture between Eastern and Western Churches over the computing of Easter. He died (probably) at Lyons. » Easter; Gnosticism; missions, Christian

Irene [iy**ree**nee] In Greek mythology, a personification of 'peace'; one of the Horae, or 'seasons'. » Horae

Ireton, Henry (1611–51) English soldier, born at Attenborough, Nottingham. Educated at Cambridge, at the outbreak of the Civil War he fought for parliament, and served at Edgehill, Naseby, and the siege of Bristol. Cromwell's son-in-law from 1646, he was one of the most implacable enemies of the King, and signed the warrant for his execution. He accompanied Cromwell to Ireland, and in 1650 became Lord Deputy. He died of the plague during the siege of Limerick. » Charles I (of England); Cromwell, Oliver; English Civil War

Irgun (Zvai Leumi) [**ir**gun zviy **loo**mee] ('National Military Organization') A Jewish commando group in Palestine, founded in 1937, whose aim was the establishment of the State of Israel by any means. Led by Menachem Begin, it was responsible for the execution of British Mandatory soldiers and of the villagers of Deir Yassin in 1948, when it numbered about 5 000. It was the nucleus for the Herut Party in Israel. » Begin; Israel [i]

Irian Jaya [ireean **jiy**ah], Eng **West Irian**, formerly **Dutch New Guinea** pop (1980) 1 173 875; area 421 981 sq km/162 885 sq ml. Province of Indonesia, comprising the W half of New Guinea and adjacent islands; mountainous and forested; Pegunungan Maoke range rises to 5 029 m/16 499 ft at Jaya Peak; part of Indonesia, 1963; ongoing separatist guerrilla movement; capital, Jayapura; copra, maize, groundnuts, tuna, pepper, gold, oil, coal, phosphate. » Indonesia [i]

iridosmine » **osmiridium**

iris (anatomy) The coloured part of the vertebrate eye, an opaque diaphragm extending in front of the lens and having a circular opening (the *pupil*). It consists of pigmental epithelium and circularly and radially arranged smooth muscle fibres. The differential contraction of these muscle fibres (under the control of the autonomic nervous system) alters pupil size and so regulates the amount of light entering the eye. Bright light decreases and dim light increases pupil size. » epithelium; eye [i]

iris (botany) A perennial, sometimes evergreen, native to N temperate regions, divisible into two groups; those with rhizomes have sword-shaped leaves in flat fans; those with bulbs have leaves narrow, channelled, or cylindrical; flowers large, showy, the parts in threes and structurally complex, often in a combination of colours with conspicuous honey guides; fruit a capsule, sometimes with brightly coloured seeds. Many species and cultivars are grown for ornament. (Genus: *Iris*, 300 species. Family: *Iridaceae*.) » bulb; cultivar; evergreen plants; flag (botany); honey guide; orris; perennial plants; rhizome

Iris In Greek mythology, the goddess of the rainbow, which seems to reach from Earth to heaven. She therefore became the messenger of the gods, especially of Zeus in Homer, and of Hera in later writers. She is depicted sitting under Hera's throne. » Hera; Zeus

Irish The Celtic language spoken in Ireland; also known as **Erse**. Designated the first official language of the Republic of Ireland, there are over a million speakers, and an active literary tradition. Most speakers of Irish as a mother tongue come from the W fringes of the country, which have been designated as an area of protection for the language, the *Gaeltacht*. Irish is taught in the schools, and language planning has introduced a standard grammar and simplified spelling system. » Celtic languages; Irish literature

Irish elk A giant fossil deer that ranged through open woodland from Ireland to Siberia and China during the Pleistocene epoch; enormous, palmate antlers of stags could span 3.7 m/12 ft, used to establish dominance over herd. (Genus: *Megaloceros*.) » deer; fossil; Pleistocene epoch

Irish Famine The widespread starvation of Irish peasantry which followed the effects of potato blight in 1845–7, and the consequent destruction of the crop. Because of starvation and emigration (to Britain and the USA), the population of Ireland fell by almost 25% between 1845 and 1851. The British government was widely blamed by the emigrants for the disaster. » potato

Irish literature A literature with two distinct traditions; the native Irish Gaelic, and the Anglo-Irish. Irish remained oral later than any other European literature. Not only the early, short prose sagas (such as the famous *Tain Bo Cuailuge* (The Cattle-Raid of Cooley) but also mediaeval lyrics and still later odes and panegyrics were kept alive by recitation. Political persecution also drove Irish literature underground. The Gaelic League (1893) promised an Irish revival, but conditions have never proved favourable. Meanwhile, many celebrated Anglo-Irish writers (eg Swift, Sterne, Wilde, Shaw) wrote entirely within the English tradition. But with the Irish revival, the poet Yeats and the dramatists Synge and O'Casey drew inspiration from Irish sources; and the novels of the self-exiled James Joyce are all set in Dublin. This re-rooting in Ireland is also evident in several contemporary Irish poets, such as Seamus Heaney (1939–); and in the work of another celebrated self-exile, Samuel Beckett, who writes in both English and French. » Beckett; English literature; Gaelic; Irish Republic [i]; Joyce, James; O'Casey; ode; panegyric; saga; Shaw, George Bernard; Sterne; Swift; Synge; Wilde; Yeats

Irish National Liberation Army (INLA) The military wing of the Irish Republican Socialist Party, a small paramilitary group which commits few terrorist attacks, but is noted for the ruthless nature of those it does carry out. Probably created by former members of the Official IRA disenchanted with the 1972 ceasefire, it was responsible for the killing of the Conservative MP Airey Neave (Mar 1979). It suffered internal feuds in the 1980s. » IRA; Irish Republican Socialist Party

Irish Republic or **Ireland**, Gaelic **Éire [airuh]**, official name **Republic of Ireland** pop (1990e) 3 509 000; area 70 282 sq km/27 129 sq ml. Republic occupying S, C, and NW Ireland, divided into 26 counties grouped into the four provinces of Ulster, Munster, Leinster, and Connacht; separated from Great Britain by the Irish Sea and St George's Channel; bounded NE by Northern Ireland, part of the UK; capital, Dublin; chief towns include Cork, Limerick, Waterford, Galway, Drogheda, Dundalk, Sligo; timezone GMT; population largely Celtic; official languages, Irish Gaelic and English; main Gaelic-speaking area (W) known as the *Gaeltacht*; main religion, Roman Catholic (95%); unit of currency, the Irish pound (*punt*).

Physical description and climate. Mountainous landscapes in W, part of the Caledonian system of Scandinavia and Scotland, with quartzite peaks weathered into conical mountains such as Croagh Patrick (765 m/2 510 ft); younger mountain system in S, rising W towards Macgillycuddy's Reeks Mts, creating a landscape of ridges and valleys; lowlands in the E, drained by slow-moving rivers such as the Shannon (S), Liffey (E), and Slaney (SE); mild and equable climate; rainfall heaviest in W, often over 3 000 mm/120 in; drier in E, Dublin annual average 785 mm/30 in.

History and government. Occupied by Goidelic-speaking Celts during the Iron Age; high kingship established c.AD 200, capital at Tara (Meath); conversion to Christianity by St Patrick, 5th-c, becoming a centre of learning and missionary activity; SE attacked by Vikings, c.800; Henry I of England declared himself lord of Ireland, 1171, but English influence restricted to area round Dublin (the Pale); Henry VIII took the title 'King of Ireland', 1542; Catholic rebellion suppressed by barbarous campaign of Oliver Cromwell (1649–50) during English Civil War; supporters of deposed Catholic King James II defeated by William III at the Battle of the Boyne (1690); following a century of suppression, struggle for Irish freedom developed in 18th–19th-c, including such revolutionary movements as Wolfe Tone's United Irishmen (1796–8), and later Young Ireland (1848) and the Fenians (1866–7); Act of Union, 1801; Catholic Relief Act (1829), enabling Catholics to sit in parliament; Land Acts (1870–1903), attacking Irish poverty; 1846 famine, reduced population by half; two Home Rule Bills introduced by Gladstone (1886, 1893); third Home Rule Bill passed in 1914, but never came into effect because of World War 1; armed rebellion, 1916; republic proclaimed by Sinn Féin, 1919; partition proposed by Britain, 1920; treaty signed, 1921, giving dominion status, subject to right of Northern Ireland to opt out; this right exercised, and frontier agreed, 1925; renamed Éire, 1937; left Commonwealth, 1949; a president (head of state) elected for seven years; National Parliament (*Oireachtas*) includes a House of Representatives (*Dáil Éireann*) of 166 elected members, and a 60-member Senate (*Seanad Éireann*); a prime minister (*taoiseach*) is head of government.

□ international airport

Economy. Two-thirds covered by improved agricultural land, with much of the remainder used for rough grazing of sheep and cattle; mainly mixed pastoral farming with some arable cropping; forestry developed since 1950s; fishing; metals, food, drink, tobacco, textiles; recent growth in light engineering, synthetic fibres, electronics, pharmaceuticals, plastics; major tourist area; hydroelectricity on main rivers; several peat-fired power stations; Kinsale natural gas field near Cork; member of the EEC in 1973. » Cromwell, Oliver; Dublin (city); Fenians; Gladstone; Grattan; Henry I (of England); Henry VIII; Ireland [i]; Irish; Irish Famine; Irish literature; Land League; Northern Ireland; O'Connell; Parnell; Patrick, St; Sinn Féin; Tone; William III; Young Ireland; RR25 national holidays; RR53 political leaders

Irish Republican Army » **IRA**

Irish Republican Socialist Party A political party formed in 1974 largely as a breakaway group from the official Sinn Féin, who disagreed with its political strategy and the ceasefire. Its most prominent member was Bernadette McAliskey. It was involved in a feud with the Official IRA in the 1970s, and subsequently moved closer to the Provisional Sinn Féin. » IRA; Irish National Liberation Army; McAliskey; Sinn Féin

Irish Sea area 103 600 sq km/39 990 sq ml. Arm of the Atlantic Ocean between Ireland and Great Britain; 210 km/130 ml long by 225 km/140 ml at its widest point; linked to the Atlantic by the North Channel, St George's Channel, and Celtic Sea. » Atlantic Ocean

Irish setter A breed of dog, developed in Ireland, similar to the English setter but more slender, with a glossy chestnut-brown coat; hair forming fringes on tail, underside, and backs of legs; also known as **red setter**. » dog; setter

Irish terrier An active medium-sized terrier with a coarse reddish-tan coat; ears soft, held high; tip of muzzle with a surrounding brush of longer hair; tail docked, but left longer than in most terriers. » dog; terrier

Irish wolfhound The tallest domestic breed of dog (shoulder height, 775 mm/30½ in); very old breed, used for hunting by the Celts; long (usually grey) coat; soft ears; similar to the deerhound, but less slender. » deerhound; hound

Irkutsk [irkutsk] 52°18N 104°15E, pop (1989) 635 000. Capital city of Irkutskaya oblast, S Siberian Russia; at the confluence of the Irkut and Angara Rivers; founded as a fortress, 1661; airport; on the Trans-Siberian Railway; university (1918); one of the largest economic centres of E Siberia; centre for fur-purchasing and gold transshipment; foodstuffs, ship repairing, woodworking, heavy machinery, machine tools. » Russia; Trans-Siberian Railway

iron Fe (from Lat *ferrum*), element 26, a metal with density of 7.8 g/cm^3, melting point 1 535°C. It is the fourth most common element in the Earth's crust, not found uncombined except in some meteorites. Learning to recover (*smelt*) it from its ores (mainly the oxide Fe_2O_3) was a major step in human civilization. This operation is still done largely by reduction using carbon. Most iron is used as metal, usually alloyed with some quantities of other elements, especially carbon and silicon. Steel is iron alloyed with other metals, mainly vanadium, chromium, manganese, and nickel. In its compounds, iron shows both +2 and +3 oxidation states, and is an essential element in biology, particularly as part of haemoglobin. » blast furnace [i]; chemical elements; corrosion; RR90

Iron Age » **Three Age System**

iron-bark » **gum tree**

Iron Cross A military decoration (an iron cross edged with silver) instituted in Prussia in 1813 and reinstated by Hitler as a German medal in 1939. The ribbon (worn) is black, white, and gold. » decoration

iron curtain A term used to describe the separation of certain E European countries from the rest of Europe by the political and military domination of the Soviet Union. It was first used by Nazi propaganda minister Goebbels in 1943, and became widely known after Churchill used it in a speech in 1946. » Churchill, Winston; Goebbels; Soviet Union [i]

iron lung » **respirator**

Ironbridge A historic industrial town in the Severn R gorge, 21 km/13 ml SE of Shrewsbury, Shropshire, the birthplace of England's Industrial Revolution. In 1709 iron was first smelted with coke nearby at Coalbrookdale, and in 1778–9 Europe's first iron bridge was cast and erected here; 196 ft (59.8 m) long, its centre span 100 ft (30.5 m) and its rise 45 ft (13.7 m), the weight precisely recorded as 378.5 tons (384.6 tonnes). Since 1968 it has been the focus of a successful open-air museum on the model of colonial Williamsburg. Ironbridge Gorge is a world heritage site. » bridge (engineering) [i]; Industrial Revolution; Williamsburg

ironclad A 19th-c term for warships which were either protected by iron plates or built entirely of iron, and more recently of steel. The first ironclad was the French frigate *La Gloire* of 1859, followed one year later by Britain's HMS *Warrior*. » warships [i]

Ironside, William Edmund, 1st Baron (1880–1959) British field marshal, born at Ironside, Aberdeenshire. He served as a secret agent disguised as a railwayman in the Boer War, held several staff appointments in World War 1, and commanded the Archangel expedition against the Bolsheviks (1918). He was Chief of the Imperial General Staff at the outbreak of World War 2, and placed in command of the Home Defence Forces (1940). The 'Ironsides', fast light-armoured vehicles, were named after him. He was made a peer in 1941. » civil defence; World War 2

irony One of the most complex forms of literary expression, more a habit of mind than a rhetorical figure, requiring continual alertness on the part of the reader for proper interpretation. Irony is not simply saying one thing and implying the opposite; the name for this crude form is *sarcasm*. Irony invites the reader to consider several shades of meaning simultaneously, some of which is elided or cancelled out in the process. The meaning of irony lies precisely in the tension between single statement and multiple meaning. It was suggested by Kierkegaard that the finest irony is undecipherable as such – which comes close to the position of the Romantic ironist, who writes with a keen sense of the double-sidedness of truth and the irreducible ambiguity of language itself. This conception is also referred to as *cosmic* or *philosophical* irony. » figurative language; Kierkegaard; Swift; Voltaire

Iroquois [**ir**uhkwoy] A N American Indian people concentrated in the Great Lakes area. Mostly settled in villages in longhouses, the women farmed, and the men hunted, fished, traded, and defended the communities from attack. They fought many wars with their neighbours, enslaving captives or absorbing them into the community. Population c.21 500. » American Indians; Iroquois Confederacy

Iroquois Confederacy A confederation of Iroquois groups during the 17th–18th-c in upper New York State: the Mohawk, Oneida, Onondaga, Cayuga, and Seneca, later joined by the Tuscarora; also known as the **Iroquois League** or the 'Six Nations'. United largely for defence and for control of the fur trade, they defeated most of their Indian rivals, and prevented the settlement of Europeans in the NE. The League broke up during the American Revolution, and they were finally defeated in 1779. Some groups settled on reservations; others went to Canada. » Iroquois

irradiance » **radiometry** [i]

irrational numbers » **numbers**

irrationalism Any of a variety of challenges to the adequacy of human reason. **1** The world itself is unintelligible or absurd (existentialism). **2** Human reason is inadequate to understand the world, be it intelligible or not (Nietzsche and others). **3** Humans ought to follow their impulses, not reason (Rousseau and others). » existentialism; Nietzsche; rationalism; Rousseau, Jean Jacques

Irrawaddy, River Major river dissecting Myanmar N–S, formed in Kachin state, N Burma, by the meeting of the Mali Hka and Nmai Hka; flows S through gorges, then W and S to form a delta beginning 290 km/180 ml from the sea; empties into Andaman Sea in a broad front of tidal forests spreading for 260 km/160 ml; easternmost arm of delta linked to Rangoon by canal; chief tributary, R Chindwin; navigable to Bhamo (1 300 km/800 ml inland); length c.1 600 km/1 000 ml; with the Nmai Hka, c.2 000 km/1 300 ml; large proportion of population in valley and delta; major rice-growing region. » Burma [i]

Irredentists In the new nations of 19th–20th-c Europe, supporters of the acquisition, by negotiation or more usually conquest, of 'unredeemed' territory. The term is most commonly applied to the Italians, who after 1870 sought 'redemption' of Italian-speaking lands still under Austrian rule, and to the Greeks, who sought to incorporate Greek-speaking, Turkish-controlled areas into the new Greek kingdom. » Risorgimento

irrigation The application of water to soil and crops. In some desert areas all the moisture requirements for plant growth may be provided through irrigation, with water being supplied via a complex canal and irrigation channel network. In other areas irrigation is used to achieve optimal growth and high quality produce, especially in the horticulture sector. In dry areas water may be applied by flooding or through inter-row channels. More general application techniques include rain guns, sprinklers and, more expensively, drip lines, which provide water to plants and trees on an individual basis. This latter system also facilitates the application of nutrients and other chemicals, along with the water in the irrigation lines. » desert

Irtysh, River [ir**tish**] Chief tributary of the R Ob, in Kazakhstan and Russia; rises in N China on the W slopes of the Mongolian Altai Mts; flows W to enter L Zaysan, then generally NW to join the R Ob at Khanty Mansiysk; length, 4 248 km/2 640 ml; hydroelectric power stations serve the non-ferrous mineral industry. » Ob, River

Irvine, Andy, properly **Andrew (Robertson)** (1951–) British rugby player, born in Edinburgh, Scotland. Educated at George Heriot's and Glasgow Universities, his club rugby was played with Heriot's Former Pupils. An outstanding fullback, he played for Scotland 50 times between 1979 and 1982. During his international career he scored a world record 301 points for Scotland and the British Lions, touring with the Lions in 1974, 1977, and 1980. » rugby football

Irving, Sir Henry, originally **John Henry Brodribb** (1838–1905) British actor and theatre manager, born at Keinton-Mandeville, Somerset. He went on stage in 1856, appeared in Sunderland, Edinburgh, Manchester, and Liverpool, and in 1866 made his London debut at the St James's Theatre. In 1871 he transferred to the Lyceum, and gained a reputation as the greatest English actor of his time. In 1878 he began a theatrical partnership with Ellen Terry which lasted until 1902. In 1895 he became the first actor to receive a knighthood, and died at Bradford, Yorkshire. » Terry; theatre

Irving, Washington (1783–1859) US man of letters, born in New York City. He studied law, travelled throughout Europe, was admitted to the Bar in 1806, and began writing in 1807. Under the pseudonym of **Geoffrey Crayon** he wrote *The Sketch Book* (1819–20), a miscellany containing such items as 'Rip Van Winkle' and 'The Legend of Sleepy Hollow'. He lived largely in Europe (1815–32), and was later appointed Ambassador to Spain (1842–6). He died at Tarrytown, New York. » American literature

Isaac [**iy**zak] Biblical character, son of Abraham by Sarah, through whose line of descent God's promises to Abraham were seen to continue. He was nearly sacrificed by Abraham at God's command (*Gen* 22). He fathered Esau and Jacob by his wife Rebecca, but was deceived into passing his blessing on to his younger son Jacob. » Abraham; Bible; Esau; Jacob

Isaacs, Alick (1921–67) British biologist, born in Glasgow, where he graduated. His early work in virology, and especially on influenza, led to his appointment as head of the World Influenza Centre in London from 1950. In 1957, with Swiss virologist Jean Lindenmann he described a novel protein, *interferon*, a natural antiviral agent, whose potential use in therapy has been much studied ever since. He died in London. » influenza; interferons

Isabella I (of Castile), byname **Isabella the Catholic** (1451–1504) Queen of Castile (1474–1504), the daughter of John II, King of Castile and Leon. In 1469 she married Ferdinand V of Aragon, with whom she ruled jointly from 1479. During her reign, the Inquisition was introduced (1478), the reconquest of Granada completed (1482–92), and the Jews expelled (1492). She sponsored the voyage of Christopher Columbus to the New World, and died at Medina del Campo. » Columbus, Christopher; Inquisition

Isabella of France (1292–1358) Daughter of Philip IV of France, who in 1308 married at Boulogne Edward II of England. She became the mistress of Roger Mortimer, with whom she overthrew and murdered the King (1327). Her son, Edward III, had Mortimer executed in 1330, and Isabella was sent into retirement, eventually to join an order of nuns. » Edward II/III; Mortimer

Isaiah, Hebrew **Jeshaiah** [iyziya] (8th-c BC) The first in order of the major Old Testament prophets, son of Amoz. A citizen of Jerusalem, he began to prophesy c.747 BC, and exercised his office until at least the close of the century. According to tradition, he was martyred. » Isaiah, Book of; prophet

Isaiah or **Isaias, Book of** [iyziya] A major prophetic work in the Hebrew Bible/Old Testament, ostensibly from the prophet Isaiah, active in Judah and Jerusalem in the latter half of the 8th-c BC during a period of Assyrian threats. Many scholars doubt the unity of the contents, with Chapters 40–55 considered a much later exilic work looking forward to Judah's restoration and called *Deutero-Isaiah* ('Second Isaiah') and Chapters 56–66 either as part of Deutero-Isaiah or as a distinct *Trito-Isaiah* ('Third Isaiah'). » Isaiah; Micah, Book of; Old Testament

Isaias » **Isaiah, Book of**

ISBN » **International Standard Book Numbering**

ischaemic/ischemic heart disease » **coronary heart disease** [i]

Isherwood, Christopher (William Bradshaw) (1904–86) British novelist, born at Disley, Cheshire. Educated at Repton, Cambridge, and London, his first novel was published in 1928. His best-known works, *Mr Norris Changes Trains* (1935) and *Goodbye to Berlin* (1939), were based on his experiences (1930–3) as an English tutor in the decadence of post-slump Berlin, and later inspired *Cabaret* (musical, 1966; film, 1972). In collaboration with Auden, a school friend, he wrote three prose-verse plays with political overtones. He also travelled in China with Auden in 1938 and wrote *Journey to a War* (1939). In 1940 he went to California as a Hollywood scriptwriter, and in 1946 took US citizenship. He died at Santa Monica, California. » Auden; English literature; novel

Ishmael [**ish**mayel] Biblical character, the son of Abraham by Hagar, his wife's maid; expelled into the desert with his mother Hagar from Abraham's household after the birth of Isaac. He is purported to have fathered 12 princes, and is considered the ancestor of the Bedouin tribes of the Palestinian deserts (the Ishmaelites). Mohammed considered Ishmael and Abraham as ancestors of the Arabs, and as associated with the construction of the Kaba at Mecca. » Abraham; Bible; Hagar; Isaac; Islam; Kaba

Ishtar [**ish**tah] Originally a Mesopotamian mother-goddess of love and war; also known as **Astarte**; later the goddess of love, identified with the planet Venus. She travelled to the Underworld to rescue her consort Tammuz, an event commemorated in annual ceremonies. » Gilgamesh; Mesopotamia; Tammuz

Isidore of Seville, St (c.560–636), feast day 4 April. Spanish ecclesiastic, encyclopedist, and historian, born either at Seville or Carthagena. Archbishop of Seville in c.600, his episcopate was notable for the Councils at Seville (618 or 619) and Toledo (633). A voluminous writer, his most influential work was the encyclopedia, *Etymologies*. He died at Seville and was canonized in 1598. » Council of the Church

isinglass [**iy**zingglahs] A pure gelatin found in fish. Its particular use, for which other gelatins are not suitable, is in the clarification of fermented beverages, presumably due to its fibrous structure. The name is also applied to a form of mica, with similar appearance. » gelatin; micas

Isis [**iy**sis] Ancient Egyptian goddess, wife of Osiris and mother of Horus, sometimes portrayed with horns and the Sun's disc. In Hellenistic and Roman times, she was a central figure in mystery religions, and was associated with magical beliefs. » Osiris

Islam [iz**lahm**] The Arabic word for 'submission' to the will of God (Allah), the name of the religion originating in Arabia during the 7th-c AD through the Prophet Mohammed. Followers of Islam are known as Muslims, or Moslems, and their religion embraces every aspect of life. They believe that individuals, societies, and governments should all be obedient to the will of God as it is set forth in the Koran, which they regard as the Word of God revealed to his Messenger, Mohammed. The Koran teaches that God is one and has no partners. He is the Creator of all things, and holds absolute power over them. All persons should commit themselves to lives of grateful and praise-giving obedience to God, for on the Day of Resurrection they will be judged. Those who have obeyed God's commandments will dwell for ever in paradise, but those who have sinned against God and not repented will be condemned eternally to the fires of hell. Since the beginning of creation God has sent prophets, including Moses and Jesus, to provide the guidance necessary for the attainment of eternal reward, a succession culminating in the revelation to Mohammed of the perfect word of God.

There are five essential religious duties known as the 'Pillars of Islam'. (1) The *shahada* (profession of faith) is the sincere recitation of the two-fold creed: 'There is no god but God' and 'Mohammed is the Messenger of God'. (2) The *salat* (formal prayer) must be performed at fixed hours five times a day while facing towards the holy city of Mecca. (3) Alms-giving through the payment of *zakat* ('purification') is regarded primarily as an act of worship, and is the duty of sharing one's wealth out of gratitude for God's favour, according to the uses laid down in the Koran. (4) There is a duty to fast (*saum*) during the month of Ramadan. (5) The *Hajj* or pilgrimage to Mecca is to be performed if at all possible at least once during one's lifetime. *Shari'a* is the sacred law of Islam, and applies to all aspects of life, not just religious practices. It describes the Islamic way of life, and prescribes the way for a Muslim to fulfil the commands of God and reach heaven. There is an annual cycle of festivals, including Hijra, the beginning of the Islamic year, and Ramadan, the month during which Muslims fast during the hours of daylight. There is no organized priesthood, but great respect is accorded the Hashim family, descendants of Mohammed, and other publicly acknowledged holy men, scholars, and teachers, such as mullahs and ayatollahs.

There are two basic groups within Islam. Sunni Muslims are in the majority, and they recognize the first four caliphs as Mohammed's legitimate successors. The Shiites comprise the largest minority group, and regard the imam as the principal religious authority. There are a number of subsects, including the Ismailis (one group of which, the Nizaris, regard the Aga Khan as their imam), and the Wahhabis, a reform movement begun in the 18th-c. There are over 700 million Muslims throughout the world. » Ahmadiyya; Allah; ayatollah; Black Muslims; dervish; Druze; hajj; imam; jihad; Kaba; Koran; mahdi; Mecca; Mohammed; mullah; Muslim Brotherhood; Shiites: Sunnis; Wahhabis

Islamabad 33°40N 73°08E, pop (1981) 201 000. Capital city of Pakistan, on the R Jhelum; a modern planned city, built since 1961; head of navigation for larger vessels in the Vale of Kashmir; two universities (1965, 1974); centre of agricultural region; shrine of Bari Imam; museum of folk and traditional heritage. » Pakistan [i]

Islamic architecture An architectural form at first deriving from converted Christian or pagan buildings, its distinctive features appearing after the 8th-c, such as the horseshoe arch, masonry tunnel vaults, rich carved surface decoration, mosaics, and paint. Minarets, attached to mosques and used to call followers to prayer, were developed during the Arab Umayyad dynasty; amongst the most noteworthy later mosques are those at Tabriz, Persia (1204), and those of the Sultan Baybars, Cairo (1267–9). » arch[i]; Indian architecture; Islam; Persian architecture; Ummayyad Mosque; vault[i]

Islamic art An essentially ornamental and abstract style of art, in contrast to the Christian emphasis on figurative art, created largely in the service of the Islamic religion. It began in the 7th-c and spread W to Spain and E to India and China. » figurative art; Islam

Islamic law » **Shari'a**

island A piece of land totally surrounded by water, in an ocean, sea, or lake. It may be formed by: (i) remnants of former high land cut off from the mainland by a rise in sea level, or by subsidence, as with the islands of the Aegean, and the Western Is of Scotland; (ii) volcanic eruptions on the ocean floor, as with the Hawaiian Is and Iceland; (iii) deposition of sediment, as with the Frisian Is; and (iv) coral islands. » atoll; island arc; RR12

island arc Oceanic islands occurring in arc-shaped chains, such as the Aleutians, Mariana, Lesser Antilles, S Sandwich, and Tonga-Kermadec Is. They usually contain active volcanoes, and are adjacent to deep ocean trenches. The theory of plate tectonics maintains that island arcs are formed by volcanism generated as the rigid plates making up the Earth's surface are recycled into the Earth's interior beneath the trenches. » plate tectonics[i]; volcano

Isle of Man » **Man, Isle of**

Isle of Wight » **Wight, Isle of**

Ismail Pasha [ismaheel] (1830–95) Khedive of Egypt, born in Cairo, the second son of Ibrahim Pasha. Educated at St Cyr, France, in 1863 he became Deputy of the Ottoman Sultan, and was granted the title of Khedive in 1866. His massive development programme included the building of the Suez Canal, which was opened in splendour in 1869. The accumulation of a large foreign debt led to European intervention; he was deposed by the Ottoman Sultan, and replaced by his eldest son, Tewfik. He died in exile in Istanbul. » Egypt[i]; Suez Canal

Ismailis [izmayeeleez] Adherents of a secret Islamic sect, one of the main branches of the Shiites; also known as the 'Seveners'. It developed from an underground movement (c.9th-c), reaching political power in Egypt and N Africa in the 10th–12th-c. It distinguished between inner and outer aspects of religion, was critical of Islamic law, and believed that in the eventual new age of the seventh imam, a kind of universal religion would emerge that was independent of the laws of all organized religions. Thus it welcomed adherents of other religions, but retained its own secret traditions and rites. » imam; Islam; Shiites

Ismailiya or **Ismailia** [izmiyleea] 30°36N 32°15E, pop (1976) 145 978. Capital of Ismailiya governorate, NE Egypt; on W bank of Suez Canal by L Timsah, 72 km/45 ml NNW of Suez; founded in 1863 as a base for constructing the Canal; railway; market gardening in irrigated area. » Suez Canal

isobar **1** In meteorology, a line on a weather map joining places of equal barometric pressure. Because of variations in barometric pressure with altitude, recordings from different elevations are corrected and adjusted to pressure at sea level. The closer the lines are together, the stronger the pressure gradient force, and therefore the stronger the winds. » atmospheric pressure; bar; isoline; wind[i] **2** In thermodynamics, a line of constant pressure on a graph, depicting the relationship between volume and temperature. » thermodynamics

Isocrates [iysokrateez] (436–338 BC) Greek orator and prose writer, born and died in Athens. In his youth, he joined the circle of Socrates, but abandoned philosophy for speech writing. He then became an influential teacher of oratory (c.390 BC), and presented rhetoric as an essential foundation of education. » Greek literature; rhetoric

isocyanate » **fulminate**

isoelectronic Having the same number of electrons. Examples of isoelectronic ions and atoms are O^{2-}, F^-, Ne, Na^+, and Mg^{2+}, each with 10 electrons; the molecules N_2O and CO_2 are also isoelectronic, with 22 electrons.

isohyet [iysohhiyuht] A line on a weather map joining places receiving equal amounts of rainfall. » isoline; rainfall

isolating language » **analytic language**

isolation A location designed to accommodate either highly infective patients or those susceptible to infection from others. The entrance to the unit, through which gowned attendants gain access to the patients and all sanitized supplies are delivered, is separated from the exit through which leave contaminated materials, including attendants who have been in contact with the patients. The direction of the flow of air can also be controlled to avoid contamination by airborne micro-organisms. » infection

isolationism A foreign policy strategy of withdrawing from international affairs as long as the country's interests are not affected. It is a means of avoiding involvement in international conflicts, and implies neutrality in most cases. It was practised most notably by the USA, which kept out of the League of Nations and World War 2 until attacked by the Japanese.

isoline A line on a map which joins places of equal value; also known as an **isopleth**. For example, on a temperature map, places recording the same temperature are joined by an isotherm. » isobar; isohyet; isotherm; map

isomers [iysuhmerz] Substances having the same molecular formula but with the atoms connected differently. The main types are: (1) *structural isomers*, such as ethanol (CH_3CH_2OH) and methyl ether (CH_3OCH_3), with different connectivities, (2) *geometrical isomers*, such as maleic and fumaric acid, where two different arrangements arise because of restricted rotation about a bond, and (3) *optical isomers*, such as the two forms of lactic acid, where the isomers are mirror images of one another. » molecule

isometrics A form of physical exercise in which muscles are contracted, but not allowed to move the associated joints. Muscles are used in this way when exerting force on a closed door or fixed bar. Isometric exercises are often undertaken to strengthen muscles not much used in everyday movements. » muscle[i]

isopentane » **pentane**

isopleth » **isoline**

Isopoda [iysopuhda] A diverse order of crustaceans characterized by a flattened body and seven similar pairs of thoracic legs; typically bottom-living in aquatic habitats, sometimes parasitic on fishes and crustaceans; some, the woodlice, are highly successful in terrestrial habitats. (Class: *Malacostraca*.) » crustacean; woodlouse

isoprene [iysuhpreen] C_5H_8, IUPAC 2-methylbuta-1,3-diene, boiling point 34°C. A liquid, the monomer of which natural rubber may be considered an addition polymer. It is also the basic unit from which terpene molecules are constructed. » addition reaction; elastomers; rubber; terpene

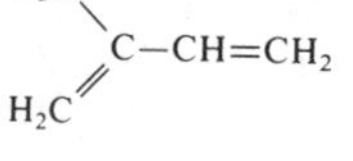

isopropyl » **propyl**

Isoptera [iysoptuhra] » **termite**

isospin In particle and nuclear physics, a vector quantum number conserved in strong interactions only, useful in determining allowed reactions and classifying particles; sometimes called **isotopic spin**. For example, neutrons and protons both have an isospin vector of length ½ unit that points up for protons and down for neutrons. The independence of strong nuclear force on the orientation of this vector corresponds to the independence of the force on electric charge. It is modelled on the spin quantum number. » nucleon; particle physics; quantum numbers; strong interaction; vector

isostasy [iysostuhsee] A theory describing the state of mass balance in the Earth's crust which can be considered as less dense blocks floating on the denser semi-molten mantle. Thus high mountains must be regions where the crust is thickest, with deep roots extending into the mantle. Also, continents uplift (*elastic rebound*) when material is removed by erosion or an overburden of ice is melted away, as at the end of an ice age. » Ice Age; orogeny

isotherm **1** In meteorology, a line on a weather map joining places of equal temperature. » isoline; temperature **2** In thermodynamics, a line of constant temperature on a graph, depicting the relationship between volume and pressure. » isothermal process; thermodynamics

isothermal process In thermodynamics, a process in which the temperature is constant whilst the system changes. Examples include melting and boiling. » heat; isotherm; latent heat

isotope separation The separation of an isotopic mixture into its component isotopes. The charged ions of isotopes are deflected in electric and magnetic fields by differing amounts, depending on their mass – an effect exploited in the mass spectrometer. The rate of diffusion of a gas of isotopic mixture depends on the isotope mass, exploited in gaseous uranium hexafluoride for the enrichment of nuclear fuel. » ion; isotopes; mass spectrometer

isotopes Species of the same element that are chemically identical, having the same proton number, but of different atomic masses due to a differing number of neutrons in the nucleus. All elements have isotopes. Many elements occur naturally as a mixture of isotopes. » chemical elements; isotope separation; mass spectrometer; nuclear structure; nuclide; radioisotope

isotopic spin » **isospin**

isotropic A term used to describe a material or feature whose properties are the same in all directions. For example, metals are isotropic, since their properties (eg conductivity and tensile strength) are the same throughout. The term contrasts with **anisotropic**, where the properties are not the same in all directions. An example is wood, which is stronger along the grain than across it. Anisotropy in certain crystals causes bifringence. » bifringence; crystals

Israel, Hebrew **Yisrael**, official name **State of Israel**, Hebrew **Medinat Israel** pop (1990e) 4 822 000, excluding E Jerusalem and Israeli settlers in occupied territories; area within the boundaries defined by 1949 armistice agreements 20 770 sq km/ 8 017 sq ml. State in the Middle East, divided into six districts, plus the occupied territories of Judaea-Samaria and Gaza; bounded W by the Mediterranean Sea, N by Lebanon, NE by Syria, E by Jordan, and SW by Egypt; capital, Jerusalem; chief towns, Tel Aviv-Yafo, Haifa, Beersheba, Acre, Holon; timezone GMT +2; population mainly Jewish (83%), Arab (11%); chief religions, Judaism (85%), Islam (11%), Christianity and others (4%); official languages, Hebrew, Arabic; unit of currency, the shekel.

Physical description and climate. Extends 420 km/261 ml N–S; width varies from 20 km/12 ml to 116 km/72 ml; narrow coastal plain crossed by several rivers; mountainous interior, rising to 1 208 m/3 963 ft at Mt Meron; mountains in Galilee and Samaria, dissected by faults, dropping E to below sea-level in the Jordan–Red Sea rift valley; R Jordan forms part of E border; Negev desert (S) occupies c.60% of the country's area; typically Mediterranean climate in N and C, with hot, dry summers and warm, wet winters; temperatures at Tel Aviv, 14°C (Jan), 27°C (Jul), average annual rainfall 550 mm/22 in; rainfall heavier inland, with occasional snow; low rainfall in Negev, decreasing in the S.

History and government. Zionist movement founded by Theodor Herzl, end of the 19th-c; thousands of Jews returned to Palestine, then part of the Ottoman Empire; Britain given League of Nations mandate to govern Palestine and establish Jewish national home there, 1922; Nazi persecution of Jews in the 1930s greatly increased Jewish immigration; British evacuated Palestine, and Israel proclaimed independence, 1948; invasion by Arab nations, resulting in armistice, 1949; Six-Day War (1967) brought Israeli control of the Gaza Strip, Sinai Peninsula as far as the Suez Canal, West Bank of the R Jordan including the E sector of Jerusalem, and the Golan Heights in Syria; Camp David conference between Egypt and Israel (1978); Israeli withdrawal from Sinai, 1979; invasion of Lebanon, forcing the PLO to leave Beirut, 1982–5; renewed tension

□ international airport

since 1988, with uprising of Arabs in occupied territories (the *intifada*); a parliamentary democracy with a prime minister and cabinet, and a unicameral 120-member parliament (*Knesset*), elected for a 4-year term; president elected for a maximum of two 5-year terms.

Economy. Over 90% of exports are industrial products, including polished diamonds, transportation equipment, plastics, processed foods, textiles, chemicals, electronics, medical engineering, agricultural equipment, computers, alternative energy sources; major tourist area, primarily to the religious centres; copper, potash, phosphates; citrus fruits, melons, avocados, flowers, cotton, sugar beet, vegetables, olives, tobacco, bananas, beef and dairy products; a world leader in agro-technology, with areas of intensive cultivation; major irrigation schemes, including the 'National Water Carrier' project to transfer water from L Tiberias in the N to the Negev desert in the S; the *kibbutz* system produces c.40% of food output, but in recent years has turned increasingly towards industry. » Arab–Israeli Wars; East Bank; Galilee; Gaza Strip; Golan; Hebrew; Hebrew literature; Jerusalem; Jordan, River; Judaism; Judea; Negev; Tel Aviv-Yafo; Tiberias, Lake; West Bank; RR25 national holidays; RR53 political leaders

Israel, tribes of In the Bible, a confederacy of twelve tribes generally traced to Jacob's twelve sons – six by Leah (Reuben, Simeon, Levi, Judah, Issachar, Zebulun), two by Rachel (Joseph, Benjamin), two by Rachel's maid Bilhah (Dan, Naphtali), and two by Leah's maid Zilpah (Gad, Asher); the name *Israel* had been given to Jacob (*Gen* 32.28) after the story of his wrestling with a divine being. During the settlement of Canaan and the Transjordan, the tribes were allocated portions of land (*Josh* 13–19); but the Levites, a priestly class, had no allocation and possibly were never a 'tribe' as such, and Joseph's 'tribe' was actually two tribes, traced to his two sons Ephraim and Manasseh (*Gen* 48). The number of tribes was thereby maintained as 'twelve'. Once the monarchy was established in Israel (c.10th-c BC), the tribal confederation effectively ended, although it still played a role in Jewish religious thought. » Asher/Benjamin/Dan/Gad/Issachar/Joseph/

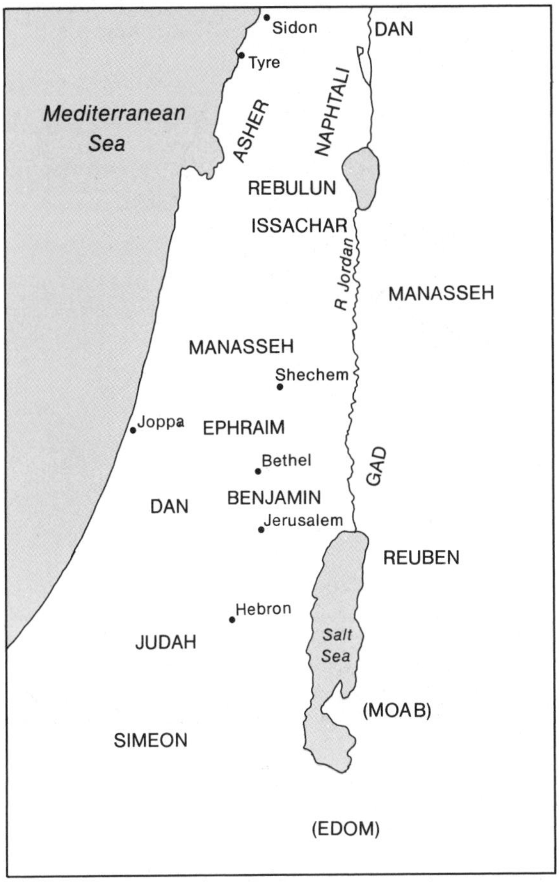

Israel during the period of the Judges – Approximate tribal areas

Judah / Levi / Naphtali / Reuben / Simeon / Zebulun, tribe of; Bible; Jacob; Ten Lost Tribes of Israel

Issachar, tribe of [isakah] One of the twelve tribes of ancient Israel, said to be descended from Issachar, one of Jacob's sons by his wife Leah. Its territory included the central plain of Jezreel between Mt Tabor and Mt Gilboa. » Israel, tribes of

issuing house A merchant bank which specializes in the issue of shares and bonds on the stock market. Over 50 banks belong to the Issuing Houses Association in the UK. » merchant bank

Istanbul [istan**bul**] or **Stamboul**, formerly **Byzantium** (c.660 BC–AD 330), **Constantinople** (330–1930) 41°02N 28°57E, pop (1980) 4 445 793. Capital city of Istanbul province, NW Turkey, on the Golden Horn and on both sides of the Bosporus; the only city in the world situated on two continents; chief city and seaport of Turkey; commercial and financial centre; the part corresponding to historic Constantinople is on the European side; founded and renamed by Constantine I in AD 330 on the site of ancient Byzantium, becoming the new capital of the Roman Empire; remains of ancient Constantinople are a world heritage site; see of the patriarch of the Greek Orthodox Church and of the Armenian Church; airport; railway (once noted as the E terminus of the Orient Express, and still an important rail junction; three universities (1453, 1773, 1944); suspension bridges (first in 1973) link European and Asian sections; commerce, textiles, shipbuilding, food processing, leather, tobacco, cement, glass; a major tourist area; Topkapi Palace (15th-c), Hagia Sophia Basilica (6th-c), Blue Mosque of Sultan Ahmet Camii, Mosque of Süleyman the Magnificent (16th-c), Roman cisterns, covered bazaar; International Istanbul Festival (Jun–Jul). » Bosporus Bridge; Constantine I (Emperor); Hagia Sophia; Turkey [i]

Isthmian Games In ancient Greece, one of the main Pan-Hellenic contests, held every other year near the Isthmus of Corinth. They were in honour of the god Poseidon, and consisted of athletic contests, horse-racing, and poetical and musical competitions. » Corinth; Olympia (Greece); Pythian Games

Istria, Serbo-Croatian **Istra** area 3 160 sq km/1 220 sq ml. Peninsula at the N end of the Adriatic Sea, Yugoslavia; occupied by Croats, Slovenes, and Italians; formerly part of the Italian province of Venezia Giulia; ceded to Yugoslavia, 1947 (apart from Trieste); chief town, Pula; tourist area. » Trieste; Yugoslavia [i]

Itaipu Dam [eetiypoo] A major earth- and rock-fill gravity buttress dam on the R Paraná at the Brazil–Paraguay frontier; completed in 1985; height 189 m/620 ft. It has the capacity to generate 12 600 megawatts of hydroelectricity, and is claimed to be the largest hydroelectric complex in the world. » dam; Paraná, River

Italian » **Italian literature; Romance languages**

Italian art The central tradition in European art, and the most powerful source of stylistic influences from the late Middle Ages to the 18th-c, affecting all other culture. Mediaeval Italy saw classical motifs re-used for Christian subjects, while antique figure sculpture dominated styles and standards for 1500 years. The succession of great masters begins with Giotto in the early 14th-c and continues unbroken down to Canova (died 1822). Italy was never unified during that time, and Florentine art developed very differently from that of Venice, Rome, or Bologna. » Canova; Christian art; Etruscan art; Florentine School; Giotto; Italy [i]; Mannerism; metaphysical painting; Renaissance art; Sienese School; Venetian School

Italian literature After some allegorical romances written under French influence in the 13th-c, Italian literature came to precocious maturity the next century with the work of Dante (*Divina Commedia*, c.1300), Petrarch, and Boccaccio (*Decameron*, 1348–58). These great poets and humanists had imitators but no real successors until the Renaissance. Then, the court of Florence and Naples produced many spirited writers, while at Ferrara Boiardo wrote the *Orlando Innamorato* (1486), Ariosto provided a more famous sequel, the *Orlando Furioso* (1516), and Tasso wrote the *Gerusalemme Liberata* (1575). Machiavelli's cynical treatise *Il Principe* (1532, The Prince) and Aretino's licentious *Letters* (published 1609) are also an index of the times. A further long period of relative decline was punctuated by the scientific and philosophical works of Galileo and Vico, and Goldoni's comedies. The Romantic movement brought the anguished lyrics of Leopardi, and Manzoni's historical novel *I Promessi Sposi* (1825–7, The Betrothed). The Realist novel took root in Sicily with Giovanni Verga (1840–1922) and in Sardinia with Grazia Deledda (1875–1936, Nobel Prize, 1926). After *Six Characters in Search of an Author* (1920), Luigi Pirandello conducted a single-handed revival of the Italian theatre, which has been followed up by the radical plays of Dario Fo (eg *The Accidental Death of an Anarchist*). Significant 20th-c Italian novelists have included Italo Svevo, Alberto Moravia, Ignazio Silone, and Italo Calvino; while the poets Quasimodo and Montale have both won a Nobel Prize. » allegory; Ariosto; Boccaccio; Boiardo; Calvino; Dante; Galileo; humanism; Italy [i]; literature; Machiavelli; Montale; Moravia, Alberto; Petrarch; Pirandello; Quasimodo; Realism; Renaissance; Romanticism (literature); Silone; Svevo; Tasso; Vico

Italian millet » **millet**

Italian Wars A series of conflicts lasting from 1494 to 1559 (Treaty of Cateau-Cambrésis) between the French Valois monarchs and the Habsburgs for the control of Italy. Both houses laid claim to the throne of the Kingdom of Naples, but after seven phases of warfare, involving a host of different monarchs and states, Spain emerged victorious. » Habsburgs

Italic languages The early languages spoken in the area of modern Italy, now extinct. The major language of the group was *Latin*, the language of Rome and the surrounding provinces, evidenced in inscriptions from the 6th-c BC, and in literature from the 3rd-c BC; it is used now only in formulaic contexts of religion, and in public (usually governmental) declamations. » Latin literature; Romance languages

italic script A sloping style of handwriting introduced by Aldus Manutius of Venice in c.1500, which was later introduced into printing. Today, it has a wide range of functions, including the identification of foreign words, quoted forms, book titles, emphatic utterance, and special emotional effects. » Aldus Manutius; typography

Italy, Ital **Italia**, official name **Italian Republic**, Ital **Repubblica Italiana** pop (1990e) 57 512 000; area 301 225 sq km/116 273 sq ml. Republic of S Europe, comprising the boot-shaped peninsula extending S into the Mediterranean Sea, as well as Sicily, Sardinia, and some smaller islands; divided into 20 regions; bounded W by the Tyrrhenian Sea, NW by France, N by Switzerland and Austria, NE by Yugoslavia, E by the Adriatic Sea, and S by the Ionian Sea; capital, Rome; chief cities, Milan, Turin, Genoa, Naples, Bologna, Palermo, Florence; timezone GMT +1; official language, Italian, with German also spoken in the Trentino-Alto Adige, French in Valle d'Aosta, and Slovene in Trieste-Gorizia; chief religion, Roman Catholicism; unit of currency, the lira.

Physical description. Italian peninsula extends c.800 km/500 ml SE from the Lombardy plains; Apennines rise to peaks above 2 000 m/6 500 ft; Alps (N) form an arc from Nice to Fiume, highest peaks along Swiss–French frontier, at Mt Blanc (4 807 m/15 771 ft) and the Matterhorn (4 477 m/14 688 ft); broad, fertile Lombardo–Venetian plain in basin of R Po; several lakes at foot of the Alps, including Maggiore, Como, and Garda; flat and marshy on Adriatic coast (N); on the Riviera (W), coastal mountains descend steeply to the Ligurian Sea; island of Sicily separated from the mainland by the 4 km/2½ ml-wide Strait of Messina; includes limestone massifs of Monti Nebrodi and the volcanic cone of Mt Etna (3 323 m/10 902 ft); Sardinia rises to 1 835 m/6 020 ft at Monti del Gennargentu; chief rivers include the Po, Tiber, Arno, Volturno, Liri, and Adige.

Climate. Great variation with relief and latitude; rainfall on R Po plain is well distributed throughout the year; hot and sunny summers, short and cold winters; higher areas of peninsular Italy are cold, wet, often snowy; coastal regions have a typical Mediterranean climate, with warm, wet winters and hot, dry summers; Adriatic coast colder than the W coast, and receives less rainfall; long hours of sunshine in extreme S during summer.

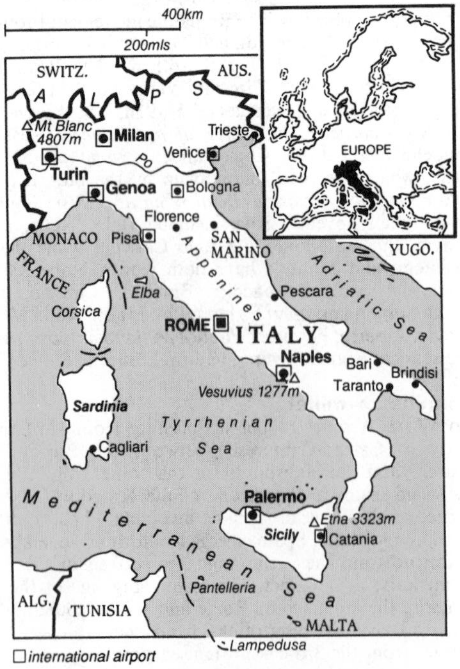

History and government. In pre-Roman times, inhabited by the Etruscans (N), Latins (C), and Greeks (S); most regions part of the Roman Empire by 3rd-c BC; invaded by barbarian tribes in 4th-c AD, last Roman emperor deposed in 476; later ruled by the Lombards and by the Franks under Charlemagne, who was crowned Emperor of the Romans in 800; part of the Holy Roman Empire under Otto, 962; conflict between popes and emperors throughout Middle Ages; dispute between Guelphs and Ghibellines, 12th-c; divided amongst five powers, 14th–15th-c (Kingdom of Naples, Duchy of Milan, republics of Florence and Venice, the papacy); major contribution to European culture through the Renaissance; numerous republics set up after French Revolution; Napoleon crowned King of Italy, 1805; 19th-c upsurge of liberalism and nationalism (*Risorgimento*); unification achieved by 1870 under Victor Emmanuel II of Sardinia, aided by Cavour and Garibaldi; colonies established in Eritrea (1870–89) and Somaliland (1889); attempt to secure a protectorate over Abyssinia defeated at Adowa (1896); fought alongside Allies in World War 1; Fascist movement brought Mussolini to power, 1922; conquest of Abyssinia (1935–6) and Albania (1939); alliance with Hitler in World War 2 led to the end of the Italian Empire; a democratic republic since 1946, when the monarchy was abolished; Parliament consists of a 630-member Chamber of Deputies and a 315-member Senate, both bodies elected for five years; a president serves a 7-year term, and appoints a prime minister; continued political instability, with over 45 governments in power since the formation of the republic.

Economy. Industry largely concentrated in the N; poorer agricultural region in the S; machinery, vehicles, iron and steel, chemicals, food processing, textiles, machine tools (world's fifth largest producer), footwear, tourism; iron ore, lead, oil, natural gas, sulphur, mercury; Po valley a major agricultural region, with wheat, maize, sugar beet, potatoes, rice, beef, dairy farming; foothills of the Alps, apples, peaches, walnuts, wine; further S, citrus fruits, vines, tomatoes, olives, tobacco. » Apennines; Cavour; fascism; Garibaldi; Ghibellines; Guelphs; Holy Roman Empire; Italian art/literature; Mussolini; Po, River; Renaissance; Roman history [i]; Rome; Sardinia; Sicily; Victor Emmanuel II; RR26 national holidays; RR53 political leaders

itch An irritating sensation in the upper surface of the skin. It may become a distressing complaint, also known as **pruritus**, which may be localized to one area (eg lice, scabies) or generalized, in which case the skin may appear normal. It occurs in a number of metabolic disorders, such as lymphomas and obstructive jaundice. Occasionally the complaint is the result of a psychoneurosis. Many skin diseases are associated with itching. » jaundice; lymphoma; scabies; skin [i]

itch mite A parasitic mite found in humans; causes itching by burrowing into the horny layer of skin; females lays eggs in burrows; larvae and nymphs also feed on skin; also known as **scabies**. (*Sarcoptes scabiei*. Order: *Acari*.) » mite; parasitology; scabies

Ito, Hirobumi [eetoh] (1838–1909) Japanese statesman and Premier (1885–8, 1892–6, 1898, 1900–1), born in Choshu province. He visited Europe and the USA on several occasions, drafted the Meiji constitution (1889), and played a major role in abolishing Japanese feudalism and building up the modern state. He was assassinated at Harbin by a supporter of Korean independence. » Meiji Restoration

Itúrbide, Agustín de [eetoorbithay] (1783–1824) Mexican general, born at Morelia. He became prominent in the movement for Mexican independence, and made himself Emperor as Agustín I (1822–3). He was forced to abdicate, travelled in Europe, and was executed on his return to Mexico, at Padilla.

IUD » **contraception**

IUPAC The acronym of **International Union of Pure and Applied Chemistry**, best known as the more-or-less acknowledged authority on chemical nomenclature. Its system, which requires frequent change, attempts to provide clear rules for naming compounds unambiguously.

Iuppiter » **Jupiter** (mythology)

Ivan III, byname **the Great** (1440–1505) Grand Prince of Moscow (1462–1505), born and died in Moscow. He succeeded in ending his city's subjection to the Tartars, and gained control over several Russian principalities. In 1472 he assumed the title of 'Sovereign of all Russia', and adopted the emblem of the two-headed eagle of the Byzantine Empire. » Golden Horde

Ivan IV, byname **the Terrible** (1530–84) Grand Prince of Moscow (1533–84), born near Moscow, the first to assume the title of 'tsar' (Lat *Caesar*). He subdued Kazan and Astrakhan, made the first inroads into Siberia, and established commercial links with England. In 1564 the treachery of one of his counsellors caused him to see treachery everywhere, and he embarked on a reign of terror, directed principally at the feudal aristocracy (boyars). He nonetheless did much for Russian culture and commerce. He died in Moscow. » boyars

Ivanovo, formerly **Ivanovo-Voznesensk** (1871–1932) [eevanuhvuh] 57°00N 41°00E, pop (1983) 474 000. Capital city of Ivanovskaya oblast, C European Russia; on R Uvod, 318 km/198 ml NW of Moscow; founded, 1871; noted for its revolutionary activities in the 1880s, 1905, and 1917; railway; historic centre of Russia's cotton-milling; textiles, machines, chemicals, wood products, foodstuffs. » Russia

Ivanovo churches [ivahnuhvuh] A series of cells, chapels, and churches cut out of the rock face on the banks of the Rusenski Lom R, near the village of Ivanovo in NE Bulgaria. The complex, which is now a world heritage site, was constructed by monks during the 13th-c and 14th-c. » Bulgaria [i]

Ives, Charles (Edward) (1874–1954) US composer, born at Danbury, Connecticut. He studied music at Yale, and worked in insurance till 1930, when he retired through ill health. His compositions were mainly written before 1915, and are firmly based in the American tradition. They include four symphonies, chamber music, and many songs. In 1947 he was awarded the Pulitzer Prize for his 3rd Symphony (composed 1904). He died in New York City.

Iviza » **Ibiza**

ivory Pieces of walrus and elephant tusk, regarded as precious material by many societies throughout the world. Carved ivory ornaments, jewellery and religious objects were produced in China from about the 15th-c BC, and later by the Greeks and Romans in Europe. Most of the finest small-scale sculptures to survive from the mediaeval period are carved from ivory, and it continued to be widely used for luxury goods until modern concern for wildlife conservation strictly curtailed its supply. » elephant; walrus

IVY LEAGUE

INSTITUTION	FOUNDED
Harvard University, Cambridge, Massachusetts	1636
Yale University, New Haven, Connecticut	1701
University of Pennsylvania, Philadelphia, Pennsylvania	1740
Princeton University, Princeton, New Jersey	1746
Columbia University, New York City, New York	1754
Brown University, Providence, Rhode Island	1764
Dartmouth College, Hanover, New Hampshire	1769
Cornell University, Ithaca, New York	1865

Ivory Coast » **Côte d'Ivoire** [i]

ivy An evergreen woody climber, growing to 30 m/100 ft, native to Europe and W Asia; adhesive aerial roots; leaves dark green often with pale veins; those of juvenile, climbing shoots palmately 3–5-lobed; those of mature, non-climbing shoots, oval, entire; flowers greenish-yellow, 5-petalled, petals 3–4 mm/0.12–0.16 in, in rounded umbels produced on non-climbing shoots; fruits berry-like, black, ribbed, poisonous. (*Hedera helix*. Family: *Araliaceae*.) » climbing plant; evergreen plants; palmate; umbel

Ivy League A group of long-established and prestigious colleges in NE USA. The league was formally established in 1956 to oversee inter-collegiate sports. » university

Iwo Jima [eewoh jeema] area c.21 sq km/8 sq ml. The most important and largest of the Volcano Is; in the W Pacific Ocean, 1 222 km/759 ml S of Tokyo; 8 km/5 ml long; maximum width 4 km/2½ ml; rises to 167 m/549 ft at Suribachi-yama, an extinct volcano; coastguard station (N); scene of major battle of World War 2 (1944–5), when the heavily fortified Japanese air base was taken in a 3-month campaign; returned to Japan, 1968; sugar, sulphur. » Volcano Islands

Ixion [ikseeon] In Greek mythology, a King of Thessaly, the first murderer; also the father of the Centaurs. For attempting to rape Hera he was bound to a wheel of fire, usually located in the underworld. » centaur

Ixtaccihuatl, Aztec **Iztaccihuatl** [eestaseewatl] 19°11N 98°38W. Dormant volcano in C Mexico; rises to 5 286 m/17 342 ft, 56 km/35 ml SE of Mexico City; irregular-shaped, snow-capped volcano with three summits; situated in Ixtaccihuatl-Popocatépetl National Park, area 257 sq km/99 sq ml, established in 1935. » Mexico [i]; volcano

Izabal, Lake (Span **Lago de**) [eesaval] Lake in Izabal department, E Guatemala; drains into an inlet of the Caribbean Sea, via the R Dulce; area 1 000 sq km/400 sq ml; length 48 km/30 ml; width 24 km/15 ml; the largest lake in the country, serving as an important commercial waterway. » Guatemala [i]

Izanagi no Mikoto and **Izanami no Mikoto** Respectively, a Japanese male and female god. In the creation myth these were the first beings who created islands in the water and the other gods. Izanami died when she gave birth to fire. Izanagi followed her to the land of the dead (Yomi), but she turned against him and pursued him. Finally he had to block the exit from Yomi with a large rock. Izanami then became the goddess of the underworld.

iz(z)ard [izuhd] » **goat**

Izmir [eezmeer], formerly **Smyrna** 38°25N 27°10E, pop (1980) 1 226 060. Seaport capital of Izmir province, W Turkey, on an inlet of the Aegean Sea; third largest city in Turkey; severely damaged by earthquakes, 1928, 1939; airfield; railway; university (1955); brewing, electronics, packaging, foodstuffs, steel, engines, cement, plastics, paper; largest poultry and egg farm in the Middle East; Kadifekale fortress (4th-c BC), Roman remains; annual international fair. » Turkey [i]

J

j-curve In economics, the shape of the curve in a diagram showing balance of trade statistics over time, after a currency has been devalued. The purpose of the devaluation is to improve a country's trade balance. Initially, however, it can deteriorate. The curve, therefore, starts by moving downwards for a few months, before changing direction and moving upwards as planned. ≫ balance of payments

jabiru [**jab**iroo] A name used for several species of stork; especially *Jabiru mycteria* of C and S America; also the **saddle-bill stork** (*Ephippiorhyncus senegalensis*) from S Africa, and the **black-necked stork** (*Ephippiorhyncus asiaticus*) from India to N Australia. (Family: *Ciconiidae*.) ≫ stork

Jabneh [**jab**ne] or **Jamnia** An ancient city on the coastal plain E of Jerusalem and S of modern Tel Aviv, referred to occasionally in writings of the Biblical and Maccabean periods. It achieved special prominence in early Judaism after the fall of Jerusalem (AD 70), when Rabban Johanan ben Zakkai asked the Roman Emperor for the city, and re-established the Sanhedrin council there for a time. Famous Jewish scholars gathered there to lay the foundations for the Mishnah and engage in study of the Torah. ≫ Akiva ben Joseph; Johanan ben Zakkai; Judaism; Mishnah; Torah

jacamar [**jak**amah] A bird native to the New World tropics; long bill and tail; iridescent plumage; inhabits forests; eats insects caught in flight; nests on ground in burrow. (Family: *Galbulidae*, 15 species.)

jacana [**jak**ana] A bird native to the tropics world-wide; inhabits freshwater lakes and ponds; eats small aquatic animals and plants; resembles rails, but not related; toes extremely long; walks on floating vegetation; also known as **lily-trotter** or **lotus bird**. (Family: *Jacanidae*, 8 species.) ≫ rail

jacaranda A small deciduous tree growing to 12 m/40 ft; leaves pinnately divided into segments, which in turn are pinnately divided into numerous small, oval leaflets; inflorescences pyramidal; flowers drooping, funnel-shaped, blue. Native to Argentina, it has been widely planted in warm regions as an ornamental and street tree. (*Jacaranda mimosifolia*. Family: *Bignoniaceae*.) ≫ deciduous plants; inflorescence [i]; pinnate; tree [i]

jacinth [**ja**sinth] A rare, red orange or yellow gemstone variety of the mineral zircon. ≫ zircon

Jack-go-to-bed-at-noon ≫ **goatsbeard**

Jack Russell A small terrier, developed in Britain by Rev John Russell (1795–1883); sent into foxes' burrows; originally fox-like in size, but white (to avoid confusion with the fox); now smaller, with shorter legs; often dark. ≫ dog; fox; terrier

Jack the Ripper Unidentified English murderer, who between August and November 1888 murdered and mutilated six prostitutes in the East End of London. The murderer was never discovered. The affair roused much public disquiet, provoked a violent press campaign against the CID and the Home Secretary, and resulted in some reform of police methods.

jackal A member of the dog family, resembling a large fox in appearance and habits; three African species: the **black-backed jackal** (*Canis mesomelas*), **side-striped jackal** (*Canis adustus*), and **simien(ian) jackal** (*Canis simensis*); also, the **golden jackal** (*Canis aureus*) from N Africa to SE Asia. ≫ aardwolf; Canidae; fox

jackass ≫ **kookaburra**

jackdaw Either of two species of bird, genus *Corvus*: the omnivorous jackdaw (*Corvus monedula*), from N Africa, Europe, and W Asia; and the insect-eating **daurian jackdaw** (*Corvus dauuricus*), from E Asia. Both nest in holes.

Jacklin, Tony, properly **Anthony** (1944–) British golfer, born at Scunthorpe, Humberside. He won the 1969 British Open at Royal Lytham (the first British winner for 18 years), and in 1970 won the US Open at Hazeltine (the first British winner for 50 years). He turned professional in 1962, and won the Jacksonville Open in 1968, the first Briton to win on the US Tour. A former Ryder Cup player, he was appointed captain of the European team in 1983. ≫ golf

jackrabbit ≫ **hare**

Jackson, Andrew, byname **Old Hickory** (1767–1845) US statesman and seventh President (1829–37), born at Waxhaw, North Carolina. He trained as a lawyer, and became a member of Congress for Tennessee (1796), Senator (1797), and a judge of its supreme court (1798–1804). In the war of 1812 against Britain, he was given command of the South, and became famous for his defence of New Orleans (1815). His election as President was the result of a campaign in which he gained the support of the mass of voters – a new development in US politics which came to be called 'Jacksonian democracy'. He retired in 1837, and died near Nashville, Tennessee. ≫ War of 1812

Jackson, Glenda (1936–) British actress, born in Birkenhead. She trained in London, and became a leading member of the Royal Shakespeare Company before appearing in films in 1967, winning two Oscars for *Women in Love* (1969) and *A Touch of Class* (1973). She has continued to portray complex characterizations on stage and screen, such as the poet Stevie Smith, whom she played first in the theatre and then in the film *Stevie* (1979), and has made several television appearances. Later films include *Beyond Therapy* (1985) and *Business as Usual* (1986).

Jackson, Helen (Maria) Hunt, *née* **Fiske** (1830–85) US writer and campaigner for Indian rights, born at Amherst, Massachusetts. She embarked on a literary career after losing her husband and two sons. She moved W in 1873, and after remarrying became interested in the Indians' cause, on which she was outspoken. Her foremost works were the nonfiction *A Century of Dishonor* (1881) and the novel *Ramona* (1884). She died in San Francisco. ≫ civil rights; Indian Wars

Jackson, Jesse (Louis) (1941–) US clergyman and politician, born at Greenville, North Carolina. Educated at the University of Illinois and Chicago Theological Seminary, he was ordained a Baptist minister in 1968. He was an active participant in the civil rights movement, and organized Operation PUSH (People United to Save Humanity) in 1971. In 1984 and 1988 he sought the Democratic nomination for the presidency, winning considerable support, and becoming the first Black American to mount a serious candidacy for the office. ≫ civil rights; Democratic Party

Jackson, Reggie, properly **Reginald** (1946–) US baseball player, born at Wyncote, Pennsylvania. In the 1977 World Series he equalled Babe Ruth's 51-year-old record for hitting three home runs in one game. He started his League career with Kansas City in 1967, and also played for Oakland, the Yankees, and (from 1982) the California Angels. ≫ baseball [i]

Jackson, Thomas Jonathan, byname **Stonewall** (1824–63) Confederate general in the US Civil War, born at Clarksburg, West Virginia. In 1851 he became a professor at the Virginia Military Institute. During the Civil War, he took command of the Confederate troops at Harper's Ferry on the secession of Virginia, and commanded a brigade at Bull Run, where his firm stand gained him his byname. He showed tactical superiority in the campaign of the Shenandoah valley (1862), and gained several victories, notably at Cedar Run, Manassas, and Harper's Ferry. He was accidentally killed by his own troops at Chancellorsville. » American Civil War

Jackson 32°18N 90°12W, pop (1980) 202 895. Capital of state in Hinds County, C Mississippi, USA, on the Pearl R; largest city in the state; established as a trading post (Le Fleur's Bluff), 1792; state capital, 1821; named after President Andrew Jackson; much of the city destroyed by Sherman's forces during the Civil War, 1863; airfield; railway; university; oil, natural gas, food processing, timber, metal and glass products; many civil rights demonstrations in the 1960s; 'Casey' Jones buried here; Dixie Livestock Show (Feb). » American Civil War; civil rights; Jackson, Andrew; Mississippi

Jacob Biblical character, son of Isaac, patriarch of the nation Israel. He supplanted his elder brother Esau, obtaining his father Isaac's special blessing and thus being seen as the inheritor of God's promises. He was re-named *Israel* (perhaps meaning 'God strives' or 'he who strives with God') after his struggle with a divine being. By his wives Leah and Rachel and their maids he fathered 12 sons, to whom Jewish tradition traced the 12 tribes of Israel. » Bible; Esau; Isaac; Israel, tribes of [i]

Jacobean Style English early Renaissance architecture from the period 1603–25. The name derives from King James I of that period. The style is characterized by a symmetry of facades, large windows and, in the case of manor houses such as Hatfield (1608–12), E- or H-shaped plans. » Elizabethan Style; Renaissance architecture

Jacobins (French history) [**jak**uhbinz] A radical political group in the French Revolution, originally the Club Breton in Versailles, but renamed after transferring to the premises of the Dominican or 'Jacobin' fathers in Paris (1789). After successive purges, the club became the instrument of the Reign of Terror under Robespierre's dictatorship (1793–4), the name being associated thereafter with left-wing extremism. » French Revolution [i]; left wing; Robespierre

Jacobins (religion) » **Dominicans**

Jacobites Those who supported the claim of the Catholic James II, and his successors, to the British throne. The Jacobites launched two rebellions, in 1715 and 1745, against the Protestant Hanoverian succession, and in the period 1714–60 some British Tory politicians had Jacobite sympathies. » Fifteen Rebellion; Forty-five Rebellion; James II (of England)

Jacobsen, Arne (1902–1971) Danish architect and interior designer, born in Copenhagen. Educated at the Royal Danish Academy, he designed many private houses, including those for Bellevue seaside resort near Copenhagen. In 1943 he escaped to Sweden from Nazi rule. In 1956 he was appointed professor of architecture at the Royal Danish Academy. His later works include the SAS building, Copenhagen (1959) and St Catherine's College, Oxford (1964). He died in Copenhagen.

Jacopo della Quercia [yak**oh**poh dela **kwair**cha] (c.1374–1438) Italian sculptor, born and died in Siena. His greatest works include the city's fountain (the 'Fonte Gaia', executed 1414–19) and the reliefs on the portal of San Petronia, Bologna. » relief sculpture; Sienese School; Renaissance

Jacopone da Todi » **Todi, Jacopone da**

Jacquard, Joseph Marie [zhak**ah**] (1752–1834) French silk-weaver, born in Lyons. His invention (1801–8) of the Jacquard Loom enabled an ordinary workman to produce highly intricate weaving patterns. Napoleon rewarded him with a small pension, but the silk weavers themselves were long opposed to his machine. By the time of his death, at Oullins, his machine was in almost universal use. » weaving

Jacquerie [**zhak**uhree] (1358) A serious peasant rebellion in NE France, noted for its savagery. Started by mercenaries following the English victory at Poitiers (1356), it degenerated (May 1358) into bitter violence between the oppressed peasantry, aggrieved Parisians, and their noble overlords; the latter massacred the insurgents indiscriminately at Meaux and Clermont-en-Beauvaisis (Jun 1358).

jade A semi-precious stone, either of two distinct mineral species: the relatively rare *jadeite* (a green pyroxene) which is often translucent, and *nephrite* (a variety of amphibole) which has a waxy lustre. Commonly green or white in colour, it is often used in ornamental carvings. Nephrite was in use for ritual objects in China by the 3rd millennium BC, the rarer jadeite in Europe for axes in the later 4th/3rd millennium. Though worked in Mexico from c.1500 BC, New World jadeite reached the West only after the Spanish Conquest (AD 1519), and China even later, c.1780. » amphiboles; gemstones; pyroxenes; Plate V

jaeger » **skua**

Jaffa » **Tel Aviv-Yafo**

Jagger, Mick » **Rolling Stones**

Jagiellons [yag**yel**uhnz] The ruling dynasty of Poland-Lithuania, Bohemia, and Hungary, which dominated EC Europe from the Baltic to the Danube in the 15th–16th-c. Founded when Jagiello, Grand Duke of Lithuania, became King of Poland (1386–1434), it flourished under his acquisitive successors until Sigismund II Augustus (reigned 1548–72) died without heirs.

jaguar A big cat, found from S USA to N Argentina; coat with rings of dark blotches surrounding dark spots; some individuals almost black; inhabits woodland and savannah near water; swims and climbs well; eats peccaries, capybaras, other mammals, birds, fish, turtles. (*Panthera onca*.) » Felidae

jaguarundi or **jaguarondi** [jagwa**run**dee] A member of the cat family, found from S USA to Paraguay; short legs; long body; grey or reddish-brown (red form formerly called *Eyra cat*); inhabits woodland margins; eats birds and small mammals; once trained by Mayans to control rodents. It is an unusual cat, in that it may chase prey for up to 1.6 km/1 ml, and sometimes eats fruit. (*Felis yagouaroundi*.) » Felidae; Mayas

Jainism [**jiy**nizm] An indigenous religion of India which regards Vardhamana Mahavira (599–527 BC), said to be the last Tirthankara, as its founder. Jains believe that salvation consists in conquering material existence through adherence to a strict ascetic discipline, thus freeing the 'soul' from the working of karma for eternal all-knowing bliss. Liberation requires detachment from worldly existence, an essential part of which is the practice of Ahimsa, non-injury to living beings. The ascetic ideal is central to both monastic and lay Jainism, although final renunciation is possible only within the former. They number about 3 million. » Ahimsa; karma; Tirthankara

Jaipur [**jiy**poor] 26°53N 75°50E, pop (1981) 1 005 000. Capital of Rajasthan state, NW India, SW of Delhi; founded, 1727; railway; university (1947); textiles, metallurgy, stone carving, jewellery; Maharaja's palace, Sawai Man Singh Museum, Hawa Mahal (1739), Jantar Mantar observatory (1726); known as the 'pink city' since 1875, when Sawai Ram Singh had all the buildings of the bazaar painted pink. » Rajasthan

Jakarta or **Djakarta** [jak**ah**ta], formerly **Batavia** 6°08S 106°45E, pop (1980) 4 576 009. Seaport capital of Indonesia; on NW coast of Java, at mouth of R Liwung on Jakarta Bay; largest Indonesian city; developed as a trading post, 15th-c; headquarters of Dutch East India Company, 17th-c; capital, 1949; airport; railway; 11 universities (1950–60); timber, textiles, shipbuilding, paper, iron, rubber, tin, oil, coffee, palm oil, tea; Istiqlal Mosque; 90 m/295 ft high national monument; Taman Mini provincial exhibition. » East India Company, Dutch; Indonesia [i]

Jakobson, Roman (1896–1982) Russian theoretician of linguistics, born in Moscow. The founder of the Moscow Linguistic Circle (which generated Russian Formalism), he moved in 1920 to Czechoslovakia (starting the Prague Linguistic Circle), and finally in 1941 to the USA, where he taught at Harvard and the Massachusetts Institute of Technology until his death in Boston. His many books and hundreds of papers on language have had a great general influence on linguistic and literary thought: see his *Selected Writings* (8 vols, 1962–88). » Formalists; linguistics; literary criticism; structuralism

jalap A perennial climber with tuberous roots and twining annual stems; leaves heart-shaped–triangular; flowers funnel-shaped, pinkish-purple; native to Mexico. The resinous roots yield a purgative drug. (*Ipomaea purga*. Family: *Convolvulaceae*.) » climbing plant; perennial; resin; tuber

Jamaica pop (1990e) 2 391 000; area 10 957 sq km/4 229 sq ml. Island in the Caribbean Sea, situated 160 km/100 ml W of Haiti and 144 km/89 ml S of Cuba; divided into three counties; capital, Kingston; chief towns, Montego Bay, Spanish Town;

timezone GMT − 5; chief ethnic groups, African (76%), Afro-European (15%); official language, English, with Jamaican Creole widely spoken; chief religion, Christianity; unit of currency, the Jamaican dollar of 100 cents; third largest island in the Caribbean; maximum length, 234 km/145 ml; width, 35–82 km/22–51 ml; mountainous and rugged, particularly in the E, where the Blue Mts rise to 2 256 m/7 401 ft; over 100 small rivers, several used for hydroelectric power; humid and tropical climate at sea-level, more temperate at higher altitudes; coastal temperatures 21–34°C, mean annual rainfall 1 980 mm/78 in; virtually no rainfall on S and SW plains; lies within the hurricane belt; visited by Columbus in 1494; settled by Spanish, 1509; West African slave labour imported for work on sugar plantations from 1640; British occupation, 1655; self-government, 1944; independence, 1962; a governor-general appoints a prime minister and cabinet; a bicameral parliament consists of an elected 60-member House of Representatives and a nominated 21-member Senate; plantation agriculture still employs about a third of the workforce; sugar, bananas, citrus fruits, coffee, cocoa, ginger, coconuts, pimento; second largest producer of bauxite in the world; alumina, gypsum, cement, fertilizer, textiles, foodstuffs, rum, chemical products, tourism. » Columbus, Christopher; Kingston (Jamaica); slave trade; RR26 national holidays; RR53 political leaders

James I (of England) (1566–1625) The first Stuart King (1603–25), also King of Scotland (1567–1625) as **James VI**, the son of Mary, Queen of Scots, and Henry, Lord Darnley, born in Edinburgh Castle. On his mother's forced abdication, he was proclaimed King, and brought up by several Regents. When he began to govern for himself, he ruled through his favourites, which caused a rebellion, and a period of imprisonment. In 1589 he married Princess Anne from Kristiania. Hating Puritanism, he managed in 1600 to establish bishops in Scotland. On Elizabeth's death, he ascended the English throne as great-grandson of James IV's English wife, Margaret. At first well received, his favouritism again brought him unpopularity. He died at Theobalds, Hertfordshire. » Authorized Version of the Bible; Buckingham, George Villiers; Cecil, Robert; Mary, Queen of Scots

James II (of England) (1633–1701) King of England and Ireland (1685–8), also King of Scotland, as **James VII**, the second son of Charles I, born in London. Nine months before his father's execution he escaped to Holland. At the Restoration (1660) he was made Lord High Admiral of England, and commanded the fleet in the Dutch Wars; but after becoming a convert to Catholicism he was forced to resign his post. The national ferment occasioned by the Popish Plot (1678) became so formidable that he had to retire to the Continent, and several unsuccessful attempts were made to exclude him from the succession. During his reign his actions in favour of Catholicism raised general indignation, and William, Prince of Orange, his son-in-law and nephew, was formally asked by leading clerics and landowners to invade. Deserted by ministers and troops, James escaped to France, where he was warmly received by Louis XIV. He made an ineffectual attempt to regain his throne in Ireland, which ended in the Battle of the Boyne (1690), and remained at St Germain until his death. » Dutch Wars; Popish Plot; Stuart, James; William III

James IV (of Scotland) (1473–1513) King of Scots (1488–1513), the eldest son of James III. He became active in government at his accession, at the age of 15, and gradually exerted his authority over the nobility. In 1503 he married Margaret Tudor, the eldest daughter of Henry VII – an alliance which led ultimately to the union of the crowns. However, he adhered to the French alliance when Henry VIII joined the League against France, and was induced to invade England by the French. He was defeated and killed, along with the flower of his nobility, at the Battle of Flodden, Northumberland. » Henry VII/VIII; Scotland [i]

James V (of Scotland) (1512–42) King of Scots (1513–42), the son of James IV. An infant at his father's death, he grew up amid the struggle between the pro-French and pro-English factions in his country. In 1536 he visited France, marrying Magdeleine, the daughter of Francis I (1537), and after her death, Mary of Guise (1538). War with England followed from the French alliance (1542), and after an attempt to invade England, he was routed at Solway Moss. He retired to Falkland Palace, Fife, where he died soon after the birth of his daughter Mary (later, Mary, Queen of Scots). » Scotland [i]

James ('brother' of Jesus), known also as **St James (the Just)** (1st-c), feast day 1 May. Listed with Joseph, Simon, and Judas (*Matt* 13.55) as a 'brother' of Jesus of Nazareth, and identified as the foremost leader of the Christian community in Jerusalem (*Gal* 1.19, 2.9; *Acts* 15.13). He is not included in lists of the disciples of Jesus, and should not be confused with James son of Alphaeus or James son of Zebedee, but did apparently witness the resurrected Christ (1 *Cor* 15.7). He showed Jewish sympathies over the question of whether Christians must adhere to the Jewish law. According to Josephus, he was martyred by stoning (c.62). » James, Letter of; Jesus Christ

James (son of Alphaeus), also known as **St James (the Less)** (1st-c) One of the twelve apostles. He may be the James whose mother Mary is referred to at the crucifixion of Jesus. » apostle; crucifixion

James (son of Zebedee), also known as **St James (the Great)** (1st-c), feast day 25 July. One of Jesus' twelve apostles, often listed with John (his brother) and Peter as part of an inner group closest to Jesus. They were among the first called by Jesus, and were with Jesus at his Transfiguration and at Gethsemane. He and his brother John were also called *Boanerges* ('sons of thunder'). According to *Acts* 12.2, he was martyred under Herod Agrippa I (c.44). » apostle; John, St (son of Zebedee)

James, Letter of New Testament writing attributed to 'James', who was considered in early tradition to be James the brother of Jesus, but who today is often considered an unknown late 1st-c author, in view of the distance from Pauline theology and polemic in the writing. The letter's recipients are described only as 'the twelve tribes in the Dispersion'. It emphasizes a variety of ethical teachings, but was sometimes criticized (most notably by Luther) for lacking a distinctively Christian message and for its un-Pauline emphasis on 'works' rather than 'faith'. » James ('brother of Jesus'); Luther; New Testament; Paul, St

James, Henry (1843–1916) US novelist, born in New York City. After travelling widely in the USA and Europe, and studying law at Harvard, he began to write literary reviews and short stories. His work as a novelist falls into three periods. In the first, he is mainly concerned with the impact of American life on the older European civilization, as in *Roderick Hudson* (1875), *Portrait of a Lady* (1881), and *The Bostonians* (1886). From 1869 he made his home in England, chiefly in London and in Rye, Sussex. His second period is devoted to purely English subjects, such as *The Tragic Muse* (1890) and *The Spoils of Poynton* (1897). He reverted to Anglo-American attitudes in his last period, which includes *The Wings of a Dove* (1902) and his masterpiece, *The Ambassadors* (1903). The acknowledged master of the psychological novel, he was a major influence on 20th-c writing. He died at Rye, Sussex. » American literature; novel

James, Jesse (Woodson) (1847–1882) US Wild West outlaw, born in Clay County, Missouri. After fighting with a guerrilla group in the Civil War, he and his brother, **Frank** (1843–1915) led numerous bank, train, and stagecoach robberies in and around Missouri before Jesse was murdered for a reward by Robert Ford, a gang member. Frank gave himself up soon after, stood trial, was released, and lived the rest of his life on the family farm.

James, P(hyllis) D(orothy), pseudonym of **Phyllis Dorothy White** (1920–) British detective-story writer, born at Oxford, and educated at Cambridge High School. She worked as a National Health Service administrator (1949–68), and then at the Home Office (1968–9), first in the Police Department, then in the children's division of the Criminal Department. The experience has provided the backgrounds of several of her novels, such as *Shroud for a Nightingale* (1971), *Death of an Expert Witness* (1977), and *Innocent Blood* (1980). » detective story

James, William (1842–1910) US psychologist and philosopher, born in New York City, the brother of the novelist Henry James. Educated in New York and in Europe, he received a medical degree from Harvard (1869), where he began teaching anatomy and physiology (1873), and philosophy (1879). His books include *The Principles of Psychology* (1890), *The Will to Believe and Other Essays in Popular Philosophy* (1897), and *The Varieties of Religious Experience* (1902). He helped found the American Society for Psychical Research, and published numerous papers on the subject. He died at Chocorua, New Hampshire. » James, Henry; parapsychology; pragmatism

Jameson Raid An expedition against the South African Republic (Dec 1895–Jan 1896), which was supposed to link up with a revolt by White workers on the Rand and topple the government of President Kruger. Leander Starr Jameson (1853–1917), administrator for the South Africa Company at Fort Salisbury, led a detachment of British South Africa Police into the Transvaal, but they were easily defeated and arrested. The German Kaiser, Wilhelm II, sent a telegram of congratulation to Kruger, and the incident caused a major government crisis in Britain as well as contributing to the tensions that led to the Boer War. » Boer Wars; Kruger; South Africa [i]

Jamestown (St Helena) 15°56S 5°44W, pop (1987) 1 302. Seaport capital and only town on the British island of St Helena in the S Atlantic; passenger and cargo services to the UK and S Africa. » St Helena

Jamestown (USA) A deserted 25 ha/62 acre town, 24 km/15 ml inland from Chesapeke Bay, Virginia, USA, the site of the first successful British settlement in America. Excavated archaeologically 1934–56, it was founded in 1607 by 105 settlers as James Fort, but after 1699 was superseded as the capital of Virginia by Williamsburg, and abandoned. » Williamsburg

Jammu-Kashmir [**jam**oo kash**meer**] pop (1981) 5 981 600; area 101 283 sq km/39 095 sq ml. State in the extreme N of India; bounded N by the July 1972 line of control (separating territory claimed by both India and Pakistan), W by Pakistan, E by China; crossed by several mountains and rivers; part of the Mughal Empire, 1586; Afghan rule, 1786; annexed to the Sikh Punjab, 1819; Kashmir asked for agreements with both India and Pakistan at independence, 1947; attacked by Pakistan, and acceded to India; further hostilities, 1965, 1972; summer capital, Srinagar; winter capital, Jammu; governed by a 36-member Legislative Council and a 76-member Legislative Assembly; rice, wheat, maize, fruit, forestry, crafts; manufacturing industry largely in Jammu; horticulture widespread in Kashmir. » India [i]; Pakistan [i]

Jamnia » **Jabneh**

Jan Mayen [yahn **mi**yuhn], formerly Eng **Hudson's Tutches** area 380 sq km/147 sq ml. Norwegian volcanic island in the Arctic Ocean, 480 km/298 ml E of Greenland, 576 km/358 ml NNE of Iceland; length 53 km/33 ml; highest point, Beerenberg (2 277 m/7 470 ft); discovered by Henry Hudson in 1608; annexed to Norway, 1929; radio and meteorological stations. » Norway [i]

Janáček, Leoš [**ya**nahchek] (1854–1928) Czech composer, born at Hukvaldy, Moravia. He became choirmaster in Brno, where he eventually settled after studying at Prague and Leipzig, and became professor of composition (1919). Devoted to the Czech folksong tradition, he wrote several operas, a mass, instrumental chamber pieces, and song cycles. He died at Ostrava, Czechoslovakia.

Jane, Frederick Thomas (1865–1916) British naval author, journalist, and artist, born at Upottery, Devon. He worked first as an artist, then as a naval correspondent on various periodicals. He founded and edited *Jane's Fighting Ships* (1898) and *All the World's Aircraft* (1909), the annuals by which his name is best known. » warships [i]

janissaries An elite force of Turkish soldiers established in the 14th-c. Throughout their history they mutinied several times, and were finally suppressed after a revolt in Constantinople in 1826. » army

Jansen, Cornelius (Otto) [**yahn**sen, **jan**sen] (1585–1638) Dutch Roman Catholic theologian, founder of the reform movement known as **Jansenism**, born at Acquoi. He studied at Utrecht, Louvain, and Paris, became professor of theology at Louvain (1630), and Bishop of Ypres (1636), where he died just after completing his 4-volume work, *Augustinus* (published 1640). This sought to prove that the teaching of St Augustine on grace, free will, and predestination was opposed to the teaching of the Jesuit schools. The book was condemned by Pope Urban VIII in 1642, but the controversy raged in France for nearly a century, when a large number of Jansenists emigrated to the Netherlands. » Roman Catholicism

jansky [**yan**skee] A unit used in radio astronomy to measure the power received at the telescope from a cosmic radio source. 1 jansky (Jy) $= 10^{-26} \mathrm{W m^{-2} Hz^{-1} sr^{-1}}$. » Jansky; radio astronomy

Jansky, Karl Guthe [**yan**skee] (1905–50) US radio engineer, born at Norman, Oklahoma. His fundamental discovery (1932) was of radio waves from outer space, while working on interference suffered by radio reception. This discovery allowed the development of radio astronomy during the 1950s. He died at Red Bank, New Jersey. » jansky; radio astronomy

Januarius, St, Ital **San Gennaro** (?–c.305), feast day 19 September. Italian Christian martyr, Bishop of Benevento, who was martyred at Pozzuoli. His body is preserved in Naples Cathedral, with two phials supposed to contain his blood. The solid matter in the phials is said to liquefy on his feast day, and at several other times during the year. » Christianity

Janus (astronomy) [**jay**nuhs] The tenth natural satellite of Saturn, discovered in 1980; distance from the planet 151 000 km/94 000 ml; diameter 200 km/120 ml. » Saturn (astronomy); RR4

Janus (mythology) [**jay**nuhs] An ancient Roman divinity who guards the 'gate' or the door; there is no Greek equivalent. Because one goes out to begin an action, Janus became the god of beginnings; he is the first god named in a list, and the god of the first month (January). He is always depicted in art with two faces, one at the back of the head.

Japan, Jap **Nippon** or **Nihon** pop (1990e) 123 692 000; area 381 945 sq km/147 431 sq ml. Island state comprising four large islands (Hokkaido, Honshu, Kyushu, Shikoku) and several small islands off the E coast of Asia; divided into nine regions; bounded W by the Sea of Japan, Korea Strait, and East China Sea, E by the Pacific Ocean, and N by the Tsugaru-kaikyo Strait; capital, Tokyo; chief cities include Yokohama, Osaka, Nagoya, Sapporo, Kyoto; timezone GMT +9; population over 99% Japanese; official language, Japanese; chief religions, Shinto, Buddhism; unit of currency, the yen.

Physical description. Islands consist mainly of steep mountains with many volcanoes; Hokkaido (N) central range runs N–S, rising to over 2 000 m/6 500 ft, falling to coastal uplands and plains; Honshu, the largest island, comprises parallel arcs of mountains bounded by narrow coastal plains; includes Mt Fuji (3 776 m/12 388 ft); heavily populated Kanto plain in E; Shikoku and Kyushu (SW) consist of clusters of low cones and rolling hills, mostly 1 000–2 000 m/3 000–6 000 ft; Ryukyu chain of volcanic islands to the S, largest Okinawa.

Climate. Oceanic climate, influenced by the Asian monsoon; heavy winter rainfall on W coasts of N Honshu and in Hokkaido; short, warm summers in N, and severe winters, with heavy snow; Akita (N Honshu), average daily temperature of

−5–2°C (Jan), 19–28°C (Aug), rainfall minimum 104 mm/4 in (Feb–Mar), maximum 211 mm/8.3 in (Sep); variable winter weather throughout Japan, especially in N and W; typhoons in summer and early autumn; mild and almost subtropical winters, with light rainfall, in S Honshu, Shikoku, and Kyushu; summer heat often oppressive, especially in cities.

History and government. Originally occupied by the Ainu; developed into small states, 4th-c; Yamato dynasty dominant, 5th-c; culture strongly influenced by China, 8th–12th-c; ruled by feudal shoguns for many centuries; little contact with the West until the Meiji Restoration, 1868; successful wars with China, 1894–5, and Russia, 1904–5; Korea annexed, 1910; occupied Manchuria, 1931–2; entered World War 2 with surprise attack on the US fleet at Pearl Harbor, Hawaii, 1941; occupied British and Dutch possessions in SE Asia, 1941–2; pushed back during 1943–5; atomic bombs on Hiroshima and Nagasaki, 1945; strong economic growth in 1960s; a constitutional monarchy with an emperor as head of state, and a prime minister and cabinet; bicameral Diet (*Kokkai*), with a 512-member House of Representatives (*Shugiin*) elected every four years and a 252-member House of Councillors (*Sangiin*) elected every six years.

Economy. Limited natural resources, with less than 20% of the land under cultivation; intensive crop production (principally of rice); timber, fishing, metallurgy, engineering, electrical goods, electronics industries, vehicles, petrochemicals, shipbuilding, textiles, chemicals. » Ainu; Fuji, Mount; Hokkaido; Honshu; Japanese; Japanese architecture/art/literature/music; Kyushu; Meiji Restoration; Shikoku; Shogun; Tokyo; World War 2; RR26 national holidays; RR53 political leaders

Japan, Sea of Area 1 012 900 sq km/390 900 sq ml. Arm of the Pacific Ocean, bounded by S and N Korea (SW), Russia (N and W), and the islands of Japan (E and S); NE-flowing warm current keeps coastal conditions ice-free as far N as Vladivostok (Russia). » Pacific Ocean

Japanese The language of Japan, spoken by c.118 million in Japan, and a further 2 million elsewhere, mainly in the USA and Brazil. The relationship of Japanese to other languages is uncertain, though it is thought to resemble the Altaic family more than others. It has written records from the 8th-c in Chinese characters (*kanji*), which remain the basis of one of the Japanese writing systems. » Altaic; ideography; Japanese literature; kanji; syllabary

Japanese architecture The architecture of Japan, largely deriving from China, based on the column and wooden frames with non-structural wood and paper infill. Unique characteristics are delicate and intricate naturalistic decorations; dominant, projecting roofs of various materials; and an ordered disposition of columns, posts, cornice brackets, and cornice rafters. The earliest surviving buildings are religious, such as the Horyuji Buddhist monastery (7th-c AD). Houses are usually of one-storey design based on a rectangular plan. The arrival of Frank Lloyd Wright and Antonin Raymond at the beginning of the 20th-c marked the start of an increasing Westernization of Japanese architecture, culminating in the Corbusier-influenced Olympia Sports Stadium, Tokyo (1963–4), architect Kenzo Tange, and the Metabolist work of Kisho Kurokawa and Arata Isozaki since the 1960s. » Chinese architecture; column; Japan [i]; Metabolism; Wright, Frank Lloyd

Japanese art The art associated with Japan, which has always depended upon the techniques and styles of China, but is distinguished by its enthusiasm for surface pattern, its emphasis on technical virtuosity, and its fondness for strong colours. Its most characteristic achievements have been in the fields of colour-prints (the names of Utamaro, Hokusai, and Hiroshige are familiar in the West), painted scrolls, pottery, lacquer, and decorative metal-work. Buddhism reached Japan in the 6th-c AD, bringing with it Korean craftsmen under whose influence a great school of religious sculpture emerged, while Zen, another import from China, deeply affected painting. » Chinese art; Hiroshige; Hokusai; Japan [i]; origami [i]; ukiyo-e; Utamaro

Japanese cedar An evergreen conifer native to Japan; narrowly conical, leaves scale-like but long-pointed, spirally arranged; cones scales with spines. It is an important forest tree in Japan, and also widely used in gardens and temples. Elsewhere, it is much planted for timber. (*Cryptomeria japonica*. Family: *Taxodiaceae*.) » conifer; evergreen plants

Japanese deer » **sika**

Japanese literature After some centuries of oral literature, the earliest surviving Japanese work is the *Kojiki*, a story of the creation of the world and of the Japanese race, which dates from AD 712; closely followed by the *Nihon Shoki* (720, Chronicles of Japan). Emancipation from Chinese influence was illustrated by the significant 8th-c anthology of poetry, the *Man'yo-shu* (Collection of the Myriad Leaves), whereas another anthology from the same period, the *Kaifuso*, was written by courtiers in Chinese. The 10th-c collection *Kokin-shu* stands comparison with the *Man'yo-shu*. Murasaki Shikibu's early 11th-c *Monogatari* (Tale of Genji) is one of the masterpieces of Japanese literature, its realism followed up by the tradition of the *zuihitsu* or occasional journal which was written (often by women) for the next two centuries. Buddhism influenced the 12th-c *Ujishui* tales, and the wars of that time are also reflected in many gloomy and introspective narratives. The same atmosphere pervades the next important anthology of poetry, the *Shin Kokin Shu* (1205), and also the celebrated Noh plays of the 14th–15th-c, with their high stylization and conscious artifice.

After a period of destructive wars, the 17th-c witnessed a literary revival linked to the new mercantile class, whose values are reflected in the novels of Ihara Saikaku (1642–93). Matsuo Basho (1644–94) perfected and popularized the *haiku*, and Chikamatsu Monzaemon (1653–1725) introduced the Kabuki plays, often using puppets. Western influence transformed Japanese literature from the mid-19th-c. Mori Ogai (1863–1922) had lived in Germany, and Natsume Sozeki (1867–1916) in England: they revalued the novel, which quickly achieved decadence with Nagai Kafu (1879–1959) and Tanizaki Jur'ichiro (1886–1965). Proletarian literature emerged in the 1920s and 1930s, and new, freer verse forms were introduced. But the prevalent nihilism of modern Japanese literature may be reflected in the suicides of several leading writers, including Akutugawa Ryunosuke (in 1927) and Mishima Yukio (in 1970). » Basho; bunraku; Chinese literature; decadence; haiku; Japan [i]; Kabuki; Mishima; nihilism; Noh

Japanese music The feudalism that isolated Japan from the rest of the world from the late 12th-c to the late 19th-c allowed a slow but unhindered development of traditional musical genres. The most important were: the accompanied chants of the Shinto and Buddhist religious ceremonies; *gagaku*, the traditional court music played by ensembles of string, wind, and percussion instruments; and music for the Noh and Kabuki theatres. There was also a rich repertory of music for individual instruments such as the koto, shamisen, and shakuhachi (a bamboo flute). Since the Meiji Restoration (1868), traditional music has been preserved mainly as a museum culture, while Western pop and art music have increasingly taken its place in the everyday experience of the urban Japanese. » ethnomusicology; Japan [i]; Kabuki; koto; Noh; shamisen

Japanese quince » **japonica**

Japanese tosa » **mastiff**

japanning A European substitution for Oriental lacquer, produced with layers of copal varnish. Instructions for decorating furniture were published by John Stalker and George Parker in the *Treatise of Japaning and Varnishing* (1688). Japanned tinwares were produced commercially in Pontypool and Usk in the late 18th-c, and copied in Birmingham in the 19th-c. » kauri gum; lacquer

Japheth [**jay**feth] Biblical character, one of the sons of Noah who survived the Flood, the brother of Shem and Ham. He is portrayed as the ancestor of peoples in the area of Asia Minor and the Aegean (*Gen* 10). » Bible; Flood, the; Noah

Japonaiserie A term used for the imitation of Japanese motifs, patterns, and compositions by European artists from the mid-19th-c to the early 20th-c. Whistler and van Gogh were among those inspired, in particular by coloured woodcuts. » chinoiserie; Japanese art

japonica A deciduous, sometimes spiny shrub, native to E Asia; leaves oval to oblong with small teeth; flowers 5-petalled, bowl-shaped, scarlet, produced on old wood; also known as **flowering** or **Japanese quince**. It is cultivated for ornament. (*Chaenomeles speciosa*. Family: *Rosaceae*.) » deciduous plants; shrub

Jaques-Dalcroze, Emile [zhahk dahl**krohz**] (1865–1950) Swiss music teacher and composer, born in Vienna. He studied composition, and became professor of harmony at Geneva, where he originated eurhythmics, a method of expressing the rhythmical aspects of music by physical movement. In 1914 he became head of a school of eurhythmic instruction at Geneva, and worked there until his death. » eurhythmics

Jarash [**ja**rash], ancient **Gerasa** 32°10N 35°50E. Village in Irbid governorate, East Bank, NW Jordan; 35 km/22 ml N of Amman; site of old city of Gerasa; paved streets and colonnades, temples, theatres, baths, and a triumphal arch. » Jordan [i]

Jarrell, Randall (1914–65) US poet, born at Nashville, Tennessee, and brought up in California. He was educated at Vanderbilt and later taught for many years at North Carolina. He wrote an early campus novel, *Pictures from an Institution* (1954), and published several volumes of criticism. A dozen volumes from *Blood for a Stranger* (1942) to *The Lost World* (1966) feature in the *Complete Poems* (1971). He died at Chapel Hill, North Carolina. » American literature; Lowell, Robert; poetry

Jarrow March (Oct 1936) A march to London by unemployed workers in the Durham shipbuilding and mining town, to put the unemployed case. Jarrow was among the towns worst affected by the Depression, and the march took place at a time when the economy was recovering in much of the rest of the country. It alerted the more prosperous South and Midlands to the intractable problems of depressed areas. » Great Depression

Jarry, Alfred (1873–1907) French writer, born at Laval. Educated at Rennes, his satirical play, *Ubu-Roi*, was first written when he was 15; later rewritten, it was produced in 1896. He wrote short stories, poems, and other plays in a Surrealist style, inventing a logic of the absurd which he called *pataphysique*. He became an alcoholic, and died in Paris. » French literature; satire; Surrealism

Jaruzelski, General Wojciech (Witold) [yaru**zel**skee] (1923–) Polish general, Prime Minister (1981–5), head of state (1985–), and President (1989–), born near Lublin. He became Chief of General Staff (1965), Minister of Defence (1968), a member of the Politburo (1971), and Prime Minister after the resignation of Pinkowski in 1981. Later that year, in an attempt to ease the country's economic problems and to counteract the increasing political influence of the free trade union *Solidarity*, he declared a state of martial law, which was lifted in 1982. He became president in 1989. » Poland [i]; Solidarity

jasmine A slender shrub or woody climber, some evergreen; flowers tubular with spreading lobes; fruit a berry. **Winter jasmine** (*Jasminum nudiflorum*), an evergreen shrub native to China, has leaves with three leaflets, and bright yellow flowers in winter. **Summer jasmine** (*Jasminum officinale*), a deciduous climber native to Asia, has pinnate leaves, and fragrant white flowers in summer. (Genus: *Jasminum*, 300 species. Family: *Oleaceae*.) » climbing plant; deciduous plants; evergreen plants; pinnate; shrub

Jason [**jay**sn] In Greek legend, the son of Aeson, King of Iolcos. When Pelias usurped the kingdom, Jason was taken away and educated by Chiron. He returned to the city wearing only one sandal, so fulfilling a prophecy which endangered Pelias. He was therefore sent on the quest of the Golden Fleece, leading the Argonauts to Colchis; there he obtained the fleece with Medea's assistance. Later he deserted her for Glauke, and died sitting under the wreck of the *Argo*, whose stern-post fell on him. » Argonauts; Golden Fleece; Medea

jasper A red variety of chalcedony. » chalcedony

Jaspers, Karl (Theodor) [**yas**perz] (1883–1969) German existentialist philosopher, born at Oldenburg. He studied law at Heidelberg and Munich, then medicine at Berlin, Göttingen, and Heidelberg, where he joined the psychiatric clinic (1909–15), and became professor of psychology (1916) and philosophy (1921). His main work is the 3-volume *Philosophie* (1932), a systematic exposition of existential philosophy. With the advent of Nazism, he was removed from his chair (1937) and had his work banned, but he nonetheless stayed in Germany, and for his uncompromising stand was awarded the Goethe Prize in 1947. He then became professor at Basle (1948), where he died. » existentialism

Jataka [**jah**taka] Stories of the Buddha's previous births, contained in the Buddhist Sutra literature. » Buddha; Buddhism

jaundice A condition in which there is a rise in the amount of bile pigments (bilirubin and biliverdin) in the blood. These stain the skin and other tissues, including the whites of the eyes, a greenish-yellow colour. Jaundice arises as a result of (1) excessive breakdown of the blood pigment, haemoglobin (*haemolytic jaundice*), when abnormally large amounts of bile pigments are produced, saturating the capacity of the liver to excrete them, (2) severe liver disease, when the liver's capacity to eliminate bile pigments from the blood to the intestine is reduced, and pigments accumulate in the body, and (3) obstruction to the passage of bile pigments out of the liver through the common bile duct, such as by a gallstone. » bile; biliary system; blood; liver; phototherapy

Jaurès, (Auguste Marie Joseph) Jean [**zhoh**res] (1859–1914) French socialist leader, writer, and orator, born at Castres. He lectured on philosophy at Toulouse, became a Deputy (1885), co-founded the socialist paper *L'Humanité* (1904), and was the main figure in the founding of the French Socialist Party. He was assassinated in Paris. » socialism

Java [**jah**va], Indonesian **Jawa** pop (1980) 91 269 528; area 132 187 sq km/51 024 sq ml. Island of Indonesia, in the Greater Sunda group, SE of Sumatra and S of Borneo; one of the most densely populated islands in the world; major cities include Jakarta, Bandung, Surabaya; mountainous, rising to 3 371 m/11 059 ft at Gunung Sumbung; covered with dense rainforest; 115 volcanic peaks, 15 still active; tobacco, rubber, tea, textiles, timber, rice, maize, sugar; noted for its batik method of cloth decoration. » batik; Indonesia [i]; Jakarta; Javanese; Javanese music

Java Man The first known fossil of *Homo erectus*, found in Java in 1891 by the Dutch anatomist Eugène Dubois (1858–1940). It was long known by the name he gave it: *Pithecanthropus erectus*. » Homo [i]

Java Sea Sea of SE Asia, bounded N by Borneo, S by Java, and

W by Sumatra; linked to the Celebes Sea by the Makassar Strait.

Javanese The largest ethnic group of Java, Indonesia. Their language (Javanese), a member of the Indo-Pacific family, is spoken throughout Java and in parts of Indonesia, and has a literary tradition dating from the 8th-c; but its use in writing is diminishing because of pressure from the standard language, Bahasa Indonesia. The people are Muslim with some Hindu traditions retained from an earlier period. Population c.65 million. » Bahasa Indonesia; Indo-Pacific languages; Java

Javanese music Music and dance are of prime importance in the cultural life of Java. Ensemble music predominates, the most important being the classical gamelan, composed mainly of percussion instruments. The larger gamelans, some of them of great antiquity, are divided into two sets of instruments, each with its own tuning system (*slendro* and *pelog*). The music they play, although highly sophisticated and rhythmically complex, is mainly anonymous and was transmitted orally until the late 19th-c. Since then some systems of skeletal notation have been introduced. » ethnomusicology; Java

javelin throw An athletics field event of throwing a spear-like javelin. The javelin consists of three parts; the pointed metal head, the shaft, and the grip. The men's javelin is 2.6–2.7 m/8.5–8.9 ft in length, and weighs 800 g/8 lb; the women's javelin is 2.2–2.3 m/7.2–7.5 ft in length, and weighs at least 600 g/1.3 lb. With the javelin in one hand, the competitor runs to a specified mark and throws it; for the throw to count, the metal head must touch the ground before any other part. The first mark made by the head is the point used for measuring the distance achieved. The current world record for men is 87.66 m/287 ft 7in, achieved by Jan Zelezńy (Czechoslovakia, born 16 Jun 1966) on 31 May 1987 at Nitra, Czechoslovakia (using a new style javelin introduced in 1986); for women it is 78.90 m/258 ft 10 in, achieved by Petra Felke (East Germany, born 30 Jul 1959) on 29 July 1987 at Leipzig, Germany. » athletics

jaw The upper and lower bones surrounding the mouth, which contain the teeth. The upper jaw (*maxilla*) is usually firmly fixed to the face, while the lower jaw (*mandible*) moves against it. The jaws move against each other during the chewing and grinding of food. The mandible also moves during speech. » mouth; teeth [i]

Jawlensky, Alexej von [yav**len**skee] (1864–1941) Russian painter, born at Kuslovo. He studied at St Petersburg Academy and in Munich, and developed his own brightly-coloured Fauvist style by c.1905. After c.1913 he came under Cubist influence, and painted simpler, more geometrical arrangements using more subdued colours. He died at Wiesbaden. » Cubism; Fauvism; Russian art

jay A name used for many birds, usually of the crow family (*Corvidae*, 42 species), especially the **common jay** (*Garrulus glandiarus*) from N areas of the Old World. The **blue jay** of India (not that of N America) is a roller (Family: *Coraciidae*). **Jay-thrushes** are babblers (Family; *Timaliidae*). » babbler; crow; roller

Jay, John (1745–1829) US statesman and jurist, born in New York City. Educated at King's (now Columbia) College, New York, he was admitted to the Bar (1768), elected to the Continental Congress (1774–5), and became President of Congress (1778), Secretary for Foreign Affairs (1784–9), Chief Justice of the Supreme Court (1789–95), and Governor of New York (1795–1801). He then retired to his farm, and died at Bedford, New York. » American Revolution; Jay's Treaty

Jay's Treaty (1794) An agreement between the USA and Britain to end the British occupation of NW military posts on US territory, and for altering the terms of US commerce with Britain and its colonies. Negotiated by John Jay, it was very unpopular with the US public, and was instrumental in the formation of the Democratic-Republicans as an opposition party. » Jay

Jayawardene, Junius Richard [jaya**wah**duhnay] (1906–) Sri Lankan statesman and President (1978–89), born and educated in Colombo, where he studied law. A member of the State Council (1943) and the House of Representatives (1947), he became Honorary Secretary of the Ceylon National Congress (1940–7), Minister of Finance (1947–53), Vice-President of the United National Party, Deputy Leader of the Opposition (1960–5), Opposition Leader (1970–7), Prime Minister (1977–8), and finally President. » Sri Lanka [i]

jazz A type of music developed from ragtime and blues in the S states of the USA during the second decade of the 20th-c. It originated among Black musicians, but was soon taken up by Whites also and spread throughout the USA and abroad, influencing such composers of 'serious' music as Milhaud, Ravel, Stravinsky, and Walton. What constitutes jazz is notoriously difficult to define, but prominent features of the earliest New Orleans jazz included *syncopation* (strongly accented rhythms which conflict with the basic pulse of the music), collective *improvisation*, and the exploitation of unusual timbres and extreme ranges in an ensemble which consisted typically of clarinet, trumpet (or cornet), trombone, piano, double bass (played pizzicato), guitar, and drums. At least one of these elements is usually present in later jazz, which has developed many different styles. » bebop; blues; cool jazz; Dixieland; improvisation; ragtime; rhythm and blues; salsa; third stream

jazz dance N American form of vernacular dancing performed to the rhythms of jazz. It is a style that swings, owing its origins to African and Caribbean forms of dance, blended with European influences. It is a popular dance style, used in musical shows on Broadway and in the UK (eg *Cats*). » African dance; Caribbean dance

Jean de Meun [zhẽ duh **moẽ**] (c.1240–1305) French poet, born in Meung-sur-Loire. He completed the *Roman de la Rose* (Romance of the Rose) begun by Guillaume de Lorris 50 years earlier, adding another 18 000 to the existing 4 000 lines, and extending the original allegory to include more ethical and philosophical material on the subject of love. He died in Paris. » allegory; Guillaume de Lorris

Jeans, Sir James (Hopwood) (1877–1946) British astrophysicist and popularizer of science, born at Ormskirk, Lancashire. He taught at Cambridge (1904–5, 1910–12) and Princeton (1905–9), where he was professor of applied mathematics, then became a research associate at Mt Wilson Observatory, Pasadena until 1944. He made important contributions to the theory of gases, quantum theory, and stellar evolution, and became widely known for his popular exposition of physical and astronomical theories. He was knighted in 1928, and died at Dorking, Surrey. » gas **1**; quantum field theory; stellar evolution

jebeer » **dorcas gazelle**

Jedda or **Jeddah** 21°29N 39°16E, pop (1982) 1 200 000. Seaport in Mecca province, WC Saudi Arabia; on the E shore of the Red Sea, 64 km/40 ml W of Mecca; Saudi Arabia's commercial capital and largest port; port of entry on pilgrimage route to Mecca; W section stands on land reclaimed from the Red Sea; airport; university (1967); shipping, steel, cement, oil refining; walled city. » Mecca; Saudi Arabia [i]

jeep The name given to a general purpose (GP) light vehicle developed in World War 2 for the United States Army. It became particularly renowned for its exceptional sturdiness and capability for operating on rough terrain, because of its high clearance and 4-wheel drive. After the War, its easy availability, alongside its technical features, laid down the standard against which later specialized rough-terrain working vehicles (eg the Land Rover) developed. With the boom in leisure in the 1970s, there arose a market for non-working rough-terrain vehicles in the USA, and thence worldwide, which led to the manufacture of such types as the Range Rover. » car [i]

Jefferson, Thomas (1743–1826) US statesman and third President (1801–9), born at Shadwell, Virginia. Educated at the College of William and Mary, he became a lawyer (1767), joined the revolutionary party, took a prominent part in the first Continental Congress (1774), and drafted the Declaration of Independence. He was Governor of Virginia (1779–81), Minister in France (1785), and Secretary of State (1789). Vice-President under Adams (1797–1801), he then became President. Events of his administration included the war with Tripoli, the Louisiana Purchase (1803), and the prohibition of the slave trade. He retired in 1809, but continued to advise as an elder statesman. He died at Monticello, Virginia. ≫ Adams, John; Louisiana Purchase

Jefferson City 38°34N 92°10W, pop (1980) 33 619. Capital of state in Cole County, C Missouri, USA, on the Missouri R; city status, 1839; railway; university (1866); government services, agricultural trade. ≫ Missouri

Jeffreys (of Wem), George, 1st Baron (1648–89) English judge, born near Wrexham. Called to the Bar in 1668, he rose rapidly, was knighted (1677), and became Recorder of London (1678). He was active in the Popish Plot prosecutions, became Chief Justice of Chester (1680), baronet (1681), and Chief Justice of the King's Bench (1683). In every state trial he proved a willing tool of the crown, and was raised to the peerage by James II (1685). His journey to the West country to try the followers of Monmouth earned the name of the 'bloody assizes' for its severity. He was Lord Chancellor (1685–8), but on James's flight was imprisoned in the Tower, where he died. ≫ James II (of England); Popish Plot

Jeffries, John (1744–1819) American balloonist, a Boston physician who settled in England after the American Revolution. He made the first balloon crossing of the English Channel with Blanchard in 1785. ≫ ballooning; Blanchard

Jehovah [je**hoh**va] Term used since the 11th-c as a form of the Hebrew name for Israel's God 'Yahweh'. It is formed from a combination of the Latinized consonants of the Hebrew word *YHWH* with the vowels of the Hebrew word *Adonai* ('Master, Lord'). ≫ Yahweh

Jehovah's Witnesses A millenarian movement organized in the USA in 1884 under Charles Taze Russell (1852–1916). They adopted the name Jehovah's Witnesses in 1931; previously they were called 'Millennial Dawnists' and 'International Bible Students'. They have their own translation of the Bible, which they interpret literally. They believe in the imminent second coming of Christ, avoid worldly involvement, and refuse to obey any law which they see as a contradiction of the law of God – refusing, for example, to take oaths, enter military service, or receive blood transfusions. They publish *The Watchtower*, meet in Kingdom Halls, and all 'witness' through regular house-to-house preaching. They number about 1 million. ≫ millenarianism

Jellicoe, John Rushworth, 1st Earl (1859–1935) British admiral, born at Southampton. He became Third Sea Lord (1908), and was Commander-in-Chief at the outbreak of World War 1. His main engagement was the Battle of Jutland (1916), for which at the time he was much criticized. Promoted First Sea Lord, he organized the defences against German submarines, and was made Admiral of the Fleet (1919). He later became Governor of New Zealand (1920–4). Created an earl in 1925, he died in London. ≫ Boxer Rising; World War 1

jellyfish A typically bell-shaped, marine coelenterate with a ring of marginal tentacles and a central mouth on undersurface of bell; body displays a 4-part radial symmetry; endodermal gastric tentacles present in gut; represents the medusa phase of the coelenterate life cycle, the polyp phase being reduced or absent. (Phylum: *Cnidaria*. Class; *Scyphozoa*.) ≫ coelenterate; medusa; polyp

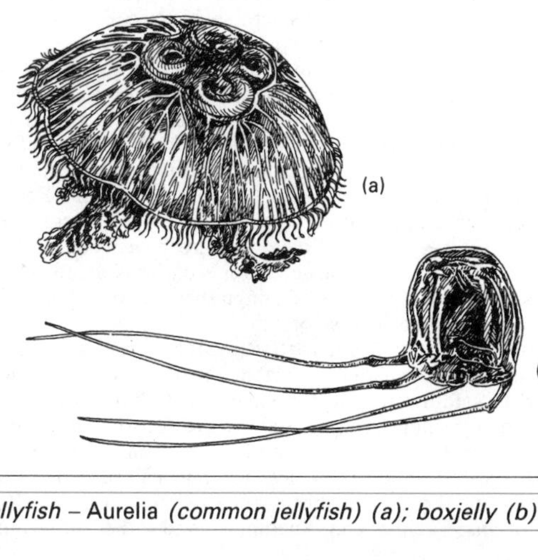

Jellyfish – Aurelia *(common jellyfish) (a); boxjelly (b)*

Jenkins, Roy (Harris), Baron (1920–) British politician, born at Abersychan, Monmouthshire. Educated at Cardiff and Oxford, he became a Labour MP in 1948, and was Minister of Aviation (1964–5), Home Secretary (1965–7), Chancellor of the Exchequer (1967–70), Deputy Leader of the Labour Party in opposition (1970–2) and again Home Secretary (1974–6). He resigned as an MP in 1976 to take up the presidency of the European Commission (1977–81). Upon his return to Britain, he co-founded the Social Democratic Party (1981), and became its first leader, standing down after the 1983 election in favour of David Owen. Defeated in the 1987 election, he was given a life peerage and also became chancellor of Oxford University. ≫ Labour Party; Owen, David; Liberal Party (UK); Social Democratic Party

Jenkins' Ear, War of A war between Britain and Spain starting in 1739, and soon merging into the wider War of the Austrian Succession (1740–8). Some of the violent anti-Spanish indignation in Britain that provoked the war was due to Captain Robert Jenkins, who claimed to have had an ear cut off by Spanish coastguards in the Caribbean. ≫ Austrian Succession, War of the

Jenner, Edward (1749–1823) British physician, the discoverer of the vaccination for smallpox, born at Berkeley, Gloucestershire. He studied in London, then began to practise at Berkeley (1773). In 1796 he inoculated a child with cowpox, then two months later with smallpox, and the child failed to develop the disease. His discovery was violently opposed at first, but within five years vaccination was being practised throughout the civilized world. He died at Berkeley. ≫ smallpox; vaccination

Jennings, Pat(rick) (1945–) Irish footballer, born at Newry, Co Down. Britain's most capped footballer, he played for Northern Ireland 119 times. He started his career with Newry Town before joining Watford, moved to Tottenham Hotspur in 1974, and became their regular goalkeeper for over 10 years before joining Arsenal in 1977. He made a total of 747 Football League appearances, and won several cup winner's medals. He retired in 1986. ≫ football [i]

jerboa A mouse-like rodent; moves by jumping (may leap 3 m/10 ft); hind legs at least four times as long as front legs; ears large; long tail, with long hairs at tip; eats seeds, plants, or insects; does not drink; also known as **desert rat**. (Family: *Dipodidae*, 31 species.) ≫ rodent

Jeremiah or **Jeremias, Book of** [jeruh**miy**a] A major prophetic work of the Hebrew Bible/Old Testament, attributed to the prophet Jeremiah, who was active in Judah c.627–587 BC and who died apparently after fleeing to Egypt from Jerusalem. The work is notable for its record of the prophet's inner struggles, persecution, and despair. Warnings of disaster for Judah's immorality and idolatry are tempered only briefly by support for King Josiah's reforms; the warnings anticipate the fall of Jerusalem (587 BC) and the Babylonian Captivity of the Jews. The present book probably results from a complex history of transmission. ≫ Baruch; Josiah; Lamentations of Jeremiah; Old Testament

Jeremiah, Letter of [jeruh**miy**a] In the Roman Catholic Bible, Chapter 6 of the Book of Baruch; for Protestants, a separate work in the Old Testament Apocrypha. It is ostensibly a letter from the prophet Jeremiah to Jewish captives in Babylon (c.597 BC) warning them against idolatry. Today it is often considered to derive from the later Hellenistic period, possibly in Maccabean times. ≫ Apocrypha, Old Testament; Baruch; Jeremiah, Book of; Maccabees

Jeremias ≫ **Jeremiah, Book of**

Jerez (de la Frontera), also **Xeres** [**he**reth] 36°41N 6°07W, pop (1981) 176 238. Picturesque town a few miles inland from Cádiz, Andalusia, S Spain, giving its name to sherry; airport; noted centre for sherry, wine, and brandy; horse breeding; Fiesta of the Horse (May), wine festival (Sep). ≫ Andalusia; sherry; Spain [i]

Jericho [jerikoh], Arabic **Eriha**, Hebrew **Yeriho** 31°51N 35°27E.

Oasis town in Jerusalem governorate, Israeli-occupied West Bank, W Jordan, 36 km/22 ml NE of Jerusalem; site of the world's earliest known town, continuously occupied c.9000–1850 BC; a tell (mound), area 4–5 ha/10–12 acres, encircled by a 3 m/10 ft-thick wall, and provided with a solid defensive tower still standing 8.5 m/28 ft high; 20th-c excavations have revealed 20 successive settlement layers; scene of famous siege during the Israelite conquest of Canaan, when it is said that the walls fell down at the shout of the army under Joshua; Mount of the Temptation (NW); ruins of palace of Qirbat al-Mafyar (724). » Canaan; Israel [i]; Joshua, Book of; tell; West Bank

Jerome, St, originally **Eusebius Hieronymus** (c.342–420), feast day 30 September. Christian ascetic and scholar, born at Stridon, Dalmatia. After living for a while as a hermit, he was ordained in 379, and became secretary to Pope Damasus (reigned 366–84). He moved to Bethlehem in 386, where he wrote many letters and treatises, commentaries on the Bible, and, notably, made the first translation of the Bible from Hebrew into Latin (the *Vulgate*). He died at Bethlehem. » Bible; Christianity

Jerome, Jerome K(lapka) (1859–1927) British humorous writer, novelist, and playwright, born at Walsall, Staffordshire, and brought up in London. He was successively a clerk, schoolmaster, reporter, actor, and journalist, then became joint editor of *The Idler* (1892) and started his own weekly, *To-Day*. His *Three Men in a Boat* (1889) established itself as a humorous classic. » English literature

Jersey pop (1980) 76 100; area 116 sq km/45 sq ml. Largest of the Channel Is, lying W of Normandy; chief languages, English with some Norman-French; airport; ferries to UK and France; capital, St Helier; noted for its dairy farming (Jersey cattle) and potatoes; tourism; Jersey Zoological Park founded by Gerald Durrell in 1959; underground German headquarters from World War 2. » Channel Islands [i]

Jerusalem, Hebrew **Yerushalayim** 31°47N 35°15E, pop (1982) 424 400. Capital city of Jerusalem district and the State of Israel; a holy city of Christians, Jews, and Muslims, on the E slope of the Judean range; the old city is a world heritage site, surrounded by a fortified wall and divided into four quarters (Armenian, Muslim, Christian, Jewish); part of Roman Empire (1st-c BC); under Turkish rule until conquered by Crusaders, and Kingdom of Jerusalem established, 1099; retaken by Turks, 1187, and again in 16th-c until 1917; capital of Palestine (1922–48); divided between Israel and Jordan by 1949 armistice; declared capital of Israel, 1950; E Jerusalem annexed after Six-Day War, 1967; airfield; railway; Hebrew University (1925); government services, tourism, light industry; citadel (24 BC), 12th-c Cathedral of St James, Temple Mount, El Aqsa Mosque (705–15), Dome of the Rock (685–705), Western Wall, Antonia Fortress (37–4 BC), Church of the Holy Sepulchre, Garden of Gethsemane, Tomb of the Kings, Mount of Olives. » Dome of the Rock; Gethsemane; Israel [i]; Olives, Mount of; Temple, Jerusalem; Western Wall

Jerusalem artichoke A large perennial growing to 2.8 m/9.2 ft, a native of N America; numerous underground stolons have potato-like tubers at their tips, persisting through the winter; leaves lance-shaped, coarsely toothed; flower heads 4–8 cm/1½–3 in across, yellow, surrounded by dark green pointed bracts. Introduced to Europe in the 16th-c, it has been cultivated for its edible tubers (Jerusalem artichokes) containing inulin, a source of the sugar fructose. (*Helianthus tuberosus*. Family: *Compositae*.) » bract; fructose; perennial; stolon; tuber

Jespersen, (Jens) Otto (Harry) [yespuhsn] (1860–1943) Danish philologist, born at Randers. He studied at Copenhagen, where he became professor of English (1893–1925). He wrote several major works on grammar, invented an international language, Novial, and contributed to the development of phonetics and linguistics. He died at Roskilde. » linguistics

Jesuit Estates Act An act of 1888 introduced by the Quebec government of Honoré Mercier, following arbitration by Pope Leo XIII, which assessed the value of Crown Lands in Canada claimed by the Jesuits, and assigned a financial settlement to the Order and the Catholic Church of more than $300 000. The act stimulated discontent and protest among the Orangemen in Canada. » Jesuits

Jesuits A religious order, the **Society of Jesus (SJ)**, founded in 1540 by Ignatius de Loyola. A non-contemplative order, it demands strict obedience, compliance with Ignatius' Spiritual Exercises, and special loyalty to the pope. Its aim is missionary in the broadest sense, ministering to society in many ways, especially in education, where it has founded several colleges and universities throughout the world. Jesuits have been leading apologists for the Roman Catholic Church, particularly at the time of the Counter-Reformation. » Counter-Reformation; Loyola, Ignatius de; missions, Christian; pope; Roman Catholicism

Jesus Christ or **Jesus of Nazareth** The central figure of the Christian faith, whose role as 'Son of God' and whose redemptive work are traditionally considered fundamental beliefs for adherents of Christianity. 'Christ' became attached to the name 'Jesus' in Christian circles in view of the conviction that he was the Jewish Messiah ('Christ').

Jesus of Nazareth is described as the son of Mary and Joseph, and is credited with a miraculous conception by the Spirit of God in the Gospels of Matthew and Luke. He was apparently born in Bethlehem c.6–5 BC (before the death of Herod the Great in 4 BC), but began his ministry in Nazareth. After having been baptized by John in the Jordan (perhaps AD 28–29, *Luke* 3.1), he gathered a group of 12 close followers or disciples, the number perhaps being symbolic of the 12 tribes of Israel and indicative of an aim to reform the Jewish religion of his day.

The main records of his ministry are the New Testament Gospels, which show him proclaiming the coming of the kingdom of God, and in particular the acceptance of the oppressed and the poor into the kingdom. He was mainly active in the villages and country of Galilee rather than in towns and cities, and was credited in the Gospel records with many miraculous healings, exorcisms, and some 'nature' miracles, such as the calming of the storm. These records also depict conflicts with the Pharisees over his exercise of an independent 'prophetic' authority, and especially over his pronouncing forgiveness of sins; but his arrest by the Jewish priestly hierarchy appears to have resulted more directly from his action against the Temple in Jerusalem. The duration of his public ministry is uncertain, but it is from John's Gospel that one gets the impression of a 3-year period of teaching. He was executed by crucifixion under the order of Pontius Pilate, the Roman procurator, perhaps because of the unrest Jesus' activities were causing. The date of death is uncertain, but is usually considered to be in 30 or 33. Accounts of his resurrection from the dead are preserved in the Gospels, Pauline writings, and Book of Acts; Acts and the Gospel of John also refer to his subsequent ascension into heaven.

The New Testament Gospels as sources for the life of Jesus have been subject to considerable historical questioning in modern Biblical criticism, partly in view of the differences amongst the Gospel accounts themselves (with the differences between John's Gospel and the other three often casting doubt on the former). Form criticism has drawn attention to the influences affecting the Jesus-traditions in the period before the Gospels were written, and when traditions were being transmitted mainly in small units by word of mouth. Redaction criticism has, in addition, drawn attention to the creative role of the Gospel writers. Some scholars have been pessimistic about efforts to reconstruct the life of Jesus at all from our Gospel sources, and have distinguished between the 'Jesus of history' and the 'Christ of faith', with only the latter being theologically significant for faith. More recent scholars have often attached greater importance to the historical Jesus for Christian faith, and in particular efforts have been made to present a credible hypothesis about the historical Jesus in terms of the social, political, and cultural situation in Judaism in the early 1st-c. Limited references to Jesus can also be found in works of the Jewish historian Josephus and the Roman historians Tacitus and Suetonius; and other noncanonical

Christian traditions circulated about Jesus, many of which are late and probably spurious. » Christianity; crucifixion; Gospels, apocryphal/canonical; John, St (the Baptist); Mary (mother of Jesus); Messiah; Pharisees; Pilate

jet A resinous, hard, black variety of lignite, formed from wood buried on the sea floor. It is often polished, and used in jewellery. » coal

jet engine An engine that accelerates a fluid into its surrounding environment to form a fast-moving jet. The reaction felt by the engine to this expulsion is the *thrust force*, which acts in the opposite direction to the jet. This reactive thrust force is the propulsion force of the engine. Although by definition a rocket motor and a ship's propeller produce thrust in this way, the term is usually taken to apply to air-breathing engines such as turbojets and ramjets. » after burning; engine; gas turbine; propeller; ramjet

jet lag Unpleasant mental and bodily sensations associated with fatigue, inability to concentrate, and impaired judgment, induced by rapid air travel through several time zones. The condition subsides usually within a few days, and appears to be related to a disturbance in biological circadian rhythms. » biological rhythm

jet stream A narrow band of high velocity, westerly winds found at or just below the top of the troposphere at c.9 000–15 000 m/30 000–50 000 ft. Maximum velocities are 100–150 ml per hour (c.45–70 m per sec), but may increase to 300 ml per hour (c.135 m per sec) in winter. Jet streams are found in both hemispheres. » general circulation model; geostrophic wind; Rossby waves [i]; troposphere; wind [i]

jetfoil A hydrofoil with a waterjet form of propulsion. Water is sucked in from the sea and expelled at great pressure through the after foils. Jetfoil craft have operated a successful ferry service across the English Channel, though the service was withdrawn for economic reasons. » hydrofoil

jew's harp A simple musical instrument held between the player's lips and teeth. A flexible metal tongue is set in motion with the hand, and the pitch and timbre of its vibrations controlled by the mouth. The origin of the name itself is unknown. » idiophone

Jhelum, River [jayluhm] River in Asia, the most westerly of the five rivers of the Punjab, Pakistan; rises in the Himalayas, flows NW through the Vale of Kashmir, then W and generally S to meet the R Chenab SW of Jhang Maghiana; length 725 km/450 ml; source of many canals and irrigation systems of the Punjab plain. » Pakistan [i]

Jiang Jieshi [jyang jye**shee**] or **Chiang Kai-shek** [chang kiy **shek**] (1887–1975) Revolutionary leader of 20th-c China, the effective head of the Nationalist Republic (1928–49), and head thereafter of the emigré Nationalist Party regime in Taiwan. Born into a merchant family in Zhejiang, he interrupted his military education in Japan to return to China and join the Nationalist revolution. In 1918 he joined the separatist revolutionary government of Sun Yixian (Sun Yat-sen) in Canton, where he was appointed Commandant of the new Whampoa Military Academy. After Sun's death (1925), he launched an expedition against the warlords and the Beijing (Peking) government, entering Beijing in 1928, but fixed the Nationalist capital at Nanjing (Nanking). During the ensuing decade the Nationalist Party steadily lost support to the Communists. When Japan launched a campaign to conquer China (1937), Nationalist resistance was weak. Defeated by the Communist forces, he was forced to retreat to Taiwan (1949), where he presided over the beginnings of Taiwan's 'economic miracle'. He died at Taipei. His son, **Jiang Jingguo** (Chiang Ching-kuo, 1918–), became Prime Minister in 1971 and President in 1978. » communism; Guomindang; Sun Yatsen; Taiwan [i]

Jiang Jingguo (Chiang Ching-kuo) » **Jiang Jieshi**

Jiang Qing or **Chiang Ch'ing** [jyang **ching**] (1914–91) Chinese politician, born in Zhucheng, Shandong province. She trained in drama and literature, and became an actress in Shanghai. In 1936 she went to Yenan to study Marxist-Leninist theory, met Mao Zedong (Mao Tse-tung), and became his third wife in 1939. She was attached to the Ministry of Culture (1950–4), and in the 1960s began her attacks on bourgeois influences in the arts and literature. One of the leaders of the Cultural

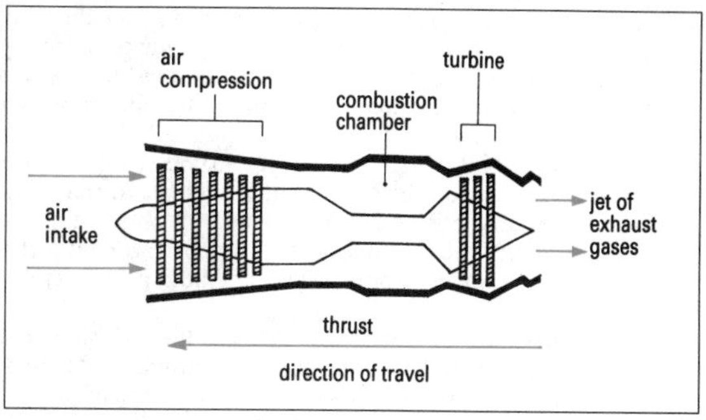

Jet engine

Revolution (1965–9), she was elected to the Politburo (1969), but after Mao's death (1976) was arrested with three others – the 'Gang of Four' – imprisoned, expelled from the Communist Party, and tried in 1980. She was sentenced to death, though the sentence was later suspended. » Cultural Revolution; Gang of Four; Mao Zedong

Jiddah » **Jedda**

jig A dance of Great Britain and Ireland, especially one including vigorous leaps. The French *gigue* is probably derived from it. Several different types are recorded from the 16th-c to the 19th-c, many of them known also as hornpipes, reels, strathspeys, etc. » gigue

jihad (Arabic 'struggle') [jee**had**] The term used in Islam for 'holy war'. According to the Koran, Muslims have a duty to oppose those who reject Islam, by armed struggle if necessary, and jihad has been invoked to justify both the expansion and defence of Islam. Islamic states pledged a jihad against Israel in the Mecca declaration of 1981, though not necessarily by military attack. » Islam; Koran; Mecca

Jilong [jee**lung**], also **Keelung** or **Chi-lung**, Jap **Kirun**, formerly Span **Santissima Trinidad** 25°06N 121°34E, pop (1982e) 351 707. Independent municipality and second largest seaport in Taiwan; on N coast of Taiwan I, overlooking the East China Sea; occupied by the Spanish and Dutch, 17th-c; occupied by the Japanese, 1895–1945; destroyed by earthquake, 1867; naval base; shipbuilding, fishing, chemicals, coal. » Taiwan [i]

Jim Crow Laws A nickname for US state laws passed after the end of slavery to keep Black people in a segregated subordinate condition. They were abolished in the mid-20th-c as a result of popular protest, Supreme Court decisions, and federal policies. » civil rights; slave trade

Jiménez, Juan Ramón [himayneth] (1881–1958) Spanish lyric poet, born at Moguer, Huelva, which he made famous by his delightful story of the young poet and his donkey, *Platero y Yo* (1914, Platero and I), one of the classics of modern Spanish literature. He abandoned law studies and settled in Madrid, where he began to write poetry, such as *Sonetos espirituales* (1916, Spiritual Sonnets). In 1936 he left Spain because of the Civil War and settled in Florida. In his last period he emerged as a major poet, and was awarded the Nobel Prize for Literature in 1956. He died at San Juan, Puerto Rico. » poetry; Spanish Civil War; Spanish literature

jimson weed » **thorn apple**

Jinan [jee**nahn**], **Tsinan**, or **Chi-nan**, byname **City of Springs** 36°41N 117°00E, pop (1984e) 1 394 600. Capital of Shandong province, E China; founded in 8th-c BC; commercial centre in the Tang dynasty (618–907); airfield; railway; metallurgy, chemicals, textiles, paper, flour; wheat, corn, cotton, tobacco, peanuts, fruit; over 100 natural springs at Daming L; dam on Yellow R for flood control and irrigation. » China [i]; Tang dynasty

Jindyworobak An Australian nationalist literary movement of the 1930s. Influenced by D H Lawrence and the Australian writer P R Stephensen (1901–65), the movement drew inspiration from Aboriginal legends. It produced some notable poets, such as Ian Mudie (1911–70) and Roland Robinson (1912–). » Australian literature; Lawrence, D H

jinja [**jin**ja] A Shinto shrine or sanctuary. It may be a small roadside shrine, a larger building surrounded by smaller buildings, or a large group of temple buildings surrounded by a wooded area. Its central feature is the *honden*, the main dwelling of the deity, containing a single chamber in which is housed the sacred symbol. » Shinto

Jinja [**jin**ja] 0°27N 33°14E, pop (1983e) 45 060. City in Busoga province, Uganda; on the N shore of L Victoria at the outflow of the Victoria Nile River, 80 km/50 ml E of Kampala; power station at Owen Falls; second largest city in Uganda; airfield; railway; textiles, metal products, grain milling, petrol depot. » Uganda [i]

Jinnah, Muhammad Ali (1876–1948) Indian Muslim politician and founder of Pakistan, born in Karachi. Educated in Bombay and London, he was called to the Bar in 1897, and practised in Bombay. He became a member of the Indian National Congress (1906) and the Muslim League (1913), and supported Hindu-Muslim unity until 1930, when he resigned from the Congress in opposition to Gandhi's policy of civil disobedience. His advocacy of a separate state for Muslims led to the creation of Pakistan in 1947, and he became its first Governor-General. He died in Karachi. » Gandhi; Indian National Congress; Pakistan [i]

jinni (plural **jinn**), or **genie** In Arab mythology a supernatural creature that could take human or animal form and then interfered, often vengefully, in human affairs. Jinn can inhabit stones, trees, fire and air. They are frequently mentioned in the Koran and in the collection of oriental tales called *The Arabian Nights*. » Arabian Nights; Koran

jird » **gerbil**

Jizo [jee**zoh**] (Jap polite form *ojizosan*; Sanskrit, Ksitigarbha Bodhisattva). In Japan, the Buddhist patron deity of children. Wayside stone *jizo* are common in town and country. Sometimes decked out with colourful clothing, they are offered flowers. Nowadays old coffee jars, etc are used as vases. » Buddhism

Joachim of Fiore or **Floris** [**joh**akim] (c.1135–1202) Italian mystic, born in Calabria. In 1177 he became abbot of the Cistercian monastery of Corazzo, and later founded a stricter Order, the *Ordo Florensis*, which was absorbed by the Cistercians in 1505. He is known for his mystical interpretation of history, recognizing three ages of increasing spirituality: the Age of the Father (the Old Testament), the Age of the Son (the New Testament and the period to 1260), and the Age of the Spirit, a period of perfect liberty, which would emerge thereafter. He died at Fiore. » Bible; Cistercians

Joad, C(yril) E(dwin) M(itchinson) (1891–1953) British controversialist and popularizer of philosophy, born at Durham. Educated at Blundell's School and Oxford, he was a civil servant (1914–30), then joined the philosophy department at Birkbeck College, London. He wrote 47 highly personal books, notably *Guide to Philosophy* (1936), and was a fashionable atheist until his last work, *Recovery of Belief* (1952). He is also remembered for his highly successful BBC Brains Trust comment, 'It all depends what you mean by ...'. He died in London.

Joan, Pope (800–900) Fictitious personage long believed to have been, as John VII, Pope (855–58). One legend claims she was born at Mainz, and elected Pope while in male disguise. Her reign is said to have ended abruptly when she died on giving birth to a child during a papal procession. » pope

Joan of Arc, St, Fr **Jeanne d'Arc**, byname **the Maid of Orleans** (c.1412–31), feast day 30 May. French patriot and martyr, who halted the English ascendancy in France during the Hundred Years' War, born into a peasant family at Domrémy. At the age of 13 she heard the voices of Saints Michael, Catherine, and Margaret bidding her rescue France from English domination. She was taken to the Dauphin, and eventually allowed to lead the army assembled for the relief of Orleans. Clad in a suit of white armour and flying her own standard, she entered Orleans (1429), forced the English to retire, and took the Dauphin to be crowned Charles VII at Rheims. She then set out to relieve Compiègne, but was captured and sold to the English by John of Luxembourg. Put on trial (1431) for heresy and sorcery, she was found guilty by an English-dominated court, and burned. She was canonized in 1920. » Charles VII; Hundred Years' War

Job, Book of [johb] A major book of the wisdom literature of the Hebrew Bible/Old Testament, named after its hero and probably drawing on old popular traditions, but in its present form showing evidence of several additions. It is composed of narrative and speeches in which the poet tackles the question of the meaning of undeserved suffering and of faith; despite the advice of his friends, Job persists in his struggles until presented with the inscrutable majesty of God directly. » Old Testament; prophet; theodicy; wisdom literature

Jocasta [joh**kas**ta] In Greek legend, the wife of King Laius of Thebes and mother of Oedipus, later unwittingly becoming the wife of her son; she is called **Epikaste** in Homer. She bore Oedipus four children – Eteocles, Polynices, Antigone, and Ismene – and killed herself when she discovered her incest. » Oedipus

Jochum, Eugen [**yokh**uhm] (1902–87) German conductor, born at Babenhausen. He studied in Augsburg (1914–22) and Munich (1922–4), and became musical director of the Hamburg Staatsoper and conductor of the Hamburg Philharmonic Orchestra (1934–49). In 1949 he returned to Munich, where he conducted the Bavarian Radio Symphony Orchestra, and where he died.

Jockey Club The controlling body for horse racing in Britain, founded c.1750 at the Star and Garter Coffee House, Pall Mall, London. In 1968 the Jockey Club and National Hunt Committee amalgamated. » horse racing

Jodl, Alfred [**yoh**dl] (1890–1946) German general, born at Aachen. An artillery subaltern in World War 1, he became general of artillery in 1940, the planning genius of the German High Command and Hitler's chief adviser. He was found guilty of war crimes at Nuremburg (1946) and executed. » Hitler; World War 2

Jodrell Bank 53°13N 2°21W. Observatory station in Macclesfield district, Cheshire, NWC England; 5 km/3 ml NE of Holmes Chapel. » Cheshire; observatory [i]

Joel, Book of One of the twelve so-called 'minor' prophetic writings of the Hebrew Bible/Old Testament, attributed to Joel, of whom nothing is known, but who is today usually assigned to the post-exilic period (c.400–350 BC), a prophet with a strong interest in priesthood and the Jerusalem Temple cult. It contains a notable reference to a locust plague, warning Judah of a devastating coming judgment and of the final 'Day of the Lord' when Israel's enemies will be destroyed. » Old Testament; prophet; Temple, Jerusalem

Joffre, Joseph Jacques Césaire [**zhofr**] (1852–1931) French general, born at Rivesaltes. He joined the army in 1870, and rose to be French Chief-of-Staff (1914) and Commander-in-Chief (1915), carrying out a policy of attrition against the German invaders of France. He was made Marshal of France (1916) and President of the Allied War Council (1917). He died in Paris. » World War 1

Johanan ben Zakkai, Rabban [**yoh**hanan ben **za**kiy] (1st-c) Prominent Jewish teacher and leader of the reformulation of Judaism after the fall of Jerusalem (70), who helped to found rabbinic Judaism. His early career was apparently in Galilee, although there are also traditions of his legal disputes with the Sadducees in Jerusalem before its fall. Afterwards he was instrumental in reconstituting the Sanhedrin council in Jabneh. » Akiva ben Joseph; Jabneh; Judaism; rabbi; Sadducees

Johannesburg [joh**han**izberg], Afrikaans [yoh**han**uhsberkh], abbreviated **Jo'burg** 26°10S 28°02E, pop (1985) 1 609 408 (metropolitan area). Largest city of Transvaal province, South Africa, 50 km/31 ml SSW of Pretoria; altitude 1 665 m/5 462 ft; South Africa's largest city; founded in 1886 after the discovery of gold in the Witwatersrand; airport; railway; two universities (1922, 1966); commerce (stock exchange), chemicals, textiles, clothing, leather products, engineering, diamond cutting, gold mining; art gallery, civic centre, several museums. » South Africa [i]; Soweto; Transvaal; Witwatersrand

Johannsen, Wilhelm Ludvig (1857–1927) Danish botanist and geneticist, born and died in Copenhagen, where he became professor of agriculture. His pioneering experiments with princess beans laid the foundation for later developments in the genetics of quantitative characters. The terms *gene*, *phenotype*, and *genotype* are due to him. He died in Copenhagen. » gene

Johanson, Donald (Carl) (1943–) US anthropologist, born in Chicago. His spectacular finds (1972–7) of fossil hominids 3–4 million years old at Hadar in the Afar triangle of Ethiopia generated worldwide interest. They include 'Lucy', a unique female specimen that is half complete, and the so-called 'First Family', a scattered group containing the remains of 13 individuals. Since 1981 he has been director of the Institute of Human Origins, Berkeley, California. » anthropology; Australopithecus; Dart, Raymond

John, byname **John Lackland** (1167–1216) King of England (1199–1216), the youngest son of Henry II, born at Oxford, and one of the least popular monarchs in English history. He tried to seize the crown during Richard I's captivity in Germany (1193–4), but was forgiven and nominated successor by Richard, who thus set aside the rights of Arthur, the son of John's elder brother Geoffrey. Arthur's claims were supported by Philip II of France, and after Arthur was murdered on John's orders (1203), Philip marched against him with superior forces, and conquered all but a portion of Aquitaine (1204–5). In 1206 John refused to receive Stephen Langton as Archbishop of Canterbury, and in 1208 his kingdom was placed under papal interdict. He was then excommunicated (1209), and finally conceded (1213). His oppressive government, and failure to recover Normandy, provoked baronial opposition, which led to demands for constitutional reform. The barons met the King at Runnymede, and forced him to seal the Great Charter (Magna Carta) (June 1215), the basis of the English constitution. His repudiation of the Charter precipitated the first Barons' War (1215–17). He died at Newark. » Barons' War; Langton, Stephen; Magna Carta; Richard I

John II, byname **the Good** (1319–64) King of France (1350–64), the son of Philip VI, born near Le Mans. In 1356 he was taken prisoner by Edward the Black Prince at the Battle of Poitiers, and carried to England. After the treaty of Brétigny (1360) he returned home, leaving his second son, the Duke of Anjou, as a hostage. When the duke broke his parole and escaped (1363), John chivalrously returned to London, and died there. » Edward the Black Prince

John, St or **John, son of Zebedee** (1st-c), feast day 27 December. One of the twelve apostles, son of Zebedee, and the younger brother of James, a Galilean fisherman; one of the inner circle of disciples who were with Jesus at the Transfiguration and Gethsemane. *Acts* and *Galatians* also name him as one of the 'pillars' of the early Jerusalem Church. Some traditions represent him as having been slain by the Jews or Herod Agrippa I; but from the 2nd-c he was said to have spent his closing years at Ephesus, dying there at an advanced age, after having written the Apocalypse, the Gospel, and the three Epistles which bear his name (although his authorship of these works has been disputed by modern scholars). » apostle; Herod Agrippa I; James (son of Zebedee); Jesus Christ; John, Letters of; John, Gospel according to; Revelation, Book of

John, St, byname **the Baptist** or **Baptizer** (1st-c), feast day 24 June. Prophetic and ascetic figure referred to in the New Testament Gospels and in Josephus' *Antiquities*, the son of a priest named Zechariah; roughly contemporary with Jesus of Nazareth. A story of his birth to Elizabeth, cousin of Mary the mother of Jesus, is recorded in *Luke* 1. He baptized Jesus and others at the R Jordan, but his baptism seemed mainly to symbolize a warning of the coming judgment of God and the consequent need for repentance. He was executed by Herod Antipas, but the circumstances differ in the accounts of Josephus and the Gospels. He is treated in the New Testament as the forerunner of Christ, and sometimes as a returned Elijah (*Matt* 11.13–14). » Herod Antipas; Jesus Christ; Josephus; New Testament

John XXII (c.1249–1334) French Pope (1316–34), one of the most celebrated of the Popes of Avignon, born at Cahors. He intervened in the contest for the Imperial Crown between Louis of Bavaria and Frederick of Austria, supporting the latter. A long contest ensued both in Germany and Italy between the Guelph (papal) party and the Ghibelline (imperial) party. In 1327 Louis entered Italy, was crowned Emperor at Rome, and deposed the Pope, setting up an antipope (1328). Although Guelphic predominance at Rome was later restored, John died at Avignon. » antipope; Ghibellines; Guelphs; pope

John XXIII, originally **Angelo Giuseppe Roncalli** (1881–1963) Italian Pope (1958–63), born at Sotto il Monte. He was ordained in 1904, served as a chaplain in World War 1, and was subsequently Apostolic Delegate to Bulgaria, Turkey, and Greece. Patriarch of Venice in 1953, he was elected Pope in 1958 on the twelfth ballot. The convenor of the 21st Ecumenical Council, he died in Rome. » ecumenism; pope; Vatican Councils

John, Gospel according to New Testament book, known also as the **Fourth Gospel**, distinct from the other three ('synoptic') gospels because of its unique theological reflections on Jesus as the Son of God and the divine Word come from God, and its records of Jesus' sayings and deeds. It is strictly anonymous, although *John* 21.24 associates it with 'the disciple whom Jesus loved', traditionally held to be John the son of Zebedee but often disputed today. » Gospels, canonical; Jesus Christ; John, St (son of Zebedee); New Testament

John, Letters of Three relatively short New Testament writings, the latter two of which have the form of a letter addressed from 'the Elder', but the first of which lacks direct references to its writer or recipients. They were traditionally considered the work of the author of the Fourth Gospel, but today they are more usually assigned to a later stage of the 'Johannine community'. 1 and 2 *John* confront the problem of a schism within this Christian community, apparently over false teachings about the importance of Jesus' work on Earth and the significance of sin for Christians. 3 *John* appears to be a private letter addressing problems with a local church leader called Diotrephes. » John, Gospel according to; New Testament

John, Augustus (Edwin) (1878–1961) British painter, born at Tenby, Pembrokeshire, Wales. He studied in London and Paris, and made an early reputation with his etchings (1900–14). His favourite themes were gipsies, fishing folk, and naturally regal women, as in 'Lyric Fantasy' (1913), and he painted portraits of several political and artistic contemporary figures, such as Shaw, Hardy, and Dylan Thomas. He died at Fordingbridge, Hampshire. » English art; etching

John, Elton, stage name of **Reginald Kenneth Dwight** (1947–) British rock singer and pianist, born at Pinner, Middlesex. He played the piano by ear from age four, and studied at the Royal Academy of Music at 11. In 1967, he and Bernie Taupin began writing songs such as 'Rocket Man', 'Honky Cat', and 'Goodbye Yellow Brick Road'. Their publisher pressed John to perform them, for which he obscured his short, plump, myopic physique in clownish garb that included huge glasses, sequinned and fringed jump suits, and ermine boots. The top pop star of the 1970s, he later became director and owner of the Watford Football Club and a stock-market speculator. » pop music

John, Otto [yohn] (1909–) West German ex-security chief, the defendant in a major postwar treason case. In 1944 he was part of the plot against Hitler, after which he escaped to Britain. In 1950 he was appointed to the West German Office for the protection of the constitution. In 1954 he mysteriously disappeared from West Berlin, and later broadcast for the East German communists. In 1956 he returned to the West, was arrested, tried, and imprisoned. His defence was that he had been drugged, driven to the communist sector, held prisoner, and forced to make broadcasts until he managed to escape. Released in 1958, he still protests his innocence. » communism

John Birch Society A moderately-sized, extreme right-wing pressure group in the USA which promotes conservative ideas and policies, and is strongly patriotic and anti-communist. Founded in 1958, the name derives from a US missionary and intelligence officer, killed by Chinese communists on 25 August 1945, who was seen by the Society as the first hero of the Cold War. » Cold War; Republican Party; right wing

John Bull A personification of the typical Englishman, or of England itself, first depicted in *The History of John Bull* by

Arbuthnot. In many political cartoons of the 18th-c and 19th-c, he is drawn as a short stocky figure, often wearing a waistcoat showing the British flag. » Arbuthnot

John Henry The hero of an American ballad, who pits himself against a steam drill, succeeds in crushing more rock than the machine, but dies from the effort. He is known as 'the Negro Paul Bunyan'. » ballad; folklore

John of Austria, Don, Span **Don Juan** (1547–78) Spanish soldier, the illegitimate son of the Emperor Charles V, born at Regensburg, Germany. He defeated the Moors in Granada (1570) and the Turks at Lepanto (1571). In 1573 he took Tunis, and was then sent to Milan and (1576) to the Netherlands as Viceroy. He planned to marry Mary, Queen of Scots, but died of typhoid at Namur. » Lepanto, Battle of; Mary, Queen of Scots

John of Damascus, St or **John Damascene** (c.675–c.749), feast day 4 December. Greek theologian and hymn writer of the Eastern Church, born at Damascus. He was educated by the Italian monk, Cosmas, and defended the use of images in church worship during the iconoclastic controversy. His later years were spent in a monastery near Jerusalem, where he was ordained. » Christianity; iconoclasm

John of Gaunt (1340–99) Duke of Lancaster, the fourth son of Edward III, and ancestor of Henry IV, V, and VI, born at Ghent, Flanders. In 1359 he married his cousin, Blanche of Lancaster, and was created duke in 1362. After her death (1369), he married Constance, daughter of Pedro the Cruel of Castile, and assumed the title of King of Castile, though he failed by his expeditions to oust his rival, Henry of Trastamare. In England he became highly influential as a peacemaker during the troubled reign of Richard II. He was made Duke of Aquitaine by Richard (1390), and sent on several embassies to France. On his second wife's death (1394) he married his mistress, Catherine Swynford, by whom he had three sons; from the eldest descended Henry VIII. He died in London. » Richard II

John of Leyden (1509–36) Dutch Anabaptist leader, born at Leyden. He worked as a tailor, merchant, and innkeeper, and became noted as an orator. Turning Anabaptist, he went to Münster, became head of the movement, and set up a 'kingdom of Zion', with polygamy and community of goods. In 1535 the city was taken by the Bishop of Münster, and John and his accomplices were executed. » Anabaptists; Zion

John of Nepomuk, St (c.1330–93), feast day 16 May. Patron saint of Bohemia, born at Pomuk, near Pilsen. He studied at Prague, and became confessor to Sophia, wife of Wenceslaus IV. For refusing to betray the confession of the Queen, he was tortured and drowned. He was canonized in 1729. » Christianity

John of the Cross, St, originally **Juan de Yepes y Álvarez** (1542–91), feast day 14 December. Spanish Christian mystic and poet, the founder with St Teresa of the Discalced Carmelites, born at Fontiveros, Ávila. He became a Carmelite monk in 1563, and was ordained in 1567. Imprisoned at Toledo (1577), he wrote a number of poems, such as *Canto espiritual* (The Spiritual Canticle), which are highly regarded in Spanish mystical literature. After escaping, he became Vicar Provincial of Andalusia (1585–7), and died in seclusion at the monastery of Úbeda. He was canonized in 1726. » Carmelites; monasticism; poetry; Teresa of Ávila, St

John o'Groats [jonuh**grohts**] Locality in NE Highland region, NE Scotland; on Pentland Firth, 23 km/14 ml N of Wick; often mistakenly thought to be the northernmost point on mainland UK; 'from Land's End to John o' Groats', a common phrase for the length of Britain (970 km/603 ml apart); no remains of the octagonal house said to have been built here by Dutchman John de Groot, who settled in Scotland in the 16th-c. » Highland; Scotland [i]

John Paul I, originally **Albino Luciani** (1912–78) Italian Pope (Aug–Sep 1978), born near Belluno. Educated at the Gregorian University in Rome, he was ordained in 1935. He became a parish priest and teacher in Belluno, vicar general of the diocese of Vittorio Veneto (1954), a bishop (1958), Patriarch of Venice (1969), and a cardinal (1973). He became the first pope to use a double name (from his two immediate predecessors, John XXIII and Paul VI). He died only 33 days later, the shortest pontificate of modern times. » pope

John Paul II, originally **Karol Jozef Wojtyla** (1920–) Polish Pope (1920–), born at Wadowice, the first non-Italian pope in 450 years. He was educated in Poland, ordained in 1946, and became professor of moral theology at Lublin and Cracow. Archbishop and Metropolitan of Cracow (1964–78), he was created cardinal in 1967. Noted for his energy and analytical ability, his pontificate has seen many foreign visits, in which he has preached to huge audiences. In 1981 he survived an assassination attempt, when he was shot in St Peter's Square by a Turkish national, Mehmet Ali Agca, the motives for which have remained unclear. A champion of economic justice and an outspoken defender of the Church in communist countries, he has been uncompromising on moral issues. » pope

Johns, Jasper (1930–) US painter, born at Allendale, South Carolina. After studying at the University of South Carolina, he became a painter in New York City in 1952, and was attracted by the Dadaist ideas of Marcel Duchamp. Because conventional art critics placed so much emphasis on 'self-expression' and 'originality', he chose to paint flags, targets, maps, and other pre-existing images in a style deliberately clumsy and banal. » action painting; Dada; Duchamp

Johnson, Amy (1903–41) British aviator, born at Hull, Yorkshire. She flew solo from England to Australia (1930), to Japan via Siberia (1931), and to Cape Town (1932), making new records in each case. A pilot in Air Transport Auxiliary in World War 2, she was drowned after baling out over the Thames estuary. » aircraft [i]

Johnson, Andrew (1808–75) US statesman and 17th President (1865–9), born at Raleigh, North Carolina. With little formal schooling, he became Alderman and Mayor in Greenville, Tennessee, and a member of the Legislature (1835), State Senate (1841), and Congress (1843). He was Governor of Tennessee in 1853, and a Senator in 1857. During the Civil War he was made Military Governor of Tennessee (1862), and Vice-President (1865). On Lincoln's assassination (1865), he became President. A Democrat, his conciliatory policies were opposed by Congress, who wished to keep the Southern states under military government. He vetoed the congressional measures, was impeached, brought to trial, and acquitted. He died at Carter Station, Tennessee. » American Civil War; Democratic Party; Lincoln, Abraham

Johnson, Dame Celia (1908–82) British actress, born at Richmond, Surrey. Well-established on the stage, she had leading roles in Noel Coward's war-time films *In Which We Serve* (1942) and *This Happy Breed* (1944), and is best remembered for her performance in *Brief Encounter* (1945). Her later film appearances were infrequent, among them *The Prime of Miss Jean Brodie* (1968), but she continued in the theatre and on television until very shortly before her death in London.

Johnson, Lyndon B(aines), byname **LBJ** (1908–73) US statesman and 36th President (1963–9), born at Stonewall, Texas. Educated at Southwest Texas State Teachers College, he was a teacher and congressman's secretary before being elected a Democrat representative in 1937. He became a Senator in 1948, and an effective leader of the Democratic majority. Vice-President under Kennedy in 1960, he was made President after Kennedy's assassination, and was returned to the post in 1964 with a huge majority. His administration passed the Civil Rights Act (1964) and the Voting Rights Act (1965), which helped the position of Blacks in US society. However, the escalation of the war in Vietnam led to active protest and growing unpopularity, and after 1969 he retired from active politics. He died at San Antonio, Texas. » civil rights; Kennedy, John F; Vietnam War

Johnson, Pamela Hansford (1912–81) British novelist, born and died in London. Best known for her portrayal of her native postwar London, her books include *An Avenue of Stone* (1947), *The Unspeakable Skipton* (1958), *A Bonfire* (1981), and several works of nonfiction, such as her study of the Moors murders, *On Iniquity* (1967). In 1950 she married the novelist C P Snow. » English literature; novel; Snow, C P

Johnson, Samuel, byname **Dr Johnson** (1709–84) British lexicographer, critic, and poet, born at Lichfield, Staffordshire.

The son of a bookseller, he was educated at Lichfield and Oxford, where he left before taking a degree, and became a teacher. In 1737 he went to London, and worked as a journalist. From 1747 he worked for eight years on his *Dictionary of the English Language*, started the moralistic periodical, *The Rambler* (1750), and wrote his prose tale of Abyssinia, *Rasselas* (1759). In 1762 he was given a crown pension, which enabled him to figure as arbiter of letters and social personality, notably in The Literary Club, of which he was a founder member (1764). In 1765 he produced his edition of Shakespeare, from 1772 engaged in political pamphleteering, in 1773 went with Boswell on a tour of Scotland, and wrote *Lives of the Poets* (1779–81). He died in London. His reputation as man and conversationalist outweighs his literary reputation, and for the picture of Johnson in society we are indebted above all to Boswell. » Boswell; dictionary; literary criticism

Johnson, Uwe (1934–84) German novelist, born in Pomerania (now part of Poland), and educated at Rostock and Leipzig. He left East for West Germany after completing his first novel *Mutmassungen Uber Jakob* (Speculations about Jakob) in 1959. His second and third novels, *Das dritte Buch uber Achim* (1961, The Third Book about Achim), and *Zwei Ansichten* (1965, Two Views), develop the theme of the relation between the two Germanies. He later moved to university posts in the USA, and then to England, but published no fiction after 1965. He died at Sheerness, Isle of Sheppey. » German literature; novel

Johnston Islands 16°45N 169°32W; pop (1981e) 1 000; area 2.5 sq km/1 sq ml. Coral atoll enclosing four islets in the C Pacific Ocean, 1 150 km/715 ml SW of Honolulu; discovered, 1807; claimed by Hawaii, 1858; taken over by US Navy, 1934; now used as a store for poisonous gas; airfield. » Pacific Ocean

Johor or **Johore** [juh**haw**] pop (1980) 1 580 423; area 18 985 sq km/ 7 328 sq ml. State in S Peninsular Malaysia, occupying the entire S tip of the peninsula; bounded W by the Strait of Malacca, E by the S China Sea; separated from Singapore by the Johor Strait; capital, Johor Baharu; tin, bauxite, rubber, oil palm, pineapple, pepper, timber. » Malaysia [i]

Johor Baharu [juh**haw bah**roo] 1°29N 103°44E, pop (1980) 246 395. Capital of Johor state, S Peninsular Malaysia, 365 km/227 ml SE of Kuala Lumpur; connected to Singapore by causeway; trading centre, tourism; Grand Palace (19th-c), Abu Bakar mosque, Johor Safariworld (SE Asia's only safari park), Fiesta Village. » Johor; Malaysia [i]

joint The region of contact between bones of the body. Some bones articulate at movable joints, others at only slightly movable joints, and others at immovable joints. The shape of the articular surfaces, and the structure and arrangement of the ligaments that unite the bones at the joint, principally determine the amount of movement which may occur. Three distinct classes of joint are recognized. **Fibrous joints** allow almost no movement, because the two bones are held firmly together by fibrous tissue. These include *sutures* (between the skull bones, allowing no movement), *gomphoses* (between the roots of the teeth and the alveolar bone, allowing minimal movement), and *syndesmoses* (where the fibrous tissue is much greater, allowing some movement, as between the lower end of the adult tibia and fibula). **Cartilaginous joints** unite the two bones by a continuous plate of hyaline cartilage, with or without an intervening fibrocartilaginous disc. They include the joints which occur in the median plane of the body, such as those between the bodies of the vertebrae. **Synovial joints** are specialized to allow free movement, and constitute the majority of permanent joints with the limbs. Several types can be identified according to the shape of their articulating surfaces, which in turn determines the type of movement possible at the joint: *plane* joints (eg the acromio-clavicular joint), *saddle* joints (eg the carpo-metacarpal joint of the thumb), *hinge* joints (eg the elbow joint), *pivot* joints (eg the superior radio-ulnar joint), and *ball-and-socket* joints (eg the hip joint). » arthritis; bone; bursitis; dislocation (medicine); ligament; osteoarthritis; sprain; synovitis; vertebral column

Joint European Torus (JET) A research facility in nuclear fusion comprising a large tokamak-type experimental fusion reactor, which became operational in 1983 at Abingdon, Oxfordshire, UK. It is funded by the countries of the European Community plus Sweden and Switzerland. » nuclear fusion; tokamak

Joinville, Jean, Sire de [zhwĩveel] (c.1224–1317) French historian, born at Joinville, Champagne. He took part in the unfortunate crusade of Louis IX (1248–54), in which the army was defeated, and he and Louis were imprisoned at Acre, and ransomed. He returned with Louis to France, and lived partly at court, partly on his estates. Throughout the crusade he kept notes on the events, which he later wrote up in his *Histoire de Saint Louis* (completed by 1309). He died at Joinville. » Crusades [i]; Louis IX

Joliot-Curie, Irène, *née* **Curie** (1897–1956) French physical chemist, the daughter of Pierre and Marie Curie, born and died in Paris. She worked as her mother's assistant at the Radium Institute, taking charge of the work in 1932. In that year she discovered, with her mother, the penetration of atomic nuclei by neutrons, and in 1934 she and her husband succeeded in producing radioactive elements artificially, for which they received the 1935 Nobel Prize for Chemistry. » Curie, Marie; Joliot-Curie, Frédéric; radioactivity

Joliot-Curie, (Jean) Frédéric, original surname **Joliot** (1900–58) French physical chemist, born in Paris. He studied at the Sorbonne, where in 1925 he became assistant to Madame Curie, and in 1926 married her daughter, Irène, with whom he shared the 1935 Nobel Prize. Professor at the Collège de France (1937), he became a strong supporter of the Resistance movement during World War 2, and a member of the Communist Party. After the liberation he became high commissioner for atomic energy (1946–50). President of the communist-sponsored World Peace Council, he was awarded the Stalin Peace Prize in 1951. » Joliot-Curie, Irène

Jolson, Al, stage name of **Asa Yoelson** (1886–1950) US singer, born in St Petersburg, Russia, and raised in Washington and New York. His sentimental songs, such as 'Mammy', 'Sonny Boy', and 'Swanee', delivered on one knee, arms outstretched, brought tears to the eyes of vaudeville audiences in the 1920s. He called himself 'the World's Greatest Entertainer' and, for a time, others agreed. In 1927, he starred in *The Jazz Singer*, the first motion picture with sound. Years after his popularity waned, his career revived briefly with the release of the films, *The Jolson Story* (1946) and *Jolson Sings Again* (1949). He died in San Francisco. » vaudeville

Jomon [yoh**mon**] A broad term used to describe prehistoric Japan c.10 000–300 BC and all archaeological remains of the period. Over 10 000 sites are known, with five main periods: *Initial* (10 000–5000), *Early* (5000–3500), *Middle* (3500–2500), *Late* (2500–1000), and *Final* (1000–300). The name derives from the cord-decorated (*jomon*) pottery excavated from the Omori shell mounds near Tokyo in 1877. » Kofun

Jonah or **Jonas, Book of** One of the twelve so-called 'minor' prophetic writings of the Hebrew Bible/Old Testament, unusual for its narrative about the reluctance of the prophet himself in preaching to the city of Nineveh. It includes the famous legend of Jonah's being swallowed by and saved from a 'great fish'. Although the story is set in the mid-8th-c BC, the work is probably post-exilic; it emphasizes Israel's role in addressing the heathen nations, and thus implicitly opposes Jewish exclusivism. » Nineveh; Old Testament; prophet

Jonas » **Jonah, Book of**

Jonathan (c.11th-c BC) Biblical character, the son and heir of Saul (the first King of Israel) and loyal friend of David. He is portrayed in 1 *Sam* as a cunning soldier, but he faces conflicting loyalties when he continues his friendship with David in spite of Saul's mounting hostility to David. David succeeds Saul as King of Israel, since Jonathan was killed in the battle of Gilboa against the Philistines. » David; Old Testament; Saul

Jones, Bobby, properly **Robert (Tyre)** (1902–71) US golfer, born and died at Atlanta, Georgia, regarded as the greatest golfer in the history of the sport. An amateur throughout his career, he won the British Open three times (1926–7, 1930) and the US Open four times (1923, 1926, 1929–30). He also won the US Amateur Title five times and the British Amateur title once. In 1930 he took the Amateur and Open titles of both countries, the game's greatest Grand Slam. He was responsible for the founding of the US Masters at Augusta. » golf

Jones, Daniel (1881–1967) British phonetician. He trained as a lawyer, and then became lecturer (1907) and professor (1921–49) of phonetics at London. He wrote phonetic readers for several languages, compiled the *English Pronouncing Dictionary* (1917), and produced several influential textbooks. His 'cardinal vowels' act as a reference system for the description of the vowels of real languages. He was secretary (1928–49) and president of the International Phonetic Association. » cardinal vowels; phonetics

Jones, Ernest (1879–1958) British psychoanalyst, born at Llwchwy, Glamorgan, Wales. Educated at Cardiff, he worked as a physician in London, where he came into contact with the work of Freud, and became his lifelong disciple and personal friend. He introduced psychoanalysis to the UK and USA, founding the British Psychoanalytical Society in 1913, and was founding editor of the International Journal of Psychoanalysis (1920–33). He was later professor of psychiatry at Toronto and director of the London Clinic for Psychoanalysis. He died in London. » Freud, Sigmund; psychiatry

Jones, Henry, byname **Cavendish** (1831–99) British writer on whist and other games, born in London. He trained as a doctor in London, and practised surgery (1852–69). The author of manuals on several games, he is mainly remembered for his codification of the rules of whist (1862). His pseudonym derives from the name of the first whist club he went to in London. » whist

Jones, Inigo (1573–1652) The first of the great English architects, born in London. He studied landscape painting in Italy, and from Venice introduced the Palladian style into England. In 1606 James I employed him in arranging the masques of Ben Jonson, and he introduced the proscenium arch and moveable scenery to the English stage. In 1615 he became surveyor-general of the royal buildings. He designed the Queen's House at Greenwich, the Banqueting House in Whitehall, and laid out Covent Garden and Lincoln's Inn Fields. He died in London. » stage

Jones, Jack, properly **James (Larkin)** (1913–) British trade unionist, born in Liverpool. He was general secretary of the Transport and General Workers Union (1969–78), favouring the decentralization of trade union power to the local branch, and had some influence on the Labour government's policies of 1974–6. Made a Companion of Honour in 1978, his autobiography, *Union Man*, was published in 1986. » trade union

Jones, Mary Harris, byname **Mother Jones** (1830–1930) US labour agitator, born in Co Cork, Ireland. She migrated to the USA via Canada, lost her family to an epidemic in 1867, and her home to the Chicago fire of 1871, and thereafter devoted herself to the cause of labour. Homeless after 1880, she travelled to areas of labour strife, especially in the coal industry, and was imprisoned in W Virginia on a charge of conspiracy to murder in 1912, at the age of 82. Freed by a new governor, she returned to labour agitation, which she continued almost until her death, at Silver Spring, Maryland.

Jones, (John) Paul, originally **John Paul** (1747–92) US naval commander, born at Kirkbean, Kirkcudbrightshire, Scotland. Apprenticed as sailor boy, he made several voyages to America, and in 1773 inherited a property in Virginia. He joined the navy at the outbreak of the War of Independence, and performed a number of daring exploits off the British coast, capturing and sinking several ships. He died in Paris. » American Revolution

Jones, Sir William (1746–94) British Orientalist, born in London. Educated at Harrow and Oxford, he was called to the Bar (1774), became a judge in the Supreme Court in Bengal (1783), and was knighted. He devoted himself to Sanskrit, whose startling resemblance to Latin and Greek he pointed out in 1787. He died in Calcutta. » family of languages [i]; Sanskrit

Jongkind, Johan Barthold [yongkint] (1819–91) Dutch painter, born near Rotterdam. He studied at The Hague, but moved to Paris in 1846, establishing close links with French art. He was a friend of Eugène Boudin, and exhibited with the Barbizon painters. An important precursor of Impressionism, he influenced the young Monet. He died at Côte-Saint-André. » Barbizon School; Boudin; Impressionism (art); Monet

Jönköping [yernkerping] 57°45N 14°10E, pop (1982) 107 123. Industrial town and capital of Jönköping county, S Sweden; at S end of L Vättern; charter, 1284; railway; focus point for agriculture and forestry; textiles, machinery, paper. » Sweden [i]

Jonson, Benjamin (Ben) (1572–1637) English dramatist, born in London. Educated at Westminster School, he worked as a bricklayer, did military service in Flanders, and joined Henslowe's company of players, where he killed a fellow player in a duel. His *Every Man in his Humour*, with Shakespeare in the cast, was performed in 1598. After some less successful works, including two Roman tragedies, he wrote his four chief plays: *Volpone* (1606), *The Silent Woman* (1609), *The Alchemist* (1610), and *Bartholomew Fair* (1614). He wrote several masques before 1625, when the death of James I ended his period of court favour. A major influence on 17th-c poets (known as the 'tribe of Ben'), he died in London. » drama; English literature; masque; Shakespeare [i]

Jooss, Kurt [johs] (1901–79) German dancer, choreographer, teacher, and director, born in Wasseralfingen. He studied ballet before meeting Laban, with whom he then worked. He was appointed director of the dance department at the Essen Folkwang School in 1927, from which the dance theatre company developed. His best-known work, *The Green Table*, was made in 1932. He left Germany in 1933 for England where he formed a new group, Ballets Jooss, and toured extensively. He returned to Essen in 1949, and retired in 1969, but his works continue to be mounted by his daughter **Anna Markard** (1931–). He died in Heilbronn. » ballet; Laban; modern dance

Joplin, Scott (1868–1917) US composer and pianist, born at Texarkana, Arkansas. He gained fame as a pianist in Chicago and St Louis in the 1890s, but he longed for recognition as a serious composer. His 'Maple Leaf Rag' (1899) made ragtime music a national craze, and was the first of his several popular rags. He died in New York City. Ragtime experienced a revival in the 1970s, and Joplin's music (especially 'The Entertainer') became more widely known. » ragtime

Jordaens, Jakob [yawdahns] (1593–1678) Flemish painter, born in Antwerp. He became a member of an Antwerp Guild in 1616, and from 1630 came under the influence of Rubens, who obtained for him the patronage of the Kings of Spain and Sweden. He painted several altarpieces, and became known for his scenes of merry peasant life, such as 'The King Drinks' (Brussels). After Rubens' death, he was considered the greatest painter in Antwerp, where he died. » altarpiece; Flemish art; Rubens

Jordan, (Marie Ennemond) Camille [zhawdã] (1838–1922) French mathematician, born at Lyons, who became professor at the Ecole Polytechnique and at the Collège de France. He applied group theory to geometry, wrote on the theory of linear differential equations, and on the theory of functions, which he applied to the curve which bears his name. He died in Milan. » equations; function [i]; geometry

Jordan, Dorothea, *née* **Bland** (1762–1816) Irish actress, born near Waterford. She made her debut in Dublin in 1777, and appeared with great success at Drury Lane in 1785. For nearly 30 years she kept her hold on the public mainly in comic tomboy roles. In 1790 commenced her connection with the Duke of Clarence, afterwards William IV, which endured until 1811, and by whom she had 10 of her 15 children. In 1814, she retired to St-Cloud, France, where she died. » theatre; William IV

Jordan, official name **Hashemite Kingdom of Jordan**, Arabic **Al Mamlaka al Urduniya al Hashemiyah** pop (1990e) 3 169 000; area 96 188 sq km/37 129 sq ml (including 6 644 sq km/2 565 sq ml in the West Bank). Kingdom in the Middle East, divided into eight governorates (*muhafazas*); bounded N by Syria, NE by Iraq, E and S by Saudi Arabia, and W by Israel; capital, Amman; chief cities, Irbid, Zarqa, Salt, Karak, Aqaba; time-zone GMT +2; population mainly of Arab descent; chief

religion, Islam (Sunni, 95%), with Christian and other minorities; official language, Arabic; unit of currency, the Jordanian dinar.

Physical description and climate. Divided N–S by Red Sea–Jordan rift valley, much lying below sea-level, lowest point −400 m/−1 312 ft at the Dead Sea; main area of irrigated cultivation, El Ghor (N); sides of the rift rise steeply through undulating hill country to heights above 1 000 m/3 200 ft; land levels out to the Syrian desert (E), sandy in the S, hard and rocky further N; highest point, Mt Ram (1 754 m/5 754 ft); c.90% of Jordan is desert, annual rainfall below 200 mm/8 in; summers uniformly hot and sunny; typically Mediterranean climate elsewhere, with hot, dry summers and cool, wet winters; temperatures at Amman, 7.5°C (Jan), 24.9°C (Jul), average annual rainfall 290 mm/11.4 in.

History and government. Part of Roman Empire; Arab control, 7th-c; centre of Crusader activity, 11th–12th-c; part of Turkish Empire from 16th-c until during World War 1; area divided into Palestine (W of R Jordan) and Transjordan (E of R Jordan), administered by Britain; Transjordan independence, 1946; British mandate over Palestine ended, 1948, with newly-created Israel fighting to control West Bank area; armistice in 1949 left Jordan in control of West Bank; West and East Banks united within Jordan, 1951; Israel control of West Bank after Six-Day War, 1967; civil war, following attempts by Jordanian army to expel Palestinian guerrillas from West Bank, 1970–1; amnesty declared, 1973; claims to the West Bank ceded to the Palestine Liberation Organization, 1974; links with the West Bank cut, 1988, prompting the PLO to establish a government in exile; a monarchy, in which the king is head of state and of government; parliament consists of a 30-member Senate and an elected 80-member House of Representatives.

Economy. Oil, cement, potash, phosphate (world's third largest exporter); light manufacturing; cereals, vegetables, citrus fruits, olives; major investment in Jordan valley agricultural development. ≫ Amman; Arab–Israeli Wars; East Bank; PLO; West Bank; RR26 national holidays; RR54 political leaders

Jordan, River River in the Middle East; rises in several headstreams in the Anti-Lebanon mountains on the Lebanon–Syria border; flows over 320 km/200 ml S through L Tiberias and El Ghor to the Dead Sea; N half of the river forms part of the Israel–Jordan and Israel–Syria borders; S half separates the East Bank of Jordan from the Israeli-occupied West Bank. ≫ Israel [i]; Jordan [i]

Joseph Biblical character and subject of many stories in *Gen* 37–50; the 11th son of Jacob, but the first by his wife Rachel. He is depicted as Jacob's favourite son (marked by the gift of a multicoloured coat) who was sold into slavery by his jealous brothers, yet who by prudence and wisdom rose from being a servant to high office in Pharaoh's court, with special responsibility for distributing grain supplies during a time of famine. Eventually he is portrayed as reconciled with his brothers, who come to Egypt to escape the famine. His sons, Ephraim and Manasseh, were blessed by Jacob, and became ancestors of two of the tribes of Israel. ≫ Israel, tribes of [i]; Jacob; Old Testament

Joseph II (1741–90) Holy Roman Emperor (1765–90), the son of Francis I and Maria Theresa, born in Vienna. Until his mother's death (1780) he was co-Regent, and his power was limited to the command of the army and the direction of foreign affairs. A sincere enlightened despot, he was known as 'the revolutionary emperor' for his programme of modernization. He was determined to assert Habsburg leadership, but some of his ambitious plans were thwarted variously by the diplomatic obstruction of France, Prussia, the United Provinces, and Britain, by war (with Prussia in 1778–9 and Turkey in 1788) and by insurrection (in the Netherlands in 1787, Hungary 1789, and the Tyrol 1790). He died in Vienna. ≫ enlightened despot; Habsburgs

Joseph, St (1st-c BC), feast day 19 March. Husband of the Virgin Mary, a carpenter at Nazareth, who last appears in the Gospel history when Jesus is 12 years old. He is never mentioned during Jesus's ministry, and must be assumed to have already died. ≫ Jesus Christ; Mary (mother of Jesus)

Joseph, Sir Keith (Sinjohn), Baron (1918–) British Conservative politician, born in London. Educated at Harrow and Oxford, he was called to the Bar (1946) then became an MP (1956). A former Secretary of State for Social Services (1970–4) and Industry (1979–81), he then held the Education and Science portfolio (1981–6). He was given an overall responsibility for Conservative policy and research in 1975, and with Margaret Thatcher founded the Centre for Policy Studies. He became a life peer in 1987. ≫ Conservative Party; Thatcher

Joseph, Père, byname **Eminence Grise** ('Grey Eminence'), originally **François Joseph le Clerc du Tremblay** (1577–1638) French diplomat and mystic, born in Paris. He became a Capuchin in 1599, and Cardinal Richelieu's secretary in 1611. His byname derives from his contact with Richelieu (the 'Red Eminence'), for whom he went on several important diplomatic missions, especially during the Thirty Years' War. He died at Rueil. ≫ Capuchins; Richelieu; Thirty Years' War

Joseph, tribes of Although Joseph was the eleventh son of Jacob, his descendants were not usually described as 'the tribe of Joseph', one of the twelve tribes of Israel, but were represented by two tribes – Manasseh and Ephraim, Joseph's two sons who were blessed by Jacob (*Gen* 48–9). It is uncertain whether a single 'tribe of Joseph' ever existed, since reference is often to 'the *tribes* of Joseph'. ≫ Ephraim/Manasseh, tribe of; Israel, tribes of [i]; Jacob; Joseph; Old Testament

Joseph of Arimathea, St (1st-c), feast day 17 March (W), 31 July (E). A rich Israelite, a secret disciple of Jesus, and a councillor in Jerusalem. He went to Pontius Pilate and begged the body of Jesus, burying it in his own rock-hewn tomb. He is frequently referred to in later Christian literature. ≫ Jesus Christ; Pilate

Joséphine, *née* **Marie Josèphe Rose Tascher de la Pagerie** (1763–1814) First wife of Napoleon Bonaparte, and French Empress, born at Trois-Ilets, Martinique. In 1779 she married the Vicomte de Beauharnais, who was executed during the French Revolution (1794). She married Napoleon in 1796, and accompanied him on his Italian campaign, but soon returned to Paris. At Malmaison, and afterwards at the Luxembourg and the Tuileries, she attracted round her the most brilliant society of France. The marriage, being childless, was dissolved in 1809. She retained the title of Empress, and died at Malmaison. ≫ Napoleon I

Josephson, Brian (David) (1940–) British physicist, born in

Cardiff, Wales. He was educated at Cambridge, where he became professor of physics in 1974. In 1962, while a research student, he deduced the existence of **Josephson effects** used in certain superconducting devices. He shared the Nobel Prize for Physics in 1973. » Josephson junction; superconductivity

Josephson junction A thin layer of insulating oxide material between two superconducting electrodes, used mainly in measuring magnetic fields; devised by British physicist Brian Josephson. At sufficiently low temperatures, electron-pairs pass through the insulating portion by quantum tunnelling. A magnetic field applied to the junction modifies the current through the oxide layer, allowing the junction to operate as a high-speed switch, potentially useful in computers. » Josephson; quantum tunnelling; superconducting quantum interference device; superconductivity

Josephus, Flavius [johseefuhs], originally **Joseph ben Matthias** (c.37–?) Jewish historian and soldier, born in Jerusalem, who commanded a Galilean force during the Jewish Revolt against Rome in 66. He cunningly gained favour upon surrendering to the Romans, and went to Rome, where he produced several writings on Jewish history and religion, including *History of the Jewish War* (75–9) and *Antiquities of the Jews* (93). He died in Rome. » Roman history [i]

Joshua, Heb **Yehoshua** In the Old Testament, the son of Nun, of the tribe of Ephraim, who during the 40 years' wanderings of the Israelites acted as 'minister' of Moses, and upon Moses' death was appointed to lead the people into Canaan. The Book of Joshua is named after him. » Joshua, Book of; Moses

Joshua or **Josue, Book of** A book of the Hebrew Bible/Old Testament named after its main hero, Joshua (originally Hoshea, but renamed by Moses). It continues the stories of the Pentateuch, beginning with the death of Moses, and presents narratives of how Israel conquered the land W of the Jordan from the Canaanites after 40 years of wandering in the desert. It ends with the death of Joshua after the conquest and the apportionment of the land among the tribes of Israel. The author is anonymous, and the present form of the work seems to be composed of several distinct strands of tradition. » Deuteronomistic History; Israel, tribes of [i]; Old Testament; Pentateuch

Josiah [johsiya] (7th-c BC) Biblical character, King of Judah (c.639–609 BC), a favourite of the Deuteronomistic historians because of his religious reforms (2 *Kings* 22–3; 2 *Chron* 34–5), allegedly based on the discovery of 'the book of the law' in the 18th year of his reign. He is credited with destroying pagan cults and attempting to centralize worship in Jerusalem and the Temple. He died in battle against the Egyptians at Megiddo. » Deuteronomistic History; Esdras/Jeremiah/Zephaniah, Books of; Old Testament

Josquin Desprez [zhoskī daypray] (c.1440–1521) French composer, possibly a pupil of Ockeghem. He was a singer at Milan Cathedral (1459–72), and was subsequently in the service of the Sforza family. From 1486 until at least 1494 he was a member of the papal chapel in Rome. After a few years in France and Ferrara, he spent the last years of this life (from 1504) as provost in Condé, where he died. One of the greatest masters of Renaissance polyphony, he left about 20 masses and numerous motets. » Ockeghem; polyphony

Jostedalsbreen or **Jostedalsbre** [yostuhdalsbrayn] area 486 sq km/188 sq ml. Ice field on the Jostedalsbreen plateau, W Norway, 160 km/100 ml NE of Bergen; length 96 km/60 ml; width 24 km/15 ml; height 2 044 m/6 706 ft; largest ice field in Europe, with a thickness of 300 m/1 000 ft; village of Jostedal lies at its E foot. » Norway [i]

Josue » **Joshua, Book of**

Jotunheimen [yohtoonhiymn] or **Jotunheim** Highest mountain range in Europe, SC Norway; extends c.112 km/70 ml between Sogne Fjord and the upper Gudbrandsval; more than 250 peaks over 1 900 m/6 200 ft, and over 60 glaciers; rises to 2 470 m/8 104 ft at Glittertind; many associations with folk legends and the scene of Ibsen's *Peer Gynt*. » Glittertind; Ibsen

joule [jool] SI unit of energy, work done, and quantity of heat; symbol J; named after British physicist James Joule; defined as the work done by a force of 1 newton applied over a distance of 1 metre in the direction of the force. » calorie [i]; energy; heat; phytic acid; units (scientific); work; RR70

Joule, James (Prescott) [jool] (1818–89) British physicist, born at Salford, Lancashire. He studied chemistry, and in a series of experiments (1843–78) showed that heat is a form of energy, and established the mechanical equivalent of heat. This became the basis of the theory of the conservation of energy. He also worked with Lord Kelvin on temperature change in gases, and formulated the absolute scale of temperature. He died at Sale, Cheshire. » energy; joule; Joule–Thomson effect; Kelvin

Joule–Thomson effect The change in temperature of a gas when passed through a nozzle and allowed to expand; named after British physicists James Joule and William Thomson (Lord Kelvin). For a gas already at low temperature, the expansion produces further cooling, a property exploited in the liquification of oxygen and nitrogen. For a gas above a certain temperature (the inversion temperature for that gas), the effect causes warming. Oxygen and nitrogen have inversion temperatures of 620°C and 348°C respectively. » cryogenics; gas **1**; Joule; Kelvin

journalism The practice and profession of producing material of current interest for the press and broadcasting. Originally limited to the written word (*print journalism*), but now extended to the spoken word on radio and television (*broadcast journalism*) and pictures (*photojournalism*), the term applies to the collecting, working up, and editing of material, especially news. Journalism has its own trade unions, professional associations, codes of conduct, awards, and training schemes. Its laudable claim to 'Fourth Estate' status is often compromised by its collusion with those with power in society, invasions of personal privacy, and 'chequebook journalism' ('revelations' bought at great expense). » newspaper

Jouvet, Louis [zhoovay] (1887–1951) French actor and theatre/film director, born at Crozon. He studied as a pharmacist but took to the stage, touring the USA with Jacques Copeau's company (1918–19). He became stage-manager (1922) and director (1924) of the Comédie des Champs Elysées. He was the first to recognize Giraudoux, all but one of whose plays he produced. In 1934 his company transferred to the Théâtre de l'Athénée, and he became professor at the Paris Conservatoire. He died in Paris. » drama; Giraudoux; theatre

Jovian (c.331–64) Roman emperor (363–4), appointed by the army in Mesopotamia on Julian's death in battle. He was immediately forced to make a humiliating peace with Shapur II, ceding great tracts of Roman territory to Sassanian Persia, and agreeing to pay her a subsidy. » Julian; Shapur II

Joyce, James (Augustine Aloysius) (1882–1941) Irish writer, born in Dublin. Educated at Dublin, he went in 1903 to Paris to study medicine, and then took up voice training for a concert career. Back in Dublin, he published a few stories, but, unable to make a living by his pen, left for Trieste to tutor in English. Dublin saw him for the last time in 1912, when he started the short-lived Volta Cinema Theatre. He went to Zürich (1915), where he formed a company of Irish players, settled in Paris (1920–40), then returned to Zürich, where he died. His early work includes short stories, *Dubliners* (1914), and *Portrait of the Artist as a Young Man* (1914–5). His best-known book, *Ulysses*, appeared in Paris in 1922, but was banned in the UK and USA until 1936. *Work in Progress* began to appear in 1927, and finally emerged as *Finnegans Wake* (1939). His work revolutionized the novel form, partly through the abandonment of ordinary plot for 'stream of consciousness', but more fundamentally through his unprecedented exploration of language. » deconstruction; Freud, Sigmund; Irish literature; novel; stream of consciousness

Joyce, William, byname **Lord Haw-Haw** (1906–46) British traitor, born in New York City. As a child he lived in Ireland and in 1922 his family emigrated to England. In 1937, he founded the fanatical British National Socialist Party, and fled to Germany before war broke out. Throughout World War 2, he broadcast from Radio Hamburg propaganda against Britain, gaining his byname from his upper-class drawl. He was captured by the British at Flensburg, and was tried and executed in London. » World War 2

Juan Carlos I (1938–) King of Spain (1975–), born in Rome, the son of Don Juan de Borbón y Battenberg, Count of Barcelona (1908–), and the grandson of Spain's last ruling monarch, Alfonso XIII (1886–1941). He was educated in Switzerland, and from 1948, by agreement between his father and General Franco, in Spain. He earned commissions in the army, navy, and air force (1955–9), and studied at the University of Madrid (1959–61). In 1962 he married Princess Sophia of Greece, and they have three children. In 1969 Franco named him as his eventual successor, and he was proclaimed King on Franco's death in 1975. Instead of upholding the Franco dictatorship (as had been intended), he decisively presided over Spain's democratization, helping to defeat a military coup (1981) and assuming the role of a constitutional monarch. » Franco; Spain [i]

Juan Fernández Islands [**hwan** fer**nan**dez] Group of three islands in Valparaíso province, Chile, in the Pacific Ocean, 640 km/398 ml W of mainland; Más a Tierra, Más Afuera, Santa Clara; total area 181 sq km/70 sq ml; Alexander Selkirk shipwrecked on Más a Tierra in 1704 for four years (basis of Defoe novel, *Robinson Crusoe*). » Chile [i]; Defoe

Juárez, Benito (Pablo) [**hwah**res] (1806–72) Mexican national hero and President (1861–72), born of Indian parents near Oaxaca. His ideas for reform forced him to live in exile (1853–5), but he then joined the new Liberal government. During the civil war of 1857–60, he assumed the presidency, and was elected to that office on the Liberal victory (1861). The French invasion under Maximilian forced him to the far north, from where he directed resistance until the defeat of Maximilian in 1867. He died in office in Mexico City. » Maximilian, Ferdinand Joseph; Mexico [i]

Jubilees, Book of An account purporting to be an extended revelation to Moses during his 40 days on Mt Sinai, a book of the Old Testament Pseudepigrapha, perhaps from the mid-2nd-c BC. Its name is derived from the division of time into 'jubilees' (49 years, representing 7 weeks of years), but it has also been called the *Little Genesis* or the *Testament of Moses*. It retells *Gen* 1 to *Ex* 12 (the Creation to the Passover), amplifying the account and emphasizing separation from non-Jews, loyalty to the Jewish religious law, and the importance of secret traditions for readers of its own times. » Moses; Pseudepigrapha

Judah, tribe of [**joo**da] One of the twelve tribes of ancient Israel, said to be descended from Jacob's fourth son by his wife Leah. Its territory originally extended S of Jerusalem, bounded on the W by the Mediterranean and on the E by the Dead Sea, but later it was restricted. » Jacob; Judah, Kingdom of; Israel, tribes of [i]; Old Testament

Judah, kingdom of [**joo**da] An ancient Jewish state which incorporated the tribal areas of Judah and Benjamin, established when the united monarchy split into the kingdoms of Judah (in the S) and Israel (in the N) in the late 10th-c BC after the reign of Solomon. Each kingdom had separate kings, with Jerusalem being in the kingdom of Judah. Both Judah and Jerusalem fell to the Babylonians in 587 BC. » Benjamin/Judah, tribe of; Israel, tribes of [i]; Old Testament

Judaism The religion of the Jews, central to which is the belief in one God, the transcendent creator of the world who delivered the Israelites out of their bondage in Egypt, revealed his law (*Torah*) to them, and chose them to be a light to all humankind. The Hebrew Bible is the primary source of Judaism. Next in importance is the *Talmud*, which consists of the *Mishnah* (the codification of the oral Torah) and a collection of extensive early rabbinical commentary. Various later commentaries and the standard code of Jewish law and ritual (*halakhah*) produced in the late Middle Ages have been important in shaping Jewish practice and thought.

However varied their communities, all Jews see themselves as members of a community whose origins lie in the patriarchal period. This past lives on in its rituals, and there is a marked preference for expressing beliefs and attitudes more through ritual than through abstract doctrine. The family is the basic unit of Jewish ritual, though the synagogue has come to play an increasingly important role. The Sabbath, which begins at sunset on Friday and ends at sunset on Saturday, is the central religious observance. The synagogue is the centre for community worship and study. Its main feature is the 'ark' (a cupboard) containing the hand-written scrolls of the Pentateuch. The rabbi is primarily a teacher and spiritual guide. There is an annual cycle of religious festivals and days of fasting. The first of these is Rosh Hashanah, New Year's Day; the holiest day in the Jewish year is Yom Kippur, the Day of Atonement. Other annual festivals include Hanukkah and Pesach, the family festival of Passover.

Modern Judaism is rooted in rabbinic Judaism, and its historical development has been diverse. Today most Jews are the descendants of either the *Ashkenazim* or the *Sephardim*, each with their marked cultural differences. There are also several religious branches of Judaism. *Orthodox* Judaism (19th-c) seeks to preserve traditional Judaism. *Reform* Judaism (19th-c) represents an attempt to interpret Judaism in the light of modern scholarship and knowledge – a process carried further by *Liberal* Judaism. *Conservative* Judaism attempts to modify orthodoxy through an emphasis on the positive historical elements of Jewish tradition. Anti-Semitic prejudice and periods of persecution have been a feature of the Christian culture of Europe, and increased with the rise of European nationalism, culminating in the Nazi Holocaust. Its effect has been incalculable, giving urgency to the Zionist movement for the creation of a Jewish homeland, and is pivotal in all relations between Jews and non-Jews today. There are now over 14 million Jews. » Abraham; Akiva ben Joseph; Amidah; Ark of the Covenant; Ashkenazim; Bar Mitzvah; Bible; covenant **2**; Diaspora, Jewish; Gemara; Halakhah; Hanukah; Hasidism; Hillel I; Holocaust; Israel [i]; Kabbalah; Kaddish; Kiddush; menorah; Messiah; messianism; midrash; Mishnah; Moses; Passover; patriarch; Pentateuch; rabbi; Reform Judaism; sabbath; Sephardim; Shema; Star of David; synagogue; Talmud; Tannaim; tefellin; Temple, Jerusalem; Torah; Tosefta; Yom Kippur; Zionism; RR22–23

Judas Iscariot [**joo**das is**ka**riuht] (1st-c) One of the twelve disciples of Jesus, usually appearing last in the lists in the synoptic Gospels (*Mark* 3.19), identified as the one who betrayed Jesus for 30 pieces of silver by helping to arrange for his arrest at Gethsemane by the Jewish authorities (*Mark* 14.43–6). Other traditions indicate his role as treasurer (*John* 13.29) and his later repentance and suicide (*Matt* 27.3–10, *Acts* 1.16–19). 'Iscariot' may mean 'man of Keriot', 'assassin', or 'man of falsehood'. » apostle; Gethsemane; Gospels, canonical; Jesus Christ

judas tree A deciduous tree growing to 10 m/30 ft, native to the Mediterranean region, and often planted as an ornamental; leaves suborbicular, heart-shaped at the base; pea-flowers pink, usually appearing before the leaves; pods up to 10 cm/4 in long. By tradition, this is the tree from which Judas Iscariot hanged himself. (*Cercis siliquastrum*. Family: *Leguminosae*.) » deciduous plants; Judas Iscariot; tree [i]

Jude, St (1st-c), feast day 28 October (W), 19 June or 21 August (E). One of the twelve apostles, probably the Judas who was one of the 'brethren of the Lord', the brother of James. A New Testament letter is named after him, but the authorship of the work is disputed. He is traditionally thought to have been martyred in Persia with St Simon, whose feast is held on the same day. » apostle; Jesus Christ; Jude, Letter of

Jude, Letter of A brief New Testament writing, considered one of the 'catholic' or 'general' letters, attributed to Jude the brother of James and thus of Jesus of Nazareth, but believed by many today to originate from very late in the 1st-c AD. The work strongly warns an unspecified readership about false teachers, who are portrayed as immoral, intemperate, and divisive, and who perhaps represented libertine, gnostic views. The canonicity of the letter was long disputed in the early Church. » Gnosticism; James ('brother of Jesus'); New Testament

Judea [joo**dee**a] Roman–Greek name for S Palestine, area now occupied by SW Israel and W Jordan; southernmost of the Roman divisions of Palestine; rises to 1 020 m/3 346 ft in the S near Hebron; chief town, Jerusalem; following 1948–9 war, W region became part of Israel, and E region part of Jordan; since 1967, West Bank and E Jerusalem occupied by Israel. » Israel [i]; Jordan [i]; West Bank

Judea-Samaria » **West Bank**

judge A public officer with authority to adjudicate in both civil and criminal disputes; in some jurisdictions (eg the USA) this authority is limited to a single branch of law (eg administrative law judges). In the UK, judges are appointed by the Crown on the advice of the prime minister in the case of the Court of Appeal and House of Lords; on the advice of the Lord Chancellor in the case of High Court and circuit judges. Judges are appointed from the ranks of experienced barristers, though in England and Wales experienced solicitors may be appointed as circuit judges. Senior judges (other than the Lord Chancellor, a government minister) can be removed only on an address presented by both Houses of Parliament; this rule is intended to secure the independence of the judiciary. Circuit judges (as magistrates) can be removed by the Lord Chancellor for incapacity or misbehaviour. » circuit; Court of Appeal; High Court of Justice; recorder

Judges, Book of A book of the Hebrew Bible/Old Testament, with 'judges' referring to the tribal heroes (such as Deborah, Gideon, and Samson) whose acts of leadership are described. It relates to the unstable period between the initial conquest of Palestine by the Israelites and the establishment of the monarchy over Israel, and it attempts to draw moral lessons from the contrasting examples of good and bad leadership. Its stories probably underwent editing at several stages of Israel's history. » Deuteronomistic History; Old Testament

judicial review In England and Wales, a legal means of obtaining remedies in the High Court against inferior courts, tribunals, and administrative bodies; a similar procedure is available in other jurisdictions. The court may make various orders, including *certiorari* (which quashes a decision), *mandamus* (to compel a duty to be carried out), and *prohibition* (to stop an intended action). Damages may also be awarded. » damages; High Court of Justice

Judith, Book of Book of the Old Testament Apocrypha (or deuterocanonical writings recognized by the Catholic Church), possibly dating from the Maccabean period (mid-2nd-c BC). It tells the story of how Judith, an attractive and pious Jewish widow, saved the city of Bethulia from siege by the Assyrian army (ostensibly c.6th-c BC) by beheading Holofernes, its general, in his tent once she had beguiled and intoxicated him. » Apocrypha, Old Testament; Maccabees

judo An unarmed combat sport, developed in Japan, and useful in self-defence. The present-day sport was devised by Dr Jigoro Kano, (1860–1938), headmaster of two leading Japanese schools, who founded the Kodokan school in 1882. Contestants wear a *judogi* (loose fitting suit) and compete on a mat to break their falls. They are graded in their abilty from 5th to 1st Kyu, and then 1st Dan to the highest, 12th Dan. Only Kano has been awarded the 12th Dan. Different coloured belts indicate a fighter's grade. » martial arts; RR114

Jugendstil » **Art Nouveau**

Juggernaut (Sanskrit 'protector of the world') [**juh**gernot] A Hindu deity equated with Vishnu. His temple is at Puri in E India, and is noted for its annual festival. » Hinduism; Vishnu

Jugoslavia » **Yugoslavia** [i]

jugular veins Blood vessels draining the structures of the head and neck. The **internal** jugular vein returns blood from the brain, face, and much of the neck (particularly the deeper structures). It begins at an opening in the base of the skull (the *jugular foramen*) and ends by joining the subclavian vein (returning blood from the upper limb) to form the brachiocephalic vein. The **external** jugular vein returns blood from the scalp and superficial aspects of the neck. The **anterior** jugular veins are found close to the midline at the front of the neck, and drain into the external jugular vein. » neck

Jugurtha (c.160–104 BC) King of Numidia (118–105 BC), after whom the Jugurthine War (112–104 BC) is named. Rome's difficulty in defeating him provided Marius with a launching pad for his career, and led to important reforms in the Roman army. Jugurtha's surrender to Marius' deputy, Sulla, ended the war, but was the starting point of the deadly feud between Marius and Sulla which plunged Rome into civil war 20 years later. » Marius; Numidia; Sulla

jujitsu The Japanese art of offence and self-defence without weapons, used by the Samurai. Jujitsu forms the basis of many modern forms of other combat sports, such as judo, aikido, and karate. It is thought to have been introduced into Japan by a Chinese monk, Chen Yuan-ping, at the turn of the 17th-c. » aikido; judo; karate; martial arts; samurai

jujube [**joo**joob] A deciduous shrub growing to 9 m/30 ft, native to the E Mediterranean region; characteristic zig-zag stem and paired spines, one hooked, one straight; leaves oval; flowers yellow; olive-like fruits black. It is cultivated for its edible fruits. (*Z jujuba.* Family: *Rhamnaceae.*) » deciduous plants; lotus; shrub

Julia The name of numerous ladies of the Julian gens, notably **1** the wife of Marius and aunt of Julius Caesar; **2** the daughter of Augustus by his first wife Scribonia (39 BC–AD 14), banished for adultery in 2 BC; **3** the daughter of **2** and Agrippa (c.19 BC–AD 28); her disgrace and banishment somehow involved the poet Ovid. » Herod Agrippa I; Marius; Ovid

Julian, byname **the Apostate**, properly **Flavius Claudius Julianus** (332–63) Roman emperor (361–3), the son of a half-brother of Constantine the Great. Appointed deputy emperor (Caesar) in the West by his cousin Constantius II (355), he served with great distinction on the Rhine, and was proclaimed emperor (Augustus) by his adoring troops in 360. As emperor, he publicly proclaimed himself a pagan (hence his nickname) and initiated a vigorous policy of reviving the old pagan cults, though without persecuting Christians. He was killed in battle against the Sassanid Persians. » Constantine the Great; Sassanids

Julian Alps, Slovenian **Julijske Alpe** Mountain range in NW Yugoslavia and NE Italy; a SE extension of the Alpine system, bounded to the N by the Karawanken Alps; rises to 2 863 m/9 393 ft at Triglav, the highest peak in Yugoslavia. » Alps

Julian calendar A calendar established in 46 BC by Julius Caesar, further modified in AD 8, when leap years were correctly implemented, then used in Catholic Europe until 1582, when it was replaced by the Gregorian calendar. Since 153 BC, the year had slipped by 3 months, relative to the seasons, because of manipulations by political opportunists (to shorten officials' terms of office). Caesar ended this confusion, inserting an extra 67 days into 43 BC, and decreeing a year of 365 days, with an extra day every fourth year, initially by using February 24 twice. The Julian year is 11 minutes longer than the tropical year, and by the 15th-c its March 11 was falling 10 days later than the true equinox. » Caesar; Gregorian calendar; tropical year

Julian date The number of days that have elapsed since 1200 GMT on 1 January 4713 BC. This consecutive numbering of days gives a calendar independent of month and year used for analysing periodic phenomena, especially in astronomy. The Julian day which began at noon on 1 January 1990 was 2 447 891. Devised in 1582 by Joseph Justus Scaliger (1540–1609), it has no connection with the Julian calendar. » calendar

Julian of Norwich, Lady (c.1342–1413) English mystic who probably lived in isolation outside St Julian's Church, Norwich. Her work, *Sixteen Revelations of Divine Love*, based on her own religious experiences, has been a lasting influence on theologians stressing the power of the love of God. » mysticism

Juliana, Louise Emma Marie Wilhelmina (1909–) Queen of the Netherlands (1948–80), born at The Hague. Educated at Leyden, she became a lawyer,. and in 1937 married Prince Bernhard zur Lippe-Biesterfeld; they have four daughters. On the German invasion of Holland (1940), Juliana escaped to Britain and later resided in Canada. She returned to Holland in 1945, and became Queen on the abdication of her mother, Wilhelmina. She herself abdicated in favour of her eldest daughter, Beatrix. » Beatrix; Bernhard Leopold

Julunggul » **Rainbow Snake**

July Days (2–5 Jul 1917) Anti-government demonstrations in Petrograd marking a decisive stage in the Russian Revolution. Demonstrators demanded Russia's withdrawal from World War 1, the overthrow of the provisional government, and the transfer of 'All power to the soviets'. Lenin judged the time for a proletarian-socialist revolution to be premature, and urged restraint. » April Theses; February Revolution; Lenin; October Revolution; Russian Revolution

July Revolution (1830) A three-day revolt in Paris which ended the Bourbon Restoration, forcing the abdication of the reactionary Charles X (reigned 1824–30). It resulted in the establishment of a more liberal regime dominated by the wealthy bourgeoisie, the so-called *July Monarchy*, under the Orleanist, Louis Philippe, 'King of the French'. » Bourbons; Charles X (of France); Louis Philippe

Jumblat, Kemal (1919–77) Lebanese socialist politician and hereditary Druze chieftain, born in the Chouf Mts. He founded the Progressive Socialist Party in 1949, held several Cabinet posts (1961–4), and was Minister of the Interior (1969–70). The Syrian intervention on the side of the Christians in 1976 was a response to the increasing power of his authority in partnership with the Palestinians. He was assassinated in an ambush outside the village of Baaklu in the Chouf Mts. His son **Walid**, became leader of the Druze after his death. » Druze; Lebanon [i]; socialism

Jumna, River » **Yamuna, River**

jumping bean A seed of *Sebastiania pringlei*, a Mexican shrub of the spurge family (*Euphorbiaceae*). It provides food for the larva of the small moth *Carpocapsa solitaris*, which occupies the seed. Warmth intensifies movement of the larva, causing the 'bean' to jump or jerk erratically. » moth; seed; shrub; spurge

jumping hare » **springhaas**

jumping mouse A mouse-like rodent, native to N America (3 species) and China (1 species); long rear legs; may leap 3 m/10 ft; does not dig burrows; may hibernate for nine months; eats seeds and insects. (Family: *Zapodidae*, 4 species.) » mouse (zoology)

jumping plant louse » **psyllid**

June Days (1848) A violent episode in the French Revolution of 1848, when working-class radicals resisted the dissolution of the National Workshops in Paris. They were crushed by the National Guard and troops of the Republican government under the direction of General Louis Eugène Cavaignac (1802–57), thus exacerbating class divisions in France for generations. » Revolutions of 1848

June War » **Arab-Israeli Wars**

Juneau [joonoh] 58°18N 134°25W, pop (1980) 19 528. Seaport capital of state in SE Alaska, USA, on Gastineau Channel; developed as a gold-rush town after 1880; airport; trade centre, with an ice-free harbour; salmon and halibut fishing, lumbering, tourism; House of Wickersham; Salmon Derby (Aug). » Alaska

Jung, Carl (Gustav) [yung] (1875–1961) Swiss psychiatrist, born at Kesswil. He studied medicine at Basle, and worked at the Burghölzli mental clinic in Zürich (1900–9). He met Freud in Vienna in 1907, became his leading collaborator, and was president of the International Psychoanalytic Association (1911–14). He became increasingly critical of Freud's approach, and *Wandlungen und Symbole der Libido* (1911–12, The Psychology of the Unconscious) caused a break in 1913. He then developed his own theories, which he called 'analytical psychology' to distinguish them from Freud's psychoanalysis and Adler's individual psychology. Jung's approach included a description of psychological types ('extraversion/introversion'); the exploration of the 'collective unconscious'; and the concept of the psyche as a 'self-regulating system' expressing itself in the process of 'individuation'. He held chairs at Basle and Zürich, and died at Küsnacht, Switzerland. » Freud, Sigmund; psychoanalysis

Jungfrau [**yung**frow] 46°33N 7°58E. Mountain peak in the Bernese Alps, SC Switzerland; height 4 158 m/13 642 ft; mountain railway to near the summit; first ascended in 1811. » Bernese Alps

jungle fowl A pheasant native to E India and SE Asia; gregarious; inhabits forest and scrub; eats grain, shoots, berries, and insects; ancestral to the domestic fowl. The name is also used in Australia for the megapode *Megapodius freycinet*. (Genus: *Gallus*, 4 species.) » domestic fowl; megapode; pheasant

junior high school » **high school**

juniper An evergreen coniferous tree or shrub native to most of the N hemisphere; leaves of two kinds, needle- or scale-like, in some species on the same tree; cones fleshy, berry-like. The timber is durable; the foliage yields an oil used in perfume; and the berries are used to flavour gin. (Genus: *Juniperus*, 60 species. Family: *Cupressaceae*.) » conifer; evergreen plants; gin; red cedar **2**; shrub; tree [i]

Junkers Prussian aristocrats whose power rested on their large estates, situated predominantly to the E of the R Elbe, and on their traditional role as army officers and civil servants. Their position came increasingly under threat in late 19th-c Germany as a result of industrialization, but they jealously safeguarded their privileges and power. » Prussia

Juno (astronomy) The third asteroid to be discovered, in 1804. Its diameter is 247 km/153 ml. » asteroids

Juno (mythology) In Roman mythology, the supreme goddess, and the wife of Jupiter. Originally an ancient Italian deity associated with the Moon and the life of women, she was later identified with Hera. » Hera (mythology); Jupiter (mythology)

Jupiter (astronomy) The fifth planet from the Sun, and the innermost of the giant outer planets. It contains two-thirds of the matter in the Solar System, apart from the Sun. It was observed for centuries by astronomers, including Galileo, who discovered four moons later named after him. In recent years it has been observed in close-up by Pioneer 10 and 11 spacecraft and by Voyagers 1 and 2. Its basic characteristics are: mass 1.901×10^{27} kg; equatorial radius 71 398 km; polar radius 66 770 km/41 490 ml; mean density 1.33 g/cm^3; rotational period 9 h 55 min 29 sec; orbital period 11.9 years; inclination of equator to orbit 3.07°; mean distance from the Sun 5.203 AU. It is made primarily of hydrogen (82%) and helium (17%), and believed to have an innermost core of terrestrial composition of 5 to 10 Earth masses, a large outer core of hydrogen and helium in a metallic phase, a liquid hydrogen/helium mantle, and a deep gaseous atmosphere. The planet has a significant internal source of heat, and radiates twice as much heat from inside as it receives from the Sun.

The face of the planet is covered by clouds, organized into bands, called *belts* and *zones*. Zones are light, and cold (−130°C) because they are high in the atmosphere; belts are darker and warmer clouds (−40°C) at a lower elevation; and a third, warmer level of clouds has also been observed (20°C). The uppermost clouds are inferred to be solid ammonia, the middle clouds ammonium hydrosulphide, and the lowest clouds water. The rotation period at the poles is five minutes longer than that at the equator – a differential which contributes to the formation of a richly coloured banded structure in the cloudy atmosphere. Complex currents and vortices are observed within the bands, including a long-lived atmospheric storm called the **Great Red Spot**. The Jovian moons number at least 16, including the four large Galilean satellites, which are distinct worlds in themselves and lie in near-circular orbits in an equatorial plane. A dark ring of dust around the planet was discovered by Voyager, bounded at its outer edge by a small

Jungle fowl

moon (radius 10–15 km/6–10 ml), and containing within it another small moon which may be the source of the ring dust. » Galilean moons; Galileo project; Pioneer programme; planet; Solar System; Voyager project [i]; RR4

Jupiter (mythology) or **Iuppiter** The chief Roman god, equivalent to Greek Zeus, originally a sky-god with the attributes of thunder and the thunderbolt. He is sometimes given additional names (eg Jupiter Optimus Maximus). Roman generals visited his temple to do him honour. » Zeus

Jura Mountains [joora] Limestone mountain range in E France and W Switzerland, on Franco-Swiss border, forming a plateau 250 km/155 ml long by 50 km/31 ml wide; highest point in France, Crêt de la Neige (1 718 m/5 636 ft), in Switzerland, Mt Tendre (1 682 m/5 518 ft); forested slopes, with poor pasture; caving, winter sports. » France [i]; Switzerland [i]

Jurassic period [joorasik] A geological period of the Mesozoic era extending from c.213 to 144 million years ago; characterized by large reptiles on land, sea, and air, with shallow seas rich in marine life (eg ammonites), and the appearance of the first birds; mammals still primitive. » Archaeopteryx; geological time scale; Mesozoic era; RR16

jurisdiction **1** The competence of a particular court to hear a case. » court of law **2** The geographical area covered by a particular legal system; this is not necessarily the same area as that of the national political unit. For example, in the UK, the jurisdiction of England and Wales is separate from that of Scotland; and in the USA, the individual states constitute separate jurisdictions.

jurisprudence The philosophy of law. As with philosophy generally, jurisprudence has concerned itself not only with what is, but what ought to be, with inevitably an ideological dimension. It has some claim to be regarded as a science of law, in that it seeks to ascertain regularities in human behaviour: judicial behaviourists claim good success rates in predicting the outcome of legal decision-making. » law

jury A group of persons, generally 12 (15 in Scotland), used to try the facts of a criminal or civil case. In England and Wales, for example, jurors are chosen from the electoral roll, and must be aged between 18 and 65. Juries are used to try criminal cases in the Crown Court. They are not used for most civil cases, though some tort cases (eg defamation) must be heard before a jury. A majority verdict (10 to 2) is now permitted. Certain people are ineligible for jury service (eg members of the judiciary, the clergy, and the mentally ill) or may be excused (eg MPs, doctors), or disqualified (eg if previously convicted of certain types of offence). Jurors may also be 'challenged' by defence lawers, and rejected. » Crown Court; defamation

Jussieu [**zhü**syer] The name of a family of French botanists, notably **Bernard de Jussieu** (c.1699–1777), who created the botanical garden at Trianon for Louis XV, and adopted a system which has become the basis of modern natural botanical classification. His brother **Antoine** (1686–1758) was a physician and professor at the Jardin des Plantes, Paris. His nephew, **Antoine Laurent** (1748–1836), was also professor at the Jardin, and elaborated his uncle's system in *Genera Plantarum* (1778–9). » botany

Just in Time system » Kanban system

justice of the peace (JP) A judicial appointment in England and Wales, also known as a magistrate. JPs are appointed, and may be removed, by the Lord Chancellor. Their principal function is to preside in the *magistrates' courts*, administering immediate (or *summary*) justice in the majority of cases, and committing the most serious cases for further trial elsewhere. Each magistrate exercises his or her functions for a particular commission area. JPs are not necessarily legally qualified – most are not – though the absence of a legal qualification is not quite as surprising as it seems, as most cases involve disputes about the facts and not the law. A legally qualified clerk advises on the law. When trying cases, a JP sits with at least one other colleague. Magistrates now receive basic training, but no salary. » stipendiary magistrate; summary trial

justiciar In mediaeval times, the chief administrative and judicial officer of the English crown, who also acted as vice-regent during the king's absences overseas. The history of the office can be followed from Bishop Roger of Salisbury (died 1139) to 1234 and then, after a long break (1234–58), to 1265, when it finally lapsed. » Burgh; Walter, Hubert

Justin (Martyr), St (c.100–c.165), feast day 14 April (W) and 1 June (E). One of the Fathers of the Church, born at Sichem, Samaria. He was converted to Christianity, studied Stoic and Platonic philosophy, and founded a school of Christian philosophy at Rome, where he wrote two 'Apologies' on Christian belief (150–60). He is said to have been martyred at Rome. » Christianity; Fathers of the Church; Platonism; Stoicism

Justinian, properly **Flavius Petrus Sabbatius Justinianus** (c.482–565) Roman emperor (527–65), the protégé of his uncle, the Byzantine Emperor, Justin (518–27). At first co-emperor with Justin, on his death he became sole ruler. Along with his wife Theodora, he presided over the most brilliant period in the history of the late Roman Empire. Through his generals, Belisarius and Narses, he recovered N Africa, Spain, and Italy, and carried out a major codification of the Roman law. He died at Constantinople. » Belisarius; Byzantine Empire; Justinian Code; Narses; Theodora

Justinian Code The Emperor Justinian's great codification of Roman law, carried out under the direction of Tribonian and published in four sections in the 530s AD. Also known as the *Corpus Juris Civilis*, it is regarded as the pinnacle of Roman Law. » Justinian

jute An annual growing to 3.5 m/11½ ft, a relative of the lime tree, and native to S Asia; leaves ovoid; flowers in axils of leaves, yellow. The stems, soaked and beaten to separate the fibres, are used in hessian and sacking. (*Corchorus capsularis*. Family: *Tiliaceae*.) » annual; lime (botany)

Jutes A Germanic people whose original homeland was the N part of the Danish peninsula (Jutland). The tradition preserved by Bede, that Jutes participated in the 5th-c Germanic invasions of Britain and settled in Kent and the Isle of Wight, is confirmed by archaeological evidence. » Anglo-Saxons; Bede

Jutland, Battle of (1916) A sea battle of World War 1, in which Admiral Jellicoe led the British Grand Fleet from Scapa Flow and intercepted the German High Seas Fleet off the W coast of Jutland, Denmark. Though the battle itself was inconclusive, German naval chiefs withdrew their fleet to port, and turned to unrestricted submarine warfare as a means of challenging British command of the sea. » Jellicoe; World War 1

Juvenal, in full **Decimus Junius Juvenalis** (c.55–c.130) Roman lawyer and satirist, born at Aquinum, Italy. He served as tribune in the army, and under Domitian was banished to Egypt for some years for his satirical writing. His 16 verse satires (c.100–128) deal with a wide range of subjects, notably the corruption and immorality of the times. » Latin literature; satire

juvenile delinquency The anti-social behaviour of young people which may or may not be criminal. Theories explaining juvenile delinquency abound in criminology and sociology. Many account for such youthful misconduct in terms of playfulness, rebelliousness, frustration, or as a form of working-class rebellion against the inequities and frustrations of capitalism. Criminal statistics indicate that some groups tend towards greater delinquency than others; this may, however, reflect the fact that certain groups (eg young Blacks) receive a greater amount of attention and even hostility from law enforcement agencies. » labelling theory

juvenilia The very early works of writers who later become well-known. Jane Austen's *Minor Works* (published 1932) contain extensive entertaining examples, as do the Brontë sisters' Gondal writings, surviving in miniature bound books. » Austen; Brontë, Anne/Charlotte/Emily; literature

Juventud, Isla de la [**eel**ya thuh la yooven**tood**] ('isle of youth'), formerly **Isle of Pines** pop (1981) 57 879; area 2 199 sq km/849 sq ml. Province of Cuba, an island 97 km/60 ml off SW coast; capital, Nueva Gerona; formerly used as penal colony; new name in 1958, to recognize young people's contribution to development; rises to 416 m/1 365 ft at Sierra de Canada; fine beaches on S coast; tourism; grapefruit, mangoes, oranges. » Cuba [i]

K

K2 or **Mount Godwin-Austen** Second highest mountain in the world and highest in the Karakoram range, NE Pakistan; height 8 611 m/28 250 ft; named for English topographer Henry Godwin-Austen; the second peak to be measured in this range (hence, K2). » Himalayas

Kaba, Kaaba, or **Kaʿbah** [**ka**ba] The most sacred sight in Islam, situated within the precincts of the Great Mosque at Mecca, Saudi Arabia. It is a small cube-shaped building, unadorned except for the sacred Black Stone, a meteorite, set into the E corner of its walls. Earlier shrines on this spot were important centres of pilgrimage even in pre-Islamic times, but in AD 630 Mohammed stripped the Kaba of its pagan decorations and it became the spiritual centre of Islam. The stone, or *qibla*, is the focus-point to which Muslims turn when they pray. » Islam; Mecca

Kabbalah [kab**bah**la] (Heb 'tradition') Jewish religious teachings originally transmitted orally, predominantly mystic in nature, and ostensibly consisting of secret doctrines. It developed along two lines – the 'practical', centring on prayer, meditation, and acts of piety; and the 'speculative' or 'theoretical', centring on the discovery of mysteries hidden in the Jewish Scriptures by special methods of interpretation. » Judaism; Zohar

Kabuki [ka**boo**kee] Originally a city entertainment in Japan, particularly popular from 1650 to 1850, which performed for commercial gain during the five seasonal festivals. A play in numerous acts, arranged into four parts and designed to last from dawn to dusk, was presented in a manner which allowed an audience to watch, talk, and picnic in a holiday mood throughout the day. A complete play is nowadays rarely performed, and the spectacular resources of Kabuki are employed to present selected acts or highlights from the traditional repertoire. » bunraku; Noh; puppetry

Kabul [**kah**bul] 34°30N 69°10E, pop (1984e) 1 179 341. Capital city of Afghanistan, and capital of Kabul province, E Afghanistan; on R Kabul in a high mountain valley, commanding the approaches to the Khyber Pass; capital of Mughal Empire (1504–1738); modern state capital in 1773; captured in 1839 and 1879 by the British during the Afghan Wars; university (1931); airport; wool, cloth, sugar-beet, plastics, leather goods, furniture, glass, soap, heavy industry; power production increased 25% in 1984 by the opening of a gas turbine plant. » Afghanistan [i]

Kabyle [kuh**beel**] A Berber people of Algeria. Organized into different castes with serfs, they speak Kabyle, a Hamito-Semitic language, and are predominantly Muslims. They live in villages, grow grains and olives, and herd goats. Population c.2 million. » Algeria [i]; Berber

Kádár, János [**kah**dah] (1912–89) Hungarian statesman, Premier (1956–8, 1961–5) and First Secretary (1956–88), born at Kapoly. He joined the (illegal) Communist Party in 1931, and was arrested several times. He became a member of the Central Committee (1942) and the Politburo (1945), and Minister of the Interior (1949), but was arrested for anti-Stalinist views (1951–3). When the anti-Soviet uprising broke out in 1956, he was a member of the 'national' government of Imre Nagy, but then formed a puppet government which repressed the uprising. He resigned in 1958, becoming Premier again in 1961. His long reign as Party Secretary ended in 1988. » communism; Hungarian uprising; Nagy; Stalin

Kaddish [ka**deesh**] (Aramaic 'holy') An ancient Jewish congregation prayer, mostly in Aramaic, which marks the closing parts of daily public worship, praising the name of God and seeking the coming of the kingdom of God. There are variations in its use, but it is mostly recited while standing and facing Jerusalem. It has affinities with the Christian formulation of the Lord's Prayer. » Judaism; Lord's Prayer; prayer

kaffir corn » **sorghum**

Kafka, Franz (1883–1924) Austrian novelist, born in Prague, Czechoslovakia. He studied law, became an official in an insurance company (1907–23), moved to Berlin, but soon after succumbed to tuberculosis. His short stories and essays, such as *Die Verwandlung* (1916, The Metamorphosis), appeared in his lifetime, but his three unfinished novels were published posthumously by his friend Max Brod: *Ein Prozess* (1925, The Trial), *Das Schloss* (1926, The Castle), and *Amerika* (1927). He has influenced many authors with his vision of society (often called 'Kafkaesque') as a pointless, schizophrenically rational organization, with tortuous bureaucratic and totalitarian procedures, psychological labyrinths, and masochistic fantasies, into which the bewildered individual has strayed. He died near Vienna. » Beckett; Camus; German literature; novel

kagu [**kah**goo] A ground-dwelling bird native to New Caledonia; slate grey with short tail, pointed bill, and long erectile crest on head; virtually flightless; inhabits forests; eats worms, insects, and snails; once abundant, but now endangered. (*Rhynochetos jubatus*. Family: *Rhynochetidae*.)

Kaieteur Falls [**kiy**uhtoor] Waterfall in C Guyana, on the R Potaro; nearly five times the height of Niagara, with a sheer drop of 226 m/742 ft from a sandstone tableland c.100 m/350 ft wide into a wide basin where the water drops a further 22 m/72 ft; discovered in 1870; set in the 116 sq km/45 sq ml Kaieteur National Park, established in 1929. » Guyana [i]

Kaikoura Ranges [kiy**koh**ra] Mountain ranges in NE South Island, New Zealand; two parallel ranges, the Inland Kaikoura and the Seaward Kaikoura; length 40 km/25 ml, separated by the Clarence R; highest peak, Mt Tapuaenuku (2 885 m/9 465 ft) in the Inland Kaikoura. » New Zealand [i]

Kailas Range » **Gangdise Shan**

Kailasa Temple The most famous of the 34 Hindu, Buddhist, and Jain cave temples and monasteries at Ellora, Maharashtra, India. The edifice, which was built in the 8th-c, represents Shiva's Himalayan home of Mt Kailasa, and is renowned for its sculptures and friezes. » Ajanta Caves

Kairouan [kayr**wan**] 35°42N 10°01E, pop (1984) 72 254. Capital of Kairouan governorate, NE Tunisia, 130 km/81 ml S of Tunis; founded in 671; capital of the Aglabite dynasty, 9th-c; carpets, crafts; an important Muslim holy city; Great Mosque, the oldest in the Maghreb; carpet museum; archaeological site of Reqqada nearby. » Islam; Tunisia [i]

Kaiser The title assumed (Dec 1870) by the Prussian king, William (Wilhelm) I, following the unification of Germany and the creation of the German Empire. He was succeeded on his death in 1888 by his son Frederick (Friedrich) III, who survived him by only three months, and then by his grandson William (Wilhelm) II, who ruled until his enforced abdication in 1918. » William I/II (Emperors)

Kaiser, Georg [**kiy**zuh] (1878–1945) German dramatist, born at Magdeburg. He worked in Buenos Aires as a clerk, returned to Germany in ill health, and began to write plays which established him as a leader of the Expressionist movement, such as *Von Morgens bis Mitternachts* (1916, From Morn to Midnight), *Gas I* (1918), and *Gas II* (1920). His work was banned by the Nazis, and he left Germany in 1938. He died at Ascona, Switzerland. » drama; Expressionism; German literature

Kakadu [kaka**doo**] National park in Arnhem Land, Northern Territory, Australia; a world heritage site; bordered N by the

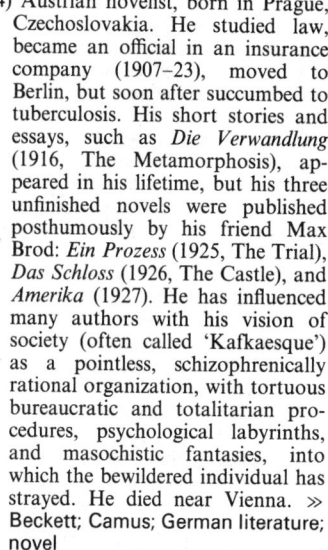

Van Diemen Gulf; includes the Jim Jim and Twin Falls; Aboriginal rock paintings found here, 18 000 years old; area 6 144 sq km/2 372 sq ml. » Northern Territory

kakapo [**kah**kapoh] A flightless, ground-dwelling parrot, native to New Zealand, also known as an **owl parrot**; face with owl-like array of radiating feathers; nocturnal; inhabits mountain forest; eats fruit, shoots, moss, and fungi; seriously endangered. (*Strigops habroptilus*. Family: *Psittacidae*.) » parrot

kakee » **persimmon**

Kakopetria [kakoh**pe**tria] 34°59N 32°54E. Summer resort town in Nicosia district, Cyprus; tomb of Archbishop Makarios III; nearby are the Byzantine churches of Lagoudhera and Stavros tou Ayiasmati. » Cyprus [i]; Makarios III

kala-azar [kahla **azah**] » **leishmaniasis**

Kalahari Desert region of Africa, in SW Botswana, SE Namibia and N Cape Province, South Africa; between Orange and Zambezi Rivers; area c.260 000 sq km/100 000 sq ml; elevation generally 850–1 000 m/2 800–3 280 ft; mainly covered with grass and woodland; bare sand in extreme SW, where annual rainfall below 200 mm/8 in; higher rainfall in the N, with savannah woodland; annual average rainfall over whole area, 150–500 mm/6–20 in; frosts common in dry season; sparsely inhabited by nomads; game reserve in S. » Botswana [i]; Khoisan; Namibia [i]

kalanchoe [kaluhn**koh**ee] A succulent herb or shrub, native mainly to tropical Africa and Madagascar; rather variable in appearance, but often with leaves blotched or marked with brown. In many species, the leaf-margins bear plantlets which drop off and grow into new plants. (Genus: *Kalanchoe*, 125 species. Family: *Crassulaceae*.) » herb; shrub; succulent

kale A very hardy mutant of cabbage with dense heads of plain or curled, green or purple leaves. It is widely grown as a vegetable and fodder crop. The leaves are sometimes called *borecole*. (*Brassica oleracea*, variety *acephala*. Family: *Cruciferae*.) » cabbage; hardy plants

Kalevala [**kah**levahla] The name given to a compilation of Finnish legends, published by Elias Lönnrot in 1835, and now regarded as the Finnish national epic. The poem is in a trochaic metre, imitated by Longfellow in *Hiawatha*. » Vainamoinen

Kalgoorlie or **Kalgoorlie–Boulder** 30°49S 121°29E, pop (1981) 19 848. Gold-mining town in Western Australia, 550 km/340 ml E of Perth; gold discovered here, 1887–8; 60% of Australia's gold mined in the suburb of Boulder; Kalgoorlie and Boulder amalgamated, 1966; between them lies the 'Golden Mile', a square mile of ground, rich in gold; airfield; railway; a Flying Doctor centre; located in the middle of infertile desert, water has to be piped in from Mundaring Weir near Perth. » Australian gold rush; Western Australia

Kali [**kah**lee] The Hindu goddess of destruction, who is also represented as the Great Mother, the giver of life. She is the consort of Shiva. » Hinduism; Shiva

Kalidasa (c.5th-c) Indian poet and dramatist, best known through his drama *Abhijnana-Sakuntala* (The Recognition of Sakuntala). Also attributed to him are two other plays, two epic poems, and a lyric poem. » Indian literature; poetry

Kalimantan [kali**man**tan] Group of four provinces in the Indonesian part of Borneo: **Kalimantan Berat**, **West Kalimantan**, or **West Borneo**, pop (1980) 2 986 068, area 146 760 sq km/56 649 sq ml, capital Pontianak; **Kalimantan Selatan**, **South Kalimantan**, or **South Borneo**, pop (1980) 2 064 649, area 37 660 sq km/14 537 sq ml, capital Banjarmasin; **Kalimantan Tengah**, **Central Kalimantan**, or **Central Borneo**, pop (1980) 954 353, area 152 600 sq km/58 904 sq ml, capital Palangkaraya; **Kalimantan Timur**, **East Kalimantan**, or **East Borneo**, pop (1980) 1 218 016, area 202 440 sq km/78 142 sq ml, capital Samarinda; coffee, copra, pepper, coal, timber, rubber, diamonds, gold; an active guerrilla separatist movement. » Borneo; Indonesia [i]

Kalinin, Mikhail Ivanovich [kah**lee**nin] (1875–1946) Soviet statesman, formal head of state after the 1917 Revolution and during the years of Stalin's dictatorship (1919–46), born at Tver. A peasant and metal-worker, he entered politics as a champion of the peasant class, and won great popularity. He became President of the Soviet Central Executive Committee (1919–38), and of the Presidium of the Supreme Soviet (1938–46). He died in Moscow. » Stalin

Kalmar or **Calmar** 56°39N 16°20E, pop (1982) 53 497. Capital town of Kalmar county, SE Sweden; on the Kalmar Sound, opposite Öland I; site of the Union of Kalmar; railway; glass, foodstuffs, shipbuilding, engineering, vehicles; castle (11th-c). » Kalmar Union; Sweden [i]

Kalmar Union The dynastic union of Denmark, Norway, and Sweden achieved at Kalmar, Sweden, where in 1397 Eric of Pomerania was crowned king of all three kingdoms. In 1523 Sweden broke away from the Union, which was dominated by Denmark, but Norway was united with Denmark until 1814. » Gustavus I

Kaluza-Klein theory [ka**looza kliyn**] A 5-dimensional theory, a variant of general relativity, which attempts the unification of gravitation and electromagnetism; after Polish physicist Theodor Kaluza (1921) and Swedish physicist Oskar Klein (1926). It was revived in the 1980s with further dimensions added to incorporate nuclear interactions. The extra dimensions are assumed to be of a size tending to Planck length, hence unobservable. The theory has no experimental support. » general relativity; grand unified theories; Planck length

Kama [**kah**ma] The Hindu god of love; also, one of the four ends of life in Hindu tradition. In this view, the pursuit of love or pleasure, both sensual and aesthetic, is necessary for life, but should be regulated by considerations of dharma. » dharma; Hinduism

Kamchatka [kam**chat**ka] area 270 033 sq km/104 233 sq ml. Large peninsula in Kamchatskaya oblast, E Siberian Russia, separating the Sea of Okhotsk (W) from the Bering Sea (E); extends c.1 200 km/750 ml S from the Koryakskiy Khrebet range to Cape Lopatka; width, 130–480 km/80–300 ml; volcanic C range, with several cones still active; highest peak, Klyuchevskaya Sopka (4 750 m/15 584 ft); abundant hot springs; chief population centre, Petropavlovsk-Kamchatskiy. » Russia

Kamenev, Lev Borisovich, original surname **Rosenfeld** (1883–1936) Soviet politician, born in Moscow. He was an active revolutionary from 1901, and was exiled to Siberia in 1915. Liberated during the Revolution (1917), he became a member of the Communist Central Committee. Expelled from the Party as a Trotskyist in 1927, he was readmitted the next year but again expelled in 1932. He was shot in Moscow for allegedly conspiring against Stalin. » Russian Revolution; Stalin; Trotsky

kamikaze (Jap 'divine wind') A term identifying the volunteer suicide pilots of the Japanese Imperial Navy, who guided their explosive-packed aircraft onto enemy ships in World War 2. They emerged in the last year of the Pacific War, when Allied forces were closing on the Japanese homeland. » World War 2

Kammersee [**kam**erzay] » **Attersee**

Kampala [kam**pah**la] 0°19N 32°35E, pop (1983e) 454 974. Capital of Uganda, close to the N shore of L Victoria; founded, late 19th-c; capital, 1963; airport at Entebbe; railway; Makerere University (1922); banking, administration, fruit and vegetable trade, tea blending and packing, brewing, textiles, coffee, petrol depot; two cathedrals. » Uganda [i]

Kampong Saom » **Kompong Som**

Kampuchea » **Cambodia** [i]

kana » **syllabary**

Kananga [ka**nang**ga], formerly **Luluabourg** (to 1966) 5°53S 22°26E, pop (1976e) 704 211. Capital of Kasai Occidental region, WC Zaire, on R Lulua; scene of a mutiny by Congo Free State troops, 1895; airfield; railway; commerce, agricultural trade, diamonds. » Zaire [i]

Kanarese » **Kannada**

Kanban system A Japanese manufacturing system, also called the 'Just in Time' system (*Kanban*, 'signboard'). First introduced at the Toyota Motor Co after World War 2, its aim is efficient manufacturing without large warehouses. Parts are supplied to the production line 'just in time'. *Kanban* cards show when boxes need refilling by parts makers. The idea has been extremely successful, and has since spread to the West.

Kanchenjunga » **Kangchenjunga**

Kandahar [kanda**hah**] 31°36N 65°47E, pop (1984e) 203 177. Capital of Kandahar province, S Afghanistan; on the ancient trade routes of C Asia, and fought over by India and Persia; capital of Afghanistan 1748–73; occupied by the British (1839–42, 1879–81) during the Afghan Wars; airfield; woollen cloth, silk, felt; market for sheep, wool, grain, tobacco, fresh and dried fruits. » Afghanistan [i]

Kandinsky, Wasily or **Vasily (Vasilyevich)** (1866–1944) Russian painter, born in Moscow. He spent his childhood in Italy, and his early work was done in Paris. In Russia (1914–21) he founded the Russian Academy and became head of the Museum of Modern Art. In 1922 he was in charge of the Weimar Bauhaus, moved to Paris in 1933, and became a naturalized French citizen in 1939. He had a great influence on young European artists, and was a leader of the Blaue Reiter group. He died at Neuilly-sur-Seine, France. » Bauhaus; Blaue Reiter, der; Russian art

Kandy [**kan**dee], byname **City of the Five Hills** 7°17N 80°40E, pop (1981) 97 872. Capital of Kandy district, Sri Lanka, looped by the R Mahaweli, 116 km/72 ml NE of Colombo; royal city until 1815; commercial centre for tea-growing area; focal point of the Buddhist Sinhalese culture; Dalada Maligawa (Temple of the Tooth), where the eye tooth of Buddha is enshrined; Peradeniya Botanical Gardens; Esala Perahera religious festival (Jul–Aug). » Buddha; Sri Lanka; Temple of the Tooth

Kanem A mediaeval Sudanic state based to the N of L Chad, and dominating the E trade across the Sahara to Fezzan. It had its origins in the 9th-c, embraced Islam in the 11th-c, conquered Fezzan in the 13th-c, and controlled trade to Egypt and the Red Sea. It declined as a result of dynastic quarrels, but its power was recreated at Bornu in the 16th-c. » African history; Islam

Kang Teh » **Pu Yi**

Kang Yuwei or **K'ang Yu-wei** [kang yoo**way**] (1858–1927) Leader of the Hundred Days of Reform in China (1898). In 1895, he organized thousands of young scholars to demand drastic national reforms. The young Emperor Zai Tian summoned him to implement reforms as the first step to creating a constitutional monarchy, but the movement was ended when Ci Xi seized the Emperor, executed six of the young reformers, and punished all who had supported them. Kang and his disciple Liang Qichao escaped to Japan with foreign help. He returned to China in 1914, and died at Tsingtao, Shandong. » Ci Xi; Hundred Days of Reform; Zai Tian

kangaroo A marsupial, usually with long hind legs used for hopping, short front legs, and a long stiff tail (held against the ground as a prop when stationary; held horizontally to counterbalance the weight of the front of the body when hopping); young (a *joey*) develops in a pouch on the mother's abdomen; large species tend to be called *kangaroos*, smaller species *wallabies*; inhabits grassland or woodland; some species climb trees. (Family: *Macropodidae*, 50 species.) » marsupial [i]; rat kangaroo; tree kangaroo; wallaroo

kangaroo paw An evergreen perennial native to SW Australia; c.1 m/3¼ ft high; leaves sword-shaped, sheathing at the base; flowers in branched inflorescence, zygomorphic, often brightly coloured; the woolly, curved tube ending in 6 claw-like lobes resembling a paw. (Genus: *Anigozanthus*, 10 species. Family: *Haemadoraceae*.) » evergreen plants; inflorescence [i]; perennial; zygomorphic flower

kangaroo rat A squirrel-like rodent, native to N America; hind legs longer than front legs; long tail with long hairs at tip; moves by hopping. (Genus: *Dipodomys*, 22 species. Family: *Heteromyidae*.) » rodent; squirrel

Kangchenjunga or **Kanchenjunga, Mount** [kanchen**jung**ga], Tibetan **Gangchhendzönga**, Nepali **Kumbhkaran Lungur** 27°42N 88°09E. Mountain on the border between Nepal and the Sikkim state of India, in the Himalayan range; third highest mountain in the world; five peaks, the highest at 8 586 m/28 169 ft; Zemu glacier on the E slope; scaled by the Charles Evans British Expedition in 1955, which turned back a few metres from the summit at the request of the Sikkim authorities, for whom the mountain is sacred. » Himalayas

KaNgwane [kahng**wah**nay] pop (1984e) 377 898. National state or non-independent Black homeland in Natal province, South Africa; self-governing status, 1971; chief town, Eerstehoek. » apartheid; South Africa [i]

kanji [**kan**jee] A character in Chinese writing, as used in Japan. Schoolchildren learn the Ministry of Education's basic 1 800 Chinese characters, plus 200 names; 46 hiragana (simplified phonetic characters for Japanese syllables); 46 katakana (further simplified syllabic characters, used for foreign words); and romaji (the Roman alphabet). Kanji are slightly simpler than the Chinese originals, and are pronounced differently. » syllabary

Kankan [kan**kan**] 10°22N 9°11W, pop (1972) 85 310. Capital of Haute-Guinée region, E Guinea, on the R Milo; second largest town in Guinea; railway terminus; commercial and transportation centre; light industry, crafts; national police school. » Guinea [i]

Kannada [**kan**ada] A Dravidian language of S India; also known as **Kanarese**, spoken mainly in the state of Karnataka. It has about 25 million speakers, and has written records from the 5th-c AD. » Dravidian languages

Kano [**kah**noh] 12°00N 8°31E, pop (1981e) 545 000. Capital of Kano state, N Nigeria, 1 130 km/700 ml NE of Lagos; ancient Hausa settlement; modern city founded in the 19th-c, becoming a major terminus of trans-Saharan trade; city walls nearly 18 km/11 ml long, 12 m/40 ft thick at the base, and up to 12 m/40 ft high; airport; railway; university (1975); food processing, brewing, textiles, leather, groundnuts, cattle, glass, metals, chemicals. » Nigeria [i]

Kanpur [**kahn**poor], formerly **Cawnpore** 26°35N 80°20E, pop (1981) 1 688 000. City in Uttar Pradesh, N India; on R Ganges, 185 km/115 ml NW of Allahabad; ceded to the British, 1801; entire British garrison massacred during the Indian Mutiny, 1857; airfield; railway; university (1966); major trade and industrial centre; chemicals, jute, textiles, food products, chemicals. » Uttar Pradesh

Kansas [**kan**sas] pop (1987e) 2 476 000; area 213 089 sq km/82 277 sq ml. State in C USA, divided into 105 counties; the 'Sunflower State'; part of the Louisiana Purchase, 1803; virtual civil war in 1854–6 over whether it should be a free or slave state; 34th state admitted to the Union (as a free state), 1861; capital, Topeka; other major cities, Wichita and Kansas City; the Missouri R forms part of the E state border; the Republican and Smoky Hill Rivers join to form the Kansas R, which meets the Missouri at Kansas City; the Arkansas R also crosses the state; highest point Mt Sunflower (1 227 m/4 025 ft); land rises steadily from prairies (E) to semi-arid high plains (W); suffered severe land erosion in the 1930s (part of the Dust Bowl); nation's leading wheat producer; grain sorghum, corn, hay; major cattle state; aircraft, chemicals, processed foods, machinery; petroleum, natural gas, helium. » Louisiana Purchase; Topeka; United States of America [i]; RR38

Kansas City (Kansas) 39°07N 94°38W, pop (1980) 161 087. Seat of Wyandotte County, E Kansas, USA; port at the junction of the Kansas and Missouri Rivers, adjacent to Kansas City, Missouri; settled by Wyandotte Indians, 1843; sold to the US government, 1855; railway; together with its sister city, a major commercial and industrial centre; market for surrounding agricultural region; stockyards, grain elevators; automobiles, metal products, processed foods, machinery, petroleum; major league teams, Royals (baseball), Chiefs (football); Agricultural Hall of Fame. » Kansas

Kansas City (Missouri) 39°06N 94°35W, pop (1980) 448 159. River port city in Jackson County, W Missouri, USA; on the S bank of the Missouri R, adjacent to its sister city, Kansas City, Kansas; town of Kansas established, 1838; city status, 1853; present name, 1889; airport; railway; university (1929); automobiles and parts, metal products, electronics, processed foods, machinery, oil refineries, railway shops; large stockyards and grain elevators; the nation's leading winter-wheat market; jazz centre in the 1930s–40s; Nelson Art Gallery, Atkins Museum of Fine Arts. » Missouri

Kant, Immanuel [kant] (1724–1804) German philosopher, born in Königsberg, where he spent his entire life. He studied at the university, becoming professor of logic and metaphysics in 1770. His main work, now a philosophical classic, is the *Kritik der reinen Vernunft* (1781, Critique of Pure Reason), in which he provided a response to the empiricism of Hume. His views on ethics are set out in the *Grundlagen zur Metaphysik der Sitten* (1785, Foundations of the Metaphysics of Morals) and the *Kritik der praktischen Vernunft* (1788, Critique of Practical Reason), in which he elaborates on the Categorical Imperative as the supreme principle of morality. In his third and last Critique, the *Kritik der Urteilskraft* (1790, Critique of Judgment), he argued that aesthetic judgments, although universal, do not depend on any property (such as beauty or sublimity) of the object. His thought exerted tremendous influence on subsequent philosophy. » Categorical Imperative; Hume, David; idealism; Neo-Kantianism

Kantianism » **Neo-Kantianism**

Kanto earthquake The worst Japanese earthquake of modern times, occurring in E Japan in 1923 at a time of day when lunch was cooking over fires. Strong winds spread the flames, and about 100 000 people were killed. Old Tokyo and Yokohama were destroyed. » RR14

Kanuri [ka**nu**ree] A Nilo-Saharan-speaking people of Bornu, NE Nigeria, and SE Niger. Well-known as traders, they formed the empire of Bornu, at its zenith during the 16th-c. Muslim since the 11th-c, they have a highly stratified social organization. Population c.3.3 million. » Niger [i]; Nigeria [i]

Kao-hsiung » **Gaoxiong**

Kao Kang » **Gao Gang**

Kaolan » **Lanzhou**

kaolin [**kay**ohlin] A pure clay formed by the decomposition of feldspar in granite, and composed chiefly of the mineral *kaolinite*, a hydrous aluminium silicate; also known as **china clay**. It is used in the manufacture of fine porcelain, and as a filler in paper making and paints. » clay; feldspar; fireclay

Kapil Dev (Nihanj) (1959–) Indian cricketer, born at Chandigarh, Punjab. An all-rounder, he made his first-class debut for Haryana at the age of 16, and played county cricket in England for Northamptonshire and Worcestershire. He led India to victory in the 1983 World Cup, and set a competition record score of 175 not out against Zimbabwe. In 1983 he became the youngest player (at 24 yr 68 days) to perform a Test double of 2 000 runs and 200 wickets (surpassing Ian Botham). » Botham; cricket (sport) [i]

kapok tree [**kay**pok] One of various members of the baobab family, with fruits containing seeds embedded in cotton-like fibres, used as fillings for cushions, etc. The principal species are the **silk-cotton tree** (*Ceiba pentandra*) from tropical America, but cultivated in W Africa, and the **cotton tree** (*Bombax ceiba*) from India and Ceylon. (Family: *Bombacaceae*.) » baobab

Kara-Kum [kara **koom**], Russ **Peski Karakumy** area c.300 000 sq km/120 000 sq ml. Extensive desert in Turkmenia, between the Caspian Sea (W) and the R Amudarya (N and E); crossed (SE) by the Trans-Caspian railway. » Turkmenia

Karachi [ka**rah**chee] 24°51N 67°02E, pop (1981) 5 103 000. Provincial capital of Sind province, SE Pakistan; on the Arabian Sea coast, NW of the mouths of the Indus; Pakistan's principal seaport; founded, 18th-c; under British rule from 1843; former capital, 1947–59; airport; railway; university (1951); trade in cotton, grain, skins, wool; chemicals, textiles, plastics, shipbuilding; tomb of Quaid-i-Azam, Mohammad Ali Jinnah, founder of Pakistan; national museum. » Pakistan [i]

Karageorge, Turk **Karadjordje**, also **Czerny George**, originally **George Petrović** (1766–1817) Leader of the Serbians in their struggle for independence, born at Viševac, Serbia, known as 'Black George' because of his dark complexion. He led a revolt against Turkey, and in 1808 was elected Governor and recognized as Prince of Serbia by the Sultan. When Turkey regained control of Serbia (1813) he was exiled, and on his return was murdered at the instigation of his rival, Prince Milosch.

Karajan, Herbert von [**ka**rayan] (1908–89) Austrian conductor, born in Salzburg. He studied there and in Vienna, and conducted at the Städtisches Theater, Ulm (1928–33), at Aachen (1934–8), and at the Berlin Staatsoper (1938–42). After the war he was not permitted to work until 1947, having been a member of the Nazi Party, but in 1955 he was made principal conductor of the Berlin Philharmonic, and it is with this orchestra that he was mainly associated until his resignation in 1989. He also conducted frequently elsewhere, and was artistic director of the Salzburg Festival (1956–60) and of the Salzburg Easter Festival (from 1967). He died near Salzburg.

karakul [**ka**rakl] A breed of sheep native to Asia; also known as **caracul**. The name is also used for the skin of a young lamb of this breed, and for cloth which resembles this fur. » sheep

Karamanlis, Konstantinos, also **Caramanlis** (1907–) Greek statesman, Prime Minister (1955–63, 1974–80), and President (1980–5), born at Próti, Macedonia. A former lawyer, he was elected to parliament in 1935, became Minister of Public Works (1952), then Prime Minister, and formed his own Party, the National Radical Union. During his administration, Greece signed a Treaty of Alliance with Cyprus and Turkey. After his Party's election defeat in 1963 he left politics and lived abroad, but returned to become Premier again in 1974, when he supervised the restoration of civilian rule after the collapse of the military government. He then served as President. » Greece [i]

karate A martial art of unarmed combat, dating from the 17th-c, which was developed in Japan in the present century; its name was adopted in the 1930s. The aim is to be in total control of the muscular power of the body, so that it can be used with great force and accuracy at any instant. Experts may show their mental and physical training by performing such acts of strength as breaking various thicknesses of wood; but in fighting an opponent, blows do not actually make physical contact. Levels of prowess are symbolized by coloured belts, as in other martial arts. » martial arts; RR114

Karawanken Alps [karava**ng**ken], Serbo-Croatian **Karavanke** Mountain range of the E Alps on the border between Yugoslavia and Austria, mostly in the Austrian state of Kärnten; an extension of the Carnic Alps; highest peak, Hochstuhl (2 238 m/7 342 ft); road from Klagenfurt to Ljubljana via the Loibl Tunnel. » Alps; Carnic Alps

Karelia, Russ **Karelskaya** pop (1981e) 746 000; area 172 400 sq km/66 560 sq ml. Constituent republic of Russia; bounded W by Finland and E by the White Sea; in mediaeval times, an independent state with strong Finnish associations; under Swedish domination, 17th-c; annexed by Russia, 1721; constituted as a Soviet Socialist Republic, 1923; many lakes and rivers; heavily forested; mining, timber, cereals, fishing. » Russia

Karen Sino-Tibetan-speaking, ethnically-diverse groups of S Burma. With Burmese independence (1948), fighting broke out between government and groups identifying themselves as Karen, wanting autonomy. Sometimes divided into White Karen and Red Karen, they have united in common opposition to Burmese control. In the late 1980s many fled to refugee camps in Thailand. » Burma [i]; Sino-Tibetan languages

Kariba Dam A major concrete arch dam on the Zambezi R at the Zambia/Zimbabwe border, impounding L Kariba; completed in 1959; height 128 m/420 ft; length 579 m/1 900 ft. It has the capacity to generate 705 megawatts of hydroelectricity. » dam; Zambezi, River

Karloff, Boris, originally **William Pratt** (1887–1969) British film star, born in London. Educated at London University, he emigrated to Canada in 1909 and joined a touring company. He spent ten years in repertory companies, then went to Hollywood, and after several silent films made his name as the monster in *Frankenstein* (1931). His career was mostly spent in popular horror films, but he returned to the stage in 1941. He died at Midhurst, W Sussex.

Karlovy Vary [**kah**lovee varee], Ger **Karlsbad** 50°14N 12°53E, pop (1984) 59 183. Town in Západočeský region, Czech Republic, W Czechoslovakia; on R Ohre, W of Prague; airport; railway; kaolin, glass, footwear, mineral water; famous health resort with hot alkaline springs. » Czechoslovakia [i]

Karlsbad » **Karlovy Vary**

Karlsruhe [**kahlz**roouh] 49°03N 8°23E, pop (1983) 270 300. Capital of Karlsruhe district, Germany; port on R Rhine, 56 km/35 ml S of Mannheim; former capital of Baden; railway; university (1825); oil refining, machine tools, chemicals, tyres, machinery, defence equipment, rubber products, dairy produce; palace (1752–85). » Germany [i]

karma [kahma] (Sanskrit 'action' or 'work') In Indian tradition, the principle that a person's actions have consequences meriting reward or punishment. Karma is the moral law of cause and effect by which the sum of a person's actions are carried foward from one life to the next, leading to an improvement or deterioration in that person's fate. » bodhisattva; Brahmanism; Buddhism; Hinduism; Jainism; Mahayana

Karnataka, formerly **Mysore** pop (1981) 37 043 451; area 191 773 sq km/74 024 sq ml. State in SW India; bounded W by the Arabian Sea; formed as Mysore under the States Reorganization Act of 1956, bringing the Kannada-speaking population of five states together; official language, Kannada; renamed Karnataka, 1973; crossed by numerous rivers; bicameral legislature comprises a 63-member Legislative Council and an elected 225-member Legislative Assembly; capital, Bangalore; rice, groundnuts, silk, cotton, coffee, sandalwood, bamboo; gold, silver, iron ore, manganese, limestone, chromite; iron and steel, engineering, electronics, chemicals, textiles, cement, sugar, paper. » Bangalore; India [i]; Kannada

Karnische Alpen » **Carnic Alps**

Karoo [karoo] Dry steppe country in Cape province, South Africa, from the Orange R down to the Cape; Karoo National Park covers 180 sq km/70 sq ml of the arid region called the Great Karoo; established in 1979. » South Africa [i]

Kárpathos [kahpathos], Ital **Scarpanto**, ancient **Carpathus** pop (1981) 4 645; area 301 sq km/116 sq ml. Mountainous, elongated island of the Dodecanese group, E Greece, in the Aegean Sea, between Rhodes and the E end of Crete; length 48 km/30 ml; rises to 1 216 m/3 989 ft; capital, Pigadhia; numerous bathing beaches. » Dodecanese; Greece [i]

Karst, Slovenian **Kras**, Ital **Carso** Barren, stony limestone plateau in the Dinaric Alps of NW Yugoslavia; extending c.80 km/50 ml from the R Isonzo (NW) to the Kvarner Gulf (SE); notable caves at Postojna; the name has come to be used in geography to describe limestone topography of this kind. » Dinaric Alps; karst region

karst region A distinctive landscape associated with limestone regions, and characterized by the complete absence of surface drainage and its replacement by a drainage system through vertical cracks, underground channels, and planes of weakness in the rock. Sink holes, labyrinths of passages, caves with stalactites and stalagmites, and underground lakes are typical features. The name derives from an area in Adriatic Yugoslavia, where this landscape is found. » limestone

karting Motor racing of small four-wheeled vehicles, usually with single-cylinder and two-stroke engines. They are raced in categories dependent on engine size. Karts can have either body-less tubular frames or, in top-class competitions, sophisticated streamlined bodies. » motor racing

karyology [karioluhjee] The branch of cytology dealing with the study of nuclei inside cells, especially with the structure of chromosomes. It includes the determination of numbers and sizes of chromosomes, the identification of sex chromosomes, the study of chromosome banding using staining techniques, and the study of the nucleic acids involved. » chromosome [i]; cytology; nucleic acids

Kashmir » **Jammu-Kashmir**

Kasparov, Gary (Kimovich) (1963–) Azerbaijani chess player, born at Baku. When he beat Anatoliy Karpov for the world title (Nov 1985) he became the youngest world champion, at the age of 22 yr 210 days. He has successfully defended his title, and is the highest-ranked active player, with a ranking of 2 760. » chess

Kassel 51°19N 9°32E, pop (1983) 190 400. Cultural, economic, and administrative centre of Kassel district, Germany; on the R Fulda, 114 km/71 ml WNW of Erfurt; an important traffic junction; badly bombed in World War 2; railway; university (1971); mineral salts, dairy products, natural gas and oil, locomotives, vehicles, machinery, cloth, optical and geodetic instruments; Wilhelmshöhe (health resort), Gallery of Old Masters in the Schloss Wilhelmshöhe, Schloss Wilhelmsthal (11 km/7 ml NW); Kurkonzerte in Wilhelmshöhe Park (May–Sep), modern art exhibition (Jul–Sep). » Germany [i]

Kästner, Erich (1899–1974) German writer, born in Dresden. He was a teacher and journalist, then turned to writing poetry and novels. He is best known for his children's books, which include *Emil und die Detektive* (1928, Emil and the Detectives). After World War 2, he became magazine editor of *Die Neue Zeitung*, and founded a paper for children. He died in Munich.

katabatic wind A local downslope wind which develops in a valley. At night, surface air over mountain ridges cools faster than air above the valley floor. Thus, colder and denser air flows from high elevations to valley bottoms. Downslope winds also flow from mountainous areas to adjacent lowlands: the chinook wind of the Rockies and the Föhn wind of the European Alps are warm katabatic winds; the Mistral of the Rhône Valley, France, is a cold katabatic wind. » anabatic wind; Föhn/Foehn wind; Mistral; wind [i]

Katanga The southernmost province of Zaire, rich in minerals. In 1960, when the Congo (Zaire) achieved independence from Belgium, Katanga (now Shaba) attempted to secede under the leadership of Moise Tshombe (1919–). In the ensuing chaos the government of Patrice Lumumba was overthrown. Lumumba was assassinated in 1961, and the unitary state was later recreated under the military leadership of President Mobutu (1930–). » Lumumba; Zaire [i]

Kathak The newest form of Indian classical dance, found in NW India, more relaxed in performance than the older forms such as Bharata Natyam. It is often secular rather than religious, using a dramatic story-telling form that may include improvisation. It is strongly rhythmic. » Indian dance

Kathakali [katakahli] Epic theatre from the SW coastal region of India in which troupes of actors, in stylized make-up and costume, enact dramas based on the Ramayana and Mahabharata, using music, song, dance, and an elaborate system of hand symbols equivalent to speech. » Indian dance/theatre

Katherine Gorge National park in Northern Territory, Australia; spectacular gorges on the Katherine R, up to 60 m/200 ft high; many Aboriginal rock drawings; area 1 800 sq km/700 sq ml. » Aborigines; Northern Territory

Kathmandu or **Katmandu** [katmandoo], formerly **Kantipur** 27°42N 85°19E, pop (1981) 195 260. Capital and principal city of Nepal; 121 km/75 ml from the Indian frontier in the Kathmandu Valley, altitude 1 373 m/4 504 ft; on the ancient pilgrim and trade route from India to Tibet, China, and Mongolia; built in its present form, 723; Gurkha capital, 1768; British seat of administration, 18th-c; university (1959); commercial centre, religious centre, tourism; Machendra Nath Temple, Hanuman Dhoka Palace, Kasthamanadap temple, Swayambhunath (Buddhist shrine), Pashupatinath Temple (centre of an annual pilgrimage), natural history museum; the Vale of Kathmandu is a world heritage site. » Nepal [i]

Katowice [katoveetsay], Ger **Kattowitz** 50°15N 18°59E, pop (1983) 361 300. Capital of Katowice voivodship, S Poland; centre of the Upper Silesian Industrial Region; airport; railway; two universities (1945, 1968); coal mining, iron and steel, zinc works, chemicals, optics, fertilizer; Kościuszko Park, cathedral; drama festival (Nov). » Poland [i]

katydid [kaytidid] A large, grasshopper-like insect in which sound communication is well-developed; characterized by a sword-shaped egg-laying tube; c.5 000 species, mostly plant feeders. (Order: *Orthoptera*. Family: *Tettigoniidae*.) » grasshopper

Katyn massacre [katin] A massacre of 4 000 Polish army officers in May 1940 in the Katyn forest near Smolensk, Byelorussia. The officers were shot and buried, and their mass graves were discovered by German occupying forces in 1943. Soviet authorities have persistently denied responsibility for the massacre, blaming it on the Germans. In 1989 the Soviet-Polish historical commission (set up in 1987 to establish the truth) reported that the crime was most probably committed by the Soviet security service (NKVD). » World War 2

Katz, Sir Bernard (1911–) British biophysicist, born in Leipzig, Germany. Educated at Leipzig and London, he carried out research in London (1935–9) and Sydney (1939–42), and became professor of biophysics at London (1952–78) and then an honorary research fellow. Knighted in 1969, in 1970 he shared the Nobel Prize for Physiology or Medicine for his studies on how transmitter substances are released from nerve terminals. » Axelrod; neurotransmitter; von Euler

Kauai [kowiy], formerly **Kaieiewaho** pop(1980) 39 082; area 1 692 sq km/653 sq ml. Island of the US state of Hawaii; forms Kauai county with Niihau I; chief town, Lihue; sugar; tourism. » Hawaii (state)

Kaufmann, George S(imon) (1889–1961) US playwright, born in Pittsburgh. He worked as a journalist, then collaborated with others in several Broadway hits, such as *You Can't Take it with You* (1936), which won the Pulitzer Prize, and *The Man Who Came to Dinner* (1939). Several of his musicals have been filmed. He died in New York City. » Broadway

Kaunas [kownas], formerly **Kovno** 54°52N 23°55E, pop(1983) 395 000. Ancient town and river port in Lithuania; on the R Neman at its confluence with the R Vilnya; capital of independent Lithuania, 1918; airfield; railway; chemicals, radio engineering, machines, clothing, foodstuffs, woodworking; ancient centre of several artistic trades; castle (13th–17th-c), Massalski Palace (17th-c), Vytautas church (1400). » Lithuania

Kaunda, Kenneth (David) [kahoonda] (1924–) Zambian statesman and President (1964–), born at Lubwa. He became a teacher, founded the Zambian African National Congress (1958), and was subsequently imprisoned. Elected President of the United National Independence Party in 1960, he played a leading part in his country's independence negotiations, and became the country's first President. » Zambia [i]

Kaunitz(-Rietberg), Wenzel Anton, Fürst von ('Prince of') [kownits reetberg] (1711–94) Austrian statesman and Chancellor (1753–92), born and died in Vienna. He distinguished himself at the Congress of Aix-la-Chapelle (1748), and as Austrian Ambassador at the French court (1750–2). As Chancellor, he instigated the Diplomatic Revolution, and directed Austrian politics for almost 40 years under Maria Theresa and Joseph II. He was a liberal patron of arts and sciences. » Maria Theresa

kauri gum A commercially important resin obtained from kauri pine, used mainly in paint and in the manufacture of linoleum. **Copal** is the name for the fossilized gum often found in large quantities on the sites of ancient forests, said to be superior to fresh gum. » kauri pine; resin

kauri pine An evergreen conifer related to araucaria, native to SE Asia and Australasia. It is the source of an important resin as well as timber. One species, *Agathis australis*, is an important forest tree in New Zealand. (Genus: *Agathis*, 20 species. Family: *Araucariaceae*.) » araucaria; kauri gum; resin

kava A Polynesian beverage made by fermenting chewed or grated, peeled roots of *Piper methysticum*, a relative of black pepper. The drink is narcotic and sedative as well as intoxicating. » narcotics; pepper **1**

Kawasaki [kawasakee] 35°32N 139°41E, pop(1980) 1 040 802. Capital of Kanagawa prefecture, Kanto region, E Honshu, Japan; S of Tokyo, on W shore of Tokyo-wan Bay; railway; iron, steel, shipbuilding, machinery, chemicals, textiles. » Honshu

Kay, John » **Arkwright, Richard**

kayak [kiyak] A small double-ended craft of Eskimo design, similar to a canoe, but enclosed except for a very small cockpit. It is made effectively watertight by a detachable spray deck attached to the body of the paddler. It is usually propelled with a double-ended paddle. » canoe

Kaye, Danny, professional name of **Daniel Kominski** (1913–87) US stage, radio, and film actor, born in New York City. In 1943 he made his first film, *Up in Arms*, following it with *Wonder Man* (1944), which made his reputation as a film comedian, together with international success in *The Secret Life of Walter Mitty* (1946). Other films include *The Inspector General* (1950) and *Hans Christian Andersen* (1952). He received an Honorary Oscar in 1955, and in later years worked unceasingly for international childrens' charities, especially UNICEF. He died in Los Angeles.

Kazakh or **Kazak** [kazak] A Turkic-speaking Mongoloid people of Kazakhstan and adjacent areas in China. Traditionally nomadic pastoralists, in the 19th-c many settled and grew crops. After the Russian Revolution (1917), wealthy Kazakh herders fled to Sinkiang (China) and Afghanistan. Apart from one group, the remaining nomads in Russia were forced onto collective cattle farms; in China, many are still nomadic. Population c.6.5 million in Kazakhstan and 800 000 in China. » Kazakhstan; nomadism; pastoralism

Kazakhstan [kazakstahn], Russ **Kazakhskaya** or **Kazakh** pop(1989) 16 536 000; area 2 717 300 sq km/1 048 878 sq ml. Republic bounded E by China and W by the Caspian Sea; second largest republic in the former USSR; steppeland (N) gives way to desert (S); lowest elevation, near the E shore of the Caspian Sea (132 m/433 ft below sea-level); mountain ranges in the E and SE; chief rivers, the Irtysh, Syr-Darya, Ural, Emba, Ili; largest lake, L Balkhash; became a constituent republic, 1936; independence movement, 1990–1; capital, Alma-Ata; chief towns, Karaganda, Semipalatinsk, Chimkent, Petropavlovsk; coal, iron ore, bauxite, copper, nickel, oil; oil refining, metallurgy, heavy engineering, chemicals, leatherwork, footwear, food processing; cotton, fruit, grain, sheep. » Kazakh; Soviet Union [i]

Kazan, Elia, originally **Elia Kazanjoglous** (1909–) US stage and film director, born in Constantinople, Turkey. His family went to the USA in 1913, and he was educated at Williams College and Yale. He acted in minor roles before becoming a theatre director, particularly known for his productions of plays by Arthur Miller and Tennessee Williams, and for co-founding the Actors' Studio (1947). He began as a film director in 1944, and won Oscars for *Gentleman's Agreement* (1948) and *On the Waterfront* (1954). His novels include the autobiographical *America, America* (1962, filmed 1964). » Actors' Studio; Miller, Arthur; theatre; Williams, Tennessee

Kazan [kazan] 55°45N 49°10E, pop(1989) 1 094 000. River-port capital of Tatarskaya, E European Russia; on the R Volga at its confluence with the R Kazanka; founded, 13th-c; airport; railway; university (1804); important industrial and cultural centre of the Volga region; chemicals, engineering, instruments, machines, fur, leather, foodstuffs; Cathedral of the Annunciation (19th-c), Governor's Palace (1845–8). » Russia

Kazanlak tomb A 4th-c BC Thracian tomb located near Kazanlak in the department of Stara Zagora, Bulgaria; a world heritage site. The tomb is noted for the frescoes which decorate the burial chamber and vaulted corridor within. It was discovered in 1944. » Thrace

Kazantzakis, Nikos (1883–1957) Greek writer, born at Heraklion, Crete. He studied law at Athens, spent some years travelling in Europe and Asia, and published his first novel in 1929. He is best known for the novel *Vios kai politia tou Alexi Zormpa* (1946, Zorba the Greek, filmed 1964) and the long autobiographical narrative poem, *Odissa* (1938, The Odyssey, a Modern Sequel). He died at Freiburg-im-Breisgau, Germany. » novel; poetry

Kaziranga [kazirangga] National park on the S bank of the Brahmaputra R in Assam, India; area 430 sq km/166 sq ml; established in 1908 to protect the great Indian rhino and the swamp deer; a world heritage site. » Brahmaputra, River

kazoo or **bazouka** A child's musical instrument, consisting of a short metal tube flattened at one end, with a hole in the top covered by a disc of membrane. This imparts a buzzing edge to the tone when the player sings or hums into the flattened end. A similar effect may be obtained with a piece of paper round the edge of a comb. » membranophone

kea A large, stocky, dull-coloured parrot native to S New Zealand; male with long upper bill; inhabits forest or open country; eats fruit, leaves, insects, or carrion; scavenges on refuse dumps; nests in hole. (*Nestor notabilis*. Family: *Psittacidae*.) » parrot

Kean, Edmund (c.1789–1833) British actor, born in London. He became a strolling player, and after 10 years in the provinces made his first appearance at Drury Lane as Shylock (1814). A period of great success followed as a tragic actor, but because of his irregularities he gradually forfeited public approval, his reputation being finally ruined when he was successfully sued for adultery in 1825. He died at Richmond, Surrey. » theatre

Keating, Tom (1918–84) British artist and forger, born in London. A self-confessed 'art imitator', he claimed to have produced some 2 000 fakes in 25 years. His activity came to light in 1976, when a group of 13 drawings in imitation of Samuel Palmer came on to the market and aroused suspicions. Keating was arrested and charged with conspiracy and criminal deception, but charges were dropped when his health declined. He became a celebrity, making a television series, and writing (with Geraldine and Frank Norman) a book, *The Fake's Progress*.

Keaton, Joseph Francis (Buster) (1895–1966) US film comedian, born at Pickway, Kansas. He joined his parents in vaudeville at the age of three, developing great acrobatic skill. He then went to Hollywood and made his film debut in *The Butcher Boy* (1917). Renowned for his 'deadpan' expression under any circumstances, he starred in and directed such classics as *The Navigator* (1924) and *The General* (1926). His reputation went into eclipse with the advent of talking films until many of his silent masterpieces were re-released in the 1950s and 1960s, and he began to appear in character roles in current films. He received a special Academy Award in 1959 for his 'unique talents', and died at Woodland Hills, California.

Keats, John (1795–1821) British poet, born in London. Educated at Enfield, he became a medical student in London (1815–17). Leigh Hunt introduced him to other young Romantics, including Shelley, and published his first sonnets in the *Examiner* (1816). His first book of poems (1817), containing the long mythological poem *Endymion* (1818), was fiercely criticized, but he was nonetheless able to produce *Lamia and Other Poems* (1820), a landmark in English poetry, which contains his romances 'The Eve of St Agnes' and 'Lamia', and his major odes. Seriously ill with consumption, he sailed for Italy, and died in Rome. His *Letters* (1848) are among the most celebrated in the language. » English literature; Hunt, Leigh; poetry; Romanticism (literature)

Keble, John (1792–1866) British Anglican churchman and poet, born at Fairford, Gloucestershire. Educated at Oxford, he was ordained in 1816, became a college tutor (1818–23), and professor of poetry (1831–41). In 1827 his book of poems on the liturgical year, *The Christian Year*, was widely circulated. His sermon on 'National apostasy' (1833) began the Oxford Movement, encouraging a return to High Church ideals, and his circle issued the 90 *Tracts for the Times*. In 1835 he moved to the Hampshire living of Hursely, where he remained until his death. Keble College, Oxford, was erected in his memory. » Church of England; Oxford Movement; poetry

Kebnekaise [**keb**nuhkiysuh] 67°55N 18°35E. Peak in the Kjölen Mts, NW Sweden; height 2 111 m/6 926 ft; highest peak in Sweden; several glaciers. » Sweden [i]

keck » **cow parsley; hogweed**

Kedah [kay**dah**] pop (1980) 1 077 815; area 9 425 sq km/3 638 sq ml. State in NW Peninsular Malaysia; bounded E by Thailand and W by the Strait of Malacca; governed by Thailand from early 19th-c until 1909, when it came under British rule; capital, Alor Setar; rice, rubber, tin, tungsten. » Malaysia [i]

Keeler, Christine » **Profumo, John**

Keeling Islands » **Cocos Islands**

Keelung » **Jilong**

keeshond [**kay**shond] A small, sturdy spitz breed of dog from Holland; grey with dark tinges; head dark with pale rings around eyes; coat very thick, especially around neck; tail tightly curled; formerly used as a guard dog, especially on barges. » dog; spitz

kefir [**ke**feer] A fermented milk originating in the Caucasus. Traditionally made from camel's milk, it is now made from cow's milk, and can be mild, medium, or strong, depending on the degree of fermentation. » milk

Keflavik [kyeplav**eek**] 64°01N 22°35W, pop (1983) 6 886. Fishing port in Suđurland region, SW Iceland; 48 km/30 ml SW of Reykjavík; important trade centre since the 16th-c; first modern freezing plant started in 1929; airport. » Iceland [i]

Keitel, Wilhelm [**kiy**tl] (1882–1946) German field marshal, born at Helmscherode. He joined the army in 1901, and became an artillery staff officer in World War 1. An ardent Nazi, he was made Chief of the Supreme Command of the Armed Forces (1938). In 1940 he signed the Compiègne armistice with France, and in 1945 was one of the German signatories of surrender in Berlin. He was convicted of war crimes at Nuremberg, and executed. » Nazi Party; World War 2

Kékes, Mount [**kay**kesh] Mountain in N Hungary; highest peak in the Matra Mts and in Hungary, rising to 1 014 m/3 327 ft. » Hungary [i]

Kelantan [kuh**lan**tan] pop (1980) 859 270; area 14 796 sq km/ 5 711 sq ml. State in NE Peninsular Malaysia; bounded N by Thailand and E by the South China Sea; drained by the R Kelantan and its tributaries; governed by Thailand from early 19th-c until 1909, when it came under British rule; capital, Kota Baharu; rice, rubber, copra, tin. » Malaysia [i]

Keldysh, Mstislav (Vsevoldvich) (1911–78) Latvian mathematician and space programme leader, born in Riga. Educated at Moscow, he conducted aeronautical research at Zhukovskii Aero-Hydrodynamics Institute (from 1934) and at Steklow Mathematics Institute (from 1939). He was a leading figure in the development of the theory of rocketry and in the emergence of the USSR in space exploration, He died in Moscow. » rocket; Soviet space programme

Keller, Helen (Adams) (1880–1968) US deaf and blind author and educator, born at Tuscumbia, Alabama. She lost her sight and hearing after an illness at 19 months, but was educated by **Anne Mansfield Sullivan** (later Mrs Macy), who taught her to speak, read, and write. She obtained a degree in 1904, and became distinguished as a lecturer and writer. The story of her life was dramatized by William Gibson in *The Miracle Worker* (1959, Pulitzer Prize 1960, filmed 1962).

Kelley, Florence (1859–1932) US social reformer, born at Girard, Illinois. She studied at Cornell and Leipzig, where she translated Engels and was converted to socialism. Becoming interested in child labour, she was appointed chief factory inspector of Illinois, meanwhile acquiring a law degree from Northwestern. In 1899 she went to New York and became general secretary of the National Consumers' League, which for the rest of her life she used as a platform for agitation on factory conditions. » Engels; socialism; women's liberation movement

Kellogg–Briand Pact A proposal made in 1927 by French Foreign Minister Aristide Briand (1862–1932) to US Secretary of State Frank B Kellogg (1856–1937) that the two countries should sign a pact renouncing war as an instrument of national policy. At Kellogg's suggestion, a Paris conference in 1928 formally condemned recourse to war, and the pact was subsequently signed by 65 states (the **Pact of Paris**). However, there was no machinery for punishing aggressors.

Kells, Gaelic **Ceanannus Mór** 53°44N 6°53W, pop (1981) 2 623. Urban district in Meath county, Leinster, E Irish Republic; on R Boyne NW of Dublin; noted for its monastery (founded by St Columba) and the remains of five Celtic crosses; *Book of Kells* (now in Trinity College, Dublin) produced there c.800. » Columba, St; Irish Republic [i]; Meath

Kelly, Gene (1912–) US actor, dancer, and film director, born in Pittsburgh, where he ran a dance school before moving to Broadway. His stage success in *Pal Joey* led to a Hollywood debut in *For Me and My Gal* (1942), followed by a long series of musicals in which he was often co-director and choreographer, such as *An American in Paris* (1951), and *Singin' in the Rain* (1952). In 1951 he received a Special Academy Award for his versatility. Since the 1960s he has worked mainly as a director.

Kelly, Grace » **Rainier III**

Kelly, Ned (Edward) (1855–80) Australian bushranger, born at Beveridge, Victoria. He was a horse-thief who (from 1878) became a bushranger in Victoria and New South Wales, working with a gang whose daring robberies received widespread publicity. His trademark was his home-made armour, which has since entered Australian iconography in the paintings of Sydney Nolan. Captured at Glenrowan, he was hanged at Melbourne. » bushrangers

keloid [**kee**loyd] The overgrowth of scar tissue (fibroblasts and collagen) in response to a surgical or accidental wound of the skin. It appears as a raised, warm, reddened, tender lump along the line of the wound. » skin [i]

kelp A large brown seaweed common in lower inter-tidal and sub-tidal zones in colder seas; life cycle involves alternation between a filamentous form (gametophyte) and a large robust form (sporophyte) differentiated into a holdfast, narrow stalk (*stipe*) and a flattened blade. (Division: *Phaeophyceae*. Order: *Laminariales*.) » alternation of generations; seaweed

kelpie (folklore) A water-demon of Scottish folklore, usually in the shape of a horse, that haunts fords and lures travellers to their death by drowning. A kelpie might sometimes do a miller a good turn by keeping his mill working through the night. » folklore

kelpie (zoology) A breed of dog developed in Australia as a sheepdog from imported Scottish sheepdogs; medium size with thick, coarse coat and bushy tail; muzzle pointed; ears erect; also called **Australian kelpie**. » dog; sheepdog

kelvin Base SI unit of thermodynamic temperature; symbol K; defined as the fraction 1/273.16 of the thermodynamic temperature of the triple point of water; named after Lord Kelvin; always written K, not °K. » Kelvin; phases of matter [i]; temperature [i]; thermodynamics; units (scientific); RR79

Kelvin (of Largs), William Thomson, 1st Baron (1824–1907) British mathematician and physicist, born in Belfast, N Ireland. Educated at Glasgow and Cambridge, he became professor of natural philosophy at Glasgow (1846). He designed several kinds of electrometer, and his sounding apparatus and compass were widely adopted. In pure science, he carried out fundamental research into thermodynamics, helping to develop the law of the conservation of energy, and the absolute temperature scale (now given in degrees Kelvin). He also presented the dynamical theory of heat, developed theorems for the mathematical analysis of electricity and magnetism, and investigated hydrodynamics, particularly wave-motion and vortex-motion. In 1892 he was created a peer with the title of Lord Kelvin. He died at Netherhall, Ayrshire. » electricity; kelvin; magnetism; temperature [i]; thermodynamics

Kemble The name of a famous British acting family of the 18th-c. The founding member was **Roger** (1721–1802), a travelling manager, whose children were **John Philip** (1757–1823), **Stephen** (1758–1822), **Charles** (1775–1854), and Sarah (1775–1831). Charles' daughter, **Frances Ann**, known as **Fanny** (1809–93), became one of the leading actresses of the 19th-c. » Siddons; theatre

Kemi, River [kemee], Finnish **Kemijoki**, Swedish **Kemiä** River in Lappi province, N Finland, rising near the Russian border; flows S then W to meet the Gulf of Bothnia at Kemi; length 480 km/300 ml; longest river in Finland. » Finland [i]

Kempe, Margery (c.1373–c.1440) English religious mystic, wife of a burgess of Lynn, mother of 14 children. Her spiritual autobiography, *The Book of Margery Kempe* (c.1432–6) recounts her religious experiences, and her pilgrimages to Jerusalem, Rome, and elsewhere. » mysticism

Kempe, Rudolf [**kem**puh] (1910–76) German conductor, born near Dresden, where he studied at the Musikhochschule. He played the oboe in orchestras at Dortmund and Leipzig before making his debut as a conductor in 1935. He then worked at Leipzig and, after the war, at Dresden and Munich. He later appeared frequently at Covent Garden, London, and was principal conductor of the Royal Philharmonic Orchestra (1961–75) and then of the BBC Symphony Orchestra until his death, in Zürich.

Kempe, Will(iam) (c.1550–c.1603) English comic actor, a leading member of Shakespeare's company in the last decade of the 16th-c. When the Chamberlain's Men moved to the Globe, he forsook the stage, and in 1600 performed a 9-day Morris dance from London to Norwich. » Shakespeare [i]; theatre

Kempis, Thomas à or **Thomas Hemerken** (1379–1471) German religious writer, so called from his birthplace, Kempen. In 1400 he entered the Augustinian convent of Agnietenberg near Zwolle, was ordained in 1413, chosen sub-prior in 1429, and died there as superior. His many writings include the influential devotional work *Imitatio Christi* (c.1415–24, The Imitation of Christ). » Christianity

Kenai bear » **brown bear**

kendo The Japanese martial art of sword fighting, now practised with *shiani*, or bamboo swords. The earliest reference to the art is in AD 789. The object is to land two scoring blows on the opponent's target area. *Kendokas* (participants) wear traditional dress of the Samurai period, including face-masks and aprons, and are graded according to ability from 6th to 1st Kyu, and then from 1st to 10th Dan. » martial arts; samurai

Kendrew, Sir John Cowdery (1917–) British biochemist, born at Oxford. He was educated at Clifton and Cambridge, where he became a fellow (1947–75), and carried out research into the chemistry of the blood. For his discovery of the structure of myoglobin, he shared the Nobel Prize for Chemistry in 1962. Knighted in 1974, he became director-general of the European Molecular Biology Laboratory at Heidelburg (1975–82), and president of St John's College, Oxford (1981–7). » blood

Keneally, Thomas (Michael) [kuh**nee**lee] (1935–) Australian novelist, born in Sydney, and educated at Strathfield, New South Wales. His novels are frequently historical, and include *Gossip from the Forest* (1975), about the armistice negotiations in November 1918, and *Schindler's Ark* (1982), the story of a German industrialist who saved the lives of Polish Jews during the early 1940s. » Australian literature; novel

Kennedy, Edward M(oore) (1932–) US politician, born at Brookline, Massachusetts. Educated at Harvard and the University of Virginia, he was called to the Bar in 1959, and elected a Democratic Senator in 1962. In 1969 he became the youngest ever majority whip in the US Senate, but his involvement the same year in a car accident at Chappaquiddick, in which a girl companion (Mary Jo Kopechne) was drowned, dogged his subsequent political career, and caused his withdrawal as a presidential candidate in 1979. » Democratic Party

Kennedy, John F(itzgerald) (1917–63) US statesman and 35th President (1961–3), born at Brookline, Massachusetts. Educated at Harvard and London, he joined the navy in 1941 and became a torpedo boat commander in the Pacific. His *Profiles in Courage* (1956) won the Pulitzer Prize. Elected Democrat Representative (1947) and Senator (1952) for Massachusetts, in 1960 he was the first Catholic, and the youngest person, to be elected President. His 'new frontier' in social legislation involved a federal desegregation policy in education, and civil rights reform. He displayed firmness and moderation in foreign policy, in 1962 inducing Russia to withdraw its missiles from Cuba, and achieving a partial nuclear test-ban treaty with Russia in 1963. On 22 November, he was assassinated by rifle fire while being driven in an open car through Dallas, Texas. The alleged assassin, Lee Oswald, was himself shot and killed at point blank range two days later during a jail transfer. In 1953 Kennedy had married **Jacqueline Lee Bouvier** (1929–), who in 1968 married Aristotle Onassis. » Bay of Pigs; civil rights; Kennedy, Robert F; Oswald, Lee Harvey

Kennedy, Joseph P(atrick) (1888–1969) US businessman and diplomat, born in Boston, Massachusetts. The grandson of an Irish Catholic immigrant, he was educated at Harvard, and became a multimillionaire in the 1920s. During the 1930s he was a strong supporter of Roosevelt and the 'New Deal', being rewarded with minor administrative posts, and the ambassadorship to Britain (1938–40). In 1914 he married **Rose Fitzgerald**, daughter of a local politician, John F Fitzgerald, also of Irish immigrant descent. They had nine children, including four sons, at whose political disposal he placed his fortune. The eldest, **Joseph Patrick** (1915–44), was killed in a flying accident while on naval service in World War 2. The others achieved international political fame. » Kennedy, Edward M/John F/Robert F; Roosevelt, Franklin D

Kennedy, Robert F(rancis) (1925–68) US politician, born at Brookline, Massachusetts. Educated at Harvard and the University of Virginia, he served at sea (1944–6), was admitted to the Bar (1951), and became a member of the staff of the Senate Select Committee on Improper Activities (1957–9). An efficient manager of his brother's presidential campaign, he became an energetic Attorney-General (1961–4), notable in his dealings with civil rights problems, and Senator for New York from 1965. On 5 June 1968, after winning the Californian primary election, he was shot, and died the following day. His assassin,

Sirhan Bishara Sirhan, a 24-year-old Jordanian-born immigrant, was sentenced to the gas chamber in 1969. » civil rights; Kennedy, John F

Kennedy Space Center, John F US space centre situated on Merrit I and Cape Canaveral (known as Cape Kennedy 1963–73) off the E coast of Florida. Since the late 1950s Cape Canaveral has been used as the principal launch site for the US space exploration programme conducted by NASA from its headquarters on Merrit I. » NASA

Kennelly, Arthur E(dwin) (1861–1939) US electrical engineer, born in Bombay, India. In 1894 he founded a consultancy firm in Philadelphia, where he developed new mathematical analyses of electrical circuits, and in 1902 discovered the ionized layer in the atmosphere, sometimes named after him. He died in Boston, Massachusetts. » Heaviside layer

Kenneth I, called **MacAlpin** (d.858) King of the Scots of Dal Riata (from 841) and King of the Picts (from c.843). He combined the territories of both peoples in a united kingdom of Scotia (Scotland N of the Forth-Clyde line). » Picts

Kensington and Chelsea 51°30N 0°12W, pop (1987e) 133 100. Borough of C Greater London, England; N of R Thames; Kensington granted the designation 'Royal Borough' by Edward VII in 1901; railway; Kensington Palace, Kensington Gardens, Chelsea Royal Hospital, Victoria and Albert Museum, Science Museum, British Museum (Natural History); Nottingham House (birthplace of Queen Victoria); Crufts dog show (Feb), Chelsea antiques fair (Mar, Sep), Ideal Home Exhibition (Mar), Chelsea Flower Show (May), Royal Tournament (Jul), Smithfield agricultural show (Dec). » London [i]

Kent, Edward (George Nicholas Paul Patrick), Duke of (1935–) British prince, the eldest son of Duke George Edward Alexander Edmund (1902–42), who was the fourth son of King George V and Queen Mary. He was commissioned in the army in 1955, and in 1961 married **Katharine Worsley** (1933–). They have three children: **George Philip Nicholas, Earl of St Andrews** (1962–), **Helen Marina Lucy, Lady Helen Windsor** (1964–), and **Nicholas Charles Edward Jonathan, Lord Nicholas Windsor** (1970–). He retired from the army in 1976. » Alexandra, Princess; Kent, Prince Michael of

Kent, Prince Michael of (1942–) British prince, the younger brother of Edward, Duke of Kent. He married in 1978 **Baroness Marie-Christine von Reibniz**, and their children are **Frederick Michael George David Louis, Lord Frederick Windsor** (1979–) and **Gabriella Marina Alexandra Ophelia, Lady Gabriella Windsor** (1981–). » Kent, Edward, Duke of

Kent, William (1685–1748) English painter, landscape gardener, and architect, born at Bridlington, Yorkshire. He studied in Rome, and became the principal exponent of the Palladian style of architecture in England. His best-known work is the Horse Guards block in Whitehall. He died in London. » Palladianism

Kent pop (1987e) 1 510 500; area 3 731 sq km/1 440 sq ml. County in SE England, divided into 14 districts; bounded N by the R Thames estuary and E by the English Channel; rises to 251 m/823 ft in the North Downs; The Weald in the SW; drained by Thames, Medway, and Stour Rivers; high chalk cliffs, especially at Dover; county town, Maidstone; principal cross-Channel ports, Dover, Folkestone, Ramsgate, Sheerness; tourism, fruit and hops ('the Garden of England'), cattle and sheep, grain, vegetables, cement, paper, shipbuilding, fishing, electronics, pharmaceuticals, oil. » England [i]; Maidstone

Kentucky pop (1987e) 3 727 000; area 104 658 sq km/40 410 sq ml. State in EC USA, divided into 120 counties; the 'Bluegrass State'; part of the territory ceded by the French (1763); explored by Daniel Boone from 1769; the first permanent British settlement at Boonesborough, 1775; included in US territory by the Treaty of Paris, 1783; originally part of Virginia; admitted to the Union as the 23rd state, 1792; capital, Frankfort; major cities, Louisville and Lexington; rivers include the Mississippi (part of the SW border), Ohio (part of the NW and N border), Tennessee, Cumberland, Kentucky, and Big Sandy with its tributary, the Tug Fork (part of the E border); Cumberland Mts in the SE; highest point Mt Black (1 263 m/4 144 ft); the C plain is known as Bluegrass country; to the W and E are rough uplands with vast coal reserves; in the SW corner are floodplains bounded by the Ohio, Mississippi, and Tennessee Rivers; famous for the distilling of Bourbon whiskey (still the country's leading producer), and for its thoroughbred racehorses; tobacco, cattle, dairy produce, soybeans; machinery, electrical equipment, processed foods, chemicals, fabricated metals; the nation's leading coal producer; petroleum, natural gas; Mammoth Cave National Park; the Kentucky Derby for three-year-olds is the nation's oldest continuously held classic horse race. » Boone; Frankfort; Mammoth Cave; United States of America [i]; RR38

Kentucky and Virginia Resolutions (1798) Declarations by two state legislatures that the Alien and Sedition laws violated the US Constitution. They were written by Thomas Jefferson (Kentucky) and James Madison (Virginia). » Alien and Sedition Acts; Jefferson; Madison, James

Kenya, official name **Republic of Kenya** [**ken**ya], formerly [**kee**nya] pop (1990e) 24 872 000; area 564 162 sq km/217 766 sq ml. Republic of E Africa, divided into eight provinces; bounded S by Tanzania, W by Uganda, NW by Sudan, N by Ethiopia, NE by Somalia, and E by the Indian Ocean; capital, Nairobi; chief towns include Mombasa, Kisumu, Nakuru, Machakos; timezone GMT +3; chief ethnic groups, Kikuyu (21%), Luhya (14%), Luo (13%), Kalejin (11%), Kamba (11%); chief religions, Christianity (66%), local beliefs (26%); official languages, English and Swahili, with many tribal languages spoken; unit of currency, the Kenya shilling.

Physical description and climate. Crossed by the Equator; SW plateau rises to 600–3 000 m/2 000–10 000 ft, includes Mt Kenya (5 200 m/17 058 ft) and the Aberdare range; Great Rift Valley (W) runs N–S; dry, arid semi-desert in the N, generally under 600 m/2 000 ft; L Turkana, largest body of water in the N; Chalbi desert SE of the lake; coastal strip S of R Tana typified by coral reefs, mangrove swamps, and small island groups; tropical climate on coast, with high temperatures and humidity; Mombasa, average annual rainfall 1 200 mm/47 in, average daily temperatures 27–31°C; annual rainfall decreases from 500 mm/20 in (S) to 250 mm/10 in (far N); frost and snow in the high mountains.

History and government. Very early fossil hominids found in the region by anthropologists; coast settled by Arabs, 7th-c;

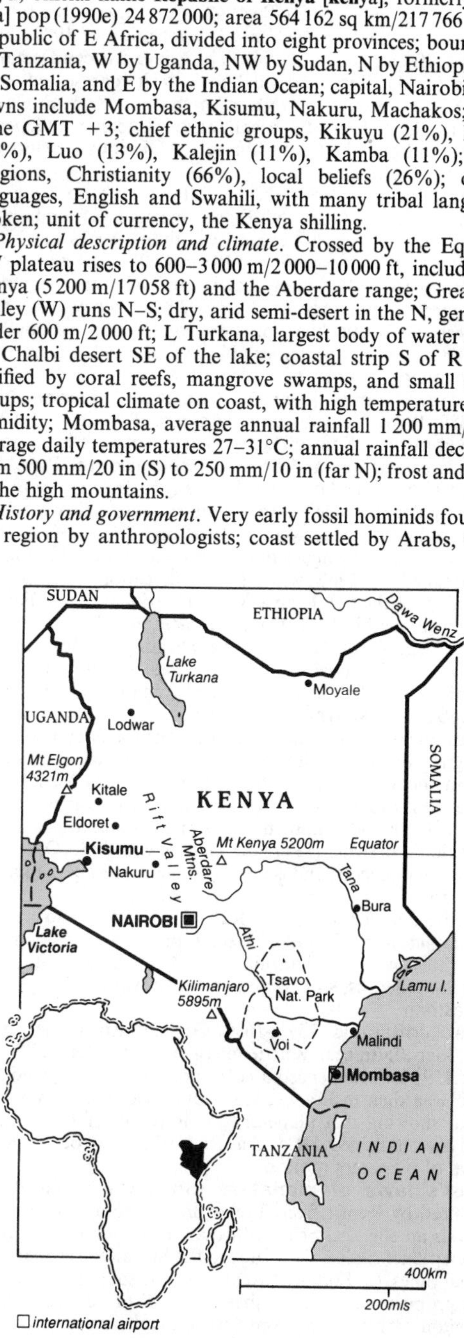

Portuguese control, 16th–17th-c; British control as East African Protectorate, 1895; British colony, 1920; independence movement led to the Mau Mau rebellion, 1952–60; independence, 1963; first leader, Jomo Kenyatta; governed by a president elected for a 5-year term, with a unicameral National Assembly of 202 members.

Economy. Agriculture accounts for a third of national income; coffee, tea, sisal, pyrethrum, cashew nuts, rice, wheat, maize, sugar cane; food processing, textiles, chemicals, cement, steel, paper, metal products, car assembly, oil refining, consumer goods, tobacco, rubber; reserves of soda ash, fluorspar, salt, diatomite, limestone, lead, gemstones, silver, gold; 14 national parks attract large numbers of tourists. » Kenyatta; Leakey; Mau Mau; Nairobi; Rift Valley; RR26 national holidays; RR54 political leaders

Kenya African National Union (KANU) The party which led Kenya to independence in 1963. It was founded in 1960 as a successor to the Kikuyu Central Association of 1929 and the Kenya African Union of 1947. The **Kenya African Democratic Union** (KADU) was a rival body which represented mainly non-Kikuyu groups. KANU won the first Kenyan election, with President Kenyatta becoming the leader of independent Kenya, although he tried to bring KADU into a coalition. » Kenya [i]; Kenyatta

Kenya, Mount 0°10S 37°18E. Extinct volcano cone in C Kenya; 112 km/70 ml NNE of Nairobi; second highest mountain in Africa; comprises three peaks of Batian 5 199 m/17 057 ft), Nelion (5 188 m/17 021 ft), and Lenana (4 985 m/16 355 ft); many lakes and glaciers; summit of Kilimanjaro often visible 323 km/200 ml away, one of the longest confirmed lines of sight on Earth; national park of 588 sq km/227 sq ml established in 1949. » Kenya [i]; Kilimanjaro, Mount

Kenyatta, Jomo [kenyata], originally **Kamau Ngengi** (c.1889–1978) Kenyan statesman and President (1964–78), born at Mitumi, Kenya. Educated at a Scots mission school, he studied at London, and became president of the Pan-African Federation. In the late 1940s his Kenya African Union advocated total independence in a unitary state. He was charged with leading the Mau Mau terrorist organization (a charge he denied), and was sentenced to seven years' hard labour in 1952, then exiled. In 1960, while still in detention, he was elected president of the new Kenya African National Union Party. He became an MP in 1961, Prime Minister in 1963, and President of the Republic of Kenya in 1964. He adopted moderate social and economic policies, and succeeded in conciliating many members of the Kenyan White community. He died at Mombasa. » Kenya [i]; Mau Mau

Kenzo, byname of **Kenzo Takada** (1940–) Japanese fashion designer, born in Kyoto. After studying art and graduating in Japan, he worked there for a time but produced freelance collections in Paris from 1964. He started a shop called Jungle Jap in 1970, and is known for his innovative ideas and use of traditional designs. He creates clothes with both Oriental and Western influences, and is a trend-setter in the field of knitwear. » fashion

Keoladeo National park in Rajasthan, India, also known as **Bharatpur**; area 29 sq km/11 sq ml; provides breeding grounds for thousands of migrating birds from Siberia and China, including herons, storks, and cranes; a world heritage site. » Rajasthan

Kepler, Johannes (1571–1630) German astronomer, born at Weil-der-Stadt, near Württemberg, and educated at Tübingen. In c.1596 he commenced a correspondence with Tycho Brahe, who was then in Prague, and from 1600 worked on Brahe's data, showing that planetary motions were far simpler than had been imagined. He died at Regensburg. » Brahe; Kepler's laws of planetary motion

Kepler's laws of planetary motion Fundamental laws deduced by Kepler from Tycho Brahe's data. (1) Each planet travels an elliptical orbit with the Sun at one focus. (2) For a given planet radius, the vector to the Sun sweeps equal areas in equal times. (3) For any two planets, the squares of the periods are proportional to the cubes of the distances from the Sun. Newton derived these from first principles using gravitational theory. » Brahe; gravitation; Kepler; Newton, Isaac; planet; vector (mathematics)

Kerala [kerala] pop(1981) 25 403 217; area 38 864 sq km/15 001 sq ml. State in S India, bounded W by the Arabian Sea; capital, Trivandrum; governed by a 140-member unicameral legislature; crossed by several rivers; created out of the former state of Travancore–Cochin under the 1956 States Reorganization Act; rice, tapioca, coconut, oilseeds, sugar cane, pepper, rubber, tea, coffee; teak, sandalwood, ebony, blackwood; textiles, ceramics, fertilizer, chemicals, glass, electrical goods, paper; ivory carving, weaving, copper and brass ware, furniture. » India [i]; Trivandrum

keratin [keratin] A tough, fibrous protein synthesized by the outer layer of the skin (*epidermis*) of vertebrates. It is the major component of hair, nails, claws, horns, feathers, scales, and the dead outer layers of cells of skin. » protein

keratosis Small dark scaly lesions on exposed parts of the skin, commonly found in individuals over 60 years of age and in younger white-skinned residents in sunny climates. A minority become malignant tumours (skin cancer). » melanoma; tumour

Kerensky, Alexandr Fyodorovich (1881–1970) Russian socialist, born at Simbirsk (now Ulyanovsk). He studied law in St Petersburg, and took a leading part in the 1917 Revolution, becoming Minister of Justice (Mar), War (May), and Premier (Jul) in the provisional government. He crushed Kornilov's military revolt (Aug), but was deposed (Oct) by the Bolsheviks, and fled to France. In 1940 he went to Australia and in 1946 to the USA, and wrote several books on the Revolution. He died in New York City. » Bolsheviks; Mensheviks; October/Russian Revolution; socialism

Kérkira » **Corfu**

Kerkuane Punic town in N Tunisia, founded in the 5th-c BC and abandoned c.140 BC after the destruction of Carthage; a world heritage site. It was a small settlement of identical houses, each with its own private bath. A necropolis was discovered nearby in 1968. » Carthage; Punic Wars

kermes [kermiz] A scale insect that feeds mainly on oaks; some species produce galls; lays up to 5 000 eggs in protected brood chambers; c.70 species in the N hemisphere. A red dye can be extracted from dried bodies of the insect. (Order: *Homoptera*. Family: *Kermesidae*.) » gall; scale insect

Kermode, Frank [kermohd] (1919–) British literary critic, born in the Isle of Man and educated at Douglas and Liverpool. He served in the Royal Navy (1940–6), and has since held posts at several universities in England and the USA. His works include *Romantic Image* (1957), *The Sense of an Ending* (1967), *The Genesis of Secrecy* (1979), and *Forms of Attention* (1985). » literary criticism

Kern, Jerome (David) (1885–1945) US songwriter, born and died in New York City. After studying at the New York College of Music and briefly in London and Heidelberg, he worked as a rehearsal pianist. His first complete score for a musical play, *The Red Petticoat*, was in 1912, followed by a string of successful Broadway shows. His greatest musical was *Show Boat* (1928, book and lyrics by Hammerstein). *Roberta* (1933) included three of his finest songs: 'Smoke Gets in Your Eyes', 'Yesterdays', and 'The Touch of Your Hand'. » Hammerstein; musical

kerosene or **paraffin** A petroleum distillation product, with larger molecules and consequently less volatility than the fraction used for gasoline (petrol). Formerly used widely as a fuel for domestic lighting, it is now an important source of domestic heating, and is the main fuel for jet engines. An early source, developed in the mid-19th-c and still exploited commercially, was oil-bearing shale. » alkanes; fuel

Kerouac, Jack, originally **Jean Louis** (1922–69) US author, born at Lowell, Massachusetts. His first novel, *The Town and the City* (1950), was written in a conventional style which he abandoned in *On the Road* (1957), a spontaneous work expressing the youthful discontent of the 'beat' generation. Later works in this vein, all autobiographical in character, include *The Subterraneans* (1958) and *Big Sur* (1962). He died at St Petersburg, Florida. » beat generation

Kerr, John (1824–1907) British physicist, born at Ardrossan,

Strathclyde. He studied at Glasgow, where he assisted Lord Kelvin. Despite a heavy teaching load in a teachers' training college, he carried out valuable research on polarized light in magnetic and electric fields, and the **Kerr effects** which result. He died in Glasgow. » Kelvin; light

Kerr cell » **electro-optic effects**

Kerry, Gaelic **Chiarraighe** pop (1981) 122 770; area 4 701 sq km/ 1 815 sq ml. County in Munster province, SW Irish Republic; bounded W by Atlantic Ocean; rises to Slieve Mish Mts on N side of Dingle Bay and Macgillycuddy's Reeks on S side; watered by Feale and Blackwater Rivers; capital, Tralee; chief towns include Killarney (notable lakeland area) and Listowel; tourism, fishing, textiles. » Killarney; Irish Republic [i]; Munster; Tralee

kerygma [ke**rig**ma] (Gr 'proclamation', 'that which is announced', often referring to the content of a priestly or prophetic proclamation.) In the New Testament it often refers to the Apostles' announcement of the saving nature of Jesus' death and resurrection (1 *Cor* 15.3–5), so that Jesus becomes not just the proclaimer of salvation but that which is proclaimed. » apostle; Jesus Christ; mythology

Kesey, Ken [**kee**zee] (1935–) US novelist, born in Colorado and educated at the University of Oregon. His reputation is based on his first novel *One Flew Over the Cuckoo's Nest* (1962; film, 1975), a black comedy set in a mental institution and based on the author's experience as an aide on the psychiatric ward of a veterans' hospital. » American literature; novel

Kesselring, Albert (1885–1960) German air commander in World War 2, born at Markstedt, Bavaria. He led the Luftwaffe attacks on France and (unsuccessfully) on Britain. In 1943 he was made Commander-in-Chief in Italy, and in 1945 in the West. Condemned to death as a war criminal in 1947, he had his sentence commuted to life imprisonment, but was released in 1952. He died at Bad Nauheim, Germany. » air force; World War 2

kestrel A falcon of worldwide genus *Falco* (13 species), especially *Falco tinnunculus*; inhabits open country and cultivation, occasionally forest; eats insects and small vertebrates; catches prey on ground after hovering. (Family: *Falconidae*.) » bird of prey; falcon

ketch A two-masted fore- and aft-rigged sailing vessel. The shorter (after-) mast, called the *mizzen*, is placed in position forward of the rudder post. By contrast, in a **yawl**, this mast is placed abaft the rudder post. » yacht [i]

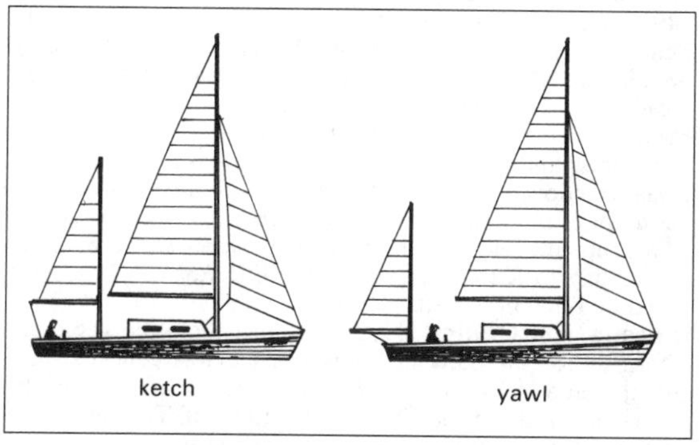

ketone [**kee**tohn] IUPAC **alkanone**. An organic compound containing a carbonyl (C=O) group bonded to two other carbon atoms. The simplest example is acetone (CH_3COCH_3). » carbonyl

Kettering, Charles Franklyn (1876–1958) US engineer, born and died at Loudonville, Ohio. In 1912 he invented the electric starter motor for cars, first installed in the Cadillac. He also discovered the cause of 'knocking' in car engines, produced a quick-drying paint for cars, and invented the refrigerant known as Freon®. » CFCs; knocking

kettledrum » **timpani**

Kew Gardens The Royal Botanical Gardens at Kew, Surrey, England. The gardens, which were inherited by George III from his mother, expanded and flourished under the direction of Sir Joseph Banks (1743–1820). In 1841 it was given to the nation. It now occupies 120 ha/300 acres, and is the premier botanical institution in the world. » botanical garden

key » **tonality**

key grip » **grip**

keyboard instrument A musical instrument in which the different pitches are controlled by means of a keyboard, ie a succession of levers arranged (for acoustical, historical, or practical reasons) in two rows. The front row produces the notes of the diatonic C major scale, the rear the pitches in between; played in order from left to right, they produce an ascending 12-note chromatic scale. In modern keyboards the front keys are white, the rear ones black; in some earlier instruments the colours are reversed, while in the case of the organ pedalboard there is usually no colour differentiation. Keyboards are integral to many aerophones (eg the accordion), chordophones, (eg the piano), and electrophones (eg the synthesizer). The term **keyboards** is also often used as a collective term for all the electronic keyboard instruments (electric pianos, electronic organs, and synthesizers) in a pop group. » accordion; aerophone; celesta; chordophone; clavichord; electrophone; glockenspiel; harpsichord; ondes Martenot; organ; piano; spinet; synthesizer; virginals

Keynes (of Tilton), John Maynard, 1st Baron (1883–1946) British economist, born at Cambridge. Educated at Eton and Cambridge, he became one of the 'Bloomsbury group', and lectured in economics. In both World Wars he was an adviser to the Treasury. The unemployment crises inspired his two great works, *A Treatise on Money* (1930) and the revolutionary *General Theory of Employment, Interest and Money* (1936). His views on a planned economy influenced Roosevelt's 'New Deal' administration. He was created a peer in 1942, and died at Firle, Sussex. » Keynesian; New Deal

Keynesian [**kayn**zian] A follower and exponent of the economic concepts propounded by British economist J M Keynes in the 1930s. The 'Keynesian revolution' is so-called because it radically changed the view of how economies should be managed, particularly in relation to the notion of full employment. Prior to Keynes, the classical school of economics believed that economies would tend towards full employment equilibrium. Keynesian thinking challenged this, with a view based on the experience of Western economies after World War 1, that economies could be in equilibrium at less than full employment. Unless demand in the economy is stimulated, growth and therefore full employment are not possible. Keynesian theories were subject to critical appraisal in the 1960s and 1970s by Monetarists. Many argue that the fundamental theory holds good, but does not fully address current economic problems, such as inflation. » Chicago School; Keynes; monetarism; Neo-Keynesianism

keystone The distortion of a projected image in which the vertical sides of a rectangle converge. The effect is caused by the optical axis of projection not meeting the screen at right angles. » cinematography [i]

Keystone A production company of silent films (1912–19), founded by Mack Sennett. It specialized in knock-about comedy shorts, especially those featuring the **Keystone Kops** troupe. » cinema

KGB An acronym of **Komitet Gosudarstvennoy Bezopasnosti** ('Committee for State Security'), after 1953 one of the Soviet Union's two secret police organizations with joint responsibility for internal and external order and security. Its tasks included the surveillance of key members of the Communist Party, the administration, and the military; the monitoring and regulation of dissidents; and espionage and subversion abroad. It was abolished following the failed 1991 coup in the USSR. » intelligence service; Soviet Union [i]

Khajuraho [kaji**rah**hoh] A group of 20 Hindu temples in Madhya Pradesh, India; a world heritage site. The temples were constructed, mainly of sandstone, in 950–1050. The sculptures which embellish their internal and external walls are reckoned masterpieces of erotic art. » Madhya Pradesh

Khalid or **Khaled, ibn Abdul Aziz** (1913–82) King of Saudi Arabia (1975–82), the fourth son of the founder of the Saudi dynasty. He ascended the throne after the assassination of his brother, Faisal; and his caution and moderation served as a stabilizing factor in the Middle East. His personal influence was seen in the halting of the Lebanese Civil War (1975–6), and in his country's disagreement with the other members of OPEC over oil price increases. He died at Taif, Saudi Arabia. » OPEC

Khama, Sir Seretse [**kah**ma] (1921–80) African statesman and President of Botswana (1966–80), born at Serowe, Bechuanaland (now Botswana). Educated in Africa and at Oxford, he became a lawyer, and after marrying an Englishwoman, Ruth Williams (1948), was banned from the chieftainship and the territory of the Bamangwato. Allowed to return as a private citizen in 1956, he became active in politics, and was restored to the chieftainship in 1963. He was the first Prime Minister of Bechuanaland in 1965, and first President of Botswana. Knighted in 1966, he died at Gaborone, Botswana. » Botswana [i]

Khamsin A hot, dry dust-laden SE wind which blows from desert areas in N Africa and Arabia. The word means 'fifty', as it regularly blows for a 50-day period. » Sirocco; wind [i]

Khan, (Muhammad) Ayub (1907–74) Pakistani soldier and President (1958–69), born at Abbottabad. Educated at Aligarh Muslim University and Sandhurst, he served in World War 2, and was the first Commander-in-Chief of Pakistan's army (1951). He became President in 1958 after a bloodless coup, and introduced a system of Basic Democracies. Following widespread civil disorder, he resigned in 1969, and martial law was re-established. He died at Islamabad. » Pakistan [i]

Khan, Jahangir (1963–) Pakistan squash rackets player, born in Karachi. A member of a prolific squash-playing family, he won three world amateur titles (1979, 1983, 1985), a record six World Open titles (1981–5, 1988), and eight consecutive British Open titles (1982–9). He was undefeated from April 1981 to November 1986, when he lost to Ross Norman (Australia) in the World Open final. » squash rackets

Kharga, El [**kah**ga] or **Al Kharijah** 25°27N 30°32E. Capital of Al-Wadi Al-Jadid governorate, SC Egypt; in the Great Oasis, Egypt's largest oasis; railway; dates, figs, olives; ruins of Temple of Hibis (now a Christian necropolis, c.500 BC) and Nadura (Christian convent, c.AD 150). » Egypt [i]

Kharkov [**khah**kuhf], Ukrainian **Kharkiv** 50°00N 36°15E, pop (1989) 1 611 000. Capital city of Kharkovskaya oblast, Ukraine, on tributaries of the R Severskiy Donets; founded as a fortress, 1655–6; badly damaged in World War 2; airport; railway junction; university (1805); Donets Basic coalfield nearby; heavy engineering, machines, metalworking, foodstuffs, building materials; Pokrovskii cathedral (1689), Uspenskii cathedral (1821–41). » Ukraine

Khartoum or **El Khartûm** [kah**toom**] 15°33N 32°35E, pop (1984e) 476 218. Capital of Sudan, near the junction of the White Nile and the Blue Nile Rivers, 1 600 km/1 000 ml S of Cairo (Egypt); founded, 1820s; garrison town in 19th-c; scene of the British defeat against the Mahdi, in which General Gordon was killed, 1885; city regained by Lord Kitchener, 1898; airport; railway; university (1955); major communications and trade centre; headquarters of the Bank for African Development; regarded as the economic link between the Arab countries (N) and the African countries (S); commerce, food processing, textiles, glass; oil pipeline runs NE to Port Sudan; three cathedrals, mosques, Sudan National Museum. » Gordon, Charles George; Kitchener, Herbert; Mahdi; Sudan [i]

khat [kaht] A shrub (*Catha edulis*) growing in E Asia and the SW part of the Arabian peninsula, whose leaves are chewed for their stimulant effect. The active principle is cathinone, whose properties are similar to amphetamine. » amphetamine; betel-nut

Khatchaturian, Aram (1903–1978) Russian composer, born at Tiflis. He was a student of folksong, and an authority on oriental music. His compositions include three symphonies, concertos, ballets, instrumental music, and film scores. He died in Moscow.

khedive An ancient Persian title acquired from the Ottoman Sultan by the effectively independent Viceroy of Egypt, Ismail, in 1867. It was used until Egypt became a British protectorate (1914). » Ismail Pasha

Khmer [kmair] An Austro-Asiatic language, spoken by over 5 million people; also known as **Cambodian**. It is the official language of Cambodia. Inscriptions date from the 6th–7th-c AD. » Austro-Asiatic languages

Khmer Empire An empire in SE Asia, founded in the 7th-c, with its capital at Angkor from 802 onwards. In the 11th–12th-c it included S Laos, a large part of Thailand, and Cambodia. It was overthrown by the Thais in the 15th-c. » Angkor Thom

Khmer Rouge A Cambodian communist guerrilla force which opposed the right-wing government that deposed Prince Sihanouk in 1970, and the subsequent US invasion of Cambodia. After gaining control in 1975, its government, led by Pol Pot, set about a drastic transformation of 'Democratic Kampuchea', involving mass forced evacuation from the towns to the countryside, the creation of agricultural co-operatives, and the execution of thousands of 'bourgeois elements'. In 1978, Vietnam invaded Cambodia, and the Khmer Rouge were ousted, retiring to the Thai-Cambodian border region. Following the Vietnamese withdrawal in 1989, they have mounted a major offensive, especially in the W and S provinces. Western intelligence estimates suggest that the force consists of 20–35 000 armed men, with 50–100 000 refugees in Khmer Rouge-controlled camps along the border and in Thailand. Pol Pot is still regarded as the overall leader; other senior personnel include the deputy leader Ieng Sary (1930–), guerrilla commander Son Sen (1930–), and the leader of Khmer Rouge delegations at international conferences, Khieu Samphan (1931–). » Cambodia [i]; Pol Pot

Khoisan [**koy**san] A collective term for the San (Bushmen) and Khoi (Hottentot) peoples of S Africa. The San were formerly hunter-gatherers, with a poor material culture but a rich oral literature and accomplished rock art. They once populated most of EC and S Africa, but today are marginalized in the Kalahari Desert of Botswana. Many now work for African or White cattle-farmers. The Khoi were traditionally pastoralists, and today are represented only by groups of mixed ancestry in Namibia. They were devastated by a smallpox epidemic in 1713, and their culture collapsed. There are no evident racial differences between the groups. Population c.100 000. » click language; pastoralism

Khomeini, Ayatollah Ruhollah (1900–89) Iranian religious and political leader, born at Khomeyn, Iran. A Shiite Muslim who was bitterly opposed to the pro-Western régime of Shah Mohammed Reza Pahlavi, he was exiled to Turkey and Iraq in 1964, and from Iraq to France in 1978. He returned to Iran amid great popular acclaim in 1979 after the collapse of the Shah's government and became virtual head of state. Under his leadership, Iran underwent a turbulent 'Islamic Revolution' in which a return was made to the strict observance of Muslim principles and traditions. In 1979, a new Islamic constitution was sanctioned, into which was incorporated his leadership concept of the *Vilayet-i faqih* (Trusteeship of the Jurisconsult). This supreme religious and political position was recognized as belonging to Khomeini, as was the title *Rabhar* (Leader). He died in Teheran. » Iran [i]; Islam; Pahlavi

Khorana, Har Gobind (1922–) Indian-US molecular biologist, born at Raipur (now in Pakistan). He was educated in the Punjab and in Europe before moving to the USA, from 1970 working at the Massachusetts Institute of Technology. His research into nucleic acids and the genetic code attracted especial notice in 1970, when he achieved the first synthesis of an artificial gene. He shared the Nobel Prize for Physiology or Medicine in 1968. » DNA [i]; gene; molecular biology

Khrushchev, Nikita Sergeevich [krush**chof**] (1894–1971) Soviet statesman, First Secretary of the Soviet Communist Party (1953–64), and Prime Minister (1958–64), born at Kalinovka. Joining the Bolshevik Party in 1918, he fought in the Russian Civil War and rose rapidly in the party organization. In 1939 he was made a full member of the Politburo and of the Presidium of the Supreme Soviet. In 1953, on the death of Stalin, he became First Secretary of the Communist Party of the Soviet Union, and three years later at the 20th Party Congress denounced Stalinism and the 'personality cult'. Among the events of his administration were the 1956 Poznan riots and Hungarian uprising, and the failed attempt to install missiles in Cuba (1962). He was deposed in 1964, replaced by Brezhnev and Kosygin, and went into retirement. He died in Moscow. » Brezhnev; Cuban missile crisis; Hungarian uprising; Kosygin; Stalin

Khyber Pass [**kiy**buh] A defile through the Safed Koh mountain range on the frontier between Pakistan and Afghanistan. A route favoured through history by both traders and invaders, it is 45 km/28 ml long, and reaches heights of 1 280 m/3 518 ft.

kiang [kiang] » **ass**

kibbutz plural **kibbutzim** A Jewish co-operative settlement in Israel which is self-supporting in terms of food supplies and many other goods. Kibbutzim spread in the 1950s as part of Israeli attempts at self-sufficiency. One of their distinctive features has been the collective responsibility members take for child rearing: rather than being cared for in nuclear family units, the young are looked after by the elder children. This is to allow the kibbutzim women as much opportunity as possible to engage in the organization of commune life on equal terms with the men. » collective farm; farmer co-operative; Israel [i]

Kidd, William, byname **Captain Kidd** (c.1645–1701) Scottish privateer and pirate, born (probably) at Greenock. He saw much privateering service, and gained a high reputation for courage. In 1696 he was commissioned to suppress piracy, and reached Madagascar, but then turned pirate himself. After a two years' cruise he returned to the West Indies, and venturing to Boston, was arrested, sent to England, and hanged in London.

Kiddush [kid**ush**] (Heb 'sanctification') A prayer usually recited by the head of the family over a cup of wine at the start of a meal in the home on the eve of a Sabbath or festival. Sometimes used also in synagogues to consecrate the Sabbath or a festival. In addition, a 'minor' Kiddush is often said over a beverage or bread before the first meal on the following morning of such events. » Judaism; prayer; Sabbath

kidney bean » **haricot bean**

kidney failure A disorder in which the ability of the kidney to excrete end products of protein metabolism (eg urea, creatinine, hydrogen ions) is severely reduced, and they accumulate in the blood to produce the clinical state of uraemia. The condition when persistent is the end result of several chronic diseases. It can also occur acutely, when it is often potentially reversible. » dialysis; kidneys; protein; uraemia

kidney machine » **dialysis**

kidneys The urine-producing organs of vertebrates. In humans the symmetrical, bean-shaped kidneys are situated in the upper rear part of the abdomen, one each side of the vertebral column. The ureter conveys urine to the bladder. Each kidney has a suprarenal (adrenal) gland immediately above, weighs about 130 gm/4.6 oz, is enclosed by connective tissue, and is supported by fat. Each consists of approximately one million **nephrons** (the functional units) and supporting tissue. The nephrons eliminate unwanted substances from the blood, but retain important body constituents (eg glucose, sodium, and potassium), so maintaining the volume and composition of body fluids within normal limits. The kidneys also produce important agents (eg renin, erythropoietin, prostaglandins), which are transported in the blood to their target organs. » abdomen; adrenal glands; colic; glomerulonephritis; kidney failure; pyelonephritis; transplantation; urinary stones; urine; Plate XII

Kiel [keel] 54°02N 10°08E, pop (1983) 248 400. Port and capital of Schleswig-Holstein province, Germany; at S end of the Kieler Förde, an arm of the Baltic Sea; badly bombed in World War 2; railway; university (1665); ferry service to Scandinavia; naval base; shipbuilding, engineering, precision instruments, fish processing, oil, railway vehicles, telephone systems, marine electronics, armaments; Schloss (13th-c); Kiel Week, sailing regattas and cultural events (Jun). » Germany [i]

Kielder Water [**keel**der] Reservoir in Northumberland, NE England; one of the largest artificial lakes in Europe, supplying water to the industrial NE; built 1974–82 by damming R North Tyne; first regional water grid system in UK; planting of nearby **Kielder Forest** begun in 1922; area with other Border forests, 650 sq km/250 sq ml; largest area of planted forest in Europe. » England [i]; Tyne, River

Kierkegaard, Sören (Aabye) [**keer**kuhgahd] (1813–55) Danish philosopher and theologian, born in Copenhagen, where he studied theology, philosophy, and literature. He criticized purely speculative systems of thought, such as Hegel's, as irrelevant to existence-making choices. For Hegel's rationalism, Kierkegaard substituted the disjunction *Enten-Eller* (1843, Either/Or). In *Afsluttende uvidenskabelig Efterskrift* (1846, Concluding Unscientific Postscript), he attacked all philosophical system building, and formulated the thesis that subjectivity is truth. A major influence on 20th-c existentialism, he died in Copenhagen. » existentialism; Hegel

Kiesinger, Kurt Georg (1904–88) West German Conservative statesman and Chancellor (1966–9), born at Ebingen. Educated at Berlin and Tübingen, he practised as a lawyer (1935–40), and served during World War 2 at the Foreign Office on radio propaganda. Interned after the war until 1947, he was exonerated of Nazi crimes. In 1949 he became a member of the *Bundestag*, and succeeded Erhard as Chancellor (1966). Long a convinced supporter of Adenauer's plans for European unity, he formed with Brandt a government combining the Christian Democratic Union and the Social Democrats, until in 1969 he was succeeded as Chancellor by Brandt. » Adenauer; Brandt; Erhard; Germany [i]

Kiev, also **Kiyev** [kyef], Ukrainian **Kiyiv** 50°28N 30°29E, pop (1989) 2 587 000. Capital city of Ukraine, on R Dnieper; earliest centre of Slavonic culture and learning; founded, 6th–7th-c; capital of mediaeval Kievan Russia, 9th-c; capital of Ukraine SSR, 1934; besieged and occupied by Germany in World War 2; airport; railway; university (1834); major industrial, cultural, and scientific centre; chemicals, clothing, knitwear, leatherwork, footwear, instruments; opera and ballet companies, St Sofia cathedral (1037), Zabrovsky Gate (1746), Monastery of the Caves (1051), All Saints Church (17th-c), Vydubetsky Monastery (1070–7). » Russian history; Ukraine

Kikuyu [ki**koo**yoo] A Bantu-speaking agricultural people of the C highlands of Kenya, and the country's largest ethnic group. During the 1950s they were involved in the Mau Mau uprising against European colonialists; after Kenya's independence (1963) they provided many of the country's political leaders. Population c.3.5 million. » Bantu-speaking peoples; Kenya [i]; Kenyatta; Mau Mau

Kildare [kil**dair**], Gaelic **Chill Dara** pop (1981) 104 122; area 1 694 sq km/654 sq ml. County in Leinster province, E Irish Republic; watered by Liffey and Barrow Rivers; low-lying C plain known as the Curragh; capital, Naas; chief towns include Kildare, Athy, Droichead Nua; farming, cattle, horse breeding; national stud at Tully, racecourse at the Curragh. » Irish Republic [i]; Leinster; Naas

Kilimanjaro, Mount [kiliman**jah**roh] 3°02S 37°20E. Mountain on the frontier between Tanzania and Kenya, E Africa; height 5 895 m/19 340 ft; highest point on the African continent; glaciated double-peaked massif of volcanic origin, capped by the dormant cone of Kibo peak and the jagged extinct Mawenza peak; first climbed in 1889; Kilimanjaro national park is a world heritage site. » Kenya, Mount; Tanzania [i]

Kilkenny (city), Gaelic **Cill Choinnigh** 52°39N 7°15W, pop (1981) 16 886. Capital of Kilkenny county, Leinster, SE Irish Republic, on R Nore; railway; clothing, footwear, brewing; Kilkenny College and design workshops; cathedrals, town hall (Tholsel), 18th-c Kilkenny Castle, Bishop Rothe's house; Kilkenny Arts Week (Aug). » Irish Republic [i]; Kilkenny (county)

Kilkenny (county), Gaelic **Chill Choinnigh** pop (1981) 70 806; area 2 062 sq km/796 sq ml. County in Leinster province, SE Irish Republic; fertile county watered by R Nore; Slieve Ardagh Hills rise W; capital, Kilkenny; agriculture, livestock. » Irish Republic [i]; Kilkenny (city); Leinster

Killarney, Gaelic **Cill Airne** 52°03N 9°30W, pop (1981) 9 083. Resort town in Kerry county, Munster, SW Irish Republic; centre of scenic lakeland area; railway; engineering, container cranes, hosiery; pan-Celtic week with Celtavision Song Contest (May); Killarney regatta (Jul); Kerry boating carnival (Sep). » Irish Republic [i]; Kerry

killer whale A toothed whale, worldwide in cool coastal waters; length, 9–10 m/30–33 ft; black with white underparts; white patches on head; dorsal fin narrow and vertical (tallest in males); eats marine mammals, birds, fish, and squid (groups may attack baleen whales). (*Orcinus orca.*) The name is also used for the **false killer whale** (*Pseudorca crassidens*) and the **pygmy killer whale** (*Feresa attenuata*). (Family: *Delphinidae.*) » grampus; whale [i]

killifish Small colourful carp-like freshwater fish widespread in tropical and warm temperate regions; jaws bearing small teeth; lacks bony linkage between swim bladder and inner ear; popular as an aquarium fish; also called **top minnows**. (Family: *Cyprodontidae.*) » carp

Killy, Jean Claude [keelee] (1943–) French alpine skier, born at Val d'Isère. He left school at 16 to join the French ski team, and won all three alpine skiing titles at the 1968 Olympics. He was combined world champion in 1966 and 1968, and downhill champion in 1966. Winner of the inaugural World Cup overall title in 1967, he retained the title the following year, when he won 12 races. He retired after the 1968 Olympics, and went to live in the USA. » skiing

kiln An oven for baking clay for bricks or pottery, or the clay and lime for cement, usually constructed of fireclay or resistant alloys. The term is also used for ovens operating at low temperatures for the drying of hops or grain. » clay; hops

kilobyte » **byte**

kilocalorie » **calorie** [i]

kilogram Base SI unit of mass; symbol kg; defined as equal to the international prototype of the kilogram, a platinum-iridium bar kept at the International Bureau of Weights and Measures; commonly used as **gram** (g, 1/1 000 kg) and **tonne** (t, 1 000 kg); 1 kg = 2.205 pounds. » mass; units (scientific); RR70

kilohm » **ohm**

kilometre » **metre** (physics)

kiloparsec » **parsec**

kiloton (of TNT) A measure of explosive power; symbol kT; one kiloton equivalent to the explosive power of 1 000 tons of TNT; used to describe the destructive power of nuclear weapons, which range from 10 kT to thousands of kT; one **megaton**, MT, equals 1 000 kT. » explosives; TNT [i]; units (scientific)

kilowatt » **watt**

kilowatt-hour The total energy consumed by a device of power one kilowatt operating for one hour; symbol kWh; equal to 3.6×10^6 J (joule, SI unit); standard unit for the electricity supply industry. » electricity; units (scientific); watt

Kilvert, Francis (1840–79) British clergyman, whose *Diary* (1870–9), discovered in 1937, is an important historical document of his period, describing his daily life as a curate and vicar.

Kim Il-sung, originally **Kim Song-ju** (1912–) North Korean soldier, statesman, Prime Minister (1948–72), and President (1972–), born near Pyongyang. He founded the Korean People's Revolutionary Army in 1932, and led a long struggle against the Japanese. He proclaimed the Republic in 1948, and has been effective head of state ever since. He was re-elected President in 1982, having named his son as his eventual political successor. » Korea, North [i]

Kimberley 28°45S 24°46E, pop (1980) 144 923. City in Cape province, South Africa, 450 km/280 ml SW of Johannesburg; major diamond-mining centre since its foundation, 1871; under siege in the Boer War (1899–1900); airfield; railway; diamonds, metal products, furniture, clothing, cement; the Big Hole (formerly, Kimberley Mine), 800 m/2 625 ft deep and 500 m/1 640 ft across, said to be the biggest artificial hole on Earth; two cathedrals, Bantu Gallery. » Boer Wars; Kimberley, Siege of; South Africa [i]

Kimberley, Siege of (1899–1900) One of the three sieges of the second Boer War, in which Boer forces attempted to pen up their British opponents and secure control of vital lines of communication. The siege lasted from the middle of October 1899 until February 1900, when the town was relieved by General French. » Boer Wars; French, John; Kimberley

Kimono

kimono [kimohnoh] Japanese traditional costume, today mostly worn for special occasions, such as weddings and the tea ceremony, or informally. It is not worn to work except by Buddhist priests, waitresses in traditional style restaurants, and a few others. Plain colours are for men; bright for girls and young women. The *obi* (waist sash) for women is frequently of an expensive material.

Kinabalu, Mount (Malay **Gunong**) [kinabahloo] 6°03N 116°32E. Mountain in Sabah state, E Malaysia, in the Crocker Range; highest peak in SE Asia, 4 094 m/13 432 ft; within the Kinabalu National Park. » Malaysia [i]

kinaesthesis/kinesthesis [kinuhstheesis] Perceived sensations of position and movement of body and limbs, and of the force exerted by muscles. The sense organs responsible are in the skin and joints and, more importantly, in the muscles themselves. The term **proprioception** has a somewhat wider application: it includes information about posture and movement not consciously perceived, as well as the senses of balance, rotation, and linear acceleration vertically and horizontally, resulting from stimulation of the vestibular organs of the inner ear. » ear [i]; muscle

kindergarten A nursery school for children under the age at which they must legally attend school. In many countries the kindergarten is organized on informal lines, with the emphasis on social development as well as on preparation for formal schooling. Provision of preschool education varies from near universal availability to very low. » nursery school; pre-school education

kine pox » **cow pox**

kinematics » **dynamics**

kinescoping A US term for the recording of a television or video programme on cinematograph film. » telerecording

kinesics [kiyneeziks] The study of visual body language as communication. Kinesics is concerned partly with the conventional movements and gestures that convey deliberate messages, and also with the way facial expressions, body movements, and posture provide patterns of involuntary clues to the emotional state of the person observed, and to the nature of social interaction. It particularly studies the way winks, eyebrow movements, smiles, waving, finger gestures, and other movements of the face and limbs vary in meaning between different cultures. » non-verbal communication

kinetic To do with motion; in chemistry, to do with the speed of reactions. Mixtures which reach equilibrium quickly are called **labile**; those which react slowly **inert**.

kinetic art A term applied to certain types of modern art, especially sculptures, which move. For example, the hanging mobiles of the US sculptor Alexander Calder (1898–1976), all the parts of which revolve separately to create changing patterns in space, usually rely on air currents, but some kinetic works are connected to a motor. » mobile

kinetic energy Energy associated with an object's motion; a scalar quantity; symbol *K*, units J (joule). For an object of mass *m* moving with velocity *v*, kinetic energy $K = mv^2/2$. A change in kinetic energy is work done to the object by a force. » energy; work

kinetic energy weapons Weapons which achieve their destructive effect by the sheer force of their impact; distinguished, in the terminology of modern warfare, from those which do damage by blast and heat (*chemical energy* or *explosive* weapons) on arrival at the target. An arrow fired from a bow or a bullet fired from a gun is a kinetic energy weapon, as is a solid-shot anti-tank round, fired at high velocity from a gun barrel. » chemical warfare; directed energy weapons; kinetic energy; rail gun

kinetic theory of gases A classical theory of gases in which a gas is assumed to comprise large numbers of identical particles which undergo elastic collisions and obey Newtonian mechanics. The statistical application of the laws of mechanics gives the relationships between the bulk thermodynamic properties of a gas and the motion of gas particles. » diffusion (science); Maxwell-Boltzmann distribution; mean free path; statistical mechanics; thermodynamics

King, Billie Jean, *née* **Moffitt** (1943–) US lawn tennis player, born at Long Beach, California. She won the ladies doubles title at Wimbledon in 1961 (with Karen Hantze) at her first attempt, and between 1961 and 1979 won a record 20 Wimbledon titles, including the singles in 1966–8, 1972–3, and 1975. She also won 13 US titles (including four singles), four French titles (one singles), and two Australian titles (one singles). » tennis, lawn [i]

King, Cecil (Harmsworth) (1901–) British newspaper proprietor, nephew of the Harmsworth brothers. He joined the *Daily Mirror* in 1926, became chairman of Daily Mirror Newspapers Ltd and Sunday Pictorial Newspapers Ltd (1951–63), and chairman of the International Publishing Corporation and Reed Paper Group (1963–8). » Harmsworth, Alfred

King, Francis (Henry) (1923–) British novelist and short-story writer, born in Switzerland, and educated at Shrewsbury and Oxford, after a childhood spent partly in India. He worked for the British Council in Greece, Egypt, and Japan (1945–64), during which time he wrote several novels, including *The Needle* (1975), *Act of Darkness* (1983), and *Voices in an Empty Room* (1984). » English literature; novel

King, Martin Luther (1929–68) US Black minister, born at Atlanta, Georgia. He studied at Morehouse College and Boston University, set up his first ministry at Montgomery, Alabama, and became a leader of the civil rights movement. In 1964 he received the Kennedy Peace Prize and the Nobel Peace Prize. His greatest successes came in challenging the segregation laws of the South. After 1965, he turned his attention to social conditions in the North, which he found less tractable. He was assassinated in Memphis, Tennessee; his assassin, **James Earl Ray**, was apprehended in London, and in 1969 was sentenced in Memphis to 99 years. » civil rights; Vietnam War

King, W(illiam) L(yon) Mackenzie (1874–1950) Canadian Liberal statesman and Prime Minister (1921–6, 1926–30, 1935–48), born at Berlin (modern Kitchener), Ontario. He studied law at Toronto, and became an MP (1908), Minister of Labour (1909–11), and Liberal leader (1919). His view that the dominions should be autonomous communities within the British Empire resulted in the Statute of Westminster (1931). He resigned from office in 1948, and died at Kingsmere, Quebec. » Canada [i]

King Charles spaniel A breed of dog developed in Britain; a small active spaniel with short legs and long ears; also known as the **Cavalier King Charles spaniel**. » dog; spaniel

king cobra The world's largest venomous snake (length, up to 5.5 m/18 ft), native to India and SE Asia; inhabits forests, especially near water; eats snakes (including venomous species) and monitor lizards; female builds nest on ground and coils on top to incubate eggs; also known as **hamadryad**. (*Ophiophagus hannah*.) » cobra

king crab » **horseshoe crab**

King James Bible » **Authorized Version of the Bible**

King Philip's War (1675–6) An attempt by the Indians of C New England to stop further White expansion. It was led by Metacom (Philip), chief of the Wampanoags, who tried to build an inter-tribe coalition. The Indians lost, and were killed or enslaved. » Indian Wars

king's evil » **scrofula**

King William's War (1689–97) The first of the great wars between France and England for the control of N America. Known in Europe as the War of the League of Augsburg, it was settled by the Treaty of Ryswick (1697). » Augsburg, League of; William III

kingcup A perennial growing in wet marshy places throughout the N hemisphere; leaves glossy, kidney-shaped; flowers cup-shaped, golden-yellow, up to 5 cm/2 in across; also called **marsh marigold**. (*Caltha palustris*. Family: *Ranunculaceae*.) » perennial

kingdom (biology) The highest category into which organisms are classified. Traditionally two kingdoms have been recognized – *Plantae* (plants) and *Animalia* (animals) – but increasing knowledge of micro-organisms has made it difficult to fit them into this system. Modern systems recognize five kingdoms: *Monera* (comprising the procaryotes such as bacteria and blue-green algae), *Protista* (comprising the eucaryotic protozoans and some flagellated algae and fungi), *Fungi* (the eucaryotic fungi that lack flagella at all stages of their life cycle), *Plantae*, and *Animalia*. » animal; eucaryote; flagellum; fungus; plant; procaryote; Protozoa; systematics; taxonomy

kingfisher A bird found almost worldwide (especially Old World tropics); short-tailed, with large head; bill usually long, straight; occupies diverse habitats, usually (but not necessarily) near water. Some species eat only fish; most eat insects and small vertebrates. (Family: *Alcedinidae*, c.85 species.) » kookaburra

Kings, Books of A pair of books of the Hebrew Bible/Old Testament, consisting of a compilation of stories about the kings and prophets of Judah and Israel from the enthronement of Solomon to the fall of the kingdom of Israel in c.721 BC, and the final collapse of Judah and Jerusalem in c.587/6 BC. It is part of the Deuteronomistic History, probably once connected to the books of Samuel, and in some Catholic versions entitled 3 and 4 *Kings*. It is strongly critical of idolatry, apostasy, and religious fragmentation away from the Jerusalem Temple cult. » Ahab; Deuteronomistic History; Elijah; Elisha; Old Testament; Samuel, Books of; Solomon (Old Testament); Temple, Jerusalem

Kingsley, Charles (1819–75) British author, born at Holne vicarage, Dartmoor, Devon. Educated at Cambridge, he was ordained in 1842, and lived as curate and rector of Eversley, Hampshire. A 'Christian Socialist', he was much involved in schemes for the improvement of working-class life, and his social novels, such as *Alton Locke* (1850), had great influence at the time. His best-known works are *Westward Ho!* (1855), *Hereward the Wake* (1866), and his children's book, *The Water Babies* (1863). In 1860 he was appointed professor of modern history at Cambridge, and in 1873 chaplain to the Queen. He died at Eversley. » English literature; novel

Kingston (Canada) 44°14N 76°30W, pop (1981) 52 616. Town in SE Ontario, SE Canada; at the NE end of L Ontario, where it joins the St Lawrence R; site of former fort (Fort Frontenac); founded in 1784 by United Empire Loyalists; Canadian naval base in War of 1812; capital of United Canada, 1841–4; railway; Royal Military College (1876); Queen's University (1841); textiles, chemicals, mining machinery, aluminium products, food processing; Pump House Steam Museum, Fort Henry. » Canada [i]; Ontario

Kingston (Jamaica) 17°58N 76°48W, pop (1982) 524 638. Capital city and commercial centre of Jamaica; on N side of a landlocked harbour, SE coast; founded, 1693; capital, 1870; airport; railway; Institute of Jamaica (1879); University of the West Indies (1948); agricultural trade, oil refining; St Peter's Church (1725), coin and note museum, national gallery, Hope Botanical Gardens, Tuff Gong International studio built by reggae star Bob Marley. » Jamaica [i]; Marley

Kingston-upon-Hull » **Hull**

Kingstown 13°12N 61°14W, pop (1984) 32 600. Capital and main port of St Vincent, Windward Is, on SW coast; airfield;

bananas, copra, arrowroot, cotton; beach resorts nearby; botanical gardens (1763), St George's Cathedral, courthouse. » St Vincent

kinkajou [**king**kajoo] A nocturnal mammal native to C and S America; superficially monkey-like, with a round head, small rounded ears, short face, large eyes, and long clasping tail; eats mainly fruit; also known as **honey bear** or **potto**. (*Potos flavus*. Family: *Procyonidae*.) » mammal [i]; monkey [i]

Kinkakuji or **Golden Pavilion** [kin**ka**kujee] A three-tiered gilded pavilion built in 1394 by Ashikaga Yoshimitsu (1358–1408) in a lakeside setting at Kyoto, Japan. The present building dates from 1955; it is a faithful reconstruction of the original which was burnt down. » Kyoto

Kinnock, Neil (Gordon) (1942–) British Labour politician, born at Tredegar, Monmouthshire. Educated at Cardiff, he became an MP in 1970, joined the Labour Party's National Executive Committee (1978), and was chief Opposition spokesman on education (1979–83). A skilful orator, he was elected Party leader following Michael Foot in 1983. » Foot; Labour Party

kinnor A musical instrument of the ancient Hebrews – a type of lyre plucked with the fingers or a plectrum. The word is also the modern Hebrew name for the violin. » lyre; plectrum; string instrument 2 [i]

Kinsey, Alfred Charles (1894–1956) US zoologist and social scientist, born at Hoboken, New Jersey, and educated at Brunswick and Harvard. Best known for his controversial studies *Sexual Behaviour of the Human Male* (1948) and *Sexual Behaviour of the Human Female* (1953), he founded the Institute for Sexual Research at Indiana University, which holds extensive data on human sexual habits. He died at Bloomington, Indiana. » social science

Kinshasa [kin**sha**sa], formerly Belgian **Léopoldville** (to 1964) 4°18S 15°18E, pop (1981e) 2 338 246. River-port capital of Zaire; on the Zaire R opposite Brazzaville (Congo); founded by Stanley, 1887; capital of Belgian colony, 1926; US troops stationed here during World War 2; airport; railway; university (1954); commerce, food processing, textiles, chemicals, brewing. » Stanley, Henry Morton; Zaire [i]

kinship Relationships between people which follow upon descent from a common ancestor. In every human society common descent (*consanguinity*) is thought to mark off a special category of kin, relationships with whom are different in kind from relationships with non-kin. Further significant distinctions may be made between relatives traced through the father and through the mother, between closer and more distant kin, and between kin of different generations. In small-scale, less mobile, pre-industrial societies, kinship relationships may provide the primary basis for association. Systems vary considerably in terms of residence patterns, marriage laws, and inheritance. » family; marriage; matrilineal descent

Kintai Bridge [kin**tiy**] 'Bridge of the Brocade Sash', famous for the grace of its five arches. Built at Iwakuni, Japan, in 1673, the original wood, bronze, and iron structure was swept away in 1950. The present bridge is a replica. » bridge (engineering) [i]

Kintyre Peninsula in Strathclyde, SWC Scotland; bounded by the North Channel and the Atlantic Ocean (W) and the Firth of Clyde (E); runs S to the **Mull of Kintyre** from a narrow isthmus; 64 km/40 ml long; average width 13 km/8 ml; chief town, Campbeltown. » Scotland [i]; Strathclyde

Kipling, (Joseph) Rudyard (1865–1936) British writer, born in Bombay, India. Educated at boarding school in England, he returned in 1880 to India, where he worked as a journalist. His satirical verses and short stories, such as *Plain Tales from the Hills* (1888) and *Soldiers Three* (1889) won him a reputation in England, to which he returned in 1889 and settled in London. His verse collections *Barrack Room Ballads* (1892) and *The Seven Seas* (1896) were highly successful, as were the two *Jungle Books* (1894–5), which have become classic animal stories, *Kim* (1901), and the *Just So Stories* (1902). He was awarded the Nobel Prize for Literature in 1907, and died in London. » English literature; satire; short story

Kipping, Frederick (Stanley) (1863–1949) British chemist, born in Manchester. He studied in Manchester and Germany, and worked in Nottingham (1897–1936) as professor of chemistry. He is now best known as the founder of silicone chemistry, although the technical uses for silicones were developed by others from 1940 onwards. He died at Criccieth, Wales. » silicone

Kirchhoff, Gustav (Robert) [**keerkh**hohf] (1824–87) German physicist, born at Königsberg. After lecturing at Berlin (1947), he became professor of physics at Breslau (1850) and Heidelberg (1854), and in 1875 of mathematical physics at Berlin. He investigated electrical networks, heat, and optics, and with Bunsen developed the technique of spectroscopy, with which they discovered caesium and rubidium. He died in Berlin. » Bunsen; Kirchhoff's laws; spectroscopy

Kirchhoff's laws Laws applying to direct current theory, stated by German physicist Gustav Kirchhoff in 1846. At any point where three or more components join, the total current into the junction is zero; and, for a closed circuit loop, the sum of all potential differences around the loop is zero. Useful in circuit analysis, the laws are the direct consequences of charge and energy conservation. » current (electricity); Kirchhoff; potential difference

Kirchner, Ernst Ludwig [**kirkh**ner] (1880–1938) German artist, born at Aschaffenburg. He studied architecture at Dresden, but then turned to painting, and became the leading spirit in the formation of the Expressionist group, Die Brücke (1905–13). Many of his works were confiscated by the Nazis as degenerate in 1937, and he committed suicide near Davos, Switzerland. » Brücke, die; Expressionism; German art

Kirghizia [kir**gi**zia], Russ **Kirgizskaya** or **Kirgiziya** pop (1989) 4 290 000; area 198 500 sq km/76 621 sq ml. Republic in NE Middle Asia; bounded SE and E by China; largely occupied by the Tien Shan Mts, highest point within the republic at Pik Pobedy (7 439 m/24 406 ft); chief river, the Naryn; largest lake, L Issyk-Kul; proclaimed a constituent republic, 1936; independence, 1991; capital, Bishkek (Frunze); metallurgy, machines, coal, natural gas, textiles, food processing, gold; wheat, cotton, tobacco, animal husbandry; nomadic Kirgiz people comprise a third of the population. » Soviet Union [i]

Kiribati, formerly **Gilbert Islands**, official name **Republic of Kiribati** [**ki**ribas] pop (1990e) 71 100; total land area 717 sq km/ 277 sq ml. Group of 33 low-lying coral islands scattered over c.3 million sq km/1.2 million sq ml of the C Pacific Ocean; comprises the Gilbert Group, Phoenix Is, and eight of the 11 Line Is; capital, Tarawa; timezone GMT −12; population chiefly Micronesian; main languages, Gilbertese and English; chief religion, Christianity; unit of currency, the Australian dollar; islands seldom rise to more than 4 m/13 ft, usually consisting of a reef enclosing a lagoon; Banaba rises to 87 m/285 ft; maritime equatorial climate in C islands, tropical further N and S; average annual temperature 27°C; average annual rainfall 1 020 mm/40 in (near Equator), 3 050 mm/ 120 in (extreme N and S); rainy season (Nov–Apr); periodic drought in some islands; Gilbert and Ellice Is proclaimed a British protectorate, 1892; annexed, 1915; Ellice Is severed links with Gilbert Is to form separate dependency of Tuvalu, 1975; Gilbert independence as Kiribati, 1979; a sovereign and democratic republic, with a president and an elected 39-member House of Assembly; phosphates, copra, coconuts, bananas, pandanus, breadfruit, papaya, sea fishing. » Kiritimati; Line Islands; Pacific Ocean; Phoenix Islands; Tuvalu; RR26 national holidays; RR54 political leaders

Kiritimati, Eng **Christmas Island** 2°00N 157°30W, pop (1985) 1 737; area 390 sq km/150 sq ml. Largest atoll in the world, one of the Line Is, Kiribati, C Pacific Ocean, 2 000 km/1 250 ml S of Honolulu; indented on the E by the Bay of Wrecks; visited by Captain Cook, 1777; annexed by the British, 1888; used as an air base; nuclear testing site in late 1950s; coconut plantations. » Cook, James; Kiribati; Line Islands

Kirkwall 58°59N 2°58W, pop (1981) 5 995. Port capital of Orkney, N Scotland; on island of Mainland, between Wide Firth (N) and Scapa Flow (S); airport; fishing, textiles, tourism, oil; Earl Patrick's palace (1607), St Magnus Cathedral (1137–1200), Tankerness House (1574), museum of Orkney life. » Orkney; Scotland [i]

Kirov, Sergey Mironovich [**ki**rof] (1886–1934) Russian revolutionary and politician, born at Urzhun, and educated at Kazan. He played an active part in the October Revolution and Civil War, and during the 1920s held a number of leading provincial Party posts. In 1934 he became a full member of the central Politburo and at the 17th Party Congress was elected a Secretary of the Central Committee. Later that year he was assassinated at his Leningrad headquarters, possibly at the instigation of Stalin, and his death served as the pretext for a widespread campaign of reprisals. He was buried in Red Square, Moscow. » Bolsheviks; Bukharin; communism; October Revolution; Stalin; Trotsky

Kisalföld [**kees**holfuld], Eng **Little Alföld** Flat, lowland geographical region in NW Hungary; bounded by the R Danube, the Hungarian Alps and the Transdanubian Central Mountain Range. » Hungary [i]

Kisangani [keesan**gah**nee], formerly **Stanleyville** (to 1966) 0°33N 25°14E, pop (1976e) 339 210. Capital of Haut-Zaire region, NC Zaire; on the Zaire R, 1 250 km/775 ml NE of Kinshasa; founded by Stanley, 1882; airport; university (1963); agricultural trade, textiles, brewing, furniture. » Zaire [i]

Kissinger, Henry A(lfred) (1923–) US academic and statesman, born at Fürth, Germany. His family emigrated to the USA in 1938 to escape the Nazi persecution of Jews. He was educated at Harvard, and after war service he worked for a number of public agencies before joining the Harvard faculty (1962–71). He became President Nixon's adviser on national security affairs in 1969, was the main American figure in the negotiations to end the Vietnam War (for which he shared the 1973 Nobel Peace Prize), and became Secretary of State in 1973, serving under Nixon and Ford. His 'shuttle diplomacy' was aimed at bringing about peace between Israel and the Arab states, and resulted in a notable improvement in Israeli-Egyptian relations. After leaving public office (1977), he became professor of diplomacy at Georgetown, and established Kissinger Associates, a consulting firm. » Arab-Israeli Wars; Ford, Gerald R; Nixon, Richard M; Vietnam War

Kistna, River » **Krishna, River**

kit A small violin, with usually four strings and a narrow body, in use from the 16th-c to the 19th-c, especially (though not exclusively) by dancing masters. » string instrument **1** [i]; violin

kit-cat portrait A life-size half-length portrait painted on a canvas 36 × 28 in (c.90 × 70 cm). The term derives from Kneller's series of portraits painted c.1700–17 of the members of the Kit-cat Club in London (now in the National Portrait Gallery). » English art; Kneller

Kita-Kyushu [**kee**ta **kyoo**shoo] 33°52N 130°49E, pop (1980) 1 065 078. City in Fukuoka prefecture, N Kyushu, Japan; comprises former towns of Tobata, Kokura, Moji, Wakamatsu, and Yawata; airport; railway; Japan's leading centre for chemicals and heavy industry. » Kyushu

Kitchen Cabinet An informal group of advisers surrounding a US president. The term originated in the mid-19th-c in the administration of President Jackson. » Jackson, Andrew

Kitchener (of Khartoum and of Broome), (Horatio) Herbert, 1st Earl (1850–1916) British field marshal and statesman, born near Ballylongford, Kerry, Ireland. He joined the Royal Engineers in 1871, and served in Palestine (1874), Cyprus (1878), and the Sudan (1883). By the final rout of the Khalifa at Omdurman (1898), he won back the Sudan for Egypt, and was made a peer. Successively Chief-of-Staff and Commander-in-Chief in South Africa (1900–2), he brought the Boer War to an end, and was made viscount. He then became Commander-in-Chief in India (1902–9), Consul-General in Egypt (1911), and Secretary for War (1914), for which he organized manpower on a vast scale ('Kitchener armies'). He was lost with HMS *Hampshire*, mined off the Orkney Is. » Boer Wars; World War 1

kite A hawk of the subfamily *Milvinae* (**true kites**) or *Elaninae* (**white-tailed kites**), found worldwide; the most varied and diverse group of hawks; eats insects, snails, and small vertebrates, or scavenges. (Family: *Accipitridae*, c.27 species.) » hawk; snail kite

kithara A musical instrument of classical antiquity, resembling a

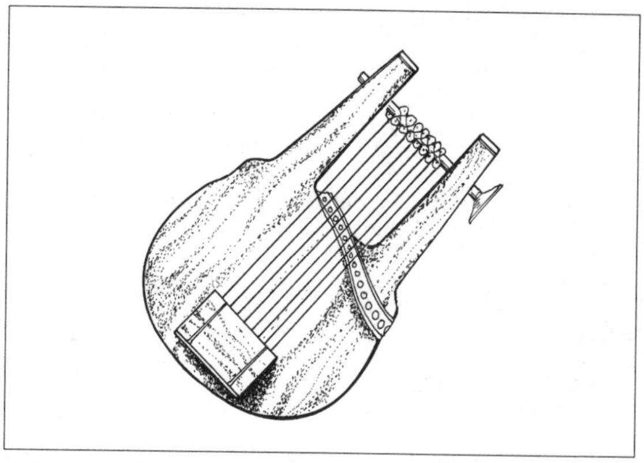

Kithara

lyre. It had a wooden resonator (usually rectangular) from which two arms (usually hollow) extended upwards, and were connected by a crossbar from which between three and eleven strings were stretched to the base of the resonator. These strings were plucked with a plectrum. The lyre, a smaller instrument, had a resonator of tortoise-shell. » lyre; plectrum; string instrument **2** [i]

kittiwake Either of two species of marine bird, genus *Rissa*: the **black-legged kittiwake** (*Rissa tridactyla*), from N areas of the N oceans; and the **red-legged kittiwake** (*Rissa brevirostris*), from the Bering Sea. They spend much time at sea, and nest on cliffs in large numbers. (Family: *Laridae*.) » gull

Kitwe [**keet**way] 12°48S 28°14E, pop (1980) 314 794. Modern mining city in Copperbelt province, Zambia; Zambia's second largest town; extended in 1970 to include several townships; railway; copper, electrical equipment, paint, fibreglass, food processing, iron foundry, furniture, clothing, plastics; Mindolo Ecumenical Centre. » Copperbelt; Zambia [i]

Kitzbühel [**kitz**büel] 47°27N 12°23E, pop (1981) 7 840. Winter sports resort and capital of Kitzbühel district, Tirol, C Austria, in the Kitzbüheler Alps, on the route to the Thurn Pass; mining of copper and silver in the 16th–17th-c; railway; health resort, tourism, casino; Kitzbühel Fair (Aug). » Alps

kiva [**kee**va] A subterranean circular room c.5–14 m/16–46 ft in diameter and 2.5 m/8 ft high, with a ceiling hatch and access ladder, used by the prehistoric Anasazi Indians of the American SW for meetings, rituals, storytelling, weaving, and crafts. Inside is a firepit and *sipapu*, a small hole in the floor symbolizing the point at which the ancestral Anasazi emerged from the underworld. » Anasazi; Pueblo (Indians)

Kivi, Aleksis, pseudonym of **Alexis Stenvall** (1834–72) Finnish dramatist and novelist, born at Nurmijärvi. He wrote penetratingly of Finnish peasant life, notably in *Seitsemän veljestä* (1870, Seven Brothers), and is now recognized as one of his country's greatest writers. He died insane, poverty-stricken, and unrecognized, at Tuusula. » drama; novel

Kivu, Lake [**kee**voo] area 4 750 sq km/1 800 sq ml. Lake in EC Africa; highest lake in the Albertine Rift, on the frontier between Zaire and Rwanda; length, c.95 km/60 ml; width, 50 km/30 ml; altitude, 1 460 m/4 790 ft; drains into L Tanganyika via the Ruzizi R; contains Idiwi I (S); European discovery by German explorer Count von Gotzen. » Africa; Rift Valley

Kiwanis International » **service club**

kiwi A flightless nocturnal bird; native to New Zealand; small eyes; acute sense of smell (rare in birds); long curved bill with nostrils at tip; strong legs; tail and wings not visible through thick, shaggy plumage; usually inhabits woodland; eats worms, other invertebrates, and berries; nests in burrow. Its egg is the largest, relative to body size, of any bird (25% of the female's weight). (Genus: *Apteryx*, 3 species. Family: *Apterygidae*.)

kiwi fruit A woody climber, native to China, and also called **Chinese gooseberry**, but cultivated on a commercial scale in New Zealand, hence the better-known name; leaves rough, oval to heart-shaped; flowers creamy, 6-petalled, in axillary clusters; fruit oblong-oval, furry with reddish-green hairs, flesh green, sweet, with surrounding black seeds. (*Actinidia chinensis*. Family: *Actinidiaceae*.) » climbing plant

Kizil Irmak ('red river') [**kuzul irmak**], ancient **Halys** Longest river of Turkey; rises in the Kizil Dağ, NC Turkey, and flows in a wide arc SW then generally N to enter the Black Sea N of Bafra; length 1 355 km/842 ml; important source of hydro-electric power. » Turkey [i]

Kjölen Mountains [**kyer**luhn] or **Kolen Mountains** Mountain range along the boundary between NE Norway and NW Sweden; rises to 2 111 m/6 926 ft at Kebnekaise, Sweden's highest peak; source of many rivers flowing SE to the Gulf of Bothnia. » Sweden [i]

Klammer, Franz (1953–) Austrian alpine skier, born at Mooswald. He was the Olympic downhill champion in 1976, and the World Cup downhill champion five times (1975–8, 1983). In 1974–84 he won a record 25 World Cup downhill races. » skiing

Klaproth, Martin Heinrich [**klap**roht] (1743–1817) German chemist, born at Wernigerode. After working as an apothecary, he became a teacher of chemistry, and the first professor of chemistry at Berlin. He devised new analytical methods, and discovered zirconium, uranium, strontium, and titanium. He died in Berlin. » chemical elements

Klee, Paul [klay] (1879–1940) Swiss artist, born at München-buchsee, near Bern. He studied at Munich and settled there, becoming a member of the Blaue Reiter group (1911–12). He then taught at the Bauhaus (1920–32), and after returning to Bern (1933) many of his works were confiscated in Germany. His early work consists of bright watercolours, but after 1919 he worked in oils, producing small-scale, mainly abstract pictures, as in his 'Twittering Machine' (New York). He died at Muralto-Locarno, Switzerland. » abstract art; Bauhaus; Blaue Reiter, der; etching; watercolour

Klein, Calvin (Richard) (1942–) US fashion designer, born in New York City. He graduated from the Fashion Institute of Technology in 1962, and set up his own firm in 1968. He quickly achieved recognition, becoming known for under-statement, and for the simple but sophisticated style of his clothes, including 'designer jeans'. » fashion

Kleist, (Bernd) Heinrich (Wilhelm) von [klyist] (1777–1811) German dramatist and poet, born at Frankfurt an der Oder. He left the army in 1799 to study, and soon devoted himself to literature. His best plays are still popular, notably *Prinz Friedrich von Homburg* (1821). His novellas, such as *Michael Kohlhaas* (1810–11), also became well known. He committed suicide at Wannsee. » drama; German literature; poetry

Klemperer, Otto (1885–1973) German conductor, born at Breslau. He studied at Frankfurt and Berlin, first appeared as a conductor in 1906, made a name as a champion of modern music, and was appointed director of the Kroll Opera in Berlin (1927–31). Nazism drove him to the USA, where he directed the Los Angeles Symphony Orchestra (1933–9). In his later years, he concentrated mainly on the German classical com-posers, and was particularly known for his interpretation of Beethoven. He also composed six symphonies, a mass, and Lieder. He died in Zürich. » Beethoven; Lied

Klimt, Gustav (1862–1918) Austrian painter, born at Baum-garten, Vienna. The leading master of the Vienna Sezession, Klimt began with a firm of decorators painting nondescript murals for museums and theatres, but in 1900–3 he painted some murals for the University of Vienna in a new and shocking Symbolist style which caused great controversy. His portraits combine realistically-painted heads with flat abstract backgrounds. He died in Vienna. » Sezession; Symbolists

Klinger, Friedrich Maximilian von (1752–1831) German playwright and romance writer, born at Frankfurt am Main. He became an actor, joined the Russian army, rising to the rank of general, held various government posts, and became curator of the University of Dorpat (1803–17). The 'Sturm-und-Drang' school was named after one of his tragedies. He died at Dorpat, Estonia. » German literature; Sturm und Drang

klipspringer A dwarf antelope native to Africa S of the Sahara; thick yellow-grey speckled coat; black feet; stands on points of small peg-like hooves; short vertical horns; rounded ears with dark radiating lines; inhabits rock outcrops in scrubland. (*Oreotragus oreotragus*.) » antelope

Klondike gold rush A flood of prospectors (largely US) when gold was discovered in Canada Yukon Territory in 1896. The rush lasted for five years, generated an estimated $50 million in gold, established the town of Dawson, and invigorated the economies of British Columbia, Alberta, Alaska, and Washing-ton State. » Yukon

Klopstock, Friedrich Gottlieb (1724–1803) German poet, born at Quedlinburg. Inspired by Virgil and Milton, he began *Der Messias* (The Messiah) as a student at Jena (1745), completing it in 1773. He lived in Copenhagen (1751–71), then moved to Hamburg, where he died. Regarded in his own time as a great religious poet, he helped to inaugurate the golden age of German literature, especially by his lyrics and odes. » German literature; Milton; ode; poetry; Virgil

Klosters [**kloh**sterz] 46°54N 9°54E. Alpine winter skiing resort in Graubünden canton, E Switzerland; on R Landquart, NE of Davos, with which it shares snowfields; comprises the villages of Platz, Dörfli, and Brücke; Kloster Pass (12 km/7 ml E) leads to Austria; children's ski school. » Alps

Kluane National park in SW Yukon territory, NW Canada; contains part of the St Elias Mts, rising to 5 950 m/19 521 ft at Mt Logan; area 22 015 sq km/8 498 sq ml; established in 1972; along with the Wrangell–St Elias park, forms the world's largest nature reserve, on both sides of the US/Canadian border; a world heritage site. » Yukon

klystron A device for amplifying microwave beams, in which energy is transferred to the microwave beam via its modulation of an electron beam passing through resonance cavities. It is used in particle accelerators and radar, and may also be used as a producer of microwaves. » electron; microwaves

knapweed The name for many species of *Centaurea*, mostly perennials; characterized by the hard, rounded flower heads surrounded by many closely overlapping bracts which often terminate in a fringed papery border with comb-like teeth; florets purple or yellow. (Genus: *Centaurea*. Family: *Compositae*.) » bract; floret; perennial

knee Commonly used to refer to the region around the knee-cap (*patella*); more specifically, in anatomy, the largest joint in the human body, being the articulation between the femoral projections (*condyles*) and the tibial plateaux, and including the joint between the patella and the femur. It allows a wide range of movement, yet still retains a high degree of stability, because of the presence and arrangement of the ligaments of the joint. It contains the medial and lateral *menisci* (pieces of fibrous tissue between the femur and tibia), which help compensate for the differences in shape between the surfaces, aid in joint lubrica-tion, assist in weight-bearing, and act as shock absorbers. » femur; housemaid's knee; joint; tibia; Plate XIII

Kneller, Sir Godfrey, originally **Gottfried Kniller** (1646–1723) English portrait painter, born at Lübeck, Germany. He studied at Amsterdam and in Italy, went to London in 1676, and in 1680 was appointed court painter. He was knighted in 1692, and made a baronet in 1715. His best-known works are his 48 portraits of members of the Whig 'Kit-Cat Club' (1702–17), and of nine sovereigns. He died in London. » English art; kit-cat portrait

Knesset [**kne**set] The 120-member Israeli parliament. Its term of office is four years, and the country's President is elected by the Knesset for five years. » Israel [i]

knight In the UK, a title of honour granted as a reward for services (Fr *Chevalier*, Ger *Ritter*); originally (in the Middle Ages) men who formed an elite cavalry. The ideal of knight-hood involved the maintenance of personal honour, religious devotion, and loyalty to one's lord. This ideal was most nearly achieved at the time of the Crusades (11th-c–13th-c). » (Orders of) Bath/British Empire/Companions of Honour/ Garter/St Michael and St George/Thistle; Hospitallers; knight bachelor; Templars; Légion d'Honneur

Knight, Dame Laura (1877–1970) British artist, born at Long Eaton, Derbyshire. Educated at Nottingham, she married her fellow student, portrait painter **Harold Knight** (1874–1961). She produced a long series of oil paintings of the ballet, the circus and gipsy life, in a lively and forceful style, and also executed a number of watercolour landscapes. She was made a Dame in 1929. » English art

knight bachelor (KB) In the UK, the lowest, but most ancient, form of knighthood, originating in the reign of Henry III. A KB is not a member of any order of chivalry. » knight

Knights Hospitallers/of Jerusalem/of Malta/of Rhodes » **Hospitallers**

Knights of Labor (1878–93) A US industrial union that tried to organize all workers in support of a large-scale political and social programme, regardless of age, race, and colour. The knights reached a membership of 700 000 in 1886, but then declined.

Knights Templars » **Templars**

knitting An ancient craft used for making fabric by linking together loops of yarn using two or three hand-held needles. The first knitting machine was invented by English clergyman William Lee (c.1550–c.1610). Machines are now used to produce complex knitted garments and fabrics of many kinds, but they cannot create all the intricate designs that are commonly produced by skilled hand knitters. The manufacture of knitted fabrics in tubular form is known as *circular knitting*; such fabrics are often used in underwear and sportswear. » yarn

knocking An audible shuddering sound produced by an engine, because of the uneven burning of its air/fuel mixture. A high-compression ratio spark ignition engine gives good fuel consumption for a given power output. However, a high-compression ratio also interferes with the fuel's combustion process, leading to uneven ignition, unsteady combustion, and eventually damage. Diesel engines tend to have knocking characteristics opposite to those of a spark ignition engine. To overcome these problems, antiknocking fuels are used. » antiknock; diesel engine

Knossos [**kno**suhs] An Aegean Bronze Age town at Kephala, NC Crete, noted for the sophistication of its art and architecture. Flourishing c.1900–1400 BC, the settlement covered c.50 ha/125 acres, its mansions and houses linked by paved roads and dominated by the 19 000 sq m/4.7 acre Minoan palace discovered in 1899, and later partly reconstructed by Sir Arthur Evans. The traditional association with Minos, the labyrinth of Theseus, and the Minotaur has no historical basis. » Evans, Arthur; Minoan civilization; Minotaur

knot Either of two species of sandpiper, genus *Calidris*: the widespread **knot** or **red knot** (*Calidris canutus*); and the **eastern knot** or **great knot** (*Calidris tenuirostris*) from E regions of the Old World. (Genus: *Calidris*, 2 species.) » sandpiper

knotgrass A spreading annual, a very widespread weed; each node of the stem enclosed in a silvery sheath; leaves small, elliptical, with small pink or white flowers in the axils. (*Polygonum aviculare*. Family: *Polygonaceae*.) » annual

Know-Nothing movement (1856) The popular name for the anti-immigrant American Party in 19th-c USA. It was so called from the response members were instructed to give to questioning: 'I know nothing'.

knowledge-based system A computer system which allows access to a set of knowledge and related rules, and which can be used by people not familiar with the subject. For example, a railway timetable could be incorporated into a knowledge-based system which could readily provide optimum routes for specific journeys. » artificial intelligence; expert system

Knox, John (c.1513–72) Scottish Protestant reformer, born near Haddington, Lothian. A Catholic priest, he acted as notary in Haddington (1540–3), and in 1544 was influenced by George Wishart to work for the Lutheran reformation. After Wishart was burned (1546), Knox joined the reformers defending the castle of St Andrews, and became a minister. After the castle fell to the French, he was kept a prisoner until 1549, then became a chaplain to Edward VI, and was consulted over the Second Book of Common Prayer. On Mary's accession (1553), he fled to Dieppe, and then to Geneva, where he was much influenced by Calvin. He returned to Scotland in 1555 to preach, and then again in 1559, where he won a strong party in favour of reform, and founded the Church of Scotland (1560). He played a lasting part in the composition of *The Scots Confession*, *The First Book of Discipline*, and *The Book of Common Order*. He died in Edinburgh. » Book of Common Prayer; Calvin; Church of Scotland; Mary, Queen of Scots; Reformation; Wishart

Knox, Ronald (Arbuthnot) (1888–1957) British theologian and essayist, born in Birmingham. He was educated at Eton and Oxford, where he became a lecturer (1910), but resigned in 1917 on being converted to Catholicism, was ordained, and appointed Catholic chaplain to the University (1926–39). He wrote an influential translation of the Bible, and several works of apologetics, as well as detective novels. He died at Mells, Somerset. » apologetics; Bible; Roman Catholicism; theology

koala [koh**ah**la] E Australian marsupial; thick soft grey or grey-brown fur with white chest; round head with small eyes, erect fluffy ears, large dark nose pad; tail not obvious; first two fingers oppose other three when climbing; female with pouch opening backwards; eats leaves (mainly of eucalyptus trees); also known (incorrectly) as a **koala bear**. (*Phascolarctos cinereus*. Family: *Phascolarctidae*.) » marsupial [i]

koatimundi » **coati**

kob A grazing antelope native to C Africa; reddish-brown (male may be black) with white throat and black marks on legs; female without horns; male with thick neck and lyre-shaped horns ringed with ridges. (*Kobus kob*, 10 subspecies.) » antelope

Kobe [**koh**bay] 34°40N 135°12E, pop (1980) 1 367 390. Port capital of Hyogo prefecture, C Honshu, Japan, W of Osaka; Japan's leading commercial port; continuing land reclamation on seaward side of the city; railway; two universities (1948, 1949); shipbuilding, iron and steel, chemicals, saké; harbour and naval museum, Museum of Namban Art, Minatogawa Shrine; Nankosai Festival of Minatogawa Shrine (May). » Honshu

Koblenz » **Coblenz**

Koch, Ed(ward) (1924–) US politician, born and educated in New York City. He practised law and became a member of the City Council (1967). Elected to Congress as a Democrat in 1969, he became Mayor of New York in 1978, and in the 1980s was a widely known political figure in the USA. » Democratic Party

Koch, (Heinrich Hermann) Robert [kokh] (1843–1910) German bacteriologist, born at Klausthal. Educated at Göttingen, he became a physician and surgeon, and settled in Wollstein. He discovered the tuberculosis bacillus (1882), and led a German expedition to Egypt and India, where he discovered the cholera bacillus (1883). He became professor and director of the hygienic institute at Berlin (1885), and director of the new institute for infectious diseases (1891). Winner of the 1905 Nobel Prize for Physiology or Medicine, and the major figure in medical bacteriology, he died in Baden-Baden. » cholera; tuberculosis

Köchel, Ludwig Ritter von [**ker**khuhl] (1800–77) Austrian musicologist, born at Stein. A botanist by training, he is known as the compiler of the catalogue of Mozart's works, which he arranged in chronological order, giving them the numbers (K1, etc) commonly used to identify them today. He died in Vienna. » Mozart

Kodály, Zoltán [**koh**diy] (1882–1967) Hungarian composer, born at Kecskemét. He studied at the Budapest Conservatory, where he became professor. Among his best-known works are the *Háry János* suite (1926) and several choral compositions, especially his *Psalmus Hungaricus* (1923) and *Te Deum* (1936). He also published editions of folk songs with Bartók. He died in Budapest. » Bartók

Kodiak bear » **brown bear**

Kodiak Island 57°20N 153°40W, pop (1984) 13 389. Island in the Gulf of Alaska, USA; 160 km/100 ml long; scene of the first settlement in Alaska (by the Russians, 1784); till 1804 the centre for Russian interests in the USA and of the fur trade; dairying, cattle and sheep raising, fur trapping, fishing, farming; home of the Kodiak brown bear (grizzly), the largest living carnivore. » Alaska

Koechlin, Pat » **Smythe, Pat**

koedoe » **kudu**

Koestler, Arthur [**kers**ler] (1905–83) Hungarian-born and naturalized British author and journalist, born in Budapest. He studied science at Vienna, embraced the cause of Zionism, and became a journalist and editor. His masterpiece is the political novel *Darkness at Noon* (1940). His nonfiction books and essays deal with politics, scientific creativity, and parapsychology, notably *The Act of Creation* (1964), and he wrote several autobiographical volumes. He and his wife were active members of the Voluntary Euthanasia Society, and, after he developed a terminal illness, they committed suicide. » English literature; euthanasia; novel; parapsychology

Koffka, Kurt (1886–1941) German psychologist, born in Berlin. At the University of Giessen (1911–24) he helped to conduct experiments in perception, which led to the founding of the *Gestalt* school of psychology. In 1927 he moved to the USA, becoming professor of psychology at Smith College. He died at Northampton, Massachusetts. » Gestalt psychology

Kofun [**koh**fuhn] The burial-mounds characteristic of early historic Japan, which have given their name to the archaeological period AD c.300–700. The most spectacular, keyhole-shaped and moated like that of the Emperor Suinin in the Nara Basin, measure over 400 m/1 300 ft in length. Large hollow clay *haniwa* models of heavily armed warriors were often placed on top or inside. » Nara

Koh-i-noor (Hindi, 'mountain of light') A famous Indian diamond with a history dating back to the 14th-c. It was presented to Queen Victoria in 1850, and is now among the British crown jewels. » crown jewels; diamond

Koheleth » **Ecclesiastes, Book of**

Kohl, Helmut (1930–) German statesman and Chancellor (1982–), born at Ludwigshafen am Rhein. Educated at Frankfurt and Heidelberg, he became a lawyer, and joined the Christian Democrats. In 1976 he moved to Bonn as a member of the Federal Parliament, became Leader of the Opposition, and his Party's candidate for the Chancellorship. After the collapse of the Schmidt coalition in 1982, Kohl was installed as interim Chancellor, and in the elections of 1983 he formed a government which has since adopted a central course between political extremes. » Christian Democrats; Germany [i]; Schmidt

Köhler, Wolfgang [**ker**ler] (1887–1967) German psychologist, born at Tallinn, Estonia. Educated at Berlin, he lectured at Frankfurt (1911), and participated in experiments which led to the formation of the school of *Gestalt* psychology. Professor of psychology at Berlin in 1921, he emigrated to the USA in 1935, where he taught at Swarthmore College, Pennsylvania until 1955, and at Dartmouth College, New Hampshire, from 1958. He died at Enfield, New Hampshire. » Gestalt psychology

kohlrabi [**kohl**rabee] A variety of cabbage with a very short, swollen, green or purple stem resembling a turnip. It is eaten as a vegetable. (*Brassica oleracea*, variety *caulorapa*. Family: *Crucifereae*.) » cabbage; turnip

Kokoschka, Oskar [ko**kosh**ka] (1886–1980) British artist, born at Pöchlarn, Austria. He studied at Vienna (1904–8), and taught at the Dresden Academy of Art (1919–24). He travelled widely, and painted many Expressionist landscapes in Europe. In 1938 he fled to England, becoming naturalized in 1947. From 1953 he lived in Switzerland, and died at Villeneuve. » Expressionism

kola or **cola** An evergreen tree native to tropical Africa. The woody fruits contain glossy nuts high in caffeine, which is released when the nuts are chewed. It is not cultivated, but the nuts of several species are much used in trade, and are an important part of local diet in W Africa. (Genus: *Cola*, 125 species. Family: *Sterculiaceae*.) » caffeine; evergreen plants; nut; tree [i]

Kola Peninsula [**ko**la], Russ **Kol'skiy Poluostrov** Peninsula in Murmanskaya oblast, NW European Russia, forming the NE extension of Scandinavia; length, 400 km/250 ml; width, 240 km/150 ml; separates the Barents Sea (N) from the White Sea (S); numerous rivers and small lakes; NE is tundra-covered while the SW is forested; road and rail transport confined to the W; rich mineral deposits. » Russia

Kolbe, Maksymilian (Maria), St (1894–1941), feast day 14 August. Polish Franciscan priest, born near Lodz. He joined the Franciscans in 1907, and studied at the Gregorian University in Rome. In 1917 he founded a devotional association, the Militia of Mary Immaculate, was ordained in 1918, and became director of a religious centre and publishing company. He was arrested by the Gestapo in 1939, and again in 1941, and imprisoned in Auschwitz, where he gave his life in exchange for one of the condemned prisoners, Franciszek Gajowniczek. He was canonized in 1982.

Kolchak, Alexander Vasilevich (1874–1920) Russian admiral and leader of counter-revolutionary (White) forces during the Russian Civil War, born in the Crimea. He fought in the Russo-Japanese War (1904–5), and in 1916 became Commander of the Black Sea fleet. After the 1917 Revolution he established an anti-Bolshevik government in Siberia, and proclaimed himself 'Supreme Ruler' of Russia. He was captured and shot by Red Army forces in Irkutsk. » Russian Civil War; Russian Revolution; Russo-Japanese War; White Russians

Kolekole » **Haleakala Crater**

Kolen Mountains » **Kjölen Mountains**

Köln » **Cologne**

Kolyma [kuhl**ima**] A gold-producing area around the valley of the R Kolyma which leads to the Arctic Ocean. Used in Stalin's time as a forced labour camp, it is estimated that up to four million people died there as a result of the conditions. » gulag; Stalin

Kolyma, River [kuhl**ima**] River in E Russia, rising in the SE Khrebet Cherskogo, N of the Sea of Okhotsk; flows generally N and NE to enter the E Siberian Sea, forming a delta W of Ambarchik; length, 2 513 km/1 562 ml. » Russia

Komodo [kuh**moh**doh] Small island in Nusa Tenggara Timur province, Indonesia; part of the Lesser Sunda Is; national park established in 1980, area 375 sq km/145 sq ml; home of the Komodo dragon. » Indonesia [i]; Komodo dragon [i]; Sunda Islands

Komodo dragon A rare SE Asian monitor lizard, native to the islands of Komodo, Flores, Pintja, and Padar (Indonesia); the world's largest lizard (length, up to 3 m/10 ft); climbs and swims well; inhabits grassland; often kills pigs and deer; capable of killing an adult water buffalo; occasionally attacks and kills people; also known as **Komodo lizard** or **ora**. (*Varanus komodoensis*.) » Komodo; monitor lizard

Komodo dragon

Kompong Som or **Kampong Saom** 10°38N 103°30E. Seaport in S Cambodia, on Gulf of Thailand; a new city, completed in 1960; chief deepwater port and commercial centre of Cambodia; airfield; railway; oil refining, tractors, fish processing, agricultural trade. » Cambodia [i]

Komsomol The All-Union Leninist Communist League of Youth, founded in 1918, incorporating almost all persons between the ages of 14 and 28. Its purpose being the socialization of youth in the thought and ways of the Communist Party. It disbanded in 1991. » Communist Party of the Soviet Union

Kon Tiki [kon **tee**kee] A balsa wood raft built in 1947 by Thor Heyerdahl. He and five others sailed 6 000 km/3 800 ml from S America to Polynesia in the 13.7 m/45 ft long raft to prove his theories on the migration of early man. The vessel is now preserved in an Oslo museum. » Heyerdahl

Konev, Ivan Stepanovich [**kon**ef] (1897–1973) Soviet military commander and Marshal of the Soviet Union (1944), born at

Lodeyno. He was drafted into the Tsarist army in 1916, and joined the Red Army in 1918. During World War 2 he commanded several different fronts against the Germans. He then became Commander-in-Chief, Ground Forces (1946–50), first Deputy Minister of Defence, and Commander-in-Chief of the Warsaw Pact forces (1956–60). He died in Moscow and was buried in Red Square. » communism; Russian Civil War; World War 2

Kongo An African kingdom situated to the S of the R Congo which by the 15th-c had a coastline of 250 km/150 ml and reached inland for 400 km/250 ml. It was already involved in trade in ivory, copper, and slaves when the Portuguese arrived in the area in 1482. Some of its kings accepted Christianity, but it was disrupted by the stepping up of the slave trade, and declined during the 18th-c when the Portuguese turned their attention S to Angola. » African history; Congo; slave trade

kongoni » **hartebeest**

Konstanz » **Constance**

Konya [**kon**ya], ancient **Iconium** 37°51N 32°30E, pop (1980) 329 139. Holy city and capital of Konya province, SC Turkey, 260 km/162 ml S of Ankara; visited by St Paul; order of the Whirling Dervishes founded here by Islamic mystical poet, Mevlana; airfield; railway; trade centre of a rich agricultural and livestock-raising region; carpets, textiles, leather; notable Seljuk architecture; annual ceremony of the dance to commemorate the death of Mevlana (Dec). » dervish; Paul, St; Turkey [i]

kookaburra Either of two species of bird of the kingfisher family: the **laughing kookaburra** or **laughing jackass** (*Dacelo novaeguinae*) from Australia; and the **blue-winged kookaburra** or **howling jackass** (*Dacelo leachii*) from Australia and New Guinea. They inhabit dry forest and savannah, eat insects and small vertebrates, and have loud laugh-like cries. (Family: *Alcedinidae*.) » kingfisher

Kópavogur [**kop**avogur] 64°06N 21°56W, pop (1983) 14 433. Second largest town in Iceland, in Suðurland region, SW Iceland; developed since 1945 to house people working in Reykjavík. » Iceland [i]; Reykjavík

kopje » **tor**

Koran or **Qu'ran** [**kurhan**] The sacred book of Islam. It is held to be the direct word of God, inscribed in heaven, and revealed piecemeal to the Prophet Mohammad as a message for all humanity. The text itself is regarded as sacred. » Allah; Islam; Mohammad

Korda, Sir Alexander, originally **Sándor Laszlo Korda** (1893–1956) Hungarian film producer, born at Turkeÿe. First a newspaperman in Budapest, he became a film producer there, then in Vienna, Berlin, and Hollywood, where he directed for First National. He moved to the UK, and in 1932 founded London Film Productions and Denham studios. His many films as producer include *The Private Life of Henry VIII* (1932), which he also directed, *The Thief of Baghdad* (1940), *The Third Man* (1949), and *Richard III* (1956). Knighted in 1942, he died in London.

Kordestan » **Kurdistan**

Korea or **South Korea**, official name **Republic of Korea**, Korean **Tae Han Minguk** pop (1990e) 42 795 000; area 98 913 sq km/ 38 180 sq ml. Republic of E Asia occupying the S half of the Korean peninsula; consists of nine provinces and four special cities with provincial status (Seoul, Inchon, Taegu, Pusan); bordered W by the Yellow Sea, E by the Sea of Japan, S by the Korean Strait, and N by North Korea, from which it is separated by a demilitarized zone at 38°N; capital, Seoul; timezone GMT +9; population mainly Korean, with a small Chinese minority; official language, Korean; chief religions Confucianism, Shamanism, Christianity, Buddhism; unit of currency, the won; an official observer at the United Nations, not holding UN membership.

Physical description. Taebaek Sanmaek range runs N–S along the E coast, reaching heights of over 900 m/3 000 ft; descends through a series of ridges to broad, undulating coastal lowlands; c.3 000 islands off the W and S coasts; largest is Cheju do, which contains Korea's highest peak, 1 950 m/ 6 398 ft; extreme continental climate, with cold winters and hot summers; typhoons can arrive in wettest months (Jun–Sep);

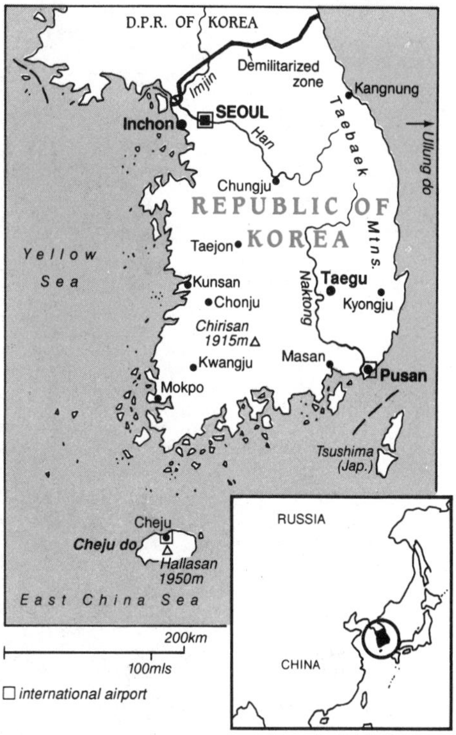

average daily temperatures at Seoul −9–0°C (Jan), 22–31°C (Aug); rainfall minimum 20 mm/0.8 in (Feb), maximum 376 mm/14.8 in (Jul).

History and government. Ruled by the ancient Choson dynasty until 1st-c BC; split into three rival kingdoms, united in 668 by the Silla dynasty; succeeded by the Koryo dynasty, 935; Yi dynasty, 1392–1910; independence recognized by China, 1895; annexation by Japan, 1910; entered by Russia (from N) and USA (from S) to enforce the Japanese surrender, dividing the country by the 38th parallel; North Korean forces invaded, 1950; UN forces assisted South Korea in stopping the advance, 1950–3; military coup, 1961; assassination of Park Chung Hee, 1979; summit talks with North Korea, 1990; governed by a president, elected indirectly by a 5 000-member electoral college for a single 5-year term; leads and appoints a State Council; a 299-member National Assembly is elected for four years.

Economy. Light consumer goods, with a shift towards heavy industries; petrochemicals, textiles, electrical machinery, footwear, steel, ships, fish; one of the world's largest deposits of tungsten; only a fifth of Korea suitable for cultivation; rice, barley, wheat, beans, grain, tobacco; cattle, pigs, poultry, fishing. » Korean; Korean War; Seoul; RR26 national holidays; RR54 political leaders

Korea, North, official name **Democratic People's Republic of Korea**, Korean **Choson Minjujuui In'min Konghwaguk** pop (1990e) 22 937 000; area 122 098 sq km/47 130 sq ml. Socialist state in East Asia, in the N half of the Korean peninsula; divided into nine provinces; bordered N by China, NE by Russia, W by Korea Bay and the Yellow Sea, and E by the Sea of Japan; separated from South Korea to the S by a demilitarized zone of 1 262 sq km/487 sq ml; capital, P'yongyang; timezone GMT +9; official language, Korean; traditional religions, Buddhism and Confucianism, but religious activities now minimal; unit of currency, the won of 100 chon.

Physical description and climate. On a high plateau occupying the N part of a mountainous peninsula which projects SE from China; many areas rise to over 2 000 m/7 000 ft; falls NW to the Yalu R valley; lower mountains and foothills (S) descend to coastal plains, wider in the W; temperate climate, with warm summers and severely cold winters; rivers freeze for 3–4 months, and ice blocks harbours; daily temperatures at P'yon-

gyang, −3°C to −13°C (Jan), 20–29°C (Jul–Aug); average rainfall 11 mm/0.4 in (Feb), 237 mm/9.3 in (Jul).

History and government. Korean Peninsula conquered by Chinese, 1392; formally annexed by Japan, 1895; N area occupied by Soviet troops, meeting US troops from the S along latitude 38°N; Korean War, 1950–3; demilitarized zone established, 1953; reunification talks (1980) broken off by North Korea; summit talks with South Korea, 1990; governed by a Supreme People's Assembly of 655 members, elected every four years; power in hands of the Korean Workers' (Communist) Party, which elects a Central Committee, and whose leader is the president.

Economy. Traditionally agricultural population on low coastal zones in the E and W; extensive destruction during the Korean War, but rapid recovery with Soviet and Chinese aid; Western technology and increased military spending in the 1970s resulted in considerable overseas debts; machine building, chemicals, mining, metallurgy, textiles, food processing; coal, phosphates, iron, magnesium, tungsten, copper, lead, zinc; c.48% of workforce employed in agriculture, generally on large-scale collective farms; rice, maize, vegetables, livestock, wheat, barley, rape, sugar, millet, sorghum, beans, tobacco; timber, fishing. » communism; Korean; Korean War; P'yongyang; RR54 political leaders

Korean A language of uncertain origin, showing resemblances to the Altaic family and to Japanese. It is spoken by over 50 million people in N and S Korea (where it is the official language), China, Japan, and Russia. » Altaic; Japanese

Korean War (1950–3) A war between communist and non-communist forces in Korea, which had been partitioned along the 38th parallel in 1945 after Japan's defeat. The communist North invaded the South in 1950 after a series of border clashes, and a United Nations force intervened, driving the invaders back to the Chinese frontier. China then entered the war, and together with the N Koreans occupied Seoul. The UN forces counter-attacked, and by 1953, when an armistice was signed, had retaken all territory S of the 38th parallel. » Korea [i]; Korea, North [i]; MacArthur, Douglas; United Nations

Kórinthos » **Corinth**

Kornberg, Arthur (1918–) US biochemist, born in New York City. He was a researcher at the National Institutes of Health in Maryland (1942–53), then became professor of microbiology at Washington University, St Louis (1953–9), and professor of biochemistry at Stanford (from 1959). In 1959 he shared the Nobel Prize for Physiology or Medicine for showing how DNA molecules are duplicated in bacterial cells, and replicating this process in the test tube. » DNA [i]

Korolyov, Sergei (Pavlovich) [**ko**rolyof] (1907–66) Russian rocketry pioneer, aerospace engineer, and space programme leader, born in Zhitomir, and educated in Odessa, Kiev, and Moscow. He was the leader of the team that developed and launched the first Soviet liquid-fuelled rocket (1933), and during World War 2 he worked on aircraft jet-assisted take-off systems. Later, he developed the first Soviet intercontinental ballistic missile, and was leader of the Soviet space programme. He died in Moscow. » jet engine [i]; rocket; Soviet space programme

Koror [**koh**raw] 7°21N 134°31E. Capital town of Belau, W Pacific Ocean, on Koror I; airport on neighbouring island of Babeldoab; tuna, copra, boatbuilding; Belau National Museum. » Belau

korrigum » **topi**

Kós » **Cos**

Kosciusko, Mount [koseeu**hs**koh] 36°28S 148°17E. Highest mountain in Australia (2 228 m/7 310 ft); in the Snowy Mts of the Australian Alps, New South Wales; within a National Park (6 458 sq km/2 493 sq ml); a popular winter sports area. » Australia [i]

Kościuszko or **Kościusko, Thaddeusz (Andrzej Bonawentura)** [kosh**chyoosh**koh] (1746–1817) Polish general and patriot, born near Slonim, Lithuania. In 1792, he achieved fame for his defence of Dubienka against a superior force of Russians, and in 1794 became head of the national movement. His defeat of the Russians at Raclawice was followed by a rising in Warsaw; he established a provisional government, but was defeated at Maciejowice (1794) and taken prisoner until 1796. In 1816 he settled at Soleure in Switzerland, where he died. » Bar, Confederation of; Poland, Partitions of

Köseg [**ku**seg] 47°14N 16°37E, pop (1984e) 14 000. Historic town in Vas county, W Hungary; at the foot of the Alps, close to the Austrian frontier; highest town in Hungary; Jurisich Square, castle with Jurisich Miklós Museum. » Hungary [i]

kosher Food fulfilling the requirements of Jewish Law, including the manner of preparation. In orthodox Judaism, only certain animals, which must be ritually slaughtered, may be eaten. » Judaism

Košice [**ko**shitsuh], Ger **Kaschau**, Hungarian **Kassa** 48°43N 21°14E, pop (1984) 214 270. Industrial capital of Východoslovenský region, Slovak Republic, E Czechoslovakia; on R Hornad; fifth largest city in Czechoslovakia; formerly part of Hungary; airport; railway; technical university (1952); iron and steel, textiles, chemicals, tobacco, brewing; 13th-c St Elizabeth Cathedral. » Czechoslovakia [i]

Kosrae, formerly **Kusaie** pop (1980) 5 522; area 100 sq km/ 40 sq ml. Island group, one of the Federated States of Micronesia, W Pacific; capital, Lelu; part of the Trust Territory of the Pacific Is until 1977; airport on Kosrae I; tourism. » Micronesia, Federated States of

Kossuth, Lajos [**ko**sooth] (1802–94) Hungarian statesman, a leader of the 1848 Hungarian Revolution, born at Monok. He practised law, and became a political journalist, for which he was imprisoned (1837–40). In 1847, he became Leader of the Opposition in the Diet; and in 1848 demanded an independent government for Hungary. At the head of the Committee of National Defence, he was appointed Provisional Governor of Hungary (1849), but internal dissensions led to his resignation, and he fled to Turkey, and then to England. He died in Turin. » Hungary [i]; Revolutions of 1848

Kosygin, Alexei Nikolayevich (1904–80) Russian statesman and Premier (1964–80), born in St Petersburg. Educated in Leningrad, he joined the army in 1919, and the Communist Party in 1927. Elected to the Supreme Soviet (1938), he held a variety of industrial posts, becoming a member of the Central Committee (1939–60) and the Politburo (1946–52). Chairman of the State Economic Planning Commission (1959–60), and first Deputy Prime Minister (with Mikoyan) from 1960, he succeeded Khrushchev as Chairman of the Council of Ministers in 1964. He resigned in 1980 because of ill health, and died soon after, in Moscow. » communism; Khrushchev; Mikoyan

koto A Japanese zither, about 185 cm/6 ft long, with 13 silk strings stretched across movable bridges which allow a variety of tunings. It is placed on the floor; the player sits cross-legged or kneels before it, and plucks the strings with three plectra on the right hand, using the left to control the pitch by pressing on the strings. » plectrum; string instrument **2** [i]; zither

Kotor A region of both natural and culturo-historical interest, located on the Gulf of Kotor on the Yugoslav coast; a world heritage area. The area is noted for its plant and marine life, and for its historic settlements, which have played a decisive role in the cultural and artistic development of the Balkans. » Yugoslavia [i]

Kotzebue, August (Friedrich Ferdinand) von [**kotz**uh-byoo] (1761–1819) German dramatist, born at Weimar. He worked in government service in Russia, and wrote about 200 poetic dramas, notably *Menschenhass und Reue* (1789–90, trans The Stranger), as well as tales, satires, and historical works. While on a mission for Emperor Alexander I, he was assassinated at Mannheim by a radical student as an alleged spy. » drama; German literature

Koulouri » **Salamis** (Greece)

koumiss or **kumiss** A fermented drink obtained from ass or mare milk. Originally made by nomadic peoples of C Asia (eg the Tartars), it has been used both as medicine and beverage.

Koussevitsky, Sergei [koosuh**vit**skee] (1874–1951) Russian conductor, born at Tver. He studied in Moscow and gained a wide reputation as a double bass virtuoso before he formed his own orchestra and took up conducting. He was conductor of the Boston Symphony Orchestra (1924–49), and established a Music Foundation which commissioned works from several major composers. He took US nationality in 1941 and died in Boston.

Kowloon, also **Jiulong** area 11 sq km/4 sq ml. Peninsula and region of the British Crown Colony of Hong Kong; one of the most densely populated areas in the world (28 500 people per sq km in 1981); railway link to Guangzhou (Canton); site of Hong Kong's airport; Victoria Harbour lies between the peninsula and Hong Kong I. » Hong Kong [i]

Kozhikode [**koh**zhuhkohd], formerly **Calicut** 11°15N 75°43E, pop (1981) 546 000. Port city in Kerala, SW India; on the Malabar Coast of the Arabian Sea, 530 km/329 ml WSW of Madras; trade centre since the 14th-c; Vasco da Gama's first Indian port of call, 1498; railway; university (1968); textiles, trade in timber, spices, tea, coffee, cashew nuts; gave its name to calico cotton. » Kerala; Gama, Vasco da

Kraepelin, Emil [**kray**puhlin] (1856–1928) German psychiatrist, who graduated at Würzburg in 1878, and became renowned for his work on the classification of mental disorders, published originally in his *Kompendium der Psychiatrie* (1883, Compendium of Psychiatry). He became professor of psychiatry at three universities, finally in 1904 at Munich, where he died. » psychiatry

Krafft-Ebing, Richard von (1840–1902) German psychiatrist, born at Mannheim. Educated in Germany and Switzerland, he became professor of psychiatry at Strassburg (1872), and at Vienna (1889). A specialist in nervous diseases, he was an early investigator of sexual disorders. He died near Graz, Austria. » psychiatry

kraft process A paper pulp-making process, which uses sodium hydroxide and sodium sulphate instead of sulphite. The pulp is stronger and less crude than that made by the sulphite process. The name derives from Swedish *kraft* 'strong'. » paper [i]

krait [kriyt] A venomous Asian snake of genus *Bungarus* (several species); related to the cobra, but smaller and lacks a 'hood'; causes many deaths each year in India. The name is also used for sea snakes of genus *Laticauda*. » cobra; sea snake; snake

Kraków or **Cracow** [**kra**kuf], Ger **Krakau**, ancient **Cracovia** 50°04N 19°57E, pop (1983) 735 200. Industrial capital of Kraków voivodship, S Poland, on R Vistula; third largest city in Poland; capital, 1305–1609; airport; railway; Jagiellonian University, one of the oldest in Europe (1364); technical university (1945); includes Nowa Huta industrial centre, 10 km/6 ml E; pig iron, metallurgy, chemicals, food processing, clothing, printing; cathedral (14th-c), royal castle, city museum; Churches of St Andrew, SS Peter and Paul, St Barbara, the Virgin Mary; Market Square (14th-c), a world heritage site; Kraków Days (Jun). » Poland [i]

Krasnoyarsk [krasnuh**yahsk**] 56°08N 93°00E, pop (1989) 912 000. Fast-growing river-port capital of Krasnoyarskiy kray, W Siberian Russia, on the R Yenisey; founded as a fortress, 1628; grew rapidly after discovery of gold in the area, 19th-c; airport; on the Trans-Siberian Railway; university (1969); heavy machinery, grain harvesters, electrical goods, steel, aluminium. » Russia

Krebs, Sir Hans Adolf (1900–81) German physiologist, born at Hildesheim. He began his research at Freiburg, but was forced to emigrate to England in 1933, where he continued his work at Cambridge, then Sheffield (1935–54) and Oxford (1954–67). He shared the Nobel Prize for Physiology or Medicine in 1953 for his work on the nature of metabolic processes. He was knighted in 1958, and died in Oxford. » Krebs cycle

Krebs cycle A sequence of biochemical reactions in biological systems which results in the release of large amounts of energy; named after Hans Adolf Krebs, and also called the **citric acid cycle**. It is the final pathway for the oxidation of the fuel molecules, ie carbohydrates, fats, and proteins. » Krebs; metabolism

Kreisler, Fritz [**kriy**sler] (1875–1962) Austrian violinist, born in Vienna. After studying at the Conservatoires of Vienna and Paris, he toured the USA (1888–9), and then studied medicine and art. He became internationally known as a violinist, and also composed violin pieces, a string quartet, and an operatta, *Apple Blossoms* (1919), which was a Broadway success. He became a US citizen in 1943, and died in New York City.

Kremlin The mediaeval citadel of a Russian town, generally used with reference to the Kremlin at Moscow, which occupies a wedge-shaped 36 ha/90 acre site by the Moscow R. The Moscow Kremlin, which was built in the 12th-c, was subsequently altered and embellished so that its palaces and cathedrals reflect a variety of architectural styles. It was the residence of the Czars until 1712, and in 1918 became the political and administrative headquarters of the USSR. » Moscow

Kreutzer, Rodolphe [**kroy**tzuh] (1766–1831) French violinist, born in Versailles. He studied with his father, and from 1784 until 1810 was one of the leading concert violinists in Europe; he also taught at the Paris Conservatoire (1793–1826), conducted at the Opera (from 1817), and composed. He became friendly with Beethoven, who dedicated a sonata to him. He died in Geneva. » Beethoven; violin

krill A typically oceanic, shrimp-like crustacean, length up to 50 mm/2 in; gills exposed beneath margins of its hard covering (carapace); feeds on minute plant plankton; often migrates to surface, massing into vast aggregations that form the main food source of baleen whales. (Class: *Malacostraca*. Order: *Euphausiacea*.) » crustacean; plankton; shrimp; whale [i]

Krishna [**krish**na] According to Hindu tradition, the eighth incarnation, in human form, of the deity Vishnu. A great hero and ruler, the Mahabharata tells the story of his youthful amorous adventures, which is understood to symbolize the intimacy between the devotee and God. His story reaches its climax when, disguised as a charioteer in an eve-of-battle dialogue with Arjuna, he delivers the great moral discourse of the Bhagavadgita. » avatar; Bhagavadgita; bhakti; Hare Krishna movement; Hinduism; Vishnu

Krishna or **Kistna, River** [**krish**na] River in S India; rises in the Western Ghats, 65 km/40 ml E of the Arabian sea; length 1 300 km/800 ml; flows generally SE through Maharashtra and Andhra Pradesh to enter the Bay of Bengal; its source is sacred to Hindus. » Hinduism; India [i]

Krishna Menon, V(engalil) K(rishnan) (1896–1974) Indian politician and diplomat, born at Calicut, Malabar. Educated at Madras and London, he became a history teacher and barrister. In 1929 he was Secretary of the India League and the mouthpiece of Indian nationalism in Britain. He was India's first High Commissioner in London (1947), and the leader of the Indian delegation to the United Nations (1952). As Defence Minister (1957–62), he came into conflict with Pakistan over Kashmir. He died in New Delhi. » India [i]; nationalism

Krishnamurti, Jiddu (1895–1986) Indian theosophist, born in

Madras. He was educated in England by Annie Besant, who in 1925 proclaimed him the Messiah. Later he rejected this persona, dissolved The World Order of the Star in the East (founded by Dr Besant), and travelled the world teaching and advocating a way of life and thought unconditioned by the narrowness of nationality, race, and religion. He set up the Krishnamurti Foundation, and wrote several books on philosophy and religion. He died at Ojai, California. » Besant, Annie; theosophy

Kristiansen, Ingrid, *née* **Christensen** (1956–) Norwegian athlete. A former cross-country skiing champion, and now an outstanding long-distance runner, she is the only person to hold world best times for the 5000 m, 10000 m, and marathon, which she achieved in 1985–6. In 1986 she knocked 45.68 sec off the world 10000 m record, and easily won the European title. She has won most of the world's major marathons, including Boston, Chicago, and London, and was the world cross-country champion in 1988. » athletics; marathon

Kristianstad [kristy**an**stad] 56°02N 14°10E, pop (1982) 69207. Seaport and capital of Kristianstad county, S Sweden, on R Helge; founded by Denmark, 1614; ceded to Sweden, 1658; taken by the Danes, 1676–8; earliest example of Renaissance town-planning in N Europe; engineering, textiles, sugar. » Sweden [i]

Kropotkin, Pyotr or **Peter Alekseyevich, Knyaz** ('Prince') (1842–1921) Russian geographer and anarchist, born in Moscow, and educated at St Petersburg. In 1872 he associated himself with the extremist section of the International, and was imprisoned (1874). He escaped to England (1876), then to Switzerland and to France, where he was imprisoned again for anarchism (1883–6). Settling in England, he wrote on anarchism, social justice, and many topics in biology, literature, and history. He returned to Russia in 1917, and died near Moscow. » anarchism; communism; International

Kru A Kwa-speaking people of Liberia and Côte d'Ivoire, famous as fishermen and stevedores throughout W Africa from Senegal to Cameroon. Land shortages have forced many into cities, and the largest settlement of Kru is now in Monrovia, Liberia. Population c.1.2 million. » Côte d'Ivoire [i]; Liberia [i]

Kruger, Stephanus Johannes Paulus (Paul), byname **Oom ('Uncle') Paul** (1825–1904) Afrikaner statesman and President (1883–1902) of the South African Republic, born at Colesberg, Cape Colony. He took part in the Great Trek of the 1830s, becoming leader of the independence movement when Britain annexed Transvaal (1877). In the first Boer War (1881), he was head of the provisional government, and in 1883 became President of the South African Republic. During the second Boer War (1899–1902), he came to Europe to seek (in vain) alliances against Britain, making his headquarters at Utrecht. He died at Clarens, Switzerland. » Boer Wars; Great Trek

Kruger National Park A game reserve in Transvaal, S Africa. Founded in 1898 as the Sabi Game Reserve, in 1926 it was renamed in honour of Paul Kruger. The sanctuary covers about 20700 sq km/8000 sq ml, and is one of the largest national parks in the world. » Kruger; Transvaal

Krugerrand A gold coin of the Republic of South Africa, one ounce in weight, named after the Boer statesman, Paul Kruger (the *rand* being the unit of South African currency). Krugerrands are minted for issue overseas, and are bought for investment; they are not part of the everyday currency of South Africa. » Kruger

krypton Kr, element 36, the fourth of the noble gases. It liquefies at −150°, and makes up about 0.0001% of the atmosphere. It forms few compounds, the most stable being a fluoride, KrF_4. » chemical elements; noble gases; RR90

Ku Klux Klan The name of successive terrorist organizations in the USA, thought to derive from Greek *kyklos* 'circle'. The first was founded after the Civil War (1861–5) to oppose Reconstruction and the new rights being granted to Blacks: the members, disguised in robes and hoods, terrorized Blacks and their sympathizers in the country areas of the South. It faded after Federal measures were passed against it, but was re-established in a stronger and wider-based form after World War 1. This time its targets were Catholics, foreigners, Jews, and organized labour, as well as Blacks. It gained great political power, but the movement ended by 1944. It was revived by the fear of communism in the 1950s, then by opposition to the civil rights movements in the 1960s. Much violence was unleashed in the South before strong measures from the federal government (under President Johnson) imposed some control. » civil rights; Johnson, Lyndon B; terrorism

Kuala Lumpur [**kwah**la **lum**poor] 3°08N 101°42E, pop (1980) 937875. Capital of Malaysia, in Wilayah Persekutuan federal territory, E Peninsular Malaysia; large Chinese and Indian population; former capital of Selangor; capital of Federated Malay States, 1895; airport; railway; university (1962); technical university (1954); commercial centre; trade in rubber, tin; national mosque, Sri Mahamariamman (Hindu temple, 1873), national museum, national museum of art, Selangor Turf Club, Mimaland recreational complex; annual Malaysian golf tournament. » Malaysia [i]

Kubelík, Rafael (Jeronym) (1914–) Czech-Swiss conductor, born at Býchory. He studied at Prague Conservatory, conducted the Czech Philharmonic Orchestra, and by 1939 had established an international reputation. He conducted at Chicago (1950–3), Covent Garden (1955–8), with the Bavarian Radio Orchestra (1961–80), and at the Metropolitan Opera in New York (1972–4). His compositions include operas, symphonies, and concertos. He became a Swiss national in 1973.

Kubitschek (de Oliveira), Juscelino [**koob**shek] (1902–76) Brazilian statesman and President (1956–61), born at Diamantina, Minas Gerais. He studied medicine at Belo Horizonte, Paris, and Berlin. His government sponsored rapid economic growth and the dramatic building of a new capital, Brasília. He died in a car accident in Rio de Janeiro. » Brazil [i]

Kublai Khan [**koo**bliy kahn] (1214–94) Mongol emperor of China (1279–94), the grandson of Genghis Khan. An energetic prince, he suppressed his rivals, adopted the Chinese mode of civilization, encouraged men of letters, and made Buddhism the state religion. He established himself at Cambaluc (modern Beijing), the first foreigner ever to rule in China, and ruled an empire which extended as far as the R Danube. The splendour of his court was legendary. » Genghis Khan; Polo, Marco

Kubrick, Stanley [**koo**brik] (1928–) US screen writer, film producer, and director, born in New York City. After directing *Spartacus* (1960), he went to the UK, where he made a series of unusual features in several film genres: *Lolita* (1962), black comedy in *Dr Strangelove* (1964), psychedelic science fiction in *2001: A Space Odyssey* (1965), urban violence in *A Clockwork Orange* (1971), a period piece in *Barry Lyndon* (1975), and a horror film in *The Shining* (1980). A later production is *Full Metal Jacket* (1987).

kudu or **koedoe** [**koo**doo] A spiral-horned antelope native to Africa; greyish-brown with thin vertical white lines; female horns small or absent; male horn length up to 1.6 m/5¼ ft; inhabits dense undergrowth; two species: the **greater** and the **lesser kudu**. (Genus: *Tragelaphus*.) » antelope

Kuei-yang » **Guiyang**

Kuiper, Gerard Peter [**kiy**puh] (1905–73) US astronomer and founder of modern planetary astronomy, born in Harencarspel, Netherlands. Educated at Leyden, he went to the USA (1933) and acquired citizenship (1937), became director of the Yerkes and McDonald Observatories (1947–9), and founded the Lunar and Planetary Laboratory, Arizona (1960). He pioneered the spectroscopy of planetary atmospheres, and laid the groundwork for early exploration missions of the space age. He died in Mexico City. » planet; Solar System

kulaks The most progressive stratum of the late 19th-c and early 20th-c Russian peasantry. The kulaks developed after the emancipation of the serfs, and engaged in capitalist farming and entrepreneurial activities. During the collectivization of agriculture in the 1930s, Stalin 'liquidated' the kulaks as a class – a process known as *dekulakization*. » capitalism; Russian history; Stalin

kulan [**koo**lan] » **ass**

Kulturkampf [kul**toor**kampf] In the German Empire, a 'cultural conflict' between the Prussian state and the Roman Catholic Church. It was inspired by Bismarck's suspicion of

Catholics' extra-German loyalties, and involved discriminatory legislation against the Church's position within Prussia. Most intense during 1870–8, it gradually subsided following the election of Pope Leo XIII (1878), and effectively ended by 1886. » Bismarck; Roman Catholicism

Kumasi [koo**mah**see], bynames **Garden City, City of the Golden Stool** 6°45N 1°35W, pop (1982) 439 717. Capital of Ashanti region, SC Ghana, 180 km/112 ml NW of Accra; second largest city in Ghana; centre of the Ashanti kingdom since the 17th-c; centre of Ghanaian transport network; airfield; railway; university (1951); National Cultural Centre, including zoo, art gallery, open-air theatre; nearby Bonwire, woodcarving and cloth centre; large market centre for cocoa-growing region. » Ashanti; Ghana [i]

kumquat or **cumquat** [**kuhm**kwot] A spiny evergreen shrub related to and closely resembling citrus, native to E and SE Asia, and cultivated elsewhere; fruits look and taste like tiny oranges, and are often candied. (Genus: *Fortunella*, 6 species. Family: *Rutaceae*.) » citrus; evergreen plants; shrub

Kun, Béla (1886–c.1939) Communist leader, born at Szilágycseh, Transylvania. He was a journalist, soldier, and prisoner in Russia (1916), where he joined the Bolsheviks. In 1919 he set up in Hungary a Soviet republic, but his policy of nationalization alienated much of the population. His regime was overthrown after only five months, and he was forced to flee to Vienna. He then returned to Russia, and was killed in one of the Stalinist purges of the late 1930s. » Hungary [i]; Stalin

Kundera, Milan [**kuhn**daira] (1929–) Czechoslovak novelist, born at Brno and educated in Prague. He lectured in Cinematographic Studies in Prague until he lost his post after the Russian invasion of 1968. His first novel, *Zert* (1967, The Joke), was a satire on Czechoslovakian-style Stalinism. In 1975 he fled to Paris, where he has lived ever since. He came to prominence in the West with *Kniha smichu a zapomneni* (1979, The Book of Laughter and Forgetting). *Nesnesitelna lehkost byti* (The Unbearable Lightness of Being) appeared in 1984, and was filmed in 1987. » Czechoslovak literature; novel; satire

kung fu A form of Chinese unarmed combat dating from the 6th-c, when it was practised at the Shaolin Temple. There are many forms; the best known is *wing chun*, popularized by the actor Bruce Lee in several films. » martial arts

Kunlun Shan Mountain range in W China; extends 2 500 km/1 500 ml along border of Xinjiang province and Xizang autonomous region (Tibet); divides E to form the Altun Shan and Hoh Xil Shan ranges; rises to 7 723 m/25 338 ft at Muztag peak. » China [i]

Kunming, formerly **Yunnan** 25°04N 102°41E, pop (1984e) 1 355 300. Capital of Yunnan province, S China, on Yunnan plateau; altitude 1 894 m/6 214 ft; major market and transport centre from 279 BC; spring-like weather and scenery ('City of Eternal Spring'); airfield; railway; university (1934); agricultural university; minerals, engineering, metallurgy, food processing, chemicals, textiles; Qiongzhu Si (Bamboo Temple), 11 km/7 ml W; Stone Forest, 126 km/78 ml SE. » China [i]

Kuomintang » **Guomindang**

Kurchatov, Igor (Vasilevich) (1903–60) Russian physicist, born at Sim, Russia. He was appointed director of nuclear physics at the Leningrad Institute (1938) and later of the Soviet Atomic Energy Institute. He was the leading figure in the building of Russia's first atomic (1949) and thermonuclear (1953) bombs. He became a member of the Supreme Soviet in 1949, and died in Moscow. » atomic bomb

Kurdistan or **Kordestan** [koordi**stahn**] pop (1982) 782 440; area 24 998 sq km/9 649 sq ml. Province in NW Iran, bounded W by Iraq; capital, Sanandaj; inhabited by Kurds, who also occupy parts of NE Iraq, SE Turkey, and NE Syria; in 1920 a Kurdish autonomous state was agreed at the Treaty of Sèvres, but the terms were never carried out. » Iran [i]; Kurds

Kurds A nationalistic W Iranian-speaking ethnic group settled in neighbouring mountainous areas of Anatolia, Iraq, Iran and Turkey (including some in Syria and Armenia), an area which they themselves call **Kurdistan**, and numbering 9–10 million. They were originally pastoral nomads with some agriculture, but the creation of national boundaries after World War 1 restricted their seasonal migrations, and most are now urbanized. They have been Sunni Muslims since the 7th-c AD. They are politically oppressed in Turkey, and have suffered religious persecution in Iran, especially after the Iranian revolution of 1979. In Iraq, the Kurds' failure to achieve autonomous status for Kurdistan during the 1970s resulted in hostilities between Kurds and government forces, especially after the 1991 Gulf War. » ethnic group; Iranian languages; nomadism; pastoralism; Sunnis

Kurgan culture The semi-nomadic population of the S Russian steppes in the fourth millennium BC, characterized archaeologically by burials sprinkled with red ochre beneath a barrow mound or *kurgan*. They were for long held responsible for the dissemination across Europe from c.3000 BC of the Indo-European family of languages, a view now largely discredited. » Indo-European languages

Kuril Islands, Russ **Kurilskiye Ostrova** [ku**reel**] area 15 600 sq km/6 000 sq ml. Archipelago off the E Russian coast, between the N Pacific Ocean (E) and the Sea of Okhotsk (W); extends c.1 200 km/750 ml from the S tip of Kamchatka Peninsula to the NE coast of Hokkaido I, Japan; rises to 2 339 m/7 674 ft; over 50 islands, actively volcanic, with hot springs; visited in 1634 by the Dutch; divided between Russia and Japan, 18th-c; all ceded to Japan, 1875; occupied by Soviet troops, 1945; part of the USSR, 1947; claimed by Japan. » Russia

Kurosawa, Akira [kooruh**sah**wa] (1910–) Japanese film director, born in Tokyo. He began as a painter, and joined a cinema studio in 1936, making his first feature film (*Sanshiro Sugata*) in 1943. He is renowned for his adaptation of the techniques of the Noh theatre to film-making, in such films as *Rashomon* (1951), which won the Venice Film Festival prize, and *The Seven Samurai* (1954). Also characteristic are his literary adaptations, such as *The Throne of Blood* (1957, from *Macbeth*) and *The Lower Depths* (1957, from Dostoyevsky). Later films include *Kagemushi* (1980) and *Ran* (1985). » Noh

Kush An independent kingdom on the Nile which emerged from the Egyptian province of Nubia in the 11th-c BC. In the 8th-c BC Kush conquered Egypt, and established the 25th dynasty which ruled until the Assyrian conquest in 671–666 BC. The Kush kings became Egyptianized, but after their withdrawal from Egypt in the 7th-c BC they moved to the more southerly capital of Meroe, where there were good supplies of iron ore and timber. It became an important centre of iron smelting, and large slag heaps can still be seen there. » African history; Axum

Kutab Minar » **Qutb Minar**

Kutch, Rann of, Kachch, Cutch area 9 000 sq km/3 474 sq ml. Region of salt marsh in the Indian state of Gujarat and Sind province, Pakistan; bounded W by the Arabian Sea and N by the Thar Desert; once a shallow arm of the Arabian Sea; great accumulations of salt on the surface when dry; inundated during SW monsoon; scene of Indo-Pakistani fighting in 1965. » Gujarat; Sind

Kutiyattam [kootiy**ah**tam] An Indian theatrical tradition found in Kerala, and believed to be a surviving example of the style of Sanskrit theatre . » Sanskrit theatre

Kutuzov, Mikhail Ilarionovich, Knyaz ('Prince') [koo**too**zof] (1745–1813) Russian field marshal, born at St Petersburg. He distinguished himself in the Turkish war, and in 1805 commanded against the French, but was defeated at Austerlitz. In 1812, as Commander-in-Chief, he fought Napoleon obstinately at Borodino, and obtained a major victory over Davout and Ney at Smolensk. He died during the pursuit of Napoleon's forces, at Bunzlau, Silesia. » Alexander I; Napoleonic Wars; Russo-Turkish Wars

Kuwait, official name **State of Kuwait**, Arabic **Dowlat al Kuwait** [koo**wayt**] pop (1990e) 2 014 135; area 17 818 sq km/6 878 sq ml. Independent state at head of Arabian Gulf, bounded N and W by Iraq, S by Saudi Arabia, and E by the Arabian Gulf; capital, Kuwait City; chief ports, Shuwaikh, Mina al Ahmadi; timezone GMT +3; population 41.5% Kuwaiti, 40% other Arab; chief religion, Islam; official language, Arabic; unit of currency, the dinar; consists of mainland and nine offshore islands; terrain flat or gently undulating, rising SW to 271 m/889 ft; Wadi al Batin on W border with Iraq; low ridges in NE

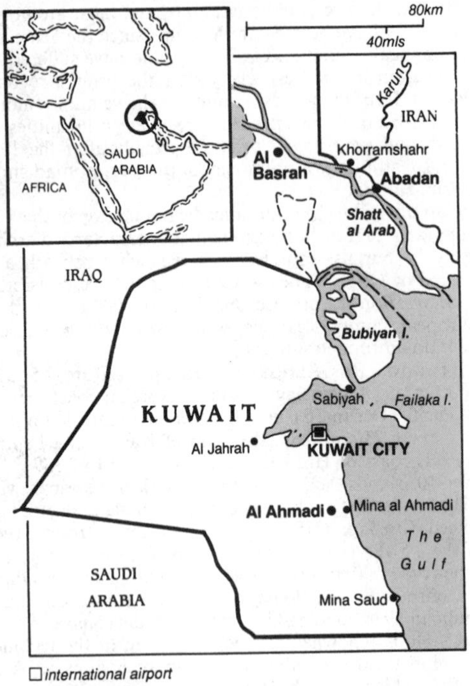

generally stony with sparse vegetation; hot and dry climate, average annual rainfall 111 mm/4 in; summer temperatures very high, often above 45°C (Jul–Aug); winter daytime temperatures can exceed 20°C; humidity often over 90%; sandstorms common all year; port founded in the 18th-c; Britain responsible for Kuwait's foreign affairs, 1899; British protectorate, 1914; independence, 1961; emir is head of state, governing through an appointed prime minister and Council of Ministers; invasion and annexation by Iraq (Aug 1990), leading to Gulf War (Jan-Feb 1991), with severe damage to Kuwait City and infrastructure; Kuwaiti government-in-exile in Saudi Arabia; large refugee emigration; major post-war problem, including burning of oil wells by Iraq (all capped by Nov 1991), and pollution of Gulf waters by oil; traditional economy, pearl diving, seafaring, boatbuilding, fishing, nomadic herding; oil discovered, 1938, and now provides 95% of government revenue; petrochemicals, fertilizers, construction materials, asbestos, batteries; active programme of economic diversification, creating a post-oil high-technology state; agriculture gradually expanding; dates, citrus fruits, timber, livestock, poultry. » Kuwait City; RR26 national holidays; RR54 political leaders

Kuwait City, Arabic **Al Kuwayt**, formerly **Qurein** 29°20N 48°00E, pop (1981) 276 356. Capital city of Kuwait, on S shore of Kuwait Bay; developed in late 1940s after discovery of oil; suburban port of Shuwaikh, SW; airport; ferry service to Failaka I; university (1966); centre for communications, banking, investment centre; shipbuilding; severely damaged in Gulf War, 1991. » Kuwait [i]

Kuybyshev [**koo**ibishef], formerly (to 1935) and from 1991 **Samara** 53°10N 50°10E, pop (1989) 1 257 000. River-port capital of Kuybyshevskaya oblast, EC European Russia; on the R Volga where it meets the R Samara; founded as a fortress, 1586; Soviet government transferred here in World War 2, 1941–3; airport; railway; university (1969); machines, metalworking, oil refining, foodstuffs. » Russia

Kuznets, Simon (Smith) (1901–85) US economist and statistician, born at Pinsk, Belorussia. Going to the USA as a young man, he worked with the National Bureau of Economic Research (1927–71). He combined a concern for facts and measurement with creative and original ideas on economic development and social change, such as the 20-year 'Kuznets cycle' of economic growth. He won the Nobel Prize for Economics in 1971. » economics

Kuznets Basin Basin of the Tom R in Kemerovo oblast, Russia; stretches from Tomsk SE to Novokuznetsk; a major industrial zone, with rich deposits of coal and iron ore. » Russia

Kuznetsov, Alexander (Vasilievich) [kuz**nets**of] (1929–79) Ukrainian writer, born in Kiev. He published short stories as early as 1946, but first came to public notice in the USSR with the short novel *Prodolzheniye legendy* (1957, The Continuation of a Legend). He is best known for *Babi Yar* (1966), a novel about the massacre of Ukrainian Jews by the German SS in 1941. Kuznetsov defected to England in 1969, changing his name to A Anatoli. » Babi Yar; novel; Russian literature

Kwakiutl [kwak**eeoo**tl] A N Pacific Coast American Indian group living on the coast of British Columbia as fishermen and traders. They were famed for their woodwork, frequently painted in bright colours, including masks, totem poles, war canoes, whale hunting vessels, and decorative boxes. Some art is still produced for the tourist trade. They also had elaborate dances and ceremonies, including the potlatch. » American Indians; Northwest Coast Indians; potlatch

KwaNdebele [kwahnde**be**lay] pop (1985) 235 855; area 2 860 sq km/1 104 sq ml. National state or non-independent Black homeland in Transvaal province, NE South Africa; situated NE of Johannesburg and E of Pretoria; self-governing status, 1981; chief town, Moutjana. » apartheid; South Africa [i]

Kwang-chow » **Guangzhou**

kwashiorkor [kwashi**aw**kuh] A nutritional disorder of young children, stemming from an inadequate intake of protein in the diet, usually with an adequate calorie intake. It frequently begins after weaning in Africa. Failure to thrive, apathy, oedema, and diarrhoea are characteristic. » calorie [i]; protein

KwaZulu [kwah**zoo**loo] pop (1985) 3 747 015. National state or non-independent Black homeland in Natal province, E South Africa; close to the Indian Ocean between the Transkei and Durban; self-governing status in 1971. » apartheid; South Africa [i]

Kyd, Thomas (1558–94) English dramatist, born and died in London. He was probably educated at Merchant Taylors' School, and brought up as a scrivener under his father. His tragedies early brought him reputation, especially *The Spanish Tragedy* (c.1592). He has been credited with a share in several plays, and may have written an earlier version of *Hamlet*. Imprisoned in 1593 on a charge of atheism, he died in poverty. » drama; English literature; tragedy

Kyoga, Lake [kee**oh**ga] area 4 427 sq km/1 709 sq ml. Lake in C Uganda, N of Kampala; the Victoria Nile R passes through from L Victoria. » Uganda [i]

Kyogen [**kyoh**gen] Comic plays often performed between Japanese Noh plays. » Noh

Kyoto [**kyoh**toh] 35°02N 135°45E, pop (1980) 1 473 065. Capital of Kyoto prefecture, C Honshu, Japan; SW of Lake Biwa; founded, 8th-c; capital of Japan, 794–1868; railway; university (1897); university of industrial arts and textiles (1949); electrical goods, machinery, silk, crafts; over 2 000 temples and shrines; Nijo-jo Castle (1603), containing the Imperial Palace; Kinkakuji, the Golden Pavilion (1394), Ryoanji temple (1450, later rebuilt), Daitokuji monastery (14th-c), Kiyomizu dera temple (8th-c), Sanjusangen do (12th-c); Mikayo Odori cherry blossom dance (Apr), Kamogawa Odori (May, Oct), Aoi (hollyhock) Matsuri processions (May); Mifune Matsuri boat festival (May), Gion Matsuri parade (Jul), Jidai Matsuri parade (Oct). » Honshu; Kinkakuji; Nijo-jo Castle

Kyushu [**kyoo**shoo] pop (1980) 12 966 000; area 42 084 sq km/ 16 244 sq ml. Island region in Japan; southernmost and most densely populated of the four main islands; four volcanic ranges, rising to 1 935 m/6 348 ft at Mt Miyanoura-dake on Yaku-shima I (S); subtropical climate; heavily forested apart from the NW, which is an extensive rice-growing area; major industrial towns include Fukuoka, Kita-Kyushu, Oita, Kagoshima, Nagasaki; many spas; rice, grain, sweet potatoes, fruit, silk, timber, fishing, porcelain. » Japan [i]

Kyzyl-Kum [**kizil kum**], Russ **Peski Kyzylkum** Extensive desert in Kazakhstan and Uzbekistan, between the Amudarya (W) and Syr-Darya (E) Rivers; extends SE from the Aral Sea; rises to 922 m/3 025 ft in the C; partially covered with sand dunes. » Kazakhstan; Uzbekistan

L

L'Anse aux Meadows [**lahns** oh **med**ohz] An isolated Norse settlement of nine turf-built houses on Epaves Bay, Newfoundland, Canada, discovered in 1961 by Helge and Anne Ingstad. Dated by radiocarbon to c.970–1000 AD, the settlement proves that the Vikings reached N America in pre-Columbian times. It has been designated a National Park and a world heritage site. » Vikings; Vínland

L-dopa or **levodopa** A drug used very effectively in the treatment of Parkinson's disease, reducing symptoms in more than two-thirds of patients. Shortly after its introduction in the late 1960s some reports stated that it increased male libido in a minority of patients. Although this probably related to the clinical improvement of the patients rather than the drug itself, L-dopa was exploited briefly (and wrongly) as an aphrodisiac. » aphrodisiacs; Parkinson's disease

L'Ouverture, Toussaint » **Toussaint L'Ouverture**

La Bruyère, Jean de [brü**yair**] (1645–96) French writer, born in Paris. He studied law, and was chosen to help in educating the Dauphin. For a time he was treasurer at Caen, and became tutor to the Duc de Bourbon. His major work is the satirical *Caractères de Théophraste*... (1688, Characters of Theophrastus...), which gained him a host of implacable enemies as well as an immense reputation. He died at Versailles. » French literature; satire; Theophrastus

La Fayette, Marie Madeleine (Pioche de Lavergne), Comtesse ('Countess') (1634–93) French novelist and reformer of French romance writing, born and died in Paris. She married the Comte de La Fayette in 1655, and at 33 formed a liaison with La Rochefoucauld, which lasted until his death in 1680. Her major novel is *La Princesse de Clèves* (1678), a vivid picture of the court life of her day. She died in Paris. » French literature; La Rochefoucauld; novel

La Fontaine, Jean de (1621–95) French poet, born at Château-Thierry. He early devoted himself to the study of old writers and to verse writing. His *Contes et nouvelles en vers* (1665, Tales and Novels in Verse) was followed by his major work, the collection of over 200 verse stories, *Fables choisies mises en vers* (1668, Selected Fables in Verse). He died in Paris. » French literature; poetry

La Guardia, Fiorello H(enry) (1882–1947) US lawyer and politician, born in New York City, where he spent the whole of his career. He became deputy Attorney-General (1915–17), and sat in Congress as a Republican (1917–21, 1923–33). A popular Mayor (1933–45), he initiated housing and labour safeguards schemes. One of the city airports is named after him. He died in New York City. » Republican Party

La, Las, Los (as name of town, river, etc) » also under initial letter of the following word

La Paz [la **pas**] 16°30S 68°10W, pop(1982) 881 404. Regional capital and government capital of Bolivia, La Paz department, W Bolivia; highest capital in the world, altitude 3 665 m/12 024 ft; Mt Illimani (6 402 m/21 004 ft) towers above the city to the SE; founded by Spanish, 1548; airport (Kennedy International, formerly El Alto); railway; university (1830); copper, wool, alpaca; cathedral, Presidential Palace (Palacio Quemado), National Congress, National Art Museum, Monastery of San Francisco; skiing nearby at world's highest ski run, Mt Chacaltaya. » Bolivia [i]; Sucre

La Plata [la **pla**ta] 34°52S 57°55W, pop(1980) 560 341. Port and capital of Buenos Aires province; on the R Plate, SW of Buenos Aires; founded in 1882; three universities (1884, 1965, 1968); named **Eva Perón** (1946–55); railway; main outlet for produce from the pampas; trade in refrigerated meat, grain, oil; oil refining; museum of natural history; zoological gardens; observatory; Garden of Peace, with each country in the world represented by one flower. » Argentina [i]; Plate, River

La Rochefoucauld, François, 6th Duke [**rosh**fookoh] (1613–80) French writer, born in Paris. An active member of the opposition to Cardinal Richelieu, he was forced to live abroad (1639–42). He then joined in the Fronde revolts (1648–53), and was wounded at the siege of Paris. He retired to the country in 1652, returning to the court on Mazarin's death in 1661. His major works were written while in retirement: *Mémoires* (1664) and the epigrammatic collection, *Réflexions*, commonly known as the *Maximes* (1665, Maxims). He died in Paris. » French literature; Frondes; Mazarin; Richelieu

La-sa » **Lhasa**

La Salle, (René) Robert Cavelier, Sieur de (1643–87) French explorer, born at Rouen. He settled in Canada in 1666, and descended the Ohio and Mississippi to the sea (1682), naming the area Louisiana (after Louis XIV of France). In 1684 he fitted out an expedition to establish a French settlement on the Gulf of Mexico. He spent two years in fruitless journeys, his harshness embittering his followers, and he was murdered near the Brazos R, Texas. » Louisiana

La Scala or **Teatro Alla Scala** ('theatre at the stairway') [la **skah**la] The world's most famous opera house, built (1776–8) on the site of the Church of Santa Maria della Scala in Milan, Italy. It was severely damaged by bombing in World War 2, and reopened in 1947. » opera

La Tène [la **ten**] A prehistoric site on the shores of L Neuchâtel, Switzerland, with rich votive deposits of decorated weapons and brooches excavated from 1858. Its name is commonly used to describe the later European Iron Age that succeeded Halstaat culture c.500 BC and survived until the coming of the Romans. Hillforts, increasing trade and warfare, the development of towns and coinage, and a vigorous curvilinear art style are characteristic features of the period. » Maiden Castle; Manching; Three Age System

La Vallière, Louise Françoise de la Baume le Blanc, Duchesse de ('Duchess of') [laval**yair**] (1644–1710) Mistress of Louis XIV of France (1661–7), born at Tours. She was maid of honour to Henrietta Anne of England, Duchess of Orleans, before becoming the royal mistress. She bore the King four children, and remained at court reluctantly after Mme de Montespan superseded her (1667). Eventually she was allowed to retire to a Carmelite nunnery in Paris (1674), where she died. » Louis XIV

La Venta An Olmec ceremonial centre in Tabasco province, Mexico, occupied c.900–400 BC, but now destroyed by oil operations. Supported by an estimated hinterland population of c.18 000, its linear complex of platforms, plazas, and 34 m/112 ft high Great Pyramid covered 5 sq km/2 sq ml. Of particular note are its carved stone pillars, pavements, colossal heads, and votive figurines of basalt, serpentine, and jade, now displayed at Parque La Venta, near the original site. » Olmecs; San Lorenzo

Laban, Rudolf von (1879–1958) Hungarian dancer, choreographer, and dance theoretician, born in Pozsony, now Bratislava. He studied painting, acting, and dancing in Paris, toured Europe and N Africa as a dancer, founded a school in Munich in 1910, and worked in many German cities as a choreographer and teacher. He organized the dance items for the 1936 Olympic Games, but left Germany for England in 1938. As the leader of the C European dance movement he was instrumental in the development of modern dance as a theatre form. His theoretical writings and notation system (**Labanotation**) have had substantial impact on approaches to movement in education, therapy, industry, and dance. He died in Weybridge, Surrey. » choreography; dance notation [i]; modern dance

labelled compound A compound containing a larger amount than usual of a particular isotope of an element. These may be radioactive isotopes, or stable isotopes detectable by spectroscopy. Widely used isotopes include deuterium and ^{13}C. » isotopes; spectroscopy

labelling theory The view, developed primarily during the 1950s and 1960s in American criminology, that certain people and their behaviour come to be 'labelled' by law enforcement agencies as in some way 'deviant' or 'criminal'. Labelling theorists argue that one must look at those doing the labelling – the law-makers and community at large – and not just the law-breakers. » deviance

Labiche, Eugène (Marin) [la**beesh**] (1815–88) French playwright, born and died in Paris. He trained as a lawyer, and worked as a journalist, before turning to literature. He wrote over 100 comedies, farces, and vaudevilles, such as *Le Chapeau de paille d'Italie* (1851, The Italian Straw Hat) and *Le Voyage de M Perrichon* (1860, The Journey of M Perrichon). » comedy; French literature

labile [**lay**biyl] » **kinetic**

Labor Day » **Labour Day**

labor union » **trade union**

labour/labor A three-stage process by which a pregnant woman expels her baby and other products of conception from the uterus through the vagina. The first stage consists of uterine muscle contractions with progressive relaxation and dilatation of the cervix, so creating a passage to the vagina. The second stage consists of the descent of the baby through the widely dilated cervix and the vagina; the expulsive process is reinforced by the mother's voluntary efforts. The third stage consists of the expulsion of the placenta, or afterbirth. Labour pains are due to the muscular contractions. » obstetrics; pregnancy [i]; uterus [i]; vagina

Labour/Labor Day A day of celebration, public demonstrations and parades by trade unions and labour organizations, held in many countries on 1 May, or the first Monday in May; in the USA, Canada and Bermuda it is the first Monday in September, and in New Zealand the fourth Monday of October.

Labour Party A British socialist/social democratic political party, originally formed in 1900 as the Labour Representation Committee to represent trade unions and socialist societies as a distinct group in Parliament. Twenty-six MPs were elected in 1906, and the name changed to the Labour Party. In 1922 it overtook the Liberals as the main opposition party, and the first minority Labour government was elected in 1924, lasting eleven months. The first majority Labour government (1945–51) established the welfare state and carried out a significant nationalization programme. Since then Labour have been in office 1964–70 and 1974–9. The breakaway social democratic movement of the 1980s hurt the Party's electoral chances throughout that decade. Outside Parliament, the annual conference and the National Executive Committee share policy making, though their influence is greater in opposition. The leader and deputy leader are elected annually when in opposition by an electoral college composed of trade unions, constituency parties, and the Parliamentary Labour Party. The British Labour Party has been little influenced by Marxism, unlike the corresponding parties in Europe. » Marxism; social democracy; socialism

labour/labor relations » **industrial relations**

labour/labor theory of value An economic theory that the relative prices of articles (their value) are determined by the relative quantity of labour put into them. The view was first propounded by Ricardo in 1817; but it is now generally recognized that other factors determine value, notably demand and supply. » Ricardo, David

Labrador Area 285 000 sq km/110 000 sq ml. Part of Newfoundland province, E Canada; bounded E by the Labrador Sea; separated from Newfoundland by the Strait of Belle Isle; mainly a barren plateau, part of Canadian Shield; heavily indented E coast; many lakes; fishing, iron ore, hydroelectric power; interior region awarded to Newfoundland, 1927, disputed by Quebec. » Newfoundland

Labrador retriever A breed of dog, developed in Britain from imported Newfoundland dogs and local breeds; large, with muscular legs and body; long tail and muzzle; short, pendulous ears; thick fawn or black (occasionally brown) coat; also known as **labrador**. » dog; retriever

Labrador Sea Arm of the Atlantic Ocean between Newfoundland and Greenland; depths fall from the continental shelves below 3 200 m/10 500 ft towards the Mid-Oceanic Canyon; cold SE-flowing Labrador Current brings icebergs, while warm NW-flowing W Greenland Current helps modify the climate of the SW shore of Greenland. » Atlantic Ocean

laburnum A deciduous tree growing to 7 m/2¾ ft, native to S and C Europe, and commonly planted as an ornamental; leaves divided into three leaflets; pea-flowers yellow, numerous, in pendent leafy clusters; pods up to 6 cm/2½ in long, hairy when young; seeds black; also called **golden rain** or **golden chain**. All parts but especially the seeds are extremely poisonous. Garden plants are often the hybrid *Laburnum* × *watereri*. (*Laburnum anagyroides*. Family: *Leguminosae*.) » deciduous plants; tree [i]

lac insect A bug that lives in clusters on twigs of trees; females legless, with reduced antennae; body enclosed in a protective shell of resinous secretion from which shellac is made. (Order: *Homoptera*. Family: *Kerridae*.) » shellac

Lacaille, Nicolas Louis de [la**kiy**] (1713–62) French astronomer, born at Rumigny. He travelled to S Africa (1750–5) to draw up the first reliable catalogue of S hemisphere stars, and named 14 new constellations. He died in Paris. » constellation; star

Laccadive Islands » **Lakshadweep**

lace An ornamental fabric in which a large number of separate threads are twisted together into a decorative network. Lace is often used for the edges of items of clothing or furnishing, such as collars, cuffs, tablecloths, and altar cloths, but whole garments or covers (eg curtains) can be made in this way. Hand-made lace is still widely produced, but machines have been making lace since 1808.

lacecap » **hydrangea**

Lacedaemon [lase**dee**muhn] The official name in antiquity for the Spartan state. It comprised the districts of Laconia and Messenia. » Laconia; Messenia; Sparta (Greek history)

Lacerta [la**ser**ta] ('lizard') A smallish, faint N constellation. It includes the object BL Lacertae, the prototype of a class of quasar-like objects. » constellation; quasar; RR8

lacewing A medium to large insect possessing two pairs of similar, membraneous wings, each with a lacework of veins; adults and larvae predatory, with simple, biting mouthparts; feed mainly on sap-sucking insects; pupation typically occurs inside a silk cocoon. (Order: *Neuroptera*.) » insect [i]; larva; pupa

Lachesis » **Moerae**

Lachlan River River in New South Wales, Australia; rises in the Great Dividing Range, N of Canberra; flows 1 484 km/922 ml to join the Murrumbidgee R. » New South Wales

Laclos, Pierre (Ambroise François) Choderlos de [la**kloh**] (1741–1803) French soldier, novelist, and politician, born at Amiens. He is remembered for his masterpiece, *Les Liaisons dangereuses* (1782, Dangerous Acquaintances), a novel in letters providing a cynical, detached analysis of personal and sexual relationships. He died at Taranto, in the Parthenopean Republic. » French literature; novel

Laconia [la**koh**nia] In ancient Greece, the SE portion of the Peloponnese, of which Sparta was the principal settlement. » Sparta (Greek history)

lacquer A hard waterproof substance made from the resin of the *Rhus vernicifera* tree. A very ancient Chinese invention, it can be coloured, polished, carved, and used to decorate wooden vessels and furniture.

lacquer tree A deciduous tree growing to c.9 m/30 ft, native to China and Japan; leaves pinnate, leaflets oval; flowers tiny, 5-petalled, yellowish, in drooping clusters; also called **varnish tree**. A resin obtained from cuts in the stem is a major constituent of Chinese and Japanese lacquer. (*Rhus verniciflera*. Family: *Anacardiaceae*.) » deciduous plants; pinnate; resin

Lacroix, Christian [**lak**rwa] (1951–) French couturier, born at Arles, Provence. He studied fashion history from 1973, intending to become a museum curator, but then joined Hermès, the leather firm, and worked with Guy Paulin, ready-to-wear designer. In 1981 he joined Jean Patou, which showed his first collection in 1982. In 1987 he left Patou and, with other partners, opened the House of Lacroix in Paris. He made his name with ornate and frivolous clothes. » fashion; Patou

lacrosse A stick-and-ball field game derived from the N American Indian game of *baggataway*. Because the stick resembled a bishop's crozier, French settlers called the game *La Crosse*. Played since the 15th-c, the game spread to Europe in the early part of the 19th-c, and to Britain in 1867. It is a team game played with 10 on each side (at international level women have 12 per side) on a pitch measuring 100–110 m/110–120 yd by 55–75 m/60–85 yd. The object is to score goals by throwing the ball into the goal using the lacrosse racket, or *crosse*. The crosse is at least 0.9 m/3 ft in length with a triangular net attached to the end in which to catch the ball. » RR115

lactation The process of suckling a new-born infant. During pregnancy, milk-producing glands in the breasts proliferate, and hormones from the front pituitary stimulate the secretion of milk, which is further augmented when the infant suckles. » breast feeding; pituitary gland

lactic acid CH_3–CH(OH)–COOH, IUPAC **2-hydroxypropanoic acid**. An acid which takes its name from milk, where it is formed on souring. It is an important stage in the breakdown of carbohydrates during respiration. It has two enantiomeric forms, both found in nature. » chirality [i]; enantiomer; glycolysis; IUPAC

lactone A ring compound formed by internal ester formation in a compound containing both an acid and an alcohol function.

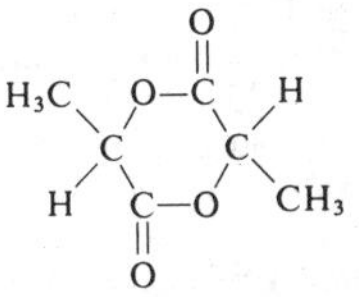

The lactone of lactic acid is shown in the illustration above. » ester [i]; ring

lactose $C_{12}H_{22}O_{11}$. A sugar occurring in the milk of all mammals. It is a disaccharide, a combination of glucose and galactose, and scarcely sweet-tasting. » disaccharide; glucose [i]

lactose intolerance A condition arising from inadequate amounts of the enzyme lactase in the lining of the intestine, in the face of excessive intake of lactose, usually in the form of milk. It causes abdominal distension, colic, and diarrhoea. » lactose

Ladoga, Lake, Russ **Ozero Ladozhskoye**, Finnish **Laatokka** area 17 700 sq km/6 832 sq ml. Largest lake in Europe, in European Russia, close to the Finnish border; length, 219 km/136 ml; maximum depth, 230 m/755 ft; over 90% of the outflow via the R Neva into the Gulf of Finland; c.660 islands; navigation difficult in winter because of ice and storms; extensive network of canals. » Russia

Lady chapel A chapel dedicated to the Virgin Mary. It is usually built behind the main altar, and forms an extension to the main building. » Gothic architecture; Mary (mother of Jesus)

Lady Day » **Annunciation**

lady's mantle A dome-shaped perennial, native to N temperate regions and tropical mountains; leaves palmate, lobes often shallow, softly hairy; flowers in clusters, small, numerous, green or yellowish; epicalyx four lobes, four sepals, petals absent. (Genus: *Alchemilla*, 250 species. Family: *Rosaceae*.) » epicalyx; palmate; perennial; sepal

lady's slipper A N temperate orchid in which the lower lip (*labellum*) of the flower is sac-like; also called **moccasin flower**. Insects visiting the flower enter the labellum, but can leave only via a hole at the base, squeezing past both stigma and anthers, and thus pollinating the flower. (Genus: *Cypripedium*, 35 species. Family: *Orchidaceae*.) » orchid [i]; stigma

lady's smock » **cuckoo flower**

ladybird A rounded, convex beetle usually red, black, or yellow with a pattern of spots or lines; adults and larvae typically active predators, feeding mostly on aphids and other plant pests; also known as a **ladybug**. If provoked, some exhibit active bleeding of a sticky, irritating fluid from knee joints and spines. (Order: *Coleoptera*. Family: *Coccinellidae*.) » aphid; beetle; larva

ladybug » **ladybird**

Ladysmith, Siege of (1899–1900) One of the three sieges of the second Boer War in which Boer forces attempted to pen up their British opponents, and around which many of the actions of the war took place. An attempt to relieve the town was frustrated at the Battle of Spion Kop (Jan 1900), but General Sir Redvers Buller (1839–1908) succeeded in raising the siege on 28 February 1900. » Boer Wars; Kimberley/Mafeking, Siege of

Laënnec, René Théophile Hyacinthe [lahe**nek**] (1781–1826) French physician, born at Quimper. From 1799 an army doctor, in 1814 he became editor of the *Journal de Médecine* and physician to the Salpêtrière, and in 1816 chief physician to the Hôpital Necker, where he invented the stethoscope, and worked on tuberculosis, peritonitis, and chest diseases. He died at Kerlouanec. » auscultation

laetrile [**lay**triyl] A trademark used for the drug *amygdalin*, a compound capable of producing cyanide in the body. It is contained in certain fruit stones, such as the apricot. Laetrile has been promoted as vitamin B_{17} and as a cure for cancer. Its curative value has been widely denied, and many have been convicted for so using it. » cancer; cyanide; vitamins [i]

Lafayette, Marie Joseph (Paul Yves Roch Gilbert du Motier), Marquis de (1757–1834) French soldier and politician, born at Chavagniac into an ancient noble family. After a period at court, he fought in America against the British during the War of Independence (1777–9, 1780–2), and became a hero and a friend of Washington. A liberal aristocrat, in the National Assembly of 1789 he presented a draft of a declaration of the Rights of Man, based on the US Declaration of Independence. Hated by the Jacobins for his moderation, he defected to Austria, returning to France during the Consulate. During the Restoration he sat in the Chamber of Deputies (1818–24), became a radical leader of the Opposition (1825–30), and commanded the National Guard in the 1830 Revolution. He died in Paris. » American Revolution; Declaration of the Rights of Man and Citizen; French Revolution [i]; Jacobins (French history)

lager » **beer**

Lagerkvist, Pär (Fabian) (1891–1974) Swedish writer, born at Växjö. He studied at Uppsala, and began his literary career as an Expressionist poet with *Angest* (1916, Anguish), emphasizing the catastrophe of war. His works include *Bödeln* (1934, The Hangman), *Dvärgen* (1944, The Dwarf), and *Barabbas* (1951). He received the Nobel Prize for Literature in 1951, and died in Stockholm. » Expressionism; novel; Swedish literature

Lagerlöf, Selma (Ottiliana Lovisa) [**lah**gerlerf] (1858–1940) Swedish novelist, born in Värmland. She became a schoolteacher, and sprang to fame with *Gösta Berling's Saga* (1891). Her fairy tales and romances earned her the 1909 Nobel Prize for Literature – the first woman to receive the distinction. She died at Mårbacka. » novel; Swedish literature

lagomorph [**lag**uhmawf] An order of mammals comprising rabbits, hares, and pikas; virtually worldwide (not native to Australasia, but now introduced); related to rodents; long soft fur, long ears, short tails, fully-furred feet, slit-like nostrils which can be closed; eat coarse plant material; also eat some of their own faeces to ensure that nourishment is extracted from the food. (Order: *Lagomorpha*, 58 species.) » hare; pika; rabbit; rodent

lagoon A shallow body of sea water separated from the open sea by island barriers. Coastal lagoons occur in regions where little surface run-off enters the sea. Organic reefs may also form lagoons, as is the case at coral atolls and barrier reefs. » atoll; barrier islands; spit

Lagos [**lay**gos] 6°27N 3°28E, pop(1975e) 1060848. Chief port and former capital (to 1982) of Nigeria, 120 km/75 ml SW of Ibadan; on Lagos I (8 km/5 ml long and 1.6 km/1 ml wide), connected to the mainland by two bridges; port facilities at Apapa and Tin Can I; settled c.1700; slave trade centre until the mid-19th-c; occupied by the British, 1851; colony of Lagos, 1862; part of the S Nigeria protectorate, 1906; capital of Nigeria, 1960–82; airport; university (1962); tanker terminal; metals, chemicals, fish, gas, brewing, tourism; national museum, palace, racecourse. » Abuja; Nigeria [i]

Lagrange, Joseph Louis, Comte ('Count') [la**grãzh**] (1736–1813) Italian-French mathematician and astronomer, born at Turin. In 1766 he became director of the Berlin Academy, where he published papers on many aspects of number theory, mechanics, the stability of the Solar System, and algebraic equations. His major work was the *Mécanique analytique* (1788, Analytical Mechanics). After the Revolution he was appointed professor of mathematics at the Ecole Polytechnique, and head of the commission which developed the metric system of units (1795). Napoleon made him a member of the Senate and a Count. He died in Paris, and was buried in the Panthéon. » equations; Euler-Lagrange equations; Lagrangian; Lagrangian points; mechanics; number theory

Lagrange's equations » **Euler-Lagrange equations**

Lagrangian [la**gron**jian] The difference between kinetic energy K and potential energy V; symbol L, units J (joule); $L=K-V$; after French mathematician Joseph Lagrange. It is the fundamental expression of the properties of a mechanical system, from which equations of motion can be derived using Euler-Lagrange equations. » action; Euler-Lagrange equations; Hamiltonian; Lagrange

Lagrangian points Five points in the plane of revolution of two bodies (eg Earth and the Moon, the Sun and Jupiter) where gravitational forces balance so as to allow a small third body to remain in equilibrium. For example, the Trojan asteroids are found in stable orbits at L-4 and L-5 points, forming an equilateral triangle with the Sun and Jupiter. » asteroids; gravity; Lagrange

Laguna, La [la la**goo**na] 28°29N 16°19W, pop(1981) 112635. Second largest town and former capital of Tenerife I, Canary Is; bishopric; university (1701); textiles, brandy, leather, tobacco; cathedral (16th-c), Church of the Conception (1502). » Canary Islands

Lahore [la**haw**] 31°34N 74°22E, pop(1981) 2922000. City in Punjab province, Pakistan, between the Ravi and the Sutlej Rivers, 1030 km/640 ml from Karachi; second largest city in Pakistan; taken in 1849 by the British, who made it the capital of Punjab; railway; two universities (1882, 1961); trade and communications centre; textiles, carpets, footwear, electrical goods, railway engineering, metal goods; considered the cultural capital of Pakistan; museum, Badshahi Mosque, Wazir Khan Mosque, Shalimar Gardens, royal fort of Akbar; a world heritage site. » Pakistan [i]

laissez-faire (Fr 'leave alone to do') [laysay **fair**] An economic doctrine advocating that commerce and trade should be permitted to operate free of controls of any kind. It was a popular view in the mid-19th-c. The phrase was coined by Disraeli, relating to the work of Richard Cobden and John Bright. » Manchester School

Laius [**li**yuhs] In Greek legend, a king of Thebes, son of Labdacus and father of Oedipus; he married Jocasta, and was warned by an oracle that their son would destroy him. This happened when Oedipus, assumed to be dead, returned from Corinth and accidentally killed Laius during a quarrel on the road. » Jocasta; Oedipus

lake A body of water surrounded by land, and lying in a hollow which may be caused by Earth movement, as in rift valleys, or by glaciation, volcanic craters, or the collapse of the roof of limestone caves. Saltwater lakes may be parts of seas or oceans cut off by Earth movement, or formed in areas of low rainfall where mineral salts can accumulate due to evaporation. » RR12

Lake District Part of Cumbria, NW England; area of c.1800 sq km/700 sq ml noted for its scenery; a system of glaciated valleys and ribbon lakes; lakes include Windermere, Derwent Water, Ullswater, Bassenthwaite, Thirlmere, Buttermere, and Coniston Water; L Windermere, largest lake in England; mountains include Scafell (highest peak in England), Skiddaw, Helvellyn; chief towns include Keswick, Windermere, Ambleside, Grasmere; area associated with Wordsworth, Coleridge, Southey, Ruskin; national park, established in 1951, protects 866 sq km/334 sq ml; walking, climbing, water sports; farming, quarrying, forestry. » Coniston Water; Helvellyn; Lake poets; Ruskin; Scafell; Skiddaw; Ullswater; Windermere, Lake

lake dwellings » **Glastonbury lake village; Swiss lake dwellings**

Lake Placid 44°18N 74°01W, pop(1980e) 2490. Resort in Essex county, N New York State, USA; in the Adirondack Mts, 65 km/40 ml SW of Plattsburg on Mirror Lake; scene of Winter Olympic events (1932, 1980). » New York (state); Olympic Games

Lake poets A phrase used (sometimes disparagingly) to refer to those poets who took up residence in the English Lake district in the early 19th-c. Wordsworth and Coleridge were the best known. » Coleridge; English literature; poetry; Romanticism (literature); Wordsworth, William

Lakeland terrier A medium-sized terrier developed in the English Lake District to hunt foxes; coarse coat, very thick on the legs, forehead, and muzzle. » dog; terrier

Laker, Jim, properly **James (Charles)** (1922–86) British cricketer, born at Saltaire, Yorkshire. He made test cricket history at Old Trafford in 1956 when he took 19 Australian wickets for 90 runs, including 10 in one innings. Three weeks earlier, playing for his county (Surrey) also against the Australians, he also took 10 wickets in an innings. He took 193 wickets in 46 test matches and during his career (1946–64) took 1944 wickets (average 18.41). One of the finest off-spin bowlers to play for England, he retired in 1959, but made a comeback with Essex. He died in London. » cricket [i]

Lakshadweep, formerly (to 1973) **Laccadive Islands** [**lahk**-shadweep] pop(1981) 40237; area 32 sq km/12 sq ml. Union territory of India, comprising 10 inhabited and 17 uninhabited coral islands in the Arabian Sea 300 km/190 ml off the Malabar Coast of Kerala; Amindivi Is (N), Laccadive (Cannanore) Is (S); Minicoy I further S; ruled by British, 1792; ceded to India, 1956; centre of administration on Kavaratti I; population mainly Muslim; coconuts, coir, bananas, fishing, tourism. » India [i]

Lakshmi The Hindu goddess of prosperity, the consort of Vishnu, sometimes called 'the lotus-goddess'. She is associated with Diwali, the autumn festival of lights. » Diwali; Hinduism; Vishnu

Lalande, Joseph Jérôme Le Français de [la**lãd**] (1732–1807) French astronomer, born at Bourg-en-Bresse. From 1795 he was director of the Paris Observatory. He wrote several major texts on astronomy, and produced the most comprehensive star catalogue of his time (1801). He died in Paris. » astronomy; parallax

Lalibela churches A group of 11 churches in the holy city of Lalibela, C Ethiopia; a world heritage monument. The buildings, which date from c.13th-c BC, are remarkable for the ingenuity and artistry of their execution. Each is hewn from a single rock, hollowed and sculpted to look as if it were constructed from separate stones. » Ethiopia [i]

Lalique, René [la**leek**] (1860–1945) French jeweller and glassware designer, born at Ay. He studied in Paris and London, and founded his own business in Paris in 1885. His glass designs, decorated with relief figures, animals, and flowers, were an important contribution to the Art Nouveau movement. He died in Paris. » Art Nouveau

Lally, Thomas Arthur, Comte de ('Count of') (1702–66) French general, son of an Irish Jacobite, born at Romans. He accompanied Prince Charles Edward to Scotland in 1745, and in 1756 became Commander-in-Chief in the French East Indies. Active against the British in the Seven Years' War, he was defeated, and capitulated in 1761. On returning to France, he was accused of treachery, and was executed in Paris. In 1778 a royal decree declared the condemnation unjust. » Saxe; Seven Years' War; Stuart, Charles

Lamaism [**lah**mahizm] The religion of Tibet, a form of Mahayana Buddhism. Buddhism entered Tibet in the 7th-c, where it was opposed by the traditional Bon religion. It was not until the next century, when the Indian missionary Padmasambhava combined elements of both religions, that Lamaism developed. Later the reformer Tsong Kha Pa (1357–1419) founded a school called the Gelu, and its heads acquired the title of Dalai Lama, eventually becoming the spiritual and temporal rulers of Tibet, a position they held until 1959. Upon the death of a reigning Lama, a search is conducted to find an infant who is his reincarnation. » Buddhism; Dalai Lama; Mahayana; Panchen Lama

Lamarck, Jean Baptiste (Pierre Antoine) de Monet, Chevalier de (1744–1829) French naturalist and pre-Darwinian evolutionist, born at Bazentin. After serving in the French army, he developed an interest in botany, publishing *Flore française* (1773, French Flora), which was immediately successful. In 1774 he became keeper of the royal garden, and in 1793 professor of invertebrate zoology at the Museum of Natural History, Paris. His major work was the *Histoire des animaux sans vertèbres* (1815–22, Natural History of Invertebrate Animals). He died, blind and in poverty, in Paris. » evolution

Lamartine, Alphonse (Marie Louis) de [lamah**teen**] (1790–1869) French poet, statesman, and historian, born at Mâcon. His best-known work was his first volume of lyrical poems, *Méditations poétiques* (1820). He became a diplomat at Naples and Florence, became a member of the provisional government in the 1848 Revolution, and acted as Minister of Foreign Affairs. He then devoted himself to literature, publishing several historical and other works. He died at Passy. » French literature; poetry

lamb » **sheep**

Lamb, Charles (1775–1834) British essayist, born in London. Educated at Christ's Hospital, he worked as a clerk for the East India Company (1792–1825). He achieved a success through the joint publication with his sister of *Tales from Shakespeare* (1807), and they followed this by other works for children. In 1818 he published his collected verse and prose, and was invited to join the staff of the new *London Magazine*. This led to his best-known works, the series of essays under the pen name of **Elia**. He resigned his post in 1825 because of ill health, and died at Edmonton, Middlesex. » English literature; poetry

Lamb, Henry (1883–1960) British painter, born in Adelaide, Australia. He studied at Manchester University Medical School and at Guy's Hospital before taking up painting. He exhibited with the Camden Town Group, and was an official war artist (1940–4). His best-known work is the portrait of Lytton Strachey (1914, Tate). He died at Salisbury, Wiltshire. » Camden Town Group

Lambert, Constant (1905–51) British composer, conductor, and critic, born and died in London. He studied at the Royal College of Music, London, became conductor of the Sadler's Wells Ballet (1928–47), and was also known as a concert conductor and music critic, notably in *Music Ho!* (1934). His best-known composition is the choral work in jazz idiom, *The Rio Grande* (1927), and his other works include ballets, a cantata, and a concerto for piano and chamber orchestra.

Lambert, Johann Heinrich (1728–77) German mathematician, born at Mülhausen. Largely self-educated, he worked as a secretary and tutor, and in 1764 moved to Berlin, where Frederick the Great became his patron. He first showed how to measure scientifically the intensity of light (1760), and demonstrated that pi is an irrational number (1768). The unit of light intensity is named after him. He died in Berlin. » numbers; pi [i]

Lambert, John (1619–84) English general, born at Calton, Yorkshire. He studied law, then joined the parliamentary army in the English Civil War, commanding the cavalry at Marston Moor (1644), and participating in several victories. He headed the cabal which overthrew Richard Cromwell (1659), and virtually governed the country with his officers as the 'Committee of Safety'. At the Restoration (1661) he was tried, and imprisoned on Drake's I, Plymouth, until his death. » English Civil War; Restoration

Lambeth Conferences Gatherings of bishops of the Anglican Communion throughout the world at the personal invitation of the Archbishop of Canterbury for consultations, but without legislative powers. The first conference was held at the instigation of the Provincial Synod of the Church of Canada in 1867 at Lambeth Palace, the London house of the Archbishop of Canterbury, and although the interval between conferences has varied, it is normally convened every ten years. Recent meetings have lasted about a month, and have considered not only internal Anglican matters (such as the ordination of women) and theological issues, but also social issues (such as race relations and human rights). » Anglican Communion; bishop; Church of England

lamellibranch [la**mel**ibrangk] » **bivalve**

Lamentations of Jeremiah A book of the Hebrew Bible/Old Testament, probably dated shortly after the Babylonian conquest of Jerusalem (c.587/586 BC), attributed in tradition to the prophet Jeremiah, but not of the same style as the Book of Jeremiah. It consists of five poems lamenting the destruction of Jerusalem, expressing the distress of its people, and petitioning God for its restoration. The first four poems are acrostics, with the stanzas beginning with successive letters of the Hebrew alphabet. » acrostic; Jeremiah, Book of; Old Testament

Lamian War [**lay**mian] (323–322 BC) The unsuccessful revolt of the Greek states from Macedon after the death of Alexander the Great. It was so called from the town of Lamia in Thessaly, which was the scene of a protracted siege. » Macedon

Laminaria [lamin**air**ia] » **kelp**

Lammas [**la**mas] In the UK, a former church festival (1 Aug); its name is derived from the Old English word *hlāf-mæss* 'loaf-mass', the festival originally being held in thanksgiving for the harvest, with the consecration of loaves made of flour from the newly-harvested wheat. It is a quarter-day in Scotland. » quarter-day

lammergeier [**lam**uhgiyuh] An Old World vulture, native to S Europe, Africa, India, and Tibet, also known as the **bearded vulture**; grey back; reddish head and underparts; white chest, on which it rubs reddish iron oxide dust; dark 'beard' of stiff feathers; inhabits mountains; eats carrion, especially bones, which it breaks by dropping them from the air onto rocks. (*Gypaetus barbatus*. Family: *Accipitridae*.) » vulture

lamp shell An unsegmented, marine invertebrate possessing a bivalved shell and a long stalk (*pedicel*); typically found attached to a substrate or in a burrow in sediment; feeds using an array of tentacles (the *lophophore*) around the mouth; contains c.350 living species found from the inter-tidal zone to deep-sea; over 12 000 fossil species described. (Phylum: *Brachiopoda*.) » bivalve

Lampedusa, Giuseppe (Tomasi), Duke of Palma [lampuh**doo**za] (1896–1957) Italian writer, born at Palermo, Sicily. His only complete work, *Il gattopardo* (The Leopard), was published posthumously in 1958. A collection of autobiographical and fictional pieces, *Racconti*, was published in 1961. He died in Rome. » Italian literature; novel

lamprey Primitive jawless fish found in marine and adjacent fresh waters of the N Atlantic; length up to 90 cm/36 in; mouth sucker-like with rasping teeth; adults feed on body fluids of other fish; may be a serious pest to local fisheries. (*Petromyzon marinus*. Family: *Petromyzonidae*.)

LAN » **local area network**

Lanai [la**niy**] pop (1980) 2 119; area 365 sq km/140 sq ml. Island of the US state of Hawaii; part of Maui county; chief town, Lanai City; pineapples. » Hawaii

Lancashire Pop (1987e) 1 381 300; area 3 063 sq km/1 182 sq ml. County of NW England, divided into 14 districts; bounded W by the Irish Sea; Pennines in the E; drained by the Lune and Ribble Rivers; county town, Lancaster; other chief towns include Blackpool, Blackburn, Burnley; ports at Heysham, Fleetwood; world centre for cotton manufacture in 19th-c; textiles, footwear, fishing, mining, tourism, aerospace, electronics; Forest of Bowland. » England [i]; Preston

Lancaster, Osbert (1908–86) British cartoonist and writer, educated at Oxford and at the Slade School of Art. His lifelong passion was architecture, and 1934–9 he was on the staff of the

Architectural Review. He began drawing cartoons for the *Daily Express* in 1939, creating Maudie Littlehampton and other characters, and he also worked as a theatrical designer (from 1951). He was knighted in 1975. » cartoon (art)

Lancaster (UK) 54°03N 2°48W, pop (1981) 44 447. County town in Lancaster district, Lancashire, NW England; on R Lune, 32 km/20 ml N of Preston; chartered 1193; city status 1937; port trade declined with river silting; university (1964); railway; paper, textiles, plastics, chemicals; 12th-c castle, on site of Roman fort; Priory Church of St Mary (15th-c). » Lancashire

Lancaster (USA) » **Lincoln** (USA)

Lancaster, Duchy of » **Duchy of Lancaster**

Lancaster, House of The younger branch of the Plantagenet dynasty, founded by Edmund 'Crouchback', the younger son of Henry III and first earl of Lancaster (1267–96), whence came three kings of England: Henry IV (1399–1413); Henry V (1413–22); and Henry VI (1422–61, 1470–1). » Edward IV; Henry IV/V/VI (of England); Plantagenets; Roses, Wars of the; York, House of

Lancaster House Agreement An agreement which ended the war in Zimbabwe and created a new constitution under which the country would be given independence in April 1980. An election, held under British supervision, was won by the Zimbabwe African National Union under the leadership of Robert Mugabe. » Mugabe; Patriotic Front (Zimbabwe); Zimbabwe [i]

lancehead viper » **fer-de-lance**

lancelet » **amphioxus**

Lancelot, Sir or **Launcelot du Lac** The most famous of King Arthur's knights, though he is a relatively late addition to the legend. He was the son of King Ban of Benwick, the courtly lover of Guinevere, and the father of Galahad by Elaine. In spite of his near-perfection as a knight, he was unable to achieve the Grail adventure; he arrived too late to help Arthur in the last battle. » Arthur; Galahad, Sir; Grail, Holy

lancet A sharp pointed arch in a building, mainly used in Early English architecture of the 13th-c. It may also refer to a tall and narrow pointed-arch window of the same period. » Early English style; Gothic architecture

Lanchester, Frederick William (1868–1946) British car and aeronautics pioneer, born at Lewisham, near London. Best known for his work (1899–1914) with the Lanchester Motor Company, he was also consultant to Daimler and later on diesel engines. In 1907–8 he published two important books on flight, which had considerable influence on other pioneers. He died in Birmingham. » aircraft [i]; diesel engine

Lanchow » **Lanzhou**

Land, Edwin (Herbert) (1909–91) US inventor and physicist, born at Bridgeport, Connecticut. Educated at Harvard, he co-founded laboratories at Boston in 1932, and produced the light-polarizing filter material 'Polaroid' in 1936. His 'Land Polaroid' camera (1947) was a system of instant photography, with developing agents incorporated in the film itself. He is also known for his research into the nature of colour vision. » photography; Polaroid

Land Acts, Irish A succession of British Acts passed in 1870, 1881, 1903, and 1909 with the objective first of giving tenants greater security and compensation for improvements, and later of enabling tenants to buy the estates they farmed. The Acts also aimed at reducing nationalist grievances. » Land League; nationalism

Land Art » **Earthworks**

land crab A true crab that has colonized the land; breathes by means of gills, protected from drying out by a chamber formed from the margins of its hard covering (carapace); feeds on fallen fruit, carrion, and other detritus; returns to sea to spawn and for early larval development. (Class: *Malacostraca*. Order: *Decapoda*.) » crab; larva

Land League An association formed in Ireland in 1879 by Michael Davitt to agitate for greater tenant rights, in particular the '3 Fs': *fair rents*, to be fixed by arbitration if necessary; *fixity of tenure* while rents were paid; and *freedom* for tenants to sell rights of occupancy. Gladstone conceded the essence of these demands in the 1881 Land Act. » Davitt; Gladstone; Land Acts, Irish

land registration A legal procedure in which ownership of land (*title*) is officially registered. In England and Wales, this is with the *Land Registry*, though registration is not yet compulsory in all areas. Registration simplifies the procedure whereby land is transferred from vendor to purchaser. The registered proprietor (the owner) proves his or her title by reference to the appropriate entry on the register. Instead of traditional title deeds, there is a land certificate issued by the registry. In the USA, all states have recording systems for instruments affecting the title to land, but recording is generally not a condition of conveying between parties. » conveyance; lease

Land's End, ancient **Bolerium** 50°03N 5°44W. Cornwall, SW England; a granite headland, the W extremity of England; Longships lighthouse lies offshore. » Cornwall

Landau, Lev Davidovich, byname **Dev** (1908–68) Russian theoretical physicist, born at Baku. Educated at Baku and St Petersburg, he worked at the Bohr Institute in Copenhagen, and became professor of physics at Moscow (1937). He received the Nobel Prize for Physics in 1962 for work on theories of condensed matter, particularly helium. He died in Moscow. » helium; physics

Landé g-factor » **g-factor**

landing craft Small warships configured for the landing of troops and vehicles on hostile shorelines. They are typically flat-bottomed boats with a bow ramp from which infantry and armour can go directly into the assault. » warships [i]

Landor, Walter Savage (1775–1864) British writer, born at Warwick. He was expelled from both Rugby and Oxford, and lived for many years on the Continent. He wrote poems, plays, and essays, but is mainly remembered for his prose dialogues, *Imaginary Conversations* (1824–9). He died in Florence. » English literature

Landowska, Wanda (Louise) [lan**dof**ska] (1879–1959) Polish pianist, harpsichordist, and musical scholar, born in Warsaw. In 1900 she went to Paris, and in 1913 became professor of the harpsichord at the Berlin Hochschule. In 1927 she established in Paris her Ecole de Musique Ancienne, where she gave specialized training in the performance of old works. In 1940 she fled from Paris, and settled in the USA. She died at Lakeville, Connecticut. » harpsichord

landrace A type of domestic pig; long, pale body with large pendulous ears; bred mainly for bacon; three breeds: *Scandinavian* (reared indoors) and the hardier *British lop* (or *long white national lop-eared*) and *Welsh*. » pig

landrail » **corncrake**

landscape gardening The art of laying out gardens and estates for aesthetic or spiritual effect. A variety of techniques (including terracing, the use of artificial mounds, still and running water, walls, and trees), disseminated mainly from the Near and Middle East, have in different combinations and with different emphases developed into several distinct styles. In Japan the naturalistic use of trees and water evolved into a highly stylized and religiously significant arrangement of natural elements. In 18th-c Europe, formal landscaping (best characterized by the work of Le Nôtre, who made heavy use of symmetry, topiary, and artificial ornament) gave way to an artfully informal naturalism, seen particularly in the work of Kent, Repton, and Capability Brown. » Brown, Lancelot; Kent, William; Le Nôtre; Repton

landscape painting The representation of natural history in art. Trees, rivers, mountains, etc have featured in the backgrounds of pictures since ancient times, but the depiction of unified landscape for its own sake, frequently with a moral dimension, dates only from the 16th-c. » Barbizon/Danube/Hudson River School; Impressionism (art); painting; Picturesque; seascape painting; staffage; veduta

Landseer, Sir Edwin (Henry) (1802–73) British artist, born in London. Trained by his father to sketch animals from life, he exhibited at the Royal Academy when only 13. Dogs and deer were his main subjects, and several of his pictures are located in the highlands of Scotland. His paintings include 'Monarch of the Glen' (1851), and his most famous sculptures are the bronze lions in Trafalgar Square (1867). He was elected a member of the Royal Academy in 1831, knighted in 1850, and died in London. » English art

Landsteiner, Karl (1868–1943) Austrian pathologist, born in Vienna. A research assistant at the Vienna Pathological Institute (1898–1908), he became professor of pathological anatomy at Vienna (1909–19), and was a member of the Rockefeller Institute for Medical Research, New York (1922–43). He won the 1930 Nobel Prize for Physiology or Medicine for his discovery of the four different types of human blood and of the Rh factor. He died in New York City. » blood types; rhesus factor

Lane, Sir Allen, originally **Allen Lane Williams** (1902–70) British publisher and pioneer of paperback books, born in Bristol. Educated at Bristol, in 1919 he was apprenticed to The Bodley Head, where he eventually became chairman. In 1935 he formed Penguin Books Ltd, a revolutionary step in the publishing trade. He began by reprinting novels in paper covers at 6d (2½p) each, expanding to other series such as non-fictional Pelicans and children's Puffins. He was knighted in 1952, and died at Northwood, Middlesex. » book

Lang, Fritz (1890–1976) US film director, born in Vienna. Educated at Vienna, he became a painter, and after World War 1 moved to Berlin, where he began to make films, notably *Metropolis* (1926). In 1933 he refused the post of head of the German film industry, fleeing to Paris and the USA. His later films include his portrayal of mob rule, *Fury* (1936), as well as several thrillers and westerns. He died in Los Angeles.

Lange, David (Russell) [**lang**ee] (1942–) New Zealand statesman and Prime Minister (1984–9), born in Auckland. A lawyer by profession, he entered parliament in 1977, became leader of the Labour Party in 1983, and Prime Minister in the fourth Labour government. He is respected for his skill in oratory and debate. » New Zealand [i]

Langer, Susanne K(nauth) (1895–1985) US aesthetician, born in New York City. She was educated at Harvard, where she taught until 1942, subsequently holding posts at Columbia University (1945–50) and Connecticut College (1954–62). Much influenced by Ernst Cassirer, she wrote widely on aesthetics and the analysis of language, notably in *Philosophy in a New Key* (1942) and *Feeling and Form* (1953). She died at Old Lyme, Connecticut. » aesthetics; Cassirer

Langland or **Langley, William** (c.1332–c.1400) English poet, born (probably) at Ledbury, Herefordshire. Little is known about his life, but he is thought to have been a clerk and a minor cleric who lived many years in London in poverty. He is credited with the authorship of the great mediaeval alliterative poem on the theme of spiritual pilgrimage, *Piers Plowman*. » English literature; poetry

Langley, Samuel Pierpont (1834–1906) US astronomer and aeronautics pioneer, born at Roxbury, Massachusetts. He practised as a civil engineer and architect in Chicago and St Louis, and in 1867 became professor of astronomy at Western University, Pennsylvania. He invented the bolometer for measuring the Sun's radiant heat, and was the first to build a heavier-than-air flying machine. He died at Aiken, South Carolina.

Langmuir, Irving (1881–1957) US physical chemist, born in New York City. Educated at Columbia and Göttingen, he was attached to the General Electric Company (1909–50), becoming associate director of the research laboratory in 1932. He won the Nobel Prize for Chemistry in 1932 for his work on solid and liquid surfaces. His many inventions include the gas-filled tungsten lamp and atomic hydrogen welding. » tungsten

Langobards » **Lombards**

Langton, Stephen (c.1150–1228) English theologian, educated at the University of Paris. Pope Innocent III made him a cardinal in 1206, and Archbishop of Canterbury in 1207. His appointment was resisted by King John, and Langton was kept out of the see until 1213, living mostly at Pontigny. He sided warmly with the barons against John, and his name is the first of the subscribing witnesses of Magna Carta. He died at Slindon, Sussex. » Magna Carta; John

Langtry, Lillie, *née* **Emilie Charlotte Le Breton**, byname **The Jersey Lily** (1853–1929) British actress, born in Jersey, Channel Is. One of the most noted beauties of her time, she married Edward Langtry in 1874, made her first important stage appearance in 1881, and managed the Imperial Theatre. Widowed in 1897, she married Hugo Gerald de Bathe in 1899, and became well-known as a racehorse owner. She died in Monte Carlo. » theatre

language 1 A species-specific communicative ability, restricted to humans, which involves the use of sounds, grammar, and vocabulary, according to a system of rules. Though other animals can communicate vocally and by gesture, they are restricted to a particular set of messages, genetically given, which cannot be creatively varied. » linguistics **2** An individual manifestation of **1**, found within a particular community. The concept of 'a language' is not always easy to define, since it is not solely a linguistic matter. Even the apparently common-sense requirement that speakers of 'the same' language should be able to understand one another (that their dialects should be mutually intelligible) does not always obtain. In most of W Europe, the situation is straightforward, because language boundaries tend to coincide with the boundaries of nation-states, and the languages of France, Germany, Italy, etc are not mutually intelligible. But in Scandinavia, political autonomy in Norway and Sweden has led to Norwegian and Swedish being called separate 'languages', despite the fact that they are largely mutually intelligible. In China, the opposite situation obtains: varieties which occur are called 'dialects' of the Chinese language, despite the fact that several are not mutually intelligible. This comes about because they all use the same writing system, which is seen as a unifying factor. The designation of 'language' status is therefore dependent on a wide variety of social, linguistic, and political considerations, and as a result, estimates of the number of living languages in the world (usually ranging between 4 000 and 6 000) are inevitably uncertain, and should be accepted with caution. » African/Australian/Austro-Asiatic/Austronesian/Dravidian/Indo-European/Indo-Pacific/Sino-Tibetan/Uralic languages; family of languages; sign language

language isolates Languages which have no certain historical or structural affiliation with any other languages. Languages may be so classified simply because too little is known about them. There are some well-documented instances, however, which defy classification. » Basque; Japanese; Korean

language laboratory A room made up of banks of booths, each one containing a cassette recorder for a student's use, connected to a central console. At the console, a language instructor monitors the performance of students as they listen to taped exercises and record their responses to them. The system is useful for administering repetition exercises, pronunciation drills, and tests of a student's mastery at all levels of language. Its great advantage is that the students are each able to advance at their own pace. Modern laboratories are now often equipped with video recorders and various kinds of computational aids. » language; learning

Languedoc [lãguh**dok**] Former province between the R Rhône, Mediterranean, and Guyenne and Gascogne, S France; Cévennes Mts in the E; name derived from the local variety of language, *langue d'oc* (Provençal); centre of wine production. » France [i]

langur [lang**goor**] An Old World monkey, native to S and SE Asia; prominent dark 'eyebrows'; slender hand with short thumb; long tail; inhabits forests; eats leaves; two genera: **langur** (*Presbytis*, 15 species) and **snub-nosed langur** (*Pygathrix*, 4 species). The latter name (along with **pig-tailed langur**) is also used for a relative of the proboscis monkey (*Nasalis concolor*). » entellus; Old World monkey; proboscis monkey

Lanier, Sidney [la**neer**] (1842–81) US poet, born at Macon, Georgia. Among his writings are a novel and several works of criticism, but he is best remembered for his poems. He believed in a scientific approach to poetry, breaking away from traditional metrical techniques and making it more akin to musical composition, as seen in 'Corn' and 'The Symphony' (1875). He died at Lynn, N Carolina. » American literature; poetry

lanner falcon A large falcon native to S Europe and Africa; inhabits desert and open country; eats mainly birds. (*Falco biarmicus*. Family: *Falconidae*.) » falcon

lanolin [**lan**uhlin] A waxy material occurring naturally in wool. It is a mixture of esters of cholesterol with stearic, palmitic, and oleic acids. It forms strong emulsions with water, and is used in toilet preparations and ointments. » emulsion (chemistry); ester [i]

Lansbury, George (1859–1940) British politician, born near Lowestoft. Active as a radical since boyhood, he became a convinced socialist in 1890 and a Labour MP in 1910, resigning in 1912 to stand in support of women's suffrage. He was defeated and not re-elected until 1922. He founded and edited the *Daily Herald* (1912–22), and became Commissioner of Works (1929) and Leader of the Labour Party (1931–5). He died in London. » Labour Party; MacDonald, Ramsay; radicalism; socialism

Lansing 42°44N 84°33W, pop (1980) 130 414. Capital of state in Ingham County, SC Michigan, USA, on the Grand R; railway; car and truck manufacturing centre; machinery and fabricated metals. » Michigan

lanternfish Any of the small deep-sea fishes of family *Myctophidae* (6 genera), widely abundant in the world's oceans, typically at depths of 500–1 000 m/1 600–3 300 ft, but may migrate to the surface at night; length up to 15 cm/6 in; head blunt, eyes large, body with numerous light organs in characteristic patterns.

lanthanides [**lan**thaniydz] or **rare earth elements** Elements with atomic numbers from 58–72 inclusive. They have very similar chemistry, mainly forming compounds in which they show oxidation state +3. They usually occur together in mixed oxides in nature, and are separated only with difficulty. » actinides; chemical elements; RR90

Lanzhou [lan**joh**], **Lanchow**, or **Kaolan** 36°01N 103°19E, pop (1984e) 1 455 100. Capital of Gansu province, NC China, on the upper Yellow R; airfield; railway; university (1946); centre for China's atomic energy industry since 1960; trade in wheat, millet, tobacco, sorghum, melons; oil refining, metallurgy, light engineering, textiles; Gansu province museum. » China [i]

Lao Zi or **Lao-tzu** ('Old Master') (c.6th-c BC) The sage and recluse, **Lao Tan**, the reputed founder of Taoism, probably a legendary figure. If the legends derive from a historical person, we know nothing about him. He is represented as the older contemporary of Confucius, against whom most of his teaching is directed. The *Tao Te Ching* or the *Lao Tzu*, the most venerated of the three classical texts of Taoism, is attributed to him, though it dates from much later. It may have been the work of a single author, but it is more likely an anthology. » Confucianism; Taoism

Laocoon [**lay**okohon] In Greek mythology, a Trojan prince, a priest of Apollo, who objected to the plan to bring the Wooden Horse into Troy. Two serpents came out of the sea and killed him, together with his two sons. » Trojan Horse

Laoighis [**lay**ish] or **Leix** [layks], formerly **Queen's County** pop (1981) 51 171; area 1 720 sq km/664 sq ml. County in Leinster province, SC Irish Republic; watered by R Nore; Slieve Bloom Mts rise in NW; capital, Portlaoighise; agriculture, livestock; huge tracts of peat used to fuel power stations. » Irish Republic [i]; Portlaoighise

Laos [lows], official name **Lao People's Democratic Republic**, Lao **Sathalanalat Paxathipatai Paxaxôn Lao** pop (1990e) 4 024 000; area 236 800 sq km/91 405 sq ml. Republic in SE Asia, divided into 13 provinces (*khouèng*); bounded E by Vietnam, S by Cambodia, W by Thailand, and N by Burma and China; capital, Vientiane; chief towns, Luangphrabang, Pakse, Savannakhét; timezone GMT +7; E area largely depopulated by war; ethnic groups include 60% Laotian, 35% hill tribes; official language, Lao; chief religions, Buddhism, animism; unit of currency, the kip of 100 att; landlocked country on the Indochinese Peninsula; dense jungle and rugged mountains (E), rising to 2 751 m/9 025 ft; Mekong R flows NW–SE, following much of the W frontier with Thailand; monsoonal climate (heaviest, May–Sep); average annual temperatures in Vientiane, 14–34°C; visited by Europeans, 17th-c; dominated by Thailand in 19th-c; French protectorate, 1893; occupied by Japanese in World War 2; independence from France, 1949; civil war, 1953–75, between the Lao government, supported by USA, and the communist-led Patriotic Front (*Pathet Lao*), supported by North Vietnam; monarchy abolished and communist republic established, 1975; headed by a president and governed by a prime minister, who is also secretary-general of the Central Committee of the Lao People's Revolutionary Party; agricultural economy suffered severely in the civil war; rice, coffee, tobacco, cotton, spices, opium; tin, iron ore, potash; forestry, rubber, cigarettes, matches, textiles, foodstuffs. » Vientiane; RR55 political leaders

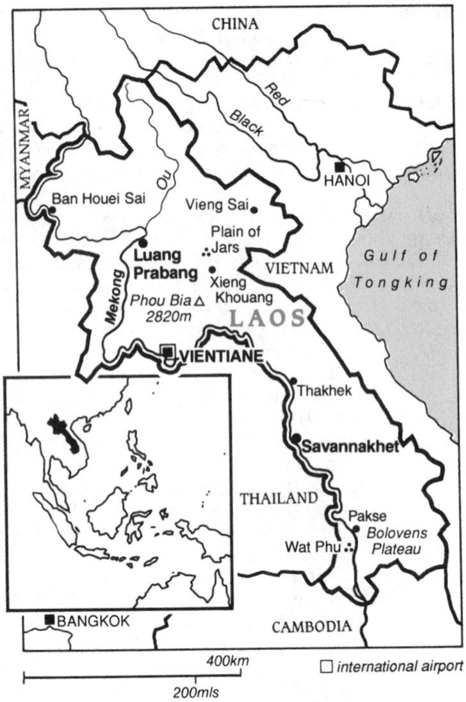

lap dissolve » **dissolve**

lapis lazuli [lapis **laz**yuliy, **laz**yulee] A deep-blue ornamental stone, principally lazurite (a silicate of sodium and aluminium), found in metamorphosed limestones. It was formerly the source of the blue pigment ultramarine, now made synthetically. » silicate minerals; Plate IV

Lapita people [la**pee**ta] Austronesian-speaking voyagers, ancestors of the Polynesians. Some of them, after moving southwards through Melanesia, travelled E from Vanuatu to the then uninhabited groups of Fiji and Tonga about 1500 BC. Evidence of their movements is mostly provided by archaeological remains, especially pottery. » Polynesia

Lapiths [**lap**iths] In Greek mythology, a people of Thessaly, mentioned in several legends. Perithous, King of the Lapiths, invited the Centaurs to his wedding with Hippodameia. A terrible fight took place between the two groups, in which the Centaurs were defeated. » centaur

Laplace, Pierre Simon, Marquis de [lap**las**] (1749–1827) French mathematician and astronomer, born at Beaumont-en-Auge. He studied at Caen, and mastered mathematics, applying this knowledge to physical astronomy, particularly the stability of orbits in the Solar System. His 5-volume *Mécanique céleste* (1799–1825, Celestial Mechanics) is a landmark in applied mathematics. He entered the Senate in 1799, and was made a peer in 1815. He died in Paris. » Jupiter (astronomy); Lagrange; Solar System

Lapland, Swedish **Lappland**, Finnish **Lapin Lääni** pop (1982) 198 011, area 98 938 sq km/38 190 sq ml. Province of N Finland, bounded W by Sweden, NW by Norway, and E by Russia; mainly within Arctic Circle; largely tundra (N), forest (S), and mountains (W); occupies c.30% of total area of Finland; Mt Haltia on frontier with Norway; provincial capital, Rovaniemi; considerable emigration to the S in recent years; chromium, iron mining; farming, fishing, trapping. The area generally called Lapland also includes large parts of Norway, Sweden, and Russia. » Finland [i]; Lapp; Rovaniemi; tundra

Lapp A people living in the sparsely populated N areas of

Finland, Sweden, Norway, and Russia, mostly within the Arctic Circle, with more than half in Norway. They speak Lapp, a Uralic language, although most are bilingual and some speak only the national language of the country. They have probably been in the area for 2000 years, but originally were more widely dispersed. Lapps are mainly Lutheran Christians, but in Finland and Russia many belong to the Russian Orthodox Church. Most are fishermen, while others farm, breed reindeer, are foresters, and work in factories. Population c.30000. » ethnic group; Lapland; Uralic languages

laptop computer A small light-weight computer, usually powered by internal batteries, which can easily be carried around and used comfortably on the user's lap. They became generally available in the mid-1980s. » computer

lapwing A plover, especially the **common lapwing** (*Vanellus vanellus*); inhabits grassland, cultivation, water edges, and swamps. (Genus: *Vanellus*, 10 species. Family: *Charadriidae*.) » peewit; plover

larch A deciduous conifer native to colder parts of the N hemisphere; long shoots rough-textured with persistent bases of fallen leaves; short shoots with tufts of needles. It tolerates intense cold, but needs full light to grow well. Often dominant in N forests, it is widely planted for timber. (Genus: *Larix*, 10–12 species. Family: *Pinaceae*.) » conifer; deciduous plants

lard A fat produced from pigs, widely used in cooking and baking, and also in the preparation of certain perfumes and ointments. **Lard oil** is used as a lubricant and in soap manufacture.

Lardner, Ring(gold) (Wilmer) (1885–1933) US writer, born in Michigan. He earned his living as a sports columnist in Chicago and New York before publishing his first collection of short stories *You Know Me, Al* (about baseball) in 1916. Between then and 1929 he wrote prolifically in a variety of forms: novels, plays, satirical verse (*Bib Ballads*, 1915), and an autobiography, *The Story of a Wonder Man* (1927), but is mainly appreciated for his short stories. He died at East Hampton, New York. » American literature; short story

Lares [**lah**reez] Minor Roman deities. Normally associated with the household was the guardian of the hearth (*lar familiaris*), but there were also guardians of crossroads (*lares viales*) and of the State (*lares praestites*). » Penates

lark A small, dull-coloured songbird, mainly Old World, especially Africa; inhabits open country; eats seeds and insects; nests on ground. The name is also used for the **lark quail** (Family: *Turnicidae*); the **meadowlark** (Family: *Icteridae*); and the **mudlark** (Family: *Grallinidae*). (Family: *Alaudidae*, 75 species.) » button quail; magpie; meadowlark; mudlark; skylark

lark quail » quail

Larkin, Philip (1922–85) British poet and novelist, born in Coventry, Warwickshire. Educated at Oxford, he worked as a librarian at Wellington (Shropshire), Leicester, Belfast, and (from 1955) Hull University. His collections of poems include *The Less Deceived* (1955), *The Whitsun Weddings* (1964), and *High Windows* (1974). His *Collected Poems* appeared in 1988. He also wrote two novels, a book on jazz criticism, and edited the *Oxford Book of Twentieth Century English Verse* (1973). He died in Hull. » English literature; poetry

larkspur An annual native to the N hemisphere; related and very similar to delphiniums, and sometimes included in that genus, but generally smaller; flowers blue, pink, or white, borne in short spikes. (Genus: *Consolida*, 40 species. Family: *Ranunculaceae*.) » annual; delphinium

Larnaca [**lah**naka], Gr **Larnax**, Turkish **Larnaka**, **Iskele** 34°55N 33°36E, pop (1973) 19608. Port and capital town of Larnaca district, S Cyprus, on Larnaca Bay; SW of Dhekelia British base; airport; old Turkish fort (1625), now a museum. » Cyprus [i]

Larousse, Pierre (Athanase) (1817–75) French lexicographer and encyclopedist, born at Toucy. He studied at Versailles, became a teacher, and began his linguistic research in Paris in 1840. He wrote several grammars, dictionaries, and other textbooks, notably his *Grand dictionnaire universel du XIXe siècle* (15 vols, 1865–76). He died in Paris. » dictionary

larva A general term for a stage in an animal's development between hatching and the attainment of the adult form, or maturity. Larval stages are often typical of the group, such as the caterpillar larva of butterflies, the nauplius larva of crustaceans, and the cercaria larva of digenetic flukes. Larvae often occupy a different habitat from the adults, and serve as a dispersal stage in the life cycle. » life cycle

laryngitis Acute or chronic inflammation of the larynx, with swelling of the vocal cords. It often accompanies infection elsewhere in the respiratory tract, such as common cold or bronchitis. » larynx

larynx That part of the air passage lying in humans between the trachea (below) and the oropharynx (above), situated in the middle of the front of the neck; also called the 'voice box', because it contains the *vocal folds* or *cords*, responsible for the production of sounds. It consists of a framework of cartilages joined together by a number of ligaments and capable of movement with respect to each other. It is attached by muscles to the hyoid bone, and so moves upwards on swallowing. The prominent hard projection in the front of the neck, especially in males (the *Adam's apple*), is part of the thyroid cartilage. The larynx acts as a valve to prevent the passage of food and liquids into the airways below (failure to do so results in choking, and the expulsion of the offending material). It may also be modified to control the expulsion of air from the lungs (by changing the size of the glottis) and to change the pitch of the sound (by altering the length and tension of the vocal folds). The deeper voices of males (which develop at puberty) result from their having a larger larynx and longer vocal folds than females. » cartilage; croup; glottis; laryngitis; trachea; vocal cords

Las Casas, Bartolomé de (1474–1566) Spanish missionary priest, the 'Apostle of the Indians', born at Seville. He sailed in the third voyage of Columbus (1502) to Hispaniola, was ordained (1512), and travelled to Cuba (1513). His desire to protect the natives from slavery led him to visit the Spanish court on several occasions. Appointed Bishop of Chiapa, he was received (1544) with hostility by the colonists, returned to Spain, and resigned his see (1547). He died in Madrid. » Columbus, Christopher; missions, Christian; slave trade

Las Cruces [las **kroo**sez] 32°19N 106°47W, pop (1980) 45086. Seat of Dona Ana County, S New Mexico, USA, on the Rio Grande; founded, 1848; railway; university (1888); White Sands Missile Range nearby, a major military and NASA testing site, where the first atomic bomb was tested; name commemorates massacre of 40 travellers by Apache Indians in 1830; Enchilada Fiesta (Oct). » atomic bomb; NASA; New Mexico

Las Palmas (de Gran Canaria) [las **pal**mas] pop (1981) 756353; area 4072 sq km/1572 sq ml. Spanish province in the Canary Is, comprising the islands of Gran Canaria, Lanzarote, and Fuerteventura; tourism, shipyards, mineral water, cement, livestock, textiles, fruit and vegetables, metal products, food processing; capital, Las Palmas (de Gran Canaria), pop (1981) 366454, resort and seaport (Puerto de la Luz); airport; tourism, trade in sugar, tomatoes, bananas; Columbus's House, cathedral, hermitage of San Telmo, Church of San Francisco; Los Reyes Magos (Jan), Winter Festival (Feb–Mar), Festival of Spain (Apr–May). » Canary Islands

Las Vegas (Span 'the meadows') [las **vay**gas] 36°10N 115°09W, pop (1980) 164674. Seat of Clark County, SE Nevada, USA; largest city in the state; named after the natural meadows which served as camping sites on early trails to the W; settled by Mormons, 1855–7; purchased by a railway company, 1903; city status, 1911; airport; railway; university (1957); noted for its gaming casinos and 24-hour entertainment; commercial centre for a mining and ranching area; printing and publishing, chemicals, glass products; Mormon Fort, Liberace Museum. » casino; Mormons; Nevada

Lascaux [las**koh**] A small, richly-decorated Palaeolithic cave of c.15000 BC near Montignac, Dordogne, SW France, renowned for its naturalistic mural paintings and engravings of animals – cows, bulls, horses, bison, ibex, musk-ox, and reindeer. Found by schoolboys in 1940 and opened to the public in 1947, it was closed permanently in 1963 when humidity changes threatened the paintings. A replica was opened nearby in 1984. » Magdalenian; rock art; Three Age System

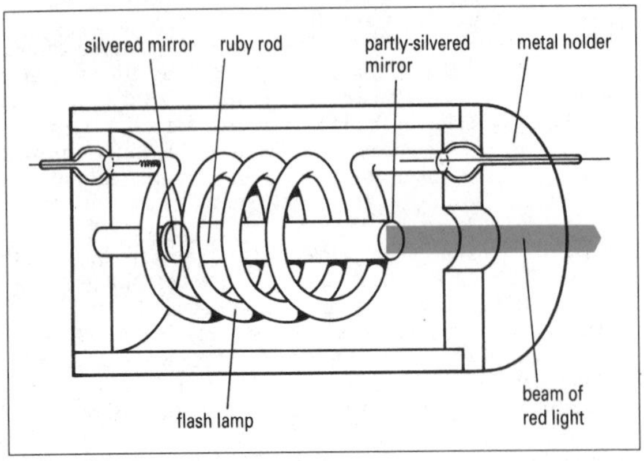

Section through a ruby laser

laser A device which produces light, infrared, or ultraviolet radiation with special properties, using a system of excited atoms; the name is an acronym of *light amplification by the stimulated emission of radiation*. The first laser was built in 1960 by US physicist Theodore Maiman (1927–), following theoretical work by Charles Townes and Arthur Schawlow. Atoms absorb energy in well-defined amounts, raising electrons to excited states; the electrons are said to move from one energy level to a level of higher energy. Usually an electron returns to its original level after less than 10^{-8} seconds, releasing energy as a photon of light. If another photon, of energy similar to that of the photon about to be released, strikes the excited atom, then photon production is more rapid; this is called *stimulated emission* (after Einstein, 1917). The result is two photons identical in phase moving in the same direction. Should these photons themselves interact with more excited atoms, eventually a cascade of identical photons will be produced, all moving in one direction. Laser action depends on the choice of special atomic systems for which an energy supply is able to raise large numbers of atoms to excited states, ready to emit photons when stimulated. Mirrors at either end of the laser reflect light end-to-end inside the laser to maintain its action. At one end, the mirror is partially transparent, allowing a portion of the light to escape to produce a laser beam. Typically, energy is supplied to the laser by electrical discharge or a powerful light source.

Laser light is monochromatic (all one colour), coherent (in step), produced as a beam which does not spread, and travels large distances undiminished in intensity. The light is produced either as a continuous beam or as pulses. Intensities of up to 10^{20}W/m^2, and pulses of less than 10^{-14}sec, have been produced. The many uses of lasers include supermarket bar code scanners, welding, surveying, phototherapy in medicine, eye surgery, hologram production, and directed energy weapons. » chemical laser; coherence; dye laser; energy level; free electron laser; laser cooling/mass spectrometer/printer/scanning; photomultiplier; photon; semi-conductor laser; X-ray laser

laser cooling A technique for reducing the velocity of atoms or ions by bombardment with laser light; used in atom and ion traps. When a laser photon strikes an oncoming atom, the photon is absorbed and subsequently re-emitted in some random direction, reducing the atom's velocity. Many such cycles allow atom velocity to be reduced from hundreds to tens of metres per second in a thousandth of a second. The atoms absorb laser photons only while moving towards the laser. » atom trap; ion trap; laser [i]

laser mass spectrometer A mass spectrometer which uses a laser to convert a sample for analysis into a form which can pass through the analysing system. Mass spectrometry needs a pure and uncontaminated source of matter propelled to the system, which deflects different components of the sample in slightly different directions. Lasers can be used particularly for the non-destructive evaporation of the sample, providing a highly localized action on the specimen without disturbing the mounting or medium. » laser [i]; mass spectrometer

laser printer A type of printer which uses a small laser to generate characters. It generally operates using xerographic principles, and is capable of producing very high quality typescript and graphics. Early laser printers were relatively expensive, but decreasing costs are establishing them as an economic means of fast, quiet printing. » laser [i]; printer, computer; xerography [i]

laser scanning 1 Causing a laser beam to scan, ie move in such a way as to point in all directions in succession. The direction of the beam may need to be varied for some uses (eg in radar). This can be done by electro-acoustic methods (using the vibration of a medium at or near the source), or by electro-optical methods (such as electrically modifying the effect on a polarized beam of some transparent cell in its path). **2** Scanning with a laser. A digital recording (yielding an eventual sound or visual signal), consisting of pits in a metallized plastic disc, is scanned by a laser beam. The response of the beam is received by a photodetector, analysed, and reproduced aurally or visually. » laser [i]

Lashley, Karl S(pencer) (1890–1958) US psychologist, born at Davis, Virginia. Educated at Johns Hopkins University, he taught at the universities of Minnesota (1920–9), Chicago (1929–35), and Harvard (1935–55). In 1942 he became director of the Yerkes laboratories of primate biology in Florida. A specialist in genetic psychology, he made valuable contributions to the study of the localization of brain function. He died in Paris. » brain [i]; laterality

Lasker, Emmanuel (1868–1941) German chess player and mathematician, born at Berlinchen, Prussia. He won the world championship in 1894, retaining it until 1921, when he was defeated by Capablanca. Educated as a mathematician, he left Germany in 1933, and finally settled in the USA, continuing to play chess until his late 60s. He died in New York City. » chess

Laski, Harold (Joseph) (1893–1950) British political scientist and socialist, born in Manchester. Educated at Manchester and Oxford, he lectured at several US universities before joining the London School of Economics (1920), where he became professor of political science in 1926. The development of his political philosophy, a modified Marxism, can be seen in his many books, such as *Authority in the Modern State* (1919) and *A Grammar of Politics* (1925). He died in London. » Marx; socialism

Laski, Marghanita (1915–88) British novelist and critic, born in Manchester, the niece of Harold Laski. Educated at Oxford, her first novel, *Love on the Supertax*, appeared in 1944; later novels included *Little Boy Lost* (1949) and *The Victorian Chaise-longue* (1953). She wrote extensively for newspapers and reviews, and published a number of critical works. She died in Dublin. » English literature; Laski, Harold; literary criticism; novel

Lassa fever An infectious disease caused by a virus confined at the present time to sub-Saharan W Africa. It is associated with pharyngitis, muscle pain, and high fever, and carries a high mortality. » virus

Lassus, Orlandus, or **Orlando di Lasso** (c.1532–94) Flemish composer, born at Mons. He wrote several masses, motets, and psalms, and also a large number of madrigals and songs in French and German. He visited Italy, Belgium, and France, and from 1556 lived largely in Munich, where he died.

Last Supper In the New Testament Gospels, the last meal of Jesus with his disciples on the eve of his arrest and crucifixion. In the three synoptic gospels, this is considered a Passover meal, and is significant for Jesus' words over the bread and cup of wine, where he declares 'This is my body' and 'This is my blood of the covenant which is poured out for many' (*Mark* 14.22–4). John's gospel dates the meal before the Passover day, and gives no record of these words. The event is commemorated in the early Church's celebration of the Lord's Supper (1 *Cor* 11), and subsequently in the sacrament of Holy Communion. » Eucharist; Gospels, canonical; Jesus Christ

latent heat Heat absorbed or released when a substance

undergoes a change of state at a constant temperature, such as solid to liquid (*latent heat of fusion*) or liquid to gas (*latent heat of vaporization*); symbol *L*, units J (joule). For ice at 0°C, the latent heat of fusion is 3.35×10^5J/kg; for water, heat of vaporization at 100°C is 2.26×10^6J/kg. » boiling point; heat; isothermal process; melting point

latent image The invisible image formed in a photographic emulsion by its exposure to light. It is made visible by development when the light-affected silver halide grains are converted to black metallic silver. » photography

laterality or **lateralization** A characteristic of the human brain, in which the left and right cerebral hemispheres are specialized for different functions; also known as **hemispheric specialization**. In the majority of both right- and left-handed people, the left hemisphere is specialized for language functions: speaking, understanding, reading, and writing. The right hemisphere is specialized for the perception of complex patterns, both visual (eg faces) and tactile. Normally, the two hemispheres work together, sending information from one to the other by way of complex brain connections. » brain [i]; language

Lateran Church of St John The oldest of the four patriarchal basilicas of Rome, the episcopal seat of the pope as Bishop of Rome. Until the 14th-c, when it was destroyed by fire, it was the centre of the Roman Catholic world. The present building dates from the 16th-c. » pope; Roman Catholicism

Lateran Councils A series of councils of the Church held at the Lateran Palace, Rome, between the 7th-c and the 18th-c. Those held in 1123, 1139, 1179, and especially 1215 are the most significant. The Fourth or Great Council defined the doctrine of the Eucharist ('transubstantiation'), and represents the culmination of mediaeval papal legislation. » Council of the Church; Eucharist; pope; transubstantiation

Lateran Treaty (1929) An agreement between the Italian fascist state and the papacy, ending a church-state conflict dating from 1870. Italy recognized the sovereignty of Vatican City, and Catholicism as the country's only religion; the papacy recognized the Italian state, and accepted the loss of other papal territories as irreversible. The treaty was confirmed in the Italian constitution of 1948. » fascism; papacy; Papal States

laterite Tropical soil in which seasonal fluctuations of groundwater have concentrated aluminium and iron oxide, forming a thick, hard, reddish layer. It is often used as roadstone. » groundwater; soil

latex A milky fluid found in special cells or ducts (*lactifers*) and present in many different plants. It is usually white, but can be colourless, yellow, orange, or red, and contains various substances in solution or suspension, such as starch, sugars, alkaloids, and rubber. In some cases it may be involved with nutrition of the plant or represent waste products, but the exact function is unknown. » alkaloids; chicle; gutta percha; papaw; poppy; rubber; spurge; starch; sugars

lathe A common machine tool used to shape workpieces of various materials. These are held in the jaws of the lathe's chuck, and rotated under power. The tools for boring, threading, cutting, or facing the workpiece are brought into contact with it either manually or under machine control. » machine tools

lathyrism A permanent paralysis, caused by excessive intake of a vetch crop (*Lathyrus sativus*). It is sown together with wheat in many parts of Africa and Asia, so that if dry weather prevents wheat growth, the vetch will perform satisfactorily in its place. » vetch

Latimer, Hugh (c.1485–1555) English Protestant reformer and martyr, born at Thurcaston, Leicestershire. He was educated at Cambridge, and appointed a university preacher in 1522. Converted to Protestantism, he was one of the divines who examined the lawfulness of Henry's marriage, and declared on the King's side. In 1535 he was made Bishop of Worcester, but opposed the Six Articles of Henry VIII, for which he was imprisoned in 1536, 1546, and 1553. He became known as a preacher under Edward VI, but under Mary was tried for heresy and was burned at Oxford. » Edward VI; Henry VIII; Protestantism; Reformation

Latin » **Italic/Romance languages; Latin literature**

Latin America The 18 Spanish-speaking republics of the W hemisphere, together with Portuguese-speaking Brazil (the largest Latin-American country) and French-speaking Haiti. The name first came into use in France just before 1860. » Latin-American Free Trade Association/literature

Latin-American Free Trade Association (LAFTA) An economic association of Latin-American countries set up by the Treaty of Montevideo in 1960; its members are Argentina, Bolivia, Brazil, Chile, Colombia, Ecuador, Mexico, Paraguay, Peru, Uruguay, and Venezuela. It aimed at eliminating tariffs and other trade barriers by gradual reduction over a 12-year period. Progress has been made, but not as fast as had been hoped.

Latin-American literature There were some remarkable writers in both Spanish and Portuguese from the S American continent in the late 19th-c, including the poet and novelist Machado de Assiz (1839–1908) in Brazil, the poet José Hernández (1834–86) in the Argentine, and the early modernist Rubén Darío (1867–1916) in Nicaragua. But it is in the 20th-c that Latin-American literature has commanded world attention. This was first achieved in poetry. Major writers include the Chilean Gabriela Mistral (1889–1957) and the immensely popular Pablo Neruda (1904–73), who both won the Nobel prize; the Peruvian exile Cesar Vallejo (1882–1938), the Mexican Octavio Paz (1914–), and the Nicaraguan Sergio Ramírez. After World War 2 it was the sophisticated short fictions of Jorge Luis Borges (1899–1986) that captured the imagination, and exercised a powerful influence. The 'magic realism' of later novelists has been attributed to the volatile politics of the region. Among the best-known are the Argentinian Julio Cortázar (1914–84; eg *Hopscotch*, 1963), the Columbian García Márquez (1928–; eg *A Hundred Years of Solitude*, 1967), and the Mexican Carlos Fuentes (1928–; *The Death of Artemio Cruz*, 1962). The Brazilian Jorge Amado (1912–) wrote, in exile, from a more explicit ideological position: and the Peruvian Mario Vargas Llosa (1936–) is likewise deeply involved in politics. » novel; poetry; Portuguese literature; Realism; Spanish literature; Borges; Darío; Mistral, Gabriela; Neruda

Latin literature Oratory was respected from the earliest days of republican Rome (from 500 BC), and hymns and songs graced popular festivals; but Latin literature emerged in the pre-Classical period (250–85 BC), when many experiments were made on Greek models. The most significant writers of this time were the comic dramatists Plautus and Terence, the poet Ennius, who introduced the hexameter, and the satirist Lucilius (180–102 BC), of whose works only fragments survive. During the last century BC, the greater sophistication of poets such as Catullus and Lucretius heralded the Golden Age of Latin literature, which was fulfilled by the refinement of Latin prose in the oratory of Cicero, and the historical and philosophical writings of Caesar and Sallust (86–34 BC). The 45 years of the Augustan Age, from Actium (31 BC) to the death of Augustus (AD 14), witnessed a remarkable output of poetry: the odes and epistles (as well as the satires) of Horace, the *Georgics* and the posthumous *Aeneid* of Virgil, the love poetry and the *Metamorphoses* of Ovid, and the elegies of Propertius and Tibullus. The prose writings of Livy, the greatest Roman historian, also form part of this peak of achievement. After a barren period, the death of Nero (AD 68) brought Martial's brilliant epigrams and the more sober work of the elder Pliny and Quintilian. Classical Latin literature concludes with the writers of the 'Silver Age' under Trajan and Hadrian (98–138). These include the greatest Roman satirist, Juvenal; the historian Tacitus; the master of the private letter, the younger Pliny; and the biographer Suetonius. » classicism; comedy; elegy; epigram; Greek literature; oratory; Caesar; Catullus; Cicero; Ennius; Horace; Juvenal; Livy; Lucretius; Martial; Ovid; Plautus; Pliny the Elder/Younger; Propertius; Suetonius; Tacitus; Terence; Tibullus; Virgil

Latinus [latiynuhs] In legends of early Rome, the ancestor and eponymous King of the Latins. He was either descended from Circe (according to Hesiod) or from Faunus (according to Virgil). In the *Aeneid*, Latinus gives his daughter Lavinia to Aeneas. » Hesiod; Virgil

latitude and longitude Two dimensions used in mapping. The **latitude** of a point on the Earth's surface is the angular

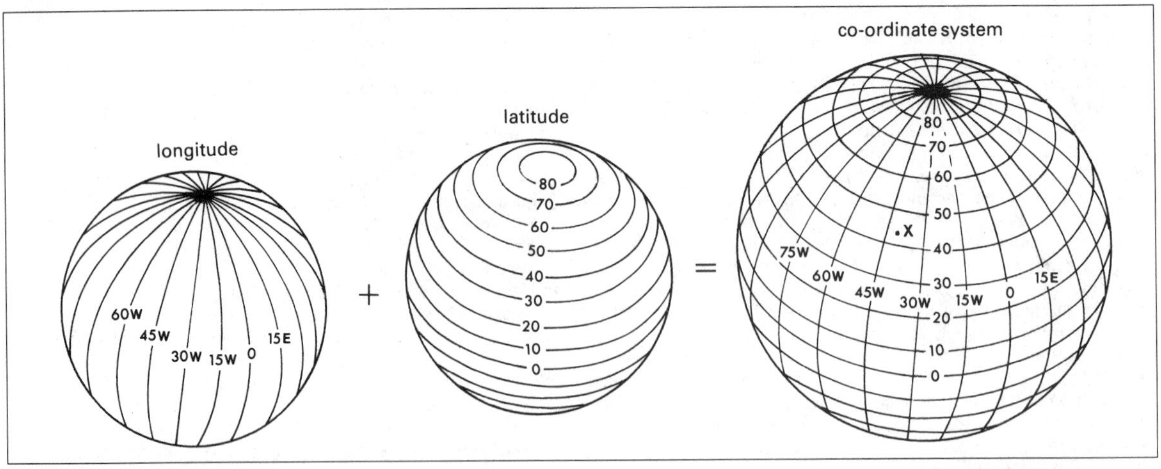

Lines of longitude and latitude give a co-ordinate system that permits the location and identification of all points on the Earth's surface (measured in degrees °, minutes ′, and seconds ″). The point x would have the following co-ordinate locations: 44°10′10″N, 39°25′40″W

distance, N or S from the Equator (at latitude 0°); the Poles are at latitude 90°; lines (*parallels*) of latitude are parallel circles running E–W joining points of equal latitude. The distance between 1° of latitude varies slightly, because the Earth is not a perfect sphere. At the Equator, it is 110.551 km/68.694 ml; at latitude 45° it is 111.130 km/69.053 ml; and near the Poles it is 111.698 km/69.406 ml. Important lines of latitude are the Tropic of Cancer (23.5° N), Tropic of Capricorn (23.5° S), the Arctic Circle (66.5° N), and the Antarctic Circle (66.5° S). Lines (*meridians*) of **longitude** are great circles running N–S and meeting at the Poles; the longitude is measured as an angular distance from the Greenwich meridian defined as 0° up to 180° E or W. At the Equator, the distance between lines of longitude 1° apart is 111.32 km/69.172 ml. This is reduced to 78.848 km/48.995 ml at latitude 45°, and is zero at the Poles. » cartography; Earth [i]; great circle

Latium [**lay**shuhm] In antiquity, the area SE of Rome between the Apennine Mts and the sea. It was the territory of the Latini, Latin-speaking peoples of whom the Romans are the most famous. Densely populated in early Roman times, by the imperial period it had become the recreation area of the Roman rich who filled it with luxurious villas. » Tusculum

Latour, Maurice Quentin de [la**toor**] (1704–88) French pastellist and portrait painter, born at St Quentin. He studied in Paris, and from 1737 exhibited many portraits, including those of Louis XV, Madame de Pompadour, Voltaire, and Rousseau. He became portraitist to the king (1750–73), and died at St Quentin. » French art

Látrabjarg [lowtra**byark**] 65°30N 24°32W. Westernmost point of Iceland, and one of the highest cliff faces in the world; in Vestfirðir region, W Iceland; British trawler *Dhoon* ran aground below the cliff in 1947, the entire crew being saved by men lowered down the cliff on ropes in one of the world's greatest rescue achievements. » Iceland [i]

lattice energy The energy required to convert one mole of an ionic solid to gaseous ions. Its value can be estimated reasonably for many compounds, and used to calculate other energies. » Born-Haber cycle

Latvia, Latvian **Latvija**, Russ **Latviskaya** pop (1990e) 2 700 000; area 63 700 sq km/24 600 sq ml. Republic in NE Europe, bounded W and NW by the Baltic Sea; flat, glaciated region; NW coast indented by the Gulf of Riga; chief river, the Daugava; over 40% forested; incorporated into Russia, 1721; independent state, 1918; proclaimed a Soviet Socialist Republic, 1940; occupied by Germany in World War 2; growth of a new nationalist movement in the 1980s; declared independence, 1991; well-developed national folklore, particularly in the 1860s when the Latvian theatre was founded in Riga (1868); capital, Riga; chief towns Daugavpils, Liepaja; machines, metalworking, instruments, electrical engineering, electronics, chemicals, furniture, knitwear, food processing, fishing; cattle, pigs, oats, barley, rye, potatoes, flax. » Baltic languages; Soviet Union [i]

Latvian » **Baltic languages**

Latynina, Larissa (Semyonovna), *née* **Diril** [lat**ee**nina] (1935–) Ukrainian gymnast, born at Kharsan. In 1956 and 1964 she collected 18 Olympic medals, a record for any sport, winning nine golds. During her 13-year career she won 24 Olympic, World, and European titles. She retired in 1966. » gymnastics

Laud, William (1573–1645) Archbishop of Canterbury, born at Reading, Berkshire. Educated at Oxford, he was ordained in 1601. His learning and industry brought him many patrons, and he rapidly received preferment, becoming King's Chaplain (1611), Bishop of St David's (1621), Bishop of Bath and Wells and a Privy Councillor (1626), Bishop of London (1628), and Archbishop of Canterbury (1633). With Strafford and Charles I, he worked for absolutism in Church and state. In Scotland, his attempt (1635–7) to Anglicize the Church led to the Bishops' Wars. In 1640 the Long Parliament impeached him. He was found guilty, and executed on Tower Hill. » absolutism; Bishops' Wars; Charles I (of England); Church of England; Long Parliament; Strafford

Lauda, Niki [**low**da] (1949–) Austrian racing driver, born in Vienna. He was three times world champion, in 1975, 1977 (both Ferrari), and 1984 (Marlboro-McLaren). He survived a horrific crash at the Nurburgring, Germany, in 1976, and despite bad burns returned and nearly won the world championship again. He retired in 1979, but made a comeback in 1982, when he won his third world title. He retired again in 1985 after 25 career wins, and became the proprietor of Lauda-Air. » motor racing

laudanum [**law**danuhm] A preparation of opium introduced by Paracelsus in the early 16th-c. Addiction to laudanum was socially acceptable until the early 19th-c, when the invention of the hypodermic syringe and needle made narcotic addiction more serious. » drug addiction; narcotics; opium; Paracelsus

Lauder, Sir Harry (MacLennan) (1870–1950) British comic singer, born in Edinburgh, Scotland. He began on the music hall stage as an Irish comedian, but made his name as a singer of Scots songs, many of which he wrote himself, such as 'Roamin' in the Gloamin''. He was knighted in 1919 for his work in organizing troop entertainments in World War 1. He died near Strathaven, Lanarkshire. » music hall

Lauderdale, John Maitland, Duke of (1616–82) Scottish statesman, born at Lethington, East Lothian. He was an ardent supporter of the Covenanters (1638), and in 1643 became a Scottish Commissioner at Westminster. Made earl in 1645, he was taken prisoner at Worcester (1651), and imprisoned. At the Restoration (1660) he became Scottish Secretary of State. A

Privy Councillor, he was a member of the Cabal advisers to Charles II, and was created duke in 1672. He died at Tunbridge Wells, Kent. » Cabal; Covenanters; English Civil War; Restoration

laughing gas » **nitrous oxide**

laughing jackass/kookaburra » **kookaburra**

Laughton, Charles [lawtn] (1899–1962) British actor, born at Scarborough, Yorkshire. He first appeared on the stage in 1926, appeared with the Old Vic Company, and gave many renowned Shakespearean performances, including Macbeth and Lear. He began to act in films in 1932, and portrayed a wide range of memorable roles, such as Henry VIII in *The Private Life of Henry VIII* (1933) and Captain Bligh in *Mutiny on the Bounty* (1935). He became a US citizen in 1950, and died in Hollywood.

Launceston [lonsestn] 41°25S 147°07E, pop (1981) 64 555 (Greater Launceston). City in Tasmania, Australia, at the confluence of the N Esk, S Esk, and Tamar Rivers; second largest city in Tasmania; airfield; railway; timber, engineering, textiles, brewing; Cataract Gorge (with suspension bridge and chair-lift). » Tasmania

launch opportunity The dates between which launches can take place to insert an interplanetary spacecraft on a minimum energy transfer orbit to a planet; typically 10 to 20 days in duration. Launches are not practicable at other times because of launch vehicle performance limitations. Because Earth and the target planet are both orbiting the Sun, launch opportunities occur at intervals that repeat cyclically: for the other outer planets, they occur about every 12–13 months, for Mars every 26 months, for Venus every 19 months, and for Mercury also every 19 months (but due to the 7° inclination of Mercury's orbit to the ecliptic, practical opportunities are every 36 months). » launch window; planet; Solar System

launch vehicle A rocket-propelled vehicle used to carry aloft spacecraft from the Earth's surface, generally consisting of several 'stages' which separate sequentially as fuel in each is consumed. The thrust is provided by the controlled explosive burning of liquid fuels (eg kerosene and oxygen, hydrogen and oxygen) or solid propellants (typically a synthetic rubber fuel mixed with an oxidized powder). The technique derived from weapon delivery systems developed during and after World War 2, and was pioneered by Konstantin Tsiolkovsky in the USSR, Robert Goddard in the USA, and Wernher von Braun in Germany. » European Space Agency; geosynchronous Earth orbit; low Earth orbit (LEO); Space Organizations Worldwide; space shuttle [i]; spacecraft; *see illustration p. 688*

launch window The time during a given day when a spacecraft may be launched on its desired trajectory. It can last from minutes to more than an hour, depending on the mission and, for interplanetary launches, on an exact date within the launch opportunity. There are two windows during each 24-hour period, one of which may be impractical because of other factors, such as launch safety for night launches. » launch opportunity

Laurasia The name given to the N 'supercontinent' comprising present-day N America, Europe, and Asia, excluding India, which began to break away from the single land mass Pangaea about 200 million years ago. The S supercontinent was Gondwanaland. » continental drift; Gondwanaland

laurel A name applied to various unrelated trees and shrubs which have glossy, leathery, evergreen leaves, but mainly to members of the large family *Lauraceae* in which the tissues contain numerous oil cavities and are aromatic. » evergreen plants; greenheart; shrub; sweet bay; tree [i]

Laurel and Hardy US comedians who formed the first Hollywood film comedy team. The 'thin one', **Stan Laurel** (1890–1965), originally **Arthur Stanley Jefferson**, was born at Ulverston, Lancashire. He began in a British touring company, went to the USA in 1910, and worked in silent films from 1917. The 'fat one', **Oliver Hardy** (1892–1957), born near Atlanta, Georgia, left college to join a troupe of minstrels before drifting into the film industry. They came together in 1926. They made many full-length feature films, but their best efforts are generally thought to be their early (1927–31) shorts. Their contrasting personalities, general clumsiness, and disaster-packed predicaments made them a universally popular comedy duo. Laurel died at Santa Monica, and Hardy at Hollywood, California.

Lauren, Ralph [loruhn], originally **Lifschitz** (1939–) US fashion designer, born in New York City. He attended nightschool for business studies, and worked as a salesperson in Bloomingdales. In 1967 he joined Beau Brummel Neckwear, and created the Polo range for men, later including womenswear. He is famous for his American styles, such as 'prairie look' and 'frontier fashions'. » fashion

Laurentian Shield » **Canadian Shield**

Laurier, Sir Wilfrid (1841–1919) Canadian statesman and Prime Minister (1896–1911), born at St Lin, Quebec. He became a lawyer, a journalist, and a member of the Quebec Legislative Assembly. He entered Federal politics in 1874, and became Minister of Inland Revenue (1877), leader of the Liberal Party (1887–1919), and the first French-Canadian and Roman Catholic to be Prime Minister of Canada (1896). A firm supporter of self-government for Canada, in his home policy he was an advocate of compromise and free trade with the USA. He died in Ottawa. » Canada [i]

laurustinus [loruhstiynuhs] A dense evergreen shrub or small tree, growing to 7 m/23 ft, native to S Europe; leaves oval, shiny; flowers 5-petalled, white, in clusters 4–9 cm/1½–3½ in across; fruit berry-like, dark, metallic blue. It is grown for ornament, but often fails to fruit in cooler regions. (*Viburnum tinus*. Family: *Caprifoliaceae*.) » evergreen plants; shrub; tree [i]

Lausanne [lohzan] 46°32N 6°39E, pop (1980) 127 349. Tourist resort, convention centre, and capital of Vaud canton, W Switzerland; on N shore of L Geneva, 51 km/32 ml NE of Geneva; two airfields; railway junction; university (1891); clothing, confectionery, printing, leather; seat of the International Olympic Committee; Mon Repos Park, with Olympic Museum; cathedral (1275), town hall (17th-c), Bishop's Palace; Fête of Lausanne (Jun), biennial Festival of Tapestry. » Switzerland [i]

Lautréamont, Comte de ('Count of') [lohtrayamõ], pseudonym of **Isidore Ducasse** (1846–70) French poet, born in Montevideo, Uruguay. He went to France as an adolescent, and published the sequence of prose poems *Les Chants de Maldoror* (The Songs of Maldoror) in 1868. *Poésies* were published in 1870, the year he died in Paris. His work was a significant influence on the Surrealists and other Modernist writers. » French literature; Modernism; poetry; Surrealism

lava Hot molten rock erupted onto the Earth's surface from a volcano. On solidification it forms volcanic igneous rocks such as rhyolite, andesite, or basalt. Lava temperature and viscosity depends on its chemical composition, with the more silica-rich lava being cooler (around 900°C) and more viscous than basic lavas (temperature up to 1100°C), which flow more freely, forming volcanoes with gentle slopes. » igneous rock; magma; volcano

Laval, Pierre (1883–1945) French statesman and Prime Minister (1931–2, 1935–6), born at Châteldon. He became a lawyer, Deputy (1914), and Senator (1926), before serving as Premier (1931–2, 1935–6). From a position on the left, he moved rightwards during the late 1930s, and in the Vichy government was Pétain's deputy (1940), then his rival. As Prime Minister (1942–4), he openly collaborated with the Germans. Fleeing after the liberation to Germany and Spain, he was brought back, charged with treason, and executed in Paris. » Pétain; Vichy

lavallier » **microphone** [i]

lavender A small aromatic shrub, native mainly to Mediterranean and Atlantic islands, typical of dry scrub; young stems square; leaves narrow, sometimes deeply lobed, greyish, in opposite pairs; flowers 2-lipped, lavender or mauve, in dense spikes. It is widely cultivated for ornament, and as the source of oil of lavender for the perfume industry and for pot-pourri. (Genus: *Lavandula*, 28 species. Family: *Labiatae*.) » shrub

Laver, Rod(ney George), byname **The Rockhampton Rocket** (1938–) Australian lawn tennis player, born at Rockhampton, Queensland. The first person to achieve the Grand Slam twice

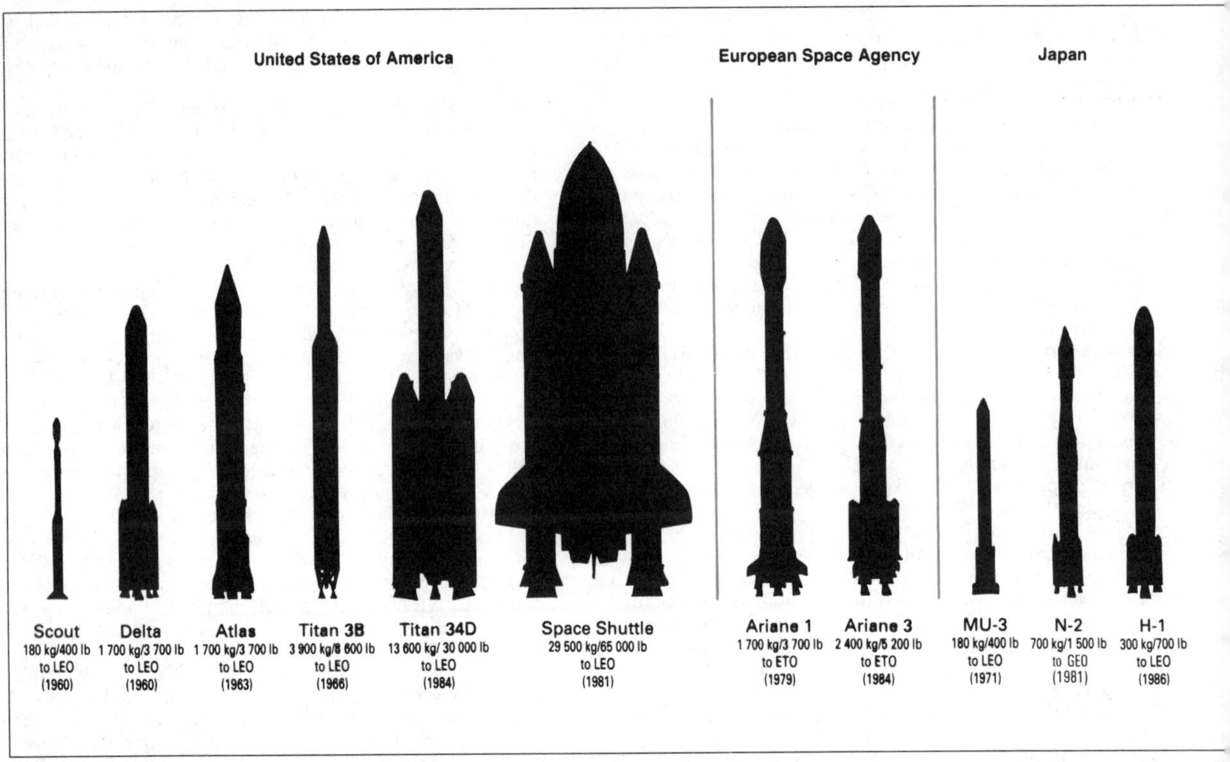

International space launchers – The major launch vehicles in use, as of March 1988. The data refer to lift capacity (given in kg/lb, in most cases to the nearest hundred) and year of launch.

(1962, 1969), he turned professional in 1963, and dominated the professional circuit. He won four singles titles at Wimbledon (1961–2, 1968–9), and was the first to win there when it went open in 1968. Left-handed, he was a very aggressive player. » tennis, lawn [i]

Lavoisier, Antoine Laurent [lavwazyay] (1743–94) French chemist, regarded as the founder of modern chemistry, born in Paris. In 1788 he showed that air is a mixture of gases which he called oxygen and nitrogen, thus disproving the earlier theory of phlogiston. His major work is the *Traité élémentaire de chimie* (1789), containing the ideas which set chemistry on its modern path. He also devised the modern method of naming chemical compounds, and was a member of the commission which devised the metric system. Despite his many reforms, he was guillotined in Paris on a contrived charge of counter-revolutionary activity. » air; chemical elements; oxygen; phlogiston theory; thermochemistry

law Specifically, a rule of conduct laid down by a controlling authority; generally, the whole body of such rules, recognized and enforced by society in the courts. Laws are made by the body recognized as having the constitutional authority to make them, ie the legislature. In common law systems, the courts are particularly influential in developing the law; although they may be said to interpret the law, the accretion of case decisions can be regarded as effectively creating the law, even though (as in the UK) parliament is sovereign. In states with a written constitution, such as the USA, the Supreme Court may have the power to declare particular laws unconstitutional, ie inconsistent with the provisions of the constitution. » administrative/brehon/civil/criminal/international/Salic/space law; jurisprudence; Law Commission; sea, law of the; Supreme Court

Law, (Andrew) Bonar (1858–1923) British statesman and Prime Minister (1922–3), born in New Brunswick, Canada. Educated in Canada and Glasgow, he was an iron merchant in Glasgow, became a Unionist MP in 1900, and in 1911 succeeded Balfour as Unionist leader. He acted as Colonial Secretary (1915–16), a member of the War Cabinet, Chancellor of the Exchequer (1916–18), Lord Privy Seal (1919), and from 1916 Leader of the House of Commons. He retired in 1921 through ill health, but returned to serve as Premier for several months in 1922–3. He died in London. » Balfour

Law, William (1686–1761) English divine, born and died at Kingscliffe, Northamptonshire. Educated at Cambridge, he became a fellow (1711), and was ordained, but was forced to resign on refusing to take the oath of allegiance to George I. He wrote several treatises on Christian ethics and mysticism, notably the *Serious Call to a Devout and Holy Life* (1729), which influenced the Wesleys. » Christianity; ethics; George I; mysticism; Wesley, John

Law Commission Body established by the Law Commissions Act (1965) for England and Wales and for Scotland, appointed by the Lord Chancellor from the judiciary and from practising and academic lawyers. Its function is to examine the law with a view to reform and codification, and to suggest the removal of obsolete and anomalous rules. While influential, it has no power to change the law. » law; Lord Chancellor

Law Society The professional body for solicitors in England and Wales; a separate Law Society exists for Scotland. It has disciplinary powers relating to solicitors' conduct, and prescribes the rules governing their admission to practice. More generally, it promotes the interests of the profession as a whole, as seen in its attempts to secure greater rights for its members to be heard in the courts (*rights of audience*). » solicitor

Lawler, Ray(mond Evenor) (1921–) Australian playwright, born in Melbourne. He was a factory-hand at 13, but then became an actor with the National Theatre Company in Melbourne. He achieved international fame with his play about the outback, *Summer of the Seventeenth Doll* (1955), in which he took the leading role. His work was influential in introducing greater realism into Australian drama.

Lawrence, D(avid) H(erbert) (1885–1930) British poet and novelist, born at Eastwood, Nottinghamshire. The son of a miner, he became a schoolmaster, and after the success of his first novel, *The White Peacock* (1911), decided to live by writing. He eloped with Frieda von Richthofen in 1912, and

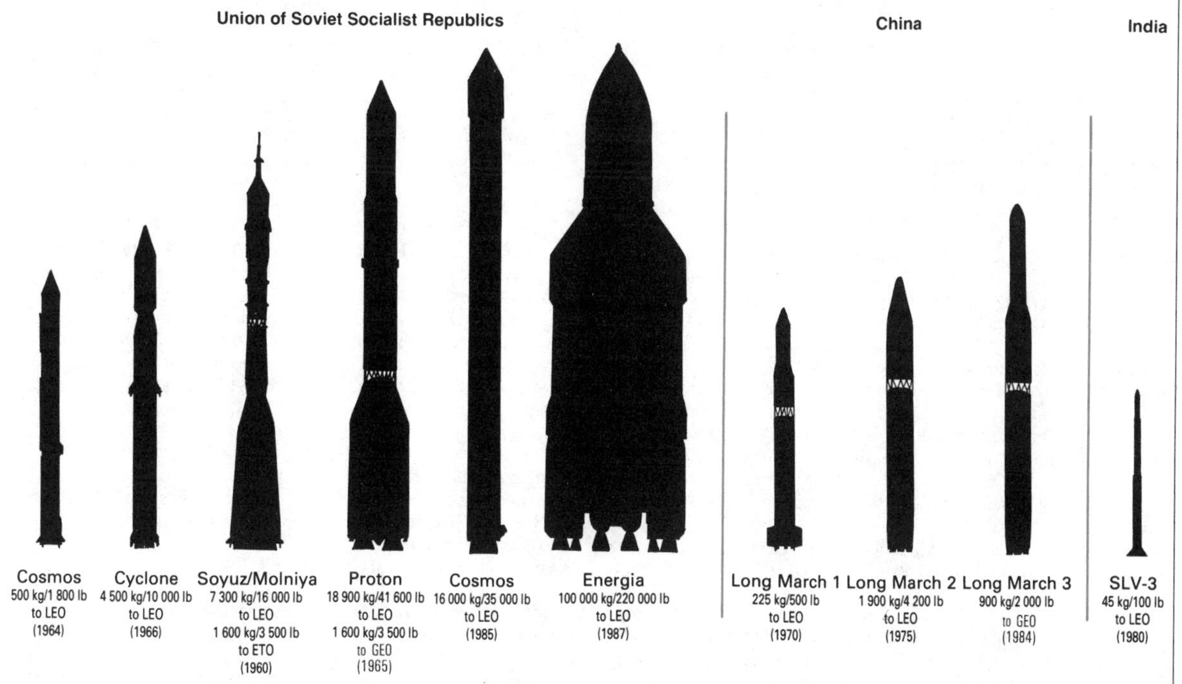

LEO Low Earth Orbit (c.200 km/125 ml) GEO Geosynchronous Earth Orbit (36 000 km/22 500 ml)
ETO Elliptical Transfer Orbit (intermediate between LEO and GEO)

travelled in Europe. He achieved fame with *Sons and Lovers* (1913), but was prosecuted for obscenity after publishing *The Rainbow* (1915). He left England in 1919, living in Italy, Australia, the USA, and Mexico, and returning to Italy for health reasons in 1921. He was further prosecuted for obscenity over the publication in Florence of *Lady Chatterley's Lover* (1928), and over an exhibition of his paintings in London the same year. His collected poems were also published in 1928. Other major novels include *Women in Love* (1921) and *The Plumed Serpent* (1926). He also wrote many short stories, short novels, and travel books. His letters are an important part of his output, over 5 000 being included in the latest edition (7 vols, 1979–). He died at Vence, France. » English literature; novel

Lawrence, Ernest O(rlando) (1901–58) US physicist, born at Canton, S Dakota. He taught at Yale and Berkeley, where in 1936 he was appointed director of the radiation laboratory, having constructed the first cyclotron for the production of high energy atomic particles. He was awarded the Nobel Prize for Physics in 1939, and died at Palo Alto, California. » cyclotron

Lawrence, T(homas) E(dward), byname **Lawrence of Arabia** (1888–1935) British soldier and author, born at Tremadoc, N Wales. Before World War 1 he travelled in the Middle East, studying Crusader castles and participating in the excavation of Carchemish. In 1914 he joined military intelligence and was sent to Cairo, where he became a member of the Arab Bureau. In 1916 he was appointed the British liaison officer to the Arab Revolt, led by Feisal, the son of the Sherif of Mecca, and was present at the taking of Aqaba in 1917 and of Damascus in 1918. He was an adviser to Feisal at the Paris Peace Conference and a member of the Middle East Department at the Colonial Office (1921). His account of the Arab Revolt, *Seven Pillars of Wisdom*, abridged by himself as *Revolt in the Desert*, became one of the classics of war literature. His exploits received so much publicity that he became a legendary figure, and he attempted to escape his fame by enlisting in the ranks of the RAF (1922) as J H Ross, in the Royal Tank Corps (1923) as T E Shaw, and again in the RAF in 1925. He retired in 1935 and was killed in a motor-cycling accident near his cottage in Dorset. » World War 1

Lawson, Nigel (1932–) British Conservative politician, educated at Westminster and Oxford. He spent some time working for various newspapers and also for television (1956–72), and during this time edited the *Spectator* (1966–70). Elected to parliament in 1974, when the Conservatives returned to office he became Financial Secretary to the Treasury (1979–81), Energy Secretary (1981–3), and Chancellor of the Exchequer (1983–9). During his time at the Exchequer, Britain saw lower direct taxes, but high interest rates and record trade deficits. » Conservative Party

Lawson cypress A species of false cypress, identifiable by the parsley-like scent of its bruised foliage; extremely variable in height, shape, branching, and colour; native to SW Oregon and NW California, but one of the most widely cultivated conifers with c.200 named cultivars. (*Chamaecyparis lawsoniana*. Family: *Cupressaceae*.) » conifer; cultivar; false cypress

laxative A drug which causes emptying of the bowels; also known as a **purgative**. Laxatives are overused for the treatment of constipation, which is usually cured by a high fibre diet. Except when medically recommended, they do more harm than good. Examples include castor oil and diphenylmethane. » castor-oil plant; fibre

Laxness, Halldór (Gudjónsson Kiljan) (1902–) Icelandic writer, born in Reykjavik. He travelled in Europe and the USA after World War 1, and became a Catholic, but in 1927 was converted to socialism. His works include *Salka Valka* (1934), a story of Icelandic fishing folk, and the epic *Sjálfstaet folk* (1934–5, Independent People). He was awarded the Nobel Prize for Literature in 1955. » Icelandic literature; novel

lay-planning or **laying up** A technique in industrial garment-making which permits the simultaneous cutting of many garment pieces, achieved by laying a number of fabric pieces on top of each other. Lay planning is done to ensure economy of fabric use. By carefully arranging the pattern pieces on the fabric, the minimum quantity of fabric is used.

Layamon (early 13th-c) English priest and poet, who lived at Ernley (now Areley), on the R Severn, Worcestershire. He wrote an amplified imitation of Wace's *Brut d'Angleterre*, recounting the history of England from the arrival of a legendary Trojan, Brutus, down to the 7th-c AD. It is one of the first poems written in Middle English, and contains a great deal of material on the Arthurian legends. » Arthur; English literature; Wace

layering A means of propagating plants by burying a stem in the soil while it is still attached to the plant. The buried portion forms roots, and eventually a separate plant. » vegetative reproduction

Lazarists A religious order, founded in France at the priory of St Lazare, Paris, in 1625 by St Vincent de Paul; properly known as the **Congregation of the Mission (CM)**; also called the **Vincentians**. Originally missionaries to rural districts and educators of the clergy, they now have foundations worldwide. » missions, Christian; Vincent de Paul, St

Le Brun, Charles (1619–90) French historical painter, born in Paris. He studied in Rome, and became a major influence on 17th-c French art. He helped to found the Academy of Painting and Sculpture in 1648, was the first director of the Gobelins tapestry works (1662), and was employed by Louis XIV in the decoration of Versailles (1668–83). He died in Paris. » French art; Gobelins; Louis XIV

Le Carré, John [luh **ka**ray], pseudonym of **David John Moore Cornwell** (1931–) British novelist, born in Poole, Dorset. Educated at Sherborne, Berne, and Oxford, he taught at Eton before entering the British Foreign Service in Bonn and Hamburg, resigning in 1964 to become a full-time writer. His first published novel, *Call for The Dead* (1961) introduced his 'anti-hero' George Smiley, who appears in most of his stories. Among his successes are *The Spy Who Came In From The Cold* (1963), *Tinker, Tailor, Soldier, Spy* (1974), and *The Perfect Spy* (1986). Many of his novels have been successfully filmed or televised. » novel; spy story

Le Corbusier » **Corbusier, Le**

Le Fanu, (Joseph) Sheridan [**lef**uhnyoo] (1814–73) Irish novelist and journalist, born in Dublin. He studied law, then became a journalist, writing for the *Dublin University Magazine*, of which he was editor and later, proprietor. His novels include *The House by the Churchyard* (1863) and *Uncle Silas* (1864). He also wrote short stories, mainly of the supernatural, such as *In a Glass Darkly* (1872). The owner of several newspapers, he died in Dublin. » novel; short story

Le Havre, formerly **Le Havre-de-Grace** [luh **hah**vruh] 49°30N 0°06E, pop (1982) 200 411. Commercial seaport in Seine-Maritime department, NW France; on the English Channel, on N side of R Seine estuary, 176 km/109 ml WNW of Paris; naval base under Napoleon I; Allied base in World War 1; largely rebuilt since heavy damage in World War 2; chief French port for transatlantic passenger liners; ferry service to England; machinery, cars; trade in tropical goods, oil (pipeline to Paris); mediaeval town of Harfleur to the E; Church of St Joseph. » Napoleon I

Le Mans [luh **mã**], ancient **Oppidum Suindinum** 48°00N 0°10E, pop (1982) 150 931. Commercial city and capital of Sarthe department, NW France; on R Sarthe, 187 km/116 ml SW of Paris; ancient capital of Maine; fortified by the Romans, 3rd–4th-c; railway junction; centre of commerce and agricultural trade; motor vehicles; Cathedral of St Julien (11th–15th-c), Notre-Dame-de-la-Coutore (11th-c); annual 24-hour motor race (Jun). » motor racing

Le Nain [luh **nã**] A family of French painters: three brothers, **Antoine** (c.1588–1648), **Louis** (c.1593–1648), and **Mathieu** (c.1607–77). All were born at Laon, but worked in Paris from c.1630, and all were foundation members of the Académie in 1648. Louis is considered the best, with his large genre-scenes and groups of peasants painted in beautiful greyish greens and browns. 'The Forge' (Louvre) may have been painted by Louis and Mathieu together, for the brothers seem occasionally to have collaborated. » French art; genre painting

Le Nôtre, André [luh **noh**truh] (1613–1700) The creator of French landscape gardening, born and died in Paris. He designed the gardens at Versailles, and laid out St James's Park in London. His formal gardens were widely imitated throughout Europe. » landscape gardening

Le Sage or **Lesage, Alain René** [luh **sazh**] (1668–1747) French novelist and dramatist, born at Sarzeau, Brittany. He studied law in Paris, then turned to literature. He wrote a large number of satirical comedies, mainly adaptations of Spanish sources, but is best-known for his picaresque 4-volume novel *Histoire de Gil Blas de Santillane* (1715–35, The Adventures of Gil Blas of Santillane). He died at Boulogne. » drama; French literature; novel; satire

Leach, Johnny, properly **John** (1922–) British table tennis player, born at Romford, Essex. He won the world singles title in 1949 and 1951, and was a member of England's winning Swaythling Cup team in 1953. During 12 years as an England international (1947–59), he represented his country 152 times. He became England's nonplaying captain upon retirement, and team manager in 1968, giving up his post in 1970 to concentrate on his sports goods firm. » table tennis

Leacock, Stephen (Butler) (1869–1944) Canadian economist and humorist, born at Swanmore, Hampshire, UK. His family emigrated to Canada when he was six. He became a teacher, then lectured at McGill University, where he was head of the department of economics and political science (1908–36). His popular short stories, essays, and parodies include *Literary Lapses* (1910) and *Nonsense Novels* (1911). He died in Toronto. » Canadian literature; parody

lead Pb (Lat *plumbum*) element 82, a soft, dense (11.5 g cm^{-3}) metal, melting point 328°C. Its main natural source is the sulphide (PbS). Its good corrosion resistance and easy workability led to its early use in plumbing and for corrosive liquids containers, with considerable toxic results, as it is slowly oxidized in the presence of air and water. It is used in quantity for the production of accumulators (storage batteries) and tetra-ethyl lead. » chemical elements; metal; tetra-ethyl lead; RR90

lead poisoning A disease acquired by swallowing or inhaling lead, which is deposited in bones. It causes abdominal colic, anaemia, and mental confusion. Some evidence suggests that lesser degrees of poisoning (eg from lead in the atmosphere, from car exhaust fumes, or in water supplies) impair brain development in children and lower IQ. Formerly a common industrial disease, it is now rare. » IQ; lead

Leadbelly, byname of **Huddie Ledbetter** (1888–1949) US folk and blues singer, and guitarist, born at Mooringsport, Louisiana, and raised in Texas. By 16, he mastered six- and twelve-string guitars, accordian, harmonica, and piano, and became a wandering musician all over the US South. At 17 he killed a man in a fight and was sentenced to 36 years in prison. After six years, he sang for the warden and was pardoned. In 1930, he stabbed a man and was sentenced to 10 years, but folklorist Alan Lomax got him a pardon after five years, and took him to New York City, where he made several recordings. He died in New York City. » blues; jazz; Lomax, Alan

leaf The main photosynthetic organ of green plants, divided into a blade (*lamina*) and a stalk (*petiole*). The lamina is usually

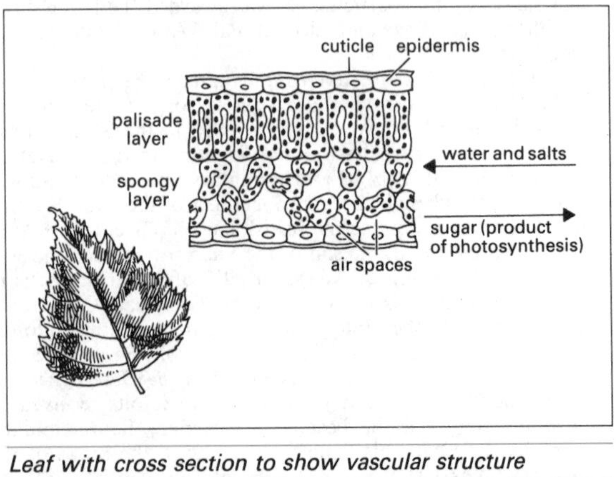

Leaf with cross section to show vascular structure

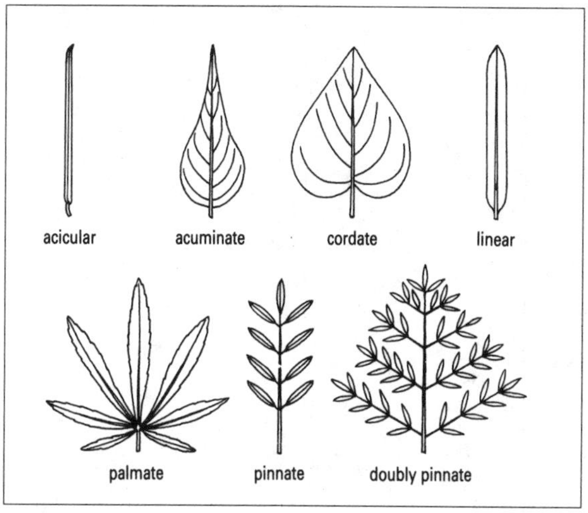

Leaf types

broad and thin, to present maximum surface area to sunlight and allow easy diffusion of gases and water vapour to and from the leaf. It is composed of several distinct layers of tissues: the *epidermis* protects the inner tissues – the *palisade layer*, which is the primary site of photosynthesis, and the spongy *mesophyll*, which has large air spaces and is the primary site of gas exchange. A network of vascular tissue, the *veins*, transports water and sap to and from the leaf. The epidermis secretes a waxy cuticle, mostly impervious to water and gases which enter and leave via pores (*stomata*) concentrated in the lower surface of the leaf.

The main source of water loss for a plant is due to transpiration via the leaves. This is minimized by the waxy cuticle, and by the opening and closing of the stomata in response to changes in humidity. Other modifications to reduce water-loss are found particularly in plants from dry or cold regions, including reduction in leaf size, inrolled margins to protect stomata, and regular shedding of leaves during unfavourable seasons. Some plants have replaced their leaves entirely with less vulnerable photosynthetic organs, such as green stems. Leaves range from a few mm to 20 m in length, exhibit a great variety of shapes, and may be entire, toothed, lobed, or completely divided into separate *leaflets*. These characters and the arrangement of the leaves on the stem are diagnostic for many plant groups. Leaves may also have specialized functions, such as water-storage in succulents, traps in carnivorous plants, and tendrils in climbers. » bract; cotyledons; palmate; photosynthesis; pinnate; stomata; tendril

leaf beetle A robust, often brightly coloured beetle; most are surface feeders on plant leaves; larvae grub-like, feeding on leaves, or are root and stem borers; c.35 000 species, including the Colorado potato beetle. (Order: *Coleoptera*. Family: *Chrysomelidae*.) » beetle; Colorado beetle; larva

leaf hopper A small, hopping insect that feeds by sucking sap or cell contents of plants; causes damage by direct feeding, by toxic secretions, and by transmitting viral diseases; c.20 000 species, including many serious pests affecting economically important crops. (Order: *Homoptera*. Family: *Cicadellidae*.) » insect [i]; virus

leaf insect A large, flattened insect with broad, flattened extensions on its legs, giving its entire body a leaf-like appearance. About 50 species are found mainly in SE Asia and New Guinea. (Order: *Phasmoptera*. Family: *Phyllidae*.) » insect [i]

leaf miner An insect larva that eats its way through leaf tissues between upper and lower surfaces of the leaf, leaving spaces (*mines*) behind; most have flattened bodies and wedge-like heads; leaf miners are mostly the larvae of flies, moths, and beetles. » insect [i]; larva; leaf [i]

leaf monkey » **langur**

leafcutter ant A fungus-feeding ant; foraging workers cut leaves to provide the basic material for a fungus garden inside their soil nest; workers harvest fungus to feed larvae; c.200 species, mostly found in the New World tropics. (Order: *Hymenoptera*. Family: *Formicidae*.) » ant; fungus; larva

leafcutter bee A solitary bee that cuts pieces of leaf to line or close its nest. It can be an important pollinator of plants, such as alfalfa. (Order: *Hymenoptera*. Family: *Megachilidae*.) » bee

League of Nations An international organization whose constitution was drafted at the Paris Peace Conference in 1919, and incorporated into the peace treaties. The main aims were to preserve international peace and security by the prevention or speedy settlement of disputes and the promotion of disarmament. It operated through a Council, which met several times a year, and an annual Assembly, which met at its Geneva headquarters. The USA refused to join, but there were 53 members by 1923, including the UK, France, Italy, and Japan. Germany joined in 1926, and Russia in 1934, but Germany and Japan withdrew in 1933, and Italy in 1936. It became increasingly ineffective in the later 1930s, and after World War 2 transferred its functions to the United Nations. » Paris Peace Conference; United Nations

League of Rights An Australian populist right-wing organization, founded in 1960 by Eric Butler (1916–), who had been engaged in similar activities since 1934. The League, which operates on the fringe of conservative politics, supports God, Queen, the Commonwealth of Nations, apartheid, and private enterprise. It opposes fluoridation of water supplies, communism, bureaucracy, and Asian immigration. » Liberal Party (Australia)

Leakey, L(ouis) S(eymour) B(azett) (1903–72) British anthropologist, born at Kabete, Kenya. Educated at Cambridge, he took part in several archaeological expeditions to E Africa, and became curator of the Coryndon Memorial Museum at Nairobi (1945–61). His great discoveries took place in E Africa, where in 1959 he and his wife **Mary Douglas Leakey** (1913–, *née* Nicol) unearthed the skull of *Zinjanthropus*. In 1964 they found the remains of *Homo habilis*, and in 1967 of *Kenyapithecus africanus*. He died in London. Their son, **Richard (Erskine Frere) Leakey** (1944–), has continued to make further important finds in the area. » *Homo* [i]; Zinjanthropus

Lean, David (1908–) British film director, born in Croydon, Greater London, and educated at Reading. Noel Coward and the Cineguild group gave him co-direction of *In Which We Serve* (1942), and for them he directed and co-scripted *This Happy Breed* (1944), *Blithe Spirit*, and *Brief Encounter* (both 1945). His interpretations of Dickens in *Great Expectations* (1946) and *Oliver Twist* (1948) were acclaimed as classics, and in the 1950s he produced three great epics: *The Bridge Over the River Kwai* (1957), *Lawrence of Arabia* (1962), and *Doctor Zhivago* (1965). Later films were *Ryan's Daughter* (1970) and *A Passage to India* (1984).

Leander » **Hero and Leander**

leap year A year of 366 days, with a day added to the month of February; any year whose date is a number exactly divisible by four is a leap year, except years ending in 00, which must be divisible by 400 to be accounted leap years. The extra day is added every four years to allow for the difference between a year of 365 days and the actual time it takes the Earth to circle the Sun (approximately 365¼ days). The system was introduced to the Western Julian calendar in its final form in AD 8, and modified by the Gregorian calendar of 1582. » Julian calendar

Lear A legendary King of Britain, first recorded in Geoffrey of Monmouth, though his name resembles that of the Celtic god of the sea. The son of Bladud, he reigned for sixty years. In his old age two of his daughters, Goneril and Regan, conspired against him, but the third daughter, Cordelia, saved him and became queen after his death. (The story is changed by Shakespeare, so that she died before his eyes.) Leicester is named after him. » Bladud

Lear, Edward (1812–88) British artist and author, born in London. From the age of 15 he lived by his drawing, and after 1837 lived mainly abroad, where he painted many landscapes. He is remembered more for his illustrated books of travels, and for his books of nonsense verse, beginning with the *Book of Nonsense* (1846), written for the Earl of Derby's grandchildren. His later years were spent in Italy, and he died at San Remo.

learning The acquisition of knowledge and/or behavioural tendencies as a result of specific experiences in an individual's life. It is distinguished from behavioural changes due to motivation (an individual's varying physiological state, needs, desires) or maturation (the growth and development of body structures and functions, such as the appearance of sexual responsiveness at puberty). Imprinting, habituation, and conditioning are examples of very general widespread types of learning. Psychological **learning theories** aim to discover the general laws and properties of such simple, universal processes. Some cases of learning, however, are thought to involve more unusual special-purpose systems, such as song-learning by many birds, and language acquisition by children. » artificial intelligence; conditioning; imprinting

lease A legal arrangement, also known as a **tenancy**, whereby the *lessor* (or landlord) grants the *lessee* (or tenant) the right to occupy land for a defined period of time. The period may be fixed (eg 10 years) or periodic (eg weekly). » land registration; property

leaseback An economic operation where a business sells an asset (such as property), the buyer renting (ie leasing) the asset back to the business. The firm continues to have use of the asset, but also has cash from the proceeds of the sale which it can use in other ways. » lease

leasehold » **freehold**

least-action principle A fundamental principle in mechanics which states that a mechanical system evolves in such a way that its action is as small as possible. The principle allows the derivation of Euler-Lagrange equations. Fermat's principle is a special case applicable to optics. The Feynman path integral is the quantum version. » action; Euler-Lagrange equations; Fermat's principle [i]

leather Animal skin rendered durable and resistant to wear and degeneration by tanning. The skin is limed to remove hair, cleaned of flesh, and then soaked in solutions of extracts of bark, galls, or other vegetable products which contain tannins (tannic acids widely distributed in nature) or chrome salts. It is finished mechanically according to use. The properties of leather are due to its fibrous and porous structure, and to its resistance to deterioration on repeated wetting and drying. *Morocco* leather is a goat skin, repeatedly polished. *Chamois* leather was originally from the chamois deer, but most is now from other skins split and tanned for softness. Synthetic materials with a porous structure resembling leather are now made. » tannins

leatherback turtle A sea turtle, worldwide in warm seas; the largest turtle (length, over 1.5 m/5 ft); no shell (adult has only small bony plates embedded in leathery skin); seven ridges along back; long front limbs (over 2.5 m/8 ft tip to tip); no claws; weak jaws; eats jellyfish; also known as **leathery turtle**. (*Dermochelys coriacea*. Family: *Dermochelyidae*.) » turtle (reptile)

leatherhead » **friarbird** [i]

leatherjacket » **cranefly**

Leavis, F(rank) R(aymond) (1895–1978) British critic, born in Cambridge, where he was educated, worked, and died. After service in World War 1, he became a lecturer in English at Emmanuel College (1925), and was later a fellow of Downing College (1936–52). He edited the journal *Scrutiny* (1932–53), and wrote several major critical works, notably *New Bearings in English Poetry* (1932), *The Great Tradition* (1948), and *The Common Pursuit* (1952). Throughout his work he stresses the moral value of literary study, and his re-assessments of such major figures as Joseph Conrad and D H Lawrence were to prove extremely influential. » Conrad; Lawrence, D H; literary criticism

Leavitt, Henrietta Swan (1868–1921) US astronomer, born at Lancaster, Massachusetts. She spent much of her career at Harvard College Observatory, where her work on variable stars established the distance scale of the universe. She died at Cambridge, Massachusetts. » Cepheid variable; universe

Lebanon, Fr **Liban**, official name **Republic of Lebanon**, Arabic

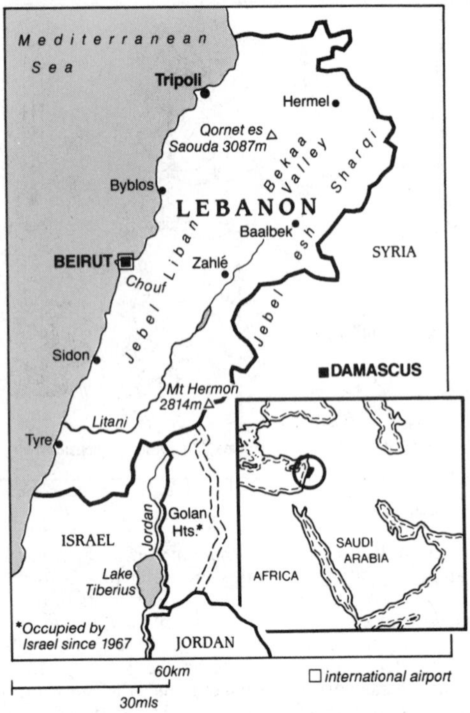

Al-Jumhouriya al-Lubnaniya pop (1990e) 2 965 000; area 10 452 sq km/4 034 sq ml. Republic on the E coast of the Mediterranean Sea, SW Asia; divided into five regional governments (*moafazats*); bounded N and E by Syria, and S by Israel; capital, Beirut; chief towns Tripoli, Sidon, Zahle; timezone GMT +2; population mainly Arab (93%), with several minorities; official language, Arabic; chief religions, Christianity and Islam; unit of currency, the Lebanese pound.

Physical description and climate. Narrow Mediterranean coastal plain rises gradually E to the Lebanon Mts, which extend along most of the country, peaks including Qornet es Saouda (3 087 m/10 128 ft); arid E slopes fall abruptly to the fertile El Beqaa plateau, average elevation 1 000 m/3 300 ft; Anti-Lebanon range in the E; R Litani flows S between the ranges; Mediterranean climate, varying with altitude, with hot, dry summers and warm, moist winters; average annual rainfall at Beirut, 920 mm/36 in; average temperatures, 13°C (Jan), 27°C (Jul); much drier and cooler in the Beqaa valley, irrigation being essential (annual rainfall, 380 mm/15 in).

History and government. Part of the Ottoman Empire from 16th-c; after the massacre of (Catholic) Maronites by (Muslim) Druzes in 1861, Maronite area around Jabal Lubnan granted special autonomous status; Greater Lebanon, based on this area, created in 1920 under French mandate; Muslim coastal regions incorporated, despite great opposition; constitutional republic, 1926; independence, 1941; Palestinian resistance units established in Lebanon by late 1960s, despite government opposition; raids into Israel, followed by reprisals; several militia groups developed in the mid-1970s, notably the Shiite Muslim Afwaj al-Muqawama al-Lubnaniya (AMAL) and the Muslim Lebanese National Movement (LNM); Syrian-dominated Arab Deterrent Force (ADF) created to prevent Palestinian fighters gaining control; following terrorist attacks, Israel invaded S Lebanon, 1978, 1982; siege of Palestinian and Syrian forces in Beirut led to the withdrawal of Palestinian forces, 1982; unilateral withdrawal of Israeli forces brought clashes between the Druze (backed by Syria) and Christian Lebanese militia; ceasefire announced in late 1982, since broken many times; international efforts to achieve political settlement so far unsuccessful; Syrian troops entered Beirut in 1988 in an attempt to restore order; constitution (in semi-suspension since 1988) provides for a Council of Ministers, president (a Maronite Christian elected for a 6-year term), prime minister (a Sunni Muslim), cabinet, and 108-member parliament equally divided between Christians and Muslims; timetable for militia disarmament introduced, 1991.

Economy. The commercial and financial centre of the Middle East, until the civil war, which severely damaged economic infrastructure and reduced industrial and agricultural production; oil refining, cement, textiles, chemicals, food processing, service industries; citrus fruits, apples, grapes, bananas, sugar beet, olives, wheat; tourist industry has virtually collapsed; irrigation projects under way to harness the waters of the Litani R. » Arab–Israeli Wars; Beirut; Druze; Islam; Israel [i]; PLO; Shiites; Sunnis; Syria [i]; RR26 national holidays; RR55 political leaders

Lebanon Mountains, Arabic **Jebel Liban** Mountain range in Lebanon; extending c.160 km/100 ml NNE–SSW parallel to the Mediterranean coast; separated from the Anti-Lebanon range to the E by the fertile El Beqaa valley; rises to 3 087 m/10 128 ft at Qornet es Saouda; grapes, olives, apples on lower slopes. » Lebanon [i]

Lebensraum (Ger 'living space') A slogan adopted by German nationalists (especially Nazis) in the 1920s and 1930s to justify the need for German territorial expansion into E Europe. They argued that Germany was over-populated, and needed more agriculturally productive land to guarantee future food supplies for an expanded German population. » nationalism; Nazi Party; World War 2

Lebowa [le**boh**a] pop (1985) 1 835 984. National state or non-independent Black homeland in N Transvaal province, NE South Africa; situated NE of Pretoria; self-governing status, 1972. » apartheid; South Africa [i]

Lechtal Alps [**lekh**tal], Ger **Lechtaler Alpen** Mountain range of the E Alps in Tirol state, W Austria; rises to 3 036 m/9 960 ft at Parseierspitze; numerous lakes, including the Spullersee; the Arlberg (W) is a major skiing area. » Alps

lecithin [**le**suhthin] » choline

Leconte de Lisle, Charles Marie René [luh**kõt** duh **leel**] (1818–94) French poet, born at Saint-Paul, Réunion. After some years of travel, he settled to a literary life in Paris, where he exercised a profound influence on all the younger poets, headed the school called *Parnassiens*, and succeeded to Victor Hugo's chair at the Academy in 1886. His poetry was published in four major collections between 1858 and 1895. He died near Paris. » French literature; Hugo; poetry

LED » light-emitting diode

Leda (astronomy) The thirteenth natural satellite of Jupiter, discovered in 1974; distance from the planet 11 110 000 km/ 6 904 000 ml; diameter 20 km/12 ml. » Jupiter (astronomy); RR4

Leda (mythology) [**lee**da] In Greek mythology, the wife of Tyndareus, and mother, either by him or Zeus, of Castor and Pollux, Helen, and Clytemnestra. A frequent subject in art is Zeus courting Leda in the form of a swan; Helen was believed to have been hatched from an egg, preserved at Sparta into historic times. » Castor and Pollux; Clytemnestra; Helen

Lederberg, Joshua (1925–) US geneticist, born at Montclair, New Jersey. He held chairs of genetics at Wisconsin and Stanford. In 1946 he helped to show that some bacteria reproduce sexually, and went on to initiate the fields of bacterial genetics and (1952) genetic engineering. He shared the Nobel Prize for Physiology or Medicine in 1958, and became president of Rockefeller University in 1978. » bacteria [i]; expert system; genetics [i]

Ledoux, Claude-Nicolas [luh**doo**] (1736–1806) French architect, born at Dormans-sur-Marane. He studied at Paris, and was the most successful of the French Neoclassical architects, becoming royal architect to Louis XVI in 1773. His designs include the saltworks at Arc-et-Senans (1775–9) and the unrealized ideal city of Chaux, published in 1804. He died in Paris. » Arc-et-Senans; architecture; Neoclassicism (art and architecture)

Lee (of Asheridge), Jennie, Baroness (1904–88) British socialist politician, born at Lochgelly, Fife. The daughter of a Scottish miner, she was educated at Edinburgh and made her own way in left-wing politics, becoming the youngest elected woman MP (1929–31). She married Aneurin Bevan in 1934. Re-elected to parliament in 1945, she became Minister for the Arts (1967–70), and was given the task of establishing the Open University. She retired from the House of Commons in 1970 to be made a life peer. » Bevan; Labour Party; socialism

Lee, Laurie (1914–) British writer, born in Slad, Gloucestershire. Educated at the village school and in Stroud, he worked as a scriptwriter for documentary films during the 1940s, and travelled widely. A nature poet of great simplicity, he is best known for his autobiographical stories of childhood and country life, *Cider With Rosie* (1959), *As I Walked Out One Midsummer Morning* (1969), and *I Can't Stay Long* (1975). » English literature; novel

Lee, Robert E(dward) (1807–70) US Confederate general, born at Stratford, Virginia. Educated at West Point, he received a commission in the engineers, and in 1861 was made Commander-in-Chief of the Virginia forces. He was in charge of the defences at Richmond, and defeated Federal forces in the Seven Days' battles (1862). His strategy in opposing General Pope, his invasion of Maryland and Pennsylvania, and other achievements are central to the history of the war. In 1865, he surrendered his army to General Grant at Appomattox Courthouse, Virginia. After the war, he became president of Washington College at Lexington, where he died. » American Civil War; Brown, John

Lee, Tsung-Dao (1926–) Chinese physicist, born in Shanghai. Educated at Jiangxi and Zhejiang University, he emigrated to the USA in 1946, studied at Chicago, then lectured at Berkeley, Princeton, and Columbia University, where he became the Enrico Fermi professor of physics in 1963. With Yang he disproved the parity principle, for which they shared the Nobel Prize for Physics in 1957. » parity (physics); Yang

leech A specialized ringed worm related to the earthworms; body highly contractile, usually with a sucker at each end; many are blood-feeders on vertebrate hosts, others are predators of invertebrates; found in aquatic and damp terrestrial habitats. (Phylum: *Annelida*. Subclass: *Hirudinea*.) » earthworm; worm

leechee » litchi

Leeds 53°50N 1°35W, pop (1981) 451 841. City in Leeds borough, West Yorkshire, N England; on the R Aire, 315 km/ 196 ml NNW of London; sixth largest city in England; ford across the R Aire in Roman times; in the 18th-c became an important centre of cloth manufacture; birthplace of Lord Darnley (Temple Newsam); incorporated by Charles I in 1626; canals link to Liverpool, Goole; university (1904); railway (important early freight and passenger centre); textiles, clothing, leather, chemicals, furniture, plastics, paper, electrical equipment; Civic Hall (1933), Town Hall (1858), art gallery, Churches of St John (1634) and St Peter (1841), Kirkstall Abbey (1147); Leeds Music Festival (every 3 years, Apr); International Pianoforte Competition (every 3 years, Sep); film festival. » Darnley; Yorkshire, West

leek A perennial with strap-shaped, sheathing leaves in two rows, and white flowers sometimes mixed with bulbils. Its origin is unknown, but it is probably derived from the wild leek of Europe (*Allium ampeloprasum*), and is now cultivated as a vegetable (*Allium porrum*). (Family: *Liliaceae*.) » allium; bulbil; perennial; vegetable

Leeuwarden [**lay**vahdn], Frisian **Liouwert** 53°12N 5°48E, pop (1984e) 85 435. Capital city of Friesland province, N Netherlands, on the R Ee; railway; canal junction; economic and cultural capital of Friesland; major cattle market; dairy products, flour milling, glass, tourism; former centre for gold and silverware; Grote Kerk (13th–16th-c), Frisian museum. » Friesland; Netherlands, The [i]

Leeuwenhoek, Antony van [**lay**wenhook] (1632–1723) Dutch scientist, born and died at Delft. He was a clerk in an Amsterdam cloth warehouse until 1654, and then became at Delft a renowned microscopist, the first to observe bacteria, protozoa, spermatozoa, and features of the blood. His *Opera* appeared at Leyden (1719–22). » microscope

Leeward Islands (Caribbean), Span **Islas de Sotavento** Island group of the Lesser Antilles in the Caribbean Sea, N of the Windward Is; from the Virgin Is (N) to Dominica (S); sheltered from the NE prevailing winds; the name was formerly used by the Spanish to include the Greater Antilles; also formerly a division of the West Indies Federation (1958–62), comprising Anguilla, Antigua and Barbuda, British Virgin Is, Montserrat, St Kitts, Nevis, Redonda, and Sombrero. » Antilles; West Indies Federation

Leeward Islands (French Polynesia), Fr **Iles sous le Vent** pop (1981e) 20 000; area 507 sq km/196 sq ml. Island group of the Society Is, French Polynesia; comprises the volcanic islands of Huahine, Raiatea, Tahaa, Bora-Bora, and Maupiti, with four small uninhabited atolls; chief town, Uturoa (Raiatea); copra, vanilla, pearls. » French Polynesia; Society Islands

Left Bank The south bank of the R Seine in Paris, an area occupied by numerous educational establishments, including the University of Paris (now scattered across the city) and the Ecole des Beaux Arts. As a result, it is noted as a haunt of writers and intellectuals. » Paris, University of

left wing A place on the political continuum, ranging from left to right, occupied by those with radical, reforming, and progressive attitudes towards social change and the political order. The term encompasses many shades of opinion, but generally includes a commitment to greater equality, liberty, and a belief in social progress through political action. » centre, the; right wing

leg A term commonly used to refer to the whole of the lower limb, primarily used for support and movement; more precisely, in anatomy, the region between the knee and ankle joints, distinguished from the *thigh* (between the hip and knee joints) and the *foot* (beyond the ankle joint). It articulates with the trunk via the *pelvic girdle* (the hip bones and sacrum). The bones are the *femur* in the thigh, the *tibia* and *fibula* in the leg, and the *tarsals*, *metatarsals*, and *phalanges* in the foot. The muscles on the front of the thigh and leg cause the extension at the knee and ankle joints and of the toes; those on the back of the thigh and leg cause opposite movements. The muscles within the foot also move the toes. » femur; fibula; foot; Plate XIII

legacy » **property**

Legacy In Australia, an organization (called at first the Remembrance Club) founded in 1922 by Major-General Sir John Gellibrand. It cares for the families of servicemen who have died as a result of war.

Legal Aid A British scheme which provides the public with advice and assistance from solicitors, and aid with representation at civil and criminal trials. Civil legal aid is administered by the Law Society under general guidance from the Lord Chancellor; help is means-tested, and a contribution may be required. A person seeking criminal legal aid applies to the court (in Scotland, to the Legal Aid Board), which may grant such aid if it is both needed and in the interests of justice to grant it; the court may order a contribution. » Law Society; Lord Chancellor; solicitor

legend A vague term, either referring to stories of ancient heroes, saints, or ordinary men and women which have been handed down by oral or written tradition; or simply to fairy stories. It is usually, but not always, distinguished from *myth*, which deals with gods; and opposed to *history*, which is subject to critical judgment. Nevertheless, because ancient peoples were not given to fiction, in the modern sense of the term, a legend often contains a kernel of truth. » mythology

Legendre, Adrien Marie [luhzh**ã**druh] (1752–1833) French mathematician, born at Toulouse. He studied at Paris, and became professor of mathematics at the military school (1775) and at the Ecole Normale (1795). He made major contributions to number theory and elliptical functions, but due to the jealousy of his colleague Laplace, he received little recognition or reward for his work. He died in Paris. » Laplace; number theory

Léger, Fernand [**lay**zhay] (1881–1955) French painter, born in Argentan. He studied in Paris, and helped to form the Cubist movement, but later developed his own 'aesthetic of the machine', as in 'Contrast of Forms' (1913, Philadelphia). He worked in New York and Paris, and also designed sets for ballets and films. He died at Gif-sur-Yvette. » Cubism; French art

leghorn A small breed of domestic fowl; named after Legorno (now Livorno) in Italy. » domestic fowl

Leghorn, Ital **Livorno** 43°33N 10°18E, pop (1981) 175 741. Port and capital of Livorno province, W Tuscany, Italy; on the low-lying coast of the Tyrrhenian Sea, SW of Pisa; railway; ferries to Bastia in Corsica; linked with the R Arno by canal; shipbuilding, engineering, cement, soap, straw hats, trade in wine, olive oil, marble; 17th-c cathedral. » Tuscany

legion The principal unit of the Roman army. It was made up of ten cohorts, each one of which was divided into six centuries. » century

Légion d'Honneur ('Legion of Honour') In France, a reward for civil and military service created by Napoleon I in 1802. The president of the Republic is grand master, and the five grades are chevalier, officer, commander, grand officer, and grand cross. The ribbon is scarlet. » decoration; Napoleon I

Legion of Mary An organization founded in Ireland in 1921 to enable lay members of the Roman Catholic Church to engage in apostolic (missionary and charitable) work within the community. It was inspired by writings devoted to the Virgin Mary by St Louis Marie Grignon de Montfort (1673–1716). » Mary (mother of Jesus); Roman Catholicism

legionella A bacterium that occurs naturally in freshwater habitats, living and multiplying inside amoebae. It can become infective to humans and, when inhaled, can cause legionnaire's disease. » amoeba; bacteria [i]; legionnaire's disease

legionnaire's disease A serious form of pneumonia caused by the bacterium *Legionella pneumophilia*. The organisms are transmitted by water droplets from shower heads, humidifiers, and cooling towers. It is so named because the first outbreak affected members of the American Legion in Philadelphia. » legionella; pneumonia

legislature The institution recognized as having the power to pass laws. In the UK the legislature is the Queen-in-Parliament, comprising the monarch, the House of Lords, and the House of Commons. The role of the monarch in this respect is now purely formal. In the USA, the President has a qualified power of veto over bills from Congress. » delegated legislation; parliament

legitimacy The legal status of a child at birth. A child is legitimate if born when its parents are validly married to each other, and the child is the biological issue of the couple. A person born illegitimate may be legitimized by the subsequent marriage of his or her parents. In addition, an adopted child is regarded as the legitimate child of adoptive parents, as is a child born to a wife who has been artificially inseminated, provided that the husband has consented to this procedure. » adoption; artificial insemination

legitimate theatre/theater Serious drama rather than variety; originally a term for the productions mounted by the patent theatres in London, as opposed to those put on at the 'illegitimate' theatres, where to circumvent legislation plays had to contain music, dance, or some 'non-dramatic' element. » patent theatre

legume A dry, 1–many-seeded fruit of the pea family (*Leguminosae*). When ripe it splits into two valves, each bearing alternate seeds. The splitting may be explosive, or the valves may twist to help scatter the seeds. Many kinds are eaten as vegetables. » fruit; pea [i]; vegetable

Lehár, Franz (1870–1948) Hungarian composer, born at Komárom. He studied at the Prague Conservatory, and became a military band conductor in Vienna. His works include two violin concertos, but he is best known for his operettas, which include *The Merry Widow* (1905) and *The Count of Luxembourg* (1909). He died at Bad Ischl, Austria.

Lehmann, Lilli [**lay**man] (1848–1929) German soprano, born in Würzburg. She was taught singing by her mother, and made her debut at Prague in 1865. She sang in Danzig, Leipzig, London, New York, and elsewhere, and took part in the first performance of Wagner's *Ring* (1876) at Bayreuth. She died in Berlin. » Wagner

Lehmann, Lotte [**lay**man] (1888–1976) German soprano, born in Perleberg. She studied in Berlin, made her debut in Hamburg in 1910, and sang at the Vienna Staatsoper (1914–38). She also appeared frequently at Covent Garden and at the New York Metropolitan, and was noted particularly for her performances in operas by Richard Strauss, including two premieres. She took US nationality, and in 1951 retired to Santa Barbara, where she died. » Strauss, Richard

Leibniz, Gottfried Wilhelm [**liyb**nits] (1646–1716) German rationalist philosopher and mathematician, born in Leipzig. He studied at Leipzig and Altdorf, and took a position at the court of the Elector of Mainz. Sent to Paris on a political mission, he studied Cartesianism and mathematics, and invented a calculating machine. He visited London in 1673, and became involved in a controversy over whether he or Newton was the inventor of the infinitesimal calculus. In 1676 he became librarian to the Duke of Brunswick at Hanover. A man of diverse interests, he induced Frederick I to found the Academy of Sciences in Berlin (1700), of which he became first president. Unpopular with George of Hanover, he was left behind when the court moved to London, and was allowed to die without recognition at Hanover. His great influence, especially upon Russell, was primarily as a mathematician and as a pioneer of modern symbolic logic. » calculus; logic; rationalism (philosophy); Russell, Bertrand

Leicester, Robert Dudley, Earl of [**les**ter] (c.1532–88) English nobleman, the favourite and possibly the lover of Elizabeth I. He became Master of the Horse, Knight of the Garter, a privy councillor, baron, and finally Earl of Leicester (1564). He continued to receive favour in spite of his unpopularity at court and a secret marriage in 1573 to the Dowager Lady Sheffield. In 1578 he bigamously married the widow of Walter, Earl of Essex; yet Elizabeth was only temporarily offended. In 1585 he commanded the expedition to the Low Countries, but was recalled for incompetence in 1587. He was nonetheless appointed in 1588 to command the forces against the Spanish Armada, and died later that year at Cornbury, Oxfordshire. » Elizabeth I; Spanish Armada

Leicester [**les**ter], Lat **Ratae Coritanorum** 52°38N 1°05W, pop (1987e) 279 700. City and county town of Leicestershire, C England; 160 km/99 ml N of London; an important royal residence in mediaeval times; charter granted by Elizabeth I (1589); university (1957); railway; hosiery, knitwear, footwear, engineering; many Roman remains; 14th-c Cathedral of St Martin, Churches of St Margaret, St Mary de Castro, and St Nicholas; 17th-c Guildhall, Belgrave Hall museum. » Britain, Roman; Leicestershire

Leicestershire [**les**tersheer] pop (1987e) 879 400; area 2 553 sq km/985 sq ml. County of C England, divided into nine districts; includes former county of Rutland; drained by the R Soar; county town Leicester; chief towns include Market Harborough, Loughborough; agriculture, livestock, cheese (Stilton), coal mining, limestone, engineering, hosiery, footwear; Charnwood Forest, Vale of Belvoir. » England [i]; Leicester

Leiden » **Leyden**

Leif Eriksson [layv] Icelandic explorer, the son of Eric the Red, the first European to reach America. He Christianized Greenland, and c.1000 discovered land which he named Vinland after the vines he found growing there. It is still uncertain where Vinland actually is, some saying Labrador or Newfoundland, others Massachusetts.

Leigh, Vivien, originally **Vivien Mary Hartley** (1913–67) British actress, born in Darjeeling, India. After a convent education in England, she trained in London, and was put under contract by Alexander Korda, playing in *Fire Over England* (1937) against Laurence Olivier, whom she subsequently married (1940–60). While in Hollywood with him, she was given the star role of Scarlett O'Hara in *Gone With the Wind* (1939), for which she was awarded an Oscar. Major starring parts followed, notably in *Lady Hamilton* (1941), *Anna Karenina* (1948), and *A Streetcar Named Desire* (1951), which gained her another Oscar. She continued on the stage during the 1950s but her later years were beset by ill health, and she died in London of tuberculosis.

Leinster [**len**ster] pop (1981) 1 790 521; area 19 633 sq km/7 578 sq ml. Province in E Irish Republic; comprises the counties of Louth, Meath, Westmeath, Longford, Offaly, Kildare, Dublin, Laoighis, Wicklow, Carlow, Kilkenny, and Wexford; capital, Dublin. » Irish Republic [i]

Leipzig [**liyp**zig], ancient **Lipsia** 51°20N 12°23E, pop (1982) 558 414. Capital of Leipzig county, SE Germany; second largest city of former East Germany; airport; railway; Karl Marx University (1409); college of technology; commercial centre, mechanical engineering, machine tools, furs, printing and publishing; St Thomas's Church, museum of fine art, Battle of the Nations monument, Renaissance town hall, Lenin Memorial, Dimitrov museum; Documentary and Short Film Week; centre for education and music (associations with Bach and Mendelssohn); annual trade fairs. » Bach, Johann Sebastian; Germany [i]; Mendelssohn

Leipzig, Battle of (1813) The overwhelming defeat of Napoleon's forces by the armies of the Fourth Coalition, also called the **Battle of the Nations**. Heavily outnumbered by the Allied force of Austrians, Prussians, Russians, and Swedes, Napoleon tried to withdraw, but his troops were badly mauled; he effectively surrendered French control E of the Rhine. » Napoleonic Wars

leishmaniasis [leeshman**iy**asis] A group of conditions caused by the protozoa *Leishmania* conveyed by sandflies, occurring on the Mediterranean shores, Africa, and S Asia; also known as **kala-azar**. The *skin form* of the disease occurs as pimples (*papules*) which enlarge and ulcerate. The *visceral form* is a generalized febrile disease affecting the liver, spleen, and lymph nodes. » fever; lymph; Protozoa

leitmotif [**liyt**mohteef] A short musical motif associated with a character, object, or attribute, which returns at appropriate places in an opera or oratorio. The use of the device is particularly associated with Wagner. » idée fixe; opera; oratorio; Wagner

Leitrim [**lee**trim], Gaelic **Liathdroma** pop (1981) 27 609; area 1 526 sq km/589 sq ml. County in Connacht province, Irish Republic, stretching SE from Donegal Bay; bounded NE by N Ireland; capital, Carrick-on-Shannon; coarse angling on R Shannon and L Allen; cattle, sheep, potatoes, oats; considerable land drainage in recent times. » Connacht; Irish Republic [i]

Lely, Sir Peter, originally **Pieter van der Faes** (1618–80) Dutch painter, born at Soest, Westphalia. He studied at Haarlem, and c.1641 settled in London as a portrait painter, being employed by Charles I, Cromwell, and Charles II, for whom he became court painter. His 13 Greenwich portraits of English admirals (1666–7) are among his best works. He was knighted in 1679, and died in London.

Lemaître, Georges (Henri) [luh**mair**truh] (1894–1966) Belgian astronomer, born at Charleroi. Ordained a priest in 1923, he studied at Cambridge, UK, and at the Massachusetts Institute of Technology, and became professor of astronomy at Louvain from 1927. His most important paper led to the concept of the Big Bang theory of the universe. He died at Louvain. » Big Bang; cosmology

Léman, Lac » **Geneva, Lake**

lemma » **theorem**

lemming A mouse-like rodent of the tribe *Lemmini* (9 species); large powerful head, long fur, short tail; prone to large fluctuations in numbers. The **Norway lemming** (*Lemmus lemmus*) undergoes a population 'explosion' every 3–4 years. When this happens there is a mass migration, thought to be a response to overcrowding (not food shortage). The direction of migration appears random, and sometimes groups reaching large water bodies, including the sea, will swim offshore and drown in large numbers. This is accidental, not 'suicide'. » mouse (zoology); rodent

Lemnos [**leem**nos], Gr **Límnos** pop (1981) 15 721; area 476 sq km/184 sq ml. Greek island in the N Aegean Sea, off the NW coast of Turkey; length 40 km/25 ml; rises to 430 m/1 411 ft; airfield; capital, Kastron; several Neolithic remains. » Greece [i]; Three Age System

lemon A citrus fruit 6–12.5 cm/2½–4¾ in in diameter; ovoid, with thick, bright yellow rind and sour pulp. (*Citrus limoni*. Family: *Rutaceae*.) » citrus; lime (botany) **2**

lemon sole Common European flatfish found in shelf waters from N Norway to the Bay of Biscay; body oval, length up to 65 cm/26 in; mouth small; brown with a mosaic of yellow and green patches; feeds mainly on polychaetes; valuable food fish taken by trawl and nets (seines). (*Microstomus kitt*. Family: *Pleuronectidae*.) » flatfish

lemon thyme » **thyme**

lemon verbena A deciduous shrub native to Chile; lemon-scented foliage; heads of small, 2-lipped, purplish flowers. (*Lippia citriodora*. Family: *Verbenaceae*.) » deciduous plants; shrub

lemur [leemuh] A primitive primate from Madagascar; large eyes and pointed snout; most species with long tail; 27 species in three families: **lemur** (*Lemuridae*), **mouse (or dwarf) lemur** (*Cheirogaleidae*), and **leaping lemur** (*Indriidae*). » colugo; indri; prosimian

Lena, River [lyena] River in Siberian Russia; rises in the Baykalskiy Khrebet, and flows generally NE and N to enter the Laptev Sea in a wide swampy delta, NW of Tiksi; length, 4 400 km/2 700 ml; coal, oil, gold nearby. » Russia

Lenclos, Anne [lãkloh], byname **Ninon de** (1620–1705) French courtesan of good family, born and died in Paris. Her lovers included several leading members of the aristocracy, as well as political and literary figures. She was nearly as celebrated for her manners as for her beauty. The most respectable women sent their children to her to acquire taste, style, and politeness.

Lend-Lease Agreement The means by which the USA lent or leased war supplies and arms to Britain and other countries during World War 2. The Act was passed by Congress in March 1941, when British reserves were almost exhausted. Up to the end of August 1945, the UK received about £5 000 million worth of materials. » World War 2

Lendl, Ivan [lendl] (1960–) Czech lawn tennis player, born at Ostrava. He dominated male tennis in the 1980s, winning the singles title at the US Open (1985–7), French Open (1984, 1986–7), and Australian Open (1989), and becoming the Masters champion (1986–7) and the World Championship Tennis champion (1982, 1985). As of 1989 he had failed to take the Wimbledon singles title. » tennis, lawn [i]

Leng, Virginia, *née* **Holgate** (1955–) British three-day eventer, born in Malta. The European junior champion in 1973, she won the team gold at the senior championship in 1981, 1985, and 1987, and individual titles in 1985 (on *Priceless*) and 1987 (on *Night Cap*). She won the World Championship team gold in 1982 and 1986, and the individual title in 1986 on *Priceless*. She also won at Badminton (1985), and three times at Burghley (1983–4, 1986). » equestrianism

Lenglen, Suzanne [lãlã] (1899–1938) French lawn tennis player, born at Compiègne. She was the woman champion of France (1920–3, 1925–6), and her Wimbledon championships were the women's singles and doubles (1919–23, 1925), and the mixed doubles (1920, 1922, 1925). In 1920 she was Olympic champion. She became a professional in 1926, toured the US, and retired in 1927 to found the Lenglen School of Tennis in Paris. She died in Paris. » tennis, lawn [i]

length contraction » **Lorentz contraction**

Lenin, Vladimir Ilyich, originally **V I Ulyanov** (1870–1924) Russian Marxist revolutionary and politician, born at Simbirsk and educated at the Universities of Kazan and St Petersburg, where he graduated in law. From 1897 to 1900 he was exiled to Siberia for participating in underground revolutionary activities. At the Second Congress of the Russian Social Democratic Labour Party (1903) he caused the split between the Bolshevik and Menshevik factions. Following the February 1917 revolution, he returned to Petrograd from Zürich, and urged the immediate seizure of political power by the proletariat under the slogan 'All Power to the Soviets'. In October he led the Bolshevik revolution and became head of the first Soviet government. At the end of the ensuing Civil War (1918–21) he introduced the New Economic Policy, which his critics in the Party saw as a 'compromise with capitalism' and a retreat from strictly socialist planning. On his death, his body was embalmed and placed in a mausoleum near the Moscow Kremlin, where it still lies. In 1924 Petrograd (formerly St Petersburg) was renamed Leningrad in his honour. » April Theses; Bolsheviks; February Revolution; Lenin Mausoleum; Mensheviks; October Revolution; Russian Civil War; Russian Revolution

Lenin Library The national library and depository of Russia, and one of the most extensive libraries in the world. When it was established in Moscow in 1917, confiscated private collections formed the bulk of its holdings. It now houses over 28 million books and periodicals. » Lenin; library; Moscow

Lenin Mausoleum The tomb of Lenin, designed by Aleksey V Shchuser and built in 1930 in Red Square, Moscow. The granite building contains the Soviet leader's burial vault, where his embalmed body may be viewed by the public. » Lenin; Red Square

Lenin, Peak, Russ **Lenina, Pik**, formerly **Mt Kaufmann** 39°21N 73°01E. Highest peak in the Alayskiy Khrebet, and second highest in Russia; height, 7 134 m/23 405 ft; first climbed in 1928.

Leningrad [leningrad], Russ [lyaynyingrat], formerly **St Petersburg** (1703–1914), later **Petrograd** (1914–24), and named **St Petersburg** again in 1991 59°55N 30°25E, pop (1989) 4 456 000. Seaport capital of Leningradskaya oblast, NW European Russia; on the R Neva, at the head of the Gulf of Finland; largest Russian Baltic port (frozen, Jan–Apr) and second largest Russian city; former capital of the Russian Empire (1712–1918); founded by Peter the Great, 1703; leading centre in the October Revolution, 1917; scene of a major siege by Germany in World War 2 (1941–4), in which nearly a million died; airport; railway junction; university (1819); Academy of Sciences (1726); nuclear power equipment, ships, tractors, machine tools, precision optical instruments, solar research; Winter Palace (1754–62, rebuilt 1839), St Isaac Cathedral (19th-c), Kazan Cathedral (1801–11), Fortress of Peter and Paul (1703), St Nicholas Navy Cathedral (1753–62); over 60 museums; White Nights art festival (Jun). » Hermitage; Peter and Paul Fortress; Peter I; October Revolution; Russian history; Russia

Leninism » **Marxism-Leninism**

Lennon, John » **Beatles, The**

Leno, Dan [leenoh], stage name of **George Galvin** (1860–1904) British comedian, born in London, who began as a singer and dancer at the age of four, and was a champion clog-dancer by 18. He appeared for many years in the annual pantomime at Drury Lane. A thin, small man, his foil was the huge, bulky Herbert Campbell. When Campbell died in 1904 after an accident, Leno pined and died in London six months later. » pantomime; theatre

lens A transparent optical element comprising two refracting surfaces, at least one of which is curved; parallel light rays passing through the lens may converge (and focus at a point) or diverge, depending on the lens shape. Lenses are characterized by their *focal length* (the distance at which the image of a distant object is most sharply defined) and their *aperture* or *f-number* (the light transmission). They are widely used in optical instruments, binoculars, projectors, and cameras, and are usually made of glass, sometimes of plastic. » aberrations 1 [i]; camera; optics [i]; refraction [i]

Lent In the Christian Church, the weeks before Easter, observed as a period of prayer, penance and abstinence in commemoration of Christ's 40-day fast in the wilderness (*Matt* 4.2); in the Western Churches, Lent begins on Ash Wednesday; in the Eastern Churches, it begins eight weeks before Easter. » Ash Wednesday; Easter

lenticel A small pore in a stem or root, with a similar role to that of stomata in leaves, allowing the passage of gases to and from tissues. » pneumatophore; stomata

lentil An annual growing to c. 40 cm/15 in; leaves pinnate with 3–8 pairs of oblong leaflets, and terminating in a tendril; pea-flowers white, veined with lilac, borne 1–3 on a long stalk; pods rectangular with 1–2 disc-shaped seeds. It is of unknown origin, but has been cultivated since ancient times as a food plant. Its seeds (lentils) are rich in protein. (*Lens culinaris*. Family: *Leguminosae*.) » annual; pinnate; protein; vegetable

lentivirus A virus which resembles other members of the retrovirus family (*Retroviridae*), both chemically and morphologically, but does not induce tumour formation. Many lentiviruses have been linked to the causation of chronic diseases, such as arthritis, progressive pneumonia, and slow neurological diseases. » retrovirus; tumour

Lenya, Lotte [**len**ya] (1898–1981) Austrian singer, born in Vienna. She studied dancing in Zürich (1914–20), and then moved to Berlin, where she took up acting and, in 1926, married Kurt Weill. She made an international reputation as Jenny in Weill's *Die Dreigroschenoper* (1928, The Threepenny Opera). She later took US nationality, and died in New York City. » Weill

Lenz's law [lentz] A law in physics: in electromagnetic induction, any induced current always flows in a direction so as to oppose its source; formulated in 1833 by German physicist Heinrich Lenz (1804–65). Were this not so, perpetual motion machines could be built. The law is responsible for speed self-regulation in electric motors. » electromagnetic induction

Leo (Lat 'lion') A N constellation. It is a summer sign of the zodiac, lying between Cancer and Virgo. Easy to recognize (the lion's head looks like a sickle), its brightest star is Leo, 26 parsecs distance. **Leo Minor** ('little lion') is a hard-to-see constellation near Leo. » constellation; RR9

Leo I (the Great), St (c.390–461), feast day 11 April (W), 18 February (E). Pope (440–61), and one of the most eminent of the Latin Fathers. He summoned the Council of Chalcedon (451), where the intention of his 'Dogmatical Letter', defining the doctrine of the Incarnation, was accepted. He also made treaties with the Huns and Vandals in defence of Rome, where he died. » Fathers of the Church; Incarnation; pope

Leo III, St (c.750–816), feast day 12 June. Italian Pope (795–816), born and died in Rome. In 799, opposition to his election forced him to flee from Rome to the protection of Charlemagne. After returning safely, he crowned Charlemagne Emperor of the West (800), thus initiating the Holy Roman Empire. He was canonized in 1673. » Charlemagne; Holy Roman Empire; pope

Leo III (Emperor) (c.680–741) Byzantine Emperor (717–41), born in Syria. He reorganized the army and financial system, and in 718 repelled a formidable attack by the Arabs on Constantinople. In 726 he prohibited the use of images in public worship, which led to more than a century of controversy. In 740 he defeated the Arabs at Amorium, thus halting their incursions into Asia Minor. He died in Constantinople. » iconoclasm

Leo X, originally **Giovanni de' Medici** (1475–1521) Italian Pope (1513–21), born in Florence. His vast project to rebuild St Peter's, and his permitting the preaching of an indulgence in order to raise funds, provoked the Reformation, leading to Luther's excommunication in 1520. He died in Rome. » indulgences; Luther; Reformation

León (Mexico) [lay**on**] 21°06N 101°41W, pop (1980) 655 809. Town in Guanajuato state, SC Mexico; 200 km/124 ml N of Morelia; altitude 1 804 m/5 919 ft; railway; commercial centre, shoes, leather work, including decorated saddles. » Mexico [i]

León (Spain) [lay**on**] 42°38N 5°34W, pop (1981) 131 132. Capital of León province, Castilla-León, NW Spain; at the junction of the Torio and Bernesga Rivers, 333 km/207 ml NW of Madrid; bishopric; capital of a mediaeval kingdom; railway; anthracite, glass, leather, iron, timber; cathedral (13th–14th-c), town walls, San Isidore, Monastery of St Mark; Fiestas of St John and St Peter (Jun), Foro and Oferta pageant in the cathedral (Aug). » Spain [i]

Leonardo da Vinci (1452–1519) Italian painter, sculptor, architect, and engineer, born at Vinci. About 1470 he entered the studio of Andrea del Verrocchio, and in 1482 settled in Milan, where he painted his 'Last Supper' (1498) on the refectory wall of Santa Maria delle Grazie. In 1500 he entered the service of Cesare Borgia in Florence as architect and engineer, and with Michelangelo decorated the Sala del Consiglio in the Palazzo della Signoria with historical compositions. About 1504 he completed his most celebrated easel picture, 'Mona Lisa' (Louvre). In 1506 he was employed by Louis XII of France, and in 1516 was given a pension by Francis I. Very few of his paintings have survived. His notebooks contain original remarks on most of the sciences, including biology, physiology, hydrodynamics, and aeronautics. He died at Cloux, France. » Borgia, Cesare; Italian art; Michelangelo

Leoncavallo, Ruggero (1857–1919) Italian opera composer, born at Naples. He studied at Naples, and wrote a number of operas, of which only *I Pagliacci* (1892) achieved lasting success. He died near Florence.

Leonidas [lee**on**idas] (?–480 BC) King of Sparta (c.491–480 BC), hero of the Persian Wars. He perished at Thermopylae along with his entire bodyguard of 300, fighting vainly to check the Persian advance into C Greece. » Persian Wars; Thermopylae

Leonids [**lee**uhnidz] A meteor shower due around 17 November that fails most years but is spectacular at 33-year intervals, when thousands can be seen per hour. The next major sighting will be 1999. » meteor

Leontief, Wassily [lee**on**tyef] (1906–) US economist, born in St Petersburg, Russia, and educated there and in Berlin. He held chairs at Harvard (1946–75) and New York (1983–), and 1975–84 was director of the Institute of Economic Analysis at New York University. In 1973 he was awarded the Nobel Prize for Economics for developing the input-output method of economic analysis, used in more than 50 industrialized countries for planning and forecasting. » economics

leopard A member of the cat family, found from Siberia to Africa; solitary; inhabits diverse habitats; reddish or yellowish brown with small empty rings of dark blotches; black individuals (**black panthers**) sometimes found in dense forests; eats mainly small grazing mammals and monkeys; stores carcasses in trees. (*Panthera pardus*.) » Felidae

leopard cat A member of the cat family, native to E Asia and offshore islands (the most common wild cat in SE Asia); pale with dark bars and spots; inhabits woodland; eats small mammals, birds, reptiles, fish; swims well. (*Felis bengalensis*.) » Felidae

leopard seal An Antarctic true seal; slim with pointed head; dark grey above, pale beneath with dark spots; lives along edge of pack ice; eats mainly penguins (may shake them, literally, out of their skins); also eats other seals, fish, and carrion; only seal in which female is larger than male; also known as **sea leopard**. (*Hydrurga leptonyx*.) » seal (biology)

Leopold I (Emperor) (1640–1705) Holy Roman Emperor (1658–1705), born in Vienna, the second son of Ferdinand III and the Infanta Maria Anna. He was elected to the crowns of Hungary (1655) and Bohemia (1657), and succeeded to the Imperial title in 1658. In 1666 he married his niece, Margaret Theresa, second daughter of Philip IV of Spain. After her early death (1673) he took a second Habsburg bride, Claudia Felicitas, before his third marriage (1676) to Eleonore of Palatinate-Neuburg, by whom he had two sons, the future Emperors Joseph I and Charles VI. Committed throughout his long reign to the defence of the power and unity of the House of Habsburg, he faced constant external threats from the Ottoman Turks and the King of France, in addition to the hostility of the Hungarian nobility. Treaties of neutrality (1667, 1671) between Leopold and Louis XIV of France gave way to military conflict over the Rhine frontier (1674–9, 1686–97), as the issue of the Spanish inheritance loomed closer. To substantiate the rights of his son, Charles, against the French claimant, Leopold took the Empire into the Grand Alliance (1701). He died in Vienna while his armies were still deeply involved in the War of the Spanish Succession (1701–13) and the Hungarian revolt of Rákóczi (1703–11). » Habsburgs; Louis XIV; Rákóczi; Spanish Succession, War of the

Leopold I (of Belgium) (1790–1865) First King of the Belgians (1831–65), son of Francis, Duke of Saxe-Coburg and uncle of Queen Victoria, born at Coburg, Germany. In 1816 he married Charlotte, daughter of the future George IV of England, and lived in England after her death in 1817. He declined the crown of Greece (1830), but the following year was elected King of the Belgians. His second marriage to Marie Louise of Orleans, daughter of Louis Philippe, ensured French support for his new kingdom against the Dutch. An influential force in European diplomacy prior to Bismarck's ascendancy, he died at Laeken, Belgium. » Belgium [i]; Bismarck

Leopold II (1835–1909) King of the Belgians (1865–1909), born in Brussels, the son of Leopold I. His chief interest was the expansion of Belgium abroad. In 1879 he founded a company to develop the Congo, and in 1885 became King of the Congo Free State, which was annexed to Belgium in 1908. He died at Laeken, Belgium. » Belgium [i]; Congo [i]

Leopold III (1901–83) King of the Belgians (1934–51), born and died in Brussels, the son of Albert I. On his own authority he ordered the capitulation of the Belgian army to the Germans (1940), thus opening the way to Dunkirk. He then remained a prisoner in his own palace at Laeken until 1944, and afterwards in Austria. On returning to Belgium in 1945, he was finally forced to abdicate in favour of his son Baudouin. » World War 2

Léopoldville » **Kinshasa**

Lepanto, Battle of (1571) The defeat of the Turkish navy in the Gulf of Corinth, ending the Turks' long-standing domination of the E Mediterranean. It was inflicted by the Christian forces of Spain and the Italian states in coalition, following the fall of Cyprus to the Turks in 1569. » John of Austria

Lepenski Vir [luh**pen**skee **veer**] A small prehistoric settlement of hunter-fisher-gatherers on the banks of the R Danube in the Iron Gates Gorge, Yugoslavia. Seven phases of occupation with 136 buildings of c.6500–5500 BC have been identified since excavations began in 1965. Of outstanding importance are its 53 abstract and representational sandstone sculptures of humans and animals, the earliest monumental sculpture in Europe. » hunter-gatherers

Lepidodendron [lepidoh**den**druhn] A fossil clubmoss which was widely distributed during the late Palaeozoic era; tall, up to 30 m/100 ft, and dichotomously branched plants bearing diamond-shaped leaf scars and large cones. » clubmoss; fossil; Palaeozoic era

Lepidoptera [lepi**dop**tuhra] A large order of insects comprising the 165 000 species of butterflies and moths; adults have two pairs of membraneous wings covered with scales; forewings and hindwings coupled together; mouthparts typically modified as a slender sucking proboscis; caterpillar larvae usually plant feeders with chewing mouthparts. » butterfly; caterpillar; insect [i]; larva; moth

Lepidus, Marcus Aemilius (?–c.13 BC) Aristocratic Roman politician of the civil war era (49–31 BC), who first rose to prominence under Caesar, becoming his deputy at Rome. He reached the high point of his career in 43 BC, when he formed the second triumvirate with Antonius and Octavian. Outmanoeuvred by Octavian in the power struggle of the 30s BC he retired from active politics, but remained head of state religion (Pontifex Maximus) until his death. » Antonius; Augustus; Caesar; triumvirate

leprechaun [**lep**rekawn] A fairy of Irish folklore, traditionally a tiny old man occupying himself with cobbling, and the possessor of a crock of gold whose whereabouts he could be persuaded to reveal by threats of violence. » fairies; folklore

leprosy An ancient chronic infectious disease due to *Mycobacterium leprae* that still affects 20 million people mainly in tropical Asia and Africa, C and S America, and endemic in the Middle East and S Europe; also known as **Hansen's disease**, after Norwegian bacteriologist Armauer Hansen (1841–1912), who discovered the bacillus in 1879. The organisms show a predilection for the skin, peripheral nerves, and upper respiratory tract. Onset of the disease is gradual, with the development of an area of numbness in the skin, followed by nodules on the external surfaces of the limbs, and enlarged nerves that are easily felt. The lining of the mouth and nose develops ulcers, and there are deformities in cartilage and bones. Drug treatment is complex and prolonged, but the condition tends to disappear with improved socio-economic conditions. » infection

Leptis Magna or **Lepcis Magna** 32°59N 14°15E. An ancient seaport of N Libya, the site of spectacular Roman remains; now a world heritage site. Founded by the Phoenicians as a trading post perhaps as early as the 7th-c BC, the city's greatest days came in the 3rd-c AD, after one of its citizens, Septimius Severus, became Roman emperor. » Libya [i]; Phoenicia

lepton In particle physics, a collective term for all those particles of half integer spin (ie fermions) not affected by strong interactions. The leptons are electrons, muons, and taus, and their respective neutrinos. » particle physics

Lepus [**lee**puhs] (Lat 'hare') A constellation in the S, easy to see near Orion. » constellation; Orion; RR9

Lermontov, Mikhail (Yurevich) (1814–41) Russian author, born in Moscow. He studied at Moscow and at the military cavalry school of St Petersburg. He started writing at an early age, but much of his work was not published until his later years. He is best known for his novel *Geroy nashego vremeni* (1840, A Hero of Our Time). He was killed in a duel at Pyatigorsk. » Russian literature

Lerwick 60°09N 1°09W, pop (1981) 7 561. Capital of Shetland, N Scotland; on E Mainland, by Bressay Sound; airfield; ferry terminus from Scottish mainland; fishing, oil supply services, woollens; museum; Fort Charlotte (1665), Clickhimin Broch (Iron Age); Up-Helly-Aa festival (Jan). » Scotland [i]; Shetland

lesbianism A sexual attraction and expression between women, which may or may not involve the complete exclusion of men as potential sexual partners. As with male homosexuality, lesbianism has become increasingly politicized in the latter part of the 20th-c, often linked, though not invariably, with feminism. » feminism; homosexuality

Lesbos, Gr **Lesvos** pop (1981) 104 620; area 1 630 sq km/629 sq ml. Greek island in the E Aegean Sea, off NW coast of Turkey; third largest island of Greece; length 61 km/38 ml; hilly, rising to 969 m/3 179 ft; in classical times, a centre of Greek lyric poetry; chief town, Mitilini; cereals, grapes, olives, fishing, tourism. » Greece [i]; Greek literature

Lescot, Pierre [**les**koh] (c.1510–78) French Renaissance architect, born and died in Paris. Among his works are the screen of St Germain l'Auxerrois, the Fontaine des Innocents, and the Hôtel de Ligneris. His masterpiece was the Louvre, one wing of which he completely rebuilt. » Louvre

Leskovac or **Leskovats** [**les**kuhvats] 43°00N 21°57E, pop (1981) 159 001. Town in SE Serbia republic, Yugoslavia, 37 km/23 ml S of Niš; railway; wine trade, soap, furniture, textiles; nearby 6th-c Byzantine ruins of Caračin Grad; international textile fair (Jul). » Serbia; Yugoslavia [i]

Lesotho, official name **Kingdom of Lesotho** [le**soo**too] pop (1990e) 1 760 000; area 30 460 sq km/11 758 sq ml. S African kingdom completely bounded by South Africa; capital, Maseru; timezone GMT +3; population mainly Bantu (Basotho); chief religion, Christianity (80%); official languages, Sesotho, English; unit of currency, the loti (maloti); 230 km/143 ml E–W, 200 km/124 ml N–S; Drakensberg Mts in NE and E, highest peak Thabana-Ntlenyana (3 482 m/11 424 ft); Mulati Mts run SW from the NE border, forming a steep escarpment; population mainly lives W of the highlands, altitude 1 500–1 800 m/5 000–6 000 ft; serious soil erosion, especially in W; main rivers, the Orange and the Caledon; mild and dry winters; warm summer season (Oct–Apr); lowland summer maximum temperature, 32.2°C, winter minimum −6.7°C; annual average rain-

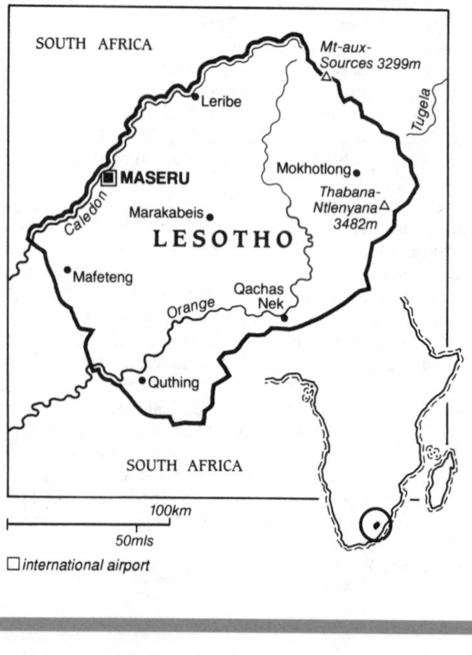

fall, 725 mm/29 in; originally inhabited by hunting and gathering bushmen; Bantu arrived, 16th-c, and Basotho nation established; incorporated in Orange Free State, 1854; under British protection as Basutoland, 1869; independence, 1960; Kingdom of Lesotho, 1966; a hereditary monarchy, with king assisted by a 6-member Military Council and a Council of Ministers; king lost effective power, 1990; transition to democracy planned for 1992; economy based on intensive agriculture and male contract labour working in South Africa; maize, sorghum, wheat, peas, beans, barley, cattle; diamonds, food processing, textiles, electrical consumer goods, carpets, pharmaceuticals, jewellery, crafts, tractor assembly, wool, mohair. » Bantu-speaking peoples; Maseru; South Africa [i]; RR26 national holidays; RR55 political leaders

less developed country (LDC) A nation with a very low standard of living; often referred to as a 'Third World' country. The term has supplanted 'underdeveloped country' since 1971, when the United Nations Conference on Trade and Development identified several nations with a per capita gross national product of $100 or less, a gross domestic product in manufactures of less than 10%, and a literacy rate of 20% or less. Some 30 countries are currently included in this classification. » developing countries; International Bank for Reconstruction and Development; Three Worlds theory

Less Favoured Areas (LFAs) Areas established in 1975 under a European Community directive to provide assistance to farmers in order to conserve the countryside, protect coastlines, and preserve areas of tourist potential. In the UK, most LFAs are in upland regions, where capital grants are available for such work as land drainage. » Environmentally Sensitive Areas

Lesseps, Ferdinand (Marie), Vicomte ('Viscount') **de** (1805–94) French engineer, born at Versailles. After holding several diplomatic posts in Europe, in 1854 he began to plan the Suez Canal, finally built 1860–9. He was knighted, and received several other honours. In 1881 work began on his scheme for a Panama Canal; but in 1892–3 the management was charged with breach of trust, and Lesseps and his son, Charles, were found guilty. He died near Guilly. » Suez Canal

lesser celandine A perennial species of buttercup, common in damp woods and meadows throughout Europe and W Asia; leaves heart-shaped, glossy dark-green; flowers with 8–12 golden-yellow petals which turn white as they fade. (*Ranunculus ficaria*. Family: *Ranunculaceae*.) » buttercup; perennial

Lessing, Doris (May) (1919–) South African writer, born at Kermanshah, Iran. Her family moved to Southern Rhodesia in 1924, where she began to write while living on the family farm. In 1952 *Martha Quest* appeared, the first novel in her 5-book sequence *The Children of Violence*, completed in 1969 with *The Four-Gated City*. *The Golden Notebook*, her best-known novel, appeared in 1962. She has written several books of short stories, and her later writing includes a number of science-fiction works and the novel *The Good Terrorist* (1985). » African/English literature; novel; science fiction; short story

Lessing, Gotthold (Ephraim) (1729–81) German writer and man of letters, born at Kamenz, Saxony. He studied theology at Leipzig, then moved to Berlin and Wittenberg. While secretary to the governor of Breslau, he wrote *Laokoon* (1766, Laocoön), a critical treatise defining the limits of poetry and the plastic arts. His *Minna von Barnhelm* (1767) is the first German comedy on the grand scale. He died at Braunschweig. » drama; German literature; literary criticism; tragedy

Lethe [**lee**thee] In the Greek and Roman Underworld, the name of a slow-moving river. When the souls of the dead drank from it, they forgot their lives on Earth. The word means 'forgetfulness', ie oblivion.

Leto [**lee**toh] or **Latona** In Greek mythology, a Titaness, the mother by Zeus of the twins Apollo and Artemis. They were born at Delos, because in her jealousy Hera would allow no land to harbour Leto; luckily, at that time Delos was a floating island. » Hera

letter » **alphabet** [i]

letterpress A form of printing in which the image to be communicated is placed on a relief surface of metal or wood,

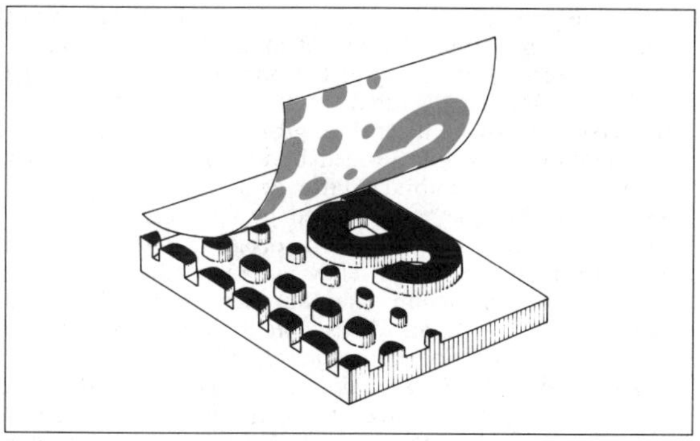

The letterpress process – Ink is carried on the surface of the image in raised relief

and transferred as an inked impression to the printing foundation, usually paper. To be read correctly on the paper, the printing image has to be reversed from left to right. It may be engraved or cast on the face of the types for individual characters, lines of type ('slugs'), plates ('blocks') for individual pictorial elements, or flat or curved plates each reproducing a whole page or sequence of pages. » printing [i]

letters of credit Documents issued by banks which give the bearer the authority to draw a stated sum of money on the bank or its agencies. They are especially used abroad, as a means of paying for foreign goods. A *confirmed* letter of credit is one which has been recognized by the paying bank. An *irredeemable* letter cannot be cancelled, whereas a *revocable* letter may be.

lettres de cachet [letruh duh ka**shay**] A royal order of the French kings, sealed with the monarch's private seal, issued for the arrest and imprisonment of individuals during the *ancien régime*. The practice was abolished in the French Revolution (1790). » *ancien régime*; French Revolution [i]

lettuce An annual or perennial, very widespread but mostly N temperate; leaves often prickly-margined; flower heads small, often in clusters, yellow or blue. The well-known garden lettuce (*Lactuca sativa*) is of uncertain origin, and unknown in the wild, but has a long history of cultivation. It is an important salad plant, its numerous cultivars being divided into two main groups: *cos*, with upright heads of crisp oblong leaves, and the round-headed *cabbage* types, with broadly rounded leaves, often softer-textured and convoluted. (Genus: *Lactuca*, 100 species. Family: *Compositae*.) » annual; cultivar; perennial; vegetable

leucocytes Blood cells without respiratory pigments, also known as **white blood cells**, whose function is to combat injury and bacterial, parasitic, and viral infection. In vertebrates the major types are *granulocytes*, sometimes called *polymorphs* (neutrophils, eosinophils, basophils) and *agranulocytes* (lymphocytes, monocytes). *Neutrophils* enter tissues from the blood, and consume and destroy invading bacteria. *Eosinophils* counteract allergy-inducing irritants released from mast cells, and also destroy parasitic worms. *Basophils* (which contain histamine and heparin) appear to be involved in allergic reactions. Some *lymphocytes* secrete antibodies, giving the body resistance to bacteria and certain viruses; others secrete chemicals involved in the resistance to viruses, some cancer cells, and tissue transplantation. *Monocytes* consume and destroy bacteria, and remove cellular debris from areas of infection and inflammation. » blood; lymphocyte

leucotomy » **psychosurgery**

leukaemia/leukemia A group of malignant disorders of the white cells of the blood which tends to be progressive and fatal. The cause is unknown, but they are associated with exposure to ionizing radiation, cytotoxic drugs, and benzene in industry. The occurrence of the disease in clusters has suggested an infective cause. Depending on the type of white blood cell involved, it may be acute in onset and short-lived (eg *acute lymphoblastic leukaemia*) or slow in onset and prolonged (eg *chronic lymphocytic leukaemia*). The more acute the disorder, the more primitive is the white cell involved. Diagnosis of the cell type is important, because it influences the treatment. It usually necessitates biopsy of the bone marrow, where many white cells are manufactured. » biopsy; blood; radiation

leukotrienes [lyookohtriynz] A group of five or more local hormones (*paracrines*), formed by an enzyme (lipoxygenase) from the same membrane fatty acid (arachidonic acid) as prostaglandins. They are released by mast cells, neutrophils, and other leucocytes, and are involved in inflammatory and hypersensitivity reactions. They act to produce chemotaxis, bronchiolar constriction, and an increase in blood vessel permeability. » anaphylaxis; arachidonic acid; asthma; chemotaxis; paracrine; prostaglandins

Leuven [lervuhn], Fr **Louvain**, Ger **Lowen** 50°53N 4°42E, pop (1983e) 85 068. University town in Brabant province, Belgium, on both banks of the R Dijle; old town, circular in shape, once surrounded by moats; centre of cloth trade in Middle Ages; largely destroyed in World War 1; Catholic University (1425), reorganized into French- and Dutch-speaking divisions since 1970; railway; beer and soft drinks, fertilizers, animal feedstuffs; town hall (1448–63), Church of St Peter (15th–16th-c), Church of St Michael (1650–6), Premonstratensian Abbey of the Park to the SE (1129). » Belgium [i]

Levant, The [luhvant] A general name formerly given to the E shores of the Mediterranean Sea, from W Greece to Egypt. The **Levant States** were Syria and Lebanon, during the period of their French mandate (1920–41). » Lebanon [i]; mandates; Syria [i]

Levellers A radical political movement during the English Civil War and the Commonwealth. It called for the extension of manhood franchise to all but the poorest, religious toleration, and the abolition of the monarchy and the House of Lords. Led by John Lilburne (c.1614–57), Richard Overton (c.1631–64), and William Walwyn (1600–80), it was supported by 'agitators' in the parliamentary army 1647–9, and defeated at Burford (May 1649). » Commonwealth (English history); English Civil War; Lilburne

Leven, Loch [leevuhn] Largest freshwater loch in lowland Scotland; in Perth and Kinross district, Tayside; drained by R Leven (SE); area 13.7 sq km/5.3 sq ml; famous for its trout fishing and its associations with Mary Queen of Scots who abdicated the throne during her imprisonment here in 1567–8; nature reserve; should be distinguished from loch of same name in Lochaber district, Highland region. » Mary, Queen of Scots; Scotland [i]; Tayside

Leverhulme (of the Western Isles), William Hesketh Lever, 1st Viscount [leeverhyoom] (1851–1925) British soap manufacturer, born at Bolton, Lancashire. In 1884 he began to turn a small soap works into a national business, through skilled advertising and continuous consideration for the customer, and developed Port Sunlight as a model industrial village. He was made a baron in 1917, and a viscount in 1922. He died in London. » soap

Leverrier, Urbain Jean Joseph [luhveryay] (1811–77) French astronomer, born at St Lô. Interested in planetary motions, he correctly predicted the existence of Neptune in 1846, and became director of the Paris Observatory (1854–70). He died in Paris. » Adams, John Couch; Neptune (astronomy)

Levi [leeviy] Biblical character, the third son of Jacob by his wife Leah. It is debated whether his descendants ever formed one of the 12 tribes of Israel descended from Jacob's sons. Although they were called a tribe, no territory was apparently allocated to them (*Josh* 13.14), and they seem to have been a kind of priestly class. Moses is later depicted as a descendant of Levi. » Israel, tribes of [i]; Jacob; Levites

Levi, Primo [layvee] (1919–87) Italian novelist, born, educated, and died in Turin. One of the survivors of Auschwitz, he returned to Italy in 1945. All of his novels are attempts to understand the nature of Nazi barbarity and the variety of responses to it evinced by its victims. *Si questo i un Uomo* (1947, If this is a Man), was the first of these. With *La trenga* (1963, The Truce), its sequel, it has acquired the status of a classic treatment of the concentration camps. » Italian literature; Nazi Party; novel

Levi-Montalcini, Rita [levee montalcheenee] (1909–) Italian neurophysiologist, born in Rome. Graduating in medicine at Rome when World War 2 began, she had to go into hiding as a non-Aryan; her early research was done in her bedroom on the neuro-embryology of the chick. In the USA for a while from 1947, she discovered nerve growth factor. She retired in 1979 from directing the Rome Cell Biology Laboratory, and shared the Nobel Prize for Physiology or Medicine in 1986. » nerve growth factor; neurology

Lévi-Strauss, Claude [layvee strows] (1908–) French social anthropologist, born in Brussels, Belgium. He studied law and philosophy, before turning to anthropology. In 1950 he became director of studies at the Ecole Pratiques des Hautes Etudes in Paris, and in 1959 professor of social anthropology at the Collège de France. He has been a major influence on contemporary anthropology, establishing a new method for analysing various collective phenomena such as kinship, ritual, and myth. His major 4-volume study *Mythologiques* (1964–72) studied the systematic ordering behind codes of expression in different cultures. » anthropology; mythology; structuralism

Leviathan [luhviyathan] A rare Hebrew loan-word of uncertain derivation, apparently used to refer to a kind of sea or river monster (*Psalms* 104.26; also *Isa* 27.1; *Psalms* 74.14). In *Job* 41, it seems nearer a crocodile; but Ugaritic parallels suggest it may have been a mythical supernatural figure, a sea dragon, perhaps symbolic of chaos or evil. » Old Testament

levirate A marriage custom or law which expects a widow to marry a brother (either real or a close relative classified as such) of her deceased husband. In some instances, the brother stands in proxy for the deceased, and all his children are regarded as children of the dead man, so no new marriage is entered into. A **sororate** is a custom whereby a man has the right to marry his wife's sister, though this normally applies only if the wife is childless or dies young. » marriage

Levites [leeviyts] Descendants of the Biblical character Levi (one of Jacob's sons), who apparently formed a class of auxiliary ministers dedicated to the care of the Tabernacle and eventually the Jerusalem Temple (*Num* 3.5–10). This role is distinct from that of the Aaronic priesthood itself, but the division between priest and Levite is blurred, and it is arguable that such distinctions arose only in later exilic times. » Aaron; Levi; Leviticus, Book of; Zadokites

Leviticus, Book of [levitikuhs] A book of the Hebrew Bible/Old Testament, the third book of the Pentateuch, the English title referring to the priestly traditions of the Levites. It was probably compiled during the exile from earlier materials, despite the traditional attribution to Moses. It continues from the end of the Book of Exodus, and contains directions about offerings (Chapters 1–7), priesthood (8–10), purity laws (11–15), and the Day of Atonement (16), followed by a major section called the 'holiness code' (17–26) and an appendix (27). » Levites; Old Testament; Pentateuch

levodopa » **L-dopa**

levorotatory » **optical activity**

Lewis, Carl (1961–) US athlete, born at Birmingham, Alabama. He won the long jump gold medal at the 1981 World Cup, and three golds in the inaugural World Championships in 1983. He emulated Jesse Owens's record by winning four gold medals at the 1984 Olympic Games, and won two more at the 1988 Olympics. » athletics; Owens, Jesse

Lewis, C Day » **Day-Lewis, C**

Lewis, C(live) S(taples) (1898–1963) British mediaevalist and Christian apologist, born in Belfast, Northern Ireland. Educated privately, he served in World War 1, and then studied at Oxford, where he was a lecturer (1925–54), becoming professor of Mediaeval and Renaissance English at Cambridge in 1954. His critical study, *The Allegory of Love*, was awarded the Hawthornden Prize (1936). His best-known book is *The Screwtape Letters* (1942), one of several works which expound issues of Christian belief and practice. He is also known for his children's stories of the land of Narnia, beginning with *The Lion, the Witch, and the Wardrobe* (1950), and his science fiction books, such as *Out of the Silent Planet* (1938). He died at Oxford. » literary criticism; science fiction

Lewis, G(ilbert) N(ewton) (1875–1946) US physical chemist, born at Weymouth, Massachusetts. Educated at Harvard,

Leipzig, and Göttingen, he spent most of his career at Berkeley, California. His best-known work, published during World War 1, developed the notions of chemical bonding between atoms, and the sharing of electrons (*covalence*), which were of fundamental importance in the development of chemical theory. » acid; base (chemistry); chemical bond; valence

Lewis, Matthew Gregory, byname **Monk Lewis** (1775–1818) British novelist, born in London. Educated at Westminster, Oxford, and Weimar, in 1794 he went as an attaché to The Hague, and there wrote his best-known work, the Gothic novel *The Monk* (1795). In 1812 he inherited estates in Jamaica, and died while returning from a visit there. » Gothic novel

Lewis, Meriwether (1774–1809) US explorer, born at Charlottesville, Virginia. He grew up in the wilderness, served in the army, and became private secretary to President Thomas Jefferson for two years (1801). With William Clark he was joint leader of the first overland transcontinental expedition to the Pacific coast and back (1804–6). From 1808, he was governor of Louisiana Territory. He died near Nashville, Tennessee. » Clark, William

Lewis, (Harry) Sinclair (1885–1951) US novelist, born at Sauk Center, Minnesota. Educated at Yale, he became a journalist and wrote several minor works before *Main Street* (1920), the first of a series of best-selling novels satirizing the materialism and intolerance of American small-town life. *Babbitt* (1922) still lends its title as a synonym for middle-class American philistinism. Other works of this period are *Martin Arrowsmith* (1925), *Elmer Gantry* (1927), and *Dodsworth* (1929). He won the 1930 Nobel Prize for Literature. His reputation declined after 1930, and he lived mainly abroad, dying near Rome. » American literature; novel

Lewis, (Percy) Wyndham (1882–1957) British artist, writer, and critic, born on a yacht in the Bay of Fundy, Maine. He studied at the Slade School of Art, London, and with Ezra Pound founded *Blast*, the magazine of the Vorticist school. His writings include the satirical novel *The Apes of God* (1930) and the multi-volume *The Human Age* (1955–6), as well as literary criticism, such as *Men Without Art* (1934), and autobiographical books, such as *Blasting and Bombardiering* (1937). His paintings include works of abstract art, a series of war pictures, and portraits. He died in London. » English literature; novel; Pound; satire; Vorticism

Lewis and Clark Expedition » **Clark, William; Lewis, Meriwether**

Lewis with Harris area 2 134 sq km/824 sq ml. Island in the Western Isles, NW Scotland; largest and northernmost of the Hebrides; separated from the mainland (W) by the North Minch; Lewis (N) linked to Harris (S) by a narrow isthmus; chief towns Stornoway, Tarbert; fishing, crofting, tweeds. » Hebrides; Western Isles

lexeme The basic unit in the meaning system of a language. It represents the constant semantic element in a set of related forms (eg *think*, *thinks*, *thought*, *thinking*), independently of the grammatical variations possible in the language. **Lexicology** is the study of a language's vocabulary, investigating the structure of word sets and relationships, and determining the structural similarities and differences between the vocabularies of different languages. Words for colour, kinship terms, and food frequently display cross-linguistic differences. For example, both Welsh and English have words for *brother* and *sister*, but Welsh has terms for male (*cefnder*) and female (*cyfnither*) cousins, where English has only the one word. » semantics

lexicography » **dictionary**

lexicology » **lexeme**

Lexington 42°27N 71°14W, pop (1980) 29 479. Town in Middlesex County, NE Massachusetts, USA, 16 km/10 ml NW of Boston; the American War of Independence started here (19 Apr 1775), when minutemen resisted British soldiers marching to seize stores at Concord. » American Revolution; Revere

Lexington and Concord, Battle of (19 Apr 1775) The first armed conflict of the US War of Independence, fought in Massachusetts after British troops tried to seize supplies stored at the village of Concord. » American Revolution

Leyden, Dutch **Leiden** [**liy**dn] 52°09N 4°30E, pop (1984e) 176 360. University city in South Holland province, W Netherlands, on the R Oude Rijn; charter, 1266; famous for its weaving, 14th-c; besieged for a year by the Spaniards (1573), relieved when William the Silent ordered the dykes to be cut enabling the Dutch fleet to sail to the city walls; as a reward for their bravery the citizens were given Holland's first university, 1575; hardware, machinery, printing; birthplace of several painters, notably Rembrandt; Gemeenlandshuis van Rijn (1596), Weighhouse (1658), Church of St Pancras (15th-c), Church of St Peter (1315), town hall (17th-c), municipal museum (1869). » Netherlands, The [i]; Rembrandt; William I (of the Netherlands)

Leyden jar The earliest device for storing electric charge, named after the University of Leyden, where it was invented in 1746. A glass jar was coated inside and outside with metal foils, which were connected by a rod passing the insulating stopper. The jar was usually charged from an electrostatic generator, and was an early form of capacitor. » capacitance; electricity

leyland cypress An inter-generic hybrid of garden origin between the false cypress and the cypress. Its appearance depends on which species is the female parent, but it is always columnar in outline, hardy and vigorous. Clones with grey or green foliage are the most common. First raised in 1888, it is much used nowadays for fast-growing hedges. (× *Cupressocyparis leylandii*. Family: *Cupressaceae*.) » clone; cypress; false cypress

Lhasa or **La-sa** [**lah**sa], byname **The Forbidden City** 29°41N 91°10E, pop (1983e) 104 800. Capital of Xizang autonomous region (Tibet), SW China; altitude 3 600 m/11 800 ft; airfield; ancient centre of Tibetan Buddhism, with many temples and holy sites; closed to foreigners in 19th-c; Chinese occupation, 1951; many monks have fled (including the Dalai Lama), especially after uprising in 1959; Potala fortress (17th-c), including Red Palace, former home of the Dalai Lama; Drepung Monastery (1416), still an active lamisary; Jokhang Temple (6th-c), containing the Sakyamuni Buddha; light industry, crafts. » Buddhism; China [i]; Dalai Lama; Potala Palace; Tibet

Lhasa apso [**lah**sa **ap**soh] A toy breed of dog developed in Tibet; small with dense coat of stiff straight hair parted along spine; usually golden (but other colours possible); head with mass of hair covering eyes; ears pendulous. » dog

Li Bo, Li Po, or **Li T'ai Po** [**lee poh**] (c.700–62) Chinese poet, born in Szechwan. He led a dissipated life at the Emperor's court, and later became a member of a wandering band calling themselves 'The Eight Immortals of the Wine Cup'. Regarded as the greatest poet of China, he wrote colourful verse of wine, women, and nature. It is said that he was drowned while attempting to kiss the Moon's reflection. » Chinese literature

Li Dazhao or **Li Ta-chao** [lee da**jow**] (1888–1927) One of the founders of the Chinese Communist Party, whose interpretation of Marxism as applied to China had a profound influence on Mao Zedong (Mao Tse-tung). Appointed head librarian of Beijing (Peking) University and professor of history (1918), he had the young Mao Zedong as a library assistant, and founded one of the first of the communist study circles which in 1921 were to form the Communist Party. In 1927, when the Manchurian military leader Chang Tso-lin, then occupying Beijing, raided the Soviet Embassy, Li was captured and executed. » communism; Mao Zedong; Marxism

Li Lisan or Li Li-san [lee li**san**] (1900–67) Chinese Communist Party leader, and effective head of the Party (1928–30), born in Hunan province. He achieved what has since become known as the 'Li Lisan line', in which the Party's weak and undeveloped military forces were used in futile attempts to capture cities. His authoritarian methods alienated his fellow leaders. He was demoted in 1930, and lived in the Soviet Union until 1945. Thereafter he was employed by the Chinese Communist Party in various minor roles. » communism

Li Ta-chao » **Li Dazhao**

liane [li**ahn**] or **liana** [li**ah**nuh] A woody climber growing from the ground to the top of the tree canopy, where it branches out and produces flowers. Many reach considerable heights, especially in tropical forests, where they are abundant. » climbing plant

Libby, Willard Frank (1908–80) US chemist, born at Grand Valley, Colorado. He studied and lectured at Berkeley, California, and was involved in atom bomb research at Columbia

(1941–5). He was professor of chemistry at Chicago (1945–54), a member of the US Atomic Energy Commission (1954–9), and professor of chemistry at Los Angeles (1959–76). He won the Nobel Prize for Chemistry in 1960 for his part in the invention of the carbon-14 method of dating. He died in Los Angeles. » radiocarbon dating

libel A defamatory statement published in permanent form. By statute this is extended to include broadcast by wireless telegraphy (radio, television), and words spoken during the public performance of a play; also, the libel need not involve words – a sculpture or painting may be libellous. The expression is not used in Scottish law. » defamation; slander

Liberal Party (Australia) Australia's largest conservative political party, formed by R G Menzies in 1944 from existing conservative groups. It built up a mass following in the late 1940s, and was victorious in 1949. It stayed in power until 1966, and was then in coalition with the Country Party until 1972 and again in 1975–83. Under Menzies (Prime Minister, 1949–66), the Party followed policies of economic growth and conservative pragmatism, espousing private enterprise. Support surged in the mid-1970s, but in the 1983 elections it was unable to match the resurgent Labor Party. Nevertheless, by 1988 the Liberal Party still had 100 000 members, and remains the main alternative to the Australian Labor Party. » Australian Labor Party; League of Rights; Menzies; National Party (Australia)

Liberal Party (UK) A British political party, originating in the 1860s, whose electoral appeal was to the new middle classes and working-class elite of skilled artisans. Its first major victory came one year after the 1867 Reform Act. The Liberals and Conservatives were the two major parties until 1922, when the Labour Party overtook the Liberals in popular support, since when their status has declined to a centrist minority party. Espousing the values of individual and economic freedom combined with social justice, it played a significant part in the development of the welfare state. After the formation of the Social Democratic Party (SDP) in 1980, the Liberal Party entered into an electoral 'Alliance', and in 1987 voted to merge with the SDP, subsequently forming the **Social and Liberal Democratic Party**. » Conservative Party; Labour Party; liberalism; Social Democratic Party

Liberal Republican Party (1872) An insurgent movement in the US Republican Party. It was opposed to reconstruction policies in the South, and to the notorious corruption in the administration of President Grant (in office 1869–77). » Grant, Ulysses S; Reconstruction; Republican Party

liberalism A political philosophy developed largely in the 18th–19th-c associated with the rise of the new middle classes, challenging the traditional monarchical, aristocratic, or religious views of the state. Liberals sought political power to match economic power, and argued for secular, constitutional, and parliamentary governments. Classical liberalism argues for limited government, and the values traditionally espoused are those of freedom – of the individual, religion, trade and economics (expressed in terms of *laissez faire*), and politics. In the 20th-c, liberalism in most countries has been overtaken by socialism as the major radical challenge to conservative parties, and has come to occupy a position in the centre ground, finding it difficult to establish a firm electoral base. In some countries (eg the UK), liberals have combined traditional values with a belief in the need for governmental intervention to overcome social injustice. » laissez-faire; Liberal Party (UK)

liberation theology A style of theology originating in Latin America in the 1960s, and later becoming popular in many developing countries. Accepting a Marxist analysis of society, it stresses the role and mission of the Church to the poor and oppressed in society, of which Christ is understood as liberator. Its sympathy for revolutionary movements led to clashes with established secular and religious authorities. » Jesus Christ; Marxism; theology

Liberia, official name **Republic of Liberia** [liybeeria] pop (1990e) 2 595 000; area 113 370 sq km/43 800 sq ml. Republic in W Africa, bounded NW by Sierra Leone, N by Guinea, E by the Côte d'Ivoire, and S by the Atlantic Ocean; capital, Monrovia; chief towns, Harper, Greenville, Buchanan, Robertsport; time-

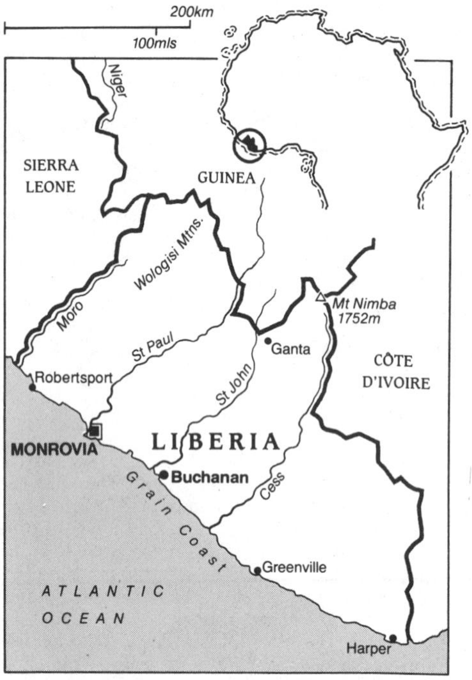

☐ international airport

zone GMT; population mainly indigenous tribes (95%), remainder being repatriated slaves from the USA (Americo-Liberians); official language, English, with many local languages spoken; chief religions, local beliefs; unit of currency, the Liberian dollar; low coastal belt with lagoons, beaches, and mangrove marshes; rolling plateau (500–800 m/1 600–2 600 ft) with grasslands and forest; land rises inland to mountains, reaching 1 752 m/5 748 ft at Mt Nimba; rivers cut SW down through the plateau; equatorial climate, with high temperatures and abundant rainfall; rainfall declines from S to N; high humidity during rainy season (Apr–Sep), especially on coast; average annual rainfall at Monrovia, 4 150 mm/163 in; mapped by the Portuguese, 15th-c; created as a result of the activities of several US philanthropic societies, wishing to establish a homeland for former slaves; founded in 1822; constituted as the Free and Independent Republic of Liberia, 1847; military coup and assassination of president, 1980, established a People's Redemption Council, with a chairman and a cabinet; new constitution, 1984, with an elected 26-member Senate and 64-member House of Representatives; civil war, followed by arrival of West African peace-keeping force, 1990; economy based on minerals, especially iron ore; gold, diamonds, platinum group metals, barite, titanium, zirconium, rare-earth metals, clay; two-thirds of the population rely on subsistence agriculture; rubber, timber, palm oil, rice, cassava, coffee, cocoa, coconuts; largest merchant fleet in the world, including the registration of many foreign ships. » Monrovia; slave trade; RR26 national holidays; RR55 political leaders

libertarianism 1 A metaphysical doctrine, held by Sartre and others, which maintains that free actions cannot be completely caused; human freedom is incompatible with universal causal determinism. **2** A political philosophy, held by Russo-US novelist Ayn Rand (1905–82) and others, which claims that the only justified function of the state is to provide protection; the promotion of other goals is an intrusion on individual rights. » determinism; Sartre

Liberty Bell » **Independence Hall**

liberty, equality, fraternity The motto of the French Republic; adopted in June 1793, it remained the official slogan of the state until the Bourbon Restoration (1814). It was re-adopted during the Second Republic (1848–51), and has remained the national slogan from 1875, except during the German Occupation (1940–4). » French Revolution [i]

Liberty, Statue of The representation of a woman holding aloft a torch, which stands at the entrance to New York harbour; a world heritage site. The idea for 'Liberty Enlightening the World' was conceived in France; it was designed by the French sculptor Bartholdi, and shipped to New York to be assembled and dedicated in 1886. The statue is 40 m/152 ft high. » Bartholdi

Libra [**lee**bra] (Lat 'scales') An inconspicuous S constellation. It is an autumn sign of the zodiac, lying between Virgo and Scorpius. » constellation; zodiac [i]; RR9

librarianship » **library science**

library A building or room containing a collection of books, records, photographs, etc, organized to facilitate consultation or borrowing by private individuals or the public; also, the collection itself. Libraries date from the earliest recorded times, being known in several ancient countries of the Middle East, such as Babylonia, Egypt, and Mesopotamia. There were famous libraries at Alexandria, Athens, and Rome. In Christian Europe, libraries were usually attached to monasteries; secular collections emerged during and after the Renaissance, several of which have provided the basis of major modern libraries, such as the Bodleian at Oxford. Libraries can be classified according to their size and importance, and whether they are public or privately owned, are general or specialized in coverage, offer a lending or reference-only service, and permit open or closed access. Other varieties include subscription libraries and mobile libraries (often found in country areas). An international library network now exists. » Bodleian/British/Lenin library; Bibliothèque Nationale; Library of Congress; library science; National Library of Australia

Library of Congress The US depository and largest library in the world, founded in 1800 in Washington, DC. The library provides bibliographical and cataloguing services for libraries throughout the world, but its main function is the provision of reference materials for the US Congress. It has holdings of over 20 million books and 30 million manuscripts. » library; Washington

library science The study of all aspects of library functions. It covers such topics as selection and acquisition policy, classification systems, and cataloguing, as well as bibliography and administration. As a discipline in its own right, library science, or **librarianship**, is a late 19th-c development. » library

libration A slight irregularity in the motion of the Moon which makes it look as if it is oscillating. The phenomenon is useful to observers on Earth, because it lets them see around the *limb*, or outer edge, of the Moon as it runs ahead or behind in its orbit. These librations mean that, over a period of time, 59% of the Moon is visible from Earth. » Moon

Libreville [leebruh**veel**] 0°30N 9°25E, pop (1985e) 350 000. Capital of Gabon, W Africa, at the mouth of R Gabon, 520 km/325 ml NW of Brazzaville; founded in 1849 as a refuge for slaves freed by the French; occupied by the British and Free French, 1940; airport; railway; university (1970); commercial and administrative centre; timber, cement, ceramics, food and drink processing, oil exploration; Cathedral of Sainte-Marie, museum, art gallery; first Central African Games held here, 1976. » Gabon [i]

Librium » **benzodiazepines**

Libya, official name **Socialist People's Libyan Arab Jamahiriya** pop (1990e) 4 206 000; area 1 758 610 sq km/678 823 sq ml. N African state, divided into 10 provinces; bounded NW by Tunisia, W by Algeria, SW by Niger, S by Chad, SE by Sudan, E by Egypt, and N by the Mediterranean Sea; capital, Tripoli; chief towns, Misratah, Benghazi, Sabha; timezone GMT + 1; chief ethnic groups, Berber and Arab (97%); chief religion, Islam (mainly Sunni); official language, Arabic; unit of currency, the Libyan dinar of 1 000 millemes.

Physical description and climate. Mainly low-lying Saharan desert or semi-desert; land rises (S) to over 2 000 m/6 500 ft in the Tibesti massif; highest point, Pic Bette on the Chad frontier (2 286 m/7 500 ft); water limited to infrequent oases; Mediterranean climate on coast; Tripoli, average annual rainfall 385 mm/15 in, average maximum daily temperatures 16–30°C; annual rainfall in desert seldom over 100 mm/4 in; temperatures in S over 40°C for three months of the year.

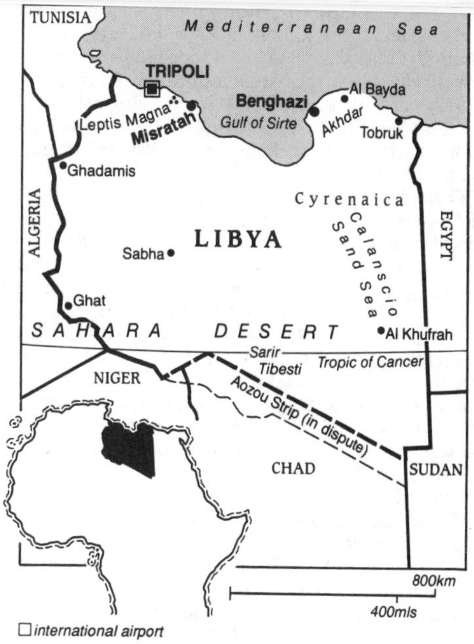

History and government. Controlled at various times by Phoenicians, Carthaginians, Greeks, Vandals, and Byzantines; Arab domination during 7th-c; Turkish rule from 16th-c until Italians gained control in 1911; named Libya by the Italians, 1934; heavy fighting during World War 2, followed by British and French control; independent Kingdom of Libya, 1951; military coup established a republic under Muammar Gaddafi, 1969; governed by a Revolutionary Command Council; foreign military installations closed down in early 1970s; government policy since the revolution based on the promotion of Arab unity and the furtherance of Islam; relations with other countries strained by controversial activities, including alleged organization of international terrorism; diplomatic relations severed by UK after the murder of a policewoman in London, 1984; Tripoli and Benghazi bombed by US Air Force in response to alleged terrorist activity, 1986; two Libyan fighter planes shot down by aircraft operating with US Navy off N African coast, 1989.

Economy. Once a relatively poor country, with an agricultural economy based on barley, olives, fruit, dates, almonds, tobacco; economy transformed by discovery of oil and natural gas, 1959; natural gas liquefaction plant, iron ore, gypsum, sulphur; cement, petroleum processing, iron, steel, aluminium, food processing, textiles, crafts; cattle, sheep, goats, with nomadic farming in S. » Gaddafi; Islam; Sahara Desert; Tripoli (Libya); RR26 national holidays; RR55 political leaders

lice » **louse**

lichen [**liy**kuhn, **li**chin] A type of composite organism formed as an association between a fungus (the *mycobiont*) and an alga or blue-green bacterium (the *phycobiont*). The body (*thallus*) may be encrusting, scale-like, leafy, or even shrubby, according to species. The fungal partner typically belongs to *Ascomycetes*. Many lichens are very sensitive to atmospheric pollution and can be used as indicators. » algae; blue-green bacteria; fungus

Lichtenstein, Roy (1923–) US painter, born in New York City. He studied at the Art Students' League, New York (1939) and at Ohio State College, and taught at Ohio State, New York State, and Rutgers. Since the early 1960s he has produced many of the best-known images of American Pop Art, especially frames from comic books complete with speech balloons, enlarged onto canvases and painted in primary colours in a hard-edged style imitated from cheap printing techniques. The Tate Gallery's huge 'Whaam!' (1963) is a characteristic example. » Pop Art

licorice » **liquorice**

Liddell Hart, Sir Basil (Henry) (1895–1970) British military journalist and theorist, born in Paris. Educated at St Paul's and Cambridge, he was wounded as an infantry officer in World War 1. He joined the Army Education Corps, then became military correspondent for the *Daily Telegraph* (1925–35) and *The Times* (1935–9), advocating the principles of modern mobile warfare. He was knighted in 1966, and died at Marlow, Buckinghamshire.

Lie, Trygve (Halvdan) [lee] (1896–1968) Norwegian lawyer, the first Secretary-General of the United Nations, born in Oslo. Educated at Kristiania, he became a Labour member of the Norwegian parliament and held several posts, before fleeing with the government to Britain in 1940, where he acted as its Foreign Minister until 1945. Elected UN Secretary-General in 1946, he resigned in 1952 over Soviet opposition to his policy of intervention in the Korean War. He died at Geilo, Norway. » Korean War; United Nations

lie detector An instrument supposed to indicate whether a person to which it is applied is responding truthfully to questions; also known as a *polygraph*. Involuntary physiological reactions detected by electrodes attached to the subject's skin indicate stresses. Its validity is not universally acknowledged nor accepted judicially.

Liebig, Justus von, Baron [**lee**bikh] (1803–73) German chemist, born at Darmstadt. He studied at Bonn and Erlangen, and in 1822 went to Paris, where he worked with Gay-Lussac. In 1824 he became professor of chemistry at Giessen, and in 1852 at Munich. He investigated many aspects of organic, animal, and agricultural chemistry, and developed new techniques for carrying out analyses, such as the distillation equipment known as **Liebig's condenser**. He was created baron in 1845, and died in Munich. » biochemistry; chemistry

Liechtenstein [**likh**tnshtiyn], official name **Principality of Liechtenstein**, Ger **Füstentum Liechtenstein** pop (1990e) 28 700; area 160 sq km/62 sq ml. Independent Alpine principality in C Europe, divided into the districts of Oberland (Upper Country) and Unterland (Lower Country); lies between the Austrian province of Vorarlberg (E) and the Swiss cantons of St Gallen and Graubünden (W); fourth smallest country in the world; land boundary 76 km/47 ml; capital, Vaduz; timezone GMT +1; population of Alemannic origin; official language, German; chief religion, Roman Catholicism (87%); unit of currency, the Swiss franc; bounded W by the R Rhine; mean altitude, 450 m/1 475 ft; forested mountains rise to 2 599 m/8 527 ft in the Grauspitz; mild climate, influenced by warm S wind (Föhn); average high temperature in summer, 20–28°C; average annual rainfall, 1 050–1 200 mm/41–47 in; formed in 1719; part of Holy Roman Empire until 1806; a constitutional monarchy ruled by the hereditary princes of the House of Liechtenstein; governed by a prime minister, four councillors, and a unicameral parliament (*Landtag*) of 25 members elected for four years; industrial sector developing since 1950s, export-based, centred on specialized and high-tech production; metalworking, engineering, chemicals, pharmaceuticals, textiles, ceramics, foodstuffs; international banking and finance, postage stamps, tourism; vegetables, corn, wheat, potatoes, grapes, timber. » Föhn; Vaduz; RR26 national holidays; RR55 political leaders

Lied [leet] (plural **Lieder**) A song with German words. In certain contexts the word implies a simple folksong (or a song in folk style), as distinct from the more ambitious and 'arty' *Gesang*; but *Lied* is generally used with reference to the solo songs with piano of the great German Romantic composers. » Brahms; Schubert; Schumann, Robert; Wolf, Hugo

Liège [lyairzh], Flemish **Luik**, Ger **Lüttich** 50°38N 5°35E, pop (1982) 211 528. River port and capital city of Liège province, E Belgium, at confluence of Ourthe and Meuse Rivers; bishopric; university (1817); fifth largest city in Belgium; railway; centre of former coal-mining area; blast furnaces, metalworking, civil engineering, textiles, foodstuffs, electronics, chemicals, glassware, arms; Church of St Jacques (11th-c, rebuilt 1513–38), Palace of Justice (1526–40), Gothic St Paul's Cathedral. » Belgium [i]

Lif [leef] and **Lifthrasir** [**leef**thrahser] In Norse mythology, the mother and father of the new race of human beings after Ragnarok (the last battle). The names presumably mean 'life' and 'strong life'. » Ragnarok

Lifar, Serge [lifar] (1905–86) Russian dancer and choreographer, born at Kiev. He was a student and friend of Diaghilev, whose company he joined in 1923. He scored his first triumph as a choreographer in Paris with *Créatures de Promethée* (1929) and became the guiding genius behind the Paris Opéra (1929–58). He wrote several works on ballet, including a biography of Diaghilev (1940), and died at Lausanne, Switzerland. » ballet; Ballets Russes; Diaghilev

life The state or property of organisms which, by their metabolic processes, use substances from their environment for the purposes of growth, the maintenance of their functional systems, the repair of their own structure, and for reproducing themselves. All life forms on Earth are based on nucleic acids, either deoxyribonucleic acid (DNA) or ribonucleic acid (RNA), which carry their hereditary genetic information. Life on Earth is thought to have originated about 4 000 million years ago in conditions in which the primordial atmosphere contained the basic constituents of organic matter (methane, ammonia, hydrogen, and water vapour). These underwent a process of chemical evolution using energy from the Sun and electric storms, combining into more and more complex molecules until self-replicating nucleic acids developed. » biology; life cycle; metabolism; nucleic acids

life assurance or **life insurance** Insurance related specifically to protection against financial hardship arising from a person's premature death. Named dependants are paid a specified sum on the death of the insured person. If the agreement is a 'term' policy, this sum is paid to the policy holder on surviving to the end of the term. » insurance

life cycle The complete series of stages through which an organism passes, from the formation of an individual by the fertilization of gametes produced by one generation, through to maturation and the production of gametes by that individual, and to its eventual death. In vertebrates there is usually a simple life cycle from fertilization to death, but in lower animals and plants the life cycle is often complex, involving the alternation of sexually reproducing and asexually reproducing generations which may or may not be similar in appearance. » alternation of generations; fertilization; gamete; neoteny

life imprisonment A sentence involving imprisonment for the remainder of the convicted person's life. In the UK, it is the sentence for murder, and the maximum sentence for certain other crimes such as manslaughter and rape. In practice, the sentence may not be for life. The prisoner may be released on licence by the Home Secretary on the advice of the Parole Board, with consultation of the Lord Chief Justice and, if possible, the trial judge. When passing this sentence, the trial judge may recommend a minimum term of imprisonment, though this is not binding on the Home Secretary. » manslaughter; murder; rape (law)

lifeboat A vessel designed specifically for saving life at sea; also, a craft carried by sea-going vessels to save the lives of personnel in the event of abandoning ship. Lionel Lukin is believed to have been the first to build a lifeboat, in 1786, basing it at Bamburgh Head, Northumberland. Several countries now run lifeboat services; some are government controlled, and others are voluntary or semi-voluntary. Many are modelled on the British RNLI. Only the Chinese lay claim to pre-dating the British, by organizing a river rescue service as early as 1737. » Royal National Lifeboat Institution (RNLI)

LIFFE » **futures**

Liffey, River [**li**fee] River in E Irish Republic, rising in N Wicklow county; flows W, NE, and E through Dublin to meet the Irish Sea at Dublin Bay; length 80 km/50 ml; crossed by the Grand Canal. » Dublin (city); Irish Republic [i]

lifting body A spacecraft designed for controlled atmospheric flight following entry from space. The aerodynamic configuration is designed to withstand entry loads and also to generate significant lift. The NASA space shuttle orbiter is an example. Similar concepts are under development in Russia and in Europe. » space shuttle [i]

ligament A tough band of tissue connecting bones (eg across joints) or supporting internal organs (eg peritoneal ligaments).

Ligaments are generally composed of inextensible collagen arranged in parallel bundles, but some contain a significant amount of elastic tissue, which allows limited movement to occur. When associated with joints they can vary from the thickenings of the joint capsule to substantial extra- or intracapsular structures, their thickness being directly related to the forces they are required to resist. They act to prevent mechanical disruption at joints, and as sensory organs for the perception of movement and joint position. » bone; collagens; joint; peritoneum

ligand A molecule or ion bonded to another. It is most often used to describe species bonded to the central metal ion in a co-ordination compound. » co-ordination compounds

liger A member of the cat family, resulting from the mating of a male lion with a female tiger. The offspring produced when a male tiger mates with a female lion is called a **tigon**. » Felidae; lion; tiger

Ligeti, György (Sándor) (1923–) Hungarian-born composer, born at Dicsöszent-márton. He studied and later taught at the Budapest Music School. After leaving Hungary in 1956, he worked at the electronics studio in Cologne, and settled in Vienna, where he developed an experimental approach to composition. His first large orchestral work, *Apparitions* (1958–9), made his name widely known. In *Aventures* (1962) he uses his own invented language of speech sounds. He has also written a choral Requiem, a cello concerto, and music for harpsichord, organ, and wind and string ensembles.

light The visible portion of the electromagnetic spectrum, corresponding to electromagnetic waves ranging in wavelength from approximately 3.9×10^{-7}m (violet) to 7.8×10^{-7}m (red) (corresponding frequencies 7.7×10^{14}Hz and 3.8×10^{14}Hz, respectively). Different wavelengths of light are perceived by humans as different colours. *White light* is composed of light of different wavelengths (colours), as may be seen by dispersing the beam through a prism. Light of a single colour is called *monochromatic*, a term sometimes taken to mean a single wavelength (which is unachievable). The best source of monochromatic light is the laser.

Light as an electromagnetic wave was deduced by James Clerk Maxwell: he derived an expression for the velocity of electromagnetic waves, using electric and magnetic quantities only, which equals the velocity of light (2.998×10^8m/s). Interactions with matter (in particular, the photoelectric effect) show that light can also be viewed as composed of particles (*photons*) of definite energy; the polarization of light as a wave effect translates into the spin properties of photons. The modern description of light is as particles whose behaviour is governed by wave principles according to the rules of quantum theory. In geometrical optics (eg lens systems), light is thought of as rays, travelling in straight lines, causing shadows for opaque objects; these rays change direction when passing between regions of different refractive index.

Light comes from many sources. Light bulbs produce light from electrically heated filaments; thermal energy causes the motion of atoms and electrons in the filament, producing thermal radiation with a frequency spectrum related to the temperature of the filament; for filament temperatures of a few hundred degrees Celsius, the radiation produced is mostly infrared; for higher temperatures (c.3 000°C for household bulbs), light is produced. Mercury arc lamps produce light by electrical discharge (the arc) in mercury vapour. Fluorescent lamps rely on electrical excitation in a gas to produce ultraviolet radiation, which in turn causes the phosphor coating on a glass tube to emit visible light by fluorescence. Electrical discharge in gases (eg neon signs) or the application of heat to substances often produces light having specific spectra; this is related to the atomic structure of the substance, and is explained in terms of quantum theory. » atomic spectra [i]; attenuation; birefringence; blackbody radiation; Čerenkov radiation; coherence; diffraction [i]; electromagnetic radiation [i]; energy level; ether; fluorescence; interference [i]; laser [i]; luminescence; optics [i]; photoelectric effect; photo-ionization; photometry [i]; photon; polarimetry; polarization [i]; quantum mechanics; spectrum; stroboscope; velocity of light; Plate X

light emitting diode (LED) A tiny semiconductor diode which emits light when an electric current is passed through it. It is used in electronic calculator displays and digital watch read-outs, where the digits are made up from the diodes. The colour of the light emitted depends on the material of the crystal. » semiconductor diode

light year The distance travelled through empty space in one tropical year by any electromagnetic radiation: 9.4605×10^{12} km. It is widely used in literature of all types, but never in fact used by astronomers, who prefer the parsec. » light; parsec; tropical year; units (scientific)

lightning A visible electric discharge in the form of a flash of light which results from charge separation in a thundercloud. There are two parts to the flash: the first is from the cloud to the ground or tall structure; the second is the return stroke from ground to cloud. The reflection of lightning on surrounding clouds, in which the illumination is diffused, is known as **sheet lightning**. » lightning conductor

lightning bug » **firefly**

lightning conductor A means of protecting buildings and tall structures from lightning strikes; also called a **lightning rod**. It consists of a metal rod or strip, usually made of copper, placed at the highest point of a building. The lower end of the rod is connected to earth by a low-resistance cable. A lightning flash hitting the rod will be given a safe passage along this line of least resistance to the ground. » lightning

lightpen A computer input device used in conjunction with a visual display unit (VDU). The pen is held against the screen of the VDU and its exact position can be detected by the computer. It can be used to generate or to alter information on the screen. » input device

Lights, Feast of » **Hanukkah**

lignite » **coal**

lignum vitae [**lig**nuhm **viy**tee] An evergreen tree growing to c.10 m/30 ft, native to W Indies; bark pale, smooth; leaves pinnate with oval leaflets; flowers blue, 5-petalled. It is a source of durable timber. (*Guaiacum officinale*. Family: *Zygophyllaceae*.) » evergreen plants; pinnate; tree [i]

Ligurian Sea [liy**gyu**rian] Arm of the Mediterranean Sea, bounded N and E by NW Italy and S by Corsica and Elba; chief ports include Genoa, Livorno, Bastia. » Mediterranean Sea

lilac A deciduous shrub or small tree, native to the Balkans; growing to 3–7 m/10–23 ft, domed and suckering freely; leaves oval to heart-shaped, in opposite pairs; flowers in dense, conical inflorescences, tubular with four spreading lobes, lilac or white, fragrant; fruit a pointed capsule. A widely cultivated garden ornamental, its botanical name should not be confused with the syringa or mock orange of horticulture. (*Syringa vulgaris*. Family: *Oleaceae*.) » deciduous plants; inflorescence [i]; mock orange; shrub; tree [i]

Lilburne, John (c.1614–57) English revolutionary, born near London, who became a leading figure in the Levellers during the English Civil War. Imprisoned by the Star Chamber in 1638, he rose in the parliamentary army, but resigned from it in 1645. He then became an indefatigable agitator, and was repeatedly imprisoned for his pamphlets. He died at Eltham, Kent. » English Civil War; Levellers

Lilienthal, Otto [**leel**yentahl] (1849–96) German aeronautical inventor, born at Anklam. He studied bird flight in order to build heavier-than-air flying machines resembling the birdman designs of Leonardo da Vinci. He made many short flights in his machines, but crashed to his death near Berlin in 1896. » aeronautics; Leonardo da Vinci

Lilith [**li**lith] In Jewish legend, the first wife of Adam; or, more generally, a demon woman. » Adam and Eve

Lille [leel], formerly Flemish **Lisle**, **Ryssel**, ancient **Insula** 50°38N 3°03E, pop (1982) 174 039. Industrial and commercial city and capital of Nord department, N France; near the Belgian frontier, 208 km/129 ml NNE of Paris; badly damaged in both World Wars; road and rail junction; university (1560); part of the main industrial centre of N France; textiles, tents, sugar-processing, hygiene goods, foodstuffs, chemicals, engineering, metalworking, printing, brewing; Gothic Church of St-Maurice, 16th-c Church of Ste-Catherine; cathedral (begun,

1854), 16th-c citadel, Palais des Beaux-Arts; international trade fair (Apr).

Lillie, Beatrice (Gladys) (1898–1989) Canadian revue singer, born in Toronto. After an unsuccessful start as a drawing-room ballad singer, she became renowned from 1914 in music hall and the new vogue of 'intimate revue'. After World War 2 she continued to work on the stage, in international revues, and in films, such as *Thoroughly Modern Millie* (1967). She died at Henley, Oxfordshire.

Lilongwe [lee**long**gway] 13°58N 33°49E, pop(1984e) 172 000. Capital of Malawi, SE Africa, in Central region, on R Lilongwe; altitude 1 100 m/3 600 ft; capital since 1975; airport; railway; seeds, tobacco, light engineering, clothes, tourism, commerce. » Malawi [i]

lily A perennial with a bulb formed from swollen, overlapping, scale-like leaves, native to N temperate regions; stem erect, unbranched, with numerous narrow, alternate, or whorled leaves; flowers with six perianth-segments, large, terminal, often hanging; usually trumpet-shaped or with perianth rolled back to resemble a Turk's cap; in a wide range of colours, mostly white, yellow to red, purple, and often spotted; stamens long, protruding. Many species are prized for their beautiful and often fragrant flowers. The name 'lily' is often applied to various other plants. (Genus: *Lilium*, 80 species. Family: *Liliaceae*.) » African lily; bulb; day lily; perennial; perianth; stamen

lily-of-the-valley A perennial growing to 20 cm/8 in, native to Europe and Asia; rhizomatous; leaves elliptical, in pairs, the stalks sheathing; inflorescence slender, 1-sided; flowers drooping, globular bells with six short lobes, white, fragrant; berries red. It is cultivated for ornament, and as source of perfume. (*Convallaria majalis*. Family: *Liliaceae*.) » inflorescence [i]; perennial; rhizome

lily-trotter » **jacana**

Lima [**lee**ma] 12°06S 77°03W, pop(1981) 4 164 597. Federal capital of Peru; on both sides of the R Rímac, at the foot of the Cerro San Cristóbal; founded by Pizarro, 1535; chief city of Spanish S America until independence; devastated by earthquake, 1746; airport; railway; 10 universities; vehicles, textiles, foodstuffs, paper; cathedral (16th-c), Palacio del Gobierno, archbishop's palace, Unity Hall, Santo Domingo Church (1549), San Francisco Church (1674), the National Museum of Art, Museum of Peruvian Culture, Parque de las Leyendas; Pacific International Fair (Nov). » Peru [i]; Pizarro

Lima bean A twining annual or perennial, native to tropical S America; leaves with three leaflets; pea-flowers white or yellowish, in long clusters from the axils of the leaves; pods up to 12.5 cm/5 in long, oblong, containing 2–4 flattened, whitish seeds; also called **butter bean**. It is widely grown in the tropics and subtropics for the edible seeds (beans). Cultivars with red, brown, purple, and black seeds are also grown. (*Phaseolus lunatus*. Family: *Leguminosae*.) » annual; cultivar; perennial

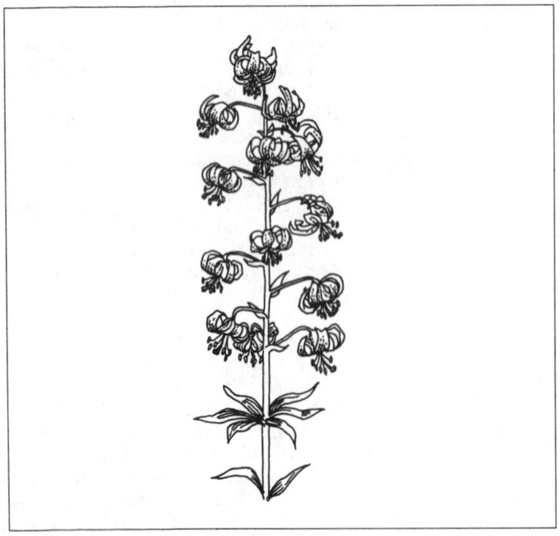

Lily – Lilium martagon (Turk's cap lily)

Limassol [**lim**asol], Gr **Lemesos**, Turkish **Limasol** 34°41N 33°02E, pop(1973) 79 641. Port and capital town of Limassol district, S Cyprus; on Akrotiri Bay, NE of Akrotiri; influx of Greek Cypriot refugees since 1974 Turkish invasion has dramatically increased population; airfield; wine-making, export of fruit and vegetables, distilling; 14th-c castle; spring carnival; arts festival (Jul); wine festival (Sep). » Akrotiri; Cyprus [i]

limbo In mediaeval Christian theology, the abode of souls excluded from the full blessedness of the divine vision, but not condemned to any other punishment. They included unbaptised infants and Old Testament prophets. » Christianity; purgatory

lime (botany) **1** A deciduous N temperate tree; leaves heart-shaped, often sticky with honey-dew caused by aphids; flowers fragrant, white, 5-petalled, in pendulous clusters; fruits rounded, the whole cluster with a wing-like bract which aids in dispersal; also called **linden**. Common lime (*Tilia* × *europaea*) is a hybrid often planted as a street tree. (Genus: *Tilia*, 50 species. Family: *Tiliaceae*.) » aphid; basswood; bract; deciduous plants; hybrid; tree **2** A citrus fruit resembling lemon, but smaller and more globose. *Citrus aurantifolia* has sour red fruits. *Citrus limetta*, the sweet lime, with sweeter, greenish fruits, is possibly a mutant of lemon. (Family: *Rutaceae*.) » citrus; lemon

lime (chemistry) Mainly calcium oxide or hydroxide, produced by heating limestone above 800°C, expelling carbon dioxide. Some of the calcium may be replaced by magnesium. The dry product is called *quicklime*; the addition of water converts the oxide to hydroxide or 'slaked' lime. » calcium; limestone

limerick The limerick, it would appear,/Is a verse form we owe Edward Lear:/Two long and two short/Lines rhymed, as was taught,/And a fifth just to bring up the rear. » Lear, Edward; verse

Limerick (county), Gaelic **Luimneach** pop(1981) 161 661; area 2 686 sq km/1 037 sq ml. County in Munster province, SW Irish Republic; bounded N by R Shannon; capital, Limerick; dairy farming, hydroelectric power (Ardnacrusha), lace. » Irish Republic [i]; Limerick (city)

Limerick (city), Gaelic **Luimneach** 52°40N 8°38W, pop(1981) 75 520. County borough and river-port capital of Limerick county, Munster, SW Irish Republic; industrial city at head of Shannon Estuary; founded, 1197; scene of major sieges by Cromwell and William III; railway; teacher training college; trade in farm produce, flour milling, brewing, fishing, lace; Belltable arts centre, St Mary's Cathedral (12th-c), St John's Cathedral (19th-c), remains of city walls, King John's Castle, treaty stone; festival of Irish dancing and Gaelic drama (Mar); Seisiún, traditional Irish entertainment (summer). » Cromwell, Oliver; Limerick (county); William III

limestone A sedimentary rock consisting mainly of carbonates, primarily calcite (calcium carbonate, $CaCO_3$) or dolomite ($CaMg(CO_3)_2$), with detrital sand or clay as impurities. Most limestones are organically formed from the secretions, shells, or skeletons of plants and animals such as corals and molluscs. Inorganic limestones are formed by precipitation from water containing dissolved carbonates. Limestone is of economic importance as a building material, and as a source of lime and cement. » calcite; carbonates; Karst region; oolite; stalactites and stalagmites; travertine

limit In mathematics, a value approached by a variable. The variable may be the sum of a number of terms of a sequence, eg if $S_n = 1 + \frac{1}{2} + \frac{1}{4} \ldots \frac{1}{2^n}$, as n becomes large (ie $n \rightarrow \infty$), S approaches the value 2. Or the variable y may be dependent on another variable x, and may approach a limit as x approaches a given value, eg if $y = 2 + 1/x$, y approaches the value 2 as x becomes large. The idea of a limit is fundamental to calculus and other branches of mathematics.

limitation clause » **exemption clause**

limitation of actions Legal rules which require civil actions to be brought within specific time limits; in the USA, usually referred to as the statute of limitations. Periods vary greatly across jurisdictions and types of actions. In England and Wales, for tort and simple contract, the period is six years from the cause of action, though for personal injuries and death the period is three years. These periods may be extended in certain circumstances. Some jurisdictions impose time limits on the prosecution of criminal offences. » contract; tort

limner A painter of portraits 'in little', ie in miniature. Nicholas Hilliard's treatise *The Art of Limning* (c.1600) describes the highly specialized techniques required by the limner, following Holbein's approach. » Holbein; miniature painting

Limoges [lee**mohzh**], ancient **Augustoritum Lemovicensium**, later **Lemovices** 45°50N 1°15E, pop (1982) 144 082. Ancient town and capital of Haute-Vienne department, C France; in R Vienne valley, 176 km/109 ml NE of Bordeaux; Gallic tribal capital, destroyed 5th-c; sacked by the English, 1370; road and rail junction; university (founded 1808); meteorological observatory; rapid post-war expansion; famed for manufacture of enamels and porcelain since 18th-c; electrical fittings, shoes; uranium mined near Ambazac; Gothic Cathedral of St-Etienne (begun, 1273); Church of St-Pierre-du-Queyroix (13th-c belfry), Church of St-Michel-des-Lions (14th–16th-c). » porcelain

limonite A general name for a rock rich in hydrous iron oxides, formed by the tropical weathering of iron ore. It is formed in bogs (*bog ore* or *brown ore*). » iron

Limousin [**li**moozĩ] or **Limosin, Léonard** (c.1505–77) French painter in enamel, born at Limoges. He flourished at the French court (1532–74), and was appointed by Francis I head of the royal factory at Limoges. He was also known as a painter in oils. » Francis I; French art

limpet A primitive snail with a simple flattened, conical shell; lives attached to rocks by its muscular foot; found in the intertidal zone or shallow seas; typically feeds at night, grazing algae off rocks using a band of teeth (*radula*). (Class: *Gastropoda*. Order: *Archaeogastropoda*.) » algae; shell; snail

Limpopo, River [limp**oh**poh], also **Crocodile River** River in South Africa, Botswana, Zimbabwe, and Mozambique, SE Africa; length c.1 600 km/1 000 ml; rises in the S Transvaal, N of Johannesburg; follows the Botswana–Transvaal and Transvaal–Zimbabwe borders; enters Mozambique at Pafuri, and flows into the Indian Ocean 130 km/80 ml NE of Maputo; Vasco da Gama named it the Rio do Espiritu Santo in 1497. » Africa; Gama

Lin Biao or **Lin Piao** [lin **byow**] (1908–71) One of the leaders of the Chinese Communist Party and a Marshal of the Red Army, born in Hupeh province. He became Minister of Defence in 1959, and in 1968 replaced the disgraced Liu Shaoqi as heir apparent to Mao Zedong (Mao Tse-tung). He was one of the promoters of the Cultural Revolution of 1966, and appears to have been a patron of extreme left-wing factions. In 1971, after a political struggle, he was killed in a plane crash in Mongolia, apparently in the course of an attempt to seek refuge in the USSR. » Cultural Revolution; Liu Shaoqi; Mao Zedong

linac » **linear accelerator**

Linacre, Thomas (c.1460–1524) English humanist and physician, born at Canterbury, Kent. He studied at Oxford and Padua, travelled widely in Italy (1485–97), and c.1501 became a tutor to Henry VII's son, Arthur. He was King's Physician to Henry VII and Henry VIII, and founded the Royal College of Physicians. In 1520 he took Catholic orders. One of the earliest champions of the New Learning, he died in London. » Galen; Henry VII; Renaissance

Lincoln, Abraham (1809–65) US Republican statesman and 16th President (1861–5), born near Hodgenville, Kentucky. Elected to the Illinois legislature in 1834, he became a lawyer in 1836. A decade later, he was elected to a single term in Congress, where he spoke against the extension of slavery, and in 1860 was elected President on a platform of hostility to slavery's expansion. When the Civil War began (1861), he defined the issue in terms of national integrity, not anti-slavery, a theme he restated in the Gettysburg Address of 1863. Nonetheless, the same year he proclaimed freedom for all slaves in areas of rebellion. He was re-elected in 1864, and after the final Northern victory he intended to reunite the former warring parties on the easiest possible terms; but on 14 April 1865 he was shot at Ford's Theatre, Washington, by an actor, John Wilkes Booth, and died next morning. » American Civil War; Booth, John Wilkes

Lincoln (USA), formerly **Lancaster** (to 1867) 40°49N 96°41W, pop (1980) 171 932. Capital of state in Lancaster County, SE Nebraska, USA; state capital in 1867, when it was renamed after President Lincoln; railway; two universities (1867, 1887); trade in grain and livestock; planetarium, art gallery, sculpture garden. » Lincoln, Abraham; Nebraska

Lincoln (UK) 53°14N 0°33W, pop (1987e) 79 600. County town of Lincolnshire, EC England; on the R Witham, 230 km/143 ml N of London and 64 km/40 ml from the North Sea; an important centre of the wool trade in the Middle Ages; railway; pharmaceuticals, vehicles, radios, engineering; parts of 3rd-c Roman wall remain; Lincoln Castle; cathedral (1073), including Wren Library (contains an original Magna Carta manuscript); cycle of mystery plays (Jun–Jul). » Lincolnshire; Magna Carta; mystery play

Lincoln Center for the Performing Arts A group of theatres, recital halls, etc erected to the W of Broadway, New York City. The complex, completed in 1969, comprises the New York State Theater, Avery Fisher Hall, the Metropolitan Opera House, Vivien Beaumont Theater, Alice Tully Hall, the Juilliard School for the Performing Arts, and the Library and Museum of the Performing Arts. » New York City; theatre

Lincoln Memorial A monument in Washington, DC dedicated in 1922 to President Abraham Lincoln. The building (designed on the plan of a Greek temple by Henry Bacon) houses the statue of Lincoln (6 m/19 ft high) by Daniel Chester French (1850–1931). » Lincoln, Abraham

Lincoln's Inn » **Inns of Court**

Lincolnshire [**ling**knsheer] pop (1987e) 574 600; area 5 915 sq km/2 283 sq ml. Flat agricultural county in EC England, divided into seven districts; bounded E by the North Sea; drained by the Welland, Witham, and Trent Rivers; Fens drained in 17th-c; county town Lincoln; chief towns include Grantham, Gainsborough, Spalding; intensive farming, horticulture, tourism. » England [i]; Fens; Lincoln (UK)

Lind, Jenny, originally **Johanna Maria Lind** (1820–87) Swedish soprano, born in Stockholm. She trained in Stockholm and Paris, made her debut in Stockholm in 1838, and attained great popularity everywhere, becoming known as the 'Swedish nightingale'. After 1856 she lived in England, and became professor of singing at the Royal College of Music (1883–6). She died at Malvern, Worcestershire.

Lindbergh, Charles A(ugustus) (1902–74) US aviator, born in Detroit. He made the first solo nonstop transatlantic flight (New York–Paris, 1927), in the monoplane *The Spirit of St Louis*. His book of that name gained the Pulitzer Prize in 1954. His young son was kidnapped and murdered in 1932, the most publicized crime of the 1930s. He later became an aeronautics consultant, and died in Maui, Hawaii. » aeronautics

Lindemann, Frederick Alexander » **Cherwell, Viscount**

linden » **lime** (botany) **1**

Lindisfarne An island off the NE coast of England, 15 km/9 ml SE of Berwick-upon-Tweed, renowned for its monastery founded from Iona by St Aidan in AD 634, burnt by Danish Vikings in 793, and ultimately abandoned c.875; also known as **Holy Island**. It was a notable centre of early English Christianity and learning, its most famous bishop being the ascetic St Cuthbert. The Lindisfarne Gospels were illuminated here, probably in the 690s, by Eadfrith (Bishop, 698–721). The island (area 10 sq km/3¾ sq ml) is accessible from the mainland at low water by a causeway (1954). » Aidan, St; Cuthbert, St; Iona; Vikings

Lindow Man » **bog burials**

Lindrum, Walter (1898–1960) Australian billiards player, born at Kalgoorlie, regarded as the world's greatest billiards player. In 1932, at Thurston's Hall, London, he set the current world break record of 4 137 while playing Joe Davis. He competed in only two world championships (1933–34), and won both. He retired from competitive play in 1950, and died near Brisbane. » billiards; Davis, Joe

line-engraving A method of intaglio printing, the metal plate being cut with a burin. The technique originated in 15th-c Germany, and the greatest early master was Martin Schongauer (1450–91). » burin; engraving; intaglio

Line Islands pop (1985) 2 508. Coral island group of Kiribati, C and S Pacific Ocean; largest **N Line Is** are Kiritimati (Christmas I) (390 sq km/150 sq ml), Fanning I (34 sq km/13 sq ml), and Washington I (9.6 sq km/3.7 sq ml), inhabited by coconut plantation workers; **S Line Is**, worked for guano in the past, now uninhabited; three of the N group are US territories. » Kiribati

line printer A type of printer, usually associated with larger computer systems, which prints a complete line of information at a time. It is very fast, especially when compared with printers that print one character at a time. Their principal advantage is speed, and they tend to be economic only in commercial situations where there is a heavy printing load. » printer, computer

lineage » **descent**

Linear A A system of writing found throughout Minoan Crete. It was used mainly by administrators in the compilation of inventories. » Linear B; Minoan civilization

linear accelerator A particle accelerator comprising a straight vacuum tube along which charged particles are accelerated by a sequence of cylindrical electrodes; also called **linac**. At the Stanford Linear Accelerator Center in the USA is a linear accelerator approximately 3 km/2 ml long. » particle accelerators

Linear B A system of writing found on clay tablets at Mycenaean palace sites. Deciphered in the 1950s by Michael Ventris, it is (unlike Linear A) an early form of Greek. » Linear A; Mycenaean civilization

linen Yarn and fabrics made from flax fibres, probably the earliest textile made from plants. Linen was made in ancient Egypt, and the Romans brought flax-growing to Britain. Linen fabrics and yarns are fine, strong, and lustrous, but are less used today because of their poor easy-care properties. » flax

ling (botany) » **heather 1**

ling (fish) Slender-bodied fish of the cod family, abundant in offshore waters of the NE Atlantic from Norway to the Bay of Biscay at depths of 300–400 m/1 000–1 300 ft; length up to 2 m/6½ ft; mottled brownish green on back; fished commercially, mainly on lines. (*Molva molva*. Family: *Gadidae*.) » cod

lingam [**ling**gam] The principal symbolic representation of the Hindu deity Shiva, a phallic shaped emblem. The female equivalent is the *yoni*, the shaped image of the female genitalia. » Hinduism; Shiva

lingua franca [**ling**gwa **frang**ka] An auxiliary language used for routine and often restricted purposes by people who speak different native languages. English and French are frequently used for this purpose in many parts of the world. German is an important lingua franca in E Europe, and Swahili in E Africa. English is an occupational lingua franca in several domains, such as in international air traffic control. » auxiliary language

linguistic philosophy A philosophical movement exemplified in the later writings of Wittgenstein and the work of Ryle and Austin. Its chief methodological assumption was that traditional philosophical problems arise from inattention to the ordinary use of language; the philosopher's task is to diagnose and resolve the problems by exposing that inattention. » Austin, J L; Ryle, Gilbert; Wittgenstein

linguistics The scientific study of language. The discipline is concerned with such matters as providing systematic descriptions of languages, investigating the properties of language structures as communicative systems, exploring the possibility that there are universals of language structure, and accounting for the historical development of linguistic systems. **Applied linguistics** is the application of linguistics to the study of such language-based fields as foreign language teaching and learning, speech pathology, translation, and dictionary writing.

The 19th-c saw the flowering of comparative philology, which studied the historical development of language families. Modern linguistics is generally said to have begun with the posthumous publication of Ferdinand de Saussure's *Cours de Linguistique Générale* (1916, Course in General Linguistics), which introduced the essential distinction between *diachronic* (historical) linguistics, and *synchronic* (descriptive) linguistics, and laid the foundation for the era of **structural linguistics**, which dominated the first half of the 20th-c. Structuralists (notably US linguist Leonard Bloomfield) stressed the uniqueness of language systems, and the need to base structural descriptions on observed evidence alone. The major development in the second half of the 20th-c has been the emergence of generative grammar, originally proposed by US linguist Noam Chomsky in *Syntactic Structures* (1957), and since elaborated in a wide range of works. Since the 1960s, several developments of and alternatives to Chomsky's original model have been proposed. Also, many points of contact between linguistics and other academic areas have been explored, leading to the growth of such 'hybrid' fields as *sociolinguistics* and *psycholinguistics*. » applied/bio-/comparative/computational/mathematical/neuro-/psycho-/socio-/statistical/text- linguistics; Chomsky; diachrony; dialectology; grammar; phonetics; phonology; pragmatics; semantics; Saussure; stylistics

linkage The occurrence of two genes together on a chromosome sufficiently close to each other as to cause a tendency for them to be transmitted together in inheritance. Several genes close together are known as a **linkage group**. » chromosome [i]; gene

linkage politics A mode of analysis which attempts to explain the behaviour of a political system by reference to the phenomena occurring in the wider international environment. Linkage politics may be broken down into three types of observed or hypothesized behaviour of political systems: reactive, emulative, and penetrative.

Linklater, Eric (Robert) (1899–1974) British novelist, born at Dounby, Orkney, Scotland. Educated at Aberdeen, he studied medicine, then English, served in World War 1, became a journalist in Bombay (1925–7), and an English lecturer at Aberdeen. While in the USA (1928–30) he wrote *Poet's Pub* (1929), the first of a series of satirical novels which include *Juan in America* (1931) and *Private Angelo* (1946). He died at Aberdeen. » English literature; novel; satire

Linnaeus, Carolus or **Carl** [linayuhs], Swed **Carl von Linné** (1707–78) Swedish botanist, the founder of modern taxonomic botany, born at Råshult. He was educated at Lund and Uppsala, where in 1730 he was appointed a botany assistant. He travelled widely on botanical exploration in Swedish Lapland, Holland, England, and France. In his *Systema Naturae Fundamenta Botanica* (1735), *Genera Plantarum* (1737), and *Species Plantarum* (1753) he expounded his influential system of classification, based on plant sex organs, and in which names consist of generic and specific elements, with plants grouped hierarchically into genera, classes, and orders. He practised as a physician in Stockholm, and in 1742 became professor of botany at Uppsala. He was ennobled in 1757, and died at Uppsala. » botany

linnet Any of three species of finch, genus *Carduelis*, especially the **Eurasian linnet** (*Carduelis cannabina*); native to Europe, N Africa, and W Asia; inhabits open country; eats seeds and insects. (Family: *Fringillidae*.) » finch

linoleic acid » **arachidonic acid**

linsang [**lin**sang] A carnivorous mammal of family *Viverridae*; inhabits forest and builds nest from leaves; three species: the SE Asian **Oriental linsang**, which includes the **banded linsang** (*Prionodon linsang*) and the **spotted linsang** (*Prionodon pardicolor*); and the **African linsang** or *oyan* (*Poiana richardsoni*). » carnivore [i]; Viverridae [i]

Linz [lints] 48°18N 14°18E, pop (1981) 199 910. Industrial town and capital of Oberösterreich, N Austria; situated on both banks of the R Danube, centre of a rich agricultural region; extensive port installations; University of Social and Economic Sciences (1966); third largest city in Austria; iron and steel, fertilizers, tobacco, chemicals, pharmaceuticals; many historical buildings, including early 16th-c castle, Martinskirche (oldest preserved church in Austria), Landhaus (former seat of the state assembly); museums, art galleries, theatres, opera house; Bruckner Festival (Sep). » Austria [i]; Bruckner

lion A member of the cat family, native to Africa and NW India (in prehistoric times was almost worldwide); brown; male with mane of long dark hair; inhabits grassland and open woodland; often territorial; lives in 'prides' averaging 15 individuals; the only cat that hunts in groups; eats mainly large grazing mammals. (*Panthera leo*.) » Felidae; liger

Lions Clubs, International Association of » **service club**

lip reading The act of observing the movements of a speaker's mouth in order to understand what is being said. It is a skill practised mostly by the deaf and hard-of-hearing, but is also used to some degree by those working in factories and other environments where noise is a problem. » deafness

lipase [**li**payz] An enzyme that stimulates the breakdown of triglycerides (esters of fatty acids) into fatty acids and glycerol; for example, pancreatic lipase secreted into the duodenum promotes the breakdown of dietary fats. » enzyme; triglyceride

Lipchitz, Jacques (1891–1973) French sculptor, born at Druskininkai, Lithuania. He moved to Paris in 1909, and became an exponent of Cubism. In the 1930s he developed a more dynamic style which he applied to bronze figure and animal compositions. He moved to New York in 1941, and died at Capri, Italy. » Cubism; French art; sculpture

Lipizzaner [lipit**sah**ner] A breed of horse, developed at Lipizza in Austria in the 16th-c from the Andalusian horse; height, 15–16 hands/1.5–1.6 m/5–5¼ ft; grey or pale brown; famous as the *white horses of Vienna*, where the stallions are used at the Spanish Riding School. » Andalusian horse; Spanish Riding School

lipogram [**lip**ohgram] A text composed with the intentional omission of a particular letter of the alphabet throughout. The 5th-c BC Greek poet Tryphiodorus wrote an epic of 24 books, each omitting a different letter of the Greek alphabet. » univocalic

Lippershey, Hans (c.1570–1619) Dutch lens grinder, born at Wesel, Germany. He has been called the inventor of the telescope, but this is unproven. Certainly, in 1608 he offered the government of the Netherlands what we would now call a refracting telescope, and shortly afterwards others, such as Galileo, constructed similar devices. » Galileo; telescope [i]

Lippi, Filippino (c.1458–1504) Italian painter, born at Prato, near Florence. Probably a pupil of his father, c.1484 he completed the frescoes in the Brancacci Chapel in the Carmine, Florence, left unfinished by Masaccio. His easel pictures include 'The Vision of St Bernard' (c.1480). He died in Florence. » fresco; Italian art; Lippi, Filippo; Masaccio

Lippi, Fra Filippo, byname **Lippo** (c.1406–69) Italian religious painter, born in Florence. He was much patronized by the Medici family. His greatest work was on the choir walls of Prato cathedral, begun in 1452. He later abducted and was eventually allowed to marry a nun, Lucrezia, who was the model for many of his Madonnas, and the mother of his son, Filippino. His later works are deeply religious and include a series of 'Nativities'. He was working in the cathedral at Spoleto when he died. » Italian art; Lippi, Filippino

Lippmann, Walter (1899–1974) US journalist, born in New York City. He was educated at Harvard, joined the editorial staff of the *New York World* until 1931, then became a special writer for the *Herald Tribune*. His daily columns became internationally famous, and he won many awards, including the Pulitzer Prize for International Reporting (1962). The author of several books, such as *Public Opinion* (1922) and *The Cold War* (1947), he died in New York City. » journalism

liqueur A spirit, usually distilled from grain, mixed with syrup, and with the addition of fruits, herbs, or spices to infuse a strong aroma and taste. Liqueurs have a high alcohol content, and are usually drunk in small quantities after a meal. Examples include Cointreau, Bénédictine, and Chartreuse (France), Cherry Heering (Denmark), Tia Maria (Jamaica), and Drambuie (Scotland).

liquid A dense form of matter which is able to flow but unable to transmit twisting forces; density typically a few per cent less than the corresponding solid. It is virtually incompressible; the atoms are constantly changing position in a random way. There is no ordering of atoms, unlike many solids, except for a slight degree of short-range order. Highly viscous liquids are similar in structure to amorphous solids. » amorphous solid; boiling point; fluid mechanics; liquid crystals; melting point; phases of matter [i]; viscosity

liquid crystals Many organic materials, crystalline in the solid state, which form a partially ordered state (the *liquid crystal state*) upon melting, and become true liquids only after the temperature is raised further. Liquid crystals have directional properties, and so are birefringent. Their optical transparency can be reduced by applying electric fields, a property extensively exploited in displays for watches, calculators, and other electronic devices. » birefringence; crystals; electro-optic effects; liquid

liquidation » **bankruptcy**

liquidity In business and banking, actual money, or assets that are easily convertible into money. Firms need to be sufficiently liquid to be able to pay off debts, to be able to buy assets when required, and to be covered in case of emergencies. **Liquid assets** are cash, short-term investments, and debtors (ie amounts due from customers). The notion is used in economics in relation to the study of money supply in the economy. » liquidity preference; money supply

liquidity preference A concept introduced by J M Keynes to explain the demand for money, referring to the percentage of assets held in the form of cash or 'near money' by an individual, bank, or company. The intention is to avoid tying up money in fixed assets, or long-term investments which may not be easily realizable, or which may lose value (such as shares in a company). » Keynes; liquidity

liquorice or **licorice** A perennial growing to 1 m/1¼ ft, native to SE Europe and W Asia; creeping rhizomes; leaves pinnate with 9–17 elliptical-oblong leaflets; pea-flowers whitish-violet, in long-stalked, spike-like inflorescences. Often cultivated, its roots are a source of liquorice, used medicinally and as a confectionary ingredient. (*Glycyrrhiza glabra*. Family: *Leguminosae*.) » inflorescence [i]; perennial; pinnate; rhizome

Lisbon, Port **Lisboa**, ancient **Olisipo** or **Felicitas Julia** 38°42N 9°10W, pop (1981) 812 400. Seaport and capital of Portugal, on N bank of R Tagus; largest city in Portugal; settlement in Roman Empire; occupied by Moors, 8th-c; Portuguese capital, 1256; devastated by earthquake, 1755; Chiado shopping district of old town destroyed by fire, 1988; archbishopric; airport; railway; university (1911); steel, textiles, chemicals, shipbuilding, wine, cork, olive oil, fishing; 16th-c Tower of Belém and Jerônimos Monastery, a world heritage site; cathedral (1344), Church of São Roque, São Jorge Castle, National Museum of Art, botanical garden. » Belém Monastery; Portugal [i]

Lisdoonvarna [lishdoon**vah**na] 53°02N 9°17W, pop (1981) 607. Spa town 37 km/23 ml NW of Ennis, Clare county, Munster, W Irish Republic; leading sulphur spring health centre; Lisdoonvarna fair (Oct), with its famous mating game when shy bachelors go in search of a wife; 3-day folk festival (Jul). » Clare; Irish Republic [i]

LISP An acronym of **LISt Processing**, a high-level computer programming language designed for use with non-numeric data. It differs radically from traditional programming languages, and is widely used in artificial intelligence applications. » artificial intelligence; programming language

Lissitsky, El, properly **Eleazar** (1890–1941) Russian painter, born at Polschiroc. He studied engineering at Darmstadt before meeting Malevich, under whose influence he took up painting in a totally abstract style, based on arrangements of simple lines, planes, and cubes. Professor of architecture and graphic arts at Vitebsk (1919), he became a leading Constructivist. He died in Moscow. » abstract art; Constructivism; Malevich; Suprematism

Lister (of Lyme Regis), Joseph, 1st Baron (1827–1912) British surgeon, born at Upton, Essex, the son of Joseph Jackson Lister. Educated at London, he became professor of surgery at Glasgow (1859), Edinburgh (1869), and London (1877). His great work was the introduction (1860) of the use of antisepsis, which revolutionized modern surgery. He was made a baronet (1883) and baron (1897), and died at Walmer, Kent. » Lister, Joseph Jackson

Lister, Joseph Jackson (1786–1869) British microscopist, born and died in London. In 1826 James Smith (?–1870) built a much improved microscope to Lister's design, and this was used a year later to produce the first competent article on histology. In 1830 Lister described a principle which for the first time allowed microscope objectives to be made to satisfactory scientific standards. » histology; microscope; optics [i]

listeria [listeeria] A genus of typically rod-shaped bacteria, of uncertain taxonomic position; typically motile by means of flagella, and exhibiting a tumbling motion; grows best in the presence of small quantities of oxygen; some strains cause food poisoning. » bacteria [i]; flagellum

Liszt, Franz (1811–86) Hungarian composer and pianist, born at Raiding. He studied and played at Vienna and Paris, touring widely in Europe as a virtuoso pianist. From 1835 to 1839 he lived with the Comtesse d'Agoult, by whom he had three children. He gave concerts throughout Europe, and in 1847 met Princess Carolyne zu Sayn-Wittgenstein with whom he lived until his death. In 1848, he went to Weimar, where he directed the opera and concerts, composed, and taught. His works include twelve symphonic poems, masses, two symphonies, and a large number of piano pieces. In 1865 he received minor orders in the Catholic Church, and was known as Abbé. He died at Bayreuth, where he is buried. » symphonic poem

litany A form of prayer used in public or private worship. Supplications or invocations are made by the priest or minister, to which the congregation replies with a fixed formula. » liturgy; prayer

litchi, litchee, leechee, or **lychee** An evergreen tree native to China; leaves pinnate; flowers white, starry; fruit 2.5–4 cm/1–1½ in long, ovoid with warty, horny, red-brown rind enclosing an ivory, fleshy aril and a single glossy brown seed. The edible aril tastes like both grapes and melon. (*Litchi chinensis*. Family: *Sapindaceae*.) » aril; evergreen plants; pinnate; tree [i]

literacy The ability to read and write in a language. Discussion of the problem of **illiteracy**, both within a country and on a world scale, is complicated by the difficulty of measuring the extent of the problem in individuals. The notion of **functional literacy** was introduced in the 1940s, in an attempt to identify minimal levels of reading/writing efficiency in a society, such as being able to read road signs, shop labels, and newspapers, and to write one's name; but defining even minimal levels is difficult, especially today, with increasing demands being made on people to be literate in a wider range of contexts. Current world estimates suggest that c.900 million adults are illiterate to a greater or lesser extent. In the UK, figures were being cited in the 1980s of c.2 million illiterate people, or 3½% of the population; in the USA, estimates have varied between 10% and 20%. In some Third World countries, the figures may be as high as 80%. National literacy campaigns in several countries have raised public awareness, and standards are slowly rising. » dyslexia; oracy

literary criticism The explication and evaluation of works of literature, a task as old as literature itself. Criticism has traditionally proposed three main questions concerning (1) the truth, (2) the function, and (3) the formal qualities of literature. Addressed by Plato and Aristotle, these set the parameters until Neoclassical times. With the Romantic movement came a new interest in the genesis of a work of literature, subsequently reinforced by Symbolism and psychoanalysis and (from different directions) by Marxist and sociological analysis. The influence of 20th-c linguistics and structuralism has given new impetus to the formal approach, emphasizing the role of the reader in producing meaning via the exchange of cultural codes. » Aristotle; classicism; comparative literature; deconstruction; Formalists; literature; Neoclassicism (art and architecture); Plato; Romanticism (literature); structuralism; feminist/Freudian/New/textual criticism

literary prizes Annual awards, accompanied usually by money prizes, given in many countries, including France, the UK, and USA. Best-known are the Nobel Prize for Literature (international), the Booker Prize (UK, fiction), the Prix Goncourt (France), the Pulitzer Prize (USA), and the Whitbread Literary Awards (UK, five categories). » RR101

literature The collective writings proper to any language or nation. World literature includes all these in translation. The term *literature* is a site of ideological conflict; it may be taken to refer exclusively to those canonical works in the established genres which 'have pleased many and pleased long' (Dr Johnson), or inclusively to the sum total of writings which are read, even the most ephemeral, such as comics and newspapers. Essays, letters, memoirs, historical, biographical and travel writings, occasional verse, etc, will be considered 'literature' depending on the point of view. Fundamental questions are addressed by Jean-Paul Sartre in *What is Literature?* (1948). The term is also used to refer to the body of secondary writings on a given subject, as in 'medical literature', 'ornithological literature'. » African/American/Arabic/Australian/Canadian/Caribbean / Celtic / Chinese / comparative / Czechoslovak / Danish/English/French/German/Greek/Hebrew/Icelandic/Indian/Irish/Italian/Japanese/Latin/Latin-American/Norwegian / Persian / Polish / Portuguese / Russian / Scottish / Spanish/Swedish/Welsh literature; autobiography; biography; comedy; detective story; epic; fable; juvenilia; literary critiscism/prizes; novel; ode; panegyric; parody; pastoral; philiopic; poetry; prose; prose poem; romance; Romanticism (literature); satire; science fiction; short story; tragedy; tragicomedy; Western

litharge [lithahj] Lead(II) oxide (PbO); a bright yellow pigment used in paints. » lead; oxide

lithium Li, element 3, melting point 181°C. The lightest of the alkali metals; not common, but found widely in several minerals, after they are converted to the chloride (LiCl), the element being obtained by electrolysis. Its compounds are used in organic synthesis: lithium aluminium hydride ($LiAlH_4$) is a powerful reducing agent. Its salts, such as Li_2CO_3, have found application as anti-depressants in psychiatry. » alkali; anti-depressants; chemical elements; electrolysis [i]; RR90

lithography A method of printing in which the design is not cut into the plate or block, but executed with a special greasy crayon on the surface of a stone slab. The stone is treated to fix the design, and water is applied. The water is repelled by the grease, but dampens the porous stone. Printing ink will now adhere to the grease but not to the wet stone, and so the design can be printed. The technique was invented by Aloys Senefelder in 1796, using limestone as the image surface, and direct impression to paper. *Stereolithography* is a modern technique which gives a three-dimensional quality and a solidity to the image produced. » offset lithography; printing [i]; Senefelder; surface printing

lithosphere Part of the Earth, consisting of the crust and the solid outermost layer of the upper mantle, extending to a depth of around 100 km/60 ml. » Earth [i]

Lithuanian » **Baltic languages**

Lithuania, Lith **Lietuva**, Russ **Litovskaya** or **Litva** pop (1990e) 3 700 000; area 65 200 sq km/25 167 sq ml. Republic in NE Europe; bounded SW by Poland and W by the Baltic Sea; glaciated plains cover much of the area; chief river, the Neman; united with Poland, 1385–1795; intensive russification led to revolts in 1905 and 1917; occupied by Germany in both World Wars; proclaimed a republic, 1918; annexed by the USSR, 1940; growth of nationalist movement in the 1980s; declared independence in 1990; capital, Vilnius; chief towns, Kaunas, Klaipeda, Špiauliai; electronics, electrical engineering, computer hardware, instruments, machine tools, shipbuilding, synthetic fibres, fertilizers, plastics, food processing, oil refining; cattle, pigs, poultry. » Soviet Union [i]

litmus A complex vegetable dye traditionally used as a pH indicator. It is red in acid solutions and blue in alkaline ones. » pH

litre Unit of volume; symbol l; defined as the volume of a cube of side 10 cm; a litre of water has a mass of one kilogram; a cubic metre contains 1 000 litres; in medicine, **millilitre** (ml, 1/1 000) is a common measure; 1 litre = 1.76 pints (UK)/2.11 pints (US). » units (scientific); RR70

Little Bighorn, Battle of the (25 Jun 1876) The engagement between US cavalry, under General Custer, and the Sioux and Cheyenne, under Sitting Bull and Crazy Horse. The Indians destroyed Custer's force. Issues behind the battle included Custer's bloody dawn attack on a Cheyenne village at the

Washita in 1868, and his sponsorship in 1875 of White invasion of the Black Hills, sacred to the Sioux. » Cheyenne (Indians); Custer; Indian Wars; Sioux; Sitting Bull

little boatman/captain/corporal » **schipperke**

little owl A typical owl of genus *Athene* (2 species), especially the **little owl** (*Athene noctua*), native to C and W Asia, Europe, and Africa, and introduced in New Zealand and the UK; inhabits open country, forest, and towns; eats insects, small mammals, occasionally birds or carrion. The **Rodriguez little owl** (*Athene murivora*) is extinct. (Family: *Strigidae*.) » owl

Little Rock [litl rok] 34°45N 92°16W, pop (1980) 158 461. Capital of state in Pulaski County, C Arkansas, USA; largest city in the state, and a port on the Arkansas R; settled, 1821; railway; university; processing of fish, beef, poultry, bauxite, timber; in 1957 Federal troops were sent to the city to enforce a 1954 US Supreme Court ruling against segregation in schools; Territorial Restoration, old statehouse; Riverfest (May). » Arkansas; civil rights

Littlewood, (Maudie) Joan (1914–) British theatre director, born in London. She trained at the Royal Academy of Dramatic Art, and with Ewan MacColl (1915–) founded in Manchester the Theatre of Action (1934) and the Theatre Union (1936). Out of this pioneering work in left-wing, popular theatre was formed the Theatre Workshop in 1945. After settling at the Theatre Royal Stratford East in 1953, her productions included *The Hostage* (1958) and *Oh What A Lovely War* (1963). » theatre; Theatre Workshop

littoral zone » **benthic environments**

liturgical movement A movement to reform the worship of the Christian Church by promoting more active participation by laity in the liturgy. Beginning in 19th-c France in the Roman Catholic Church, it became influential and effective in the mid-20th-c in other Churches, often through the World Council of Churches and the ecumenical movement. » ecumenism; liturgy; Roman Catholicism; World Council of Churches

liturgy (Gr *leitourgia*, 'duty, service') The formal corporate worship of God by a Church. It includes words, music, actions, and symbolic aids, and in Christian form is derived from Jewish ritual. Liturgies exist in a wide variety of prescribed forms, reflecting the needs and attitudes of different religious communities. » liturgical movement

Litvinov, Maxim Maximovich (1876–1951) Soviet diplomat, born at Bielostok, Russian Poland. He was Bolshevik Ambassador in London (1917–18), Deputy Commissar (1921) then Commissar (1930) for Foreign Affairs, Ambassador to the USA (1941), and Vice-Minister of Foreign Affairs (1942–6). A strong advocate of co-operation between the Soviet Union and the West, he died in Moscow. » Bolsheviks

Liu Shaoqi or Liu Shao-ch'i [lyoo show**chee**] (1898–1969) Leading figure in the Chinese communist revolution, born in Hunan. He was educated in the USSR, returned to China in 1922, and became a communist trade-union organizer. In 1939 he joined Mao Zedong (Mao Tse-tung) at Yanan, where he emerged as the chief Party theorist on questions of organization. In 1943 he became Party Secratry, and succeeded Mao in 1959. After the Cultural Revolution (1966), the extreme left made Liu their principal target, and in 1968 he was stripped of all his posts and dismissed from the Party. He died at K'ai-feng, Honan. » Cultural Revolution; Great Leap Forward; Mao Zedong

Liupanshui [lyoopan**shway**] or **Suicheng** 25°45N 104°40E, pop (1984e) 2 166 400. City in Guizhou province, S China; W of Guiyang; railway. » China [i]

Live Aid » **Geldof, Bob**

liver In vertebrates, a large, unpaired gland, with digestive functions, situated in the upper part of the left-hand side of the abdominal cavity under cover of the ribs, separated from the thoracic contents by the diaphragm. It is attached to the abdominal wall and the stomach, and divided into four lobes. The liver performs many important functions. It secretes bile, which is emptied into the duodenum (via the common bile duct), and facilitates the digestion and absorption of fats. It deals with the newly absorbed products of digestion (eg the formation of glycogen or fats from monosaccharides, the release of glucose into the blood stream). It manufactures the anticoagulant heparin and other plasma proteins. It stores glycogen, fat, iron, copper, and the vitamins A, D, E and K. It detoxifies harmful substances such as drugs and toxins, and consumes and destroys red blood cells. » abdomen; cirrhosis; digestion; gland; hepatitis; jaundice; Reye's syndrome; Plate XII

liver fluke Leaf-like, parasitic flatworm, with a mouth sucker on its cone-shaped front end; life cycle complex, involving a snail as intermediate host in which asexual multiplication takes place; final host is a vertebrate, often sheep; can be a serious pest of domesticated animals. (*Fasciola hepatica*. Phylum: *Platyhelminthes*. Class: *Trematoda*.) » flatworm; parasitology

Liverpool, Robert Banks Jenkinson, 2nd Earl of (1770–1828) British statesman and Tory Prime Minister (1812–27), born and died in London. Educated at Charterhouse and Oxford, he entered parliament in 1790, and was a member of the India Board (1793–6), Master of the Royal Mint (1799–1801), Foreign Secretary (1801–4), Home Secretary (1804–6, 1807–9), and Secretary for War and the Colonies (1809–12). He succeeded his father as Earl of Liverpool in 1807. As Premier, he oversaw the final years of the Napoleonic Wars and the War of 1812–14 with the USA. He resigned after a stroke early in 1827. » Napoleonic Wars; Tories

Liverpool 53°25N 2°55W, pop (1987e) 476 000. Seaport in Merseyside, NW England; on the right bank of the R Mersey estuary, 5 km/3 ml from the Irish Sea and 312 km/194 ml NW of London; founded in the 10th-c, became a borough in 1207 and a city in 1880; port trade developed in the 16th–17th-c; importance enhanced in the 18th-c by the slave trade and the Lancashire cotton industry; major world trading centre and the UK's most important seaport for Atlantic trade; railway; container terminal (1972); linked to Birkenhead under the R Mersey by road and rail tunnels (1934, 1971); ferries to Belfast, Dublin, Isle of Man; airport; university (1903); trade in petroleum, grain, ores, non-ferrous metals, sugar, wood, fruit, and cotton; Catholic cathedral, modern design by Frederick Gibberd on earlier classical foundation by Edward Lutyens (consecrated 1967); Anglican cathedral, designed by Giles Gilbert Scott (begun 1904, completed 1980); Royal Liver Building (landmark at Pier Head), St George's Hall, Albert Dock redevelopment, Maritime Museum, Tate in the North (1987), Walker Art Gallery, Merseyside Innovation Centre, Speke Hall; Royal Liverpool Philharmonic Orchestra; home of the Beatles (museum, 1984), and many other pop groups; Liverpool and Everton football clubs; International Garden Festival held here in 1984; Grand National steeplechase at Aintree (Apr). » Beatles, The; Mersey, River; Merseyside; slave trade

Liverpool poets A group of poets writing out of Liverpool after the success of the Beatles in the 1960s, when the city was referred to by Allen Ginsberg as 'the cultural centre of the Universe'. The best-known are Adrian Henri (1932–), Roger McGough (1937–), and Brian Patten (1946–); selections are given in *The Mersey Sound* (1967). » Beatles, The; Ginsberg

liverwort A small, spore-bearing, non-vascular plant of the Class *Hepaticae*, closely related to mosses and hornworts. They are divided into two types, depending on their gametophytic form: **thalloid** liverworts have a flattened, often lobed or branched body (the *thallus*); **foliose** or leafy liverworts have slender, creeping stems with three rows of leaves, of which usually only two develop fully. They have single-celled, root-like rhizoids which anchor the plant to the ground, but do not absorb water. The sporophyte consists of a stalked, star-shaped capsule containing spores and sterile structures (*elaters*). When the spores are mature the stalk elongates, the capsule opens, and the elaters help disperse the spores. Liverworts also reproduce by means of *gemmae*, multicellular discs which are budded off and develop into new plants. Liverworts are found almost everywhere, but are very vulnerable to drying out, and thus restricted to damp, shady habitats. (Class: *Hepaticae*.) » bryophyte; gametophyte; gemma; hornwort; moss; rhizoid; spore; sporophyte

livery companies In the UK, charitable and professional associations in the City of London, which have developed from the craft and trade guilds of the Middle Ages. The twelve 'great' companies (nominated in 1514) are the mercers, grocers, drapers, fishmongers, goldsmiths, merchant taylors, skinners, haberdashers, salters, ironmongers, vintners, and clothworkers. Some of these are famous for their educational foundations. » London [i]

livestock farming The farming of domestic animals, especially cattle, sheep, pigs, poultry, and horses. The term is also applied to other animals producing food, fibre, skins, or pulling power in the farm context. » animal husbandry; factory farming; transhumance

Livia (58 BC–AD 29) Augustus' wife (39 BC–AD 14) and key backroom figure in the early days of the Roman Empire. The mother of Tiberius by her first husband, Tiberius Claudius Nero, she plotted strenuously to ensure his succession, thus gaining from her great-grandson, the future Emperor Caligula, the nickname 'Ulysses in Petticoats'. » Augustus; Caligula; Roman history [i]; Tiberius

living fossil A species that has persisted to modern times with little or no detectable change over a long period of time, and typically sharing most of its characters only with otherwise extinct organisms (fossils). The coelacanth discovered off the coast of South Africa in 1939 is a typical example of a living descendant of a group previously thought to be extinct. » crossopterygii; extinction; fossil

Living Newspaper A unit of the Federal Theater Project and the style of documentary theatre it espoused, which dramatized current social and political issues in short immediate sketches. Joseph Losey was a creative exponent of the form. » Losey; theatre

living stone A perennial native to S Africa and adapted to very dry, desert conditions. It consists of a single, annual pair of succulent leaves, grossly swollen with water, and more or less fused together; the daisy-like flower appears between the leaves. Each species is associated with a particular kind of rock, and has leaves coloured to resemble that rock and no other – a rare example of plant mimicry. (Genus: *Lithops*, 50 species. Family: *Aizoaceae*.) » mimicry; perennial; succulent

Living Theatre/Theater A theatre begun by Judith Malina and Julian Beck in 1947 as an Off-Broadway venture. It became one of the best-known and most-attacked of the radical cultural experiments that swept the USA and much of Europe during the 1960s and early 1970s. Its main feature was a conscious refusal to separate the art of theatre from the art of living. » Broadway; theatre

Livingstone, David (1813–73) British missionary and traveller, born at Low Blantyre, Lanarkshire, Scotland. He trained as a physician at Glasgow, and was ordained in the London Missionary Society in 1840. He worked for several years in Bechuanaland, then travelled N (1852–6), discovering L Ngami and the Victoria Falls. He led an expedition to the Zambezi (1858–63), and discovered L Shirwa and L Nyasa. In 1866 he returned to Africa to establish the sources of the Nile, but the river he encountered proved later to be the Congo. On his return after severe illness to Ujiji, he was found there in 1871 by Stanley, sent to look for him by the *New York Herald*. He again set out to find the Nile, but died at Chitambo (now in Zambia). He is buried in Westminster Abbey. » Nile, River; Stanley

Livingstone daisy A sprawling annual with succulent leaves and stems, native to arid parts of S Africa; flowers daisy-like, in various colours from yellow and pink to mauve, opening only in full, bright sunlight. It is sometimes referred to by the old botanical name **mesembryanthemum**. (*Dorotheanthus bellidiflorus*. Family: *Aizoaceae*.) » annual; daisy; succulent

Livius » Livy

Livonian Knights Brothers of the Knighthood of Christ in Livonia, commonly known as the **Sword-Brothers**, founded c.1202 to convert the pagan Latvians; then, from 1237 to its dissolution in 1561, members of the Livonian branch of the Teutonic Knights. By the 14th-c they controlled the E Baltic lands of Courland, Estonia, and Livonia. » Crusades [i]; Teutonic knights

Livorno [leevawnoh] » Leghorn

Livy, properly **Titus Livius** (c.59 BC–AD 17) Roman historian, born and died at Patavium (Padua). He went to Rome, and was admitted to the court of Augustus, but took no part in politics.

Lizards – Flying lizard (a); tuatara (b)

His history of Rome, from its foundation to the death of Drusus (9 BC), comprised 142 books, of which 35 have survived. The work was a great success during his lifetime, and was a major influence on subsequent historical writing.

lizard A reptile, found worldwide except in the coldest regions. Some have no obvious limbs and resemble snakes; but most differ from snakes in having eyelids and an obvious ear opening. Many species can voluntarily break off their tail to distract predators (a new tail grows). Only 2% of species are primarily vegetarian. (Suborder: *Sauria* or *Lacertilia*. Order: *Squamata*, c.3 750 species.) » agamid; chameleon; gecko; gila monster; glass snake; monitor lizard; reptile; sand lizard; skink; slowworm; snake

Lizard Point 49°56N 5°13W. Cornwall, SW England; the most S point on the UK mainland, near Lizard Town. » Cornwall

Ljubljana [lyooblyahna], Ital **Lubiana**, ancient **Emona** 46°00N 14°30E, pop (1981) 305 211. Capital of Slovenia republic, N Yugoslavia; on Sava and Ljubljanica Rivers, 120 km/75 ml WNW of Zagreb; founded, 34 BC; capital of the former Kingdom of Illyria, 1816–49; badly damaged by earthquake, 1895; ceded to Yugoslavia, 1918; airport; railway; university (1595); textiles, paper, chemicals, food processing, electronics; education and convention centre; Tivoli sports park, national museum, castle, cathedral, Ursuline church; Alpe-Adria International Trade Fair (Apr), Ljubljana Festival (Jul–Aug), International Festival of Graphic Art (alternate years Jun–Aug), International Wine Fair (Aug), flower show (Sep), International 'Ski Expo' Fair (Nov). » Slovenia; Yugoslavia [i]

llama A member of the camel family, found in the C Andes; domesticated c.4 500 years ago; used mainly as a beast of burden; long flat-backed body with long erect neck and long ears; dense coat; two breeds: *chaku* and *ccara*. (*Lama glama*.) » Camelidae

Llanfairpwllgwyngyll, in full **Llanfairpwllgwyngyllgogerychwyrndrobwllllantysiliogogogoch** ('St Mary's Church in the hollow of the white hazel near a rapid whirlpool and the Church of St Tysilio by the red cave') [lhanviyrpulh**gwing**ihl] 53°13N 4°12W. Village in Ynys Môn (Anglesey), Gwynedd, NW Wales, UK; W of Menai Bridge; gained notoriety through the extension of its name (to 58 letters) by a poetic cobbler in the 18th-c, probably to attract visitors; tourism; Marquis of

Anglesey's Column (1816); Plas Newydd stately home nearby; first Women's Institute in Britain founded here, 1915. » Menai Straits; Ynys Môn

Llangefni [lhangevnee] 53°16N 4°18W, pop (1981) 4625. Town in Ynys Môn district, Gwynedd, NW Wales, UK, on the R Cefni; administrative centre for the island; market, agricultural implements, livestock. » Ynys Môn

Llangollen [lhangolhen] 52°58N 3°10W, pop (1981) 3072. Town in Glyndŵr district, Clwyd, NE Wales, UK; on the R Dee, 15 km/9 ml SW of Wrexham; hide and skin dressing, printing, crafts, agricultural trade, tourism; 14th-c St Collen's Church, 14th-c bridge; Valle Crucis abbey nearby (c.1200), and Eliseg's Pillar (8th–9th-c cross); Plâs Newydd, headquarters of the Welsh National Theatre since 1943; site of annual international musical eisteddfod since 1947. » Clwyd; eisteddfod

Llano Estacado ('staked plain') [lahnoh estakahdoh] Vast semi-arid S portion of the Great Plains, in E New Mexico and W Texas, USA; flat, windswept grasslands broken by streams; formerly devoted to cattle raising; natural gas, oil fields, irrigated farming. » Great Plains

llanos [lyahnos] The savannah grasslands of the plains and plateaux of the Orinoco region (Colombia, Venezuela), northern S America. Traditionally it was an important livestock farming area, and there have been recent schemes to re-establish cattle ranching following a decline in the early 20th-c. » savannah

Llewellyn, Richard [hlooelin], pseudonym of **Richard Dafydd Vivian Llewellyn Lloyd** (1907–83) Welsh author, born at St David's, Pembrokeshire. After service with the regular army and a short spell as a film director, he became a best-selling novelist with *How Green was my Valley* (1939). Among his later works are *Up, into the Singing Mountain* (1963) and *I Stand On A Quiet Shore* (1982). He died in Dublin. » Welsh literature; novel

Lleyn Peninsula [lheen] Peninsula in Dwyfor county, Gwynedd, NW Wales, UK; separates Cardigan Bay and Tremadog Bay (S) from Caernarfon Bay (N); chief towns, Pwllheli, Porthmadog; agriculture, tourism. » Gwynedd

Llosa, Mario Vargas [lyohsa] (1936–) Peruvian novelist, born at Arequipa. He was educated at military school in Lima, and lived in Paris, London, and Barcelona before returning to Peru in 1974. His novels include *La ciudad y los perros* (1962, The City of Dogs) and *Pantaleon y las visitidores* (1973, Captain Pantoja and the Special Service). » Latin-American literature; novel

Lloyd, Harold (1893–1971) US film comedian, born at Burchard, Nebraska. He started as a film extra in 1913, and subsequently made hundreds of short silent comedies, adopting from 1917 his character of the unassuming 'nice guy' in horn-rimmed glasses and a straw hat. He made a few full-length features in the 1920s, notably *Safety Last* (1923) and *Welcome Danger* (1929), but he made few appearances after the coming of sound films. He died at Beverley Hills, California.

Lloyd, Marie, originally **Matilda Alice Victoria Wood** (1870–1922) British music-hall entertainer, born and died in London. She made her first appearance at the Royal Eagle Music Hall in 1885, and became one of the most popular of all music-hall performers. Among her most famous songs were *Oh, Mr Porter* and *My Old Man Said Follow the Van*. » music hall; theatre

Lloyd-George (of Dwyfor), David, 1st Earl (1863–1945) British Liberal statesman and Prime Minister (1916–22), born in Manchester of Welsh parentage. Educated in Wales, he became a solicitor, and in 1890, as a strong supporter of Home Rule, an MP for Caernarvon Boroughs (a seat he was to hold for 55 years). He was President of the Board of Trade (1905–8), and Chancellor of the Exchequer (1908–15). His 'people's budget' of 1909–10 was rejected by the House of Lords, and led to a constitutional crisis and the Parliament Act of 1911, which removed the Lords' power of veto. He became Minister of Munitions (1915), Secretary for War (1916), and superseded Asquith as coalition Prime Minister, carrying on a forceful war policy. After World War 1, he continued as head of a coalition government dominated by Conservatives. He negotiated with Sinn Féin, and conceded the Irish Free State (1921) – a measure which brought his downfall. Following the 1931 general election, he led a 'family' group of Independent Liberal MPs. He was made an earl in 1945, and died at Ty-newydd, Caernarvonshire, Wales. » Asquith; Boer Wars; Liberal Party (UK); Sinn Féin; World War 1

Lloyd's An international market for insurance, based in London. It originated in Edward Lloyd's coffee house in Tower Street in the City of London, from 1688. Anyone wishing to insure a ship or its cargo would seek out individuals willing to 'underwrite the risk' – or pay for any losses sustained to the items insured. By the early 1700s Lloyd's became a private club, with its members owning and controlling operations. In 1871 the Lloyd's Act was passed, setting a legal framework on its activities. All kinds of insurance are now handled worldwide, with some three-quarters of all business from outside the UK. The members (*underwriters*) of Lloyd's are organized into syndicates, and risks are spread among the members of the syndicate so that no single individual carries too large a risk personally. There is, however, no limit to a member's liability. *Lloyd's List* is London's oldest daily newspaper, providing in particular an information service on shipping matters. *Lloyd's Shipping Index* gives daily information about the worldwide movements of over 20000 merchant vessels. » insurance; Lloyd's Register of Shipping; Lutine Bell

Lloyd's Register of Shipping A publication which catalogues information about the construction and characteristics of individual vessels, to help insurance underwriters. Known as the Underwriters' Register, or 'Green Book', it was first published in 1760, but has been published by a separate organization from Lloyd's since 1834. 'A1 at Lloyd's' refers to the top grade of the classification made by the Register, indicating that the vessel is in first-class order. » insurance; Lloyd's

Lloyd Webber, Andrew (1948–) British composer, born in London. He met Tim Rice in 1965, and together they wrote a 'pop oratorio' *Joseph and the Amazing Technicolour Dreamcoat* (1968) which was extended and staged in 1972. Their greatest success was the 'rock opera' *Jesus Christ Superstar* (staged 1971, filmed 1973). His later musicals include *Evita* (1978), *Cats* (1981), *Starlight Express* (1983), and *The Phantom of the Opera* (1986). His *Requiem* appeared in 1984. His brother **Julian** (1951–) is a cellist. » musical

Llull or **Lull, Ramón** Eng **Raymond Lully**, byname **The Enlightened Doctor** (c.1232–1315) Catalan theologian and philosopher, born at Palma, Majorca. He served as a soldier and led a dissolute life, but from 1266 gave himself up to asceticism, became a Franciscan, and went on a spiritual crusade to convert the Mussulmans. His major work is the *Ars Magna* (The Great Art), condemned in 1376 for its attempt to link faith and reason, but later viewed more sympathetically. He travelled widely, and was allegedly killed on missionary work in Bugia (Bougie), Algeria. His followers, known as **Lullists**, combined religious mysticism with alchemy. » alchemy; Franciscans; monasticism; mysticism; theology

Llullaillaco, Cerro [yooyiyyakoh] 24°43S 68°30W. Snow-capped extinct volcano on the Chile–Argentina border; 300 km/186 ml W of Salta (Argentina); height 6723 m/22057 ft; Socampa Pass and railway are to the NE. » Andes

Llywelyn [hlooelin] The name of two Welsh princes. **Llywelyn ap Iorwerth** or **Llywelyn the Great** (?–1240) successfully maintained his independence against King John and Henry III, and gained recognition of Welsh rights in the Magna Carta (1215). He died at Aberconwy. **Llywelyn ap Gruffydd** (?–1282) helped the English barons against Henry III, and opposed Edward I, who forced his submission. He was slain near Builth, at which point Wales lost her political independence. » Edward I; Henry III (of England); John; Magna Carta

loach Slender-bodied freshwater fish of the family *Cobitidae* (7 genera), found in rivers and lakes throughout Europe and Asia; length commonly less than 10 cm/4 in; mouth fringed with barbels; popular amongst aquarists; includes the colourful **collie loach** (*Acanthophthalmus kuhlii*) and **tiger loach** (*Botia macracantha*).

loam An easily worked soil, composed of varying mixtures of sand, clay, and humus. Sandy loams are often favoured by horticulturalists because of their good draining qualities and the possibility of producing crops early in the season. » humus; soil

Lobachevski, Nikolai Ivanovich (1793–1856) Russian mathematician, born at Makariev. He was educated at Kazan, where he became professor of mathematics (1816) and rector (1827). In 1829 he published the first geometry on non-Euclidean principles, but the significance of his work was not appreciated until after his death. He died at Kazan. » geometries, non-Euclidean

lobbying Originating in 19th-c USA, attempts by organized groups to influence elected representatives through personal contacts in the 'lobbies' of legislative buildings. Contemporary usage has broadened the term to incorporate making demands upon civil servants, state institutions, and influencing public opinion. Significant in all liberal democracies, many groups now employ paid, professional lobbyists. » democracy; pressure group

lobefish Any of the mainly fossil bony fishes belonging to the *Sarcopterygii*, but including also the extant lungfishes (*Dipnoi*) and the coelacanth (*Crossopterygii*); characteristic fleshy bases to the paired fins. » bony fish

lobelia [loh**beel**ia] A large and very diverse genus, ranging from small annuals to shaggy, columnar perennials reaching several metres high; found almost everywhere, but mostly tropical and subtropical, especially in the New World; leaves alternate, simple; flowers twisted through 180°, usually red, blue, or violet, zygomorphic with five fused petals forming a curved, 2-lipped tube. Many are cultivated for ornament. They occupy a wide range of habitats: several are aquatic, while the giant lobelias are restricted to individual mountains of E Africa. Many contain deadly alkaloids; just the scent of the Chilean *Lobelia tupa* is said to cause poisoning. (Genus: *Lobelia*, 200–300 species. Family: *Campanulaceae*.) » alkaloid; annual; perennial; zygomorphic flower

lobotomy » psychosurgery

lobster A large marine crustacean with a well-developed abdomen and the front pair of legs modified as pincers (*chelipeds*); chelipeds asymmetrical, one for crushing and one for cutting; feeds at night on molluscs and carrion; length up to 60 cm/2 ft; eggs carried in masses stuck to abdominal legs of female; found in holes and crevices in shallow coastal seas; caught commercially using pots or wickerwork traps (creels). (Class: *Malacostraca*. Order: *Decapoda*.) » crustacean; spiny lobster

lobster claw » parrot's bill

local area network (LAN) A system which allows communication between computers situated within a well-defined geographical area, and which does not use the public telephone system. By contrast, a **long-distance network** allows computer communication over a very wide geographical area, generally using the telephone system. » acoustic coupler; computer; electronic mail; packet switching

local education authority (LEA) A regional government organization responsible for education in its area. In the UK, this is usually a city or county council. The elected members of the LEA are local politicians; they decide policy, stand for election, and receive no payment other than attendance allowances. It also comprises professional officers, responsible for the day-to-day running of the education system in their area. » education

local government A set of political institutions constitutionally subordinate to the national, provincial, or federal government, with delegated authority to perform certain functions within territorially-defined parts of the state. Sovereign authority remains with the higher levels of government, which may create, dissolve, or change local structures and add to or take away their powers and functions. Some of the services most commonly provided by local government include education, public transport, roads, social services, housing, leisure and recreation, public health, and water. The rationale for local government includes the need for local participation, achieved through direct or indirect elections, and in local authorities' revenue-raising powers. Although considerable discretion may be granted to local authorities in some political systems, conflict with the centre can occur. This is usually centred around the extent of legitimate democratic authority possessed by local government derived from the electoral process, as different views exist about whether local government should be an agent or partner of central government. » borough; centralization; council; parish council

Local Group The family of galaxies to which the Milky Way, Magellanic Clouds, and the Andromeda galaxy belong. It sprawls over 1 megaparsec, and contains 3 large spiral galaxies, 11 irregular dwarfs, and 14 ellipticals – about 5×10^{12} solar masses in all. » Andromeda (astronomy); galaxy; Magellanic Clouds; Milky Way

Locarno Pact An agreement reached in 1925 at an international conference held at Locarno, Italy, guaranteeing post-1919 frontiers between France, Belgium, and Germany, and the demilitarization of the Rhineland. The treaty was signed by France, Germany, and Belgium, and guaranteed by Britain and Italy. Germany also signed arbitration conventions with France, Belgium, Poland, and Czechoslovakia; and France signed treaties of mutual guarantee with Poland and Czechoslovakia.

locational analysis The study of the spatial patterning of features on the Earth's surface, a major component of human geography in the UK and USA in the 1960s and 1970s. By establishing general models and laws, and continually testing these, locational analysis seeks to explain the factors accounting for the regularity with which spatial arrangements (eg the location of particular types of business) occur. » geography

Loch Ness Monster » Ness, Loch

Lochner, Stefan [**lokh**nuh] (c.1400–51) German painter, born at Meersburg, on L Constance. He may have studied in the Netherlands before settling in Cologne c.1440, where he became the principal master of the Cologne School, marking the transition from the Gothic style to naturalism. His best-known work is the great triptych, 'Adoration of the Kings', now in Cologne Cathedral. He died at Cologne. » German art; Gothic; naturalism

lock A device for securing objects, usually doors on houses or safes. It is normally a mechanical device operated by levers and

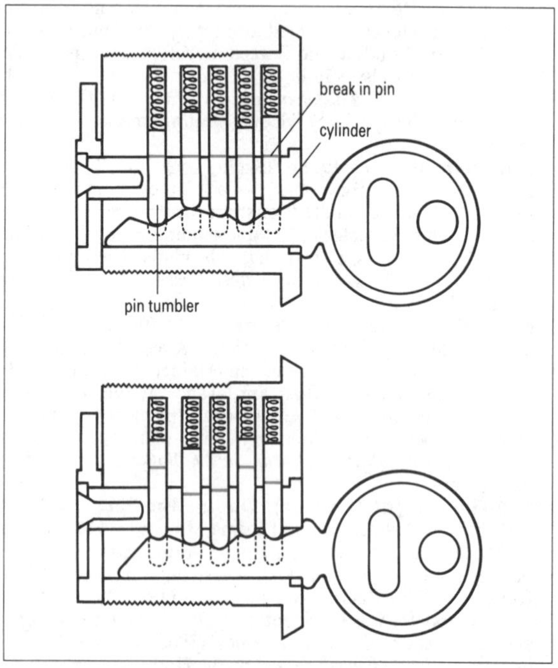

Yale lock – In a Yale lock (devised by US locksmith Linus Yale Jr in the 1880s), a set of pins inside a cylinder is raised to a predetermined height by a key with a serrated edge. This enables the cylinder to be turned, and the lock opens. If the wrong key is used, the pins are not pushed to their correct heights, and the lock remains closed.

keys, but many are nowadays magnetically or electronically operated, and can be computer controlled. Time locks can be opened only at certain predetermined times of the day. » Bramah

Locke, John (1632–1704) English empiricist philosopher, born at Wrington, Somerset. Educated at Westminster School and Oxford, in 1667 he joined the household of Anthony Ashley Cooper, later first Earl of Shaftesbury, and through him gained an interest in philosophy. In 1672, Locke became secretary of the Board of Trade, lived in France for health reasons (1675–9), then moved to Holland. He returned to England in 1689, and became a commissioner of appeals, retiring in 1691 to Oates, Essex, where he died. His major work, the *Essay Concerning Human Understanding* (1690), accepted the possibility of rational demonstration of moral principles and the existence of God, but its denial of innate ideas, and its demonstration that 'all knowledge is founded on and ultimately derives itself from sense...or sensation', was the real starting point of British empiricism. His treatises *On Government* (1689) were also influential, and his sanctioning of rebellion was an inspiration for both American and French revolutionaries. » empiricism

Lockerbie A Scottish Borders town, the scene of Britain's worst air disaster, when a Pan Am Boeing 747 flying from Frankfurt to New York via London crashed on 21 December 1988. There were no survivors. The total death toll was 270, including townspeople killed by plane debris which demolished houses. The explosive device which led to the disaster was incorporated into a radio-cassette player placed in the baggage hold, thought to have been taken on board at Frankfurt. It remains unclear which terrorist group was responsible for the disaster.

lockjaw » **tetanus**

lockout An industrial situation in which a company refuses to allow its workforce into the premises. It is an extreme measure, used infrequently in negotiations, especially with trade unions, to persuade the workforce to accept the company's terms of employment. » industrial action

Lockyer, Sir Joseph Norman (1836–1920) British astronomer, born at Rugby. In 1868 he detected an element, which he called helium, in the Sun's atmosphere. He founded and then edited for 50 years the scientific journal *Nature*. He was knighted in 1897, and died at Salcombe Regis, Devon. » helium

locomotive The vehicle that provides the tractive force to haul trucks and carriages on a railway. The locomotive can be powered by a steam engine, an internal combustion engine, an electric motor, or some combination of these power sources. If it is propelled by steam, the steam is generated in a boiler mounted on the locomotive and normally burning coal. If it is propelled by an electric motor, the electricity is taken either from a special rail or from overhead lines. The normal internal combustion engine used for propulsion is the diesel engine, which may drive the locomotive directly through suitable gears, or sometimes in diesel-electric configuration. In the latter case the diesel engine is used to drive a generator whose electricity drives an electric motor, which in turn drives the locomotive and its load.

The world's first locomotive was built by Richard Trevithick in 1801, and although many famous locomotives (such as 'Puffing Billy' and 'Locomotion') were used on railways to haul coal after that time, it was not until 1829 that the 'Rocket' won the Rainhill trials and inaugurated the full-time carriage of passengers. A number of British locomotives were exported to the USA from 1829, the first US-built locomotive ('Best Friend of Charleston') being built in 1831. By the mid-19th-c, the steam locomotive had developed into a form which did not change substantially thereafter, although there were many individual variations. The front wheels were small and swivelled, allowing the locomotive to enter a bend; the main driving wheels were coupled to each other, and driven directly by the steam engine itself; and the rear wheels supported the firebox. This led to the description of locomotives by their wheel arrangements; for example, 2–6–2 refers to two leading wheels (one on each side), six drive wheels, and two trailing wheels.

During the 20th-c the steam locomotive has been progressively displaced as the main type of locomotive by diesel, diesel-electric, and electric motive power, the last countries to still use steam locomotives extensively being South Africa and China. In an effort to counter the competition posed by road transport, new types of propulsion are currently under test, such as the use of linear electric motors for propulsion coupled with magnetic levitation. Countries that have investigated or are investigating these new systems are the UK, Germany, and Japan. » diesel/internal combustion engine; railway; Stephenson, George; Trevithick; *see illustration p 716*

locust Any of several species of grasshoppers, with a 2-phase life cycle. At low population density they are solitary in behaviour and show camouflaged coloration, but at high density they become brightly coloured and gregarious. These individuals swarm and migrate, often causing massive destruction of crops and natural vegetation. The main species are the **migratory locust**, the **desert locust**, and the **red locust**. (Order: *Orthoptera*. Family: *Acrididae*.) » grasshopper

locust tree » **carob; false acacia**

lodestone » **magnetite**

Lodge, David (1935–) British novelist and critic, born at Dulwich, Greater London. Educated at London, he taught at Birmingham University (1960–87). Three early realist novels give place to parodic fictions in pursuit of literature itself, including *Changing Places* (1975) and *Small World* (1984). The real world returns in *Nice Work* (1988), a rewrite of the 19th-c industrial novel. » English literature; novel; parody

Lodge, Henry Cabot (1850–1924) US Republican Senator, historian, and biographer, born in Boston, Massachusetts. He was assistant editor of the *North American Review*, but from 1878 his career was mainly political, becoming a Senator in 1893. He led the opposition to the Treaty of Versailles (1919) and prevented the USA joining the League of Nations in 1920. He died at Cambridge, Massachusetts. » League of Nations

Lodge, Thomas (c.1558–1625) English dramatist, romance writer, and poet, born in London, and educated at Merchant Taylors', Oxford, and Lincoln's Inn. His best-known work is the pastoral romance, *Rosalynde* (1590), which was the source of Shakespeare's *As You Like It*. He died in London. » English literature; pastoral; Shakespeare [i]

Łódź [wudsh] 51°49N 19°28E, pop (1983) 848 600. Industrial capital of Łódź voivodship, C Poland; second largest city in Poland; charter, 500; development since 1820 through the textile industry; railway; two universities (1945); textiles, chemicals, electrical engineering, textile machinery, transformers, radios; film studios; museums of art, archaeology, ethnography, central textile industry; botanical gardens; artistic spring festival (May). » Poland [i]

loerie » **turaco**

Loess Plateau, [**loh**is] Chinese **Huangtu Gaoyuan** Plateau in NC China; area 400 000 sq km/150 400 sq ml; altitude 800–2 000 m/2 600–6 500 ft; covered with a layer of wind-blown loamy deposit (*loess*), generally 100 m/325 ft deep, but much deeper in places; serious soil erosion; trees and grass now being planted to help conserve soil and water. » China [i]; soil

Loewe, Frederick [loh] (1904–88) US composer, born in Berlin. He went to the USA in 1924, and worked as a composer on a number of Broadway musicals. Those he wrote in collaboration with Alan Jay Lerner (1918–86), including *Brigadoon* (1947) and *My Fair Lady* (1956), were particularly successful, as also was the film *Gigi* (1958), for which he wrote the score. He died in Palm Springs, California.

Löffler, Friedrich (August Johannes) (1852–1915) German bacteriologist, born at Frankfurt an der Oder. Educated at Würzburg and Berlin, he became a military surgeon, professor at Greifswald (1883), and from 1913 director of the Koch Institute in Berlin. He first cultured the diphtheria bacillus (1884) discovered by Klebs, and called the 'Klebs-Löffler bacillus', and also prepared a vaccine against foot-and-mouth disease (1899). He died in Berlin. » diphtheria

Lofoten Islands [loh**foh**tn] area 1 425 sq km/550 sq ml. Mountainous island group in the Norwegian Sea, off the NW coast of Norway, separated from the mainland by Vest Fjord; major fishing grounds nearby; fish processing. » Norway [i]

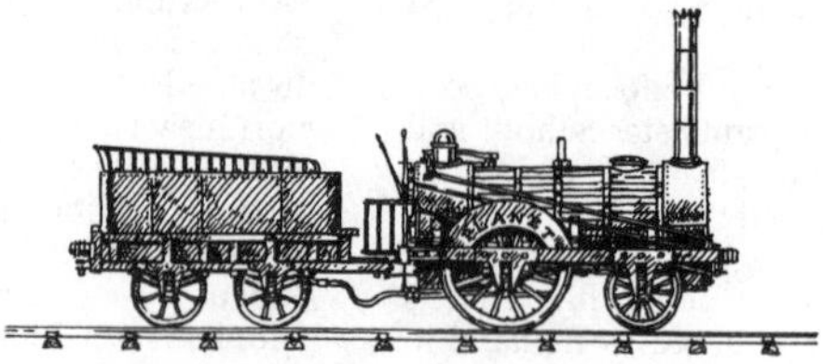

Stephenson's 'Planet', supplied to the Liverpool and Manchester Railway in 1830.

New York Central and Hudson River Rail Road No 999, which achieved a world record of 112.5 mph/181 kph in 1893.

Streamlined A4 Pacific Class 'Quicksilver' designed in 1935 for the London and North Eastern Railway.

British Rail Advanced Passenger Train, which in 1973 achieved the world record for diesel-powered locomotives of 142 mph/230 kph.

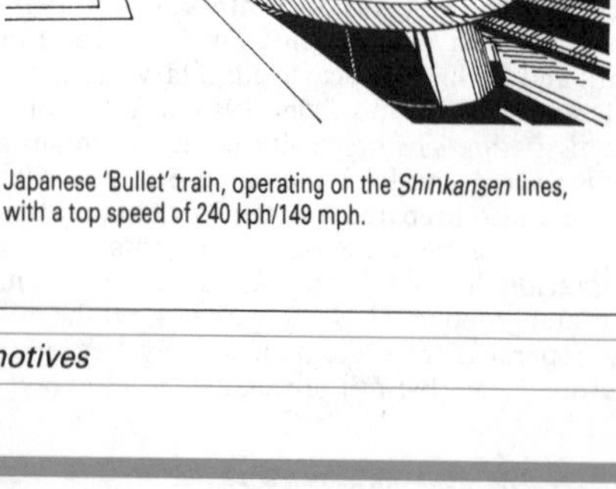

Japanese 'Bullet' train, operating on the *Shinkansen* lines, with a top speed of 240 kph/149 mph.

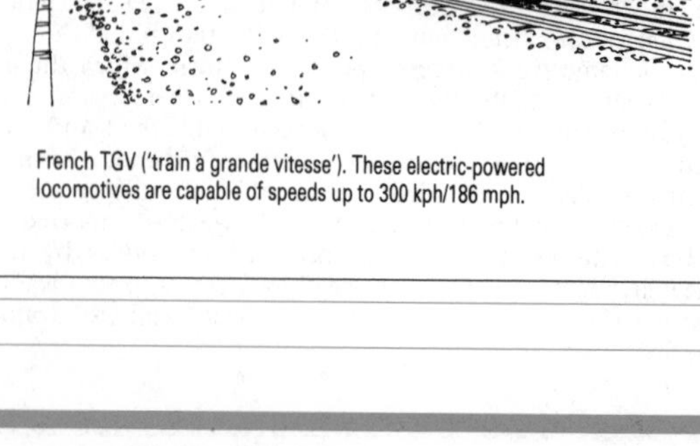

French TGV ('train à grande vitesse'). These electric-powered locomotives are capable of speeds up to 300 kph/186 mph.

Locomotives

Lofty-Flinders Ranges, Mount Mountain ranges in South Australia state, Australia; extending 800 km/500 ml N from Cape Jervis to the N end of L Torrens, running roughly N–S; the Mt Lofty Ranges are in the S, comparatively low, rising to Mt Lofty (727 m/2 385 ft); Flinders Ranges in the N include a national park (802 sq km/310 sq ml), rising to St Mary Peak (1 166 m/3 825 ft); unusual basins (notably Wilpena Pound) with multi-coloured rock faces and wild flowers; numerous examples of Aboriginal art, some 10 000 years old; copper, coal, and gold have been mined here; popular tourist area. » Aborigines; South Australia

Logan, Mount 60°34N 140°24W. Highest mountain in Canada, and second highest in N America; rises to 5 950 m/19 521 ft in the St Elias Mts, SW Yukon territory; to the N of the Seward Glacier, in Kluane National Park. » Canada [i]

logarithm The power *n* to which a number *a* must be raised to equal another number *b*, ie 'the logarithm to the base *a* of *b*': $a^n = b \Rightarrow \log_a b = n$; for example, since $10^2 = 100$, $\log_{10} 100 = 2$. From the definition, the *logarithmic function* is the inverse of the exponential function. Properties of the logarithmic function can be deduced from the laws of indices, and include: $\log(ab) = \log a + \log b$, and $\log(a/b) = \log a - \log b$. These properties enabled logarithms to be used extensively as calculating aids before the advent of computers. Logarithms base *e* are called *natural* or *Napierian* logarithms, denoted by ln; logarithms base 10 are denoted by lg. » base (mathematics); exponential function; index/indices; Napier, John

loggia [**loh**jia] A gallery in a building, behind an open arcade or colonnade, and facing onto a garden, street, or square. It is sometimes a separate structure. » colonnade

logic The systematic study of inference. Logicians seek not to describe the way people do in fact reason, but to specify the principles of correct reasoning and diagnose patterns of incorrect reasoning. All cases of inference are either deductive or inductive. **Deductive logic** is the study of those inferences that are valid (or invalid) in virtue of their structure, not their content. 'Hydrogen and Oxygen are elements; therefore Hydrogen is an element' and 'London and New York are planets; therefore London is a planet' have the same structure, '(A & B); therefore A'; and any inference with that structure is valid. Logicians can thus investigate validity by means of constructing abstract formal languages: this is the enterprise of **symbolic logic**. Such languages either specify a set of axioms and depict valid inferences as theorems, or specify a set of obviously valid inferential rules which allow one to discover less obviously valid inferences.

There are two major parts of elementary deductive logic. **Propositional logic** is that part which deals with inferences involving simple sentences in the indicative mood joined by such connectives as *not* (negation), *and* (conjunction), *or* (disjunction), and *if…then* (conditional). Any such inference can be determined to be valid or invalid by a mechanical algorithm. **Predicate logic** (also known as *quantification theory*) presupposes propositional logic; it deals with sentences in the indicative mood involving such quantifying terms as *some*, *all*, and *no*. Thus, 'All cats are mammals, and no mammals are worms; therefore no black cats are worms' is a (valid) inference in predicate logic. Although many kinds of inference in predicate logic can be determined to be valid or invalid by mechanical means, not all can; there is no general decision procedure for predicate logic. Logicians are also concerned to portray logical truth, the sentences that are true solely in virtue of their structure; in propositional logic they are the *tautologies*. The investigation of deductive inference has also been extended beyond propositional and predicate logic to include *modal logic*, which treats the notions of necessity and possibility; *epistemic logic*, the logic of knowledge and belief; *many-valued logic*, which allows some sentences to be assigned a designation other than true or false; and *tense logic*, which analyses inferences involving such temporal notions as past, present, and future.

Inductive logic is the study of inferences which are not deductively valid, but are such that the premisses, if true, would increase the likelihood of the truth of the conclusion. Many typical inductive inferences can be represented by the scheme '*n* percent of all observed (tested, sampled) As are Bs; therefore *n* percent of all As whatsoever are Bs', and are thus deductively invalid. Nevertheless the premisses of a correct inductive inference give good reason to believe that the conclusion is true. The rigorous study of inductive logic leads quickly to issues in probability theory and statistics. There is no unified theory of incorrect inference, since there seems to be no limit to the variety of ways in which people can reason faultily. Logicians have catalogued some of the more salient ways, thus producing a significant literature on fallacies.

In antiquity, logic was chiefly studied by Aristotle, who wrote the first systematic treatises on the subject, and by the earlier Stoics, who studied propositional logic with great sophistication. The period 3rd–12th-c AD was mostly a time of consolidation and transmission of this ancient material. By contrast, scholastic philosophy in the 12th–15th-c was characterized by intense activity in logic and in the related fields of philosophy of logic and semantic theory. Such endeavours were viewed as sterile by the Renaissance philosophers, and the discipline lay dormant from the Renaissance to the 19th-c, since when it has flourished. » Boole; Cantor; de Morgan; deduction; fallacy; Frege; Gödel, Kurt; induction (logic); inference; modal logic; Peirce, C S; Russell, Bertrand; Tarski; tautology; Whitehead

logical positivism A philosophical movement beginning with the 'Vienna Circle' in the 1920s under the leadership of Moritz Schlick and Rudolf Carnap. Positivism rejected traditional philosophy insofar as it did not possess scientific rigour; metaphysical, ethical, and religious pronouncements were branded as meaningless because their truth or falsity was unverifiable. » Ayer; Carnap; Schlick; verificationism; Vienna Circle

logicism » reductionism

logography The study of writing systems in which the symbols (*logographs* or *logograms*) represent whole words, or, in some cases, components of words. A few logographs are found in European languages, such as & ('and'), ÷ ('divided by'), @ ('at'), and £ ('pound'); but Chinese and Japanese are the most famous examples of a logographic writing system. Though originally derived from ideographs, the symbols of these languages now stand for words and syllables, and do not refer directly to concepts or things. » graphology; ideography; pictography [i]

Lohengrin [**loh**engrin] In Germanic legend, the son of Parsifal. He leaves the temple of the Grail and is carried to Antwerp in a boat drawn by swans. There he saves Princess Elsa of Brabant, and is about to marry her; but she asks forbidden questions about his origin, and he is forced to leave her, the swan-boat taking him back to the Grail temple. » Perceval, Sir

Loire, River [lwah], ancient **Liger** River in E France, rising in the Massif Central; flows N and NW to Orléans, then turns W to empty into the Bay of Biscay by a wide estuary below St-Nazaire; longest river in France; length 1 020 km/634 ml; canal link to R Seine; valley known for its vineyards; several important chateaux. » France [i]

Loki [**loh**kee] A mischievous Norse god; originally a Giant, he was later accepted into the company of the gods. Although he plays tricks on them, he is also able to save them from danger by his cleverness. However, after contriving the death of Balder, he was tied to a rock where he will stay until Ragnarok. » Balder; Germanic religion; Hel; Ragnarok

Lollards A derisive term applied to the followers of the English theologian John Wycliffe (14th-c). The movement, responsible for the translation of the Bible into the vernacular, was suppressed; however, it continued among the enthusiastic but less literate of society, generally anticlerical in attitude, and prepared the way for the Reformation in England. » Bible; Reformation; Wycliffe

Lomax, Alan (1915–) US ethnomusicologist and folklorist, born at Austin, Texas. He accompanied his father, **John Avery Lomax** (1867–1948), to Southern prison camps to record songs and tales. They discovered Leadbelly in prison, and arranged for his pardon. In 1938 Lomax interviewed Jelly Roll Morton, obtaining an oral record of early jazz which appeared first as Lomax's book *Mister Jelly Roll* (1950) and later as a series of recordings. In 1951–8 he turned his attention to Europe, recording songs and tales in England, Italy, and Spain. » ethnomusicology; jazz; Leadbelly; Morton, Jelly Roll

Lombard, Peter, byname **Magister Sententiarum** ('Master of Sentences') (c.1100–64) Italian theologian, born near Novara, Lombardy. He studied at Bologna, Reims, and Paris, and, after holding a chair of theology there, became Bishop of Paris in 1159. His byname stems from his collection of sentences from Church Fathers on points of Christian doctrine. His work was the standard textbook of Catholic theology down to the Reformation. » Fathers of the Church; Roman Catholicism

Lombard League A coalition of N Italian cities, established in 1167 to assert their independence as communes (city-republics) against the German emperor, Frederick I Barbarossa. The League, of which new versions were later formed, set a model for inter-city alliances, and underlined the rising political importance of urban communities in the mediaeval West. » Frederick I/II (Emperors)

Lombardo, Pietro (c.1435–1515) Italian sculptor and architect. He came originally from Lombardy, was working in Padua in 1464, and settled in Venice c.1467. He ran the most important workshop in Venice, specializing in tomb sculpture. The Church of Santa Maria dei Miracoli (1481–9) was his design. In its building and decoration he was assisted by his sons **Tullio** (c.1455–1532) and **Antonio** (c.1458–1516?). He died in Venice. » Renaissance; Venetian School

Lombards A Germanic people settled in Hungary – their name deriving from the long beards (*langobardi*) they traditionally wore – who invaded N Italy in AD 568 under their king, Alboin. They founded a new capital at Milan, and in time controlled most of the peninsula except for the S and the area around Ravenna. Their kingdom was annexed by Charlemagne in 774, but the Lombard duchies (Benevento, Spoleto) survived as autonomous entities until the 11th-c. » Charlemagne; Ravenna; Visigoths

Lombardy [**lom**buhdee], Ital **Lombardia** pop (1981) 8 891 652; area 23 833 sq km/9 199 sq ml. Region of N Italy; capital, Milan; chief towns, Brescia, Pavia, Varese; S Lombardy, highly developed industrial and agricultural region (plain of R Po); tourism important around the Alpine lakes and in the mountains. » Italy [i]; Lombards

Lombardy poplar A form of poplar with upswept branches and a distinctive narrow columnar crown; named from plants originating in N Italy, and brought to Britain in the 18th-c. The trees are almost invariably male. They are resistant to air pollution, and are often planted. (*Populus nigra*, cultivar *Italica*. Family: *Salicaceae*.) » poplar; tree [i]

Lombroso, Cesare (1836–1909) Italian founder of the science of criminology, born at Verona. After working as an army surgeon, he became professor of mental diseases at Pavia, director of an asylum at Pesaro, and professor of forensic medicine (1876), psychiatry (1896), and criminal anthropology (1906) at Turin. His theory (now discredited) postulated the existence of a criminal type distinguishable from a normal person. He died at Turin. » forensic medicine

Lomé [**loh**may] 6°10N 1°21E, pop (1983) 366 476. Seaport capital of Togo; important market centre, noted for its marble, gold, and silver crafts; airport; railway junction; university (1965); oil refining, steel processing, tourism; location of trade conventions in 1970s and 1980s arranged between African, Caribbean, and EEC states. » Togo [i]

Lomond, Loch [**loh**muhnd] Largest lake in Scotland, and largest stretch of inland water in the UK; 32 km/20 ml NW of Glasgow; area 70 sq km/27 sq ml; 34 km/21 ml long; narrow in the N, opening out to 8 km/5 ml at the S end; up to 190 m/625 ft deep; hydroelectricity in NW; outlet is R Leven (S); major tourist area; pleasure cruises. » Scotland [i]

London, Jack, pseudonym of **John Griffith Chaney** (1876–1916) US novelist, born in San Francisco. He was successively sailor, tramp, and gold miner before he took to writing, using his knowledge of the Klondyke in the highly successful *Call of the Wild* (1903), and of the sea in *Sea-Wolf* (1904). He also wrote the more serious political novel, *The Iron Heel* (1907), and an autobiographical tale of alcoholism, *John Barleycorn* (1913). He died at Glen Ellen, California. » American literature; novel

London, Lat **Londinium** (in the 4th-c, **Augusta**) 51°30N 0°10W, pop (1987e) 6 770 400 (Greater London), 4 700 (City of London). Capital city of England and the UK; on the R Thames in SE England; **Greater London** consists of 32 boroughs and the City of London, area 1 579 sq km/609 sq ml; from 1st–5th-c, a Roman town (c.43 AD), situated where the Thames narrowed to its lowest convenient crossing; sacked by Boadicea (c.61); later surrounded by a defensive wall, fragments of which remain; developed as the leading trade and administrative centre of England; received charter privileges in 1067; mayoralty established in 1191; major building programmes in Middle Ages; extended W, especially in 16th-c; Great Plague (1665), Great Fire (1666), followed by major reconstruction; many squares laid out in 17th–18th-c; in 17th-c developed into a major trade centre and became one of the world's largest cities; severe damage especially to City and East End in World War 2 (the Blitz), with much subsequent rebuilding; administered by London County Council (1888–1963) and by the Greater London Council until 1986, its functions then transferring to the boroughs and other bodies; **City of London**, occupying site of the old mediaeval city N of the Thames, is the financial and business centre, including the Bank of England, Stock Exchange, and Royal Exchange; National Westminster Building (1977) is the tallest building in London (183 m/600 ft); **City of Westminster** is the administrative and judicial centre, including the Houses of Parliament, Buckingham Palace, and government departments; the **West End** is the main shopping and entertainment centre, around Oxford Street, Piccadilly, and Regent Street; outer boroughs comprise mixed residential and industrial developments; extensive dockland, much now scheduled for redevelopment; headquarters of Port of London Authority; major railway terminuses (Euston, King's Cross, Paddington, St Pancras, Victoria, Waterloo); extensive underground system (known as 'the Tube') run by London Transport Executive; main airports at Heathrow (W) and Gatwick (S), also at London City, Luton (N), and Stansted (E); central bridges across R Thames include Westminster (1750), Blackfriars (1769), Waterloo (1817), and Southwark (1819); markets (Billingsgate, Smithfield; Nine Elms at Vauxhall, replacing Covent Garden, now a tourist centre); parks (Battersea/Hyde/Regent's/St James's Parks, Kensington Gardens); zoological gardens at Regent's Park; leading cultural centre, with many theatres, museums (British/London/Natural History/Science/Victoria and Albert), galleries (National/National Portrait/Tate Galleries, Courtauld Institute), concert halls (Albert/Queen Elizabeth/Royal Festival/Wigmore Halls, Barbican Centre), churches and cathedrals (Saint Paul's/Westminster Cathedrals; Westminster Abbey and St Margaret's Church, a world heritage site); BBC Symphony/London Philharmonic/London Symphony/Royal Philharmonic Orchestras; Royal Shakespeare Company/Opera House (Covent Garden)/Ballet (Sadler's Wells)/Academy of Music/College of Music/Academy of Dramatic Art; centre for radio (Broadcasting House), television, and the press (traditionally at Fleet Street, now largely elsewhere); Central Criminal Court (Old Bailey), Planetarium, Madame Tussaud's; leading medical centre, with several major hospitals, and Harley Street (private practices); leading educational centre, with several constituent colleges of London University (from 1836), and many other institutions, including City and Brunel Universities (both 1966); Trooping of the Colour on the Queen's official birthday (Jun); procession to the Royal Courts of Justice (Lord Mayor's Show) (Nov). » Big Ben; Billingsgate Market; British Museum; Buckingham Palace; Covent Garden; Downing Street; East End; Hampton Court; Houses of Parliament; Hyde Park; Imperial War Museum; Inns of Court; London Bridge/Contemporary Dance Theatre/Festival Ballet/Group/Museum/University [i]; Mayfair; Monument; National Gallery; National Portrait Gallery; Natural History Museum; Old Bailey; Oval, the; Royal Opera House; St James's Palace; St Paul's Cathedral; Science Museum; Smithfield; Tate Gallery; Temple; Temple Bar; Tower Bridge; Tower of London; Victoria and Albert Museum; Wembley Stadium; Westminster Abbey; Whitehall; Adam, Robert; Boadicea; Britain, Roman; Jones, Inigo; Nash, John; Wren, Christopher

LONDON

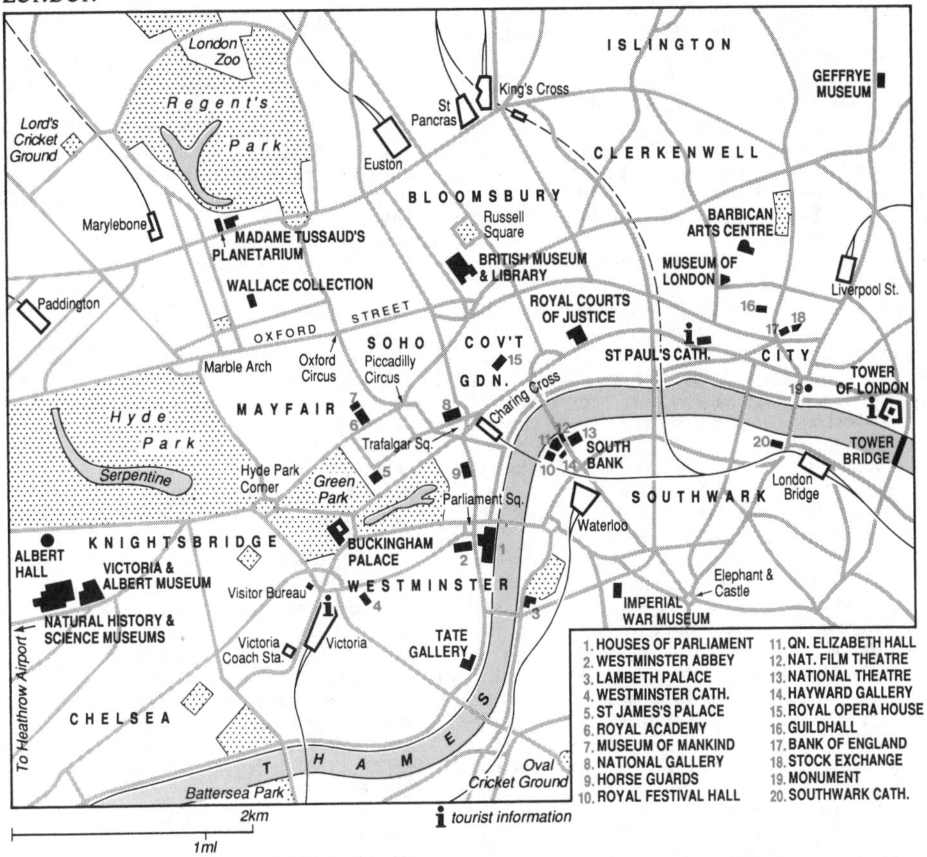

London Bridge A bridge over the R Thames linking Southwark with the City of London. Early wooden structures were replaced in the 12th-c by a 19-arch stone bridge bearing shops and houses. This was superseded in 1831 by a 5-arch bridge which was dismantled and sold to Lake Havasu City, Arizona, in 1968. It was replaced by a concrete structure. » London [i]

London clubs » **club**

London Contemporary Dance Theatre A dance company founded in London in 1967 by the philanthropist, Robin Howard, under the artistic direction of Robert Cohan. Cohan has created many works for the company, which tours widely and has major London seasons. In the 1980s it expanded its repertoire to include popular works based on jazz steps and street dance. The **London Contemporary Dance School** trains dancers, and the company offers a training ground for choreographers. » London [i]; modern dance

London Festival Ballet A company which emerged from Markova and Dolin's groups of Ballets Russes dancers in 1950, and which has attracted wide audiences by its popular dancers and guest stars. It offers regular London seasons and extensive tours, mainly performing the classics, but with some works by modern choreographers. It has offered a programme for schools since the late 1970s. » ballet; London [i]; Markova

London Group A society of British artists founded in 1913 by Nash, Epstein, Fry, and others; its first president was Harold Gilman (1878–1919). It held regular exhibitions for half a century. » English art; Epstein; Fry, Roger Eliot; London [i]; Nash, Paul

London Missionary Society (LMS) Formed in London in 1795 by evangelical Protestants to undertake missionary work in the Pacific islands. It was particularly successful in Tahiti (1797), the Cook Is (1821), Samoa (1830), and Papua New Guinea (1871). The LMS also came to operate in other parts of the world, including Africa. » Evangelicalism

London Museum A museum at London Wall in the City of London, created from the former London and Guildhall museums and opened in 1975. It covers the history of London from prehistoric times to the present day. » London [i]

London plane » **plane tree**

London pride A mat-forming perennial with rosettes of paddle-shaped, blunt-toothed leaves; flowers in sprays on erect stems growing to 30 cm/12 in, white to pinkish with red spots. It is a hybrid of unknown origin, widely grown in gardens. (*Saxifraga × umbrosa*. Family: *Saxifragaceae*.) » perennial; saxifrage

London University A federation of colleges, medical schools and research institutions established as a university in London in 1836. In addition to the medical schools of the London teaching hospitals, several major institutions form part of the university. » London [i]

Londonderry » **Derry**

LONDON UNIVERSITY

COLLEGE	FOUNDED
Royal Veterinary College	1791
Birkbeck College	1823
University College	1826
King's College (merged with Queen Elizabeth College and Chelsea College 1985)	1829
Goldsmiths' College	1891
London School of Economics	1895
Imperial College of Science and Technology	1907
School of Oriental and African Studies	1916
Royal Holloway and Bedford New College (founded through merger of Bedford College and Royal Holloway College)	1985
Queen Mary and Westfield College (founded through merger of Queen Mary College and Westfield College)	1989

lone pair Two valence electrons of an atom not involved in bonding to another. They affect the shape of a molecule, and often become involved in a co-ordinate bond. » co-ordination compounds; hydrogen bond

Long Beach 33°47N 118°11W, pop(1980) 361 334. City in Los Angeles County, SW California, USA, on San Pedro Bay; developed rapidly after the discovery of oil, 1921; railway; university (1949); oil refining; diverse manufacturing; tourist centre; a long bathing beach; location for the British cruise liner *Queen Mary*, now a museum-hotel-convention centre; Long Beach Marine Stadium (scene of the 1932 Olympic boating events). » California

long-distance network » **local area network**

Long Island area 3 600 sq km/1 400 sq ml, length 190 km/118 ml. Island in SE New York State, USA, E of New York City; bounded N by Long Island Sound; separated from the Bronx and Manhattan by the East River, and from Staten I by the Narrows; comprises the New York State counties of Kings (includes Brooklyn), Nassau, Queens, Suffolk; many residential towns and resort beaches; contains John F Kennedy airport; settled by the Dutch in 1623, and by the English c.1640; site of the Battle of Long Island (1776) in the US War of Independence, when British forces under Howe defeated American forces under Washington. » American Revolution; Howe, William; New York (state); Washington, George

long jump An athletics field event in which the contestant has a running stride to the take-off mark and must then jump as far as possible into a sandpit. The length of the jump is measured from the nearest break in the sand made by any part of the competitor's body, to the front of the take-off line. It is sometimes called the **broad jump**. The current world record for men is 8.90 m/29 ft 2½ in, achieved by Bob Beamon (USA, born 29 Aug 1946) on 18 October 1968 at Mexico City, and for women is 7.45 m/24 ft 5½ in, achieved by Heike Dreschler (*née* Daute) (East Germany, born 16 Dec 1964) on 21 June 1986 at Tallinn, Estonia, and also on 3 July 1986 at Dresden, Germany; and by Jackie Joyner-Kersee (USA, born 3 Mar 1962) on 14 August 1987 at Indianapolis, USA. » athletics; triple jump

Long March The long trek in China, covering over 8 000 km/5 000 ml, made by approximately 100 000 communists under Mao Zedong (Mao Tse-tung) to reach their base in Shaanxi from the Jiangxi Soviet, which had been encircled by nationalist government troops. It began in October 1934 and lasted about a year. » Mao Zedong

Long Parliament An English parliament called (Nov 1640) by Charles I after his defeat by the Scots in the second Bishops' War. It was legally in being 1640–60, but did not meet continuously. It attacked prerogative rights and alleged abuses of power by the King and his ministers, and abolished the Court of Star Chamber, the Councils of the North and for Wales, and the Ecclesiastical Court of High Commission (1641), the bishops and the Court of Wards (1646), and the monarchy and the House of Lords (1649). Moderates were eliminated in Pride's Purge (Dec 1648), and the remaining Rump was dismissed by Cromwell in 1653. The Rump was recalled in the death-throes of the Protectorate (May 1659), and all members in December 1659. » Bishops' Wars; Pride, Thomas; Rump Parliament

long-range navigation system » **loran**

long-tailed tit A small bird of the long-tailed **titmouse** family; native to Europe and Asia; black, white, and pink; body shorter than long straight tail; inhabits scrub and woodland; eats seeds, buds, and insects. (*Aegithalos caudatus*.) » tit

longbow An English bow with a shaft of yew-wood 1.5 m/5 ft long, which could fire an arrow capable of penetrating plate armour at 400 yd (365 m). It dominated the battlefield for 200 years from 1300, proving decisive at the Battles of Crécy, Poitiers, and Agincourt. » crossbow

Longchamp » **Bois de Boulogne**

Longfellow, Henry Wadsworth (1807–82) US poet, born at Portland, Maine. Educated at Brunswick, Maine, he spent three years in Europe, and became professor of modern languages and literature at Harvard (1836–54). *Voices of the Night* (1839), his first book of verse, made a favourable impression, and this was followed by several other works, notably *Evangeline* (1847), a tale of the French exiles of Acadia, and *The Song of Hiawatha* (1855). He died at Cambridge, Massachusetts. » American literature; poetry

Longford (county), Gaelic **Longphuirt** pop(1981) 31 140; area 1 044 sq km/403 sq ml. County in NW Leinster province, C Irish Republic; drained by R Shannon and its tributaries; crossed by the Royal Canal; hilly in NW; capital, Longford; sheep, cattle, oats, potatoes. » Irish Republic [i]; Longford (city)

Longford (city), Gaelic **Longphort** 53°44N 7°47W, pop(1981) 6 548. Capital of Longford county, NW Leinster, C Irish Republic; on R Camlin and a branch of the Royal Canal; former literary centre; railway; St Mel's Cathedral; Tullynally Castle at Castlepollard. » Longford (county)

Longhi or **Falca, Pietro [longgee]** (1702–85) Italian painter, born and died in Venice. He worked as a silversmith, then became a painter, excelling in small-scale pictures of Venetian life. Most of his work is in Venetian public collections. He died at Venice. His son, **Alessandro** (1733–1813) was a portrait painter. » Italian art

Longinus, Dionysius [lon**jiy**nuhs] (c.213–73) Greek Neoplatonic rhetorician and philosopher. He taught rhetoric in Athens, settled at Palmyra, and became chief counsellor to Queen Zenobia, for which Emperor Aurelian beheaded him. He is the supposed author of the treatise on excellence in literature, *On the Sublime*, which influenced many Neoclassical writers, such as Dryden and Pope. » Greek literature; Neoclassicism (art and architecture); Neoplatonism; rhetoric

longitude » **latitude and longitude** [i]

longitudinal wave » **wave** (physics) [i]

Longman, Thomas (1699–1755) British publisher, born in Bristol. He bought a bookselling business in Paternoster Row in 1724, and shared in publishing such works as Ephraim Chambers's *Cyclopaedia*, and Johnson's *Dictionary*. He was the founder of the British publishing house that still bears his name.

longship A vessel used by the Vikings in their voyages of exploration, plunder, and conquest. The largest were 45 m/150 ft in length, made of overlapping wooden planks ('clinker built'), very strong, and propelled by both oars and sail. They usually carried 30 or 40 men, but there was room for more (such as captured Saxon maidens), and the larger vessels may well have carried twice this number. » ship [i]; Vikings

longshore transport The movement of sediment particles along a beach in response to wave activity. The particles may be transported along the beach face, being rolled up and down at an angle with the waves (*beach drift*). They may also be transported in suspension by the turbulent water in the surf zone as it moves along the beach (the *longshore current*). » beach; spit; wave (oceanography)

longsightedness » **eye** [i]

Lonsdale, Dame Kathleen, *née* **Yardley** (1903–71) British crystallographer, born at Newbridge, Co Kildare, Ireland. The family came to the UK in 1908 and she graduated in physics in London in 1922. She spent 20 years at the Royal Institution, and became professor of chemistry at University College, London (1946–68). From the 1920s she applied X-ray crystal diffraction to determine chemical structures. She was made a Dame in 1956, and died in London. » crystallography; X-rays

Lonsdale Belt In boxing, a championship belt awarded to a fighter who wins a British title fight. If he wins three fights in one weight division, he is allowed to keep the belt permanently. The wins do not necessarily have to be in succession. It is named after the 5th Earl of Lonsdale, who presented the first belt to the National Sporting Club in 1909. The British heavyweight boxer Henry Cooper (1934–) is the only man to have won three Lonsdale Belts outright. » boxing [i]; Cooper, Henry

loofah An annual climbing vine with tendrils, native to the tropics; leaves heart-shaped; flowers yellow, funnel-shaped; fruit marrow-like, up to 30 cm/12 in long, roughly cylindrical. The familiar sponge-like item of bathrooms is the fibrous vascular tissue of the fruit left when the soft parts are removed. (*Luffa cylindrica*. Family: *Cucurbitaceae*.) » climbing plant; marrow (botany); vascular tissue

look-and-say A method of teaching reading through whole-word recognition, linking the form with a visual stimulus, and using frequently occurring short words (eg *go*, *see*) as a prelude to introducing longer words of which they may form component parts. The aim is to teach words as meaningful entities, rather than as sequences of meaningless phonic syllables. » phonics

loon » **diver**

looper The caterpillar larva of a geometrid moth, characterized by its looping locomotion pattern; possesses only one pair of pro-legs and one pair of claspers; body held rigid at rest, resembling a twig; also known as **inch worm**. (Order: *Lepidoptera*. Family: *Geometridae*.) » caterpillar; geometrid moth; larva

Lope de Vega » **Vega (Carpio), Lope de**

loquat [**loh**kwat] A small evergreen tree with very hairy twigs, native to China, but widely grown in S Europe; leaves coarse, reddish, hairy beneath; flowers white, fragrant, in terminal clusters; fruits 3–6 cm/1¼–2½ in, round, yellowish-orange, flesh sweet and edible; one or more seeds. (*Eriobotrya japonica*. Family: *Rosaceae*.) » evergreen plants; tree [i]

loran An acronym for **long-range navigation system**. Radio pulses emitted at fixed intervals by pairs of transmitters define a grid pattern, over a very large area, not in two sets of straight lines but in sets of intersecting hyperbolae. The timing of the reception of these paired pulses by an aircraft or ship indicates its position on the network. » hyperbola (mathematics) [i]; radio

Lorca, Federico García (1899–1936) Spanish poet, born at Fuente Vaqueros. His best-known works are his gypsy songs, *Canciones* (1927, Songs) and *Romancero Gitano* (1928, 1935, The Gypsy Ballads). He also wrote several successful plays, including the folk trilogy *Bodas de Sangre* (1933, Blood Wedding), *Yerma* (1934), and *La Casa de Bernarda Alba* (1936, The House of Bernarda Alba). He was shot at Granada by nationalists at the beginning of the Spanish Civil War. » poetry; Spanish literature

Lord Chancellor The head of the judiciary of England and Wales and of Scotland, a member of the cabinet, and the person who presides over the House of Lords. As someone who holds prominent positions in all three branches of government, his office is a clear exception to the doctrine of the separation of powers. The Lord Chancellor appoints, and may dismiss, magistrates and circuit judges. » justice of the peace; Lords, House of; separation of powers

Lord Chief Justice In the UK, the head of the Queens Bench Division of the High Court; also the president of the Criminal Division of the Court of Appeal. » Court of Appeal; High Court of Justice; judge

Lord Howe Island 31°33S 159°04E, pop (1982) 420. Volcanic island in the Pacific Ocean, 702 km/436 ml NE of Sydney; part of New South Wales; area 16.6 sq km/6.4 sq ml; rises to 866 m/2 841 ft at Mt Gower; discovered 1788; a popular resort island; a world heritage site. » New South Wales

Lord-Lieutenant [lawd lef**ten**ant] In the UK, the sovereign's permanent representative in a county or county borough of England, Wales, or Northern Ireland, or in a part of one of the Scottish regions. The lordly prefix is by custom only, and the office is now primarily one of honour.

Lord Lyon King of Arms » **heraldry [i]**

Lord's Cricket Ground A cricket ground founded by Thomas Lord (1755–1832) in 1814 in NW London. It is the home of the Marylebone Cricket Club (MCC) and the Middlesex County Cricket Club, and the recognized administrative and spiritual home of national and international cricket. Its cricketing treasures include the Ashes. » Ashes; cricket [i]

Lord's Prayer A popular prayer of Christian worship, derived from *Matt* 6.9–13 and (in different form) *Luke* 11.2–4; also known as the **Pater Noster** ('Our Father'). It is a model for how Jesus' followers are to pray, consisting (in Matthew) of three petitions praising God and seeking his kingdom, followed by four petitions concerning the physical and spiritual needs of followers. The closing doxology ('For thine is the kingdom...') was apparently added later in Church tradition. » Jesus Christ; Kaddish; prayer

lords-and-ladies A perennial native to Europe and N Africa, with glossy dark-green arrowhead-shaped leaves and poisonous scarlet berries; also called **cuckoo-pint**. The complex inflorescence consists of a cylindrical spadix the colour of dead meat, which becomes warm and emits a rotting scent to attract flies. These crawl into the bulbous base of the pale green spathe enclosing the male and female flowers, and are trapped by a ring of guard hairs. The flies pollinate the female flowers and collect pollen from the male flowers, but can escape only when the spadix collapses and the hairs wither after pollination. (*Arum maculatum*. Family: *Araceae*.) » arrowroot; inflorescence [i]; perennial; pollination; spadix; spathe

Lords, House of The non-elected house of the UK legislature. Its membership (currently c.1200) includes hereditary peers and life peers (including judicial members – the *Lords of Appeal in Ordinary*); also the two archbishops and certain bishops of the Church of England. The House can no longer veto bills passed by the House of Commons, with the exception of a bill to prolong the duration of a parliament. Its functions are mainly deliberative, its authority based on the expertise of its membership. The House of Lords also constitutes the most senior court in the UK. Appeals heard by the House are confined to matters of law. » Commons, House of; legislature; Lord Chancellor; parliament; woolsack

Lorelei [**lor**eliy] The name of a precipitous rock on the Rhine near St Goar, dangerous to boatmen and celebrated for its echo. The story of the siren of the rock whose songs lure sailors to their death dates only from 1800. » Rhine, River

Loren, Sophia, originally **Sofia Scicolone** (1934–) Italian film actress, born in Rome and brought up in poverty near Naples. As a film extra she became the protégée of the producer Carlo Ponti, who later married her, and through him gained small film parts in the 1950s, and the lead in *The Pride and the Passion* (1957) and other US productions. Her performance under the direction of De Sica in *La Ciociara* (1961, Two Women) won her an Oscar. She played the part of her own mother as well as herself in *Sophia, Her Own Story* (1981).

Lorentz, Hendrik Antoon (1853–1928) Dutch theoretical physicist, born at Arnhem. Educated at Leyden, he became professor of mathematical physics there in 1878. He shared the Nobel Prize for Physics in 1902 for his theory of electromagnetic radiation, which prepared the way for Einstein's theory of relativity. He died at Haarlem. » electromagnetism; Lorentz contraction; special relativity [i]

Lorentz contraction The apparent contraction of objects in their direction of motion when their velocity is comparable to the velocity of light, as described by special relativity; named after Dutch physicist Hendrik Lorentz, and also known as the Lorentz–FitzGerald contraction, after Irish physicist George FitzGerald (1851–1901), who made this proposal independently in 1889. » Lorentz; special relativity [i]; velocity

Lorenz, Konrad (Zacharias) (1903–89) Austrian zoologist, a founder of the science of ethology, born and died in Vienna. His work in the late 1930s, with that of Tinbergen and others, favoured the investigation of animal behaviour in the wild. He shared the 1973 Nobel Prize for Physiology or Medicine. His books include *On Aggression* (1963), *King Solomon's Ring* (1949), and *Civilised Man's Eight Deadly Sins* (1974). » ethology; Tinbergen

Lorenzetti, Ambrogio (c.1290–c.1348) Italian artist, born at Siena. He worked at Cortona and Florence, but is best known for his allegorical frescoes in the Palazzo Pubblico at Siena. His brother, **Pietro** (c.1280–c.1348), also belonged to the Sienese School, working also at Arezzo and at Assisi, where he painted dramatic frescoes of the 'Passion' in the Lower Church of San Francesco. » fresco; Italian art; Sienese School

Lorenzo Monaco (Ital 'Lorenzo the monk'), originally **Piero di Giovanni** (c.1370–c.1425) Italian painter, born at Siena. His pictures, usually on a small scale, are represented in both the Uffizi and Louvre galleries. His major work is the 'Coronation of the Virgin' (1413, Florence). He became a monk in 1391, and lived mainly at a monastery in Florence, where he died. » Italian art; Sienese School

lorikeet » **lory**

loris A primitive primate, native to forests in S and SE Asia; no tail; pale face with dark rings around large eyes; slow climbers; three species: **slender loris** (*Loris tardigradus*) with long thin legs; **slow loris** or **cu lan** (*Nycticebus coucang*), and **lesser slow loris** (*Nycticebus pygmaeus*). (Family: *Lorisidae*.) » prosimian

Lorraine, Claude » **Claude Lorraine**

Lorraine [lorayn], Ger **Lothringen** pop (1982) 2 319 905; area 23 547 sq km/9 089 sq ml. Region and former province of NE France, comprising departments of Meurthe-et-Moselle, Meuse, Moselle, and Vosges; bordered by the Plaine de Champagne (W), Vosges (E), Ardennes (N), and Monts Faucilles (S); frequent source of Franco-German conflict; duchy since the 10th-c; part of France, 1766; ceded to Germany as part of Alsace-Lorraine, 1871; returned to France after World War 1; chief towns, Metz, Nancy, Luneville, Epinal; corn, fruit, cheese; iron ore, coal, salt; mineral springs. » Alsace

Lorraine, Cross of A cross with two horizontal crosspieces. The symbol of Joan of Arc, it was adopted by the free French forces leader (Charles de Gaulle) in 1940. » RR93

lory [lawri] A parrot of the subfamily *Loriinae* (c.60 species), found from SE Asia to Australia; eats mainly pollen and nectar, but also insects and seeds; tongue has brush-like tip. Smaller species are called **lorikeets**. (Family: *Psittacidae*.) » parrot

Los Alamos [los alamos] 35°52N 106°19W, pop (1980) 1 039. Community in Los Alamos County, N New Mexico, USA; 56 km/35 ml NW of Santa Fe in the Jemez Mts; a nuclear research centre since 1943; the first nuclear weapons were developed here during World War 2; government control ended in 1962. » atomic bomb; New Mexico; nuclear weapons

Los Angeles, Victoria de (1923–) Spanish soprano, born in Barcelona. She made her debut in Madrid (1944) and soon achieved international recognition as both a concert and an operatic singer. She is noted particularly for her 19th-c Italian roles and for her performances of Spanish songs. » opera

Los Angeles 34°04N 118°15W, pop (1980) 2 966 850. Seaport capital of Los Angeles County, California, USA; founded by the Spanish, 1781; originally called **Nuestra Señora Reina de Los Angeles**; captured from Mexico by the US Navy, 1846; established, 1850; grew after the arrival of the Southern Pacific Railroad and the discovery of oil nearby in 1894; has absorbed several towns, villages, and independent cities; third largest US city; three airports (Los Angeles, Long Beach, Santa Clara); railway; five universities; harbour on San Pedro Bay, 40 km/25 ml S of city centre; major industrial and research centre; military and civil aircraft, machinery, petroleum products, electronic equipment, glass, chemicals, oil refining, fish canning and distributing; high density of road traffic; smog a major problem; major tourist area; major league teams, Dodgers (baseball), Clippers, Lakers (basketball), Raiders, Rams (football), Kings (ice hockey); district of Hollywood a major centre of the US film and television industry; Los Angeles County Museum of Art; 28-storey City Hall; Old Mission Church (c.1818), now a museum; La Brea Tar Pits; Hollywood Bowl; Hollywood Wax Museum; Universal Film Studios; Disneyland; scene of summer Olympic Games 1984. » California; Disney; Hollywood; smog; Watts Towers

Losey, Joseph (Walton) (1909–84) US film director, born at La Crosse, Wisconsin. He worked first on the stage, and moved to films in 1938 as an editor and writer. His first feature was the pacifist allegory *The Boy with Green Hair* (1945). Blacklisted as a suspected communist by the McCarthy Committee, he came to England in 1952, where he made *The Servant* (1963) and *The Go-Between* (1971), as well as the quite untypical *Modesty Blaise* (1966). From the mid-1970s he worked mostly in France, where his last film was *La Truite* (1982, The Trout). He died in London. » McCarthy, Joseph R

Lossiemouth [loseemowth] 57°43N 3°18W, pop (1981) 6 847. Port town in Moray district, Grampian region, NE Scotland; fishing, tourism; air force base nearby (often involved in air-sea rescue); birthplace of Ramsay Macdonald. » Grampian; Macdonald, Ramsay; Scotland [i]

lost generation A term applied by Gertrude Stein to a group of US expatriates (including herself) living in Paris in the 1920s, among them Ezra Pound, Ernest Hemingway, and Scott Fitzgerald. Their work reflects the breakdown of order and values after World War 1. » American literature; Fitzgerald, Scott; Hemingway; Pound; Stein, Gertrude

Lost World Name given by novelist Arthur Conan Doyle to an imaginary range of mountains where prehistoric animals survived into the 20th-c; based on Col Percy Fawcett's description of the Ricardo Franco Hills in the Mato Grosso state of W Brazil. » Brazil; Doyle

Lot Biblical character, portrayed in *Genesis* as the nephew of Abraham who separated from him and settled in Canaan, near Sodom. Stories describe his rescue from the wickedness of that place by Abraham and two angels. Symbolic of backsliding, Lot's wife is described as looking back during this escape and being turned into 'a pillar of salt'. Lot was named also as the ancestor of the Moabites and Ammonites. » Abraham; Old Testament; Sodom and Gomorrah

Lotharingia Originally, the kingdom of Lothar II (855–69), great-grandson of Charlemagne; subsequently, though disputed with France, two duchies of the kingdom of Germany. Only one, Upper Lotharingia (modern Lorraine), survived the 12th-c, and it was eventually incorporated into France (1766). » Charlemagne

Lothian [lohthian] pop (1981) 738 372; area 1 755 sq km/677 sq ml. Region in E Scotland, divided into four districts; bounded N by the Firth of Forth, NE by the North Sea; Pentland and Moorfoot Hills in the S; Lammermuir Hills in the SW; capital, Edinburgh; major towns include Livingston, Musselburgh, Haddington, Dalkeith, Penicuik; agriculture, tourism, open-cast coal-mining, whisky, engineering. » Edinburgh; Scotland [i]

Loti, Pierre [lohtee], pseudonym of **Louis Marie Julien Viaud** (1850–1923) French novelist, born at Rochefort. He joined the navy, and his voyages provide the scenes for most of his writings. His best-known works are the semi-autobiographical *Rarahu* (1880), and his descriptive study of Breton fisher life, *Pêcheur d'Islande* (1886, Fisherman of Iceland). He died at Hendaye, France. » French literature; novel

Lotophagi » **lotus-eaters**

Lots, Feast of » **Purim**

Lotto, Lorenzo (c.1480–1556) Italian religious painter, born in Venice. He worked in Treviso, Bergamo, Venice, and Rome, and became known for his altarpieces and portraits. In 1554 he became a lay brother in the Loreto monastery, where he died. » altarpiece; Italian art

lotus The name given to three different plants. The sacred lotus of Egypt (*Nymphaea lotus*) is a species of water lily. The sacred lotus of India and China (*Nelumbium nuciferum*), traditionally associated with the Buddha, is also an aquatic plant, but with circular leaves which have the stalks attached in the centre of the blade, and pink and white flowers. The lotus of classical times (*Zizyphus lotus*) is a type of jujube from the Mediterranean region. » jujube; water lily

lotus bird » **jacana**

lotus-eaters or **Lotophagi** [luhtofuhjiy] In Homer and Tennyson, a fabulous people encountered by Odysseus, living on 'a flowery food' which makes those who eat it forget their own country, and wish to live always in a dreamy state. Odysseus had to force his men to move on. » Odysseus

Louangphrabang or **Luang Prabang** 19°53N 102°10E, pop (1984) 44 000. Town in W Laos, on R Mekong, at head of navigation; former capital (1946–75); centre of agricultural region; Buddhist pagodas. » Laos [i]

loudspeaker or **speaker** A device which converts electrical energy into sound waves. The loudspeaker is fed a current having frequencies and amplitudes proportionate to some original sound waves. It reconverts these signals, radiating a new set of sound waves which reproduce at a listener's ears as nearly as possible the acoustic experience of the original performance. The majority of loudspeakers use the electromagnetic principle. An alternating signal current passes through one or more voice coils set in powerful permanent magnetic fields. The alternating magnetic fields which result cause the coils (and the diaphragm or cone to which each one is fixed) to move to and fro in vibration, and it is this mechanical vibration that regenerates the sound waves. » electromagnetism; microphone [i]; sound recording

Louganis, Greg(ory) [**loo**ganis] (1960–) US diver, born at El Cajon, California, of Samoan and Swedish ancestry. In the 1983 world championships, his routine won him more than 700 points for his 11 dives, the first man to achieve such a score. He was Olympic champion (1984, 1988), platform world champion (1978, 1982, 1986), and springboard champion (1982, 1986). » swimming

Louis II (1845–86) King of Bavaria (1864–86), born in Nymphenburg, the son of Maximilian II. A German patriot of romantic disposition, he devoted himself to patronage of Wagner and his music. Siding with Prussia (1870–1) against France, he took Bavaria into the new German Reich. Later he adopted the life of a recluse, and in 1886 was declared insane; shortly after, he drowned himself in the Starnberger L, near his castle of Berg. » Prussia; Reich; Wagner

Louis IX, St (1214–70), feast day 25 August. King of France (1226–70), born at Poissy, near Paris, the son of Louis VIII. By his victories he compelled Henry III of England to acknowledge French suzerainty in Guienne (1259). He led the Seventh Crusade (1248), but was defeated in Egypt, taken prisoner, and ransomed. After returning to France (1254), he carried out several legal reforms, and fostered learning, the arts, and literature. He embarked on a new Crusade in 1270, and died of plague at Tunis. He was canonized in 1297. » Crusades [i]; Henry III (of England)

Louis XII (1462–1515) King of France (1498–1515), born at Blois, the son of Charles, Duke of Orléans, to whose title he succeeded in 1465. He commanded the French troops at Asti during Charles's invasion of Italy (1494–5) before succeeding him to the French throne (1498) and marrying his widow, Anne of Brittany. He proved a popular ruler, concerned to provide justice and avoid oppressive taxation. His Italian ambitions brought him into diplomatic and military involvement with Ferdinand II of Castile (1500–12), who finally outmanoeuvred Louis with the formation of the Holy League (1511). Meanwhile, Louis had foiled the Emperor Maximilian's dynastic designs on Brittany, but paid the price when his forces were driven from Italy (1512) and then defeated by an Anglo-Imperial alliance at the Battle of Guinegate (1513). To guarantee peace, Louis married Mary Tudor, sister of Henry VIII (1514), but died in Paris shortly afterwards. » Ferdinand (of Castile); Holy League; Maximilian I

Louis XIII (1601–43) King of France (1610–43), born at Fontainebleau, the eldest son of Henry IV and Marie de Médici. He succeeded to the throne on the assassination of his father (1610), but was excluded from power, even after he came of age (1614), by the Queen Regent. She arranged Louis's marriage to Anne of Austria, daughter of Philip III of Spain (1615). In 1617 Louis took over the reins of government, and exiled Marie de Médici to Blois (1619–20). By 1624 he was entirely dependent upon the political acumen of Richelieu, who became his Chief Minister. Various plots to oust the Cardinal were foiled by the King's loyalty to his Minister, whose domestic and foreign policies seemed to fulfil the royal ambition for great achievements. Louis's later years were enhanced by French military victories in the Thirty Years' War against the Habsburgs, and by the birth of two sons in 1638 and 1640, including the future Louis XIV. He died at St-Germain-en-Laye. » Huguenots; Richelieu; Thirty Years' War

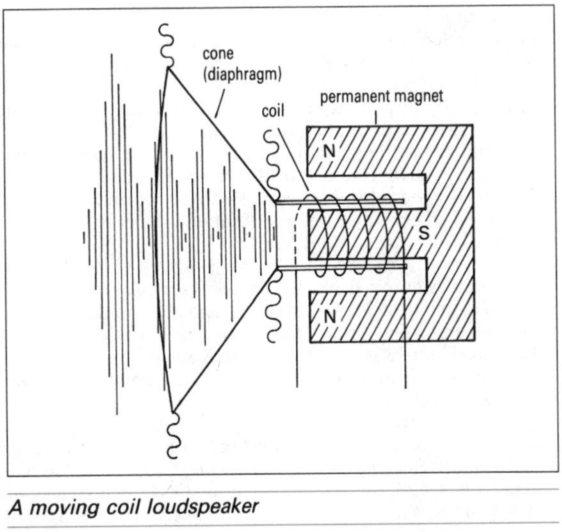

A moving coil loudspeaker

Louis XIV, bynames **Louis the Great** or **The Sun King ('Le Roi Soleil')** (1638–1715) King of France (1643–1715), born at St Germain-en-Laye, the son of Louis XIII, whom he succeeded at the age of five. During his minority (1643–51) France was ruled by his mother, Anne of Austria, and her Chief Minister, Cardinal Mazarin. In 1660 Louis married the Infanta Maria Theresa, elder daughter of Philip IV of Spain, through whom he was later to claim the Spanish succession for his second grandson. In 1661 he assumed sole responsibility for government, advised by various royal councils. His obsession with France's greatness led him into aggressive foreign and commercial policies, particularly against the Dutch. His patronage of the Catholic Stuarts also led to the hostility of England after 1689; but his major political rivals were the Austrian Habsburgs, particularly Leopold I. From 1665 Louis tried to take possession of the Spanish Netherlands, but later became obsessed with the acquisition of the whole Spanish inheritance. His attempt to create a Franco-Spanish Bourbon bloc led to the formation of the Grand Alliance of England, the United Provinces, and the Habsburg Empire, and resulted in the War of the Spanish Succession (1701–13). In his later years Louis was beset by other problems. His determination to preserve the unity of the French state and the independence of the French Church led him into conflict with the Jansenists, the Huguenots, and the papacy, with damaging repercussions. His old age was overshadowed by military disaster and the financial ravages of prolonged warfare. Yet Louis was the greatest monarch of his age, who established the parameters of successful absolutism. In addition, his long reign marked the cultural ascendancy of France within Europe, symbolized by the Palace of Versailles, where he died, to be succeeded by his great-grandson as Louis XV. » absolutism; Augsburg, League of; Bourbons; Colbert, Jean Baptiste; Dutch Wars; Fouquet, Nicolas; Frondes; Leopold I (Emperor); Louvois; Maintenon; Mazarin; Spanish Succession, War of the; Stuarts

Louis XV, byname **Louis le Bien-Aimé** ('Louis the Well-Beloved') (1710–74) King of France (1715–74), born and died at Versailles, the son of Louis, Duc de Bourgogne and Marie-Adelaide of Savoy, and the great-grandson of Louis XIV, whom he succeeded at the age of five. His reign coincided with the great age of decorative art in the Rococo mode (dubbed the Louis XV style). Until he came of age (1723) he was guided by the Regent, Philippe d'Orléans, and then by the Duc de Bourbon, who negotiated a marriage alliance with Maria Leczczynska, daughter of the deposed King Stanislas I of Poland. In 1726 Bourbon was replaced by the King's former tutor, the elderly Fleury, who skilfully steered the French state until his death (1744). Thereafter Louis vowed to rule without a First Minister, but allowed the government to drift into the hands of ministerial factions, while indulging in secret diplomatic activity, distinct from official policy, through his own network of agents. This system – *le secret du roi* – brought confusion to French foreign policy in the years prior to the Diplomatic Revolution (1748–56), and obscured the country's interests overseas. Instead, France was drawn into a trio of continental wars during Louis's reign, which culminated in the loss of the French colonies in America and India (1763). In 1771 Louis tried to introduce reforms, but these came too late to staunch the decline in royal authority. He was succeeded by his grandson, Louis XVI. » Austrian Succession, War of the; Choiseul-Amboise; du Barry; Fleury; Poland, Partitions of; Pompadour; Rococo; Seven Years' War

Louis XVI (1754–93) King of France (1774–93), born at Versailles, the third son of the Dauphin Louis and Maria Josepha of Saxony, and the grandson of Louis XV, whom he succeeded in 1774. He was married in 1770 to the Archduchess Marie Antoinette, daughter of the Habsburg Empress Maria Theresa, to strengthen the Franco-Austrian alliance. He failed to give consistent support to ministers who tried to reform the outmoded financial and social structures of the country, such as Turgot (1774–6) and Necker (1776–81). He allowed France to become involved in the War of American Independence (1778–83), which exacerbated the national debt. Meanwhile, Marie Antoinette's propensity for frivolous conduct and scandal helped to discredit the monarchy. To avert the deepening social and economic crisis, he agreed in 1789 to summon the States General. However, encouraged by the Queen, he resisted demands from the National Assembly for sweeping reforms, and in October was brought with his family from Versailles to Paris as hostages to the revolutionary movement. Their attempted flight to Varennes (Jun 1791) branded the royal pair as traitors. Louis reluctantly approved the new constitution (Sep 1791), but his moral authority had collapsed. In August an insurrection suspended Louis's constitutional position, and in September the monarchy was abolished. He was tried before the National Convention for conspiracy with foreign powers, and was guillotined in Paris. » French Revolution [i]; Marie Antoinette; Necker; Turgot

Louis (Charles) XVII (1785–95) Titular King of France (1793–5), born at Versailles, the second son of Louis XVI and heir to the throne from June 1789. After the execution of his father (Jan 1793) he remained in the Temple prison in Paris. His death there dealt a blow to the hopes of Royalists and constitutional monarchists. The secrecy surrounding his last months led to rumours of his escape, and produced several claimants to his title. » French Revolution [i]

Louis XVIII, also **Louis Stanislas Xavier, Comte de** ('Count of') **Provence** (1755–1824) King of France in name from 1795 and in fact from 1814, born at Versailles, the younger brother of Louis XVI. He fled from Paris in June 1791, finally taking refuge in England, becoming the focal point for the Royalist cause. On Napoleon's downfall (1814) he re-entered Paris, and promised a Constitutional Charter. His restoration was interrupted by Napoleon's return from Elba, but after Waterloo (1815) he again regained his throne. His reign was marked by the introduction of parliamentary government with a limited franchise. He died in Paris. » French Revolution [i]; Napoleon I

Louis, Joe [loois], byname of **Joseph Louis Barrow**, also called **The Brown Bomber** (1914–81) US boxer, born at Lexington, Alabama. He was the US amateur light-heavyweight champion in 1934, and turned professional the same year. He beat James J Braddock (1905–74) for the world heavyweight title in 1937, and held the title for a record 12 years, making a record 25 defences. He retired in 1949, but made a comeback in 1950. He lost the world title fight to Ezzard Charles (1921–75), and had his last fight against Rocky Marciano in 1951. In all, he won 63 of his 66 contests. He died at Las Vegas, Nevada. » boxing [i]; Marciano

Louis Napoleon » **Napoleon III**

Louis period styles A range of classical, Baroque, and Rococo stylistic variations used in the 17th-c and 18th-c, and particularly associated with the reign of Louis XIV of France. They are broadly characterized by lavish and ornate internal decoration and comparatively restrained facades and formal gardens; in the case of the Palais de Versailles (1661–1756), it also involved enormous amounts of labour, materials, and money. » Baroque (art and architecture); classicism; Renaissance architecture; Rococo

Louis Philippe, byname **The Citizen King** (1773–1850) King of the French (1830–48), born in Paris, the eldest son of the Duke of Orléans, Philippe Egalité. At the Revolution he entered the National Guard, and with his father renounced his titles to demonstrate his progressive sympathies. He joined the Jacobin Club (1790), and fought in the Army of the North before deserting to the Austrians (1793). He lived in Switzerland (1793–4), the USA, and England (1800–9), and in 1809 moved to Sicily and married Marie Amélie, daughter of Ferdinand IV of Naples and Sicily. He returned to France in 1814, but fled to England again in the Hundred Days. On the eve of Charles X's abdication (1830) he was elected Lieutenant-General of the kingdom, and after the Revolution was given the title of King of the French. He strengthened his power by steering a middle course with the help of the upper bourgeoisie; but political corruption and industrial and agrarian depression (1846) caused discontent, and united the radicals in a cry for electoral reform. When the Paris mob rose (1848), he abdicated, escaped to England, and died at Claremont, Surrey. » Bourbons; French Revolution [i]; Hundred Days; Jacobins (French history); July Revolution; Revolutions of 1848

Louisiade Archipelago [looeezee**ahd**] pop (1980) 16 496; area 1 553 sq km/599 sq ml. Mountainous island group in Papua New Guinea, SE of New Guinea; comprises the islands of Tacuta, Rossel, and Misima, with numerous other small islands and coral reefs; named in 1768 after Louis XIV of France; gold has been worked on Tacuta. » Papua New Guinea

Louisiana [loozee**an**a] pop (1987e) 4 461 000; area 123 673 sq km/47 752 sq ml. State in S USA, divided into 64 parishes; the 'Pelican State'; name (after Louis XIV of France) originally applied to the entire Mississippi R basin, claimed for France by La Salle, 1682; most of the E region ceded to Spain in 1763, then to the USA in 1783; W region acquired by the USA in the Louisiana Purchase, 1803; admitted to the Union as the 18th state, 1812; seceded from the Union, 1861; re-admitted, 1868; experienced an economic revolution in the early 1900s when large deposits of oil and natural gas were discovered; capital, Baton Rouge; other major cities, New Orleans and Shreveport; bounded S by the Gulf of Mexico; rivers include the Mississippi (large delta area in the S), Red, Sabine, and Pearl; highest point Mt Driskill (162 m/532 ft); vast coastal areas of marsh, lagoon, and fertile delta lands; further inland are plains and low rolling hills; over half the land area forested, supporting a major lumber and paper industry; highly productive in agriculture; soybeans, rice, sugar cane, sweet potatoes, cotton, cattle, dairy products; fishing, particularly for shrimps and oysters; a major source of pelts, especially muskrat; second only to Texas in oil and natural gas production (mainly offshore); oil refineries and petrochemical plants in several cities; leads the nation in salt and sulphur production; foods, clay, glass, transportation equipment; tourism increasing; world famous for the jazz music which grew up in and around New Orleans; special population groups of Creoles (French descent) and Cajuns (descendants of French Acadians driven from Canada by the British in the 18th-c). » Baton Rouge; jazz; La Salle; Louisiana Purchase; New Orleans; United States of America [i]; RR38

Louisiana Purchase (1803) The sale by France to the USA of an area between the Mississippi R and the Rocky Mts for $15 000 000. The purchase gave the USA full control of the Mississippi Valley. » Louisiana

Louisville [**loo**eevil] 38°15N 85°46W, pop (1980) 298 451. Seat of Jefferson County, NW Kentucky, USA; port at the Falls of the Ohio R; settled, 1778; named after Louis XVI of France; city status, 1828; largest city in the state; University of Louisville (1798), the oldest municipal US university; a major horse breeding centre; important shipping point for coal; whiskey, cigarettes, machinery, electrical appliances, fabricated metals, foods; JB Speed Art Museum, Kentucky Railway Museum, Kentucky Derby Museum; Kentucky Derby (May) at Churchill Downs. » Kentucky

Lourdes [loordz] 43°06N 0°00W, pop (1982e) 18 000. Town and important site of Roman Catholic pilgrimage in Hautes-Pyrénées department, S France; Bernadette Soubirous was led by a vision of the Virgin Mary to the springs at the Grotte de Massabielle in 1858; Basilica of the Rosary (1885–9), Church of St-Pie-X (completed, 1958). » Bernadette, St; Mary (mother of Jesus)

lourie » **turaco**

louse A secondarily wingless insect, parasitic on warm-blooded vertebrates. **Sucking lice** (Order: *Anoplura*) suck blood of mammals; length up to 6 mm/¼ in; bodies flattened, legs with claws for attaching to host; eyes reduced or absent; c.300

Lovebird

species. They include two varieties of human louse: **head lice** (*Pediculus humanus capitis*) and **body lice** (*Pediculus humanus humanus*), both transmitted by direct contact; lay eggs (*nits*) on hair and clothing; can transmit typhus and other diseases. **Biting lice** (Order: *Mallophaga*) live mostly on birds, have biting mouthparts for feeding on feathers; c.2 700 species, a few found on mammals, feeding on hair. » booklouse; insect [i]; psyllid

Louth [lowth], Gaelic **Lughbhaidh** pop (1981) 88 514; area 821 sq km/317 sq ml. County in NE Leinster province, Irish Republic; bounded N by N Ireland and E by Irish Sea; capital, Dundalk; cattle, oats, potatoes. » Dundalk; Irish Republic [i]

Loutherbourg, Philip James de [**loo**terboorg] (1740–1812) French scene designer, born at Strasbourg. After working in Paris, he was employed by Garrick at the Drury Lane Theatre (1771–81). His innovations in scene design and particularly in stage lighting laid the foundations for the development of pictorial illusion and the picture-frame concept in stagecraft. He abandoned theatre in 1781 to develop and exhibit his Eidophusikon, a model stage displaying panoramic transformations through the use of transparencies and coloured plates. He died at Chiswick, Greater London. » Garrick; proscenium; theatre

Louvain [loovĩ] » **Leuven**

Louvois, François Michel le Tellier, Marquis de [loov**wah**] (1641–91) French statesman and Secretary of State for War under Louis XIV, born in Paris. He proved an energetic minister in the War of Devolution (1668), reforming and strengthening the army. His work bore fruit in the Dutch War, ending with the Peace of Nijmegen (1678). He was recognized as a brilliant administrator and the King's most influential minister in the years 1683–91. He died at Versailles. » Dutch Wars; Louis XIV; Nantes, Edict of

Louvre [**loo**vruh] The national museum of art in Paris, and one of the finest art collections in the world. Built for Francis I in 1546, the Louvre was added to by successive French monarchs. The Grande Galerie of the Louvre was officially opened to the public in 1793. » Francis I

lovage A strong-smelling perennial growing to 2.5 m/8 ft, native to Iran; leaves divided into large oval coarsely toothed leaflets; flowers small, greenish-yellow, in umbels up to 10 cm/4 in across; fruit ellipsoid with narrowly winged ribs. It is often cultivated and used for flavouring. (*Levisticum officinale*. Family: *Umbelliferae*.) » perennial; umbel

love apple » **tomato**

love-in-a-mist An annual native to Europe and W Asia; finely-divided, feathery leaves and bracts; large, pale blue flowers; a globular, papery capsule. (*Nigella damascena*. Family: *Ranunculaceae*.) » annual; bract

lovebird A small parrot native to Africa and Madagascar; inhabits woodland, brush, and open country; eats seeds and berries; forms large flocks; female sometimes larger than male; a popular cage bird. They preen one another, hence the name, which is also used for the budgerigar. (Genus: *Agapornis*, 9 species. Family: *Psittacidae*.) » budgerigar; parrot

Lovecraft, H(oward) P(hillips) (1890–1937) US short-story writer, born at Providence, Rhode Island, where he spent his life as an invalid. His reputation as a skilful practitioner of the tale of horror is almost entirely posthumous, based on a selection of his stories published as *The Outsider and Others* (1939). » American literature; short story

Lovelace, Richard (1618–57) English Cavalier poet, born (possibly) at Woolwich, near London, and educated at Charterhouse and Oxford. During the Civil War, he was twice imprisoned, and spent his estate in the King's cause. In 1642 he wrote 'To Althea, from Prison' ('Stone walls do not a prison make...'), and in 1649 published his best-known work, *Lucasta*. He died in London. » Cavaliers; English literature; poetry

Lovell, Sir (Alfred Charles) Bernard (1913–) British astronomer, born at Oldham Common, Gloucestershire. Educated at Bristol, he became a lecturer in physics at Manchester (1936), then worked at the Air Ministry on radar during World War 2. In 1951 he became professor of radio astronomy at Manchester, and later director of the Nuffield Radio Astronomy Laboratories at Jodrell Bank. He is distinguished for his pioneering work in radio telescope design, space research, and the physics of radio sources. He was knighted in 1961. » radio astronomy

Low, Sir David (Alexander Cecil) (1891–1963) British political cartoonist, born at Dunedin, New Zealand. He worked for several newspapers in New Zealand and for the *Bulletin* of Sydney, before coming in 1919 to the *Star* in London. In 1927 he joined the staff of the *Evening Standard*, for which he drew some of his most successful cartoons, including the creation of the notable Colonel Blimp. From 1953 he worked with *The (Manchester) Guardian*. Knighted in 1962, he died in London.

Low Countries A term used to refer to the Netherlands and Belgium. It derives its name from the low-lying coastal plain of both countries.

low Earth orbit (LEO) A spacecraft orbit about the Earth typically used for manned missions and for Earth remote-sensing missions; the minimum altitude above the surface is c.200 km/125 ml to minimize drag effects of the Earth's atmosphere. The inclination of orbit is chosen to allow the ground track of the spacecraft to pass over regions of interest; polar inclination orbits are needed for complete global coverage. Typical orbital periods are c.100 min; circular velocity c.7.8 km/4.9 ml per sec. Depending on altitude, the orbit may eventually decay, causing the spacecraft to re-enter Earth's atmosphere and burn up; because of the occasional destruction of spacecraft in LEO there is an increasing accumulation of tiny debris particles there, a new hazard to spacecraft. » escape velocity; geosynchronous Earth orbit; launch vehicle [i]

low-level language A computer language in which each instruction has a single machine-code equivalent, such as assembly language. Programs written in low-level languages can be run only on computers using the same type of processor. » assembly language; high-level language; machine code; processor

lowan » **mallee fowl**

Lowell, Amy (1874–1925) US Imagist poet, born at Brookline, Massachusetts. Privately educated, and a great traveller, she began to write poetry in her late twenties, producing volumes of free verse which she named 'unrhymed cadence' and what she called 'polyphonic prose', as in *Sword Blades and Poppy Seed* (1914). She also wrote several critical volumes, and a biography of Keats. She died at Brookline. » American literature; Imagism; metre (literature); poetry

Lowell, Percival (1855–1916) US astronomer, born in Boston, and educated at Harvard. In 1894 he established the Lowell Observatory at Flagstaff, Arizona. He is somewhat notorious for his observations alleging canals on Mars, and sparked speculation about the existence of Martians; but he correctly predicted the existence of Pluto. He died at Flagstaff. » Mars (astronomy); Pluto (astronomy); Tombaugh

Lowell, Robert (Traill Spence) (1917–77) US poet, born in Boston, Massachusetts. Educated at Harvard University and Kenyon College, Ohio, he published his first volume of poetry, *Land of Unlikeness*, in 1944. His early poems, intricate and symbolic, show a preoccupation with his New England background and his conversion to Catholicism. With *Life Studies* (1959), he began to write poems on painfully autobiographical subjects, giving rise to the style of 'confessional' poetry, also evident in *Notebook* (1969), *History* (1973), and *Day by Day* (1977). He died in New York City. » American literature; confessional poetry; poetry

Lowestoft [**loh**istoft] 52°29N 1°45E, pop (1981) 59 875. Port town and resort in Waveney district, Suffolk, E England; on North Sea, 62 km/38 ml NE of Ipswich; Lowestoft Ness the most E point in England; railway; transport equipment, fishing and fish processing, radar and electrical equipment, yachting, tourism; Royal Naval Patrol Service Memorial. » Suffolk

Lowry, L(aurence) S(tephen) (1887–1976) British artist, born in Manchester, where he trained, while working as a clerk. From the 1920s he produced many pictures of the Lancashire industrial scene, mainly in brilliant whites and greys, peopled with scurrying ant-like men and women. A major retrospective exhibition of his work was held at the Royal Academy in the year of his death. » English art

Lowry, (Clarence) Malcolm (1909–57) British novelist, born at New Brighton, Merseyside. He left school to go to sea and, after an 18-month journey to the East, returned to England, where he was educated at Cambridge. His reputation is based on *Under the Volcano* (1947), a novel set in Mexico, where he lived 1936–7. He also wrote *Ultramarine* (1933), based on his first sea voyage, and several other novels published posthumously, such as *Dark is the Grave Wherein my Friend is Laid* (1968). He spent most of his writing years in British Columbia, Canada, but died in England, where he lived from 1954. » English literature; novel

Loyalists Refugees from the 13 British American colonies who fled to Britain, New Brunswick, Nova Scotia, Prince Edward Island, and Canada as a result of the American War of Independence. Some 45 000 settled in British North America, including White farmers, pro-British Iroquois, and Black ex-slaves. » American Revolution

Loyalty Islands, Fr **Iles Loyauté** pop (1976) 14 518; area 1 981 sq km/765 sq ml. Group of coral islands in the SW Pacific Ocean, 128 km/79 ml E of New Caledonia, comprising Ouvéa, Lifu, Mare, Tiga, and many small islets; dependency of the Territory of New Caledonia; capital, We (Lifu I); coconuts, sandalwood, copra. » New Caledonia

Loyola, Ignatius de [loy**oh**la], originally **Iñigo López de Recalde** (1491 or 1495–1556), feast day 31 July. Spanish theologian and founder of the Jesuits, born at his ancestral castle of Loyola in the Basque province of Guipúzcoa. He became a soldier, was wounded, and while convalescing read the lives of Christ and the saints. In 1522 he went on a pilgrimage to Jerusalem, studied in Alcalá, Salamanca, and Paris, and in 1534 founded with six associates the Society of Jesus. Ordained in 1537, he went to Rome in 1539, where the new order was approved by the Pope. The author of the influential *Spiritual Exercises*, he died in Rome, and was canonized in 1622. » Francis Xavier, St; Jesuits; missions, Christian

Lozi [**loh**zee] or **Barotse** A cluster of Bantu-speaking agricultural and cattle-herding people of W Zambia, formerly Barotseland, living in the floodplain of the upper Zambezi. During the colonial period, they were controlled by indirect rule, so that their kingship and distinctive institutions survived. Population c.325 000. » African history; Bantu-speaking peoples; indirect rule; Zambia [i]

LSD or **lysergic acid diethylamide** A hallucinogen which was a popular drug of abuse in the 1960s and early 1970s, taken as 'microdots' and known as 'California sunshine', 'white lightning', 'purple haze', or simply 'acid'. In 1943 the Swiss chemist Albert Hoffmann (1906–) discovered its powerful effect after taking a dose in the course of his work for the Sandoz drug company. At one time LSD was recommended by some psychologists for use during psychotherapy. The cult of LSD-taking was promoted by Dr Timothy Leary (1920–), who was dismissed from his post as clinical psychologist at Harvard in 1963. » hallucinogens; psychotherapy

Lu Xun or **Lu Hsün** [loo **shoon**] (1881–1936) Chinese writer, born at Shao-hsing, Chekiang. In 1913 he became professor of Chinese literature at Beijing (Peking), and later held posts at Amoy and Canton. His career as an author began with a short story, *Diary of a Madman* (1918), which was an immediate success, as was his 1921 book, *The True Story of Ah Q*. He also wrote critical essays and translations. Now regarded as a revolutionary hero, he died in Shanghai. » Chinese literature

Luanda [**lwan**da], formerly also **Loanda**, Port **São Paulo de Loanda** 8°50S 13°15E, pop (1982e) 700 000. Seaport capital of Angola, on Bay of Bengo, SW Africa; on the R Cuanza estuary 530 km/329 ml SSW of Kinshasa, Zaire; founded in 1575, the centre of Portuguese administration from 1627; a major slave trading centre with Brazil in 17th–18th-c; university (1962); airport; railway; oil refining, export of minerals and agricultural produce; cathedral, governor's palace, São Miguel fortress. » Angola [i]

Luang Prabang » **Louangphrabang**

Luba-Lunda Kingdoms A succession of African states occupying territory in what is now Zaire. They were powerful by the 17th-c, involved in slave and ivory trading with the Portuguese and later with Zanzibar. The Luba states were relatively unstable, but the Lunda Empire seems to have consolidated its power through trade. The central Lunda state did not survive the ending of the Angolan slave trade in the 1840s, and the others fell to European imperialism. » African history; slave trade; Zaire [i]

Lubbock, Sir John, 1st Baron Avebury (1834–1913) British archaeologist, biologist, and politician, born in London. He became an MP in 1870, and initiated over a dozen Acts of Parliament, including Bank Holidays ('St Lubbock's Days') in 1871. In science his work was on human prehistory in Europe, and also on social insects, where he devised new methods of study. He died at Kingsgate Castle, Kent. » entomology

Lübeck 53°52N 10°40E, pop (1983) 216 100. Commercial and manufacturing seaport in E Schleswig-Holstein province, Germany; on R Trave, 56 km/35 ml NE of Hamburg; major city in the Hanseatic League; railway; important Baltic port; machinery, aeronautical and space equipment, steel, ironwork, tiles, foodstuffs, fish canning, shipbuilding; birthplace of Thomas Mann; Holstentor (1477), town hall (13th–15th-c), St Mary's Church (13th–14th-c), Holy Ghost hospital (13th-c), cathedral (1173); noted for its red wine trade and its marzipan; the Hanseatic City is a world heritage site. » Germany [i]; Hanseatic League; Mann

Lubitsch, Ernst (1892–1947) German film director, born in Berlin. In Hollywood from 1923, he established himself as the creator of witty sophisticated light comedies in a unique style. The availability of sound gave rein to the full development of 'the Lubitsch touch' throughout the 1930s, from *The Love Parade* (1929) to *Ninotchka* (1939). He received a Special Academy Award in 1947 for his contributions over 25 years. He died in Hollywood shortly after.

Lublin [**lub**yeen] 51°18N 22°31E, pop (1983) 320 200. Capital of Lublin voivodship, E Poland, on a plateau crossed by the R Bystrzyca; a castle town, gaining urban status in 1317; Poland's first Council of Workers' Delegates formed here, 1918; railway; university (1918); food processing, lorries, agricultural machinery; castle, Kraków Gate, cathedral (16th-c), St Brigittine's convent, Bernardine monastery. » Lublin, Union of; Poland [i]

Lublin, Union of [**lub**yeen] (1569) An Act uniting Poland and the Grand Duchy of Lithuania. The Union, separately confirmed by the Polish and Lithuanian assemblies (*sejms*), completed the formal unification of the two states begun in the 14th-c. It established a common political system and currency, and a Commonwealth headed by a king jointly elected by the Polish and Lithuanian aristocracy. » Jagiellions; Lublin

lubricant A substance used to reduce friction between two surfaces moving in contact with each other. It is most often a liquid, such as a mineral or vegetable oil, but it can be a solid, such as a wax and, importantly, graphite. Some conditions call for special lubricants; for example, molybdenum sulphite is useful at high temperatures. Gases (eg air, helium) can be used, the gas being pumped into the bearing to maintain sufficient pressure between the faces. » graphite; wax

Lubumbashi [lubum**ba**shee], formerly **Elisabethville** (to 1966) 11°40S 27°28E, pop (1976e) 451 332. Capital of Shaba region,

SE Zaire; on R Lualaba, close to the Zambian frontier; founded, 1910; airport; railway; university (1955); copper mining and smelting, food processing; cathedral. » Zaire [i]

Lucas van Leyden, or **Lucas Jacobsz** (1494–1533) Dutch painter and engraver, born at Leyden. He practised almost every branch of painting, and as an engraver ranks but little below Dürer, by whom he was much influenced. His masterpiece is the triptych, 'The Last Judgment' (1526, Leyden). He died at Leyden. » Dutch art; engraving

Luce, Henry R(obinson) (1898–1967) US magazine publisher and editor, born in Shandong province, China, to a missionary family. Educated at Yale, he co-founded and edited *Time* (1923), which aimed to present news in narrative style. Later he founded *Fortune* (1930), *Life* (1936), *Sports Illustrated* (1954), and in the 1930s inaugurated the radio programme 'March of Time', which became cinema newsreels in 1935. He died at Phoenix, Arizona.

lucerne A bushy perennial growing to 90 cm/3 ft; leaves with three leaflets, broadest and toothed towards the tip; pea-flowers purple or blue, in dense spike-like inflorescences; fruit a spiral pod with 1½–3 coils; also called **alfalfa**. Its origin is unknown, but it is now an important forage crop, widely introduced in temperate regions. (*Medicago sativa*, subspecies *sativa*. Family: *Leguminosae*.) » inflorescence [i]; perennial

Lucerne [loo**sern**], Ger **Luzern** 47°03N 8°18E, pop (1980) 63 278. Resort capital of Lucerne canton, C Switzerland, on W shore of L Lucerne, 40 km/25 ml SSW of Zürich; developed as a trade centre on the St Gotthard route; railway junction; lake steamers; engineering, tourism; Lion Monument, painted footbridge (16th-c), cathedral (17th-c), town hall (17th-c); Lucerne Music Festival (Aug), folk festivals, winter carnival. » Switzerland [i]

Lucerne, Lake, Ger **Vierwaldstätter See** area 114 sq km/44 sq ml. Irregular and indented lake in C Switzerland; fourth largest of the Swiss lakes; length 38 km/24 ml; maximum depth 214 m/702 ft; main arm runs E and SE from Lucerne, then S in a narrower arm, the Urner See; associated with the origins of the Swiss Confederation and the legend of William Tell; resorts on its shores include Weggis, Gersau, Brunnen, Vitznau. » Lucerne; Switzerland [i]; Tell, William

Lucian (c.117–180) Greek rhetorician, born at Samosata, Syria. He practised as an advocate in Antioch, travelling widely in Asia Minor, Greece, Italy, and Gaul. He then settled in Athens, where he devoted himself to philosophy, and produced a new form of literature – humorous dialogue. His satires include *Dialogues of the Gods* and *Dialogues of the Dead*. In his later years, he spent some time attached to the court in Alexandria, then returned to Athens, where he died. » Greek literature; rhetoric; satire

Lucifer » **Devil**

Lucknow [**luhk**now] 26°50N 81°00E, pop (1981) 1 007 000. Capital of Uttar Pradesh, NC India; 410 km/255 ml SE of New Delhi, on R Gomati; capital of the Kingdom of Oudh, 1775–1856; capital of the United Provinces, 1877; British garrison besieged for five months during the Indian Mutiny (1857); focal point of the movement for an independent Pakistan; airfield; railway; university (1921); paper, chemicals, railway engineering, carpets, electrical products; Imamabara Mausoleum (1784), British Residency (1800), palaces, royal tombs. » Indian Mutiny; Uttar Pradesh

Lucretia [loo**kree**sha] or **Lucrece** According to Roman legend, the wife of Collatinus. She was raped by Sextus, son of Tarquinius Superbus; after telling her story, she committed suicide. The incident led to the expulsion of the Tarquins from Rome. » Roman history [i]; Tarquinius Superbus

Lucretius, in full **Titus Lucretius Carus** (1st-c BC) Latin poet and philosopher. His major work is the 6-volume hexameter poem *De rerum natura* (On the Nature of Things). Little is known about his life; one story, found in St Jerome, recounts that a love potion drove him insane, and that he committed suicide. » Latin literature; poetry

Lucullus, Lucius Licinius (c.110–57 BC) Roman politician and general, famous for his victories over Mithridates VI, and also for his enormous wealth, luxurious lifestyle, and patronage of the arts. He is believed to have introduced the cherry to Italy from Asia Minor, the scene of his greatest military triumphs and administrative reforms. » Mithridates VI Eupator; Pompey

Lud According to Geoffrey of Monmouth, a legendary King of Britain who first walled the principal city, from that time called Kaerlud after him, and eventually London. He is buried near Ludgate, which preserves his name.

Luddites The name given to the group of workers who in 1811–12 destroyed newly-introduced textile machinery in Nottingham, Yorkshire, and Lancashire. Their fear was that the output of the equipment was so much faster than the output of a hand-loom operator that many jobs would be lost. Known as 'the Luds', after their leader, Ned Ludd, the movement ended with a mass trial in York in 1813; many were hanged or transported to Australia. The term has since been used to describe any resistance to technological innovation.

Ludendorff, Erich von (1865–1937) German general, born near Posen. He became Chief-of-Staff under Hindenburg, defeated the Russians at Tannenberg (1914), and conducted the 1918 offensives on the Western front. In 1923 he was a leader in the unsuccessful Hitler putsch at Munich, but was acquitted of treason. He became a Nazi, but from 1925 led a minority party of his own. He died in Munich. » Hindenburg, Paul von; Nazi Party; World War 1

Luderitz [**lü**duhrits], formerly **Angra Pequena** 26°38S 15°10E, pop (1978) 6 460. Seaport in SW Namibia, on Luderitz Bay, an inlet of the Atlantic Ocean; Diaz landed here in 1486; first German settlement in SW Africa, 1883; taken by South African forces during World War 1; railway; fishing. » Diaz, Bartolomeu; Namibia [i]

Ludlow 52°22N 2°43W, pop (1981) 8 130. Historic market town in Shropshire, WC England; on R Teme, 38 km/24 ml S of Shrewsbury; developed in the 12th-c around a Norman fortress; clothing, agricultural machinery, precision engineering; 11th-c Ludlow Castle, 12th–14th-c Church of St Lawrence, Reader's House. » Shropshire

Ludwig, Karl Francis Wilhelm (1816–95) German physiologist, born at Witzenhausen. As professor (mainly at Leipzig) he did much to create modern physiology, devising methods which did much to illuminate respiration, the function of the blood, and the action of the kidneys and heart. By his death, in Leipzig, almost every leading physiologist had studied with him. » blood; physiology; respiration

Ludwigshafen or **Ludwigshafen am Rhein** [**lud**vikshahvn am riyn] 49°29N 8°27E, pop (1983) 157 400. Commercial and manufacturing river port in E Rheinland-Pfalz province, Germany; on W bank of the R Rhine, opposite Mannheim; railway; chemicals, resins, plastics, dyestuffs, pharmaceuticals, fertilizers, consumer goods. » Germany [i]

Luftwaffe The correct name for the German Air Force, re-established in 1935 under Göring, in contravention of the Treaty of Versailles. Dominant in the years of German victory in World War 2, the Luftwaffe had all but ceased to exist by 1945, having lost some 100 000 aircraft. The Federal Republic of Germany's air force, also known as the Luftwaffe, was re-established in 1956, and today is a critical element in NATO, operating over 600 combat aircraft. » air force; Britain, Battle of; Göring; NATO; V-1

Lug [lookh], **Lugh**, or **Lugus** In Irish mythology, the god of the Sun, the divine leader of the Tuatha De Danann, who led his people to victory over the Formorians. » Tuatha De Danann

Lugano [loo**gah**noh] 46°01N 8°57E, pop (1980) 27 815. Resort town in Ticino canton, S Switzerland, on N shore of L Lugano (area 49 sq km/19 sq ml); on N–S road and rail route over the St Gotthard Pass; third largest financial centre in Switzerland; clothing, engineering, tourism; town hall (1844), Cathedral of St Lawrence (13th-c). » Switzerland [i]

lugeing Travelling across ice on a toboggan sled, usually made of wood with metal runners. The rider sits upright or lies back, as opposed to lying on the stomach in tobogganing. In competitive lugeing, competitors race against the clock on a predetermined run of at least 1 000 m/1 094 yd. The luge is approximately 1.5 m/5 ft in length, and is steered by the feet and a hand rope. Competitions are held for single- and two-seater luges. » bobsledding

Lugo [**loo**goh], Lat **Lucus Augusti** 43°02N 7°35W, pop(1981) 73 986. Capital of Lugo province, Galicia, NW Spain; on R Minho, 511 km/317 ml NW of Madrid; bishopric; railway; electrical equipment, leather, trade in cattle, cheese; hot springs nearby; town walls, cathedral (12th-c); Fiestas of St Froilan (Oct). » Galicia; Spain

lugworm A large annelid worm that burrows in soft inshore or estuarine sediments; feeds on deposited organic matter; breathes using external gills along body; widely used as fishing bait. (Class: *Polychaeta*. Order: *Capitellida*.) » annelid

Luhya [**loo**ya] A cluster of small groups of Bantu-speaking agricultural and trading people of SW Kenya. Each group is traditionally autonomous, forming a national group only during the 1940s in order to be more effective politically. Many now work in the cities. Population c.1.9 million. » Bantu-speaking peoples; Kenya [i]

Luik [loyk] » **Liège**

Lukács, Georg or **György** [**loo**kach] (1885-1971) Hungarian Marxist philosopher and critic, born and died in Budapest. He took a degree in jurisprudence at Budapest (1906), then studied at Berlin and Heidelberg. He became a member of the Hungarian Communist Party in 1918, spent several years in Vienna (1919–29) and Moscow (1933–45), then returned to Budapest to a chair of aesthetics. He was a major figure in the articulation of the Marxist theory of literature and socialist realism, especially through his work on the novel, as in *Die Theorie des Romans* (1920, The Theory of the Novel). » literary criticism; socialist realism

Luke, St (1st-c), feast day 18 October. New Testament evangelist, a Gentile Christian, perhaps 'the beloved physician' and companion of St Paul (*Col* 4.14, *Phil* 24), but this is disputed. Church tradition made him a native of Antioch in Syria, and a martyr. He is first named as author of the third Gospel in the 2nd-c, and tradition has ever since ascribed to him both that work and the Acts of the Apostles. » Acts of the Apostles; Luke, Gospel according to; Paul, St

Luke, Gospel according to New Testament writing, one of the four canonical Gospels, and the first part of a two-fold narrative that includes the Book of Acts. It is anonymous, but traditionally considered the work of 'Luke', a Gentile convert, physician, and friend of Paul. The Gospel is noteworthy for its stories of the births of Jesus and John the Baptist (*Luke* 1–2), Jesus' promises to the poor and oppressed, the extensive so-called 'travel narrative' (*Luke* 9–19) containing many popular parables and sayings, and its special accounts of Jesus' passion and resurrection. » Acts of the Apostles; Gospels, canonical; Luke, St; New Testament

Lull, Ramón » **Llull, Ramón**

Lully, Jean Baptiste [**loo**lee], originally **Giovanni Battista Lulli** (1632–87) French composer, born at Florence. He came as a boy to Paris, and was finally, after much ambitious intriguing, made operatic director by Louis XIV (1672). He composed many operas, in which he made the ballet an essential part, and also wrote church music, dance music, and pastorals. He died in Paris.

Lully, Raymond » **Llull, Ramón**

Luluabourg » **Kananga**

lumbago An imprecise term used to indicate pain or discomfort in the back over the lumbar region, without identifying or defining a specific cause. » vertebral column

lumbar puncture The introduction of a needle between the vertebrae in the lower back (the *lumbar* region) into the narrow space lying between the inner two layers of membranes surrounding the spinal cord and its nerve roots. Its purpose is to obtain a sample of cerebrospinal fluid for examination in the diagnosis of infections (eg meningitis) or of bleeding (eg subarachnoid haemorrhage). » cerebrospinal fluid; vertebral column

Lumbini [luhm**bee**nee] Town and centre of pilgrimage in the W Terai of Nepal, 431 km/268 ml SW of Kathmandu; the birthplace of Buddha; preserved here are the broken Ashokan Pillar, the remains of a monastery, and images of Maya Devi (Buddha's mother); the town is being developed with the help of international aid. » Buddha; Nepal [i]

lumen [**loo**min] SI unit of luminous flux; symbol lm; defined as the luminous flux emitted from a light source of intensity one candela into a solid angle of one steradian. » photometry [i]; units (scientific); RR70

Lumière, Auguste (Marie Louis) [lüm**yair**] (1862–1954) French inventor of photographic equipment, along with his brother, **Louis Jean** (1864–1948), both born at Besançon. In 1893 they developed a cine camera, the *cinématographe*, and showed the first motion pictures using film projection in 1895. They also invented the Autochrome screen plate for colour photography in 1903. They died at Lyon and Bandol, respectively. » cinematography [i]; colour photography

luminaires Artificial light sources used in photography and video. Flood lights give general illumination over a wide area; directional **spot** lights can be adjusted from an intense narrow beam, 'full spot', to a wider 'flood' setting. Hinged flaps, termed 'barndoors', are used to limit the illuminated area.

luminance The component of a video signal which determines the brightness of an image point. It contrasts with *chrominance*, which specifies its colour. » luminous intensity; television

luminescence The emission of light from a substance for reasons other than heating, classified according to energy source. **Photoluminescence** corresponds to a bombardment with light, exploited in zinc sulphide-based paints, which continue to glow after the external light source is removed. **Bioluminescence** is observed in fireflies and glow worms, resulting from chemical reactions. Energy is absorbed by atoms of the substance, raising the electrons to an excited state. After a short time, the electrons return to an unexcited state, giving off light. Solids which luminesce are called *phosphors*. » bioluminescence; energy level; fluorescence; light; phosphorescence

Luminism In art, a term formerly applied to the brilliant, high-key effects of light found in the work of painters such as the Impressionists. Since the 1960s, however, the term has been used for moving patterns of light projected mechanically to create 'light spectacles'. Light has in fact been used as an artistic medium since the 18th-c; a 'colour organ' linked to music was demonstrated in 1734. » Impressionism (art)

luminosity The intrinsic or absolute amount of energy radiated per second from a celestial object. Luminosity is related to the surface area and surface temperature of a star; two stars with the same surface temperatures but different luminosities must differ in size. Stars vary greatly in their observed luminosities, from one million times more to one thousand million times less than the Sun. In astronomy, luminosity is measured in *magnitudes*. » magnitude; star; RR5

luminous flux The total flow of visible light available for illumination from some source, taking into account the source's ability to generate visible light; symbol Φ, unit lm (lumen). Luminous flux from a 60 watt incandescent bulb is about 600 lm, and considerably more from a 60 watt fluorescent tube. » light; photometry [i]

luminous intensity The flow of visible light capable of causing illumination, emitted from a source per unit solid angle; symbol I, unit cd (candela). It takes account of the fact that although two sources may produce the same total light output, one may produce a single strong beam. It is independent of distance from source. A related quantity is **luminance**, formerly called **brightness**, symbol L, units cd/m^2, the luminous intensity per square metre. The luminance of a clear blue sky is approximately 4000 cd/m^2. » light; photometry [i]

lumpsucker Heavy-bodied fish widespread in the N Atlantic and Arctic Oceans; length up to 60 cm/2 ft; body rounded, bearing rows of spiny plates and with a large underside sucker; feeds on a variety of invertebrates and small fish; marketed commercially, salted or smoked, in some areas. (*Cyclopterus lumpus*. Family: *Cyclopteridae*.)

Lumumba, Patrice (Hemery) [lu**mum**ba] (1925–61) Congolese statesman and Prime Minister (1960–1), born at Katako Kombe. He became the leader of the Congolese national movement, and Premier when the Congo became an independent republic in 1960 (now Zaire). Almost immediately the country was plunged into chaos by warring factions; he was deposed after four months, and soon after assassinated, at Katanga. » Congo [i]

Luna programme A highly successful evolutionary series of

Soviet lunar missions carried out between 1959 and 1976. Luna 2 (1959) was the first spacecraft to impact the Moon; Luna 3 (1959) acquired the first pictures of the lunar farside; Luna 9 (1966) achieved the first soft landing, and returned the first TV pictures from the surface; Luna 10 (1966) achieved the first lunar orbit; Luna 16 (1970) achieved the first automated lunar soil sample return to Earth (repeated by Luna 20 (1972) and Luna 24 (1976)); and Luna 17 (1970) deployed the first automated surface rover – Lunakhod 1 (repeated by Luna 20, which deployed Lunakhod 2). » Moon; Soviet space programme

Lunar Orbiter programme A series of US spacecraft, managed by NASA's Langley Research Center, used to survey the Moon at high resolution from a lunar orbit, prior to the crewed Apollo landings. Launched 1966–7, and equipped only with cameras, it provided the database for a selection of Apollo landing sites. Lunar Orbiters 1 to 5 were all successful, providing the principal source of lunar geological mapping coverage for science analysis until at least the mid-1990s, when the next phase of lunar exploration may begin. Precision tracking mapped the lunar gravity field, discovering mass concentrations ('mascons') under the lunar seas. » Apollo programme; NASA; Moon

Lund 55°42N 13°10E, pop (1982) 79 791. Ancient city in Malmöhus county, SW Sweden, NE of Malmö; intermittently under Danish rule prior to 1658; bishopric; university (1666); technical institute (1961); railway; paper, textiles, furniture, printing, publishing, sugar; cathedral (1080). » Sweden [i]

Lunda » **Luba-Lunda Kingdoms**

Lundy Island Island in the Bristol Channel, off the NW coast of Devon, SW England; 19 km/12 ml NNW of Hartland Point; noted for its interesting flora and birdlife; two lighthouses; area 9.6 sq km/3.7 sq ml; National Trust area, since 1969. » Bristol Channel

lune In mathematics, a crescent-shaped region bounded by circular arcs. The notion is often associated with the Greek mathematician Hippocrates of Chios (5th-c BC), who proved that the sum of the areas of the lunes on the two shorter sides of a right-angled triangle is equal to the area of the triangle. » geometry; quadrature

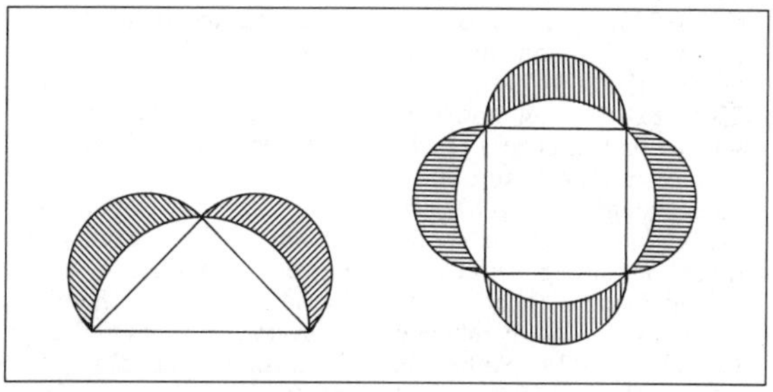

Lunes of a circle

Lüneburger Heide ('Luneburg Heath') [lünuhberguh hiyduh] A region of moorland and forest lying between the R Aller and R Elbe in W Germany, where Field Marshal Montgomery accepted the capitulation of the German Army (4 May 1945). » Montgomery, Bernard Law

lungfish Any of a small group of freshwater fishes, the only living representatives of an order that flourished from the Devonian to Triassic periods; has a pair of lungs on the underside of the gut and connected to the oesophagus, as in higher vertebrates; gills much reduced; includes the African lungfish (family: *Protopteridae*), Australian lungfish (family: *Ceratodontidae*), and S American lungfish (family: *Lepidosirenidae*). » Devonian/Triassic periods; lungs

lungs The organs of respiration, where the exchange of oxygen and carbon dioxide between the blood and air takes place. They are present in terrestrial vertebrates (reptiles, birds, mammals) and some fish (eg lungfish). In humans the paired lungs lie free within the *pleural cavities* of the thorax, except for the attachment by their roots to the trachea and the heart by the bronchi and blood vessels respectively. Each lung is highly elastic, and appears mottled dark grey because of the accumulation of atmospheric particles (in the newborn they are pink). Each is covered by a thin, moist membrane which secretes a watery fluid (*surfactant*) that facilitates movement during breathing. The lungs are divided into a number of lobes, each of which is further subdivided; each lobe receives a *bronchus* (*bronchiole* when the lobules become small) and blood vessels (a branch of the pulmonary artery, a tributary of the pulmonary vein). The subdivisions continue until the respiratory bronchioles divide into a cluster of *alveoli* (thin-walled air-filled spaces surrounded by a capillary bed) where gaseous exchange occurs. At rest, the volume of air passing in and out of the lungs at each breath is about 500 ml: this can increase eightfold during extreme exertion. » asphyxia; emphysema; empyema; heart [i]; pleurisy; pneumoconiosis; pneumonia; pneumothorax; respiration; trachea; tuberculosis; Plate XII

lungwort A perennial growing to 30 cm/12 in, with creeping rhizome, native to Europe; leaves broadly oval, often spotted with white; flowers 1 cm/0.4 in diameter, tubular or funnel-shaped, pink or reddish, changing to blue with age. (*Pulmonaria officinalis*. Family: *Boraginaceae*.) » perennial; rhizome

Luo A Nilotic-speaking people of W Kenya. Unlike most other Nilotes, who are traditionally pastoralists, the Luo are mainly farmers and fishermen, but many are employed as migrant labourers throughout E Africa. They are the second largest ethnic group in Kenya, and politically a significant opposition to the ruling party. Population c.2.2 million. » Kenya [i]; Nilotes

Luoyang [loh**yang**] or **Honan** 34°47N 112°26E, pop (1984e) 1 023 900. Town in Henan province, NC China; capital of ancient China during the E Zhou dynasty (770–256 BC); railway; trade in wheat, sorghum, corn, sesame, peanuts, cotton; mining equipment, glass, construction equipment, light engineering; Wangcheng (Royal Town) Park, Luoyang museum; 8 km/5 ml NE, Baimasi (White Horse) Temple (founded AD 75); 14 km/9 ml S, Longmen Caves, with c.100 000 images and statues of Buddha (5th–7th-c). » Buddhism; China [i]

Lupercalia [looper**kay**lia] An ancient festival of purification and fertility. It was held every year in ancient Rome (on 15 Feb) at a cave on the Palatine Hill called the Lupercal.

lupin A large group of annual and perennial herbs or (less commonly) shrubs, native to America and the Mediterranean region; leaves palmately divided with up to 15 narrow leaflets; pea-flowers in long, terminal, often showy spikes, blue, pink, yellow, or white; pods splitting open explosively to release the seeds. Several species are grown for fodder and green manure. Highly prized as ornamentals, garden plants are usually of hybrid origin. Particularly popular are **Russell** hybrids, which come in a wide range of colours, but are often short-lived. (Genus: *Lupinus*, 200 species. Family: *Leguminosae*.) » annual; herb; palmate; perennial; shrub

Lupus [**loo**puhs] (Lat 'wolf') A small S constellation with bright stars and naked-eye doubles. » constellation; RR9

lupus erythematosus » **systematic lupus erythematosus**

lupus vulgaris [**loo**puhs vuhl**gah**ris] Tuberculosis of the skin, now rare in countries in which pulmonary tuberculosis is well-controlled. It causes ulceration and scarring of the skin of the face or neck, and when untreated results in great disfigurement. » tuberculosis

lurcher A cross-bred dog formerly kept by poachers for catching rabbits and hares; usually a cross between a greyhound and a collie. » collie; dog; greyhound

Lusaka [loo**sa**ka] 15°26S 28°20E, pop (1980) 538 469. Capital of Zambia; replaced Livingstone as capital of former N Rhodesia, 1935; capital of Zambia, 1964; airport; railway; university (1965); banking, administration, agricultural trade, cement, chemicals, insecticides, clothing, metal and plastic products; cathedral (1957), geological survey museum, national archives, Munda Wanga Gardens, zoo. » Zambia [i]

Lusitania [loosi**tay**nia] A Cunard passenger liner of 31 000 tons gross, sunk in the Irish Sea in 1915 by a German U-boat with great loss of life. Her sinking caused worldwide anger. The

Germans claimed she was carrying armaments, but this was officially denied by the British.

lute A European musical instrument, descended from the Arabian ʿud, in use from the Middle Ages to the 18th-c, and revived in modern times for performing early music. It had a large pear-shaped body, a flat soundboard, a wide neck and fingerboard with gut frets, and a pegbox set at a 90° angle to the neck. By the 16th-c there were normally six courses of 'stopped' strings (ie fingered by the left hand to produce different pitches); lower 'open' (ie unstopped) strings were later added. Players plucked the strings with their right hand. » chitarrone; pipa; shamisen; sitar; string instrument 2 [i]; tablature; theorbo; ʿud

luteinizing hormone (LH) [**lyoo**tiniyzing] A chemical substance (a glycoprotein gonadotrophin) secreted by the front lobe of the pituitary gland in vertebrates. In female mammals it is involved in the final maturation of ovarian follicles, the start of ovulation, and the initial formation of the *corpus luteum*. In males, it stimulates the interstitial cells of the testes to secrete testosterone: accordingly, it is also known in males as *interstitial cell-stimulating hormone* (ICSH). » follicle-stimulating hormone; gonadotrophin; pituitary gland

Luther, Martin (1483–1546) German religious reformer, born at Eisleben. He spent three years in an Augustinian monastery, obtained his degree at Erfurt, and was ordained in 1507. His career as a reformer began after a visit to Rome in 1510–11, where he was angered by the sale of indulgences. In 1517 he drew up 95 theses on indulgences, which he nailed on the church door at Wittenberg. Violent controversy followed, and he was summoned to Rome to defend his theses, but did not go. He then began to attack the papal system more boldly, and publicly burned the papal bull issued against him. An order was issued for the destruction of his books; he was summoned to appear before the Diet at Worms, and was put under the ban of the Empire. In 1525 he married a former nun, Katharina von Bora. The drawing up of the Augsburg Confession, where he was represented by Melanchthon, marks the culmination of the German Reformation (1530). He died at Eisleben, and was buried at Wittenberg. His translation of the Bible became a landmark of German literature. » Augsburg Confession; bull; Eucharist; indulgences; Lutheranism; Melanchthon; Reformation

Lutheranism Churches derived from the Reformation of Martin Luther, and the doctrine which they share. Lutheran Churches originally flourished in Germany and Scandinavia, then in other parts of Europe; later, through immigration from Europe, in the USA, and through missionary activity in Africa and Asia. The doctrine is based on the Augsburg Confession (1530), the Apology (1531), Luther's two Catechisms, and the Formula of Concord (1577). It emphasizes justification by faith alone, the importance of scripture, and the priesthood of all believers. Three sacraments are recognized: baptism, Eucharist, and penance. The Lutheran World Federation, a free association of Lutheran Churches, was founded in 1947, and is the largest of the Protestant confessional families. » Augsburg Confession; Luther; Protestantism; sacrament

Luthuli, Albert » **Lutuli, Albert**

Lutine Bell [**loo**teen] A bell formerly rung at Lloyd's of London insurer's offices to announce the loss of a ship or other news of great importance to the underwriters. With regard to overdue vessels, it was rung once for bad news and twice for good news. The bell belonged to a vessel (HMS *Lutine*) carrying gold bullion which foundered off the Dutch coast in 1799; the loss of the gold fell upon the underwriters. Nowadays it is rung mainly on ceremonial occasions. » insurance; Lloyd's

Luton [**loo**tn] 51°53N 0°25W, pop (1987e) 165 300. Industrial town in Bedfordshire, SC England; 45 km/28 ml NW of London; railway; airport; engineering, clothing, hats, motor vehicles; 13th–15th-c Church of St Mary; Luton Hoo (3 km/1¾ ml S), within a park laid out by Capability Brown. » Bedfordshire; Brown, Lancelot

Lutosławski, Witold [lootuh**slav**skee] (1913–) Polish composer, born in Warsaw, where he studied music at the Conservatory and mathematics at the University. His works include the *Variations on a Theme of Paganini* (1941) for two pianos, three symphonies, concertos, songs, and chamber music. He has been very influential as a teacher.

Lutuli or **Luthuli, Albert (John Mvumbi)** (?1899–1967) African resistance leader, born in Rhodesia. Educated at an American mission school near Durban, he spent 15 years as a teacher before being elected tribal chief of Groutville, Natal. Deposed for anti-apartheid activities, he became President-General of the African National Congress, and dedicated himself to a campaign of nonviolent resistance, for which he was awarded the Nobel Peace Prize in 1960. He died at Stanger, South Africa. » apartheid

Lutyens, Sir Edwin (Landseer) (1869–1944) British architect, born in London. He studied at the London Royal College of Art, and became known as a designer of country houses. His best-known projects are the Cenotaph, Whitehall (1919–20), and the laying out of New Delhi, with its spectacular Viceroy's House (1912–30). His project for a Roman Catholic cathedral in Liverpool was incomplete at his death, in London.

lux SI unit of illuminance; symbol lx; defined as one lumen of luminous flux incident on one square metre. » photometry [i]; units (scientific); RR70

Luxembourg (city) 49°37N 6°08E, pop (1981) 78 924. Capital of Luxembourg, on the Alzette and Petrusse Rivers; residence of the Grand Duke of Luxembourg and seat of government; also site of the Court of Justice of the European Communities, the General Secretariat of the European Parliament, the Consultative Committee, the European Investment Bank, the European Monetary Fund, and the Coal and Steel Union; airport; railway; steel, chemicals, textiles, food processing; Musée de l'Etat with the 8th-c Echternach stone; international trade fair (May), Schobermesse amusement fair and market (Aug). » European Parliament; Luxembourg (country) [i]

Luxembourg (country) or **Luxemburg** [**luhk**smberg], official name **Grand Duchy of Luxembourg**, Fr **Grand-Duché de Luxembourg**, Ger **Gross-Herzogtum Luxemburg**, Letzeburgish **Grousherzogdem Lëtzebuerg** pop (1990e) 379 000; area 2 586 sq km/998 sq ml. Independent, constitutional monarchy in NW Europe, divided into three districts; bounded E by Germany, W by Belgium, and S by France; capital, Luxembourg; chief towns, Esch-sur-Alzette, Dudelange, Differdange; timezone GMT +1; languages, French, German, Letzeburgish; a quarter of the population is foreign; chief religion, Roman Catholicism (97%); unit of currency, the French franc; divided into the two natural regions of Ósling (N), wooded, hilly land, average height 450 m/1 475 ft, and Gutland, flatter, average height 250 m/820 ft; drier and sunnier in the S, but winters can be severe; made a Grand Duchy by the Congress of Vienna, 1815; granted political autonomy, 1838; recognized as a neutral independent state, 1867; occupied by Germany in both World Wars; joined Benelux economic union, 1948; neutrality abandoned on joining NATO, 1949; a hereditary monarchy with the Grand Duke as head of state; Parliament has a Chamber of Deputies with 64 members elected every five years and a State Council with 21 members appointed for life; head of government is the Minister of State; important international centre, based in city of Luxembourg; iron and steel, food processing, chemicals, tyres, metal products, engineering; mixed farming, dairy farming, wine, forestry, tourism. » Benelux; Luxembourg (city); RR26 national holidays; RR55 political leaders

Luxembourg, Palais du Since 1958, the seat of the French Senate in Paris. The palace was built in 1613–14 by Salomon de Brosse (1565–1626) for Henri IV's Florentine widow, Marie de Medicis; its design was based on that of the Pitti Palace. It was altered and enlarged in the 19th-c. » Paris [i]; Pitti Palace

Luxembourg Accord » **European Community**

Luxemburg, Rosa (1871–1919) German revolutionary, born in Russian Poland. She became a German citizen in 1895, and emigrated to Zürich in 1889, where she studied law and political economy. With the German politician, Karl Liebknecht (1871–1919), she formed the Spartacus League, which later became the German Communist Party. She was arrested and murdered during the Spartacus revolt in Berlin. » Marxism

Luxor [**luhk**saw], Arabic **El Uqsor**, **Al-Uqsur** 25°41N 32°24E, pop (1983e) 113 400. Winter resort town in Qena governorate,

EC Egypt; on E bank of R Nile, 676 km/420 ml S of Cairo; known as Thebes to the Greeks; numerous tombs of pharaohs in Valley of the Kings; Theban ruins, Temple of Luxor (built by Amenhotep III); one of the obelisks was removed to the Place de la Concorde in Paris. » Amenhotep III; Egypt [i]; pharaoh

Luzon [loo**zon**] pop (1980) 23 900 000; area 108 130 sq km/ 41 738 sq ml. Largest island of the Philippines; bounded W by the South China Sea, E by the Philippine Sea, N by the Luzon Strait; many bays and offshore islets; Cordillera Central rises to 2 929 m/9 609 ft in the NW at Mt Puog; Sierra Madre in the NE; largest lake, Laguna de Bay; occupied by Japanese in World War 2; chief city, Manila; grain; sugar cane, timber, hemp, chromite, tourism. » Manila; Philippines [i]

Lvov, Giorgiy Yevgenievich, Knyaz ('Prince') (1861–1925) Russian liberal politician, born at Popovka. Educated at Moscow, he joined the civil service, then entered local government and became a minister. He was head of the first and second provisional governments after the February Revolution of 1917, but his moderate policies and popular opposition to Russia's war effort led to the collapse of his government. He was succeeded by Kerensky, and arrested by the Bolsheviks, but escaped to Paris, where he died. » Bolsheviks; Kerensky; Russian Revolution

Lvov [li**vof**], Polish **Lwow**, Ger **Lemberg**, Ukrainian **Lwiw** 49°50N 24°00E, pop (1989) 790 000. Capital city of Lvovskaya oblast, Ukraine; close to the Polish border, near the R Poltva; founded, 1256; important centre on the Black Sea–Baltic trade route; ceded to Poland after World War 1; ceded to USSR, 1939; airfield; railway junction; university (1661); oil refining, machines, heavy engineering, clothing, knitwear, pottery, footwear; centre for Ukrainian culture; St Yuri's Uniate Cathedral, Church of the Assumption (16th-c). » Ukraine

Lyallpur » **Faisalabad**

lycanthropy [liy**kan**thruhpee] In popular superstition, the assumption by humans of the shapes of other animals, typically the most dangerous beast of the area. In Europe and N Asia it is usually a wolf or bear, in India and other parts of Asia a tiger, and in Africa a leopard.

lychee » **litchi**

Lycurgus [liy**ker**guhs] The name of various Greeks, including, in mythology, **1** The King of Thrace who opposed Dionysus and was blinded, **2** The founder of the Spartan constitution, with its military caste-system. (The date when this originated has been much disputed, and is now thought to be c.600 BC, much too late for the legendary Lycurgus to have participated.) » Sparta (Greek history)

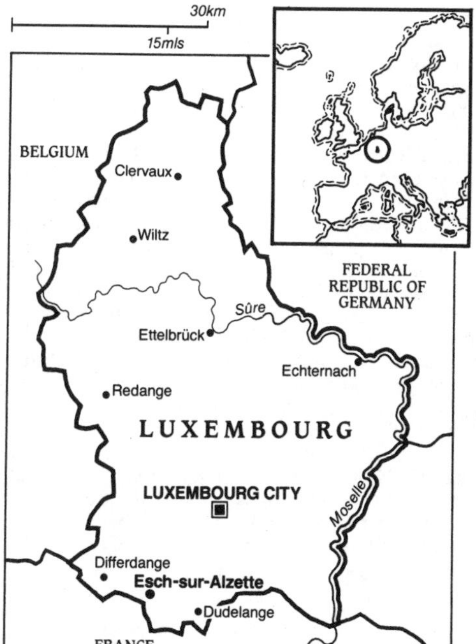

□ international airport

Lydgate, John (c.1370–c.1451) English poet, born at Lydgate, Suffolk. He became a Benedictine monk, travelled in Europe, and was prior of Hatfield Broadoak in 1423. A court poet, he received a pension in 1439, but died in poverty, at Bury St Edmunds. His major works are the narrative poems, *The Troy Book*, *The Siege of Thebes*, and the *Fall of Princes*, in which the influence of Chaucer is marked. » Chaucer; English literature; poetry

Lydia [**li**dia] In antiquity, the area of W Asia Minor lying inland of Ionia. Its capital was Sardis. At the height of its power in the 7th-c and 6th-c BC, it was the centre of an empire which stretched from the Aegean to C Turkey. Conquered by the Persians in 546 BC, it lost its political independence for ever, and was ruled in succession by Persians, Seleucids, Attalids, and Romans. » Ionia; Persian Empire

Lyly, John [**li**lee] (c.1554–1606) English writer, born in the Weald of Kent. He studied at both Oxford and Cambridge, and was for a while an MP (1597–1601). He is remembered for the style of his writing, as seen in his two-part prose romance, *Euphues* (1578, 1580), which led to the term 'euphuism', referring to an artificial and extremely elegant language, with much use made of complex similes and antithesis. He died in London. » drama; English literature; euphuism

lymph A clear, colourless tissue fluid comprising protein, water, and other substances derived from blood, and conveyed in an independent system of thin-walled vessels. It drains from the body tissues back to the vascular system by vessels which empty into the subclavian veins. It contains lymphocytes for destroying infective organisms, and after a meal, fats (absorbed from the intestine for transport to the vascular system). » blood; lymphocyte; lymphogranuloma venereum; protein; scrofula

lymphocyte [**lim**fuhsiyt] A type of white blood cell (*leucocyte*), present in blood and lymph vessels and in organized lymphoid tissues, ie spleen and lymph nodes. Lymphocytes are classified as bone marrow-derived B lymphocytes (*B cells*) and thymus-derived T lymphocytes (*T cells*). B lymphocytes mature in bone marrow, and include the precursors of plasma cells, the producers of antibodies. T lymphocytes mature in the thymus from precursor cells that have migrated from bone marrow, and may help (*helper T cells*) or inhibit (*suppressor T cells*) B cells. T lymphocytes also include the precursors of *cytotoxic T cells* which directly kill virus-infected cells without the use of antibodies. The immunodeficiency seen in HIV infection (AIDS) results primarily from a loss of T helper cells as a result of the selective infection of the T cell population by the virus, which leads to their destruction. » AIDS; antibodies; leucocytes; lymph; lymphoid tissue; lymphoma

lymphogranuloma venereum [limfohgranyoo**loh**ma ve**neer**iuhm] A sexually-transmitted disease caused by *Chlamydia trachomatis*. Genital ulceration is followed by enlargement of lymph nodes draining the initial site of the infection. It responds to antibiotics. » chlamydia; lymph; urinary system

lymphoid tissue Lymphocyte-containing tissues such as lymph nodes, spleen, thymus, tonsils, and Peyer's patches of the small intestine. It forms part of the body's defence against foreign organisms, such as bacteria, toxins, and viruses. » antibodies; Hodgkin's disease; lymphocytes

lymphoma (non-Hodgkin's) The malignant proliferation of lymphoid cells, usually of lymphocytes (B-cell type); the condition merges with lymphocytic leukaemias. Unlike Hodgkin's disease, non-Hodgkin's lymphoma is widespread when first diagnosed, and can be distinguished by the absence of multinucleated cells. » Hodgkin's disease; leukaemia; lymphocyte

Lynch, Jack, properly **John** (1917–) Irish politician and Prime Minister (1966–73, 1977–9), born and educated at Cork. Following a career in the Department of Justice (1936), he was called to the Bar (1945). Elected an MP in 1948, he held ministerial posts in Lands (1951), the Gaeltacht (1957), Education (1957–9), Industry and Commerce (1959–65), and Finance (1965–6), before becoming Prime Minister. Perceived as a strong supporter of the Catholic minority in Ulster, he drew criticism from both Ulster and mainland Britain. He lost the premiership in 1973, regained it four years later, but in 1979 resigned both the post and the leadership of Fianna Fáil. He retired from politics in 1981. » Fianna Fáil; Gaelic; Haughey; Northern Ireland [i]

lynx A nocturnal member of the cat family, native to the northern N Hemisphere; plain brown or with dark spots; very short tail; tips of ears tufted; cheeks with long 'whiskers'; inhabits scrubland and coniferous forest; eats birds, rodents, hares, rabbits, young deer; two species: **lynx** (*Felis lynx*), and the rare **Spanish lynx** (*Felis pardina*.) » bobcat; Felidae

Lynx A N constellation introduced in 1690, near to Ursa Major. It is not easy to recognize. » constellation; Ursa Major; RR9

Lyon, John (1962–) British boxer, born at St Helens, Merseyside. An outstanding amateur boxer, he is the only man to win eight Amateur Boxing Association titles – the light-flyweight title 1981–4 and the flyweight title 1986–9. He also won the 1986 Commonwealth Games flyweight title. » boxing [i]

Lyons [leeõ], Fr **Lyon**, ancient **Lugdunum** 45°46N 4°50E, pop (1982) 418 476. Manufacturing and commercial capital of Rhône-Alpes region, SC France; at confluence of Rhône and Saône Rivers; third largest city in France; city centre on peninsula between rivers, linked by many bridges; Roman capital of Gaul, centre of military highway network; airport; road and rail junction; metro; archbishopric; two universities (1875, 1896); business and commercial centre; leading centre of French textile industry, particularly silk production; pharmaceuticals, electrical products, tinned milk, vehicles, armaments, nuclear equipment, chemicals, metallurgy; international exhibition hall (Eurexpo); 17th-c Palais St-Pierre, Church of St-Nizier, Hôtel de Ville (1646–72), 12th–15th-c Cathedral of St-Jean, 19th-c Basilica of Notre-Dame-de-Fourvière (1872–96); Olympic swimming pool and artificial ski piste. » Gaul

Lyons, Sir John (1932–) British linguist, born in Manchester. Educated at Cambridge, he taught linguistics at London (1957–61) and Cambridge (1961–4), before becoming professor of linguistics at Edinburgh (1964–76) and Sussex (1976–84), and Master of Trinity Hall, Cambridge (1984–). A specialist in semantics and linguistic theory, his major publications include *Semantics* (2 vols, 1977) and *Language, Meaning and Context* (1980). He was knighted in 1987. » linguistics; semantics

Lyons, Joseph Aloysius (1879–1939) Australian statesman and Prime Minister (1931–9), born at Stanley, Tasmania. Educated at the University of Tasmania, he became a teacher, entering politics in 1909 as Labor member in the Tasmanian House of Assembly. He held the post of Minister of Education and Railways (1914–16), and was Premier (1923–9). In the Federal parliament, he was in turn Postmaster-General, Minister of Public Works, and Treasurer. In 1931 he founded the United Australian Party, and became Prime Minister until his death, in Sydney. » Australia [i]

lyophilization or **freeze drying** The process for the removal of solvent or adherent water from materials (eg blood plasma, foodstuffs, beverage bases) while in a frozen condition. The material is frozen and held at a temperature just high enough to prevent sublimation (eg evaporation direct from the solid state without passing through a melting phase). » food preservation

Lyra ('harp') A small but obvious N constellation. It includes the fifth brightest star, Vega, as well as the prototype variable RR Lyrae, and the *Ring nebula*; a planetary nebula 700 parsecs away. Vega, 8 parsecs distance, was the Pole Star c.15 000 years ago. » constellation; Polaris; variable star; RR9

lyre A musical instrument of great antiquity, with a resonator, two arms, and a crossbar. Gut strings, from three to twelve in number, were stretched from the front of the resonator to the crossbar, and plucked with a plectrum. The tortoise-shell resonator of the classical lyre distinguishes it from the larger kithara, with its wooden rectangular soundbox. » crwth; kinnor; kithara [i]; plectrum; string instrument 2 [i]

lyrebird Either of two species of a shy, ground-feeding, Australian bird, genus *Menura*: the **superb lyrebird** (*Menura novaehollandiae*; and **Albert's lyrebird** (*Menura alberti*); long legs; flies poorly but runs well; tail of male shaped like lyre; spectacular display and song; mimics complex sounds; inhabits mountain forest with rock outcrops; eats small invertebrates. (Family: *Menuridae*.)

Lysenko, Trofim (Denisovich) [liy**seng**koh] (1898–1976) Ukrainian biologist and plant physiologist, born at Karlovka. Educated at Uman and Kiev, he gained a reputation in crop husbandry during the famine of the 1930s, and built up a quasi-scientific creed that heredity can be changed by good husbandry. Using political affiliation rather than scientific recognition for advancement, he became director of the Academy of Agricultural Sciences (1938–56, 1958–62), and in 1948, with the approval of the Communist Party, declared the accepted Mendelian theory erroneous, and banished many outstanding Soviet scientists. He resigned in 1962, on grounds of ill health, and after Khrushchev's downfall was relieved of his post as head of the Institute of Genetics (1965). He died in Kiev. » genetics [i]; Mendel's laws

Lysias [liseeas] (c.450–380 BC) Greek orator, who settled in Athens about c.440. The Thirty Tyrants in 404 stripped him and his brother Polemarchus of their wealth, killed Polemarchus, and forced him to flee to Megara. After their fall (403), he returned to prosecute Eratosthenes, who was chiefly to blame for his brother's murder. He then practised with success as a writer of speeches for litigants. » Thirty Tyrants

Lysithea [liysi**thee**a] The tenth natural satellite of Jupiter, discovered in 1938; distance from the planet 11 720 000 km/7 283 000 ml; diameter 40 km/25 ml. » Jupiter (astronomy); RR4

lysosome [**liy**suhsohm] A membrane-bound sac which contains numerous enzymes capable of digesting a wide variety of substrates. Lysosomes are found within cells, and are probably formed by the Golgi body. They are involved in the digestion of food and in the destruction of bacteria in white blood cells. » blood; digestion; enzyme; Golgi body

lysozyme [**liy**suhziym] An enzyme present in tears, saliva, sweat, milk, and nasal and gastric secretions; also known as *muramidase*. It destroys bacterial cell walls by digesting their polysaccharide component. » disaccharide; enzyme

Lytham St Anne's [**lith**am] 53°45N 3°01W, pop (1981) 40 136. Resort town in Blackpool urban area and Fylde district, Lancashire, NW England; on the R Ribble estuary, 20 km/12 ml W of Preston; railway; championship golf course; engineering. » Lancashire

Lyttleton, Humphrey [**lit**ltuhn] (1921–) British jazz trumpeter and bandleader, born at Windsor, Berkshire. He formed a band in 1948, and became the leading figure in the British revival of traditional jazz. His group expanded to an octet, emulating Ellington's early ensembles, and then modernized even further, to the horror of many fans of traditional jazz. He responded with a satirical book *I Play As I Please* (1954). He retained his stature, and increased the tolerance for more modern jazz styles in Britain. » Ellington; jazz

Lytton (of Knebworth), Edward George Earle Bulwer-Lytton, 1st Baron (1803–73) British writer and politician, born in London. Educated at Cambridge, he published his first collection of poetry in 1820, and wrote many popular novels, especially on historical themes, such as *The Last Days of Pompeii* (1834) and *Harold* (1843), as well as plays and essays. He became an MP (1831), baronet (1838), Colonial Secretary (1858–9), and baron (1866). He died at Torquay, Devon. » English literature; novel; poetry

M

M-II The trade name for a videotape recording system of broadcast standard introduced in 1986 by Matsushita. It uses ½ inch metal particle tape at a speed of 6.63 cm/sec in a cassette 189 × 104 × 25 mm, with component recording of luminance and compressed chrominance on adjacent parallel tracks. » videotape recorder

M'Naghten rules [muhk**nawtn**] A legal set of principles which state that a defendant may not be convicted if insanity is proved. The rules provide that accused persons must show that they suffer from a defect of reason arising from serious mental disease; also that, because of this, they did not know what they were doing or did not know that what they were doing was wrong. The rules were developed subsequent to the 19th-c murder trial of Daniel M'Naghten, a case in which insanity was proved. They serve as the legal standard for insanity in Britain, Canada, and many US jurisdictions. » murder

M'Zab Valley An oasis in a fertile gorge along the Oued M'zab watercourse in the Saharan region of C Algeria; a world heritage site. The area was settled in the 11th-c by the M'zabites, a nonconformist Islamic sect who came here to escape persecution. It is renowned for its five ancient towns, its 4 000 wells, and its palm groves. » Algeria [i]; Islam

Maasai » **Masai**

Maastricht [**mahs**trikht], ancient **Traieclum ad Mosam** or **Traiectum Tungorum** 50°51N 5°42E, pop (1984e) 157 329. Capital city of Limburg province, S Netherlands, on the R Maas; commercial hub of an area extending well into Belgium; railway junction; noted for its vegetable and butter markets; paper, packaging, leatherwork, brewing, printing, ceramics, glass, tourism; St Pietersburg underground gallery; Church of St Servatius (6th-c), Romanesque basilica (10th–11th-c). » Netherlands, The [i]

Maazel, Lorin [mah**zel**] (1930–) US conductor, born at Neuilly, France. His family moved to the USA when he was a child, and he studied in Pittsburgh, making his debut as a violinist in 1945 and as a conductor in 1953. He directed the Deutsche Oper Berlin (1965–71), the Cleveland Orchestra (1972–82), and the Vienna Staatsoper (1982–4). Since 1986 he has been conductor of the Pittsburgh Symphony Orchestra.

Mac surnames » also under **Mc**

MAC (Multiplex Analogue Components) A system of colour television transmission in which coded signals representing luminance, chrominance, and sound, along with synchronizing data, are sent in succession as separate components during each TV line. The system requires greater bandwidth than normal, but offers enhanced definition and picture quality. » colour television [i]

McAdam, John (Loudon) (1756–1836) British inventor of the 'macadamizing' system of road-making, born at Ayr, Scotland. He went to New York City in 1770, became a successful merchant, and returned to Scotland in 1783. He was made surveyor (1816) to the Bristol Turnpike Trust, and his advice was widely sought. Impoverished through his labours, he petitioned parliament in 1820, was given a grant in 1825, and made surveyor-general of metropolitan roads. He died at Moffat, Dumfriesshire.

macadamia nut [maka**day**mia] An evergreen tree growing to c.20 m/65 ft, native to NE Australia, and cultivated in Australia and Hawaii; leaves up to 30 cm/12 in, lance-shaped, widest above middle, rigid and sometimes prickly, in whorls of 3–4; flowers in long, drooping spikes, 2.5 cm/1 in in diameter, zygomorphic with four creamy perianth segments; fruits green, splitting to reveal round, edible nut. (*Macadamia integrifolia.* Family: *Proteaceae.*) » evergreen plants; perianth; tree [i]; zygomorphic flower

Macao [ma**kow**], Port **Macáu** pop (1989e) 484 000; area 16 sq km/6 sq ml. Overseas province of Portugal; a flat, maritime tropical peninsula in SE China and the nearby islands of Taipa and Colôane; on the Pearl R delta, 64 km/40 ml W of Hong Kong; airport; capital, Nome de Deus de Macau; population largely Chinese (99%); official language, Portuguese, with Cantonese generally spoken; chief religions, Buddhism, Roman Catholicism; unit of currency, the pataca of 100 avos; ferry links with Hong Kong; a Chinese territory under Portuguese administration; right of permanent occupation granted to Portugal in 1887; Governor appointed by Portugal, with a 23-member Legislative Assembly; textiles, electronics, toys, tourism, gambling, fishing; several fortresses, Jaialai Palace; grand prix racing. » China [i]; Portugal [i]

macaque [ma**kahk**] An Old World monkey, native to S and SE Asia (18 species) and NW Africa (*Barbary ape*); legs and arms of equal length; tail often short; lives in trees or on ground (depending on species); buttocks with naked patches. (Genus: *Macaca*, 19 species.) » barbary ape; Old World monkey; rhesus monkey

macaroni » **pasta**

MacArthur, Douglas (1880–1964) US general, born at Little Rock, Arkansas. Educated at West Point, he joined the US army engineers, and in World War 1 served with distinction in France. In 1941 he became commanding general of the US armed forces in the Far East, and from Australia directed the recapture of the SW Pacific (1942–5). He formally accepted the Japanese surrender, and commanded the occupation of Japan (1945–51), introducing a new constitution. In 1950 he led the UN forces in the Korean War, defeating the North Korean army, but was relieved of command when he tried to continue the war against China. He died in Washington, DC. » Korean War; World War 2

Macassar » **Makassar Strait; Ujung Padang**

Macaulay, Dame (Emilie) Rose (1889–1958) British novelist, essayist, and poet, born at Rugby, Warwickshire. She began writing while an Oxford undergraduate, her first book appearing in 1906. She won a considerable reputation as a social satirist, with such novels as *Dangerous Ages* (1921). Her best-known novel is *The Towers of Trebizond* (1956). Two posthumous volumes, *Letters to a Friend* (1961–2), describe her return to the Anglican faith. She was made a Dame in 1958, and died in London. » English literature; novel; satire

Macaulay (of Rothley), Thomas Babington Macaulay, 1st Baron (1800–59) British essayist and historian, born at Rothley Temple, Leicestershire. He was educated privately and at Cambridge, where he became a fellow. Called to the Bar in 1826, he had no liking for his profession, and turned to literature. He also became an MP (1830), and established his powers as an orator in the Reform Bill debates. After a period in Bengal (1834–8), he became Secretary of War (1839–41), and wrote the highly popular *Lays of Ancient Rome* (1842). His major work, the *History of England from the Accession of James II*, was published between 1848 and 1861, the fifth volume unfinished. He became a peer in 1857, and died in London.

macaw A large parrot native to the Caribbean, and to C and tropical S America; inhabits woodland or savannah; eats fruit, seeds, and nuts; nests in holes. (Genera: *Ara*, *Anodorhynchus*, *Cyanopsitta*, c.16 species.) » parrot

Macbeth (?–1057) King of Scots (1040–57), the legend of whose life was the basis of Shakespeare's play. The mormaer (provincial ruler) of Moray, he became King after slaying Duncan I in battle near Elgin, and in 1050 went on a pilgrimage to Rome. He was defeated and killed by Duncan's son, Malcolm Canmore, at Lumphanan, Aberdeenshire. » Malcolm III

Maccabees [**mak**abeez] An important Jewish family, and those of its party (also known as the **Hasmoneans**) who initially resisted the influences of Greek culture on Israel and its religion during Syrian rule over Palestine. **Judas Maccabeus** (or **ben Mattathias**) led a revolt in 168 BC by attacking a Jewish apostate, and it was continued by his sons through a kind of guerrilla warfare. It resulted eventually in semi-independence from Syrian control, with Jonathan and Simon beginning a Hasmonean dynasty of high priestly rulers which lasted until the rise of Herod the Great under Roman patronage (c.37 BC). » Hasidim; Herod the Great; Hyrcanus I, John; Maccabees, Books of the

Maccabees or **Machabees, Books of the** [**mak**abeez] Four writings, the first two being part of the Old Testament Apocrypha (or deuterocanonical works of the Roman Catholic canon) and the last two being assigned to the Old Testament Pseudepigrapha. 1 *Mac* is a historical narrative concerned with the victories of Judas Maccabeus and his family in 2nd-c BC Palestine, leading eventually to Jewish semi-independence from Syrian control. 2 *Mac* roughly parallels 1 *Mac* 1–7, but is of less certain historical value. 3 *Mac* narrates stories of Jewish resistance before the Maccabean period, particularly in Egypt under Ptolemy IV Philopater (reigned 221–204 BC). 4 *Mac* presents vivid descriptions of tortures and martyrdoms during the early years of the Maccabean revolt, formulated to commend certain theological and philosophical ideals. » Apocrypha, Old Testament; Maccabees; Pseudepigrapha

MacCaig, Norman (Alexander) (1910–) British poet, born and educated in Edinburgh, Scotland. He worked for many years as a schoolmaster, and later at the University of Stirling. His collections include *Rings on a Tree* (1968), *The Equal Skies* (1980), *Voice-Over* (1988), and *Collected Poems* (1985). » poetry; Scottish literature

macchia [**ma**kia] » **maquis**

MacDiarmid [mak**dir**mid], **Hugh**, pseudonym of **Christopher Murray Grieve** (1892–1978) British poet, born at Langholm, Dumfriesshire, Scotland. He served in both World Wars, and worked as a journalist in the 1920s. In 1922 he founded and edited the *Scottish Chapbook*, where he published his own distinctive poems, such as 'A Drunk Man Looks at the Thistle' (1926) and 'In Memoriam James Joyce' (1955). A founder-member of the Scottish National Party, he dedicated his life to the regeneration of the Scottish literary language. He died in Edinburgh. » nationalism; poetry; Scottish literature

Macdonald, Flora (1722–90) Scottish heroine, born in South Uist. After the rebellion of 1745, she conducted the Young Pretender, Charles Edward Stuart, disguised as 'Betty Burke', to safety in Skye. For this she was imprisoned in the Tower of London, but released in 1747. She married in 1750, and in 1774 emigrated to North Carolina, where her husband fought in the War of Independence. When he was captured (1779), Flora returned to Scotland, to be rejoined there in 1781 by her husband. They settled at Kingsburgh, Skye, where she died.

Macdonald, Sir John A(lexander) (1815–91) Canadian statesman and Prime Minister (1857–8, 1864, 1867–73, 1878–91), born in Glasgow. His family emigrated in 1820, and he was educated in law at Kingston. Entering politics in 1843, he became leader of the Conservative Party and joint premier in 1856. He was instrumental in bringing about the confederation of Canada, and in 1867 formed the first government of the new Dominion. The 'Pacific scandal' brought down his government in 1874, but he regained the premiership in 1878. He died in Ottawa.

MacDonald, (James) Ramsay (1866–1937) British statesman and Prime Minister (1924, 1929–31, 1931–5), born at Lossiemouth, Morayshire, Scotland. He had little formal education, worked as a clerk, then joined the Independent Labour Party in 1894, eventually becoming its leader (1911–14, 1922–31). He became an MP in 1906, and was Prime Minister and Foreign Secretary of the first British Labour government. He met the financial crisis of 1931 by forming a largely Conservative 'National' government, most of his Party opposing; and in 1931 reconstructed it after a general election. Defeated by Shinwell in the 1935 general election, he returned to parliament in 1936, and became Lord President. He died on his way to S America. » Labour Party; Shinwell

MacDonnell Ranges Mountain ranges in Northern Territory, C Australia; extend 320 km/200 ml W from Alice Springs; rising to 1 524 m/5 000 ft at Mt Liebig, the highest point in the state. » Northern Territory

mace A spice obtained by grinding up the red, net-like aril which surrounds the seed of the nutmeg tree (*Myristica fragrans*). Like nutmeg, mace is poisonous if consumed in large quantities because of the presence of a narcotic. » aril; nutmeg; spice

Macedon [**ma**sedon] In antiquity, the territory to the N of Greece abutting on to the NW corner of the Aegean. Regarded by the Greeks as backward, Macedon did not attract much notice until the military and diplomatic genius of Philip II (359–336 BC) transformed her into the most powerful state in the whole of Greece. Under Alexander the Great, the Persian Empire was overthrown; but with his death (323 BC) decline set in, and eventually Macedon, like the rest of his western empire, fell to the Romans. It became a Roman province in 146 BC. » Lamian War; Roman history [i]

Macedonia (Greece) [masuh**doh**nia], Gr **Makedhonia** pop (1981) 2 121 953; area 34 177 sq km/13 192 sq ml. N region of Greece, from the Albanian frontier (W) to the R Nestos (E), and from the Yugoslav frontier (N) to Mt Olympus (S); capital, Thessaloniki; chief towns, Kavalla, Drama, Edhessa, Kastoria; mountainous, with fertile plains; ancient sites include Pella (former capital) and Vergina; livestock, grain, tobacco, olives, grapes. » Greece [i]; Mount Athos; Vergina

Macedonia (Yugoslavia) [masuh**doh**nia], Serbo-Croatian **Makedonija** pop (1981) 1 909 112; area 25 713 sq km/9 925 sq ml. Republic in S Yugoslavia, bounded W by Albania, S by Greece, E by Bulgaria, and N by Serbia; capital, Skopje; chief towns include Bitola, Gostivar, Tetovo, Kumanovo; populated by Slavs, Serbs, Albanians, and Turks; incorporated into Serbia after the Balkan Wars; declaration of independence, 1991; market gardening. » Skopje; Yugoslavia [i]

Macgillycuddy's Reeks [makg**il**ikuhdeez **reeks**] Mountain range in Kerry county, Munster, SW Irish Republic, rising to 1 041 m/3 415 ft at Carrantuohill, highest peak in Irish Republic. » Irish Republic [i]

Mach, Ernst [mahkh] (1838–1916) Austrian physicist and philosopher, born in Turas, Moravia. He studied at Vienna, and became professor of mathematics at Graz (1864), of physics at Prague (1867) and of philosophy at Vienna (1895). He experimented with supersonic projectiles and the flow of gases, and influenced aeronautical design and the science of projectiles. His writings greatly influenced Einstein and laid the foundations of logical positivism. He died at Haar, Germany. » aerodynamics [i]; logical positivism; Mach number; Mach's principle

Mach number [mak] Unit of velocity; symbol Ma; defined as the ratio of velocity of an object to that of sound in some medium, usually air; named after Austrian physicist Ernst Mach; an aircraft travelling at Ma 1 has velocity 331.5 m per sec, the velocity of sound in air. » Mach; sound; units (scientific); velocity

Mach's principle [maks] In physics, an argument that the acceleration of an object cannot be measured relative to absolute space, but must instead be measured against all matter in the universe. The inertia of an object is determined by all matter around it, and has no meaning in empty space. The argument, propounded by Austrian physicist Ernst Mach in 1863, influenced Einstein's development of general relativity. » general relativity; inertia; Mach; mass

Machabees » **Maccabees, Books of the**

Machaut, Guillaume de » **Guillaume de Machaut**

Machel, Samora Moïsés [ma**shel**] (1933–86) The leader of the guerrilla campaign against Portuguese rule in Mozambique, and first President of Mozambique (1975–86). He was commander-in-chief of the army of Frente de Libertação de Moçambique (FRELIMO) (1966–70), President of FRELIMO from 1970, and became President of Mozambique following its independence. Although a Marxist, he established warm relations with Western governments, and attempted an accommodation with the South African regime. He was killed in an air crash over South African territory. » Marxism; Mozambique [i]

Machiavelli, Niccolò (di Bernardo dei) [makeea**ve**lee] (1469–1527) Italian statesman and political theorist, born in Florence. He travelled on several missions in Europe for the republic (1498–1512). On the restoration of the Medici, he was arrested on a charge of conspiracy (1513), and although pardoned, was obliged to withdraw from public life. He devoted himself to literature, writing historical treatises, poetry, short stories, and comedies. His masterpiece is *Il Principe* (1532, The Prince), whose main theme is that all means may be used in order to maintain authority, and that the worst acts of the ruler are justified by the treachery of the governed. It was condemned by the Pope, and its viewpoint gave rise to the adjective 'machiavellian'. His writings were not published until 1782. » Charles V (Emperor); Medici; political science

machine An assembly of connected parts arranged to transmit or modify force to perform useful work. All machines are based on six types: (1) lever; (2) wheel and axle; (3) pulley; (4) inclined plane; (5) wedge; and (6) screw. The wheelbarrow, human arm, and crowbar are all levers. Wheel and axles are used to raise loads by pulling a rope attached to the axle. Pulleys work in the same way, but the force and movement of load may be in different directions. Inclined plane and screw are used to move heavy weights with little effort. Wedges exert large sideways forces. The mechanical advantage can be determined for each type. » mechanical advantage/engineering; pulley; tools

machine code The fundamental binary-coded instructions which can be directly understood and acted on by a computer. Programmers seldom write directly in machine code; instead they use either the assembly language for the specific computer or one of the many available high-level languages. » assembly language; high-level language

machine-gun A gun firing a rifle calibre bullet with an automated ammunition feed and firing cycle, allowing sustained automatic fire with the operator needing to do no more than squeeze the trigger and ensure there is enough ammunition. Multi-barrel weapons such as the Gatling gun appeared in the mid-19th-c, but it was the American inventor Hiram Maxim who hit on the principle of using the force of recoil to power the automatic cycle in his water-cooled weapon, to eject the spent cartridge, chamber a new one, close the breech block, and fire. Machine-guns made a huge impact on warfare, their firepower consigning the infantry of 1914–18 to positional trench warfare. But lighter, air-cooled weapons were on the way, using gas bled off from the firing cycle as their operating power source, producing such weapons of World War 2 as the British Bren gun and the German MG 34. Machine-guns are still an important weapon of world armies, although weapons technology has produced lightweight assault rifles, themselves capable of sustained automatic fire. » Bren gun; Browning automatic rifle; Maxim; rifle; submachine-gun

machine tools A variety of powered machines used in industry to work and shape components made of metal or other material, and operated either manually by skilled operators or under the control of other machines or computers. They include lathes, planes, saws, and milling machines. Finer tolerances and greater repeatability of product is possible with machine tools than with old hand tools, and their development during the Industrial Revolution made mass production and the concept of replaceable parts possible. » Industrial Revolution; lathe

Machu Picchu [**ma**choo **pee**choo] Ruined Inca city in SC Peru; a world heritage site; on the saddle of a high mountain with terraced slopes falling away to the R Urubamba; comparatively well-preserved because it was never found by the Spaniards; discovered in 1911 by US explorer Hiram Bingham; ruins consist of staircases, temples, terraces, palaces, towers, fountains, and a famous sundial; Museo de Sitio museum; near the Urubamba is the Temple of the Moon; approached from Cuzco by rail. » Incas; Peru [i]

Macintosh, Charles (1766–1843) British manufacturing chemist, who in 1823 patented in Glasgow, Scotland, a method of waterproofing fabric, to which he gave his name. The technique involved the use of rubber dissolved in a naphtha solution to cement two pieces of cloth. Raincoats were often thereafter called 'macintoshes'. » fabrics; naphtha; rubber

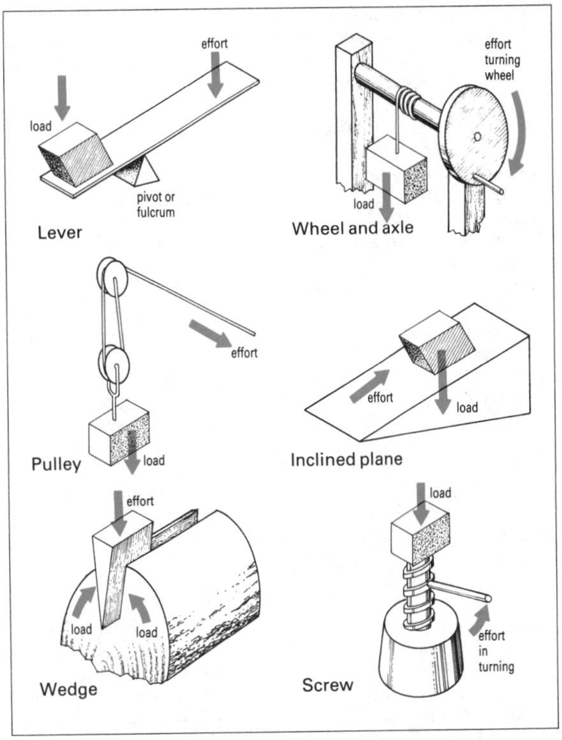

Machine – Six types

Macke, August [**mak**uh] (1887–1914) German Expressionist painter, born at Meschede. He studied at Düsseldorf and designed stage scenery. Profoundly influenced by Matisse, he and Franz Marc founded the Blaue Reiter group. He was a sensitive colourist, working in watercolour as well as oil, and remained attached to the kind of subject matter favoured by the Impressionists: figures in a park, street scenes, children, and animals (eg 'The Zoo', 1912). He was killed in action at Champagne, France. » Blaue Reiter, der; Expressionism; Marc; Matisse

Mackenzie, Sir (Edward Montague) Compton (1883–1972) British writer, born in West Hartlepool, County Durham. Educated at Oxford, he began on the stage, but turned to literature, publishing his first novel in 1911. He served at Gallipoli in World War 1, and in 1917 became director of the Aegean Intelligence Service in Syria. He wrote a large number of novels, notably *Sinister Street* (1913–14) and *Whisky Galore* (1947). He lived in Scotland after 1928, and became a strong nationalist. Knighted in 1951, he died in Edinburgh. » nationalism; novel; Scottish literature

Mackenzie, William Lyon (1795–1861) Canadian politician, born in Dundee. He emigrated to Canada in 1820, established the *Colonial Advocate* in 1824, and entered politics in 1828. In 1837 he published in his paper a declaration of Canadian independence, headed a band of reform-minded insurgents, and after a skirmish with a superior force, fled to the USA, where he was imprisoned. He returned to Canada in 1849, becoming a journalist and MP (1850–8). He died in Toronto. » Canada [i]

Mackenzie Range Mountain range in Northwest Territories, NW Canada; extends c.800 km/497 ml SE–NW; rises to 2 972 m/9 750 ft at Keele Peak; watershed for tributaries of Mackenzie and Yukon Rivers; Nahanni nature park in the S. » Canada [i]; Rocky Mountains

Mackenzie River River in Northwest Territories, NW Canada;

issues from W end of Great Slave Lake; flows NW to enter the Beaufort Sea through a wide delta near the boundary with Yukon territory; length 4 241 km/2 635 ml; navigable in summer (Jun–Oct); hydroelectricity; oil and mineral transportation. » Northwest Territories

mackerel Surface-living fish widespread and locally abundant in the N Atlantic; undertakes long seasonal migrations; length up to 60 cm/2 ft; body slender, rounded in section, tail deeply forked, small finlets between dorsal and anal fins; bright blue or green with dark blue or black bars, underside silvery white; extensively fished commercially using nets or lines; changes in distribution and migration patterns led to a failure of the major fisheries off Cornwall and the Minch, Scotland, during the 1970s. The name is also used for other species in the families *Scombridae* and *Scomberesocidae*. (*Scomber scombrus*. Family: *Scombridae*.)

mackerel shark Large powerful shark found in open ocean waters of the N Atlantic and Mediterranean; feeds mostly on fish and squid; not normally offensive; good sport fish, and taken commercially on long lines; also called **porbeagle**. (*Lamna nasus*. Family: *Lamnidae*.) » shark

mackerel sky A patterning of cirrocumulus and altocumulus clouds resembling fish markings. These are found at altitudes above 5 000 m/16 000 ft. » altocumulus clouds; cirrocumulus clouds; cloud [i]

Mackerras, Sir Charles [ma**ker**as] (1925–) Australian conductor, born at Schenectady, New York. He studied in Sydney (where he lived from the age of two) and in Prague, and has since lived mainly in England. He has been musical director of the Sadler's Wells (later English National) Opera (1970–9), of the Sydney Symphony Orchestra (since 1982) and of the Welsh National Opera (since 1986). He was knighted in 1979.

Mackintosh, Charles Rennie (1868–1928) British architect and designer, born in Glasgow, Scotland. He studied at Glasgow and became a leader of the 'Glasgow Style', a movement related to Art Nouveau. As well as interiors and furniture, his designs include the Glasgow School of Art (1896–9 and 1906–9) and Hill House, Helensburgh (1902–3). He left Glasgow in 1904 and eventually settled in London, where he died. His designs for jewellery and furniture enjoyed a renewed vogue in the 1980s. » Art Nouveau

Maclean, Alistair [ma**klayn**] (1922–87) British author, born in Glasgow, Scotland. He served in the Royal Navy (1941–6), and then studied at Glasgow. In 1954, while a teacher, he won a short-story competition, then wrote the novel *HMS Ulysses* (1955), which became an immediate best-seller. He followed it with *The Guns of Navarone* (1957), and turned to the full-time writing of what he calls 'adventure stories', with fast-moving intricate plots and exotic settings, such as *Ice Station Zebra* (1963), *Where Eagles Dare* (1967), and *San Andreas* (1984). Most have made highly successful films. » novel

Maclean, Donald (Duart) [ma**klayn**] (1913–83) British traitor, born in London. He was educated at Cambridge, where he studied at the same time as Burgess and Philby, and was similarly influenced by communism. He joined the diplomatic service in 1935, serving in Paris, Washington (1944–8), and Cairo (1948–50), and from 1944 acted as a Soviet agent. He became head of the American Department of the Foreign Office, but by 1951 was a suspected traitor, and in May of that year, after Philby's warning, disappeared with Burgess to the USSR. He died in Moscow. » Burgess, Guy

MacLeish, Archibald (1892–1982) US poet, born at Glencoe, Illinois. He trained as a lawyer, was librarian of Congress (1939–44), and became professor of rhetoric at Harvard (1949–62). His first volume of poetry appeared in 1917, and he won Pulitzer Prizes for *Conquistador* (1932), *Collected Poems 1917–52* (1953), and his social drama in modern verse, *J.B.* (1959). A close supporter of Roosevelt, he was Assistant Secretary of State (1944–5). He died in Boston. » American literature; poetry; Roosevelt, Franklin D

MacLeod, Iain (Norman) [muh**klowd**] (1913–70) British Conservative politician, born at Skipton, Yorkshire. Educated at Cambridge, he became an MP (1950), Minister of Health (1952–5), Minister of Labour (1955–9), Secretary of State for the Colonies (1959–61), and Chairman of the Conservative Party (1961–3). Refusing to serve under Home (he had supported Butler's claim), he spent two years editing the *Spectator* (1963–5). When Heath became leader, MacLeod was appointed Shadow Chancellor (1965–70), and after the Conservative victory (1970) became Chancellor of the Exchequer. However, a month later he died in London. » Conservative Party; Heath, Edward; Home of the Hirsel

Macleod, J(ohn) J(ames) R(ickard) [muh**klowd**] (1876–1935) British physiologist, born at Cluny, Perthshire, Scotland. Educated at Aberdeen, Leipzig and Cambridge, he became professor of physiology at Cleveland, Ohio (1903), Toronto (1918), and Aberdeen (1928). In 1922 he was a member of the group who discovered insulin, for which he shared the 1923 Nobel Prize for Physiology or Medicine. He died in Aberdeen. » Banting; insulin

MacMahon, Marie Edme Patrice Maurice de [mak**mahn**], **Duc de** ('Duke of') **Magenta** (1808–93) French Marshal and second President of the Third Republic, born at Sully, descended from an Irish Jacobite family. He was a commander in the Crimean War (1854–6), and for his services in the Italian campaign (1859) was made Marshal and a duke. In the Franco-Prussian War (1870–1) he was defeated at Wörth and surrendered at Sedan. After the war he suppressed the Commune (1871), and succeeded Thiers as President (1873). Failing to assume dictatorial powers, he resigned in 1879, thus ensuring the supremacy of parliament. He died at Loiret. » Commune of Paris; Franco-Prussian War; Thiers

Macmillan, Daniel (1813–57) British bookseller and publisher, born at Upper Corrie, Arran, Scotland. A bookseller's apprentice, in 1843 he and his brother, **Alexander** (1818–96), opened a bookshop in London. They then moved to Cambridge, and branched out into publishing, first educational and religious works, and then English classics. The company became one of the world's largest publishing houses. He died at Cambridge. » book

Macmillan, Sir (Maurice) Harold, 1st Earl of Stockton (1894–1986) British Conservative statesman and Prime Minister (1957–63), born in London. Educated at Eton and Oxford, he became an MP in 1924. He was Minister of Housing (1951–4) and Defence (1954–5), Foreign Secretary (1955), Chancellor of the Exchequer (1955–7), and succeeded Eden as Premier. He gained unexpected popularity with his infectious enthusiasm, effective domestic policy ('most of our people have never had it so good'), and resolute foreign policy, and he was re-elected in 1959. After several political setbacks, he resigned through ill health in 1963, and left the House of Commons in 1964. He became chancellor of Oxford University in 1960, an earl in 1984, and died at Chelwood Gate, West Sussex. » Conservative Party; Eden

Macmillan, Sir Kenneth (1929–) British ballet dancer, choreographer, and ballet company director. He joined the Sadler's Wells Theatre Ballet in 1946, and began to choreograph in 1953. He directed the Berlin opera (1966–9), and became artistic director of the Royal Ballet in 1970, and its principal choreographer in 1977. His works include *Romeo and Juliet* (1965), *Manon* (1974), and Meyerling (1978). He was knighted in 1983. » ballet; choreography; Royal Ballet

MacMillan, Kirkpatrick (1813–78) British blacksmith, born in Dumfriesshire, Scotland. In 1837 he built a 'dandy' horse – a kind of bicycle on which the rider pushed himself along with his feet. Two years later he had applied the crank to his machine to make the world's first pedal cycle, with wooden frame and iron-tyred wheels. » bicycle

MacNeice, Louis (1907–63) British writer, born in Belfast, Northern Ireland. Educated at Oxford, he lectured at Birmingham (1930–6) and London (1936–40), and was closely associated with the British left-wing poets of the 1930s, especially Auden. His books of poetry include *Letters from Iceland* (1937), *Autumn Journal* (1939), *The Burning Perch* (1963), and *Collected Poems* (1966). He died in London. » Auden; English literature; poetry

Mâcon [ma**kõ**], ancient **Matisco** 46°19N 4°50E, pop (1982) 39 866. Manufacturing city and capital of Saône-et-Loire department, C France, on the W bank of the R Saône; episcopal see from the 6th-c until the Revolution; road and rail junction;

commercial centre of major wine area; textiles, agricultural machinery, casks; remains of 12th-c cathedral; birthplace of Lamartine; prehistoric site at Solutre, 8 km/5 ml W. » French Revolution [i]; wine

Maconchy, Dame Elizabeth (1907–) British composer, who studied at the Royal College of Music, London, and in 1929 went to Prague, where her first major work, a piano concerto, was performed in 1930. She has written much chamber music, and also choral, operatic, and ballet music, as well as orchestral works and songs. She was made a Dame in 1987. Her daughter, Nicola LeFanu (1947–), is also a composer.

Macquarie, Lachlan [muh**kwo**ree] (1761–1824) British soldier and colonial administrator, born on Ulva, off Mull, Scotland. He became Governor of New South Wales in 1810 after the deposition of Bligh. He raised the colony to a state of lawfulness and prosperity, but his liberal policies towards ex-convicts united his opponents, and caused his resignation. He returned to Britain in 1821, and died in London. The Lachlan and Macquarie Rivers and Macquarie I were named after him. » Bligh; New South Wales

Macquarie Island 54°30N 158°56W. Island lying 1 345 km/835 ml SW of Tasmania, Australia; area 123 sq km/47 sq ml; average height 240 m/800 ft, rises to 425 m/1 400 ft; meteorological and geological research stations; nature reserve (1933); breeding ground of royal penguin; colony of fur seals re-established here 1956. » Tasmania

macramé [ma**krah**mee] A type of coarse lace produced by knotting and plaiting, which enjoyed a widespread revival in the mid-19th-c. It was used to make decorative fringed borders for costumes as well as furnishings such as window blinds, antimacassars, and cushions. » lace

Macready, William Charles (1793–1873) British actor and theatre manager, born in London. He became an actor in his father's company (1810), and by 1837 had established himself as the leading English actor, notable for his Shakespearian roles. He became manager of Covent Garden in 1837, and of Drury Lane in 1841. His last visit to the USA (1849) was marked by riots arising from the ill-feeling borne towards him by the US actor, Edwin Forrest. He retired in 1851, and died at Cheltenham, Gloucestershire. » Forrest; theatre

macro-photography or **photomacrography** The photography of small objects or details in extreme close-up using normal camera lenses, in contrast to *photomicrography*, which uses a microscope lens. In practice, macro lens settings allow focusing down to a subject distance of 1–2 cm. » camera; lens; photomicrograph

macrobiotics A 'perfect diet', influenced by Zen Buddhist philosophy at the turn of the century, thought to improve health and prolong life. All foods are seen as either *yin* (eg fruit) or *yang* (eg bread), and a strict balance of intake is prescribed. Seven levels of a macrobiotic diet are established, with the role of cereals increasing from 40% to up to 100% of the foods eaten. Such a diet is low in quality protein and has been associated with several cases of malnutrition in the USA, especially in children subjected to such diets by over-enthusiastic parents. » diet; malnutrition; yin and yang

macroeconomics » economics

macronutrients » nutrients

mad cow disease » bovine spongiform encephalopathy

Madagascar, official name **Democratic Republic of Madagascar**, Malagasy **Repoblika Demokratika n'i Madagaskar** pop (1990e) 11 980 000; area 592 800 sq km/228 821 sq ml. Island republic in the Indian Ocean, separated from E Africa by the Mozambique Channel; divided into six provinces; world's fourth largest island; length (N–S) 1 580 km/982 ml; capital, Antananarivo; chief towns, Toamasina, Mahajanga, Fianarantsoa, Antseranana, Toliara; timezone GMT +3; population mainly Malagasy tribes; official language, Malagasy, with French widely spoken; chief religions, Christianity (40%), local beliefs; dissected N–S by a ridge of mountains rising to 2 876 m/9 436 ft at Maromokotra; cliffs (E) drop down to a coastal plain through tropical forest; terraced descent (W) through savannah to the coast, heavily indented in the N; temperate climate in the highlands; average annual rainfall 1 000–1 500 mm/40–60 in; tropical coastal region, annual rain-

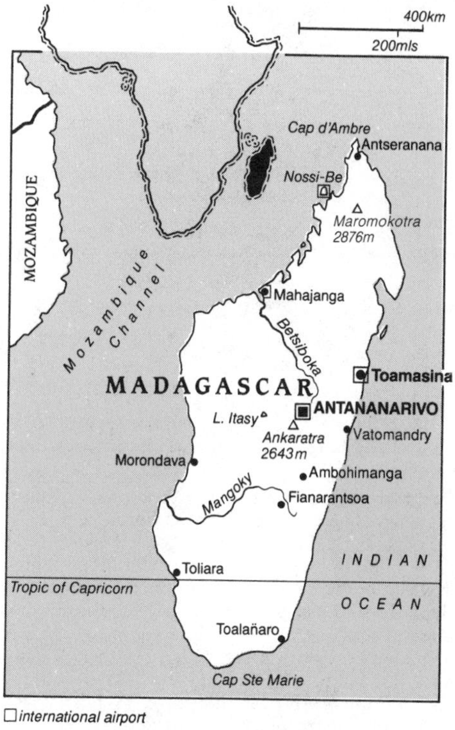

fall at Toamasina (E), 3 500 mm/140 in; settled by Indonesians (1st-c AD) and by African traders (8th-c); visited by Portuguese, 16th-c; French established trading posts, late 18th-c; claimed as a protectorate, 1885; autonomous overseas French territory (Malagasy Republic), 1958; independence, 1960; became Madagascar, 1977; governed by a president, elected for seven years, who appoints a Council of Ministers and is guided by a 20-member Supreme Revolutionary Council; 137-member National People's Assembly elected every five years; chiefly agricultural economy; rice, manioc, coffee, sugar, vanilla, cloves, cotton, peanuts, sisal, tobacco, livestock; food processing, tanning, cement, soap, glassware, paper, textiles, oil products; graphite, chrome, coal, bauxite, ilmenite, semi-precious stones. » Antananarivo; RR26 national holidays; RR56 political leaders

Madagascar jasmine » stephanotis

Madara Rider An 8th-c bas-relief, carved out of the sheer cliff face in the village of Madara, E Bulgaria; a world heritage monument. The near life-size sculpture depicts a man on horseback trampling a lion beneath his horse's hooves. » bas relief; Bulgaria [i]

Madariaga y Rojo, Salvador de [maṯhar**yah**ga] (1886–1978) Spanish diplomat and writer, born at Coruña. Educated at Madrid and Paris, he became a journalist in London (1916–21), a member of the League of Nations secretariat (1922–7), professor of Spanish studies at Oxford (1928–31), and Spanish Ambassador to the USA (1931) and France (1932–4). During 1933 he was briefly Minister of Education in the Spanish Republican government. An opponent of the Franco regime, he was in exile 1936–76. The author of many historical works, especially on Spain and Spanish-America, he died at Locarno, Switzerland. » Franco; League of Nations; Spain [i]

madder An evergreen perennial, native to the Mediterranean; stems 4-angled, trailing or scrambling by means of small downwardly-directed hooks; leaves narrow, stiff, in whorls of 4–6; flowers small, yellow, 5-petalled; berries reddish-brown. The roots produce the dye alizarin. (*Rubia tinctoria*. Family: *Rubiaceae*.) » dyestuff; evergreen plants; perennial

Madeira (Islands) [ma**dee**ra] or **Funchal Islands**, Port **Ilha de Madeira** 32°45N 17°00W, pop (1980) 254 880. Main island in an archipelago off the coast of N Africa, 990 km/615 ml SW of

Lisbon; name often given to the group as a whole; several islands uninhabited; occupied by the Portuguese, 16th-c; capital, Funchal; highest point, Pico Ruivo de Santana (1 861 m/6 106 ft); sugar cane, fruit, farming, fishing, wine, embroidery, crafts, tourism. » Funchal; Portugal [i]

Madeira, River [madayra] River in NW Brazil, the longest tributary of the Amazon, and third longest river in S America; flows N along the Bolivia–Brazil border, then NE to join the Amazon 152 km/94 ml E of Manaus; length with its headstream, the Mamoré, is over 3 200 km/2 000 ml; navigable from Pôrto Velho. » Amazon, River; Brazil [i]

Maderna, Bruno (1920–73) Italian composer and conductor, born in Venice. A child prodigy violinist, he studied composition and conducting, wrote music for films and radio, and taught at the Venice Conservatory. In 1954 he became involved with electronic music, founding with Berio the Studio di Fonologia Musicale of Italian Radio. He died at Darmstadt, Germany. » Berio; electronic music

Madhya Pradesh [madya pradaysh] pop (1981) 52 131 717; area 442 841 sq km/170 937 sq ml. State in C India, between the Deccan and the Ganges plains; largest state in India; crossed by numerous rivers; ruled by the Gonds, 16th–17th-c, and Mahrattas, 18th-c; occupied by the British, 1820; called Central Provinces and Berar, 1903–50; formed under the States Reorganization Act, 1956; capital, Bhopal; governed by a 90-member Upper House and an elected 320-member Lower House; major irrigation schemes; sugar cane, oilseed, cotton, forestry; steel, electrical engineering, aluminium, paper, textiles, machine tools, food processing, handicrafts; coal, iron ore, manganese, bauxite. » Bhopal; India [i]

Madison, James (1751–1836) US statesman and fourth President (1809–17), born at Port Conway, Virginia. He entered politics in 1776, played a major role in the Constitutional Convention of 1787, which framed the Federal constitution, and collaborated in the writing of *The Federalist Papers*. He was elected to the first national congress, and became a leader of the Jeffersonian Republican Party. He was Secretary of State under Jefferson, and President himself for two terms from 1809. His period in office saw the European wars, which were destructive of American commerce, and conflict with Britain (1812). He died at Montpelier, Virginia. » Constitutional Convention; War of 1812

Madison 43°04N 89°24W, pop (1980) 170 616. Capital of state in Dane County, S Wisconsin, USA; on L Mendota and L Monona; state capital, 1836; city status, 1856; airfield; railway; university (1836); trading and manufacturing centre in agricultural region; farm machinery, medical equipment; World Dairy Exposition (Oct). » Wisconsin

Madison Avenue A street in Manhattan, New York City, extending N to the R Harlem from Madison Square. With its glittering skyscrapers and expensive boutiques, it is seen as the centre of the advertising industry. » New York City

Madras [madras] 13°08N 80°19E, pop (1990) 5 360 000. Capital of Tamil Nadu, SE India; on R Coom, 1 360 km/845 ml SW of Calcutta; fourth largest city in India, and chief port of Tamil Nadu; founded by the British, 17th-c; airport; railway; university (1857); textiles, chemicals, tanning, glass, engineering, jewellery, clothing, cars, bicycles; trade in leather, wool, cotton, tobacco, mica, magnesite; Fort St George (1639), Kapaleeswara temple, Pathasarathy temple (8th-c), San Thome Cathedral; St Mary's Church (1680), thought to be the oldest Anglican church in Asia; Mount St Thomas nearby, traditional site of martyrdom of the apostle. » Tamil Nadu

Madrid [madrid] 40°25N 3°45W, pop (1981) 3 188 297. Industrial capital and largest city of Spain; in C Spain, on R Manzanares; altitude, 655 m/2 149 ft, the highest capital city in Europe; archbishopric; airport; railway; metro; two universities (1508, 1968); textiles, engineering, chemicals, leather goods, agricultural trade; site of a Moorish fortress until 11th-c; under siege for nearly three years in the Civil War; capital (replacing Valladolid), 1561; El Escorial, a world heritage site; Royal Palace (18th-c), Prado Museum, Lazaro Galdiano Museum, El Retiro Park, archaeological museum, national library; Fiesta of Almudena (Nov), pilgrimage of St Isidore (May). » Prado; Spain [i]; Spanish Civil War

madrigal A polyphonic song, usually secular and without instrumental accompaniment. It was cultivated especially in Italy during the 16th-c by Palestrina, Lassus, Gabrieli, Marenzio, and others, and is characterized by a judicious mixture of contrapuntal and chordal style and by serious, Petrarchan, and usually amorous verses. In the early 17th-c, Italian madrigals, notably those of Monteverdi, absorbed some Baroque features, including solo vocal writing, continuo accompaniment, and instrumental obbligatos, and were superseded by the new cantata. » Baroque (music); polyphony; Byrd; Gabrieli, Andrea; Gibbons, Orlando; Lassus; Monteverdi; Palestrina; Petrarch; Weelkes; Wilbye

Madura foot » **mycetoma**

Madurai [madooriy] 9°55N 78°10E, pop (1981) 904 000. City in Tamil Nadu, S India; on the R Voigai, 425 km/264 ml SW of Madras; capital of the Pandyan kingdom and the Nayak dynasty; occupied by the British, 1801; airfield; railway; university (1966); silk and muslin weaving, woodcarving, brassware, trade in coffee, tea, cardamom; large Dravidian temple complex (14th–17th-c). » Tamil Nadu

Madurese An Austronesian-speaking people of the island of Madura, Kangean Is, and nearby coastal areas of NE Java, Indonesia. They cultivate rice and raise export cattle on Madura, and are well-known in Java as migrant labourers, traders, fishermen, and sailors. Population c.5 million. » Austronesian languages; Java

Maecenas, Gaius (Cilnius) [miyseenas] (?–8 BC) Roman politician of ancient Etruscan lineage, who together with Agrippa played a key role in the rise to power of Octavian/Augustus, and his establishment of the empire after 31 BC. Besides being a trusted counsellor and diplomatic agent, he also helped the new regime by his judicious patronage of the arts, encouraging such poets as Horace, Virgil, and Propertius. » Agrippa, Marcus Vipsanius; Augustus; Horace; Propertius; Roman history [i]; Virgil

maenads [meenads] In Greek mythology, 'mad women', who followed Dionysus (Bacchus) on his journeys; they were dressed in animal-skins, and so strong that they could uproot trees and kill wild animals, eating the flesh raw. They are also known as **Bacchae** or **Bacchantes**.

Maes, Nicholas [mahs] (1634–93) Dutch painter, born at Dordrecht. He studied in Rembrandt's studio in Amsterdam (c.1648–50), returning to Dordrecht by 1654. He specialized in small genre subjects, especially kitchen scenes (eg 'Woman Scraping Parsnips', 1655, National Gallery, London), and old women praying. After a visit to Antwerp (c.1665), he turned to portraiture in a style derived from van Dyck. In 1673, he settled in Amsterdam, where he died. » genre painting; Rembrandt; van Dyck

Maes Howe [mayz how] A chambered tomb of the early 3rd millennium BC on Orkney, N Scotland, outstanding for its construction and preservation. Beneath a mound 35 m/115 ft in diameter, a 7.3 m/24 ft long drystone-walled entrance passage gives onto a cross-shaped burial chamber with a corbelled vault 3.8 m/12 ft high. Above the door slab is a slot allowing the setting Sun to penetrate the burial chamber at the midwinter solstice. Inside are 24 runic inscriptions scratched by Viking raiders in the mid-12th-c AD. » chambered tomb; corbelling; runes [i]; solstice; Vikings

maestà [miy**sta**] (Ital 'majesty') In art, the Virgin represented as Queen of Heaven, flanked by angels and saints. The most splendid examples were painted in Italy in the 13th–14th-c by Cimabué, Duccio, and Martini. » altarpiece; Mary (mother of Jesus); Cimabué; Duccio di Buoninsegna; Martini

Maeterlinck, Count Maurice [**may**tuhlingk] (1862–1949) Belgian writer, born at Ghent. He studied law at Ghent, but became a disciple of the Symbolist movement, and in 1889 produced his first volume of poetry, *Les Serres chaudes* (Hot House Blooms). His plays include *Pelléas et Mélisande* (1892), on which Debussy based his opera. *La Vie des abeilles* (1901, The Life of the Bee) is one of many popular expositions of scientific subjects, and he also wrote several philosophical works. He was awarded the Nobel Prize for Literature in 1911, made a count in 1932, and died in Nice, France. » French literature; Symbolism

Mafeking, Siege of (1899–1900) The most celebrated siege of the second Boer War. Colonel Robert Baden-Powell and a detachment of British troops were besieged by the Boers from October 1899 until May 1900. The news of their relief aroused public hysteria in Britain, the celebrations being known as 'mafficking'. The truth about the siege was rather different from the heroic action depicted by the British press. It is now known that the White garrison survived in reasonable comfort as the result of appropriating the rations of the Blacks, who were faced either with starvation or with running the gauntlet of the Boers by escaping from the town. » Baden-Powell; Boer Wars; Kimberley/Ladysmith, Sieges of

Magallanes-La Antártica Chilena [magal**ya**nays la an**tar**teeka chee**lay**na] Region of S Chile extending S from 48°40′S; comprises the provinces of Ultima Esperanza, Magallanes, Tierra del Fuego and Antártica Chilena; Chile lays claim to the slice of Antarctica between 53°W and 90°W; capital, Punta Arenas; sheep, cattle, forestry, oil, natural gas, food canning; several national parks; Cueva de Miladón, where remains of *Mylodon listai* found, c.8 000 years old. » Chile [i]; Punta Arenas; Tierra del Fuego

Magdalena, River (Sp **Río**) [magda**lay**na] Major river of Colombia, rising in the Cordillera Central; flows N 1 610 km/1 000 ml to enter the Caribbean 14 km/9 ml NW of Barranquilla in a wide delta; navigable for most of its course; fertile valley in upper and mid course, producing coffee, sugar cane, tobacco, cacao, cotton. » Colombia [i]

Magdalenian [magda**leen**ian] The last Upper Palaeolithic archaeological culture of W Europe, named after the cave of La Madeleine, Dordogne, SW France, excavated in 1863. Many sites dated c.16 000–10 000 BC are known from Spain, France, Belgium, Britain, Germany, Switzerland, and Czechoslavakia. Most notable are the painted caves of Lascaux and Altamira. » Altamira; Lascaux; Palaeolithic art; Three Age System

Magdeburg [**mahk**duhboork] 52°08N 11°36E, pop (1982) 287 579. River-port capital of Magdeburg county, C Germany; on R Elbe WSW of Berlin; former capital of Saxony, and important mediaeval trading town at centre of N German plain; access to the Ruhr and Rhine Rivers via the Mittelland Canal; badly bombed in World War 2; railway; college of medicine; college of technology (1953); iron and steel, engineering, chemicals, sugar refining, textiles; 13th–16th-c cathedral. » Germany [i]; Saxony

Magellan, Ferdinand [ma**jel**an] Port **Magalhães**, (c.1480–1521) Portuguese navigator, born near Villa Real. After serving in the East Indies and Morocco, he offered his services to Spain. He sailed from Seville (1519) around the foot of S America (Cape of the Virgins), to reach the ocean which he named the Pacific (1520). He was killed in the Philippines, but his ships continued back to Spain (1522), thus completing the first circumnavigation of the world. The Strait of Magellan is named after him.

Magellan project A US space mission, managed by NASA's Jet Propulsion Laboratory, planned to map Venus at sub-kilometre resolution using side-looking radar from a Venus orbit. Radar is used because of the global cloud cover, the created images being interpreted much as are television images. The technique of Venus radar mapping was pioneered by Soviet Venera 15 and 16 spacecraft in 1983. The Magellan project aims for higher resolution data and global coverage. A single spacecraft was launched using the NASA Shuttle in May 1989 and images were returned to Earth in the latter half of 1990. » NASA; Venera programme; Venus (astronomy)

Magellanic Clouds Two dwarf galaxies, satellites of the Milky Way, visible as cloudy patches in the S night sky, first recorded by Magellan in 1519, c.55 000 parsecs away, and containing a few thousand million stars. They are of immense astrophysical importance, because the individual stars within them can be studied, and they are essentially all at the same distance from us. This removes a great source of uncertainty compared to the situation within our own Galaxy, where actual distances to individual stars are hard to determine. » galaxy; Magellan; Milky Way

Magen David » **Star of David**

Magendie, François [mazh**ã**dee] (1783–1855) French physiologist and physician, born in Bordeaux. As professor of anatomy in the Collège de France (1831), he studied nerve physiology, the veins, and was the first to experiment on hypersensitivity to foreign substances (anaphylaxis). His research demonstrated the functional differences in the spinal nerves, and the effects of drugs on the body. He died at Sannois. » nervous system

Maggiore, Lake (Ital **Lago**) [maja**w**ray], ancient **Verbanus Lacus** area 212 sq km/82 sq ml. Second largest of the N Italian lakes; N end in the Swiss canton of Ticino; length 60 km/37 ml; width 3–5 km/1¾–3 ml; maximum depth 372 m/1 220 ft; major tourist area; lake resorts include Ispra, Stresa, Arona, and (Swiss) Locarno; Borromean Is on W arm of the lake. » Italy [i]

maggot The grub-like larval stage of many true flies. (Order: *Diptera*.) » fly; larva

Maghreb, Eng **Maghrib** area c.9 million sq km/3.5 million sq ml. Area of NW Africa including the countries of Morocco, Algeria, and Tunisia; largely occupied by sedentary and nomadic Berbers of the Kabyle, Shluh, and Tuareg groups. In Arabic, it refers to Morocco only. » Africa

Magi [**may**jiy] **1** A Greek term used in antiquity with a variety of connotations: magi were members of the priestly clan of the Persians, but classical Greek and Roman writers used the term in a derogatory sense and with no necessary connection with Persia to refer to sorcerers and even 'quacks'. **2** A group of unspecified number guided by a mysterious star (*Mat* 2.1–12), who came from 'the East' and presented gifts to the infant Jesus in Bethlehem, after inquiring of his whereabouts from Herod. Origen (3rd-c AD) suggests they were three because of the three gifts of gold, frankincense, and myrrh. Tertullian (c.160–220 AD) deduced that they were kings. Later Christian tradition named them as Gaspar, Melchior, and Balthasar. » Jesus Christ; Matthew, Gospel according to

magic Beliefs and practices which promise a power to intervene in natural processes, but which have no scientific basis. Two common principles of magical belief are that 'like affects like' – that a cloud of smoke rising to the sky will bring rain, for example; and that 'part affects whole' – so that by burning a person's hair-cuttings, for instance, that person will be damaged. In modern industrial societies, belief in magic remains strong, since it offers some hope that malign chance can be combated. Everywhere, magical beliefs are strongest in situations of uncertainty – as Hume remarked, when he commented on the notorious superstitiousness of sailors. » Hume, David

magic mushroom The British liberty cap mushroom *Psilocybe semilanceata* which contains the hallucinogen *psilocybin*. Its use is cultish among young people, who take it as an infusion, adding it to boiling water, in which the active ingredients dissolve. » hallucinogens; mushroom

magic numbers » **nuclear structure**

Maginot Line [**ma**zhinoh] French defensive fortifications stretching from Longwy to the Swiss border, named after

André Maginot (1877–1932), French Minister of Defence (1924–31). The line was constructed (1929–34) to act as protection against German invasion, but Belgium refused to extend it along her frontier with Germany. The German attack of 1940 through the Low Countries largely by-passed the Maginot Line, whose name became synonymous with passive defence and defeatism. » World War 2

magistrate » **justice of the peace; stipendiary magistrate**

Maglemosian [magluh**moh**zian] A N European Mesolithic culture extending from Britain to S Scandinavia and NW Russia c.8000–5600 BC; its name derives from the Danish *Magle Mose* ('Great Bog') on Zeeland, where notable early finds were made. Fishing, fowling, and the hunting of elk and wild cattle constituted its subsistence base – activities archaeologically attested by finds of bows and arrows, barbed spear and harpoon heads, fish hooks, nets, traps, and boats. » Three Age System

magma Molten rock, formed by the partial melting of the Earth's mantle. Under certain geological conditions it may migrate upwards and solidify within the crust to form an igneous intrusion, or may reach the surface, where it loses its volatile constituents and is erupted as lava. » igneous rock; lava

Magna Carta The 'Great Charter', imposed by rebellious barons on King John of England in June 1215, designed to prohibit arbitary royal acts by declaring a body of defined law and custom which the king must respect in dealing with all his free subjects. The principle that kings should rule justly was of long standing, but in Magna Carta the first systematic attempt was made to distinguish between kingship and tyranny. While failing to resolve all the problems raised by the nature of the English crown's relations with the community, it endured as a symbol of the sovereignty of the rule of law, and was of fundamental importance to the constitutional development of England and other countries whose legal and governmental systems were modelled on English conventions. » Barons' War; John

Magna Graecia [**gri**ysha] Literally, 'Great Greece'; the collective name in antiquity for the Greek cities of S Italy. Most (eg Cumae, Sybaris) were founded by settlers from mainland Greece and the Aegean area, but some were offshoots of the Greek colonies in Italy themselves (eg Naples was founded by Cumae, and Paestum by Sybaris). » Cumae; Greek history; Sybaris

Magnani, Anna [many**ah**nee] (1908–73) Italian actress, born in Alexandria, Egypt. Raised in poverty, she first made her living as a night-club singer, but married the director Alessandri and worked in films from 1934, achieving recognition in Rossellini's *Roma città aperta* (1945, Rome, Open City). She won an Oscar for her first Hollywood film *Rose Tattoo* (1955), but much of her later work was for the Italian stage and television, although she appeared in *Fellini's Roma* (1972). She died unexpectedly in Rome following a minor operation.

magnesia Magnesium oxide (MgO), also called **periclase**; a white solid, melting point 2 850°, obtained from heating magnesium carbonate, used as a heat-resisting material. **Milk of magnesia** is a suspension of hydrated magnesia, magnesium hydroxide ($Mg(OH)_2$), used as a laxative. » magnesium

magnesite A magnesium carbonate ($MgCO_3$) mineral formed by the alteration of magnesium-rich rock by fluids. It forms pale, massive ore deposits which are an important source of magnesium. » magnesium

magnesium Mg, element 12, melting point 649°C. A silvery metal, always found combined in nature, but mainly as the carbonate in magnesite ($MgCO_3$) and dolomite ($CaMg(CO_3)_2$). In practice, magnesium is obtained by electrolysis of $MgCl_2$ obtained from brines. It is used in alloys for its lightness (density 1.7 g/cm^3), and for flares and flash bulbs because of the bright white light produced by its very exothermic reaction with oxygen. In its compounds, it almost always shows oxidation state +2; salts of Mg^{2+} are, after those of Ca^{2+}, the main cause of hard water. Hydrated magnesium sulphate is known as *Epsom salts*. » chemical elements; electrolysis [i]; Grignard; magnesia; RR90

magnet A source of magnetic field; always with two poles, named N (north) and S (south), since no isolated single pole exists; like poles repel; opposite poles attract. A permanent magnet is usually made from a ferromagnetic material which at some time has been exposed to a magnetic field. An *electromagnet* is some suitable core material around which is wrapped a current-carrying coil. » ferromagnetism; magnetism; magnetic monopole

magnetic cooling A technique used to cool a sample to temperatures as low as 10^{-3}K (approximately −273°C). If a paramagnetic sample is cooled by conventional means whilst subjected to a magnetic field, and is then thermally insulated and the field removed, the individual magnetic moments in the material are free to become disordered, but in doing so they take up heat from the sample, causing it to cool. This is an adiabatic process, as no heat flows into or out of the sample. » adiabatic process; heat; paramagnetism

magnetic declination The direction of the Earth's magnetic field in terms of the angle, measured in the horizontal plane, which the field makes with the meridian, ie the deviation of the field from true N; also termed the magnetic *variation*. » geomagnetic field

magnetic dip The direction of the Earth's magnetic field in terms of the angle at which the field is inclined to the horizontal; also termed the magnetic *inclination*. » geomagnetic field

magnetic dipole moment » **magnetic moment**

magnetic disk A disk coated with magnetizable material on one or both sides. Magnetic disks are an important type of computer storage medium. Data is written to or read from a set of concentric tracks on the disk by magnetic read/write heads. Two general classes exist: the so-called *hard* disks made of rigid material, and *floppy* disks made of flexible plastic. Disks may be removable from the disk drive (eg floppy disks) or non-removable (eg Winchester disks). In comparison with magnetic tapes, data can be very rapidly retrieved from magnetic disk media. » Bernoulli disk; floppy disk; hard disk; magnetic tape **2**; minidisk; Winchester disk

magnetic domain In a ferromagnetic material, a region in which individual atomic magnetic moments are all aligned parallel, even in the absence of an external field. In unmagnetized material, the direction of magnetic orientation of different domains is unrelated; in magnetized material, they are parallel. » ferromagnetism; magnetic moment

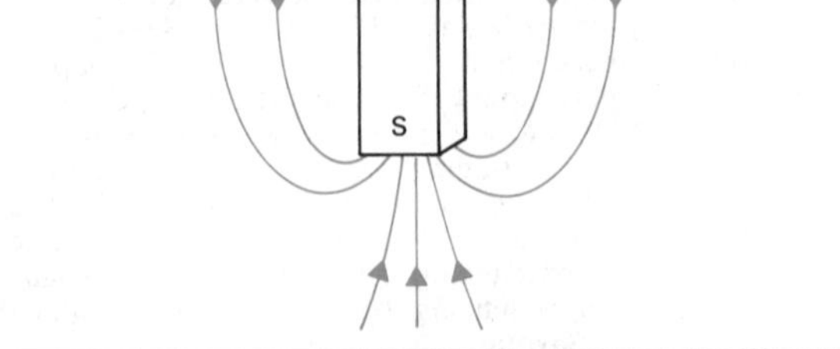

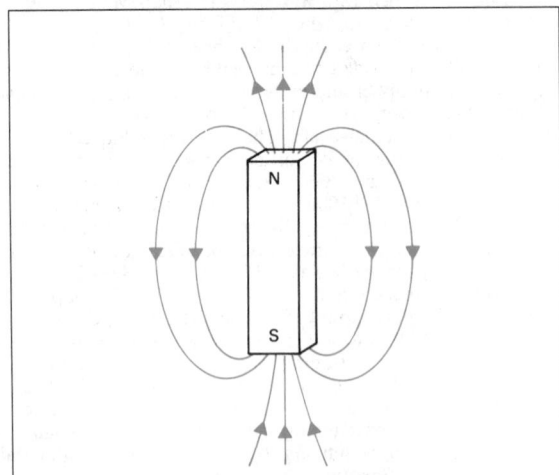

A permanent bar magnet showing lines of magnetic field; N and S denote north and south poles respectively

magnetic field A region of magnetic influence around a magnet, moving charge, or current-carrying wire; denoted by B (units, tesla), the magnetic flux density, and by H (units, A/m), the magnetic field strength. There are many technological applications, including generators and motors. » magnetism

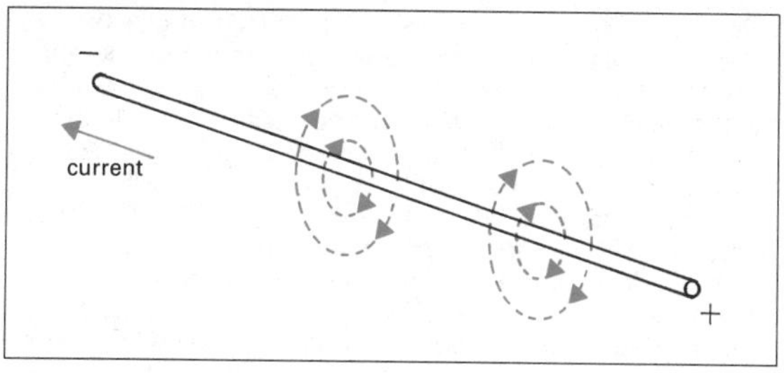

Lines of magnetic field circulate around current-carrying wires

magnetic flux The flow of magnetic influence from the N to S poles of a magnet, or around a current-carrying wire; symbol Φ, units Wb (weber). It is the product of magnetic flux density B (sometimes called 'magnetic field') and area. B is related to magnetic field intensity H via permeability μ: $B=\mu H$. » flux (physics); magnetic field [i]; magnetism; permeability

magnetic hysteresis In ferromagnetic materials such as iron, the dependence of the magnetic field in the material on the magnetizing field and prior magnetization. It is an important source of energy loss in transformers and motors. » magnetization

magnetic moment A property of magnets, currents circulating in loops, and spinning charged particles that dictates the strength of the turning force exerted on the system by a magnetic field, B; symbol μ, units A.m^2 (amp.metre-squared) or J/T (joule per tesla); a vector quantity; also called the **magnetic dipole moment**. Turning force (torque), Γ, is $\Gamma=\mu B\sin\theta$, where θ is the angle between μ and B directions.

Spinning charged particles such as electrons and protons behave like minute current-carrying coils, and so have magnetic moments. Neutrons, despite having zero net charge, also have a magnetic moment, since they spin and are composed of charged particles; their magnetic moment is exploited in neutron diffraction experiments. Atomic nuclei have magnetic moments which are exploited in nuclear magnetic resonance. For certain atoms, the magnetic moment contributions from various electrons, either from their spins or motion about the atomic nucleus, do not cancel. Such atoms have large net atomic magnetic moments, which form the basis of magnetic properties of bulk materials such as paramagnetism and ferromagnetism.

For a magnet in a magnetic field, a force acts that tries to align its poles in the direction of the field (which is how a compass works). Spinning particles precess in a magnetic field, ie the direction of their spins (hence magnetic moments) rotates about the field direction. The magnetic moment of the electron (9.285×10^{-24}J/T) is due solely to the fact that the electron is a spinning charge. For comparison, this is equivalent to a current loop the size of an atomic nucleus carrying a current of 300 000 A. The magnetic moment of a single loop of radius 1 cm carrying a current of 1 A is 3×10^{-4} J/T. » Bohr magnetron; couple; diamagnetism; electromagnetism; ferromagnetism; g-factor; gyromagnetic ratio; magnetic domain; magnetic resonance; magnetization; magnon [i]; moment [i]; neutron diffraction; paramagnetism; precession; torque [i]

magnetic monopole A lone magnetic pole – non-existent, according to classical electromagnetism. British physicist Paul Dirac proposed that monopoles could be present in quantum theories (1931), and they have been predicted in modern gauge theory (1974). Unified theories of fundamental forces predict monopoles of mass 10^{16} greater than proton mass. No monopoles have ever been detected. » Dirac; gauge theory; grand unified theories; magnet

magnetic permeability » **permeability**

magnetic poles The two points on the Earth's surface to which a compass needle points. The N and S magnetic poles have geographical co-ordinates 78½°N 69°W and 78½°S 111°E, and move very slowly with time. » geomagnetic field

magnetic resonance A resonance effect in which atoms or nuclei precessing in a magnetic field absorb energy from incident radio waves; also called **spin resonance**. The magnetic moments of atoms and nuclei precess about the direction of an applied magnetic field. When such a system is subjected to radio waves of certain frequencies related to the precession frequency, a resonance condition is satisfied, and energy is absorbed from the radio beam. The effect provides the basis for important analytical techniques in chemistry. » magnetic moment; nuclear magnetic resonance; paramagnetic resonance; precession

magnetic storm A disturbance in the Earth's magnetic field causing global disruption of radio signals and the occurrence of auroras. There is a tendency for such events to be periodic. They are caused by the interaction of charged solar particles with the Earth's magnetic field. » aurora; geomagnetic field

magnetic susceptibility The ratio of magnetization M to magnetic field strength H; symbol κ, expressed as a pure number. It expresses the dependence of a magnetic field in a material on an external field which results only from current in the magnetizing coils. It is related to permeability, and constant except for ferromagnetic materials. » ferromagnetism; magnetism; magnetization; permeability

magnetic tape 1 A clear plastic film coated with crystalline magnetic particles embedded in varnish, first demonstrated as an effective sound recording and reproducing medium in the 1930s. It came increasingly into use after World War 2, and has more recently been extended to video recording, and data storage for computers. Professional recording practice of the 1980s employs multiple-track open-reel tape, storing the sounds in digital form, whilst domestic use came to be dominated by the compact cassette introduced first by Philips in 1964. To the convenience of the latter has been added increasing quality with new coatings (chrome dioxide, metal) and noise reduction systems. » Dolby system; sound recording; tape recorder; videotape **2** A storage medium used on larger computers, the most common being 2 400 ft (c.750 m) reels of 0.5 in (12.7 mm)-wide tape. In recent years, smaller format magnetic cartridge tape systems have been used as archiving ('back-up') systems for microcomputers, especially those employing Winchester disks. Another variation has been the use of standard audio tapes for digital data storage in low-cost microcomputer systems; but the decreasing cost of floppy disk systems is gradually ousting the rather unreliable audio-tape system. All magnetic-tape systems are relatively slow, compared to magnetic disks, since the access time required to obtain a particular piece of information depends on its position on the tape. » computer; magnetic disk; microcomputer; tape recording

magnetic vector potential A vector quantity whose rate of change with distance is related to magnetic field in a complex way; symbol A, units Wb/m (weber per metre). Electric current is the source for A, as electric charge is for electrostatic potential. A supports a special transformation (a *gauge transformation*) which leaves the related magnetic field equations unchanged. » gauge theory; magnetic field [i]

magnetism Phenomena associated with magnetic fields and magnetic materials, and the study of such phenomena. All magnetic effects ultimately stem from moving electric charges, and all materials have magnetic properties. Electric coils, currents in wires, and permanent magnets are all sources of magnetic field. » diamagnetism; degaussing; electrical and magnetic properties of solids; electromagnetism; ferromagnetism; magnet; magnetic cooling/domain/field [i] /flux/hysteresis/moment/susceptibility/vector potential; magnetization; paramagnetism; permeability; screening; solenoid

magnetite or **lodestone** An iron oxide mineral (Fe_3O_4) with a very strong natural magnetism. It is a valuable ore of iron. » iron; spinel

magnetization Magnetic moment per unit volume, resulting from the individual magnetic moments contributed by molecules of the material; symbol M, units A/m; expresses how much a material is magnetized. For diamagnetic materials, magnetization opposes the external field; for paramagnetic materials, it reinforces it. In these cases, the magnetization is proportional to the external field. For ferromagnets this proportionality fails, and M can be large, even with no external field. » magnetic hysteresis/moment/susceptibility; magnetism

magneto A simple machine which generates alternating current, using the principle that a current is generated when a conductor moves through a magnetic field. One type comprises a coil of thin wire spinning between the poles of a powerful horseshoe magnet. It is used with combustion engines to provide the power for the sparking plugs. » electricity; internal combustion engine; magnetism

magneto-fluid-mechanics » **magnetohydrodynamics**

magneto-optical effects » **Faraday effect; Zeeman effect**

magnetohydrodynamics The mechanics of electrically conducting fluids, such as liquid metals and plasmas when subject to electric and magnetic fields; also called **magneto-fluid-mechanics**. The study is relevant to plasma nuclear fusion, liquid metal cooling systems, and electrical power generation from hot plasmas. » electromagnetic pump; fluid mechanics; plasma (physics)

magnetosphere The region surrounding Solar System bodies having magnetic fields, in which the field is confined under the influence of the streaming solar wind. It is a teardrop-shaped region whose size and shape are constantly readjusting to the variations of the solar wind. Charged particles from both solar wind and Earth's atmosphere are stored in the terrestrial magnetosphere, which has been extensively explored since van Allen 'radiation belts' were discovered by Explorer 1 in 1958. Stored particles are periodically ejected into N and S regions of the atmosphere along the magnetic field and accelerated to high speeds by mechanisms which are poorly understood. Collisions with atmospheric atoms cause emissions of light seen as aurora. Other planets known to have magnetospheres include Jupiter, Saturn, Uranus, and Mercury. » atmospheric physics; aurora; Explorer 1; solar wind; van Allen radiation belts

magnetostriction The change in length of ferromagnetic materials when subject to a magnetic field. For example, nickel will contract along the field direction, and expand in the transverse direction. The effect results from the alignment of magnetic domains under the influence of the external field. It is exploited in ultrasonic transducers. » electrical and magnetic properties of solids; ferromagnetism; transducer; ultrasound

magnetron A device for generating microwaves. It comprises an evacuated chamber with a central cathode surrounded by a circular anode. Electrons expelled from the cathode circle it under the influence of electric and magnetic fields. Microwave production results from resonances between the moving electrons and cavities in the anode. Developed during the 1940s for radar, it is today widely used in microwave ovens. » anode; cathode; microwaves

magnification A measure of an optical system's power to reduce or enlarge an image. For a simple lens, magnification equals the ratio of the angle subtended at the eye without the lens to the angle subtended at the eye with the lens. It is approximately equal to the ratio of size of image to size of object. » lens; optics [i]

Magnitogorsk [mag**nyi**tuhgorsk], formerly **Magnitnaya** 53°28N 59°06E, pop (1983) 419 000. Industrial town in Chelyabinskaya oblast, SW Siberian Russia, on the R Ural; built, 1929–31; airfield; railway; iron and magnetite deposits; one of the largest centres of the Russian metallurgical industry; clothing, footwear; Palace of Metallurgists (1936). » Russia

magnitude A measure of the apparent or absolute brightness of a celestial object, first used (120 BC) by Hipparchus, who referred to the brightest stars as 'first magnitude' and the dimmest as 'sixth magnitude'. The system was given a scientific basis in 1854: equal magnitude steps are in logarithmic progression, such that a magnitude difference of one unit corresponds to a brightness ratio of 2.512, and five magnitudes correspond to a ratio of 100 in actual brightnesses. The zero of the magnitude scale is essentially arbitrary. The **apparent magnitude** of a star is its brightness measured at the Earth, which depends on distance and luminosity. More useful physically is **absolute magnitude**; this is the observed apparent magnitude converted to what the object would have at an (arbitrary) distance of 10 parsecs. Properties of stars and galaxies can be properly compared only via absolute magnitudes. » Hipparchos; luminosity; star; RR5

magnolia A deciduous or evergreen shrub or tree native to E North America and E Asia; leaves often glossy; flowers generally large, cup-shaped, with several whorls of white or pink perianth segments; fruit an almost cone-like strobilus of many carpels. Many species are popular ornamentals. Various characteristics, including the construction of its flower and fruit, make them often regarded as the most primitive flowering plants. (Genus: *Magnolia*, 80 species. Family: *Magnoliaceae*.) » carpel; deciduous plants; evergreen plants; perianth; shrub; strobilus; tree [i]

magnon In magnetic materials, oscillation in the relative orientations of atomic spins, which correspond to magnetization waves. A magnon is a quantum spin wave, appearing as particles capable of scattering with neutrons. Experimentally observable, it is important in understanding the thermodynamic and magnetic properties of magnetic materials. » magnetism; phonon

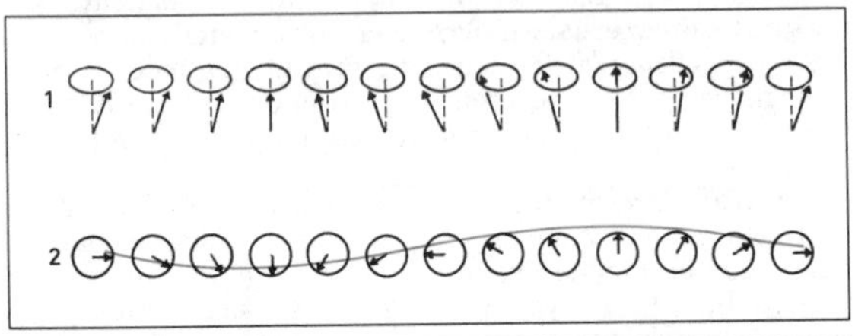

1 Spin vectors on a line of adjacent atoms in magnetic material
2 The same line of atoms viewed from above. A wave can be associated with these spins

Magog » **Gog and Magog**

magot [ma**goh**] » **Barbary ape**

magpie A bird of the crow family (13 species); especially the **black-billed magpie** (*Pica pica*). The name is also used for black-and-white birds in the families *Cracticidae* (the **bell/black-backed/white-backed magpie**), *Anatidae* (the **magpie goose**), *Estrildidae* (the **magpie mannikin**), *Grallinidae* (the **magpie lark**), *Sturnidae* (the **magpie starling**), *Thraupidae* (the **magpie tanager**), and *Turdidae* (the **magpie robin**). » crow; goose; lark; robin; starling; tanager

Magritte, René (François Ghislain) (1898–1967) Belgian painter, born at Lessines. He trained in Brussels, became a commercial artist, and in 1924 was a leading member of the Belgian Surrealist group. Apart from a brief Impressionist phase in the 1940s, he remained constant to Surrealism, producing such works as 'The Wind and the Song' (1928–9) and 'The Human Condition' (1934, 1935). Acclaimed in the USA as an early innovator of the Pop Art of the 1960s, he died in Brussels. » Pop Art; Surrealism

Magyar A Uralic language spoken as a national language by about 11 million people in Hungary, and by a further three million in the surrounding areas. » Uralic languages

mah-jong or **mah-jongg** A Chinese game, originally played with cards, introduced to the West under its present name after World War 1. It is usually played by four people using 144 small tiles divided into six suits. (Sets containing 136 tiles and five suits are also used.) The aim is to collect sequences of tiles, in the manner of rummy card games. In 1937 the National Mah-Jong League was founded in the USA. The name means 'sparrow', a bird of mythical great intelligence, which appears on one of the tiles. » rummy

Mahabalipuram monuments [ma**hah**baleepuram] A collection of Hindu monolithic temples and cave temples at Mahabalipuram in Tamil Nadu, S India; a world heritage site. The temples date from the 7th–8th-c, and are noted for their rich carvings, particularly the rock sculpture known as 'The Descent of the Ganges' or 'Arjuna's Penance'. » Hinduism; Tamil Nadu

Mahabharata [mahah**bah**rata] The sacred book of the Hindus, its 110 000 couplets making it the longest epic in the world. Dating back to the first millennium BC, it was orally transmitted and not printed until the 19th-c. The central plot concerns the conflict between the Kurus (spirits of evil) and Pandus (spirits of good). » epic; Hinduism; Indian literature; Ramayana

Mahamuni Pagoda or **Arakan Pagoda** A temple built near Mandalay, Burma, by King Bodawpaya in 1784 to house the famous 'Mahamuni', a 4 m/13 ft high image of Buddha probably cast in Arakan in the 2nd-c. The statue has been covered with gold leaf to a depth of several centimetres by Buddhist pilgrims. » Buddha; Mandalay

Maharashtra [ma**hah**rashtra] pop (1981) 62 693 898; area 307 762 sq km/118 796 sq ml. State in W India, bounded W by the Arabian Sea; crossed by several mountain ranges and rivers; ruled by the Muslims, 14th–17th-c; British control, early 19th-c; became a state in 1960; capital, Bombay; governed by a 78-member Legislative Council and an elected 287-member Legislative Assembly; rice, sugar cane, groundnuts, cotton; textiles, electrical equipment, machinery, chemicals, oil products; industry largely in Bombay, Poona, and Thana; coal, chromite, iron ore, bauxite. » Ajanta Caves; Bombay; India [i]

Maharishi (Sanskrit, 'great sage') [maha**ri**shee] The Hindu title for a guru or spiritual leader. In the West, the teaching of Transcendental Meditation by the Maharishi Mahesh Yogi is well known. » guru; Transcendental Meditation

Mahayana (Sanskrit, 'greater vehicle') [maha**yah**na] The form of Buddhism commonly practised in China, Tibet, Mongolia, Nepal, Korea, and Japan. It dates from about the 1st-c, when it arose as a development within Buddhism in N India. It emphasizes various forms of popular devotion based on its theory of the bodhisattvas. » bodhisattva; Buddhism

Mahdi (Arabic, 'divinely guided one') [**mah**dee] The name given by Sunni Muslims to those who periodically revitalize the Muslim community. Sunnis look forward to a time before the Last Day when a Mahdi will appear and establish a reign of justice on Earth. Shiites identify the Mahdi with the expected reappearance of the hidden Imam. Many Muslim leaders have claimed the title, such as Mohammed Ahmed, who established a theocratic state in the Sudan in 1882. His great-grandson, Sadiq al-Mahdi, became Prime Minister of the Sudan in 1986. » imam; Islam; Mohammed Ahmed; Shiites; Sunnis

Mahé 4°41S 55°30E; pop (1985e) 65 245; area 153 sq km/59 sq ml. Main island of the Seychelles, Indian Ocean; c.1 600 km/1 000 ml E of Mombasa (Kenya); Victoria, capital of the Seychelles, on the NW coast; airport; tourism; Morne Seychelles National Park. » Seychelles

Mahler, Gustav (1860–1911) Czech-Austrian composer, born in Kalist, Bohemia. He studied at the Vienna Conservatory, and worked as a conductor, becoming artistic director of the Vienna Court Opera in 1897. He resigned after 12 years to devote himself to composition and the concert platform. His mature works consist entirely of songs and nine large-scale symphonies, with a tenth left unfinished. He is best known for the song-symphony *Das Lied von der Erde* (1908–9, The Song of the Earth). He died in Vienna.

mahlstick A stick, with a pad at one end, on which the painter steadies his hand while executing delicate passages in his picture. Mahlsticks can occasionally be seen in artists' self-portraits. » painting

mahogany An evergreen tree native to C America and the Caribbean Is; leaves pinnate; flowers 5-petalled, yellowish, in loose clusters. It is one of several timbers commercially called mahogany, a reddish wood of high quality; heavy, hard, and easily worked. (*Swietenia mahagani*. Family: *Meliaceae*.) » evergreen plants; pinnate; tree [i]

Mahomet » **Mohammed**

Mahon, Derek [mahn] (1941–) British poet, born and educated in Belfast, Northern Ireland. He travelled to N America, returning to Belfast in 1967, and moved to London in 1970. His collections include *Night-Crossing* (1969), *Lives* (1972), *The Snow Party* (1975), and *The Hunt By Night* (1983). » poetry

mahonia » **Oregon grape**

Mahratta » **Maratha**

Maiden Castle A spectacular Iron Age hillfort near Dorchester, Dorset, UK, its multiple earthwork ramparts and ditches enclosing 18 ha/44 acres, and having an internal perimeter of 2.5 km/1.6 ml. Constructed after 350 BC on the site of an earlier Neolithic camp, the existing defences date to c.150 BC, their complex entrances remodelled c.70 BC. Capital of the native tribe of the Durotriges, it is thought to have been captured by Vespasian's Second Legion following the Roman invasion of Britain in AD 43, and abandoned. » Three Age System; Vespasian

maidenhair fern A graceful and delicate perennial fern, found almost everywhere, but especially in the tropics; fronds with slender, black, wiry stalks; leaflets stalked, irregularly fan-shaped, the margins turned under and bearing sori. (Genus: *Adiantum*, 200 species. Family: *Polypodiaceae*.) » fern; perennial; sorus

maidenhair tree » **ginkgo**

Maidstone 51°17N 0°32E, pop (1981) 87 068. County town in Maidstone district, Kent, SE England; on the R Medway, S of Chatham; birth place of William Hazlitt; railway; paper, fruit canning, brewing, cement, confectionery; 14th-c All Saints Church, 14th-c Archbishop's palace, Chillington Manor, Tyrwhitt Drake museum of carriages.

Mailer, Norman (1923–) US writer, born in Long Branch, New Jersey. Educated at Harvard, he served as an infantryman (1944–6), and in 1948 published *The Naked and the Dead*, a panoramic World War 2 novel. His later novels, such as *American Dream* (1964), had a more mixed reception. Identified with many of the US liberal protest movements, he has also written political studies, such as *The Armies of the Night* (1968, Pulitzer Prize in 1969). Later works include *Ancient Evenings* (1983) and *Tough Guys Don't Dance* (1984). » American literature; novel

Maillol, Aristide (Joseph Bonaventure) [ma**yol**] (1861–1944) French sculptor, born at Banyuls-sur-Mer. He studied at the Ecole des Beaux-Arts, and spent some years designing tapestries. The latter half of his life was devoted to the representation of the nude female figure in a style of monumental simplicity and classical serenity. He died near Banyuls-sur-Mer. » French art

mailmerge A word-processing facility which allows inserts to be placed in a standard document. It is widely used for the bulk mailing of circulars in letter form, as it gives these the semblance of having been individually produced. » word processor

Maiman, Theodore H(arold) (1927–) US physicist, born in Los Angeles. He studied physics at Colorado and Stanford, and joined Hughes Research Laboratories, Miami, in 1955. He was much interested in the maser, devised in 1953 to produce coherent microwave radiation. He improved its design, and by 1960 devised the first working laser, which gave coherent visible light. From the 1960s he founded companies to develop laser devices, and in 1977 joined TRW Electronics of California. » laser [i]; maser; Schawlow

Maimonides, Moses [miy**mon**ideez], originally **Moses ben Maimon** (1135–1204) Jewish philosopher, born at Córdoba. He studied Aristotelian philosophy and Greek medicine from Arab teachers, and migrated to Egypt, where he became physician to Saladin. A major influence on Jewish thought, he wrote an important commentary on the Mishna, and a great philosophical work, the *Dalālat al-hā'irin* (Guide of the Perplexed), arguing for the reconciliation of Greek philosophy and religion. He died in Cairo. » Mishnah

main sequence In astronomy, a broad band in the Hertzsprung-Russell diagram, in which most stars lie. A star spends most of its life on this main sequence, while it burns hydrogen to helium. Once the hydrogen in the core is consumed, the star evolves away from the main sequence, becoming first a red giant. The Sun is a main sequence star. » helium; Hertzsprung-Russell diagram [i]; hydrogen; red giant

Mainbocher [manboh**shay**], byname of **Main Rousseau Bocher** (c.1890–1976) US fashion designer, born in Chicago. He studied and worked in Chicago and Paris, eventually becoming a fashion artist with *Harper's Bazaar* and, later, editor of French *Vogue* until 1929. He started his couture house in Paris in 1930, one of his creations being Mrs Wallis Simpson's wedding dress. He opened a salon in New York City in 1940, which continued until 1971. He died in Munich. » Edward VIII; fashion

Maine pop (1987e) 1 187 000, area 86 153 sq km/33 265 sq ml. New England state in the NE corner of the USA, divided into 16 counties; bounded N and E by Canada; the 'Pine Tree State'; explored by the Cabots in the 1490s; settled first by the French in 1604, and by the English in 1607; separated from Massachusetts in 1820, when admitted to the Union as 23rd state; capital, Augusta; largest town, Portland; the Kennebec and Penobscot Rivers run S to the Atlantic Ocean; crossed by the Appalachian Mts which rise to 1 605 m/5 266 ft at Mt Katahdin in Baxter State Park; dotted with over 1 600 lakes, largest L Moosehead; N 80% forested; S coastal strip mainly arable; main industries agriculture (especially potatoes), forestry, fishing. » Augusta (Maine); United States of America [i]; RR38

mainframe computer A somewhat dated term still used to refer to very large capacity computers, and to distinguish them from the smaller computers now widely available. However, the distinction between mainframe and other computers is not always clear. The term **minicomputer**, for example, is sometimes used to refer to computers which do not fall into the category of either microcomputer or mainframe computer. » microcomputer

mainstreaming The introduction of children with special educational needs, many of whom were formerly known as 'handicapped', into ordinary schools. In both the USA and UK, it was decided in the late 1970s and early 1980s to reduce the number of such children who attended special schools. The argument in favour was that many children in special schools were set targets which were too low, and also that they would gain from being educated alongside so-called 'normal' children. Reservations were expressed about most schools' ability, without substantial training for staff and extra resources, to offer skilled specialist help to children with different needs. » special education; streaming

maintained school A school which receives its money from a local education authority. It is often known popularly as a 'state school', though this term is inappropriate in a country where the state does not run schools. » independent schools; public school

maintenance Money payments paid by one marriage partner to help support the other during or following legal separation or divorce. The payments are often referred to as *alimony*, but terminology varies (eg it is *periodical allowance* in Scotland). » divorce

Maintenon, Madame de, [mĩtuhnõ] byname of **Françoise d'Aubigné, Marquise de Maintenon** (1635–1719) Second wife of Louis XIV of France, born at Niort. In 1652 she married the crippled poet, Paul Scarron, and on his death was reduced to poverty. In 1669 she took charge of the King's two sons by Mme de Montespan, and moved with them to the court in 1673. By 1674 the King's generosity enabled her to purchase the estate of Maintenon, near Paris, which was converted to a marquisate. After the Queen's death (1683) Louis married her secretly. On the King's death (1715) she retired to the educational institution for poor girls which she had founded at St-Cyr (1686), where she died. » Louis XIV; Montespan; Scarron

Mainz [miynts], Fr **Mayence** 50°00N 8°16E, pop (1983) 186 400. Old Roman city and capital of Rheinland-Pfalz province, Germany; on left bank of R Rhine opposite mouth of R Main; important traffic junction and commercial centre; railway; university (1477); headquarters of radio and television corporations; centre of the Rhine wine trade; glass materials, electronics, publishing; Gutenberg set up his printing press here; cathedral (mostly 11th–13th-c); Mainzer Fastnacht (Shrovetide); tourist river cruises along the Rhine to Cologne. » Germany [i]; Gutenberg

maiolica [mayolika] Tin-glazed earthenware produced in Italy since before 1400. In the Renaissance period the decoration was often similar to the work of the most important contemporary Italian painters of complex religious and secular scenes. » Renaissance

maize The only cereal native to the New World, originally tropical and developed as a major food crop from wild types by the Indians of C America; also called **sweet corn** and **Indian corn**. Modern strains are suitable for temperate regions. It is a robust annual; male flowers in a terminal tassel; females forming a woody cob, bearing rows of plump, white, yellow, red, or purple grains. It is eaten ripe or unripe as a vegetable. The grains and foliage are used for animal fodder, and it also yields flour, starch, syrup, alcohol, and paper. (*Zea mays*. Family: *Gramineae*.) » annual; cereals; grass [i]; vegetable

majlis [**maj**lees] The meetings of the ruler and his advisers in countries of the Arabian Gulf.

Major, John (1943–) British politician, born in London. He had a career in banking before becoming an MP in 1976. He rose to become Chief Secretary to the Treasury, was unexpectedly made Foreign Secretary in Margaret Thatcher's Cabinet reshuffle in 1989, and soon after replaced Nigel Lawson as Chancellor of the Exchequer. He won the leadership contest following Mrs Thatcher's resignation, and became Prime Minister in November 1990. » Conservative Party; Lawson; Thatcher

Majorca [mayawka], Span **Mallorca**, ancient **Balearis Major** pop (1981) 561 215; area 3 640 sq km/1 400 sq ml. Largest island in the Balearics, W Mediterranean, 240 km/150 ml N of Algiers; tree-covered Sierra del Alfabia rises to 1 445 m/4 741 ft at Torrellas; taken in 1229 by James I of Aragón; in the Middle Ages, famous for its porcelain (majolica); chief town, Palma; popular tourist resort; pottery, brandy, jewellery, mining, sheep, timber, fishing; many Roman, Phoenician, and Carthaginian remains. » Balearic Islands; Spain [i]

majuscule [**ma**juhskyool] A form of writing in which the letters are of uniform height, as if contained within a pair of horizontal lines. Usually called CAPITAL letters, the Greek and Roman alphabets were originally written in this way. It is contrasted with the later system known as **minuscule**, in which parts of the letters extend above and below the horizontal lines ('small letters'), eg *h*, *g*. Minuscule writing was a gradual development, in regular use for Greek by the 7th–8th-c AD. The 'dual alphabet', using both capital and small letters, dates from the 8th-c. » graphology

Makale » **Mekele**

Makarios III, originally **Mihail Khristodoulou Mouskos** (1913–77) Archbishop and Primate of the Orthodox Church of Cyprus, and President of Cyprus (1960–74, 1974–77), born at Ano Panciyia. He was ordained priest in 1946, elected Bishop of Kition in 1948, and Archbishop in 1950. He reorganized the Enosis (Union) movement, was arrested and detained in 1956, but returned to a tumultuous welcome in 1959 to become chief Greek-Cypriot Minister in the new Greek-Turkish provisional government. Later that year he was elected President. He died at Nicosia. » Cyprus [i]; Enosis

Makassar » **Ujung Padang**

Makassar or **Macassar Strait** [ma**ka**sah] Indonesian **Selat**, Stretch of water between the islands of Borneo in the W and Sulawesi (Celebes) in the E, linking the Java Sea (S) to the Celebes Sea (N); length 720 km/447 ml. » Indonesia [i]

Makonde [ma**kohn**day] A Bantu-speaking agricultural group of N Mozambique and SE Tanzania. Many work as migrant labourers on the E African coast. They lack any centralized political system, and are famous as woodcarvers, often drawing on Makonde folklore for themes. Population c.1 million. » Bantu-speaking peoples; Mozambique [i]; Tanzania [i]

Maksutov telescope An optical telescope in which the principal image-forming lens and mirror surfaces are spherical, and therefore easy to make. The design was published in the USSR by D D Maksutov in 1944. » telescope [i]

Makua A Bantu-speaking agricultural people of N Mozambique and S Tanzania. Strongly influenced by E African coast Arabs, many converted to Islam. Population c.3.8 million. » Bantu-speaking peoples; Islam; Mozambique [i]; Tanzania [i]

Malabo, formerly **Clarencetown** or **Port Clarence**, and **Santa Isabel** 3°45N 8°50E, pop (1983) 24 100. Seaport capital of Equatorial Guinea, W Africa; on island of Bioko, Gulf of Guinea; founded by British in 1827; airfield; coffee, cocoa, timber trade. » Bioko; Equatorial Guinea [i]

malabsorption The failure of intestinal absorption of nutrients taken as food. In general, this results in diarrhoea, abdominal pain and distension, loss of weight, anaemia, and features of specific vitamin deficiencies. Underlying causes include the tropical disease sprue, which may have an infective cause; abnormal bacterial proliferation in the small intestine, due to congenital or acquired blind loops of intestine; Crohn's disease, a non-specific chronic inflammation of the alimentary tract that affects young people; and pancreatic disease. The most important cause in the UK is coeliac disease. » coeliac disease; Crohn's disease; intestine

Malacca or **Melaka** [malaka] pop (1980) 446 769; area 1 657 sq km/640 sq ml. State in SW Peninsular Malaysia; bounded W by the Strait of Malacca; one of the former Straits Settlements; capital, Malacca, pop (1980) 88 073; centre of a great trading empire since the 15th-c; Islam spread from here throughout the Malayan Peninsula; held at various times by the Portuguese, Dutch, and British; large Chinese population; rubber, tin, rice; state museum, St John's Fort, St Peter's Church (1710), Cheng Hoon Teng Temple (oldest Chinese temple in Malaysia), Kampung Kling Mosque, Vinayagar Moorthi Temple. » Malaysia [i]

Malacca, Strait of Channel between the Malaysia Peninsula and the Indonesian island of Sumatra; 800 km/500 ml long by 50–320 km/30–200 ml wide; links the Andaman Sea to the S China Sea; an important shipping lane; largest port, Singapore.

Malachi [**ma**lakhiy] or **Malachias, Book of** The last of the twelve so-called 'minor' prophetic writings of the Hebrew Bible/Old Testament; probably anonymous, since 'Malachi' in Hebrew means 'my messenger'; possibly the work of a 'cult prophet' in view of the strong criticism of priestly neglect of cultic requirements. Usually dated c.510–460 BC, in the period before the reforms of Ezra and Nehemiah, it stresses the need for faithfulness to the covenant with Yahweh, the need for fidelity in marriage, and the threat of a coming day of judgment. » Old Testament; prophet; Yahweh

malachite [**ma**lakiyt] A hydrated copper carbonate mineral ($Cu_2CO_3(OH)_2$) found in weathered copper ore deposits. It is bright green in colour. » copper; Plate IV

malachite green [**ma**lakiyt] A green dye, named for its similarity in colour to the mineral malachite; there is no structural

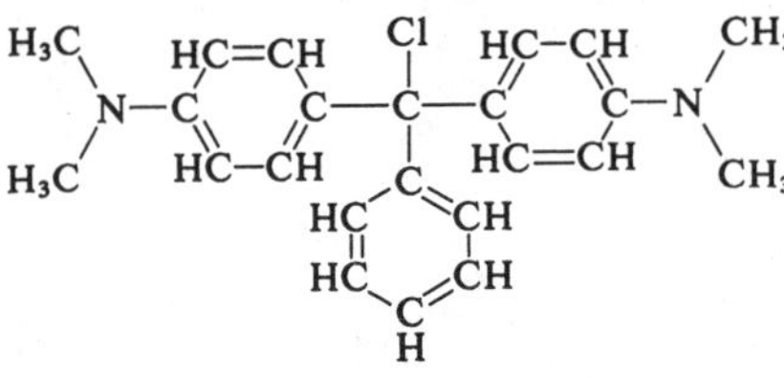

relationship. It is an example of a large class of dyes called *triphenylmethanes* on account of their structure. » dyestuff; malachite

Malachy, St (c.1094–1148), feast day 3 November. Irish churchman, born at Armagh. He became Abbot of Bangor (1121), Bishop of Connor (1125), and Archbishop of Armagh (1134). In 1140 he journeyed to Rome, visiting St Bernard at Clairvaux, and on his return (1142) introduced the Cistercian Order into Ireland. In 1148 he went to France, and died at Clairvaux. » Bernard of Clairvaux, St; Cistercians

Málaga [**ma**laga], ancient **Malaca** 36°43N 4°23W, pop (1981) 503 251. Port and capital of Málaga province, Andalusia, S Spain; at the mouth of R Guadalmedina, 544 km/338 ml S of Madrid; founded by the Phoenicians, 12th-c BC; part of Spain, 1487; bishopric; airport; railway; car ferries to Casablanca, Tangier, Genoa; university (1972); tourism, textiles, beer, wine, chemicals, food processing, fruit trade; birthplace of Picasso; Moorish Alcazaba, cathedral (16th–18th-c), Roman theatre, fine arts museum; Fiestas of La Virgen del Carmen (Jul), fair (Aug), Festival of Spain (Aug–Sep), Costa del Sol Rally (Dec). » Andalusia; Picasso; Spain [i]

Malagasy The peoples of the island of Madagascar, comprising about 50 ethnic groups, of diverse origins, but the strongest element from Indonesia; Malagasy languages are Malayo-Polynesian. There are also Swahili and Bantu groups from the African mainland in the NW, where there is a strong Muslim minority. The traditional economy is based on agriculture, with rice grown as a staple, and cattle farming important in many areas. Before colonial rule groups were politically autonomous, and mostly lacking centralized organization, except for the Merina of the central highlands, who established a powerful kingdom in the 16th-c. Most Malagasy are Protestant Christians. Population c.9 million. » Madagascar [i]

Malamud, Bernard [**ma**lamood] (1914–86) US novelist and short-story writer, born and died in New York City, and educated at Columbia University. His early novels *The Natural* (1952) and *The Assistant* (1957) combine realistic descriptions of life among poor Jewish immigrants in New York City, and an element of fantasy that reappears in his short stories, such as *The Magic Barrel* (1958). *The Fixer* (1967) is a more directly serious depiction of Jewish life in Czarist Russia. Later novels include *Pictures of Fidelman* (1965) and *Dublin's Lives* (1979). » American literature; novel

malamute [**ma**lamyoot] » **Alaskan malamute**

Malan, Daniel F(rançois) [ma**lan**] (1874–1959) South African statesman and Prime Minister (1948–54), born at Riebeek West, Cape Province. Educated at Stellenbosch and Utrecht, in 1905 he joined the ministry of the Dutch Reform Church, but in 1915 left to become editor of *Die Burger*, the Nationalist newspaper. He became an MP in 1918, and in 1924 held the portfolios of the Interior, Education, and Public Health. In 1939 he founded with Hertzog the Nationalist Party, was Leader of the Opposition, and in 1948 became Premier and Minister for External Affairs, introducing the controversial apartheid policy. He died at Stellenbosch. » apartheid; Hertzog

Mälar, Lake [**me**lah], Swed **Mälaren** area 1 140 sq km/440 sq ml. Lake in SE Sweden, extending 113 km/70 ml inland from the Baltic Sea; city of Stockholm on both sides of the strait connecting the lake with the Baltic Sea. » Stockholm; Sweden [i]

malaria A disease caused by infection with one of four species of *Plasmodium* transmitted by the bite of infected mosquitoes (*Anopheles*). The disease is endemic or sporadic through most of the tropics and subtropics. Infections with *Plasmodium vivax* and *ovale* give rise to bouts of fever every alternate day; *Plasmodium malariae* causes fever every third day. *Plasmodium falciparum* infection is the most serious, giving rise to more continuous fever, jaundice, and cerebral infection, and may be rapidly fatal. Diagnosis is best made by determining which parasite is involved in a drop of blood examined under the microscope. Several effective drugs are available for treatment. » Anopheles; blackwater fever; mosquito; spleen

Malatesta Lords of the state of Rimini in NE Italy from the 13th-c to the 16th-c; among the most durable of several families of *signori* who dominated political life in the Italian Renaissance. Originally the political 'vicars' of the papacy, the Malatesta state was overthrown in 1500 by a coalition of the papacy and the French. » Papal States

Malawi, official name **Republic of Malawi** [ma**lah**wee] pop (1990e) 8 830 000; area 118 484 sq km/45 735 sq ml. SE African republic, divided into three regions and 24 districts; bounded SW and SE by Mozambique, E by L Nyasa (L Malawi), N by Tanzania, and W by Zambia; capital, Lilongwe; chief towns, Blantyre, Limbe, Salima; timezone GMT +2; population largely Bantu; chief religions, Protestantism (55%), Roman Catholicism (20%), Islam (20%); official languages, English, Chichewa; unit of currency, the kwacha of 100 tambala; crossed N–S by the Great Rift Valley, containing Africa's third largest lake, L Nyasa (L Malawi); high plateaux on either side (900–1 200 m/3 000–4 000 ft); Shire highlands (S) rise to nearly 3 000 m/10 000 ft at Mt Mulanje; tropical climate in S, with high year-round temperatures, 28–37°C; average annual rainfall, 740 mm/30 in; more moderate temperatures in C; higher rainfall in mountains overlooking L Nyasa, 1 500–2 000 mm/60–80 in; visited by the Portuguese, 17th-c; European contact established by David Livingstone, 1859; Scottish church missions in the area; claimed as the British

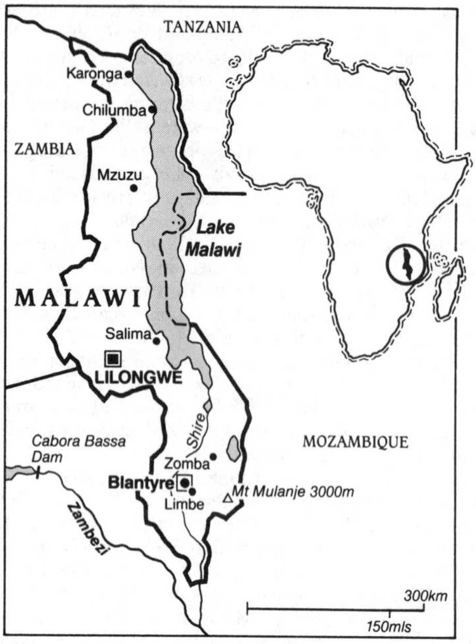

□ international airport

Protectorate of Nyasaland, 1891; British colony, 1907; in the 1950s joined with N and S Rhodesia to form the Federation of Rhodesia and Nyasaland; independence, 1964; republic, 1966; governed by a president, elected for five years (though the first president, Dr Banda, was elected for life in 1970); there is a cabinet and a 112-member National Assembly; economy based on agriculture, which employs 90% of the population; tobacco, sugar, tea, cotton, groundnuts, maize; textiles, matches, cigarettes, beer, spirits, shoes, cement. » Banda; Lilongwe; Livingstone, David; RR26 national holidays; RR55 political leaders

Malawi, Lake » **Nyasa, Lake**

Malay (people) A cluster of Malay-speaking (Austronesian) peoples of the Malay Peninsula (where they are 54% of the population), and neighbouring islands and territory, including parts of Borneo and Sumatra. Most became Hindu before being converted to Islam in the 15th-c, and Hindu Indian influence on their culture is still strong. Most Malay villages are along the rivers and coasts in jungle territory. They grow wet rice and rubber, a major cash crop. » Austronesian languages; Islam; Malay (language)

Malay (language) The language of the Malay Peninsula, which has provided the modern standard language, **Bahasa Indonesia**. A pidginized form, **Bazaar Malay**, has been a lingua franca in the region for many centuries, before the advent of Western trade and colonialism. A further variety, **Baba Malay**, is used by Chinese communities in Malaysia. Inscriptions in Malay date from the 7th-c AD. » Bahasa Indonesia; Malay (people)

Malay bear » **sun bear**

Malayalam The Dravidian language associated with the S Indian state of Kerala. It has about 25 million speakers. » Dravidian languages; Kerala

Malaysia [malayzha] pop (1990e) 17 886 000; area 329 749 sq km/127 283 sq ml. Independent federation of states in SE Asia, comprising 11 states and a federal territory in Peninsular Malaysia, and the E states of Sabah and Sarawak on the island of Borneo; capital, Kuala Lumpur; chief cities, George Town, Petaling Jaya, Ipoh, Melaka, Johor Baharu, Kuching, Kota Kinabalu; timezone GMT +8; ethnic groups include Malay (59%), Chinese (32%), Indian (9%); official language, Bahasa Malaysia (Malay), but Chinese, English, and Tamil also spoken; several world religions practised; unit of currency, the Malaysian ringgit.

Physical description. Mountain chain of granite and limestone running N–S, rising to Mt Tahan (2 189 m/7 182 ft); narrow E and broader W coastal plains; peninsula length 700 km/435 ml, width up to 320 km/200 ml; mostly tropical rainforest and mangrove swamp; coastline of long, narrow beaches; chief river, the Pahang (456 km/283 ml); Sarawak, on NW coast of Borneo, has a narrow, swampy coastal belt backed by foothills rising sharply towards mountain ranges on the Indonesian frontier; Sabah, in NE corner of Borneo, has a deeply indented coastline and narrow W coastal plain, rising sharply into the Crocker Range, reaching 4 094 m/13 432 ft at Mt Kinabalu, Malaysia's highest peak; tropical climate strongly influenced by monsoon winds; high humidity; average annual rainfall in the peninsula, 260 mm/10 in (S), 800 mm/32 in (N); Sarawak, 470–670 mm/19–26 in; Sabah, 260–670 mm/10–26 in; average daily temperatures, 21–32°C in coastal areas, 12–25°C in the mountains.

History and government. Part of Srivijaya Empire, 9th–14th-c; Hindu and Muslim influences, 14th–15th-c; Portugal, the Netherlands, and Britain vied for control from the 16th-c; Singapore, Malacca, and Penang formally incorporated into the British Colony of the Straits Settlements, 1826; British protection extended over Perak, Selangor, Negeri Sembilan, and Pahang, constituted into the Federated Malay States, 1895; protection treaties with several other states (Unfederated Malay States), 1885–1930; occupied by Japanese in World War 2; after the war, Sarawak became a British colony, Singapore became a separate colony, the colony of North Borneo was formed, and the Malay Union was established, uniting the Malay states and Straits Settlements of Malacca and Penang; Federation of Malaya, 1948; independence, 1957; constitutional monarchy of Malaysia, 1963; Singapore withdrew from the Federation, 1965; governed by a bicameral Federal Parliament (*Majlis*), consisting of a 69-member Senate (*Dewan Negara*) elected for six years and a 177-member House of Representatives (*Dewan Rakyat*) elected for five years; head of state is a monarch elected for five years by his fellow sultans; advised by a prime minister and cabinet.

Economy. Discovery of tin in the late 19th-c brought European investment; rubber trees introduced from Brazil; rice, palms, timber, fishing; iron ore, ilmenite, gold, bauxite, oil, natural gas; textiles, rubber and oil products, chemicals, electronic components, electrical goods, tourism. » Johor; Kedah; Kelantan; Kuala Lumpur; Malacca; Negeri Sembilan; Pahang; Penang; Perak; Perlis; Sabah; Sarawak; Selangor; Singapore; Terengganu; RR26 national holidays; RR56 political leaders

Malcolm III, called **Canmore** ('large headed') (c.1031–93) King of Scots (1058–93), the son of Duncan I, who was slain by Macbeth in 1040. He returned from exile in 1054, and con-

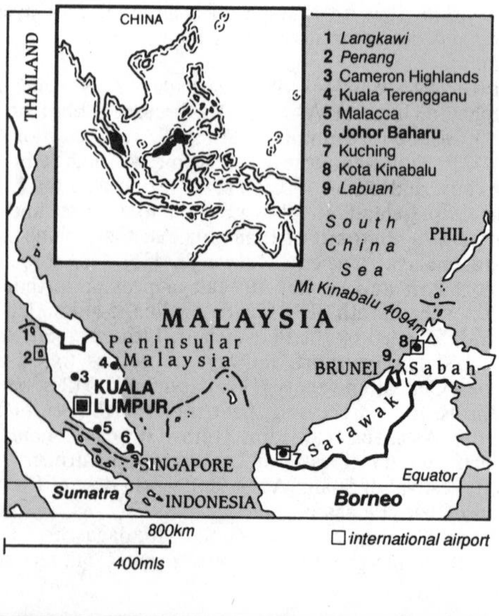

□ international airport

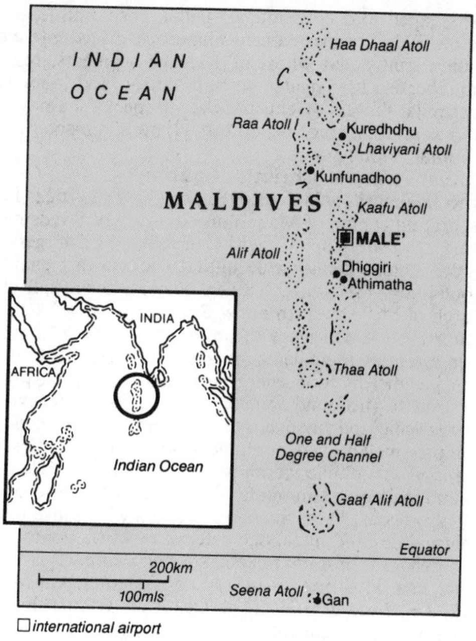

quered S Scotland; but he did not become King until he had defeated and killed Macbeth (1057), and disposed of Macbeth's stepson, Lulach (1058). He married as his second wife the English Princess Margaret (later St Margaret), sister of Edgar the Atheling, and launched five invasions of England between 1061 and his death in a skirmish near Alnwick, Northumberland. » Macbeth; Northumbria

Malcolm, George (1917–) British harpsichordist and conductor, born in London. He studied at the Royal College of Music and at Oxford, and was Master of the Music at Westminster Cathedral (1947–59), since when he has earned a wide reputation as a freelance harpsichord soloist and a conductor. » harpsichord

Maldives [**mol**diyvz], formerly **Maldive Islands**, official name **Republic of Maldives**, Divehi **Divehi Jumhuriya** pop (1990e) 214 000; land area 300 sq km/116 sq ml. Island archipelago in the Indian Ocean; 670 km/416 ml SW of Sri Lanka; comprises 1 190 islands, 202 inhabited; 823 km/511 ml N–S, 130 km/81 ml E–W at its greatest width; divided into 19 administrative atolls; capital, Malé; timezone GMT +5½; population mostly of Aryan origin; official language, Divehi, but English widely spoken; official religion, Islam (Sunni); unit of currency, the Maldivian rupee (*rufiyaa*) of 100 laaris; small and low-lying islands, with sandy beaches fringed with coconut palms; generally warm and humid; affected by SW monsoons (Apr–Oct); average annual rainfall, 2 100 mm/83 in; average daily temperature, 22°C; former dependency of Ceylon; British protectorate, 1887–1965; independence, 1968; governed by a president, elected every five years, a ministers' *Majlis* (cabinet), and a citizens' *Majlis* of 48 members elected for five years; breadfruit, banana, mango, cassava, sweet potato, millet; fishing, shipping, tourism. » Indian Ocean; Islam; Malé; RR26 national holidays; RR56 political leaders

Malé [**ma**lee], Divehi **Daviyani** 4°00N 73°28E, pop (1985e) 38 000; area 2 sq km/0.77 sq ml. Chief atoll and capital of the Maldives; over 700 km/435 ml WSW of Sri Lanka; airport; commercial centre; trade in breadfruit, copra, palm mats. » Maldives

Malebranche, Nicolas [**mal**brãsh] (1638–1715) French philosopher, born and died in Paris. He joined the Oratorians (1660), and studied theology until Descartes' works drew him to philosophy. His major work is *De la recherche de la vérité* (1674, Search after Truth), which defends many of Descartes' views. » Descartes; occasionalism

maleic acid [mal**ay**ik] $C_4H_4O_4$, IUPAC **cis-butenedioic acid**, melting point 139°C. A geometrical isomer of fumaric acid, but as the carboxyl groups are on the same side of the double bond, it forms an internal hydrogen bond, indicated in the formula, and thus has a much lower melting point than fumaric acid. It easily forms an anhydride by the loss of a water molecule with the formation of a ring. » acid; anhydride; fumaric acid; IUPAC

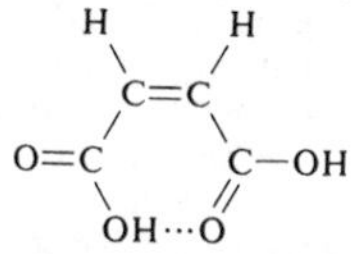

Malenkov, Giorgiy Maksimilianovich [**mal**yenkof] (1901–79) Soviet politician and Premier (1953–5), born at Orenburg. He joined the Communist Party in 1920 and was involved in the collectivization of agriculture and the purges of the 1930s under Stalin. He became a member of the Politburo and Deputy Premier in 1946, succeeding Stalin as Party First Secretary and Premier in 1953. In 1955 he resigned as Premier, admitting responsibility for the failure of Soviet agricultural policy, and in 1957 was sent to Kazakhstan as manager of a hydroelectric plant. He died in Moscow. » communism; Khrushchev; Stalin

Malesherbes, Chrétien (Guillaume de Lamoignon) de [mal**zairb**] (1721–94) French statesman, born in Paris. In 1744 he became a counsellor of the Parlement of Paris, and in 1750 was made chief censor of the press. At Louis XVI's accession (1774) he was made Secretary of State for the royal household, instituting prison and legal reforms in tandem with Turgot's economic improvements. He resigned in 1776 on the eve of Turgot's dismissal. Despite his reforming zeal, he was mistrusted as an aristocrat during the Revolution. Arrested as a Royalist (1794) he was guillotined in Paris. » French Revolution [i]; Louis XVI; Turgot

Malevich, Kazimir [mal**yay**vich] (1878–1935) Russian painter, born in Kiev. He studied in Moscow in 1902, and together with Mondrian was one of the earliest pioneers of pure abstraction, founding the Suprematist movement. He claimed to have painted the first totally abstract picture, a black square on a white background, as early as 1913. Certainly he was exhibiting similar work by 1915, and went on to paint a series entitled 'White on White'. He died in St Petersburg. » abstract art; Suprematism

Mali, official name **Republic of Mali**, Fr **République de Mali** [**mah**lee] pop (1990e) 8 150 000; area 1 240 192 sq km/478 714 sq ml. Republic in W Africa, divided into six regions; bounded NE by Algeria, NW by Mauritania, W by Senegal, SW by Guinea, S by Côte d'Ivoire, SE by Burkina Faso, and E by Niger; capital, Bamako; chief towns include Ségou, Mopti,

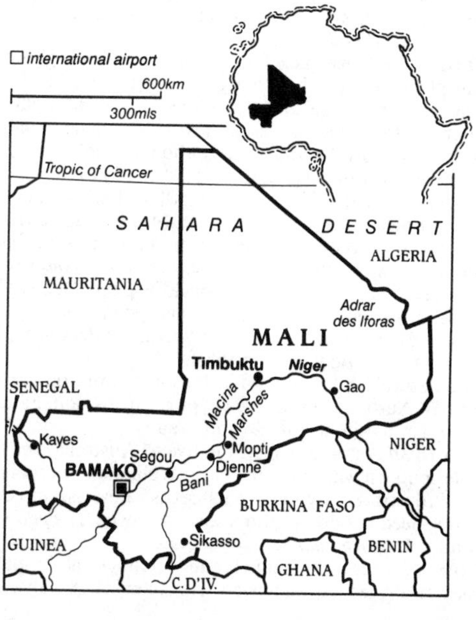

Sikasso, Kayes, Gao, Timbuktu; timezone GMT; chief ethnic groups, Mande tribes; official language, French, with local languages widely spoken; chief religion, Islam (90%); unit of currency, the Mali franc; landlocked country on the fringe of the Sahara; lower part of the Hoggar massif (N); arid plains 300–500 m/1 000–1 600 ft; mainly savannah land in the S; main rivers the Niger and Sénégal; featureless desert land (N) with sand dunes, little rainfall, and extremes of temperature; a Sahelian transition zone over a third of the country, with a 3-month rainy season; further S, increased rainfall (Jun–Oct), c.1 000 mm/40 in; mediaeval state controlling the trade routes between savannah and Sahara, reaching its peak in the 14th-c; important in the Islamicization of W Africa; governed by France, 1881–95; territory of French Sudan (part of French West Africa) until 1959; partnership with Senegal as the Federation of Mali, 1959; separate independence, 1960; governed by a president, elected every six years, and an 82-member National Assembly; economy mainly subsistence agriculture; sorghum, millet, rice, maize, cotton, groundnuts; crops severely affected by drought conditions; small amounts of marble, limestone, bauxite, nickel, manganese; fishing, livestock, food processing, textiles, leather, cement; some tourism. » African history; Bamako; Islam; Sahara Desert; sahel; Senegal [i]; Songhai; Timbuktu; RR26 national holidays; RR56 political leaders

malic acid HOOC–CH_2–CH(OH)–COOH, IUPAC **2-hydroxybutanedioic acid**, melting point 100°C. An acid found in unripe fruit, especially apples. Loss of water produces maleic and fumaric acids. » acid; fumaric acid; IUPAC; maleic acid [i]

Malinke [ma**ling**kay] or **Mandingo** A cluster of autonomous Mande-speaking agricultural peoples of Mali, Guinea, Senegal, and neighbouring areas. All groups are under the authority of a hereditary noble class. Malinke groups founded the Mandingo Empire of Mali (13th–16th-c). Population c.1.5 million. » Mande

Malinowski, Bronisław (Kasper) [mali**nof**skee] (1884–1942) Polish anthropologist, born in Kraków. Educated at Kraków and Leipzig, in 1910 he went to London, and taught at the London School of Economics, where he became a professor in 1927. In 1938 he went to the USA, where he accepted a post at Yale. He was the pioneer of 'participant observation' as a method of fieldwork (notably, in the Trobriand Is), and a major proponent of functionalism in anthropology. He died at New Haven, Connecticut. » anthropology; structuralism

Malipiero, (Gian) Francesco [mali**pyay**roh] (1882–1973) Italian composer, born in Venice. He studied in Vienna, Venice, and Bologna, visited Paris, and became professor of composition at the Parma Conservatory (1921), and director of institutes at Padua and (1939) Venice. He wrote symphonic, operatic, vocal, and chamber music, and edited Monteverdi and Vivaldi. He died at Treviso.

mallard A dabbling duck found near water throughout the N hemisphere; blue patch on wing; male with green head and thin white neck ring; the ancestor of nearly all domestic ducks. Originally the name was used only for the male. (*Anas platyrhynchos*. Family: *Anatidae*.) » dabbling duck

Mallarmé, Stéphane [malah**may**] (1842–98) French Symbolist poet, born in Paris. He taught English in Paris and elsewhere, visiting England on several occasions. He translated the poems of Poe, and in his own writing became a leader of the Symbolist school. His works include *Hérodiade* (1864), *L'Après-midi d'un faune* (1865, published 1876), which inspired Debussy's prelude, and the remarkable experimental poem, *Un Coup de dés* (1914, A Dice-Throw). He died at Valvins. » Debussy; French literature; Poe; poetry; Symbolism

mallee A scrubland vegetation zone in the semi-arid parts of SE and SW Australia. Dwarf eucalyptus shrubs dominate, growing to 2 m/6 ft in height. » gum tree

mallee fowl A megapode bird native to Australia; brown with white spots on wings; inhabits dry scrubland, especially **mallee scrub** (dwarf eucalyptus); eats seeds, flowers, insects, and lizards; need not drink; also known as **lowan**. (*Leipoa ocellata*. Family: *Megapodiidae*.) » megapode

mallow N temperate annual and perennial herb; palmately lobed or divided leaves; flowers with an epicalyx, calyx and five heart-shaped to deeply notched petals, rose, purple, or white, often with dark veins; stamens numerous, united into a central column; fruit a flat whorl of 1-seeded segments, resembling small cheeses. It is related to both cotton and hibiscus, with very similar flowers. (Genus: *Malva*, 40 species. Family: *Malvaceae*.) » annual; epicalyx; cotton [i]; herb; hibiscus; palmate; perennial; sepal; stamen

Mallowan, Max » **Christie, Agatha**

Malmö [**mal**mer] 55°35N 13°00E, pop (1982) 230 022. Fortified seaport and capital of Malmöhus county, SW Sweden; on The Sound opposite Copenhagen, Denmark; third largest city in Sweden; under Danish rule until 1658; railway; engineering, shipbuilding, foodstuffs, textiles, cement; town hall (16th-c); Church of St Peter (14th-c). » Sweden [i]

malnutrition A deficiency of protein or of one or more of the other essential ingredients of a diet. Undernutrition occurs when insufficient food energy is taken, and when prolonged may lead to profound weight loss. The insufficiency may be more specific and involve one or several vitamin deficiencies. Examples include water-soluble vitamins (B-vitamins, C, folates) and fat-soluble vitamins (A, D, E). Electrolyte deficiencies and inadequate amounts of essential fatty and amino acids may also occur. These may give rise to a wide range of clinical abnormalities and metabolic defects. » kwashiorkor; marasmus; pellagra; protein; rickets; scurvy; vitamins [i]

Malory, Sir Thomas (?–1471) English writer, known for his work, *Le Morte d'Arthur* (The Death of Arthur). From Caxton's preface, we are told that Malory was a knight, that he finished his work in the ninth year of the reign of Edward IV (1469–70), and that he 'reduced' it from some French book. Probably he was the Sir Thomas Malory (d. 1471) of Newbold Revel, Warwickshire, whose quarrels with a neighbouring priory and (probably) Lancastrian politics brought him imprisonment. » Arthur; Caxton; English literature

Malraux, André (Georges) [mal**roh**] (1901–76) French statesman and novelist, born and died in Paris. He studied oriental languages and spent much time in China, where he worked for the Guomindang and was active in the 1927 revolution. He also fought in the Spanish Civil War, and in World War 2 escaped from a prison camp to join the French resistance. He was Minister of Information in de Gaulle's government (1945–6) and Minister of Cultural Affairs (1960–9). He is known for his novels, notably *La Condition humaine* (1933, Man's Fate), winner of the Prix Goncourt, and *L'Espoir* (1937, Man's Hope). » French literature; novel

malt sugar » **maltose**

Malta, official name **Republic of Malta**, Maltese **Repubblika ta' Malta**, ancient **Melita** pop (1990e) 353 000; area 316 sq km/122 sq ml. Archipelago in the C Mediterranean Sea, comprising the islands of Malta (246 sq km/95 sq ml), Gozo (67 sq km/26 sq ml), and Comino (2.7 sq km/1 sq ml), with some un-

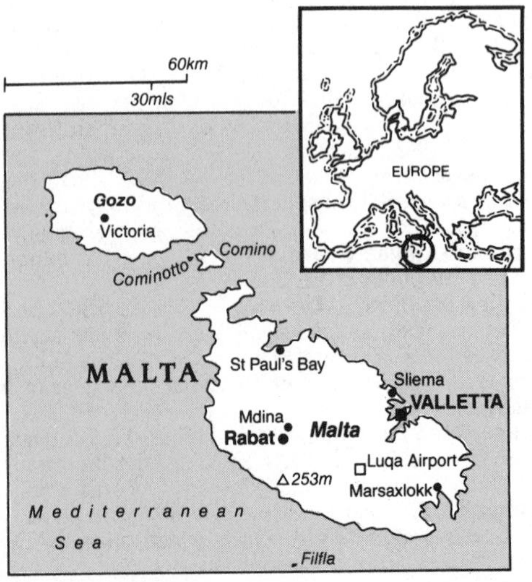

inhabited islets; 93 km/58 ml S of Sicily, 290 km/180 ml E of Tunisia; capital, Valletta; chief towns, Sliema, Birkirkara, Qormi, Rabat; timezone GMT +2; airport; population European; languages, English and Maltese; chief religion, Roman Catholic Apostolic; unit of currency, the Maltese pound; generally low-lying; highest point, 253 m/830 ft; no rivers or mountains; well-indented coastline; dry summers and mild winters; average annual rainfall c.400 mm/16 in; average daily winter temperature, 13°C; controlled at various times by Phoenicia, Greece, Carthage, and Rome; conquered by Arabs, 9th-c; given to the Knights Hospitallers, 1530; British Crown Colony, 1815; important strategic base in both World Wars; for its resistance to heavy air attacks, the island was awarded the George Cross in 1942; achieved independence, 1964; republic, 1974; British Military Facilities agreement expired, 1979; governed by a president, prime minister, cabinet, and a 65-member House of Representatives elected for five years; tourism and ship repair are the major industries; naval dockyards now converted to commercial use; developing as a transshipment centre for the Mediterranean; tobacco, canned foods, light engineering products, textiles, paints, detergents, plastic and steel goods; potatoes, tomatoes, onions, wheat, barley, grapes, oranges, cut flowers; cattle, sheep, goats, poultry. » Comino; Gozo; Maltese (language); Valletta; RR26 national holidays; RR56 political leaders

Maltese (zoology) A small toy spaniel developed in Italy (name probably derived from the Sicilian town of Melita); colour uniform; hair straight, coat very long and thick, reaching ground; legs short, hidden by coat. » dog; spaniel

Maltese (language) A language spoken by 300 000 people on the island of Malta, related to the W dialects of Arabic. It has changed substantially from the linguistic structure of its source, through the influence of the Romance languages. It is the only variety of Arabic written in the Roman alphabet. » Arabic; Malta [i]; Romance languages

Malthus, Thomas Robert (1766–1834) British economist, born near Dorking. Educated at Cambridge, he was ordained in 1797, and in 1798 published anonymously his *Essay on the Principle of Population*, which argued that the population has a natural tendency to increase faster than the means of subsistence, and that efforts should be made to cut the birth rate, either by self-restraint or birth control – a view which later was widely misrepresented under the name of Malthusianism. In 1805 he became professor of political economy in the East India College at Haileybury, where he wrote *Principles of Political Economy* (1820) and other works. He died near Bath.

maltose [**mawl**tohs] $C_{12}H_{22}O_{11}$. A condensation dimer of two molecules of glucose which are produced when it is hydrolyzed; also known as **malt sugar**. It is derived from the limited hydrolysis of starch, of which it is the repeating unit. » condensation (chemistry); dimer; glucose [i]; hydrolysis; starch

Malvern or **Great Malvern** [**mol**vern] 52°07N 2°19W, pop (1981) 30 470. Town in Malvern Hills district, Hereford and Worcester, WC England; popular health resort in the Malvern Hills, 12 km/7 ml SW of Worcester; railway; engineering, plastics, tourism; Malvern College (public school); Elgar lived and is buried here; Malvern Festival (May). » Elgar; Hereford and Worcester

Malvinas » Falkland Islands

Mamaev Kurgan [**mam**yef koor**gan**] or **Mamai Hill** An area in the heart of Volgograd, Russia, and the scene of the most severe conflict during the Battle of Stalingrad (1942–3). The Soviet victory is commemorated by the Motherland monument, a 52 m/171 ft statue designed by E V Vuchetich, which dominates the hill, and the dead are mourned in the Square of Heroes and the Square of Grief below. The Mamaev Kurgan memorial was erected in 1963–7. » Stalingrad, Battle of; Volgograd

Mamai Hill » Mamaev Kurgan

mamba A venomous African snake of the family *Elapidae*; may climb trees; eats lizards and birds; strong venom; not usually aggressive (although the fastest snake ever recorded was a black mamba which reached 11 kph/7 mph while chasing a man who had been teasing it); two species: the **black mamba** (*Dendroaspis polylepis*), correctly the **black-mouthed mamba**, with body dark brown or grey, never black; and the **green mamba** (*Dendroaspis angusticeps*). » snake

Mamluks or **Mamelukes** Slave soldiers who constituted the army of the Ayyubid sultanate established in Egypt by Saladin in the 1170s. Their commanders (*amirs*) created a professional army of high quality. In 1250 they overthrew the Ayyubids, and established Muslim dynasties until conquered by the Turks in 1516–17. They continued to rule in Egypt with Ottoman blessing until their massacre by Mohammed Ali in 1811. » Ottoman Empire; Saladin

mammal An animal characterized by having mammary glands in the female, along with several other features: a covering of hair (very sparse in some mammals); each side of the lower jaw formed from one bone (the *dentary*); three small bones in the middle ear (the hammer, anvil, and stirrup); seven vertebrae in the neck (only six in the manatee); and no nucleus in the red blood cells. Whales, dugongs, and manatees have lost their hind legs. Mammals are divided into **placental mammals**, in which the young develop in a womb (the *uterus*) where they are nourished from the blood of the mother and are born at an advanced stage of development; **marsupials**, in which the young are not nourished in a womb but are born at a very early developmental stage and develop outside the mother's body, usually in a pouch, nourished with milk from the mammary gland; and **monotremes** (or **egg-laying mammals**), in which the young hatch from an egg outside the body of the mother and are then nourished with milk. (Class: *Mammalia*, c.4 000 species.) » animal; Bovidae; Camelidae; deer; insectivore; marsupial [i]; monotreme; Mustelidae; panda; tree shrew; *see illustration p 750*

mammary gland In female mammals, a gland responsible for the production and release of milk to feed their young. The number varies between 2 and 20. They are located on the surface of the chest or abdomen, and may be concentrated into an udder. They are probably derived from highly modified sweat glands. » breast milk; gland

mammoth A specialized elephant originating in Africa, which spread in the early Pleistocene epoch through Eurasia and N America. The woolly mammoth was abundant in tundra regions, had long hair and a thick fat layer for insulation, fed on grasses and legumes in summer, and on shrubs and bark in winter. It died out c.12 000 years ago. (Order: *Proboscidea*.) » elephant; Pleistocene epoch; tundra

Mammoth Cave A system of subterranean passages and caverns created by limestone erosion and extending over 484 km/301 ml in W Kentucky. The area was designated a National Park in 1936, and is a world heritage site. » Kentucky; mammoth

mammoth tree A massive evergreen conifer confined to the W slopes of the Sierra Nevada Mts, California; also called **giant redwood, California big tree** or **wellingtonia**. It is sometimes claimed as the oldest living organism; age estimates range from 400–4 000 years. Several of the finest specimens are named after famous Americans. (*Sequoiadendron giganteum*. Family: *Taxodiaceae*.) » conifer; evergreen plants

Man, Isle of pop (1981) 64 679; area 572 sq km/221 sq ml. British island in the Irish Sea, W of England and E of N Ireland; rises to 620 m/2034 ft at Snaefell; airport; ferries; capital, Douglas; other towns, Castletown, Peel, Ramsey; ruled by the Welsh, 6th–9th-c, then by the Scandinavians, Scots, and English; purchased by the British Government between 1765 and 1828; the island has its own parliament, the bicameral Court of Tynwald, which consists of the elected House of Keys and the Legislative Council (composed of the Lieutenant-Governor, the President, the Lord Bishop of Sodor and Man, the Attorney-General, and seven members elected by the House of Keys); acts of the British parliament do not generally apply to Man; Manx survived as an everyday language until the 19th-c; tourism, agriculture, light engineering; used as a tax haven; Tynwald Hill, where all acts of the Manx parliament must be proclaimed; annual Tourist Trophy motorcycle races. » Celtic languages; Douglas; United Kingdom [i]

Mana Pools area 2 196 sq km/848 sq ml. National park in N Zimbabwe; a world heritage site; established in 1963; partly

platypus
squirrel
hare
kangaroo
hedgehog
dugong
rhesus monkey
armadillo
bear
pangolin
humpback whale
mouflon
colugo
rhinoceros
African elephant
hyrax
aardvark
walrus
Not to scale

Mammals

bordered NW by the R Zambezi, the frontier with Zambia; extensive wildlife; in the dry season animals migrate towards the river in huge numbers. » Zimbabwe [i]

Managua [ma**na**gwa] 12°06N 86°18W, pop(1981) 819 679. Commercial centre and capital city of Nicaragua, on the S shore of Lago de Managua, 45 km/28 ml inland from the Pacific Ocean; badly damaged by earthquake in 1931 and 1972, and by civil war in the late 1970s; airport; railway; university (1961); textiles, matches, cigarettes, cement; archaeological site of Huellas de Acahualinca nearby; Fiesta of Santo Domingo (Aug). » Nicaragua [i]

manakin A small bird native to C and tropical S America; short bill, wings, and (usually) tail; toes partially joined; inhabits forests; eats insects and small fruits picked in flight; noted for its complex display. (It should not be confused with the mannikin.) (Family: *Pipridae*, c.53 species.) » mannikin

Manama [ma**na**ma], Arabic **Al Manamah** 26°12N 50°38E, pop(1981) 121 986. Seaport capital of Bahrain, on N coast of Bahrain I in the Arabian Gulf; connected by a causeway with Muharraq I to the NE; a free trade port with facilities at Mina Sulman near Sitra Wharf; oil refining, commerce, banking. » Bahrain [i]

Manas A wildlife sanctuary in Assam, on the Indian border with Bhutan; a world heritage site. Occupying jungle-clad hills in the watershed of the Mana, Beki, and Hakua Rivers, it is noted as a refuge for a wide variety of bird and animal life, particularly the rare pygmy hog and golden langur. » Assam

Manasseh, Prayer of [ma**na**se] Short, eloquent writing of the Old Testament Pseudepigrapha (but often considered part of the Apocrypha even though not clearly in the Septuagint), ostensibly the work of Manasseh, a notoriously wicked king of Judah (c.687–642 BC), expressing his personal confession of sin and petition for pardon. Most scholars date the work from the 2nd-c BC to the 1st-c AD, considering it a late elaboration based on parts of 2 *Chron* 33. » Apocrypha, Old Testament; Pseudepigrapha

Manasseh, tribe of [ma**na**se] One of the twelve tribes of ancient Israel, but said to be descended from Joseph's elder son, who with Ephraim was adopted by Jacob to share in his blessing (*Gen* 48–9). Perhaps originally it was a half tribe. Its territory in C Palestine extended on both sides of the Jordan R, located between the tribes of Ephraim and Issachar in the W. » Israel, tribes of [i]; Joseph, tribe of

manatee [mana**tee**] An aquatic mammal, found from Brazil to SE USA, and in W Africa; inhabits shallow coastal seas and rivers; large rounded body; short head with square muzzle; front legs are flippers; no hind legs; tail ends in a flat horizontal disc; eats underwater plants. (Order: *Sirenia*. Family: *Trichechidae*, 3 species.) » mammal [i]

Manaus or **Manáos** [ma**nã**os] 3°06S 60°00W, pop(1980) 611 736. River-port capital of Amazonas state, N Brazil, on the N bank of the R Negro just above its influx into the Amazon; the collecting point for produce of a vast area; founded 1660; free zone established, 1967; airfield; university (1965); timber, rubber, natural fibres, nuts; Teatro Amazonas opera house (1896, rebuilt 1929 and 1974), seats over 1 000; folklore festival (Jun). » Amazon, River; Brazil [i]

Manchester, Lat **Mancunium** 53°30N 2°15W, pop(1987e) 450 100. Metropolitan district in Greater Manchester urban area, NW England, on the R Irwell, 256 km/159 ml NW of London; Roman town, located at a major crossroads; became centre of local textile industry in 17th-c, and focal point of English cotton industry during the Industrial Revolution; became a city in 1853; University of Manchester (1880), University of Manchester Institute of Science and Technology (1824); railway; airport; connected to the Irish Sea by the 57 km/35¼ ml Manchester Ship Canal (1894); UK's second largest commercial centre; textiles, chemicals, engineering, paper, foodstuffs, rubber, electrical equipment, printing; cultural centre for NW; art gallery, Royal Exchange (theatre), Cotton Exchange (leisure centre); Hallé Orchestra; 15th-c cathedral; Chetham's Hospital and Library, the oldest public library in England; Free Trade Hall (1843); Liverpool Road Station, the world's oldest surviving passenger station. » Industrial Revolution; Manchester, Greater; Manchester Ship Canal

Manchester, Greater pop(1987e) 2 580 100; area 1 287 sq km/497 sq ml. Metropolitan county of NW England, consisting of 10 boroughs (Bolton, Bury, Manchester, Oldham, Rochdale, Salford, Stockport, Tameside, Trafford, Wigan); metropolitan council abolished in 1986; county town, Manchester; Ship Canal, Old Trafford cricket ground. » Manchester

Manchester School A group of economists, working from Manchester, England, in the early 19th-c, who advocated free trade and laissez-faire. The focus of their attention was the repeal of the Corn Laws: the *Anti-Corn Law League* was headed by Bright and Cobden. » Bright, John; Cobden; Corn Laws; Manchester

Manchester Ship Canal An artificial waterway in the UK linking Manchester with the Mersey estuary. The canal, which is 57 km/35 ml long, was opened in 1894 and allowed the city to develop as a sea port. » canal; Manchester

Manching A massive hillfort of the Middle La Tène period (2nd–1st-c BC) near Ingolstadt, Bavaria, S Germany. The native capital of the Vindelici and one of Europe's earliest towns, it was a major trading centre, manufacturing iron, glass, pottery, leather, and textiles, and minting coins. » La Tène; Maiden Castle

Manchu Originally a people of Tartar stock from Manchuria (an area that included present-day Liaoning, Jilin, and Heilongjiang) who ruled all China from 1644 to 1911 under the Qing dynasty. (Both Qing and Man mean 'pure'.) There are now about 2.5 million Man people in China. » Altaic; Manchuria; Qing dynasty

Manchukuo or **Manzhouguo** A Japanese puppet-state established in 1932 in Manchuria, which Japanese forces had invaded in 1931. Henry Puyi, the last Qing emperor, was its nominal head. The regime ended with the defeat of Japan in 1945. » Manchuria; Pu Yi; Sino-Japanese Wars **2**

Manchuria Former region of NE China; mountainous area, sparsely populated by nomadic tribes; Manchus overthrew Ming dynasty to become the last Chinese emperors (Qing dynasty, 1644–1911); vast natural resources of timber and minerals (coal, iron, magnesite, oil, uranium, gold); Russian military control, 1900; captured by Japan, 1932, and part of puppet state of Manchukuo; Russian control re-asserted, 1945; Chinese sovereignty recognized, 1950, but border area with Russia a continuing focus of political tension. » China [i]; Manchukuo; Pu Yi; Qing dynasty

Mandaeans [man**dee**anz] A small Gnostic sect in Iran and Iraq who believe that the spiritual soul will be freed from its imprisonment in the evil material world by the redeemer, Manda d'Hayye ('the knowledge of life'). » Gnosticism; sect

mandala [**man**dala] Circular designs in Hindu and Buddhist religious art, representing the universe or other aspects of their beliefs. They are used as a focus and aid to concentration in worship and meditation. » Buddhism; Hinduism

Mandalay [manda**lay**] 21°57N 96°04E, pop(1983) 417 226. River-port capital of Mandalay division, C Myanmar; on R Irrawaddy, N of Rangoon; airfield; railway; university (1964); commercial centre, tourism; Kuthodaw Pagoda contains 729 marble slabs on which are inscribed the entire Buddhist canons; Shwenandaw Kyaung monastery; old city of Pagan to the W, founded 109 AD, contains largest concentration of pagodas and temples in Myanmar (mainly 11th–13th-c). » Buddhism; Burma [i]; Mahamuni Pagoda

mandarin A citrus fruit with yellow to deep orange-red fruits, very like small oranges but with thin, loose rind. It includes satsumas and tangerines. (*Citrus reticulata*. Family: *Rutaceae*.) » citrus; orange; satsuma; tangerine

Mandarin » **Chinese**

mandarin duck A perching duck native to E Asia, and introduced in N Europe; male multicoloured with shaggy head and sail-like feathers on wings; inhabits fresh water among trees; eats seeds, small fish, and insects; nests in hole in tree; also known as **mandarin**. (*Aix galericulata*.) » perching duck

mandates A system under which former territories of the German and Ottoman Empires were to be administered by the victorious powers of World War 1 under international supervision. The mandates were granted by the League of Nations, and annual reports had to be submitted to its Permanent

Mandates Commission. Britain and France acquired mandates in the Middle East (Palestine, Iraq, Transjordan, Syria, Lebanon) and Africa (Tanganyika, Togo, Cameroun) while Belgium acquired Rwanda-Urundi, South Africa acquired South-West Africa, and Australia and New Zealand acquired New Guinea and Western Samoa. The functions of the Commission were later taken over by the Trusteeship Council of the United Nations. » League of Nations; United Nations

Mande A cluster of Mande-speaking agricultural peoples of W Sudan, Sierra Leone, Liberia, and Côte d'Ivoire. They founded the mediaeval empires of Ghana and Mali, and were also important traders. They include the Bambara (well-known for their art), Dyula (Islamic converts who dominated the African end of the Sahara trade), Malinke, Mende, and Soninke. » Bambara; Malinke

Mandela, Nelson [man**de**la] (1918–) African Nationalist leader, born in Transkei, South Africa. He was a lawyer in Johannesburg, then joined the African National Congress in 1944. For the next 20 years he directed a campaign of defiance against the South African government and its racist policies, orchestrating in 1961 a three-day national strike. In 1964 he was sentenced to life imprisonment for political offences. He has continued to be such a potent symbol of Black resistance that the 1980s saw a co-ordinated international campaign for his release. His wife **Winnie** has also frequently been subjected to restrictions on her personal freedom. He was released from prison in February 1990, after President F W de Klerk had unbanned the ANC, removed restrictions on political groups, and suspended executions. Mandela was elected President of the African National Congress in 1991. » African National Congress; apartheid; racism; South Africa [i]

Mandelstam, Osip [**man**duhlstam] (1891–1938) Russian poet, born of Jewish parents in Warsaw, and brought up in St Petersburg. His early success with *Kamen* (1913, Stone), *Tristia* (1922, Sad Things), and *Stikhotvorenia 1921–25* (1928, Poems) was followed by suspicion and arrest (1934) by the Soviet authorities. His death was reported from Siberia in 1938. His *Sobranie sochineny* (Collected Works) were published in three volumes (1964–71). After his death, his wife, Nadezhda, wrote their story in *Hope Against Hope* (1970). » poetry; Russian literature

Mandeville, Jehan de, or **Sir John** (14th-c) The name assigned to the compiler of a famous book of travels, published apparently in 1366, and soon translated from the French into many languages. It seems to have been written by a physician, Jehan de Bourgogne, or Jehan à la Barbe, who died at Liège in 1372, and who is said to have revealed on his death-bed his real name of Mandeville, explaining that he had had to flee from his native England for a homicide. Some scholars, however, attribute it to Jean d'Outremeuse, a Frenchman.

Mandingo » **Malinke**

mandolin A plucked string instrument, about 60 cm/2 ft long, developed in the 18th-c from the earlier mandora and mandola. It has a pear-shaped body somewhat like a lute's, a fretted fingerboard, and a pegbox set back at an angle. There are four pairs of steel strings, tuned like a violin's and played with a plectrum. » plectrum; string instrument **2** [i]

mandrake A thick-rooted perennial, native to Europe; leaves in a rosette; flowers blue; berries yellow to orange. Once widely regarded for its medicinal and narcotic properties, it has been the subject of many superstitions, such as the claim that it screams when uprooted. (*Mandragora officinalis*. Family: *Solanaceae*.) » narcotics; perennial

mandrill A baboon native to W African forests; stocky with short limbs and thick coat; tail minute; buttocks red-blue; naked face with scarlet muzzle and bright blue, ridged cheeks (especially in male); lives on ground in small family groups. (*Mandrillus sphinx*.) » baboon; drill

maned jackal » **aardwolf**

maned sheep » **aoudad**

Manet, Edouard [**ma**nay] (1832–83) French painter, born in Paris. Intended for a legal career, he became an artist, and exhibited at the Salon in 1861. His 'Déjeuner sur l'herbe' (1863, Luncheon on the Grass), which scandalized the traditional classicists, was rejected, and, although the equally provocative 'Olympia' was accepted in 1865, the Salon remained hostile and Manet's genius was not recognized until after his death. He exhibited in the *Salon des Refusés*, and helped to form the group out of which the Impressionist movement arose, as seen in his 'Bar at the Folies Bergères' (1882). He died in Paris. » French art; Impressionism (art); Salon

mangabey [**mang**gabee] An Old World monkey, native to tropical Africa; slender with long tail, long coat; pronounced whiskers on sides of face; inhabits forests; some species spend time on the ground. (Genus: *Cercocebus*, 4 species.) » Old World monkey

manganese Mn, element 25, melting point 1 244°C. A transition metal, density about 7.4 g cm^{-3}, always found combined in nature, but mainly as the dioxide, MnO_2. The metal is produced by heating this to give Mn_3O_4, and then reducing with aluminium. The metal, which has three irregular structures not found for any other metal, is mainly used in alloy steels. It forms a wide range of compounds, commonly showing oxidation states +2, +3, +4, +6, and +7. The last is found in *permanganates*, which contain the ion MnO_4^-. Potassium permanganate is a convenient and strong oxidizing agent in aqueous solution. » alloy; chemical elements; metal; oxidation; RR90

manganese nodules Nodule-shaped masses of metal oxides a few centimetres across, which form at the sea floor. They were first discovered by the HMS *Challenger* expedition in 1873, and have now been found to occur widely in all the major ocean basins except the Arctic. They are also known as *ferromanganese* or *polymetallic* nodules because of their mixture of metal oxides. Though primarily iron and manganese-rich, some nodules contain copper, nickel, cobalt, titanium and other economically valuable metals. Recent interest in the commercial exploitation of nodules helped spark the Law of the Sea treaty. » oxide; sea, law of the

Mangbetu [mang**be**too] A cluster of C Sudanic-speaking peoples in NE Zaire. In the 19th-c they were a powerful kingdom ruled by an aristocracy to which alone the name Mangbetu is properly given. They are renowned for their craftmanship, especially in wood and iron. Population c.1 million. » Zaire [i]

mange A contagious skin disease of domestic animals. It results from infestation with several types of mites which burrow into the skin, causing itching and irritation. » itch; mite; skin [i]

mange tout [mãzh **too**] » **pea** [i]

mangel-wurzel » **beet**

mango An evergreen tree growing to 18 m/60 ft, native to SE Asia; leaves roughly oblong; flowers tiny, white, with 4–5 petals; fleshy fruit 7–10 cm/2¾–4 in, oval to kidney-shaped, yellow flushed with red. It is grown for the sweet-tasting, edible fruit. (*Mangifera indica*. Family: *Anacardiaceae*.) » evergreen plants; tree [i]

mangosteen A small evergreen tree native to Malaysia; leaves up to 20 cm/8 in, oval to elliptical; flowers red, 4-petalled; fruit round, with thick purplish rind and sweet, white, edible flesh. (*Garcinia mangostana*. Family: *Guttifereae*.) » evergreen plants; tree [i]

mangrove Any of several unrelated tropical and subtropical trees, all sharing similar structure and biology, growing on coastal and estuarine mud-flats. All possess either aerial roots or *pneumatophores*, special breathing roots which help aerate the root system in swampy ground. The seeds germinate while still on the parent tree, allowing them to become quickly established when shed in the shifting tidal environment. Mangroves often cover extensive tracts, forming a distinctive vegetation type. (Main Genera: *Rhizophora*, 7 species, and *Brugeria*, 6 species, Family: *Rhizophoraceae*; and *Avicennia*, 14 species, Family: *Avicenniaceae*.) » root (botany); tree [i]

mangrove snake Any snake usually found in the trees of mangrove swamps. The name is used especially for several SE Asian snakes of the family *Colubridae*: the **mangrove tree snake** (*Boiga dendrophila*), the **white-bellied mangrove snake** (*Fordonia leucobalia*), and **Gray's mangrove snake** (*Myron richardsonii*). » snake

Manhattan pop (1980) 1 428 285, area 57 sq km/22 sq ml. An island forming one of the five boroughs of the City of New

York, New York State, E USA; at the N end of New York Bay, bounded W by the Hudson R; co-extensive with New York County; settled by the Dutch as part of New Netherlands in 1626, bought from local Indians for trinkets and cloth worth c.$24; taken by the British in 1664; major financial and commercial centre based around Wall Street and the World Trade Center; headquarters of the United Nations; Broadway, Empire State Building, Greenwich Village; three universities (1754, 1831, 1848); named after a local tribe of Indians. » New York City; United Nations

Manhattan project The codename for the most secret scientific operation of World War 2, the development of the atomic bomb, undertaken successfully in the USA from 1942 onwards. The project culminated in the detonation of the first atomic weapon at Alamogordo, New Mexico (16 Jul 1945). » atomic bomb

manic depressive psychosis A severe illness with repeated episodes of depressed and/or elevated mood. There is often the loss of normal social inhibitions, irritability, hyperactivity, elation, accelerated thought and speech, delusions, and occasionally hallucinations in the manic episodes. In the depressive phase there is loss of energy, feelings of worthlessness, and altered physiological functioning, such as disturbed sleep. » depression (psychiatry); mental disorders

Manichaeism [manikeeizm] or **Manichaeanism** A religious sect founded by the prophet Manes (or Mani) (c.216–76), who began teaching in Persia in 240. His teaching was based on a primaeval conflict between the realms of light and darkness, in which the material world represents an invasion of the realm of light by the powers of darkness. The purpose of religion is to release the particles of light imprisoned in matter, and Buddha, the Prophets, Jesus, and finally Manes have been sent to help in this task. Release involved adherence to a strict ascetic regimen. The Zoroastrians condemned the sect and executed Manes, but it spread rapidly in the West, surviving until the 10th-c. » Augustine, St (of Hippo); Zoroastrianism

Manila [manila] 14°36N 120°59E, pop (1980) 1 630 485. Capital of the Philippines, on R Pasig, Manila Bay, SW Luzon I; founded, 1571; important trade centre under the Spanish; occupied by the British 1762–3; taken by the USA during the Spanish-American War, 1898; badly damaged in World War 2; airport; railway; several universities (earliest, 1611); shipbuilding, chemicals, textiles, timber, food processing. » Philippines [i]

Manila hemp » abaca

manioc » cassava

Manipur [manipoor] pop (1981) 1 433 691; area 22 356 sq km/8 629 sq ml. State in NE India; British rule in 1891; administered from the state of Assam until 1947, when it became a union territory; became a state in 1972; capital, Imphal; governed by a 60-member Legislative Assembly; weaving, sugar, cement; wheat, maize, pulses, fruit, bamboo, teak; problems of soil erosion being reduced by terracing of valley slopes. » India [i]

Manipuri A form of Indian dance from the hill region of NE India. It has two strands: a ritualistic form, dedicated to the god Shiva and incorporating stories of immortal lovers; and social forms performed at major festivals, such as the New Year (in mid-April). Unusually, in Indian dance, the face is not used for expressive purposes. » Indian dance

Manitoba [manitohba], formerly **Red River Settlement** (to 1870) pop (1981) 1 026 241; area 649 950 sq km/250 945 sq ml. Province in C Canada; boundaries include Hudson Bay (NE) and USA (S); known as the 'land of 100 000 lakes', the result of glaciation, notably Lakes Winnipeg, Winnipegosis, Manitoba; drained by several rivers flowing into L Winnipeg or Hudson Bay; land gradually rises in W and S to 832 m/2 730 ft at Mt Baldy; capital, Winnipeg; major town, Brandon; cereals (especially wheat), livestock, vegetables, fishing, timber, hydroelectric power, food processing, mining (oil, gold, nickel, silver, copper, zinc), machinery, tourism; trading rights given to Hudson's Bay Company, 1670; several forts established because of English–French conflict, including Fort Rouge, 1738 (site of Winnipeg); French claims ceded to the British under the Treaty of Paris, 1763; settlement on the Red R from 1812, with many Scottish and Irish settlers; joined the confederation, 1870, provoking insurrection under Riel; boundaries extended, 1881 and 1912; major development of area after railway reached Winnipeg in the 1880s; governed by a lieutenant-governor and an elected 57-member Legislative Assembly. » Canada [i]; Métis; Red River Rebellion; Riel; Winnipeg

manitou [manitoo] A term used by the Algonkin Indians of the E Woodlands of N America to designate the supernatural world and to identify any manifestation of it, such as spirits encountered in visions, or certain powers of nature. Human beings and animals may also exhibit the 'spirit' of manitou. » Algonkin

Manizales [maneesalays] 5°03N 75°32W, pop (1985) 327 806. Capital of Caldas department, C Colombia; in Cordillera Central at 2 153 m/7 064 ft; founded, 1848; railway; university (1950); centre of coffee area; textiles, leather, chemicals; experimental coffee plantation and freeze-dried coffee plant at Chinchiná; Teatro de los Fundadores; cathedral (unfinished); skiing and mountain climbing at Nevado del Ruiz; coffee festival (Jan). » Colombia [i]

Mankowitz, (Cyril) Wolf [mankohvits] (1924–) British author, playwright, and antique dealer, born in London. An authority on Wedgwood, his publications in the art domain include *The Concise Encyclopedia of English Pottery and Porcelain* (1957). His fiction includes the novel *A Kid for Two Farthings* (1953), the play *The Bespoke Overcoat* (1954), and the films *The Millionairess* (1960), *The Long, the Short, and the Tall* (1961), and *Casino Royale* (1967). » novel; Wedgwood, Josiah

Mann, Thomas (1875–1955) German novelist, born at Lübeck. He left school at 19, and spent some time at Munich University before joining his brother, **Heinrich** (1871–1950), also a writer, in Italy. There he wrote his early masterpiece, *Buddenbrooks* (1901), tracing the decline of a family over four generations. He produced several short stories and novellas, such as *Der Tod in Venedig* (1913, Death in Venice), and then wrote *Der Zauberberg* (1924, The Magic Mountain), for which he won the Nobel Prize for Literature in 1929. He left Germany for Switzerland in 1933, settling in the USA in 1936. He returned to Switzerland in 1947, and produced his greatest work, a modern version of the mediaeval legend, *Doktor Faustus* (1947). He died near Zürich. » German literature; novel; novella; satire; short story

manna The name of several edible plant products, some of which have been proposed as the biblical food dropped from heaven during the Israelites' flight from Egypt. Lichen (*Lecanora esculenta*) from Asia Minor, the source of lichen bread and manna jelly, curls into balls when dry and blows in the wind. Stems of tamarisk (*Tamarisk mannifera*) produce a honey-like substance in response to scale insect attack. » lichen; Old Testament; tamarisk

manna ash A species of ash, native to the Mediterranean, and often planted in streets and parks, displaying large clusters of fragrant flowers with creamy-white petals. The dried sap is rich in the sugar-alcohol mannitol, and forms the manna of commerce. (*Fraxinus ornus*. Family: *Oleaceae*.) » ash; manna

Mannerheim, Carl Gustav (Emil), Baron von [manerhiym] (1867–1951) Finnish soldier, statesman, and President (1944–6), born at Villnäs. When Finland declared her independence (1918), he became Supreme Commander and Regent. Defeated in the presidential election of 1919, he retired into private life, but returned as Commander-in-Chief against the Russians in the Winter War of 1939–40. He continued to command the Finnish forces until 1944, when he became President of the Finnish Republic until 1946. He died at Lausanne, Switzerland. » Finland [i]; World War 2

Mannerism A form of art and architecture prevalent in France, Spain, and especially Italy during the 16th-c, characterized by the playful use of classical elements and *trompe l'oeil* effects in irrational or dramatic compositions. Vasari (1550) used the word *maniera* for a type of refined and artificial beauty, as seen in such works as Raphael's 'St Cecilia' and Michelangelo's 'Victory'. In art, leading Mannerists included Giulio Romano, Pontormo, and Parmigiano, whose pictures are painted with jewel-like colours, and sculptors such as Cellini. In architecture, the style is typified by the Laurentian Library vestibule, Florence (1526), architect Michaelangelo. » Baroque (art and architecture); Italian art; Renaissance architecture/art; *trompe l'oeil*; Cellini; Giulio Romano; Michelangelo; Parmigiano; Pontormo; Raphael; Vasari

Mannheim [**man**hiym] 49°30N 8°28E, pop (1983) 299 700. Commercial and manufacturing river port in Karlsruhe district, Germany; on right bank of R Rhine, at the outflow of the canalized R Neckar, 70 km/43 ml SW of Frankfurt; one of the largest inland harbours in Europe; seat of the Electors Palatine (18th-c), when it became a cultural centre; badly bombed in World War 2; railway; university (1907); machinery, vehicles (Daimler-Benz), electrical engineering, oil refining, chemicals, pharmaceuticals, plastics, sugar refining, cables, tourism; castle, town hall, National Theatre, Reiss Museum; folk festival (May). » Germany [i]

mannikin A small seed-eating bird, native to Africa S of Sahara, India, and SE Asia; inhabits forest, open country, and cultivation. (Genus: *Lonchura*, 23 species. Family: *Estrildidae*.)

Manning, Henry Edward (1808–92) British Roman Catholic cardinal, born at Totteridge, Hertfordshire. Educated at Harrow and Oxford, he became a priest in the Church of England in 1833, became a Catholic in 1851, and in 1865 was appointed Archbishop of Westminster. At the Council of 1870, he was a zealous supporter of the infallibility dogma; and, named cardinal in 1875, he continued as a leader of the Ultramontanes. He died in London. » infallibility; Ultramontanism

manometer A device for measuring pressure exerted by or within a fluid (gas or liquid). It usually refers to various U-tube methods, pressure being shown by the difference in the height of the fluid (such as mercury) in the two arms of a U-tube, one arm being connected to the fluid whose pressure is being measured. The term is also sometimes used for other types of pressure gauge, in which pressure is exerted on a surface linked mechanically or electrically with an indicator or recorder.

manor A basic feature of English society from the 11th-c to the 15th-c, which poses many problems of definition. The 'typical' manor used to be regarded as an agricultural estate coincident with the village, and comprising the lord's estate (*demesne*) or home farm, attached villein tenements providing labour services on the demesne, and free tenements owing rents. In reality, there was a pronounced lack of uniformity. Manors, which might be concentrated or dispersed, frequently cut across villages; some consisted solely or largely of demesne; others contained only peasant tenements; and labour dues, often commuted for money by the 13th-c, varied widely in their onerousness. » Domesday Book; feudalism; villein

Manpower Services Commission (MSC) A UK quango, established in 1974, with responsibility for the provision of employment and training services. Staffed by civil servants, it was headed by a Commission comprising a full-time chairman and part-time members from employer, employee, local authority and education organizations. In 1988 the employment and training service functions were returned to the Department of Employment, and the MSC ceased to exist. » quango

Mansard [**man**sah] or **Mansart, François** (1598–1666) French architect, born in Paris. He brought a simplified adaptation of the Baroque style into use in France, designed Sainte Marie de la Visitation (1632) and other Paris churches, several chateaux, and made fashionable the high pitched type of roof which bears his name. » Baroque (art and architecture)

Mansfield, Katherine, pseudonym of **Kathleen Middleton Murry**, *née* **Beauchamp** (1888–1923) British short-story writer, born in Wellington, New Zealand. In 1908 she settled in Europe, and married John Middleton Murry in 1918. Her chief works are *Bliss* (1920), *The Garden Party* (1922), and *Something Childish* (1924). She died near Fontainebleau, France. » English literature; Murry, John Middleton; short story

manslaughter A form of unlawful homicide, covering a wide spectrum of culpability; known as *culpable homicide* in Scottish law. Mitigating factors, such as provocation, may reduce an offence from murder to manslaughter; grossly negligent behaviour which results in unintended death may also constitute the offence. There is a separate offence of causing death by reckless driving. In the USA, reckless homicide is the primary instance of manslaughter in many jurisdictions. » homicide; murder

manta ray Largest of the devil rays, exceeding 6 m/20 ft in width and 1 300 kg/2 800 lb in weight; mouth broad, situated across front of head; feeds on plankton and small fish filtered from water passing over gill arches. (Genus: *Manta*. Family: *Mobulidae*.) » devil ray

Mantegna, Andrea [man**tayn**ya] (1431–1506) Italian painter, born near Vicenza. He was the pupil and adopted son of Francisco Squarcione (1394–c.1468), who founded the Paduan school. In 1460 he settled in Mantua, where his major works included nine tempera pictures representing the 'Triumph of Caesar' (1482–92). He was also an engraver, architect, sculptor, and poet. He died at Mantua. » Italian art; tempera

mantis A medium to large insect that has a well-camouflaged body and a mobile head with large eyes; waits motionless for insect prey to approach before striking out with its grasping, spiny forelegs; c.1 800 species, in some of which the female eats the male head-first during copulation. (Order: *Mantodea*.) » insect [i]; praying mantis

mantis shrimp A shrimp-like crustacean, found in abundance in shallow tropical seas; c.350 species, all fierce, grasping predators, typically inhabiting burrows or crevices from where they emerge to spear or smash prey with their powerful claws. (Class: *Malacostraca*. Order: *Stomatopoda*.) » crustacean; shrimp

Mantle, Mickey (Charles) (1931–) US baseball player, born at Spavinaw, Oklahoma. A great outfielder and batter, he was a member of the great New York Yankees team of the 1950s. The American League's Most Valuable Player in 1956, he once hit a home run measured at a record 177 m/565 ft. » baseball [i]

Mantoux test [man**too**] Intradermal injection of an extract prepared from tuberculosis bacilli. The skin reaction measures the immune response to tuberculosis. When positive, the patient is known to suffer from or to have suffered from tuberculosis. It is named after French physician Charles Mantoux (1877–1947). » immunity; injection; tuberculosis

mantra [**man**tra] The belief among Hindus and Buddhists that the repetition of a special phrase, word, or syllable in meditation and devotion helps to concentrate the mind and aids the development of spiritual power. A disciple of a spiritual leader may be given an individual mantra as an initiation. » Buddhism; Hinduism

Mantua [**man**tyooa], Ital **Mantova** 45°10N 10°47E, pop (1981) 60 866. Capital town of Mantua province, Lombardy, N Italy, on R Mincio; founded in Etruscan times; railway; sugar refining, brewing, tanning, printing, tourism; birthplace of Virgil nearby; ringed by ancient walls and bastions; Church of Sant'Andrea (1472–94), cathedral (10th–18th-c), Palazzo Ducale, Castello San Giorgio (1395–1406). » Gonzaga; Lombardy; Virgil

Manu (Hinduism) [ma**noo**] In Hindu mythology, the forefather of the human race, to whom the Manu Smirti ('Lawbook of Manu') is attributed. » Hinduism

Manú (Peru) [ma**noo**] area 15 328 sq km/5 917 sq ml. National park in SE Peru; a world heritage site; established in 1973. » Peru [i]

Manuel I » **Emanuel I**

Manuzio » **Aldus Manutius**

Manx cat A breed of domestic cat, native to the Isle of Man; a British short-haired type; thick double-layered coat; no tail (but this does not always breed true, as some kittens may have tails or stumps of tails); also known as a **rumpy**. » cat

many body theory In physics, a general term describing attempts to explain the properties of systems of a number of interacting particles or objects, irrespective of the type of particles and the form of interaction between them. Nucleons moving in the nucleus, electrons around the atom, and planets moving around the Sun are examples where many-body approximation techniques can be used. » chaos; mechanics; statistical mechanics

many worlds interpretation In physics, a proposal that, when a measurement is performed on a quantum system, all possible outcomes of the measurement actually occur; made by

US physicist Hugh Everett in 1957. This contrasts with the conventional view, that only one state of many possible states is observed. The many-worlds view leads to the conclusion that the universe is constantly dividing to give vast numbers of alternative universes which co-exist but do not interact with one another, and that we live in a single one of these many universes. The theory does resolve difficulties in the quantum theory of measurement, but in a philosophically dubious manner. » quantum mechanics

Mao Zedong or **Mao Tse-tung** [mow dzi**dung**] (1893–1976) Leader and leading theorist of the Chinese Communist revolution which won national power in China in 1949. Born in Hunan province, the son of a farmer, at the age of 12 he sought an education in Changsha, where he was introduced to Western ideas. After graduating from a teachers' training college there, he went to Beijing (Peking), where he came under the influence of Li Dazhao. He took a leading part in the May Fourth Movement, then became a Marxist and a founding member of the Chinese Communist Party (1921). During the first united front with the Nationalist Party, he concentrated on political work among the peasants of his native province, and advocated a rural revolution, creating a rural Soviet in Jiangxi province in 1928. After the break with the Nationalists in 1927, the Communists were driven from the cities, and with the assistance of Chu Teh, he evolved the guerrilla tactics of the 'people's war'. In 1934 the Nationalist government was at last able to destroy the Jiangxi Soviet, and in the subsequent Long March the Communist forces retreated to Shaanxi to set up a new base.

When in 1936, under the increasing threat of Japanese invasion, the Nationalists renewed their alliance with the Communists, Mao restored and vastly increased the political and military power of his Party. His claim to share in the government led to civil war; the regime of Jiang Jieshi (Chiang Kai-shek) was ousted from the Chinese mainland; and the new People's Republic of China was proclaimed (1 Oct 1949) with Mao as both Chairman of the Chinese Communist Party and President of the Republic. He followed the Soviet model of economic development and social change until 1958, then launched his Great Leap Forward, which encouraged the establishment of rural industry and the use of surplus rural labour to create a new infrastructure for agriculture. The failure of the Great Leap lost him most of his influence, but by 1965, with China's armed forces securely in the hands of his ally Lin Piao, he launched a Cultural Revolution, and the Great Leap strategy was revived (though with new caution) when the left wing was victorious in the ensuing political struggles (1965–71). He died in Beijing (Peking) after a prolonged illness, which may well have weakened his judgment during his last years. A strong reaction set in against the excessive collectivism and egalitarianism which had emerged, but his anti-Stalinist emphasis on rural industry and on local initiative was retained and strengthened by his successors. » communism; Cultural Revolution; Great Leap Forward; Long March; Maoism; May Fourth Movement; soviet

Maoism Specifically, the thought of Mao Zedong (Tse-tung), and more broadly a revolutionary ideology based on Marxism-Leninism adapted to Chinese conditions. Maoism shifted the focus of revolutionary struggle from the urban workers or proletariat to the countryside and the peasantry. There were three main elements: strict Leninist principles of organization, Chinese tradition, and armed struggle as a form of revolutionary activity. Mao gained political power in 1949 through a peasant army, his slogan being 'Political power grows through the barrel of a gun'. While there were attempts to take account of the views of the masses, the Chinese Communist Party was organized along strict centralist, hierarchical lines, and increasingly became a vehicle for a personal dictatorship. In domestic terms Mao pursued a radical and far-reaching attempt to transform traditional Chinese society and its economy, using thought reform, indoctrination, and the psychological transformation of the masses. Maoism was regarded in the 1960s at the height of the Cultural Revolution as a highly radical form of Marxism-Leninism that was distinct from the bureaucratic repression of the Soviet Union, and had a strong appeal among the New Left. Since his death, his use of the masses for political purposes, his economic reforms, and his conception of political power have been increasingly criticized inside and outside China as seriously misguided and too rigid. » Cultural Revolution; Mao Zedong; Marxism-Leninism

Maoris Polynesian people who were the original inhabitants of New Zealand. The first of them arrived, probably from the Marquesas, about AD 800, bringing with them dogs and rats, and some cultivated plants, including the kumara (sweet potato). They also ate fern roots, fish, and birds, including the large flightless moa, which they hunted to extinction. By 1200 they had explored the whole country, and by 1800 numbered over 100 000. They were skilful carvers of wood and greenstone (jade). Politically they were divided into loose tribes linked by trade and sporadic warfare, and ruled by hereditary chiefs. In the 19th-c they came to be outnumbered and dominated by European (*pakeha*) settlers. Their culture declined; they lost most of their land; and by 1896 their population had shrunk to 42 200. There has been some improvement in the 20th-c. Numbers have risen (279 000 in 1981), and since the 1970s they have become politically more assertive. The Maori language has been officially encouraged, and they have obtained the return of some of their land. » Anglo-Maori Wars; Polynesia

map The graphic representation of spatial information about a place on a plane surface through the use of symbols and signs. Maps are generally produced for specific purposes (eg *cadastral* maps show land ownership; *topographical* maps show relief and terrain features; and *thematic* maps illustrate particular features, such as maps of population density). The earliest surviving maps are of estates of wealthy Babylonians (c.2500 BC) on clay tablets. The European traditions of map making date back to the Ancient Greeks. » cartography; isoline; map projection [i]; surveying; topography

map projection The method of portraying the spherical surface of the Earth on a flat surface. Because a sphere is three-dimensional in form, and a map two-dimensional, there is inevitably some distortion: the representation of distance (true

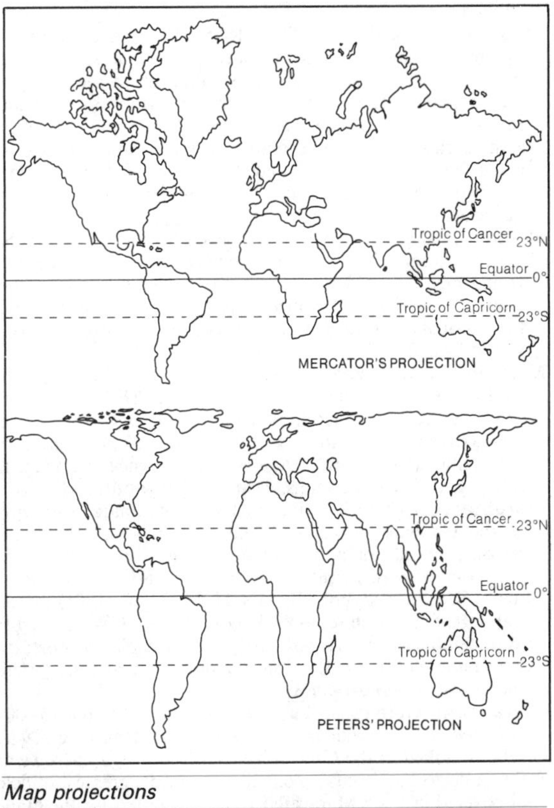

Map projections

scale), direction (true bearing), area, and shape cannot be shown correctly together on the same map. Consequently different map projections have been developed, according to purpose, which show for example true distance, or true area. The greatest distortions occur when a large area, such as the whole of the Earth's surface, is being mapped. For the mapping of smaller areas, such as topographical maps, a compromise is made to minimize the distortion of all four properties. » equal area/Mercator's/Peters' projection

maple A large genus of deciduous trees, native to N temperate regions; leaves variable in shape but typically palmately lobed with 3–13 toothed lobes, sometimes pinnate; flowers in clusters, small, greenish, purple, or red; characteristic fruit of two winged seeds fused at base, eventually splitting apart, the wings acting as propellers. Many species produce striking autumn colours, especially reds and purples, and are planted for ornament. Maple syrup is obtained from the sap of the **sugar maple** (*Acer saccharum*). (Genus: *Acer*, 200 species. Family: *Aceraceae*.) » box elder; deciduous plants; palmate; pinnate; sycamore; tree [i]

Mappa Mundi [**ma**pa **mun**dee] (Lat 'map of the world') A celebrated 13th-c map of the world, owned by Hereford Cathedral, Hereford, UK. The map is on vellum, measuring 163 × 137 cm/64 × 54 in, and shows the world as a round plate, with Jerusalem centrally located and Britain on its fringes. It comprises c.500 illustrations, and gives information on routes of pilgrimage, trade and travel, architecture, place names, history, mythology, flora, and fauna. In 1988 there was a public outcry over proposed plans to sell the map, to help raise funds for the Cathedral. The proposal was subsequently withdrawn, following assistance given by the National Heritage Memorial Fund. » Hereford

Maputo [ma**poo**toh], formerly **Lourenço Marques** (to 1976) 25°58S 32°32E, pop (1980) 755 000. Seaport capital of Mozambique, on Maputo Bay, 485 km/301 ml E of Johannesburg; visited by the Portuguese, 1502; explored by the trader Lourenço Marques; capital of Portuguese East Africa, 1907; airport; railway; university (1962); steel, textiles, ship repair, footwear, cement, furniture; an outlet for several SE African countries. » Mozambique [i]

maquette [ma**ket**] A small model made by a sculptor as a preliminary study or sketch for a full-size work. A maquette is usually in clay, wax, or plaster. » sculpture; sketch

maquis [ma**kee**] The evergreen scrub vegetation of the Mediterranean region; also known as **macchia**. The vegetation includes spiny shrubs and many aromatic species. In some areas it may result from overcultivation and overgrazing. It is equivalent to the chaparral of N America. » chaparral; evergreen plants; garrigue

Maquis [ma**kee**] The local name given to the dense scrub in Corsica; adopted in German-occupied France by groups of young men who hid in the hills and forests to escape forced labour in Germany. Organized into resistance groups, they led the national rising against the Germans on and after D-Day. » World War 2

Mar del Plata [**mah** thel **pla**ta] 38°00S 57°30W, pop (1980) 407 024. Port on the Atlantic coast in SE Buenos Aires province, E Argentina; founded in 1874; one of the prime holiday resorts of S America, with 8 km/5 ml of beaches; two universities (1958, 1962); railway; airfield; meat packing, fish canning, tourism; museums, casino. » Argentina [i]

marabou A large stork native to Africa S of Sahara; also known as the **marabou stork**; head and neck naked; inhabits dry regions; eats carrion and small animals; nests in trees. (*Leptoptilos crumeniferus*. Family: *Ciconiidae*.) » adjutant; stork

Maracaibo [mara**kiy**boh] 10°44N 71°37W, pop (1981) 890 553. Capital of Zulia state, NW Venezuela, on NW shore of L Maracaibo; second largest city in Venezuela; airport; two universities (1891, 1973); oil production and processing, petrochemicals. » Venezuela [i]

Maracaibo, Lake (Span **Lago de**) [mara**kiy**boh] area 13 000 sq km/5 000 sq ml. Lake in NW Venezuela; length, c.210 km/130 ml; linked to the Gulf of Venezuela through narrows and the Tablazo Bay; contains one of the world's greatest oilfields, discovered in 1917; Maracaibo Lowlands noted for the highest annual average temperatures in Latin America. » Venezuela [i]

maracas A pair of rattles, originally gourds filled with dried seeds, used as a rhythm instrument in Latin American and occasionally Western orchestral music. » idiophone

Maradona, Diego [mara**do**na] (1960–) Argentine footballer, born at Lanus, near Buenos Aires. He became Argentine's youngest ever international in 1977, transferred to Boca Juniors for £1 million as a teenager, and in June 1982 became the world's most expensive footballer when he joined Barcelona for £5 million. He broke the record again in 1984 when the Italian club Napoli paid £6.9 million for him. He captained Argentina to their second World Cup in 1986. » football [i]

maral » **red deer**

Maralinga 30°13S 131°24E. Ghost town, South Australia, on the E Nullarbor Plain, N of the transcontinental railway; area used by the British as a nuclear testing site in the 1950s. » South Australia

Marañón, River (Span **Río**) [mara**nyohn**] River in Peru, one of the Amazon's major headstreams; rises in the Andes, 137 km/85 ml E of the Pacific; joins the R Ucayali to form the Amazon 88 km/55 ml SSW of Iquitos; estimated length is 1 600 km/1 000 ml; navigable as far as the Pongo de Manseriche gorge. » Peru [i]

marasmus [ma**raz**muhs] The childhood equivalent of adult starvation, usually occurring after six months of life, and caused by insufficient intake of protein and of energy. Affected children are extremely thin and wizened. » diet; protein

Marat, Jean Paul [**ma**ra] (1743–93) French revolutionary politician, born at Boudry, Switzerland. He studied medicine at Bordeaux, and lived in Paris, Holland, and London. At the Revolution he became a member of the Cordelier Club and established the radical paper *L'Ami du Peuple* (The Friend of the People). His virulence provoked hatred, and he was several times forced into hiding. Elected to the National Convention, he became a leader of the Mountain, and advocated radical reforms. After the King's death he was locked in a struggle with the Girondins, and was fatally stabbed in his bath by a Girondin supporter, Charlotte Corday; thereafter he was hailed as a martyr. » French Revolution [i]; Girondins; Mountain, the

Maratha or **Mahratta** [ma**rah**ta] Marathi-speaking people of Maharashtra, W India (though sometimes the name refers only to the Maratha caste in the region). They include a group of castes who are mainly peasant farmers, soldiers, and landowners. Historically they are famed as warriors and for promoting Hinduism. Population c.41 million. » caste; Hinduism; Maharashtra

Maratha Kingdom [ma**rah**ta] A W Indian regional power, founded by Maratha warrior-leader Shivaji (1627–80), which filled the vacuum left by Mughal decline. It later became a confederacy of leading families (Bhonsle, Gaekwad, Holkar, Sindhia) under hereditary chief ministers (Peshwas). The kingdom was defeated by Afghans at Panipat (1761). It sought British protection but was destroyed by British intervention in 1818.

Marathi » **Indo-Aryan languages**

marathon A long-distance running race, normally on open roads, over the distance 42 km 195 m/26 ml 385 yd. The race was introduced at the first modern Olympic Games in 1896 to commemorate the run of the Greek courier (according to legend, Pheidippides) who ran the c.24 ml/39 km from Marathon to Athens in 490 BC with the news of a Greek victory over the Persian army. After proclaiming the victory, he collapsed and died. The current marathon distance was first used at the 1908 London Olympics, its exact distance being fixed so that competitors could finish in front of the royal box. The distance was standardized in 1924. It is now a popular event for the non-competitive enthusiast. The London marathon attracts more than 20 000 entrants each year. In the 1980s, the **half-marathon** also became very popular, over the distance 21 km/13 ml 192½ yd. » Marathon, Battle of

Marathon, Battle of (490 BC) The decisive Athenian victory over the Persians on the E coast of Attica, which brought the First Persian War to an end. » marathon; Persian Wars

Marbella [mah**bay**ya] 36°30N 4°57W, pop (1981) 67 822. Port and resort on the Costa del Sol, Málaga province, Andalusia, S Spain; watersports; large bathing beaches; tourism, iron and steel, furniture; Fiesta del Sol (Jan), Fiestas of San Bernabe (Jun), Semana del Sol (Aug), Costa del Sol Rally (Dec). » Costa del Sol; Spain [i]

marble A metamorphic rock formed by the recrystallization of limestone and dolomite. It is white when pure, but its impurities give it a distinctive coloration. It is easily sculpted and polished, and is also used as a building stone. » dolomite; limestone; metamorphic rock

Marburg [**mah**boork] 50°49N 8°36E, pop (1983) 79 100. City in Giessen district, West Germany; on the R Lahn, 74 km/46 ml N of Frankfurt; railway; university (1527); pharmaceuticals, optical equipment; St Elizabeth's Church (1235–83), Gothic castle (15th–16th-c). » Germany, West [i]

Marburg disease » green monkey disease

Marc, Franz (1880–1916) German artist, born in Munich. He studied at Munich and also in Italy and France, and helped to found the Blaue Reiter group in Munich in 1911. Most of his paintings were of animals (eg 'Tower of the Blue Horses') portrayed in forceful colours. He was killed at Verdun. » Blaue Reiter, der; German art

Marc Antony » Antonius, Marcus

marcasite [**mah**kuhsiyt] An iron sulphide mineral (FeS_2) with the same chemical composition as pyrite, but formed at lower temperatures. It is found in sedimentary rocks, and is also associated with major ore deposits of the Mississippi Valley. » pyrite; sedimentary rock

Marceau, Marcel (1923–) French mime artist, born in Strasbourg. He studied at Paris, and in 1948 founded the *Compagnie de Mime Marcel Marceau*, of which he was the director until 1964. The leading exponent of the art of mime, his white-faced character, Bip, became famous from his appearances on stage and television throughout the world. Since 1978 he has been head of the *Ecole de Mimodrame Marcel Marceau*. » mime; theatre

Marcellus, Marcus Claudius 1 (c.268–208 BC) Roman general of the time of the Second Punic War. Nicknamed the 'Sword of Rome', his main exploits were the defeat of the Insubrian Gauls (222 BC) and the capture of Syracuse (212 BC). » Punic Wars **2** (42–23 BC) Nephew of the Emperor Augustus by his sister Octavia, and his first intended successor. His early death was widely regarded as a national calamity. » Augustus

march Music designed to accompany soldiers marching in step, and therefore virtually always in duple or quadruple metre and (except for funeral marches) in a moderate or quick tempo. Concert pieces in march style include the 'Marche au supplice' in Berlioz's *Symphonie fantastique* (1830) and Elgar's five *Pomp and Circumstance* marches (1901–7). » Berlioz; Elgar

March on Rome The largely symbolic culmination of the pseudo-revolutionary process surrounding Italian fascism's entry into goverment and Mussolini's appointment (1922) as premier. Planned as part of an insurrection which only half occurred, the actual march was a celebration of a victory achieved by nominally constitutional means. » fascism; Mussolini

March Through Georgia (1864) A campaign in the American Civil War by the Northern army under General Sherman, resulting in devastation of the area between Atlanta and the ocean. In military terms it completed the task of splitting the Confederacy on an E–W line. » American Civil War; Sherman

Marches, the The area of EC Italy between the Apennines and the Adriatic Sea, centred on Ancona. Except for the narrow coastal plain, it is mostly mountainous.

marchioness » marquess

Marciano, Rocky, originally **Rocco Francis Marchegiano** (1923–69) US heavyweight boxing champion, born at Brockton, Massachusetts. He became a professional in 1947, and made his name by defeating the former world champion, Joe Louis, in 1951. He won the world title from Jersey Joe Walcott the following year, and when he retired in 1956 was undefeated as world champion, with a professional record of 49 bouts and 49 victories. He died in an air crash at Newton, Iowa. » boxing [i]; Louis, Joe

Marco Polo's sheep » argali

Marconi, Guglielmo (1874–1937) Italian inventor, born in Bologna. He successfully experimented with wireless telegraphy in Italy and England, succeeded in sending signals across the Atlantic in 1901, and was awarded the Nobel Prize for Physics in 1909. He was created a marquis, became a senator (1929), and died in Rome. » telegraphy

Marcos, Ferdinand (Edralin) (1917–1989) Philippines politician and President (1965–86), born at Ilocos Norte. He trained as a lawyer, and as a politician obtained considerable US support as an anti-communist. His regime as President was marked by increasing repression, misuse of foreign financial aid, and political murders (notably, the assassination of Benigno Aquino in 1983). He declared martial law in 1972, but was overthrown in 1986 by a popular front led by Corazon Aquino. He went into exile in Hawaii, where he and his wife, Imelda, fought against demands from US courts investigating charges of financial mismanagement and corruption. He died in Honolulu. » Aquino; Philippines [i]

Marcus Aurelius Antoninus » Aurelius

Marcuse, Herbert (1898–1979) US Marxist philosopher, born in Berlin. He was educated at Berlin and Freiburg, becoming an influential figure of the Frankfurt School. He fled to Geneva in 1933, and after World War 2 moved to the USA, working in intelligence. He later held posts at Columbia (1951), Harvard (1952), Brandeis (1954), and in 1965 at California, as professor of philosophy. His books include *Reason and Revolution* (1941) and *Eros and Civilization* (1955). He died in Munich, Germany. » Frankfurt School; libertarianism; Marx

Mardi Gras [**mah(r)**dee **grah**] The French name (literally 'fat Tuesday') for Shrove Tuesday, the day before the beginning of Lent; Mardi Gras carnivals, beginning some time before Shrove Tuesday, are held in various places; among the most famous are those of Rio de Janeiro and New Orleans. » Lent; Shrove Tuesday

Marduk [**mah**duhk] Originally the patron deity of the city of Babylon. He later became the supreme god of Babylonia, taking over the functions of Enlil. » Babylon; Enlil

mare's tail An aquatic perennial native to Europe, Asia, and N Africa; stems growing to 150 cm/5 ft, usually less, emerging above water; narrow leaves in whorls of 6–12; flowers tiny, green, on emergent portion of stem. (*Hippuris vulgaris*. Family: *Hippuridaceae*.) » perennial

Marfan's syndrome An inherited disease of connective tissue in which arms and legs grow to abnormal lengths; also known as **arachnodactyly**. The fingers are long and spidery, joints are excessively mobile, and there is a lack of subcutaneous tissue. Affected individuals are underweight in spite of being extremely tall. It is named after French paediatrician Bernard Jean Antoinin Marfan (1858–1942). » tissue

Margaret (1353–1412) Queen of Denmark, Norway, and Sweden, born at Søborg, Denmark. She became Queen of Denmark in 1375, on the death of her father, Waldemar IV, without male heirs; by the death of her husband, Haakon VI, in 1380, she became ruler of Norway; and in 1388 she aided a rising of Swedish nobles against their King, Albert of Mecklenburg, and became Queen of Sweden. She had her infant cousin, Eric of Pomerania, crowned King of the three kingdoms at Kalmar in 1397, but remained the real ruler of Scandinavia until her death at Flensburg. » Kalmar Union

Margaret (Rose), Princess (1930–) British princess, second daughter of George VI and sister of Queen Elizabeth II, born at Glamis Castle, Scotland. In 1955, when she was third in succession to the throne, she denied rumours of her possible marriage to Group-Captain Peter Townsend (a divorcé), amid a great deal of publicity and concern that a constitutional crisis could be precipitated by such a marriage. In 1960 she married Antony Armstrong-Jones, who was created Viscount Linley and Earl of Snowdon in 1961. The former title devolved upon their son, **David Albert Charles** (1961–). They also have a daughter, **Sarah Frances Elizabeth** (1964–). The marriage was dissolved in 1978. » Snowdon, Earl of

Margaret, St (c.1045–93), feast day 10 or 16 June. Scottish Queen, born in Hungary, who came to England, but after the Norman Conquest fled to Scotland with her boy brother,

Edgar Atheling. She married the Scottish King, Malcolm Canmore, and did much to civilize the realm, and to assimilate the old Celtic Church to the rest of Christendom. She died in Edinburgh, and was canonized in 1250. » Christianity; Edgar the Atheling; Malcolm III

Margaret of Anjou (1429–82) Queen Consort of Henry VI of England from 1445, the daughter of René of Anjou. Because of Henry's madness, she became deeply involved in political life, and during the Wars of the Roses, was a leading Lancastrian. Defeated at Tewkesbury (1471), she was imprisoned in the Tower for four years, until ransomed by Louis XI. She then retired to France, and died at the castle of Dampierre, near Saumur. » Henry VI; Roses, Wars of the

Margaret Tudor (1489–1541) Queen of Scotland, the eldest daughter of Henry VII, born in London. She became the wife of James IV of Scotland (1503) and the mother of James V, for whom she acted as Regent. After James IV's death in 1513 she married twice again, to the Earl of Angus (1514) and Lord Methven (1527). She was much involved in the political intrigues between the pro-French and pro-English factions in Scotland, but lacking Tudor shrewdness, she was discredited (1534). She died at Methven Castle, Perth. Her great-grandson was James I of England and VI of Scotland. » Tudors

margarine A butter-substitute that does not contain dairy fat, usually made from vegetable oils and skimmed milk, and supplemented with vitamins A and D. In the 1860s a French chemist, Hippolyte Mège-Mouriès (1817–80), extracted a fraction of beef fat at 30–40°C which he termed *oleo-margarine*. This was used as the basis of a butter substitute until 1903, when a process of hardening vegetable oils by hydrogenation was patented. Since then, butter substitutes have developed in sophistication, although most of these are still based on hydrogenated vegetable or marine oils. The degree of hydrogenation of the original oil determines how much remains of the original polyunsaturates. » hydrogenation; polyunsaturated fatty acids; vitamins [i]

margay [**mah**gay] A rare member of the cat family, found from N Mexico to N Argentina; pale with ring-like dark spots; inhabits forest; hunts in trees; rear feet adapted for climbing (capable of rotating through 180°); sometimes reared as pets. (*Felis wiedii*.) » Felidae

marginal cost In economics, the cost of producing one extra unit, or the total cost saved if one less unit is produced. In accountancy, it is the variable cost of producing a unit. *Marginal costing* is a system where only variable costs (ie costs which vary directly with the volume made or sold, such as materials) are related to the unit. *Fixed costs* (ie those remaining unchanged whatever the volume, such as rent) are not allocated to the unit.

marginal productivity An economic concept defining the additional output (*marginal output*) generated by the last, additional input of labour (or other input). The concept is used as a theory of wage determination, in that firms employ workers only as long as the revenue from the marginal worker is greater than his or her cost. » diminishing returns, law of

Margrethe II (1940–) Queen of Denmark, born in Copenhagen, the daughter of Frederick IX, whom she succeeded in 1972. Educated at Copenhagen, Aarhus, Cambridge, Paris, and London, she qualified as an archaeologist. In 1967 she married a French diplomat, Count Henri de Laborde de Monpezat, now **Prince Henrik of Denmark**. Their children are the heir apparent, **Prince Frederik André Henrik Christian** (1968–) and **Prince Joachim Holger Waldemar Christian** (1969–). » Denmark [i]

marguerite [mahguh**reet**] » **ox-eye daisy**

Mari [**mah**ree] The most important city on the middle Euphrates in the third and second millennia BC until its destruction c.1759 BC by the Babylonians. It was the centre of a vast trading network in NW Mesopotamia. Since 1933, c.20 000 cuneiform tablets dating from c.18th-c BC have been discovered, providing a great deal of information about the period. Although no mention is made of any actual Biblical character or place, several offer interesting parallels to practices in the patriarchal period of Israel's history. » Babylonia; cuneiform [i]; Mesopotamia; patriarch **1**

maria [**ma**riya] (singular **mare** [**mah**ray]) Dark regions mainly on the nearside of the Moon. They are flat plains of basalt formed 3–3.9 billion years ago. Dense concentrations of material beneath the maria are known as *mascons*. » basalt; Moon

Maria Theresa (1717–80) Archduchess of Austria, Queen of Hungary and Bohemia (1740–80), the daughter of Emperor Charles VI, born and died in Vienna. In 1736 she married Francis, Duke of Lorraine, and in 1740 succeeded her father in the hereditary Habsburg lands. Her claim, however, led to the War of the Austrian Succession, during which she lost Silesia to Prussia. In 1741 she received the Hungarian crown, and in 1745 her husband was elected Holy Roman Emperor. Although her Foreign Minister, Kaunitz, tried to isolate Prussia by diplomatic means, military conflict was renewed in the Seven Years' War, and by 1763 she was finally forced to recognize the status quo of 1756. In her later years she strove to maintain international peace, and reluctantly accepted the partition of Poland (1772). » Austrian Succession, War of the; Frederick II (of Prussia); Habsburgs; Poland, Partitions of; Seven Years' War

Mariana Islands, in full **Commonwealth of the Northern Mariana Islands** pop (1988e) 30 000; area 471 sq km/182 sq ml. Group of 14 islands in the NW Pacific, c.2 400 km/1 500 ml E of the Philippines; capital, Saipan; mainly volcanic (three still active); includes Saipan, Tinian, Rota, Pagan, Guguan; held by the USA under UN mandate after World War 2 as part of the US Trust Territory of the Pacific Is, 1947–78; self-governing commonwealth of the USA, 1978–90; trusteeship ended, 1990; tourism, sugar cane, coconuts, coffee. » mandates; United States Trust Territory of the Pacific Islands

Marianas Trench An oceanic trench running SW to N off the I of Guam and the N Marianas Is, Pacific Ocean. Its deepest point, Challenger Deep, 11 034 m/36 201 ft, is the Earth's maximum ocean depth. » Pacific Ocean

Marie Antoinette (Josèphe Jeanne) (1755–93) Queen of France, born in Vienna, the daughter of Maria Theresa and Francis I, and sister of Leopold II. She was married to the Dauphin, afterwards Louis XVI (1770), to strengthen the Franco-Austrian alliance, and exerted a growing influence over him. Capricious and frivolous, she aroused criticism by her extravagance, disregard for conventions, devotion to the interests of Austria, and opposition to reform. From the outbreak of the French Revolution, she resisted the advice of constitutional monarchists (eg Mirabeau), and helped to alienate the monarchy from the people. In June 1791 she and Louis tried to escape from the Tuileries to her native Austria, but were apprehended at Varennes and imprisoned in Paris. After the King's execution, she was arraigned before the Tribunal and guillotined. » French Revolution [i]; Louis XVI; Mirabeau

Marie de France (12th-c) French poet, born in Normandy. She spent much of her life in England, where she wrote several verse narratives based on Celtic stories. Her *Lais*, dedicated to 'a noble king' (probably Henry II), were a landmark in French literature. » French literature; poetry

Marie de Médicis Ital **Maria de' Medici**, (1573–1642) Queen Consort of Henry IV of France, born in Florence, the daughter of Francesco de' Medici, Grand Duke of Tuscany. She married Henry in 1600, following his divorce from his first wife, Margaret, and gave birth to a son (later Louis XIII) in 1601. After her husband's death (1610) she acted as Regent, but her capricious behaviour and dependence on favourites led to her confinement in Blois when Louis assumed royal power (1617). She continued to intrigue against Louis and her former protégé, Richelieu, who had become the King's adviser. She was banished to Compiègne, but escaped to Brussels (1631). Her last years were spent in poverty, and she died in Cologne. » Louis XIII; Medici; Richelieu

Marie Louise (1791–1847) Empress of France, born in Vienna, the daughter of Francis I of Austria. She married Napoleon in 1810 (after his divorce from Josephine), and in 1811 bore him a son, who was created King of Rome and who became Napoleon II. On Napoleon's abdication she returned to Austria. By the Treaty of Fontainebleau (1814) she was awarded the

Duchies of Parma, Piacenza, and Guastalla in Italy, where she died. » Napoleon I

marigold The name applied to several different species of the daisy family, *Compositae*. » African/corn/pot marigold

marihuana or **marijuana** » **cannabis**

marimba In modern orchestras and pop groups, a percussion instrument resembling a xylophone, with slender wooden bars and metal resonators, but with a lower compass and played with soft beaters. » percussion [i]; xylophone

Mariner programme A series of increasingly complex 3-axis stabilized spacecraft launched by NASA to begin the exploration of the inner and outer Solar System. The programme included the first planetary flyby (Mariner 2, Venus, Dec 1962), the first planetary orbiter (Mariner 9, Mars, Nov 1971), the first mission to Mercury (Mariner 10, Mar 1974, Sep 1974, and Mar 1975), and the first detailed observations of Jovian, Saturnian, and Uranian systems (Mariner *Jupiter-Saturn* – renamed *Voyager* – 1979–86). The spacecraft were built and operated by NASA's Jet Propulsion Laboratory and derived from the early lunar impact spacecraft *Ranger*. The Viking Mars orbiter is also a member of the Mariner family. » NASA; Solar System

Marines Soldiers, under naval command, who nevertheless are equipped and organized to make war on land. Originally posted in small units aboard warships, in the two world wars, Marines have been used as combat forces in their own right, specializing in such operations as commando raiding and amphibious assault. » army; navy; Royal Marines; US Marines

Marinetti, Filippo Tommaso (Emilio) (1876–1944) Italian writer, born in Alexandria, Egypt. He studied in Paris and Genoa, and published the manifesto for Futurism in 1909. In his writings he glorified war, the machine age, speed, and 'dynamism', and condemned all traditional forms of literature and art. His ideas influenced several painters and sculptors. He died at Bellagio, Italy. » Futurism; Italian literature

Marini, Marino [mar**ee**nee] (1901–66) Italian sculptor, born at Pistoia. He was trained at the Academy of Fine Art in Florence, and won prizes at the Rome Quadriennale in 1935 and at the Venice Biennale in 1952. He worked mainly in bronze in a traditional figurative style, his favourite subjects including horses and riders, portraits, and dancers. » bronze; Italian art

Marino, Dan (1961–) US footballer, born in Pittsburgh. An outstanding quarterback with the Miami Dolphins, in the 1984 season he gained 5084 yards passing to create a National Football League record. He completed a record 29 passes in the 1985 Super Bowl, and in 1986 established a record for the most passes completed in a season, 378. » football [i]

marionettes » **puppetry**

Maritain, Jacques [mar**ee**tĩ] (1882–1973) French Catholic philosopher, born in Paris, and educated at Paris and Heidelberg. He early abandoned Bergsonism for orthodox neo-Thomism, and became a Catholic in 1906. He was professor of philosophy at the Institut Catholique in Paris (1913–40), also taught at Toronto, Columbia, Chicago, Notre Dame, and Princeton (1948–60), and was French ambassador to the Vatican (1945–8). His philosophical writings include *Les degrés du savoir* (1932, The Degrees of Knowledge), but he is best-known outside France for his many writings on art, politics, and history. He died at Toulouse. » Aquinas; Bergson

Maritime Trust A national organization in the UK to restore, maintain, and display ships of historic or technical importance. It has preserved many ships including HMS *Warrior*, and is now restoring Captain Scott's *Discovery*. It was set up in 1969, on the initiative of Prince Philip.

Marius, Gaius (157–86 BC) Roman general and politician from Arpinum, of comparatively humble extraction, whose military talents and ruthless ambition enabled him to rise to the very top at Rome, where he held an unprecedented number of consulships (seven) and married into the heart of the aristocracy – the Julian gens. Famous in his lifetime for his victories over Jugurtha (105 BC), the Teutones (102 BC), and the Cimbri (101 BC), it was by his army reforms that he made his greatest impact on the state. His final years were dominated by his rivalry with Sulla. The violence with which he recaptured Rome for Cinna from the forces backing Sulla (87 BC) permanently damaged his reputation. » Cinna; Jugurtha; Roman history [i]; Sulla

Marivaux, Pierre (Carlet de Chamblain de) [**ma**reevoh] (1688–1763) French dramatist, born and died in Paris. He published a burlesque of the *Iliad*, in 1716, and wrote many comedies on romantic themes, such as *Le Jeu de l'amour et du hasard* (1730, The Game of Love and Chance) and the unfinished *La Vie de Marianne* (1731–41, The Life of Marianne). His affected style, full of witty plays on words, came to be known as 'Marivaudage'. » drama; French literature

marjoram [**mah**juhruhm] A somewhat bushy perennial, native to limestone and chalky soils in Europe, the Mediterranean, and Asia; stems square; leaves oval, in opposite pairs; flowers small, 2-lipped, white or purplish-pink, in dense spikes. It is cultivated as a culinary herb, often under the name **oregano**. The plants grown in warm countries are the most strongly aromatic. (*Origanum vulgare*. Family: *Labiatae*.) » herb; perennial

Mark Antony » **Antonius, Marcus**

Mark, Gospel according to The second book of the New Testament canon, the shortest of the four gospels, and argued by many scholars also to be the earliest; anonymous, but traditionally attributed to John Mark. Because it contains less teaching material than the other Gospels, it places relatively greater emphasis on Jesus' passion, and draws attention to the mystery of his role and activities. It is noteworthy also for its abrupt beginning (compared with the other Gospels) and for disputes concerning the original ending of the Gospel. » Gospels, canonical; Mark, St; New Testament

Mark, St or **John Mark** feast day 25 April. Described in the New Testament as 'John whose surname was Mark' (*Acts* 12.12, 25), a helper of the apostles Barnabas and Paul during their first missionary journey, but the cause of a split between Barnabas and Paul over the question of his loyalty; later commended in *Col* 4.10 and 2 *Tim* 4.11. He is often considered the Mark who is accredited in 2nd-c traditions with the writing of the second Gospel, described by Papias (early 2nd-c bishop in Asia Minor) as 'the interpreter of Peter'. » Barnabas; Mark, Gospel according to; Paul, St

Markarian galaxy » **galaxy**

market economy An economic system where prices, wages, and what is made and sold are determined by market forces of supply and demand, with no state interference. The contrast is with a *command economy*, where the state takes all economic decisions. Most Western economies these days are mixed, with varying degrees of state control. » free trade; laissez-faire; market forces

market forces or **market mechanism** The network of interactions between buyers and sellers which determines the price and quantity of products and goods, prices being set by the forces of supply and demand. The process assumes that there is no interference by, for example, government.

market gardening The intensive production of horticultural crops on small-holdings, especially fruit and vegetables for local markets. It may incorporate pick-your-own enterprises, where labour is scarce. » horticulture; humus; intensive farming

market research A technique to find out more about the market in which a business is operating, or may operate in the future. Survey techniques are often used, seeking the opinions of individuals who might be buyers, and providing information about the potential size and characteristics of a particular market segment. Market research also enables advertising agencies to target their campaigns more accurately. » marketing

marketing The management of a business with the customer in mind. It aims to identify a market where a potential exists for profitable business, and to take the necessary steps to satisfy that market by careful planning of the 'marketing mix' or the 'Four Ps': product, price, place, and promotion (including advertising). » market research; marketing board; telemarketing

marketing board A statutory body which has the power to

control some aspect(s) of production, processing, or marketing for a specific commodity. It is usually created through a majority vote of producers and financed through compulsory levy. Most commonly used to manage the marketing and promotion of agricultural commodities, it may also fund research and the collection and dissemination of information. Marketing boards are used widely throughout the non-communist world, and are particularly common in N America. » agriculture

markhor [**mah**kaw] A wild goat native to the mountains of S Asia; the largest goat; male with long beard covering throat; long horns extremely thick, close (or joined) at base, with sharp spiral ridge around outside; inhabits woodlands. (*Capra falconeri*.) » goat

Markievicz, Constance (Georgine), Countess [mah**kyay**vich] (1868–1927) Irish nationalist, the daughter of Sir Henry Gore-Booth of Co Sligo, who married Polish Count Casimir Markievicz. She fought in the Easter Rising (1916), and was sentenced to death but reprieved. Elected the first British woman MP in 1918, she did not take her seat, but was a member of the Dáil from 1923. » Easter Rising; nationalism

Markov chain In mathematics, a chain of events in which the probability of moving from one state to another depends on the existing state. These are often displayed in matrices, and a two-state Markov chain, one in which there are two possible states at each stage, is illustrated by the matrix $\begin{pmatrix} a & 1-a \\ 1-b & b \end{pmatrix}$

For example, a man travels home from work either by car or by train. If he travels by car any one day, the probability that he travels by car the next might be 0.4; if he travels by train one day, the probability that he travels by train the next might be 0.3. These would be shown in the transition matrix $\begin{pmatrix} 0{\cdot}4 & 0{\cdot}6 \\ 0{\cdot}7 & 0{\cdot}3 \end{pmatrix}$

The notion is named after the Soviet mathematician Andrei Andreevich Markov (1856–1922). » matrix; probability of an event

Markova, Dame Alicia [mah**koh**fa], originally **Lilian Alicia Marks** (1910–) British prima ballerina, born in London. She danced with the Diaghilev company 1925–9, and appeared at Sadler's Wells in the early 1930s. Her career included periods in Monte Carlo, New York, and London, the latter with Sadler's Wells (later, the Royal Ballet) and the London Festival Ballet. She retired in 1962, was created a Dame in 1963, and became director of the Metropolitan Opera Ballet (1963–9). » ballet; London Festival Ballet; Royal Ballet

Marks (of Broughton), Simon, 1st Baron (1888–1964) British businessman, born in Leeds. In 1907 he inherited the 60 Marks and Spencer 'penny bazaars', which his father Michael had built up from 1884. In collaboration with Israel (later Lord) Seiff (1899–1972), his brother-in-law, he took Marks and Spencer from a policy of 'Don't ask the price – it's a penny' to become a major retail chain. 'Marks and Sparks' used their considerable purchasing power to encourage British clothing manufacturers to achieve demanding standards, and the 'St Michael' brand label became a guarantee of high quality at a reasonable price. He was knighted in 1944 and created a baron in 1961. He died in his company's London head office. » Sieff

marl Carbonate-rich clay deposits formed by the weathering of impure limestones. » clay; limestone

Marlborough, John Churchill, 1st Duke of (1650–1722) English general, born at Ashe, Devon. He was commissioned as an ensign in the Guards (1667), and fought in the Low Countries. In 1678 he married Sarah Jennings (1660–1744), a close friend and attendant of Princess Anne, and was further promoted. On James II's accession (1685), he was elevated to an English barony and given the rank of general. He took a leading part in quelling Monmouth's rebellion at Sedgemoor but, concerned for the integrity of the Anglican Church under James, deserted to the Prince of Orange in 1688, and served the Protestant cause in campaigns in Ireland and Flanders. Under Queen Anne he was appointed Supreme Commander of the British forces in the War of the Spanish Succession, and he became Captain-General of the Allied armies. His military flair and organization skills resulted in several great victories – Donauwörth and Blenheim (1704), Ramillies (1706), Oudenarde and the capture of Lille (1708) – for which he was richly rewarded with Blenheim Palace and a dukedom. Forced by political interests to align himself with the Whig war party (1708), his influence waned with theirs after 1710. When his wife fell from royal favour, the Tories pressed for his downfall. He was dismissed on charges of embezzling, and left England for continental Europe (1712), returning after George's accession (1714). Though restored to his former offices, his health was impaired, and he died at Windsor, Berkshire. » Anne; Blenheim Palace; Monmouth; Spanish Succession, War of the; Tories; Whigs; William III

Marley, Robert (Nesta), byname **Bob** (1945–81) Jamaican singer, guitarist, and composer of reggae music, born near Kingston. In 1965, tourists started bringing back stories about, and cheap records by, Bob Marley and his band, the Wailers. Their music (reggae) developed political themes with an artless lyricism and infectious rhythms, and in the 1970s he brought it around the world. He was a disciple of Rastafarianism, and a charismatic spokesman not only for his religion but also his culture and generation. He died of cancer, apparently at Jack's Hill, Jamaica. » Rastafarianism; reggae

marlin Any of several large, fast-swimming, highly agile billfishes widespread in warm seas; length up to 4.5 m/14¾ ft; very important commercially, and highly prized as sport fish, especially the **blue marlin** (*Makaira nigricans*) and the **striped marlin** (*Tetrapturus audax*). (Genera: *Makaira, Tetrapturus*. Family: *Istiophoridae*.) » billfish

Marlowe, Christopher (1564–93) The greatest of Shakespeare's predecessors in English drama, born at Canterbury, Kent, and educated there and at Cambridge. His *Tamburlaine the Great* (c.1587) shows his discovery of the strength and variety of blank verse, and this was followed by *The Jew of Malta* (c.1590), *The Tragical History of Dr Faustus* (c.1592), partly written by others, and *Edward II* (c.1592). He wrote several translations and poems, such as the unfinished *Hero and Leander*; and much of his other work has been handed down in fragments. He led an irregular life, and was on the point of being arrested for disseminating atheistic opinions when he was fatally stabbed at Deptford, near London, in a tavern brawl. » drama; English literature; Shakespeare [i]

Marmara [**mah**mara] or **Marmora, Sea of**, Turkish **Marmara Denizi**, ancient **Propontis** area 11 474 sq km/4 429 sq ml. Sea in NW Turkey, between Europe (N) and Asia (S); connected (E) with the Black Sea through the Bosporus and (W) with the Aegean Sea through the Dardanelles; length, c.200 km/125 ml; Istanbul is on its NE shore; Marmara I (from which the sea gets its modern name) is in the W, a source of marble, slate, and granite. » Bosporus; Dardanelles; Istanbul; Turkey [i]

Marmes Man Prehistoric human remains found in 1965 on R J Marmes's ranch in Washington, USA. About 11 000 years old, they rank as early evidence for the peopling of N America from E Asia. » *Homo* [i]

marmoset [**mah**muhset] A monkey-like primate, native to S America; thick fur, long tail; head may have ornamental tufts; thumb not opposable; nails long, curved, pointed; inhabits tropical forest. (Family: *Callitrichidae*, 17 species.) » monkey [i]; tamarin; titi

marmot [**mah**muht] A large, ground-dwelling squirrel native to Europe, Asia, and N America; length, c.750 mm/30 in; inhabits open country; lives in burrows; hibernates for up to 9 months; eats vegetation and insects. (Genus: *Marmota*, 11 species.) » squirrel; woodchuck

Marne, Battle of the (1914) A battle early in World War 1, in which General Joffre's French armies and the British Expeditionary Force halted German forces which had crossed the Marne and were approaching Paris, thus ending German hopes of a swift victory. The German line withdrew across the R Aisne, dug in, and occupied much the same positions until 1918. » British Expeditionary Force; Joffre; World War 1

Marne, River, ancient **Matrona** River in C France rising in the Langres Plateau; flows NW and W across Champagne to meet the R Seine near Paris; length 525 km/326 ml; navigable to St Dizier; scene of two major battles in World War 1 (1914, 1918). » World War 1

Maronite Church A Christian community originating in Syria in the 7th-c, claiming origin from St Maro (died 407). Condemned for its Monothelite beliefs in 680, the Church survived in Syria and elsewhere, and since 1182 has been in communion with the Roman Catholic Church. » Monothelites

Marprelate Tracts Seven pamphlets covertly published in London, 1587–9. The pseudonymous author, 'Martin Marprelate', satirized the Elizabethan Church and bishops, and favoured a Presbyterian system. One alleged author, John Penry (1559–93), was executed; another, John Udall (1560–92), died in prison; a third, Job Throckmorton (1545–1601), successfully refuted the accusations. The Tracts led to statutes against dissenting sects and sedition (1593). » Presbyterianism

Marquesas Islands [mah**kay**saz], Fr **Iles Marquises** pop (1983) 6 548; area 1 189 sq km/459 sq ml. Mountainous, wooded volcanic island group of French Polynesia, 1 184 km/736 ml NE of Tahiti; comprises Nuku Hiva (where Herman Melville lived), Ua Pu, Ua Huka, Hiva Oa (where Gauguin painted), Tahuata, Fatu Hiva, and five smaller uninhabited islands; acquired by France, 1842; chief settlement, Taiohae (Hiva Oa); copra, cotton, vanilla. » French Polynesia; Gauguin; Melville

marquess (or **marquis**, feminine **marchioness**) In the UK, a nobleman holding a title in the second rank of the peerage. The word is derived from Lat. *marchio* and originally denoted a commander of a march, or frontier area. » peerage; titles [i]

marquetry Veneers (thin sheets of highly polished woods of different colours) applied to furniture in ornamental patterns, frequently of fruit, flowers, and foliage. A popular technique throughout W Europe in the later 17th–18th-c, it became particularly widely used in England after the accession of William and Mary in 1688. The finest examples were by French cabinetmakers of the reigns of Louis XIV, XV, and XVI. **Parquetry** is marquetry arranged in geometrical patterns, sometimes to give an effect of perspective. It was popular in England in the second half of the 17th-c.

Márquez, Gabriel García [mah**keth**] » García Márquez, Gabriel

marquis » marquess

Marrakesh or **Marrakech** [mara**kesh**] 31°49N 8°00W, pop (1982) 439 728. City in Tensift province, C Morocco; in N foothills of the Haut Atlas, 240 km/150 ml S of Casablanca; one of Morocco's four imperial cities, founded in 1062; second largest city in Morocco; airport; railway; university; leather, carpets, tourism; Koutoubia mosque (12th-c); Medina, a world heritage site. » Morocco [i]

marram grass A tough perennial with creeping rhizomes, native to coasts of W Europe; leaf-blades inrolled, panicles spike-like. It is a pioneer colonizer, adapted to dry conditions, and able to withstand burial by drifting sand. It is often planted on dunes as a sand-binder. (*Amophila arenaria*. Family: *Gramineae*.) » grass [i]; panicle; perennial; rhizome

marriage In anthropology, the legitimate long-term mating arrangement institutionalized in a community. If a union is called marriage, this implies that husband and wife have recognized claims over their partners, often including material claims; and it gives the children born of such a union a special, preferential status. Marriage also creates relationships of affinity between a person and his or her spouse's relatives, and perhaps even directly between the relatives of the husband and wife. In many parts of the world a man may legitimately marry more than one wife (*polygyny*), but it is very unusual for a woman to be permitted more than one husband (*polyandry*). Polygyny is often associated with the payment of a bride-price by the groom or his family to the relatives of the bride. In other societies the wife may bring a dowry to her husband, particularly where a woman is expected to marry into a higher social class.

Not every woman is marriageable: some are ruled out by incest restrictions; others by virtue of religion, social class, ethnicity, and (above all) by age, since almost universally the bride is expected to be younger than her husband. The actual pool of marriageable women is in practice often very restricted. Anthropologists have made a special study of societies where there is also a positive requirement, or a preference, for marriage with a woman who stands in a particular kinship relationship to her prospective husband. Many Muslim communities, for example, favour marriage between a man and his father's brother's daughter. In a number of other societies there is a strong preference for marriage with a mother's brother's daughter. The contemporary Western belief that a young man or woman should be free to choose their own marriage partner is historically most unusual. In most societies – and historically in many Western communities – these decisions have been taken by the older generation. » divorce; endogamy and exogamy; kinship; levirate; polygamy

marrow (anatomy) » **bone marrow**

marrow (botany) A trailing or climbing vine, native to America, long cultivated as a vegetable; leaves palmately-lobed; male and female flowers yellow, 12.5 cm/5 in in diameter, funnel-shaped; fruit up to 90 cm/3 ft or more long, cylindrical, oval, or round; rind green or yellow, leathery, smooth or rough, with thick flesh surrounding numerous seeds. (*Cucurbita pepo*. Family: *Cucurbitaceae*.) » climbing plant; courgette; palmate; squash (botany); vegetable

Marryat, Frederick (1792–1848) British naval officer and novelist, born in London. He joined the navy (1806–30), and served in many parts of the world. He then became a man of letters, writing a series of novels on sea life, notably *Peter Simple* (1833) and *Mr Midshipman Easy* (1834). He toured the USA, then retired (1843) to a small farm at Langham, Norfolk, where he farmed and wrote stories for children, the best known being *The Children of the New Forest* (1847). He died at Langham. » novel

Mars (astronomy) The fourth planet from the Sun; the outermost of the terrestrial-type planets, with an eccentric orbit at a mean distance of 1.52 AU, and a diameter about half that of Earth. Its basic planetary characteristics are: mass 6.42×10^{23} kg; mean density 3.93 g/cm^3; equatorial gravity 370.6 cm/s^2; day (sidereal) 24 h 37 min 22 sec; year 687 days; obliquity 23°59′; orbital eccentricity 0.093. A characteristically red planet, known to the ancients, it has been the subject of popular interest as a possible abode of life. There are two small natural satellites, Phobos and Deimos. Modern understanding dates back to the first spacecraft flyby of the planet in 1965 (NASA's Mariner 4) with later knowledge derived from Mariners 6 and 7, from the first planetary orbiter Mariner 9, and from Viking landers and orbiters. It is a dry, cold planet with a thin, 95% carbon dioxide atmosphere. The atmospheric circulation has similarities to Earth's, but is marked by annual episodes of violent dust-storm activity that often escalate to planet-wide storms.

There is a complex surface of cratered uplands, lowland plains, and massive volcanic regions. The tilt of the rotational axis is similar in magnitude to Earth's, and leads to marked seasonal variations. Seasonal polar caps of carbon dioxide grow to middle latitudes by the end of winter. There is an apparently permanent cap of water ice at the N pole. Polar regions show extensive sedimentary deposits with periodic layering – apparent evidence of periodic climate change. A variety of channel-like features (the 'canals') are observed – 'runoff' channels a few tens of kilometres long and having tributaries; 'outflow' channels of great size (tens of kilometres wide and hundreds long); and 'fretted' channels that are wide and steep-walled. The 'runoff' channels provide suggestive evidence that water once flowed on Mars early in the planet's history, when the climate might have been more clement.

Volcanism is widespread, especially in the regions of Tharsis and Elysium. Tharsis volcanos are the largest and youngest, and lie on a pronounced crustal bulge – Olympus Mons reaches 27 km/16 ml in height, is c.700 km/435 ml across, and is capped by a caldera 80 km/50 ml across. The Valles Marineris is an equally spectacular canyon system, stretching a quarter of the way around the planet (over 4 000 km/2 500 ml), measuring 150–700 km/100–450 ml in width, and reaching depths of 2–7 km/1–4 ml. Soil coloration is due to the oxidation of iron minerals. Viking lander soil analysis revealed no organic material, even from meteorite falls, and indicates that the soil/atmospheric chemistry destroys organics. It is thought highly unlikely that Mars is, today, an abode for life. The possibility of biotic or prebiotic molecular evolution in earlier eras remains an intriguing question. » Deimos; Mariner/Mars programme; Phobos; planet; Solar System; Viking project; volcano; RR4

Mars (mythology) The Roman god of war, second only to Jupiter. The month of March is named after him. His mythology is borrowed from Ares, though various annual ceremonies at Rome indicate that he was originally an agricultural deity who guarded the fields. » Ares

Mars programme A Soviet series of robotic Mars exploration projects (1962–74), including flybys, orbiters, and hard-landers. It was less successful than other Soviet planetary missions. Mars 5 (1974) returned images from Mars orbit. The Soviets resumed Mars exploration in 1988, with dual launches of new generation interplanetary spacecraft to orbit Mars, rendezvous with moon Phobos, and land capsules on Phobos. One spacecraft (Phobos 2) successfully achieved the rendezvous, but was lost before a landing could be attempted. » Deimos; Mars (astronomy); Phobos; Soviet space programme

Marseille [mahsay], also Eng **Marseilles**, ancient **Massilia** 43°18N 5°23E, pop (1982) 878 689. Principal commercial port and capital of Bouches-du-Rhône department, S France; on NE shore of the Gulf of Lyons, 130 km/81 ml WSW of Nice; second largest city in France and leading port of the Mediterranean; founded c.600 BC by Greeks; Old Port (Vieux Port) on a rocky peninsula; airport; railway; metro; archbishopric; university; shipbuilding, chemicals, trade in minerals, oil refining, engineering, soap, glass, cigarettes, beverages, dairy produce, trade in fruit, wine, olive oil, vegetables, spices, hides; known for its bouillabaisse (fish soup); Church of St-Victor (11th–14th-c), 19th-c neo-Byzantine basilica of Notre-Dame-de-la-Garde, town hall (1663–83), Cathédrale de la Major (1852–93), 11th–12th-c Cathédrale St-Lazare, Musée des Beaux-Arts, New Harbour (Port Moderne); Basin de la Joliette used by passenger ships; international trade fair (Apr–Sep). » France [i]; Mediterranean Sea

Marsh, Dame Ngaio (Edith) [**ni**yoh] (1899–1982) New Zealand detective-story writer, born and died in Christchurch. She came to England in 1928, and published her first novel, *A Man Lay Dead*, in 1934. It was followed by a series of novels and short stories featuring Superintendent Roderick Alleyn of Scotland Yard. These include *Vintage Murder* (1937), *Opening Night* (1951), and *Black as He's Painted* (1974). She was made a Dame in 1948. » detective story

marsh gas » **methane** [i]

marsh harrier A hawk found throughout the Old World; brown body, paler head, and grey tail; inhabits marshland (sometimes grassland in Australasia); eats frogs and other small animals; nests among reeds; also known as **swamp hawk**. (*Circus aeruginosus*. Family: *Accipitridae*.) » harrier (bird); hawk

marsh marigold » **kingcup**

marsh samphire » **glasswort**

marsh tern » **tern**

Marsh test A test for arsenic and antimony involving the reduction of their compounds to volatile AsH_3 and SbH_3, which deposit the metals as a mirror on a glass surface. It is named after British chemist James Marsh (1794–1846), assistant to Michael Faraday at the Royal Military Academy, London. » antimony; arsenic; Faraday

Marshall, George C(atlett) (1880–1959) US general and statesman, born at Uniontown, Pennsylvania. Educated at the Virginia Military Institute, he became Chief-of-Staff (1939–45), and directed the US Army throughout World War 2. After two years in China as special representative of the President, he became Secretary of State (1947–9) and originated the Marshall Aid plan for the postwar reconstruction of Europe. He was awarded the Nobel Peace Prize in 1953, and died in Washington, DC. » Marshall Plan

Marshall, John (1755–1835) American jurist, born near Germantown, Virginia, the foremost chief justice in the history of the US Supreme Court. In the 1790s he became a supporter of the nationalist measures of Washington and Hamilton, and was named chief justice by the outgoing President John Adams in 1801. From then until his death he dominated the Supreme Court, establishing the American doctrine of the judicial review of federal and state legislation. He died in Philadelphia. » Adams, John; American Revolution; Hamilton, Alexander; Washington, George

Marshall, Thurgood (1908–) US lawyer and jurist, born in Baltimore, Maryland. Educated at Lincoln and Howard universities, he joined the legal staff of the National Association for the Advancement of Colored People, and argued many important civil rights cases. He served as a judge of the US Court of Appeals (1961–5), and as Solicitor-General of the United States (1965–7), before becoming the first Black Justice of the US Supreme Court. He resigned in 1991. » civil rights

Marshall Islands land area c.180 sq km/70 sq ml; pop (1989e) 38 000. Archipelago in the C Pacific Ocean, part of the US Trust Territory of the Pacific Is; two parallel chains of coral atolls, called Ratik (E) and Ralik (W), extending c.925 km/800 ml in length; islands include Kwajalein and Jaluit (chief town, Majuro); US nuclear weapon tests held on Bikini and Enewetak atolls, 1946–62; Micronesian population, chiefly Christian, speaking English and Marshallese; explored by the Spanish, 1529; Trust Territory, 1947–78; self-governing republic, 1979; compact of free association with the USA, 1982; Trusteeship ended, 1990; governed by a president, elected by a 33-member parliament; farming, fishing, tropical agriculture. » United States Trust Territory of the Pacific Islands

Marshall Plan The popular name for the *European Recovery Program*, a scheme for large-scale, medium-term US aid to war-ravaged Europe, announced in 1947 by US Secretary of State, George Marshall. 'Marshall Aid' was rejected by the USSR and the Eastern bloc, but during 1948–50 it materially assisted W Europe's economic revival. » Marshall, George C

Marston, John (1576–1634) English dramatist, born at Wardington, Oxfordshire. He was educated at Oxford, and wrote several plays published between 1602 and 1607, notably *The Malcontent* (1604), and *Eastward Ho!* (1605), a satirical comedy written with Chapman and Jonson. In 1607 he gave up playwriting, took orders (1609), and held the living of Christ Church, Hampshire (1616–31). He died in London. » Chapman; drama; English literature; Jonson; satire

Marston Moor, Battle of (1644) A major conflict in the English Civil War, in which a force of 27 000 parliamentary and Scottish troops defeated 18 000 royalists. The royalist cavalry was led by Prince Rupert; the parliamentary horse by Oliver Cromwell. The defeat led to the fall of the royalist stronghold of York, and the virtual collapse of Charles I's cause in the N. » English Civil War

marsupial A mammal, native to Australasia and the New World; young often develop in a pouch which opens forwards (climbing species) or backwards (burrowing species); vagina is branched; penis usually forked; second and third toes of foot often small and joined, forming a comb for grooming. (Order: *Marsupialia*, 266 species.) » bandicoot; dasyure; honey possum; kangaroo; koala; mammal [i]; marsupial mole; numbat; opossum; phalanger; possum; Tasmanian devil; thylacine [i]; wombat [i]; yapok; *see illustration p 763*

marsupial mole An Australian marsupial; mole-like with pale yellow coat; eyes and ears hidden by fur; nose pad enlarged to cover front of head; large claws for digging; tail very short; female with pouch opening backwards; inhabits dry sandy areas; burrows collapse behind them as they dig. (*Notoryctes typhlops*. Family: *Notoryctidae*.) » marsupial [i]; mole (zoology)

Martello towers Small circular forts with thick walls. Many were erected on the S and SE coast of England in the early 19th-c to provide observation posts and defence against a projected French invasion. The name comes from Cape Mortella, Corsica, where such a tower was captured by a British Fleet in 1794.

marten A mammal of genus *Martes* (7 species), native to

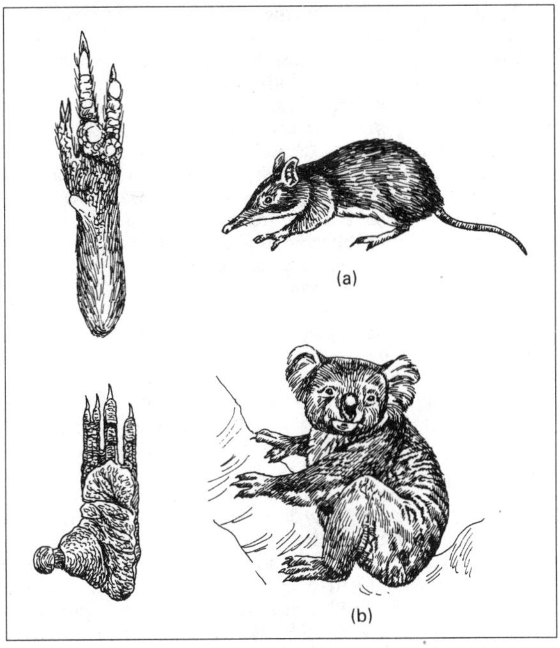

Marsupials – Bandicoot (a) and koala (b), showing feet adapted as grooming combs.

Europe, Asia, and N America; solid body with sharp nose and long bushy tail; usually inhabits upland forests; eats small mammals, birds, and carrion. (Family: *Mustelidae*.) » Mustelidae; pine marten; sable

martensite The principal component of hard steel, formed by quenching from high temperatures. It consists of intergrown plate-like crystals with a distorted cubic structure arising from the presence of carbon atoms in the iron structure. » steel

Martha's Vineyard Island in the Atlantic off the SE coast of Massachusetts, USA; part of Duke's County; area 280 sq km/108 sq ml; chief town, Edgartown; former whaling and fishing centre; summer resort; so called because the first English settlers found an abundance of wild grapes growing here. » Massachusetts

Martial, properly **Marcus Valerius Martialis** (c.40–c.104) Latin poet and epigrammatist, born in Spain. He went to Rome in 64, and became a client of the influential Spanish house of the Senecas, through which he found a patron in Calpurnius Piso. He is remembered for his 12 books of epigrams, mainly satirical comments on contemporary events and society. He returned to Spain, and died at Bilbilis. » epigram; Latin literature; satire; Seneca, Lucius Annaeus

martial arts Styles of armed or unarmed combat developed in the East. In modern times most of these arts have developed into popular sports in the West. » aikido; judo; jujitsu; karate; kendo; kung fu; ninjutsu; taekwondo

martial law The imposition of military rule on the civilian population, either by the leader of an occupying army, or by a territory's own government. In the latter case, it most commonly occurs after there has been a military coup or during a period of colonial rule. Many countries' constitutions have provision for the introduction of martial law in times of foreign threats and emergencies, although in many liberal democracies there are severe restrictions on its implementation which render it largely impractical. The military in such countries can, however, be more readily mobilized in support of the civil authorities.

martin A bird of the swallow family (23 species). Those with short tails are usually called 'martins', those with long tails 'swallows'. The names are not applied consistently. » swallow

Martin, St (c.316–c.400), feast day 11 November (W), 12 November (E). Patron saint of France, born at Sabaria, Pannonia. Educated at Pavia, he travelled to Gaul, and c.360 founded the first monastery there, near Poitiers. In 371–2 he was drawn by force from his retreat, and made Bishop of Tours. He died at Candes. » monasticism

Martin, Pierre Emile [mahtĩ] (1824–1915) French engineer, born at Bourges. In 1863 he was licensed to build a Siemens furnace, and is regarded as the inventor of the Siemens–Martin open-hearth steel process. He died at Fourchambault, near Nevers. » Bessemer process; steel

Martín de Porres, St [**poh**res] (1579–1639) S American saint, who spent his entire life in the Dominican Order in Lima, Peru, ministering to the sick and poor. He was also noted for his way with animals. Beatified in 1837, he was canonized in 1962. » Dominicans

Martin du Gard, Roger [mahtĩ dü **gah**] (1881–1958) French novelist, born at Neuilly. He is known for his 8-novel series *Les Thibault* (1922–40), dealing with family life during the first decades of the present century. Author also of several plays, he was awarded the Nobel Prize for Literature in 1937, and died at Bellême. » French literature; novel

Martin Luther King's Birthday The birthday (15 Jan) of the Black US civil rights leader, commemorated in about half of the US States. There are several variations on the name of the day, and the date of the celebration also varies, from State to State. » King, Martin Luther

Martini, Simone (c.1284–1344) Italian painter, born at Siena. The most important artist of the 14th-c Sienese School, his work is notable for its grace of line and use of colour. He worked at Assisi (1333–9), and then at the Papal court at Avignon until 1344. His 'Annunciation' is in the Uffizi Gallery. He died at Avignon, Provence. » Italian art; Sienese School

Martinique [mahtee**neek**] pop (1989e) 337 000; area 1 079 sq km/416 sq ml. Island in the Windward group of the Lesser Antilles, E Caribbean, between Dominica and St Lucia; since 1946, an overseas department of France; capital, Fort-de-France; timezone GMT −4; population mainly of African or mixed descent; chief religion, Roman Catholicism; official language, French, with creole widely spoken; unit of currency, the French franc; length, 61 km/38 ml; width, 24 km/15 ml; rises steeply from the sea, particularly on N coast; highest point, Mt Pelée (1 397 m/4 583 ft); tropical climate with high humidity; average temperature at Fort-de-France, 21–29°C (Jan–Mar), 23–31°C (Jun–Oct); wet season (Jul–Nov); visited by Columbus, 1502; French colony, 1635; overseas department of France, 1946; administered by a commissioner general and a 41-member Regional Council, both elected for up to six years; economy based largely on agriculture; sugar cane, bananas, rum, pineapples; construction, distilling, cement, oil refining, light industry, tourism. » Fort-de-France; Pelée, Mount; Windward Islands

Martinmas In the UK, the feast of St Martin (11 Nov), a day on which traditionally rents were paid, servants hired, and livestock slaughtered for winter salting; a quarter-day in Scotland. » quarter-day

Martinů, Bohuslav [**mah**tinoo] (1890–1959) Czech composer, born at Polička. He worked as a violinist until in 1924 his ballet *Ishtar* attracted attention. In 1940 he went to the USA. A prolific composer, his music includes symphonies, concertos, ballets, and operas, and ranges from orchestral works in 18th-c style to modern programme pieces evoked by unusual stimuli, such as football and aeroplanes. From 1957 he lived in Switzerland, and died at Liestal.

Marvell, Andrew (1621–78) English poet, born at Winestead, Yorkshire. Educated at Hull and Cambridge, he travelled widely in Europe (1642–6), worked as a tutor, and became Milton's assistant (1657). He is remembered for his pastoral and garden poems, notably 'To his Coy Mistress'. After becoming an MP (1659), his writing was devoted to pamphlets and satires attacking intolerance and arbitrary government. He died in London. » English literature; metaphysical poetry; Milton; pastoral

Marx, Karl (Heinrich) (1818–83) German founder of modern international communism, born at Trier, the son of a Jewish lawyer. He studied law at Bonn and Berlin but took up history, Hegelian philosophy and Feuerbach's materialism. He edited a radical newspaper, and after it was suppressed, moved to Paris

(1843) and Brussels (1845). There, with Engels as his closest collaborator and disciple, he reorganized the Communist League, which met in London in 1847. In 1848 he finalized the *Communist Manifesto* (1848), which attacked the state as the instrument of oppression, and religion and culture as ideologies of the capitalist class. He was expelled from Brussels, and in 1849 settled in London, where he studied economics, and wrote the first volume of his major work, *Das Kapital* (1867). He died in London, with this work unfinished. » communism; Engels; Feuerbach; Hegel; Marxism; Marxism-Leninism

Marx Brothers US family of film comedians, born in New York City, comprising **Julius** (1895–1977), or **Groucho**; **Leonard** (1891–1961), or **Chico**; **Arthur** (1893–1961), or **Harpo**; and **Herbert** (1901–79), or **Zeppo**. They began their stage career in vaudeville in a team called the Six Musical Mascots, which included their mother, Minnie (?–1929), and an aunt; another brother, **Milton** (?1897–1977), known as **Gummo**, left the act early on. They later appeared as the Four Nightingales, and finally as the Marx Brothers. Their main reputation was made in a series of films, such as *Animal Crackers* and *Monkey Business* (both 1932). Herbert retired from films in 1935, but the others had several further successes, such as *A Day at the Races* (1937). Each had a well-defined stencil: Groucho with his wisecracks; Chico, the pianist with his own technique; and Harpo, the dumb clown and harp maestro. The team broke up in 1949, and the brothers led individual careers. Chico and Harpo died in Hollywood, Groucho in Los Angeles, and the others in Palm Springs, California.

Marxism The body of social and political thought informed by the writings of Karl Marx. It is essentially a critical analysis of capitalist society contending that such societies are subject to crises which create the conditions for proletarian revolutions and the transformation to socialism. Much of Marx's writing, especially *Das Kapital*, was concerned with the economic dynamics of capitalist societies, seeing the state as an instrument of class rule supporting private capital and suppressing the masses. Because of private capital's need to earn profits or extract surplus value, wages have to be kept to a subsistence minimum. This produces economic contradictions, because it restricts the purchasing power of workers to consume the goods produced. Capitalism is, therefore, inherently unstable, being subject to crises of booms and slumps. Marx's view was that these crises would become increasingly worse, and eventually lead to revolution, whereby the working class would seize the state and establish a dictatorship of the proletariat, productive power would be in public hands, and class differences would disappear (socialism). This classless society would eventually lead to the withering away of the state, producing a communist society. Marxism has sought to popularize and extend this method of analysis to contemporary conditions. In particular, Western Marxism has examined the impact of state intervention in smoothing out the crises of capitalism and establishing a legitimacy for the existing capitalist order through its control over education and the media. In non-industrialized societies Marxism has been adapted to account for revolution in countries where there is no extensive development of capitalism, in contrast to Marx's view of history. It is generally recognized that Marx's writings regarding the transformation to socialism and the nature of socialism lacked detail. In consequence, Marxism has adopted a wide range of interpretations. » Marx; Marxism-Leninism; Neo-Marxism

Marxism-Leninism A distinct variant of Marxism formulated by Lenin, who prior to the Bolshevik revolution argued for direct rule by workers and peasants, and advocated direct democracy through the soviets (councils). In practice, the Bolshevik revolution did not produce a democratic republic, but gave a 'leading and directing' role to the party, seen as the vanguard of a working class which had insufficient political consciousness to forge a revolution; such a well-organized and disciplined party, operating according to the principles of democratic centralism, would be able to exploit the revolutionary situation. Leninist principles of a revolutionary vanguard have become the central tenet of all communist parties. All are organized according to the idea of democratic centralism which affords the leadership, on the grounds of their revolutionary insight, the right to dictate party policy, to select party officials from above, and to discipline dissenting party members. Lenin modified Marx's theory of historical materialism, contending that revolutionary opportunities should be seized when they arose, and not when the social and economic conditions of capitalist crisis leading to proletarian revolution existed. He also developed a theory of imperialism which held that it was the last stage of a decaying capitalism. This was used to justify revolution in feudal Russia, because it was an imperial power, and since then to justify communist intervention in underdeveloped countries as part of the struggle between socialism and imperialism. » Lenin; Maoism; Marxism; Russian Revolution

Mary (mother of Jesus) (?–c.63) Mother of Jesus Christ; also entitled **Our Lady** or **the Blessed Virgin Mary**. In the New Testament she is most prominent in the stories of Jesus' birth (Matthew and Luke) where the conception of Jesus is said to be 'of the Holy Spirit' (*Matt* 1.18), and she is described as betrothed to Joseph. She only occasionally appears in Jesus' ministry, but in *John* 19.25 she is at the Cross and is committed to the care of one of the disciples. According to the Acts of the Apostles, she remained in Jerusalem during the early years of the Church, and a tradition places her tomb in Jerusalem. She has become a subject of devotion in her own right, especially in Roman Catholic doctrine and worship, and apocryphal traditions were attached to her in works such as the *Gospel of Mary* and *Gospel of the Birth of Mary*. The belief that her body was taken up into heaven is celebrated in the festival of the Assumption, defined as Roman Catholic dogma in 1950. Her Immaculate Conception has been a dogma since 1854. Belief in the apparitions of the Virgin at Lourdes, Fatima, and in several other places attracts many thousands of pilgrims each year. In Roman Catholic and Orthodox Christianity, she holds a special place as an intermediary between mankind and God. » Assumption; Hail Mary; Immaculate Conception; Jesus Christ; New Testament; Orthodox Church; Roman Catholicism; rosary

Mary I (1516–58) Queen of England and Ireland (1553–8), born at Greenwich, the daughter of Henry VIII by his first wife, Catherine of Aragon. A devout Catholic, during the reign of Edward, her half-brother, she lived in retirement, refusing to conform to the new religion. Despite Northumberland's conspiracy to prevent her succession on Edward's death (1553), she relied on the support of the country, entered London and ousted Lady Jane Grey. Thereafter she proceeded cautiously, repealing anti-Catholic legislation and reviving Catholic practices, but her intention was to restore papal supremacy with the assistance of Cardinal Pole, and to cement a Catholic union with Philip II of Spain. These aspirations provoked Wyatt's rebellion, followed by the execution of Jane Grey and the imprisonment of Mary's half-sister, Elizabeth, on suspicion of complicity. Mary's unpopular marriage to Philip (1554) was followed by the persecution of some 300 Protestants, which earned her the name of 'Bloody Mary' in Protestant hagiography, though her direct responsibility is unproven. Broken by childlessness, sickness, grief at her husband's departure from England, and the loss of Calais to the French, she died in London. » Cranmer; Edward VI; Grey, Lady Jane; Henry VIII; Latimer; Philip II (of Spain); Pole; Reformation; Ridley

Mary II » **William III**

Mary, Queen, formerly **Princess of Teck** » **George V**

Mary, Queen of Scots (1542–87) Queen Consort of France (1559–60), daughter of James V of Scotland by his second wife, Mary of Guise, born at Linlithgow Palace, Scotland. Queen of Scotland at a week old, her betrothal to Prince Edward of England was annulled by the Scottish parliament, precipitating war with England. After the Scots' defeat at Pinkie (1547), she was sent to the French court and married the Dauphin (1558), later Francis II, but was widowed at 18 (1560) and returned to Scotland (1561). Ambitious for the English throne, in 1565 she married her cousin, Henry Stuart, Lord Darnley, a grandson of Margaret Tudor, but disgusted by his debauchery, was soon alienated from him. The vicious murder of Rizzio, her Italian secretary, by Darnley and a group of Protestant nobles in her presence (1566) confirmed her insecurity. The birth of a son, the future James VI, failed to bring a reconciliation. While ill with smallpox, Darnley was mysteriously killed in an explosion at Kirk o' Field (1567); the chief suspect was the Earl of Bothwell, who underwent a mock trial and was acquitted. Mary's involvement is unclear, but she consented to marry Bothwell, a divorcee with whom she had become infatuated. The Protestant nobles under Morton rose against her; she surrendered at Carberry Hill, was imprisoned at Loch Leven, and compelled to abdicate. After escaping, she raised an army, but was defeated again by the confederate lords at Langside (1568). Placing herself under the protection of Queen Elizabeth, she found herself instead a prisoner for life. Her presence in England gave rise to countless plots to depose Elizabeth and restore Catholicism. Finally, after the Babington conspiracy (1586) she was brought to trial for treason, and executed in Fotheringay Castle, Northamptonshire. » Babington; Bothwell; Darnley; Elizabeth I; Morton, James Douglas; Rizzio

Mary Magdalene New Testament character; *Magdalene* possibly means 'of Magdala', in Galilee. *Luke* 8.2 reports that Jesus exorcized seven evil spirits from her; thereafter she appears only in the narratives of Jesus' passion and resurrection where, seemingly with other women, she appears at the Cross and later at the empty tomb. *John* 20 relates a private encounter with the resurrected Jesus (*Matt* 28.9). Her identification with Mary the sister of Martha (*John* 11–12) is very tenuous. » Jesus Christ; New Testament

Mary Rose A warship built in 1511 for Henry VIII and rebuilt in 1536. In 1545, whilst in action against the French off Portsmouth, she capsized and sank with the loss of most of her crew. Her remains were salvaged in 1982 in a complex and much-publicized operation, and are now exhibited at Portsmouth. » Wasa

Maryland pop (1987e) 4535000; area 27090 sq km/10460 sq ml. State in E USA, divided into 23 counties and one city; the 'Old Line' or 'Free State'; the first settlement (1634) located at St Mary's (state capital until 1694); seventh of the original 13 states to ratify the Constitution, 1788; gave up territory for the establishment of the District of Columbia; abolished slavery, 1864; capital, Annapolis; major city, Baltimore (85% of the population live in this area); bounded E by Delaware and the Atlantic Ocean; Chesapeake Bay stretches N through the state, almost splitting it in two; the Potomac R forms most of the S border; the Susquehanna and Patuxent Rivers cross the state, emptying into Chesapeake Bay; highest point Mt Backbone (1024 m/3360 ft); to the N and W is the rolling Piedmont, rising up to the Blue Ridge and Pennsylvania Hills; to the S and E is Chesapeake Bay with indented shores forming a popular resort area; the Eastern Shore with over 12000 sq km/4500 sq ml of forest is noted for its scenic beauty; iron and steel, shipbuilding, electrical equipment, machinery, processed foods; poultry, dairy products, corn, soybeans, tobacco. » Annapolis; Baltimore; District of Columbia; United States of America [i]; RR38

Masaccio [mazatchoh], byname of **Tomasso di Giovanni** (1401–28?) Italian painter, born at San Giovanni Valdarno. A pioneer of Renaissance painting in a powerful, austere, and realistic style, he worked in Florence, where he executed frescoes, in collaboration with Masolino. He died in Rome, a major influence on Michelangelo, Raphael, and other great masters. » Florentine School; fresco; Italian art; Masolino

Masada [masahda] or **Mezada** A Roman hilltop fortress established 37–31 BC by the Palestinian ruler Herod in barren mountains W of the Dead Sea; within Israel since 1947. Seized by zealots during the First Jewish Revolt in AD 66–70, it was taken by the Roman army in 73 after a lengthy siege which culminated in the mass suicide of all 400 defenders. As a political symbol of Jewish solidarity and resistance down the ages, it remains unparalleled. » Herod the Great; Judaism; Roman history [i]

Masai or **Maasai** [masiy] A people of the Rift Valley area of Kenya and Tanzania, speaking a Nilotic language. They are nomadic and semi-nomadic cattle herders, organized in a complex age-set system which provided warriors under control of ritual leaders. In some regions they are being encouraged to turn to sedentary farming. Population c.230000. » African history; Kenya [i]; nomadism; Tanzania [i]

Masaryk, Thomáš (Garrigue) (1850–1937) First President of the Czech Republic (1918–35), born at Hodonin, Moravia. An ardent Slovak, while in exile during World War 1 he organized the Czech independence movement. He was re-elected President on three occasions, before retiring in his mid-80s. He died at Lány. » Czechoslovakia [i]

Mascagni, Pietro [maskanyee] (1863–1945) Italian composer, born at Leghorn. In 1890 he produced his highly successful one-act opera, *Cavalleria Rusticana*. His many later operas failed to repeat this success, though arias and intermezzi from them are still performed. He died in Rome.

Mascarene Islands [mazkereen], Fr **Archipel des Mascareignes** Island group in the Indian Ocean, 700–800 km/450–500 ml E of Madagascar; includes Réunion, Mauritius, and Rodrigues; named after the 16th-c Portuguese navigator, Mascarenhas. » Mauritius [i]; Réunion; Rodrigues Island

mascon » **maria**

Masefield, John (1878–1967) British poet and novelist, born at Ledbury, Herefordshire. After serving in the merchant navy, he spent three years in New York, then returned to England in 1897, becoming a journalist. His sea poetry includes *Salt Water Ballads* (1902) and *Dauber* (1913), and his narrative poetry *Reynard the Fox* (1919). He also wrote novels, such as *Sard Harker* (1924), and plays, such as *The Trial of Jesus* (1925). He became poet laureate in 1930, and died near Abingdon, Berkshire. » English literature; novel; poetry

maser A device which produces microwaves from excited atoms or molecules, devised in 1954 by US physicist Charles Townes and others; the name is an acronym of *microwave amplification by the stimulated emission of radiation*. The first device relied on thermally excited ammonia molecules; other gases such as hydrogen are now also used. Masers employ the same physical principles as lasers, but produce lower frequency radiation. They are used as sensitive low-noise amplifiers for radar and satellite communications. » laser [i]; microwaves; Townes

Maseru [maseeroo] 29°19S 27°29E, pop (1982) 288951. Capital of Lesotho; on the R Caledon, 130 km/81 ml E of Bloemfontein (South Africa); altitude 1506 m/4941 ft; founded, 1869; airport; railway terminus; university (1964); experimental crop station; administration, commerce, diamond processing, tourism. » Lesotho [i]

Mashhad [mashhad] or **Meshed** 36°16N 59°34E, pop (1983) 1119748. Capital city of Mashhad district, Khorasan, NE Iran; near the Turkmenia border, just S of the R Kashaf; second largest city in Iran; industrial and trade centre; airport; railway; university (1956); carpets, gemstones; 9th-c shrine of Imam Ali Reza. » Iran [i]; Islam

masochism » **sadomasochism**

Masolino, originally **Tommaso di Cristoforo Fini** (c.1400–c.47) Florentine artist, born at Panicale, Romagna. He was a distinguished early Renaissance painter, who entered the painters' guild in Florence in 1423. He collaborated with Masaccio in the Brancacci chapel. His frescoes in Castiglione d'Olona were discovered only in 1843. He also worked in Hungary and Rome, and died probably in Florence. » Florentine School; fresco; Italian art; Masaccio

mason bee A solitary bee that collects soft malleable materials such as mud, resin, or chewed leaves, and shapes them into a nest either inside an existing hole in timber or under stones, or on branches or exposed rock surfaces. (Order: *Hymenoptera*. Family: *Megachilidae*.) » bee

Mason-Dixon Line The border between Maryland and Pennsylvania, drawn in 1763–7 by British astronomer Charles Mason (1730–87) and his colleague Jeremiah Dixon (of whom little is known). It is regarded as the boundary of 'the South'.

Masoretes or **Massoretes** [masohreets] (Heb 'transmitters of tradition') Jewish scholars considered responsible for preserving traditions regarding the text of the Hebrew Bible, and especially for creating a system of vowel signs to reflect the pronunciation of the Hebrew consonantal text in their day. The resulting vocalized text (c.9th–10th-c) was known as the Masoretic Text, the basis for the text of the Hebrew Bible normally used today. » alphabet [i]; Hebrew; Old Testament

masque An aristocratic celebration composed of poetry, song, dance and (usually) elaborate mechanical scenery, unified by a theme or emblematic story. It was often performed at banquets when the masked performers would engage spectators in the fictitional game, and encourage participation in the dancing. The Royal masques of Tudor and Stuart England are best-known for the collaboration of Ben Jonson and Inigo Jones. » drama; Jones, Inigo; Jonson; theatre

mass An intrinsic property of all matter and energy, the source of gravitational field; symbol m, units kg (kilogram). It is perceived as an object's weight (the downward-acting force due to gravity) or its inertia (its reluctance to change its motion). The mass of an object increases with its velocity, according to special relativity, tending towards infinity as the object's velocity approaches the speed of light. » centre of mass; density; gravitation; inertia; Mach's principle; mass-energy relation; mechanics; weight

Mass (Lat *missa*, from *missio* 'dismissal') The sacrament of the Eucharist (Holy Communion) in the Roman Catholic Church and some other churches. Bread and wine are consecrated by a priest, and the elements (usually bread alone) distributed among the faithful. According to the doctrine of the Council of Trent (counteracting the teaching of the 16th-c Reformers) the bread and wine become the body and blood of Christ (*transubstantiation*), and the sacrament is to be understood as a divine, propitiatory sacrifice. Masses perform different functions in the life of the Church, eg a Requiem Mass for the dead, a Nuptial Mass for a marriage. » Eucharist; Jesus Christ; Roman Catholicism; sacrament; transubstantiation

mass action, law of A law in chemistry: the rate of reaction of a substance is proportional to its 'active mass', or essentially its concentration. Hence, the speed of a simple chemical reaction is proportional to the product of the concentrations of the reactants. Most chemical reactions must, however, be analysed in terms of a sequence of such simple reactions.

mass-energy relation A relationship in physics, stated by Einstein, expressed as $E=mc^2$, where E is energy, c is the velocity of light, and m is mass, as measured for a moving object. It corresponds to the statement that all energy has mass (rather than 'mass and energy are interconvertible'). In typical nuclear decay, the sum of the masses of decay fragments as measured at rest is less than the initial rest mass by the amount E/c^2, where E is the energy evolved in the process. In general, energy and mass are conserved, rest mass is not. » Einstein; energy; mass; pair production; special relativity [i]; velocity of light

mass media » **media**

mass number » **nucleon number**

mass observation A set of social research techniques developed in the late 1930s for gathering a substantial amount of data on the lives of 'ordinary' people, including ethnographic community studies using informal interviews, participant observation, and similar methods. Both professional and lay volunteer observers and informants were used to produce a broad, richly detailed profile of a number of urban communities. Today the technique is less fashionable, though the revolution in communications technology makes the approach more feasible. » ethnography; participant observation; sociology

mass spectrometer A machine for measuring the proportions and masses of the atomic species in some sample; invented in 1919 by British scientist Francis Aston (1877–1945). Ions formed from a gaseous sample are passed through a magnetic field, where they are deflected by an amount depending on their mass. Different isotopes can be distinguished. It is an important analytical device for determining atomic and isotopic compositions. » atomic physics; ion; isotopes

Massachusetts pop (1987e) 5 855 000, area 21 455 sq km/8 284 sq ml. New England state in NE USA, divided into 14 counties; the 'Bay State' or 'Old Colony'; third most densely populated state; one of the original states of the Union, sixth to ratify the Constitution; capital, Boston; major towns Cambridge, Springfield, Worcester; rises from an indented coastline to a stony, upland interior and gentle, rolling hills to the W; Connecticut R flows N–S across the W part of the state, Housatonic R flows S near the W border, Merrimack R enters the Atlantic Ocean in the NE; Berkshire Hills rise between the Housatonic and Connecticut Rivers; highest point Mt Greylock (1 049 m/3 442 ft); electronics, printing and publishing, timber, nursery and greenhouse produce, vegetables, cranberries; many coastal resorts; Pilgrim Fathers settled at Plymouth in 1620; first shots of the War of Independence fired at Lexington in 1775. » American Revolution; Boston; Pilgrim Fathers; United States of America [i]; RR38

Massawa [masa**h**wa] or **Mitsiwa** 15°37N 39°28E, pop (1982e) 36 839. Seaport in Eritrea region, N Ethiopia, on Red Sea coast, 65 km/40 ml NE of Asmara; occupied by Italy, 1885; capital of Italian Eritrea until 1897; largely rebuilt after earthquake in 1921; railway; commercial centre; fish and meat processing, cement, salt, tourism; naval base. » Eritrea; Ethiopia [i]

Masséna, André [masayna] (1758–1817) Leading French general of the Revolutionary and Napoleonic Wars, born in Nice. He distinguished himself in Napoleon's Italian campaign (1796–7), defeating the Russians at Zürich (1799), and successfully defending Genoa (1800). He was created Marshal of the Empire in 1804, took command of the army in Italy, and after further successes was made Duke of Rivoli (1807). After the Austrian campaign (1809) he was made Prince of Essling. However, forced to retreat in the Iberian Peninsula by Wellington's forces, in 1810 he was relieved of his command. He died in Paris. » Bourbons; French Revolutionary Wars; Hundred Days; Napoleonic Wars

Massenet, Jules (Emile Frédéric) [**ma**suhnay] (1842–1912) French composer, born near St Etienne. He studied at the Paris Conservatoire, where in 1878–96 he was professor. He made his name with the comic opera *Don César de Bazan* in 1872. Several other operas followed, including *Manon* (1884), and he also wrote oratorios, orchestral suites, music for piano, and songs. He died in Paris.

Massey, Raymond (Hart) (1896–1983) Canadian actor, born in Toronto. He made his debut in 1922, and played several leading parts in the theatre, cinema, and television. He is best known for his role as Dr Gillespie in the long-running *Dr Kildare* series during the 1960s. He became a US citizen in 1944, directed many Broadway plays, and died in Los Angeles.

Massey, William Ferguson (1856–1925) New Zealand statesman and Prime Minister (1912–25), born at Limavady, Londonderry, Northern Ireland. He went to New Zealand and became a farmer. Elected to the House of Representatives, he became Opposition leader and then Prime Minister, an office he held until his death, in Wellington. » New Zealand [i]

Massif Central [**ma**seef sõ**tral**] Area of ancient rocks in SEC France, occupying about a sixth of the country; generally over 300 m/1 000 ft; highest peak, Puy de Sancy in the Monts Dore (1 885 m/6 184 ft); massive limestone beds with gorges, crags, and caves, as well as volcanic rocks such as the Monts Dômes; source of Loire, Allier, Cher, and Creuse Rivers; farming, several industrial centres, tourism; winter sports at Le Mont-Dore, Super-Besse, Super-Lioran. » France [i]

Massine, Léonide [maseen], originally **Leonid Fyodorovich Miassin** (1896–1979) Russian dancer and choreographer, born in Moscow. He was principal dancer and choreographer with Diaghilev (1914–21, 1925–8) and the Ballet Russe de Monte Carlo (1938–43), and produced and danced in many ballets in Europe and the USA. He also choreographed several controversial 'symphonic ballets', such as *Choreartium* (1933), which was danced to Brahms's fourth symphony. He died in Cologne, Germany. » ballet; Ballets Russes

Massinger, Philip (1583–1640) English dramatist, born near Salisbury, Wiltshire. He left Oxford without a degree, and became a playwright. In later years he wrote many plays single-handed, but much of his work is a collaboration with others, particularly Fletcher. His most masterly comedies are *The City Madam* (1632) and *A New Way to Pay Old Debts* (1633). He died in London. » drama; English literature; Fletcher

Massys or **Matsys, Quentin** (c.1466–c.1530) Flemish painter, born at Louvain. In 1491 he joined the painters' guild of St Luke in Antwerp. His pictures are mostly religious, treated with a reverent spirit, but with decided touches of realism. His many portraits include the notable 'Erasmus'. He died in Antwerp. » Flemish art

mast cells Cells with granules containing histamine, heparin, and other chemicals. They are absent from blood, but present in the loose connective tissue surrounding the blood vessels and lymphatics, especially in the respiratory and digestive tracts. Tissue injury and infection causes the release of the granular contents, resulting in inflammatory and allergic responses. » antibodies; heparin; histamine; leucocytes; urticaria

mastaba [**ma**staba] An ancient Egyptian funerary tomb built of brick or stone; rectangular, flat-topped with sloping sides. An outer chamber for offerings links to an inner chamber, and from there a shaft leads downwards to the actual grave below ground level. » Egyptian architecture

mastectomy » **breast cancer**

master An artistic status achieved within the mediaeval guild system. Artists and craftsmen followed several years' apprenticeship before becoming 'masters', through production of a 'masterpiece'. Only then could they open workshops of their own and take apprentices. The term **Old Master** is used loosely to refer to any major painter from Giotto to Cézanne, regarded as a model of traditional excellence. » bottega

Masters The popular name for the **US Masters** golf tournament, played every April over four rounds of the course at Augusta, Georgia. An invitational event, only the world's top players take part. The Masters was the idea of the former leading US amateur golfer Robert Tyre ('Bobby') Jones (1902–71), who lived in Georgia. The first Masters was in 1934, and won by Horton Smith (USA). The winner receives a coveted green jacket as part of the prize. » golf

Masters, Edgar Lee (1869–1950) US author, born at Garnett, Kansas. He became a lawyer, and wrote several plays and novels, but is mainly remembered for his satirical *Spoon River Anthology* (1915), epitaphs in free verse dealing with the lives of people in the Midwest. He died in Philadelphia. » American literature

mastic An evergreen shrub, sometimes small tree growing to 8 m/26 ft, native to the Mediterranean region; leaves pinnate with 6–12 leaflets on a winged stalk; flowers tiny, in dense axillary heads; fruits round, red becoming black, very aromatic. The mastic resin is used both in medicine, and as a varnish sealant. (*Pistacia lentiscus*. Family: *Anacardiaceae*.) » evergreen plants; pinnate; resin; shrub; tree [i]

mastiff A large domestic dog; originally any large dog, but now restricted to three breeds: the **Old English mastiff** (short pale coat, long legs and tail, heavy head with short pendulous ears, deep muzzle and jowls), the rare **Tibetan mastiff**, and the **Japanese tosa**. The name is also used in **bullmastiff**. » bullmastiff; dog; Great Dane

Mastodon A browsing, elephant-like mammal found in woodland savannahs during the Miocene epoch, almost worldwide in distribution; became extinct in the Pleistocene epoch; characterized by dentition; often with upper and lower pairs of tusks, lower tusks sometimes shovel-like. (Order: *Proboscidea*.) » elephant; mammal [i]; Miocene/Pleistocene epoch

mastoid process The large bony prominence behind the ear. It is part of the temporal bone, and contains air cells (*mastoid air cells*) which communicate with the middle ear cavity. It gives attachment to the *sternomastoid* muscle (which in thin individuals stands out as it passes downwards and medially towards the sternum). » ear [i]; mastoiditis; skull

mastoiditis Acute bacterial inflammation in the honeycomb of air-containing spaces within the mastoid bone. Formerly a common complication of infection in the nose or throat, the use of antibiotics has greatly reduced its frequency. Complications of mastoiditis include meningitis, brain abscess, and deafness. » mastoid process

Mastroianni, Marcello (1923–) Italian film actor, born at Fontana Liri. His film career began in 1947, and leading roles under the directors Visconti, in *Le Notte Bianche* (1957, White Nights) and Fellini, in *La Dolce Vita* (1959, The Sweet Life) and *Otto e Mezzo* (1963, 8½) established him as an international star. He appeared several times with Sophia Loren, and in later years he has taken to character roles, as in *Blood Feud* (1981) and *Occhi Ciornie* (1987, Black Eyes).

masturbation A normal process in which there is manual or mechanical stimulation of the sex organs for the purpose of sexual gratification. It is usually accompanied by sexual fantasies. » voyeurism

Mata Hari, stage name of **Margaretha Geertruida Zelle** (1876–1917) Dutch spy, born at Leeuwarden, Holland. She married a Dutch army officer in 1895, and lived in Indonesia until 1902. After the marriage broke up, she became a dancer in Paris, and adopted her stage name (Malay 'eye of the day'). She was found guilty of espionage for the Germans during World War 1, and was shot in Paris.

Matabeleland [mata**bee**leeland] Region of W and S Zimbabwe, between the Zambezi and Limpopo Rivers; named after the Matabele Bantu, a Zulu tribe originally located in Natal and the Transvaal; acquired by the British South Africa Company, 1889; part of Southern Rhodesia, 1923; chief town, Bulawayo. » Bulawayo; Zimbabwe [i]; Zulu

matamata [mata**ma**ta] A side-necked turtle from S America; large head shaped like an arrow-head; shell with a jagged irregular surface, often with a growth of water weed; lies camouflaged on river beds and ambushes passing fish. (*Chelus fimbriatus*. Family: *Chelidae*.) » Chelonia [i]

Matamata

materialism The metaphysical view that everything is composed exclusively of physical constituents located in space and time. Materialists thus deny the existence of such abstract entities as numbers and sets, and claim that mental phenomena can be accounted for without positing the existence of anything non-physical. » dialectical materialism; idealism

materials science The study of the engineering properties of materials, as dictated by their microscopic structure. It draws on standard mechanical testing techniques from engineering, and methods of structural study derived from physics and chemistry (eg electron microscopy), to understand how bonds are formed between different components of material. It has been responsible for the development of several new materials, such as conducting rubber, metallic glasses, ceramics for use in car engines, special metals for aircraft, and the fibreglass and carbon fibre composites used in sports equipment. » rheology; solid-state physics

mathematical linguistics The study of language using mathematical concepts, of particular importance in the formalization of linguistic theory within generative grammar. Statistical techniques are also widely employed, eg in the study of the frequency and distribution of specific forms in texts, to decide cases of uncertain authorship (**statistical linguistics**). » generative grammar; statistics

mathematical logic The application of mathematical rigour and symbolic techniques to the study of logic – for example, the development of formal languages and axiom systems for constructing logical proofs – which in turn has had the effect of imposing more rigour on the study of the foundations of mathematics. Modern work in the field was inspired by Frege, and carried forward by Whitehead and Russell, Gödel, Tarski, and Church. » Frege; logic; mathematics

mathematics A systematic body of knowledge built on certain axioms and assumptions, principally relating to numbers and spatial relationships. Thus, **arithmetic** was developed from the natural (or counting) numbers (1, 2, 3, 4...) to negative integers (−3, −2, −1...), rationals (−¾, −½, ½...), irrationals ($\sqrt{2}$...), and transcendentals (π, e...). **Geometry** was developed from Euclid's axioms, and later from variants of them. **Algebra** was generalized from arithmetic algebra, where an unknown x represented a number, to abstract algebras, in which not only were the operations defined differently (eg multiplication is not necessarily commutative, $a \times b$ is not equal to $b \times a$), but the operations themselves are not defined on numbers, eg Boolean algebra is defined on sets.

Virtually all civilizations had some idea of counting, albeit as a one-to-one correspondence between the number of animals to be counted and the number of marks on a stick. The idea of a number came next, then that of a numeral to represent that number; but by c.1000 BC peoples such as the Chinese, Hindus, Babylonians, and Egyptians had made significant advances in arithmetic. The study of geometry was developed by the Greeks from c.600 BC, with Thales of Miletus, Pythagoras, and their disciples developing it from stated axioms; much of their work was summarized in Euclid's *Elements* (c.300 BC). The greatest mathematician of pre-Christian times was Archimedes. The invention of algebra is credited to the Moors (notably al-Khawarizmi, c.800 AD), who had also introduced to Europe the system of numerals on which our present system is based.

Euclidean geometry had been virtually exhausted by the 17th-c, but Descartes' invention of co-ordinate geometry opened exciting new prospects, and later Gauss, Lobachevski, and others varied the postulates on which Euclidean geometry was based. The invention of the calculus by Newton and Leibnitz enabled scientists to solve a vast range of physical problems, including the motion of the celestial bodies. In 17th-c France, Fermat and Pascal pioneered the study of probability, furthered by Abraham Demoivre (1667–1754, a close friend of Isaac Newton), and others. The 19th-c saw Gauss, the greatest mathematician of that century, contribute to almost every field of mathematics then known, his own favourite being number theory. At the same time, abstract ideas were being developed, such as set theory by Cantor, group theory by Evariste Galois (1811–32), and matrix algebra. Developments in the past 40 years have been stimulated by the electronic computer, advances being made in fields as diverse as numerical analysis and the theory of fractals.

Abstract ideas in mathematics may be classified as **pure mathematics**, and their applications as **applied mathematics**; but it is remarkable how many abstract ideas (eg set theory, matrix algebra) have had practical applications (the pattern of a snowflake, electrical networks) and how practical problems (eg the fair distribution of lottery prizes) have stimulated abstract ideas (the concept of a random number). Since the 1960s, many new topics (set theory, matrices, and vectors) have been taught in schools. These are sometimes, usually abusively, called 'new maths'. » algebra; arithmetic; differential calculus; games, theory of; geometry; integral calculus [i]; new mathematics; number theory; statistics; topology; trigonometry; Archimedes; Cantor; Descartes; Euclid; Fermat; Gauss; Leibniz; Lobachevski; Newton, Isaac; Pascal; Pythagoras; Thales

Mather, Cotton (1662–1728) American colonial minister, born and died in Boston, Massachusetts. Educated at Harvard, he became the foremost Puritan minister in New England during his time. A polymath, he reported on American botany, and was one of the earliest New England historians. But his reputation suffered lasting disfigurement because of his involvement in the Salem witchcraft trials of 1692. » Puritanism; Salem

Mathias, William (James) (1934–) British composer, born in Whitland, Carmarthenshire, Wales. He studied in London, and was lecturer (1959–68) and then professor (1970–87) at University College, Bangor. His works include an opera *The Servants* (1980), two symphonies, several concertos, and much chamber music. Among his choral works is an anthem written for the wedding ceremony of the Prince and Princess of Wales (1981). » anthem; Charles, Prince of Wales

Matisse, Henri (Emile Benoît) [matees] (1869–1954) French artist, born at Le Cateau. He studied at Paris, and from 1904 became the leader of the Fauves. Although he painted several pictures influenced by Cubism and Impressionism, his most characteristic paintings display a bold use of brilliant areas of primary colour, organized within a rhythmic two-dimensional design. During the early 1930s he travelled in Europe and the USA, and in 1949 he decorated a Dominican chapel at Venice. He died in Nice. » Cubism; Fauvism; French art; Impressionism (art)

Matlock 53°08N 1°32W; pop (1981) 13 867. County town in West Derbyshire district, Derbyshire, C England; 14 km/9 ml SW of Chesterfield; railway; transport equipment, engineering; formerly a spa town. » Derbyshire

Mato Grosso, formerly **Matto Grosso** [**mat**oh **gro**soh] pop (1980) 1 138 691; area 881 000 sq km/340 000 sq ml. State in Centro-Oeste region, CW Brazil, bordered SW by Bolivia; drained by tributaries of the Amazon (N), Paraguay (S), and Araguaia (E); half the area under forest; 611 sq km/236 sq ml Cará-Cará biological reserve in the SW (1971); Xingu National Park in the NE; capital, Cuiabá; food processing; cattle, coffee, cotton, timber, rubber, metallurgy; states of Mato Grosso (N) and Mato Grosso do Sul (S) separated in 1979; the name also given to the whole plateau area in the S (the Planalto de Mato Grosso), which extends beyond the state. » Brazil [i]

Matra Mountains Mountain range in N Hungary; a S spur of the Carpathian Mts; rises to 1 014 m/3 327 ft at Mt Kékes, highest peak in Hungary. » Hungary [i]

matrilineal descent A descent system in which family or clan membership, inheritance, and succession is traced through the mother's daughters. It does not mean that women control all property, or hold all positions of authority. One of the most famous examples was found on the Trobriand Is, New Guinea. » descent; kinship

matrix In mathematics, an ordered array of numbers subject to certain laws of composition. These laws can be demonstrated

by the matrices $A = \begin{pmatrix} a & b \\ c & d \end{pmatrix}$ and $B = \begin{pmatrix} p & q \\ r & s \end{pmatrix}$.

We define addition by $A + B = \begin{pmatrix} a+p & b+q \\ c+r & d+s \end{pmatrix}$

and multiplication by $A \cdot B = \begin{pmatrix} ap+br & aq+bs \\ cp+dr & cq+ds \end{pmatrix}$

Matrices can have any number of rows and columns, a matrix with m rows and n columns being called an *m by n* (written $m \times n$) matrix. **Matrix algebra** was developed by Cayley and other mathematicians in the 19th-c in an attempt to develop a non-commutative algebra, as $\mathbf{A.B} \neq \mathbf{B.A}$ in general. Matrices have in the past 40 years been found to have many applications, such as in probability theory (Markov chains), electricity, and the theory of games. » algebra; Cayley, Arthur; determinant

Matsys, Quentin » **Massys, Quentin**

matte shot A motion picture scene in which a mask, or matte, restricts the image area exposed so that a second image can be added subsequently. The matte may be a card or metal cut-out mounted in front of the lens during photography, or a strip of film with opaque and transparent areas used during printing. » special effects

Matteotti, Giacomo [matayo**tt**ee] (1885–1924) Italian politician, born at Fratta Polesine. A member of the Italian Chamber of Deputies, in 1921 he began to organize the United Socialist Party. He was an outspoken opponent of Mussolini's fascists (1922–4). His protests against fascist election outrages in 1924 led to his murder in Rome, provoking a crisis which nearly brought the fascist regime to an end. » fascism; Mussolini

matter The substances of which everything in the universe is composed. At one level, this is taken to mean atoms bound together into bulk matter. At the ultimate level, matter means the spin ½ particles such as electrons and quarks, bound together by spin 1 force particles such as photons and gluons. » phases of matter [i]; particle physics

Matterhorn, Fr **Mont Cervin**, Ital **Monte Cervino** 45°59N 7°39E. Mountain peak in Switzerland, SW of Zermatt; in the Pennine Alps, on the Swiss–Italian border; height, 4478 m/14691 ft; first climbed by British mountaineer Edward Whymper in 1865. » Alps

Matthew, St (1st-c), feast day 21 September (W), 16 November (E). One of the twelve apostles, a tax gatherer before becoming a disciple of Jesus, identified with Levi in *Mark* 2.14 and *Luke* 5.27. According to tradition he was the author of the first Gospel, a missionary to the Hebrews, and suffered martyrdom, but nothing is known with certainty about his life. » Jesus Christ; Matthew, Gospel according to

Matthew, Gospel according to The first work of the New Testament canon; one of the four canonical Gospels, until this century widely thought to have been the earliest Gospel written; anonymous, but 2nd-c traditions assign it to the apostle and former tax-collector, Matthew. It is noteworthy for its story of the magi at Jesus' birth, its wealth of moral instruction (as in the Sermon on the Mount), and its emphasis on Jesus as the fulfilment of the Old Testament expectations. » Matthew, St; New Testament; Gospels, canonical; Magi **2**; Sermon on the Mount/Plain

Matthew Paris (c.1200–59) English chronicler and Benedictine monk. Although he probably cared most about the history of his own monastery, St Albans Abbey, he gave in his main work (*Chronica Majora*) the fullest available account of events in England between 1236 and 1259, as well as interesting details on many other European countries. He is especially famous for his maps and drawings. » Benedictines

Matthews, Sir Stanley (1915–) British footballer, born at Hanley, Staffordshire. He started his career with Stoke City in 1931, before a controversial transfer to Blackpool in 1947. Medals eluded him until 1953, when he played a significant role in the Football Association Cup Final, a game which has been called 'The Matthews Final'. He returned to Stoke in 1961, and continued to play First Division football until after he was 50. He played for England 54 times, was twice the Footballer of the Year (1948, 1963), and was the inaugural winner of the European Footballer of the Year award in 1956. He later managed Port Vale, was knighted in 1965, and now lives in Canada. » football [i]

Matthias I, byname **Corvinus** Hung **Mátyás Corvin** (c.1443–90) King of Hungary (1458–90), born at Koloszvár, the second son of János Hunyady. He drove back the Turks, and made himself master of Bosnia (1462), Moldavia and Wallachia (1467), Moravia, Silesia, and Lusatia (1478), Vienna, and a large part of Austria proper (1485). He greatly encouraged arts and letters, founded the Corvina library, promoted industry, and reformed finances and the system of justice; but his rule was arbitrary and his taxes heavy. He died in Vienna. » Hunyady

MATV (Master Antenna Television) The use of a single antenna to serve a number of TV receivers. The system can be introduced directly, as in an apartment block, or from a central station by way of a cable distribution service. » television

Mau [mow] A nationalist movement (1926–35) challenging New Zealand colonial rule in W Samoa. On 'Black Sunday' (28 Dec 1929) police fired on a peaceful crowd and killed eight Mau supporters. W Samoa was ruled by New Zealand from 1914 to 1961. » nationalism; New Zealand [i]

Mau Mau A secret society which led a revolt of the Kikuyu people of Kenya in the 1950s. It began in 1952, with the murder of White settlers and Kikuyu 'loyalists'. British troops were deployed in its suppression, but the cost in men and money convinced Britain that decolonization was imperative. » Kenyatta; Kenya African National Union; Kikuyu

Maudling, Reginald (1917–79) British Conservative politician, born and died in London. He was educated at Merchant Taylors' and Oxford, called to the Bar (1940), and became an MP in 1950. He became Minister of Supply (1955–7), Paymaster-General (1957–9), President of the Board of Trade (1959–61), Colonial Secretary (1961–2), Chancellor of the Exchequer (1962–4), and Deputy Leader of the Opposition (1964). In 1970 he was Home Secretary in the Heath government, but resigned in 1972, when he became implicated in the bankruptcy proceedings of architect John Poulson. » Conservative Party; Heath

Mauger, Ivan (Gerald) [**may**jer] (1939–) New Zealand speedway rider, born at Christchurch. He rode for Wimbledon, Rye House, Eastbourne, Newcastle, Belle Vue, Exeter, and Hull between 1957 and 1982, and won the world individual title a record six times (1968–70, 1972, 1977, 1979). He also won two pairs world titles, four team titles, and the world long track title twice. » speedway

Maugham, W(illiam) Somerset [mawm] (1874–1965) British author, born in Paris. He was educated at Canterbury and Heidelberg, and qualified as a surgeon in London. He published his successful first novel, the lurid *Liza of Lambeth*, in 1897. After initial difficulty, he achieved success with his plays, four running simultaneously in London in 1908. His later works include the novels *Of Human Bondage* (1915), *The Moon and Sixpence* (1919), *Cakes and Ale* (1930), and *The Razor's Edge* (1945). He is best known for his short stories, several of which were filmed, such as *Quartet* (1949). In 1928 he settled in the South of France, but was forced to live in the USA during most of World War 2. He died in Nice. » drama; English literature; short story

Maui [**mow**ee] pop (1980) 62775; area 1885 sq km/728 sq ml. Second largest island of the US state of Hawaii; forms Maui County with the islands of Lanai and Molokai; chief town Wailuku; resort at Kanapali; former capital of Hawaii at Lahaina; rises to 3055 m/10023 ft at Haleakala; has the only railway in the Pacific; sugar, tourism. » Hawaii (state)

Mauna Kea [**mow**na **kay**a] 19°50N 155°28W. Dormant volcano in NC Hawaii, USA; rises to 4201 m/13783 ft; highest island mountain in the world; numerous cinder cones; snow-capped in winter; several large telescopes at the summit. » Hawaii (state); Mauna Kea Observatory; volcano

Mauna Kea Observatory [**mow**na **kay**a] The best accessible site for ground-based astronomy between 320 nm and 1 mm wavelengths, located on Mauna Kea, Hawaii. The observatory comprises telescopes on the summit (4205 m/13800 ft) and shield of the dormant volcano, among the most powerful of their kind. These include the CFHT (optical, Canada/France), UKIRT (infrared, UK), IRTF (infrared, NASA), CSO (submillimetre, California Institute of Technology), JCMT (submillimetre, Canada/Netherlands/UK), and the Keck telescope, the world's largest optical telescope (10 m/400 in), being constructed by the California Institute of Technology and the University of California. » observatory [i]; telescope [i]

Mauna Loa [**mow**na **loh**a] 19°28N 155°35W. Active volcano in C Hawaii, USA; in Hawaii Volcanoes National Park; rises to 4169 m/13678 ft; numerous craters, notably Kilauea, the second largest active crater in the world (containing Halemaumau fiery pit); on its summit is Mokuaweoweo Crater, also large and active; last erupted 1984. » Hawaii (state); volcano

Maunder diagram or **butterfly diagram** A diagram which plots the location of sunspots on the Sun as a function of date, and is useful for tracking the 1-year solar cycle of activity. It is named after British astronomer E W Maunder of the Royal Greenwich Observatory, who started solar observations in 1873, and published the original version of this chart in 1904. » sunspot

Maundy Thursday [**mawn**dee] The Thursday before Easter, so called from Latin *mandatum*, 'commandment', the first word of the anthem traditionally sung on that day. In memory of Christ's washing his disciples' feet (John 13.4-10) it was once the custom for monarchs to wash the feet of poor people on Maundy Thursday; in Britain, special money (**Maundy money**) is given by the sovereign to the same number of elderly poor people as there are years in the sovereign's age.

Maupassant, (Henry René Albert) Guy de [**moh**pasã] (1850–93) French novelist and short-story writer, born near Dieppe. He was educated at Rouen and spent his life in Normandy. After serving as a soldier and a government clerk, he took to writing, and joined the Naturalist group led by Zola. His stories range from the short tale of one or two pages to the full-length novel. His first success, *Boule de suif* (1880, Ball of

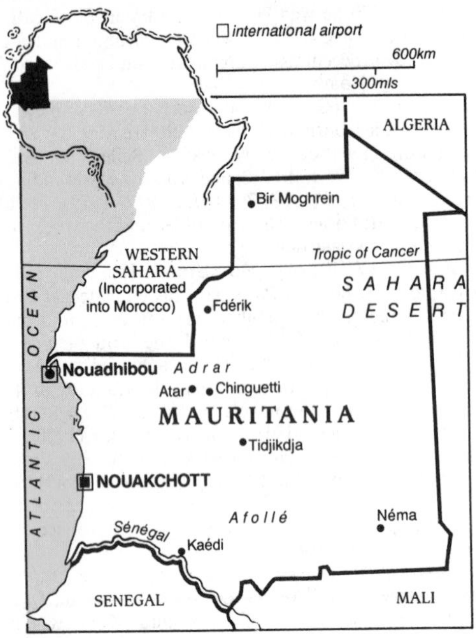

Fat), was followed by a decade in which he wrote c.300 short stories, as well as such novels as *Une Vie* (1883, A Woman's Life) and *Bel-Ami* (1885). In 1892, he was committed to an asylum in Paris, where he died. » French literature; Naturalism; short story; Zola

Maupertuis, Pierre Louis Moreau de [**moh**pertwee] (1698–1759) French astronomer and mathematician, born at St Malo. A strong supporter of Newton's physical theories, he was made a member of the Royal Society of London in 1728, and president of the Berlin Academy in 1745. He is best known for his 'principle of least action' in explaining the paths of moving bodies. In 1753 he settled in Basle, where he died. » least-action principle; Newton, Isaac

Mauriac, François [**moh**reeak] (1885–1970) French novelist, born in Bordeaux. Of Roman Catholic parentage, he is regarded as the leading novelist of that faith, dealing with the themes of temptation, sin, and redemption, set within Bordeaux provincial life. His main works include the novels *Le Baiser au lépreux* (1922, The Kiss to the Leper), *Thérèse Desqueyroux* (1927), and *Noeud de vipères* (1932, Vipers' Tangle), and his play *Asmodée* (1938). He won the 1952 Nobel Prize for Literature, and died in Paris. » French literature; novel; Roman Catholicism

Maurice, Prins van Oranje, Graaf van Nassau ('Prince of Orange, Count of Nassau') (1567–1625) Son of William the Silent, born at Dilenburg. He was elected stadtholder of Holland and Zeeland (1587) and later (1589) of Utrecht, Overyssel, and Gelderland, also becoming Captain-General of the armies of the United Provinces during their War of Independence from Spain. He checked the Spanish advance, and by his steady offensive (1590–1606) liberated the N provinces of the Netherlands from Spain. In the renewed conflict with the Habsburgs, he commanded the new republic, seeking help from England and France (1524). He died in the Hague. » Habsburgs; United Provinces of the Netherlands

Maurists [**maw**rists] A French Benedictine congregation of St Maur, founded in the early 17th-c. The monks were chiefly noted for their literary and historical work. Suspected of being influenced by Jansenism, they were eventually dissolved in 1818. » Benedictines; Jansen; monasticism

Mauritania [moritaynia], Fr **Mauritanie,** Arabic **Muritaniyah,** official name **Islamic Republic of Mauritania,** Fr **République Islamique de Mauritanie** pop(1990e) 1 990 000; area 1 029 920 sq km/397 549 sq ml. Republic in NW Africa, divided into 12 regions and a capital district; bounded SW by Senegal, S and E by Mali, NE by Algeria, N by Western Sahara, and W by the Atlantic Ocean; capital, Nouakchott; chief towns, Nouadhibou, Atar, Fderik, Kaédi, Rosso, Zouîrât; timezone GMT; chief ethnic groups, Moor (30%), Black (30%), mixed (40%); official religion, Islam; official language, Arabic, with French and local languages also spoken; unit of currency, the ouguija of 5 khoum; Saharan zone in N two-thirds of the country, with sand dunes, mountainous plateaux, and occasional oases; coastal zone, with minimal rainfall, little vegetation; Sahelian zone, with savannah grasslands; Sénégal R zone, the chief agricultural region; highest point, Kediet Ijill (915 m/3 002 ft) in the NW; dry tropical climate, with sparse rainfall, highest in the *Chemama* zone (S) with 300–600 mm/12–24 in annually; rainfall in the Sahel zone decreases N; humid but temperate on coast, annual rainfall less than 25 mm/1 in; temperatures of over 49°C in the Sahara; visited by Portuguese, 15th-c; French protectorate within French West Africa, 1903; French colony, 1920; independence, 1960; Spanish withdrew from Western Sahara in 1976, and Mauritania occupied large area in the S under the name of Tiris el Gharbia; renounced all rights in 1979, after conflict with the Frenta Polisario guerrillas; military coup, 1979; new constitution in 1991; governed by an executive president (6-year term), who appoints a prime minister, National Assembly, and Senate; 80% of population rely on subsistence agriculture; livestock, cereals, vegetables, dates; crop success constantly under threat from drought; mining based on vast iron ore reserves, also copper and gypsum; fish processing, gum arabic, textiles, cement, bricks, paints, industrial gas. » Nouakchott; Sahara Desert; sahel; Western Sahara; RR26 national holidays; RR56 political leaders

Mauritius [mo**rish**uhs] pop(1990e) 1 080 000 (excluding Rodrigues I); area 1 865 sq km/720 sq ml. Small island in the Indian Ocean, c.800 km/500 ml E of Madagascar; includes c.20 surrounding islets, and the dependencies of Rodrigues I, Agalega Is, and Cargados Carajos Is (St Brandon Is); sovereignty of Tromelin I in dispute between France and Mauritius; 61 km/38 ml long by 47 km/29 ml wide; capital, Port Louis; timezone GMT +4; over two-thirds of the population are Indo-Mauritians; official languages, French, English; chief religions, Hinduism (over 50%), Christianity (30%), Islam (17%); unit of currency, the Mauritius rupee of 100 cents; no standing defence forces; volcanic island, with a central plateau reaching 550–730 m/1 800–2 400 ft (S); falls steeply to narrow coastlands in S and SW; highest peak, Piton de la Petite Rivière Noire (826 m/2 710 ft); dry lowland coast, with wooded savan-

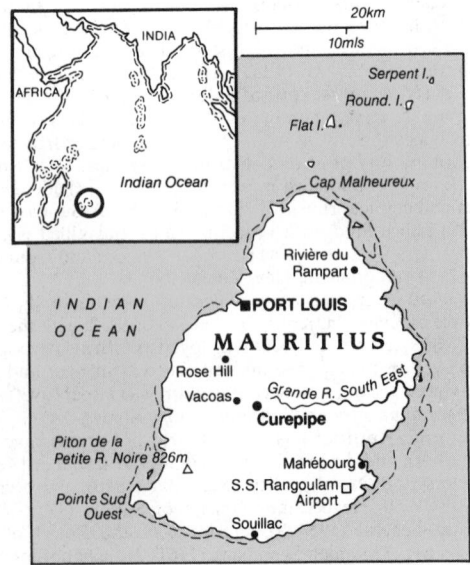

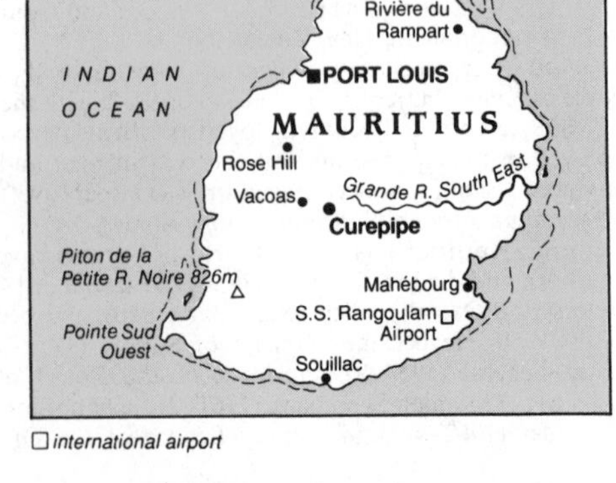

nah, mangrove swamp, and (E) bamboo; surrounded by coral reefs enclosing lagoons and sandy beaches; tropical-maritime climate, mean temperatures at sea-level 26°C (Nov–Apr), 22°C (May–Oct); humidity increases with altitude; average rainfall, 850 mm/34 in (NW), 5 000 mm/200 in (C plateau); visited by the Portuguese and Dutch, 16th-c; settled by the French, 1722; ceded to Britain, 1814; governed jointly with Seychelles as a single colony until 1903; independent sovereign state within the Commonwealth, 1968; monarch represented by a governor-general; prime minister presides over a cabinet, responsible to the Legislative Assembly of 70 members (62 elected every five years); sugar-cane industry employs over a quarter of the workforce; knitwear, clothing, diamond-cutting, watches, rum, fertilizer, tea, tobacco, potatoes, vegetables, fishing, tourism. » Port Louis; Rodrigues Island; Seychelles; RR26 national holidays; RR56 political leaders

Maurois, André [**moh**rwa], pseudonym of **Emile Herzog** (1885–1967) French novelist and biographer, born at Elbeuf. During World War 1 he was a liaison officer with the British army, and began his literary career with a book of shrewd and affectionate observation of British character, *Les Silences du Colonel Bramble* (1918, The Silence of Colonel Bramble). His many biographies include studies of Shelley (1923), Disraeli (1927), Voltaire (1935), and Proust (1949). He died in Paris. » biography; French literature; novel

Mauroy, Pierre (1928–) French politician and Prime Minister (1981–4). He was a teacher before becoming involved with trade unionism and socialist politics, and was prominent in the creation of a new French Socialist Party in 1971. He became mayor of Lille in 1973, and was elected to the National Assembly the same year. A close ally of Mitterand, Mauroy acted as his spokesman during the socialists' successful election campaign. » Mitterand; socialism

mausoleum » **Gur Amir; Lenin Mausoleum; Qin Shi Huang Mausoleum; Taj Mahal**

Mausolus, Tomb of [**mow**zuhluhs] A huge, ornate tomb built at Halicarnassus in SW Asia Minor around 350 BC by Mausolus' widow, Queen Artemisia II of Caria (reigned c.353–350 BC). It is the source of the word 'mausoleum'. » Roman architecture; Seven Wonders of the Ancient World

Maw, (John) Nicholas (1935–) British composer, born at Grantham, Lincolnshire. He studied in London (1955–8) and Paris (1958–9) and has taught at Cambridge and Yale Universities. His music, traditional in idiom but original in expression, includes two operas – *One Man Show* (1964) and *The Rising of the Moon* (1970) – two string quartets, and many orchestral works.

Maxim, Sir Hiram (Stevens) (1840–1916) British inventor, born at Sangersville, Maine, USA. He became a coachbuilder, and from 1867 took out patents for gas apparatus, electric lamps, and other devices. He is best known for the invention of the first fully automatic machine-gun (1883). He became a British subject in 1900, was knighted in 1901, and died in London. » machine-gun

maximal aerobic power The highest oxygen uptake an individual can achieve during physical work while breathing air at sea-level, commonly used as a test of cardiovascular fitness; also known as **maximal oxygen uptake**. Genetic constitution is the most important determining factor, but the level can still be raised by appropriate training. » aerobics

Maximilian I (1459–1519) Holy Roman Emperor (1493–1519), born Archduke of Austria at Weiner Neustadt, the eldest son of Emperor Frederick III and Eleanor of Portugal. Elected King of the Romans (1486), he inherited the Habsburg territories and assumed the Imperial title in 1493. He pursued an ambitious foreign policy, based on dynastic alliances, with far-reaching results for Habsburg power. His marriage to Mary of Burgundy brought his family the Burgundian inheritance, including the Netherlands, followed by union with the Spanish kingdoms of Castile and Aragon when the Spanish crown passed to his grandson, Charles (1516). A double marriage treaty between the Habsburgs and the Jagiellons (1506) eventually brought the union of Austria-Bohemia-Hungary (1526). He was involved in conflict with the Flemish, the Swiss, the German princes, and especially with the Valois Kings of France. Financial difficulties weakened his campaigns, and he was later forced to cede Milan (1504) to Louis XII. He incurred the hostility of the Venetians, and despite the League of Cambrai (1508), suffered defeat. He died at Wels, leaving his extended empire to his grandson, as Charles V. » Habsburgs; Holy Roman Empire; Jagiellons; Valois

Maximilian, Ferdinand Joseph (1832–67) Emperor of Mexico (1864–7), born in Vienna, the younger brother of Emperor Francis Joseph I, and an archduke of Austria. In 1863, he accepted the offer of the crown of Mexico, supported by France; but when Napoleon III withdrew his troops, he refused to abdicate, made a brave defence at Querétaro, and was betrayed and executed. » Juárez; Mexico [i]; Napoleon III

maxwell » RR70

Maxwell, James Clerk (1831–79) British physicist, born in Edinburgh, Scotland. Educated at Edinburgh and Cambridge, he became professor at Aberdeen (1856) and London (1860), and the first professor of experimental physics at Cambridge (1871), where he organized the Cavendish Laboratory. In 1873 he published his great *Treatise on Electricity and Magnetism*, which treats mathematically Faraday's theory of electrical and magnetic forces. He also contributed to the study of colour vision, and to the kinetic theory of gases, but his greatest work was his theory of electromagnetic radiation, which established him as the leading theoretical physicist of the century. He died at Cambridge. » electromagnetism; Maxwell–Boltzmann distribution

Maxwell, (Ian) Robert (1923–91) British publisher and politician, born in Czechoslovakia. Self-educated, he served in World War 2, then founded the Pergamon Press. A former Labour MP (1964–70), he had many business interests, including film production and television, and was chairman of the Mirror group of newspapers.

Maxwell–Boltzmann distribution A description of the distribution of energy amongst the atoms or molecules of a (perfect) gas; made by British physicist James Clerk Maxwell and Austrian physicist Ludwig Boltzmann in 1868. It is essential to understanding how the bulk thermodynamic properties of a gas are related to the behaviour of large numbers of individual gas atoms. » Boltzmann; ideal gas; kinetic theory of gases; Maxwell, James Clerk; statistical mechanics

Maxwell Davies, Sir Peter (1934–) British composer, born in Manchester. He studied at Manchester, Rome, and Princeton, and was composer-in-residence at the University of Adelaide in 1966. His works include *Taverner* (1972) and three other operas, *Eight Songs for a Mad King* (1969), symphonies, and concertos. Since 1970 he has worked mainly in Orkney, frequently using Orcadian or Scottish subject matter for music. He was knighted in 1987.

may » **hawthorn**

May Fourth Movement A student demonstration in Beijing (Peking) on 4 May 1919 which crystallized the political and cultural aspirations of those who struggled for a new China. Originally a protest against the Japanese takeover of Germany's rights in Shandong (agreed by the Western powers at the Versailles Peace Conference), the movement spread nationwide, rallying students and intellectuals across a broad political spectrum. » China [i]; Versailles, Treaty of

Mayakovsky, Vladimir (Vladimirovich) (1894–1930) Russian poet, born at Bagdadi, Georgia. He began writing at an early age, and was regarded as the leader of the Futurist school. During the Russian Revolution (1917) he emerged as the propaganda mouthpiece of the Bolsheviks, and also wrote two satirical plays. He committed suicide in Moscow. » Futurism; poetry; Russian literature; Russian Revolution

Mayas [**mi**yaz] The best-known civilization of the classic period of Middle America (250–900). The Maya rose to prominence around 300 in present-day S Mexico, Guatemala, N Belize, and W Honduras. Inheriting the inventions and ideas of earlier civilizations, such as the Olmec and Teotihuacan, they developed astronomy, calendrical systems, hieroglyphic writing, and ceremonial architecture, including pyramid temples. The tropical rainforest area was cleared for agriculture, and rain water was stored in numerous reservoirs. They also traded with other distant people, clearing routes through jungles and swamps. Most people farmed, while centres such as Tikal and Bonampak were largely ceremonial and political, with an elite of priests and nobles ruling over the countryside. Maya civilization started to decline, for reasons unknown, around c.900, although some peripheral centres still thrived, under the influence of Mexico. » American Indians; hieroglyphics [i]; Olmecs

maybug » **cockchafer**

Mayer, Louis B(urt), originally **Eliezer Mayer** (1885–1957) US film producer, born in Minsk, Russia. After his family emigrated to the USA, he became involved in cinema management. He set up a film production company in Los Angeles in 1919, and in 1924 became vice-president of the newly merged group, Loew's Metro-Goldwyn-Mayer. In charge of the studios for more than 25 years, he exercised enormous personal power at the cost of becoming one of Hollywood's best-hated moguls. He died in Los Angeles.

Mayfair A district in London where throughout the 17th-c a fair was held in May. It became a fashionable residential area in the late 19th-c and early 20th-c, but is now largely given over to offices. It lies between Piccadilly and Oxford St to the N and S, and between Hyde Park and Regent St to the E and W. » London [i]

Mayflower A three-masted carrack in which the Pilgrim Fathers, about a hundred in number, sailed from Plymouth in 1620. The ship was only 27.5 m/90 ft in length, and the voyage took 66 days. » carrack; Plymouth (UK)

mayfly A winged insect with a short adult life. Mayflies live as aquatic larvae for up to four years, then emerge as non-feeding, flying adults that survive only 2–72 hours, during which time mating takes place. (Order: *Ephemeroptera*, c.2 000 species.) » insect [i]; larva

Mayo, Charles Horace (1865–1939) US surgeon, born at Rochester, Minnesota. Educated at Chicago, he practised surgery with his father, **William Worrall Mayo** (1819–1911), and brother, **William James Mayo** (1861–1939), and organized the Mayo Clinic within what is now St Mary's Hospital, Rochester. The Mayo Foundation for Medical Education and Research was set up in 1915. His son, **Charles William Mayo** (1898–1968), also became a surgeon. The family were pioneers in the practice of group medicine. » goitre

Mayo [**may**oh], Gaelic **Mhuigheo** pop (1981) 114 766; area 5 398 sq km/2 084 sq ml. County in Connacht province, W Irish Republic; bounded N and W by the Atlantic Ocean; drained by R Moy (noted for salmon fishing); Achill I lies off W coast; Nephin Beg Range to the NW; capital, Castlebar; sheep and cattle farming, potatoes, oats; Knock, scene of apparition of Virgin Mary in 1879, major place of pilgrimage, served by new airport; Croagh Patrick, Ireland's holy mountain, scene of annual pilgrimage (Jul). » Castlebar; Irish Republic [i]; Mary (mother of Jesus)

mayor The political head of a town or city government. The name is used in a vast range of political systems, but the role and to some extent the status of mayors vary considerably. In some cases the mayor can have significant executive powers of decision-making and appointment, while in others the position is one of chairing local councils while enjoying few special powers; in a few instances the role is largely a ceremonial one. Whatever their actual powers, they are inevitably seen by the local population as the key political figure in the community.

Mayotte [**may**ot], Eng **Mahore** pop (1989e) 78 000; area 374 sq km/144 sq ml. Small island group of volcanic origin, E of the Comoros Is at the N end of the Mozambique Channel, W Indian Ocean; administered by France; two main islands; Grande Terre (area 360 sq km/140 sq ml), rising to 660 m/ 2 165 ft at Mt Benara; La Petite Terre or Ilot de Pamandzi (area 14 sq km/5 sq ml); capital, Dzaoudzi; chief languages, French, Mahorian; French colony, 1843–1914; attached with the Comoros Is to Madagascar; overseas territory of France; when the rest of the group became independent in 1974, Mayotte voted to remain a French dependency; airport; fishing, vanilla, coffee, copra, ylang-ylang. » Comoros; Dzaoudzi; France [i]

maypole dance A 19th-c Victorian entertainment of dancing round a maypole, of uncertain origin. It is often danced by young girls holding ribbons attached to the pole. Performances take place on such occasions as well-dressing – fertility celebrations at a water source – and May Queen festivals. » Ruskin; traditional dance

Mays, Willie (Howard) (1931–) US baseball player, born at Westfield, Alabama. An outstanding batter, fielder, and base runner with the San Francisco Giants and New York Mets (1951–73), he was the leading all-round player of the era, and the Most Valuable Player of the Year in the National League in 1954 and 1965. He was one of the few players to achieve more than 3 000 hits and 600 home runs. » baseball [i]

Mazarin, Jules, Cardinal [**ma**zarĩ], originally **Giulio Mazarini** (1602–61) Neapolitan cleric, diplomat, and statesman, born at Pescine. He studied at Rome and in Spain, became Papal Nuncio to the French court (1634–6) and entered the service of Louis XIII in 1639. Through the influence of Richelieu he was elevated to cardinal, succeeding his mentor as First Minister in 1642. After Louis's death (1643), he retained his authority under the Queen-Regent, Anne of Austria. Blamed by many for the civil disturbances of the Frondes, he twice fled the kingdom, and returned to Paris in 1653 after the nobles' revolt had been suppressed. His foreign policy was more fruitful: he concluded the Peace of Westphalia (1648), whose terms increased French prestige, and negotiated the Treaty of the Pyrenees (1659), ending the prolonged Franco-Spanish conflict. He died at Vincennes. » Anne of Austria; Bourbons; Frondes; Louis XIII; Richelieu

Mazatlán [masat**lan**] 23°11N 106°25W, pop (1980) 249 988. Seaport in Sinaloa state, W Mexico; on the Pacific coast S of the Gulf of California; airfield; railway; largest Mexican port on the Pacific Ocean; main industrial and commercial centre in the W; fishing, textiles, sugar refining, distilling, trade in tobacco and bananas, tourism. » Mexico [i]

mazurka A quick Polish dance in triple metre, with a strong accent on the second or third beat. Chopin wrote numerous examples for piano solos. » Chopin

Mazzini, Giuseppe [mat**zee**nee] (1805–72) Italian patriot and republican, born in Genoa. Trained as a lawyer, he became an ardent liberal, founded the Young Italy Association (1833) and, expelled from France, travelled Europe advocating republicanism and insurrection. In 1848 he became involved in the Lombard revolt, and collaborated with Garibaldi in attempting to keep the patriot struggle alive in the Alps. In 1849 he became one of the triumvirate governing the Roman Republic, overthrown after two months by French intervention. During the events of 1859–60 he and his supporters worked strenuously but vainly to make the new Italy a republic. He died at Pisa. » Garibaldi; Italy [i]; Risorgimento

Mbabane [mba**ba**nay] 26°18S 31°06E, pop (1986) 38 290. Capital of Swaziland, 320 km/200 ml E of Johannesburg (South Africa) and 160 km/100 ml WSW of Maputo (Mozambique); capital, 1902; administrative and commercial centre; iron ore; less stringent gaming laws bring tourists from South Africa to the town's casino. » Swaziland [i]

MBE » **British Empire, Order of the**

Mboya, Tom, properly **Thomas Joseph Mboya** [muh**boy**a] (1930–69) African Nationalist leader, born near Nairobi, Kenya. Educated at Mangu, he joined the Kenya African Union, and after this Party was suppressed, became Secretary of the Kenya Federation of Labour, and a campaigner for independence. In 1960 he was General Secretary of Kenyatta's Kenya African National Union, and became Minister of Labour (1962–3), Justice (1963–4), and Economic Development and Planning (1964–9). He was assassinated in Nairobi. » Kenya African National Union; Kenyatta

Mc surnames » also under **Mac**

McAliskey, Bernadette Josephine, *née* **Devlin** (1947–) Irish political activist, brought up in Dungannon, Co Tyrone. Educated at Dungannon and Belfast, while at university she became the youngest MP in the House of Commons since William Pitt, when she was elected as an Independent Unity candidate in 1969. Her aggressive political style led to her arrest while leading Catholic rioters in the Bogside, and she was sentenced to nine months' imprisonment. In 1971 she lost Catholic support when she gave birth to an illegitimate child; she married two years later, and was defeated in the February 1974 general election. She was a founder member of the Irish Republican Socialist Party (1975). » IRA; Northern Ireland [i]

McBride, Willie John, properly **William James** (1940–) Irish rugby union player, born at Toomebridge, Co Antrim. A lock forward, he made a record 17 appearances for the British Lions, and played for Ireland 63 times. He toured with the Lions in 1966, 1968, 1971, and 1974, and was tour captain in 1974 (to South Africa) and manager in 1983 (to New Zealand). Most of his club rugby was played for Ballymena. » rugby football

MCC An acronym of **Marylebone Cricket Club**, whose headquarters are at Lord's Cricket Ground, N London. It was founded in 1787 by a group of noblemen headed by the Earl of Winchilsea, Lord Charles Lennox, the Duke of York, and the Duke of Dorset. It retained responsibility for the making of cricket laws until 1969. » cricket (sport) [i]; Lord's Cricket Ground

McCarthy, Eugene J(oseph) (1916–) US politician, born at Watkins, Minnesota. Educated at St John's College and the University of Minnesota, he taught political science, and entered the House of Representatives as a Democrat in 1949. In 1958 he was elected Senator from Minnesota, and in 1968 challenged President Johnson for the presidential nomination, on a policy of opposition to the Vietnam War. Although Johnson stood down, McCarthy did not gain the nomination. He left the Senate in 1970 to devote himself to teaching and writing, though he mounted an independent presidential campaign in 1976. » Democratic Party; Johnson, Lyndon B; Vietnam War

McCarthy, Joseph R(aymond) (1909–57) US Republican politician and inquisitor, born at Grand Chute, Wisconsin. Educated at Marquette University, Milwaukee, he became a circuit judge in 1939, and after war service was elected Senator (1945). He achieved fame for his unsubstantiated accusations in the early 1950s that 250 communists had infiltrated the State Department, and in 1953 became chairman of the powerful Permanent Subcommittee on Investigations. By hectoring cross-examination and damaging innuendo he arraigned many innocent citizens and officials, overreaching himself when he came into direct conflict with the army. This kind of anti-communist witchhunt became known as 'McCarthyism'. Formally condemned by the Senate, he lost power, and died at Bethesda, Maryland. » communism; Un-American Activities Committee

McCarthy, Mary (Therese) (1912–89) US novelist and critic, born at Seattle, Washington. She was brought up in Minneapolis, educated at Vassar College, and worked as a publisher's editor, theatre critic, and teacher, before writing her first novel, *The Company She Keeps*, in 1942. Her other novels include *The Groves of Academe* (1952), *The Group* (1963), and *Cannibals and Missionaries* (1979). She has also published critical works, travel books, and the autobiographical *Memories of a Catholic Girlhood* (1957). » American literature; novel

McCartney, Paul » **Beatles, The**

McClellan, George B(rinton) (1826–85) US Federal general in the Civil War, born in Philadelphia, and educated at West Point. When the war began, he drove the enemy out of West Virginia, and was called to Washington to reorganize the army of the Potomac. His Virginian campaign ended disastrously at Richmond (1862). He forced Lee to retreat at Antietam, but failed to follow up his advantage, and was recalled. In 1864 he opposed Lincoln for the presidency, and in 1877 was elected Governor of New Jersey. He died at Orange, New Jersey. » American Civil War

McClintock, Barbara (1902–) US plant geneticist, born at Hartford, Connecticut. She studied at Cornell, where she later taught. Working at the Cold Spring Harbor Laboratory from the 1940s, she discovered and studied a new class of mutant genes in maize, concluding that the function of some genes is to control other genes, and that they can move on the chromosome to do this. She received the first unshared Nobel Prize for Physiology or Medicine to be awarded to a woman, in 1983. » chromosome [i]; gene

McClung, Nellie (Letitia), *née* **Mooney** (1873–1951) Canadian suffragist, writer, and public speaker, born at Chatsworth, Ontario. Educated in Manitoba, she rose to prominence through the Women's Christian Temperance Union and the suffrage movement, and was elected to the Alberta Legislative Assembly (1921–6). She died in Victoria, British Columbia. » women's liberation movement

McClure, Sir Robert (John le Mesurier) (1807–73) Irish explorer, born at Wexford. He joined the navy in 1824, and served in an expedition to the Arctic in 1836. He was with the Franklin expedition in 1848–9, and again in 1850, when he commanded a ship that penetrated E to the coast of Banks Land, where he was icebound for nearly two years. Rescued by another ship which had travelled from the W, he thus became the first person to accomplish the Northwest Passage. He died in London. The McClure Strait is named after him. » Franklin, John; Northwest Passage

McCormack, John (1884–1945) US tenor, born in Athlone. He studied in Milan, made his London debut in 1907, and sang at Covent Garden, appearing also in oratorio and as a Lieder singer. He toured the USA and Australia, and became a US citizen in 1917, turning to popular sentimental songs. He was raised to the papal peerage as a count in 1928, and died near Dublin.

McCormick, Cyrus H(all) (1809–84) US inventor of the reaper, born in Rockbridge Co, Virginia. He continued experiments begun by his father, and produced a successful model in 1831, at the age of 22. He made his first sale in 1840, and moved to Chicago in 1847, where he manufactured more than six million harvesting machines during his lifetime. He died in Chicago. » combine harvester [i]

McCullers, Carson, *née* **Smith** (1917–67) US author, born in Columbus, Georgia. Educated at Columbia and New York, she began to write realistic, tragic, and often symbolic novels, notably *The Heart is a Lonely Hunter* (1940), and *The Member of the Wedding* (1946, filmed 1952). Known also for her short stories and plays, she died at Nyack, New York. » American literature; novel

McEnroe, John (Patrick) (1959–) US lawn tennis player, born at Wiesbaden, Germany. He reached the semifinal at Wimbledon as a prequalifier in 1977, turned professional in 1978, and engaged in a great Wimbledon final with Björn Borg in 1980. He won the Wimbledon title three times (1981, 1983–4), the US singles four times (1979–81, 1984), and seven Grand Slam doubles events with Peter Fleming. He was also Grand Prix winner in 1979 and 1984–5, and World Championship Tennis champion in 1979, 1981, and 1983–4. Throughout his professional career, his outbursts on court have been the source of much adverse publicity. He is married to film actress Tatum O'Neal. » Borg; tennis, lawn [i]

McGonagall, William (1830–1902) Scottish doggerel poet, the son of an Irish weaver. He went from Dundee to Edinburgh, where he gave readings in public houses, published broadsheets of topical verse, and was lionized by the legal and student fraternity. His poems are uniformly bad, but possess a disarming naïveté and a calypso-like disregard for metre which still never fail to entertain.

McGovern, George S(tanley) (1922–) US Democratic politician, born at Avon, South Dakota. Educated at Northwestern University, became professor of history and government at Dakota Wesleyan University. He was a member of the House of Representatives (1956–61) and Senator for South Dakota (from 1963). He sought the Democratic presidential nomination in 1968, and opposed Nixon in the 1972 presidential election, but was defeated. He tried again for the presidential nomination in 1984, but withdrew. » Democratic Party; Nixon, Richard M; radicalism

McKay, Heather (Pamela), *née* **Heather Pamela Blundell** (1941–) Australian squash rackets player, born at Queanbeyan, New South Wales. She won the British Open in 16 successive years (1962–77), and 14 Australian titles (1960–73), and was World Champion in 1976 and 1979. Between 1962 and 1980 she was unbeaten in women's squash. She moved to Canada in 1975, and became Canadian racketball champion. » squash rackets

McKinley, William (1843–1901) US Republican statesman and 24th President (1897–1901), born at Niles, Ohio. He served in the Civil War, then became a lawyer. He was elected to Congress in 1877, and in 1891 was made Governor of Ohio, his name being identified with the high protective tariff carried in the McKinley Bill of 1890. He secured a large majority in 1896 and again in 1900 as the representative of a gold standard and high tariffs. In his first term, the war with Spain (1898) took place, with the conquest of Cuba and the Philippines. He was shot by an anarchist at Buffalo. » Republican Party

McKinley, Mount 63°04N 151°00W. Mountain in SC Alaska, USA; in Denali National Park and Preserve; highest peak in the USA and in N America; covered almost completely by glaciers; consists of two peaks (6 194 m/20 321 ft, 5 934 m/19 468 ft); Indian name Denali; first climbed (1913) by Hudson Stuck (US). » Alaska

McLuhan (Herbert) Marshall [muhk**loo**uhn] (1911–80) Canadian critic and cultural theorist, born in Edmonton, Alberta. He studied English at Manitoba and Cambridge, became professor at Toronto in 1946, and founder-director of the University of Toronto's Centre for Culture and Technology (1963). He held controversial views on the effect of the communication media on the development of civilization, claiming that it is the media *per se*, not the information and ideas which they disseminate, that influence society. His books include *The Gutenberg Galaxy* (1962) and *The Medium is the Massage* (1967). He died in Toronto. » literary criticism; mass media; semiotics

McNamara, Robert S(trange) (1916–) US Democratic politician and businessman, born in San Francisco. After service in the air force (1943–6), he worked his way up in the Ford Motor Company to president by 1960, and in 1961 joined the Kennedy administration as Secretary of Defense, being particularly involved in the Vietnam War. In 1968 he resigned to become president of the World Bank (a post he held until 1981). In the 1980s he emerged as a critic of the nuclear arms race. » Democratic Party; Kennedy, John F; nuclear weapons; Vietnam War

McPherson, Aimee Semple (1890–1944) US religious leader, born near Ingersoll, Ontario, Canada, the founder of the Church of the Foursquare Gospel. She became an evangelical Christian at the age of 17, and married the man who had converted her. She went to China with her husband as a missionary in 1910, but after his death there returned to the USA. She flourished as an evangelist, preaching a simple gospel of personal salvation. She died at Oakland, California. » evangelicalism

McQueen, Steve, originally **Terence Steven McQueen** (1930–80) US actor, born in Indianapolis. After a delinquent youth he took up acting on stage and television, and from 1955 was recognized as a film star with a reputation as a tough unconventional rebel, both on and off the screen. Typical of his successes were *The Magnificent Seven* (1960), *Bullitt* (1961), and *An Enemy of the People* (1977). He died from cancer at Juarez, Mexico.

ME syndrome An abbreviation for **myalgic encephalomyelitis syndrome**, a condition following certain viral infections which cause self-limited feverish illnesses. It is characterized by weakness, diffuse muscle pains, depression, and headaches, which persist for several months and which ultimately resolve. In the absence of evidence of viral involvement, such features are thought by some doctors to be psychological in origin. » neurasthenia

mead An alcoholic beverage derived from fermented honey. It was widely drunk in Anglo-Saxon England, and was known as *hydromel* by the Romans. » honey

Mead, Margaret (1901–78) US anthropologist, born in Philadelphia. Educated at Columbia, she carried out a number of field studies in the Pacific before World War 2, writing both academic and popular books, such as *Coming of Age in Samoa* (1928) and *New Lives for Old* (1956). She held a position for many years at the American Museum of Natural History, but increasingly she became a freelance media heavyweight, one of the most famous women of her generation, particularly well known for her views on educational and social issues. She died in New York City. » anthropology

Meade, James Edward (1907–) British economist, born at Swanage, Dorset. He was a member (latterly director) of the economic section of the Cabinet Office (1940–6), then professor of economics at the London School of Economics (1947–57) and of political economy at Cambridge (1957–68). A prolific writer, his principal contributions are in the area of international trade. He shared the Nobel Prize for Economics in 1977. » economics

Meade, Richard (John Hannay) (1938–) British equestrian rider, born at Chepstow, Gwent, Wales. One of Britain's most successful Olympians, he won three gold medals – the Three Day Event team golds in 1968 and 1972, and the individual title in 1972 (on *Laurieston*). He also won world championship team gold medals (1970, 1982), European championship team gold medals (1967, 1971, 1981), Burghley in 1964 (on *Barberry*), and Badminton in 1970 (on *The Poacher*) and 1982 (on *Speculator III*). » equestrianism

meadow grass A perennial grass with creeping, rooting stems forming rather stiff tufts; variable and widespread throughout the temperate N hemisphere. It is important as a pasture grass. (*Poa pratensis*. Family: *Gramineae*.) » blue grass; grass [i]; perennial

meadow saffron A plant with corms, native to Europe; leaves 12–30 cm/5–12 in, lance-shaped, glossy, absent when flowers appear in autumn; flowers lilac, goblet-shaped, the six perianth-segments fused below to form a tube 5–20 cm/2–8 in long; fruit ripening in spring as leaves appear; also called **autumn crocus**. It is the source of the alkaloid colchicine, used in genetic research to inhibit chromosome separation. (*Colchicum autumnale*. Family: *Liliaceae*.) » alkaloids; chromosome [i]; corm; perianth; saffron

meadow-sweet An erect perennial growing to 120 cm/4 ft, native to Europe, W Asia, and N Africa; leaves pinnate with pairs of small leaflets alternating with five pairs of large ones; flowers 5-petalled with reflexed sepals, creamy, fragrant, forming an irregular terminal mass, carpels spirally twisted. (*Filipendula ulmaria*. Family: *Rosaceae*.) » carpel; perennial; pinnate; sepal

meadowlark A bird native to the New World; plumage streaked and mottled on back; inhabits grassland and cultivation; eats insects and seeds; nests on ground. (Genus: *Sturnella*, 5 species. Family: *Icteridae*.) » lark

Meads, Colin (Earl), byname **Pinetree** (1936–) New Zealand rugby union player, born at Cambridge, Waikato. A prop forward, he wore the All Black jersey in 133 representative matches, including a record 55 in Test Matches between 1957 and 1971. He is now a sheep farmer. » rugby football

mealworm The larva of a darkling ground beetle, *Tenebrio molitor*, which feeds on stored flour; a cylindrical larva up to 25 mm/1 in long, well-adapted to life in very arid conditions. (Order: *Coleoptera*. Family: *Tenebrionidae*.) » ground beetle; larva

mealybug A scale insect that infests all parts of its host plants; adult female flattened, males enclosed in cocoon-like sac; can lay eggs or bear live young; c.1 100 species distributed worldwide, including many pests of cultivated plants. (Order: *Homoptera*. Family: *Pseudococcidae*.) » scale insect

mean In mathematics, the sum of n scores, divided by n; colloquially called the 'average'. The **arithmetic mean** is obtained by adding a set of scores and dividing the total by the number of scores; for example, the arithmetic mean of the scores 6, 2, 8, 4 is 5 ($6+2+8+4=20$; $20\div4=5$). If the scores are $x_1, x_2, x_3, \ldots x_n$, the mean m is $\frac{1}{n}(x_1+x_2+x_3\ldots x_n)$, written $\sum_{i=1}^{n} x_i$. The **geometric mean** of n scores is the nth root of the product of those scores; for example, the geometric mean of

2,9,12 is 6, since $2 \times 9 \times 12 = 216$, and $\sqrt[3]{216} = 6$. The n numbers $a_1, a_2, a_3, \ldots a_n$, have the geometric mean $\sqrt[n]{a_1 a_2 a_3 \ldots a_n}$. » mode (mathematics); statistics

mean free path The average distance travelled by some atom or molecule before colliding with another, typically about 60 nm in gases; symbol l, units m (metre). It is important in understanding the properties of gases, such as diffusion, and the movement of such particles as electrons and neutrons through solids. » atom; kinetic theory of gases

mean life In atomic, nuclear, and particle physics, the average time taken for an excited atom to lose energy or for a particle to decay; symbol τ, units s (second). It is related to half-life $T_{1/2}$ by $T_{1/2} = \tau \log 2 = .693\tau$; $1/\tau$ is the decay rate. » half-life

means test A method of assessing an individual or family's eligibility for some kind of financial assistance, used by government agencies and local authorities. The 'means' refers to a person's income and other sources of money. Aid is given on a sliding scale, and above a certain level no help is given. The expression is used infrequently nowadays, because of its emotive overtones, and has largely been replaced by 'assessment'.

measles A widespread viral childhood disease spread by airborne infected droplets. It begins with catarrhal symptoms followed by the development of a generalized blotchy red rash. Complications include secondary bacterial middle-ear infection, and pneumonia. Diffuse viral infection of the brain (*encephalitis*) also occurs rarely. The condition is common in developed countries, and carries a low mortality; however, in developing countries it is severe, with a high mortality. » German measles; virus

meat The edible muscle of animals, the most common forms including beef, pork, bacon, lamb, and poultry. The flesh of many other species is also eaten as meat, including the horse, buffalo, camel, dog, rabbit, and monkey. Meat is rich in protein, iron, and zinc. The level of fat surrounding meat is determined by age and the method of husbandry. » protein; sausage; vegetarianism

Meath [meeth], Gaelic **na Midhe** pop (1981) 95 419; area 2 339 sq km/903 sq ml. County in Leinster province, E Irish Republic; bounded E by Irish Sea; drained by Boyne and Blackwater Rivers; crossed by the Royal Canal; former kingdom; capital, Trim; sheep, cattle, potatoes, oats. » Irish Republic [i]

Mecca [meka], Arabic **Makkah**, ancient **Macoraba** 21°30N 39°54E, pop (1974) 366 800. Islamic holy city in Mecca province, WC Saudi Arabia; 64 km/40 ml E of its Red Sea port, Jedda; birthplace of Mohammed and site of the Kaba, the chief shrine of Muslim pilgrimage; between 1.5 and 2 million pilgrims visit Mecca annually; city closed to non-Muslims; large bazaars, Al-Harram Mosque with the Kaba and sacred Black Stone. » Islam; Kaba; Mohammed; Saudi Arabia [i]

mechanical advantage The ratio of the load to effort of a machine; for example, the weight lifted by a lever divided by the effort required. It is an essential property of a machine, which can be less than, equal to, or greater than 1. » machine [i]

mechanical engineering The branch of engineering concerned with the design, construction, and operation of machines of all types. It is also concerned with the production and application of mechanical power. Hence mechanical engineers design, operate, and test engines that produce power from steam, petrol, nuclear energy, and other sources, and a wide range of associated equipment. The field became a separate branch of engineering when steam power was introduced into manufacturing in the 1800s. » engineering; machine [i]

mechanical hysteresis » **elastic hysteresis**

mechanical properties of matter Properties such as tensile strength and stiffness, dictated by the nature of the bonds between atoms of the material. These bonds also control whether the material is metallic, crystalline, glass-like, or of some other character. » bulk modulus; creep; elasticity; fracture (physics); hardness; high pressure physics; isotropic; plastic deformation; Poisson's ratio; rheology; shear modulus; solid-state physics; tensile strength; toughness; yield stress; Young's modulus

mechanics The study of the motion of objects as a result of the forces acting on them. Motion in a straight line is called *linear* or *rectilinear* motion, and is described using mass m, velocity v, acceleration a, momentum p, and force F; *rotational* motion is described using moment of inertia I, angular velocity ω, angular acceleration α, angular momentum L, and torque Γ. **Quantum mechanics** governs objects the size of atoms (10^{-10}m) or less. **Classical mechanics** corresponds to all other aspects of mechanics, and includes **Newtonian mechanics, celestial mechanics** (the motion of stars and planets), general relativity, **fluid mechanics**, and **relativistic mechanics** (for objects moving at high velocity). » acceleration; angular momentum; ballistics; centre of gravity/mass; Coriolis force [i]; dynamics; energy; equilibrium; Euler–Lagrange equations; fluid mechanics; force; friction; general relativity; least-action principle; mass; momentum; Newtonian mechanics; precession; quantum mechanics; statistical mechanics; torque [i]; velocity

mechanism The view that everything in nature can be explained by means of deterministic causal processes, most clearly exemplified in Newtonian mechanics. Mechanism denies the need for teleological explanations and vitalistic claims that biological processes are not entirely physical. Because it is deterministic, it is incompatible with orthodox interpretations of quantum mechanics. » determinism; mechanics; Newton, Isaac; teleology; vitalism

mechanization The use of machines wholly or partly to replace the human operator. Unlike automation, in which there is no reference to the operator at all, mechanization requires some input from people, in terms of feeding in data and giving instructions. Early mechanization replaced the craftsman by the machine operator, and involved the use of machines such as levers and pulleys. Computers are the major example of modern mechanization and automation. » automation; computer; machine [i]

Mechnikov or **Metchnikoff, Ilya** (1845–1916) Russian biologist, born at Ivanovka, Ukraine. He became professor of zoology and comparative anatomy at Odessa (1870), and in 1888 joined Pasteur in Paris. He shared the 1908 Nobel Prize for Physiology or Medicine for his work on immunology, in which he discovered the cells (*phagocytes*) which devour infective organisms. He died in Paris. » blood; immunology; Pasteur

Mecklenburg Declaration of Independence (1775) Resolutions adopted in Mecklenburg County, N Carolina, during the American Revolution, denying all British authority. The resolutions were ignored by the Continental Congress, which at that point was much more interested in reconciliation with Britain than in independence from it. » American Revolution; Continental Congress

Mecoptera [muh**kop**tuhra] » **scorpion fly**

medal A piece of metal, often in the form of a coin or cross, bearing a device or inscription, struck or cast in commemoration of an event or as a reward for merit. Medals may be awarded for personal bravery (eg Victoria Cross, Medal of Honor), for participation in an event or battle (eg Victoria Medal, awarded to soldiers of all Allied nations in World War 1), or for sports (eg Olympic gold, silver, and bronze medals). » decoration; *see illustration p.776*

Medal of Honor (MH, MOH) In the USA, the highest decoration awarded for heroism, instituted in 1861; it is worn on a blue ribbon decorated with white stars. » decoration

Medawar, Sir Peter (Brian) [**med**awah] (1915–87) British zoologist, born in Rio de Janeiro. Educated at Marlborough and Oxford, he became professor of zoology at Birmingham (1947–51), professor of comparative anatomy at London (1951–62), and director of the National Institute for Medical Research, London (1962–71). He shared the 1960 Nobel Prize for Physiology or Medicine for his discovery of acquired immunological tolerance. Well known for his general books on the nature of science, he was knighted in 1965, and died in London. » immunology

Medea [me**dee**a] In Greek mythology, a witch, the daughter of Aeetes, the King of Colchis, who assisted Jason in obtaining

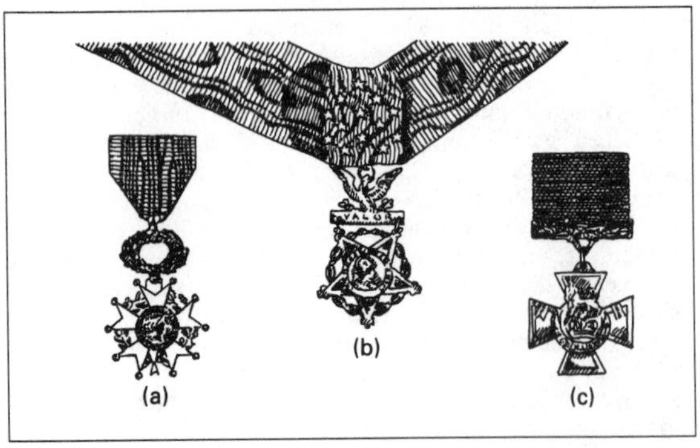

Medals – Legion of Honour, France (a); Medal of Honor, USA (b); Victoria Cross, UK (c)

the Golden Fleece. On their return to Iolcos, she renewed the youth of Aeson, and tricked the daughters of Pelias into performing a similar ritual, so that they destroyed their own father. When deserted by Jason at Corinth, she fled in her aerial chariot after killing her children. » Golden Fleece; Jason

Medellín [medelyeen] 6°15N 75°36W, pop(1985) 2068892. Industrial and commercial capital of Antioquia department, NWC Colombia; second largest city in Colombia, and leading industrial centre; airport; railway; five universities; coffee trade, steel, textiles, chemicals, pharmaceuticals, food processing; rubber, wood, and metal products; new cathedral of Villanueva in Parque Bolívar; Museo El Castillo, Museo Folklórico Tejicondor, zoo. » Colombia [i]

Medes [meedz] An ancient people living to the SW of the Caspian Sea, often wrongly identified with the Persians. At their peak in the 7th-c and 6th-c BC, they conquered Urartu and Assyria, and extended their power as far west as C Turkey. In the E they ruled most of Iran. Their Empire passed to the Persians c.550 BC. » Assyria; Persian Empire; Urartu

media A collective term for television, radio, cinema, and the press. Although each medium of mass communication has always had its own distinctive output, technology, and industrial structure, the media are nowadays often discussed as a single entity. Among the reasons for this are their combined importance as providers of entertainment and information, their presumed power to mould public opinion and set moral and aesthetic standards, the growth of cross-ownership among the various sectors, and their often parasitic interest in each others' personalities and problems. » advertising; broadcasting; journalism

median In mathematics, the middle score, when the scores are arranged in order of size; for example, the scores 1,5,3,7,2 are re-arranged 1,2,3,5,7, and the middle score is 3. If we have an even number of scores, the median is the mean of the two middle scores; thus for 1,4,5,2, the median is $\frac{1}{2}(2+4)$, ie 3. For a continuous distribution, the median M is such that half the scores are less than M, and half greater. » mean; mode; statistics

medical insurance » **health insurance**

Medicaid and **Medicare** Two US schemes to provide health care, introduced by the federal government in 1965. **Medicaid** is operated by state governments, and provides financial assistance to low-income persons covering physician, hospital, and other medical needs. **Medicare** is for persons over the age of 65, providing for basic hospital insurance and supplementing insurance for doctors and other health care services. » medicine

Medici [maydeechee] Fr **Médicis**, A banking family which virtually ruled Florence from 1434 to 1494, though without holding formal office. They were overthrown by the republic in 1494, but restored to power in 1512, and from 1537 became hereditary dukes of Florence, and from 1569 Grand Dukes of Tuscany. They were patrons of artists, including Botticelli and Michelangelo (who later designed their 16th-c funerary chapel). » Catherine de' Medici; Florence; Leo X; Marie de Médicis

medicine The science and practice of preventing, alleviating, and curing human illness. From the earliest times, trial-and-error revealed plants and parts of animals to be poisonous, edible, or useful in disease; this led to medical folklore and herbal remedies. Prior to the scientific revolution of the last century, attempts to cope with serious disease were frustrated by the lack of a satisfactory theory of disease or knowledge of causes. Although the study of anatomy grew rapidly from the time of Aristotle and the Alexandrian medical school in 300 BC, physiology and ideas of organ function remained rudimentary. Speculations untested by experiments were by present-day standards grotesque, and gave rise to such practices as trephining, bleeding, cupping, and purging, often accompanied by magic rituals and incantations. Nevertheless in a few societies doctors accurately recorded relevant events, such as Indian physicians who in 1000 BC were listing features of several common disabling diseases. The major contribution of Greek medicine was in the field of medical ethics, and the Hippocratic code of conduct is still invoked today. Roman medicine was pre-eminent in public health, with its emphasis on clean water, sewage disposal, and public baths. The emphasis by early Christians on miracles was balanced by the impulse to comfort and nurse the sick. Arabian medicine made significant contributions to chemistry and drugs, and set up the first organized medical school in Salerno. From there the torch was passed to Padua, where Vesalius corrected the anatomical misconceptions of Galen, and thereafter to Montpelier, Leyden, Edinburgh, and London.

The major medical discovery of the 17th-c was the circulation of the blood; 100 years later, oxygen and its relationship to blood. In the 18th-c, clinical bedside teaching became the favoured method of doctor training, as it is today. The value of post-mortem studies was demonstrated by Morgagni in Padua. New methods of examination were introduced, notably the stethoscope (by Laennec) and percussion of the chest. Jenner showed the benefit of vaccination to prevent smallpox. The germ theory of disease dominated the 19th-c, and Pasteur virtually created the science of bacteriology, from which Lister was inspired to develop the concept of antisepsis. By the end of the century, mosquitoes were known to carry malaria and yellow fever. Röntgen discovered X-rays, and the Curies radium. Freud developed psychiatry.

Progress in the 20th-c has been unparalleled, being distinguished by the growth in modern technology and the development of rigorous experimental testing. Thus the claim for the efficacy of a new drug, for example, does not rest on anecdote, but on carefully planned double-blind animal and human trials in statistically-controlled populations. Progress was stimulated rather than hindered by World Wars 1 and 2, in such areas as rehabilitation after injury, blood transfusion, anaesthesia, and chemotherapy, including the development of antibiotics and vitamins and the discovery of insulin and cortisone. New concepts have included genetic disease, the baleful effects of some lifestyles and environmental pollution, vaccination for the majority of infectious disease, artificial organ and life support systems, organ transplantation, and the science of immunology. » British/American Medical Association; alternative/community/forensic/preventive/space physiology and/sports medicine; epidemiology; General Medical Council; geriatrics; gynaecology; haematology; National Health Service; neurology; nursing; obstetrics; oncology; ophthalmology; orthopaedics; paediatrics; pathology; perinatology; serology; surgery; Curie; Freud, Sigmund; Jenner; Laënnec; Lister, Joseph; Morgagni; Pasteur; Röntgen; Vesalius

Medicine Hat 50°03N 110°41W, pop(1984) 41493. Town in SE Alberta, S Canada, on S Saskatchewan R; railway arrived, 1873; city status, 1906; airfield; natural gas, glass blowing, chemical fertilizers, petrochemicals, clay products; Dinosaur Provincial Park, 104 km/65 ml W; oldest rodeo in Alberta (Jul). » Alberta

medick An annual and perennial, native to Europe, W Asia, and N Africa; leaves with three toothed leaflets; pea-flowers small, mostly yellow; fruit usually a spirally coiled pod, often spiny, less commonly sickle-shaped. (Genus: *Medicago*, 100 species. Family: *Leguminosae*.) » annual; perennial

Medina, Arabic **Madinah, Al** 24°35N 39°52E, pop (1974) 198 200. Islamic holy city in Medina province, Saudi Arabia; 336 km/209 ml N of Mecca; second most important holy city of Islam (after Mecca), containing the tomb of Mohammed; after his flight from Mecca, Mohammed sought refuge here; important pilgrimage trade, served by the Red Sea port of Yanbu al-Bahr; city closed to non-Muslims; airfield; Islamic university (1961); centre of a large date-growing oasis, producing also fruit, grain, clover; numerous mosques, Islamic monuments. » Islam; Mohammed; Saudi Arabia [i]

meditation Devout and continuous reflection on a particular religious theme, practised in many religions and serving a variety of aims, such as deepening spiritual insight, or achieving union with the divine will. Some religions hold that disciplined breathing, posture, and ordering of thoughts deepen meditation. » religion

Mediterranean Sea, ancient **Mediterraneum** or **Mare Internum** area 2 510 000 sq km/968 900 sq ml. World's largest inland sea, lying between Africa, Asia, and Europe; connected with the Atlantic by the 14.5 km/9 ml-wide Straits of Gibraltar, with the Black Sea by the Dardanelles, Sea of Marmara, and Bosporus, and with the Indian Ocean by the Suez Canal and Red Sea; subdivided into the Ligurian, Adriatic, Aegean, Ionian and Tyrrhenian Seas; length, 3 860 km/2 400 ml; maximum width, 1 610 km/1 000 ml; maximum depth, 4 405 m/14 452 ft; higher salinity than the Atlantic; 'Mediterranean climate' of hot, dry summers (intensified by the Sirocco wind) and mild winters with rainstorms; seaboard highly favoured as holiday and health resort; maritime highway since ancient times for the Phoenicians, Greeks, Venetians, and Crusaders, connecting Europe with the E; eclipsed during 14th–16th-c because of Turkish dominance and opening of ocean highway around Africa; Suez Canal (1869) restored much of its importance; pollution a major problem; strategic importance demonstrated during and after World War 2. » Sirocco; Suez Canal

medium (art) The liquid into which pigment is mixed to make paint. Its purpose is to enable the pigment to be spread on the surface of the picture, and to stick. Various substances have been used for this, including oil, glue, size, egg, vegetable gum, and wax. » acrylic/oil painting; paint; tempera

medium (parapsychology) Especially in spiritualism, a person through whom spirits of the dead are claimed to demonstrate their presence by means of spoken or written messages (via **mental mediums**), or apparently paranormal physical effects (via **physical mediums**). » automatic writing; ectoplasm; materialism; paranormal; seance; spiritualism

Medjugorje [medyoo**gor**ye] Village in Bosnia and Herzegovina republic, W Yugoslavia, S of Mostar; since 1981, claimed to be the scene of regular appearances by the Virgin Mary to a group of local children; now a major site of pilgrimage, having attracted over 10 million visitors in the 1980s. » Bosnia and Herzegovina; Mary (mother of Jesus); Yugoslavia [i]

medlar A small deciduous tree or shrub, growing to 6 m/20 ft, native to SE Europe, and cultivated and naturalized elsewhere; leaves oblong, yellowish; flowers solitary, 3–6 cm/1¼–2½ in in diameter, white; sepals leafy, longer than petals; fruit 2–3 cm/¾–1¼ in, brown, becoming soft and edible when over-ripe. (*Mespilus germanica*. Family: *Rosaceae*.) » deciduous plants; sepal; shrub; tree [i]

Médoc [**may**dok] District in Gironde department, SW France; flat alluvial plain on W bank of Gironde estuary, N of Bordeaux; bounded W by the Atlantic Ocean; famous for its clarets, notably at Haut-Médoc; chief towns, Lesparre and Pauillac. » France [i]; wine

medulla oblongata [me**duh**la oblong**gah**ta] The rear part of the brainstem, continuous with the pons (above) and with the spinal cord (below). It contains the 'vital centres' (so-called because damage to them is often fatal) concerned with the reflex control of the cardiovascular and respiratory systems. It also helps to govern swallowing, sneezing, coughing, and vomiting. » brainstem

medusa [me**dyoo**za] The free-swimming phase in the life cycle of a coelenterate. The body is typically discoid or bell-shaped, usually radially symmetrical, with marginal tentacles and a centrally located mouth on the underside. The medusa contains the reproductive organs, and is the sexual phase in the coelenterate life cycle. » coelenterate; life cycle; polyp (marine biology)

Medusa [me**dyoo**za] In Greek mythology, the name of one of the Gorgons, whose head is portrayed with staring eyes and snakes for hair. » Gorgon; Perseus (mythology)

Medway Towns pop (1981) 216 694. Urban area in Kent, SE England; includes Gillingham, Rochester, Chatham, and Strood on the R Medway, E of London; railway. » Kent

Mee, Arthur (1875–1943) British journalist, editor, and writer, born near Nottingham. He is most widely known for his *Children's Encyclopaedia* (1908) and *Children's Newspaper*, as well as a wide range of popular works on history, science, and geography.

Meegeren, Han van » **van Meegeren, Han**

meerkat A mongoose native to S Africa; three species: the **suricate** or **slender-tailed meerkat** (*Suricata suricata*); the **yellow** or **thick-tailed meerkat**, or **yellow mongoose** (*Cynictis penicillata*); and the **gray meerkat** or **Selous mongoose** (*Paracynictis selousi*). » mongoose; Viverridae [i]

meerschaum [**meer**shuhm] or **sepiolite** A hydrated magnesium silicate mineral, which forms fine, fibrous masses like white clay and is easily carved. It is porous when dry, and is used for pipe bowls. Asia Minor is the main source. » silicate minerals

megabyte » **byte**

megalith (Gr *mega* 'large' + *lithos* 'stone') In European prehistory, a monument built of large, roughly-dressed stone slabs; sometimes called a **cromlech**. Most are of Neolithic date. Outside Europe, comparable (though unrelated) megalithic monuments are found in S India, Tibet, SE Asia, Japan, and Oceania. » chambered tomb; menhir; stone circles; Three Age System

Megaloceros [mega**lo**suhruhs] » **Irish elk**

megalomania An extremely inflated view of one's own significance and abilities. This may take on a delusional quality in which, for example, the individual may believe himself to be Jesus Christ. In this situation the description of the thoughts is referred to as *delusions of grandeur*.

Megaloptera [mega**lop**tuhra] » **alderfly; dobsonfly**

megaparsec » **parsec**

megapode An Australasian ground-living bird; usually inhabits rainforest; eats mainly fruit and insects; sturdy body with large legs and feet; eggs usually incubated by natural heat in mound of decaying vegetation; young fly within hours of hatching; also known as **mound bird**, **mound builder**, or **incubator bird**. It includes **scrub-fowl** of the genus *Megapodius*. (Family: *Megapodiidae*, 12 species.) » brush turkey; jungle fowl [i]

megastructure An architectural structure of gigantic proportions, usually of the 20th-c and fantastical in nature. It is designed to contain all the requirements for human existence in one monumental building, effectively forming artificial land, as in the high-density projected 'Arcologies' by architect Paolo Soleri for up to six million inhabitants.

Megatherium [mega**theer**iuhm] The largest ground sloth, found in C and S America during the Pleistocene epoch; a two-legged browser and grazer in grassy woodlands and pasture; forelimbs large, hindlimbs short but massive; toes clawed; walked on outer edge of foot. (Order: *Xenarthra*.) » Pleistocene epoch; sloth

megaton » **kiloton**

megavitamin therapy A dietary supplement aimed at providing therapeutic doses of a vitamin. The amount of a nutrient, including vitamins, recommended for daily consumption is liberally calculated to take into account almost everybody – even those with very high requirements. If vitamins are taken above this level by a factor of two, the dose can be considered a megavitamin dose. Because many vitamins are toxic, the use of megavitamin supplements is undesirable. » nutrients; vitamins [i]

megawatt » **watt**

Megiddo In antiquity, an important town in N Palestine controlling the main route from Egypt to Syria. Under Israelite control from around 1000 BC, it was rebuilt by Solomon (c.970–933 BC) as a military and administrative centre. Among its most impressive remains are the 9th-c stables of the Israelite kings.

megohm » ohm

Meidan Emam [**may**dan e**mam**] A public square built in Isfahan, C Iran, by Abbas I (1571–1629) in the late 16th-c; a world heritage site. The square is flanked by four notable buildings: the former Royal Mosque, the Sheikh Lotfollah Mosque, the Ali Qapu Palace, and the gateway to the Qeyssariyeh. » Iran [i]

Meiji Restoration (1868) [**may**jee] An important point in Japanese history, when the last Shogun was overthrown in a short civil war, and the position of the emperor (Meiji, the title of Mutsuhito, who ruled until 1912) was restored to symbolic importance. Powerful new leaders set about making Japan into an industrial state. The four hereditary classes of Tokugawa Japan were abolished. New technology and technical experts were brought from the West. » daimyo; Meiji Tenno; samurai; Shogun

Meiji Shrine [**may**jee] An important pilgrimage centre in Tokyo. The shrine was completed in 1920 and dedicated to Emperor Meiji. The present building is a reconstruction of the original which was destroyed in World War 2. » Meiji Tenno; Tokyo

Meiji Tenno [**may**jee] ('emperor'), **Mutsuhito** [mootsoo**hee**toh] (1852–1912) Emperor of Japan who became the symbol of Japan's modernization. He is commemorated by the Meiji Shrine and the Meiji Memorial Picture Gallery, Tokyo, and a large mausoleum at Momoyama, near Kyoto. » Ito; Meiji Restoration/Shrine; Tokugawa

Meiningen Players The private theatre company of the Duke of Saxe-Meiningen which, through its European tours of the 1880s, influenced the development of Western theatre. The advantages of the unifying hand of a director could be seen in the organization of the crowd scenes and the integration of scenic design with the movements of the actors. » theatre

meiosis [miy**oh**sis] One of the principal mechanisms of nuclear division in living organisms, resulting in the formation of gametes (in animals) or sexual spores (in plants). During meiosis a diploid nucleus (ie one possessing a double set of chromosomes) undergoes two successive divisions. This results in the production of four cells, each receiving only one member of each chromosome pair. The halving of chromosome numbers compensates for the doubling that occurs when two haploid gametes (ie each possessing a single set of chromosomes) unite to form a zygote during sexual reproduction. The phases of meiosis are *leptotene* (the appearance of chromosomes as threads in the nucleus), *zygotene* (the pairing of chromosomes to form bivalents), *pachytene* (the separation of bivalents), and *diplotene* (the moving apart of chromosomes). Meiosis is an important process in sexual reproduction, providing the opportunity for recombination to occur, as genetic material can be exchanged by crossing over between homologous chromosomes during the pachytene phase. » cell; chromosome [i]; gamete; genetics [i]; homology; mitosis; nucleus (biology)

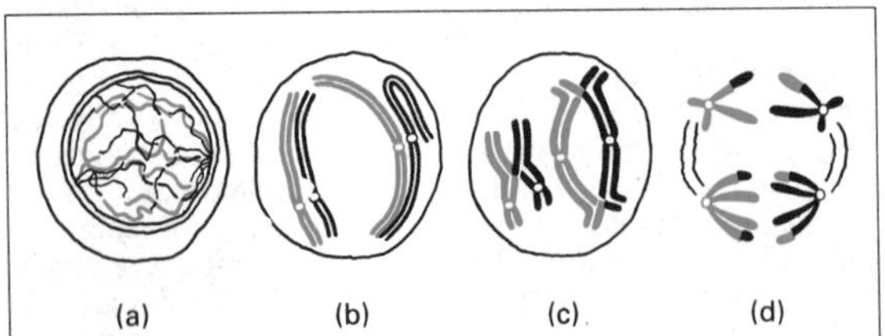

Four stages in meiosis – leptotene (a); zygotene (b); pachytene (c); diplotene (d)

Meir, Golda, [may**eer**] *née* **Goldie Mabovich**, later **Goldie Myerson** (1898–1978) Israeli politician and Prime Minister (1969–74), born in Kiev. Her family emigrated to Milwaukee, USA, when she was eight. She married in 1917 and settled in Palestine in 1921. She was Israeli Ambassador to the Soviet Union (1948–9), Minister of Labour (1949–56), and Foreign Minister (1956–66). As Prime Minister, her efforts for peace in the Middle East were halted by the fourth Arab-Israeli War (1973). She died in Jerusalem. » Arab-Israeli Wars; Israel [i]

Meissen porcelain Porcelain made at Meissen, near Dresden; the first factory in Europe to make true hard paste porcelain. The secret was discovered in c.1710 by Johann Friedrich Böttger (1682–1719). The factory was the most influential in Europe, and is still in production. » porcelain

Meissner effect [**miys**ner] In superconductivity, the exclusion of magnetic fields from the body of the superconducting material; discovered by German physicist Walther Meissner in 1933. If a block of metal is placed in a magnetic field, the field will exist throughout the material. When the temperature is lowered to below a certain substance-dependent critical temperature, the field vanishes from inside the material, being forced to flow round it. » superconductivity

Meissonier, (Jean Louis) Ernest [**may**sonyay] (1815–91) French painter, born at Lyons. His works were largely of military and historical scenes, painted with careful attention to detail, including several of the Napoleonic era. He died in Paris. » French art

Meistersinger [**miy**sterzinger] German guilds of the 14th–16th-c devoted to the encouragement of poetry and music in strict traditional forms. Their activities form the basis for Wagner's opera *Die Meistersinger von Nürnberg* (1868). » Minnesinger; Wagner

Meitner, Lise [**miyt**ner] (1878–1968) Austrian physicist, born and educated in Vienna. She became professor of physics at Berlin, and a member (1917–38) of the Kaiser Wilhelm Institute for Chemistry. In 1917 she shared with Hahn the discovery of the radioactive element protactinium, and became known for her work in nuclear physics. She left Germany for Sweden in 1938, becoming a Swedish citizen the following year. With her nephew O R Frisch she devised the idea of nuclear fission in late 1938. She retired to England in 1960, and died at Cambridge. » Frisch, Otto Robert; Hahn; nuclear physics

Mekele or **Makale** [ma**ka**lay] 13°32N 39°33E, pop (1984e) 61 580. Capital of Tigray region, NE Ethiopia; airport; salt trade, resin; major refugee centre during the severe drought of 1983. » Ethiopia [i]; Tigray

Meknès [**mek**nes] 33°53N 5°37W, pop (1982) 319 783. City in Centre-Sud province, N Morocco; in the Moyen Atlas, 50 km/31 ml WSW of Fez; one of Morocco's four imperial cities, founded in the 12th-c; several palaces built under Moulay Ismail (1672–1727) to rival the Versailles of Louis XIV; capital until 1728; railway; leather, wine, carpets, pottery; Musée des Arts Marocains, Bou Inania Médersa (14th-c, religious college), Grand Mosque, Moulay Ismail's tomb, gardens of El Haboul. » Morocco [i]

Mekong River [**mee**kong], Chin **Langcang Jiang** River in Indo-China, SE Asia; rises on the Xizang Plateau, China, as the Zi Qu and Za Qu, which join as the Langcang Jiang; flows S and SW, forming the boundary between Laos and Burma, SE to form the Laos–Thailand boundary, then generally E and S into Cambodia and Vietnam, splitting into four major tributaries at its delta on the South China Sea; linked to the Tonlé Sap lake in C Cambodia, which acts as its flood reservoir during the wet season; length c.4 000 km/2 500 ml; navigable for c.550 km/340 ml. » Indo-China

Melaka » Malacca

Melanchthon, Philipp [mel**angk**thon], originally **Philipp Schwarzerd** (1497–1560) German religious reformer, born at Bretten, the Palatinate; his name is a Greek translation of his German surname, 'black earth'. Educated at Heidelberg and Tübingen, he became professor of Greek at Wittenberg in 1516 and Luther's fellow worker. His *Loci Communes* (1521) is the first great Protestant work on dogmatic theology, and the Augsburg Confession (1530) was composed by him. He may have died at Wittenberg. » Augsburg Confession; Luther; Reformation; theology

Melanesia One of the three broad geographical-cultural areas of the Pacific. It includes the islands of New Guinea, the Solomons, Vanuatu, and New Caledonia. (Fiji is more usually included in Polynesia.) The peoples of Melanesia typically have dark skin, kinky hair, large jaws, and a high incidence of blood group B. Numerous languages are spoken among them. The name comes from Greek *melas*, 'black' and *nesos*, 'island'. » Micronesia; Oceania; Polynesia

melanins [**mel**aninz] Dark brown pigments which in different concentrations give coloration (shades of yellow and brown) to the eyes, skin, hair, feathers, and scales of many vertebrates. They are present in the pigment-bearing cells (*melanophores*) of amphibians, reptiles, and fish, as well as in the outer skin cells (*melanocytes*) of mammals. In humans they help protect the skin against the damaging effects of sunlight (ultraviolet radiations). The amount present in the skin is determined by both genetic and environmental factors. » albinism; birthmark; melanocyte-stimulating hormone; melanoma; skin [i]

melanocyte-stimulating hormone (MSH) A type of hormone (a polypeptide) present in the intermediate lobe of the pituitary gland of vertebrates; also known as **intermedin**. It stimulates the synthesis and dispersion of melanins. » hormones; melanins; peptide

melanoma A pigmented tumour due to overgrowth of melanin-producing cells in the basal cell layer of the skin. A proportion become malignant, enlarge rapidly, and spread to other parts of the body (*malignant melanoma*). » keratosis; melanins

melatonin A hormone produced from serotonin, mainly within the pineal gland. Little is known about its precise function. Its secretion from the pineal gland and its concentration within blood both fluctuate, being highest during darkness. In humans it may be associated with the synchronization of circadian rhythms. » circadian rhythm; hormones; pineal gland; serotonin

Melba, Dame Nellie, originally **Helen Mitchell**, married name **Armstrong** (1861–1931) Australian prima donna, born near Melbourne; her professional name derives from the city. She appeared at Covent Garden in 1888, and the purity of her coloratura soprano voice won her worldwide fame. She was created a Dame in 1918, and died in Sydney. 'Peach Melba' and 'Melba toast' were named after her.

Melbourne, William Lamb, 2nd Viscount (1779–1848) British statesman and Whig Prime Minister (1834, 1835–41), born in London. Educated at Eton, Cambridge, and Glasgow, he became an MP in 1805, and Chief Secretary for Ireland (1827–8). Succeeding as second viscount (1828), he became Home Secretary (1830–4) under Grey. He formed a close, almost avuncular relationship with the young Queen Victoria. Defeated in the election of 1841, he resigned and thereafter took little part in public affairs. He died near Hatfield, Hertfordshire. His wife (1785–1828) wrote novels as **Lady Caroline Lamb**, and was notorious for her nine months' devotion (1812–13) to Lord Byron. » Chartism; Grey, Charles; Victoria; Whigs

Melbourne 37°45S 144°58E, pop (1986) 2942000. Port and state capital in Victoria, Australia; on the Yarra R, at the head of Port Phillip Bay; founded in 1835, named after the British Prime Minister, Lord Melbourne; state capital, 1851; capital of Australia, 1901–27; scene of first Federal Parliament, 1901; Melbourne statistical division contains 56 areas; two airports; railway; underground; three universities (1855, 1958, 1964); Australia's biggest cargo port; major financial and communications centre; heavy engineering, textiles, paper, electronics, chemicals, foodstuffs, metal processing, cars, shipbuilding; two cathedrals; Melbourne Cricket Ground; Flemington racecourse (holds the Melbourne Cup horse race); Moomba 10-day festival of street parades, sporting events and cultural activities (Mar); Melbourne Royal Agricultural Show (Sep); Melbourne Cup Day (Nov); site of 1956 summer Olympic Games. » Melbourne Cup; Victoria (Australia)

Melbourne Cup Australia's principal horse race, first run in 1861, for 3-year-olds and upwards. It is now run over 3200 m (2 ml) of the Flemington Park racecourse in Victoria. Held on the first Tuesday in November, Melbourne Cup day is a social occasion like Royal Ascot. » horse racing

Melchett, Baron » **Mond, Ludwig**

Melchites [**mel**khiyts] Christians who follow the Byzantine rite, and who belong to the Patriarchates of Alexandria, Antioch, and Jerusalem. During the 5th-c, they supported the Byzantine emperor in his opposition to the Monophysites (hence their name, which is from the Syriac word for 'royalist'). » Monophysites; Orthodox Church

Meleager [meleeayger] A Greek hero, at whose birth the Moerae appeared and prophesied that he would die when the brand then on the fire had burnt away. His mother, Althaea, removed it and kept it. When the quarrel over the Calydonian boar took place and her brothers were killed, she threw the brand onto the fire, so that he died.

Melies, Georges (1861–1938) French illusionist and film maker, born in Paris, where he made his name as a stage magician. Immediately after the invention of the cinema, he began making short films, and from 1895 was a pioneer in trick cinematography to present magical effects. He fell into obscurity after 1913, and died in poverty in Paris. » special effects

Melilla [may**leel**ya], ancient **Russadir** 35°21N 2°57W, pop (1981) 53593 (with Ceuta). Free port and modern commercial city on N African coast of Morocco; with Ceuta, forms a region of Spain; founded as a port by the Phoenicians; free port since 1863; re-occupied by Spain in 1926; airport; car ferries to Málaga; trade in iron ore; naval shipyard; old town, Church of the Purisima Concepción (16th-c). » Ceuta; Spain [i]

melilot [**mel**ilot] Typically an annual or biennial, native to Europe, Asia, and N Africa, often smelling strongly of new-mown hay on drying; leaves with three toothed leaflets; pea-flowers small, yellow or white, in long, narrow, spike-like inflorescences. Several species are grown for fodder, and it is also used for flavouring cheeses. (Genus: *Melilotus*, 20 species. Family: *Leguminosae*.) » annual; biennial; inflorescence [i]

Mellon, Andrew W(illiam) (1855–1937) US financier, philanthropist, and politician, born in Pittsburgh. He inherited a fortune from his father, with which he established himself as a banker and industrial magnate. Entering politics, he became Secretary of the Treasury in 1921 and made controversial fiscal reforms. He was Ambassador to the UK in 1932–3. He endowed the National Gallery of Art in Washington, and died at Southampton, New York.

melodrama A theatrical genre in vogue after the French Revolution and popularized by Pixerécourt (1773–1884), which became a mass entertainment in Europe and the USA throughout the 19th-c. Originating in operatic theatre, melodrama is a style which emphasizes the depiction of story, the creation of suspense, and the use of sensational episodes. » drama

melody A basic constituent of music, being a succession of pitches arranged in some intelligible order. In Western music, melody is found independently of music's other basic elements (harmony and rhythm) only in plainchant and some folksong. Between c.1675 and 1925, melodic inspiration (a gift for composing 'good tunes') became more and more highly prized as the token of a composer's originality. Since then, many composers have sought to express their musical personalities in other ways, through the use of texture, rhythm, etc. » harmony; music; plainchant; rhythm

melon A trailing or climbing vine with tendrils, probably native to Africa, but cultivated from early times; leaves heart-shaped, palmately-lobed; male and female flowers yellow, c.3 cm/1¼ in in diameter, funnel-shaped; fruit up to 25 cm/10 in long, round or ovoid; rind green or yellow, leathery, sometimes with a net pattern; flesh thick, sweet, surrounding numerous seeds. The types include canteloupe, casaba, honeydew, and musk. (*Cucumis melo*. Family: *Cucurbitaceae*.) » climbing plant; palmate

Melos [**mee**los], Gr **Mílos** area 151 sq km/58 sq ml. Southwesternmost island of the Cyclades, Greece, in the S Aegean Sea; main town, Plaka; minerals, fruit, olives, cotton, tourism;

'Venus de Milo' sculpture (Louvre, Paris) discovered here in 1820. » Cyclades

Melpomene [mel**pom**inee] The Greek Muse of tragedy. » Muses

meltdown A catastrophic event in a nuclear reactor. If control of the release of thermal energy is lost, the temperature of the reacting core rises to a point at which the fuel rods melt, and radioactive material may be released into the environment. » Chernobyl; nuclear reactor [i]; radioactivity

melting point The temperature at which a solid becomes liquid. If heat is applied to a solid, its temperature rises until the melting point is reached, when heat energy is then absorbed to form liquid from the solid. Temperature continues to rise once the melting is complete. » latent heat; phases of matter [i]

Mélusine In French folklore, a half-human fairy who locked her father into a mountain and was condemned to change into a serpent from the waist down every Saturday. Her husband, Raymond de Poitiers of Lusignan, broke his promise never to see her on Saturdays, and she disappeared, to be heard lamenting whenever one of her descendants was about to die. » folklore

Melville, Herman (1819–91) US novelist, born and died in New York City. He became a bank clerk, but in search of adventure joined a whaling ship bound for the South Seas (1841). His journeys were the subject matter of his first novels, *Typee* (1846) and *Omoo* (1847). He married in 1847, and in 1850 took a farm near Pittsfield, Massachusetts, where he wrote his masterpiece, *Moby Dick* (1851), a classic among sea stories. After 1857 he wrote only some poetry, leaving his long story, *Billy Budd, Foretopman* in manuscript. » American literature; novel

membrane potential The voltage differential maintained across the plasma membranes of most living cells, with the inside of the cell being negatively charged with respect to the outside; also known as *transmembrane potential*. Its magnitude is determined by differences in the concentrations of ions on the two sides of the membrane, varying from about −9 to −100 mv according to the nature of the cell. » action potential; cell; ion

membranophone Any musical instrument in which the sound is generated by the vibrations of a stretched membrane. The most important are the various kinds of drum. Membranophones form one of the main categories in the standard classification of Hornbostel and Sachs (1914). » drum; kazoo; musical instruments; percussion [i]; tambourine

Memlinc or **Memling, Hans** (c.1440–94) Flemish religious painter, born at Seligenstadt. He lived mostly at Bruges, and was perhaps a pupil of Roger van der Weyden. His works include the triptych of the 'Madonna Enthroned' at Chatsworth (1468) and the 'Marriage of St Catherine' (1479). He was also an original and creative portrait painter. » Flemish art; Weyden

Memnon [**mem**non] In Greek mythology, a prince from Ethiopia, the son of Eos and Tithonus, who was killed at Troy by Achilles. The Greeks thought that one of the gigantic statues at Thebes represented him; it gave out a musical sound at sunrise. » Achilles

Memorial Day A national holiday in the USA, held on the last Monday in May in honour of American war dead; originally instituted as **Decoration Day** in 1868 in honour of soldiers killed in the American Civil War.

memory The ability to access information in the mind relating to past events or experiences. Theories of memory deal with the causes of memory loss (pure decay or interference from other material), and the possibility that there may be two or more distinct stores from which information decays at different rates (**short-** and **long-term** memory). They also analyse the distinction between **episodic** memory (memory for specific events experienced by the individual) and **semantic** memory (knowledge), and the way incoming information and previous knowledge interact in language comprehension and problem solving ('working memory'). Practical issues include the reliability of eye-witnesses' memories (eye-witnesses are easily biased by information they receive after the witnessed event). » amnesia; cognitive psychology; mental imagery; memory, computer

memory, computer A part of a computer which stores, either permanently or temporarily, programs and data. There are two basic types of internal memory used in digital computers: **Random Access Memory** (RAM) and **Read-Only Memory** (ROM) or variants thereof. All are available as integrated circuits which allow very rapid data transfer between the memory and the central processing unit. » auxiliary store; bubble memory; buffer (computing); cache memory; central processing unit; EAROM; EPROM; PROM; RAM; ROM

Memphis (ancient Egypt) An important town in ancient Egypt on the W bank of the Nile, S of the Delta. The capital of Lower Egypt under the pharaohs, it declined in importance under the Ptolemies, who made Alexandria their capital instead. The necropolis of Memphis is at Saqqarah. » pharaoh; Ptolemy I Soter; Saqqarah [i]

Memphis (USA) [**mem**fis] 35°08N 90°03W, pop (1980) 646 356. Seat of Shelby County, SW Tennessee, USA; a port on the Mississippi R; largest city in the state; site of military fort, 1797; city established, 1819; captured by Union forces during the Civil War (battle of Memphis, 1862); severe yellow-fever epidemics in the 1870s; airfield; railway; two universities (1848, 1912); important market for cotton, hardwood lumber, livestock, poultry; food and paper products, chemicals, textiles, fabricated metals; Martin Luther King Jr assassinated here (1968); Graceland, home of Elvis Presley; Beale Street, made famous by W C Handy and regarded as the birthplace of the blues; Mud Island Park. » American Civil War; blues; King, Martin Luther; Presley; Tennessee

Menai Straits [**men**iy] Channel separating Ynys Môn (Anglesey) from the mainland of NW Wales, UK; length 24 km/15 ml; width varies from 175 m/575 ft to 3.2 km/2 ml; crossed by the Menai Suspension Bridge, built by Telford (1819–26), length 176 m/580 ft, and the Britannia railway/road bridge (1980), rebuilt after fire in 1970 seriously damaged the original tubular railway bridge of Robert Stephenson (1846–9). » Stephenson, Robert; Telford, Thomas; Ynys Môn

Menander (c.343BC–291BC) Greek comic dramatist, born in Athens. Only a few fragments of his work were known until 1906, and in 1957 the complete text of the comedy *Dyskolos* (The Bad-Tempered Man) was found in Geneva. He was drowned while swimming at the Piraeus, the port of Athens. » comedy; Greek literature; poetry

menarche [**men**ahkee] The first menstrual bleeding of the human female, which occurs during puberty (10 to 15 years of age depending on nutritional and emotional status). It signifies the approach of reproductive maturity, but does not indicate the attainment of full fertility, which is delayed until the adult pattern of pituitary and gonadal hormone secretion is established, and menstrual cycles become regular. » menstruation

Menchik-Stevenson, Vera (Francevna) (1906–44) Russian-British chess player, born in Moscow. She became a naturalized British subject on her marriage in 1937. Recognized as the finest of all female chess players, she held the world title from 1927 (the first champion) to 1944, when she was killed during a London air-raid. » chess

Mencius, properly **Mengzi** or **Meng-tse** (c.372–c.298 BC) A Chinese sage, born in Shantung, who founded a school modelled on that of Confucius. For over 20 years he searched for a ruler who would put into practice his system of social and political order; but, finding none, he retired in order to write. After his death his disciples collected his sayings and published them as the *Book of Meng-tse*. » Confucianism

Mencken, H(enry) L(ouis) (1880–1956) US philologist, editor, and satirist, born and educated in Baltimore. He became a journalist and literary critic, and greatly influenced the US literary scene in the 1920s. His major work, *The American Language*, was first published in 1918, and in 1924 he founded the *American Mercury*, editing it until 1933. He died in Baltimore. » comparative linguistics; dictionary; English; satire

Mendel, Gregor Johann (1822–84) Austrian botanist, born near Odrau, Silesia. Entering an Augustinian monastery in Brünn, he was ordained a priest in 1847. After studying science at Vienna (1851–3) he returned to the monastery, and in 1868 became abbot there. Meanwhile he had been pursuing research into plant breeding, and eventually established his 'laws' governing the nature of inheritance. He died at Brno, Czechoslovakia. Recognition came many years after his death, when his key article, 'Experiments with plant hybrids' (1866), was discovered. » genetics [i]; Mendel's laws

Mendel's laws The fundamental principles governing the nature of inheritance, proposed by Austrian botanist Gregor Mendel in 1866. In a series of experiments on garden peas, he crossed varieties differing in particular features (eg tall by short), and observed the effects on the individuals in each generation. His experiments led him to compose a series of laws. The *principle of gametic purity* states that inherited pairs of factors segregate at germ cell formation and recombine at fertilization, ie that a sex cell (sperm, ovum, pollen) can carry only one from each pair of factors available to it. This showed that observable characteristics are not transmitted directly from generation to generation as previously thought, but that there are discrete factors responsible for their appearance. The *law of independent segregation* states that when more than one pair of factors are involved in a cross, each pair segregates independently of the others. The mechanisms which Mendel described in his laws remain the basis for all modern genetics, though they have been refined. » Correns; de Vries, Hugo; gene; genetics [i]; Mendel

Mendeleyev, Dmitri Ivanovich [mende**lay**ef] (1834–1907) Russian chemist, born at Tobolsk. He became a teacher, then studied at Odessa, St Petersburg, and Heidelberg, becoming professor of chemistry at St Petersburg from 1866. He devised the periodic classification (or table) by which he predicted the existence of several elements which were subsequently discovered. It forms the central concept in modern inorganic chemistry. Element 101 (*mendelevium*) is named after him. He died in St Petersburg. » periodic table

Mendelssohn(-Bartholdy), (Jakob Ludwig) Felix [**men**duhlsuhn] (1809–47) German composer, the grandson of Moses Mendelssohn, born the son of a Hamburg banker who added the name Bartholdy. Among his early successes as a composer was the *Midsummer Night's Dream* overture (1826). In London in 1829 he conducted his C minor symphony. A tour of Scotland in the summer inspired him with the *Hebrides* overture and the *Scottish Symphony*. He founded an Academy of Arts at Berlin in 1841, and a music school at Leipzig in 1843. Other major works include his oratorios *St Paul* (1836) and *Elijah* (1846). He died soon after at Leipzig.

Mendelssohn, Moses [**men**duhlsuhn] (1729–86) German philosopher, literary critic, and biblical scholar, born at Dessau. He studied at Berlin, and later became the partner of a rich silk manufacturer. A zealous defender of enlightened monotheism, he was an apostle of deism. His major works include *Phädon* (1767), on the immortality of the soul, and *Jerusalem* (1783). He died in Berlin. » deism

Menderes, Adnan [**men**derez] (1899–1961) Turkish statesman and Prime Minister (1950–60), born near Aydin. Though educated for the law, he became a farmer, and entered politics in 1932, at first in opposition, then with the party in power under Atatürk. In 1945 he was one of the leaders of the new Democratic Party and became Prime Minister when it came to power. He was deposed in an army coup, put on trial, and hanged at Imrali. » Atatürk, Mustapha Kemal

Mendès-France, Pierre [**mãdez frãs**] (1907–82) French statesman and Prime Minister (1954–5), born and died in Paris. He entered parliament in 1932, and in 1941 escaped to join the Free French forces in England. He was Minister for National Economy under de Gaulle in 1945, and became a prominent member of the Radical Party. As Prime Minister, he ended the war in Indo-China, but his government was defeated on its N African policy. A firm critic of de Gaulle, he lost his seat in the 1958 election. » de Gaulle; France [i]; Vichy

Mendicant Orders (Lat *mendicare*, 'to beg') Religious Orders in which friars were not permitted to hold property, either personally or in common. Such Orders were able to survive only through the charity of others. » Augustinians; Carmelites; Dominicans; Franciscans; monasticism; Orders, Holy

Mendip Hills Hill range in Somerset and Avon, SW England; extending 37 km/23 ml NW–SE from Weston-super-Mare to near Shepton Mallet; rises to 326 m/1 069 ft at Blackdown; includes limestone caves of Cheddar Gorge; traces of former Roman lead mines. » Cheddar; England [i]

Mendoza [men**th**ohsa] 32°48S 68°52W, pop (1980) 596 796. Capital of Mendoza province, W Argentina; at foot of Sierra de los Paramillos range, on the R Tulumaya; altitude 756 m/2 480 ft; colonized by Chile in 1561; belonged to Chile until 1776; destroyed by fire and earthquake in 1861; four universities (1939, 1959, 1960, 1968); airport; railway; trading and processing centre for a large, irrigated agricultural area, dealing mainly in wine; annual wine festival (Feb). » Argentina [i]

Menelaus [meni**lay**uhs] In Greek legend, the younger brother of Agamemnon. He was King of Sparta, and married to Helen. He took part in the Trojan War and was delayed in Egypt on his return. Finally he settled down at Sparta with Helen again. » Agamemnon; Helen; Proteus; Trojan War

Mengistu, Haile Mariam (1941–) Ethiopian leader, born in Addis Ababa, Chairman of the Provisional Military Administrative Council (1977–87), and President (since 1987). He trained at Guenet military academy, and took part in the attempted coup against Haile Selassie in 1960, but was not put on trial. In 1977, after a further coup, he became undisputed ruler. He models himself on Fidel Castro, and has set out to create a socialist state in Ethiopia aligned with the communist bloc. » Castro; Derg; Ethiopia [i]; Haile Selassie I; socialism

Mengs, Anton Raphael (1728–79) German painter, born at Aussig, Bohemia. He settled in Rome, where under Winckelmann's influence he directed a school of Neoclassical painting. In Madrid (1761–70, 1773–6) he decorated the dome of the grand salon in the royal palace with the 'Apotheosis of the Emperor Trajan'. He died in Rome. » German art; Neoclassicism (art and architecture); Winckelmann

menhir [**men**eer] (Welsh *maen* 'stone' + *hir* 'long') In European prehistory, a single standing stone or megalith. A striking example is the tapering granite pillar at Locmariaquer near Carnac, Brittany, known as 'Le Grand Menhir Brisé'; now lying in four pieces, this formerly stood 20 m/67 ft high and weighed an estimated 256 tonnes. » megalith

Ménière's disease [muhn**yair**] Paroxysmal attacks of vertigo (a subjective sense of rotation), usually abrupt in onset, accompanied by tinnitus and progressive deafness, and sometimes associated with sweating, nausea, pallor, and vomiting. It is a disorder of the inner ear of unknown cause, affecting mainly middle-aged and elderly persons. It is named after French physician Prosper Ménière (1799–1862). » deafness; ear [i]; tinnitus

meningitis An infection of the membranes (pia and arachnoid) covering the brain. It may be caused by bacteria (eg *Neisseria meningitis*, pneumococci, haemophylus, tuberculosis, or other species, by viruses, and more rarely by fungi (eg *Cryptococcus*). Entrance of the infectious agent is by way of the nose or by the blood stream. **Viral meningitis** is usually short-lived and harmless; **bacterial meningitis** is more serious and may cause death. The onset is usually sudden, with headache, fever, stiffness of the neck on flexion, and dislike of the light (*photophobia*). Diagnosis is made by lumbar puncture which allows the organism to be identified and appropriate antibiotics given. » brain [i]; lumbar puncture

meniscus [muh**nis**kuhs] » **surface tension** [i]

Mennonites [**men**uhniyts] Dutch and Swiss Anabaptists who later called themselves Mennonites after one of their Dutch leaders, Menno Simons (1496–1559). They adhere to the Confession of Dordrecht (1632), baptise on confession of faith, are pacifists, refuse to hold civic office, and follow the teachings of the New Testament. Most of their 1 million adherents live in the USA. » Anabaptists

Menon, Krishna » **Krishna Menon**

menopause Strictly defined as the cessation of menstruation, but more commonly used to refer to the period of time (up to eight years prior to the cessation of menstruation) when the menstrual cycle becomes less regular, due to the loss of responsiveness of the ovaries to gonadotrophins; also known as **climacteric**. Even though menstruation may be irregular, reproductive capacity is not lost. The complete cessation of menstruation usually occurs between 45 and 50 years. It is often accompanied by physical (sweating, hot flushes, vaginitis) and psychogenic (depression, insomnia, fatigue) disturbances, which generally respond to oestrogen therapy. Menopause is unique to the human female, but its significance is unclear. » gonadotrophin; menstruation; oestrogens

menorah [muh**noh**ra] A candelabrum of seven branches, with three curving upwards on each side of a central shaft, an ancient symbol of Judaism, and the official symbol of the modern State of Israel. In the Bible, it was originally part of the furnishings of the Tabernacle in the wilderness, and eventually of the Jerusalem Temple. The Hanukkah candleholder has eight arms, and in many synagogues the arms number other than seven, so as to avoid direct imitation of that in the Temple (forbidden in the Talmud). » Judaism; Tabernacle; Temple, Jerusalem

menorrhagia [menuh**ray**jia] Excessive menstrual bleeding. It commonly results from local abnormalities of the uterus, but also arises from disorders of the hormones controlling normal menstruation. » menstruation

Menotti, Gian Carlo (1911–) US composer, born in Cadegliano, Italy. He settled in the USA at 17, and achieved international fame with a series of operas that began with *Amelia goes to the Ball* (1937). *The Consul* (1950) and *The Saint of Bleecker Street* (1954) both won Pulitzer Prizes. *Amahl and the Night Visitors* (1951) was a successful television opera. In 1958 he established the Festival of Two Worlds at Spoleto, Italy.

Mensa (Lat 'table') An inconspicuous constellation in the S sky. It was named by Lacaille after Table Mountain, Cape Province, South Africa, where he had an observatory. » constellation; Lacaille

Mensa International An organization of people whose members are admitted only after they 'have established by some standard intelligence test, that their intelligence is higher than 98% of the population'. Founded in England in 1945, branches now exist in over 60 countries. » intelligence

Mensheviks (Russ 'minority-ites') Members of the moderate faction of the Marxist Russian Social Democratic Labour Party, led by J Martov (pseudonym of Yulii Osipovich Tsederbaum, 1878–1923), which split with Lenin's Bolsheviks at the party's second congress in 1903. The Mensheviks opposed Lenin's policies on party organization and his revolutionary tactics. In 1917 some Mensheviks joined the provisional government. » Bolsheviks; Lenin; Russian Revolution

menstruation A periodic discharge from the vagina of blood, mucus, and debris from the disintegrating mucous membrane of the uterus, in response to hormone changes when the ovum is not fertilized. It lasts 3–5 days. In women of child-bearing age (13–50 years), it occurs at approximately four-week intervals, reflecting the changing hormone production in the ovaries. The first menstrual period in life is known as *menarche*, the last as *menopause*. Menstruation does not occur during pregnancy, and for some time after (up to three months), because of the change in balance of reproductive hormones. Menstrual regularity may be disrupted by a number of factors, of which nutritional status and emotion are perhaps the most common. It also occurs in monkeys and apes. » amenorrhea; dysmenorrhea; Graafian follicle; lactation; menarche; menopause; menorrhagia

mental disorders A group of conditions with psychological or behavioural manifestations which may be accompanied by impaired functioning. This may be a result of current distress or an increased risk of morbidity or mortality. The range of causes includes biological, psychological, genetic, social, and physical disturbances. The features of a mental disorder exclude normal reactions to distressing events and deviant behaviours. The disorders do not have discrete boundaries, nor do people suffering from the same disorder necessarily display many features in common. Examples include anxiety, dementia, drug addictions, eating disorders, schizophrenia, and sleep disorders. Mental retardation and disorders of development are usually considered separately. » anorexia nervosa; bulimia nervosa; complex; conversion (psychiatry); dementia; mental handicap; neurosis; paranoia; psychiatry; psychosis; schizophrenia

mental handicap A condition in which people have an intelligence quotient of less than 70, with deficits in their ability to live independently, evidenced before age 18. Four types are generally recognized: *mild* (IQ 50–70), *moderate* (IQ 35–49), *severe* (IQ 20–34), and *profound* (IQ<20). The cause is unknown in c.75% of cases. Theories include currently undetectable brain damage and environmental deprivation. Known causes include genetic conditions (eg Down's syndrome), infectious diseases (eg rubella), and noxious chemicals (eg thalidomide). Accidents are one of the major causes in early childhood. » intelligence

mental imagery The experience of vivid, perceptual-like activity in the mind, in the absence of a corresponding external stimulus; usually but not exclusively visual. It is useful as a memory aid; for example, imageable words are better remembered. » memory

mentalism A form of entertainment in which a magician fakes special mental powers, such as psychic ability or mathematical genius. There are numerous techniques involved, including the use of confederates, subtle cues, and sleight of hand. » paranormal

menthol $C_{10}H_{20}O$, a terpene alcohol, melting point 43°C. A waxy solid, the main constituent of oil of peppermint, it is used as a flavouring, a mild antiseptic, a decongestant, and a local anaesthetic. Its structure is closely related to that of camphor. » alcohols; camphor [i]; terpene

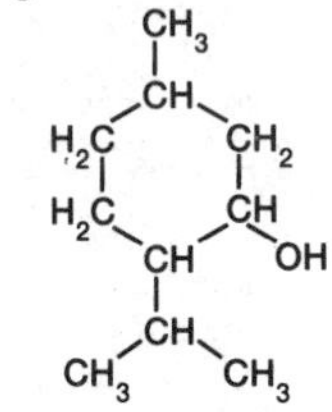

menu (computing) A set of options presented to the user by a computer program. A program which communicates with the user solely by providing choices from interlinked menus is said to be **menu-driven**. » program, computer

Menuhin, Yehudi [**men**yooin] (1916–) US-British violinist, born in New York City. At the age of seven he appeared as soloist with the San Francisco Symphony Orchestra. This was followed by appearances all over the world as a prodigy, and he won international renown as a virtuoso violinist. He reserved an honorary knighthood in 1965, and was made a member of the Order of Merit in 1987. He took British nationality in 1985. His sister **Hephzibah** (1920–81) was a gifted pianist. » violin

Menzies, Sir Robert (Gordon) (1894–1978) Australian statesman and Prime Minister (1939–41, 1949–66), born at Jeparit, Victoria. He practised as a barrister before entering politics, becoming an MP in the Victorian parliament in 1928, and moving to the Federal House of Representatives in 1934. He was Commonwealth Attorney-General (1935–39), and Prime Minister twice – first as head of the United Australia Party, then as head of the Liberal Party, which he formed in 1944. He was knighted in 1963, retired in 1966, and died in Melbourne. » Liberal Party (Australia); Suez Crisis

Mercator, Gerhardus, originally **Gerhard Kremer** or **Cremer** (1512–94) Flemish mathematician, geographer, and mapmaker, born at Rupelmonde, Flanders, and a student at Louvain. The projection which has since borne his name was used in his map of 1569. He died at Duisberg. » map projection [i]; Mercator's map projection

Mercator's map projection A map projection devised in 1569 by Gerhardus Mercator, which was the first of real use for navigation purposes. It is based on parallels equal in length to that of the Equator. The distance between the meridians is stretched away from the Equator. As a result, a line of constant bearing appears as a straight line on Mercator's projection, rather than the curved line on a globe. The major distortion is that area is exaggerated at high latitudes; for example Greenland appears as large as S America even though it is only c.10% of the latter's area. » map; map projection [i]; Mercator; meridian

Mercedario, Cerro [mersay**da**rioh] 31°58S 70°10W. Andean peak rising to 6770 m/22211 ft in San Juan province, W Argentina, near the Chilean border. » Andes

Mercer, David (1928–) British dramatist, born at Wakefield,

Yorkshire. Educated in Newcastle, he became a teacher, then turned to writing. His plays include *Ride a Cock Horse* (1965), *After Haggerty* (1970), and *Cousin Vladimir* (1978). He has also written screenplays (eg *Morgan*, 1965; *Family Life*, 1972) and many TV plays. » drama; English literature; theatre

mercerizing The chemical treatment of cotton with strong alkalis, to make it stronger, lustrous, and more silk-like. The process was devised in 1844 by English chemist John Mercer (1791–1866). » alkali; cotton [i]

Merchant Adventurers Local guilds exporting woollen cloth from 14th-c London. Formed in 1407, they increasingly dominated trade at the expense of smaller ports; from 1496, their headquarters were in Antwerp. Although numbering only a few dozen, they were important in economy and finance until the mid-17th-c, because woollen cloth was the country's leading export. » guilds

merchant bank A UK bank specializing in trading and company financial matters; similar to a US *investment bank*. The term is traditionally used to describe members of the Accepting Houses Committee, dealing primarily with bills of exchange. Its functions include financing overseas trade; raising new finance for companies; helping exporters hedge against currency fluctuations; advising companies on mergers and takeovers; and issuing and marketing Eurodollars and other Eurocurrency. » accepting house; bill of exchange; investment bank; issuing house

Merchant Navy The commercial ships of a nation, a term first used by King George V in a speech in 1922. The mercantile marine was classed as an armed service throughout World War 2, and developed a highly efficient manning and recruiting service which was reconstituted for peace time. In 1939 there were over 9 000 ships in Britain's Merchant Navy. In 1988 the number had dwindled to 2 142. » navy

Mercia A kingdom of the Anglo-Saxon heptarchy, with its main centres at Tamworth, Lichfield, and Repton. Mercian supremacy over the other Anglo-Saxon kingdoms reached its height under Offa, whom Charlemagne treated as an equal, but by the early 10th-c Mercia had been brought under the direct rule of Wessex. » Anglo-Saxons; Offa; Wessex

Merckx, Eddy, byname **The Cannibal** [merks] (1945–) Belgian cyclist, born at Woluwe St Pierre, near Brussels. He won the Tour de France a record-equalling five times (1969–72, 1974), the Tour of Italy five times, and all the major Classics, including the Milan-San Remo race seven times. World Amateur Road Race champion in 1964, he won the professional title three times. He won more races (445) and more classics than any other rider. He retired in 1978 and established his own bicycle manufacturing company. » cycling

Mercouri, Melina, originally **Anna Amalia Mercouri** (1923–) Greek film actress, born in Athens. She started in films in 1955, and found international fame in 1960 with *Never on Sunday*. Always politically involved, she was exiled from Greece (1967–74), during which time she played in several British and US productions, such as *Topkapi* (1964) and *Gaily, Gaily* (1969). She returned to be elected to parliament in 1977, and became Minister of Culture from 1981.

mercury Hg (Lat *hydrargyrum*), element 80, melting point −39°C, boiling point 357°C. Silver in colour, unique among metals by being a liquid at normal temperatures; also known as **quicksilver**. A relatively unreactive metal, it is found free in nature, but is much more common as the sulphide (HgS), called *vermilion* when used as a pigment. This is roasted in air to give the metal directly: $HgS + O_2 \rightarrow Hg + SO_2$. The metal is used in both temperature- and pressure-measuring equipment. In its compounds, it shows oxidation states +1 and +2, the +1 state being the unusual dimeric ion Hg_2^{2+}. Hg_2Cl_2 was formerly much used as a purgative; the fulminate, $Hg(CNO)_2$, is a detonator. The vapour and soluble salts are toxic and cumulative; a particularly virulent form in the environment is the ion CH_3Hg^+. » chemical elements; metal; pigments; RR90

Mercury (astronomy) The innermost planet of the Solar System; an airless, lunar-like body with the following characteristics: mass 3.28×10^{26}g; radius (equatorial) 2 440 km/1 516 ml; mean density 5.5 g/cm^3; rotational period 59 days; orbital period 88 days; obliquity ~0°; orbital eccentricity 0.206; mean distance from the Sun 57.9×10^6 km. It has a relatively high orbital ellipticity and slow rotation rate, making three rotations for every two revolutions about the Sun. The equatorial surface temperatures reach 430°C, while on the night side temperatures may drop to −180°C. It has a weak magnetic field (c.1% of Earth's), and a very tenuous sodium atmosphere. It is a high temperature 'end member' of the family of planets, with a greater proportion of iron (65–70% by mass) than others, and the correspondingly highest density. One hemisphere of the surface was mapped by Mariner 10 (1974–5), the other is still unknown. It has an apparently lunar-like crust, shaped by asteroidal bombardment and episodes of volcanic flooding. Its most notable surface feature is the 1 300 km/800 ml diameter impact basin *Caloris*. Planet-wide evidence of crustal faulting in the form of elongated scarps suggests tidal despinning early in its history because of the Sun's gravitational interaction. » Mariner programme; planet; Solar System

Mercury (mythology) or **Mercurius** A Roman god, principally of trading, who was identifed with Hermes, and inherited his mythology. » Hermes (mythology)

Mercury programme The first US crewed spaceflight programme, the precursor to the Gemini and Apollo programmes, using a one-man crew. The first suborbital flight (5 May 1961) was piloted by Alan Shepard; the first orbital flight (20 Feb 1962) by John Glenn. The spacecraft demonstrated a life support system and the basic elements of recovery – retro-rocket de-orbit, drag braking re-entry, and water landing and recovery. There were two suborbital flights, and four orbital flights. » Apollo programme; astronaut; Gemini programme; space physiology and medicine

Meredith, George (1828–1909) British novelist, born in Portsmouth, Hampshire. He was educated privately and in Germany, began to study law, then turned to journalism and letters. He achieved popularity with *The Egoist* (1879) and *Diana of the Crossways* (1885). His main poetic work is *Modern Love* (1862), based partly on his first, unhappy marriage. He died at Box Hill, Surrey. » English literature; novel

merganser [mer**gan**suh] A sea duck native to the N hemisphere and SE Brazil; slender serrated bill; inhabits marine and inland waters; dives for food; eats fish and crustaceans; also known as **saw-bill**. (Genus: *Mergus*, 5 species. Subfamily: *Anatinae*. Tribe: *Mergini*.) » diving duck; duck

merger A business arrangement in which two companies bring together their operations and form a single company. The share capital of the two companies is replaced by an issue of shares in the new company, shareholders of the old companies receiving new shares on a formula basis. The extent to which operations are merged depends on the nature of the companies, ranging from total merging (as when two building firms merge) to the merging of head office activities only (where the two firms are in different business sectors). » Monopolies Commission

meridian At any location, the great circle on the Earth at right angles to the Equator passing from N to S Poles. All celestial objects reach their highest point in the sky here, and the Sun is on the meridian at local noon. » latitude and longitude [i]; meridian circle

meridian circle A telescope specially designed to observe celestial objects only when they cross the meridian; also called a **transit circle**. On a fixed E–W axis which can swing only N–S, it is used for timing the passage of stars across the local meridian. In the past of crucial importance for determining star positions, it is now used for tracking the irregular rotation of the Earth. The excellent instrument at Greenwich, near London, secured the selection of Greenwich as the prime meridian in 1884. » meridian; telescope [i]

Mérimée, Prosper [mereemay] (1803–70) French novelist, born in Paris. He studied law, and held posts in the ministries of the navy, commerce, and the interior, becoming a Senator in 1853. He wrote novels and short stories, archaeological and historical dissertations, and travels. His novels include *Colomba* (1841) and *Carmen* (1843), the source of Bizet's opera. He died at Cannes. » Bizet; French literature; novel

merino A breed of sheep which produce a heavy thick white fleece of very high quality. Originating in Spain, merinos are now found in many parts of the world, being well adapted to hot climates. Australia is by far the largest producer of merino wool.

meristem A region of growth or potential growth in a plant, such as the tips of shoots and roots, or buds. It consists of actively dividing cells (the *initials*) and their undifferentiated daughter-cells which will form the new tissues. » auxins; cambium

Merleau-Ponty, Maurice [mairloh põtee] (1908–61) French phenomenological philosopher, born at Rochefort-sur-mer. He studied at the Ecole Normale Supérieure in Paris, and with Sartre and de Beauvoir helped to found the journal *Les Temps modernes* (1945). He held posts at Lyons (1948) and the Sorbonne (1949), and was appointed to the chair of philosophy at the Collège de France in 1952. His books include *La Structure du comportement* (1942, The Structure of Behaviour) and *Phénoménologie de la perception* (1945, The Phenomenology of Perception). » de Beauvoir; phenomenalism; phenomenology; Sartre

merlin A small falcon native to the N hemisphere; lacks white cheeks of other falcons; inhabits open country, hills, and desert; eats mainly birds (some small mammals and insects); nests on ground or in abandoned nests of other species in trees; also known as **pigeon hawk**. (*Falco columbarius*. Family: *Falconidae*.) » falcon

Merlin In the Arthurian legends, a good wizard or sage whose magic was used to help King Arthur. He was the son of an incubus and a mortal woman, and therefore indestructible; but he was finally entrapped by Vivien, the Lady of the Lake, and bound under a rock for ever. He was famous for his prophecies. » Arthur; incubus

Merneptah (13th-c BC) King of Egypt (1236–1223 BC), the son of Rameses II. He is famous principally for his great victory near Memphis over the Libyans and Sea Peoples (1232 BC). » Sea Peoples

Meroe » **Kush**

meroplankton » **plankton**

Merovingians [merohvinjiuhnz] The original Frankish royal family, formerly chiefs of the Salians, named after the half-legendary Merovech or Meroveus (the 'sea-fighter'). Clovis was the first Merovingian king to control large parts of Gaul; the last to hold significant power was Dagobert I (died 638), though the royal dynasty survived until Childeric III's deposition in 751. » Carolingians; Clovis I; Franks; Huns

Mersey, River [merzee] River in NW England; formed at junction of Goyt and Etherow Rivers; flows 112 km/70 ml W past Warrington, Runcorn, Birkenhead, and Liverpool to form a wide estuary into the Irish Sea at Liverpool Bay; tributaries include the Weaver and Irwell Rivers and the Manchester Ship Canal. » England [i]

Merseyside pop (1987e) 1 456 800; area 652 sq km/252 sq ml. Former county of NW England, comprising five boroughs; created 1974 from parts of Lancashire and Cheshire; on both sides of the R Mersey estuary; chemicals, vehicles, electrical equipment; metropolitan council abolished in 1986; chief town Liverpool; Prescot Museum, Croxteth Hall and Country Park, Speke Hall. » England [i]; Liverpool; Mersey, River

Meru, Mount In Hindu cosmology, a mythical golden mountain (popularly identified with one of the Himalayan peaks), considered the central axis of the universe and the paradisial abode of the gods. It is the subject of many myths, also in Buddhism. Brahma's square city of gold is said to be found at its summit; beneath the mountain are said to be seven underworlds. » Hinduism

mesa [maysa] An area of high, flat land (tableland) with steep escarpments formed by the remnants of horizontal resistant rocks, and underlain by softer rock. Further erosion forms buttes. » butte

Mesa Verde [maysa verday] (Sp 'green table') An area of precipitous canyons and wooded volcanic mesa in SW Colorado, USA, 55 km/34 ml W of Durango; a world heritage site. The most visited archaeological site in the USA, and a National Park since 1906, it is renowned for its Anasazi Indian cliff-dwellings – notably the four-storey Cliff Palace of the 13th-c AD, which has 220 rooms and 23 kivas, and held an ancient population of c.250–350. » Anasazi; kiva

mescal » **century plant**

mescal button » **peyote**

mescalin(e) [meskalin, meskaleen] A hallucinogenic drug from the Mexican cactus *Lophophora williamsi*, also known as *Anhalonium lewinii*. Having been used for centuries for its ability to cause hallucinations, it was made famous in the 1950s by Aldous Huxley in *The Doors of Perception*, and was widely used during the 'psychedelic era' of the 1960s. » cactus [i]; hallucinogens; Huxley, Aldous

mesembryanthemum » **Livingstone daisy**

Meshed » **Mashhad**

Mesmer, Franz Anton (1734–1815) Austrian physician and founder of mesmerism, born near Constance. He studied medicine at Vienna, and about 1772 claimed that there exists a power, which he called 'magnetism', that could be used to cure diseases. In 1778 he went to Paris, where he created a sensation; but in 1785 a learned commission reported unfavourably, and he retired into obscurity in Switzerland. He died at Meersburg. » hypnosis

Mesoamerica or **Middle America** The area covered by C America and Mexico together. Because Mexico is geographically a part of N America, this term is often used to identify features of cultural or historical importance which both regions share. » Chichén Itzá; Monte Albán; Teotihuacán

Mesoamerican ballgame A ritual athletic contest of notable brutality, widespread in Mexico from c.1000 BC to the Spanish Conquest in 1519. Played with a large, solid rubber ball by two opposing teams on a purpose-built court – at Chichén Itzá 83 m/272 ft by 61 m/200 ft with walls 8 m/27 ft high – the ball represented the Sun, the court the cosmos. Post-game ceremonies included the sacrifice of the losers. » American Indians; Hohokam; Mayas

Mesolithic » **Three Age System**

meson [meezon] In particle physics, a collective term for strongly interacting sub-atomic particles having integer spin, each comprising a quark-antiquark pair. Mesons, especially pi-mesons (pions), are responsible for holding together protons and neutrons in atomic nuclei. » boson; CP violation; particle physics; pion

mesopelagic zone The depth zone in the open sea extending from just beneath the epipelagic zone down to a depth of approximately 1 000 m/3 000 ft. In this depth range, not enough light penetrates for photosynthesis, but there may be enough light for vision. The zone also includes the main ocean thermocline and the zone of minimum dissolved oxygen for most parts of the world's oceans. » pelagic environments; photosynthesis; thermocline

Mesopotamia Literally, 'the land between the rivers'; the name in antiquity for the area between the Tigris and Euphrates. It was conventionally divided into two: **Lower Mesopotamia**, the home of the Sumerian and Babylonian civilizations, stretched from the alluvial plain at the head of the Persian Gulf to Baghdad (C Iraq); **Upper Mesopotamia**, the home of the Assyrians, extended from Baghdad to the foothills of E Turkey. Historically, the former is more important: here the world's first urban civilization emerged during the fourth millennium BC. » Assyria; Babylonia; Eridu; Sumer; Ur; Uruk

mesosaurus A lightly built, aquatic reptile known from the late Carboniferous to the early Permian periods in S America and S Africa; up to 1 m/3 ft long; lived in freshwater. (Class: *Anapsida*. Order: *Mesosauria*.) » Carboniferous/Permian period; reptile

mesosphere A region of the atmosphere from c.50–80 km/30–50 ml, separated from the stratosphere below by the stratopause, and from the thermosphere above by the mesopause. It is characterized by rapidly falling temperature with height, from around 0°C to −100°C. Pressure is very low, from c.1 mb at 50 km/30 ml to 0.01 mb at 80 km/50 ml. » atmosphere [i]; stratosphere; thermosphere

Mesozoa [mezuhzoha] A small phylum of multicellular animals found as internal parasites of marine invertebrates such as cephalopod molluscs; covered by hair-like cilia; body organized into two layers, not differentiated into tissues. » Cephalopoda [i]; parasitology; phylum

Mesozoic era [mezoh**zoh**ik] A major division of geological time extending from c.250 million to 65 million years ago; subdivided into the Triassic, Jurassic, and Cretaceous periods. It was the age of the giant reptiles and the beginning of mammalian life. » Cretaceous/Jurassic/Triassic period; geological time scale; RR16

Messager, André (Charles Prosper) [**mes**azhay] (1853–1929) French composer and conductor, born at Montluçon. He wrote several operettas, popular in France and England, and three ballets, notably *Les Deux Pigeons* (1886, The Two Pigeons). He died in Paris.

Messenia [mes**ee**nia] In ancient Greece, the SW part of the Peloponnese. Conquered by the Spartans in the 8th-c and 7th-c BC, its inhabitants were reduced to a state of serfdom called *helotry*. They regained their independence in 369 BC with Theban help. » Sparta (Greek history); Thebes

Messerschmitt, Willy, properly **Wilhelm** (1898–1978) German aviation designer and production chief, born at Frankfurt-am-Main. In 1923 he established the Messerschmitt aircraft manufacturing works, and during World War 2 supplied the Luftwaffe with its foremost types of combat aircraft. From 1955 he worked in the aircraft and automobile industry. He died in Munich. » aircraft [i]

Messiaen, Olivier (Eugène Prosper Charles) [**mes**iã] (1908–) French composer and organist, born at Avignon. He studied at the Paris Conservatoire, and taught at the Schola Cantorum. Taken prisoner at the outbreak of World War 2, he was repatriated in 1942, and became professor of harmony at the Conservatoire. His music, which has evolved new methods of pitch organization and intricate mathematical rhythmic systems, is motivated by religious mysticism and a keen interest in birdsong. He has also been a profoundly influential teacher.

Messiah [muh**si**ya] (Heb 'anointed one') In Jewish writings from c.2nd-c BC onwards, one who would help deliver Israel from its enemies, aid in its restoration, and establish a worldwide kingdom. Many different representations of this figure can be discovered in early Judaism and Christianity. In Christian thought, the role is interpreted as fulfilled in Jesus of Nazareth: 'Christ' is derived from the Greek rendering of the Hebrew word for 'messiah'. » Christianity; David; Jesus Christ; Judaism; messianism

messianism Jewish movements expressing the hope for a new and perfected age. Jewish Orthodoxy reflects this through traditional beliefs in the coming of a personal Messiah who would re-establish the Temple in Jerusalem and from there rule over a redeemed world. Reformed Judaism anticipates the world's perfection by the example of Judaism in human achievements such as social reforms and justice, though still concerned with preserving the identity of the Jewish race within existing states. In contrast, Zionism places emphasis on the physical restoration of the Jewish state in Palestine and the return of exiled Jews there. » Judaism; Messiah; Temple, Jerusalem; Zionism

Messier, Charles [**mes**yay] (1730–1817) French astronomer, born at Badonviller. He had a keen interest in comets, discovering 15, and is mainly remembered for the Messier Catalogue of 108 star clusters, nebulas, and galaxies. Objects were given alphanumeric names (M1, M2, etc), which continue to be used in astronomy. He died in Paris. » comet; galaxy; nebula; star cluster

Messina, Strait of, ancient **Fretum Siculum** Channel between Sicily and the Italian mainland, separating the Ionian and Tyrrhenian Seas; minimum width (N) 3 km/1¾ ml; length 32 km/20 ml; chief ports, Messina (Sicily) and Reggio di Calabria (mainland). » Italy [i]; Sicily

metabolism The complete range of biochemical processes taking place within living organisms. It comprises those processes which produce complex substances from simpler components, with a consequent use of energy (**anabolism**), and those which break down complex food molecules, thus liberating energy (**catabolism**).

In the context of nutrition, it refers to an efficient way of burning food calories to give the body the energy it needs for its various functions. These include walking, running, and all forms of physical exertion, as well as the maintenance of the body's vital functions, such as the heart beat. **Basal metabolism** is the minimum energy expenditure needed to maintain all the vital functions of the body, such as heart beat, urine formation, respiration, and brain function. This can be viewed as the energy expended during sleep, or while the body is resting. In the latter case, the energy expended is approximately 1 kilocalorie per minute – slightly more for men and less for women. » biochemistry; mitochondrion; nutrition; specific dynamic action

Metabolism A Japanese architectural concept and group originally founded in 1960 by Kiyonori Kitukake, Kisho Kurokawa, and Noburo Kawazoe. It is characterized by the use of forms strongly reminiscent of science fiction, and by the synthesis of the public realm with private spaces. The latter often consist of minimal, high-technology capsules. » Japanese architecture

metaethics » **ethics**

metahistory A branch of historical study concerned with the philosophy of history and with the formulation of laws governing the process of change. It also includes a critique of the nature of history, and the means by which historical reasoning is conducted. » history

metal An element whose solid phase is characterized by high thermal and electrical conductivities. Pure metals are all hard, lustrous, opaque, cold to the touch, and more or less malleable. The large majority of the elements are metals, and metallic properties increase from lighter to heavier elements in each group of the periodic table and from right to left in each row. » chemical elements; metallic glass; metallurgy; oxide; solid; RR90

metal fatigue A weakness which develops in a metal structure that has been subjected to many repeated stresses, even though they may be intermittent. As a result, the structure may fail under a load which it could initially have sustained without fracture. The condition was known and studied in the late 19th-c, but it became a subject of particularly serious study after the Comet aircraft disaster of 1954. The causes of metal fatigue remain obscure, but experiment and design now aim at obviating it. » metal

metallic glass Metal in an amorphous condition (ie the atoms of the metal have no regular or crystalline arrangement); first produced in 1960 by US materials scientist William Klement (1937–). Metals, normally crystalline in internal structure, can be converted to this condition (analogous to that of glass) by the rapid cooling of a melt, or by very fine subdivision. Metallic glasses are useful for transformer cores, and for forming (by powder metallurgy methods) very strong components such as gears. » amorphous solid; glass [i]; powder metallurgy

metallography The study of the structure of metals, usually implying the use of microscopy or X-ray diffraction. A metal has several kinds of structure, arising from grain, crystalline structure, and the inclusion of impurities. Many types of examination may be made. In microscopic methods, pioneered in Sheffield in the 1860s by English chemist Henry Clifton Sorby (1826–1908), a polished etched surface is examined at several degrees of magnification. For electron microscopy, a plastic impression is made for use as the specimen. X-ray diffraction may be used to study internal atomic arrangements. » electron microscope [i]; metallurgy; microscope; X-ray diffraction

metalloids Elements midway between being metals and nonmetals. They make a diagonal band across the periodic table, and are generally considered to include boron, silicon, germanium, arsenic, antimony, tellurium, and polonium. » chemical elements; metal; RR90

metallurgy The technique and science of extracting metals from their ores, converting them (often as alloys with other metals) into useful forms, and establishing the conditions for their fabrication. Metallurgy is one of the most ancient arts. Traditional methods were transformed in the latter half of the 19th-c by the application of chemistry, physics, and microscopy. The changes undergone by metals during fabrication and treatment are now important aspects of metallurgy, as are the physics and chemistry of corrosion prevention. The development of metallurgical theory has promoted the growth of a wide practice of testing and inspection. » corrosion; metallography; ore; X-rays

metamorphic rock Rock formed by the alteration of pre-existing rock by intense heat and/or pressure, and often accompanied by the action of hot fluids in the Earth's crust. The changes characteristically involve the growth of new minerals that are stable under these conditions, and a change of texture. *Contact metamorphism* is localized, and produced by the heat of an igneous intrusion. *Regional metamorphism* is associated with large-scale mountain-building processes in the crust. Slates, schists, and gneisses are characteristic rocks formed at progressively higher grades of metamorphism. » gneiss; orogeny; schist; slate

metamorphosis In biology, an abrupt structural change, as seen in the marked changes during the development of an organism, especially the transformation from larva to adult, or from one larval stage to the next. Metamorphosis may be progressive, such as the transformation of tadpole into frog, or may involve an intermediate quiescent phase within a cocoon or chrysalis, during which tissue reorganization takes place. » biology; larva

metaphor (Gr 'carrying from one place to another') A figurative device in language where something is referred to, implicitly, in terms of something else: the Moon is a goddess, life a dark wood, the world a stage. An explicit comparison ('Life, like a dome of many-coloured glass') is a *simile*. Language is essentially metaphoric, making different aspects of experience intelligible in terms of each other. It is for this reason that metaphor is considered essential to poetic expression: enabling us 'To see a world in a grain of sand/And Heaven in a wild flower;/Hold infinity in the palm of your hand,/And eternity in an hour' (Blake). » Blake, William; figurative language; imagery; metonymy; poetry

metaphysical painting A modern art movement which flourished c.1915–18 in Italy. It was founded by Chirico, who painted mysterious empty landscapes inhabited by tailors' dummies, and classical busts casting threatening shadows. » Chirico; Italian art; modern art; Surrealism

metaphysical poetry A term applied to some English poetry of the late 16th-c and early 17th-c, on account of its use of unusual and sometimes difficult ideas in relation to emotional states. Dryden remarked that the chief proponent of the genre, John Donne, 'affects the metaphysics', and Dr Johnson referred to the way in which in this poetry 'heterogeneous ideas are yoked by violence together'. » English literature; imagery; poetry; Cowley; Crashaw; Donne; Herbert, George; Marvell; Vaughan

metaphysics The branch of philosophy which deals with questions about what sorts of things exist (ontology) and how they are related. The term, which originally meant 'after physics', was used by Hellenistic philosophers to name a collection of Aristotle's texts; it then came to acquire the sense 'beyond physics'. *Monists* claim that only one sort of thing really exists; some monists are materialists, others are idealists. *Pluralists* claim that two or more sorts of things ultimately exist; the most familiar variety is a dualism of matter and mind. » Aristotle; determinism; dualism; essentialism; free will; idealism; materialism; monism; ontology; pluralism (philosophy)

Metastasio, Pietro, originally **Pietro (Armando Domenico) Trapassi** (1698–1782) Italian poet, born in Rome. A precocious gift for improving verses gained him a patron in Gravina, a lawyer, who educated him, and left him his fortune (1718). He gained his reputation by his masque, *The Garden of Hesperides* (1722), wrote the libretti for 27 operas, including Mozart's *Clemenza di Tito*, and in 1729 became court poet at Vienna, where he died. » Italian literature; masque; opera; poetry

metastasis [mitastuhsis] The occurrence of tumour tissue in organs distant from the site of the primary tumour. It is characteristic of malignant tumours, where malignant cells are transported by way of the blood stream or lymphatics. » cancer

metatheory In general, any theory whose subject matter is another theory. In logic, it is the investigation of various properties of a formal language, such as whether the language is consistent (no contradiction can be derived from its assumptions) and complete (every logical truth can be derived from its assumptions). » logic

Metaxas, Ioannis [metaksas] (1870–1941) Greek general and dictator (1936–41), born in Ithaka. He fought against the Turks in 1897, studied military science in Germany, and in 1913 became Chief of the General Staff. On the fall of King Constantine I in 1917 he fled to Italy, but returned with him in 1921. In 1935 he became Deputy Prime Minister, and as Premier in 1936 established a fascist dictatorship. He led the resistance to the Italian invasion of Greece in 1940. He remained in office until his death, in Athens. » Constantine I (of Greece); Greece [i]

metazoan [metazohan] A multicellular animal with its body organized into specialized tissues and organs; a member of the subkingdom *Eumetazoa*. » kingdom

Metchnikoff » **Mechnikov**

meteor A streak of light seen when dust, sand, or grit (a **meteoroid**) burns up in the Earth's atmosphere; popularly known as a *shooting star*. A **meteor shower** can be seen when the Earth passes through a trail of dust left by a comet in interplanetary space. An unusual number of meteors (tens per hour) can then be seen emanating from the same part of the sky (the *radiant*). » cosmic dust; meteorite; Perseids

Meteor Crater or **Barringer Crater** An impact crater 1.3 km/0.8 ml across near Flagstaff, Arizona; estimated age 20 000 years. Its origin was determined by geologist Eugene Shoemaker in the 1950s, thereby illuminating the significance of meteoritic impacts on the history of Earth and the planets. It is believed to be the result of the impact of a meteorite c.10 m/11 yd across. » asteroids; meteorite; Tunguska event

Meteora [metayora] 39°44N 21°38E. Rock formations in Trikala department, N Greece, rising to 300 m/1 000 ft from the Pinios plain; site of monasteries, first settled 9th-c AD. » Greece [i]

meteoric water » **groundwater**

meteorite A lump of interplanetary rock that survives a high-speed passage through the atmosphere and hits the ground. Meteorites mostly derive from asteroids, with a few from the Moon and possibly even from Mars. The types are stony, iron, and stony-iron; some have intriguing inclusions of organic material. They often show clear signs of heat abrasion. The biggest known (60 tonnes) was found in Kansas; and Meteor Crater, Arizona, was formed by a meteorite. The oldest is dated at 4.7 billion years. A meteorite is known as a **meteoroid** while travelling in space. » Allende meteorite; asteroids; meteor; Meteor Crater

meteoroid » **meteorite**

meteorology The scientific study of global atmospheric processes: the receipt of solar radiation, evaporation, evapotranspiration, and precipitation, and the determination of, and changes in, atmospheric pressure (and, therefore, wind). Meteorology is generally concerned with the short-term processes (ie hours and days rather than months and seasons) operating in the troposphere and mesosphere, which are the atmospheric layers of the Earth's weather systems. Satellites are now the main source of meteorological data, the first purpose-built device being the American *Tiros I*, launched in 1960. The data are used for weather forecasting, and in meteorological and climatological research. » atmosphere [i]; atmospheric pressure; climate; evaporation; evapotranspiration; insolation; mesosphere; precipitation; Stevenson screen; troposphere; weather; wind [i]

methanal » **formaldehyde**

methane [meethayn, methayn] CH_4. The simplest of the alkane or paraffin hydrocarbons; the tetrahedral shape of methane is fundamental to all organic compounds. Formed by the anaerobic decomposition of organic matter, it is the main constituent of natural gas, and was originally called **marsh gas**. » hydrocarbons; gas 2 [i]

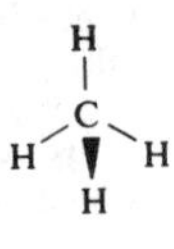

methanogen » **Archaebacteria**

methanoic acid » **formic acid**

methanol [methanol] CH_3OH, also called **methyl** or **wood alcohol**, boiling point 65°C. A colourless liquid, originally produced by the dry distillation of wood, but now synthesized from hydrogen and carbon monoxide. It is an important starting chemical in synthesis, a solvent, and a denaturing agent for ethyl alcohol. It is poisonous, causing blindness and eventually death when drunk. » methylated spirits

Method, the Both a style of acting and a system of training for the working actor, developed in the USA by Lee Strasberg. He was inspired by what he knew of Stanislavski's system, particularly that part which is concerned with the actor's work on himself. The method stresses inner motivation and psychological truth. A well-known exponent of this style is Marlon Brando. » Actors' Studio; Stanislavski; Strasberg

Methodism A Christian denomination founded in 1739 by John Wesley as an evangelical movement within the Church of England, becoming a separate body in 1795. The movement spread rapidly as he travelled the country on horseback and sent other evangelical leaders to the American colonies, where the movement flourished. In the 19th-c, doctrinal disputes caused divisions both in Britain and the USA. These were healed in Britain in 1932, and partially so in the USA, with the uniting of the three main bodies of Methodists. The principal doctrines of the Church are laid down in Wesley's sermons, his notes on the New Testament, and his Articles of Religion. There are 25 million Methodists worldwide. » Church of England; evangelicalism; Wesley, John

Methodius, St » **Cyril and Methodius, Saints**

Methuen [**meth**yooin] , originally **Stedman, Sir Algernon Methuen Marshall** (1856–1924) British publisher, born in London. He was a teacher of Classics and French (1880–95), and began publishing as a sideline in 1889 to market his own textbooks. His first publishing success was Kipling's *Barrack-Room Ballads* (1892), and he published works of Belloc, Chesterton, Conrad, Masefield, R L Stevenson, and Oscar Wilde. He was created a baronet in 1916. » publishing

Methuselah [mi**thoo**zuhla] The eighth and longest-lived of the Hebrew patriarchs, who lived before the Flood. His supposed 969 years makes him the paragon of longevity. » patriarch 1

methyl alcohol » **methanol**

methyl orange [**mee**thiyl, **me**thil] A dye of the diazo type, containing the group –N=N–. It is a pH indicator, being red in its acid form and yellow-orange in base, the change occurring about pH 4. » dyestuff; pH

methylated spirits Ethyl alcohol with additives to make it poisonous and unpalatable, and hence unsuitable for beverage use; also called *denatured alcohol.* Its major ingredients are methanol, pyridine, and benzene. » ethanol

methylbenzene » **toluene**

methylbutane » **pentane**

Metis (astronomy) [**mee**tis] A tiny natural satellite of Jupiter, discovered in 1979; distance from the planet 128 000 km/79 000 ml; diameter 40 km/25 ml. » Jupiter (astronomy); RR4

Métis [**may**tee] The mixed blood offspring of French-Canadian and native Indian marriages; the descendants of the coureurs de bois. » coureurs de bois; Northwest Rebellion; Red River Colony; Red River Rebellion

metonymy [mi**ton**uhmee] (Gr 'name change') The substitution of an attribute of something for the thing itself, such as *the stage* for the theatrical profession, *the crown* for royal powers. It can be compared with **synechdoche** (Gr 'taking up together'), where the part stands for the whole: *hand* for man, *head* for cattle. » figurative language; metaphor

metre (literature) (Gr *metron* 'measure') The recurrence of a rhythmic pattern in poetry, within the line and over larger units (*stanzas*). The subject is problematical, because different languages measure different things to establish metre. In the classical languages, it is length (or 'quantity'); in Chinese, it is pitch; in Japanese, the syllable; in Germanic languages, stress. French metre respects classical quantity. Some English metre works by stress count, overriding the syllable (as in Old English poetry, Hopkins), some by counting both stressed and unstressed syllables (as in the traditional iamb, dactyl, etc). But there is no definitive system of English prosody. » alexandrine; blank verse; heroic couplet; iamb; poetry; verse

metre (physics) Base SI unit of length; symbol m; defined as 1 650 763.73 wavelengths in vacuum of the radiation corresponding to the transition between the levels $2p_{10}$ and $5d_5$ of the krypton-86 atom; commonly used as **kilometre** (km, 10^3 m), **centimetre** (cm, 1/100 m) and **millimetre** (mm, 1/1000 m). » units (scientific)

metric In mathematics, a rule for measuring distance along curves and angles between curves in some space, and containing information on the curvature of the space. It is central to general relativity, which establishes equations relating the metric (and hence curvature) to matter distribution. » Euclid; general relativity; Minkowski space

metronome A device for indicating and determining the tempo of a musical work. The type in common use, patented in 1815 by Johann Nepomuk Maelzel (1770–1838), works like a pendulum clock; its rate of swing, and therefore of 'tick' also, is controlled by an adjustable weight on the upper extension of the pendulum arm, visible outside the wooden box which encloses the rest.

Metropolitan Opera House The chief opera house in New York City, housing the Metropolitan Opera Association. It opened in 1883, and soon acquired an international reputation. In 1966 it moved from its Broadway location to the Lincoln Center. » Bing; Lincoln Center for the Performing Arts; Toscanini; Walter, Bruno

Metropolitan Museum of Art A museum opened in New York City in 1872. It houses a vast and comprehensive collection displaying the artistic achievements of many cultures, ancient and modern. » museum; New York City

Metternich, Klemens (Wenzel Nepomuk Lothar), Fürst von ('Prince of') (1773–1859) Austrian statesman, born in Coblenz. He studied at Strasbourg and Mainz, was attached to the Austrian embassy at The Hague, and became Austrian Minister at Dresden, Berlin, and Paris. In 1809 he was appointed Foreign Minister, and negotiated the marriage between Napoleon and Marie Louise. He took a prominent part in the Congress of Vienna, and between 1815 and 1848 was the most powerful influence for conservatism in Europe, contributing much to the tension that produced the upheaval of 1848. After the fall of the Imperial government in that year, he fled to England, and in 1851 retired to his castle of Johannesberg on the Rhine. He died in Vienna. » Vienna, Congress of; Revolutions of 1848

Metz [mets], ancient **Divodurum Mediomatricum** 49°08N 6°10E, pop (1982) 118 502. Fortified town and capital of Moselle department, NE France; on R Moselle near German border, 285 km/177 ml ENE of Paris; strategic focus of crossroads; residence of Merovingian kings, 6th-c; later, part of Holy Roman Empire; taken by France, 1552; part of Germany from 1871 until after World War 1; scene of major German defence in 1944 invasion; World War 1 military cemetery nearby; airport; road and rail junction; bishopric; university (1971); trade in coal, metals, wine; brewing, tanning, foodstuffs, cement, footwear; Gothic Cathedral of St-Etienne (1250–1380), St-Pierre-aux-Nonnains (7th-c), Eglise Ste-Thérèse, town hall (18th-c), Porte des Allemands (13th-c); Mirabelle Plum Festival (Sep). » Holy Roman Empire; Merovingians; World War 2

Meung, Jean de [merng], or **Jean Clopinel** (c.1250–1305) French satirist, who flourished in Paris under Philip the Fair. He translated many books into French, but his great work is the lengthy continuation (18 000 lines) of the *Roman de la Rose*, in which he replaced allegory by satirical pictures of actual life and an encyclopedic discussion of contemporary learning. » French literature; poetry; satire

Meuse, River [merz], Dutch **Maas**, ancient **Mosa** River in NE France, Belgium, and the Netherlands, rising on the Langres Plateau, NE France; flows N through the Ardennes into Belgium, then W into the Netherlands as the Maas; enters the North Sea through Hollandsch Diep in the Rhine delta; length 950 km/590 ml; navigable for 578 km/359 ml; scene of severe fighting during the German invasions in both World Wars. » Belgium [i]; France [i]; Netherlands, The [i]

Mexican architecture The architecture associated with Mexico. The Spanish conquest of C America led to the introduction of W European architectural forms, first Gothic, then Spanish Renaissance and the Baroque, typified by Mexico Cathedral, Mexico City (1563–1667). In the 20th-c, the influence of the

French Beaux Arts was quickly replaced by International Style tenets. Since the 1950s, the work of Felix Candela and Pedro Ramirez Vásquez has met with increasing recognition, as have the simple vernacular building forms developed by Luis Barragán and others during the 1920s. » architecture; Beaux-Arts; International Style; Mexican art

Mexican art The art associated with Mexico. Before the Spanish conquest (1520–42), the Aztecs produced powerful religious sculpture in stone, richly ornamental frescoes, and polychrome pottery. Since the Revolution (1910), artists such as José Clementi Orozco (1883–1949), David Alfaro (1898–1974), and Diego Rivera (1886–1957) have dedicated their talents to overtly political ends, painting huge murals for the edification of the masses. Modern Mexican art is strongly figurative, tending to caricature, and draws on popular rather than 'high art' traditions. » Pre-Columbian art and architecture

Mexican War (1846–8) A war between Mexico and the USA, declared by the US Congress after it received a message from President Polk calling for war. The war began in territory disputed between Texas (annexed by the USA but claimed by Mexico) and Mexico. US troops invaded the heart of Mexico and forced a capitulation in which Mexico ceded most of the present-day SW United States. » Guadalupe Hidalgo, Treaty of; Polk; Wilmot Proviso

Mexican Wave A spectacular wavelike motion of people standing up and sitting down in sequence, normally at sporting events. It was widely seen during the 1986 FIFA World Cup in Mexico, hence its name; but since then, it has become popular at many sporting events. Major events also often devise carefully choreographed movements of spectators, sometimes holding coloured display items; these first came to prominence at the Moscow Olympics of 1980.

Mexico, Span **México**, official name **United Mexican States**, Span **Estados Unidos de México** pop (1990e) 81 885 000; area 1 978 800 sq km/763 817 sq ml. Federal republic in S North America; divided into 31 states and the federal district of Mexico City; bounded by the USA (N), the Gulf of California (W), the Pacific Ocean (W, SW), Guatemala and Belize (S), and the Gulf of Mexico (E); capital, Mexico City; timezones GMT −8 to −6; chief ethnic groups, Indian–Spanish (60%), Amerindian (30%); official language, Spanish; chief religion, Roman Catholicism (97%); unit of currency, the peso of 100 centavos.

Physical description. Bisected by the Tropic of Cancer; at S end of the N American Western Cordillera; narrow coastal plains border the Pacific Ocean and Gulf of Mexico; land rises steeply to a C plateau, rising to c.2 400 m/7 800 ft around Mexico City; bounded by the Sierra Madre Occidental (W) and

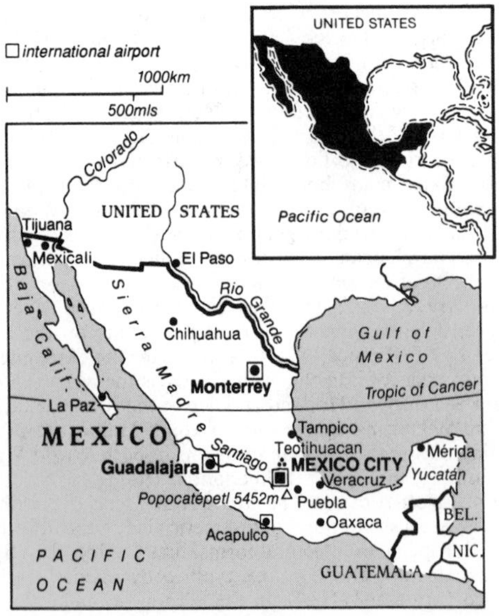

Sierra Madre Oriental (E); volcanic peaks to the S, notably Citlaltépetl (5 699 m/18 697 ft); limestone lowlands of the Yucatán peninsula stretch into the Gulf of Mexico (SE); region subject to earthquakes.

Climate. Great climatic variation between coastlands and mountains; desert or semi-desert conditions in NW; Guaymas, average daily temperature 13–23°C (Jan–Dec), 27–35°C (Aug), average rainfall 91 mm/3.6 in (Aug), 0 mm (Feb); typically tropical climate on E coast; generally wetter on S coast; average annual rainfall at Acapulco, 1 400 mm/55 in; extreme temperature variations in N, very cold in winter, very warm in summer; Mexico City, altitude 2 200 m/7 200 ft, temperatures 6–19°C (Dec–Jan), 13–24°C (Jul), rainfall maximum 170 mm/6.7 in (Jul), minimum 5 mm/0.2 in (Feb).

History and government. Centre of Indian civilizations for over 2 500 years; Gulf Coast Olmecs based at La Venta, Zapotecs at Monte Albán near Oaxaca, Mixtecs at Mitla, Toltecs at Tula, Maya in the Yucatán, Aztecs at Tenochtitlán; Spanish arrival, 1516; Cortés came ashore near Veracruz, 1519, destroying the Aztec capital within two years; Viceroyalty of New Spain established; struggle for independence from 1810; federal republic, 1824; lost territory to the USA in 1836 and after the Mexican War, 1846–8; civil war, 1858–61; occupation of Mexico City by French forces in 1863, with Archduke Maximilian of Austria declared Emperor; withdrawal of French and execution of Maximilian, 1867; revolution, 1910–17; governed by a president, elected for six years, a cabinet, and a bicameral Congress with a 64-member Senate elected for six years and a 400-member Chamber of Deputies elected for three years.

Economy. Wide range of mineral exports; major discoveries of oil and natural gas in the 1970s (now world's fourth largest producer); fluorite and graphite (world's leading producer); gold, silver, lead, zinc, arsenic, cadmium, phosphates, sulphur, copper, antimony, iron, salt; sugar, maize, coffee, tobacco, fruit; large petrochemical industry; iron, steel, aluminium, vehicles, cement, food processing, textiles, clothing, crafts, cotton, cattle, machinery, fishing, tourism. » Aztecs; Cortés; Maximilian, Ferdinand Joseph; Mayas; Mexican architecture/art/War; Mexico City; Olmecs; Toltecs; Zapotecs; RR26 national holidays; RR56 political leaders

Mexico City, Span **Ciudad de México** 19°25N 99°10W, pop (1980) 9 373 353. Federal district and capital of Mexico; in C Mexico, altitude 2 200 m/7 200 ft, in a small, intermontane basin, area 50 sq km/20 sq ml; largest city in the world; oldest capital in continental America; built on the site of the Aztec capital, Tenochtitlán; city centre a world heritage site; capital of the Viceroyalty of New Spain for 300 years until independence; airport; railway; seven universities; vehicles, iron and steel, chemicals, tobacco, glass, food processing, textiles; cathedral (16th–19th-c), National Palace (1692), Castle of Chapultepec (now the national museum of history), national museum of anthropology; ruins of Teotihuacán, 40 km/25 ml NE; location of 1968 summer Olympic Games; scene of a major industrial accident (Nov 1984), when a liquefied gas tank exploded at the San Juan Ixhuatepec storage facility; major earthquake (Sep 1985) killed c.20 000. » Mexico [i]

Mexico, Gulf of area 1 507 600 sq km/581 900 sq ml. Gulf on the SE coast of N America, forming a basin enclosed by the USA (N) and Mexico (E) as far as the Yucatán Peninsula; deepest point, Sigsbee Deep (3 878 m/12 723 ft); receives the Mississippi and Rio Grande del Norte Rivers; low, sandy shoreline with many marshes, lagoons, deltas; oil and natural gas resources on continental shelves.

Meyerbeer, Giacomo [**mi**yerbayr], originally **Jakob Liebmann Meyer Beer** (1791–1864) German operatic composer, born in Berlin. After studying in Italy, he produced operas in the new (Rossini's) style, which at once gained a cordial reception. He then studied French opera, writing the highly successful *Robert le Diable* (1831) and *Les Huguenots* (1836). In 1842 he was appointed *Kapellmeister* at Berlin, but later returned to Paris, where he died. » opera; Rossini

Meyerhold, Vsevolod (Emilievich) [**ma**yerhold] (1874–1940) Russian actor and theatre director, born at Penza. He joined the Moscow Art Theatre as an actor, and was appointed by Stanislavsky as director of the new Studio on Povarskaya Street in 1905. He later became director of the Theatre of the Revolution (1922–4) and of the Meyerhold Theatre (1923–38). He was arrested in 1939 after delivering a defiant speech at a theatre conference, and either died in a labour camp or was executed. » biomechanics; Stanislavsky; theatre

Mezada » **Masada**

mezereon [muhzeeriuhn] A small deciduous shrub growing to c.1 m/3¼ ft, native to chalky areas in Europe and Asia; leaves oval, entire; flowers pink-purple, sometimes white, tubular with four spreading lobes, fragrant, appearing before the leaves. It is often cultivated for ornament. (*Daphne mezereon*. Family: *Thymeleaceae*.) » deciduous plants; shrub

mezzanine [mezaneen] An intermediate low-storey floor in a building, placed within a higher storey. Also known as an **entresol**, it is often used to create extra space within an existing building, and to act as a means of regulating access and circulation.

Mezzogiorno [metzohjeeawnoh] Geographical region comprising all the regions of S Italy excluding Sardinia and the provinces of Latina, Frosinone, and Rieti in S Latium; a largely agricultural area; name ('midday') refers to the heat of the region; a special development area. » Italy [i]

mezzotint A technique of engraving which gives tonal rather than linear effects, and which was therefore very suitable for reproducing oil paintings. Invented c.1640, it was rendered obsolete by photography in the 19th-c. » engraving; oil painting

mi lou » **Père David's deer**

Miami [miyamee] 25°47N 80°11W, pop (1980) 346 865. Seat of Dade County, SE Florida, USA; a port on Biscayne Bay, at the mouth of the Miami R; settled around a military post in the 1830s; since 1945, one of the country's most famous and popular resorts; airport; railway; major tourist industry with extensive recreational facilities (nearly 6 million visitors each year); the processing and shipping hub of a large agricultural region; printing and publishing, fishing, clothing, aluminium products, furniture, transportation equipment; air gateway to Latin America; large numbers of immigrants (nearly half the metropolitan population is Hispanic); major league team, Dolphins (football); Dade County Art Museum, Seaquarium, Villa Vizcaya, the Everglades, Biscayne Boulevard; Orange Bowl Festival (Dec). » Florida; Miami Beach

Miami Beach 25°47N 80°08W, pop (1980) 96 298. Town in Dade County, SE Florida, USA, on an island across Biscayne Bay from Miami; area developed in 1920s; railway; connected to Miami by four causeways; popular year-round resort, famous for its 'gold coast' hotel strip. » Florida; Miami

Miao A Sino-Tibetan-speaking mountain people of SE Asia and S China, constituting many different groups, each with its own language or dialect, customs, and dress. They are agricultural, growing opium as a cash crop. Population more than 4 million, mostly in China. » Sino-Tibetan languages

Micah [miyka] or **Micheas, Book of** One of the twelve so-called 'minor' prophetic books of the Hebrew Bible/Old Testament, attributed to the prophet Micah of Moresheth-gath (in the hill country of Judah), a contemporary of Isaiah in Judah and active in the late 8th-c BC. The work is noted for its attack on social injustices against the poorer classes, as well as for predicting the punishment of Samaria and Jerusalem because of the sins of their people. Some parts of the work may be of later date (6th–5th-c BC). » Isaiah, Book of; Old Testament; prophet

micas [miykuhz] An important group of common rock-forming minerals characterized by a layer structure which gives the crystals a platy form and a perfect basal cleavage. Micas are chemically complex hydrous sheet silicates, commonly containing aluminium, potassium, sodium, magnesium, and iron. Important members are *muscovite* (white mica), a light, silvery-coloured potassium aluminium silicate, and *biotite*, which is dark brown, and contains additional iron and magnesium. » silicate minerals

Michael (1921–) King of Romania (1927–30, 1940–7), born at Sinaia, the son of Carol II. He came to the throne on the death of his grandfather Ferdinand I, his father having renounced his own claims in 1925. In 1930 he was supplanted by Carol, but again made King in 1940 when the Germans gained control of Romania. In 1944 he helped to overthrow the dictatorship of Antonescu, and declared war on Germany. Forced in 1945 to accept a communist-dominated government, he was later compelled to abdicate (1947), and has since lived in exile near Geneva. » Antonescu; Carol II; Romania [i]

Michael (angel) An angel described as the guardian of Israel (*Dan* 10, 12). He appears as a great patron, intercessor, and warrior in later Jewish non-canonical works (eg 1 *Enoch*, the Ascension of Isaiah, the War Scroll at Qumran). In *Jude* 9, he is depicted as an 'archangel' disputing with the Devil over Moses' body, and in *Rev* 12.7 as warring against 'the dragon'. In the later Christian Church, the benefits of his patronage were claimed by Christians, and his feast day is 'Michaelmas Day'. » angel; Gabriel

Michael VIII Palaeologus (c.1225–82) Eastern Roman Emperor (1259–82), born at Nicaea. He distinguished himself as a soldier, and was made Regent for the heir to the throne, John Lascaris, whom he ultimately deposed and banished. His army took Constantinople in 1261, thus re-establishing the Byzantine Empire. He died in Thrace.

Michaelmas daisy A large group of perennial cultivars of aster, mostly derived from the N American *Aster novi-belgii*; stems tall, erect; leaves alternate; flower heads daisy-like, often in large clustered inflorescences; spreading outer florets blue, pink, red, or white; inner disc florets yellow. (Genus: *Aster*. Family: *Compositae*.) » aster; cultivar; floret; inflorescence [i]; perennial

Michaelmas Day [miklmas] In the Christian Church, the feast of St Michael and All Angels (29 Sep); a quarter-day in England and Wales. » quarter-day

Micheas [mikayas] » **Micah, Book of**

Michelangelo, properly **Michelangelo di Lodovico Buonarroti Simoni** (1475–1564) Italian sculptor, painter, and poet, born at Caprese, Tuscany. As a boy he was placed in the care of a stonemason at Settignano, and in 1488 spent three years at Florence with Ghirlandaio. He received the patronage of Lorenzo de' Medici, and after his death (1492) spent three years in Bologna. His 'Cupid' was bought by Cardinal San Giorgio, who summoned him to Rome (1496), where he stayed for four years. He then returned to Florence, where he sculpted the marble 'David'. Though he did not wholly neglect painting, his genius was essentially plastic, and he was far more interested in form than in colour. In 1503 Julius II summoned him back to Rome, where he was commissioned to design the Pope's tomb; but interruptions and quarrels left him able to complete only a fragment. Instead, he was ordered to decorate the ceiling of the Sistine Chapel with paintings, which he did with reluctance in 1508–12. In 1528 danger to Florence forced him to the science of fortification, and when the city was besieged (1529) he was foremost in its defence. His last pictorial achievement was 'The Last Judgment' (1537), and the next year he was appointed architect of St Peter's, to which he devoted himself until his death, in Rome. » Ghirlandaio; Italian art; Renaissance; sculpture

Michelin, André [meeshlĩ] (1853–1931) French tyre manufacturer, born and died in Paris. He and his younger brother **Edouard** (1859–1940) established the Michelin tyre company in 1888, and were the first to use demountable pneumatic tyres on motor cars. They also initiated the production of high-quality road maps and guide books. » tyre

Michelson, A(lbert) A(braham) (1852–1931) US physicist, born at Strelno, Prussia. His family emigrated to the USA, where he became professor of physics at Chicago in 1892. He developed an interferometer, and did important work on the spectrum, but is chiefly remembered for his experiment with US chemist **Edward Williams Morley** (1838–1923) to determine ether drift, the negative result of which set Einstein on the road to the theory of relativity. The first US scientist to win a Nobel Prize (1907), he died at Pasadena, California. » ether 2; special relativity [i]

Michigan [mishigan] pop (1987e) 9 200 000; area 151 579 sq km/58 527 sq ml. State in NC USA, divided into 83 counties; split into two peninsulas by L Michigan and L Huron; the 'Great

Lake State' or the 'Wolverine State'; 26th state admitted to the Union, 1837; settled by the French, 1668; ceded to the British, 1763; handed over to the USA in 1783 and became part of Indiana Territory; Territory of Michigan established, 1805; boundaries greatly extended in 1818 and 1834; capital, Lansing; other major cities include Detroit, Grand Rapids, Warren and Flint; the Montreal, Brule, and Menominee Rivers mark the Wisconsin border; the border with Canada is formed by the St Clair R (between L Huron and L St Clair) and the Detroit R (between L St Clair and L Erie); 99 909 sq km/38 565 sq ml of the Great Lakes lie within the state boundary; highest point Mt Curwood (604 m/1 982 ft); the upper peninsula and N part of the lower peninsula are mainly forested, containing several state parks; a major tourist area; the S part of the state is highly industrialized; motor vehicles and parts, machinery, cement, iron and steel (second in the country for iron ore production); corn and dairy products. » Detroit; Great Lakes; Lansing; United States of America [i]; RR38

Michigan, Lake Third largest of the Great Lakes (area 58 016 sq km/22 394 sq ml) and the only one lying entirely within the USA; 494 km/307 ml long; maximum width 190 km/118 ml; maximum depth 281 m/922 ft; Green Bay indents the Wisconsin shore; linked in the NE with L Huron via the Strait of Mackinac; linked to the Mississippi by canals and rivers; ports include Michigan City, Gary, Chicago, Evanston, Waukegan, Kenosha, Racine, Milwaukee, Manitowoc, Escanaba, Muskegon, Grand Haven. » Great Lakes

Michiko » **Akihito**

Mickiewicz, Adam (Bernard) [mits**kyay**vich] (1798–1855) The national poet of Poland, born near Novogrodek, Lithuania. Educated at Vilna, he published his first poems in 1822. After travelling in Germany, France, and Italy he wrote his masterpiece, the epic *Pan Tadeusz* (1834, Thaddeus). He taught at Lausanne and Paris, and in 1853 went to Italy to organize the Polish legion. He died in Constantinople. » Napoleon III; poetry; Polish literature

MICR (Magnetic Ink Character Recognition) » **character recognition**

micro-organism An organism of microscopic size, typically not visible to the unaided eye; commonly includes bacteria, blue-green bacteria, yeasts, and some other fungi, viroids, and viruses; also referred to as **microbes**. » algae; bacteria [i]; fungus; lichen; Protista; viroid; virus; yeast

microbe » **micro-organism**

microchip A tiny wafer of semiconductor material, such as silicon, processed to form an integrated circuit. Using large scale integration (LSI) or very large scale integration (VLSI), up to 100 000 transistors can be built into the chip. It can do the work of thousands of individual electronic devices. When memory and logic circuits are built in, it becomes known as a **microprocessor**. The costs of microchip technology are relatively small. As a result, microprocessors are now commonly used in calculators, washing machines, video games, and even on credit cards. » integrated circuit; semiconductor; silicon

microclimatology The study of climatic conditions in small areas on or near to surfaces where plants and animals live. The microclimate of an area is determined by the processes operating at the surface: the absorption of solar radiation by plants and soil; the use of heat in evaporation and evapotranspiration; and the effect of air flowing across the surface. » climate; evaporation; evapotranspiration

microcomputer A computer based on a single chip microprocessor plus necessary memory and input and output devices. The term (often abbreviated to **micro**) was first applied to the small desktop computers which first appeared in the 1970s, based originally on 8-bit microprocessors. Since then 16-bit single chip microprocessors have become widely available, and the power and speed of microcomputers based on these have increased dramatically. The distinction in terms of performance between microcomputers and minicomputers is no longer clear. » microchip; mainframe computer

microeconomics » **economics**

microelectronics A branch of electronics concerned with producing and using microcircuits – miniaturized electronic circuits consisting of tiny transistors, integrated circuits, and other electronic components often contained in one microchip. Microelectronic circuiting is used in computers, inertial guidance systems, and spacecraft. » electronics; integrated circuit; microchip; printed circuit; transistor

microfarad » **farad**

microfilm Black-and-white photographic material of extremely fine grain and high resolution for document copying on a greatly reduced scale. Microfilms are usually read by enlarged projection. » photocopying

microfloppy disk » **minidisk**

microgravity A state of free-fall weightlessness experienced in spacecraft. In Earth orbit, the force of gravity is counter-balanced by centrifugal acceleration due to rotation; equivalently, an object in orbit around the Earth may be considered to be always falling towards Earth, while Earth's curvature causes its surface to retreat at the same rate. In practice, due to gravitational effects of the spacecraft itself, and accelerations produced by spacecraft altitude control, it is difficult to obtain less than one-millionth Earth gravity for experimentation. There are limited opportunities for microgravity experiments in the small space stations presently available. » Skylab project; Spacelab; space station

microlight » **hang glider** [i]

micrometer [miy**krom**iter] A gauge for making precise measurements of size, consisting of a spindle moved by a finely-threaded screw. An object is held between the screw's spindle and anvil. The leg of the micrometer is calibrated so that the size of the object can be read from the scale on the barrel.

micrometre » **micron**

microminiaturization The construction of very small electronic circuits and systems to save weight, size, and cost. This process began with the replacement of valves by transistors in the early 1950s, and continued with the development of integrated circuits. It is used extensively in satellite technology and computers. » electronics; integrated circuit; transistor

micron Unit of length; symbol μ; defined as one micrometre or 10^{-6} m; commonly used in biological sciences. » units (scientific)

Micronesia A collection of island groups in the N Pacific. Included are the Marianas, Carolines, Marshalls, Kiribati (Gilbert Is), and Nauru. Most are of atoll formation, and very small. Their small size and limited resources, and the distances between them, ensured that the power of traditional chiefs was both limited and localized. The people are outwardly similar to Melanesians and Polynesians, but analysis of their blood typing suggests that they are a distinctive racial grouping. The name comes from Greek *micros*, 'small' and *nesos*, 'island'. » atoll; Melanesia; Polynesia

Micronesia, Federated States of land area 700 sq km/270 sq ml. Group of four states in the W Pacific Ocean (Yap, Truk, Ponape, Kosrae) formerly belonging to the US Trust Territory of the Pacific Is; compact of free association with the USA, 1982; trusteeship ended, 1990. » Kosrae; Ponape; Truk; Yap

micronutrients » **nutrients**

microphone A device that converts acoustic waves in air to electrical signals for transmission, recording, and reproduction. First developed by Bell and Edison in 1876–7 for telephony, microphones are widely employed in telecommunications, sound recording, and hearing aids. In all types, impinging sound waves cause corresponding oscillations of a diaphragm. These movements in their turn vary a resistance (*carbon microphones*, as in telephone receivers), capacitance (*condenser microphones*), electromagnetic field (*dynamic* and *coil microphones*), or the shape of a piezo-electric crystal (*crystal microphones*), each producing a variation in electrical output.

There are various patterns of reception: *omni-directional*, more or less equally sensitive in all directions; *bi-directional* with marked front and rear sensitivity in a figure-of-eight pattern; and *uni-directional*, in which the sensitivity falls off to each side in a cardioid pattern. This last characteristic is further emphasized by a slotted tube in front of the diaphragm in the highly-directional gun- or rifle-microphone. A *lavallier* [laval**yay**] is a small personal microphone worn by the speaker on a neck-cord or coat lapel, allowing freedom of movement. » Bell, Alexander Graham; Edison; loudspeaker [i]; piezo-electric effect; sound recording; telephone

microprocessor » **microchip; microcomputer**

microscope An optical instrument for producing enlarged images of minute objects. The compound microscope, in which a second lens further magnifies the image produced by a primary lens, was invented in the Netherlands in the late 16th-c; after 1830 it was widely used, following Joseph Lister's refinements which minimized chromatic and spherical distortions. The effectiveness of compound light microscopes is limited by the resolving power of the lens; magnifications can be achieved up to a maximum of 1 000. Electron microscopes use a beam of electrons instead of light, thus allowing viruses and other molecular phenomena to be studied at magnifications of over 50 000. » electron microscope [i]; field ion microscope; Lister, Joseph Jackson; optics [i]

Microscopium (Lat 'microscope') A small S constellation, which is difficult to see. It was introduced in the 18th-c. » constellation; RR9

microsurgery The performance of surgical procedures under microscopic control, involving very small structures; examples include the joining of tiny blood vessels severed by injury, or operations on the inner ear. Miniaturized precision surgical instruments are employed. » surgery

microteaching A technique used in the training of teachers which involves the trainee practising a specific teaching skill (such as questioning or explaining) for a short time with a small group of children, receiving feedback such as a tutor's comments, a written appraisal, or seeing a videotape of the mini-lesson. A second attempt follows with another small class. » education

microtone A musical interval smaller than a semitone. Microtones are indigenous to some musical cultures, especially in the East, and they occur naturally in the harmonic series. In Western art music, where the smallest interval is normally the semitone, some 20th-c composers (eg Hába, Bloch, Bartók, Boulez) have used microtones (especially quarter-tones) for their exotic effect or to extend their means of expression. » harmonic series; scale [i]

microwave background radiation A weak radio signal that comes from the entire universe, discovered in 1965 by Arno Penzias and Robert Wilson of the AT&T Bell Laboratories in New Jersey. It has a spectrum identical to a perfect black body a mere 2.7 degrees above absolute zero. This is the temperature of our universe, measured far from any stars. The character of the radiation is almost the same in every direction, apart from a slight asymmetry due to the motion of our Galaxy relative to the radiation. The microwave background is a relic of an early very hot phase in the universe, a fossil of the Big Bang itself. » Big Bang; spectrum; universe

microwave link Communication using radio transmission at frequencies above 1 GHz, usually by highly directional beams between dish antennae. The method is important in telephone transmission, and also in television distribution, both for temporary outside broadcast links to the main studio and as permanent stages in a broadcast network. » dish; microwaves

microwave oven An oven, first constructed in 1947, which uses microwave radiation (electromagnetic waves) to heat food. The radiation used (wavelength 0.12 m) penetrates inside food, where it is absorbed primarily by water molecules, causing heat to spread through the food. This penetration effect makes heating much faster than in conventional ovens. Microwave ovens are sometimes combined with conventional ovens to provide quick heating plus surface browning. Many materials, such as glass and ceramics, are unaffected by microwave radiation. » microwaves; electromagnetic radiation [i]

microwaves Electromagnetic radiation of wavelength between 1 mm and 10 cm, less than radio waves and more than infrared. They are produced by klystrons and magnetrons, and used in radar, communications, and microwave ovens. » electromagnetic radiation [i]; klystron; magnetron; maser; microwave background radiation; microwave link/oven; waveguide

micturition » **urine**

Mid Glamorgan pop (1987e) 534 700; area 1 018 sq km/393 sq ml. County in S Wales, UK, divided into six districts; created in 1974; bounded SW by the Bristol Channel; drained by Taff, Rhymney, Ogmore Rivers; administrative centre, Cardiff; other chief towns, Aberdare, Merthyr Tydfil, Bridgend, Pontypridd; farming, engineering, coal, textiles, electrical goods, vehicle components; castle at Caerphilly. » Cardiff; Wales [i]

Midas [**miy**das] A legendary King of Phrygia, of whom many stories are told. In one story, as a reward for helping the satyr, Silenus, Dionysus gave Midas a wish, and he asked that anything he touched should turn to gold. However, this caused so many difficulties (eg in eating and drinking) that he asked to be released; he was told to bathe in the River Pactolus, which thereafter had golden sands. » Dionysus

Middle Ages The period of European history between the collapse of the Roman Empire in the West and the Renaissance (c.500–c.1500); sometimes, however, the term is restricted in its use to the four or five centuries after the year 1000. By the early 16th-c, humanists regarded the civilization that followed the fall of Rome as distinctly different from the classical culture that preceded it and the classical revival of their own day. The notion of a separate but inferior mediaeval civilization has since been transformed into a more positive appreciation of the age and its achievements, notably the emergence of national states, the vigour of cultural life, and the spiritual attainments of the Church in what was above all an age of faith. Though a more or less well-defined period between ancient and modern times, it has no obvious beginning, still less an obvious end. » Crusades [i]; Dark Ages; feudalism; Renaissance; Roman history [i]; serfdom

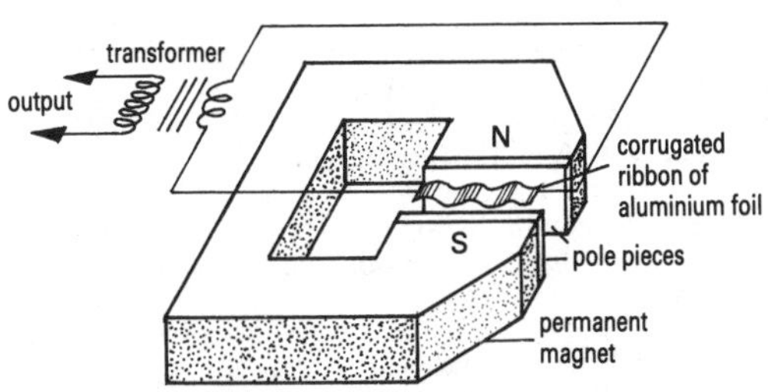

Ribbon microphone A thin strip of corrugated metal foil suspended between two magnetic pole pieces acts as both diaphragm and conductor.

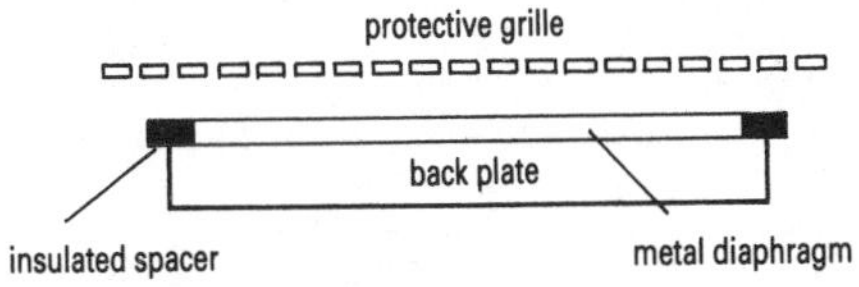

Condenser or **capacitor microphone** Sound waves cause the thin electrically-charged metal diaphragm to vibrate, varying the capacitance between it and the fixed back plate.

Two types of microphone

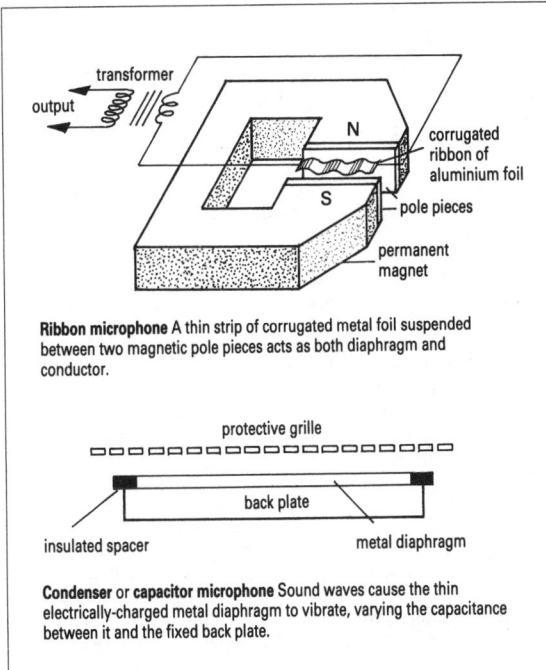

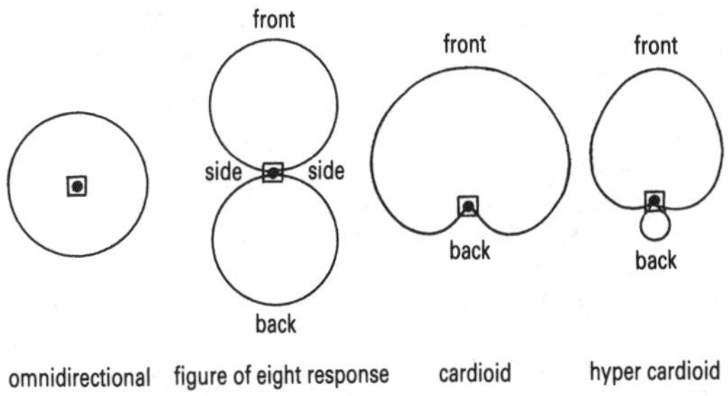

Types of microphone response

Middle America A geographical region encompassing Mexico, Central America, and the West Indies; includes the Gulf of Mexico and the Caribbean.

middle school A type of school in the UK for children aged 8–12 or 9–13. The former are regarded as primary, the latter as secondary schools. » primary education; secondary education

Middle Temple » **Inns of Court**

Middle West or **Midwest** The region of the USA comprising the states between the Great Lakes and the upper Mississippi R valley: Illinois, Indiana, Iowa, Kansas, Minnesota, Missouri, Nebraska, Ohio, and Wisconsin. Much of this area is within the corn belt agricultural region. » corn belt

Middlesborough [**mid**lzbruh] 54°35N 1°14W, pop (1981) 150 430. Port town in Middlesborough district, Cleveland, NE England; on the R Tees estuary; developed around the iron industry in the 19th-c; part of the Teeside conurbation; railway; iron and steel, engineering, chemicals, fertilizer; Town Hall (1846). Custom House (1840); Captain Cook birthplace museum.

Middleton, Thomas (c.1570–1627) English dramatist, born in London. He collaborated in many plays, such as *The Honest Whore* (1604, with Dekker), and was often employed to write the Lord Mayor's pageant. His own works include the satirical *A Game at Chess* (1624), and the posthumously published tragedies *Women Beware Women* (?1621) and *The Changeling* (1622), in which William Rowley (c.1585–c.1642) collaborated. He died at Newington Butts, Surrey. » Dekker; drama; English literature

Midgard [**mid**gahd] Middle Earth, the land in which human beings live, according to Norse mythology. » Yggdrasil

midge A small, delicate fly that gathers in vast swarms at dusk near standing water; adults gnat-like but non-biting, as mouthparts are poorly developed; larvae typically aquatic, feeding on algae or detritus, occasionally predatory. (Order: *Diptera*. Family: *Chironomidae*, c.5 000 species.) » biting/gall midge; bloodworm; fly; larva

midget » **dwarfism**

Midianites [**mid**ianiyts] An ancient semi-nomadic people dwelling in the desert area of the Transjordan; in *Gen* 25, reputedly descended from the offspring (Midian) of one of Abraham's concubines (Keturah). Later they are portrayed as enticing the Israelites into idolatry, but are overcome by Gideon (*Jud* 6–8). They were noted for their use of camels in raids. » Abraham; Judges, Book of

Midland Canal » **Mittelland Canal**

midnight sun A phenomenon during the summer period within the Arctic and Antarctic circles, when the Sun remains continuously above the horizon. Correspondingly, there is an equal period in winter when the Sun does not rise at all. » equinox; solstice

midrash [**mid**rash] In general terms, teaching linked to a running exposition of scriptural texts, especially found in rabbinic literature. The scriptural interpretation is often a relatively free explanation of the text's meaning, based on attaching significance to single words, grammatical forms, or similarities with passages elsewhere so as to make the text relevant to a wide range of questions of rabbinic interest. The term can also apply to the genre of rabbinic writings which consist of such interpretations. » Judaism

midshipman Bottom-dwelling fish found on or in muddy bottoms along Atlantic and Pacific coasts of N America; length up to 35 cm/14 in; head rather flattened, body tapering to tiny tail fin; dorsal and anal fins long; underside bearing numerous small light organs; may produce audible grunts or whistles. (Genus: *Porichthys*. Family: *Batrachoididae*.)

midsummer The summer solstice or 'longest day', which falls in the northern hemisphere on 21 or 22 June, depending on the locality. Ceremonies in honour of the Sun have been held on this day from the earliest times. **Midsummer Day**, a quarter-day in England and Wales, is 24 June. It is preceded by **Midsummer Night**, when supernatural beings are said to roam abroad. » quarter-day; solstice

Midway Islands 28°15N 177°25W; pop (1981) 2 300; area 3 sq km/1 sq ml. Circular atoll enclosing two small islands in the C Pacific Ocean 1 850 km/1 150 ml NW of Oahu, Hawaii; annexed by USA, 1867; submarine cable station since 1905; commercial aircraft stopover since 1935; military airbase since 1941; Allied air victory in the Battle of Midway (1942) was a turning point in World War 2. » Pacific Ocean

midwife toad A European frog of the family *Discoglossidae*; lives away from water; may dig burrows; mates on dry land; male wraps eggs around his legs and carries them until they hatch, then puts tadpoles in water; two species: the **common midwife toad** (*Alytes obstetricans*) and the **Iberian midwife toad** (*Alytes cisternasii*.) » frog

Mies van der Rohe, Ludwig [**mees** van der **roh**er] (1886–1969) German architect and designer, born at Aachen. He was trained in Berlin (1908–11) and became one of the greatest 20th-c architects, his designs including the German Pavilion for the Barcelona Exhibition (1929) and the Seagram Building, New York (1956–9). He was director of the Bauhaus at Dessau and Berlin (1930–3), and moved to the Illinois Institute of Technology, Chicago, in 1938. He died in Chicago. » Bauhaus

mignonette [minyuh**net**] An annual native to N Africa; leaves lance-shaped; spikes of creamy, fragrant flowers; petals 4–7, lobed, those at the back larger with deeper, more numerous lobes. (*Reseda odorata*. Family: *Resedaceae*.) » annual

migraine A recurrent, usually one-sided headache, often accompanied by vomiting and a disturbance of vision which takes the form of bright streaks of light. It tends to occur in young people, lasts a few hours, and lessens in severity and frequency with age. In the majority of cases the condition, though troublesome, is benign. It is believed to arise from the constriction of arterioles within the brain followed by their dilatation. Some foods containing substances affecting the degree of constriction of blood vessels appear to be responsible in some cases. » headache

migration 1 In anthropology and sociology, a movement of population within or between countries. Migration within countries has been preponderantly towards urban centres, seen possibly by migrants as attractive alternatives to rural over-population and its associated deprivation. International migration (*emigration*) may be a response to other factors, such as political threats against minority groups or warfare. Migrants may not always be given the right to settle in those regions to which they travel, and may be treated as temporary refugees or stateless migrant labourers. In advanced, prosperous societies there has been a considerable out-migration of people from the cities to the surrounding countryside, a phenomenon known as 'population turnaround'. » demography; nomadism; population; refugees; resocialization; transhumance **2** In biology, the movement of organisms or their dispersal stages (seeds, spores, or larvae) from one area to another. It includes one-way movement into and out of an area, but is commonly restricted to the periodic two-way movements that take place over relatively long distances and along well-defined routes. Such seasonal migration between summer and winter feeding areas, for example, is usually triggered by day length. » ethology

Mihailović, Dragoljub, byname **Drazha** [me**hiy**lohvich] (1893–1946) Serbian soldier, born at Ivanjica. He rose to the rank of colonel in the Yugoslav army, and in 1941 remained in Yugoslavia after the German occupation, forming groups (*Chetniks*) to wage guerrilla warfare. He later allied himself with the Germans and then with the Italians to fight the communists. He was executed in Belgrade by the Tito government for collaboration. » Chetniks; Tito; World War 2

Mikonos or **Mykonos** [**mee**kuhnos] pop (1981) 5 503; area 85 sq km/33 sq ml. Island of the Cyclades, Greece, in the Aegean Sea; airfield; ferry service to Delos and other islands; several noted resorts; Agios Panteleimon monastery, many churches built by sailors. » Cyclades; Greece [i]

Mikoyan, Anastas Ivanovich (1895–1970) Soviet politician, born at Sanain, Armenia. A member of the Central Committee in 1922, he supported Stalin against Trotsky, and in 1926 became Minister of Trade, doing much to improve Soviet standards of living, and introducing several ideas from the West. He was Vice-Chairman of the Council of Ministers (1955–64), and President of the Presidium of the Supreme

Soviet (1964–5). He died in Moscow. » communism; Stalin; Trotsky

Milan, Ital **Milano** 45°28N 9°12E, pop (1981) 1 604 773. Commercial city and capital of Milan province, Lombardy, N Italy, on R Olna; Gallic town, taken by the Romans in 222 BC; later the chief city of the Western Roman Empire; from 12th-c, ruled by the dukes of Milan; Duchy of Milan held by Spain, 16th-c; ceded to Austria, 1713; capital of Kingdom of Italy, 1805–14; held by Austria, 1815–60; linked by shipping canals with the Ticino and Po Rivers, and with Lakes Maggiore and Como; two airports (Malpensa, Linate); railway junction; underground; two universities (1920, 1923); a leading financial and commercial centre; textiles, iron and steel, metalworking, cars, chemicals, pharmaceuticals, electrical apparatus, data processing equipment, foodstuffs, engineering, publishing; Churches of San Lorenzo (early Christian), Sant'Ambrogio (founded 386); Santa Maria delle Grazie (15th-c, with Leonardo da Vinci's 'Last Supper' on the wall of the adjoining convent), a world heritage site; Gothic cathedral (14th-c), Palazzo dell'Ambrosiana (1603–9), Castello Sforzesco (1368), La Scala opera house (1776–8); Milan trade fair (Apr). » Italy [i]; La Scala; Leonardo da Vinci

mildew Any fungal disease of a plant in which the thread-like fungal strands (together forming the mycelium) are visible on the leaves of the host plant as pale or white patches. » fungus; plant

Mildura [mil**dyoo**ra] 34°14S 142°13E, pop (1983e) 16 920. Town in NW Victoria, Australia, on the Murray R; railway; airfield; citrus growing, wine; Aboriginal Arts Centre; the bar in the Mildura Working Men's Club is said to be the longest in the world at 90.8 m/298 ft with 27 beer taps. » Victoria (Australia)

Miletus [miy**lee**tuhs] A prosperous, commercially-oriented, Greek city-state in Ionia on the W coast of Asia Minor. It was the birth-place of Thales, one of the Seven Wise Men of Greece, and is commonly regarded as the cradle of Western philosophy. » Ionia; Naukratis; Thales

milfoil » **yarrow**

Milhaud, Darius [**mee**yoh] (1892–1974) French composer, born at Aix-en-Provence. He studied at the Paris Conservatoire, and for a time was a member of *Les Six*. In 1940 he went to the USA, where he became professor of music at Mills College, California (1940–7), and afterwards lived in both France and the USA. He was a prolific composer, writing several operas, ballets, and symphonies, and orchestral, choral, and chamber works. He died in Geneva. » *Six, Les*

Militant Tendency A British political group which came to prominence in the 1980s. Ostensibly, *Militant* is a newspaper published by Labour Party members espousing Marxist positions. In practice, critics have argued, the newspaper is a front for a 'party within a party', a separate organization of revolutionary Trotskyists who have entered the Labour Party (*entryism*) to use its organizational base for its own political ends. To all intents and purposes Militant is a cover for the Revolutionary Socialist League, the original British section of the Fourth International. In the 1980s, its supporters infiltrated a number of local Labour Parties and the Young Socialists (its youth wing). Fearing the adverse electoral publicity resulting from Militant activities, the Labour Party moved to expel members of Militant on the grounds that they were members of a separate political party, which is against the Party's constitution. Many of those expelled took the Party to court, but their cases were not upheld. Since then, Militant's influence appears to have declined. » International; Trotskyism

military intelligence The collection and evaluation of information relevant to military decision making. Intelligence can be gathered by many means, such as listening to enemy electronic emissions (electronic intelligence, or *Elint*), monitoring signals traffic (*Sigint*), the use of surveillance satellites, and traditional espionage techniques. Most armed forces have specifically trained intelligence units attached to them (whose role would include such activities as interrogating prisoners after a battle, or listening in to enemy radar traffic), but more well-known are the national agencies which collate information at a strategic level, such as the US Defense Intelligence Agency (DIA) and the British Secret Intelligence Service (SIS). The practice of resisting and frustrating hostile attempts to gain military, political, or scientific intelligence is known as **counter-intelligence**. » Elint; RECONSAT

military monkey » **patas monkey**

military science The theoretical study of warfare and of the strategic, tactical, and logistic principles behind it. Studied from ancient times to the computerized war-game 'scenarios' of today, military science concerns itself with such unchanging principles as the primacy of the objective, concentration of force, economy of force, surprise, and manoeuvre. Notable theoreticians and writers on military science include the Chinese general Sun Tzu (c.500 BC), the German general, Karl von Clausewitz (1780–1831), and the British writer Basil Liddell Hart (1895–1972), who did much to inspire the German concept of Blitzkrieg. » blitzkrieg; Clausewitz; strategic studies

military starling » **starling**

military textiles High-performance textiles used for military purposes. Some were first used in this field, for example Orlon (for parachutes) and Kevlar (for bullet-proof vests and flash suits).

militia A military force raised (usually in times of emergency) for national defence, separate from the regular army. These national forces are raised by government decree, and can thus be distinguished from guerrilla forces. » Home Guard; national guard

milk A white or whitish liquid secreted by the mammary glands of female mammals to nourish their young. The milks of many species have been consumed by humans from earliest times, especially cow's milk, with goat's, ewe's, and buffalo milk also making a significant contribution in various parts of the world. Milk is about 88% water, 4.7% lactose, 3.3% protein, and 3.8% fat. *Cream* is the yellowish surface layer of fat which forms when milk is allowed to stand. This may be removed, leaving water emulsion and skimmed milk. Low-fat milks, which are increasing in popularity, are produced by partially removing the fat (by 50% – *semi-skimmed milk*). Butter is made by churning the cream, while both yogurt and cheese are made by fermenting milk using different bacteria. Most milks are *pasteurized* before being sold for human consumption: this greatly removes the risk of the consumer being exposed to bacteria which cause brucellosis and tuberculosis. The shelf life of milk can be greatly increased by ultra-high-temperature (UHT) treatment, although the palatability declines somewhat. » breast milk; butter; cheese; kefir; koumiss; pasteurization; UHT milk; yoghurt

milk of magnesia A suspension of magnesium hydroxide used as an antacid to sooth an acid stomach. It can also be used as a mild laxative. » hydroxide; laxative; magnesium

milkweed A latex-producing perennial, sometimes shrubby, native to America; leaves in pairs or whorls of three; flowers in small umbels, each flower with a short, tubular corolla and five stamens united with the style into a tube with five valve-like appendages. (Genus: *Asclepias*, 120 species. Family: *Asclepiadaceae*.) » latex; milkweed butterfly; perennial; petal; shrub; stamen; umbel

milkweed butterfly A large, colourful butterfly; wings brownish, bearing black and white markings; caterpillars brightly banded or striped as warning coloration; feed on milkweed plants containing chemicals that make them distasteful to predators. (Order: *Lepidoptera*. Family: *Nymphalidae*.) » butterfly; caterpillar; milkweed

milkwort A perennial herb or small shrub, found almost everywhere; leaves usually alternate; flowers in spikes, five sepals, two inner large, often petaloid and brightly coloured, enclosing three petals fused with eight stamens to form a tube. In **common milkwort** (*Polygala vulgaris*), the flowers are white, pink, or blue, sometimes all on the same plant. (Genus: *Polygala*, 500–600 species. Family: *Polygalaceae*.) » herb; perennial; sepal; shrub; stamen

Milky Way A diffuse band of light across the sky, first resolved by Galileo into a 'congeries of stars' resulting from the combined light of billions of faint stars in our Galaxy. Strictly it means the belt of light seen in the night sky, but the term is used freely, even by professional astronomers, as the name of the Galaxy to which our Sun belongs. The name, from ancient Greek, was adopted also by the Romans. » Galaxy

Mill, John Stuart (1806–73) British empiricist philosopher and utilitarian reformer, born in London. He was educated by his father, Scottish philosopher James Mill (1773–1836), under whom he began a career at the East India Company. He became an MP in 1865, supporting women's suffrage and liberalism. His major writings include *System of Logic* (1843), *Principles of Political Economy* (1848), *On Liberty* (1859), and his most widely known work, *Utilitarianism* (1863). He died at Avignon, France. » utilitarianism

Millais, Sir John Everett [**mil**ay] (1829–96) British painter, born in Southampton. He studied in London, and became a founder of the Pre-Raphaelite Brotherhood, his works in this style including the controversial 'Christ in the House of His Parents' (1850). His later work included several portraits and landscapes, and he also became well known for his woodcut illustrations for magazines. He became a baronet in 1885, and died in London. » English art; Pre-Raphaelite Brotherhood; woodcut

Millay, Edna St Vincent (1892–1950) US poet, born at Rockland, Maine. She won the Pulitzer Prize with *The Harp-Weaver* (1922). Other volumes include *Conversation at Midnight* (1937) and *The Murder of Lidice* (1942), as well as collections of lyrics and sonnets. She died at Austerlitz, New York. » American literature; poetry; sonnet

millenarianism [mili**nair**ianizm] The belief held by some Christians that there will be a thousand-year (millennium) reign of the saints, either before or immediately after the return of Christ. The belief is usually based on an interpretation of *Rev* 20. 1–7. The main body of Christians has not endorsed millenarianism, but it had its advocates from the earliest years of Christianity, and in the 19th-c there was a renewal of apocalyptical and millennial ideas, such as the Plymouth Brethren and the Adventists. In recent decades, the term has been used more broadly by social scientists, referring to any religious group looking forward to a sudden and early transformation of the world. Such movements tend to arise in periods of great social change or during social crises, and usually aim to advance a suppressed social group, as in the Melanesian cargo cults. » Adventists; Anabaptists; apocalypse; cargo cult; Plymouth Brethren

Miller, Arthur (1915–) US dramatist, born in New York City. He began to write plays while a student at Michigan, and achieved recognition with *All My Sons* (1947). *Death of a Salesman* (1949, Pulitzer Prize) brought him international recognition. Other major works include *The Crucible* (1953), *A View from the Bridge* (1955), and *Playing for Time* (1981). In 1956 he gained considerable publicity from his marriage to Marilyn Monroe (divorced 1961), and an appearance before the Un-American Activities Committee for alleged communist sympathies. His autobiography *Timebends* was published in 1987. » drama; theatre

Miller, Glenn (1904–44) US bandleader and trombonist, born at Clarinda, Iowa. After 10 years of playing in dance bands, he discovered a new voicing with a clarinet lead over four saxophones. His first venture as leader in 1937 failed, but he tried again the next year and enjoyed phenomenal success with his 'sweet' ensemble sound, fox-trot rhythms, and well-drilled showmanship. In 1939, his hit records included 'Moonlight Serenade' (his theme song), 'Sunrise Serenade', 'Little Brown Jug', and 'In the Mood'. He joined the US Air Force in 1942, and assembled a large orchestra in England. In December 1944, he took off for France on a flight that disappeared without a trace. Decades later, records revealed that his aeroplane was inadvertently hit by bombs jettisoned over the English Channel by Allied bombers returning from a mission over Germany. » trombone

Miller, Henry (Valentine) (1891–1980) US author, born in New York City. His early books, *Tropic of Cancer* (1934) and *Tropic of Capricorn* (1938), published in Paris, were originally banned in Britain and the USA for their sexual explicitness. Later work includes the series *Sexus* (1945), *Plexus* (1949), and *Nexus* (1960), and the Surrealist play *Just Wild About Harry* (1963). He died at Pacific Palisades, California. » American literature; novel; satire

miller's thumb » **bullhead**

millet A small-grained, rather inferior cereal from the tropics and warm temperate regions, grown in poor areas or as emergency crops mainly for animal feed and bird seed. **Common millet** (*Panicum miliaceum*) has branching heads; **foxtail** or **Italian millet** (*Setaria italica*) and **bulrush millet** (*Pennisetum glaucum*) have dense heads. (Family: *Gramineae*.) » cereals; grass [i]

Millet, Jean François [**mee**lay] (1814–75) French painter, born at Grouchy. The son of a peasant farmer, he showed an early talent for art, studied at Cherbourg, and in 1837 went to Paris, where he exhibited at the Salon in 1844. After the 1848 Revolution he settled at Barbizon, where his paintings of rustic French life included 'Sower' (1850) and 'The Gleaners' (1857). He died at Barbizon. » Barbizon School; French art; Salon

millibar » **bar** (physics)

Milligan, Spike » **Goons, the**

Millikan, Robert (Andrews) (1868–1953) US physicist, born at Morrison, Illinois. Educated at Berlin and Göttingen, he became professor of physics at Chicago (1910) and head of California Institute of Technology (1921). His oil drop experiment demonstrated that electric charge always occurs in multiples of a fixed electron charge, and measured the value of this charge; it was carried out by observing drifting oil droplets subjected to an electric field. The winner of the 1923 Nobel Prize for Physics, he died at San Marino, California. » charge; electron; fundamental constants

millilitre » **litre**

millimetre » **metre** (physics)

millipede A long-bodied, terrestrial arthropod; typically with double body segments, each bearing two pairs of walking legs; mostly small, found in soil or litter; many are able to roll into a ball or coil for protection; c.10 000 species. (Class: *Diplopoda*.) » arthropod

Mills, Sir John (1908–) British actor, born at Felixstowe, Suffolk. From a theatrical family, he started in films in the 1930s. He became much in demand for typically English roles, but his character parts were often outstanding, as in *Great Expectations* (1946) and *The History of Mr Polly* (1949). He has continued to appear in an extremely wide variety of roles, including *Ryan's Daughter* (1978), for which he was awarded an Oscar, *Gandhi* (1982), and *A Woman of Substance* (1986). He was knighted in 1976, and is the father of the actresses Hayley and Juliet Mills.

Milne, A(lan) A(lexander) (1882–1956) British author, born in London. He was educated at Westminster and Cambridge, joined the staff of *Punch*, and became well known for his light essays. In 1924 he achieved world fame with his book of children's verse, *When We Were Very Young*, written for his own son, Christopher Robin; further children's classics include *Winnie-the-Pooh* (1926) and *The House at Pooh Corner* (1928). He died at Hartfield, Sussex.

Milo or **Milon** (6th-c BC) Greek athlete, from Crotona in Magna Graecia. He was twelve times victor for wrestling at the Olympic and Pythian games, and commanded the army which defeated the Sybarites (511 BC). He carried a live ox upon his shoulders through the stadium of Olympia, and afterwards, it was said, ate the whole of it in one day. In old age he attempted to split up a tree, which closed upon his hands, and held him fast until he was devoured by wolves.

Miłosz, Czesław [**mi**wosh] (1911–) Polish poet, born at Szetejnie and brought up in Wilno, where he graduated in law. His first two volumes were published in the 1930s. During World War 2 he worked for the underground in Warsaw, and in 1960 went to live in the USA. Later volumes include *Hymn o perle* (1981, Hymn of the Pearl) and *Nieobjeta ziemia* (1986, Hymn of the Earth). He was awarded the Nobel Prize for Literature in 1980. » poetry; Polish literature

Milstein, Cesar (1927–) Argentinian-British molecular biologist, born and educated in Buenos Aires. He worked in Cambridge (1958–61), and since 1963 has been on the staff of the Medical Research Council Unit there. His main research has been into the production of monoclonal antibodies, using a method he helped to devise in 1975. He shared the Nobel Prize for Physiology or Medicine in 1984. » antibodies; immunology

Miltiades (c.550–489 BC) Athenian general, statesman, and the chief architect of the Greek victory at Marathon. He was also the father of Cimon by the Thracian princess, Hegesipyle. » Cimon; Marathon, Battle of; Persian Wars

Milton, John (1608–74) English poet, born in London, the son of a scrivener. He was educated at St Paul's School and Cambridge, then spent six years of studious leisure at Horton, which he regarded as preparation for his life's work as a poet. There he wrote *Allegro* and *Il Penseroso* (1632), *Comus* (1633), and *Lycidas* (1637). He concluded his formal education with a visit to Italy (1638–9). Becoming involved in the Civil War with revolutionary ardour, he wrote very little poetry for the next 20 years. Instead, he published a series of controversial pamphlets against episcopacy (1642), on divorce (1643), and in support of the regicides (1649), and became official apologist for the Commonwealth. Blind from 1652, after the Restoration he went into hiding for a short period, and then devoted himself wholly to poetry. The theme of his epic sacred masterpiece, *Paradise Lost*, had been in his mind since 1641. The first three books reflect the triumph of the godly; the last books, written in 1663, are tinged with despair – God's kingdom is not of this world. It was followed by *Paradise Regained* and *Samson Agonistes* (both 1674). He died at Chalfont St Giles, Buckinghamshire, widely esteemed as a poet second only to Shakespeare. » Commonwealth (English history); English Civil War; English literature; epic; poetry; Restoration

Milton Keynes [keenz] 52°03N 0°42W, pop(1981) 137 048. Industrial new town (since 1967), designed on a grid pattern, in Milton Keynes district, Buckinghamshire, SC England; 80 km/50 ml NW of London; Open University (1969); railway; wide range of light industries; festival (Feb). » Buckinghamshire

Milwaukee [milwawkee] 43°02N 87°55W, pop(1980) 636 212. Seat of Milwaukee County, SE Wisconsin, USA, on the W shore of L Michigan; major lake port; largest city in the state; founded by German immigrants in the mid-19th-c; airfield; railway; two universities (1857, 1908); heavy machinery, electrical equipment; leading manufacturer of diesel and petrol engines; home of several breweries, and famed for its beer-producing tradition; major league teams, Brewers (baseball), Bucks (basketball); Pabst Museum, brewery tours, Mitchell Park Horticultural Conservatory, Milwaukee Public Museum, art museum. » Wisconsin

Mimas [miymas] The natural satellite orbiting closest to Saturn, discovered in 1789; distance to the planet 186 000 km/116 000 ml; diameter 390 km/240 ml; orbital period 0.942 days. » Saturn (astronomy); RR4

Mimbres [mimbresh] A native Mogollon Indian culture of the Mimbres R, SW New Mexico, USA, c.1000–1250 AD. It is celebrated artistically for its painted pottery, particularly bowls bearing stylized humans and animals in black, brown, and orange on white. » Mogollon

mime In terms of ancient theatre, both a short dramatic sketch and a professional entertainer. In 20th-c theatre, it signifies the art of silent corporeal expression as espoused by Etienne Decroux and popularized by Marcel Marceau. » Decroux; Marceau; pantomime

mimicry The close resemblance of one organism (the mimic) to another (the model) in order to deceive a third. There are two main types of mimicry: *Batesian mimicry*, in which harmless or palatable species mimic a venomous or unpalatable model in order to deceive a predator; and *Mullerian mimicry*, in which several different mimic species, all of which are unpalatable, display a similar warning coloration pattern. » ethology

mimosa » **wattle** [i]

mimulus An annual or perennial, found almost everywhere, many from N America; leaves oval, in opposite pairs; flowers usually yellow with red blotches, 2-lipped, the upper lip 2-lobed, lower 3-lobed with two projecting flaps in the throat. (Genus: *Mimulus*, 100 species. Family: *Scrophulariaceae*.) » annual; perennial; musk

minaret » **Islamic architecture**

Minas Gerais [meenas zheriys] pop(1980) 13 378 553; area 587 172 sq km/226 648 sq ml. State in Sudeste region, SE Brazil; a wedge of land between Goiás (N) and São Paulo (S), known as the Triângulo Mineiro (Mineral Triangle) because it accounts for half of Brazil's mineral production; capital Belo Horizonte; coffee, iron ore, gold (the only two working mines in Brazil), diamonds, metal-working, timber, textiles, food processing, cattle, mineral waters; national monument of Ouro Prêto; 400 caves and grottoes. » Belo Horizonte; Brazil [i]; Ouro Prêto

mind An entity (also called **soul**) which originally was supposed to differentiate between animate and inanimate nature; Aristotle thought that plants and animals had souls. Later philosophers ascribed the mind only to persons, supposing it to be the thing that unifies our experiences, makes our experiences *ours* (and not some other person's), makes self-consciousness possible, initiates our actions, and makes possible our continued identity through time. Descartes claimed that an immaterial mind is what makes freedom and immortality possible. In psychology, movements such as behaviourism believe that the word can be dispensed with completely. Many psychologists are happy to use it only in an adjectival form (as in *mental tests*). Cognitive psychologists use it in a broad sense, as the software of the computer whose hardware is the brain, and also in a narrow sense, as that part of our experience which is conscious (as in 'bring to mind'). » behaviourism; cognitive psychology/science; consciousness; free will

Mindanao [minduhnahoh] pop(1980) 10 900 000; area 99 040 sq km/38 229 sq ml. Island in the S Philippines; bounded by the Celebes Sea (SW), Sulu Sea (W), and Bohol Sea (N); many bays and offshore islets; mountainous, rising to 2 954 m/9 691 ft at Mt Apo; major rivers include the Agusan and Mindanao; largest lake, Laguna Lanao; chief towns, Davao, Zamboanga; hemp, pineapples, maize, timber, gold. » Davao; Philippines [i]; Zamboanga

Mindelo [meendayloo] 16°54N 25°00W, pop(1970) 28 797. City and chief port (Porto Grande) of Cape Verde; on NW shore of São Vicente I; important refuelling point for transatlantic ships; submarine cable station. » Cape Verde [i]

Mindoro [mindohroh] pop(1980) 669 369; area 9 732 sq km/3 756 sq ml. Island of the Philippines, SW of Luzon I; bounded by the Sulu Sea (S) and South China Sea (W); rises to 2 585 m/8 481 ft at Mt Halcon; wide coastal plains to the E; chief town, Calapan; timber, coal. » Philippines [i]

Mindszenty, József, Cardinal (1892–1975) Roman Catholic Primate of Hungary, born at Mindszent, Vas. He became internationally known in 1948 when charged with treason by the communist government in Budapest. He was sentenced to life imprisonment in 1949, but in 1955 was released on condition that he did not leave Hungary. In 1956 he was granted asylum in the US legation at Budapest, where he remained as a voluntary prisoner until 1971. He spent his last years in a Hungarian religious community in Vienna. » communism; Roman Catholicism

mine An explosive munition concealed in a fixed place, which achieves its destructive effects when the target moves onto or comes near it. Mines may be planted at sea or 'sown' on land, shallowly buried underground. They are particularly useful in creating barriers which naval or land forces can cross only at their peril. » space mine

mineral oil A term used to distinguish lubricating oils of mineral origin. Early lubrication used oils of vegetable or animal origin, but the extensive development of machinery in the mid-19th-c demanded other supplies, which were found in the newly exploited subterranean sources of oil. » oil (earth sciences)

mineral waters Naturally occurring groundwaters rich in dissolved minerals derived from the rocks through which they flow. They are associated with medicinal properties, and may be used for bathing or as drinking water, depending on the composition. » groundwater

mineralocorticoids Steroid hormones synthesized and released from the adrenal cortex of many vertebrates. They are important in the body's sodium and potassium balance, and in the maintenance of extracellular fluid volume. In humans the main mineralocorticoid is aldosterone. » glucocorticoids; hormones; steroid

mineralogy The study of the chemical composition, physical properties, and occurrence of minerals. Major aspects of the subject include identification, classification and systematics, crystallography, and mineral associations in rocks and ore deposits. » minerals

minerals Naturally occurring substances, generally inorganic and crystalline, with a homogeneous structure and a chemical composition defined within specified limits; classified by chemical composition and crystal structure. They are the constituents of rocks in the Earth. *Mineral ores* are the source of most elements, and also have wide use as fluxes and catalysts in industry. Well-crystallized examples of durable minerals are often prized as gemstones. » gemstones; mineralogy; ore; silicate minerals; Plate IV

miners' right A document granting the holder the legal right to prospect and mine for minerals in Australia. Replacing a licence system after the Eureka stockade clash (1854), the new system was introduced in Victoria in 1855, and spread throughout Australia. » Eureka

Minerva [mi**ner**va] The Roman goddess of handicrafts, identified with Athena. » Athena

minesweeper A small vessel designed or adapted to cut the moorings of mines, thus allowing them to float to the surface where they are destroyed by gunfire. » mine; warships [i]

Ming dynasty (1368–1644) The last indigenous Chinese dynasty, founded by Zhu Yuanzhang, and finally replaced by the Manchu Qing dynasty, after peasant rebels had sacked Beijing (Peking) and driven the last emperor to commit suicide. Its capital was shifted from Nanjing (Nanking) to Beijing in 1420 by the Yongle emperor, who was responsible for building such monuments as the Forbidden City and the Temple of Heaven. » China [i]; Forbidden City; Qing dynasty

Mingus, Charlie, properly **Charles** (1922–79) US bassist, composer, and bandleader, born at Nogales, Arizona, and raised in Los Angeles. In New York in 1953 he began leading groups called the 'Jazz Workshop', which experimented with atonality and other devices of European symphonic music. His most powerful and individualistic music came later, such as 'Wednesday Night Prayer Meeting' (1959) and 'Fables of Faubus' (1960). He died at Cuernavaca, Mexico. » atonality; jazz

miniature camera Originally, a small still camera using short lengths of perforated 35 mm film, first produced in the mid-1920s. The term **compact camera** has been preferred, since the 1970s, involving the widespread use of small-format film, both perforated and unperforated. » camera

miniature painting A term sometimes used for the small pictures in illuminated manuscripts, and (more often, and properly) for the 'portraits in little' that were so popular in Elizabethan England. There is a comprehensive collection in the Victoria and Albert Museum, London. » limner

minicomputer » **mainframe computer**

minidisk A very compact magnetic disk storage medium for microcomputers, sometimes known as a **microfloppy disk**. There are presently at least four different sizes varying from about 2.75 to 4 in (c.7–10 cm) in diameter. Unlike the larger floppy disks, minidisks are enclosed in a rigid jacket, and are better protected from accidental damage. » floppy disk

Minimal Art A modern art movement that has flourished since the 1950s, mainly in the USA. Typical products are the blank or monochrome canvases of US painter Ad Reinhardt (1913–67), and the prefabricated firebricks of US sculptor Carl André (1935–). In all cases the art content may be described as minimal. » abstract art; De Stijl; modern art; Suprematism

minimum lending rate (MLR) Formerly the minimum rate of interest at which the Bank of England would lend to discount houses. Used as an instrument of government policy, it superseded the bank rate in 1973, and was itself superseded in 1981 by the *bank base rate*, on which all other interest rates are set. » bank base rate

minimum wage A minimum rate of pay imposed by a government in certain sectors of the economy, or in general, with the aim of raising standards of living among the poorer sections of the community. Economists argue that the interference with free market forces may lead to even less desirable results; for example, the demand for a particular type of labour may disappear altogether.

mining The extraction of useful mineral substances from the Earth, either near the surface or at some depth. It was practised in prehistoric times, widely used in classical times, and became highly developed after the introduction of mechanical power. In surface, strip, and open-cast mining, the soil is stripped away, and the ore, coal, clay, or mineral is dug directly. At greater depths the deposits are approached by horizontal tunnels dug from vertical shafts (*drifts*). Variants of these digging methods are adopted for different geological situations. Other methods of mining may be devised for particular substances. Tin ore (from Malaysia) is dredged from lake bottoms. Sulphur is raised from depth by concentric bore-holes down one of which is passed a stream of very hot water that melts the sulphur (the *Frasch process*). Salt is sometimes raised by leaching with water, and recovered by evaporation of the brine. » coal mining

minivet A small brightly-coloured bird, native to India and SE Asia; inhabits forest, scrub, and cultivation; eats insects, spiders, and buds. (Genus: *Pericrocotus*, 11 species. Family: *Campephagidae*.)

mink A mammal of genus *Mustela*; weasel-like, with a thick dark brown coat important to the fur trade (other colours produced by captive breeding); inhabits woods near water; swims well; two living species: most important commercially is the **American mink** from N America (introduced elsewhere); also, the **European mink**. The extinct **sea mink** lived along the E shore of the USA until the 1880s. (Family: *Mustelidae*.) » Mustelidae; weasel

Minkowski space [min**kof**skee] The space-time of special relativity, comprising one time and three space dimensions; formulated by Russo-German mathematician Hermann Minkowski (1864–1909). His notion of flat space (ie no gravity, so zero curvature), with a geometry expressed in a special metric, is consistent with the requirements of special relativity. It is distinct from the flat space of Newtonian mechanics. » metric; Newtonian mechanics; special relativity [i]

Minneapolis [minee**ap**uhlis] 44°59N 93°16W, pop (1980) 370 951. Seat of Hennepin County, SE Minnesota, USA; largest city in the state; a port on the Mississippi R to the W of its twin city, St Paul; part of Fort Snelling military reservation, 1819; later developed as a centre of the timber and flour milling industries; city status, 1867; airport; railway; university (1851); important processing, distributing, and trade centre for enormous grain and cattle area; machinery, electronic equipment and computers, food processing and flour milling; the financial capital of the upper Midwest, with a Federal Reserve Bank; wide streets, parks, and lakes; major league teams, Minnesota Twins (baseball), Minnesota Vikings (football), Minnesota North Stars (ice hockey); Institute of Arts, Guthrie Theatre, American Swedish Institute, Grain Exchange; Aquatennial (Jul). » Minnesota; St Paul

Minnesinger [**min**uhzinger] Aristocratic German minstrels who performed songs of courtly love in the 12th–14th-c. » Meistersinger; Walther von der Vogelweide

Minnesota [mini**soh**ta] (Siouan 'watery cloud'), pop (1987e) 4 246 000; area 218 593 sq km/84 402 sq ml. State in N USA, divided into 87 counties; bounded N by Canada; the 'North Star State' or the 'Gopher State'; 32nd state admitted to the Union, 1858; the land E of the Mississippi R included in the North-west Territory, 1787; the land to the W became part of the USA with the Louisiana Purchase, 1803; permanently settled after the establishment of Fort Snelling, 1820; area became Minnesota Territory in 1849 and a state in 1858; Sioux Indian rebellion in S Minnesota, 1862; settled by many Scandinavians in the 1880s; capital, St Paul; other major cities, Minneapolis and Duluth; Mississippi R source in the NC region; Minnesota and St Croix Rivers empty into the Mississippi; over 11 000 lakes scattered throughout the state; 5 729 sq km/22 114 sq ml of L Superior within the state boundary; Sawtooth Mts in the extreme NE; highest point Mt Eagle (701 m/2 300 ft); glaciated terrain in the N, with boulder-strewn hills, marshland, and large areas of forest; major tourist area; iron ore mined in the E mountains; prairies in the S and W; agriculture the leading industry; nation's second biggest producer of dairy products, hay, oats, rye, turkeys; processed foods, machinery, electrical equipment, paper products. » Louisiana Purchase; Minneapolis; St Paul; United States of America [i]; RR38

minnow Small freshwater fish widely distributed and locally abundant in lakes and streams of N Europe and Asia; length up to 13 cm/5 in; body slender, cylindrical, mouth small; variable greenish brown above, underside yellowish; breeding males have bright orange underside. (*Phoxinus phoxinus*. Family: *Cyprinidae*.)

Minoan art The art associated with the Minoan civilization of the Aegean, notably in Crete c.2300–1100 BC. The well-known amphora painted with an octopus and seaweed patterns attests to a powerful feeling for decoration. The frescoes in the Palace of Minos at Knossos, representing figures vaulting over the backs of charging bulls, show Egyptian influence. » Minoan civilization; Mycenaean art

Minoan civilization The brilliant Bronze Age culture which flourished in the Aegean area in the third and second millennia BC, reaching its zenith around the middle of the second millennium (1700–1450 BC). Its most impressive remains come from Crete: the large palace-like structures at Knossos, Phaestus, Mallia, and Zakron reveal a sophisticated society, a complex centrally-controlled economy, a highly developed bureaucracy, and evidence of trading contacts far beyond the Aegean itself (eg the Levant and Egypt). Minoan civilization came abruptly to an end c.1450 BC. The cause is unknown: earthquakes, tidal waves, and invading Mycenaeans are all possible. » Knossos; Mycenaean civilization

minor In the UK, a person who has not yet reached the age of 18, often referred to technically as an *infant*; in Scottish law, a distinction is drawn between *pupils* (up to age 12 for girls, 14 for boys) and *minors* (from those ages to age 18); in the USA, the age of majority varies across jurisdictions and according to different purposes. Minors cannot validly enter certain contracts, such as a contract for a loan. In the UK, a citizen who has reached the age of 18 (the *age of majority*) is entitled to vote in parliamentary and local elections and, until the age of 65, may be called on to serve as a juror. » adoption; contract; guardian; jury

minor planet » **asteroids**

Minorca [minawka], Span **Menorca**, ancient **Balearis Minor** pop (1981) 58 727; area 700 sq km/270 sq ml. Second largest island in the Balearics, W Mediterranean, NE of Majorca; length, 47 km/29 ml; breadth, 10–19 km/6–12 ml; low-lying, rising to 357 m/1 171 ft at Monte Toro; occupied by the British, 18th-c; airport at Mahón, the island capital; tourism, lead, iron, copper. » Balearic Islands

Minos [miynos] A legendary King of Crete (or several kings), preserving the memory in the Greek mind of what we now call Minoan civilization. In Greek mythology, he was the son of Zeus and Europa, and expected a tribute from Athens of fourteen youths and maidens every year. In the Underworld he became a judge of the dead. » Ariadne; Daedalus; Minotaur; Pasiphae; Theseus

Minotaur [miynotaw] The son of Pasiphae and a bull from the sea, half bull and half human; the name means Minos's bull. It was kept in a labyrinth made by Daedalus, and killed by Theseus with the help of Ariadne. » Daedalus; Pasiphae; Theseus

Minsk 53°51N 27°30E, pop (1989) 1 589 000. Capital city of Belorussia, on the R Svisloch; one of the oldest towns in the state, c.11th-c; under Lithuanian and Polish rule; part of Russia, 1793; badly damaged in World War 2; large Jewish population killed during German occupation; airport; railway junction; university (1921); machine tools, vehicles, instruments, electronics, electrical engineering; Bernardine convent (17th-c), Cathedral of the Holy Spirit (17th-c). » Belorussia

mint A perennial native to temperate regions, especially in the N hemisphere; creeping rhizomes; square stems; oval leaves in opposite pairs; whorls of small pale pink to purplish flowers, sometimes forming heads; sometimes called **balm**. Its characteristic pungent scent is due to the presence of essential oils containing menthol. Mints hybridize easily, both in cultivation and in the wild, and are grown for their culinary value as herbs and flavourings. Many have distinctive odours, including ginger mint (*Mentha × gentilis*), peppermint, eau de Cologne mint (both *Mentha × piperita*), spearmint (*Mentha spicata*), and pineapple mint (*Mentha suaveolens*). (Genus: *Mentha*, 25 species. Family: *Labiatae*.) » catmint; essential oil; herb; horehound; pennyroyal; perennial; rhizome

Mint » **Royal Mint**

Mintoff, Dom(inic) (1916–) Maltese Labour statesman and Prime Minister (1955–8, 1971–84), born at Cospicua. He was educated at Malta and Oxford, becoming a civil engineer. In 1947 he joined the Malta Labour Party, and in the first Labour government was Minister of Works and Deputy Prime Minister. As Premier, his demands for independence and accompanying political agitation led to the suspension of Malta's constitution (1959). He resigned in 1958 to lead the Malta Liberation Movement, became Opposition leader in 1962, and was elected Premier again in 1971, when he followed a policy of moving away from British influence. » Malta [i]

Minton ceramics One of the principal British potteries of the 19th–20th-c, founded in 1796 by Thomas Minton (1765–1826). They produced pottery and porcelain, making large quantities of willow pattern. Mid-19th-c wares included finely-painted pieces in the Sèvres style, and versions of maiolica. » maiolica; porcelain; pottery; Sèvres porcelain; willow pattern

minuet A French dance in triple metre and moderate tempo, popular among the European aristocracy in the 17th–18th-c. It became a standard movement in the symphony and related genres of the classical period, in the form minuet–trio–minuet. » scherzo; symphony; trio

minuscule [minuhskyool] » **majuscule**

Minutemen Militiamen, particularly in New England, who were prepared to take up arms at very short notice. They were important in the first months of the US War of Independence, before the creation of a regular Continental Army under Washington. » Bunker Hill/Lexington and Concord, Battle of; Washington, George

Miocene epoch [miyuhseen] A geological epoch of the Tertiary period, from c.24 million to 5 million years ago. It was characterized by great mountain-building episodes, which formed the Alps and Himalayas, and the development of most modern mammalian groups. » geological time scale; Tertiary period; RR16

MIPS An acronym for **millions of instructions per second**. It is a measure of the speed at which computers can operate.

Mir ('Peace') space station A Soviet space station (launched Feb 1986) which evolved from Salyut, having more power (solar panels) and more docking ports (five) than previous spacecraft, allowing for the build-up of a modular station. It is used for long-duration spaceflight experience, and biomedical, science, and applications experiments. Yuri Romanenko occupied Mir for 326 days in 1987. » Salyut space station; Soviet space programme; space station

Mira Ceti Mira [miyra seetee miyra] (Lat 'the Wonderful') A star (*omicron Ceti*) in the constellation Cetus, first recorded in 1596 and recognized as a variable in 1638. It is a red giant, varying on a cycle of 331 days from 10th magnitude (minimum) to 3rd magnitude (maximum). It reached 1.2 magnitude, one of the brightest objects in the sky, in 1779. It is the prototype for **Mira variables** – variable stars with long periods of months or more. » Cetus; magnitude; variable star

Mirabeau, Honoré Gabriel Riqueti, Comte de ('Count of') [meeraboh] (1749–91) French revolutionary politician and orator, born at Bignon. Elected to the States General by the Third Estate of Marseilles (1789), his political acumen made him a force in the National Assembly, while his audacity and eloquence endeared him to the people. He advocated a constitutional monarchy on the English model, but failed to convince Louis XVI. As the popular movement progressed, his views were also rejected by the revolutionaries. He died in Paris before the climax of the Revolution. » French Revolution [i]; Louis XVI

miracle play » **mystery play**

mirage An optical illusion caused by the refraction of light through thin surface layers of air with different temperature and hence density, causing objects near the horizon to become distorted. It appears as a floating and shimmering image on the horizon, particularly in deserts, on very hot days. » light; refraction [i]

Miranda The innermost satellite of Uranus, discovered in 1948; distance from the planet 130 000 km/81 000 ml; diameter 400 km/250 ml. Its very complex surface, observed by Voyager 1 in 1986, suggests a history of almost total destruction and subsequent re-accretion. » Uranus; Voyager project [i]; RR4

Miró, Joan [meeroh] (1893–1983) Spanish artist, born at Montroig. He studied in Paris and Barcelona, and exhibited in Paris with the Surrealists. Apart from a period in Spain (1940–4), he mainly worked in France. His paintings are predominantly abstract, and his humorous fantasy makes play with a restricted range of pure colours and dancing shapes, as in 'Catalan Landscape' (1923–4, New York). His other work includes ballet sets, sculptures, murals, and tapestries. He died in Palma, Majorca. » abstract art; Spanish art; Surrealism

mirror A smooth surface which reflects large amounts of light, usually made of glass with a highly reflective metal deposit on the front or back, or of highly-polished metal. *Plane mirrors* form a virtual image the same size as the object, but with left and right reversed. *Convex mirrors* distort the image, but *concave mirrors* with a parabolic surface are used in astronomical telescopes to collect and focus light. Large astronomical mirrors can be over 5 m/16 ft across, but mirrors of all sizes are used in optical instruments. Half-silvered mirrors are used as one-way mirrors between a well-lit and a dim room. » aberrations [i]; optics [i]; telescope [i]

MIRV An acronym for **Multiple, Independently-targeted Re-entry Vehicle**, a nuclear-armed warhead, numbers of which may be incorporated in the front end of a large ballistic missile to be dispensed over a target area. A 'MIRVed' missile may therefore make attacks on several targets at once. » ballistic missile; missile, guided; Trident missile

miscarriage » **abortion**

Mishima, Yukio, pseudonym of **Hiraoka Kimitake** (1925–70) Japanese writer, born and educated in Tokyo. His first major work was *Kamen no kokuhaku* (1949, Confessions of a Mask). His great tetralogy, *Hojo no umi* (1965–70, Sea of Fertility), spanned Japanese life and events in the 20th-c. He passionately believed in the chivalrous traditions of Imperial Japan, became expert in the martial arts, and in 1968 founded the Shield Society, dedicated to the revival of bushido. He committed suicide in Tokyo. » bushido; Japanese literature; kabuki; Noh

Mishnah [**mish**nuh] (Heb 'repetition', referring to the practice of learning by repetition) An important written collection of rabbinic laws, supplementary to the legislation in Jewish Scriptures. The laws are classified under six main headings (*sedarim*): Seeds (agricultural tithes), Set Feasts, Women, Damages, Holiness (offerings), and Purities. Although the Mishnah's general arrangement can be traced to Rabbi Akiva (c.120 AD), its final editing was due to Rabbi Judah the Prince (c.200 AD). » Akiva ben Joseph; Halakhah; Judaism; Torah

Miskolc [**meesh**kolts] 48°07N 20°50E, pop (1984e) 212 000. Capital of Borsod-Abaúj-Zemplén county, NE Hungary, on R Sajo; second largest city in Hungary; airfield; railway; technical university of heavy industry (1870); iron and steel, chemicals, food processing, textiles, wine; National Theatre; castle of Diósgyör, 15th-c church on Avas Hill, Fazola furnace. » Hungary [i]

Missal The liturgical book of the Roman Catholic Church, containing liturgies for the celebration of Mass throughout the year. It includes all the prayers, Biblical readings, ceremonial, and singing directions. » liturgy; Mass; Roman Catholicism

missile, guided A weapon system (ranging in size from a small portable antitank missile to an intercontinental ballistic missile) which has the ability to fly towards its target under its own power. Its progress is directed either by an external source of command or by an internal computer which sends electronic guidance instructions to the missile's control surfaces. » antiballistic/antitank/ballistic/cruise/high-speed antiradiation/MX/Pershing/Polaris/Trident missile; penetration aid

missions, Christian The promotion of Christian faith among non-Christian people. Missionary activity has been a permanent feature of Christianity, particularly in the Roman Catholic and Protestant Churches. In the past, it was often associated with the expansion of European or American power, but modern missions recognize the importance of early establishing indigenous churches, with worship expressed in terms of local culture. » Christianity; Paul, St

Mississippi pop (1987e) 2 625 000; area 123 510 sq km/47 689 sq ml. State in S USA, divided into 82 counties; the 'Magnolia State'; held by France, Britain, and Spain in turn, becoming part of the USA in 1795; the 20th state to join the Union, 1817; seceded, 1861; re-admitted in 1870, but White supremacy was maintained, particularly by the constitution of 1890; highest Black population of any state (35%); capital, Jackson; other chief cities Biloxi, Meridian, Hattiesburg, Greenville, Gulfport; bounded S by the Gulf of Mexico and Louisiana; main rivers the Mississippi (forms the W border), Pearl (part of S border), and Tennessee (NE border); highest point Mt Woodall (246 m/807 ft); much of the S state covered in pine woods; fertile coastal plain; land rises in the NE; major cotton-producing area between Mississippi and Yazoo Rivers; soybeans, cattle, dairy products, poultry; petroleum, natural gas (over a third of the land given over to oil and gas development); clothing, wood products, foods, chemicals; fisheries prominent along the Gulf coast; the lowest per capita income in the USA; a centre of the civil rights movement in the 1960s; Old Spanish Fort, Vicksburg National Military Park, historic Natchez. » civil rights; Jackson (Mississippi); United States of America [i]; RR38

Mississippi River River in C USA; rises in N Minnesota; flows S to form the border between the states of Minnesota, Iowa, Missouri, Arkansas, and Louisiana on the W and Wisconsin, Illinois, Tennessee, and Mississippi on the E; enters the Gulf of Mexico in SE Louisiana, near New Orleans; length 1 884 km/1 171 ml; the second longest river in the USA, excluding the Missouri; when the Missouri is considered part of the main stream, length from the Red Rock–Jefferson R is 6 019 km/3 740 ml; major tributaries the Minnesota, Des Moines, Missouri, Arkansas, and Red (on the W), and the Illinois and Ohio (on the E); drains an area of about 3.25 million sq km/2 million sq ml between the Appalachian and the Rocky Mts, including part of Alberta and Saskatchewan; several artificial levees on the banks of the lower river help to cope with flooding; delta consists of salt marsh, wooded swampland and low-lying alluvial tracts, dissected by numerous distributaries (*bayous*); practically no tides; navigable as far as Minneapolis; steamboat era in the 19th-c; now a busy commercial waterway; major ports New Orleans, St Louis, Memphis, St Paul, Minneapolis, Baton Rouge. » Missouri River; United States of America [i]

Mississippian period » **Carboniferous period**

Missoni, Tai Otavio [miso**h**nee] (1921–) Italian knitwear designer, born in Yugoslavia. He founded the Missoni company with his wife, Rosita, in Italy in 1953. At first manufacturing knitwear to be sold under other labels, they later created, under their own label, innovative knitwear notable for its sophistication, and for its distinctive colours and patterns. » fashion

Missouri [mizo**o**ree] pop (1987e) 5 103 000; area 180 508 sq km/69 697 sq ml. State in C USA, divided into 115 counties; the 'Show Me State'; became part of USA with the Louisiana Purchase, 1803; a territory in 1812, but its application for admission as a state (1817) was controversial, as it had introduced slavery; eventually admitted as the 24th state in 1821 under the Missouri Compromise; capital, Jefferson City; major cities St Louis, Kansas City, Springfield and Independence; E and W borders largely defined by the Mississippi, Missouri, and Des Moines Rivers; Ozark Plateau in the SW; highest point Mt Taum Sauk (540 m/1 772 ft); split into two parts by the Missouri R; to the N, open prairie-land with corn and livestock, particularly hogs and cattle; to the S, foothills and the Ozarks, much of which is forested; more farms than any other state except Texas; automobiles, aircraft and aerospace components, processed foods and chemicals, machinery, fabricated metals and electrical equipment; mines yield over 90% of the nation's lead; position at the junction of the nation's two greatest rivers led to its development as a transport hub, and as the starting point for the pioneering advance W across the continent. » Jefferson City; Louisiana Purchase; United States of America [i]; RR39

Missouri Compromise (1820) An agreement to admit Missouri, with slavery, and Maine (separated from Massachusetts), without it, to statehood simultaneously, in order to preserve a sectional balance in the US Senate. The compromise also forbade slavery in the rest of the Louisiana Purchase, N of 36°30. » slave trade

Missouri River Longest river in the USA, and chief tributary of the Mississippi; formed in SW Montana by the confluence of the Jefferson, Madison, and Gallatin Rivers; flows through North and South Dakota, then forms the borders between Nebraska and Kansas (W) and Iowa and Missouri (E); joins the Mississippi just N of St Louis; length 3 725 km/2 315 ml (with longest headstream, 4 125 km/2 563 ml); major tributaries the Musselshell, Milk, Yellowstone, Little Missouri, Grand (of South Dakota), Moreau, Cheyenne, Bad, White, Niobrara, James, Platte, Kansas, Grand (of Iowa and Missouri), Gasconade, Osage; used for irrigation, flood-control, and hydroelectricity; major dams the Canyon Ferry, Hauser L, Holter L, Fort Peck L, Garrison, Oahe, and Fort Randall; navigation (as far as Fort Benton) is dangerous. » Mississippi River; United States of America [i]

Misti, Volcán El or **El Misti** [**mee**stee] Dormant volcano in S Peru, in the Andean Cordillera Occidental; height, 5 843 m/ 19 170 ft; last eruption, 1600; of religious significance to the Incas; observatory established by Harvard University near its summit. » Peru [i]; volcano

Mistinguett [meest**ĩget**], stage name of **Jeanne Marie Bourgeois** (1874–1956) French dancer and actress, born at Pointe de Raquet. She made her debut in 1895, and became the most popular French music-hall artiste for the next 30 years, reaching the height of success with Maurice Chevalier at the Folies Bergère. She died at Bougival. » Chevalier; music hall; theatre

mistle thrush A thrush native to Europe (N Africa during winter), and E to Siberia and N India; cream breast with bold spots; wing feathers with pale edges; inhabits open woodlands; nests high in forks of trees; also known as **storm-cock**. *Turdus viscivorus*.) » song thrush; thrush (bird)

mistletoe A hemiparasitic evergreen shrub, native to Europe, N Africa, and Asia; stem growing to 1 m/3¼ ft, branches regularly forked; leaves leathery, yellowish, in opposite pairs; flowers small, in tight clusters of 3–5, greenish yellow, males and females on separate plants; berries white. Mistletoe usually grows on deciduous trees (often apples, but also others), rarely on evergreens. The germinating seed sends haustorial roots into the vascular system of the host, from which it draws nutrients. All members of the mistletoe family (*Loranthaceae*) are hemiparasites. The plant was venerated by the druids, who cut it ceremonially from their sacred oaks with a golden knife. It was widely held to cure sterility and counteract poisons. Nowadays it is used as a Christmas decoration. (*Viscum album*. Family: *Loranthaceae*.) » deciduous/evergreen/parasitic plants; haustorium; shrub

Mistral A strong, cool wind common in S France. It originates in the Massif Central, and blows down the Rhône Valley between the Massif Central and French Alps. When it occurs in spring it may damage early crops. A similar wind is the Bora on the Adriatic Coast of Yugoslavia. Both are examples of katabatic winds. » katabatic wind; wind [i]

Mistral, Frédéric (1830–1914) French poet, born, lived, and died at Maillane, near Avignon. He became a founder of the Provençal renaissance movement (the *Félibrige* school), and is best known for his long narrative poems, such as *Miréio* (1859) and *Calendau* (1861), and for his Provençal–French dictionary (1878–86). He won the Nobel Prize for Literature in 1904. » French literature; poetry

Mistral, Gabriela, pseudonym of **Lucila Godoy de Alcayaga** (1889–1957) Chilean writer, educationalist, and diplomat, born in Vicuña. As a teacher she won a poetry prize with her *Sonetos de la muerte* (Sonnets of Death, 1914), and the cost of publication of her first book, *Desolación* (1922, Desolation), was defrayed by the teachers of New York. She was awarded the Nobel Prize for Literature in 1945, and died at Hempstead, New York. » Latin-American literature; poetry

MIT school In linguistics, a label applied to the group of US linguists associated with the Massachusetts Institute of Technology (MIT), who have developed the concept of generative grammar, under the influence of Noam Chomsky. » Chomsky; generative grammar

Mitchell, Margaret (1900–49) US novelist, born and died in Atlanta, Georgia. She studied for a medical career, then turned to journalism, but after her marriage to J R Marsh in 1925, began the 10-year task of writing her only novel, *Gone with the Wind* (1936). This book sold eight million copies, was translated into 30 languages, and filmed. » novel

Mitchell, R(eginald) J(oseph) (1895–1937) British aircraft designer. Trained as an engineer, he was led by his interest in aircraft to join an aviation firm (1916), where he soon became chief designer. He designed seaplanes for the Schneider trophy races (1922–31) and later the Spitfire, whose triumph he did not live to see. » aircraft [i]; seaplane

mite A small, short-bodied arthropod with head and abdomen fused into a compact body; typically with four pairs of walking legs; mouthparts include a pair of fangs; c.30 000 described species, including both free-living and parasitic forms, many of which are pests of economically important crops. (Class: *Arachnida*. Order: *Acari*.) » arthropod; harvestmite; parasitology; spider mite; tick

Mitford, Nancy (1904–73) British author, born in London. She established a reputation with such witty novels as *Pursuit of Love* (1945) and *Love in a Cold Climate* (1949). Her biographies, such as *Madame de Pompadour* (1953) and *The Sun King* (1966) were also highly popular. As editor and contributor to *Noblesse Oblige* (1956), she helped to originate the 'U' (upper-class) and 'non-U' classification of linguistic usage. She died at Versailles, France. » English literature; U and non-U

mithan » gaur

Mithra or **Mithras** A god worshipped in the early Roman Empire, of Persian origin, and identified with the Sun. The cult was predominantly military, and restricted to males; it was practised in caves, and involved baptism. Other resemblances to Christianity include Mithras's miraculous birth and his adoration by shepherds. The main story was of his fight with the bull, which he conquers and sacrifices.

Mithridates VI Eupator ('the Great') (?–63 BC) King of Pontus (c.115–63 BC), a Hellenized ruler of Iranian extraction in the Black Sea area, whose attempts to expand his empire over Cappadocia and Bithynia led to a series of wars (the **Mithridatic Wars**) with Rome (88–66 BC). Though worsted by Sulla (c.86 BC) and Lucullus (72–71 BC), he was not finally defeated until Pompey took over the E command (66 BC). Mithridates avoided capture, but later took his own life. » Lucullus; Pompey the Great; Pontus; Sulla

Mitla [**meet**la] 16°54N 96°16W. Ancient city in C Oaxaca, S Mexico, in the Sierra Madre del Sur, 40 km/25 ml ESE of Oaxaca; former centre of the Zapotec civilization; well-preserved ruins include temples, subterranean tombs, and a building known as the 'hall of monoliths'. » Mexico [i]; Zapotecs

mitochondrion [miytoh**kon**driuhn] A typically oval-shaped structure, often about 2 μm long, found in large numbers in eucaryotic cells. It comprises a double membrane, the inner forming folds and ridges (*cristae*) which penetrate the central matrix. It functions as a major site for metabolic activities that release energy by the breaking down of food molecules. » eucaryote; metabolism

mitosis [miy**toh**sis] The normal process of nuclear division and separation that takes place in a dividing cell, producing two daughter cells each containing a nucleus with the same complement of chromosomes as the mother cell. During mitosis, each chromosome divides lengthwise into two chromatids, which separate and form the chromosomes of the resulting daughter nuclei. The phases of mitosis are: *prophase* (the shortening and thickening of chromosomes), *metaphase* (the arrangement of chromosomes around the equator of a spindle), *anaphase* (the separation of chromatids), and *telophase* (the chromosomes return to an extended state, and the nuclear membrane is reformed). » cell; chromosome [i]; genetics [i]; meiosis [i]

mitre/miter (Gk *mitra*, 'turban') The liturgical headwear of a bishop of the Western Christian Church. It takes the form of a shield-shaped, high, stiff hat, representing the 'helmet of salvation'. » bishop; liturgy; vestments [i]

Mitsiwa » Massawa

Mittelland (Midland) **Canal** [**mi**tuhlant] A system of German canals and rivers linking the Dortmund–Ems Canal with Magdeburg. The waterway, which together with side canals provides an important transportation network, was completed in the late 1930s. It is 325 km/202 ml in length. » canal; Rhine canals

Mitterrand, François (Maurice Marie) (1916–) French statesman and socialist President (1981–), born at Jarnac. He studied law at Paris, served with the French Forces (1939–40), escaped from capture, and was active in the Resistance. A Deputy in the French parliament almost continuously from 1946, he has held various ministerial posts. For many years he was a stubborn opponent of de Gaulle, worked for unification of the French Left, and became Secretary of the Socialist Party in 1971. Following his victory in 1981, he embarked on a programme of nationalization and job creation in an attempt to combat stagnation and unemployment. He was re-elected President in 1988. » de Gaulle; socialism

mix; mixing » dissolve; dubbing

mixed-ability groups » streaming

mixed economy » market economy

mixed tide A tidal cycle intermediate between a diurnal tide and a semi-diurnal tide. It normally exhibits two low and two high tides per lunar day, but the highs and lows are of unequal magnitude. This type of tide is common around the Pacific Ocean basin. » tide

mixture A notion distinguished in chemistry from a compound in the following respects. A *mixture of A and B* is of indefinite composition, contains properties of A and B, and is easily separated to A and B. A *compound AB* has a definite ratio of A to B, contains properties unrelated to A and B, and needs a reaction to regain A and B.

Mjøsa, Lake [**my**ersa] or **Mjøsen** area 368 sq km/142 sq ml. Elongated lake in SE Norway, from Eidsvall (S) to Lillehammer (N); length 100 km/62 ml; maximum depth 443 m/1 453 ft; Norway's largest lake; heavily stocked with trout; chief towns, Lillehammer, Hamar, Gjøvik. » Norway [i]

Mnemosyne [nee**mo**zinee] In Greek mythology, a Titaness, daughter of Earth and Heaven, and mother of all the Muses. The name means 'Memory'. » Muses

moa An extinct bird native to New Zealand; a large ratite (up to 3 m/10 ft high) with long neck and legs, no wings; slow moving; inhabited forests; ate berries, seeds, and shoots. Some may have survived into the 19th-c. (Family: *Dinornithidae*, c.12 species.) » Ratitae

Moabite Stone [**moh**abiyt] An inscribed basalt slab, discovered in 1868 and subsequently broken up, which describes the successful revolt of Mesha, king of Moab, against the Israelites during the reign of Ahab (7th-c BC) or possibly of his son Jehoram (2 *Ki* 1.1). It is important also for the linguistic and historical light cast on the Hebrew Biblical narratives. » Ahab; Old Testament

Moabites An ancient Semitic people who in Old Testament times inhabited the area to the SE of the Dead Sea. Like the Ammonites, they were believed to be descended from Lot. » Lot; Semites

Mobile [moh**beel**] 30°41N 88°03W, pop (1980) 200 452. Seat of Mobile County, SW Alabama, USA; a major US port on Mobile Bay; settled by the French, 1711; ceded to the British, 1763; city status, 1819; scene of a Federal victory at the naval battle of Mobile Bay, 1864; railway; university (1963); Alabama's only seaport; shipbuilding, oil refining, paper, textiles, aluminium, chemicals; Mardi Gras, Azalea Trail Festival (Mar–May). » Alabama

mobile A name first applied by Marcel Duchamp to the hanging wire-and-metal sculptures of Alexander Calder (1898–1976). From c.1931 Calder perfected these popular and widely-imitated abstract constructions, sometimes adding a motor, sometimes relying on air currents to set them turning. » Duchamp; kinetic art

mobile communications A system which provides a simple, convenient means of communication for people who wish to keep in touch when travelling. The first mobile communication system was ship-borne radio, and there have since been widespread developments in the field of military communications. In modern times the term also refers to personal communication systems such as CB radio, radio paging, and car and pocket phones which use cellular radio. Cellular radio employs local radio transmitters, covering small areas (*cells*), which receive and transmit calls in association with the telecommunications network. Direct-dial calls using special handsets can be made on foot, from cars and trains, and now from aircraft. » citizens' band radio; pager; pocket phone; telecommunications

Möbius, August Ferdinand [**mer**biuhs] (1790–1868) German mathematician, born at Schulpforta, Saxony. He worked on analytical geometry, topology, and theoretical astronomy, but is chiefly known for the discovery of the *Möbius strip* and the invention of the *Möbius net*, important in projective geometry. He died at Leipzig. » analytic geometry; Möbius strip [i]; topology

Möbius strip In topology, a one-sided surface bounded by a single continuous line. Take a long thin rectangle *ABCD*, and join *A* to *B*, and *C* to *D*. This forms a cylinder, with two surfaces, an inside and an outside. Now take a similar rectangle *ABCD*, and join *A* to *C*, *B* to *D*. Starting at any point *P* on the surface now formed, we can draw a continuous line over the surface to reach the point at the 'other' side of *P*. » Möbius; topology

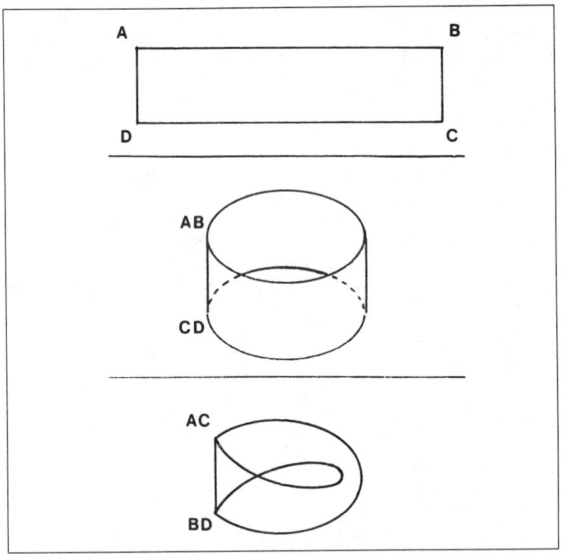

Möbius strip

Mobuto Sésé Seko, Lake » Albert, Lake

mocassin flower » lady's slipper

Moche [**mo**chay] An ancient Andean city near Trujillo, Peru, the capital c.200–550 AD of the Moche (or Mochica) state. Particularly celebrated are its twin pyramids of the Sun and Moon, the former 160 m/525 ft by 34 m/112 ft square and 40 m/130 ft high, with 130 million adobe bricks. Moche metalwork, textiles, and especially ceramics are notable. » American Indians; ceramics

mock orange A deciduous, temperate shrub, mainly from E Asia; leaves oval, opposite, with prominent veins; flowers fragrant, usually white, bowl-shaped, with four petals and numerous stamens; fruit a capsule. It is named for the resemblance of its flowers to those of the orange, but in horticulture it is sometimes called **syringa**, the botanical name for lilac. (Genus: *Philadelphus*, 75 species. Family: *Hydrangaceae*.) » deciduous plants; horticulture; lilac; orange; shrub; stamen

mockingbird A bird native to the New World; thrush-like with sharp, slightly curved bill and long tail; sings well; excellent mimic; inhabits forest and bushy areas; eats invertebrates and fruit; also known as **mocking-thrush**. (Family: *Mimidae*, 16 species.) » thrush (bird)

Mod The annual autumn musical and literary festival of Gaelic-speaking Scotland organized by An Comunn Gaidhealach (the Gaelic language society) on the model of the Welsh eisteddfod; first held in Oban in 1892. » eisteddfod; Gaelic

modal logic The study of the logic of the modal adverbs *necessarily* and *possibly*, supplemented by investigation of the notion of possible worlds; for example, if a proposition is necessarily true, it is true in all possible worlds. This has led to important debates in metaphysics and the philosophy of language. » possible worlds

mode (mathematics) In mathematics, the commonest of a set of scores; for example, the mode of 1,2,3,4,4,5 is 4. If the scores are grouped, the group with the highest frequency per unit class width is the modal class. Thus in the example

marks	0–19	20–29	30–39
frequency	8	10	8 ,

the modal class is 20–29. » mean; median; statistics

mode (music) In older musical theory, a 'manner' of distributing the notes of a scale so that the sequence of intervals varied according to which note was the *final* (ie the note on which the plainchant or, in polyphonic music, the lowest part ended). Late Renaissance theory recognized six modes (finals are shown in parentheses): Dorian (D), Phrygian (E), Lydian (F), Mixolydian (G), Aeolian (A), and Ionian (C). If the melody ranged between the final and its octave, the mode was called 'authentic'; if it ranged on either side of the final, the mode was 'plagal'. The modal system was superseded during the 17th-c by tonality. » raga; scale [i]; tonality

modelling A term used in art with two distinct meanings. **1** In painting, drawing, and photography it refers to the use of light and shade to create the effect of solid form. » hatching **2** In sculpture it refers to the technique of shaping a soft material such as clay or wax. Whereas carving removes material from an existing block, modelling builds up material, usually over a wire armature or frame. » sculpture

modello A small, but complete and detailed painting or drawing made to show to a patron before embarking on the full-size work. At this stage the patron might suggest changes. Superb oil *modelli* exist by Rubens and Tiepolo. » maquette; Rubens; sketch; Tiepolo

modem An acronym of **MOdulator/DEModulator**, a device which converts digital information from computers into electrical signals that can be transmitted over telephone lines and vice-versa. » acoustic coupler; telegraphy

moderator A person who presides over Presbyterian Church courts, such as the kirk session, presbytery, synod, or General Assembly. In Reformed Churches generally, the term is applied to the chairman of official Church gatherings. » Presbyterianism; Reformed Churches

modern art A term used widely but imprecisely to refer to all the 'progressive' movements in 19th–20th-c art. Accounts vary: some consider Goya the first modern artist; others prefer Manet. What is agreed is that towards the end of the 19th-c a number of artists, including Cézanne, Gauguin, van Gogh, Ensor, and Munch, challenged in various ways the traditional approach to painting based on such notions as naturalistic figure-drawing and Renaissance perspective. Their innovations inspired the younger generation around 1904–5 (in Paris, Rouault, Matisse, Picasso; in Dresden Kirchner, Heckel, Schmitt-Rottluff). Picasso and Braque developed Cubism (1906–8), the most widely influential of all modern movements. The Blaue Reiter group in Munich pushed further away from imitation (1912–14), and a purely abstract art soon emerged in the hands of Kandinsky and Klee. In Moscow in 1917 Malevich developed a totally abstract art which he called 'Suprematism'. By 1916 a nihilist reaction known as 'Dadaism' was already emerging in Zürich; it attacked all artistic values, but itself contributed to the ideas of the early Surrealists, who launched their first manifesto in Paris in 1924. » abstract art; Aesthetic Movement; Armory Show; art for art's sake; avant garde; Blaue Reiter, der; body art; Brücke, die; Cubism; Dada; Earthworks; Expressionism; Fauvism; Futurism; metaphysical painting; Postimpressionism; Suprematism; Surrealism; Braque; Kandinsky; Kirchner; Klee; Matisse; Picasso; Rouault

modern dance A theatre form of dance which flowered 1910–45 and continues today. It shares the revolutionary assumptions of all modern movements in the arts, rejecting the established form of dance, ballet. Greek myths, psychological states, political comment, reflections on the mechanization of life, and alienation of modern society have been common themes, demonstrating a serious modern consciousness. Isadora Duncan and Ruth St Denis are often credited with originating the modern movement in the first two decades of this century, the former in returning to natural movements, the latter in using exotic Far Eastern influences. Later, Martha Graham and Doris Humphrey emerged as major figures, each developing a particular way of moving and a distinctive repertoire. The emphasis is on expressiveness of the human body in showing emotional states, and this required a new vocabulary of movement using 'natural' actions such as walking, running, and breathing. The choreographer Rudolf Laban developed theories of movement which remain important, and a comprehensive notation system. In Germany in the 1970s–80s, Pina Bausch's dramatic theatrical works continued the modern, expressionist movement. Since the 1960s there has been a massive expansion of small modern dance companies in Europe and N America. » dance notation [i]; Duncan, Isadora; Graham, Martha; London Contemporary Dance Theatre; postmodern dance; Rambert Dance Company

Modern Movement » **Bauhaus; International Style 2**

modern pentathlon » **pentathlon**

Modernism A generic term which refers to experimental methods in different art forms in the earlier part of the 20th-c. These experiments were stimulated by a sharpened sense of the arbitrariness of existing artistic conventions, and doubts about the human place and purpose in the world. Dada, Surrealism, and various anti-genres are all manifestations of Modernism. Notable works include Joyce's *Ulysses* (1922) and T S Eliot's *Waste Land* (1922); the Cubist paintings of Picasso and Braque; and the twelve-tone music of Webern and Schoenberg. » anti-novel; Braque; Dada; Eliot, T S; Joyce, James; Picasso; Schoenberg; Surrealism; Webern

Modigliani, Franco [mohdeel**yah**nee] (1918–) US economist, born in Rome. He studied law in Rome, held chairs at several smaller institutions in the USA (1942–8), then at Illinois (1949–52), Carnegie-Mellon (1952–60), and Northwestern (1960–2) Universities, and at the Massachusetts Institute of Technology (1962–). He was awarded the Nobel Prize for Economics in 1985 for his work on personal saving and on corporate finance. » economics; Modigliani–Miller theory

Modigliani–Miller theory An economic theory developed by US economists Franco Modigliani and Merton H Miller in 1958, which broke new ground in business finance. Their thesis is that if two companies differ only in the way they are financed and in their total market value (ie the value of their shares on the stock market), then investors will sell shares in the overvalued company, and buy shares in the undervalued company until the market value for both is the same. » company; Modigliani, Franco; shares

modulation (physics) The imposition of regular changes on some background, usually a beam of particles or radiation, and often as a means of conveying information via the beam. A broadcast signal is used to modulate the electron beam inside a television set to reproduce the picture. Certain crystals and liquids when subjected to electric fields may be used to modulate beams of light. » amplitude modulation; electro-optic effects; frequency modulation

module A unit measure of proportion in architecture used to regulate all the parts of a building. In classical architecture, this was either the diameter or radius of the column at the base of the shaft. The name derives from Latin *modulus*, 'measure'. Since World War 2, it is particularly used as the common unit of measure that co-ordinates the sizes of all the components in a standardized or 'modular' building, so that they may be fitted together with maximum ease and flexibility. » column; orders of architecture [i]; prefabrication

modulus of compression » **bulk modulus**

modulus of elasticity » **Young's modulus**

modulus of rigidity » **shear modulus**

Moerae or **Moirai** [**moy**ree, **moy**riy] In Greek mythology, the fates; a trio of goddesses, mentioned in Homer, who control human destiny and sometimes overrule the gods. In later writers, they are assigned names and functions: Lachesis, [**la**kesis] ('the distributor'), who allots the destinies of human beings; Clotho, [**kloh**thoh] ('the spinner'), who spins the thread of life; and Atropos, [**a**tropos] ('the inflexible'), who cuts it. They may originally have been birth-goddesses. » Meleager

Mogadishu [moga**di**shoo], Somali **Muqdisho**, Ital **Mogadiscio** 2°02N 45°21E, pop (1982) 377 000. Seaport capital of Somalia, on the Indian Ocean coast; founded, 10th-c; taken by the Sultan of Zanzibar, 1871; sold to Italy, becoming capital of Italian Somaliland, 1905; occupied by British forces in World War 2; airport; university (1954); commerce, oil refining, uranium, food processing; fort, mosques (13th-c), cathedral (1928). » Somalia [i]

Mogadon » **benzodiazepines**

Mogao Caves [mo**gow**] A complex of 496 Buddhist cave temples on the edge of the Taklamakan desert, Gansu, China; a world heritage site. The caves were excavated from the 4th–14th-c, and are noted for their wall paintings, particularly those executed during the 6th–9th-c. » Buddhism

Mogollon [moguh**yohn**] A prehistoric culture of the American SW c. 300–1350, artistically notable for its vigorous ceramics. Extending from S Arizona and New Mexico to the Chihuahuan and Sonoran deserts of Mexico, its villages of c.15–20 pithouses were typically sited for defence on mountain-tops until c.600, when there was a movement towards river valleys to facilitate more intensive maize agriculture. The Zuni of Arizona are their modern descendants. » Anasazi; ceramics; maize; Mimbres; Zuni

Mogul » **Mughal**

mohair » **Angora goat**

Mohammed or **Mahomet** (Western forms of Arabic **Muhammad**) (c.570–632) Founder of the Islamic religion, born at Mecca, the son of Abdallaah, a poor merchant. Orphaned at six, he was cared for first by his grandfather, then by his uncle, and earned his living by tending sheep. At 25 he led the caravans of a rich widow, whom he later married. He continued as a merchant, but spent much of his time in solitary contemplation, and was moved to teach a new faith, which would dispense with idolatry, narrow Judaism, and corrupt Christianity. When he was 40, Gabriel appeared to him on Mt Hira, near Mecca, and commanded him in the name of God to preach the true religion. Four years later he was told to come forward publicly as a preacher. The basis of his teaching was the Koran, which had been revealed to him by God. He attacked superstition, and exhorted people to a pious, moral life, and belief in an all-powerful, all-just, and merciful God, who had chosen him as his prophet. God's mercy was principally to be obtained by prayer, fasting, and almsgiving. At first dismissing him as a poet, the Meccans finally rose against him and his followers. He sought refuge at Medina in 622 (the date of the Mohammedan Era, the Hegira), and assumed the position of highest judge and ruler of the city. He then engaged in war against the enemies of Islam. In 630 he took Mecca, where he was recognized as chief and prophet, and thus secured the new religion in Arabia. In 632 he undertook his last pilgrimage to Mecca, and there on Mt Arafat fixed the ceremonies of the pilgrimage (Hajj). He fell ill after his return, and when too weak to visit the houses of his nine wives, chose as his last sojourn that of Ayeshah, his best beloved, the daughter of Abu Bekr. » Islam; Koran

Mohammed II (1430–81) Ottoman sultan (1451–81), born at Adrianople. He took Constantinople in 1453, thus extinguishing the Byzantine Empire. Checked by Hunyady at Belgrade, he yet annexed most of Serbia, all of Greece, and most of the Aegean Is. Repelled from Rhodes by the Knights of St John (1479), he took Otranto in 1480, and died in a campaign against Persia. » Byzantine Empire; Hunyady

Mohammed Ahmed (1844–85) The Mahdi, born in Dongola. He was for a time in the Egyptian civil service, then a slave trader, and finally a relentless and successful rebel against Egyptian rule in the E Sudan. He made El Obeid his capital in 1883, and defeated Hicks Pasha and an Egyptian army. In 1885 Khartoum was taken, and General Gordon killed. He died later that year, at Omdurman. » Gordon, Charles George; Mahdi

Mohawk An Iroquoian-speaking, semi-sedentary, N American Indian group, living around L Champlain. A member of the Iroquois League, they were defeated by US troops in 1777, and crossed into Canada, settling permanently in Ontario, where they work as farmers and itinerant structural steel workers. Population c.6 000. » Iroquois Confederacy

Mohenjo-daro [muh**hen**joh **da**roh] A prehistoric walled city on the R Indus, in Sind, Pakistan, c.320 km/200 ml NE of Karachi; a world heritage site. Occupied c.2300–1750 BC and excavated since 1922, it covered 100 ha/250 acres and held an ancient population of c.30–40 000. Its two mounds have buildings entirely of mudbrick. To the W, there is a citadel encircled by a 13 m/42 ft-high embankment containing civic, religious, and administrative buildings (notably the 3 m/10 ft-deep Great Bath for ritual bathing). To the E, there is a regularly planned lower city of two-storied houses for the bulk of the population. » Indus Valley Civilization

Mohiniyattam A classical temple dance from India that combines elements of Bharata Natyam and Kathakali. It is a secular, flowing, graceful dance performed by women. » Indian dance

Mohism or **Moism** A Chinese philosophical tradition originating with Mo Tzu (c.470–390 BC). Unlike Confucius, Mo Tzu claimed that one should not follow traditional practices for their own sake; one should love all people equally and adopt those practices that will most benefit people. » Confucianism

Mohole An attempt by US geologists and engineers to drill a borehole into the upper mantle beyond the Mohorovicic discontinuity. It was begun in the 1950s but abandoned in 1966 due to rising costs. » Mohorovicic discontinuity

Moholy-Nagy, László [mohoy **noj**] (1895–1946) Hungarian artist, born at Bàcsborsod. He studied law in Budapest, then under the influence of Lissitzky and the Suprematists became in c.1919 an abstract painter, experimental photographer, theatrical designer, and pioneer constructivist, using translucent and transparent plastic materials; the results he called 'space modulators'. He taught at the Bauhaus (1923–8), and after emigrating he founded in 1937 the New Bauhaus in Chicago, where he died. » abstract art; Bauhaus; Constructivism; Lissitsky; Suprematism

Mohorovicic discontinuity [mohhuh**roh**vuhchich] (or **Moho**) The zone separating the Earth's crust from the mantle, characterized by an abrupt change in density and the speeds of seismic waves travelling through them. It lies at c.6 km/3.5 ml below the ocean floor but up to 70 km/45 ml below the surface of the continents. It is named after its discoverer, Croatian geophysicist Andrija Mohorovičić (1857–1936) who identified it from earthquake shock-wave data in 1909. » Earth [i]; seismology

Mohs' scale » **hardness**

Moism » **Mohism**

Mojave or **Mohave Desert** [moh**hah**vee] Desert in S California, USA, part of the Great Basin; a series of flat basins with interior drainage separated by low, bare ranges; area c.40 000 sq km; annual rainfall c.120 mm/4.7 in; agriculture only where artesian water occurs; the Mojave R flows mainly underground into the Mojave sink. » desert; Great Basin

molasses A brownish syrup, obtained as a by-product of the sugar beet or sugar cane industry; it is what remains once the sugar has been refined. It is widely used as an animal feed supplement, especially for dairy cows, and in the production of rum and treacle. » rum

Mold, Welsh **Yr Wyddgrug** 53°10N 3°08W, pop (1981) 8 505. County town of Clywd in Delyn district, Clwyd, NE Wales, UK; on the R Alyn, 18 km/11 ml WSW of Chester; railway; agricultural trade, light industry. » Clwyd

Moldavia or **Moldava**, Russ **Moldavskaya** pop (1989) 4 338 000; area 33 700 sq km/13 000 sq ml. Republic in E Europe, bounded W by Romania; hilly plain, reaching a height of 429 m/1 407 ft (C); chief rivers, the Dnestr and Prut; proclaimed a Soviet Socialist Republic, 1940; declaration of independence (as Republic of Moldava), 1991; capital, Kishinev; chief towns, Tiraspol, Bendery; wine, tobacco, food-canning, machines, electrical engineering, instruments, knitwear, textiles, fruit. » Soviet Union [i]

Moldavia and Wallachia [mol**day**via, wo**lay**kia] Two independent Balkan principalities formed in the 14th-c: Moldavia lies in NE Romania, SW of the R Prut; Wallachia lies in S Romania, S of the Transylvanian Alps. In the 16th-c they were incorporated into the Ottoman Empire, but the Russo-Turkish wars during the 18th–19th-c weakened Turkish control of the Balkans, and the two states gained autonomy under a Russian protectorate by the Treaty of Adrianople (1829). In 1862 Moldavia and Wallachia merged to form the unitary Principality of Romania; Russian Moldavia became a Soviet Socialist Republic in 1940. » Moldavia; Ottoman Empire; Romania [i]; Russo-Turkish Wars

mole (medicine) Usually a small flat congenital lesion in the skin resulting from the proliferation of small blood vessels and containing scattered pigment cells (*birthmarks*). Occasionally these are more extensive, and form raised patches (*plaques*) which may necessitate surgical removal or other treatment. » birthmark; skin [i]

mole (zoology) A mammal native to lowlands in Europe, Asia, and N America; an insectivore; dark with minute eyes, short tail; enlarged forelimbs used for digging; most moles feed in their burrows; **star-nosed mole** catches food in water; **shrew moles** feed above ground. (Family: *Talpidae*, 27 species.) » desman; insectivore; marsupial mole

mole (physics) Base SI unit of amount of substance; symbol mol; defined as the amount of substance of a system which contains as many elementary entities as there are atoms in 0.012 kg of carbon-12. » Avogadro's number; units (scientific)

mole cricket A burrowing, grasshopper-like insect; body large, to 48 mm/2 in, and heavily armoured; forelegs powerful, spade-like, used for digging; digs galleries underground; feeds on insects, seedlings and tubers; c.50 species, all of which produce sound by vibration (*stridulation*). (Order: *Orthoptera*. Family: *Gryllotalpidae*.) » cricket (entomology); grasshopper

mole rat A mouse-like rodent of family *Muridae* (16 species); three subfamilies: the **blind mole rat** from the Middle East and surrounding area (*Spalacinae*); the **E Asian** or **C Asiatic mole rat**, or **zokor** (*Myospalacinae*); and the **African mole rat** (*Tachyoryctinae*). The name is also used for the cavy-like rodent of family *Bathyergidae* (8 species), the **African mole rat** or **blesmol**. » cavy; mouse (zoology); rodent

mole viper » asp

molecular beam epitaxy A method of producing thin crystal films, in which the film composition can be carefully controlled. It relies on a number of heated sources, each of a different element, from which beams of atoms pass through an evacuated chamber and strike a crystalline target. The precise composition of the atomic layers built up on the crystal is controlled by source temperatures and systems of shutters. The method is used to produce novel semiconductor devices, such as in integrated optics and quantum Hall effect research. » crystals; electrical conduction; integrated optics; quantum Hall effect; thin films

molecular biology The study of the structure and function of the large organic molecules associated with living organisms, especially the nucleic acids (DNA and RNA) and proteins. » biology; molecule; nucleic acids; protein

molecular cloud An interstellar nebula, unusually rich in molecules (as opposed to atoms), detected from microwave radiation. The Galactic centre and Orion Nebula have very rich clouds of this sort. » molecule; nebula

molecular weight The mass of a mole of a substance, based on a mole of ^{12}C having a mass of 12 units; more accurately called the **relative molecular mass**. It is calculated in practice by summing the relative atomic masses of the atoms making up the formula of the substance. » mole (physics)

molecule A finite group of two or more atoms, which is the smallest unit of a substance having the properties of that substance. Molecular compounds include water, most organic compounds, globular proteins, and viruses. Non-molecular compounds include metals, ionic compounds, and diamond. » atom; chemical bond

Molière, originally **Jean-Baptiste Poquelin** (1622–73) French playwright, born in Paris. He began a theatre company in 1643, moving with it to the provinces in 1646, and obtaining the patronage of Philippe d'Orléans. In 1658 he played before the King, and organized a regular theatre. From the publication of *Les Précieuses ridicules* (1659, The Affected Young Ladies) no year passed without at least one major dramatic achievement, such as *L'Ecole des femmes* (1662, The School for Wives), *Tartuffe* (1664), *Le Misanthrope* (1666, The Misanthropist), and *Le Bourgeois gentilhomme* (1670). He died in Paris, after acting in a performance of his last play, *Le Malade imaginaire* (1673, The Imaginary Invalid). » comedy; drama; French literature; satire; theatre

Molina, Luis de (1535–1600) Spanish Jesuit theologian, born at Cuenca. He studied at Coimbra, and became professor of theology at Evora (1568–83). His main work was *Concordia liberi arbitrii cum gratiae donis* (1588, The Harmony of Free Will with Gifts of Grace), which presented the view (later known as **Molinism**) that predestination to eternal happiness or punishment depends on God's foreknowledge of the free determination of human will. He died in Madrid. » Jesuits; scholasticism; theology

mollusc [**mol**uhsk] An unsegmented invertebrate animal, typically with an underside muscular foot and a mantle above, covered by calcareous scales or a solid calcareous shell. A posterior cavity contains gills (*ctenidia*) for respiration. Most have a well-developed head, with eyes and a rasping jaw apparatus (*radula*). Visceral organs are typically protected by a shell secreted by the mantle. Most are free-living in aquatic or damp terrestrial habitats; some are parasitic. There are c.80 000 species. (Phylum: *Mollusca*.) » ammonite; bivalve; calcium; clam; limpet; octopus; oyster; slug; snail; squid

molly Small colourful freshwater fish found in rivers and lakes of C America; length up to 12 cm/4¾ in; greenish brown above, rows of orange spots along sides, dorsal fin with orange and black markings; popular amongst aquarists; many varieties produced through captive breeding. (*Poecilia sphenops. Family: Poeciliidae.*)

Molly Maguires A secret organization of (primarily Irish) miners, involved in industrial disputes in Pennsylvania during the 1870s. The prosecution of their leaders led to hangings and imprisonments, which crushed the group.

Molnár, Ferenc (1878–1952) Hungarian writer, born in Budapest. He studied law, became a journalist, and turned to writing. He is best known for his novel *A Pál utcai fiuk* (1907, The Paul Street Boys), and his plays *Az ördög* (1907, The Devil) and *Liliom* (1909). He moved to the USA in 1940, and died in New York City. » drama; novel

Moloch (mythology) [**moh**lok] In the Bible, a god of the Canaanites and other peoples, in whose cult children were sacrificed by fire. He is a rebel angel in Milton's *Paradise Lost*. The name is used for any excessive and cruel religion. » Milton, John

Moloch (reptile) An agamid lizard native to W Australia; entire body covered with large thorn-like spines; spiky tail shorter than head and body; inhabits deserts; eats ants; also known as **thorny devil** or **horny devil**. (*Moloch horridus*.) » agamid

Molokai [moluh**kiy**] area 670 sq km/260 sq ml. Island of the US state of Hawaii, in Maui county; Kalaupapa leper settlement on the N coast; cattle. » Hawaii (state)

Molotov [**mol**otof], originally **Skriabin, Vyacheslav Mikhailovich** (1890–1986) Russian statesman and Premier (1930–41), born at Kukaida, Vyatka. An international figure from 1939, when he became Foreign Minister (1939–49, 1953–6), he was Stalin's chief adviser at Teheran and Yalta, and was present at the founding of the United Nations (1945). After World War 1, he emerged as the uncompromising champion of world Sovietism; his *nyet* ('no') at meetings of the UN became a byword, and fostered the Cold War. He resigned in 1956, and was demoted by Khrushchev. In the 1960s he retired to his home near Moscow, where he died. » communism; Khrushchev; Stalin; United Nations

Moltke, Helmuth (Karl Bernhard), Graf von ('Count of') [**molt**kuh] (1800–91) Prussian field marshal, born at Parchim, Mecklenburg. He entered Prussian service in 1822, and became Chief of the General Staff in Berlin (1858–88). His reorganization of the Prussian army led to the successful wars with Denmark (1863–4), Austria (1866), and France (1870–1). He died in Berlin. » Prussia

Moluccas, Indonesian **Maluku**, or **Spice Islands** pop (1980) 1 411 006; area 74 505 sq km/28 759 sq ml. Island group and province of Indonesia, lying between Sulawesi (W) and New Guinea (E); includes c.1 000 islands, notably Halmahera, Seram, Buru; mostly volcanic and mountainous; visited by the Portuguese, 1512; under Dutch rule, early 17th-c; secession movement in the S Moluccas followed Indonesian independence (1949), still continuing in the Netherlands; capital, Ambon; copra, spices, sago, coconut oil, tuna. » Indonesia [i]

molybdenum [muh**lib**duhnuhm] Mo, element 42, density 10.2 g/cm^3, melting point 2 610°C. A grey metal, occurring most commonly as the disulphide, MoS_2; it is roasted in air to give MoO_3, which is then reduced with hydrogen. It is an ingredient of several steel alloys, and MoS_2 is important as a high temperature lubricant. » alloy; chemical elements; metal; RR90

Molyneux, Edward [**mol**inyoo] (1891–1974) British fashion designer, born in London. After studying art, he worked for Lucile in London and abroad. After World War 1, he opened his own house in Paris, with branches in London, Monte Carlo, Cannes, and Biarritz, becoming famous for the elegant simplicity of his tailored suits with pleated skirts, and for his evening wear. He died in Monte Carlo. » fashion

Mombasa [mom**ba**sa] 4°04S 39°40E, pop (1984e) 478 000. Seaport in Coast province, SE Kenya; Kenya's main port and second largest city; on Mombasa I, connected to mainland by Mukapa causeway; Kilindini harbour; capital of British East Africa Protectorate, 1888–1907; used as a British naval base in World War 2; airport; railway terminus; car assembly, oil refining, tourism; Fort Jesus (1593), now a museum. » Kenya [i]

moment In physics, a general term referring to a system's ability to rotate under the application of an external force. The moment of force in mechanics is called *torque*. » couple; torque [i]

moment of force » torque [i]

moment of inertia In mechanics, the notion that, for a rotating object, the turning force required to make the object turn faster depends on how the object's mass is distributed about the axis of rotation; symbol I, units kg.m^2. For example, the force needed to spin a disc more quickly about its centre will be greater if the disc's mass is concentrated towards its rim. For a uniform disc of radius r and mass m spinning horizontally about its centre, $I=mr^2/2$. » angular momentum; inertia; mass; mechanics

momentum The product of mass and velocity; symbol p, units kg.m/s; a vector quantity. 'Force equals the rate of change of momentum with time' is the proper statement of Newton's second law. For a closed system on which no forces act, momentum is conserved – an essential principle in physics. » angular momentum; mechanics; velocity

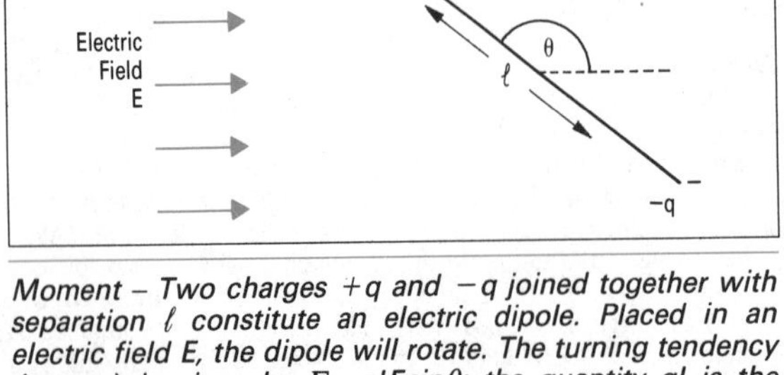

Moment – Two charges +q and −q joined together with separation ℓ constitute an electric dipole. Placed in an electric field E, the dipole will rotate. The turning tendency (torque) is given by $\Gamma = qlE\sin\theta$; the quantity ql is the electric dipole moment.

Mommsen, Theodor (1817–1903) German historian, born at Garding, Schleswig-Holstein. He studied jurisprudence at Kiel (1838–43) and classical inscriptions in Italy (1844–7), and held posts at Leipzig (1848), Zürich (1852), Breslau (1854), and Berlin (1858). His greatest work is his *Romische Geschichte* (3 vols, 1854–5, The History of Rome), in which he applied the new historical method of critical examination of sources. He won the Nobel Prize for Literature in 1902, and died near Berlin.

Mon An agricultural people of Burma and Thailand, thought to have come originally from W China, establishing a kingdom in Burma in about the 9th-c. They introduced Buddhism and Indian Pali writing into Burma, and were subjugated by the Burmese in the 18th-c. They speak an Austro-Asiatic language, also known as **Tailang**. Population c.670 000. » Austro-Asiatic languages; Burma [i]; Thailand [i]

mona monkey A W African monkey, a type of guenon; dark, with undersurface and insides of limbs white or yellow; lives in large noisy troops high in tree tops; eats plant material (especially unripe nuts), snails, and insects. (*Cercopithecus mona*.) » guenon

Monaco, official name **Principality of Monaco** [**mon**akoh] pop (1990e) 29 300; area 1.9 sq km/¾ sq ml. Constitutional monarchy on the Mediterranean Riviera, close to the Italian frontier with France; surrounded landward by the French department of Alpes-Maritimes; capital, Monaco; timezone GMT +1; population 58% French; unit of currency, the French franc; nearest airport at Nice; heliport at Fontvieille; warm, dry summers and mild winters; tourism, chemicals, printing, textiles, precision instruments, plastics, postage stamps; under protection of France since the 17th-c, apart from a period under Sardinia, 1815–61; governed by a prince as head of state, a minister of state, heading a Council of Government, and an 18-member National Council; close political ties with France; Palais du Prince (13th-c), Musée Océanographique, Jardin Exotique. » France [i]; Monte Carlo; RR26 national holidays; RR56 political leaders

monad In metaphysics, any ultimately indivisible unit of which things are composed. Leibniz argued that since anything that is extended is divisible, monads must be unextended. His monads are dynamic and conscious (to varying degrees); every mind, including God's, is a monad. » Leibniz; metaphysics

Monaghan (county) [**mon**agan], Gaelic **Mhuineachain** pop (1981) 51 192; area 1 290 sq km/498 sq ml. County in Ulster province, Irish Republic; bounded N by N Ireland; watered by R Finn; capital, Monaghan (pop (1981) 6 275); cattle, oats, potatoes; fiddler of Orie festival (Jul). » Irish Republic [i]

monarch butterfly A large, colourful butterfly; wings brownish orange, marked with black patterns; slow fliers, migrating over great distances, from Mexico to Canada. (Order: *Lepidoptera*. Family: *Nymphalidae*.) » butterfly

monarchy A political system in which a single person is a political ruler, whose position normally rests on the basis of divine authority, backed by tradition. In Europe, the democratic revolutions of the 18th–20th-c saw an end to what was until then the most widely-known form of government. A number of countries, however, maintained the position of monarch, establishing **constitutional monarchies**, where the sovereign acts on the advice of government ministers who govern on his or her behalf. The monarchy's political power is thus largely formal and its role largely ceremonial, but its influence may increase in times of political crisis or when there is a vacuum in parliamentary politics. » republic

monasticism A form of religious life found in both Christianity (mostly in Roman Catholic and Orthodox circles) and Buddhism, emphasizing the perfection of the individual either through a solitary ascetic existence or more often through life in a consecrated community. In Christianity the movement is often traced back to Antony and Pachomius of Egypt (late 3rd-c). Although initially a lay movement, it soon became dominated by clergy, often marked by voluntary poverty and a life of devotion and worship. The most significant early monastic legislation was the rule of Benedict (480–543), which became a standard in Western Christianity. In the Middle Ages, monks were increasingly involved in scholarly research and copying manuscripts. In the 13th-c several new orders emerged, known as *friars* or *mendicant orders*, which combined monastic life with missionary preaching to those outside. Periods of decline and reform followed from the 14th-c to the 16th-c. » abbey; Augustinians; Benedictines; Buddhism; Capuchins; Carmelites; Carthusians; Christianity; Cistercians; Dominicans; Franciscans; Maurists; Mendicant Orders; Passionists; Premonstratensians; Taizé

monazite [**mon**aziyt] A phosphate mineral containing rare-earth metals (*lanthanides*) such as lanthanum, cerium, yttrium and thorium, and important as the major source of these metals. It occurs in granitic rocks and placer deposits. » lanthanides; phosphate

Monck, George, 1st Duke of Albemarle (1608–70) English general, born at Great Potheridge, Devon. He fought in the Low Countries, and with the Royalists in Scotland, then joined the Commonwealth cause and served successfully in Ireland, Scotland, and in the first Dutch War (1652–4). He feared a return to Civil War during and after Richard Cromwell's regime (1658–9), and was instrumental (as commander of the army in Scotland) in bringing about the restoration of Charles II, for which he was created Duke of Albermarle. He died in London. » Charles II (of England); Dutch Wars; English Civil War

Mond, Ludwig (1839–1909) German-British chemist and industrialist, born at Kassel. He settled in England in 1864, where he perfected a sulphur recovery process, founded an alkali works, and devised a process for the extraction of nickel. He died in London. His son, **Alfred Moritz Mond, 1st Baron Melchett** (1868–1930), became Commissioner of Works (1916–21), and Minister of Health (1922), and helped to form Imperial Chemical Industries (ICI). » nickel; Solvay process; sulphur

Mondale, Walter F(rederick) (1928–) US Democratic politician, born at Ceylon, Minnesota. Educated at Macalester College and the University of Minnesota, he practised law privately, becoming Minnesota Attorney-General (1960) and US Senator (1964). He served under President Carter as Vice-President (1977–81), but failed to obtain a presidential nomination in 1980 and 1984, losing to Reagan. » Carter, Jimmy; Democratic Party; Reagan

Mondrian, Piet, [**mon**drian] originally **Pieter Cornelis Mondriaan** (1872–1944) Dutch artist, born at Amersfoort, the founder with Theo van Doesburg (1883–1931) of the De Stijl movement in architecture and painting. He worked in Paris (1919–38), subsequently going to London and New York. His rectilinear abstracts in black, white, and primary colours have had considerable influence, and he is considered the leader of Neoplasticism. He died in New York City. » De Stijl; Dutch art; Neoplasticism; Plate XI

Monet, Claude [**mon**ay] (1840–1926) French Impressionist painter, born in Paris. He exhibited at the first Impressionist exhibition in 1874; one of his works, 'Impression: soleil levant' (1872, Impression: Sunrise; Paris), gave the name to the movement. He also executed several paintings of subjects under different aspects of light, such as 'Haystacks' (1890–1, Chicago). During his last years he painted the famous series of 'Water Lilies' in his garden at Giverny, where he died. » French art; Impressionism (art); Pissarro; Plate XI

monetarism An economic policy based on the control of a country's money supply. It assumes that the quantity of money in an economy determines its economic activity, and particularly its rate of inflation. If the money supply is allowed to rise too quickly, prices will rise, resulting in inflation. To curb inflationary pressures, governments therefore need to reduce the supply of money and raise interest rates. This view was a major influence on British and US economic policy in the 1980s. » Chicago School (economics); quantity theory of money

money A generally acceptable and convenient medium of exchange, in order to avoid the problems of barter; also a representation of value and a means of storing value. It is usually in the form of coins or notes, but it can be any generally accepted object. Originally coins of gold or silver had an intrinsic value of their own; today, their intrinsic value is virtually nothing. Until the 1920s, money was backed by gold (the *gold standard*): a pound note or dollar bill could be exchanged for a small amount of gold (hence such words on banknotes as 'promise to pay') and the amount of money issued by banks was related to the amount of gold held. Money is now increasingly not in tangible form, but consists of balances in accounts at banks, exchange being by means of cheques, credit-cards or charge-cards, and by *credit-transfer*, where one account is reduced (debited) and another increased (credited) by the same amount electronically. Modern systems are reducing the dependence on cash, hence the emergence of the phrase, the 'cashless society'. Many definitions of money are in use. In the UK, for example, the narrow definition, M0, refers to the stock of notes and coins in circulation, banks' till money, and bankers' balances at the Bank of England. Also in use are M1, M2, M3, M4, and M5, each measurement containing additional items. » credit card

money market In economic terms, the supply of and demand for money. In a free market, the increasing demand for money leads to pressure to raise interest rates. If governments then raise these rates (in the UK through the Bank of England; in the USA, through the Federal Reserve Bank), the demand falls. The term also refers to the place where money is traded – banks, discount houses, and foreign exchange dealers (*money brokers*). » discount houses; interest

money-market funding An economic system created in the 1970s in the USA when interest rates were rising. Interest-rate ceilings were placed on Savings and Loan Associations (US building societies), who were thus unable to offer depositors competitive interest rates. Money-market institutions would take the deposits and invest them in short-term bonds, such as treasury bills. The system also offered limited banking facilities to investors as well as high interest rates. » interest

money spider A small, dark-coloured spider that constructs a sheet-like web on vegetation; adults hang on underside of web and run out to catch prey; very abundant in N hemisphere; can travel long distances attached to silk threads blown by the wind. The name is derived from the folk belief that a spider on one's clothes was a sign of good luck or that money was coming. (Order: *Araneae*. Family: *Liniphiidae*.) » spider

money supply The amount of money in circulation in an economy. The concept is used as a measure of economic activity and as an early indicator of economic problems. The control of money supply is considered very important by monetarists. » monetarism; money

Monge, Gaspard [mõzh] (1746–1818) French mathematician, physicist, and inventor of descriptive geometry, born at Beaune. He became professor of mathematics at Mézières (1768) and of hydraulics at the Lycée in Paris (1780). In 1795 he published his treatise on the application of geometry to the arts of construction. He was made a Senator (1805), but lost his honours at the Restoration, and died in poverty in Paris. » French Revolution [i]; geometry

Mongo A cluster of Bantu-speaking peoples of forested regions of C Zaire, organized into many small chiefdoms. They live by farming, hunting, and gathering, and have a rich oral and music tradition. Population c.500 000. » Bantu-speaking peoples; hunter-gatherers; Zaire [i]

Mongo-Ma-Loba » **Cameroon, Mount**

Mongol » **Altaic**

Mongolia, formerly **Outer Mongolia**, official name **Mongolian People's Republic**, Mongol **Bügd Nayramdakh Mongol Ard Uls** pop (1990e) 2 116 000. Republic of EC Asia, divided into 18 counties (*aimag*); bounded N by Russia and on other sides by China; capital, Ulaanbaatar; chief towns, Darhan, Erdenet; timezone GMT +7 (W), +8 (C), +9 (E); chief ethnic group, Mongol (90%); official language, Khalkha Mongol; chief religion traditionally Tibetan Buddhism; unit of currency, the tugrik of 100 möngö; landlocked mountainous country, average height 1 580 m/5 180 ft; highest point, Tavan-Bogdo-Uli, 4 373 m/14 347 ft; high ground mainly in the W, with folded mountains lying NW–SE to form the Mongolian Altai chain;

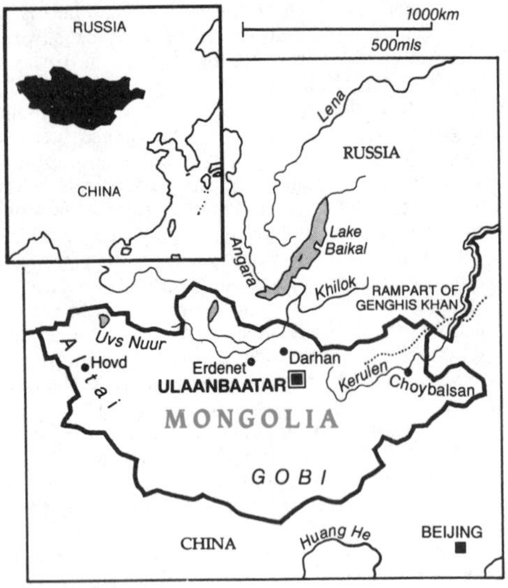

□ *international airport*

lower SE section runs into the Gobi Desert; largest lakes in the NW; major rivers flow N and NE; lowland plains mainly arid grasslands; continental climate, with hard and long-lasting frosts in winter; annual temperature at Ulaanbaatar, −27°C (Jan), 9–24°C (Jul); precipitation generally low; arid desert conditions prevail in the S; originally the homeland of nomadic tribes, which united under Ghengis Khan in the 13th-c to become part of the great Mongol Empire; assimilated into China, and divided into Inner and Outer Mongolia; Outer Mongolia declared itself an independent monarchy, 1911; Mongolian People's Republic formed in 1924, not recognized by China until 1946; governed by a 370-member Great People's Khural (parliament), elected for five years, a Council of Ministers, and a 9-member Presidium, elected for nine years; chairman of Presidium is head of state; traditionally a pastoral nomadic economy; series of 5-year plans aiming for an agricultural-industrial economy; 70% of agricultural production derived from cattle raising; foodstuffs, animal products, wool, hides, fluorspar; copper, coal, gold, tungsten, uranium, lead. » Genghis Khan; Gobi Desert; Mongols; Ulaanbaatar; RR26 national holidays; RR56 political leaders

Mongolian wild horse » **Przewalski's horse**

mongolism » **Down's syndrome**

Mongoloid Any member of the mainly N, E, and SE Asian racial groups, featuring a flattish face, high cheekbones, a fold of the upper eyelid, straight black hair, and yellowish or other medium skin pigmentation. Mongoloid peoples include the Inuit (Eskimos) of Arctic N America. » race

Mongols The general name applied to the tribes of C Asia and S Siberia who effected the violent collapse of the Abbasid Empire before converting to Islam. United under Genghis Khan in 1206, they conquered China under his grandson Kublai, who ruled as first emperor of the Yuan dynasty (1271–1368). About 3 million now live in the Chinese autonomous region of Inner Mongolia, and about 2 million in the People's Republic of Mongolia. » Abbasids; Genghis Khan; Golden Horde; Kublai Khan

mongoose A carnivorous mammal, native to S and SE Asia and Africa (introduced elsewhere); adept at killing snakes and rats, and often introduced to areas for this purpose (usually disastrously, as they also eat other mammals, birds, and birds' eggs). (Family: *Viverridae*, 36 species.) » carnivore [i]; meerkat; Viverridae [i]

monism Any metaphysical doctrine which maintains either that only one thing exists or that only one *kind* of thing exists. Parmenides held the former version, denying all plurality whatsoever. Idealists, who believe that only minds exist, and materialists, who believe that only matter exists, hold the latter version. » idealism; materialism; metaphysics; Parmenides

monitor (navy) A floating gun platform, lying low above the waterline, moving at slow speed. It achieved relatively high firepower while offering a small target silhouette. Used mainly for coastal bombardment, modern weapons have made it obsolete. The name derives from the USS *Monitor*, built by the Unionists in the American Civil War (1861–5), which fought a famous but inconclusive action against CSS *Virginia*; both were ironclads. *Monitor*, capable of only four knots, and unseaworthy, eventually foundered off Cape Hatteras nine months after the initial action. » warships [i]

monitor lizard A lizard native to Africa, S and SE Asia, and Australia; long pointed head and long neck; long tail which cannot voluntarily be shed; long claws; long forked tongue; teeth narrow with sharp cutting edges. (Genus: *Varanus*, 31 species. Family: *Varanidae*.) » Komodo dragon [i]; lizard [i]

monitorial system A concept of early 19th-c British education, developed by British educationalists Andrew Bell (1753–1832) and Joseph Lancaster (1778–1838), to train young school leavers to act as teachers' assistants or 'monitors'. It involved only a few hours' training.

monitoring service An agency responsible for systematically checking foreign broadcasts. Such work entails not only watching or listening to broadcast material, but also recording, translating, and deciphering it, where necessary. When part of a country's intelligence operations, monitoring services are cloaked in great secrecy. » cryptography

Monetary Compensation Amount » **green pound**

Monk, George » **Monck, George**

Monk, Thelonious (Sphere) (1917–82) Composer and pianist, born at Rocky Mount, North Carolina, but brought up in New York. Although once called the 'High Priest of Bebop', and credited with helping to create the jazz style of the 1940s, his angular, idiosyncratic melodies stood apart from the main currents of the day, and his audiences never quite caught up with him. He produced his most memorable compositions when he began recording as a leader (1947–52), such as 'Round Midnight' (1947), and 'Criss Cross' (1951). He died at Weehawken, New Jersey. » jazz; piano

monkey A primate of the group *Anthropoidea*; two subgroups: the **Platyrrhine** or **flat-nosed monkeys** from the New World (includes New World monkeys and marmosets), and the **Catarrhine** or **downward-nosed monkeys** from the Old World. » Anthropoidea; marmoset; New World monkey; primate; Old World monkey

(a) (b)

Monkeys – New World (a) and Old World (b)

monkey bread » **baobab**

monkey nut » **peanut**

monkey-puzzle An evergreen conifer, native to Chile and Argentina; branches in open whorls, covered with hard, sharp-pointed, triangular, overlapping leaves; also known as **Chile pine**. It is often planted in parks and gardens as a curiosity. (*Araucaria araucana*. Family: *Araucariaceae*.) » araucaria; conifer; evergreen plants

monkfish Largest of the angelsharks common in the E North Atlantic and Mediterranean; length up to 1.8 m/6 ft; body shape intermediate between sharks and rays; head flattened, mouth anterior, gill openings lateral, pectoral fins very broad, tail slender; also called **angelfish**. (*Squatina squatina*. Family: *Squatinidae*.) » angelfish

monkshood A perennial with blackish, tuberous roots, native to Europe and NW Asia; leaves deeply-divided; flowers mauve, with a cowl-shaped helmet or hood; also called **aconite**. It is used as a narcotic and painkiller, but is highly poisonous because of the presence of alkaloids, including aconitin. (*Aconitum napellus*. Family: *Ranunculaceae*.) » alkaloids; narcotics; perennial; tuber

Monmouth, James, Duke of (1649–85) Illegitimate son of Charles II of England, born in Rotterdam, the Netherlands. He was created Duke of Monmouth in 1663, and became Captain-General in 1670. He had substantial popular support, and as a Protestant became a focus of opposition to Charles II. After the discovery of the Rye House Plot (1683), he fled to the Low Countries. In 1685 he landed at Lyme Regis, and asserted his right to the crown. He was defeated at the Battle of Sedgemoor, captured, and beheaded in London. » Charles II (of England); James II (of England); Rye House Plot

Monmouth, Battle of (1778) An engagement in New Jersey between British and American troops during the US War of Independence. It was notable for Washington's suspension of General Charles Lee (1731–82) from command, and for the discipline of American troops under fire. » American Revolution; Washington, George

Monnet, Jean [**mon**ay] (1888–1979) French political economist and diplomat, born at Cognac. He introduced in 1947 the **Monnet Plan** for the modernization of French industry. He was President of the European Coal and Steel High Authority (1952–5), and of the Action Committee for the United States of Europe (1956–75). He died at Houjarray. » European Economic Community

Monoceros [muh**no**suhruhs] (Gk 'unicorn') A constellation in the Milky Way, near Orion. It is hard to pick out. » constellation; Orion; RR9

monoclonal antibody A pure antibody produced in bulk by artificial means, and used in medicine for treating diseases (eg some cancers) and in scientific research. It is produced by immunizing an animal with a particular antigen. The animal's lymphocytes which raise antibodies against the antigen are subsequently fused with myeloma cells (B-lymphocyte tumours) to form hybrid cells. These cells multiply rapidly, and produce the antibody in large amounts. » antibodies; cell; lymphocyte

monocotyledons [monuhkoti**lee**dnz] One of two major divisions of the flowering plants, often referred to simply as **monocots**; contrasting with *dicotyledons* (*dicots*). The seed embryo has only one cotyledon, and the primary root of the seedling soon withers, leaving only a fibrous root system. Monocots usually have narrow leaves with parallel unbranched veins, and flowers with parts arranged in threes or multiples of three. The vascular bundles are scattered through the stem; there is usually no cambium, and thus no secondary vascular tissue; and while there are tree-like monocots such as palms, both their manner of growth and their timber are very different from those of dicots. Monocots form a much smaller group than dicots, with about 60 families currently recognized, although some of them (eg grasses, palms, orchids, lilies) are among the largest families of flowering plants. (Subclass: *Monocotyledonae*.) » cotyledons; dicotyledons; flowering plants; vascular tissue

monoculture The growing of one type of crop on the same land, year after year. It is a common practice among cereal growers in many parts of the world, but to maintain high yields heavy use of chemical fertilizers and sprays may be necessary. The term may also refer to single-species tree plantations. » crop rotation

Monod, Jacques (Lucien) [**mon**oh] (1910–76) French biochemist, born in Paris. He became head of the cellular biochemistry department at the Pasteur Institute, Paris (1954), and professor of molecular biology at the Collège de France (1967). He shared the Nobel Prize for Physiology or Medicine in 1965 for his work on the mechanisms governing the activity of genes. He died at Cannes. » biochemistry; gene

monody In music, a single vocal or instrumental line, in contrast to polyphony. Gregorian chant and unaccompanied folksong are both examples of monody, but the term is often applied more specifically (though perhaps less accurately) to the continuo-accompanied solo vocal music of the early 17th-c. » continuo; Gregorian chant; plainchant; polyphony

monomer [**mon**uhmer] A simple molecule which can add to or condense with itself to form a *polymer*. An amino acid is a monomer of a protein; ethylene ($CH_2=CH_2$) is the monomer of polyethylene ($(-CH_2-CH_2-)_n$). » polymerization

mononucleosis, infectious » **glandular fever**

monopack » **integral tripack**

Monophysites [mo**no**fisiyts] (Gr 'one nature') Adherents to the doctrine that Christ did not have two natures after his Incarnation – one human and one divine – but rather had only one nature, which was effectively divine since the divine apparently dominated the human. This view grew out of controversies over the nature and person of Christ from the 4th–6th-c, associated especially with Eutyches (c.378–454, head of a monastery in Constantinople), and condemned by Pope Leo (449) and the Council of Chalcedon (451); yet variant forms continued to arise in subsequent centuries, especially influencing Coptic, Syrian, and Armenian churches. » Christology; heresy

Monopolies Commission or **Monopolies and Mergers Commission** A UK government body set up in 1948 as the *Monopolies and Restrictive Practices Commission*, whose powers were extended by the Restrictive Trade Practices Act (1980). It has wide powers to investigate activities which may be against the public interest, particularly with respect to mergers, takeovers, and monopoly situations. It can empower companies to sell off their operations. » merger; monopoly

monopoly A business situation where there is only one supplier of a commodity or product. It is also an economic concept used to illustrate the effect on demand and prices where there is no competition. The situation is rare in reality, apart from cases of state-owned monopolies, and where there is only one source of supply (a 'natural' monopoly). » Antitrust Acts; Monopolies Commission; monopsony

monopsony A business situation where there is only one buyer – a 'buyer's monopoly'. It is very rare on any significant scale. » monopoly

monorail A railway using a single rail for the support of the train. The rail may be above or below the train, and the train may be stabilized if necessary by guide wheels and gyroscopes. The rail may be made of steel or concrete. Considerable research has gone into investigating non-wheeled methods of support, such as using air cushions and magnetic levitation. Monorails are used almost exclusively for public transport, with the two best-known systems running in Tokyo and Seattle. » gyroscope; railway

monosaccharide [monuh**sa**kariyd] A simple sugar, the monomer of a polysaccharide, formed from it by condensation polymerization. » condensation (chemistry); glucose [i]; polysaccharides; ribose [i]; sugars

monosodium glutamate (MSG) A flavouring agent used to enhance the meat flavour of many processed foods containing meat or meat extracts. It is commonly associated with the 'Chinese Restaurant Syndrome', an array of symptoms associated with eating a Chinese meal where excess MSG has been used. All objective studies suggest that sensitivity to MSG is extremely rare. MSG is absorbed as glutamic acid, and since this is the most abundant natural amino acid in blood, it is difficult to elevate blood glutamate through ingesting MSG. Some of the reported side-effects of MSG may be due to impurities. Most are psychosomatic. » amino acid [i]; flavouring agent

monotheism The belief that only one God exists. It developed within the Jewish faith, and remains a feature of Judaism, Christianity, and Islam. It is opposed to both polytheism and pantheism. Christian belief in the Trinity is thought by Muslims and Jews to deny monotheism. » Christianity; God; Judaism; Islam; pantheism; polytheism

Monothelites A Christian group who believed that in the person of Jesus Christ there was only one will, not two (one human, one divine). They were condemned at the Council of Constantinople in 680. » Christianity; Maronite Church; Monophysites

monotreme [**mon**ohtreem] An egg-laying mammal; lays soft-shelled eggs which hatch after 10 days; suckles young for 3–6 months; no teeth as adults. (Order: *Monotremata*, 3 species.) » duck-billed platypus; echidna; mammal [i]

monotype In art, a one-off print made by painting on a sheet of glass or a metal plate, and pressing a sheet of paper against the wet surface. Castiglione used this method in the 17th-c, Blake used a form of monotype in the 18th-c, and Degas in the 19th-c, frequently in combination with other media such as pastel. » lithography; surface printing; Blake, William; Castiglione; Degas

Monroe, James (1758–1831) US statesman and fifth President (1817–25), born in Westmoreland Co, Virginia. After serving in the War of Independence, he entered politics, becoming a member of the Senate (1790–4), Minister to France (1794–6), Governor of Virginia (1799–1802), Minister in London and Madrid (1803–7), and Secretary of State (1811–17). His most popular acts as President were the recognition of the Spanish-American republics, and the promulgation of the *Monroe Doctrine*. He retired in 1825, and died in New York City. » Monroe Doctrine

Monroe, Marilyn, originally **Norma Jean Mortenson** or **Baker** (1926–62) US film star, born in Los Angeles. After a childhood spent largely in foster homes, she became a photographer's model in 1946. Following several small film parts and a studio publicity campaign, she starred in many successful films as a sexy 'dumb blonde'. Wanting more serious roles, she studied at Strasberg's Actors' Studio and went on to win acclaim in *Bus Stop* (1956). She came to London to make *The Prince and the Showgirl* (1957) with Laurence Olivier, returning after two years to Hollywood. Divorced from her third husband, Arthur Miller, in 1961, she died of an overdose of sleeping pills, and has since become a symbol of Hollywood's exploitation of beauty and youth. » Miller, Arthur; Strasberg

Monroe Doctrine A major statement of American foreign policy, proclaimed in 1823, attributed to President James Monroe, but written by Secretary of State John Quincy Adams. The doctrine was issued after renewed interest in the Americas by European powers, especially Britain and Russia, following the Spanish-American revolutions for independence. It announced (1) the existence of a separate political system in the Western hemisphere, (2) US hostility to further European colonization or attempts to extend European influence, and (3) non-interference with existing European colonies and dependencies or in European affairs. » Adams, John Quincy; Monroe, James

Monrovia [monr**oh**via] 6°20N 10°46W, pop(1981) 306 460. Seaport capital of Liberia, W Africa; 362 km/225 ml SSE of Freetown (Sierra Leone); on an area divided by lagoons into islands and peninsulas; main port and industrial sector on Bushrod Island; founded by the American Colonization Society, 1822; original name Christopolis, changed to Monrovia after the US President; airport; railway terminus; university (1862); Firestone rubber plantation and processing centre nearby; oil, cement. » Liberia [i]

Mons, Flemish **Bergen** 50°28N 3°58E, pop(1982) 93 377. Commercial and cultural city, capital of Hainaut province, S Belgium; inland harbour, handling mostly coal from the Borinage, major mining region; built on site of one of Caesar's camps; often a battlefield, notably in World War 1 (Aug 1914); railway; university (1965); textiles, leather, pharmaceuticals, metal processing, aluminium products; Gothic cathedral, town hall (15th-c); annual Battle of the Lumecon. » Belgium [i]

Monsarrat, Nicholas, pseudonym of **John Turney** (1910–79) British novelist, born in Liverpool. He was educated at Winchester and Cambridge, and abandoned law for literature. During World War 2 he served in the navy, and then wrote his best-selling novel *The Cruel Sea* (1951), which was filmed. He worked in Ottawa as director of the UK Information Office (1953–6) after holding a similar post in South Africa. He died in London. » novel

monsoon climates Climates characterized by distinct wet and dry seasons, resulting from the seasonal migration of the intertropical convergence zone and changes in wind direction; they are found in tropical areas, especially Asia. For the Asiatic monsoon, heating over the Asian landmass in summer results in low pressure over the continent. Warm, moist air is drawn in from the oceans (the SW monsoon) and rain falls. In the autumn the thermal contrast between land and sea declines, and areas of low and high pressure reverse. Cooler, drier winds blow down from the Himalayas (the NE monsoon) and persist until the spring. Much of the agriculture of Asia is dependent on the monsoon, but the timing of its arrival is variable, and if it is late there is generally less rainfall. » intertropical convergence zone; rainfall

monstera [monst**ee**ra] A tall climber or liane, native to tropical America; stems with tough aerial roots; leaves large, heart-shaped, entire when young, developing deep notches and sometimes holes as tissue between veins ceases to grow; spadix surrounded by a large, coloured spathe; also called **Swiss cheese plant**. A popular house plant, the flowers and edible fruits rarely appear when grown indoors. (*Monstera deliciosa*. Family: *Araceae*.) » climbing plant; liane; spadix; spathe

monstrance A liturgical vessel, usually of gold or silver frame with a glass window, used to display the Eucharistic host or consecrated bread. It enables the host to be venerated by worshippers. » Eucharist; liturgy; Roman Catholicism

Mont Blanc [mõ **blã**] Highest alpine massif of SE France, SW Switzerland, and NW Italy; 25 peaks over 4 000 m/13 000 ft; highest peak, Mont Blanc (4 807 m/15 771 ft); frontiers of France, Switzerland, and Italy meet at Mt Dolent (3 823 m/12 542 ft); road tunnel (12 km/7½ ml long) connects France and Italy; first climbed in 1786 by J Balmat and M G Paccard; chief resort, Chamonix. » Alps

Mont-Saint-Michel [mõ sĩ **mishel**] A rocky isle off the coast of Normandy, NW France, famous for its Gothic abbey; a world heritage site. A Benedictine settlement was first established here in the 8th-c, but the most impressive elements of the abbey date from the early 13th-c. » Benedictines; Gothic architecture; Normandy

montage **1** In art, a technique whereby illustrations or photographs are cut from papers or magazines, arranged in new ways, and mounted. A development of collage, it was used by the Dadaists and Surrealists, and persists in modern advertising. » collage; Dada; Surrealism **2** In film editing, a sequence containing a series of rapidly changing images, often dissolving together or superimposed to convey a visually dramatic effect. » editing

Montagu, Lady Mary Wortley, *née* **Pierrepont** (1689–1762) English writer, born and died in London. The daughter of the Earl of Kingston, she married **Edward Wortley Montagu** in 1712, and lived in London, where she gained a brilliant reputation among literary figures. While in Constantinople with her husband, she wrote her entertaining *Letters* describing Eastern life, and introduced inoculation for smallpox into England. She stayed in England until 1739, and then moved to Italy, returning just before her death. » English literature; smallpox

Montaigne, Michel (Eyquem) de [mõ**ten**] (1533–92) French essayist, born at the Château de Montaigne, Périgord. He received his early education at Bordeaux, studied law, and became a city counsellor. In 1571 he succeeded to the family estate, where he lived as a country gentleman until his death, apart from visits to Paris, and a tour in Germany, Switzerland, and Italy. He is remembered for his *Essais* on the ideas and personalities of the time, which introduced a new literary genre, and provided a major contribution to literary history. » French literature

Montale, Eugenio [mont**ah**lay] (1896–1981) Italian poet, born in Genoa. He was the leading poet of the modern Italian 'Hermetic' school, his primary concern being with language and symbolic meaning. His works include *Ossi di Seppia* (1925, Cuttlefish Bones) and *La bufera* (1956, The Storm). He won the 1975 Nobel Prize for Literature, and died in Milan. » Italian literature; poetry

Montana [mont**a**na] pop(1987e) 809 000; area 380 834 sq km/147 046 sq ml. State in NW USA, divided into 56 counties; the 'Treasure State'; most of the state acquired by the Louisiana Purchase, 1803; border with Canada settled by the Oregon Treaty, 1846; became the Territory of Montana 1864; gold rush after 1858 discoveries; ranchers moved into the area in 1866, taking over Indian land; conflict with the Sioux resulted in the defeat of General Custer at the Battle of the Little Bighorn, 1876; six Indian reservations now in the state; 41st state to join the Union, 1889; capital, Helena; other chief cities, Billings and Great Falls; bounded N by the Canadian provinces of British Columbia, Alberta, and Saskatchewan; fourth largest US state; crossed by the Missouri and Yellowstone Rivers; Bitterroot Range, part of the Rocky Mts, lies along much of the W border; highest point Granite Peak (3 901 m/12 798 ft); the Great Plains (E) are largely occupied by vast wheat fields and livestock farms; W dominated by the Rocky Mts, covered in dense pine forests; part of Yellowstone National Park in the S; Glacier National Park in the W; tourism a major state industry; hunting, fishing, skiing, hiking, boating (glacier lakes); copper, silver, gold, zinc, lead, manganese in the mountainous W; petroleum, natural gas, large coalmines in the E; timber, wood products, refined petroleum, processed foods; cattle, wheat, hay, barley, dairy products. » Indian Wars; Louisiana Purchase; United States of America [i]; RR39

Montanism [**mon**tanizm] A popular Christian movement derived from Montanus of Phrygia (c.170 AD) and two women, Prisca and Maximilla, whose ecstatic prophecies and literal expectation of the imminent end of the age won a wide following of churches in Asia Minor. Its austere ethical and spiritual ideals were opposed by the Catholic Church, which defended the importance of the institutional ministry and apostolic tradition. » Christianity; prophet

montbretia [mon**bree**sha] A perennial growing to 90 cm/3 ft, producing corms and spreading by stolons; leaves sword-shaped, in narrow fans; flowers 2.5–5 cm/1–2 in in diameter, orange, slightly zygomorphic, funnel-shaped, in one-sided sprays. It is a hybrid of garden origin, first raised in France in 1880. (*Crocosmia × crocosmiiflora*. Family: *Iridaceae*.) » corm; hybrid; perennial; stolon; zygomorphic flower

Montcalm (de Saint Véran), Louis Joseph de Montcalm-Grozon, Marquis of [mõ**kalm**] (1712–59) French general, born at Condiac. During the Seven Years' War, he took command of the French troops in Canada (1756), and captured the British post of Oswego and Fort William Henry. In 1758 he defended Ticonderoga, and proceeded to the defence of Quebec, where he died in the battle against General Wolfe on the Plains of Abraham. » Seven Years' War; Wolfe, James

Monte Albán [**mon**tay al**ban**] The ancient capital of the Zapotecs of S Mexico, strategically placed at an elevation of 400 m/1 300 ft above the Valley of Oaxaca; a world heritage site. In use c.400 BC–AD 800, it occupied an area of 40 sq km/15 sq ml at its peak (c. 200–700) with a population of c.20 000. Its artificially-levelled hilltop plaza (300 m/1 000 ft by 200 m/650 ft) contains platform pyramids and a ballcourt, while the slopes below are terraced to form c.2 000 house and farm plots. » Meso-American ballgame; Zapotecs

Monte Carlo [**mon**tay **kah**loh] 43°46N 7°23E. Resort town on a rocky promontory of the Mediterranean Riviera, in Monaco, on the N side of the harbour opposite the town of Monaco; famous Casino, providing c.4% of national revenue, built in 1878; Palais des Congrès (Les Spélugues); annual car rally, world championship Grand Prix motor race. » Monaco

Montefiore, Sir Moses (Haim) [monte**fyoh**ray] (1784–1885) Anglo-Jewish philanthropist, born in Leghorn, Italy. He retired with a fortune from stockbroking in 1824, and from 1829 was prominent in the struggle for the rights of Jews, making several journeys throughout Europe on their behalf. He was appointed sheriff of London, knighted in 1837, and made a baronet in 1846. He died at Ramsgate, Kent. » Zionism

Montego Bay [mon**tee**goh] , locally **Mobay** 18°27N 77°56W, pop (1982) 70 265. Port and capital city of St James parish, Cornwall county, NW coast of Jamaica; free port and principal tourist centre of the island; airport; railway; trade in bananas, sugar; Rose Hall Great House (1770), old British fort, 18th-c church. » Jamaica [i]

Montenegro [montuh**nee**groh], Serbo-Croatian **Crna Gora** pop (1981) 584 310; area 13 812 sq km/5 331 sq ml. Constituent republic in W Yugoslavia; a mountainous region bounded SW by the Adriatic Sea and SE by Albania; independent monarchy until 1918; capital, Titograd; livestock, grain, tobacco. » Titograd; Yugoslavia [i]

Montespan, Françoise Athenaïs de Rochechouart, Marquise de [mõtuhspã] (1641–1707) Mistress of Louis XIV, born at Tonnay-Charente, the daughter of the Duc de Mortemart. In 1663 she married the Marquis de Montespan and joined the household of Queen Maria Theresa as lady-in-waiting. She became the King's mistress in c.1667, and after her marriage was annulled (1674) was given official recognition of her position. She bore the King seven children who were legitimized (1673). Supplanted first by Mlle de Fontanges and later by Mme de Maintenon, she left court in 1687 and retired to the convent of Saint-Joseph in Paris, eventually becoming the Superior. She died at Bourbon-l'Archambault. » Louis XIV; Maintenon

Montesquieu, Charles-Louis de Secondat, Baron de la Brède et de [mõtuhskyuh] (1689–1755) French philosopher and jurist, born near Bordeaux. Educated at Bordeaux, he became an advocate, but turned to scientific research and literary work. He settled in Paris (1726), then spent some years travelling and studying political and social institutions. His best-known work is the comparative study of legal and political issues, *De l'esprit des lois* (1748, The Spirit of Laws), which was a major influence on 18th-c Europe. He died in Paris.

Montessori, Maria (1870–1952) Italian doctor and educationalist, born in Rome. She was educated at the University of Rome, where she was the first woman in Italy to graduate in medicine. Later, she joined the psychiatric clinic, and became interested in the problems of mentally-handicapped children. She opened her first 'children's house' in 1907, developing a system of education for children of three to six, based on freedom of movement, the provision of considerable choice for pupils, and the use of specially-designed activities and equipment. 'Montessori schools' were also later developed for older children. She left Italy in 1934, finally settling in the Netherlands. She died at Noordwijk. » education; mental handicap

Monteux, Pierre [mõ**ter**] (1875–1964) French, later US, conductor, born in Paris. He trained at the Paris Conservatoire, and began his career as a viola player. In 1914 he organized the 'Concerts Monteux', whose programmes gave prominence to new French and Russian music. He conducted several orchestras in Europe and the USA, notably the Paris and San Francisco Symphony Orchestras (1929–38, 1936–52 respectively). He died at Hancock, Maine.

Monteverdi, Claudio (1567–1643) Italian composer, born at Cremona. He became a violist, learnt the art of composition, and was appointed court musician to the Duke of Mantua (c.1590), becoming *maestro di cappella* in 1601. In 1613 he took a similar post at St Mark's, Venice, where he remained until his death. His works include eight books of madrigals, operas, and (his greatest contribution to church music) the Mass and Vespers of the Virgin (1610), which contained tone colours and harmonies well in advance of their time. » madrigal

Montevideo [montayvee**day**oh] 34°55S 56°10W, pop (1985) 1 296 089. Federal and provincial capital of Uruguay, on the R Plate; founded, 1726; capital, 1830; airport; railway; university (1849); meat packing, food processing, tanning, footwear, soap, matches, trade in meat, skins, wool; cathedral (1790–1804), several museums and parks, sports stadium (Estadio Centenario), fort on Cerro hill; the German battleship *Graf Spee* was scuttled offshore during the Battle of the River Plate (1939). » Plate, River; Uruguay [i]

Montez, Lola, originally **Marie Gilbert** (1818–61) Irish dancer and adventuress, born in Limerick. She became a dancer in London, and while touring Europe, came to Munich (1846), where she gained influence over the eccentric artist-king, Louis I (1786–1868), who created her Countess of Landsfeld. The 1848 revolution forced her to flee. She then travelled in Australia and the USA, and died in New York City. » Revolutions of 1848

Montezuma II (1466–1520) The last Mexican emperor (1502–20), a distinguished warrior and legislator, who died at Tenochtitlán during the Spanish conquest. One of his descendants was Viceroy of Mexico (1697–1701). » Cortés

Montfort, Simon de, Earl of Leicester (c.1208–65) English statesman and soldier, born at Montfort, near Paris. In 1238 he married Henry III's youngest sister, Eleanor, and as the King's deputy in Gascony (1248), put down disaffection with a heavy hand. He returned to England in 1253, became the leader of the barons in their opposition to the King, and defeated him at Lewes (1264). He then became virtual ruler of England, calling a parliament in 1265; but the barons soon grew dissatisfied with his rule, and the King's army defeated him at Evesham, where he was killed. » Barons' Wars; Henry III (of England)

Montgolfier, Joseph Michel (1740–1810) and **Jacques Etienne** [mõ**golf**yay] (1745–99) French aeronautical inventors, born at Annonay. In 1782 they constructed a balloon whose bag was lifted by lighting a cauldron of paper beneath it, thus heating the air it contained. In 1783 they achieved a flight of 9 km/5½ ml over Paris. Additional experiments were frustrated by the outbreak of the French Revolution. Joseph died at Balaruc-les-Bains, and Jacques near Annonay. » balloon

Montgomery (of Alamein), Bernard Law, 1st Viscount (1887–1976) British field marshal, born in London. Educated at St Paul's School and Sandhurst, he was commissioned into the Royal Warwickshire Regiment in 1908. In World War 2, he gained renown as arguably the best British field commander since Wellington. A controversial and outspoken figure, he was nevertheless a 'soldier's general', able to establish a remarkable rapport with his troops. He commanded the 8th Army in N Africa, and defeated Rommel at El Alamein (1942). He played a key role in the invasion of Sicily and Italy (1943), and was appointed Commander-in-Chief, Ground Forces, for the Allied invasion of Normandy (1944). On his insistence, the invasion frontage was widened, and more troops were committed to the initial assault. Criticized for slow progress after D-Day, he uncharacteristically agreed to the badly planned airborne landings at Arnhem (Sep 1944), which resulted in the only defeat of his military career. In 1945, German forces in NW Germany, Holland, and Denmark surrendered to him on Lüneberg Heath. Appointed field marshal (1944) and viscount (1946), he served successively as Chief of the Imperial General Staff (1946–8) and Deputy Supreme Commander of NATO forces in Europe (1951–8). He died near Alton, Hampshire. » D-Day; El Alamein, Battle of; Normandy Campaign; North African Campaign; World War 2

Montgomery (Alabama) 32°23N 86°19W, pop (1980) 177 857. Capital of state in Montgomery County, C Alabama, USA, on the Alabama R; state capital, 1847; the Confederate States of America formed here, 1861; occupied by Federal troops, 1865; railway; university (1874); important market centre for farming produce; cotton, livestock, dairy products; diverse industries, including machinery, glass, textiles, furniture, foods, paper; scene of the 1955 bus boycott by Blacks protesting against segregation, which contributed to the growth of the civil rights movement. » Alabama; American Civil War; civil rights

month The time for the Moon to orbit the Earth, relative to a reference point. Lunar motion is very complex. The Moon orbits the Earth in 27.32 days (relative to the stars), passing through the familiar cycle of lunar phases. The lunar month of 29.53 days is the interval between successive new Moons. Twelve lunar months is less than one solar year, so the calendar months are arbitrarily longer than lunar months.

Montherlant, Henri (Marie Joseph Millon) de [mõterlã] (1896–1972) French writer, born and died in Paris. He was severely wounded in World War 1, after which he travelled in Spain, Africa, and Italy. His major work is a 4-novel cycle, beginning with *Les jeunes filles* and *Pitié pour les femmes* (1936, trans Pity for Women). After 1942 he wrote several plays, including *Malatesta* (1946) and *Don Juan* (1958). » drama; French literature; novel

Monti, Eugenio (1928–) Italian bobsleigh driver. The winner of a record six Olympic bobsleighing medals, he won golds in the 2- and 4-man events at the 1968 Games after winning the silver in both events in 1956, and the bronze in 1964. He was also a member of 11 Italian world championship winning teams between 1957 and 1968. After retiring in 1968, he was appointed manager to the Italian national team. » bobsledding

Montoneros [monto**nai**ros] Argentine urban guerrillas claiming allegiance to Peronism and (from 1970) staging terrorist actions against the military regime then in power. Repudiated by Juan Domingo Perón himself (1974), the Montoneros renewed their attacks on the regime installed in 1976, meeting with severe repression. » Peronism

Montpelier [mont**pel**yer] 44°16N 72°35W, pop (1980) 8 241. Capital of Vermont, USA; in Washington County, N Vermont, on the Winooski R; settled, 1780; state capital, 1805; railway; Vermont College (1834); notable skiing areas nearby at Pinnacle Mt, Judgement Ridge, Glen Ellen, Bolton Valley, Sugarbush Valley, Mad River Glen; birthplace of Admiral George Dewey; textiles, machinery, wood products, granite quarrying, printing. » Vermont

Montpellier [mõpel**yay**] 43°37N 3°52E, pop (1982) 201 067. Industrial and commercial city, and capital of Hérault department, S France; 123 km/76 ml WNW of Marseilles; founded around a Benedictine abbey, 8th-c; airport; railway; bishopric; university (1289); wine trade, textiles, printing, concrete, machinery, wood products; birthplace of Comte; Gothic Cathedral of St Pierre (1364), many 17th–18th-c patricians' and merchants' houses, Doric triumphal arch (1691), Château d'Eau (aqueduct terminal); Jardin des Plantes, France's first botanical garden (1593); Musée Fabre, Atger Museum. » Comte; Gothic architecture

Montreal [montree**awl**], Fr **Montréal** [mõray**al**] 45°30N 73°36W, pop (1981) 980 354. River-port city in S Quebec province, SE Canada; on Montreal I, on the St Lawrence R (ice-free May–Nov); largest city in Canada, and second largest French-speaking city in the world; first visited by Cartier, 1535; fort, 1611; developed as a fur-trading centre; surrendered to British, 1760; capital of Canada, 1844–9; British garrison withdrawn, 1870; two airports; railway; metro; four universities (1821, 1876, 1969, 1974), two English- and two French-speaking; major commercial centre; aircraft, railway equipment, oil refining, meat packing, clothing, plastics, footwear, cement, brewing, publishing; trade in grain, timber, paper; major league teams, Montreal Expos (baseball), Montreal Canadiens (ice hockey); neo-Gothic Notre Dame Church (1829), Christ Church Cathedral, St James Cathedral, Séminaire de Saint-Sulpice (1658), Maisonneuve Monument (1895), Château de Ramezay (now a museum); location of 1967 World's Fair (Expo) and 1976 Olympic Games. » Cartier; Quebec (province)

Montreux [mõ**trer**] 46°27N 6°55E, pop (1980) 19 685. Winter sports centre and resort town in Vaud canton, SW Switzerland; at E end of L Geneva, SE of Lausanne; railway; figs, vines, walnuts, tourism; casino; 13th-c Château de Chillon nearby; Golden Rose Television Festival (spring), International Jazz Festival (Jun–Jul), music festival (Sep). » Switzerland [i]

Montrose, James Graham, 1st Marquis of (1612–50) Scottish general. Educated at St Andrews, he helped to draw up the Covenant in support of Presbyterianism. He served in the Covenanter army in 1640, but transferred his allegiance to Charles I, and led the Royalist army to victory at Tippermuir (1644). After the Royalist defeat at Naseby (1645), his army became disaffected, and his remaining force was defeated at Philiphaugh. He fled to Europe, returning to Scotland after Charles's execution to avenge his death; but his army was largely lost by shipwreck, and the remnant defeated at Invercharron (1650). He was taken prisoner, and hanged in Edinburgh. » Charles I (of England); Covenanters; English Civil War

Montserrat [montsuh**rat**], also **Emerald Isle** pop (1987) 11 900; area 106 sq km/41 sq ml. Volcanic island in the Leeward Is, Lesser Antilles, E Caribbean; 43 km/27 ml SW of Antigua; British dependent territory; capital, Plymouth; timezone GMT −4; population of mixed African and European descent; chief religion, Christianity; official language, English; unit of currency, the East Caribbean dollar; length, 18 km/11 ml; maximum width, 11 km/7 ml; mountainous, heavily forested; highest point, Chance's Peak (914 m/2 999 ft); seven active volcanoes; tropical climate, with low humidity; average annual rainfall, 1 500 mm/60 in; hurricanes occur (Jun–Nov); visited by Columbus, 1493; colonized by English and Irish settlers, 1632; plantation economy based on slave labour; British Crown Colony, 1871; joined Federation of the West Indies, 1958–62; British sovereign represented by a governor; 7-member Executive Council and a 12-member Legislative Council; tourism the mainstay of the economy, accounting for 25% of national income; cotton, peppers, market gardening, livestock, electronic assembly, crafts, rum distilling, postage stamps; island severely damaged by hurricane Hugo in 1989. » Leeward Islands (Caribbean); Plymouth (Montserrat); West Indies Federation

Monument A Doric column, surmounted by a representation of a flame-encircled globe, designed by Wren and erected (1671–7) to commemorate the Fire of London. The structure is 61.5 m/202 ft high and stands in Fish Street Hill, London. » Doric order; Fire of London; London [i]; Wren, Christopher

Moody, Dwight L(yman) (1837–99) Leading independent US evangelist, born and died at Northfield, Massachusetts. A shopman in Boston, in 1856 he went to Chicago, where he engaged in missionary work. In 1870 he was joined by **Ira David Sankey** (1840–1908), who accompanied his preaching with singing and organ playing. They toured the USA as evangelists, and in 1873 and 1883 they visited Britain. » evangelicalism; missions, Christian

Moog synthesizer » synthesizer

Moon The Earth's only natural satellite, lacking any atmosphere; about a quarter the size of the Earth, and treated as one of the family of terrestrial planets. It has the following characteristics: mass 0.073×10^{27}g; radius (equatorial) 1 738 km/1 080 ml; mean density 3.34 g/cm^3; equatorial gravity 162 cm/s; rotational period 27.3 days; orbital period 27.3 days; average distance from Earth 382 000 km/237 000 ml. Overall density is low, because of a major iron deficiency – a singularity which challenges theories of its origin. Apollo seismic measurements indicate that the interior is solid to a depth of c.1 000 km/600 ml; the nature of the core is still uncertain. There is no global magnetic field, but evidence of past magnetization is contained in individual rock samples. The equality of rotational and orbital rates is due to tidal despinning of the Moon into a stable synchronous period, and causes the same hemisphere of the Moon always to face the Earth.

The brighter surface regions (*highlands*) represent the original lunar crustal material shaped by saturation bombardment of meteoritic material. The dark surface regions (*mare* regions), located mainly on the side observable from Earth, represent basaltic (volcanic) flooding of basins created by major asteroidal impacts. Apollo and Luna sample isotopic dating places mare basalts in the range of 3–4 thousand million years, in contrast to 4.2–4.5 thousand million for highland samples. Lunar evolution models based on Lunar Orbiter mapping of the Moon and on Apollo and Luna sample analyses suggest five principal episodes: accretion and large-scale melting; crustal separation and concurrent massive meteoritic bombardment; partial melting at depth; diminished bombardment with further melting at depth and emplacement of mare basalts; and cessation of volcanism and gradual internal cooling. The current paradigm for the creation of the Moon involves the impact of a Mars-sized object with the Earth, occasioning a catastrophic disruption of the Earth, and the accretion of the Moon in Earth orbit from debris torn from the Earth's mantle. » Apollo/Luna/Lunar Orbiter/Ranger/Surveyor programme; Earth [i]; libration; planet; RR6 [i]

moon bear » black bear

moon daisy » ox-eye daisy

moonfish Large midwater fish widespread in tropical and temperate seas at depths of 100–500 m/300–1 600 ft; length up to 1.5 m/5 ft; body deep, compressed, fins well-developed, protruding mouth, lacking teeth; colour very characteristic, deep blue on back spotted with white, underside silver, fins deep red; also called **opah**. (*Lampris guttatus*. Family: *Lampridae*.)

moonrat A SE Asian insectivorous mammal; resembles closely-related hedgehogs, but lack spines and have longer tails; several species reputed to be the most evil-smelling animals (scent from anal glands resembles rotting garlic); they live alone; also known as **hairy hedgehog** or **gymnure**. (Family: *Erinaceidae*, 5 species.) » hedgehog; insectivore

moonstone A semi-precious gemstone variety of the mineral potassium feldspar. It has a pale opalescent lustre because of its fine-scale oriented microstructure, which diffracts light. » feldspar

Moore, Archie, byname of **Archibald Lee Wright** (1913/1916–) US boxer, born at Benoit, Missouri. His actual date-of-birth is uncertain (by his own account), but he is still the oldest man to hold a world title. He was 39 (or 36) when he beat Joey Maxim (1922–) for the light-heavyweight title in 1952. He had 234 professional bouts and won 199, knocking out a record 145 opponents. He lost to Cassius Clay in 1962, and retired in 1965. » Ali, Muhammad; boxing [i]

Moore, Brian (1921–) British novelist, born and educated in Belfast, Northern Ireland. He emigrated to Canada in 1948, and then lived in New York and California. His first novel, *Judith Hearne*, appeared in 1955; later works include *The Doctor's Wife* (1976) and *Black Robe* (1985), both short-listed for the Booker Prize. » novel

Moore, G(eorge) E(dward) (1873–1958) British empiricist philosopher, born in London. Educated at Dulwich College and Cambridge, he left classics for philosophy, where he first embraced and then rejected the claims of Hegelian idealism. His major ethical work was *Principia Ethica* (1903), in which he argued against the naturalistic fallacy. At Cambridge he became a lecturer in moral science (1911), professor of mental philosophy and logic (1925–39), and editor (1921–47) of *Mind*. A leading influence on the Bloomsbury group, he died in Cambridge. » Bloomsbury group; Hegel; idealism; naturalistic fallacy

Moore, Gerald (1899–1987) British piano accompanist, born at Watford, Hertfordshire. He studied music at Toronto, and established himself as an outstanding accompanist of the world's leading singers and instrumentalists, a constant performer at international music festivals, and a notable lecturer and TV broadcaster on music. He died at Penn, Buckinghamshire. » piano

Moore, Henry (Spencer) (1898–1986) British sculptor, born at Castleford, Yorkshire. He studied at Leeds and London, where he taught sculpture from 1924. He produced mainly figures and groups in a semi-abstract style based on the organic forms and rhythms found in landscape and natural rocks. His interest lay in the spatial quality of sculpture, an effect he achieved by the piercing of his figures. His major works include 'Madonna and Child' (1943–4) in St Matthew's Church, Northampton, and the decorative frieze (1952) on the Time-Life building, London. He died at Much Hadham, Hertfordshire. » abstract art; English art; sculpture

Moore, Sir John (1761–1809) British general, born in Glasgow, Scotland. From 1794 he served in many countries in Europe, and in the West Indies, but is remembered for his command of the English army in Spain (1808–9), where he was forced to retreat to Coruña. There he defeated a French attack, but was mortally wounded (as recounted in the poem by Charles Wolfe.) » Peninsular War; Wolfe, Charles

Moore, Marianne (Craig) (1887–1972) US poet, born in St Louis, Missouri, and educated at Bryn Mawr College. From 1925 to 1929 she edited *The Dial*. *Poems* (1921) was followed by *Observations* (1924) and *Selected Poems* (1935), with an introduction by T S Eliot; her *Collected Poems* appeared in 1951. She died in New York City. » American literature; poetry

moorhen Either of two species of rail, genus *Gallinula*, especially the **moorhen, common gallinule**, or **Florida gallinule** (*Gallinula chloropus*), found worldwide except Australasia; also the **lesser** or **little moorhen** (*Gallinula angulata*), found in Africa S of the Sahara; long legs and toes; inhabit water margins; related to coots. » coot; gallinule; rail

moorish idol Colourful marine fish widespread on shallow reefs in the Indo-Pacific region; length to 18 cm/7 in; body deep with tall dorsal and anal fins; mouth tubular; coloration very bold in broad black and white bands with some yellow shading. (*Zanclus cornutus*. Family: *Acanthuridae*.)

Moors Muslims from N Africa who conquered the Iberian Peninsula in the 8th-c AD. The Hispanic Christian kingdoms (Castile, above all) fought Wars of Reconquest, which by the mid-13th-c eliminated the Moors from all but the small S kingdom of Granada. Granada was conquered in 1492, and in 1502 all professed Muslims were expelled by order of Queen Isabella. » Isabella I

moose » elk

mop-head » **hydrangea**

moped [**moh**ped] A small lightweight motorcycle fitted with pedals, and capable of being pedalled if necessary. It was established as a means of personal transport before World War 2, but it was not until after the War that its economy made it attractive. This economy was achieved by lightness of design and the application of the two-stroke engine. The dividing line between a moped and a light motorcycle is very fine, but depends on the possibility of actually being able to propel the vehicle by means of its pedals. Because of its characteristics, the moped is normally used for short distance urban travel. » motorcycle

moraine A sedimentary deposit of poorly sorted rock and detritus transported by glaciers and ice-sheets. Different classes of moraine correspond to the different zones of glaciers where deposition occurs (eg terminal moraines, lateral moraines). » glaciation; till

Moral Majority A US pressure group founded in 1979 which has played a leading part in the revival of the New Right. It campaigns for the election of morally conservative politicians and for changes to public policy in such areas as abortion, homosexuality, and school prayers. It is associated with Christian fundamentalists who in the 1980s came to play a prominent role in US politics. » New Right

Moral Rearmament A movement founded by Frank Buchman in 1938 to deepen the spirituality and morality of Christians. It succeeded the 'Oxford Group Movement' (founded 1921), and the original individualistic and pietistic emphasis was expanded to include political and social concerns. » Buchman; Christianity; Pietism

moral theology A theological discipline concerned with ethical questions considered from a specifically Christian perspective. Its sources include scripture, tradition, and philosophy. In Roman Catholic teaching, it deals traditionally with God as the goal of human life, and provides instruction on spirituality and the means of grace. It is often divided into *foundational* and *special* moral theology, the former dealing with such topics as scriptural ethics, Christian anthropology, freedom, responsibility, and sin; the latter dealing with particular areas of social and political morality. Since the Second Vatican Council, it has become increasingly ecumenical, and concerned with issues such as peace, justice, and bioethics. » Christianity; ecumenism; ethics; Roman Catholicism; theology; Vatican Councils

morality play A play which dramatizes a moral argument, presenting the opposition between good and evil, often with characters who personify abstractions. The genre derived its technique from the miracle and mystery play, and its subject matter from sermons. It was popular in England in the late mediaeval and early Tudor period. Unlike the mystery play, it was not tied to religious festivals, and was performed by professional actors. » allegory; drama; mystery play

Morar, Loch Loch in W Highland region, W Scotland; SE of Mallaig, on W coast; 19 km/12 ml long; deepest loch in Britain (310 m/1 017 ft); drains into the Sound of Sleat via the R Morar. » Highland; Scotland [i]

Moravia, Alberto, pseudonym of **Alberto Pincherle** (1907–90) Italian novelist and short-story writer, born and died in Rome. He became a journalist, travelled extensively, and lived for a time in the USA. His first novel was a major success, *Gli indifferenti* (1929, The Time of Indifference), portraying in a fatalistic way the preoccupation with sex and money of bourgeois Roman society. Later works include *La disubbidienza* (1948, Disobedience) and *Racconti romani* (1954, Roman Tales). » Italian literature; novel; short story

Moravia [muh**ray**via], Czech **Morava**, Ger **Mähren** Historic province of C Czechoslovakia; bounded N by Poland, S by Austria, W by Bohemia, and E by Slovakia; separated from Slovakia by the Little and White Carpathian Mts; corridor (the Moravian Gate) provides communication link (N–S); chief towns include Brno, Ostrava, Olomouc; chief rivers include the Morava, Oder, Opava, Dyje; early mediaeval kingdom (Great Moravia), 9th-c; part of Bohemia, 1029; under Habsburg rule from early 16th-c; province of Czechoslovakia, 1918; united with Silesia, 1927–49; coal, iron ore, and other minerals. » Bohemia; Czechoslovakia [i]; Habsburgs

Moravian Brethren A Protestant body descended from an association of Brethren formed in Bohemia in 1457, and driven out in 1722 by persecution. They spread over parts of Europe, where they were influenced by Pietism. In 1734 the Moravian Church was established in N America, where most members live today. » Pietism; Protestantism

Moray, James Stuart, 1st Earl of (1531–70) Regent of Scotland (1567–70), the natural son of James V of Scotland, and half-brother of Mary, Queen of Scots. He acted as Mary's chief adviser (1560), but supported John Knox and opposed Mary's marriage to Darnley. After an attempted coup, he was outlawed and took refuge in England (1565). Pardoned the following year, he became Regent for Mary's baby son when she abdicated (1567), and defeated her army at Langside (1568). His Protestant and pro-English policies alienated some Scots nobles, and he was killed at Linlithgow by one of Mary's supporters. » Darnley; Knox, John; Mary, Queen of Scots

moray eel Any of the family *Muraenidae* of marine eels, widespread in tropical and warm temperate seas; dorsal and anal fins continuous, pelvics and pectorals absent; teeth well-developed; largest species may exceed 3 m/10 ft in length; includes *Muraena helena*, found in the Mediterranean and E Atlantic; length up to 1.3 m/4.3 ft; mottled brown and yellow; may be extremely aggressive. » fin

Mordecai [**maw**duhkiy] Biblical hero, described in the Book of Esther as a Jew in exile in Persia (c.5th-c BC) who cared for his orphaned cousin Esther and gained the favour of King Xerxes after uncovering a plot against him. He used his subsequent influence to protect Jews from an edict issued against them. The event is commemorated by the annual Jewish feast of Purim. » Esther, Book of; Old Testament

More, Henry (1614–87) English philosopher and poet, known as the 'Cambridge Platonist', born at Grantham, Lincolnshire. He was educated at Eton and Cambridge, where he became a fellow in 1639, and remained all his life. He gave himself entirely to philosophy, especially to Plato and the Neoplatonists. His works include the *Divine Dialogues* (1668). » Cambridge Platonists; Neoplatonism

More, Sir Thomas, also **St Thomas More** (1478–1535), feast day 9 July. English statesman, born in London. He was educated at London and Oxford, became a lawyer, then spent four years in a Carthusian monastery to test his vocation for the priesthood. He did not take holy orders, and under Henry VIII became Master of Requests (1514), Treasurer of the Exchequer (1521), and Chancellor of the Duchy of Lancaster (1525). On the fall of Wolsey (1529), he was appointed Lord Chancellor, but resigned in 1532 following his opposition to Henry's break with Rome. On refusing to recognize Henry as head of the English Church, he was imprisoned and beheaded. A leading humanist scholar, as revealed in his Latin *Utopia* (1516) and many other works, he was canonized in 1935. » Henry VIII; Reformation; Wolsey

Moreau, Gustave [mo**roh**] (1826–98) French painter, born in Paris, where he studied at the Ecole des Beaux-Arts. He was an eccentric Symbolist who painted colourful but usually rather sinister scenes from ancient mythology and the Bible (eg 'Salome', 1876). In 1892 he was appointed professor of painting at the Ecole des Beaux-Arts. He died in Paris. » Symbolists

morel [mo**rel**] An edible fungus; fruiting body consists of a pale stalk (*stipe*) and brownish, egg-shaped head with a pitted or ridged surface; found singly, sometimes in rings, in rich alkaline soils in woods, pastures, and bonfire sites. (*Morchella esculenta*. Subdivision: *Ascomycetes*. Order: *Pezizales*.) » fungus

morello cherry » **cherry**

Morgagni, Giovanni Battista [morgan**yee**] (1682–1771) Italian physician and pathologist, born at Forli. Educated at Bologna, he became an anatomical demonstrator, and professor of theoretical medicine at Padua in 1711. In his writings, he correlated pathological lesions with symptoms in over 700 cases, and is traditionally considered to be the 'father of morbid anatomy'. He died at Padua. » anatomy; pathology

Morgan A breed of strong horse, developed in the 19th-c in the USA; descended from one stallion called *Justin Morgan* (originally called *Figure*); height, 14–15½ hands/1.4–1.6 m/4½–5¼ ft; brown or black; good riding or carriage horse. » horse [i]

Morgan, Edwin George (1920–) British poet, born in Glasgow, Scotland, and educated at the city's university, where he later taught literature. He is a versatile writer, having produced both powerful 'social' poems (the Glasgow Sonnets in *From Glasgow to Saturn*, 1973) as well as much experimental writing, including concrete and computer poems. His work is well represented in *Poems of Thirty Years* (1982). » concrete poetry; poetry; Scottish literature

Morgan, Sir Henry (c.1635–88) Welsh buccaneer, born at Llanrhymney, Glamorgan. Kidnapped as a child in Bristol and shipped to Barbados, he joined the buccaneers, leading many raids against the Spanish and Dutch in the West Indies and Central America. His most famous exploit was the sacking of Porto Bello and Panama (1671). Transported to London under arrest (1672) to placate the Spanish, he was subsequently knighted (1674) on the renewal of hostilities. He died a wealthy planter and Deputy Governor of Jamaica. » buccaneers

Morgan, J(ohn) P(ierpont) (1837–1913) US financier, born at Hartford, Connecticut. In 1895 he founded the international banking firm of J P Morgan and Co, providing US government finance, and developing interests in steel, railroads, and shipping. He was a prominent philanthropist and art collector. His only son, **John** (1867–1943), helped to finance the Allies during World War 1.

Morgan, Thomas Hunt (1866–1945) US geneticist, born at Lexington, Virginia. He studied at Kentucky and Johns Hopkins Universities, and later taught at Columbia, New York (1904–28), and at the California Institute of Technology (1928–45). His early work was in embryology, but his fame rests on his work in genetics: he proved that Mendel's 'genetic factors' are the chromosomes, and showed the link between genes and chromosomes. He won the Nobel Prize for Physiology or Medicine in 1933. » chromosome [i]; genetics [i]; Mendel

Morgan le Fay In Arthurian legend, an enchantress, 'Morgan the Fairy', King Arthur's sister, and generally hostile towards him. She was one of the three queens who received him at his death. » Arthur

Morisot, Berthe (Marie Pauline) [**mo**reesoh] (1841–95) French painter, born at Bourges. The leading female exponent of Impressionism, her early work shows the influence of Corot, who was her friend and mentor. She herself exercised an influence on Manet, whose brother Eugène she married. She died in Paris. » Corot; French art; Impressionism (art); Manet

Morley, E W » **Michelson, A A**

Morley, Robert (1908–) British actor and writer, born at Semley, Wiltshire. He trained in London, and appeared on the London and Broadway stages. In his film career, from 1938, he played many individual character parts, including the title role in *The Trials of Oscar Wilde* (1960). He continued writing into the 1980s, and appeared in *Loophole* (1980) and *Sky High* (1986).

Mormons [**maw**muhnz] A religious movement based on the visionary experiences of Joseph Smith, who organized it as the 'Church of Jesus Christ of Latter-Day Saints' in 1830 at Fayette, New York. Smith claimed to have been led to the Book of Mormon, inscribed on golden plates and buried 1 000 years before in a hill near Palmyra, New York. An account of an ancient American people to whom Christ appeared after his ascension, it teaches Christ's future establishment of the New Jerusalem in America. It is regarded as equal with the Bible. Subjected to persecution, the Mormons moved W, and Brigham Young finally led most of them to the valley of the Great Salt Lake (1847). Mormons actively engage in missionary work and give two years' voluntary service to the Church. There are over 5 million worldwide. » Smith, Joseph; Young, Brigham

Mornay, Philippe de, Seigneur du ('Lord of') **Plessay-Marly** (1549–1623) French Huguenot leader and polemicist, born at Buhy, Normandy, and educated at Heidelberg. Converted to Protestantism in 1560, he was nicknamed the 'Pope of the Huguenots' for his role in the Wars of Religion (1562–98). A trusted counsellor of Henry of Navarre, he undertook many embassies for the Protestant cause; however, he lost the King's favour after Henry's conversion to Catholicism (1593) and played no further part in national affairs. He died at La Forêt-sur-Sèvre. » Huguenots; Religion, Wars of

morning-after pill » **contraception; DES**

morning glory An annual growing to 3 m/10 ft, native to tropical America; climbing by means of twining stems; leaves oval to heart-shaped; flowers up to 12.5 cm/5 in in diameter, funnel-shaped, blue with yellow throat, sometimes purple or red. It is a relative of the sweet potato and bindweeds, and a popular ornamental. (*Ipomaea tricolor*. Family: *Convolvulaceae*.) » annual; bindweed; climbing plant; sweet potato

morning sickness Nausea and vomiting during the first three months of pregnancy, which affects c.50% of women. It tends to subside thereafter, and is believed to result from associated hormonal changes. » pregnancy [i]

Morocco, official name **The Kingdom of Morocco**, Arabic **Al-Mamlakah al-Maghribiyah** pop (1990e) 25 113 000; area 409 200 sq km/157 951 sq ml. N African kingdom, divided into seven provinces; bounded SW by the Western Sahara, SE and E by Algeria, NE by the Mediterranean Sea, and W by the Atlantic Ocean; capital, Rabat; chief towns include Casablanca, Fez, Tangier, Meknès, Kenitra, Tétouan, Oujda; timezone GMT; population almost all of Arab-Berber origin; religion, Islam; official language, Arabic, with French also important; unit of currency, the dirham of 100 centimes.

Physical description and climate. Dominated by a series of folded mountain ranges, rising in the Haut Atlas (S) to 4 165 m/13 664 ft at Mt Toubkal; Atlas Mts descend SE to the NW edge of the Sahara Desert; broad coastal plain bounded W by the Atlantic Ocean; Mediterranean climate on N coast; settled and hot (May–Sep); average annual rainfall 400–800 mm/15–30 in, decreasing towards the Sahara, which is virtually rainless; Rabat, average maximum daily temperature 17–28°C; heavy winter snowfall in High Atlas; desert region has extreme heat in summer, with chilly winter nights.

History and government. N coast occupied by Phoenicians, Carthaginians and Romans since 12th-c BC; invasion by Arabs, 7th-c AD; European interest in the region in 19th-c; Treaty of Fez (1912) established Spanish Morocco (capital, Tétouan) and French Morocco (capital, Rabat); international zone of Tangier created, 1923; protectorates gained independence, 1956; former Spanish Sahara (Western Sahara) under joint control of Spain, Morocco, and Mauritania, 1975; became responsibility of Morocco, 1979; a 'constitutional' monarchy, but the king presides over his appointed cabinet, which is led by a prime minister; unicameral 306-member Chamber of Representatives,

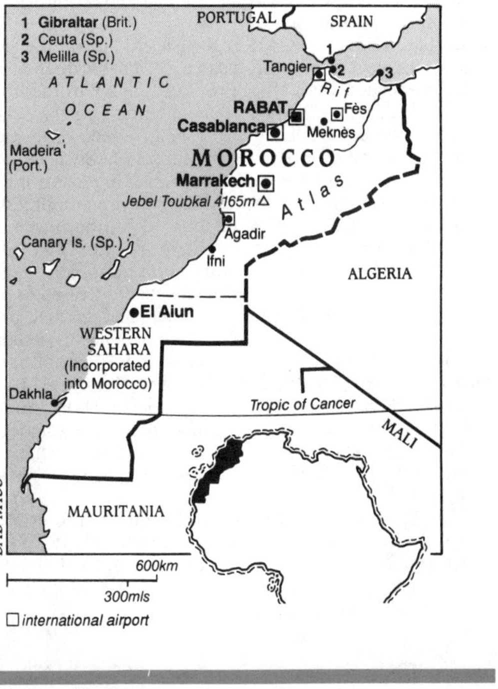

206 elected every six years, the rest chosen by an electoral college.

Economy. Over half the population engaged in agriculture; cereals (wheat and barley), citrus fruits, olives, vegetables, sugar beet, cotton, sunflowers; largest known reserves of phosphate; coal, barite, cobalt, copper, manganese, antimony, zinc, iron ore, fluorspar, lead, silver; fishing, textiles, cement, soap, tobacco, chemicals, paper, timber products, vehicle assembly, crafts; tourism centred on the four imperial cities and the warm Atlantic resorts. » Agadir incident; Tangier; Western Sahara; RR26 national holidays; RR56 political leaders

Moroni [mo**roh**nee] 11°40S 43°16E, pop (1980) 20 112. Capital of Comoros, and chief town of Grand Comore I; airport; vanilla, coffee, cacao, soft drinks, metal and wood products; several mosques; pilgrimage centre at Chiouanda. » Comoros

Morpeth 55°10N 1°41W, pop (1981) 14 496. County town of Northumberland, on the R Wansbeck, 23 km/14 ml N of Newcastle upon Tyne; railway; light engineering, market gardening, mineral water; remains of Morpeth Castle (14th-c). » Northumberland

Morpheus [**maw**fyoos] In Roman mythology, one of the sons of Somnus ('sleep') who sends or impersonates images of people in the dreamer's mind. Later, as in Spenser, he is the god of sleep. » Spenser

morphine A drug derived from opium used to ease severe pain. Because of its addictive potential, its use is controlled. In overdoses it causes death by suppressing respiration. It is also used in anti-diarrhoeal preparations. » diarrhoea; drug addiction; narcotics; opium

morpho A large to very large butterfly with bright, metallic wings; colours produced by scales on wings rather than by pigments; caterpillars with divided last abdominal segment; feeding on leguminous plants. (Order: *Lepidoptera*. Family: *Nymphalidae*.) » butterfly; caterpillar

morphology (biology) The form and structure of an individual organism, with special emphasis on its external features. » anatomy

morphology (linguistics) In linguistics, the study of *morphemes*, the smallest indivisible units of meaning in the structure of a word (eg *anti-lock-ing*, *un-worthi-ness*, *horse-s*). It recognizes such notions as roots, inflections, prefixes, suffixes, and compound words, and tries to establish the rules governing the way words are formed and inter-related within specific languages and language in general. » grammar

Morris, Robert L(yle) (1942–) US psychologist, born at Canonsburg, Pennsylvania, and educated at the University of Pittsburgh and Duke University. In 1985 he was appointed the first Koestler professor of parapsychology at the University of Edinburgh. » parapsychology

Morris, William (1834–96) British craftsman and poet, born and died near London. Educated at Marlborough and Oxford, he associated with the Pre-Raphaelite Brotherhood, then specialized in the revival of handicrafts and the art of house decoration and furnishing. In 1883 he joined the Social Democratic Federation, and then organized the Socialist League. In 1890 he set up the Kelmscott Press, issuing his own works and reprints of classics. » Arts and Crafts Movement; English art; Gothic architecture; Pre-Raphaelite Brotherhood; socialism

Morris dance A ceremonial form of traditional dance found in England. Its distinctive features are stamping and hopping performed by files of performers usually dressed in white and always carrying some prop – a stick, handkerchief, or garland. Some wear bells. They are accompanied by accordion or concertina with bass drum. » Sharp; traditional dance

Morrison (of Lambeth), Herbert Stanley, 1st Baron (1888–1965) British Labour politician, born in London. Largely self-educated, he helped to found the London Labour Party and became its secretary in 1915. First elected an MP in 1923, he was Minister of Transport (1929–31), Minister of Supply (1940), and Home Secretary (1940–5). He served in the War Cabinet from 1942, and became a powerful postwar figure, acting as Deputy Prime Minister (1945–51), but was defeated by Gaitskell for the leadership of the Labour Party in 1955. He was made a life peer in 1959, and died at Sidcup, Kent. » Gaitskell; Labour Party

Morrison, Mount » Yu Shan

Morse, Samuel (Finley Breese) (1791–1872) US artist and inventor, born at Charlestown, Massachusetts, and educated at Yale. He founded and was first president (1826–45) of the National Academy of Design at New York. He studied chemistry and electricity, and developed the magnetic telegraph (1832–5), which along with the 'Morse code' (1838) brought him honours and rewards after the opening of the first telegraph line between Washington and Baltimore (1844). He died in New York City. » Morse code; telegraphy; RR81

Morse code A binary code for the tranmission of verbal messages, devised during the 1830s by Samuel Morse. Each letter of the alphabet, numeral, and punctuation mark, is assigned a distinctive combination of (short) dots and (long) dashes. Thus the distress call SOS is rendered ··· --- ···. An improved version, known as the International Morse Code, was devised at a European conference in 1851. Morse has continued to be used in ship-to-shore communication and various other contexts, but modern telegraphy has made greater use of the more economical **Baudot code**, devised in 1874 by French engineer Jean Maurice Émile Baudot (1845–1903). In 1988, the International Maritime Organization (the United Nations body on shipping safety) agreed to introduce from 1993 the **Global Maritime Distress and Safety System**, which uses satellite technology and dispenses with the tapping out of signals by a radio operator. » Morse; RR81

mortar (building) Any one of many mixtures of lime and sand or (modern) cement and sand with water, which provide a bond between bricks, masonry, or tiles. » cement

mortar (military) A weapon, used typically by infantry forces, which projects a small bomb at a high trajectory to fall on enemy forces at short range. » bomb

mortar and pestle A device known in various forms since ancient times for grinding granular material into powder. The *mortar* is a shallow bowl of abrasive stone. The *pestle* is a conical piece of the same material with a rounded end, with which the material to be ground is forced against the bowl. Simple forms are used in the kitchen or in simple pharmacy. Modern sophisticated mechanized versions are used in industry.

mortgage [**maw**gij] An arrangement whereby a lender (the **mortgagee**) lends money to a borrower (the **mortgagor**), the loan being secured on the mortgagor's land. Mortgages have played a significant role in permitting the spread of home ownership. However, mortgages are not confined to loans used to buy property. Mortgages of chattels are possible, but the complexity of the relevant law has meant that such mortgages are uncommon. The development of hire-purchase was a response to this situation. » property

Mortier, Edouard Adolphe Casimir Joseph, Duc de Trevise ('Duke of Treviso') [**maw**tyay] (1768–1835) French soldier who fought in the Revolutionary and Napoleonic Wars, born at Cateau-Cambrésis. Promoted to general (1799) and Marshal of the Empire (1804), he campaigned in Germany, Russia, and Spain. He was Prime Minister and Minister of War (1834–5) under Louis Philippe, at whose side he was killed during an assassination attempt on the King's life in Paris. » Hundred Days; Louis Philippe; Napoleon I

Mortimer, John (Clifford) (1923–) British playwright and novelist, born in London. He was educated at Harrow and Oxford, became a barrister, and came to prominence as a dramatist with his one-act play *The Dock Brief* (1957), followed by *The Wrong Side of the Park* (1960) and *A Voyage Round My Father* (1970). Television plays and stories about the disreputable barrister Horace Rumpole began in 1978. Among his novels are *Paradise Postponed* (1985) and *Summer's Lease* (1988). » drama; English literature; novel

Morton, H(enry) V(ollam) (1892–1979) British journalist and author of many informally written travel books. He is best known for *In Search of London* (1951), and others in the *In Search of...* series.

Morton, James Douglas, 4th Earl of (c.1525–81) Regent of Scotland (1572–8) for James VI. Although a Protestant, he was made Lord High Chancellor by Mary Stuart (1563); yet he was involved in the murders of Rizzio (1566) and Darnley (1567), and played an important part in the overthrow of the Queen. He joined the hostile noble confederacy, leading its forces at Carberry Hill and Langside, and succeeded Moray as Regent. However, his high-handed treatment of the nobles and Presbyterian clergy caused his downfall (1581). He was arraigned for his part in Darnley's murder, and executed at Edinburgh. » Darnley; Mary, Queen of Scots; Moray; Rizzio

Morton, Jelly Roll, originally **Ferdinand LaMenthe** or **Lamothe** (1885–1941) Jazz composer, bandleader, and pianist, born at Gulfport, Louisiana. His genius as a jazz pioneer comes from his recordings (1923–7) while living in Chicago. His unaccompanied piano solos made best sellers of such tunes as 'King Porter Stomp', 'Wolverine Blues', and 'Jelly Roll Blues'. His orchestral arrangements for his band, the Red Hot Peppers, blended lyricism with stomping rhythms, and ensemble subtlety with improvisation. He died, all but forgotten, in Los Angeles, but his recordings were rediscovered and greeted with considerable fanfare a few years later. » jazz; Lomax, Alan; piano

Morton, John (c.1420–1500) English statesman and cardinal, born (probably) at Milborne St Andrew, Dorset. He practised as a lawyer, and adhered with great fidelity to Henry VI, but after the Battle of Tewkesbury made his peace with Edward IV, and became Master of the Rolls (1473) and Bishop of Ely (1479). Richard III imprisoned him (1483), but he escaped, and after the accession of Henry VII was made Archbishop of Canterbury (1486), Chancellor (1487), and cardinal (1493). He died at Knole, Kent. » Edward IV; Henry VII; Richard III; Roses, Wars of the

Morton, John Cameron (Andrieu Bingham Michael) (1893–1979) British author and journalist. After service in World War 1, he took to writing, publishing many books of humour, fantasy and satire, as well as several historical works. From 1924 he contributed a regular humorous column to the *Daily Express* under the name of 'Beachcomber'. » satire

mosaic The technique of making decorative designs or pictures by arranging small pieces (*tesserae*) of coloured glass, marble, or ceramic in a bed of cement. It was much used by the Romans for pavements, by the early Christians and Byzantines for murals in churches, and also by Islamic artists. Interest in mosaic revived in Italy in the later 19th-c. » Byzantine/Christian/Roman art

Mosaic Law » **Torah**

mosasaur [**moh**sasaw] A very large, marine lizard abundant in Cretaceous seas around N Europe and America; swimming mainly by movements of tail; paddle-like limbs used for steering; head long, teeth long and sharp; typically fed on fishes and other vertebrates. (Order: *Squamata*.) » Cretaceous period; lizard [i]

moschatel [mosk**a**tel] A perennial native to the N hemisphere, 5–10 cm/2–4 in high; rhizomatous; leaves divided into three toothed leaflets; flowers greenish-yellow, forming an almost square head, each face formed by a 5-petalled flower (hence the alternative name, **town hall clock**) plus a 4-petalled flower at the top. (*Adoxa moschatellina*. Family: *Adoxaceae*.) » perennial; rhizome

Moscow, Russ **Moskva** 55°45N 37°42E, pop (1989) 8 769 000. Capital and largest city of Russia, on the R Moskva; linked by canal to the R Volga; known from the 12th-c; capital of the principality of Muscovy, 13th-c; invaded by Napoleon, 1812; capital of the Russian SFSR, 1918; capital of the USSR, 1922; airport; railway; underground; two universities (1960, 1975); Academy of Sciences; solar research, clothing, footwear, textiles, oil refining, chemicals, publishing, tourism; Moscow Art Theatre, Bolshoi Theatre of Opera and Ballet, Moscow State Circus; Kremlin (1300); Spassky Tower (symbol of Moscow), Uspenski (Assumption) Cathedral (1475–9), Cathedral of the Archangel (1333, rebuilt 1505–9), Blagoveshchenski (Annunciation) Cathedral, Great Palace (1838–49), Granovitaya Palace (1487–91), Oruzheinaya Plata or Armoury (1849–51), Palace of the Patriarchs (17th-c), Red Square, St Basil's Cathedral (16th-c, now a museum), Lenin Mausoleum; numerous theatres, art galleries, museums notably the Lenin Museum and the Museum of the Revolution; scene of the 1980 Olympic Games. » Bolshoi Ballet; Kremlin; Lenin Library; Lenin Mausoleum; Red Square; Russia; St Basil's Cathedral; Tretyakov Gallery

Moscow Art Theatre Now one of the most prestigious of Russian theatrical institutions, which began in 1898 as a company of student and amateur actors. Its fame rests on its founders – Stanislavsky and Nemirovich-Danchenko – and their determined advocacy of theatre as a serious and important art; on its meticulous and innovative productions of Chekhov and Gorki; and on its studios, established from 1913 onwards for training and experimental work. » Nemirovich-Danchenko; Stanislavsky; theatre

Moselle, River [moh**zel**], Ger **Mosel**, ancient **Mosella** River in W Germany, Luxembourg, and NE France; rises in the French Vosges; flows N and NE to enter the R Rhine at Coblenz; length 514 km/319 ml; navigable length 240 km/150 ml; canalized since 1964, with a series of 10 dams to regulate its flow; a major wine area. » Germany [i]; wine

Moser-Pröll, Annemarie [**moh**zer **prerl**], *née* **Annemarie Pröll** (1953–) Austrian alpine skier, born at Kleinarl. She won a women's record 62 World Cup races (1970–9), and was overall champion (1979), downhill champion (1978, 1979), Olympic downhill champion (1980), world combined champion (1972, 1978), and world downhill champion (1974, 1978, 1980). She temporarily retired in 1975–6, after her marriage, and finally retired after the 1980 Olympics. » skiing

Moses [**moh**ziz] (probably c.13th-c BC) Major character of Israelite history, portrayed in the Book of Exodus as the leader of the deliverance of Hebrew slaves from Egypt and the recipient of the divine revelation at Mt Sinai. In Exodus, stories about his early life depict his escape from death as an infant, his upbringing in the Egyptian court, his flight to Midian, and his divine call to lead the Hebrews out of Egypt. Stories of this deliverance describe Moses predicting a series of miraculous plagues designed to persuade the Pharaoh to release the Hebrews, the Passover narrative, and the miraculous escape led by Moses through the 'sea of reeds'. Traditions then describe Moses' leadership of the Israelites during their 40 years of wilderness wanderings, his acceptance of the tablets of the Law on Sinai, and his death E of the Jordan R before the Hebrews entered Canaan. Moses was traditionally considered the author of the five books of the Law, the Pentateuch of the Hebrew

Moschatel – Plant and flower head

Bible, but this is doubted by modern scholars. » Aaron; Exodus, Book of; Judaism; Passover; Pentateuch; Sinai, Mount; Torah

Moses, Ed(win) (1955–) US athlete, born at Dayton, Ohio. The world's most successful hurdler over 400 m. Between August 1977 and June 1987 he ran a record 122 races without defeat. He was the World Cup gold medal winner at the 400 m hurdles in 1977, 1979, and 1981, the world champion in 1983, and Olympic champion in 1976 and 1984, only the US boycott of the 1980 Olympics preventing a possible hat trick. He won the bronze medal at the 1988 Olympics. Between 1976 and 1983 he broke the world record four times. » athletics

Moshoeshoe II, originally **Constantine Bereng Seeiso** (1938–) King of Lesotho. Educated at Oxford, he was installed as Paramount Chief of the Basotho people in 1960 and proclaimed King when Lesotho became independent in 1966. His desire for political involvement led to his being twice placed under house arrest, and in 1970 an eight-month exile in Holland ended when he agreed to take no further part in the country's politics. » Lesotho [i]

Moslem » **Islam**

Mosley, Sir Oswald (Ernald), 6th Baronet [**moh**zlee] (1896–1980) British politician, born in London. He was successively a Conservative, Independent, and Labour MP, and a member of the 1929 Labour government. He resigned from Labour, and founded, first, the New Party (1931), and then, following a visit to Italy, the British Union of Fascists, of which he became leader, and which is remembered for its anti-Semitic violence in the East End of London and its support for Hitler. Detained under the Defence Regulations during World War 2, he founded another racialist party, the Union Movement, in 1948. He died in Orsay near Paris, where he mainly lived after the War. » fascism; Hitler

mosquito A small, slender fly with a piercing proboscis; females feed on blood, males on plant juices; eggs laid in water; larvae aquatic, feeding by filtering plankton from water; pupa comma-shaped, active, lives beneath surface film, suspended by its breathing tube; blood-feeding females act as intermediate hosts of malaria, yellow fever, filariasis, dengue, and other disease organisms; c.3 000 species, distributed worldwide. (Order: *Diptera*. Family: *Culicidae*.) » Aedes; Culicidae; fly; larva; malaria; pupa

Mosquito Coast Undeveloped lowland area in E Honduras and E Nicaragua, C America, following the Caribbean coast in a 65 km/40 ml-wide strip of tropical forest, lagoons, and swamp; inhabited by the Meskito Indians; controlled by the British, 1665–1860; timber, bananas. » Caribbean Sea

moss A small, spore-bearing, non-vascular plant of the Class *Musci*, related to liverworts and hornworts. Mat- or cushion-forming, the visible plant is the gametophyte which begins as an undifferentiated body (*thallus*) or, more usually, a threadlike structure (*protonema*) reminiscent of a green alga. This develops into the more familiar plant with stems, simple, delicate leaves, and multicellular rhizoids. The sporophyte consists of a stalked capsule containing a central pillar and numerous spores. The capsule matures after the stalk has elongated, and the spores are released via pores, slits or, in some species, explosively. Mosses are found almost everywhere, most often in damp, shady places. However, some species are better able to withstand drying out, and a few even inhabit very dry places such as walls. (Class: *Musci*.) » algae; bryophyte; gametophyte; hornwort; liverwort; rhizoid; sporophyte

Moss, Stirling (1929–) British racing driver, born in London. He won many major races in the 1950s, including the British Grand Prix (twice), the Mille Miglia, and the Targa Florio; but he never won a world title, though was runner-up to Fangio (1955–7) and to Mike Hawthorn (1958). He won 16 races from 66 starts (1951–61). A bad crash at Goodwood in 1962 ended his career. He then became a journalist and broadcaster, returning to saloon car racing in 1980. » Fangio; motor racing

moss animal » **Bryozoa**

Mössbauer effect [**mers**bower] The recoil-free adsorption and subsequent re-emission of gamma rays by matter; discovered in 1958 by German physicist Rudolf Mössbauer (1929–). Usually after an atom has absorbed a gamma ray photon, it will re-emit the photon and recoil, thereby increasing the wavelength of the emitted radiation. Mössbauer discovered that at low temperatures atomic nuclei can absorb then re-emit gamma ray photons without recoiling individually. The recoil is passed instead to the bulk of the material, and thus has negligible effect on the emitted radiation. This finding provides the basis for a spectroscopic technique, which has been used to observe gravitational red shift as predicted by general relativity. » adsorption; gamma rays; photon; spectroscopy

Mossi A Gur-speaking people of Burkina Faso. They are sedentary farmers, comprising several chiefdoms united under a powerful paramount chief, the Morho Naba of Ouagadougou, who rules a feudally organized kingdom. Population c.1.8 million. » Burkina Faso [i]

Mosul [moh**sool**] 36°21N 43°08E, pop (1970) 293 079. Capital town of Neineva governorate, NW Iraq, on W bank of R Tigris, 352 km/218 ml NNW of Baghdad; chief town of N Mesopotamia, 8th–13th-c; airfield; railway; university (1967); agricultural market centre; power generation, oil refining, cement, textiles; ruins of ancient Nineveh nearby. » Iraq [i]; Mesopotamia

motet A sacred musical work, originating in the 13th-c and cultivated (especially at Vespers) during the Renaissance as an unaccompanied polyphonic piece, reaching its highest point of development in the works of such composers as Desprez, Lassus, Palestrina, and Byrd. After 1600, motets often included instrumental accompaniment, notably the *grands motets* of Charpentier, Lalande, and others performed at the French court, but the term continued to distinguish sacred works in Latin from others (cantatas and anthems) in the vernacular. Some German composers (notably Bach and Brahms), however, used the term *Motette* for pieces in the vernacular without independent instrumental support. » anthem; polyphony; Byrd, William; Charpentier; Josquin Desprez; Lassus; Palestrina

moth An insect belonging to the order *Lepidoptera*, which comprises the butterflies and moths. Moths are distinguished from butterflies by being active mostly at night, by folding their wings flat over the body when at rest, and by having complex comb-like tips to their antennae; but there are exceptions. » cactus/clearwing/clothes/codling/death's head/emperor/geometrid/goat/gypsy/hawk/noctuid/peppered/plume/puss/pyralid/saturnalid/swift/tiger/tineid/tussock/underwing/wax moth; butterfly; corn borer; cutworm; silkworm; Plate IX

moth owl » **owl; owlet frogmouth**

mother-in-law's-tongue A perennial native to W Africa; rhizomatous; leaves to 1 m/3¼ ft, stiff, erect, sword-shaped, fleshy, dark green with pale bands; flowers greenish white; berries orange. It is a widely-grown house plant, also called **sanseveria** and **snake plant**, from the patterning on its leaves. (*Sanseveria trifasciata*. Family: *Agavaceae*.) » perennial; rhizome

Mother Lode The gold-mining region in the W foothills of the Sierra Nevada, California, USA. It was the centre of the Californian gold rush, with peak production in 1852. » gold rush

Mother's Day A day set apart in honour of mothers: in the UK, Mothering Sunday, the fourth Sunday of Lent; in Australia, Canada and the USA, the second Sunday in May.

motherese The speech used by adults to young children while they are learning to speak; also known as **caretaker speech**. It typically has shorter expressions than the ones adults normally use, is grammatically simple, and has clear pronunciation, often with exaggerated intonation patterns. » baby talk

Motherwell, Robert Burns (1915–) US artist, born at Aberdeen, Washington. He studied philosophy at Stanford, Harvard, Grenoble, and later at Columbia, his writing contributing to the theory of modern art in the USA. He was the youngest of the group who founded the Abstract Expressionist movement in New York in the 1940s. » action painting; modern art; Surrealism

Motherwell 55°48N 4°00W, pop (1981) 30 676. Capital of Strathclyde, C Scotland; 20 km/12 ml SE of Glasgow; united with Wishaw burgh in 1920; railway; engineering; pilgrimages to Grotto of Our Lady of Lourdes at Carfin, 3 km/1¾ ml N. » Strathclyde; Scotland [i]

motion pictures » cinema; cinematography [i]

motmot A bird native to the New World tropics; related to kingfishers; tail feathers long, usually with barbless zone near tip; inhabits deep forest; eats insects, lizards, and fruit. (Family: *Motmotidae*, 8 species.) » feather [i]; kingfisher

moto-cross A specialist form of motorcycle racing over a circuit of rough terrain, and taking advantage of natural hazards such as streams and hills. The motorcycles are sturdier than those for road use, and for competition are usually categorized by engine size. The first moto-cross was held at Camberley, Surrey, in 1924. The sport is also often known as **scrambling**. » motorcycle racing

motor insurance A means of protecting a car owner from having to pay the full costs of a car accident or theft. The motorist pays an annual premium to an insurance company, and in the event of accident, damage, or theft, the company will pay the costs arising. There is usually a legal requirement to take out motor insurance on a vehicle before being permitted to drive it on public roads. Various levels of cover are available; for example, 'third party only' allows claims to be made only for damage or injury to another vehicle or road user, whereas 'comprehensive' cover provides protection against all claims. A 'no-claims bonus' entitles the insured person to a reduced premium, if no claims are made. » insurance

motor neurone disease A rare disorder of the central nervous system in which the nerve cells responsible for muscular movement slowly degenerate. Affected persons have progressive difficulty in speaking, swallowing, and moving the limbs. Intellectual powers are preserved to a late stage. The cause is unknown, and there is no effective remedy. » central nervous system

motor racing The racing of finely-tuned motor cars, which can either be purpose-built or modified production vehicles. The most popular form of motor racing is Formula One grand prix racing for high-powered purpose-built cars which can average more than 150 mph/240 kph. A season-long world championship (Mar–Nov), it involves usually 16 races at different venues worldwide. Other popular forms include formula 3000, formula three, rallying, sports car, Indy car racing in the USA, Formula Ford, hill climbing, and production car races. A dangerous sport, safety precautions are very strict in all countries where racing takes place. The first race was in 1894, from Paris to Rouen; the first grand prix was the French, in 1906. Past famous races include the Mille Miglia in Italy and Targa Florio in Sicily. Current famous races include the Le Mans 24-hour endurance race, the Monte Carlo Rally, the Paris to Dakar Rally, and the Indianapolis 500. » drag racing; karting; rally; stock-car racing; RR115

motorcycle A two-wheeled vehicle designed to carry a rider and frequently a passenger for transport and pleasure, using a two- or four-stroke internal combustion engine to drive the rear wheel, with steering being accomplished by the rider turning the front wheel. A sidecar was often fitted to provide extra passenger accommodation, but this has become increasingly rare since the 1960s. The range, style, and design of motorcycles has varied enormously since they became a practical proposition in the mid-1890s. Since the 1960s, motorcycle production has been dominated by a number of Japanese firms, such as Honda and Yamaha. » bicycle; internal combustion engine; moped; motorcycle racing/trials; tyre

motorcycle racing The racing of motorcycles, first organized by the Automobile Club de France in 1906, from Paris to Nantes and back. The most famous races are held on the roads of the Isle of Man each June, and are known as the *TT* (*Tourist Trophy*) races; first held in 1907. A season-long grand prix world championship takes place each year, and a series of races is held for each of the following engine-size categories: 80 cc, 125 cc, 250 cc, 500 cc, and sidecar. Other forms of motorcycle racing include speedway moto-cross (scrambling), and motorcycle trials riding. » moto-cross; motorcycle; motorcycle trials; speedway; RR115

motorcycle trials One of the oldest forms of motorcycle competition. Trials riding is a severe test of the machine's durability, held over tough predetermined courses normally 50–60 km/30–40 ml in length. The Scottish Six Days Trial is the toughest trial in the world. The test calls for all the riders' skills of balance, as well as speed, because they must remain on their machines over rugged undulating surfaces. » motorcycle; motorcycle racing

Mott, Lucretia (1793–1880) US abolitionist and feminist, born at Nantucket, Massachusetts. A Quaker, she became deeply involved in anti-slavery agitation in the 1830s, helping to organize the American Anti-Slavery Society (1833) and the Anti-Slavery Convention of American Women (1837). She was one of the driving forces at the world's first women's rights convention, held at Seneca Falls, New York, in 1848. She died near Abington, Pennsylvania. » Friends, Society of; slave trade; women's liberation movement

Mott, Sir Nevill (Francis) (1905–) British physicist, born in Leeds. He was educated at Cambridge, where he spent most of his career. His early research ranged over atomic collisions, the photographic process, and the properties of crystals, but his most familiar work dates from the 1950s and was concerned with fundamental studies on semiconductors and disordered systems. He shared the Nobel Prize for Physics in 1977. » crystals; semiconductor

motte and bailey A quickly constructed earth and timber fortification of Norman date. It consisted of an artificial mound or *motte* – characteristically shaped like an upturned basin – surrounded by a ditch, a separately defended outer court or *bailey* adjoining to one side. Common particularly in England in the late 11th-c and 12th-c, four examples are depicted on the Bayeux Tapestry. » Bayeux Tapestry; Normans

mouflon [**moo**flon] A wild sheep with a short tail and thick curling horns; short dark fleece with white legs and underparts; two species: **Asiatic mouflon** or **red sheep** (*Ovis orientalis*), the ancestor of domestic sheep, from the mountains of SW Asia; and the **mouflon** or **European mouflon** (*Ovis musimon*) from Corsica and Sardinia (introduced elsewhere). » sheep

mould Any fungus, particularly one with an abundant, woolly mycelium of thread-like strands, often with visible spore-bearing structures. » fungus

moulting The shedding of an external covering, such as the periodic loss of hair by mammals and feathers by birds. Feather shedding and replacement in birds is usually gradual and does not affect flight, but in some birds (eg ducks) all flight feathers are shed simultaneously, and the bird is temporarily flightless. The shedding of the hard outer covering (*exoskeleton*) of arthropods is known as *ecdysis*. » arthropod; feather [i]; hair

mound bird/builder » megapode

Mount Athos, Gr **Agíon Óros** pop (1981) 1 472; area 336 sq km/130 sq ml. Autonomous administration in Macedonia region, Greece; Mt Athos, rising to 1 956 m/6 417 ft, is the 'Holy Mountain' of the Greek Church, associated with the monastic order of St Basil since the 9th-c; declared a theocratic republic in 1927. » Greece [i]; Greek Orthodox Church

Mount Li The burial place of Qin Shihuangdi, the first Emperor of China (259–210 BC); a world heritage site. On the Wei R 32 km/20 ml E of Xi'an, Shaanxi, it is renowned for the discovery in 1974 of a life-size army of c.7 500 painted terracotta figures deployed in military formation in chambers underground. Pit 1 (210 m/690 ft by 60 m/200 ft) holds an armed infantry unit of c.6 000, in 11 parallel corridors, with crossbowmen and six chariots containing officers at the head. Pit 2 has c.1 400 cavalry and 90 chariots drawn by four-horse teams arranged in 14 corridors. » Great Wall of China; Qin dynasty; terracotta

Mount of Olives » Olives, Mount of

Mount Palomar Observatory An observatory in S California, the site of the 5 m Hale reflector telescope (1948), which has made numerous contributions to observational astronomy and cosmology. The 48 in Schmidt telescope at this observatory is used to survey the sky photographically. The first Palomar Optical Sky Survey in the 1950s is a primary database used by all observatories. A second epoch survey using new photographic emulsions has commenced. Measurement of plates from both epochs will enable the proper motions of thousands of stars to be calculated. » observatory [i]; Schmidt telescope; telescope [i]

Mount Sinai » **Sinai, Mount**

Mount Vernon The family home of George Washington on the Potomac R in Virginia. The 18th-c building and its gardens were purchased by the Mount Vernon Ladies' Association in 1858, and furnished and decorated as in Washington's time. Washington and his wife, Martha, are buried there. » Washington, George

Mount Wilson and Las Campanas Observatories Observatories at Mt Wilson, near Pasadena, California, funded by the Carnegie Institution, Washington DC, USA, established in 1904. The main telescope of 2.5 m (1908) contributed to our knowledge of the distant galaxies in the early 20th-c, and is still in use; its observations in the 1920s established that the universe is expanding. Observing conditions in recent years have been severely affected by the night sky brightness of the West Coast urban areas. » telescope [i]

mountain ash » **rowan**

mountain avens [avinz] A dwarf, creeping, evergreen shrub to 8 cm/3 in, native to arctic regions and high mountains; leaves oval with rounded teeth; flowers 7–10-petalled, white, heliotropic; fruits with feathery plume. The flowers act as parabolic mirrors, raising the temperature at the centre several degrees above ambient, thus attracting pollinating insects and enabling them to be more active in the warmth. (*Dryas octopetala*. Family: *Rosaceae*.) » avens; evergreen plants; shrub; tropism

mountain beaver A squirrel-like rodent, native to the Pacific coast of N America; not a true beaver; the most primitive living rodent; stocky with a minute hairy tail; white spot under each ear; inhabits burrows in cool moist regions (not necessarily mountains); also known as **sewellel**, **boomer**, or **whistler**. (*Aplodontia rufa*. Family: *Aplodontidae*.) » beaver; rodent; squirrel

mountain goat » **Rocky Mountain goat**

mountain laurel A coarse, evergreen shrub or small tree, native to N America; leaves elliptical, leathery; flowers saucer-shaped, 5-lobed, white, pink, or red; also called **calico bush**. (*Kalmia latifolia*. Family: *Ericaceae*.) » evergreen plants; shrub; tree [i]

mountain lion » **cougar**

mountain sheep » **bighorn**

Mountain, the A group of Jacobin extremist deputies in the French Convention, led by Robespierre, so-called because they sat high up at the back of the Assembly where they overlooked their political opponents, the Girondins, and the uncommitted majority who were known collectively as 'the Plain'. » French Revolution [i]; Girondins; Jacobins (French history); Plain, the; Robespierre

mountaineering The skill of climbing a mountain aided by ropes and other accessories, such as crampons. It is a very dangerous pastime if undertaken with the wrong pre-approach and equipment. The most popular form in the UK is *rock climbing*; *snow and ice climbing* is practised on the higher peaks of the world. For tall peaks, the climb can take weeks, and often assistance is needed from guides, such as the Sherpas who assist with climbs in the Himalayas. All the world's highest peaks have now been conquered, and present-day mountaineering expeditions aim to climb previously untried routes. Major climbs include: Mont Blanc (1786, Michel Paccard, Jacques Balmat), The Matterhorn (1865, Edward Whymper), Annapurna I (1950, Maurice Herzog, Louis Lachenal), Everest (1953, Edmund Hillary, Tenzing Norgay), and K2 (1954, Achille Compagnoni, Lino Lacedelli).

Mountbatten (of Burma), Louis (Francis Albert Victor Nicholas), 1st Earl (1900–79) British admiral of the fleet and statesman, born at Windsor, Berkshire, the younger son of Prince Louis of Battenberg (later Louis Mountbatten, Marquess of Milford Haven) and Princess Victoria of Hesse, the granddaughter of Queen Victoria. Educated at Osborne and Dartmouth, he joined the Royal Navy in 1916. In World War 2 he became chief of Combined Operations Command (1942), and played a key role in preparations for D-Day. In 1943 he was appointed Supreme Commander, SE Asia, where he defeated the Japanese offensive into India (1944), and worked closely with Slim to reconquer Burma (1945). He received the Japanese surrender at Singapore, and in 1947 was sworn in as last Viceroy of India prior to independence. Created an earl in 1947, he returned to the Admiralty, and became First Sea Lord (1954) and Chief of the Defence Staff (1959). Retiring in 1965, he remained in the public eye, and was assassinated by Irish terrorists while fishing off Mullaghmoor near his summer home, Classiebawn Castle, Co Sligo. » Combined Operations Command; D-Day; Slim; World War 2

Mountbatten, Prince Philip » **Edinburgh, Duke of**

Mourne Mountains [mawn] Mountain range in SE Co Down, SE Northern Ireland; extends 24 km/15 ml from Carlingford Lough NE to Dundrum Bay; a granitic hill range which supplies most of Belfast's water; rises to 852 m/2 795 ft at Slieve Donard. » Northern Ireland [i]

mourning dove A dove native to N America and the Caribbean; short legs, thin bill, and long tail; inhabits woodland, semi-desert, and town outskirts; eats seeds and invertebrates; nests in trees, buildings, or on ground. (*Zenaida macroura*. Family: *Columbidae*.) » dove

mouse (computing) A computer input device which can be moved around on a flat surface causing a cursor to move around the computer screen in response. It usually has at least one selection button, and can be used to choose options pointed to on the screen. » input device

mouse (zoology) A name used for many small unrelated species in the rodent family, found worldwide, especially for members of genus *Mus* (36 species throughout Old World); **house mouse** (*Mus musculus*), from Asia, has dispersed globally in association with humans; spreads some diseases, but is not as guilty as rats; the white **laboratory mouse** is a form of *Mus musculus*. (Family: *Muridae*.) » deer mouse; dormouse; fieldmouse; gerbil; hamster; harvest mouse; jumping mouse; lemming; rat; rodent; vole

mouse deer » **chevrotain**

mouse hare » **pika**

mousebird » **coly**

Moussorgsky, Modest (Petrovich) [moosawgskee] (1839–81) Russian composer, born at Karevo. Educated for the army, he resigned through ill health and began to study music under Balakirev. A member of the Glinka-inspired nationalist group in St Petersburg, he first made a name with his songs; but his masterpiece is the opera *Boris Godunov* (1874). His piano suite *Pictures from an Exhibition* (1874) has also kept a firm place in the concert repertoire. He died in St Petersburg. » Balakirev; Glinka

Mousterian [moosteerian] A European archaeological culture of the Middle Palaeolithic Age (c.70 000–40 000 BC), named after the cave at Le Moustier, Dordogne, SW France, excavated from c.1863. Its stone tools are probably the work of Neanderthal peoples. Comparable material is also found in the Middle East and N Africa. » Neanderthal man; Three Age System

mouth The first part of the gastro-intestinal tract; the space bounded by the lips, cheeks, and palate, lined with mucous membrane, and containing the teeth, the tongue, salivary glands, nerves, and blood vessels. In mammals one of its characteristic features is the movable muscular lips and cheeks, which are intimately related to chewing, and in humans to speech. It is continuous behind with the upper part of the pharynx. » alimentary canal; cleft lip and palate; cold sore; pharynx; salivary glands; teeth [i]; tongue

mouth organ » **harmonica**

mouth-to-mouth respiration » **artificial respiration** [i]

mouthbrooder Freshwater fish widespread in C Africa and along the Nile; length up to 50 cm/20 in; body deep, compressed; feeds on a variety of aquatic invertebrates; female broods eggs in mouth; an important food fish in some areas. (*Sarotherodon niloticus*. Family: *Cichlidae*.)

movement In music, a self-contained section of a longer work, such as a concerto or symphony. It may be linked to the movement that precedes or follows it, with which it is usually contrasted in tempo or key (often both). » concerto; sonata; symphony

movies » cinema; cinematography [i]

Movietone The trade name for one of the first sound-on-film recording and reproducing systems, launched by Fox in 1927. It was used initially for newsreels, and subsequently for all their feature film production. » cinema; sound film

Moynihan, Daniel P(atrick) (1927–) US academic and politician, born at Tulsa, Oklahoma. Educated at the City College of New York and Tufts University, he taught at Syracuse, Harvard, and the Massachusetts Institute of Technology. He served in the administrations of Presidents Johnson and Nixon, acquiring notoriety as the author of *The Negro Family: The Case for National Action* (1965). He became Ambassador to India (1973–4), and won a seat in the US Senate from New York as a Democrat in 1976. » Democratic Party; Johnson, Lyndon B; Nixon, Richard M

Mozambique [mohzam**beek**], official name **Republic of Mozambique**, Port **República de Moçambique** pop (1990e) 15 696 000; area 789 800 sq km/304 863 sq ml. SE African republic, divided into 10 provinces; bounded S by Swaziland, SW by South Africa, W by Zimbabwe, NW by Zambia and Malawi, N by Tanzania, and E by the Mozambique Channel and the Indian Ocean; capital, Maputo; chief towns, Nampula, Beira; timezone GMT +2; chief ethnic groups, the Makua-Lomwe (37%), Shona (10%), Thonga (23%); chief religions, local beliefs (60%), Christianity (30%); official language, Portuguese, with Swahili widely spoken; unit of currency, the escudo of 100 centavos.

Physical description and climate. Main rivers, the Zambezi and Limpopo, providing irrigation and hydroelectricity; S of the Zambezi the coast is low-lying, with sandy beaches and mangroves; low hills of volcanic origin inland; Zimbabwe plateau further N; N of the Zambezi, a more rugged coast, backed by a narrower coastal plain; savannah plateau inland, mean elevation 800–1 000 m/2 600–4 300 ft; highest peak, Mt Binga, 2 436 m/7 992 ft; tropical coastal lowland climate, with relatively low rainfall; average annual rainfall at Beira, 1 520 mm/60 in; maximum daily temperatures, 25–32°C; in drier areas of interior lowlands, rainfall decreases to 500–750 mm/20–30 in; one rainy season (Dec–Mar).

History and government. Originally inhabited by Bantu peoples from the N, 1st–4th-c AD; coast settled by Arab traders; visited by Portuguese explorers by the late 15th-c; part of Portuguese India since 1751; Mozambique Portuguese East Africa, late 19th-c; overseas province of Portugal, 1951; independence movement formed in 1962, the Frente de Libertação de Moçambique (FRELIMO), with armed resistance to colonial rule; independence, 1975; continuing civil war, with first peace talks in 1990; a socialist one-party state, 1975–90; new constitution, 1990; president rules with an Assembly of the Republic; free elections planned.

Economy. Badly affected by drought (1981–4), internal strife, and a lack of foreign exchange; 85% of the population involved with agriculture; cashew nuts, tea, cotton, sugar cane, copra, sisal, groundnuts, fruit, maize, rice, cassava, tobacco; forestry, livestock; reserves of gemstones, diamonds, iron ore, copper, marble, alabaster, aluminium, fluorspar, coal, tin, gold. » Maputo; Zambezi, River; RR26 national holidays; RR56 political leaders

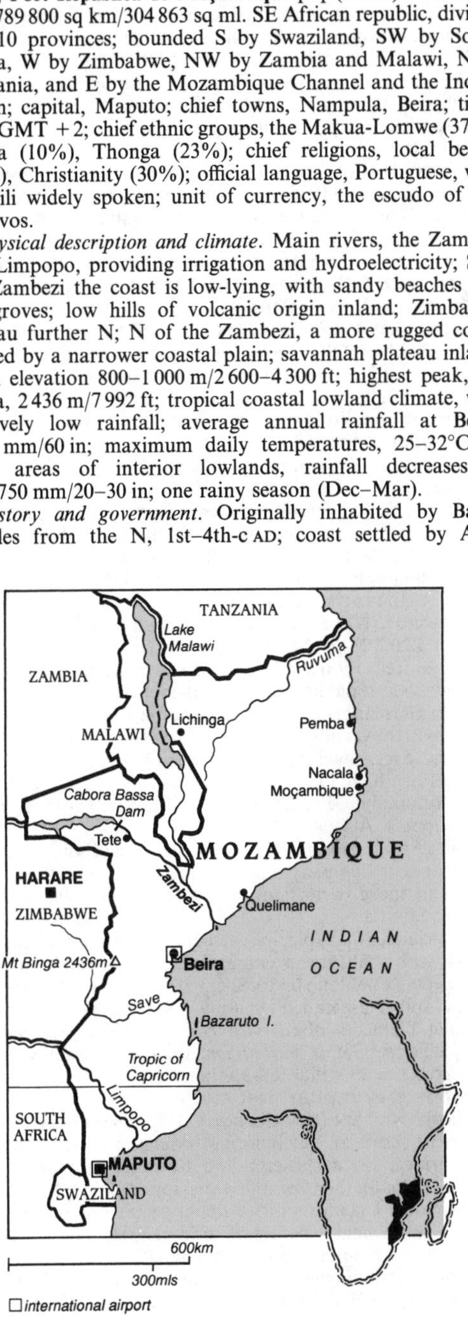

Mozart, (Johann Chrysostom) Wolfgang Amadeus [**moh**tsaht] (1756–91) Austrian composer, born in Salzburg, the son of the violinist and composer Leopold Mozart (1719–87). A child prodigy, he made his first professional tour (as a pianist) through Europe when he was six. He was a prolific composer, and travelled widely, but failed to find a permanent position. After some years in Salzburg as *Konzertmeister* to the Archbishop, he resigned (1781) and settled in Vienna. His operas *The Marriage of Figaro* (1786) and *Don Giovanni* (1787) made it impossible for the court still to overlook the composer, and he was appointed court composer to Joseph II in 1787. He wrote over 600 compositions (indexed by Köchel), including 41 symphonies, and many concertos, string quartets, and sonatas. In writing the Requiem Mass commissioned for Count Walsegg, he felt he was writing his own requiem; he died before it was finished. » concerto; Köchel; symphony

Mubarak, (Mohammed) Hosni (Said) [moo**ba**rak] (?1928–) Egyptian statesman and President (1981–), born at al-Minufiyah. A former pilot and flying instructor, he became Commander of the Egyptian Air Force, and Vice-President under Sadat (1975). After Sadat's assassination (1981), he continued the same domestic and international policies, including firm treatment of Muslim extremists, and the peace process with Israel. » Egypt [i]; Sadat

mucous membrane A sheet of fibrous tissue that lines every cavity or canal of the body which opens to the exterior (eg the alimentary and urogenital tracts). It consists of a surface layer of epithelium, and an underlying connective tissue layer (the *lamina propria*). The surface may contain simple glands. It provides a barrier between the cells that form the body and the external environment. » epithelium; gland; purpura

mudfish » bowfin

mudhopper Very distinctive fish widespread in the Indo-Pacific; locally common on mud flats of estuaries and mangrove swamps, living much of the time out of water; length 15–25 cm/6–10 in; eyes raised on top of head; paired fins used as props and for locomotion across the mud; also called **mudskipper**. (*Periophthalmus koelreuteri* and *Periophthalmodon schlosseri*. Family: *Gobiidae*.)

mudlark Either of two species of bird of genus *Grallina*, also known as **mudnester** or **mudnest builder**: the black-and-white **magpie lark** (*Grallina cyanoleuca*), from open woodland in Australia; and the **torrent lark** (*Grallina bruijni*), from mountain streams in New Guinea. They build nests from mud, hence the name. (Family: *Grallinidae*.) » lark

mudnest builder/mudnester » mudlark

mudpuppy A salamander from N America; spends entire life in water; brown-grey with feathery gills; limbs with four toes; deep narrow tail; inhabits diverse waterbodies; eats invertebrates and fish. (*Fecturus maculosus*. Family: *Proteidae*.) » salamander [i]

mudskipper » mudhopper

muezzin [moo**ee**zin] In Islam, an official of the mosque who issues the call to prayer to the faithful. The name means 'announcer'. » Islam

mufti A man trained in the *Shariʿa*, or Muslim divine law, and who can give legal opinions (*fatwa*) on questions. » Islam

Mufulira [moofoo**lee**ra] 12°30S 28°12E, pop (1980) 149 778.

Mining city in Copperbelt province, Zambia; fourth largest city in Zambia; world's second largest underground copper mine nearby; railway; clothing, explosives. » Copperbelt; Zambia [i]

Mugabe, Robert (Gabriel) [moog**ah**bay] (1924–) Zimbabwean statesman, first Prime Minister (1980–), and President (1987–), born at Kutama, Southern Rhodesia. Largely self-educated, he became a teacher. After short periods in the National Democratic Party and Zimbabwe African People's Union (ZAPU) he was briefly detained, but escaped to co-found, in 1963, the Zimbabwe African National Union (ZANU). After a 10-year detention in Rhodesia (1964–74), he spent five years in Mozambique gathering support in preparation for independence (1980). Mugabe's ZANU and the ZAPU forces of Joshua Nkomo united in 1976 to form the Patriotic Front and, later, a coalition government. A Marxist, Mugabe advocates the transformation of Zimbabwe into a one-party state. » Nkomo; Patriotic Front; Rhodesia; Zimbabwe [i]

mugger A rare crocodile native to India and Sri Lanka; formerly common in the R Ganges; broad snout; young may be 1 m/3 ¼ ft long after only one year. (*Crocodylus palustris.*) » crocodile

Mughal or **Mogul Empire** An important Indian Muslim state (1526–1857), founded by Babur (1526–30). It temporarily declined under Humayun (1530–40), who lost control to the Afghan chieftain Sher Shah (1540–5). His son, Akbar (1556–1605), defeated the Afghan challenge at Panipat (1556) and extended the empire to include territory between Afghanistan and Deccan. This was a period of religious freedom, in which a policy of conciliation was pursued with the Rajput states. Akbar was succeeded by Jehangir (1605–27) and Shah Jehan (1627–58). Its last great emperor was Aurangzeb (1658–1707), who extended the limits of the empire further south; however, religious bigotry alienated non-Muslim supporters and undermined the empire's unity. The Empire disintegrated under Maratha and British pressure. By the mid-18th-c it ruled only a small area around Delhi. Its last emperor, Bahadur Shah II (1837–57) was exiled by the British to Rangoon after the 1857 uprising. » Akbar the Great; Indian Mutiny; Maratha Kingdom

mugwort An aromatic perennial growing to 120 cm/4 ft, native to many temperate areas; leaves deeply divided, dark green above, silvery with woolly hairs below; flower heads reddish-brown, numerous but rather insignificant, crowded on long leafy stems. The young leaves are used as a condiment for goose, duck, and pork. (*Artemisia.* Family: *Compositae.*) » perennial

mugwump A name for Independent Republicans in the US election of 1884 who preferred reform to party discipline, particularly on the question of ending the spoils system. They included the journalist E L Godkin (1831–1902) and the prominent office-holders George William Curtis (1824–92), Carl Schurz (1829–1906), and Charles Francis Adams (1807–86). » Republican Party; spoils system

Muhammad » **Mohammed**

Muharram [mu**ha**ram] The first month of the Muslim year; also used as the name of a religious celebration, especially among Shiite Muslims, held then in commemoration of the death of Husain, grandson of Mohammed, with processions in which the faithful beat their breasts or whip themselves. » Mohammed; Shiites; RR22

Muir, Edwin (1887–1959) British poet, born at Deerness, Orkney, Scotland. He married in 1919, and migrated to Prague, where with his wife he produced translations of Kafka and other authors. He also worked in Rome, Scotland, and Harvard (1955–6, as professor of poetry). His poems appeared in eight slim volumes, dating from 1925, notably in *The Voyage* (1946) and *The Labyrinth* (1949), and he also wrote several critical works. He died near Cambridge, UK. » poetry; Scottish literature

Muir, Jean (1933–) British fashion designer, born in London. Employed by Liberty from 1950, then by Jaeger from 1956, she started on her own as Jane & Jane in 1961. In 1966 she established her own company, Jean Muir. Her clothes are noted for their classic shapes and for their softness and fluidity. » fashion

Mujahadeen [moojaha**deen**] ('holy warriors') Muslim guerrillas who resisted the Soviet occupation of Afghanistan after the invasion (Dec 1979). Based in Iran and Pakistan, they formed various armed bands united by their common aim of defeating the invaders, and the conflict was proclaimed a *jihad* ('holy war'). The Russians withdrew from Afghanistan in 1989, and the Mujahadeen subsequently experienced much internal dissent over their role in the country's future. » Afghanistan [i]; Islam

mujtahid [mooj**tah**hid] A man who exercises personal interpretation of the *Shariᶜa* or Muslim divine law. Shiism allows such interpretations, while Sunnism has usually refused them. » Islam; Shariᶜa; Shiites; Sunnis

Mukden » **Shenyang**

mulberry A deciduous tree, of oriental origin, but long cultivated; heart-shaped, toothed leaves; male and female flowers in separate catkin-like spikes; individual fruits juicy, coalescing so that the whole spike forms the 'berry'. The **black mulberry** (*Morus nigra*) has purplish fruits. The leaves of the **white mulberry** (*Morus alba*) are food for silkworms. (Genus: *Morus*, 10 species. Family: *Moraceae.*) » deciduous plants; silkworm; tree [i]

Muldoon, Robert David (1921–) New Zealand statesman and Prime Minister (1975–84), born in Auckland. He served in World War 2, trained as an acccountant, and became a National Party MP in 1960. After five years as Minister of Finance, he became deputy Prime Minister in 1972, and party leader in 1974. He remained as an MP after his period as Prime Minister. » New Zealand [i]

mule (textiles) A spinning frame invented by Samuel Crompton in 1782, which fully mechanized the hand spinning process. It was regarded as a hybrid of two previous inventions, hence its name. Mainly used for woollen spinning, it is still used for some high-quality yarns. » Crompton, Samuel; Industrial Revolution; spinning

mule (zoology) An animal produced from the mating of a male donkey with a female horse. If a male horse mates with a female donkey the result is a **hinny**. Both are usually sterile, and have the front end resembling the father and the rear end resembling the mother. » donkey; horse [i]

Mulhouse [muhl**ooz**], Ger **Mulhausen** 47°45N 7°21E, pop (1982) 113 794. Industrial and commercial river port in Haut-Rhin department, NE France; on R Ill and Rhine-Rhône Canal, 35 km/22 ml S of Colmar; second largest town in Alsace; imperial free city from 1308; allied with the Swiss, 1515–1648; independent republic until 1798, then voted to become French; under German rule in 1871, reverting to France in 1918; railway; university; linen-weaving and spinning, printed fabrics, dyes, machinery, chemicals, fertilizers, cars; Renaissance town hall (1552), Church of St-Etienne, Musée National de l'Automobile, French Railway Museum, 31-storey Tour de l'Europe. » Alsace

mullah (Arabic, 'master') [**mu**la] In Islam, a scholar, teacher, or man of religious piety and learning. It is also title of respect given to those performing duties related to Islamic Law. » Islam; Shariᶜa

mullein [**mu**luhn] Typically a biennial or perennial, often very hairy, with a tall, erect stem, native to Europe and Asia; rosette leaves oval to oblong up to 50 cm/20 in or more; flowers in long dense spike, 5-petalled, yellow, pink, purple, or white; the stamen filaments often with conspicuous white, yellow, or purple hairs. (Genus: *Verbascum*, 360 species. Family: *Scrophulariaceae.*) » biennial; perennial; stamen

mullet » **grey mullet; red mullet**

Mulliken, Robert (Sanderson) (1896–1986) US chemist and physicist, born at Newburyport, Massachusetts. Educated at Cambridge, Massachusetts, and Chicago, he taught at New York (1926–8), then became professor at Chicago. He won the 1966 Nobel Chemistry Prize for his work on chemical bonds and the electronic structure of molecules. He died at Arlington, Virginia. » chemical bond; molecule

Mullingar [muhlin**gah**], Gaelic **Muileann Cearr** 53°32N 7°20W, pop (1981) 11 703. Market town and capital of Westmeath county, Leinster, E Irish Republic; on the Royal Canal, WNW of Dublin; railway; cattle trade; cathedral. » Irish Republic [i]; Westmeath

Mulready, William (1786–1863) Irish painter, born at Ennis, Co Clare. He studied at the Royal Academy, London, and specialized in genre paintings, becoming best known for his rural scenes, such as 'Interior of an English Cottage' (1828). He also worked at portrait and book illustration, and designed the first penny postage envelope (1840). He died in London. » genre painting

Mulroney, (Martin) Brian (1939–) Canadian politician and Prime Minister (1984–), born at Baie Comeau, Quebec. He studied law at Laval University, taking up a career first in law, then in business. He became leader of the Progressive Conservative Party in 1983, and won a landslide election victory in 1984. His measures have included the Meech Lake Accord (1987), which proposed constitutional changes regarding the position of French-speaking Quebec, and a free trade agreement with the USA (1988) » Canada [i]

multi-vision The audio-visual presentation from groups of slide projectors programmed to show a complex sequence of images on a very wide screen with accompanying sound from tape recording. The pictures can be separate or blended together to fill the whole screen, with fast or slow dissolves between successive images and superimposed effects. » audiovisual aids; slide

multicultural education The education together of more than one cultural or ethnic group. The term is also used to describe education which stresses pluralism, and the contribution to learning which can come from many social and cultural sources, not solely the predominant national one. » education

multilateralism In economics, support for an economic trading system where many countries are encouraged to trade with each other (multilateral trade). The notion is usually contrasted with **bilateralism**, where there is an agreement between two countries to trade with each other on special terms, usually in the form of reduced tariffs, or on favourable financial terms. It was a common form of trading agreement in the 1930s, and is nowadays used mainly in relation to foreign aid. A *bilateral monopoly* exists where there is only one buyer and one seller of a commodity, product, or service. » foreign aid; tariff

multilingualism » **bilingualism**

multinational corporations » **transnational corporations**

multiple sclerosis A disease associated with loss of the normal coating of neurones (*myelin*) in the brain and spinal cord, which affects about 1 in 2 000 people in the UK. There is a genetic susceptibility, and one theory of its cause is that the process is auto-immune. Clinical features are diverse, and include weakness of the limbs, double vision, dimness of vision, vertigo, a sensation of pins and needles, and inability to co-ordinate movements (*ataxia*), all of which can be transient but recurrent, and slowly become more severe. » auto-immune diseases; neurone [i]

multiple star Three or more stars gravitationally bound in complex orbits. The star complex Alpha Centauri is an example of such a system. » Centaurus; star

multipolarity A theory of international politics which contends that power is likely to become concentrated in the hands of a few major powers: the USA, W Europe, USSR, Japan, and China. It superseded the idea of **bipolarity**, which had currency in the 1950s, where power was said to be concentrated in the hands of the two superpowers. Multipolarity gives greater emphasis to economic power relative to military (especially nuclear) power, hence the inclusion of Japan and W Europe. It is suggested that a multipolar system leads to more flexible and stable relationships in international politics.

Mumford, Lewis (1895–1990) US sociologist and author, born at Flushing, New York. Educated at New York City, he became a literary critic and journal editor, and began to write on architecture and urbanization in such works as *The Story of Utopias* (1922) and *The City in History* (1961), stressing the unhappy effects of technology on society. A prolific author, he held academic posts at several universities, including the chair of city and regional planning at Pennsylvania (1951–9). His autobiography was published in 1975. » sociology

mummers In mediaeval England, masked actors who entered houses during winter festivals, diced in silence, distributed gifts, and danced. In the 18th-c the mummers' Christmas play evolved, based on a legend of St George, with a duel between champions ending in the death of one of them and his revival by a doctor.

mumps A viral, feverish infection spread by droplets, especially common among children and young adults. A characteristic feature is pain and swelling of one or both parotid glands near the angle of the jaw; the testes, pancreas, and ovaries may also be affected. The parotid gland swelling usually subsides in a few days. » gland; virus

Munch, Edvard [moongk] (1863–1944) Norwegian painter, born at Löten. He studied at Oslo, travelled in Europe, and settled in Norway in 1908. While in Paris, he was influenced by Gauguin. He was obsessed by subjects such as death and love, which he illustrated in an Expressionist Symbolic style, using bright colours and a tortuously curved design, as in 'The Scream' (1893). His engravings influenced Die Brücke in Germany. He died near Oslo. » Brücke, Die; Expressionism; Gauguin; Symbolism

Münchhausen, (Karl Friedrich Hieronymus), Baron von [**münsh**howzn] (1720–97) German soldier, born and died at Bodenwerder, Hanover. He served in Russian campaigns against the Turks, and became proverbial as the narrator of ridiculously exaggerated exploits. The best of the material attributed to him was written by **Rudolf Erich Raspe** (1737–94), who became professor of archaeology at Cassel. » German literature

Münchhausen's syndrome [**münsh**howzn] In medicine, individuals who wander the country and present themselves at different hospitals with different but spurious physical complaints, many of which need investigation to establish their false nature. It is named after an 18th-c baron, notorious for his tales and romances. » Münchhausen

Muncie 40°12N 85°23W, pop (1980) 77 216. Seat of Delaware County, E Indiana, USA, on W fork of the White R; settled, 1824; city status, 1865; railway; university (1918); electrical equipment, glassware, furniture, vehicle parts; represented as the 'average American town' in the 1929 sociological study *Middletown* by R & H Lynd. » Indiana

Munda An Austroasiatic-speaking people settled in hilly and forested regions of E and C India. Physically indistinguishable from Indians, and culturally similar to other Indians, they have retained a separate identity and religion. Population c.5 million. » Austroasiatic languages

mung bean A bushy annual growing to 90 cm/3 ft or more, native to tropical Asia; leaves with three hairy leaflets; pea-flowers yellow, in small stalked clusters; pods slender, up to 15-seeded. It is widely cultivated, especially in the Orient for the edible pods and nutritious seeds eaten boiled, or germinated to produce 'bean sprouts'. (*Vigna radiata*. Family: *Leguminosae*.) » annual

Munich [myoonikh], Ger **München** 48°08N 11°35E, pop (1983) 1 284 300. Capital of Bavaria province, Germany, on the R Isar; third largest city in Germany; founded, 1158; capital of Bavaria, from 1506; home of the Nazi movement, 1920s; badly bombed in World War 2; railway; university (1471); technical university (1868); chemicals, pharmaceuticals, cosmetics, rubber, precision engineering, machinery, vehicles, aircraft, defence systems, printing and publishing, clothing, foodstuffs, brewing, wine, agricultural produce; Church of St Peter (1181), town hall (1470), cathedral (15th-c), Nymphenburg Palace (17th-c), opera house, art gallery; Oktoberfest (beer festival); site of summer Olympic Games (1972). » Bavaria; Germany [i]; Nazi Party; Pinakothek, Alte

Munich Agreement An agreement signed (29 Sep 1938) at a conference in Munich by British Prime Minister Chamberlain, French Prime Minister Daladier, Mussolini, and Hitler. The Sudeten area of Czechoslovakia was to be ceded to Germany, and the rest of Czechoslovakia was to be guaranteed against unprovoked aggression. Neither Czechoslovakia nor Russia were invited to the conference, or were consulted about the agreement. » Chamberlain, Neville; Daladier; Hitler; Mussolini

Munich Putsch The abortive attempt by Hitler to overthrow the state government of Bavaria in 1923, as a prelude to the March on Berlin and the establishment of the Nazi regime in Germany. It was supported by General Ludendorff, but badly planned, and it disintegrated in the face of firm Bavarian police action. Hitler was tried for treason, and sentenced to five years' imprisonment. » Hitler; Ludendorff; Nazi Party

Munnings, Sir Alfred (1878–1959) British painter, born in Suffolk. A specialist in the painting of horses and sporting pictures, he became president of the Royal Academy (1944–9), and was well known for his forthright criticism of modern art. » English art

Munro, H(ector) H(ugh), pseudonym **Saki** (1870–1916) British writer, born at Akyab, Burma. He went to London c.1900, and became a journalist. He is best known for his humorous and macabre short stories, such as *Reginald* (1904) and *The Chronicles of Clovis* (1911). His novels, such as *The Unbearable Bassington* (1912), show him as a social satirist of the contemporary upper-class Edwardian world. He was killed on the French front in World War 1. » short story; satire

Munsell colour system A system for measuring and naming colours, devised by US painter Albert H Munsell (?–1918). The Munsell Book of Colour contains 1 200 samples grouped according to minimum discriminable intervals of hue, saturation, and brilliance. » light; spectrum

Munster pop (1981) 998 315; area 24 127 sq km/9 313 sq ml. Province in S Irish Republic; bounded S and W by the Atlantic Ocean; comprises the counties of Clare, Cork, Kerry, Limerick, Tipperary (N and S Ridings), and Waterford; a former kingdom. » Irish Republic [i]

Münster [**mün**ster] 51°58N 7°37E, pop (1983) 273 500. Capital city of Münster district, Germany; on the R Aa and the Dortmund-Ems Canal, 125 km/78 ml NNE of Cologne; member of the Hanseatic League; capital of former province of Westphalia; Treaty of Westphalia (1648) signed here; bishopric; railway; university (1780); service industries, civil engineering, gases; cathedral (1225–65). » Germany [i]; Hanseatic League

muntjac or **muntjak** A true deer, native to India and SE Asia; face with 'V'-shaped ridge; arms of 'V' continued as freely projecting bony columns; ends of columns in male bearing short antlers; both sexes with projecting canine teeth; call resembles a dog barking; also known as **barking deer** or **rib-faced deer**. (Genus: *Muntiacus*, 5 species.) » antlers [i]; deer

Müntzer, Thomas [**münt**suh] (c.1489–1525) German preacher and Anabaptist, born at Stolberg. He studied theology, and in 1520 began to preach at Zwickau, but his socialism and mystical doctrines soon brought him into conflict with the authorities. In 1525 he was elected pastor of the Anabaptists of Mülhausen, where his communistic ideas soon aroused the whole country. A leader of the Peasants' Revolt (1524–5), he was captured at the Battle of Frankenhausen, and executed at Mühlhausen. » Anabaptists; Peasants' Revolt; Reformation

muon A fundamental particle, produced in weak radioactive decays of pions; symbol μ; mass 106 MeV; charge -1; spin ½. It behaves like a heavy electron, but decays to an electron and neutrinos. It was discovered in 1937 by US physicist Carl Anderson (1905–) in cosmic ray experiments. » fundamental particles; lepton; pion

mural A painting or carving on a wall. Murals, representing human and animal motifs as well as pure pattern, have existed since prehistoric times, and various techniques have been used. A great deal of impressive wall decoration survives from the Ancient Near East: the Egyptians, for instance, used distemper or gouache for decorating their tombs, while the Babylonians and Assyrians made extensive use of stone low-relief sculpture. Although Greek wall-painting has almost all perished, we know a good deal about the various styles of Roman wall decoration from the excavations at Pompeii, Herculaneum, and Stabiae (2nd-c BC–AD 79). Both fresco and mosaic were employed: mosaic was much favoured during the Byzantine period in Italy, fresco during the later Middle Ages and Renaissance. » fresco; mosaic; relief sculpture

muramidase » lysosyme

Murasaki, Shikibu (978–c.1031) Japanese court lady and author, born and died at Kyoto. She wrote the saga *Genji Monagatari* (The Tale of Genji), a classic of Japanese literature, and considered to be the world's earliest novel. » Japanese literature; novel

Murat, Joachim [**mür**a] (1767–1815) French Marshal and King of Naples (1808–15), born at La Bastide-Fortunière. He enlisted in the cavalry on the eve of the French Revolution (1787), and was promoted to general of division in the Egyptian campaign (1799). He married Napoleon's sister, Caroline, after helping him become First Consul. After failing to gain the Spanish crown (1808), he was proclaimed King of the Two Sicilies. After taking part in the Russian campaign, he won Dresden and fought at Leipzig, but concluded a treaty with the Austrians, hoping to save his kingdom. On Napoleon's return from Elba, he recommenced war against Austria, but was twice defeated and failed to recover Naples. He was captured and executed at Pizzo, Calabria. » Napoleon I; Napoleonic Wars

Murcia Eng [**mer**sha], Span [**moor**thya] pop (1981) 957 903; area 11 313 sq km/4 367 sq ml. Region and province of SE Spain; thinly populated, except in the river valleys; oranges, lemons, dates, coastal tourism, lead, zinc, iron; capital, Murcia, pop (1981) 288 631, on R Segura; former capital of Moorish kingdom; bishopric; airport; railway; university (1915); agricultural market, silk, textiles, flour, pharmaceuticals, tinned food, leather goods; cathedral (14th-c), Salzillo museum; Spring Festival, Our Lady of La Fuensanta (Sep). » Spain [i]

murder Unlawful homicide other than manslaughter, infanticide (where separately recognized, as in England and Wales), or causing death by reckless driving. In England and Wales, a person can be convicted of murder only where the crime was committed with malice aforethought; also the victim must have died within a year and a day of the commission of the crime. In many US jurisdictions (and also in Scotland), the notion of 'malice aforethought' has been discarded: in these jurisdictions, murder is homicide committed purposefully or knowingly. In the UK, the sentence on conviction is life imprisonment, but in several countries there is provision for capital punishment. » capital punishment; infanticide; life imprisonment; manslaughter

Murdoch, (Jean) Iris (1919–) British novelist and philosopher, born in Dublin, Ireland. Educated at Bristol and Oxford, she worked at the Treasury (1938–42) and for a United Nations relief organization (1944–6), and from 1948 taught at Oxford. A professional philosopher, she took up novel-writing as a hobby, producing a series of successful books exploring human relationships with subtlety and humour, such as *Under the Net* (1954), *The Bell* (1958), *The Black Prince* (1973), *The Sea, The Sea* (1978, Booker Prize), and *The Philosopher's Pupil* (1983). She has also written plays and several philosophical and critical studies. » English literature; novel

Murdoch, (Keith) Rupert (1931–) US media proprietor, born in Melbourne, Australia. Educated at Oxford, he worked for two years on the *Daily Express*, returning to Australia in 1952, where he inherited *The News* in Adelaide on the death of his father. He built a substantial newspaper and magazine publishing empire in Australia, the USA, Hong Kong, and the UK, including the *Sun*, the *News of the World*, and *The Times* and its related publications in Britain. He also has major business interests in other media industries, especially television, films, and publishing, in three continents. He became a naturalized US citizen in 1985. » broadcasting; newspaper; media

Murdock, William (1754–1839) British engineer and inventor of coal gas for lighting, born near Auchinleck, Ayrshire, Scotland. In 1784 he constructed in Cornwall a high-pressure engine to run on wheels, an oscillating engine, and a new method of wheel rotation. His distillation of coal to make coal gas began at Redruth in 1792. He died in Birmingham. » coal gas; engine; gas **2** [i]

murex [**myoor**eks] A carnivorous marine snail, characterized by its elaborate shell bearing spiny outgrowths; many species feed on bivalve molluscs, forcing the valves apart and eating the contents; species of Mediterranean murex are the principal source of Royal Purple dye. (Class: *Gastropoda*. Order: *Neogastropoda*.) » bivalve; carnivore [i]; gastropod; shell; snail

Murillo, Bartolomé Esteban [moo**reel**yoh] (1617–82) Spanish painter, born and died in Seville. In 1645 he painted 11

remarkable pictures for the convent of San Francisco, and was made head of the school there. He founded the Academy of Seville in 1660. After this came his most brilliant period, including several pieces for the almshouse of St Jorge (1661–74). His pictures naturally fall into two groups: scenes from low society, mostly executed early in his life, and religious works. He died after a fall from a scaffold while painting an altarpiece in Cadiz. » Spanish art

Müritz, Lake, Ger **Müritz-See** Lake in Neubrandenburg county, Germany; largest natural lake in former East Germany; area 117 sq km/45 sq ml. » Germany [i]

Murmansk [**moor**mansk], formerly **Romanov-na-Murmane** (to 1917) 68°59N 33°08E, pop (1983) 405 000. Seaport capital of Murmanskaya oblast, Russia; on the E coast of Kola Bay, 50 km/31 ml from the open sea; founded, 1916; most important Russian fishing port (ice-free); airfield; railway; fishing, fish processing, shipbuilding and repairing, tourism. » Russia

Murray, (George) Gilbert (Aimé) (1866–1957) British classical scholar, author, and lifelong Liberal, born in Sydney, Australia. Educated at Merchant Taylors' and Oxford, he became professor of Greek at Glasgow (1889–99) and at Oxford (1908–36). His work as a classical historian and translator of Greek dramatists brought him acclaim as the leading Greek scholar of his time. He was also President of the League of Nations Union (1923–38). He died at Oxford. » Greek literature

Murray, Sir James (Augustus Henry) (1837–1915) British philologist and lexicographer, born at Denholm, Roxburghshire, Scotland. He was a grammar school teacher for 30 years (1855–85), during which time he established his scholarly reputation with a work on Scots dialects (1873). His major project, the editing of the Philological Society's New English Dictionary, was begun at Mill Hill (1879). He edited about half the work himself, and created the organization and the inspiration for its completion (in 1928). He died at Oxford. » comparative linguistics; dialectology; dictionary; English

Murray, Len, properly **Baron Lionel Murray of Telford** (1922–) British trade unionist, born in Shropshire. Educated at London and Oxford, he became general secretary of the Trades Union Congress (1973–84), and was made a life peer in 1985. His main publication is *Trade Unions and the State* (1970). » trade union

Murray cod Large freshwater fish found in rivers and lakes of Australia; length up to 1.8 m/6 ft; body robust with large head and powerful jaws; dark green mottled with blue; good sport fish. (*Maccullochella macquariensis.* Family: *Serranidae.*)

Murray River Longest river in Australia; rises in the Australian Alps near Mt Kosciusko; length 2 570 km/1 600 ml; enters the Southern Ocean at Encounter Bay SE of Adelaide; forms the border between New South Wales and Victoria for 1 930 km/1 200 ml; receives the Darling R 640 km/400 ml from its mouth (the Murray–Darling is 3 750 km/2 330 ml long); the river system extends into four states, covering a seventh of the continent; used extensively for irrigation and hydroelectric power; navigation now generally confined to tourist steamers; major tributaries the Darling, Murrumbidgee, Mitta Mitta, Goulburn, Campaspe, Loddon. » Australia [i]

Murrow, Edward (Egbert) R(oscoe) (1908–65) US broadcasting journalist, born at Greensboro, Carolina. He joined the CBS radio network in 1935 as director of talks and education, but made his name as a radio journalist during the Battle of Britain and the Blitz. In 1946 he was appointed CBS vice-president and director of public affairs. In 1961 he was appointed director of the US Information Agency. He died at Pawling, New York. » broadcasting; journalism

Murrumbidgee River [muhruhm**bi**jee] River in New South Wales, Australia; rises in the Snowy Mts; flows 1 759 km/1 093 ml N through Australian Capital Territory, then W to join the Murray R on the Victoria border; major tributary the Lachlan R; floodplain irrigates a large agricultural basin. » Murray River; New South Wales

Murry, John Middleton (1889–1957) British writer and critic, born in London. His poetry, essays, and criticism had a strong influence on the young intellectuals of the 1920s. The husband of Katherine Mansfield, he introduced her work in *The Adelphi*, of which he was editor (1923–48). He became a pacifist, and editor of *Peace News* (1940–6). A later interest in agriculture led to his starting a community farm in Norfolk. He died at Bury St Edmunds, Suffolk. » literary criticism; Mansfield, Katherine

Mururoa [muhruhr**oh**a] pop (1985) 3 000. Remote atoll in French Polynesia, used by France as a nuclear testing site. Between 1966 and 1974 tests were carried out in the atmosphere; since then they have been held underground within an extinct volcano. » French Polynesia

Musca (Lat 'fly') A small S constellation near Crux. » constellation; Crux; RR9

muscarine [**muhs**karin, **muhs**kareen] A substance isolated from the poisonous mushroom *Amanita muscaria.* Peoples of E Siberia used dried mushrooms for their intoxicating effects. In W Europe, extracts were used as fly-killing agents (the common name for the mushroom is *fly-agaric*). Purified muscarine has been formative in constructing the theory of information transmission in nerves. » fly agaric; mushroom; neurone [i]

Muscat [**muhs**kat], Arabic **Masqat** 27°37N 58°36E, pop (1974e) 25 000. Seaport capital of Oman, on a peninsula in the Gulf of Oman; occupied by the Portuguese, 1508–1650; a former commercial centre, with much trade now lost to Matrah; airport; residence of the Sultan; natural gas, chemicals; two forts (16th-c). » Oman [i]

muscle A contractile tissue consisting of fibres bound together by connective tissue and specialized to convert chemical energy into mechanical energy for movement. It is traditionally classified as skeletal, smooth, and cardiac, depending on certain characteristics, but recently myoepithelial cells (of sweat glands) have become recognized as a type of muscle. **Skeletal muscle** is generally attached to bone, and being under central nervous control is principally concerned with voluntary movement. There are two types of skeletal muscle fibre: *red fibres* contain large amounts of myoglobin, which provides the fibre with a store of oxygen, and are generally more numerous in postural muscles, while *white fibres* are found in muscles performing rapid movements. **Smooth muscle** is present mainly in the walls of hollow structures (eg the gut, uterus, blood vessels, ducts). Contraction and relaxation of the fibres is slower than in skeletal muscle, and may be spontaneous or controlled by the autonomic nervous system. **Cardiac muscle** is present only in the heart: its continuous rhymical contraction is

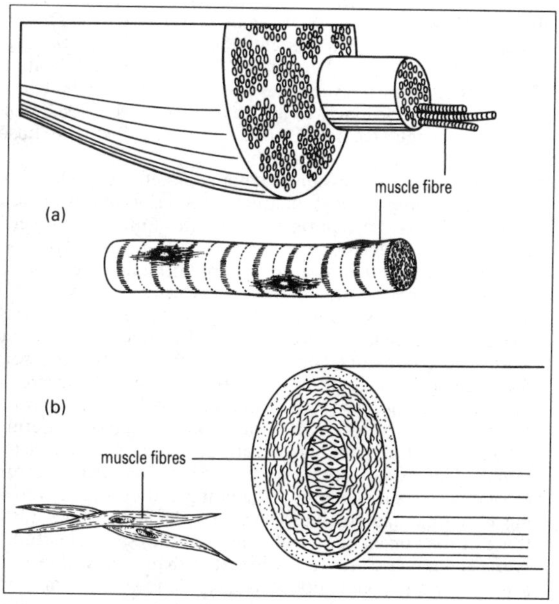

Section through skeletal muscle (a) and smooth muscle – a blood vessel (b), with detail of muscle fibres

due to the presence of pacemaker cells modulated by the autonomic nervous system as well as by circulating adrenaline. » bone; colic; cramp; fibrositis; heart [i]; isometrics; muscular dystrophy; myasthenia gravis; pacemaker; paralysis; rheumatism; Plate XII

muscovite » **micas**

muscovy duck A large duck native to C and tropical S America; wild male black/green with white patches on wing; dark bare skin on face; inhabits water in woodland; eats plants, seeds, small fish, and insects, especially termites. Domestic breeds are grey, white, or speckled, with a scarlet skin patch. It is the only duck other than the mallard to be domesticated. (*Cairina moschata.* Family: *Anatidae.*) » duck; perching duck

muscular dystrophy A genetically-determined group of disorders in which muscles undergo progressive degeneration and increase of fibrous tissue (*fibrosis*). The nervous system is not involved. The condition appears early in life, and causes symmetrical weakness and wasting of groups of muscles, such as those of the lower limbs, shoulder, girdle, and face. In one form of the disease (*Duchenne* type), the muscle cell membrane lacks a specific protein (*dystrophin*), which normally prevents the muscle structure from being destroyed by its own contractions. » muscle [i]

Muses In Homer, the nine daughters of Zeus and Mnemosyne, who inspire the bard. In later writers they are located on Helicon and Parnassus, and are associated with fountains, such as the Pierian Spring. They were then given names and functions, though there are variations: *Calliope*, epic poetry; *Clio*, history; *Erato*, lyric poetry, hymns; *Euterpe*, flute; *Melpomene*, tragedy; *Polyhymnia*, acting, music, dance; *Terpsichore*, lyric poetry, dance; *Thalia*, comedy; *Urania*, astronomy.

museum » **art gallery; Ashmolean/British/Imperial War/London/Natural History/Peace Memorial/Science/Victoria and Albert Museum; Hagia Sophia; Louvre; Pergamum** (East Berlin); **Pinakothek, Alte; Pitti Palace; Prado; Terme; Uffizi**

Museum of London » **London Museum**

Musgrave Ranges [**muhz**grayv] Mountain ranges in South Australia, close to the Northern Territory border; extend 80 km/50 ml; rise to 1 440 m/4 724 ft at Mt Woodroffe, highest point in the state. » South Australia

mushroom The cultivated mushroom, *Agaricus bisporus*; fruiting body comprises a short white stalk (*stipe*) and rounded cap with brownish gills on the underside; also used as a general name for any similar-shaped fungus. (Subdivision: *Basidiomycetes.* Order: *Agaricales.*) » Basidiomycetes; fungus

Musial, Stan (1920–) US baseball player, born at Donora, Pennsylvania. He spent his entire career with the St Louis Cardinals, making his debut in 1941. He topped the National League's batting list seven times (1943–57) and was three times the Most Valuable Player of the Year. He retired in 1962 with a National League record of 3 630 hits to his credit. » baseball [i]

music An orderly succession of sounds of definite pitch, whose constituents are melody, harmony, and rhythm. Almost as fundamental to a perception of the nature of music, however, is *articulation*, which embraces not only the phrasing, dynamics, etc that breathe life into a musical performance, but also the composer's creative use of silence. Music, even when it is imagined silently without an interpreter, exists in time, which means that, except for certain types of composition in which words are paramount (such as operatic recitative and some plainchant), virtually all musical structures entail a degree of audible repetition, even if this cannot always be fully grasped at a first hearing. Music is therefore a kind of aural patterning rather than aural painting – abstract rather than representational. This is not to deny its capacity to elicit a strong emotional response, mainly by creating and eventually resolving harmonic and rhythmic tensions which somehow mirror those of the human body and mind, but the essential nature of music is possibly closer to mathematics than to any of its sister arts. » arrangement; conservatory; dance; harmony; jazz; melody; music theatre; musical instruments/notation; musicology; musique concrète; opera; polyphony; rhythm; singing; tonality; African/Chinese/Japanese/Javanese music; aleatory / chamber / classical / computer / electronic / folk / gospel/pop/programme/rock music; Baroque (music); Impressionism (music); Neoclassicism (music); Romanticism (music); RR91

music hall Mass entertainment of the Victorian era which developed in the music rooms of London taverns. After Charles Morton organized a building specifically for this purpose alongside his tavern in 1849, such special 'halls' were opened throughout the country, 'worked' by itinerant performers who perfected short turns with stage business and comic songs to suit their individual style. » burlesque; Folies-Bergère

music theatre A staged performance of a dramatic kind, with music and (usually) singing. The term is applied mainly to small-scale avant-garde works written since World War 2 which reject the aims and values of traditional opera, but it might be extended to include such earlier works as Stravinsky's *The Soldier's Tale* and the musical plays of Brecht and Weill. » opera; theatre; Brecht; Stravinsky; Weill

musical A distinctive genre of musical comedy, where a strong story is fused with a musical score and professional choreography, found in both theatre and cinema. Feature films with spectacular show-business song-and-dance themes followed rapidly on the introduction of sound-film in 1927, with the direct transcription of theatrical productions or built around a backstage story. For the cinema audiences of the depressed 1930s and the war-restricted 1940s, lavish musicals provided outstanding popular escapism. Their appeal has decreased in recent years, except for transfers of established stage successes or as vehicles for current pop stars. » cinema; musical comedy

musical comedy A show derived from burlesque and light opera in the 1890s. The formative productions at the Gaiety Theatre in London had their counterpart across the Atlantic, and this kind of entertainment proved popular in England and the USA for some 40 years. » burlesque; vaudeville

musical glasses An instrument, also known as the **glass harmonica**, consisting of glass vessels of various sizes and pitches which were struck or stroked to produce musical, bell-like sounds. Various types, including Franklin's 'armonica' (1761) were popular in the 18th-c, and several composers, including Mozart, wrote music for them. » Franklin, Benjamin; idiophone; Mozart

musical instruments Devices for producing musical sounds, among the oldest cultural artefacts known. They have changed and developed over the ages in response to technical advances, the discovery of new materials, the invention of new designs, and the expressive demands of composers. Many old instruments have become obsolete, or have been revived in modern times for performing early music. The instruments of the modern symphony orchestra are commonly divided into four types: woodwind, brass, percussion, and strings; it is in that order (reading from top to bottom) that they are grouped in orchestral scores. Another way of classifying all instruments (not merely those of the orchestra) would be according to the method of playing them: whether they are bowed, blown, struck, plucked, strummed, or (as with keyboard instruments) touched. However, a different classification, now generally regarded as standard, was devised by musicologists Erich von Hornbostel (1877–1935) and Kurt Sachs (1881–1959), and published in the *Zeitschrift für Ethnologie* in 1914. Building on the work of Charles Victor Mahillon (1841–1924), they divided instruments into four main classes according to the physical characteristics of the sound source (ie the vibrating agent): *aerophones* (in which the sound is generated by air), *chordophones* (by one or more strings), *idiophones* (by the body of the instrument itself), and *membranophones* (by a stretched membrane). To these a fifth class has since been added: *electrophones*, in which the sound is produced by electromagnets, oscillators, or other non-acoustic devices. Each class is then subdivided according to other characteristics. » aerophone; chordophone; electrophone; idiophone; membranophone; music; orchestra; percussion [i]; transposing instrument; brass/reed/string/woodwind instrument [i]

musical notation The modern method of notating music on

five-line staves (*staff notation*) is a development of a mediaeval system for the preservation and uniform dissemination of plainchant. Until the 13th-c only the pitch, and not the length, of notes was indicated, but the development of polyphony in the later Middle Ages necessitated the invention of some form of notation showing note length. Other ways of notating music have included several systems of tablature. » music; plainchant; polyphony; tablature; tonic sol-fa; RR91

musicology The scientific and scholarly study of music, embracing the recovery and evaluation of source material, the study of music's historical context, the analysis of particular works and repertories, and several other disciplines. Modern musicology may be said to have originated in the Enlightenment, with the compilation of dictionaries (such as J G Walther's *Musikalisches Lexikon*, 1732; J-J Rousseau's *Dictionnaire*, 1768), the writing of music histories (such as those by Burney and Hawkins), and the publication of specialized journals. Such activities proliferated in the 19th-c, when German scholars took the lead with carefully prepared collected editions (of Handel, Bach, Palestrina, etc). Modern musicologists need to command many specialized skills, including a knowledge of palaeography, paper-types, watermarks, and rastrology (the study of how music staves are drawn). It is an advantage if they are good practical musicians as well. » ethnomusicology; music; palaeography

Musil, Robert (Elder von) [moozil] (1880–1942) Austrian novelist, born at Klagenfurt of Austrian-Czech descent. His masterpiece is a very long, unfinished novel *Der Mann ohne Eigenschaften* (The Man without Qualities), written between 1930 and 1942, but not translated into English until 1969. During the Anschluss he fled to England, where he died in poverty. » Anschluss; German literature; novel

musique concrète Music composed of 'natural' (ie non-electronic but not necessarily musical) sounds, which are then mixed and manipulated on tape and heard through loudspeakers. Both the term and the technique originated with French composer Pierre Schaeffer (1910–) in the 1940s. » electronic music

musk A species of mimulus with yellow flowers, native to N America from British Columbia to the California region. It was formerly cultivated for the musky scent given off by sticky hairs on all parts of the plant, but this characteristic has been lost, and the plants are nowadays scentless. (*Mimulus moschatus*. Family: *Scrophulariaceae*.) » mimulus

musk deer A deer native to wet mountain forests in E Asia; rear legs longer than front legs; kangaroo-like head has no antlers; male with long canine teeth and gland on abdomen, producing a pungent oily jelly (*musk*); musk collected and used in perfumes to make the scent longer-lasting. (Genus: *Moschus*, 3 species. Family: *Moschidae*.) » antlers [i]; deer

musk ox A large goat antelope, native to the Arctic tundra of N America; very thick long shaggy dark-brown coat; short pale brown legs with splayed hooves; head large, held low, with flat horns meeting in mid-line as a helmet, horn tips curving forwards; lives in herds. (*Ovibos moschatus*.) » antelope

muskeg The poorly drained sphagnum moss peat bog and marshland found in the tundra and taiga areas of N Canada. It is underlain by permafrost, the upper surfaces of which partially thaw in summer, providing good breeding conditions for mosquitoes. » Barren Grounds; permafrost; taiga; tundra

muskellunge [**muh**skuhluhnj] Largest of the pike fishes confined to well-weeded habitats in the Great Lakes of N America and associated rivers; length up to 2.4 m/8 ft; an agile predator, much prized by anglers as a sport fish. (*Esox masquinongy*. Family: *Esocidae*.) » pike

musket A heavy firearm, the most important infantry weapon from the late 17th-c to the mid-19th-c, dominant particularly in the Napoleonic era. Smooth-bored and muzzle-loading, the musket required a high degree of training to operate. It was inaccurate, requiring massed ranks of infantrymen firing their muskets in volleys at short range to prove effective. » arquebus; firearms

Muskie, Edmund S(ixtus) (1914–) US politician and statesman, born at Rumford, Maine. He studied at Bates College and Cornell, and after war service and private law practice he entered the Maine legislature in 1947. He became Governor (1955–9) and US Senator (1959–80) for Maine, resigning to accept appointment as Secretary of State under President Carter. He was Democratic candidate for the vice-presidency in 1968. » Carter, Jimmy; Democratic Party

muskrat A large nocturnal water rat native to N America; tail flattened from side to side; thick fur exploited commercially; has a musky smell; inhabits wetlands; builds 'houses' (large domes of vegetation and mud); also known as **musquash**. (*Ondatra zibethicus*.) The name **round-tailed muskrat** is used for the Florida water rat (*Neofiber alleni*). » rat; water rat

Muslim » **Islam**

Muslim art » **Islamic art**

Muslim Brotherhood An Islamic movement, founded in Egypt in 1928 by an Egyptian schoolteacher, Hasan al-Banna, its original goal being the reform of Islamic society by eliminating Western influences and other decadent accretions. Subsequently, it became more radical, and its goal of a theocratic Islamic state found support in many other Sunni countries. » Islam; Sunnis

musquash » **muskrat**

mussel A sedentary bivalve mollusc found in estuaries and shallow seas, attached to the substrate by means of tough filaments (*byssus* threads); feeds by filtering particles of matter from water passing over gills; commonly used for human consumption. (Class: *Pelecypoda*. Order: *Mytiloida*.) » bivalve; mollusc

Musset, (Louis Charles) Alfred de [**mü**say] (1810–57) French poet and dramatist, born and died in Paris. From 1830 he devoted himself to an 'armchair theatre', with plays intended for reading only (though several were later staged successfully). In 1833 he met the novelist George Sand, and there began the stormy love affair which coloured much of his work after that date, notably in his autobiographical novel *La Confession d'un enfant du siècle* (1835, The Confession of a Child of his Time). » drama; French literature; poetry; Romanticism (literature); Sand

Mussolini, Benito (Amilcare Andrea), byname **Il Duce** ('The Leader') (1883–1945) Italian Prime Minister (1922–43) and dictator, born at Predappio, Romagna. In 1919 he helped found the *Fasci di Combattimento* as a would-be revolutionary force, and in 1922 became Prime Minister, his success symbolized by the March on Rome (Oct 1922). By 1925 he had established himself as dictator. His rule saw the replacement of parliamentarism by a 'Corporate State' and an officially totalitarian system; the establishment of the Vatican state (1929); the annexation of Abyssinia (1935–6) and Albania (1939); and the formation of the Axis with Germany. His declaration of war on Britain and France exposed Italy's military unpreparedness, and was followed by a series of defeats in N and E Africa and in the Balkans. Following the Allied invasion of Sicily (Jun 1943), and with his supporters deserting him, he was overthrown and arrested (Jul 1943). Rescued from imprisonment by German paratroopers, he was placed in charge of the puppet Italian Social Republic, but in 1945 he was captured by the Italian Resistance and shot. » Axis Powers; fascism; totalitarianism; World War 2

Mussorgsky » **Moussorgsky**

mustang A breed of horse, developed naturally in N America as a wild horse; descended from Spanish horses introduced by the Conquistadors; first horses used by American Indians; height, 14–15 hands/1.4–1.5 m/4½–5 ft; used for riding. » horse [i]

Mustapha Kemal Atatürk » **Atatürk, Mustapha Kemal**

mustard An erect annual growing to 1 m/3¼ ft; deeply lobed leaves; yellow, cross-shaped flowers. Commercial mustard is produced from ground seeds of two species cultivated on a large scale: **white mustard** (*Brassica alba*) is native to Europe; **black mustard** (*Brassica nigra*), origin unknown but widely naturalized, also yields mustard oil. (Family: *Cruciferae*.) » annual; brassica

mustard gas A light-yellow, oily liquid which becomes a gas above 14°C, acting as a powerful vesicant (producer of blisters) that attacks the human skin, eyes, and lungs. It was first used as a poison gas on the battlefield of Ypres by the Germans in July 1917. Chemically, it is 2,2′-dichlorodiethylsulphide,

$(Cl–CH_2–CH_2)_2S$, boiling point 216°. » chemical warfare; poison gas

Mustelidae [muhs**tel**uhdee] A family of carnivorous mammals (67 species), found worldwide except in Australasia and Madagascar; usually with long thin body, short legs, long tail. » badger; carnivore [i]; fisher; grison; mammal [i]; marten; mink; otter; polecat; skunk; stoat; weasel; wolverine

mutation An abrupt change in the physical characteristics of an organism (*phenotype*) due to a change in its hereditary material. In **chromosomal** mutations, there is a deletion, breakage, or rearrangement of chromosome material. In **molecular** mutations, there is a physico-chemical change in the DNA sequence, either within a codon, or involving the loss, duplication, or rearrangement of longer sections of DNA. An example of the first would be a baby born with the 'cat-cry' syndrome in a family with no history of any chromosomal disorder, where the mutation would be a deletion of the short arm of a chromosome 5. An example of the second would be a baby born with or developing Duchenne muscular dystrophy in a family with no previous history. » chromosome [i]; DNA [i]; muscular dystrophy

mute swan The largest swan (up to 15 kg/33 lb), native to Europe and Asia, and introduced in the USA; inhabits lakes, often near habitation; eats water plants; orange bill with black swelling at base; does not 'honk' when flying; feet black. One form with pink feet is called the **Polish swan**. (*Cygnus olor*. Family: *Anatidae*.) » swan

muttonbird The alternative name of the **short-tailed shearwater** (*Puffinus tenuirostris*) from S Australia and the Pacific, or the **sooty shearwater** (*Puffinus griseus*) from New Zealand. The young of both are harvested commercially as food and for their down. » petrel; shearwater

mutual fund » **open-ended investment company**

mutualism An association between two different species of organisms in which both species benefit from the relationship. Usage is sometimes restricted to those obligatory relationships where neither species can survive in the absence of the other. The relationship between termites and the protozoans living in their gut is mutualistic: the protozoans digest the cellulose in wood and make its nutrients available to the termites, receiving in return a suitable protected environment and a supply of food. » commensalism; symbiosis

Muzorewa, Abel (Tendekayi) [moozuh**ray**wa] (1925–) Zimbabwean clergyman and politician, born at Umtali, Southern Rhodesia. Ordained in 1953, he studied in the USA and became a bishop of the United Methodist Church in 1968. In 1971 he became President of the African National Council, but was unable to control the more aggressive Nationalist personalities, which led to the 1975 split into Muzorewa and Nkomo factions. He continued to be involved in the transition to majority rule, and was Prime Minister of 'Zimbabwe Rhodesia' for six months in 1979. After independence his United African National Council was defeated by the Patriotic Front of Mugabe and Nkomo. » Mugabe; Nkomo; Patriotic Front; Zimbabwe [i]

MX missile An abbreviation used for **Missile Experimental**, the codename of a US third-generation land-based intercontinental ballistic missile. Under development from the late 1960s, it was eventually deployed as the 'Peacekeeper' missile from 1987 onwards in land-based silos in the US mid-West. This followed much political and strategic debate about the best way of basing these very large and very powerfully armed long-range missiles, to keep them out of reach of a potential Soviet 'first strike'. Eventually it was decided to base 100 in fixed underground silos. » intercontinental ballistic missile; missile, guided

My Lai incident [mee**liy**] The massacre of several hundred unarmed inhabitants of the S Vietnamese village of My Lai by US troops (Mar 1968), an incident exposed by *Life* magazine photos in 1969. The officer responsible, Lieutenant Calley, was court-martialled in 1970–1. » Vietnam War

Myall Creek massacre In Australian history, the massacre of 28 Aborigines in NE New South Wales (1838) by a party of assigned convicts for an alleged attack on cattle. Seven of the men charged with the massacre were found guilty and hanged. The accused attracted considerable support from other colonists, who regarded Aborigines as less than human; thereafter the murder of Aborigines was carefully concealed. » Aborigines

Myanmar » **Burma** [i]

myasthenia gravis [miyas**thee**nia **grah**vis] A condition characterized by the inability to sustain a contraction of voluntary (*somatic*) muscles. It results from the presence of an auto-antibody which blocks the action of motor nerve impulses that initiate muscle contraction. The muscles become rapidly fatigued, but recover temporarily after a period of rest. » muscle [i]

Mycenae [miy**see**nee] A fortified town in the Argolid, associated in Greek tradition with Agamemnon, the conqueror of Troy. While its extensive Bronze Age remains do indicate that Mycenae was the seat of a powerful warrior chieftain in the 16th-c BC, this is no longer thought to be that of Agamemnon himself. » Agamemnon; Argolid; Mycenaean art/civilization; Trojan War

Mycenaean architecture » **Cretan and Mycenaean architecture**

Mycenaean/Mycenean art [miysi**nee**an] The art of Homeric (ie late Bronze Age) Greece. Minoan influence was strong, as in the famous gold cup from Vaphio (c.16th–12th-c BC) with its vigorous representation of bulls captured in nets (National Museum, Athens). » Greek art; Minoan art; Mycenae

Mycenaean/Mycenean civilization A brilliant Bronze Age culture which flourished in Greece and the Aegean in the second millennium, reaching its high point in Greece in the 13th-c BC. Important sites are Mycenae, Pylos, and Tiryns. These show the existence in Greece of the palace system of government with its complex redistributive economy, found earlier in Minoan Crete. An important difference, however, is the existence in Mycenaean society of a distinct warrior class. The chief Mycenaean palace sites were destroyed or abandoned towards the end of the 13th-c. Inner-state strife may have been the cause; invading Dorians are no longer considered responsible. » Cretan and Mycenaean architecture; Minoan civilization; Mycenae; Mycenaean art; Pylos; Three Age System; Tiryns

mycetoma [miysi**toh**ma] A painless swelling arising from a specific fungal infection (*Eumycetes* or *Actinomycetes*) which becomes matted together with soft body tissues. The fungus often enters the body through the skin by a thorn, and so the lesion occurs commonly in the feet or legs; it is also known as **Madura foot**. There may be deeply penetrating chronic abscesses, and the discharge of pus. » abscess; actinomycosis; fungus

mycology [miy**kol**uhjee] The study of fungi, including the identification, description and classification of the great diversity of fungi. Fungi are usually only identifiable when they are fruiting, as their vegetative bodies consist of a mass of filamentous threads (*hyphae*), and are similar in appearance in the majority of species. » fungus

mycoplasma The smallest, self-replicating micro-organisms, usually 150–300 nm in diameter. A distinct nucleus is lacking, as are cell walls. They vary in shape from spherical to filamentary. There are c.60 species, all except one being parasitic on vertebrates, plants, and insects. (Kingdom: *Monera*. Class: *Mollicutes*. » micro-organism; spiroplasm

mycorrhiza [miykuh**riy**za] A common symbiotic association formed between a fungus and the roots of a plant. In **ectotrophic** mycorrhiza, found in many trees, the fungus grows mainly outside the root, forming a sheath and replacing the root hairs; in **endotrophic** mycorrhiza, found in orchids and heaths, the fungus grows within and between the cells of the root. Mycorrhizal systems have enhanced absorption abilities, and infected plants compete better than non-infected ones, while the fungus benefits from nutrients supplied by the plant. In many cases the plants which form these associations will not grow properly – if at all – in the absence of the fungal partner. » fungus; parasitic plant; root (botany); symbiosis

myelin [**miy**uhlin] A soft, white substance (a complex of protein-lipids) forming a multi-layered insulating sheath around the large-diameter axons of vertebrate and crustacean neurones.

This increases the speed of conduction of the action potential along the axon. The progressive breakdown of the sheath is associated with the disruption of normal neurone conduction (as in human multiple sclerosis). » action potential; neurone [i]; neuropathology

myeloma The excessive proliferation of antibody-producing plasma cells (derived from B-lymphocytes). These cells infiltrate the bone marrow, and may lead to tender local tumours in the skeleton. » plasma (physiology)

Myers, Frederic William Henry (1843–1901) British psychical researcher, poet, essayist, and (from 1872) school inspector, born at Keswick, Cumbria, and educated at Cambridge. In 1882 he helped found the Society for Psychical Research, and for the rest of his life was one of its most productive researchers. He died in Rome. » parapsychology

Mykonos » **Mikonos**

mynah/myna A bird of the starling family (13 species), native to India and SE Asia, and introduced widely elsewhere; inhabits forest and cultivation, often near habitation; eats mainly fruit, grain, and insects. » hill mynah; starling

myocardial infarction The death of muscle cells of the heart, occurring when the demand for oxygen by the cardiac muscles outstrips supply. It may be preceded by attacks of angina pectoris. The cardinal symptom is pain over the chest, which unlike that of angina does not subside with rest but persists for several hours. Effects vary with the site and extent of the muscle involved. It may cause little bodily disturbance beyond a few days of tiredness, or lead to heart failure, cardiac irregularities, and cardiac arrest with sudden death. Complete recovery is also possible. » angina; atherosclerosis; coronary heart disease [i]

Myolodon [miyo**l**uhduhn] The last of the ground sloths, surviving in Patagonia until recent times, now extinct; samples of its red-haired skin with embedded bony structures have been found in caves. (Order: *Xenarthra*.) » sloth

myopia » **eye** [i]

Myrdal, (Karl) Gunnar (1898–1987) Swedish economist, politician, and international civil servant. He was educated at Stockholm, where he became professor of political economy (1933), and was also executive secretary of the UN Economic Commission for Europe. He shared the Nobel Prize for Economics in 1974, principally for his work on the critical application of economic theory to Third World countries. » Three Worlds Theory

Myriapoda [miriapuhda] A diverse group of terrestrial arthropods containing the millipedes (class: *Diplopoda*), centipedes (class: *Chilopoda*), and two small classes, *Symphyla* and *Pauropoda*. All have a segmented trunk that is not differentiated into thorax and abdomen. » arthropod; centipede; millipede

Myrmidons [**mer**midnz] In Greek legend, a band of warriors from Thessaly who went to the Trojan War with Achilles. » Achilles

myrobalan » **cherry plum**

Myron (5th-c BC) Greek sculptor, born in Eleutherae. A contemporary of Phidias, he lived in Athens. He worked in bronze, and is known for the celebrated 'Discobolos' (Discus Thrower). » Greek art; Phidias; sculpture

myrrh 1 A spiny, deciduous shrub, native to Africa and W Asia; leaves oval or widest above the middle; flowers tiny, males and females on separate plants. Several species from E Africa and Arabia exude the aromatic resin myrrh used in incense and perfume. (Genus: *Commiphora*, 185 species. Family: *Burseraceae*.) » deciduous plants; resin; shrub **2** » sweet cicely

Mysore [miy**saw**] 12°17N 76°41E, pop (1981) 476 000. City in Karnataka state, SW India; 850 km/528 ml SSE of Bombay; formerly the dynastic capital of Mysore state; founded, 16th-c; railway; university (1916); textiles, food processing, chemicals; known as 'the garden city of India' because of its wide streets and numerous parks; maharaja's palace, within an ancient fort (rebuilt, 18th-c); statue of Nandi (sacred bull of Shiva) on Chamundi Hill (SE), a place of pilgrimage. » Karnataka

mystery play A mediaeval play based upon a Biblical episode. Cycles of plays (notably, York and Wakefield) tell a continuous story, often portraying the Christian vision from the Creation to the Day of Judgment. These plays, and the later **miracle plays** on the Virgin and saints' lives, represent an important phase in the evolution of secular drama from religious ritual. » Bible; drama; morality play

mystery religions Religious cults of the Graeco-Roman world, full admission to which was restricted to those who had gone through certain secret initiation rites or mysteries. The most famous were those of Demeter at Eleusis in Greece, but the cults of Dionysus, Isis, and Mithras also involved initiation into mysteries. » Eleusinian mysteries

mysticism The spiritual quest in any religion for the most direct experience of God. Characteristically, mysticism concentrates on prayer, meditation, contemplation, and fasting, so as to produce the attitude necessary for what is believed to be a direct encounter with God. Christian mysticism tends to focus on the person and sufferings of Christ, attempting to move beyond image and word to the immediate presence of God. In contrast with other forms of mysticism, Christian mystics reject the idea, common in some other religions, of the absorption of the individual into the divine, and retain the distinction between the individual believer and God. Notable Christian mystics include such diverse figures as St Augustine, St Francis of Assisi, and St Teresa of Avila. » Augustine, St (of Hippo); Francis of Assisi, St; God; meditation; prayer; religion; Teresa of Avila, St

mythology The traditional stories of a people, often orally transmitted. They usually tell of unbelievable things in a deliberate manner, so that a 'myth' can mean both 'an untrue story', and 'a story containing religious truth'. The subject-matter of myths is either the gods and their relations with human or other beings, or complex explanations of physical phenomena. Until recently *mythology* meant Greek mythology, which is distinct in its concentration on stories of heroes and heroines, and its avoidance of the bizarre episodes in contemporary Near Eastern myths. Greek mythology was largely derived from Homer; it referred to a specific historical period (before the Trojan War); and it was, to a certain extent, rationalized and beautified by later writers. The use of this mythology in Elizabethan and Romantic poets indicates a wish to break out of narrowly Christian patterns of behaviour. Some writers (such as Blake and Yeats) have created mythical systems of their own by synthesizing disparate mateials. Recent scholarship has been either folklorist or structuralist, finding unexpected parallels in myths from widely different sources, and showing their function in determining social behaviour. » allegory; demythologizing; figurative language; folklore; Greek/Latin literature; legend; structuralism

myxoedema/myxedema [miksuh**dee**ma] The deposition of a substance (*mucopolysaccharide*) under the skin, which causes thickening, swelling, and pallor of the face, and a characteristic facial appearance. It is almost invariably associated with severe primary hypothyroidism. » hypothyroidism; polysaccharides; thyroid hormone

myxomatosis [miksuhma**toh**sis] A contagious viral disease of rabbits, characterized by the presence of jelly-like tumours (*myxomata*); harmless to cottontails (occurs naturally in the S American forest rabbit, or tapiti (*Sylvilagus brasiliensis*), but is fatal to European rabbits); introduced to Australia in 1951 to control the vast population of introduced rabbits; devastated wild rabbit populations in Europe in the 1950s. » cottontail; rabbit; virus

N

N'Djamena [njameena], formerly **Fort Lamy** 12°10N 14°59E, pop(1984e) 402 000. Capital of Chad, NC Africa, and capital of Chari-Baguirmi prefecture, WC Chad; at confluence of Logone and Chari Rivers; junction of caravan routes; founded by French, 1900; bombed by Italians, 1942; airport; university (1971); trade in cotton, cattle; several research institutes; National Museum. » Chad [i]

Naas [nays], Gaelic **Nás na Riogh** 53°13N 6°39W, pop(1981) 8 345. Market town and capital of Kildare county, Leinster, Irish Republic; on branch of the Grand Canal, SW of Dublin; former capital of the kings of Leinster; noted horse-racing area. » Irish Republic [i]; Kildare

Nabis (Heb 'prophet') A small group of artists working in Paris c.1890–c.1900 under the influence of Gauguin. Its leading members were Denis, Bonnard and Vuillard. » French art; Intimisme; Post-Impressionism; Bonnard; Denis; Gauguin; Vuillard

Nablus [nabloos] 32°13N 35°16E, pop(1971e) 44 200. Capital town of Nablus governorate, Israeli-occupied West Bank, NW Jordan; 48 km/30 ml N of Jerusalem; market centre for the surrounding agricultural region; wheat, olives, sheep, goats; Great Mosque (rebuilt, 1167, as Crusader church); Jacob's Well nearby. » Israel [i]; Jordan [i]

Nabokov, Vladimir (Vladimirovich) [nabohkof] (1899–1977) US author, born in St Petersburg, Russia. After moving to England, he studied at Cambridge, and in 1940 settled in the USA, where he became a research fellow in entomology at Harvard, and in 1948 professor of Russian literature at Cornell. A considerable Russian author, he established himself also as a novelist in English, notably with his controversial book *Lolita* (1955), dealing with the desire of a middle-aged intellectual for a 12-year-old girl. His later work includes *Pale Fire* (1962) and *Ada* (1969), and he is also known for his short stories. He died at Montreux, Switzerland. » English literature; novel; Russian literature; short story

nadir A point on the celestial sphere immediately below an observer, therefore unobservable. Its opposite, the point vertically above the observer, is the **zenith**. » celestial sphere

Naevius, Gnaeus [nayviuhs] (c.264–194 BC) Latin poet and dramatist, born (probably) in Campania. A plebeian, he satirized the Roman nobles in his plays, and was compelled to withdraw from Rome, ultimately retiring to Utica in Africa, where he died. Fragments of an epic on the Punic War, *De Bello Punico*, are extant. » drama; poetry; Punic Wars; Roman literature; satire

naevus » **birthmark**

Nafud [nafood] Desert area in N part of the Arabian Peninsula; c.290 km/180 ml long and 225 km/140 ml wide; occasional violent windstorms have formed crescent-shaped dunes, rising to heights of c.200 m/600 ft; dates, vegetables, barley, and fruit are grown in oases, especially near the Hejaz Mts. » Arabia; desert

Nag Hammadi texts [nahg hamahdee] A library of religious texts recorded in Coptic and discovered in 1945 in Egypt near the town of Nag Hammadi. It consists of some 12 books containing 52 tractates, the scriptures of the Christian Gnostic movement in Egypt, although some works are neither openly 'Gnostic' or 'Christian' but are rather of a philosophical or Jewish character. It is valuable evidence for this early form of 'heretical' Christianity, and contains many previously-unknown works. » Christianity; Coptic Church; Gnosticism

Nagaland [nahgaland] pop(1981) 773 281; area 16 527 sq km/6 379 sq ml. State in NE India; administrative centre, Kohima; governed by a 60-member State Assembly; rice, sugar cane, pulses, forestry, weaving; former territory of Assam; became a state in 1961; strong movement for independence amongst Naga tribesmen; talks with the Naga tribes underground movement resulted in the Shillong Peace Agreement, 1975. » India [i]

Nagarjuna [nagahjoona] (c.150–c.250) Indian Buddhist monk-philosopher. He was the founder of the Madhyamika or Middle Path school of Buddhism. » Buddhism

Nagasaki [nagasakee] 32°45N 129°52E, pop(1980) 447 091. Capital of Nagasaki prefecture, W Kyushu, Japan; visited by the Portuguese, 1545; centre for Christian missionaries from 16th-c; target for the second atomic bomb of World War 2 (9 Aug 1945), killing or wounding c.75 000, and destroying over a third of the city; airport; railway; university (1949); fishing, shipbuilding, engineering, metal products; stone bridges across the R Nakajima, including Spectacles Bridge (1634); Sofukuji pavilions; peace statue in Peace Park; Suwa Shrine festival (Oct). » Kyushu

Nagoya [nagoya] 35°08N 136°53E, pop(1980) 2 087 902. Port capital of Aichi prefecture, C Honshu, Japan, on NE shore of Ise-wan Bay; founded as a castle, 17th-c; fifth largest city of Japan; munitions centre, heavily bombed in World War 2; airport; railway; two universities (1939, 1950); engineering, metal products, bicycles, watches, sewing machines, textiles; Nagoya Castle (rebuilt, 1959), Atsuta Shrine (c.1st-c), Tokugawa art museum. » Honshu

Nagpur [nahgpoor] 21°08N 79°10E, pop(1981) 1 298 000. City in Maharashtra, WC India; on R Pench, 675 km/419 ml ENE of Bombay; founded, 18th-c; scene of the final British overthrow of the Mahrattas, 1817; former capital of Berar and Madhya Pradesh states; airfield; railway; university (1923); cotton textiles, paper, metallurgy, trade in oranges. » Maharashtra

Nagy, Imre [noj] (1895–1958) Hungarian statesman and Prime Minister (1953–5), born at Kaposvar. He had a minor post in the Béla Kun revolutionary government in Hungary, but in 1929 fled to the USSR. Returning with the Red Army (1944), he became Minister of Agriculture, and as Premier introduced milder political control. When Soviet forces began to put down the 1956 revolution, he appealed to the world for help, but was displaced by the Soviet puppet János Kádár, and executed in Budapest. » Hungarian uprising; Kádár; Kun; Russian Revolution

Nahanni National park in NW Canada; area 4 770 sq km/1 842 sq ml; habitat of the peregrine falcon, golden eagle, grey wolf, and grizzly bear, as well as many other rare species; a world heritage site. » Canada [i]

Nahum, Book of [nayhuhm] One of the twelve so-called 'minor' prophetic writings of the Hebrew Bible/Old Testament, attributed to a prophet named Nahum, about whom little else is known. The oracle vigorously announces the imminent downfall of Assyria and the destruction of Nineveh (612 BC), which is interpreted as the Lord's judgment upon its wickedness and as good news for Judah. It was perhaps intended to encourage Judean stirrings for independence from the occupying power. » Nineveh; Old Testament; prophet

naiad [niyad] In Greek mythology, a nymph who inhabits springs, rivers, and lakes. » nymph (mythology)

nails Rectangular plates of horny tissue found on the back of the end bones (*phalanges*) of each digit. They are a specialized modification of the outer two layers of the epidermis. Each nail is partly surrounded by a fold of skin (the *nail wall*) and is firmly anchored to the underlying *nail bed*. They grow at c.1 mm/0.04 in per week, faster in summer than in winter. » hand; foot

Naipaul, V(idiadhar) S(urajprasad) [niy**pawl**] (1932–) West Indian novelist, born at Chaguanas, Trinidad, and educated at Port of Spain and at Oxford. He has lived in England since 1950, travelling widely and recording his experiences of foreign societies in such books as *The Middle Passage* (1962, on the West Indies) and *An Area of Darkness* (1964, on India). His early short stories were collected in *Miguel Street* (1959), and a sequence of comic novels set in Trinidad concluded with *A House for Mr Biswas* (1961). Later novels revealed a darker vision and a sense of the wider, often political, ramifications of the experiences recorded in them, as in *The Mimic Men* (1967) and *A Bend in the River* (1979). » Caribbean literature; novel; short story

Nairobi [niy**roh**bee] 1°17S 36°50E, pop (1984e) 1 161 000. Province and capital of Kenya; on the central Kenya plateau, 450 km/280 ml NW of Mombasa; largest city in E Africa; former seat of the British governor of Kenya; airport; railway; university (1956); centre of communications and commerce; textiles, chemicals, glass, agricultural trade; headquarters of the United Nations Environment Programme Secretariat; cathedral (1963), Sikh temple, national museum (including largest collection of African butterflies in the world), Snake Park. » Kenya [i]

naive art » **primitivism**

Nakasone, Yasuhiro [naka**soh**nay] (1918–) Japanese political leader, statesman, and Prime Minister (1982–8), born in Gumma Prefecture, E Japan. Educated at Tokyo University, he was a junior naval officer in World War 2, and entered the Ministry of Home Affairs in 1945. Elected to the Diet at age 29 for the Liberal-Democratic (Conservative) Party, he held a range of ministerial posts (1959–82). As Premier, he supported the renewal of the US–Japan Security Treaty, and maintained close relations with US President Reagan. » Japan [i]; Reagan

Namaqualand [na**ma**kaland], Afrikaans [na**ma**kwalant] Region in S Namibia and W South Africa; comprises **Little Namaqualand**, extending S from the Orange R, chief town Springbok, and **Great Namaqualand**, extending N from the Orange R, chief town Keetmanshoop; European presence since 1665; indigenous peoples known as Namaquas or Nama; diamond mines. » Namibia [i]

Namath, Joe, properly **Joseph (William)** (1943–) US footballer, born at Beaver Falls, Pennsylvania. He joined the New York Jets from the unbeaten University of Alabama team in 1964, and became one of the leading quarterbacks in the 1960s. His lifestyle outside football attracted a great deal of publicity, and after his retirement (1978) he remained in the public eye with appearances in films and on television. » football [i]

Namen [**na**men] » **Namur**

Namib Desert [**na**mib] Desert in W Namibia, along most of the Atlantic seaboard of Namibia; length, c.1 300 km/800 ml; width, 50–160 km/30–100 ml; contains the highest sand dunes in the world. » Namibia [i]

Namibia [na**mib**ia], formerly **South-West Africa** (to 1968), earlier **German South-West Africa** pop (1990e) 1 300 000; area 823 144 sq km/317 734 sq ml. Republic in SW Africa, divided into 22 administrative districts; bounded N by Angola, NE by Zambia, E by Botswana, S by South Africa, and W by the Atlantic Ocean; capital, Windhoek; chief towns include Luderitz, Keetmanshoop, Grootfontein; timezone GMT −2; population mainly African (85%), chiefly Ovambo; official languages, Afrikaans, English; unit of currency, the South African rand.

Physical description and climate. Desert along the Atlantic Ocean coast; inland plateau, mean elevation 1 500 m/5 000 ft; highest point, Brandberg (2 606 m/8 550 ft); Kalahari Desert to the E and S; Orange R forms S frontier with South Africa; low rainfall on coast, higher in interior; average annual rainfall at Windhoek, 360 mm/14 in; average maximum daily temperature, 20–30°C.

History and government. British and Dutch missionaries from late 18th-c; German protectorate, 1884; mandated to South Africa by the League of Nations, 1920; UN assumed direct responsibility in 1966, changing name to Namibia in 1968, and recognizing the Southwest Africa People's Organization (SWAPO) as representative of the Namibian people; South Africa continued to administer the area as Southwest Africa; Administrator-General appointed by South Africa, advises an 18-member elected Legislative Assembly and a 12-member Ministerial Council; SWAPO commenced guerrilla activities in 1966; bases established in S Angola, involving Cuban troops, in 1970s; interim administration installed by South Africa, 1985; full independence, 1990; governed by an executive president, elected for a five-year term, assisted by a cabinet headed by a prime minister; the lower house of the bicameral parliament is a 72-member elected National Assembly, serving for five years; the upper house representing regional leaders will be created in 1992.

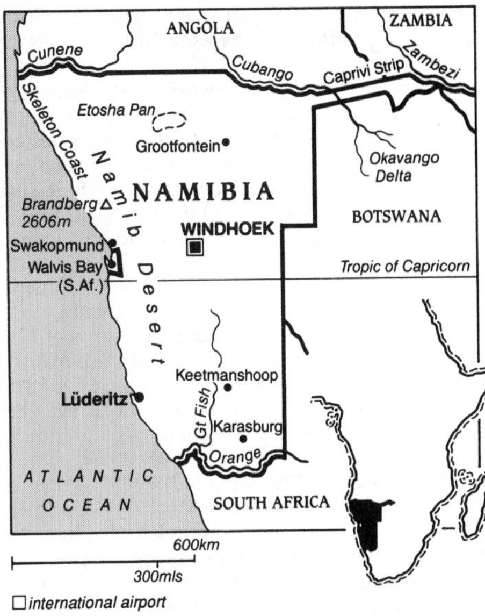

Economy. Agriculture employs c.60% of the population; White-owned livestock ranches; indigenous subsistence farming in the N; major world producer of diamonds and uranium; copper, lead, zinc, arsenic, cadmium, salt, silver, tin, tungsten; fishing, food processing, brewing, plastics, furniture, textiles. » Angola [i]; Kalahari; Namib Desert; South Africa [i]; Southwest Africa People's Organization; Windhoek

Namier, Sir Lewis (Bernstein) [**nay**mier], originally **Ludwik Bernstein Niemirowski** (1888–1960) British historian, born near Warsaw. He came to England in 1906, was educated at Oxford, and took British nationality. He became professor of modern history at Manchester (1931–52), creating a school of history in which the emphasis was on detailed analysis of events and institutions, particularly parliamentary elections, so as to reveal the entire motivation of the individuals involved in them. He died in London.

Namur, Flemish **Namen** 50°28N 4°52E, pop (1982) 102 075. Capital city of Namur province, Belgium, at confluence of Sambre and Meuse Rivers; key strategic point of the Belgian defence line on the R Meuse; conquered by the Germans in 1914 and 1940; railway; private university (1831); glass, porcelain, enamel, paper, steel; cathedral (1751–67), citadel (17th-c). » Belgium [i]

Nana Sahib, byname of **Brahmin Dundhu Panth** (c.1820–c.1859) Indian rebel, the adopted son of the ex-peshwa of the Marathas, who became known as the leader of the Indian Mutiny in 1857. On its outbreak he was proclaimed peshwa, and was held responsible for the massacres at Cawnpore (Kanpur). After the rebellion he escaped into Nepal. » Indian Mutiny

Nanak [**na**nak] (1469–1539) Founder of Sikhism, born near Lahore, present-day Pakistan. A Hindu by birth and belief, he fell under Muslim influence, and denounced many Hindu practices as idolatrous. His doctrine, set out later in the *Adi-Granth*, sought a fusion of Brahmanism and Islam on the grounds that both were monotheistic, although Nanak's own ideas leaned rather towards pantheism. He died at Kartarpur, Punjab. » Adi Granth; Brahmanism; Hinduism; Islam; pantheism; Sikhism

NANC An acronym for **non-adrenergic, non-cholinergic**: a description of autonomic nerve fibres in which the neurotransmitter is neither noradrenaline nor acetylcholine. Important areas supplied by such nerves include the airways, bladder, intestine, and genitals. Possible NANC transmitters include some purines (eg adenosinetriphosphate) and various peptides (eg vasoactive intestinal polypeptide). » autonomic nervous system; peptide; purine

Nanchang or **Nan-ch'ang** 28°38N 115°56E, pop (1984e) 1 088 800. Industrial capital of Jiangxi province, SE China; founded 201 BC during the E Han dynasty; scene of Nanchang Uprising (1927), when peasants defeated Nationalist forces; airfield; railway; university; distribution centre for kaolin pottery; cotton, machinery, paper, food processing, chemicals; Jiangxi provincial museum; Bada Shanren Exhibition Hall. » China [i]

Nancy [**nã**see] 48°42N 6°12E, pop (1982) 99 307. Manufacturing city and capital of Meurthe-et-Moselle department, NE France; on R Meurthe and Marne-Rhine Canal, 285 km/177 ml E of Paris; former capital of Lorraine; part of France, 1766; road and rail junction; episcopal see; university (1572); iron and steel, boilers, catering equipment, glass, footwear, tobacco, yeast, brewing; 17th-c town hall, 13th-c ducal palace, 15th-c Eglise des Cordeliers, 14th-c Porte de la Craffe, cathedral (1703–42); noted for its 18th-c Baroque architecture: Place Stanislas, Place de la Carrière, and Place d'Alliance comprise a world heritage site. » Lorraine

nandu » **rhea**

Nanjing or **Nanking** [nan**king**], formerly **Chian-ning** 32°03N 118°47E, pop (1984e) 2 207 500. Capital of Jiangsu province, SE China, on the Yangtze R; founded, 900 BC; capital of China 220–589, 907–79, 1928–49; centre of Taiping Rebellion; river port and trade centre; open port after the Opium War (1842); airfield; railway; university (1902); coal, metallurgy, petroleum refining, engineering, shipbuilding; many historical sites and relics; Nanjing museum, Zhongshanling mausoleum (in memory of Sun Yatsen), Mingxiaoling (Ming Emperor's Tomb), Zijin mountain observatory and museum, Yuhuatai Park. » China [i]; Opium Wars; Taiping Rebellion

Nanking » **Nanjing**

Nanning or **Nan-ning** 22°50N 108°06E, pop (1984e) 902 900. Capital of Guangxi autonomous region, S China; China's most southerly city; founded during the Yuan dynasty; military supply town during Vietnam War; closed to foreigners until 1977; airfield; railway; agricultural trade; food processing, coal, bauxite, leather, paper, machinery; Dragon Boat Regatta (May–Jun). » China [i]; Yuan dynasty

Nansen, Fridtjof (1861–1930) Norwegian explorer, scientist, and statesman, born and died near Oslo. Educated at Oslo and Naples, in 1882 he travelled into the Arctic regions, and in 1888 made an E–W journey across Greenland. His greatest scheme was to reach the N Pole by letting his specially built ship, the *Fram*, get frozen into the ice N of Siberia and drift with a current setting towards Greenland. In this way he reached in 1895 the highest latitude till then attained, 86° 14N. He became professor of zoology (1897) and of oceanography (1908) at Oslo, and was Norwegian Ambassador in London (1906–8). In 1922 he won the Nobel Peace Prize for Russian relief work. » Poles

Nantes [nãt], Breton **Naoned**, ancient **Condivincum**, later **Namnetes** 47°12N 1°33W, pop (1982) 247 227. Manufacturing and commercial seaport, and capital of Loire-Atlantique department, W France; at head of Loire estuary, 171 km/106 ml W of Tours; seventh largest city in France; 16th–18th-c centre of sugar and ebony trade; France's leading port in 18th-c; 19th-c decline, halted by construction of harbour at St-Nazaire and river dredging; major bomb damage in World War 2; railway; university (1962); oil refining, sugar refining, boatbuilding, tobacco, soap, textiles, food products, building materials; birthplace of Jules Verne; Gothic Cathedral of St-Pierre-et-St-Paul, museum of fine arts, Château des Ducs (10th-c, rebuilt 1466), where Edict of Nantes was signed. » Gothic architecture; Nantes, Edict of; Verne

Nantes, Edict of [nãt] (1598) A law promulgated by Henry IV of France granting religious and civil liberties to his Huguenot subjects at the end of the Wars of Religion. Richelieu annulled its political clauses (1629) as a threat to the integrity of the state; and the same motive led Louis XIV to order the infamous revocation of the edict (1685). » Henry IV (of France); Huguenots; Louis XIV; Religion, Wars of; Richelieu

Nantucket (Algonquian 'narrow-tidal-river-at'), pop (1980) 5 087. Island in the Atlantic off the SE coast of Massachusetts, USA; with Muskeget and Tuckernuck Is, forms Nantucket County; area 122 sq km/47 sq ml; formerly an important whaling centre; now a summer resort. » Massachusetts

Naomi [nay**oh**mee] (Heb 'my delight') Biblical character described in the stories of the Book of Ruth as the mother of Ruth and Orpah. After Naomi was widowed, she returned from Moab to Bethlehem with her daughter, and attempted to arrange the marriage of Ruth with Boaz, one of the secondary kinsmen of Naomi's deceased husband. The offspring of this union was said to be the grandfather of David. » David; Old Testament; Ruth, Book of

napalm [**nay**pahm] A munition (usually air-launched in canisters by aircraft) containing petroleum gel which uses flame for its destructive effects. It is designed for use against hard targets such as bunkers and armoured vehicles. Chemically, it is an aluminium soap of naphthenic and palmitic acids (which give the substance its name). » aluminium; gel

Napata [na**pah**ta] An ancient city, situated on the W bank of the Nile in what is now the Sudan. It was the capital of the kingdom of Cush c.750–590 BC. Although political dominance passed to Meroe in that year, Napata remained the religious capital. » Cush

Naphtali, tribe of [**naf**talee] One of the twelve tribes of ancient Israel, said to be descended from Naphtali, Jacob's second son by Bilhah (Rachel's maid). Its tribal territory was in N Palestine, immediately W of the Sea of Galilee and upper Jordan R. The tribe is described in the Book of Judges as consisting of courageous warriors. » Jacob; Israel, tribes of [i]; Old Testament

naphtha [**naf**tha] A mixture of hydrocarbons obtained either from coal tar or from petroleum. It has a boiling range of about 100–180°C. Naphtha from coal tar is mainly aromatic, containing much toluene, while that from petroleum is mainly aliphatic. » aliphatic compound; aromatic compound; hydrocarbons

naphthalene [**naf**thaleen] $C_{10}H_8$, melting point 80°C. A white, waxy solid, containing two fused benzene rings; obtained from the distillation of coal tar. It forms many derivatives, and is important as a starting material in the synthesis of dyestuffs and plastics. It is familiar as the main ingredient of mothballs. » aromatic compound; benzene [i]

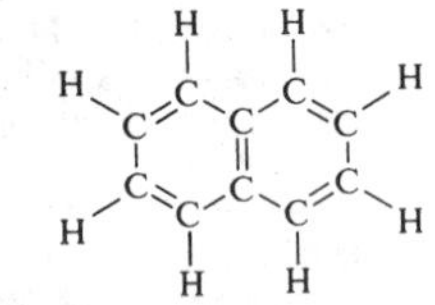

naphthol [**naf**thol] $C_{10}H_7OH$. Two isomeric phenols, obtained by substituting –OH for one hydrogen atom of naphthalene. Both are present in coal tar, and are starting materials for dyes. » isomers; phenol

Napier, John (1550–1617) Scottish mathematician, the inventor of logarithms, born and died near Edinburgh. Educated at St Andrews, he travelled in Europe, then settled down to a life of literary and scientific study. He described his famous invention in *Mirifici Logarithmorum Canonis Descriptio* (1614, Description of the Marvellous Canon of Logarithms), and also devised a calculating machine, using a set of rods, called 'Napier's Bones'. » logarithm

Napier [**nay**pyer] 39°29S 176°58E, pop (1988e) 52 100. Seaport in Hawke Bay on the E coast of North Island, New Zealand; largely destroyed by earthquake in 1931; a modern seaside city built largely on reclaimed land; airfield; railway; centre of a rich farming area; electronics, food processing, trade in wool, meat, fruit, pulp, tobacco. » New Zealand [i]

Naples, Ital **Napoli**, Lat **Neapolis** 40°50N 14°15E, pop (1981)

1 212 387. Seaport and capital city of Naples province, Campania, SW Italy; on the Tyrrhenian Sea, 189 km/117 ml SE of Rome; founded c.600 BC by refugees from Greek colony of Cumae; capital of Napoleon's Parthenopean Republic (1799) and of the Sicilian kingdom (1806); joined Kingdom of Italy, 1860; severely damaged in World War 2, and by earthquakes, 1980; archbishopric; airport; railway; car ferries to Sardinia and Sicily; university (1224); commerce, textiles, cars, aerospace, glass, tourism; several areas economically deprived; Cathedral of San Gennaro (13th–15th-c), Church of San Lorenzo Maggiore (1266–1324), Porta Capuana (15th–16th-c), Church of San Giovanni a Carbonara (14th-c), national museum; folk song festival (Sep). » Campania; Italy [i]; Napoleon I; Pompeii

Napoleon I (Fr Napoléon Bonaparte, Ital **Napoleone Buonaparte**) (1769–1821) French general, consul, and Emperor (1804–15), a titanic figure in European history, born at Ajaccio, Corsica. He entered the military schools at Brienne (1779) and Paris (1784), commanded the artillery at the siege of Toulon (1793), and was promoted brigadier-general. In 1796 he married Josephine, widow of the Vicomte de Beauharnais, and soon after left for Italy, where he skilfully defeated the Piedmontese and Austrians, and made several gains through the Treaty of Campo Formio (1797). Intending to break British trade by conquering Egypt, he captured Malta (1798), and entered Cairo, defeating the Turks; but after the French fleet was destroyed by Nelson at the Battle of the Nile, he returned to France (1799), having learned of French reverses in Europe. The *coup d'état* of 18th Brumaire followed (9 Nov 1799) in which Napoleon assumed power as First Consul, instituting a military dictatorship. He then routed the Austrians at Marengo (1800), made further gains at the Treaty of Luneville (1801), and consolidated French domination by the Concordat with Rome and the Peace of Amiens with England (1802).

Elected consul for life, he assumed the hereditary title of Emperor in 1804. His administrative, military, educational, and legal reforms (notably the *Code Napoléon*) made a lasting impact on French Society. War with England was renewed, and extended to Russia and Austria. Forced by England's naval supremacy at Trafalgar (1805) to abandon the notion of invasion, he attacked the Austrians and Russians, gaining victories at Ulm and Austerlitz (1805). Prussia was defeated at Jena and Auerstadt (1806), and Russia at Friedland (1807). After the Peace of Tilsit, he became the arbiter of Europe. He then tried to cripple England with the Continental System, ordering the European states under his control to boycott British goods. He sent armies into Portugal and Spain, which resulted in the bitter and ultimately unsuccessful Peninsular War (1808–14).

In 1809, wanting an heir, he divorced Josephine, who was childless, and married the Archduchess Marie Louise of Austria, a son being born in 1811. Believing that Russia was planning an alliance with England, he invaded, defeating the Russians at Borodino, before entering Moscow, but he was forced to retreat, his army broken by hunger and the Russian winter. In 1813 his victories over the allied armies continued at Lützen, Bautzen, and Dresden, but he was routed at Leipzig, and France was invaded. Forced to abdicate, he was given the sovereignty of Elba (1814). The unpopularity which followed the return of the Bourbons motivated him to return to France in 1815. He regained power for a period known as the Hundred Days, but was defeated by the combination of Wellington's and Blücher's forces at Waterloo. He fled to Paris, abdicated, surrendered to the British, and was banished to St Helena, where he died. » Alexander I; Blücher; Bourbons; Continental System; French Revolution [i]; Hundred Days; Joséphine; Napoleon II/III; Napoleonic Wars; Nelson, Horatio; Peninsular War; Waterloo, Battle of; Wellington, Duke of

Napoleon II, originally **François Charles Joseph Bonaparte** (1811–32) Son of Napoleon I by the Empress Marie Louise, born in Paris. Styled King of Rome at his birth, after his father's abdication he was brought up in Austria and in 1818 given the title of the Duke of Reichstadt, though allowed no active political role. He died at Schönbrunn. » Napoleon I

Napoleon III, until 1852 **Louis-Napoleon**, in full **Charles Louis Napoleon Bonaparte** (1808–73) Third son of Louis Bonaparte, King of Holland (the brother of Napoleon I) and Hortense Beauharnais; President of the Second French Republic (1850–2) and Emperor of the French (1852–70). Born in Paris, he was brought up in Switzerland, and after the death of the Duke of Reichstadt (1832) became the head of the Napoleonic dynasty. He made two abortive attempts on the French throne (1836, 1840), for which he was imprisoned at Ham, near Amiens. He escaped to England (1846), but when the Bonapartist tide swept France after the 1848 Revolution he was elected first to the Assembly and then to the Presidency (1848). Engineering the dissolution of the constitution, he assumed the title of Emperor, and in 1853 married Eugénie de Montijo de Guzman (1826–1920), a Spanish countess, who bore him a son, the Prince Imperial (1856). He actively encouraged economic expansion and the modernization of Paris, while externally the Second Empire coincided with the Crimean conflict (1854–6), the expeditions to China (1857–60), the annexation (1860) of Savoy and Nice, and the ill-starred intervention in Mexico (1861–7). Encouraged by the Empress Eugénie, he unwisely declared war on Prussia in 1870 and suffered humiliating defeat, culminating in the Battle of Sedan. Confined at Wilhelmshohe until 1871, he went into exile in England, living at Chislehurst, Kent, until his death. » Franco-Prussian War; Haussmann; Napoleon II; Revolutions of 1848

Napoleonic Wars (1800–15) The continuation of the Revolutionary Wars, fought to preserve French hegemony in Europe. They were initially a guarantee for the political, social, and economic changes of the 1789 Revolution, but increasingly became a manifestation of Napoleon's personal ambitions. The wars began with Napoleon's destruction of the Second Coalition (1800); after a peaceful interlude (1802–3) Britain resumed hostilities, prompting Napoleon to prepare for invasion, and encouraging the formation of a Third Coalition (1805–7). While Britain retained naval superiority (1805), Napoleon established territorial domination, sustained by economic warfare, resulting in the invasions of Spain (1808) and Russia (1812). Gradually the French were overwhelmed by the Fourth Coalition (1813–14); the Hundred Days' epilogue ended with Waterloo (1815). » Confederation of the Rhine; Continental System; Grand Alliance, War of the; Hundred Days; Leipzig/Trafalgar/Waterloo, Battles of; Paris, Treaties of **2**; Peninsular War; Vienna, Congress of; Alexander I; Barclay de Tolly; Blucher; Charles XIV; Francis II; Frederick-William III; Gneisenau; Godoy; Kutuzov; Louis XVIII; Masséna; Napoleon I; Nelson, Horatio; Ney; Pius VII; Soult; Stein, Baron von; Villeneuve; Wellington, Duke of

nappe A large-scale geological fold structure in which rocks have been overturned and transported several kilometres or more by compressional stresses during mountain-building processes. The Alps consist of several such nappes. » Alps; orogeny

Nara [**nah**ra] 34°41N 135°49E, pop (1980) 297 953. Capital of Nara prefecture, S Honshu, Japan, 29 km/18 ml E of Osaka; first capital of Japan, 710; cultural and religious centre; centre of Japanese Buddhism; railway; women's university (1908); textiles, dolls, fans; Daibutsu-den (Great Buddha Hall) in Todaiji (East Great Temple, founded 743), housing bronze statue of Buddha (22 m/72 ft tall); Nara national museum, Shoso-in (8th-c), Kasuga-taisha shrine; Horyuji (6th-c) nearby, oldest temple complex in Japan, and the oldest wooden buildings in the world. » Buddhism; Honshu; Horyuji Temple

Narayan, R(asipuram) K(rishnaswami) [nar**a**yan] (1906–) Indian novelist and short-story writer, born in Madras, and educated there and in Mysore. The action of his first novel, *Swami and Friends* (1935) takes place in the fictional S Indian town of Malgudi, the setting of most of his subsequent fiction, all of it in a comic form. It includes *Mr Sampath* (1949) and *The Vendor of Sweets* (1967). » Indian literature; novel

Narayanganj [nar**a**yangganj] 23°36N 90°28E, pop (1981) 405 562. City in Narayanganj district, SE Bangladesh; on R Meghna, E of Dhaka; river port for Dhaka, and one of the busiest trade centres; collection centre for jute, hides, and skins; major industrial region, including jute mills, cotton textiles, leather, glass, shoes. » Bangladesh [i]; Dhaka

narcissism A condition of self-infatuation stemming from difficulties at an early stage of psychological development. It may manifest as exhibitionism, indifference to criticism, a presumption of special entitlement, and fantasies of unlimited sexual prowess, intelligence, or attractiveness. » inferiority complex

narcissus [nahsisuhs] A bulb native to Europe, the Mediterranean region, and W Asia; leaves strap-shaped; flowers solitary or several on a long stalk, central trumpet or cup (the *corona*), surrounded by six spreading perianth-segments, white, yellow, or pink; the corona often contrasting, sometimes red. Horticulturally a division is made into *daffodils*, with the corona equalling or longer than the perianth, and *narcissi*, with the corona shorter than the perianth. Many species and numerous cultivars are grown in gardens and for the cut-flower trade. (Genus: *Narcissus*, 60 species. Family: *Amaryllidaceae*.) » bulb; cultivar; daffodil; perianth

Narcissus [nahsisuhs] In Greek mythology, a beautiful youth who fell in love with his reflection in a pool; he pined away and was changed into a flower. Ovid says this was because of his cruelty to Echo. » Echo

narcolepsy An extreme tendency towards excessive sleepiness often associated with cataplexy, and in which sleep onset is accompanied by dreaming. Sleep paralysis and hypnagogic (during the process of falling asleep) hallucinations are accompanying features. Genetic factors have recently been shown to be involved. » cataplexy; sleep

narcotics Drugs related to morphine which, in the literal sense, induce narcosis, or stupor. In common parlance the term has been adopted to include all addictive drugs. Narcotics such as morphine, heroin, and cocaine are used illegally for the euphoric sensations they induce, and are highly addictive. » analgesics; cannabis; cocaine [i]; drug addiction; heroin; laudanum; morphine; opium

Narmada [nahmada] or **Narbada, River** River of India, rising in the Maikala range of Madhya Pradesh; flows generally WSW across Gujarat to meet the Gulf of Cambay; length 1 245 km/774 ml; a sacred river to Hindus; many pilgrimage centres and bathing ghats along its course. » Hinduism; India [i]

Narnia [nahnia] A mythical country, the scene of a sequence of novels by C S Lewis, beginning with *The Lion, The Witch, and The Wardrobe* (1950). » Lewis, C S

narrowcasting » **broadcasting**

Narses (c.478–573) Famous general of the Emperor Justinian, and rival of Belisarius. He reasserted Byzantine control over Rome and Italy by his victories over the Ostrogoths (550–4). » Belisarius; Justinian; Ostrogoths

narthex A transverse vestibule in a basilica church, either inside and before the nave, or outside the main facade. Alternatively, it may refer to any enclosed, covered space before the main entrance. » basilica; church [i]; nave

Narvik [nahvik] 68°26N 17°25E, pop (1980) 19 339. Seaport in Nordland county, N Norway; at W end of a peninsula in the Ofoten Fjord, opposite the Lofoten Is; airfield; terminus of the Lappland railway from the Kiruna iron-ore mines in Sweden; ice-free harbour; occupied by Germany, 1940; scene of World War 2 naval battles in which two British and nine German destroyers were lost. » Norway [i]

narwhal [nahwuhl] A small toothed whale, native to the Arctic seas; mottled brown; no dorsal fin; two teeth (at front of upper jaw); in male, left tooth grows forwards forming a straight tusk half as long as body; eats fish, squid, and crustaceans. (*Monodon monoceros*. Family: *Monodontidae*.) » whale [i]

NASA (National Aeronautics and Space Administration) An independent agency of the US Government responsible for the civil space programme. It was established in 1958 by President Eisenhower based on the old National Advisory Committee for Aeronautics (NACA). Its headquarters is in Washington DC, where programme plans originate. Individual projects are implemented at different Field Centers: *Ames Research Center* (Mountain View, California) for aeronautics; *Goddard Space Flight Center* (Greenbelt, Maryland) for astronomy and Earth sciences; *Jet Propulsion Laboratory* (Pasadena, California) for Solar System exploration; *Johnson Space Center* (Houston, Texas) for manned missions; *Kennedy Space Center* (Cape Canaveral, Florida) for launch operations; *Langley Research Center* (Norfolk, Virginia) for aeronautics; *Lewis Research Center* (Cleveland, Ohio) for space technologies; and *Marshall Space Flight Center* (Huntsville, Alabama) for launch vehicles and space science. » Apollo/Gemini/Lunar Orbiter/Mariner/Mercury/Observer/Pioneer/Ranger/Surveyor (programmes); Apollo-Soyuz/Galileo/Magellan/Skylab/Viking/Voyager [i] (projects); Deep Space Network; Search for Extraterrestrial Intelligence; space exploration; space shuttle [i]; Space Organizations Worldwide

Naseby, Battle of (14 Jun 1645) A major conflict of the English Civil War in the E Midlands. The Royalist forces of Charles I, outnumbered by two to one, were defeated by Parliament's 'New Model' Army led by Fairfax, with Cromwell commanding the cavalry. Royalist cavalry, led by Prince Rupert, left the main battle, fatally weakening Charles's forces. » English Civil War

Nash, John (1752–1835) British architect and city planner, born in London. His country house designs brought him to the attention of the Prince of Wales, and he was engaged (1811–25) to plan the layout of the new Regent's Park. He recreated Buckingham Palace, designed the Marble Arch which originally stood in front of it, laid out Trafalgar Square and St James's Park, and rebuilt Brighton Pavilion in oriental style. The skilful use of terrain and landscape features in his layouts marks him as one of the greatest town planners. He died at Cowes, Isle of Wight. » London [i]

Nash, (Frederic) Ogden (1902–71) US humorous writer, born at Rye, New York. Educated at Harvard, he worked in advertising, editing, and teaching before joining the *New Yorker* (1931), where his verse was first published. His subject matter was the everyday life of middle-class America, which he described in a witty and acute manner, in an idiosyncratic style involving long digressions and striking rhyme schemes. His collections include *Hard Lines* (1931) and *Marriage Lines* (1964). He died in Baltimore. » American literature

Nash, Paul (1889–1946) British painter, born in London. Educated at St Paul's and the Slade School, London, he became an official war artist in 1917. He won renown as a landscape painter, and also practised scene painting, commercial design, and book illustration. Experiments in an abstract manner were followed by a phase of Surrealism until, in 1939, he again filled the role of war artist, with such pictures as 'Battle of Britain' and 'Totes Meer' (1940–1, Tate, London). He died at Boscombe, Hampshire. » abstract art; English art; landscape painting; Surrealism

Nash, Richard, byname **Beau Nash** (1674–1762) Welsh dandy, born in Swansea. Educated at Carmarthen and Oxford, he held a commission in the army, and studied law. He then made a shifty living by gambling, but in 1705 became master of ceremonies at Bath, where he conducted the public balls with a splendour never before witnessed. His reforms helped to transform Bath into a leading fashionable centre, and although he died a pauper he was buried in pomp in Bath Abbey. » Bath

Nashe or **Nash, Thomas** (1567–1601) English dramatist and satirist, born at Lowestoft, Suffolk. Educated at Cambridge, he travelled in France and Italy, and then went to London as a writer, where he plunged into the Martin Marprelate controversy, displaying a talent for vituperation, attacking the Puritans in *Pierce Penilesse* (1592). Other works include the satirical masque, *Summer's Last Will and Testament* (1592), and the picaresque tale, *The Unfortunate Traveller* (1594). His satirical play *The Isle of Dogs* (1597), now lost, was suppressed, and he was imprisoned. He died at Yarmouth, Norfolk. » drama; English literature; Marprelate Tracts; masque; picaresque novel; satire

Nashville 36°10N 86°47W, pop (1980) 455 651. Capital of state in Davidson County, N Tennessee, USA; port on the Cumberland R; settled as Nashborough, 1799; renamed Nashville, 1784; state capital, 1843; merged with Davidson, 1963; airfield;

railway; three universities (1867, 1872, 1909); chemicals, glass, clothing, publishing, railway engineering; famed for its music industry (country and western); centre for religious education; the Capitol (tomb of James K Polk), Country Music Hall of Fame, Opryland USA (family entertainment complex); Country Music Fan Fair (Jun). » country and western; Natchez Trace; Polk; Tennessee

Nasik [**nah**sik] 20°02N 75°30E, pop (1981) 916 000. City in Maharashtra state, WC India, on a tributary of the Darna R, 145 km/90 ml NE of Bombay; a holy place of Hindu pilgrimage; cattle, poultry, brassware, printing; many Vishnuite temples and shrines; Buddhist caves, 2nd-c AD. » Hinduism; Maharashtra

Nassau (Bahamas) [**na**saw] 25°05N 77°20W, pop (1980) 10 213. Capital of the Bahamas on NE coast of New Providence I; frequented by pirates during the 18th-c and captured briefly by Americans in 1776; Fort Nassau (1697), Fort Charlotte (1787–94), and Fort Fincastle (1793) built to protect the city from Spanish invasion; airport; a popular winter tourist resort. » Bahamas [i]; New Providence

Nassau (European history) A Burgundian noble family, who rose as servants of the Habsburgs, then rebelled against their authority in the Low Countries. They were made *stadtholders* of Holland, Zeeland, and Friesland, Counts of Nassau, and Princes of Orange by Charles V. The heirs to the titles, William of Orange (1533–84), and his brother Louis (1538–74), Count of Nassau, supported and led the Dutch Revolt (1566–1648) against their former masters. » Habsburgs

Nasser, Gamal Abdel (1918–70) Egyptian statesman, Prime Minister (1954–6), and President (1956–70), born in Alexandria. An army officer, he became dissatisfied with the corruption of the Farouk regime, and was involved in the military coup of 1952. He assumed the premiership in 1954, and then presidential powers, deposing his fellow officer, General Mohammed Neguib (1901–). Officially elected President in 1956, he nationalized the Suez Canal, which led to Israel's invasion of Sinai, and the intervention of Anglo-French forces. He aimed to build a N African Arab empire, and in 1958 created a federation with Syria, the United Arab Republic, but Syria withdrew in 1961. After the six-day Arab-Israeli War (1967), heavy losses on the Arab side led to his resignation, but he was persuaded to stay on, and died still in office in Cairo. » Egypt; Farouk I

Nasser, Lake, Arabic **Buheiret En Naser** Lake in S Egypt; length 500 km/310 ml; area c.5 000 sq km/1 930 sq ml; created after building the Aswan High Dam (1971); named after former President of Egypt. » Aswan High Dam; Egypt [i]; Nasser

nastic movement A non-directional plant response to an external stimulus, such as the opening and closing of flowers and the collapse of leaflets of the sensitive plant. It is attained by differential growth, or by controlled water movement within specialized cells. » auxins; sensitive plant; tropism

nasturtium [nas**ter**shuhm] An annual and perennial, trailing or climbing by twining leaf-stalks, native to Mexico and temperate S America; leaves rounded or lobed, stalk attached to centre of blade; flowers large, slightly zygomorphic, roughly trumpet-shaped with five petals and a backward-projecting spur, in shades of yellow, orange, and scarlet. Various species and numerous cultivars are grown for ornament. (Genus: *Tropaeolum*, 90 species. Family: *Balsaminaceae*.) » annual; cultivar; perennial; zygomorphic flower

Natal (Brazil) [na**tahl**] 5°46S 35°15W, pop (1980) 376 446. Port capital of Rio Grande do Norte state, NE Brazil; on the Atlantic coast at mouth of R Potengi, N of Recife; airfield; railway; university (1958); trade in sugar, cotton; textiles; Marine Research Institute at Praia da Areia Preta; rocket base of Barreira do Inferno, 20 km/12 ml S; cathedral, 16th-c fort, folk museum. » Brazil [i]

Natal (South Africa) [na**tahl**] pop (1985) 2 145 018; area 91 355 sq km/35 263 sq ml. Smallest province in South Africa; bounded E by the Indian Ocean, N by Mozambique and Swaziland, and SW by Lesotho; Drakensberg Mts follow the NW frontier; capital, Pietermaritzburg; chief towns include Durban, Ladysmith; annexed to Cape Colony, 1844; separate colony, 1856; Zululand province annexed, 1897; joined Union of South Africa, 1910; sugar cane, citrus, grain, vegetables, chemicals, paper, food processing, iron and steel, oil refining, explosives, fertilizers, meat canning. » Durban; Pietermaritzburg; South Africa [i]

NATIONAL ANTHEM/SONG

COUNTRY	TITLE	COMPOSER	ADOPTED
Australia	Advance Australia Fair*	Peter Dodds McCormick	1977
Canada	O Canada	Calixa Lavallée	1980
France	La Marseillaise	Claude-Joseph Rouget de Lisle	1795
Japan	Kimigayo ('His Majesty's Reign')	Hayashi Hiromori	not officially adopted
West Germany	Deutschland-lied ('Song of Germany')	Haydn	1950
UK	God Save the Queen/King	*not known*	18th-c
USA	The Star-Spangled Banner	John Stafford Smith	1931
USSR	Gimn Sovetskogo Soyuza ('Hymn of the Soviet Union')	*not known*	1944

*National tune. The official anthem is *God Save the Queen/King*, played when a regal or vice-regal personage is present.

Nataraja [nata**rah**ja] One of the names of the Hindu deity, Shiva. As the Lord of the Dance he dances the creation of the universe. » Hinduism; Shiva

Natchez Trace A road built by the US Army in the early 19th-c to link Nashville, Tennessee, with the then pioneer outpost of Natchez in Mississippi, 725 km/450 ml distant. The road, which follows an earlier American Indian track, was designated a national parkway in 1939. » Nashville

Nathanael (Heb 'God has given') New Testament character appearing only in *John* 1.45–51, 21.2. He is said to have been brought to Jesus by Philip, and is one of the first to confess Jesus as 'Son of God, King of Israel'. He does not appear by this name in any list of disciples in the synoptic Gospels, however; possibly he was not one of the twelve or even a historical individual at all, despite some attempts to identify him with Bartholomew or Matthew in the synoptic lists of the twelve disciples. » apostle; Jesus Christ; John, Gospel according to

Nation of Islam » **Black Muslims**

National Academy of Design The main official academy of art in the USA. Founded in 1826, it still exists as an exhibiting society for the more traditionally-minded artists.

national accounts A set of accounts showing how a nation's wealth has been generated and used. The amount of money generated by a nation in a year in the form of wages, rents, interest, and profits is known as the **national income**. The **national debt** is the amount of money borrowed by a government over the years. The total interest payable on government borrowing is known as *debt servicing*. » gross domestic product; interest

National Aeronautics and Space Administration » **NASA (National Aeronautics and Space Administration)**

national anthem » **panel** (above)

national archives » archives

National Association for the Advancement of Colored People (NAACP) A pressure group in the USA which aims to extend awareness among the country's Black population of their political rights. It has successfully used the courts, in the face of opposition from politicians, to remove certain legal barriers to the equal rights of Blacks. » Black consciousness; civil rights

National Audubon Society A US private conservation organization named after the US artist and naturalist, John James Audubon. It manages more than 60 wildlife sanctuaries in the USA. » Audubon; conservation (earth sciences)

National Council of the Churches of Christ in the USA An association of Protestant, Eastern Orthodox, and National Catholic Churches formed in 1950 in the USA. Affiliated to the World Council of Churches, it is committed to the principle of manifesting the oneness of the Church of Christ. » Christianity

national debt » **national accounts**

National Economic Development Council (NEDC), byname **Neddy** A UK forum set up in 1962 where government, industry, and unions could meet to discuss economic affairs. The Council is supported by a secretariat, the National Economic Development Office (NEDO). Many 'little Neddies' were created, relating to specific industries. » quango

National Front (NF) A strongly nationalist political party in Britain which centres its political programme on opposition to immigration, and calls for the repatriation of ethnic minorities even if they were born in the UK. The party was created in 1960 by the merger of the White Defence League and the National Labour Party, and in its early years was a small neo-Nazi grouping. In the mid- and late 1970s it had some minor impact in elections and its membership grew. It tried to develop a more respectable face and recruited some members from the right of the Conservative Party to widen its base beyond hard-line neo-fascists. Its political appeal declined with the election of a Conservative government in 1979, and it has largely withdrawn from any move to enter the mainstream of politics. Many of the Front's leaders are avowedly racist and anti-semitic, and many of those associated with the party are widely believed to be involved in racial and latterly football violence. » neofascism

National Gallery An art gallery in London housing the largest collection of paintings in Britain, and one of the finest collections in the world. It was opened in 1824 in Pall Mall, but moved to its present premises in Trafalgar Square in 1838. » London [i]

National Gallery of Art A gallery endowed by Andrew W Mellon and opened in Washington, DC in 1941. Although the museum is a branch of the Smithsonian Institution, it is administered independently. » Mellon; Smithsonian Institution

National Geographic Society In the USA, a scientific and educational organization, founded in 1890. The knowledge gained from the exploration and research it funds is published in its monthly journal *National Geographic*. » geography

National Grid Reference System A unique grid reference for mapping purposes for any part of the UK, using letters and numbers. The country has been divided by the Ordnance Survey into a number of grid squares, 100 x 100 km (62.14 ml), each with its own identifying letters. Each square is further subdivided into numbered 1 km (0.62 ml) squares. » grid reference; northing; Ordnance Survey

national guard A militia or reserve military force. The US National Guard is organized on a state-by-state basis, its members voluntarily enlisting for military training and for service in aiding the civil power when called upon by the state governor. » militia

National Health Service (NHS) A system of health care established in the UK in 1948. World War 2 revealed the need for reform of the health and hospital services which had served up to that time. The new service was to be, and largely remains, a free service available to the whole population, without income limit, and funded out of general taxation. Existing municipal and voluntary hospitals were nationalized and came under the control of regional Health Boards (subsequently called Area Health Committees). Hospital consultants and specialists were salaried (full-time and part-time). General practitioners (GPs) remained self-employed, but were organized by local general medical practice committees, and received capitation fees based on the number of individuals who registered with them as patients. GP services are now largely based on a growing number of Health Centres which accommodate small groups of doctors sharing supportive services. The NHS is supported by nurses, technical and scientific staff, and ancillary workers, and is the largest single employer of labour in the UK. » medicine

National Heritage Memorial Fund A fund set up in 1980 by the National Heritage Memorial Act as a memorial to those who have died in service for the UK. It is the successor of the National Land Fund, and is administered by the Department of the Environment. The fund is used for the purpose of helping in the acquisition, maintenance, and preservation of land, buildings, and objects of outstanding scenic, historic, architectural, artistic, and scientific interest. » conservation (earth sciences); environmentalism

national hunt racing » **horse racing**

national insurance The sum levied on all working people by the state as an insurance against sickness and unemployment. The amount is a percentage of pay, supplemented by a contribution from the employer. Receipts are collected by the employer and passed on to the government. The individual receives benefit in the form of state medical treatment, sick pay, or unemployment benefit. » insurance; social security

National Library of Australia One of Australia's principal libraries, established in 1901 as the parliamentary library of the new federal government. In 1912, it became entitled to a copy of all Australian material. Re-housed in Canberra in 1968, it now holds over four million items. » library

National Park According to the United Nations, an area of educational and scientific importance for habitat and wildlife, of great beauty, and of recreational value, but which has suffered little human impact, so remaining a relative wilderness. It should also be protected from resource development and be relatively unpopulated. Examples include Yosemite National Park, USA, and Wood Buffalo National Park, Canada. According to these criteria, the National Parks of England and Wales do not qualify for inclusion in the United Nations list, because they are situated near populated areas where forestry, agriculture, and limited industrial activities are permitted. National Parks date back to 19th-c USA, where the first was established at Yellowstone, Montana, in 1872. The first parks in England and Wales were designated in 1951, and by 1988 there were ten. There are none in Scotland. » Countryside Commission for England and Wales; wildlife refuge

National Party (Australia) The third largest party in Australia since 1920, originally named the **County Party**. It grew out of rural dissatisfaction with the way governments had favoured urban areas, and concern over loss of population to the towns. The Party is conservative in social matters, generally favours policies of free trade and low tariffs, and supports government public expenditure. Since 1923 it has been in coalition with the Conservative Party. The National Party achieved its greatest success when it governed with the Liberal Party nationally (1949–72). It has been most dynamic in Queensland under Premier Johannes Bjelke-Peterson (1968–87), where it has ruled in its own right since 1983, the only state where this has happened. In 1988, the Party claimed the largest membership of any Australian political party (140 000), but attracted the lowest vote of the three largest parties (11.5%) in the 1987 national election. » Liberal Party (Australia)

National Physical Laboratory A state laboratory established in 1900 at Teddington, near London, to research and develop industrial and scientific standards of measurement.

National Portrait Gallery A gallery of portraits of distinguished people in British history. Opened in London in 1859, it was moved to its present position adjoining the National Gallery in 1895. » National Gallery

national product » **gross domestic product**

National Radio Astronomy Observatory The principal

radio astronomy observatory of the USA, with telescopes at Green Bank, West Virginia (a 91 m dish) and Socorro, New Mexico (Very Large Array), and headquarters at Charlottesville, Virginia. In 1988 its 91 m/300 ft dish, used since 1963, collapsed without warning from metal fatigue, fortunately without injuring the astronomers using it at the time. » metal fatigue; observatory [i]; radio astronomy

National Road A road built in the early 19th-c from Cumberland, Maryland, to Vandalia, Illinois, and eventually to St Louis, Missouri. Its construction and repair were financed initially by government sales of land, but in the 1830s this became the responsibility of the states through which it passed. The National Road played an important role in the expansion of the West.

National Security Adviser A member of staff who is responsible for advising the US President on security matters. He is regarded as a senior figure in the White House; his views sometimes serve to balance or compete with those of the secretary of state.

National Security Council A body created by Congress in 1947 to advise the US President on the integration of domestic, foreign, and military policies relating to national security. It was designed to achieve effective co-ordination between the military services and other government agencies and departments, and is composed of the President, Vice-President, Secretary of State, Secretary of Defense, and Director of the Office of Emergency Planning. » Congress

national service » **conscription**

National Socialism » **Nazi Party**

National Socialist German Worker's Party » **Nazi Party**

National Society for the Prevention of Cruelty to Children » **NSPCC**

national theatre A theatre which is endowed by the state and is usually situated in the national capital. Today found throughout the world, such endowed companies have a long history in many European countries (the National Theatre in Stockholm, for example, opened in 1773). In Britain, though advocated from the time of Garrick, a National Theatre was not inaugurated until 1962, under the direction of Laurence Olivier. Peter Hall replaced Olivier in 1973; and since 1976 the company has occupied its own building on the South Bank. » Habima; Olivier, Laurence; theatre

National Trust In the UK, a charity founded in 1895 with the full name 'The National Trust for Places of Historic Interest and Natural Beauty'. Its membership stands at over 1 million, making it the largest and most influential conservation body in Britain. The Trust owns historic houses, gardens, and sites of natural beauty, which it opens to the public; those who are not members pay a fee to enter. It has a branch for US members, the Royal Oak. The National Trust for Scotland is a separate organization run on similar lines. » conservation (earth sciences); English Heritage

National Youth Dance A Trust which organizes an annual festival for youth dance companies from across Britain to work with top professional choreographers and teachers. The National Youth Dance Theatre has been in existence since 1985. It auditions countrywide, selecting 25 dancers aged 16–20 to tour with a programme of commissioned works. Its artistic director is John Chesworth. » ballet; modern dance

nationalism A political doctrine which views the nation as the principal unit of political organization. Underlying this is the assumption that human beings hold the characteristic of nationality, with which they identify culturally, economically, and politically. A primary aim of nationalists, therefore, is to secure the right to belong to an independent state based on a particular national grouping. Nationalism is thus associated with attempts by national groupings to secure independence from dominance by other nation-states and to maintain that position against threats to it. It is often associated with the struggle against colonialism. More broadly, nationalism can be seen as a general political stance which holds that the principal aim of political activity should be to serve the national interest as opposed to that of a particular class or grouping. In practice, the national interest is, except in extreme cases such as war, open to different interpretations, and nationalism is often no more than an attempt to give legitimacy to a particular political standpoint. Nationalism, with the exception of anti-colonial movements, is based around a conservative, and sometimes romantic political philosophy that emphasizes the nation's past. » conservatism; Plaid Cymru; Scottish National Party; self-determination; separatism

nationalization Taking into public ownership an entire industry, normally a public utility. Nationalization takes place with social as well as commercial objectives. The main reasons are that an industry (a) is crucial to the economy and in need of government direction, (b) is a natural monopoly, (c) has suffered a period of decline which needs to be reversed, (d) produces a good or service which would not be available to all areas if commercial profit were the only criterion for supply, and (e) is important to national defence. There is also the view, based on a socialist ideology, that public ownership is desirable to prevent the earning of private profit extracted from labour and the concentration of economic power in private hands. Nationalized industries in the UK are normally constituted as *public corporations* accountable to a government minister. » privatization; socialism

Nations, Battle of the » **Leipzig, Battle of**

Native American Church An indigenous 19th-c religious movement among N American Indians, combining native religion with certain elements of Christianity; formally founded in 1918. Its main ritual centres on the sacramental and curative use of the non-narcotic hallucinogen mescaline, derived from the peyote plant. » American Indians; mescaline

Nativity, the The story of the miraculous birth of Jesus of Nazareth to Mary, the accompanying events of which are variously described in the opening chapters of the Gospels of Matthew and Luke. Although the year of Jesus' birth is unknown, it is usually fixed at c.6 BC, two years before the death of Herod the Great (Matt 2.1, 16–20). The observance of the birth, the festival of Christmas, has been celebrated since the 4th–5th-c on 25 December throughout most of Christendom. » Christmas; Jesus Christ; New Testament

NATO An acronym of **North Atlantic Treaty Organization**. An organization established by a treaty signed in 1949 by Belgium, Canada, Denmark, France, Iceland, Italy, Luxembourg, the Netherlands, Norway, Portugal, the UK, and the USA; Greece and Turkey acceded in 1952, West Germany in 1955, and Spain in 1982. NATO is a permanent military alliance established to defend W Europe against Soviet aggression. The treaty commits the members to treat an armed attack on one of them as an attack on all of them, and for all to assist the country attacked by such actions as are deemed necessary. The alliance forces are based on contributions from the member countries' armed services and operate under a multi-national command. The remit includes the deployment of nuclear, as well as conventional, weapons. Its institutions include a Council, an International Secretariat, the Supreme Headquarters Allied Powers, Europe (SHAPE), and various committees to formulate common policies. In the 1970s and 1980s, NATO policy of a first-strike nuclear attack to fend off a Soviet conventional attack became controversial in W Europe, where many thought it increased the possibility of nuclear war. In 1966 France under de Gaulle withdrew all its forces from NATO command, but it remains a member. After the 1989 changes in E Europe, a NATO summit in London (Jul 1990) began the process of redefining NATO's military and political goals. » nuclear weapons

natterjack A European true toad; rough green s .in with thin yellow line along spine; short legs; inhabits sandy areas; the loudest European toad (croak may be heard 2 k.n/1¼ ml away). (*Bufo calamita*.) » frog

Natufian [natoofeeuhn] A Mesolithic culture of SW Syria, Lebanon, and Palestine (c.10 000–8000 BC), named after the Palestinian site of Wādi en-Natūf. Though largely restricted to 65 km/40 ml of the Mediterranean coast, animal herding, the harvesting of wild cereals, and increasingly permanent settlement point to incipient agriculture. Open sites like Jericho were occupied, as well as caves and rock shelters. » Jericho; Three Age System

natural childbirth Successful labour entirely without or with minimal use of drugs or outside assistance. Exercises to strengthen the abdominal muscles and to encourage relaxation of the pelvic muscles are undertaken throughout pregnancy. It is facilitated by a full awareness of the nature of childbirth, and by developing psychological attitudes which reduce anxiety and fear, and increase pain tolerance. It is best acceded to by the doctor or midwife in the absence of evidence of physical disorder either of the mother or foetus, and when the mother is strongly motivated to carry it out. » labour; pregnancy [i]

natural gas Gas which occurs in subterranean accumulations, often in association with petroleum deposits. It mainly consists of simple hydrocarbons, mostly methane, with some propane; there may also be nitrogen, helium, and hydrogen sulphide. 'Wet gas' has recoverable amounts of higher hydrocarbons (eg butane, pentane) which have commercial value as Liquefied Petroleum Gas. Natural gas is one of the most widely-used and versatile of fuels, and a source of other chemicals. When used as a gas supply, it is adulterated with other gases to give it an odour. » gas **2** [i]; methane [i]; petroleum

Natural History Museum The popular name for the British Museum (Natural History), housed since 1881 in S Kensington, London. The exhibition was originally built up in the 17th–18th-c around the collections of Sir Hans Sloane and Sir Joseph Banks. » Banks, Joseph; British Museum; museum; Sloane, Hans

natural justice A legal concept involving two main principles: everyone should have a right to be heard in his or her own case; and judges should be unbiased in hearing a case. These rules apply not only to those accused before courts, but also to those persons subject to the decisions of bodies acting judicially. An interested party alleging lack of natural justice may seek a judicial review. » High Court of Justice; judicial review

natural law 1 Any law in the natural sciences, such as Newton's laws of mechanics or Mendel's laws of inheritance. **2** In ethics and legal theory, any law which prescribes how people ought to behave, the source of which is supposed to be nature itself, independent of and superior to human legislation. Natural law theories have been used to attempt to justify many different political institutions, from absolute monarchy to doctrines of natural rights. Although many such theorists (eg Aquinas) have conceived of God as a divine legislator, others (eg the Stoics) do not necessarily maintain a theistic belief. » Aquinas; ethics; Stoicism

natural selection The complex process by which the totality of environmental factors determines the non-random and differential reproduction of genetically different organisms. It is viewed as the force which directs the course of evolution, by preserving those variants or traits best adapted to survive. » evolution

natural units A system of units used in particle physics in which equations are simplified by setting $c = (h/2\pi) = 1$, where c is the velocity of light and h is Planck's constant; requires that both length and time have units of one divided by mass. » equations; light; particle physics; Planck's constant; units (scientific); RR78

Naturalism (art) A term used in art criticism for the faithful copying of nature, with no attempt to 'improve' or idealize the subject; used in this sense in 1672 by Giovanni Pietro Bellori (1615–96) to characterize the work of Caravaggio and his followers. It later became used to describe the incorporation of scientific method into art, especially literature. This was advocated by the French novelist Emile Zola in the late 19th-c, at a time when confidence in science ran high. Zola claimed the writer should be a dispassionate observer of phenomena, his imagination a laboratory. The Naturalist movement provided a philosophical framework for the earlier Realist initiative, but was soon undermined by Symbolist ideas. Naturalism had an after-life in England (with Bennett), in the USA (with Dreiser), and in Germany (with Hauptmann). » Bennett, Arnold; Caravaggio; Comte; Dreiser; French literature; Hauptmann; Realism; Symbolism; Zola

naturalism (philosophy) **1** The meta-ethical position that the truth or falsity of moral judgments can be determined by empirical means; a simple version might maintain that '*x* is good' is equivalent to '*x* is pleasant' (Bentham). **2** The general philosophical position that all phenomena can be made intelligible by science. » Bentham; ethics

naturalistic fallacy According to Moore, the mistake of thinking that goodness is some natural property of things, such as their capacity to produce pleasure. It is sometimes more generally characterized as the alleged mistake of inferring normative conclusions from factual premises – an 'ought' from an 'is'. » egoism; Moore, G E

Nature Conservancy Council A British government agency responsible for wildlife and nature conservation, originally established as the Nature Conservancy in 1949. The Council manages National Nature Reserves, selects and schedules Sites of Special Scientific Interest to planning authorities, owners, and occupiers, and offers management agreements for these where needed. It also undertakes research on conservation issues. » conservation (earth sciences); Nature Reserve; Sites of Special Scientific Interest

Nature Reserve A protected area for the conservation and management of wildlife and habitat. In the UK these range from National Nature Reserves, established by the Nature Conservancy Council, to reserves managed by the National Trust, local authorities, and county naturalist trusts. By 1985 there were 200 National Nature Reserves, which represent the best-known examples of coastal, freshwater, marshland, bog, moorland, heathland, grassland, woodland, and alpine habitats. » conservation (earth sciences); endangered species; habitat loss; Nature Conservancy Council; wildlife refuge

Naukratis [**naw**kratis] A Greek town in the Delta of Egypt, established by the Milesians c.675 BC. It was the commercial and industrial centre of the Greeks in Egypt until the foundation of Alexandria by Alexander the Great (c.331 BC). » Miletus

Nauru, official name **Republic of Nauru** [na**oo**roo] 0°32S 166°56E; pop (1990e) 9 000; area 21.3 sq km/8.2 sq ml; circumference 20 km/12 ml. Small isolated island in the WC Pacific Ocean, 42 km/26 ml S of the Equator and 4 000 km/2 500 ml NE of Sydney, Australia; government offices in Yaren district (no capital city as such); timezone GMT +11½; several small scattered settlements; half population Nauruans, remainder Australians and New Zealanders, Chinese, other Pacific islanders; language, Nauruan, with English widely understood; religion, mostly Protestant, also Roman Catholic; Australian currency used; ground rises from sandy beaches to give fertile coastal belt, c.100–300 m/300–1 000 ft wide, the only cultivable soil; central plateau inland, highest point 65 m/213 ft, mainly phosphate-bearing rocks; tropical climate, average daily temperatures 24.4–33.9°C, humidity 70–80%, annual rainfall 1 524 mm/60 in, mainly in the monsoon season (Nov–Feb), with marked yearly deviations; under German administration from the 1880s until 1914; after 1919, League of Nations mandate, administered by Australia; movement for independence by the 1960s; self-government, 1966; full independence, 1968; unicameral parliament of 18 members, elected every three years; parliament elects a president, who appoints a cabinet; economy based on phosphate mining, but reserves now very limited, and over 60% of revenue from phosphate exports invested to provide future income; coconuts, some vegetables; tourism; tax haven. » mandates; Pacific Ocean; RR26 national holidays; RR56 political leaders

Nausicaa [naw**si**kaya] In Homer's *Odyssey*, the daughter of King Alcinous. When Odysseus landed in Phaeacia, alone and naked, she was doing the laundry by the sea-shore; she took him home to her father's palace. » Odysseus

nautilus [**naw**tiluhs] A primitive cephalopod mollusc with an external spiral shell containing gas in its chambers; numerous tentacles present around mouth; four gills; eyes like a pinhole camera in design, without lenses; only a single living genus known, but the group has an extensive fossil record. (Class: *Cephalopoda*. Subclass: *Nautiloidea*.) » Cephalopoda [i]; mollusc; shell

Navajo or **Navaho** Athapascan-speaking N American Southwest Indians, who migrated to the SW some time after 1000 AD, and who are today the largest Indian group in the USA, numbering c.97 000. They carried out raids on Spanish settlers in the area, but were themselves eventually defeated by US troops

(1863–4), and settled in 1888 on a reservation in Arizona (presently 15 million acres). Many work as itinerant labourers throughout the SW, and some have settled in the cities and on irrigated farming lands. » American Indians; Southwest Indians

Navaratri [navarahtree] A Hindu festival held in the autumn (Asvina S 1–10) in honour of the goddess Durga, and also commemorating the victory of Rama over Ravana, the Demon King; also known as **Durga Puja [durgah poojah]**. » Hinduism; RR23

Navarre [navah], Span **Navarra** pop (1981) 507 367; area 10 421 sq km/4 022 sq ml. Region and former kingdom of N Spain, co-extensive with the modern province of Navarre; early centre of resistance to the Moors; united with Castile, 1515; capital, Pamplona; cereals, vegetables, vines, food canning, cement, footwear, textiles, clothes, electrical equipment, iron and steel, furniture, metal products. » Pamplona; Spain [i]

nave The W part of a church open to the laity, as opposed to the chancel or choir. More specifically, it refers to the middle section of the W limb between the side aisles. » chancel; church [i]

navel » umbilical cord

Navier–Stokes equation An important but complex equation describing the mechanics of a viscous fluid, relating changes in the velocity of the fluid to the pressure and viscous forces acting on it; formulated by French engineer Claude Navier (1785–1836) and British mathematician George Stokes (1819–1903). It can be solved only for certain special cases. » fluid mechanics; viscosity

Navigation Acts Protective legislation in Britain passed between 1650 and 1696, designed to increase England's share of overseas carrying trade. The laws stated that all imports to England had to be in English ships or in those of the country of origin. The laws were frequently contentious in the 18th-c, adding to the 13 American colonies' sense of grievance against the mother country. They were not repealed until 1849. » American Revolution; free trade

navigation satellite An artificial object placed in orbit around the Earth, which acts as an aid to navigation. By giving position references and acting as signal relays, navigators of aeroplanes and ships can obtain an accurate fix on their position. » satellite

Navratilova, Martina [navratilohva] (1956–) US lawn tennis player, born in Prague, Czechoslovakia. The winner of a record-equalling nine singles titles at Wimbledon (1978–9, 1982–7, 1990), she has won 53 Grand Slam events, including 18 doubles with Pam Shriver. Also the winner of the Virginia Slims championship (1981, 1983–6), she is the most prolific winner in women's tennis. She became a naturalized American in 1981. » tennis, lawn [i]

navy The branch of the armed forces whose main function is the projection of military power at and by sea. The role of naval forces is manifold, primarily the protection of lines of communication for the safe transport of troops and supplies (and its converse, denying the enemy the freedom of the seas). In the two World Wars, naval power was of critical importance, with the added dimensions of submarine, amphibious, and carrier warfare. Since the 1960s, with the advent of the ballistic missile-firing submarine, navies have had the additional responsibility of nuclear deterrence. » Marines; Royal Australian Navy; Royal Navy; warships [i]

Naxos [naksos] pop (1981) 14 037; area 428 sq km/165 sq ml. Largest island of the Cyclades, Greece, in the S Aegean Sea; length 35 km/22 ml; width 26 km/16 ml; rises to 1 002 m/3 287 ft; chief town, Naxos; wine, emery, tourism. » Cyclades; Greece [i]

Nazarenes A derisive nickname given to a group of German artists in Rome 1810–c.1820. Leading members, including Johann Friedrich Overbeck (1789–1869), Franz Pforr (1788–1812), and Peter von Cornelius (1783–1867), were inspired by 15th-c styles, and dedicated to the revival of mediaeval and Renaissance religious art. » Renaissance art

Nazareth, Hebrew **Nazerat** 32°41N 35°16E, pop (1982) 44 900. Capital town of Northern district, N Israel; above the Jezreel plain; mainly Christian population; home of Jesus for most of his life; tourism, market centre; Church of the Annunciation, Church of St Joseph. » Israel [i]; Jesus Christ

Nazca [naska] A pre-Columbian culture located along the S Peruvian coast, and flourishing between c.200 BC and AD 500. It was noted for its distinctive style of pottery and large-scale 'lines' (best seen from the air) on the desert surface.

Naze, the, Norwegian **Lindesnes** or **Lindesnas** 57°59N 7°03E. Cape on the S extremity of Norway, projecting into the North Sea at the entrance to the Skagerrak; first beacon light in Norway established here. » Norway [i]

Nazi Party A German political party which originated as the German Worker's Party, founded in 1919 to protest against the German surrender of 1918 and the Treaty of Versailles, and renamed the *Nationalsozialistische Deutsche Arbeiterpartei* (National Socialist German Worker's Party, or Nazi Party) in 1920. Adolf Hitler became the Party's leader the following year. Its ideology was extremely nationalist, imperialist, and racist, maintaining that the world was divided into a hierarchy of races: Aryans, of whom Germans were the purest example, were the supreme culture-bearing race, while the Jews were the lowest. It was also contended that the Jews were intent on world conquest through infesting the Aryan race. This set of ideas was set out by Hitler in *Mein Kampf* (1925). It was not until the 1930s that the Nazi Party gained a position of significant support: in 1932 with 37.3% of the vote they became the largest party in the Reichstag. Support came from people of all backgrounds, but was most prominent among Protestants, the middle class, and the young. In 1933 Hitler was appointed Chancellor in a coalition government, a position from which he, aided by the Party, was able to build up a personal dictatorship, through legal measures, terror, and propaganda. Once in power, the Nazis ruthlessly crushed opposition, indoctrinated the public with their ideas, engaged in extensive rearmament, and in the late 1930s invaded Austria, the Sudetenland, and the rest of Czechoslovakia, which according to the ideology was necessary for obtaining land for the 'master race'. During World War 2, their actions included slave labour, plunder, and mass extermination. Nazism as a political ideology is now viewed very much as the expression of extreme inhumanity, fanatical nationalism, and the logic of nihilism. » fascism; Hitler; imperialism; nationalism; nihilism; racism

Ndebele [nduhbeelee] or **Matabele** A Bantu-speaking people of SW Zimbabwe and N South Africa, originating in the 19th-c as an offshoot of Nguni groups who moved N, conquering some of the indigenous Shona peoples, and establishing a highly stratified state. In the 1890s they resisted White pioneers' encroachment on their land, but were ruthlessly suppressed. Population c.1.5 million. » Bantu-speaking peoples; Nguni; Shona; Zulu

Ndola [ndohla] 13°00S 28°39E, pop (1980) 282 439. Capital of Copperbelt province, C Zambia, 275 km/171 ml N of Lusaka; airport; railway; technical college; commercial centre of a major mining area; cement, oil refining, paint, adhesives, tyres, furniture, clothing, mining equipment, food processing. » Copperbelt; Zambia [i]

Neagh, Lough [lokh nay] area 396 sq km/153 sq ml. Large lake in C Northern Ireland; length, 29 km/18 ml; width, 18 km/11 ml; largest lake in the British Isles; well-known for its eels; outlet is the R Bann, which flows N to the coast; lignite mining around the lake. » Northern Ireland [i]

Neanderthal Man [neeandertahl] *Homo sapiens neanderthalensis*, a stocky, muscular, upright, beetle-browed, large-nosed, chinless subspecies of *Homo sapiens*; height 1.7 m/5 ft 7 in; weight 70 kg/154 lb; brain capacity 1 500 cc. The subspecies lived c.250 000–30 000 years ago in Europe and SW Asia. » *Homo* [i]

neap tide An especially small tidal range occurring twice monthly. It is produced by the tidal forces of the Sun and Moon acting in opposition. These minimum monthly tides occur when the Moon is in its first and third quarters. » spring tide; tide

near-death experience (NDE) A striking experience sometimes reported by those who have recovered from being close to death. It generally includes an out-of-the-body experience in which one travels through a dark void or tunnel towards a bright light, and then may encounter religious figures or deceased loved ones. It is often accompanied by strong feelings of peacefulness. » out-of-the-body experience

nearsightedness » eye [i]

Neblina, Pico da [**pee**koh da neb**lee**na] 1°45N 66°01W. Mountain in Amazonas state, N Brazil; rises to 3 014 m/9 888 ft in the Serra Imeri range on the frontier with Venezuela; now known to be the highest mountain in Brazil; situated in a 22 000 sq km/8 500 sq ml national park established in 1979. » Brazil [i]

Nebraska [nuh**bras**ka] pop (1987e) 1 594 000; area 200 342 sq km/77 355 sq ml. State in C USA, divided into 93 counties; the 'Cornhusker State'; part of the Louisiana Purchase, 1803; Bellevue first permanent settlement; became a territory stretching to the Canadian border in 1854, but its area was reduced in 1863; the 37th state admitted to the Union, 1867; in the same year the Union Pacific Railroad completed its transcontinental line, resulting in a land boom; capital, Lincoln; other chief cities, Omaha and Grand Island; Missouri R forms the E border; Platte R crosses the state to empty into the Missouri; highest point Johnson Township (1 654 m/5 426 ft); E region undulating fertile farmland, growing corn; further W, on the Great Plains, grass cover helping to stabilize eroded land; in the far W, foothills of the Rocky Mts; agriculture dominates the economy; cattle (second largest producer in the country), corn, hogs, wheat, grain sorghum; food processing, electrical machinery, chemicals. » Lincoln (USA); Louisiana Purchase; United States of America [i]; RR39

Nebuchadnezzar or **Nebuchadrezzar** (c.630–562 BC) King of Babylon (605–562 BC), the son of Nabopolassar, founder of the New Babylonian Empire, and the most famous king of Babylon. Under him, Babylonian civilization reached its height, and its empire extended as far as the Mediterranean. In the West, he is remembered chiefly for his deportation of the Jews to Babylonia (586 BC). » Babylonia; Babylonian Exile; Chaldaeans

nebula Any celestial object that appears as a hazy smudge of light in an optical telescope, its usage pre-dating photographic astronomy. It is now more properly restricted to true clouds of interstellar matter. » Crab nebula; Orion

neck That part of the body which connects the head and the thorax as well as the upper limbs to the trunk. The various structures within the neck are contained within coverings of connective tissue (*fascia*), organized in well-defined sheets and membranes. The most superficial cylindrical layer of fascia encloses and covers all structures within the neck (except the platysma muscle, which lies in the subcutaneous tissue). Deeper layers of fascia surround specific structures. The cylindrical organization of these various fasciae emphasizes that they form longitudinal compartments transmitting structures from one region to another. The neck contains the continuations of many structures: the vertebral column, alimentary and respiratory tracts, blood vessels and their branches, lymph nodes and lymphatic vessels, groups of muscles, and several cranial and cervical nerves. » blood vessels [i]; jugular veins; larynx; tissue; trachea; vagus; vertebral column; Plate XII

Necker, Jacques (1732–1804) French statesman and financier, born in Geneva, Switzerland. Initially a banker's clerk, he moved to Paris (1762), founded a bank, and became a wealthy speculator. By 1776–7 he became Director of the French Treasury and Director-General of Finances. He attempted some administrative reforms, but tried to finance French involvement in the War of American Independence by heavy borrowing, while concealing the large state deficit. He was dismissed in 1781, but recalled in 1788 to deal with the impending financial crisis. He summoned the States General, but his proposals for social and constitutional change aroused royal opposition. He was dismissed and hastily recalled (1789), but finally resigned in 1790. He retired to his estate near Geneva, where he died. » Louis XVI

nectar A sugary fluid secreted by specialized glands (*nectaries*) usually found in flowers, sometimes also in other organs, and used to attract insect pollinators. » flower; pollination

nectarine A smooth-skinned variety of peach. (*Prunus persica*, variety *nectarina*. Family: *Rosaceae*.) » peach

Neddy » **National Economic Development Council**

Needham, Joseph (1900–) British specialist in China and historian of science, educated at Oundle and Cambridge, where he became a Fellow (1924–66), Master of Gonville and Caius College (1966–76), and director of the Needham Research Institute (from 1976). He trained as a biochemist, and published a pioneering *History of Embryology* (1934) before developing a consuming interest in the Chinese tradition of science, technology, and medicine. His major work is *Science and Civilisation in China* (7 vols, 1954). » China [i]

needlefish Slender-bodied fish with very long jaws forming a narrow bill; widespread in tropical and warm temperate seas; dorsal and anal fins placed close to tail; includes W Atlantic, *Strongylura marina*, a voracious surface-living predator; length up to 1.2 m/4 ft; also called **garfish**. (Family: *Belonidae*.)

Neer, Aernout (Aert) van der (c.1603–77) Dutch painter, who took up painting in his 30s when living in Amsterdam, but his work never sold well, and he went bankrupt in 1661. He specialized in wintery river scenes, especially at night, the emphasis almost always on the beautifully-observed effect of the Moon peering through ragged clouds. He died in Amsterdam. » landscape painting

Nefertiti [nefuh**tee**tee] (14th-c BC) Egyptian queen, the consort of Akhenaton. She is immortalized in the beautiful sculptured head found at Amarna in 1912, now in the Berlin museum. » Akhenaton

negative An image in which the tonal scale of the original scene is inverted, light areas being reproduced as dark and vice versa. In a **colour negative** the hues of the original are also represented in their complementary colours. Film exposed in a camera is usually processed to yield a negative, from which a positive print must be made to reproduce the original scene. » film; photography

negative income tax A scheme where the poorest sections of the community receive a state-funded 'income support payment' instead of various grants and supplementary benefits. The notion applies to low-earning workers, and is intended to raise their income to a suitable level. » income tax

Negeri Sembilan [nuh**gree** suhmbee**lahn**] pop (1980) 551 442; area 6 643 sq km/2 564 sq ml. State in SW Peninsular Malaysia; bounded W by the Strait of Malacca, SE by Malacca, NW by Selangor, NE by Pahang; capital, Seremban; rubber, rice, tin. » Malaysia [i]

Negev Hilly desert region of S Israel, extending in a wedge from Beersheba in the N to Eilat on the Gulf of Aqaba; hilly in the S, reaching 1 935 m/6 348 ft at Har Ramon; N irrigated by a conduit leading from L Tiberias; increasing kibbutz settlement. » Israel [i]; kibbutz

negligence A tort applicable to a very wide range of situations. To succeed in negligence, the plaintiff must prove that the defendant owed him or her a duty of care; that the duty was breached in this instance; and that the breach caused damage to the plaintiff. Road accidents are a common source of negligence claims. It is not sufficient to show that there has been an incident; negligence must be proved. In the case of pure economic loss, where no physical damage is involved (eg poor investment advice), it will also be generally necessary to establish a special relationship based on reliance by the plaintiff on the defendant's actions or statements. » damages; no-fault principle; tort

Negoiul, Mount [ne**goy**ul] 45°35N 24°31E. Mountain in the Transylvanian Alps of SC Romania, rising to 2 548 m/8 359 ft; highest mountain in Romania. » Transylvanian Alps

Negro, River (Argentina)(Span **Río**) [**nay**groh] Patagonian river in SC Argentina; formed by junction of Neuquén and Limay Rivers; flows S and SE to the Atlantic 32 km/20 ml SE of Viedma; navigable for 400 km/250 ml upstream; used for hydroelectric power; vineyards in irrigated valleys; length of the Neuquén-Negro, 1 130 km/702 ml. » Argentina [i]; Patagonia

Negro, River (Brazil)(Port **Rio**) [**neg**roh] Important N tributary of the Amazon, N Brazil; rises in SE Colombia, flows generally SE through the Amazon tropical rainforest, joining the Amazon 18 km/11 ml below Manaus; length c. 2 253 km/1 400 ml; a major transport channel, connected to the Orinoco R via the Casiquiare Canal; contains numerous islands; up to

32 km/20 ml wide above Manaus, narrows to 2.5 km/1½ ml at its mouth. » Amazon, River; Brazil [i]

Negroid Someone of African origin with dark skin, curly hair, broad nose and lips, and slim body build. Most Negroes now prefer to call themselves *Blacks*; but not all Blacks (dark-skinned people) come from Africa. » race

Nehemiah, Book of [neehuh**miy**a] A book of the Hebrew Bible/Old Testament, originally joined to the Book of Ezra, and probably also to 1 and 2 Chronicles. This historical writing was named after a Jewish official of the King of Persia, Nehemiah, who apparently led a return to Judea by Jewish exiles in Persia. He had two periods of governorship in Judea during the reign of Artaxerxes I (465–424 BC) or possibly Artaxerxes II (404–359 BC). There is some chronological confusion in the work, because of the presence of some sections which appear to belong to the Book of Ezra. » Ezra, Book of; Old Testament

Nehru, Jawaharlal [**nai**roo], byname **Pandit** (Hindi 'teacher') (1889–1964) Indian statesman and Prime Minister (1947–64), born at Allahabad. Educated at Harrow and Cambridge, he became a lawyer, and served in the Allahabad High Court. He joined the Indian Congress Committee (1918), was influenced by Gandhi, and was imprisoned several times by the British. In 1929 he was elected President of the Indian National Congress. In 1947 he became India's first Prime Minister and Minister of External Affairs, following a policy of neutrality during the Cold War. He introduced a policy of industrialization, reorganized the states on a linguistic basis, and brought the dispute with Pakistan over Kashmir to a peaceful solution. He died in New Delhi. » Gandhi; Indian National Congress; Pakistan [i]

Nei Mongol » **Inner Mongolia**

nekton Swimming marine organisms, capable of locomotion for extended periods of time at speeds greater than those of ocean currents; distinct from plankton, which are drifters. Nekton range in size from tiny fish to giant sperm whales. » plankton

Nelson, (John) Byron (1912–) US golfer, born at Fort Worth, Texas. He won a record 18 tournaments on the US Professional Golfers Association (PGA) tour in 1945, 11 of them successive, and also won the US Open (1939), the US PGA Championship (1940, 1945), and the US Masters (1937, 1942) – a total of 54 US Tour events (the fifth all-time best). He captained the 1965 US Ryder Cup team at Birkdale, and became a notable golf teacher and broadcaster after he retired from tournament play. » golf

Nelson, Horatio, Viscount (1758–1805) British admiral, born at Burnham Thorpe, Norfolk. He joined the navy in 1770, and was sent to the West Indies (1784) to enforce the Navigation Act against the newly independent United States. There he married Frances Nisbet (1761–1831), and in 1787 retired with her to Burnham Thorpe. In 1794 he commanded the naval brigade at the reduction of Bastia and Calvi, where he lost the sight of his right eye, and in an action at Santa Cruz had his right arm amputated. In 1798 he followed the French fleet to Egypt, destroying it at Aboukir Bay. On his return to Naples, he fell in love with Emma, Lady Hamilton, and began a liaison with her which lasted until his death. In 1801 he was made Rear-Admiral, and led the attack on Copenhagen. Previously created a baron, he then became a viscount, and Commander-in-Chief. In 1805 he gained his greatest victory, against the combined French and Spanish fleet at Trafalgar. During the battle he was mortally wounded on his flagship, HMS *Victory*. His body was brought home and buried in St Paul's. » Aboukir Bay, Battle of; Hamilton, Emma; Hood, Samuel; Napoleonic Wars; Trafalgar, Battle of

Nelson Lakes area 961 sq km/371 sq ml. National park, N South Island, New Zealand; contains Rotoiti and Rotoroa lakes; surrounded by rugged, forest-clad mountains rising to over 1 800 m/6 000 ft; established in 1956. » New Zealand [i]

nematode An unsegmented worm, typically circular in section; body covered with cuticle; head end with terminal mouth, surrounded by lips and three rings of sense organs; abundant in aquatic sediments, in soil, and as parasites of plants and animals; c.12 000 species described; also known as **eelworms**, **roundworms** and **pinworms**. (Phylum: *Nematoda*.) » Ascaris; filariasis; worm

Nematomorpha [nematuh**maw**fa] » **horsehair worm**

Nemertea [ne**mer**tia] » **ribbon worm**

nemesia [ni**mee**zhuh] An annual growing to 60 cm/2 ft, native to S Africa; leaves oblong, toothed; flowers with 2-lobed upper lip and large, spreading 3-lobed lower lip, in a range of colours. It is a popular garden plant, especially in dwarf forms. (*Nemesia strumosa*. Family: *Scrophulariaceae*.) » annual

Nemesis [**ne**muhsis] In Greek mythology, the goddess of retribution. She primarily represents the penalty the gods exact for human folly.

Nemirovich-Danchenko, Vladimir (Ivanovich) [nye**miruh**vich dan**chen**koh] (1858–1943) Russian theatre director, writer, and teacher, born at Ozurgety. Co-founder with Stanislavsky of the Moscow Art Theatre, he became sole director following the latter's death in 1938. Among his most notable productions were *The Brothers Karamazov* (1910) and *Nikolai Stavrogin* (1913). After 1919, his interest in opera led to some of his most original work as a director. He died in Moscow. » Chekhov; Gorky; Moscow Art Theatre; opera; theatre

Nemrut Dag The mountain site of the tomb-sanctuary of King Antiochus of Commagene (64–32 BC), S Anatolia, Turkey; a world heritage monument. The peak is 220 m/722 ft above sea-level, while the tomb is a conical tumulus 50 m/160 ft high and 150 m/500 ft in diameter at its base. » Anatolia

nene [**nay**nay] » **Hawaiian goose**

Nenets A Uralic-speaking ethnic group living in N Russia, originally known a **Samoyed** or **Yurak**. They are reindeer keepers, and also fishermen and hunters (of wild reindeer). Formerly nomadic, they are now settled in villages. Population c.30 000. » nomadism; Uralic languages

Nennius (8th-c) Welsh writer, the reputed author of *Historia Britonum*. The book gives the mythical account of the origins of the Britons, the Roman occupation, the settlement of the Saxons, and closes with King Arthur's 12 victories. » Arthur; Welsh literature

Neoclassicism (art and architecture) A classical revival affecting all the visual arts, including architecture and the decorative arts, which flourished from c.1750 onwards, lasting well into the 19th-c. A reaction against the decorous excesses of Baroque and the 'frivolity' of Rococo, it began in Rome, but spread throughout W Europe and N America. Partly inspired by the excavations at Pompeii, Herculaneum, and Paestum, it received its theoretical underpinning from Winckelmann, whose essay on the 'noble simplicity and calm grandeur' of Greek art (1755) was followed by a pioneering history of antique art (1764). In painting, the style reached its peak in the powerful and dramatic works of David (eg 'Oath of the Horatii', 1784), while the rather frigid side of Neoclassicism is well exemplified by the sculpture of Canova. In architecture, theorists proposed a reasoned approach based on the 'primitive hut' and clear structural principles. The buildings are usually characterized by pure geometric form, restrained decoration, unbroken contours, an overall severe appearance, and sometimes monumental proportions. The chief exponents were Etienne Louis Boullée and Claude Nicolas Ledoux in France, and John Soane in England. » Canova; classical revival; classicism; David, Jacques Louis; rationalism (philosophy); Rococo; Winckelmann

Neoclassicism (music) A 20th-c music movement which sought to restore the ideals, and to some extent the style and vocabulary, of the 18th-c classical period. Since Bach often provided the model for Neoclassical works, the movement might be as accurately described as 'neo-Baroque', but its main motivation was in any case anti-Romantic. It is associated particularly with Stravinsky's middle-period works (c.1920–30), but touched many other composers, including Prokofiev and Hindemith. » classical music; Bach, Johann Sebastian; Stravinsky

neo-corporatism » **corporatism**

Neoexpressionism A vague term sometimes used for all forms of abstract art which are regarded as conveying strong emotions, or which seem to have been produced by the artist in a heightened emotional state. Examples include Kandinsky's work after c.1920, or US Action Painting. » abstract art; action painting; Kandinsky

neofascism Fascist ideas and movements that have continued after the demise of the inter-war fascist dictatorships. Apart from considerably less political influence, it is hard to detect significant differences between contemporary fascism and its earlier counterparts. Neofascism in W Europe has, however, been opposed to immigration from former colonial and Mediterranean countries, and has used this as a major campaigning platform. » fascism

Neo-Freudian Applied to psychoanalysts who base their theories and practice on those elaborated by Freud, but who have made specific modifications to Freud's theories. They include the German psychoanalyst Karen Horney (1885–1952) and the American psychiatrist Harry Stack Sullivan (1892–1949), but not Freud's contemporaries. » Freud, Sigmund

Neoimpressionism » Divisionism

Neo-Kantianism A movement in several different German universities between 1870 and 1920, divided on many issues, but united against the speculative metaphysics of Hegel on the grounds that it was inadequate to account for mathematical and scientific knowledge. Neo-Kantians generally tried to reinstate Kant's epistemology, but disagreed about Kant's metaphysics. » Hegel; Kant; metaphysics

Neo-Keynesianism or **new Keynesianism** A term introduced in 1982 by the British economist Sir James Meade (professor of political economy at Cambridge, 1957–69), related to the economic theories of J M Keynes, but modified to apply to the economic situation of the time. The approach recognizes three government economic targets: growth, balance of payments equilibrium, and adequate investment. These aims can be met by tax policy, exchange rates, and interest rates. » Keynesian

Neolithic » Three Age System

neologism [nee**ol**uhjizm] A term referring to any newly-coined word, usually identifying a new concept. In the 1980s, English neologisms included *stagflation*, *yuppie*, *glitz*, *pocketphone*, and *user-friendly*. The term is also used in the field of language pathology, where it refers to the coining of a word of obscure or no meaning; the phenomenon is found in aphasia, schizophrenia, and several other disorders. » aphasia; lexeme; schizophrenia

Neo-Malthusianism A modern version of the theory of Malthus, that excessive poverty and mortality in populations results from imbalance between population size and available resources. It is used by some conservative theorists with reference to the Third World today. » Malthus; population; Three Worlds Theory

Neo-Marxism The doctrines of Marxists who draw upon Marx's early writings, which had a more romantic and utopian emphasis than his later works concerned with economics and historical materialism. Strongly influenced by Hegelian philosophy, a key feature of Neo-Marxism is its self-critical approach, which accepts the need for a review of theory, rather than a rigid acceptance of dogma, as prevalent under Soviet communism. This critical approach, at its peak in the 1960s and 1970s, has seen a number of competing schools. » Frankfurt School; Hegel; Marxism; New Left

neon Ne, element 10. The second noble gas, forming c.0.002% of the atmosphere, and obtained by the fractional distillation of liquid air. It forms no known compounds, and is used mainly in gas discharge tubes and gas lasers, where it emits a characteristic red glow. » chemical elements; noble gases; RR90

neopentane » pentane

neoplasm » tumour

Neoplasticism A term invented c.1917 by Mondrian to describe his own particularly severe form of abstract art. He permitted only primary colours, black, white, and grey, and restricted his shapes to squares or rectangles defined by vertical and horizontal lines. » De Stijl; Mondrian

Neoplatonism A school of philosophy founded by Plotinus (205–270), lasting into the 7th-c, which attempted to combine doctrines of Plato, Aristotle, and the Pythagoreans. Basic to Plotinus's philosophy is The One, whence emanate Intelligence (which contains the Platonic ideas) and Soul (which includes individual souls). » Plotinus

Neoptolemus [neeop**tol**emuhs] In Greek legend, the son of Achilles and Deidameia, his original name being Pyrrhus. He went with Odysseus to persuade Philoctetes to come to Troy. At the end of the war he killed Priam and enslaved Andromache; for this, Apollo prevented him from reaching his home, and he was killed in a dispute at Delphi. The name means the 'young warrior'. » Achilles; Andromache; Philoctetes; Priam

neorealism A style of film-making which arose in Italy soon after World War 2, emphasizing themes of social reality even in fictional stories, rather than the escapism of artificial middle-class drama. It used actual settings and non-professional artists, at least in minor roles. » cinema

neoteny [nee**ot**uhnee] A relative slowing down of bodily (*somatic*) development, so that sexual maturity is attained in an organism while retaining some juvenile characters. In an evolutionary perspective, this gives rise to descendants that retain as adults juvenile features of their ancestors. An example is the Mexican axolotl, a newt which becomes sexually mature before metamorphosing into the adult, so that it retains juvenile characters, such as external gills, even as an adult. » axolotl; evolution; life cycle

Neo-Thomism [neeoh**toh**mizm] A philosophical movement in the late 19th-c and 20th-c which sought to revive interest in the thought of St Thomas Aquinas. 'Thomism' was declared the official theology of the Roman Catholic Church in 1879, and Neo-Thomism (and the natural theology associated with it) remains an important feature of Roman Catholic and some Anglican thought. » Aquinas; Roman Catholicism; theology

Nepal [ne**pawl**, nay**pal**], official name **Kingdom of Nepal**, Nepali **Sri Nepala Sarkar** pop (1990e) 18 910 000; area 145 391 sq km/ 56 121 sq ml. Independent kingdom lying along the S slopes of the Himalayas, C Asia; divided into 14 zones; bounded N by the Tibet region of China, E and S by India; capital, Kathmandu; chief towns include Patan and Bhadgaon; timezone GMT +5½; official language, Nepali; chief religion, Hinduism (90%), the only official Hindu kingdom in the world; unit of currency, the Nepalese rupee; landlocked, length E–W 880 km/547 ml, width 144–240 km/90–150 ml N–S; rises steeply from the Ganges Basin; high fertile valleys in the 'hill country' at 1 300 m/4 300 ft, notably the Vale of Kathmandu (a world heritage site); dominated by the glaciated peaks of the Himalayas, highest Mt Everest, 8 848 m/29 028 ft; climate varies from subtropical lowland, with hot, humid summers and mild winters, to an alpine climate over 3 300 m/10 800 ft, where peaks are permanently snow-covered; temperatures at Kathmandu, 40°C (May), 1.6°C (Dec); monsoon season during summer (Jun–Sep), with average annual rainfall decreasing from 1 778 mm/70 in (E) to 889 mm/35 in (W); originally a

□ international airport

group of independent hill states, united in the 18th-c; parliamentary system introduced in 1959, replaced in 1960 by a partyless system of *panchayats* (village councils); a constitutional monarchy ruled by a hereditary king; period of unrest (Apr 1990) was followed by a reduction of the king's powers, a new constitution (Nov), and fresh elections (1991); one of the least developed countries in Asia; agriculture employs 90% of the people; rice, wheat, jute, millet, maize, wheat, barley, sugar cane; few minerals exploited commercially, though there are deposits of coal, copper, iron, mica, zinc, and cobalt; agricultural and forest-based goods, jute, handicrafts, carpets, medicinal herbs, ready-made garments, shoes, woollen goods; hydroelectric power developing; tourism becoming increasingly important. » Everest, Mount; Himalayas; Kathmandu; RR26 national holidays; RR56 political leaders

nephanalysis (Gr *nephos* 'cloud') A meteorological term for the study of clouds, in particular the amount and frequency of different cloud forms. Satellite imagery of cloud cover is often used in weather forecasting. » cloud [i]

nephrite » **jade**

nephritis » **glomerulonephritis**

nephrons » **kidneys**

nephrotic syndrome A clinical syndrome which results from the loss of large amounts of plasma proteins in the urine, leading to a fall in their concentration in the blood and to generalized oedema. » oedema; plasma (physiology)

Neptune (astronomy) The eighth planet from the Sun, the outermost of the four 'gas giant' planets; discovered in 1846 as a prediction which would explain anomalies in the observed orbit of Uranus; encountered by Voyager 2 (24 Aug 1989), closest approach 5 000 km/3 000 ml. There are at least eight moons, including Triton, which has an atmosphere, and Nereid. Its main characteristics are: mass 17.2 times that of Earth; radius 25 225 km/15 675 ml; mean density 1.5 g/cm^3; rotational period 0.67 days; orbital period 164.82 years; inclination of equator 29°; eccentricity of orbit 0.010; mean distance from Sun 30.06 AU. It is an apparent twin of Uranus internally, composed of hydrogen and helium, but with much more carbon, nitrogen, and oxygen than Jupiter and Saturn. It is thought to lack sharp internal boundaries between a rock-rich core, an ice-rich mantle, and a deep atmosphere. Its bluish-green coloration is produced by methane in the upper atmosphere. It has cirrus clouds of methane above high-level clouds of methane and ammonia, with lower water clouds. There are storm systems resembling Jupiter's, including a Great Dark Spot in the S hemisphere. It has a magnetic field of 0.2 gauss, tilted 60° from the rotation axis. There are two main rings (53 000 km/33 000 ml and 63 000 km/40 000 ml from Neptune's centre) and one diffuse inner ring. The outer ring has clumpy sections, probably associated with small moonlets. » Nereid; planet; Solar System; Triton (astronomy); Voyager project [i]

Neptune (mythology) The Roman water-god (the Romans originally had no sea-gods). He was later identified with Poseidon, whose characteristics and mythology he acquired. » Poseidon

Nereid [**nee**reeid] The second substantial natural satellite of Neptune, discovered in 1949; distance from the planet 5 510 000 km/3 424 000; diameter c.300 km/190 ml, but estimates vary greatly, depending on reflectivity. It has a highly inclined (27°), eccentric orbit about Neptune, and may be a captured object. » Neptune (astronomy); RR4

nereid [**nee**reeid] In Greek mythology, a sea-nymph, one of the 50 or (in some accounts) 100 daughters of Nereus and Doris. They lived with their father in the depths of the sea. Thetis and Galatea were nereids. » Nereus

Nereus [**nee**reeuhs] In Greek mythology, a sea-god, the wise old man of the sea who always tells the truth. Heracles had to wrestle with him to find the location of the Golden Apples. » Heracles

Nergal [**ner**gahl] The Mesopotamian god of the Underworld; at first, a solar deity capable of killing enormous numbers of people in the heat of noon-day. He forced Ereshkigal, the original goddess of the Underworld, to share her power with him. » Mesopotamia

Neri, St Philip (1515–95), feast day 26 May. Italian founder of the Oratory, born in Florence. He spent many years at Rome in works of charity and instruction, and in solitary prayer. In 1551 he became a priest, and gathered around him a following of disciples which in 1563 became the Congregation of the Oratory. The community was finally established at Vallicella. He died in Rome, and was canonized in 1622. » Oratorians

neritic zone The marine life zone in the water over the continental shelves. It is strongly influenced by its proximity to land, hence neritic organisms must be able to tolerate greater change in temperature and salinity than oceanic organisms. » oceanic zone

Nernst, Walther Hermann (1864–1941) German physical chemist, born at Briesen, W Prussia. He was professor of chemistry at Göttingen (1891) and Berlin (1905), and director of the Berlin Physical Institute (1925). He proposed the heat theorem (the third law of thermodynamics) in 1906, and also investigated the specific heat of solids at low temperature in connection with quantum theory. He won the Nobel Prize for Chemistry in 1920, and died in Berlin. » photochemistry; quantum field theory; thermodynamics

Nero, properly **Nero Claudius Caesar**, originally **Lucius Domitius Ahenobarbus** (37–68) Roman emperor (54–68), the son of Gnaeus Domitius Ahenobarbus and the younger Agrippina, daughter of Germanicus. He owed his name and position to the driving ambition of his mother, who engineered his adoption by the Emperor Claudius, her fourth husband. Initially his reign was good, thanks to his three main advisers: his mother, the philosopher Seneca, and the Praetorian Prefect Burrus. But after her murder (59), and their fall from favour, Nero, more interested in sex, singing, acting, and chariot-racing than government, neglected affairs of state, and corruption set in. He was blamed for the Great Fire of Rome (64), despite assiduous attempts to make scapegoats of the Christians. A major plot to overthrow him (the Conspiracy of Piso) was formed (65) but detected, and Rome had to endure three more years of tyranny before he was toppled from power by the army, and forced to commit suicide. » Agrippina the Younger; Claudius; Poppaea Sabina; Seneca, Lucius Annaeus

Neruda, Pablo (Neftali Reyes) (1904–73) Chilean poet and diplomat, born at Parral. Educated at Santiago, he made his name with *Veinte poemas de amor ya una canción desesperada* (1924, Twenty Love Poems and a Song of Despair). From 1927 he held diplomatic posts in various E Asian and European countries. Returning to Chile in 1943, he joined the Communist Party, and was elected to the Senate in 1945. He travelled in Russia and China (1948–52), and was later the Chilean Ambassador in Paris (1970–2). His other works include *Residencia en la tierra* (1925–31, Residence on Earth) and *Canto General* (1950, General Song). He won the Nobel Prize for Literature in 1971, and died in Santiago. » Latin-American literature; poetry

nerve (cell) » **neurone** [i]

nerve gas an agent of chemical warfare, whose deadly effects are achieved by attacking the human body's central nervous system. Paralysis and death come within seconds of absorption (which may be via the skin). » chemical warfare

nerve growth factor (NGF) A biologically active peptide found widely (eg in the eye, heart, salivary glands, vas deferens) in many animals, including humans. It controls the growth and development of sympathetic nervous tissue and some sensory neurones. It is classified as a hormone by some authorities. » neurone [i]; peptide

Nervi, Pier Luigi (1891–1979) Italian architect, born at Sondrio. He studied as an engineer, set up as a building contractor, and achieved an international reputation by his designs for the Olympic Games in Rome (1960). He also designed the exhibition halls at Turin (1948–50), the Pirelli building (the first skyscraper in Italy, 1955), and San Francisco Cathedral (1970). He died in Rome.

nervous system That part of the body concerned with controlling and integrating the activity of its various parts, providing a mechanism whereby the animal can respond to a changing external environment but still maintain a relatively constant internal environment. It is composed of nerves (*neurones*) and supporting cells. The transfer of information between nerve cells (at *synapses*) is usually by the release of small quantities of *transmitter substances*. Communication with other body tissues may be by the direct release of transmitter substances on to the tissue (usually in the presence of some other substance, such as an enzyme) or by the release of hormones into the blood stream (either directly from the nervous system or from endocrine glands under its control).

In all activities involving the nervous system, regardless of their complexity, there are three components involved: a *receptive* or *sensory* component, an *integrative* component, and an *effector* or *motor* component. In higher animals, the integrative component has undergone the greatest development, and forms the major part of the nervous system. In its simplest form, as in coelenterates, the nervous system merely consists of a diffuse network of interconnecting cells. With increasing complexity of the animal, the network becomes organized into a longitudinal cord. This is followed by the grouping and centralization of the motor and sensory cells, and the eventual development of a large integrating centre (the brain). In mammals the nervous system is divided into **central** and **peripheral** parts, both parts working together as a functioning unit: the central part comprises the brain and spinal cord, while the peripheral part comprises the remainder. » brain [i]; central nervous system; neuralgia; neurology; neurone [i]; neuropathology; neuropathy; neurophysiology; neurotoxins; neurotransmitter; paralysis; peripheral nervous system; sciatica; shingles; synapse; tetanus

Nesbit, E(dith), maiden and pen name of **Mrs Hubert Bland** (1858–1924) British writer, born in London. Educated at a French convent, she began her literary career by writing poetry, but is best remembered for her children's stories, which reacted against the moralizing then prevalent. They include *The Story of the Treasure Seekers* (1899), *The Wouldbegoods* (1901), and *The Railway Children* (1906). She died at New Romney, Kent.

Nesebar A town, formerly Menebria, situated on the E coast of Bulgaria; a world heritage site. It has a wealth of ancient buildings and archaeological sites which testify to its 3 000-year history as a Thracian settlement, a Greek colony, and a Byzantine city. » Bulgaria [i]; Thrace

Ness, Loch Loch in Highland region, N Scotland; extending NE from Fort Augustus along the Great Glen to 9 km/6 ml SW of Inverness; 38 km/24 ml long; average width 2 km/1¼ ml; maximum depth 230 m/755 ft (near Castle Urquhart); part of the Caledonian Canal; drained by R Ness (N) to the Moray Firth; said to be inhabited by a 12–15 m/40–50 ft-long 'monster'; several unconfirmed sightings, but no clear results from scientific investigations; Loch Ness Monster Exhibition Centre at Drumnadrochit (W shore). » Caledonian Canal; Highland; Scotland [i]

Nesselrode, Karl (Robert Vasilyevich), Graf ('Count') [nesel**roh**duh] (1780–1862) Russian diplomat, born in Lisbon, Portugal. He represented Russia at the Congress of Vienna (1814–15), and was one of the most active diplomats of the Holy Alliance. He became Foreign Minister in 1822, and dominated Russian foreign policy for 30 years. His Balkan policy of trying to curb France's influence over the Ottoman Empire contributed to the outbreak of the Crimean War (1853). He died in St Petersburg. » Crimean War; Nicholas I; Vienna, Congress of

nest A domicile or home constructed, typically by birds, for the purpose of containing and protecting eggs and young; young birds before they leave the nest are known as *nestlings*. They may continue to be fed by their parents even after leaving the nest. Young birds that remain in the nest for a prolonged period after hatching are known as *nidicolous*; those that leave soon after hatching are known as *nidifugous*. » bird [i]

Nestor [**nes**taw] A senior Greek leader in the Trojan War, the son of Neleus. In the *Iliad*, Homer portrays him as a long-winded sage, whose advice is often not taken. In the *Odyssey*, he is still living at Pylos, where a Mycenaean palace was discovered in the 1930s. » Trojan War

Nestorians Followers of Nestorius, Bishop of Constantinople (died c.451), who is alleged to have taught the doctrine, later declared heretical, of two persons (one human, one divine) as well as two natures in the incarnate Christ. They formed a separate Church which survived in parts of Persia. » Christians of St Thomas; Christology; heresy

netball A women's 7-a-side court game invented in the USA in 1891 and developed from basketball. The court is 100 ft (30.5 m) long and 50 ft (15.25 m) wide. The object is to score goals by throwing the ball through the opponent's net, which is attached to a circular hoop suspended on a post 10 ft (3.05 m) high. Players must not run with the ball. » basketball; RR116

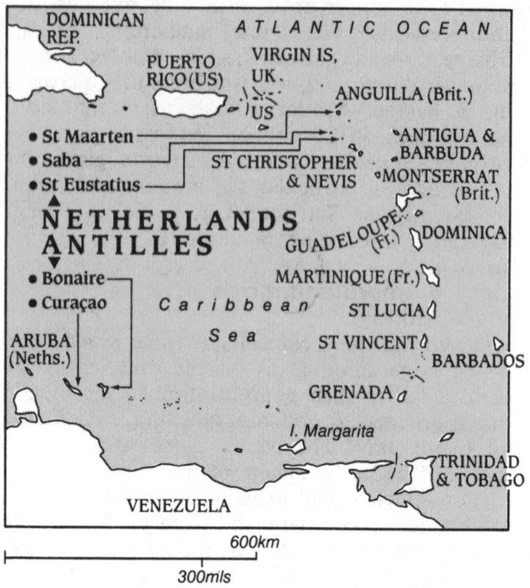

Netherlands Antilles [anti**leez**], Dutch **Nederlandse Antillen** pop (1989e) 183 000; area 993 sq km/383 sq ml. Islands in the Caribbean Sea, comprising the Southern group (Leeward Is) of Curaçao (444 sq km/171 sq ml), Aruba (193 sq km/74 sq ml), and Bonaire (288 sq km/111 sq ml), 60–110 km/37–68 ml N of the Venezuelan coast, and the Northern group (Windward Is) of St Maarten (34 sq km/13 sq ml), St Eustatius (21 sq km/8 sq ml), and Saba (13 sq km/5 sq ml), E of Puerto Rico; an autonomous region of the Netherlands; capital, Willemstad; timezone GMT −4; 85% of the population of mixed African descent; official language, Dutch, with English and Papiamento widely spoken; unit of currency, the Antillian guilder; tropical maritime climate, average annual temperature of 27.5°C; average annual rainfall varies from 500 mm/20 in (S) to 1 000 mm/40 in (N); visited by Columbus, initially claimed for Spain; occupied by Dutch settlers, 17th-c; sovereign of the Netherlands is head of state, represented by a governor, a Council of Ministers, and a unicameral legislature (*Staten*) of 22 members, elected every four years; economy based on refining of crude oil imported from Venezuela; salt, phosphate; aim of industrial diversification, especially tourism; rum distilling, textiles, petrochemicals, beverages, ship repairing. » Aruba; Bonaire; Curaçao; Willemstad

Netherlands, Austrian and Spanish Ten provinces in the S of the Low Countries, predominantly Catholic, and united to Spain through Emperor Charles V, who inherited them from his grandfather Maximilian. They remained Spanish after the Dutch secession (1648), were ceded to the Austrian Habsburgs by the Treaty of Utrecht (1713), and achieved independence from Austria (1794) in the French Revolutionary Wars. » Charles V (Emperor); Habsburgs; United Provinces of the Netherlands

Netherlands East Indies The name applied to Indonesia until 1945, when Dr Sukarno declared independence: the area included the islands of Java, Sumatra, the Celebes, most of Borneo, the Molveens, and Bali. The Dutch recognized Indonesia's independence in 1948. » Indonesia [i]; Sukarno

Netherlands, The or **Holland**, Dutch **Nederland**, official name **Kingdom of the Netherlands**, Dutch **Koninkrijk der Nederlanden** pop (1990e) 14 934 000; area 33 929 sq km/13 097 sq ml. Maritime kingdom of NW Europe, divided into 12 provinces; bounded N and W by the North Sea, E by Germany, and

S by Belgium; also includes the islands of the Netherlands Antilles in the Caribbean; European coastline 451 km/280 ml; capital, Amsterdam; seat of government, The Hague; largest city, Rotterdam; chief towns, Utrecht, Haarlem, Eindhoven, Arnhem, Groningen; timezone GMT +1; population mainly of Germanic descent; official language, Dutch; chief religions, Roman Catholicism (40%), Dutch Reformed Church and other Protestant churches (31%); unit of currency, the gulden (guilder) of 100 cents.

Physical description and climate. Generally low and flat, except SE, where hills rise to 321 m/1 053 ft; much of the coastal area lies below sea-level, protected by coastal dunes and artificial dykes; without these, two-fifths of the country would be submerged; 27% of the land area is below sea-level, an area inhabited by c.60% of the population; cool, temperate, maritime climate; average temperature 1.7°C (Jan), 17°C (Jul); annual rainfall exceeds 700 mm/27 in, distributed fairly evenly throughout the year.

History and government. Part of Roman Empire, to 4th-c AD; part of Frankish Empire by 8th-c; incorporated into the Holy Roman Empire; lands passed to Philip II, who succeeded to Spain and the Netherlands, 1555; attempts to stamp out Protestantism led to rebellion, 1572; seven N provinces united against Spain, 1579; United Provinces independence, 1581; overrun by the French (1795–1813), who established the Batavian Republic; united with Belgium as the Kingdom of the United Netherlands until 1830, when Belgium withdrew; neutral in World War 1; occupied by Germany, World War 2, with strong Dutch resistance; joined with Belgium and Luxembourg to form the Benelux economic union, 1948; conflict over independence of Dutch colonies in SE Asia in late 1940s; a parliamentary democracy under a constitutional monarchy; government led by a prime minister; States-General (*Staten-Generaal*) consists of a 75-member Chamber, elected for six years, and a 150-member Chamber, elected for four years.

Economy. Rotterdam and the newly-constructed Europort are major European ports of transshipment, handling goods for EEC member countries; Amsterdam a world diamond centre; highly intensive agriculture; world's largest exporter of dairy produce; animal husbandry, horticulture (area under glass has doubled since the 1950s), potatoes, sugar beet, grains; engineering, chemicals, oil products, natural gas, foodstuffs, electrical and high technology goods, fishing, tourism. » Amsterdam; Benelux; Dutch; Dutch art/Reformed Church/Wars; Hague, The; Netherlands Antilles/East Indies; Philip II (of Spain); Revolt of the Netherlands; United Provinces of the Netherlands; RR26 national holidays; RR57 political leaders

nettle » **dead-nettle; stinging nettle**

nettle rash » **urticaria**

network » **local area network**

Neuchâtel [nershatel], Ger **Neuenburg** 44°60N 6°56E, pop (1983e) 33 321. Capital town of Neuchâtel canton, W Switzerland, on W shore of L Neuchâtel, 40 km/25 ml W of Bern; railway; university (1909); research centre for the Swiss watch industry; scientific instruments, electronics, tobacco, wine trade; university church (13th-c), castle (mainly 16th-c). » Switzerland [i]

Neuchâtel, Lake (Fr **Lac de**) [nershatel] area 218 sq km/84 sq ml. Largest lake to lie wholly within Switzerland, running SW–NE at the foot of the Jura Mts, W Switzerland; major wine-growing area; boat services link lakeside towns; chief towns on the shore include Neuchâtel (NW) and Yverdon (S). » Neuchâtel; Switzerland [i]

Neue Künstlervereinigung [noyer **kunst**lerfri**y**nigung] (Ger 'new association of artists') A group of modern 'fauvist' artists founded in Munich in 1909. Leading members included Vasily Kandinsky (1866–1944), Alexey von Jawlensky (1864–1941), and Gabriele Münter (1877–1962). » Blaue Reiter, der; Fauvism; German art; Kandinsky

Neue Sachlichkeit [noyer **sakh**likhkiyt] (Ger 'new objectivity') A movement in German art c.1920, a reaction against the abstract and expressionist tendencies of modern art and a return to 'true objectivity', ie a kind of literal and deliberately seamy realism. The chief exponents of this short-lived style were Georg Grosz (1852–1944), and Otto Dix (1898–1969).

Neumann, (Johann) Balthasar (1687–1753) German architect, born at Eger. At first a military engineer, after visiting Paris he turned to architecture, and became professor at Würzburg. He designed many outstanding examples of the Baroque style, notably Würzburg Palace and Schloss Bruchsal. He died at Würzburg. » Baroque (art and architecture)

Neumann, Johann (John) von (1903–57) US mathematician, born in Budapest. He escaped from Hungary during the communist regime (1919), studied at Berlin and Zürich, and in 1931 became professor at Princeton. He wrote a major work on quantum mechanics (1932), and participated in the atomic bomb project at Los Alamos during World War 2, providing a mathematical treatment of shock waves. His mathematical work on high-speed calculations for H-bomb development contributed to the development of computers, and he also introduced game theory (1944), which was a major influence on economics. He died in Washington, DC. » computer; games, theory of; quantum field theory

neuralgia Pain arising from a sensory nerve, and felt over the surface of the body supplied by the affected nerve. In the most common type, **trigeminal neuralgia**, the cause is unknown. Pain, usually severe and paroxysmal, is felt over the forehead, face, or jaw supplied by one or more of the branches of the trigeminal (Vth cranial) nerve. Other forms include **post-herpetic neuralgia**, which may follow herpes zoster, and **brachial neuralgia**, affecting the nerves of the upper arm (the brachial plexus), often arising from abnormal pressure on the spinal nerves in the neck; it results in aching and pain over the shoulder and down the arms. » arm; nervous system

neurasthenia A neurosis which takes the form of complaints of excessive fatigue and tiredness. No physical cause of the condition has been found. » neurosis

neuritis » **neuropathy**

neuroanatomy » **anatomy**

neurohormone A chemical messenger secreted by nerve cells and carried by the blood to the target cells, where its effects are mediated. For example, two neurohormones secreted by the neurohypophysis (a collection of nerve terminals) of the pituitary gland are *antidiuretic hormone* and *oxytocin*, which promote water re-absorption by kidneys and milk ejection from breasts, respectively. » antidiuretic hormone; hormones; oxytocin

neurolinguistics The study of the neurological basis of language use: in particular, how the brain controls the processes of speech and comprehension. Important data comes from the study of clinical linguistic conditions (eg aphasia, stuttering) and everyday 'errors', such as hesitations and slips of the tongue, which throw light on the way in which the basic speech system can break down. » brain [i]; clinical linguistics; neurology

neurology The branch of medicine which deals with the study of physical diseases of the central nervous system (the brain and spinal cord) and its peripheral nerves. » medicine; nervous system; neuropathy; neuropathology

neurone/neuron The functional unit of the nervous systems of animals; also known as a **nerve cell**. Neurones process and transmit information to target tissues (other neurones, muscles, glands) usually through the mediation of chemicals (*neurotransmitters*). Vertebrate neurones typically consist of a cell body (with a well-developed nucleus surrounded by a mass of cytoplasm), an *axon* (with terminal branches specialized to carry information from the cell body across connections to target tissues), and *dendrites* (projecting from the cell body and receiving information from axon terminals of other neurones for integration by the neurone). Most invertebrate neurones lack dendrites. » multiple sclerosis; nervous system; neurotransmitter; synapse

neuropathology The study of the disease processes which affect the nervous system. These include haemorrhage in various parts of the brain, infections and tumours of the brain and its enveloping membranes, degenerative disorders such as Parkinsonism and dementia, metabolic disorders, neuropathies, and demyelinating disorders such as multiple sclerosis. » myelin; nervous system; neuropathy

neuropathy A term which covers all pathological processes that affect peripheral somatic and autonomic nerves, including inflammation of the nerves (**neuritis**). Very many disorders affect peripheral somatic nerves and induce similar clinical features. These consist of the sensation of pins and needles (*paraesthesiae*), loss of sensation, and muscle weakness. Very often the most distal part of the nerve in the extremities (hands and feet) are affected first or most severely. Causes include ischaemia (diabetes and polyarteritis), vitamin deficiencies (B and B_{12}), alcoholism and other poisons, infections such as leprosy, and some viruses. When there is widespread involvement of many nerve fibres, the condition is known as **polyneuropathy**. » nervous system

neurophysiology The study of the functions of the nervous systems of animals. Neurophysiologists use a variety of methods to elucidate aspects of nervous function. Common techniques are ablation (the removal or destruction of nervous tissue); the electrical stimulation of, or recording from, single nerve cells (eg squid axons, retinal photoreceptors) and groups of nerve cells (eg the basal ganglia and motor cortex areas of mammalian brains), using electrodes; and techniques borrowed from other disciplines (eg computer-assisted tomography, histofluorescence techniques, autoradiography). » action potential; autoradiography; brain [i]; nervous system; patch clamp analysis; tomography

neuropsychology The study of psychological phenomena in the light of what is known about brain organization and function. Neuropsychologists are often concerned with patients suffering from brain damage. The aim of their work is to identify these patients' disabilities, discover methods of rehabilitation, and use this information to make inferences about the functioning of the normal mind and brain. » agnosia; amnesia; aphasia; brain [i]; dyslexia; psychology

Neuroptera [nyoo**rop**tuhra] An order of primitive winged insects, including the snakeflies, lacewings, and antlions; typically two pairs of similar wings with lace-like veins; mouthparts of a simple, biting type; adults and larvae typically feed on sap-sucking insects. » antlion; insect [i]; lacewing; larva; snakefly

neurosis A mental illness often associated with high levels of anxiety and representing exaggerated and/or unconscious ways

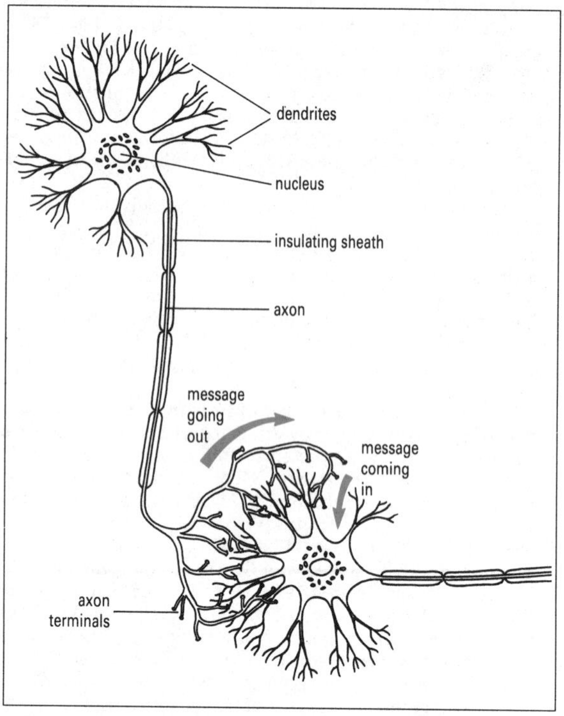

Vertebrate neurones

of dealing with conflicts. The symptoms are distressing to the individual and considered to be unacceptable. The condition is enduring, and throughout reality testing remains intact. Examples include hypochondriasis, obsessive-compulsive disorders, and phobic disorders. » mental disorders; phobia [i]; psychosis

neurotoxins Naturally-occurring or synthetic substances which specifically or predominantly affect the nervous system. Examples are aconitum (from aconite), an early poison used by ancient warriors on darts and spears, chickpeas (resulting in lathyrism), synthetic organophosphorous compounds (eg nerve gas), and toxins of bacterial origin such as tetanus toxin and the toxin of *Clostridium botulinum*, one of the most powerful poisons known. » botulism; nervous system

neurotransmitter A chemical substance (eg acetylcholine, noradrenaline) released as a messenger from nerves. It enables the transmission of a nervous impulse across the narrow gap (*synapse*) between a nerve ending and a muscle, gland, or another nerve. Its rapid breakdown by enzymes or its re-uptake by the nerve terminates its effect. » acetylcholine; NANC; nervous system; noradrenaline

neutrality In foreign policy, a situation where a state will not provide military and sometimes diplomatic support to another state. When the term refers simply to a state's policy, it is synonymous with *neutralism*, but it also has a more precise legal meaning. Under international laws of neutrality, a non-belligerent enjoys certain rights and obligations in times of war. It may not permit the use of its territory as a base for military operations nor furnish military assistance to the belligerents. A neutralized state enjoys the right of passage on the open seas for its non-military goods. It may, however, show sympathy with one belligerent as long as this is not reflected in its actions. A member of an alliance may remain neutral in a conflict between another member of the alliance and a third state, if the alliance is not established for the purposes of conflict with that third state (eg members of NATO during the UK's conflict with Argentina over the Falkland Is.) » non-aligned movement

neutralization In acid-base reactions, the mixing of chemically equivalent amounts of acid and base to give a solution near pH 7. Weak, non-toxic acids and bases are often used to neutralize spills, since excess will not cause the inverse problem to that being treated. » acid; base (chemistry); pH

neutrino A fundamental particle; symbol *ν*; mass not known exactly, but small, possibly zero; charge 0; spin ½, with spin direction always opposing the direction of motion; senses only gravitational and weak nuclear forces; produced in weak radioactive decays; very unreactive and difficult to detect. Three species of neutrino are known, corresponding to the electron, muon, and tau. Neutrinos were predicted by Austro-Swiss physicist Wolfgang Pauli in 1930, and first observed in 1956 in nuclear reactor experiments. » fundamental particles; lepton; neutrino astronomy; Pauli; weak interaction

neutrino astronomy A term applied to attempts to detect neutrinos from the Sun, to discover the conditions existing in the solar core. Experiments conducted since the 1960s have shown a detected rate rather less than predicted by theories of nucleosynthesis. » astronomy; neutrino; nucleosynthesis

neutron A component particle of the atomic nucleus; symbol n; mass 1.675×10^{-27}kg (939.6 MeV), charge 0, spin ½; held in the nucleus by strong nuclear force; discovered by British physicist James Chadwick in 1932. Free neutrons decay to protons, electrons, and antineutrinos, with a half-life of 10.1 minutes. » magnetic moment; nuclear structure; nucleon; neutron bomb/diffraction/star; quark

neutron bomb More precisely an **enhanced radiation (ER) weapon**, a nuclear munition small enough to be used on the battlefield, fired as an artillery shell or short-range missile warhead, which on detonation produces radiation effects rather than blast and heat. The destructive effect is therefore aimed against living things (such as the crews of tanks inside their machines, which the gamma radiation released on detonation can penetrate) rather than vehicles and buildings. » bomb; neutron; radiation

neutron diffraction An interference effect using neutrons scattered from different layers of atoms in a solid, giving distinctive intensity patterns which can be used to determine the solid's structure. Because neutrons have a magnetic moment but no electric charge, they are useful in determining the magnetic aspects of structure. » magnetic moment; neutron; solid

neutron star A star that has collapsed so far under gravity that it consists almost entirely of neutrons. Once the nuclear fuel in a star is exhausted, it cools and contracts. Stars of more than 1.5 solar masses shrink until pressure between the neutrons balances the inward pull of gravity. They are only 10 km/6 ml across, and have a density of 10^{17}kg m^{-3} at this stage. Formed in supernova explosions, they are observed as pulsars. » gravity; neutron; pulsar; supernova

Nevada [nuh**vah**da] pop (1987e) 1 007 000; area 286 341 sq km/ 110 561 sq ml. State in W USA, divided into 16 counties and one independent city; the 'Sage Brush State', 'Battle Born State', or 'Silver State'; part ceded by Mexico to the USA in the Treaty of Guadalupe Hidalgo, 1848; included in Mormon-ruled Utah Territory, 1850; settlement expanded after the Comstock Lode silver strike, 1859; a separate territory, 1861; joined the Union as the 36th state, 1864; capital, Carson City; other major cities, Las Vegas and Reno; rivers include the Colorado (part of the Arizona border) and Humboldt; L Pyramid and L Winnemucca in the W; L Tahoe on the Californian border; highest point Boundary Peak (4 006 m/ 13 143 ft); mainly within the Great Basin, a large arid desert interspersed with barren mountain ranges; an area of internal drainage, with most of the rivers petering out in the desert or ending in alkali sinks; in the rain shadow of the Sierra Nevada Mts of California; the driest of all the states; mostly unpopulated and uncultivated, with a few oases of irrigation; Hoover Dam creates L Mead; mining (mercury, barite, and several other minerals); a major gold supplier; oil discovered 1954; agriculture not highly developed; cattle, sheep, dairy products, hay, alfalfa; food processing, clay and glass products, chemicals, copper smelting, electrical machinery, lumber; tourism, notably the shores of L Tahoe, Death Valley National Monument (partly in Nevada), and the gambling resorts of Las Vegas and Reno (which attract around 20 million visitors each year; gaming taxes a primary source of state revenue). » Carson City; Great Basin; Guadalupe Hidalgo, Treaty of; Las Vegas; United States of America [i]; RR39

Nevado » **under accompanying name**

Never Never Land Area of Northern Territory, Australia, SE of Darwin; chief town, Katherine; first explored by Leichardt in 1844; featured in Mrs Aeneas Gunn's book, *We of the Never Never*.

nevus » **birthmark**

New Amsterdam » **New York City**

New Britain, formerly **Neu-Pommern** pop (1984e) 227 100; area 37 799 sq km/14 590 sq ml. Largest island of the Bismarck Archipelago, Papua New Guinea; separated from New Ireland by St George's Channel; Solomon Sea (S) and Bismarck Sea (N); length, 480 km/298 ml; width, 80 km/50 ml; capital, Rabaul; oil palm, copra, cocoa, coconuts, timber, copper, gold, iron, coal. » Bismarck Archipelago

New Brunswick pop (1981) 696 403; area 73 440 sq km/ 28 355 sq ml. Province in E Canada, boundaries include the USA (W), Gulf of St Lawrence (E), and Bay of Fundy (S); forested, rocky land, generally low-lying, rising in the NW; several rivers and lakes, especially Grand Lake (area 174 sq km/67 sq ml); capital, Fredericton; major towns include St John and Moncton; paper and wood products, potatoes, seafood, mining (zinc, lead, silver, potash, bismuth), tourism, food processing, dairy products, livestock, poultry; known as Acadia, first settled by French fur traders; ceded to Britain by the Treaty of Utrecht (1713); many United Empire Loyalist immigrants, and separation from Nova Scotia, 1783; joined confederation, 1867; governed by a lieutenant-governor and an elected 58-member Legislative Assembly. » American Revolution; Canada [i]; Fredericton

New Caledonia, Fr **Nouvelle Calédonie** pop (1989e) 158 000; area 18 575 sq km/7 170 sq ml. Territory in the SW Pacific Ocean, 1 100 km/680 ml E of Australia, comprising New Caledonia, Loyalty Is, Isle des Pins, Isle Bélep, and the uninhabited Chesterfield and Huon Is; capital, Nouméa; timezone GMT +11; chief ethnic groups, Melanesians (43%), Europeans (37%); official language, French, with English widely spoken; chief religion, Roman Catholicism; unit of currency, the French Pacific franc; long, narrow main island, 400 km/250 ml in length; rises to 1 639 m/5 377 ft at Mt Panie; C mountain chain; dry W coast covered mostly by gum-tree savannah; tropical E coast; mild Mediterranean-type climate; average temperatures 19.9°C (Jul), 25.8°C (Jan); warm and humid; visited by Captain Cook, 1774; annexed by France as a penal settlement, 1853; French Overseas Territory, 1946; governed by a high commissioner and four Regional Councils, members of which serve on the national 46-member Territorial Council; serious disturbances in the mid-1980s when indigenous Melanesians began their struggle for independence; French referendum in 1988 will allow New Caledonia to vote on self-determination in 1998; beef, pork, poultry, coffee, maize, fruit, vegetables; copra, nickel (world's third largest producer), chrome, iron; chlorine and oxygen plants, cement, soft drinks, clothing, foodstuffs, tourism. » Cook, James; France [i]; Nouméa; Pacific Ocean

New Comedy Athenian comic theatre of the late 4th-c and early 3rd-c BC, exemplified in the work of Menander and the Roman imitations of Plautus and Terence. » Menander; Plautus; Terence; Old Comedy

New Criticism A critical theory and method which concentrates on the text itself, the 'words on the page', to the exclusion of extrinsic information. It was developed by such critics as Cleanth Brooks (1906–) and John Crowe Ransom (1888–1974) in the USA in the 1930s and 1940s, under the influence of Symbolist and Russian Formalist ideas; and in its turn provided a theoretical basis for the technique of 'practical criticism'. » American/English literature; Formalists; literary criticism; Symbolism

New Deal The administration and policies of US President Roosevelt, who pledged a 'new deal' for the country during the campaign of 1932. He embarked on active state economic involvement to combat the Great Depression, setting the tone in a hectic 'first hundred days'. Although some early legislation was invalidated by the Supreme Court, the New Deal left a lasting impact on US government, economy, and society, not least by the effective creation of the modern institution of the presidency. Major specific initiatives included the National Industrial Recovery Act (1933), the Tennessee Valley Authority (1933), the Agricultural Adjustment Act (1933), the National Youth Administration (1935), the National Labor Relations Act (1935), and the Social Security Act (1935). Historians often distinguish the 'first New Deal' (1933–4), concerned primarily with restarting and stabilizing the economy, from the 'second New Deal' (1935–9), aimed at social reform. From 1940 onwards Roosevelt was primarily concerned with foreign affairs. » Roosevelt, Franklin D

New Delhi » **Delhi**

New England Confederation (1643–84) An agreement of the American colonies of Massachusetts, Plymouth, Connecticut, and New Haven to establish a common government for the purposes of war and Indian relations. The Confederation declined in importance after 1664.

New English Art Club A British society founded in 1886 by a group of artists whose 'progressive work', largely inspired by recent French painting, was being rejected by the Royal Academy. Leading members included George Clauser (1852–1944), Wilson Steer (1860–1942), John Singer Sargent (1856–1925), John Lavery (1856–1941), and Walter Richard Sickert (1860–1942). » Camden Town Group; English art

New English Bible An English translation of the Bible from the original languages undertaken by an interdenominational committee of scholars under the auspices of the University Presses of Cambridge and Oxford since 1948. The first edition of the New Testament was completed in 1961, and the first complete Bible was produced in 1970. The goal was to present the text in good English literary idiom rather than in 'Biblical English', and to reflect the results of recent Biblical scholarship. It was substantially revised in 1989 under the title of the **Revised English Bible**. » Bible

New Forest An area of heath, woodland, and marsh covering c.37 300 ha/92 200 acres of S Hampshire, England; a popular tourist area. William the Conqueror appropriated the area for his new 'forest' (royal hunting land) in 1079. Known for its ponies, it is now administered by ten Verderers, the head Verderer being appointed by the Crown. » Crown Estate; Hampshire

New Forest pony A breed of horse, developed naturally in the New Forest, England, from many breeds roaming the area; classed as two types: **Type A** (height, 12–13½ hands/1.2–1.37 m/4–4½ ft) and the more solid **Type B** (height, 13½–14½ hands/1.37–1.47 m/4½–4¾ ft). » horse [i]

New France N American colonies claimed by France from the 16th-c, including Canada, Acadia, and Louisiana. Their economy was based largely on the fur trade, subsistence agriculture, and fisheries. The population totalled 70 000 at its peak. Canada and Acadia were lost to the British incrementally up to 1763; Louisiana was sold to the USA in 1803. » Acadia; Louisiana Purchase

New Frontier The administration and policies of US President Kennedy (1961–3). It was characterized by a high international profile and a liberal domestic stance. » Kennedy, John F

New General Catalogue (NGC) An astronomical catalogue published in 1888 by J L E Dreyer, Armagh Observatory, N Ireland, listing 7 840 nebulas, galaxies, and clusters. The numbering system is still regularly used by professional astronomers. » astronomy; Dreyer

New Granada, Span **Nueva Granada** The official name in the Spanish-American Empire for the area now covered by the Republic of Colombia. It was also the name (1739–1810) of a Spanish viceroyalty embracing Venezuela and Quito in addition to New Granada. » Colombia [i]

New Grange A megalithic passage grave of c.3200 BC in the Boyne R valley, Ireland, 40 km/25 ml N of Dublin. The 19 m/60 ft slab-roofed passage gives onto a cross-shaped burial chamber with a 6 m/20 ft high corbelled vault, the earthen mound above being c.80–85 m/260–280 ft in diameter and c.11 m/36 ft high, retained by a kerb and sheathed with white quartz pebbles. At the winter solstice, the Sun could shine through a slot above the entrance to illuminate the burial chamber. The pecked abstract ornament of the kerb, passage, and chamber is amongst Europe's finest prehistoric art. » chambered tomb; corbelling; Maes Howe; megalith; solstice

New Guard In Australian history, an extreme right-wing organization formed in New South Wales in 1932 by Eric Campbell, which claimed 100 000 members by 1933. Its principal achievement was the disruption of the official opening of Sydney Harbour Bridge (1932). In some respects a fascist organization, the Guard was defunct by 1935. » fascism; Sydney Harbour Bridge

New Hampshire pop (1987e) 1 057 000, area 24 032 sq km/9 279 sq ml. State in NE USA, divided into 10 counties; bounded N by Canada; the 'Granite State'; explored by Champlain and Pring, 1603–5; first settlement at Little Harbor, 1623; ninth of the original 13 states to ratify the Federal Constitution; capital, Concord; chief cities Manchester, Nashua, Portsmouth; Connecticut R forms the W border; Merrimack R flows S through the C into Massachusetts; forested mountains in the N (White Mts), highest point Mt Washington (1 917 m/6 289 ft); the S largely devoted to arable farming and grazing; chief agricultural products dairy and greenhouse products, maple syrup, hay, apples, eggs; diverse manufacturing industries, tourism, forestry. » Champlain; Concord (New Hampshire); United States of America [i]; RR39

New Haven, formerly **Quinnipiac** (to 1640) 41°18N 72°55W, pop (1980) 126 109. Port town in New Haven County, S Connecticut, USA; on Long Island Sound; founded by Puritans, 1638; joint capital of state with Hartford, 1701–1873; railway; Yale University (1701); diverse industrial development; inventions developed here include vulcanized rubber (Charles Goodyear) and the repeating revolver (Samuel Colt); firearms, aircraft parts, hardware. » Colt; Connecticut; Goodyear; Puritanism

New Hebrides » **Vanuatu**

New Ireland, formerly **Neu-Mecklenburg** pop (1984e) 70 800; area 8 647 sq km/3 338 sq ml. Second largest island in the Bismarck Archipelago, Papua New Guinea, separated from New Britain (SW) by St George's Channel; length, 480 km/298 ml; average width, 24 km/15 ml; capital, Kavieng; tuna fishing, copra. » Bismarck Archipelago

New Jersey pop (1987e) 7 672 000, area 20 168 sq km/7 787 sq ml. State in E USA, divided into 21 counties; the 'Garden State'; one of the original states of the Union, third to ratify the Federal Constitution; colonized after the explorations of Verrazano (1524) and Hudson (1609); capital, Trenton; other major cities Newark, Jersey City, Paterson, Elizabeth; Hudson R follows the NE border, and the Delaware R the W border; Appalachian Highlands fall down through Piedmont Plateau to low coastal plains, broken by ridges of the Palisades; highest peak Mt High Point (550 m/1 804 ft); 40% of the land forested, mostly in the SE; NE highly industrialized and densely populated; the rest mainly arable and grazing, producing dairy products, hay, soybeans; a major industrial and commercial area; chemicals, pharmaceuticals, electronics, metals, machinery, textiles, processed foods; many tourist centres. » Hudson, Henry; Trenton; United States of America [i] RR39

New Jerusalem, Church of the A religious sect based on the teachings of the Swedish scientist and seer, Emmanuel Swedenborg, who believed he had direct contact with the spiritual world through visionary experiences. There he saw that a first dispensation of the Christian Church had ended and a new one was beginning, the 'New Jerusalem'. His first church was organized in London in 1783. » spiritualism; Swedenborg; theosophy

New Left A neo-Marxist movement which espoused a more libertarian form of socialism compared to orthodox Marxism. In part, it was inspired by the earlier writings of Marx, which were essentially humanistic, and the ideas of Italian politician Antonio Gramsci (1891–1937) regarding the importance of ideological hegemony. It also drew on dialectical sociology and radical forms of existentialism. It is, however, difficult to pinpoint any central ideas specific to the New Left. The movement had some influence in the 1960s, particularly in student politics and in opposition to the Vietnam War, but it never became an effectively organized political force. Its importance in the 1980s declined, and it gave way in part to the New Right. » existentialism; Neo-Marxism; New Right; sociology

new mathematics A term used to denote mathematical topics which are introduced into the school curriculum later than other more traditional activities, and which are thus usually less familiar to parents and the general public. The actual mathematics is not in itself 'new', and would include such topics as 'tessellations' (the fitting together of regularly chequered pattern shapes), and learning to draw a Venn diagram showing the separateness or overlapping of sets. » mathematics; set

New Mexico pop (1987e) 1 500 000; area 314 914 sq km/121 593 sq ml. State in SW USA, divided into 32 counties; the 'Land of Enchantment'; first explored by the Spanish in the early 1500s; first White settlement at Santa Fe, 1609; governed by Mexico from 1821; ceded to the USA in the Treaty of Guadalupe Hidalgo, 1848; organized as a territory (1850), including Arizona and part of Colorado; admitted to the Union as the 47th state, 1912; capital, Santa Fe; other main cities Albuquerque, Las Cruces, Roswell; over a third of the population Hispanic; bounded S by Texas and Mexico; rivers include the Pecos and the Rio Grande (forms part of S border); highest point Wheeler Peak (4 011 m/13 160 ft); mainly broad deserts, forested mountain wildernesses, and towering barren peaks; isolated mountain ranges, part of the Rocky Mts, flank the Rio Grande; forests mainly in the SW and N; mostly semi-arid plain with little rainfall; farming in the well-irrigated valley of the Rio Grande; cattle, dairy products, sheep, hay, wheat, cotton; processed foods, chemicals, electrical equipment, lumbering; nation's chief producer of uranium, potash, perlite; oil, coal, natural gas; tourism important (warm, dry climate and striking scenery); the Carlsbad Caverns National Park, Aztec Ruins, White Sands, Chaco Canyon, Gila Cliff Dwellings, Gran Quivira; several military establishments and atomic energy centres; Los Alamos atomic research centre built 1943; first atomic bomb explosion at White Sands proving grounds, July 1945; several mountain Indian reservations. » Guadalupe Hidalgo, Treaty of; Santa Fe; United States of America [i]; RR39

New Model Army An English army established by Parliament (15 Feb 1645) to strengthen its forces in the Civil War against Royalists. The county and regional armies of Essex, Manchester, and Waller were merged into a successful national force. The cavalry and artillery were augmented; the battle tactics of Gustavus Adolphus adopted; discipline and pay improved; and religious toleration introduced. » English Civil War; Gustavus II

New Netherland A Dutch colony in the valley of the Hudson R. The first settlement was Fort Orange (Albany), founded in 1617; Nieuw Amsterdam (New York City) followed in 1624. Conquered by the English and named New York in 1664, it was reconquered in 1674 after a second brief period of Dutch rule. Initially established on feudal social lines, the colony prospered on the basis of the fur trade. » New York

new novel » **nouveau roman**

New Orleans [awleenz] 29°58N 90°04W, pop (1980) 557 515. Parish seat of Orleans parish, SE Louisiana, USA, between the Mississippi R and L Pontchartrain; 'Crescent City', located on a bend in the river; founded by the French, 1718; capital of French Louisiana, 1722; ceded to Spain, 1763; passed to the US in the Louisiana Purchase; French influence still evident in the city today; prospered in the 19th-c as a market for slaves and cotton; gained a lasting reputation for glamour and wild living; fell to Union troops during the Civil War; industrial growth in the 20th-c after the discovery of vast deposits of oil and natural gas in the region; jazz music originated in New Orleans in the late 1800s among Black musicians; airport; railway; five universities; one of the nation's busiest ports, at the head of the Mississippi; oil and petrochemical industries; shipbuilding yards; major league team, Saints (football); the French Quarter, the Cabildo, St Louis Cathedral, Jazz Museum, Isaac Delgado Museum of Art; Mardi Gras (Feb–Mar), Jazz and Heritage Festival (Apr). » jazz; Louisiana

New Providence pop (1980) 135 437; area 207 sq km/80 sq ml. Island in the NC Bahamas, on the Great Bahama Bank; length 32 km/20 ml; capital Nassau; contains more than half the total population of the group; airport; popular tourist resort. » Bahamas [i]; Nassau (Bahamas)

New Right A wide-ranging ideological movement associated with the revival of conservatism in the 1970s and 1980s, particularly in the UK and USA. Its ideas are most prominently connected with classical liberal economic theory from the 19th-c. It is strongly in favour of state withdrawal from ownership, and intervention in the economy in favour of a free-enterprise system. There is also a strong moral conservatism – an emphasis on respect for authority, combined with a strong expression of patriotism and support for the idea of the family. Politically, the New Right adopts an aggressive style which places weight on pursuing convictions rather than on generating a consensus. In the USA in the 1980s it has been associated with the emergence of Christian fundamentalism (eg the Moral Majority). » conservatism; fundamentalism; Moral Majority

New Ross, Gaelic **Baila Nua** 52°24N 6°56W, pop (1981) 6 141. Mediaeval town and river port in Wexford county, Leinster, SE Irish Republic; on R Barrow, NE of Waterford; home of the Kennedy family in Dunganstown, 8 km/5 ml S; J F Kennedy Memorial Park nearby. » Irish Republic [i]; Kennedy, John F; Wexford (county)

New Siberian Islands, Russ **Novosibirskiye Ostrova** area 28 250 sq km/10 900 sq ml. Uninhabited Russian archipelago in the Arctic Ocean, between the Laptev Sea (W) and the E Siberian Sea (E), NE Russia; rises to 374 m/1 227 ft; chief islands are Kotelnyy, Faddeyevskiy, and New Siberia; separated from the Lyakhov Is (S) by the Proliv Sannikova strait; mammoth fossils. » Russia

New South Wales pop (1986) 5 605 300; area 801 428 sq km/309 400 sq ml. State in SE Australia, bordered E by the South Pacific Ocean and Tasman Sea; the first British colony, named by Captain Cook, who landed at Botany Bay, 1770; first settlement at Sydney, 1788; comprises 12 statistical divisions; coastal lowlands give way to tablelands, formed by the Great Dividing Range (highest point Mt Kosciusko, 2 228 m/7 310 ft); fertile irrigated plains further W comprise two-thirds of the state; main coastal rivers the Hawkesbury, Hunter, Macleay, Clarence; main inland rivers the Darling, Murray, Murrumbidgee, Lachlan, Macquarie-Bogan; capital, Sydney; principal towns Newcastle, Wollongong; beef cattle, dairy farming, wool, cereals, fishing, forestry, textiles, electrical machinery, chemicals, food processing; lead, zinc, and coal mining; the most populous and most heavily industrialized state in Australia; state holidays Bank Holiday (Aug); Labour Day (Oct). » Australia [i]; Cook, James; Sydney

New Spain, Span **Nueva España** The formal title of the Spanish viceroyalty covering the area of modern Mexico. » Mexico [i]

New Style date The dating system which followed the adoption of the Gregorian calendar by Great Britain and its American colonies (14 Sep 1752); previous dates are referred to as **Old Style** dates. The new system eliminated 11 days to get in step with Europe, and moved the day on which the count of years changes from the Feast of the Assumption (25 Mar) back to 1 January. » Gregorian calendar

New Sweden A Swedish colony, founded at Fort Christina (Wilmington) on the Delaware R in 1633, with Dutch investment and involvement. It was absorbed by New Netherland in 1655. » New Netherland

New Territories area 950 sq km/367 sq ml. Region of the British Crown Colony of Hong Kong; N of the Kowloon Peninsula, bounded N by China; includes part of the mainland and over 200 islands; leased to Britain until 1997, when Hong Kong is restored to China, under the Sino-British Agreement of 1984. » Hong Kong

New Testament Along with the Old Testament, the sacred literature of Christianity. It is called 'New Testament' because its writings are believed to represent a new covenant of God with his people, centred on the person and work of Jesus Christ, as distinct from the old covenant with Israel which is described in the 'Old Testament'. The 27 New Testament writings were originally composed in Greek, mainly in the

1st-c AD, unlike the Old Testament writings which are primarily in Hebrew and from earlier centuries. The New Testament writings are usually grouped as follows: 4 Gospels (Matthew, Mark, Luke, John), the Acts of the Apostles, 13 letters attributed to Paul (Romans, 1 and 2 Corinthians, Galatians, Ephesians, Philippians, Colossians, 1 and 2 Thessalonians, 1 and 2 Timothy, Titus, Philemon), the Letter to the Hebrews, 7 General or 'Catholic' letters (James; 1 and 2 Peter; 1, 2 and 3 John; Jude) and the Book of Revelation. This corpus largely achieved recognition in the Christian Church by the end of the 2nd-c, but a few works continued to be contested in later centuries. » Acts of the Apostles; Apocrypha, New Testament; Bible; Gospels, canonical; Hebrews, Letter to the; James/John/Jude/Peter, Letters of; Pauline Letters; Revelation, Book of

new town A British solution to problems of city growth: a planned, self-contained settlement designed to relieve urban congestion. Some (eg Peterborough) incorporated existing settlements; others (eg Peterlee) were built on new sites. Dating from the 1946 New Towns Act, 14 were designated between 1947 and 1950, and seven more since then. They incorporate features designed to ensure independence from the parent community, minimum commuting, and a balance of social groups. Examples include Cumbernauld, Cwmbran, Harlow, and Milton Keynes. » expanded town; garden city; green belt

new universities Universities built to accommodate the expanding numbers entering higher education in Britain during the postwar period: Keele (1949); Sussex (1961); Essex (1961); York (1963); Lancaster (1964); East Anglia (1964); Kent (1965); Warwick (1965); Stirling (1967); Open (1969). The term does not generally include those 19th-c colleges which were converted into universities in the 20th-c, such as Newcastle and Bath. » red-brick universities

New Wave » Nouvelle Vague

New World monkey A monkey inhabiting C and S America; nostrils wide apart and opening to the side (unlike Old World monkeys); thumb not opposable; some species with prehensile (grasping) tails. (Family: *Cebidae*, 32 species.) » capuchin; douroucouli; howler monkey; monkey [i]; saki; spider monkey; squirrel monkey; titi; woolly monkey

New Year's Day The first day of the year (1 Jan) in countries using the Gregorian calendar. Communities using other calendars celebrate New Year on other dates: the Jewish New Year, for example, is Rosh Hashanah (1 Tishri), which comes in September or October, and the Chinese New Year falls between 21 January and 19 February. » Gregorian calendar RR22

New York (state) pop (1987e) 17 825 000; area 127 185 sq km/ 49 108 sq ml. State in NE USA, divided into 62 counties; the 'Empire State'; second most populous state; one of the original states of the Union, 11th to ratify the Federal Constitution; explored by Hudson and Champlain, 1609; Dutch established posts near Albany, 1614, settled Manhattan, 1626; New Netherlands taken by the British, 1664; capital, Albany; Hudson R flows S through the E state, St Lawrence R part of the N border, Delaware R part of the S border; Adirondack Mts rise in the N, Catskill Mts in the S; highest point in the Adirondacks at Mt Marcy (1 629 m/5 344 ft); state contains 11 334 sq km/4 375 sq ml of the Great Lakes, as well as L Oneida and the Finger Lakes in the C; extensive woodland and forest in the NE, elsewhere a mixture of cropland, pasture, and woodland; clothing, pharmaceuticals, publishing, electronics, automotive and aircraft components; dairy products, corn, beef. » Albany (USA); Champlain; Erie Canal; Hudson, Henry; New York City; United States of America [i]; RR39

New York City or **New York** 40°43N 74°00W, pop (1980) 7 071 639. County seat of New York County, SE New York, USA; at the mouth of the Hudson R; largest city in the USA and largest port, with 1 200 km/750 ml of waterfront, including that in neighbouring New Jersey; originally the site of a trading post established in 1609 by Henry Hudson; colonized by the Dutch and named New Amsterdam; captured by the British in 1664 and named New York after the King's brother, the Duke of York; scene of the reading of the Declaration of Independence (4 Jul 1776); held by the British throughout the War of Independence; George Washington inaugurated here as first US president; rapid commercial and industrial growth after the opening of the Erie Canal, 1825; movement away from the city to the suburbs by many middle-class residents since World War 2; emergency loans saved city from bankruptcy in mid-1970s; divided into five boroughs, each co-extensive with a county – Bronx (Bronx Co), Brooklyn (Kings Co), Manhattan (New York Co), Queens (Queens Co), Staten Island (Richmond Co); eight universities; railway; two airports (La Guardia, Kennedy); major world financial centre, with Stock Exchange in Wall Street; advertising, the media, printing and publishing, textiles, food processing, metal products, scientific equipment, vehicles, shipbuilding, machinery, pharmaceuticals; major league teams, Mets, Yankees (baseball), Knickerbockers (basketball), Giants, Jets (football), Islanders, Rangers (ice hockey); the country's centre for fashion, arts, and entertainment, with many museums and galleries; Central Park. » Broadway; Brooklyn Bridge; Cloisters, the; Empire State Building; Greenwich Village; Liberty, Statue of; Lincoln Center for the Performing Arts; Madison Avenue; Metropolitan Museum of Art; New York (state); Rockefeller Center; Times Square; United Nations; Verrazano-Narrows Bridge; Wall Street; World Trade Center

New York School A term sometimes applied rather loosely (for it was never a school in the formal sense) to the group of US painters who, after 1945, centred around Jackson Pollock (1912–56), Arshile Gorky (1904–48), Willem de Kooning (1904–), and Mark Rothko (1903–70). » action painting; school (art)

New Zealand pop (1990e) 3 389 000; area 268 812 sq km/ 103 761 sq ml. Independent state, comprising a group of islands in the Pacific Ocean SW of Australia, divided into 13 statistical divisions; bounded W by the Tasman Sea and E by the South Pacific Ocean; consists of two principal islands (North and South) separated by the Cook Strait, and several minor islands; total length, 1 770 km/1 100 ml; capital, Wellington; chief towns, Auckland, Christchurch, Dunedin, Hamilton; timezone GMT +12; chief ethnic groups, European (87%), Maori (9%); official language, English; chief religion, Christianity (81%); unit of currency, the New Zealand dollar of 100 cents; North Island mountainous in the centre, with many hot springs; peaks rise to 2 797 m/9 176 ft at Mt Ruapehu; South Island mountainous for its whole length, rising in the Southern Alps to

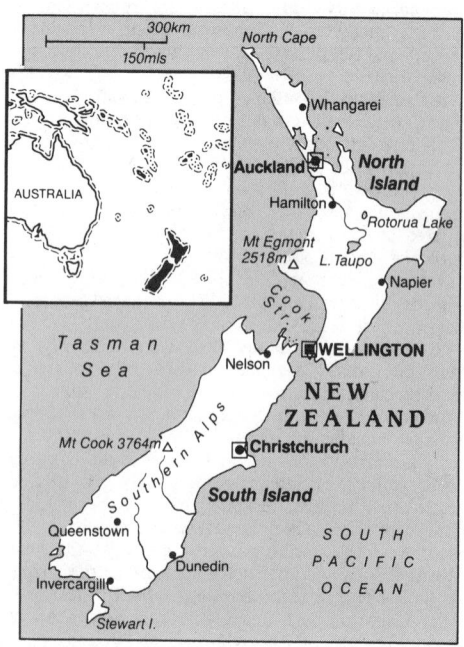

3 764 m/12 349 ft at Mt Cook; many glaciers and mountain lakes; largest area of level lowland is the Canterbury Plain, E side of South Island; highly changeable weather, with all months moderately wet; almost subtropical in N and on E coast, with mild winters and warm, humid summers; Auckland daily temperatures, 8–13°C (Jul), 16–23°C (Jan), average monthly rainfall 145 mm/5.7 in (Jul), 79 mm/3.1 in (Dec–Jan); lower temperatures in South Island; settled by Maoris from SE Asia before 1350; first European sighting by Abel Tasman in 1642, named Staten Landt; later known as Nieuw Zeeland, after the Dutch province; sighted by Captain Cook, 1767; first settlement, 1792; dependency of New South Wales until 1841; outbreaks of war between immigrants and Maoris, 1860–70; Dominion of New Zealand, 1907; independent within the Commonwealth, 1947; governed by a prime minister, cabinet, and unicameral 97-member House of Representatives; elections every three years; economy based on farming, especially sheep and cattle; one of the world's major exporters of dairy produce; third largest exporter of wool; kiwi fruit, venison, mohair, textiles, timber, food processing; substantial coal and natural gas reserves; 80% of electricity supplied by hydroelectric power; tourism a growing sector. » Cook, James; Maoris; North Island; South Island; Tasman; Wellington; RR26 national holidays; RR57 political leaders

Newark (UK), properly **Newark-on-Trent** **[nyoouhk]** 53°05N 0°49W, pop (1981) 33 390. Town in Newark district, Nottinghamshire, C England; at junction of a branch of the Trent and Devon Rivers, 25 km/15 ml SW of Lincoln; railway; foodstuffs, brewing, engineering, agricultural machinery, gypsum, limestone; Newark Castle place of King John's death; repeatedly under siege in Civil War. » English Civil War; John; Nottinghamshire

Newark (USA) 40°44N 74°10W, pop (1980) 329 248. Seat of Essex County, NE New Jersey, USA; port on the Passaic R and Newark Bay; largest city in the state; an important road, rail, and air centre; settled by Puritans from Connecticut, 1666; city status, 1836; airport; railway; university (1934); chemicals, electrical equipment; insurance and financial centre; linked to New York City by underground rail; Trinity Cathedral, Newark Museum. » New Jersey; Puritanism

Newcastle » **Cavendish, William; Pelham, Thomas**

Newcastle (Australia) 32°55S 151°46E, pop (1986) 429 300. City in New South Wales, Australia, on the E coast, 160 km/100 ml N of Sydney; founded as a penal settlement, 1804; scene of Australia's biggest earthquake (1989); airfield; railway; university (1965); coal mining, iron and steel, shipbuilding, railway engineering, chemicals, fertilizers, textiles; trade in coal, grain, wool, dairy produce. » New South Wales

Newcastle (UK) **[nyookahsl]**, locally **[nyookasl]**, properly **Newcastle upon Tyne**, Lat **Pons Aelii**, Anglo-Saxon **Monkchester** 54°59N 1°35W, pop (1981) 203 591. Administrative centre of Tyne and Wear, NE England; part of Tyneside urban area; 440 km/273 ml N of London, on R Tyne, crossed by seven bridges; cultural, commercial, and administrative centre for the NE of England; founded 11th-c, a castle for defence against the Scots; city status 1882; university (1963); railway; underground; ferries to N Europe; heavy engineering, shipbuilding, aircraft, chemicals, pharmaceuticals, coal trade; Stephenson's iron works established here (1820s); 12th-c castle keep, 15th-c Cathedral of St Nicholas, Roman Catholic Cathedral (1844), art gallery, museums, Guildhall (1658). » Stephenson, George; Tyne and Wear

Newcastle disease » **fowl pest**

Newcomen, Thomas (1663–1729) English inventor, born at Dartmouth, Devon. By 1698 he had invented the atmospheric steam engine, and from 1712 this device was being used for pumping water out of mines. He died in London. » steam engine

Newfoundland (Canada) **[nyoofuhnland]** pop (1981) 567 681; area 405 720 sq km/156 648 sq ml. Province in E Canada, consisting of the island of Newfoundland and the coast of Labrador, separated by the Strait of Belle Isle; a roughly triangular island, rising to 814 m/2 671 ft (W); mainly a rolling plateau with low hills; a deeply indented coastline; several peninsulas, lakes, and rivers; Gros Morne National Park on W coast (area 1 942 sq km/750 sq ml, established 1970); capital St John's; food processing, pulp and paper, mining (iron ore), fishing, oil, hydroelectric power, dairy products, poultry; Vikings thought to have visited Labrador c.1000 AD; discovery by Cabot, 1497; British sovereignty declared, 1583 (Britain's first colony); self-governing colony, 1855; placed under a Commission of Government appointed by Britain, 1934; voted to unite with Canada, 1949; governed by a lieutenant-governor and an elected 58-member House of Assembly. » Cabot, John; Canada [i]; Labrador; St John's

Newfoundland (zoology) A breed of dog, developed in Newfoundland; large, very thick-set, with an enormous heavy head; broad deep muzzle and small ears and eyes; very thick, black, double-layered, water-resistant coat; webbed feet. » dog

Newgate From the 13th-c to 1902, the main prison of the City of London, whence many convicted criminals were taken to Tyburn for hanging. It became a generic description for a prison. » London [i]

Newman, John Henry, Cardinal (1801–90) British theologian, born in London. Born into a Calvinist family, he was educated at Oxford, became a fellow of Oriel College, and was ordained in 1824. He became a vigorous member of the Oxford Movement, composing a number of its tracts, notably Tract 90, which argued that the intention of the Thirty-nine Articles was Catholic in spirit. This led to the end of the Movement, and his own conversion to Catholicism in 1845. He went to Rome, and joined the Oratorians, returning to set up his own community in Birmingham. He published several essays, lectures, and sermons, as well as a spiritual autobiography, *Apologia pro Vita Sua* (1864). A moderate in the controversies of the Vatican Council, he was made a cardinal in 1879. He died in Birmingham. » Church of England; Oratorians; Oxford Movement; Pusey; Roman Catholicism

Newman, Paul (1925–) US film actor, born in Cleveland, Ohio. He started in stage repertory and television, and moved to films in the mid-1950s. His good looks and rugged individualism have brought continued success in a wide range of parts, as in *Cat on a Hot Tin Roof* (1958), *Cool Hand Luke* (1967), *Butch Cassidy and the Sundance Kid* (1969), *The Sting* (1973), and *The Verdict* (1982), and directed *The Glass Menagerie* (1987). In addition to winning several Oscars, he was given an Honorary Academy Award in 1986. He also directs, and has been active politically in the civil rights movement.

Newport (Isle of Wight) 50°42N 1°18W, pop (1981) 20 324. River port, market town, and county town in Medina district, I of Wight, S England; on the R Medina, 8 km/5 ml from its mouth; Parkhurst prison nearby; construction equipment, valves, printing; 12th-c Carisbrooke Castle. » Wight, Isle of

Newport (USA) 41°29N 71°19W, pop (1980) 29 259. Seat of Newport County, SE Rhode Island, USA; port at the mouth of Narragansett Bay; settled, 1639; city status, 1853; haven for religious groups, including Quakers and Jews; railway; several US Navy establishments; shipbuilding, electrical goods, jewellery, precision instruments; many palatial mansions (eg the Breakers), the sloop *Providence*, Tennis Hall of Fame; Newport Jazz Festival held here 1954–71; music festival (Jul); yachting (including America's Cup races). » Rhode Island

Newport (Wales), Welsh **Casnewydd** 51°35N 3°00W, pop (1981) 116 658. Town in Newport district, Gwent, SE Wales, UK; on the R Usk, 32 km/20 ml WNW of Bristol; railway; steel, aluminium, electronics, chemicals, market gardening.

Newport News 36°59N 76°25W, pop (1980) 144 903. Seaport and independent city, SE Virginia, USA, at the mouth of the James R; railway; shipbuilding; Mariners' Museum, War Memorial Museum of Virginia. » Virginia

news agency An organization providing a general or specialized news service. Agencies range from large, publicly-quoted companies (eg Reuters) and state-owned concerns (eg TASS) to small private operations. Clients, especially the media, subscribe to the continuous (*wire*) service provided by the major agencies, or buy individual items locally. » Agence France Press; Associated Press; Reuter; TASS; Xinhua

newspaper A regularly published account of recent events. Modern newspapers are printed, usually by offset lithography, on large sheets, folded once and inserted one within another, and published at daily, weekly or (occasionally) monthly frequencies. Predecessors of the modern newspaper included official information sheets, as in the Roman *Acta Diurna*, hung in public places, and mediaeval manuscript news pamphlets, printed in Germany and the Netherlands. The modern newspaper can be traced back to the British publications, the *Corante* (1621) and *Weekly Newes* (1622). Many publications were suppressed during the 17th-c, but censorship was relaxed after the 1688 revolution. The first daily paper was the *Daily Courant* (1702), and the first true evening paper the *Courier* (1792). The reign of George III was marked by bitter conflict over the freedom of the press, not least the reporting of speeches in the House of Commons. In the USA the first newspapers (in Boston, 1689) avoided controversy, but the *Boston Gazette* (and the *Massachusetts Spy* 1770) engaged in anti-British political debate.

In the 19th-c, fast rotary presses, the change to cheap paper, and the abolition of the Stamp Duty (1855) encouraged a great growth in publication. Technical improvements since then have successively brought in mechanized metal typesetting, photo-engraved illustrations, phototypesetting, offset lithography, and facsimile transmission of text and pictures. The revolution in newsgathering and editorial preparation has equalled the technical advances. Recent developments include the use of electronic databases, facilities for journalists to type stories straight into the phototypesetter computer, make-up screens on which whole pages can be laid out and reviewed, and the inclusion of four-colour half-tone illustrations. Newspaper design and marketing has seen rapid development in the 20th-c, with the tabloid circulation wars, price competition, and a reduction in the number of newspapers published. » censorship; journalism; news agency; printing [i]; publishing

newt An amphibian of order *Urodela*; resembles the salamander, but adults spend summer or entire year in water; breeds in water; young (called the *eft* stage) live on land for 1–7 years. (Genera: *Triturus*, *Taricha*, *Notophthalmus*, *Pleurodeles*, *Echinotriton*. Family: *Salamandridae*.) » amphibian; salamander [i]

newton SI unit of force; symbol N; named after Isaac Newton; defined as the force which causes an acceleration of 1 m/s^2 for an object of mass 1 kg. » force; Newton, Isaac; units (scientific); RR70

Newton, Sir Isaac (1642–1727) English physicist and mathematician, born at Woolsthorpe, Lincolnshire. Educated at Grantham and Cambridge, in 1665–6 the fall of an apple is said to have suggested the train of thought that led to the law of gravitation. He studied the nature of light, concluding that white light is a mixture of colours which can be separated by refraction, and devised the first reflecting telescope. He became professor of mathematics at Cambridge in 1669, where he resumed his work on gravitation, expounded finally in his *Philosophiae naturalis principia mathematica* (1687, Mathematical Principles of Natural Philosophy), which established him as the greatest of all physical scientists. In 1696 he was appointed warden of the Mint, and was master of the Mint from 1699 till the end of his life. He also sat in parliament on two occasions. During his life he was involved in many controversies, notably with Leibniz over the question of priority in the discovery of calculus. He was knighted in 1705, and died in London. » differential calculus; Flamsteed; gravitation; Leibniz; light; Newton's laws; Newtonian mechanics; optics [i]; refraction [i]; telescope [i]

Newton's laws The basic expression of Newtonian mechanics; formulated in 1687 by Isaac Newton. *First law*: the velocity of an object does not change unless a force acts on it. *Second law*: a force F applied to an object of mass m causes an acceleration a according to $F = ma$. *Third law*: every action has an equal and opposite reaction. » force; inertia; mass; momentum; Newtonian mechanics

Newtonian mechanics A theory of mechanics which considers the relationships between force and motion for 'everyday' objects, ie objects much larger than atoms and moving slowly relative to the speed of light; formulated by Isaac Newton. The theory is expressed as Newton's three laws of motion. Time is regarded as fixed and absolute, the same for all observers, and distinct from space; mass and energy are separate. » mechanics; Newton, Isaac; Newton's laws; time

Newtonian telescope The first usable astronomical telescope with a parabolic mirror rather than a lens to focus light, and an internal flat mirror to deflect the image to an eyepiece, thus eliminating colour distortions. This optical arrangement is still popular for low-cost amateur telescopes. » telescope [i]

Ney, Michel, Duke of Elchingen (1769–1815) French Marshal, born at Saarlouis. He fought in the Revolutionary Wars, became a general of division in 1799, and a Marshal of the Empire. Created Duke of Elchingen (1805), he distinguished himself at Jena (1806), Eylau, and Friedland (1807). He commanded the third corps of the Grand Army in the Russian campaign (1813), for which he received the title of Prince of Moskowa. After Napoleon's abdication (1814) he accepted the Bourbon restoration, but instead of obeying orders to retake Bonaparte (1815), Ney deserted to his side and led the centre at Waterloo. On Louis XVIII's second restoration, he was condemned for high treason, and shot in Paris. » French Revolutionary Wars; Napoleon I; Napoleonic Wars; Waterloo, Battle of

Ngorongoro Crater [unggohronggohroh] Crater in N Tanzania, in the Rift Valley; its rim is at an altitude of c.2 100 m/6 900 ft, and its floor lies c.600 m/2 000 ft below this level; area, c.260 sq km/100 sq ml; centre of a conservation region, a world heritage site, covering 7 800 sq km/3 000 sq ml; provides a cattle-farming area for the Masai, and a wildlife range for wildebeeste, gazelle, zebra. » Olduvai Gorge; Rift Valley; Tanzania [i]

Nguni [uhngoonee] A cluster of Bantu-speaking peoples of S Africa. Originally occupying present-day Natal and Transkei, they expanded rapidly in the early 19th-c in a series of migrations. The main groups today include the Zulu, Swazi, and Xhosa of South Africa and Swaziland; the Ndebele of Zimbabwe; and the Ngoni of Zambia, Malawi, and Tanzania. All groups are organized under the control of powerful chiefs aided by councils. In South Africa they lost much of their land and power to Europeans from the 18th-c onwards. Population c.7 million. » Bantu-speaking peoples; Ndebele; Swazi; Xhosa; Zulu

nhandu » **rhea**

niacin » **nicotinic acid**

Niagara Falls Two waterfalls in W New York, USA and S Ontario, Canada; between L Erie and L Ontario, on the international border; American Falls 55.5 m/182 ft high, 328 m/1 076 ft wide; Canadian Falls, known as Horseshoe Falls, 54 m/177 ft high, 640 m/2 100 ft wide; separated by Goat Island; Cave of the Winds behind the American Falls; Rainbow Bridge (1941) between Canada and USA below the falls; part of the flow above the Canadian Falls diverted to supplement the shallower US Falls; mean daily flow over both falls before diversion c.5 000 cu m/200 000 cu ft; world-famous tourist attraction since early 19th-c, developed after railway arrived, 1836; twin resort towns of Niagara Falls in Ontario and New York; scene of many daredevil exploits, such as the tightrope crossing by Blondin (1859) and Annie Edson Taylor's 'shooting' of the Horseshoe Falls in a sealed barrel in 1901. » Blondin; New York (state); Ontario

Niamey [neeamay] 13°32N 2°05E, pop (1983) 399 100. River-port capital of Niger; 800 km/500 ml NNW of Lagos (Nigeria); airport; railway terminus; university (1971); textiles, metals, food processing, ceramics, plastics, chemicals, pharmaceuticals; markets selling cloth, leather, iron and copper craftwork; national museum, zoo, botanical gardens. » Niger [i]

Niarchos, Stavros (Spyros) [niahkos] (1909–) Greek ship-owner, born in Athens. After serving in World War 2 in the Royal Hellenic navy, he became the controller of one of the largest independent fleets in the world, pioneering the construction of supertankers, in competition with his brother-in-law Aristotle Onassis. He is also a major art collector. » Onassis; tanker

Nias [neeas] Island in the Indian Ocean, 125 km/78 ml off the W coast of Sumatra, Indonesia; 240 km/159 ml long by 80 km/50 ml wide; airfield; chief town, Gunungsitoli; populated by the agricultural Niah tribe; headhunting and human sacrifice recorded here as late as 1935; notable prehistoric stone sculptures. » Indonesia [i]

Nibelungen [neebelungen] In mediaeval German legends, a race of dwarfs who live in Norway and possess a famous treasure. The *Nibelungenlied* recounts how Siegfried obtained the treasure and his later misfortunes. Wagner conflated this with other legends for his opera cycle. » Brunhild; German literature; Gudrun; Sigurd; Wagner

Nicaea, Council of 1 (325) The first ecumenical Council of the Church, called by Emperor Constantine to settle the doctrinal dispute between the Arians and the Orthodox on the person of Christ. » Arius; Christology; Council of the Church **2** (787) A Council of the Church called to deal with the question of the veneration of images. » iconoclasm

Nicaragua [nikar**a**gwa], official name **Republic of Nicaragua**, Span **República de Nicaragua** pop (1990e) 3 871 000; area 148 000 sq km/57 128 sq ml. Largest of the Central American republics, divided into 16 departments; bounded N by Honduras and S by Costa Rica; capital, Managua; chief towns, León, Granada, Masaya, Chinandega, Matagalpa, Corinto; timezone GMT −6; population mainly of mixed Indian, Spanish, and African descent; chief religion, Roman Catholicism; official language, Spanish; unit of currency, the córdoba of 100 centavos; mountainous W half, with volcanic ranges rising to over 2 000 m/6 500 ft (NW); two large lakes, Lago de Nicaragua and Lago de Managua, in a broad structural depression extending NW–SE behind the coastal mountain range; rolling uplands and forested plains to the E; many short rivers flow into the Pacific Ocean and the lakes; tropical climate, average annual temperatures 15–35°C according to altitude; rainy season (May–Nov) when humidity is high; temperatures at Managua, 26°C (Jan), 30°C (Jul), average annual rainfall 1 140 mm/45 in; colonized by Spaniards, early 16th-c; independence from Spain, 1821; left the Federation of Central America, 1838; dictatorship under Anastasio Somoza, 1938; Sandinista National Liberation Front seized power, 1979, and established a socialist junta of national reconstruction; under the 1987 constitution, a president and a 96-member national Constituent Assembly are elected for 6-year terms; former supporters of the Somoza government (the Contras), based in Honduras and supported by the USA, carried out guerrilla activities against the junta from 1979; ceasefire and disarmament agreed, 1990; agriculture accounts for over two-thirds of total exports; cotton, coffee, sugar cane, rice, corn, beans, shellfish, tobacco, bananas, livestock; oil, natural gas, gold, silver; food processing, chemicals, metal products, textiles, beverages. » Managua; Somoza; RR26 national holidays; RR57 political leaders

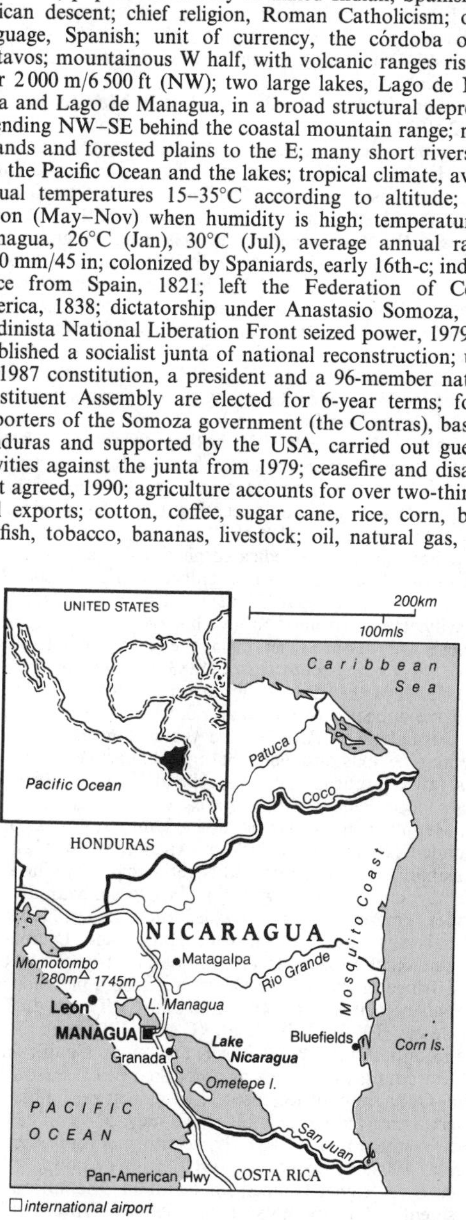

□ *international airport*

Nicaragua, Lago de or **Gran Lago** area 8 026 sq km/3 098 sq ml. Largest lake of Nicaragua and C America, separated from the Atlantic Ocean (W) by a 15 km/9 ml-wide isthmus; length 148 km/92 sq ml; width 55 km/34 ml; contains over 300 small islands, notably Isla de Ometepe, with two volcanoes; Granada is on the NW shore. » Nicaragua [i]

Nice [nees], Ital **Nizza**, ancient **Nicaea** 43°42N 7°14E, pop (1982) 338 486. Fashionable coastal resort on the Mediterranean Sea, and capital of Alpes-Maritimes department, SE France; encircled by hills on the Baie des Anges, 157 km/98 ml ENE of Marseilles; fifth largest city in France; airport; railway; university (1965); leading tourist centre; textiles, perfume, soap, olive oil, fruit, furniture; flower market in old town; cathedral (1650), several 17th–18th-c Baroque churches, 17th-c Palais Lascaris, Palais de la Mediterranée, Palais des Expositions, 19th-c opera house, casinos, palm-lined Promenade des Anglais; Carnival (before Lent), book festival (May), international dog festival (Jun); ballet festival (Jul–Aug). » Mediterranean Sea

Nicene Creed [n**iy**seen] An expanded formal statement of Christian belief, based on the creed of the first Council of Nicaea (325). This is still publicly recited as part of the Eucharistic liturgies of the Orthodox and Roman Catholic Churches, as well as many Protestant Churches. » Christianity; Eucharist; liturgy; Nicaea, Council of

Nichiren Buddhism [nichir**e**n] A sect founded by the Japanese Buddhist reformer Nichiren (1222–82); sometimes called the **Lotus** sect, because of his claim that the Lotus Sutra contained the ultimate truth. He attacked other forms of Buddhism, and called the nation to convert to true Buddhism. There are almost 40 subsects today. » Buddhism; Soka Gakkai

Nicholas I (1796–1855) Emperor of Russia (1825–55), born near St Petersburg, the third son of Paul I. An absolute despot, he engaged in wars with Persia and Turkey, suppressed a rising in Poland, and attempted to Russianize all the inhabitants of the empire. He helped to quell the 1848 Hungarian insurrection, and drew closer the alliance with Prussia. The re-establishment of the French empire confirmed these alliances, and led him to think of absorbing Turkey; but the opposition of Britain and France brought on the Crimean War, during which he died, in St Petersburg. » Crimean War; Napoleon III; Nesselrode, Karl

Nicholas II (1868–1918) The last emperor of Russia (1895–1917), born near St Petersburg, the son of Alexander III. His reign was marked by the alliance with France, an *entente* with Britain, a disastrous war with Japan (1904–5), and the establishment of the national assembly, or Duma (1906). He took command of the Russian armies against the Central Powers in 1915. Forced to abdicate at the Revolution, he was shot with his family by the Red Guards at Ekaterinburg. » Russian Revolution

Nicholas, St (4th-c), feast day 6 December. Bishop of Myra, Lucia, and patron saint of Russia, widely associated with the feast of Christmas. He was imprisoned under Diocletian and released under Constantine, and his supposed relics were conveyed to Bari in 1087. He is the patron of youth, merchants, sailors, travellers, and thieves. His identification with Father Christmas began in Europe, and spread to America, where the name was altered to *Santa Claus*. The tradition of exchanging gifts on Christmas Day derives from a legend of his benevolence. » Christmas; Constantine I (Emperor); Diocletian

Nicholas of Cusa » **Nicolaus of Cusa**

Nicholson, Ben (1894–1982) British artist, born at Denham, Buckinghamshire. Largely self-taught, he travelled widely in Europe, and gained an international reputation as an abstract artist. Although he produced several purely geometrical paintings and reliefs, he generally used as a starting point conventional still-life objects. Three times married, his second wife was Barbara Hepworth. He died in London. » abstract art; English art; Hepworth

Nicholson, Jack (1937–) US film actor, born at Neptune, New Jersey. His early parts were in minor horror and rebel youth quickies, but success came with a character part in *Easy Rider* (1969), and he has since created a versatile range of antiheroes, winning an Oscar for *One Flew over the Cuckoo's Nest* (1975). Notable performances have included *The Shining* (1980), *The Postman Always Rings Twice* (1981), *Terms of Endearment* (1984), and *The Witches of Eastwick* (1986). He also writes scripts, and occasionally directs.

Nicias (?–413 BC) Wealthy Athenian politician and general, prominent during the Peloponnesian War. A political moderate, he was opposed to the strident warmongering of Cleon and Alcibiades, and in 421 BC arranged the short-lived peace named after him. Appointed commander in Sicily in 416 BC, his lack of sympathy with his mission, along with bad luck, ill health, and sheer incompetence, led to the total destruction of the Athenian forces and his own death at the hands of the Syracusans. » Alcibiades; Cleon; Peloponnesian War

nickel Ni, element 28, density 8 g cm^{-3}, melting point 1 450°C. A silvery metal, most commonly obtained from pentlandite, a complex sulphide of nickel and iron; it occurs uncombined only in some meteorites. The metal, which is weakly ferromagnetic, forms a protective oxide coating, and is used in coinage and cutlery, both as the free metal and as an alloy with copper (*German silver*). It is also an important catalyst for hydrogenation (*Raney nickel*), and is an ingredient of many stainless steels. Its compounds mainly show oxidation state +2. » chemical elements; metal; RR90

nickel-silver » **Britannia metal**

Nicklaus, Jack (William) (1940–) US golfer, born at Columbus, Ohio, the most successful golfer of the postwar era. He won the US Amateur title in 1959 and 1961, then turned professional. Runner-up to Arnold Palmer in the 1960 US Open, as amateur, he has since won all the world's major tournaments: the British Open (1966, 1970, 1978), the US Open (1962, 1967, 1972, 1980), the US Professional Golfers Association tournament a record-equalling five times (1963, 1971, 1973, 1975, 1980), and the US Masters a record six times (1963, 1965–6, 1972, 1975, 1986). His win in 1986 was at the age of 46 yr 82 days, the oldest winner of the event. His 18 professional majors is a world record. He is still playing, but is also involved in golf course and golf club design. » golf; Palmer, Arnold

Nicobar Islands » **Andaman and Nicobar Islands**

Nicolai, (Carl) Otto (Ehrenfried) (1810–49) German composer and conductor, born at Königsberg. He studied in Berlin and Rome, becoming court conductor in Vienna (1841) and conductor of the Berlin Opera (1847). His opera *The Merry Wives of Windsor* was produced in Berlin just before his death.

Nicolaus of Cusa (1400–64) German cardinal and philosopher, born at Cusa, Trier. He studied at Heidelberg and Padua, and took a prominent part in the Council of Basle. Ordained in 1440, he became a cardinal in 1448, and as papal legate visited Constantinople to promote the union of the Eastern and Western Churches. A Renaissance scientist in advance of his time, he wrote on astronomy, mathematics, philosophy, and biology. He died at Todi, Papal States. » Renaissance

Nicomedia [niykoh**mee**dia] In antiquity, the capital first of the kingdom and then of the Roman province of Bithynia. Under Emperor Diocletian (AD 284–316), it was the capital of the E half of the Roman Empire. » Bithynia

Nicosia [niko**see**a], Gr **Levkosia**, Turkish **Lefkosa**, ancient **Ledra** 35°11N 33°23E, pop (1982) 161 100. Capital city of Republic of Cyprus; on R Pedias, in the C of Mesaoria plain; capital since 12th-c; 'Green Line' divides the city into northern (Turkish) and southern (Greek) sectors; agricultural trade centre; textiles, food processing, cigarettes; old city surrounded by Venetian-built walls (late 16th-c); technical institute (1968); Cathedral of St John; International State Fair and Nicosia Art Festival (May). » Cyprus [i]

nicotine $C_{10}H_{14}N_2$. An alkaloid derived from pyridine, found in the leaves of the tobacco plant. It is a poisonous and addictive material, usually indulged in for its relaxing properties. It is also used as an insecticide. » alkaloids; drug addiction; pyridine [i]; smoking; tobacco

nicotinic acid A B-vitamin found usually in plants and animals, important in the production of energy inside cells. It usually exists in the form of *nicotinamide*, and can be synthesized from the amino acid tryptophan, but at relatively low rates; nonetheless its level in foods is usually expressed as nicotinic acid equivalents (nicotinic acid + 0.017 tryptophan). In cereals, nicotinic acid is present as *niacytin*, a biologically inactive form. It becomes available on heating the cereal with lime, a practice adopted by S American Indians to prevent pellagra. » enzyme; pellagra; vitamins [i]

Niebuhr, Barthold Georg [**nee**boor] (1776–1831) German historian, born in Copenhagen, Denmark. Educated at Kiel, London, and Edinburgh, in 1816 he became Prussian Ambassador at the Vatican, and on his return in 1823 lectured at Bonn. His main work, the *Römische Geschichte* (1811–32, History of Rome), based on the constructive analysis of historical source material, marked him out as a founder of the 19th-c school of German historical scholarship. He died in Bonn. » Prussia; Stein, Baron von

Nielsen, Carl (August) [**neel**suhn] (1865–1931) Danish composer, born at Nørre-Lyndelse. He studied at the Copenhagen Conservatory (1884–6), and became conductor at the Royal Theatre (1908–14) and with the Copenhagen Musical Society (1915–27). He is particularly known for his six symphonies, and he also wrote concertos, choral and chamber music, the tragic opera *Saul and David* (1902), the comic opera *Masquerade* (1906), and a huge organ work, *Commotio* (1931). He died in Copenhagen.

Niemöller, (Friedrich Gustav Emil) Martin [**nee**merluh] (1892–1984) German Lutheran pastor, born at Lippstadt, Westphalia. He was a leading submarine commander in World War 1, then studied theology, and was ordained in 1924, becoming pastor at Berlin-Dahlem in 1931. Summoned with other Protestant Church leaders before Hitler, he publicly opposed the Nazi regime, and was arrested and placed in concentration camps until 1945. In 1945 he was responsible for the 'Declaration of Guilt' by the German Churches for not opposing Hitler more strenuously, but he also condemned the abuses of the de-Nazification courts. He later became Church President of the Evangelical Church in Hesse and Nassau (1947), and President of the World Council of Churches (1961). He died at Wiesbaden, Germany. » Lutheranism; Nazi Party; World Council of Churches

Nietzsche, Friedrich (Wilhelm) [**nee**chuh] (1844–1900) German philosopher and critic, born at Röcken, Saxony, the son of a Lutheran pastor. He was a strongly religious child and a brilliant undergraduate, accepting the professorship of classical philology at Basle (1869–79) before graduating. Influenced by Schopenhauer, he dedicated his first book, *Die Geburt der Tragödie* (1872, The Birth of Tragedy) to his friend Wagner, whose operas he regarded as the true successors to Greek tragedy. He determined to give his age new values, Schopenhauer's 'will to power' serving as the basic principle. His major work, *Also sprach Zarathustra* (1883–5, Thus Spake Zarathustra) develops the idea of the 'overman'. Much of his esoteric doctrine appealed to the Nazis, and he was a major influence on existentialism. After twelve years of insanity, he died at Weimar. » existentialism; Schopenhauer; Wagner

Niger [**niy**jer], official name **Republic of Niger**, Fr **République de Niger** pop (1990e) 7 779 000; area 1 186 408 sq km/457 953 sq ml. Republic in W Africa, divided into seven departments; bounded NE by Libya, NW by Algeria, W by Mali, SW by Burkina Faso, S by Benin and Nigeria, and E by Chad; capital, Niamey; chief towns, Agadez, Diffa, Dosso, Maradi, Tahoua, Zinder; timezone GMT +1; chief ethnic group, Hausa (54%); official language, French, with Hausa and Djerma widely spoken; chief religion, Islam; unit of currency, the franc CFA; on S fringe of the Sahara Desert, on a high plateau; Hamada Manguene plateau (far N); Aïr massif (C); Ténéré du Tafassasset desert (E); W Talk desert (C and N); water in quantity found only in the SW (R Niger) and SE (L Chad); one of the hottest countries of the world; marked rainy season in the S (Jun–Oct); rainfall decreases N to almost negligible levels in desert areas; annual rainfall at Niamey, 554 mm/22 in; occupied by the French, 1883–99; territory within French West Africa, 1904; independence, 1960; military coup, 1974; governed by a Higher Council for National Orientation led by a president who appoints a Council of Ministers; elected

□ international airport

National Assembly, 1989; constitution suspended, 1991; economy dominated by agriculture and mining; groundnuts, cotton, cowpeas, gum arabic, livestock; production badly affected by severe drought conditions in the 1970s; uranium, tin, phosphates, coal, salt, natron; building materials, textiles, food processing. » Hausa; Niamey; Sahara Desert; sahel; RR26 national holidays; RR57 political leaders

Niger, River [**niy**jer] River in W Africa; length c.4 100 km/2 550 ml; third longest river in Africa; rises 280 km/175 ml from the Atlantic coast; flows NE through Guinea and Mali; dammed at Markala and Sansanding in Mali; splits into several courses and a cluster of lakes in the Macina depression; part of Niger's SW border with Benin; dammed to form the Mainji reservoir, Nigeria; flows SE and S, spreading into a delta c.320 km/200 ml across, entering the Gulf of Guinea; known as **Upper Niger** or Djoliba as far as Timbuktu, **Middle Niger** from there to Jebba in W Nigeria, and **Lower Niger** or Kovarra (Kawarra, Kwara) from Jebba to its delta; navigable in sections and seasonally; frequently interrupted by rapids; first explored by Mungo Park, 1795–6. » Africa; Park, Mungo

Niger-Congo languages The largest language family in Africa, with 1 000 languages spread over almost the entire continent S of the Sahara. The largest group is the *Benue-Congo*, which comprises c.700 languages; of these, c.500 belong to the *Bantu* group, including Swahili, Xhosa, and Zulu. Non-Bantu languages belonging to the group are found in Nigeria, notably Efik and Tiv. » African languages; Bantu-speaking peoples

Nigeria, official name **Federal Republic of Nigeria** pop (1990e) 119 812 000; area 923 768 sq km/356 574 sq ml. Republic in W Africa, divided into 19 states and a federal capital district; bounded W by Benin, N by Niger, NE by Chad, E by Cameroon, and S by the Gulf of Guinea; capital, Abuja; chief towns include Lagos, Ibadan, Ogbomosho, Kano, Oshogbo, Ilorin, Abeokuta, Port Harcourt; timezone GMT +1; over 250 tribal groups, notably the Hausa and Fulani (N), Yoruba (S), and Ibo (E); chief religions, Islam (c.50%), Christianity (34%); official language, English, with Hausa, Yoruba, Edo, and Ibo widely used; unit of currency, the naira of 100 kobos.

Physical description and climate. Maximum length, 1 000 km/650 ml, width 1 100 km/700 ml; long sandy shoreline with mangrove swamp, dominated by R Niger delta; undulating area of tropical rainforest and oil palm bush behind the coastal strip; open woodland and savannah further N; edge of the Sahara Desert (far N), gently undulating savannah with tall grasses; numerous rivers, notably the Niger and Benue; Gotel Mts on SE frontier, highest point, Mt Vogel (2 024 m/6 640 ft); two rainy seasons in coastal areas; wettest part the Niger delta and the mountainous SE frontier, annual rainfall above 2 500 mm/100 in, decreasing W; Ibadan (SE), average daily maximum temperature 31°C, average annual rainfall 1 120 mm/44 in; dry season in the N (Oct–Apr), when little rain falls.

History and government. Centre of the Nok culture, 500 BC–AD 200; several African kingdoms developed throughout the area in Middle Ages (eg Hausa, Yoruba); Muslim immigrants, 15th–16th-c; European interests in gold and the slave trade; British colony at Lagos, 1861; protectorates of N and S Nigeria, 1900; amalgamated as the Colony and Protectorate of Nigeria, 1914; federation, 1954; independence, 1960; federal republic, 1963; military coup, 1966; E area formed Republic of Biafra, 1967; civil war, and surrender of Biafra, 1970; military coups 1983 and 1985; a president rules with an 18-member Armed Forces Ruling Council, which appoints a Council of Ministers.

Economy. Based on agriculture, until oil production began in the late 1950s; oil provides c.90% of exports; half the population still engaged in agriculture; cocoa, rubber, palm oil, groundnuts, cotton, yams, cassava, rice, sugar cane, tobacco; fishing, livestock, forestry; natural gas, coal, tin, lead, zinc, lignite, iron ore, columbite (world's largest supplier), tantalite, limestone, marble; food, pulp and paper, textiles, rubber, sugar, beer, vehicles, pharmaceuticals. » Abuja; African history; Biafra; Lagos; Niger, River; RR26 national holidays; RR57 political leaders

night ape/monkey » **douroucouli**

night blindness Reduced ability to adapt to the dark and to see in dim light, resulting from lack of vitamin A (retinol). This vitamin is an essential component of rhodopsin, upon which colour vision in the retina depends. » eye [i]; vitamins [i]

night heron A short, stocky heron, found worldwide; inhabits water margins; eats small aquatic animals; usually feeds at night. (Tribe: *Nycticoracini*, 8 species.) » heron

Night of the Long Knives The event which took place in Germany (29–30 Jun 1934) when the SS, on Hitler's orders, murdered Röhm and some 150 other leaders of the Sturmabteilung (SA 'storm troopers'). The aim was to crush the political power of the SA and to settle old political scores. It has been estimated that up to 1 000 of Hitler's political opponents and rivals were killed. » Brownshirts; Hitler; Röhm, Ernst

nighthawk » **goatsucker**

Nightingale, Florence, byname **Lady of the Lamp** (1820–1910) British hospital reformer, born in Florence, Italy. She trained as a nurse at Kaiserswerth and Paris, and after the Battle of Alma (1854) led a party of 38 nurses to organize a nursing department at Scutari, where she soon had 10 000

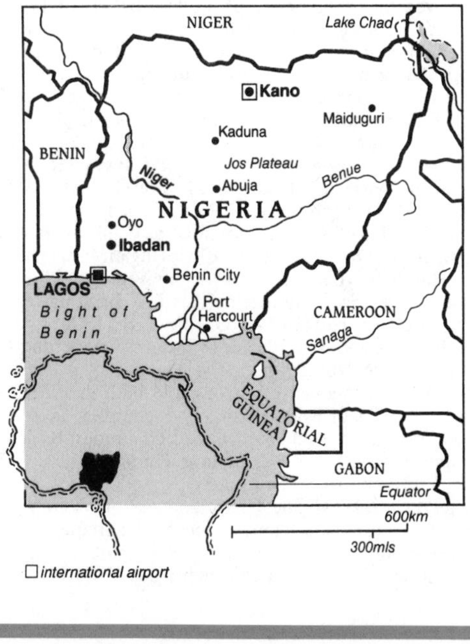

□ international airport

under her care. She returned to England in 1856, where she formed an institution for the training of nurses at St Thomas's Hospital, and spent several years on army sanitary reform, the improvement of nursing, and public health in India. She died in London. » Crimean War

nightingale Either of two species of thrush of the genus *Luscinia*, native to Europe, Asia, and N Africa; mid-brown with paler breast; renowned for its song; often sings at night. The **nightingale** (*Luscinia megarhynchos*) is found in dry woods and hedgerows; the **thrush nightingale**, or **nightingale thrush** (*Luscinia luscinia*), in damp woodland near water. (Family: *Turdidae*.) » thrush (bird)

nightjar A nocturnal bird of the widespread family *Caprimulgidae* (c.70 species); mottled brown with short bill; spends day camouflaged on ground or along branch; inhabits woodland or desert; eats insects. The name is also used for the **tree nightjar** (Family: *Nyctibiidae*) and the **owlet nightjar** (Family: *Aegothelidae*). » frogmouth; goatsucker; oilbird

nightshade » deadly nightshade; woody nightshade

nihilism (Latin *nihil* 'nothing') A term made popular by Turgenev's *Fathers and Sons*, referring to any outlook that denies the possibility of justifying moral values. It came to characterize several members of the Russian radical intelligentsia, including Nikolai Chernyshevski (1828–89) and Dmitri Pisarev (1840–68), who advocated the total annihilation of all existing institutions in the name of unrestricted individual freedom. » Turgenev

Niigata [neeg**a**ta] 37°58N 139°02E, pop(1980) 457785. Port capital of Niigata prefecture, N Honshu, Japan; on the Sea of Japan at the mouth of R Shinano; airport; railway; university (1949); oil refining, machinery, chemicals, textiles. » Honshu

Nijinska, Bronislava [nizh**in**ska] (1891–1972) Russian ballet dancer and choreographer, born in Minsk, the sister of Vaslav Nijinsky. She studied at St Petersburg, and became a soloist with the Maryinski company. She danced with the Diaghilev company in Paris and London (1909–14) before returning to Russia during World War 1, where she danced and started a school in Kiev. She joined Diaghilev in 1921 as principal choreographer. After working in Buenos Aires and Paris, she briefly formed her own company (1932), and after 1938 lived and worked mainly in the USA. Two works have been revived, and are highly regarded: *Les Noces* (1923) and *Les Biches* (1924). » ballet; choreography; Diaghilev; Nijinsky

Nijinsky, Vaslav [nizh**in**ski] (1890–1950) Russian dancer, born in Kiev. He studied at St Petersburg, and first appeared in ballet at the Maryinski Theatre. He danced in Paris with Diaghilev's company in 1909, and in 1911 appeared as Petrouchka in the first performance of the Fokine/Stravinsky ballet. Diaghilev encouraged his choreography, which foreshadowed the development of modern ballet. In 1913, his *Le sacre du printemps* was regarded as outrageous. He was interned in Hungary during the early part of World War 1, rejoined Diaghilev for a world tour, but retired in 1917 as a result of schizophrenia. He then lived in Switzerland, France, and finally London, where he died. » ballet; choreography; Diaghilev; Stravinsky

Nijmegen or **Nimeguen** [**niy**muhkhn, **niy**maygn], Ger **Nimwegen**, ancient **Noviomagus** 51°50N 5°52E, pop(1984e) 233992. City in S Gelderland province, E Netherlands; on the R Waal, 19 km/12 ml S of Arnhem; founded as a hilltop Roman fort, AD 69; former residence of the Carlovingian kings; member of the Hanseatic League; railway; university (1923); metal-working, electrical engineering, textiles, printing, foodstuffs, chemicals; town hall (16th-c), Groote Kerk (13th-c); remains of Charlemagne's Valkhof Palace (8th-c). » Charlemagne; Hanseatic League; Netherlands, The [i]

Nijo-jo Castle [nij**oh**joh] A stronghold built in 1603 in Kyoto, Japan, by Tokugawa Ieyasu. The complex is set in fine landscaped gardens and surrounded by a moat; it includes the Ninomaru Palace and the famous Karamon gate (originally from Fushimi Castle). » Kyoto

Nike [**niy**kee, **nee**kay] The Greek goddess of Victory, either in war or in an athletic contest. She is the frequent subject of sculpture, often shown as a winged figure, as in Nike of Samothrace. The Roman equivalent was Victoria.

Nile, Battle of the » Aboukir Bay, Battle of

Nile, River [niyl], Arabic **Nahr En Nil** River in E and NE Africa; longest river in the world; length from its most remote head-stream (Luvironza R), 6695 km/4160 ml; Luvironza rises in SC Burundi, and flows generally NE and N under various names, entering L Victoria in W; Victoria Nile flows N through L Kyoga into NE end of L Albert; Albert Nile flows N through NW Uganda, becoming known as the White Nile at the Sudanese frontier; joined by the Blue Nile at Khartoum, to become the Nile proper, c.3000 km/1900 ml from its delta on the Mediterranean Sea; joined (E) by R Atbara, the only significant tributary; on entering Egypt, flows into L Nasser, created by the Aswan High Dam; opens out into a broad delta N of Cairo, from Alexandria (W) to Port Said (E), 250 km/155 ml E–W and 160 km/100 ml N–S; flows through two mouths (Rosetta and Damietta), both c.240 km/150 ml long; Egypt's population and cultivated land almost entirely along the floodplain; European discovery of Blue Nile's source made by James Bruce, 1768–73; L Victoria established as Nile's main reservoir by J H Speke, 1858. » Albert/Blue/Victoria/White Nile; Aswan High Dam; Bruce, James; Egypt [i]; Speke

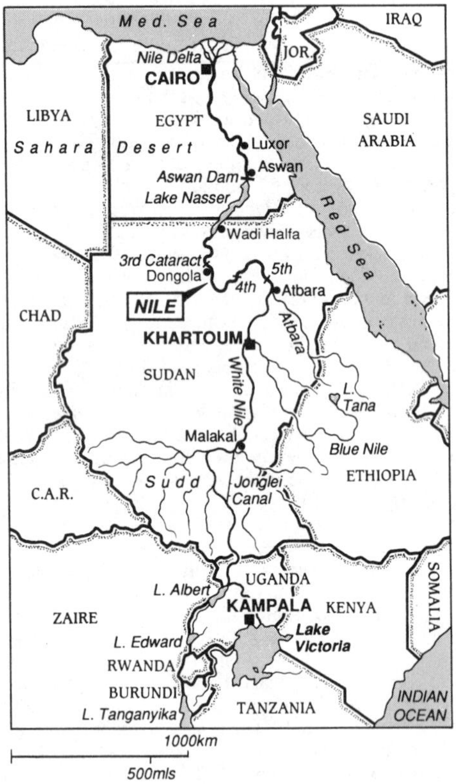

nilgai [**nil**giy] An Indian spiral-horned antelope, the largest Indian antelope; male bluish with short slightly curved horns, tuft of dark hairs on throat; female brown without horns; also known as **blue bull** or **bluebuck** (*Boselaphus tragocamelus*.) The name *bluebuck* is also used for an extinct African antelope (*Hippotragus leucophaeus*). » antelope

Nilgiri Hills [**neel**giree] Hills linking the Eastern Ghats with the Western Ghats, Tamil Nadu state, S India; connected to the S Deccan Plateau; highest point, Doda Betta (2636 m/8648 ft); many coffee and tea plantations. » Ghats

Nilotes [niy**loh**teez] Peoples of NE Africa who originated in the Nile regions and moved S probably before the 16th-c. Pastoralists, they mingled with agriculturalists creating new ethnic groupings. The Acholi and Alur of N Uganda, and the Luo who inhabit the E shores of L Victoria, all belong to this group. It is also thought that some Nilotic migrants, known as the

Bito, became the aristocracies of some of the states of Uganda, notably Buganda, Bunyoro, and Toro. » African history; Luo; pastoralism; Uganda [i]

Nilsson, (Märta) Birgit (1918–) Swedish soprano, born at Karup. She studied in Stockholm and made her debut there in 1946. Her international reputation developed in the 1950s, particularly in Wagnerian roles, and she retired in 1982. » opera; Wagner

nimbostratus clouds Dark-grey, rain-producing clouds of the stratus family. They are found at relatively low layers of the atmosphere, c.1 000 m–3 000 m/3 000–9 000 ft. Cloud symbol: Ns. » cloud [i]; nimbus clouds; stratus clouds

nimbus Another word for the halo, circular or square, which surrounds the heads of sacred persons in much religious art. Originating on Greek vases, it is common in Roman art, from whence it was taken over by the early Christians. Buddha, too, occasionally has a nimbus. » Christian art; Roman art

nimbus clouds Clouds which produce rain or snow. For example, cumulonimbus clouds form from convectional cooling and are associated with thunderstorms, while nimbostratus clouds give more or less continuous rain. » cloud [i]; cumulonimbus clouds; nimbostratus clouds

Nîmes [neem], ancient **Nismes** or **Nemausus** 43°50N 4°23E, pop (1982) 129 924. Ancient town and capital of Gard department, S France; 102 km/63 ml NW of Marseilles; principal city of Roman Gaul; Protestant stronghold in 16th-c; Pacification of Nîmes signed here, 1629; airport; railway; bishopric; textiles, clothing, footwear, carpets, agricultural machinery, trade in grain, wine, brandy, fruit; centre of silk industry (cloth 'de Nîmes', name later contracted to 'denim'); birthplace of Alphonse Daudet; Roman buildings and monuments, amphitheatre (1st-c), Maison Carrée (Corinthian temple, now a museum), tower remains on Mont Cavalier, Temple of Diana, 11th-c Cathedral of St-Castor; summer courses in archaeology. » Daudet; denim; Gaul; Gard, Pont du; Roman architecture

Nimitz, Chester William [**nim**its] (1885–1966) US admiral, born at Fredericksburg, Texas. He trained at the US Naval Academy, served mainly in submarines, and by 1938 had become Rear-Admiral. Chief of the Bureau of Navigation during 1939–41, he then commanded the US Pacific Fleet, his conduct of naval operations being a major factor in the defeat of Japan. He was made Fleet Admiral (1944), Chief of Naval Operations (1945–7), and Special Assistant to the Navy Secretary (1947–9). He died near San Francisco. » World War 2

Nimrod In the Table of Nations (*Gen* 10), purportedly the son of Cush and great-grandson of Noah. He was a legendary warrior and hunter, and allegedly one of the first to rule over a great empire after the Flood, becoming King of Babylon and S Mesopotamia as well as of Assyria, where he is said to have founded Nineveh. In some rabbinic traditions, he was also considered the builder of the Tower of Babel (*Gen* 11), but it is uncertain whether he was a historical individual at all. » Babel, Tower of; Flood, the; Nineveh

Nimrud The Upper Mesopotamian city which became the royal seat and military capital of the Assyrian Empire in the 9th-c BC. » Assyria

Nineteen Counties An unsuccessful attempt by the government of New South Wales to limit the spread of settlement. The counties were proclaimed by Governor Darling in 1829, covering 9 million ha/22 million acres, and bounded (N) by the Manning R, (W) by the Wellington Valley, (S) by the Goulburn Plains, and (E) by the Pacific Ocean. The boundaries of the counties were ignored, and Pastoralists 'squatted' on the land outside them. In 1836 Governor Bourke permitted squatters to graze their sheep outside the counties for an annual licence fee. In 1847, the Nineteen Counties were absorbed into a new administrative division of the Colony. » New South Wales

ninety-five theses A series of points of academic debate with the Pope, posted by Martin Luther on the church door at Wittenberg in 1517. They attacked many practices of the Church, including indulgences and papal powers. This act is generally regarded as initiating the Protestant Reformation. » indulgences; Luther; pope; Protestantism; Reformation

Nineveh [**nin**eve] One of the most important cities of ancient Assyria, located E of the Tigris, and the site of royal residences from c.11th-c BC. It was founded in pre-historic times, although some Biblical legends associate its origin with Nimrod, and the temple of Ishtar is noted there in the Code of Hammurabi. It was at its height of importance in the 8th–7th-c BC under Sennacherib, but fell in 612 BC to the Medes and Persians. Its royal libraries, containing thousands of clay tablets, are one of the best surviving sources for ancient Mesopotamian history. » Assyria; Mesopotamia; Nimrod

Ningbo, **Ningpo**, or **Yin-hsien** 29°54N 121°33E, pop (1984e) 615 600. Port city in Zhejiang province, E China, at confluence of Fenghua, Tong, and Yuyao Rivers; traditional outlet for silk and porcelain; designated a special economic zone; railway; fishing, food processing, shipbuilding, textiles, high technology; Tianyi Ge Library (1561, oldest in China); Tianfeng Ta pagoda (1330). » China [i]

ninjutsu An armed Japanese martial art, whose origins are obscure because of the secrecy surrounding the Ninja, who were assassins. In the 1980s it became popular as a cult in the cinema and video world. » martial arts

Niobe [**niy**ohbee] In Greek mythology, the daughter of Tantalus and the wife of Amphion. She had twelve children (or more) and said she was better than any mother, including Leto. This provoked Leto's children, Apollo and Artemis, who killed all (or most of) the children, and turned the weeping Niobe into a weeping rock on Mt Sipylos. » Leto

Niokolo-Koba [nyokohloh **koh**ba] area 9 130 sq km/3 524 sq ml. National park and game reserve in E Senegal, W Africa; established in 1953; principally watered by the R Gambia; Mt Asirik rises to 311 m/1 020 ft; a world heritage site. » Senegal [i]

Nippur The religious centre of the Sumerians, where their kings were crowned and perhaps also buried. It was never a political capital, but the seat of the god, Enlil, the head of the Sumerian pantheon. » Mesopotamia; Sumer

Nirvana [ner**vah**na] In Buddhism, the attainment of supreme bliss, tranquillity, and purity, when the fires of desire are extinguished. The goal of Buddhists, it is neither personal immortality nor the annihilation of the self, but more like absorption into the infinite. » Buddha; Buddhism

Niš or **Nish** [neesh], ancient **Naisus** 43°20N 21°54E, pop (1981) 230 711. Industrial town in SEC Serbia republic, Yugoslavia, on R Nišava; formerly a stronghold on the road to Byzantium; occupied by Bulgaria until 1918; airfield; railway; university (1965); locomotives, wine, grain, cattle trade, electronics; open-air theatre, Tower of Skulls, Turkish citadel; Constantine's villa at Mediana; film festival. » Serbia; Yugoslavia [i]

nisnas monkey » **patas monkey**

nit An egg laid by a louse of the order *Phthiraptera*, especially used of eggs of the human head and body lice. » louse

Niterói [neetay**roy**] 22°54S 43°06W, pop (1980) 382 736. Port in Rio de Janeiro state, SE Brazil, on SE shore of Guanabara Bay opposite Rio de Janeiro; founded 1573; former state capital; connected to Rio by a bridge, length 14 km/9 ml; railway; university (1960); commerce, shipbuilding, canning, fishing, tourism; colonial forts of Santa Cruz (16th-c), Barão do Rio Branco (1633), Gragoatá, Nossa Senhora da Boa Viagem; Church of Boa Viagem (1633); archaeological site and museum. » Brazil [i]; Rio de Janeiro

nitrate The salt of nitric acid, containing the NO_3^- ion, or a compound containing the covalently bonded $-O-NO_2$ group. Potassium and sodium nitrates occur in nature (*saltpetre* or *Chile saltpetre*), and are used in food preservation, fertilizers, and explosives. Organic nitrates are highly explosive. » nitric acid; nitrite; nitro-; salt

nitre [**niy**tuh] » **potassium**

nitric acid HNO_3, melting point −42°C. A strong, oxidizing acid, made commercially by the oxidation of ammonia (the Ostwald process), the overall reaction being: $NH_3 + 2O_2 \rightarrow HNO_3 + H_2O$. It is important in the manufacture of agricultural chemicals and explosives. » acid; ammonia

nitric oxide NO, boiling point −152°C. A colourless gas, an intermediate in the oxidation of ammonia to nitric acid. It reacts spontaneously with oxygen to give nitrogen dioxide (NO_2). » gas **1**; oxidation

nitrite The salt of nitrous acid (HNO_2), containing the ion NO_2^-, or a compound containing covalently bonded $-O-N=O$. Nitrites are the most effective means of reducing the growth of the bacteria causing botulism. Sodium nitrite plays a particular role in food preservation. » botulism; food preservation; nitrate; nitro-; salt

nitro- The name for the group $-NO_2$, isomeric with the nitrite group, but bonded through nitrogen. Most organic nitro-compounds are explosive, such as trinitrotoluene. *Nitroglycerine* is better called *glyceryl trinitrate*, as it is the nitrate ester of glycerol. It is mixed with sawdust or other filler to make dynamite. » explosives; nitrate; nitrite

nitrocellulose A chemical compound formed by the action of nitric acid on cellulose; first made in 1845 by German chemist Christian Friedrich Schonbein (1799–1868). Its explosive properties proved unmanageable until about 20 years later, when it was turned into the form known as *gun-cotton*. Mixed with nitroglycerine, it forms the main constituent of some blasting explosives and propellants. Some forms of cellulose nitrate, less explosive but still highly inflammable, were for many years used in plastics and as a film base. » cellulose; explosives; nitroglycerine; plastics

nitrogen N, element 7, boiling point −196°C. In the form of diatomic molecules (N_2), it is the most abundant gas in the atmosphere, of which it makes up 78%. It is obtained by the fractional distillation of air. The strength of the triple bond in $N{\equiv}N$ makes the gas almost inert, and it is commonly used when an inert atmosphere is required. Conversion of nitrogen to water-soluble forms, such as ammonia and nitrates, is called **nitrogen fixation**. This can be carried out by soil bacteria, and industrially by the Haber process. Most other compounds of nitrogen, especially nitrites and nitrates, are derived from ammonia. The main uses of its compounds are in agricultural fertilizers and in explosives, which make use of the large amount of energy released when N_2 is reformed. » chemical elements; gas **1**; Haber–Bosch process; nitrogen cycle [i]; nitrogen fixation; RR90

nitrogen cycle The dynamic system of changes in the nature of nitrogen-containing compounds circulating between the atmosphere, the soil, and living organisms. It includes the fixation of gaseous molecular nitrogen into nitrogenous compounds by micro-organisms, lightning, or other processes; the oxidation of ammonia to nitrite, and nitrite to nitrate by aerobic organisms (*nitrification*); the decomposition of organic matter by putrefaction; and the eventual release of gaseous nitrogen by the reduction of nitrates and nitrites, typically by anaerobic micro-organisms (*denitrification*). » aerobe; nitrogen

nitrogen fixation A means of converting atmospheric nitrogen to compounds usable as fertilizers. The need for such means, in the face of potential food shortage for a growing population, was seen to be an acute world problem in the late 19th-c. Attention was called to it in a famous speech to the British Association by Sir William Crookes in 1898. Nitrogen, which is essential for the nutrition of plants, is not directly absorbed by them from the atmosphere. In nature, soil bacteria carry out the necessary conversion of gaseous nitrogen to assimilable compounds. The best solution to the problem was that of Haber and Bosch (via ammonia); most nitrogenous fertilizers are now derived from atmospheric nitrogen through this type of fixation process. » Crookes; fertilizer; Haber–Bosch process; nitrogen

nitroglycerine An explosive liquid made by the action of nitric acid (mixed with sulphuric acid) on glycerol. When first made in 1846 by Italian chemist Ascanio Sobrero (1812–88), it was considered impossibly dangerous, but was put to some use with careful handling. Then from 1867 Nobel made its use more general by mixing it with moderators. It is a constituent of several mixed explosives (eg gelignite). » explosives; glycerol; nitric acid; Nobel

nitrous oxide Boiling point −88°C. Dinitrogen oxide, N_2O, isoelectronic with carbon dioxide; also called **laughing gas**. It has a slightly sweet odour, and is used as a general anaesthetic for short periods, especially in dentistry. It is produced by the decomposition of ammonium nitrate: $NH_4NO_3 \rightarrow N_2O + 2H_2O$. » anaesthetics, general; nitrogen; oxide

Niue [neeooay] 19°02S 169°55W; pop (1989e) 2 100; area 263 sq km/101 sq ml. Coral island in the S Pacific Ocean, 2 140 km/1 330 ml NE of New Zealand; main settlement, Alofi; timezone GMT +12; chief religion, Christianity; official language, English; New Zealand currency used; mainly coral, with a flat, rolling interior and porous soils; highest point, 70 m/230 ft; subtropical and damp climate; hurricanes in the hot season (Dec–Mar); rainfall throughout the year; visited by Captain Cook, 1774; European missionaries in mid-19th-c; British protectorate, 1900; annexed to New Zealand, 1901; since 1974, internal self-government in free association with New Zealand, which still maintains responsibility for defence

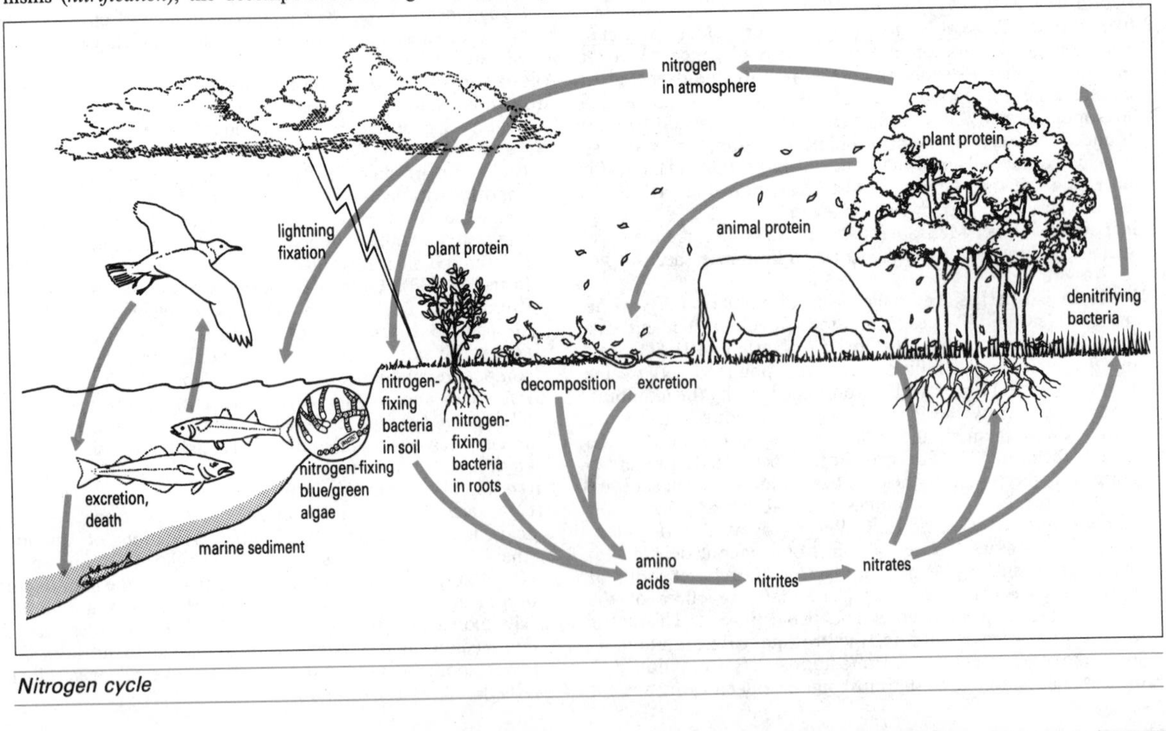

Nitrogen cycle

and foreign affairs; governed by an elected 24-member Legislative Assembly, headed by a premier; mainly agricultural economy; passionfruit, copra, bananas, crafts. » Cook, James; New Zealand [i]; Pacific Ocean

Niven, David (1910–83) British film actor, born in London. Educated at Stowe and Sandhurst, he served in the army until 1930. He had his first leading parts in *Dodsworth* (1936) and *The Prisoner of Zenda* (1937), becoming established in urbane romantic roles with an English style. Early in World War 2 he enlisted in the Commandos, becoming a Colonel. Later successes included *A Matter of Life and Death* (1946), *Around the World in 80 Days* (1956), *Separate Tables* (1958), for which he won an Oscar, and the adventure stories *The Guns of Navarone* (1961) and *55 Days at Peking* (1963). He died in Switzerland.

nix or **nixie** In European folk-tales, a water-sprite, who occasionally entraps people into her pool; not to be confused with the deity Nyx in Greek mythology.

Nixon, Richard M(ilhous) (1913–) US statesman and Republican President (1969–74), born in Yorba Linda, California. Educated at Whittier College and Duke University, he became a lawyer, served in the US Navy, and was elected to the House of Representatives in 1946, becoming Senator in 1950, and Vice-President in 1952. He lost the 1960 election to Kennedy, but won in 1968, and was re-elected in 1972. He resigned in 1974 under the threat of impeachment after several leading members of his government had been found guilty of involvement in the Watergate affair, but was given a full pardon by President Ford. He withdrew from public life, but in the late 1980s emerged as an author on world affairs and an elder statesman in the Republican Party. » Ford, Gerald R; Kennedy, John F; Khrushchev; Republican Party; Watergate

Nizhny Novgorod » **Gorky**

Nkomo, Joshua (Mqabuko Nyongolo) [nuh**koh**moh] (1917–) Zimbabwean politician, born at Semokwe, Matabeleland. Educated mainly in South Africa, in 1952 he became a member of the African National Congress, and in 1961 President of the Zimbabwe African People's Union (ZAPU). There followed a long period during which he was placed under government restrictions, but in 1976 he formed the Popular Front with Robert Mugabe to press for Black majority rule in an independent Zimbabwe, and was given a Cabinet post in the Mugabe government in 1980. However, tension between his party and Mugabe's led to his dismissal in 1982. Although Nkomo's native Matabeleland continued to harbour dissidents from Mugabe's rule, some reconciliation was achieved as Zimbabwe moved towards a one-party state. » Mugabe; Patriotic Front; Zimbabwe [i]

Nkrumah, Kwame [nuh**kroo**ma] (1909–72) Ghanaian statesman, Prime Minister (1957–60), and President (1960–6), born at Nkroful, Gold Coast. He studied in both the USA and UK, returning to Ghana in 1947, and in 1949 formed the nationalist Convention People's Party. In 1950 he was imprisoned, but elected to parliament while still in jail. Released in 1951, he became leader of business in the Assembly, and then Premier. Called the 'Gandhi of Africa', he was a significant leader both of the movement against White domination and of Pan-African feeling. He was the moving spirit behind the Charter of African States (1961). Economic reforms led to political opposition and several attempts on his life, interference with the judiciary, and the formation of a one-party state in 1964. His regime was overthrown by a military coup during his absence in China. He sought asylum in Guinea, where he was given the status of co-head of state, and died in Bucharest. » Ghana [i]

no-fault principle In law, the principle that it should be possible to claim compensation for injury without proving fault against a defendant. In an action for negligence, it is necessary to prove that the damage was caused through a breach of a duty of care owed to the plaintiff by the defendant; if the defendant is not shown to be at fault, the case fails. The no-fault principle seeks to fill this gap by means of an insurance scheme. The compensation scheme for personal injuries in New Zealand is a notable example of the principle in operation. » damages; negligence

Noah [**noh**a] Biblical character, depicted as the son of Lamech; a 'righteous man' who was given divine instruction to build an ark in which he, his immediate family, and a selection of animals were saved from a widespread flood over the Earth (*Gen* 6–9). In the Table of Nations (*Gen* 10), Noah's sons (Japheth, Ham, and Shem) are depicted as the ancestors of all the nations on Earth. A similar flood legend was told of a Babylonian character, Utanapishtim, in the Gilgamesh Epic. » Flood, the; Genesis, Book of; Gilgamesh Epic

Nobel, Alfred (Bernhard) (1833–96) Swedish inventor and manufacturer, born in Stockholm. He discovered how to make a safe and manageable explosive (dynamite), and also invented blasting-jelly and several kinds of smokeless powder. He died at San Remo, Italy. » explosives; Nobel Prizes

Nobel Prizes Prizes awarded each year from the income of a trust fund established by the will of Swedish scientist and industrialist Alfred Nobel to those who, in the opinion of the judges, have contributed most in the fields of physics, chemistry, physiology or medicine, literature, and peace. A sixth prize, for economics, is now awarded by the Swiss National Bank. Each prizewinner receives a gold medal, and a sum of money. » Nobel; RR100

Nobile, Umberto [**noh**beelay] (1885–1978) Italian airman, born at Lauro. A general in the Italian air force, and a professor of aeronautical engineering at Naples, he built the airships *Norge* and *Italia*. Wrecked in *Italia* when returning from the N Pole (1928), he was held responsible for the disaster, and resigned his commission, but was later reinstated. He died in Rome. » aeronautics; airship; Amundsen

noble gases The eighth or zeroth group of the periodic table; also called the **rare** or **inert gases**. They are all gases at normal temperatures, and were called 'noble' because they were long thought to form no chemical compounds. » argon; gas **1**; helium; krypton; neon; radon; xenon

noble metals Metals which are intrinsically unreactive and not readily subject to corrosion. Gold, silver, and the 'platinum metals' are the best examples. Metals such as aluminium and chromium, whose corrosion resistance is due to an adhering coat of oxide, are called *passive*. » corrosion; metal

Nobunaga, Oda [noboo**nah**ga] (1534–82) The first of the three great historical unifiers of Japan, followed by Hideyoshi and Tokugawa, born into a noble family near Nagoya. He became a general, and occupied the old capital, Kyoto, in 1568, destroying the power of the Buddhist Church, and favouring Christianity as a counter-balance. He built Azuchi Castle, near Kyoto, as his headquarters. He was assassinated by one of his own generals, in Kyoto. » daimyo; Hideyoshi; Tokugawa

Noctiluca [nokti**loo**ka] An unusually large, single-celled marine organism; a dinoflagellate, moving by means of whip-like flagella; bioluminescent, producing flashes of light when disturbed; feeds mainly by ingestion of small particles. (Class: *Dinophyceae*.) » flagellum

noctilucent cloud Very high altitude (80 km/50 ml) dusty clouds visible as a rippled or veiled structure after sunset from about May to August in the N hemisphere. They consist of water ice frozen onto a dust core. » cloud [i]

noctuid moth [**nok**tyooid] Any of a large family, the *Noctuidae*, of typically drab, nocturnal moths (Order: *Lepidoptera*); larvae feed on leaves, flowers, and buds, or bore into plant stems; c.21 000 species, many of which cause serious damage to crops, including cutworms and armyworms; also known as the **owlet moth**. » cutworm; larva; moth

noctule A type of bat, native to Asia, Europe, Madeira, and the Azores; dark or yellow brown; inhabits woodland but may feed in open areas; often eats beetles (once observed to eat mice). (Genus: *Nyctalus*, 5 species. Family: *Vespertilionidae*.) » bat

nocturnal In astronomy, an instrument analogous to a sundial, consisting of an arm and a disc, used to determine local time at night. It works by aligning the arm parallel to the Pointers in Ursa Major, and reading the time from engraved scales. » sundial

nocturne A piece of music, usually in a meditative, languid style. The title has been used for piano pieces by John Field (its inventor), Chopin, and Fauré, and for orchestral pieces by Mendelssohn and Debussy. » Chopin; Debussy; Fauré; Field, John; Mendelssohn

noddy » **tern**

Noel-Baker (of the City of Derby), Philip (John), Baron (1889–1982) British Labour politician, born and died in London. Educated at Cambridge, he captained the British Olympic team in 1912. He served on the secretariat of the League of Nations (1919–22), became professor of international relations at London (1924–9), and an MP (1929–31, 1936–70). He was Secretary of State for Air (1946–7), and of Commonwealth Relations (1947–50), and Minister of Fuel and Power (1950–1). He was awarded the Nobel Peace Prize in 1959, and created a life peer in 1977. » Labour Party; League of Nations

Noh Classical theatre of Japan in which imitation, gesture, dance, mask-work, costume, song, and music are fused in a concise stage art. The philosophy, style and much of the repertoire was established by Kan'ami (1333–84) and his son Zeami (1363–1443). Five schools of Noh exist, and most of the plays they perform were written before 1600. » Japan [i]

Nolan, Sir Sidney (Robert) (1917–) Australian painter, born in Melbourne. Largely self-taught, he took up full-time painting in 1938, and made his name with a series of 'Ned Kelly' paintings, begun in 1946, following this with an 'explorer' series. He first went to Europe in 1950, and although he has worked in Italy, Greece and Africa, he remains best known for his Australian paintings. He is also a theatrical designer and book illustrator. He was knighted in 1981. » Australian art; Kelly, Ned

Nolde, Emil, pseudonym of **Emil Hansen** (1867–1956) German artist, born at Nolde. He was one of the most important Expressionist painters, his powerful style being summed up by the phrase 'blood and soil'. He was a member of Die Brücke (1906–7), and produced a large number of etchings, lithographs, and woodcuts. He died at Seebüll, Germany. » Brücke, die; Expressionism; German art

Nollekens, Joseph (1737–1823) British Neoclassical sculptor, born and died in London. He spent 10 years in Rome, returning to London in 1770, where he executed likenesses of most of his famous contemporaries, such as Goldsmith, Johnson, Fox, Pitt, and George III. » English art; Neoclassicism (art and architecture)

nomadism A way of life characterized by moving from one place to another, with no fixed residence, though often temporary centres. Mobility may be cyclical or periodic, determined by the availability of food supplies, rainfall, weather, employment, etc. Most nomadic people (eg the Bedouin, the Kirghiz) are either hunter-gatherers or pastoralists. Some are described as **semi-nomadic** (eg the Fulani), as they remain settled in one area for a span of time and cultivate crops. As various governments have restricted movements of people, nomadism has declined in recent decades. » Bedouin; hunter-gatherers; pastoralism

nominalism Any metaphysical theory which claims that only individual things exist; there are no universals such as properties. Thus 'red' in 'this rose is red' either refers to nothing, or it simply names this rose again, or it refers to the individual patch of redness in this rose. » metaphysics

non-aligned movement A movement of states which positively espoused the position of not taking sides in the major division within world politics between the USA and USSR. Non-alignment differs from neutralism in that it is associated with moves to mediate between the superpowers, and aims to make a direct contribution to the achievement of peace. The neutrality of non-aligned states is supposed to afford them increased diplomatic influence. Attempts in the early 1960s to give impetus to the movement by Mediterranean, African, and Asian countries were badly shaken by superpower hostility. However, a number of recently de-colonized countries have favoured non-alignment as a mark of their independence. » neutrality

Non-Co-operation Movement An unsuccessful nationalist campaign (1919–22) led by M K Gandhi and Congress to force the British to grant Indian independence. It was strengthened by joining forces with Indian Muslims campaigning against British policy towards the Ottoman Empire. The movement involved the boycott of Government institutions and foreign goods, and was abandoned when the protest became violent. » Gandhi

Nonconformists Originally, those Protestants in England and Wales in the 17th-c who dissented from the principles of the Church of England. It has subsequently been applied to such denominations as Baptists, Congregationalists, and Methodists, and generally refers to Christians who refuse to conform to the doctrine and practice of an established or national Church. » Christianity; Church of England; Dissenters

non-Euclidean geometries » **geometries, non-Euclidian**

nonfigurative art » **abstract art**

non-flam » **safety film**

nonjurors Those who refused to swear an oath of loyalty to William III and Mary II in 1689, since to do so would infringe the divine right of monarchical succession. Most were clerics, including Archbishop William Sancroft of Canterbury (1617–93), five other bishops, and about 400 clergy. They were deprived of their offices. » William III

nonlinear physics The study of systems in which the response to a stimulus is not directly proportional to the size of the stimulus. For example, when small weights are suspended from a spring, doubling the weight doubles the extension (Hooke's law) and the system is termed linear. If too much weight is added, the extension is not governed by such a simple law: the system is nonlinear. A pendulum undergoing large swings is a nonlinear system. High intensity light, such as laser light, induces nonlinear responses when interacting with atoms. » cavitation; chaos; physics; shock wave

Nono, Luigi (1924–) Italian composer, born in Venice, where he attended the Conservatory. A leading composer of electronic, aleatory, and serial music, he is also a politically committed artist. *Il canto sospeso* (1955–6, The Suspended Song), based on the letters of victims of wartime oppression, brought him to international notice. » aleatory music; electronic music; serialism

non-objective art » **abstract art**

Nonpartisan League An organization of farmers, founded in 1915 in N Dakota and spreading across the N wheat belt. Quasi-socialist, the League advocated public ownership of public utilities. It declined after 1920, in part because of opposition to involvement in World War 1.

Non-Proliferation Treaty (NPT) A treaty signed in 1968 by the USA, Soviet Union, UK, and an open-ended list of over 100 other countries. It seeks to limit the spread of nuclear weapons by restricting their transfer by the signatories, and for non-nuclear weapon states to pursue only peaceful uses of nuclear energy. » nuclear weapons

non-renewable resources Resources (ie objects of material or economic use to society, such as minerals, timber, and fish) which have evolved or formed over such long time periods that their exploitation is not sustainable. They cannot be used without danger of exhaustion because of the timescale needed for new stocks to form. Examples include fossil fuel deposits (coal, oil, gas) and mineral deposits (iron, gold). Some non-renewable resources can be recycled (eg metallic ores). » fossil fuel; recycling; renewable resources

nonsense verse Verse which is written in defiance of sense and logic to satisfy the ear and the spirit rather than the intelligence. Edward Lear (1812–88) wrote famous examples, as did Lewis Carroll in the two *Alice* books. » Carroll; Lear, Edward; limerick

non-sporting dog A category of domestic dog; name used for breeds bred as pets/companions (except very small such breeds, which are called **toy dogs**); includes dogs formerly bred for sport (eg bulldog, some poodles); sometimes includes **working dogs** (eg collies). » bulldog; collie; dog; Pekingese; Pomeranian; poodle; silky terrier; sporting dog

nonverbal communication (NVC) Those forms of interpersonal communication beyond the spoken or written word; often referred to as body language. The messages communicated may be deliberate (eg winking or bowing), or unintentional (eg blushing or shivering). Cultural codes largely determine what meaning, if any, there is in a facial expression, gesture, or posture. » kinesics; proxemics

non-woven fabrics Fabrics constructed from sheets of fibres, with or without fibre orientation, by stitching, glueing, or otherwise bonding the fibres together. Such non-woven fabrics are widely used as low-cost or disposable products, such as curtaining, medical textiles, and cleaning cloths.

noosphere [nohuhsfeer] A term associated with the philosophical theology of Teilhard de Chardin, referring to the moment of 'threshold of consciousness' reached in the increasingly complex evolution of the cosmos. After this point, the evolutionary process may be consciously directed. » evolution; Teilhard de Chardin; theology

Nootka An American Indian group of the Northwest Pacific Coast, on the W side of Vancouver I. They were famous as whalers, using dugout canoes and harpoons, and became wealthy during the late 18th-c through the fur trade. » American Indians; Northwest Coast Indians

Nor-wester » **Föhn/Foehn wind**

noradrenaline (UK) [naw(r)**adren**alin]/**norepinephrine** (US) [naw(r)uhpi**nef**rin] A chemical substance (a catecholamine) which functions in many animals as a neurotransmitter in the sympathetic nerves and brain, released (in association with adrenaline) from the adrenal medulla. Its widespread actions include cardiac stimulation, blood vessel constriction, and the relaxation of the bronchioles and gastro-intestinal tract. Within the brain, it is involved in the regulation of body temperature, food and water intake, and cardiovascular and respiratory control. » adrenaline; catecholamine; neurotransmitter

Norbertines » **Premonstratensians**

Nordenskjöld, (Nils) Adolf Erik, Baron [**naw**duhnsherl] (1832–1901) Swedish-Finnish Arctic navigator, born in Helsinki. Educated at Helsinki, he moved to Sweden in 1858. He made several expeditions to Spitsbergen, and accomplished (1878–9) the navigation of the Northeast Passage, from the Atlantic to the Pacific along the N coast of Asia. He died at Dalbyö. » Northeast Passage

Nordic Relating to N Europe's Germanic peoples, notably Scandinavians. Typical individuals are tall and long-headed, with blue eyes, and pale skin and hair. » race

Nördliche Kalkalpen [**noed**likhuh kal**kal**pen] Mountain range of the E Alps in C Austria, rising to 2 995 m/9 826 ft at Hoher Dachstein. » Alps

norepinephrine » **noradrenaline**

Norfolk, Duke of » **Howard, Thomas**

Norfolk (UK) [**naw**fuhk] pop (1987e) 736 200; area 5 368 sq km/ 2 072 sq ml. Flat, arable county in E England, divided into seven districts; low-lying, with fens in W; Norfolk Broads in E; drained by Yare, Ouse, Waveney, and Bure Rivers; county town, Norwich; other chief towns King's Lynn and Great Yarmouth, a major resort and fishing port; offshore natural gas; agriculture, turkeys, fishing, tourism; Grime's Graves (Neolithic flint mines), Sandringham royal residence, Shrine of Our Lady of Walsingham, Halvergate Marshes wildlife preserve. » Norwich

Norfolk (USA) 36°51N 76°17W, pop (1980) 266 979. Seaport and independent city, SE Virginia, USA, on the Elizabeth R; settled, 1682; city status, 1845; centre of fighting in the American Revolution and the Civil War; largest city in the state; airfield; railway; Norfolk State College (1935); headquarters of the US Atlantic Fleet, largest naval base in the world; shipbuilding, automobiles, chemicals machinery, trade in coal, grain, tobacco, timber, vegetables; Chrysler Museum, Douglas MacArthur Memorial, Hampton Roads Naval Museum, Botanical Gardens; Azalea Festival (Apr). » American Civil War; American Revolution; Virginia

Norfolk Island 29°04S 167°57E, pop (1981) 2175; area 35 sq km/ 13 sq ml; length 8 km/5 ml. Fertile, hilly island in the W Pacific Ocean, 1 488 km/925 ml NE of Sydney, Australia; a British penal settlement in 1788–1806 and 1826–55; many people from the Pitcairn Is transferred here, 1856; an Australian external territory since 1913, governed by the Norfolk Island Legislative Assembly, and represented in Australia by an Administrator appointed by the Governor-General; English and Tahitian spoken; postage stamps, tourism. » Australia [i]; Pacific Ocean

Noriega, Manuel (Antonio) (1939-) The ruling force behind the Panamanian presidents (1983–9), he had been recruited by the CIA in the late 1960s, and supported by the US government until 1987. Alleging his involvement in drug trafficking, the US authorities ordered his arrest in 1989: 13 000 US troops invaded Panama to support the 12 000 already there. He surrendered in January 1990 after taking refuge for 10 days in the Vatican nunciature, and was taken to the USA for trial.

norm-referenced test A test which compares candidates with each other, usually spreading marks over a normal distribution, with most in the middle and few at each extreme. Most conventional tests which give percentages of A to E grades are of this kind. » criterion-referenced test

Norma (Lat 'level') A small S hemisphere constellation. » constellation; RR9

Norman architecture The form of architecture prevalent in 11th-c and 12th-c England, corresponding to the European Romanesque. The most notable example is Durham Cathedral (1093–1133). » Gothic/Romanesque architecture

Norman Conquest A fundamental watershed in English political and social history, though some of its consequences are much debated. It not only began the rule of a dynasty of Norman kings (1066–1154), but entailed the virtual replacement of the Anglo-Saxon nobility by Normans, Bretons, and Flemings, many of whom retained lands in N France. Moreover, between 1066 and 1144 England and Normandy were normally united under one king-duke, and the result was the formation of a single cross-Channel state. The Angevin conquest of Normandy (1144–5) and takeover of England (1154) ensured that England's fortunes would continue to be linked with France, even after the French annexation of Normandy in 1204. » Angevins; Domesday Book; Hastings, Battle of; Henry I (of England); Hundred Years' War; Stephen; William I/II (of England)

Normandy, Fr **Normandie** Former duchy and province in NW France, along the littoral of the English Channel between Brittany and French Flanders; now occupying the regions of Haute-Normandie and Basse-Normandie; leading state in Middle Ages; William Duke of Normandy conquered England in 1066; focus of English–French dispute in 12th–14th-c, until became part of France in 1449; scene of Allied invasion, 1944; fertile agricultural area; sheep, dairy farming, flax, fruit. » Normandy Campaign; William I

Normandy Campaign (1944) A World War 2 campaign which began on D-Day (6 Jun 1944). Allied forces under the command of General Eisenhower began the liberation of W Europe from Germany by landing on the Normandy coast between the Orne R and St Marcouf. Artificial harbours were constructed along a strip of beach so that armoured vehicles and heavy guns could be unloaded. Heavy fighting ensued for three weeks, before Allied troops captured Cherbourg (27 Jun). Tanks broke through the German defences, and Paris was liberated (25 Aug), followed by the liberation of Brussels (2 Sep), and the crossing of the German frontier (12 Sep). » D-Day; Eisenhower; World War 2

Normans By the early 11th-c, a label (derived from 'Northmen', ie Vikings) applied to all the people inhabiting Normandy, a duchy (and later province) in N France, though probably only a small element was actually of Scandinavian descent. During the second half of the 11th-c and the first decade of the 12th-c, their achievements, especially as conquerors, were remarkable. They completed the conquest and aristocratic colonization of England and a large part of Wales, established a kingdom in S Italy and Sicily, and founded the Norman principality of Antioch. They also fought against the Muslims in Spain and settled peacefully in Scotland. » Bohemond I; David I; Guiscard; Norman Conquest; Rollo; Vikings

Norns In Norse mythology, the equivalent of the Fates, three sisters who sit under the tree Yggdrasil and spin the web of Destiny, including that of individual human beings. Even Odin cannot unpick the web of the Norns. Their names are Urd (who knows the past), Verlandi (the present), and Skuld (the future). They also water the principal root of the world-tree. » Odin; Parcae; Yggdrasil

North, Frederick, 8th Lord North (1732–92) British statesman and Prime Minister (1770–82), born and died in London. He became a Lord of the Treasury (1759) and Chancellor of the Exchequer (1767), and as Prime Minister brought George III a period of political stability. He was widely criticized both for failing to avert the Declaration of Independence by the N American colonies (1776) and for failing to defeat them in the subsequent war (1776–83). He annoyed the King by resigning in 1782, then formed a coalition with his former Whig opponent, Fox (1783), but it did not survive royal hostility. After this coalition was dismissed (1783), he remained an opposition politician until his death. » American Revolution; Fox, Charles James; George III

North, Sir Thomas (?1535–?1601) English translator, born in London. A lawyer, diplomat, and soldier, he is known for his translation of Plutarch's *Lives of the noble Grecians and Romans* (1579), which Shakespeare used in many of his plays. He was knighted c.1597. » Plutarch; Shakespeare [i]

North African Campaign (1940–3) A campaign fought during World War 2 between Allied and Axis troops. After an initial Italian invasion of Egypt, Italian forces were driven back deep into Libya, and Rommel was sent to N Africa with the specially trained Afrika Corps to stem a further Italian retreat. The British were driven back to the Egyptian border, though they defended Tobruk. They counter-attacked late in 1941, and fighting continued the following year, with Rommel once more gaining the initiative. In October, British troops under Montgomery defeated Rommel at the Battle of El Alamein, and drove the German troops W once more. In February 1943, the Germans attacked US troops in Tunisia, were driven back, and finally 250 000 Axis troops, half of them German, were caught in a pincer movement by Allied forces advancing from E and W. » Afrika Corps; El Alamein, Battle of; Axis Powers; Montgomery, Viscount; Rommel

North America Third largest continent, extending 9 600 km/6 000 ml from 70°30N to 15°N; area c.24 million sq km/9¼ million sq ml; separated from Asia by the Bering Strait; bounded by the Beaufort Sea (NW), Arctic Ocean (N), Baffin Bay and Davis Strait (NE), Atlantic Ocean (E), and Pacific Ocean (W); includes Canada, USA, and Mexico; numerous islands, including Baffin I, Newfoundland, and the West Indies; ranges include the Rocky Mts, Alaska Range (including Mt McKinley, highest point), and Appalachian Mts; major lake system, the Great Lakes; major rivers include the Mississippi, Missouri, Rio Grande, and St Lawrence. » Canada [i]; McKinley, Mount; Mexico [i]; United States of America [i]

North Atlantic Treaty Organization » **NATO**

North Cape, Norwegian **Nordkapp** 71°10N 25°48E. Cape on N Magerøy I, N Norway; considered to be the most northerly point of Europe. » Norway [i]

North Carolina pop (1987e) 6 413 000; area 136 407 sq km/52 669 sq ml. State in SE USA, divided into 100 counties; the 'Tar Heel State' or 'Old North State'; unsuccessful settlement on Roanoke I in the 1580s; part of the Carolina grant given by Charles II, 1663; named North Carolina 1691; a royal province, 1729; twelfth of the original 13 states to ratify the Constitution, 1789; withdrew from the Union after the Declaration of Mecklenburg, 1861; slavery abolished, 1865; re-admitted to the Union, 1868; capital, Raleigh; other major cities Charlotte, Greensboro, Winston-Salem, Durham; bounded E by the Atlantic Ocean; crossed by the Roanoke and Yadkin (becomes the Pee Dee) Rivers; highest point Mt Mitchell (2 037 m/6 683 ft); a chain of coastal islands with constantly shifting sand dunes, enclosing several lagoons; a major tourist area; flat, swampy, mainland coastal strip; low land gives way to the rolling hills of the Piedmont; fast-flowing rivers provide hydroelectric power for manufacturing industries; in the W the Blue Ridge and Great Smoky Mts; four national forests; 40% of all US tobacco; cotton, silk goods, synthetic fibres, furniture, electrical machinery, chemicals; poultry, corn, soybeans, peanuts, hogs; feldspar, mica, lithium. » Raleigh (North Carolina); United States of America [i]; RR39

North Dakota [da**koh**ta] pop (1987e) 672 000; area 183 111 sq km/70 702 sq ml. State in NC USA, divided into 53 counties; 'Sioux State', 'Flickertail State'; became part of USA in the Louisiana Purchase, 1803; included in Dakota Territory, 1861; separated from South Dakota to become the 39th state admitted to the Union, 1889; capital, Bismarck; other chief cities Fargo, Grand Forks, Minot; sparsely populated; crossed by the Missouri R; the Red R follows the E state border; highest point White Butte (1 069 m/3 507 ft); semi-arid conditions in the W; cultivation possible only in river valleys, rest of the land covered in short prairie grasses, where cattle are grazed; E region a flat fertile plain, covered almost entirely by crops, chiefly spring wheat, barley, sunflowers, and flaxseed (nation's leading producer of all these crops); major cattle state; oil (NW) and lignite coal (W); processed foods and machinery; several Indian reservations. » Bismarck (USA); Louisiana Purchase; United States of America [i]; RR39

North Downs Way Long-distance footpath in S England; length 227 km/141 ml; follows the crest of the North Downs from Farnham to Dover. » Downs

North German Confederation The state system and constitutional arrangement created in 1866 by Bismarck, Chancellor of Prussia, following the Prussian defeat of Austria and the dissolution of the German Confederation. Utterly dominated by Prussia, the new Confederation was itself dissolved with the creation of the German Empire in 1871. » Austro-Prussian War; Bismarck; German Confederation; Prussia

North India, Church of A Church established in Nagpur in 1970 by the union of six different, originally missionary churches in India, including the Anglicans, United Church of North India, Methodists, Baptists, Brethren, and Disciples of Christ. Its constitution combines episcopal and conciliar government. » Christianity; ecumenism; episcopacy

North Island pop (1981) 2 322 989; area 114 834 sq km/44 326 sq ml. The smaller but more densely populated of the two major islands of New Zealand; separated from South Island by the Cook Strait; irregularly shaped with a long peninsula projecting NW; several mountain ranges; highest volcanic mountain, Ruapehu (2 797 m/9 176 ft); contains the largest of New Zealand's lakes, L Taupo (606 sq km/234 sq ml); many hot springs, NC; fertile plains in the coastal areas; chief towns include Wellington, Auckland, Napier, Hastings, New Plymouth, Palmerston North; wine, farming, horse breeding, fruit, coal, natural gas; spas and health resorts; Maoris mostly live on North Island. » Maoris; New Zealand [i]

North Korea » **Korea, North** [i]

North Pole » **Poles**

North Sea area 520 000 sq km/201 000 sq ml. Arm of the Atlantic Ocean between continent of Europe (E) and UK (W), from Shetland Is (N) to Straits of Dover (S); bounded by the UK, Norway, Denmark, the Netherlands, Germany, Belgium, and France; length c.950 km/600 ml; maximum width 650 km/400 ml; depths of 660 m/2 165 ft near Norwegian coast; generally shallow, lying on wide continental shelf; irregular sea floor, shallowed by banks running across from Yorkshire coast (eg Dogger Bank); important fishing grounds; territorial disputes led to the Cod Wars of the 1960s and 1970s between Iceland and UK; extensive offshore oil and gas exploitation; some land reclamation in the Dutch polder area; high tides sometimes cause flooding in E England and Netherlands. » Atlantic Ocean

North Sea oil Oil and gas deposits in the sedimentary rocks below the North Sea, first discovered in 1969 in Norwegian waters (the Ekofisk field) and in 1975 in the UK sector. The sea-bed is divided into national territories, with UK and Norway controlling most of the oilfields. By 1981 the UK had become a net exporter of crude oil. Reserves are estimated at 12 billion barrels. » North Sea; oil (earth sciences)

North York Moors National park in North Yorkshire and Cleveland, England; area 1 432 sq km/553 sq ml; established in 1952; follows the coast N of Scarborough to Hambleton Hills (W); headlands and sandy beaches, open moorland and wooded valleys; Mount Grace Priory, Rievaulx Abbey, Byland Abbey. » Cleveland (UK); Yorkshire, North

North Yorkshire » **Yorkshire, North**

Northampton 52°14N 0°54W, pop (1981) 155 694. County town in Northampton district, Northamptonshire, C England; on R Nene, SE of Coventry and 97 km/60 ml NW of London; originally a Saxon town; Thomas à Becket tried here in 1164; destroyed by fire in 1675; designated a 'new town' in 1968; railway; footwear, leather goods, cosmetics, vehicle parts; 12th-c Church of the Holy Sepulchre, one of four round

churches in England; All Saints' Church and the Church of St Peter. » Northamptonshire

Northamptonshire pop (1987e) 561 800; area 2 367 sq km/ 914 sq ml. Agricultural county in C England, divided into seven districts; drained by the Welland and Nene Rivers; county town, Northampton; cereals, livestock, sugar beet, potatoes, iron mining, shoemaking, printing, engineering. » England [i]; Northampton

Northcliffe, Lord » Harmsworth, Alfred

Northeast Passage A shipping route through the S Arctic Ocean along the N coast of Europe and Asia, connecting the Atlantic and Pacific Oceans. Its crossing was first attempted in 1550, but it was not successfully travelled until 1878–9. A regular shipping lane is maintained by Russia.

Northern Ireland, also **Ulster** pop (1981) 1 481 959; area 14 120 sq km/5 450 sq ml (including 663 sq km/256 sq ml of inland water). Constituent division of the United Kingdom of Great Britain and Northern Ireland, traditionally divided into six counties, now 26 districts; occupies the NE part of Ireland, centred on Lough Neagh; Mourne Mts in the SE; capital, Belfast; other chief towns, Derry, Lisburn, Ballymena, Armagh; timezone GMT; chief religions, Roman Catholicism (28%), Presbyterianism (23%), Church of Ireland (19%); agriculture, linen, shipbuilding, textiles, engineering, chemicals, service industries; economy badly affected by the sectarian troubles since 1969.

History and government. Separate parliament established in 1920, with a 52-member House of Commons and a 26-member Senate; Protestant majority in the population, generally supporting political union with Great Britain; many of the Roman Catholic minority look for union with the Republic of Ireland; violent conflict between the communities broke out in 1969,

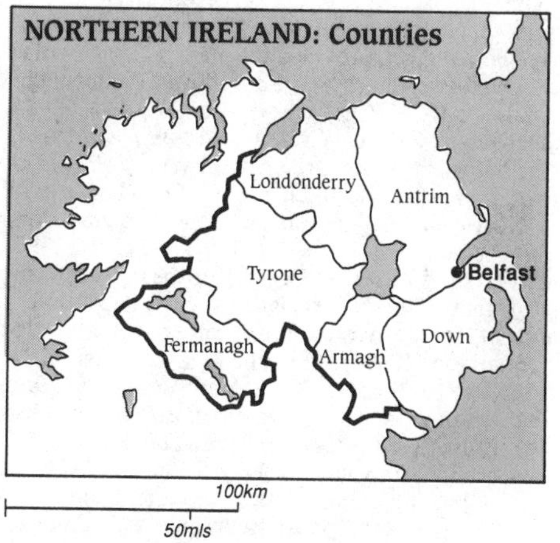

leading to the establishment of a British army peace-keeping force; sectarian murders and bombings continued both within and outside the province, notably in London and (in the late 1980s) in British military bases in Europe; as a result of the disturbances, parliament was abolished in 1973; powers are now vested in the UK Secretary of State for Northern Ireland; formation of a 78-member Assembly, 1973; replaced by a Constitutional Convention, 1975; Assembly re-formed in 1982, but Nationalist members did not take their seats; under the 1985 Anglo-Irish agreement, the Republic of Ireland was given a consultative role in the government of Northern Ireland; all Northern Ireland MPs in the British Parliament resigned in protest, 1986; the agreement continued to attract controversy in the late 1980s. » Anglo-Irish Agreement; Belfast; INLA; IRA; Irish Republic [i]; Stormont; RR41

northern lights » aurora

Northern Territory pop (1986) 158 400; area 1 346 200 sq km/ 520 000 sq ml. One of the three mainland territories of Australia, covering about a sixth of the continent; part of New South Wales, 1824; annexed by South Australia, 1863; transferred to Federal Government control, 1911; achieved self-government, 1978; bordered N by the Arafura Sea and the Gulf of Carpentaria; mainly within the tropics; from Arnhem Land in the N the land rises S to the Macdonnell Ranges, reaching 1 524 m/5 000 ft at Mt Liebig; good pasture land in the N (Barkly Tableland), largely flat and arid in the S (Simpson Desert); many islands off the N coast (notably Groote Eylandt, Melville and Bathurst Is); Ayers Rock in Uluru national park; major rivers in the N the Victoria, Daly, South Alligator, East Alligator, McArthur, Roper; rivers in the interior flow only after heavy rain; capital and chief port, Darwin; chief towns Alice Springs, Katherine, Nhulunbuy; beef cattle, fishing, minerals (bauxite, bismuth, uranium, gold, manganese, copper), oil, gas; many Aboriginal settlements; Aboriginal art found throughout the area; state holidays: May Day, Picnic Day (Aug). » Aborigines; Australia [i]; Ayers Rock; Darwin

Northern War » Great Northern War

northing A grid line which runs W to E on a map, but which is numbered northwards. It is related to the **easting**, a grid line which runs N to S, and which is numbered eastwards. The northing number associated with a place is always given after the number of the easting when citing a grid reference. » grid reference; map; National Grid Reference System

Northumberland, Dukes of » Percy

Northumberland pop (1987e) 300 900; area 5 032 sq km/ 1 942 sq ml. County in NE England, divided into six districts; bounded N by Scotland, E by the North Sea; Pennines in the W; rises in the N to 755 m/2 477 ft at The Cheviot; drained by the Tyne, Blyth, Wansbeck, Coquet, Aln, and Till Rivers; Holy I and the Farne Is lie off the coast; Kielder Water (artificial lake, 1982); county town, Morpeth; chief towns include Berwick-upon-Tweed, Ashington, Blyth, Alnwick; sheep, barley, oats, fishing, forestry, coal; many Roman remains, especially Hadrian's Wall; castles at Alnwick and Bamburgh. » England [i]; Morpeth

Northumberland National Park National park in NE England; area 1 031 sq km/398 sq ml; established in 1956; bounded S by Hadrian's Wall and N by the Cheviot Hills. » Hadrian's Wall

Northumbria The largest kingdom of the Anglo-Saxon heptarchy. In the 7th-c it established a broad dominance in Britain both N and S of the Humber, while in the 8th-c the Northumbrian monasteries gained a European-wide reputation for sanctity and learning. The kingdom came to an end in 876, and by the 12th-c Northumbria was equivalent to the earldom or county of Northumberland. » Anglo-Saxons; Edwin, St

Northwest Coast Indians N American Indians living along the Pacific coastline from Alaska to NW California, consisting of a number of different groups, who were wealthy, hierarchical, and had highly developed artistic traditions. They included the Haidas, Tsimshians, Kwakiutls, Nootkas, Tlingits, and Yuroks. One of their famous ceremonial institutions was the potlatch. Many died in the conflict with White settlers and traders, and their way of life was eroded. » Haida; Hupa; Kwakiutl; Nootka; potlatch; Tlingit; totem pole

Northwest Company A trading partnership based in Montreal and Fort William, Canada, from the 1780s to 1821. It combined Scottish/Loyalist management with French-Canadian fieldworkers, and competed fiercely for the fur resources of the British North West along a chain of land forts. The 'Nor'Westers' merged into the Hudson's Bay Company in 1821. » Hudson's Bay Company

Northwest Frontier pop (1981) 11 061 000; area 74 521 sq km/28 765 sq ml. Federal province in Pakistan; bounded W and S by Afghanistan and N by India; crossed by the R Indus; linked to Afghanistan by the Khyber Pass, and thus of strategic importance; inhabited mainly by the Pathans, renowned for their warlike character; capital, Peshawar; livestock, grains, tobacco, fruit. » Khyber Pass; Pakistan [i]; Peshawar

Northwest Ordinance » **Ordinance of 1787**

Northwest Passage A route through the S Arctic Ocean, Arctic Archipelago, N Canada, and along the N coast of Alaska. From the 16th-c attempts were made to find it, but not until 1903–6 was it first traversed by Amundsen. The first commercial ship, an ice-breaking tanker, completed the route in 1969. » Amundsen; Franklin, John; Frobisher

Northwest Rebellion A rebellion in 1885 along the N and S branches of the Saskatchewan R in Canada. Continuing Dominion neglect of Métis complaints lingering from the Red River Rebellion led to the return from exile in Montana of Louis Riel. Métis forces clashed with North-West Mounted Police at Duck Lake. Dominion troops were hurried to the region along the newly-completed Canadian Pacific Railway, where they confronted and defeated the Métis guerrillas under Riel and Gabriel Dumont, along with their native allies, the Cree, led by Big Bear and Poundmaker. Riel was captured and hanged at Regina. The event aggravated French–English tensions in the rest of Canada. » Canadian Pacific Railway; Métis; Red River Rebellion; Riel, Louis

Northwest Territories pop (1981) 45 471; area 3 426 320 sq km/1 322 902 sq ml. Canadian territory extending over the N of Canada, consisting of the Arctic islands, the islands in Hudson and Ungava Bays, and the land N of 60°N, between Hudson Bay and the Yukon territory; sparsely populated, two-thirds nomadic Indians and Eskimos; capital, Yellowknife (since 1967); mining (lead, zinc, gold), handicrafts, fur products, fishing, tourism, oil; land held by the Hudson's Bay Company (Rupert's Land and North West Territory) changed to the present name on entering Canadian federation, 1870; present form of administration adopted, 1905; governed by a commissioner and an elected 24-member Legislative Assembly. » Canada [i]; Hudson's Bay Company; Yellowknife

Norway, Norwegian **Norge**, official name **Kingdom of Norway**, Norwegian **Kongeriket Norge** pop (1990e) 4 246 000; area 323 895 sq km/125 023 sq ml. NW European kingdom, occupying the W part of the Scandinavian peninsula, divided into 19 counties (*fylker*); bounded N by the Arctic Ocean, E by Sweden, Finland, and Russia, W by the North Sea, and S by the Skagerrak; capital, Oslo; chief towns, Bergen, Trondheim, Stavanger, Kristiansand; timezone GMT + 1; official language, Norwegian, in the varieties of Bokmål and Nynorsk; most of the population of Nordic descent; Lapp minority in far N; chief religion, Evangelical-Lutheran (95%); unit of currency, the krone of 100 øre; a mountainous country; Kjölen Mts form the N part of the boundary with Sweden; Jotunheimen range in SC Norway; extensive plateau regions, especially in SW and C; much of the interior over 1 500 m/5 000 ft; numerous lakes, the largest being L Mjøsa (368 sq km/142 sq ml); major rivers include the Glåma, Dramselv, Lågen; irregular coastline with many small islands and long deep fjords; the two largest island groups (NW) are Lofoten and Vesterålen; Arctic winter climate in the interior highlands, with snow, strong winds, and severe frosts; comparatively mild conditions on coast; rainfall heavy on W coast; average annual rainfall at Bergen, 1 958 mm/77 in; colder winters and warmer, drier summers in S lowlands; a united kingdom achieved by St Olaf in the 11th-c, whose successor, Cnut, brought Norway under Danish rule; united with Sweden and Denmark, 1389; annexed by Sweden as a reward for assistance against Napoleon, 1814; growing nationalism resulted in independence, 1905; declared neutrality in

both World Wars, but occupied by Germany 1940–4; a limited, hereditary monarchy; government led by a prime minister; parliament (*Storting*) comprises an upper house (*Lagting*) and a lower house (*Odelsting*); members elected every four years; economy based on the extraction and processing of raw materials, using plentiful hydroelectric power; oil, natural gas, paper and paper products, industrial chemicals, basic metals, shipbuilding, engineering, food processing, fishing, tourism; less than 3% of the land is under cultivation; barley, hay, oats; area covered with productive forests was 21% in 1985. » Canute; Lapland; Norwegian literature; Oslo; Vikings; RR26 national holidays; RR57 political leaders

Norway spruce The most common species of spruce, native to Europe and planted on a vast commercial scale. It is a source of timber, pitch, spruce beer, and, in Britain, Christmas trees. (*Picea abies*. Family: *Pinaceae*.) » spruce

Norwegian » **Germanic languages; Scandinavian languages**

Norwegian literature The ballads, folk songs, and legends of the later Middle Ages, taken by Norwegian colonists to Iceland, provided the materials for the great sagas in Old Norse. Copenhagen provided the literary focus until the 18th-c; modern Norwegian literature followed independence from Denmark in 1814. Poet Henryk Wergeland (1808–45) and his novelist sister Camilla Collett (1813–95) expressed the new nationalist spirit, where Johan Welhaven (1807–73) looked to former links. Henryk Ibsen (1828–1906) began with themes from Norwegian legend, but moved to contemporary subjects for his best-known plays (eg *Hedda Gabler*, 1890), as did Björnstjerne Björnson (1832–1910); these transformed European drama. The Norwegian novel of this time was also important, in the hands of Alexander Kielland (1849–1906) and Jonas Lie (1833–1908). The greatest name in Norwegian literature since then is Knut Hamsun (1859–1952), whose vitalist fiction anticipated 20th-c themes. But novelists such as Sigrid Undset (1882–1949), Olav Duun (1876–1939), Johan Borgen (1902–) and latterly Dag Solstad (1941–), and poets such as Olaf Bull (1883–1933) and the libertarian socialist Arnulf Overland (1889–1968) continue a distinguished tradition. » Björnson; Danish/Icelandic/Swedish literature; Ibsen; Hamsun; Norway [i]; saga; Undset; Wergeland

Norwegian Sea N Atlantic sea bounded by NW coast of Norway and E coast of Iceland; depths in the Norwegian Basin reach 1 240 m/4 068 ft, and in the Jan Mayen Fracture Zone, close to the continental shelf, 2 740 m/8 989 ft; generally ice-free because of influence of warm N Atlantic Drift. » Atlantic Ocean

Norwich [**no**rich] 52°38N 1°18E, pop (1981) 122 890. County town in Norwich district, Norfolk, E England; near the confluence of the Yare and Wensum Rivers, 160 km/99 ml NE of London; provincial centre for the largely agricultural East Anglia; major textile centre in 16th–17th-c; University of East Anglia (1963); North Sea reached via R Yare and Great Yarmouth (32 km/20 ml E); railway; commerce, engineering, printing, chemicals, electrical goods, silk, foodstuffs, trade in grain and livestock; Norman cathedral (1096), Church of St Peter Mancroft (1430–55). » Norfolk

Norwich School A group of provincial English landscape painters, in oil and watercolour, working in Norwich 1803–34. Leading masters were Cotman and Crome. » Cotman; Crome; English art; landscape painting; school (art)

nose The protrusion from the front of the face above the mouth and below the eyes. Part of the respiratory tract, it consists of an external part (with a skeleton of bone and cartilage) and an inner cavity. The nasal cavity has a large surface area, because of the presence of scrolls of bone (the *conchae*) projecting into it from the side walls. It is mainly covered with respiratory epithelium, except in its most superior part where the epithelium is specialized to subserve the sense of smell. The functions of the nasal cavity are olfaction (smell) and changing the nature of the inspired air. Various glands moisten the air, and produce a sticky substance which traps inspired particles (afterwards conveyed by cilia towards the nasopharynx for swallowing). The rich vascular network also warms the air. Because of this network, the nose has a tendency to bleed profusely if it is hit. » epithelium; pharynx; respiration; sinus

noseeum [nohs**ee**uhm] » **biting midge**

Nostradamus or **Michel de Notredame** (1503–66) French astrologer, born at St Remy, Provence. He became a doctor of medicine in 1529, and after practising in several cities, set himself up as a prophet c.1547. His *Centuries* of predictions in rhymed quatrains (1555–8), expressed generally in obscure and enigmatical terms, brought him a great reputation. Charles IX on his accession appointed him physician-in-ordinary. He died at Salon.

note-cluster In music, a group of adjacent notes, especially on a keyboard instrument, sounded together for their percussive or sonorous effect. Clusters are associated with some 20th-c composers, such as Cowell and Bartók, but they appear also in the sonatas of Scarlatti. » harmony; keyboard instrument; Bartók; Cowell; Scarlatti, Domenico

nothosaur [**no**thuhsaw] A long-necked, marine reptile; flourished during the Triassic period, but extinct by the early Jurassic period; limbs well adapted for swimming. (Order: *Sauropterygia*. Suborder: *Nothosauria*.) » Jurassic period; reptile; Triassic period

notochord [**noh**tuhkawd] A rod-like structure which extends almost the entire length of the body in larvae and some adult chordates. It lies behind the gut, but below the nerve cord, providing flexible support for the body. It is replaced by the vertebral column in most vertebrates, but retained throughout life in certain marine animals (eg cephalochordates, lampreys). » Chordata; lamprey; larva; vertebral column

Notre Dame (de Paris) [**no**truh **dam** duh pa**ree**] An early Gothic cathedral on the Ile de la Cité in Paris. It was commissioned by Maurice de Sully, Bishop of Paris, in 1159 and constructed over a period of two centuries (1163–1345). The tremendous weight of its masonry has caused it to subside several feet. » cathedral; Paris [i]

Nottingham, Anglo-Saxon **Snotingaham** or **Notingeham** 52°58N 1°10W, pop (1981) 272 141, urban area 598 867. County town in Nottingham district, Nottinghamshire, C England; on the R Trent, 200 km/124 ml NNW of London; university (1948); founded by the Danes; became a city in 1897; Civil War started here in 1642; connected to both the Irish and North Seas by canal; railway; cigarettes, lace (former major centre), textiles, tanning, engineering, bicycles, furniture, typewriters, printing, pharmaceuticals; 17th-c Nottingham Castle, 15th-c St Mary's Church; Theatre Royal, Playhouse; nearby, Newstead Abbey (home of Byron) and Eastwood (home of D H Lawrence); Goose Fair during the first week in Oct. » Byron; Lawrence, D H; Nottinghamshire

Nottinghamshire pop (1987e) 1 007 800; area 2 164 sq km/835 sq ml. County in the R Trent basin of C England, divided into eight districts; Pennines in W, remains of Sherwood Forest in SW; county town, Nottingham; chief towns include Worksop, Newark, Mansfield; arable and dairy farming, coal, gypsum, limestone, textiles, chemicals. » Dukeries, the; England [i]; Nottingham; Robin Hood

Notungulata [notuhngyoo**lah**ta] A large order of extinct, S American, plant-eating mammals, known from the late Palaeocene to the Pleistocene epochs; typically with short skulls; ear structure unique in having two large chambers; third digit of feet forming main axis. » herbivore; mammal [i]; Palaeocene/Pleistocene epoch

Nouadhibou [nooadee**boo**], Fr **Port Étienne** 20°54N 17°00W, pop (1976) 21 961. Seaport capital of Dakhlet-Nouadhibou region, Mauritania, at N end of the Bay of Levrier; Mauritania's main seaport; linked by rail to the iron ore mines near Zouîrât; airport; iron ore trade, fish processing and refrigeration, industrial gas. » Mauritania [i]

Nouakchott [**nwak**shot] 18°09N 15°58W, pop (1982e) 150 000. Capital of Mauritania, near the Atlantic coast; harbour 7 km/4 ml SSW; founded on an important caravan route, 1960; airport; salt, cement, insecticides, matches, trade in gums and grains; camel markets. » Mauritania [i]

Nouméa [noo**may**a], formerly **Port de France** 22°16S 166°26E, pop (1983) 60 112. Seaport capital of New Caledonia; capital, 1854; US air base in World War 2; airport; tourism, nickel, chrome, iron, manganese; cathedral. » New Caledonia

nouveau roman [**noo**voh roh**mã**] (Fr 'new novel') A type of novel written (and theorized) by French novelists of the 1950s in reaction against established fictional forms. The idea was to replace the cloying human perspective with a colder, more objective, less compromised narrative. Writers include Michel Butor, Alain Robbe-Grillet, and Nathalie Sarraute. » Butor; French literature; novel; Realism; Robbe-Grillet; Sarraute

nouvelle cuisine A movement away from the elaborate food of classical cuisine to a simpler, more natural presentation. The approach began in the 1970s, and was given emphasis by the French chef Michel Guérard (1933–). The first consideration is the quality of the fresh produce, with the aim of achieving lightness by using less fat and no flour in sauces. The movement has also been influenced by the Japanese style of food presentation.

Nouvelle Vague The 'New Wave' group of young French film directors of the late 1950s and 1960s, who wished to discard many of the conventional formulae of the current cinema. They used the freedom of light-weight hand-held cameras outside the studio, with innovative story lines and unconventional editing and sound. » cinema

nova In a binary star system near the end of its life, the phenomenon where one star becomes a giant, and its atmosphere spills over to its companion, a white dwarf. A nuclear explosion is triggered on the white dwarf, whose luminosity increases up to 10 000 times (10 magnitudes) for a few months. The phenomenon can recur. » binary star; giant star; white dwarf

Nova Scotia [**noh**va **skoh**sha] pop (1981) 847 442; area 55 490 sq km/21 424 sq ml. Province in SE Canada; boundaries include the Atlantic Ocean (E, S, W), Bay of Fundy (W), Northumberland Strait (N), and Gulf of St Lawrence (NE); includes Cape Breton I to the NE, separated by the Strait of Canso, 3 km/1¾ ml wide, connected by causeway; province linked to the Canadian mainland by the isthmus of Chignecto; deeply indented coastline, low hill ranges, many lakes and small rivers; capital, Halifax; other chief towns, Dartmouth, Sydney, Glace Bay, Truro, New Glasgow; dairy farming, fruit, fishing (especially lobster), timber, coal, gypsum, tin, tourism; probably first visited by Vikings and European fishermen; settled by the

French as Acadia, 1604–5; mainland assigned to England in the Treaty of Utrecht (1713), Cape Breton I remaining French until 1763; many United Empire Loyalists settled here after the American Revolution; Cape Breton I a separate province from 1784, re-incorporated into Nova Scotia, 1820; joined the Canadian federation, 1867; governed by a lieutenant-governor and an elected 52-member House of Assembly. » Acadia; American Revolution; Canada [i]; Cape Breton Island; Halifax

Novalis, pseudonym of **Friedrich Leopold von Hardenberg, Baron** (1772–1801) German Romantic poet, born at Oberwiederstedt, Saxony. He studied law, and became a government auditor at Weissenfels. Known as the 'prophet of Romanticism', he is best known for his *Geistliche Lieder* (1799, Sacred Songs) and *Hymnen an die Nacht* (1800, Hymns to the Night). He died at Weissenfels, Saxony. » German literature; poetry; Romanticism (literature)

Novaya Zemlya [**no**vaya zim**lya**] area 81 279 sq km/31 374 sq ml. Archipelago in the Arctic Ocean, between the Barents Sea (W) and Kara Sea (E), NW Russia; two large islands separated by a narrow strait; numerous offshore islands; length, 960 km/596 ml; glaciated land (N) gives way to tundra lowland (S); an extension of the Ural Mts, rising to heights above 1 000 m/3 000 ft; some settlement on heavily indented W coast; copper, lead, zinc, asphaltite; used for thermonuclear testing. » Russia; Ural Mountains

novel A work of fiction, most often in prose. The term (literally meaning 'new' or 'news') came into general use in the 18th-c to describe that form of fiction, deriving from classical epic and romance but incorporating features from other modes such as autobiography and travel writing, which centred on the life of an individual, as in *Robinson Crusoe* and *Tom Jones*. Satisfying the taste of the new reading public for a personal perspective on familiar and unfamiliar experiences, the novel quickly became the dominant literary form in the West; and such writers as Dickens and George Eliot, Balzac and Zola, Dostoevsky and Tolstoy, helped create the moral and imaginative climate of their age. While retaining its traditional function, in the 20th-c the novel has been developed (some would say destroyed) by persistent experimentation, by (among others) Joyce, Proust, Virginia Woolf, Nabokov, Cortazar, and Calvino. » epic; epistolary/Gothic novel; individualism; literature; novella; roman fleuve; short story

novel proteins Proteins derived from processed or textured vegetable proteins or from bacterial or fungal proteins; also known as **single-cell proteins**. The micro-organisms can be grown on a wide variety of industrial waste products, such as hydrocarbon waste from petroleum, or grain waste from milling; they are then harvested, and their protein isolated for animal or human nutrition. » protein

novella (Ital 'tale', 'news') Originally a short story, as in Boccaccio's *Decameron*. The term is now used to define (if somewhat precariously) a prose fiction which is longer than a short story but shorter than a novel. » novel; short story

Novello, Ivor, originally **David Ivor Davies** (1893–1951) British actor, composer, songwriter, and dramatist, born in Cardiff, Wales. He was educated at Oxford, where he was a chorister. His song 'Keep the Home Fires Burning' was one of the most successful of World War 1. He first appeared on the regular stage in London in 1921, and enjoyed great popularity, his most successful works being the 'Ruritanian' musical plays such as *The Dancing Years* (1939) and *King's Rhapsody* (1949). He died in London.

Novgorod [**nof**guhruht] 58°30N 31°20E, pop (1983) 210 000. Capital city of Novgorodskaya oblast, NW European Russia; on R Volkhov, 6 km/4 ml from L Ilmen; one of the oldest cities in the USSR, known in the 9th-c; badly damaged in World War 2; railway; centre of an important agricultural area; electrical engineering, woodworking, ship repairing, foodstuffs, tourism; St Sophia's Cathedral (1045–50), Dukhov monastery (12th-c); since 1945, major excavations of deep waterlogged deposits, revealing two-storied log cabin houses of the mediaeval town, arranged along timber roadways. » Russia

Novi Sad [**no**vee **saht**], Ger **Neusatz** 45°15N 19°51E, pop (1981) 257 685. Commercial and industrial capital of the autonomous province of Vojvodina, N Serbia republic, Yugoslavia; on R Danube; formerly an important stronghold against the Turks; railway; university (1960); wine, fruit and vegetable trade, leather, textiles, tobacco; Niška Banja health resort nearby; bishop's palace, Petrovaradin castle, cathedral; international agricultural show (May), Danube international rowing regatta (Aug), autumn fair (Oct). » Serbia; Yugoslavia [i]

novocaine A proprietary name for *procaine*, a local anaesthetic. Procaine was first manufactured in 1905 to displace cocaine, whose stimulant and addictive properties were disadvantageous. *Lignocaine* is now more frequently used. » anaesthetics, local

Novosibirsk [novuhsyi**byeersk**], formerly **Novonikolaevsk** 55°00N 83°05E, pop (1989) 1 436 000. River-port capital of Novosibirskaya oblast, S Siberian Russia, on the R Ob; founded, 1893; on the Trans-Siberian Railway; university (1959); leading economic centre of Siberia; Kuznetsk Basin coal and iron deposits nearby; machines, metallurgy, chemicals, foodstuffs. » Russia

Noyes, Alfred (1880–1958) British poet, born in Wolverhampton, Staffordshire. His first book of poetry was completed while studying at Oxford, which he left without taking a degree. His most successful work deals with the sea and the Elizabethan tradition, notably the epic *Drake* (1908). Having married an American, he travelled in the USA, and became visiting professor of poetry at Princeton (1914–23). In 1922 appeared *The Torchbearers*, a panegyric in blank verse on the hitherto comparatively unsung men of science. He died on the Isle of Wight. » English literature; poetry

NSPCC An acronym for the **National Society for the Prevention of Cruelty to Children**, a child welfare society, founded in 1884 as the London Society for the Prevention of Cruelty to Children. The NSPCC has over 200 inspectors in England, Wales, and N Ireland who investigate reports of cruelty to, and neglect of, children. In Scotland, the Royal Scottish Society for the Prevention of Cruelty to Children (also founded in 1884, 60 field workers) performs a similar function.

NTSC National Television Systems Commission, responsible for the coding system for colour television introduced in the USA in 1954, and since then generally adopted throughout the Americas and Japan for all 525-line 60 Hz transmission. The two colour difference signals are 90° out of phase and combined to form the chrominance signal. The colour of the final picture is critically dependent on the correct phase relation being maintained throughout broadcast transmission, and the receiver requires a hue control. » colour television [i]; PAL; SECAM

Nu, U [oo **noo**] (1907–) Burmese statesman and Prime Minister (1948–56, 1957–8, 1960–2), born at Wakema. Educated at Rangoon, he became a teacher, and in 1934 came to prominence through student political movements. Imprisoned by the British for sedition (1940), he was released by the Japanese and served in Ba Maw's puppet administration. In 1946 he became president of the Burmese Constituent Assembly, and the first Prime Minister of the independent Burmese Republic (1948). He was finally overthrown by a military coup in 1962, and imprisoned, but released in 1966. He then lived abroad, organizing resistance to the military regime, but returned to Burma in 1980 to become a Buddhist monk. » Burma [i]

Nubian Desert [**nyoo**bian] area c.400 000 sq km/155 000 sq ml. Desert in NE Sudan; a sandstone plateau between the Red Sea and the R Nile; the ancient state of Nubia occupied the area from the First Cataract of the Nile to Khartoum. » Sudan [i]

Nubian monuments A group of world heritage monuments around L Nasser in Ethiopia, many of which were rescued from flooding during the construction of Aswan High Dam. They include the 13th-c BC temples of Ramses II at Abu Simbel; Philae, the island of sanctuaries, sacred to Isis from the 4th-c BC; Amada, with its temples from the 15th-c and 13th-c BC; Kalabsha, built during the reign of Augustus; the 11th-c monastery of St Simeon; and 11th–12th-c Islamic cemeteries. » Abu Simbel; Aswan High Dam; Augustus; Isis

nuclear disarmament A political movement which emerged soon after the advent of nuclear weapons, demanding their control, the limitation of their spread to non-nuclear weapon states, and their eventual abolition. Although the US and Soviet governments have had some success in reaching arms limitation treaties, such as the Partial Test-Ban Treaty (1963), the Anti-Ballistic Missile Treaty (1972), and the Intermediate range Nuclear Forces (INF) agreement (1987), mass political movements such as the British Campaign for Nuclear Disarmament (CND) have continued to attract support. » Non-Proliferation Treaty; Nuclear Test-Ban Treaty; nuclear weapons

nuclear family » family

nuclear fission The splitting of a heavy atomic nucleus into two approximately equal portions, with the emission of free neutrons and energy; discovered by Italian physicist Enrico Fermi in 1934. Induced fission is initiated by collisions with neutrons. Spontaneous fission is comparatively rare. Fission in uranium and plutonium forms the basic mechanism of nuclear power and atomic bombs. » atomic bomb; chain reaction; Fermi; nuclear physics; nuclear reactor [i]

nuclear fusion The fusing together of two light-weight atomic nuclei, typically isotopes of hydrogen or lithium, having a total rest mass which exceeds that of the products. The mass difference is made up by energy released in the process. To initiate fusion, the reacting species must be brought close enough together so that short-range nuclear forces come into play, as is possible in the high-temperature environments of the Sun and nuclear explosions. Fusion reactors attempt to reproduce such conditions in a controlled way. The chief experimental fusion reactors are the Joint European Torus in the UK, the Tokamak Fusion Test Reactor at Princeton, USA, and JT60 near Tokyo, Japan. » cold fusion; deuterium; hydrogen bomb [i]; Joint European Torus; nuclear physics; plasma (physics); tokamak; tritium

nuclear magnetic resonance (NMR) An analytic technique, important in chemistry, which relies on magnetic resonance involving protons. A sample is subjected to a magnetic field, causing the proton magnetic moments to precess. A variable frequency radio signal is applied, and the spectrum of absorbed frequencies measured. This spectrum reflects the proton's environment, so indicating the sample's structure. NMR is an important imaging technique in medicine, complementary to X-ray imaging. » magnetic moment/resonance; precession; proton

nuclear magnetron » **Bohr magnetron**

nuclear physics The study of the properties and composition of the atomic nucleus. Early nuclear physics experiments include the study of natural radioactivity, and British physicist Ernest Rutherford's demonstration of the existence of the nucleus in 1911. Modern experiments include the study of rapidly rotating 'superdeformed' nuclei, and of dense nuclear matter (quark-gluon plasma) formed by collisions of heavy nuclei. The nucleus is probed using X-rays, neutrons, mesons, and electrons. The applications of nuclear physics include nuclear power, nuclear weapons, and radio-isotopes in medicine. » atomic physics; cross section; nuclear fission/fusion/structure; nucleus (physics); radioactivity; scattering

nuclear power » **nuclear fission/fusion/reactor [i]**

nuclear reactor A device for producing a continuous supply of heat energy from controlled radioactivity. Certain radioactive atomic nuclei, on being struck by neutrons, generate additional neutrons. This is self-sustaining if the speed of the neutrons is not too great. A nuclear reactor therefore has (i) a 'fuel', which may be uranium 235 or 238, or plutonium 239; (ii) a moderator, to control the speed and number of neutrons; and (iii) a heat exchange system, to utilize the heat generated (generally by operating the steam-driven turbines of a conventional electric power station). A **boiling water reactor** uses the cooling water itself as the source of steam for the turbines. In a **pressurized water reactor**, the coolant is water under such pressure that it reaches a high temperature without evaporation, and is used to heat boiler water via a heat exchanger. A **gas-cooled reactor** uses carbon dioxide or some other gas as a coolant, heating turbine water via a heat exchanger. A **fast reactor** has no moderator, and generally uses liquid sodium as a coolant. A **breeder reactor** uses uranium 238 enriched with plutonium 239; it produces more Pu 239, and is the type of reactor used to generate material for atomic weapons. Some nuclear reactors are built and used solely for research purposes. » containment building; meltdown; nucleonics; plutonium; radioactivity; uranium

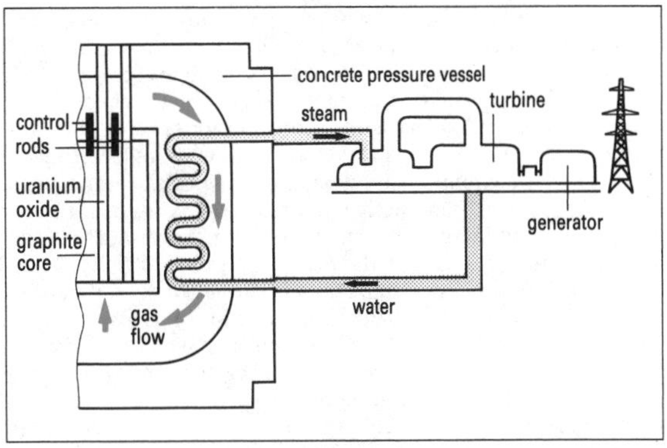

Advanced Gas-cooled Reactor (AGR) – Section through an electricity-generating power station

nuclear structure The structure of the atomic nucleus, composed of protons and neutrons, not necessarily in equal numbers. Often the number of neutrons is larger, especially for the nuclei of heavier elements; many such materials are radioactive as nuclei, with a preponderance of relatively unstable neutrons. The density of all nuclei is approximately the same. Most nuclei have net angular momentum and magnetic moment, and may have excited states with transitions from high to low energy states accompanied by the emission of gamma photons. Certain nuclei having special values of proton number Z and neutron number N (the so-called 'magic numbers') are especially stable, which supports the *shell model* of nuclear structure. Other features of nuclear structure are best understood in terms of a *liquid drop model*, which views the nucleus as a homogenous drop of 'nuclear liquid'. » isotopes; neutron; nuclear physics; nucleus (physics); pion; proton

Nuclear Test-Ban Treaty A 1963 treaty prohibiting the testing of nuclear weapons on or above the surface of the Earth, originally put forward by the USA, USSR, and UK as an indirect means of slowing down the proliferation of countries with nuclear weapons. The impact of the treaty has been somewhat diminished by its boycott by two nuclear nations, France and China. » nuclear disarmament/weapons

nuclear weapons Weapons of mass destruction employing the energy-liberating nuclear phenomena of fission or fusion for their effects. According to their size and the means of delivery, they may be classified as **tactical** short-range weapons for use against enemy battlefield forces; **theatre** medium-range weapons for use against deep military targets; and **strategic** long-range weapons for use against enemy cities and command centres. » atomic bomb; hydrogen bomb [i]; missile, guided; Non-Proliferation Treaty; nuclear disarmament; SIOP

nucleic acids Large molecules which store genetic information, produced by living cells, and composed of a chain of nucleotides. Two forms are found: deoxyribonucleic acid (DNA) and ribonucleic acid (RNA), which may be either single- or double-stranded. DNA is found primarily in the nucleus, but also in small quantities in mitochondria and other structures. RNA is found in the nucleus and cytoplasm. » cell; DNA [i]; molecule; nucleotide; RNA

nucleolus A clearly defined and typically spherical structure within the nucleus of a eucaryotic cell, functioning as the site of the origin of ribosomes. It is composed of densely packed fibres and granules, rich in RNA and protein. » eucaryote; nucleus (biology)

nucleon A collective term for both proton and neutron. It was suggested by German physicist Werner Heisenberg in 1932 that protons and neutrons appear to the strong nuclear force as two possible states of a single underlying particle. This particle, called the nucleon, was described in terms of a new quantum number called isospin. » isospin; nucleon number

nucleon number The total number of protons plus neutrons in an atomic nucleus; symbol A; also called the **mass number**. This total differs for different isotopes, and so is useful for labelling them. The number of neutrons equals A − Z, where Z is the proton number. » nucleon; proton number

nucleonics The technology associated with nuclear reactors and their functioning. It entails the study of the techniques of assembling the radioactive material safely and in a form allowing it to produce its energy, the transfer of heat energy to boilers and turbines for the production of electricity, and the installation of all these units in structures which will be safe in normal use and in the event of malfunction. It is also concerned with the design and use of instruments which monitor and control radioactivity, as well as with the disposal of radioactive waste material. » nuclear reactor [i]

nucleophile An entity with an excess of electrons which tends to react at a positively charged centre. Anions and molecules with lone pairs of electrons (eg H_2O and NH_3) are nucleophiles.

nucleosynthesis The creation of chemical elements by nuclear reactions in stars and other cosmic explosions. Current theory suggests the very early universe consisted only of hydrogen and helium. Hydrogen burning in stars, and nuclear explosions at the end of a star's life, have formed all other elements by transmutation. Carbon atoms in the ink on this page were made billions of years ago in an exploding star by fusing together three helium nuclei at a temperature of 10^{7-8} degrees. » chemical elements; helium; hydrogen

nucleotide A portion of a nucleic acid consisting of a purine or pyrimidine base, a sugar molecule, and a phosphate group bonded together. There are four principal nucleotides in DNA: deoxyadenylic, deoxycytidylic, deoxyguanylic, and deoxythmidylic acids. When the phosphate is missing, the residue is called a *nucleoside*. » DNA [i]; purines; pyrimidines

nucleus (astronomy) **1** The central core of a comet, about 1–10 km/½–6 ml across, consisting of icy substances and dust. » comet **2** The central part of a galaxy or quasar, possibly the seat of unusually energetic activity within the galaxy. » galaxy; quasar

nucleus (biology) The chromosome-containing structure found in the great majority of non-dividing eucaryotic cells; delimited from the surrounding cytoplasm by a double membrane; typically ovoid or spherical, sometimes irregularly shaped. The nucleus is essential for the long-term survival of the cell. However, it disappears temporarily during cell division, and may be lost in certain mature cells, such as mammalian red blood cells. » cell; chromosome [i]; cytoplasm; eucaryote; nucleolus

nucleus (physics) The core of an atom, comprising various numbers of protons and neutrons, making up c.99.975% of an atom's mass. The number of protons equals the total positive charge of the nucleus, and equals the number of electrons in a complete atom. The nuclear components are bound together by strong nuclear force, sufficient to overcome electrical repulsions between the protons. The nucleus diameter is approximately 10^{-14}m. The nucleus of common hydrogen is a single proton; the nucleus of uranium-238 contains 92 protons and 146 neutrons. » atom; nuclear physics; nuclear structure

nuclide In nuclear physics, a nucleus having a particular number of protons and neutrons. The proton number (lower) and nucleon number (upper) must both be given. For example, the two nuclides corresponding to two of the isotopes of carbon are $_6C^{12}$ and $_6C^{14}$, which both contain 6 protons, but 6 and 8 neutrons respectively. » isotopes; nuclear physics; transmutation

Nudibranchia [nyoodi**brang**kia] » **sea slug**

nuée ardente ('burning cloud') [**nüay** ah**dẽnt**] An incandescent cloud of hot gas and volcanic ash erupted from a volcano and travelling at great speed down its flanks. » volcano

Nueva Esparta [**nway**va es**pah**ta] pop (1980) 196 911; area 1 149 sq km/443 sq ml. State consisting of Caribbean islands, off the coast of Venezuela; consists of Margarita I, Coche, and several smaller islands; capital, La Asunción; fishing, pearling, tourism. » Caribbean Sea

Nuffield, William Richard Morris, 1st Viscount (1877–1963) British motor magnate and philanthropist, born in Worcestershire. He started in the cycle business at Cowley, Oxford, and became the first British manufacturer to develop the mass production of cheap (Morris) cars. He was made a baronet in 1929 and a viscount in 1934. In 1943 he established the Nuffield Foundation for medical, scientific, and social research. He died near Henley-on-Thames, Oxfordshire. » foundation, philanthropic

Nuffield Radio Astronomy Laboratories An institution at Jodrell Bank, Cheshire, UK, founded in 1945, operated by the University of Manchester. It contains the first fully steerable radio telescope (76 m), completed in 1957, now called the Lovell telescope. It is responsible for the MERLIN array telescope, with antennae throughout England, as well as an educational centre and a public planetarium. » radio astronomy; telescope [i]

nuisance A tort which involves unreasonable interference with the use or enjoyment of neighbouring property, such as by noise, smell, or smoke. The interference must be substantial to be actionable. Nuisance can also be committed against certain rights over land, such as a right of support of buildings. A nuisance affecting a number of people may amount to the crime of public nuisance, as in the obstruction of a road. » easement; tort

Nuku'alofa [**noo**kooalohfah] 21°09S 175°14W. Port and capital town of Tonga, S Pacific; on Tongatapu I, 690 km/430 ml SE of Suva, Fiji; university; coconut processing; royal palace (1867). » Tonga

Nullarbor Plain [**nuhl**abaw] Vast plateau in SW South Australia and S Western Australia, between the Great Victoria Desert and the Great Australian Bight; extends 480 km/300 ml W from Ooldea, South Australia to Kalgoorlie, Western Australia; maximum height 305 m/1 000 ft; consists of sand dunes and sparse vegetation; crossed by the Trans-Australian Railway, the world's longest straight stretch of railway (478 km/297 ml); Nullarbor national park on the coast (area 2 319 sq km/895 sq ml). » Australia [i]

nullification A US legal doctrine that a state has the power to render laws of the federal government void within its borders. It was first tested by S Carolina during the 'Nullification Crisis' in 1832, over the issue of enforcing a federal tariff. That immediate issue was resolved by the Jackson administration's Force Bill. But in larger terms the problem was not resolved until the Civil War, and in some ways until the civil rights movement. » civil rights

numbat An Australian marsupial; narrow pointed head with horizontal black line through eye; shoulders reddish-brown; hindquarters with grey and white hoops; long bushy grey tail; female without a pouch; inhabits woodlands; eats termites; also known as **banded anteater** or **marsupial anteater**. (*Myrmecobius fasciatus*. Family: *Myrmecobiidae*.) » marsupial [i]

number line In mathematics, a straight line marked at equal intervals to show the positive and negative numbers. » numbers; straight line

number theory The abstract study of the relationship between numbers, by which is meant positive rational numbers. An early problem was one of several solved by Diophantus: 'Find three numbers such that their sum is a perfect square, and the sum of any two is a perfect square' (41,80,320). In the 17th-c Fermat proved many results in number theory, leaving us his famous 'last theorem'. The following theorem is said to have been his own favourite. 'All the primes greater than 3 can be divided into two classes, those such as 5,13,17,29,37... of the form $4n+1$, where n is an integer), and those such as 7,11,19,23,31... of the form $4n+3$. All the primes of the first class, and none of the second, can be expressed as the sum of two squares, eg $5=1^2+2^2, 13=2^2+3^2, 17=1^2+4^2$.' German mathematician Gauss asserted: 'Mathematics is the queen of the sciences, and the theory of numbers is the queen of mathematics.' » amicable numbers; Diophantus; Fermat's last theorem; Gauss; numbers; prime number

numbers A concept used initially in counting, to compare the sizes of groups of objects. **Natural numbers** (or *cardinal numbers*) are the numbers used in counting, 1,2,3,4,5... These are always *whole numbers*. The set of *integers* comprises all the natural numbers (the *positive integers*), *zero*, and the *negative numbers*... −3, −2, −1. The **rational numbers** are all the numbers that can be expressed in the form m/n, where m and n are two integers, positive or negative. Rational numbers include *proper fractions* (those whose numerator is less than their denominator, eg $^3/_8$) and *improper fractions* (those whose numerator is greater than their denominator, eg $^8/_3$). **Mixed numbers** are the sum of an integer and a proper fraction, eg 2½. *Decimal fractions* are those with denominator a power of 10, written as 0.3, 0.345, etc. *Recurring decimals* are decimal fractions where a sequence of digits is repeated, eg 0.037037037..., which can be written $0.\dot{0}3\dot{7}$, and is equal to $^{37}/_{999}$, or $^1/_{27}$. All recurring decimals can be expressed as rational numbers.

Irrational numbers are all real numbers that are not rational. Some can be expressed as the roots of algebraic equations with rational coefficients, eg $\sqrt{3}$ is a root of $x^2=3$. Those that cannot be so expressed are called **transcendental numbers**, eg π, e, e^2. **Real numbers** are all numbers that do not contain an **imaginary number** (a square root of a negative number). The positive square root of −1 is denoted by i (occasionally j). **Complex numbers** have a real and an imaginary part, eg $3+4i$. Either part of a complex number can be zero, so that all real numbers can be considered to be complex. Nearly all real numbers are transcendental – a surprising proposition, but true, for π, π^2, π^3..., etc are all transcendental numbers. To any non-transcendental number, say k, there correspond an infinite number of transcendentals, such as $k+\pi$, $k+\pi^2$, $k+\pi^3$,.... » amicable numbers; complex number; numeral; perfect numbers

Numbers, Book of A book of the Hebrew Bible/Old Testament, the fourth book of the Pentateuch; entitled in the Hebrew text 'In the Wilderness' or 'And He Spoke', but called 'Numbers' in Greek tradition because of the census of the tribes recorded in the first chapters. It describes the wilderness wanderings of Israel after the Exodus, starting with the preparations for leaving Sinai, and including the journeys to Kadesh-barnea and to the Transjordan prior to the entry into Canaan. Moses is the dominant character in the narrative, but there is also much ritual and legal material (often assigned to the Priestly source). » Moses; Old Testament; Pentateuch

numeral In mathematics, the symbol used to represent a number. The commonest system of numerals today is the Hindu-Arabic, possibly invented by the Hindus and brought to Europe by the Arabs. This uses the symbols 0,1,2,3,...9 and the idea of place-value to represent each whole number. Other systems of numerals include the Roman and the Greek. The latter used the letters of the alphabet to represent the numbers, α (alpha) for 1, β (beta) for 2,... with ι (iota) for 10, κ (kappa) twenty,... and ρ (rho) for 100. As there were only 24 letters in the Greek alphabet, even for some numbers below 1 000 it was necessary to use obsolete characters. » numbers; Roman numerals; RR77

numerical analysis Methods of calculation involving successive approximations, such as iterative methods. For example, to find $\sqrt{10}$ to any required degree of accuracy, if x_n is a good approximation to $\sqrt{10}$, use the algorithm

$$x_{n+1} = \frac{1}{2}\left(x_n + \frac{10}{x_n}\right)$$

to find x_{n+1}, a better approximation. Great developments have been made recently in this field, encouraged by the suitability of computers for numerical methods. » trapezium rule [i]

numerical control The branch of computer science related to the computer control of machine tools in the manufacturing industry. Analog, digital, and hybrid computers have all been used in this area, although digital computers now predominate. » computer science; digital computer

Numidia The Roman name for the region in N Africa to the W and S of Carthage. It roughly corresponds to modern Algeria.

numismatics The study and collecting of coins, notes, and other similar objects, such as medals. The first known coins were issued by the Lydians of Anatolia in the 7th-c BC. The first containing an accurate likeness of a reigning English monarch were minted in 1504, with the head of Henry VII. The first coins with milled edges were minted in France in 1639. The history of coin collecting dates from the Italian Renaissance, one of the first collectors being the 14th-c poet, Petrarch. Collectors in the 17th-c were the first to catalogue their collections. Coin collectors worldwide were brought together in 1936, when the International Numismatics Foundation was set up. Most museums now have extensive collections.

nummulites An important group of fossil protozoans known from the middle Palaeocene to the middle Oligocene epochs; shells disc-shaped, many-chambered, and containing calcium. They are used as zone fossils in stratigraphic analysis. » fossil; Oligocene epoch; Palaeocene epoch; Protozoa; stratigraphy; RR16

nun A member of a religious order of women living under vows of poverty, chastity, and obedience. The term includes women living in enclosed convents, as well as sisters devoted to service of the sick or poor. » monasticism; Orders, Holy; Ursulines

Nuremberg [**nyoo**ruhmberg], Ger **Nürnberg** 49°27N 11°05E, pop (1983) 476 400. Commercial and manufacturing city in Mittelfranken district, Germany; on the R Pegnitz and the Rhine-Main-Danube Canal, 147 km/91 ml NNW of Munich; second largest city in Bavaria; scene of Mastersingers' contests during the Renaissance; annual meeting place of Nazi Party after 1933; badly bombed in World War 2; scene of German war criminal trials (1945–6); railway; electronics, electrical equipment, pharmaceuticals, metal products, cars, office machinery, toys, foodstuffs, brewing; birthplace of Albrecht Dürer and Hans Sachs; Lawrence's Church (13th–15th-c), Imperial Castle; Annual International Toy Fair. » Bavaria; Dürer; Germany [i]; Nazi Party; Nuremberg Laws/ Trials; Sachs, Hans

Nuremberg Laws Two racial laws promulgated in Nuremberg in 1935 at a Reichstag meeting held during a Nazi Party rally. The first deprived of German citizenship those not of 'German or related blood', the second made marriage or extra-marital relations illegal between Germans and Jews. The laws were the first steps in the process of separating off Jews and other 'non-Aryans' in Nazi Germany. » Nazi Party

Nuremberg Trials Proceedings held by the Allies at Nuremberg after World War 2 to try Nazi war criminals, following a decision made in 1943. An International Military Tribunal was set up in August 1945, and sat from November until October 1946. Twenty-one Nazis were tried in person, including Goering and Ribbentrop (who were sentenced to death), and Hess (who was given life imprisonment). » Goering; Hess, Rudolf; Nazi Party; Nuremberg; Ribbentrop

Nureyev, Rudolf (Hametovich) (1938–) Russian ballet dancer, born at Irkutsk, Siberia. He studied at the Leningrad Choreographic School, and became a soloist with the Kirov Ballet. While touring with the Ballet in 1961, he obtained political asylum in Paris. He made his debut at Covent Garden with the Royal Ballet in 1962, and became Fonteyn's regular partner. His virtuosity and expressiveness made him one of the greatest male dancers of the 1960s, in both classical and modern ballets. He began to choreograph and dance for many European companies, and became ballet director of the Paris Opera in 1983. » ballet; Fonteyn; Royal Ballet

Nurmi, Paavo (Johannes) [**ner**mee] (1897–1973) Finnish athlete, born at Turku. He won nine gold medals at three Olympic Games (1920–8), and set 22 world records at distances ranging from 1 500–20 000 m. His first world record was in 1921, when he clocked 30 min 40.2 sec for the 10 000 m. He retired from racing in 1933, and died in Helsinki. His statue stands outside the Helsinki Olympic Stadium. » athletics

Nürnberg » **Nuremberg**

nurse shark Very large inoffensive shark found in shallow waters of the tropical and subtropical Atlantic; length up to 4 m/13 ft; head broad with conspicuous barbels close to nostrils, fins broad; yellowish brown. (*Ginglymostoma cirratum*. Family: *Orectolobidae*.) » shark

nursery rhymes Traditional jingles, essentially adult-inspired, passed on from parent to child as nursery entertainment. Most date from no earlier than the 18th-c; some celebrate contemporary personalities; some are 'counting-out' rhymes, chanted while selecting a 'victim' from a group. Included in the earliest printed collections (1744 and 1780) are: 'Little Tommy Tucker', 'Ba, Ba, Black Sheep', 'There was a Little Man', 'Sing a Song of

Sixpence', 'Who Killed Cock Robin?', 'Jack and Jill', 'Ding Dong Bell' and 'Hush-a-bye Baby'.

nursery school A school for children under the age at which schooling becomes compulsory. The teachers are usually trained, by comparison with *playgroups*, which make greater use of volunteer helpers. Provision varies, when it is non-statutory, according to where one lives. » playgroup; pre-school education

nursing The branch of medicine which provides care for the sick and injured, and assumes responsibility for the physical, social, and spiritual needs of patients that encourage recovery. Nurses comprise the largest single group of health workers. In developed countries the profession undergoes formal training prior to registration. They do not have the authority to prescribe specific medical or surgical remedies or drugs, but assist doctors and surgeons in carrying out treatment and help to monitor its effects. With advances in medical practice, many nurses have become specialized in one of several subdisciplines, including hospital, paediatric, psychiatric, home-visiting, and intensive care nurses. They also have responsibility for training junior nurses and nursing aides in practical procedures, and in encouraging self-help and self-care by patients themselves where this is feasible. » medicine; Nightingale; St John ambulance brigade

nut A dry, non-splitting fruit with a woody shell, often seated in a cup-like structure and containing several seeds, only one of which develops fully. In non-specialist use, the term is often applied to any woody fruit or seed. » Brazil nut; fruit; hazel; seed; walnut

nutation In astronomy, the irregular 'nodding' of a rotation axis, particularly for Earth, discovered in 1743 by British astronomer James Bradley (1693–1762). It has an amplitude of 9 arc seconds and a period of 18.6 years, and results from small differences in the gravitational field of the Sun and Moon on the Earth due to variations in their distances. » gravitation

nutcracker Either of two species of crow of the genus *Nucifraga*: the **nutcracker** (*Nucifraga caryocatactes*) of Europe and Asia; and **Clark's nutcracker** (*Nucifraga columbiana*) of western N America. They inhabit coniferous forest, and eat insects, seeds, and young birds. (Family: *Corvidae*.) » conifer; crow

nuthatch A small bird of the family *Sittidae* (c.23 species), inhabiting rocks or woodland in the N hemisphere; short tail, sharp straight bill; eats insects (sometimes nuts); hunts by walking 'head first' down treetrunks or rock faces. The name is also used for the **coral-billed nuthatch** (Family: *Hyposittidae*) and the **pink-faced nuthatch** (Family: *Daphoenosittidae*). » wallcreeper

nutmeg An evergreen tree growing to 9 m/30 ft, native to the Moluccas, Indonesia; leaves oblong, fragrant; flowers waxy, yellow, 3-lobed bells; fruit 5–9 cm/2–3½ in, fleshy, pear-shaped, containing a single, large seed (the nutmeg) surrounded by a red aril from which mace is made. Both spices contain a narcotic, and are poisonous in large quantities. (*Myristica fragrans*. Family: *Myristicaceae*.) » aril; evergreen plants; mace; narcotics; tree [i]

nutria » **coypu**

nutrients All components of foods and all diet supplements which fall into one or other of the following categories. **Macronutrients** are energy proteins, carbohydrates, and fats; **micronutrients** are minerals, vitamins, and various chemical substances present in tiny quantities (the *trace elements*). Dietary fibre is not a nutrient.

nutrition The scientific study of all aspects of what organisms (in particular, human beings) eat. It involves the analysis of what people eat, the psychology of why they eat, what happens to food in the body, and how the balance of food affects health. Nutrition is deeply rooted in biochemistry and physiology, but also involves chemistry, psychology, sociology, economics, agriculture, and medicine. An expert in nutrition is known as a **nutritionist** (often wrongly referred to as a 'nutritionalist'). » biochemistry; physiology

Nuzi An ancient town in Upper Mesopotamia, E of the Tigris. It was a flourishing Hurrian community in the second millennium BC, with strong commercial interests. » Hurrians

nyala An African spiral-horned antelope; greyish-brown with thin vertical white lines; male with shaggy coat; two species: **nyala** (*Tragelaphus angasi*), found in dense undergrowth near water in SE Africa; and **mountain nyala** (*Tragelaphus buxtoni*), from high forest in Ethiopia. » antelope

Nyasa [niasa] or **Malawi, Lake**, Mozambique **Niassa** Area 28 500 sq km/11 000 sq ml. Lake in SEC Africa; third largest lake in Africa, in the S section of the Great Rift Valley; within Malawi and Mozambique, and bordering Tanzania; 580 km/365 ml long; 24–80 km/15–50 ml wide; altitude, 437 m/1 434 ft; navigation possible over the whole of the lake; sometimes known as the 'Calendar Lake' because it is 365 miles long and 52 miles across, at its widest point; a world heritage site. » Rift Valley

Nyerere, Julius (Kambarage) [niyreeree] (1922–) Tanzanian statesman and President (1962–85), born at Butiama, L Victoria. He became a teacher at Makerere, then studied at Edinburgh. On his return, he reorganized the nationalists into the Tanganyika African National Union (1954) of which he became President, and in 1960 became Chief Minister. He was Premier when Tanganyika was granted internal self-government (1961), and President on independence (1962). In 1964 he negotiated the union of Tanganyika and Zanzibar, as Tanzania. He led his country on a path of socialism and self-reliance, but his policies failed, and he retired in 1985. » Arusha Declaration; Tanzania [i]

nylon A generic term for the most widely-produced type of synthetic fibre, used commercially since 1938. It is a polyamide whose lightness and elasticity make it available for use both in fibre and solid form. It is also an extremely strong and hard-wearing material. Its uses are therefore varied, including ropes, tyre cords, engineering components, furnishings, and apparel. » polyamides

nymph (entomology) A feeding and growth stage in the development of insects, between hatching and the reorganization involved in attaining adulthood. The term is used only of those insects in which the wings develop gradually and externally. » insect [i]; life cycle

nymph (mythology) In Greek mythology, one of the 'young women', nature-spirits, who live in streams (*naiads*), trees (*hamadryads*), the sea (*nereids*), as well as rocks and mountains; also those of a particular locality, who sometimes have a special name. They are long-lived but not immortal, and are fond of music and dancing. Unfortunately, people who see them become *nympholept*, filled with madness. » dryad; hamadryad (mythology); naiad; nereid

nymphalid butterfly A butterfly of the family *Nymphalidae*; typically colourful, with long hair-like scales; forelegs reduced, non-functional; eggs ribbed; caterpillars with spines; c.8 200 species, including admirals, emperors, fritillaries, and tortoiseshell butterflies. (Order: *Lepidoptera*). » butterfly; caterpillar

Nymphenburg porcelain Porcelain made at the Nymphenburg factory near Munich, which from 1753 produced fine table wares and figures. Their most celebrated modeller was Franz Anton Bustelli (1723–63), who made elegant Rococo miniature sculptures of stylized humans in contemporary dress. » porcelain; Rococo

nymphomania » **satyriasis**

Nyoro A Bantu-speaking agricultural people of W Uganda. The original feudal kingdom of Bunyoro-Kitara was founded in the 14th–15th-c with a pastoralist ruling class (Hima) and farming peasants (Iru). It was the most powerful kingdom in the area during the 19th-c, but was destroyed by the British in the 1890s. The kingship was abolished by the Ugandan government in 1966. Population c.400 000. » Bantu-speaking peoples; Uganda [i]

Nyx » **nix**

O

O'Brien, Edna (1932–) Irish novelist, born in Tomgraney, Co Clare. Her novels, which include *The Country Girls* (1960), *Girls in their Married Bliss* (1963), and *The Girl with Green Eyes* (1965), are characterized by their frank depiction of female sexuality and their lyrical powers of natural description. » Irish literature; novel

O'Brien, Flann, pseudonym of **Brian O'Nuallain** (1911–66) Irish writer, born in Strabane, Co Tyrone, and educated at University College, Dublin. As 'Myles na Gopaleen' he made regular satirical contributions to the *Irish Times*. His first novel, *At Swim-Two-Birds* (1939), combines satire with wild fantasy and farce. His later works include *The Hard Life* (1960) and *The Dalkey Archive* (1964), and display a less exuberant, darker comic vision. His Gaelic second novel, *An Beal Bocht* (1941, trans The Poor Mouth) was published in 1973. He died in Dublin. » Irish literature; novel

O'Brien, William (1852–1928) Irish journalist and nationalist, born at Mallow, Co Cork. He became editor of the weekly *United Ireland*, and sat in parliament as a Nationalist (1883–95). Several times prosecuted, and imprisoned for two years, he later returned to parliament (1900–18), and founded the United Irish League (1898) and the All-for-Ireland League (1910). He died in London.

O'Casey, Sean, originally **John Casey** (1884–1964) Irish playwright, born in Dublin. His early plays, dealing with low life in Dublin, such as *The Shadow of a Gunman* (1923) and *Juno and the Paycock* (1924), were written for the Abbey Theatre. He was awarded the Hawthornden Prize in 1926. His more experimental and impressionistic later work includes *Cock-a-doodle Dandy* (1949) and *The Bishop's Bonfire* (1955). He died at Torquay, Devon. » Abbey Theatre; drama; Irish literature

O'Connell, Daniel, byname **the Liberator** (1775–1847) Irish Catholic political leader, born near Cahirciveen, Co Kerry. He became a lawyer, and in 1823 formed the Catholic Association, which successfully fought elections against the landlords. His election as MP for Co Clare precipitated a crisis in Wellington's government, which eventually granted Catholic Emancipation (1829), enabling him to take his seat in the Commons. In 1840 he founded the Repeal Association, and agitation to end the union with Britain increased. In 1844 he was imprisoned for 14 weeks on a charge of sedition. In conflict with the Young Ireland movement (1846), and failing in health, he left Ireland in 1847, and died in Genoa, present-day Italy. » Catholic Emancipation; Wellington, Duke of

O'Connor, Feargus Edward (1794–1855) Irish Chartist leader, born at Connorville, Co Cork. He studied at Dublin, became a lawyer, and entered parliament in 1832. Estranged from O'Connell, he devoted himself to the cause of the working classes in England. His Leeds *Northern Star* (1837) became the most influential Chartist newspaper. He attempted, without great success, to unify the Chartist movement via the National Charter Association (1842), and presented himself as leader of the Chartist cause. Elected MP for Nottingham in 1847, in 1852 he became insane, and died in London. » Chartism; O'Connell

O'Connor, Sandra Day (1930–) US lawyer and jurist, born at El Paso, Texas. She studied at Stanford, and after practising law she entered Arizona politics as a Republican, becoming majority leader in the State Senate before moving to the state bench. In 1981 President Reagan named her as the first woman justice of the US Supreme Court. » Reagan; Republican Party

O'Flaherty, Liam (1897–1984) Irish writer, born in the Aran Is, Galway. He fought in the British army during World War 1, and on the Republican side in the Irish civil war. His novels include *The Informer* (1926), which was a great popular success, *The Assassin* (1928), and *Land* (1946), and he also wrote several collections of short stories. He died in Dublin. » Irish literature; novel

O'Hara, John (Henry) (1905–70) US novelist and short-story writer, born at Pottsville, Pennsylvania. He spent his early life as a journalist before writing his first novel *Appointment in Samarra* (1934). His writing is characterized by its documentary realism and command of detail, features which led to several novels being made into successful films, such as *Butterfield 8* (1935; film, 1960) and *Ten North Frederik* (1955; film, 1958). *Pal Joey* (1940) was adapted by the author and others into a celebrated musical comedy. He died at Princeton, New Jersey. » American literature; novel; short story

O'Higgins, Bernardo (1778–1842) Chilean revolutionary, born at Chillán, Chile. The son of an Irish-born Governor of Chile and Viceroy of Peru, he was educated in Peru and England, and played the major role in the Chilean struggle for independence. He became the first leader of the new Chilean state in 1817, but his reforms caused antagonism, and he was deposed in 1823, thereafter living in exile in Peru, where he died. » Chile [i]

O'Keefe, Georgia (1887–1986) US painter, born at Wisconsin. She studied at the Art Institute of Chicago (1905–6) and the Art Students' League in New York City (1907–8). As early as 1915 she pioneered abstract art in America (eg 'Blue and Green Music', 1919, Art Institute of Chicago) but later moved towards a more figurative style, painting flowers and architectural subjects, frequently with a Surrealist flavour. After 1949 she lived in New Mexico. She won many awards, and a retrospective exhibition was held in New York in 1970. She died at Santa Fe. » abstract art; Surrealism

O'Neill, Eugene (Gladstone) (1888–1953) US playwright, born in New York City. After a fragmentary education, he took various menial jobs and became a sailor, before beginning to write plays. He joined the Provincetown Players in 1915, for whom *Beyond the Horizon* (1920, Pulitzer Prize) was written. His best-known works are *Desire Under the Elms* (1924), *The Iceman Cometh* (1946), and *Long Day's Journey into Night* (1957, Pulitzer Prize), and he also wrote several plays using experimental techniques. He was the first US dramatist to win the Nobel Prize for Literature, in 1936. He died in Boston. » American literature; drama; Provincetown Players

O'Neill (of the Maine), Terence (Marne), Baron (1914–) Ulster politician and Prime Minister (1963–9), born in Co Antrim. He was educated at Eton, and served in the Irish Guards during World War 2. A member of the Northern Ireland parliament (1946–70), he held junior posts before becoming Minister for Home Affairs (1956), Finance (1956–63), and then Prime Minister. A supporter of closer cross-border links with the Republic, he angered many Unionists. Following a general election in 1969, dissension in the Unionist Party increased, and he resigned the premiership soon after. Made a life peer in 1970, he continued to speak out on Northern Ireland issues. » Northern Ireland [i]

Oahu [oha**h**hoo] pop (1980) 797 367; area 1 526 sq km/589 sq ml. Third largest island of the US state of Hawaii; part of Honolulu County; chief town Honolulu; rises to 1 233 m/4 045 ft at Kaala; sugar, fruit, tourism; naval base at Pearl Harbor. » Hawaii (state); Honolulu

oak A large genus of often massive and long-lived trees and also small shrubs, native to the N hemisphere; leaves deciduous or evergreen, usually shallowly-lobed or with wavy margins; flowers tiny, perianth 4–7-lobed, males in catkins, females solitary or in clusters; fruit an acorn seated in a scaly cup. It is a traditional source of excellent timber, and also of cork and bark for tanning. Some N American species are planted for their fine autumn colours. **Oak-apples** are woody galls produced by wasp larvae. (Genus: *Quercus*, 450 species. Family: *Fagaceae*.) » acorn; deciduous plants; evergreen plants; gall; perianth; shrub; tree [i]

Oak Ridge 36°01N 84°16W, pop (1980) 27 662. Town in Anderson County, E Tennessee, USA, on the Clinch R; founded by the US Government in 1942 to house workers developing the uranium-235 and plutonium-239 isotopes for the atomic bomb; the community was kept secret until after the first bombs were dropped in 1945; centre of atomic energy and nuclear physics research; nuclear fuel, nuclear instruments, electronic instrumentation; American Museum of Atomic Energy. » atomic bomb; Tennessee

Oakland 37°49N 122°16W, pop (1980) 339 337. Port capital of Alameda County, W California, USA, on the E shore of San Francisco Bay; founded, 1850; linked by the San Francisco–Oakland Bay Bridge (1936); airports (Oakland, Hayward); railway; vehicles, chemicals, paint, food processing, metal products, office equipment; observatory; art gallery; museums; major league teams, A's (baseball), Golden State Warriors (basketball). » California

Oakley, Annie, originally **Phoebe Anne Oakley Moses** (1860–1926) US sharpshooter and Wild West performer, born near Woodland, Ohio. After an unhappy childhood, she married a sharpshooter, Frank E Butler, and began touring with him, adopting the name Oakley. She won fame in Buffalo Bill's Wild West Show, but her career ended when she was injured in a train crash in 1901. She died at Greenville, Ohio. » Cody

Oaks » Classics

oarfish Very long ribbon-shaped fish widespread in tropical and warm temperate seas; length up to 7 m/23 ft; body extremely slender, compressed, tapering posteriorly; dorsal fin extending full length of body, tail fin absent, pelvis reduced to long filaments. (*Regalecus glesne*. Family: *Regalecidae*.)

OAS The acronym for the **Organisation de l'Armée Secrète** ('Secret Army Organization'), the clandestine organization of French Algerians, led by rebel army generals Jouhaud and Salan, active (1960–2) in resisting Algerian independence. It caused considerable violence in Algeria and metropolitan France until thrown into rapid decline by the Franco-Algerian cease-fire (Mar 1962), Salan's capture (Apr 1962), and Algerian independence (Jul 1962). » Algeria [i]; FLN

Oates, Lawrence (Edward Grace) (1880–1912) British explorer, born in London. Educated at Eton, he joined the army and served in South Africa. In 1910 he joined Scott's Antarctic Expedition in charge of the ponies, and was one of the party of five to reach the S Pole in 1912. On the return journey the explorers became weatherbound. Lamed by severe frostbite, and convinced that his condition would fatally handicap his companions' prospect of survival, he walked out into the blizzard, sacrificing his life. » Scott, R F

Oates, Titus (1649–1705) English conspirator and perjurer, born at Oakham, Rutland. Educated at Cambridge, he took Anglican orders, but was dismissed from his curacy for misconduct. In 1677 he fabricated a 'Popish Plot', supposedly directed at the life of Charles II. He feigned conversion to Catholicism, and for a while attended the Jesuit seminaries of Valladolid and St Omer. When the plot was made public, he became the hero of the day; but two years later he was found guilty of perjury, flogged, and imprisoned for life. The Revolution of 1688 set him at liberty, and he was granted a pension. He died in London. » Charles II (of England); Popish Plot

oath A solemn expression from a person giving evidence in court or making a sworn written statement. The traditional wording is 'I swear by Almighty God that the evidence which I shall give shall be the truth, the whole truth, and nothing but the truth'. Alternatively, it is possible to *affirm*, that is to solemnly promise to tell the truth. Other traditional or religious practice may be recognized; for example a Chinese witness may break a plate to emphasise solemnity. » court of law; perjury

oats A cereal, probably native to the Mediterranean basin, and cultivated in temperate regions, especially in the N hemisphere, tolerating a wide climatic range, and growing where other cereals fail. Its inflorescence is a graceful, spreading panicle. It is an important human and animal food, though less so in recent times. It is rich in protein, but unlike wheat cannot be used for bread. (*Avena sativa*. Family: *Gramineae*.) » cereals; grass [i]; inflorescence [i]; panicle; protein; wheat

Ob, River [op] Chief river of the W Siberian Lowlands, C Russia; formed by the union of the Biya and Katun Rivers, in the N foothills of the Altay Mts; flows generally NW and W to the mouth of the R Irtysh at Khanty-Mansiysk; turns N and divides into numerous channels, to enter Ob Bay, an inlet of the Kara Sea; length, 3 650 km/2 268 ml; with the R Irtysh, its chief tributary, length 5 570 km/3 461 ml, the world's fourth longest river; frozen for 5–6 months of the year; important transport route; vast oil reserves within its basin. » Russia

Obadiah, Book of [ohbadiya] One of the twelve so-called 'minor' prophetic writings of the Hebrew Bible/Old Testament, and the shortest book of the Hebrew Bible; named after the otherwise unknown prophet, whose name means 'Servant of God'; sometimes called **Book of Abdias**. The work may have originated soon after the fall of Jerusalem in 587/6 BC, but it is not always seen as a unified composition deriving from one time. It prophesies the fall of Edom in retribution for taking sides against Jerusalem, predicting judgment on the nations and the restoration of Israel at the final day of the Lord. » Edomites; Old Testament; prophet

Obelia [ohbeelia] A genus of marine invertebrate animals; a hydroid, living in colonies, commonly found growing on seaweeds in the inter-tidal zone on shores; polyps on erect stems connect by root-like horizontal branches; a horny sheath (theca) forms a protective cup around each polyp; free-swimming medusa stage. (Phylum: *Cnidaria*. Class: *Hydrozoa*.) » Hydrozoa; medusa; polyp

obelisk A tall pillar, usually made of granite, square in section, tapering upwards, and ending in a small pyramid. Obelisks were common in ancient Egypt, being used for commemorative or religious purposes. Well-known examples are Cleopatra's Needles (c.1475 BC), one of which is now located on the Victoria Embankment, London, the other in Central Park, New York City. » Egyptian architecture

Oberon (astronomy) The outermost satellite of Uranus, discovered in 1787 by Herschel; distance from the planet 583 000 km/362 000 ml; diameter 1 600 km/1 000 ml. » Herschel; Uranus (astronomy); RR4

Oberon (mythology) [ohberon] In European literature, the name of the king of the fairies, as in Shakespeare's *A Midsummer Night's Dream* and Wieland's *Oberon*. » fairies; Titania

Oberpfälzer Wald [ohberfeltser vahlt] Low NW section of the Bohemian Forest, between the Fichtelgebirge and Bavarian Forest; highest peak in former West Germany, the Entenbuhl (901 m/2 956 ft). » Bohemian Forest

obesity An excessive amount of body fat, with the affected person being overweight; the most common nutritional disease in affluent societies. It is associated with a high mortality, and predisposes to the development of several potentially serious diseases. Obesity arises because of an imbalance of energy intake over expenditure, but many factors influence its development in the individual case. Endocrine and genetic factors are important, but the extent to which the level of physical activity (notably basal or resting activity) over extended periods of time plays a part is controversial. Other theories include the idea that obese people suffer from a metabolic defect that causes reduced energy expenditure, compared with less obese individuals. » fat 2

objective test A test which is scored according to strict rules, rather than on the subjective judgment of the tester. The scorer usually operates to a marking system based on predetermined acceptable answers. Often the test will be scored by someone other than the person who gave it, for even greater objectivity. » criterion-referenced test

obliquity of the ecliptic The angle at which the celestial equator intersects the ecliptic, now decreasing by 0.47 arc seconds per year, due to precession and nutation. It varies

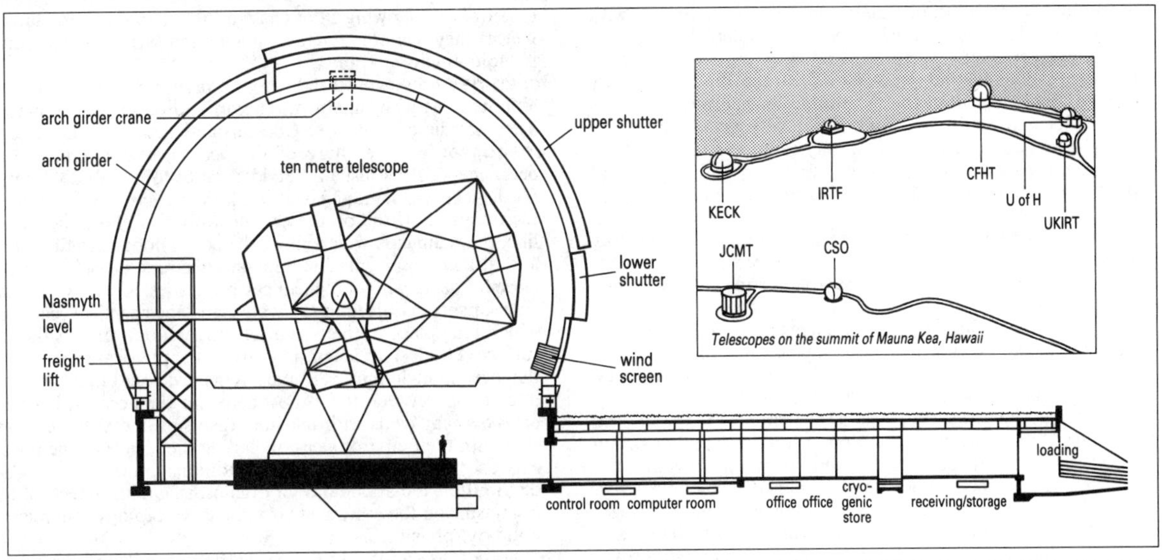

Observatory – Elevation view of the Keck telescope dome and support buildings on Mauna Kea, Hawaii. The inset shows the position of telescopes on the site – JCMT: James Clark Maxwell Telescope (Canada, Netherlands, UK); IRTF: Infra Red Telescope facility (NASA); CSO: California Submillimetre Observatory (University of California); CFHT: Canada–France–Hawaii Telescope; U of H: University of Hawaii 2.2 m Telescope; UKIRT: United Kingdom Infrared Telescope.

between 21°55′ and 24°18′. Its value in AD 2000 will be 23°26′20″. » celestial equator; nutation; precession of the equinoxes

obo [**oh**boh] A term derived from 'oil/bulk ore', a vessel designed to carry oil and bulk ore either together or separately. This is a relatively new class of vessel, first built in the mid-1960s. Total obo tonnage in 1988 was 20.03 million gross tons. » ship [i]

oboe A musical instrument made of wood in three jointed sections, opening to a small bell; it is fitted with a double reed. It first appeared in recognizable form in the mid-17th-c and was widely used in the 18th-c. Since then its mechanism has been developed, particularly by the addition of keys. In the orchestra it is normally the oboe that sets the pitch for the other instruments. A lower-pitched instrument, the **oboe d'amore**, was also used in the 18th-c, but fell into disuse later. » cor anglais; reed instrument; woodwind instrument [i]

observatory The instruments and associated buildings for conducting astronomical research of any kind. This broad definition includes the structures of native proto-astronomers, such as the builders of Stonehenge and Meso-American pyramids, the great mountain observatories of professionals in Hawaii, Australia, and Chile, the backyard shed of the keen amateur, and satellites carrying telescopes far above the atmosphere. Modern optical observatories are situated on mountain tops to get above cloud and light pollution, with oceanic islands being particularly satisfactory. The astronomers at most large observatories welcome enquiries from the general public, and many are open for self-guided tours. Local astronomical societies, listed in the phone book, often have observatories where it is possible to view the planets, stars, and galaxies on clear nights. » astronomy; IRAM; Nuffield Radio Astronomy Laboratories; telescope [i]; Arecibo/Byurakan Astrophysical/European Southern/Mauna Kea/Mount Palomar/Mount Wilson and Las Campanas/National Radio Astronomy/Royal Greenwich/Siding Spring Observatory; Royal Observatory, Edinburgh

Observer programme A planned series of relatively simple 3-axis stabilized US planetary spacecraft designed to further explore the inner Solar System, beginning with the Mars orbital mission to be launched in 1992. It is managed and operated by NASA's Jet Propulsion Laboratory. » Mars (astronomy); NASA

obstetrics The medical and surgical care of pregnancy and childbirth. It involves the prenatal care and assessment of the woman's ability to undergo labour, the assessment of the size and health of the foetus in the womb, the detection of diseases related to pregnancy (eg eclampsia), the diagnosis of the position of the foetus in the uterus, and the conduct of the delivery via the vagina. In special circumstances, delivery may need to be assisted by the use of obstetrical forceps to ease the passage of the head through the pelvic outlet, by vacuum extraction, or by caesarian section. Also important are the control of pain, the use of drugs to influence uterine contraction, and the diagnosis and treatment of complications during pregnancy and in the following period. » caesarian section; eclampsia; labour; pregnancy [i]

ocarina A simple, egg-shaped musical instrument belonging to the flute family, with a protruding mouthpiece, six finger-holes, and two thumb holes. It is made from terracotta, and is played by children, and also as a folk instrument. » flute; terracotta; woodwind instrument [i]

Occam, William of » **Ockham, William of**

occasionalism An attempted solution to the mind-body problem created by Cartesian dualism, put forward by Malebranche and others. Physical bodies and human minds have no intrinsic power to continue to exist from one moment to the next, let alone interact; all causal power is supplied directly by God. » Cartesian philosophy; dualism; Malebranche

occluded front A meteorological term, also called an **occlusion**, used to describe the situation in a depression when the cold front catches up with the warm front, and lifts the warm air off the ground. The depression then fills in, and atmospheric pressure rises. » depression (meteorology) [i]; front

occultation An astronomical phenomenon observed when a planet or moon passes across the line of sight to a star. It is useful for getting information on the atmosphere of the body causing the occultation. The rings round Uranus were detected when the planet occulted light from a bright star. » Uranus (astronomy)

occultism Activities purporting to achieve communication with the supernatural. The term includes magic, divination, certain types of spiritualism, and witchcraft. Occult knowledge is often held to be secret, for initiates only. » magic; spiritualism; witchcraft

occupational diseases Diseases which arise out of the course of employment; also known as **industrial disease**, in the context of industrial work. They have been recognized from antiquity and throughout history: Ecclesiastes recognized that blacksmiths suffered from deafness because of the noise of their work; Venetian gilders suffered from mercury poisoning; and the Industrial Revolution caused atmospheric pollution with many toxic substances. Such conditions affect almost every bodily system. Many chemicals and dyes induce dermatitis. Inhalation of industrial products affects the lungs, and may lead to pneumoconiosis or asbestosis. Agricultural workers may suffer damage from the inhalation of vegetable dust and fungal spores. Ionizing radiation may cause leukaemia. Compressed air workers suffer damage to their ears and fingers; and welders may damage their eyes. Health workers can acquire infections. Liver disease may follow exposure to organic solvents. Such events have led to the development of *industrial medicine*, by which environmentally-produced disease is identified, indices of well-being of vulnerable groups are established and monitored, and the limiting factors in the environment or work place which cause disorder are defined. In most countries there are arrangements for the compensation of those who suffer from occupational diseases. » community medicine; decompression sickness; pneumoconiosis; silicosis

occupational psychology The application of psychological methods to the study and resolution of problems in industry in the widest sense. It includes the study of work skills and the working environment, vocational guidance, personnel selection, all forms of training, principles of management, organization structure and function, principles of advertising and salesmanship, and consumer motivation, preference, and satisfaction. » ergonomics; psychology

occupational therapy The provision of practical facilities to acquire or develop a skill for those who are disabled or who suffer from a long-continued illness. Activities include the provision of jigsaw puzzles and material for basket-making, opportunities for amateur dramatics, and access to vocationally-orientated workshops.

ocean thermal energy conversion (OTEC) A technique for converting difference in ocean temperature between warm surface waters and cold deeper waters into a usable energy resource. A typical OTEC plant might use tropical ocean surface water to evaporate ammonia, which would cause a turbine to generate electricity. Cold deep water would be used to condense the ammonia to start the cycle again. Part of the electrical power is used to operate pumps to bring the cold water to the ocean surface. » electricity; energy

oceanarium » **aquarium**

Oceania [ohsheeahnia], also **Oceanica** A general name applied to the isles of the Pacific Ocean, including Polynesia, Melanesia, Micronesia, Australasia, and sometimes the Malaysian islands. » Pacific Ocean

oceanic ridges Giant undersea mountain ranges, rising above the surrounding sea floor 1–4 km/½–2½ ml, which wind their way around the globe for over 80 000 km/50 000 ml and cover 35% of the sea floor. Average depth of a ridge crest is c.2.5 km/1.5 ml; ridge width is 2 000–4 000 km/1 250–2 500 ml, with the relief becoming more subdued away from the crest as the surface slopes down to the ocean basin. The axes of all oceanic ridges are offset by numerous fractures called *transform faults*, which are seismically active, being the sites of numerous shallow earthquakes. The Mid-Atlantic Ridge is the best-known ridge system, divided into *crest* and *flank* provinces. The crest province consists of a *high fractured plateau*, *rift mountains*, and a *rift valley* which lies along the axis of the ridge, 25–50 km/15–30 ml wide, and 1–2 km/½–1 ml deeper than the adjacent mountains. A series of steps going from the high fractured plateau to the ocean basin forms the flank province. The overall gradient of this ridge is 1:100. The East Pacific Rise, on the other hand, is a wide, low bulge with a gradient of 1:500. It further differs from the Mid-Atlantic Ridge in having no prominent valley along its crest.

Large areas of the sea floor which rise more than several hundred metres above the level of the ocean basin floor are **oceanic rises**. Unlike ridge systems, these features are generally aseismic, lacking significant earthquake activity. Examples are the Ninety East Ridge in the Indian Ocean, Jan Mayen Ridge in the N Atlantic, and the Shatsky Rise in the N Pacific.

oceanic rise » **oceanic ridges**

oceanic zone The marine life zone of the open ocean past the edge of the continental shelf. Oceanic organisms live in an environment showing little change in temperature or salinity, hence they cannot tolerate fluctuations. » neritic zone; pelagic environments

Oceanides [ohseeanideez] In Greek mythology, the innumerable nymphs who inhabit the ocean and other watery places. They are the daughters of Oceanus and Tethys. » Oceanus

oceanography The study of the oceans, also referred to as **oceanology**. It is usually divided into four sub-disciplines. **Geological oceanography** deals with the structure and origin of the ocean floor, the processes which operate along the shoreline, the sediments which cover the ocean floor, and the origin and distribution of marine mineral resources. **Chemical oceanography** deals with the chemical properties of sea water, the components dissolved in sea water, and the chemical reactions which take place in the ocean, at the sea floor, and at the sea surface. **Physical oceanography** covers the physical processes in the ocean, including ocean currents, waves, tides, and the interaction between the atmosphere and the ocean. **Biological oceanography** deals with marine organisms and their relationship with their environment, including the effects of the physical, chemical, and geological conditions in the sea on the distribution and abundance of organisms, and the effects of the organisms on the marine environment. » biology; chemistry; geology; physics

Oceanus [ohseeanuhs] In Greek mythology, a Titan, the son of Uranus and Gaia. He is a benign god who personifies the stream of Ocean which was assumed to surround the world, as known to the Greeks. » Titan

ocelot [osuhlot] A rare member of the cat family, found from S USA to N Argentina; pale with dark spots and lines; inhabits diverse habitats; eats small mammals, birds, snakes, and fish; sometimes reared as pets; also known as **painted leopard** or **tigrillo**. (*Felis pardalis*.) » Felidae

ochre Earth consisting of a mixture of hydrated iron oxides and clay, light yellow to brown in colour. It is ground to a powder and used as a pigment. » hematite; limonite

Ockeghem, Joannes [ikegem] (c.1410–c.97) Flemish composer, born probably at Termonde. In 1452 he became a court musician to Charles VII, Louis XI, and Charles VIII of France, and played a major role in the stylistic development of church music in the 15th-c. Renowned as a teacher, he died at Tours.

Ockham or **Occam, William of** (c.1285–c.1349) English scholastic philosopher, born in the village of Ockham, Surrey. He entered the Franciscan order, and studied theology at Oxford. Summoned to Avignon (1324) to respond to charges of heresy, he became involved in a dispute between the Franciscans and Pope John XXII over apostolic poverty. He fled to Bavaria in 1328, where he remained until 1347, writing treatises on papal v. civil authority. He probably died of the Black Plague, in Munich. » Franciscans; Ockham's Razor

Ockham's Razor 'Do not multiply entities beyond necessity'; a theory should not propose the existence of anything more than is needed for its explanations. Also called the Principle of Parsimony, it is attributed to the 14th-c philosopher, William of Ockham. » Ockham

octadecanoic acid » **stearic acid**

octane number The measure of ability of a fuel to resist knocking (premature ignition) in the cylinder of an internal combustion engine. The properties of a mixture of iso-octane (which resists knocking) and heptane (which knocks easily) are matched to the behaviour of the fuel under test. » cetane number; internal combustion engine; knocking

Octans (Lat 'octant') An inconspicuous S constellation. » constellation; RR9

octet A group of eight; used in chemistry for the elements between boron and calcium (atomic numbers 5 to 20), whose most stable compounds have an octet of valence electrons associated with each atom, either by ion formation or by sharing electrons in covalent bonding. An octet of valence electrons is also called a *noble gas configuration*. » chemical elements; valence

October Revolution (1917) The overthrow of the Russian provisional government by Bolshevik-led armed workers (Red Guards), soldiers, and sailors (25–26 Oct 1917). The revolution was organized by the Military Revolutionary Committee of the

Petrograd Soviet. The members of the provisional government were arrested and replaced by the Soviet of People's Commissars (*Sovnarkom*), chaired by Lenin – the first Soviet government. » April Theses; Bolsheviks; February Revolution; July Days; Lenin; Russian history

October War » **Arab-Israeli Wars**

octopus A carnivorous marine mollusc with a short, sac-like body and eight arms largely connected by webbing; reaches 5.4 m/18 ft in length, and with a maximum outstretched armspan of nearly 9 m/30 ft; shell usually absent; contains a funnel, used for swimming by jet propulsion; prey caught using suckers on arms; when alarmed, may eject a cloud of ink. (Class: *Cephalopoda*. Order: *Octopoda*.) » Cephalopoda [i]; mollusc

octopush A form of hockey played underwater, first introduced in South Africa in the 1960s. Teams consist of six players who use miniature hockey sticks and a puck replacing the ball. To score a goal, the puck must hit the opposing end of the swimming pool. » hockey [i]

odd function » **even functions [i]**

ode (Gr 'song') A lyric poem, usually of some length and formal complexity. The form of the ode is not prescribed, but determined in each case by the theme, subject, and situation. Pindar in Greek, Horace in Latin, Keats in English, and Claudel in French were notable practitioners. » Claudel; Horace; Keats; Pindar; poetry

Odense [**oh**densuh] 55°24N 10°25E, pop (1983) 170 648. Port and chief town on Fyn I, Denmark; third largest city of Denmark; railway; university (1964); engineering, foodstuffs, textiles, timber; St Knud's Church (reconstructed 13th-c), 18th-c palace; birthplace of Hans Andersen. » Andersen; Denmark [i]

Oder-Neisse Line The Polish–German border, drawn by the Allies (1944–5), and involving the transfer to Poland of large areas of pre-war Germany. A source of contention between the German Federal Republic and the German Democratic Republic, it was finally recognized by the former in 1970. » Germany [i]; Poland [i]

Oder, River [**oh**der], Czech, Polish **Odra**, ancient **Viadua** River in C Europe rising in E Sudetes Mts of Czechoslovakia; flows N through Poland, eventually following the East German frontier to meet the Baltic Sea near Szczecin; length 854 km/531 ml; navigable for 711 km/442 ml; canal links to W and E Europe. » Poland [i]

Odessa [oh**de**sa] 46°30N 30°46E, pop (1989) 1 115 000. Seaport capital of Odesskaya oblast, Ukraine, on NW shore of the Black Sea; centre of the battleship *Potemkin* mutiny in the 1905 Revolution; railway; university (1865); naval base and home port for a fishing and Antarctic whaling fleet; leading Black Sea port, trading in grain, sugar, machinery, coal, oil products, cement, metals, jute, timber; icebreakers ensure that the port is ice-free throughout the year; large health resorts nearby; fishing, solar research, machines, oil refining, metalworking, chemicals; Uspensky Cathedral (1855–69). » Revolution of 1905; Ukraine

Odets, Clifford [o**dets**] (1903–63) US playwright and actor, born in Philadelphia. In 1931 he joined the Group Theatre, New York, under whose auspices his early plays were produced. The most important US playwright of the 1930s, his works are marked by a strong social conscience formed out of the conditions of the Great Depression of that time. They include *Waiting for Lefty* (1935) and *Golden Boy* (1937). In the late 1930s he moved to Hollywood, where he wrote many film scenarios, and there he died. » American literature; drama; Great Depression; theatre

Odin [**oh**din] In Norse mythology, the All-Father, the god of poetry and the dead; also known as **Woden** (English) or **Wotan** (German). He gave one eye to the Giant Mimir in exchange for wisdom. He rides the eight-legged horse Sleipnir, and keeps two ravens to bring him news. Often he wanders the world as a hooded one-eyed old man. » Germanic religion; Valhalla

Odissi A soft, lyrical and erotic style of classical dance for women. It is found in E India. » Indian dance

Odo of Bayeux (c.1036–97) Bishop of Bayeux (1049–97) and Earl of Kent, the half-brother of William the Conqueror. He rebuilt Bayeux cathedral and may have commissioned the Bayeux tapestry. He died in Palermo, during the first crusade. » Bayeux Tapestry; William I (of England)

Odoacer or **Odovacer** [ohdoh**ay**ser] (?–493) Germanic warrior who destroyed the W Roman Empire, and became the first barbarian King of Italy (476–93). An able ruler, he was challenged and overthrown by the Ostrogothic King Theoderic (489–93) at the instigation of the E Roman Emperor, Zeno. » Roman history [i]; Romulus Augustulus; Theodoric

Odonata [**oh**donata] » **damselfly; dragonfly**

Odysseus [o**dis**yoos] A Greek hero, known in Latin as **Ulixes**, from which Ulysses is derived. The son of Laertes, King of Ithaca, he took part in the Trojan War, where he was respected for his intelligence. (In later writers he is made cunning and devious.) He took ten years to return from Troy, encountering many romantic adventures, described in Homer's *Odyssey*. Eventually he returned to Ithaca, slaughtered the suitors who were besieging his wife Penelope, and, to appease Poseidon, the main cause of his troubles, set out to find a country where the oar on his shoulder would be taken for a winnowing-fan. Dante and Tennyson credit him with one final journey of exploration into the Atlantic Ocean. » Charybdis; Circe; lotus-eaters; Nausicaa; Penelope; Philoctetes; Polyphemus; Scylla; Sirens; Telemachus

oedema/edema [uh**dee**ma] The generalized accumulation of excess amounts of body fluids (water and salts) within and around the tissues of the body. In the majority of cases, it is caused by heart, kidney, or liver failure.

Oedipus [**ee**dipuhs] In Greek legend, a Theban hero of whom it was foretold that he would kill his father and marry his mother. He was exposed at birth, and lamed with a spike through his feet (his name means 'swell-foot'). Brought up in Corinth, he fled from his adoptive parents when an oracle revealed his destiny. On the way to Thebes he killed his father Laius by chance, and, having guessed the riddle of the sphinx, was made the new ruler of the city and married its queen, Jocasta. When all was revealed, he blinded himself. He died either at Thebes (Homer) or at Colonus in Attica (Sophocles). » Jocasta; Laius; Oedipus complex; sphinx

Oedipus complex A psychoanalytic term describing the erotic feelings of a son for his mother, and an associated sense of competitiveness towards the father. The female equivalent is the **Electra complex**, describing a daughter's jealousy of her mother, love for her father, and blame for the mother's depriving her of a penis. Both terms were coined by Freud. » castration anxiety; Freud, Sigmund; Oedipus

Oehlenschlager, Adam (Gottlob) [**er**luhnshlayger] (1779–1850) Danish poet, born at Vesterbro. He studied law at Copenhagen, but turned to writing, becoming the leader of the Danish Romantic movement. His fame rests mainly on his 24 tragedies, beginning with *Hakon Jarl* (1807), based on the life of a national hero. In 1810 he was made professor of aesthetics at Copenhagen, where he died. » Danish literature; poetry; Romanticism (literature); tragedy

Oersted, Hans Christian [ersted] (1777–1851) Danish physicist, born at Rudkøbing. He became professor at Copenhagen (1806), where in 1820 he discovered the magnetic effect of an electric current. He died in Copenhagen. » electromagnetism; RR70

Oesling » **Ösling**

oesophagus/esophagus [ee**so**faguhs] A long, muscular tube passing from the lower part of the pharynx through the thorax to the stomach; also known as the **gullet**. In adult humans it is c.24 cm/9.5 in long. The most muscular part of the digestive tract, it squeezes solids and liquids (taken in by the mouth) by waves of contraction of its muscle layers towards the stomach. During its course it has several constrictions, which are of clinical importance because ingested material will be momentarily held up on its way to the stomach; consequently there will be a greater degree of damage to the lining membrane at these points, should corrosive materials (eg turpentine) be swallowed. » pharynx; stomach

oestrogens/estrogens [**ee**struhjuhnz] Steroid sex hormones (eg *oestradiol*, *oestriol*, *oestrone*) produced in the ovary, placenta, testis, and adrenal cortex. They are responsible for the development of female secondary sexual characteristics in humans, as well as promoting sexual readiness (*oestrus*, eg in rats and mice), and preparing the uterus for implantation. They are used in oral contraceptives and in the treatment of certain cancers (eg of the prostate). They are also found in plants. » androgens; contraception; hormones; pregnancy [i]; puberty; steroid [i]

oestrus/estrus [eestruhs] The period of maximum sexual receptivity, or heat, in female mammals. It is usually also the time of release of the egg from the ovary. » Graafian follicle; ovary

Off-Broadway » **Broadway**

Offa (?–796) King of Mercia (757–96). He was the greatest Anglo-Saxon ruler in the 8th-c, treated as an equal by Charlemagne. Styling himself 'King of the English', he asserted his authority over all the kingdoms S of the Humber, and treated their rulers as subordinate provincial governors. He was responsible for constructing Offa's Dyke, and established a new currency based on the silver penny which, with numerous changes of design, remained the standard coin of England for many centuries. His reign represents an important but flawed attempt to unify England, with the Mercian supremacy collapsing soon after his death. » Anglo-Saxons; Charlemagne; Egbert; Mercia; Offa's Dyke

Offa's Dyke An interrupted linear earthwork 130 km/80 ml long – the gaps originally thick forest – linking the R Dee near Prestatyn, N Wales, with the Severn Estuary at Chepstow. Erected in the late 8th-c AD by Offa, King of Mercia, to define the W boundary of his kingdom, it marks the traditional boundary between England and Wales. Offa's Dyke Path, opened in 1971, follows most of its course, the bank still standing 3–4 m/10–13 ft high in places. » Anglo-Saxons; Offa

offal All the organs of slaughtered animals other than muscles and bones. Several of these organs (such as the liver and kidneys) are eaten; others (such as the gut) are discarded.

Offaly, Gaelic **Ua bhFailghe** [ofalee] pop (1981) 58 312; area 1 997 sq km/771 sq ml. County in Leinster province, C Irish Republic; bounded W by R Shannon; Slieve Bloom Mts rise in the SW; capital, Tullamore; cattle, grain; large tracts of peat used as fuel for power stations. » Irish Republic [i]; Tullamore

Offenbach, Jacques, originally **Jakob Eberst** (1819–80) German-Jewish composer, born in Cologne. He came to Paris in 1833, directing the Théâtre-Français orchestra in 1848, and becoming manager of the *Bouffes parisiens* in 1855. He composed many light, lively operettas, such as *Orphée aux enfers* (1858, Orpheus in the Underworld). He also produced one grand opera, *Les Contes d'Hoffmann* (The Tales of Hoffmann), which was not produced until 1881, after his death, in Paris. » opera buffa

Office, Divine or **Holy** In the pre-Reformation Western Church and in the Roman Catholic Church, prayers which must be said by priests and religious every day, originally at fixed hours. The practice dates from early monasticism, and derives from Jewish tradition. » Breviary; Benedict, St; monasticism

Office of Management and Budget The office which the US president uses to control the financial operations of government, created in 1970 out of the Bureau of the Budget. In recent times, particularly under President Reagan, it has been used more overtly as an instrument of policy, by controlling domestic spending. It is an important political arm of the presidency and not just a technical budget advisory office. » Reagan

offset lithography A form of printing in which the image to be communicated, having first been created by photographic means on a printing plate, is transferred to a rubber 'blanket' cylinder and then to the printing substrate (normally paper, but also metal and plastic). Offset-litho printing presses are either sheet-fed (printing one or more pages or other images at a time, in one or more colours, on cut sheets of the paper or other substrate), or reel- or web-fed (printing on a continuous reel, which is cut up after printing). » lithography; printing [i]

Ogaden [ogaden] Geographical area in SE Ethiopia; dry plateau intermittently watered by Fafen Shet and Jerer Rivers; part of Abyssinia, 1890; part of Italian East Africa, 1936–41; largely inhabited by Somali-speaking nomads; area claimed by Somalia in 1960s; Somali invasion in 1977 repulsed by Ethiopian forces; fighting continued throughout the 1980s. » Ethiopia [i]; Somalia [i]

Ogam or **Ogham** A writing system used from around the 4th-c AD for writing Irish and Pictish. Memorial inscriptions occur on stone monuments, particularly in Ireland and S Wales. The alphabet has 20 letters composed of sets of parallel straight lines (numbering from one to five), cut to and across the vertical corners of stone monuments, some lying horizontally and others falling diagonally from left to right. » alphabet [i]

Ogbomosho [ogbomohshoh] 8°05N 4°11E, pop (1981e) 590 600. Market town in Oyo state, W Nigeria, 88 km/55 ml NNE of Ibadan; third largest city in Nigeria; agricultural trade, crafts, cloth, shoes, tobacco; festivals of Ebo Oba Ijeru (Feb), Egungun (Jul), and Ashun (Aug). » Nigeria [i]

Ogden, C(harles) K(ay) (1889–1957) British linguistic reformer, born at Fleetwood, Lancashire. Educated at Cambridge, he founded the *Cambridge Magazine* (1912–22), and in 1917 the Orthological Institute. In the 1920s he conceived the idea of Basic English, a simplified form of English with only 850 words, to provide a practical means of international communication. He developed the approach with the help of I A Richards, and by the 1940s it was attracting considerable interest. He died in London. » artificial language; English; Richards, I A

Ogdon, John (Andrew Howard) (1937–89) British pianist, born at Mansfield Woodhouse, Nottinghamshire. He studied in Manchester, and in 1962 was joint prizewinner in the Tchaikovsky Competition in Moscow. He had a powerful technique, a remarkable memory, a huge repertory, and he also composed, his works including a piano concerto. Illness forced him to give up playing for several years. He died in London. » piano

Ogham » **Ogam**

Ogilvy, Mrs Angus » **Alexandra, Princess**

Ohio (state) [ohhiyoh] pop (1987e) 10 784 000; area 107 041 sq km/41 330 sq ml. State in E USA, divided into 88 counties; the 'Buckeye State'; visited by La Salle in 1669 and settled by fur traders from 1685; 17th state to join the Union, 1803; capital, Columbus; other chief cities Cleveland, Cincinnati, Toledo, Akron, Dayton; part of the Allegheny plateau; drained by the Muskingum, Scioto, and Great Miami Rivers which flow to meet the Ohio R and L Erie; grain, soybeans, vegetables, dairy cattle, livestock; coal (E and SE Appalachian coalfield), natural gas, stone, sand, gravel; major industrial centre, including steel, metal products, vehicles, paper, chemicals, rubber, clothing, electrical goods, foodstuffs. » Columbus; La Salle; United States of America [i]; RR39

Ohio Company 1 Virginia-based speculators who acquired a Crown grant of 200 000 acres (80 000 ha) in 1749 in the area

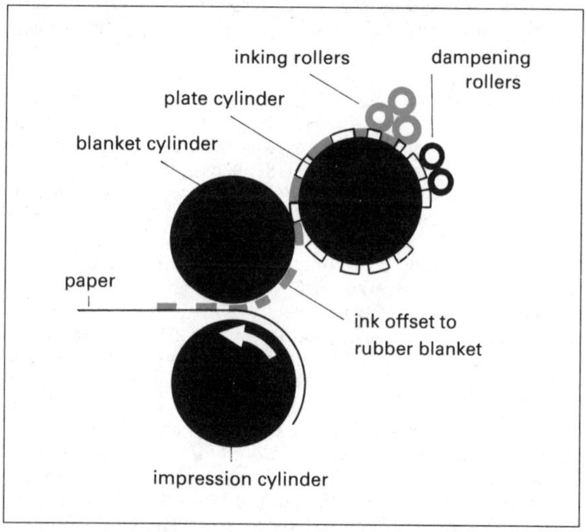

An offset litho press

between the Ohio R, Great Kanawha R, and Allegheny Mts. **2** An organization of speculators in 1786 who used depreciated currency and securities to acquire large amounts of Ohio land. They were indirectly responsible for the passage of the Ordinance of 1787, establishing a political basis for Westward expansion. » Ordinance of 1787

Ohio River River in EC USA; formed at Pittsburgh by the union of the Monongahela and Allegheny Rivers; flows generally SW for 1 578 km/980 ml to join the Mississippi at Cairo, Illinois; forms the state boundary between Ohio, Indiana, and Illinois (N) and West Virginia and Kentucky (S); chief tributaries the Kanawha, Licking, Kentucky, Tennessee (left); the Scioto, Miami, Wabash (right); navigable all the way, with the help of a canal at Louisville; length 2 101 km/1 306 ml (including the Allegheny). » United States of America [i]

Ohm, Georg Simon (1787–1854) German physicist, born at Erlangen, Bavaria. In 1817 he became professor of mathematics at Cologne, and in 1849 at Munich, his main discoveries being in the field of electricity. He died in Munich. » ohm; Ohm's law

ohm SI unit of electrical resistance; symbol Ω; a resistance of 1 ohm exists between two points of a conductor if a potential difference of 1 volt causes a current of 1 amp to flow between them; named after German physicist Georg Ohm; commonly used as **kilohms** (kΩ, 10^3 ohms) and **megohms** (MΩ, 10^6 ohms). » electricity; Ohm; resistance; units (scientific); RR70

Ohm's law In electrical circuits, the result that potential difference U and current I satisfy $U=IR$ for resistance R; for alternating current circuits, $U=IZ$, where Z is impedance; stated by German physicist Georg Ohm in 1827. » electricity; impedance; Ohm; resistance

ohmmeter A small portable instrument for measuring resistances in an electrical circuit. It consists of an ammeter together with one variable and one fixed resistance. The unknown resistance is found by measuring the difference in current flow between closed circuit conditions and when the unknown resistance is introduced between the connectors of the ohmmeter. » electricity; ohm; resistance

Ohrid [**okh**rid] 41°06N 20°49E, pop (1981) 64 245. Town in SW Macedonia republic, Yugoslavia, on the shores of L Ohrid; airfield; tourism, fishing, agriculture; old town, a world heritage site; Cathedral of St Sophia, St Clement's Church (13th-c), castle; old town festival (May, Aug), Balkan folk festival (Jul), summer festival (Jul–Aug). » Macedonia (Yugoslavia)

Ohrid, Lake, Serbo-Croatian **Ohridsko Jezero** [**okh**rid] Lake situated on the frontier between Albania and Yugoslavia to the E of Elbasan; area 350 sq km/135 sq ml; two-thirds in Yugoslavia; boat service joining the picturesque town of Ohrid, now a national monument, to Sveti Naum at the S end; tourist resort at Struga. » Albania [i]; Yugoslavia [i]

oil (botany) A fluid secreted by special glands in many plants, often forming food reserves in fruits and seeds such as olives, palms, rape, and flax. Volatile *essential oils* are produced by aromatic plants, especially in dry regions, and may help reduce transpiration or provide protection against animals. *Edible oils* are obtained from many plants, including soy beans, maize, olives, sunflowers, coconut, and rapeseed. » essential oil; palm oil; transpiration; triglyceride

oil (earth sciences) A fossil fuel that is chemically a complex mixture of hydrocarbons, formed from organic remains by the action of heat and pressure over millions of years; known as *natural* or *crude* oil. It occupies the pore spaces between grains in sedimentary rock, and accumulates when its upward migration is trapped by a suitable impervious 'cap' rock. It occurs together with natural gas and solid hydrocarbons (collectively termed *petroleum*) as well as water. When refined it is used as a primary fuel for industry, and hence has great economic importance. » hydrocarbons; North Sea Oil; petroleum

oil beetle A brightly-coloured beetle; adults produce a chemical (*cantharidin*) that causes skin blisters; larvae louse-like, feeding on insect eggs or on food stores in bees' nests. (Order: *Coleoptera*. Family: *Meloidae*, c.3 000 species.) » beetle; larva; louse

oil painting A method of painting which employs drying oils (such as linseed oil) in the medium. In use since Roman times for decorating shields, etc, the technique was perfected and adapted to painting pictures in the 15th-c. » glaze; medium (art); paint; painting

oil palm A tree reaching 15 m/50 ft, native to tropical Africa; leaves 4.5 m/15 ft, feathery. The numerous oval, orange fruits are rendered down for oil. (*Elaeis guineensis*. Family: *Palmae*.) » palm; tree [i]

oil pollution Damage to the seas and coasts as a result of major oil spillages from oil tankers. In 1967, the Torrey Canyon spilt more than 100 000 tons of oil off the Cornish coast. In 1978, the Amoco Cadiz ran aground off Brittany, losing 220 000 tons of oil. In March 1989 the supertanker Exxon Valdez ran aground on an Alaskan reef, spilling 11 million gallons of crude oil into the fishing waters of Prince William Sound, putting the fishing industry at risk and devastating wildlife over an area of 2 500 sq km/1 000 sq ml. The consequences of such pollution are long-lasting, because of the contaminated food chain. » food chain; oil (earth sciences); pollution

oilbird A nightjar-like bird, native to northern S America and Trinidad; roosts in caves; uses echolocation; eats fruit picked in flight; also known as the **guacharo**, or **diablotin**. It is the only nocturnal fruit-eating bird. Its fledglings are very fat, and were formerly boiled to extract oil, used as cooking oil. (Family: *Steatornithidae*, *Steatornis caripensis*.) » nightjar

Oireachtas [**erakh**tas] An annual Irish gathering organized, on the lines of the Welsh eisteddfod, by the Gaelic League; first held in 1898. » eisteddfod

Oistrakh, David (Feodorovitch) (1908–74) Russian violinist, born in Odessa. He studied at the Odessa Conservatory, went to Moscow (1928), and became professor at the Conservatory there in 1934. He made several concert tours in Europe and the USA, and was awarded the Stalin (1945) and Lenin (1960) Prizes. He died in Amsterdam. His son **Igor Davidovitch** (1931–), born at Odessa, is also a noted violinist. » violin

Ojibwa [oh**jib**wa] An Algonkian-speaking N American Indian group originally concentrated around L Superior and L Huron, called **Chippewa** by the Europeans. Hunters and nomads, they were impoverished following the decline of the fur trade. Population c.42 000. » American Indians

Ojos del Salado, Cerro [**ohkh**ohs thel sa**lath**oh] 27°05S 68°35W. Andean peak rising to 6 908 m/22 664 ft on the Argentina–Chile border; second highest peak in the W hemisphere, after Aconcagua. » Andes

okapi [oh**kah**pee] A mammal of the giraffe family, native to Zaire; reddish-brown with long neck, large ears, and extremely long tongue (can lick its own eyes); face and lower legs pale; upper legs and hindquarters with thin horizontal stripes; male with two blunt 'horns'; inhabits dense wet forest; eats leaves and fruit. (*Okapia johnstoni*.) » giraffe

Okavango, River [ohka**vang**goh] Third largest river in S Africa, flowing through Angola, Namibia, and Botswana; rises in C Angola, and flows SE then S to enter the sea in a wide delta (c.15 000 sq km/6 000 sq ml), containing forest, swamp, marsh, and lagoon, a major wildlife area; flooding here fills nearby rivers and sometimes L Ngami; length 1 600 km/1 000 ml.

Okayama [ohka**ya**ma] 34°40N 133°54E, pop (1980) 545 765. Port capital of Okayama prefecture, SW Honshu, Japan, 112 km/70 ml W of Osaka; railway; university (1949); commerce, cotton, porcelain; dominated by the 'Castle of the Crow' (16th-c), Koraku-en Gardens (17th-c). » Honshu

Okeechobee, Lake [ohkee**choh**bee] Lake in SC Florida, USA; linked to the Atlantic by the St Lucie and Miami Canals; largest lake in S USA (area 815 sq km/315 sq ml, maximum depth 4.6 m/15 ft); rivers drain S through the Everglades. » Everglades; Florida

Okefenokee Swamp [ohkuhfuh**noh**kee] (Muskogean 'water-shaking') Area of swamp land in SE Georgia and NE Florida, USA; drained SW by the Suwannee R; important wildlife refuge; tourist centre. » Florida; Georgia

Oki Archipelago, Jap **Oki Retto** [**oh**kee] area 375 sq km/145 sq ml. Island group in Chugoku region, Japan; in the Sea of Japan, 56 km/35 ml N of SW Honshu; includes Dogo (largest island) and Dozen (group of three islands); generally mountainous and forested; Dogo rises to 608 m/1 995 ft; timber, fishing; chief town and port, Saigo on Dogo. » Japan [i]

Okinawa (Bolivia) [ohkeen**awa**] pop(1984e) 5 600. Town in Santa Cruz department, C Bolivia; established by Japanese settlers in 1954; population of 4 000 Bolivians and 1 600 Japanese. » Bolivia [i]

Okinawa (Japan) [ohkee**na**wa] pop(1980) 1 107 000; area 2 246 sq km/867 sq ml. Region of Japan comprising the S part of the Ryukyu group; bounded W by the East China Sea, E by the Pacific Ocean; island of Okinawa is the largest in the group (area 1 176 sq km/454 sq ml), 528 km/328 ml SSW of Kyushu; taken by the USA in World War 2; returned to Japan, 1972; capital, Naha; rice, sugar cane, fish, sweet potatoes. » Japan [i]

Oklahoma [ohkla**hoh**ma] (Muskogean 'red people'); pop(1987e) 3 272 000; area 181 083 sq km/69 919 sq ml. State in SW USA, divided into 77 counties; the 'Sooner State'; mostly acquired by the USA in the Louisiana Purchase, 1803; Indians forced to move here in the 1830s (Indian Territory); Allem Wright, a Choctaw chief, coined the name to describe the land held by his people; Indians then lost the W region to Whites (Oklahoma Territory, 1890); merged Indian and Oklahoma territories admitted into the Union as the 46th state, 1907; capital, Oklahoma City; other major cities Tulsa and Lawton; rivers include the Red (forms the S border), Arkansas, Canadian, Cimarron; Ouachita Mts in the SE; Wichita Mts in the SW; highest point Black Mesa (1 516 m/4 974 ft); in the W, high prairies part of the Great Plains; major agricultural products livestock and wheat; cotton, dairy products, peanuts; large oil reserves and associated petroleum industry; machinery, fabricated metals, aircraft. » Indian Wars; Louisiana Purchase; Oklahoma City; United States of America [i]; RR39

Oklahoma City 35°30N 97°30W, pop(1980) 403 213. State capital in Oklahoma County, C Oklahoma, USA, on the N Canadian R; settled around a railway station, 1889; state capital, 1910; developed rapidly after oil discovered, 1928; largest city in the state; airport; railway; university (1911); oil production; distribution and processing centre for livestock, grain, cotton; aircraft, machinery, electrical equipment; Tinker Air Force Base; National Cowboy Hall of Fame, Western Heritage Centre, state historical museum; festival of arts (Apr), Quarter Horse Show (Nov). » Oklahoma

Öland [**er**land] pop(1984e) 23 874; area 1 344 sq km/519 sq ml. Elongated Swedish island in the Baltic Sea, off the SE coast of Sweden; separated from the mainland by Kalmar Sound; length, 136 km/84 ml; largest island in Sweden; chief town, Borgholm; potatoes, sugar beet, cattle, sugar refining, quarrying; Borgholm castle (12th–13th-c). » Sweden [i]

Olav V (1903–91) King of Norway (1957–91), born near Sandringham, Norfolk, the only child of Haakon VII and Maud, daughter of Edward VII. Educated in Norway and at Oxford, he was appointed head of the Norwegian Armed Forces in 1944, escaping with his father to England on the Nazi occupation, returning in 1945. In 1929 he married **Princess Martha** (1901–54) of Sweden, and had two daughters and a son, **Harald** (1937–), who succeeded him. » World War 2

Olbers' paradox A paradox expressed in 1826 by German astronomer Heinrich Wilhelm Olbers (1758–1840): why is the sky dark at night? In an infinitely large, unchanging, universe populated uniformly with stars and galaxies, the sky would be dazzling bright, which is not the case. This simple observation implies that the universe is not an infinite static arrangement of stars. In fact, modern cosmology postulates a finite expanding universe. » universe

Old Bailey A street in the City of London, and, by association, the Central Criminal Court located there. The first courthouse was erected in 1539. The present building dates from 1907; the bronze statue of Justice surmounting its dome is a notable London landmark. » Crown Court; London [i]

Old Believers Russian Orthodox traditionalists who rejected the reforms instituted in 1666. Although persecuted, they survived, established their own hierarchy in 1848, and were recognized by the state in 1881. » Russian Orthodox Church

Old Catholics A group of Churches separated at various times from the Roman Catholic Church, including the Church of Utrecht (separated 1724), and German, Austrian, and Swiss Catholics who refused to accept papal infallibility (1870); also some former Poles and Croats in N America. They enjoy intercommunion with Anglicans. » Anglican Communion; infallibility; Roman Catholicism

Old Church Slavonic » **Slavic languages**

Old Comedy Athenian comic theatre of the 5th-c BC. It has a unique structure that includes an *agon* (a contest) and a *parabasis* (a choral address to the audience on a contemporary social issue). The only complete plays extant are by Aristophanes. » Aristophanes; New Comedy

Old English sheepdog A breed of dog, developed in Britain in the 18th-c to protect cattle; large with hindquarters higher than shoulder; covered in long, untidy coat, often hiding ears and eyes; usually white with large dark patches; short tail. » dog; sheepdog

Old High German » **Germanic languages**

Old Masters » **master**

Old Persian » **Iranian languages**

Old Style date » **New Style date**

Old Testament The sacred literature of Judaism, in which the corpus of writings is known simply as the Jewish Scriptures or Hebrew Bible, or even sometimes the Torah; it was also adopted by Christians as part of their sacred writings, and they began to call it the 'Old Testament' as distinct from the Christian writings that constitute the 'New Testament'. The canon of the Jewish religious community, which was fixed c.100 AD, was arranged into three parts – the **Law**, the **Prophets**, and the **Writings** – although the precise arrangement and divisions of the books have varied through the centuries. The Law consists of the five books of the Pentateuch (Genesis, Exodus, Leviticus, Numbers, Deuteronomy). The Prophets have been divided since about the 8th-c AD into the *former* and *latter* prophets: the former prophets consist of the narratives (presumed written by prophets) found in Joshua, Judges, Samuel, and Kings, and the latter prophets consist of Isaiah, Jeremiah, Ezekiel, and the Book of the Twelve Prophets (Hosea, Joel, Amos, Obadiah, Jonah, Micah, Nahum, Habakkuk, Zephaniah, Haggai, Zechariah, Malachi). The Writings contain all remaining works: Psalms, Proverbs, Job, Song of Songs, Ruth, Lamentations, Ecclesiastes, Esther, Daniel, Ezra-Nehemiah, and Chronicles.

All the books of the Hebrew Bible appear in the versions of the Old Testament used by Protestant Churches today, but divided so as to number 39 in total. Roman Catholic versions of the Old Testament, however, accept 46 works, the additions not appearing in the Hebrew Bible but being found in Greek versions and the Latin Vulgate. These extra works are considered part of the Old Testament Apocrypha by Protestants. » Apocrypha, Old Testament; Bible; Christianity; Judaism; Lamentations of Jeremiah; New Testament; Pentateuch; Pseudepigrapha; Song of Solomon; Torah; Amos/Chronicles/Daniel/Deuteronomy/Ecclesiastes/Esther/Exodus/Ezra/Genesis/Habbakuk/Haggai/Hosea/Isaiah/Jeremiah/Job/Joel/Jonah/Joshua/Judges/Kings/Leviticus/Malachi/Micah/Nahum/Nehemiah/Numbers/Obadiah/Proverbs/Psalms/Ruth/Samuel/Shephariah, Books of

Old World monkey A monkey of family *Cercopithecidae* (76 species); nostrils close together and opening downwards or forwards (unlike New World monkeys); tails never grasping, sometimes short; buttocks may have naked patches of skin; some species ground-dwelling. » baboon; colobus; guenon; langur; macaque; mangabey; monkey [i]; New World monkey; patas monkey; proboscis monkey; talapoin

Oldcastle, Sir John (c.1378–1417) English Lollard leader and knight. After serving in the Scottish and Welsh wars, and becoming an intimate of Henry V when Prince of Wales, he was tried and convicted on charges of heresy in 1413. He escaped from the Tower, and conspired with other Lollards to capture Henry V at Eltham Palace, Kent, and take control of London. The rising was abortive. Oldcastle remained free until caught near Welshpool in 1417, and was hanged and burned. Shakespeare's Falstaff is based partly on him. » Henry V; Lollards

Oldenburg, Claes (1929–) US sculptor, born in Stockholm, Sweden. He studied at Yale, graduating in 1950. In his work he blends Surrealism and Pop Art, especially in his giant models of everyday objects made of canvas stuffed with foam rubber and painted in bright colours (eg 'Giant Ice Cream Cone', 1962). » Pop Art; Surrealism

Oldfield, Bruce (1950–) British fashion designer, born in London. He taught art, then studied fashion in Kent and in London, after which he became a freelance designer. He designed for Bendel's store in New York City, sold sketches to St Laurent, and showed his first collection in London in 1975. His designs include evening dresses for royalty and screen stars, and ready-to-wear clothes. » fashion

Olduvai Gorge [**ol**dooviy] A gorge within the Ngorongoro conservation area of the Rift Valley, N Tanzania. It is of great archaeological importance as the source of some of the oldest known 'human' remains, notably the Leakeys' 1959 discovery of the skull of *Zinjanthropus boisei* ('nutcracker man'), and remains of *Australopithecus*, *Homo habilis*, and *Homo erectus*. » *Homo* [i]; Leakey; Ngorongoro Crater; Rift Valley; Tanzania [i]

oleander [oli**an**duh] An evergreen shrub growing to 5 m/16 ft, native to the Mediterranean region; leaves lance-shaped, leathery; flowers 4 cm/1½ in diameter, in terminal clusters, tubular with five spreading lobes, pink or white. It is widely cultivated in warm regions as an ornamental; all parts are poisonous. Cultivars have larger (often double) flowers, ranging from white to crimson or purple. (*Nerium oleander*. Family: *Apocynaceae*.) » cultivar; evergreen plants; shrub

oleaster [oli**as**tuh] A deciduous, sometimes thorny, shrub or tree growing to 13 m/42 ft, native to W Asia; leaves narrow, dull green above, covered with minute silvery scales beneath; flowers 1 cm/0.4 in long, tubular with four spreading lobes, silver outside, yellow inside, fragrant; berries silvery-yellow. (*Elaeagnus angustifolia*. Family: *Eleagnaceae*.) » deciduous plants; shrub; tree [i]

olefin(e)s [**oh**luhfinz] » **alkenes**

Oléron, Ile d' [eel **do**layrõ], ancient **Uliarus** Wooded fertile island in E Bay of Biscay, W France; France's second largest off-shore island (after Corsica); 3 km/1¾ ml from mainland; linked by modern toll-bridge; area 175 sq km/68 sq ml; length 30 km/19 ml; main towns, Le Château d'Oléron, St-Pierre d'Oléron; oysters, farming, tourism. » Biscay, Bay of

oligarchy In ancient Greece, the term applied to city-states such as Corinth and Thebes, where political power was in the hands of a minority of its male citizens. They contrasted with democracies such as Athens and Argos, where power was held by the majority. » Greek history; polis

Oligocene epoch [**ol**iguhseen] A geological epoch of the Tertiary period from c.37 million to 25 million years ago, and characterized by colder climate, the general retreat of the seas, and the evolution of many modern mammals. » geological time scale; Tertiary period; RR16

oligomer [**ol**iguhmer] A small polymer, generally consisting of 3–10 monomer units; examples include oligopeptides and oligosaccharides. » carbohydrate; peptide

oligopoly An economic situation where an industry is dominated by a few suppliers. In economic theory, it constitutes one type of imperfect competition. » monopoly; perfect competition

olingo [o**ling**goh] A nocturnal mammal, native to C and N South America; superficially resembles the lemur; pale brown with small rounded ears, large eyes and very long, darkly banded tail; inhabits trees; eats mainly fruit. (Genus: *Bassaricyon*, 5 species. Family: *Procyonidae*.) » lemur

Oliphant, Sir Mark (Marcus Laurence Elwin) (1901–) Australian nuclear physicist, born in Adelaide. He studied at Adelaide and Cambridge, joined the Cavendish Laboratory, and became Professor at Birmingham (1937). He worked on the atomic bomb project at Los Alamos (1943–5), became Australian member of the United Nations Atomic Energy Commission (1946), and research professor at Canberra (1950). He was knighted in 1959. » atomic bomb

Olivares, Gaspar de Guzman y Pimental, Conde-Duque de ('Count-Duke of') [oli**vah**rez] (1587–1645) Spanish statesman, favourite and Chief Minister of Philip IV (1623–43), born in Rome. He cultivated the arts, and tried to modernize Spain's anachronistic administration and to build up military resources, but his introduction of the Union of Arms brought revolts in Portugal and Catalonia (1640–3). He took Spain into renewed conflict with the United Provinces and challenged France over the Mantuan Succession (1628–31) and in the Thirty Years' War (1635–48). After the Spanish fleet was destroyed at the Battle of the Downs (1639) and Roussillon was overrun by the French, he was dismissed (1643), and died in exile at Toro. » Habsburgs; Philip IV; Thirty Years' War

olive shell A carnivorous or scavenging marine snail found in warm seas; usually active at night, moving around at a depth of 1–2 cm/0.4–0.8 in below the surface of the sediment; prey caught using a large muscular foot. (Class: *Gastropoda*. Order: *Neogastropoda*.) » carnivore [i]; gastropod; snail

olive tree A long-lived evergreen tree native to the Mediterranean region, growing to 15 m/50 ft; trunk silvery, gnarled with numerous cavities; leaves opposite, narrow, pointed, leathery, dark green above, pale beneath; flowers small, white, four petals; fruit succulent, oily, green, ripening over one year to black. The wild form (variety *sylvestris*) is bushy with spiny branches and small fruits; the cultivated olive (variety *europaea*) has been grown since early times as an important source of olive oil obtained from pressed fruit. The fruits are also pickled, both green and ripe. The trees yield timber. (*Olea europaea*. Family: *Oleaceae*.) » evergreen plants; tree [i]

Olives, Mount of or **Mount Olivet** [**ol**ivet] A rocky outcrop overlooking the Old City of Jerusalem across the Kidron Valley, a site of sanctuaries during the reigns of David and Solomon, and a traditional Jewish burial ground. In Jesus' ministry this marks the location of his discourse about the coming of the end of the age (*Mark* 13). It is also near the site of the Garden of Gethsemane where Jesus was arrested, and the supposed location of the ascension of the risen Jesus (*Acts* 1.6–12). » David; Gethsemane; Jerusalem; Jesus Christ; Solomon

Olivier (of Brighton), Laurence (Kerr), Baron (1907–89) British actor, producer, and director, born at Dorking, Surrey. He trained in London, and began his career at Birmingham in 1926, joining the Old Vic company, London, in 1937. He played all the great Shakespearean roles, while his versatility was underlined by his virtuoso display in *The Entertainer* (1957) as a broken-down low comedian. After war service he became in 1944 co-director of the Old Vic. His films include *Henry V*, *Hamlet*, and *Richard III*. Divorced from his first wife, **Jill Esmond** in 1940, in the same year he married English actress **Vivien Leigh** (1913–67), whose film career included the role of Scarlett O'Hara in *Gone With the Wind*. They were divorced in 1960, and in 1961 he married English actress **Joan Plowright** (1929–). In 1962 he became Director of the Chichester Theatre Festival and (1963–73) of the National Theatre. After 1974 he appeared chiefly in films and on television, notably in *Brideshead Revisited* (1982) and *King Lear* (1983). He was knighted in 1947, and made a life peer in 1970. He died at Steyning, West Sussex. » National Theatre; theatre

olivine A silicate mineral ranging in composition from Fe_2SiO_4 (*fayalite*) to Mg_2SiO_4 (*forsterite*); glassy, hard, and typically olive-green in colour. It is important in rocks poor in silica, and is a primary constituent of the upper mantle of the Earth. Its gem quality crystals are termed *peridot*. » silicate minerals

olm A salamander, native to underground limestone caves in Yugoslavia and NE Italy; spends entire life in water; thin pale body (length, up to 300 mm/12 in), red feathery gills, extremely thin limbs, no eyes. (*Proteus anguinus*. Family: *Proteidae*.) » salamander [i]

Olmecs Members of a highly elaborate Middle American Indian culture on the Mexican Gulf Coast, at its height 1200–600 BC. The Olmecs influenced the rise and development of the other great civilizations of Middle America. They probably had the first large planned religious and ceremonial centres, at San Lorenzo, La Venta, and Tres Zapotecs, where the resident elite and their families lived, served by much larger populations dispersed throughout the lowland area. The centres had temple mounds, monumental sculptures, massive altars, and sophisticated systems of drains and lagoons. They were probably also the first people in the area to devise glyph writing and the 260-day Mesoamerican calendar. » American Indians; hieroglyphics [i]

Olympia (Greece), Gr **Olímbia** 37°38N 21°39E. Village and national sanctuary in Ilia department, S Greece, on N bank of R Alfios; chief sanctuary of Zeus, from c.1000 BC; site of the Panhellenic religious festival held every four years from 776 BC, the ancestor of the modern Olympic Games; railway; major excavations in 19th-c; Temple of Zeus (5th-c BC), Hera's Temple, Stadium. » Greece [i]; Isthmian Games; Olympic Games; Pythian Games; Zeus, statue of

Olympia (USA) 47°03N 122°53W, pop (1980) 27 447. Seaport capital of Washington State and Thurston County, W Washington, USA; at the S end of Puget Sound, at the mouth of Deschutes R; founded at the end of the Oregon Trail, 1850; capital of Washington Territory, 1853; railway; lumbering, fishing, mining. » Oregon Trail; Washington (state)

Olympians In Greek mythology, a collective name for the major gods and goddesses, who were thought to live on Mt Olympus, the highest mountain in Ancient Greece, situated in a range between Macedonia and Thessaly.

Olympic Games A sports gathering held every four years by athletes from all over the world, each celebration taking place at a different venue. They evolved from the Ancient Greek Games, held at Olympia, which go back at least to the 8th-c BC. They were banned in AD 393 by the Christian Emperor Theodosius I, probably because of their pagan practices, and were revived in 1896 by French educator Pierre de Fredi, Baron de Coubertin (1863–1937), with Athens as the first venue. Today, more than 6 000 competitors from nearly 100 nations compete at each games, in more than 20 different sports. Since 1924 a separate Winter Olympic Games has been staged, and is held in the same year as the Summer Games. The Games are governed by the International Olympic Committee. » RR102

Olympic National Park National park in the Olympic Mountains, Washington, USA; area 3 678 sq km/1 420 sq ml; a world heritage area; noted for the variety of its scenery, which includes glaciers and a stretch of the Pacific coastline, and as a refuge for the rare Roosevelt elk. » Washington (state)

Olympus, Mount (Cyprus) [uhl**limp**uhs] Mountain in the Troödos range of C Cyprus, rising to 1 951 m/6 401 ft; highest peak on the island. » Cyprus [i]

Olympus, Mount (Greece), Gr **Ólimbos** [uhl**limp**uhs] Range of mountains between Macedonia and Thessalia regions, N Greece, highest point, Mitikas (2 917 m/9 570 ft); traditionally the abode of the dynasty of gods headed by Zeus. » Greece [i]; Zeus

Olympus Mons [uhl**limp**uhs **monz**] A huge volcanic mountain on Mars, lying on the edge of a region of intense Martian volcanism ('Tharsis'), a broad upwarp in the crust. It is enormous by terrestrial standards, with a summit 25 km/15.5 ml high, and a diameter of 700 km/435 ml. It is accompanied by three other huge volcanoes on the Tharsis bulge, each with summits about 17km/10.5 ml high. It was discovered by Mariner 9 orbiter in 1972, and extensively studied by Viking orbiters, but was previously known to astronomers as a region of persistent brightenings ('Nix Olympica'), now realized to be diurnal cloud formations. » Mariner programme; Mars (astronomy); Mauna Loa; Viking project

Olynthus [o**lin**thuhs] In antiquity, the chief city-state on the Chalcidic peninsula in the N Aegean. It was destroyed in 348 BC by its former ally, Philip II of Macedon, for deserting his cause and throwing in its lot with Athens. » Macedon

Om [om, ohm] A mystical and sacred monosyllable in Hindu tradition, the sound of which was believed to have a divine power. It was used at the beginning and end of prayers, as a mantra for meditation, and as an invocation itself. In the Upanishads it is mentioned as the primary sound syllable. » Hinduism; Upanishads; RR93

Omagh [oh**mah**], Gaelic **An Omaigh** 54°36N 7°18W, pop (1981) 14 627. County town of Tyrone, WC Northern Ireland, on R Strule; footwear, engineering, salmon fishing, dairy produce, tourism; inside the 19th-c Catholic parish church is the Black Bell of Drumragh (9th-c). » Tyrone

Omaha (Indians) A Siouan-speaking N American Plains Indian group, originally from the Atlantic seaboard, who migrated to Minnesota but in the late 17th-c were pushed into Nebraska by Dakotas, where they farmed and hunted buffalo. In 1854 they sold most of their land to White settlers, but were granted some land by the government in 1882. Population c.1500 on reservations in Nebraska. » American Indians; Plains Indians

Omaha (Nebraska) [**oh**maha] 41°17N 96°01W, pop (1980) 314 255. Seat of Douglas County, E Nebraska, USA; a port on the Missouri R; fur-trading post established here, 1812; city status, 1867; largest city in the state; airport; railway; two universities (1878, 1908); major livestock market and meat-processing centre; farm machinery, electrical equipment, fertilizers; centre for medical treatment and research; air force base; Joslyn Art Museum, aerospace museum, Boys Town; College World Series (Jun). » Nebraska

Oman, formerly **Muscat and Oman**, official name **Sultanate of Oman** [oh**man**] pop (1990e) 1 468 000; area 300 000 sq km/115 800 sq ml. Independent state in the extreme SE corner of the Arabian peninsula; bounded NW by the United Arab Emirates, N and W by Saudi Arabia, SW by Yemen, NE by the Gulf of Oman, and SE and E by the Arabian Sea; capital, Muscat; chief towns, Matrah, Nizwa, Salalah; timezone GMT +4; population mainly Arabic; official language, Arabic; chief religion, Ibadhi Muslim; unit of currency, the Omani rial; the tip of the Musandam peninsula in the Strait of Hormuz is separated from the rest of the country by an 80 km/50 ml strip belonging to the United Arab Emirates; Hajar range runs NW–SE parallel to the coast; several peaks in the Jabal Akhdar over 3 000 m/10 000 ft; alluvial plain of the Batinah in E and N; vast sand desert in NE; a desert climate with much local variation; hot and humid coast (Apr–Oct), maximum 47°C; hot and dry interior; relatively temperate in mountains; light monsoon rains in S (Jun–Sep); dominant maritime power of the W Indian Ocean in 16th-c; internal dissension (1913–20) between supporters of the Sultanate and members of the Ibadhi sect who wanted to be ruled exclusively by their religious leader; separatist tribal revolt (1964) led to a police coup that installed the present Sultan in 1970; an independent state ruled by a sultan who is both head of state and premier; oil discovered in 1964, now provides over 90% of government revenue; natural gas an important source of industrial power; attempts made to diversify the economy; copper smelting, date processing, banana packing, electric wire and cables, paper bags; c.70% of the population relies on agriculture; alfalfa,

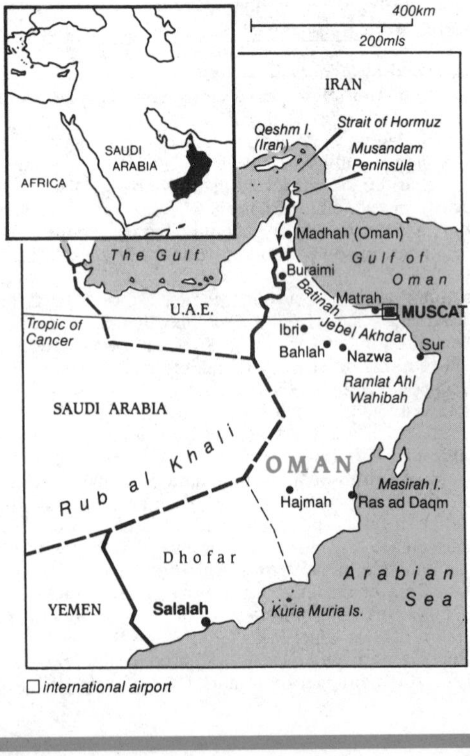

□ international airport

wheat, tobacco, fruit, vegetables, fishing. » Muscat; RR26 national holidays; RR58 political leaders

Oman, Gulf of NW arm of the Indian Ocean, lying between Oman and Iran; linked to the Arabian Gulf by the Strait of Hormuz, and (SE) to the Arabian Sea; vital waterway for ocean traffic to and from the Gulf states; 480 km/300 ml long. » Hormuz, Strait of; Indian Ocean

Omar or **Umar** (c.581–64) The second caliph (634–44), the father of one of Mohammed's wives, who succeeded Abu-Bekr. He built up an empire comprising Persia, Syria, and all N Africa. He was assassinated at Medina by a slave. » Abu-Bekr; Mohammed

Omar Khayyám (c.1050–c.1123) Persian astronomer-poet, born and died at Nishapur. Summoned to Merv by the sultan, he reformed the Muslim calendar, and was known to the Western world as a mathematician, until in 1859 Edward FitzGerald published a translation of his *Rubáiyát* ('Quatrains'). The work is now regarded as an anthology of which little or nothing may be by Omar. » Persian literature

ombudsman An official who investigates complaints regarding administrative action by governments – so-called 'mal-administration'. The complaint may not necessarily be confined to illegal action, but can cover broader injustices in administrative decisions. Most ombudsmen's powers are of necessity widely defined, but they normally do not investigate issues that can be considered by the courts or tribunals. Their findings do not have the force of law, and are put in the form of reports from which it is hoped remedial action will result. The first such institution was created in Sweden at the beginning of the 19th-c, and today most countries have followed the lead, with the exception of those in C and S America and communist states. » Parliamentary Commissioner for Administration

Omdurman [**om**doorman] 15°37N 32°29E, pop (1983) 526 287. Major suburb of Khartoum, C Sudan; connected to the main city by a tramline bridge over the White Nile; military headquarters of Mohammed Ahmed, 1884; captured by the British, 1898; university (1961); agricultural trade, textiles, crafts; ruins of the Mahdi's tomb. » Sudan [i]

Omdurman, Battle of [**om**doorman] (1898) An engagement outside Khartoum, across the Nile, which confirmed the British reconquest of the Sudan. The British campaign under Kitchener had been authorized in 1895, and instituted with powerful Anglo-Egyptian forces in 1896. The overwhelming defeat of the massed forces of the Khalifa (the successor of the Mahdi), with many casualties, illustrated the power of modern weapons. » Fashoda; Kitchener; Mohammed Ahmed

OMNIMAX » **IMAX**

omnivore Any animal, or human, whose diet includes both the flesh of animals and vegetable material; there may be specialized teeth to deal with the varied foodstuffs. The term contrasts with *carnivore* (a flesh-eater, such as the lion) and *herbivore* (a plant-eater, such as the cow). » carnivore [i]; herbivore

Omo National park in S Ethiopia; area 4 015 sq km/1 550 sq ml; lower valley, a world heritage site. » Ethiopia [i]

Omsk 55°00N 73°22E, pop (1989) 1 148 000. River-port capital of Omskaya oblast, W Siberian Russia; at the confluence of the Irtysh and Om Rivers; founded as a fortress, 1716; the greenest city in Siberia with 25 sq km/10 sq ml of boulevards and gardens; airport; on the Trans-Siberian Railway; university (1974); oil refining, chemicals, engineering, clothing, footwear. » Russia; Trans-Siberian Railway

onager [**on**ajuh] » **ass**

Onassis, Aristotle (Socrates) (1906–75) Greek millionaire shipowner, born in Smyrna, Turkey. At 16 he left Smyrna for Greece as a refugee, and from there went to Buenos Aires, where later he was Greek consul for a time. He bought his first ships in 1932–3, built up one of the world's largest independent fleets, and became a pioneer in the construction of supertankers. His first marriage ended in divorce in 1960, and after a long relationship with Maria Callas, in 1968 he married **Jacqueline Bouvier Kennedy**, the widow of US President John F Kennedy. He died in Paris.

oncogene A gene which causes a normal cell to develop into a cancerous cell. Its effects are often the result of chromosomal re-arrangement, so that in its new location it escapes the control mechanisms previously present, and is actively transcribed. In Burkitt's lymphoma, for example, the common translocation brings the oncogene *c-myc* on chromosome 8 to the vicinity of an immunoglobin gene on chromosome 14. » cancer; cell; gene

oncology The branch of medicine concerned with the nature and origin of tumours, including the study of their natural history and response to treatment by drugs, surgery, or by ionizing radiation (radioactive substances or X-rays). » cancer; medicine

ondes Martenot [õd **mah**tuhnoh] An electronic musical instrument invented in 1928 by Maurice Martenot; the name derives from Fr *ondes* '[musical] waves'. A keyboard, capable of producing a vibrato, is played by the right hand; the left operates the controls for timbre and dynamics. The sound is heard through loudspeakers, often of unusual design. The instrument has been used especially by French composers, including Messiaen and Boulez. » electrophone; keyboard instrument; Boulez; Messiaen

One Thousand Guineas » **Classics**

Onega, Lake [on**yeg**a], Russ **Ozero Onezhskoye** area 9 720 sq km/3 752 sq ml. Second largest lake in Europe, NW European Russia, close to the Finnish border; between L Ladoga (S) and the White Sea (NE); length, 250 km/155 ml; maximum depth, 120 m/394 ft; narrow bays (N) extend up to 112 km/70 ml inland; numerous islands (N); connected by canal to the R Volga and the White Sea; chief ports include Petrozavodsk, Voznesenye, Povenets; freezes over (Nov–May). » Russia

Oneida [ohni**yi**da] An Iroquoian-speaking N American Indian agricultural group, the smallest tribe of the Iroquois League, originally based in C New York State. They supported the colonists during the American Revolution and were attacked by pro-British Iroquois. They later divided into factions settling in Ontario, Wisconsin, and New York. Population c.5 700. » American Indians; Iroquois Confederacy

onion Any of several species of the Genus *Allium*, probably originating in Asia, and all grown as vegetables. The ordinary onion (*Allium cepa*) has solitary, globular, or flask-shaped bulbs, often of great size; flattened, tubular leaves semi-circular in cross-section; and inflated stalks bearing white flowers. **Spanish onion** is a variety with white-skinned bulbs; the **shallot** a variety with clusters of small, oval bulbs. **Egyptian** and **everlasting onions** are varieties with narrow bulbs growing in clumps, and bulbils mixed with the flowers. **Welsh onion** (*Allium fistulosum*) has narrow bulbs, leaves circular in cross-section, and yellowish flowers. (Family: *Liliaceae*). » allium; bulb; bulbil

Onnes, Heike Kamerlingh [**oh**nes] (1853–1926) Dutch physicist, born at Groningen. Educated at Heidelberg and Groningen, he became professor of physics at Leyden. He was the first to produce liquid helium, and worked in low-temperature physics, discovering the phenomenon of superconductivity. In 1913 he was awarded the Nobel Prize for Physics, and died at Leyden. » helium; superconductivity

onomastics The study of the history, development, and geographical distribution of proper names. All categories of names are included, such as people's first names and surnames, place names, home names, and the names of boats, trains, and pets. » semantics

onomatopoeia [onuhmatuh**pee**a] (Gr 'name-making') The imitation of a natural (or mechanical) sound in language. This may be found in single words (*screech*, *babble*, *tick-tock*) or in longer units. It is especially heard in poetry, where Pope said that 'The sound must give an echo to the sense'; for example, 'the slithering and grumble/as the mason mixed his mortar' (Seamus Heaney). Japanese has over three times as many onomatopoeic expressions as English, and uses them to express a much wider range of meanings, eg *fura-fura* ('roam') and *dabu-dabu* ('baggy'). » poetry

onsen [**on**sen] A Japanese hot spring. The country's volcanic geography means there are many hot spring resorts, or spas, a favourite destination of private or company excursions. Some springs are supposed to have medicinal properties. *Onsen* hotels can have public baths as large as swimming pools.

Ontario pop (1981) 8 625 107; area 1 068 580 sq km/412 578 sq ml. Province in SE Canada; boundaries include Hudson Bay (N), James Bay (NE), and USA (S), largely via the Great Lakes; rocky Canadian Shield in N, with clay belt suitable for farming; several rivers flow into Hudson and James Bays, the St Lawrence, and the Great Lakes; many lakes; N area sparsely populated, densely wooded; capital, Toronto; major cities include Ottawa, Thunder Bay, Hamilton; wealthiest, most populated, and second largest province; tobacco, corn, livestock, poultry, dairy products, fur, vehicles and parts, food processing, iron and steel, machinery, mining (nickel, copper, uranium, zinc, gold, iron), hydroelectricity; widely explored by French fur traders and missionaries, 17th-c; British territory, 1763; many United Empire Loyalist immigrants after the American War of Independence; constituted as Upper Canada, 1791; separatist rebellion, 1837–8; joined to Lower Canada, 1840; modern province established at time of confederation, 1867; governed by a lieutenant-governor and a 125-member legislature. » American Revolution; Canada [i]; Ottawa; Toronto

Ontario, Lake Smallest of the Great Lakes, N America, on US–Canadian border; length 311 km/193 ml; breadth 85 km/53 ml; maximum depth 244 m/800 ft; area 19 011 sq km/7 338 sq ml, just over half in Canada; connected (SW) with L Erie via the Niagara R and the Welland Ship Canal; outlet, the St Lawrence R (NE); canals link with Hudson R, L Huron, and Ottawa; ports include Kingston, Hamilton, Toronto, Rochester, Oswego; never ice-bound. » Great Lakes; St Lawrence River; Welland Ship Canal

ontological argument An argument for God's existence, allegedly based on logic alone, presented by St Anselm, Descartes, and others. According to Anselm, God is the being than which nothing greater can be conceived. If God did not exist, something greater than he could be conceived; therefore God must exist. » Anselm, St; God

ontology In metaphysics, the investigation of what sorts of things exist most fundamentally. For example, a materialist ontology claims that matter is the only fundamentally existing thing, so that anything else alleged to exist must either not really exist or be accounted for in exclusively materialistic terms. » metaphysics; monism; pluralism (philosophy)

Onychophora [oni**kof**uhra] A sub-phylum of primitive arthropods, comprising the velvet worms; sometimes classified as a separate phylum. » Peripatus; velvet worm

onyx » **agate**

oolite [**oh**uhliyt] A limestone composed of *ooliths*, ie rounded grains made of concentric layers of radiating fibres of carbonate, usually aragonite or calcite. It is formed by the precipitation and growth of consecutive layers of carbonate on a nucleus of a sand or shell fragment, as it is moved about on a warm, shallow sea floor. Coarser oolites (>3 mm/0.12 in diameter) are termed *pisolites*. » aragonite; calcite; limestone

Oort cloud [awt] A hypothesized source of the long-period comets; a spherical 'halo' about the Sun at a distance of c.50 000 AU; named after Dutch astronomer Jan Hendrik Oort (1900–), who first noted the clustering of aphelia of new comets in this region. It is at the boundary of the Sun's gravitational sphere of influence, about a third of the distance to the nearest star. Comets are believed to have originated in the outer Solar System 4.6 thousand million years ago when the system was being formed, and to have been scattered outward by the gravitational effects of the giant planet. » astronomical unit; comet; periapsis; Solar System

Oostende [ohs**ten**duh] » **Ostend**

Op Art An abbreviation for **Optical Art**, a modern art movement which exploits the illusionistic effects of abstract spiral or wavy patterns, stripes, spots, etc. Hungarian-born French painter Victor Vasarely (1908–) and British painter Bridget Riley (1931–) are leading exponents. » abstract art; modern art

opah [**oh**puh] » **moonfish**

opal A natural form of amorphous (non-crystalline) silica (SiO_2), containing varying amounts of water, and formed at relatively low temperatures from solutions associated with igneous activity and supersaturated in silica. It is usually white, but gems have a characteristic play of rainbow colours. The best occurrences are in Australia. » gemstones; silica; Plate V

OPEC (Organization of Petroleum Exporting Countries) [**oh**pek] An international economic organization set up in 1960 with its headquarters in Vienna; the longest-surviving major cartel. It consists of 13 oil-producing countries: the founder members were Iran, Iraq, Kuwait, Saudi Arabia, and Venezuela; and they have since been joined by Algeria, Ecuador, Gabon, Indonesia, Libya, Nigeria, Qatar, and the United Arab Emirates (formerly Abu Dhabi). Its purpose is to co-ordinate the petroleum policy of members to protect their interests, especially in relation to the fixing of prices for crude oil and the quantities to be produced. » cartel

open-cast mining » **mining**

open cluster A young family (10–250 million years) of a few dozen stars formed simultaneously and still physically close together; also called a **galactic cluster**. There are c.1 000 in our Galaxy. Pleiades and Hyades are examples visible to the naked eye. » Hyades; Pleiades (astronomy); star

Open Door US foreign policy towards China, formulated in response to the weakness of the late Chinese empire. Announced in March 1900, the Open Door policy sought to preserve Chinese integrity by opposing the development of spheres of influence dominated by particular countries.

open-ended investment company or **mutual fund** An investment company which pools the funds of its shareholders, and invests in a diversified portfolio of stocks and shares. It grows by continually offering new shares for sale. A UK example is the unit trust company. Such a company contrasts with a **closed-end** investment company, which has a fixed amount of share capital. » investment company; unit trust

open enrolment A policy which permits parents to enrol their child at any school which has a place available. This is in contrast with a policy based on strictly defined geographical catchment areas. » education

open government A demand made by several groups in the 1970s and 1980s, particularly in the UK, for less secrecy in policy making. Such groups press for reform of the 'catch-all' Section 2 of the Official Secrets Act, and the introduction of a Freedom of Information Act. The UK government introduced reform proposals in the late 1980s, but critics argued that these were likely to prove even more restrictive.

open-hearth process A steel-making process devised in 1860 by William Siemens (1823–83) and first successfully operated in 1864 by Pierre Émile Martin (1824–1915). The molten pig iron from which the steel is to be made is not in direct contact with the fuel providing the heat, but only with the hot flames from combustion which play on a shallow hearth containing pig-iron, scrap, and a flux. The steel can be withdrawn continuously. It will operate with iron derived from ores, with which the Bessemer process is ineffective. » Bessemer process; iron; Siemens; steel

open-market operations An economic situation where a central bank actively engages in selling or buying government bonds to influence liquid reserves in the banks. If the central bank buys securities, the money paid out increases the commercial banks' reserves, and therefore the amount of money that can be lent, and vice-versa. The opposite consequences obtain when the central bank engages in selling. » liquidity

open plan An arrangement of rooms in a building in which the internal doors and walls have been reduced to a minimum, or even omitted altogether. It is particularly associated with the International Style architecture of the 1920s and 1930s, and subsequently with offices and private housing of the period after World War 2.

open-plan school A school with few interior walls or box-shaped classrooms. Instead, open-plan areas permit freedom of movement and team teaching. Usually there are special areas for noisier activities or for painting and drama, as well as a resources centre. » open plan

open shop » **closed shop**

open stage Any stage in a theatre building which is in the same space as the auditorium, and which has no part of the acting or scenic area separated from the audience by a wall or an abrupt variation in ceiling height. » theatre in the round

Open Theater A US experimental theatre company which

performed from 1963 until 1973. Under the leadership of Joseph Chaikin, it concentrated on extending the actor's resources for image-making and encouraged collaboration, through a creative rehearsal period, between actors and writers. » Chaikin; theatre

Open University An institution of higher education, such as has been established in a number of countries, which enables students to study for a degree without attendance. Courses are usually based on a credit system, and the student graduates when sufficient credits have been amassed. The teaching is frequently carried out through correspondence units and broadcast or taped supporting programmes, though often with some face-to-face tutoring at local study centres. Entry qualifications are often more permissively framed than in conventional universities, and in many cases no formal qualifications are required, because beginners can take foundation or access courses. » credits; School of the Air; university

opera A stage work in which music plays a continuous or substantial role. The genre originated in Florence c.1600, and was well established throughout Italy by the end of the 17th-c; by the middle of the 18th-c it had conquered most of W Europe. In Italy, opera, whether serious or comic, has usually been sung throughout; elsewhere other types have developed which alternate songs with spoken dialogue (*semi-opera* in England, *opéra comique* in France, *Singspiel* in Germany). The history of opera has largely been one of reforms introduced to correct an imbalance between the demands of music and those of the drama. Wagner's music dramas aimed at a *Gesamkunstwerk* which united the arts of music, poetry, gesture, and painting. The hope was that this would provide the 'music of the future'; but the course of opera since then has been dictated as much by financial as by artistic considerations. » aria; chamber opera; comic opera; La Scala; leitmotif; music theatre; opera buffa; opéra comique; opera seria; operetta; overture; recitative; Royal Opera House; semi-opera; Singspiel; Sydney Opera House; vaudeville; Wagner; zarzuela

opera buffa Italian comic opera, especially of the 18th-c, with dialogue in recitative. Mozart's *Le nozze di Figaro* (1786, The Marriage of Figaro) is an outstanding example of the genre. » opera; Mozart; recitative

opéra comique French opera, with spoken dialogue, originally comic but later including such dramatic operas as Bizet's *Carmen* (1875). » Bizet; opera

opera seria Italian serious opera of the 18th-c and early 19th-c, exhibiting a rigid separation of aria (and the occasional ensemble) and recitative. It reached its highest point of development as a poetic form in the librettos of Metastasio, and as a musical genre in Mozart's *Idomeneo* (1781) and *La clemenza di Tito* (1791). » aria; Metastasio; Mozart; opera; recitative

operant A term of instrumental learning, introduced by US psychologist B F Skinner. An *operant* is an action which has an effect on the environment, and which can be modified according to its consequences. » conditioning; instrumental learning; Skinner

operating system A computer program which supervises the running of all other programs on a computer. Common microprocessor operating systems are CP/M and MS DOS. » DOS

operationalism A programme enunciated by P W Bridgman in 1927 which identifies scientific concepts with the sets of physical operations used to measure them; length, for example, is nothing more than what is specified by the activities of measurement. In psychology, operationalists sought to replace private mental states with the experimental measurement of behaviour. » Bridgman

operetta Light opera, with spoken dialogue and usually dancing, exemplified in the stage works of Offenbach, Strauss, and Sullivan. » opera; Offenbach; Strauss, Johann (the Younger); Sullivan, Arthur

operon A group of closely linked genes which affect different steps in a single metabolic sequence and which function as an integrated unit. The term was introduced by the French geneticist, François Jacob, in 1960. » gene; metabolism

Ophir [**oh**fer] A land of unknown location, mentioned in the Bible as famous for its resources of gold; 1 *Kings* 9–10, 22 suggest that it was reached from Palestine by ship, so it is variously placed in Arabia, India, or E Africa. Solomon is said to have sent a fleet there from Ezion-Geber, but the fame of the 'gold of Ophir' is known also from archaeological inscriptions. » Bible; Solomon

Ophites [**oh**fiyts] Gnostic sects who accorded special significance to the serpent. Some groups regarded it as an object of worship; others regarded it as a hostile power. » Gnosticism

Ophiuchus [ofee**yoo**kuhs] ('serpent bearer') A large constellation on the celestial equator. » constellation; RR9

ophthalmia Inflammation of the conjunctival membrane covering the eye in the newborn (*ophthalmia neonatorum*) or arising as a consequence of injury to the other eye (*sympathetic ophthalmia*). » conjunctivitis; eye [i]

ophthalmology The branch of medical practice concerned with disorders and diseases of the eyes. It includes general or systemic diseases that may affect the eye, and their medical and surgical treatment. » eye [i]; medicine

Ophuls or **Opüls, Max**, originally **Max Oppenheimer** (1902–57) Franco-German film director, born in Saarbrücken, who chose French nationality in the plebiscite of 1934. He worked in films from 1930, first in Germany and later in France. In 1941 he emigrated to the USA, and in 1947–49 made *The Exile*, *Caught*, and *The Reckless Moment*. He then returned to France where he made his greatest successes, *La Ronde* (1950, The Round) and *Lola Montez* (1955). He died soon after in Hamburg.

Opie, John (1761–1807) British portrait and historical painter, born near St Agnes, Cornwall. His portraits interested his teacher John Wolcot (1738–1819), by whom he was taken to London to become the 'Cornish Wonder', producing such works as 'The Murder of Rizzio' (1787). He became professor of painting at the Royal Academy in 1805, and died in London. » English art

opinion poll The taking of opinions from a representative and systematically-drawn sample of the electorate regarding their voting intentions, their views of political leaders, and wider political attitudes. Polls originated in the USA in the 1930s, and today are commonplace both at and between elections. Although based on small samples, they are accurate within a few per cent, but often people misunderstand precisely what they are measuring, and opinions can change. There is concern that the publishing of polls forecasting the results of elections could themselves influence voting intentions, and some countries restrict poll publication before an election.

opioid peptides A family of chemical substances (peptides), including *enkephalins*, *endorphins*, and *dynorphins*, which are found in the brain, spinal cord, pituitary gland, gastro-intestinal tract, and adrenal medulla; also known as **endogenous opioids**. In the brain and spinal cord they appear to be neurotransmitters or neuromodulators involved in pain perception. Central nervous system effects in humans include potent analgesia, euphoria, and respiratory depression. They are probably also involved in gut motility and pituitary hormone release. » endorphins; neurotransmitter; pain; peptide; receptors

Opitz (von Boberfeld), Martin (1597–1639) German poet, born at Bunzlau, Silesia. Educated at Frankfurt, Heidelberg, and Leyden, he served several German princes, and became historiographer to Wladyslaw IV of Poland. He wrote in a scholarly and stilted style which influenced German poetry for 200 years, and introduced Renaissance poetic thinking into Germany. He died at Danzig. » German literature; poetry; Renaissance

opium The dried extract of the unripe seed capsules of the opium poppy, *Papaver somniferum*, which contains several narcotic alkaloids, including morphine. It was used by many ancient cultures including the Babylonians, Egyptians, Greeks, and Romans for its properties of relieving pain, inducing sleep, and promoting psychological effects of peace and well-being. In China, opium smoking followed a ban on tobacco smoking introduced in the mid-17th-c; in 1840 the move to ban opium smoking precipitated the Opium Wars. Opium is still occasionally used as an anti-diarrhoeal preparation. » alkaloids; narcotics; opium poppy; Opium Wars

opium poppy A bluish or greyish-green annual growing to 1 m/3¼ ft, native to Europe and Asia; leaves oblong, shallowly lobed, clasping stem; flowers 4-petalled; capsule pepper-pot shaped, with a ring of pores around the rim. In the garden form (subspecies *hortense*), the flowers are mauve with a dark centre; in the drug-producing form (subspecies *somniferum*), the flowers are white. Opium is obtained by making incisions in the young fruit capsules, which weep latex containing the drug. The refinement of raw opium yields other drugs, such as morphine. (*Papaver somniferum*. Family: *Papaveraceae*.) » annual; latex; morphine; opium; poppy

Opium Wars Two wars (1839–42, 1856–60) between Britain and China, fought over the question of commercial rights in China, specifically relating to the opium trade. The British were victorious on each occasion, and gained increased access to China through the Treaties of Nanjing (Nanking) (1842) and Tianjin (Tientsin) (1858). » Arrow War; treaty ports

Oporto, Port **Porto** [uh**paw**toh] 41°08N 8°40W, pop(1981) 350 200. Capital of Oporto district, N Portugal; 318 km/198 ml N of Lisbon, on N bank of R Douro near its mouth; second largest city in Portugal; bishopric; railway; university (1911); port wine, fruit, olive oil, cork; cathedral (13th-c), stock exchange palace, Clerigos Tower; festival of São João (Jun). » Portugal [i]

opossum [uh**po**suhm] A marsupial of family *Didelphidae* (75 species), native to the New World; hind foot with opposable 'thumb', and lacking the 'comb' of many Australian marsupials; most climb trees; often have grasping tail; not all females have pouches; New World marsupials called opossums; Australian marsupials of similar appearance called **possums**. The name is also used for 7 species of New World **shrew** or **rat opossums** (family: *Caenolestidae*). » marsupial [i]; possum

Oppenheimer, J(ulius) Robert (1904–67) US nuclear physicist, born in New York City. He studied at Harvard, Cambridge (UK), Göttingen, Leyden, and Zürich, then joined the California Institute of Technology (1929). He became director of the atom bomb project at Los Alamos (1943–5), chairman of the advisory committee to the US Atomic Energy Commission (1946–1952), and professor of physics at the Institute for Advanced Study, Princeton (1947). Opposing the hydrogen bomb project, in 1953 he was suspended from secret nuclear research as a security risk, but was awarded the Enrico Fermi prize in 1963. He retired in 1966, and died at Princeton, New Jersey. » atomic bomb; hydrogen bomb [i]

opposition (astronomy) The moment when a planet is opposite the Sun, as observed in our sky. It crosses the meridian at local midnight, which is therefore the best time for observing. » planet; meridian; Sun

opposition (politics) The right of parties and political movements not holding government office to criticize the government and seek to replace it by offering alternative policies. In democratic systems the *Opposition* normally consists of those parties which oppose the government through parliamentary channels, their activities being regarded as a necessary activity, and recognized in parliamentary and electoral procedures. Opposition can also occur from parties or movements outside parliament, either because they are too weak or not inclined to gain parliamentary representation. Interest groups may oppose governments on specific issues. In non-democratic systems, oppositions are often outlawed and sometimes repressed, although covert opposition continues. » parliament

Ops The Roman goddess of plenty, the consort of Saturn, identified with Rhea. » Rhea

optical activity The ability of certain materials to rotate the plane of polarization of light passing through them. The degree of rotation depends on the thickness of material traversed. Substances which rotate light clockwise (when looking along the beam towards the light source) are termed *dextrorotatory*; those which rotate to the left, *levorotatory*. Sugar, quartz, and turpentine are optically active. » chirality [i]; Faraday effect; light; polarization [i]

optical character reader (OCR) A machine which can read standard texts into a computer using a combination of optical and computer techniques. » character recognition

optical fibres Fibres of transparent optical material, usually glass, for transmitting images or data. Each fibre consists of a core and an outer cladding of lower refractive index: light travels through the core and is contained within it by refraction (total internal reflection) at the core/cladding boundary. In telecommunications, optical fibres, made from very pure materials, transmit data very long distances (up to 50 km/30 ml at one stretch). Optical fibre cables contain bundles of very thin fibres allowing high transmission capacity combined with flexibility. Because of the flexibility and small diameter of the optical fibre bundle, the technique is also used in medicine for viewing inaccessible parts of the body (*endoscopy*). » endoscopy; light; telecommunications

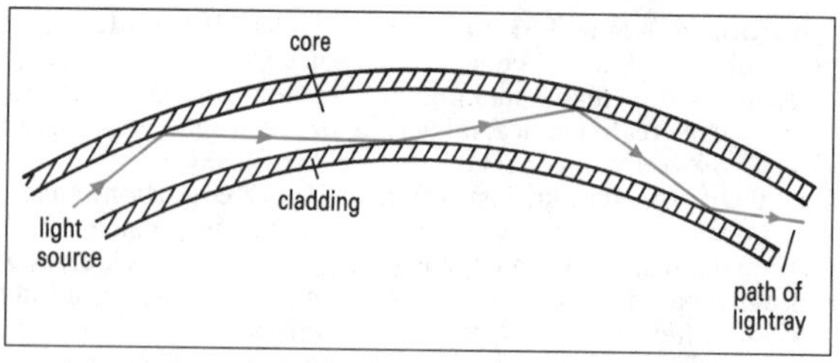

Section through optical fibre

optical sensing Sensors which detect light and convert it into electrical signals. Human eyes are very adaptable optical sensors, able to respond to a wide range of light levels: the light stimulation results in electrical impulses to the brain, which are then interpreted. Artificial optical sensors include photoelectric cells and photographic light meters. » electricity; eye [i]; light; photoelectric cell

optical stress analysis » photoelasticity

optics The study of light and of instruments using light. The subject has a long history. Mirrors were used by the ancient Egyptians c.2000 BC, and Greek philosophers developed simple theories of light (the law of reflection being stated by Euclid in 300 BC). The Greeks also knew of lenses (burning glasses) and studied refraction. The idea of using lenses to correct vision is probably due to Roger Bacon (13th-c). Galileo devised one of the earliest telescopes (1609); and Newton built the first reflecting telescope (1668). The compound microscope (consisting of two or more elements) is thought to have been invented c.1590 by Dutch spectacle-maker Zacharias Janssen (1588–1632). The modern formulation of geometrical optics, including reflection and refraction, began in the early 17th-c. Geometrical optics treats light as rays which travel in straight lines, changing direction only at the interface between materials. Diffraction was noted later that century, leading to early ideas that light may be wave-like. The *wave* theory of light was supported by the work of Dutch physicist Christian Huygens, but opposed by Isaac Newton, who maintained that light was composed of particles called corpuscles (the *corpuscular* theory). The demonstration by British physicist Thomas Young of interference effects in light (1804) supported the wave theory. Light as a (transverse) wave provided an explanation of the polarization effects observed by Newton and Huygens in calcite crystals. The modern understanding of light embraces both wave and particle viewpoints. The 'rays' of geometrical optics correspond to the direction of wave propagation. Physical optics includes wave effects.

Modern optical developments include optical fibres and their use in communications; optical logic elements and potentially optical computers; the application of Fourier analysis techniques, in particular spatial filtering (eg allowing the removal of unwanted horizontal lines from photographs); the mass production of plastic lenses with complicated curved surfaces; lasers; and holography. » aberrations **1** [i]; diffraction [i]; holography; Huygens' principle [i]; integrated optics; interference [i]; laser [i]; lens; light; magnification; mirror; optical fibres [i]; polarization [i]; refraction; telescope [i]; velocity of light; wave (physics) [i]

option (economics) A market in commodities or stocks and shares, where there is an opportunity to buy or sell at a specified price regardless of whether the price rises or falls

OPTICS

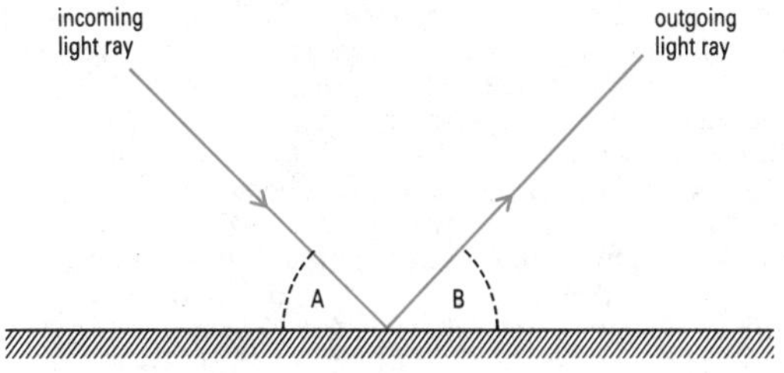

Fig 1 – A reflection at a mirror. The Law of Reflection says that angles A and B are the same.

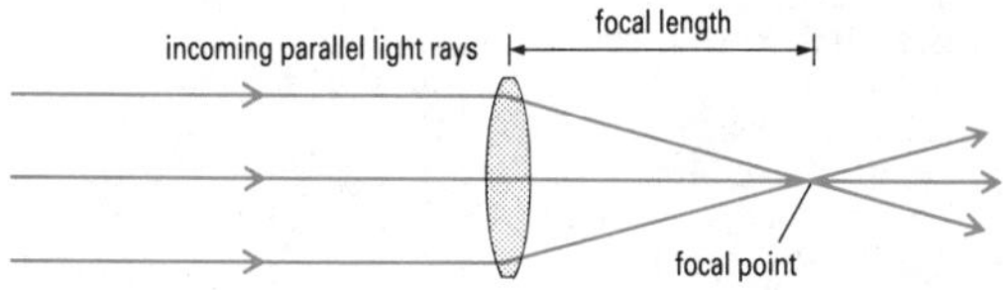

Fig 2 (a) – A double-convex converging lens.

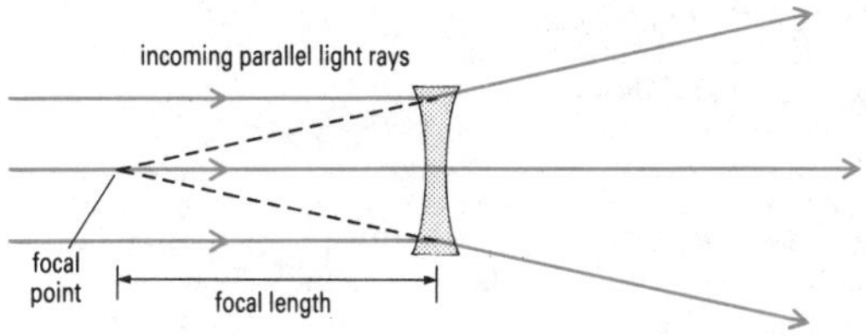

Fig 2 (b) – A double-concave diverging lens.

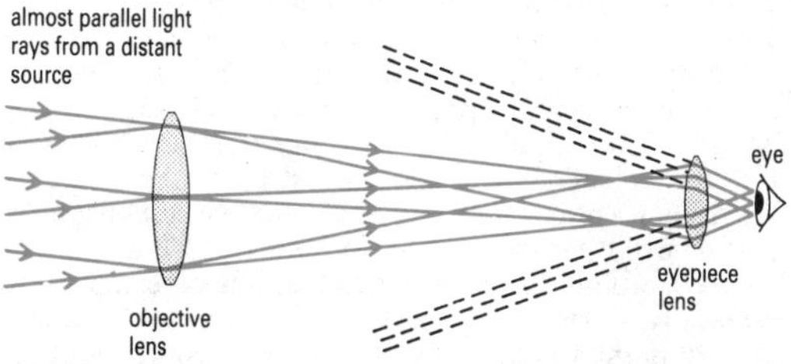

Fig 3 – A basic telescope. A long focal length objective lens and a short focal length eyepiece are required.

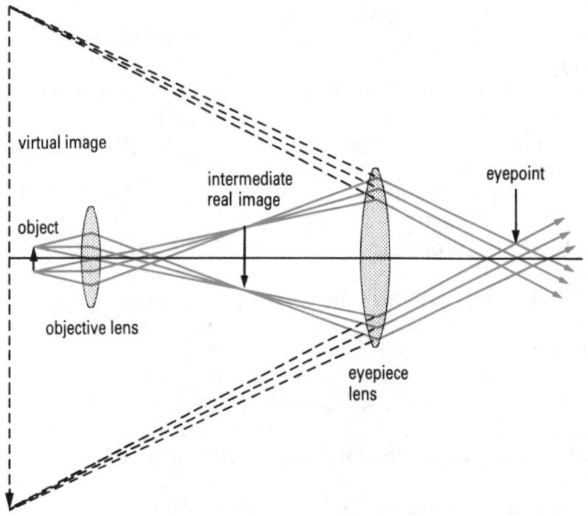

Fig 4 – A basic compound microscope. The object lens forms an enlarged real image of the object, which is then viewed via the eyepiece. A short focal length objective lens and eyepiece are required. A 'virtual image' is an image which cannot be projected on to a screen.

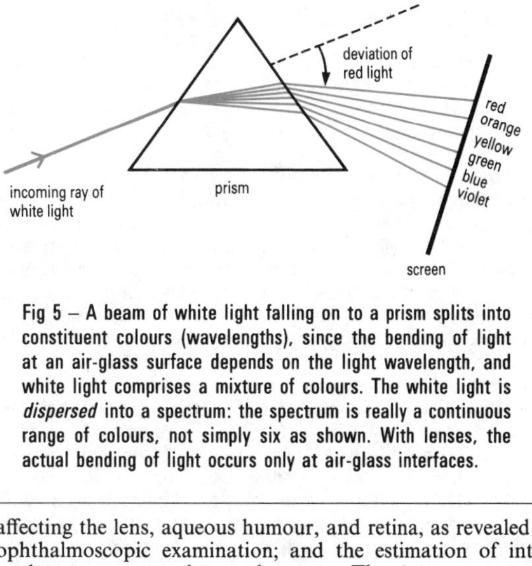

Fig 5 – A beam of white light falling on to a prism splits into constituent colours (wavelengths), since the bending of light at an air-glass surface depends on the light wavelength, and white light comprises a mixture of colours. The white light is *dispersed* into a spectrum: the spectrum is really a continuous range of colours, not simply six as shown. With lenses, the actual bending of light occurs only at air-glass interfaces.

subsequently. The present market in share and stock options (*traded options*) started in Chicago in 1973 and in London in 1978. Options are available only on shares of a few very large companies, and there is a nine-month time limit in which they must be exercised. The operation is considered highly speculative. » shares; stocks

optoelectronics The study of the production and control of light by electronic devices, such as semiconductor lasers, liquid crystals, and light-emitting diodes. It provides the technology for electronic displays in watches and calculators, and the interconversion of optical and electronic signals in optical fibre communications. » electronics; integrated optics; liquid crystals; optical fibres [i]

optometry The assessment of the function of the eye with special reference to errors of refraction, and the provision of appropriate corrective lenses and spectacles. It also now includes the specialized examination of the eye to diagnose a wide range of defects, such as disorders of fields of vision; disorders affecting the lens, aqueous humour, and retina, as revealed by ophthalmoscopic examination; and the estimation of intraocular pressure to detect glaucoma. These assessments are carried out by qualified and registered *optometrists*. » eye [i]; glaucoma; ophthalmology

opuntia [**opuhn**shuh] A large genus of cacti with stems made up of flattened, spiny, pear-shaped segments; native to the Americas, but widely introduced elsewhere. They spread easily, forming impenetrable thickets and often becoming troublesome weeds. They are sometimes cultivated for their juicy fruits, or grown as hedging plants and ornamentals. *Opuntia cochenillifera* is a food plant for cochineal insects. (Genus: *Opuntia*, 250 species. Family: *Cactaceae*.) » cactus [i]; prickly pear

Opus Dei [**oh**puhs **day**ee] (Lat 'work of God') **1** The title of a Roman Catholic society, founded in 1928, to promote the exercise of Christian virtues by individuals in secular society. In some countries and at certain periods (eg Spain in the mid-

20th-c) it acquired a measure of political power. » Roman Catholicism **2** A term formerly used by the Benedictines, referring to the divine office, to express the duty of prayer. » Benedictines; prayer

ora » **Komodo dragon** [i]

orache [orich] A genus of annuals and perennials, found almost everywhere, some forming small shrubs; the whole plant often mealy white; flowers tiny, green, males with five perianth-segments, females enclosed in two small bracts. The garden form of the annual **common orache** (*Atriplex patula*) is rich in vitamin C, and was once used as a vegetable. (Genus: *Atriplex*, 200 species. Family: *Chenopodiaceae*.) » annual; bract; perennial; perianth; shrub; vitamins [i]

oracle Divine prophetic declarations about unknown or future events, or the places (such as Delphi) or inspired individuals (such as the sibyls) through which such communications occur. In ancient Greek stories, these revelations were usually given in response to questions put to the gods. In Biblical traditions, however, oracles are sometimes distinguished from 'prophecies', in that the latter are unsolicited, although the Old Testament also testifies to interrogations of the divine being. Sometimes oracles were not expressed as verbal messages, but were associated with casting lots or other methods of the divination of signs. » Delphi; God; prophet; Sibyl

Oracle The teletext system operated by the UK Independent Broadcasting Association as a commercial service since 1981. The name is an acronym of *Optional Reception of Announcements by Coded Line Electronics*. » Ceefax; teletext

oracle bones Inscribed shoulder blades of pig, ox, and sheep (later tortoise shells) used for divination by the Shang monarchs of Anyang, N China, c.1850–1030 BC. The patterns of cracks made by hot brands applied to the bones were read as guidance from royal ancestors, this information being recorded alongside, using an ideographic script of 3 000 characters – the earliest-known Chinese writing. Since 1928 c.200 000 bones have been recovered. » Chinese; ideography

oracy The ability to express oneself coherently and to listen with good comprehension. The fostering of these skills has come to be seen as an important goal of childhood education, alongside the traditional focus on reading and writing. The term itself was coined on analogy with *literacy* and *numeracy*. » education; literacy

oral contraceptives » **contraception**

oral history The means of discovering information about the past by interviewing subjects, a technique increasingly used since the 1970s by social historians and anthropologists to augment the written record, especially in areas where 'orthodox' sources are deficient or unobtainable. Some argue that oral history is now a discipline in its own right, rather than simply a means of acquiring information. » anthropology; history

oral surgery » **dentistry**

Oran [orahn] or **Wahran** 35°45N 0°38W, pop (1984e) 450 000. Seaport in Oran department, N Algeria, N Africa; 355 km/221 ml W of Algiers; founded 8th-c; first ruled by Arabs, then Spaniards (1509–1708), Turks (1708–32), and French (1831–1962); landing point for Allied forces in World War 2; former French naval base nearby at Mers el Kabir; university (1965); airport; railway; iron, textiles, food processing, footwear, cigarettes; trade in grain, wool, vegetables, esparto grass; 16th-c Santa Cruz fortress, municipal museum. » Algeria [i]

orang-utan An ape native to forests of Sumatra and Borneo; height, 1.5 m/5 ft; sparse covering of long shaggy red-brown hair; armspan up to 2.25 m/7½ ft; adults with large naked 'double chin'; adult male with large naked fatty folds around face; sleeps in trees. (*Pongo pygmaeus*.) » ape

orange A citrus fruit 7–10 cm/2¾–4 in in diameter, globular with thick, often rough rind. The familiar edible fruit is the **sweet orange** (*Citrus sinensis*). The **Seville orange** (*Citrus aurantium*) has sour fruits, and is cooked for marmalade. **Bergamot orange** (*Citrus bergamia*) is grown as a source of bergamot oil, obtained from the rind of the yellow fruit, and oil of Neroli from the flowers. (Genus: *Citrus*. Family: *Rutaceae*.) » citrus; mandarin

Orange, Princes of » **William I** (of the Netherlands); **William III**

Orange [orãzh] 44°08N 4°48E, pop (1982) 17 745. Town in Vaucluze department, SE France, on the R Rhône, N of Avignon; market centre, glass, food processing; developed around a group of Roman monuments, now a world heritage site; vast well-preserved theatre, with 4 m/12 ft statue of Augustus (probably late 1st-c BC); 18 m/60 ft-high triumphal arch, commemorating Julius Caesar's victories over local Gauls. » Augustus; France [i]; Caesar

Orange Free State pop (1985) 1 776 903; area 127 993 sq km/ 49 405 sq ml. Province in EC South Africa; bounded S by the Orange R, NW by the Vaal R, and SE by Lesotho; capital, Bloemfontein; many settlements date from the Great Trek of 1831; claimed by British as the Orange River Sovereignty, 1848; independence, 1854; joined Union of South Africa as Orange Free State, 1910; a largely rural province; grain, livestock; oil, agricultural equipment, fertilizers, wool, clothing, cement, pharmaceuticals, pottery. » Bloemfontein; Great Trek; South Africa [i]

Orange Order An association that developed from the Orange Society, which had been formed in 1795 to counteract growing Catholic influence in Ireland and 'to maintain the laws and peace of the country and the Protestant constitution'. The name was taken from the Protestant Dutch dynasty represented by William III. Organized in 'Lodges', it provided the backbone of resistance to Home Rule proposals from the mid-1880s, and has operated as organized Protestantism in Northern Ireland since partition. » Protestantism; William III

Orange River, Afrikaans **Oranjerivier** River in Lesotho, South Africa, and Namibia; rises in the Drakensberg Mts in NE Lesotho, and flows S into South Africa, then generally W and NW, following the border between South Africa and Namibia, to enter the Atlantic Ocean at Alexander Bay; length 2 090 km/1 300 ml; dammed in several places as part of the **Orange River Project** (begun 1963) to provide irrigation and power. » Lesotho [i]; Nambia [i]

Oratorians 1 A community of priests, followers of St Philip of Neri (16th-c), living together without vows, and devoted to prayer, preaching, and attractive services of worship. They still flourish in many countries, including Italy, France, and England where they were introduced by Cardinal Newman. » Neri; Newman, John Henry; prayer **2** Priests of the French Oratory, or **Oratory of Jesus Christ**, founded in 1611 and re-established in 1852. This community is noted for educating priests and furthering popular devotion. » Jesus Christ; priest

oratorio A non-liturgical, quasi-dramatic sacred work, usually for solo voices, chorus, and orchestra. It takes its name from the Italian 'prayer-hall' in which the earliest oratorios were performed in the mid-17th-c, but until c.1750 it existed also in secular settings as an alternative to the serenata and opera, especially during Lent. Handel's oratorios, originally performed in the London theatres, represent this type at its finest, but by the time they influenced Haydn's *The Creation* (1798) the oratorio had come to be regarded as a religious rather than a dramatic work, and since then cathedral festivals have frequently provided the occasion for an oratorio performance. Among composers of oratorio after Haydn, Mendelssohn and Elgar were particularly important. » Elgar; Handel; Haydn; Mendelssohn

oratory The art and practice of public speaking. Effective oratory requires that the choice of language, its style, and mode of delivery should be appropriate for a given audience, location, and occasion. Its major forms (legal, political, ceremonial) can be traced back to earliest times, notably to the Greek orators of the 4th-c BC (eg Demosthenes), and the Roman orators of the 1st-c BC (eg Cicero). Other categories developed later, such as religious oratory, following the rise of Christianity and other religions, and commercial oratory. In modern times, oratory continues to be effectively practised, as can be seen in the speeches of Hitler, Churchill, and Martin Luther King Jr, and the radio or television debates and 'fireside chats' used by leading politicians. » Cicero; Demosthenes; rhetoric

orb weaver A spider that spins orb-shaped webs; legs armed with many long spines; fangs with many teeth; prey caught in web are cut out and wrapped in silk. (Order: *Araneae*. Family: *Araneidae*.) » spider

orbit The path followed by any celestial object or satellite moving through a gravitational field. For the case of two bodies only, the orbit can be calculated analytically with arbitrary precision, and is one of the conic sections: parabola, ellipse, or circle. For three or more, the problem is immensely complex, and has to be solved numerically by computer. A **geostationary orbit** is one followed by a satellite above the Equator at 35 900 km, where it keeps in exact step with the Earth's rotation and is thus always in the same part of the sky. This is essential for satellite communications and television. » conic sections [i]; gravitation; satellite

Orcagna, Andrea, originally **Andrea di Cione** [awk**an**ya] (c.1308–68) Italian painter, sculptor, and architect, born in Florence. A member of a family of painters, his greatest paintings are frescoes, an altarpiece in Santa Maria Novella, and 'Coronation of the Virgin' (National Gallery, London). Many consider him second in the 14th-c only to Giotto, who influenced him. » altarpiece; fresco; Giotto; Italian art

orchestra Originally the name for the semi-circular space in front of a stage, later extended to the body of instrumentalists that performed there. Large instrumental ensembles were often used in the Renaissance period, but these were not orchestras in the modern sense of a regular constituted body of string players, with additional woodwind, brass, and percussion as required. Opera 'orchestras' in the mid-17th-c were mostly small, with only one player to a part, and the development of the orchestra took place mainly in the courts, those of London, Paris, and Vienna being particularly important. The advent of the concerto in the late 17th-c stimulated the formation of four-part string orchestras in all the major musical centres, and by the end of the 18th-c the standard orchestra for the symphonies of Haydn and Mozart included also pairs of flutes, oboes, bassoons, horns, trumpets, timpani, and (sometimes) clarinets. Each section expanded further during the 19th-c, and the modern symphony orchestra of about 100 players will normally include 60 or more string instruments, triple or quadruple woodwind and brass, and (in addition to the instruments mentioned above), at least three trombones, tuba, harp, and a vast array of percussion. » concerto; musical instruments; orchestration; Philharmonic Society; promenade concert

orchestration The scoring of a piece of music for the instruments of the orchestra. The study of orchestration as a discipline separate from composition originated in the 19th-c, when one of the most influential treatises was written on the subject by Berlioz (1843). » Berlioz; musical instruments; orchestra

orchid A monocotyledonous plant belonging to the family *Orchidaceae*, one of the largest and most advanced flowering plant families, containing some 17 000 species. Orchids are found in virtually all parts of the world except Antarctica, but are especially abundant in the tropics. Nearly half the species are epiphytic; the remainder are terrestrial, a few Australian species even having a completely subterranean life-cycle. All are perennial herbs with sometimes tuberous rhizomes. The epiphytic species have clinging and aerial roots as well as normal feeding roots. A common feature is the development of *pseudobulbs* – cylindrical or bulb-like swellings of the stems just above soil level, which store nutrients and water, and from which leaves and flowers arise. The fleshy, frequently spotted or blotched leaves sheath the stem at their bases.

Orchids are best-known for their complex, often spectacular and exotic flowers, and for their highly developed pollination mechanisms. The flower typically consists of a slender ovary surmounted by three petaloid sepals and two similar petals, with the third petal forming a lower lip or *labellum* which differs from the others in form and colour. It is variously expanded, enlarged, lobed, frilled, or divided, sometimes spurred, and usually strikingly marked or ornamented. Within the flower the three stigmas and one or two stamens are fused into a column, the exact form of which depends greatly on the pollinator species to which these organs must be presented. Insects, bats, and even frogs may act as pollinators, and many are species specific. The pollen is usually held in sticky, stalked masses called *pollinia*, which become attached with special quick-setting glue to the pollinator. Despite pollinator specificity, orchids interbreed with great facility, and very many hybrids are known in the wild as well as in cultivation.

Orchid seeds take up to 18 months to ripen, and up to four years to reach the flowering stage. They are minute, with a poorly developed embryo, and germination is successful only if mycorrhizal fungi are present. Because of these problems, commercial orchid breeding relies heavily on tissue culture and similar propagation techniques. Orchids exert a strong fascination for many people, and numerous species are now commonly cultivated, with whole societies devoted to their study and care. (Family: *Orchidaceae*.) » bee orchid; cattleya;

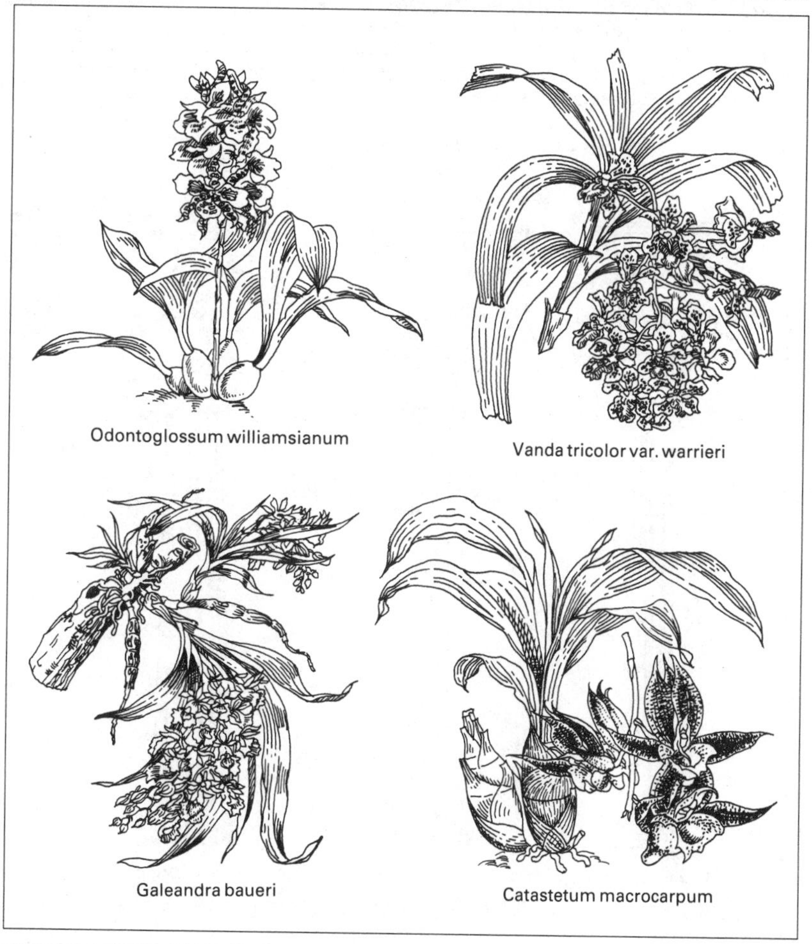

Orchids

cymbidium; epiphyte; flower [i]; helleborine; herb; lady's slipper; monocotyledons; mycorrhiza; perennial; pheromone; pollination; rhizome; twayblade; vanilla

Orczy, Emmuska, Baroness [awtsee] (1865–1947) British writer, born in Tarnaörs, Hungary. Educated in Brussels and Paris, she studied art in London. *The Scarlet Pimpernel* (1905) was her first success, followed by many popular adventure romances. She died in London. » novel

Order in Council In British government, legislation made by the Monarch in Council allowed by act of parliament, but which does not need to be ratified by parliament. It is the main means through which the powers of the royal prerogative are exercised. In practice the decisions are taken by government ministers, not by the monarch. » Parliament

Order of Merit (OM) In the UK, an order for distinguished men and women for whom a knighthood might not be appropriate. Instituted by Edward VII in 1902 and limited to 24 members, it comprises a military and a civil class. The ribbon is blue and scarlet. » decoration

order of reaction The dependence of a rate of reaction on the concentration of a reactant. A reaction whose rate varies directly with concentration is said to be *first order*; if as the square of the concentration, *second order*; and so on. The overall order of reaction is the sum of the orders with respect to each reactant. » mass action, law of

ordered pairs In mathematics, pairs of numbers, say (a,b) and (c,d) which are only equal if $a=c$, $b=d$. Rational numbers are examples of ordered pairs, as 2/3 is not the same as 3/2. Further examples are the Cartesian co-ordinates of points in a plane, for the point (3,4) is not the same as the point (4,3). Ordered triples, etc are defined similarly. » Cartesian co-ordinates

Orders » **(Orders of) Australia/Bath/British Empire/Canada/Companions of Honour/Garter/Royal Victorian /St Michael and St George/Thistle**

Orders, Holy Grades of ministry in Orthodox, Roman Catholic, and Anglican Churches. **Major Orders** consist of ordained ministers, bishops, priests, and deacons (and, in the Western Church, subdeacons). **Minor Orders** include, in the Western Church, lectors, porters, exorcists, acolytes; in the Eastern Church, subdeacons. Major Orders constitute the hierarchy of the Church, to be distinguished from the laity. A distinction is also drawn between **First Orders** (fully professed men), **Second Orders** (fully professed women), and **Third Orders** (those affiliated usually to one of the Mendicant Orders). A member of a Third Order (a 'Tertiary') may live in a religious community, or in the world. » bishop; Church of England; deacon; Mendicant Orders; Orthodox Church; priest; Roman Catholicism; Tertiaries

orders of architecture The arrangement of the parts of a column and an entablature in classical architecture according to one of five accepted principles, or orders: Tuscan, Doric, Ionic, Corinthian, Composite. Originally developed by the ancient Greeks, the earliest surviving codification is by the 1st-c Roman Vitruvius, subsequently analysed in much greater detail by European architectural theorists from the Renaissance onwards. » Composite/Corinthian/Doric/Ionic/Tuscan order; column; entablature; frieze; Greek/Renaissance/Roman architecture

Ordinance of 1787 An Act of the American Continental Congress establishing procedures by which newly-settled Western territories could enter the American union on the basis of full political equality with the original states. It was one of several **Northwest Ordinances** passed in 1784–7. » Continental Congress

ordinary language philosophy » **linguistic philosophy**

Ordnance Datum (OD) The mean sea level in the UK, used as a fixed reference from which the elevations of all points in the country are surveyed. It was determined by hourly measurements of sea level made between 1915 and 1921 at Newlyn, Cornwall. The equivalent in the USA is the **Sea Level Datum**, calculated from the mean sea level for the whole US coastal area. » benchmark; surveying

Ordnance Survey of Great Britain The survey and mapping agency established by the 1841 Ordnance Survey Act, although founded initially in 1791 as the Trigonometrical Survey. Maps were originally produced at a scale of 1:63 360 (1 in to the ml) and are now available at a number of scales. The basic scales

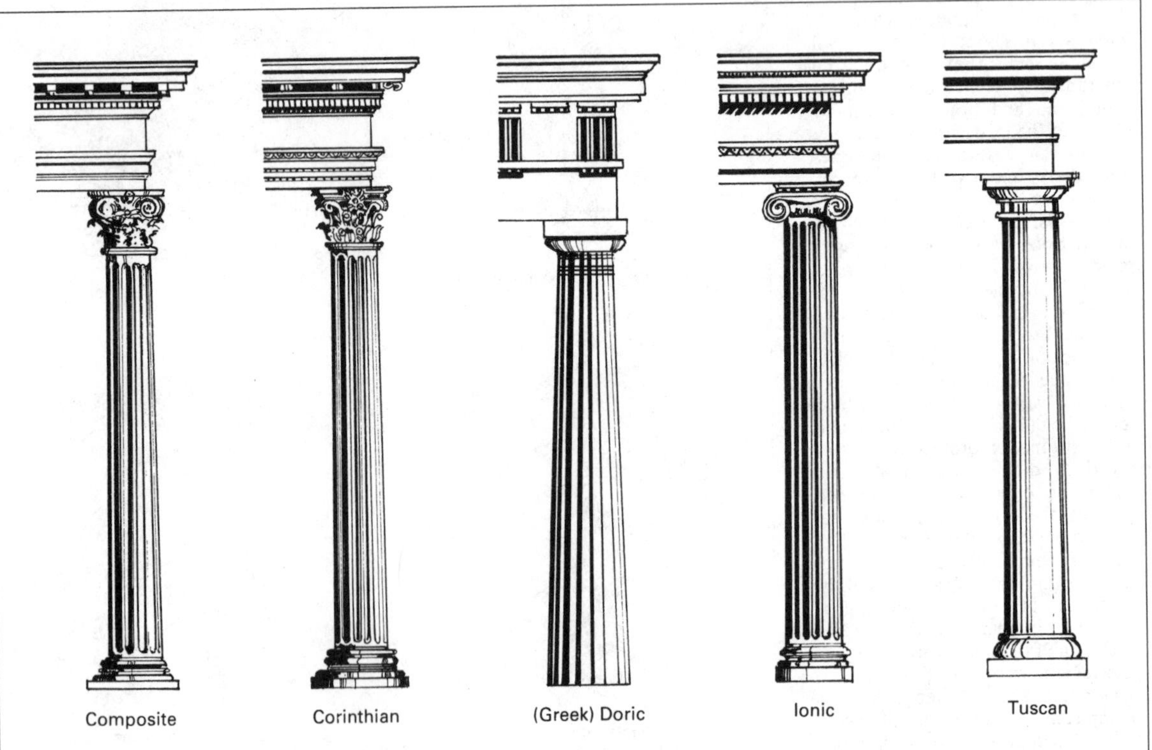

The five orders of architecture

(which are metric, with 1 representing 1 cm) are 1:1 250 (c.50 inches to the mile), 1:2 500 (c.25 inches to the mile) and 1:10 000, which supersedes the 1:10 560 (c.6 inches to the mile). These are produced by ground fieldwork, topographical survey, and aerial photography, kept up-to-date by a system of continuous revision. All other map series (1:25 000, 1:50 000, and 1:250 000) are derived from the detail of the basic maps. The survey also produces archaeological and historical maps. The Ordnance Survey of N Ireland is separate. » cartography; map; National Grid reference system; surveying

Ordovician period [awduh**vish**ian] The second of the geological periods of the Palaeozoic era, extending from c.505 million to 438 million years ago. All animal life was restricted to the sea; numerous invertebrates flourished, including graptolites, trilobites, brachiopods, and corals; and the first vertebrates appeared (jawless fish). The proto-Atlantic ocean opened. » geological time scale; Palaeozoic era; RR16

ore A mineral deposit from which metallic and non-metallic constituents can be extracted. Ores may be formed directly from crystallizing magma, or precipitated from hydrothermal fluids associated with igneous activity or concentrated in alluvial deposits after weathering. » magma; minerals

Örebro [eruhbroh] 59°17N 15°13E, pop (1982) 117 258. Capital city of Örebro county, SC Sweden; at W end of L Hjälmaren, 160 km/100 ml W of Stockholm, at mouth of R Svartån; former meeting place of the parliament (*Riksdag*); railway; university (1967); machinery, chemicals; St Nicholas's Church (18th-c), castle (16th-c, restored 19th-c), town hall (1856–62). » Sweden [i]

oregano [orig**ah**noh] » **marjoram**

Oregon pop (1987e) 2 724 000; area 251 409 sq km/97 073 sq ml. State in NW USA, divided into 36 counties; the 'Beaver State'; established as a fur-trading post on the site of the present town of Astoria, 1811; occupied by both Britain and the USA, 1818–46, when the international boundary was settled on the 49th parallel; became a territory, 1848; joined the Union as the 33rd state, 1859; population grew after 1842 with settlers following the Oregon Trail, and again in the late 19th-c after the completion of the transcontinental railway; capital, Salem; chief cities Albany, Eugene, Springfield; bounded W by the Pacific Ocean; rivers include the Columbia, Snake, Willamette; split by the Cascade Range; fertile Willamette R valley in the W, with the Coast Ranges beyond; High Desert in the E, a semi-arid plateau used for ranching and wheat-growing; Blue Mts and Wallowa Mts in the NE; Fremont Mts and Steens Mts in the S; highest point Mt Hood (3 424 m/11 234 ft); several small lakes in the S, including Upper Klamath L and L Albert; about half the area forested; produces over a quarter of the USA's softwood and plywood; electronics, food processing, paper, fishing; livestock, wheat, dairy produce, fruit, vegetables; major tourist region; Crater Lake National Park in the SW. » Oregon boundary dispute; Oregon Trail; Salem (Oregon); United States of America [i]; RR39

Oregon boundary dispute A disagreement between the British and US governments over the frontier between respective possessions on the W coast of N America. Britain claimed the NW basin of the Columbia R to its mouth at Fort Vancouver, while the US sought a much more northerly boundary. The Oregon Treaty (1846) settled on the 49th parallel, dipping S at Juan de Fuca Strait to maintain British claims to Vancouver Island. Residual disputes over the disposition of the Gulf/San Juan Is in the strait were settled by arbitration in 1872. » Oregon

Oregon grape An evergreen shrub, native to western N America; leaves glossy, with ovoid, spiny leaflets; flowers yellow, in short spikes; edible berries c.8 mm/0.3 in, blue-black with a whitish bloom. (*Mahonia aquifolium*. Family: *Berberidaceae*.) » evergreen plants; shrub

Oregon Trail The main route for emigration to the far W of the USA in the 1840s. The trail began at Independence, Missouri, crossed the Rockies at South Pass in Wyoming, and terminated at the mouth of the Columbia R. » Oregon

Orestes [oresteez] In Greek legend, the son of Agamemnon and Clytemnestra. After his father's murder he went into exile, but returned to kill Aegisthus and his mother, for which he was pursued by the Erinyes. His character was made psychologically interesting by the Greek tragic poets. » Aegisthus; Agamemnon; Clytemnestra; Electra; Erinyes

orfe [awf] Freshwater fish widespread in lowland rivers and lakes of E Europe and C Russia; length up to 40 cm/16 in; greenish brown on back, sides silver, underside white; also known as **ide**; **golden orfe** is an ornamental variety with orange coloration. (*Leuciscus idus*. Family: *Cyprinidae*.)

Orff, Carl (1895–1982) German composer, born and died in Munich. He studied at Munich, where in 1925 he helped to found the Günther music school. The influence of Stravinsky is apparent in his compositions. He is best known for his operatic setting of a 13th-c poem, *Carmina Burana* (1937); later works include *Oedipus* (1959), and *Prometheus* (1966). » Stravinsky

organ The name of various types of musical instruments, but without further qualification referring to an instrument in which air from a windchest, fed by bellows, is released under pressure into metal or wooden pipes of various lengths and bores by the action of keys operated by the player's fingers or feet. The ranks of pipes, which vary in pitch, volume, and timbre according to their length, material, width of bore, and the method by which the air is made to vibrate in them, are brought into action by means of drawknobs (or *stops*); the player can select a *registration* (or combination of stops) appropriate to the music he wishes to play.

The earliest organs had only one manual keyboard. Most modern church organs have at least two: a 'Great' and, above that, a 'Swell', so called because the pipes it operates are enclosed within a shuttered swell-box, enabling gradations of volume to be made without changing the stops. Large organs have also a 'Choir' manual below the Great, and very large instruments often have a fourth or even a fifth manual situated above the Swell. In addition, a pedalboard, operated by the feet, is provided, and couplers enable pipes belonging to one keyboard to be sounded on another.

The cinema organ, with its distinctive 'voicing' and its special effects (train hooter, telephone bell, etc) was developed in the early 20th-c, especially by the Wurlitzer Company in the USA, to accompany silent films and to play popular medleys during intervals. In electronic organs, an invention of the 1920s, the pipes are replaced by other means of tone production, such as electromagnets and oscillators. Since they occupy only a small space and are inexpensive compared to a pipe organ, they have been installed in many churches, and are popular as domestic instruments, as well as in pop and rock groups. » aerophone; barrel organ; calliope; electrophone; hydraulis; keyboard instrument; reed organ

organ-grinder's monkey » **capuchin**

organic architecture A conception of architecture in which elements are placed in harmony rather than in juxtaposition with each other. It usually involves the rejection of classical notions of a given set of rules or solutions, and instead treats form as something latently present in the problem at hand. In particular, it is concerned with the relation of human beings and the building to the rest of nature. Stylistically, it ranges from the ornate naturalistic decoration of Antonio Gaudí to the geometric compositions of Alvar Aalto. » Aalto; Art Nouveau; Gaudí; Expressionism

organic chemistry That part of chemistry which deals specifically with the structures and reactions of the compounds of carbon. Since carbon has a tendency to form chains and rings to a far greater extent than other elements, its compounds are much more numerous than those of the other elements. » carbon; chemistry

organic farming Farming without synthetic chemical fertilizers, sprays, or pharmaceuticals. Fertility is maintained through the addition of animal manures and composts, and through rotations which include nitrogen-fixing plants such as clover. Weeds and diseases are controlled through rotations and cultivations, including hand weeding. In some countries there is a premium market for certified organic produce, including livestock products which are guaranteed to have been fed exclusively on organically grown feedstuffs. Nutritionally, organic food is no different from ordinary food; but its taste may be superior. » fertilizer

Organisation de l'Armée Secrète » OAS

Organisation Européene pour la Recherche Nucléaire (CERN) (European Organization for Nuclear Research) The principal European centre for theoretical and experimental research in particle physics, supported by most European countries; located in Geneva; founded in 1954. Its facilities include high and low energy proton and antiproton accelerators, and an electron-positron collider. » particle accelerators; particle physics

Organization for Economic Co-operation and Development (OECD) An international organization set up in 1961 to assist member states to develop economic and social policies aimed at high sustained economic growth with financial stability. Its 24 members are Australia, Austria, Belgium, Canada, Denmark, Finland, France, Germany, Greece, Iceland, Ireland, Italy, Japan, Luxembourg, The Netherlands, New Zealand, Norway, Portugal, Spain, Sweden, Switzerland, Turkey, the UK, and the USA. It is located in Paris.

Organization for European Economic Co-operation (OEEC) An organization established in 1948 by 16 W European countries and by the occupying forces on behalf of West Germany. Its formal aims were to promote trade, stability, and expansion, and it provided a framework for handling aid from the USA. It was replaced in 1961. » Marshall Plan; Organization for Economic Co-operation and Development

Organization of African Unity (OAU) An organization founded in 1963 by representatives of 32 African governments meeting in Addis Ababa, which dedicated itself to the eradication of all forms of colonialism in Africa. By seeking to perpetuate the territorial integrity of African states, it accepted the often artificial boundaries created by the Partition of Africa. It played some part in pressing forward the process of decolonization, particularly through the United Nations Special Committee, but has been less active in recent years. It had 51 members in 1990. » Africa, Partition of

Organization of American States (OAS) A regional agency established in 1948 for the purpose of co-ordinating the work of a variety of inter-American agencies, recognized within the terms of the United Nations Charter. The Organization operates through the Inter-American Conference, which meets every five years to decide issues of policy; consultative meetings of foreign ministers, which decide on more pressing matters; a council of representatives of all member states; its central organ, the Pan-American Union; and a series of special conferences and inter-governmental organizations. The vast majority of states within the Americas are members. » Pan-American Union; United Nations

Organization of Arab Petroleum Exporting Countries (OAPEC) An organization formed under the umbrella of the Organization of Petroleum Exporting Countries (OPEC) in 1968 by Saudi Arabia, Kuwait, and Libya, with its headquarters in Kuwait. By 1972 all the Arab oil producers had joined. » OPEC

Organization of Central American States An agency established in 1951 by Costa Rica, El Salvador, Guatemala, Honduras, and Nicaragua (Panama refused to join) to promote economic, social, and cultural co-operation. In 1965 this was extended to include political and educational co-operation. The Organization has also been involved in legal reform.

Organization of Petroleum Exporting Countries » OPEC

organum [**aw**gunum] An early type of mediaeval polyphony in which one or more parts were added to a plainchant, moving mainly in parallel intervals with it. » plainchant; polyphony

Orhon Gol, River [awkon **gol**] River in Mongolia; flows for 1 117 km/694 ml from the NE edge of the Gobi Desert to the W of Altanbulag, where it joins the Selenge R. » Mongolia

oribi [**o**ruhbee] A dwarf antelope, native to Africa S of the Sahara; pale brown with tufts of long hairs on the knees; naked glandular area beneath each ear; males with short spike-like horns; inhabits grasslands. (*Ourebia ourebi.*) » antelope

Oriental dance The dance styles of the Far East, essentially religious in origin and highly stylized in performance, through the use of symbolic arm gestures and facial expressions. In China, dance is mainly secondary to drama and opera, but it appears within both these genres. Buddhist connections give rise to such forms as the lotus, butterfly, lion, and stilt dances. Japanese dance remains substantially intact from its 7th-c court form of *bugaku*. The 15th-c Noh drama has a danced concluding section which is economic in style, demonstrating control and repose. *Kabuki* is the popular later 16th-c amalgam of drama, music, and dance – a flamboyant spectacle based on traditional stories told in a realistic manner. » Kabuki; Noh

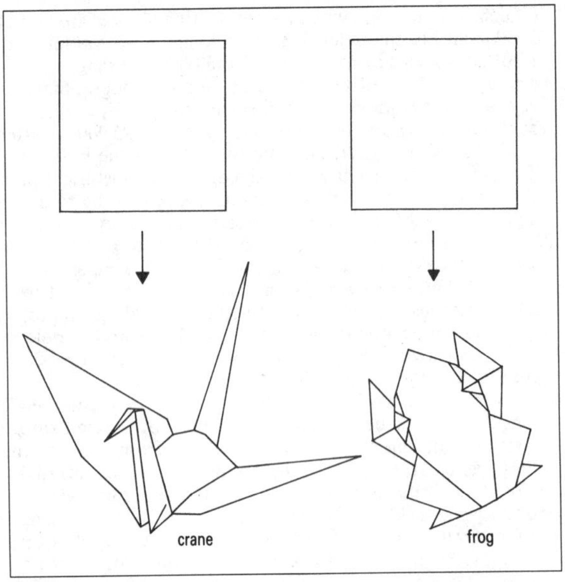

Origami figures – The crane is usually the first one taught

orienteering A form of cross-country running with the aid of a map and compass. The sport was devised by Swedish youth leader Ernst Killander in 1918, and based on military training techniques. Popular in the Nordic countries, it developed as an international sport in the 1960s. Competitors have to reach specifically designated control points on the course by using their map and compass, and skill in using these is as important as athletic stamina. » RR116

origami The art of making models of animals or other objects by folding sheets of paper into shapes with the minimum use of scissors or other implements. It originated in the 10th-c AD in Japan, where it is widely practised. In many countries, it is used primarily as an educational aid for young children.

Origen [**oh**rigen] Christian Biblical scholar and theologian of Alexandria, Egypt, who became head of the catechetical school in Alexandria. He was a layman until c.230, when he was ordained in Palestine. Exiled from Alexandria by Bishop Demetrius, he established a new school in Caesarea. He was imprisoned during the persecution under Decius in 250, and died soon afterwards. His writings were prolific, but his views on the unity of God and speculations about the salvation of the devil were condemned by Church Councils in the 5th–6th-c.

original sin The traditional Christian doctrine that, by virtue of the Fall, every human being inherits a 'flawed' or 'tainted' nature in need of regeneration and with a disposition to sinful conduct. There have been various interpretations of the Fall and humanity's sinful condition, ranging from the literal to various symbolic accounts. » Christianity; grace; sin

oriole A bird of the Old World family *Oriolidae* (**Old World orioles**, 28 species) or the New World family *Icteridae* (**American Orioles**, c.90 species). The name is also used for the **oriole finch** (Family: *Fringillidae*). » blackbird; bobolink; grackle; redwing

Orion (astronomy) [o**riy**uhn] Perhaps the most conspicuous of all constellations, although only 26th in size. Equatorial, and thus visible in both hemispheres, with bright stars Rigel and Betelgeuse (1st magnitude) poised above brilliant Sirius in Canis Major. It is a dominant sight in the mid-winter sky of the N hemisphere. The **Orion nebula** is found in the 'sword' of

Orion. It is the nearest and brightest emission nebula, 500 parsecs away, visible to the naked eye, and a veritable cosmic factory, making new stars and interstellar molecules. It is a strong radio and infrared source. Even binoculars will show its structure. » Betelgeuse; constellation; infrared radiation; Rigel; Sirius; Plate I; RR9

Orion (mythology) [**ori**yuhn] In Greek mythology, a gigantic hunter, beloved by Eos and killed by Artemis. He was changed into a constellation, and this generated further astronomical stories – for example, that he pursues the Pleiades. » Artemis; Eos; Pleiades

Orissa [uh**ri**sa] pop(1981) 26272054; area 155782 sq km/ 60132 sq ml. State in E India, bounded E by the Bay of Bengal; ceded to the Mahrattas, 1751; taken by the British, 1803; subdivision of Bengal until 1912, when province of Bihar and Orissa created; separate province, 1936; became a state, 1950; capital, Bhubaneswar; governed by a 147-member Legislative Assembly; R Mahanadi dammed to form the Hirakaud Reservoir (1957), largest earth dam in the world; rice, wheat, oilseed, sugar cane, jute, forestry, fishing; chromite, dolomite, graphite, iron ore, limestone; cement, fertilizer, sugar, glass, machinery, textiles, crafts; tourism in the Golden Triangle (Konark, Puri, Bhubaneswar). » India [i]

Orkney [**awk**nee] pop(1981) 19056; area 976 sq km/377 sq ml. Group of islands off NE Scotland; separated from Scottish mainland (S) by the Pentland Firth; 15 main islands (especially Mainland, South Ronaldsay, Sanday, Westray, Hoy), and many smaller islands; c.20 islands inhabited; generally low-lying, with steep cliffs on W side; capital, Kirkwall, on Mainland; Norse dependency from 9th-c; annexed by Scotland from Norway and Denmark, 1472; fishing, farming, weaving; North Sea oil terminal on Flotta; oil service bases on Mainland and Hoy; several prehistoric remains, notably Standing Stones at Stenness (W Mainland), c.3000 BC, and Neolithic village at Skara Brae (W Mainland); isolated stack (height 137 m/449 ft), Old Man of Hoy (NW of Hoy); Scapa Flow, sea area within the islands, used in World Wars 1 and 2 as a major naval anchorage; German Fleet surrendered there in 1918, but in 1919 was scuppered by its skeleton crews. » Scotland [i]; Skara Brae

Orlando 28°33N 81°23W, pop(1980) 128291. Seat of Orange County, C Florida, USA; settled c.1844; airfield; railway; tourism, aerospace, and electronic industries, trade in citrus fruit and vegetables; Walt Disney World. » Disney; Florida

Orléans, Charles, Duc d' ('Duke of') (1391–1465) French poet, born in Paris. In 1406 he married his cousin Isabella, widow of Richard II of England. He commanded at Agincourt (1415), was taken prisoner and carried to England, where he lived for 25 years, composing courtly poetry in French and English. Ransomed in 1440, he then maintained a kind of literary court at Blois. He died at Amboise, his son becoming Louis XII. » Agincourt, Battle of; French literature; poetry

Orléans, Louis Philippe Joseph, Duc d' ('Duke of'), byname **Philippe Egalité** ('equality') [**aw**layã] (1747–93) French Bourbon prince, born at Saint-Cloud, the cousin of King Louis XVI and father of Louis Philippe. He became the Duc de Chartres in 1752 and inherited his father's title in 1785. At the Revolution he proved a strong supporter of the Third Estate against the privileged orders, and in 1792 renounced his title of nobility for his popular name. At the Convention he voted for the King's death but was himself arrested after the defection of his eldest son to the Austrians (1793), and guillotined. » French Revolution [i]; Louis XVI; Marie Antoinette

Orleans [aw**lee**uhnz], Fr **Orléans,** ancient **Aurelianum** 47°54N 1°52E, pop(1982) 105589. Ancient town and capital of Loiret department, C France; on right bank of R Loire, 92 km/57 ml SSW of Paris; associated with Joan of Arc, 'The Maid of Orleans', who raised the English siege here in 1429; road and rail junction; bishopric; university (1309); centre of fruit and vegetable region; textiles, clothing, blankets, food processing, sparkling wines, agricultural equipment; 13th–16th-c cathedral, 16th-c town hall, episcopal palace, museum of fine art; Feast of Joan of Arc (May). » Hundred Years' War; Joan of Arc

Orléans, House of The junior branch of the Valois and Bourbon dynasties in France, the title of which fell to four individual lines: Philippe de Valois, created Duke in 1344 but died without issue; Louis I de Valois (1372–1407), whose descendants held the title until 1544; Gaston (1608–60), the Bourbon third son of Henry IV, made Duke in 1626; and Louis XIV's younger brother Philippe (1640–1701), from whom descended the Regent Orléans (1674–1723), Philippe 'Égalité' (1747–93), who died in the French Revolution, and Louis Philippe (1773–1850), 'King of the French'. The latter's son was the last to hold the ducal title. » Bourbons; Louis Philippe; Orléans, Louis Philippe Joseph; Valois

Ormandy, Eugene [**aw**mandee] (1899–1985) US conductor, born in Budapest, where he studied the violin. He was an orchestral player in Berlin before emigrating to the USA in 1921, becoming a US citizen in 1927. He conducted the Minneapolis Symphony Orchestra (1931–6) and the Philadelphia Orchestra (1936–80). He died in Philadelphia.

ormer » **abalone**

ormulu A gilded metal alloy of copper, zinc, and tin used in France since the 17th-c for candelabra, clocks, and other decorative luxury objects, and for mounting elaborate furniture. It was adopted more sparingly in England from the mid-18th-c. » alloy

Ornithischia [awni**thiski**a] The bird-hipped dinosaurs, characterized by the backwards pointing pubis bone in the pelvic girdle, similar to that of birds. They comprise four exclusively plant-eating groups: the ankylosaurs, the ceratopsians, the stegosaurs, and the ornithopods such as the hadrosaurs and Iguanodon. » ankylosaur; dinosaur [i]; hadrosaur; Iguanodon; Protoceratops; Stegosaurus; Triceratops

Ornitholestes [awnithuh**les**teez] » **Coelurus**

ornithology The study of birds. It includes observations on the evolutionary relationships of the different groups, the distribution of species and populations, ecology, conservation, migration, behaviour of individuals, birdsong, anatomy, physiology, biochemistry, and genetics. More than most other scientific disciplines, ornithology has benefited from the enthusiastic involvement of amateurs and the co-ordination of their observations. » bird [i]

orogeny A period of mountain-building involving intense deformation and subsequent uplift of rocks when crustal plates collide. The plate boundaries define an *orogenic belt* which forms a fold-mountain chain. Metamorphism and igneous intrusion take place at depth in the orogenic belt. Examples include the Pacific belt, where the continental crust collides with the oceanic crust, and the Himalayas, which resulted from the collision of the Indian and Asian continental plates. » igneous rock; intrusive rock; plate tectonics [i]

orographic rain A type of precipitation which occurs when an airstream crosses a mountain barrier. It is forced to rise, cool, and (if moist) condense. Rain falls on the windward side of the barrier, and dry air descends on the leeward or sheltered side. » condensation (physics); Föhn wind; precipitation

Oromo » **Galla**

Orozco, José Clemente [o**ros**koh] (1883–1949) Mexican painter, born at Zapotlán, Jalisco. He studied engineering and architectural drawing in Mexico City, and then art at the Academia San Carlos (1908–14). He was one of the greatest mural painters of the 20th-c, decorating public buildings in Mexico and the USA, his powerful realistic style, verging on caricature, acting as a vehicle for his revolutionary socialist ideas. He died in Mexico City. » Mexican art; socialism

Orpheus [**aw**fyoos] A legendary Greek poet from Thrace, able to charm beasts and even stones with the music of his lyre. In this way he obtained the release of his wife Eurydice from Hades. He was killed by the maenads, and his head, still singing, floated to Lesbos. » Eurydice; Hades; maenads

Orphism A modern art movement which flourished c.1912, experimenting with pure colour in ways that heralded abstract painting. The leading exponent was Delaunay. » abstract art; Delaunay; modern art

orris A white-flowered species of iris, with fleshy rhizomes which provide **orris root**, used in perfumery. (*Iris germanica*, variety *florentina*. Family: *Iridaceae*.) » iris; rhizome

Ortega y Gasset, José [aw**tay**ga ee ga**set**] (1883–1955) Spanish philosopher and existentialist humanist, born in Madrid. Educated at Madrid and in Germany, he became professor of metaphysics at Madrid (1910). His critical writings on modern authors made him an influential figure, and his *La rebelión de las masas* (1930, The Revolt of the Masses) foreshadowed the Civil War. He lived in exile in S America and Portugal (1936–48), and died in Madrid. » existentialism

Ortelius (1527–98) The Latinized name of the cartographer and engraver **Abraham Ortel**, born and died at Antwerp. He was trained as an engraver, and c.1560 became interested in map-making. His *Theatrum Orbis Terrarum* (1570, Epitome of the Theatre of the World) was the first great atlas. » cartography; engraving

orthicon An electron tube used extensively in early television cameras, but now superseded by photoconductive vidicon tubes or charge-coupled devices. The orthicon tube made broadcast television practical, converting the optical image into an electrical signal. » camera; charge-coupled device; television

orthoclase [awthuhklayz] A form of the mineral potassium feldspar; usually pink and a primary constituent of granite. » feldspar; granite

orthodontics » **dentistry**

Orthodox Church or **Eastern Orthodox Church** A communion of self-governing Churches recognizing the honorary primacy of the Patriarch of Constantinople and confessing the doctrine of the seven Ecumenical Councils (from Nicaea I, 327, to Nicaea II, 787). It includes the patriarchates of Alexandria, Antioch, Constantinople, and Jerusalem, and the Churches of Russia, Bulgaria, Cyprus, Serbia, Georgia, Romania, Greece, Poland, Albania, and Czechoslovakia. It developed historically from the Eastern Roman or Byzantine Empire. In doctrine it is strongly trinitarian, and in practice stresses the mystery and importance of the sacraments, of which it recognizes seven. Episcopal in government, the highest authority is the Ecumenical Council. » Council of the Church; episcopacy; Greek Orthodox Church; Russian Orthodox Church; patriarch; sacrament; Trinity

orthopaedics/orthopedics The branch of surgery concerned with injuries and disorders affecting the skeleton, ie the bones and joints and associated connective tissues and muscle tendons. It includes the diagnosis and treatment of fractures and dislocations, the correction of congenital and acquired deformities and abnormalities of posture, and the surgical re-alignment or replacement of diseased or damaged joints by artificial prostheses. It also provides surgical and medical treatment for tumours and bone infections, for complaints such as backache and sciatica, and for prolapsed intervertebral and degenerative disorders of the spine. » bone; dislocation (medicine); fracture (medicine); skeleton; vertebral column

Orthoptera [awthoptuhra] An order of medium-to-large insects found in all terrestrial habitats, from soil burrows to tree canopies; hindlegs usually modified for jumping; forewings leathery or parchment-like; many produce sound by rubbing their limbs or wings (*stridulation*). » cricket (entomology); grasshopper; katydid; locust

ortolan [awtuhlan] A bunting found from Europe to Mongolia (winters in N Africa), inhabiting bushy open country, rocky hillsides, and cultivation; eats seeds and insects. also known as the **ortolan bunting** or **garden bunting**. (*Emberiza hortulana*.) » bunting

Orton, Joe (1933–67) British dramatist, born in Leicester, and educated at the Royal Academy of Dramatic Art, London. His first stage play, *Entertaining Mr Sloane* (1964), was in the style of absurdist drama; but this was quickly followed by several more extreme, erotic, and anarchic farces, among them *Loot* (1964) and *What the Butler Saw* (1967). He was murdered by his lover in London. » absurdism; drama; English literature

Orust [ooruhst] area 346 sq km/134 sq ml. Swedish island in the Kattegat, off SW coast of Sweden; separated from the mainland by a narrow channel 1.6–5 km/1–3 ml wide; length, 22 km/14 ml; width, 16 km/10 ml; second largest island in Sweden. » Sweden [i]

Orwell, George, pseudonym of **Eric Arthur Blair** (1903–50) British novelist and essayist, born at Motihari, Bengal. Educated at Eton, he served in Burma in the Indian Imperial Police (1922–7), and was wounded in the Spanish Civil War. He developed his own brand of socialism in *The Road to Wigan Pier* (1937) and many essays, and also wrote four novels in the 1930s, notably *Coming up for Air* (1939). During World War 2, he was a war correspondent. He is best known for his satire of totalitarian ideology in *Animal Farm* (1945), and the prophetic novel, *Nineteen Eighty-Four* (1949). He died in London. » English literature; novel; satire; socialism; Spanish Civil War; totalitarianism

oryx [oriks] A grazing antelope with very long slender horns; pale with striking white and dark markings on face and underparts; three species: the **oryx** (also known as the **Cape oryx**, **beisa oryx**, **fringe-eared oryx**, or **gemsbok**) (*Oryx gazella*) and the **scimitar** or **white oryx** (*Oryx dammah*), both from Africa; and the **Arabian** or **white oryx** (*Oryx leucoryx*) from the Middle East. » antelope

Osaka [ohsaka], formerly **Naniwa** 34°40N 135°30E, pop (1980) 2 648 180. Port capital of Osaka prefecture, S Honshu, Japan, on NE shore of Osaka-wan Bay; developed around a castle, built 16th-c; city almost completely destroyed in World War 2; now third largest city in Japan; airport; railway; subway; several universities; part of the Osaka–Kobe industrial area; steel, textiles, chemicals, brewing, cars, printing; famous puppet theatre; Osaka Castle, municipal museum, electric science museum, Fujita museum, Shintennoji temple (6th-c), Sumiyoshi Shrine (present buildings, 1808); Tenjin Matsuri river races (Jul). » Honshu; Kobe

Osborne, John (James) (1929–) British playwright and actor, born in London. *Look Back in Anger* (1956) and *The Entertainer* (1957), with Sir Laurence Olivier playing Archie Rice, established him as the leading younger exponent of British social drama. The 'hero' of the first, Jimmy Porter, became the prototype 'Angry Young Man'. Among other works are *Luther* (1961), *Inadmissible Evidence* (1964), *A Patriot for Me* (1965). » Angry Young Men; drama; English literature; Olivier; theatre

Oscar The familiar name for the statuettes awarded annually by the American Academy of Motion Picture Arts and Sciences for outstanding performances and creative and technical achievement in films shown during the preceding year. The title was reputedly given by a secretary at the Academy, who said that the figure reminded her of her Uncle Oscar. » RR101

oscillation A repetitive periodic change. Electrical currents in radio receivers oscillate, for example. Mechanical oscillations, such as those in a building caused by passing traffic or in a plucked guitar string, are usually called *vibrations*. » damping; oscillator; periodic motion

oscillator A circuit for converting direct current (DC) into alternating current (AC), of a required frequency. Part of the output is returned via a feedback circuit to the input. By varying the components of the feedback circuit, the oscillator can be 'tuned' to a certain frequency. » electricity; oscillation; superheterodyne

Osee » **Hosea, Book of**

osier A species of willow-forming shrub or small tree, growing to 3–5 m/10–16 ft; native to Europe and Asia, and often grown as a source of *withies*, long pliant stems produced in numbers when the plants are coppiced and used, for example, in basket-work. (*Salix viminalis*.) » shrub; tree [i]; willow

Osiris [ohsiyris] Ancient Egyptian god, the husband of Isis. Originally he was the king of Egypt; his brother Seth murdered him and scattered the pieces of his body. These were collected by Isis; and Osiris, given renewed life, was made the king of the Underworld. After the cult of the dead was developed during the Middle Kingdom, Osiris was seen as the judge of the soul after death. » Isis

Ösling or **Oesling** [osling] Geographical region in the Ardennes, N Luxembourg; wooded and less fertile than the Gutland ('good land') to the S, but largely agricultural; occupies 828 sq km/320 sq ml (32%) of Luxembourg. » Luxembourg [i]

Oslo, formerly **Christiania** or **Kristiania** [ozloh] 59°55N 10°45E, pop (1983) 448 775. Capital city of Norway, at the head of Oslo Fjord, SE Norway; founded, 11th-c; under the influence of the Hanseatic League, 14th-c; destroyed by fire, 1624; rebuilt by

Christian IV of Denmark and Norway and renamed Christiania; cultural revival, 19th-c; capital, 1905; renamed Oslo, 1925; bishopric; airports; railway; university (1811); metalworking, foodstuffs, clothing, shipbuilding, trade in timber, paper; largest port in Norway, the base of a large merchant shipping fleet; cathedral (17th-c), royal palace (1825–48), Akershus Castle (13th-c), Norwegian folk museum, national gallery, national theatre. » Hanseatic League; Norway [i]

osmiridium A naturally occurring alloy of osmium and iridium in which the iridium content is less than 35%; *iridosmine* has osmium greater than 35%. It occurs with platinum ores. » alloy; platinum

osmosis » osmotic pressure

osmotic pressure [oz**mo**tik] The pressure that must be exerted in a solution containing a given concentration of solute separated from a sample of the pure solvent by a membrane permeable only to the solvent, in order to prevent the solvent's passage through the membrane. It is usually directly proportional to the concentration, and thus may be used to determine the molecular weights of unknown solutes. Exerting a pressure greater than the osmotic pressure causes the solvent to pass from the solution to the solvent; this 'reverse osmosis' is a method of purifying water. Osmosis is an important process in living organisms, especially aquatic organisms. Many are **osmoregulators**, maintaining the osmotic concentration of their body fluids at a level independent of that of the surrounding medium. » colligative properties: solution

Osnabrück [**ohz**nabrük] 52°17N 8°03E, pop (1983) 156 100. Manufacturing city in SW Lower Saxony province, Germany, 48 km/30 ml NE of Münster; badly bombed in World War 2; railway; linked to the Mittelland Canal; bishopric; university (1973); iron and steel, machine tools, cars, textiles, paper; cathedral (13th-c), episcopal palace (17th-c). » Germany [i]

osprey A large bird of prey, inhabiting sea coasts or inland waters world-wide, also known as **fish hawk** or **fish eagle**; dives on fish, grasping them in its talons; soles of feet have spines to aid grip. (*Pandion haliaetus*. Family: *Pandionidae*.) » bird of prey

Ossa, Mount Highest mountain in Tasmania (1 617 m/5 305 ft); within the Cradle Mt–L St Clair national park (area 1 319 sq km/509 sq ml). » Tasmania

Ossian or **Oisín** Legendary Irish poet and warrior, the son of the 3rd-c hero Fingal or Fionn MacCumhail. The Scottish poet **James Macpherson** (1736–96) professed to have collected and translated his works, though it was later shown that the poems, such as the epic *Fingal*, were largely of his own devising. Nonetheless they were well received in Europe, and influenced the Romantic movement. » Irish literature; Romanticism

Ossory An ancient Irish kingdom, co-extensive with the diocese of Ossory (seat, Kilkenny), conquered by Anglo-Norman invaders in the late 12th-c. The most powerful families in the area were the Marshals, Earls of Pembroke, Wales, and Lords of Leinster (1199–1245), and the Butlers, created Earls of Ormond (1328) and Ossory (1528).

Ostade, Adriaen van [os**tah**duh] (1610–85) Dutch painter and engraver, born and died at Haarlem. He was a pupil of Hals, and his use of chiaroscuro shows the influence of Rembrandt. His subjects are taken mostly from everyday peasant life. His brother, **Isaak** (1621–49), treated similar subjects, but excelled at winter scenes and landscapes. » chiaroscuro; Dutch art; Hals; Rembrandt

Ostend, Flemish **Oostende**, Fr **Ostende** 51°13N 2°55E, pop (1982) 69 331. Seaport in West Flanders province, W Belgium, on the North Sea coast; principal ferry port for England (Dover and Folkestone); most important seaport and largest seaside resort in Belgium; headquarters of the Belgian fishing fleet; railway; shipbuilding, fish processing, soap; spa resort, promenade, casino, racecourse, Chalet Royal; Blessing of the Sea (Jul). » Belgium [i]

osteoarthritis A common disease of joints of both man and animals; also known as **osteoarthrosis**. Over 80% of those over middle age are affected. The condition is a primary degeneration and disintegration of the articular cartilage, which tends to

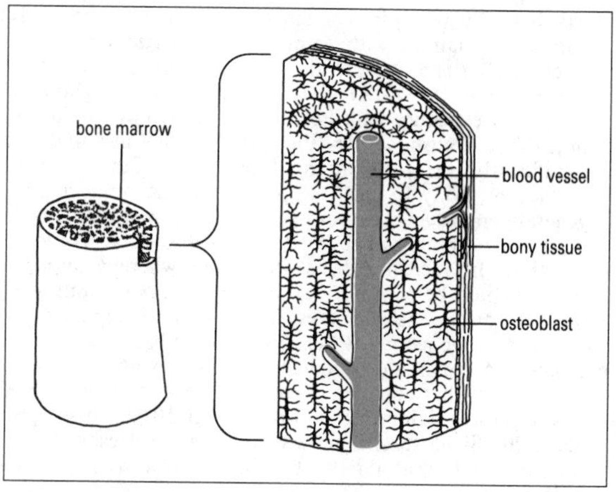

Section through a long bone

affect the weight-bearing joints such as the hips; but no joint is immune. The cause is unknown, though wear and tear is often invoked. Osteoarthritis may occur at an earlier age in joints affected by bone fracture or by other diseases, such as rheumatoid arthritis, in which the alignment of joint surfaces has been affected. The main symptom is pain and stiffness of the joint. When this is severe and affects the hip joint, replacement by an artificial 'ball and socket' joint of steel and polyethelene is successful in the great majority of cases. » arthritis; bone; joint

osteology The scientific study of bone and bones, involving both their microscopic and macroscopic structure. It is used in anthropology for species identification and carbon dating, in clinical medicine for the assessment of development and nutritional status of the individual, and in forensic medicine for the reconstruction and sexing of victims.

osteomalacia [ostiohma**lay**sha] A metabolic disorder of bone caused by a lack of vitamin D. In children and adolescents, normal growth is retarded, and the condition is called *rickets*. In adults, the bones become thinner and often show small fractures at points of stress, such as in the pelvis. Generalized bone and muscle pain are common symptoms. » bone; rickets; vitamins [i]

osteomyelitis [ostiohmiyuh**liy**tis] Infection within bone. It arises either as a result of blood-borne infection (eg tuberculosis), or less commonly following direct injury. Many pus-producing organisms may be responsible, but occasionally actinomycosis and fungi may be involved. » actinomycosis; bone; fungus; pus

osteopathy [osti**op**athee] A system of treatment originally based on the belief that abnormalities in the skeletal system are responsible for a wide range of diseases by interfering with the blood supply to the region affected. Today less ambitious claims are made, and osteopaths concentrate on the treatment of backache, and pains in the legs, neck, and head. Like chiropractors they use massage and manipulation, stretch various joints, and apply high-velocity thrusts. Most of the evidence of their success is anecdotal, and today there is no clear distinction between chiropractic and osteopathy. » alternative medicine; bone; chiropractic; skeleton

osteoporosis [ostiohpuh**roh**sis] Thinning and weakening of bones because of a loss of calcium from their substance. It is identified by standardized X-ray techniques, from which reduction in bone density can be assessed. It tends to occur in elderly women, and appears related to a reduction in the level of sex hormones. Sex hormone replacement therapy is thought to be effective in preventing osteoporosis in menopausal women. » bone; calcium; Cushing's disease

Ostia The ancient town situated at the mouth of the Tiber in W Italy. It was Rome's main naval base during the Punic Wars. Under the Roman empire, it was the main port; here the precious grain cargoes were unloaded and warehoused before being taken up the Tiber to the capital. » Punic Wars

Ostpolitik The policy initiated in West Germany in the 1960s to normalize relations with communist countries which recognized the German Democratic Republic (GDR), and to reduce hostility between West Germany and its Eastern neighbours. It led to peace treaties with Poland and the USSR, the recognition of the Polish border (the Oder-Neisse Line) and, most significantly, the recognition of the GDR. Largely masterminded by Willy Brandt, the policy had the broader aim of generally improving relations between West and East, and can be viewed as a forerunner of detente. » Brandt, Willy; detente

ostracism In ancient Athens, the means whereby unpopular citizens could be banished for up to ten years without loss of property or citizenship. Votes were cast by writing on *ostraka* (potsherds) the names of the citizens to be banished.

ostracod A small, short-bodied crustacean with a hinged bivalved shell that completely encloses the body; legs typically adapted for walking over substrate; over 10 000 fossil species and 5 700 living species known from marine, freshwater, and occasionally terrestrial habitats. (Class: *Ostracoda*.) » bivalve; crustacean

Ostrava [ostrava] 49°50N 18°13E, pop (1984) 323 732. Industrial capital of Severomoravský region, Czech Republic, C Czechoslovakia; near junction of Oder and Ostravice Rivers; fourth largest city in Czechoslovakia; important strategic position in mediaeval times; airport; railway; metal industries, coal mining, chemicals, machinery, rolling stock. » Czechoslovakia [i]

ostrich The largest living bird (height up to 2.75 m/9 ft); unable to fly; fastest animal on two legs (c.70 kph/45 mph); largest egg of any living bird (the same volume as 40 hen's eggs); inhabits dry areas of Africa; eats plants and some lizards. The **American ostrich** is an obsolete name for the rhea. (*Struthio camelus*. Family: *Struthionidae*.) » rhea

Ostrogoths A Germanic people, forming one of the two great Gothic tribes, who entered Italy in 489 and established a kingdom under Theodoric, traditionally a descendant of the Ostrogothic chieftain Hermanaric, defeated by the Huns in 375. The kingdom collapsed in the mid-6th-c, but was revived by the Lombards. » Belisarius; Goths; Lombards; Theodoric

Oswald, St (c.605–42), feast day 5 August. Anglo-Saxon King of Northumbria (633–41), the son of Ethelfrith of Benicia. Having been converted at Iona, he established Christianity in Northumbria with St Aidan's help. He fell in battle with the pagan King Penda. » Aidan, St; Anglo-Saxons; Christianity

Oswald, Lee Harvey (1939–63) The alleged killer of President Kennedy, born in New Orleans. A Marxist and former US Marine, he lived for a while in the USSR (1959–62). Two days after the assassination, he was killed at Dallas by nightclub owner Jack Ruby (1911–67), before he could stand trial. » Kennedy, John F

oswega/oswego tea [osweeguh] » **bergamot 1**

Otis, Elisha Graves (1811–61) US inventor, born at Halifax, Vermont. In 1852, when building a new factory in Yonkers, New York City, he designed and installed the first lift (or *elevator*) to incorporate an automatic brake. The device quickly became established, thus paving the way for the development of the skyscraper. He died at Yonkers, New York.

Ottawa 45°25N 75°43W, pop (1981) 295 163. Capital of Canada, in SE Ontario, SE Canada, on the Ottawa R at its junction with the Rideau R; founded as Bytown, 1826; present name, 1854; capital of United Provinces, 1858; national capital, 1867; two-thirds English-speaking, one-third French; airport; railway; two universities (1848, 1942); pulp and paper, aluminium, steel, bronze, clothing, food processing, watches and clocks, glass; Peace Tower in parliament buildings, 88 m/289 ft high; Eternal Flame on Parliament Hill, lit 1967; National War Memorial, War Museum, National Library, National Gallery of Canada, National Museum of Man, National Museum of Natural Sciences, Museum of Science and Technology; Changing of the Guard on Parliament Hill, Tulip Festival (May). » Canada [i]; Ontario

Ottawa River, Fr **Rivière des Outaouais** Canadian river, the largest tributary of the St Lawrence; rises in the Canadian Shield, flows W, then S and SE to the St Lawrence SW of Montreal; length 1 271 km/780 ml; forms the Ontario–Quebec border for most of its course; hydroelectric power; connected to L Ontario via the Rideau Canal; its river valley was an important early travel route. » Canada [i]; Canadian Shield; St Lawrence River

Ottawa Agreements A series of agreements concluded in Canada in 1932 at an economic conference held between Britain and its Dominions at the height of the world depression. The conference decided in favour of a limited amount of imperial preference following the adoption of a new protective tariff by the British government earlier that year. » Great Depression; tariff

otter A mammal of family *Mustelidae*; streamlined, with a flattened muzzle; brown with paler underparts; tail thick at base; feet usually webbed; inhabits streams and lakes; eats fish and invertebrates; 12 species in genera *Lutra* (**river otters**), *Aonyx* (**clawless otters**), and *Pteronura* (the **giant otter**). » Mustelidae; sea otter

otter hound A breed of dog, used in Britain since the 14th-c to hunt otters; excellent sense of smell; large, with short erect tail, large head, and long, pendulous ears; coat coarse, wiry, water-resistent; feet webbed. » dog; hound; otter

otter shrew A mammal of the tenrec family (3 species); an insectivore, native to WC Africa; resembles the otter, with brown back and white underparts, small eyes, long flat muzzle, and tail flattened from side to side. » insectivore; otter; tenrec

Otto I, byname **the Great** (912–73) King of the Germans (from 936) and Holy Roman Emperor (from 962). He subdued many turbulent tribes, maintained almost supreme power in Italy, and encouraged Christian missions to Scandinavian and Slavonic lands. He died at Memleben, Thuringia. » missions, Christian

Otto, Nikolaus August (1832–91) German engineer, born near Schlangenbad. In 1876 he invented the four-stroke internal combustion engine, the sequence of operation of which is named the **Otto cycle** after him. He died at Cologne. » internal combustion engine

otto » **attar**

Ottoman Empire A Muslim empire founded c.1300 by Sultan Osman I (1259–1326), and originating in Asia Minor. Ottoman forces entered Europe in 1345, conquered Constantinople in 1453, and by 1520 controlled most of SE Europe, including part of Hungary, the Middle East, and N Africa. Following the 'golden age' of Sulaiman the Magnificent, the empire began a protracted decline. During the 19th-c and early 20th-c, Ottoman power was eroded by the SE European ambitions of Russia and Austria, the N African ambitions of France, Britain, and Italy, the emergence of the Balkan nations, and internal loss of authority. It joined the Central Powers in 1914, and collapsed with their defeat in 1918. » Islam; Sulaiman I; Young Turks

Ottonian art Art of the 10th–11th-c in Germany, named after the Holy Roman Emperors Otto I–III. Carolingian elements are combined with early Christian and Byzantine motifs. The bronze doors of Hildesheim Cathedral (1015), with their expressive biblical scenes, attest to the high standards achieved. » Byzantine/Carolingian/Christian/German art; Otto I

Otway, Thomas (1652–85) English dramatist, born at Trotton, Sussex. Educated at Winchester and Oxford, he left without a degree, and became a writer. He translated Racine and Molière, and wrote Restoration comedies, but his best-known works are the tragedies *The Orphan* (1680) and *Venice Preserved, or a Plot Discovered* (1682). He died in London. » drama; English literature; tragedy

Ötztal Alps [ertstal], Ger **Ötztaler Alpen** Mountain range in Tirol state, W Austria, rising to 3 774 m/12 382 ft at Wildspitze, Austria's second highest peak. » Alps

Ouagadougou [wagadoogoo] 12°20N 1°40W, pop (1985) 442 223. Capital of Burkina Faso, W Africa; part of the Ivory Coast until 1947; capital of Mossi empire from 15th-c; captured by French, 1896; airfield; terminus of railway line from Abidjan (Nigeria); university (1969); textiles, soap, vegetable oil; trade in groundnuts, millet, livestock; neo-romanesque cathedral; palace of Moro Naba (Mossi Emperor). » Burkina Faso [i]

Oudenaarde, Fr **Audenarde** 50°50N 3°37E, pop (1982) 27 226. Town in East Flanders province, W Belgium; site of defeat of

French by Marlborough and Prince Eugene (1708); railway; traditional centre for carpet-weaving and tapestries; town hall (1526–37), Church of Onze Lieve Vrouw Pamele (begun 1235). » Belgium [i]

Ouija board [**wee**ja, **wee**jee] A board bearing letters, words, and numbers, upon which an indicator such as an upturned glass is placed. Several people rest their fingers on the indicator, which then moves without their conscious volition across the board. It can then purportedly spell out messages which provide information about events or situations unknown to the people present. It is alleged that information may also be received from deceased persons. The word originates from the French and German words for *yes* (*oui* and *ja*).

Oulu [**ow**loo], Swedish **Uleaborg** 65°00N 25°26E, pop (1982) 96 199. Seaport and capital of Oulu province, W Finland, on the Gulf of Bothnia, at mouth of R Oulu; established, 1605; destroyed by fire, 1822; airfield; railway; university (1958); shipbuilding, timber; Tar Ski Race, cross-country ski race founded in 1889; Oulu Music Summer (Jul–Aug). » Finland [i]

ounce (zoology) » **snow leopard**

ounce (physics) » RR70

Our Lady » **Mary** (mother of Jesus)

Ouranus » **Uranus**

Ouro Prêto [ohroh **pray**toh], formerly **Vila Rica** Town founded in 1711 in Minas Gerais, the mining area of NE Brazil; a world heritage site; centre of gold and diamond trading during the colonial era, with wealth reflected in its architecture; showcase of the work of the sculptor Antonio Francisco Lisboa (1738–1814). » Minas Gerais

Ouse, River [ooz] **1** River in East Sussex, S England; rises 10 km/6 ml SSW of Crawley and flows E and S for 48 km/30 ml to meet the English Channel at Newhaven. **2** River in Yorkshire, NE England; formed at the junction of the Ure and Swale Rivers near Boroughbridge; flows 96 km/60 ml SE to meet the R Trent where it becomes the Humber estuary. **3** River rising NW of Brackley in Northamptonshire, C England; flows 256 km/159 ml past Buckingham and Bedford and through the S fenland, to meet the Wash NNW of King's Lynn; also known as the **Great Ouse**. **4** Tributary of the Great Ouse river, E England; flows 38 km/24 ml W along part of the Norfolk–Suffolk border to meet the Great Ouse at Brandon Creek; also known as the **Little Ouse**. » England [i]

ousel » **ouzel**

out-of-the-body experience (OOBE or **OBE)** An experience in which people have the sensation that their consciousness exists in a separate location from their body, such that they perceive their surroundings as if their consciousness actually had left their body. The experience often feels as real to them as normal everyday life reality. » astral projection

ouzel or **ousel** A thrush (*Turdus torquatus*), native to Europe, N Africa, and SW Asia; dark with pale wings and white crescent on breast; inhabits high moorland and hillsides; also known as the **ring ouzel**. The name was formerly used for the blackbird *Turdus merula*. **Water-ouzel** is used for the unrelated dipper (*Cinclus cinclus*). » blackbird; dipper; thrush (bird)

ouzo A traditional Greek spirit flavoured with aniseed, and usually drunk with water. » spirits

Oval, the One of the largest cricket grounds in England, located at Kennington, S London. It is owned by the Duchy of Cornwall, and is the headquarters of Surrey County Cricket Club. » cricket (sport) [i]; Duchy of Cornwall; London [i]

Ovamboland [oh**vam**bohland] Region in N Namibia, extending W along the Namibia–Angola frontier from the Okavango R; Etosha national park in the S; chief indigenous peoples, the Ovambo; area of conflict since the 1970s between SWAPO guerrilla forces based in S Angola and South African forces. » Angola [i]; Namibia [i]; South-West Africa People's Organization

ovary The reproductive organ in a female animal in which the eggs are produced, and which may also produce hormones. Ovaries are typically paired, and release their eggs down *oviducts* or Fallopian tubes. In plants, the hollow base of the carpel, containing the ovules, is termed the ovary. Its wall contributes to the fruit containing the seeds. » carpel; Fallopian tubes; flower [i]; gonad; Graafian follicles

over-the-counter drugs (OTCs) Those drugs which may be purchased directly from a pharmacy without a prescription, such as aspirin. Some problems arise with OTCs such as their inappropriate use (eg an overdose) and their dangerous interactions with some prescription drugs. » pharmacy

over-the-counter (OTC) trading Trading in stocks and shares other than via the stock exchange. Over-the-counter shares are issued by companies too small for Stock Exchange listing; they are often considered to be a very risky investment. Dealing in these shares takes place through companies specializing in this type of stock, and not through a stockbroker. In the USA, the National Association of Securities Dealers' Automated Quotations (NASDAQ) has been described as an 'electronic over-the-counter stock market': the system does not work through the New York Stock Exchange, but directly by computer to brokers and market makers. » shares; stocks

Overland Telegraph A telegraph line linking Australia with the outside world; opened in 1872. The line crossed the centre of Australia, and covered 3 175 km/1 972 ml between Port Augusta (South Australia) to Darwin (Northern Territory), where it joined an undersea cable to Java. » telegraphy

overpopulation A density of population such that the available resources of an area are unable to support the resident people; contrasted with **underpopulation**, where the area is able to support a greater density. It is impossible to derive a precise figure for overpopulation, as the concept is subjective and rarely related to any agreed minimum standard of living. It is important to take account of the area under consideration. For example, the crude population density of Chad is only 3.8 people per sq km/9.8 per sq ml, yet the country could be regarded as overpopulated because the harsh physical conditions mean that the land is unable to support that density. The daily (1978–80) per capita calorific intake was 1 808, which is 76% of the United Nations Food and Agricultural Organization recommended minimum requirement. » population [i]; population density

overture An orchestral prelude to an opera or other work, or (since the early 19th-c) an independent, usually descriptive, concert piece of similar length. The 'French overture' of the 17th–18th-c consisted of a slow section followed by a quick one, often ending with a partial return of the opening material; the contemporary 'Italian overture' was on the pattern fast–slow–fast. » opera; programme music

Ovid, in full **Publius Ovidius Naso** (43 BC–AD 17) Latin poet, born at Sulmo, in the Abruzzi. He trained as a lawyer, but devoted himself to poetry, and visited Athens. His first success was the tragedy *Medea*, followed by *Heroides*, love letters from legendary heroines to their lords. His major poems are the 3-book *Ars Amatoria* (Art of Love) and the 15-book *Metamorphoses*, a collection of stories in which a transformation (metamorphosis) plays some part. In AD 8 he was banished, for some reason unknown, to Tomi on the Black Sea, where he died. » Latin literature; metre (literature); poetry

Oviedo [ovyaythoh] 43°25N 5°50W, pop (1981) 184 473. Capital of Oviedo province, Asturias, NW Spain, 451 km/280 ml NW of Madrid; bishopric; airport; railway; university (1608); former capital of Asturias; commerce, cement, pharmaceuticals, domestic appliances, metal products; cathedral (14th-c); Fiesta of La Ascension (May), Fiesta of San Mateo (Sep). » Asturias; Spain [i]

Ovimbundu A Bantu-speaking agricultural people of the Benguela Highlands of Angola, comprising some 20 indigenous chiefdoms. They formerly traded over much of C Africa, and supplied slaves to the Portuguese. Population c.1.9 million. » Angola [i]; Bantu-speaking peoples

ovo-lacto vegetarians » **vegetarianism**

ovulation » **Graafian follicle**

ovule The female sex-cell of seed plants which, after fertilization, forms the seed. In gymnosperms the ovules lie exposed on the scales of the female cone; in flowering plants they are enclosed within an ovary. » flowering plants; gymnosperms; ovary; placenta (botany)

ovum » **egg**

Owen, (Dr) David (Anthony Llewellyn) (1938–) British politician, born in Plymouth, and educated at Cambridge and

London. He trained in medicine, then became an MP (1966) and Under-Secretary to the Navy (1968). He was Secretary for Health (1974–6), and Foreign Secretary (1977–9). One of the so-called 'Gang of Four' who formed the Social Democratic Party (SDP) in 1981, he succeeded Roy Jenkins as its leader in 1983. Following the Alliance's disappointing result in the 1987 general election, he opposed Liberal leader David Steel over the question of the merger of the two parties. In 1988, after the SDP voted to accept merger, Owen led the smaller section of the party to an independent existence. » Jenkins; Steel, David; Social Democratic Party

Owen, Robert (1771–1858) British social reformer, born and died at Newtown, Montgomeryshire, Wales. In 1800 he became manager and part owner of the New Lanark cotton mills, Lanarkshire, where he set up a social welfare programme, and established a 'model community'. His socialistic theories were put to the test in other experimental communities, such as at Orbiston, near Glasgow, and New Harmony in Indiana, but all were unsuccessful. He was later active in the trade-union movement, and in 1852 became a spiritualist.

Owen, Wilfred (1893–1918) British poet of World War 1, born at Oswestry, Shropshire, killed in action on the Western Front. His poems, expressing a horror of the cruelty and waste of war, were edited by his friend Siegfried Sassoon in 1920. Several of them were set to music by Benjamin Britten in his *War Requiem* (1962). » Britten; English literature; poetry; Sassoon

Owens, Jesse, properly **James Cleveland** (1913–80) US athlete, born at Danville, Alabama. Within 45 min on 25 May 1935 at Ann Arbor, Michigan, he set five world records (100 yds, long jump, 220 yds, 220 yds hurdles, 200 m hurdles). His long jump record of 26 ft 8¼ in stood for 25 years. In 1936 he showed his dominance at the Berlin Olympics, much to Hitler's annoyance, when he won four gold medals, a feat equalled only in 1984, by Carl Lewis. He died at Tucson, Arizona. » athletics; Lewis, Carl

owl A predatory nocturnal bird, found world-wide; large head and broad flat face; forwardly directed eyes; acute sight and hearing; kills prey with talons and swallows whole, regurgitating bones, fur, etc as pellets. There are two families: **typical owls** (*Strigidae*, c.120 species) and **barn owls**, **grass owls**, and **bay owls** (*Tytonidae*, 11 species). *Tytonidae* differ in having smaller eyes, long slender legs, a serrated middle claw, and a heart-shaped face. Some typical owls have ear-like tufts on their head. The name *owl* is also used for unrelated **moth owls** of the family *Aegothelidae*. (Order: *Strigiformes*.) » barn/burrowing/eagle/fish/grass/hawk/little/scops/tawny owl; bird of prey; owlet frogmouth

owl monkey » douroucouli

owl parrot » kakapo

owlet frogmouth A nightjar-like bird found from Tasmania to New Guinea; small with long tail; inhabits forests; eats insects; also known as **owlet nightjar** or **moth owl**. (Genus: *Aegotheles*, 8 species. Family: *Aegothelidae*.) » nightjar

owlet moth » noctuid moth

owlet nightjar » nightjar; owlet frogmouth

ox A ruminant mammal of genus *Bos* (5 species); an artiodactyl. The name is used especially for the domestic bullock used as a draught animal. » artiodactyl; aurochs; banteng; bull; cattle; gaur; mammal [i]; ruminant [i]; yak

ox-eye daisy A variable clump-forming perennial, growing to 1 m/1¼ ft, native to Europe; lower leaves spoon-shaped with toothed margins; flower heads up to 5 cm/2 in or more across, long-stalked, solitary; spreading outer florets white, inner disc florets yellow; also called **marguerite** and **dog** or **moon daisy**. It is widely grown as a garden ornamental and for cut flowers, and was formerly used as a medicinal herb. (*Leucanthemum vulgare*. Family: *Compositae*.) » herb; perennial

oxalic acid [oksalik] IUPAC **ethanedioic acid**, HOOC–COOH, colourless crystals; melting point of the dihydrate is 101°C. It occurs in many plants, especially rhubarb, and is poisonous. It is a moderately strong acid, partially neutralized solutions having a pH of about 2.5. Its salts, *oxalates*, form chelates with transition metals, and are thus useful in removing rust and blood stains from clothing. » acid; crystals; pH

oxalis A perennial, sometimes an annual, found almost everywhere, but many native to S America and S Africa; leaves clover-like with three (sometimes more) leaflets, often folding up at night; flowers 5-petalled, funnel-shaped; fruits with catapult mechanism for dispersing seeds. Some species are grown as ornamentals. Several are serious weeds. (Genus: *Oxalis*, 800 species. Family: *Oxalidaceae*.) » annual; perennial; wood sorrel

Oxenstjerna or **Oxenstern, Axel, Greve** ('Count') (1583–1654) Swedish statesman, born near Uppsala. From 1612 he served as Chancellor, and negotiated peace with Denmark, Russia, and Poland; and though he sought to prevent Gustavus Adolphus from plunging into the Thirty Years' War, he supported the war effort, even after the King's death (1632). During most of the minority of Queen Christina he was effective ruler of the country (1636–44), vindicating his policies by the terms of the Peace of Westphalia (1648). He died in Stockholm. » Gustavus II; Thirty Years' War

OXFAM A British charity based in Oxford, dedicated to alleviating poverty and distress throughout the world. Founded as the Oxford Committee for Famine Relief in 1942, most of its funds are now used to provide long-term development aid to the Third World countries. Over 700 OXFAM shops now exist throughout the UK. » Three Worlds Theory

Oxford, Lat **Oxonia** 51°46N 1°15W, pop (1981) 99 195. County town in Oxford district, Oxfordshire, SC England; on Thames and Cherwell Rivers, 80 km/50 ml WNW of London; 12th-c university, granted its first official privileges in 1214; Royalist headquarters in Civil War; airfield; railway; industry located in the suburb of Cowley (notably vehicles); steel products, electrical goods, paper; 12th-c cathedral, colleges, Bodleian Library (1488), Sheldonian Theatre (1664–8), Ashmolean Museum, Radcliffe Camera; Sunrise Service (May Day); Eights Week (Jun–Jul); St Giles Market (Sep). » Ashmolean Museum; Bodleian Library; Oxford University [i]; Oxfordshire

Oxford, Provisions of (1258) A baronial programme imposing constitutional limitations on the English crown. Henry III had to share power with a permanent council of barons, parliaments meeting three times a year, and independent executive officers (chancellor, justiciar, treasurer). In 1261 the Pope absolved Henry from his oath to observe the Provisions. » Barons' War; Henry III (of England)

Oxford Movement A movement within the Church of England, beginning in 1833 at Oxford, which sought the revival of high doctrine and ceremonial; also known as **Tractarianism**. Initiated by 'tracts' written by Keble, Newman, and Pusey, it opposed liberal tendencies in the Church and certain Reformation emphases. It led to Anglo-Catholicism and ritualism, and has remained influential in certain quarters of Anglicanism. » Anglo-Catholicism; Church of England; Keble; Newman, John Henry; Pusey

Oxford University The oldest university in Britain, having its origins in informal groups of masters and students gathered in Oxford in the 12th-c. The closure of the University of Paris to Englishmen in 1167 accelerated Oxford's development into a *universitas*. Prestigious university institutions include the Bodleian Library, the Ashmolean Museum, and the Oxford University Press (founded in 1585). » Ashmolean Museum; Bodleian Library; Paris, University of

Oxfordshire pop (1987e) 578 000; area 2 608 sq km/1 007 sq ml. County in the S Midlands of England, divided into five districts; Cotswold Hills to the NW, Chiltern Hills to the SW; county town Oxford; agriculture, vehicles, paper, textiles; River Thames, Vale of the White Horse; Atomic Energy Authority laboratories at Culham. » Chiltern Hills; Cotswold Hills; England [i]; Joint European Torus; Oxford; Thames, River

oxidation The loss of electrons, always accompanied by reduction, the gain of the same electrons. Chemical reactions in which electrons are transferred from one atom to another are called **oxidation-reduction** or **redox** reactions. Elements in compounds are conveniently given an **oxidation state** or **oxidation number** which relates to their redox properties. These states may usually be assigned by the following rules: (1) oxygen is -2 except in the element (O) and in peroxides (-1); (2) hydrogen is $+1$ except in the element (O) and saline hydrides

(−1); (3) halogens bonded to elements other than oxygen are −1; (4) other elements are calculated to make the sum of all the oxidation states of the atoms in an ion or molecule equal to the net charge. Thus, the oxidation state of Mn in MnO_4^- is +7, and the average for sulphur in $S_2O_3^{2-}$ is +2. The oxidation state is expressed using Roman numerals, as in manganese(VII) or Mn^{VII}. » electron; reduction

oxide A compound of oxygen, especially one containing the ion O^{2-}. Oxides of non-metals are called **acidic oxides**, as they react with water to give acids; for example, sulphur trioxide (SO_3) gives sulphuric acid (H_2SO_4); carbon dioxide (CO_2) gives carbonic acid (H_2CO_3). **Oxides of metals** are basic, and react with water to give hydroxides, such as sodium oxide (Na_2O) gives sodium hydroxide (NaOH). **Amphoteric oxides** are those like aluminium oxide (Al_2O_3), which reacts with strong acid as a base and with strong base as an acid. » aluminium; oxygen

oxidizing agent A substance which oxidizes another in a chemical reaction, being itself reduced in the process. The most important is oxygen gas (O_2), which is reduced to water when it oxidizes a metal. » oxidation; reduction

oxlip A perennial with a rosette of crinkled leaves, drooping flowers at the tip of a common stalk, and a tubular calyx. The true oxlip (*Primula elatior*), from C and N Europe, has pale yellow flowers all hanging on one side of the stalk. A plant referred to as the **common oxlip** is a hybrid between the cowslip and the primrose (*Primula veris × vulgaris*), similar to the cowslip but with larger, paler flowers. (Family: *Primulaceae*.) » cowslip; perennial; primrose; sepal

oxopropanoic acid » **pyruvic acid**

oxpecker An African bird of the starling family; narrow but deep bill, short legs, and stiff tail; inhabits grassland; clings to large mammals, especially ungulates; eats flies and ticks from host's skin; also known as **tickbird**. (Genus: *Buphagus*, 2 species.) » starling; tick; ungulate

Oxus, River » **Amudarya, River**

oxyacetylene welding A technique much used in cutting metal and in joining two pieces of metal by melting them together at the point of contact (*welding*). The temperature obtained by burning acetylene with oxygen is the highest obtainable by any gas-oxygen flame (over 3 200 degrees).

oxygen O, element 8, boiling point −183°C. By far the commonest element in the Earth's crust, of which it makes up nearly 50%; in various combined forms it also constitutes 21% of the atmosphere as diatomic molecules (O_2). The presence of this oxygen is brought about by photosynthesis; without it, all the oxygen in the atmosphere would quickly react with other substances. All higher forms of life depend on oxygen. The element boils at 13°C higher than nitrogen, and is isolated by the fractional distillation of air. Liquid oxygen is pale blue in colour, and is used as an oxidant. Oxygen occurs widely in organic and inorganic compounds, mainly showing oxidation state −2. » chemical elements; nitrogen; oxygen cycle; ozone; photosynthesis; RR90

OXFORD UNIVERSITY

COLLEGE	FOUNDED	COLLEGE	FOUNDED
University College	1249	Pembroke	1624
Balliol	1263	Worcester	1714
Merton	1264	St Catherine's	1868
St Edmund Hall	1278	Keble	1870
Exeter	1314	Hertford	1874
Oriel	1326	Lady Margaret Hall[1]	1878
Queen's	1340	Somerville[1]	1879
New	1379	St Hugh's[1]	1886
Lincoln	1427	St Hilda's[1]	1893
All Souls	1438	St Peter's	1929
Magdalen	1458	Nuffield[2]	1937
Brasenose	1509	St Antony's	1950
Corpus Christi	1517	St Anne's[1]	1952
Christ Church	1546	Linacre[2]	1962
Trinity	1554	Wolfson[2]	1965
St John's	1555	St Cross[2]	1965
Jesus	1571	Green[2]	1979
Wadham	1612		

[1] *Women's colleges* [2] *Graduate colleges*

oxygen cycle The dynamic system of changes in the nature of oxygen-containing compounds circulating between the atmosphere, the soil, and living organisms. The oxygen cycle is interwoven with other cycles, such as the nitrogen cycle and the global water cycle. The main biological phase involves the use of gaseous oxygen during respiration in animals and plants, with the consequent production of water and carbon dioxide, and the use of these products by green plants during photosynthesis, resulting in the liberation of gaseous oxygen. » nitrogen cycle [i]; oxygen; photosynthesis

oxytocin [okseetohsin] A chemical substance (a peptide) present in the rear part of the pituitary gland (the *neurohypophysis*) of many vertebrates. In humans, it is a hormone produced in the hypothalamus, but stored in and released from the pituitary gland. In lactating females it is released when the newborn suckle, thereby promoting milk-ejection. It also induces contractions of the uterus during labour. Its role in males is unknown. » hormones; hypothalamus; peptide

oyan » **linsang**

oyster Bivalved mollusc with unequal valves, the left valve typically being cemented to a hard substrate; shell valves closed by a single muscle; often cultured for human consumption, regarded as a delicacy. (Class: *Pelecypoda*. Order: *Ostreoida*.) » bivalve; mollusc

oystercatcher A large plover-like bird, inhabiting coasts world-wide (except mid-ocean and polar regions) and cultivated areas; black, or black-and-white; long reddish bill and legs; eats invertebrates, especially bivalve shellfish; also known as the **sea pie**. (Genus: *Haematopus*, 4 species. Family: *Haematopodidae*.) » plover

Oz, Amos (1939–) Israeli novelist, born in Jerusalem, and educated there and at Oxford. His novels describe the tensions of life in modern Israel, and include *Ma'kom aher* (1966, Elsewhere, Perhaps), *Mikha'el sheli* (1968, My Michael), and *Po y-sham be-Erets Yisre'el bis-setary* (1982, In the Land of Israel). » Hebrew literature; novel

ozalid process » **photocopying**

Ozark Mountains (Fr *aux arks*, 'at the arks'). Highlands in SC USA, between the Arkansas and Missouri Rivers; area c.129 500 sq km/50 000 sq ml, altitude generally 300–360 m/1 000–1 200 ft; Boston Mts rise to 747 m/2 450 ft; hydroelectricity from Bagnell Dam (Lake of the Ozarks); mining, forestry, tourism. » United States of America [i]

ozone A form of oxygen having molecules O_3. It is formed by the action of ultraviolet radiation on ordinary oxygen, and is a gas, boiling point −112°. It is unstable and a strong oxidizing agent, with bacteriocidal properties, but is corrosive to humans in any but very low concentration. Its presence in the upper atmosphere is important in protecting the Earth from excessive ultraviolet radiation. » CFCs; oxygen; ozone layer

ozone layer The part of the stratosphere at a height of c.22 km/14 ml in which the gas ozone (O_3) is most concentrated. It is produced by the action of ultraviolet light from the Sun on oxygen (O_2) in the air. The ozone layer shields the Earth from the harmful effects of solar ultraviolet radiation, but can be decomposed by complex chemical reactions, notably involving chlorofluorocarbons (CFCs), used as the pressurized propellant in some aerosol sprays, in refrigerating systems, and in the production of foam packaging. International concern over the appearance of a 'hole' in the ozone layer over the Antarctic reached a peak in the mid-1980s, and led to a movement for the withdrawal of CFC-producing devices. In 1987 the Montreal Protocol was signed by around 40 countries to limit their use, with the intention that by 1999 worldwide consumption of CFCs should be 50% of 1986 levels. In 1989, the European Community meeting in Brussels agreed to cut CFC consumption by 85% as soon as possible, and altogether by the end of the century. » atmosphere [i]; CFCs; fluorocarbons; greenhouse effect; ozone; Plate II

P

Pabst, G(eorg) W(ilhelm) (1895–1967) German film director, born at Raudnitz (now in Czechoslovakia). He began directing in 1923, and his darkly realistic, almost documentary style was acclaimed in *Die Liebe der Jeanne Ney* (1927, The Love of Jeanne Ney); other works include his pacifist *Westfront 1918* (1930) and his great co-production with France *Kameradschaft* (1931, Comradeship), all examples of the New Realism. After World War 2 he continued to direct for a few years, re-creating the last days of Hitler in *Der Letzte Akt* (1955, The Last Act). He died in Vienna.

paca [**pa**ka] A cavy-like rodent native to C and S America; inhabits forests near water; resembles the agouti, but with a larger snout, and body marked with pale spots and horizontal lines. (Genus: *Cuniculus*, 2 species. Family: *Dasyproctidae*.) » agouti; cavy; pacarana; rodent

pacarana [pakar**a**na] A rare cavy-like rodent; resembles the paca, but has a short bushy tail; also known as **false paca** or **Branick's paca**. (*Dinomys branickii*. Family: *Dinomyidae*.) » paca

pacemaker A cell or object that determines the rhythm at which certain events occur. In vertebrates, pacemaker cells are present in the heart and in the longitudinal muscle of the stomach and ureter. Such cells depolarize and repolarize spontaneously at basic rhythms (which can be modified by the autonomic nervous system), thereby establishing the rate of contraction. In patients with heart block (a malfunction of the sino-atrial node or conducting system) artificial pacemakers (usually battery-operated and implanted under the skin) stimulate the heart electrically to restore and maintain higher rates of cardiac contraction. » heart [i]; nervous system

Pachelbel, Johann [**pakh**elbel] (c.1653–1706) German composer and organist, born and died in Nuremberg. He held a variety of organist's posts before (1695) returning to Nuremberg as organist of St Sebalds' Church. His best-known composition is the Canon in D Major. His works profoundly influenced J S Bach. » Bach, Johann Sebastian

pachinko [pa**chin**koh] The Japanese game of pinball, the word coming from the sound of a steel ball running round a pinball machine. Many pachinko halls are found in all Japanese towns, with bright lighting, neon signs, and loud music. They have row upon row of vertically installed machines, with facing seats for customers. It is Japan's most popular relaxation, highly profitable for hall owners. » yakuza

Pachomius, St (4th-c), feast day 9 May. Egyptian hermit who superseded the system of solitary recluse life by founding (c.318) the first monastery, on an island in the Nile. His monastic rule is extant only in a 5th-c translation by St Jerome. » Jerome, St; monasticism

pachyderm [**pa**kiderm] A mammal of the (now obsolete) group *Pachydermata* ('with thick skin'). The name was used for those ungulates which do not 'chew the cud', especially the elephants, but also rhinoceroses, hippopotamuses, horses, pigs, and other perissodactyls. » perissodactyl [i]; ruminant [i]; ungulate

Pacific Islands » **United States Trust Territory of the Pacific Islands**

Pacific Ocean area c.166 241 000 sq km/64 169 000 sq ml. Ocean extending from the Arctic to the Antarctic, between N and S America (E) and Asia and Oceania (W); covers a third of the Earth and almost half the total water surface area; S part sometimes known as the South Sea; chief arms, the Bering, Ross, Okhotsk, Japan, Yellow, E China, S China, Philippine, Coral, Tasman, Arafura, and Celebes Seas; narrow continental shelves on E shores, wider on W; rim of volcanoes ('Pacific Ring of Fire'), deep open trenches, and active continental margins; sea-floor contraction, Pacific and N American Plates converging at 5.2–5.6 cm/2.05–2.2 in per year (NW), also at the Nazca Plate (SE), 17.2 cm/6.8 in per year; greatest known depth, Challenger Deep in the Marianas Trench, 10 915 m/35 810 ft; major ridge system, the E Pacific Ridge (Albatross Cordillera); ocean floor largely a deep sea-plain, average depth 4 300 m/14 100 ft; many islands, either volcanic (eg Hawaii) or coral, mainly in the E section; Spain, Portugal, UK, and Netherlands held colonies from the 17th-c, France and Russia in the 18th-c, and USA, Germany, and Japan in the 19th-c; commercial importance has increased since opening of Panama Canal (1920). » continental drift; plate tectonics [i]

Pacific scandal Funds of around $350 000 supplied by railroad promoters to the Conservative Party of Canada during the general election of 1872. The discovery of widespread attempts to use the money for bribing the electorate led to the resignation of the Macdonald government in 1873. » Macdonald, John A

Pacific, War of the (1879–83) A war fought by Chile with Peru and Bolivia (in alliance since 1873), arising out of Chilean grievances in the Atacama desert, then Bolivian-held. Chile won command of the sea in the early months of the war, and sent large expeditions to Peru, occupying the capital, Lima (Jan 1881). Peace treaties gave Chile large territorial gains. » Bolivia [i]; Chile [i]; Peru [i]

pacifism The doctrine of opposition to all wars, including civil wars. Its most obvious feature is the personal commitment to non-participation in wars, except possibly in a non-combatant role. Pacifists also advocate efforts to maintain peace and support disarmament, especially through the strengthening of international organizations and law. They have long been associated with Christian sects, but in the 20th-c they include many who oppose war from secular moral bases. Pacifism is often associated with support for non-violent political action. A more limited form is **nuclear pacifism**, which is opposed to nuclear, but not conventional, war. » war

pack rat A rat native to C and N America; grey-brown with pale undersides; tail may be bushy or naked; builds nests with whatever is available, including man-made items; also known as **trade rat** or **wood rat**. (Genus: *Neotoma*, 20 species.) » rat

packet switching An efficient method of directing digitally-encoded data communications over a network from source to receiver. The message is broken into small 'packets', which are sent over the network and reconstituted into the full message at the destination. Network resources are used only when data is actually being sent, and the circuit can be shared. » local area network

Pact of Paris (1927) » **Kellogg–Briand Pact**

Padang [pa**dang**] 1°00S 100°21E, pop (1980) 196 339. Capital of Sumatra Barat province, Indonesia; main seaport on the W coast of Sumatra; third largest city in Sumatra; airfield; railway; university (1956); outlet for exports of rubber, copra, tea, coffee at Telukbajur, 6 km/4 ml S. » Sumatra

paddle tennis A bat-and-ball game played as singles or doubles, invented in the USA c.1920. It is played on a court which is half the size of lawn tennis with a wooden bat (the paddle) and a sponge ball. In most respects the rules are the same as lawn tennis. » platform tennis; tennis, lawn [i]

paddlefish Archaic sturgeon-like freshwater fish of family *Polyodontidae*, with only two living representatives; *Polyodon spathula* (length up to 2 m/6½ ft), found in the Mississippi basin, USA; *Psephurus gladius* (length up to 7 m/23 ft), from

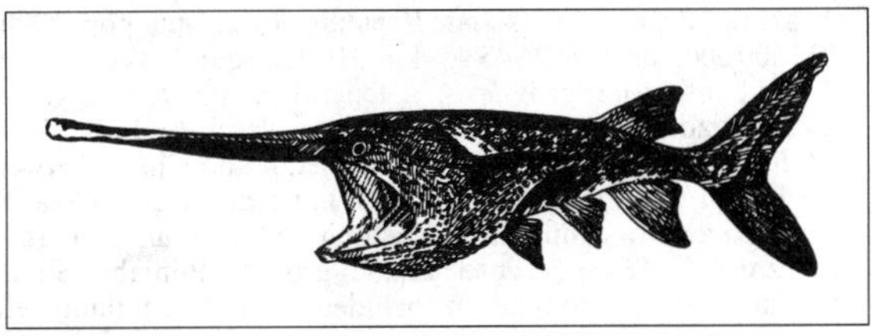

Paddlefish

the Yangtze R, China; head produced into a long snout; known as fossils from the Eocene and Upper Cretaceous periods. » Cretaceous period; Eocene epoch; sturgeon

Paderewski, Ignacy (Jan) [paduh**ref**skee] (1860–1941) Polish pianist, composer, and patriot, born at Kuryłowka, Podolia. He studied at Warsaw, becoming professor in the Conservatoire (1878), and a virtuoso pianist, appearing throughout Europe and the USA. In 1919 he was one of the first premiers of Poland, but soon retired from politics, lived in Switzerland, and resumed concert work. He was elected president of Poland's provisional parliament in 1940, and died in New York City. » piano; Poland [i]

Padua, [**pad**yooa] Ital **Padova**, ancient **Patavium** 45°24N 11°53E, pop (1981) 234 678. Capital town of Padua province, Veneto, NE Italy; 30 km/19 ml W of Venice, on the R Bacchiglione; railway junction; 16th-c university; textiles, machinery, motorcycles, tourism; birthplace of Livy and Mantegna; Church of Sant'Antonio (1232–1307), with tomb of St Antony of Padua, a pilgrimage site; cathedral (16th-c), Donatello's equestrian statue of Gattamelata (1447), Church of the Eremitani (13th-c), oldest botanical garden in Europe (1545); trade fair (Jun). » Antony of Padua, St; Donatello; Italy [i]; Livy; Mantegna

paediatrics/pediatrics The medical care of infants and children, and the study of the diseases which affect them. It encompasses the care of the newborn child, including problems such as failure to breathe, jaundice, failure to thrive, congenital malformations, and special care units. In older children many common diseases behave differently from the same condition in adult life, and require specialized attention. *Community paediatrics* is a developing branch of the discipline, covering such aspects as behavioural disorders and child abuse. » congenital abnormality/deformity; medicine

paedophilia/pedophilia A sexual interest in children (of either sex). Active interference is illegal, and there is often long-term psychological trauma experienced by the child. It has been suggested that paedophiles act in the way they do because they have difficulties in establishing normal adult relationships, and find children less threatening.

Paestum [**pee**stuhm] An ancient Greek town in SW Italy in the region of Naples, founded c.600 BC by Sybaris. It was renowned in antiquity for its magnificent Doric temples, impressive remains of which still survive. » Sybaris

Páez, José Antonio [**pi**yes] (1790–1873) Venezuelan general and President, born in Aragua, Venezuela. He commanded forces of *llaneros* ('cowboys') in the war of independence as principal lieutenant of Simón Bolívar. On the break-up of Grancolombia, he became President of Venezuela (1831) and ruled the country until the late 1840s, again assuming power 1861–3. He died in exile in New York City. » Spanish-American Wars of Independence; Venezuela [i]

Paganini, Niccolò (1782–1840) Italian violin virtuoso, born at Genoa. He gave his first concert in 1793, and began professional tours in 1797, visiting (1828–31) Austria, Germany, Paris, and London. His dexterity and technical brilliance acquired an almost legendary reputation. He revolutionized violin technique, his innovations including the use of stopped harmonics. He also composed six violin concertos, and other works for violin. » violin

Page, Sir Frederick Handley (1885–1962) British pioneer aircraft designer and engineer, born at Cheltenham, Gloucestershire. In 1909 he founded the firm of aeronautical engineers which bears his name. His twin-engined 0/400 (1918) was one of the earliest heavy bombers, and his Hampden and Halifax bombers were used in World War 2. His civil aircraft include the Hannibal, Hermes, and Herald transports. He was knighted in 1942, and died in London. » aircraft [i]

pager A small radio receiver used in one-way communication to alert an individual or deliver a short message; not normally used with voice transmission. A radio-paging system has three parts: a pager, a radio transmitter, and an encoder. It works within a small area using one low-power transmitter, or over larger areas using multiple transmitters. » mobile communications; radio

Paget's disease A chronic disorder of the adult skeleton, of unknown origin, in which normal bone growth and replacement is disturbed; named after English surgeon James Paget (1814–99), and also known as **osteitis deformans**. As a result, some bones or parts of bones become overcalcified and dense, and others become demineralized. It causes bone pains. » bone; skeleton

pagoda [pa**goh**da] A Buddhist reliquary cairn or mound (*stupa*), modified by Chinese architectural principles, and developed over time into the stone, brick, and wooden pagodas found throughout E Asia. It is a multi-storied tower, with each storey having a roof of glazed tiles. » Buddhism; stupa

Pahang [pa**hang**] pop (1980) 768 801; area 35 965 sq km/13 882 sq ml. State in E Peninsular Malaysia, bounded E by the South China Sea; watered by R Pahang; formerly part of the kingdom of Malacca; capital, Kuantan; timber, rubber, tin, rice, tourism. » Malaysia [i]

Pahang, River Longest river in Peninsular Malaysia; flows 456 km/283 ml E into the South China Sea, S of Kuantan. » Malaysia [i]

Pahari An Indo-Aryan-speaking agricultural people of Nepal and the adjoining Himalayan region of India. They are predominantly Hindu, but with a less elaborate caste system than most other Hindus. Population c.10 million. » caste; Indo-Aryan languages; Nepal [i]

Paharpur Vihara [pahahpoor vi**hah**ra] The ruins of a Buddhist monastery (*vihara*) at Paharpur, NW Bangladesh; a world heritage site. Said to have been founded by King Dharma Aal in AD 700, this is the largest Buddhist building S of the Himalayas, and a major archaeological site. » Buddhism

Pahlavi, Mohammad Reza (1919–80) Shah of Persia, who succeeded on the abdication of his father, Reza Shah, in 1941. His reign was for many years marked by social reforms, but during the later 1970s protest at Western-style 'decadence' grew among the religious fundamentalists. He was forced to leave Iran in 1979. He was admitted to the USA for medical treatment, and lived in Egypt until his death. » Iran [i]; Khomeini

Pahsien » **Chongqing**

Päijänne, Lake [**pi**yanu] Lake in SC Finland; largest single lake in Finland; area 1 090 sq km/420 sq ml; drained S to the Gulf of Finland by R Kymi; boat and hydrofoil service links Jyväskylä and Lahti. » Finland [i]

pain An unpleasant sensation – in the simplest case, the stimulation of nerve endings by a strong stimulus, such as heat, cold, pressure, or tissue damage. Pain receptors are located over most of the body surface and at many internal sites. When stimulated, they initiate reflex responses within the spinal cord, and convey information to the brain, where pain is perceived. The degree of pain is determined not only by the intensity of the stimulus, but also by psychological factors which can increase or decrease the release of pain-killing peptides (endorphins and enkephalins) within the brain and spinal cord. Pain which disappears with healing is called *acute*. *Chronic* pain persists after healing (eg pain from a phantom limb), suggesting a pain memory stored in the brain. Many factors modify pain experience. In combat, wounds may not be painful. Stimulation of one body region can reduce pain in another. The converse also happens: recurrent pain in one area can sensitize other areas to become trigger zones, where even a light touch can trigger pain. In *referred pain*, pain from an internal organ is felt as if located in a skin area supplied by the same nerve which supplies the organ (eg angina pain from heart muscle is felt in the left arm). Acute pain is protective: people born with insensitivity to pain inflict serious injuries on themselves. » analgesics; nervous system; opioid peptides; substance P

Paine, Thomas (1737–1809) British radical political writer, born at Thetford, Norfolk. In 1774 he sailed for Philadelphia, where his pamphlet *Common Sense* (1776) argued for complete independence. He served with the American army, and was made Secretary to the Committee of Foreign Affairs. In 1787 he returned to England, where he wrote *The Rights of Man* (1791–2), in support of the French Revolution. Arraigned for treason, he fled to Paris, where he was elected a Deputy to the National Convention, but imprisoned for his proposal to offer the King asylum in the USA. At this time he wrote *The Age of Reason*, in favour of deism. Released in 1796, he returned to the USA in 1802, and died in New York City. » deism; French Revolution [i]; radicalism

paint A colouring substance consisting of two basic elements, pigment and medium. Pigments have been derived from earths (eg yellow ochre), minerals (eg malachite), and dyes (organic, and since the mid-19th-c, synthetic). These are reduced to powder, and dispersed in whatever medium (eg oil) the artist is using. » acrylic painting; airbrush; bitumen; fixative; fresco; glaze; gouache; impasto; medium (art); oil painting; painting; palette; sinopia; tempera; underpainting; watercolour

painted lady A medium-sized butterfly; wings brick red with black patches, and white patches on point of forewings; caterpillar blackish green, with branching spikes, up to 50 mm/2 in long. (Order: *Lepidoptera*. Family: *Nymphalidae*.) » butterfly; caterpillar

painted leopard » **ocelot**

painter » **cougar**

painting An art which originated in prehistoric times; but the modern sense of the word, the skilful arrangement of colours on a surface to create an independent work, has been current only since the Renaissance. In many societies, including that of mediaeval Europe, painting has been devoted largely to religious ends; but the Romans decorated their houses with secular murals, and from the 15th-c onwards various types of painting have developed: history, portrait, landscape, genre, and still life. » action/genre/landscape/seascape painting; art; cabinet picture; paint; panorama; still life

pair production The production of an electron-positron pair from a high energy X-ray or gamma ray photon, in which the photon loses energy equivalent to at least double the mass of an electron. It occurs in the passage of gamma rays through matter, and is the principle mechanism of high energy gamma ray absorption. » gamma rays; mass-energy relation; photon

Paisley, Bob, properly **Robert** (1919–) British football manager, born at Hetton-le-Hole, Durham. A player with the amateur side Bishop Auckland, he joined Liverpool in 1939, and spent nearly 50 years at the club. It was during his spell as manager (1974–83) that Liverpool enjoyed their greatest years, and became the most successful club side in England. Manager of the Year on six occasions, he is still involved with the club as director and adviser. » football [i]

Paisley, Rev Ian (Richard Kyle) (1926–) Northern Ireland militant Protestant clergyman and politician, born at Armagh. An ordained minister since 1946, he formed his own Church (the Free Presbyterian Church of Ulster) in 1951, and from the 1960s became deeply involved in Ulster politics. He founded the Protestant Unionist Party and stood as its MP for four years until 1974, since when he has been the Democratic Unionist MP for North Antrim. He has been a member of the European Parliament since 1979. A rousing orator, he is strongly pro-British, and fiercely opposed to the IRA, Roman Catholicism, and the unification of Ireland. » European Parliament; IRA; Presbyterianism

Paiute [piy**oo**t] Two separate Numic-speaking American Indian groups, traditionally hunter-gatherers, divided into the S Paiute (Utah, Arizona, Nevada, California) and the N Paiute (California, Nevada, Oregon); also disparagingly termed 'Diggers'. The S Paiute, who had relatively peaceful relations with Whites, were put into reservations in the 19th-c. The N group fought intermittently with White prospectors and farmers until 1874, when the US government appropriated their land. Population c.5 000, in or near reservations. » American Indians

Pakistan, official name **Islamic Republic of Pakistan** pop (1990e) 122 600 000; area 803 943 sq km/310 322 sq ml. Asian state, divided into four provinces, a federal capital territory, and federally administered tribal areas; bounded E by India, W by Afghanistan and Iran, N by Tadzhikistan and China; between the Hindu Kush mountain range (N) and the Arabian Sea (S); disputed area of Jammu and Kashmir (N); capital, Islamabad; timezone GMT +5; chief ethnic groups, Punjabi, Sindhi, Pathan, Baluchi; population includes nearly five million refugees from Afghanistan; official languages, Urdu and English, with several local languages spoken; chief religion, Islam (97%); unit of currency, the Pakistan rupee of 100 paisas.

Physical description and climate. Largely centred on the alluvial floodplain of the R Indus; bounded N and W by mountains rising to 8 611 m/28 250 ft at K2; mostly flat plateau, low-lying plains, and arid desert to the S; climate dominated by the Asiatic monsoon; cool with summer rain and winter snow in the mountains; temperatures at Islamabad, maximum 40°C (Jun), minimum 2°C (Jan); average monthly rainfall, 12 mm/½ in (Nov), 258 mm/10 in (Aug); hot summers and cool dry winters in the upland plateaux; rainy season (Jun–Oct).

History and government. Walled cities at Mohenjo-Daro, Harappa, and Kalibangan, remains of Indus valley civilization over 4 000 years ago; Muslim rule under the Mughal Empire (1526–1761); British rule over most areas, 1840s; separated from India to form a separate state for the Muslim minority, 1947; consisted of **West Pakistan** (Baluchistan, North-West Frontier, West Punjab, Sind) and **East Pakistan** (East Bengal), physically separated by 1 610 km/1 000 ml; occupied Jammu and Kashmir, 1949 (disputed territory with India, and the cause of wars in 1965 and 1971); proclaimed an Islamic republic, 1956; differences between E and W Pakistan developed into civil war, 1971; E Pakistan became an independent state (Bangladesh); military coup by General Zia ul-Haq in 1977, with execution of former Prime Minister Bhutto in 1979, despite international appeals for clemency; governed by an elected president and a bicameral federal parliament.

Economy. Agriculture employs 55% of the labour force; concentrated on the floodplains of the five major rivers of Pakistan, and supported by an extensive irrigation network; wheat, cotton, maize, sugar cane, rice; cotton production important, supporting major spinning, weaving, and processing industries; textiles, food processing, tobacco, engineering, cement, fertilizers, chemicals; natural gas, limestone, gypsum, iron ore, rock salt, uranium. » Bangladesh [i]; Bhutto;

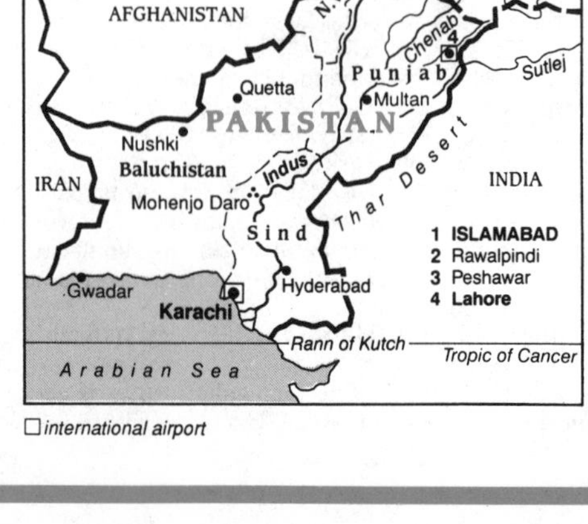

□ *international airport*

India [i]; Indus Valley Civilization; Islam; Islamabad; Mughal Empire; Zia-Ul-Haq; RR26 national holidays; RR58 political leaders

PAL An acronym for **Phase Alternating Line**, the coding system for colour television developed in Germany and the UK from 1965, and widely adopted for 625-line 50 Hz transmission in Europe and many other parts of the world. To overcome the critical phase relation of the colour difference signals in the NTSC system, their phase is reversed line by line so that small differences are cancelled out; no hue control is necessary in the receiver. » colour television [i]; NTSC; SECAM

pala [**pah**la] An altarpiece consisting of a single large picture, instead of several small ones; also known as a *pala d'altare*. The type first appeared in Florence c.1430. » altarpiece

Palach, Jan (1948–69) Czech philosophy student, who, as a protest against the invasion of Czechoslovakia by Warsaw Pact forces (Aug 1968), burnt himself to death in Wenceslas Square, Prague (Jan 1969). He became a hero and symbol of hope, and was mourned by thousands. Huge popular demonstrations marking the 20th anniversary of his death were held in Prague in 1989.

Palaeocene/Paleocene epoch [**pal**eeohseen] The first of the geological epochs of the Tertiary period, from c.66 million to 55 million years ago. The vast majority of dinosaurs had disappeared, and mammals suddenly diversified. » geological time scale; Tertiary period

palaeoclimatology/paleoclimatology An interdisciplinary subject which studies past climatic conditions, and attempts to model the responsible atmospheric processes. It involves components of a wide range of academic disciplines. » archaeology; botany; climate; geography; geology; glaciology; oceanography

palaeoecology/paleoecology [palioheekoluhjee] The application of ecological concepts to the study of the interactions between members of fossil communities and their environment. The basic assumption is that the animals and plants of the geological past lived under essentially the same conditions as their living relatives. A palaeoecological study of a fossil community would involve the construction of a faunal and floral list, an assessment of the relative abundances of these organisms, and some interpretation of their feeding (*trophic*) relationships, as in any ecological study. » ecology; fossil

palaeogeography/paleogeography The study of the geography of former geological periods. This is achieved through the reconstruction of prevailing geographical conditions from the presence of fossils and an interpretation of the environment under which rocks were formed. » geography; geology

palaeography/paleography The study of the styles of handwriting used by scribes in ancient and mediaeval times. The aim is to establish the provenance or authenticity of specific texts, by relating the hand of a particular scribe, in a particular document, to the styles prevailing in the relevant historical period. There are many pitfalls for the palaeographer: the earliest manuscripts had no spaces between words; documents were made available only by laborious copying; scribes frequently miscopied (often, they were not conversant with the language of the text they were copying), and abbreviations were often used, which could lead to ambiguity, eg Latin *imperator* ('emperor') might appear as *imp*. » chirography

Palaeolithic/Paleolithic » **Three Age System**

Palaeolithic/Paleolithic art The art of the Old Stone Age, created c.30 000 years ago, the oldest known. Preserved in limestone caves in France and Spain are impressive murals representing hunting scenes, with realistic drawings of horses, bulls, and many animals now extinct or no longer found in Europe. Small sculptures were also made, the best-known being the 'Venus of Willendorf', a stylized 11.5 cm/4½ in stone carving of a pregnant woman. Such works were not made as 'art' in the modern sense; the paintings are often found only in virtually inaccessible chambers deep within the ground, and were presumably done for magical purposes. » Altamira; Breuil; Lascaux; Three Age System

palaeomagnetism/paleomagnetism The magnetism preserved in rocks which contain iron-bearing minerals such as magnetite and hematite. It results from the alignment of the internal magnetic fields of the mineral grains to the prevailing Earth's field during the formation of the rock, either by sedimentation, crystallization from a magma, or chemical reaction. By measuring the direction of this 'fossil magnetism' in rocks, it is possible to measure the palaeolatitude at which the rock formed, and the position of the Earth's Poles at the time. » magnetism

palaeontology/paleontology The study of fossils; especially, the reconstruction of the organism from its fossil remains and the study of the processes of fossilization. » fossil

palaeopathology/paleopathology The study of ancient human diseases using skeletal material and, where it survives through mummification or bog preservation, soft tissue. Arthritis, tuberculosis, leprosy, syphilis, tumours, dental disease, fractures, and congenital deformities can be diagnosed, as well as dietary deficiency diseases, such as rickets and yaws. Relative frequencies of occurrence and life-expectancy statistics throw light on ancient demography. » bog burials; demography; medicine; trepanning; Pazyryk

Palaeozoic/Paleozoic era [paleeoh**zoh**ik] A major division of geological time extending from c.590 million to 250 million years ago; subdivided into the Cambrian, Ordovician, and Silurian periods (the **Lower Palaeozoic** era), and the Devonian, Carboniferous, and Permian periods (the **Upper Palaeozoic** era). » geological time scale; RR16

palaeozoology/paleozoology [paliohzoo**ol**uhjee] The study of animal fossils, including their tracks and other trace fossils, such as burrows and faeces. » fossil; zoology

palantype The UK trade name of a shorthand typewriter; known by the trade name **stenotype** in the USA. Using a silent keyboard, the operator produces on bands of paper a phonetic version of ongoing utterances (eg court proceedings). Both hands are used, and several keys are pressed simultaneously. The output is later transcribed to produce a normal typescript. » phonetics; shorthand [i]

palate A structure forming the roof of the mouth and the floor of the nasal cavity. A complete palate is a characteristic of mammals, being associated with the ability to suck. It is divided into the **hard palate**, towards the front (formed by bone) and the mobile fibro-muscular **soft palate**, towards the back (which is continuous with the hard palate). The soft palate hangs downwards into the pharynx (separating its nasal and oral parts), and consists mainly of muscle attached to a fibrous base. It may be tensed and raised to close off the nasopharynx, as in swallowing or when producing certain sounds. The muscles of the soft palate pass to both the pharynx and the tongue. Failure of the two halves of the palate to meet and fuse in the midline gives rise to the condition of *cleft palate*. » cleft lip and palate; mouth; pharynx

Palatinate, the A German Rhenish principality, capital Heidelberg. Acquired by the Wittelsbach family (1214), it was elevated to an imperial Electorate by the Golden Bull of 1356, and became increasingly wealthy and important in the 13th–15th-c. After the introduction of Calvinism by Frederick III (reigned 1559–76), it was the leading Protestant German state and head of the Protestant Union (1608), before its division and systematic devastation in the Thirty Years' War (1618–48) and later by France (1685). In the 18th-c it lost significance, being successively re-unified as a single state (1706), linked dynastically with Bavaria (1777), and occupied by the French (1793–4). Shared between Baden and Bavaria (1815), it was finally absorbed into the German Reich (1871). » Heidelberg; Protestantism; Reich; Thirty Years' War

Palau » **Belau**

Palawan [pa**lah**wan], formerly **Paragua** (1902–5) area 11 780 sq km/4 547 sq ml; pop (1980) 311 548. Island of the W Philippines; long, narrow, with a mountain chain running almost the whole length; Mindoro I to the NE, separated by Mindoro Strait; bounded by the Sulu Sea (E) and South China Sea (W); rises in the S to 2 054 m/6 739 ft at Mt Mantalingajan; chief town, Puerto Princesa; timber, chromite, fishing. » Philippines [i]

Pale The 'land of peace' where English rule prevailed in late mediaeval Ireland. It shrank during this period because of aggrandizement by Anglo-Irish nobles (the earls of Desmond,

Kildare, and Ormond), and continued to diminish until its reconquest under Henry VIII. It was defined as the four counties of Dublin, Kildare, Louth, and Meath in 1464, but the Act of 1495 under Poynings' rule showed a smaller area. » Ireland [i]; Poynings' Law

Palembang [pa**lem**bang] 2°59S 104°45E, pop (1980) 582 961. River-port capital of Sumatra Selatan province, Indonesia; on R Musi, S Sumatra I; former capital of the Sriwijaya Empire (7th–12th-c); airfield; university (1960); oil refining, trade in oil, rubber, fertilizers, textiles. » Sumatra

Palenque [pa**leng**kway] A Mayan city of 600–800 AD on the slopes of the Chiapas Mts, S Mexico, celebrated for its beauty and distinctive architecture: a world heritage site. Its monuments include a labyrinthine palace complex; temple pyramids of the Sun, Cross, and Foliate Cross; and the Temple of Inscriptions, built to house the tomb of Pacal, ruler of Palenque 615–84. » Mayas

Paleo-, paleo- » **Palaeo-, palaeo-**

Palermo [pa**ler**moh] 38°08N 13°23E, pop (1981) 701 782. Seaport and capital of Palermo province, on N coast of Sicily, Italy; founded by Phoenicians, 8th-c BC; archbishopric; airport; railway; ferries; university (1777); shipbuilding, steel, glass, chemicals, furniture, tourism, trade in fruit, wine, olive oil; cathedral (12th-c), Church of San Cataldo, ruined Church of San Giovanni degli Eremiti (1132), Church of La Mortorana (1143), Teatro Massimo (1875–97); trade fair (May–Jun). » Sicily

Palestine » **Jordan [i]; Zionism**

Palestine Liberation Organization » **PLO**

Palestrina, (Giovanni Pierluigi da) (1525–94) Italian composer, born at Palestrina. At Rome he learned composition and organ playing, and in 1544 became organist and *maestro di canto* at the cathedral of St Agapit, Palestrina. In 1551 he became master of the Julian choir at St Peter's, the first of several appointments in Rome. He composed over 100 masses, motets, hymns, and other church pieces, and in 1577 began a revision of the Gradual (which he later abandoned). He died in Rome, the most distinguished composer of the Renaissance.

palette In art, a term with two main senses: **1** A flat wooden plate, oval or rectangular, on which painters arrange their colours. **2** The range of colours used by an artist. Thus, Rembrandt's palette was occasionally restricted to just four or five basic colours, while an Impressionist might use a dozen. By extension, this sense has come to be used in computing, referring to the range of colours available on a computer using computer graphics. » computer graphics; Impressionism (art); paint; Rembrandt

Palgrave, Francis Turner (1824–97) British poet and critic, born at Great Yarmouth, Norfolk. He studied at Oxford, worked as a civil servant in the education department, and became professor of poetry at Oxford (1886–95). He is best known as the editor of the *Golden Treasury of Lyrical Poetry* (1875), which influenced poetic taste for many years. He died in London. » literary criticism; poetry

palindrome A word or phrase which reads the same backwards as forwards, such as 'madam', 'radar', and 'Draw, o coward!'. Longer sequences are usually nonsensical, but there are exceptions, as in: 'Doc, note, I dissent. A fast never prevents a fatness. I diet on cod'.

palio An Italian festival held annually in several cities. Palios were first held in mediaeval times, the highlight being the bareback horse races in which jockeys race for the *palio* (a silk standard bearing a painted image of the Virgin Mary). The most famous is the Palio of Siena, first held in 1482.

Palissy, Bernard (c.1509–89) French potter, born at Agen. He began as a glass-painter, then in 1568 settled at Saintes, where he devised new techniques for glazing earthenware. His products, bearing in high relief plants and animals coloured to represent nature, soon made him famous; and, though imprisoned as a Huguenot in 1562, he was speedily released and taken into royal favour. In 1564 he established his workshop at the Tuileries, and was specially exempted from the massacre of St Bartholomew (1572). In 1588 he was again arrested as a Huguenot, and died in prison in Paris. » glaze

Palladianism An architectural style of the 17th-c and 18th-c derived from the Renaissance buildings and writing of Andrea Palladio, and characterized by the use of symmetrical planning and the slightly Mannerist application of Roman architectural forms. Especially popular in England, it was first used by Inigo Jones for the Banqueting House, London (1619–22), and followed and promoted by the publications of Lord Burlington. The style was also used in Italy, Germany, Holland, Russia, and the USA. » Jones, Inigo; Mannerism; Palladio; Renaissance architecture

Palladio, Andrea, originally **Andrea di Pietro della Gondola** (1508–80) Italian architect, born and died at Vicenza. He founded modern Italian architecture, as distinguished from the earlier Italian Renaissance. The 'Palladian' style, modelled on the ancient Roman, can be seen in many palaces and villas in the Vicenza region, notably the Villa Rotonda (1550–1). *I quattro libri dell' architettura* (1570, The Four Books of Architecture) greatly influenced his successors. » Palladianism

Palladium In Greek legend, an image of Pallas Athene which fell from heaven, and became 'the luck of Troy'. Odysseus and Diomedes stole it, and it was supposed to have reached Argos, Athens, or Sparta. The Romans believed Aeneas had brought it to Rome. » Athena

Pallas The second asteroid to be found (1802), 608 km/378 ml across. » asteroids

Pallas's cat A member of the cat family, found from SE Siberia to Iran; same size as the domestic cat; heavy body; short legs; thickest coat of any wild cat; silvery grey or dirty brown; inhabits open and rocky country; lives in a den; eats small mammals and birds. (*Felis manul*.) » Felidae

pallium or **pall** A circular white woollen band with six purple crosses, signifying episcopal power and union with the Holy See (of Rome). It is worn by the pope, and by archbishops to whom he grants the right. » archbishop; pope; Roman Catholicism; vestments [i]

palm A woody plant found throughout the tropics, with a few species reaching warm temperate regions, typical of and prominent on oceanic islands. Palms are monocotyledons, and display the typical characters of parallel-veined leaves and floral parts arranged in whorls of three, or multiples of three. Some species are climbers, but most are trees and, as is typical in monocots, lack secondary growth from a vascular cambium. Unlike dicot trees, which increase in size and girth each year, palms achieve their full diameter as seedlings, subsequent growth increasing their height only.

The trunk is covered with old leaf-sheaths, or their scars, and has a crown of leaves. At the tip is a single, large, apical bud; if the bud is removed or damaged, the plant dies. Leaves are mostly fan- or feather-shaped, with numerous, pleated segments, and can reach 20 m/65 ft in length. The huge inflorescences can contain an estimated 250 000 flowers; in some species they are produced only once, after which the plant dies. Such a massive burst of flowering requires great energy, and in these species the trunk often contains large quantities of starch or sugar. The fruits are 1-seeded berries, dry, fleshy or fibrous, oily rather than starchy, often brightly coloured, sometimes very hard. They show a great size range, and include the world's largest seed, that of the *coco de mer* (20 kg/44 lb, c.50 cm/20 in long).

Palms are of immense ecomonic importance, especially in the tropics, where they provide a range of basic products, including vegetables, starch, fruits and nuts, timber, fibre, sugar, alcohol, and wax. They are a very old plant group; fossils of a salt water palm, *Nypa*, date from 100–110 million years ago, making it the seventh oldest-known flowering plant. (Family: *Palmae*.) » cambium; climbing plant; fan palm; inflorescence [i]; monocotyledons; tree [i]

palm oil A major edible oil, obtained from the flesh of the fruit of several types of palm tree. It is produced in large quantities, and widely used for the manufacture of margarines, as well as in soap, candles, and lubricating greases. » margarine; oils, edible

Palm Springs 33°50N 116°33W, pop (1980) 32 271. Resort city in Riverside County, S California, USA, in the N Coachella Valley; founded, 1876; developed as a luxurious desert resort in the early 1930s; airfield; nearby Palm Canyon (an ancient grove of native palms), Tahquitz Bowl (a natural amphitheatre); hot springs; golf courses. » California

Palm Sunday In the Christian Church, the Sunday before Easter, commemorating the entry of Jesus into Jerusalem, when the crowd spread palm branches in front of him (*Mark* 11, *John* 13). » Easter; Jesus Christ

Palma (de Mallorca) [**pal**ma] 39°35N 2°39E, pop (1981) 304 422. Seaport and chief city of Majorca I, Balearic Is; bishopric; airport; university (1967); shipyard, footwear, metalwork, beer, clothes, pottery, tourism; Bellver Castle (14th-c), Church of St Francis, cathedral (13th–16th-c), Spanish Pueblo open-air museum. » Majorca

palmate In botany, the shape of a leaf in which four or more leaflets arise from the same point, and spread like the fingers of a hand. » leaf [i]

Palmer, Arnold (Daniel) (1929–) US golfer, born at Latrobe, Pennsylvania. US Amateur champion in 1954, he won the Canadian Open (1955), the British Open (1961–2), the US Open (1960), and the US Masters (1958, 1960, 1962, 1964). The first golfer (1968) to win $1 million in his career, he has since been involved in various business enterprises. » golf

Palmerston (of Palmerston), Henry John Temple, 3rd Viscount (1784–1865) British statesman and Liberal Prime Minister (1855–8, 1859–65), born at Broadlands, Hampshire. Educated at Edinburgh and Cambridge, he became a Tory MP in 1807, served as Secretary of War (1809–28), joined the Whigs (1830), and was three times Foreign Secretary (1830–4, 1835–41, 1846–51). His brusque speech, assertive manner, and robust defences of what he considered to be British interests abroad secured him the name of 'Firebrand Palmerston'. Home Secretary in Aberdeen's coalition (1852), he became Premier in 1855, when he vigorously prosecuted the Crimean War with Russia. He died at Brocket Hall, Hertfordshire. » Aberdeen, Earl; Crimean War; Liberal Party (UK); Tories; Wellington, Duke of; Whigs

Palmerston (Australia) » **Darwin** (Australia)

Palmerston North 40°20S 175°39E, pop (1988e) 67 700. City on SW coast of North Island, New Zealand, NE of Wellington; airfield; railway; university (1926); agricultural research centre; dairy products, pharmaceuticals, textiles, electrical goods; Manawatu rugby museum. » New Zealand [i]

palmitic acid [pal**mi**tik] $C_{15}H_{31}COOH$, IUPAC **hexadecanoic acid**, a saturated fatty acid, melting point 63°C. It is obtained from many animal and plant sources, especially milk and palm oil (from which the name is derived). » carboxylic acids; IUPAC; napalm; soap

Palmyra (Pacific Ocean) [pal**mi**yra] 5°52N 162°05W. Uninhabited atoll enclosing 50 small islets in the Pacific Ocean 1 600 km/1 000 ml S of Honolulu; annexed by USA, 1912; important air transport base in World War 2; since 1962 under jurisdiction of US Department of the Interior; site for nuclear waste disposal since 1986. » Pacific Ocean

Palmyra (Roman history) [pal**mi**yra] In Roman times, a flourishing oasis town on the E fringe of the Empire, whose wealth came from controlling the desert trade routes between N Syria and Babylonia. At the height of its power in the 3rd-c AD, it briefly ruled the E half of the Empire, before being brought to heel and destroyed by the Romans in 273. » Petra

palomino [paluh**mee**noh] A horse with a distinctive type of colouring, found in various breeds, and actively selected by some breeders, especially in the USA; pale golden brown with white mane and tail (occasionally white on face or legs); also known as **California sorrel**. » horse [i]

Palouse » **Appaloosa**

palynology [payli**nol**uhjee] The analysis of pollen grains preserved in ancient sediments and soils to reconstruct variations in vegetation over time; blanket bog, acid moorland podzols, and lake deposits provide particularly good data. The impact of prehistoric peoples and early agriculture on the natural environment is a subject of much contemporary interest. » archaeology; pollen [i]

pampa(s) The extensive grassland (prairie) region of Argentina and Uruguay around the R Plate estuary. It is a major centre for cattle ranching. » prairie; steppe

pampas cat A member of the cat family native to S America; same size as the domestic cat; thick greyish brown or pale coat, marked with spots and lines; inhabits forest and grassland; eats small mammals (eg guinea pigs) and birds. (*Felis colocolo*.) » Felidae

pampas grass A large perennial grass forming dense tufts of arching bluish leaves and tall, erect stems 3 m/10 ft high, bearing silvery-white, sometimes pink, plume-like panicles. Native to Brazil, Argentina and Chile, it is widely grown as an ornamental. (*Cortaderia selloana*. Family: *Gramineae*.) » grass [i]; panicle; perennial

Pamplona [pam**ploh**na], Lat **Pampeluna** or **Pompaelo** 42°48N 1°38W, pop (1981) 183 126. Capital of Navarre province, N Spain; on R Arga, 407 km/253 ml N of Madrid; archbishopric; capital of the Kingdom of Navarre, 10th-c; airport; railway; university (1952); agricultural centre, paper, rope, pottery, chemicals, kitchenware; cathedral (14th–15th-c), museum; Fiesta of San Fermin (Jul), with bull-running in the streets; Chiquita (Sep). » Navarre; Spain [i]

Pamporovo [pampuh**roh**voh] 41°43N 24°39E. International ski resort in Smolyan province, S Bulgaria; 15 km/9 ml N of Smolyan in the Rhodopi Mts; altitude 1 650 m/5 413 ft; on Snezhanka ('snow white') Peak there are several ski runs up to 3 800 m/12 500 ft in length. » Bulgaria [i]

Pan A Greek god, the 'nourisher' of flocks and herds, originally a rural goat-god from Arcadia, depicted with goat-like ears, horns, and legs. His pan-pipe is made of reeds, and he can cause groups of people to be seized with uncontrollable fear ('panic'). » Selene; Syrinx

Pan-Africanism A movement founded by US and W Indian Blacks to promote the interests of Black people everywhere. It held meetings in 1900, 1919 (in association with the Peace Conference at Versailles), and 1945, and influenced the intellectual development of nationalism in Africa. Nasser made Cairo a centre of Pan-African influence, a role subsequently taken over by Addis Ababa. » African history; Black consciousness; Nasser

Pan-American Games A multi-sport competition for athletes from N, S and C American nations. First held at Buenos Aires, Argentina, in 1951, they now take place every four years.

Pan-American Highway A network of designated roads extending 27 000 km/17 000 ml across the Americas from Alaska to Chile. The proposal, which was put to the 5th International Conference of American States in 1923, was originally for a single route, but several alternative routes have since been designated.

Pan-American Union An organization founded in 1890 to foster political and economic co-operation among American states, and to draw N and S America closer together; first called the **International Bureau for American Republics**. Until World War 2 the Union concluded many agreements covering trade, migration, and neutrality zones around their coasts, despite fears among many members of domination by the USA. In 1948 it became part of the wider Organization of American States, and now forms its permanent administrative and advisory machinery. It has four departments: economic and social affairs; international law; cultural affairs; and administrative services. » Organization of American States

pan-and-scan A method of adapting a wide-screen motion picture to the narrower video format by selecting a limited area of the frame covering the most important action, which is continuously followed as though by 'panning' a camera. The selection is in fact made electronically in the telecine process. » cinematography [i]; telecine

Pan Gu The first being of the Chinese creation myth. He breaks open the primal egg from within, holds up the sky, and prevents it from bearing down upon the Earth. Then the world is made from parts of him, so that his body becomes the mountains, his hair the stars, and his eyes the Sun and Moon.

Panama, Span **Panamá**, official name **Republic of Panama**, Span **República de Panamá** pop (1990e) 2 418 000; area 77 082 sq km/29 753 sq ml. Republic occupying the SE end of the isthmus of C America, divided into nine provinces and one Indian territory; bounded N by the Caribbean Sea, S by the Pacific Ocean, W by Costa Rica, and E by Colombia; capital, Panama City; chief towns, David, Colón, Santiago; timezone GMT −5;

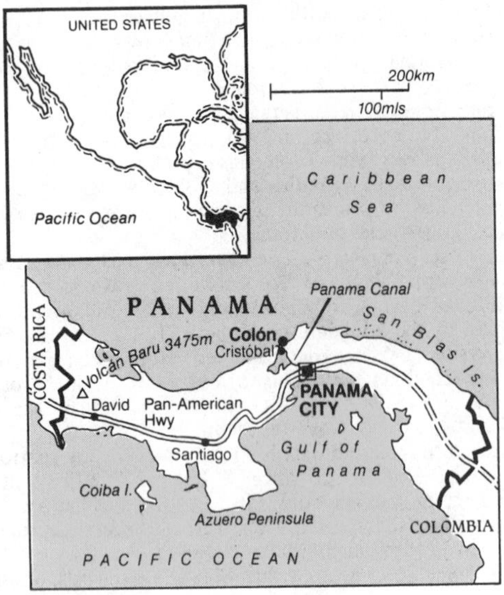

□ international airport

chief ethnic groups, mixed Spanish–Indian (70%), West Indian (14%); official language, Spanish; chief religion, Roman Catholicism; unit of currency, the balboa of 100 centesimos; mostly mountainous; Serranía de Tabasará (W) rises to over 2 000 m/6 500 ft; Azuero peninsula in the S; lake-studded lowland cuts across the isthmus; dense tropical forests on the Caribbean coast; tropical climate, mean annual temperature 32°C; average annual rainfall at Colón, 3 280 mm/130 in; at Panama City, 1 780 mm/70 in; visited by Columbus, 1502; under Spanish colonial rule until 1821; joined the Republic of Greater Colombia; separation from Colombia after a US-inspired revolution, 1903; assumed sovereignty of the 8 km/5 ml-wide Canal, previously administered by the USA, 1979; governed by a president, elected for five years, and a cabinet, with a 67-member Legislative Assembly, but the military have been the ruling force led by Manuel Noriega until 1989; economy centred mainly on the Canal and the ports of Colón and Panama; Canal revenue accounts for four-fifths of the country's wealth; great increase in banking sector since 1970; attempts to diversify include oil refining, cigarettes, clothing, beverages, construction materials, paper products, shrimps, tourism; copper, gold, silver deposits; bananas, coffee, cacao, sugar cane. » Colombia [i]; Noriega; Panama Canal; Panama City; RR26 national holidays; RR58 political leaders

Panama Canal A canal bisecting the Isthmus of Panama and linking the Atlantic and Pacific Oceans. It is 82 km/51 ml long, and 150 m/490 ft wide in most places; built by the US Corps of Engineers (1904–14). In 1979, US control of the Panama Canal Zone (8 km/5 ml of land flanking the canal on either side) was passed to the Republic of Panama, who have guaranteed the neutrality of the waterway itself when operational control of the canal is passed to them in 2000. » Panama [i]

Panama City, Span **Panamá** 8°57N 79°30W, pop (1980) 389 172. Capital city of Panama, on the N shore of the Gulf of Panama, near the Pacific end of the Panama Canal; founded, 1673; airport; railway; two universities (1935, 1965); industrial and transportation centre of Panama; on the Pan-American Highway; Church of San José. » Panama [i]

Panathenaea [pana**the**niya] A festival held annually at Athens in honour of Athene, the patron goddess of the city. It consisted of a procession from the town to the Acropolis, the sacrifice at the great altar there of a hekatomb (100 cattle), and then athletic contests. » Acropolis

Pancake Day » **Shrove Tuesday**

Panchen Lama [**pan**chen **lah**ma] A spiritual leader and teacher in Tibetan Buddhism, second in importance to the Dalai Lama, and said to be the reincarnation of the Buddha Amitabha. The late Panchen Lama (1938–89), the 10th reincarnation, became the ward of the Chinese in his childhood, and some Tibetans disputed his status. » Dalai Lama; Lamaism

pancreas A soft gland made up of small lobes (*lobules*) associated with the alimentary canal of vertebrates with jaws, having both endocrine and exocrine secretions. It consists of the *islets of Langerhans* (the endocrine part) and the *secretory alveoli* (the exocrine part). In humans it is c.12–15 cm/4.5–6 in long, and lies on the rear abdominal wall in front of the upper two lumbar vertebrae, extending to the left. The secretory alveoli produce an alkaline mixture of digestive enzymes (the **pancreatic juices**), which are discharged into the duodenum. The islets of Langerhans (consisting of A, B, and D cells in humans) synthesize and secrete hormones involved in carbohydrate metabolism. » alimentary canal; diabetes mellitus; duodenum; endocrine glands; gland

panda A mammal of family *Ailuropodidae*, related to raccoons and bears; inhabits bamboo forests in mountains; two species: **giant panda** (*Ailuropoda melanoleuca*) from China; bear-like with large round head; white with black legs, shoulders, chest, ears, and area around eyes; front paw with elongated wrist bone which acts like a sixth digit; grasps bamboo shoots between this extra 'thumb' and the first and second true digits; also the **red panda**, **lesser panda**, or **cat bear** (*Ailurus fulgens*) found from S China to N Burma; raccoon-like; red-brown with black underparts and tail tip; dark rings around tail; white markings on face. » bear; mammal [i]; raccoon

Pandarus [**pan**daruhs] In Homer's *Iliad*, a Trojan prince, killed by Diomedes. In later developments of the story of Troilus and Cressida, he became her uncle and their 'go-between' (hence 'pander'). » Cressida; Troilus

Pandit, Vijaya Lakshmi, *née* **Swarup Kumari Nehru** (1900–) Indian politician and diplomat, born at Allahabad, the sister of Nehru. Leader of the Indian United Nations delegation (1946–8, 1952–3), she also held several ambassadorial posts (1947–51). In 1953, she became the first woman President of the UN General Assembly, and Indian High Commissioner in London (1954–61). » Nehru

Pandora [pan**daw**ra] In Greek mythology, the first woman, made by Hephaestus, and adorned by the gods with special qualities; she was sent to be the wife of Epimetheus. Zeus gave her a box (or she found a storage-jar) from which all the evils which plague mankind came out; only Hope was left in the bottom of the box. The name means 'all gifts'. » Prometheus

panegyric A speech, poem, or song of praise addressed to an individual, group, or institution. Examples include Pliny's eulogy of Trajan, and Mark Antony's oration on Caesar in Shakespeare's *Julius Caesar*. Less creditable instances are addresses by authors to patrons, and periodic tributes to royalty by the English poets laureate.

Pangaea [pan**jee**a] The name given to the hypothesized 'supercontinent' comprising Gondwanaland and Laurasia which made up the Earth's continental crust before the Jurassic period. It then began to split, as a result of continental drift, eventually forming the present-day distribution of the continents. » continental drift; Gondwanaland; Jurassic period; Laurasia

pangamic acid A component of many seeds, whose chemical name is n-di-isopropyl-glucuronate. Although it is promoted as a vitamin (B_{15}), pangamic acid serves no known nutritional function. » vitamins [i]

pangolin [pang**goh**lin] A mammal native to Africa and S and SE Asia; pointed head with small eyes; long broad tail; long tongue and no teeth; eats ants and termites; covered in large overlapping horny plates (resembles a tiled roof); curls into an armoured ball; the only member of order *Pholidota*; also known as **scaly anteater**. (Genus: *Manis*, 7 species.) » anteater

pangram A meaningful sentence which contains all the letters of the alphabet, ideally only once each. A familiar example, though with duplications, is the typists' test sentence *The quick brown fox jumped over the lazy dog*. A 26-letter English pangram (albeit with rather obscure words) is *Veldt jynx grimps waqf zho buck*.

Panhandle Any territory comprising a narrow strip of land running out from a large area in the shape of a pan handle; in the USA, applied to areas in (1) NW Texas (the Texas Panhandle), (2) NW Oklahoma, (3) N Idaho, (4) NE West Virginia (Eastern Panhandle), (5) N West Virginia, (6) SE Alaska, (7) Nebraska, and (8) an extension of the Golden Gate Park in San Francisco. » United States of America [i]

panicle A branched, racemose type of inflorescence, in which each branch is itself a racemose. The term is often used for any complexly-branched inflorescence. » inflorescence [i]

Paninari An Italian youth cult of the 1980s named from the sandwich bars where its members gathered. They wore expensive 'designer' clothes (from the US and Italy), presenting a tough militaristic image – leather jackets, belts with large buckles, dark glasses – which accorded with their right-wing views.

Panjabi » **Indo-Aryan languages**

Pankhurst, Emmeline, *née* **Goulden** (1858–1928) British suffragette, born in Manchester. In 1905 she organized the Women's Social and Political Union, and fought for women's suffrage by violent means, on several occasions being arrested and going on hunger strike. After the outbreak of World War 1, she worked instead for the industrial mobilization of women. She died in London. Of her daughters and fellow workers, **Dame Christabel** (1880–1958) turned later to preaching Christ's Second Coming; and **Sylvia** (1882–1960) diverged to pacificism, internationalism, and Labour politics. » women's liberation movement

panorama In art, a painting of a landscape which is too large to be viewed all at once but which is either unrolled before the spectator, bit by bit, or displayed all around a room, which may be circular in plan. The huge panorama of Scheveningen by Hendrik Willem Mesdag (1831–1915) is one of the tourist attractions of the Hague. » painting

panpipes A musical instrument made of various lengths of hollowed cane or wood joined together in a row. The player blows across the top to sound a different pitch from each pipe. Of great antiquity, panpipes are still widely used in certain folk cultures, such as those of S America. » woodwind instrument [i]

pansy Any of several species of violet, in which the flat, 5-petalled flowers are held in a vertical plane and often resemble a face, the effect being heightened by honey-guide markings on the petals. The cultivated pansy, developed as a cottage garden flower c.1830, has large flowers with overlapping petals in a wider range of colours. (Genus: *Viola*. Family: *Violaceae*.) » heartsease; honey guide; violet

pantheism The belief that God and the universe are ultimately identical. It may equate the world with God or deny the reality of the world, maintaining that only the divine is real and that sense experience is illusory. It is a characteristic feature of Hinduism and certain schools of Buddhism. » Buddhism; God; Hinduism; Spinoza

pantheon A temple dedicated to all gods. The term is often used to refer specifically to the Pantheon at Rome, erected by Hadrian (AD 100–125), and now the Santa Maria Rotunda. » Roman architecture

panther A member of the cat family, but not a distinct species. The name is used for the black form of the leopard (especially in the combination **black panther**) or as an alternative name for the cougar. » cougar; Felidae; leopard

pantomime A theatrical term used to describe the silent narration and dramatization of a story through gesture and movement, often by a single performer. Also, a Christmas play, loosely connected to a fairy-tale or nursery-rhyme, which was developed in Victorian and Edwardian Britain. » harlequinade; mime

pantonality An attribute of music which fluctuates rapidly from one key centre to another, so that it cannot be said to be in any particular key. Some late Wagner and early Schoenberg works might be described as pantonal. » tonality; Schoenberg; Wagner

pantothanic acid A B-vitamin which acts as a co-factor in several enzyme reactions. Because it is found so widely in nature, a deficiency in humans has not yet been recorded. » enzyme; vitamins [i]

Panzer (Ger 'armour') A term used in the German armed forces, applied to warships (*Panzerschiffe*, 'armoured ship') but more particularly to armoured fighting vehicles. The Panzer divisions (essentially tank forces) were the most important component of the German army's fighting strength during World War 2. » armoured fighting vehicle; warships [i]

Papa Doc » **Duvalier, Françøis**

papacy » **pope**

Papago [**pa**pagoh] A Uto-Aztecan-speaking N American Indian group who lived on the Arizona-Mexico border. Semi-nomadic wild food gatherers, they later raised cattle and had a few crops. Population c.16 500, concentrated on three reservations in Arizona. » American Indians

Papal States The 'States of the Church', straddling rural, mountainous areas of C Italy, comprised of territories received by treaties and donations in the Middle Ages. The papal government was often ineffective, and relied upon local lords (Malatesta of Rimini, Montefeltro of Urbino) who were appointed as 'vicars in temporal matters'. Annexed in 1870, the papacy refused to recognize their loss until the Lateran Treaty (1929), which established the Vatican papal state. » Lateran Treaty; Malatesta; pope

papaw [puh**paw**] A small, unbranched tree growing to 6 m/20 ft, with very soft wood and copious latex; a crown of long-stalked, palmate leaves up to 75 cm/30 in wide; flowers yellow, males and females on separate plants; fruit up to 30 cm/12 in long, oval, yellow; also called **papaya** and **pawpaw**. Its origin is unknown, but it is possibly a hybrid. It is widely cultivated throughout the tropics for its juicy but bland fruits. Latex from the leaves and young fruits contains the enzyme *papain*, which is used in the medical, meat, and leather industries. (*Carica papaya*. Family: *Caricaceae*.) » enzyme; latex; palmate; tree [i]

papaya » **papaw**

Papeete [papaya**ay**tay] 17°32S 149°34W, pop (1977) 62 735. Capital and chief port of French Polynesia, on NW coast of Tahiti; airport; copra, vanilla, mother-of-pearl. » French Polynesia; Tahiti

Papen, Franz von [**pah**puhn] (1879–1969) German politician, born at Werl, Westphalia. He was military attaché in Mexico and Washington, Chief-of-Staff with a Turkish army, and in 1921 took to centre party politics. He was Hindenburg's Chancellor (1932), Hitler's Vice-Chancellor (1933–4), and Ambassador to Austria (1936–8) and Turkey (1939–44). Taken prisoner in 1945, he was acquitted at the Nuremberg Trials. He died at Obersasbach. » Hindenburg, Paul von; Hitler; Nuremberg Trials

paper Material in sheet form used for a wide range of functions, notably writing, drawing, printing, and packaging. Probably a 2nd-c AD Chinese invention, paper was originally produced from pulped rags or plant fibres. It was introduced to mediaeval Europe by the Moors, eventually superseding parchment as the standard material for written and printed documents. From the 19th-c, wood pulp and cellulose have largely been used in its manufacture, but plant fibres (eg esparto grass) and rags continue to be used, especially for paper of strength or high quality, and the recycling of waste paper nowadays is increasingly practised on ecological grounds. Early paper was hand made, and consisted of single sheets. Machines for making continuous rolls (or *webs*) of paper were introduced in France at the end of the 18th-c. » ink; parchment; pen; pencil; printing [i]; *see illustration p.904*

paper-bark birch A species of birch with peeling white bark, which is used to make canoes. It is native to N America. (*Betula papyrifolia*. Family: *Betulaceae*.) » birch

paper nautilus [**naw**tiluhs] An octopus-like marine mollusc; two tentacles modified in the female to secrete a fragile external egg case, the so-called shell; female c.30 cm/12 in long, male only 1 cm/0.4 in long; widely distributed in tropical and subtropical seas. (*Argonauta*. Class: *Cephalopoda*.) » mollusc; octopus

Paphos [**pa**fos] 34°45N 32°23E, pop (1973) 8 984. Holiday resort and capital town of Paphos district, SW Cyprus, on the Mediterranean Sea; capital of Cyprus during Roman times; old city founded probably in Mycenaean period, a world heritage site; remains of Roman villa (House of Dionysos), 7th-c

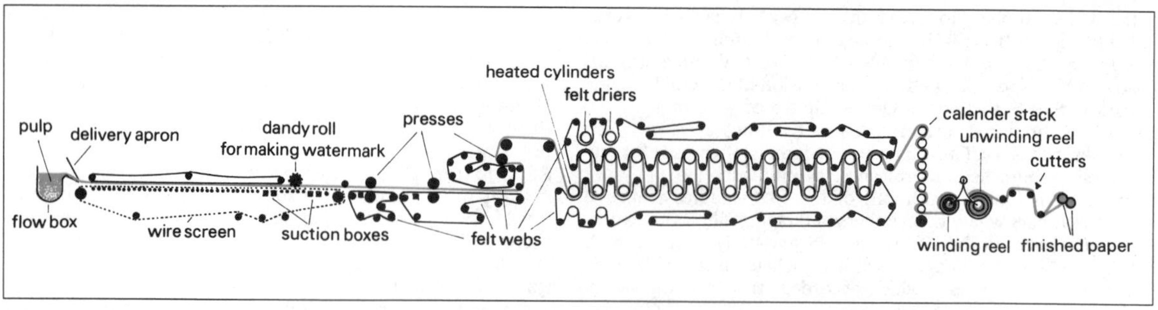

The Fourdrinier paper-making machine, invented by French engineer Henry Fourdrinier (1766–1854) and his brother, Sealy, and introduced into England in 1803. The fibres are first separated and soaked to produce paper pulp, which is then filtered to make a fibre sheet. Most of the water is removed by pressing and suction. The sheet is carried by an endless reel of felt around a long series of steam-heated cylinders, which dry out the remaining water. The dry sheet then passes through a set of smoothing rollers (calendars), which provide the finished quality. Further processes, such as glazing or sizing, can be applied for special purposes.

Byzantine castle, 3rd-c BC 'Tombs of the Kings', Saranda Kolones (remains of Byzantine castle), Chrysopolitissa Basilica (early Christian basilica). » Cyprus [i]; Mycenae

papilionid butterfly [papilyuhnid] A butterfly of the family *Papilionidae*; medium to very large, and often brightly-coloured; hindwings commonly extended into tails; adults and caterpillars usually distasteful to predators; c.550 species, including swallowtails, Apollo butterflies, and the birdwings. (Order: *Lepidoptera*.) » butterfly; caterpillar

papilloma Localized overgrowths of cells of the surface of tissues such as the skin, intestinal lining, or bladder. Many papillomas are benign, but some tend to recur and become malignant.

papillon [papilon] A toy breed of dog developed in France several centuries ago; small with long fine coat thickest on chest, neck, and upper legs; ears with fringes of hair, resembling a butterfly's wings. » dog; non-sporting dog

Papineau, Louis Joseph (1786–1871) French-Canadian politician, born in Montreal. The speaker of Lower Canada's House of Assembly (1815–37), he opposed union with Upper Canada, and agitated for a greater degree of governmental independence from Britain. His leadership of the *Patriotes* during the Rebellions of 1837 led to charges of treason. He escaped to Paris, but returned to Canada under amnesty in 1845, and died at Montebello, Quebec. » Rebellions of 1837

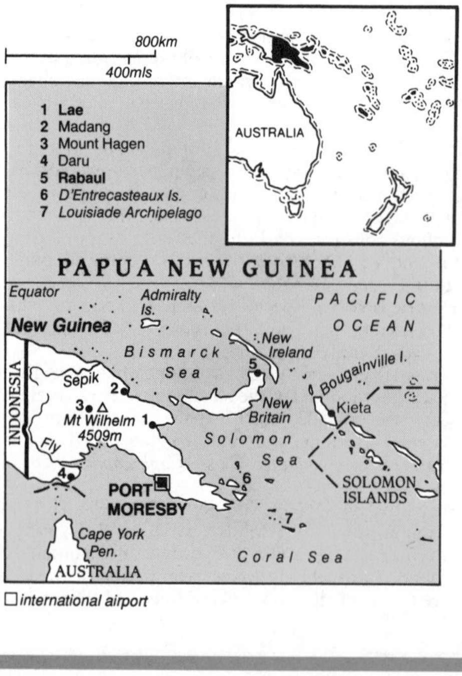

Papp, Joseph, originally **Papirofsky** (1921–91) US theatre director, born in New York City. He founded the New York Shakespeare Festival in 1954, where he carried out most of his work, apart from a period at the Lincoln Center (1973–7). Notable productions include *Cymbeline* (1954), *Twelfth Night* (1963), *Hamlet* (1967), and *Measure for Measure* (1985). » theatre

Pappus of Alexandria (AD 4th-c) Greek mathematician, whose 8-book *Synagoge* (Collection) is extant in an incomplete form. Most of our knowledge of ancient Greek mathematics derives from his work.

paprika » **pepper 1**

Papua New Guinea, official name **Independent State of Papua New Guinea** pop (1990e) 3 671 900; area 462 840 sq km/178 656 sq ml. Island group in the SW Pacific Ocean, 160 km/100 ml NE of Australia, comprising the E half of the island of New Guinea, the Bismarck and Louisiade Archipelagos, the Trobriand and D'Entrecasteaux Is, and other off-lying groups; divided into 19 provinces and a national capital district; capital, Port Moresby; chief towns, Lae, Madang, Rabaul; timezone GMT +10; chief ethnic group, Melanesian; chief religions, Christianity, magico-religious beliefs; official language, pidgin English, with c.750 other languages spoken; complex system of mountains, with snow-covered peaks rising above 4 000 m/13 000 ft; highest point, Mt Wilhelm (4 509 m/14 793 ft); large rivers flow to the S, N, and E; mainly covered with tropical rainforest; vast mangrove swamps along coast; archipelago islands are mountainous, mostly volcanic, and fringed with coral reefs; typically monsoonal climate, with temperatures and humidity constantly high; average temperature range, 22–33°C; high rainfall, averaging 2 000–2 500 mm/80–100 in; British protectorate in SE New Guinea, 1884; some of the islands under German protectorate, 1884; German New Guinea in NE, 1899; German colony annexed by Australia in World War 1; Australia mandated to govern both British and German areas, 1920; combined in 1949 as the United Nations Trust Territory of Papua and New Guinea; independence within the Commonwealth, 1975; a governor-general represents the British Crown; governed by a prime minister and cabinet, with a unicameral 109-member National Parliament elected for five years; over two-thirds of the workforce engaged in farming, fishing, forestry; yams, sago, cassava, bananas, vegetables, copra, coffee, cocoa, timber, palm oil, rubber, tea, sugar, peanuts; copper, gold, hydroelectric power, natural gas; food processing, brewing, tourism. » Bismarck Archipelago; Bougainville; mandates; Port Moresby; RR26 national holidays; RR58 political leaders

papyrus [papiyruhs] An aquatic perennial, native to N Africa; stems growing to 4 m/13 ft, triangular in cross-section; leaves grass-like; flowers tiny, yellowish, lacking perianth, in spikelets forming large spherical heads. The ancients made paper by pressing wet strips of the pithy stems side by side. (*Cyperus papyrus*. Family: *Cyperaceae*.) » paper [i]; perennial; perianth

par value » **parity** (economics)

parable A metaphor in narrative form (although sometimes considered a simile) with the purpose not so much of imparting propositional truths or general moral lessons as challenging the perspective of the hearer. In the Bible, parables are frequently used by Jesus in his preaching about the kingdom of God, and include well-known stories about the Good Samaritan, the Prodigal Son, the Sower, and many others. These parables were often subjected to allegorical interpretation by the Church fathers. » Jesus Christ; metaphor; New Testament

parabola In mathematics, the locus of a point whose distance from a fixed point S (the *focus*) is equal to its distance from a fixed line l (the *directrix*). It is one of the classical conic sections. The parabola has the property that the tangent at any point P is equally inclined to the line PS, and the line through P parallel to the x-axis of the parabola. Thus rays emitted from S and reflected by the curve will be parallel. This notion underlies the technique for obtaining parallel rays of light, and for transmitting parallel radio waves. » conic sections [i]; geometry; hyperbola [i]

Paracas A barren peninsula on the S coast of Peru, renowned for its ornate prehistoric pottery and colourful embroidered textiles. Most of the artefacts have been recovered from mummified burials and dated c.600–100 BC.

Paracelsus, byname of **Philippus Aureolus Theophrastus Bombasttus von Hohenheim** (1493–1541) Swiss alchemist and physician, born at Einsiedeln. He travelled widely in Europe and the Middle East, learning a great deal about alchemy, and acquiring great fame as a medical practitioner (1526). He became town physician and lecturer at Basle in 1527, but he burned the works of Galen, and admitted barber surgeons to his lectures, which caused his departure in 1538. He then travelled through Europe until settling at Salzburg in 1541, where he died. In spite of his attraction to alchemy and mysticism, he introduced laudanum, sulphur, lead, and mercury into Western therapeutics. He rejected authoritarian knowledge, and encouraged research. » Galen

paracetamol [para**see**tamol] A mild pain killer commonly used for headache, menstrual pain, etc. It will also reduce body temperature during fever. Although very safe, overdose leads to irreversible liver damage. » analgesics; aspirin; liver

parachuting The act of jumping out of an aircraft and eventually landing with the aid of a parachute. As a sport, the competitor free-falls for a few thousand feet before opening the chute, normally at approximately 750 m/2 500 ft. In competition, the object is to land within a predetermined target area. Parachuting first became popular as a variety act. French aeronaut André-Jacques Garnerin (1769–1823) made the first recorded descent over Paris in October 1797, when he was released from a balloon. » skydiving

paracrine A chemical messenger (eg prostaglandins, pancreatic somatostatin, kinins) synthesized by specific cells and released into the extracellular fluid for transport to adjacent cells, where it has a regulatory effect. It is rapidly inactivated by local enzymes. It may function as a hormone, a neurohormone, an autocrine, or a neurotransmitter elsewhere in the body. By convention, neurotransmitters themselves are not classified as paracrines. » hormones; neurohormone

Paradise A term, probably of Persian origin, referring to a walled garden or park; in the Bible, applied variously to the Garden of Eden (*Gen* 2–3, in the Septuagint only) and to forests, but only later to a blessed, future heavenly state and place of bliss (2 *Cor* 12.4; *Rev* 2.7). In ancient and modern thought, paradise has been visualized not only as gardens, but also as mountains and islands. » Bible; Eden, Garden of; heaven

paradox An absurd result implied by plausible but quite often unstated principles. 'This sentence is false' seems to be false if and only if it is true. The study of paradoxes has led to insights in logic and mathematics. The form is also often used in literary expression (eg 'Freedom is slavery', George Orwell). » figurative language; logic; rhetoric

paraffin » **kerosene**

paraffin wax Solid hydrocarbon wax, originally produced from shale c.1850, but now made from petroleum. It is used for

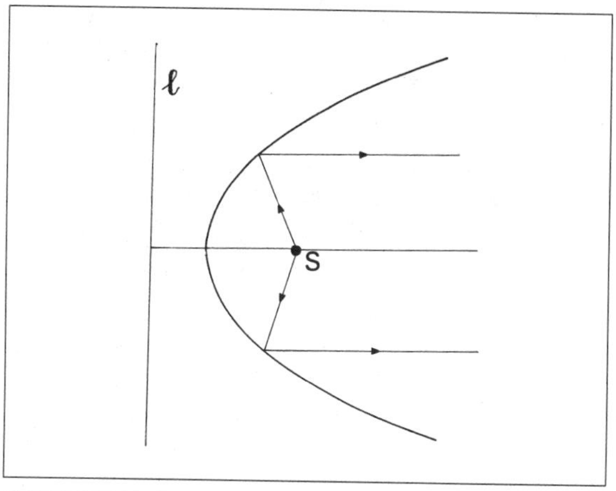

Parabola, focus S, directrix l. Reflexive property

candles (for which it was socially very useful in the later 19th-c), waterproofing, textile conditioning, polishes, and ointments. It owes some of its properties to its micro-crystalline structure. » petroleum; wax

Paraguay, official name **Republic of Paraguay**, Span **República del Paraguay** [**pa**ragwiy] pop (1990e) 4 279 000; area 406 750 sq km/157 000 sq ml. Landlocked country in C South America; divided into two regions, 19 departments, and the national capital; bordered N by Bolivia and Brazil, S by Argentina; capital, Asunción; 10 river ports; timezone GMT −3; population mainly mixed Spanish–Guaraní (95%); official language, Spanish, but Guaraní also spoken; chief religion, Roman Catholicism (97%); unit of currency, the guaraní of 100 centimos; divided into two regions by the R Paraguay; mostly at altitudes below 450 m/1 450 ft; bordered S and E by R Paraná; Gran Chaco in the W, mostly cattle country or scrub forest; more fertile land in the E; Paraná Plateau at 300–600 m/1 000–2 000 ft, mainly wet, treeless savannah; tropical NW, with hot summers and warm winters; annual rainfall 750 mm/30 in (S), 1 250 mm/50 in (extreme N); temperate SE, with rainfall up to 1 750 mm/70 in; minimum winter temperature at Asunción, 12°C, maximum summer temperature, 35°C; originally inhabited by Guaraní Indians; arrival of the Spanish, 1537; arrival of Jesuit missionaries, 1609; indepen-

dence from Spain, 1811; War of the Triple Alliance against Brazil, Argentina, and Uruguay, 1864–70, when Paraguay lost over half of its population; regained disputed territory in 1935 after the 3-year Chaco War with Bolivia; civil war, 1947; General Alfredo Stroessner seized power in 1954, and was appointed President, being forced to stand down following a coup in 1989; agriculture employs 40% of the labour force; oilseed, cotton, wheat, manioc, sweet potato, tobacco, corn, rice, sugar cane; livestock rearing; meat packing, pulp, timber, textiles, fertilizers, cement, kaolin, glass. » Asunción; Chaco War; Gran Chaco; Guaraní; Paraguay, River; Stroessner; Triple Alliance, War of the; RR26 national holidays; RR58 political leaders

Paraguay, River (Span **Río**), Port **Rio Paraguai** [para**gwiy**] River in C South America; a chief tributary of the R Paraná; rises in Brazil (Mato Grosso), flows S, forming part of Brazil–Bolivia, Brazil–Paraguay, and Paraguay–Argentina borders, flowing into the Paraná above Corrientes, Argentina; length 2 300 km/1 450 ml; used widely by local river traffic. » Paraná, River; South America

Paraguayan War » **Triple Alliance, War of the**

parakeet The name used for some small parrots with long pointed tails (c.37 species). » parrot; swift

paraldehyde [par**al**duhhiyd] $(C_2H_4O)_3$. A large molecule (a trimer) of acetaldehyde, a liquid boiling at 128°C. Acetaldehyde is conveniently stored in this form, from which it is regenerated by heating with acid. » acetaldehyde; polymerization

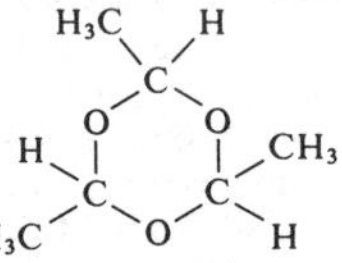

Paralipomenon [paraliy**pom**enuhn] » **Chronicles, Books of**

parallax An apparent displacement in the position of any celestial object caused by a change in the position of the observer; specifically, a change because of the motion of the Earth through space. It is often loosely used by astronomers to be synonymous with distance, because it is inversely proportional to distance.

parallel computing » **parallel processing**

parallel distributed processing » **connectionism**

parallel processing The use of two or more processors simultaneously to carry out a single computing task, each processor being assigned a particular part of the task at any given time. This differs from conventional single-processor computing, where the whole task is carried out sequentially by the one processor. Parallel processing does have inherent programming and supervisory difficulties, but promises greatly increased computing speeds at least for certain types of task. The Transputer has been designed to take advantage of parallel processing. » Transputer

paralysis Loss of movement resulting from interference with the nerve supply to a muscle or muscles. It may arise from destruction of the motor nerve cells in the brain (eg *hemiplegia*, in which muscles on one side of the body are affected), or in the spinal cord (eg infantile paralysis). *Paraplegia* refers to the loss of muscle power affecting both lower limbs, and is usually caused by injury to the spinal cord. In *quadriplegia* all four limbs are affected. » brain [i]; muscle [i]; nervous system

paramagnetic resonance Magnetic resonance exhibited by atoms of paramagnetic substances, having magnetic moments due to unpaired electrons; also called **electron paramagnetic resonance** or **electron spin resonance**. It can be used to study the nature of chemical bonds in a sample, and is an important analytical technique in chemistry, biology, and medicine. » magnetic moment/resonance; paramagnetism

paramagnetism A magnetic effect present in many materials (eg aluminium and oxygen at room temperature) in which individual atoms' magnetic moments align in support of an applied magnetic field, the material being attracted towards the source of the applied field. It is characterized by positive magnetic susceptibility, and exploited in magnetic cooling. » Curie's law; magnetic cooling; magnetic moment; magnetism; paramagnetic resonance; permeability

Paramaribo [parama**ree**boh] 5°54N 55°14W, pop (1980) 192 810. Federal capital of Suriname; chief port and only large town of Suriname, on the R Suriname; founded by the French, 1540; capital of British Suriname, 1650; under Dutch rule, 1816; airport; university (1968); trade in bauxite, coffee, timber, fruit; People's Palace (former Governor's Mansion), Fort Zeelandia, cathedral (19th-c). » Suriname [i]

Paramecium [para**mee**siuhm] A single-celled micro-organism, ovoid in shape, length up to 0.33 mm/0.013 in; cells contain two types of nucleus (macronucleus and micronucleus); feeds by ingestion of bacteria; hair-like processes (cilia) arranged uniformly over cell surface; common in aquatic habitats. (Phylum: *Ciliophora*.) » cell; nucleus (biology)

parana pine » **araucaria**

Paraná, River (Span **Río**), in Brazil **Alto Parana** Major river of S America; forms with its tributaries (notably the Paraguay) and the R Uruguay, S America's second largest drainage system; rises in SEC Brazil and flows generally S along Paraguay's E and S border into Argentina, where it joins the Uruguay after 3 300 km/2 000 ml to form the R Plate estuary on the Atlantic; dammed at various points for hydroelectricity, with a major scheme at Itaipu in Brazil. » Itaipu Dam; Paraguay, River; Plate, River

paranoia An excessive tendency to suspiciousness and sensitivity to being rebuffed. Paranoid individuals may presume by merely seeing a police car that there is an elaborate plot to put them in jail, and that the plot has been directed by an unknown authority. This definition is of a symptom, but in addition the term has been used to describe a syndrome, and in this sense it was brought into common usage by the German physician Karl Ludwig Kahlbaum (1828–99) in 1863. » mental disorders

paranormal Beyond the bounds of what can be explained in terms of currently-held scientific knowledge. Thus, to describe an event as paranormal requires that all other possible explanations for the event, based on known principles, be ruled out. However, the use of the term does not imply that the eventual explanation, as science discovers more about allegedly paranormal events, will be non-physical; it allows for the possibility that new discoveries in physics may account for events which are now classified as paranormal. This is in contrast with the term *supernatural*, which implies a non-physical explanation for events that lie forever beyond natural laws. » parapsychology

paraplegia » **paralysis**

parapsychology The scientific study of certain aspects of the paranormal, primarily those in which an organism appears (i) to receive information from its environment through some presently not understood means (also known as *extrasensory perception*, or ESP), or (ii) to exert an influence on its environment through some presently not understood means (also known as *psychokinesis*, or PK), in the laboratory or in everyday life. Although the terms *parapsychology* and *psychical research* are roughly equivalent, some topics considered to be the subject matter of psychical research in its early days, such as hypnosis, had become part of 'orthodox' psychology and medicine by the time the term *parapsychology* came into use, and so the latter incorporates only those topics which seem to have a paranormal component according to today's knowledge.

In addition, the term has tended to be applied to studies of the paranormal which have used scientific methodology, no doubt because it was popularized in the English-speaking world by J B Rhine, who in the 1930s gained prominence with his application of laboratory methods. Publication of the positive results of Rhine's research had considerable impact on scientists, although interest declined when others found it difficult to repeat his results themselves. In the present day, the reality of paranormal phenomena remains controversial, but increasingly sophisticated approaches to experimentation offer hopes of increasing the level of repeatability between different laboratories. Meanwhile, the scientific approach of parapsychology appears to be gaining respectability, with the acceptance of the Parapsychological Association as an affiliate by the American Association for the Advancement of Science in 1969, and the establishment of the Koestler Chair of Parapsychology at the University of Edinburgh in 1985. » extrasensory perception; paranormal; psi; psychokinesis; Rhine, J B

parasitic plant A plant which obtains some or all of its food and/or shelter from another plant. The arrangement may be temporary or permanent. **Obligate parasites** can survive only by this means; **facultative parasites** are more flexible, and under certain conditions are able to survive without the host, for example by changing to a saprophytic lifestyle. Many fungi and some plants have adopted this lifestyle. Among flowering plants total parasites include broomrapes, rafflesias, and dodders. They are brown or reddish, completely lacking chlorophyll, have very reduced leaves and roots, and hence are unable to manufacture any food of their own. Rafflesias are unusual within flowering plants in being **endoparasites**, living entirely within the host's tissues, except for the flowers, which break out through the body of the host in order to be pollinated and to shed their seeds. Broomrapes and dodders are examples of **ectoparasites**, living outside the host, but attached to it by modified feeding organs (*haustoria*) which penetrate the host vascular system to draw off nutrients.

A much larger group are the semi-parasitic plants, which possess green leaves and are able to manufacture at least some nutrients, but have root systems capable of forming haustorial attachments, usually to other root systems, and thus supplement their food supply from a host. They are termed **hemiparasites**, and include mistletoe and eyebrights. Not all plants that augment their food supply from outside sources are parasites. Some, such as orchids and members of the pea family, live together in a relationship of symbiosis; others are saprophytes; and a few are predatory. » broomrape; carnivorous plant; dodder; eyebright; mistletoe; mycorrhiza; rafflesia; root nodule; saprophyte; symbiosis

parasitology The study of organisms which live on and at the expense of another living creature (the *host*) and of their interactions. Strictly these organisms include both harmless and disease-producing viruses and bacteria, but common usage restricts the study to (1) *protozoa* such as *Amoeba*, *Giardia*, *Trichomonas*, *Trypanosoma*, *Leishmania*, and *Toxoplasma*, (2) worms such as round and flat worms, tapeworms, *Trichinella*, *Schistosoma*, *Echinococcus*, and others, and (3) *arthropods* which cause harm to humans by producing venom, sucking blood, and carrying disease (eg mosquitoes, sandflies, and lice), or merely by inhabiting the skin and causing itching (eg scabies). » arthropods; protozoa; worm

parasympathetic nervous system » **autonomic nervous system**

parathormone » **parathyroid hormone**

parathyroid glands In humans, a set of glands, usually four in number, closely associated with the back of the thyroid gland within its capsule. Each gland consists of *chief* cells, which produce parathyroid hormone, and *oxyphil* cells, whose function is unknown. The removal of all parathyroid glands in mammals causes death within a few days. » parathyroid hormone; thyroid gland

parathyroid hormone A chemical substance (a polypeptide) synthesized and secreted by the chief cells of the parathyroid glands, released in response to lowered blood calcium levels; also known as **parathormone**. It has the opposite effect to calcitonin: it raises extracellular calcium levels by stimulating the removal of calcium from bone and from the renal tubule into the blood, and it promotes the conversion of vitamin D to an active form, which stimulates intestinal calcium absorption. » calcitonin; parathyroid glands; peptide

paratyphoid fever A generalized infection by a species of *Salmonella*, related to but less serious than that responsible for typhoid fever. It is usually acquired through contaminated food or drink. » typhoid fever

Parcae [**pah**see, **pah**kiy] The fates. The name originally referred to a Roman birth-goddess. She was later trebled, and identified with the Moerae, the goddesses who allot the destiny of human beings. » Moerae

parchment A prepared but untanned animal skin, usually of a sheep, goat, or calf, developed by the Greeks c.2nd-c BC as a medium of writing. In mediaeval Europe, before the introduction of paper, parchment was used for manuscripts and later for printed books. Nowadays, its use is reserved for commemorative and other important documents. A high quality, fine-grained parchment is known as *vellum*. » paper [i]

parchment-bark » **pittosporum**

parchment worm A filter-feeding bristleworm that inhabits a leathery or parchment-like tube embedded in soft sediment; fragile body divided into three distinct regions; c.45 species, all marine. (Class: *Polychaeta*. Order: *Chaetopterida*.) » bristleworm; worm

pardalote » **diamondbird**

parenteral nutrition » **intravenous feeding**

Pareto, Vilfredo (1848–1923) Italian economist and sociologist, born in Paris. Educated at Turin, he became professor of political economy at Lausanne, writing textbooks on the subject, in which he demonstrated a mathematical approach. In sociology, his *Trattato di sociologica generale* (1916, The Mind and Society), with its theory of governing elites, anticipated some of the principles of fascism. He died in Geneva. » fascism; sociology

Paricutín [pareekoo**teen**] 19°29N 102°17W. Active volcano in W Michoacán, WC Mexico; height 2 774 m/9 101 ft; 1943 eruption buried the Indian town of San Juan; church spires are all that can be seen of the former village. » Mexico [i]; volcano

Paris (mythology) In Greek mythology, a prince of Troy, the son of Priam and Hecuba; also called Alexander. Because of a prophecy, he was exposed at birth on Mt Ida, where he was loved by Oenone, a nymph. There he also chose Aphrodite as the fairest of three goddesses ('the judgment of Paris'). She offered him the most beautiful woman in the world; he abducted Helen, and so caused the Trojan War. He was wounded by Philoctetes, and in his death-agony asked Oenone for help, which she refused. » Eris; Helen; Trojan War

Paris, Matthew » **Matthew Paris**

Paris (France), Ancient **Lutetia** 48°50N 2°20E, pop (1982) 2 188 918. Capital of France and of Ville de Paris department, on R Seine; originally a Roman settlement; capital of Frankish kingdom, 6th-c; established as capital, 987; R Seine spanned here by 30 bridges, oldest the Pont Neuf (1578–1604); tourist river boats ('bateaux mouches'); bounded by Bois de Boulogne (W), Bois de Vincennes (E); divided into 20 arrondissements; 'Left Bank' (formerly associated with the aristocracy) and 'Right Bank' (formerly associated with the middle class); headquarters of many international organizations (notably UNESCO); airports at Orly (S), Charles de Gaulle (Roissy) and Le Bourget (NE); main railway stations, Gare du Nord, Gare de l'Est, Gare d'Austerlitz, Gare de Lyon, Gare St-Lazare, Gare Montparnasse; métro; Sorbonne University (12th-c); one of the world's main tourist centres, with famous hotels, nightclubs, theatres, restaurants, and shops; world centre of high fashion and production of luxury goods; wide range of heavy and light industry in suburbs; *Right Bank*: Arc de Triomphe, Champs Elysées, Place de la Concorde, Centre Pompidou (1977), Louvre, Church of La Madeleine, Montmartre, Basilica of Sacré Cœur, L'Opéra (1861–75), Tuileries gardens; *Left Bank*: Eiffel Tower (1889), Hôtel des Invalides, Jardins des Plantes (1626), Luxembourg Palace, Notre-Dame Cathedral (1163), Montparnasse and Latin Quarter, associated with artists and writers; horse racing at Longchamp, Vincennes, Auteuil; international air show at Le Bourget (every second June), Festival du Quartiers du Marais (Jun–Jul), international film festival (Oct). » Arc de Triomphe; Bibliothèque Nationale; Bois de Boulogne; Centre Beaubourg; Eiffel Tower; Elysée, Palais de l'; Folies-Bergère; France [i]; Gobelins; Halles, Les; Haussmann; Invalides, Hôtel des; Left Bank; Louvre; Luxembourg, Palais du; Notre Dame; Paris, University of; Quai d'Orsay; Tuileries; Versailles; *see map p 908*

Paris, School of In art history, a term with two applications: in the 13th-c, when Paris was the European centre for illuminated manuscripts; and in the 20th-c, when Paris was the focus of most of the modern art movements (c.1900–50). » French art; modern art; school (art)

PARIS

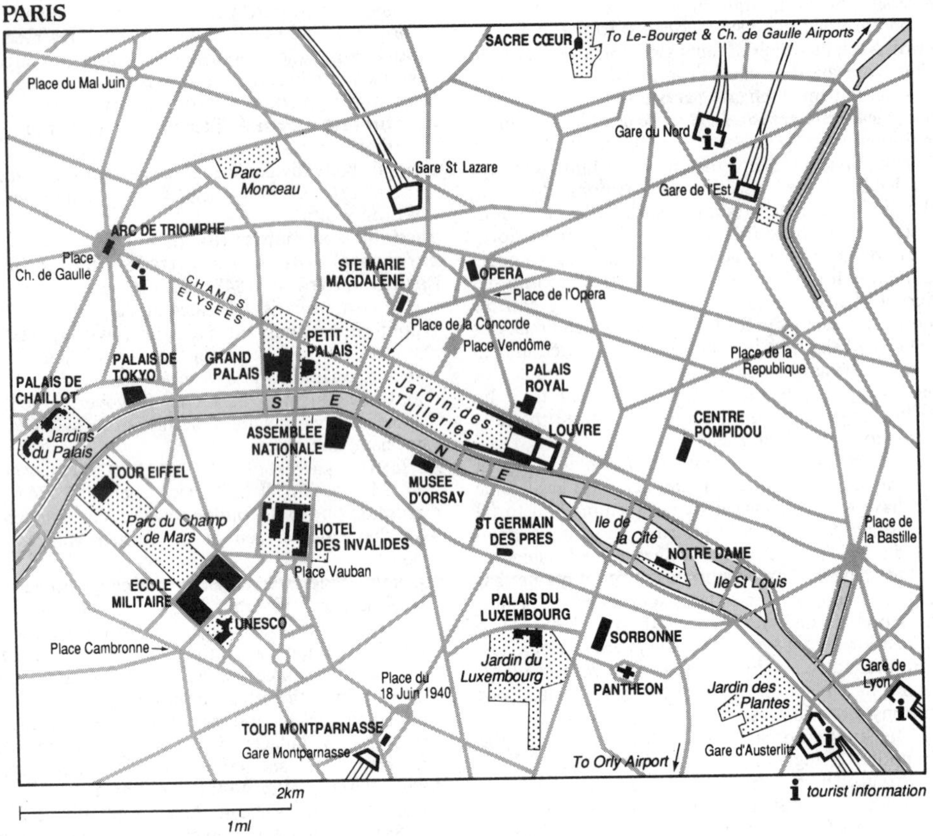

Paris, Treaties of 1 (1761–3) The peace settlement ending the Seven Years' War (1756–63), signed by Britain, France, and Spain. Spain surrendered Florida to the British, but received the Louisiana Territory and New Orleans from France, and Havana and Manila from Britain. In exchange for minor concessions, France ceded Canada, America E of the Mississippi, Cape Breton and the St Lawrence islands, Dominica, Tobago, the Grenadines, and Senegal to Britain. In the short term, Britain was isolated by the French determination for revenge, but the final consequence was British colonial supremacy. » Seven Years' War 2 (1814–15) Successive peace settlements involving France and the victorious coalition of Britain, Austria, Prussia, Russia, Sweden, and Portugal, restoring the Bourbon monarchy to France in place of the Napoleonic Empire, before and after the Hundred Days (1815). In 1815 a large indemnity and army of occupation replaced the generous terms of 1814. » Bourbons; Hundred Days; Napoleonic Wars

Paris, Treaty of (1951) » **European Coal and Steel Community**

Paris, University of A university founded c.1170 on the left bank of the R Seine in Paris. Thomas Aquinas, Bonaventure, and Alexander of Hales were among those who taught there during the 13th-c, and in 1253 the prestigious college of Sorbonne was founded as part of the University by Robert de Sorbon (1201–74). In the 14th-c it was pre-eminent amongst European universities. As a result of student demands for educational reform in May 1968, the University was reorganized into 13 independent faculties, known as *Universités de Paris I à XIII*. » Paris [i]; university

Paris Pacts (1954) A series of amendments and protocols to the Treaty of Brussels and the Brussels Treaty Organization. Italy and the Federal Republic of Germany became members of what became known as the Western European Union. Germany agreed not to manufacture atomic, bacteriological, or chemical weapons, thus clearing the way for its rearmament and membership of NATO. » Brussels, Treaty of; Kellogg-Briand Pact; NATO

Paris Peace Conference 1 (1919–20) A meeting of 32 'allied and associated powers' who met in Paris to draw up a peace settlement after World War 1. Five treaties were concluded – with Germany (Treaty of Versailles, 1919), Austria (Treaty of St Germain, 1919), Hungary (Treaty of Trianon, 1920), Bulgaria (Treaty of Neuilly, 1919), and Turkey (Treaties of Sèvres, 1920, and Lausanne, 1923). » Versailles, Treaty of; World War 1 2 (1946) A meeting of the five members of the Council of Foreign Ministers (UK, France, USA, Russia, China) and 16 other nations involved in the war against the Axis Powers. It drew up peace treaties with Bulgaria, Finland, Hungary, Romania, and Italy. Despite repeated divisions, agreement was finally reached and the treaties signed in the spring of 1947. » Axis Powers; World War 2

parish council The smallest unit of local elective government in the UK, dating back to the 16th-c and originally based on an area covered by one church. It is not normally elected along party political lines, but has close links with the local community. Councils of this kind have various names in different countries, such as community councils, townships, rural communes, and (in India) panchayats. » council; local government

parity (economics), abbreviation **par** An economic term used when currencies are based on a gold standard, **par value** being determined by the gold content of the unit of currency. In addition, the par value of a share or stock unit of a company is its nominal value. » purchasing power parity

parity (physics) In quantum mechanics, a quantity which monitors the behaviour of a system under change from left- to right-handed co-ordinates; symbol P. A multiplicative parity quantum number can be ascribed to quantum systems and particles, and is conserved by electromagnetic and strong nuclear forces but not by weak nuclear force. Weak radioactive decays have an overall handedness; neutrinos are described as left-handed. » CP violation; neutrino; quantum numbers; weak interaction

parity check A simple means of detecting errors in transmitted binary data. Each byte contains a **parity bit** which is set to indicate whether the byte contains an odd or even number of 1s. This bit is then checked on reception to ensure that it is consistent. This simple system will not detect all errors, eg it will detect if one bit is in error but not if two are in error. Much more complicated and reliable systems are now in general use. » bit; byte

Park, Mungo (1771–1806) British explorer of Africa, born at Fowlshiels, Selkirk, Scotland. He became a surgeon at Edinburgh, and in 1792 served on an expedition to Sumatra. In 1795–6 he made a journey along the Niger R, as recounted in *Travels in the Interior of Africa* (1799). He settled as a surgeon in Peebles, then in 1805 undertook another journey to the Niger. They reached Bussa, where he was drowned following an attack by natives.

Parker, Charlie, properly **Charles (Christopher), Jr**, byname **Bird** or **Yardbird** (1920–55) US jazz saxophonist, born in Kansas City, Kansas, and raised in Kansas City, Missouri. He worked with Jay McShann's orchestra, and his first recordings in 1941 already reveal technical grace on the alto saxophone and melodic inventiveness. In New York, he joined Dizzy Gillespie, Thelonious Monk, and other musicians in expanding the harmonic basis for jazz. The new music, called 'bebop', developed an adventuresome young audience at the end of World War 2. He began using heroin as a teenager, and died at 34, in New York City. In 1988 the film *Bird*, directed by Clint Eastwood, presented an entertaining but sanitized version of his life. » bebop; jazz; saxophone

Parker, Dorothy, *née* **Rothschild** (1893–1967) US writer, born at West End, New Jersey. She worked as a drama critic for *Vanity Fair* and the *New Yorker*, then became a freelance writer, noted for her satirical humour, as shown in such verse collections as *Enough Rope* (1926), and such short stories as *Here Lies* (1939). She died in New York City. » American literature; satire

Parker, Matthew (1504–75) The second Protestant Archbishop of Canterbury, born at Norwich, Norfolk. He was chaplain to Anne Boleyn (1535), and held several church posts, becoming Dean of Lincoln. Deprived of his preferments by Queen Mary, he was made Archbishop of Canterbury by Elizabeth I (1559). He strove to bring about more general conformity, adopting a middle road between Catholic and Puritan extremes, and was in charge of the formulation of the Thirty-nine Articles (1562). He died in London. » Church of England; Elizabeth I; Protestantism; Thirty-nine Articles

Parkes, Sir Henry (1815–96) Australian statesman, born at Stoneleigh, Warwickshire. He emigrated to New South Wales in 1839, and became a well-known journalist in Sydney. A member of the colonial parliament in 1854, from 1872 was five times Premier of New South Wales. In 1891 he helped draft a constitution for a federated Australia. Knighted in 1877, he died in Sydney. » Australia [i]; federalism

Parkinson, C(yril) Northcote (1909–) British writer, historian, and political scientist, born at Barnard Castle, Durham. Educated at Cambridge and London, he taught in England and (1950–8) Malaya, and was also visiting professor at Harvard and Illinois. He has written many works on historical, political, and economic subjects, but achieved wider renown by his serio-comic tilt at bureaucratic malpractices in *Parkinson's Law: the Pursuit of Progress* (1957). 'Parkinson's Law' – that work expands to fill the time available for its completion, and subordinates multiply at a fixed rate, regardless of the amount of work produced – has passed into the language.

Parkinson's disease A disorder of the central nervous system in which the neurones of tbe basal ganglia are specifically affected; also known as **paralysis agitans**, and named after British physician James Parkinson (1755–1824). These neurones secrete dopamine as their neurotransmitter, and its lack affects the ability to control muscle movement and tone. There is no paralysis, but muscles become more rigid, facial expression is lost, and a 'pill-rolling' tremor of the hands develops. The intellect is preserved. Relief is obtained by providing dopamine as a drug, or by the introduction of dopamine-secreting brain tissue obtained from aborted foetuses. » central nervous system; dopamine

Parlement [**pah**luhmẽ] The French court of law in *ancien régime* France, originally a single institution, the *Parlement* of Paris, which developed from the mediaeval King's Court or *curia regis*, and subsequently assumed both political and judicial functions. Between the 14th-c and 17th-c a network of provincial *parlements* emerged, but all were abolished in 1790. » *ancien régime*; law

parliament The general term in most English-speaking countries for the national legislative body, normally elected by popular vote. Its role is to pass legislation and keep a check on the activities of the government or executive. In a parliamentary governmental system it is also responsible for choosing and sustaining a government, though the individual members of the government will be chosen by the prime minister. In some presidential systems (eg France) parliament can also be integral to supporting the government, but not the president, who is elected separately and who can be a member of a party which does not hold a parliamentary majority. In other systems, the executive may exist independently of the parliament, as is the case with the US president. In the UK, parliament is constituted by the House of Lords and the elected House of Commons. Proposed laws must go through a defined procedure in both Houses and receive the royal assent, before becoming statutes. » bicameral system; Bundestag; Commons/Lords, House of; Congress; legislature; unicameral system

Parliamentary Commissioner for Administration The British ombudsman for central administration, established in 1967, who examines complaints of maladministration. The Commissioner is a servant of parliament and works closely with a House of Commons select committee. Peers have no access to him; all complaints have to be channelled through MPs. » ombudsman; select committee

Parma [**pah**ma] 44°48N 10°19E, pop (1981) 179 019. Capital city of Parma province, Emilia-Romagna, N Italy; on R Parma, 126 km/78 ml SE of Milan; major cultural centre in Middle Ages; railway; university (1502); agricultural trade, oil refining, foodstuffs, pasta, cheese (Parmesan), perfume; baptistery (12th–13th-c), cathedral (12th-c), Palazzo della Pilotta (begun 1583), Church of the Madonna della Steccata (1521–39), modelled on St Peter's in Rome. » Italy [i]

Parmenides [pah**men**ideez] (c.515–c.445 BC) The most influential of the Presocratic philosophers, a native of the Greek settlement of Elea in S Italy, and founder of the Eleatic school. He is the first philosopher to insist on a distinction between the world of appearances and reality. » Eleatics; Presocratics

Parmigiano [pahmi**jah**noh] or **Parmigianin**, byname of **Girolamo Francesco Maria Mazzola** (1503–40) Italian painter of the Lombard School, born at Parma. He began to paint at Parma, moving to Rome in 1523, but was forced to flee to Bologna when the city was sacked in 1527. At Bologna he painted his famous Madonna altarpiece for the nuns of St Margaret before returning to Parma in 1531. He died at Casalmaggiore. » altarpiece; Italian art; Mannerism

Parnassians A group of poets in 19th-c France, associated with the journal *Le Parnasse Contemporain* (1866–76); among them Charles Leconte de Lisle (1818–94), José Heredia (1842–1905), and Sully-Prudhomme (1839–1907). In reaction against Romanticism, and in the scientific spirit of the age, they favoured a more austere and objective poetry. » French literature; Leconte de Lisle; poetry; Romanticism (literature); Sully-Prudhomme

Parnell, Charles Stewart (1846–91) Irish politician, born at Avondale, Co Wicklow. He studied at Cambridge, and in 1875 became an MP, supporting Home Rule, and gained great popularity in Ireland by his audacity in the use of obstructive parliamentary tactics. In 1878 he was elected President of the Irish National Land League, and in 1886 allied with the Liberals in support of Gladstone's Home Rule Bill. He remained an influential figure until 1890, when he was cited as co-respondent in a divorce case, and was forced to retire as leader of the Irish nationalists. He died at Brighton, Sussex. » Gladstone; Liberal Party (UK); nationalism; Phoenix Park murders

parody (Gr 'burlesque poem/song') An imitation of a literary work, or form, usually for comic and satirical purposes. Good parody requires both skill and sympathy with the 'target' – some of the best (Cervantes, Shakespeare, Henry James) is self-parody. Much Modernist art has a parodic element; arguably inevitable at a late, self-conscious stage of culture. » comedy; literature; Modernism; satire

parole A conditional release given to a prisoner who still has part of a sentence left to serve. In the UK, for example, prisoners may be considered for parole after one third of the sentence (or six months, if longer) has been completed. A local review committee reports to the Parole Board which then advises the Home Secretary. In certain cases, the minister may act on the advice of the local committee alone. Release is conditional, and those paroled are supervised by a probation officer. » sentence

Paros [**pay**ros] area 195 sq km/75 sq ml; pop (1981) 7 881. Third largest island of the Cyclades, Greece, in the S Aegean Sea, W of Naxos; chief town, Parikia; beaches at Drios, Alikes, Pisso Livadi; famous for its marble and churches. » Cyclades; Greece [i]

parousia [paroo**see**a] (Gr 'coming', 'arrival', 'presence') In Christian thought, normally the future return or 'second coming' of Christ, which will be marked by a heavenly appearance, God's judgment of all humanity, and the resurrection of the dead. Belief in the imminence of Christ's return is particularly prominent in Paul's letters. Protracted delay of the event eventually led to some reformulation of the belief, although some Christian movements continue to await the literal fulfilment of this predicted event and the signs associated with it. » Christianity; eschatology; Jesus Christ; Paul, St

parquetry » **marquetry**

Parr, Catherine (1512–48) Sixth wife of Henry VIII, the daughter of Sir Thomas Parr of Kendal. She married first Edward Borough, then Lord Latimer, before becoming Queen of England (1543). A learned, tolerant, and tactful woman, she persuaded Henry to restore the succession to his daughters, and showed her stepchildren much kindness. Very soon after Henry's death (1547) she married a former suitor, Lord Thomas Seymour of Sudeley, and died in childbirth the following year at Sudeley Castle, near Cheltenham. » Henry VIII

Parra, Violeta [**pa**ra] (1917–67) Internationally celebrated Chilean folklorist, songwriter, and singer, born at San Carlos, Chile. She had a varied career, including a period in Paris (1961–5), and her work inspired the New Chilean Song movement of the later 1960s. She committed suicide in Santiago. » folk music

parrot A colourful bird, native to warm regions world-wide; bill large, hooked; nostrils on fleshy band (*cere*); inhabits forests or open country; eats mainly fruit and seeds (some insects); manipulates food with foot; good at mimicking human voice. (Family: *Psittacidae*, c.330 species.) » budgerigar; cockatiel; cockatoo; kakapo; kea; lory; lovebird [i]; macaw; parakeet; rosella

parrot disease » **psittacosis**

parrot's bill An evergreen shrub, growing to 3.5 m/11 ft or more, native to New Zealand; also called **glory pea** and **lobster claw**, referring to the curiously-shaped, long curving lower petals of the flowers; leaves pinnate; flowers to 6.5 cm/2½ in, long, scarlet, in large pendulous clusters. (*Clianthus puniceus*. Family: *Leguminosae*.) » evergreen plants; pinnate; shrub

parrotfish Colourful fish belonging to the family *Scaridae* (4 genera), in which jaw teeth are fused into a parrot-like beak used for scraping algal and coral growth from reefs; flat grinding teeth; body compressed, length 20–100 cm/8–40 in. The name is also used for the Indo-Pacific family *Oplegnathidae*.

Parry, Sir (Charles) Hubert (Hastings) (1848–1918) British composer, born at Bournemouth, Hampshire. Educated at Eton and Oxford, he became professor in the Royal College of Music (1883), and professor of music at Oxford (1900). He wrote three oratorios, an opera, five symphonies, and many other works, but is best known for his unison chorus 'Jerusalem' (1916), sung as an unofficial anthem at the end of each season of Promenade Concerts in London. He died at Rustington, Sussex.

Parry, Joseph (1841–1903) British musician, born at Merthyr Tydfil, Glamorgan, Wales. He studied at the Royal Academy of Music, London, and became professor at University College, Cardiff. He composed oratorios, operas, and songs, and became one of the leading hymn-writers in the Welsh tradition, his best-known hymn tune being *Aberystwyth*. He died at Penarth, Glamorgan.

parsec (**pc**) A unit of length, used for distances beyond the Solar System. The term is a contraction of **parallax second**, and is the distance at which the astronomical unit (AU) subtends one second of arc; it equals 206 265 AU, 3.086×10^{13} km, 3.26 light years. (The light year is never used in professional astronomy.) The larger units **kiloparsec** (kpc) and **megaparsec** (Mpc) for 1 000 and 1 000 000 pc respectively are also widely used in galactic and extragalactic contexts. » astronomical unit; units (scientific)

Parseeism [**pah**seeizm] The religion of the descendants of the ancient Zoroastrians, who fled Persia after its conquest and settled in India in the 8th-c AD. They live mainly in the region round Bombay, and preach a rule of life conforming to the purity of Ahura Mazda. » Ahura Mazda; Zoroastrianism

Parsifal » **Perceval, Sir**

parsing The analysing and labelling of the grammatical components of a sentence, according to their function within some grammatical framework, such as 'subject', 'verb', and 'object'. Thus, in one widely used system, a sentence such as *The cat sat on the dog* would be parsed as Subject + Predicate, with the Predicate parsed into Verb + Adverb Phrase, viz. *The cat + sat + on the dog*. Further divisions would identify the definite articles and preposition. Exercises of this kind were universally practised in schools during the 19th-c and in the first half of the 20th-c, but fell into disfavour during the 1950s because of their mechanical, uninspiring techniques. During the 1980s a move to re-introduce some form of parsing, as an antidote to the perceived widespread ignorance of grammar, received increasing support. » constituent analysis [i]; grammar

parsley A biennial or perennial, growing to 75 cm/30 in; leaves triangular, shining, divided into wedge-shaped segments, lobed and also often curly in cultivated varieties; flowers yellowish, in long-stemmed, flat-topped umbels up to 5 cm/2 in across, petals notched; fruit ovoid. Its origin is uncertain, but it is widely cultivated as a flavouring. (*Petroselinum crispum*. Family: *Umbelliferae*.) » biennial; cow parsley; perennial; umbel

parsnip A biennial growing to 1.5 m/5 ft, native to Europe and W Asia, and introduced in N and S America and Australasia; leaves divided into oblong-oval toothed segments up to 10 cm/4 in long; flowers yellow, without sepals, in umbels 3–10 cm/1¼–4 in across; fruit ellipsoid, broadly winged. It is grown commercially for the sweet, fleshy tap-roots, which are eaten as a vegetable and used as fodder for livestock. (*Pastinaca sativa*. Family: *Umbelliferae*.) » biennial; sepal; umbel

parson bird » **tui**

Parsons, Talcott (1902–79) US sociologist, born at Colorado Springs, Colorado. Educated at Amherst College, the London School of Economics, and Heidelberg, he became one of the most prominent US sociologists, based throughout his career at Harvard. He developed a functionalist analysis of social systems through his principal publications, *The Structure of Social Action* (1939) and *The Social System* (1951). He died at Cambridge, Massachusetts. » functionalism; sociology

parthenocarpy » **fruit**

parthenogenesis [pahthuhnoh**jen**uhsis] The development of an individual from an egg without fertilization by a male gamete (*sperm*). Eggs that develop parthenogenetically are usually diploid (possessing two chromosome sets) and genetically identical with the mother. Many organisms (eg water fleas) pass through several parthenogenetic generations consisting only of females, but will produce males and reproduce sexually at the onset of adverse environmental conditions. » fertilization; gamete; genetics [i]; water flea

Parthenon The principal building of the Athenian Acropolis, a Doric temple of Pentelic marble dedicated to Athena Parthenos (the Maiden); a world heritage site. It was built 447–433 BC to the plans of Ictinus and Callicrates under the supervision of Phidias, the sculptor responsible for its 9 m/30 ft high gold and ivory cult statue. Converted subsequently into a church, then a mosque, it was reduced by explosion to a shell in 1687 whilst housing a powder magazine during the Turkish-Venetian war. » Acropolis; Athena; Doric order; Elgin marbles; Erechtheum; Phidias

Parthians The inheritors of the E territories of the Seleucids, from the 3rd-c BC ruling an empire that stretched from the Euphrates to the Indus. Rome's main rivals for power in the east, they resisted conquest by her in the 50s BC, but failed in their turn to take over her E provinces. In the end, both had to settle for uneasy co-existence. » Hatra

participant observation A research technique in social science in which the researcher observes social action directly by becoming a member of the group under observation. Such membership may be overt (ie the observer tells the group that he/she is a researcher) or covert (ie the observer adopts a role in the group to disguise this fact). » mass observation; role; social science

particle accelerators Machines for accelerating charged sub-atomic particles, usually electrons or protons, to high velocity. The basic configurations are straight (linear accelerators) or circular (synchrotrons). In the latter, magnetic fields control the beam path. Both use radio-frequency electric fields to provide acceleration. The beams of particles collide either with stationary targets (eg liquid hydrogen) or another on-coming particle beam (colliding beam machines). » cyclotron; linear accelerator; Organisation Européene pour la Recherche Nucléaire; klystron; particle detectors; particle physics; synchrotron [i]; van de Graaff generator

particle beam weapons The use of high-energy sub-atomic particles, generated in nuclear accelerators and turned into a directable beam, as a practical weapon. One of the goals of late 20th-c military research is to prove the technology of this approach, which would be used, for example, to shoot down missiles in space. » directed energy weapons

particle detectors Devices for detecting and identifying sub-atomic particles in particle physics experiments. They are designed to measure total energy, charge to mass ratio, velocity, position, and time. Since no single instrument can perform all these tasks, detectors often comprise several distinct units, each performing a different task. » bubble chamber; cloud chamber; Čerenkov radiation; particle accelerators; particle physics; photomultiplier; proportional counter; scintillation counter

particle physics The study of the fundamental components of matter and the forces between them; also called **high energy physics** or **elementary particle physics**. Most particle physics experiments involve the use of large particle accelerators, necessary to force particles close enough together to produce interactions. All theories in particle physics are quantum theories, in which symmetry is of central importance.

The material world is composed of atoms. Each atom in turn comprises a central nucleus surrounded by electrons, and the nucleus is composed of protons and neutrons. These protons, neutrons, the particles from which they are made, and other related objects are the entities studied in particle physics. Sub-atomic particles thought to be indivisible into smaller particles are known as *fundamental particles*: these are the matter particles (quarks, neutrinos, electrons, muons, and taus) and the force particles (gluons, photons, W and Z bosons, and gravitons). The important forces acting between these particles are the electromagnetic, strong nuclear, and weak nuclear forces. Gravity is ignored.

By the mid-1930s, protons, neutrons, and electrons were all known; nuclear fission had been observed; and the subject of nuclear physics was established. Particle physics explores the structure of matter at one level beneath nuclear physics. The earliest particle physics experiments involved measuring tracks left by cosmic rays in photographic emulsions. In this way muons (1937) and pions (1947) were discovered. Originally the pion was thought to be the fundamental carrier of nuclear force, in line with an early theory of nuclear force proposed by Japanese physicist Hideki Yukawa in 1935. This view has now been superseded, although in low energy nuclear physics the force between protons and neutrons can be discussed in terms of mediation by pions.

During the 1950s, further cosmic ray studies and early accelerator experiments revealed other particles of various masses. Some exhibited unusual or 'strange' behaviour. Such particles were produced easily, suggesting they formed via strong interactions, but decayed slowly via weak interactions. A new quantum number called *strangeness*, conserved in strong but not in weak interactions, was invented to explain these results. Other similar quantum numbers having equally unlikely names have subsequently been introduced to account for observed particle interactions. During the 1950s and 1960s, many particles and resonances were discovered, including the antiproton (confirming that antiparticles exist) and the neutrino.

A scheme of particle classification based on symmetry, in which particles were labelled by quantum numbers such as isospin and strangeness, was introduced in 1961 by US physicist Murray Gell-Mann (1929–) and Israeli physicist Yuval Ne'emann (1925–). In 1964 Gell-Mann and US physicist George Zweig (1937–) proposed quarks as abstract entities underlying symmetry patterns. However, experiments (1968) at the Stanford Linear Accelerator Center in the USA, which involved firing electrons at protons, suggested that objects within protons have the properties of quarks. Although no quarks have ever been observed directly, it is widely assumed they are the ultimate components of protons, neutrons, and most other sub-atomic particles.

The full theory of strong interaction, in which the strong force between quarks is carried by gluons, dates from 1973, and is called **quantum chromodynamics**. Weak interactions governing radioactive decay are understood in terms of the decay of individual quarks. For a neutron decaying to a proton (plus electron and antineutrino), a single u quark in the proton decays to a d quark plus electron and antineutrino. The weak force is carried by W and Z particles, and is well described by Glashow-Weinberg-Salam theory (1968). Purely electromagnetic interactions are described by quantum electrodynamics. Current research focuses on resolving difficulties in existing theories, constructing unified theories of strong, weak, and electromagnetic forces, and incorporating gravity to give a complete theory of the physical universe. » cosmic rays; cross section; forces of nature [i]; gauge theory; Gell-Mann; Glashow-Weinberg-Salam theory; grand unified theories; nuclear physics; particle accelerators; particle detectors; quantum electrodynamics/field theory/gravity; relativistic quantum mechanics; sub-atomic particles; strong interaction; tachyon; weak interaction; Yukawa

partita In music of the Baroque period, **1** one of a set of instrumental variations (*partite*), such as Bach's *Partite diverse* on the chorale melody 'O Gott, du frommer Gott'; **2** a set of instrumental dances, such as Bach's three partitas for violin and six for keyboard. » Bach, Johann Sebastian; suite; variations

partition coefficient » distribution coefficient

partnership A form of business organization where the owners share all the profits – or take all the losses – according to some predetermined formula. Liability is normally unlimited, but sometimes a 'limited partnership' is set up. There are usually not more than twenty partners, though larger partnerships do exist, as in the case of solicitors and firms of chartered accountants.

partridge A drab, plump, short-tailed bird of the pheasant family (84 species); found from Europe to SE Asia, and in Africa; inhabits open country (sometimes tropical rainforest); eats insects when young, plant material as adult. » francolin; pheasant; tinamou

Partridge, Eric (Honeywood) (1894–1979) British lexicographer, born near Gisborne, New Zealand. Educated at Queensland and Oxford, he served in World War 1, and lectured at Manchester and London. After serving in the RAF in World War 2, he became a freelance author and lexicographer, specializing in studies of style, slang, and colloquial language, notably *Dictionary of Slang and Unconventional English* (1937) and *Usage and Abusage* (1947). He died at Moretonhampstead, Devon. » dictionary; English

Pasadena (California) [pasa**dee**na] 34°09N 118°09W, pop (1980) 118 550. Resort city in Los Angeles County, SW California, USA, in the San Gabriel foothills; founded, 1874; railway; electronics, aerospace; Pasadena Art Museum, Civic Centre; Tournament of Roses, Rose Bowl football game. » California

Pasargadae [pa**sah**gadiy] The site in S Iran chosen by Cyrus the Great in 546 BC to be the capital of the new Achaemenid empire. It was also the site of Cyrus' tomb. » Achaemenids; Cyrus II; Persian Empire

pascal SI unit of pressure; symbol Pa; named after French mathematician Blaise Pascal; defined as the pressure due to a force of 1 newton acting on an area of 1 square metre. » Pascal; pressure; units (scientific); RR70

PASCAL A high-level computer programming language, named after the French mathemetician, Blaise Pascal, which was developed from ALGOL in the late 1960s. It has become a popular language in the educational field, and is widely used with microcomputers. » microcomputer; Pascal; programming language

Pascal, Blaise [pas**kahl**] (1623–62) French mathematician, physicist, theologian, and man-of-letters, born at Clermont-Ferrand. In 1647 he invented a calculating machine, and later the barometer, the hydraulic press, and the syringe. Until 1654 he spent his time between mathematics and the social round in Paris, but a mystical experience that year led him to join his sister, who was a member of the Jansenist convent at Port-Royal, where he defended Jansenism against the Jesuits in *Lettres provinciales* (1656–7). Fragments jotted down for a case book of Christian truths were discovered after his death, in Paris, and published as the *Pensées* (1669). » Euclid

Pascua, Isla de » **Easter Island**

Pashtun or **Pathan** [pa**tahn**] A cluster of Pashto-speaking agricultural and herding people of NW Pakistan and SE Afghanistan; possibly originally from Afghanistan, with several groups migrating to Pakistan in the 13th–16th-c. Traditionally warriors, many are employed in the national armies. They are the most numerous and dominant group in Afghanistan, numbering 6.2 million; 6.7 million live in Pakistan.

Pašić, Nikola [**pa**sheetch] (c.1846–1926) Serbian statesman, born at Zaječar. Condemned to death in 1883 for his part in the plot against King Milan, he survived on the accession of King Peter to be Prime Minister of Serbia (five times, from 1891) and later of Yugoslavia (1921–4, 1924–6), which he helped to found. He died in Belgrade. » Serbia; Yugoslavia [i]

Pasiphae (astronomy) [pa**si**fayee, pa**si**fiy] The eighth natural satellite of Jupiter, discovered in 1908; distance from the planet 23 500 000 km/14 603 000 ml; diameter 50 km/30 ml. » Jupiter (astronomy); RR4

Pasiphae (mythology) [pa**si**fayee] In Greek mythology, the daughter of Helios, and wife of Minos, king of Crete. She loved a bull sent by Poseidon, and became the mother of the Minotaur. » Minotaur

Pasmore, (Edwin John) Victor (1908–) British artist, born at Chelsham. One of the founders of the Euston Road School (1937), he became an art teacher and after World War 2 began to paint in a highly abstract style, in which colour is often primarily used to suggest relief. His works include 'Rectangular Motif' (1949) and 'Inland Sea' (1950, Tate). » abstract art; English art; Euston Road School

Pasolini, Pier Paulo (1922–75) Italian film director, born in Bologna. He became a Marxist following World War 2, moved to Rome, and began to write novels. In the 1950s he also worked as a film scriptwriter and actor. He made his debut as director in 1961, and became known for such films as *Il Vangelo secondo Matteo* (1964, The Gospel According to St Matthew), *Il Decamerone* (1972, The Decameron), and *The Canterbury Tales* (1973). He was murdered at Ostia, near Rome.

Passion flower

passacaglia [pasa**kahl**ya] A musical structure in which a continuously repeated bass line or harmonic progression provides the basis for a set of uninterrupted variations. Bach's C minor Passacaglia for organ is a well-known example. » Bach, Johann Sebastian; variations

passage rites » **initiation rites**

Passchendaele, Battle of [**pash**uhndayl] (1917) The third battle of Ypres during World War 1; a British offensive which was continued despite no hope of a break-through to the Belgian ports, the original objective. It was notable for appallingly muddy conditions, minimal gains, and British casualties of at least 300 000. In the final action, Canadians captured the village of Passchendaele, 10 km/6 ml NE of Ypres. » World War 1; Ypres, Battles of

passenger pigeon An extinct long-tailed pigeon from eastern N America; formed flocks of millions of birds; inhabited forests; nested in trees; migrated; hunted to extinction in the wild by 1894. The last specimen died in Cincinnati Zoo (1 Sep 1914, at 1 pm). (*Ectopistes migratorius*.) » pigeon

passerine Any bird of the worldwide order *Passeriformes* ('perching birds'); includes the **songbirds** (suborder: *Oscines*); comprises more than half the living species of birds; four toes, one pointing backwards and opposing the others; wing has 9–10 primary feathers; tail usually with 12 main feathers. They are land birds, crossing seas only when migrating. » songbird

passion flower A large genus of climbers with twining tendrils, native to America, a few to Asia and Australia; leaves oval, crescent-shaped or deeply palmately-lobed; flowers large, showy, with five coloured sepals alternating with five petals, said to symbolize the crucifixion, with the inner corona of filaments representing the crown of thorns, and the styles the cross and nails; yellow or purple edible berry (known as **passion fruit** or **granadilla**), up to 10 cm/4 in long. (Genus: *Passiflora*, 500 species. Family: *Passifloraceae*.) » climbing plant; corona (botany); granadilla; palmate; sepal; style (botany)

passion fruit » **passion flower** [i]

Passionists A religious order, founded in Italy in 1720 by St Paul of the Cross; properly known as the **Congregation of the Barefooted Clerics of the Most Holy Cross and Passion of our Lord Jesus Christ**. With houses in Europe and the USA, their declared objective is to maintain the memory of Christ's sufferings and death. » Jesus Christ; monasticism

passive smoking Inhalation by non-smokers of tobacco smoke introduced into the atmosphere by smokers. Evidence suggests that this gives rise to a small increase (c.10%) in the probability of developing carcinoma of the lung. » cancer

Passover An annual Jewish festival, occurring in March or April (15–22 Nisan), commemorating the exodus of the Israelites from Egypt; named from God's passing over the houses of the Israelites when he killed the first-born children of the Egyptians (*Exodus* 13); also known as Pesach [**pay**sakh]. » Judaism; RR23

pasta A mixture of water, wheat flour (hard), and occasionally egg, originating in Italy. The dough is extended through dies of various shapes, and dried to provide a wide variety of types (eg canneloni, farfalle, fettucine, fusilli, lasagne, macaroni, noodles, ravioli, tagliatelle, tortellini, and vermicelli). Pastas are rich in carbohydrates, and are often served with a meat-based sauce. » carbohydrate; durum; semolina

pastel Powdered pigment mixed with a little gum or resin and shaped into sticks like crayons. The artist works directly onto the paper, which may be slightly tinted, without using a medium of any sort. Pastel painting enjoyed a considerable vogue in the 18th-c, especially in France. » medium (art); paint

Pasternak, Boris (Leonidovich) (1890–1960) Russian lyric poet, novelist, and translator of Shakespeare, born in Moscow. During the Stalin years he became the official translator into Russian of several major authors, such as Shakespeare, Verlaine, and Goethe. His major work, *Dr Zhivago*, caused a political furore, and was banned in the USSR, but was an international success after its publication in Italy in 1957. Expelled by the Soviet Writers' Union in 1958, he was compelled to refuse the Nobel Prize for Literature, and died near Moscow. » novel; poetry; Russian literature

Pasteur, Louis [pas**ter**] (1822–95) French chemist and microbiologist, born at Dôle. He studied at Besançon and Paris, and held academic posts at Strasbourg, Lille, and Paris, where in 1867 he became professor of chemistry at the Sorbonne. He established that putrefaction and fermentation was caused by micro-organisms, thus providing an impetus to microbiology. In a famous experiment in 1881, he showed that sheep and cows 'vaccinated' with the attenuated bacilli of anthrax received protection against the disease. In 1888 the Institut Pasteur was founded at Paris for the treatment of rabies, and he worked there until his death. » pasteurization; rabies

pasteurization A mild heat treatment used to kill micro-organisms in milk. The process heats the milk at 63–66°C for 30 minutes or 72°C for 15 seconds. This destroys pathogenic bacteria, and somewhat aids the shelf-life of the milk. It was discovered by the French chemist, Louis Pasteur, after whom it was named. » milk; Pasteur; UHT-milk

Paston Letters An invaluable collection of over 500 letters of a 15th-c gentry family from Norfolk, England, providing pictures of family life, estate management, local feuds, and national politics during the Wars of the Roses (1455–87). They are particularly valuable because the Pastons were of middling rank and, therefore, were more typical of landed society than the great lords dominant on the national scene. » Roses, Wars of the

pastoral (Lat 'pertaining to shepherds') A poem or other work expressing love of and longing for an idealized rural existence. Deriving from Theocritus, whose faithful lovers Daphnis and Chloe have become proverbial, the pastoral mode has been much imitated and adapted. Other forms include the pastoral romance and drama. » eclogue; poetry; Theocritus

Pastoral Letters or **Pastoral Epistles** Three New Testament writings – the First and Second Letters to Timothy and the Letter to Titus – so named since about the 18th-c because they purport to give Paul's advice to his colleagues Timothy and Titus about Church leadership. Their direct authorship by Paul, however, is now widely doubted on grounds of vocabulary, theology, and setting. » New Testament; Paul, St; Pauline Letters

pastoral staff A crook-shaped stick carried by bishops; otherwise called a **crozier**. The symbol of episcopal office, it represents the rod of correction and the crook of care. » bishop; liturgy

pastoralism A way of life characterized by keeping herds of animals, such as cattle, sheep, camels, reindeer, goats, and llamas. It is common in dry, mountainous, or severely cold climates not suitable for agriculture, although some groups combine pastoralism with agriculture. Many pastoralists are nomadic, having to move around in search of good grazing ground, but the amount of nomadism varies considerably, some living in settled areas for most of their lives. Because they travel around and can use their animals to transport goods, many pastoralists have become important long-distance traders. During the colonial period, pastoral migration and movements were severely curtailed in many parts. As agriculture expanded into areas which had previously served pastoralists (eg in Masailand, Kenya), pastoral communities found themselves confined to a diminishing area, which was inadequate, particularly in the dry season. As a result, many pastoralists have been victims of devastating famines. » nomadism

Patagonia [patag**oh**nia] area 489 541 sq km/188 963 sq ml; pop (1980) 790 803. Region of S Argentina, comprising the provinces of Chubut, Rio Negro, Santa Cruz, and the territory of Tierra del Fuego; name sometimes applied to the whole of the S part of S America, including Chilean territory; in 1520 Magellan sailed along the Patagonian coast, passing through the strait now bearing his name; a semi-arid tableland rising in terraces from the Atlantic coast to the base of the Andes; several rivers; chief towns include Rawson, Ushuaia, Comodoro Rivadavia, Rio Gallegos, and the resort town of Bariloche; sheep, oil, iron ore, coal, copper, uranium, manganese; irrigated crops; many immigrants in 19th-c. » Argentina [i]

Patan [**pa**tan], also **Lalitpur** 27°40N 85°20E, pop (1971) 48 577. City in C Nepal, 5 km/3 ml SE of Kathmandu, in the Kathmandu Valley; founded, 7th-c; built in a circular plan with Buddhist stupas on the four points of the compass; capital of the Nepali kingdom, 17th-c; captured by the Gurkhas, 1768; wool, leather; centre of the Banra sect of goldsmiths and silversmiths; known as the 'city of artists'; 16th-c Palace of the Malla Kings, Temple of Lord Krishna, Royal Bath (*Tushahity*). » Nepal [i]; stupa

patas monkey [pa**tah**] An Old World monkey native to grasslands of W and C Africa; coat red-brown; male with mane of long hairs and white moustache; can run at up to 50 kph/30 mph; also known as **red guenon**, **military monkey**, **hussar monkey**, or **nisnas monkey**. (*Erythrocebus patas*.) » Old World monkey

patch clamp analysis An electrophysiological technique which isolates a small area of the plasma membrane of a living, excitable cell (eg a muscle, nerve, or gland cell), and studies single receptors within it, with respect to their interaction with chemical transmitters, hormones, drugs, or other substances applied directly to them. » cell; neurophysiology; receptors

patchouli A shrubby aromatic perennial growing to 1 m/1¼ ft or more, native to the tropics and subtropics of SE Asia; stems square; leaves oval, toothed, in opposite pairs; flowers white, tubular, 2-lipped, in whorls. It yields an aromatic essential oil used in perfumery. (*Pogostemon cablin*. Family: *Labiatae*.) » essential oil; perennial; shrub

paten A circular metal plate, often of silver or gold, on which bread is placed at the celebration of the Eucharist. » Eucharist

Patenier, Joachim (?–c.1524) Flemish painter, born (possibly) at Bouvignes or at Dinant. He became a master in the Antwerp guild in 1515. He painted fantastic spiky mountains and rich green valleys according to a simple three-part scheme; brown foreground, green middle ground, and pale blue distance. Very few pictures are known to be definitely his work. » Flemish art; landscape painting

patent medicine A medicine for which a patent was granted, or one to which the preparer affixed his or her name to indicate sole rights of sale. Patent medicines stemmed from the 1624 Statute of Monopolies in England which granted 14 years of protected monopoly for the sale of a branded medicine. Preparers of these medicines had the right to use 'secret ingredients', until the Pharmacy and Medicines Act of 1941 required their disclosure for safety reasons. The sale of patent medicines expanded rapidly in the 18th-c, and English patent medicines were popular in the USA by mid-century. In the 19th-c, US-produced patent medicines took over the market. In 1796, Samuel Lee, Jnr became the first American to patent a medicine: 'Bilious Pills'. By 1804 there were already more than 80 patent medicines, promoted aggressively by newspaper advertising, signboards, pamphlets, and tours. » pharmacy

patent theatre A theatre with Letters Patent from the Crown granting it the privilege of presenting plays publicly in London. Two such companies, ultimately resident at Covent Garden and Drury Lane, held these exclusive rights from 1660 until 1843, though Samuel Foote was granted a Patent at the

Haymarket for the summer months from 1766. » Legitimate theatre; theatre

Pater, Walter (Horatio) [paytuh] (1839–94) British critic and essayist, born in London. He was educated at Canterbury and Oxford, where he worked as a scholar, and became known with his *Studies in the History of the Renaissance* (1873). His philosophic romance *Marius the Epicurean* (1885) appealed to a wider audience, dealing with the spread of Christianity in the days of the catacombs. He developed a highly polished prose style, and exercised considerable influence on the aesthetic movements of his time. He died at Oxford. » aesthetics; literary criticism

Pater Noster » **Lord's Prayer**

Paterson, A(ndrew) B(arton), byname **Banjo** (1864–1941) Australian journalist and poet, born at Narrambia, New South Wales. He was a World War 1 correspondent and the author of several books of light verse, including *The Animals Noah Forgot* (1933), but is best known as the author of 'Waltzing Matilda'. He died in Sydney. » Australian literature

Paterson, William (1658–1719) British financier, born at Tinwald, Dumfriesshire, Scotland. He spent some years in the West Indies, and then promoted a scheme for a colony at Darien, Central America. After making a fortune by commerce in London, he founded the Bank of England, and was one of its first directors (1694). He sailed with the expedition to Darien (1698), and after its failure returned in ill health to England (1699). In 1715 the government awarded him an indemnity for his Darien losses. » Bank of England

Paterson's curse A herb (*Echium lycopsis*) introduced into Australia c.1869, named after a landowner in Victoria thought to have been responsible for its spread. A noxious weed in agricultural areas, it is also known as 'Salvation Jane' and 'Lady Campbell Weed'.

Pathan » **Pashtun**

Pathé, Charles [patay] (1863–1957) French film pioneer, born in Paris. In 1896 he founded Société Pathé Frères with his brothers Emile, Théophile, and Jacques, first for cinema presentation, but expanding into manufacture. By 1912 it had become one of the largest film production organizations in the world, including a hand-colouring stencil process, Pathécolor. They introduced the newsreel in France in 1909, and shortly after in the USA and Britain, as well as the screen magazine *Pathé Pictorial*. Charles retired in 1929, but the company continued, and in England became Associated British Pathé Ltd in 1949. He died in Monte Carlo.

pathology The scientific study of disease in humans and other living organisms. It involves the application of a wide range of analytical techniques to body fluids, body cells, and tissues. Originally limited to gross post-mortem dissection of the body, ready access to blood and to tissue biopsies today allows the investigation of the living person. It encompasses the study of the causes of diseases, the detection of micro-organisms and of chromosome and enzyme defects, the microscopic (including ultramicroscopic) study of cells and tissues, cell culture and immunological reactions, and microchemical analyses. » biopsy; medicine

Patmore, Coventry (Kersey Dighton) (1823–96) British poet, born at Woodford, Essex. He was a library assistant at the British Museum, and associated with the Pre-Raphaelite Brotherhood. His major work, *The Angel in the House* (1854–62), describing the intimacies of a rectory courtship, was followed by the death of his wife in 1862, and his conversion to Catholicism. Thereafter he wrote mainly on mystical or religious themes, as in *The Unknown Eros* (1877). He died at Lymington, Hampshire. » English literature; poetry; Pre-Raphaelite Brotherhood

Patmos area 34 sq km/13 sq ml; pop (1981) 2 534. Island of the Dodecanese, Greece, in the Aegean Sea, off W coast of Turkey; chief town, Hora; St John the apostle lived here for two years; Monastery of St John (19th-c); resort beaches. » Dodecanese; Greece [i]; John, St (son of Zebedee)

Patna [patna] 25°37N 85°12E, pop (1981) 916 000. Winter capital of Bihar, E India; on S bank of R Ganges, 467 km/290 ml NW of Calcutta; on site of ancient city of Pataliputra, capital of 6th-c Magadha kingdom; French trading post, 1732; university (1917); major rice-growing region; noted for its handicrafts (brassware, furniture, carpets); Sikh temple, mosque of Sher Shah. » Bihar

Paton, Alan (Stewart) (1903–88) South African writer and educator, born in Pietermaritzburg. He began as a teacher, and in 1935 became principal of the Diepkloof Reformatory, where he was known for the success of his enlightened methods. From his deep concern with the racial problem in South Africa sprang several novels, notably *Cry the Beloved Country* (1948) and *Too Late the Phalarope* (1953). He was president of the Liberal Association of South Africa (1953–68). » African literature; apartheid; novel

Patou, Jean [patoo] (1880–1936) French fashion designer, born in Normandy. The son of a prosperous tanner, in 1907 he joined an uncle who dealt in furs. In 1912 he opened Maison Parry in Paris, and in 1913 sold his collection outright to an American buyer. After war service he successfully opened again as a couturier in 1919. He was noted for his designs for sports stars, actresses, and society women, and for his perfume 'Joy'. He died in Paris. » fashion

patriarch 1 The head of a family or tribe. In Biblical literature, usually applied either to the ten purported ancestors of the human race prior to the Flood (*Gen* 5), or more commonly to Abraham, Isaac, Jacob, and Jacob's twelve sons (*Gen* 12–50). The twelve tribes of Israel are traced to the twelve sons of Jacob. » Bible; Flood, the; Israel, tribes of [i] **2** An ecclesiastical title used since about the 6th-c for the bishops of the five important ecclesiastical centres of the early Christian Church: Alexandria, Antioch, Constantinople, Jerusalem, and Rome. These bishops exercised influence and jurisdiction over the churches in the areas surrounding their cities. » bishop; Christianity

patricians In ancient Rome, the members of a select number of aristocratic clans or *gentes*, such as the Julii. The precise origins of this elite are obscure and still much debated. » plebeians

Patrick, St (c.385–c.461), feast day 17 March. Apostle of Ireland, born (perhaps) in S Wales. At 16 he was carried to Ireland by pirates, and sold to an Antrim chief. Six years later he escaped, and became a monk in France. Ordained a bishop at 45, he then became a missionary to Ireland (432), travelling widely among the chiefs, and fixed his see at Armagh (454). He died at Saul (Saulpatrick), and was probably buried at Armagh. The only authentic literary remains of the Saint are his *Confession* and a letter addressed to a British chieftain, Coroticus. » missions, Christian; monasticism

Patriotic Front (Zimbabwe) A union of nationalist movements formed to respond to efforts by US Secretary of State Henry Kissinger to find a solution to the problem of White minority rule in Rhodesia (Zimbabwe), entrenched since the Unilateral Declaration of Independence (Nov 1965). The guerrilla forces of the Zimbabwe National Liberation Army and the Zimbabwe People's Revolutionary Army stepped up their action, and by 1979 the White Rhodesian leader, Ian Smith, was forced into an internal settlement. An election brought Bishop Abel Muzorewa to power as the country's first African prime minister, but the guerrilla campaign continued. In 1980 the Lancaster House Agreement created fresh elections, in which the Patriotic Front won 87% of the votes. The Front broke up, but Nkomo and Mugabe were later reconciled in moves towards the creation of a one-party state. » Great Zimbabwe; Kissinger; Mugabe; Muzorewa; nationalism; Nkomo; Smith, Ian; Zimbabwe [i]

patristics » **Fathers of the Church**

Patroclus [patrokluhs] In Greek legend, the son of Menoetius; the faithful follower of Achilles at Troy. He went into battle wearing Achilles' armour, but was cut down by Hector. His death made Achilles return to the battle. » Achilles; Myrmidons

Patrons of Husbandry » **Granger movement**

Pattadakal An old town in Karnataka, SW India, which reached the height of its glory in the 7th–8th-c, when most of its temples (now designated world heritage monuments) were built. The most notable is the Lokeshwari or Virupaksha temple, a huge structure with sculptures that narrate episodes from Hindu epics. » Karnataka

Pattaya [pahtiya] 12°57N 100°53E. Beach resort in E Thailand; on the NE shore of the Gulf of Thailand S of Bang Phra; the 'Riviera' of Thailand, with resort facilities. » Thailand [i]

pattern recognition » **character recognition**

Patton, George (Smith) (1885–1945) US general, born at San Gabriel, California. Trained at West Point, he became one of the most daring and flamboyant US combat commanders in World War 2. He played a key role in the Allied invasion of French N Africa (1942), led the US 7th Army in its assault on Sicily (1943), commanded the 3rd Army in the invasion of France, and contained the German counter-offensive in the Ardennes (1944). He was fatally injured in a motor accident near Mannheim, and died at Heidelberg. » Bulge, Battle of the; Normandy Campaign; World War 2

Pau [poh] 43°19N 0°25W, pop (1982) 85 766. Economic centre and capital of Pyrénées-Atlantiques department, SW France; on right bank of R Gave de Pau, 174 km/108 ml S of Bordeaux; former capital of Béarn province, 1464; health resort, winter sports centre; road and rail junction; engineering, textiles, brewing, tanning, tourism; natural gas nearby; birthplace of Henry IV of France, Charles XIV of Sweden; 12th–15th-c castle, Musée des Beaux-Arts, Musée Bernadotte, Boulevard des Pyrénées. » Charles XIV; Henry IV (of France)

Paul I (of Greece) (1901–64) King of the Hellenes (1947–64), born and died in Athens. In 1922 he served with the Greek navy against the Turks; but in 1924, when a Republic was proclaimed, went into exile. In 1935 he returned to Greece as crown prince. In World War 2 he served with the Greek general staff in the Albanian campaign, and was in exile in London (1941–6). His reign covered the latter half of the Greek Civil War (1946–9) and its difficult aftermath; during the early 1960s his personal role, and that of his wife Queen Frederika, became sources of bitter political controversy. » Greece [i]; World War 2

Paul III, originally **Alessandro Farnese** (1468–1549) Pope (1534–49), born at Canino, Papal States. The first of the popes of the Counter-Reformation, in 1538 he issued the bull of excommunication and deposition against Henry VIII of England, and also the bull instituting the Order of the Jesuits in 1540. He summoned the Council of Trent (1545), and died in Rome. » Counter-Reformation; Henry VIII; Jesuits; pope; Trent, Council of

Paul VI, originally **Giovanni Battista Montini** (1897–1978) Italian Pope (1963–78), born at Concesio. He studied at Rome, was ordained in 1920, and entered the Vatican diplomatic service, where he remained until 1944. As Archbishop of Milan, he became known for his liberal views and support of social reform. Made cardinal in 1958, he succeeded John XXIII, many of whose opinions he shared. He travelled more widely than any previous pope, and initiated important advances in the move towards Christian unity. He died at Castel Gandolfo. » ecumenism; John XXIII; pope

Paul, St, also known as **Saul of Tarsus** (?–c.62/65) Apostle to the Gentiles and important theologian of the early Christian Church, born of Jewish parents at Tarsus, Cilicia. He apparently trained as a rabbi in Jerusalem, becoming a fervent Pharisee and persecutor of Christians. On his way to Damascus (c.34–35), he was converted to Christianity by a vision of Christ, and after several months in Nabatea began to preach the Christian message and undertake missionary journeys, first in Cyprus, Antioch of Pisidia, Iconium, Lystra, and Derbe. Around 48–51, he had to address an apostolic conference in Jerusalem on the disputed issue of how Gentiles and Jews were to be admitted to the Church (*Gal* 2.1–10; *Acts* 15.1–21), and a form of resolution was apparently reached which allowed him to continue his mission to the Gentiles, although a later dispute with Peter did arise in Antioch.

The precise chronology of his missionary activities is confused, but other journeys took Paul, with Silvanus (Silas), to Asia Minor and through Galatia and Phrygia to Macedonia and Achaia, where in Corinth he was especially successful. An extensive mission was also undertaken in Ephesus, amid many difficulties, leading eventually to a final visit to Macedonia and Corinth. On his return to Jerusalem, he was apparently imprisoned for two years, following disturbances against him by the Jews. He was transferred to Caesarea and to Rome after appealing to Caesar; and according to later tradition, he was executed by Nero (although some traditions suggest that he was released and went to Spain). Thirteen New Testament letters are traditionally attributed to him, as well as some extracanonical works. » Acts of the Apostles; Christianity; New Testament; Pauline Letters

Pauli, Wolfgang (1900–58) Austrian-Swiss theoretical physicist, born in Vienna. He studied at Munich and Copenhagen, in 1925 formulating the 'exclusion principle' in atomic physics, and in 1931 postulating the existence of an electrically neutral particle (the neutrino), later confirmed by Fermi. Winner of the 1945 Nobel Prize for Physics, he died in Zürich. » Fermi; nuclear physics; Pauli exclusion principle

Pauli exclusion principle The principle that no two electrons (or other fermions) may occupy exactly the same quantum state; formulated by Austro-Swiss physicist Wolfgang Pauli in 1925. The principle is necessary to explain why electrons in atoms do not all collapse into a single state. It is a fundamental principle of quantum theory. » boson; fermions; Pauli; quantum mechanics

Pauline Letters or **Pauline Epistles** A set of New Testament writings ascribed to the apostle Paul, usually numbering 13, excluding the letter to the Hebrews which rightly does not claim Pauline authorship. Modern scholars are confident of Paul's authorship in only 7 cases (Romans, 1 and 2 Corinthians, Galatians, Philippians, 1 Thessalonians, and Philemon), and debate the authenticity of 2 Thessalonians, Colossians, Ephesians, and the Pastoral Letters. The widely accepted writings were actual letters to specific churches and situations in areas where Paul had a pastoral or missionary interest, and were not general systematic treatises. » Colossians/Corinthians/Ephesians/Galatians/Philemon/Philippians/Romans/Thessalonians, Letters to (the); New Testament; Pastoral Letters; Paul, St

Pauling, Linus (Carl) (1901–) US chemist, born at Portland, Oregon. Educated at Oregon and California, he studied at several centres in Europe, becoming a professor of chemistry at the California Institute of Technology in 1927. He applied quantum theory to chemistry, and was awarded the Nobel Prize for Chemistry in 1954 for his contributions to the theory of valency. His work on molecular structure (mainly using X-ray diffraction) revolutionized both inorganic chemistry and biochemistry. He became a controversial figure from 1955 as the leading scientific critic of US nuclear deterrent policy, forcibly setting out his views in *No More War* (1958). Awarded the Nobel Peace Prize in 1962, he is the first person to have won two full Nobel Prizes. » protein; valence

pavane A stately dance of the 16th–17th-c, probably of Italian origin; the name may derive from the town of Padua. It was often linked to a livelier dance, generally in triple time, known as a *galliard* (from Fr 'merry').

Pavarotti, Luciano (1935–) Italian tenor, born at Modena. He won the international competition at the Teatro Reggio Emilia in 1961, and made his operatic debut there the same year. He performed with the La Scala tour of Europe 1963–4, and made his US debut in 1968. He is internationally known as a concert performer, and has made many recordings and television appearances.

Pavese, Cesare [pavayzay] (1908–50) Italian novelist, born at Cuneo, Piedmont, and educated in Turin. He worked as a translator and publisher before turning to writing. His short stories, such as *La bella estate* (1949, The Beautiful Summer), were well-received, but he is best known for his novel *La luna e i falò* (1950, The Moon and the Bonfires). He committed suicide in Turin. His unsentimental celebration of Italian rural life exerted a strong influence on later Italian fiction and film making. » Italian literature; novel

Pavia [paveea], ancient **Ticinum** 45°12N 9°09E, pop (1981) 85 029. Capital town of Pavia province, Lombardy, N Italy, on R Ticino; linked with Milan by canal; railway; university (1361); iron and steel castings, textiles, sewing machines; cathedral (begun 1487), Church of San Michele (1155), Church of San Pietro in Ciel d'Oro (1132, restored 19th-c). » Lombardy

Pavlov, Ivan (Petrovich) (1849–1936) Russian physiologist, born near Ryazan. He studied at St Petersburg, Breslau, and Leipzig, then returned to St Petersburg, where he became professor (1891) and director of the Institute of Experimental Medicine (1913). He worked on the physiology of circulation and digestion, and from 1902 studied what later became known as Pavlovian or classical conditioning in animals, summarizing this work in *Lectures on Conditioned Reflexes* (1926). A major influence on the development of behaviourism in psychology, he was awarded the Nobel Prize for Physiology or Medicine in 1904, and died in St Petersburg. » behaviourism; conditioning; psychology

Pavlova, Anna [**pav**lohva] (1881–1931) Russian ballerina, born in St Petersburg. She studied at the Marinsky Theatre, and joined the Imperial Ballet in 1899. In 1909 she travelled to Paris with the Ballets Russes, and after 1913 danced with her own company in reduced versions of the classics in many parts of the world. *Le Cygne* (1907), known as 'The Dying Swan', was choreographed for her by Fokine, and she wrote her own ballet *Autumn Leaves* (1918). She died in The Hague. » Ballets Russes; Fokine

Pavo (Lat 'peacock') [**pah**voh] A small constellation, a handful of bright stars in the S hemisphere. » constellation; RR9

pawnbroking A system of money-lending in which an article, usually personal property, is deposited with an agent (the pawnbroker) as security for the loan. The article can be redeemed within a given time on repayment of the loan plus interest. Articles of low value which are unredeemed at the end of the period become the property of the pawnbroker; larger-value items may be sold in order to repay the loan. The system has a very long history, and was popular with the poorer classes in earlier times. It has declined in recent years with the growth of hire-purchase and easier credit facilities.

pawpaw » **papaw**

Paxton, Sir Joseph (1801–65) British gardener and architect, born near Woburn, Bedfordshire. He was a working gardener to the Duke of Devonshire, at Chiswick and Chatsworth, where he remodelled the gardens, and built the conservatory and lily house. He designed a building for the Great Exhibition of 1851 (nicknamed the 'Crystal Palace'), which he re-erected in Sydenham (destroyed by fire in 1936). He died at Sydenham, Kent. » landscape gardening

pay TV The non-broadcast distribution of video entertainment to a restricted audience of subscribers who pay for the programmes viewed. The programmes are received either by individual cable connection or by scrambled microwave or satellite transmission requiring a rented decoder. » television

Payachata, Nevados de [paya**cha**ta] 18°10S 69°10W. Andean massif on Chile–Bolivia border; 129 km/80 ml WNW of Arica; includes two snow-capped peaks, Cerro de Pomarepe (6 240 m/20 472 ft) and Cerro de Parinacota (6 342 m/20 807 ft). » Andes

PAYE An abbreviation of **pay as you earn**, a UK taxation system whereby income tax is deducted from a worker's pay by an employer before handing over the wage. The employer is therefore responsible for collecting the tax on behalf of the government. The amount to be collected is determined from tables issued by the tax authorities, and by reference to each person's *tax code*, calculated at the start of each fiscal year. » income tax

Payton, Walter (1954–) US footballer, born at Columbia, Mississippi. In his career with the Chicago Bears (1975–88), he rushed for 16 726 yards, a National Football League record. In one game (1977) he rushed for a record 275 yards. His record of 125 touchdowns (1975–87) is second only to that of Jim Brown. » football [i]

Paz, Octavio (1914–) Mexican poet, born and educated in Mexico City. A career diplomat, he served as the Mexican ambassador to India (1962–8), and taught at Texas, Harvard, and Cambridge Universities. He is a writer of great energy and versatility, with 30 volumes from 1933; his *Collected Poems* (1957–87), in Spanish and English, were published in 1988. He has also written important prose works, notably *Tiempo Nublado* (1984, trans One Earth, Four or Five Worlds). » Latin-American literature; poetry; RR100 Nobel Prizes

Paz Estenssoro, Víctor [pas esten**soh**roh] (1907–) Bolivian revolutionary and politician, born at Tarija, Bolivia, founder of the National Revolutionary Movement in 1941. Following the 1952 Revolution he served as President (1952–6, 1960–4), being ousted by a military coup. He returned as President in 1985. » Bolivia [i]

Paz, La » **La Paz**

Pazyryk [pa**zuh**rik] In the Altai Mts, C Siberia, a group of frozen tombs of prehistoric nomad chieftains perfectly preserved by permafrost since their deposition in timber-lined burial chambers in the 4th-c BC. Embalmed, tattooed bodies survived, as well as furniture, wooden plates, horse trappings, clothing, felt rugs, and Chinese silk. Cannabis-smoking equipment was also recovered. » permafrost; Scythians

PC » **personal computer**

PCP » **angel dust**

pea A botanical term used as a suffix, referring to several plants of the family *Leguminosae*, but especially to members of the genus *Pisum*. The distinctive flower is typical of most of the family, having an upright petal (the standard), two spreading petals (the wings), and two lower petals which are partly joined along their length, and surround the ovary and stamens (the keel); the whole is sometimes rather butterfly-like in appearance. The best-known species are **sweet pea** (*Lathyrus odoratus*) and **garden pea** (*Pisum sativum*), a climbing annual growing to 2 m/6½ ft, native to S Europe and N Africa; leaves with 1–3 pairs of oval leaflets and a terminal branched tendril; flowers up to 3.5 cm/1½ in long, white, pink or purplish, in small clusters of 1–3; pods up to 12 cm/4¾ in long, oblong, containing up to 10 seeds. It has been cultivated since prehistoric times for the edible seeds (*peas*) eaten as a vegetable, fresh, dried, frozen, or canned. Many cultivars are also widely grown, including the smaller-seeded *petit pois*, and also *mange tout*, where the whole pod is consumed. (*Pisum sativum*. Family: *Leguminosae*.) » annual; climbing plant; cultivar; ovary; stamen

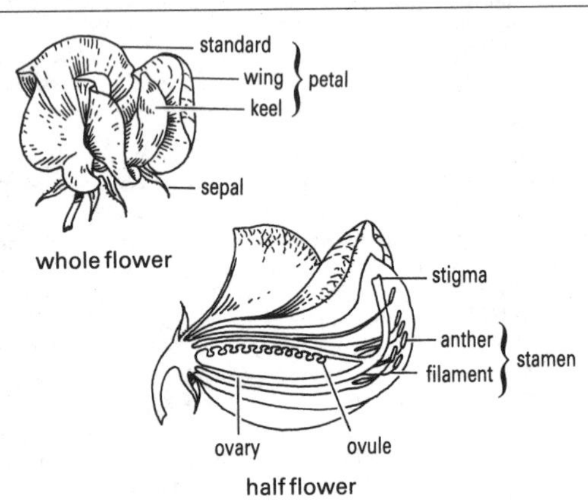

Pea flower

pea crab A small crab that lives inside marine bivalve molluscs, such as mussels and oysters, usually in shallow waters; pale in colour; last pair of legs armed with hooks for holding onto the host. (Class: *Malacostraca*. Order: *Decapoda*.) » bivalve; crab

Peace Corps An agency of volunteers funded by the US government, established in 1961. Volunteers numbered more than 10 000 in 52 countries in 1966, but in the 1980s the corps was asked to leave some countries hostile to US policies. Development has paralleled that of similar agencies in France, Germany, and the UK, with more emphasis now on the recruitment of skilled, mature volunteers. » Voluntary Service Overseas

Peace Memorial Museum A museum in the Heiwa Koen ('Peace Park'), Hiroshima, Japan, housing information and exhibits chronicling the effects of the atomic bomb which destroyed the city in 1945. » Hiroshima; museum

Peace River River in W Canada, rising in the Omineca Mts, British Columbia, as the Finlay R; flows SE, then E and N to enter the Slave R near its outflow from L Athabasca; length 1 923 km/1 195 ml to the head of Finlay R; used for hydroelectricity. » Canada [i]

peace studies Educational courses designed to explore the role of the military in society, international strategic relationships, and those conditions that most promote peace and human welfare in society. They have a strong association with the liberal left tradition in academia, and are therefore viewed with some suspicion by orthodoxy. » left wing; military science

peach A small deciduous tree, growing to 6 m/20 ft; leaves elliptical to oblong, pointed, toothed; flowers pink, rarely white, appearing before leaves; fruit globular, velvety 4–8 cm/1½–3 in, yellow flushed red with thick sweet flesh, stone grooved. Its origin is obscure: possibly native to China, it has long been cultivated, often as an espalier. (*Prunus persica*. Family: *Rosaceae*.) » deciduous plants; nectarine; prunus; tree [i]

peacock Either of two species of pheasant (genus: *Pavo*) from the forests of India and SE Asia: especially the **Indian peafowl** (*Pavo cristatus*); also *Afropavo congensis* from the Congo basin; alternatively known as **peafowl**; the female sometimes called **peahen**. The two species can interbreed. The name is also used for **peacock pheasants** of the genus *Polyplectron* (6 species). » pheasant

Peacock, Thomas Love (1785–1866) British novelist, born at Weymouth, Dorset. He entered the service of the East India Company (1819–56) after producing three satirical romances, *Headlong Hall* (1816), *Melincourt* (1817), and *Nightmare Abbey* (1818), and later produced four other works along similar lines. In each case a company of humorists meet in a country house, and the satire arises from their conversation rather than from character or plot. He died at Lower Halliford, Middlesex. » English literature; novel; satire

peacock butterfly A medium-sized butterfly with a prominent eyespot on each reddish-brown wing; caterpillars feed on stinging nettles; early caterpillars spin silk webs on nettle leaves. (Order: *Lepidoptera*. Family: *Nymphalidae*.) » butterfly; caterpillar

peacocking The methods used by illegal land occupiers ('squatters') to protect their holdings from the Free Selection Acts in New South Wales and Victoria from the 1860s. A common method was to retain areas with water or good pastures, making the rest of the land useless for closer settlement. Another method was to use agents or 'dummies' to buy up land on the squatters' behalf. Because of the dryness of much of Australia, 'peacocking' often succeeded. The allusion is to the eye-like markings on the tail of a peacock: the squatters 'picked the eyes' (ie the most desirable parts) out of the land. » free selection

peafowl » **peacock**

Peak District National park in NC England; area 1 404 sq km/542 sq ml; established in 1951; mainly in Derbyshire, with parts in adjacent counties; limestone uplands and woodlands (S, E); limestone caves, major tourist attraction, notably at Peak Cavern, near Castleton; moorlands and crags (N), walking and climbing area; highest point, Kinder Scout, 727 m/2 088 ft. » Derbyshire

Peake, Mervyn (1911–68) British author and artist, born at Kuling, S China, where his father was a missionary. Educated in China and Kent, he became a painter, and taught at the Westminster School of Art. He is best known for his Gothic fantasy trilogy of novels: *Titus Groan* (1946), *Gormenghast* (1950), and *Titus Alone* (1959), and his novel *Mr Pye* (1953). He also published books of verse, and illustrated several classics and children's books. He died at Burcot, Oxfordshire. » English literature; Gothic novel

peanut An annual, growing to 50 cm/20 in, native to S America; leaves divided into four elliptical or oval leaflets; pea-flowers yellow, growing downwards after fertilization and drawing the young pods into the soil, where they ripen underground; also called **groundnut** or **monkey nut**. It is widely grown for the edible seeds (*peanuts*), used in confectionary and as a source of peanut oil. (*Arachis hypogaea*. Family: *Leguminosae*.) » annual

peanut worm An unsegmented marine worm that lives in burrows in sediment, in calcareous rock, or in coral; body usually divided into stout trunk and slender retractable proboscis, encircled by tentacles; gut U-shaped; larvae found in plankton. (Phylum: *Sipuncula*, c.320 species.) » calcium; coral; larva; plankton; worm

pear A deciduous, usually thorny tree or shrub, native to Europe and Asia; leaves narrowly lance-shaped to broadly oval; flowers white or pinkish, in flat-topped clusters, appearing before or with the leaves; fruit round or top-shaped as well as pear-shaped. Its characteristic gritty texture is caused by the presence of stone-cells in the flesh of the fruit. It is widely grown as an orchard tree and ornamental. (Genus: *Pyrus*, 30 species. Family: *Rosaceae*.) » deciduous plants; shrub; tree [i]

Pearl Harbor Inlet occupied by a US naval base on the island of Oahu in the US Pacific Ocean state of Hawaii; adjacent to Honolulu; 1887 treaty granted the USA rights as a coaling and repair base; naval base established, 1908; the bombing of the base by the Japanese (7 Dec 1941), sinking or disabling 19 ships and 120 aircraft, brought the USA into World War 2. » Hawaii (state); World War 2

Pearl Islands, Span **Archipiélago de las Perlas** pop (1980) 2 942. Panamanian island group in the Gulf of Panama, C America; over 180 islands, the largest being Isla del Rey, chief town San Miguel; pearl fishing in colonial times; now a wide range of fishing. » Panama [i]

Pearl River » **Zhu Jiang**

pearlfish Elongate and very slender fish widespread in tropical and warm temperate seas, living inside sea cucumbers, sea urchins, and other marine invertebrates; length up to 30 cm/12 in; tail pointed, dorsal and anal fins long, pelvics absent; includes European *Echiodon drummondi*. (Family: *Carapidae*, 2 genera.)

pearlite A type of steel formed by an intimate intergrowth of iron with iron carbide. It has a lustrous sheen. » iron; steel

Pears, Sir Peter (Neville Luard) [peerz] (1910–86) British tenor, born at Farnham, Surrey. He was organ scholar at Oxford, then studied singing (1933–4) at the Royal College of Music, London. He toured the USA and Europe with Benjamin Britten, and in 1943 joined Sadler's Wells. In 1946 he helped Britten found the English Opera Group, and was co-founder with him of the Aldeburgh Festival (1948). He was knighted in 1978, and died at Aldeburgh, Suffolk. » Britten

Pearse, Patrick (or **Pádraic**) **Henry** (1879–1916) Irish writer, educationist, and nationalist, born and died in Dublin. A barrister, he was a leader of the Gaelic League, and editor of its journal. Having commanded the insurgents in the Easter Rising of 1916, he was proclaimed president of the provisional government. After the revolt had been quelled, he was court-martialled and shot, along with his brother, William. » Easter Rising

Pearson, Lester B(owles) (1897–1972) Canadian statesman and Prime Minister (1963–8), born at Newtonbrook, Ontario. Educated at Toronto and Oxford, he was leader of the Canadian delegation to the United Nations, becoming president of the General Assembly in 1952–3. Secretary of State for External Affairs (1948–57), his efforts to resolve the Suez Crisis were rewarded with the Nobel Peace Prize in 1957. As Prime Minister, he introduced a comprehensive pension plan, socialized medicine, and the maple leaf flag. He died in Ottawa. » Suez Crisis

Peary, Robert Edwin (1856–1920) US admiral and explorer, born at Cresson Springs, Pennsylvania. He made eight Arctic voyages to the Greenland coast, in 1891–2 arriving on the E coast by crossing the ice. In 1909 he led the first expedition to the N Pole, though his achievement was disputed by his fellow-explorer Frederick Cook, who claimed to have reached the Pole in 1908 – a claim generally discredited. Peary died in Washington, DC. » North Pole

Peary Land Region of N Greenland on the Arctic Ocean, forming a mountainous peninsula; its N cape, Kap Morris Jesup, is the most northerly point of land in the Arctic; not covered by ice; explored by Peary in 1892 and 1900. » Greenland [i]; Peary

Peasant's Revolt An English popular rising of June 1381, among townsmen as well as peasants, based in Essex, Kent, and London, with associated insurrections elsewhere. It was precipitated by the three oppressive poll taxes of 1377–81, the underlying causes being misgovernment, the desire for personal freedom, and an assortment of local grievances. It was quickly suppressed. » poll tax; Tyler, Wat; villein

Peasants' War (1524–5) Probably the largest peasant uprising in European history, raging through Germany, from the Rhineland to Pomerania. It sought to defend traditional agrarian rights against lords and princes, and appealed to notions of divine law fostered by the Lutheran Reformation. It was denounced by Luther, and brutally suppressed by the princes. » Luther; Reformation; Swabia

peat The partially decomposed remains of plants which accumulate and are preserved in waterlogged conditions in areas of cool, humid climate. Because it is an anaerobic environment, it is a good medium for the preservation of archaeological remains and also bodies, such as Grauballe Man (1540–1740 years old) in Denmark. It is the first stage in the formation of coal, and is widely used as a form of fuel (eg in Ireland and Russia). » coal

pecan A deciduous tree growing to 45 m/150 ft, native to eastern N America; leaves pinnately divided into toothed leaflets; flowers small, green, lacking petals; males in catkins, females in clusters; nut 4–5 cm/1½–2 in, roughly oblong, reddish-brown, edible. (*Carya pecan*. Family: *Juglandaceae*.) » deciduous plants; pinnate; tree [i]

peccary [**pek**aree] A mammal native to forest and dry scrubland in C and S America; an artiodactyl, a New World equivalent of the Old World pig, but smaller, with three (not four) toes on each hind foot; tusks grow downwards (not upwards). (Family: *Tayassuidae*, 3 species.) » artiodactyl; pig

Peckinpah, Sam (1925–84) US film director, born at Fresno, California. He started work on television Westerns, and directed his first feature, *The Deadly Companions*, in 1961. He portrayed a harshly realistic view of the lawless US West, accentuating the inherent violence, as in *Major Dundee* (1965) and *The Wild Bunch* (1969). His personal life was equally turbulent, his heavy drinking and quarrels with the studios restricting his creative output in his later years, and although he retired to a mountain retreat in 1978, he died in Los Angeles not long after.

Pecos River [**pee**kos] River in S USA; rises in New Mexico in the Sangre de Cristo Mts; flows S through Texas to join the Rio Grande NW of Del Rio; length 1 490 km/925 ml; used for irrigation. » United States of America [i]

Pécs [paych], Ger **Fünfkirchen**, Lat **Sopianae** 46°05N 18°15E, pop (1984e) 175 000. Industrial capital of Baranya county, S Hungary; capital of E Pannonia under Roman rule; bishopric; university (1367, refounded 1922), university of medicine (1923); centre of a noted wine-producing area; leather, coal. » Hungary [i]

pectin A complex molecule (a homopolysaccharide) especially rich in galacturonic acid. It functions as a cement-like material in plant cell walls, particularly young primary cell walls, and is abundant in fruits such as apples. » galactose; molecule; polysaccharides

pediatrics » **paediatrics**

pediment (architecture) In classical architecture, a triangular section of wall above the entablature and enclosed by the sloping cornices, ie a low pitched gable. A **broken pediment** is one where the sloping sides do not meet at the apex. » cornice; entablature; frieze

pediment (earth science) A gently sloping surface cut into bedrock where there is a change in gradient, such as at the foot of a steep mountain slope, and extending towards an alluvial or river plain. There is some controversy as to their origin: competing explanations include erosion by rivers flowing from the mountainous area, and the transport of soil downslope by running water not confined to channels. » erosion

pedology The study of soil as a natural phenomenon, including its formation, development, and physical characteristics. It embraces soil mapping, the study of soil formation and development, and the subdisciplines of soil chemistry, soil physics, and soil microbiology. The term derives from Greek *pedon* 'ground'. » soil; soil science

pedometer A device for counting the number of paces taken by the wearer. It usually consists of a free pendulum, operating a ratchet, which moves a toothed wheel one tooth per pace; this is then connected to a dial counter. The device will be calibrated to correspond to the length of the user's pace.

pedophilia » **paedophilia**

Pedro I (1798–1834) The first Emperor of Brazil (1822–31), born in Lisbon, the second son of John VI of Portugal. He fled to Brazil with his parents on Napoleon's invasion, and became Prince Regent there when his father returned to Portugal (1821). Liberal in outlook, he declared for Brazilian independence in 1822, and was crowned as Pedro I. Local dissensions caused his abdication in 1831, when he withdrew to Portugal, becoming Pedro IV of Portugal on the death of his father. He abdicated in favour of his daughter, and died in Lisbon. » Brazil [i]

Peebles 55°39N 3°12W, pop (1981) 6 692. Capital of Tweeddale district, Borders, SEC Scotland; on R Tweed, 33 km/20 ml S of Edinburgh; textiles, tourism; Tweeddale museum; mediaeval Neidpath Castle nearby; 13 km/8 ml ESE, Traquair House (oldest inhabited house in Scotland); birthplace of William and Robert Chambers. » Borders; Chambers Robert/William; Scotland [i]

Peel, Sir Robert (1788–1850) British statesman and Prime Minister (1834–5, 1841–6), born near Bury, Lancashire. Educated at Harrow and Oxford, he became a Tory MP in 1809. He was made Secretary for Ireland (1812–18), where he displayed a strong anti-Catholic spirit, and was fiercely attacked by O'Connell, earning the nickname 'Orange Peel'. As Home Secretary (1822–7, 1828–30), he carried through the Catholic Emancipation Act (1829) and reorganized the London police force ('Peelers' or 'Bobbies'). As Prime Minister, his second ministry concentrated upon economic reforms, but his decision to phase out agricultural protection by repealing the Corn Laws (1846) split his Party, and precipitated his resignation. He remained in parliament as leader of the 'Peelites' (1846–50), and died in London after a riding accident. » Corn Laws; Melbourne, Viscount; O'Connell, Daniel; Tories; Whigs

Peele, George (c.1558–98) English dramatist, born in London. Educated at Oxford, he moved to London where for 17 years he lived a Bohemian life as actor, poet, and playwright. His best-known works are *The Arraignment of Paris* (1584), a dramatic pastoral containing ingenious flatteries of Elizabeth, and the historical play, *Edward I* (1593). » drama; English literature; pastoral

peepul A species of strangler fig, native to SE Asia, and regarded as sacred in India; also called **pipal** or **bo-tree**. (*Ficus religiosa*. Family: *Moraceae*.) » fig

peerage In the UK, holders of the title of duke, marquis, earl, viscount, and baron/baroness (whether hereditary or for life), who make up, in that order of precedence, the titled nobility. Their privileges have been reduced; the two main ones remaining are their right to sit in the House of Lords, and their exemption from jury service. The Peerage Act 1963 permits a person inheriting a peerage to disclaim it for life, as did Lord Benn and Lord Home, without the subsequent descent of the peerage being affected. » titles [i]

peewit An alternative name for the lapwing (*Vanellus vanellus*); also known as **pewit**. It was formerly an alternative name for the **black-headed gull** (*Larus ridibundus*). » gull; lapwing

Pegasus (astronomy) (Lat 'winged horse') The seventh largest constellation, conspicuous in the N hemisphere » constellation; RR9

Pegasus (mythology) In Greek mythology, a winged horse, which sprang from the body of the Medusa after her death. Bellerophon caught it with Athene's assistance. Various fountains sprang from the touch of its foot, such as Hippocrene on Mt Helicon. Finally it was placed in the sky as a constellation. » Bellerophon

pegmatite Very coarse-grained igneous rocks with varied and sometimes exotic mineralogy due to concentrations of the rarer elements. They are commonly associated with the later stages of granite crystallization in dykes and sills, and are the source of many gem-quality and uncommon minerals. » gemstones; granite; igneous rock

Peirce, C(harles) S(anders) (1839–1914) US philosopher and logician, born at Cambridge, Massachusetts. Educated at Harvard, he worked with the Coastal and Geodesic Survey (1861–91), and was a lecturer at Johns Hopkins (1879–84), but devoted most of his time to philosophy, and spent the rest of his life in almost complete seclusion. He is known for his contributions to pragmatism, including the development of a pragmatic theory of meaning; and he also worked on mathematical logic. He died near Milford, Pennsylvania. » pragmatism

Peirls, Sir Rudolph (Ernest) [piylz] (1907–) German-British theoretical physicist, born and educated in Berlin. He travelled widely before becoming a professor at Birmingham (1937–63), Oxford (1963–74), and the University of Washington, Seattle (1974–7). He applied quantum theory to solids and to magnetic effects, and then turned to nuclear physics. In 1940 with Frisch he reported to the British government that an atomic bomb based on uranium fission was feasible, and worked on this (the Manhattan project) throughout World War 2. » atomic bomb; Frisch, Otto Robert; nuclear fission

pekan » **fisher**

Peking » **Beijing**

Peking Man Fossils of *Homo erectus* found before World War 2 in a cave near Beijing (Peking), and originally named *Sinanthropus pekinensis*. Their likely age is 350 000 years. » *Homo* [i]

Pekingese A toy breed of dog, developed in China 2 000 years ago; long body with short legs; tail curved over back; long, pendulous ears; flat face, muzzle virtually non-existent; coat very long, fine, thickest on neck and chest; also known as **peke**. » dog; non-sporting dog

Pelagianism » **Pelagius**

pelagic environments The marine life zone in the water, as opposed to the environments at the sea floor (*benthic*). Pelagic environments have been subdivided into *neritic* and *oceanic*, based on proximity to land, and into *epipelagic* and *mesopelagic*, based on depth. » benthic environments; epipelagic/mesopelagic/neritic/oceanic zone

Pelagius [puhlayjiuhs] (c.360–c.420) A British or Irish monk, who settled in Rome c.400, where he disputed with St Augustine on the nature of grace and original sin. His view that salvation can be achieved by the exercise of human powers (**Pelagianism**) was condemned as heretical by Councils in 416 and 418, and he was excommunicated and banished from Rome. Nothing more is known of him after that date. » Augustine, St (of Hippo); Christianity; heresy; original sin

pelargonium An annual or perennial, native mainly to S Africa; often slightly succulent, leaves rounded or ivy-shaped, variously lobed; flowers in a range of colours in clusters. They include the so-called 'geraniums' of horticulture, which fall into three main types: **regals** have spectacular flowers; **zonals** have leaves with bands of colour; and **ivy-leaved** have lobed leaves and trailing stems. (Genus: *Pelargonium*, 250 species. Family: *Geraniaceae*.) » annual; cranesbill; perennial

Pelasgians [pelazgianz] The name given by the Greeks to the indigenous, pre-Greek peoples of the Aegean region.

Pelau » **Belau**

Pelé, byname of **Edson Arantes do Nascimento** (1940–) Brazilian footballer, widely held to be the best player in the game's history, born at Três Corações. He made his international debut at age 16, and at 17 appeared for Brazil in the 1958 World Cup Final, scoring two goals in the 4–2 win over Sweden. He won a second winner's medal in 1962, and a third in 1970. His first-class career was spent at Santos (1955–74) and with the New York Cosmos (1975–7). He appeared in 1 363 first-class games (1955–77) and scored 1 281 goals. He is a national hero in Brazil. » football [i]

Pelecypoda [peluhsipuhda] » **bivalve**

Pelée, Mount, Fr **Montagne Pelée** [pelay] 14°18N 61°10W. Active volcano on Martinique I, E Caribbean; height, 1 397 m/4 583 ft; erupted in 1902 killing over 26 000 people in the town of St Pierre. » Martinique; volcano

Peleus [peeliuhs] In Greek mythology, the King of Phythia in Thessaly, who had to capture Thetis, a nereid, before he could marry her. The gods attended the wedding feast. He was the father of Achilles. » Achilles; Eris; Thetis

Pelham, Henry » **Pelham, Baron Thomas Pelham-Holles**

Pelham, Baron Thomas Pelham-Holles, 1st Duke of Newcastle (1693–1768) English statesman and Prime Minister (1754–6, 1757–62), who became Earl of Clare (1714) and Duke of Newcastle (1715). A Whig and a supporter of Walpole, in 1724 he became Secretary of State, and held the office for 30 years. He succeeded his brother, **Henry Pelham** (c.1695–1754) as Premier, and was extremely influential during the reigns of George I and II. In 1757 he was in coalition with Pitt during the Seven Years' War, but resigned in 1762 after hostility from the new King, George III. He died in London. » George I/II/III (of Great Britain); Pitt (the Elder); Seven Years' War; Walpole, Robert; Whigs

pelican A large aquatic bird from warm regions worldwide; bill long, with lower part sack-like; face naked; eats fish and crustaceans. (Genus: *Pelecanus*, 8 species. Family: *Pelecanidae*.) » bird [i]

pellagra [puhlaygra] A nutritional disease which results from a deficiency of niacin (a vitamin of the B group). It occurs in Africa or as a result of malabsorption of food. In severe form it is characterized by dermatitis, diarrhoea, and dementia. » vitamins [i]

Pelopidas (c.410–364 BC) Theban general and statesman who, together with his friend Epaminondas, established the short-lived Theban hegemony over Greece in the 360s BC. After playing a prominent part in the Theban victory over Sparta at Leuctra (371 BC), he subsequently operated mainly to the N of Greece in Thessaly and Macedonia. » Epaminondas; Sparta (Greek history); Thebes

Peloponnese [pelopuhneez], Gr **Pelopónnisos** pop (1981) 1 012 528; area 21 379 sq km/8 252 sq ml. Peninsular region of Greece, the most southerly part of the Greek mainland, to which it is linked by the Isthmus of Corinth; bordered N by a range of hills, highest peak Killini (2 376 m/7 795ft); chief towns, Argos, Corinth, Patras, Pirgos, Sparta, Calamata; a popular holiday region. » Greece [i]

Peloponnesian War [peloponeeshan] (431–404 BC) The war waged throughout the Greek world on land and sea by the Spartans and their allies. The underlying cause was Athenian imperialism and the fear this produced in the chief mainland city-states, notably Corinth and Sparta itself. Despite its length, there were few decisive engagements; in fact so evenly balanced were the two sides that the war ended only when the Persians intervened and threw their weight behind the Spartans. The result was defeat for the Athenians, the dismantling of their empire, and the installation in Athens of a Spartan-backed puppet regime, the so-called Thirty Tyrants. » Sparta (Greek history); Thirty Tyrants

Pelops [pelops] In Greek mythology, the son of Tantalus. As a child, his father served him up to the gods; Demeter ate part of his shoulder, but it was replaced with ivory and Pelops was brought back to life. In order to marry Hippodameia, he bribed Myrtilus, the charioteer of her father Oenomaus, to put a wax linch-pin in his chariot-wheel; after Oenomaus' death he also killed Myrtilus, and this brought a curse upon Atreus and Thyestes, his sons. » Atreus; Thyestes

pelota The generic name for various hand, glove, racket, or bat-and-ball court games which all developed from the French *jeu de paume* ('palm [of hand] game'). The most popular form is *Pelote Basque*, which was first played in the Basque region on the French/Spanish border. It uses a walled court, known as a *trinquete*. Players wear a shaped wicker basket attached to their forearm in which they catch and propel the ball. Pelota is one of the world's fastest games.

Peltier effect » **thermoelectric effects**

pelvis **1** The region of the trunk that lies below the abdomen. It contains part of the gastro-intestinal tract (coils of the small intestine, caecum and appendix, sigmoid colon, and rectum), part of the urinary system (the bladder), and some of the genital organs (the ovaries and uterus in females; the vas deferens, seminal vesicles, and prostate gland in males). » abdomen **2** A ring of bone which serves to transmit forces from the lower limbs to the trunk. It consists of the two hip bones, the sacrum, and the coccyx. It gives attachment to the muscles of the trunk and lower limbs. » bone; coccyx; hip; pyelonephritis; sacrum; Plate XIII

pelycosaur [puhl**ik**uhsaw] A carnivorous fossil reptile known from the Carboniferous to the late Permian periods, mostly in N America; skull mammal-like with a single opening behind orbit for insertion of jaw muscles; typically with expanded sail along back, used for temperature regulation and possibly for signalling. (Subclass: *Synapsida*. Order: *Pelycosauria*.) » Carboniferous period; fossil; Permian period; reptile

Pemba pop (1985e) 256 950; area 981 sq km/379 sq ml. Island region of Tanzania, in the Indian Ocean, N of Zanzibar and E of Tanga; capital, Chake Chake; cloves (world's largest producer), copra. » Tanzania [i]

Pembrokeshire Coast National park in Wales; area 579 sq km/ 223 sq ml; established in 1952; long stretches of coastline alternating between cliffs and sandy beaches; includes Milford Haven harbour, St David's Cathedral, several Norman castles. » Wales [i]

pen A writing or drawing implement used with ink. The modern pen developed from brushes (as used in Chinese calligraphy), reeds, and quills. By the mid 19th-c, metal pen nibs fixed to wooden stems had largely replaced quill pens, though they also needed to be dipped continually in ink. This problem was finally solved by the end of the century with the invention of the *fountain pen*, with its reservoir and capillary action. The ball-point pen has remained in common use since the late 1930s, through rivalled by the felt-tip pen from the 1960s. » Biró; ink; quill

PEN Initials standing for 'poets, playwrights, editors, essayists, novelists', an international association, founded by C A Dawson Scott in 1921, to promote friendship and understanding between writers, and defend freedom of expression within and between all nations. Publications include *PEN International* (reviews), and *PEN New Fiction* and *PEN New Poetry*, in alternate years. » censorship; literature

Penal Laws Collectively, statutes passed against the practice of Roman Catholicism in Britain and Ireland, when Catholic nations were perceived as a threat in the 16th–17th-c. They prevented Catholics from voting and holding public office. Fines and imprisonment were prescribed for participation in Catholic services, while officiating priests could be executed. The laws were repealed in stages, from the late 18th-c, the last not until 1926. » Catholic Emancipation; Roman Catholicism

penal settlements Places of secondary punishment in Australia where convicts found guilty of serious offences were sent; also used for colonial criminals sentenced to transportation, and (after 1842) for British convicts transported for life. About 10% of the 162 000 convicts transported to Australia spent some time in these settlements, which were mainly at Newcastle (1801–24), Port Macquarie (1821–30), Morton Bay (1825–38), Macquarie Harbour (1822–33), Port Arthur (after 1830), and Norfolk I (after 1825). Life in these settlements varied from hard to savage, with hard labour and frequent and severe floggings; the last three named had deservedly fearsome reputations. » transportation

penance (Lat *poena*, 'punishment') Both the inner turning to God in sorrow for sin, and the outward discipline of the Church in order to reinforce repentance by prayer, confession, fasting, and good works. In the Orthodox and Roman Catholic Churches, penance is a sacrament. » confession; God; sacrament

Penang [pe**nang**], also **Pulau Pinang** pop (1980) 900 772; area 1 044 sq km/403 sq ml. State in NW Malaysia; a coastal strip on the NW coast of the Malay Peninsula and the island (*pulau*) of Penang in the Strait of Malacca; first British settlement in Malaya; capital, George Town; rice, rubber, tin. » George Town (Malaysia); Malaysia [i]

Penates [pen**ay**teez, pen**ah**teez] In Roman religion, the guardians of the storeroom; 'Lares and Penates' were the household gods. The *penates publici* were the 'luck' of the Roman state, originally brought by Aeneas from Troy and kept at Lavinium. » Lares

pencil In art, originally a brush, a meaning still found in the 18th-c. Drawing sticks of graphite encased in wood were in use by the 17th-c, but modern hard and soft pencils, in which the graphite is mixed with clay and fired in a kiln, were first devised in France c.1790 by French inventor Nicholas-Jacques Conté (1755–1805). Readily erasable, the pencil lends itself to sketches and temporary notes, and is widely used by artists and draftsmen, as well as for everyday purposes. The term 'lead pencil' is a misnomer, arising from the early belief that graphite was a type of lead. The hardness of a pencil depends on the amount of clay used along with the graphite, and is indicated by a hardness rating, such as 8B (very soft) to 10H (very hard). The blackness of a pencil depends on the size and number of particles it deposits when making a mark. A wide range of coloured pencils is also manufactured, especially for children. » graphite; silverpoint

Penda (c.575–655) King of Mercia (c.632–55), who established mastery over the English Midlands, and was frequently at war with the kings of Northumbria. His forces defeated and killed Edwin at Hatfield in Yorkshire (633), and also Edwin's successor, Oswald, when he invaded Penda's territories (642); but Penda was himself slain in battle near Leeds while campaigning against Oswald's successor, Oswiu. » Anglo-Saxons; Edwin, St; Mercia; Northumbria

Penderecki, Krzysztof [penduh**ret**skee] (1933–) Polish composer, born at Debica. He studied in Kraków, and became a leading composer of the Polish avant garde, exercising considerable influence as a teacher. He first attracted international attention with his *Threnody for the Victims of Hiroshima* (1960). Later works include the opera *The Devils of Loudon* (1969), two further operas, a St Luke Passion, and several other orchestral and vocal compositions. » avant garde

pendulum In its simplest form, a weight, suspended by a wire or rod from a firm support, and allowed to swing freely to and fro under the influence of gravity. For a support of length l, the time taken for a there-and-back complete swing, the period T, is $T = 2\pi\sqrt{l/g}$, where g is acceleration due to gravity. The period does not depend on the weight of the bob nor on the size of the swing (for small swings), which is why pendulums are used in clocks. » Foucault pendulum; non-linear physics; periodic motion; torsion

Penelope In Greek legend, the wife of Odysseus, who faithfully waited 20 years for his return from Troy. She tricked her insistent suitors by weaving her web (a shroud for Odysseus' father, Laertes, which had to be finished before she could marry), and undoing her work every night. » Odysseus

penetrance The extent to which a gene can be seen in the phenotype. A gene is *fully* penetrant if all individuals carrying it show its effects, as in Huntington's chorea. A gene is of *reduced* penetrance if it has no detectable effect in some individuals proved by pedigree studies to be carrying it, as in brachydactyly (abnormal shortness of fingers and toes). » gene; phenotype

penetration aid Devices built into the 'front-end' of a nuclear-armed missile which, when the real warheads separate from their carrier (known as the *post boost-vehicle*), fly out and on to confuse enemy radars into believing that they are real rather than dummy warheads. This makes interception by anti-ballistic missile defences much more difficult. » missile, guided; radar

Penghu or **P'eng-hu Qindao** [peng**hoo**], Span, Port **Pescadores** pop (1982e) 104 083; area 127 sq km/49 sq ml. Island archipelago and county of Taiwan, in the Taiwan Strait, astride the Tropic of Cancer; consists of 64 islands, a third uninhabitable; 85% of the population lives on the largest island, Penghu; Penghu Bay Bridge is the largest inter-island bridge in the Far East (5 541 m/18 179 ft long); fishing, vegetables, coral; many temples (oldest, 1593 in honour of Matsu, Goddess of the Sea). » Taiwan [i]

penguin A flightless sea-bird, native to S hemisphere; wings modified as flippers; feathers small, waterproof; mouth lined with fleshy, backward-pointing spines; eats fish, squid, krill, etc. (Family: *Spheniscidae*, 18 species.) » bird [i]; emperor penguin; fairy penguin

penicillin An antibiotic produced by the mould *Penicillium*. In 1928 at St Mary's Hospital, London, Fleming first noted its activity against the bacterium *Staphylococcus* when his culture plate accidentally became contaminated with the mould. The work was taken up and developed 10 years later by Florey, Chain, and others at Oxford. Its remarkable clinical activity in infectious diseases was first demonstrated in 1941. Today penicillin is still one of the most important antibiotics. Several types are used, such as ampicillin and benzylpenicillin (Penicillin G). » antibiotics; drug resistance; Chain; Fleming, Alexander; Florey

Penicillium A fungus with a white network of filaments (*mycelium*) bearing greenish powdery masses (*conidia*) on its surface; grows on decaying organic matter; many species produce important antibiotics, such as penicillin. (Subdivision: *Ascomycetes*. Order: *Eurotiales*.) » antibiotics; fungus; penicillin

Peninsular Campaign (1862) In the American Civil War, an extended attempt by the Union army under General McClellan to take Richmond, Virginia (the Southern capital), by moving up the peninsula between the James and York Rivers. The effort failed, but Confederate troops were unable to drive the Northerners off the peninsula. » American Civil War; McClellan, George B; Seven Days Battles

Peninsular War (1808–14) The prolonged struggle for the Iberian peninsula between the occupying French and a British army under Wellington (formerly Wellesley), supported by Portuguese forces. Known in Spain as the *War of Independence* and to Napoleonic France as 'the Spanish ulcer', it started as a Spanish revolt against the imposition of Napoleon's brother Joseph as King of Spain, but developed into a bitter conflict, as British troops repulsed Masséna's Lisbon offensive (1810–11) and advanced from their base behind the Torres Vedras to liberate Spain. Following Napoleon's Moscow campaign (1812), French resources were over-extended, enabling Wellington's army to invade SW France (1813–14). » Bonaparte, Joseph; Masséna; Napoleonic Wars; Wellington, Duke of

penis A part of the male urogenital system composed mainly of erectile tissue and traversed by the *urethra*. It has a fixed root and a mobile body. The erectile tissue consists of three longitudinal columns (two *corpora cavernosa* and the *corpus spongiosum*). The urethra traverses the corpus spongiosum, which is considerably smaller than the corpora cavernosa. The free end of the corpus spongiosum expands to form the *glans penis* (which has the slit-like external urethral orifice near its summit). The erectile masses at the root of the penis are covered on their outer surfaces by muscle. The skin over the body of the penis is thin, delicate, freely mobile, and largely free from hairs. Towards the base of the glans penis it forms a free fold (the *foreskin*) which overlaps the glans to a variable extent (the foreskin is surgically removed in circumcision so that the glans is always visible). The size of the penis varies with the amount of blood trapped within the erectile tissue. Erection builds up as a consequence of various sexual stimuli (pleasurable sights, sound, smell, and other psychic stimuli) reinforced by direct sensory touch (of the body and genital skin). This results in an increase in length and diameter of the penis until it assumes the erect position. Once the climax of sexual excitement is reached, and ejaculation takes place, it returns to its flaccid state. In some mammals (eg dog, bear, baboon) a bone (the *os penis*) develops in the septum between the two corpora cavernosa. » gonorrhoea; impotence; semen; syphilis; testis; urinary system; venereal disease

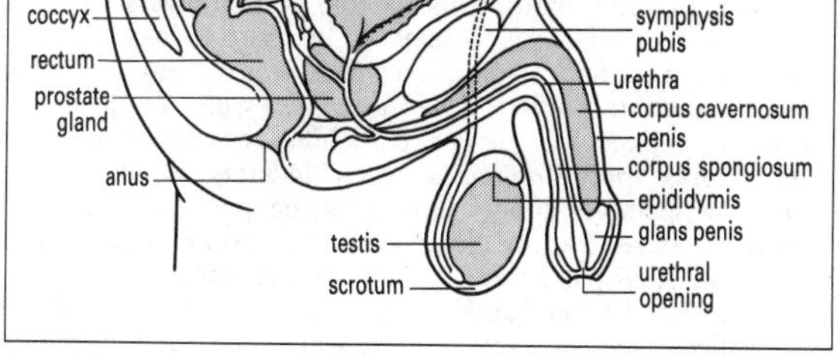

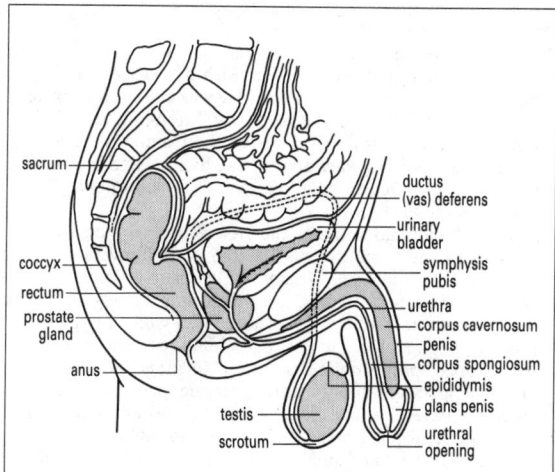

Main male organs of reproduction and surrounding structures

penitential psalms A set of seven Old Testament psalms – *Psalms* 6, 32, 38, 51 (*Miserere*), 102, 130 (*De Profundis*) and 143, although differently numbered in the Vulgate and many Catholic versions – which have been used in Christian liturgy since at least the early Middle Ages, when they were regularly recited on Fridays during Lent. They are mainly laments, although not all are directly concerned with repentance of sin. » Old Testament; Psalms, Book of

Penn, William (1644–1718) English Quaker leader and founder of Pennsylvania, born in London. Sent down from Oxford for his opposition to Anglicanism, he joined the Quakers in 1666, was imprisoned for his writings (1668), and while in the Tower wrote the most popular of his books, *No Cross, no Crown*. In 1681 he obtained a grant of land in N America, which he called Pennsylvania in honour of his father. He sailed in 1682, and governed the colony for two years. After his return, he supported James II, and worked for religious tolerance. He made a second visit to Pennsylvania (1699–1701), and died in Buckinghamshire. » Friends, Society of; James II (of England); Pennsylvania; William III

Penney, William (George), Baron (1909–91) British physicist, born in Gibraltar. Educated at London, Wisconsin, and Cambridge, he became professor of mathematics at London, and worked at Los Alamos on the atom bomb project (1944–5). He later became director of the Atomic Weapons Research Establishment at Aldermaston (1953–9), and chairman (1964–7), of the UK Atomic Energy Authority (1964–7). He was the key figure in the UK's success in producing its own atomic (1952) and hydrogen bombs (1957). Knighted in 1952, he was created a life peer in 1967, and became Rector of Imperial College London (1967–73). » atomic bomb

Pennines or **Pennine Chain**, byname **the backbone of England** Mountain range in N England; extends S from Northumberland to Derbyshire; fold of carboniferous limestone and overlying millstone grit, worn into high moorland and fell; separated from the Cheviot Hills (N) by the Tyne Gap; dissected by the Yorkshire Dales (S); rises to 893 m/2 930 ft at Cross Fell; main watershed for rivers of N England; **Pennine Way** footpath extends 402 km/250 ml from Derbyshire to the Scottish Borders. » Cheviot Hills; England [i]

Pennsylvania [pensil**vay**nia] pop (1987e) 11 936 000; area 117 343 sq km/45 308 sq ml. State in E USA, divided into 67 counties; the 'Keystone State'; one of the original states of the Union, second to ratify the Federal Constitution; first settled by the Swedish, 1643; taken by the Dutch, and then by the British in 1664; region given by King Charles II to William Penn, 1681; scene of many battles in the American Revolution and Civil War; capital, Harrisburg; other major cities Philadelphia, Pittsburgh, Erie; Delaware R forms the E border; other rivers the Susquehanna, Allegheny, Monongahela, the latter two forming the Ohio R at Pittsburgh; major industrial state; coal mining, oil drilling; steel and other metals, machinery, electrical equipment; dairy products, grain, vegetables, apples, hay, tobacco, grapes. » American Civil War; American Revolution; Harrisburg; Penn; United States of America [i]; RR39

Pennsylvania, University of » Ivy League [i]

Pennsylvanian period » Carboniferous period

pennyroyal A species of mint native to Europe and the Mediterranean, with creeping, mat-forming stems, pale green leaves, mauve flowers, and strong, slightly peppermint, scent. It is used for soups and stuffings, and is sometimes grown as a lawn plant. (*Mentha pulegium*. Family: *Labiatae*.) » mint

pension A payment made to an individual who has retired from work, on a weekly or monthly basis, related to the wage or salary being earned before retirement. *Company pension schemes* operate by receiving contributions from employees and employers; the funds are invested, and the pensions are paid from the proceeds of the investment. In the UK, a *state-pension scheme* (SERPS, or State Earnings Related Pension Scheme) is available for individuals without a company pension. The state also pays a basic old-age pension. Private pensions are schemes where the individual secures a pension privately, using the investment process. » annuity

Pentagon The central offices of the US military forces and the Defense Department, in Arlington, Virginia. The complex, which was designed by G E Bergstrom and built 1941–3, covers 10 ha/29 acres. It is composed of five 5-storey, concentric, pentagonal buildings. » Arlington

pentameter (Gr 'five measures') A line of verse of five feet: 'The lyf so short, the craft so long to lerne'. Since Chaucer (quoted here), and in this form (the iambic pentameter), it has been the most common verse form in English. » blank verse; Chaucer; iamb; metre (literature); poetry; verse

pentane C_5H_{12}, an alkane hydrocarbon with five carbon atoms. There are three structural isomers: **(n-)pentane**, $CH_3CH_2CH_2CH_2CH_3$ (boiling point 36°C); **isopentane** (IUPAC **methylbutane**), $CH_3CH_2CH(CH_3)CH_3$ (boiling point 28°C); and **neopentane** (IUPAC dimethylpropane), $CH_3C(CH_3)_2CH_3$ (boiling point 10°C). » alkanes; hydrocarbons; IUPAC

Pentateuch [**pen**tatyook] The five Books of Moses in the Hebrew Bible/Old Testament, comprising Genesis, Exodus, Leviticus, Numbers, and Deuteronomy; also called by Jews the *Torah*. Although attributed to Moses since ancient times, the works as a whole are believed by modern scholars to be composed of several discrete strands of traditions from various periods (such as an early Judean source 'J'; a N Israelite source 'E'; a priestly source 'P', perhaps from exilic times; and a source 'D' responsible for most of Deuteronomy). Together they trace Israel's origins from the earliest times, through the patriarchs, to the Exodus and Sinai periods prior to the entry to Canaan; they also contain much cultic and legal instruction. » Moses; Old Testament; patriarch **1**; Torah

pentathlon 1 A track-and-field event involving five disciplines, generally contested by women. Each competitor attempts to gain as many points as possible at each event according to performance. The events are the 100 m hurdles, shot put, high jump, long jump, and 800 m. It was replaced by the seven-event *heptathlon* in 1981. **2** Another form is the **modern pentathlon**, a five-sport competition based on miltary training. The events are cross-country riding on horseback, epée fencing, pistol shooting, swimming, and cross-country running. » fencing; heptathlon; high jump; hurdling; long jump; shooting (recreation); shot put; swimming; RR115

pentatonic scale A musical scale with five notes in the octave, most commonly equivalent to the 1st, 2nd, 3rd, 5th, and 6th degrees of the major scale. » scale [i]

Pentecost [**pen**tuhkost] **1** The Jewish feast of Shabuoth. » Shabuoth **2** A festival day in the Christian calendar, some 50 days after the death and resurrection of Jesus (seven weeks after Easter Sunday), commemorating the event in *Acts* 2 when the Holy Spirit was said to have come upon Jesus' apostles in Jerusalem, enabling them to 'speak in other tongues' to those present. In *Acts* 2.1, this occurred on the Jewish feast of Pentecost. In the English Church, this day is sometimes called 'Whitsunday'. The term *Pentecost* may also be used for the entire period between Easter Sunday and Pentecost Sunday. » Christianity; Holy Spirit; Pentecostalism; Whitsunday

Pentecostal Churches » **Pentecostalism**

Pentecostalism [pentikostalizm] A modern Christian renewal movement inspired by the descent of the Holy Spirit experienced by the Apostles at the first Christian Pentecost (*Acts* 2). It is marked by the reappearance of speaking in tongues, prophecy, and healing. The movement began in 1901 at Topeka, Kansas, USA, and became organized in 1905 at Los Angeles. Rejected by their own churches, new churches were established, commonly called 'Pentecostal', and since then their missionary zeal has reached every part of the world. Pentecostal churches are characterized by a literal interpretation of the Bible, informal worship during which there is enthusiastic singing and spontaneous exclamations of praise and thanksgiving, and the exercise of the gifts of the Holy Spirit. There are over 22 million Pentecostals worldwide. Since the 1960s, Pentecostalism (usually referred to as 'charismatic renewal') has appeared within the established Protestant, Roman Catholic, and Greek Orthodox Churches. » charismatic movement; Christianity; faith healing; Holy Spirit; Pentecost

Pentheus [**pen**thiuhs] In Greek mythology, a king of Thebes who did not welcome Dionysus. Disguising himself as a woman, he tried to spy on the orgiastic rites of the maenads, who tore him to pieces, his mother leading them on. » Dionysus; maenads

pentyl » **amyl**

penumbra 1 An area of partial shadow on the Earth during a total eclipse of the Sun. In this zone, observers see a partial eclipse only. » eclipse **2** The lighter periphery of a sunspot, surrounding the umbra. » sunspot

Penzance [pen**zans**] 50°07N 5°33W, pop (1981) 19 579. Town in Kerrier district, Cornwall, SW England; chief resort town of 'the Cornish Riviera', 40 km/25 ml SW of Truro; railway; ferry and helicopter services to Scilly Is; tourism, horticulture, clothing; Chysauster Iron Age village (N). » Cornwall

Penzias, Arno Allan [**pen**zias] (1933–) US astrophysicist, born in Munich, Germany. He fled with his parents to the USA in the 1930s, and studied at Columbia University, New York (1962), having joined Bell Laboratories in 1961. Using a large radio telescope, he and his colleagues detected residual radiation from the 'Big Bang' at the origin of the universe. He shared the Nobel Prize for Physics in 1978. » Big Bang; cosmology

peony A perennial herb or shrub, native to Europe (especially Greece), Asia, and western N America; leaves divided into lobed leaflets; flowers large, showy, ranging in colour from white or yellow to pink or red, up to 15 cm/6 in across, with 5–10 petals and numerous stamens. Many species, hybrids, and cultivars are grown as ornamentals. (Genus: *Paeonia*, 33 species. Family: *Peoniaceae*.) » cultivar; herb; perennial; shrub; stamen

people's democracy A term applied by communist regimes to themselves, where they have some form of machinery for mass participation in government, but do not hold democratic elections. Given the very restricted opportunity afforded to the people to make any choices, the term is something of a misnomer. » communism

People's Liberation Army (PLA) A Chinese army numbering over 3 million troops, a significant political as well as military force. In recent years its political role has been somewhat reduced. » Cultural Revolution

People's Party » **Populist Party**

Pepin III, byname **the Short** (c.715–68) King of the Franks (751–68), the founder of the Frankish dynasty of the Carolingians, the father of Charlemagne. He was chosen King after the deposition of Childeric, the last of the Merovingians. He led an army into Italy (754), and defeated the Lombards. The rest of his life was spent in wars against the Saxons and Saracens. He died at Saint-Denis, near Paris. » Carolingians; Charlemagne; Franks

pepper 1 An annual native to the New World tropics. Related to the potato and tomato, it has similar white flowers but entire, glossy leaves and large, fleshy, edible berries in a variety of shapes and colours. Its hot, spicy flavour is due to the chemical *capsaicin*, contained in the placenta. Used whole or ground into powder, peppers include paprika, chilies, cayenne pepper, and red pepper, plus numerous purely local types; the familiar green peppers are simply unripe red peppers. (Genus: *Capsicum*, 50 species. Family: *Solanaceae*.) » annual; ovary; potato; tomato **2** A tropical shrub or climber with long, slender spikes of minute flowers and small hard fruits. The dried, unripe fruits are called *black peppercorns*. Removal of the outer layer yields *white peppercorns*. Both are used whole or ground as spice or condiment. (*Piper nigrum*. Family: *Piperaceae*.) » climbing plant; shrub; spice

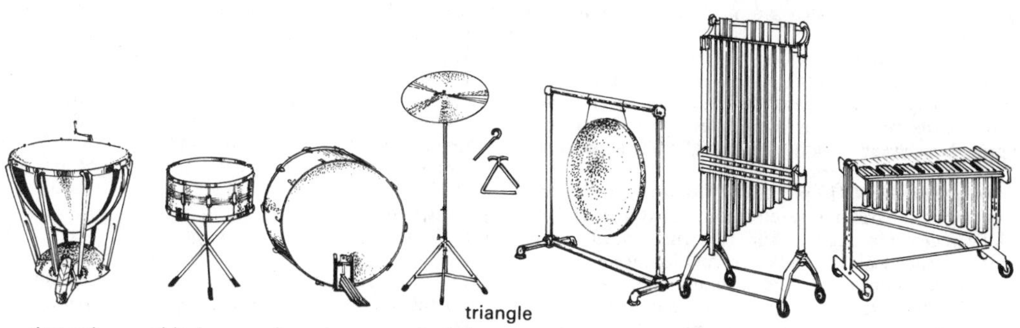

Percussion instruments (to scale)

peppered moth A moth found in two colour forms: white wings with dark speckling, and dark wings with white speckling. It is regarded as a classic example of industrial melanism, ie birds selectively prey upon a light form when settled on a dark (polluted) background, and upon a dark form settled on a light (unpolluted) background, so that the dark form predominates in polluted industrial areas. (Order: *Lepidoptera*. Family: *Geometridae*.) » moth

pepperidge » **tupelo**

peppermint » **mint**

pepsin A digestive enzyme, present in the gastric juice of vertebrates, which breaks down dietary protein into polypeptides of various sizes. It is secreted into the cavity of the stomach by the chief cells of the stomach, as an inactive pro-enzyme precursor (*pepsinogen*), and converted into pepsin by gastric HCl. It is active only in the acid environment of the stomach. Seven related pepsins have been identified in humans. » digestion; enzyme; peptide

peptic ulcer The erosion and ulceration of a small part of the lining of either the stomach or duodenum. » duodenum; stomach; ulcer

peptide A molecule obtained by the partial hydrolysis of proteins, a short chain (oligomer) of amino acids. Longer polymers (generally 50 or more amino acids) are called **polypeptides** or proteins. The amide linkage in proteins is known as a **peptide linkage**. » amino acid [i]; hydrolysis; oligomer; protein

Pepys, Samuel (1633–1703) English naval administrator and diarist, born and died in London. Educated at London and Cambridge, after the Restoration he rose rapidly in the naval service, and became Secretary to the Admiralty in 1672. His Diary runs from 1 January 1660 to 31 May 1669 – a detailed personal record and a vivid picture of contemporary life, notably of the great plague, the burning of London, and the arrival of the Dutch fleet (1665–7). It was written in cipher, and not decoded until 1825. » Restoration

Perak [**pe**rak] pop (1980) 1 743 655; area 21 005 sq km/8 108 sq ml. State in W Peninsular Malaysia; bounded W by the Strait of Malacca; watered by the R Perak; capital, Ipoh; one of the wealthiest states in Malaysia since the discovery of tin in the 1840s; Kinta Valley, the leading tin-mining area; rubber, coconuts, rice, timber. » Malaysia [i]

Perceval, Sir, or **Parsifal** In the Arthurian legends, a knight who went in quest of the Holy Grail. In the German version (*Parzival*) his bashfulness prevented him from asking the right questions of the warden of the Grail castle, so that the Fisher King was not healed. » Arthur; Grail, Holy

Perceval, Spencer (1762–1812) British statesman, and Prime Minister (1809–12), born in London. Educated at Harrow and Cambridge, he was called to the Bar (1786), and became an MP (1796). He was Solicitor-General (1801), Attorney-General (1802), and Chancellor of the Exchequer (1807), before becoming Premier. He was an efficient administrator, and his Tory government was firmly established, when he was shot while entering the House of Commons by a bankrupt Liverpool broker, John Bellingham. » Tories

perch Name used for many of the freshwater fish in families *Percidae* and *Centropomidae*, as well as several similar species in other groups; includes European *Perca fluviatilis*, widespread in lakes and quiet rivers; deep bodied, length up to 50 cm/20 in; green and brown with dark vertical bands; popular with anglers, and fished commercially in some areas.

Percheron [**per**shuhron] A heavy breed of horse, developed in France, with much Arab blood; height, 15½–17 hands/ 1.6–1.7 m/5.1–5.5 ft; black or grey; deep, solid body with strong neck and short, very muscular legs; the most popular heavy draught horse worldwide. » Arab horse; horse [i]

perching duck Duck of the tribe *Cairinini* (8 species), including the genera *Aix*, *Nettapus*, *Callonetta*, *Cairina*, *Chenonetta*, and *Sarkidiornis*. They nest in holes or (**muscovy duck**) in hollows. The tribe also includes four species of geese, called **perching geese**.) » duck; goose; mandarin duck; muscovy duck; teal

percussion A category of musical instruments, essentially idiophones and membranophones, which are played by being struck or shaken. Some produce notes of definite pitch (eg timpani, xylophone); others do not (eg cymbals, side drum). The percussion instruments commonly used in the modern orchestra are those illustrated above; except for the side drum and timpani, they are all idiophones. » bruitisme; celesta; cymbals; glockenspiel; gong; hi-hat cymbals; idiophone; marimba; membranophone; musical instruments; side drum; snare drum; steel band; timpani; triangle (music); tubular bells; vibraphone; wood block; xylophone

percussion cap A small container holding an explosive charge – a development of firearm technology in the early 19th-c which led to the modern centre-fire cartridge used in small arms. The fall of a hammer ignites the percussion cap, which in turn detonates the main propellant charge in the cartridge. » firearms

Percy A noble N England family, whose founder, **William de Percy** (c.1030–96), went to England with the Conqueror. The most famous member of the family was **Henry** (1364–1403), the famous 'Hotspur', who fell fighting against Henry IV at Shrewsbury. His father, who had helped Henry of Lancaster to the throne, was dissatisfied with the King's gratitude, and with his son plotted the insurrection. » Henry IV (of England)

Père David's deer A true deer native to China, extinct in the wild for nearly 2 000 years; a herd survived in the Chinese Imperial Hunting Park until 1900; descendants of these now in parks and zoos; large with long tail; antlers may grow twice in one year, tines pointing backwards; original habitat unknown, but broad feet and willingness to swim suggest wetlands; also known as **mi lou**. (*Elaphurus davidianus*.) » antlers [i]; deer

peregrine falcon A fast, agile falcon, found virtually worldwide, often near sea cliffs or in mountains; eats birds; dives vertically on prey, or chases in flight; also known as **duck hawk**. A popular choice for falconry, its numbers are declining because of insecticide poisoning, as they feed on seed-eating birds which have eaten treated grain. (*Falco peregrinus.*) » falcon

perennial A plant which lives for at least several years. **Herbaceous perennials** die back to ground level each year, surviving as underground organs such as bulbs or rhizomes. **Woody perennials** retain their aerial stems, which put out further growth each year. » annual; biennial; bulb; herbaceous plants; rhizome

perestroika [pere**stroy**ka] The process of 'reconstructing' Soviet society through a programme of reforms initiated from 1985 by General Secretary Gorbachev. Such reforms, meant to be consistent with the ideals of the 1917 revolution, were directed at relaxing state controls over the economy, eliminating corruption from the state bureaucracy, and democratizing the Soviet communist party and the workplace to strengthen workers' control. » Communist Party of the Soviet Union; glasnost; Gorbachev

Pérez de Cuéllar, Javier (1920–) Peruvian diplomat, born in Lima. After a period as Peru's first Ambassador to the USSR, he became a representative to the United Nations in 1971, and was appointed Secretary-General in 1982. He played a prominent role in trying to secure a peaceful solution to the Falklands Crisis. » Falklands War; United Nations

perfect competition A market situation described in economic theory where there are many buyers, many sellers, products are indistinguishable from each other, and there is perfect knowledge. The actions of any one individual cannot affect the market. » commodity market; monopoly; oligopoly

perfect numbers In mathematics, a number where the sum of its divisors is equal to the number itself. Thus the divisors of 6 are 1,2,3, and $1+2+3=6$; the divisors of 28 are 1,2,4,7,14, and their sum is 28; the next perfect number is 496. In Euclid's *Elements* a formula is given for finding perfect numbers: if 2^n-1 is prime, then $2^{n-1}(2^n-1)$ is a perfect number. » Euclid; numbers

performance » **competence**

Pergamum or **Pergamon** (Asia Minor) An ancient city in NW Asia Minor, which in Hellenistic times was the capital of the Attalids. Under their patronage it became a major centre of art and learning; its school of sculpture was internationally renowned, and its library came second only to that of Alexandria. » Attalids; Bergama; Hellenistic Age

Pergamum (Berlin, East) A branch of the Staatliche (state) museum in Berlin, E Germany, housing one of the world's finest collections of Greek, Roman, Middle Eastern, and Eastern art and antiquities. The Pergamum altar, erected in the 2nd-c BC at the Greek settlement of Pergamum in Turkey, is on display there. » Berlin, East; museum

Pergolesi, Giovanni Battista [pergoh**lay**zee] (1710–36) Italian composer, born at Jesi. He attended the Conservatorio dei Poveri di Gesù Cristo at Naples, became a violinist, and in 1732 was appointed *maestro di cappella* to the Prince at Naples. His comic intermezzo *La Serva Padrona* (1732) was highly popular, and influenced the development of opera buffa. He wrote much church music, and in 1736 he left Naples for a Capuchin monastery at Pozzuoli, where he composed his great *Stabat Mater*, and where he died. » opera buffa

peri [**pee**ree] In Persian mythology, the generic name given to a good fairy or genie. Peri-Banou, for example, was the name of a beautiful fairy in *The Arabian Nights*. » fairies

perianth The two outer whorls of floral parts (sepals and petals) taken together. When the whorls are not clearly distinguishable from each other, the individual parts are referred to as **perianth-segments**. When the entire perianth is petaloid, as in many monocot flowers, the individual segments are sometimes termed *tepals*. » flowering plants; monocotyledons; sepal

periapsis The closest point of approach of an orbiting body (planet, comet, spacecraft, etc) to the primary body; contrasted with **apoapsis**, the furthest point. For orbits about the Sun, **perihelion** is the point of closest approach; **aphelion** the furthest distance. For orbits about the Earth, the lowest point is **perigee**; the furthest distance **apogee**. » ephemeris

periclase » **magnesia**

Pericles [**per**ikleez] (c.495–429 BC) Athenian general and statesman of the aristocratic Alcmaeonid family, who presided over the 'Golden Age' of Athens, and was virtually its uncrowned king (443–429 BC). Politically a radical, he helped push through the constitutional reforms that brought about full Athenian democracy (462–461 BC). A staunch opponent of Sparta, it was his unremitting hostility to her and her allies that brought about the Peloponnesian War (431–404 BC). » Alcmaeonids; Delian League; Greek history; Peloponnesian War; Sparta (Greek history); Thucydides

peridot » **olivine**

peridotite A coarse-grained igneous rock rich in the mineral olivine together with pyroxene and other ferromagnesian minerals. It is thought to be a major constituent of the Earth's mantle. » igneous rock; olivine; pyroxenes

perigee » **periapsis**

Périgord [**pay**reegaw] Part of the former province of Guyenne, SW France, now mostly in the department of Dordogne; chief town, Périgueux; extensively forested, chalky area, known for truffles; Palaeolithic (Perigordian) caves near Montignac, Rouffignac, and Le Bugue. » Guyenne; Périgueux; Three Age System

perihelion » **periapsis**

perinatal mortality rate » **infant mortality rate**

perinatology The study of disorders of the newborn that occur in the perinatal period, ie in the period shortly before birth and during the first four weeks of life. It includes the care of such disorders as failure to breathe and distressed breathing, bleeding, jaundice of the newborn, and birth injuries. » obstetrics

period (physiology) » **menstruation**

period (geology) » **geological time scale**

periodic function In mathematics, a function such that $f(x+a)=f(x)$ for all x. If a is the smallest positive constant for which this is true, a is called the period. The commonest periodic functions are sine and cosine; the period of sin kx is $2\pi/k$. » function (mathematics) [i]

periodic motion Any motion which repeats itself in a regular way, such as the swing of a pendulum, a weight bouncing on a spring, or wave motion. It is characterized by time T, the time taken for a complete cycle, and a restoring force that is always directed towards some rest position, resulting in motion about that rest position. » mechanics; oscillation; pendulum; simple harmonic motion; wave (physics) [i]

periodic table The method of listing the chemical elements in terms of increasing atomic number, so that the rows represent increasing occupancy of an electron subshell, and the columns represent equivalent numbers of valence electrons. The original table of Mendeleyev (1869) was based on atomic weight, but had several successes in predicting the existence and chemical properties of undiscovered elements. » chemical elements; Mendeleyev; RR90

periodicals Magazines and journals published at advertised intervals. No rigid distinction can be drawn: magazines are generally published speculatively by commercial publishers and sold retail in newsagents, bookshops, and bookstalls; journals are edited and published by or for institutions, clubs, and societies for sale predominantly to their members. However, many magazines may be bought on subscription. The weekly *Tatler* (1709–11) and *Spectator* (1711–14) were the earliest periodicals, quickly achieving considerable circulations. In the 18th-c, c.800 magazine titles were published, the longest-running being the *Gentleman's Magazine* (1731–1907). In the present century, there has been a great increase in the number of weekly and monthly magazines published, and in the range of their subject matter. Similarly, journal publishing has increased, sponsored by learned societies, commercial and university-press publishers, and government and other official bodies. A recent development is the electronic journal, which may be received on-line direct to the subscriber's computer, and which may or may not be accompanied by the publication of a printed form of the same text. » Addison, Joseph; publishing

periodontics » **dentistry**

Peripatus [puh**ri**patuhs] A velvet worm typically found in humid forest litter; body segmented, length up to 150 mm/6 in;

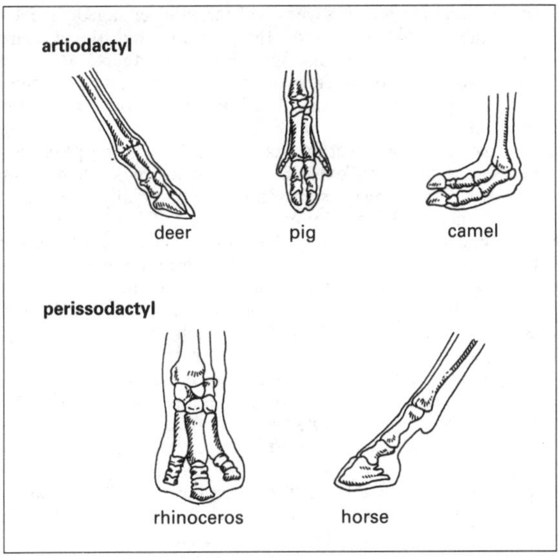

Perissodactyl and artiodactyl hooves

head with a pair of antennae and jaws; legs lobe-like; mostly nocturnal, feeding on invertebrates. (Phylum: *Arthropoda.* Subphylum: *Onychophora.*) » velvet worm

peripheral nervous system A collection of cells arranged into a large number of nerves which connect the central nervous system with other tissues of the body. It is divided into a **somatic** part, which in humans comprises the 12 pairs of *cranial nerves* and some 31 pairs of *spinal nerves*, all of which are involved in voluntary acts, and an **autonomic** part involved in involuntary (automatic) responses. » autonomic nervous system; nervous system

periscope An optical instrument for viewing an object concealed from view by a barrier (usually higher than the observer's eye-level). The basic principle is the use of two mirrors, parallel but separated by some distance: light from the object being observed reaches the first mirror, is reflected downwards, then reflected again at the second mirror, its whole path being somewhat in the form of a Z. The efficiency of the instrument may be assisted by additional optical devices such as an internal telescope or range finder system, as in the periscope used in a submerged submarine for viewing an object above sea-level, or in tanks for steering. » mirror

perissodactyl [puhrisoh**dak**til] ('odd-toed ungulate') A hoofed mammal of order *Perissodactyla* (16 species); foot with one or three functional toes (the first absent on all feet, the fifth absent on hindfeet); weight carried on toe 3 or toes 2–4. » artiodactyl; horse [i]; mammal [i]; rhinoceros; tapir; ungulate

peristyle [**pe**ristiyl] A series of columns surrounding an open court, temple, or other building. It is particularly used in classical architecture, such as the Lincoln Memorial, Washington (1911–22), architect Henry Bacon. » column

peritoneum [perituh**nee**uhm] The fluid-secreting lining of the abdominal cavity and part of the pelvic cavity. During embryonic development it becomes twisted and folded, because of the relative growth of different parts of the gastro-intestinal tract. The majority of the tract is suspended from the rear abdominal wall by folds of peritoneum. Peritoneal ligaments attach lesser mobile structures to the abdominal walls. » abdomen; pelvis; peritonitis

peritonitis Inflammation of the peritoneum, caused by infection or by irritant substances. The peritoneum may be regarded as the 'policeman' of the abdomen, in the sense that infection from the stomach or intestine (as occurs in a perforation) causes layers of the peritoneum to stick to each other and confine the infection to a limited area; for example, a perforated appendix may lead to a localized appendiceal abscess. Sometimes however the infection spreads throughout the peritoneal cavity, resulting in a generalized peritonitis, which is an acute surgical emergency with a high mortality. The surface of the peritoneum is very large, and generalized infection leads to the exudation of large volumes of fluid from the circulation, and so to shock. Chemical irritants to the peritoneum include gastric hydrochloric acid, bile juice leaking from a perforated duodenal ulcer, or pancreatic enzymes released into the peritoneum following acute pancreatitis. » abdomen; peritoneum

periwinkle (botany) An evergreen, creeping shrub, native to Europe, W Asia, and N Africa, and widely cultivated; slender, arching, or trailing stems; leaves oval, in opposite pairs; flowers white, mauve, or blue-purple, tubular with five flat, asymmetric lobes. (Genus: *Vinca*, 5 species. Family: *Apocynaceae.*) » evergreen plants; shrub

periwinkle (marine biology) A marine snail commonly found in the inter-tidal zone on shores; shells lack a mother-of-pearl layer; aperture closed off by a horny plate (*operculum*) on the foot; feeds by grazing on seaweeds and lichens. (Class: *Gastropoda.* Order: *Mesogastropoda.*) » shell; snail

Perlis [**per**lis] pop (1980) 144 782; area 818 sq km/316 sq ml. State in NW Peninsular Malaysia, bounded N by Thailand, SW by the Strait of Malacca; smallest state in Malaysia; Langkawi Is lie offshore; capital, Kangar; rice, rubber, coconuts, tin. » Malaysia [i]

Perm, formerly **Molotov** 58°01N 56°10E, pop (1989) 1 091 000. Industrial capital city of Permskaya oblast, NE European Russia, on R Kama; founded, 1723; airfield; railway; university (1916); heavy engineering, chemicals, oil refining, clothing, footwear. » Russia

permafrost Perennially frozen ground in low temperature regions of the Earth. It is underlain at depth by unfrozen ground, and also overlain by an active surface layer which thaws in summer and refreezes in the autumn. The pressure produced by the downfreezing from the surface on the unfrozen and moisture-laden lower part of this active zone may be released by cracking of the frozen surface layer, causing severe problems for the construction of roads, buildings, and pipelines. Also the removal of insulating vegetation in permafrost regions deepens the active zone by melting the permafrost, often resulting in subsidence at the surface.

permalloy An alloy of iron and nickel, which is easily magnetized and demagnetized. » alloy; iron; nickel

permanent magnet » **magnet**

permanent set » **plastic deformation**

permeability The ratio of magnetic flux density B in some material to the applied magnetic field strength H; symbol μ, units H/m (henry per metre); $B = \mu H$. The permeability of the vacuum $\mu_0 = 4\pi \times 10^{-7}$ H/m is a fundamental constant appearing throughout magnetism. Equivalently, permeability μ is the ratio of magnetic field (the magnetic flux density B) produced in a material enclosed by some solenoid to the magnetic field that would be produced in empty space within the same solenoid, all multiplied by μ_0. For paramagnetic materials, μ is larger than μ_0, and the field in the material is larger than the corresponding field in empty space. For diamagnetic materials, μ is less than μ_0, and the field is reduced. For ferromagnetic materials, μ is usually much larger than μ_0, and the field much larger. The property is related to magnetic susceptibility. » diamagnetism; ferromagnetism; magnetic susceptibility; magnetism; solenoid

Permian period A geological period of the Upper Palaeozoic era, extending from c.286 million to 250 million years ago. It was marked by the extinction of many groups of marine invertebrate animals and the diversification of reptiles. There were hot deserts in many parts of the Earth, with periods of glaciation in the S continents. » geological time scale; Palaeozoic era; RR16

permittivity A measure of the degree to which molecules of some material polarize (align) under the influence of an electric field; symbol ε, units F/m (farad per metre). The permittivity of the vacuum $\varepsilon_0 = 8.854 \times 10^{-12}$F/m is a universal constant appearing throughout electricity. For dielectric materials, ε is a material-dependent constant (the dielectric constant for that material under specified conditions) multiplied by ε_0. » dielectric; electricity

permutational art A form of modern art in which certain

features of the work are subject to change. Such changes (size, arrangement, number of parts, etc) may be predetermined by the artist (as in computer graphics) or left to chance. » computer art; modern art

Perón, (Maria) Eva (Duarte de), byname **Evita** (1919–52) The second wife of Argentine President Juan Perón, born at Los Toldos. A radio and screen actress before her marriage in 1945, she became a powerful political influence and a mainstay of the Perón government. She was idolized by the poor, and after her death, in Buenos Aires, support for her husband waned. Her body was stolen, taken to Europe, and kept in secret until 1976. The successful musical *Evita* (1979) was based on her life. » Perón, Juan

Perón, Isabelita (1931–) The popular name of **Maria Estela Martínez de Perón**, a dancer, born in La Rioja province, Argentina. She became the third wife of Juan Perón in 1961, living with him in Spain until his return to Argentina as President in 1973, when she was made Vice-President. She took over the presidency at his death in 1974, but her inadequacy in office led to a military coup in 1976. She was imprisoned for five years, and on her release settled in Madrid. » Perón, Juan

Perón, Juan (Domingo) (1895–1974) Argentine soldier and President (1946–55, 1973–4), born in Lobos. He took a leading part in the army coup of 1943, gained widespread support through his social reforms, and became President in 1946. He was deposed and exiled in 1955, having antagonized the Church, the armed forces, and many of his former Labour supporters. He returned in triumph in 1973, and won an overwhelming electoral victory, but died the following year. » Argentina [i]; Perón, Isabelita/Eva; Peronism

Peronism A heterogeneous Argentine political movement formed in 1945–6 to support the successful presidential candidacy of Juan Domingo Perón and his government thereafter. The movement later underwent division, some left-wing Peronists forming the Montoneros guerrilla group, but it survived Perón's death (1974). Despite continued internal disputes, the party made a good showing in the congressional elections of 1986. The ideology of Peronism (formally labelled Justicialism in 1949) has proved difficult to describe, and can perhaps best be viewed as a unique amalgam of nationalism and social democracy, strongly coloured by loyalty to the memory of Perón. » Argentina [i]; Montoneros; Perón, Juan

peroxide A compound containing the ion O_2^{2-} or the group –O–O–. **Hydrogen peroxide** (H_2O_2) is an important oxidizing agent and bleach. Organic peroxides are explosive. » group; ion; oxidizing agent

Perpendicular style The form of English Gothic architecture prevalent from the late 14th-c to the 16th-c, derived from the Decorated style. It is characterized by a stress on horizontals and slender verticals, large expanses of windows, simple window tracery and, in particular, fan vaults. The most dramatic example is King's College Chapel, Cambridge (1446–1515). » Decorated style; Early English style; Gothic architecture; tracery [i]; vault [i]

perpetual motion Literally, motion which is never ending. The term usually refers to 'perpetual motion machines' that invariably violate energy conservation and represent their inventors' optimism. An example would be a car powered by a windmill whose blades are driven by the flow of air due to the car's motion. Superfluidity and the flow of electrical current in superconductors are examples of literal perpetual motion. » energy

Perpignan [**per**peenyã] 42°42N 2°53E, pop (1982) 113 646. Market town and resort capital of Pyrénées-Orientales department, S France; near the Spanish border, 154 km/96 ml S of Toulouse; settled in Roman times; capital of former province of Roussillon; chartered, 1197; scene of Church Council, 1408; united to France, 1659; road and rail junction; university (14th-c); trade in olives, fruit, wine; tourism; citadel (17th–18th-c), chateau (14th-c, now a museum), town hall (13th–17th-c), Cathedral of St-Jean (14th–17th-c), Church of St-Jacques (14th–18th-c), Church of Notre-Dame-la-Réal (14th-c); Midsummer Festival (Jun). » Councils of the Church

Perrault, Charles [pe**roh**] (1628–1703) French writer, born and died in Paris. He became a lawyer, and in 1663 was a secretary to Colbert. He wrote several poems, and engaged in debate over the relative merits of the ancients and the moderns, but is best known for his eight fairy tales, the *Contes de ma mère l'oye* (1697, trans Tales of Mother Goose), which included 'The Sleeping Beauty' and 'Red Riding Hood'. » Colbert; folklore

perry An alcoholic beverage made from fermenting pears. Sour pears contain a high level of tannin, which make them unsuitable for eating. Perry is produced commercially in Germany and France, and is very popular in the UK. » tannins

Perry, Fred(erick John) (1909–) British lawn tennis and table tennis player, born at Stockport, Cheshire. He won the world table tennis title in 1929, and the men's lawn tennis singles title at Wimbledon in 1934–6, the last British male champion. He also won the singles title at the French, Australian, and US championships, and was the first man to win all four major titles. He later became a US citizen and served with the US armed forces. A notable writer, he is proprietor of a famous sports goods firm. » table tennis; tennis, lawn [i]

Perseids [per**see**idz] A major meteor shower visible for up to two weeks before and after peaking on 12 August each year, the date on which the Earth crosses the orbit. The maximum hourly rate is c.70 meteors. This show is associated with a comet of 1862, and is believed to be stony debris left by the comet as it traced its orbit. » meteor; RR5

Persephone [per**se**fuhnee] In Greek mythology, the daughter of Demeter and Zeus, originally called Kore ('maiden'); known as **Proserpine** in Latin. She was gathering flowers at Enna in Sicily when Hades abducted her and made her queen of the Underworld. There she ate the seeds of the pomegranate, which meant (in fairy lore) that she was bound to stay; but a compromise was arranged so that she returns for half of every year (an allegory of the return of Spring). » Demeter

Persepolis [per**se**polis] The site in the mountains of Iran of the palaces and graves of the Achaemenid rulers of Persia; a world heritage site. Selected originally by Darius I, the site was extensively developed by his successors Xerxes and Artaxerxes. It was sacked by Alexander the Great in 331 BC. » Achaemenids; Persian Empire

Perseus (astronomy) [**per**siuhs] A N hemisphere constellation, in the Milky Way. Fairly easy to see, it includes a double cluster of stars visible to the naked eye. » Algol; constellation; Milky Way; RR9

Perseus (mythology) [**per**siuhs] In Greek mythology, the son of Zeus and Danae. Danae's father put her and the young Perseus in a chest which floated to Seriphos, and he grew up on the island. The king ordered Perseus to fetch the head of Medusa, otherwise he would take Danae by force. With Athene's help Perseus asked the way of the Graiae, killed the Gorgon, and used its head to rescue Andromeda and save his mother. » Andromeda; Graiae; Gorgon

Pershing, John J(oseph), byname **Black Jack** (1860–1948) US general, born at Laclede, Missouri. He trained at West Point, and served in several Indian Wars, in the Cuban War (1898), in the Russo-Japanese War (1904–5), and in Mexico (1916). In 1917 he commanded the American Expeditionary Force in Europe, and after the war became Chief-of-Staff (1921–4). He died in Washington, DC. » World War 1

Pershing missile A medium-range, land-based missile with a nuclear warhead, deployed by the US Army in West Germany from 1983 onwards as part of NATO's theatre nuclear force modernization programme. The Pershing II supplanted the earlier Pershing I. » missile, guided

Persia » Iran [i]

Persian » Iranian languages

Persian architecture The architecture associated with Iran (Persia). The earliest examples are fortified buildings in W Iran, from the 8th-c–7th-c BC. Later buildings of the Achaemenid and Sassanian dynasties disclose an architecture heavily dependent on columns and thick walls, made of stone and mudbricks and brilliantly decorated with reliefs, glazed bricks, and carved stucco. Most impressive is the Palace of Persepolis (c.518–460 BC), including the 'Hall of the Hundred Columns' throne room. Persia also contributed the cruciform mosque to Islamic architecture, such as the Masjid-i-Shah, Isfahan

(1612–38). » column; Islamic architecture; stucco; Sumerian and Assyrian architecture

Persian art The art associated with Iran (Persia), which has flourished since remote antiquity. Pottery dating from 4000–3000 BC is decorated with abstract and stylized animal designs, which were soon adapted by craftsmen in bronze and gold. Alexander the Great's conquest (333 BC) introduced new ideas, including Greek conventions for drapery and gestures. The Sassanian period (AD 224–642), one of the most creative periods of all, reacted by reviving traditional forms. The Arab conquest (7th-c) introduced Islamic ideas: splendid mosques were built, and calligraphy and manuscript illumination flourished. » calligraphy; Islamic art; Sassanids

Persian cat A type of long-haired domestic cat; round head and short face; many breeds. The name was formerly used for any long-haired cat, and is still used in the USA for breeds which in Britain are called *long-hairs* (eg *blue Persian = blue long-hair*). » cat

Persian Empire An empire created by the Achaemenids in the second half of the 6th-c BC through their conquests of the Medes, Babylonians, Lydians, and Egyptians, extending from NW India to the E Mediterranean. Although it was overthrown by Alexander the Great in the 330s BC, its administrative structure, the satrapal system, survived. » Achaemenids; Babylonia; Bactria; Lydia; Medes; Persian Wars; satrapy

Persian Gulf » Arabian Gulf

Persian literature A literature which begins with 10th-c court poetry, represented by Rudagi (died 954). Firdausi (935–1020) composed the *Shahnama* or Book of Kings, the vast national epic on legends of Iran, establishing a Golden Age that lasted until the 15th-c. Earlier in this period we have the quatrains or *rubaiyyat* of the mathematician Omar Khayyam (1034–1130), the odes or *qasida* of Anvari (12th-c) and Khaqani (1106–85), and the *mathnavi*, narrative poems on a complex rhyme scheme, of Nizami (1141–1202). The influence of Islamic mysticism is evident later, in the *mathnavi* of Jalal-ud-din Rumi (c.1326–c.90), whose collection *Divan* has been frequently translated; and the lyrical poems of Jami (1414–92). Important prose works were written on science by Avicenna (980–1037), on religion by Ghazzali (1058–1111), and on ethics – the celebrated *Gulistan* – by Saadi (1184–1291). Prose was also used for biographical and historical writings. Drama and prose fiction were introduced from the West in the late 19th-c, and there are now some interesting short-story writers. » Arabic/Indian literature; mysticism; Avicenna; Firdausi; Hafiz; Omar Khayyam

Persian Wars The name given to the two punitive expeditions launched by the Persian kings, Darius I and Xerxes, against Greece in 490 and 480–479 BC. The first was in retaliation for Greek intervention in the Ionian revolt of 499 BC, and was directed only at Athens and Eretria; it ended in catastrophe for the Persians at Marathon. The second was to wipe out the disgrace of Marathon; it ended in the twin defeats for the Persians at Plataea and Mycale. » Eretria; Marathon, Battle of; Plataea; Salamis; Thermopylae

persimmon [puh**sim**uhn] Any of several species of ebony, widely cultivated for their fleshy berries, which are edible but very astringent until fully ripe; also called **date plums**. The best-known are the Chinese or Japanese persimmon, or **kakee** (*Diospyros kaki*), fruit 7.5 cm/3 in, globose, yellow to orange, native to E Asia; the **American persimmon** (*Diospyros virginiana*), fruit c.3.5 cm/1½ in diameter, orange, native to N America; and the **common date plum** (*Diospyros lotus*), fruit 1.5 cm/0.6 in, yellow or blue-black, native to Asia. (Family: *Ebonaceae*.) » ebony

person-centred therapy » client-centred therapy

personal computer (PC) A term used to describe microcomputers in general, and also used by the firm of IBM in its range of microcomputers. However, with microcomputers becoming increasingly powerful and widely used in industry and commerce, the initial significance of the term has begun to wane. » microcomputer

personalism Any metaphysical theory which maintains that everything that exists is either a person or an aspect of a person. Many personalists reject Hegel's kind of idealism, which maintained that all persons are merely manifestations of one absolute mind; they claim instead that reality is a plurality of persons. » Hegel; idealism; metaphysics

personality A set of individually evolved characteristic patterns of behaviour which determine daily functioning on both conscious and unconscious levels. It is said to represent the balance between innate drives and a combination of conscience and external controls. A **personality disorder** is said to exist when features of personality limit the formation and maintenance of satisfying interpersonal relationships. As a result of inflexible and/or maladaptive personality traits, the individual's ability to function is impaired, or there is extreme objective distress. The description of personality disorders varies greatly in different psychiatric classifications. Examples include dependent and schizoid personalities. » introversion/extraversion; schizophrenia; Type A/Type B personality

perspective In art, any method whereby the illusion of depth is achieved on a flat surface. Various methods have existed in addition to the 'scientific' one-point system invented by Brunelleschi c.1420. Most are based on the fact that objects appear smaller in proportion to their distance from the beholder, and that receding parallel lines appear to meet on the horizon at what is called the 'vanishing point'. The Greeks developed scientific perspective as a by-product of their interest in optics and geometry, but it was unknown to the Egyptians. Alberti, Uccello, Dürer, and Leonardo were pioneers of the theory of perspective, and many textbooks were written on the subject in the 17th–18th-c. » anamorphosis; illusionism; Alberti; Brunelleschi; Dürer; Leonardo da Vinci; Uccello

Perspex The proprietary name for a flat sheet form of polymethylmethacrylate resin, of notably high transparency. It first gained importance through its use for aircraft windows in World War 2. » resin

perspiration » sweat

Perth (Australia) 31°58S 115°49E, pop (1986) 1 025 300. State capital of Western Australia, near the mouth of the Swan R; the commercial, cultural, and transportation centre on the W coast; founded, 1829; city status, 1856; rapid development after the discovery of gold and the opening of Fremantle harbour (1897); fifth largest city in Australia; airport; railway; two universities (1911, 1975); two cathedrals; textiles, clothes, cement, furniture, motor vehicles, gold mining, agricultural trade; Western Australian Museum; Old Court House; the most isolated of Australia's state capitals (Adelaide is 2 250 km/1 400 ml away); scene of the Commonwealth and Empire Games 1962. » Western Australia

Perth (Scotland) 56°24N 3°28W, pop (1981) 43 010. Capital of Perth and Kinross district, Tayside, E Scotland; on R Tay, 50 km/31 ml N of Edinburgh; scene of assassination of James I (1437); railway; whisky, insurance, glass making, printing, agricultural supplies, tourism; Balhousie castle, art gallery and museum, St John's Kirk (15th-c); festival of arts (May); agricultural show (Jun). » Scotland [i]; Tayside

perturbation In astronomy, any small deviation in the equilibrium motion of a celestial object caused by a change in the gravitational field acting on it. Two bodies in mutual orbit trace a perfect ellipse. Any deviations from such a path indicate the presence of further objects. Perturbations in the orbit of Uranus led directly to the discovery of Neptune in 1846. » ellipse; Neptune (astronomy); Uranus (astronomy)

perturbation theory A mathematical technique frequently used to obtain approximate solutions to equations describing physical systems that are too complicated to solve exactly. The problem is rewritten in two portions: one which can be solved exactly, and a smaller part (the *perturbation*) which allows the calculation of corrections to the first answer in terms of a sequence of ever-decreasing terms. The technique is essential in many branches of physics, particularly quantum theory. » equations; Feynman diagrams [i]; physics

pertussis » whooping cough

Peru, official name **Republic of Peru**, Span **República de Peru** pop (1990e) 22 332 000; area 1 284 640 sq km/495 871 sq ml. Republic on the W coast of S America, divided into one province and 24 departments; bordered by Ecuador (N), Colombia (NW), Brazil and Bolivia (W), and Chile (S); capital,

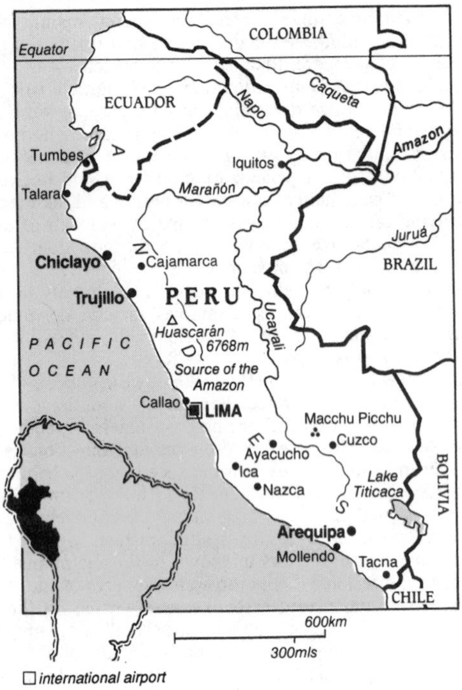

Lima; timezone GMT −5; chief ethnic groups, Indian (45%), mixed Indian and European (37%); official languages, Spanish and Quechua; chief religion, Roman Catholicism; unit of currency, the new sol of 100 centimos.

Physical description and climate. Arid plains and foothills on the coast, with areas of desert and fertile river valleys; C sierra, average altitude 3 000 m/10 000 ft, contains 50% of the population; rivers cut through the plateau, forming deep canyons; forested Andes and Amazon basin (E), with major rivers flowing to the Amazon; mild temperatures all year on coast; dry, arid desert in the S; Andean temperatures never rise above 23°C; large daily range, with night frost in dry season; single rainy season (Nov–Mar); typically wet, tropical climate in Amazon basin, temperatures warm to hot throughout the year.

History and government. Highly developed Inca civilization; arrival of Spanish, 1531; Viceroyalty of Peru established; gold and silver mines made Peru the principal source of Spanish power in S America; independence declared, 1821; frequent border disputes in 19th-c (eg War of the Pacific, 1879–83); clashes between Ecuador and Peru continued in recent decades; several military coups; terrorist activities by Maoist guerrillas; bicameral Congress consists of a 60-member Senate and a 180-member National Chamber of Deputies elected every five years; an elected president appoints a Council of Ministers.

Economy. One of the world's leading producers of silver, zinc, lead, copper, gold, iron ore; 80% of Peru's oil extracted from the Amazon forest; cotton, potatoes, sugar, rice, grapes, fruit, olives; sheep, cattle; steel, iron, vehicles, tyres, cement, wool, fishmeal, fish canning; fishing severely affected by the adverse weather conditions of 1982–3 and by continuous overfishing; tourism, especially to ancient sites. » El Niño; Incas; Lima; RR26 national holidays; RR58 political leaders

Perugia [pay**roo**ja] 43°07N 12°23E, pop (1981) 142 348. Capital town of Perugia province, Umbria, Italy, on a hill c.300 m/1 000 ft above the Tiber valley, 141 km/88 ml N of Rome; founded by Etruscans; taken by Romans, 310 BC; archbishopric; railway; university (1276); agricultural trade, textiles, furniture, chocolate, tourism; Cathedral of San Lorenzo (15th-c), town hall (13th-c), Arco d'Augusto (Etruscan town gate), Church of San Pietro dei Cassiensi; jazz festival (summer); music festival (Sep). » Umbria

Perugino [peroo**jee**noh] ('the Perugian'), byname of **Pietro di Cristofero Vannucci** (c.1450–1523) Italian painter, born at Città della Pieve, Umbria. He established himself in Perugia, and in Florence (1486–99) he had Raphael as a pupil. He painted several frescoes in the Sistine Chapel at Rome, notably 'Christ Giving the Keys to Peter' (1481–2). He died of the plague, near Perugia. » fresco; Italian art; Raphael

Perutz, Max (Ferdinand) (1914–) British scientist, born in Vienna. Educated at Vienna and Cambridge, he worked at the Cavendish Laboratory on the molecular structure of haemoglobin, using the technique of X-ray diffraction. He became director of the Medical Research Council's unit for molecular biology, shared the Nobel Prize for Chemistry in 1962, and was awarded the Order of Merit in 1988. » haemoglobin; X-ray diffraction

Pesach » **Passover**

Peshawar [puh**shah**wa] 34°01N 71°40E, pop (1981) 555 000. Capital of North-West Frontier province, Pakistan; 172 km/107 ml W of Islamabad and 16 km/10 ml E of the Khyber Pass; city of the Pathan people; under Sikh rule, early 19th-c; occupied by the British, 1849; airfield; railway; university (1950); major trade centre on the Afghan frontier; textiles, leather, food processing, copperware; Balahisar fort, Mosque of Mahabat, Qissa Khawani bazaar. » Khyber Pass; Pakistan [i]

Pestalozzi, Johann Heinrich [pesta**lot**see] (1746–1827) Swiss educationalist, a pioneer of mass education for poor children, born in Zürich. He worked as a farmer (1769), then tried to educate waifs and strays in his home (1774). After several failed attempts, he managed to open a school at Berthoud (Burgdorf), where he wrote *Wie Gertrud ihre Kinder lehrt* (1801, How Gertrude Educates her Children), the recognized exposition of the Pestalozzian method, in which the process of education is seen as a gradual unfolding, prompted by observation, of the child's innate faculties. He died at Brugg. *Pestalozzi International Children's Villages* have been established at Trogen, Switzerland (1946) and Sedlescombe, Surrey, UK (1958). » education

pesticide Any chemical substance used to kill insects, rodents, weeds, fungi, or other living things which are harmful to plants, animals, or foodstuffs. » fungicide; herbicide; insecticide

Pétain, (Henri) Philippe [pay**tĩ**] (1856–1951) French soldier and statesman, born at Cauchy-à-la-Tour. During World War 1 he became a national hero for his defence of Verdun (1916), and was made Commander-in-Chief (1917) and Marshal of France (1918). When France collapsed in 1940, he negotiated the armistice with Germany and Italy, and became Chief of State, establishing his government at Vichy. His aim to unite France under the slogan 'Work, Family and Country', and keep it out of the war, involved active collaboration with Germany. After the liberation, he was tried in the French courts, his death sentence for treason being commuted to life imprisonment on the Ile d'Yeu, where he died. His role remains controversial, and some still regard him as a patriot rather than a traitor. » Vichy; World War 2

petal One of the second whorl of flower parts, collectively termed the *corolla*. It is usually large and brightly coloured to attract pollinators, but is sometimes pale, reduced, or absent. » flower [i]

Peter I, byname **the Great** (1672–1725) Tsar of Russia (1682–1721) and Emperor (1721–5), born in Moscow, the son of Tsar Alexey and his second wife, Natalia Naryshkin. He was joint Tsar with his mentally retarded half-brother, Ivan, under the regency of their sister, Sophia (1682–9). On Ivan's death (1696) he became sole Tsar, and embarked on a series of sweeping military, fiscal, administrative, educational, cultural, and ecclesiastical reforms, many of them based on W European models. All classes of society suffered from the impact of the reforms and the brutality of their implementation; his own son, Alexey, died under torture (1718), suspected of leading a conspiracy against his father. Peter fought major wars with the Ottoman Empire, Persia, and in particular Sweden, which Russia defeated in the Great Northern War. This victory established Russia as a major European power, and gained a maritime exit on the Baltic coast, where Peter founded his new capital, St Petersburg. He failed to nominate a successor, and on his death was succeeded by his wife, Catherine. » Great Northern War; Romanovs; Sophia Alexeyevna

Peter, St (1st-c), feast day 29 June. One of the twelve apostles of Jesus, named originally as **Simeon** or **Simon bar Jona** ('son of Jonah'), a fisherman living in Capernaum during the public ministry of Jesus, but renamed by Jesus as **Cephas** or Peter (meaning 'rock') in view of his leadership amongst the disciples. In the Gospels he is often the spokesman for the other disciples, and leader of the inner group which accompanied Jesus at the Transfiguration and Gethsemane. Immediately after Jesus' resurrection and ascension, Peter appears also as the leader of the Christian community in Jerusalem; later he may have engaged in missionary work outside Palestine, certainly visiting Antioch, but little is directly known of these activities. Tradition says that he was executed with his head downward in Rome; his presence in Rome was in fact uncertain, but he is regarded by the Roman Catholic Church as the first Bishop of Rome. Two New Testament letters bear his name, but the authenticity of both is often disputed; other apocryphal writings also exist in his name, such as the Acts of Peter and the Apocalypse of Peter. » Acts of the Apostles; apostle; Jesus Christ; Peter, Letters of

Peter, Letters of New Testament writings attributed to the apostle Peter, although both are widely considered by modern scholars to be pseudonymous. The first letter claims to be written from 'Babylon' (possibly a cipher for Rome) to Christians in Asia Minor, encouraging them to stand fast amidst persecution, and reminding them of their Christian vows and obligations. It has been variously dated between the Neronian persecution of 64 AD and the Domitian persecution c.95 AD. The second, shorter letter yields no direct references to its situation, but appears to oppose teachers who deny the second coming of Christ and espouse gnostic-tending doctrines. It is sometimes dated in the first half of the 2nd-c, and its canonical status was at times disputed in the early Church. » Domitian; Gnosticism; Nero; New Testament; Peter, St

Peter Lombard » Lombard, Peter

Peter the Hermit (c.1050–c.1115) French monk, a preacher of the first Crusade, born at Amiens. He served as a soldier, became a monk, and in 1095 preached throughout Europe, generating enthusiastic support for the Crusade. He led the second army, which reached Asia Minor, but was defeated by the Turks at Nicaea. He then accompanied the fifth army in 1096, which reached Jerusalem. He died near Huy, Flanders. » Crusades [i]; monasticism

Peter and Paul Fortress A stronghold founded in 1703 by Peter the Great on a small island in the Neva R delta, and around which the city of St Petersburg sprang up. The fortress, which was notorious throughout the 19th-c for its political prison, has been a museum since 1922. » Leningrad

Peterloo Massacre (1819) The name given to the forcible break-up of a mass meeting about parliamentary reform held at St Peter's Fields, Manchester. The Manchester Yeomanry charged into the crowd, killing eleven people. The incident strengthened the campaign for reform. 'Peterloo' was a sardonic pun on the Waterloo victory of 1815. » Reform Acts

Peters' map projection An equal area map projection, produced in 1973 by German cartographer and mathematician, Arno Peters (1916–). It shows continents and oceans in proportion to their relative sizes, allowing comparisons to be made. More traditional projections exaggerate the importance of the N hemisphere (eg in maps based on Mercator's Projection, the N hemisphere covers two thirds of the map area and the S hemisphere the remaining third). The Peters' projection avoids the Eurocentric view of the world, and shows the densely populated equatorial regions in correct proportion to each other. » map projection [i]; Mercator's map projection

Petersburg 37°14N 77°24W, pop(1980) 41 055. Independent city, E Virginia, USA, on the Appomattox R; besieged by Union forces in the Civil War (1864–5) until the Confederate army retreated, to surrender at Appomattox; railway; tobacco market, optical equipment, luggage; Center Hill Mansion, Old Blandford Church, Siege Museum, Petersburg National Battlefield Site. » American Civil War; Virginia

Peterson, Oscar (1925–) Canadian jazz pianist, born in Montreal. He could already play the piano when he began formal studies at 6, his extraordinary keyboard facility winning him numerous awards and making him a local celebrity. In 1949 he became an international star when he joined a concert tour called 'Jazz at the Philharmonic' in New York. He travels globally, and has recorded both as soloist and accompanist more than any musician in history. » jazz; piano

Petipa, Marius (1818–1910) French dancer, ballet master, and choreographer, born in Marseilles. After touring France, Spain, and the USA as a dancer, he went to St Petersburg in 1847 to join the Imperial Ballet. He became ballet master in 1869, and between then and his retirement (1903) he created 46 original ballets, the most famous being Tchaikovsky's *The Sleeping Beauty* (1890) and *Swan Lake* (1895). He died at Gurzuf, Russia. » ballet

Petit, Roland [puh**tee**] (1924–) French choreographer and dancer, born in Paris. He trained at the Paris Opéra Ballet, and became its leading dancer in 1943. In 1948 he founded Ballets de Paris de Roland Petit, which toured widely in Europe and the USA. He created a repertory of new ballet, and was also responsible for the ballet sequences in the film *Hans Christian Andersen* (1952), danced by his wife, **Zizi Jeanmaire**. In 1972 he founded the Ballet de Marseille, and is its director. » ballet

petit mal [petee **mal**] **» epilepsy**

petit pois [petee **pwah**] **» pea** [i]

petition of right » Crown Proceedings Act

Petöfi, Sándor [**pe**terfee] (1823–49) Hungarian poet, born at Kiskörös. He was successively actor, soldier, and literary hack, but by 1844 had secured his fame as a poet, his most popular work being *János vitéz* (1845, Janos the Hero). In 1848 he threw himself into the revolutionary cause, writing numerous war songs, and fell in battle at Segesvár. » poetry; Revolutions of 1848

Petra [**pee**tra], Arabic **Wadi Musa** 30°20N 35°26E. Ancient rock-cut city in Maan governorate, East Bank, SW Jordan; capital of the Nabataean Arabs until their conquest by Rome in the early 2nd-c AD; wealthy commercial city for several centuries, controlling the international spice trade; approached only via a series of narrow ravines; numerous temples, tombs, houses, shrines, altars, and a great theatre carved out of red sandstone cliffs; a world heritage site. » Jordan [i]; Palmyra (Roman history)

Petrarch, in full **Francesco Petrarca** (1304–74) Italian poet and scholar, born at Arezzo. He studied at Bologna and Avignon, where he became a churchman. In 1327 at Avignon he first saw Laura (possibly Laure de Noves, married in 1325 to Hugo de Sade) who inspired him with a passion which has become proverbial for its constancy and purity. As the fame of his learning grew, royal courts competed for his presence, and in 1341 at Rome he was crowned poet laureate. The earliest of the great Renaissance humanists, he wrote widely on the classics, but he is best known for the series of love poems addressed to Laura, the *Canzoniere*. He left Avignon in 1353 after Laura's death, and lived the rest of his life in N Italy, dying at Arquà near Padua. His writing proved to be a major influence on many authors, notably Chaucer. » Chaucer; humanism; Italian literature; poetry; Renaissance

petrel A sea-bird of the order *Procellariiformes* (**tubenoses**): small species called *petrels*; larger species called *albatrosses*. They include fulmars, prions, shearwaters, gadfly petrels (all from the family *Procellariidae*), storm petrels (*Hydrobatidae*), and diving petrels (*Pelecanoididae*). Their body contains much fat; sailors used to push a wick through the bird and use it as a candle. » albatross; fulmar; muttonbird; prion; shearwater; storm petrel; tubenose

Petrie, Sir (William Matthew) Flinders (1853–1942) British archaeologist and Egyptologist, born at Charlton, Kent. He surveyed Stonehenge (1874–7), but turned from 1881 entirely to Egyptology, beginning by surveying the pyramids and temples of Giza, and excavating the mounds of Tanis and Naucratis. The author of more than 100 books, he became professor of archaeology at London (1892–1933), continuing excavations in Egypt and Palestine until well into his 80s. He died in Jerusalem. » archaeology; pyramid

petrified forest The results of a fossilizing process in which wood is gradually replaced by silica, commonly chalcedony or opal, by the infiltration of mineral-rich water. The fine structural detail may be perfectly preserved during the process, as in the Petrified Forest National Park in Arizona, USA (area 377 sq km/145 sq ml, established 1962). » silica

petrochemicals Organic chemicals made from products of the petroleum industry or from natural gas. It is possible to make them all from other source materials, but the petroleum source is cheap and plentiful, and simple chemical reactions on distillates provide materials for conversion to plastics, fibres, detergents, etc. Many important solvents are the direct products of distillation. » natural gas; petroleum

petrocurrency or **petro-dollar** A currency surplus available in oil-producing countries on their balance of payments, which is surplus to their own requirements; sometimes termed 'footloose' money. The term came to prominence after the 1973 oil crisis. The currency is available for investment elsewhere, mainly in the USA and W Europe. Funds are usually held in US dollars, pounds sterling, or West German deutschmarks. » currency; dollar

petrogenesis » **petrology**

petrography » **petrology**

petrol (UK) or **gasoline (US)** A liquid fuel for use in those internal combustion engines in which the fuel-air mixture is ignited by a spark. It consists of a mixture of many volatile hydrocarbons derived from the distillation and cracking of petroleum. It normally contains additives such as lead compounds to improve performance (the prevention of premature ignition) or rust inhibitors. In the 1980s, environmental concern led to a rapid increase in the use of unleaded petrol. » catalytic converter; diesel engine; internal combustion engine; petroleum

petroleum Crude oil, probably of biological origin, occurring as accumulations under impervious rock. Normally liquid, it ranges from being light and mobile to very viscous, and is often associated with gas or water. Its main constituents are a variety of hydrocarbons, but there may also be sulphur, nitrogen, or oxygen compounds. It is found chiefly in the USA, several republics of the former USSR, Middle East, Venezuela, North Africa, and the North Sea. » hydrocarbons; oil

petrology The study of rocks: their composition, mineralogy, mode of occurrence, and origin. The subdisciplines include *sedimentary*, *igneous* and *metamorphic* petrology. **Petrography** is concerned with the textural and mineralogical description of rocks, often studied by optical microscopy of thin slices, while **petrogenesis** is concerned with their origin. » rock

Petronius Arbiter (1st-c AD) Latin writer, supposed to be the Gaius Petronius whom Tacitus calls *arbiter elegantiae* ('arbiter of taste') at the court of Nero. He is generally believed to be the author of *Satyricon*, a satirical romance in prose and verse about the licentious life of the upper class in S Italy, fragments of which have been preserved. Accused of conspiring against Nero, he committed suicide. » Nero; Latin literature; satire

Petrov affair The defection by Soviet embassy third secretary, Vladimir M Petrov, in Canberra in April 1954; he was granted political asylum by the Australian government. The Soviet government tried to fly Petrov's wife back to Moscow, but the aircraft was intercepted at Darwin, and she too was granted asylum. Later the Petrovs revealed they had been spying in Australia, and in one of their documents they implicated two members of the staff of Dr H V Evatt, the Federal leader of the Labor opposition. Evatt defended his staff before a Royal Commission (1954–5), but it refused to clear them. The affair helped to split the Labor Party and kept it from winning national government for nearly 20 years. » Australian Labor Party

petunia A bushy, free-flowering annual, native to S America, with large, funnel-shaped flowers. It is a relative of the potato, and a popular garden plant grown for its brightly coloured, often striped flowers. (*Petunia hybrida*. Family: *Solanaceae*.) » annual; potato

Peul » **Fulani**

Pevsner, Antoine (1886–1962) Franco-Russian sculptor, born at Oryol, Russia. In Moscow he helped to form the Suprematist group, but in 1920 broke away to issue the *Realist Manifesto* with his brother, Naum Gabo. Exiled from Russia, he migrated to Paris. Several of his completely nonfigurative constructions (mainly in copper and bronze) are in the Museum of Modern Art, New York. He died in Paris. » Constructivism; Gabo; Suprematism

Pevsner, Sir Nikolaus (Bernhard Leon) (1902–83) German art historian, born in Leipzig. He lost his post at Göttingen on the advent of Hitler, and went to Britain, where he became an authority on (especially English) architecture, and professor of fine art at Cambridge (1949–55). His best-known works are *An Outline of European Architecture* (1942), and the 50-volume Penguin series, *The Buildings of England* (1951–74). He was knighted in 1969, and died in London.

pewit » **peewit**

pewter A grey alloy consisting mainly of tin with other constituents. Lead was formerly used, to increase hardness, but because of its toxicity this has now been replaced by antimony. Pewter is traditionally used in candlesticks, drinking vessels, and other utensils. » alloy; antimony; lead; tin

peyote or **peyot** [pay**oh**tee] A small cactus native to Mexico and Texas; stem globular, bluish, with tufts of hairs but no spines; also called **mescal button**. It was used by American Indians to produce a drug containing the hallucinogen *mescalin*, used in religious rites. (*Lophophora williamsii*. Family: *Cactaceae*.) » cactus [i]; hallucinogens

pH A measure of the acidity of a solution; it is approximately the negative of the common logarithm of the concentration of hydrogen ions in a solution. For water, the product of the concentrations of hydrogen and hydroxide ions is about 10^{-14} at normal temperatures, so the pH of an aqueous solution must be between -1 (10 molar strong acid) and 15 (10 molar strong base). A neutral solution has pH = 7. » acid; base (chemistry); buffer; litmus

Phaedra [**fee**dra] In Greek legend, the daughter of Minos and the second wife of Theseus. While he was away she fell in love with her step-son Hippolytus. He rejected her, so she accused him of trying to rape her. Theseus called on Poseidon to punish him with death, after which Phaedra hung herself in remorse. » Hippolytus; Theseus

Phaedrus or **Phaeder** (1st-c AD) The translator of Aesop's fables into Latin verse, born a slave in Macedonia. He went to Italy, where he was the freedman of Emperor Augustus, and published five books of fables, many his own invention, which were still widely read in mediaeval Europe. » Aesop; Latin literature

Phaeophyceae [feeoh**fi**ysee-ee] The class of seaweeds comprising the brown algae; also known as the **Phaeophyta**. » brown algae; seaweed

Phaethon [**fay**ithohn] or **Phaeton** [**fay**iton, **fay**ton] In Greek mythology, the son of Helios the Sun-god and Clymene. He found his way to his father's palace and asked to drive the chariot of the Sun. He swung it too near the Earth, and so Zeus destroyed him with a thunderbolt. He fell into the R Eridanos.

phagocyte [**fag**uhsiyt] Any cell which engulfs and usually digests particles, micro-organisms (bacteria), or harmful cells. Many unicellular animals are phagocytic. In most multicellular animals, phagocytes fulfil a protective and cleansing role. In humans and other mammals, they occur in the blood (neutrophils, basophils, and monocytes), connective tissue, and the reticulo-endothelial system (tissue macrophages). » bacteria [i]; epithelium

phalanger [fa**lan**juh] An Australasian nocturnal marsupial; thick fur, small ears, large forward-facing eyes, long grasping tail (often naked at tip); inhabits trees; eats mainly plant material; also known as **cuscus**. (Genus: *Phalanger*, 10 species. Family: *Phalangeridae*.) » flying phalanger; marsupial [i]

Phalaris (?–c.554 BC) Greek tyrant of Acragas (modern Agrigento) in Sicily, notorious for his cruelty. On his overthrow, he suffered the same fate as his former victims: he was roasted alive in a brazen bull. » Greek history

phalarope [**fal**uhrohp] A sandpiper of the genus *Phalaropus* (3 species), widespread; breeds in N hemisphere, winters in S tropics; adapted for swimming; inhabits shallow water. The larger female is more colourful than the male, and takes several mates. » sandpiper

Phanerozoic time [fanuhruhz**oh**ik] A geological term used to describe the period of c.590 million years from the end of the Precambrian era to the present. Phanerozoic rocks were once thought to be the only ones which contain fossils. » geological time scale; Precambrian era; RR16

Phar Lap New Zealand chestnut gelding which became Australia's most famous racing horse in the late 1920s and early 1930s. He won 37 of his 51 races in this period, but his greatest win was the 1930 Melbourne Cup. Taken to N America, he won a major race in Mexico but died several weeks later in San Francisco, probably from eating highly fermentable green pasture and not, as widely believed, from poisoning by US gangsters. The autopsy showed his heart was twice normal size. » horse racing

pharaoh The title applied to the god-kings of ancient Egypt from the New Kingdom (c.1500 BC) onwards. Pharaohs were the chief mediators between their mortal subjects and the gods, and after death were believed to become gods themselves, as their mummified forms show; all have the attributes of the god Osiris – plaited beard, crook, and flail. Best-known of the New Kingdom pharaohs are Tutankhamun (c.1352 BC), Rameses II (the pharaoh of the Exodus), and Rameses III (the conqueror of the Sea Peoples). » Abu Simbel; Egyptian history, Ancient [i]; Sea Peoples

Pharaoh hound A medium-sized breed of dog, developed in Egypt; similar in stature to the greyhound, but with ears large, broad, pointed, and held erect; coat short, reddish-brown or white with grey or reddish patches. » dog; greyhound

Pharaoh's rat » **ichneumon** (mammal)

Pharisees [f**a**riseez] An influential minority group within Palestinian Judaism before 70 AD, mainly consisting of laymen; possibly originating out of the Hasidim who opposed the political aspirations of John Hyrcanus I (c.2nd-c BC). They were noted for their separation from the common people, and for their punctilious observance of written and oral laws regarding ritual purity, cleansings, and food laws, assuming even the obligations placed upon priests. In the New Testament Gospels, they are often portrayed as the opponents of Jesus. After the fall of Jerusalem in 70, it was from Pharisaic circles that the rabbinic movement arose. » Hasidim; Hyrcanus I, John; Jesus Christ; Judaism; rabbi; Sadducees

pharmacology A branch of medical science which studies the actions, uses, and undesirable side-effects of drugs. The first descriptions of remedies from plant sources were made by the ancient Greeks: Dioscorides' *De Materia Medica* (c.AD 60) was the first basic pharmacopoeia. The subject became a scientific discipline in the 19th-c, when pioneers began to study more precisely the physiological actions of purified drugs. Magendie performed one of the first experimental analyses of the actions of a pure drug (strychnine), and described the actions and uses of various others in his *Formulaire* (1821). Building on this approach, German scientists developed the subject in both the commercial and academic worlds from the late 19th-c. Oswald Schmeideberg (1838–1921) researched the actions of digitalis and muscarine; Hans Horst Meyer (1853–1939) the mechanism of action of anesthetics. Paul Ehrlich (1854–1915) contributed to the modern theory of drug action by defining the interactions between drugs and their target tissues as being the same as those involved in conventional chemical bonds. John J Abel (1857–1938) returned to the USA after studying in Germany, and was a major influence on the development of the subject there. Pharmacological research is carried out in drug companies, universities, and research institutes, and has led to the development of over 200 essential drugs, as defined by the World Health Organization. In recent years, specialized branches have developed, such as molecular pharmacology, immunopharmacology, and neuropharmacology, which cross the boundaries of other biological disciplines. » Ehrlich; Magendie; pharmacopoeia; toxicology

pharmacopoeia [fahmakuhp**ee**a] A book of standards for drugs, advising on identity, purity, and identification. In most countries there is an official pharmacopoeia, and any dispensed drug must comply with its standards. » pharmacology

pharmacy Originally the science of preparing, compounding, and dispensing medicines. Since more potent drugs have become available (mid-1940s), the scope of pharmacy has become increasingly concerned with more clinical functions, such as the checking of doses and drug interactions. » apothecary; patent medicine; pharmacology; prescription

Pharos of Alexandria A marble watch tower and lighthouse on the island of Pharos in the harbour of Alexandria, built by Ptolemy II (285–246 BC). It was the first of its kind. » Seven Wonders of the Ancient World

pharyngeal tonsils » **adenoids**

pharyngitis A sore throat; one of the commonest medical complaints, usually the result of bacterial or viral infection of the lining tissues of the pharynx. » pharynx

pharynx A space consisting of membrane-covered muscle situated behind and communicating with the nose, mouth, and larynx. It extends from the base of the skull, and is continuous with the oesophagus below. The nasal part of the pharynx receives the opening of the Eustachian tube. In the oral part, the digestive and respiratory tracts cross, and during swallowing, respiration is temporarily suspended. In the lower part, the narrow slits on either side of the larynx (the *piriform fossae*) are the regions where sharp objects (eg large fish bones) may become lodged if swallowed. The upper areas contain accumulations of lymphoid tissue (the tonsils) which, it is thought, help to guard against airborn infection. » adenoids; Eustachian tube; larynx; lymphoid tissue; pharyngitis; respiration

phase **1** In wave motion, the fraction of a wave cycle completed by a time variable, where one complete cycle corresponds to 2π radians; alternatively, an argument of a function describing a wave. The phase difference, ϕ radians, represents the degree to which one wave leads or lags behind another; for $\phi = 0$ or 2π, the waves are in phase; for $\phi = \pi$, the waves are antiphase. **Phase shift** refers to a change in phase, eg by π radians for light waves reflected by a mirror. Two waves having a constant phase difference are called *coherent*. » coherence; wave (physics) [i] **2** In circuit theory, current and potential difference may be out-of-phase. If these are changing in time in a periodic way, then the maximums in current flowing through components such as inductors and capacitors will occur at different times from maximums in potential difference across these components. There will be a phase difference between the two. » current; potential difference **3** In relation to matter, the different states: solid, liquid, and gas. » phases of matter [i]

phase transition » **phases of matter** [i]

phases of matter The three possible states of matter: solid, liquid, and gas. The phase of a particular substance depends on temperature and pressure. A change from one phase to

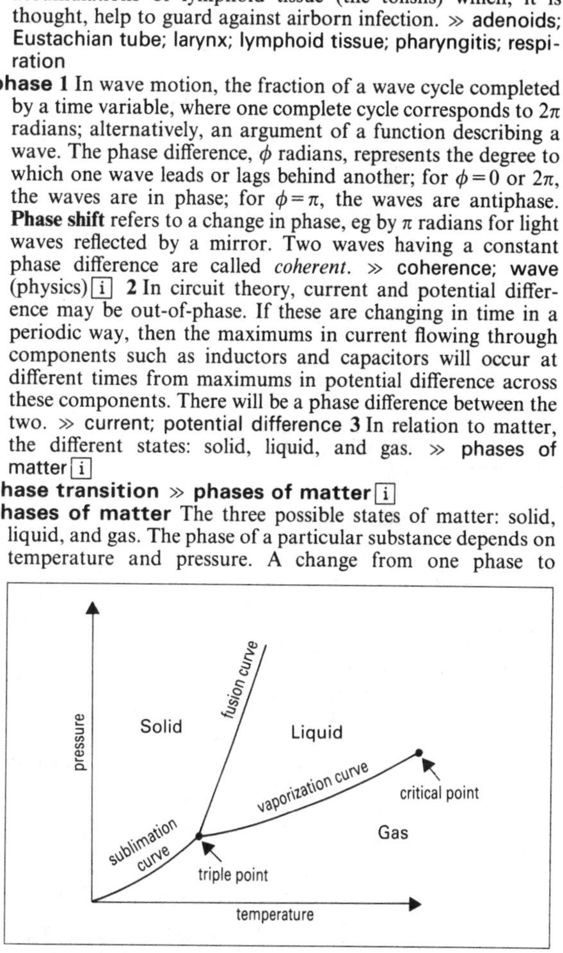

A typical phase diagram showing the phases of a substance for various temperatures and pressures. A substance melts from solid to liquid, for example, at temperatures and pressures defined by the fusion curve. The triple point *is the only temperature and pressure where all three phases coexist. Liquid and gas phases are distinct only for temperatures and pressures less than the critical point; at temperatures higher than this critical temperature, gas cannot be liquified.*

another, as in boiling or melting, is called a **phase transition.** » critical phenomena; gas 1; liquid; solid

Phasmida [fazmida] An order of large insects with either elongate bodies and limbs (stick insects) or flattened, leaf-like bodies and limbs (leaf insects); length up to 300 mm/1 ft; c.2 500 species, all of which are foliage feeders, mostly tropical or subtropical in distribution. » insect[i]

phatic communion A use of language which is not intended for giving or getting information, but for setting up social relationships, or being polite. It includes many formulae for greeting and leave-taking, as well as dance-hall routines (*Do you come here often?*) and conversations about the weather.

pheasant A large, plump, ground-feeding bird, native to Africa (1 species) and Asia, and introduced elsewhere; short wings and fast, low flight; male brightly-coloured with long tail; inhabits woodland or scrub; eats plant material and insects; many species bred and hunted for sport. (Family: *Phasianidae*, 48 species.) » francolin; jungle fowl[i]; partridge; peacock; quail; tragopan

phenanthrene [fenanthreen] $C_{14}H_{10}$, melting point 101°C. A crystalline solid, an aromatic hydrocarbon containing three fused benzene rings. It occurs in coal tar, and it and its

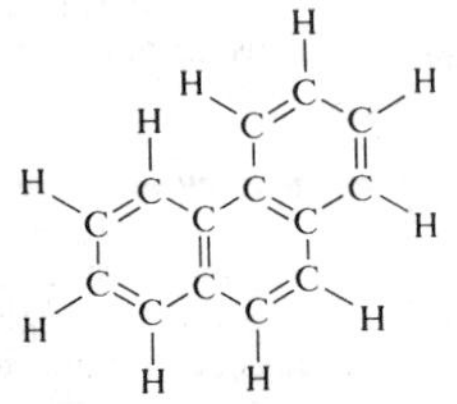

derivatives are suspected of being carcinogenic. The bond pictured uppermost in the illustration is easily broken, yielding derivatives of diphenyl (C_6H_5–C_6H_5). » aromatic compound; hydrocarbons

phencyclidine » **angel dust**

phenobarbitone » **barbiturates**

phenol [feenol, fenohl] C_6H_5OH, IUPAC **hydroxybenzene**, also called **carbolic acid**, used as an antiseptic where its corrosive properties are not a problem. A major constituent of coal tar, it is also synthesized in large quantities, as it has applications in the manufacture of fibres, resins, dyes, drugs, and explosives. » corrosion; IUPAC

phenology [finoluhjee] The branch of biology which studies the timing of natural phenomena. Examples include seasonal variations in vegetation, and their relationship with weather and climate. » biology; photoperiodism

phenomenalism A philosophical doctrine, elements of which can be found in Berkeley and Hume, which maintains that physical objects are just collections of sense data lodged in individual minds. Since it implies that objects cease to exist when unperceived, some phenomenalists, such as A J Ayer, have recast the doctrine so that propositions about objects can be translated into propositions about actual or hypothetical experiences. » Ayer; Berkeley, George; Hume, David

phenomenology A philosophical movement begun by Husserl, and furthered by Max Scheler (1874–1928), Heidegger, Sartre, and Maurice Merleau-Ponty (1908–61). Its method is to describe carefully the processes involved in perceiving, thinking, and acting, suspending from this description all assumptions about existence and causation; the result is supposed to be non-empirical, intuitive knowledge of the essences of things. » Heidegger; Husserl; Sartre

phenothiazines [feenohthiyazeenz] A class of drugs introduced in the 1950s and used in the treatment of psychiatric disorders such as schizophrenia and mania. Chlorpromazine (Largactil) was the first example. » psychiatry; schizophrenia

phenotype » **genotype**

phenyl [feeniyl, fenil] C_6H_5–. A group derived by the removal of one hydrogen atom from a benzene ring. » benzene[i]; ring

phenylamine » **aniline**

phenylketonuria [fenilkeetuhnyooria] A genetically determined defect in the metabolism of phenylalanine (an amino acid contained in protein). Phenylalanine accumulates in the body, and may cause mental deficiency. It can be detected in infancy by a screening test applied to urine. » amino acid[i]

phenylmethanal » **benzaldehyde**

phenylmethyl » **benzyl**

pheromone [feruhmohn] A chemical substance secreted to the outside by an animal, which has a specific effect on another member of the same species. **Releasing** pheromones elicit a particular behavioural response, such as mating or aggression. **Priming** pheromones cause a change in the physiology of the recipient, such as an effect on reproductive hormones. Pheromones are common in insects; they are also found in rodents and monkeys, and more may be discovered. They are exploited in agriculture to control the time and frequency of mating in farm animals, and the movement of insects. » hormones; physiology

Phi Beta Kappa » **fraternity and sorority**

Phidias [fiydias] (5th-c BC) The greatest sculptor of Greece, born in Athens. He received from Pericles a commission to execute the chief statues for the city, and became superintendent of all public works. He constructed the Propylaea and the Parthenon, carving the gold and ivory Athena there and the Zeus at Olympia. Charged by his enemies with appropriating gold from the statue, he disappeared from Athens, presumably into exile. » Greek art; Parthenon; sculpture

Philadelphia 39°57N 75°10W, pop (1980) 1 688 210. Major deep-water port in Philadelphia County, SE Pennsylvania, USA, at the confluence of the Schuylkill and Delaware Rivers; noted centre for culture, education, and medical research; fourth largest city in the USA; first settled by Swedes in the 1640s; British settlement organized by William Penn in 1681, and the town laid out in 1682; many Scottish and Irish immigrants settled in the 18th-c; birthplace of the nation, where the Declaration of Independence signed, 1776; Constitutional Convention met here and adopted the Constitution of the United States, 1787; US capital, 1790–1800; heavily involved in the anti-slavery movement and the Civil War; site of Centennial Exposition, 1876; airport; railway; four universities (1740, 1851, 1884, 1891); financial centre; textiles, machinery and electronic equipment, chemicals, printing and publishing; service economy supplanting the dwindling manufacturing industry; naval dockyard; major league teams, Phillies (baseball), 76ers (basketball), Eagles (football), Flyers (ice hockey); Liberty Bell (Independence Hall), Pennsylvania Academy of the Fine Arts (oldest art museum in USA), Museum of Art, Franklin Institute Science Museum and Planetarium, Independence National Historical Park. » American Revolution; Independence Hall; Penn; Pennsylvania

philadelphus [filadelfuhs] » **mock orange**

philately The collecting of stamps, one of the world's most popular hobbies, particularly with schoolboys. The biggest collection in the world can be found in the British Museum. Stamps issued and stamped by the post office on their first day of issue (*first-day covers*) are increasingly popular. The first stamp-collector is thought to have been John Tomlynson, who started collecting stamps on 7 May 1840, the day after the issue of the world's first postage stamp, the penny black.

Philby, Kim, byname of **Harold Adrian Russell Philby** (1912–88) British double agent, born in Ambala, India. He was educated at Westminster and Cambridge, where, like Burgess, Maclean, and Blunt, he became a communist. Already recruited as a Soviet agent, he was employed by the British Secret Intelligence Service (MI6), from 1944–6 as head of anti-communist counter-espionage. He was First Secretary of the British embassy in Washington, working in liasion with the CIA (1949–51), and from 1956 worked in Beirut as a journalist. In 1963 he disappeared to Russia, where he was granted citizenship. » Blunt; Burgess, Guy; communism; Maclean, Donald

Philemon and Baucis [fileemuhn, bawsis] An old couple, man and wife, who were the only ones to entertain the Greek gods Zeus and Hermes when they visited the Earth to test people's hospitality. In return they were saved from a flood, made priest and priestess, and allowed to die at the same time, when they were changed into trees. » Hermes (mythology); Zeus

Philemon, Letter to [fiyleemuhn] The shortest of Paul's letters, usually accepted as genuinely from the apostle to an individual

Christian named Philemon, whose runaway slave Onesimus had been converted by Paul in prison. Paul asks Philemon to forgive and receive Onesimus as a fellow Christian, and not to seek punishment under Roman law. It dates perhaps from the late 50s to the early 60s. » New Testament; Paul, St; Pauline Letters

Philip II (of France) (1165–1223) King of France (1179–1223), born in Paris, the son of Louis VII. His reign formed a key period in the development of the mediaeval kingdom of France. He embarked on the Third Crusade in 1190, but returned the following year to concentrate on attacking the continental lands of the Angevin kings of England. When he died at Mantes, near Paris, Capetian power was firmly established over most of France. » Angevins; Capetians; Crusades [i]; John

Philip II (of Macedon) (382–336 BC) King of Macedon (359–336 BC), the father of Alexander the Great. He used his military and diplomatic skills first to create a powerful unified state at home (359–353 BC), then to make himself the master of the whole of independent Greece. His decisive victory at Chaeronea (338 BC) established Macedonian hegemony there for good. The planned Macedonian conquest of Persia, aborted by his assassination in 336 BC, was eventually carried out by his son. » Aeschines; Alexander the Great; Demosthenes; Greek history; Macedon

Philip II (of Spain) (1527–98) King of Spain (1556–98) and Portugal (as Philip I, 1580–98), born at Valladolid, the only son of Emperor Charles V and Isabella of Portugal. Following the death of his first wife, Maria of Portugal, at the birth of their son, Don Carlos (1545), he married Mary I (1554), becoming joint sovereign of England. Before Mary's death (1558) he had inherited the Habsburg possessions in Italy, the Netherlands, Spain, and the New World. To seal the end of Valois-Habsburg conflict, he married Elizabeth of France (1559), who bore him two daughters. His brief fourth marriage to his cousin, Anna of Austria (1570) produced another son, the future Philip III. As the champion of the Counter-Reformation, he tried to destroy infidels and heretics alike. He sought to crush Protestantism, first in the Low Countries (from 1568), then in England and France. The destruction of the Armada (1588) and the continuing revolt of the Netherlands, along with domestic economic problems and internal unrest, suggest a reign marked by failure. However, among his political achievements were the curbing of Ottoman seapower after the Battle of Lepanto (1571) and the conquest of Portugal (1580). He died at his monastic palace of El Escorial. » Alva; Counter-Reformation; Habsburgs; Lepanto, Battle of; Mary I; Revolt of the Netherlands; Spain [i]; Spanish Armada; Valois

Philip V (1683–1746) First Bourbon King of Spain (1700–46), born at Versailles, the grandson of Louis XIV and Maria Theresa, and great-grandson of Philip IV of Spain. After a long struggle with the rival Habsburg candidate of the Spanish succession, he gained the throne at the Peace of Utrecht (1713), but lost the Spanish Netherlands and Italian lands. Twice married, he fell under the influence of his second wife, Elizabeth Farnese of Parma, whose desire to secure Italian possessions for her sons brought Spain into conflict with Austria, Great Britain, France, and the United Provinces. He died in Madrid. » Bourbons; Habsburgs

Philip VI (1293–1350) First Valois King of France (1328–50), the nephew of Philip IV, who became King on the death of Charles IV. His right was denied by Edward III of England, son of the daughter of Philip IV, who declared that females, though excluded by the Salic law, could transmit their rights to their children. The Hundred Years' War with England thus began (1337), and in 1346 Edward III landed in Normandy, defeating Philip at Crécy, just as the Black Death was about to spread through France. He died near Paris. » Black Death; Edward III; Hundred Years' War; Valois

Philip, Prince » **Edinburgh, Duke of**

Philip, St (1st-c), feast day 1 May (W) or 14 November (E). One of the disciples of Jesus, listed among the twelve in *Mark* 3.14 and *Acts* 1, but especially prominent in John's Gospel, where he is said to come from Bethsaida in Galilee, leads Nathanael to Jesus (1.43), is present at the feeding of the 5000 (6.1) and brings 'the Greeks' to Jesus (12.21). His later career is unknown, but traditions suggest he was martyred on a cross. He is probably not to be confused with Philip 'the Evangelist' (*Acts* 6.5). » apostle; Jesus Christ; John, Gospel according to

Philip the Good (1396–1467) Duke of Burgundy (1419–67), born at Dijon, the grandson of Philip the Bold. He at first recognized Henry V of England as heir to the French crown, but concluded a separate peace with the French in 1435. Philip created one of the most powerful states in later mediaeval Europe. A committed crusader, he maintained a fleet for operations against the Ottoman Turks. He died at Bruges. » Crusades [i]; Henry V; Hundred Years' War

Philippi, Battle of [filipiy] (42 BC) The decisive battle in N Greece in which Antony and Octavian (later the emperor Augustus) defeated Brutus and Cassius, and thus avenged the murder of Julius Caesar. » Antonius, Marcus

Philippians, Letter to the [filipianz] New Testament writing, widely accepted as genuinely from the apostle Paul to a Christian community that he had founded earlier at Philippi in Macedonia, although the unity of the work has been debated. Writing while imprisoned (mid-50s AD?), Paul thanks them for a gift sent to him, appraises them of his situation and difficulties, warns them of sectarian teaching, but generally displays a warm regard for their commitment. » New Testament; Paul, St; Pauline Letters

philippic A denunciation in speech or writing, direct and often abusive. The term derives from Demosthenes' orations (c.350 BC) attacking Philip of Macedon. Cicero's *In Verrem* (70 BC), Swift's *Drapier's Letters* (1724), and the *Letters* of Junius (1769–72) are notable examples. » Demosthenes; literature; panegyric; rhetoric

Philippines [filuhpeenz], official name **Republic of the Philippines**, Span **Republica de Filipinas** pop (1990e) 61 480 000; area 299 679 sq km/115 676 sq ml. Republic consisting of an archipelago of more than 7 100 islands and islets, NE of Borneo and S of Taiwan; divided into 72 provinces; major islands, Luzon, Mindanao, Samar, Palawan, Mindoro, Panay, Negros, Cebu, Leyte, Masbate, Bohol; separated from Borneo by the Sulu Sea; bounded E by the Philippine Sea and W by the South China and Luzon Seas; capital, Manila; chief cities,

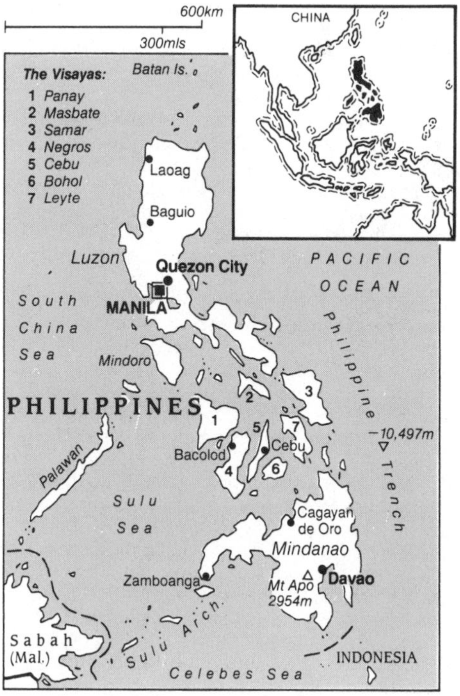

□ international airport

Quezon City, Basilan, Cebu, Bacolod, Davao, Iloilo; timezone GMT +8; chief ethnic group, Filipino, with several minorities; official language, Pilipino, with English and many local languages also spoken; chief religion, Roman Catholicism; unit of currency, the peso of 100 centavos; largely mountainous, with N–S ridges rising to over 2 500 m/8 000 ft; narrow coastal margins and broad interior plateaux; forests cover half the land area; some islands ringed by coral reefs; lowlands have a warm and humid tropical climate throughout the year, average 27°C; average rainfall at Manila, 2 080 mm/82 in; affected by cyclonic storms; claimed for Spain by Magellan, 1521; ceded to the USA after the Spanish–American War, 1898; became a self-governing Commonwealth, 1935; occupied by the Japanese in World War 2; independence, 1946; communist guerrilla activity in N; Muslim separatist movement in S; martial law following political unrest, 1972–81; exiled political leader Benigno Aquino assassinated on returning to Manila in 1983; coup in 1985 ended the 20-year rule of President Ferdinand Marcos; new constitution, 1987; attempted coup, 1989, with continuing political unrest; governed by a president and a bicameral legislature, the Congress, comprising a Senate of 24 members elected for five years, and a House of Representatives with up to 250 members serving for three years; farming employs nearly half the workforce; rice, maize, pineapples, mangos, vegetables, livestock, sugar, tobacco, rubber, coffee, abaca, coconuts; lumber, veneer, plywood; oil, copper, lead, iron, nickel, chromite, gold; textiles, oil products, food processing, electronics, vehicles, fishing, tourism. » Aquino; Luzon; Magellan; Manila; Marcos; Mindanao; Mindoro; Palawan; Spanish–American War; Visayan Islands; RR26 national holidays; RR59 political leaders

Philistines The ancient warlike inhabitants of the coastal area of the SE Mediterranean between present-day Jaffa and Egypt. They were constantly at odds with the Israelites of the hinterland – a struggle epitomized by the stories of Samson and of David and Goliath. » David; Israel, tribes of [i]; Samson

Phillips, Mark » Anne, Princess

Phillips' curve In economics, the shape of a curve in a diagram which shows the relationship between inflation and levels of unemployment. It derives from the work of British economist A W Phillips (1914–75) in the early 1960s. » inflation

Philo Judaeus [**fiy**loh joo**day**uhs] (c.20 BC–c.AD 40) Hellenistic Jewish philosopher, born and died in Alexandria. His work brought together Greek philosophy and the Hebrew scriptures. His commentaries on the Pentateuch interpret it according to the philosophical ideas of Plato and Aristotle; their doctrines in turn were modified by him in the light of scripture. When over 50, he formed part of a deputation to Emperor Caligula in support of Jewish rights. » Judaism; Old Testament

Philoctetes [filok**tee**teez] A Greek hero, the son of Poeas, who inherited the bow of Heracles and its poisoned arrows. On the way to Troy he was bitten by a snake, and the wound stank, so that he was left behind on the island of Lemnos. It was prophesied that only with the arrows of Heracles could Troy be taken, so Diomedes and Odysseus came to find Philoctetes. His wound was healed and he entered the battle, killing Paris. » Heracles; Trojan War

philodendron [filuh**den**druhn] An evergreen shrub, climber, or epiphyte with both clinging and aerial roots, native to warm regions of the New World; leaves varying with species, age, and position on plant, lance- to spear- or heart-shaped, sometimes deeply lobed; flowers tiny, grouped in a spadix surrounded by a large, showy spathe. Many are popular house plants. (Genus: *Philodendron*, 275 species. Family: *Araceae*.) » climbing plant; epiphyte; evergreen plants; shrub; spadix; spathe

Philomela and Procne [filuh**mee**la, **prok**nee] or **Philomel, Progne** In Greek mythology, the daughters of Pandion, King of Athens. Procne married Tereus, King of Thrace, who raped Philomela and removed her tongue; but she was able to tell Procne by a message in her embroidery. So Procne served up her son Itys, or Itylos, in a meal to his father. While pursuing the sisters, the gods changed Tereus into the hoopoe, Philomela into the swallow, and Procne into the nightingale. In Latin authors, the birds of the sisters are reversed.

Philosophes [filo**zof**] The leaders of the French Enlightenment – political commentators, writers, and propagandists – who were critical of the *ancien régime* and advocates of rational criteria. Their great collective work was the *Encyclopédie*. » Alembert; *ancien régime*; Diderot; Encyclopaedists; Enlightenment; Montesquieu; Voltaire

philosophy Literally the love of wisdom, philosophy deals with some of the most general questions about the universe and our place in it. Is the world entirely physical in its composition and processes? Is there any purpose to it? Can we know anything for certain? Are we free? Are there any absolute values? Philosophy differs from science, in that its questions cannot be answered empirically or by experiment; and from religion, in that its purpose is entirely intellectual, and allows no role for faith or revelation. Philosophy tends to proceed by an informal but rigorous process of conceptual analysis and argument. Philosophers have also questioned the nature of their own enterprise: what philosophy is or should be is itself a philosophical issue.

The major branches of philosophy are *metaphysics*, the inquiry into the most general features, relations, and processes of reality; *epistemology*, the investigation of the possibility, types, and sources of knowledge; *ethics*, the study of the types, sources, and justification of moral values and principles; and *logic*, the analysis of correct and incorrect reasoning. Philosophical issues can arise concerning other areas of inquiry, for example, in art, law, religion, and science; the issues tend to be ramifications of one or more of the four major branches.

Western philosophy began with the Presocratics in the 6th-c BC in the Greek-speaking region around the Aegean Sea and southern Italy. Ancient philosophers such as Plato and Aristotle probed virtually every area of knowledge; there was as yet no distinction between philosophy and science. As Christianity became an important social force in Europe and N Africa (2nd-c–5th-c AD), apologists such as St Augustine began to synthesize ancient philosophy with the Christian world-view, a process that continued throughout the Middle Ages. With the scientific revolution of the 16th-c and 17th-c, the physical sciences began to separate from philosophy, and philosophers such as Descartes, Locke, and Leibniz began to assess the philosophical implications of the new scientific results. In the 19th-c and early 20th-c, psychology established itself as a discipline distinct from philosophy. This process of continued separation of disciplines from philosophy raises the question whether philosophy has a subject-matter proper to itself. The perennial nature of the questions mentioned above suggests that it does; moreover, as new subject matters emerge, new philosophical issues typically arise with respect to them. Two contemporary examples are *hermeneutics*, conceived most generally as the study of the interpretation of such meaning-laden phenomena as language, works of art, and social practices; and *cognitive science*, the investigation of how the results of neurophysiology, psychology, linguistics, and computer simulation shed light on the workings of the mind. » Aristotle; Augustine, St (of Hippo); Descartes; epistemology; ethics; Leibniz; Locke, John; logic; metaphysics; Plato; Presocratics

Phipps, Sir William (1651–95) US colonial governor, born at Pemaquid, Maine. He was successively shepherd, carpenter, and trader, and in 1687 recovered treasure from a wrecked Spanish ship off the Bahamas. This gained him a knighthood and the appointment of Provost-Marshal of New England, and in 1692 he became Governor of Massachusetts. The force behind the Salem witchcraft trials of 1692 burned itself out when Sir William's wife was accused of witchcraft. He died in London. » Salem

Phiz » Browne, Hablot Knight

phlebitis [fli**biy**tis] Inflammation of a vein, commonly associated with varicose veins, or following thrombosis of the blood within veins, when it is referred to as **thrombophlebitis**. The veins of the leg are commonly affected, and the disorder may follow childbirth, a surgical operation, or stagnation of the blood from a prolonged dependency on the legs, such as during a long journey. Severe degrees of phlebitis may lead to ulceration of the overlying skin and oedema of the affected leg. An embolism is a potentially lethal complication after surgery. » pulmonary embolism; thrombosis; varicose veins; vein

phloem [**floh**em] Tissue, composed of conducting cells and often supporting fibres, which transports sap from the leaves to other parts of a plant. It is either located in the vascular bundles or forms the inner bark of woody plants. It is complementary to xylem, but composed of living cells. » vascular tissue; xylem

phlogiston theory [fluh**jis**tn] A theory, popular in the 18th-c, to explain combustion as the loss of a substance (*phlogiston*) to the atmosphere. The theory was strongly defended, but became increasingly untenable as it became clear that the products of combustion always weigh more than the material burnt.

phlogopite [**flog**uhpiyt] A member of the mica group of minerals, common in igneous rocks. Its composition is similar to biotite. » micas

phlox A mat-forming to erect annual and perennial, almost exclusively native to N America and Mexico; leaves in opposite pairs; flowers tubular with five notched lobes, often white, pink, or blue, sometimes fragrant, in dense terminal heads. (Genus: *Phlox*, 67 species. Family: *Polemoniaceae*.) » annual; perennial

Phnom Penh [(p)nom **pen**] 11°35N 104°55E, pop (1983e) 500 000. River port capital of Cambodia, at the confluence of Mekong R and Tonlé Sap (lake); founded by the Khmers, 1371; capital, 1434; abandoned as capital several times, but became permanent capital in 1867; under Japanese occupation in World War 2; after the communist victory of 1975, the population was removed to work in the fields; railway; several universities; commerce, food processing, textiles; royal palace, several museums and pagodas; current population uncertain, because of continuing refugee problem. » Cambodia [i]

phobia A situation in which anxiety is elicited but which is not specifically dangerous. Avoidance behaviour usually occurs. The major forms of phobia are *simple* phobia (in which people are afraid of a specific object or situation) and *social* phobia (in which they are concerned about their behaviour in front of others). » neurosis; *see panel p 936*

Phobos [**foh**bos] One of the two natural satellites of Mars, discovered in 1877; distance from the planet 938 000 km/583 000 ml; diameter 27 km/17 ml; orbital period 7 hr 39 min. Close approaches by Viking Orbiter spacecraft have revealed irregular cratered, dark surfaces with low densities, suggesting a similarity to carbonaceous meteorites and primitive asteroids. Phobos 2 spacecraft achieved a rendezvous with Phobos in April 1989. » asteroids; Deimos; Mars (astronomy); Mars programme; meteorite; Viking project; RR4

Phocis [**foh**kis] The region in C Greece to the W of Boeotia, in which Delphi and the Delphic oracle were situated. » Delphi, oracle of

Phoebe (astronomy) [**fee**bee] The ninth natural satellite of Saturn, discovered in 1898; distance from the planet 12 950 000 km/8 047 000 ml; diameter 160 km/100 ml; orbital period 550.40 days. » Saturn (astronomy); RR4

Phoebe (mythology) [**fee**bee] In Greek mythology, a Titaness, identified with the Moon. Later she was confused with Artemis. » Artemis

Phoenicia [fuh**nee**sha] The narrow strip in the E Mediterranean between the mountains of Lebanon and the sea, where the cities of Arad, Byblos, Sidon, and Tyre were located. It derived its name from the Phoenicians; descendants of the Canaanites, they were the dominant people of the area from the end of the second millennium BC, and this was their base first for trading all over the Mediterranean and then, from the 8th-c BC, for establishing trading posts and colonies in the W Mediterranean, such as Leptis Magna and Carthage in N Africa. From here came their most important contribution to Western culture – the alphabet. » alphabet [i]; Byblos; Canaan; Phoenician; Punic Wars; RR81

Phoenician [fuh**nee**shan] An extinct language of the Semitic family. Its consonantal alphabet was adapted by the Greeks, through the addition of vowel symbols, and ultimately it became the model for all Western alphabets. » Afro-Asiatic languages; alphabet [i]; Phoenicia

Phoenix (astronomy) [**fee**niks] A S hemisphere constellation. » constellation; RR9

phoenix/phenix (mythology) [**fee**niks] A legendary bird, which lives a long time. It kills itself on a funeral pyre, but is then reborn from the ashes. The idea of resurrection appealed to Christian allegorists.

Phoenix (USA) [**fee**niks] 33°27N 112°04W, pop (1980) 789 704. State capital in Maricopa County, SC Arizona, USA, on the Salt R; largest city in the state; settled, 1870; state capital, 1889; airport; railway; hub of the rich Salt River Valley; important centre for data-processing and electronics research; computer components, aircraft, machinery, food products, textiles; popular winter and health resort, with its dry, sunny climate; major league team, Suns (basketball); Heard Museum of Anthropology and Primitive Arts, Pueblo Grande Museum, Desert Botanical Garden, Pioneer Arizona Museum; Cowboy Artists Exhibition (Nov). » Arizona

Phoenix Islands pop (1985) 24 (all on Kanton I). Coral island group of Kiribati, S Pacific Ocean, c.1 300 km/800 ml SE of the Gilbert Is; formerly an important source of guano; most inhabitants were resettled in the Solomon Is in 1978. » Kiribati

Phoenix Park murders The murder in Dublin on 6 May 1882 of the recently appointed Chief Secretary for Ireland, Lord Frederick Cavendish (1836–82), and his Under-Secretary, Thomas Henry Burke (1829–82), by a terrorist nationalist group called 'The Invincibles'. More murders followed during the summer. The British government responded with a Coercion Act. Five of the Phoenix Park murderers were arrested and hanged. » nationalism

phoneme The smallest unit in the sound system of a language, capable of signalling a difference of meaning between words. For example, the English words *pail* and *tail* are distinguished by the initial consonant phonemes /p/ and /t/. The same phoneme will vary in its phonetic character, depending on the context in which it occurs; /t/, for instance, is pronounced with lips spread, in the word *tan*, but with lips rounded in *too*. These phonetic variants of a phoneme are known as **allophones**. The number of phonemes in a language varies greatly, from less than a dozen to well over 100. English has about 44 (depending on the accent and the method of analysis used). No two languages or dialects have the same phonemic system. » phonetics; phonology

phonetics The study of the range of sounds which can be produced by the human vocal organs. **Articulatory** phonetics studies the movements of the vocal organs (such as the tongue, lips, and larynx); **acoustic** phonetics, the physical properties of the sound waves produced in speech; and **auditory** phonetics, the way in which the listener uses ear and brain to decode sound waves. Any study of speech which employs instruments to measure such features as airflow or the frequencies of sound waves is known as **instrumental** phonetics, and these studies typically take place within **experimental** phonetics. The study of the properties of speech as a human capacity is known as **general** phonetics, while other studies describe the particular range of phonetic characteristics in specific languages (**descriptive** phonetics). » phonology; linguistics

phonics A general method of teaching children to read by recognizing the relationship between individual letters and sounds. It builds up the pronunciation of new words by saying them sound by sound, as with the one-to-one correspondences between *cat* and [k-a-t]. More complex correspondences are gradually introduced, such as between the split sequence *a...e* and the pronunciation [ay] in *dame*. Many phonic approaches have now been devised. » look-and-say

phonograph The first practical device for recording and reproducing sounds stored as grooves cut in cylinders, mainly of wax, rotated beneath a stylus by hand or clockwork. Demonstrated by Edison in 1877, it was initially intended as an office dictating machine, but came to be widely applied in home musical entertainment during the next half-century. » Edison, Thomas Alva; gramophone; sound recording

phonology The study of the sound system of a language, and of the general properties of sound systems. The human vocal apparatus is capable of a wide variety of speech sounds, but only a small number is used distinctively in any one language. Phonologists study the way the sound segments (or *phonemes*) are organized in languages (*segmental* phonology), and also the patterns of pitch, loudness, and other voice qualities which can

AN A TO Z OF PHOBIAS

TECHNICAL TERM	EVERYDAY TERM	TECHNICAL TERM	EVERYDAY TERM	TECHNICAL TERM	EVERYDAY TERM	TECHNICAL TERM	EVERYDAY TERM
acero-	sourness	claustro-	closed spaces	hypno-	sleep	ourano-	heaven
achulo-	darkness	cnido-	stings	ideo-	ideas	pan- (panto-)	everything
acro-	heights	cometo-	comets	kakorraphia-	failure	partheno-	girls
aero-	air	cromo-	colour	karagalo-	ridicule	patroio-	heredity
agora-	open spaces	cyno-	dogs	keno-	void	penia	poverty
aichuro-	points	demo-	crowds	kineso-	motion	phasmo-	ghosts
ailouro-	cats	demono-	demons	klepto-	stealing	phobo-	fears
akoustico-	sound	dermato-	skin	kopo-	fatigue	photo-	light
algo-	pain	dike-	injustice	kristallo-	ice	pnigero-	smothering
amaka-	carriages	dora-	fur	lalio-	stuttering	poine-	punishment
amatho-	dust	eisoptro-	mirror	linono-	string	poly-	many things
andro-	men	elektro-	electricity	logo-	words	poto-	drink
anemo-	wind	entomo-	insects	lysso- (mania)	insanity	pterono-	feathers
angino-	narrowness	eoso-	dawn	mastigo	flogging	pyro-	fire
anthropo-	man	eremo-	solitude	mechano-	machinery	rypo-	soiling
antlo-	flood	erete-	pins	metallo-	metals	Satano-	Satan
apeiro-	infinity	ereuthro	blushing	meteoro-	meteors	sela-	flash
arachno-	spiders	ergo-	work	miso-	contamination	sidero-	stars
astheno-	weakness	geno-	sex	mono-	one thing	sito-	food
astra-	astral	geuma-	taste	musico-	music	sperma- (spermato-)	germs
ate-	ruin	grapho-	writing	muso-	mice	stasi-	standing
aulo-	flute	gymnoto-	nudity	necro-	corpses	stygio- (hade-)	hell
Auroro-	Northern Lights	gyno-	women	nelo-	glass	syphilo-	syphilis
bacillo-	microbes	hamartio-	sin	neo-	newness	thalasso-	sea
baro-	gravity	hapto-	touch	nephelo-	clouds	thanato-	death
baso-	walking	harpaxo-	robbers	noso- (patho-)	disease	thasse-	sitting
batracho-	reptiles	hedono-	pleasure	ocho-	vehicles	theo-	God
belone-	needles	haemato-	blood	odonto-	teeth	thermo-	heat
bronto-	thunder	helmintho-	worms	oiko-	home	toxi-	poison
cheima-	cold	hodo-	travel	olfacto-	smell	tremo-	trembling
chiono-	snow	homichlo-	fog	omato-	eyes	triskaideka-	thirteen
chrometo-	money	horme-	shock	oneiro-	dreams	zelo-	jealousy
chrono-	duration	hydro-	water	ophido-	snakes	zoo-	animals
chrystallo-	crystals	hypegia-	responsibility	ornitho-	birds	xeno-	strangers

EVERYDAY TERM	TECHNICAL TERM	EVERYDAY TERM	TECHNICAL TERM	EVERYDAY TERM	TECHNICAL TERM	EVERYDAY TERM	TECHNICAL TERM
air	aero-	fire	pyro-	mice	muso-	smothering	pnigero-
animals	zoo-	flash	sela-	microbes	bacilli-	snakes	ophidio-
astral	astra-	flogging	mastigo-	mirrors	eisoptro-	snow	chiono-
birds	orthino-	flood	antlo-	money	chrometo-	soiling	rypo-
blood	hemato-	flute	aulo-	motion	kineso-	solitude	eremo-
blushing	ereutho-	fog	homichlo-	music	musico-	sound	akoustico-
carriages	amaka-	food	sito-	narrowness	angino-	sourness	acero-
cats	ailouro-	fur	dora-	needles	belone-	spiders	arachno-
closed spaces	claustro-	germs	sperma- (spermato-)	newness	neo-	standing	stasi-
clouds	nephelo-	ghosts	phasmo-	Northern Lights	Aurora-	stars	sidero-
cold	cheima-	girls	partheno-	nudity	gymnoto-	stealing	klepto-
colour	cromo-	glass	nelo-	one thing	mono-	stings	cnido-
comets	cometo-	God	theo-	open spaces	agora-	strangers	xeno-
contamination	miso-	gravity	baro-	pain	algo-	string	linono-
corpses	necro-	heat	thermo-	pins	erete-	stuttering	lalio-
crowds	demo-	heaven	ourano-	pleasure	hedono-	syphilis	syphilo-
crystals	chrystallo-	heights	acro-	points	aichuro-	taste	geuma-
darkness	achluo-	hell	stygio- (hade-)	poison	toxi-	teeth	odonto-
dawn	eoso-	heredity	patroio-	poverty	penia-	thirteen	triskaideka-
death	thanato-	home	oiko-	punishment	poine-	thunder	bronto- (tonitro)
demons	demono-	ice	kristallo-	reptiles	batracho-	touch	hapto-
disease	noso-, patho-	ideas	ideo-	responsibility	hypegia-	travel	hodo-
dogs	cyno-	infinity	apeiro-	ridicule	katagalo-	trembling	tremo-
dreams	oneiro-	injustice	dike-	robberies	harpaxo-	vehicles	ocho-
drinks	poto-	insanity	lysso- (mania-)	ruin	ate-	void	keno-
duration	chrono-	insects	entomo-	Satan	Satano-	walking	baso-
dust	amatho-	jealousy	zelo-	sea	thalasso-	water	hydro-
electricity	elektro-	light	photo-	sex	geno-	weakness	astheno-
everything	pan- (panto-)	machinery	mechano-	shock	horme-	wind	anemo-
eyes	omato-	man	anthropo-	sin	hamartio-	women	gyno-
failure	kakorrphia-	many things	poly-	sitting	thasso-	words	logo-
fatigue	kopo-	men	andro-	skin	dermato-	work	ergo-
fears	phobo-	metals	metallo-	sleep	hypno-	worms	helmintho-
feathers	pterono-	meteors	meteoro-	smell	olfacto-	writing	grapho-

extend over syllables, phrases, and sentences (*non-segmental* or *suprasegmental* phonology). » graphology; linguistics; phoneme; phonetics

phonon A wave which passes like a ripple through a solid, causing momentary displacement of atoms. Phonons are the quantum of lattice vibration, and exhibit particle-like properties, including the ability to scatter other particles, as observed in neutron diffraction. » magnon [i]; neutron diffraction; quasi-particles; thermal conduction

phosphate The salt of phosphoric acid, usually containing one of the tetrahedral ions PO_4^{3-}, HPO_4^{2-}, or $H_2PO_4^-$. Phosphates occur in various minerals, especially apatite, and are mined for use as fertilizers. Solutions containing mixtures of the ions HPO_4^{2-} and $H_2PO_4^-$ are buffered at $pH \approx 7$. » buffer (chemistry); pH; phosphoric acid; superphosphates

phospholipid A special category of fats where a part of the molecule (the head) is highly polar and thus, unlike most fats, soluble in water (*hydrophilic*), while the remainder (the tail) is highly insoluble (*hydrophobic*). The head varies from one phospholipid class to another. Phospholipids are the main components of all biological membranes. In addition, they store arachidonic acid, a precursor of the prostaglandins. » arachidonic acid; prostaglandins

phosphor » luminescence

phosphorescence Light produced by an object excited by a means other than heat, where the light emission continues after the energy source has been removed; a type of luminescence. The emission may continue for a fraction of a second or for hours, depending on the substance. » light; luminescence

phosphoric acid H_3PO_4. A tri-basic acid, with three series of salts. It is generally a syrupy liquid, very hygroscopic; dehydration gives phosphorus pentoxide (P_2O_5), itself an excellent drying agent. » acid; deliquescent; phosphate

phosphorus P, element 15, the second element of the nitrogen group. It is not found free in nature, but may be prepared both as a very reactive, molecular, white form (P_4), melting point 44°C, and as a variety of less reactive, high-melting polymeric solids with colours ranging from red to black. It is found in many minerals, particularly apatite, mainly as calcium phosphate. The white form of the element is prepared by the reduction of calcium phosphate with carbon. It reacts spontaneously with air to give phosphorus pentoxide (P_2O_5), the anhydride of phosphoric acid. Phosphorus in compounds shows oxidation state +3 or (more commonly) +5. It is essential to life, being required for DNA. Industrial uses for phosphorus compounds include matches and agricultural fertilizers. » anhydride; chemical elements; DNA [i]; nitrogen; polymerization; RR90

photic zone » epipelagic environments

photino » supersymmetry

Photius [**foh**tiuhs] (c.820–91), feast day 6 February (E). Patriarch of Constantinople (858–67, 877–86), born in Constantinople. On the deposition of Ignatius from the patriarchate, he was hurried through all the stages of holy orders, and installed in his stead. In 862, Pope Nicholas I called a Council at Rome, which declared Photius's election invalid, and reinstated Ignatius. Supported by the Emperor, Photius assembled a Council at Constantinople (867), which withdrew from communion with Rome. He was then deposed and reinstated on several occasions, and excluded the *Filioque* clause from the Creed (879). In 886 he was finally exiled to Armenia, where he died. » Filioque

photocell A device sensitive to light which responds to radiation with an electrical effect. It is generally based on a semiconductor (eg selenium, germanium or silicon, suitably prepared or modified). The radiation releases bound electrons, and, according to the constitution of the cell, the result may be a change in conductivity, the production of an electromotive force, or some other effect. In everyday life, such a device is encountered in apparatus, such as doors actuated by the interruption of a beam of light. » semiconductor

photochemistry The study of chemical reactions brought about by the absorption of visible and ultraviolet light, and of those reactions that produce light. Reactions of the first type include those which can be used to convert light energy into electrical energy in solar cells. The decomposition or dissociation of molecules by exposure to light is known as **photolysis**. » light

photoconductivity The increase in conductivity of a material (usually a semiconductor, such as silicon or germanium arsenide) resulting from the exposure to light. Incoming light photons above a certain energy level cause the production of electron-hole pairs that aid conduction. The effect is exploited in light-sensitive detectors and switches, and in television cameras. » electrical conduction; light; photo-ionization

photocopying The photographic reproduction of written, printed, or graphic work. Two processes can be used. In **xerography** an image of the original is focused on to a photosensitive surface (a selenium plate or cylinder), which converts light into electric charge. This electrostatic image attracts charged ink powder, and the image is then permanently fixed by heating. The **ozalid process** (also called the **diazo process**) uses paper coated with diazonium compounds. This is exposed to ultraviolet light through a transparent original. Only the diazo in the shadows of the original is developed by ammonia vapour to give a positive print. » xerography [i]

photoelasticity The change in the light-transmitting properties of a solid (eg glass or plastic) caused by stress; also called **mechanically induced birefringence**. It alters the polarization of transmitted light, and is observable by placing a suitable material between crossed Polaroids (ie having the transmission directions at right angles) and stressing the material. The coloured patterns formed are useful in engineering stress analysis. » birefringence; light; Polaroid; stress (physics)

photoelectric cell A device with electrical properties whose operation depends on the amount of light falling on it. Photoelectric cells include *photovoltaic cells*, which convert light radiation into electricity, and *photoconductive cells*, whose conductivity increases as more light falls on them. They are used in light meters (eg in photography), light detectors (eg in burglar alarms), and spacecraft power supplies. » electricity; optical sensing; selenium cell

photoelectric effect The emission of electrons from the surface of a metal as a result of irradiation with light. No electrons are emitted unless the wavelength of the light is less than some critical value, which depends on the material; and the energy of the emitted electrons depends not on the intensity of the light but on its wavelength. The correct interpretation, that light must comprise well-defined units having energy related to wavelength (photons, quanta of light), is due to Einstein (1905). The effect was discovered by German physicist Heinrich Hertz in 1887, and was crucial to the development of quantum theory. » Einstein; electron; field emission; Hertz; photoemission spectroscopy; photo-ionization; photomultiplier; photon; secondary emission; thermionics; wavefunction

photoemission spectroscopy A technique for studying the structure of atoms and molecules. Electromagnetic radiation directed on to a sample causes the emission of electrons, which are then detected. The use of X-rays allows the study of inner electrons; ultraviolet rays allow the study of bonding electrons. » atom; electron; molecule; photoelectric effect; spectroscopy

photoengraving Techniques for the creation of metal printing plates on cylinders carrying the image of continuous-tone ('line') and half-tone text and, particularly, illustrations for letterpress and gravure printing. Film produced by photographing the image to be communicated is exposed on the metal plate, which is already coated with a light-sensitive solution. After exposure and subsequent etching, the printing image will remain in relief on a letterpress plate, or etched into a gravure cylinder. » gravure; letterpress [i]

photogrammetry The use of photographic records to determine precise measurements. It is principally applied in map-making by aerial survey, but is also used for medical, forensic, and architectural purposes, where dimensional grids may be included or superimposed. » aerial photography

photography The recording and reproduction of images on light-sensitive materials by chemical processes. In 1816 Joseph Niepce (1765–1833) in France tried to record the optical image formed in a camera obscura, and by 1839 Daguerre had established a reliable process. About the same time in England, Fox Talbot discovered the process of developing and fixing the exposed image as a negative and making a positive print. Scott Archer (1813–87) in 1848 invented the collodion 'wet plate', and dry plates coated with sensitized emulsion were produced commercially in the mid-1870s, followed by celluloid-based film from 1889.

In a camera, light reaching the photo-sensitive emulsion containing silver halide crystals forms a latent (invisible) image, which can be made visible by chemical development, reducing the exposed crystals to black metallic silver. The remaining unaffected halide is then removed by fixing to leave a permanent negative record of the exposure. By exposing another photo-sensitive material to light passing through this negative, a print can be made which, after developing and fixing, yields a positive image representing the original scene. In a reversal system, the film exposed in the camera is processed to produce a positive rather than a negative image by removing the initially exposed halide. » aerial/colour/electronic/high-speed/schlieren/stereoscopic/time-lapse photography; camera; Daguerre; Talbot

photo-ionization The production of ions by light or other electromagnetic radiation of sufficient energy to remove an electron from an atom. For example, the Earth's ionosphere is caused by ultraviolet light forming ions from atoms in the atmosphere. Light falling on semiconductors causes the production of charge-carrying electrons and holes that are essential to solar cells. » ion; photoconductivity; photoelectric effect; photovoltaic effect

photoluminescence » luminescence

photolysis » photochemistry

photomacrography » macro-photography

photomechanical reproduction The multiple printing of photographs in ink on paper, usually from metal or plastic plates in which the image is made up of solid dots. Gradation in the picture is produced by variations in the dot size, not the density of the ink. Plates are prepared by re-photographing flat copy through a screen with a line-ruling appropriate to the printing process and product: from 65–100 lines per cm for newsprint; up to 120–180 per cm for high quality book illustration. For colour reproduction, separate plates are made for each of the inks to be used, normally yellow, magenta, cyan, and black. » gravure; letterpress [i]; lithography

photometry The measurement of light and its rate of flow. In contrast to radiometry, photometry considers visible frequencies only, and takes account of the uneven sensitivity of the eye to light of different frequencies. Photometric quantities (see table) are measured using **photometers**. The technique is important in photography and lighting design. » illuminance; light; luminous flux/intensity; radiometry [i]

PHOTOMETRY

PHOTOMETRIC QUANTITIES	SYMBOLS	UNITS	CORRESPONDING RADIOMETRIC QUANTITIES
luminous flux	Φ	lumen (lm)	radiant power
luminous intensity	I	candela (cd)	radiant intensity
luminance	L	cd/m^2	radiance
illuminance	E	lux (lx)	irradiance

photomicrograph A photograph of an object as observed through a microscope. Optical means can provide magnifications up to about ×2 000, and techniques such as dark-ground illumination, phase contrast, and polarization in colour can be recorded. For an electron microscope, the scanned image must be photographed from a high-resolution display tube, using long exposure time to eliminate scanning line-structure; magnifications of $\times 10^6$ or more can be achieved. » macro-photography; microscope

photo-montage An assembly of selected images achieved either by physically mounting cut-out portions of prints on a backing, or by combination printing from several separate negatives in succession. It is widely used in the preparation of advertising display material, and sometimes for artistic creations. » photography

photomultiplier A device for the electronic detection of light. Incoming light causes the emission of electrons from a surface via the photoelectric effect. A sequence of electrodes accelerates away the electrons, and gives a measurable current which signals the detection of a photon. » particle detectors; photoelectric effect

photon The quantum or particle of light. Light and all other electromagnetic radiation comprises a stream of photons, each of which has energy $E=h\nu$, where h is Planck's constant and ν is frequency. Photons of yellow light have energy 3.4×10^{-19}J. A household light emits c.10^{20} photons every second. Photons have no (rest) mass and are spin 1. In quantum theory they transmit electromagnetic force. » light; quantum mechanics

photoperiodism The response of an organism to periodic changes, either in light intensity or, more usually, in the duration of the light period (daylength) in a natural or artificial light-dark cycle. Photoperiodism controls the timing of many events in the annual life cycle of plants, and in the seasonal reproductive cycles of some animals. » life cycle; phenology; phytochrome

Photorealism A style of modern painting, also called *Hyperrealism* or *Superrealism*. Pictures, often quite large, are meticulously painted in a style of extreme naturalism like a sharply-focused coloured photograph. Photorealism has flourished since the 1960s, especially in the USA. » modern art; naturalism

photosphere The visible surface of the Sun or a star. About 500 km/300 ml thick, it is the zone where the Sun's layers progress from being completely opaque to radiation to being transparent, hence the zone from which the light we see actually comes. The temperature is c.6 000 K. When viewed at very high resolution, the photosphere has a mottled appearance (*granulation*). » Sun

photosynthesis The complex process in which light-energy is used to convert water and carbon dioxide into simple carbohydrates. Light-absorbing pigments, notably chlorophyll, found in chloroplasts, are essential to the process, which can be carried out only by green plants and photosynthetic bacteria. Plants are the main source of atmospheric oxygen, released as a by-product of photosynthesis. » carbohydrate; carbon; chlorophyll; light; oxygen

phototherapy Body exposure to cool blue light (420–480 nm), free of ultraviolet light. It is used in the treatment of jaundice occurring in the newborn. The pigment bilirubin is degraded into water-soluble products that are more readily eliminated in the urine. » jaundice; light

phototypesetter A machine for composing type and creating an image of the composed type on film or paper, ready for exposure to a plate for printing. The individual characters may be stored in the machine either as images on film, or digitally within the machine's computer memory; they may be exposed one after another, or line by line using a raster scan; the light source may be a flash, cathode-ray tube, or laser-beam. » printing [i]

photovoltaic effect The production of electrical current by light falling on some material, usually a semiconductor. The charge carriers are produced by photo-ionization. To produce a useful current, this must occur at a p–n semiconductor junction, so that the potential difference across the junction separates the charge carriers. The effect is the basic mechanism of solar cells. » electrical conduction; electromotive force; photo-ionization; semiconductor; solar cell

phrenology The analysis of mind and character by the study of the shape and contours of the skull. It is based on the belief that this reflects the degree of development of the underlying regions of the brain, particularly those areas concerned with higher mental functions. It was popular in Europe during the early 19th-c. » brain [i]; skull

Phrygia [**fri**jia] The name of the kingdom in antiquity with whom the legendary Midas is associated. At its widest extent around the beginning of the first millenium, it consisted of the C plateau of Asia Minor and its W flank. After its conquest by

Lydia in the 6th-c BC, it never regained its political independence. » Lydia

Phryne [**fri**ynee] (4th-c BC) A famous Greek courtesan of antiquity, who reputedly was Praxiteles' model for his statue of Aphrodite. Accused of profaning the Eleusinian Mysteries, she was defended by the orator Hyperides, who threw off her robe, showing her loveliness, and so gained the verdict. » Praxiteles

Phuket [poo**ket**], formerly **Salang** or **Junkseylon** Largest island of Thailand, in the Andaman Sea, 900 km/560 ml S of Bangkok; a resort area; notable limestone caves and columns at Phang Nga Bay; marine biological centre; major outlet to the Indian Ocean; vegetarian festival (Oct). » Thailand [i]

phylloxera [filok**seera**] A dwarf, aphid-like insect that can kill grape vines; some larvae are short-beaked, and cause galls on vine leaves; others are long-beaked and suck at roots. (Order: *Homoptera*. Family: *Phylloxeridae*.) » aphid; gall; insect [i]; larva; wine

phylogeny [fiy**loj**uhnee] The relationships between groups of animals as determined by their evolutionary history, so that groups are linked together on the basis of the recency of common ancestry. This is assessed primarily by the recognition of shared derived characters. The pattern of evolutionary relationships within and between groups can be depicted in the form of a branching diagram (an evolutionary tree) showing the lines of descent. » evolution

phylum [**fiy**luhm] In animal classification, one of the major groupings, forming the principal category below *kingdom*, and comprising classes and lower categories. Phyla represent the major types of animals, each having its own basic structural plan that is clearly different from that of other phyla. » kingdom; systematics; taxonomy

physalis [**fi**suhlis] A soft-leaved annual or perennial; found almost everywhere, but many species native to America; salver-shaped, 5-petalled flowers, in which the calyx becomes enlarged and bladder-like, enclosing the berry in fruit. Several are important local crops. (Genus: *Physalis*, 100 species. Family: *Solanaceae*.) » annual; perennial; sepal

physical chemistry The study of the dependence of physical properties on chemical composition, and of the physical changes accompanying chemical reactions. » chemistry; physics

physical medicine » **physiotherapy**

physicalism A philosophical position which maintains that any empirical proposition can be stated in a language that makes reference only to physical objects and events, or more stringently, to the objects and events recognized by physics. Physicalism was championed by such logical positivists as Otto Neurath (1882–1945) and Rudolf Carnap (1891–1970). The term is sometimes also used as a synonym for materialism. » Carnap; empiricism; materialism; physics

physics The study of matter and forces, at the most basic level. Physics as a discernible discipline began during the Renaissance, with Copernicus' model of planetary motion and Galileo's mechanics. Astronomy and mechanics continued to dominate the field, with the work of Newton, Kepler, and others; Newton and Leibniz developed calculus, which Newton used to express his theorems of mechanics. Galileo, Newton, and Kepler all studied optics. Huygens was the first to envisage light as a wave, an idea strongly disputed by Newton. Galileo built one of the earliest telescopes, and the compound microscope was (probably) invented c.1590 by Zacharias Janssen. Thermodynamics dates from the work of Carnot, Joule, and others in the 19th-c. About this time, steam power was becoming important: Watt introduced his improved steam engine in 1769, and Stephenson's 'Rocket', a steam-powered railway engine, dates from 1829. Franklin was the first to clarify the idea of electric charge; the electric battery was invented by Volta. The foundation of modern electromagnetism was laid by Ampère and Faraday, and electric motors and dynamos were invented at this time.

Newton's mechanics dominated physics for two centuries, and was in part responsible for a mechanistic philosophy that attempted to explain all phenomena in terms of mechanics. The physicists' view of the world has changed dramatically due to two major developments in the early part of the 20th-c. The first was Einstein's theory of special relativity, which grew in part from Maxwell's work in electromagnetism in the second half of the 19th-c. From the special theory, Einstein went on to his general theory of relativity, a theory of gravity, which was possible only because of mathematical developments by Riemann in the study of geometry. The second was the development of quantum theory and atomic theory by Schrödinger, Bohr, and many others. This was made possible by work in thermodynamics, electromagnetism, and the new radiations. It has led to modern solid state physics, as well as atomic, nuclear and particle physics. From these have developed electronics and hence computers, lasers, nuclear power, and much more. » atomic/atmosphere/high pressure/non-linear/particle/solid state/surface physics; acoustics; astrophysics; conservation laws; cryogenics; dimensional analysis; electromagnetism; energy; fluid mechanics; force; forces of nature [i]; fundamental constants; general relativity; matter; mechanics; optics [i]; perturbation theory; plasma (physics); quantum mechanics; scattering; special relativity [i]; statistical mechanics; thermodynamics; vacuum; wave (physics) [i]; Ampère; Bohr; Carnot, Nicholas; Copernicus; Einstein; Faraday; Franklin, Benjamin; Galileo; Huygens; Joule; Kepler; Leibniz; Maxwell, James Clerk; Newton, Isaac; Riemann; Schrödinger; Stephenson, George; Volta; Watt

Physiocrats A group of French economic and political thinkers of the later 18th-c, led by Quesnay, and committed to *a priori* principles of reason and natural law. Their theories made them critics of internal trade barriers, and controls and advocates of systematic economic reform. » economics; natural law; Quesnay

physiological psychology The study of the physiological processes in brain and body which underlie behaviour and psychological experience. This includes the physiology of the senses, the study of the electrical and chemical activity of the brain, the effects of drugs and hormones, the physiological correlates of mental disorders, and the consequences of brain damage. » physiology; psychology

physiology An experimental science concerned with the study of the functions of living things. Its scope is wide: some studies are concerned with processes that go on in cells (eg phagocytosis, photosynthesis); others with how tissues or organs work, and how they are controlled and integrated within the whole organism; yet others deal with how living things respond to their environments. Physiology makes use of many investigative procedures including those employed in the related disciplines of biochemistry, biophysics, cell biology, histology, and pharmacology. » biology; histology; pharmacology; physiological psychology

physiotherapy The application of physical treatment to restore the function of muscles and joints after injury, surgery, or disease. Treatment varies widely, but includes active and passive exercises, massage, and the application of heat by infrared and short-wave diathermy. Wasting and weakness of muscle from enforced disuse (eg following a fracture) occurs very rapidly, and associated joints become stiff. Graded exercises over long periods are essential if proper function is to be restored. Post-operative or bed-ridden individuals are prone to chest infection, and deep-breathing exercises with pummelling of the back of the chest encourages the expectoration of retained secretions. Exercises are also applied to paralysed limbs following nerve injury or strokes. » diathermy; muscle [i]

phytic acid A store of phosphorus present in most cereals and legumes; also called *inositol hexaphosphate*. This acid can bind such minerals as calcium, iron, and zinc, and reduce their bioavailability. Thus, iron is less available from vegetable sources than from animal sources. However, its availability can be increased by consuming vitamin C at the same time. » inositol; phosphorus; vitamins [i]

phytochrome [**fiy**tuhkrohm] A pigment found in most groups of plants, which is involved in photoperiodic responses. A protein compound, it exists in two forms which absorb different kinds of light, and acts as a switch mechanism linked to environmental light conditions, such as daylength. It controls many activities, such as flowering and growth. » photoperiodism; pigments

phytogeography The study of the factors responsible for the past and present distribution of plants on the Earth's surface. It is part of the larger discipline of biogeography. » biogeography; geography; zoogeography

phytoplankton » plankton

phytosaur [**fiy**tuhsaw] An extinct reptile with a crocodile-like body; teeth inserted in sockets (*thecodontic*); known from the late Triassic period of N America, Europe, and Asia. (Subclass: *Archosauria*.) » reptile; Triassic period

pi (π) [piy] In mathematics, the ratio of a circle's circumference to its diameter, (3.14159...). This was often taken to be 3 (for example, in the Old Testament, 1 *Kings* 7.23; 2 *Chron* 4.2). The Egyptians (in the Rhind papyrus) used $\pi \approx (4/3)^4 \approx 3.1604$. By successive approximations of inscribed and circumscribed polygons, Archimedes proved that $223/71 < \pi < 22/7$, ie $3.1408 < \pi < 3.14285$. The Chinese, c.500 knew that $\pi \approx 355/113 \approx 3.1415929...$ – an approximation whose digits (1,1,3,3,5,5) make it easy to recall. » Archimedes; circle; circumference; geometry

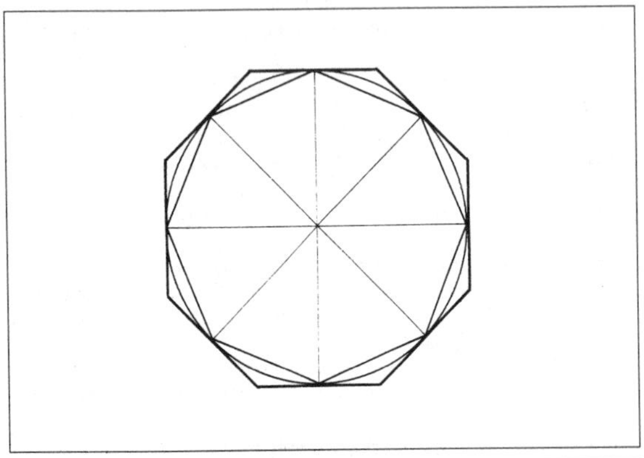

Inscribed and circumscribed polygons, for approximations to π

pi-meson » pion

Piacenza [pya**chent**sa], ancient **Placentia** 45°03N 9°41E, pop (1981) 109 039. Capital town of Piacenza province, Emilia-Romagna, N Italy; on R Po, 61 km/38 ml SW of Milan; railway; agricultural trade and machinery, pasta, leather goods; Palazzo Gotico (begun 1281), cathedral (begun 12th–13th-c), Church of Sant'Antonino (11th–12th-c), Church of Santa Maria di Campagna (1522–8); well-preserved circuit of 16th-c walls. » Italy [i]

Piaf, Edith, originally **Edith Giovanna Gassion** (1915–63) French singer, born and died in Paris. She began singing in music hall and cabaret, where she became known as *Piaf* (Parisian argot 'little sparrow'). She appeared in stage-plays and films, but is mainly remembered for her songs, with their undercurrent of sadness and nostalgia, such as 'La vie en rose' and 'Non, je ne regrette rien'. After a severe illness she made a successful return to the stage in 1961, but died two years later.

Piaget, Jean [**pjah**zhay] (1896–1980) Swiss psychologist, born at Neuchâtel. He studied at Neuchâtel, Zürich, and Paris, becoming professor of child psychology at Geneva in 1929, and at the Centre of Genetic Epistemology in 1955. He is best known for his research on the development of cognitive functions in children, in such pioneering studies as *La Naissance de l'intelligence chez l'enfant* (1948, The Origins of Intelligence in Children). He died in Geneva. » cognitive/Piagetian psychology

Piagetian psychology [peea**zhet**ian] A psychological approach which aims to understand the persistent philosophical problem of how, as biological organisms, people acquire knowledge; derived from the work of Swiss psychologist, Jean Piaget. For Piagetians, development involves the gradual acquisition of logical abilities, which we gain simply through interacting with the environment. Babies, for example, have to learn that objects and people still exist when they cannot be seen. School-aged children have to discover the principles of perspective-taking and conservation, which reflect an ability to reconcile two conflicting pieces of information. Largely as a result of Piaget's ideas, primary education now relies much upon self-discovery, since the theory holds that children progress through a set sequence of intellectual stages which cannot be rushed. » developmental psychology; egocentrism; Piaget

piano The most important domestic and recital instrument for over 200 years, first made by Cristofori in Florence in the last years of the 17th-c. The main difference between its mechanism and that of the earlier clavichord is that the hammers (tipped with felt) rebound after they have struck the string, and this made possible the dynamic contrasts from which the instrument derived its full name ('pianoforte' = quiet/loud). During the 19th-c a succession of famous makers, including John Broadwood (1732–1814), Sébastien Erard (1752–1831), Karl Bechstein (1826–1900), Julius Ferdinand Blüthner (1824–1910), and Heinrich Engelhard Steinway (1797–1871), developed the piano to increase its volume and sustaining power, extend its compass, and refine its action (especially in the direction of rapid articulation).

The earliest pianos were built with the strings extending away from the keyboard, as in the harpsichord and the modern grand, or (in the case of the 'square' piano) at right-angles to the keys, as in the clavichord. In the 19th-c the upright model, with the strings set perpendicularly, was developed in response to the need for a sonorous, full-compass instrument that could stand in a small room. The modern piano is fitted with a mechanism operated by two pedals: the left ('soft') pedal makes the tone quieter; the other sustains it after the keys have been released. Some modern grand pianos have a third, central pedal which allows the player to sustain some notes while dampening others. In modern pianos all but the very lowest (single) strings are tuned in pairs, or threes, an important consideration in the case of some types of popular music, for which pianos are often tuned with the unisons slightly but perceptibly out of tune, giving a distinctive 'honky-tonk' timbre. » clavichord; Cristofori; keyboard instrument; player piano; prepared piano

pianola A trade name for a type of player piano manufactured by the Aeolian Corporation in the USA. » player piano

piapiac [peea**pee**ak] A crow native to C Africa; black with thick black bill and very long tail; inhabits open country and palm trees; eats insects (sometimes taken from the backs of large mammals) and palm fruit. (*Ptilostomus afer*. Family: *Corvidae*.) » crow

Piatra or **Piatra-Neamţ** [**pya**tra nyamts] 46°53N 26°23E, pop (1983) 102 584. Industrial town and capital of Neamţ county, NE Romania, on R Bistriţa; railway; chemicals, food processing, textiles, pharmaceuticals; Bistriţa monastery (1402). » Romania [i]

pica [**piy**ka] The consumption of non-food items, including in particular the consumption of soil, known as **geophagia** or **geophagy**. Animals deprived of some minerals may chew at non-foods to overcome their deficiency. Among humans, geophagy is especially common in W Africa, where village industries exist to supply the demand for rock-based pellets.

Picabia, Francis [pee**kah**bia] (1879–1953) French artist, born and died in Paris. He was one of the most anarchistic of modern artists, involved in Cubism, Dadaism, and Surrealism. He helped to introduce Dadaism to New York in 1915. His anti-art productions, often portraying senseless machinery, include 'Parade Amoureuse' (1917), and many of the cover designs for the American anti-art magazine *291*, which he edited. » Cubism; Dada; French art; Surrealism

Picardy [**pi**kadee], Fr **Picardie** pop (1982) 1 740 321; area 19 399 sq km/7 488 sq ml. Region and former province of N France, comprising departments of Aisne, Oise, and Somme; bounded NW by the English Channel; flat landscape, crossed by several rivers (eg Somme, Oise) and canals; chief towns, Abbeville, Amiens, St-Quentin, Laon, Beauvais, Compiègne; chemicals, metalworking; scene of heavy fighting during World War 1. » World War 1

picaresque novel (Sp *picaro* 'rogue') A novel which dealt originally with the comic misfortunes of a low-life character, as in the anonymous Spanish *Lazarillo de Tormes* (1553). It is now applied more loosely to the miscellaneous adventures of any character living on his wits, and often on the road. » anti-hero; novel; Spanish literature

Picasso, Pablo (Ruiz y) [pi**ka**soh] (1881–1973) Spanish artist, born at Málaga, the dominating figure of early 20th-c art. He studied at Barcelona and Madrid, and in 1901 set up a studio in Montmartre, Paris. His 'blue period' (1902–4), a series of striking studies of the poor in haunting attitudes of despair and gloom, gave way to the gay, life-affirming 'pink period' (1904–6), full of harlequins, acrobats, and the incidents of circus life. He then turned to brown, and began to work in sculpture. His break with tradition came with 'Les Demoiselles d'Avignon' (1906–7, New York), the first exemplar of analytical Cubism, a movement which he developed with Braque (1909–14). From 1917 he became associated with Diaghilev's Ballets Russes, designing costumes and sets. His major creation is 'Guernica' (1937, Madrid), expressing in synthetic Cubism his horror of the bombing of this Basque town during the Civil War. During World War 2 he was mostly in Paris, and after the liberation joined the communists. A great innovator, he also illustrated classical texts, and experimented in sculpture, ceramics, and lithography. He died at Mougins, France. » Ballets Russes; Braque; Cubism; Diaghilev; Spanish Civil War; Plate XI

Piccard, Auguste [pee**kah**] (1884–1962) Swiss physicist, born in Basle. He studied at Zürich, and became professor of applied physics at Brussels in 1922. In 1932 he ascended 16 940 m/55 563 ft into the stratosphere, and in 1948, explored the ocean depths off W Africa in a bathyscaphe of his own design. He retired in 1954, and died at Lausanne. His twin brother, **Jean (Felix)** (1884–1963) became a chemical engineer in the USA, where he also made pioneer balloon ascents. His son **Jacques (Ernest Jean)** (1922–) was a member of the team which established a world record by diving 10 900 m/35 800 ft in the US bathyscaphe *Trieste* into the Marianas Trench of the Pacific Ocean (1960). » bathyscaphe; ballooning

piccolo A small transverse flute pitched one octave higher than the standard instrument. » flute; transposing instrument; woodwind instrument [i]

Pichincha [pee**cheen**cha] 0°10S 78°35W. Andean volcano in Pichincha province, NC Ecuador; 10 km/6 ml NW of Quito; rises to 4 794 m/15 728 ft; last eruption, 1881, and still emits gases; site of decisive battle (1822) in fight for independence. » Andes

pick-up A term from the electrical period of recorded sound reproduction, describing the stylus, cantilever, and cartridge of a record player (or turntable). The undulations in the record groove are first converted into stylus lever vibrations. The light, stiff cantilever (typically aluminium or boron) conveys these movements to the cartridge, which may be of the moving magnet, moving coil, moving iron, piezo-electric, or electrostatic type. The resulting electrical oscillations are then sent via the amplifier to the loudspeakers. The development of the long-playing record and subsequently of stereophonic recordings required the development of diamond styli with progressively smaller tips. » record player; sound recording

pickerel Small freshwater pike found in slow weedy streams and lakes in E North America; length up to c.30 cm/12 in; feeds on small fish and invertebrates. (*Esox americanus*. Family: *Esocidae*.) » pike

picketing The action by a trade union in an industrial dispute to try to persuade fellow-workers and others not to go to work, or do business with the company involved in the dispute. Pickets stand outside the gates of the factory or offices, and lobby all who would go in. Trade union legislation in the UK now limits picketing to the place where the picket actually works (*primary picketing*), and requires that it be carried out peacefully. Employers may be able to take legal action to stop other forms of action, such as the picketing of locations where the company in dispute is not directly involved (*secondary picketing*), or the use of *flying pickets*, workers not employed by the company in dispute, who are nonetheless ready to travel to the scene of the industrial action to help in the picketing. » industrial action

Pickford, Mary, originally **Gladys Mary Smith** (1893–1979) US actress, born in Toronto. She made her first film in 1913, and quickly gained the title of 'America's sweetheart', playing an innocent heroine in many silent films. A co-founder of United Artists Corporation (1919), she retired in the 1930s, and died at Santa Monica, California. » silent film

Pico de Orizaba » **Citlaltépetl**

Pico della Mirandola, Giovanni (1463–94) Italian Renaissance philosopher, born at Mirandola, Ferrara. He studied in Italy and France, and in 1486 offered to defend 900 theses on Christian theology at Rome, but the debate was forbidden on the grounds that some of the theses were heretical (a charge from which he was absolved in 1493). His philosophy was an attempt to combine the insights of many of his predecessors. He wrote Latin epistles and elegies, a series of Italian sonnets, and a major study of free will, *De hominis dignitate oratio* (1486, Oration on the Dignity of Man). He died in Florence. » Renaissance

picofarad » **farad**

picric acid $C_6H_2(NO_2)_3OH$, 2,4,6-trinitrophenol, melting point 122°C. A yellow solid, made by nitrating phenol. A weak acid, but stronger than phenol, it is a yellow dye and an explosive. » phenol; TNT [i]

pictography The study of writing systems, which make use of symbols called **pictographs** or **pictograms** – direct, stylised representations of objects in the real world, drawn in outline. Pictographic writing is the oldest form of writing known, and occurs very widely throughout the world; the earliest discovered in Egypt is dated to c.3000 BC. Pictographs must be sufficiently suggestive of their referents to be recognized unambiguously. They have one potential advantage over other writing systems, in that they represent objects, and not linguistic elements; in this way, they are independent of any specific language system, and might be thought to cross over language boundaries. However, they are difficult to interpret outside the artistic and other representational conventions specific to the culture in which they were devised; consequently very many remain undeciphered, because we cannot be certain what a particular arrangement of lines and curves stands for. They are inherently ambiguous linguistically, too; for example, they cannot convey when an event occurred, or whether it is completed, on-going, or to happen in the future. » graphology; hieroglyphics [i]; ideography

Pictor (Lat 'easel') A small inconspicuous S constellation, near

PICTOGRAPHY

Some of the pictographic symbols used on seals and tablet in the early Minoan period in Crete. Over 100 symbols represent human figures, body parts, animals, and other everyday objects. Not everything is immediately recognizable, showing that there has been some development towards an ideographic system.

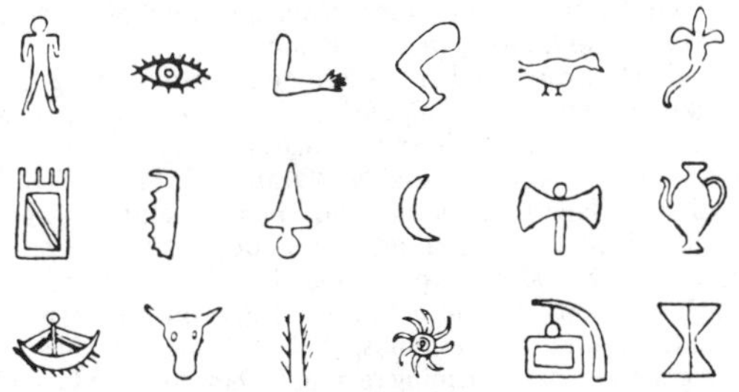

Some modern pictographic road signs

the Large Magellanic Cloud. » constellation; Magellanic Clouds; RR9

Picts (Lat *picti* 'painted people') A general term coined by the Romans in the 3rd-c for their barbarian enemies in Britain N of the Antonine Wall, and then used to describe the subjects of kings ruling N and S of the E Grampians. The name derives from the local custom of body tattooing. They disappear from history soon after being united with the Scots under Kenneth I. Traces of their language and art – notably the enigmatic Pictish symbol stones – survive. » Antonine Wall; Britain, Roman; Kenneth I

Picturesque A word used vaguely nowadays to mean 'as pretty as a picture', but in the 18th-c much discussed as an aesthetic category in its own right, somewhere between 'beautiful' and 'sublime'. It was applied mainly to rugged landscapes with rocks, waterfalls, and winding paths. » landscape painting

piculet » **woodpecker**

piddock A marine bivalve mollusc that bores into hard substrates such as chalk or wood on the lower shore in shallow waters; lives in a hollowed-out chamber in the substrate; takes in water by means of long siphons. (Class: *Pelecypoda*.) » bivalve; mollusc

pidgin A language with a highly simplified grammar and vocabulary, the native language of no one, which develops when people who lack a common language attempt to communicate. Pidgins flourish in areas of trade contact, and were particularly common in the East and West Indies, Africa, and the Americas, based on English, French, Spanish, and Portuguese, during the days of colonial exploration. Some pidgins have developed into important systems of communication, such as Tok Pisin in Papua New Guinea, which is used on the radio and in the press. Pidgins become *creoles* when they are used by people as a mother-tongue. » creole; language

Pied Piper of Hamelin In German legend a 13th-c piper who charmed Hamelin's rats out of the city with his pipe-music. He was refused his fee, and in revenge lured all the children away from the city. Goethe and Robert Browning tell the tale; the legend may have its roots in the Children's Crusade of 1212. » Children's Crusade

Piedmont [**peed**mont], Ital **Piemonte** pop (1981) 4 479 031; area 25 400 sq km/9 804 sq ml. Region of N Italy; centre of Italian unification in 19th-c; capital, Turin; chief towns, Cuneo, Saluzzo, Asti, Alessandria; bounded (S) by the Appenines and (N, W) Alps; industries (metalworking, machinery, cars, textiles, leather, foodstuffs) around Turin, Ivrea, Biella; fruit-growing, arable farming, cattle in Po valley; tourism in hill regions. » Italy [i]

Piedras, Las [las **pyay**dras] 34°42S 56°14W, pop (1985) 57 711. Town in Canelones department, Uruguay; railway; wine, fruit, cattle. » Uruguay [i]

Piero della Francesca [fran**chay**ska] (c.1420–92) Italian painter, born and died at Borgo San Sepolcro. He is known especially for his series of frescoes, 'The Legend of the True Cross' (1452–66) at the church of San Francesco in Arezzo. He also wrote a treatise on geometry and a manual on perspective. » Florentine School; fresco; Italian art

Piero di Cosimo, originally **Piero de Lorenzo** (c.1462–c.1521) Italian painter, born and died in Florence. His later work, influenced by Signorelli and Leonardo, is largely devoted to mythological scenes, notably 'Death of Procris' (c.1500, National Gallery, London) and 'Perseus and Andromeda' (c.1515, Uffizi). » Italian art; Leonardo da Vinci; Signorelli

Pierre 44°22N 100°21W, pop (1980) 11 973. Capital of state in Hughes County, C South Dakota, USA, on the Missouri R; founded as a railway terminus, 1880; state capital, 1889; centre of a grain and dairy farming region; L Oahe and the Oahe Dam nearby. » South Dakota

Pierrot An evocative fictional character with a rich theatrical, literary, and artistic history. Originally Pedrolino, a servant role in the *commedia dell' arte*, Pierrot gained his white face and white floppy costume on the French stage. His childlike manner and his pathos, dumb and solitary, was the creation of the great 19th-c pantomimist Deburau. » *commedia dell' arte*; pantomime

pierrot show A British form of concert party created, due to the popularity of Pierrot, in the 1890s. Dressed in white or black, with pompoms, ruffs, and – for the men – a dunce's cap, the pierrot-troupes performed their form of variety on the beaches and piers of seaside towns. » Pierrot

pietà In art, the representation of the dead Christ mourned by angels, apostles, or holy women. Michelangelo's famous marble 'Pietà' (c.1500) in St Peter's shows Christ lying peacefully in the lap of his mother, represented as young and beautiful; but most representations of the subject are dramatic and emotional. » Jesus Christ; Michelangelo

Pietermaritzburg [peeter**ma**ritzberg] or **Maritzburg** 30°33S 30°24E, pop (1980) 178 972. Capital of Natal province, E South Africa, 73 km/45 ml WNW of Durban; founded by Boers from Cape Colony, 1838; railway; university (1910); centre of rich farming area; footwear, aluminium, rubber, furniture, rice; Voortrekker Museum, Macrorie House Museum. » Afrikaners; Natal (South Africa)

Pietism Originally, a movement within Lutheranism in the 17th-c and 18th-c stressing good works, Bible study, and holiness in Christian life. It was a reaction against rigid Protestant dogmatism, and influenced other groups, such as Moravians, Methodists, and Evangelicals. » Lutheranism; Methodism; Moravian Brethren

piezo-electric effect [piy**eet**zoh i**lek**trik] The appearance of an electric field in some material as a result of the application of stress, as in quartz and bone. Stress distorts the crystals, causing unbalanced electrical forces in the material. The effect is exploited in gas cooker lighters, load sensors, and transducers. » electric field; stress (physics); transducer

pig A mammal native to woodland in Europe, S Asia, and Africa; an artiodactyl; stout body with short legs and coarse hair; short thin tail; face in front of ears and small eyes very long; snout muscular, flattened, disc-like (often used for digging); lower and/or upper canine teeth may form upward-pointing tusks; eats plant and animal food; male called *boar*, female called *sow*, young called *piglets*; also known as **hog** or **swine**. The name *pig* is usually used for the domestic pig (*Sus scrofa*). (Family: *Suidae*, 9 species.) » artiodactyl; babirusa; landrace; warthog; wild boar

pig-iron The product of the blast furnace. The molten iron is run into channels which have moulds led off them, fancifully likened to pigs in a litter. This cast-iron has a high proportion of carbon (c.4%) which has to be reduced to under 1% to form steel. » blast furnace [i]; steel

pigeon A bird of the widespread family *Columbidae* (c. 255 species); plump with round bill; nostrils on fleshy band (*cere*); strong flier; inhabits diverse areas; eats fruit, seeds, and some invertebrates; many domestic breeds. The name is also used for the **pigeon guillemot** (Family: *Alcidae*) and the **Cape pigeon** (Family: *Procellariidae*). » dove; guillemot; passenger pigeon; petrel; rock dove; wood pigeon

pigeon hawk » **merlin**

Piggott, Lester (Keith) (1935–) British jockey, born at Wantage, Berkshire. He rode his first winner at the age of 12, and his first Epsom Derby winner in 1954 on *Never Say Die*. He subsequently rode a record nine winners of the race, and a record 29 English Classic winners between 1954 and 1985. During his career (1948–85) he rode 4 349 winners in Britain, a figure bettered only by Gordon Richards, and was champion jockey 11 times. After retiring, he took up training at Newmarket, but was imprisoned (1987–8) for tax offences. » Classics; horse racing; Richards, Gordon

pigments Colouring materials. (1) **Biological** pigments are substances, usually similar to dyestuffs, which give colour to tissues. (2) **Industrial** pigments give colour and opacity to paints, plastics, and other materials by being dispersed through them. A good pigment must be suitably stable to light and chemical attack. » skin [i]

pignut » **earthnut**

pigweed » **amaranth**

pika [**pee**ka, **piy**ka] A mammal of order *Lagomorpha*, native to C and NE Asia and W North America; resembles a small rabbit, with short legs, short rounded ears, and minute tail; inhabits rocky areas or open country; also known as **cony**, **coney**, **rock rabbit**, **slide rat**, **little chief hare**, **mouse hare**, **haymaker**, **squeak**

rabbit, **whistling hare**, or **calling hare**. (Family: *Ochotonidae*, 14 species.) » hyrax; lagomorph

pike Any of the large predatory freshwater fish of the family *Esocidae*; distinguished by an elongate body with dorsal and anal fins set close to the tail; snout pointed, jaws large; includes familiar *Esox lucius*, found in well-weeded rivers and lakes throughout N Europe, Russia, and N America; length up to 1.5 m/5 ft; mottled greenish brown; feeds on fish and other aquatic vertebrates, including birds; highly prized by anglers.

pikeperch » **zander**

piket » **skunk**

pilaster [pilaster] A rectangular pillar that projects only slightly from the wall of a building. In classical architecture it is usually designed according to one of the five orders. » orders of architecture [i]

Pilate, Pontius, properly **Pontius Pilatus** (1st-c) Roman appointed by Tiberius in c.26 as prefect of Judea, having charge of the state and the occupying military forces, but subordinate to the legate of Syria. Although based in Caesarea, he also resided in Jerusalem, and was noted for his order to execute Jesus of Nazareth by crucifixion at the prompting of the Jewish authorities. He caused unrest by his use of Temple funds to build an aqueduct, by his temporary location of Roman standards in Jerusalem, and by his slaughter of Samaritans in 36 (for which he was recalled). » Annas; Jesus Christ; Roman history [i]

pilchard Small herring-like surface-living fish widespread and locally abundant in the E North Atlantic and Mediterranean; length up to 25 cm/10 in; greenish blue above, underside silver; important commercial fish, usually canned for marketing; also called **sardine**. The name is also used for several similar clupeid species in the genera *Sardinella* and *Sardinops*. (*Sardina pilchardus*. Family: *Clupeidae*.) » herring

piles » **haemorrhoids**

Pilgrim Fathers The English religious dissenters who established Plymouth Colony in America in 1620, after crossing the Atlantic aboard the *Mayflower*; 102 sailed, and one was born at sea. They originally came from Lincolnshire, but had spent an extended period in the Netherlands before migrating to America. » Mayflower

Pilgrim's Way A long-distance footpath in Surrey and Kent, S England, opened in 1972. The path is pre-Roman; its name derives from the popular belief that it was used by mediaeval pilgrims travelling from Winchester to Canterbury.

Pilgrimage of Grace (Oct 1536–Jan 1537) A major Tudor rebellion in England, a series of armed demonstrations in six N counties. It was directed against the policies and ministers of Henry VIII, and combined upper-class and popular discontent over religious and secular issues. It was led by Lord Thomas Darcy (1467–1537), Robert Aske (?–1537), and 'pilgrims' carrying banners of the Five Wounds of Christ. » Henry VIII

pill » **contraception**

Pillars of Hercules The ancient mythological name for the promontories flanking the Strait of Gibralter: the Rock of Gibralter and Cueta, N Africa. They guard the entrance to the Mediterranean Sea. » Mediterranean Sea

pillars of Islam » **Islam**

pilot whale A toothed whale of family *Delphinidae*; black with bulbous overhanging snout; eats squid (and some fish); two species: **long-finned pilot whale**, **blackfish**, or **ca(a)'ing whale** (*Globicephala melaena*) from N Atlantic and cool temperate S oceans; **Pacific pilot whale** (*Globicephala sieboldii*) from tropical and warm temperate oceans. » whale [i]

pilotfish Marine fish which derives its name from the behaviour of juveniles that swim alongside ships or larger fish such as sharks; adults tend to be solitary; length up to 60 cm/2 ft; greyish blue on back with banding on sides; widely distributed in tropical and warm temperate seas. (*Naucrates ductor*. Family: *Carangidae*.)

pilotis [pilotee, piloteez] Posts or columns used on the ground floor of a building to raise most of the main body to first-floor level, thus leaving unenclosed space below. Usually slender and circular in section, they are particularly associated with the work of the 20th-c architect Le Corbusier. » column; Corbusier, Le; International Style **2**

Pilsen » **Plzeň**

Piłsudski, Józef (1867–1935) Polish Marshal and statesman, born near Vilna, and educated at the University of Kharkov. Often imprisoned in the cause of Polish independence, he was leader of the Polish Socialist Party (1892), and formed a band of troops which fought on the side of Austria during World War 1. He declared Poland's independence in 1918, and served as President until 1922. He returned to power in 1926 by means of a military coup, and established a dictatorship. He died in Warsaw. » Poland [i]; socialism

Piltdown Man A supposed early fossil man found in 1912 near Piltdown, Sussex, England; named *Eoanthropus* ('Dawn Man'). Later study proved the find a forgery, with a modern human cranium and the jawbone of an orang-utan. » *Homo* [i]

pimento » **allspice**

pimpernel A sprawling annual weed; cosmopolitan; leaves paired, shiny, oval; flowers on long slender stalks, five petals. Scarlet and blue pimpernels are different coloured forms of the same plant. (*Anagallis arvensis*.) » annual

PIN An acronym of **Personal Identification Number**; a unique number allocated to the users of computer-based equipment which allows the identity of each user to be established. It is often used in modern banking systems, where users can draw cash from machines on presentation of their card plus their PIN.

pin-yin » **Chinese**

Pinakothek, Alte [altuh peenakohtek] A museum founded in 1836 in Munich, Germany. It houses one of the finest collections of German, Dutch, Flemish, and Spanish paintings from the 14th-c to the 18th-c. The adjacent **Neue Pinakothek** was established in 1853, and houses 19th-c and 20th-c paintings and sculptures. » Munich; museum

pinchbeck An alloy of copper and zinc, but with less zinc than in brass. It is named after London watchmaker Christopher Pinchbeck (1670–1732) who used it to simulate gold. » alloy; brass; copper; zinc

Pinckney, Charles Cotesworth (1746–1825) US statesman, born and died at Charleston, South Carolina. Educated at Oxford, he became a lawyer. He was Washington's aide-de-camp at Brandywine and Germantown, but was taken prisoner at the surrender of Charleston (1780). A member of the convention that framed the US constitution (1787), he introduced the clause forbidding religious tests. He was twice Federalist candidate for the presidency (1804–8). » American Revolution

Pincus, Gregory Goodwin (1903–67) US biologist, born at Woodbine, New Jersey. He followed his father by graduating in agriculture, then studied biology at Cambridge, Berlin, and Harvard before setting up his own consultancy. Inspired in 1951 by the birth control campaigner Margaret Sanger (1883–1966), he concentrated on reproduction, and found that some of the new synthetic hormones controlled fertility effectively. Field trials in 1954 were successful, leading to the development of the contraceptive pill. He died in Boston, Massachusetts. » contraception; hormones

Pindar (c.522–c.440 BC) The chief lyric poet of Greece, born near Thebes. Educated in Athens, he became famous as a composer of odes for people in all parts of the Greek world. Although he wrote for all kinds of circumstances, only his *Epinikia* (Triumphal Odes) have survived entire, four books celebrating the victories won in the Olympian, Pythian, Nemean, and Isthmian games. He died at Argos. » Greek literature; ode; poetry

Pindus Mountains, Gr **Píndhos Óros** Mountain range in WC and NW Greece; length c.500 km/310 ml, from the Albanian frontier to near the Gulf of Corinth; highest peak, Smolikas (2 633 m/8 638 ft); watershed between rivers flowing to the Aegean Sea and to the Ionian Sea. » Greece [i]

pine A large genus of evergreen conifers widespread throughout the N hemisphere. The branches and twigs are in whorls, each whorl representing one year's growth. The leaves are of three kinds: (1) seedling leaves, narrow, toothed; (2) adult scale leaves, borne on long shoots but soon falling; (3) adult needle leaves in bundles of 2, 3, or 5, according to species, borne on short shoots in the axils of the scale leaves. The cones are woody, at least two years old when ripe. Pines are of great commercial importance, and are planted on a vast scale. The timber is resistant to decay because of a high content of resin, rich in oil of turpentine. This yields turpentine, tar, and pitch on distillation, and is also the source of the distinctive foliage scent. (Genus: *Pinus*, 70–100 species. Family: *Pinaceae*.) » conifer; evergreen plants; leaf [i]; resin

pine marten A marten often found in trees; brown with pale markings on undersurface; nests in holes; two species: **European pine marten** (*Martes martes*) from coniferous and deciduous forests in Europe and Asia, and **American pine marten** (*Martes americana*) from coniferous forests of N America. » marten

pineal gland [**pin**ial] A small gland of vertebrates situated above the third ventricle of the brain, and separated from the brain by the blood-brain barrier. It synthesizes the hormone *melatonin*, whose release is under the control of sympathetic fibres, and whose activity is synchronized with the light-dark cycle. It has an important role in determining seasonal breeding patterns in some mammals. » biological rhythm; blood-brain barrier; brain [i]; melatonin

pineapple An evergreen perennial native to S America; leaves stiff, arching, sword-shaped, spiny, grey-green; flowers 3-petalled, blue, in a dense cone-like inflorescence topped by a leafy spire; individual fruits fusing to form a fleshy, yellow multiple fruit up to 30 cm/12 in long. It is an important crop in much of the tropics. The cultivars include seedless forms, and variegated ornamentals. The juice from the fruit is rich in vitamins A and B. (*Ananas comosus*. Family: *Bromeliaceae*.) » bromeliad; cultivar; evergreen plants; inflorescence [i]; perennial; vitamins [i]

pineapple mint » **mint**

Pinero, Sir Arthur (Wing) [pi**nay**roh] (1855–1934) British playwright, born and died in London. He studied law, but in 1874 made his debut on the stage at Edinburgh, and in 1875 joined the Lyceum company. He wrote several farces, but is best known for his social dramas, notably *The Second Mrs Tanqueray* (1893), which made him the most successful playwright of his day. He was knighted in 1909. » drama

pingo An Inuit word used to describe an ice-cored hill found in areas of permafrost. As an ice lens forms in the ground, it pushes the overlying earth up into a mound. Pingos in the Northwest Territories, Canada, can reach 70 m/230 ft in height. » permafrost

pink An annual, biennial, or perennial herb with grass-like, paired, often bluish leaves, native to the temperate N hemisphere; flowers with short, tubular epicalyx and tubular calyx; five petals, spreading, toothed or slightly frilly, pink, also red or white, often scented. Many species are cultivated in gardens. The genus includes the well-known carnations and sweet williams of horticulture. (Genus: *Dianthus*, 300 species. Family: *Caryophyllaceae*.) » annual; biennial; carnation; epicalyx; herb; horticulture; perennial; sweet William

pink salmon Comparatively small salmon species native to the N Pacific, but now introduced to the Atlantic; length up to 75 cm/30 in; dorsal surface with small black spots; spawning males have a distinctive humped back and red coloration; commercially important as a food fish. (*Oncorhynchus gorbuscha*. Family: *Salmonidae*.) » salmon

Pinkerton, Allan (1819–84) US detective, born in Glasgow, Scotland, UK. He was a Chartist who in 1842 settled at Dundee, Illinois, became a detective and deputy-sheriff, and in 1850 founded the Pinkerton National Detective Agency. He headed a Federal intelligence network during the Civil War, and his agency later took a leading part in breaking up the Molly Maguires and in policing other labour disputes. He died in Chicago. » Molly Maguires

pinnate The shape of a leaf divided into several lobes or leaflets arranged in two opposite rows along the stalk. In **bi-pinnate** leaves, the leaflets are themselves pinnate. » leaf [i]

Pinochet (Ugarte), Augusto [**pee**nuhshay] (1915–) Chilean dictator, born in Valparaíso. A career army officer, he led the military coup overthrowing the Allende government (1973), establishing himself at the head of the ensuing military regime. In 1980 he enacted a constitution giving himself an eight-year presidential term (1981–9). A plebiscite held in 1988 rejected his candicacy as President beyond 1990. » Allende; Chile [i]

pinochle [**pee**nuhkl] A card game derived from bézique. Two packs of 24 cards are used, all cards from 2–8 having been discarded. The object is to win tricks, as in whist, and to score points according to the cards won. Cards have the following values: ace–11, ten–10, king–4, queen–3, jack–2, nine–0. » bézique; playing cards; whist

pint » **litre**

pinta [**pin**ta] An infection with a non-venereal spirochaete, a bacterium endemic in C and S America. It causes a number of skin lesions depending on the stage of the illness. » bacteria [i]

pintail A dabbling duck of genus *Anas* (3 species): two are native to S America and the Caribbean; one to the N hemisphere (*Anas acuta*). The male has long central tail feathers. *Anas acuta* may be the most abundant duck in the world. » dabbling duck

Pinter, Harold (1930–) British playwright, born in London. He became a repertory actor, wrote poetry, then turned to drama. His first major play, *The Birthday Party* (1958), was badly received, but was revived after the success of *The Caretaker* (1960). Later plays include *The Homecoming* (1965), *Old Times* (1971), and *No Man's Land* (1975), and he has written many television and film scripts. An explicit commitment to radical political causes is evident in the short prison play *Mountain Language* (1988). » drama; English literature

pinworm » **nematode**

pion [**pi**yon] A strongly interacting sub-atomic particle of the meson family; symbol π; three possible charges: $+1$, -1 (π^+, π^-, mass 140 MeV each), and 0 (π^0, mass 135 MeV); spin zero; also called a **pi-meson**. Charged pions decay to muons and neutrinos; neutral pions decay to gamma rays. Discovered in cosmic ray experiments in 1947, in nuclear physics pions are carriers of strong nuclear force. » meson; nuclear physics; particle physics

Pioneer programme A series of relatively simple spin-stabilized spacecraft launched by the USA 1958–78. Pioneers 1 to 3 were Air Force 'lunar' flights that were only partially successful. Pioneers 4 to 9 explored the interplanetary medium from orbits around the Sun at about the same distance as Earth. Pioneers 10 and 11 (launched in 1972 and 1973) achieved the first flybys of Jupiter (Dec 1973, Apr 1974) and of Saturn (Pioneer 11 in 1979), and the first exploration of the boundary of the Sun's influence (heliopause). Pioneer 12 was the first US Venus orbiter, and Pioneer 13's four probes successfully explored Venus' atmosphere (1978). Since 1970, the programme has been managed and operated by NASA's Ames Research Center. » NASA; planet

pipa A Chinese lute with a pear-shaped body, short neck, fretted soundboard, and four silk strings plucked with the fingernails. » lute; string instrument **2** [i]

pipal » **peepul**

Pipe Rolls Records of the English Exchequer containing county by county the annual accounts of sheriffs and other royal officials. They were so called because they consisted of sheets of parchment rolled into the shape of pipes. The earliest Pipe Roll to survive is that of 1130, and they form a virtually complete series from 1156 until discontinued in 1832.

pipefish Distinctive fish with a very slender segmented body, small mouth on a tubular snout, and delicate fins; with seahorses and seadragons, comprises the family *Syngnathidae* (11 genera); feeds on plankton and fish larvae; length up to 60 cm/2 ft, typically much smaller; eggs carried by males, in some species within a special brood pouch. » fish [i]

Piper, John (1903–) British artist, born at Epsom, Surrey. An abstract artist in the 1930s, he developed a representational style, as seen in his pictures of war damage, and his topographical pictures, notably the watercolours of 'Windsor Castle' commissioned by the Queen in 1941–2. He is also known for his theatre sets, as well as the stained glass design in Coventry Cathedral. » abstract art; English art; watercolour

Piper, Leonora E (1857–1950) US medium, discovered in 1885 by William James. Mrs Piper's trance speech and writing were studied extensively (1885–1911) by James and other members of the American and British Societies for Psychical Research. She became for William James his 'white crow', when he became convinced of the paranormal origin of some of her trance utterances. » James, William; medium (parapsychology)

Piper Alpha An oil-drilling platform in the North Sea, off the coast of Scotland, which was destroyed by an explosion in July 1988. The disaster killed 167, and resulted in insurance claims approaching 1.5 thousand million dollars.

pipes of Pan » **panpipes**

pipistrelle [pipistrel] A bat of family *Vespertilionidae*; genus *Pipistrellus* (46 species), found worldwide except S America; includes the smallest bats; among the first bats to fly in the evening; erratic in flight; also genus *Glischropus* (2 species), called **thick-thumbed pipistrelles**. » bat

pipit A wagtail of worldwide genus *Anthus* (34 dull-coloured species), or the more colourful African genera *Tmetothylacus* (1 species) and *Macronyx* (8 species, the 'longclaws'). They sing during fluttering, descending flights. » wagtail

Piquet, Nelson [peekay], byname of **Nelson Souto Maior** (1952–) Brazilian motor racing driver, born in Rio de Janeiro. He changed his name so that his parents would not find out about his racing exploits. He was British Formula Three champion in 1978, and world champion in 1981, 1983 (both Brabham), and 1987 (Williams). He won 20 races from 157 starts between 1978 and 1988. » motor racing

Piraeus [piyreeuhs], Gr **Piraiéus** 37°57N 23°42E, pop (1981) 196 389. Major port in Attica department, Greece; on a hilly peninsula, 8 km/5 ml SW of Athens; the port of Athens since the 5th-c BC; main harbour, Kantharos, with two ancient harbours still used on the E coast; rail terminus; ferries to the Greek islands; Navy Week (Jun–Jul). » Athens; Greece [i]

Pirandello, Luigi (1867–1936) Italian author, born at Girgenti, Sicily. He studied at Rome and Bonn, becoming a lecturer in literature at Rome (1897–1922). After writing several realistic novels and short stories, he turned to the theatre, becoming a leading exponent of the 'grotesque' school of contemporary drama. Among his plays are *Six Characters in Search of an Author* (1920) and *Enrico IV* (1922). In 1925 he established a theatre of his own in Rome, where he died. In 1934 he was awarded the Nobel Prize for Literature. » drama; Italian literature

Piranesi, Giovanni Battista or **Giambattista** [peeranayzee] (1720–78) Italian architect and copper-engraver of Roman antiquities, born in Venice. He settled in Rome in 1745, where he developed original techniques of etching, and produced c.2000 plates of the city, both in ancient times and in his own day. A major influence on classical archaeology and Neoclassicism, he died in Rome. » etching; Italian art; Neoclassicism (art and architecture)

piranha [pirahna] Any of several voracious predatory freshwater fishes widespread in rivers of S America; body deep and robust; length up to 60 cm/2 ft; strong jaws and sharp interlocking teeth; extremely aggressive flesh-eating fish, often feeding in large shoals. » fish [i]

Pirani gauge An instrument for measuring the degree of vacuum. Electrically heated thin wire, initially in equilibrium, loses heat faster or slower as pressure changes; consequent change in the resistance of the wire is thus a measure of the change of pressure of the surrounding gas. » vacuum

Pire, Dominique (Georges) [peer] (1910–69) Belgian Dominican priest and educator, born at Dinant. He lectured at Louvain (1937–47), and worked in the resistance during World War 2. He was awarded the 1958 Nobel Peace Prize for his scheme of 'European villages' for elderly refugees and destitute children. He died at Louvain. » Dominicans

Pisa [peeza] 43°43N 10°24E, pop (1981) 104 509. Capital town of Pisa province, Tuscany, W Italy, on both banks of the R Arno, 10 km/6 ml from the Ligurian Sea; formerly a major port, now distanced from the sea through river silting; archbishopric; airport; railway; university (1343); glass, motorcycles, yachts, tourism; birthplace of Galileo; cathedral (11th–12th-c), baptistery (12th–14th-c), Campo Santo cemetery; campanile (the 'Leaning Tower', 1173–1350), 55 m/180 ft high, now in danger of collapse; Piazza del Duomo is a world heritage site; carnival (Feb); Gioco del Ponte historic boat races (Jun). » Galileo; Italy [i]

Pisanello [peezaneloh], properly **Antonio Pisano** (c.1395–c.1455) Italian medallist and painter, born in Pisa. He seems to have studied in Verona, and travelled widely, painting frescoes (all since destroyed) in the Doge's Palace at Venice (1415–20) and in the Lateran Basilica in Rome (1431–2). Little of his painting survives, but numerous drawings attest to his mastery of the International Gothic style with its precise study of costumes, birds, and animals. He died (probably) in Rome. » International Gothic; Italian art

Pisano, Andrea or **Andrea da Pontedera** (c.1270–1349) Italian sculptor, born at Pontedera. He became famous as a worker in bronze and marble, and settled in Florence, where he completed the earliest bronze doors of the baptistery (1336). In 1347 he produced reliefs and statues for the cathedral at Orvieto, where he died. » Italian art; sculpture

Pisano, Nicola (c.1225–c.78) Italian sculptor of Pisa, known for three major works in a classicizing style that anticipated the Renaissance by two centuries: the pulpit of the baptistery at Pisa (1260), the shrine of St Dominic for a church at Bologna (1267), and the pulpit of Siena cathedral (1268). » Italian art; Renaissance; sculpture

Pisces (Lat 'fishes') [piyseez] A large N constellation which lacks bright stars, and so is hard to identify. It is a winter sign of the zodiac, lying between Aquarius and Aries. » constellation; RR9

Piscis Austrinus (Lat 'southern fish') [piysis ostriynuhs] A small S hemisphere constellation, which includes the 1st magnitude star Fomalhaut. » constellation; RR9

Pisistratus [pisistratuhs] (c.600–527 BC) Tyrant of Athens (561–c.556 BC, 546–527 BC). A moderate and far-sighted ruler, he did much to improve the lot of the small farmer in Attica, and to boost Athenian trade abroad, especially in the Black Sea area. A patron of the arts, he invited the leading Greek poets of the day to settle in Athens, where he set about fostering a sense of national unity by instituting or expanding great religious and cultural festivals. He was succeeded by his sons Hippias and Hipparchus, the so-called *Pisistratidae*, but the dynasty was overthrown in 510 BC. » Greek history; tyrant

Pissarro, Camille [peesaroh] (1830–1903) French Impressionist artist, born at St Thomas, West Indies. He went in 1855 to Paris, where he was much influenced by Corot's landscapes. Most of his works were painted in or around Paris, such as 'Boulevard Montmartre' (1897, National Gallery, London). He was the leader of the original Impressionists, and the only one to exhibit at all eight of the Group exhibitions in Paris (1874–86). He also experimented with Divisionism. He died in Paris. » Corot; Divisionism; French art; Impressionism (art)

Pissis, Monte [peesees] 27°45S 68°40W. Andean peak rising to 6 858 m/22 500 ft on the border between Catamarca and La Rioja provinces, Argentina. » Andes

pistachio [pistahshioh] A small deciduous tree growing to 6 m/20 ft, native to W Asia; leaves pinnate with 3–5 leaflets and slightly winged stalk; flowers greenish, in long, loose heads; fruit 2–2.5 cm/¾–1 in, red-brown, nut-like. It is widely cultivated for its edible seeds, used in confectionery. (*Pistachio vera*. Family: *Anacardiaceae*.) » deciduous plants; pinnate; tree [i]

pistil » **carpel**

pistol A hand-held firearm first developed from 'hand-cannons' in the 14th-c. The application of the revolver principle in the 1830s made the pistol a multi-shot weapon, while the development of 'automatic' weapons around 1900 (such as the Luger and Browning) was a further refinement. » revolver

pit viper A viper of the subfamily *Crotalinae* (142 species), sometimes treated as a separate family (*Crotalidae*, with the remaining vipers called *true vipers*); absent from Africa; front of face with small heat-sensitive pit on each side; can hunt and attack in total darkness by sensing prey's body heat. » bushmaster; copperhead; cottonmouth; fer-de-lance; viper [i] *see illustration p 946*

Pitcairn Islands pop (1983) 61; area 27 sq km/10 sq ml. Island group in the SE Pacific Ocean, E of French Polynesia; comprises Pitcairn I (4.5 sq km/1.7 sq ml) and the uninhabited islands of Ducie, Henderson, and Oeno; chief settlement,

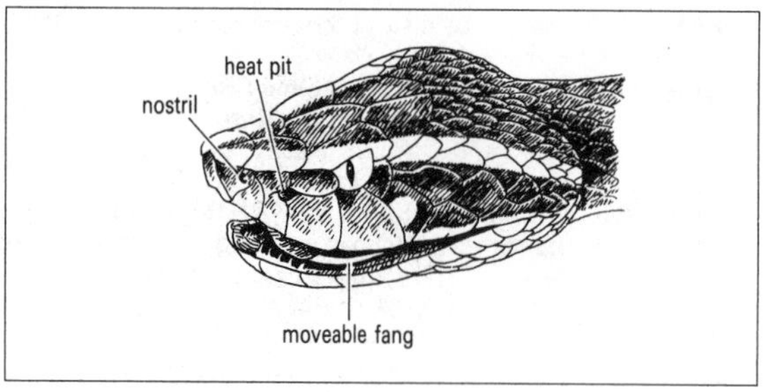

Pit viper

Adamstown; timezone GMT $-8\frac{1}{2}$; chief religion, Seventh Day Adventism; official language, English; New Zealand currency in use; volcanic islands, with high lava cliffs and rugged hills; Pitcairn I rises to 335 m/1 099 ft; equable climate, average annual rainfall 2 000 mm/80 in; average monthly temperatures, 24°C (Jan), 19°C (Jul); visited by the British, 1767; occupied by nine mutineers from HMS *Bounty*, 1790; overpopulation led to emigration to Norfolk I in 1856, some returning in 1864; transferred to Fiji, 1952; now a British Crown Colony, governed by the High Commissioner in New Zealand; Island Magistrate presides over a 10-member Council; postage stamps, tropical and subtropical crops, crafts, forestry. » Bounty Mutiny; Norfolk Island; Pacific Ocean

pitch (acoustics) An aspect of auditory sensation which makes listeners judge a sound as relatively 'high' or 'low'. The pitch at which a musical note sounds, and to which instruments are tuned, has varied considerably from one period to another, and often within a particular period. The present standard, $a' = 440$ Hz (cycles per second), was adopted by the International Organization for Standardization in 1955. Anyone who can name accurately the pitch of an isolated note is said to possess 'absolute' or 'perfect' pitch. » auditory perception

pitch (chemistry) The black, semi-solid residue left after the distillation of tar, used in bitumen and road-surfacing. It contains a complex mixture of hydrocarbons and resins, and is soluble in some organic solvents. » tar

pitchblende or **uraninite** Uranium oxide (UO_2), the chief ore of uranium; hard, very dense, and radioactive. It is found in high temperature veins related to igneous rocks. » igneous rock; uranium

pitcher plant Any of three separate families of carnivorous plants, in which the leaves are modified to form lidded pitcher traps containing water and enzymes. The pitchers are often flushed or blotched with red, and have honey glands and sometimes translucent 'windows' on the inner surface, or emit odours to attract insect prey; below the honey glands is a smooth 'slide zone' down which the insects fall. A second zone of downward-pointing hairs prevents the prey from climbing out, and it drowns in the fluid-filled base, where it is digested by the plant. The *Sarraceniaceae*, native to eastern N America, California, and tropical S America, are perennial herbs with basal rosettes of long, curved pitchers, flowers nodding, solitary or several on a leafless stem. The *Nepenthaceae*, native to the tropics of SE Asia, Australia, and Madagascar, are herbs, shrubs, often epiphytes and climbing by means of tendrils formed from an extension of the leaf midrib. In most species the end of the tendril expands to form a jug-shaped pitcher; flowers small, in spikes, males and females on separate plants; petals absent, but 4–5 sepals often brightly coloured. The *Cephalotaceae* contains a single species, the **flycatcher plant** (*Cephalotus follicularis*), native to W Australia; a perennial herb with a basal rosette in which some leaves form jug-shaped pitchers; flowers with six coloured sepals, borne on a leafless stem. » carnivorous plant; enzyme; epiphyte; herb; perennial; sepal; shrub

Piteşti [peetesht] 44°51N 24°51E, pop (1983) 149 684. Capital of Argeş county, Romania, on R Argeş; railway junction; petrochemicals, vehicles, electric motors, textiles, wine, fruit. » Romania [i]

Pithecanthropus [pithuh**kan**thruhpuhs] A name formerly used for the fossil ape-man, *Homo erectus*, which includes Java Man and Peking Man. » *Homo* [i]

Pitman, Sir Isaac (1813–97) British inventor of a shorthand system, born at Trowbridge, Wiltshire. He became a clerk, then a teacher, but was dismissed for joining the New (Swedenborgian) Church. After 1843 he specialized in the development of shorthand and spelling reform. In 1842 he brought out the *Phonetic Journal*, and in 1845 opened premises in London. Knighted in 1894, he died in Somerset. » shorthand [i]; spelling reform

Pitot tube An instrument for measuring the velocity of a flowing fluid; named after French engineer Henri Pitot (1695–1771). An open-ended tube faces the direction of the flow: the pressure observed by an attached manometer is a function of velocity. » anemometer [i]; manometer

Pitt, William, 1st Earl of Chatham, often called **Pitt the Elder** (1708–78) British statesman and orator, born in London. Educated at Eton and Oxford, he joined the army (1731) and then entered parliament for the family borough, Old Sarum (1735). He led the young 'Patriot' Whigs, and in 1756 became nominally Secretary of State, but virtually Premier. The King's enmity led him to resign in 1757, but public demand caused his recall. Again compelled to resign when his Cabinet refused to declare war with Spain (1761), he vigorously attacked the peace terms of the Treaty of Paris (1763) as too generous to France. He formed a new ministry in 1766, but ill health contributed to his resignation in 1768. He died in the House of Lords. His eldest son, **John, 2nd Earl of Chatham** (1756–1835), commanded the luckless Walcheren Expedition (1809). His second son, **William**, was twice Prime Minister. » Pitt (the Younger); Seven Years' War; Whigs

Pitt, William, byname **the Younger** (1759–1806) British statesman and Prime Minister (1783–1801, 1804–6), born at Hayes, Kent, the second son of the Earl of Chatham (William Pitt, the Elder). Educated at Cambridge, he studied law, but then became an MP (1781), his first post being Chancellor of the Exchequer under Shelburne (1782). He became First Lord of the Treasury (1783), and was confirmed as Prime Minister at the election of 1784. His first ministry lasted for 18 years, during which he carried through important reforms, his policy being influenced by the political economy of Adam Smith. He negotiated coalitions against France (1793, 1798), but these had little success. After the Irish rebellion of 1798, he proposed a legislative union which would be followed by Catholic emancipation. The union was effected in 1800, but Pitt resigned office in 1801 rather than contest George III's hostility to emancipation. He resumed office in 1804. He drank very heavily, and this contributed to his early death, in London, while he was still Prime Minister. » Fox, Charles James; George III; Napoleonic Wars; Shelburne; Smith, Adam

Pitti Palace A palace in Florence, Italy, designed by Brunelleschi in the 15th-c. It was originally the residence of the Grand Dukes of Tuscany and (1866–70) of Victor Emanuel II. The palace now houses museums of silverware and of modern art, and the Palatine Gallery, a magnificent art collection principally of Italian masters. » Brunelleschi; museum; Victor Emanuel II

pittosporum [pito**spo**hruhm] An evergreen shrub or small tree mostly native to Australasia but also to parts of Africa and Asia; leaves leathery; flowers 5-petalled, purple, white, or greenish-yellow, and often fragrant; also called **parchment-bark**. (Genus: *Pittosporum*, 150 species. Family: *Pittosporaceae*.) » evergreen plants; shrub; tree [i]

Pittsburgh 40°26N 80°01W, pop (1980) 423 938. County seat of Allegheny County, W Pennsylvania, USA; at the confluence of the Allegheny and Monongahela Rivers where they form the Ohio R; Fort Duquesne built here by the French; taken by the British and renamed Fort Pitt, 1758; city status, 1816; airport; railway; three universities (1787, 1878, 1900); city's traditional steel industry largely replaced by service industries; machinery, chemicals; third largest US corporate headquarters; noted for recent urban redevelopment and a dramatic reduction in air and water pollution; major league teams, Pirates (baseball), Steelers (football), Penguins (ice hockey); Carnegie Institute,

Frick Art Museum, Point State Park, Heinz Hall, Phipps Conservatory; arts festival (Jun). » Pennsylvania

pituitary gland A vertebrate endocrine gland situated within the skull in a small concavity on the sphenoid bone, and connected to the hypothalamus by the infundibulum; also known as the **hypophysis**. Anatomical differences exist between species, but it generally consists of two parts – an *adenohypophysis* at the front, and a *neurohypophysis* at the back. It acts mainly by controlling the activities of all the other endocrine glands. » acromegaly; dwarfism; endocrine glands; lactation; neurohormone

Pius V, originally **Michele Ghislieri** (1504–72), feast day 30 April. Italian Pope (1566–72), born near Alessandria. He became a bishop in 1556, and a cardinal in 1557. As Pope, he implemented the decrees of the Council of Trent (1545–63), excommunicated Queen Elizabeth I (1570), and organized the expedition against the Turks, resulting in the naval engagement of Lepanto (1571). He was canonized in 1712. » Lepanto, Battle of; Trent, Council of

Pius VII, originally **Gregorio Barnaba Chiaramonti** (1742–1823) Italian Pope (1800–23), born at Cesena, Papal States. Ordained in 1758, he became a cardinal in 1785. He arranged a concordat with Napoleon, and in 1804 was compelled to consecrate him as Emperor. In 1809 the French annexed the Papal States; Pius was removed to Grenoble, then to Fontainebleau, and forced to sign a new concordat sanctioning the annexation. The fall of Napoleon (1814) allowed his return to Rome, and papal territory was restored by the Congress of Vienna. He died in Rome. » Napoleon I; pope; Vienna, Congress of

Pius IX, originally **Giovanni Maria Mastai-Ferretti**, byname **Pio Nono** (1792–1878) Italian Pope (1846–78), born at Senigallia, Papal States. He became Archbishop of Spoleto in 1827, and a cardinal in 1840. He introduced several reforms, but after the 1848 revolutions (during which he was forced to flee from Rome) he became progressively more conservative, and condemned modernism in theology. He decreed the dogma of the Immaculate Conception in 1854, and called the Vatican Council (1869–79), which proclaimed papal infallibility. He refused to recognize the new state of Italy, into which Rome was incorporated in 1870, after which he lived a voluntary 'prisoner' within the Vatican until his death. His pontificate is the longest in papal history. » Immaculate Conception; infallibility; pope; Revolutions of 1848; theology

Pius XI, originally **Ambrogio Damiano Achille Ratti** (1857–1939) Italian Pope (1922–39), born at Desio, near Milan. Ordained in 1879, he was a great linguist and scholar, and librarian of the Ambrosian (Milan) and Vatican libraries. He became Cardinal Archbishop of Milan in 1921. As Pope, he signed the Lateran Treaty (1929), which brought into existence the Vatican State, and made concordats with many countries. He died in Rome. » pope; Vatican City

Pius XII, originally **Eugenio Maria Giuseppe Giovanni Pacelli** (1876–1958) Italian Pope (1939–58), born in Rome. Ordained in 1899, he became a papal diplomat, cardinal (1929), and Secretary of State to the Holy See. During World War 2 under his leadership the Vatican did much humanitarian work, notably for prisoners of war and refugees. There has been continuing controversy, however, over his attitude to the treatment of the Jews in Nazi Germany, critics arguing that he could have used his influence with Catholic Germany to prevent the massacres, others that any attempt to do so would have proved futile and might have worsened the situation. In the postwar years he was particularly concerned with the plight of persecuted churchmen in communist countries. He died at Castel Gandolfo. » Nazi Party; pope

pixel From *pic*ture *el*ement, the smallest resolved unit of a video image which has specific luminance and colour. Its proportions are determined by the number of lines making up the scanning raster and the resolution along each line. » raster; television

Pizarro, Francisco [peet**hah**roh] (c.1478–1541) Spanish conquistador, born at Trujillo. He served in Italy, and with the expedition which discovered the Pacific (1513). In 1526 he and Almagro sailed for Peru, and in 1531 began the conquest of the Incas. He killed the Inca king, Atahualpa, then worked to consolidate the new empire, founding Lima (1535) and other cities. Dissensions between Pizarro and Almagro led to the latter's execution. In revenge, Almagro's followers assassinated Pizarro at Lima. » Almagro; Incas

PK » **psychokinesis**

placebo [pla**see**boh] An inactive substance given as a drug to a patient, who may benefit from the belief that the drug is active. Because patients can improve under this illusion, in most countries new drugs are tested for clinical efficacy in trials where a placebo is given to one group. The active drug must prove itself to be more efficacious than the placebo. » experimental psychology

placenta (anatomy) An organ which develops in the uterus of all pregnant mammals, except marsupials. It is attached to the uterus of the mother, and connected to the foetus by the umbilical cord. It subserves the needs of the developing foetus by allowing maternal and foetal blood to come into close association for the exchange of respiratory gases, nutrients, and waste products. It secretes a number of hormones (such as oestrogen and progesterone) essential for pregnancy. » chorionic villus sampling; hormones; metabolism; umbilical cord; uterus [i]

placenta (botany) Tissue to which the ovules or spores of plants are attached. The arrangement of ovules is termed **placentation**, and is an important diagnostic character in many plants. » ovule; spore

Placid, Lake » **Lake Placid**

Placodermi [**plak**uhdermee] An extinct class of primitive, jawed fishes known primarily from the Devonian period, mostly dwelling on sea bottom; large head covered by shield composed of bony plates; body depressed, heavily armoured. » Devonian period; fish [i]

plagioclase [**play**jeeuhklayz] » **feldspar**

plague The most notorious epidemic disease of all time, caused by infection with *Yersinia* (formerly *Pasteurella*) *pestis*, carried by fleas that infest rodents and squirrels which then bite humans. The features are those of a severe infection with the development of 'buboes', ie swollen, acutely inflamed lymph nodes; hence the name **bubonic plague**. A pneumonic form which spreads rapidly between people occurs in an epidemic. Outbreaks of plague (*black death*) afflicted communities over many centuries, and in the middle of the 14th-c, wave after wave of the disease killed half of the population of Europe. Today it occurs only in isolated cases or as small local outbreaks. » infection; lymph

plaice Common European flatfish widespread in continental shelf waters from N Norway to the Mediterranean; length up to 90 cm/3 ft; both eyes on right side; upper surface brown with orange spots, underside white; support very important commercial fisheries, especially around the British Is. (*Pleuronectes platessa*. Family: *Pleuronectidae*.) » flatfish

Plaid Cymru [pliyd **kuhm**ree] The Welsh National Party, founded in 1925, with the aim of achieving independence for Wales. It stands for election throughout Wales, but finds support mainly in the N of the country. It had one MP following the 1987 general election, and has never had more than three. » nationalism

Plain, the Known as the *Marais*, the majority of deputies in the French Revolutionary Convention, politically uncommitted to a particular faction, although broadly aligned with the Girondins. They were ultimately outmaneouvred by extremists, the Jacobins of the Mountain. » French Revolution [i]; Girondins; Mountain, the

plainchant The unaccompanied, single-strand music to which the mass and other parts of the Roman liturgy were sung (and to some extent still are). It is notated, without precise indications of rhythm, on a four-line staff. » chant; Gregorian chant; liturgy; monody; organum; sequence (music) 1

Plains Indians N American Indian groups who lived on the Great Plains between the Mississippi R and the Rocky Mts in the USA and Canada. Most were nomadic or semi-nomadic buffalo hunters living together in small bands, and engaged in various conflicts with one another. Their lives were dramatically changed by the introduction of horses by the Spanish, which led to intensified warring between groups, and hunting over much greater expanses. Eventually the buffalo was exterminated, and White settlers finally destroyed their power, placing the surviving Indians in reservations. » American Indians; Cheyenne (Indians); Comanche; Crow; Hidatsa; nomadism; Omaha; Sioux

plains wanderer A small, plump, ground-dwelling bird from open country in SE Australia; mottled plumage; four toes on each foot; eats insects, seeds, and plants; also known as the **collared hemipode**. (*Pedionomus torquatus*. Family: *Pedionomidae*.)

plainsong » **plainchant**

plaintiff » **defendant**

planarian [planairian] A free-living predatory flatworm commonly found in aquatic and damp terrestrial habitats; intestine divided into an anterior and front posterior branches; feeds using a posteriorly-directed pharynx. (Phylum: *Platyhelminthes*. Order: *Tricladida*.) » flatworm; intestine; pharynx

Planchon, Roger [plãshõ] (1931–) French theatre director, playwright, and actor, born in the Ardèche. He founded a theatre company in a disused printing works in Lyons in 1952, moving to the Théâtre de la Cité in Villeurbanne in 1957. His company was the recipient of the title, subsidy, and touring obligations of the Théâtre National Populaire in 1972. » theatre

Planck, Max (Karl Ernst Ludwig) (1858–1947) German theoretical physicist, the formulator of the quantum theory, born at Kiel. He studied at Munich and Berlin, where he became professor of theoretical physics (1889–1926). His work on the second law of thermodynamics and blackbody radiation led him to abandon classical Newtonian principles and formulate the quantum theory (1900), for which he was awarded the Nobel Prize for Physics in 1918. Several research institutes now carry his name. He died at Göttingen, Germany. » Planck length; Planck's constant; quantum field theory

Planck length A length scale thought to be of importance in quantum gravity, which may represent the shortest possible distance between points; equals $\sqrt{Gh/2\pi c^3}$, where G is the gravitational constant, h is Planck's constant, and c is the velocity of light; value 1.62×10^{-35} m; stated by German physicist Max Planck. The corresponding Planck mass is 2.1×10^{-8} kg. » Planck; quantum gravity

Planck mass » **Planck length**

Planck's constant A fundamental constant appearing in all equations of quantum theory; symbol h, value 6.626×10^{-34} J.s (joule.second); introduced by German physicist Max Planck in 1900, via the study of blackbody radiation. It relates the energy E of a quantum of light to its frequency ν by $E=h\nu$. » blackbody radiation; fundamental constants; Planck; quantum mechanics

plane (mathematics) In mathematics, a surface such that if any two points in that surface are joined by a straight line, all the points on the straight line lie on the surface. This can be seen as a generalization in three-dimensional space of a straight line. Two planes are either parallel or meet in a straight line. A plane is uniquely determined by three points not in a straight line, or by two straight lines meeting in a point, or by a point in the plane and a direction perpendicular to the plane. The equation of a general plane in rectangular Cartesian co-ordinates is $ax+by+cz+d=0$. » polyhedron; straight line

plane tree A tall, long-lived deciduous tree, native to S Europe, Asia, and especially N America; distinctive flaking bark, revealing large creamy or pink patches; leaves palmately lobed; fruiting heads pendulous globes, persisting on the tree through the winter. The **London plane** (*Platanus × hispanica*) is a garden hybrid resistant to air pollution, widely planted in city streets. (Genus: *Platanus*, 10 species. Family: *Platinaceae*.) » deciduous plants; palmate; tree [i]

planet A non-luminous body gravitationally bound to the Sun or a star, and rotating in orbit in a prograde direction (ie counter-clockwise, viewed from N). The basic distinction between a star and a planet is that a star generates its own heat and light, through nuclear reactions, whereas a planet shines only through reflected light. The theory of planetary formation suggests that they condense from material left over during primary star formation. They should therefore be common, but they are extremely hard to detect, being so much fainter than their parent stars. They were detected around one other star in 1988. In the Solar System there are nine major planets and innumerable minor planets, or *asteroids*. Large numbers of comets are stored in a spherical shell (the *Oort Cloud*) at great distances from the Sun, some of which occasionally enter the inner Solar System and a few of which (the periodic comets) are trapped there. The major planets comprise two types; the inner *terrestrial* planets (Mercury, Venus, Earth, Mars), and the giant gaseous *outer* planets (Jupiter, Saturn, Uranus, Neptune), together with unique, distant Pluto. All except Mercury and Venus have associated moons or, for the outer planets, systems of moons. All are believed to have been formed about 4.6 thousand million years ago, soon after the formation of the Sun from a collapsing cloud of gas and dust.

The inner planets are dense, and made primarily of metals and of metal silicates. They are internally differentiated into zones: an iron-rich *core*, an iron-magnesium silicate *mantle*, and a *crust* of lighter metal silicates. Venus, Earth, and Mars have atmospheres believed to be outgassed from the interiors over geological time. The outer planets are much less dense, and made primarily of gases and ices together with a core equivalent to a large terrestrial planet. They are also internally differentiated into zones: an outer core of hydrogen in a solid phase, a mantle of liquid hydrogen/helium, and a deep gaseous atsmosphere. Jupiter is by far the most massive planet, containing over two-thirds of the material in the Solar System apart from the Sun. Many searches have been made for a tenth planet in our Solar System; if it exists, it is small and very remote. » asteroids; Earth [i]; Jupiter/Mars/Mercury/Neptune/Pluto/Saturn/Uranus/Venus (astronomy); Moon; Oort cloud; Solar System; star

planetarium A special building with a dome in which a projector produces an impression of the stars in the night sky. Planetary motions and many sorts of astronomical phenomena can be demonstrated for teaching and entertainment purposes. A famous example is the London Planetarium.

planetary nebula A shell of glowing gas surrounding an evolved star, from which it was ejected. There is no connection with planets: the name derived from the visual similarity at the telescope between the disc of such a nebula and the disc of a planet. They are late stages in the evolution of stars 1–4 times as massive as the Sun. Some thousands are known in our Galaxy. » stellar evolution

planimeter A mathematical instrument for measuring the area enclosed by an irregular curve. A pointer moved around the perimeter is connected by lever arms to an integrating mechanism.

plankton Organisms without effective means of locomotion; drifters. They have been subdivided into plant (*phytoplankton*) and animal (*zooplankton*) types. Some plankton are capable of limited swimming ability, but cannot move faster than the ocean currents in which they may be carried, hence they cannot effectively swim. Most plankton are microscopic in size. Some are the larval stages of organisms with larger, more mobile adult phases (*meroplankton*); examples include sea urchins, starfish, bivalves, and larval fish. Others remain planktonic for their entire life cycle (*holoplankton*); examples include copepods, arrow worms, and krill. » hydrobiology; nekton

planographic printing » **printing** [i]

plant An organism which typically uses sunlight as an energy source via photosynthetic pathways involving the green pigment chlorophyll (kingdom: *Plantae*). Plants are mostly non-motile and lack obvious excretory and nervous systems, and sensory organs. They are eucaryotic, and typically possess cell walls composed largely of cellulose. Traditionally the chlorophyll-containing single-celled algae have been regarded as plants, even though they may be motile and can feed by ingesting organic matter. The fungi have also been grouped with plants, although they lack chlorophyll and feed by absorbing organic substances. » algae; botany; carnivorous/climbing/herbaceous/parasitic/pitcher/vascular plant; cell; chlorophyll; eucaryote; fungus; kingdom; photosynthesis

plant hopper A small, hopping insect that feeds by sucking sap or cell contents of plants; c.1 300 species, including pests of economically important crops, such as rice and sugar cane. (Order: *Homoptera*. Family: *Delphacidae*.) » insect [i]

Plantagenets The name given by historians to the royal dynasty in England from Henry II to Richard II (1154–1399), then continued by two rival houses of younger lines, Lancaster and York, until 1485. The dynasty was so called because, allegedly, Henry II's father Geoffrey, count of Anjou, sported a sprig of broom (Old Fr, *plante genêt*) in his cap. » Edward I/II/III; English history; Henry III (of England); John; Richard I

plantain **1** Typically an annual or perennial, sometimes a shrub, often a weed; very widespread; a rosette of narrow, lance-shaped to broadly oval, strongly veined leaves; flowers tiny, with four brownish or green, membranous petals, packed into a dense, erect spike. (Genus: *Plantago*, 265 species. Family: *Plantaginaceae*.) » annual; perennial; shrub; weed **2** » banana

plantain-eater » **turaco**

plantain lily » **hosta**

plantation A system of agriculture generally found in the tropics and subtropics. Plantations were a product of colonialism – large, company-owned, and labour intensive. With the independence of former colonies many plantations were nationalized, and some divided into smaller units. Plantation farming is associated with the production of cash crops such as coffee, tea, rubber, and cotton, which are suited to such farming because of the delay between planting and first harvesting. The term is also applied to planted and managed forests in temperate regions. » agriculture; colony

Plantation of Ireland The colonization and conquest of Ireland, begun in 1556 and continued to 1660; at first mainly English, but Scottish settlers came to Ulster 1608–11. The policy led to rebellions by the native Irish and Anglo-Irish aristocracy (1563–9, 1580–3, 1598–1603, 1641) and the eventual conquest of Ireland under Cromwell, in which possibly two-thirds of the Irish died. » Cromwell, Oliver

plasma (physics) A fourth state of matter comprising a fluid of ions and free electrons, formed for example by the extreme heating of a gas, and characterized by powerful electrical forces between the particles. Fluorescent lights and the interiors of stars contain plasmas. Plasma properties are studied in **plasma physics**. The main interest is the creation of controlled nuclear fusion, with the ultimate aim of power generation. The principal features are the containment of the plasma using magnetic fields (*plasma confinement*) and the heating of the plasma by passing electrical currents through it, by injecting particles into it, or by the application of radio-frequency waves. » electron; ion; nuclear fusion; magnetosphere; tokamak

plasma (physiology) The fluid portion of whole blood, in which the blood cells are suspended. It transports nutrients, metabolic waste products, and chemicals involved in the clotting process, as well as hormones and drugs to their target cells. It clots readily, and can be obtained by centrifuging or sedimentation. » blood; blood products; myeloma; nephrotic syndrome; plasmapheresis

plasmapheresis [plazma**fer**uhsis] or **plasma exchange** The circulation of whole blood outside the body, during which centrifugal force separates the cellular component and plasma, which is discarded and replaced by fresh plasma or plasma albumin. The purpose is to remove a damaging plasma component such as an abnormal antibody. » blood; myasthenia gravis; plasma (physiology)

Plasmodium [plaz**moh**diuhm] A genus of parasitic protozoans containing the micro-organisms that cause malaria in humans; life cycle complex, involving stages in an intermediate host, the mosquito, and stages in the blood or other organs of a final vertebrate host. (Phylum: *Apicomplexa*. Class: *Sporozoa*.) » life cycle; malaria; mosquito; parasitology; Protozoa

Plassey, Battle of [**pla**see] (1757) A decisive British victory under Clive over Nawab Siraj ud Daula, Nawab of Bengal, India. Clive's success was aided by the treachery of Nawab's general, Mir Jafar, whom the British subsequently placed on the throne. The victory was an important step in the British acquisition of Bengal. » Clive; East India Company, British

plaster » **gypsum**

plastic deformation The irreversible deformation of a material stressed to beyond its elastic limit (*yield point*). Further increases in stress cause disproportionately large deformations until a fracture point is reached. *Ductile* materials are those which undergo large plastic deformations (eg most metals); *brittle* materials undergo small plastic deformations. » elasticity; fracture (physics); rheology; stress (physics)

plastic surgery The grafting of skin and subcutaneous tissue from a healthy site on the body to one that has suffered damage from disease, trauma, or burns. The manoeuvre is sometimes carried out in several stages, and its purpose is to cover areas denuded of skin and to fill in areas deficient in tissue. It also includes surgical operations undertaken for cosmetic purposes, such as face lifting, reshaping noses, and removing unsightly fat. » surgery

plastics Originally any soft, formable material; now commonly used for synthetic organic resins which can be softened by heating, and then shaped or cast. Some (called *thermoset*, eg phenol-formaldehyde resin) are then resistant to softening on further heating; others (called *thermoplastic*, eg polyethylene and polystyrene) may be repeatedly softened. Plastics may be designed with almost any desired property, ranging from great heat stability to rapid natural decomposition in soil, and from being a good electrical insulator to a conductor. » resin

Plataea [plat**ee**a] **1** A Greek city-state in Boeotia, which shared with Athens the honour of defeating the Persians at Marathon. **2** The site in 479 BC of a decisive Greek victory over the Persians. » Boeotia; Marathon; Persian Wars

plate **1** A photographic material with a sensitive emulsion coated on a sheet of glass. » emulsion **2** In special effects cinematography, a positive picture print on slide or film, used in back projection and similar processes as the background scene against which the foreground action is to appear. » special effects

Plate, River, Span **Río de la Plata** A wide, shallow estuary of the Paraná and Uruguay Rivers on the E coast of S America, between Argentina (S and W shore) and Uruguay (N shore); area 35 000 sq km/13 510 sq ml; length 320 km/200 ml; width 220 km/140 ml at its mouth and 45 km/28 ml at Buenos Aires; European discovery, 1516; Buenos Aires on S shore, Montevideo on N shore; scene of a naval engagement (Dec 1939) between three out-gunned British cruisers and the formidable German pocket-battleship *Graf Spee* (**Battle of the River Plate**); the *Graf Spee* inexplicably disengaged, and was trapped in the neutral port of Montevideo, to be scuttled a few days later. » battleship; Paraná, River; Uruguay, River

plate tectonics A model of the structure and dynamics of the Earth's crust, developed in the 1960s to explain and relate observations such as continental drift, mid-ocean ridges and ocean trenches, the distribution of earthquakes, and volcanic activity. The theory proposes that the Earth's lithosphere is made up of a number of relatively thin, rigid plates which may include both continental and ocean crust and which move relative to one another. Plate boundaries are defined by major earthquake zones and belts of volcanic activity. New plate material is generated by basaltic lava erupted along mid-ocean ridges and eventually consumed at subduction zones at the site of deep ocean trenches. Plate collisions result in the formation of mountain belts such as the Alps and Himalayas. Plate motion is most probably driven by convection currents within the mantle on which the plates float. » continental drift; Earth [i]; earthquake; lithosphere; orogeny; sea-floor spreading; subduction zone [i]; *see map p 950*

Plateau Indians N American Indian groups who lived on the plateau between the Rocky Mts and the Cascade Range. Most groups lived in camps during the summer, hunting and fishing; during the severe winters, they sheltered in earth lodges in permanent villages located along the rivers. This way of life was radically affected by fur traders and trappers arriving from the E and bringing in European diseases, to which many succumbed, and weapons. In the 18th-c, Plains Indians introduced horses, and during the 19th-c European settlers and prospectors fought with the Indians over land. In the ensuing wars, most groups were decimated, and the survivors forced into reservations. » American Indians; Chinook; Salish

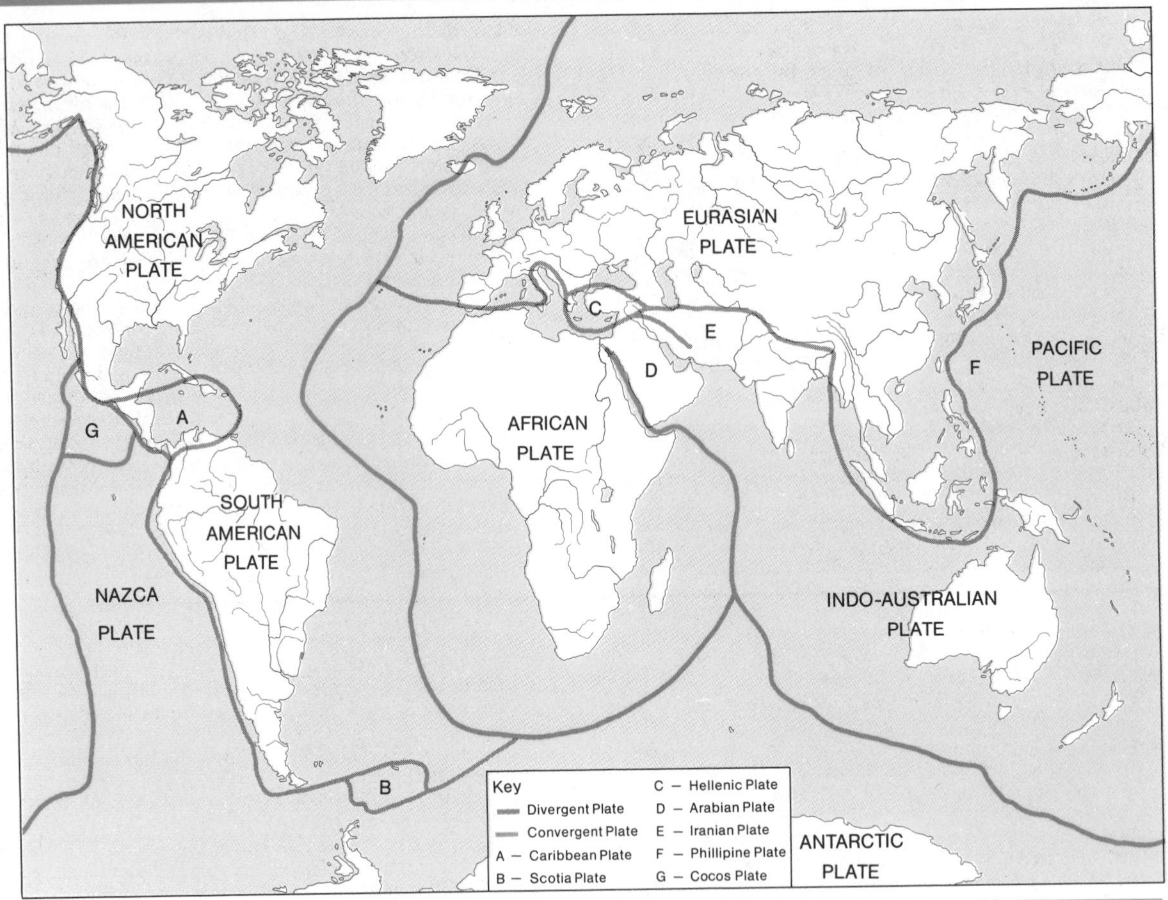

Major lithospheric plates

platelets Small disc-like structures (2–4 μ in diameter) found in the blood of all mammals, produced in bone marrow. They contain factors important in the arrest of bleeding (eg serotonin), and in wound healing (eg platelet-derived growth factor). The number of circulating platelets is regulated by a hormone (*thrombopoietin*) of unknown origin. Any deficiency (*thrombocytopenia*) results in severe bleeding, either spontaneously or when wounded. » bone marrow; haemostasis

platform tennis A variation of paddle tennis, a cross between lawn tennis and squash rackets. Side walls can be used to bring the ball into court. It is a popular indoor winter sport in the USA, where the US Platform Tennis Association was formed in 1934. » paddle tennis; squash rackets; tennis, lawn [i]

Plath, Sylvia (1932–63) US poet, born in Boston, and educated there and at Cambridge, Massachusetts. She married Ted Hughes in 1956. They lived in Spain and the USA, returning to England in 1959. Her first collection *The Colossus* appeared in 1960, and a novel *The Bell Jar* in 1963, shortly before she committed suicide in London. A posthumous volume, *Ariel*, was published in 1965, containing many of the poems by which she is known. Her *Collected Poems*, edited by Ted Hughes, appeared in 1981. » English literature; Hughes, Ted; poetry

platinum Pt, element 78, density 21.5 g/cm^3, melting point 1 772°C. A precious metal, which occurs occasionally uncombined but more importantly as a sulphide. It is a valuable impurity in nickel deposits, and is generally found along with the other *platinum metals*. Similar to gold in its unreactivity, it is used for jewellery and for laboratory vessels. It is also an important catalyst for hydrogenations; finely divided platinum can absorb large volumes of hydrogen gas. » chemical elements; hydrogenation; metal; platinum metals; RR90

platinum metals A series of elements which occur together in nature, and have similar properties: ruthenium (Ru), rhodium (Rh), palladium (Pd), osmium (Os), iridium (Ir), and platinum (Pt). » chemical elements; RR90

Plato (c.427–347 BC) Athenian philosopher, born possibly in Athens of an aristocratic family, but little is known of his early life. He became a disciple of Socrates, who appears in most of Plato's 35 dialogues. He travelled widely, then before 368 BC founded his own Academy at Athens, where he remained for the rest of his life, apart from visits to Syracuse. The chronology of the dialogues is a vexed subject, but they may be grouped into the *early* dialogues, in which the main interlocutor is Socrates, and the main interest is the definition of moral concepts (eg piety in *Euthyphron*, courage in *Laches*); the *middle* dialogues, in which Plato increasingly outlines his own doctrines (eg the doctrine of learning as recollection in the *Meno*, and the theory of forms in the *Republic*); and the *later* dialogues, which express his rigorous self-criticism (eg the *Parmenides* and the *Sophist*).

Plato is particularly known for his theory of ideas, or *forms*: the world of transient, finite, ever-changing objects of sense experience is to be distinguished from that of the timeless, unchanging, universal forms, which are the true objects of knowledge. There is, for example, a universal form of 'equality' that all equal things in the sensible world imperfectly resemble. Our knowledge of the forms cannot come from sense experience, so if we do know of them, we must be recalling them from a time before our souls were in their present bodies. Plato's influence has been universal, extending through his pupil and disciple, Aristotle, and the Stoics into Christian theology via Philo Judaeus, Neoplatonism, and St Augustine. From the Renaissance on, his thought was repeatedly revived. » Aristotle; Neoplatonism; Platonism; Philo Judaeus; Socrates; Stoicism

Platonic solids In mathematics, solids whose faces are congruent regular polygons. There are five such solids: the *tetrahedron* (four faces, each an equilateral triangle); the *cube* (six faces, each a square); the *octahedron* (eight faces, each a pentagon); the *dodecahedron* (twelve faces, each a hexagon); and the *icosahedron* (twenty faces, each an equilateral triangle). All five were described by Plato, who showed how to construct models of the solids using triangles, squares, and pentagons for their faces. » Plato; polygon

Platonism Any philosophical position which includes many of the central features of Plato's philosophy. These include a belief in a transcendent realm of abstract, perfect entities; the inferiority of the physical world; the power of reason to know these perfect entities; and bodily separability and the immortality of the soul. » Neoplatonism; Plato

Platyhelminthes [plateе**hel**minths] A phylum of flattened, worm-like animals comprising parasitic groups, such as the tapeworms (class *Cestoda*) and flukes (class *Trematoda*), and free-living groups, such as the planarians (class *Tricladida*). » fluke; parasitology; planarian; systematics; tapeworm; worm

platypus » **duck-billed platypus**

Plautus, Titus Maccius [**plaw**tuhs] (c.250–184 BC) Roman comic dramatist, born at Sarsina, Umbria. He worked in the theatre, then in foreign trade, before beginning to write plays (c.224 BC). About 130 plays have been attributed to him, but many are thought to be the work of earlier dramatists which he revised. Varro limited the genuine comedies to 21, and these 'Varronian comedies' are the ones which have survived. Extremely popular, and still being acted five centuries later, the plays are full of robust life and vigorous dialogue, and were influential on many other dramatists, such as Shakespeare and Molière. » comedy; drama; Molière; Latin literature; Shakespeare [i]; Varro

Player, Gary (Jim) (1935–) South African golfer, born in Johannesburg, the only golfer to win a major tournament in each of four decades (1950s–1980s). His first major success was the 1959 British Open, a title he also won in 1968 and 1974. He was the first non-American for 45 years to win the US Open (1965), and the first to win the US Professional Golfers Association title (1962, regained 1972) and the US Masters (1961, regained 1974, 1978). He won the South African Open 12 times, and the world match-play title a record five times. He now breeds horses in South Africa, and plays golf on the US Seniors Tour. » golf

player piano A mechanism attached to a piano (or a piano fitted with such a mechanism) in which a perforated roll passes over a brass 'tracker bar' and causes those keys to be depressed to which the perforations correspond. The mechanism is driven by suction generated by pedals operated by the player's feet. In the earliest models, made from c.1890 onwards, tempo, dynamics, and 'expression' were at the command of the player, but later they were incorporated into the rolls themselves, some of which were cut by such artists as Gershwin and Rachmaninov. The popularity of the player piano declined in the 1920s and 1930s as other means of mechanical reproduction were developed. » keyboard instrument; piano; Gershwin; Rachmaninov

Playfair, John (1748–1819) British mathematician and geologist, born at Benvie, near Dundee, Scotland. He studied at St Andrews, and became joint professor of mathematics at Edinburgh (1785) and professor of natural philosophy (1805). He wrote an important textbook on geometry, and also investigated glaciation and the formation of river valleys. He died in Edinburgh. » geometry; glaciation

playgroup An informal gathering of children under normal school age, and many of their parents, where the emphasis is on play and enjoyment of each other's company. There are usually rules governing the running of such groups, mainly about the suitability of premises, health aspects, and the ratio of adults to children, but though playgroup leaders may be trained people, many of the helpers are volunteer parents themselves. » kindergarten; nursery school

playing cards Small rectangular cards used for playing card games. A standard pack contains 52 cards divided into four *suits*; hearts, clubs, diamonds, and spades. Each suit is subdivided into 13 cards numbered as follows: ace, 2–10, and the court (or picture) cards, jack, queen, and king. Most packs also contain two cards known as jokers, which can be given any value, but they are used in very few games. The earliest playing cards were used in China in the 10th-c. When they first appeared in Europe (in Italy) in the 14th-c, the pack consisted of 78 cards. It was standardized at 52 in the 15th-c. » baccarat; bézique; blackjack; bridge (recreation); canasta; chemin de fer; cribbage; hazard; pinochle; poker; pontoon; rummy; whist

plebeians [ple**bee**anz] In early Rome, citizens other than the patricians, who were the ruling elite. By the late Republic, some plebeian clans (such as the Claudians) had come to be part of the ruling aristocracy, and the distinction between them and the patricians became blurred. » patricians

plebiscite » **referendum**

Plecoptera [pluh**kop**tuhra] » **stonefly**

plectrum A short length of metal, tortoise-shell, ivory, plastic, or other material worn on the fingers or held between them, to pluck a string instrument such as the guitar and mandolin. » string instrument 2 [i]

Pléiade, La [la play**ad**] (Fr 'the Pleiades') A group of French poets of the 16th-c who sought to emancipate the French language (and literature) from mediaevalism by introducing Greek and Latin models. The best known were Ronsard (1524–85) and du Bellay (1522–60), whose *Défense et illustration de la langue française* (1549) served as a manifesto. » Bellay; French; French literature; poetry; Ronsard

Pleiades (astronomy) [**plee**adeez, **pliy**adeez] An open cluster of stars in Taurus, familiarly known as the **Seven Sisters**, although only six stars are readily visible to the naked eye, while people with sharp vision claim to see twice as many. The most prominent of the open clusters, it was noted as early as 2357 BC in literature and mythology. The cluster is 20 million years old, and contains 3 000 stars. Distance: 120 parsecs. » open cluster; Taurus

Pleiades (mythology) [**pliy**adeez] In Greek mythology, the seven daughters of Atlas and Pleione: Maia, Taygete, Elektra, Alkyone, Asterope, Kelaino, and Merope. After their deaths they were changed into the star-cluster of the same name. » Orion (mythology)

pleiotropy [**pliy**uhtropee] The multiple effects of a single gene on the phenotype (the observed characteristics of an organism). The 'vestigial' gene in *Drosophila*, a genus of fruit fly, markedly reduces the size of the wings, but also modifies the balancers (*halteres*), changes the direction of particular bristles, and alters the number of egg strings in the ovaries, together with other changes. The genes for human syndromes are mostly pleiotropic; for example, the gene for arachnodactyly (Marfan's syndrome) produces not only the slender spidery physique, with elongation especially of the end portions of the limbs, but also joint hypermobility, often dislocation of the lens of the eye, and diseases of the heart. » Drosophila [i]; gene; Marfan's syndrome

Pleistocene epoch [**pliy**stohseen] The earlier of the two geological epochs of the Quaternary period, from 2 million to 10 000 years ago; termed the *Ice Age* in the N hemisphere, where it was characterized by several periods of glacial advance and retreat. It was marked by the extinction of mammals such as the mammoth and the mastodon, and the evolution of man and familiar mammalian life. » geological time scale; glaciation; Ice Age; Quaternary period; RR16

Plekhanov, Giorgiy Valentinovich [ple**kah**nof] (1856–1918) Russian Marxist philosopher, historian, and journalist, 'the father of Russian Marxism', born at Gundalovka. He left Russia in 1880, and in 1883 founded the first Russian Marxist group, the Liberation of Labour Group, in Geneva, where he remained until 1917. He was a major intellectual influence on the young Lenin, but sided with the Mensheviks against Lenin's Bolsheviks, and denounced the October Revolution. He then moved to Finland, where he died. » Bolsheviks; Lenin; Mensheviks; October Revolution; Russian Revolution

plesiosaur [**ples**iohsaw] A marine reptile known from the Mesozoic era; body broad and compact, with large limbs developed as paddles; neck typically long, head small with a long snout bearing sharp teeth for feeding on fish; short-necked forms known as *pliosaurs*. (Order: *Sauropterygia*.) » Mesozoic era; pliosaur; reptile

pleurisy Inflammation of membranes in the chest cavity (*pleura*) by micro-organisms, especially bacteria or viruses. It induces sharp pain on one or other side of the chest, aggravated by breathing. The pain often lessens with the passage of time, as fluid is exuded and separates the layers of pleura. » empyema; lungs

Plimsoll, Samuel (1824–98) British social reformer, 'the sailors' friend', born in Bristol, He became an MP in 1868, and having accumulated a large file on the unseaworthiness of ships, caused the Merchant Shipping Act (1876) to be passed. Every owner was ordered to mark upon the side of a ship a circular disc (the **Plimsoll line**), with a horizontal line drawn through its centre, down to which the vessel might be loaded. It was legally enforced in 1894.

Pliny (the Elder), in full **Gaius Plinius Secundus** (23–79) Roman scholar, born at Novum Comum (Como), Gaul. Educated at Rome, he served in the army in Germany, and later settled in Como, where he devoted himself to study and writing. Nero appointed him procurator in Spain, and through his brother-in-law's death (71) he became guardian of his nephew, Pliny (the Younger), whom he adopted. He continued his studies, and wrote a 37-volume encyclopedia, the *Historia Naturalis* (77, Natural History), his only work to survive. In 79 he was in command of the Roman fleet when the great eruption of Vesuvius was at its height. He landed at Stabiae (Castellamare), to observe more closely, and was killed. » Latin literature

Pliny (the Younger), in full **Gaius Plinius Caecilius Secundus** (c.62–114) Roman writer and administrator, born at Novum Comum (Como), Gaul, who became the adopted son of Pliny the Elder. He became a lawyer and a highly proficient orator, much in demand. He served as a military tribune in Syria, and progressed to be quaestor, praetor, and (100) consul, holding several posts throughout the empire. He died in Bithynia. He was the master of the epistolary style, his many letters providing an insight into the life of the upper class in the 1st-c. » Latin literature

Pliocene epoch [**pli**yohseen] The last of the geological epochs of the Tertiary period, from 5 million to 2 million years ago and immediately preceding the Pleistocene Ice Age. » geological time scale; Tertiary period; RR16

pliosaur [**pli**yuhsaw] A powerfully built plesiosaur known from Mesozoic seas; a short neck and an enormous head; predatory on large aquatic animals. (Order: *Sauropterygia*.) » Mesozoic era; plesiosaur

PLO (Palestine Liberation Organization) An organization, founded in 1964, consisting of several of the Palestinian groups opposed to Israel; its leader is Yasser Arafat. In 1974 the Arab Summit in Rabat, Morocco, affirmed the right of the Palestinian people to establish an independent national authority under the leadership of the PLO in its role as sole legitimate representative of the Palestinian people. However, some Palestinian groups have remained independent, notably the Popular Front for the Liberation of Palestine. The PLO has been responsible for several terrorist actions of recent years. In 1982 its forces were expelled from Lebanon. » Arafat; Fatah

Ploieşti [ploy**esht**] 44°57N 26°01E, pop (1983) 229 945. Capital of Prahova county, SC Romania; railway; major centre for the petroleum industry, with pipelines to Giurgiu, Bucharest, and Constanţa; oil refining, oilfield equipment, petrochemicals, textiles, paper, furniture. » Romania [i]

Plotinus [plo**tiy**nus] (205–70) Greek philosopher, the founder of Neoplatonism, born possibly at Lycopolis in Egypt. He studied in Alexandria and Persia, and settled in Rome in 244, where he became a popular lecturer, advocating asceticism and the contemplative life. When 60 years old, he attempted to found a platonic 'Republic' in Campania, but died at Minturnae. His 54 works were edited by his pupil, Porphyry, who arranged them in six groups of nine books, or *Enneads*. He greatly influenced early Christian theology. » Neoplatonism; Plato; Porphyry

plough An implement used for turning over the soil into ridges and furrows, so that surface vegetation is buried and seed-bed preparation can begin. Modern ploughs are made of steel and are tractor-drawn. They commonly turn between two and six furrows in one pass. » stump-jump plough; tractor

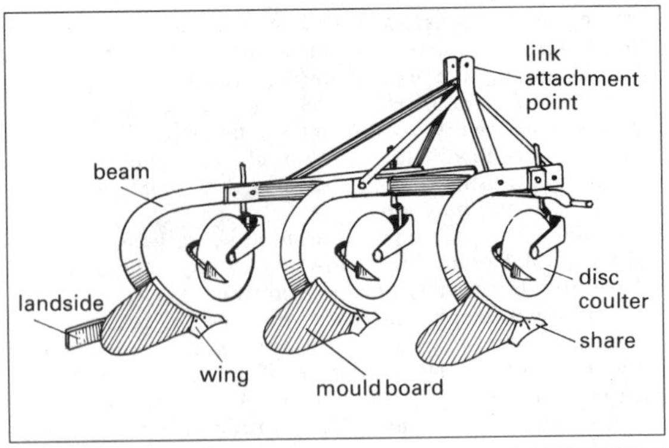

A three-furrow mounted plough, showing the three ploughing bodies attached to a steel frame. Each body consists of a coulter, *which cuts a vertical slice, and a* share, *which makes a horizontal cut underneath; the slice is then turned by the* mould board. *The lateral accuracy and stability of each body is maintained by a* landside.

Plough, the A familiar pattern of seven bright stars within Ursa Major; also called the **Big Dipper** (chiefly US) and **Charles' Wain**. The two stars furthest from the handle, Merak and Dubhe (the Pointers), point almost directly to Polaris, the North Star. » Polaris; Ursa Major

Plough Monday The Monday after Twelfth Day, traditionally the time when ploughmen and others resumed work after the Christmas festivities.

Plovdiv [**plov**dif], formerly **Philippopoli**, Lat **Evmolpia** or **Trimontium** 42°08N 24°25E, pop (1981) 358 176. Capital of Plovdiv province, C Bulgaria; on the R Maritsa, 156 km/97 ml SE of Sofia; airport; railway; second largest city in Bulgaria; metal products, food processing, textiles, chemicals; trading centre for livestock and tobacco; Roman amphitheatre; Old Plovdiv has many buildings from the Middle Ages and the National Revival Period. » Bulgaria [i]

plover A small to medium-sized bird, found worldwide; short tail, long legs; bill straight, same length as head; inhabits shores, grasslands, or deserts; eats invertebrates; moves by repeated short runs and pauses; includes lapwings and dotterels. The name is also used for the **crab-plover** (Family: *Dromadidae*), the **Egyptian plover** (*Glareolidae*), the **upland plover** (*Scolopacidae*), the **Norfolk plover** and **stone-plover** (*Burhinidae*), *and the* **quail-plover** (*Turnicidae*). (Family: *Charadriidae*, 63 species.) » dotterel; lapwing; oystercatcher; thick-knee; wrybill

Plowright, Joan » **Olivier, Laurence**

plum Any of various species of the genus *Prunus*. The widely grown plum of orchards (*Prunus domestica*) is a small deciduous tree or shrub; white blossom appearing simultaneously with leaves; ovoid yellow, red, purplish, or black fruit; sweet flesh enclosing a large stone. It is thought to be a hybrid between the sloe and the cherry plum. (Family: *Rosaceae*.) » blackthorn; bullace; cherry plum; damson; deciduous plants; prunus; shrub; tree [i]

plume moth A delicate, long-legged moth which holds its rolled wings sideways, at an angle to its body, when at rest; wings often divided; caterpillars small and spiny. (Order: *Lepidoptera*. Family: *Pterophoridae*, c.500 species.) » caterpillar; moth

pluralism (philosophy) Any metaphysical theory which is committed to the ultimate existence of two or more kinds of things. For example, mind–body dualists, such as Descartes, are pluralists. » Descartes; dualism; metaphysics; monism

pluralism (politics) Both a description of and prescription for circumstances where political power is widely dispersed, so that no one interest group or class predominates. The principal conditions for pluralism are free elections, many and overlapping interests, low barriers to ways of organizing pressure on government, and a state that is responsive to popular demands. The term is commonly applied to liberal democracies, where it is argued that the large number of pressure groups complement electoral politics in allowing citizens to get their preferences reflected in government decisions. However, the argument that pluralism is democratic is criticized by some on the grounds that social and economic inequalities make political competition unequal. » democracy; polyarchy

Plutarch, Gr **Ploutarchos** (c.46–c.120) Greek historian, biographer, and philosopher, born at Chaeronea, Boeotia. Educated in Athens, he paid several visits to Rome, where he gave public lectures in philosophy. His extant writings comprise *Opera Moralia*, a series of essays on ethical, political, religious, and other topics, and several historical works, notably *Bioi paralleloi* (Parallel Lives), a gallery of 46 portraits of the great characters of preceding ages, each book consisting of a Greek and a Roman figure, sharing some resemblance. North's translation of this work into English (1579) was the source of Shakespeare's Roman plays. » Greek literature; North, Thomas

Pluto (astronomy) The ninth and most distant planet from the Sun, smaller than our Moon, discovered in 1930 by Clyde Tombaugh after an extensive search. It is an anomalous planet in the outer Solar System, bearing no resemblance to the 'gas giants'. It is accompanied by a large moon, Charon, discovered in 1978. The two objects may be escaped satellites of Neptune. Pluto's known characteristics are: mass 0.0025 of Earth; radius 1 122 km/697 ml; mean density 1.99 g/cm^3; inclination of equator 90°; rotational period 6.387 days; orbital period 248.6 years; eccentricity of orbit 0.248; mean distance from the Sun 39.53 AU. It is an extremely difficult object to study telescopically. Possibly akin to the larger moons of the gas giants, it has a notably low density, suggesting the admixture of significant quantities of methane ice in its make-up. There is a thin atmosphere of methane gas, and evidence for distinct reflectivity differences on the surface. Surface temperatures are c.55°C. Pluto is unlikely to be visited by a reconnaissance spacecraft in the foreseeable future because of the extreme trip times required, using presently available launch and propulsion systems. A large space telescope may provide the next breakthrough in knowledge. » Charon (astronomy); planet; Solar System; Tombaugh

Pluto (mythology) In Greek mythology, originally the god of wealth, **Plutos**; but Hades was also called Pluton, 'the Rich One', perhaps to avoid naming him. The name later became a synonym for Hades. » Hades

plutocracy A political system ruled by the wealthy. It is difficult to identify any example of a country that has strictly been a plutocracy, and no set of rulers would ever claim to be plutocrats. The label is commonly used in a looser sense to mean a government heavily influenced by wealth, or as a term of abuse.

plutonic rock An igneous rock which has a coarse grain size because of the slow crystallization of magma at depth in the Earth's crust. Granites and gabbros are typical plutonic rocks. » gabbro; granite; igneous rock

plutonium Pu, element 94, essentially a synthetic element, density 19.8 g/cm^3, melting point 641°C. It was first prepared in a nuclear reactor in 1940 by a neutron bombardment of uranium. Its most stable isotope (^{238}Pu) has a half-life of nearly 25 000 years. It forms an extensive series of compounds with oxidation states mainly +3, +4, and +6, but is mainly important as a fissile nuclear fuel. » chemical elements; nuclear reactor [i]; uranium

Plymouth (Montserrat) 16°44N 62°14W, pop (1980) 3 343. Port and capital town of Montserrat, Lesser Antilles, E Caribbean; on the SW tip of the island; tourism, crafts, agricultural trade. » Montserrat

Plymouth (UK) [**plim**uhth] 50°23N 4°10W, pop (1981) 242 560. Seaport in Plymouth district, Devon, SW England; on Plymouth Sound, at the confluence of the Tamar and Plym Rivers, 340 km/211 ml SW of London; home port of Sir Francis Drake; Pilgrim Fathers set out from here in the *Mayflower* (1620); much rebuilding after severe bombing in World War 2; a major base for the Royal Navy; ferry links to Santander (Spain), Roscoff, and St Malo; railway; airfield; light industries; Plymouth Hoe, where Drake is said to have finished his game of bowls before leaving to fight the Spanish Armada; Eddystone Lighthouse at entrance to harbour; navy week (Aug). » Devon; Drake; Pilgrim Fathers; Spanish Armada

Plymouth (USA) 41°57N 70°40W, pop (1980) 35 913. Seat of Plymouth County, SE Massachusetts, USA; on Plymouth Bay; first permanent European settlement in New England, founded by Pilgrims in 1620; railway; fishing, textiles, rope, tourism; Plymouth Rock, replica *Mayflower II*, 'living history' community at Plimouth Plantation. » Massachusetts; Pilgrim Fathers

Plymouth Brethren A religious sect founded by a group of Christian evangelicals in 1829 at Dublin, Ireland. It spread to England, where in 1832 a meeting was established at Plymouth. Millenarian in outlook, the sect is characterized by a simplicity of belief, practice, and style of life based on the New Testament. By 1848 they had split into the 'Open' and the 'Exclusive' Brethren. » Christianity; evangelicalism; millenarianism

Plynlimon Fawr [plin**li**muhn **vowr**] 52°28N 3°47W. Mountain rising to 752 m/2 467 ft on the Dyfed–Powys border, C Wales, UK; 23 km/14 ml ENE of Aberystwyth. » Wales [i]

Plzeň [**puhl**zen], Ger **Pilsen** 49°40N 13°10E, pop (1984) 174 094. Modern industrial capital of Západočeský region, Czech Republic, W Czechoslovakia; at junction of Uhlava, Uslava, Radbuza and Mze Rivers, SW of Prague; railway; beer (Pilsen lager), metallurgy, aircraft, armaments, motor vehicles, chemicals, clothing. » Czechoslovakia [i]

pneumatophore A root with numerous lenticels which projects into the air some distance from the plant. It aids aeration of the root system in plants such as mangroves, which grow in swampy or water-logged ground. » lenticel; mangrove; root (botany)

pneumococcus A common name for the bacterium *Streptococcus pneumoniae*, one of the causative agents of pneumonia. (Kingdom: *Monera*. Family: *Streptococcaceae*.) » bacteria [i]; streptococcus

pneumoconiosis [nyoomohkoni**oh**sis] A lung disease caused by the inhalation of air containing dust particles, which are dispersed throughout the lungs and set up foci of scarring (*fibrosis*). A common industrial disorder, it occurs among coal and other miners and sand blasters. Silica, asbestos, and berylium may also be responsible in addition to coal dust. A cough and progressive shortness of breath are common. » lungs; occupational disease

pneumonia Inflammation of the lungs from infection by bacteria or viruses. In contrast to bronchitis, the infection involves the terminal alveolar saccules deep in the lungs where oxygen exchange normally takes place. The alveoli become inflamed, fill with fluid and inflammatory cells, and become waterlogged. This imperils gaseous exchange, and a fall in the oxygen content of the blood occurs. It is usually an acute illness of sudden onset, often with shortness of breath and pleurisy. When the inflammatory reaction involves one or more lobes or parts of a lobe, the pneumonia is referred to as **lobar pneumonia**. A further type is **bronchopneumonia**, where patches of infection are scattered throughout both lungs. » bronchitis; lungs; pleurisy

pneumothorax The occurrence of air between the two layers of pleura surrounding each lung (the *pleural space*). This separates the two layers and, depending on the amount, impairs ventilation. The air may enter the pleural space from the lung through an area of pleural weakness (*spontaneous pneumothorax*) or be introduced from the outside by a wound of the chest wall. » lungs

Po, River, ancient **Padus**, Gr **Eridanos** [poh], Ital [po] River in N Italy, rising in the Cottian Alps near the French frontier; flows generally E to enter the Adriatic Sea, 56 km/35 ml S of Venice; length 652 km/405 ml; longest river in Italy; its valley is the most fertile agricultural region in the country; irregular flow, tending to silt up and alter its course; artificial embankments below Piacenza since ancient times. » Italy [i]

Pobedy, Peak (Russ **Pik**) 42°25N 80°15E. Highest peak in the Tien Shan range, on the China–Kirghizia frontier; height, 7 439 m/24 406 ft. » Tien Shan

Pocahontas (1595–1617) Indian princess, the daughter of an Indian chief, Powhatan, who twice saved the life of Captain John Smith, leader of a group of colonists who settled in Chesapeake Bay in 1607. Cajoled to Jamestown in 1612, she embraced Christianity, was baptised Rebecca, married an Englishman, John Rolfe (1585–1622), and went to England with him in 1616. Having embarked for Virginia, she died off Gravesend the next year. She left one son; several Virginia families claim descent from her. » Powhatan Confederacy

pochard A duck of the world-wide tribe *Aythyini* (15 species), comprising the diving-duck genera *Aythya* and *Netta*. It nests on the ground. » diving duck; white-eye

Pockels cell » **electro-optical effects**

pocket borough British parliamentary boroughs, especially before the First Reform Act (1832), which were directly controlled by one landed proprietor. The number of voters in such boroughs was usually very small, making control easier. The number of seats controlled by leading landowners was an indication of their political power in the 18th-c. » parliament; Reform Acts

pocket gopher A squirrel-like rodent, native to N and C America; rat-like with large head and strong jaws; cheeks infolded as fur-lined 'pockets'; digs burrows with incisor teeth; inhabits open country; also known as **pouched rat** or **gopher**. (Family: *Geomyidae*, 34 species.) » gopher; rodent; squirrel

pocket phone A portable telephone handset, used with a cellular radio or other mobile communication system, small enough to fit into the pocket. It enables users to make direct-dial telephone calls wherever they are. » mobile communications; telephone

Podgorniy, Nikolay Victorovich [podg**aw**nee] (1903–) Soviet politician, party official, and Chairman of the Presidium of the Supreme Soviet (1965–77), born in Karlovka, the Ukraine. In 1930 he joined the Communist Party, and after World War 2 took a leading role in the economic reconstruction of the liberated Ukraine. He held various senior posts (1950–65), and after the dismissal of Khrushchev (1964) became Chairman of the Presidium. He was relieved of his office in 1977 and replaced by Brezhnev, since when he has lived in retirement. » Brezhnev; communism; Khrushchev

podiatry [puh**di**yatree] » **chiropody**

Poe, Edgar Allan (1809–49) US poet and story writer, born in Boston, Massachusetts. Orphaned at three, he was adopted and brought up partly in England. He began to write poetry, became a journalist in Richmond, then settled in Philadelphia, where he worked for literary magazines, published *Tales of the Grotesque and Arabesque* (1840), and several short stories, notably 'The Murders in the Rue Morgue' (1841), the first detective story. His weird and fantastic stories, dwelling by choice on the horrible, were both original and influential. In 1844 he moved to New York, where his poem 'The Raven' (1845) won immediate fame. His wife died in 1847, after which he wrote little. He became mentally disturbed, and attempted suicide in 1848. After a temporary recovery, he died in Baltimore. » American literature; detective story; Gothic novel; poetry; short story

Poet Laureate The post appointed by the British sovereign with the duty (no longer obligatory) of writing verse upon significant royal and national occasions. The first was John Dryden, who held office 1668–88. From then until the 19th-c the post was held by inferior poets, but it gained great prestige with the tenure (1850–96) of Alfred Lord Tennyson. » RR100

poetic licence The poet's practice of taking liberty with known facts in the interests of telling a more interesting or more effective story. The historical Hotspur was 20 years older than Prince Henry; in *Henry IV*, for dramatic purposes, Shakespeare makes them the same age. The term can also refer to licence taken, for poetic effect, with the rules of grammar. » figurative language; poetry; Realism

poetry (Gr *poiein* 'to make') Originally, any creative literary work; the term is still so defined in Shelley's *Defence of Poetry* (1821). With the development and diversification of literary forms, 'poetry' came to be used for metrical composition in any mode, as distinct from writing in prose. But the weakening of such distinctions (with the prose poem and the poetic novel) has meant that a strict separation is not maintainable, the only evident distinction being between prose and verse. The term therefore has resumed an evaluative rather than descriptive significance, and is often used for any literary work of a distinctly imaginative or elaborate kind. The theory and practice of poetry, concerning itself with such fundamental questions as what poetry is, what it does, and how it should be written, is known as **poetics**. » concrete/confessional/Georgian/metaphysical/pop/skaldic poetry; Cavalier/Lake/Liverpool poets; ballad; ballade; imagery; literature; Parnassians; poetic licence; prose

Poggio (Bracciolini), Giovanni Francesco [**pod**joh] (1380–1459) Florentine humanist, born at Terranuova, Tuscany. His research took him to many European libraries, where he recovered the manuscripts of several Classical Latin writers. In 1453 he retired to Florence, and became chancellor and historiographer to the republic. His writings include letters, moral essays, invectives, and most notably the *Liber Facetiarum*, a collection of humorous stories, mainly against monks and secular clergy. He died in Florence. » humanism; Latin literature

Pogonophora [poguh**nof**uhra] » **beardworm**

poikilotherm [poy**kil**uhtherm] An animal that has no internal mechanism for regulating body temperature, so that it fluctuates with changes in ambient temperatures. It is often termed *cold-blooded*, but body temperatures may be maintained at a high level as a result of activity, or by behaviour patterns such as basking. » temperature [i]

Poincaré, (Jules) Henri [**pwĩ**karay] (1854–1912) French mathematician, born at Nancy. He was educated at Paris, where he became professor in 1881. He was eminent in physics, mechanics, and astronomy, and contributed to many fields of mathematics, especially the theory of functions. Well-known for his popular expositions of science, he died in Paris. » function (mathematics) [i]

Poincaré, Raymond (Nicolas Landry) [**pwĩ**karay] (1860–1934) French statesman, Prime Minister (1912–13, 1922–24, 1926–9), and President (1913–20), born at Bar-le-Duc. He studied law, then became a Deputy (1887) and Senator (1903), held ministerial posts in Public Instruction, Foreign Affairs, and Finance, and was three times Premier, and President of the Third Republic during World War 1. He occupied the Ruhr in 1923, and his National Union ministry averted ruin in 1926. He died in Paris. » France [i]

poinsettia [poyn**set**ia] A deciduous shrub native to Mexico. The flower is in fact a specialized inflorescence (*cyathium*) with large vermillion bracts resembling petals. Pot plants are commonly treated with growth retardant to retain shape and stature. (*Euphorbia pulcherrima*. Family: *Euphorbiaceae*.) » bract; deciduous plants; inflorescence [i]; shrub; spurge

point-to-point Horse races for amateur riders over a cross-country course, normally on farmland. They are organized by hunts, and the horses used are regular hunting horses. Original courses went from one point to another, hence the name, but are now often over circular or oval courses with a mixture of artificial and natural fences. » horse racing

Pointe-à-Pitre [pwĩt a **pee**truh] 16°14N 61°32W, pop (1982) 53 165. Seaport and capital town of Guadeloupe, on SW coast of island of Grande-Terre; largest town in Guadeloupe; airport; commercial centre, agricultural trade, tourism. » Guadeloupe

Pointe-Noire [pwĩt **nwah**] 4°48S 11°53E, pop (1980) 185 105. Seaport in Kouilou province, SW Congo, W Africa; on the Atlantic coast 385 km/239 ml WSW of Brazzaville; W terminus of railway from Brazzaville; harbour facilities begun in 1934, completed after 1945; airfield; centre of Congo's oil industry; oil refining, banking, timber, shoes. » Congo [i]

pointer A sporting dog belonging to one of several breeds developed to detect game; stands rigidly, like a statue, with the muzzle pointing towards the prey animal. » English pointer; griffon; setter; sporting dog

Pointers » **Plough, the**

Pointillism » **Divisionism**

Poiret, Paul [pwa**ray**] (1879–1944) French fashion designer, born and died in Paris. The son of a cloth merchant, he started to make sketches and sell them, eventually joining Doucet in 1896, and later Worth. In 1904 he set up on his own. He loosened and softened women's clothes, producing a more natural outline; his 'hobble' skirts became famous. In 1914 he was the first President of Le Syndicat de Défense de la Grande Couture Française, formed to protect the copyright of couturiers. >> fashion

poise [pwahz] Unit of (dynamic) viscosity; symbol *P*; a viscosity of 1 poise equals a pressure of 0.1 of a pascal applied for 1 second; named after French physician Jean-Louis-Marie Poiseuille. >> units (scientific); viscosity; RR70

poison-arrow frog >> **arrow-poison frog**

poison gas Chemical munitions fired in artillery shells or released from containers which spread toxic or disabling gases onto the battlefield. Such gases (used in World War 1) included mustard, phosgene, and chlorine. >> chemical warfare

poison ivy A shrub or woody vine, native to N America; a very variable plant, the leaves with three leaflets, smooth and glossy or hairy, toothed or lobed, sometimes resembling oak leaves, hence the alternative name, **poison oak**; flowers white. All parts produce a resin containing the chemical urushinol, which is poisonous to the touch, causing severe dermatitis. The resin is non-volatile, and can be carried on clothing, soil, and even smoke, and take effect far from the plant itself. (*Rhus toxicodendron*. Family: *Anacardiaceae*.) >> dermatitis; resin; shrub; sumac

poison oak >> **poison ivy**

Poisson, Siméon Denis [**pwa**sõ] (1781–1840) French mathematician, born at Pithiviers. He studied medicine but then turned to mathematics, becoming professor at the Ecole Polytechnique in 1806. He is known for his research into celestial mechanics, electromagnetism, and also probability, where he established the law governing the distribution of large numbers (the **Poisson distribution**). He died at Sceaux. >> electromagnetism; mechanics; Poisson's ratio; statistics

Poisson's ratio The (negative) ratio of strain in a direction perpendicular to an applied stress to the strain in the direction of the stress; symbol μ, expressed as a number; stated by French mathematician Siméon Poisson. It expresses the decrease in diameter of a rod stretched lengthways. Typical values are between 0.1 and 0.4. >> mechanical properties of matter; Poisson; strain; stress (physics)

Poitiers [**pwa**tyay] 46°35N 0°20E, pop (1982) 82 884. Market town and capital of Vienne department, W France; 160 km/99 ml ESE of Nantes; Roman settlement; former capital of ancient province of Poitou; site of French defeat by English (1356); road and railway junction; bishopric; university (1431); chemicals, hosiery, trade in honey, wine, wool; 4th-c Baptistry (France's oldest Christian building), 12th–13th-c Cathedral of St-Pierre, 11th–12th-c Church of Notre-Dame-de-la-Grande, town hall (1869–76) containing the Musée des Beaux-Arts, 11th–12th-c Romanesque Church of St-Hilaire-le-Grand. >> France [i]; Poitou

Poitou [pwa**too**] Former province in W France, now occupying the departments of Vendée, Deux-Sèvres, and Vienne; chief town, Poitiers; held by England until 1369. >> Poitiers

poker A gambling card game for 2 to 8 players which started in the USA in the 19th-c. The object is to get (or convince your opponents that you have) a better hand than them. Hands are ranked, the best hand being a Royal Flush, ie 10-Jack-Queen-King-Ace all of the same suit. There are several varieties of poker, the most popular being 5-card draw, 5-card stud, and 7-card stud. >> dice; playing cards

pokeweed A herbaceous perennial, native to N America; stems c.2 m/6½ ft; leaves oval; flowers small, white, 4-lobed, in dense spikes; berries dark purple with poisonous seeds. The leaves are used in salads. The berries yield a red dye, hence the alternative name, **red ink plant**. (*Phytolacca americana*. Family: *Phytolaccaceae*.) >> herbaceous plant; perennial

Pokhara Valley [**poh**kara] Valley in Nepal, C Asia, 203 km/126 ml NW of Kathmandu; town of Pokhara at an altitude of 913 m/2 995 ft; centre of one of Nepal's Development Regions; dominated by the Himalayas, notably Machhapuchhre, height 7 993 m/26 223 ft; road and air flights from Kathmandu; several lakes; fishing, boating, trekking. >> Himalayas; Nepal [i]

Pol Pot (1926–) Cambodian politician, born in Kompong Thom Province. He was active in the anti-French resistance under Ho Chi-Minh, and in 1946 joined the pro-Chinese Communist Party. He then studied in Paris (1949–53), worked as a teacher (1954–63), and became leader of the Khmer Rouge guerrillas, defeating Lon Nol's military government in 1976. As Prime Minister, he set up a totalitarian regime which caused the death, imprisonment, or exile of millions. Overthrown in 1979, when the Vietnamese invaded Cambodia, he withdrew to the mountains to lead the Khmer Rouge forces. >> Cambodia [i]; Khmer Rouge

Poland, Polish **Polska**, official name **The Republic of Poland**, pop (1990e) 38 070 000; area 312 612 sq km/120 668 sq ml. Republic in C Europe, divided into 49 voivodships (provinces); bounded N by the Baltic Sea, W by Germany, E by Lithuania, Belorussia, and Ukraine, and S by Czechoslovakia; coastline 491 km/305 ml; capital, Warsaw; chief towns include Łódź, Kraków, Wrocław, Poznań, Gdańsk, Katowice, Lublin; timezone GMT + 1; population mainly Polish, of W Slavic descent; chief religion, Roman Catholicism (95%); unit of currency, the złoty of 100 groszy.

Physical description and climate. Mostly part of the great European plain, with the Carpathian and Sudetes Mts (S) rising in the High Tatra to 2 499 m/8 199 ft at Mt Rysy; Polish plateau to the N, cut by the Bug, San, and Vistula Rivers; richest coal basin in Europe in the W (Silesia); lowlands with many lakes N of the plateau; flat Baltic coastal area, with sandy heathland and numerous lagoons; main rivers, the Vistula and Oder; rivers often frozen in winter, and liable to flood; forests cover a fifth of the land; continental climate, with severe winters and hot summers; rain falls chiefly in summer, seldom exceeds 650 mm/25 in annually.

History and government. Emergence as a powerful Slavic group, 11th-c; united with Lithuania, 1569; weakened by attacks from Russia, Brandenburg, Turkey, and Sweden; divided between Prussia, Russia and Austria, 1772, 1793, 1795; semi-independent state after Congress of Vienna, 1815; incorporated into the Russian Empire; independent Polish state after World War 1; partition between Germany and the USSR,

□ international airport

1939; invasion by Germany, 1939; major resistance movement, and a government in exile during World War 2; People's Democracy established under Soviet influence, 1944; rise of independent trade union, Solidarity, in 1980; Solidarity leaders detained, and state of martial law imposed, 1981–3; worsening economic situation, with continuing unrest in 1980s; loss of support for communist government and major success for Solidarity in 1989 elections; constitution amended in 1989 to provide for a 2-chamber legislature, comprising a 460-member lower assembly (the *Seym*) and a 100-member Senate.

Economy. Nearly 50% of the land under cultivation; rye, wheat, barley, oats, potatoes, sugar beet; bacon, eggs, geese, turkeys, pork; major producer of coal; lead, zinc, sulphur, potash, copper; shipbuilding, vehicles, machinery, electrical equipment, food processing, textiles. » Jagiellons; Poland, Partitions of; Polish literature; Solidarity; Warsaw; RR26 national holidays; RR59 political leaders

Poland, Partitions of Agreements between Russia, Austria, and Prussia to partition and take over Poland in the late 18th-c. There were three partitions (1772, 1793, 1795), under the provisions of which Poland lost its independent statehood, and its territories were divided between the three empires. Throughout the 19th-c, the Poles constantly struggled for national liberation and political autonomy. » Poland [i]

Polanski, Roman (1933–) Franco-Polish film director, scriptwriter and actor, born in Paris of Polish parents. Brought up in Poland, he started film work there as an actor, then writer and director, his first feature *Nóz w Wodzie* (1962, The Knife in the Water), finding international recognition. He worked in Britain in 1965, and made his first Hollywood film *Rosemary's Baby* in 1968, exploring, as in his previous productions, the nature of evil and personal corruption. After the murder of his wife in the Manson killings in 1969, he went through a troubled period and left the USA under a cloud, but created controversial interpretations of *Macbeth* (1971) in England and *Tess* (1979) in France. Later productions include *The Vampires' Ball* (1980) and *Frantic* (1988).

Polanyi, Michael [po**lan**yee] (1891–1976) Hungarian physical chemist and social philosopher, born in Budapest. He studied at Budapest and Karlsruhe, lectured at Berlin, emigrated to Britain after Hitler's rise to power, and became professor of physical chemistry (1933–48) and of social studies (1948–58) at Manchester. He did notable work on reaction kinetics and crystal structure, and wrote much on the freedom of scientific thought, philosophy of science, and social science. » crystals; social studies

polar bear A bear native to the Arctic ice pack and surrounding seas; white with long neck and small head; swims well; eats mainly seals, also small mammals, birds, reindeer (can outrun reindeer over short distances), fish, vegetation. (*Thalarctos maritimus*.) » bear

Polar Circle » **Arctic Circle**

polar co-ordinates In mathematics, a method of determining the position of a point P by its distance r from a pole O and the angle θ between OP and a base line. This system is particularly convenient for points related to one fixed point, eg the polar equation of a circle centre O is merely $r=a$; the polar equation of a circle passing through O, base line the diameter through O, is $r=2a\cos\theta$. Loops and similar curves have easy polar equations, eg $r=a\sin n\theta$. » Cartesian co-ordinates

Polar Front The main area of frontal weather systems in the N Pacific and N Atlantic. It forms the boundary between polar (cold) and subtropical (warmer) air masses, along which depressions or cyclones develop. The position of the front is associated with the polar jet stream, and shifts according to season. In winter it is further S (40°–50°N), and frontal activity is responsible for the cold, wet weather of N Europe. In summer it migrates N, and its location is more variable. » depression (meteorology) [i]; front; general circulation model; jet stream

polar molecule » **electric dipole moment**

polarimetry An analytic technique in which linearly polarized light is passed through an optically active sample, and the degree of rotation of the plane of polarization is measured. It is used especially in chemistry and biology to identify and measure concentrations of transparent solutions, such as sugar solutions. » Faraday effect; optical activity; polarization [i]

Polaris [puh**lah**ris] The brightest star in the constellation Ursa Minor, currently lying (by chance) within 1° of the N celestial pole; also called the **Pole Star**. Its altitude is approximately equal to the latitude of the observer. This star was much used for simple navigation. » Poles

Polaris missile A first-generation US submarine-launched ballistic missile under development from the mid-1950s. The US Navy's first Polaris deterrent patrol was made in 1960, and the system was operational with the Royal Navy in 1968. It is no longer operational with the US Navy, but a modified version with three separate warheads and advanced penetration aids will continue with the Royal Navy's four Polaris-equipped submarines, until replaced by the Trident system. » ballistic missile; penetration aid; Trident missile

polarity In chemistry, a permanent property of a substance, implying an inherent separation of electric charge. The notion contrasts with **polarizability**, which is an induced property of a substance, implying an easy separation of charge. » dipole; van der Waals interaction

polarization A property of (transverse) waves in which wave oscillations occur in a direction which is either constant or varies in a well-defined way. Illustration (a) shows a wave moving in x-direction along a rope, polarized in the y direction, and Illustration (b) in the z-direction. These are both linear polarizations, since each portion of rope moves up and down in straight lines. General linear polarization can be represented as a sum of x and z polarizations, not necessarily in equal amounts. The x and z polarized waves may be combined such that they are not in step, ie their phases differ. The y polarized wave may lead the x wave by a phase difference of $\pi/2$, corresponding to elliptical polarization, ie when looking back along the direction of motion, the rope traces out an ellipse. The precise shape of the ellipse depends on the phase difference and amplitudes of the two waves. A special case is equal amplitude linear waves, differing in phase by $\pi/2$, which gives circular polarization. If, when looking back along the direction of motion, the rope appears to move clockwise, the polarization is described as right circular; if anticlockwise, it is left circular. A plate with a slit cut in it placed in the path of a wave will allow that portion of the wave in the direction of the slit to pass; the slit acts as a polarizer. Corresponding polarization effects to those oberved in the rope can be seen elsewhere. Polarization in electromagnetic radiation (including light) is dictated by the electric part of the wave. Skylight, reflected light, and scattered light are all (partially) polarized. » birefringence; Faraday effect; optical activity; polarimetry; Polaroid; Zeeman effect

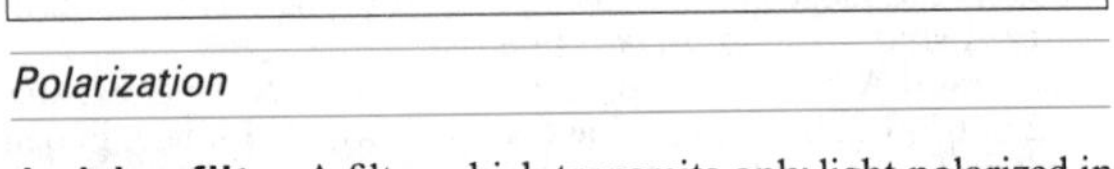

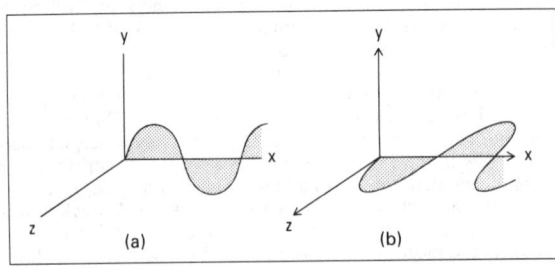

Polarization

polarizing filter A filter which transmits only light polarized in a specific dimension. It is used in general photography to suppress specular reflections from glass or water surfaces and to darken blue skies. Other applications include stereoscopy, stress analysis, and mineral structures in photomicrography. » filter; photomicrograph; stereoscopic photography

polarography The study of the relationship between current and voltage in an electrochemical cell. Generally, the voltage of a working electrode relative to a standard reference is changed systematically in an electrolysis cell while the current passing is measured. Sharp rises in current at particular voltages are characteristic of specific ions in solution, and may be used in both qualitative and quantitative analysis. » cell; electrolysis [i]

Polaroid 1 A trade name for doubly refracting material; developed by US physicist Edwin Land in 1938. A plastic sheet is strained so as to align its molecules, thus making it refract light in two slightly different directions. It is familiar in sun-glasses to reduce the glare from light polarized on reflection, and is also used in some optical equipment. » polarization [i]; refraction [i] 2 The trade name of an instant photography system developed by Land for black-and-white (1948) and colour (1963). The film is processed with viscous chemical reacting substances applied in the camera immediately after exposure. » Land; photography

polder A Dutch term for a flat area of land reclaimed from the sea or a river floodplain, and protected from flooding by dykes (eg the partial reclamation of the Zuider Zee in the Netherlands). They are often below sea level, so pumping is needed to keep them clear of water. » dam; Zuider Zee

pole » **magnetic poles; Poles**

Pole, Reginald (1500–58) English Roman Catholic churchman and Archbishop of Canterbury, born at Stourton Castle, Staffordshire. Educated at Oxford and Padua, he received several Church posts, and was at first high in Henry VIII's favour; but after opposing the King on divorce, he left for Italy, and lost all his preferments. In 1536 the Pope made him a cardinal, and in 1554, in the reign of the Catholic Queen Mary, he returned to England as papal legate. He became one of her most powerful advisers, returned the country to Rome, and became Archbishop of Canterbury. He died in London on the same day as Mary. » Henry VIII; Mary I; Reformation

Pole Star » **Polaris**

pole vault An athletics field event; a jumping contest for height using a fibreglass pole for leverage to clear a bar. In competition the bar is raised progressively, and each competitor has three attempts to clear the height before attempting a new height. The current world record is 6.03 m/19 ft 9½ in, achieved by Sergey Bubka (USSR, born 4 Dec 1963) on 23 June 1987 at Prague, Czechoslovakia. » athletics

polecat A mammal of family *Mustelidae*; resembles a large weasel (length, 600 mm/24 in); dark with pale marks on face and ear tips; two species: **European polecat**, **foul marten**, **foumart**, or **fitchet** (*Mustela putorius*); **steppe polecat** (*Mustela eversmanni*) from Asia. The name is also used for the **marbled polecat** of genus *Vormela*; for the zorilla; and (in the USA) for skunks of genus *Mephitis*. » ferret; Mustelidae; skunk; weasel; zorilla

Poles The two diametrically opposite points at which the Earth's axis cuts the Earth's surface; known as the **geographical poles**. The N Pole is covered by the Arctic Ocean, and the S Pole by the land mass of Antarctica. The **magnetic poles** are the positions towards which the needle of a magnetic compass will point. They differ from the geographical poles by an angle known as the *declination* or *magnetic variation*, which itself varies at different points of the Earth's surface and at different times. The S Pole was first reached by Amundsen on 14 December 1911, a month before the British team, led by Scott, which arrived on 17 January 1912; the N Pole was first reached by Robert E Peary on 6 April 1909. » Amundsen; Earth [i]; magnetic poles; Peary; Scott, Robert

policy unit A small group of officials in a government department, or other public agency, whose role is to supply information, advice, and analysis to policy makers, normally politicians. The main idea behind the unit is to have officials concentrating on strategic issues free from other responsibilities.

Polignac, Auguste Jules Armand Marie, Prince de [poleenyak] (1780–1847) French statesman, born at Versailles. Arrested for conspiring against Napoleon (1804), he became a peer at the Bourbon Restoration. A committed exponent of papal and royal authority, he received the title of prince from the Pope in 1820. English Ambassador in 1823, he became in 1829 head of the last Bourbon ministry, which promulgated the St Cloud Ordinances that cost Charles X his throne (1830). He was imprisoned until 1836, then lived in exile in England, returning in 1845 to Paris, where he died. » Bourbons; Charles X (of France); July Revolution

poliomyelitis An infection by a virus that predominantly affects the motor neurone cells in the spinal cord, the axons of which supply the muscles; also known as **infantile paralysis**. Access to the central nervous system is via the nasopharynx. The features are those of an infectious disease with fever and headache, which may subside, but which in some cases is followed by weakness in a single group of muscles followed by widespread muscle paralysis. Occasionally involvement of the brain stem results in respiratory paralysis and death. A vaccine taken by mouth is effective. » Sabin; Salk; spinal cord; virus

polis (plural **poleis**) [polis/polays] Conventionally translated 'city-state', the principal political and economic unit of classical Greece. There might be differences of political colouring between one polis and another. Some (eg Athens) were full-blown democracies, while others (eg Corinth, Thebes, Sparta) were more oligarchical in character. But all possessed the same basic organs of government – an assembly of male citizens, an advisory council, and elected executive officers. Always self-governing, they were usually economically self-sufficient as well. » Corinth; oligarchy; Sparta (Greek history); Thebes

Polish » **Polish literature; Slavic languages**

Polish Corridor An area of formerly German territory granted to Poland by the Treaty of Versailles (1919). It linked the Polish heartland with the free city of Danzig, but divided E Prussia from the rest of Germany. Its recovery was one of Hitler's aspirations during the late 1930s, thereby contributing to the outbreak of World War 2. » Hitler; Poland [i]

Polish literature The *Bogurodzica*, a late 14th-c hymn to the Virgin, initiates a literature which reflects Polish history, at the crossroads (often the battleground) of East and West. The 'father of Polish literature', Rej (1509–69), bridged the mediaeval and early modern world, while Copernicus (1473–1543) still wrote in Latin; the poet Jan Kochanowski (1530–84) was the first Renaissance figure. The 17th-c Baroque was well adapted to the tensions of the time, reflected in the poetry of Jan Morsztyn (1621–93), the epic chronicles (1660–1) of Samuel Twardowski, and the memoirs of Jan Pasek (1636–1701). The later 18th-c was a period of intense activity, with the first theatre opening (in Warsaw) in 1765, and a new readership eager for the novels, plays, poems, and satires of such writers as the poet-priest Ignacy Krasicki (1735–1801) and Julian Niemcewicz (1757–1841). The early 19th-c finds three great Romantic poets writing in exile: the national poet Adam Mickiewicz (1798–1855), Juliusz Słowaci (1808–49), and Zygmunt Krasiński (1812–59); while the Modernist precursor Cyprian Norwid (1821–83) endured both exile and neglect.

Political realities ushered in the novel, in the hands of Eliza Orzeskowa (1841–1910), Boleslaw Prus (1845–1912), and Henryk Sienkiewicz (1846–1916; Nobel Prize, 1905). The writers of Young Poland, before 1918, reflected the experimentalism of the time; among them the poet Jan Kasprowicz (1860–1926), the novelist Stefan Żeromski (1864–1925), and the innovatory dramatist Stanislaw Wyspiański (1868–1907). Between the wars, independent Poland produced many important novelists, including Maria Dabrowska (1889–1965), Michał Choromański (1904–72), Witold Gombrowicz (1904–69), and Jerzy Andrzejewski (1909–83); also the poetry of Julian Tuwim (1894–1953) and the Surrealist theatre of Stanisław Witkiewicz (1885–1939). Since 1945, writers such as the novelist Tadeusz Konwicki (1926–), poets Zbigniew Herbert (1924–) and Czesław Miłosz (1911–), the playwright Sławomir Mrożek (1930–), and Stanisław Lem (1921–), with his prophetic science fiction, have expressed an embattled but undefeated consciousness. » Copernicus; Herbert, Zbigniew; Mickiewicz; Miłosz; Poland [i]; Sienkiewicz

Polish swan » **mute swan**

Politburo The Political Bureau of the Central Committee of the Communist Party of the Soviet Union; at various times, known as the **Presidium**. It was the highest organ of the party, and, therefore, of the entire Soviet political system. Elected by the Central Committee, there were twelve members plus seven candidate members who had no votes, but in practice membership was decided by the politburo itself under the General

Secretary, who presided over it. Its functions may be compared to those of a cabinet, though its authority varied over the years, becoming more firmly established during the Brezhnev era. » Brezhnev; cabinet; Communist Party of the Soviet Union

political action committee A non-party organization in the USA, which contributes money to candidates for public office. Since 1971 each committee has been able to give only $5 000 per election to each candidate. The committees are created by various organized interests, such as unions, trade associations, and groups with strong political beliefs. There is increasing concern about their 'buying' influence.

political economy The name given to economics in the late 18th-c and early 19th-c. The term has not been much used in the present century, apart from in professorial titles, reflecting the fact that the scope of economics is today much wider, dealing with many more issues than national economic affairs and the role of government. The name does however indicate that economics is not an exact science, but a social science which often has to take into account 'political' considerations. » economics

political science The academic discipline which describes and analyses the operations of government, the state, and other political organizations, and any other factors which influence their behaviour, such as economics. A major concern is to establish how power is exercised, and by whom, in resolving conflict within society. There is a range of approaches, some of which draw upon other academic studies, such as sociology, economics, and psychology, and which can be regarded as sub-disciplines of the subject. Two general trends may be recognized. *Empirical analysis* draws conclusions by observing and generating data about state organizations and wider societal groupings and their interrelationships. *Political theory* (of which *political philosophy* is a sub-branch) has two principal concerns: the clarification of values in order to demonstrate logically the purpose of political activity, and thereby the way in which society 'ought' to proceed (eg in allocating resources); and the rigorous derivation and testing of theories drawn from empirical research. » community politics; geopolitics; political sociology

political sociology The academic study of the relationship between social structures and political behaviour. It seeks to explain political phenomena in terms of social factors, in particular social conflict and consensus. Its range of coverage is extensive and growing, having established itself since the war as a separate field of study. Much of the work is based upon the comparative analysis of different countries.

politics » **political science**

Polk, James K(nox) (1795–1849) US statesman and 11th President (1845–9), born in Mecklenburg Co, North Carolina. Admitted to the Bar in 1820, he entered Congress as a Democrat (1825), and became Governor of Tennessee (1839). During his presidency, Texas was admitted to the Union (1845), and after the Mexican War (1846–7) the USA acquired California and New Mexico. The Oregon boundary was settled by a compromise with England. He also condemned the antislavery agitation, and was committed to state rights, a revenue tariff, and an independent treasury. He died at Nashville, Tennessee, » Mexican War

polka A quick dance of Bohemian origin, in duple metre, with an accent on the second beat. It was a favourite 19th-c ballroom dance, and numerous examples were composed by the Strauss family. » Strauss, Johann (the Elder)

poll » **opinion poll**

poll tax » **community charge**

pollack Cod-like fish found in inshore waters of the N Atlantic from Norway to the Mediterranean; length up to 1.3 m/4¼ ft; lower jaw protrudes beyond upper; chin barbel absent; greenish brown on back, sides pale yellow, underside white; feeds mainly on other fishes; taken commercially by net and on lines; also popular with sea anglers. (*Pollachius pollachius*. Family: *Gadidae*.) » cod

Pollaiuolo, Antonio [poliywoloh] (c.1432–98) Italian goldsmith, sculptor, and painter, born in Florence. He cast sepulchral monuments in St Peter's, Rome, for two popes, and was one of the first painters to study anatomy and apply it to his art. He died in Rome. His brother, **Piero** (c.1443–c.96), was associated with him in his work. » Florentine School; Italian art

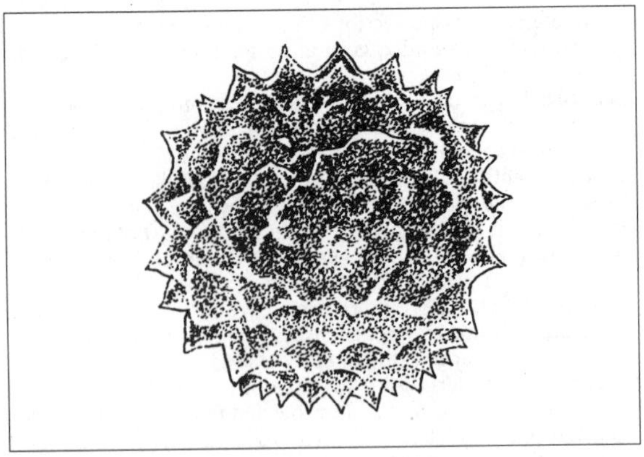

Magnified pollen grain

pollen The male sex-cells of seed plants, produced in large numbers in the anthers of flowering plants and the pollen-sacs of gymnosperms. On reaching the stigma of a flower or the scale of a female cone, the pollen grain grows a tube through which its contents are transferred to fertilize the ovule. Pollen grains vary greatly in size, shape, and surface sculpturing, which may all play a part in dispersal. Windborne pollen is smooth and light; that carried by insects is often heavier and sticky. The outer coat of the grain (*exine*) is very resistant to decay, and pollen can be used to investigate the vegetation of prehistoric times. » flowering plants; gymnosperms; ovule; pollination; stigma

pollen analysis » **palynology**

pollination The transfer of pollen from anther to ovary within a flower, necessary for fertilization and seed production. It is usually a complex and sophisticated process, demanding structural and physiological specialization within the flower, and often involving outside agents, principally insects, birds, wind, or water. The entire package of adaptations and modifications found in any particular flower may be referred to as the *pollination syndrome*. The control of outside agents such as animals may be achieved by the use of very specific signals from the flower (eg colour, scent) to stimulate responses only in specific pollinators, thus increasing the chances of successful transfer, and requiring relatively low pollen production. Inanimate agents such as wind and water are much more haphazard, and plants using them must produce larger amounts of pollen to ensure success. Pollination may occur between the stamens and ovary of the same flower, but in the interests of outbreeding, many species have one or more mechanisms to prevent this, including the spatial arrangement and differential ripening of the floral parts, and chemical compatability systems which prevent pollen of the wrong sort from fertilizing the ovules. » flowering plants; nectar; ovary; pollen; stamen

polliwog or **polliwig** » **tadpole**

pollock » **saithe**

Pollock, (Paul) Jackson (1912–56) US artist, born at Cody, Wyoming, the leading exponent of action painting in the USA. His art developed from Surrealism to abstract art and the first drip paintings of 1947. This technique he continued with increasing violence and often on huge canvases, such as 'One', which is 5 m/17 ft long. He died at E Hampton, New York. » abstract art; action painting; Surrealism

pollution The direct or indirect introduction of a harmful substance into the environment. The degree of pollution depends on the nature and amount of the pollutant, and the location into which it is introduced; fertilizers become pollutants when used to excess, and when they become concentrated in run-off water entering streams. Different categories of pollution include air pollution (eg acid rain), freshwater pollution (eg discharge of chemical effluent from industry into rivers), marine pollution (eg oil spills from tankers), noise pollution (eg from aircraft), land pollution (eg the burial of toxic waste), and visual pollution (eg the intrusion of industry into an area of scenic beauty). » acid rain [i]; eutrophication; hazardous substances; oil pollution; radioactive waste; waste disposal

Pollux » Gemini

pollywog or **pollywig** » tadpole

Polo, Marco (1254–1324) Merchant and traveller, born and died in Venice. His father and uncle, after a previous visit to Kublai Khan in China (1260–9), made a second journey (1271–5), taking Marco with them. Marco became an envoy in Kublai's service, and served as Governor of Yang Chow. He left China in 1292, and after returning to Venice (1295), fought against the Genoese, but was captured. During his imprisonment, he compiled an account of his travels: *Il milione* (The Million, trans The Travels of Marco Polo), which became widely read. » Kublai Khan

polo A stick-and-ball game played on horseback by teams of four. When the side lines of the ground are boarded, the playing area measures 274 m/300 yd by 146 m/160 yd, making it the largest of all ball games. The object is to strike the ball with a hand-held mallet into the opposing goal, which measures 7.3 m/8 yd wide by 3 m/10 ft high. Each game is divided into seven-minute periods known as *chukkas*. The number of chukkas varies according to each competition. Polo was first played in C Asia c.500 BC, its name deriving from the Tibetan *pulu*. » water polo; RR116

polonaise A Polish dance in a moderate triple metre. Chopin wrote some famous examples for piano, but the dance itself dates from the 16th-c or earlier. » Chopin

Polonnaruwa [pohluhn**nah**ruva] 7°56N 81°02E, pop (1981) 11 636. Capital of Polonnaruwa district, Sri Lanka, on the N shore of L Parakrama Samudra; many buildings of the 11th–14th-c, when it was the island's capital; a world heritage site; King Parakrama Bahu's Palace, Kumara Pokuna; formerly fortified by three concentric walls. » Sri Lanka [i]

Poltava [pul**ta**va] 49°35N 34°35E, pop (1983) 290 000. Industrial capital city of Poltavskaya oblast, Ukraine, on R Vorskla; one of the oldest settlements in the Ukraine, known since the 7th-c; site of Swedish defeat by Peter the Great, 1709; railway; agricultural trade, machinery, metalworking, foodstuffs, clothing, glass; cathedral of the Krestovozdvizhenskii monastery (1689–1709). » Ukraine

poltergeist Unusual apparently paranormal physical disturbances, such as movement and/or breakage of objects, malfunctioning of electrical devices, and loud raps, which seem to depend upon the presence of a particular living person. This individual is often referred to as the 'agent' or 'focus'. » paranormal; psychokinesis

polyamides Large molecules formed by the condensation polymerization of diamines with dicarboxylic acids (eg 1,6-diaminohexane, $H_2NCH_2CH_2CH_2CH_2CH_2CH_2NH_2$ with 1,6-hexanedioic acid, $HOOCCH_2CH_2CH_2CH_2COOH$ to give nylon). These complementary molecules give the same type of amide linkage as that found in natural protein fibres, such as silk and wool, where the monomers are amino acids. » amides; amino acid [i]; polymerization

polyanthus [poli**an**thuhs] A garden hybrid derived mainly from the primrose and the cowslip, with the large flowers of the former, borne in heads like the latter. (*Primula × polyanthus*. Family: *Primulaceae*.) » cowslip; primrose

polyarchy A political term characterizing the processes and institutions of modern, Western, liberal democracies. The main features of polyarchies are opposition and the absence of strictly hierarchical organizations. They tend to be segmented, with people participating in political processes of direct interest to them; but universal elections remain of importance. » democracy; liberalism; pluralism

Polybius [puh**lib**iuhs] (c.200–after 118 BC) Greek politician, diplomat, and historian from Megalopolis in the Peloponnese, who wrote of the rise of Rome to world power status (264–146 BC). Only five of the original 40 books survive. The 18 years he spent in Rome as a political hostage (168–150 BC) gave him a unique insight into Roman affairs, and led to lasting friendships with some of the great figures of the day, notably Scipio Aemilianus. » Roman history [i]; Scipio Aemilianus

polycarbamates » polyurethanes

Polycarp, St (c.69–c.155), feast day 23 February. Greek Bishop of Smyrna, who bridges the little-known period between the age of his master, the apostle John, and that of his own disciple Irenaeus. His only extant writing is the *Epistle to the Philippians*. He visited Rome to discuss the question of the timing of Easter, and was martyred on his return to Smyrna – an event graphically described in an early document, *The Martyrdom of Polycarp*. » Irenaeus, St; John, St

polycentrism A political term, first used by the Italian communist party leader, Palmiro Togliatti (1893–1964) after the 20th Congress of the Soviet Communist Party (1956), to indicate the growing independence of communist parties from the Soviet Party after the Stalin era. The trend began in Yugoslavia under Tito, and was adopted to varying degrees by other national parties as a means of taking account of local conditions. » Marxism-Leninism; Stalinism; Tito

polychromy In art, the practice of colouring sculpture; also in architecture, the employment of coloured marbles, bricks, flint, stone, etc on buildings for decorative effect. » architecture; sculpture

Polyclitus [polee**kliy**tus] (5th-c BC) Greek sculptor from Samos, a contemporary of Phidias, known for his statues of athletes, which were often copied. One of his greatest works is the bronze 'Doryphorus' (Spear Bearer). » Greek art; Phidias; sculpture

Polycrates [po**li**krateez] (6th-c BC) Tyrant of Samos (540–522 BC), one of the earliest of the Greek tyrants, a great ruler who turned Samos into a major naval power, the ally of Egypt, Cyrene, and later Persia, and made her the cultural centre of the E Aegean. Among the poets who enjoyed his patronage was Anacreon. » Anacreon; tyrant

polycythaemia/polycythemia [poleesiy**thee**mia] An excessive number of circulating red blood cells. It arises as a result of oxygen deficiency, as occurs for example by living at high altitudes, and rarely as a spontaneous disease of unknown cause. » blood

polyembryony [poli**em**brionee] The formation of numerous embryos from a single fertilized egg (*zygote*), ovule, or other cell. » egg; embryo; ovary

polyesters Large molecules formed by the condensation polymerization of dialcohols with dicarboxylic acids (eg ethylene glycol $HOCH_2CH_2OH$ with terephthalic acid $HOOC–C_6H_4–COOH$ to give terylene). Synthetic fibres include Terylene (ICI) and Dacron (Du Pont): they impart crease-resistant and easy-care properties to domestic textiles. Their high strength, abrasion resistance, and chemical inertness are also exploited industrially – for example, combined with other plastics and glass fibre, as reinforced plastic for construction. » ester [i]; polymerization

polyethylene A family of thermoplastics of a waxy nature, made by subjecting ethene (ethylene) to high pressures at moderate temperatures; commonly known as **polythene**. Valuable as an insulator, it is easy to work into vessels with high chemical resistance, and was important in the development of radar. » ethylene; radar; thermoplastic

polygamy A form of marriage where a person has more than one spouse at the same time. The concept includes *polygyny*, the most common, where a man has more than one wife, and *polyandry*, where a woman has more than one husband. » marriage

polygene [**po**lijeen] A gene of small effect, acting in combination with many others and not individually detectable. Variation in observable characteristics is of two types: *discrete* (eg blood groups A or O), where assignment is to one category or another; and *quantitative* (eg stature) where measurement is against a continuous scale without distinct categories. Inheritance of the latter type of character is thought to be by polygenes. » gene

polygon In mathematics, a plane figure whose boundaries are segments of straight lines. If there are n sides of the polygon, the sum of the interior angles is $(2n-4)$ right angles. A **regular polygon** has sides equal in length, and all the interior angles at the vertices are equal. A regular polygon with three sides is an equilateral triangle; one with four sides is a square. There is an infinite number of regular figures. » geometry; plane; polyhedron; polytope

polyhedron In mathematics, a solid completely bounded by plane surfaces. It can be proved that there are only five regular polyhedra, those bounded by congruent regular polygons. If there are v vertices, e edges, f faces, and a angles in a polyhedron, $v+f-e=2$ (Euler's formula), and $a=2e$, $a\geqslant 3f$, $v\leqslant e$, $f\leqslant \frac{2}{3}e$, $f\leqslant 2v-4$. Polyhedra are of great importance in crystallography and mineralogy. » Platonic solids; plane; polygon

Polyhymnia [poleehimnia, polimnia] In Greek mythology, one of the Muses, associated with dancing or mime. » Muses

polymerization The forming of a large molecule, a **polymer**, by the combination of smaller ones (*monomers*). Combinations of two molecules are called **dimers**; of three, **trimers**. Small polymers (usually of 3–10 monomers) are known as **oligomers**. The monomers may be all of the same type, as in polyethylene, or they may be two complementary molecules, as in polyester or polyamide formation. There are two main types of reaction: *condensation*, in which a side product is formed, and *addition*, in which it is not. Polymers may contain anything from 100 to over 10 000 monomer residues. » addition reaction; condensation (chemistry); polyamides; polyesters; polysaccharides; protein; resin

polymethylmethacrylate » **Perspex**

polymorph In chemistry, one of several forms of crystal structure with the same chemical composition, such as graphite and diamond. » allotrope

polymorphism In biology, the coexistence of two or more genetically distinct forms of an organism within the same interbreeding population, where the frequency of the rarest type is not maintained by mutation alone. The polymorphism may be balanced and persist over many generations, or may be transient. Human eye colour is an example of a readily observable polymorphism, but there are many invisible polymorphisms detectable only by special techniques, such as DNA analysis. » DNA [i]; genetics [i]; mutation

polymyositis [poleemiyohsiytis] A rare diffuse disorder of muscle, connective tissue, and skin, in which an auto-immune process may play a part. » auto-immune diseases

Polynesia A large triangular area in the EC Pacific extending from Hawaii in the N, to New Zealand in the S, and to Easter I in the E. Among other island groups, it includes Tuvalu (Ellice), Tokelau, Samoa, Tonga, Cook Is, Marquesas, and Society Is (Tahiti). The striking cultural, linguistic, and physical similarities between the people of these islands are due to their common descent from the Lapita people who first settled in Tonga. Polynesians are typically of medium height, stocky build, with light-to-medium skin colour, and little body hair; there is a high rate of blood group N, a low rate of B, and an absence of Rh-negative. » Lapita people; Melanesia; Micronesia; Oceania

polyneuropathy » **neuropathy**

Polynices or **Polyneices** [poliniyseez] A Greek hero, the second son of Oedipus, who led the Seven against Thebes. Creon's refusal to bury him led eventually to the death of Antigone. » Antigone; Creon; Eteocles; Seven against Thebes

polynomial An algebraic expression containing several terms added to or subtracted from each other, eg $a+2b-3c$. If these terms are multiples of powers of a single variable, say x (eg $a_0x^n+a_1x^{n-1}+a_2x^{n-2}+\ldots a_n$), the polynomial is said to be of degree n in x. A polynomial of degree 2 is a *quadratic*; of degree 3 is a *cubic*. » algebra; equations; quadratic equation

polyp (marine biology) The individual, soft-bodied, sedentary form of a coelenterate; body consists of a cylindrical trunk with an apical mouth surrounded by tentacles; attached basally in solitary forms, or to a branching tubular system in colonies. (Phylum: *Cnidaria*.) » coelenterate; medusa

polyp (medicine) A small tumour growing from the lining surface of an organ, such as the large intestine, nose, or larynx. It may bleed and need surgical removal. Often benign, it may become malignant or recurrent. » tumour

polypeptide » **peptide**

Polyphemus [polifeemuhs] In Greek mythology, one of the Cyclopes, who imprisoned Odysseus and some of his companions in his cave. They blinded his one eye, and told Polyphemus that 'No one' had hurt him. As a result, when he called on the other Cyclopes for help, and they asked who had attacked him, they did not understand his answer. Odysseus' band escaped by hiding under the sheep when they were let out of the cave to graze. » Cyclops; Galatea

polyphony Music in more than one part. In general usage the term implies counterpoint, rather than simple chordal texture (*homophony*). One might thus talk of 'Renaissance polyphony' with reference to the masses, motets, and madrigals of the 16th-c, but not of 'Romantic polyphony' with reference to 19th-c music as a whole, even though virtually all Romantic music is in the strictest sense polyphonic. » counterpoint; melody; monody; Romanticism (music)

polyploidy [poliploydee] The condition in which an individual has more than the normal two sets of homologous chromosomes found in diploid organisms; particularly common in plants. It is caused by replication of the entire chromosome set within the nucleus, but without any subsequent nuclear division. It includes triploid (three sets), tetraploid (four sets), and octoploid (eight sets). » chromosome [i]; homology; nucleus (biology)

polypody A perennial fern with creeping rhizomes, found almost everywhere; often epiphytic; fronds solitary, deeply lobed or divided; sori without indusia, forming 1–3 rows on the underside of the frond. (Genus: *Polypodium*, 75 species. Family: *Polypodiaceae*.) » epiphyte; fern; perennial; rhizome; sorus

polypropylene A thermoplastic made by passing propene (propylene) over a phosphoric acid catalyst at a moderately high temperature, or by passing propene into heptane with a catalyst. It is useful as a moulding material, or as an extruded film. » thermoplastic

polysaccharides [poleesakariydz] Large carbohydrate molecules resulting from the condensation polymerization of sugars to form ether linkages between the monosaccharide units. Hydrolysis of a polysaccharide leads to the forming of simpler sugars. Common polysaccharides include starch and cellulose, both polymers of glucose. » carbohydrate; condensation (chemistry); disaccharide; sugars

polystyrene » **styrene**

polytechnic An institution of higher education devoted to the teaching of many subjects, as opposed to a *monotechnic*, such as a college of education, which teaches only one kind of course. What distinguishes it from a university is that more of its courses have a strong vocational bias, often involving actual work experience during the course. However, it is not exclusively devoted to vocational work, and may offer liberal studies as well. Research is also undertaken, especially in conjunction with industry. » university; vocational education

polytetrafluorethylene (PTFE) A thermosetting plastic polymer with important surface-modifying properties. PTFE has a low coefficient of friction which makes it valuable in non-lubricated bearings, ski-surfaces, etc. Its anti-stick properties make it useful in cooking utensils. It has a high chemical resistance, a high softening point, and is a good insulator. » plastics; polymerization; thermoset

polytheism The belief in or worship of many gods, characteristic not only of primitive religions but also of the religions of classical Greece and Rome. It is an attempt, contrasting with monotheism, to acknowledge a divine presence in the world. » animism; monotheism; pantheism

polythene » **polyethylene**

polytonality The property of music in which two or more keys are used simultaneously. In Holst's *Terzetto* (1924), the parts for flute, oboe, and viola are each written in a different key. » bitonality; Holst

polytope In mathematics, the four-dimensional analogue of a polyhedron. With each point in 2-dimensional space, we can associate a number-pair (x,y); with each point in 3-dimensional space, we associate the ordered triple (x,y,z), so we are encouraged to go on and think of n-dimensional space as ordered sets of numbers $(x_1, x_2, x_3, \ldots x_n)$. This leads at once to

4-dimensional space. Regular polytopes have 3-dimensional regular polygons as their 'faces'; it has been proved that whereas there are only five regular polygons in 3-dimensional space, there are six regular polytopes in 4-dimensional space, and three in 5-dimensional space. » hypercube [i]; polyhedron

polyunsaturated fatty acids Dietary fats largely comprised of glycerol combined with three fatty acids, the whole molecule being a *triglyceride*. Fatty acids can be *saturated*, *mono-unsaturated*, or *polyunsaturated* depending on the number of carbon-to-carbon bonds which are not fully saturated with hydrogen atoms. The greater the number of such unsaturated bonds, the more polyunsaturated the fat. Polyunsaturated fats are liquid at room temperature, and are industrially hydrogenated to produce a harder, more saturated fat used in many margarines. An adequate intake of these fats can contribute to the maintenance of acceptable levels of blood cholesterol. All marine oils, and most vegetable oils (but not palm and coconut oils) are polyunsaturated fats. The main such fat in nature is linoleic acid, an essential component of the human diet (one of the **essential fatty acids**); it is needed for the synthesis of arachidonic acid and prostaglandins, but is obtainable only from vegetable oils. We require c.3% of our daily calories to come from linoleic acid. » arachidonic acid; carboxylic acids; cholesterol; margarine; prostaglandins

polyurethanes [poleeyo**oo**ruhthaynz] or **polycarbamates** Large molecules formed from the addition polymerization of butane-1,4-diol and hexane-1,6-di-isocyanate, which give light-weight flexible or rigid foams. They are widely used in coatings and adhesives, and the flexible form is found in swim-suits and corsets. Their combustion releases very poisonous isocyanate fumes, which leads to restrictions on their use (eg in furnishings). » addition reaction; fulminate

polyuria » **diabetes mellitus**

polyvinylacetate A polymer of vinyl acetate monomer ($CH_2COO.CH=CH_2$) used in adhesives, plasticizers, and concrete additives. » polymerization; vinyl

polyvinylchloride (PVC) A family of polymers of vinyl chloride ($CH_2=CHCl$). It is generally mixed with additives or fillers to give materials useful for their limited flexibility, such as floor coverings, luggage, furnishing, and electric wire coating. » polymerization; vinyl

polywater A temporary excitement of the 1960s, when a silicate gel was mistaken for a new polymorph of water, with apparent formula about H_8O_4. Had this existed and been stable with respect to ordinary water, a catalyst might have been discovered which would have ended life on Earth by converting all water to this form! » gel; polymorph

Pombal, Sebastião (José) de Carvalho (e Mello), Marquês de ('Marquis of') (1699–1782) Portuguese statesman, born near Coimbra. He became Ambassador to London (1739) and Vienna (1745), and Secretary for Foreign Affairs (1750). He showed great resourcefulness in replanning the city of Lisbon, following the disastrous earthquake of 1755, and was made Prime Minister in 1756. He opposed church influence, reorganized the army, and improved agriculture, commerce, and finance. He was made count (1758) and marquis (1770), but fell from office on the accession of Maria I (1777). He died at Pombal. » Lisbon

pomegranate A deciduous, sometimes spiny, shrub or tree growing to 9 m/30 ft, native to SW Asia, and cultivated in Europe since ancient times; leaves up to 8 cm/3 in, shiny, oblong, opposite; flowers 2–4 cm/¾–1½ in, calyx and petals scarlet; fruit 5–8 cm/2–3 in, globose with yellow or reddish, leathery skin; seeds numerous, each embedded in translucent, purplish, juicy and sweet flesh. (*Punica granatum*. Family: *Punicaceae*.) » deciduous plants; sepal; shrub; tree [i]

Pomerania [pomuh**ray**nia], Ger **Pommern**, Polish **Pomorzr** Region of NC Europe along the Baltic Sea from Stralsund (East Germany) to the R Vistula in Poland; a disputed territory, 17th–18th-c; divided among Germany, Poland, and the free city of Danzig, 1919–39; divided between East Germany and Poland, 1945; many lakes; chief towns, Gdańsk, Szczecin, Koszalin. » Germany [i]; Poland [i]

Pomeranian A toy breed of dog developed from spitz breeds in Britain during the 19th-c; thick double-layered coat, longest on neck, legs and rear end; tail curled only at tip, carried across the back. » dog; non-sporting dog; spitz

Pomona [puh**moh**na] Roman goddess of fruit-trees and their fruit, especially apples and pears.

Pompadour, Jeanne Antoinette Poisson, Marquise de, byname **Madame de Pompadour** (1721–64) Mistress of Louis XV, born in Paris. A woman of remarkable grace, beauty, and wit, she became a queen of fashion, and attracted the eye of the King at a ball. Installed at Versailles (1745), and ennobled as Marquise de Pompadour, she assumed the entire control of public affairs, and for 20 years swayed state policy, appointing her own favourites. She founded the royal porcelain factory at Sèvres, and was a lavish patroness of architecture, the arts, and literature. Blamed for French defeats in the Seven Years' War, she died at Versailles. » Louis XV; Seven Years' War

pompano [**pom**panoh] Any of several large deep-bodied marine fish which with jacks and scads comprise the family *Carangidae* (11 genera); body typically compressed, head with steep profile, tail deeply forked; widespread in open oceanic waters, especially of warm seas; many are excellent sport and food fishes.

Pompeii, Ital **Pompei** [pomp**ay**ee], Ital [pom**pay**] 40°45N 14°27E, pop (1981) 22 896. Ruined ancient city in Naples province, Campania, SW Italy, at the S foot of Vesuvius, 20 km/12 ml SE of Naples; an important port and agricultural, wine, and perfume centre in Roman times; damaged by a violent earthquake in AD 63; great eruption of Vesuvius in AD 79 covered the whole city with a layer of ashes and pumice-stone 6–7 m/20–23 ft deep; systematic excavation since 18th-c has revealed a city roughly elliptical in shape, 3 km/1¾ ml in circumference, with eight gates, and many buildings well-preserved by the volcanic ash; two-fifths of the city still remains buried; modern town lies to the E, with the pilgrimage church of Santuario della Madonna del Rosario. » Herculaneum; Vesuvius

Pompey the Great, properly **Gnaeus Pompeius Magnus** (106–48 BC) Roman politician and general of the late Republic, whose outstanding military talents, as shown by his victories over the Marians (83–82 BC), Sertorius (77 BC), Spartacus (71 BC), the pirates (67 BC), and Mithridates VI (66 BC), put him at the forefront of Roman politics from an early age. He was also an organizer of genius, and his settlement of the East after the Mithridatic Wars (63 BC) established the pattern of Roman administration there for well over a century. Consistently outmanoeuvred in the 50s BC by Julius Caesar, he was finally defeated by him in the Battle of Pharsalus (48 BC), and was assassinated in Egypt shortly after. » Caesar; Crassus; Marius; Mithridates VI Euphator; Roman history [i]; Spartacus; triumvirate

Pompidou, Georges (Jean Raymond) [põpeedoo] (1911–74) French statesman, Prime Minister (1962, 1962–6, 1966–7, 1967–8), and President (1969–74), born at Montboudif. He trained as an administrator, joined de Gaulle's staff in 1944, and held various government posts from 1946. He helped to draft the constitution for the Fifth Republic (1959), and negotiated a settlement in Algeria (1961) and in the student-worker revolt of 1968. He died in Paris. » de Gaulle; France [i]

Pompidou Centre » **Centre Beaubourg**

Ponape [**pon**apay] pop (1980) 22 319; area 345 sq km/133 sq ml. One of the Federated States of Micronesia, W Pacific; comprises the island of Ponape (303 sq km/117 sq ml) and eight outlying atolls; capital, Kolonia; copra, tropical fruit, tourism. » Micronesia, Federated States of

Ponce [**pon**say] 18°01N 66°36W, pop (1980) 189 046. Second largest city in Puerto Rico, E Caribbean; port at Playa de Ponce on the S coast, 70 km/43 ml SW of San Juan; airfield; iron, sugar, canning; colonial mansions, Ponce fort (1760). » Puerto Rico [i]

Ponce de León, Juan [**pon**thay thay layon] (1460–1521) Spanish explorer, born at San Servas. A page at the Aragonese court, he was a member of Columbus's second expedition (1493) and served as deputy to Ovando (1508–9), exploring and settling Puerto Rico (1510). In 1513 he discovered Florida and, while Acting Governor, occupied Trinidad, but failed to conquer his new subjects, the Carib Indians. On a second expedition to Florida (1521) he retured to Cuba, where he died from a poisoned arrow wound. » Columbus, Christopher

pond skater An aquatic bug which lives and moves over the surface of rivers, lakes, and even the ocean, supported by surface tension; its body and legs have a water repellant and unwettable surface; feeds mainly on drowning insects. (Order: *Heteroptera.* Family: *Gerridae*, c.400 species.) » bug (entomology)

pond turtle » terrapin

Pondicherry [**pon**dicheree] pop (1981) 604 136; area 492 sq km/190 sq ml. Union territory in S India; founded, 1674, the chief French settlement in India; transferred to India, 1954; union territory, 1962; capital, Pondicherry; governed by a Council of Ministers responsible to a Legislative Assembly; railway; rice, millet, groundnuts, sugar cane, cotton; textiles, paper, brewing. » India [i]

pondweed An aquatic perennial, native to freshwater habitats everywhere; submerged leaves translucent; floating leaves, if present, opaque, green; flowers inconspicuous, in oval heads, wind- or water-pollinated; seeds buoyant. (Genus: *Potamogeton*, 100 species. Family: *Potamogetonaceae.*) » perennial

Ponta Delgada [**pon**ta del**gah**da] 37°29N 25°40W, pop (1981) 21 940. Largest town in the Azores, on S coast of São Miguel I; commercial centre, tourism; Churches of São Sebastião and Pedro, Convent of Santo Andre; Cavalhadas de São Pedro mediaeval equestrian games (Jun), Divino Espirito Santo folk festival (Aug). » Azores

Ponte Vecchio [**pon**tay **vek**kyoh] A bridge across the R Arno at Florence, completed in 1345 by Taddeo Galli. The lower walkway is lined with jewellers' shops above which an upper corridor, built by Vasari, links the Pitti Palace with the Uffizi. » bridge (engineering) [i]; Florence; Pitti Palace; Uffizi; Vasari

Pontedera, Andrea da » Pisano, Andrea

Pontiac's Conspiracy (1763) An attempt by American Indians of the Ohio and Great Lakes country to drive Whites out of the area W of Niagara. It was led by Pontiac (c.1720–69), Chief of the Ottawa tribe, and inspired by the religious leader known as the Delaware Prophet. The movement reached its peak with an unsuccessful siege of Detroit, and a final peace was signed in 1766. » Indian Wars

pontoon A popular card game which is a variation of blackjack. It can be played by any small number of players, ideally six. The object is to try to obtain a total of 21 with your cards, and is thus also known as *vingt-et-un* ('twenty-one'). » blackjack; playing cards

pontoon bridge A floating bridge supported by pontoons. The structure may be temporary, as for military usage, or permanent, where deep water and adverse ground conditions make piers expensive. Typically the pontoons consist of flat bottomed boats, hollow metal cylinders, or concrete rafts. Three permanent concrete pontoon bridges cross L Washington in Seattle, USA. » bridge (engineering) [i]

Pontormo, Jacopo da, originally **Jacopo Carrucci** (1494–1557) Florentine painter, born at Pontormo. A pupil of Andrea del Sarto and other masters, his works include several frescoes, notably of the Passion (1522–5) in the Certosa near Florence, but his masterpiece is the 'Deposition' (c.1525), a chapel altarpiece in Santa Felicità, Florence. He died in Florence. » Florentine School; fresco; Italian art; Mannerism; Sarto

Pontus In antiquity, the territory in NE Asia Minor lying E of Bithynia and S of the Black Sea. In the early 1st-c BC, it was the centre of the empire of Mithridates VI, and with his defeat the area became a Roman province. » Bithynia

pony » Dales / Dartmoor / Exmoor / Highland / New Forest/polo/Shetland/Welsh pony; horse [i]

Pony Club A world-wide organization with the aim of establishing good horsemanship among children through championships and rallies. It was established in 1929. » equestrianism

pony express A rapid mail service from St Joseph, Missouri, to San Francisco, using relays of riders and horses. Established in 1860, the service was withdrawn after the completion of the first transcontinental telegraph line a year later. » telegraphy

poodle A French breed of dog, developed originally for hunting; three sizes: *standard* (taller than 380 mm/15 in), *miniature*, and *toy* (less than 280 mm/11 in); narrow head with pendulous ears; tail docked; thick coat often clipped for ornamental effect. » dog; non-sporting dog

pool An American table game played in many forms. It uses 15 balls, and a cue similar to that used in billiards and snooker. The most popular form in Great Britain is the variation known as 8-ball pool. The object is to pot all balls of your colour, and then finally the black ball (the No. 8 ball, hence the name). It is played on a table approximately half the size of a standard billiard table, with six round pockets. » billiards; snooker

Poona or **Pune** 18°34N 73°58E, pop (1981) 1 685 000. City in Maharashtra state, W India, 120 km/75 ml SE of Bombay; former capital of the Mahrattas; under British rule, 1818; important colonial military and administrative centre; airfield; railway; university (1949); cotton, engineering, munitions, chemicals, metalwork, vehicles, soap, paper; 17th–18th-c palaces and temples. » Maharashtra

Poopó, Lake (Span **Lago**) [pohoh**poh**] Lake in Oruro department, W Bolivia; 56 km/35 ml S of Oruro; second largest lake in Bolivia; area 2 512 sq km/970 sq ml; length 97 km/60 ml; width 32–48 km/20–30 ml; c.2.5 m/8.2 ft deep. » Bolivia [i]

Poor Clares » Franciscans

Poor Laws Legislation in Britain originally formulated in 1598 and 1601, whereby relief of poverty was the responsibility of individual parishes under the supervision of Justices of the Peace and the administration of Overseers. Funds were provided by local property rates. As the population grew and rates rose at the end of the 18th-c, the poor laws were increasingly criticized. The Poor Law Amendment Act of 1834 radically changed the system. » Speenhamland system; workhouse

Pop Art A modern art form based on the commonplace and ephemeral aspects of 20th-c urban life, such as soup cans, comics, movies, and advertising. Pioneer British Pop artists included Eduardo Paolozzi (1924–) and Richard Hamilton (1922–) in the mid-1950s, and leading US contributors in the 1960s include Jasper Johns (1930–), Andy Warhol (1926–87), and Roy Lichtenstein (1923–). American Pop is tougher and more deliberately shocking than British, with strong reminiscences of Dada. Humour is an important element, though art critics have been inclined to take it all very solemnly. » Dada; Surrealism

pop group An ensemble which performs pop music, pursuing one particular musical style, and adopting a corresponding image. It usually includes two or three electric guitars, drums (with other percussion), keyboards, and vocalist(s), nearly always with amplification. Several highly successful pop groups – including the Monkees in the late 1960s and Bros in the late 1980s – have assumed an image which was created by a record company, manager, or producer, and designed to appeal to a very specific adolescent market. » guitar; keyboard instrument; percussion [i]; pop music

pop music Popular commercial music, with its audience mainly amongst the young, current in the developed countries since the late 1950s. Popular music as such has a very long history: c.1900 the name 'pops' was given to a series of concerts of light music promoted annually by the Boston Symphony Orchestra. But the singular, *pop*, refers to the kind of music inaugurated by rock and roll, and which has since diversified to such an extent that it is now most easily defined in terms of its market. The Beatles in the 1960s were one of the first groups to experiment radically with the basic rock format. Since then, pop music has taken in and adapted elements from a diverse range of musical sources, including soul, reggae, country and western, and various ethnic styles. Pop musicians have also been very quick to exploit the possibilities of electronic music, particularly for such dance styles as hip-hop and rap music. Pop music is generally played, presented, and marketed for a teenage audience, with success measured in terms of the various pop charts (particularly in the UK the Music Week/Gallup/BBC chart, and in the USA the Billboard chart), which list records in order of sales attained. » Beatles, The; country and western; Eurovision Song Contest; gospel music; pop group;

punk rock; reggae; rhythm and blues; rock; salsa; soul (music)

pop poetry A term derived from 'pop [ie popular] music' in the 1970s to describe poetry written for public performance rather than for private reading. It is often topical, satirical, 'protest poetry', and accompanied by music; as with John Cooper Clarke and Lynton Kwesi Johnson (1952–). » poetry; pop music

Popayán [popa**yan**] 2°27N 76°22W, pop (1985) 156 530. Historic city and capital of Cauca department, SW Colombia; founded, 1536; serious earthquake, 1973; railway; university (1827); coffee, food processing, tanning. » Colombia [i]

pope (Lat *papa*, Gk *papas*, 'father') The title of the Bishop of Rome as head or Supreme Pontiff of the Roman Catholic Church; also, the title given to the head of the Coptic Church. The Bishop of Rome is elected by a conclave of the College of Cardinals, his authority deriving from the belief that he represents Christ in direct descendancy from the Apostle Peter, said to be the first Bishop of Rome. After the decline of the ancient churches of the Eastern Roman Empire, resulting from the spread of Islam, the pope in Rome became the undisputed centre of the Christian Church, and enjoyed considerable political power as the temporal sovereign of extensive papal states in Europe (now restricted to the Vatican City in Rome). The claim to infallibility was formalized at the First Vatican Council in 1870. » antipope; apostle; Cardinals, College of; conclave; Coptic Church; infallibility; Roman Catholicism; Vatican Councils; RR67

Pope, Alexander (1688–1744) English poet, born in London. In 1700 the family settled at Binfield, Berkshire. He suffered from poor health, and had a curvature of the spine, his diminutive stature providing a target for critics, since he was frequently engaged in literary vendettas. He became well-known as a satirical poet, and a master of the heroic couplet, notably in *The Rape of the Lock* (1712). He turned to translation to settle his finances, producing the *Iliad* (1715–20), whose success enabled him to set up a home in Twickenham. There he wrote his major poem, *The Dunciad* (1728, continued 1742), the *Epistle to Doctor Arbuthnot* (1734), the philosophical *Essay on Man* (1733–4), and a series of satires imitating the epistles of Horace (1733–8). He died at Twickenham. » English literature; heroic couplet; Horace; satire

Popish Plot An apocryphal Jesuit conspiracy in 1678 to assassinate Charles II of England, burn London, slaughter Protestants, and place James, Duke of York, on the throne. Created by opportunist rogues, Titus Oates (1649–1705) and Israel Tonge (1621–80), it resulted in 35 executions, bills in three Parliaments for the exclusion of James from the succession, and the fall of the Danby government. » Charles II (of England); James II (of England); Oates, Titus

poplar A deciduous, N temperate tree; triangular-ovoid to almost heart-shaped leaves; flowers tiny, in pendulous catkins appearing before leaves; seeds with cottony white hairs, which aid wind-dispersal and give rise to the American name **cottonwood**. Very fast-growing, it is used for cheap timber, matchwood, paper pulp, and as ornamentals. Some species (**balsam poplars**) have aromatic timber. (Genus: *Populus*, 35 species. Family: *Salicaceae*.) » aspen; deciduous plants; Lombardy poplar; tree [i]

Popocatépetl [popohka**tay**petl] 19°01N 98°38W. Dormant volcano in C Mexico, 72 km/45 ml SE of Mexico City; height 5 452 m/17 887 ft; second highest peak in Mexico, with a snow-capped symmetrical cone; crater c.1 km/¾ ml in circumference and 402 m/1 319 ft deep; last eruption, 1702; in Ixtaccihuatl-Popocatépetl National Park, area c.250 sq km/100 sq ml; established in 1935. » Mexico [i]; volcano

Poppaea Sabina [po**pay**a sa**bee**na] (?–65) Roman society beauty and voluptuary who before her marriage to the Emperor Nero (62) had been the wife of his playboy friend, the future Emperor Otho. She shared the then fashionable interest in Judaism, and has been thought by many to have encouraged Nero in his vicious attack on the Christians in the aftermath of the Fire of Rome (64). » Nero

Popper, Sir Karl (Raimund) (1902–) Austrian philosopher, born in Vienna. Educated at Vienna, he published in 1935 for the 'Vienna Circle' his first book on scientific methodology, *Die Logik der Forschung* (1934, The Logic of Scientific Discovery). He left Vienna during Hitler's rise to power, lectured in New Zealand (1937–45), finally becoming professor of logic and scientific method at London (1949–69). He was knighted in 1965. » Vienna Circle

poppy The name given to many members of the family *Papaveraceae*. All produce latex, often brightly-coloured, and have flowers with two sepals and four overlapping petals, often crumpled when they first open. » Californian/corn/horned/opium/Welsh poppy; latex

Popski's Private Army A British fighting unit in World War 2. It was raised in October 1942 by Lt-Col Vladimir Peniakoff (1897–1951), known as 'Popski', a Belgian of Russian parentage. It had a maximum strength of 195 men, and engaged in intelligence-gathering and hit-and-run attacks behind enemy lines in N Africa and Italy. » World War 2

popular front A strategy of the communist movement begun in the 1930s as a means of fostering collaboration among left and centre parties to oppose the rise of right-wing movements and regimes, most obviously fascist ones. There were popular front governments in France, Spain, and Chile. The strategy virtually died with the signing of the Nazi-Soviet Pact (1939), but re-emerged after Hitler invaded the Soviet Union. » communism; fascism

population The inhabitants of a region or country who together comprise its native and immigrant people. While it is often used to define the boundary of the citizenry of a sovereign state, it is also used more specifically to refer to a group or category of people sharing specific characteristics, eg 'the working class population', 'the coloured population', and so on. » census; demography; migration; population biology/density/genetics; *see map p 964*

population biology The branch of biology dealing with the study of the distributions of populations of living organisms in time and space. It includes the study of the dynamic changes that occur within populations, and the factors that cause those changes. » biology

population density A measure of the number of people living within a standard unit of area, useful for comparative purposes. For example, the population density of the Netherlands (1983) was 422.4 per sq km/1 094 per sq ml, and for Australia (1984) 2 per sq km/5.2 per sq ml. However, these are crude measurements, and take no account of the area of habitable land. Accordingly, population density may be calculated to relate population to cultivable land or some other economic indicator. » overpopulation

population genetics The study of the genetic constitutions of populations, the processes that affect gene and genotype frequencies, and the mathematical theorems that describe them. The basic theorems were established in the period 1908–30, with the work of British geneticists R A Fisher (1890–1962), J B S Haldane (1892–1964), and US geneticist Sewall Wright (1889–1988). The compilation of data on the gene frequencies of human populations is ongoing, with a great deal known of the distribution of gene frequencies for blood groups in different peoples, and rather less for serum proteins and enzymes. The new DNA technology suggests that variations in DNA sequences at the infra-gene level may be subject to similar processes, but the frequencies of these variant sequences (*restriction fragment length polymorphisms*) in different populations are as yet little known. » gene; genetics [i]; genotype; Haldane, J B S; recombinant DNA

populism Essentially a political outlook or mentality rather than an ideology, identified by a popular reaction to dramatic change, such as rapid industrialization. People feel that events are beyond their control, which is blamed on some conspiracy of foreigners, ethnic groups, economic interests, or intellectuals. The populist reaction is to 'regain' control from the suggested centres of power, usually through some form of participation, and to seek revenge and redemption. Beyond that, populism is an obscure and variable outlook, and has failed to establish political parties successfully. It is often found in underdeveloped countries as a reaction against more developed countries.

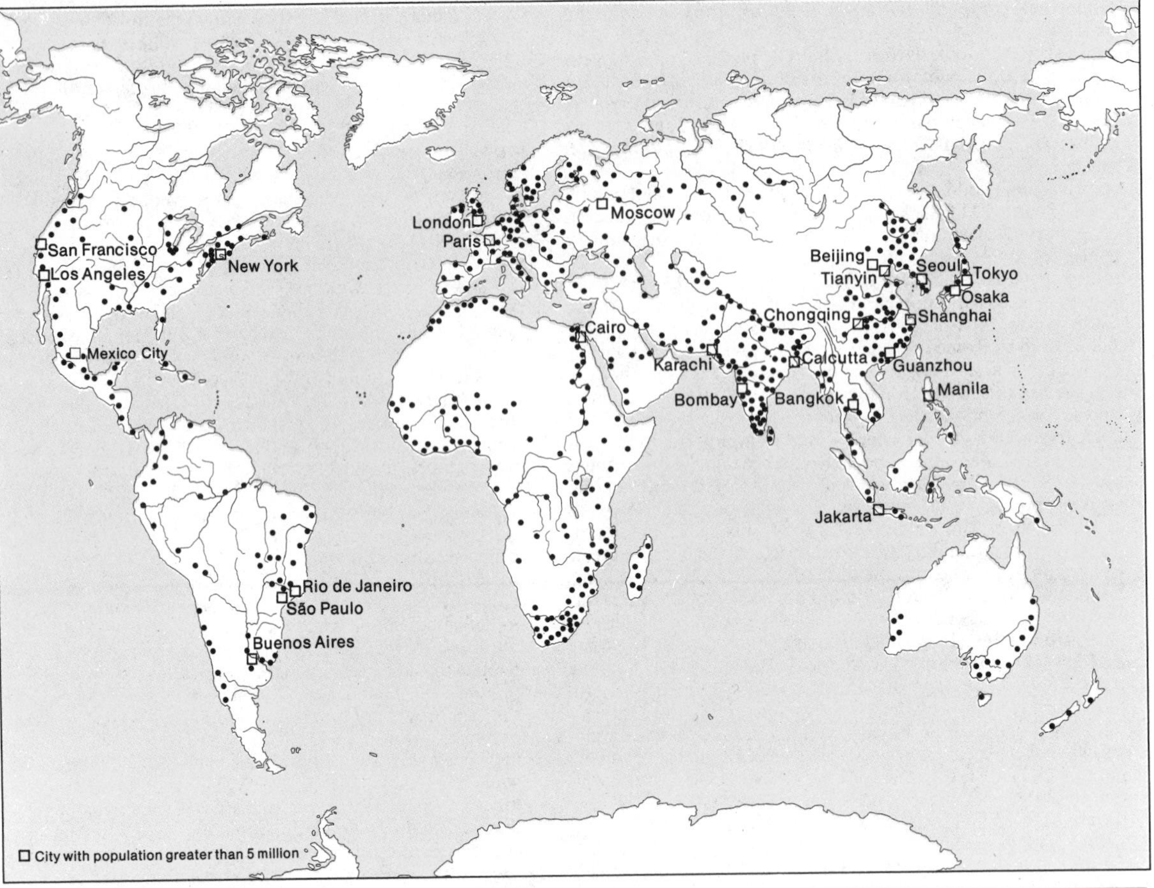

World population density map – Dots show distribution of population

Populist Party (1892–6) A US political party that grew from agrarian and labour discontent, especially in the S and mid-W; also known as the **People's Party**. In 1892 the Populists ran their own presidential candidate, who gained over a million votes. In 1896 the party endorsed the Democratic candidate William Jennings Bryan (1860–1925). » populism

porbeagle » **mackerel shark**

porcelain A hard, thin, vitreous, translucent material, contrasting with thicker, more porous pottery. Porcelain was first manufactured by the Chinese in the Sung dynasty (AD 960–1279). It found its way to W Europe from c.1300, and was prized as a semi-precious material, often mounted in gold or silver. The first European attempts to make it were at the Medici factory in Florence in the 1570s, but real success was only achieved at Meissen in the early 18th-c. » Bow/Capodimonte/Chelsea/Meissen/Nymphenburg/Sèvres/Worcester porcelain; Minton ceramics; pottery; Spode; Wedgwood, Josiah

porcupine A cavy-like rodent; some hairs modified as long sharp spines; lives in diverse habitats; 22 species in two families: ground-dwelling family *Hystricidae* (**Old World porcupines**) from Africa and S Asia, and tree-climbing family *Erithizontidae* (**New World porcupines**), widespread in the New World. » cavy; rodent

porcupinefish Large bottom-living fish widespread in shallow waters of tropical seas; length up to 90 cm/3 ft; body covered with long sharp spines; inflates body as a defence to become almost spherical with spines erect; mouth has a parrot-like beak, bearing strong crushing teeth; feeds on molluscs, echinoderms, and crustaceans. (*Diodon hystrix*. Family: *Diodontidae*.)

porgy » **sea bream**

Porifera [puhrifuhra] » **sponge**

porky » **filefish**

pornography A demeaning and sometimes violent representation of sexuality and the body, typically the woman's, through film, graphic, or written media. Most authorities distinguish between 'soft' and illegal 'hard core' pornography, but many, especially feminists, argue that the 'softer' version should be banned as well, as it too is an affront to female dignity. In the US, pornography is a major industry – bigger, for example than the film and record industries combined. There is evidence to suggest that pornographic material which shows women 'enjoying' rape, degradation, or other forms of sexual violence may encourage men to become sexually violent. » Boccaccio; censorship; Lawrence, D H; Ovid; Sade

porosity A mechanical property of solids, a measure of their ability to allow the passage of a fluid. The narrow channels that make a material porous allow it to absorb fluid via capillarity, as a sponge absorbs water. Oil exists underground in porous rock; water drains through sand. » capillarity; fractals

porphyria [pawfiria] A group of inherited disorders involving the excess production of the chemical substances known as *porphyrins*. They cause a wide range of abnormalities, including sensitivity of the skin to sunlight, pigmentation of the skin, abdominal pain, and mental confusion. » skin [i]

Porphyry (c.233–304) Neoplatonist philosopher, born at Tyre or Batanea. After studying at Athens, he went to Rome (c.263), where he studied under Plotinus, becoming his disciple and biographer. He wrote a celebrated treatise against the Christians, of which only fragments remain. His most influential work was the *Isagoge*, a commentary on Aristotle's *Categories*, widely used in the Middle Ages. » Neoplatonism; Plotinus

porpoise » **dolphin**

Porres, St Martín de » **Martín de Porres, St**

Porsche, Ferdinand (1875–1951) German automobile designer, born at Hafersdorf, Bohemia. He designed cars for

Daimler and Auto Union, then set up his own studio, and in 1934 produced the plans for a revolutionary type of cheap car with engine in the rear, to which the Nazis gave the name *Volkswagen* ('people's car'). The Porsche sports car was introduced in 1950. He died in Stuttgart. » car [i]

port A sweet, fortified wine, first produced in the upper Douro valley, N Portugal. Grapes have been grown on the steeply-terraced hillsides since the 17th-c. The wine used to be transported down the fast-flowing river to Oporto (hence the name), but is today taken by road. 'Vintage' port is unblended. All port is aged in *pipes* (115-gallon wooden barrels). » fermentation; wine

Port-au-Prince [pawt oh **prĭs**] 18°33N 72°20W, pop (1982) 763 000. Seaport capital of Haiti; on the Gulf of Gonâve, W coast of Hispaniola I; commercial and processing centre at W end of the fertile Plaine du Cul-de-Sac; airport; railway; archbishopric; university (1944); coffee, sugar; 18th-c cathedral. » Haiti [i]

Port Augusta 32°30S 137°27E, pop (1981) 15 254. Town in South Australia, at the head of the Spencer Gulf; airfield; railway; wool and grain trade, engineering; starting point for the 'Ghan' train to Alice Springs and the Indian Pacific train to Perth; base for the flying doctor service. » flying doctor service; South Australia

Port Elizabeth 33°58S 25°36E, pop (1980) 651 993 (metropolitan area). Seaport in Cape province, South Africa, on Algoa Bay, Indian Ocean, 725 km/450 ml E of Cape Town; Fort Frederick built here by British forces, 1799; founded, 1820; airfield; railway; university (1964); locomotives, motor vehicles, food processing, steel, wool, mohair, skins, tyres, citrus fruits; Addo Elephant national park nearby. » South Africa [i]

Port Harcourt [**hah**kert] 4°43N 7°05E, pop (1981e) 330 800. Seaport capital of Rivers state, S Nigeria; on R Bonny, 65 km/40 ml from the sea; Nigeria's second largest port; established in 1912; airport; railway link to the Enugu coalfields; university (1975); metals, glass, liquid propane gas, oil refining, petrochemicals, fishing. » Nigeria [i]

Port Louis [**loo**is] 20°18S 57°31E, pop (1983) 135 629. Seaport capital of Mauritius; established, 1735; trade developed until the building of the Suez Canal; university (1965); handles almost all of the trade of Mauritius; sugar, textiles, clothes, diamond cutting, watches, electrical and electronic equipment, sunglasses; two cathedrals. » Mauritius [i]

Port Moresby [**mawz**bee] 9°30S 147°07E, pop (1980) 118 429. Seaport capital of Papua New Guinea, on the S coast of New Guinea; Allied base in World War 2; airport; university (1965); base for overseas telecommunications and national broadcasting; light industry; Hiri Moale Festival (Aug–Sep), arts festival (Sep). » Papua New Guinea [i]

Port Natal » **Durban**

Port of Spain 10°38N 61°31W, pop (1980) 55 800. Seaport capital of Trinidad and Tobago, NW coast of Trinidad; capital of Trinidad, 1783; airport; principal commercial centre in the E Caribbean; oil products, rum, sugar; botanical gardens, two cathedrals, San Andres Fort (1785). » Trinidad and Tobago

Port Royal [pawt roy**al**] A French religious and intellectual community occupying the former convent of Port-Royal-des-Champs, near Paris. It was associated with the Jansenist movement, and founded by the Abbé de Saint-Cyran (1637), a friend and admirer of the theologian, Cornelius Jansen, himself a devotee of Augustinian philosophy. The community was dispersed in 1665, and the convent destroyed (1710–11). » Augustine, St (of Hippo)

Port Said [sa**eed**], Arabic **Bur Said** 31°17N 32°18E, pop (1986) 382 000. Seaport capital of Port Said governorate, NE Egypt; on Mediterranean coast at N end of Suez Canal, 169 km/105 ml NE of Cairo; founded in 1859 at beginning of Canal construction; shipping services, trade in rice, cotton, salt. » Egypt [i]; Suez Canal

Port San Carlos 51°30S 58°59W. Settlement on the W coast of East Falkland, Falkland Is; British Task Force landed near here in May 1982, during the Falklands War. » Falkland Islands; Falklands War

Port Sudan [soo**dan**] 19°38N 37°07E, pop (1983) 206 727. Seaport capital of Eastern region, Sudan, on the Red Sea coast; Sudan's main port; founded, 1906; airfield; railway; NE terminus of an oil pipeline from Khartoum; handles most of the country's trade. » Sudan [i]

porter » **beer** [i]

Porter, Cole (1892–1964) US songwriter, born at Peru, Indiana. He studied law at Harvard, served in World War 1, then studied music at the Schola Cantorum in Paris. His success as composer and lyricist came late, beginning with 'What Is This Thing Called Love?' (1930), but in the end he ranked high in the golden period of American popular song, with such pieces as 'Night and Day' (1932), 'Begin the Beguine' (1935), and 'Don't Fence Me In' (1944), and such musical comedies as *Kiss Me Kate* (1948) and *Can-Can* (1953). He died at Santa Monica, California. » musical

Porter, Sir George (1920–) British physical chemist, born at Stainforth, Yorkshire. He studied at Leeds, and worked with radar as a naval officer in World War 2. In 1945 he moved to Cambridge, where he studied very fast reactions in gases, using a combination of electronic and spectroscopic techniques. He was awarded the Nobel Prize for Chemistry in 1967. He became Director of the Royal Institution (1966–85), continuing his work on ultra-rapid chemical reactions. » gas **1**; spectroscopy

Porter, Katherine Anne (1890–1980) US novelist and short-story writer, born at Indian Creek, Texas, where she was educated privately. Apart from short stories, she is best known for a long allegorical novel, *The Ship of Fools* (1962), about a journey from Mexico to Germany on the eve of Hitler's rise to power. She died at Silver Spring, Maryland. » American literature; novel; short story

Porter, Peter (Neville Frederick) (1929–) Australian poet, born and educated in Brisbane, where he worked as a journalist before coming to England in 1951. His collections *Once Bitten, Twice Bitten* (1961) and *Poems Ancient and Modern* (1970) are descriptive and satirical of Britain in the 1960s, while later volumes such as *The Cost of Seriousness* (1978) and *The Automatic Oracle* (1987) are more reflective and elegiac. His *Collected Poems* appeared in 1983. » Australian literature; poetry; satire

portfolio theory The analysis of how investors spread their wealth among the many different possible types of investment. It is assumed that all will attempt to obtain the highest possible return on their investments, yet will wish to minimize the risks which certain investments incur. The *capital asset pricing model* analyses the relationship between risk and return; and the concept of having a balanced portfolio to achieve better-than-average results (for the market as a whole) is in common use with investment analysts. The work in this area of US economist James Tobin (1918–) secured him the Nobel Prize for Economics in 1981. » investment **1**

portico A colonnaded and roofed space attached to a building and forming an entrance way. It is usually classical in style, with detached or attached columns and a pediment above. » colonnade; column; pediment (architecture)

Portland, Duke of » **Bentinck, William Henry Cavendish**

Portland (Maine) 43°39N 70°16W, pop (1980) 61 572. Business capital and chief port of Maine, USA; seat of Cumberland County; on the coast of Casco Bay, SE of Sebago Lake; established, 1632; city status, 1832; state capital, 1820–32; railway; Westbrook Junior College (1831); fisheries, ship repair, paper, chemicals, oil trade; birthplace of Longfellow. » Longfellow; Maine

Portland (Oregon) 45°32N 122°37W, pop (1980) 366 383. Freshwater port and capital of Multnomah County, NW Oregon, USA, on the Willamette R; largest city in the state; laid out, 1845; served as a supply point in the 1850s during the California gold rush and later (1897–1900) during the Alaska gold rush; airport; railway; university (1901); machinery, electrical equipment, food processing, wood products, metal goods; trade in timber, grain, aluminium; tourism; major league team, Trail Blazers (basketball). » gold rush; Oregon

Portland, Isle of Rocky peninsula on Dorset coast, S England;

extends into the English Channel; connected to the mainland by a shingle ridge (Chesil Beach); area 12 sq km/4.6 sq ml; naval base at Portland Harbour; Portland Stone (limestone) used in many London buildings; Portland Castle built by Henry VIII (1520). » Dorset

Portland Cement » **cement**

Portlaoighise [pawt**lay**ish] or **Port Laoise**, formerly **Maryborough** 53°02N 7°17W, pop (1981) 7 756. Capital of Laoighis county, Leinster, Irish Republic; WSW of Dublin; railway; jail; small industrial estate. » Irish Republic [i]; Laoighis

Porto Novo 6°30N 2°47E, pop (1979) 132 000. Seaport capital of Benin, W Africa, on a lagoon in Ouémé province; settled by the Portuguese, centre for slave and tobacco trading; though the official capital, there is little political and economic activity, this taking place in Cotonou; railway; palm oil, cotton; Palace of King Toffa and museum. » Benin [i]; Cotonou

Porton Down A research centre established by the Ministry of Defence in Wiltshire, S England, for the investigation of biological and chemical warfare. » chemical warfare

Portree 57°24N 6°12W, pop (1981) 1 505. Port capital of Skye and Lochalsh district, Highland region, NW Scotland; on Loch Portree, on E coast; largest town on Skye. » Highland; Scotland [i]; Skye

Portrush, Gaelic **Port Rois** 55°12N 6°40W, pop (1981) 5 114. Town in Antrim, NE Northern Ireland, on the N coast; railway; engineering; tourist centre for the Giant's Causeway, 11 km/7 ml ENE. » Antrim (county); Giant's Causeway

Portsmouth (UK) 50°48N 1°05W, pop (1981) 177 905. City and seaport in Portsmouth district, Hampshire, S England; on Portsea I, 133 km/83 ml SW of London; major naval base; railway; ship repairing, electronics, engineering; ferries to the Channel Is, France, and the I of Wight; birthplace of Charles Dickens; Nelson's flagship *HMS Victory*; Tudor warship, *Mary Rose*; Royal Navy Museum; Royal Marines Museum; Southsea Castle including Round Tower and Point Battery; Fort Widney (Portsdown Hill); Navy Week (Aug). » Dickens; Hampshire; Nelson, Horatio

Portsmouth (New Hampshire, USA) 43°05N 70°45W, pop (1980) 26 254. Seaport and summer resort town in Rockingham County, SE New Hampshire, USA; on the Atlantic coast at the head of the Piscataqua R; established, 1624; city status, 1849; treaty ending the Russo-Japanese War signed here, 1905; submarine base on Seavy's I; railway; machine tools, clothing; John Paul Jones house (1758), Strawberry Banke. » Jones, Paul; New Hampshire

Portsmouth (Virginia, USA) 36°50N 76°18W, pop (1980) 104 577. Port and independent city, SE Virginia, USA, on the Elizabeth R; founded, 1752; a base for British and then Revolutionary troops during the War of Independence; evacuated and burned by Union troops during the Civil War (1861), then retaken (1862); part of a US naval complex; railway; shipbuilding (the *Chesapeake* and the ironclad *Merrimack* were built here), railway engineering, fishing; trade in tobacco and cotton. » American Civil War; American Revolution; Virginia

Portugal, official name **Republic of Portugal**, Port **República Portuguesa**, ancient **Lusitania** pop (1990e) 10 388 000; area 88 500 sq km/34 200 sq ml. Country in SW Europe on the W side of the Iberian peninsula; divided into 11 mainland provinces, and the semi-autonomous Azores and Madeira Is; bounded N and E by Spain, and S and W by the Atlantic Ocean; greatest length, 560 km/348 ml (N–S); greatest width, 220 km/137 ml; capital, Lisbon; chief towns, Oporto, Setúbal, Coimbra, Évora; timezone GMT; unit of currency, the escudo of 100 centavos; Macao still administered by Portugal; several mountain ranges formed by W spurs of the Spanish mountain system; chief range, the Serra da Estrêla (N), rising to 1 991 m/6 532 ft; four main rivers (Douro, Minho, Tagus, Guadiana) are the lower courses of rivers beginning in Spain; basically a maritime climate, with increased variation between summer and winter temperatures inland; relatively cool W coast in summer; most rainfall in winter; became a kingdom under Alphonso I, 1139; major period of world exploration and beginning of Portuguese Empire, 15th-c; under Spanish domination, 1580–1640; invaded by the French, 1807; monarchy overthrown and republic established, 1910; dictatorship of Dr Salazar, 1932–68; military coup in 1974, followed by 10 years of political unrest under 15 governments; governed by a president, elected for five years, a prime minister and Council of Ministers, and a 250-member unicameral Assembly of the Republic, elected every four years; several labour-intensive areas in the economy, such as textiles, leather, wood products, cork, ceramics; timber, wine, fish, chemicals, electrical machinery, steel, shipbuilding; copper, wolfram, tin, iron ore, pyrites, zinc, lead, barium, titanium, uranium, sodium, calcium; wheat, maize, rice, rye, beans, potatoes, fruit, olive oil, meat, dairy produce; large forests of pine, oak, cork-oak, eucalyptus, and chestnut covering about 20% of the country; tourism, especially in the S; joined the EEC in 1985. » Azores; European Economic Community; Macao; Madeira; Peninsular War; Portuguese literature; Salazar; RR27 national holidays; RR59 political leaders

□ *international airport*

Portuguese » **Portuguese literature; Romance languages**

Portuguese literature Troubadour songs from the 13th-c represent the earliest Portuguese literature. This genre flourished, to be joined by court poetry collected in the *Cancioniero Geral* (1516, General Song-Book). Saints' lives and legends were popular material. Drama developed after Gil Vicente (1470–1537), the tragedies of Antonio Ferreira (1528–69) being particularly notable. Classical influences from Italy and Spain affected court circles in the 16th-c, but Camões' *Os Lusíadas* (1572, The Lusiads), the Portuguese epic, confirmed nationalist feeling. This was depressed during Spanish rule, when even the language was threatened; but in the 18th-c Francisco do Nascimento (1734–1819) and Manuel du Bocage (1756–1805) revived earlier traditions. The Romantic movement, stimulated by the revolutionary João Almeida-Garrett (1799–1854), was represented by Alexandre Herculano (1810–77), Antero de Quental (1842–91), and Cesário Verde (1855–86). Júlio Dinis (1839–71) and Eça de Queirós (1845–1900), the 'Portuguese Zola', introduced the Realist novel, to be followed by Alves Redol (1911–). But as often happens, it is the poets who have best survived the political turmoil of the 20th-c. The most remarkable is Fernando Pessoa (1888–1935), who wrote from four different 'personalities'; but the Symbolist Eugénio de Castro (1869–1944), the speculative Teixeira de Pascões (1879–1952), José Régio (1901–69) with his explorations of loss, and Miguel Torga (1907–), with his countervailing optimism, all made important contributions. Meanwhile, two centuries of Brazilian literature have also been written in Portuguese. » Camões; Latin-American literature; literature; Pessoa; Portugal [i]; Spanish literature; Vicente

Portuguese man-of-war A jellyfish-like coelenterate which floats at the ocean surface, held up by a gas-filled float; lives in colonies; individuals within the colony are specialized for particular tasks, such as feeding or reproduction; catches prey using long stinging tentacles that hang down from the float; can inflict painful stings on swimmers. (Phylum: *Cnidaria*. Order: *Siphonophora*.) » coelenterate; jellyfish [i]

Porvoo [**paw**voh], Swedish **Borgå** 60°24N 25°40E, pop (1982) 19 195. Picturesque town in Uudenmaa province, SE Finland; near mouth of R Porvoonjoki; second oldest town in Finland, established 1346; bishopric; boat service to Helsinki; publishing, brewing, tourism; home of national poet, Johan Runeberg; cathedral (15th-c); cycle race and Porvoo day (Jun); Postmaki Festival (Jul). » Finland [i]; Runeberg

porwiggle » **tadpole**

Poseidon [puh**siy**duhn] In Greek mythology, the brother of Zeus, god of water and the sea, depicted with a trident in his hand. He is a violent god, responsible for earthquakes and similar destructive forces. He is also connected with horse-taming. » Amphitrite; Neptune (mythology)

Poseidon weed A grass-like, totally submerged, marine plant common in shallow parts of the Mediterranean sea. Leaves and rhizomes are often washed ashore in great quantities, as are **Poseidon balls**, brown globes formed of the fibrous debris by wave action. (*Posidonia marina*. Family: *Posidoniaceae*.) » grass [i]; rhizome

positivism Any philosophical position which maintains that all genuine knowledge is acquired by science, and denies the validity of metaphysical speculation. Positivism flourished in the latter half of the 19th-c; its elements can be found in such diverse thinkers as Comte, the English utilitarians, Spencer, and Mach. » Comte; logical positivism; Mach; Spencer, Herbert

positron The antiparticle partner to the electron; symbol e^+; mass and spin same as electron, but charge +1; discovered in 1932 by US physicist Carl Anderson (1905–) and British physicist Patrick Blackett (1897–1974), by observing tracks left in cloud chambers by cosmic rays. It annihilates with electrons to give gamma rays, and is emitted by some radioactive sources, such as sodium-22. It is used in positron emission tomography in medicine, and in studies of the electron properties of solids. » antiparticles; beta particle; Dirac equation

possession The alleged control of a living person by an entity lacking a physical body. In the Middle Ages, the Christian Church generally saw possession in terms of demonic control, while in other cultures, shamans who appear to be taken over by a different personality may be thought of as being controlled by (often benign) spirits. These days, cases of apparent possession are frequently interpreted as being instances of multiple personality, or indicative of some other disorder.

possible worlds A notion first used by Leibniz, who claimed that God chose to create this world because it is the best of all the infinitely many possible worlds he might have created. Contemporary philosophers have exploited the notion to develop a semantic theory for modal logic; for example, the distinction between necessary and contingent truths can be expressed as a distinction between propositions that are true in all possible worlds and propositions that are true only in some. » Leibniz; modal logic

possum An Australian marsupial of family *Burramyidae* (**pygmy possum**, 7 species), family *Pseudocheiridae* (**ringtail possum**, 16 species), family *Phalangeridae* (**scaly-tailed possum** plus 3 species of **brushtail possum**), or family *Petauridae* (**Leadbetter's possum** plus 2 species of *striped possum*). » honey possom; marsupial [i]; opossum

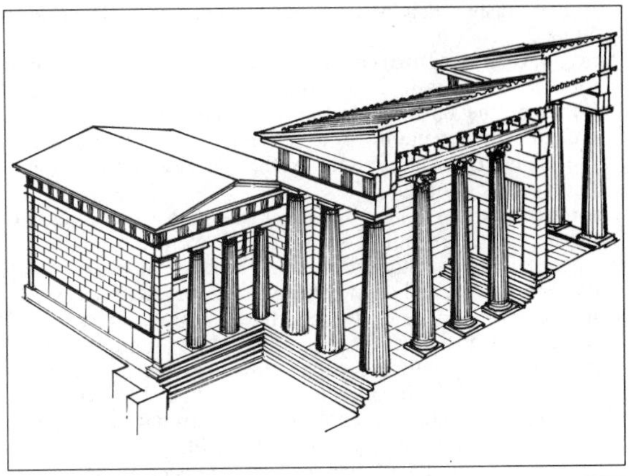

An example of post and lintel construction – Propylaea, Athens, 437–432 BC (restored)

post and lintel/lintol A form of architectural construction consisting of vertical, loadbearing posts supporting horizontal lintels to create openings. It is typified by Greek architecture, in contrast to arched or arcuated construction. The technique is also known as **trabeated** construction. » arch; Greek architecture

post office » **postal service**

postal service The collection, sorting, and delivery of mail. National postal services have existed since the early 19th-c, using a network of post offices and post boxes for the collection of letters, cards, parcels, and other missives. Deliveries are usually to-the-door, but may also be made to a private PO Box or Poste Restante at a post office. The sorting of mail has become quicker in recent years with the introduction of postal or zip codes and new electronic technology. In some countries, private operators now provide competition for the former monopoly state suppliers. Post offices may also offer a range of additional counter services, such as savings accounts and telegrams. » Hill, Rowland

poster art The development of posters as an art form, dating from the late 19th-c, when there were improvements in printing techniques, especially colour lithography. Toulouse-Lautrec was an early master who achieved some of his most striking effects through this medium; and the work of Czech artist Alphonse Mucha (1860–1939) has enjoyed a wide revival. » lithography; Toulouse-Lautrec

Postimpressionism An imprecise term coined by the art critic Roger Fry c.1910 to cover the more progressive forms of French painting since c.1880. The painters included van Gogh, Gauguin, Cézanne, and Matisse. » French art; Fry, Roger; Impressionism (art); modern art

post-industrial society An economically and technologically advanced society no longer dependent for its productivity on large-scale, labour-intensive industrial manufacture. The term was coined by the US sociologist Daniel Bell (1919–) in 1973. » sociology

postmodern dance A late 1960s form of dance based on ordinary movement rather than stylized techniques. It has links with Eastern movement forms and martial arts, and is either abstract and sparse in style (minimalist) or intensely theatrical. It sometimes carries feminist or political messages. » modern dance

Post-Modernism A term used in architecture to describe a style or concept that supersedes 20th-c modernism and the International Style in particular. Often used in a polemical and self-consciously intellectual way, it is generally applied to buildings which draw upon an eclectic range of stylistic precedents, especially classical, such as the A T & T building, New York (1978–83), architects Johnson & Burgee. In recent years the term has been increasingly used to identify a basic rejection of previously widely-held architectural beliefs. » International Style 2

postpartum haemorrhage/hemorrhage Bleeding in the mother in excess of 500 ml (c.1 pt) occurring in the first 24 hours of the birth of the baby. It has many causes, which include the retention of a placental fragment, inadequate uterine contraction after the birth, and bleeding disorders. » haemorrhage; uterus [i]

post-production The completion stages of a film after shooting up to the first public showing. The picture is finally edited to the director's satisfaction, and the original negative cut to conform; music and sound effects are recorded and mixed with the actors' dialogue in dubbing the final track. This magnetic record is transferred to a photographic sound negative for printing along with the cut picture negative to produce the *answer print*. After the director's approval, a *show print* is made for the premiere presentation. Corresponding stages are followed for a video production: the editing and sound track preparation results in the 'on-line' transfer of the original videotape to produce the final master for transmission or duplication. » film production

PostScript A computer language which has been developed to provide a uniform means of describing pages of text and/or graphics. It is widely used in desktop publishing. PostScript-compatible printers contain a microcomputer system which can interpret a PostScript program and produce the relevant printed page(s). » desktop publishing

post-traumatic stress A prolonged response to an event outside the range of normal human experience, such as wartime involvement. Key features include nightmares, flashback experiences, avoidance behaviour, lack of pleasure, and a sense of numbness.

pot marigold An annual to perennial, growing to 70 cm/27 in; slightly sticky to the touch; leaves paddle-shaped; flower heads solitary, up to 7 cm/2¾ in across; outer ray florets orange or yellow, often in several rows; fruit boat-shaped. Of unknown origin, it is a popular garden plant. The dried petals were once used for colouring butter. (*Calendula officinalis*. Family: *Compositae*.) » annual; perennial

Potala Palace An imposing 13-storey stronghold constructed on a rocky outcrop near Lhasa, Tibet, in the 17th-c. Once the religious and political centre of Tibet, the complex includes the Red Palace (former seat of the Dalai Lamas) as well as many halls, chapels, and prisons. » Dalai Lama; Lhasa

potash Potassium oxide, K_2O. The term is generally used for any potassium compounds used as fertilizers whose potassium content is reported in terms of the equivalent amount of K_2O, or about 1.2 times the percentage by weight of potassium. » fertilizer; potassium

potassium K (Lat *kalium*), element 19, melting point 63°C. One of the most reactive metals, and the third of the alkali metal group. It is not found free in nature, but mainly obtained from mineral deposits of the chloride (KCl) and the nitrate (KNO_3, also known as *nitre* or *saltpetre*). The metal is prepared by the electrolysis of molten KCl or KOH. It is an important strong reducing agent, and must be kept away from water, with which it reacts explosively. In virtually all of its compounds, it has oxidation state +1. These are mainly important as agricultural chemicals and explosives. » alkali; chemical elements; metal; nitrate; RR90

potassium-argon dating A radiometric method for dating rocks more than 100 000 years old. It uses the fact that radioactive isotope ^{40}K decays with a known half-life to yield ^{40}A, and hence the amount of each isotope in a rock can be used to determine its age. It has proved crucial for dating the early human remains found in the E African Rift Valley at such sites as Olduvai, Laetoli, Hadar, and Koobi Fora. » argon; potassium; radiometric dating

potato A well-known tuber-producing plant and staple crop throughout temperate regions of the world; an erect to somewhat sprawling perennial; pinnate leaves; clusters of drooping, white or purple flowers, with a 5-lobed corolla and five yellow stamens forming a prominent cone. The fruit is a berry similar in appearance to that of the tomato (a relative), but usually greenish, and unlike the tomato it is poisonous. The value of the potato as a vegetable lies in the stem tubers which are produced in abundance at the ends of stolons and which are rich in starch, vitamin C, and proteins. The tubers vary greatly in size, shape, colour, keeping and cooking qualities, and taste. The skins can be white, yellow to brown, pink, red, or purplish-black, and the flesh white to yellow, pink, or purple. The 'eyes' on a potato are dormant buds, which in favourable conditions give rise to new stems. Plants grown from tubers are clones of the parent; this is commercially useful, as any desired characters are conserved. There are thousands of varieties, all regarded as belonging to a single species, *Solanum tuberosum*. There are also some 160 wild species, not all closely related.

The potato is native to S America, where it has a long history as a cultivated plant, primitive varieties being a staple crop from at least AD 200. Prior to the Spanish conquest, it was confined to the high Andes from Colombia to Northern Argentina and to Chile. Exactly when and how it was introduced to Europe is still a matter for conjecture, but despite various legends it probably first arrived in Spain from Colombia or Peru c.1565, and separately in England towards the end of the 16th-c (though not, as legend would have it, brought by Sir Walter Raleigh). Whatever its exact origin, 90% of the world's production now comes from the Old World, mainly E Europe, and as a crop it is rivalled only by wheat and rice. Potatoes are susceptible to a number of diseases, including viruses and potato blight (*Phytophthora infestans*), which caused the great Irish potato famines of the mid-19th-c. Production of better quality, higher-yielding, and especially of disease-resistant strains is a priority for crop breeders. Wild species and primitive strains, many of which are disease-resistant and have other desirable traits, are nowadays recognized as being very important as a gene pool for improving modern strains. (*Solanum tuberosum*. Family: *Solanaceae*.) » cloning; perennial; petal; pinnate; potato blight; stamen; stolon; tomato; tuber

potato blight A widespread disease of potato and related plants caused by the fungus *Phytophthora infestans*, especially in wet weather; symptoms include brown patches on leaves and in tubers; white mould often visible beneath leaves. A severe outbreak in Ireland in the 1840s caused the great Irish potato famine. (Class: *Oomycetes*. Order: *Peronosporales*.) » fungus; potato

Potemkin, Grigoriy Aleksandrovich [potyo**m**kin] (1739–91) Russian field marshal, born near Smolensk. He entered the Russian army, attracted the notice of Catherine II, and became her intimate favourite, heavily influencing Russian foreign policy. There is some reason to believe they were secretly married. He distinguished himself in the Russo-Turkish Wars (1768–74, 1787–92), during which Russia gained the Crimea and the N coast of the Black Sea. He died while travelling to one of the cities he founded, Nikolaev. » Catherine II; Russo-Turkish Wars

potential A scalar quantity associated with a force whose rate of change with distance is proportional to the strength of that force; symbol V. In a gravitational field, it is the potential energy of an object of mass 1 kg; in an electric field it is the potential energy of a charge of 1 C. » charge; magnetic vector potential; potential difference/energy; potentiometer

potential difference A quantity in physics, often called **voltage**; symbol U, units V (volt). A potential difference is said to exist between two points if work must be done against an electric field to carry a charge from one point to the other. A potential difference divided by the distance between the two points gives the strength of the electric field between the points. The potential difference between the terminals of a battery indicates the battery's ability to drive current around a circuit. » electricity; electromotive force; electron volt; Kirchhoff's laws; potential

potential energy The energy stored by an object by virtue of its position in the region of influence of some force; symbol V, units J (joule). For example, an object acquires potential energy equal to the work done against the force of gravity in raising it above the Earth's surface; when released, the object falls to the ground, and its potential energy is converted into kinetic energy, the energy of motion. Work done in compressing a spring is stored as elastic potential energy in the spring. The potential energy of a positive electric charge may be increased by bringing it closer to another positive charge. » energy; potential

potentilla A large genus of annuals or perennials, sometimes creeping, rarely small shrubs, native to N temperate regions; leaves with three leaflets, or pinnately or palmately divided into leaflets; flowers with epicalyx, 4–5 sepals, 4–5 petals;. They can be roughly divided into two groups: **cinquefoils** with 5-petalled flowers, and **tormentils** with 4-petalled flowers. Several, especially the shrubby species, are widely grown ornamentals. (Genus: *Potentilla*, 500 species. Family: *Rosaceae*.) » annual; epicalyx; palmate; perennial; pinnate; sepal; shrub; tormentil

potentiometer An instrument for the accurate measurement or control of electrical potential. A known potential drop is created in a long wire by a battery, and a sliding contact is used to tap off any proportion of this drop. Potentiometers are used in electronic circuits, especially as volume controls in transistor radios. » electricity; potential; transistor

potholing » **speleology**

potlatch A feast celebrating an important event, or following personal humiliation, at which the host gives away his wealth (slaves, blankets, canoes, etc), or destroys it in front of the guests. People receiving wealth in this way would later give their own potlatches, ensuring circulation of some of the property. It was a common practice among N American Indians of the Northwest Pacific coast. » Northwest Coast Indians

Potomac River [puh**toh**mak] River in West Virginia, Virginia, and Maryland, USA; formed at the junction of two branches rising in the Allegheny Mts; flows into Chesapeake Bay; navigable for large craft as far as Washington; main tributary the Shenandoah; the Great Falls lie 24 km/15 ml above Washington. » United States of America [i]

potoroo » **rat kangaroo**

Potosí [potoh**see**] 19°34S 65°45W, pop (1982) 103 182. Capital of Potosí department, SW Bolivia; altitude 4 060 m/13 320 ft; highest city of its size in the world; founded by Spanish in 1545; major silver-mining town in 17th–18th-c, becoming the most important city in S America at the time; airfield; railway; university (1892); tin, silver, copper, lead; chief industrial centre of Bolivia; Convent of Santa Teresa (art collection); Las Cajas Reales (Cabildo and Royal Treasury); cathedral; thermal baths at the Laguna de Tarapaya; nearby mint (Casa Real de Moneda), founded 1542, rebuilt 1759, now a museum and world heritage site. » Bolivia [i]

Potsdam 52°23N 13°04E, pop (1982) 133 225. Capital of Potsdam county, EC Germany; on R Havel, W of Berlin; former residence of German emperors and Prussian kings; badly bombed in World War 2; scene of the 1945 Potsdam Conference; railway; Academy of Political Science and Law; colleges of cinematographic and television art; Central Meteorological Centre; food processing, pharmaceuticals, electrical equipment, textiles, film industry; Sans Souci palace and park (1745–7), 18th-c garrison church. » Germany [i]; Potsdam Conference; Sans Souci

Potsdam Conference A conference which met during the final stages of World War 2 (17 Jul–2 Aug 1945). Churchill (and later Attlee), Stalin, and Truman met to discuss the post-war settlement in Europe. Soviet power in E Europe was recognized, and it was agreed that Poland's W frontier should run along the Oder–Neisse line. The decision was made to divide Germany into four occupation zones. Political differences between the USA and USSR marked the start of the Cold War. » Attlee; Churchill, Winston; Cold War; Oder–Neisse line; Stalin; Truman; World War 2

Potter, (Helen) Beatrix (1866–1943) British author, born in London. She wrote many books for children, which she illustrated herself, creating such popular characters as Peter Rabbit (1900), Squirrel Nutkin (1903), and Benjamin Bunny (1904). In 1913 she married her solicitor, William Heelis, and went to live in Sawrey, in the Lake District, where she died.

Potter, Paul (1625–54) Dutch painter and etcher, born at Enkhuizen. He worked in Delft and The Hague, moving in 1652 to Amsterdam, where he died. His best pictures are small pastoral scenes with animal figures, but he also also painted large pictures, notably the life-size 'Young Bull' (1647, The Hague). » Dutch art; etching

Potter, Stephen (1900–69) British writer and radio producer. He joined the BBC in 1938, and is best known in radio as co-author with Joyce Grenfell of the *How* series. In his writing, he is remembered for his humorous studies of the art of demoralizing the opposition, such as *Gamesmanship* (1947), *Lifemanship* (1950), and *One-Upmanship* (1952). » satire

potter wasp A solitary, hunting wasp; adults make flask-shaped nests of clay and saliva; females provision nests with paralysed caterpillars or other insect larvae before egg laid; adults feed on nectar. (Order: *Hymenoptera*. Family: *Eumenidae*.) » caterpillar; wasp

Potteries, the Pop (1981) 376 764. NW Midlands urban area in the upper Trent valley of Staffordshire, C England; extends c.14 km/9 ml (NW–SE) by 5 km/3 ml (W–E); includes several towns within Stoke-on-Trent; railway; since the 18th-c, the heart of the English china and earthenware industry, based on local clay and coal. » pottery; Stoke-on-Trent

pottery Vessels made out of fired clay, produced by mankind since the earliest civilizations. They can be built, moulded, or in more sophisticated societies thrown on a wheel. Pottery tends to be soft and rather porous, and is therefore normally protected by a **glaze**, which also gives a shiny decorative appearance. Glaze is applied after the first firing, when the pot is placed in the kiln for the second time at a lower temperature. » clay; Delftware; Doulton; faience; maiolica; porcelain; Spode; stoneware; Toby jug; Wedgwood, Josiah

potto A primitive primate, native to Africa; resembles the slow loris, but has a dark face and short tail; four spines (elongated vertebrae) on back of neck. (*Perodicticus potto*. Family: *Lorisidae*.) The name **golden potto** is used for the related angwantibo.) » kinkajou; loris; prosimian

pouched rat A type of rat native to Africa; three species resemble rats, two resemble hamsters; all have internal cheek pouches; rat-like species often have blind wingless earwigs (of genus *Hemimerus*) in their fur. (Subfamily: *Cricetomyinae*, 5 species.) » hamster; pocket gopher; rat

Poulenc, Francis [**poo**lãk] (1899–1963) French composer, born and died in Paris. He became a member of *Les Six*, and was prominent in the reaction against Impressionism. His works include much chamber music and the ballet *Les Biches*, produced by Diaghilev in 1924; but he is best known for his considerable output of songs, such as *Fêtes Galantes* (1943). » Diaghilev; Impressionism (music); *Six, Les*

pound (economics) The unit of currency of the UK (the *pound sterling*), and certain other countries. The £ symbol is derived from letter *L* for *libra*, a measure of weight. It was formerly divided into 20 shillings and 240 pence; but since decimalization in 1971 it is divided into 100 pence (*new pence*). » currency

pound (physics) » **kilogram**

Pound, Ezra (Loomis) (1885–1972) US poet, born at Hailey, Idaho. Educated at Pennsylvania, he travelled widely in Europe, working as a journalist and editor, and becoming part of literary movements in London, where his publications included *Personae* (1909) and *Homage to Sextus Propertius* (1919). From 1924 he made his home in Italy, where he caused resentment by making pro-fascist broadcasts in the early stages of World War 2. In 1945 he was escorted back to the USA and indicted for treason, but was judged insane, and placed in an asylum. Released in 1958, he returned to Italy. He was an experimental poet, whom T S Eliot regarded as the motivating force behind modern poetry. His main work is *The Cantos*, a loosely-knit series of poems, which he began during World War 1, and which were published in many instalments, 1930–59. He died in Venice. » American literature; Eliot, T S; Modernism; poetry

poundal » RR71

Poussin, Nicholas [**poo**sĩ] (1594–1665) French painter, born near Les Andelys. He went to Rome in 1624, and spent the rest of his life there, apart from a short visit (1640–2) to Paris. The greatest master of French classicism, deeply influenced by Raphael and the Antique, his masterpieces include two sets of the 'Seven Sacraments' (one set on loan to Edinburgh). He died in Rome. » classicism; French art; Raphael

Poussinisme » **Rubénisme**

poverty trap An anomaly in a social welfare and taxation system which occurs when individuals, previously unemployed and claiming various social benefits, obtain work, and find that they are taxed, so ending up with less net income than before. The same situation may also apply to low-paid workers who obtain a small rise and find they have lost the right to certain benefits. » income tax

POW An acronym for **prisoner-of-war**, whose treatment was first codified by International Treaty at the Hague Conference of 1899. This stated that POWs must be humanely treated, and not obliged to divulge military information other than name, rank, and number. » Geneva convention

powder metallurgy Making metal shapes by compressing powdered metal into a finished or near-finished shape. First used for tungsten lamp filaments, it is now used for such products as tungsten carbide cutting tools and self-lubricating bearings. It can be used on iron, tin, nickel, copper, aluminium, and titanium. The powders are made a specific and regular size by atomization (cooling a spray of molten metal) or controlled chemical precipitation. The material is pressed into shape and then heat-treated (*sintered*). In an alternative method, the powder is fed from a hopper into a gap between rollers to produce a strip. The advantages of powder metallurgy are economy of manufacture and porosity where needed. » metallic glass; sintering

Powell, Anthony (Dymoke) (1905–) British novelist, born in London. Educated at Eton and Oxford, he worked in publishing and journalism. After World War 2, he wrote a major series of satirical social novels, *A Dance to the Music of Time* (1951–75) – 12 volumes covering 50 years of British upper-middle-class life and attitudes. He has also published four volumes of memoirs under the general title *To Keep the Ball Rolling* (1976–82). » English literature; novel

Powell, (John) Enoch (1912–) British Conservative politician, born in Birmingham. Educated at Birmingham and Cambridge, he was professor of Greek at Sydney (1937–9), and became an MP in 1950. He held several junior posts before becoming Minister of Health (1960–3). His outspoken attitude on the issues of non-White immigration and racial integration came to national attention in 1968, and as a consequence of this he was dismissed from the Shadow Cabinet. He was elected as an Ulster Unionist MP in October 1974, losing his seat in 1987. » Conservative Party

Powell, Michael (1905–90) British film director, scriptwriter, and producer, born near Canterbury, Kent. He worked as a director on minor productions in the 1930s, and co-directed on *The Thief of Baghdad* (1940) for Korda, who introduced him to the Hungarian scriptwriter, Emeric Pressburger (1902–88). Powell and Pressburger formed The Archers company in 1942, and for more than ten years made a series of unusual and original features, many with an exceptional use of colour, such as *Black Narcissus* (1947) and *The Tales of Hoffman* (1951). After the break-up of the partnership, Powell's productions were infrequent, including the controversial *Peeping Tom* (1960) and *The Boy Who Turned Yellow* (1972), from a script by Pressburger. He died at Avening, Gloucestersire.

power (mathematics) » **exponent**

power (physics) The rate of change of work with time; symbol P, units W (watt). To lift an object some distance into the air requires a fixed amount of work, but to do the job more quickly requires more power. » electrical power; work

powerboat racing The racing of boats fitted with high-powered and finely-tuned engines. The first boat to be fitted with a petrol engine was by Frenchman Jean Joseph Lenoir (1822–1900) in 1865, when he introduced his boat on the R Seine in Paris. The first race was c.1900, and the first race of note was from Calais to Dover in 1903. Races take place both inshore and offshore.

Powhatan Confederacy A group of Algonkin-speaking N American Indian tribes inhabiting the Tidewater region of Virginia at the time of the first White contact; named after chief Powhatan. Initially receptive, the Indians grew suspicious of the newcomers, and in 1622 and 1644 launched massive attacks on them. They were defeated both times. Over 1 000 scattered descendants of these tribes were still to be found in Virginia in the mid-20th-c. » Algonkin; American Indians; Indian Wars

Powys, John Cowper [**poh**is] (1872–1964) British writer and critic, born in Shirley, Derbyshire. Educated at Sherborne and Cambridge, he worked as a teacher and lecturer, much of the time in the USA. He wrote poetry and essays, but is best known for his long novels on West Country and historical themes, such as *A Glastonbury Romance* (1932) and *Owen Glendower* (1940). He died at Blaenau Ffestiniog, Merioneth. His brothers **Llewelyn** (1884–1939) and **Theodore Francis** (1875–1953) were also writers. » novel; Welsh literature

Powys [**pow**is] pop (1987e) 113 300; area 5 077 sq km/1 960 sq ml. Mountainous county in E Wales, UK, divided into three districts; created in 1974; bounded E by England; drained by the Usk, Wye, Taff and Tawe Rivers; Lake Vyrnwy (reservoir) source of water for Liverpool and Birmingham; capital, Llandrindod Wells; agriculture, forestry, tourism; Brecon Beacons National Park. » Wales [i]

Poyang Hu Lake in N Jiangxi province, SE China; China's largest freshwater lake; area 3 583 sq km/1 383 sq ml; much reduced from earlier size by silt deposits and land reclamation; merges with the Yangtze R in N. » China [i]

Poynings' Law Statutes enacted by the Irish Parliament at the direction of Sir Edward Poynings (1459–1521), English lord deputy, in 1494, removing its right to meet without the English government's agreement and to pass laws without prior approval. The immediate object was to crush Yorkist support, but over the long term it bolstered English claims to sovereignty and conquest. It was effectively repealed in 1782. » Roses, Wars of the

Poznań [**poz**nan], Ger **Posen** 52°25N 16°53E, pop (1983) 570 900. Capital of Poznań voivodship, W Poland, on R Warta; capital of Poland until 13th-c; bishopric; airfield; railway; two universities (1918, 1919); metallurgy, machinery, chemicals, clothing, food processing, transport; noted for its choirs and the Polish Theatre of Dance; Franciscan church (17th–18th-c), 13th-c castle with museum of crafts, national museum, Great Poland army museum, cathedral (18th-c, largely rebuilt); festival of Polish contemporary music (spring), international violin competitions (every five years), commercial fair (Jun). » Poland [i]

Prado [**prah**doh] The Spanish national museum in Madrid, housing the world's finest collection of Spanish art, as well as many exhibits from other major European schools. The gallery, which evolved from the private collections of the Spanish royal house, was opened to the public in 1819 by Ferdinand VII. » museum

Praesepe [priy**see**pee] » **Cancer**

Praetorian Guard [pree**taw**rian] An elite corps in imperial Rome – effectively, the Emperor's bodyguard. Their real influence dates from the 20s AD, when they were concentrated in a single barracks in Rome itself, and put under the control of a single commander.

Praetorius, Michael [prita**w**riuhs] (1571–1621) German composer, born in Creuzburg, Thuringia. He studied in Torgau, Frankfurt an der Oder, and Zerbst, and became court organist and (from 1604) *Kapellmeister* at the court of Wolfenbüttel, where he died. As well as being one of the most prolific composers of his time (especially of church music), he wrote an important treatise *Syntagma musicum* (1614–20).

praetors [**pree**tawz] In ancient Rome, the chief law officers of the state, elected annually, second only to the consuls in importance. The office could not be held before the age of 33. » cursus honorum

Pragmatic Sanction A Habsburg family law devised in 1713 by Charles VI to alter an earlier pact in favour of the undivided succession of his heirs, male or female, to the Habsburg lands (1713). Later, much effort was deployed in achieving internal and international guarantees for his daughter Maria Theresa's claims, though these were repudiated by Frederick II of Prussia (1740). » Frederick II (of Prussia); Habsburgs; Maria Theresa

pragmatics In linguistics, philosophy, and psychology, the study of the way context influences a person's use and understanding of language. It analyses such topics as the norms which influence linguistic behaviour (eg in addressing, replying, being polite, or being persuasive) and the rules which govern the pattern of turn-taking in conversation. The subject also includes the study of the way language is used to do things; for example, *I promise*, used in appropriate circumstances, *is* to promise. » discourse analysis

pragmatism A philosophical movement begun in the USA in the 1870s, developed by Peirce, James, and Dewey. Its most distinctive feature is the claim that the truth of a proposition depends on the inquiring and opining activities of people, although pragmatists have disagreed about the nature of this dependence. » Dewey, John; Peirce, C S; James, William

Prague, Czech **Praha** 50°05N 14°25E, pop (1984) 1 186 253. Industrial and commercial capital of Czechoslovakia, on R Vltava; important trading centre since 10th-c; capital of newly-created Czechoslovakia, 1918; occupied by Warsaw Pact troops, 1968; historical centre declared a conservation area, 1971; archbishopric; airport (Ruzyne); railway; metro; Charles University (1348); technical university (1707); chemicals, machine tools, locomotives, aircraft, glass, motorcycles, furniture, soap, perfumes; Hradčany Castle, Cathedral of St Vitus, Royal Palace (Královsky Palác), St Nicholas Cathedral, Wallenstein Palace, St George (10th-c Romanesque church), National Gallery. » Czechoslovakia [i]; Hradčany Castle

Praia [**prah**ya] 14°53N 23°30W, pop (1980) 37 500. Port and capital of the Republic of Cape Verde, on S shore of São Tiago I; airport connecting with Dakar and neighbouring islands; naval shipyard, light industry, fishing, commerce. » Cape Verde [i]

prairie The extensive grassland and treeless region of N USA and Canada. Originally the vegetation was coarse grass and habitat for the bison. Its fertile soils encouraged ploughing and cultivation, and the prairies are now a major arable area. Cattle ranching is also important. Little natural prairie survives. Prairies are known as *steppe* in Europe and Asia, and as *pampa(s)* in S America. » pampa(s); steppe

prairie chicken A grouse native to C USA; upright tail; long upright feathers on head; inflatable orange neck sacs; inhabits prairie; eats fruit, seeds, and insects. (*Tympanuchus cupido*.) » grouse

prairie dog A N American squirrel; length, up to 450 mm/18 in, with short tail; inhabits open country; digs extensive burrow systems called 'towns' (composed of 'wards' which contain social units called 'coteries'). (Genus: *Cynomys*, 5 species.) » squirrel

prairie schooner A type of wagon used by emigrants making the journey W in the 19th-c, with cloth covers stretched over hoops. They were also known as *covered wagons*, or *Conestoga wagons*, from the place in Pennsylvania where they were originally manufactured.

prairie wolf » **coyote**

Prasad, Rajendra [pra**sad**] (1884–1963) Indian statesman and President (1950–62), born at Zeradei, Bihar. He left legal practice to become a supporter of Gandhi, and was President of the Indian National Congress on several occasions between 1934 and 1948. In 1946 he was made Minister for Food and Agriculture, and became India's first President in 1950. He died at Patna. » Gandhi; Indian National Congress

Prairie dog

pratincole [**prat**ingkohl] A bird of the Old World family *Glareolidae*, sub-family *Glareolinae* (8 species); long wings, short tail; short black bill with reddish base; short legs (*Glareolus*, 7 species) or long legs (*Stiltia*); lives near water; eats insects. » courser

prawn A general name for many shrimp-like crustaceans. *Prawn* and *shrimp* are interchangeable common names, with usage varying according to local tradition. (Class: *Malacostraca*. Order: *Decapoda*.) » crustacean; shrimp

Praxiteles [prak**si**tuhleez] (4th-c BC) Greek sculptor, a citizen of Athens. His works have almost all perished, though his 'Hermes carrying the boy Dionysus' was found at Olympia in 1877. Several of his statues are known from Roman copies. » Greek art; sculpture

prayer Turning to God in speech or silent concentration. A major characteristic of most religions, it includes petition, adoration, confession, invocation, thanksgiving, and intercession. It can be silent (mental) or vocal, public or private, individual or corporate, liturgical or free. It is generally considered an essential feature of worship. » Amidah; God; Hail Mary; Kaddish; Kiddush; litany; liturgy; Lord's Prayer; Shema

praying mantis A large, green mantis which lies motionless in wait for its prey, holding its grasping forelegs in an attitude suggestive of prayer; found in Europe. (Order: *Mantodea*. Family: *Mantidae*.) » mantis

Precambrian era A geological time before the Phanerozoic, from the formation of the Earth (c.4 600 million years ago) to c.590 million years ago; subdivided into the Archean and the Proterozoic eons. Precambrian rocks outcrop over vast areas of continental interiors. » Baltic Shield; Canadian Shield; geological time scale; RR16

precession In rotational mechanics, the progressive change in orientation of the axis of rotation. For example, a child's spinning top spins about its own axis, but also wobbles or precesses about the vertical. The Earth precesses in a complicated way. » angular momentum; gyroscope; magnetic resonance; mechanics; precession of the equinoxes

precession of the equinoxes A phenomenon which results from slow changes in the direction in space of the Earth's rotation axis. The gravitational attractions of the Sun and Moon tug at the Earth's equatorial bulge, leading to a turning force or 'couple' that swings the rotation axis through a cone in space, at an angle of 23.5° to the equatorial plane, on a period of 25 800 years. An important consequence of precession is that the positions of all celestial objects change continuously: the origin of the co-ordinate system is where the Equator and ecliptic cross (the First Point of Aries) and this moves W along the ecliptic at 50 arc seconds a year. Star catalogues always list the year to which the positions apply, so that the exact position at any moment has to be computed. Another consequence is that the celestial pole describes a circle 47° in diameter, and in 13 000 years Vega, rather than Polaris, will be the North Star. » celestial sphere; equinox; First Point of Aries; Polaris; precession

precious stones » **gemstones**

precipitate Insoluble material formed during a chemical reaction in solution. Examples include the deposition of scale in a kettle and the formation of soap scum by hard water. » chemical reaction

precipitation A climatic term covering rainfall, drizzle, snow, sleet, hail, and dew. As rising air cools, it condenses around dust particles to form water droplets and clouds. If the droplet grows to a critical size, it will fall as precipitation; the type reaching the ground depends on the air temperature between the cloud and the ground. In many parts of the world, rain and snow are the main contributors, and often the words 'rainfall' and 'precipitation' are used interchangeably. » cloud [i]; condensation (physics); dew; fog; hail; rainfall; rime; sleet; snow; thunderstorm

Pre-Columbian art and architecture The arts of the N, C, and S American Indians, before the European conquests of the 16th-c. The more advanced 'high cultures' developed in the Peruvian (C Andean) area of S America and in C America and Mexico. In Peru, the Incas (15th-c) built with huge stone blocks, worked smooth and fitted tightly together. In C America, truncated pyramids served as bases for temples; the Maya (Guatemala, Honduras, Mexico) were great builders and inventive sculptors in stone, pottery, and jade, as were the Aztecs of Mexico. Most pre-Columbian cultures produced textiles and metalwork. » American Indians; Aztecs; Incas; Mayas; Mexican art/architecture; pyramid

predella A row of small pictures attached to the lower edge of an altarpiece. Predella panels normally illustrate scenes from the life of the saint who appears on the main *pala* above. » altarpiece; pala

predestination In Christian theology, the doctrine that the ultimate salvation or damnation of each human individual has been ordained beforehand. A source of endless dispute, the doctrine has been interpreted in many ways. It was first fully articulated by Augustine during his controversy with the Pelagians, who upheld the doctrine of free will. The Protestant Reformers Luther and Calvin defended the doctrine, though in varying degrees. Jakob Arminius (1560–1609) rejected the Calvinist view of predestination, and argued that the divine sovereignty was compatible with human free will. » Arminianism; Augustine; Calvin; Calvinism; free will; Luther; Lutheranism

predicate logic » **logic**

pre-eclampsia A potentially serious, abnormal condition of late pregnancy, in which blood pressure rises to above 140/90 mmHg, protein appears in the urine, and there is oedema of the limbs; also known as **pregnancy hypertension**. It is an uncommon condition, of unknown cause, but one which justifies regular surveyance throughout pregnancy. Once detected, admission to hospital and bed rest usually results in the resolution of the disorder and the birth of a normal baby; otherwise, eclampsia may develop. » blood pressure; eclampsia; pregnancy [i]

pre-emptive strike » **strategic capability**

prefabrication In architecture, the manufacture of parts or the whole of a building in a factory or other place away from the construction site. It was famously used for the rapid construction of the Crystal Palace, London (1851), architect Joseph Paxton. First considered in earnest during the 1920s, it was subsequently put into practice on a wide scale during the post-war years. Although successfully used for many building types, particularly industrial ones, the prefabricated houses of the 1950s and 1960s ('prefabs') have frequently met with great structural, water penetration, and hence social problems. Since the 1960s, the practice has been increasingly referred to as **systems building**.

prefect In local government, a senior official who is a direct agent of central government. The prefectorial system contrasts with systems of local government that allow for local participation and autonomy, and is found most notably in France since Napoleon, and in Italy since the *Risorgimento*. It has been criticized for its high degree of centralization, and the power of prefects has declined over the years.

preference shares Shares issued by a company, without voting rights, which carry a fixed rate of dividend (or interest). The holders have a prior claim on the profits of the company over ordinary shareholders. » shares

prefix » **affix**

pregnancy A physiological process in which female, live-bearing mammals nurture their developing young within the uterus; also known as **gestation**. It begins when the fertilized ovum embeds itself in the uterine wall (*implantation*), and ends with the birth of the offspring (*parturition*). During pregnancy in humans, menstruation is absent (in response to circulating hormones), the uterus enlarges, and the breasts increase in size (in preparation for lactation). The duration of pregnancy is species-specific: smaller animals with large litters generally have short gestation periods (eg hamsters, 16 days), whereas humans and African elephants have gestation periods of 266 days and 640 days respectively. » abortion; contraception; eclampsia; ectopic pregnancy; Fallopian tubes; fertility drugs; gamete intrafallopian transfer; Graafian follicle; induction (obstetrics); labour; morning sickness; natural childbirth; obstetrics; pre-eclampsia; superovulation syndrome; test-tube baby; uterus [i]

LENGTH OF PREGNANCY IN SOME MAMMALS

ANIMAL	GESTATION PERIOD*	ANIMAL	GESTATION PERIOD*
camel	406	kangaroo	40
cat	62	lion	108
cow	280	mink	50
chimpanzee	237	monkey, rhesus	164
dog	62	mouse	21
dolphin	276	opossum	13
elephant, African	640	orangutan	245–275
ferret	42	pig	113
fox	52	rabbit	32
giraffe	395–425	rat	21
goat	151	reindeer	215–245
guinea pig	68	seal, northern fur	350
hamster	16	sheep	148
hedgehog	35–40	skunk	62
horse	337	squirrel, grey	44
human	266	tiger	105–109
hyena	110	whale	365

**average number of days*

prehistoric art » **Palaeolithic art**

prejudice Making judgments about individuals based on inadequate or biased information. Indigenous racism in the USA, together with the Holocaust and the influx of refugee psychologists and sociologists into the USA in the 1930s, made the study of prejudice, especially racial prejudice, one of the key areas of social psychological research in the mid-20th-c. The search for the roots of prejudice in terms of the individual pathology of the prejudiced led to both social cognitive (the phenomenon of stereotyping) and developmental (the 'authoritarian personality') explanations. A different social climate has seen more recent attention being paid to prejudice towards women and homosexuals. Marxist and other critical theorists object to the individualism of this approach, and its failure to recognize societal and structural bases of prejudice. » Holocaust; Marxism; racism; sexism; social psychology

prelude A piece of instrumental music which precedes a longer work, such as a suite of dances or an operatic act, or is coupled with another of comparable length, especially a fugue. Until the 17th-c, independent preludes were often written, or improvised, to test an instrument's tuning, and several 19th-c composers (including Chopin) extended this tradition to sets of independent preludes in all the major and minor keys. » Chopin; fugue; suite

premenstrual tension syndrome A condition in which a variety of symptoms occur in relation to menstruation which interfere with normal life. It is of variable duration, has components that are both physical (eg constipation, abdominal pain, asthma, sleep disturbance) and mental (eg irritability, lethargy, and depression), and does not usually commence with puberty. In some societies it has been considered a cause of 'temporary insanity'. The causes are unknown, but psychological, social, and biological factors have been invoked. Treatment has included psychotherapy, progesterone hormones, and drugs to promote the passage of urine to eliminate the bloated feeling that many sufferers have. » menstruation

premier » **prime minister**

Preminger, Otto (1906–) Austrian film director and producer, born in Vienna, where he made his first film in 1932. He emigrated to the USA in 1935, and after some years of directing on the Broadway stage, made *Laura* (1944), a *film noir*, often considered his best. In the 1950s he made good use of the new wide-screen technology in such productions as *Carmen Jones* (1954) and *Bonjour Tristesse* (1959). Later films included *Porgy and Bess* (1959), *Exodus* (1960), and *The Human Factor* (1979). » cinema

premiss A sentence which is explicitly assumed in an argument. In '*Paris is larger than London; therefore London is smaller than Paris*', 'Paris is larger than London' is the only premiss. A sentence need not be true, or be believed to be true, to function as a premiss. » inference

premium bond A UK government security, introduced in 1956, and issued in numbered units of one pound. The accumulated interest on bonds sold is distributed through a lottery in the form of weekly and monthly tax-free cash prizes. Winning numbers are selected by a computer known as the Electronic Random Number Indicator Equipment (ERNIE). » bond

Premonstratensians A religious order founded by St Norbert at Prémontré, France, in 1120; also known as the **Norbertines** or **White Canons**. They are noted for parish education and mission work, and continue chiefly in Belgium. » missions, Christian; monasticism

prenatal diagnosis The assessment of the well-being of the foetus and the detection of abnormalities. Traditional clinical methods have been greatly reinforced by three recent techniques. *Ultrasound* is simple and safe, and is used later in pregnancy to establish gestational age, confirm multiple pregnancies, and detect grosser anatomical defects, such as spina bifida. *Amniocentesis* and *chorionic villus sampling*, as well as the sampling of foetal blood, are carried out at an earlier stage of pregnancy, when the information obtained may be of great value to counselling the mother with a view to obtaining an early abortion. As these methods entail some additional risks to the foetus, they tend to be used in selective cases where the transmission of genetic disease is suspected. » amniocentesis; chorionic villus sampling; genetically determined disease; obstetrics

preparatory school An independent fee-paying school for children up to the age when they might move to a public school or maintained secondary school if parents no longer wish to pay fees. It usually caters for pupils up to the age of 13. » public school; secondary education

prepared piano A piano into which extraneous objects have been inserted, usually between the strings, to alter the timbre of all or selected notes. US composer John Cage (1912–) and other avant-garde composers have used it since the 1940s. » keyboard instrument; piano

Pre-Raphaelite Brotherhood (PRB) A group of artists formed in London in 1848 with the aim of revolutionizing early Victorian art; their preference for the styles of the 15th-c (ie pre-Raphael) led to someone (it is unclear who) suggesting the name c.1847. Leading members were Millais, Hunt, and D G Rossetti. They rejected the sentimental mediaevalism and academic formulae of the time, seeking instead a new truth to nature and fresh subjects, often taken from Romantic poetry (eg Keats, Tennyson, Patmore). The public was deeply suspicious until Ruskin came to their defence. PRB pictures (the initials appear on some early pictures) are recognizable by their bright colours, hard-edged forms, shallow picture-space, and meticulous attention to detail. » English art; Hunt, William Holman; Millais; Raphael; Rossetti, Dante Gabriel; Ruskin

presbyopia » **eye** [i]

presbyter » **elder** (religion)

Presbyterianism The conciliar form of Church government of the Reformed Churches, deriving from the 16th-c Reformation led by John Calvin in Geneva and John Knox in Scotland. Government is by courts at local congregational (eg kirk session), regional (presbytery), and national (General Assembly) levels. *Elders* (ordained laymen) as well as ministers play a leading part in all courts. Through emigration and missionary activity from Scotland, Ireland, and England, Presbyterianism has spread world-wide. The World Presbyterian Alliance was formed in 1878, to be succeeded in 1970 by the World Alliance of Reformed Churches. » Calvin; elder (religion); General Assembly (religion); Knox, John; presbyter; presbytery 3; Reformation; Reformed Churches

presbytery 1 The E part of the chancel of a church, behind the choir. » church [i] 2 The traditional name for the dwelling-house of priests in the Roman Catholic Church. » priest; Roman Catholicism 3 In Presbyterianism, a church court composed of equal numbers of elders and ministers, presided over by a moderator, and overseeing a geographical grouping of congregations. » elder (religion); moderator; Presbyterianism

preschool education The provision of education for children under the statutory school age. This can either be in nursery or kindergarten, where there will usually be trained personnel, or in playgroups, where parent volunteers work with playgroup leaders. In some countries the provision of preschool education is widespread, but in others it is almost nonexistent. » kindergarten; nursery school; primary education

prescription An order for drugs written by a physician to a pharmacist, who will supply the correct medicine to the patient. Originally the sign ℞ was used to instruct the pharmacist to assemble the ingredients according to written instructions. This sign now simply indicates requests for prepared drugs. Until the 1940s prescriptions were written entirely in Latin. » pharmacy

prescriptivism An approach to language use which lays down 'rules of correctness', without taking account of real norms of usage, but by appealing to historical or imagined 'standards'. Examples of prescriptive rules in English state that one should say *I shall* not *I will* to express future time, and that one should never end a sentence with a preposition. Such rules date from the end of the 18th-c, and were widely taught in public schools during the 19th-c, thereby gaining prestige, as they came to be associated with educated speech and writing. They usually bear little correspondence to the way the majority of people speak, and the question of whether one should or should not adhere to them is thus hotly debated. » grammar

president The name used by a head of state who is not appointed on a hereditary basis. The powers and means of selection can take a variety of forms: some are elected and others appointed. A number of presidents perform a largely formal and ceremonial role, ensuring that a government is formed (eg the Irish Republic). Others share constitutionally in governing with the prime minister, cabinet, and legislature (eg France). Yet others effectively act as head of the government (eg the USA). » prime minister

Presidential Medal of Freedom (PM of F) The highest American award for civilians in peacetime, given for contributions to the interests of the USA, or to world peace, or for cultural achievements. » decoration

Presidium » **Politburo**

Presley, Elvis (Aaron) (1935–77) US rock singer, born at Tupelo, Mississippi. He began singing in his church choir and taught himself to play the guitar, his early models being Black gospel and blues singers. In 1953 he recorded some sides for Sun Records in Memphis, Tennessee, which came to the attention of the entrepreneur, Colonel Tom Parker, and led to aggressive promotion of Presley's career. In 1956, 'Heartbreak Hotel' sold millions of copies, and his performances, featuring much hip-wriggling and sexual innuendo, incited hysteria in teenagers and outrage in their parents. Although he served two years in the US Army in Germany, and became increasingly reclusive on his return to civilian life, he made 45 records that sold in the millions, including 'Hound Dog', 'Love Me Tender', and 'Jailhouse Rock'. His Hollywood films such as *Loving You* (1957), *King Creole* (1958), and *GI Blues* (1960) became enormous moneymakers. He died at Graceland, his Memphis mansion, which is now a souvenir shrine for his many fans. » pop music; rock music

Presocratics The first Western philosophers, who preceded Socrates and flourished in Greece, Asia Minor, and Italy in the 5th-c and 6th-c BC. They sought natural rather than mythological explanations for phenomena. » Anaxagoras; Anaximander; Anaximenes; Democritus; Empedocles; Heraclitus; Parmenides; Socrates

Pressburg » **Bratislava**

pressure Force per unit area; symbol p, units Pa (pascal). A given weight acting on a smaller area corresponds to larger pressure. For an object immersed in a fluid, such as water or air, pressure acts on all sides of the object. It is measured using barometers or pressure gauges. Other common units of pressure are bar and torr. » atmospheric pressure; bar (physics); barometer; force; isobar; pressure gauge; shock wave; sound; torr

pressure gauge A gauge which measures pressure in enclosed vessels and containers, such as boilers and pipes. Inside the gauge is a *Bourdon tube*, which is normally hook-shaped. When the pressure inside exceeds that outside, the tube straightens. This movement is transferred through levers and gears to move a pointer around a calibrated dial. » pressure

pressure group A voluntary organization formed to articulate a particular political interest or cause; also called an **interest group**. It can directly represent its members (a *sectional* group) or act on behalf of others (a *promotional* group). In the main, it tries to influence government and legislature, but may also attempt to influence public opinion. It differs from a political party in that it does not seek political office.

pressurized water reactor » **nuclear reactor** [i]

PRESTEL An interactive computer-based information system provided over the telephone network in the UK by British Telecom. It provides access to a wide variety of information sources. » interactive computing; viewdata

Prester John A mythical Christian priest-king of a vast empire in C Asia. Reports of his existence, wealth and military might, substantiated by a famous letter purporting to have come from him in 1165, raised the morale of Christian Europe as it faced the Muslim threat. The story almost certainly related to the Christian kingdom of Ethiopia, which had been cut off by the Islamic conquest of Egypt. 'Prester' comes from Old French *prestre*, 'priest'. » Axum; Ethiopia [i]; Islam

Preston 53°46N 2°42W, pop (1981) 126 155. Town in Preston district, Lancashire, NW England; administrative centre of Lancashire; 45 km/28 ml NW of Manchester, on the R Ribble; site of Royalist defeat in the Civil War (1648); 18th-c centre of the cotton industry; birthplace of Richard Arkwright; railway; electrical goods, engineering, textiles, plastics, chemicals; Harris museum; Preston Guild Fair every 20 years. » Arkwright; English Civil War; Lancashire

Prestonpans [prestuhn**panz**] 55°57N 3°00W, pop (1981) 7 621. Town in East Lothian district, Lothian, E Scotland; on S shore of Firth of Forth, 5 km/3 ml NE of Musselburgh; railway; coal processing; site of Scottish victory over the English (1745). » Lothian; Scotland [i]; Stuart, Charles

Prestwick 55°30N 3°12W, pop (1981) 13 599. Town in Kyle and Carrick district, Strathclyde, SW Scotland; on the W coast, 4.8 km/3 ml N of Ayr; airport (the official international gateway for Scotland); railway; aerospace engineering. » Strathclyde

Pretoria [prit**aw**ria] 25°45S 28°12E, pop (1985) 822 925 (metropolitan area). Administrative capital of South Africa, and capital of Transvaal province; 48 km/30 ml NNE of Johannesburg; altitude 1 369 m/4 491 ft; founded, 1855; capital of South African Republic, 1881; railway; two universities (1873, 1908); railway engineering, vehicles, iron and steel, chemicals, cement, leather; Voortrekker Memorial, Paul Kruger Memorial, Transvaal Museum. » South Africa [i]; Transvaal

Pretorius, Andries (Wilhelmus Jacobus) [prit**oh**riuhs] (1799–1853) Afrikaner leader, born at Graaff-Reinet, Cape Colony. A prosperous farmer, he joined the Great Trek of 1835 into Natal, where he was chosen Commandant-General. He later accepted British rule, but after differences with the Governor he trekked again, this time across the Vaal. Eventually the British recognized the Transvaal Republic, later the South African Republic, whose new capital was named Pretoria after him. He died at Magaliesberg, Transvaal. » Great Trek

Pretorius, Marthinus (Wessel) [prit**oh**riuhs] (1819–1901) Afrikaner soldier and statesman, born at Graaff-Reinet, Cape Colony, the son of Andries Pretorius. He succeeded his father as Commandant-General in 1853, and was elected President of the South African Republic (1857–71), and of the Orange Free State (1859–63). He fought against the British again in 1877, until the independence of the Republic was recognized (1881), then retired, and died at Potchefstroom. » Boer Wars

preventive medicine A branch of medical practice that is concerned with the prevention of disease. This is achieved by measures that (1) control the environment, such as clean air legislation, (2) ensure a clean and suitable food and water supply, (3) promote mass medication (eg schemes of immunization), (4) organize programmes for the eradication of disease (eg smallpox, diphtheria), and (5) promote safer life styles largely by education (eg the reduction in smoking to prevent cancer of the lung, and the promotion of condoms to reduce the possibility of AIDS). » community medicine; medicine; vaccination

Prévert, Jacques [**pray**vair] (1900–77) French poet, born at Neuilly-sur-Seine. He was involved with the Surrealists, and wrote songs, pieces for cabaret, and scenarios for Renoir; also the screenplay for *Les Enfants du Paradis* (1946, The Children of Paradise). The piquant mixture of wit and sentiment in his poetry proved very popular; collections include *Paroles* (1946, Words), *La Pluie et le beau temps* (1955, Rain and Fine Weather) and *Choses et Autres* (1972, Things and Others). He died at Omonville-la-Petite. » French literature; poetry; Renoir, Jean; Surrealism

Previn, André (George) (1929–) US conductor and composer, born in Berlin, his family fleeing to the USA in 1938. He studied music mainly in California and Paris, spent some years as a jazz pianist, and became musical director of symphony orchestras at Houston (1967–9), London (1968–79), and Pittsburgh (1976–86). He has composed musicals, film scores, and orchestral works, and achieved popular success, both on television and in the concert hall, by bringing classical music to the attention of a wide public.

Prévost (Antoine François), l'Abbé [**pray**voh] (1697–1763) French novelist, born at Hesdin, Artois. He spent some years in the army, became a Benedictine monk, then lived in exile in England and Holland. He wrote many novels and translations, but is best known for *Manon Lescaut* (1731), originally published as the final part of a 7-volume novel. Having returned to France by 1735, he was appointed honorary chaplain to the Prince de Conti. He died at Chantilly. » French literature; novel

Priam [**pri**yam] In Greek legend, the King of Troy. He was son of Laomedon, and husband of Hecuba, and is presented in the *Iliad* as an old man. When Hector was killed, he went secretly to Achilles to beg his son's body for burial. At the sack of Troy, he was killed by Neoptolemus. » Achilles; Hector; Neoptolemus; Trojan War

Pribilof Islands [**pri**bilof] Group of four islands in the Bering Sea, Alaska, USA; two inhabited (St Paul, St George); area 168 sq km/65 sq ml; centre of seal fur trade. » Alaska

price index » **retail price index**

prices and incomes policy A British government policy for managing the economy, arising out of a concern that if incomes are allowed to rise too quickly, inflationary pressures will appear, with rising prices. It is believed that control of both elements is necessary for the successful management of the economy. The opposite view is that inflation can be successfully controlled only by control of the money supply, and that regulating prices and incomes interferes with market mechanisms. Full legal backing is necessary if the policy is to be effective, and this step is opposed by some economists and trade unionists, as emerged when such a policy was used in the UK in the late 1960s and early 1970s. » stop-go policy

prickly heat A common generalized skin disorder in tropical countries that may affect local areas of skin in temperate climates. Obstruction to the ducts of sweat glands results in a crop of small red pimples (*papules*) associated with itching. » skin [i]; sweat

prickly pear A species of opuntia often cultivated for its reddish, juicy, edible fruits. (*Opuntia vulgaris*. Family: *Cactaceae*.) » opuntia

Pride, Sir Thomas (?–1658) English parliamentarian during the Civil War, born (possibly) near Glastonbury. Little is known of his early life. He commanded a regiment at Naseby (1645), and served in Scotland. When the House of Commons betrayed a disposition to effect a settlement with Charles I, he was appointed by the army (1648) to expel its Presbyterian Royalist members (**Pride's Purge**). He sat among the King's judges, and signed the death warrant. Knighted by Cromwell in

1656, he died at Worcester House, Surrey. » Charles I (of England); English Civil War

pride of India A deciduous tree growing to 15 m/50 ft, native to E Asia; leaves pinnate, leaflets toothed; inflorescence pyramidal; flowers 1 cm/0.4 in diameter, yellow, 4-petalled; fruit a papery capsule; also called **goldenrain tree**. It is widely planted for ornament. (*Koelreuteria paniculata*. Family: *Sapindaceae*.) » deciduous plants; inflorescence [i]; pinnate; tree [i]

priest The person authorized to sacrifice. In Christianity, the term derives from the Old Testament sacrificial system, and developed in the New Testament with Jesus Christ as great High Priest. Now, mainly in Roman Catholic and Orthodox usage, it refers to an ordained officer authorized to administer the sacraments, in particular the Eucharist (the sacrifice of the Mass). » Eucharist; Jesus Christ; Mass; Old Testament; Orders, Holy; sacrament

Priestley, J(ohn) B(oynton) (1894–1984) British author, born at Bradford, Yorkshire. Educated at Bradford and Cambridge, he made a reputation with his critical writings, and in 1929 his novel *The Good Companions* (1929) gained him wide popularity. It was followed by other humorous novels, such as *Angel Pavement* (1930), and he established his reputation as a dramatist with *Dangerous Corner* (1932), *Time and the Conways* (1937), and other plays on space-time themes, as well as popular comedies, such as *Laburnum Grove* (1933). He refused both a knighthood and a peerage, and died at Alveston, Warwickshire. His widow, **Jacquetta Hawkes** (1910–), is an archaeologist and writer. » drama; English literature; novel

Priestley, Joseph (1733–1804) British chemist and clergyman, born at Fieldhead, Yorkshire. In 1755 he became a Presbyterian minister, and after moving to Leeds in 1767 took up the study of chemistry. He is best known for his research into the chemistry of gases, and his discovery of oxygen. He also wrote an English grammar, and books on education and politics. His controversial views on religion and political theory (he was a supporter of the French Revolution) led him in 1794 to leave for America in fear of his life, where he was well received. He died at Northumberland, Pennsylvania. » oxygen

primary In politics, an election to choose the candidates for an election to public office. It differs from other forms of candidate selection in that the primary election is not organized by political parties, but by the government authority for which the election is to be held. The procedure is more commonly associated with the USA, but there are various forms of primary, and several ways in which political parties can be directly or indirectly involved. » political science

primary colours There are three primary colours recognized in art: red, yellow, and blue. In theory all other colours can be made by mixing these, but a good deal depends on the chemical constitution of the actual pigments employed. » complementary colour; Munsell colour system

primary education The first phase of statutory education, usually covering the years from 5 or 6 up to 11 or 12. In most countries, the emphasis is on the coverage of a wide range of subjects and themes usually taught by the class teacher. In some countries there is more specialist teaching, especially in fields such as music, mathematics, and science, and children may have specialist rather than generalist teachers for these subjects. There is also emphasis on social and personal development in the primary phase, and on 'learning by doing'. Primary schools tend to be much smaller in size than secondary schools. » pre-school education; secondary education

primate (biology) A mammal of the order *Primates* (c.180 species); most inhabit tropical forests; both eyes face forwards; hands and (usually) feet with grasping 'opposable thumb', used for climbing; cerebral hemispheres of brain well developed. Their classification is unsettled, but living species are usually placed in two suborders: the *Strepsirhini* (**prosimians**) and the *Haplorhini* (**tarsiers** and **Anthropoidea**). » Anthropoidea; ape; mammal [i]; marmoset; monkey [i]; prosimian; tarsier

primate (religion) The most senior bishop of a given area; for example, in the Church of England the Archbishop of Canterbury is primate of All England. Originally, the name applied to the metropolitan of a province, and then to the patriarch. » bishop; Church of England; patriarch **2**

prime minister The leader of and usually head of a government; also known as a **premier**. In general, prime ministers have to work through collective decision-making in a cabinet, although they can enjoy certain separate powers. In electoral systems, they are invariably the leader of the largest party or coalition in parliament; unlike presidents, their power base is more that of the party than that of personality.

prime number In mathematics, a positive integer greater than 1 that has no divisors other than 1 and itself. Primes have always had an important place in the theory of numbers. Number theorists have tried to devise functions $f(n)$ which produce only prime numbers for positive integer values of n, but so far, all have failed. The function $f(n)=n^2-n+41$ yields primes for all $n<41$; $f(n)=n^2-79n+1601$ produces primes for $n<80$. Fermat conjectured that $2^{2^n}+1$ is prime for all non-negative integer n, but this has been proved incorrect. » arithmetic, fundamental theorem of; Fermat; Goldbach's conjecture; numbers; number theory

prime rate The US bank base lending rate, at which the bank will lend to its best ('prime') customers. This rate applies to only 50 or so large US corporations, all others paying higher rates. An increase in the prime rate is a signal for all other interest rates to follow, making borrowing generally more expensive. » bank base rate; minimum lending rate

primitivism In modern art, the deliberate rejection of Western techniques and skills in the pursuit of 'stronger' effects found in such domains as African tribal or Oceanic art. The word may therefore be applied to Gauguin, and to Picasso's work from c.1906. It is sometimes referred to as 'naive art'. » Brücke, die; Expressionism; Gauguin; modern art; Picasso

Primo de Rivera (y Orbaneja), Miguel (1870–1930) Spanish general, born at Jerez de la Frontera. He served in Cuba, the Philippines, and Morocco, and in 1923 led a military coup, inaugurating a dictatorship which lasted until 1930. During 1928–9 he lost the support of the army, the ruling class, and the King, Alfonso XIII, and in 1930 gave up power. He died in Paris. His son, **José Antonio** (1903–36) founded the Spanish Fascist Party (*Falange Española*) in 1933, and was executed by the Republicans in 1936. » fascism; Spanish Civil War

primrose A stemless perennial, native to Europe, W Asia, and N Africa; a rosette of crinkled, tongue-shaped leaves; flowers long-stalked with a tubular calyx and spreading, pale yellow, rarely pink petals. It is a plant of woods and hedges, decreasing in some places because of excessive picking. The garden polyanthus is derived from a hybrid with the cowslip. (*Primula vulgaris*. Family: *Primulaceae*.) » oxlip; perennial; polyanthus; sepal

Prince Edward Island pop (1981) 122 506; area 5 660 sq km/2 185 sq ml. Province in E Canada; island in the Gulf of St Lawrence, separated from the mainland (S) by the Northumberland Strait; irregular coastline; rises to 142 m/466 ft; capital, Charlottetown; other towns include Summerside, Tignish, Souris; potatoes, tobacco, vegetables, grains, dairy products, fishing, food processing, tourism; visited by Cartier, 1534; French claim as Ile St Jean; settled by Acadians; occupied by British, 1758; annexed to Nova Scotia, 1763; separate province, 1769; modern name, after Queen Victoria's father, 1798; joined Canada, 1873; governed by a lieutenant-governor and a 32-member elected Legislative Assembly. » Canada [i]; Cartier; Charlottetown

Prince of Wales In the UK, the title conferred (by custom, not law) on the sovereign's eldest son. Wales was ruled by a succession of independent princes from the 5th-c; the first to be acknowledged by an English king was Llewelyn ap Gruffudd (reigned 1246–82) in 1267. Tradition holds that after the death of Llewelyn in battle (against the British) and the execution of his brother, Edward I presented his own infant son to the Welsh people at Caernarvon Castle as their prince. The title has been used since that time. » Charles, Prince of Wales

Princess Royal A title sometimes bestowed on the eldest, or only, daughter of a sovereign. George V's daughter Mary was Princess Royal until her death in 1965; the title was conferred by the Queen on Princess Anne in 1987. » titles [i]

Princeton 40°21N 74°40W, pop (1980) 12 035. Borough in Mercer County, WC New Jersey, USA, on the Millstone R;

founded by Quakers, 1696; scene of a British defeat by George Washington, 1777; a noted centre for education and research; university (1746); birthplace of Paul Robeson; home of Einstein after his emigration to the USA. » Einstein; Friends, Society of; Ivy League [i]; New Jersey; Robeson

principle of equivalence » **equivalence principle**

principle of least action » **least-action principle**

printed circuit A technique which replaces individual wiring between components in electronic circuits. It is made by depositing a network of thin, metallic connections on to a board, the electronic components usually being soldered to pins on the other side of the board. The technique is commonly used to mount integrated circuits or chips together on boards for use as plug-in units in computers, televisions, or other electronic components. Printed circuit boards can be mass-produced, and their use enables circuit assembly to be easily automated. » electronics; integrated circuit

printer, computer A computer output device which produces characters or graphics on paper. Many different types exist, and the optimum choice for any given situation depends on the acceptable cost, printing speed, print quality, and operating noise. » daisy wheel/dot-matrix/golf-ball/impact/ink jet/laser/line/thermal xerographic printer

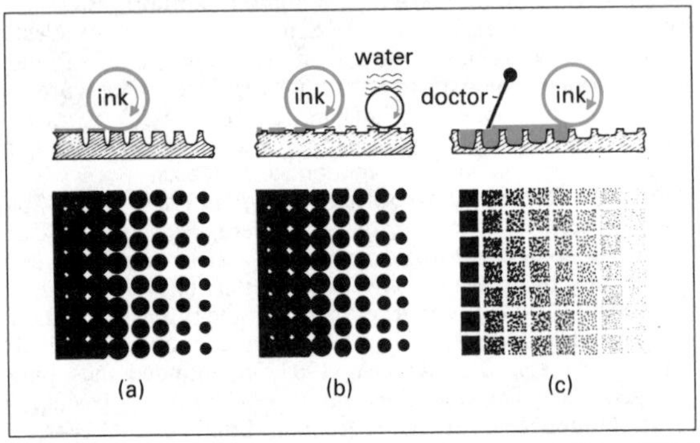

Three methods of printing: (a) The relief or letterpress process with dots of varying size. (b) The surface, lithographic, or planographic process, with the same kind of dot system as (a). (c) The recess or intaglio process, with rectangular prints varying in intensity but not in size.

printing A set of techniques for placing an image on a foundation in a controlled sequence of identical copies. The image may be verbal, illustrative or abstract, in one or many colours; the foundation is generally paper; and the colouring agent is generally ink. The techniques include *relief*, *planographic* (surface), and *intaglio* (recess) printing. The principal forms of relief printing are *letterpress* and *flexography*; those of planographic printing, *lithography* and the obsolescent *collotype*. Intaglio printing is typified by *gravure*, but most of the techniques used by artists in printmaking (engraving, drypoint, mezzotint, and etching) also fall into this category. Screen-process printing and stencilling are sometimes categorized as planographic processes, but are better viewed as unique processes.

The oldest form of printing, letterpress, depends upon pressure for the satisfactory transfer of ink to paper, so the early history of printing is the history of wooden printing presses as well as of moveable type and blocks. The wooden handpress was superseded in 1795 by the first all-metal press, the Stanhope. The 19th and 20th-c saw the development of increasingly elaborate mechanical presses capable of printing on one side, then on both sides of the sheet, in one and then two colours, and faster machines in which the relief image is carried on a curved plate attached to one of the cylinders (*flexography*). Offset lithography developed at the beginning of the 20th-c, and came into widespread use. Techniques of typesetting can now create the typographic image direct, either on film or on paper, thus cutting out the need for typesetters to set and store metal type. » gravure; letterpress [i]; lithography; phototypesetter; offset lithography [i]; screen-process printing

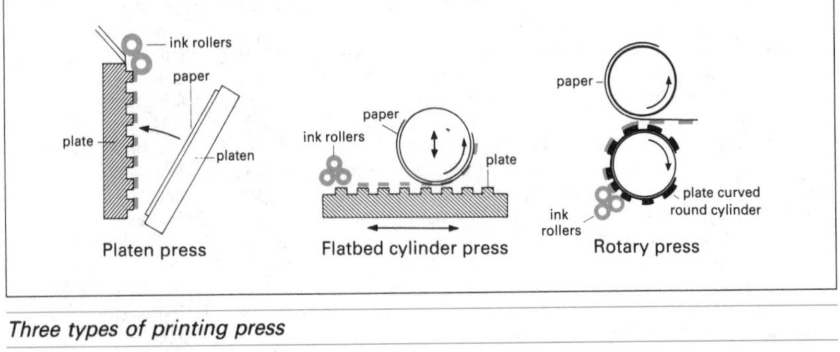

Three types of printing press

prion A petrel, native to S oceans; uses very stout bill with sieve-like edge to strain minute crustaceans from water. (Genus: *Pachyptila*, perhaps 6 species – experts disagree. Family: *Procellariidae*.) » petrel

Prior, Matthew (1664–1721) English diplomat and poet, born at Wimborne, Dorset. Educated at Westminster and Cambridge, he became an MP (1700), and carried out diplomatic work in Holland, being instrumental in concluding the Treaty of Utrecht (1713). He wrote several political and philosophical poems, but is best known for his light occasional verse, collected as *Poems on Several Occasions* (1709). » English literature; poetry

Priscian, Lat **Priscianus** (6th-c AD) Latin grammarian, born in Caesarea. He taught Latin at Constantinople, and became the best known of the Latin grammarians. His 18-volume *Institutiones Grammaticae* (Grammatical Foundations) was highly regarded in the Middle Ages. » grammar; Italic languages

prism In mathematics, a solid geometrical figure: its section is a rectilineal figure, with parallel edges. In optics, it is a transparent object used to produce or study the refraction and dispersion of light. It may be made of glass, plastic or liquid in a hollow prism. » geometry; refraction [i]; Plate X

prison That part of the penal system where criminals are held in custody for varying lengths of time determined by the courts as punishment for offences. Prisons developed rapidly from the early 19th-c; before then, banishment and corporal or capital punishment were the main ways of dealing with offenders. Subsequently, imprisonment itself came to be seen as both an adequate penalty and acceptable means of social control or 'deterrence'. Conditions in the earliest municipal prisons were usually atrocious, and were improved only through the work of penal reformers such as Elizabeth Fry. Problems of overcrowding still dog many prisons today, making efforts of rehabilitation of prisoners much more difficult. » Fry, Elizabeth; Howard, John

Priština [**preesh**tina] 42°39N 21°10E, pop (1981) 216 040. Capital town of Kosovo autonomous province, S Serbia republic, SEC Yugoslavia; former capital of Serbia; airfield; railway; university (1976); vehicle parts, crafts; many Turkish buildings, including the Sultan Murad mosque; nearby marble cave of Donje and monastery of Gračanica. » Serbia; Yugoslavia [i]

Pritchett, Sir V(ictor) S(awdon) (1900–) British writer and critic, born at Ipswich, Suffolk. Educated in London, he became a foreign newspaper correspondent, and published his first novel, *Claire Drummer*, in 1929. He became known for his critical works, such as *The Living Novel* (1946), short stories (2 vols, 1982, 1983), and travel books. He was knighted in 1975. » English literature; literary criticism; novel; short story

private enterprise An economic system where individuals, singly or collectively, may engage in a business venture using their own resources and without needing state approval or control, as long as the venture does not contravene existing laws and rules. It contrasts with *public enterprise*, where the activity is carried out by a state-owned or -controlled organization. » free enterprise

private sector Those aspects of an economy which are not controlled by the state, but which are in the hands of individuals or companies, and thereby answerable to the owners. The notion contrasts with the *public sector*. » public sector borrowing requirement

privateering » **buccaneers**

privatization The return to private ownership of organizations which are owned at present by the state. The government issues shares in the company to be privatized, and offers them for sale to the public. The company therefore becomes answerable to the shareholders and not to the government. Several cases of privatization took place in Britain in the 1980s, including British Telecom and British Gas. The government was able to raise considerable sums of money by this means, thus helping to reduce its borrowing requirements and cut tax rates. » nationalization; shares

privet A mostly temperate, evergreen or deciduous shrub or small tree; leaves opposite, leathery; flowers tubular with four spreading lobes, creamy, fragrant, in loose conical inflorescences; berries black or purple, poisonous. Several species are commonly used for garden hedges. (Genus: *Ligustrum*, c.40 species. Family: *Oleaceae*.) » deciduous/evergreen plants; inflorescence [i]; shrub; tree [i]

Privy Council A body which advises the British monarch, appointed by the crown. In previous times, particularly the Tudor period, it was a highly influential group, and might be regarded as the precursor of the cabinet. Today its role is largely formal, enacting subordinate legislation (proclamations and Orders in Council). Its membership is over 300, but the quorum is three. » cabinet; Order in Council

Prix de l'Arc de Triomphe [**pree** duh **lahk** duh **tree**ŏf] The richest horse race in Europe, held at the end of the season over 2 400 m (2 625 yds) at Longchamp near Paris on the first Sunday in October. First run in 1920, it is the leading race for inter-age horses in Europe. » horse racing

Prizren [**pree**zren] 42°12N 20°43E, pop (1981) 134 526. Town in Kosovo autonomous province, SW Serbia republic, Yugoslavia; on R Prizrenska Bistrica, near the Albanian frontier; built on the site of a Roman town (Theranda); important mediaeval trade centre; part of Albania, 1941–4; railway; tourism, gold and silver work; old town, mosques. » Serbia; Yugoslavia [i]

pro-life movement Organized opposition to the legality of induced abortion, and to laboratory experiments on human embryos. The pressure group *LIFE* draws much support from Roman Catholics, who emphasize the sanctity of foetal life. » abortion

probability of an event A number, between 0 and 1, indicating the relative likelihood of an event taking place. The early development of the subject was stimulated by an enquiry made of Pascal by his friend the Chevalier de Mere: 'Which is the more likely to occur, a throw of 6 at least once in 4 throws of a single dice, or a throw of 'double 6' at least once in 24 throws of a pair of dice?'. The resulting correspondence between Pascal and Fermat laid the foundations for the serious study of probability. » Fermat; Pascal; statistics

probate The official proving of a will. The executor of the will applies to the court (eg in England and Wales, the High Court, Family Division) for a certificate confirming the validity of the will and the authority of the executor to administer the estate of the deceased. The term is not used in all jurisdictions (eg in Scotland). » will (law)

probation A method of dealing with offenders where, instead of a sentence of imprisonment, a court may order the offender to be supervised for a fixed period by a **probation officer**. Offenders must agree to being placed on probation after the obligations under the order are explained to them. » community service order

proboscis monkey [pruh**bo**sis] An Old World monkey native to Borneo; pale with darker 'cap' on head, and dark back; long tail; protruding nose, which in adult males becomes bulbous and pendulous; excellent swimmer; inhabits forest near freshwater; eats leaves. (*Nasalis larvatus*.) » langur; Old World monkey

procaryote or **prokaryote** [proh**ka**rioht] An organism that lacks an organized nucleus separated from the surrounding cytoplasm by a nuclear membrane. They are predominantly single-celled micro-organisms, such as the bacteria and blue-green algae, or infectious agents of cells, such as the viruses. » bacteria [i]; eucaryote; nucleus (biology); virus

processing (photography) Treating exposed photographic material to produce a permanent visible image. This is normally carried out through a series of chemical reactions such as developing and fixing, interspersed with washes to remove residues, and completed by drying, so that the result may be safely handled. » development; film; photography

processionary caterpillar A caterpillar that lives in colonies with its siblings inside a silk tent constructed on its food plant. Periodically, the caterpillars leave the tents and migrate in long, nose-to-tail lines over the ground. (Order: *Lepidoptera*.) » caterpillar

Proclus (c.412–85) Greek Neoplatonist philosopher, born in Constantinople. He studied at Alexandria and Athens, and became the last head of Plato's Academy. His approach, based on Plotinus, combined the Roman, Syrian, and Alexandrian schools of thought in Greek philosophy into one theological metaphysic. His works were translated into Arabic and Latin, and were influential in the Middle Ages. He died in Athens. » Neoplatonism; Plato; Plotinus

Proconsul » **Dryopithecus**

Procop » **Prokop**

Procopius (c.499–c.565) Byzantine historian, born at Caesarea, Palestine. He studied law, and accompanied Belisarius on his campaigns against the Persians, the Vandals in Africa, and the Ostrogoths in Italy. He was highly honoured by Justinian, and seems to have been appointed prefect of Constantinople in 562. His principal works are histories of the wars, and of the court of Justinian. » Belisarius; Justinian

Procrustes [proh**kruh**steez] In the legend of Theseus, a robber, living in Attica, who made travellers lie on his bed, and either cut or lengthened them to fit it; his name means 'the stretcher'. Theseus gave him the same treatment, and killed him.

producer In the motion picture industry, the person who brings the initial concept to practical reality, organizing finance and budgetary control, choosing the director, and holding the balance between the director and other important members of the production team, including the principal artistes. Producers exercise day-to-day administration to ensure that the shooting schedule is maintained and unforeseen crises dealt with. They are also concerned with publicity and distribution for the international market, and exploitation on television and video. In major television organizations, producers tend to specialize in particular categories (eg drama, comedy, current affairs), and one producer is often in charge of a series of programmes, working with several different directors or presenters. » film production

producer gas A gas formed by passing air through hot coke, the chemical reaction being $C + \frac{1}{2}O_2 \rightarrow CO$. This reaction is exothermic, but produces gas of low calorific value – it contains about 60% nitrogen. It is often produced alternately with water gas. » coke; gas **2** [i]; water gas

productivity The ratio of output to input in an industrial context. It usually refers to the quantity of goods or commodities produced in relation to the number of employees engaged in the operation (*labour productivity*). *Total productivity* includes the input of capital also. Low productivity is the major cause of a company's decline, since it results in high costs per unit, and therefore high prices that are not competitive. The notion is important in wage negotiations: *productivity bargaining* balances a proposed increase in wages with an anticipated rise in productivity. » time and motion study

profit The difference for a company between its sales revenue and the costs attributable to those sales. Profit may be calculated before or after deducting interest payments, and before or after deducting taxation charges. The surplus may be paid out to shareholders as a dividend, or retained by the business (as *reserves*) to finance capital expenditure. **Profit sharing** is a scheme whereby a percentage of the profits of a company is given to staff in the form of an additional bonus payment; it may be in the form of cash or of shares in the company. **Profit maximization** is the economic concept that firms will aim to do everything possible to achieve the maximum possible profits – a view which is not considered realistic or possible by some authorities in economics. **Profitability** is the measurement of how effectively a company has used the resources available to it. The ratio of profit to capital employed (ie equity capital, or assets) is commonly used. » company; dividend; equity (economics); satisficing

Profumo, John (Dennis) (1915–) British Conservative politician. Educated at Harrow and Oxford, he became an MP in 1940, and held several government posts before becoming Secretary of State for War in 1960. He resigned in 1963 after admitting that he had been guilty of a grave misdemeanour in deceiving the House of Commons about the nature of his relationship with Miss Christine Keeler, who was at the time also involved with a Russian diplomat. He later sought anonymity in social and charitable services. » Conservative Party

progesterone [pruh**jes**tuhrohn] A steroid present in both sexes of all vertebrates. In mammals it is a hormone critical for the establishment and maintenance of pregnancy. In humans it is primarily secreted by the ovaries and placenta. It acts to prepare the uterus for implantation of the embryo, inhibits ovulation during pregnancy, and prepares the breasts for lactation. It also acts to raise body temperature. » gonad; hormones; pregnancy [i]; steroid [i]

program, computer A complete structured sequence of statements in a programming language or languages which directs a computer to carry out a specific task. The task of writing computer programs is known as **programming**, and the specialists who carry out this task are computer **programmers**. » programming language; systems analysis

programme music Music which paints a scene or tells a story. Among early examples are the violin concertos by Vivaldi called *The Four Seasons*, but it was in the 19th-c, with the increased resources of the symphony orchestra, that composers most widely and effectively gave musical expression to literary and other extra-musical ideas. The concert overture and the symphonic poem proved to be ideal vehicles for this, and in many cases (such as in Smetana's cycle of symphonic poems, *Má Vlast* (1874–9, My Country), they embodied nationalistic ideals and aspirations. The capability of music to convey a 'programme' without the aid of a written commentary is severely limited, but its illustrative powers have been proved many times. » overture; symphonic poem; Smetana; Vivaldi

programmed learning A form of learning developed in the 1960s, based on the behaviourist learning theories of US psychologist B F Skinner. He stressed the need for short frames of information to be given, followed by an active response and the immediate reinforcement of correct answers. The element of self-pacing was also important. Specially designed teaching machines were developed, some on a linear basis with the learner following a fixed sequence of frames, others on a branching principle which permitted a variety of paths through the programme. Though no longer as popular as it was in the 1960s, programmed learning principles have been influential in the development of microcomputer software and the interactive video disc. » behaviourism; Skinner, B F; video disc

programming language An artificial language which allows people to instruct computers to carry out specific tasks. Many programming languages have been developed; among the relatively common high-level languages are ADA, APL, ALGOL, BASIC, COBOL, CORAL, FORTH, FORTRAN, LISP, PASCAL, and PROLOG (*see separate entries*). In addition there are numerous low-level languages which, unlike high-level languages, are specific to particular processors. » assembly language; compiler; interpreter; high-level language; low-level language; program, computer

Progress spacecraft An uncrewed version of the Soviet Soyuz crewed spacecraft, modified as a resupply vehicle for the Salyut and Mir space stations. After unloading, the spacecraft is separated and removed from orbit to burn up in the atmosphere. » Soviet space programme; Soyuz spacecraft; space station

progressive education A term used to denote teaching which places greater emphasis on the wishes of the child. It usually involves greater freedom of choice, activity, and movement than traditional forms of teaching. Progressive education has been pioneered in certain schools such as Summerhill and Dartington Hall, UK, but its influences have spread to other schools, particularly in the primary sector. » education; primary education

Progressive Party (1912–16, 1924) The name used by two separate third-party political initiatives in the USA. The first, essentially a breakaway from the Republicans, centred on former president Roosevelt (in office 1901–9), who was its presidential candidate in 1912. The second developed in 1924 from midwestern farmer and labour discontent. Its presidential candidate, Senator Robert La Follette (1855–1925) of Wisconsin, won four million votes. » Republican Party; Roosevelt, Theodore

progressive taxation Tax levied at a rate which varies as the quantity taxable rises. The notion usually refers to income tax, where the higher the income the greater the rate of tax becomes. » income tax; taxation

Prohibition (1920–33) An attempt to forbid all alcoholic drinks in the USA, authorized by the 18th amendment to the Constitution (1919) and the Volstead Act (1920). Prohibition met great resistance, especially in urban immigrant communities, and generated a large bootlegging industry. It was ended by the repeal of the 18th amendment in 1933. » Anti-Saloon League

projection television A television system in which images are projected through special wide-aperture lenses on a large external screen, usually using three high-brightness cathode ray tubes in the component colours red, green, and blue. Electronic adjustment allows accurate registration of the three colour images, but the limited brightness output limits the width of an external high-reflection screen to c.4 m/13 ft. For larger areas a xenon lamp with video image modulation must be used, as in the eidophor system. » eidophor; television; xenon

projective tests In psychology, a number of somewhat contentious procedures for assessing personality. Their use involves the presentation of ambiguous, vague, or unstructured material onto which the testee is assumed to project his/her personality. They are believed capable of revealing unconscious wishes, complexes, and conflicts, but test results may be influenced by current mood and recent experiences. The most famous is the Rorschach Psychodiagnostic Technique, which required subjects to describe what they see in 10 bilaterally symmetrical inkblots. Other tests include pictures from which subjects make up stories, and the completion of incomplete sentences. » personality

projector An apparatus for presenting an enlarged image on a screen from a transparency such as a photographic slide or film. In a motion picture projector, each frame is held stationary at an illuminated aperture for a brief period, and then advanced by an intermittent sprocket or reciprocating claw, the light being cut off by a rotating shutter during the movement. The sound track on the film is reproduced at a separate sound head where the film is moved continuously at constant speed. Cinema presentation on large screens requires powerful light sources, originally carbon lamps, now xenon lamps of 2 kW to 5 kW, whose light is concentrated on the aperture by a large parabolic mirror. 35 mm film is fed and taken up on large spools, up to 4 000 ft (1 800 m) capacity, mounted above and below the projector body. Continuous loop systems are also widely employed, which can run a complete programme of 4½ hours duration with as much as 24 500 ft (7 500 m) of film fed from horizontal turntables, termed *platters*. 16 mm projectors for smaller screens generally have tungsten-halogen lamps of 250 to 500 W, and use 1 600 ft (500 m) film spools. » cinematography [i]

prokaryote » **procaryote**

Prokofiev, Sergei Sergeyevitch [pro**ko**fyef] (1891–1953) Russian composer, born at Sontsovka, Ukraine. He began to compose at the age of five, studied at the St Petersburg Conservatory, and won a reputation as a virtuoso pianist. During World War 1 he lived in London, and then moved to the USA, until returning to the USSR in 1934. He wrote many

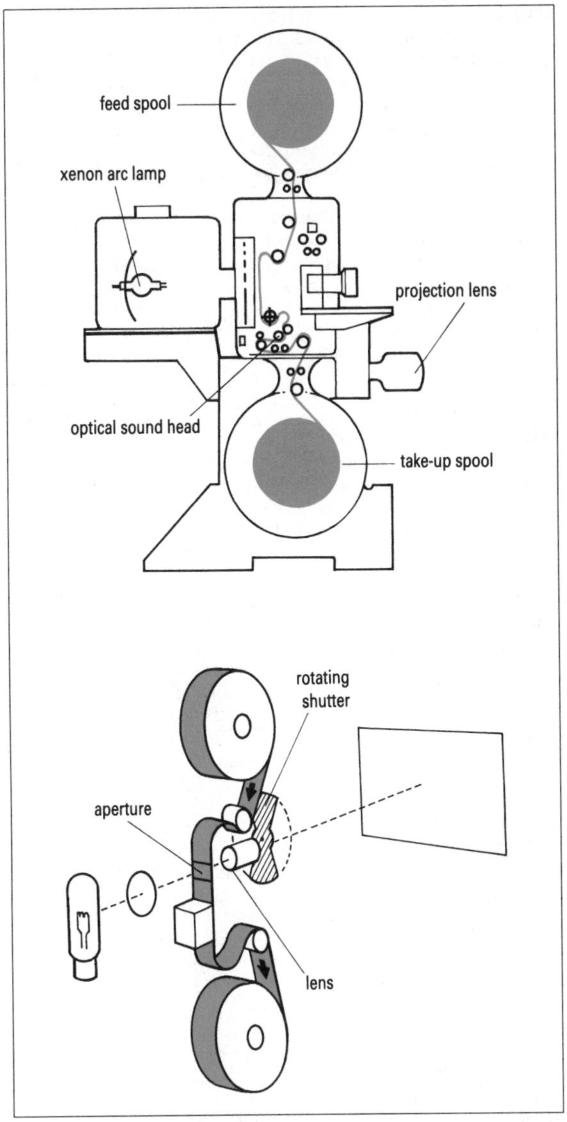

Cine projector principle – Each successive frame of the film is momentarily held stationary while its image is projected on the screen; a rotating shutter obscures the beam during the movement to the next frame.

occasional works for official celebrations, in addition to popular pieces such as *Peter and the Wolf* (1936) and film music. His works have a vast range, including seven symphonies, nine concertos, ballets, operas, suites, cantatas, sonatas, and songs. He died in Moscow.

Prokop (the Bald), or **Procop(ius)** (c.1380–1434) Bohemian Hussite leader, a follower of Žiška, and on his death, the leader of the Taborites. He carried out raids into Silesia, Saxony, and Franconia, and repeatedly defeated German armies. With his colleague, Prokop (the Younger), he fell in battle at Lipany, Hungary. » Hussites; Žiška

prolactin A hormone secreted by the front part of the pituitary gland (*adenohypophysis*) which initiates lactation in mammals and stimulates the production of another hormone, progesterone, by the corpus luteum. » corpus luteum; hormones; lactation; pituitary gland

prolapsed intervertebral disc A condition which arises when the nucleus of the disc situated between the bodies of the vertebrae is forced outwards through the surrounding joint capsule; commonly known as a **slipped disc**. It is caused by an excessive load being placed on the joints between the bodies of the spinal vertebrae, such as in heavy or awkward lifting, and is followed by sudden or rapidly developing back pain or sciatica. Common levels for disc prolapse are in the lower back (between lumbar vertebrae 4–5 and lumbar 5 and sacral vertebrae 1) and in the neck. » vertebral column

proletariat In radical and socialist philosophy, a term coined to denote the working class, ie those who live by their labour and do not own property. It is particularly important in Marxist and communist ideology, though it has no distinctive meaning from 'wage labour'. *Lumpenproletariat* was coined by Marx to refer to those in big cities from whom class identification could be expected. » Marxism

PROLOG A high-level programming language based on mathematical logic, widely used in artificial intelligence applications. It was developed at the University of Aix-Marseille in France and in the UK at Imperial College and Edinburgh University. PROLOG has, to some extent, replaced LISP. » LISP; programming language

PROM An acronym of **programmable read-only memory**, a special type of integrated circuit read-only memory (ROM) into which the user can write data after manufacture. Once written, the data cannot be altered. » EAROM; EPROM; ROM

promenade concert A musical performance, especially by an orchestra, during which some at least of the audience are offered floor space, without seats, at reduced prices. The London 'proms' were started at the Queen's Hall by Sir Henry Wood in 1895; they transferred to the Royal Albert Hall in 1941. » orchestra; Wood, Henry

Prometheus [prohmeethiuhs] In Greek mythology, a Titan, son of Iapetus and brother of Epimetheus; originally a trickster who outwits Zeus; his name means 'the foreseeing'. He made human beings out of clay, and taught them the arts of civilization. He stole fire from heaven to help mankind, whom Zeus wished to destroy, and was punished by being chained to a rock in the Caucasus; every day an eagle fed on his liver, which grew again in the night. He knew a secret which concerned Zeus' future, and bargained for his release. Heracles, passing through the Caucasus, shot the eagle and set Prometheus free. » Heracles; Loki; Pandora; Thetis

promissory note A signed document containing a written promise to undertake to pay a sum of money on or by a specific date. The document is legally binding and is signed, for example, when a bank customer takes out a loan. A particular form is a *commercial paper*, issued by large companies, which can be bought and sold. » commercial paper

pronation A movement of the forearm so that the palm of the hand is brought to face backwards, with the thumb towards the body. In this position the radius lies across the ulna. » arm; supination

prongbuck » **pronghorn**

pronghorn A N American antelope; male called **prongbuck**; pale brown with prominent eyes; female horns short; male horns with frontal 'prong' and backward curving tips; outer layer of horns shed each year; will approach moving objects (including predators); inhabits grasslands. (*Antilocapra americana*.) » antelope

proof spirit » **alcohol strength**

propane C_3H_8, boiling point $-42°C$. The third in the alkane series of hydrocarbons; a gas obtained from petroleum and natural gas, used as a fuel and a refrigerant. » alkanes; gas **2** [i]; propyl

propanone » **acetone**

propellant 1 An explosive which produces a violent but steady pressure, such as is needed to expel a projectile from a gun. Gunpowder, suitably graded, was the first. After the high explosive properties of nitroglycerine and nitrocellulose had been discovered, attempts were made to moderate their disruptive effect to make them useful as propellants. Success was achieved with various gelatinized mixtures, notably Cordite. » explosives **2** A rocket fuel which functions not by exerting pressure but by the recoil effect of the expulsion of gases at high speed (which is why a rocket can be propelled in empty space). Many forms exist, some solid, some liquid (eg hydrazine with dinitrogen tetroxide). » rocket

propeller A device used principally by ships and aeroplanes to transform the rotational energy of an engine into directed thrust. To accomplish this, the propeller is fitted with blades radiating from a central hub, each blade being of aerofoil cross section. As the propeller rotates, the water or air is accelerated backwards, producing an opposite reactive force in the propeller and its shaft. This reactive force acts in the forward direction, which is transmitted to the craft as the propulsive force. » aerodynamics [i]; aeroplane; propfan; ship [i]

Propertius, Sextus (c.48–c.15 BC) The greatest Latin elegiac poet, born (probably) at Asisium (Assisi), Italy. He travelled to Rome (c.34 BC), where he became a poet, winning the favour of Maecenas and Emperor Augustus. The central figure of his inspiration was his mistress, to whom he devoted the first of his four surviving books, *Cynthia*. Much of his work was published after his death, in Rome. » elegy; Maecenas; poetry; Latin literature

property Something owned or possessed – a notion whose precise definition varies greatly between different jurisdictions. In English law, **real property** includes lands and buildings; also, intangible interests in land, such as easements. Other kinds of property are known as **personal property**. Leases are classified as personal property, and are also referred to as 'chattels real'. **Chattels** are moveable goods, classed as personal property. A gift of personal property made by will is a **legacy**; a gift of real property made by will is a **devise**. A devise may specify the property involved; it may be worded to cover all property; or it may deal only with the residue of property, following a specific devise. **Intellectual property** is a general term covering intangible rights in the product of intellectual effort. It includes copyright in published work, and patents granted to protect new inventions. » copyright; easement; fixture; lease; mortgage; restrictive covenant

propfan An aircraft propeller designed for a turbo-engine, enabling large amounts of power to be delivered by increasing the number and area of the blades in comparison with a conventional aircraft propeller. A particular feature of such propellers is the swept back or 'skew' nature of the blades, which allows quieter operation for the rotational speeds involved. » propeller; turbine

prophet One who is inspired to reveal a message from a divine being; an important figure in many religious traditions, sometimes with cultic functions, but sometimes a lone figure opposing the established cult or social order (eg Jeremiah, Amos, and Hosea in the Old Testament). Although their messages may acquire an enduring relevance, they usually address a specific situation or problem. In the New Testament, prophets are listed after apostles in Paul's lists of Christian ministries (1 *Cor* 12.28f; *Eph* 4.11), but the problem of false prophets is also of concern in some works (*Matt* 7.15; 1 *John* 4.1). » God; New Testament; Old Testament; oracle

proportional counter A device for monitoring the path of charged particles produced in particle physics experiments. Arrays of wire electrodes give an electric field which accelerates ions produced by a passage of charged particles. The ions cause pulses in electrodes that are recorded electronically to give a map of the particle track. Drift chambers and multi-wire proportional chambers are common forms of proportional counter. » particle detectors

proportional representation Any system of voting designed to ensure that the representation of voters is in proportion to their numbers. There are many voting methods, none of which achieves perfect proportionality. In the *list system* the number of candidates on a party's list who are elected depends on the proportion of votes they receive in national elections. In the *single transferable vote*, votes are cast in multi-member constituencies and an ordered preference for all the candidates can be expressed on the ballot paper, votes being transferred from one candidate to another to enable them to gain the necessary quota to be elected. Proportional representation comes close to meeting the democratic principle of majority government; examples can be found in most W European countries (but not the UK). The case against it is that it does not in fact produce majority party government, but unstable coalitions, and breaks the bond between MPs and their constituencies.

propositional logic » **logic**

proprioception » **kinaesthesis**

propyl [**proh**piyl, **proh**pil] $CH_3CH_2CH_2$–. A group derived from propane. **Isopropyl** is the isomeric $(CH_3)_2$. Propyl and isopropyl alcohols (propan-1-ol and propan-2-ol) are both used as solvents and as substitutes for ethanol in non-beverage applications. » ethanol; propane

propylaeum or **propylaea** [prohpi**lee**um, prohpi**lee**a] An important entrance gateway or vestibule. It is usually in front of a sacred building, as on the Acropolis, Athens (437–432 BC). » Acropolis; Greek architecture

proscenium An arch and opening of a stage wall separating the auditorium of a theatre from the acting and scenic area. From its origins in the stagecraft of Peruzzi (1481–1537), Serlio (1475–1554) and others, its development, linked to a concept of theatrical illusion, dominated Western drama until the early 20th-c. In its early form, it was a frame for perspective scenery, and a permanent structure, with doors for actors' exits and entrances, embracing a deep acting area (which was also known as the proscenium). In time it became the narrowest of picture frames enclosing a common world of scenery and action. The process culminated – through the coincidence of naturalism and the ability to darken the auditorium – in the notion of the proscenium as a 'fourth wall' through which the audience, sitting in darkness, could see and eavesdrop. » open stage; stage

prose (Lat *prosa oratio* 'straightforward discourse') Non-metrical writing, or indeed speech (Molière's M Jourdain was impressed to realize that he spoke prose). There is a natural tendency to regard prose as direct and unadorned, the clear pane of expression beside the stained glass of poetry. Such limpid prose was recommended to the members of the Royal Society in 1667 – an attitude which continues to be found in such works as Ernest Gower's *Plain Words* (1948). But prose may be as elaborate, complex, and figurative as any poetry, as may be seen in the works of Cicero, Rabelais, Swift, Dickens, Proust, and Joyce. » figurative language; literature; poetry; prose poem

prose poem A composition printed continuously, as prose, but sharing many features (rhythm, imagery) with poetry. Aloysius Bertrand's *Gaspard de la nuit* (1842), followed by Baudelaire's *Petits poemes en prose* (1869), established the genre, which overlaps with the very short story, as practised by Kafka and others. » Baudelaire; Kafka; literature; poetry; prose

Proserpine » **Persephone**

prosimian A primate of the suborder *Strepsirhini* (40 species); wet nose with slit-like nostrils; tip of nose, between nostrils, with an obvious vertical groove; also known as **primitive primate**. » aye-aye; indri; lemur; loris; potto

prosody The pitch, loudness, tempo, and rhythm of speech. A particular application of prosodic study is in relation to poetry, where it provides a means of analysing the rhythmical properties of lines (*metrics*), as part of the study of versification. Prosodic features play an important role in forming the stress patterns within words and phrases, and the intonation patterns within sentences. » intonation; metre (literature)

prosopography The study of human behaviour through collective biography, aiming to explain people's actions through knowledge of their personal backgrounds – sex, education, age, wealth, class, and family relations. It was applied to 18th-c British history by Sir Lewis Namier, but found to be of limited value in periods of ideological division, such as the 16th-c and 17th-c. » Namier

Prost, Alain (1955–) French motor racing driver, born at St Chamond, the first Frenchman to win the world title. He won in 1985–6 (both for Marlboro-McLaren), and was runner-up in 1983–4 and 1988. In 1987 he surpassed Jackie Stewart's record of 27 wins, and between 1980 and 1988 won 35 races from 137 starts. His 493½ championship points is a world record. » motor racing; Stewart, Jackie

prostaglandins A family of unsaturated fatty acids produced by virtually every tissue of the body in response to particular stimuli. They are largely derived from arachidonic acid present in the plasma membrane, and probably act locally at sites of production. Their physiological role is unclear, but they are implicated in the breakdown of the corpus luteum, platelet function, the natural prevention of ulcers, and the causes of inflammation. » arachidonic acid; carboxylic acids; Graafian follicle

prostate gland A partly muscular, partly glandular, accessory male sex organ in mammals, lying within the pelvis below the bladder, encircling part of the urethra. The ejaculatory ducts also pass through the gland to enter the urethra. It is small at birth and grows rapidly during puberty to attain adult size within a year. During sexual arousal it contributes (via numerous ducts opening into the urethra) an alkaline fluid to semen, accounting for approximately one third of its volume and giving it its characteristic odour. The gland can be divided into a number of lobes: a mainly muscular lobe towards the front, lobes at the sides (enlargement of which may compress and narrow the urethra and bulge into the bladder, obstructing micturition), a middle lobe, and a lobe towards the back (often the site of cancer of the prostate). After age 50 the gland may atrophy; however, an excessive increase in the size of the side and middle lobes may also occur, compressing the urethra, and adversely affecting the functioning of the kidneys. Treatment involves the removal of part or all of the gland. » semen; urinary system

prosthesis An artificial substitute for a part of the body. Examples include a mechanical arm or leg, artificial dentures, and tooth implants. » dentistry

Protagoras [prohtaguhras] (c.490–421 BC) The earliest self-proclaimed Greek Sophist, born at Abdera. He taught mainly in Athens, presenting a system of practical wisdom fitted to train men for citizen's duties, and based on the doctrine that 'man is the measure of all things'. His doctrine that all beliefs are true was examined in great detail and rejected by Plato. All his works are lost except a fragment of his treatise *On the Gods*. He died at sea. » Sophists

protea [prohtia] A shrub or small tree, native to tropical and especially S Africa, where they are very diverse; leaves entire or divided, leathery. The large and often spectacular 'flowers' are actually inflorescences containing numerous small true flowers in the centre, surrounded by stiff, often brightly-coloured, petal-like bracts. (Genus: *Protea*, 130 species. Family: *Proteaceae*.) » bract; inflorescence [i]; shrub; tree [i]

protectionism A government policy of protecting domestic industries against foreign competition by building tariff walls or by giving subsidies to local firms. It is often used for 'infant industries' which a state wishes to see grow. The policy can lead to retaliation by other countries, so that exports are not accepted. » quotas, import; tariff

protective coloration/colouration The coloration pattern of an animal, serving a protective function. **Cryptic coloration** camouflages the animal against its background. **Disruptive coloration** delays recognition of the whole animal by attracting the predator's attention to elements of the colour pattern. **Warning coloration** is conspicuous, and advertises the unpalatable, poisonous, or otherwise harmful properties of an animal to a potential predator. » ethology; Plate IX

protectorate A territory over which the protecting state enjoys power and jurisdiction short of full sovereignty; not formally annexed, it can come about by treaty, grant, or usage. A *protected state* is a form of protectorate where the territory is more like a unified state and has its own identifiable rulers. The commonest types were the 19th–20th-c colonial protectorates, Botswana being a British example, all of which have now achieved independence. » Protectorate

Protectorate A regime established by Instrument of Government, the work of army conservatives, England's only written constitution. The Lord Protectors, Oliver Cromwell (ruled 1653–8) and his son Richard (ruled 1658–9), issued ordinances and controlled the armed forces, subject to the advice of a Council of State and with Parliament as legislative partner. It failed to win support, and its collapse led to the Restoration. » Commonwealth (English history); Cromwell, Oliver; Restoration

protein One of the three essential types of energy foods. It is a natural condensation polymer of amino acids occurring mainly as structural tissue in animals (fibrous proteins, mainly water insoluble, eg silk) but also as enzymes in both animals and plants (globular proteins, largely water soluble, eg haemoglobin). Nearly all proteins are derived from 20 amino acids. » amino acid [i]; carbohydrate; fat; peptide

Proterozoic eon The later of the two geological eons into which the Precambrian era is divided; the period of time from 2 500 million years ago until the beginning of the Cambrian period 590 million years ago. » Archaean eon; geological time scale; Precambrian era; RR16

Protestant Ethic The term coined by the German sociologist Max Weber to describe the conduct and attitudes of the non-conformist religious groups of the Reformation period, such as the Lutheran and Calvinist forms of Protestantism. Weber drew most attention to the idea common to all such groups that believers must be diligent, disciplined, and fully committed to their worldly duties and tasks in order to 'glorify God'. He argued that the sort of conduct this inspired at work and at home helped to promote the growth of industry and capitalist enterprise. The careful use of one's resources, being thrifty, investing wisely, and acting with moderation not only made good religious sense but led to sound business practice as well. » Reformation; Protestantism; Weber, Max

Protestantism The generic term for expressions of Christian faith originating from the 16th-c Reformation as a protest against Roman Catholicism. Common characteristics include the authority of scripture, justification by faith alone, and the priesthood of all believers. The original groupings were those who followed Luther, Calvin, and Zwingli, and the term now embraces most non-Roman Catholic or non-Orthodox denominations. » Anabaptists; Baptists; Calvinism; Church of Scotland; Congregationalism; Dutch Reformed Church; Episcopal Church, Protestant; Lutheranism; Nonconformists; Orthodox Church; Presbyterianism; Reformation; Roman Catholicism; Unitarians; Zwingli

proteus [prohtiuhs] A typically rod-shaped bacterium that moves by means of flagella. Many strains exhibit swarming behaviour. They are found primarily in the intestines and faeces of humans and other animals. Some species cause disease. (Kingdom: *Monera*. Family: *Enterobacteriaceae*.) » bacteria [i]; intestine

Proteus [prohtiuhs] In Greek mythology, a sea god, associated with seals, and a shape-changer; he will give answers to questions after a wrestling match. He is sometimes to be found on the island of Pharos, in Egypt, where Menelaus wrestled with him. » Menelaus

Protista [pruhtista] A kingdom of relatively simple organisms, comprising the single-celled protozoans and those algae and fungi that possess flagellated spores. They typically possess, at some stage in their life cycle, a true flagellum (a whip-like organelle containing a ring of nine microtubules surrounding two central tubules). » algae; flagellum; fungus; kingdom; Protozoa

Proto-Indo-European » **Indo-European languages**

Protoceratops [prohtuhseratops] A primitive ceratopsian dinosaur, known from the Upper Cretaceous period of E Asia; rear frill on skull well developed; teeth for shearing, and powerful enough to cope with extremely tough plants; probably lived in herds and shared common nursery sites for egg-laying. (Order: *Ornithischia*.) » Cretaceous period; dinosaur [i]

protochordate [prohtohkawdayt] An informal name for any of the chordates (phylum: *Chordata*) that lack a vertebral column. These invertebrate chordates include the amphioxus (subphylum: *Cephalochordata*) and the tunicates (subphylum: *Tunicata*). » amphioxus; Chordata; tunicate

Protocols of the Elders of Zion A fraudulent document, originally printed in Russia (1903) and much translated, ostensibly reporting discussions among Jewish elders of plans to subvert Christian civilization and erect a world Zionist state. Exposed as forgeries in *The Times* (1921), the 'Protocols' have nevertheless been, and remain, a staple of right-wing, anti-semitic propaganda. » Zionism

proton A component particle of the atomic nucleus; symbol p; mass 1.673×10^{-27} kg (938.3 MeV), charge +1, spin $\frac{1}{2}$. It is held in the nucleus by strong nuclear force, sufficient to overcome the repulsion due to other protons. Free protons are not known to decay. » deuterium; nuclear structure; nucleus (physics); proton number; quark

proton number The number of protons in an atomic nucleus, equal to the number of electrons in an atom; symbol Z; also called **atomic number**. Each element has a unique proton number. Isotopes of an element have the same proton number, but a different nucleon number. » atom; nucleon number; proton

protoplasm The complex, translucent substance that makes up every living cell. It includes the plasma membrane, but excludes such elements as ingested material and masses of secretion. In eucaryotes, protoplasm is divisible into *nucleoplasm* (the protoplasm in the nucleus) and *cytoplasm* (the protoplasm in the rest of the cell). » cell; cytoplasm; eucaryote

protostar A collapsing sphere of gas, of sufficient mass to make a star, but in which nuclear reactions have not yet started. Such objects can be detected with infrared telescopes on account of the great amount of heat released by the collapse, and the ability of infrared to pass from the centre to the outside of the gas. The phase lasts 10^5–10^7 years. » infrared astronomy; star

Protozoa A diverse group of unicellular micro-organisms found free-living, as consumers of organic matter, in all kinds of habitats, and as parasites or associates of other organisms; typically possess a single nucleus, sometimes two or more; usually reproduce by splitting in two (binary fission), but sexual reproductive processes are known to occur; includes many disease-causing organisms. » amoeba; cell; parasitology; radiolaria; reproduction; Sarcodina

protozoology The study of the *Protozoa*, a diverse group of single-celled eucaryotic micro-organisms which feed by ingesting or absorbing organic matter. » eucaryote; Protozoa

Protura [pruh**tyoo**ra] An order of small, primitively wingless insects that lack eyes and antennae; use forelegs as feelers; possess three pairs of rudimentary limbs (*styli*) on abdominal segments; found under stones and bark, or in rotting vegetation; c.120 species. » insect [i]

Proudhon, Pierre Joseph [**proo**dõ] (1809–65) French socialist and political theorist, born at Besançon. In Paris he wrote his first important book, *Qu'est-ce que la propriété?* (1840, What is Property?), affirming the bold paradox 'property is theft', because it involves the exploitation of the labour of others. He then published his greatest work, the *Système des contradictions économiques* (1846, System of Economic Contradictions). During the 1848 Revolution, the violence of his utterances brought him three years' imprisonment, and after further arrest (1858) he retired to Belgium. Amnestied in 1860, he died near Paris. » Revolutions of 1848; socialism

Proust, Marcel [proost] (1871–1922) French novelist, born at Auteuil. A semi-invalid from asthma, he was looked after by his mother, and her death in 1905 caused him to withdraw from society, living in a sound-proofed flat, and giving himself over entirely to introspection. He then devoted himself to writing, and in 1912 produced the first part of his 13-volume masterpiece, *À la recherche du temps perdu* (Remembrance of Things Past). The second volume of this work, delayed by the war, won the Prix Goncourt in 1919. The next volumes brought him an international reputation, and he was able to complete the last six volumes (but not revise them) before his death, in Paris. His massive novel, exploring the power of the memory and the unconscious, as well as the nature of writing itself, has been profoundly influential. » French literature; novel

Provence [provãs], Lat **Provincia** Former province in SE France on the Mediterranean coast, now occupying departments of Bouches-du-Rhône, Var, Basses-Alpes, and parts of Alpes-Maritimes and Vaucluse; formerly part of the kingdom of Arles; part of France, 1481; distinctive Romance dialect; coal, bauxite, lead, zinc, salt; market-gardening, grapes, olives, perfumes, tourism (especially on Riviera). » France [i]

Proverbs, Book of A book of the Hebrew Bible/Old Testament, attributed in the opening title to Solomon, but probably consisting of collected wisdom traditions from several centuries. It contains several sub-collections: Chapters 1–9 include poems about personified Wisdom, and moral admonitions of a father to his son; Chapters 10–29 present sets of individual sayings on virtues and vices with little thematic arrangement, similar to Egyptian wisdom instructions; Chapters 30–31 are two appendices, ending with a poem about the virtuous wife. » Old Testament; Solomon (Old Testament)

providence The belief that all things are ultimately ordered and governed by God towards a purpose. Some form of this belief features in Judaism, Islam, and Christianity, and is implied in the belief in the trustworthiness, goodness, and power of God. Human free-will is not generally denied, it being claimed that God either overrules it or works through it. » Christianity; God; Islam; Judaism

Providence 41°49N 71°24W, pop(1980) 156 804. Capital of Rhode Island, USA; port at the head of Providence R, in Providence County; established, 1636; city status, 1832; an early haven for religious dissenters; airport; railway; Brown University (1764); jewellery and silverware, fabricated metals, equipment; first Baptist and Unitarian churches, State Capitol, museum of art; its excellent harbour makes it a popular sailing resort, as well as a major port for oil tankers. » Dissenters; Rhode Island

Providencia » **San Andrés-Providencia**

Provincetown Players A US theatre group (1915–29) remembered for the work of its leading playwright Eugene O'Neill and designer Robert Edmond Jones. » O'Neill, Eugene; theatre

Provisional IRA » **IRA**

Provisional Sinn Féin » **Sinn Féin**

Provisions of Oxford » **Oxford, Provisions of**

proxemics [prok**see**miks] The study of how people use physical space as an aspect of non-verbal communication. It is concerned with the intimate, personal, social, and public distances that individuals, classes, and cultures maintain in their interactions with each other. Several research studies have now been made of such behaviours as how closely people sit together, how much they touch each other while talking, and how they vary their practices of hand-shaking, and significant cultural and personal differences have been demonstrated. » non-verbal communication

Proxima Centauri [**prok**sima sen**taw**ree] » **Centaurus**

Prud'hon, Pierre Paul [**prü**dõ] (1758–1823) French painter, born at Cluny. He studied in Dijon, trained with engravers in Paris, and went to Rome. He returned to work in a refined style not in accord with revolutionary Paris. Patronized, however, by the empresses of Napoleon, he was made court painter, and among his best work is a portait of Josephine. He died in Paris. » French art; Napoleon I

Prudhoe Bay [**proo**doh] Bay on N coast of Alaska, USA, on the Beaufort Sea; pipeline links Arctic oil fields with Valdez on the Gulf of Alaska. » Alaska

prunus A large genus of temperate trees and shrubs containing many well-known ornamentals and orchard fruits, such as cherry, plum, peach, and almond; flowers with five petals and usually 20 stamens; fruit a single stony seed surrounded by a fleshy outer layer. (Genus: *Prunus*, 400 species. Family: *Rosaceae*.) » almond; apricot; blackthorn; cherry; cherry laurel/plum; drupe; peach; plum; shrub; stamen; tree [i]

Prussia A N European state, originally centred in the E Baltic region as a duchy owing suzerainty to Poland. Inherited by the German house of Brandenburg in the early 17th-c, Brandenburg-Prussia was consolidated and expanded, and Polish sovereignty thrown off, by Frederick William the 'Great Elector' (1620–88). The kingdom of Prussia was founded in 1701; under Frederick William I (1713–40) and Frederick II ('the Great') (1740–86) it acquired W Prussia and Silesia, and gained considerable territory in W Germany at the Congress of Vienna (1815). During the 19th-c it emerged as the most powerful German state, and ultimately the focus of German unification. Within the German Empire (1871–1918) and the Weimar Republic (1919–33), it retained considerable autonomy and influence. As a legal entity, Prussia ceased to exist with the post-1945 division of Germany and the establishment of a revised E German-Polish frontier. » Austro-Prussian War; Franco-Prussian War; Frederick William; Frederick William III; German Confederation; North German Confederation; Zollverein

prussic acid » cyanide; hydrocyanic acid

Prynne, William (1600–69) English Puritan pamphleteer, born at Swanswick, Somerset. Educated at Oxford, he was called to the Bar, but was early drawn into controversy. In 1633 appeared his *Histrio-Mastix: the Players Scourge*, which contained an apparent attack on the Queen; for this he was tortured, fined, and imprisoned. Released in 1640 by the Long Parliament, he prosecuted Laud (1644), and became an MP (1648). Purged from the House in 1650, he was again imprisoned (1650–2). After Cromwell's death he returned to parliament as a Royalist, for which he was made Keeper of the Tower Records. He died in London. » Laud; Long Parliament; Protectorate; Puritanism

Przewalski's horse [pruhzhuh**val**skee] A rare wild horse, native to the steppes fringing the Gobi Desert; thought to be a 'steppe type' ancestor of modern domestic breeds; reddish-brown with stiff, erect black mane and white muzzle; named after 19th-c Russian soldier and explorer Nikolai Przewalski; also known as **Mongolian wild horse**, or **Asiatic wild horse**. » horse [i]; tarpan

Psalms, Book of A book of the Hebrew Bible/Old Testament, designated *tehillim* (Heb 'songs'), but the name 'Psalms' deriving from the Greek translation; also known as the **Psalter**. It consists of 150 hymns or poems of various types, including songs of thanksgiving, individual and community laments, wisdom poetry, and royal and enthronement songs. Many of the poems have individual titles and attributions, and the collection represents material from several centuries, brought together in its present form probably in the post-exilic period. The Psalter is regularly used in Jewish and Christian worship, its hymns admired for the religious insights of their composers. It was the most important type of mediaeval illustrated book. » Old Testament

Psalter » Psalms, Book of

psaltery A mediaeval zither, constructed in various shapes, with a wooden soundbox and strings played by the fingers or with a plectrum. It is considered the ancestor of the dulcimer, which replaced it in the 15th-c. The word *psaltery* was earlier used for any plucked string instrument. » dulcimer; plectrum; string instrument **2** [i]; zither

Psamtik I (?–610 BC) King of Egypt (664–610 BC) who liberated Egypt from Assyrian control, and founded the 26th dynasty. » Assyria

psephology The study of elections and voting. It is popularly associated with the analysis of voting figures and the forecasting of outcomes, but covers all aspects of elections including legal frameworks, candidate selection, sociological and geographical analysis of voting patterns, and electoral systems.

Pseudepigrapha [syooduh**pig**rafa] An ancient Jewish (and sometimes Christian) body of literature which is not part of the Jewish Scriptures or of major Christian versions of the Old Testament or of the Apocrypha, but which is similar to the Old Testament in character, in that its works claim to present a divine message, derived from Old Testament characters or ideas. Strictly the term means works 'written under a false name', but this does not adequately distinguish this literature from the Old Testament or Apocrypha. This large collection of writings spans roughly the period 200 BC–200 AD, although it was first collected by Johannes Fabricius (1668–1736). It includes apocalypses (eg 1 Enoch, 4 Ezra), testaments (eg Testaments of the 12 Patriarchs), wisdom literature, prayers and psalms (eg Prayer of Manasseh, Psalms of Solomon), and additions to Old Testament stories (eg Life of Adam and Eve). » Apocrypha, Old Testament; Bible; Jubilees, Book of; Judaism; Maccabees, Books of the; Old Testament; Manasseh, Prayer of; Solomon, Psalms of; testament literature

Pseudo-Isidorian Forgeries A collection of genuine and spurious materials made by Frankish churchmen c.850, primarily to stress the authority and independence of bishops. It incorporates forged decretals (papal decrees) which 'Isodorus Mercator' claimed to have gathered together. Regarded as authoritative by 11th-c popes, these helped justify papal claims during the Investiture Controversy. » Franks; Investiture Controversy

pseudopodium [syoodoh**poh**diuhm] A lobe-like protrusion, usually temporary, of the cell body of amoeboid cells brought about by cytoplasmic streaming. Pseudopodia function as a means of locomotion, and also as a way of feeding (by engulfing food particles). » amoeba; cell; cytoplasm

psi A parapsychological term for certain paranormal processes, embracing both extrasensory perception and psychokinesis. The term was introduced by British psychologist R H Thouless, being the letter of the Greek alphabet most appropriate to stand for things considered as psychic. » extrasensory perception; psi-missing; psychokinesis

psi-missing A parapsychological term applied to formal tests of extrasensory perception or psychokinesis in which the person being tested produces results that are actually below the level expected by chance. It is analogous to consistent 'bad luck'. » psi

psittacosis [(p)situh**koh**sis] A systemic infection associated with pneumonia, caused by a micro-organism (*Chlamydia*) contracted from infected birds; also known as **parrot disease**. The pneumonia may be severe. Chlamydial infections are best treated with the antibiotic tetracycline or one of its derivatives. » chlamydia; infection; pneumonia

Pskov School Russian icon and mural painters active c.1200–c.1500 in the city of Pskov. Byzantine influence is very evident. » Byzantine art; Russian art

psoriasis [(p)so**riy**uhsis] A common persisting or recurring skin disorder, in which small red scaly patches form in the superficial layers of the skin. The lesions particularly affect the elbows, knees, scalp, and nails. The cause is unknown, but the turnover of the basal cells of the skin is increased. The condition causes a great deal of personal distress. It rarely threatens life, but may do so when it becomes widespread and severe (*exfoliative psoriasis*). » skin [i]

Psyche [**siy**kee] In Greek mythology, 'the soul', usually represented by a butterfly. In the story told by Apuleius, she was beloved by Cupid, who hid her in an enchanted palace, and visited her at night, forbidding her to look at him. Her sisters persuaded her to light a lamp; she saw Cupid, but was separated from him, and given impossible tasks by Venus, who impeded her search for him. The story is an allegory of love and the soul. » Cupid

psychedelic art An art style that flourished in the late 1960s, influenced by the craze for hallucinatory drugs, especially LSD. Typical designs feature abstract swirls of high-key colour, sometimes accompanied by calligraphy in a curvilinear style derived from Art Nouveau. » abstract art; Art Nouveau

psychedelic drugs » hallucinogens

psychiatry A branch of medicine concerned with the study, diagnosis, prevention, and treatment of mental and emotional disorders. Its pattern of practice derives from many other disciplines (such as philosophy, psychology, biology, and ethology) and incorporates a wide range of treatment modalities. Within psychiatry, there is a range of sub-specialities including *child psychiatry*, *liaison psychiatry* (the study of patients with other physical illnesses concurrent with psychological and mental difficulties), *forensic psychiatry* (the study and treatment of patients who have broken the law), and *psychotherapy*. The range of conditions treated by psychiatrists is wide, and includes patients suffering from psychoses (in which there is a loss of contact with reality), neuroses (in which anxiety plays a major component), eating disorders, disorders of dependence, mental retardation, and sleep disorders. The term *psychiatry* was coined in 1847. Society's attitude to the mentally ill has undergone a series of changes, and has often been influenced by those working outside of the psychiatric domain. Important contributors to modern attitudes concerning the mentally ill were the French physician Philippe Pinel (1745–1826) and the British philanthropist William Tuke (1732–1822). There has been a range of contributors to various aspects of psychiatry. Freud, Adler, Jung and many others have contributed to the psychological and psychoanalytic schools. Pavlov, Skinner, Solpe, and Beck have contributed to behavioural aspects. The German psychiatrist Emil Kraepelin (1856–1926) contributed the definition of clinical syndromes. » Adler; anti-psychiatry; autism; behaviour therapy; biological psychiatry; forensic psychiatry; Freud, Sigmund; hallucination; Jung; mental disorders; neurosis; Pavlov; psychoanalysis; psychosis; Skinner

psychical research » **parapsychology**

psychoanalysis The theory and clinical practice of a form of psychology which emphasizes unconscious aspects of the mental life of an individual. The treatment, pioneered by Freud, is a form of therapy which attempts to eliminate conflict by altering the personality in a positive way. Freud introduced ideas concerning the use of the study of dreams as a way of understanding people's deeper emotions; he emphasized the introspective study of the self and, with colleagues such as Adler, Karl Abraham (1877–1925), and Jung, advanced ideas about normal and abnormal psychological processes. The first Psychoanalytic Society was in Austria, but both a combination of differences of views and wider political events led to psychoanalysis having a greater impact on N American as opposed to European psychiatry. » Adler; Freud, Sigmund; Jung; repression; unconscious

psychodrama A technique involving a combination of behavioural and psychoanalytic psychotherapy which makes use of the dramatic presentation of personal life situations. Through these, the patient learns new ways of dealing with both emotional and interpersonal problems. » dramatherapy; group therapy

psychohistory A method of historical study using psychoanalytic methods, especially those of Sigmund Freud, who attempted analyses of Leonardo da Vinci and Woodrow Wilson. Its leading practitioner is Erik H Erikson (1902–), whose *Young Man Luther* (1958) shocked traditional historians by connecting the reformer's theological breakthrough with an 'identity crisis', the result of an allegedly unhappy childhood, uneasy relations with parents as an adolescent, and chronic constipation. Psychohistory has also studied Charles I, Archbishop Laud, Gandhi, and President Nixon. While sometimes successful in showing the relationship between personalities and history, psychohistory suffers from a concentration upon individuals and from a failure to explain larger movements. » psychoanalysis

psychokinesis (PK) One of the two major categories of allegedly paranormal phenomena studied by parapsychologists (the other being extrasensory perception). It is defined as the influencing by a living agent of a physical system or object by means other than those currently understood by the physical sciences. The phenomenon was earlier referred to as **telekinesis**. » extrasensory perception; paranormal; parapsychology; psi

psycholinguistics The study of the psychology of language. Psycholinguists are variously concerned with first and second language acquisition, language production and comprehension, and linguistic deficits such as aphasia and dyslexia. The central goal of the subject is to marry the methods and theories of the linguist with those of the psychologist. For example, a linguist might propose a grammar that accurately describes the structure of English, but the psycholinguist must try to explain how such a grammar could be learned by an infant with limited perceptual and mnemonic capacities. » linguistics; psychology

psychologism Any philosophical thesis which maintains that inquiry into some field of knowledge is or should be an investigation of the workings of the mind. Some versions stress the importance of introspection; others insist only that inquiry take account of the mind's abilities and causal relations to what is known. Mill defended psychologism with respect to logic and mathematics; such attempts were attacked by Husserl and Frege. » Frege; Husserl; Mill, J S; psychology

psychology The science of mental life – a succinct definition used by US psychologist William James in 1890. Modern psychology began with the great advances in science and medicine of the 19th-c, including the work of Darwin on comparative studies of behaviour, Galton on inheritance and variation in human abilities, Helmholtz and others on the functions of the nervous system, Fechner on the basis of psychophysics, and Freud on the explanation of 'irrational' behaviour. In 1879, Wundt established in Leipzig the first laboratory entirely devoted to experimental psychology. The turn of the century saw the publication of Binet and Simon's work on testing the intelligence of French school children. Pavlov's work on the conditioned reflex had a profound influence on theories of learning and their practical applications. At the same time, Thorndike's studies of animal learning in the USA laid the basis for behaviourism, developed by Watson, and later by Skinner, in an attempt to give a complete account of human behaviour without any reference to mental states.

Contemporary psychology has seen a revival of interest in cognitive processes, with new interpretations using concepts from communication theory, information processing systems, control systems, and goal-seeking devices, and computer systems for the organization and representation of knowledge. The application of psychological methods pervades many aspects of everyday life. These methods are used, for example, in learning methods, the assessment of food preferences, the investigation of attitudes, opinions, and prejudices, the design of work and leisure environment, personnel selection and management, counselling, and therapy. » abnormal/clinical/cognitive/comparative/depth/developmental/dialectical/educational/experimental/occupational/Piagetian/physiological psychology; neuropsychology; phrenology; psychoanalysis; psychometrics; psychophysics; Binet; Darwin, Charles; Fechner; Freud; Galton; Helmholtz; Pavlov; Skinner; Watson, John B; Wundt

psychometrics A branch of psychology concerned with the measurement of psychological characteristics, especially intelligence, abilities, personality, and mood states. Psychometric tests are carefully constructed and standardized to provide measures of the highest possible reliability and validity. » factor analysis; psychology

psychometry In parapsychology, the apparent ability to gain information paranormally from an inanimate object about past events associated with it or its owner. » paranormal; parapsychology

psychopathology A term used in psychiatry and clinical psychology, referring to any form of mental illness or aberration. » psychiatry

psychopharmacology The science of the mechanisms, uses, and side-effects of drugs that modify psychological function and behaviour. » pharmacology

psychophysics Methods originated by Gustav Fechner in 1860 as an attempt to quantify, as psychophysical laws, the relationships between physical stimulation and sensations. Measures of *sensitivity* have been developed into rigorous techniques (eg using signal detection theory), nowadays used principally to establish and describe the constraints on perception provided by the sensory apparatus. *Scaling* methods, which have been controversial, assess the magnitude of the effect of different amounts of stimulation. Both types of method are also used to study more complex perceptual abilities, such as face, speech, or music perception. » auditory perception; Fechner; signal detection theory

psychophysiological disorder » **psychosomatic disorder**

psychosis A psychiatric term with a variety of uses. It is most clearly used when referring to psychiatric illnesses in which there is a loss of contact with reality, in the form of delusions or hallucinations. Less optimally, it is an indication that a psychiatric illness is severe rather than mild or moderate in its impact on the individual. It is also used with reference to two main groups of psychiatric illnesses: **organic psychoses** are caused by diseases affecting the brain; **functional psychoses** do not have a known physical cause. The term may in addition be used for illnesses in which there is a qualitative change in the emotions; those in which there is regression to immature forms of behaviour; and situations of marked withdrawal and a lack of relating to others. » hallucination; neurosis; psychiatry

psychosomatic disorder A set of real physical symptoms (eg headaches, high blood pressure) which have been caused, maintained, or exacerbated by emotional factors; also called a **psychophysiological disorder**. The cause is thought to involve intense and prolonged activity of the sympathetic branch of the autonomic nervous system in response to stress. » nervous system; psychiatry

psychosurgery A procedure in which there is surgery on a brain regarded as histologically normal, with the intention of influencing the course of a behaviour disorder. The term was first employed by the US neurologist Walter Freeman (1895–1972) and US neurosurgeon James Winston Watts (1904–) in 1942, but the procedure was first initiated by Moniz in 1935. The intention in psychosurgery is to create a lesion in the brain to remove pathological thoughts and feelings with the preservation of normal functions. These procedures were initially referred to as *lobotomy* in the USA and *leucotomy* in Europe. » mental disorders

psychotherapy The treatment of emotional problems by a trained therapist with the object of removing or modifying maladaptive feelings or behaviours and the promotion of what is referred to as 'personal growth and development'. There are various styles of treatment, including individual psychotherapy, marital counselling, family psychotherapy, and group psychotherapy. The question of the effectiveness of psychotherapy has often been raised, and there is now convincing research that in particular conditions, such as psychosomatic illnesses, psychotherapy (often using a combination of techniques) is effective in approximately two-thirds of patients. » anaclitic therapy; family therapy; group therapy; supportive psychotherapy; transactional analysis

psychotomimetic drugs » **hallucinogens**

psyllid [**sil**id] A jumping plant louse; feeds by sucking sap; some induce formation of galls on plant; immature stages almost immobile and unable to jump; c.1 300 species, distributed world-wide. (Order: *Homoptera*. Family: *Psyllidae*.) » gall; louse

Ptah [tah, ptah] An early Egyptian god associated with Memphis, and represented in human shape. Originally the creator of the world, he is later the god of craftsmanship. The name 'Egypt' is a Greek misunderstanding of 'Hut-ka-Ptah', which means 'the mansion of Ptah'. Herodotus equated him with Hephaestus. » Hephaestus; Herodotus

ptarmigan A grouse of the N hemisphere, inhabiting the high-altitude Alpine zone and tundra; moults three times a year; plumage mottled grey in summer, white in winter, with thickly feathered feet and toes acting as snowshoes. (Genus: *Lagopus*, 3 species.) » grouse

Pteranodon [te**ran**uhduhn] A huge pterosaur from the late Cretaceous period of N America; wingspan up to 7 m/23 ft; long toothless beak counterbalanced by a bony crest arising at neck joint; tail reduced to short stump; probably ate fish. (Order: *Pterosauria*.) » Cretaceous period; pterosaur; reptile

Pteraspis [te**ras**pis] A fossil jawless vertebrate; known from the late Ordovician to the Devonian periods; body eel-like, without paired fins; skeleton not composed of true bone; related to the hagfish. (Class: *Pteraspidimorphi*.) » Devonian period; hagfish; Ordovician period

pteridophyte [**te**riduhfiyt] Any spore-bearing vascular plant, in some classifications forming the Division *Pteridophyta*. They include ferns, whisk ferns, clubmosses, and horsetails. » clubmoss; fern; horsetail; spore; vascular tissue; whisk fern

pterodactyl [teruh**dak**til] » **pterosaur**

pteropod [**te**ruhpod] » **sea butterfly**

pterosaur [**te**ruhsaw] An extinct, flying reptile known from the late Triassic to the end of the Cretaceous period; ranged in size from sparrow-like to a wingspan of 15 m/50 ft; narrow, leathery wings supported by elongated fourth finger, probably flapped in active flight; bodies hairy; mostly predators; formerly known as **pterodactyls**. (Subclass: *Archosauria*. Order: *Pterosauria*.) » Cretaceous period; Pteranodon; reptile; Triassic period

Ptolemaic system [toluh**may**ik] The planetary system described in the 2nd-c AD by Claudius Ptolemaeus of Alexandria. It is Earth-centred, with the planets moving in circular orbits. Realism is added by letting each planet move on a small circle (the *epicycle*) which in turn travels along a larger circle (the *deferent*). It can predict positions to within 1° or so, and was widely used as the definitive description of the Solar System until overthrown by Copernicus in 1543. » Copernican system; planet; Ptolemy; Solar System

Ptolemy I Soter ('Saviour') [**tol**uhmee] (c.366–c.283 BC) Macedonian general, in the army of Alexander the Great, who became ruler of Egypt after Alexander's death (323 BC). In 304 BC he adopted the royal title, and thus founded the Ptolemaic dynasty. An able ruler, he secured control over Palestine, Cyprus, and parts of Asia Minor, and placed his regime everywhere on a sound military and financial basis. On his abdication in 285 BC, he was succeeded by his son, **Ptolemy II Philadelphus**, the greatest of the Ptolemaic kings. Abroad, the empire was maintained, and in Egypt, Alexandria (with its royally founded museum and library) became the chief centre for learning in the Mediterranean world. » Alexandria, Library of; Cleopatra; Pharos of Alexandria

Ptolemy or **Claudius Ptolemaeus** (c.100–168) Greek astronomer and geographer, who worked in the great library in Alexandria. Considered the greatest astronomer of late antiquity, his book *Almagest* is the most important compendium of astronomy produced until the 16th-c. His system, an Earth-centred universe, held sway until dislodged by Copernicus. » Copernicus; Ptolemaic system

Pu Yi or **P'u-i** [poo **yee**], personal name of **Hsuan T'ung** (1906–67) Last Emperor of China (1908–12) and the first of Manchukuo (1934–5), born and died in Beijing (Peking). Emperor at the age of two, after the 1912 revolution he was given a pension and a summer palace. Known in the West as Henry Puyi, in 1932 he was called from private life by the Japanese to be provincial dictator of Manchukuo, under the name of **Kang Teh**. Taken prisoner by the Russians in 1945, he was tried in China as a war criminal (1950), pardoned (1959), and became a private citizen. The story of his life was made into a successful film in 1988. » Manchukuo

puberty The period of change from childhood to adulthood, characterized by the attainment of sexual maturity and full reproductive capacity. It begins earlier in girls (about age 11) than in boys (about age 13), and lasts between 3 and 5 years. Its onset depends on both genetic and environmental influences (such as nutritional status). In both sexes there is an accelerated growth of the body (the pubertal/juvenile growth spurt), and the development of secondary sexual characteristics: the development of breasts, appearance of pubic hair, and onset of menstruation in girls; the appearance of pubic and facial hair, enlargement of the penis, and deepening of the voice in boys. » adolescence; hormones

public corporations » **nationalization**

public debt The total amount of government borrowings, both short-term, such as treasury bills, and long-term bonds; also known as the *government debt* or the *national debt*. The total UK public debt in the late 1980s was over £170 thousand million, whilst that of the USA was over $1 300 thousand million. » national accounts

public house In the UK, an establishment licensed to sell alcoholic drinks; the 'pub', also known as the 'local' is, like the café in Europe, a place to meet and relax. Many pubs have names of great antiquity, often of historical interest; the common image of the pub is of a quaint building in the country, dating from Tudor times (or earlier), but many different forms exist, and true 'traditional' pubs are becoming rarer.

Public Record Office (PRO) The British national depository of government papers, selected archives, and legal documents to be permanently preserved. It was established by Act of Parliament in 1838. The museum is now housed in a neo-classical building in Chancery Lane, London.

Public Safety, Committee of A French Revolutionary political body, set up in the war crisis (Apr 1793) to organize defence against internal and external enemies. Its members, elected by the National Convention, came to exercise dictatorial powers during the Reign of Terror, particularly under Robespierre's leadership. After his downfall (Jul 1794), its powers were strictly limited. » French Revolution [i]; Robespierre

public school In England, a fee-paying school for pupils of secondary age, often over 11 for girls and over 13 for boys; famous examples include Charterhouse, Eton, Harrow, Merchant Taylors', Radley, Roedean, Rugby, and Westminster. In the USA, it is the exact opposite: a school run by public authorities where fees are not paid. » Christ's Hospital; independent schools; maintained school

public sector borrowing requirement (PSBR) The amount of money a government needs to raise in a fiscal year by borrowing. The need results from tax revenues and other income being less than the total expenditure budgeted by the various government departments. The balance has to be borrowed, ie there is a budget deficit. This occurred in the UK in the 1970s and early 1980s, but the sale of state-owned enterprises and general economic growth led to a budget surplus in the late 1980s. In contrast, the USA Federal budget showed a huge deficit throughout the period. Reducing PSBR has been seen, in the UK, as an important means of reducing money supply, and thus a way of keeping inflation under control. » budget; inflation

publishing The complex commercial activity in which a publisher selects, edits, and designs verbal and illustrative material, arranges its manufacture, and offers it for sale. The commodity in which publishers trade is information, interpreted widely to include entertainment, verbal and visual art, and propaganda. The media employed for publication embrace books, periodicals, newspapers, television and radio, audio and video tapes and discs, optical discs such as CD-Rom, and computer-driven on-line services. The great bulk of material published at any one time is in copyright, and broadly speaking copyrights are a publisher's stock-in-trade.

The complexity and size of the publishing trade are phenomena of modern times, and have grown in parallel with the rise of the professional author, the spread of literacy, the modernization of retailing, the use of computers to assist writing and typesetting, and other such factors. All publishing is characterized by investment in plant followed by speculative mass-production. For centuries, early printers had to be publishers too, until this role was assumed by booksellers, who often collaborated to share the initial costs of printing. Most publishing houses over 100 years old have their origins in printing or bookselling or both. The trade has changed greatly since the 1950s: the largest publishers have grown, partly by natural expansion but also particularly by acquisition; medium-sized and smaller firms have merged or been taken over; but new houses continue to spring up. » book; copyright; electronic publishing; newspaper; periodicals; printing [i]

Pucci, Emilio, Marchese (Marquess) **di Barsento [poochee]** (1914–) Italian fashion designer, born in Naples. He studied in Italy and the USA, gaining a doctorate in political science in 1941. A member of the Italian ski team in 1934, in 1947 he was photographed wearing ski clothes he had designed. He then began to create and sell clothes for women, opening his couture house in 1950, and becoming famed for his use of bold patterns and brilliant colour. He became a member of the Italian parliament in 1965. » fashion

Puccini, Giacomo (Antonio Domenico Michele Secondo Maria) [puch**ee**nee] (1858–1924) Italian operatic composer, born at Lucca. An organist and choirmaster, his first compositions were for the church. In 1880 he attended the Milan Conservatory. His first great success was *Manon Lescaut* (1893), but this was eclipsed by *La Bohème* (1896), *Tosca* (1900), and *Madama Butterfly* (1904). His last opera, *Turandot*, was left unfinished at his death, in Brussels.

Pucello, Johan [p**ü**sel] (c.1300–c.55) French painter who ran an important workshop in Paris from the 1320s onwards, specializing in illuminated manuscripts. The 'Belleville Breviary' (Bibliothèque Nationale, Paris) and the 'Hours of Jeanne d'Evreux' (Metropolitan Museum, New York) are among the greatest masterpieces of early French painting, fusing Italian Renaissance with traditional French elements. » French art; International Gothic

puddling process **1** A process for converting pig-iron (high carbon) into wrought iron (very low carbon) by melting it in a small furnace in which it is worked to remove carbon (by exposure to oxidation by air) and the slag (by extrusion). This was formerly carried out by hand, but is now done mechanically. » wrought iron **2** The agitation of a concrete mix to promote settling and uniformity of texture.

Pudovkin, Vsevoied (Ilarionovich) (1893–1953) Russian film director and writer, born at Penza. He joined the State Institute for Cinematography in Moscow and in his first feature, *Mat* (1926, Mother), applied his concepts of cross-cutting and montage in editing. There followed the silent classics, *Konets Sankt-Peterburga* (1927, The End of St Petersburg) and *Potomok Chingis-Khan* (1928, Storm Over Asia), and such sound films as *Dezertir* (1933, Deserter); much of his work portrays heroic characters in the context of historical turmoil. His books and lectures also had great international influence. He died in Moscow.

Puebla or **Puebla de Zaragoza** 19°03N 98°10W, pop (1980) 835 759. Capital of Puebla state, SC Mexico; SE of Mexico City; altitude 2 150 m/7 054 ft; damaged by earthquake, 1973; railway; two universities (1937, 1940); agricultural trade, textiles, pottery, cement, onyx; famous for its glazed tiles which cover the domes of many of its 60 churches; cathedral (17th-c), Church of Santo Domingo (1659), archbishop's palace (16th-c), Teatro Principal (1790); historic centre now a world heritage site. » Mexico [i]

Pueblo (Indians) **[pwebloh]** N American Indians of SW USA, living in settlements called *pueblos* in multi-storied, permanent houses made of clay. Culturally and linguistically diverse, they are divided into E and W Pueblo, the latter including the Hopi and Zuni. They are famed for their weaving, basketry, sand paintings, and pottery, and have preserved much of their traditional culture intact. Population c.31 000. » cliff dwellings; Hopi; kiva; Southwest Indians; Zuni

***Pueblo*, USS** [**pway**bloh] A US spy ship shelled and boarded by N Koreans in 1968. She carried sophisticated electronic surveillance equipment, but being virtually unarmed was arrested and her crew detained for nearly a year. The US government was forced to sign a public apology to obtain the crew's release.

puerperal fever [pyoo**er**puhral] Any fever arising in the period immediately following childbirth. It was formerly a serious complication of childbearing, when infection was introduced to the genital tract by the hands of doctors or midwives. Today it is a rare cause of maternal death. » fever; obstetrics

Puerto Cortes [**pwair**toh kor**tays**] 15°50N 87°55W, pop (1983e) 40 249. Port town in Cortés department, NW Honduras; at mouth of R Ulúa, on the Caribbean Sea; principal port of Honduras; free zone opened in 1978; railway; oil refining. » Honduras [i]

Puerto Presidente Stroessner, Ciudad Presidente Stroessner [**pwair**toh prayseed**ayn**tay **strer**sner] 25°32S 54°34W, pop (1982) 39 676. Capital of Alto Paraná department, N Paraguay, on the R Paraná; fastest-growing city in the country, and centre for the construction of the Itaipú dam, the largest hydroelectric project in the world; a bridge links the city with Brazil and the town of Foz do Iguaçu; named after the former President of Paraguay. » Paraguay [i]

Puerto Rico, formerly **Porto Rico** (to 1932), official name **Commonwealth of Puerto Rico [pwairtoh reekoh]** pop (1990e) 3 336 000; area 8 897 sq km/3 434 sq ml. Easternmost island of

the Greater Antilles, situated between the Dominican Republic (W) and the US Virgin Is (E), c.1 600 km/1 000 ml SE of Miami; capital, San Juan; chief towns, Ponce, Bayamón, Mayaguez; timezone GMT −4; population mostly of European descent; official language, Spanish, with English widely spoken; chief religion, Roman Catholicism; unit of currency, the US dollar; almost rectangular in shape; length, 153 km/95 ml; width, 58 km/36 ml; crossed W–E by mountains, rising to 1 338 m/4 389 ft at Cerro de Punta; islands of Vieques and Culebra also belong to Puerto Rico; average annual temperature, 25°C; high humidity; originally occupied by Carib and Arawak Indians; visited by Columbus, 1493; remained a Spanish colony until ceded to the USA, 1898; high levels of emigration to the USA, 1940s–50s; became a semi-autonomous Commonwealth in association with the USA, 1952; executive power is exercised by a governor, elected for a 4-year term; a bicameral legislative assembly consists of a 27-member Senate and 51-member House of Representatives, also elected every four years; manufacturing is the most important sector of the economy; textiles, clothing, electrical and electronic equipment, food processing, petrochemicals; dairying, livestock, sugar, tobacco, coffee, pineapples, coconuts; tourism. » Antilles; San Juan; United States of America [i]

puff adder A viper which inhabits grassland; two species: the **puff adder** (*Bitis arietans*) from Africa and the Middle East; length, up to 2 m/6½ ft; very thick mottled brown body; very loud hiss; puffs up the body with air when alarmed; the **dwarf puff adder** (*Bitis peringueyi*) from SW Africa; length, 300 mm/12 in. » adder; viper [i]

puffball A globular, often spherical fruiting body of certain fungi (the gasteromycetes); found above ground; spores are released when the wall of the puffball ruptures. (Subdivision: *Basidiomycetes*. Order: *Lycoperdales*.) » Basidiomycetes; fungus

puffer Any of several stout-bodied marine and freshwater fish which can inflate the body with air or water to become almost spherical; widespread in shallow warm seas, especially over reefs and sea grass beds; body often spiny, jaws bearing four teeth forming a parrot-like beak; some organs and tissue extremely poisonous. Fishes of this family are considered a delicacy in Japan, where they are prepared by specialist chefs. (Family: *Tetraodontidae*, 7 genera.) » fish [i]

puffin Either of two species of auk, genus *Fratercula* (2 species), *Cerorhinca* (1 species), or *Lunda* (1 species); bill large, deep, multicoloured; eats young fish and sand eels; nests in burrows or rock crevices. *Cerorhinca* is nocturnal. » auk

pug A toy breed of dog developed in China; similar origins to the Pekingese, but with a short coat; now taller and heavier than the Pekingese, but face still flat, and tail carried over back. » dog; Pekingese

Pugachev, Emelyan [poogachof] (?1742–75) Russian Don Cossack, pretender to the Russian throne and leader of a mass rebellion against Catherine II (1773–5). He proclaimed himself to be Peter III, Catherine's murdered husband, and promised to restore ancient freedoms. The rebellion was marked by great ferocity, and Pugachev's name later became a byword for the spirit of peasant revolution in Russia. He was captured in 1774 and taken to Moscow where he was tortured and executed. » Catherine II; Cossacks; Razin

Pugin, Augustus (Welby Northmore) [pyoojin] (1812–52) British architect, born and died in London. Trained by his father, he worked with Charles Barry, designing a large part of the decorations and sculpture for the new Houses of Parliament (1836–7). He became a Catholic c.1833, and most of his plans were made for churches within that faith, such as the Catholic cathedral at Birmingham. He did much to revive Gothic architecture in England. » Gothic architecture; Houses of Parliament

Pugwash Conference A series of conferences first held in Pugwash, Nova Scotia, in 1957, which brought together scientists concerned about the impact on humanity of nuclear weapons. It owed much to the initiative of Bertrand Russell. The 1963 conference saw the USA give the USSR information regarding a safety system for nuclear weapons as part of an effort in arms control. » arms control; Russell, Bertrand

Pula [poola], Ital **Pola**, Lat **Pietas Iulia** 44°52N 13°52E, pop (1981) 77 278. Seaport and resort town in W Croatia republic, Yugoslavia, on the Adriatic coast; built on the site of a former Roman colony; airport; railway; car ferries to Italy; naval and commercial port, shipyards, tourism; Roman amphitheatre, Temple of Augustus, cathedral, castle (17th-c); folk displays and concerts (Jun–Aug), festival of Yugoslav feature films (Jul–Aug). » Croatia; Yugoslavia [i]

Pulci, Luigi [poolchee] (1432–84) Italian Renaissance poet, born in Florence. He is best known for his epic *Morgante Maggiore* (1481, Morgante the Giant), 1481, a burlesque with Roland for hero, one of the most valuable specimens of the early Tuscan dialect. He also produced a comic novel and several humorous sonnets. He died at Padua. » epic; Italian literature; Renaissance; sonnet

puli [poolee] A medium-sized breed of dog developed in Hungary for hunting and as a sheepdog; ears pendulous; tail curls over back; coat thick and long, covering eyes and ears, often reaching the ground and tangled into rope-like cords. » dog; sheepdog

Pulitzer, Joseph (1847–1911) US newspaper proprietor, born at Makó, Hungary. He emigrated to join the US army, was discharged in 1865, and became a reporter in St Louis. He then began to acquire and revitalize old newspapers. The *New York World* (1883), sealed his success. In his will he established annual **Pulitzer Prizes** for literature, drama, music, and journalism. He died at Charleston, South Carolina. » RR101

pulley A simple machine: a wheel with a grooved rim in which a rope can run. This changes the direction of force applied to the rope, and so can be used to raise heavy weights by pulling downwards. » machine [i]

Pullman, George M(ortimer) (1831–97) US inventor, born at Brocton, New York. In 1859 he made his first sleeping-cars on trains, and also introduced dining-cars. The Pullman Palace Car Company was formed in 1867. In 1880 he founded 'Pullman City', since absorbed by Chicago, where he died.

pulmonaria » **lungwort**

pulmonary embolism The passage of a blood clot (*thrombus*) into the arteries to the lungs. It may lodge in the main pulmonary artery and cause sudden death; smaller clots block smaller segments of lung tissue. » embolism; heart [i]

pulsar A source of cosmic radio emission, characterized by the rapidity and regularity of the bursts of radio waves it sends out. The time between successive radio pulses is 0.033 seconds for the pulsar in the Crab nebula, and 4 seconds for the slowest pulsars. Pulsars are collapsed neutron stars, having a mass similar to the Sun, but a diameter of only 10 km/6 ml or so. » Crab nebula; neutron star

pulsating star A variable star whose outer layers regularly expand and contract. Cepheid variables are of particular importance, because their period of pulsation gives a measure of absolute luminosity, and therefore enables stellar distances to be found for these stars by comparing apparent and absolute brightness. » Cepheid variable; luminosity; variable star

pulse (botany) A general name applied to peas, beans, and lentils, the edible ripe seeds of several plants of the pea family. Pulses are often rich in protein and nutritious. (Family: *Leguminosae*.) » bean; pea [i]; lentil; protein

pulse (physiology) A pressure wave generated by the ejection of blood from the left ventricle into the vascular system. The number of pulsations per minute reflects heart rate, which in humans is between 70 and 90 at rest (exercise, anger, and fever increase pulse rate, whereas fear and grief lower it). The alternate expansion and recoil of arteries lying near to the body surface can readily be felt (and sometimes seen) as a throbbing. The pulse rate is commonly taken by placing the finger tips on the inside of the forearm just above the wrist (the *radial pulse*). » blood; circulation

puma » **cougar**

pumice A very light and porous igneous rock, usually granitic in chemical composition, and formed by solidifying the froth caused by vigorous degassing of volatile substances from a lava during eruption. It is used as an abrasive. » granite; lava

pump A machine for moving a fluid or gas from one place to another; commonly used to move fluids, often water, through pipes. The simplest pump, which uses the pressure of the air, can lift water through a height of only c.10 m/33 ft. More complex pumps provide mains water for the home, and circulate water to cool car engines. *Pressure pumps* are used to blow up bicycle tyres and footballs. *Evacuation pumps* suck air from sealed containers to make a partial vacuum. The heart is also a type of pump, moving blood through the veins in the body. » machine [i]

pumpkin A trailing or climbing vine, native to America; leaves palmately-lobed; male and female flowers 12.5 cm/5 in diameter, funnel-shaped; fruit usually globular, often reaching great size and weight; rind and flesh orange, rather fibrous, surrounding numerous seeds. It is cultivated as a vegetable. (*Cucurbita maxima*. Family: *Cucurbitaceae*.) » climbing plant; palmate; squash (botany); vegetable

Punch and Judy A glove-puppet show – named after the man and wife who are its central characters – which developed in Britain from the marionette plays based on Pulcinella, the impudent hunchback of the *commedia dell' arte*. The Victorian era was the heyday of the itinerant puppeteer with his portable open-air booth, but the tradition has survived and its major features have remained constant. Being a one-man show, only two hand-puppets can appear at a given time. Punch, operated by the right hand, is a constant figure, while the challenges of the left hand introduce character after character to be defeated by Punch's anarchic vigour. » *commedia dell' arte*; puppetry

punctuation The part of a language's writing system which provides clues to the way a text is organized. Early writing systems made little or no use of punctuation. Punctuation marks were first introduced as an aid to reading a text aloud, and they retain some of that function in modern languages. They are primarily a visual prompt to the lexical and grammatical structure of a text, with two main functions. Some conventions organize the text into grammatical or semantic units, such as paragraphs and words (spaces), sentences and clauses (full-stop, comma, colon, semi-colon); parentheses and the dash can both substitute for commas, while quotation marks identify extracts of speech. Other conventions carry meaning of their own: the question mark identifies a sentence type, the apostrophe marks possession (*John's*) and contractions (*I'm, must've*), while the exclamation mark conveys such features of meaning as surprise. » graphology

Pune » **Poona**

Punic Wars The three wars fought and won in the 3rd-c and 2nd-c BC by Rome against her only remaining rival for supreme power in the W Mediterranean, the Phoenician (Punic) city, Carthage. The first (264–241 BC) resulted in Rome's acquisition of her first overseas province, Sicily, hitherto a Carthaginian territory. The second war (218–201 BC) saw Carthage surrender to Rome all her remaining overseas possessions, and become a dependent, tribute-paying ally. The third (149–146 BC) ended in the capture and total destruction of Carthage itself. » Roman history [i]

Punjab (India) [**puhn**jahb] pop (1981) 16 669 755; area 50 362 sq km/19 440 sq ml. State in NW India, bounded W and NW by Pakistan; capital (jointly with Haryana), Chandigarh; major cities include Amritsar, Jalandhar, Faridkot, Ludhiana; governed by a 117-member Legislative Assembly; wheat, maize, rice, sugar cane, cotton; textiles, sewing machines, sugar, fertilizers, bicycles, electrical goods, machine tools, scientific instruments; part of the Mughal Empire until end of 18th-c; annexed by the British after the Sikh Wars (1846, 1849); autonomous province, 1937; partitioned between India and Pakistan into East and West Punjab on the basis of religion, 1947; population c.60% Sikh in Indian Punjab, mainly Muslim in Pakistani Punjab; Indian state renamed Punjab, reformed as a Punjabi-speaking state, 1956 and 1966; Alkai Dai Party campaigns for Sikh autonomy. » India [i]; Punjab (Pakistan); Sikh Wars

Punjab (Pakistan) [**puhn**jahb] pop (1981) 47 292 000; area 205 334 sq km/79 259 sq ml. Province in Pakistan, bounded E and S by India and the Thar Desert and N by Baltistan; crossed by the Sutlej, Chenab, Jhelum, Ravi, and Indus Rivers; chiefly Muslim population; capital, Lahore; grains, cotton, sugar cane, fruit, vegetables; textiles, foodstuffs, metal goods, bicycles, machinery. » Pakistan [i]; Punjab (India)

Punjabi » **Indo-Aryan languages**

punk rock A type of anarchistic rock music, originating in the late 1970s with such groups as Generation X and the Sex Pistols. Their very loudly amplified performances were characterized by the public use of swear words, outrageous behaviour, and clothes and hairstyles which sought to challenge establishment values. » pop music; rock

punkie » **biting midge**

Punt, land of In antiquity, the area to the S of Egypt near the mouth of the Red Sea. From the third millennium BC, it was the source for the Egyptians of incense, myrrh, gold and ivory.

Punta Arenas [**pun**ta a**ray**nas] 53°09S 70°52W, pop (1982) 80 706. Port and capital of Magallanes-La Antártica Chilena region, Chile; most southerly city in Chile, on the Straits of Magellan; airfield; sheep-farming trade, exporting wool, skins, and frozen meat; crude oil; museum at Colegio Salesiano, Museo del Recuerdo, Patagonian Institute; Festival Folclórica de la Patagonia (July). » Chile [i]; Magallanes-La Antártica Chilena

pupa The life cycle stage of an insect during which the larval form is reorganized to produce the definitive adult form. It is commonly an inactive stage, enclosed in a hard shell (*chrysalis*) or silken covering (*cocoon*). » insect [i]

pupil » **eye** [i]

puppetry The art and craft of manipulating inanimate figures for performance. There are three major means of manipulation: from above, by strings, as with **marionettes**; from below, behind or beside, by inserting a hand into the costume, head or limbs of the puppet, as with **glove puppets**; and from below or behind, by a central support (sometimes with additional strings) activating the head and body, and by separate supports controlling the limbs, as with **rod-puppets**. The last method is sometimes used to manipulate two-dimensional figures so as to form silhouettes on a screen; these are known as **shadow puppets**. In the UK, puppetry is often seen only as a children's show, but in many cultures it is appreciated as a major art form, sometimes with a religious significance. » bunraku; shadow puppets

Puppis (Lat 'ship's stern') [**pup**is] A S constellation, partly in the Milky Way, which includes many notable star clusters. » constellation; Milky Way; RR9

Puranas [poo**rah**nas] In Indian tradition, a set of sacred compositions dating from the Gupta period (c.4th-c AD onwards), dealing with the mythology of Hinduism. They are very important in popular Hinduism. » Hinduism

Purcell, E(dward) M(ills) (1912–) US physicist, born at Taylorville, Illinois. He held posts at the Massachusetts Institute of Technology and Harvard, where he became professor of physics in 1949. He shared the 1952 Nobel Prize for Physics for his work on nuclear magnetic resonance, which has become a major technique in chemistry and physics. In radio-astronomy, he was the first to detect interstellar neutral hydrogen. » Bloch, Felix; nuclear magnetic resonance; nuclear physics

Purcell, Henry (1659–95) English composer, born and died in London. He was a Chapel Royal chorister, and held posts as organist there and at Westminster Abbey, as well as becoming keeper of the king's instruments (1683). Though his harpsichord pieces and his trio-sonatas for violins and continuo have retained their popularity, he is best known for his vocal and choral works. In his official capacity he produced a number of pieces in celebration of royal birthdays, St Cecilia's Day, and other occasions. He also wrote a great deal of incidental stage music, and an opera, *Dido and Aeneas* (1689).

Purchas, Samuel (1577–1626) English compiler of travel books, born at Thaxted, Essex. Educated at Cambridge, he became vicar of Eastwood (1604). His major works were *Purchas his Pilgrimage* (1613) and *Hakluytus Posthumus* (1625), based on the papers of Hakluyt and archives of the East India company. He died in London. » Hakluyt

purchase tax A type of excise tax levied on goods, and added to the price paid by the customer. It is no longer in use in the UK since the advent of Value Added Tax. >> excise tax; taxation; VAT

purchasing power parity (PPP) An economic theory that the true rate of exchange between two currencies can be determined by what can be bought with a unit of each currency. Parity is achieved when what can be purchased is the same. >> currency; parity (economics)

Pure Land Buddhism A school of Buddhism founded, it is said, by the Chinese monk, Hui Yuan (334–417). It is characterized by devotion to the Bodhisattva Amitabha, who rules over a 'pure land'. The goal of those devoted to Amitabha and the pure land is to be reborn there, and attain enlightenment. The school also spread to Japan. >> bodhisattva; Buddhism

purgative >> **laxative**

purgatory In Roman Catholic and some Orthodox teaching, the place and state in which the souls of the dead suffer for their sins before being admitted to heaven. Those in purgatory may be assisted by the prayers of the faithful on Earth. >> heaven; Orthodox Church; prayer; Roman Catholicism; sin

Purim [**pyu**rim, poo**reem**] The Jewish Feast of Lots, celebrated on 14 Adar (about 1 Mar), commemorating the deliverance of the Jews from a plot to have them massacred, as related in the Book of Esther. >> Esther, Book of; Judaism

purines [**pyoo**reenz] A group of organic bases, the most important of which are adenine and guanine, part of the nucleotide chains of DNA and RNA. >> DNA [i]; RNA

Purism A modern art movement founded in 1918 by French artist Amédée Ozenfant (1886–1966) and the architect Le Corbusier. They rejected Cubism, and sought an art of pure and impersonal forms based, however, on the observation of real things. Although no great pictures resulted, Purism influenced modern architecture and design. >> Cubism; Corbusier, Le

Puritanism The belief that further reformation was required in the Church of England under Elizabeth I and the Stuarts. It arose in the 1560s out of dissatisfaction with the 'popish elements', such as surplices, which had been retained by the Elizabethan religious settlement It was not always a coherent, organized movement; rather, a diverse body of opinions and personalities, which occasionally came together. It included the anti-episcopal Presbyterian movement of John Field (1545–88) and Thomas Cartwright (1535–1603) in the 1570s and 1580s; the separatist churches that left England for Holland and America from 1590 to 1640; the 'presbyterian', 'independent', and more radical groups which emerged during the Civil War and interregnum; and the nonconformist sects persecuted by the Cavalier Parliament's 'Clarendon Code' under Charles II. >> Church of England; Nonconformists; Restoration

Purkinje, Johannes (Evangelista) [**poor**kinyay] (1787–1869) Czech histologist and physiologist, born at Libochowitz. He graduated in 1818 with a thesis on vision, which gained him the friendship and support of Goethe. Helped by this, he became professor at Breslau and later at Prague. An early user of the improved compound microscope, he discovered a number of new and important microscopic anatomical structures, some of which are named after him. He was also a very early user of the microtome for cutting sections. He died in Prague. >> anatomy; microscope

Purple Heart (PH) In the USA. a decoration instituted in 1782 as an award for gallantry; it was revived in 1932, since when it has been awarded for wounds received in action. The ribbon is purple with white edges. >> decoration

purpura [**per**pyoora] A condition in which there is spontaneous bleeding into the skin or mucous membranes, giving rise to small scattered areas of bruising. It has many causes, including damage to small blood vessels, disorders of blood platelets, and defects in blood clotting. >> blood; mucous membrane; skin [i]

purslane A name applied to several different plants. **Common purslane** (*Portulacca oleracea*), a weed very widespread in warm regions and cultivated as a pot herb, is a fleshy-leaved annual with yellow, 4–6-petalled flowers. The related **pink purslane** (*Claytonia sibirica*), native to western N America, is an annual or perennial with long-stalked leaves and white or pink 5-petalled flowers. (Family: *Portulaccaceae*.) >> annual; herb; perennial

pus Yellow liquid often formed after localized inflammation, such as an abscess or on the surface of a wound, caused by certain bacteria (known as *pyogenic* bacteria). It consists of dead tissue, white blood cells, and micro-organisms. >> abscess; inflammation

Pusan or **Busan** [poo**sahn**] 5°05N 129°02E, pop (1984) 3 495 289. Seaport and special city in SE Korea, on SE coast on Korea Strait; Korea's second largest city; airport; railway; international ferry; hydrofoil; two universities (1946–7); engineering, shipbuilding, tourism, fishing, trade in salt, fish, rice, soybeans; municipal museum; UN Memorial Cemetery from the Korean War, Yongdu san park, Pusan Tower, T'aejongdae park, Tongnae Hot Springs nearby, Pomosa Buddhist temple nearby (founded 678). >> Korea [i]

Pusey, E(dward) B(ouverie) (1800–82) British theologian, born at Pusey, Berkshire. He was educated at Eton and Oxford, where he became professor of Hebrew (1828), a position which he retained until his death. His main aim was to prevent the spread of Rationalism in England, and he joined Newman in the Oxford Movement (1833), contributing several tracts, notably those on baptism and the Eucharist. After Newman's conversion, he became the leader of the Movement, defending his own position in several publications. An ascetic, deeply religious man, he died at Ascot Priory, Berkshire. >> Newman, John Henry; Oxford Movement; theology

Pushkin, Alexandr Sergeyevich [**push**kin] (1799–1837) Russian poet, born in Moscow. In 1817 he entered government service, but his Liberalism caused his exile to S Russia (1820) until after the accession of Nicholas I (1826). Hailed in Russia as her greatest poet, his first success was the romantic poem *Ruslan and Lyudmila* (1820), followed by the verse novel *Eugene Onegin* (1828), the historical tragedy *Boris Godunov* (1831), and several other large-scale works. He also wrote many lyrical poems, tales, and essays, and was appointed Russian historiographer. His marriage proved unhappy and led to his early death, defending his wife's honour in a duel, at St Petersburg. >> poetry; Russian literature

puss moth A prominent moth with white forewings bearing black zigzag markings; hindwings white in male, grey in female; caterpillar green with reddish head, found on willow and poplar. (Order: *Lepidoptera*. Family: *Notodontidae*.) >> caterpillar; moth

putrefaction The anaerobic decomposition of protein-rich organic matter by bacteria. It results in the formation of methane and other foul-smelling gaseous products. >> aerobe; bacteria [i]; methane [i]

putty A cement made of fine powdered chalk or white lead, mixed with linseed oil. It is used for filling wood, and for fixing glass in frames. **Putty powder** is a fine tin oxide powder used for polishing glass and granite. >> cement

Puvis de Chavannes, Pierre (Cécile) [püvee duh sha**van**] (1824–98) French painter, born in Lyons. He is best known for his murals on public buildings, notably the life of St Geneviève in the Panthéon, Paris, and the large allegorical works such as 'Work' and 'Peace' on the staircase of the Musée de Picardie, Amiens. He died in Paris. >> French art; Symbolists

Puyi >> **Pu Yi**

PVC >> **polyvinylchloride**

Pycnogonida [piknuh**gon**ida] >> **sea spider**

pyelitis >> **pyelonephritis**

pyelonephritis [piyuhlohnuh**friy**tis] A bacterial inflammation of the pelvis, the kidney, and surrounding kidney tissue, usually associated with infection in the lower urinary tract, such as the bladder. The infection usually reaches the pelvis and kidney by ascending the ureters, and is encouraged to do so by a lesion causing obstruction to the free flow of urine, such as ureteric calculi, or enlargement of the prostate. It causes an acute infection accompanied by high fever and back pain; persisting or recurrent infection may lead to renal failure. >> calculi; kidneys; pelvis; urinary system

Pygmalion [pig**may**liuhn] In Greek mythology, a king of Cyprus, who made a statue of a beautiful woman. He prayed to Aphrodite, and the sculptured figure came to life.

Pygmies A small-statured people living in C Africa (averaging 1.50 m/4.9 ft in height), the best-known of which are the forest-dwelling Mbuti of Zaire and the Twa of the Great Lakes savannas. Traditionally hunter-gatherers, most Pygmy bands live in a close relationship with non-Pygmy groups, and many have become farmers and herders in surrounding savannah areas. All speak the Bantu languages of their non-Pygmy neighbours. Population c.200 000. » hunter-gatherers

pygmy hippopotamus » hippopotamus

pygmy owl A small owl, native to the Americas, Europe, and Asia; inhabits woodland; nests in holes. (Genus: *Glaucidium*, 6 species. Family: *Strigidae*.) » owl

pylon 1 The flanking towers to the gateway of an ancient Egyptian temple; usually rectangular in plan with tapering, truncated sides. » Egyptian architecture 2 In the 20th-c, a tall, usually metal structure that carries power cables or acts as a guiding post at an airfield.

Pylos A town on the W coast of the Peloponnese, associated in Greek tradition with Nestor, a Greek chief at the time of the Trojan War. Excavations have revealed a large, unfortified Mycenaean palace there. » Mycenaean civilization

Pym, Barbara (Mary Crampton) (1913–80) British novelist, born at Oswestry, Shropshire, and educated at Liverpool and Oxford. For most of her adult life she worked at the International African Institute in London. She is best known for her series of satirical novels on English middle-class society, including *Excellent Women* (1952) and *Quartet in Autumn* (1977). She died at Oxford. » English literature; novel

Pym, John [pim] (1584–1643) English politician, born at Brymore, Somerset. He left Oxford without taking a degree, studied law, and entered parliament (1614). In 1641 he took a leading part in the impeachment of Strafford, helped to draw up the Grand Remonstrance, and in 1642 was one of the five members whom Charles I singled out by name. He stayed in London during the Civil War, and died soon after being appointed Lieutenant of the Ordnance. » English Civil War; Grand Remonstrance; Strafford

Pynchon, Thomas [**pin**chon] (1937–) US novelist, born at Glen Cove, New York, and educated at Cornell, where he studied English. He has written three novels: *V* (1963), *The Crying of Lot 49* (1966), and *Gravity's Rainbow* (1973), all of which display a preoccupation with codes, quests, and coincidences that determines the form of the narratives and the extra-personal origins of many of their characters' experiences. » American literature; novel

P'yongyang [pyuhng**yang**], Jap **Heijo** 39°00N 125°47E, pop (1981) 1 280 000. Capital of North Korea, overlooking the R Taedong; Korea's oldest city, founded allegedly in 1122 BC; capital of Choson kingdom, 300–200 BC; colony of China, 108 BC; capital of North Korea since 1948; rebuilt after the Korean War; airport; railway; university (1946); iron and steel, machinery, textiles, aircraft, sugar; 1st-c tombs. » Korea, North [i]

pyorrhoea/pyorrhea [piyuh**ree**a] **» dentistry**

pyracantha » firethorn

pyralid moth [**pi**ralid] A moth of the family *Pyralidae*; adults often slender with long hindlimbs; caterpillars typically plant feeders, sometimes scavengers or parasites; c.20 000 species, many pests of crops and dried vegetable products. (Order: *Lepidoptera*.) » caterpillar; moth

pyramid An architectural structure with a triangular, square, or polygonal base, with triangular sides meeting in a single point. In Egyptian architecture, it is a sepulchral stone monument with a square base. In Pre-Columbian architecture, it is an artificial hill with a flat top. The phrase **the Pyramids** usually refers to the Fourth Dynasty pyramids of the Giza plateau on the SW outskirts of modern Cairo. The Great Pyramid of Cheops (c. 2589–2566 BC) is 146 m/480 ft high, 230 m/755 ft square, and 2 352 000 cu m/27 688 000 cu ft in volume, made up of 2.5 million limestone blocks each of 2.5 tonnes. » Egyptian architecture; Pre-Columbian art and architecture; Ship of Cheops; sphinx

pyramids A ball game played on a standard billiard table in which 15 coloured balls, usually red, are placed in a triangle with the apex ball on the pyramid spot (the pink-ball spot). The object is to pot more balls than your opponent. Pyramids was the forerunner of snooker in the 19th-c. » snooker

Pyramus and Thisbe [**pi**ramuhs, **thiz**bee] In a story told by Ovid, two lovers who were kept apart by their parents. They conversed through a crack in the wall between their houses, and agreed to meeet at Ninus' tomb outside the city of Babylon. Finding Thisbe's blood-stained cloak, Pyramus thought she had been killed by a lion, and committed suicide. When she found him, Thisbe killed herself on his sword. The story is incorporated into Shakespeare's *A Midsummer Night's Dream*.

Pyrenean mountain dog A breed of dog developed in the Pyrenees several centuries ago to protect sheep; large powerful body with heavy head; thick, usually pale coloured, coat. » dog

Pyrenees [piruh**neez**], Fr **Pyrénées**, Span **Pirineos** Mountain range extending W–E from the Bay of Biscay to the Mediterranean Sea, separating the Iberian Peninsula from the rest of Europe; stretches 450 km/280 ml along the French–Spanish frontier; includes Andorra; highest point, Pic de Aneto (3 404 m/11 168 ft); Gouffre de la Pierre St Martin, one of the deepest caves in the world; Grotte Casteret, highest ice cave in Europe; observatory at Pic du Midi de Bigorre. » Andorra [i]; Europe

Pyrenees, Treaty of the (1659) A treaty between France and Spain ending the hostilities of the Thirty Years' War. It followed a series of Spanish Habsburg defeats since 1643 (the Austrian Habsburgs made a separate peace in the Treaty of Westphalia, 1648). The French gained border regions, but withdrew from most of Italy. It marked the end of Spanish military and political dominance in W Europe. » Habsburgs; Thirty Years' War

pyrethrum [piy**ree**thruhm] A perennial, growing to 45 cm/18 in, native to W Yugoslavia and Albania, but extensively cultivated, especially in E Africa and S America; leaves divided, silvery-grey; flower heads solitary, daisy-like, spreading outer florets white. An insecticide is prepared from the extracts of the powdered and dried flower heads. (*Tanacetum cinerariifolium*. Family: *Compositae*.) » daisy; insecticide; perennial

Pyrex A trade name for a borosilicate glass with a high silica content, some boron, and some aluminium. It is useful chemically because of its high mechanical strength, and its resistance to strong alkalis and acids. It is useful physically because of its low coefficient of thermal expansion (giving resistance to thermal shock). These properties favour its extensive domestic use. » borax; glass [i]

pyrexia » fever

pyridine [**pi**rideen] C_5H_5N, boiling point 115°C. An organic base with a vile odour. It occurs in a fraction of coal tar, and is carcinogenic. Many alkaloids are pyridine derivatives. » base (chemistry); tar

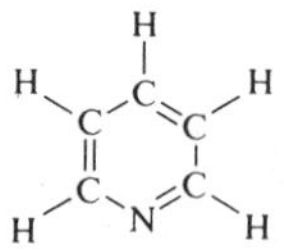

pyridoxine A B-vitamin (B_6) which exists in the form of *pyridoxine* in vegetable foods and *pyridoxal* and *pyridoxamine* in animal food. In the body, all food forms of this vitamin are converted to pyridoxal phosphate. It acts as a co-enzyme for the enzymes involved in the interconversion and metabolism of amino acids. Although a deficiency is rare, B_6 is frequently used as a vitamin supplement for the treatment of mild depression, although its efficacy for such is disputed. Prolonged excessive intakes have been associated with nervous disorders. » amino acid [i]; depression (psychiatry); enzyme; vitamins [i]

pyrimidines [pi**ri**mideenz] A group of organic bases, the most important of which are cytosine and thymine, part of the nucleotide chains of DNA and RNA. » DNA [i]; RNA

pyrite A metallic yellow iron sulphide (FeS_2) mineral, common and widespread, often occurring as well-formed cubic crystals; also termed 'fool's gold', because of its colour. It is used as a source of sulphur and in the manufacture of sulphuric acid. » gold; marcasite; sulphur

pyroclastic rock A general name given to rocks formed from fragments of lava ejected from a volcano into the atmosphere. Examples are ignimbrites, consolidated volcanic ash (*tuff*), and volcanic agglomerate. » agglomerate

pyroelectrics Crystalline materials having an overall electric dipole moment that changes with temperature but is insensitive to an applied electric field, eg lithium niobate, $LiNbO_3$. They are related to ferroelectrics. » crystals; electric dipole moment; ferroelectrics

pyrolysis The decomposition of a substance by heating in the absence of oxygen, usually resulting in simpler compounds being formed. The most important example is the pyrolysis or 'cracking' of petroleum, by which alkanes are converted into shorter alkanes and alkenes, eg propane may be converted to ethene and methane: $CH_3CH_2CH_3 \rightarrow CH_2=CH_2+CH_4$. » alkanes; petroleum

pyrometer A type of thermometer for measuring high temperatures. In the optical pyrometer, the heat colour of the hot object is compared to that of a heated filament through which a controlled current is passed. When the colours match, the sample temperature is known via the previous calibration of the filament. » blackbody radiation; thermometer

pyrope [**piy**rohp] » **garnet**

pyroxenes A large group of silicate minerals including many important rock-forming minerals; similar to amphiboles, but with a single-chain structure of silicate tetrahedra and without hydroxyl ions. Important members of the group are enstatite, diopside, augite, pigeonite, and jadeite. They are widely distributed in igneous and metamorphic rocks. » amphiboles; silicate minerals

Pyrrho [**pi**roh] (c.360–c.270 BC) Greek philosopher, born at Elis. His opinions are known from the writings of his pupil, Timon. He taught that we can know nothing of the nature of things, but that the best attitude of mind is suspense of judgment, which brings with it calmness of mind. Pyrrhonism is often regarded as the foundation of scepticism. » scepticism

Pyrrhus (c.318–272 BC) King of Epirus (modern Albania) (307–303 BC, 297–272 BC), an ambitious ruler whose aim was to revive the empire of his second cousin, Alexander the Great. Unsuccessful in this goal (283 BC), he turned to the West, where he became embroiled in Italian affairs and hence conflict with Rome. Though he won two battles against her (280–279 BC), his losses, particularly at Asculum (279 BC), were so great that they gave rise to the phrase 'Pyrrhic victory'. » Alexander the Great; Roman history [i]

pyruvic acid [piy**roo**vik] CH_3–CO–COOH, IUPAC **2-oxopropanoic acid**. The non-chiral oxidation product of lactic acid. It occurs in several metabolic reaction pathways. » chirality [i]; lactic acid

Pythagoras [piy**tha**goras] (6th-c BC) Greek philosopher and mathematician, born in Samos. He settled at Crotona, Magna Graecia, c.530 BC, where he founded a moral and religious school. He eventually fled from there because of persecution, settling at Metapontum in Lucania, where he died. Pythagoreanism was first a way of life, of moral abstinence and purification, not solely a philosophy; its teaching included the doctrine of the transmigration of souls between successive bodies. The school is best-known for its studies of the relations between numbers. Pythagorean thought exerted considerable influence on Plato's doctrines. » Plato; Pythagoras' theorem [i]

Pythagoras' theorem A mathematical proposition advanced by Pythagoras, that in any right-angled triangle, the square on the hypotenuse is equal to the sum of the squares on the other two sides. The converse of the theorem is also true: in any triangle in which the square on the longest side is equal to the sum of the squares on the other two sides, the angle opposite the longest side is a right angle. Although known to the Babylonians, tradition ascribes to Pythagoras himself the first proof, probably based on the first diagram. The commoner proof (the second diagram), proving first that the area of square *ABXY* is equal to that of the rectangle *APRS*, was given by Euclid. Pythagorean triples – three integers (eg 3,4,5) that can be the sides of right-angled triangles – have long fascinated people. The formula $2mn$, m^2+n^2, m^2-n^2 generates a sequence of Pythagorean triples; but no general formula has yet been found that will generate all Pythagorean triples. » Euclid; geometry; Pythagoras; triangle (mathematics)

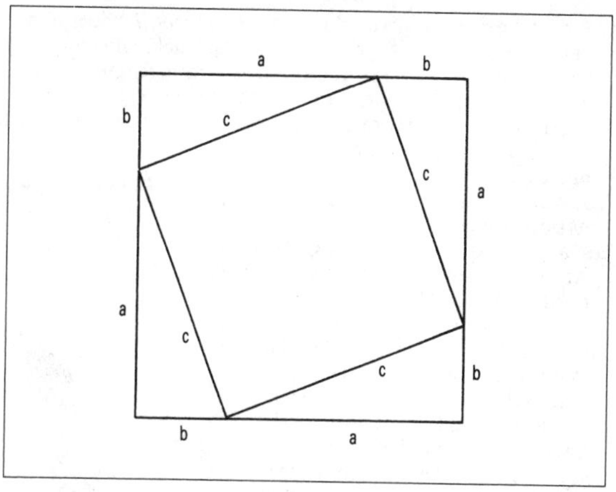

Pythagoras' theorem: $c^2=a^2+b^2$

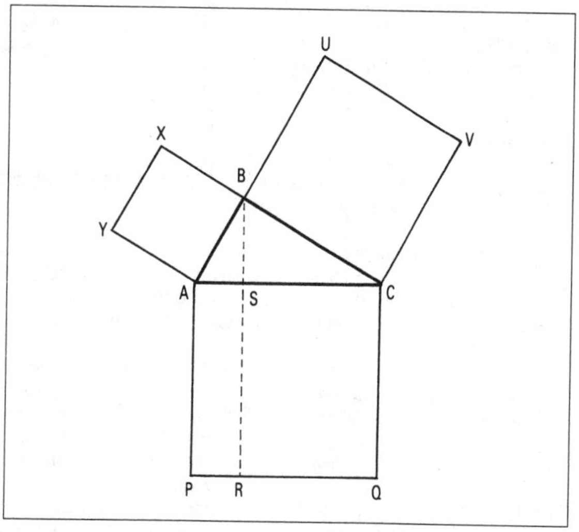

Pythagoras' theorem: $AC^2=AB^2+BC^2$

Pytheas (4th-c BC) Greek mariner, born at Massilia (Marseilles), Gaul. He sailed c.330 BC past Spain, Gaul, and the E coast of Britain, and reached the island of 'Thule', six days' sail from N Britain (possibly Iceland). His account of the voyage is lost, but referred to by several later writers.

Pythian Games In ancient Greece, one of the main Pan-Hellenic festivals, held every four years in the sanctuary of Apollo Pythios at Delphi. 'Pythios' or 'python slayer' was the name under which Apollo was worshipped there. » Delphi, Oracle of; Olympia (Greece)

Pythias (of Syracuse) » **Damon and Pythias**

python A snake of family *Pythonidae* (27 species), sometimes included in the boa family; native to Africa, S and SE Asia, Australasia, and (1 species) C America; a constrictor; minute remnants of hind limbs; eye with vertical slit-like pupil; females lay eggs and often incubate these until they hatch. » boa; constrictor

pyx A small metal box used in the Roman Catholic Church for carrying the Blessed Sacrament to the sick; also a larger receptacle for exposing the host or consecrated bread. » Eucharist; Roman Catholicism; sacrament

Pyxis [**pik**sis] » **Vela**

Q

Q fever An infection caused by *Coxiella burnettii*, widespread in nature, and carried by many insects and ticks affecting cattle and sheep. It occurs in country areas as a self-limiting flu-like illness. Endocarditis (infection of the lining of the heart and heart valves) is a serious complication. The infection can be treated by several antibiotics. » heart [i]

Qaddafi, Muammar » **Gaddafi, Muammar**

Qatar, official name **State of Qatar**, Arabic **Dawlat al-Qatar** [**ka**tah] pop (1990e) 445 000; area 11 437 sq km/4 415 sq ml. Low-lying state on the E coast of the Arabian Peninsula, comprising the Qatar Peninsula and numerous small offshore islands; bounded S by Saudi Arabia and the United Arab Emirates, elsewhere by the Arabian Gulf; capital, Doha; timezone GMT +3; population 40% Arab, 18% Pakistani, 18% Indian; official language, Arabic; chief religion, Islam; unit of currency, the riyal; the peninsula, 160 km/100 ml long and 55–80 km/34–50 ml wide, slopes gently from the Dukhan Heights (98 m/321 ft) to the E shore; barren terrain, mainly sand and gravel; coral reefs offshore; desert climate, average temperatures 23°C (winter), 35°C (summer); high humidity; sparse annual rainfall, maximum 75 mm/3 in; British protectorate after Turkish withdrawal, 1916; independence, 1971; a hereditary monarchy, with an emir who is both head of state and prime minister; Council of Ministers is assisted by a 30-member nominated Consultative Council; economy based on oil; offshore gas reserves thought to be an eighth of known world reserves; oil refineries, petrochemicals, liquefied natural gas, fertilizers, steel, cement, ship repairing, engineering, food processing, fishing; aubergines, lucerne, squash, hay, tomatoes. » Doha; RR27 national holidays; RR59 political leaders *see map p 993*

Qin dynasty [chin] (221–206 BC) The first dynasty to rule over a united China. Its founder, Qin Shihuangdi, led the state of Qin (in present-day Shaanxi) to victory over the other 'warring states', and installed a regime of strict authoritarian legalism. Its achievements included abolition of the ancient feudal order in favour of a prefectural system, the standardization of the Chinese script, weights, and measures, and the construction of roads, canals, and the Great Wall. » China [i]; Great Wall of China

Qin Shihuangdi Mausoleum The tomb of Emperor Qin Shihuangdi (259–210 BC) discovered near Lintong, Shaanxi province, China, in 1974. Excavation, which is still in progress, has revealed an army of over 6 000 life-size terracotta warriors and horses arranged as if for battle. A wealth of other items (weapons, chariots, silk and linen articles, etc) has been discovered on the site, where a museum has been erected in which to exhibit them. » mausoleum; terracotta; Xi'an

Qing dynasty [ching] (1644–1911) A dynasty of Manchu rulers in China, founded in 1616 prior to the Manchu conquest. It came to power through the collaboration of Chinese generals after peasant rebels had overthrown the Ming and invaded Beijing (Peking). Indigenous resistance continued sporadically throughout its rule, but its final decline and overthrow were hastened by the military and economic intervention of foreign imperial powers, who exercised semi-colonial control over key areas of the country from the 19th-c on. Modernization and reform programmes enjoyed only limited success, and the 1911 Revolution brought a severely weakened regime to an end. » Boxer Rising; China [i]; Hundred Days of Reform; Manchu; Ming dynasty; Taiping Rebellion

Qingdao, Tsingtao, or **Ching-tao** [ching**tow**] 36°04N 120°22E, pop (1984e) 1 229 500. Resort seaport city in Shandong province, E China, on the Yellow Sea; a small fishing village until after 1898, when developed by Germans into a modern city; occupied by Japan in World War 1; airfield; railway; cars, trains, consumer goods, brewing. » China [i]

Qinghai Hu [chinghiy **hoo**] Salt lake in NE Qinghai province, WC China; area 4 583 sq km/1 769 sq ml; altitude 3 196 m/10 485 ft; largest salt lake in China; island in centre of lake a nature protection zone, well known for its water birds. » China [i]

Qinghai–Tibet Plateau » **Tibet Plateau**

Qinhuangdao [chinwhang**dow**] 39°55N 119°37E, pop (1984e) 425 300. Port in Hebei province, N China, on NW coast of Bohai Gulf; designated a special economic zone in 1985; linked by pipeline to the Daqing oil field; railway; metallurgy, fibreglass, glass, textiles, fertilizer, chemicals; trade in fruit, chestnuts, fish, grain, coal, oil; Shan Haiguan (N), the E end of the Great Wall. » China [i]; Great Wall of China

Qoheleth [koh**hel**eth] » **Ecclesiastes, Book of**

Qom [koom] 34°39N 50°57E, pop (1983) 424 048. Industrial town in Qom district, Markazi, Iran; on R Anarbar, 120 km/75 ml SSW of Teheran; road and rail junction; gas pipeline; pilgrimage centre for Shiite Muslims; shrine of Fatima. » Iraq [i]; Islam

Quadragesima [kwodra**je**sima] In the Western Christian Church, the first Sunday in Lent, so called from its being approximately 40 days before Easter (Latin *quadrāgēsimus*, 'fortieth'). » Lent

quadratic equations » **equations**

quadrature The position of a planet or the Moon when the angular distance from the Sun, as measured from the Earth, is 90°. The Moon is at half phase when at quadrature. » Moon; planet

quadrature of the circle One of the classical problems of geometry, to draw a square equal in area to a circle, using only straight edge and compasses. Although it has been proved impossible with these instruments, many 'solutions' have been found. One of the earliest was given by the Egyptians, who used a square side equal to $(8/9)d$, where d is the diameter of the circle. This gives a square area $(64/81)d^2$, instead of $(\pi/4)d^2$, whence $\pi \approx 3.160\ldots$ » circle; geometry

quadrille A popular 19th-c dance, performed to music (often arranged from popular tunes) in a lively duple time.

quadriplegia » **paralysis**

quadrophonic sound A system attempting greater authenticity in reproducing concert-hall musical performances by the use of four signal channels and four loudspeakers placed in a square around the listener. Unconvincing results, additional equipment costs, and no single industry standard restricted this to being an episode of the 1970s. » loudspeaker [i]; sound recording

Quadruple Alliance **1** (1718) A treaty signed by Britain, France, and the Habsburg emperor, to which the Dutch were expected to accede, to ensure the principle of collective security in W Europe. It provided for mutual guarantees of titles, possessions, and rights of succession, despite Spain's hostility to Italian territorial provisions, and secured peace for a generation (1718–33). **2** (1815) A treaty signed initially by Austria, Prussia, Russia, and Britain, and acceded to by France in 1818, confirming the 1815 Paris and Vienna provisions for 20 years. It was part of Castlereagh's scheme to guarantee peace through a permanent Concert of Europe. » Castlereagh

quaestors [**kwee**stawz] Junior, annually elected, financial officers at Rome. The quaestorship was the lowest office of the 'cursus honorum' and could not be held before the age of 25.

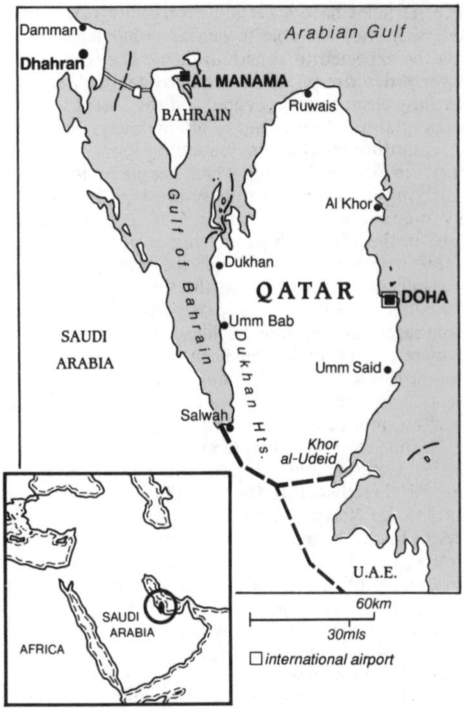

Tenure conferred automatic membership of the Senate. ≫ cursus honorum; Senate, Roman

quagga [**kwa**ga] An extinct zebra native to S Africa; stripes only on head and shoulders; brown body, white legs and tail; last individual died in Amsterdam zoo in 1883. (*Equus quagga*.) ≫ zebra

Quai d'Orsay [**kay** daw**say**] The embankment on the left bank of the R Seine in Paris, and by association the French Foreign Ministry located there. ≫ Paris [i]

quail A small, short-tailed bird of the pheasant family; native to the New World (29 species) and the Old World (10 species). Indian **bush quails** are actually small partridges. The name is also used for the unrelated **bustard/button-quail** and **lark quail/quail plover** (*Turnicidae*), the **quail dove** (*Columbidae*), **quail finch** (*Estrildidae*), and **quail thrush** (*Timaliidae*). ≫ babbler; bobwhite; button quail; dove; finch; pheasant; plover

Quakers ≫ **Friends, Society of**

quaking grass A slender grass, native to temperate regions, with pyramidal panicles of oval, flattened spikelets hanging on thread-like stalks which tremble in the slightest breeze, hence the name. (Genus: *Briza*, 20 species. Family: *Gramineae*.) ≫ grass [i]

Quality Circles Groups of 10–20 workers who were given responsibility for the quality of products in Japan after World War 2, using techniques introduced from the USA. These Circles helped make Japanese products famous for quality and reliability.

QUALY An acronym for **Quality Adjusted Life Year**; a standardized method of assessing health care on the basis of cost and benefit, which takes both life expectancy and quality of life into account.

quango A shortened form of the term **quasi-non-governmental organization**, a new type of organization which became common in the USA, being established by the private sector but largely or entirely financed by the federal government. In the UK the term has been applied to non-departmental bodies (the exact definition varies) that are neither part of a central government department nor part of local government, such as the Monopolies Commission. Many are merely advisory bodies, but a number do have important regulatory functions. In the late 1970s there was increasing concern about these bodies because of their lack of accountability, their cost, and their use as a source of patronage. The concern has declined, but quangos have not.

Quant, Mary (1934–) British designer, born in London. She studied in London, and began fashion design when she opened a shop in Chelsea in 1955. Her clothes were particularly fashionable in the 1960s, when the geometric simplicity of her designs, especially the miniskirt, and the originality of her colours became a feature of the 'swinging Britain' era. In the 1970s she extended into cosmetics and textile design. ≫ fashion

quantity theory of money An important economic theory stating that money supply (M) and its velocity of circulation (V) – how fast it changes hands – is more or less equal to the aggregate of prices (P) and the quantity of goods etc (Q) available. So, $MV = PQ$. Monetarist economists consider that the major determining factor in price rises (therefore inflation) is the money supply (M). The theory was originally devised by English economist Alfred Marshall (1842–1924) in the early 1900s. ≫ monetarism

quantum chromodynamics A widely accepted theory of strong nuclear force in which quarks are bound together by gluons; proposed in 1973; also known as **QCD**. Quarks interact because of a 'colour' quantity on each in a way analogous to the interaction between charged particles because of the charge on each particle. ≫ gauge theory; gluon; particle physics; quantum field theory; quark; strong interaction

quantum electrodynamics A modern theory of high-speed (relativistic) electromagnetic interactions, developed by US physicists Richard Feynman (1918–88) and Julian Schwinger (1918–), Japanese physicist Sinichiro Tomonaga (1906–79), and others during the 1940s; also called **QED**. Charged subatomic particles interact via photons, the quantum of electromagnetic radiation. The theory predicts the electron g-factor and atomic energy levels to high precision. It is a prototype gauge theory on which theories of nuclear forces are modelled. ≫ electrodynamics; Feynman; gauge theory; g-factor; pair production; quantum field theory

quantum field theory The most sophisticated form of quantum theory, in which all matter and force particles are expressed as sums over simple waves. It is essential for understanding the processes in which particles are created or destroyed, as when electrons and positrons annihilate at the same time, and is applied to solid state and particle physics. Quantum electrodynamics, quantum chromodynamics, and the Glashow-Weinberg-Salam theory are all quantum field theories. ≫ Feynman diagrams [i]; gauge theory; quantum mechanics; relativistic quantum mechanics; renormalization; virtual particle

quantum gravity Gravitation acting at sub-microscopic length scales where quantum effects are important. Theories of quantum gravity seek to combine features of quantum mechanics and general relativity. The proposed quantum of gravitation is gravitational interaction via the exchange of gravitons. However, the view has no experimental support, and as yet no consistent theory has been developed. ≫ general relativity; graviton; Planck length; quantum mechanics; supergravity

quantum Hall effect Regular steps in the Hall conductivity effect at low temperatures in high magnetic fields for electrons constrained to move in a plane, such as in the junction region of silicon-metal oxide semiconductor devices; first observed in 1980 by German physicist Klaus von Klitzing (1943–) and others. It results from the quantized orbiting motion of electrons in a magnetic field. The conductivity has values that are integer multiples of e^2/h, where e is the electron charge and h is Planck's constant. More recently, the fractional quantum Hall effect has been discovered, in which the conductivity has certain fractional multiples of e^2/h. ≫ Hall effect; surface physics

quantum mechanics A system of mechanics applicable at distances of atomic dimensions, 10^{-10} m or less, and providing for the description of atoms, molecules, and all phenomena that depend on properties of matter at the atomic level. Among the many technologically important applications of quantum mechanics are superconductors, lasers, and electronics. In

1900, the study of blackbody radiation (electromagnetic radiation emitted by objects on account of their temperature) led German physicist Max Planck to the idea that light is composed of photons – minute packets of light each of energy $E=h\nu$, where h is Planck's constant and ν is the frequency of light. Further evidence that light exists in packets (*quanta*) came from the photoelectric effect (1905) and the Compton effect (1923). Light, thought to be wave-like, thus appeared to behave like particles.

In 1923 French physicist Louis de Broglie suggested that matter particles may in turn behave like waves. He proposed that particles such as electrons have associated with them a wavelength λ given by $\lambda=h/p$, where p is the particle momentum. The wave-like character of electrons was confirmed in 1927 by US physicists Clinton Davisson (1881–1958) and Lester Germer (1896–1971), by diffracting electrons with crystals. In 1926, Austrian physicist Erwin Schrödinger devised an expression for the behaviour of matter waves. When applied to the hydrogen atom, Schrödinger's equation predicted spectral lines in good agreement with observation. Werner Heisenberg also devised a form of quantum mechanics equivalent to that of Schrödinger (1925), but more difficult to understand. Other essential elements of quantum mechanics are Heisenberg's uncertainty principle (1927) and Pauli's exclusion principle (1925). The development of quantum mechanics applicable to particles moving at high speed was due to British physicist Paul Dirac (1928), and is known as **relativistic quantum mechanics**. The final development of quantum theory, incorporating the creation and destruction of particles, took place during the 1940s and is called **quantum field theory**.

The wave-like nature of electrons and other particles is expressed by wavefunctions, the most fundamental way of describing either simple particles or other more complicated quantum systems. The behaviour of wavefunctions is governed by the Schrödinger equation. Particles such as electrons are no longer considered as point-like objects, but are spread out in a way governed by wavefunctions. The square of the wavefunction measures the probability of finding a particle at a given point. Quantum mechanics necessarily means dealing with a probabilistic description of nature, and thus contrasts with classical mechanics, in which the precise properties of every object are in principle calculable. The attributes of quantum systems have measurable values which are discrete. For example, the energy of an electron in an atom does not have a continuous spectrum of values, but only allows certain values; the energy is said to be *quantized*. When an electron in an excited atom jumps from one possible energy state to another of lower energy, a quantum of light is emitted. Measurements on quantum states will give one of the possible discrete values, with a probability controlled by the wavefunction. » Aharanov-Bohm effect; anthropic principle; atomic physics; Berry's phase; blackbody radiation; Broglie, Louis Victor de; Copenhagen Interpretation; correspondence principle (physics); Dirac; electron diffraction; electronic structure of solids; energy levels; laser [i]; many worlds interpretation; Pauli exclusion principle; photoelectric effect; Planck; quantum field theory/gravity/numbers/tunnelling; quasiparticles; relativistic quantum mechanics; spin; wave-particle duality; zero point energy

quantum numbers Simple numbers or vectors that specify the state of a quantum system and the results of observations performed on that system. The values are usually discrete. Charge is a simple quantum number; spin is a vector quantum number. Conservation laws are expressed in terms of quantum numbers; sub-atomic particles and atomic states are classified by quantum numbers. » bottom; charge; charm; conservation laws; energy levels; isospin; parity (physics); quantum chromodynamics; spin; strangeness; vector

quantum statistical mechanics An extension of statistical mechanics in which quantum conditions on individual particles are taken into account, especially restrictions imposed by the uncertainty principle. » Bose-Einstein statistics; Fermi-Dirac statistics; Heisenberg uncertainty principle; statistical mechanics

quantum tunnelling A feature specific to quantum systems, in which particles have a certain probability of existing beyond barriers, ie they are able to penetrate barriers that classically would be expected to constrain them. The feature arises from the wave description of quantum systems. Alpha decay, the tunnelling electron microscope, and the Josephson junction all display quantum tunnelling. » alpha decay; Josephson junction; quantum mechanics; wavefunction

quarantine A period during which people or animals suspected of carrying a contagious disease are kept in isolation. Originally quarantine was an attempt to prevent the spread of plague in the 14th-c: ships arriving at port were kept isolated and offshore for 40 days. Later the principle was applied to many infectious diseases, and the time shortened to relate to the incubation period of the particular infection. The practice is now rarely used in human illness: possible infected suspects are merely kept under medical supervision at home or in hospital. It is still applied to dogs and other animals imported from overseas to the UK as a defence against the spread of rabies; a 6-month period is normal. » rabies

quark A fundamental component of matter; symbol q. Though there is experimental support for quarks, none has been observed directly. It is thought that six quark types exist, identified by 'flavours': *up, down, strange, charm, top*, and *bottom*. Each flavour quark carries one of three possible 'colours'. Quarks have spin ½, are of indeterminate mass, and have charges of $\pm\frac{1}{3}$ or $\pm\frac{2}{3}$. For example, the up quark (u) has charge $+\frac{2}{3}$ and the down quark (d) charge $-\frac{1}{3}$. Protons comprise uud, neutrons udd. According to current theory, sub-atomic particles composed of quarks are bound together by gluons. Baryons are made of three quarks; mesons of quark/antiquark pairs. » confinement; gluon; particle physics; quantum chromodynamics

quark-gluon plasma » nuclear physics

Quarles, Francis (1592–1644) English religious poet, born near Romford, Essex. Educated at Cambridge and London, he was successively cup-bearer to the Princess Elizabeth (1613), secretary to Archbishop Ussher (c.1629), and chronologer to the City of London (1639). A royalist and churchman, many of his books and manuscripts were destroyed. His best-known work is the emblem book (a series of symbolic pictures with verse commentary), *Emblems* (1635), and a prose book of aphorisms, *Enchyridion* (1640). He died in London. » English literature; poetry

quarrying Making an open excavation for the extraction of stone for direct use, as distinct from *open-cast mining*, in which minerals are extracted for subsequent conversion. The stone may be used as it is in blocks, or crushed for such uses as a compound in concrete. » mining

quarter-day Any of the four days in the year (i.e. one every quarter year) on which rents and similar charges are traditionally paid; in England and Wales, the quarter-days are Lady Day (25 Mar), Midsummer Day (24 Jun), Michaelmas (29 Sep) and Christmas Day (25 Dec); Scottish quarter-days are Candlemas (2 Feb), Whitsunday (15 May), Lammas (1 Aug) and Martinmas (11 Nov). They are different in the USA (1 Jan, 1 Apr, 1 Jul, 1 Oct). There is much folklore and tradition behind these days, several of which display some variation in date, largely because people were formerly not exact about when the solstices and equinoxes fell. » equinox; solstice

quarter horse The oldest American breed of horse, developed for sprinting a quarter of a mile; height, 15½–16¼ hands/ 1.5–1.7 m/5.1–5.4 ft; muscular body and hindquarters; slender legs; popular with cowboys; also known as **American quarter horse**, or **short horse**. » horse [i]

quartz The crystalline form of silicon dioxide (SiO_2), one of the most common minerals in the Earth's crust. The clear crystals are known as *rock crystal*, but it is commonly white and translucent. Semi-precious varieties (eg amethyst) may be coloured. It may occur as microcrystalline varieties, such as chalcedony, agate, and flint. It is very important industrially because of its piezo-electric properties. » chalcedony; piezo-electric effect; silica; silicate minerals

quartzite A rock produced by the recrystallization of sandstone by metamorphism, and consisting of interlocking crystals of quartz (*metaquartzite*). It is also a sandstone with purely siliceous cement (*orthoquartzite*). » quartz; sandstone; silica

quasar A distant, compact object far beyond our Galaxy, which looks starlike on a photograph, but has a redshift characteristic of an extremely remote object. The word is a contraction of **quasi-stellar object**. The distinctive features of quasars are an extremely compact structure and high redshift corresponding to velocities approaching the speed of light. Implied distances run into billions of parsecs, making them the most distant and luminous objects in the universe, millions of times brighter than normal galaxies. Objects such as black holes appear capable of satisfying the energy requirements. » black hole; redshift

quasi-crystals Solid substances which on a small scale exhibit symmetries similar to those of crystals, but which lack the perfect overall ordering of true crystals. They were first observed in 1984 as an unexpected five-fold symmetry in Al_6Mn alloy. » crystals

quasi-particles Excitations that behave in a particle-like way, or real particles whose behaviour is modified by their environment. An example of the first type is the phonon, a crystal lattice vibration; an example of the second is the motion of electrons in solids, where the electrons can appear to have an effective mass far greater than a free electron mass. Other important quasi-particles are excitons and magnons. » exciton; magnon [i]; particle physics; phonon

Quasimodo, Salvatore (1901–68) Italian poet, born at Syracuse, Sicily. He studied at Palermo and Rome, and became an engineer, then turned to writing, becoming professor of literature in Milan. His early work was Symbolist in character, as in *Ed é subito sera* (1942, And Suddenly it's Evening), and he became a leader of the 'hermetic' poets. After World War 2 his poetry dealt largely with social issues, and a deep concern with the fate of Italy, as in *La Vita non e sogno* (1949, Life is not a Dream). He died in Naples. » hermetic; Italian literature; poetry

quassia [**kwo**shuh] A shrub or small tree native to tropical America; leaves pinnate; flowers tubular, red. It is cultivated for ornament, and for the bitter wood containing the chemical *quassiin*, used medicinally to counter dysentry. (*Quassia amara*. Family: *Simaroubaceae*.) » pinnate; shrub; tree [i]

Quaternary period [kwa**ter**nuhree] A geological period of the Cenozoic era extending from 2 million years ago to the present day; subdivided into the Pleistocene and Holocene epochs. It is characterized by extensive glaciations in the N Hemisphere and the emergence of mankind. » Cenozoic era; geological time scale; glaciation; RR16

quaternions In algebra, a set of four ordered real numbers subject to certain laws of composition. The laws of composition are illustrated by

$$(a,b,c,d) + (p,q,r,s) = (a+p,\ b+q,\ c+r,\ d+s) \text{ and}$$
$$(a,b,c,d).(p,q,r,s) = (ap-bq-cr-ds,\ aq+bp+cs-dr,\ ar+cp+dq-bs,\ as+br+dp-cq).$$

Quaternions were developed by William Hamilton (1803–65), and provide an example of a non-commutative algebra, as multiplication is not commutative. The name *quaternion* was suggested because there are four ordered numbers in each. » algebra; commutative operation; numbers

Quayle, (J) Dan(forth) (1947–) US politician, born in Indianapolis. Educated at DePauw and Indiana Universities, he worked as a lawyer, journalist, and public official, becoming a member of the Congress (1977–81) and Senate (1981–8). He was elected Vice-President under George Bush in 1988. » Bush, George

Quebec (province), [kwe**bek**], Fr **Québec** [kay**bek**] pop (1981) 6 438 403; area 1 540 680 sq km/594 856 sq ml. Largest province in Canada; boundaries include James and Hudson Bays (W), Hudson Strait and Ungava Bay (NE), Gulf of St Lawrence (E), and USA (S); Canadian Shield in N four-fifths, a rolling plateau dotted with lakes; tundra in extreme N; rises to 1 588 m/5 210 ft at Mont d'Iberville; Notre Dame Mts in the S; several rivers flow into the St Lawrence and James and Hudson Bays; several islands in the St Lawrence; S part intensely cultivated; most population in St Lawrence valley; capital, Quebec; major cities include Montreal, Laval, Sherbrooke, Verdun, Hull, Trois Rivières; agriculture, timber, paper, hydro-electric power, aluminium, bauxite, iron ore, copper, gold, zinc, asbestos, textiles, high-technology industries, tourism; claimed for France by Cartier, 1534; province of New France, 1608; captured by British, 1629; restored to France, 1632; transferred to Britain by Treaty of Paris, 1763; constituted as Lower Canada, 1791; province of Quebec, 1867, with English and French as official languages; strong separatist movement emerged in 1960s, but 1980 referendum decided against secession; governed by a lieutenant-governor and a 122-member elected Legislative Assembly. » Canada [i]; Cartier; Quebec (city); Seven Years' War

Quebec (city), Fr **Québec** 46°50N 71°15W, pop (1981) 166 474. Capital of Quebec province, SE Canada, on the St Lawrence R where it meets the St Charles R; built on Cape Diamond, cliff rising 100 m/328 ft; 92% French-speaking; visited by Cartier, 1535; French colony founded, 1608; taken by the English, 1629; returned to France, 1632; capital of New France, 1663; captured by the British under Wolfe, 1759; ceded to Britain, 1763; capital of Lower Canada, 1791; airport; railway; two universities (1852, 1968); shipbuilding, paper, clothing, food processing, footwear, electrical goods, tobacco, tourism; major league team (ice hockey), Quebec Nordiques; Château Frontenac (setting for World War 2 meetings with USA and UK), N America's oldest lift (links Upper and Lower Town), Musée du Fort, Citadel fortress (a world heritage site), Battlefield Park (including Provincial Museum and Plains of Abraham), Quebec Museum; Quebec Winter Carnival Canoe Race (Feb). » Abraham, Plains of; Cartier; Montcalm; Quebec (province); Wolfe, James

Quechua [**kech**ooa] A S American Indian language of the Andean-Equatorial group. The official language of the Incas, it is now spoken by 6 million from Colombia to Chile, and is widely used as a lingua franca. It has a literary history which dates from the 17th-c. » American Indians; Incas; lingua franca

Queen, Ellery (1905–) The pseudonym of two US writers of crime fiction, **Frederic Dannay** (1905–82) and his cousin **Manfred B Lee** (1905–71), both born in New York City. As business men they won a detective-story competition with *The Roman Hat Mystery* (1929), and thereafter wrote many popular books in this genre, using 'Ellery Queen' both as their pseudonym and as the name of their detective. They also used the pseudonym **Barnaby Ross** as the author of their other detective, Drury Lane. They began *Ellery Queen's Mystery Magazine* (1941) and co-founded Mystery Writers of America. Dannay died at White Plains, New York, and Lee near Waterbury, Connecticut. » detective story

Queen Anne's lace » cow parsley

Queen Anne's War (1702–1713) The second of the four intercolonial wars waged by Britain and France for control of colonial N America, known in Europe as the War of the Spanish Succession. Both sides made considerable use of Indian allies. Settled by the Treaty of Utrecht (1713), the war resulted in British control of Newfoundland, Acadia, and Hudson Bay. Britain also gained the Assiento, allowing trade with Spanish America. » Spanish Succession, War of the

Queen Anne style The architecture, furniture, and silver designed during the reign of Queen Anne (1702–14), notable for carefully calculated proportions and a lack of applied ornament. Generous Baroque shapes and robust carved legs characterized chairs, cabinets, and several other objects. The style was revived in English architecture in the second half of the 19th-c, characterized by compositions of mullioned windows, handsome brickwork, and imposingly grouped chimneys. » Anne; Arts and Crafts Movement; Baroque (art and architecture); Gothic Revival

Queen Charlotte Islands pop (1981) 5 884; area 9 790 sq km/3 779 sq ml. Archipelago of c.150 islands off the W coast of British Columbia, W Canada; extend over c.100 km/60 ml; timber, fishing. » Anthony Island; Canada [i]

Queen Elizabeth Islands area over 390 000 sq km/150 000 sq ml. Northernmost islands of the Canadian Arctic Archipelago, situated N of latitude 74°N; include Ellesmere, Devon, Prince Patrick, and Cornwallis Is, and the Sverdrup and Parry groups; named in 1953. » Canada [i]

Queen Maud Land, Norwegian **Dronning Maud Land** Main part of Norwegian Antarctic Territory (between 20°W and 45°W and S of 60°S), extending to the S Pole; claimed by Norway in 1939; scientific bases at Sanae (S Africa) and Novo Lazarevskaya (Russia). » Antarctica [i]

Queen's Award In the UK, an award given annually on the Queen's birthday (21 Apr). Established in 1965, there are now two separate awards, one for export achievement, and one for technological achievement.

Queen's Counsel (QC) A senior member of the English or Scottish Bar. A practising barrister of 10 years' standing may apply to become a Queen's Counsel (or 'take silk' – a reference to the gowns worn by such counsel). Application is made to the Lord Chancellor; a list of those selected each year is published on Maundy Thursday. » barrister; Inns of Court; Lord Chancellor

Queen Victoria water lily A giant water lily, native to the Amazon, growing in water 1–2 m/3–6 ft deep; prickly, floating leaves up to 2 m/6½ ft diameter, with upturned rim several cm deep, resembling a shallow dish; flowers up to 30 cm/12 in diameter, white, fading to purple. It was named in honour of Queen Victoria. (*Victoria amazonica*. Family: *Nymphaeaceae*.) » Victoria; water lily

Queens pop (1980) 1 891 325, area 283 sq km/109 sq ml. Borough of New York City, USA; co-extensive with Queens County; at the W end of Long Island; connected to the mainland by the Hell Gate Bridge, and with Manhattan by the Queensboro Bridge; a borough since 1898; contains the two New York airports. » Long Island; New York City

Queensberry, Sir John Sholto Douglas, 8th Marquis of (1844–1900) British aristocrat, a keen patron of boxing, who supervised the formulation in 1867 of new rules to govern that sport, since known as the **Queensberry rules**. In 1895 he was tried and acquitted for publishing a defamatory libel on Oscar Wilde – an event which led to Wilde's trial and imprisonment. » boxing [i]; Wilde

Queensland pop (1986) 2 675 300; area 1 727 200 sq km/666 900 sq ml. Second largest state in Australia; established as a penal colony, 1824; open to free settlers, 1842; part of New South Wales until 1859; contains 11 statistical divisions; bordered N by the Gulf of Carpentaria, the Torres Strait, and the Coral Sea, and E by the South Pacific Ocean; Cape York Peninsula in the N; the Great Dividing Range runs N–S, separating a fertile coastal strip to the E from dry plains to the W; tropical climate in the N; Scenic Rim Mountains on the border with New South Wales; most population in the SE; capital, Brisbane; principal cities Gold Coast, Townsville, Cairns, Ipswich, Toowoomba, Rockhampton; provides 22% of Australia's agricultural production, with sugar the main export crop; wheat, sorghum, tomatoes, citrus and tropical fruit; bauxite, coal, copper, zinc, lead, phosphate, nickel, oil, gas; machinery, chemicals, textiles, food processing, furniture, plastics, rubber products, forest products, paper, motor vehicles; total coastline 5 200 km/3 200 ml; Great Barrier Reef runs parallel to the Pacific coast; Noosa to Bribie I is known as the 'sunshine coast', while E of Brisbane to the New South Wales border is the 'gold coast', major resort areas with fine surfing beaches. » Australia [i]; Brisbane; Great Barrier Reef

Queensland arrowroot » arrowroot; canna

quelea [**kwee**lia] An African weaverbird, inhabiting grassland, woodland, and marsh; eats seeds. The **red-billed quelea** (*Quelea quelea*) is a serious agricultural pest, plaguing grain crops. (Genus: *Quelea*, 3 species.) » weaverbird

Queluz [ki**luzh**] 38°45N 9°15W, pop (1981) 46 856. Market town in Lisbon district, C Portugal, 15 km/9 ml WNW of Lisbon; Roco Palace, former summer residence of the Braganza kings; Queluz fair (Sep). » Portugal

Queneau, Raymond [ke**noh**] (1903–76) French novelist and poet, born at Le Havre, and educated at the Sorbonne. The best of his poetry is contained in *Les Ziaux* (1943) and *Si tu t'imagines* (1952, If you suppose). His novels include *Le Chiendent* (1933, The Bark Tree) and *Zazie dans le métro* (1959, Zazie), and are often self-reflective, anticipating some of the devices of the *nouveau roman*. » French literature; nouveau roman

Querétaro [ke**ray**taroh] 20°38N 100°23W, pop (1980) 293 586. Capital of Querétaro state, C Mexico, 200 km/124 ml NNW of Mexico City; altitude, 1 865 m/6 119 ft; important in the 1810 independence rising; scene of the surrender and execution of Emperor Maximilian, 1867; railway; university (1618); textiles, opals, mercury, pottery; Church of Santa Cruz, Convent of San Francisco, federal palace; agricultural fair (Dec). » Maximilian, Ferdinand Joseph; Mexico [i]

Quesnay, François [ke**nay**] (1694–1774) French physician and economist, born at Mérey. He studied medicine at Paris, and at his death was first physician to the king. But the fame of the 'European Confucius' depends on his essays in political economy. He became a leader of the *Economistes*, also called the Physiocratic School, and contributed to Diderot's *Encyclopédie*. He died at Versailles. » Diderot

Quesnel, Pasquier [ke**nel**] (1634–1719) French Jansenist theologian, born in Paris. He studied at the Sorbonne, and in 1662 became director of the Paris Oratory, where he wrote *Nouveau Testament en français avec des réflexions morales* (1687–94, New Testament in French with Thoughts on Morality). Having refused to condemn Jansenism in 1684, he fled to Brussels. Hostility to his work led to his imprisonment (1703), but he escaped to Amsterdam, where he died. » theology

Quetta [**kwe**ta] 30°15N 67°01E, pop (1981) 285 000. Capital of Baluchistan province, W Pakistan; in the C Brahui Range, 590 km/367 ml N of Karachi; altitude 1 650 m/5 500 ft; strategic location on the trade route between Afghanistan and the Lower Indus valley; controls the Bolan Pass and the Khojak Pass; acquired by the British, 1876; badly damaged by earthquake, 1935; airfield; railway; centre of a fruit-growing area; linked to Shikarpur by natural gas pipeline in 1982. » Pakistan [i]

quetzal A C American bird, inhabiting mountain forests; eats fruit, insects, frogs, lizards, and snails; male with red underparts, green head and back, and very long trailing tail; also known as the **resplendent quetzal** or **resplendent trogon**. Revered by the Mayans and Aztecs, it was associated with the god Quetzalcoatl, and is the national bird of Guatemala. Its numbers are now seriously diminishing. The name is also used for four S American species of *Pharomachrus*. (*Pharomachrus mocinno*.) » trogon

Quetzalcoatl [ketzalkoh**atl**] The feathered serpent god of the pre-Columbian Aztec and Mayan cultures of C America. Represented as the god of air and water, he is associated with the invention of the calendar and the recreation of human life. He provoked the anger of another god, and fled in a boat made of serpent skin promising to return – a promise used to advantage by the invader Cortés. » Aztecs; Cortés; Mayas

Quezaltenango [ketsalte**nang**goh] 14°50N 91°30W, pop (1983e) 65 733. Capital town of Quezaltenango department, SW Guatemala; surrounded by volcanic peaks; Guatemala's second industrial and trading centre; largely rebuilt since earthquakes of 1818 and 1902; branch of San Carlos University. » Guatemala [i]

Quezon City [**kay**son] 14°39N 121°01E, pop (1980) 1 165 865. Residential city in Capital province, Philippines; on Luzon I, NE of Manila; laid out in 1940; former capital, 1948–76; university (1908); textiles, tourism; night procession of La Naval de Manila (Oct). » Philippines [i]

quicklime » calcium

quicksilver » mercury

quickthorn » hawthorn

quill A pen made from the tapered stem of a bird's feather, especially the outer wing feathers of geese. Quills were the chief writing implement from the 6th-c AD until the advent of steel pens in the mid 19th-c. » pen

Quiller-Couch, Sir Arthur [**kwil**uh **kooch**] (1863–1944) British man of letters, born at Bodmin, Cornwall. He was educated at Clifton College and Oxford, where he became a lecturer in classics (1886–7). After literary work in London and Cornwall, he became in 1912 professor of English literature at Cambridge. He edited the *Oxford Book of English Verse* (1900) and other anthologies, and published several volumes of essays and criticism. He wrote poems, short stories, and (under the pseudonym of 'Q') several humorous novels of Cornwall and the sea. He was knighted in 1910, and died at Fowey, Cornwall. » literary criticism; novel

quillwort A spore-bearing vascular plant related to clubmosses, mostly aquatic pteridophytes distributed throughout the world; tufted leaves grass-like but cylindrical, enclosing sporangia in their swollen bases. (Genus: *Isoetes*, 75 species. Family: *Isoetaceae*.) » clubmoss; pteridophyte; selaginella; spore; vascular tissue

Quimper [kīpair] or **Quimper Corentin** 48°00N 4°09W, pop (1982) 60 162. Manufacturing and commercial capital of Finistère department, NW France; on estuary of R Odet, 179 km/111 ml W of Rennes; capital of old countship of Carnouailles; railway; pottery (Quimper or Brittany ware) since 16th-c; textiles, tourism; 13th-c Gothic Cathedral of St-Corentin; former bishop's palace (early 16th-c), now a museum; folk festival (Jul). » Gothic architecture; pottery

quince A deciduous shrub or small tree reaching 1.5–7.5m/ 5–25 ft, native to Asia; leaves oval; flowers pale pink, bowl-shaped, resembling apple blossom; fruit apple- or pear-shaped, 5–12 cm/2–4¾ in diameter in cultivated plants, fragrant but hard when ripe, mainly used in preserves. It is cultivated and naturalized in much of Europe. (*Cydonia oblonga*. Family: *Rosaceae*.) » japonica; shrub; tree [i]

Quine, Willard Van Orman (1908–) US philosopher and logician, born at Akron, Ohio. Educated at Oberlin College, Harvard, Warsaw, and Prague, he became professor of philosophy at Harvard (1948). His books include *From a Logical Point of View* (1953) and *Word and Object* (1960). His insistence that philosophy is continuous with science has been a source of controversy. » logic; semantics

quinine A drug used in the prevention of malaria, and sometimes used in its treatment. It is present in the bark of various *Cinchona* trees native to the Andes, but it is also cultivated in Ceylon, India, and Java. Pure quinine was first isolated from the bark in 1820, and this form of the drug was the only real antimalarial drug in use until the 1920s. Since the development of resistance to new synthetic antimalarial drugs, it has regained a certain popularity. » alkaloids; malaria

Quinnipiac » **New Haven**

quinoline C_9H_7N, boiling point 238°C. An organic base, related to pyridine. Both it and the isomeric *isoquinoline* are oily

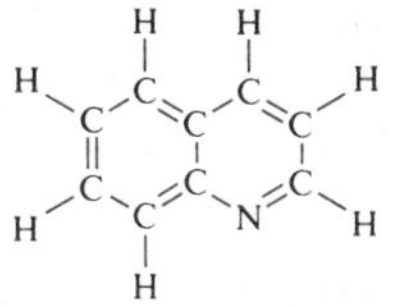

liquids, constituents of coal-tar. Quinine and other alkaloids are derivatives of quinoline. » alkaloids; base (chemistry); pyridine [i]

quinone $C_6H_4O_2$. One of two isomers derived from benzene

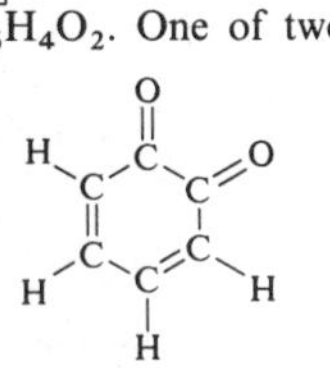

1,2-quinone

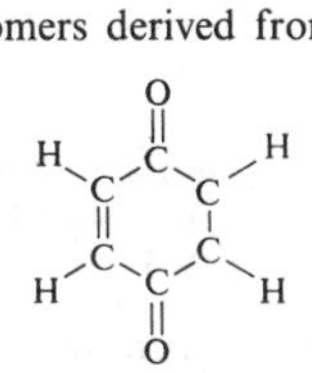

1,4-quinone

(*benzoquinones*) or derivatives of these. They are highly coloured, and a quinone group is often a chromophore of a dyestuff. » benzene [i]; chromophore; isomers

Quinquagesima [kwinkwajesima] In the Western Christian Church, the Sunday before Lent, so called from its being 50 days before Easter, counting inclusively (Latin *quinquagesimus*, 'fiftieth'). » Lent

quinsy The formation of an abscess in and around the tonsils. It is a complication of severe tonsillitis resulting from a bacterial infection. » abscess; streptococcus; tonsils

quipu [keepoo] An accounting system of knotted cords developed by the Peruvian Incas and others. The system was a complex one, with strings and knots of various lengths, shapes, and colours, and was used for keeping detailed records, such as census information, and for sending messages. » Incas

Quirigua [keereegwa] The ruins of a Maya city, dating from 600–900, in a 30 ha/75 acre forest preserve in E Guatemala; a world heritage site. The ruins are notable for their massive sandstone stelae (one is 11 m/35 ft tall), altars, and animal carvings. » Mayas

Quirk, Sir (Charles) Randolph (1920–) British grammarian and writer on the English language, born in the Isle of Man. He was educated at University College, London, where he lectured in English (1947–54), then taught at Durham (1954–60). He returned to a chair at University College (1960–81), where he also directed the Survey of English Usage. Major grammars in which he was involved are *A Grammar of Contemporary English* (1972) and *A Comprehensive Grammar of the English Language* (1985). He was Vice-Chancellor of London University (1981–5). » English language; grammar

Quisling, Vidkun (Abraham Lauritz Jonsson) [kwizling] (1887–1945) Norwegian diplomat and fascist leader, born at Fyresdal. He was Defence Minister in Norway (1931–2), founded the *Nasjonal Samling* (National Unity) in imitation of the German National Socialist Party (1933), and became puppet Prime Minister in occupied Norway. He gave himself up in May 1945, and was executed. His name has since become synonymous with 'traitor'. » fascism; World War 2

Quit India Movement A campaign launched (Aug 1942) by the Indian National Congress calling for immediate independence from Britain, and threatening mass non-violent struggle if its demands were not met. Gandhi and other Congress leaders were arrested, and the movement quickly suppressed. As a result there were two years of relative quiet in Indian politics. » Gandhi; satyagraha

Quito [keetoh] 0°14S 78°30W, pop (1982) 866 472. Capital of Ecuador in the Andean Sierra of NC Ecuador; at E foot of Pichincha volcano; altitude 2 850 m/9 350 ft, giving it a temperate climate; former Inca capital (old city designated a world heritage site); captured by Spanish, 1533; airport; railway; three universities (1769, 1869, 1946); commerce, mining (clay, sand), food processing, textiles, pharmaceuticals, iron and steel, motor vehicles; cathedral, archbishop's palace, government palace, Parque Alameda (with observatory), School of Fine Arts, church and monastery of San Francisco (1535), church and monastery of La Merced (with twin clock to London's Big Ben, 1817); Carnival (Feb). » Ecuador [i]

Qumran, community of [kumran] (c.2nd-c BC–1st-c AD) An exclusive Jewish sect, located near the NW corner of the Dead Sea, apparently closely related to the Essene sect mentioned by Josephus. They opposed the Hasmonean highpriesthood of the 2nd-c BC, and considered themselves alone to be the true Israel awaiting God's new kingdom, being kept pure by their strict practices of legal observance and community discipline. They were destroyed during the Jewish revolt of AD 66–70, but many of their writings were discovered in 1947 as part of the Dead Sea Scrolls. » Dead Sea Scrolls; Essenes; Judaism; Teacher of Righteousness

quoits An outdoor game demanding great accuracy, which involves the throwing of a metal ring at a peg. It has been a popular sport in England since the middle of the 14th-c. From quoits has developed horseshoe pitching.

quotas, import A means of restricting imports of a commodity or product by limiting the quantity that can be imported in a particular period. The aim is to protect domestic industry and preserve foreign currency reserves. They were extensively imposed in the UK in the late 1940s and 1950s, but have now been eliminated for many goods. » protectionism

Qu'ran » **Koran**

Qutb Minar or **Kutab Minar** [kutb minah] A famous city landmark in Delhi, India. Built in 1199 as a Muslim tower of victory, the Qutb Minar is 72.5 m/263 ft high. » Delhi

QwaQwa [kwakwa] pop (1984e) 178 124. National state or non-independent Black homeland in South Africa; self-governing status, 1974. » apartheid; South Africa [i]

R

Rab [rap], ancient **Arba** 44°46N 14°44E, pop (1981) 8 877. Island in the Adriatic Sea off the coast of W Croatia republic, Yugoslavia; a leading resort island since the 1950s; noted for fruit and wine. » Croatia; Yugoslavia [i]

Rabat (Malta) [ra**bat**] 35°53N 14°25E, pop (1983e) 12 121. Town in SWC Malta, 10 km/6 ml SW of Valletta; St Paul lived in a cave here during his 3-month stay on the island after shipwreck, AD 60; Roman villa and museum of Roman antiquities, St Paul's Grotto, Verdala Castle, St Agatha and St Paul's Catacombs. » Malta [i]

Rabat (Morocco) [ra**bat**] 34°02N 6°51W, pop (1982) 518 616. Capital of Morocco, 90 km/56 ml NE of Casablanca at the mouth of the Bou Regreg; one of Morocco's four imperial cities; originally a fortified monastery; city founded, 12th-c; French colonialists established a Residency-General, 1912; airport; railway; university (1957); textiles, carpets, cement bricks, flour milling; mausoleum of Mohammed V, Hassan Tower, 14th-c Chella fortress, arts museum, archaeological museum. » Morocco [i]

rabban » **rabbi**

rabbi (Heb 'my lord', or 'my master/teacher') In Judaism after AD 70, a title for accredited Jewish teachers or sages, who often exercised judicial functions too; prior to 70, used less technically as a form of respectful address, as presumably in the New Testament Gospels. The teachings of these early sages are preserved in the Mishnah, the Talmuds, and many other forms of rabbinic literature. **Rabban** is a superior form of the title, used in the Mishnah for four early scholars: Gamaliel the Elder, Johanan ben Zakkai, Gamaliel II, and Simeon ben Gamaliel II. Today rabbis also have pastoral functions and a role in worship, much like ministers or clergy of other faiths. » Judaism; Mishnah; synagogue

rabbit A mammal of the order *Lagomorpha*, family *Leporidae* (23 species); differs from the closely-related hare in several respects (different skull features, smaller, gives birth to naked young, lives in groups, burrows to produce complex warrens, lacks black ear tips); also called **con(e)y** – a name often used for rabbit skin. The **domestic rabbit**, also known as the **European rabbit or Old World rabbit** (*Oryctolagus cuniculus*), is common as a pet, with many breeds. The **white laboratory rabbit** used in medical research is a form of the domestic rabbit. The name *hare* is used in describing some species. » chinchilla rabbit; cottontail; hare; hyrax; lagomorph; myxomatosis; pika

rabbitfish » **chimaera**

Rabelais, François [ra**buh**lay], pseudonym (an anagram of his name) **Alcofribas Nasier** (?1494–?1553) French satirist, physician, and humanist, born at or near Chinon. After a period with a Franciscan order, he studied medicine at Montpellier, and became a physician at Lyons. Here he began the series of books for which he is remembered, beginning with the comic and satirical *Pantagruel* (1532) and *Gargantua* (1534), published under his pseudonym, and both highly successful, though condemned by the Church for its unorthodox ideas and mockery of religious practices. In 1546 he published his *Tiers Livre* (1546, Third Book) under his own name. It was again condemned, and he fled to Metz, where for a while he practised medicine. He later published a *Quart Livre* (1552, Fourth Book), and there is a *Cinquiesme Livre* (1564, Fifth Book), published after his death, whose authorship is uncertain. » French literature; humanism; satire

rabies A virus infection that affects a wide range of animals, such as dogs, cats, foxes, skunks, and vampire bats; also known as **hydrophobia**. It is transmitted to humans by bites and licks on skin abrasions or intact mucous membranes. The central nervous system and salivary glands are predominantly affected, leading to mental excitement, maniacal attacks, delusions, and hallucinations. The alternative name stems from the violent contractions of the diaphragm and inspiratory muscles induced by drinking. Death is almost invariable. » virus

raccoon A mammal of genus *Procyon* (7 species), native to N and C America; grey with dark bands around tail; face pale with black band across eyes; inhabits woodland and scrubland near water; eats fruit, nuts, and small animals. (Family: *Procyonidae*.) » coati

raccoon dog An E Asian member of the dog family (introduced in Russia); fox-like, with short legs and heavy body; thick yellow-brown coat; face resembles raccoon; inhabits woodland near water; eats small animals (mainly frogs) and fruit; also known in the fur trade as the **Japanese fox** or **Ussuri(an) raccoon**. (*Nyctereutes procyonoides*.) » Canidae; fox; raccoon

race A biologically distinctive human group. The concept has figured large in European thinking until recently, but most anthropologists today consider it to be of little scientific value. Biological differences result from the isolation of one breeding population, but there have been few isolated human groups in recent millennia. In the past 500 years, with the growth of imperialism, slavery, and European colonization, contacts between all human groups have been intensive; gene pools are in constant flux; and the biological differences between populations are slight. The familiar 'racial' classifications typically emphasize superficially obvious features, such as skin colour or hair type, but other genetically transmitted features, such as blood groupings, or differences in inherited enzyme deficiencies, which are more precisely measurable, tend to cross-cut the classical categories. Moreover, genetic dispositions and environment interact to produce local physical types; for example, there are clear correlations between body proportions and climatic variations.

Earlier generations of scholars assumed that biological races could be clearly demarcated, and that racial groups would vary not only in skin colour, skull shape, and so on, but also in intelligence and even in personality. Despite many attempts to establish such correlations, there seems to be no evidence that biological differences between populations have any relationship to variations in ability or character or with any cultural institutions. » anthropology; biology; genetics [i]; Mongoloid; Negroid; Nordic; racism; sociology

racehorse » **thoroughbred**

raceme » **inflorescence** [i]

racer » **black snake**

Rachel Biblical character, daughter of Laban and wife of Jacob, mother of Joseph and Benjamin. According to *Gen* 29, Jacob worked 14 years to earn Rachel as his wife, after having once been tricked into taking her elder sister Leah. At first, Rachel was said to be barren, but later she died when giving birth to her second son Benjamin. » Jacob; Joseph; Old Testament

Rachmaninov or **Rakhmaninov, Sergei Vasilyevich** [rakh**man**inof] (1873–1943) Russian composer and pianist, born at Nijni-Novgorod. He studied at St Petersburg and at Moscow, where he won the gold medal for composition. Having fled from the Russian Revolution, he settled in the USA (1918). He wrote operas, orchestral works, and songs, but is best known for his piano music, which includes four concertos, the popular *Prelude in C Sharp Minor*, and his last major work, the *Rhapsody on a Theme of Paganini* (1934) for piano and orchestra. He died at Beverly Hills, California. » piano

racial discrimination Treating someone in a particular way because of their race or ethnicity. The term is usually understood to mean negative discrimination, that is, treating people in a way which will disadvantage them relative to other social groups. Negative racial discrimination often occurs in housing and employment and is illegal in most modern societies, though often difficult to prove in a court of law. ≫ race; racism

Racine, Jean (Baptiste) [raseen] (1639–99) French dramatic poet, born at La Ferté-Milon. Educated at Beauvais and Port Royal, he went to Paris, where his verses quickly made him known. He began to write plays in 1664, his major verse tragedies including *Andromaque* (1667), *Britannicus* (1669), *Bérénice* (1679), *Bajazet* (1672), and *Phèdre* (1677). He then left the theatre, married, and lived in domestic retirement. He later wrote two religious plays on Old Testament subjects, *Esther* (1689) and *Athalie* (1691). He died in Paris, widely regarded as the master of tragic pathos. ≫ drama; French literature; tragedy

racism An ideology that claims to explain an alleged inferiority of certain racial or ethnic groups in terms of their biological or physical characteristics. Racist beliefs have been used to justify genocide, chronic poverty, and the maintenance of systems of inequality (such as S African apartheid). ≫ ethnicity; ideology; racial discrimination

rackets (UK)/**racquets** (US) A racket-and-ball game played on a walled court by two or four players. It is thought to have originated in the Middle Ages, and to have developed at the Fleet debtor's prison, London, in the 18th-c. It is regarded as the forerunner of many racket/bat and ball games. ≫ real tennis; RR116

Rackham, Arthur (1867–1939) British artist, born and educated in London. A watercolourist and book illustrator, he was well known for his typically Romantic and grotesque pictures in books of fairy tales, such as *Peter Pan* (1906) and his own *The Arthur Rackham Fairy Book* (1933). ≫ English art; watercolour

racoon ≫ **raccoon**

rad In radioactivity, an old unit for absorbed dose; symbol rad; 1 rad is equivalent to 0.01 J/kg, or 1 rad = 0.01 Gy (gray, SI unit); an abbreviation of **röntgen absorbed dose**. ≫ gray; radioactivity units [i]; units (scientific)

radar An acronym for **radio detection and ranging**, a system developed in the 1930s whereby the position and distance of objects can be determined by measuring the time taken for radio waves to be reflected and returned. *Continuous wave radar* detects returned signals by their different frequencies. *Pulsed radar* has a directional antenna which scans the area or tracks an object; the receiver converts the echo pulses to a video signal displayed on a cathode ray tube. The most usual display is the *plan position indicator* (PPI) used by air traffic control. Radar is used in navigation, air control, fire control, storm detection, and by motorway police. ≫ radio

radar astronomy The use of pulses of radio waves to detect the distances and map the surfaces of objects in the Solar System. It has been applied with great success to Venus. ≫ astronomy; Solar System

Radcliffe, Ann, *née* **Ward, Ann** (1764–1823) British novelist, born and died in London. She lived a retired life, and became well known for her Gothic novels, notably *The Romance of the Forest* (1791), *The Mysteries of Udolpho* (1794), and *The Italian* (1797). Her contemporary reputation was considerable, and she influenced Byron, Shelley, and others, many of whom imitated her 'gothick romances'. ≫ Byron; English literature; Gothic novel; Shelley, Percy Bysshe

Radek, Karl Bernhardovich [**rah**dek], originally **Sobelsohn** (1885–?1939) Russian revolutionary and politician, born at Lwów. Educated at Kraków and Bern, he became a journalist. He organized the German communists during their revolution (1918), and was imprisoned (1919). Returning to the Soviet Union, he became a leading member of the Communist International, but lost standing with his growing distrust of extremist tactics. He was charged as a Trotsky supporter, and expelled from the Party (1927–30). In 1937 he was a victim of one of Stalin's show trials. ≫ communism; Russian Revolution; Stalin; Trotsky

Radhakrishnan, Sir Sarvepalli (1888–1975) Indian philosopher, statesman, and President (1962–7), born at Tiruttani, Madras. Educated at Madras, he taught at Mysore and Calcutta Universities, and became professor of Eastern religions and ethics at Oxford (1936–52). In 1946 he was chief Indian delegate to UNESCO, becoming Chairman in 1949. A member of the Indian Assembly in 1947, he was Indian Ambassador to the Soviet Union (1949), Vice-President of India (1952–62), and President. He was knighted in 1931, and died in Madras. ≫ India [i]; UNESCO

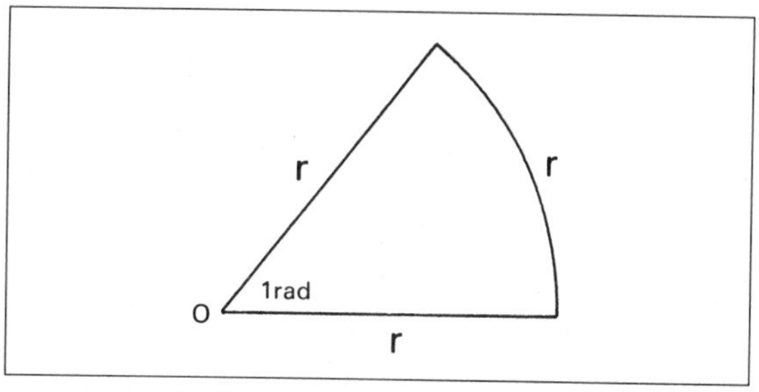

A radian

radian SI unit for measuring angles in a plane: symbol rad; 1 radian is the angle subtended at the centre of a circle by an arc along the circumference equal in length to the circle's radius; thus π radians = 180°. ≫ angle; plane; units (scientific); RR71

radiance; radiant intensity/power ≫ **radiometry** [i]

radiation A general term for the processes by which energy is lost from a source without physical contact. It refers to various radioactive and electromagnetic emissions. Heat radiation, for example, is electromagnetic radiation emitted from an object on account of its temperature. ≫ blackbody radiation; electromagnetic radiation [i]; radiation sickness; radioactivity; radiometry [i]

radiation sickness A common complication of the application of radiotherapy (ionizing radiations) to parts of the body in the course of treatment for malignant tumours. Weakness, nausea, and vomiting are common, both during and after treatment. The skin may become abnormally red in patches (*erythema*), and lesions of the mouth may occur. ≫ radiotherapy; tumour

radical An unstable molecule containing unpaired electrons (eg CH_3, methyl). The term is also used as a synonym for 'group' in the sense of 'part of a molecule'. ≫ molecule

radicalism Any set of ideas, normally of the left but not exclusively so, which argues for more substantial social and political change than is supported in the political mainstream. What is radical is a matter of judgment, and so the term is very widely applied. In a number of countries there are radical parties which are left of centre. ≫ left wing; social action

radio The transmission of sound signals through space by means of radio-frequency electromagnetic waves. In 1888 the German physicist Heinrich Hertz produced and detected radio waves, developing the equations made by James Clerk Maxwell. Gulielmo Marconi constructed a device to translate radio waves into electrical signals, and in 1901 transmitted signals across the Atlantic Ocean. Prior to World War 1, radio messages were sent between land stations and ships, and between land and aircraft. In 1918, a radiotelegraph message was transmitted from Wales to Australia. Radio broadcasting became routinely available during the 1920s, when such institutions as the BBC came into being. ≫ amplitude modulation; BBC; broadcasting; citizens' band (CB) radio; electromagnetic radiation [i]; frequency modulation; Hertz; loudspeaker [i]; Marconi; Maxwell, James Clerk; microphone [i]; modulation; radio astronomy/beacon/galaxy/waves; telegraphy; telescope [i]; thermionic valve; transistor

radio astronomy The exploration of the universe by detecting radio emission from celestial objects. The frequency range is very great, from 10 MHz to 300 GHz. A variety of antennas are used, from single dishes to elaborate networks of telescopes forming intercontinental radio interferometers. The principal sources of cosmic radio emission are the Sun, Jupiter, interstellar gas, pulsars, supernova remnants, radio galaxies, quasars, and the cosmic background radiation of the universe itself. » astronomy; radio waves

radio beacon A fixed radio transmitting station, sending out a coded signal characteristic of that station. This helps aircraft pilots and ships' captains to navigate safely, especially in bad weather conditions. Using two or more radio beacons, a direction finder aboard a vessel can accurately pinpoint the vessel's position. » direction finder; radio

radio galaxy A galaxy which is an intense source of cosmic radio waves – about one galaxy in a million. In such objects, an active galactic nucleus (almost certainly a black hole) is producing immense quantities of electrons travelling at almost the speed of light. When these encounter a magnetic field, they spiral around the field lines, emitting synchrotron radiation as radio waves. Some radio galaxies are extremely large, with radio emission coming from regions up to 300 kiloparsecs from the associated galaxy. Investigations of these objects led directly to the discovery of quasars. » black hole; galaxy; quasar; synchrotron radiation

radio telescope » telescope [i]

radio waves Electromagnetic radiation of wavelength greater than about 10 cm. It is produced by oscillating electric currents in antennas, and travels at the velocity of light. Modulated radio waves are used in communications. » amplitude modulation; attenuation; electromagnetic radiation [i]; frequency modulation; radio

radioactive dating » radiocarbon dating

radioactive fallout The radioactive substances produced by a nuclear explosion (eg above-ground weapons testing; the accident at Chernobyl nuclear power station in 1986). These substances are carried away from the explosion site by winds, and are deposited (either from dry air as particles, or dissolved in rain) causing contamination, possibly up to thousands of kilometres away. Fallout from the Chernobyl accident included caesium-134, caesium-137, iodine-131, plutonium-239, and strontium-90. » Chernobyl; nuclear reactor [i]; nuclear weapons; radioactivity

radioactive tracer A radioactive isotope of an element substituted specifically in the compound in order to 'tag' it. Much has been learned about the mechanisms of reactions in this way, as the reactant supplying a specific atom to a product can be identified. » radioactivity

radioactive waste A by-product of the many processes involved in the generation of nuclear power. Despite nearly 30 years of commercial nuclear power generation, there is no acceptable solution to the problem of radioactive waste disposal. Three levels of waste are produced: low, intermediate, and high. *Low-level* and *intermediate-level* waste is generally buried in pits: at Drigg, adjacent to the Sellafield nuclear complex in the UK, and in abandoned salt mines in Germany. *High-level* waste is generally stored in stainless steel tanks, and continually cooled. One possibility for storage is vitrification (solidification in glass), to reduce the volume of waste. Proposals exist for the burial of high-level waste either under the sea-bed or deep underground on land. The production and storage of radioactive waste is a major international environmental issue, with strong opposition from such pressure groups as Greenpeace. » Greenpeace; hazardous substances; nuclear reactor [i]; waste disposal

radioactivity The spontaneous decay of atomic nuclei, resulting in the emission of particles and energy; discovered by French physicist Antoine Henri Becquerel in 1896. The possible emissions are alpha particles, beta particles, and gamma rays. The exact moment of decay for any one nucleus cannot be predicted, though for a large sample the fraction of nuclei that will decay can be determined. Radioactivity is detected and measured using Geiger counters. » alpha decay; background radiation; Becquerel; beta decay; electron capture; gamma rays; half-life; Geiger counter [i]; nuclear physics; radioactivity units [i]; radiocarbon dating; radioisotope

radioactivity units The activity of a radioactive source expressed in *becquerels*, Bq, where 1 Bq is one decay per second. Particles from different substances may be produced in similar numbers but with very different energies. This is taken into account using a second unit, the *gray*, Gy, which measures the energy deposited in some object by the radiation: the *absorbed dose*. Different types of radiation cause different degrees of biological damage, even if the total energy deposited is the same; for example, 1 Gy of alpha radiation causes 20 times as much damage as 1 Gy of beta radiation. This potential for causing harm is expressed as *dose equivalent*, units sievert, Sv, which is the product of absorbed dose in Gy and a *relative biological effectiveness* (RBE) factor. Radiation limits for working places and the environment are expressed in Sv. Names, definitions, and units are summarized in the table. » becquerel; exposure (physics); gray; radioactivity; sievert

RADIOACTIVITY UNITS

NAME	DEFINITION	UNIT	OLD UNIT
activity	rate of disintegrations	Bq	Ci (curie)
absorbed dose	energy deposited in object, divided by mass of object	Gy	rad
dose equivalent	absorbed dose × RBE	Sv	rem

RBE	RADIATION
20	alpha
10	neutron
1	beta, gamma, X-ray

radiobiology The branch of biology concerned with the effects of radioactive materials on living organisms, and with the use of radioactive tracers to study metabolic processes. » biology; metabolism; radioactivity

radiocarbon dating A radiometric method for measuring the decay of the radioactive isotope carbon-14 in organic material up to 100 000 years old, developed in 1948–9 by US chemist Willard Libby. Living animals and plants take in carbon, which contains some radioactive carbon-14. When the organism dies, it stops taking in carbon, and as the carbon-14 decays, its proportion to the total amount of carbon decreases in a way which is directly related to the time elapsed since death. Using samples principally from wood and charcoal, the technique revolutionized archaeological dating across the world. » carbon; dendrochronology; Libby; radioactivity

radiochemistry The production and use of radioisotopes to study chemical compounds and their reactions. An example is the synthesis of compounds incorporating radioactive atoms in specific sites, to see whether those atoms are present in a product of a subsequent chemical reaction. » chemistry

radiogram A single device capable of both receiving radio broadcasts and playing gramophone records. It was developed during the 1930s, with the wider domestic use of radio sets and electricity, and incorporated a record player which made use of the radio's amplifier and speaker. Popular for its convenience and for aesthetic reasons, it was the forerunner of the music centre. » radio; record player

radiography Producing a photographic image (actually a shadow-image) of a structure which is penetrated by X-rays, gamma-rays, or electrons. These radiations are, in general, differentially absorbed by the different parts of any structure, and produce corresponding densities of exposure on a photographic film. The first radiograph was made by Röntgen in 1895, and the technique is now highly developed for medical diagnosis and for non-destructive industrial testing. In **miniature radiography**, the X-ray image on a large fluorescent screen in contact with the subject is photographed with a 35 mm camera. » auto-radiograph; gamma rays; photography; Röntgen; X-rays

radio-immunoassay A method using radioactivity-labelled material corresponding to a substance to be measured, together with a specific antibody to the substance. After mixing, the degree of binding of the antibody to the labelled substance can be estimated, and used to calculate the amount of substance present in a biological fluid, such as blood. » radioactivity

radioisotope An isotope which spontaneously undergoes radioactive decay. It may be naturally occurring or artificially produced. All isotopes of all elements with an atomic number above 83 are radioisotopes. Carbon-14 is an isotope continuously produced in the upper atmosphere by cosmic ray bombardment, and used in the technique of carbon dating. » radio-carbon dating; isotopes; RR90

radioisotope thermo-electric generator (RTG) A source of electrical power for spacecraft operating at great distances from the Sun (replacing insufficiently powerful solar arrays) or on planetary surfaces (where solar array operation is impractical). Radioactive material is used to generate heat, and electricity is generated by temperature differential across dissimilar metals. The fuel is usually plutonium-238, which has a half-life of 77 years and can therefore generate copious heat in small quantities to power spacecraft having mission lifetimes of a decade or so. RTGs have been used for many US and Soviet space missions, including Apollo seisometer packages, Viking landers, Pioneers 10 and 11, and Voyagers 1 and 2; they are also planned as the power source for Galileo and Ulysses missions. Because nuclear fuel is used, the devices are built to survive launch and spacecraft accidents, and even to withstand atmospheric re-entry. » Apollo/Pioneer programme; Galileo/Ulysses/Viking/Voyager project [i]; half-life

radiolaria [raydiuh**lai**ria] An informal grouping of marine single-celled organisms (protozoans). They have a typically spherical cell body, with an elaborate skeleton consisting of radiating spikes of silica. (Class: *Actinopoda*.) » Protozoa

radiometric dating A method for determining the absolute age of a rock by measuring the amount of radioactive element present and comparing it to the amount of stable element into which it decays. This ratio, in conjunction with the known half-life of the radiometric element, is used to calculate the age of the rock or mineral being measured. » potassium-argon/radiocarbon/rubidium-strontium/uranium-lead dating; radioactivity

radiometry The measurement of radiated electromagnetic energy, especially infrared; see table for symbols and units. **Radiant power** is the total power from a source; **radiant intensity** is radiant power per unit solid angle, and is used to describe sources that do not radiate uniformly in all directions; **radiance** is radiant intensity per unit area; **irradiance** is total power per unit area. Radiometric quantities are measured using radiometers. » electromagnetic radiation [i]; photometry [i]

RADIOMETRY

RADIOMETRIC QUANTITY	SYMBOL	UNITS
radiant power	Φ	W
radiant intensity	I	W/sr
radiance	L	W/sr.m^2
irradiance	E	W/m^2

radiosonde (radiosounding) balloon A package of instruments sent up with a weather balloon to measure pressure, temperature, and humidity as the balloon rises to high altitudes (20 000 m/65 000 ft). Pressure measurements are used to calculate altitude. Information is transmitted back to ground-receiving stations by radio signals, and the instruments are recovered after descent by parachute. A **rawindsonde** (radar wind sounding) balloon is a version of radiosonde which also measures wind speed and direction. The balloon carries a radar target so that its course can be plotted. » weather

radiotherapy The use of radiation (especially X-rays) to treat disease, especially malignant tumours, which are more sensitive to certain kinds of radiation than are normal tissues. When X-rays are used to control a tumour, they are directed into the patient in a beam from several different angles, carefully positioned so that the tumour receives the maximum concentration, leaving adjacent healthy tissues little affected. Radioactive materials can also be used (eg a tiny pellet), implanted directly into the tumour to give a carefully calculated total dose. The technique has proved particularly successful in the treatment of various kinds of cancer. » cancer; tumour; X-rays

radish An annual or biennial with a tuberous root, irregularly-lobed leaves, and cross-shaped, white to purplish flowers. Its origin is unknown, but it has been used as a vegetable since Ancient Egyptian times. Summer radishes are small and fast-growing; winter radishes large, up to 250 g/9 oz, are slower-growing. The related **wild radish** (*Raphanus raphanistrum*) has slender roots and often yellow flowers. (*Raphanus sativus*. Family: *Cruciferae*.) » annual; biennial; tuber; vegetable

radium Ra, element 88, melting point 700°C. A metal, with all its isotopes radioactive. The most stable isotope, ^{226}Ra, has a half-life of only 1 620 years, but it occurs in uranium ores as a product of radioactive decay, and its main source is extraction from these ores. Its chemical properties are similar to those of barium, but all its uses relate to its radioactivity, and it is usually used as a salt, such as $RaCl_2$. It is a source of α-particles, and combined with beryllium, a neutron source. Radium salts exhibit fluorescence, and were formerly used in luminous watch dials. » chemical elements; neutron; uranium; RR90

radius (anatomy) » **arm**

radon Rn, element 86, boiling point −62°C. The heaviest of the noble gases. It has several isotopes: that with the longest half-life (4 days) is ^{222}Rn, formed with radium. It is continuously liberated to the atmosphere by natural radioactive decay; on average, a litre of air contains about 1 000 atoms of Rn (1 part in 10^{20}). Its few compounds, mainly fluorides, are similar to those of xenon; its primary use is in radiotherapy. » chemical elements; noble gases; radium; xenon; RR90

Raeburn, Sir Henry (1756–1823) British portrait painter, born near Edinburgh, Scotland. He first produced watercolour miniatures, then worked in oils. After his marriage to a lady of means, he studied in Rome (1785–7), then settled in Edinburgh, where he painted the leading members of Edinburgh society in a typically bold, strongly-shadowed style. He was knighted in 1822, and died in Edinburgh. » miniature painting; watercolour

Raeder, Erich [**ray**der] (1876–1960) German grand admiral, born at Wandsbek. He joined the navy in 1894, and became a Chief-of-Staff during World War 1. In 1928 he was made Commander-in-Chief of the navy, a grand admiral in 1939, and in 1943 head of an anti-invasion force. At the Nuremberg Trials (1946), he was sentenced to life imprisonment, but released in 1955. He died in Kiel. » World War 2

RAF » **Royal Air Force**

raffia palm A tree growing to 7.5 m/25 ft, native to Africa; leaves 18 m/60 ft, feathery. The surface of the young leaflets is stripped to provide raffia fibre. (Genus: *Raffia*, 30 species. Family: *Palmae*.) » palm

Raffles, Sir (Thomas) Stamford (1781–1826) British colonial administrator, born at sea, off Port Morant, Jamaica. He became Lieutenant-Governor of Java (1811–16), where he completely reformed the administration. In 1816 ill-health brought him home to England, where he was knighted. As Lieutenant-Governor of Benkoelen (1818–23), he established a settlement at Singapore. He died in London. » East India Company, British

rafflesia The best-known member of an entirely parasitic family of flowering plants from the tropics and subtropics. All are obligate parasites, in which the plant is reduced to a web of cells, most closely resembling the hyphae of fungi, which spread through the body of the host plant. Only the flowers are recognizable as belonging to a flowering-plant, developing as buds within the host tissue and bursting through before opening. Some members of the family have small flowers and parasitize herbs; rafflesia, native to Malaysia, parasitizes woody vines and has enormous flowers. The flowers of *Rafflesia arnoldii* are the largest in the world, reaching 1 m/3¼ ft in diameter. They are bowl-shaped, with 4–5 spreading lobes, and are typical carrion flowers, the whole structure being fleshy, mottled, and coloured to resemble rotting meat. They produce a strong putrid smell to complete the illusion, and attract flies to pollinate them. (Genus: *Rafflesia*, 12 species. Family: *Rafflesiaceae*.) » carrion flower; fungus; parasitic plant

Rafsanjani, Ali Akbar Hashemi [rafsan**jah**nee] (1934–) Iranian political leader, born in Rafsanjan, in the 1980s the most influential figure in Iran after Khomeini, and his successor as President (1989–). He supported Khomeini after the latter's exile in 1963, and became a wealthy property speculator in the 1970s. After the 1979 revolution, he helped to found the ruling Islamic Republican Party, and in 1980 was chosen as Speaker of the Majlis (Lower House), representing the moderates who favour improved relations with the West. Since he became President, his policies have been more radical. » Iran [i]; Khomeini

raga In Indian music, the equivalent of the Western 'mode', but with broader connotations of melodic contour, performance style, ornamentation, etc. » mode (music)

ragged robin A perennial herb, native to Europe and Asia, usually in marshy or damp places; opposite leaves; flowers pink, rarely white, five petals, each divided into four narrow segments and with two cleft scales at the base, giving the 'ragged' effect. (*Lychnis flos-cuculi*. Family: *Caryophyllaceae*.) » herb; perennial

ragged school A school where education was offered free to the children of the poor, who often came to school without shoes and in ragged clothing. It was a development of the early 19th-c by John Pounds of Portsmouth (1766–1839).

Raglan (of Raglan), Fitzroy James Henry Somerset, 1st Baron (1788–1855) British general, born at Badminton, Gloucestershire. He joined the army in 1804, fought at Waterloo (1815), became an MP, and was made a baron in 1852. In 1854 he led an ill-prepared force against the Russians in the Crimea, but though victorious at Alma he did not follow up his advantage. His ambiguous order led to the Charge of the Light Brigade (1854) at Balaclava. He died at Sevastopol. His name was given to the raglan sleeve, which came into use in the 1850s. » Crimean War

Ragnarok [**rag**narok] In Norse mythology, the final battle between the gods and the monstrous forces hostile to them. Though gods and monsters die, a new world will arise. » Germanic religion; Lif

ragtime A type of syncopated US music popular from c.1890 to c.1920, when it yielded to (and influenced) the new jazz style. Despite the popularity of Irving Berlin's song, *Alexander's Ragtime Band* (1911), 'rags' were composed mainly for piano, and ragtime was popularized by Scott Joplin and other pianist-composers. Its revival in the 1970s was mainly due to the advocacy of US scholar, pianist and conductor, Joshua Rifkin (1944–). » jazz; Joplin

ragworm A free-swimming, carnivorous worm found close to the sea bed; catches prey using an outward-turning muscular tube (proboscis) armed with strong jaws; swims using lateral lobes (*parapodia*) on its body segments, armed with bristles. (Phylum: *Annelida*. Class: *Polychaeta*.) » worm

ragwort A robust biennial or perennial, growing to 1.5 m/5 ft, native to Europe and W Asia, but widely introduced elsewhere; leaves with irregularly toothed lobes; flower heads numerous, up to 2.5 cm/1 in across, bright golden yellow and daisy-like, in dense flat-topped clusters. It is poisonous to livestock if eaten in quantity, and is usually avoided by grazing cattle. (*Senecio jacobaea*. Family: *Compositae*.) » biennial; perennial

Rahman, Shaikh Mujibur [rah**mahn**] (1920–75) First Prime Minister (1972–5) and President (1975) of Bangladesh, born at Tongipara, East Bengal (now Bangladesh). After studying law at Dacca, he helped found the Awami League (1949). In 1954 he was elected to the East Pakistan Provincial Assembly, and took an oppositional role during the 1960s. In 1966 he was arrested and imprisoned for two years for provoking separatism. After winning an overall majority in the Pakistani elections of 1970, but being denied office, he launched a non-co-operation campaign which escalated into civil war and the creation of Bangladesh. After becoming President in 1975, he was overthrown and killed in a coup in Dacca. » Bangladesh [i]; Pakistan [i]

Rahner, Karl (1904–84) Leading German Roman Catholic theologian, who played a major role as consultant at the Second Vatican Council (1962–6), born at Freiburg im Breisgau. He studied at Freiburg and Innsbruck, and taught at Innsbruck, Munich, and Münster. In his voluminous writings (such as his multivolume *Theological Investigations*), he uses insights of the philosophy of existentialism while remaining true to the tradition of Aquinas. He died at Innsbruck, Austria. » Aquinas; existentialism; Vatican Councils

Raikes, Robert (1735–1811) British philanthropist and pioneer of the Sunday-School movement, born and died in Gloucester. In 1757 he succeeded his father as proprietor of the *Gloucester Journal*. His pity for the misery and ignorance of many children in his native city led him in 1780 to start a Sunday School where they might learn to read and repeat the Catechism. He lived to see such schools spread over England.

rail A bird of the world-wide family *Rallidae* (c.130 species), possibly the most widespread group of terrestrial birds; large legs, short rounded wings, and short tails; many (not all) found near water; many extinct species. The name is also used for **rail-babblers** (*Timaliidae*) and **Bensch's rail** (*Mesitornithidae*). » coot; corncrake; crake; gallinule; jacana; moorhen; takahe

rail gun 1 A heavy artillery piece mounted on a railway carriage. **2** A proposed component of SDI, a land-based, short-range system for the last-ditch defence of individual land targets. It uses electrical energy to accelerate kinetic energy munitions to very high velocities. » kinetic energy weapons; SDI

railway The general name given in the UK to a transport system that has as its central feature the operation of a locomotive hauling passenger carriages or freight trucks on specially mounted tracks or rails, called the *permanent way*. The geographical area covered by the rails forms a *rail network*, and the operation of all trains on the network together with their scheduling, control, and engineering support services form a *railway system*. N American usage retains the historical name of *railroad* to describe the above definition of railway, and uses the term *railway* to describe the permanent way, ie the rails, their fixings, and associated engineering.

The world's first railway, the Stockton and Darlington, was opened in 1825, and was used mainly for the carriage of coal and other goods, employing both steam locomotives and horses for traction. It was not until 1830, and the opening of the Liverpool and Manchester Railway, that a full passenger-carrying railway with all its associated handling features, and solely dependent on steam locomotives, became operational. From this early start, railways quickly spread across Europe and the USA, where in 1831 the 'Best Friend of Charleston' pulled the first train on US soil. By 1869 it was possible to cross the USA by rail. Railways spread across the rest of the world by colonial and trade expansion, as happened in India in 1851. However, such introductions quickly developed into different types to suit local conditions, even though most of the equipment was still manufactured in Europe or the USA and exported.

Because of the strategic nature of railways, governments have always taken a strong interest in their building and operation, and indeed most railways in the world are at present state-owned, running at a loss. These losses arise from the high cost of investment needed to replace old machinery and buildings, and the strong increase in competition from road transport. Since 1947, the entire British railway system has been state-owned, and various attempts at rationalization have been undertaken in an endeavour to reduce non-economic operation. The most famous of these rationalizations, which gave rise to a large number of line closures, was the implementation of the Beeching Report of 1963. Rather similar problems in the USA led to the formation of AMTRAK in 1971. AMTRAK is wholly owned by the US government, but unlike most nationalized railways is responsible only for intercity passenger rail services; freight is handled by private companies. It seems likely that both British Rail and AMTRAK will be privatized in the future. In an effort to counter the competition of both road transport and aircraft, new fast trains have been developed, most notably in Japan (the 'Bullet' train) and France (the TGV, short for 'Très Grande Vitesse'). The success of the TGV has led to a new network of such trains being introduced throughout France. » Canadian Pacific Railway;

locomotive [i]; Shinkansen; underground

railway signalling A system for controlling the movement of trains, formerly using flags and hand-operated mechanical signals, and in recent years electronic systems. In the UK in the 1980s, British Rail installed computer-controlled 4-aspect signalling, designed to interlock with the points system. Trackside colour light signals give the driver instructions: green (go), red (stop), double yellow (caution), single yellow (greater caution). These are supplemented by audio and visual signals in the driver's cab. Drivers must acknowledge yellow signals by braking or pressing a reset button, otherwise the train is automatically stopped. Despite these precautions, accidents still occur. A collison in Clapham, London, in 1988 was caused by defective wiring; a crash at Purley, Greater London, in 1989 was caused by a driver going through a red light. Some European countries use a system whereby a microcomputer in the cab can over-ride the driver. » railway

rain gauge A meteorological instrument used to measure the amount of rainfall for a given period. It is commonly in the form of a bucket, with an opening of known size, which funnels rain into a measuring cylinder below. To maintain standards, measurements are made at set times using standardized instruments. Automatic rain gauges recording time and amount of rain are used to calculate rainfall intensity. » rainfall

rainbow An arc of light comprising the spectral colours, formed when the Sun's rays are refracted and internally reflected by raindrops acting as prisms or lenses. It is visible when the Sun is behind the observer and the rain is in front. » spectrum

Rainbow Snake In Australian aboriginal religion, the great fertility spirit, both male and female, creator and destroyer; known as **Julunggul**. It is associated with streams and waterholes, from which it emerges in the creation-story and leaves special markings on the ground. » Aborigines

rainfall A type of precipitation in which water droplets reach the ground in liquid state. When water droplets are small, rain may be called *drizzle*. In temperate and humid regions, rainfall may form the major contribution to annual precipitation totals, while at high latitudes snow may be the main contributor. The amount of rainfall is measured with a rain gauge. » convective/orographic rain; precipitation; rain gauge; sleet

rainforest The vegetation type found in wet equatorial regions and other areas of high precipitation, such as the Coast Mountains of NW USA, and New Zealand. Tropical rainforests are characterized by a great diversity of plant and animal species, a closed canopy layer which allows little light to reach the forest floor, and rapid nutrient cycling within the forest. Despite the luxuriant growth of these forests, when cut down the soils are relatively infertile, because most of the nutrients are in the vegetation, and soils are rapidly washed away. Many of the trees have considerable commercial value (eg mahogany, teak), and large areas are being cleared. Deforestation is also occurring to create new agricultural areas (cattle ranching) and industry (mining). The United Nations Food and Agricultural Organization estimates that 100 000 sq km/40 000 sq ml are cleared each year. This rate of disappearance is alarming many conservationists, because of the extinction of unique plant and animal species. Tropical rainforests also play an important role in the global climate system, which could also be disrupted by clearance. » deforestation; selva; shifting cultivation; tropics; Plate II

Rainier III, properly **Rainier Louis Henri Maxence Bertrand de Grimaldi** [raynyay] (1923–) Prince of Monaco (1949–), born in Monaco. In 1956 he married **Grace (Patricia) Kelly** (1929–82), a US film actress, whose successful career included *High Noon* (1952), *Rear Window* (1954), and *High Society* (1956), before she retired on her marriage. There are two daughters, **Princess Caroline Louise Marguerite** (1957–) and **Princess Stephanie Marie Elisabeth** (1965–), and a son **Prince Albert Alexandre Louis Pierre** (1958–). Princess Grace died after a car accident in 1982. » Monaco

Rainier, Mount [raynyer] 46°51N 121°46W. Dormant volcano in WC Washington, USA; height 4 395 m/14 419 ft; highest point in the Cascade Range; the largest single-peak glacier system in the USA; Mt Rainier National Park; 26 glaciers, notably Emmons (c.8 km/5 ml long) and Nisqually (c.6 km/3¾ ml long). » Washington (state)

Rais or **Raiz** » **Retz, Baron**

raisins Black or white grapes, dried naturally or artificially. They have a high sugar content, and are used widely in cake and bun making to impart sweetness.

Rajasthan [**rah**jastahn] pop (1981) 34 102 912; area 342 214 sq km/132 095 sq ml. State in NW India, bounded W by Pakistan; formed in 1948; capital, Jaipur; governed by a 200-member Legislative Assembly; crossed by numerous rivers; Thar desert in the W; Anavalli range to the S; pulses, sugar cane, oilseed, cotton; textiles, cement, glass, sugar; phosphate, silver, asbestos, copper, feldspar, limestone, salt. » India [i]; Jaipur

Rakhmaninov » **Rachmaninov**

Rakoczi [rak**oh**tsee] A princely family of Hungary and Transylvania which became extinct in 1780. The most important member was the popular **Francis II** (1676–1735), who in 1703 led a Hungarian revolt against Austria. He had little success but was hailed by his countrymen as a patriot and a hero. His later years were spent as a Carmelite monk in France and in Turkey, where he died. » Hungary [i]

Raleigh or **Ralegh, Sir Walter** (1552–1618) English courtier, navigator, and author, born at Hayes Barton, Devon. Educated at Oxford, he became prime favourite of Queen Elizabeth. He was knighted in 1584, and that year sent the first of three expeditions to America. After the arrival of the Earl of Essex at court, he lost influence, and spent some years in Ireland. On his return, Elizabeth discovered his intrigue with Bessy Throckmorton, one of her maids-of-honour, and he was committed to the Tower. On his release, he married Bessy, and lived at Sherborne. He took little part in the intrigues at the close of Elizabeth's reign, but his enemies turned James I against him, and he was imprisoned (1603), his death sentence being commuted to life imprisonment. While in the Tower, he wrote his *History of the World* (1614), and several other works. Released in 1616, he made an expedition to the Orinoco in search of a gold-mine, which was a failure. His death sentence was invoked, and he was executed. » Elizabeth I; Essex, 2nd Earl of; James I (of England)

Raleigh [**rah**lee] 35°46N 78°38W, pop (1980) 150 255. Capital of state in Wake County, EC North Carolina, USA; established, 1788; named after Sir Walter Raleigh; airfield; railway; two universities (1865, 1887); foods, textiles, electrical equipment; birthplace of President Andrew Johnson. » Johnson, Andrew; North Carolina; Raleigh, Walter

rally A form of motor racing which demands skill and endurance from driver and navigator. Rallies are raced over several days (sometimes weeks) both on open roads and in forests, national parks, etc, where special stages are organized. Drivers use modified production cars. The most famous rallies are the Monte Carlo Rally, the RAC Lombard Rally, and the Safari Rally. » motor racing

ram » **sheep**

RAM An acronym of **random access memory**, a type of computer memory, usually integrated circuits, which can be read from and written to. RAM is used in all computers; data contained in RAM is lost when the electrical power is removed. » memory, computer; ROM

Ram Mohan Roy, Raja (1774–1833) Indian religious reformer, born at Burdwan, Bengal, who did much to awaken the Hindu social conscience. Of high Brahman ancestry, he came early to question his ancestral faith, and studied Buddhism in Tibet. He published various works in Persian, Arabic, and Sanskrit, with the aim of uprooting idolatry, and helped to abolish suttee. In 1820 he published *The Precepts of Jesus*, accepting the morality preached by Christ, but rejecting his deity and miracles. In 1828 he began the Brahmo Samaj association, and in 1830 was given the title of Raja. He visited England in 1831, and died in Bristol. » Brahmo Samaj; Buddhism; Hinduism; Jesus Christ; Suttee

Ram Singh [**rahm** sing] (1816–85) Sikh philosopher and reformer, born at Bhaini. As a boy, he was a member of the Namdhari movement, of which he later became leader. Having entered the army of Ranjit Singh, he formed a sect to rejuvenate Sikhism. He built up a *khalsa*, or private army, and prophesied that British rule would be broken. Following attacks on Muslims in 1872, he was exiled to Rangoon as a state prisoner. He died in Mergni, Burma. » Sikhism

Ramadan [rama**dahn**] The ninth month of the Muslim year, observed as a month of fasting during which Muslims abstain from eating and drinking between sunrise and sunset; the Ramadan fast is one of the five 'pillars', or basic duties, of Islam. » Id-ul-Fitr; Islam; RR22

Ramadan War » **Arab-Israeli Wars**

Ramakrishna [rama**krish**na] , also called **Gadadhar Chattopadhyaya** (1836–86) Hindu religious teacher, born at Hooghly, Bengal, the son of a poor Brahmin family with little formal education. He formed a religious order which bore his name, and established its headquarters in Calcutta. His most noteworthy disciple was Swami Vivekananda. He died in Calcutta. » Vivekananda

Raman, Sir Chandrasekhara (Venkata) (1888–1970) Indian physicist, born at Trichinopoly. Educated at Madras, he became professor of physics at Calcutta (1917–33) and director of the Indian Institute of Science at Bangalore. In 1929 he was knighted, and in 1930 awarded the Nobel Prize for Physics for his discoveries relating to the scattering of light. He died at Bangalore. » optics [i]

Raman scattering Light scattering from a material in which the scattered light comprises substance-dependent spectral lines centred on and symmetric about the frequency of the incident light; described by Indian physicist Chandrasekhara Raman in 1928. The frequency shift is due to an energy exchange between the incident light photons and the scattering atoms. Raman spectroscopy using lasers is an important means of studying the structure of molecules. » light; Raman

Ramanuja [ra**man**ooja] (traditionally c.1017–1137) Hindu theologian and philosopher, born at Sriperumbudur, Tamil Nadu. He organized temple worship, founded centres to disseminate his doctrine of devotion to Visnu and Siva, and provided the intellectual basis for the practice of *bhakti* or devotional worship. He died at Srirangam. » Hinduism

Ramapithecus [rama**pith**uhkuhs] A fossil ape, known from the Miocene epoch of E Europe, Asia, and E Africa; ground-dwelling, walked on all fours; jaws robust; cheek teeth large, with thick enamel; canine teeth low as in early hominids; probably fed on coarse foodstuffs gathered in mixed woodland and savannah. (Family: *Pongidae*.) » ape; Miocene epoch

Ramayana One of the two great Sanskrit epics of ancient India, which tells the story of Rama, his wife Sita, and the evil forces ranged against them. Though ascribed to the sage Valmiki, it derives from oral tradition. Its 24 000 couplets make it one-quarter the length of the *Mahabharata*. A critical edition is in progress (1958–). » epic; Hinduism; Indian literature; Mahabharata

Rambert, Dame Marie, originally **Cyvia Rambam** (1888–1982) Polish-British ballet dancer and teacher, born in Warsaw. She was sent to Paris to study medicine, but became involved in artistic circles, and instead took up dancing. In 1913 she worked on Stravinsky's *Rite of Spring* with Diaghilev's Ballets Russes. She moved to London, where she became a British citizen (1918). From 1926 she formed small companies to present classical and new ballets, promoting collaboration between painters, musicians, and choreographers. In 1935 she formed the Ballet Rambert, and remained closely associated with it through its change to a modern dance company in the 1960s. She was created a Dame in 1962, and died in London. » ballet; Ballets Russes; modern dance; Rambert Dance Company

Rambert Dance Company As Ballet Rambert, a dance company famous from the 1920s for generating new choreography and for collaborations with visual artists and musicians, inspired by Marie Rambert. It was a major classical company in the 1940s–50s, and became a streamlined modern dance company in 1966 under director Norman Morrice. A new director, Richard Alston, introduced a style derived from the US choreographer Merce Cunningham, and in 1987 changed the name to the Rambert Dance Company. » ballet; Rambert

Ramblers' Association A British federation of local rambling clubs, established in 1935. It campaigns for access to open countryside, defends outstanding landscape and rights of way, and is one of the main advocates of long-distance footpaths, such as the Pennine Way. » Pennines

Rameau, Jean Philippe [rah**moh**] (1683–1764) French composer, born in Dijon. He became an organist, and in 1722 settled in Paris, where he published his *Traité de l'harmonie* (1722, Treatise on Harmony), a work of fundamental importance in the history of musical style. He wrote many operas, notably *Hippolyte et Aricie* (1733) and *Castor et Pollux* (1737), as well as ballets, harpsichord pieces, and vocal music. He died in Paris.

Rameses or **Ramses II**, byname **the Great** (13th-c BC) King of Egypt (1304–1237 BC), whose long and prosperous reign marks the last great peak of Egyptian power. Despite his doubtful victory over the Hittites at Kadesh in N Syria (1299 BC), he managed to stabilize his frontier against them, making peace with them (1283 BC) and later marrying a Hittite princess (1270 BC). An enthusiastic builder, he has left innumerable monuments, among them the great sandstone temples at Abu Simbel. » Abu Simbel; Hittites

Rameses or **Ramses III** (12th-c BC) King of Egypt (1198–1166 BC), famous primarily for his great victory over the Sea Peoples, invaders from Asia Minor and the Aegean Is. Tradition identifies him with the Pharaoh who oppressed the Hebrews of the Exodus. » Exodus, Book of; Merneptah; Sea Peoples

ramjet A type of jet engine in which fast-moving air is slowed down by a diffuser, which produces a corresponding increase in the air's pressure. This high-pressure air then has fuel injected into it, and the mixture is continuously burned. The resulting hot gases are ejected rearwards in the form of a jet of gas. This method of jet propulsion is practical up to speeds of eight times the speed of sound. » jet engine [i]; scramjet

Ramsay, Allan (c.1685–1758) Scottish poet, born at Leadhills, Lanarkshire. By 1718 he was known as a poet, having issued several short humorous satires. His works include the pastoral comedy, *The Gentle Shepherd* (1725), and an edited collection of Scots poetry, *The Evergreen* (1724). He died in Edinburgh. His eldest son, **Allan** (1713–84), became an artist, well known for his portraits of women, who in 1767 was appointed portrait painter to George III. » pastoral; Scottish literature; poetry

Ramses » **Rameses**

Ramsgate 51°20N 1°25E, pop (1981) 37 398. Port town in Thanet district, Kent, SE England; S of Margate on the English Channel; one of the Cinque Ports; resort made popular by George IV; railway; hovercraft service to France; yachting, fishing, tourism; St Augustine's Abbey and Church; model village; Celtic cross marks the spot where St Augustine is supposed to have landed in 597. » Augustine, St (of Canterbury); Cinque Ports; George IV; Kent

Ramus, Petrus [ram**ü**], Fr **Pierre de la Ramée** (1515–72) French humanist, born at Cuts, near Soissons. Educated in Paris, he became a lecturer on classical authors, and undertook to reform the science of logic. His attempts excited much hostility among the Aristotelians and his *Dialectic* (1543) was suppressed; but in 1551 he became professor of philosophy at the Collège de France. He later became a Protestant (c.1561), fled from Paris, and travelled in Germany and Switzerland. Returning to France in 1571, he was killed in the massacre of St Bartholomew. » St Bartholomew's Day Massacre

Rancagua [ran**kag**wa] 34°10S 70°45W, pop (1982) 137 773. Capital of Cachapoal province, C Chile; S of Santiago; scene of a royalist victory (1814) in the Spanish-American Wars of Independence; railway; agricultural trade; El Teniente, world's largest underground copper mine, nearby; thermal springs of Cauquenes to the S; Merced Church (national monument); historical museum; Festival del Poroto (Bean Festival) (Feb); national rodeo championships (Mar). » Chile [i]; Spanish-American Wars of Independence

rancidity The reaction of atmospheric oxygen with fats, which reduces vitamin A and E levels in foods. Antioxidants are commonly added to foods to prevent the development of rancidity. Vitamin E is nature's own antioxidant. » antioxidants; vitamins [i]

Rand » **Witwatersrand**

random number In mathematics, a number chosen from a given set of numbers so that each has the same probability of being chosen. If the given set of numbers is the set of integers from 0 to 9 inclusive, each number has a probability of 0.1 of being chosen. A **random number table** is a table of digits chosen at random, each digit having a probability of 0.1 of being chosen, and each choice being independent of the other choices. In order to choose fairly the prize-winning numbers in a national lottery, random numbers may be generated electronically. In the UK premium bonds lottery, ERNIE stands for 'Electronic Random Number Indicator'. » numbers

random processes In physics, processes comprising a sequence of events in which the outcome of one event has no bearing on the outcome of any other; also termed **stochastic processes**. Such processes cannot be predicted exactly; for example, an atom diffusing through gas moves from one collision with a gas atom to another, giving rise to a random path. Random processes involving large numbers of particles are amenable to statistical techniques. » statistical mechanics

Randstad Urban conurbation of settlements in NW Netherlands, forming a horse-shoe shape around a central agricultural zone; contains most of the Dutch population; chief cities, Amsterdam, Rotterdam, Utrecht, The Hague. » Netherlands, The [i]

range-finder An optical device for measuring subject distance by determining the angular convergence of the lines of sight from two points a known distance apart. It is sometimes provided as a focusing aid in photography, directly coupled to the camera lens movement. » camera

Ranger programme The first US series of lunar spacecraft missions, built and managed by NASA's Jet Propulsion Laboratory, designed to study the surface characteristics of the Moon prior to the Apollo manned landings. Launched on Atlas vehicles, the spacecraft were targeted to impact the Moon after telemetering images of increasingly high resolution. The first successful mission was Ranger 7 (Aug 1964), which impacted the Moon in the Mare Nubium (Sea of Clouds) region. The following two Rangers were also successful. They were the technological forerunner to the Mariner series of planetary spacecraft. » Mariner programme; Moon

Rangoon [ranggoon], renamed **Yangon** (1989) 16°47N 96°10E, pop (1983) 2 458 712. Chief port and capital of Myanmar, in Rangoon division, S Myanmar, on R Rangoon; settlement around Dagon pagoda in 6th-c; capital, 1886; large Indian and Chinese population; airport (Mingaladon); railway; university (1920); oil, timber, rice; Sule and Botataung Pagodas (both over 2 000 years old), Shwedagon Pagoda (height 99.4 m/326 ft), reclining Buddha Image of Chauk-Htat-Gyi Pagoda, seated Buddha Image of Koe-Htat-Gyi Pagoda, Kaba Aye (World Peace Pagoda), national museum, natural history museum. » Burma [i]

Ranji [rahnjee] A sky-father in the creation stories of New Zealand Maori religion. He and the Earth-mother Papa are the creators of gods and human beings. » Maoris; New Zealand [i]

Ranjit Singh, byname **Lion of the Punjab** (1780–1839) Sikh ruler, born at Budrukhan. Succeeding his father as ruler of Lahore, he fought to unite all the Sikh provinces, and with the help of a modernized army trained by Western soldiers, became the most powerful ruler in India. In 1813 he procured the Koh-i-noor diamond from an Afghan prince, as the price of assistance in war. He died in Lahore. » Sikhism

Rank (of Sutton Scotney), J(oseph) Arthur, 1st Baron (1888–1972) British film magnate, born in Hull, Yorkshire. He became chairman of many film companies, including Gaumont-British and Cinema-Television, and did much to promote the British film industry at a time when Hollywood seemed to have the monopoly. An active supporter of the Methodist Church, he was keenly interested in social problems. He became a baron in 1957, and died at Winchester, Hampshire.

Rankine temperature » **temperature** [i]

Ransome, Arthur (Mitchell) (1884–1967) British writer, born in Leeds. Educated at Rugby, he worked for a publisher, and became a war correspondent in World War 1. He wrote critical and travel books before making his name with books for young readers, notably *Swallows and Amazons* (1931). He died in Manchester.

ransoms A perennial growing to 45 cm/18 in, native to Europe and Asia; narrow bulb consisting of a single leaf base, 2–3 broadly elliptical leaves, and a flat-topped umbel of white, star-shaped flowers. It is often found carpeting woodland floors. The whole plant smells strongly of garlic. (*Allium ursinum*. Family: *Liliaceae*). » allium; bulb; garlic; perennial; umbel

rape (botany) A biennial herb growing to 1 m/3¼ ft, related to the swede, but with a non-tuberous root; bluish-green leaves; yellow, cross-shaped flowers. It is grown for fodder and, increasingly, as a source of rape-oil, obtained from crushed seeds, and rape-seed cake, made from the residue. (*Brassica rapus*, variety *arvensis*. Family: *Cruciferae*.) » biennial; brassica; herb; swede; tuber

rape (law) The crime of forcing a woman to have sexual intercourse without her freely given consent. A genuine belief that the woman has consented is a valid defence. In the UK, the maximum sentence is life imprisonment.

Raphael [rafael], properly **Raffaello Sanzio** (1483–1520) Italian painter, born at Urbino. He studied at Perugia under Perugino, whose style is reflected in his earliest paintings, such as the 'Crucifixion' (c.1503, National Gallery, London). In c.1504 he went to Florence, where he was strongly influenced by Leonardo and Michelangelo. He completed several sweet Madonnas, as well as such works as the 'Holy Family' (Madrid) and 'The Entombment' (Borghese). In 1508 he went to Rome, where he produced his greatest works, including the frescoes in the papal apartments of the Vatican, and the cartoons for the tapestries of the Sistine Chapel. In 1514 he succeeded Bramante as architect of St Peter's. His last work, the 'Transfiguration', was nearly finished when he died, in Rome. » Bramante; cartoon (art); Italian art; Leonardo da Vinci; Michelangelo; Perugino

rare earths » **lanthanides**

rare gases » **noble gases**

Ras al Khaimah [**ras** al **khiy**ma] pop (1980) 73 700; area 1 690 sq km/652 sq ml. Northernmost of the United Arab Emirates, bounded W by the Arabian Gulf; capital, Ras al Khaimah; offshore oil production began in 1984; industrial development largely at Khor Khuwair; cement, pharmaceuticals, limestone. » United Arab Emirates [i]

Ras Shamra texts [rahs **shahm**rah] Some 350 texts, inscribed on tablets, found 1928–60 on the site of ancient Ugarit in NW Syria, many written in a previously unknown cuneiform script now described as 'Ugaritic', and others in Babylonian. The texts include several epics, with stories about the Canaanite gods El, Baal, Astarte, and Asherah. Dated c.1400 BC, they are important not only for descriptions of pre-Israelite Canaanite religious practices and ideas, but also for light shed on practices recorded in the Hebrew Bible. » Baal; Bible; Canaan; cuneiform [i]

Rasmussen, Knud (Johan Victor) (1879–1933) Danish explorer and ethnologist, born at Jacobshavn, Greenland. From 1902 he directed several expeditions to Greenland in support of the theory that the Inuit and the N American Indians were both descended from migratory tribes from Asia. In 1910 he established Thule base on Cape York, and in 1921–4 crossed by dog-sledge from Greenland to the Bering Strait. He died at Gentofte, Denmark. » Eskimo; Greenland [i]

raspberry A deciduous shrub growing to c.2 m/6½ ft, native to Europe and Asia; straight, slender prickles; woody, biennial stems from buds on the roots; leaves pinnately divided into 3–5 toothed leaflets; flowers 5-petalled, white. The red 'berry' is an aggregate of 1-seeded carpels separating cleanly from a conical receptacle when ripe. It is cultivated for fruit. (*Rubus idaeus*. Family: *Rosaceae*.) » biennial; carpel; deciduous plants; pinnate; receptacle; shrub

Raspe, Rudolf Erich » **Münchhausen, Baron von**

Rasputin, Grigoriy (?1871–1916) Russian peasant and self-styled religious 'elder' (*starets*), born at Pokrovskoye, Siberia. A member of the schismatic sect of Khlysty (flagellants), he was introduced into the royal household, where he quickly gained the confidence of the Emperor (Nicholas II) and Empress by his ability to control through hypnosis the bleeding of the haemophiliac heir to the throne, Tsarevich Alexey. He was also a notorious lecher and drunkard, and created a public scandal through the combination of his sexual and alcoholic excesses, and his political influence in securing the appointment of government ministers. He was murdered by a clique of aristocrats, led by Prince Felix Yusupov, a distant relative of the Tsar. » Nicholas II

Rastafarianism A religious movement from the West Indies, followed by c.1 million people. It largely derives from the thought of Jamaican political activist Marcus Garvey (1887–1940), who advocated a return to Africa as a means of solving the problems of Black oppression. When Haile Selassie was crowned Emperor of Ethiopia in 1930, he came to be viewed as the Messiah, with Ethiopia seen as the promised land. Rastafarians follow strict taboos governing what they may eat (eg no pork, milk, coffee); ganja (marijuana) is held to be a sacrament; they usually wear their hair in long dreadlocks; and they cultivate a distinctive form of speech. » Black consciousness; Haile Selassie I

raster The rectangular pattern of horizontal scanning lines by which the picture image is analysed in a video camera, and reproduced on the display screen of a cathode-ray tube. » scanning [i]

rat A mouse-like rodent of family *Muridae*; name used generally for many unrelated species in this family, especially for members of genus *Rattus* (c.80 species throughout the Old World); also used for some species in other families. The Malaysian **black rat**, **house rat**, or **roof rat** (*Rattus rattus*) and Chinese **brown rat**, **sewer rat**, or **Norway rat** (*Rattus norvegicus*) have dispersed globally in association with humans. Both species spread human diseases (bubonic plague was spread by fleas of the black rat). The **laboratory rat** is a white form of *Rattus norvegicus*. » bubonic plague; mouse; pouched rat; rodent; water rat

rat kangaroo An Australian marsupial, resembling a small kangaroo (head and body length up to 500 mm/20 in) but differing in the structure of the teeth and in having a more general diet; eats plant material and invertebrates; smallest species have rat-like heads. The three species of the genus *Potorous* are called *potoroos*. (Family: *Potoroidae*, 10 species.) » kangaroo; marsupial [i]

rat-tail Deep-water fish with large head and narrow tapering body; dorsal and anal fins continuous; may have light organs on underside; some species make sounds by resonating the swim bladder; also called **grenadier**. (Family: *Macrouridae*.) » fish [i]

Ratana Church A Christian sect founded in 1918 by Wiremu Ratana with the purpose of uniting the Maori people of New Zealand. Although not successful, it came to exert great political influence among Maoris. » Maoris

ratel A badger-like mammal, native to Africa and S Asia; dark brown with top of head and centre of back pale yellowish-grey; fearless, with very tough skin; eats small animals, carrion, and vegetation; follows honeyguides to beehives and takes the honey; also known as **honey badger**. (*Mellivora capensis*. Family: *Mustelidae*.) » badger; honeyguide; Mustelidae

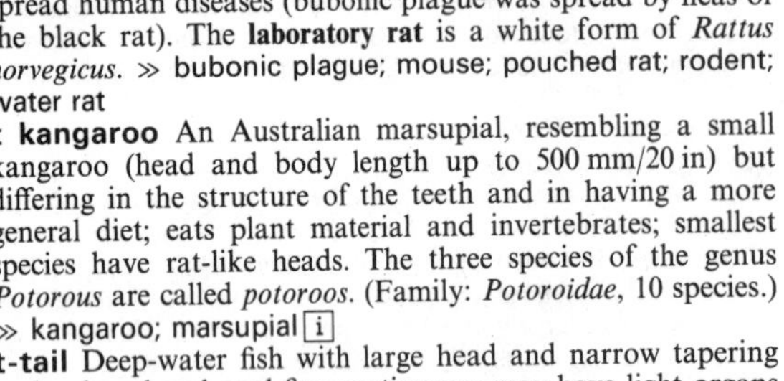

Ratel

rates Local taxation in the UK based on the value of property owned (the *rateable value*). This is determined from time to time by the local authority, who also sets an annual rate. It is used for local government expenditure on such matters as lighting, street cleaning, refuse collection, and police services. The chief disadvantage of the system is that it applies only to owners of property. An alternative method of raising money locally is the poll tax, or community charge. » community charge; taxation

ratfish » **chimaera**

Rathenau, Walther [**rah**tuhnow] (1867–1922) German industrialist and statesman, born in Berlin. He organized German war industries during World War 1, and in 1921, as Minister of Reconstruction, and after February 1922 as Foreign Minister, dealt with reparations. His attempts to negotiate a reparations agreement with the victorious Allies, and the fact that he was Jewish, made him extremely unpopular in nationalist circles, and he was murdered by extremists in the summer of 1922. » reparations; World War 1

Rathlin Island area 14 sq km/5½ sq ml. Island in N Antrim, N Northern Ireland, 5 km/3 ml NW of Fair Head; length, 8 km/5 ml; up to 5 km/3 ml wide; rises to 137 m/449 ft; St Columba founded a church here, 6th-c; ruins of a castle where Robert the Bruce is thought to have taken refuge in 1306. » Antrim (county); Bruce, Robert; Columba, St

ratio of specific heats For gases, the ratio of specific heat at constant pressure to specific heat at constant volume; symbol γ, expressed as a pure number. The former is larger, since at constant pressure gas does work expanding against its surroundings. Typical values are between 1.2 and 1.6. The ratio is related to the ideal gas constant, R, and is important in the study of the thermodynamic properties of gases. » heat capacity; ideal gas; thermodynamics

rational-emotive therapy An approach developed by US clinical psychologist Albert Ellis (1913–), based on the premise that emotional problems arise as a result of the unrealistic beliefs people hold about themselves (eg 'I must be loved by everyone', 'I must be perfect in everything I do'). Negative evaluations of the self – and consequent adverse emotions such as anxiety and depression – are thought to arise when these beliefs are not supported. By cajoling, teasing, and arguing, the therapist challenges the client's beliefs in an attempt to make them more realistic and rational. » clinical psychology

rational number » **numbers**

rationalism (architecture) A 20th-c conception of architecture which pursues the most logical possible solution to every aspect of building. Although to some extent inherent in a great part of 20th-c architecture, it is particularly associated with the work of most of the Bauhaus and International Style architects of the 1920s and 1930s, especially in Italy. » Bauhaus; functionalism (art and architecture); International Style; Neoclassicism (art and architecture)

rationalism (philosophy) A philosophical tradition which maintains that knowledge is independent of sense experience; it is usually contrasted with empiricism. Versions of it flourished with Descartes, Spinoza, and Leibniz, who maintained that all of science is a deductive system, patterned after Euclidean geometry, reflecting the fact that there is no contingency in nature. The axioms are ideas within us innately (for example, that God exists), and that a cause must be adequate to its effect. Rationalism was rejected by the empiricists, Locke, Berkeley, and Hume. The innateness of some ideas has been urged recently by Chomsky to account for language acquisition; it is not clear that this is inconsistent with empiricism. » empiricism; innateness hypothesis

Ratitae [ra**tiy**tee] (Lat *ratis* 'raft') An obsolete term for flightless running birds, such as the ostrich and emu (which are still referred to as **ratites**). With loss of flight, the breast bone in these birds has lost its keel and become flat (or 'raft-like'). » bird [i]; Carinatae

rattan palm [ruh**tan**] A large genus of tropical climbing palms with slender, extremely long stems up to 180 m/500 ft. The plants climb by means of hooked spines at the tips, or along midribs of the feathery leaves which cling to surrounding vegetation and support stems as they grow upward. The stems are stripped to make rattan canes, widely used for furniture, baskets, and other items; also the very strong malacca cane used for walking sticks. (Genus: *Calamus*, 375 species. Family: *Palmae*.) » climbing plant; palm

Rattigan, Sir Terence (Mervyn) (1911–77) British dramatist, born in London. Educated at Harrow and Oxford, he scored a great success with his comedy *French Without Tears* (1936). Since then, most of his works have been internationally acclaimed, notably *The Winslow Boy* (1946), *The Browning Version* (1948), *Separate Tables* (1954), and *Ross* (1960). He was knighted in 1971, and died at Hamilton, Bermuda. » drama; English literature

rattlesnake A New World pit viper of genus *Crotalus* (28 species); tail with a segmented rattle (except in the **Santa Catalina rattlesnake**, *Crotalus catalinensis*); rattle made from modified scales (one segment added at each moult, but old segments are lost); venom attacks blood cells. The name is also used for the **pygmy** or **ground rattlesnakes** of genus *Sistrurus* (3 species). » diamondback; pit viper [i]; sidewinder [i]

Rauschenberg, Robert [**row**shuhnberg] (1925–) US artist, born at Port Arthur, Texas. He studied art in Paris and at Black Mountain College in North Carolina, and is one of the most aggressive US modernists, whose collages and 'combines' incorporate a variety of rubbish (eg rusty metal, old tyres, stuffed birds). He is sometimes categorized as a Pop Artist, but his work has strong affinities with Dadaism and with the readymades of Marcel Duchamp. » Dada; Duchamp; Pop Art; readymade

Ravel, Maurice (1875–1937) French composer, born at Ciboure. He studied under Fauré at the Paris Conservatoire, and won recognition with *Pavane pour une infante défunte* (1899, Pavane for a Dead Princess). He wrote several successful piano pieces, *Rapsodie espagnole* (1908), and the music for the Diaghilev ballet *Daphnis et Chloé* (first performed, 1912). After World War 1, in which he saw active service, his works included the 'choreographic poem' *La Valse* (1920), the opera *L'Enfant et les sortilèges* (1925, The Child and the Enchantments), and *Boléro* (1928), intended as a miniature ballet. He died in Paris. » Diaghilev

raven A large crow, especially the **great raven** (*Corvus corax*) of the N hemisphere; other species found in the N hemisphere and Australia; omnivorous; territorial; does not nest in colonies. (Genus: *Corvus*, 9 species.) » crow

Ravenna [ra**ve**na] 44°25N 12°12E, pop (1981) 138 034. Capital town of Ravenna province, Emilia-Romagna, NE Italy; 8 km/5 ml from the Adriatic Sea, connected by canal; capital of W Roman Empire in AD 402, and of later Ostrogothic and Byzantine rulers; archbishopric; railway; oil refining, wine; Church of San Vitale (begun 526), with famous mosaics; cathedral (18th-c), octagonal baptistery (5th-c) in Church of Sant' Apollinare Nuovo, tomb of Empress Galla Placidia (5th-c), tomb of Theodoric (c.520); Dante celebrations (mid-Sep). » Italy [i]; mosaic; Ostrogoths; Roman history [i]; Theodoric

Ravi [**rah**vee] **River**, ancient **Hydraotes** River in NW India and Pakistan; one of the five rivers of the Punjab; rises in the SE Pir Panjal range; flows generally SW across the Pakistan Punjab, past Lahore, to join the R Chenab 53 km/33 ml NNE of Multan; length 765 km/475 ml; part of the border between Pakistan and India. » Punjab (India, Pakistan)

Rawalpindi [rahwal**pin**dee] 33°40N 73°08E, pop (1981) 806 000. City in Punjab province, Pakistan, 258 km/160 ml NNW of Lahore; strategically important location controlling routes to Kashmir; occupied by the British, 1849; interim capital, 1959–69; airfield; railway; military and commercial centre; oil refining, railway engineering, iron, chemicals, furniture, trade in grain, timber, wool. » Pakistan [i]

rawindsonde balloon » **radiosonde balloon**

Rawlings, Jerry J(ohn) (1947–) Ghanaian leader, born in Accra. He was at the centre of a peaceful coup in 1979, returning power to a civilian government a few months later. Despite being forcibly retired from the armed forces and discredited by the government, his popularity remained high, and he returned with his Armed Forces Revolutionary Council to seize power again at the end of 1981. » Ghana [i]

Rawsthorne, Alan (1905–71) British composer, born at Haslingden, Lancashire. He trained as a dentist, then turned to music, studying in Manchester and Berlin. He settled in London in 1935, and wrote a wide range of works, including three symphonies, eight concertos, choral and chamber music, and several film scores. He died at Cambridge.

ray Any of the numerous small to large bottom-dwelling cartilaginous fishes in families *Anacanthobatidae*, *Pseudorajidae*, *Rajidae* (skates and rays), *Gymnuridae* (butterfly ray), *Rhinopteridae*, *Mobulidae* (devil rays), *Torpedinidae* (electric rays), and *Myliobatidae* (eagle rays); front part of the body strongly flattened with broad pectoral fins; mouth and gill openings on the underside; tail typically slender and cylindrical; dorsal and tail fins very small. » cartilaginous fish; devil/electric ray; sawfish; skate; stingray

Ray, John (1627–1705) English naturalist, born and died at Black Notley, Essex. He was educated at Cambridge, where he became a fellow (1649), but lost his post at the Restoration for religious reasons. With a pupil, Francis Willughby (1635–72), he travelled widely in Europe studying botany and zoology. His classification of plants, with its emphasis on the species as the basic unit, was the foundation of modern taxonomy, his major work being the 3-volume *Historia Plantarum* (1686–1704). » taxonomy

Ray, Man, pseudonym of **Emanuel Rabinovitch** (1890–1976) US painter, sculptor, photographer and film-maker, born in Philadelphia, Pennsylvania. He studied art in New York, and became a major figure in the development of Modernism, founding the New York Dadaist movement. He experimented with new techniques in painting and photography, then moved to Paris (1921), where he became interested in films, and during the 1930s produced many photographs and 'rayographs' (photographic montages). Apart from a stay in the USA during World War 2, he settled in Paris, where he died. » Dada; Modernism

Ray, Satyajit [riy] (1921–) Indian film director, born and educated in Calcutta. His first film, *Pather Panchali* (1954, On the Road) was undertaken in his spare time with very limited finance. Its international success at the Cannes Film Festival allowed him to complete the trilogy with *Aparajito* (1956, The Unvanquished) and *Apur Sansar* (1959, The World of Apu), and he has since continued as India's leading film maker. Later features include *The Kingdom of Diamonds* (1980), *Pickoo* (1982), and *The Home and The World* (1984).

Rayleigh scattering The scattering of light by objects which are small compared to the wavelength of light; varies as (frequency)^4; described by British physicist Lord Rayleigh (1842–1919). The Rayleigh scattering of sunlight by air molecules makes the sky appear blue, since blue light is scattered more than other frequencies. » light

rayon A textile fibre formed from cellulose (a constituent of wood pulp), first produced late in the 19th-c. Improvements in manufacturing methods have made modern rayon fibres important as domestic and industrial materials. » viscose

Razi » **Rhazes**

Razin, Stepan Timofeyevich [**ra**zin], byname **Stenka** (c.1630–71) Russian Don Cossack and leader of a Cossack and peasant revolt (1670–1), directed against the boyars and landowning nobility. In April 1671 he was captured, taken to Moscow and publicly executed. He became a folk-hero celebrated in later legend and song as the embodiment of popular rebellion against authority. » boyars; Cossacks; Pugachev

razor shell A burrowing marine bivalve with two similar elongate shell valves; shell closed by two muscles; burrows actively in sand using a muscular foot. (Class: *Pelecypoda*. Order: *Veneroida*.) » bivalve; shell

razorbill An auk native to the N Atlantic; black bill, with vertical white stripe near tip; nests in colonies, often with guillemots. (*Alca torda*.) » auk; guillemot

Re [ray] or **Ra** [rah] In Egyptian religion, the ancient Sun-god of Heliopolis. As the creator, he emerged from the primaeval waters at the beginning of time. He is depicted as a falcon with the Sun's disc on his head: at night he appears as a ram-headed god who sails through the Underworld. » Amun

reactance In alternating current circuits containing inductors and capacitors, the factor which determines the phase relationship between current and voltage; symbol X, units Ω (ohms). It is an imaginary part of impedance, controlling the power input to the circuit. » alternating current; capacitance; complex number; impedance; inductance

reaction time (RT) The interval between the onset of a signal and the initiation of a voluntary response to it. The time (rarely less than a fifth of a second) varies according to the complexity of the situation, the number of possible alternative signals, and the choice of available responses. Measures of RT are used by psychologists to make inferences about processes in the central nervous system, and in applications such as the improvement of high-speed skills (eg in car-driving, piloting aircraft, ball-games). » experimental psychology

reactive armour A form of protection for military vehicles such as tanks against the kind of 'hollow-charge' warhead typically used in infantry-fired antitank missiles. This warhead is designed to burn its way through the armoured metal skin of the vehicle in a hot jet of gas and molten metal, rather than to smash its way in using simple kinetic energy. On impact from such a hollow-charge weapon, reactive armour itself detonates locally, neutralizing the attacking weapon's effects. » antitank missile; kinetic energy weapons

Read, Sir Herbert (1893–1968) British poet and art critic, born near Kirby Moorside, Yorkshire. He was an assistant keeper at the Victoria and Albert Museum, London, and then professor of fine art at Edinburgh (1931–3). He held several other academic posts, and became known as a poet and a writer on aesthetics in such works as *The Meaning of Art* (1931). He was knighted in 1953, and died at Malton, Yorkshire. » aesthetics; English literature; poetry

Reading [**red**ing] 51°28N 0°59W, pop (1981) 133 540. County town of Berkshire, S England; at the junction of the Kennet and Thames Rivers, 63 km/39 ml W of London; a centre of the textile industry in mediaeval times; railway; university (1926); rapidly developing commercial centre; brewing, boatbuilding, food processing, metal products, engineering, electronics, printing; 12th-c Benedictine abbey, burial place of Henry I; Hexagon (theatre), museum of English rural life (1951), museum of Greek archaeology. » Berkshire; Henry I (of England)

readymade In modern art, any object not made by the artist but chosen by him or her and exhibited as a 'work of art'. Thus Duchamp exhibited a bottle-rack in 1914 and (most notoriously) a urinal, which he 'signed' R. Mutt and entitled 'Fountain' in 1917. » Dada; Duchamp; modern art

Reagan, Ronald (Wilson) (1911–) US Republican statesman and 40th President, born at Tampico, Illinois. Educated at Eureka College, Illinois, he became a radio sports announcer, went to Hollywood (1937), and made over 50 films, beginning with *Love Is On the Air* (1937). Although originally a Democrat and supporter of liberal causes, he became increasingly anti-communist, and in 1962 joined the Republican Party as an extreme right-winger. He became Governor of California in 1966, stood unsuccessfully for the Republican presidential nomination in 1968 and 1976, but in 1980 defeated Jimmy Carter, and won a second term in 1984, defeating Walter Mondale. He introduced a major programme of economic changes aimed at reducing government spending and inflation, took a strong anti-communist stand, especially in the Middle East and C America, and introduced the Strategic Defence Initiative. In 1981 he was wounded in an assassination attempt. During his second term, he backed off from his previous attitude of confrontation with the USSR, reaching a major arms-reduction accord with Soviet leader Gorbachev. His domestic popularity remained high throughout his presidency, despite charges of corruption against his aides, and his own inability to get much of his programme through Congress. » Carter, Jimmy; Gorbachev; Mondale; Republican Party; SDI

real numbers » numbers

real presence The belief that the body and blood of Christ are actually present in the bread and wine at communion (Eucharist/Mass). The nature of Christ's presence became the subject of great controversy at the Reformation. » consubstantiation; Eucharist; Jesus Christ; Reformation

real tennis An indoor racket-and-ball game played on a walled court, similar to rackets, but containing specifically designed hazards. A derivation of the French *jeu de paume* ('palm [of hand] game'), which was first played in the 11th-c. The racket developed in the 16th-c, and the game became very popular in the following century. Today, however, it is a minority sport, having been eclipsed by lawn tennis and other derivatives. It is also known as 'royal' or 'court' tennis. » rackets; RR116

real-time computing A notion which applies to those computing systems where near-simultaneous response to input data is a necessary requirement; examples include air-traffic control, point-of-sale terminals, military applications, and vehicle control. Interactive computing on larger computers is generally time-shared, and does not place the user in a real-time computing environment. » interactive computing; time-sharing

Realism (art and literature) In art criticism, a term (especially with a capital R) referring to the deliberate choice of ugly or unidealized subject-matter, sometimes to make a social or political point. Thus Courbet's *Stonebreakers* (1849) represented the hardship of the poorest class in France. Realism with a small 'r' is often used rather vaguely as the opposite of 'abstract'. More generally, in literature and art, the term refers to the advocacy of verisimilitude, as encountered in the Realist movement of mid-19th-c France, which flourished (as Naturalism) in the revolutionary scientific confidence of that era. The dislocation of reality in the 20th-c has undermined conventional or 'naive' Realism, and a further qualification is now needed to make the term meaningful (eg 'surrealism', 'magic realism'). » abstract art; Ashcan School; Courbet; French literature; Naturalism; Neue Sachlichkeit; social realism; Socialist Realism; *trompe l'oeil*

realism (philosophy) **1** The philosophical doctrine, held by Aristotle, Descartes, Locke, and others, that whatever exists has its character independently of its being perceived by human or divine minds; opposed to verificationism and some versions of idealism and phenomenalism. **2** A theory about universals, held by Plato, which maintains that properties such as redness exist outside the mind; opposed to nominalism and conceptualism. **3** The philosophical thesis that scientific theories aim or should aim to depict the way the physical world really is; opposed to instrumentalism. » conceptualism; idealism; instrumentalism; nominalism; phenomenalism; verificationism

Reardon, Ray(mond) (1932–) British snooker player, born Tredegar, Monmouthshire, Wales. The first of the great snooker players of the modern era, he was dominant in the 1970s. Welsh amateur champion six times (1950–5), he turned professional in 1968, after careers as a miner and policeman. He was world professional champion six times (1970, 1973–6, 1978), and until 1982 was top of the snooker ratings. » snooker

reasoning Mental activity in which the reasoner moves from given information to a novel conclusion, in a series of steps that the reasoner can justify. Reasoning may be *deductive*, arriving at a conclusion from a set of premises (eg proving a theorem in mathematics), or *inductive*, when we try to create a new generalization based on available evidence. Psychologists have debated whether reasoning is based on some sort of internal mental logic, or whether more informal procedures (images, scenarios, or 'mental models') are used. Experimental investigations suggest that, when we attempt to reason, we are poor at handling negative information, and reluctant to seek evidence that will disconfirm currently-held beliefs. » cognitive psychology

Réaumur, René Antoine Ferchault de [**ray**ohmür] (1683–1757) French polymath, born at La Rochelle. He carried out research in metallurgy, and glassmaking, and produced a major work on entomology. His thermometer (with spirit instead of mercury) has 80 degrees between the freezing- and boiling-points. » entomology; temperature [i]

Rebellions of 1837 **1** A rebellion in Lower Canada (Quebec) generated by stalemate between the legislative council and the appointed executive council over control of provincial revenues. Led by Papineau and his Parti Patriote, it sought to dissolve the unsatisfactory imperial tie with Britain. It was crushed by government troops after several brief confrontations. **2** Later in 1837, a rebellion in Upper Canada (Ontario), which opposed the oligarchical control exercised by the Family Compact, and the position of preferment enjoyed by the Church of England. Armed Radicals led by Mackenzie marched on Toronto to seize the government, but were repulsed by pro-government troops and volunteers. Mackenzie

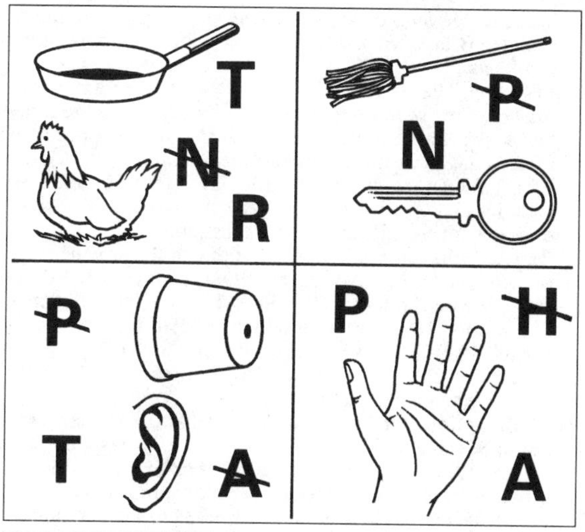

Rebus – Each square contains the name of an animal

and Papineau both fled to the USA. » Clergy Reserves; Mackenzie, William Lyon; Papineau

Reber, Grote [**ray**ber] (1911–) US radio engineer and amateur astronomer, born at Wheaton, Illinois. He built the first steerable radio telescope (1936), which produced the first maps (1944) of the radio waves from the Milky Way. » Jansky; Milky Way; radio telescope

rebus [**ree**buhs] The enigmatic representation in visual form of the sounds of a name or word. As a form of visual pun, rebuses are often used to puzzle or amuse, such as a drawing of a ray-gun (='Reagan'), or the letters CU (='see you'); some have become part of everyday writing, such as IOU (='I owe you'). They are an ancient means of communication, being found in early forms of picture-writing. » hieroglyphics [i]; pictography [i]

Récamier, Madame de [raykam**yay**], *née* **(Jeanne Françoise) Julie (Adélaide) Bernard** (1777–1849) French hostess, born in Lyons. Her salon became a fashionable meeting-place, especially for former Royalists and those opposed to Napoleon. When her husband was financially ruined, she was forced to leave Paris (1805), returning in 1815. The most distinguished friend of her later years was Chateaubriand. She died in Paris. » Chateaubriand; Napoleon I

receptacle In flowering plants, the area at the tip of the flower-stalk to which the floral parts are attached. Usually convex, it may become swollen or expanded to enclose the carpels, and play an important role in fruit formation. » carpel; flower [i]; fruit

receptors In physiology, specialized sites, usually within the cell membrane, which have evolved to bind and mediate the effects of neurotransmitters and hormones, but which also mediate the effects of many substances foreign to the body (such as drugs); also known as **binding sites**. As a consequence of the binding, intermediate factors are activated which trigger a cellular response. » cell; second messengers

recession An economic situation where demand is sluggish, output is not rising, and unemployment is on the increase. Not as severe a downturn as a depression, it is usually identified when gross domestic product declines for two successive quarters. The two most important recessions were 1974–5 and 1980–2, the latter giving rise to very high levels of unemployment throughout the Western world. » depression (economics); gross domestic product; reflation; trade cycle

Recife [ruh**see**fay] 8°06S 34°53W, pop (1980) 1 183 391. Port capital of Pernambuco state, NE Brazil, at the mouth of the R Capibaribe; consists of Recife proper (on a peninsula), Boa Vista (on the mainland), and Santo Antônio (on an island between the two), all connected by bridges; most important commercial and industrial city in the NE; airport (Guararapes); two universities (1951, 1954); sugar, sugar refining, cotton, distilling, tourism; location of first Brazilian printing house, 1706; São Francisco de Assisi Church (1612), Church of Conceição dos Militares (1708), Church of Nossa Senhora das Prazeres, Fort Brum (1629), Conco Pontas (fort, 1677), Casa da Cultura (old prison), Museu do Açúcar (Sugar Museum). » Brazil [i]

Reciprocity A movement begun in British N America during the 1840s for the bilateral reduction of tariffs between the British colonies and the USA; it resulted in the Reciprocity Treaty of 1854. The treaty negotiations represented an important step in the growth of Canadian political autonomy. Arrangements became a source of discord in Washington, however, and the Treaty was dissolved by the USA in 1866. Attempts to renew Reciprocity failed up to 1911, when the idea was finally shelved.

recitative A type of musical declamation which allows the words to be delivered naturally and quickly, and is therefore indispensable in those types of all-sung opera, oratorio, and cantata in which dialogue and narrative are interrupted by long or numerous arias. 'Simple recitative' (*recitative semplice* or *secco*) is accompanied only by continuo; 'accompanied recitativo' (*recitativo accompagnato* or *stromentato*) by the orchestra. » aria; continuo; opera; opera buffa/seria

recombinant DNA A technology by which hybrid (recombinant) nucleic acid molecules can be produced. Its development stems from the discovery of *restriction enzymes*, present in many micro-organisms, that have the property of cutting double-stranded DNA molecules at a specific sequence of 4 to 6 base pairs. Each enzyme recognizes a different base sequence. Any two DNA fragments produced by cleavage with a particular restriction enzyme can be joined and the joint resealed, so that molecules composed of DNA segments from totally unrelated organisms may be artificially recombined to produce genes which do not occur in nature. In medicine, the technique has been particularly useful for the development and application of probes, which can detect the presence of a particular disease gene in those members of the families at risk of carrying it, as in Huntington's chorea and haemophilia. » DNA [i]; enzyme; haemophilia; Huntington's chorea

recommended daily allowance (RDA) A standard against which the quantity of a population's intake of nutrients is measured. The RDA for a nutrient is calculated to allow for individuals whose metabolic requirements are naturally high. For most nutrients this is achieved by increasing the RDA from the mean requirement to the mean plus two standard deviations. Some nutritionists feel that many RDAs are set excessively high by some expert committees. » diet; mean; nutrients

RECONSAT An abbreviation of ***recon**naissance **sat**ellite*, a military space system placed into Earth orbit. It is equipped with cameras and other sensors capable of recording objects (such as military units) and activities on the ground, and relaying that information to Earth stations for analysis by intelligence experts. » military intelligence; spacecraft

reconstruction (linguistics) The process by which the sound system of an undocumented parent language can be 'constructed', by comparing the words in languages known (or suspected) to be related; also called **internal reconstruction**. Thus, the Indo-European form ***pəter* ('father') is reconstructed by comparing such variants as Latin *pater* and Gothic *fadar*. An analysis of the systematic correspondences between *p-* and *f-* in these and other related languages leads to the postulation of *p* as the earlier first consonant in these words. » Indo-European languages; phonology

Reconstruction The period after the American Civil War when the South was occupied by Northern troops, while major changes went forward in its way of life. These included the destruction of slavery and the attempted integration of the freed Black people. Reconstruction brought three amendments to the US Constitution, as well as bitter dispute over the extent of the needed changes. Resistance to it among White southerners resulted in the founding of the Ku Klux Klan in 1866. Once scorned by historians as a 'tragic era' of corruption, Reconstruction is now seen as a period of necessary but incomplete social change. The era ended in 1877, when a bargain among politicians gave a disputed presidential election to the

Republicans in return for 'home' (ie White) rule in the South. Once White rule was fully restored, a policy of racial segregation was imposed to keep Black people firmly subordinate. » American Civil War; Jim Crow Laws; Ku Klux Klan

record player The successor to the gramophone, following the advent in the 1920s of the use of electricity in the recording and reproducing processes. It was essentially a turntable, pick-up, and arm which reproduced the music or other sounds recorded on discs (gramophone records), usually through its own amplifier and speaker. » gramophone; loudspeaker [i]; pick-up; sound recording

recorder (law) In the legal system of England and Wales, a part-time judge. Those appointed are barristers or solicitors. Recorders sit mainly in the Crown Court. » Crown Court; judge

recorder (music) A type of end-blown duct flute in two or three jointed sections, with seven finger-holes and a thumb-hole. It is made of wood or (in recent times) plastic in various sizes, the most common being the *descant* and the *treble*. By the end of the 18th-c it was superseded by the transverse flute, but it has been revived in the 20th-c as a school instrument and for playing early music, and several modern composers have written for it. » flute; woodwind instrument [i]

recording » **sound recording**

rectifier A device that changes alternating current (AC), which continuously reverses direction, into direct current (DC), by allowing it to flow in one direction only. Electric lights and motors use alternating current, but in general most electronic equipment needs direct current. Semiconductor diodes can be used as rectifiers. » electricity; semiconductor diode

rectilinear motion » **mechanics**

rector In the Church of England, the parish priest receiving full tithe rents; in other Anglican churches, generally a parish priest. In Roman Catholicism, the term denotes the priest in charge of a religious house, college, or school. In some countries (eg Scotland), it refers to the senior officer of a university, elected by students. » Church of England; priest; Roman Catholicism

rectum That part of the gastro-intestinal tract between the sigmoid colon and the anal canal. When gastro-intestinal contents enter the rectum, the individual has the urge to defaecate. Partial (mucous membrane and submucosa layer) or complete (whole thickness of the rectal wall) prolapse of the rectum is relatively common, and has many causative factors (eg muscle damage during childbirth, poor muscle tone in the elderly). » alimentary canal; anus; colon; defaecation; haemorrhoids; peritoneum

recycling Putting waste substances back into productive use, a procedure advocated by many conservationists. It is a means of reducing the demand on non-renewable resources, and of preventing problems of pollution and waste disposal. Examples include the pulping of waste paper to make recycled paper, the existence of bottle banks to collect used glass, and the smelting of metals from scrap. In the UK about 62% of lead is recycled. Incentives for recycling can be provided by government subsidies or by a deposit tax on containers. » conservation (earth sciences); non-renewable resources; pollution; waste disposal

Red Adair (1915–) Texan fire-fighting specialist, called in as a troubleshooter to deal with major oil fires. In 1984 he and his team put out a major fire on an offshore rig near Rio de Janeiro, and in 1988 they were the first men to board the Piper Alpha oil rig in the North Sea after it was destroyed by an explosion. He is the subject of a film, *Hellfighter* (1968), starring John Wayne. » Piper Alpha

red admiral A large butterfly found widely in the N hemisphere; upperside of wings black with scarlet bands and patches of white and blue; caterpillars commonly found on nettles; overwinter as adults. (Order: *Lepidoptera*. Family: *Nymphalidae*.) » butterfly; caterpillar

red algae A large and diverse group of alga-like plants, ranging in form from single cells to large differentiated bodies; reddish colour stems arises from the mixture of photosynthetic pigments, chlorophyll *a*, phycobiliproteins, and carotenoids inside the cells; reproduction involves the production of an egg cell inside a specialized organ (*oogonium*) receptive to the male gamete. (Class: *Rhodophyceae*.) » algae; gamete; photosynthesis

Red Army The Red Army of Workers and Peasants (*RKKA*, *Rabochekrest'yanshi Krasny*), the official name of the army of the Soviet Union (1918–45). It was the most important land force engaged in the defeat of Nazi Germany (1941–5), and later became the most powerful land force in the world. » army

red-brick universities Those English universities founded in the late 19th-c or first half of the 20th-c in the provincial cities: Manchester (1880; new charter 1903), Liverpool (1903; affiliated to Manchester, 1884–1903), Leeds (1904; affiliated to Manchester, 1887–1904), Birmingham (1900), Sheffield (1905), Bristol (1909), Reading (1926), Southampton (1952, University College 1902), and Leicester (1957, University College 1918). » new universities; university

Red Brigades Ital **Brigate Rosse** A left-wing Italian terrorist group which began operating in 1974 as a response to the failure of the New Left, involved in bombings and killings. Its activities were largely directed at the kidnapping and killing of Italian judges, politicians, and businessmen, such as the former Italian premier Aldo Moro in 1978. Several leading members have been imprisoned, and the gang has become less prominent in recent years. » terrorism

red cedar 1 A species of *arbor vitae*, native to N America, which yields red timber. (*Thuja plicata*. Family: *Cupressaceae*.) » arbor vitae **2** The commercial name for timber from the American species of juniper, *Juniperus virginiana*, often used for pencils. » juniper

Red Crescent » **Red Cross**

Red Cross An international agency founded by the Geneva Convention (1864) to assist those wounded or captured in war. There are national branches; the British Red Cross performs relief duties throughout the world; the American Red Cross also runs a blood supply service. All branches use the symbol of the red cross on a white ground, except Muslim branches, which use the red crescent, and Iran, which uses a red lion and sun. » Dunant, Henri; Geneva Convention

red currant A species of currant native to W Europe. It produces edible red berries on old wood. The **white currant** is merely a white-berried form. (*Ribes rubrum*. Family: *Grossulariaceae*.) » currant

red deer A true deer widespread in the temperate N hemisphere (introduced in Australia and New Zealand); also known as the **Bactrian deer**, **Yarkand deer**, **maral**, **shou**, **hangul**, or (in N America) **wapiti** or **elk**; sometimes farmed; pale brown in summer, darker in winter. Each antler usually has five tines (the *Swedish* form); if each has six, the stag is a *Royal*; if each has seven, it is a *Wilson*. (*Cervus elephas*.) » antlers [i]; deer

red fox A fox native to Europe, temperate Asia, N Africa, and N America (introduced in Australia); usually red-brown with white underparts (**red fox**); sometimes black (**black fox**), silvery grey (**silver fox**), or with a black cross on the back (**cross fox**). (*Vulpes vulpes*.) » fox

red giant A cool red star, 10–100 times the radius of the Sun, but of similar mass. It develops in a late stage of stellar evolution, after the main sequence. Hydrogen in the core is exhausted, and the outer layers expand. » hydrogen; main sequence; stellar evolution

red grouse A reddish-brown grouse, native to the British Is; originally considered a separate species, *Lagopus scoticus*; now treated as a subspecies of the widespread N hemisphere **willow grouse** (*Lagopus lagopus*). » grouse

Red Guards Young radical Maoist activists (mostly students) who spread the 1966 Cultural Revolution across China, destroying whatever was 'old', and rebelling against all 'reactionary' authority. The first Red Guards were a group formed in Qinghua University in Beijing (Peking) on whom Mao bestowed his blessing (18 Aug 1966) at a mass rally in the capital. » Cultural Revolution; Mao Zedong

red-hot poker A perennial native to S Africa; leaves greyish, narrow, tapering; flowers tubular, downward-angled, red, turning orange then yellow with age, in dense, poker-shaped

Red grouse

spike on stem up to 2 m/6½ ft high. Numerous hybrids of various stature and flower colour are cultivated for ornament. (*Kniphofia uvaria.* Family: *Liliaceae.*) » perennial

red ink plant » **pokeweed**

red mullet Colourful marine fish widespread in tropical and warm temperate seas; body elongate, underside rather straight, upper surface of head strongly curved; mouth with pair of large chin barbels; includes commercially important European species, *Mullus surmuletus*; also called **goatfish**. (Family: *Mullidae*, 3 genera.)

Red River (China), Chin **Yuan Jiang**, Vietnamese **Song Hong** River rising in C Yunnan province, China, SW of Kunming; flows SE into Vietnam to meet the Gulf of Tongking in a large delta, 32 km/20 ml E of Haiphong; length, c.800 km/500 ml. » Vietnam [i]

Red River (USA) River in S USA; rises in N Texas in the Llano Estacado; forms the Texas–Oklahoma and Texas–Arkansas borders; above Baton Rouge, enters two distributaries; the Atchafalaya R flows S to the Gulf of Mexico; the Old R joins the Mississippi; length 1 966 km/1 222 ml; major tributaries the Pease, Wichita, Washita, Little, Black; used for flood-control, irrigation, hydroelectricity; navigable to Shreveport. » United States of America [i]

Red River Colony A British colony founded by the Earl of Selkirk in Rupert's Land (Manitoba) on the Assiniboine and Red Rivers in 1812. It was an English- and Gaelic-speaking colony in an area predominated by Indian and Métis fur traders and farmers. From the 1820s, anglophone Protestant 'country-born' settlers and francophone Catholic Métis developed side by side in relative harmony until 1869–70. » Métis; Red River Rebellion

Red River Rebellion A movement for self-determination in 1869–70 by the resident Métis population of Red River Colony, Canada (now Manitoba), which broke out when control over trading rights passed from the Hudson Bay Company to the Dominion of Canada. Led by Louis Riel, the Métis and anglophone 'mixed-bloods' established a provisional government (1870). Armed conflict followed, and a leader of a failed Anglo-Protestant counter-rising, Thomas Scott, was executed by the Métis. Although Canada agreed to the terms of the rebels (in the Manitoba Act, 1870), Orange opinion in Ontario was so outraged by the execution of Scott that Riel was obliged to flee the country. » Métis; Northwest Rebellion; Red River Colony; Riel

red salmon » **sockeye**

Red Sea, ancient **Sinus Arabicus** area c.453 000 sq km/175 000 sq ml. NNW arm of the Indian Ocean, between the Arabian Peninsula and Egypt, Sudan, and Ethiopia; occupies the rift valley which stretches S into the African continent; connected to the Mediterranean Sea by the Suez Canal; divided into the Gulfs of Suez and Aqaba by the Sinai Peninsula (NW); a narrow sea, up to 360 km/225 ml wide, 2 335 km/1 450 ml long; maximum depth, 2 200 m/7 200 ft near the centre; many islands; coral reefs parallel to shores; high salinity; name probably derives from reddish seaweed found here; major trade route, especially since Suez Canal (1869). » Indian Ocean; Suez Canal

red setter » **Irish setter**

red sheep » **mouflon**

Red Spot, Great » **Jupiter** (astronomy)

Red Square The central square of Moscow. Its Russian name (*krasnaya ploshchad*) derives from the Old Slavonic *krasny* ('beautiful' or 'red'). The translation of 'red' has become established only in the 20th-c. Historically the site of executions, demonstrations, and processions, the square became the scene of parades held every May and November. » Kremlin; Moscow

red squirrel A small tree-dwelling squirrel; coat reddish brown (dark brown or white forms exist); inhabits woodland, especially coniferous forest; four species: the **European red squirrel** (*Sciurus vulgaris*) from Europe and Asia, and the N American **red squirrels** or **chickarees** of genus *Tamiasciurus.* » squirrel

red valerian » **valerian**

redemption The belief that through the work of Jesus Christ humanity is enabled to be released from a state of sin to a state of grace with God. The term was originally applied to the purchase of the liberty of a slave. » atonement; grace; Jesus Christ

Redford, Robert (1936–) US actor, born at Santa Barbara, California. He dropped out of college to study art and acting, and good performances on Broadway and on television led to engagements in Hollywood, but without great success until the film version of his stage role in *Barefoot in the Park* (1968). After this, major star parts followed regularly, as in *Butch Cassidy and the Sundance Kid* (1969), *The Sting* (1973), *All the President's Men* (1976), *Out of Africa* (1985), and *Springs* (1986). As a director he made the Olympics-based skiing film *Downhill Racer* in 1969, and was awarded an Oscar for *Ordinary People* (1980).

Redgrave, Sir Michael (Scudamore) (1908–85) British actor, born in Bristol. Educated at Clifton College and Cambridge, he became a teacher, and began his acting career at the Liverpool Playhouse in 1934. His many notable stage performances included Richard II (1951), Prospero (1952), Antony (1953), and Uncle Vanya (1962), and he also had a distinguished film career, starting with his appearance in Hitchcock's *The Lady Vanishes* (1938). His autobiography *In my Mind's Eye* appeared in 1983. He was knighted in 1959, and died at Denham, Buckinghamshire. He married the actress **Rachel Kempson** (1910–) in 1935, and their three children are all actors; **Vanessa** (1937–), **Corin** (1939–), and **Lynn** (1944–). » theatre

Redgrave, Vanessa (1937–) British actress, daughter of the actor Michael Redgrave. She joined the Royal Shakespeare Company in the 1960s, and took the lead in several feature films, including *Morgan, a Suitable Case for Treatment* (1966), *The Devils* (1971), and *Julia* (1977), for which she was awarded an Oscar. Well-known for her active support of left-wing causes, her later film appearances include *The Bostonians* (1983) and *Prick Up Your Ears* (1987).

Redon, Odilon [ruhdõ] (1840–1916) French artist, born in Bordeaux. He is usually regarded as a pioneer Surrealist, because of his use of dream images in his work. He made many charcoal drawings and lithographs, but after 1900 he painted, especially in pastel, pictures of flowers and portraits in intense colour. He died in Paris. » French art; lithography; Surrealism; Symbolists

redpoll Either of two species of finch of genus *Carduelis*, especially the **common redpoll**, with subspecies **mealy redpoll**, **lesser redpoll**, and **Greenland redpoll** (*Carduelis flammea*); also the **Arctic redpoll** or **Hornemann's redpoll** (*Carduelis hornemanni*); native to the N hemisphere, and introduced in New Zealand. (Family: *Fringillidae.*) » finch

redshank Either of two species of sandpiper of genus *Tringa*, especially the **common redshank** (*Tringa totanus*), from Europe and Asia; also the **spotted redshank** (*Tringa erythropus*), from Scandinavia, Europe, and Asia; long red legs; long dark bill with red base. » sandpiper

redshift The displacement of features in the spectra of astronomical objects, particularly galaxies and quasars, towards the longer wavelengths. This is generally interpreted as a result of the Doppler effect resulting from the expansion of the universe. » Doppler effect; spectrum; universe

redstart An Old World thrush of genus *Phoenicurus* (11 species), *Sheppardia* (2 species), or *Rhyacornis* (2 species); also, a New World warbler of genus *Myioborus* (11 species) or *Setophaga* (1 species). » thrush (bird); warbler

reduced instruction set computer (RISC) A computer using a very small and relatively simple instruction set, which allows faster processing and greater compatibility in design between computers. » instruction

reducing agent A substance which reduces another in a chemical reaction, being itself oxidized in the process. An important example is hydrogen gas (H_2), which is oxidized to water when it reduces a metal oxide. » oxidation; reduction

reduction A chemical process involving the gain of electrons, always accompanied by oxidation, the loss of electrons. It often involves the gain of hydrogen or the loss of oxygen by a compound. » hydrogenation; oxidation

reductionism Any attempt to claim that the phenomena of one theory can be accounted for by another theory. Some philosophers claim that psychology and/or biology reduce to physics. *Logicism* is the thesis that mathematics reduces to logic. Some phenomenalists maintain that physical objects reduce to sense data. » phenomenalism

redundancy A business situation where workers are no longer required by a company. The reasons include a lack of demand for the products of the firm, a productivity drive, increased mechanization, or a rationalization programme. In the UK, the individuals 'laid off' often receive compensation, to a minimum laid down by the Redundancy Payments Act. » productivity

redwing A thrush native to Europe, Asia, and N Africa; speckled breast, red sides, and cream 'eye-brow'; migrates S in autumn, often with fieldfares. The name is also used for the **red-winged blackbird** (*Icteridae*) and the **redwing francolin** (*Phasianidae*). (*Turdus iliacus*.) » francolin; oriole; thrush (bird)

redwood » **coast redwood; dawn redwood**

Redwood National park in N California, USA, on the Pacific coast; protects the Coast redwood trees (*Sequoia sempervirens*), among the tallest in the world; area 228 sq km/88 sq ml. » California; redwood

reed A tall grass with far-creeping rhizomes, found almost everywhere; stout, erect stems 2–3 m/6–10 ft high; panicle nodding, soft, dull purple. It forms vast beds in swamps or shallow water, and is used for good quality thatch. (*Phragmites australis*. Family: *Gramineae*.) » grass [i]; panicle; rhizome

Reed, Sir Carol (1906–76) British film director, born and died in London. Educated at Canterbury, he became an actor and director, joining the cinema in 1930. He produced or directed several major films, such as *Kipps* (1941), *The Fallen Idol* (1948), and *Oliver!* (1968, Academy Award), but is best-known for *The Third Man* (1949), depicting the sinister underworld of postwar, partitioned Vienna, based on the book by Graham Greene. He was knighted in 1952.

Reed, Walter (1851–1902) US army physician, born in Belroi, Virginia. He was in the medical corps from 1875, and became professor of bacteriology in the Army Medical College, Washington, in 1893. In 1900 he carried out research in Cuba which showed that yellow fever was carried by mosquitoes, and was soon able to eradicate the disease from the region. He died in Washington, DC. » yellow fever

reed instrument Any woodwind instrument whose sound is produced by a stream of air causing a 'reed' (which may be of cane, metal, or plastic) to vibrate. The reed may be single (as in the clarinet), or double (as in the oboe); it may vibrate freely (as in the harmonica and the crumhorn) or be controlled by the player's lips (as in all orchestral reed instruments). Each type has a distinctive timbre, which is further affected by the size and shape of the instrument. The main orchestral reed instruments are the oboe, cor anglais, clarinet, bass clarinet, bassoon, and double bassoon. » aerophone; basset-horn; bassoon; clarinet; cor anglais; crumhorn; harmonica; oboe; reed organ; sarrusophone; woodwind instrument [i]

reed organ A musical instrument in which reeds, brought into play by means of one or more keyboards, are made to vibrate freely by air under pressure from bellows. Smaller models, such as the harmonium, have only one manual, and the bellows are powered by a foot treadle; larger ones may have two manuals and a pedalboard, the bellows being operated by a separate lever or by an electric motor. Reed organs were at one time popular as domestic instruments and also in small churches, being less expensive and requiring less space than pipe organs. In the 20th-c the demand has gradually switched to electronic organs. » accordion; concertina; harmonium; organ; reed instrument; regal

reed warbler An Old World warbler, especially the **reed warbler** (*Acrocephalus scirpaceus*) from Europe, SW Asia, and Africa; inhabits reed beds and parks; eats insects, berries, and molluscs. (Genus: *Acrocephalus*, 14 species.) » warbler

reedbuck An African grazing antelope of genus *Redunca*; pale brown with white underparts; male with horns curving forward at tip; female without horns; inhabits long grass and reeds near water; three species: **southern, mountain** and **bohor reedbucks**. » antelope

reedling A small, long-tailed babbler, native to S Asia and Europe; male pale brown with grey head and black vertical bar on face; inhabits reedbeds and swamps; eats insects, berries, and seeds; also known as the **bearded reedling**, or **bearded tit**. (*Panurus biarmicus*.) » babbler

reedmace An aquatic perennial, more or less cosmopolitan; stems robust, growing to 2.5 m/8 ft; leaves grass-like; flowers tiny, grouped into a distinctive inflorescence, the hairy female florets forming a furry, brown cylinder surmounted by a plume composed of male flowers all reduced to clusters of stamens; also called **cat's-tail, false bulrush** and, erroneously, **bulrush**. It often forms extensive reed-swamps. (*Typha latifolia*. Family: *Typhaceae*.) » bulrush; inflorescence [i]; perennial; stamen

reef » **atoll**

reefer A vessel designed to carry refrigerated cargoes in specially cooled and insulated compartments. Modern cargoes include carcases of beef, dairy produce, and most kinds of fruit. » ship [i]

reel In photography, (1) a flanged spool on which long lengths of film or tape may be wound, or (2) the roll of motion picture film that forms a convenient length for handling a section of a programme during editing and printing. A typical feature film comprises 5 or 6 reels, each between 1 600 and 2 000 ft (500 and 600 m) in length. » film

reeve » **ruff**

referendum A device of direct democracy whereby the electorate can pronounce, usually for or against, some measure put before it by government; also known as a **plebiscite**. In some countries a petition of sufficient voters can put an issue to a referendum. Most commonly referenda are held on constitutional changes, rather than on government policy. » representation

reflation In economics, government action designed to stimulate an economy which is in a period of recession. Strategies include increasing government expenditure, lowering taxes, and reducing interest rates. » recession

reflectance » **reflection**

reflecting telescope » **telescope** [i]

reflection In physics, the bouncing off from a suitable surface of a beam of light, sound, or other wave at an angle equal to that of the incident beam. Light is reflected by shiny (eg metal) surfaces, and at a change in refractive index (eg in passing from air to glass). Sound is reflected by hard, smooth surfaces and in passing through a change in air density. **Reflectance** is the measured ratio of incident intensity to reflected intensity. » mirror; refractive index; speckle pattern

reflex A rapid, involuntary, and stereotyped action made by an animal in response to a particular stimulus involving the central nervous system. An example is the rapid withdrawal of the hand after touching a very hot surface.

reflex camera A camera in which an image of the scene being photographed is shown on the viewfinder screen by way of a mirror. In **single-lens reflex** (SLR) types, the mirror is at 45° behind the camera lens and is automatically swung out of the way immediately before exposure. The **twin-lens reflex** has two matched lenses coupled for focusing, one for the viewfinder alone and the other with shutter and diaphragm for the camera proper. » camera

reflex projection In special effects cinematography, a system of front projection onto a highly reflective directional beaded screen by way of a semi-silvered mirror. Foreground action and projected background can then be photographed together through the mirror by a camera whose lens axis coincides with that of the projector – hence also known as **front axial projection.** » front projection; special effects

Reform Acts Legislation in Britain which altered parliamentary constituencies and increased the size of the electorate. The main Acts were: **1832**, which gave the vote to almost all members of the middle classes, and introduced a uniform £10 franchise in the borough; **1867**, which gave the vote to all settled tenants in the boroughs, thus creating a substantial working-class franchise for the first time; **1884**, which extended a similar franchise to rural and mining areas; **1885**, which aimed to create parliamentary constituencies of broadly equal size; **1918**, which created a universal male suffrage and gave the vote to women of 30 years and over; **1928**, which gave the vote to all adult women; and **1969**, which lowered the minimum voting age from 21 years to 18. The 1832 Reform Act was the subject of furious controversy, and was preceded by widespread radical agitation. » parliament; pocket borough; radicalism; rotten borough

Reform Judaism A movement beginning in early 19th-c Germany for the reform of Jewish worship, ritual, and beliefs in the light of modern scholarship and knowledge. Greater emphasis is placed on the ethical teachings of the prophets than on ritual law, and reason and experience are primary in the assessment of belief. » Judaism

Reformation The Protestant reform movements in the Christian Church, inspired by and derived from Martin Luther, John Calvin, and others in 16th-c Europe. A complex phenomenon, various factors are common to all reforms: a Biblical revival and translation of the Word of God into the vernacular; an improvement in the intellectual and moral standards of the clergy; emphasis on the sovereignty of God; and insistence that faith and scriptures are at the centre of the Christian message. Non-religious factors aiding the spread of the Reformation included the invention of the printing press; the political, social and economic uncertainties of the age; and a general feeling of revival caused by the Renaissance.

In Germany, Luther's 'ninety-five theses' (1517) questioned the authority of the Church and led to his excommunication. The Lutheran Church then spread rapidly, in Switzerland under Zwingli and later under Calvin, neither of whom allowed any form of worship or devotion not explicitly warranted by scripture. The authority of scripture, the cornerstone of the Reformation, required a degree of ecclesiastical authority (and power) to justify and maintain it. The doctrine of the priesthood of all believers and the importance placed on preaching the Word of God led to an educated clergy, and decentralized church communities were better able to prevent abuse of ecclesiastical privilege. In England, Henry VIII declared that the king was the supreme head of the English Church, and appropriated Church property; in 1549 the Book of Common Prayer, embodying Reformation doctrine, was published, and under Elizabeth I a strong anti-papal stance was taken. In Scotland, under the influence of Calvin and the leadership of John Knox, the Presbyterian Church of Scotland was established in 1560, and remains the national Church. The Reformation also took root as Lutheran and Reformed Churches in France, Scandinavia, Czechoslovakia, Hungary, Romania, and Poland. » Book of Common Prayer; Calvin, John; Christianity; Church of England; Church of Scotland; Henry VIII; Knox, John; Luther; ninety-five theses; Protestantism; Reformed Churches

Reformation, Catholic A 16th-c reform movement in the Roman Catholic Church, partly as a reaction to the Protestant Reformation, but partly from a desire for internal reform. The principal organ of reform was the Council of Trent, which affirmed papal authority and rejected conciliation with Protestants. » Council of the Church; pope; Reformation; Roman Catholicism

Reformed Church in America A Christian denomination established in 1628 with the organization of the Collegiate Church for the early Dutch Reformed settlers. It gained its independence in 1770, was incorporated as the Reformed Protestant Church in 1819, and adopted its current name in 1867. In 1784 it established the New Brunswick Theological Seminary, the oldest Protestant seminary in the USA. » Protestantism; Reformed Churches

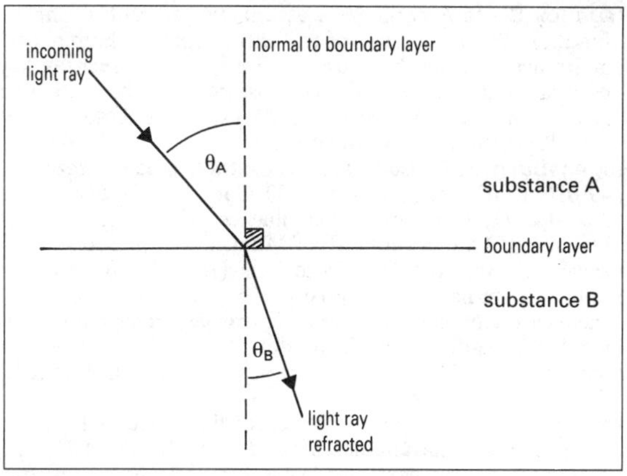

Refraction

Reformed Churches Churches deriving from Calvin's Reformation in 16th-c Geneva, adopting a conciliar or presbyterian form of Church government. They are now worldwide in extent, with most being members of the World Alliance of Reformed Churches. » Calvin, John; elder (religion); Presbyterianism; Reformation; Reformed Church in America

reformism Any doctrine or movement that advocates gradual social and political change rather than revolutionary change; most commonly applied to socialism. The underlying premise is that democratic procedures provide the most suitable means through which to build social change. » communism; revolution; social democracy; socialism

refracting telescope » **telescope** [i]

refraction A change in the direction of a wave as it passes from one medium to another in which the wave velocity is different, for example a sound wave passing from hot to cold air. It is expressed by Snell's law, $\sin \theta_A/\sin \theta_B=$constant. The illustration shows a wave having a velocity in substance B which is less than its velocity in substance A. If the wave was light and substance A was a vacuum, $\sin \theta_{vac} \sin \theta_B = n_B$, the refractive index of substance B. Light passing into a substance of higher refractive index is bent towards normal. The distortion of partially submerged objects, rainbows, and mirages are all caused by the refraction of light. » birefringence; Fermat's principle; refractive index

refractive index A measurement of the ratio of velocity of light (or other electromagnetic wave) in a vacuum to that in matter; symbol *n*; always greater than 1; n(air) = 1.0003, n(water) = 1.33, so the velocity of light in water is about 75% of that in air. » refraction [i]

refractories Materials which are neither deformed nor chemically changed by exposure to high temperatures. This makes them suitable for containers, structural materials, and components, particularly in metallurgical operations, such as furnace linings. Naturally occurring refractories include silica, fireclay, and alumina. Synthetic refractories include the high-melting carbides and nitrides used in nuclear power plant. » alumina; carbide; fireclay; silica

refuse-derived fuel 1 Garbage from which metallic and mineral inclusions have been removed, so that it can be fed into a suitably designed furnace. It is often used for generating electricity or district heating. **2** The product of small-scale fermentation of domestic and animal waste to produce gas (*methane*) for domestic use. The process has been promoted particularly in some rural areas in Third World countries. » methane [i]; Three Worlds theory

regal A small portable reed organ, in use during the 16th–17th-c. The wind pressure was maintained by two small bellows directly behind the keyboard. » reed organ

Regency Style A florid Neoclassical style current in England for about the first quarter of the 19th-c. Like the Empire Style in France, it made bold use of Greek motifs, such as key-pattern, and Egyptian devices inspired by the campaigns against Napoleon on the Nile (1798–1800). » Empire Style; Neoclassicism (art and architecture)

Regensburg, Fr **Ratisbon**, ancient **Castra Regina** [**ray**gnzboork] 49°01N 12°07E, pop (1983) 132 000. Commercial city in Oberpfalz district, Germany; at confluence of R Regen and R Danube, 104 km/65 ml NNE of Munich; well-preserved mediaeval city; Imperial Diets held here (1663–1806); bishopric; railway; river harbour; university (1962); electrical engineering, chemicals, clothing, sugar refining, carpets, river craft, brewing; Gothic cathedral (13th–16th-c), old town hall, Benedictine monastery of St Emmeram (7th-c). » Diet; Germany [i]; Gothic architecture

regent The person appointed to act for the monarch if he/she is incapacitated, unavailable, or under 18. In the UK, it is customary for the next heir to the throne to be regent: from 1811 to 1820 the Prince of Wales (later George IV) acted as regent because of the insanity of his father, George III.

reggae A type of popular music, of Jamaican origin but drawing on Afro-American traditions and influenced by rock. Many reggae songs spring from a social malaise; they are usually accompanied by electric guitars, piano, organ, and drum set. Among prominent reggae artists are Bob Marley (1945–81) and the Wailers. » Marley; pop music

Reggio di Calabria [**red**joh dee ka**la**bria] 38°06N 15°39E, pop (1981) 173 486. Seaport and capital of Reggio di Calabria province, Calabria, S Italy; on E side of the Strait of Messina; founded by Greek colonists, 8th-c BC; archbishopric; airfield; railway; ferry to Sicily; fruit, oil of bergamot. » Calabria

Reggio nell'Emilia [**red**joh nelay**mee**lia] 44°42N 10°37E, pop (1981) 130 376. Capital town of Reggio nell'Emilia province, Emilia-Romagna, N Italy; founded by the Romans; railway; agricultural trade, wine, cement, engineering; cathedral (13th-c), Church of the Madonna della Chiaira (1597–1619). » Italy [i]

Regina [re**jiy**na] 50°30N 104°38W, pop (1981) 162 613. Capital of Saskatchewan province, on Moosejaw Creek, SC Canada; founded, 1882 as capital of Northwest Territories; named in honour of Queen Victoria; capital, 1905; centre of grain, potash, and oil region; airport; railway; university (1917); grain trade, oil refining, steel, engineering, meat processing, canning; Royal Canadian Mounted Police Museum, Wascana Park, Diefenbaker Homestead, Saskatchewan Centre of Arts, Museum of Natural History; Buffalo Days (pioneer celebration, Jul), Canadian Western Agribition (autumn). » Diefenbaker; Saskatchewan

Regiomontanus, pseudonym of **Johannes Müller** (1436–76) German mathematician and astronomer, born at Königsberg (Lat *Mons Regius*, hence his byname). He studied at Vienna, and in 1471 settled in Nuremberg. He established the study of algebra and trigonometry in Germany, and wrote on a variety of applied topics. In 1474 he was summoned to Rome by Sixtus IV to help reform the calendar, and died there. » algebra; trigonometry

regionalism 1 In planning, the division of a country into regions for political, developmental, and administrative purposes. The division is based on the underlying assumption of unifying characteristics (eg social, economic) within a region. 2 A political movement whereby the inhabitants of a region stress their individual or separate identity from other regions. This can be based on factors such as linguistic differences (eg in Belgium), religious differences (eg Northern Ireland), and ethnic differences (eg the Kurdish population in Iraq).

register A variety of language defined by the social context in which it is deemed appropriate for use, such as religion, law, science, advertising, journalism, conversation. Each register can be identified by a range of linguistic features which together distinguish it from other registers in the language. Traditional religious language is usually one of the most distinctive in English, making use of such forms as *goeth*, *knowest*, *vouchsafe*, and *O*. » Seaspeak; standard language; stylistics

regolith The layer of fine powdery material on the Moon produced by the repeated impact of meteorites. It is up to 25 m/80 ft thick. Similar dust probably covers many other objects in the Solar System. » meteorite; Moon

regression One of many defence mechanisms in which the individual returns to behaviour more apposite to an earlier age. This can be a component of a psychotherapy process and can also occur in physical illness; for example, a man with a severe injury to the spine but who was able to feed himself insisted on his wife feeding him with a spoon during the acute phase of his illness. » defence mechanism; psychotherapy

Regulator Movements Rural insurgencies in S Carolina and N Carolina, just prior to independence. The S Carolina events took place in the mid-1760s, and the N Carolina movement followed a few years later, meeting military defeat in 1771. Both disputes pitched the slave-holding seacoast against small farmers of the interior, but otherwise the causes and outcomes were different. The ensuing bitterness spilled over into the American Revolution. The term *regulator* was also used elsewhere in early America to describe popular insurrectionary movements. » American Revolution

Regulus, Marcus Atilius (3rd-c BC) Roman general and statesman of the First Punic War, whose heroic death at the hands of the Carthaginians earned him legendary status. After capture by the Carthaginians, he was sent to Rome on parole to sue for peace. Having dissuaded the Senate from agreeing to their terms, he voluntarily returned to Carthage, where he was tortured to death. » Punic Wars

Rehnquist, William H(ubbs) (1924–) US jurist, born at Milwaukee, Wisconsin. Educated at Stanford and Harvard, he became a law clerk on the US Supreme Court before entering private practice. After serving as Assistant Attorney General (1969–71), he was named as an Associate Justice of the Supreme Court, and became Chief Justice in 1986.

Reich The term used to describe the German Empire. The Holy Roman Empire was regarded as the *First Reich*, and unified Germany after 1870 was referred to as the *Second Reich* (*Kaiserreich*). After 1933, the enlarged Germany envisaged in Hitler's plans was known as the *Third Reich*. » Hitler; Holy Roman Empire; Kaiser

Reichenbach, Hans [**riykh**uhnbakh] (1891–1953) German philosopher of science, born in Hamburg. Educated at Berlin, Munich, Göttingen, and Erlangen, he became professor of philosophy at Berlin (1926–33), Istanbul (1933–8), and California (from 1938). An early associate of the logical positivists, he was best-known for his *Warscheinlichkeitslehre* (1935, Theory of Probability) and *Philosophie der Raum-Zeit-Lehre* (1978, Philosophy of Space and Time). He died in Los Angeles. » conventionalism; logical positivism; probability of an event

Reichstag fire The deliberate burning down of Germany's parliament building (27 Feb 1933), shortly after the Nazi accession to power. A deranged Dutch ex-communist, van der Lubbe, was accused of arson and executed. The new Nazi government, insisting that the act was evidence of a wider communist conspiracy, used the situation to ban and suppress the German Communist Party. Communist conspiracy was certainly not behind the fire; nor, probably, were the Nazis themselves, though it was long believed to be so. It is now increasingly agreed that, however convenient the fire may have been to the regime, van der Lubbe acted alone. » communism; Nazi Party

Reign of Terror (1793–4) The extreme phase of the French Revolution, characterized by the systematic execution of political opponents of the Jacobins and supposed sympathizers of the Counter-Revolution, who were brought before the Revolutionary Tribunal and guillotined. 40 000 people are thought to have been killed in Paris and the provinces. » French Revolution [i]; Jacobins (French history)

Reims » **Rheims**

reincarnation The belief that following death, some aspect of the self or soul can be reborn in a new body (human or animal), a process which may be repeated many times. This belief is fundamental to many Eastern religions, such as Hinduism and Buddhism, and is also found in more modern, Western belief systems such as theosophy. Alleged past-life regressions, where a hypnotized person appears to 'remember' past lives, have recently fuelled Western interest in reincarnation, although such cases may only represent the person trying to meet the implied demands of the hypnotist. » Buddhism; Hinduism; theosophy

reindeer A true deer native to high latitudes of the N hemisphere (introduced on South Georgia I); first domesticated 3000 years ago; the most northerly deer, inhabiting open tundra; the only deer in which females have antlers, and the only one in which the lowest, forward-pointing tine is branched; long coat of hollow hairs; nose covered with hairs; feet make clicking sound when walking; hooves broad; in winter digs in snow with antlers to eat lichens; also known as **caribou** ('shoveller'). (*Rangifer tarandus*.) » antlers [i]; deer

Reinhardt, Django, [riynhaht] originally **Jean Baptiste Reinhardt** (1910–53) Gypsy jazz guitarist, born at Liverchies, Belgium. At 18, injury in a fire caused the fusing of the fourth and fifth fingers of his left hand, but he simply devised a new chording method for his guitar, and continued to play. He played in the Quintet of the Hot Club of France with Stephane Grapelli (1934–9), producing many renowned recordings, and became the first European jazz musician to influence the music. He died at Fontainebleau, France. » Grapelli; guitar; jazz

Reinhardt, Max [riynhaht], originally **Max Goldmann** (1873–1943) Austrian theatre manager, born at Baden, Germany. He became recognized as an innovator in theatre art and technique, often involving large-scale productions, as in *The Miracle* (London 1911), which used over 2000 actors. A co-founder of the Salzburg Festival (1920), he left Hitler's Germany in 1933, and moved to Hollywood, where he opened a theatre workshop. He died in New York City. » theatre

Reith (of Stonehaven), John (Charles Walsham), 1st Baron [reeth] (1889–1971) British statesman and engineer, born at Stonehaven, Kincardineshire, Scotland. Educated at Glasgow, he entered the field of radio communication, and became the first general manager of the BBC in 1922, and its Director General (1927–38). He was the architect of public service broadcasting in the UK. He became an MP in 1940, and was Minister of Works and Buildings (1940–2). The BBC inaugurated the Reith Lectures in 1948 in honour of his influence on broadcasting. Created baron in 1940, he died in Edinburgh. » BBC

relapsing fever A group of diseases resulting from infection with spirochaetes bacteria of the genus *Borrelia*, transmitted to humans by body lice or ticks. It tends to occur in epidemics and to afflict refugees. » bacteria [i]; lice; tick

relative atomic mass The mass of atoms, expressed in atomic mass units u, eg carbon-12 is 12.0000 u by definition, nitrogen-14 is 14.0031 u; symbol A_r; formerly called **atomic weight**. The periodic table lists masses for naturally occurring isotopic mixtures, eg naturally occurring nitrogen is 14.0067 u. » nucleon number; periodic table; RR90

relative biological effectiveness » radioactivity units [i]

relative density Density measured relative to some standard, typically water at 20°C; symbol d, expressed as a pure number; measured using hydrometers; formerly called **specific gravity**. For example, for alcohol, density $\rho = 789$ kg/m^3, d=0.791. » alcohols; density (physics); proof spirit

relativism Any philosophical position which maintains that there are truths and values, but denies that they are absolute. **Epistemological relativism**, first defended by Protagoras, asserts that all truth is necessarily relative; 'is true' is always elliptical for 'is true for *x*', where *x* might be an individual, society, or conceptual framework. **Ethical relativism**, held by the anthropologist Ruth Benedict (1887–1948) and others, comprises three doctrines, often confused: *cultural relativism*, the anthropological hypothesis that different societies have *fundamentally* different views about values; *normative relativism*, the thesis that there are no absolute values valid for all societies; and *metaethical subjectivism*, the doctrine that there can be no objective decision procedures for resolving value disputes. » epistemology; ethics; Protagoras

relativistic quantum mechanics Quantum mechanics consistent with special relativity, and thus applicable to fast-moving systems; originally developed by British physicist Paul Dirac in 1928. It predicts the observed fine detail of atomic spectra, and is essential in particle physics. » antiparticles; Bohr magnetron; Dirac; Dirac equation; quantum field theory; quantum mechanics; particle physics

relativity » general relativity; special relativity [i]

relay An electrical or solid-state device, operated by changes in input, which is used to control or operate other devices connected to the output. Most relays are used in electrical circuits, though they may have mechanical input or output. They have a range of applications in telephone exchanges, switches, and automation systems. » electricity; solid-state device

releasing factor » releasing hormone

releasing hormone One of a group of hormones secreted by the neurones of the middle ridge of the hypothalamus in response to stimuli from the brain. It is transported to the front lobe of the pituitary gland, where it stimulates or inhibits the release of pituitary hormones (eg growth-hormone-releasing hormone). Previously known as a *releasing factor*, this term is now confined to hypothalamic hormones whose chemical structures are unknown (eg prolactin-releasing factor). » dopamine; hormones; hypothalamus; pituitary gland; somatostatin

relics Material remains (eg bones, skin) of, or objects which have been in contact with, a saint or person worthy of special religious attention. In many religions, and in the Christianity of Roman Catholic and Orthodox Churches, these are objects of veneration, and the churches in which they are housed places of pilgrimage. » Orthodox Church; Roman Catholicism

relief printing A print, made from a block (usually wood or lino) which has been cut away in those parts intended to be left white; the method contrasts with intaglio or surface prints. The ink adheres to the raised (relief) parts only, and when the block is pressed against a sheet of paper only those parts print. » intaglio; printing [i]; surface printing; woodcut

relief sculpture A type of sculpture in which the forms are raised above the background, but not shaped fully 'in the round'. In *low relief* (or *bas-relief*) the design is hardly raised above the surface, as on a coin, while in *high relief* the forms may be almost free-standing, as on a Roman sarcophagus, or the pediments of many classical buildings. » bas-relief; sculpture

religion A concept which has been used to denote: (1) the class of all religions; (2) the common essence or pattern of all supposedly genuine religious phenomena; (3) the transcendant or 'this-worldly' ideal of which any actual religion is as an imperfect manifestation; and (4) human religiousness as a form of life which may or may not be expressed in systems of belief and practice. These usages suffer from a tendency to be evaluative, presuppose a commitment of some sort, or are so general as to provide little specific guidance. What is clear is that no single definition will suffice to encompass the varied sets of traditions, practices, and ideas which constitute different religions. Some religions involve the belief in and worship of a god or gods, but this is not true of all. Christianity, Islam, and Judaism are theistic religions, while Buddhism does not require a belief in gods, and where it does occur, the gods are not considered important. There are theories of religion which construe it as wholly a human phenomenon, without any supernatural or transcendent origin and point of reference, while others argue that some such reference is the essence of the matter. Several other viewpoints exist, and there are often boundary disputes regarding the application of the concept. For example, debate continues as to whether Confucianism is properly to be considered a religion; and some writers argue that Marxism is in important respects a religion. » Ahmadiyya; apologetics; Baha'i; Brahmanism; Buddhism; Christianity; comparative religion; Confucianism; cult; deism; Egyptian religion; fundamentalism; Germanic religion; God; Hare Krishna movement; Hinduism; Islam; Jainism; Jehovah's Witnesses; Judaism; Lamaism; millenarianism; monotheism; mystery religions; mysticism; Parseeism; Pentecostalism; polytheism; sect; Shinto; Sikhism; Slavic religion; Taoism; theology; voodoo; Zoroastrianism

Religion, Wars of (1562–98) A series of religious and political conflicts in France, caused by the growth of Calvinism, noble factionalism, and weak royal government. After 1559 there were a number of weak and/or young Valois kings whose mother, Catherine de' Medici, attempted abortive compromises. Calvinist or 'Huguenot' numbers increased from the 1550s, fostered by the missionary activities of Geneva. The noble factions of Bourbon, Guise, and Montmorency were split by religion as well as by family interests. Civil wars were encouraged by Philip II of Spain's support of the Catholic Guise faction and by Elizabeth I's aid to the Huguenots. They ended when Henry of Navarre returned to Catholicism and crushed the Guise Catholic League (1589–98). » Catherine de' Medici; Guise; Huguenots

rem In radioactivity, an old measure of dose equivalent; symbol rem; equal to absorbed dose in rad multiplied by relative biological effectiveness, 1 rem = 0.01 Sv (sievert, SI unit); an abbreviation of **röntgen equivalent man**. » radioactivity units [i]; sievert; units (scientific)

Remarque, Erich (Maria) [ruh**mahk**] (1898–1970) German novelist, born at Osnabrück. He joined the German army at 18, and was wounded in World War 1. After the war, he became a journalist, while working on his first novel, *Im Westen nichts Neues* (1929, All Quiet on the Western Front), which was an immediate success, and filmed in 1930. He left Germany in 1933, and his books were banned by the Nazis. In 1939 he went to the USA, becoming naturalized in 1947. He then settled in Switzerland, where he died, at Locarno. » German literature; novel; World War 1

Rembrandt (Harmenszoon van Rijn) (1606–69) Dutch painter, born at Leyden. He studied under various masters, and was introduced to Italian art. His early works include religious and historical scenes, unusual in Protestant Holland. He settled in Amsterdam (1631), where he ran a large studio and took numerous pupils. 'The Anatomy Lesson of Dr Nicolaes Tulp' (1632, The Hague) assured his reputation as a portrait painter. In 1634 he married Saskia van Ulenburgh (1613–42), and the year of her death (1642) produced his masterpiece, 'The Night Watch' (Amsterdam), which was well received, and which was followed by other important commissions. His extravagance, especially as a collector, led to bankruptcy in 1656, but he continued to work with undiminished energy and power. His preserved works number over 650 oil paintings, 2 000 drawings and studies, and 300 etchings. He died in relative obscurity, in Amsterdam. » Dutch art; Italian art

Remembrance Day In the UK, the Sunday nearest 11 November, on which are commemorated those who died in the two world wars; formerly Armistice Day. A two-minute silence is observed at 11 a.m. There are special church services, and wreath-laying ceremonies at war memorials. » Armistice Day; Veterans' Day

Remington, Eliphalet (1793–1861) US firearms manufacturer and inventor, born at Suffield, Connecticut. While still a young man he made for himself a flintlock rifle which, although not original, was very accurate. In 1828 he built a factory beside the Erie Canal, and pioneered several improvements in small arms manufacture, including a method of straightening gun barrels and the first successful cast steel rifle barrel in the USA. He died at Ilion, New York. » firearms

Remonstrants Christians adhering to the Calvinistic doctrine of Jacobus Arminius (17th-c Holland), whose followers were also known as **Arminians**. They were named after the 'Remonstrance', a statement of Arminian teaching dating from 1610. Small in number, they were influential among Baptists, and in Methodism and Calvinism. » Arminius; Baptists; Calvinism; Methodism

remora [**rem**uhra] Slender-bodied fish widespread in warm seas; large sucking disc on upper surface of head, with which it attaches firmly to other fish, especially sharks; length up to 45 cm/18 in; also called **shark-sucker**. (*Remora remora*. Family: *Echeneidae*, 3 genera, 8 species.)

remote sensing A method of measuring the characteristics of an object without touching it. The term is usually applied to images of the Earth taken by satellites, and to cameras in aircraft which can be used to map different phenomena; examples include cloud cover from METEOSAT, and land-use patterns from LANDSAT. » aerial photography; weather satellite; Plates I, II, III

Renaissance From the French for 're-birth', referring to the revival of classical literature and artistic styles at various times in European history. Such renaissances occurred in the 8th-c and 9th-c, in the 12th-c, and from the 14th-c to the 16th-c. The first, or *Carolingian*, centred upon the recovery of classical Latin texts in cathedral schools; the second was marked by the foundation of universities and the rediscovery of Aristotle's ethical and philosophical works; and the third was distinguished for the development of naturalistic works of art, the study of ancient Greek authors, above all Plato, and the critical study of Christian texts.

Although varied in content and institutional focus, all three renaissances therefore included elements of revived classicism. Yet it was the third such revival between c.1300 and c.1600 that historians since Michelet and Burckhardt in the mid-19th-c have thought marked the beginnings of modern times. Since they wrote, however, a number of criticisms have been levelled against their interpretations. One is that the two earlier renaissances diminish the supposed unique importance of the third. A second is that few major scientific and technological discoveries, which are crucial to modern societies, were made during the third renaissance. A third is that mass movements – another hallmark of 'modernity' – were almost totally absent from the third renaissance, which was a distinctly elite affair. A final objection is that Burckhardt's renaissance was almost entirely limited to N Italy.

These caveats have some validity, but they do not wholly negate Burckhardt's hypothesis. He did not deny the existence of previous classical revivals, but emphasized that classicism was just one element in the renaissance he described. At any rate, causal connections and continuities between the earlier and later renaissances have not been demonstrated. Further, Burckhardt did not claim that *all* forms of modernity were included in his renaissance. Nor did he say that N Italy was typical of all Europe; rather, the suggestion was, Italy was the starting-point for changes that eventually affected much of Europe.

Recent scholarship has indeed confirmed certain elements of the Burckhardtian theory. Chief among them is the rise of secular states and values. These changes included new institutions such as permanent embassies and spies, standing armies, and regular taxation. New attitudes were also involved. In the 14th-c, Marsiglio of Padua rejected all clerical authority; in the 15th-c, 'civic humanists' made service to the city-state a moral imperative; and in the early 16th-c, Machiavelli stated that power should be pursued without reference to Christian commandments. In philosophy, Ficino and Pico della Mirandola suggested that human perfection was possible through the intellectual study of pagan sources, as well as Christian ones, and through Platonic love. Artistic production, although its subjects often remained religious, also acknowledged secular values, as in the geometric naturalism of Piero della Francesca's paintings.

The changes brought about by the Italian Renaissance of the 14th–16th-c should not be compared with modern political and social revolutions. But it did contain fundamental changes in values and institutions, the effects of which were not confined to Europe's elites. » Aristotle; Burckhardt, Jacob; Charlemagne; classicism; Erasmus; Machiavelli, Niccolo; Pico della Mirandola; Piero della Francesca; Plato; Renaissance architecture/art

Renaissance architecture The rediscovery and application of classical and especially Roman architectural forms and principles in 15th-c and 16th-c W Europe. It is particularly associated with Italy, and the work of such architects as Alberti, Bramante, Brunelleschi, Michaelangelo, Palladio, Raphael, Guilio Romano, Guiliano da Sangallo, and Vignola. Renaissance architecture is also to be found in England, such as the Queens House Greenwich (1616), architect Inigo Jones, and in Belgium, France, Germany, the Netherlands, and Spain.

» Baroque (art and architecture); Elizabethan Style; Greek architecture; Jacobean Style; Mannerism; Palladianism; Renaissance; Roman architecture

Renaissance art A movement which began in Florence in the early 15th-c, when Masaccio, Donatello, and Brunelleschi turned to ancient Roman art and architecture for inspiration. Parallel to the new humanism in literature, a new self-consciousness arose about style. Piero della Francesca, Mantegna, and others sought classical proportions for their figures, while the new system of perspective helped to rationalize the picture-space. Ghiberti, Verrocchio, and Michelangelo were the greatest sculptors after Donatello; Leonardo and Raphael painted portraits, and religious and historical works. The period c.1500–20 is known as the **High Renaissance**. In the 16th-c, Renaissance style spread throughout Italy, especially to Venice, and to much of W Europe. » Florentine School; Fontainebleau School; Italian art; Mannerism; Renaissance; Venetian School; Brunelleschi; Donatello; Ghiberti; Leonardo da Vinci; Mantegna; Masaccio; Michelangelo; Piero della Francesca; Raphael; Verrocchio

Rendell, Ruth (1932–) British detective-story writer, born in London. She spent some time as a journalist and managing director of a local newspaper before publishing her first novel *From Doon with Death* in 1964. She has written detective stories featuring Chief Inspector Wexford (eg *Shake Hands Forever*, 1975), and mystery thrillers (eg *A Judgement in Stone*, 1977). Since 1986, she has also written under the pen name of **Barbara Vine**. » detective story

renewable resources Resources with a yield which is sustainable and which may be used without danger of exhaustion, such as solar power, wind energy, and hydroelectric power, all of which are directly or indirectly due to solar energy. Some renewable resources (eg crops, timber, fish) are sustainable in the long-term only through careful management, so that they are not overexploited (eg overcropping, overgrazing) or misused in the short-term. » alternative energy; hydroelectric power; non-renewable resources; solar power

Renfrew, (Andrew) Colin (1937–) British archaeologist, educated at St Albans and Cambridge. Much influenced by the writings of Gordon Childe, his work has ranged widely but exhibits a preoccupation with the nature of cultural change in prehistory. He has excavated in Greece (1964–76) and on Orkney (1972–4), notably at Maes Howe. Since 1981 he has been professor of archaeology at Cambridge. » archaeology; Binford; Childe; Maes Howe

Reni, Guido [**ray**nee] (1575–1642) Italian Baroque painter, born near Bologna. He studied in Bologna, and worked both there and in Rome. The fresco painted for the Borghese garden house, 'Aurora and the Hours' (1613–14) is usually regarded as his masterpiece, but some critics rank higher the unfinished 'Nativity' in San Martino at Naples. He later settled at Bologna, where he died. » Baroque (art and architecture); fresco; Italian art

renin A hormone, produced by the kidneys, which promotes the conversion of *angiotensinogen* (a plasma protein) into *angiotensin I*, the inactive precursor of the physiologically active *angiotensin II*. The function of the latter is to constrict the arterioles (thereby raising blood pressure), and to stimulate aldosterone secretion and thirst. It is the most important blood vessel contractor known. » aldosterone; artery; kidneys

Renner, Karl (1870–1950) Austrian statesman, Chancellor (1918–20, 1945), and President (1945–50). born at Unter-Tannowitz, Bohemia. He trained as a lawyer, joined the Austrian Social Democratic Party, and became the first Chancellor of the Austrian Republic. Imprisoned as a socialist leader, following the brief civil war (Feb 1934), he was Chancellor again after the War, and first President of the new Republic. He died at Doebling, Austria. » Austria [i]

Rennes [ren], Breton **Roazon**, ancient **Condate** 48°07N 1°41W, pop (1982) 200 390. Industrial and commercial city, and capital of Ille-et-Vilaine department, NW France; at confluence of canalized Ille and Vilaine Rivers, 309 km/192 ml WSW of Paris; capital of Brittany, 10th-c, and now its economic and cultural centre; largely rebuilt after major fire, 1720; badly bombed in World War 2; airport; road and rail junction; archbishopric; university (founded 1461); oil refining, textiles, chemicals, electronics, cars; Baroque town hall (1734), Palais de Justice, former abbey church of Notre-Dame (11th–13th-c), cathedral (largely rebuilt, 19th-c), La Porte Mordelaise, Thabor Gardens. » Brittany

rennet An extract derived from *rennin*, an enzyme present in the stomach of most young animals, but particularly the calf and the lamb. It causes the main milk protein casein to precipitate, thus allowing the milk to clot, forming a hard curd with the release of a watery whey rich in sugar (lactose) and whey protein. Rennet is commercially available, sometimes being used in recipes and the manufacture of cheese. » casein; milk

Rennie, John (1761–1821) British civil engineer, born at Phantassie, E Lothian, Scotland. Educated at Edinburgh, in 1791 he set up in London as an engineer, and soon became famous as a bridge-builder, constructing several bridges over the R Thames (none now remaining). He also built canals, drained fens, designed London and other docks, and improved harbours and dockyards, including the breakwater at Plymouth. He died in London. » bridge (engineering) [i]; civil engineering

Reno [**ree**noh] 39°31N 119°48W, pop (1980) 100 756. Seat of Washoe County, W Nevada, USA, on the Truckee R; settled, 1859; developed with arrival of railway, 1868; airport; university (1874); noted for its casinos; couples wanting a quick divorce drive to Reno; Reno Rodeo (Jun), National Air Races (Sep). » Nevada

Renoir, Jean [ruh**nwah**] (1894–1979) French film director, born in Paris, the son of Pierre Auguste Renoir. He fought in World War 1, and from scriptwriting turned to film-making. His major works include his antiwar masterpiece, *La Grande Illusion* (1937, Grand Illusion) and *La Règle du jeu* (1939, The Rules of the Game). He left France in 1941 during the invasion, and became a naturalized American. He continued to make films after the War, such as *French Can-Can* (1955), and worked in India and Europe. He died in Los Angeles. » Renoir, Pierre Auguste

Renoir, Pierre Auguste [ruhn**wah**] (1841–1919) French Impressionist artist, born at Limoges. He first painted porcelain and fans, beginning to paint in the open air c.1864, and from 1870 he obtained several commissions for portraits. In 1874–9 and 1882 he exhibited with the Impressionists. His picture of sunlight filtering through leaves – the 'Moulin de la Galette' (1876, Louvre) – epitomizes his colourful, happy art. His visit to Italy in 1880 was followed by a series of 'Bathers' in a more cold and classical style. He then returned to reds, orange, and gold to portray nudes in sunlight, a style which he continued to develop until his death, at Cagnes. » French art; Impressionism (art)

renormalization A mathematical procedure in quantum field theories for avoiding infinite results in calculations by a careful redefinition of basic quantities such as mass and charge. The requirement of renormalization, as displayed for example by quantum electrodynamics, is regarded as prerequisite for a useful theory. » quantum field theory

Renshaw, Willie, properly **William (Charles)** (1861–1904) British lawn tennis player, born at Cheltenham, Gloucestershire, the first great tennis champion. He started playing at Cheltenham School with his twin brother **Ernest** (1861–99), who also became a champion. Willie was Wimbledon singles champion 1881–6 and in 1899, and won the All-England doubles title with Ernest in 1884–6 and 1888–9. » tennis, lawn [i]

reparations Payments imposed on the powers defeated in war to cover the costs incurred by the victors. For example, they were levied by the Allies on Germany at the end of World War 1, though the final sum of £6 000 million plus interest was not fixed until April 1921. The Dawes (1924) and Young (1929) Plans reduced the scale of the payments, which were finally abandoned after 1932, because of the Depression. » Dawes Plan; World War 1

repertory grid A technique developed by the US psychologist George Kelly (1905–66) for eliciting a respondent's view of some aspect of the world. Respondents produce their own list of characteristics (*constructs*) on which they rate items (eg colleagues). The structure of this grid of constructs and items can be used to describe how the respondent sees the world. » psychology

replete » honey ant

representative action In English law, an action taken by one person representing a number of others who have an identical claim against the defendant; the term is not used in Scottish law; in the USA, it is usually referred to as a **class action**. For example, it might be used by one or more individual shareholders against alleged wrongdoers in control of a company. An analogous procedure is a *test action* (or *test case*), where several people agree to be bound by the result of an action brought by one or more of those persons. » defendant

Representatives, House of » **House of Representatives**

repression A psychoanalytic term representing one of many defence mechanisms. There is the unconscious exclusion of painful memories and unacceptable feelings. In psychotherapy there is often the exploration of this defence mechanism with the release of information into conscious awareness. However, in certain forms of treatment (eg repressive-inspirational group psychotherapy) there is an attempt to bolster rather than to penetrate the patient's defences. » defence mechanism; psychoanalysis; psychotherapy

reproduction The act or process or producing offspring; one of the essential properties of a living organism. Reproduction in its simplest form is an asexual process involving the division of an organism into two or more parts by fission, budding, spore formation, or vegetative propagation. Sexual reproduction involves the formation of specialized gametes (such as sperm and egg) by meiosis, and the fusion of a pair of gametes to form a zygote. In demographic research, the **reproduction rate** is the rate at which a population produces new members by birth. » biology; demography; egg; embryo; gamete; meiosis [i]

reptile An animal of the class *Reptilia* (6547 species), which evolved from primitive amphibians; most live on land; breathe with lungs, not gills; dry waterproof skin with horny scales (not separated, like those of a fish, but folds of skin); may moult outer skin regularly; one small bone (the *columella* or *stapes*) in the ear, and several bones forming either side of the lower jaw (unlike mammals); use Sun's rays to maintain body temperature; young do not develop in water (born live, or hatch from shelled eggs laid on land); classified in four orders: *Squamata* (lizards and snakes), *Chelonia* (*Testudinata* or *Testudines* – tortoises and turtles), *Crocodylia* (or *Loricata* – crocodiles, alligators, etc), and *Rhyncocephalia* (the tuatara); many extinct species, including dinosaurs, pterodactyls, plesiosaurs, and ichthyosaurs. » alligator [i]; amphibian; Chelonia [i]; crocodile; dinosaur [i]; lizard [i]; mammal [i]; moulting; palaeontology; snake; tortoise; tuatara; turtle (reptile)

Repton, Humphrey (1752–1818) British landscape-gardener, born at Bury St Edmunds, Suffolk. He completed the change from the formal gardens of the early 18th-c to the 'picturesque' types favoured later. His work can still be seen at Sheringham Hall, Norfolk, and elsewhere. He died in London. » landscape gardening

republic A form of state and government where, unlike a monarchy (which is hereditary), the head of state and leader of the government is periodically appointed under the constitution. It thus covers most modern states, and in this respect the term has lost something of its earlier meaning and appeal as an alternative to systems where political power was hereditary. Republics now vary considerably in form, ranging from liberal democratic states to personal dictatorships. » monarchy

Republican Party One of the two main parties in US politics, created in 1854 out of the anti-slavery movement that preceded the Civil War. It found almost immediate success when Lincoln was elected president in 1860, and held the presidency except for four terms until Roosevelt in 1933, when the Depression led to a major turnaround in Republican fortunes, and the Democrats became the clear majority party for 20 years. Since then there has been a period of split party control, with the Republicans often winning the presidency, and the Democrats holding the majority in Congress. Traditionally supported by voters with high income, education, and social status, its largest support is in NE industrial and W farming areas. It is identified with big business rather than unions, and with White Anglo-Saxons rather than ethnic minorities. It advocates limited central government, the protection of states' rights, and an active and interventionist foreign policy stance. In the 1980s, it became rather more conservative in outlook. » Democratic Party; mugwump; National Republican Party; Progressive Party; slave trade

requiem [**ray**kwee-em] (Lat 'rest') In the Roman Catholic Church, a Mass for the dead. In addition to its liturgical use, it has become a musical form, of which there are many outstanding examples, eg requiems by Mozart, Fauré, and Britten. » Britten; Fauré; liturgy; Mass; Mozart

reredos » **altarpiece**

resale price maintenance A device used by sellers acting together to prevent price-cutting. All agree to maintain their prices at a certain level – in effect forming a cartel. The practice was stopped in the UK by the Restrictive Trade Practices Act (1956) and the Resale Prices Act (1964). With one or two exceptions, manufacturers cannot print 'the price' of the product on their goods; they may only show a 'recommended retail price'. » cartel

reserpine [**re**serpin] A drug present in the shrub *Rauwolfia serpentina* which has been widely used for centuries in Hindu medicine for the treatment of a variety of diseases, including hypertension, insomnia, and mental disorders. More recently it has been used in the West as a sedative, and in psychosis. It has now been superseded by more potent, safer drugs. It is still sometimes used in hypertension. » hypertension; insomnia; psychosis

reserves Gold and convertible currency held by countries as a result of receiving payment for exports. Falling reserves occur as a result of imports being greater than exports. In banking, the term refers to the notes and coins banks must hold in case of a sudden demand (a 'run on the bank'). In accountancy, it refers to the profits which have been ploughed back into a company. » accountancy; balance of payments; equity (economics)

reservoir A tank or artificial lake where water is stored. Reservoirs are filled either by damming streams and rivers at times of excess flow, or by pumping water to them. The water can then be released in a controlled manner for domestic or industrial consumption, irrigation, or to generate electric power. » dam; hydroelectric power; irrigation; lake

resin A natural or synthetic polymer which softens on heating. The term is loosely used to include any polymer, as in 'ion-exchange resins'. » polymerization; rosin; shellac

resistance A measure of the potential difference U needed to produce direct current I in an electrical circuit component; symbol R, units Ω (ohm); $R = U/I$ by definition. It measures a component's ability to restrict current flow. Resistance causes energy loss from a circuit by heating. I/R is called conductance. » electrical conduction/power; impedance; Ohm's law; potential difference; resistivity; resistor

Resistencia [reseest**en**sia] 27°28S 58°59W, pop (1980) 218 438. Agricultural, commercial, and industrial capital of Chaco province, N Argentina; on the R Barranqueras; founded as Jesuit mission, mid-18th-c; airport; railway; cotton, sugar cane, cattle, timber. » Argentina [i]

resistivity The electrical resistance of a metre cube of material, constant for a given material at a specific temperature; symbol ρ, units Ω.m (ohm.metre). At 0°C, for copper (a good conductor), $\rho = 1.55 \times 10^{-8}$ Ω.m; for germanium (a semiconductor) $\rho = 0.5$ Ω.m approximately; for glass (an insulator), $\rho = 10^{11}$ Ω.m approximately. $1/\rho$ is conductivity. » electrical conduction; resistance

resistor A component in an electrical circuit designed to introduce a known resistance to the flow of current. Resistance changes with temperature rise, increasing in metals, and falling in semiconductors. It also varies with the size of the conductor, rising as it becomes longer or thinner. » electricity; resistance; semiconductor; Plate XV

Reşiţa [**re**sheetsa] 45°16N 21°55E, pop (1983) 104 902. Capital of Caraş-Severin county, W Romania, in the W foothills of the

Transylvanian Alps; railway; iron foundries opened in 1770s; metallurgy, steel, coal, iron ore, marine diesel engines, food processing. » Romania [i]

Resnais, Alain [ruhn**ay**] (1922–) French film director, born at Vannes. He studied in Paris, and made a series of prize-winning short documentaries, such as *Van Gogh* (1948, Oscar) and *Guernica* (1950). His first feature film was *Hiroshima mon amour* (1959, Hiroshima my Love), and this was followed by the controversial *L'Année dernière à Marienbad* (1961, Last Year at Marienbad), hailed as a surrealistic and dreamlike masterpiece by some, as a confused and tedious failure by others. His later films include *Mon Oncle d'Amérique* (1980, My American Uncle), *La Vie est un roman* (1983, Life is a Novel), *L'Amour à mort* (1984, Love Until Death), and *Melo* (1986).

resonance A condition obtained when the frequency of force driving an oscillating system matches a natural frequency of the system. It is characterized by especially large amplitudes of oscillation at these specific frequencies. » atomic spectra [i]; klystron; magnetic resonance; magnetron; periodic motion; resonances

resonances In particle physics, strongly interacting particle-like entities that decay after about 10^{-23} s into more stable particles. This is too short a time to correspond to a particle having a well-defined mass-energy in the usual sense. Large numbers of resonances have been detected and documented. » strong interaction; sub-atomic particles

resonant ionization spectroscopy A sensitive analytical technique for determining trace amounts of materials to better than 1 part in 10^{14}. It utilizes a pair of tuned dye lasers to ionize atoms or molecules in a vapour sample. The resulting ions are counted or passed to a mass spectrometer for identification. » spectroscopy

Respighi, Ottorino [resp**ee**gee] (1879–1936) Italian composer, born in Bologna. He studied at Bologna and St Petersburg, and in 1913 became professor of composition at the St Cecilia Academy in Rome. His works include nine operas, the symphonic poems, *Fontane di Roma* (1916, Fountains of Rome) and *Pini di Roma* (1924, Pines of Rome), and the ballet *La Boutique fantasque*, produced by Diaghilev in 1919. He died in Rome. » Diaghilev

respiration A physiological term with a range of related meanings: (1) the act of breathing, whereby terrestrial animals move air in and out of their lungs, and aquatic animals pump water through their gills; (2) the uptake of oxygen from and the release of carbon dioxide to the environment; and (3) the metabolic processes by which organisms derive energy from foodstuffs by utilizing oxygen (*aerobic respiration*), or without the involvement of oxygen (*anaerobic respiration*); often referred to as *tissue* or *cell respiration*. In humans, breathing is achieved by periodic changes in the volume of the thoracic cage (produced principally by the contraction of the diaphragm and the movement of the ribs) which draws air into the lungs (*inhalation*) or expels air from them (*exhalation*). Oxygen diffuses from the alveoli into the pulmonary capillaries, and is carried to the tissues for use in aerobic respiration. Carbon dioxide (the main end product of aerobic respiration) is carried by blood to the lungs for release into the environment. » artificial respiration [i]; diaphragm (anatomy); influenza; lungs; respirator

respirator A mechanical method of delivering oxygen and of removing carbon dioxide from a patient who is suffering from severe respiratory failure. It expands the lungs intermittently through a tube introduced into the trachea. One type of apparatus can be operated by hand when short-term ventilation is required. For more prolonged use, a number of automated machines are available. The original respirator was referred to as an 'iron lung'; this was a large box enclosing the patient's body, excluding the head and neck. Entry of air into the lungs was achieved by intermittently lowering the air pressure within the chamber, thus expanding the patient's lungs and chest. This type of respirator is no longer used. » respiration

Restoration The return of Charles II to England (Jun 1660) at the request of the Convention Parliament, following the collapse of the Protectorate regime; but many royal prerogative powers and institutions were not restored. The bishops and the Church of England returned, but Parliament took the lead in passing the Clarendon Code (1661–5) outlawing dissent from the Book of Common Prayer (1662). » Protectorate

restrictive covenant A deed whereby one person (the **covenantor**) undertakes a negative obligation for the benefit of another (the **covenantee**). In the context of land, a restrictive covenant may be transmitted to burden subsequent owners of a property – for example, a promise not to build. The term is not used in Scottish law. » covenant **1**; easement; property

resurrection A form of re-animation of a person after death, the belief in which can be traced to late Biblical Judaism and early Christianity. The nature of the new corporeality, the timing of the transformation, and the matter of whether all people would be raised from the dead or only the 'just' have been variously expressed in Jewish and Christian literature, but the emphasis on some form of revival of the body after death is distinct from many views about the immortality of the soul. Christian faith affirms the resurrection of Jesus Christ in particular, signifying God's vindication of Jesus. » Christianity; eschatology; Jesus Christ; Judaism; reincarnation; soul (religion)

retable » **altarpiece**

retail price index (RPI) A means of calculating the general trend of prices of goods and services; popularly known as the 'cost of living index'. It is used as the main indicator of inflation, and is calculated each month by identifying the prices that an average household will have paid for a basket of goods and services. Any increase or decrease is expressed in terms of an index number, where the base at a certain date was 100. If prices on average rose by 4% in the month, then the index would have moved from 100 to 104, or an equivalent amount. The 'basket' is reformed periodically to keep in line with changing consumer spending habits. » index-linking

Reticulum (Lat 'net') [ruh**tik**yuhluhm] A small S constellation near the Large Magellanic Cloud. » constellation; Magellanic Clouds; RR9

retina The innermost lining of the vertebrate eyeball, which transmits information about the visual world to the brain. It consists of an outer pigmented layer and an inner (cerebral) layer of photosensitive cells (*rods and cones*) and neurones. The cerebral layer radiates out from the *optic disc* (the region where the nerve fibres leave the eyeball to form the optic nerve) to the periphery, gradually reducing in thickness. The optic disc is non-pigmented and insensitive to light, because of the absence of both retinal layers, and is known as the *blind spot*. Within the cerebral layer is the *macula* (a small oval area in the visual axis) having a central depression (the *fovea centralis*). The fovea has the highest resolving power of any part of the retina, because it contains only tightly packed cones, which almost reach the internal surface; consequently an image on this region is least distorted. Light focused by the lens forms an inverted image on the retina. This stimulates the rods and cones to generate impulses which are transmitted via the optic nerve to reach the visual areas of the cortex for interpretation. The pigmented and cerebral layers occasionally separate, leading to partial blindness. Reattachment is often possible using cryoscopy or photocoagulation by laser beam. » eye [i]

retinol The active form of vitamin A. In the diet, retinol is found in margarines, oily fish, and dairy fats. It acts to maintain the integrity of skin and lung (epithelial tissue) and is also involved in the synthesis of visual purple, which determines our ability to adapt our vision to darkness. Vitamin A deficiency leads to a reduced ability to adapt to darkness, and a severe deficiency leads to permanent blindness. Retinol can be synthesized from dietary carotene found in carrots and green leafy vegetables – hence the belief that carrots help your eyesight. » carotene; vitamins [i]

retriever A sporting dog belonging to one of several breeds developed to assist hunters. When game has been shot, the retriever is sent to the point where it fell to collect it and bring it to the hunter. » golden retriever; griffon (mammal); Labrador retriever; sporting dog

retrograde motion A temporary E→W movement of a planet through our sky. Planetary paths are normally from W to E.

However, because the Earth is also on an orbit, the two motions sometimes combine to make the planet temporarily backtrack, and move for a time in the reverse direction. The effect is most marked for Mars. » Mars (astronomy); planet

retrovirus A virus c.100 nm in diameter, with an outer envelope enclosing the core. The genetic information is stored in a molecule of single-stranded ribonucleic acid. It is characterized by the occurrence of a special enzyme (reverse transcriptase) within the virus particle. (Family: *Retroviridae*.) » enzyme; lentivirus; RNA; virus

Returned Services League In Australia, an organization recruited from men and women with military service overseas (motto 'The price of liberty is eternal vigilance'). Its functions are social (welfare care and clubs) and political: it forms a major pressure group, with direct access to the Cabinet.

Retz, (Jean François Paul de Gondi), Cardinal de (1614–79) French prelate, born in Montmirail. He plotted against Mazarin, and exploited the parlementary Fronde (1648) to further his own interests and the power of the Church. After transferring his allegiance between the rebel factions and the crown, he received a cardinal's hat, though in 1652 he was imprisoned on Louis XIV's personal orders. After making peace with Louis in 1662, he received the abbacy of St Denis. In his last years he wrote his *Mémoires*, a classic in 17th-c French literature. » Frondes, the; Louis XIV; Mazarin; Richelieu

Retz, Rais or **Raiz, Gilles de Laval, Baron** (1404–40) Breton nobleman who fought by the side of Joan of Arc at Orleans, became Marshal of France at 25, but soon retired to his estates, where for over 10 years he is alleged to have indulged in satanism and the most infamous orgies. He was hanged and burned at Nantes, after being tried and condemned for heresy. » Joan of Arc

Reuben, tribe of [**roo**buhn] One of the twelve tribes of ancient Israel, portrayed as descended from Jacob's first son by Leah. Reuben is also said to have encouraged his brothers to cast Joseph into a pit, rather than to kill him. The tribe's territory included the region E of the Dead Sea and S of Gad. » Israel, tribes of [i]; Jacob; Old Testament

Réunion [rayoon**yon**], formerly **Bourbon** pop (1989e) 584 000; area 2 512 sq km/970 sq ml. Island in the Mascerenes archipelago, Indian Ocean, 690 km/430 ml E of Madagascar; capital, St Denis; timezone GMT +4; established as a French penal colony, 1638; overseas department, 1946; part of an administrative region, 1973; administers several uninhabited small islands nearby; several volcanoes, one active, rising to Le Piton des Neiges at 3 071 m/10 075 ft; governed by a commissioner, a 36-member General Council, and a 45-member Regional Council, both elected for 6-year terms; tourism, sugar, rum, maize, potatoes, tobacco, vanilla. » Mascarene Islands; St Denis (Réunion)

Reuter, Paul Julius, Baron von [**roy**tuh], originally **Israel Beer Josaphat** (1816–99) British founder of the first news agency, born at Kassel, Germany. Of Jewish parentage, he became a Christian and adopted his new name in 1844. He developed the idea of a telegraphic news service, and in 1851 moved his headquarters to London, becoming a naturalized British subject. His news service extended worldwide with the development of international cables. Created a baron in 1871, he died in Nice, France. » news agency; telegraphy

revelation Generally, the disclosure of what was previously unknown or not clearly apprehended, usually by divine or preternatural means. In religion, it is used to refer to disclosures by God or the divine as distinguished from that attained by the human processes of observation, experiment, and reason. » Bible; God; Koran

Revelation, Book of or **The Apocalypse of St John** The last book in the New Testament, whose author is named as 'John', an exile on the island of Patmos (1.9), although scholars differ about his precise identity, and parts of the Eastern Church were slow to accept the work as canonical. Chapters 1–3 are letters of exhortation to seven churches in Asia Minor, but Chapters 4–22 consist of symbolic visions about future tribulations and judgments marking the End times and the return of Christ. It may have been an attempt to offer hope to a church facing persecution in the early 90s. » apocalypse; eschatology; New Testament

reverberatory furnace A furnace in which the contents are not heated directly by the burning fuel, but by hot flames diverted by the roof of the furnace so as to play down on the material to be heated. Although mainly known in steel making, it is also used in other processes such as glass making or ceramics. » blast furnace [i]; ceramics; glass [i]; steel

Revere, Paul [ruh**veer**] (1735–1818) American patriot, born and died in Boston, Massachusetts. He served as a lieutenant of artillery (1756), then followed the trade of silversmith and copperplate printer. He was one of the party that destroyed the tea in Boston harbour, and was at the head of a secret society formed to watch the British. On 18 April 1775, the night before Lexington and Concord, he rode from Charleston to Lexington and Lincoln, rousing the minutemen as he went. His ride was immortalized in a poem by Longfellow. » American Revolution

reversal process A photographic method by which film exposed in a camera yields a positive picture rather than a negative. After the original negative image has been developed, it is bleached and removed, leaving the previously unexposed silver halides in the emulsion to be given a second development and form the complementary positive. With colour materials, the first development is to silver only, and after its removal the second developer forms the colour-coupled images. » film; negative

Revised English Bible » **New English Bible**

revisionism Most commonly, a doctrinal deviation from the ideological stance of a communist party or state; also, the critical re-assessment of Marxist theories. In general, the term has polemical overtones, and is applied to those thought to have broken with Marxist-Leninist orthodoxy. In the era of polycentrism it has been used by communist parties to attack each other's claims to represent the orthodox position. The term is sometimes used in much the same manner by other political parties claiming to have some deep-rooted ideological position, such as the British Labour Party. Given its negative associations, few would ever adopt the revisionist label. » communism; polycentrism

Revolt of the Netherlands (1566–1648) Uprisings and wars against Spanish Habsburg rule by 17 provinces in the Low Countries, also called the *War of Independence*, the *Eighty Years' War*, and the *Dutch Revolt*. The provinces, previously separate fiefs, were united by Charles V (reigned 1519–58). Resistance to centralization and religious persecution began in the 1550s. The wars devastated the 10 southern provinces retained by the Spanish. The rebels, led by William of Orange and his Protestant naval force of 'sea beggars' (*Watergeuzen*), took refuge in seven northern provinces, chiefly Holland, which was declared a republic in 1609, with the Orange family as *Stadtholder*. Independence was recognized by Spain in 1648. » Blood, Council of; Charles V (Emperor); Habsburgs; William I (of the Netherlands)

revolution A change of regime in a country followed by a major reconstitution of the political, social, and economic order. The emphasis is on complete change, though continuities have been a feature of almost all major revolutions. This is notable in Marxism, which not only advocates social and political change by revolution, but also how revolution comes about. Revolutions are normally viewed as involving violent overthrow and the use of force, but this is not a necessary condition. In this respect, it can be distinguished from the sudden overthrow of a ruler by force in a *coup d'état*. » French Revolution [i]; Marxism; reformism; Russian Revolution

Revolution of 1905 A series of nationwide strikes, demonstrations, and mutinies in Russia, sparked off by the massacre of peacefully demonstrating workers by soldiers in St Petersburg on 'Bloody Sunday' (9 Jan 1905). Faced with continuing popular unrest, Nicholas II was forced to make concessions, including the legalization of political parties, and elections to a national assembly – the State Duma. » duma; Nicholas II; Russian history; Russian Revolution

Revolutions of 1848 A succession of popular uprisings in various W and C European countries during 1848–9, some fuelled by political and economic grievances against established governments, often inspired by liberal and socialist ideas, others by demands for national independence from foreign rule, as in the Italian states, Bohemia, and Hungary. In France the abdication of Louis Philippe was followed by the Second Republic and the socialist experiment of National Workshops; liberal constitutions were granted in Austria and in many German states; Britain experienced Chartism. The revolutions collapsed from internal weakness or military suppression, and aroused reaction; but they presaged the ultimate triumph of nationalism, if not liberalism. » Delescluze; liberalism; Louis Philippe; Metternich; Napoleon III; nationalism; Proudhon; Schwarzenberg; Wolfe, James

revolver A single-barrelled pistol with a revolving breech containing chambers for cartridges (usually six), which automatically brings a new cartridge into alignment for firing after each shot. The first practical example was produced by Samuel Colt in 1835, using the action of cocking the firing hammer to revolve the cylinder barrel. » Colt, Samuel; pistol

rex A domestic cat with an unusually thin curly coat; a *foreign short-haired* variety; three forms: *Cornish*, *Devon* and *German*. A rex with a dark face, legs, and tail (like a Siamese) is called a **si-rex**. The name *rex* is also used for a rabbit with a short outer coat. » cat; rabbit; Siamese cat

Reye's syndrome A rare acute illness with involvement of the brain (*encephalopathy*) and the liver following an apparently viral illness in children. Some studies incriminate aspirins as a contributory factor. It is named after an Australian pathologist, R D K Reye, who wrote about the condition in 1963. » aspirin; brain [i]; liver; virus

Reykjavík [**ray**kyaveek] 64°09N 21°58W, pop (1983) 87 309. Capital and chief port of Iceland, on Faxa Bay, SW Iceland; founded, 874; chartered, 1786; seat of Danish administration, 1801; capital, 1918; seat of Icelandic parliament; Lutheran bishopric; airport; university (1911); heating system uses nearby hot springs; commerce, fishing, fish processing; national museum, Árbđjarsafn open air museum; meeting place of US and USSR leaders in October 1986 to discuss arms control. » Iceland [i]

Reynaud, Paul [ray**noh**] (1878–1966) French statesman, born at Barcelonnette. He became a barrister, and held many government posts, being Premier for a short time during the fall of France in 1940. He was imprisoned by the Germans during World War 2. Afterwards he re-entered politics, until losing his seat in 1962. He died in Paris.

Reynolds, Sir Joshua (1723–92) British portrait painter, born at Plympton, Devon. He studied art in London and in Rome (1749–52), then established himself in London, and by 1760 was at the height of his fame as a portrait painter. His works include 'Dr Samuel Johnson' (c.1756, National Portrait Gallery, London) and 'Sarah Siddons as the Tragic Muse' (1784, San Marino, California). He became the first president of the Royal Academy (1768), and was knighted in 1769. He died in London, leaving well over 2 000 works, from which 700 engravings have been executed. » English art; engraving

Reynolds' number In fluid mechanics, an empirical relationship between viscosity η and flow pattern; symbol Re, expressed as a pure number; named after British engineer Osborne Reynolds (1842–1912). For a fluid of density ρ flowing at velocity v along a pipe of diameter d, $\text{Re} = vd\rho/\eta$. An increase in the value of Re corresponds to a change in flow pattern from smooth to turbulent, such as when the Re for water changes from 200 to 3000 as water velocity is increased. » fluid mechanics; turbulence; viscosity

Reza Pahlavi, Mohammed » Pahlavi, Mohammed Reza

Rhadamanthus or **Rhadamanthys** [rada**man**thuhs] In Greek mythology, a Cretan, son of Zeus and Europa, who did not die but was taken to Elysium, where he became the just judge of the dead.

Rhaetian [reeshan] » **Romance languages**

rhapsody A piece of music in which the composer allows his imagination to range more or less freely over some theme, story, or idea, without regard for any prescribed structure. Lizst's *Hungarian Rhapsodies* and Rachmaninov's *Rhapsody on a Theme of Paganini* (a set of free variations) are examples of what is essentially a Romantic genre. » Romanticism (music); variations

Rhätikon [**ray**tikon] Mountain range of the E or Rhaetian Alps on the frontier between Austria, Switzerland, and Liechtenstein, rising to 2 965 m/9 728 ft at Schesaplana; major skiing area. » Alps

Rhazes [**ray**zeez] or **Razi**, in full **Abu Bakr Muhammad ibn Zakariya ar-Razi** (10th-c) Persian physician and alchemist, who lived in Baghdad. He gave excellent accounts of smallpox and measles, and wrote an immense Graeco-Arabic encyclopedia. This was translated into Latin, and had considerable influence on medical science in the Middle Ages.

rhea A S American ratite, resembling the ostrich, but smaller (up to 1.5 m/5 ft), duller plumage, and larger wings; inhabits open country with long-stemmed vegetation; eats plants, insects, and small vertebrates; can swim; also known as the **ema**, **nandu** (**nhandu**), or **American ostrich**. (Family: *Rheidae*, 2 species.) » ostrich; Ratitae

Rhea (astronomy) [**ree**a] The fifth natural satellite of Saturn, discovered in 1672; distance from the planet 527 000 km/ 327 000 ml. It is the second largest moon in its system, diameter 1 530 km/950 ml; orbital period 4.518 days. » Saturn (astronomy); RR4

Rhea or **Rheia** (mythology) [**ree**a] In Greek mythology, a Titan, sister and wife of Cronus, and mother of Zeus and other Olympian gods. When Cronus consumed his children, Rhea gave him a stone instead of Zeus, who was saved and later rebelled against his father. » Cronus; Zeus

Rhee, Syngman (1875–1965) Korean statesman, born near Kaesong. Imprisoned (1897–1904) for his part in an independence campaign, he later went to the USA, returning to Japanese-annexed Korea in 1910. After the unsuccessful rising of 1919, he became President of the exiled Korean Provisional Government. On Japan's surrender (1945) he returned to become the first elected President of South Korea (1948). Re-elected for a fourth term (1960), he was obliged to resign after a month following major riots and the resignation of his cabinet. He went into exile, and died in Honolulu. » Korea [i]

Rheims [reemz], Fr **Reims** [rĩs], ancient **Durocortorum**, later **Remi** 49°15N 4°02E, pop (1982) 181 985. Historic town in Marne department, NE France; on right bank of R Vesle, 133 km/83 ml ENE of Paris; bishopric since 4th-c, now an archbishopric; former coronation site of French kings; extensive damage in World War 1; scene of German surrender, 1945; road and rail junction; port on Aisne-Marne Canal; university (1967); textiles, chemicals, metallurgy, building, wholesale grocery, stained-glass workshops; major wine-producing centre (especially champagne), with an extensive network of storage caves; 13th-c Gothic cathedral (badly damaged in World War 1, now restored), 11th-c Church of St-Rémi, Musée St-Denis; Roman remains, including the Porte de Mars (2nd-c AD). » Gothic architecture; wine

Rhenish Slate Mountains, Ger **Rheinisches Schiefergebirge** Extensive plateau of Germany, dissected by the Rhine and its tributaries, between the Belgian border (W), the Lahn R (E), Bingen (S), and Bonn (N); highest peak, the Grosser Feldberg (879 m/2 884 ft) of the Taunus range. » Germany [i]; Rhine, River

rheology [ree**ol**uhjee] The study of the deformation and flow of materials subjected to force. It includes the viscosity of liquids and gases, strain and shear due to stresses in solids, and plastic deformation in metals. » mechanical properties of matter; plastic deformation; tribology; viscosity

rhesus factor A series of closely related but distinct antigens (*agglutinogens*) usually present in the plasma membranes of human red blood cells. Individuals with the factor are **Rh+**; those without are **Rh−**. An Rh− woman carrying her first Rh+ child may produce anti-Rh antibodies during the period immediately following the birth. During the next pregnancy, these antibodies may cross the placenta, and if the foetus is Rh+ they may cause haemolysis and haemolytic disease of the newborn (*erythroblastosis foetalis*). The risk is minimized by reducing the formation of maternal antibodies, achieved by the administration of anti-Rh+ antibodies to the mother immediately after the birth of the first child. In Britain 85% of the

RHINE CANALS

CANAL SYSTEM	LENGTH km/ml	BUILT
Rhine–Rhone	349/217	1784–1833
Rhine–Marne	314/195	1838–1853
Dortmund–Ems	266/165	1892–1899
Rhine–Herne	39/24	1907–1914
Rhine–Main–Danube	171/106	To be completed in 1992

The Dortmund–Ems and Rhine–Herne canals link the Rhine and the Ruhr valleys to the German port of Emden.

population is Rh+. The ratio of Rh+/Rh− differs between ethnic populations. » antibodies; blood; genetics [i]

rhesus monkey A macaque native to S Asia from Afghanistan to Indochina; stocky; sandy-brown; inhabits a wide range of habitats, including towns; used widely for medical research; also known as **rhesus macaque**. The *rhesus factor* of blood is named after this species. (*Macaca mulatta*.) » macaque

rhetoric The spoken and written language of persuasion. Rhetoric has had a chequered history. In the classical and mediaeval world, it was a formal branch of learning concerned with the techniques and devices required to persuade or convince an audience. Leading early analysts included Aristotle, Cicero, and Quintillian, who developed theories of successful speech-making. Subsequently it came to signify elaborate and pompous language, which is nonetheless empty and insincere. In recent years, however, there has been a renewed interest in its role in interpersonal and mass communication, as attention has focused on the rules and conventions that enable language and other sign systems to convey meaning, and to present a message in the most effective way. » Aristotle; Cicero; oratory; semiotics

rheumatic fever A common disease of children and adolescents in Asia and Africa, arising from an immunological reaction to preceding infection with certain strains of *Streptococcus*. It is characterized by fever, a flitting arthritis (in which pain and swelling moves from joint to joint), and inflammation of the linings of the heart (*carditis*). While joint involvement rarely leads to persisting deformity, serious rheumatic heart disease can produce distortion, narrowing, and incompetence of the valves of the heart. » chorea; heart [i]; streptococcus

rheumatism A non-specific name given to aches and pains in muscles, particularly in the shoulders and back, and common in older people. The absence of fever and serological abnormalities distinguishes the condition from inflammatory rheumatic diseases. » arthritis; muscle [i]; serology

Rhine canals » *panel on this page*

Rhine, J(oseph) B(anks) (1895–1980) US psychologist, a pioneer of parapsychology, born at Waterloo, Pennsylvania. He studied at Chicago and Harvard, and in 1927 went to Duke University, where he remained in the department of psychology until his retirement in 1965. His laboratory-devised experiments involving packs of specially designed cards established the phenomenon of extrasensory perception on a statistical basis. His books include *Extra-Sensory Perception* (1934) and *Parapsychology* (with J G Pratt, 1957). » parapsychology

Rhine, River, Ger **Rhein**, Dutch **Run**, Fr **Rhin**, ancient **Rhenus** River in C and W Europe, rising in SE Switzerland, in the Rheinwaldhorn glacier; flows N to L Constance, W to Basle, then generally N, forming part of the Germany–France border; divides into two major branches in the Netherlands, the Lek and Waal, before entering the North Sea; length, 1 320 km/820 ml; main waterway of W Europe, flowing through major industrial areas; widely connected by canals to other rivers; tourism in the Rhine Valley and on the Rhine itself. » Rhine Canals [i]

rhinoceros The second largest land animal (after the elephant), native to S and SE Asia and Africa; a perissodactyl mammal of the family *Rhinocerotidae*; skin tough, usually with few hairs; long head with small eyes placed well forward; nose with 'horn(s)' made from fibrous outgrowths of the skin; five species: **Indian** (or **greater one-horned**) **rhinoceros**, with stud-like lumps on skin; **Javan** (or **lesser one-horned**) **rhinoceros**, with smoother skin; **Sumatran** (or **Asian two-horned**) **rhinoceros**, with a covering of red-brown hair; African **black** (or **hook-lipped**) **rhinoceros** and African **white** (or **square-lipped**) **rhinoceros**, both with two horns; many extinct species; also known as **rhino**. » perissodactyl [i]; woolly rhinoceros

rhizoid A uni- or multi-cellular thread-like structure found in algae, mosses, liverworts, and the gametophytes of ferns. Rhizoids anchor the plant to the substrate and absorb water, but unlike true roots are not differentiated into separate tissues. » algae; fern; gametophyte; liverwort; moss; root (botany)

rhizome A horizontally-growing underground stem. It is either slender and fast-growing, allowing the plant to spread vegetatively, or fleshy and acting as a food store. » stem

Rhizopoda [riyzopuhda] A large group of protozoans distinguished on the basis of their types of pseudopodia; includes the amoebae and foraminiferans. » amoeba; Protozoa

Rhode Island pop (1987e) 986 000, area 3 139 sq km/1 212 sq ml. New England state in NE USA, divided into five counties; 'Little Rhody' or the 'Ocean State'; smallest US state, but the second most densely populated; one of the original states, 13th to ratify the Federal Constitution; gave protection to Quakers in 1657 and to Jews from the Netherlands in 1658; capital, Providence; major cities Warwick, Cranston, Pawtucket; rises from the Narragansett Basin in the E to flat and rolling uplands in the W; highest point Jerimoth Hill (247 m/810 ft); textiles, electronics, silverware, jewellery, potatoes, apples, corn. » Friends, Society of; Providence; United States of America [i]; RR39

Rhodes, Cecil (John) (1853–1902) South African statesman, born at Bishop's Stortford, Hertfordshire, UK. After studying in Oxford, he entered the Cape House of Assembly, securing Bechuanaland as a protectorate (1884) and the charter for the British South Africa Company (1889), whose territory was later to be named after him, as Rhodesia. In 1890 he became Prime Minister of Cape Colony, but was forced to resign in 1896 because of complications arising from the Jameson raid. He was a conspicuous figure during the Boer War of 1899–1902, when he organized the defences of Kimberley. He died at Muizenberg, Cape Colony, and in his will founded scholarships at Oxford for Americans, Germans, and colonials ('Rhodes scholars'). » Boer Wars; Jameson raid

Rhodes, Wilfred (1877–1973) British cricketer, born at Kirkheaton, Yorkshire. He played for Yorkshire and England,

and during his career (1898–1930) took a world record 4 187 wickets and scored 39 722 runs. He took 100 wickets in a season 23 times, and performed the 'double' of 1 000 runs and 100 wickets 16 times – first-class cricket records. The oldest man to play Test cricket, he was 52 yr 165 days when he played for England against the West Indies at Kingston in April 1930. Blind since 1952, he died at Bournemouth, Hampshire. » cricket (sport) [i]

Rhodes, Zandra (1940–) British fashion designer, born at Chatham, Kent. She studied textile printing and lithography at Medway College of Art, then won a scholarship to the Royal College of Art. She designed and printed textiles and, with others, opened the Fulham Road Clothes Shop, afterwards setting up on her own. She showed her first collection in 1969, and is noted for her distinctive, exotic designs in floating chiffons and silks. » fashion

Rhodes, Gr **Ródhos**, Ital **Rodi** pop (1981) 87 831; area 1 398 sq km/540 sq ml. Largest island of the Dodecanese, Greece, in the SE Aegean Sea, off SW coast of Turkey; length 72 km/45 ml; maximum width 35 km/22 ml; fourth largest Greek island; crossed by a long ridge of hills, rising to 1 215 m/3 986 ft; originally settled by Mycenean Greeks, 1400 BC; statue of the Sun-god Chares was one of the Seven Wonders of the World; Knights of the Order of St John settled here, 1309–1522; held by Italy, 1912–47; airfield; ferries to Cyprus, Italy, Turkey; capital, Rhodes, pop (1981) 40 392; wine, cereals, fruit, tobacco, tourism; acropolis, Temple of Aphrodite (3rd-c BC); Hospital of the Knights (1440–89), now an archaeological museum; Navy Week (Jun–Jul). » Dodecanese; Knights Hospitallers; Seven Wonders of the Ancient World

Rhodesian ridgeback A national breed of dog of South Africa; large muscular body with thick neck and long muzzle; ears pendulous; short golden coat; hairs along spine grow forwards, forming a ridge; originally used to hunt lions. » dog

rhododendron An evergreen shrub or small tree, sometimes an epiphyte, native to N temperate regions but concentrated in the area where the great Asian rivers break through the E Himalayas and in New Guinea, and only found on acid soils; leaves alternate, usually oval, leathery; flowers in clusters at tips of main branches, funnel or bell-shaped; sepals sometimes reduced to a rim; 5–10 petals and stamens. Several hundred cultivars are known, with flowers varying greatly in size and colour. Azaleas belong to the same genus and have the same features, except they are deciduous. (Genus: *Rhododendron*, c.1 200 species. Family: *Ericaceae*.) » azalea; cultivar; epiphyte; evergreen plants; sepal; shrub; tree [i]

Rhodope Mountains [roduhpee], Bulgarian **Rhodopi Planina** or **Despoto Planina**, Gr **Rodopi** Range of mountains stretching NW–SE in SW Bulgaria and NE Greece, rising to 2 925 m/9 596 ft at Musala; length 290 km/180 ml; a major climatic divide between C Bulgaria and the Aegean; Bulgarian forestry area. » Bulgaria [i]

Rhondda, Welsh **Ystradyfodwg** [hrontha] 51°40N 3°30W, pop (1981) 71 611. District in Mid Glamorgan, S Wales, UK; extends along the Rhondda Fawr and Rhondda Fach valleys; railway; coal mining (of less importance in recent years), light engineering, electrical goods, clothing. » Mid Glamorgan

Rhône, River River in C and SW Europe, rising in the Rhône glacier in S Switzerland, and flowing through L Geneva then W and S between the Jura and the Alps to its delta on the Mediterranean; length, 812 km/504 ml; joined at Lyons by its largest tributary, the Saône; extensive source of hydroelectricity and irrigation; strong current allows little navigation until well below Lyons; canal system between Lyons and the coast; Rhône valley an important routeway, renowned for its scenery. » France [i]

rhubarb A long-lived perennial herb, related to dock, and native to Siberia; basal leaves large, heart-shaped, wavy with green or red stalks; flowers small, white, 6-petalled, in large spreading inflorescence. A number of hybrids and cultivars are grown for the edible leaf-stalks. (*Rheum rhaponticum*. Family: *Polygonaceae*.) » cultivar; herb; inflorescence [i]; perennial

Rhyl [ril] 53°19N 3°29W, pop (1981) 23 318. Seaside resort town in Rhuddlan district, Clwyd, NE Wales, UK; in Abergele-Rhyl-Prestatyn urban area; at mouth of Clwyd R; railway; furniture, tourism; funfair, promenade, Floral Hall. » Clwyd

rhyme The repetition of the same or a similar sound, for rhetorical effect. It is a device usually associated with poetry, where the rhyming words occur at the end of a line. Rhyme was rarely found in the classical literatures, developing only with late Latin – it is suggested, to aid memorizing and recitation. There is a limitless variety of rhyme schemes, from the simple rhyming couplet to 'open' rhyme schemes such as that employed in Milton's *Lycidas*. 20th-c poets have explored half-rhyme, as in Wilfred Owen's 'Strange Meeting', where *friend/frowned* and *killed/cold* are rhymes. » heroic couplet; metre (literature); poetry; rondeau; sonnet; terza rima

rhyolite [**riy**uhliyt] A silica-rich volcanic igneous rock with a composition approximately equivalent to granite. It is fine-grained or glassy, because of rapid cooling, and occurs in several forms. » igneous rock; pumice

Rhys, Jean (1894–1979) British novelist, born at Roseau, Dominica. In 1910 she went to England, and joined a touring theatre company. After World War 1 she lived in Paris, where she wrote short stories and several novels on the theme of female vulnerability. Returning to Cornwall, she lived in retirement for nearly 30 years, then in 1966 published her best-known novel, *Wide Sargasso Sea* (a 'prequel' to Charlotte Bronte's *Jane Eyre*). She died at Exeter, Devon. » English literature; novel

rhythm The constituent of music that has to do with metre, note-lengths, and accent rather than with pitch. Music is said to be 'strongly rhythmic' when the basic pulse is firmly emphasized (as in much pop music) or when a rhythmic pattern is insistently repeated (such as 'Mars' from Holst's *The Planets*); but rhythmic subtlety in music depends more on the play between an established pulse and the melodic or harmonic accents that disturb it, or between one rhythmic pattern and another ('cross-rhythm'). » eurhythmics; music; rhythm and blues

rhythm and blues A type of popular music of the 1950s and 1960s which combined melodic and textual features of the blues with the rhythm section of a pop group (electric guitars, keyboards, and drum set). It was an important forerunner of rock and roll, and was itself superseded by soul. » blues; jazz; pop group; pop music; soul (music)

rhythm method » **contraception**

Rialto Bridge [reealtoh] A bridge spanning the Grand Canal in Venice. It was built in 1588–92 by Antonio da Ponte. » bridge (engineering) [i]; Venice

rib A curved, twisted strip of bone passing around the thorax from the vertebral column to articulate indirectly with the sternum by its costal cartilage. There are twelve pairs in humans, of which the eleventh and twelfth are not attached at the front (*floating ribs*). As they pass around the thorax the ribs curve downwards as well as forwards. They provide protection for the lungs, heart, and great vessels. During breathing they move to bring about changes in the volume of the thorax. » bone; respiration; sternum; thorax; Plate XIII

rib-faced deer » **muntjac**

Ribbentrop, Joachim von (1893–1946) German politician, born at Wesel. He became a member of the National Socialist Party in 1932, and as Hitler's adviser in foreign affairs, was responsible in 1935 for the Anglo-German naval pact. He became Ambassador to Britain (1936) and Foreign Minister (1938–45). Captured by the British in 1945, he was condemned and executed at Nuremberg. » World War 2

Ribble, River River rising in the Pennine Hills of North Yorkshire, N England; flows 120 km/75 ml S and SW past Preston to meet the Irish Sea in a broad estuary. » England [i]

ribbon worm An unsegmented, bilaterally symmetrical worm found mainly on or in shallow marine sediments, occasionally in freshwater; typically predators or scavengers that feed using an outward-turning muscular tube (proboscis); may reach lengths of over 20 m/65 ft. (Phylum: *Nemertea*.) » worm

ribbonfish Elongate slender-bodied fish widespread in the tropical and warm temperate N Atlantic, and in parts of the Indian and Pacific Oceans; length up to 2 m/6½ ft; head pointed, jaws bearing powerful teeth; body compressed and tapering, tail fin reduced or absent; dorsal fins extend entire length of body, pelvics absent; also called **scabbardfish**. (*Lepidopus caudatus*. Family: *Trichiuridae*.) ≫ fish $\boxed{i}$

Ribera, José or **Jusepe de**, byname **Lo Spagnoletto** ('The Little Spaniard') (1588–1656) Spanish painter and etcher, born at Játiva. He settled in Naples, where he became court painter. He is noted for the often gruesome realism with which he treated religious and mythological subjects, such as the martyrdom of the saints. Later works were calmer and more subtle, and include his paintings of the Passion. He died in Naples. ≫ Spanish art

riboflavin A B-vitamin (B₂), the essential active component (*co-enzyme*) involved in energy transfers in cells, found especially in green vegetables, milk, eggs, liver, and yeast. A simple deficiency of riboflavin is rare; where one occurs, it is usually associated with multiple deficiencies of several vitamins. ≫ vitamins $\boxed{i}$

ribonucleic acid ≫ RNA

ribose [riybohs] $C_5H_{10}O_5$. A pentose or 5-carbon sugar, occurring in the structure of ribonucleic acids (RNA). The atoms

$$
\begin{array}{c}
{}^{*}OH \\
| \\
CH_2 \qquad OH \\
H-C \quad O \quad C-H \\
H-C-C-H \\
HO^{*} \quad OH
\end{array}
$$

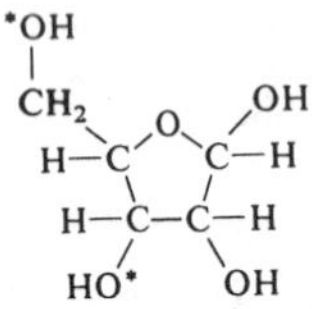

marked * in the illustration are connected to the phosphate groups in RNA. ≫ deoxyribose; RNA

Ricardo, David (1772–1823) British political economist, born in London. He set up in business as a young man, and by 1814 had made a fortune. In 1817 appeared the work on which his reputation chiefly rests, *Principles of Political Economy and Taxation*. In 1819 he became an MP, where he was influential in the free-trade movement. He died at Gatcombe Park, Gloucestershire. ≫ Smith, Adam

Ricci, Matteo [reechee] (1552–1610) Italian founder of the Jesuit missions in China, born at Macerata, Papal States. He studied at Rome, then travelled to India, where he was ordained (1580), and went on to China in 1582. He so mastered Chinese as to write works which received much commendation from the Chinese literati, and met with great success as a missionary. He died in China. ≫ China; Jesuits

Ricci, Sebastiano [reechee] (1659–1734) Italian painter, born at Belluno. He was trained in Venice and Bologna, but travelled to England, France, the Netherlands and elsewhere as one of the leading decorative painters of his day. His colourful style influenced the young Tiepolo. He died at Venice. ≫ Italian art; Tiepolo

Riccio ≫ **Rizzio**

rice An important cereal, with open panicles, drooping with numerous grains; it is the premier food plant of Asia. It is cultivated in flooded paddy fields, with many varieties adapted to different water-levels. Recent breeding programmes have produced successful, high-yielding, semi-dwarf varieties. Upland rice is low-yielding, but does not require flooding, and can be grown in cooler, drier regions. (*Oryza sativa*. Family: *Gramineae*.) ≫ cereals; grass $\boxed{i}$; panicle

Richard I, byname **Coeur de Lion** or **the Lionheart** (1157–99) King of England (1189–99), the third son of Henry II and Eleanor of Aquitaine. Of his 10-year reign, he spent only five months in England, devoting himself to crusading, and defending the Angevin lands in France. Already recognized as an outstanding soldier, he took Messina (1190), Cyprus, and Acre (1191) during the Third Crusade, and advanced to within sight of Jerusalem. On the return journey, he was arrested at Vienna (1192), and remained a prisoner of the German Emperor Henry VI until he agreed to be ransomed (1194). The rest of his reign was occupied in warfare against Philip II of France, while the government of England was conducted by the justiciar, Hubert Walter. Richard was mortally wounded while besieging the castle of Châlus, Aquitaine. ≫ Angevins; Crusades $\boxed{i}$; Henry II (of England); justiciar; Philip II (of France); Walter, Hubert

Richard II (1367–1400) King of England (1377–99), born at Bordeaux, the younger son of Edward the Black Prince, who succeeded his grandfather, Edward III, at the age of 10. He displayed great bravery in confronting the rebels in London during the Peasants' Revolt (1381); but already parliament was concerned about his favourites, and the reign was dominated by the struggle between Richard's desire to act independently, and the magnates' concern to curb his power. He quarrelled with his uncle, John of Gaunt, and his main supporters were found guilty of treason in the 'Merciless Parliament' of 1388. After Richard had declared an end to his minority in 1389, he built up a stronger following, and in 1397–8 took his revenge by having the Earl of Arundel executed, the Duke of Gloucester murdered, and several lords banished, the exiles including Gaunt's son, Henry Bolingbroke (later Henry IV). His final act of oppression was to confiscate the Lancastrian estates after Gaunt's death (1399). Having failed to restrain the King by constitutional means, the magnates resolved to unseat him from the throne. Bolingbroke invaded England unopposed, and Richard was deposed in his favour (Sep 1399). He died in Pontefract Castle, Yorkshire, possibly of starvation. ≫ Henry IV (of England); John of Gaunt; Peasants' Revolt

Richard III (1452–85) King of England (1483–5), born at Fotheringhay Castle, Northamptonshire, the youngest son of Richard, Duke of York. He was created Duke of Gloucester by his brother, Edward IV, in 1461, accompanied him into exile (1470), and played a key role in his restoration (1471). Rewarded with part of the Neville inheritance, he exercised viceregal powers in N England, and in 1482 recaptured Berwick-upon-Tweed from the Scots. When Edward died (1483) and was succeeded by his under-age son, Edward V, Richard acted first as protector; but within three months, he had overthrown the Woodvilles (relations of Edward IV's Queen), seen to the execution of Lord Hastings, and had himself proclaimed and crowned as the rightful King. Young Edward and his brother were probably murdered in the Tower on Richard's orders. He tried to stabilize his position, but failed to win broad-based support. His rival, Henry Tudor (later Henry VII), confronted him in battle at Bosworth Field, and Richard died fighting bravely against heavy odds. Though ruthless, he was not the absolute monster Tudor historians portrayed him to be. Nor is there proof he was a hunchback. ≫ Bosworth Field, Battle of; Edward IV/V; Henry VII

Richards, Frank, pseudonym of **Charles Hamilton** (1875–1961) British author of the 'Tom Merry', 'Billy Bunter' and other school-story series. He wrote for boys' papers, particularly for *The Gem* (1906–39) and *The Magnet* (1908–40). After World War 2 he published school stories in book and play form, and his *Autobiography* (1952).

Richards, Sir Gordon (1904–86) British jockey and trainer, born at Oakengates, Shropshire. Between 1921 and 1954 he rode a record 4 870 winners in Britain, and was champion jockey a record 26 times between 1925 and 1953. On 12 occasions he rode 200 winners in a season, and his 269 winners in 1947 remains a record. He won 14 English Classics between 1930 and 1953, and in 1933 rode 12 consecutive winners, including all six at Chepstow. He won his only Epsom Derby in 1953 on *Pinza*, six days after receiving a knighthood. He took up training in 1954 after retirement, and died at Kintbury, Berkshire. ≫ horse racing

Richards, I(vor) A(rmstrong) (1893–1979) British literary critic and scholar, who pioneered the detailed critical study of literary texts in the 20th-c, born at Sandbach, Cheshire. With C K Ogden he wrote *The Meaning of Meaning* (1923), followed by the influential *Principles of Literary Criticism* (1924) and *Practical Criticism* (1929). During the 1930s he helped to develop Basic English, worked in China (1929–30, 1936–38), and became professor of English at Harvard (1944), where his publications included poetry as well as critical essays. He died at Cambridge, England. ≫ New Criticism; Ogden, C K

Richardson, Henry Handel, pseudonym of **Ethel Florence Lindesay Robertson**, *née* **Richardson** (1870–1946) Australian novelist, born in Melbourne. She travelled and studied in Europe, after her marriage living in Strasbourg (1895) and then

England (1904). She attained distinction only with the third part of the trilogy *The Fortunes of Richard Mahony* (1929). She died at Fairlight, Sussex. » Australian literature; novel

Richardson, Henry Hobson (1838–86) US architect, born at Priestley Plantation, Louisiana. Educated at Harvard, he studied and worked in Paris (1860–5), then returned to the USA, where he began a Romanesque revival, designing a wide range of buildings. His chief works include Trinity Church, Boston (1878–80) and halls at Harvard University (1885–7). He died at Brookline, Massachusetts. » Romanesque architecture

Richardson, Sir Ralph (David) (1902–83) British actor, born at Cheltenham, Gloucestershire. He made his debut at the Little Theatre, Brighton, in 1921, and gained an early reputation with the Birmingham Repertory Theatre, which he joined in 1926. His association with the Old Vic company commenced in 1930, and he was asked to lead its postwar revival. His films included *Anna Karenina* and *Oh, What a Lovely War.* He was knighted in 1947, and died in London. » Olivier; Priestley, J B; theatre

Richardson, Samuel (1689–1761) English novelist, born at Mackworth, Derbyshire. He was apprenticed to a printer, married his master's daughter, and set up in business for himself in London, where he became the centre of a wide circle of friends. *Pamela* (1740), his first novel, is 'a series of familiar letters now first published in order to cultivate the Principles of Virtue and Religion', and this was the aim of all his works. He also wrote *Clarissa* (1748), published in seven volumes, and *Sir Charles Grandison* (1754). In using the epistolary method (which suggested authenticity at a time when mere fiction was frowned upon), he helped to develop the dramatic scope of the novel, then little regarded as a literary form. He died near London. » English literature; epistolary novel; Fielding, Henry; novel

Richelieu, Armand Jean du Plessis, Cardinal and Duc de ('Duke of') [**reesh**lyer] (1585–1642) French statesman and First Minister of France (1624–42), born at Richelieu, near Chinon. A protégé of the Queen Mother, Marie de' Medici, he became Minister of State (1624), and as Chief Minister was the effective ruler of France. His twin aims, to secure universal obedience to the Bourbon monarchy and to enhance France's international prestige, were achieved at the expense of recalcitrant groups in French society. His principal achievement was to check Habsburg power, ultimately by sending armies into the Spanish Netherlands, Alsace, Lorraine, and Roussillon. He died in Paris. » Academy; Bourbons; Habsburgs; Louis XIII

Richler, Mordecai (1931–) Canadian author, born in Montreal. He was brought up in Montreal's Jewish ghetto, attended university in Montreal, then lived in Paris (1951–2). His best-known novel is *The Apprenticeship of Duddy Kravitz* (1959), which was later filmed, although *St Urbain's Horseman* (1971) is a more ambitious work. He has also written essays, and scripts for the cinema, radio, and television. » Canadian literature; novel

Richmond (UK), properly **Richmond-upon-Thames** [temz] 51°28N 0°19W, pop (1987e) 163 000. Borough of SW Greater London, England; on the R Thames; includes the suburbs of Twickenham, Richmond, and Barnes; railway; engineering, plastics; Hampton Court Palace, Royal Botanic Gardens (Kew Gardens), Ham House. » London [i]

Richmond (USA) 37°33N 77°27W, pop (1980) 219 214. Port and capital of state in E Virginia, USA, on the James R; settled as a trading post (Fort Charles), 1645; state capital, 1779; scene of Virginia Convention (1788) for the ratification of the Federal Constitution; Confederate capital during the Civil War; captured by Union forces, 1865; airfield; railway; three universities (1804, 1832, 1865); corporate headquarters centre; tobacco, aluminium products, industrial fibres; Virginia Museum of Fine Arts, Museum of the Confederacy, National Battlefield Park. » American Civil War; Virginia

Richter, Hans (1843–1916) Hungarian conductor, born at Raab. He studied at Vienna, became conductor at Munich, Budapest, and Vienna, gave a series of annual concerts in London (1879–97), and was conductor of the Hallé orchestra (1897–1911). He was an authority on the music of Wagner, with whom he was closely associated in the Bayreuth festivals. He died at Bayreuth. » Wagner

Richter, Johann Paul (Friedrich), pseudonym **Jean Paul** (1763–1825) German novelist and humorist, born at Wunsiedel. He studied theology in Leipzig, then turned to literature, and after several years struggling to publish, began to teach (1787). He produced a wide range of works, achieving success with such romances as *Die unsichtbare Loge* (1793, The Invisible Lodge), *Hesperus* (1795), and the 4-volume *Titan* (1800–3). In 1804 he settled at Bayreuth, where he died. » German literature; novel

Richter, Sviatoslav (Teofilovich) (1914–) Russian pianist, born at Zhitomir. He studied at the Moscow Conservatory (1937–42), and won the Stalin Prize in 1949. He has since made extensive concert tours, with a wide repertoire, and has been associated with the music festivals at Aldeburgh and Spoleto. » piano

Richter scale A logarithmic scale, devised in 1935 by US geophysicist Charles Richter (1900–), for representing the energy released by earthquakes. A figure of 2 or less is barely perceptible, while an earthquake measuring over 5 may be destructive, and 8 or more is a major earthquake. » earthquake; RR14

Richthofen, Ferdinand (Paul Wilhelm), Baron von [**rikh**thohfn] (1833–1905) German geographer, geologist, and traveller, born at Karlsruhe. Educated at Breslau and Berlin, in 1860 he accompanied a Prussian expedition to E Asia, then travelled in Java, Siam, Burma, California (1863–8), China, and Japan (1868–72). After his return he became professor of geology at Bonn (1875), and of geography at Leipzig (1883) and at Berlin (1886), his research helping to develop the field of geomorphology. He died in Berlin. » geomorphology

ricin [**riy**sin, **ri**sin] An extremely toxic protein present in the castor bean (*Ricinus sanguineui*, Euphorbiaceae) which has been used as a deadly poison in political assassinations. It has been proposed as a chemical warfare agent. » castor-oil plant; protein; toxin

rickets A disorder of infants and growing children resulting from a deficiency in vitamin D. There is a failure to calcify the growing ends of long bones (eg the femur and radius), swelling, and enlargement of the ends of the ribs in front of the chest. Softening of the bone may also lead to deformities. » bone; osteomalacia; vitamins [i]

rickettsia [**ri**ketsia] A typically rod-shaped micro-organism with bacteria-like cell walls. Rickettsias multiply inside or in close association with cells of animal hosts. The primary hosts are usually arthropods, which often serve as carriers to vertebrate hosts. They include the causative agents of scrub typhus, trench fever, and other human diseases. (Kingdom: *Monera*. Family: *Rickettsiaceae*.) » arthropod; bacteria [i]; micro-organism

riddle An utterance, often cast in a traditional form, whose intention is to mystify or mislead; a linguistic guessing game. In Europe, riddles tend to be short questions, usually posed for humorous purposes, and generally restricted to children's games and conversation. In Africa, however, they are widely used by adults, often comprising cryptic statements of a philosophical character. In ancient Greece, they had a serious purpose, being used by judges, oracles, and others to test a person's wisdom.

Ridgeway A long-distance footpath in England running 137 km/85 ml from Beacon Hill, Buckinghamshire, to Overton Hill, Wiltshire. The modern path follows the Great Ridgeway, a prehistoric trading route (used by drovers in the 18th-c); it also follows the old Icknield Way for a stretch. » Icknield Way

riding the marches A Scottish ceremony, the equivalent of English 'beating the bounds', performed on horseback, chiefly in the towns of S Scotland. » beating the bounds

Ridley, Nicholas (c.1500–55) English Protestant martyr, born near Haltwhistle, Northumberland. Educated at Cambridge, he was ordained c.1524, and studied in Paris and Louvain (1527–30). He then held a variety of posts, including chaplain to Cranmer and Henry VIII, and Bishop of Rochester (1547). An ardent reformer, he became Bishop of London (1550), and

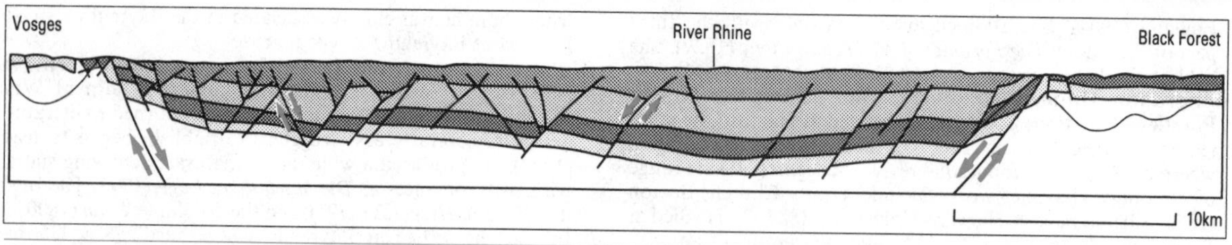

Rift valley – Rhine graben

helped Cranmer prepare the Thirty-nine Articles. On the death of Edward VI he espoused the cause of Lady Jane Grey, was imprisoned, and executed at Oxford. » Cranmer, Thomas; Grey, Jane; Reformation; Thirty-nine Articles

Riefenstahl, Leni [reefuhnshtahl], in full **Berta Helene Amalie** (1902–) German film-maker, born in Berlin. After acting in several films, she formed her own company, and made *Triumph des Willens* (1935, Triumph of the Will), a compelling record of a Nazi rally at Nuremberg. It vividly illustrated Hitler's charismatic appeal, but tainted her career, prompting criticism that she had glorified the event. *Olympia* (1938), her epic documentary of the Berlin Olympic Games, was given a gala premiere on Hitler's 49th birthday. In the 1970s she published several photographic studies of Africa. » Hitler

Riel, Louis [ree-el] (1844–85) Canadian political leader, born at St Boniface, Manitoba. He succeeded his father as a leader of the Métis, and headed the Red River Rebellion in 1869–70. As president of the provisional government, he was able to secure better terms for the new province in the Confederation. Following a period of exile in the USA, he returned to lead a second uprising of Métis (1885) in what is now Saskatchewan. His subsequent arrest and trial led to his execution at Regina. » Métis; Red River Rebellion

Riemann, (Georg Friedrich) Bernhard [reeman] (1826–66) German mathematician, born at Breselenz. Educated at Göttingen and Berlin, he became professor of mathematics at Göttingen (1859). His early work was on the theory of functions, but he is best remembered for his development of non-Euclidian geometry. He died at Selasca, Italy. » function (mathematics); integral calculus [i]; geometries, non-Euclidian

Rienzi or **Rienzo, Cola di** [ryentsee] (1313–54) Italian patriot, born in Rome. In 1347 he incited the citizens to rise against the rule of the nobles. The senators were driven out, and he was made tribune. Papal authority then turned against him, and he fled from Rome. He returned in 1354, and tried to re-establish his position, but was killed in a rising against him. Wagner's opera on his story was completed in 1840. » Italy [i]; Wagner

Riesman, David [reesman] (1909–) US social scientist, born in Philadelphia, and educated at Harvard, where he was to become professor of social sciences (1958–81). His most famous publication, *The Lonely Crowd* (1950), explored the social and psychological insecurities of the individual in mass society. He has also written extensively on policy for higher education. » social science

Rif or **Riff** A cluster of Berber agricultural and herding groups of NE Morocco. Famed as warriors, in the 1920s they defeated the Spanish, but were eventually conquered by combined French and Spanish forces in 1926. They later served in the French and Spanish regiments in Morocco. Population c.700 000. » Abd-el-Krim

rifle A type of firearm developed into a practical weapon in the mid-19th-c in which the barrel of the gun is internally grooved in a spiral form. The bullet is spun as it passes down the bore, the spin stabilizing it in flight and thus increasing its accuracy. Bolt-action magazine rifles firing smokeless powder cartridges transformed infantry firepower by the end of the 19th-c, but their technology remained more or less static until the middle of World War 2, when the gas-operated automatic rifle made its appearance. Today's military **assault rifles** are lightweight, fully automatic weapons with great range and accuracy. » bayonet; firearms

riflebird A bird of paradise, native to NE Australia and New Guinea; males with metallic plumage on throat; short rounded wings; displays high in trees; inhabits forests; eats invertebrates and fruit. (Genus: *Ptiloris*, 3 species.) » bird of paradise; rifleman

rifleman A small, wren-like bird, native to New Zealand and nearby islands; male with green back and pale underparts; inhabits woodland; feeds in trees on insects and spiders; nests in hole in tree; formerly also called **riflebird**. (*Acanthisitta chloris*. Family: *Xenicidae*.) » wren

rift valley An elongated trough in the Earth's crust bounded by normal faults; also termed a **graben**. It is a region of tension in the Earth's crust arising from crustal plates moving apart, and is associated with volcanoes, such as Kilimanjaro in the East African Rift valley. Rift valleys also form along mid-ocean ridges. » plate tectonics [i]; Rift Valley; volcano

Rift Valley or **Great Rift Valley** Major geological feature running from the Middle East S to SE Africa; from Syria (35°N) to Mozambique (20°S), covering a sixth of the Earth's circumference; a depression interrupted by plateaux and mountains; parts filled by seas and lakes; contains the Sea of Galilee, Dead Sea, Gulf of Aqaba, and Red Sea; runs between the Ethiopian highlands and the Somali plains; branches in Kenya, S of L Turkana; E branch lakes include Baringo Nakuru, Naivasha, and Magadi; W branch (also known as the Albertine Rift), along the edge of the Congo basin, includes lakes Albert, Edward, Kivu, and Tanganyika; once rejoined, the rift holds L Nyasa, follows the R Zambezi valley, and ends on the Mozambique coastal lowlands. » Africa; rift valley [i]

rig(ging) » sailing rig [i]

Riga [reega] 56°53N 24°08E, pop (1989) 915 000. Seaport capital of Latvia; on the R Daugava, near its mouth on the Gulf of Riga; founded as a trading station, 1201; member of the Hanseatic League, 1282; capital of independent Latvia, 1918–40; occupied by Germany in World War 2; airport; railway; university (1919); military base; shipbuilding, machinery, metalworking, woodworking, chemicals, electronics, fishing; cultural centre and seaside resort; Riga Castle (1330), Lutheran cathedral (13th-c, rebuilt 16th-c). » Latvia

Rigel [riyjuhl] A supergiant in Orion, the seventh brightest star in our sky, and also one of the most luminous of all stars. Distance: 270 parsecs. » Orion (astronomy); supergiant

right ascension One of the two co-ordinates, used with declination for specifying position on the celestial sphere; the celestial equivalent of longitude. It is the angular distance measured E along the celestial equator from the vernal equinox to the intersection of the hour circle passing through the body. Units are hours, minutes, and seconds, and one hour of right ascension is 15°. » celestial sphere; declination; latitude and longitude [i]

right whale A baleen whale; large head (up to 40% of total length); three species: **right whale** (*Balaena glacialis*) from temperate seas; **bowhead** or **Greenland right whale** (*Balaena mysticetus*) from the Arctic, with the longest baleen plates (4.5 m/14¾ ft) of any whale; **pygmy right whale** (*Caperea marginata*) from sub-Antarctic seas. The name is also used for **right whale dolphins** (genus: *Lissodelphis*, 2 species). (Family: *Balaenidae*.) » baleen [i]; dolphin; whale [i]

right wing One end of the political continuum, originally identifying those who supported the institutions of the monarchy during the French Revolution. In the 19th-c the term was applied to those who were conservative in their view, supporting authority, the state, tradition, property, patriotism, and institutions such as the Church and family. Those on the right were strongly opposed to socialism. In the 20th-c, while the right is still associated with such a position, it has also developed a radical, non-conservative side. On the one hand, this has been associated with extreme nationalism (fascism), and, on the other, with attempts to reverse what are viewed as socialist developments. » centre, the; conservatism; left wing; New Right; socialism

rigidity » **shear modulus**

rigor mortis A temporary stiffening of the body after death because of the depletion of adenosine triphosphate and phosphoryl creatinine within skeletal muscle fibres. The time of onset depends to some extent on the cause of death and environmental temperature, but usually begins 3 hours after death, and is completed by 12 hours. The effects persist for 3 to 4 days, after which flaccidity returns.

Rijeka [riyeka], Ital **Fiume**, Ital **Fiume** 45°20N 14°27E, pop (1981) 193 044. Seaport town in W Croatia republic, Yugoslavia; on R Rečina, where it meets Rijeka Bay on the Adriatic coast; Yugoslavia's largest port; former Roman base (Tarsatica); occupied by the Slavs, 7th-c; naval base of the Austro-Hungarian Empire until 1918; ceded to Italy, 1924; ceded to Yugoslavia, 1947; airfield; railway; ferries; university (1973); shipyards, oil refineries; Trsat castle, Jadran palace, cathedral, national museum. » Croatia; Yugoslavia [i]

Rijksmuseum ('state museum') [**riyks**moozayum] A Dutch word generally used to indicate the national art gallery in Amsterdam, the Netherlands. The collection, which is amongst the finest in Europe and is unrivalled in its holdings of Dutch masters, derives from that of the Nationale Kunst-Galerij, opened in 1800. The present building was designed by Petrus Cuypers and erected in 1877–85.

Rila Monastery A monastery in the Rila Mts, Bulgaria, founded by Ivan Rilski (876–946), which became a great spiritual centre. In the 14th-c, when it was at the height of its wealth and power, a vast monastery was erected – most of which was destroyed by fire in 1833. The present complex was built in 1834–60, and is a world heritage site.

Rila Mountains, Bulgarian **Rila Planina** [**ree**la] Range of mountains in W Bulgaria on the border with Yugoslavia, forming the NW part of the Rhodope Mts; the highest range in the Balkan peninsula, rising to 2 925 m/9 596 ft at Musala; forestry and livestock grazing. » Rhodope Mountains

Riley, Bridget (1931–) British artist, born in London. She was educated at Goldsmith's College of Art (1949–53), and at the Royal College of Art (1952–5). Her first one-woman exhibition was in London at Gallery One in 1962, followed by others worldwide. She is a leading practitioner of Op Art (eg 'Fall' 1963, Tate). » Op Art

Rilke, Rainer Maria [**ril**kuh] (1875–1926) Austrian lyric poet, born in Prague, Czechoslovakia. He studied at Prague, Munich, and Berlin. His three-part poem cycle, *Das Stundenbuch* (1905, The Book of Hours), written after visiting Russia, shows the deep influence of Russian Pietism. Mysticism was abandoned for the aesthetic ideal in *Gedichte* (1907–8, Poems), seen also in his two major works, *Die Sonnette an Orpheus* (Sonnets to Orpheus) and *Duineser Elegien* (Duino Elegies), both written in 1923. He died at Valmont, Switzerland. » German literature; Pietism; poetry

rille A winding valley, with a U-shaped cross-section, found in the lunar maria. Rilles are related to the lava tubes in volcanic regions such as Hawaii, and mark places where molten lava has flowed in the past. » lava; maria

Rimbaud, (Jean Nicolas) Arthur [**rĩ**boh] (1854–91) French poet, born at Charleville. He published his first book of poems in 1870, following this with his most popular work, *Le Bateau ivre* (1871, The Drunken Boat). In 1871 Verlaine invited him to Paris, where they led together a life of ill repute. Before the relationship ended (1873), Rimbaud wrote *Les Illuminations* (1872), a series of prose and verse poems, which show him to be a precursor of Symbolism. Disappointed at the cold reception given to his *Une Saison en enfer* (1873, A Season in Hell), he stopped writing, and spent the rest of his life wandering in Europe and Africa. He died in Marseilles. » French literature; poetry; Symbolism; Verlaine

rime A form of precipitation in which surfaces are coated in opaque ice. It forms when ice accretes on objects through the freezing, on impact, of supercooled water droplets, because the surfaces are at temperatures well below the freezing point of water. » dew point temperature; frost; precipitation

Rimsky-Korsakov, Nikolai (Andreyevich) (1844–1908) Russian composer, born at Tikhvin, Novgorod. His early musical education was perfunctory, his interest being kindled after meeting Balakirev in 1861, after which he wrote his first symphony (1865). In 1871 he was made a professor at the St Petersburg Conservatoire, where he was able to develop his technique. In 1887–8 he produced his three great orchestral masterpieces – *Capriccio Espagnol*, *Easter Festival* and *Scheherazade* – but his main works after that were operas, such as *The Golden Kestrel* (1907). Ever conscious of his bygone technical shortcomings, he rewrote almost all his early work. He died at Lyubensk. » Balakirev

rinderpest [**rin**derpest] An infectious disease of ruminant mammals; also known as **cattle plague**; characterized by blood in the faeces, fever, and swelling of the mucous membranes. » ruminant [i]

ring In chemistry, a closed group of atoms. For carbon compounds, rings of five or six atoms are the most stable.

Ring nebula » **Lyra**

ring of fire A belt of major earthquake and volcanic activity around the Pacific Ocean, defining the boundary between crustal plates. » earthquake; plate tectonics [i]; volcano

ring ouzel » **ouzel**

ringdove » **wood pigeon**

ringed lizard » **amphisbaena**

ringtail » **cacomistle**

ring-tailed monkey » **capuchin**

ringworm A common skin disease resulting from a fungal infection of the outer layers of the skin. The infection spreads outwards from a single site, forming a reddened ring, while the centre tends to heal. It commonly affects the scalp, groin, and the clefts of the toes. » athlete's foot; fungus

Rinzai Zen » **Zen Buddhism**

Rio de Janeiro, byname **Rio** 22°53S 43°17W, pop (1980) 5 090 700. Port capital of Rio de Janeiro state, SE Brazil, on the Bahia de Guanabara; covers an area of 20 km/12 ml along a narrow strip of land between mountains and sea; Pão de Açucar (Sugar Loaf Mountain) rises to 396 m/1 299 ft; airport (Galeão); two airfields; railway; metro; three universities (1920, 1940, 1950); discovered 1502; first settled by the French, 1555; taken by the Portuguese, 1567; seat of the Viceroy, 1763; capital of Brazil 1834–1960; trade in coffee, sugar, iron ore; shipbuilding, sugar refining, pharmaceuticals, textiles, food processing, engineering, printing; major international tourist centre, with famous beaches at Copacabana, Ipanema, Leblon; suburb of Santa Teresa contains many colonial and 19th-c buildings; figure of Christ on the highest peak, Corcovado (690 m/2 264 ft); monastery of São Bento (1633), 17th-c convent of Carmo, Church of Nossa Senhora da Glória do Outeiro; municipal theatre, replica of the Paris Opera House; national museum; world-famous Carnival, on the days preceding Lent, with parades, competitions, and fancy-dress balls; festival of Iemanjá (31 Dec). » Brazil [i]

Rio Grande [reeoh **grand**, **gran**day], (Mexico) **Río Bravo**, **Río Bravo del Norte**. River in SW USA and N Mexico; rises in the Rocky Mts, SW Colorado; flows SE through New Mexico, then along the Texas–Mexico border; enters the Gulf of Mexico E of Brownsville; length 3 033 km/1 885 ml; major tributaries the Pecos and Conchos; used for irrigation and flood-control; navigation forbidden by international agreement beyond Brownsville. » Mexico [i]; United States of America [i]

Río Muni [**ree**oh **moo**nee] area 26 016 sq km/10 042 sq ml. Mainland territory of Equatorial Guinea, WC Africa; bounded W by the Gulf of Guinea, E and S by Gabon, and N by Cameroon; chief town, Bata; R Mbini (Benito) flows from the mountains to the coast. » Equatorial Guinea [i]

Rioja [reeokha] pop (1981) 253 295; area 5 034 sq km/1 943 sq ml. Region of N Spain co-extensive with the modern province of Logroño; watered by the R Ebro and its tributaries; the best-known wine-producing area in Spain; capital, Logroño. » Spain [i]

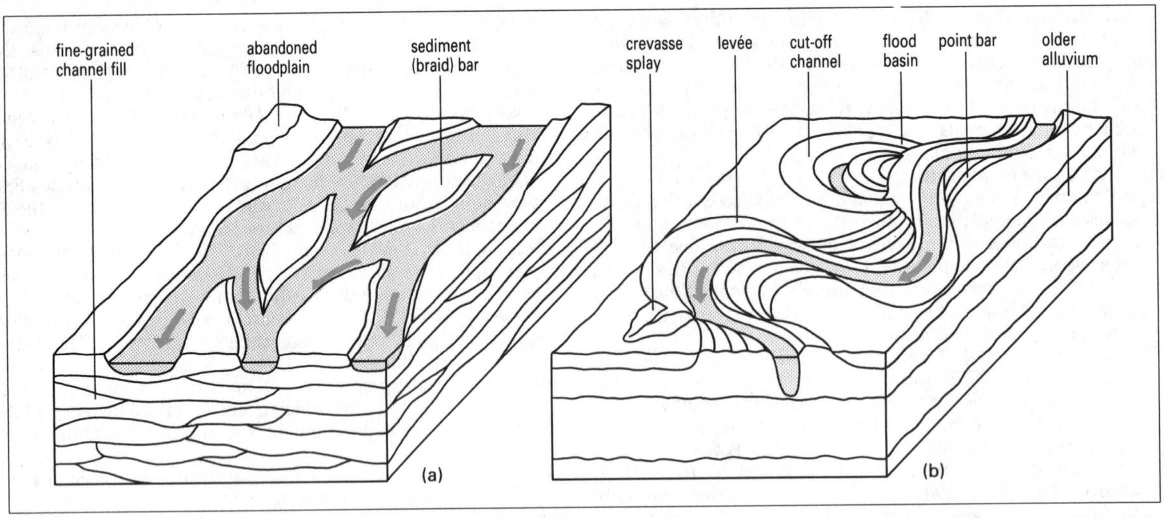

Sections of river channels showing a braided river (a) with cross-stratified gravels and sand, and a meandering river (b) with levées.

Riot Act Legislation in Britain concerned to preserve public order, first passed at the beginning of the Hanoverian era in 1714. When 12 or more people were unlawfully assembled and refused to disperse, they were, after the reading of a section of this Act by a person in authority, immediately considered felons having committed a serious crime.

ripieno [ripee**ay**noh] » **concerto grosso**

Ripon 54°08N 1°31W, pop (1981) 13 232. Town in Harrogate district, North Yorkshire, N England; reckoned to be England's second oldest town; light engineering; racecourse; Cathedral of St Peter and St Wilfrid; 13th-c Wakeman's House; Fountains Abbey ruins nearby. » Fountains Abbey; Yorkshire, North

risk analysis A technique used in insurance and in business which attempts to calculate the effect of the 'worst possible' outcome of a venture. In business, the profits from a project costing many millions of pounds are unknown, but may be very high or unacceptably low. Risk analysis looks at all possible outcomes, assigning probabilities to each so that all the options are quantified. In insurance, actuaries calculate probabilities for the purpose of determining premiums. » actuary; insurance

Risorgimento [rizawzhi**men**toh] (It 'resurgence', 'rebirth') The 19th-c movement by which Italy achieved unity and nationhood. Although its origins lay in the 18th-c Enlightenment and the Napoleonic period, the Risorgimento proper began with the 1830 revolutions and, after failure in 1848–9, reached fruition under the leadership of Piedmont/Sardinia during 1859–70. In 1859–61 the Austrians were expelled from Lombardy, and the C Italian duchies, the Papal States, and Naples/Sicily united with Sardinia to form the Kingdom of Italy. Venetia (1866) and Rome (1870) were added later. » Cavour; Garibaldi; Mazzini; Sardinia, Kingdom of; Thousand, Expedition of the; Young Italy

river A body of flowing water restricted to a relatively narrow channel by banks. It typically originates as a stream in high ground from springwater or run-off from rainwater or a glacier, and moves downhill, eroding a channel which grows as tributaries join the flow, and often carving out major valleys. In its middle stages the river flows more slowly, and meanders begin to form, while in its mature stages deposition of sediment and the formation of broad flood-plains and deltas is characteristic. Rivers are the most significant modifiers of the landscape, and their course has also determined the pattern of settlement, agriculture, and trade. » hydrology; valley; RR13

river blindness An infection caused by the filaria, *Onchocerca volvulus*, conveyed by flies that inflict a painful bite; also known as **onchocerciasis**. Eye involvement causes itching, excessive secretion of tears (*lachrymation*), inflammation of the iris, glaucoma, and blindness. » eye [i]; filariasis; glaucoma

Rivera, Diego [riv**ay**ra] (1886–1957) Mexican painter, born at Guanajuato. In 1921 he began a series of murals in public buildings depicting the life and history of the Mexican people. He also executed frescoes in the USA (1930–4), mainly of industrial life. His art is a blend of folk art and revolutionary propaganda, with overtones of Byzantine and Aztec symbolism. He died in Mexico City. » fresco; Mexican art

Riverside 33°59N 117°22W, pop (1980) 170 876. City in Riverside County, S California, USA, on the Santa Ana R; established, 1870; railway; university (1907); navel orange introduced into California here, 1873; Citrus Experiment Station (1913); food processing, electronics, mobile homes, irrigation equipment; International Raceway. » California

Riviera The Mediterranean coast between Toulon, France, and La Spezia, Italy. It is a narrow coastal strip bordered by the Alps to the N, and includes many holiday resorts.

Riyadh, Arabic **Ar Riyad** [ri**yad**] 24°41N 46°42E, pop (1984) 1 000 000. Capital city of Saudi Arabia; formerly a walled city; airport; railway; three universities (1950, 1957, 1984); communications centre; commerce, oil refining, dates, fruit, grain; over 1 000 mosques, royal palace; 'Solar Village' to the N, a prototype project for use of solar power. » Saudi Arabia [i]

Rizzio or **Riccio, David** [**rit**syoh, **reech**yoh] (?1533–66) Italian courtier and musician, born at Pancalieri, near Turin. After travelling to Scotland with the Duke of Savoy's embassy, he entered the service of Mary, Queen of Scots in 1561, became her favourite, and was made her French secretary in 1564. He negotiated her marriage with Darnley (1565), who became jealous of his influence, and plotted his death with a group of nobles, including Morton and Ruthven. Rizzio was dragged from the Queen's presence and murdered at Holyrood Palace, Edinburgh. » Darnley; Mary, Queen of Scots; Morton, James Douglas

RNA or **ribonucleic acid** The nucleic acid that is found throughout the cell, distinguished from DNA by the substitution of the pyrimidine base, uracil, for thymine. In the nucleus, **nuclear RNA** is formed as a complementary strand to a section of DNA base sequences. The intron sequences are then excised to give mature **messenger RNA**, which passes through the nuclear membrane to the ribosomes in the cytoplasm. **Transfer RNA** collects the free amino acids in the cytoplasm, and transports them to the ribosomes, where they are laid down in the sequence dictated by the messenger RNA. Thus the messenger RNA, once attached to the ribosomes, serves as a template for the production of polypeptide chains. » amino acid [i]; cell; DNA [i]; intron; peptide

ro ro [**roh**roh] A term derived from 'roll on, roll off', a vessel designed to permit vehicles to drive on and off the ship under their own power. Access to the vessel is normally made through the bow or stern doors. » ship [i]

roach Freshwater fish found in rivers and lakes of Europe; body moderately deep, length up to 45 cm/18 in; greenish brown on back, sides silver, pelvic and anal fins red; feeds on invertebrates and some plant material; popular with anglers, and fished commercially in some parts of E Europe. (*Rutilus rutilus*. Family: *Cyprinidae*.)

Roach, Hal, byname of **Harald Eugene Roach** (1892–) US film producer, born at Elmira, New York. In 1915 he formed a production company to make short silent comedies, whose players included Harold Lloyd and Will Hays, and after 1928 continued with sound. He made the comedy features *Topper* (1937) and *Topper Returns* (1941), but was unsuccessful in moving into television in the 1950s. In 1984 he was given a Special Academy Award for his achievements.

Road Town 18°26N 64°32W, pop (1983e) 3 000. Seaport and capital town of the British Virgin Is, Greater Antilles, E Caribbean; on E coast of Tortola I; agricultural trade, tourism. » Virgin Islands, British

roadrunner A ground-dwelling cuckoo, native to SW USA and C America; long tail and legs; head with short crest; inhabits dry open country; eats invertebrates, small vertebrates and eggs; territorial; nests in tree or cactus. (Genus: *Geococcyx*, 2 species.) » cuckoo

roan antelope A grazing antelope native to Africa W of the Rift Valley; also known as **horse antelope**; pale horse-like body with short mane of stiff hairs, short horns, and tips of ears with long tufts of hairs; inhabits savannah. (*Hippotragus equinus*.) » antelope; savannah

Roanoke [**roh**uhnohk] 37°16N 79°56W, pop (1980) 100 220. Independent city, SW Virginia, USA, on the Roanoke R; settled, 1740; gateway to the Shenandoah valley; airfield; railway; railway engineering, electrical equipment, furniture, textiles, metal products. » Virginia

Roaring Forties » **westerlies**

Rob Roy (Gaelic 'Red Robert'), byname of **Robert MacGregor** (1671–1734) Scottish outlaw, born at Buchanan, Stirlingshire. After his lands were seized by the Duke of Montrose, he gathered his clansmen and became a brigand. His career gave rise to many stories, often unsubstantiated, about his brave exploits, and of his generosity to the poor. Captured and imprisoned in London, he was sentenced to transportation, but pardoned in 1727. He is later thought to have become a Catholic, and died at Balquhidder, Perthshire.

Robbe-Grillet, Alain (1922–) French novelist, born at Brest. Educated in Paris, he worked as an agronomist, then in a publishing house. After his first novel, *Les Gommes* (1953, The Erasers), he emerged as the leader of the *nouveau roman* group, contributing to the form such novels as *Le Voyeur* (1955, The Voyeur) and *La Jalousie* (1959, Jealousy), and the theoretical work *Pour un nouveau roman* (1963, Towards the New Novel). He has also written essays and film scenarios, notably *L'Année dernière à Marienbad* (1961, Last Year at Marienbad). » French literature; nouveau roman; Resnais

robber crab A large terrestrial crustacean related to the hermit crab; cuticle of abdomen hard and resistant to drying out; found in tropical and subtropical areas scavenging near the sea shore; able to climb trees and to crack open coconuts, hence its alternative name of **coconut crab**. (Class: *Malacostraca*. Order: *Decapoda*.) » crab; crustacean

robber fly An active, predatory fly commonly found in open sunny habitats; forelegs robust, armed with strong bristles for gripping insect prey caught in flight; c.5 000 species, many of which mimic bees and wasps. (Order: *Diptera*. Family: *Asilidae*.) » fly

robbery A crime in which theft is coupled with force against a person, while the act is being committed. A threat of force is sufficient. » theft

Robbins, Jerome (1918–) US dancer, choreographer, and director, born in New York City, where he studied ballet and modern dance, and worked initially as an actor. He joined the American Ballet Theatre (1940), and became associate director and then director of New York City Ballet (1949–59) and ballet master (1969–). His collaboration with Leonard Bernstein resulted in his most famous musical, *West Side Story* (1957). » ballet; Bernstein, Leonard; choreography

Robbins (of Clare Market), L(ionel Charles), Baron (1898–1984) British economist and educationalist, born at Sipson, Middlesex. Professor of economics at the London School of Economics (1929–61), he directed the economic section of the War Cabinet, then became chairman of the *Financial Times* (until 1970). He also chaired the 'Robbins Committee' on the expansion of higher education in the UK (1961–4). His best-known work is *An Essay on the Nature and Significance of Economic Science* (1932). He became a life peer in 1959, and a Companion of Honour in 1968. » economics; higher education

Robert I » **Bruce, Robert**

Robert II (1316–90) King of Scots (1371–90), the son of Walter, hereditary steward of Scotland. He acted as sole Regent during the exile and captivity of David II. On David's death, he became King in right of his descent from his maternal grandfather, Robert Bruce, and founded the Stuart royal dynasty. He died at Dundonald, Ayrshire. » Bruce, Robert; David II; Stuarts

Robert, Duke of Normandy » **Henry I** (of England)

Roberts (of Kandahar, Pretoria, and Waterford), Frederick Sleigh Roberts, 1st Earl (1832–1914) British field marshal, born at Cawnpore, India. Educated at Clifton, Eton, and Sandhurst, he took an active part in the Indian Mutiny, winning the VC in 1858. He became Commander-in-Chief in India (1885–93), and served as Supreme Commander in South Africa during the Boer War, relieving Kimberley (1900). He was created earl in 1901, and died while visiting troops in the field in France. » Afghan Wars; Boer Wars; Indian Mutiny; Kimberley, Siege of

Roberts, Tom (1856–1931) Australian painter, born at Dorchester, Dorset, England. He emigrated as a child, and studied at the Carlton School of Design and at the National Gallery School, both in Melbourne, before returning to London to attend the Royal Academy Schools. His best work, which deals with pioneering life in the bush, was produced in Australia in the late 1880s and 1890s. He died in London. » Australian art

Robeson, Paul (Bustill) [**rohb**sn] (1898–1976) US Black singer and actor, born in Princeton, New Jersey. He became a lawyer, then embarked on a stage career, becoming popular as a singer. He appeared in works ranging from *Show Boat* to *Othello*, gave song recitals, notably of Negro spirituals, and appeared in numerous films. In the 1950s, his left-wing views caused him to leave the USA for Europe (1958–63). He retired after his return, and died in Philadelphia. » theatre

Robespierre, (Maximilien François Marie Isidore de) [**rohbz**pyair] (1758–94) French revolutionary leader, born at Arras. He became a lawyer, was elected to the States General (1789), became a prominent member of the Jacobin Club, and emerged in the National Assembly as a popular radical, known as 'the Incorruptible'. In 1791 he was public accuser, and in 1792 presented a petition to the Legislative Assembly for a Revolutionary Tribunal. Elected First Deputy for Paris in the National Convention, he emerged as leader of the Mountain, strenuously opposed to the Girondins, whom he helped to destroy. In 1793 he became a member of the Committee of Public Safety and for three months dominated the country, introducing the Reign of Terror and the cult of the Supreme Being. But as his ruthless exercise of power increased, his popularity waned. He was attacked in the Convention, arrested, and guillotined on the orders of the Revolutionary Tribunal. » French Revolution [i]; Jacobins (French history); Mountain, the

Robey, Sir George (1869–1954) British comedian, born at Herne Hill, Kent. He first appeared on the stage in 1891, made a name for himself in musical shows such as *The Bing Boys* (1916), and later emerged as a Shakespearean actor in the part of Falstaff. Dubbed the 'Prime Minister of Mirth', he was famous for his bowler hat, black coat, hooked stick, and thickly painted eyebrows. He was knighted in 1954, and died at Saltdean, Sussex. » theatre

robin A bird of the thrush family (44 species), usually with a red breast; especially the Eurasian/N African robin (*Erithacus* *rubecula*). The name is also used for some Australasian flycatchers (28 species) and for the **Jamaican tody** (Family: *Todidae*). » flycatcher; magpie; thrush (bird)

Robin Goodfellow In English 16th-c and 17th-c superstition, a mischievous fairy who would do housework if duly rewarded. He was also called Puck or Hobgoblin, and his name held sufficient terror for nurses to use it as a threat to naughty children. His characteristic activities are listed in *A Midsummer Night's Dream* (2.i). » fairies

Robin Hood A legendary 13th-c outlaw who lived in Sherwood Forest in the English N Midlands, celebrated in ballads dating from the 14th-c. He protected the poor, and outwitted, robbed, or killed the wealthy and unscrupulous officials of Church and state. The legend may have had its origins in the popular discontent that led to the Peasants' Revolt of 1381. » Peasants' Revolt

Robinson, Edward G, originally **Emmanuel Goldenberg** (1893–1973) US film actor, born in Bucharest, Romania, of Jewish parents who emigrated to the USA in 1903. He started in silent films, but became famous as the gangster Rico in *Little Caesar* (1930), a typecasting which dogged him for many years. His dramatic scope constantly expanded, but his support of democratic causes brought disfavour at the time of the McCarthy witch-hunts. Susbsequently he continued in strong character parts, many of his later appearances being in international co-productions. He received a Special Academy Award in 1972 not long before his death in Los Angeles. » McCarthy, Joseph R

Robinson, Edwin Arlington (1869–1935) US poet, born at Head Tide, Maine; Gardiner, in the same state, is the protoype of the 'Tilbury Town' of his poems. Educated at Harvard, he settled in New York City, where he began to write. He won Pulitzer Prizes for his *Collected Poems* (1922), *The Man Who Died Twice* (1925), and *Tristram* (1928), one of his several modern renderings of Arthurian legends. He died in New York City. » American literature; Arthur; poetry

Robinson, (William) Heath (1872–1944) British artist, cartoonist, and book illustrator, born and died in London. He trained in London, and illustrated several popular books, such as *Arabian Nights* (1899). His fame rests mainly on his humorous drawings satirizing the machine age, displaying 'Heath Robinson contraptions' of absurd and complicated design, but with highly practical and simple aims, such as the raising of one's hat. » English art

Robinson, Joan V(iolet) (1903–83) British economist, born at Camberley, Surrey. She was educated at Cambridge, where she taught at the university (1931–71). In 1965 she succeeded her husband as professor of economics. She was one of the most influential economic theorists of her time, and a leader of the Cambridge School, which developed macro-economic theories of growth and distribution, based on the work of Keynes. She died at Cambridge. » Keynes; macro-economics

roble beech A tree similar to the beech, and replacing that genus in the S hemisphere. It differs chiefly by having nuts in threes, enclosed in spiny or scaly case. (Genus: *Nothofagus*, 35 species. Family: *Fagaceae*.) » beech; nut

robotics (cybernetics) The application of automatic machines (*robots*) to perform tasks traditionally done by humans. Robots are widely used in industry to perform simple repetitive tasks accurately and without tiring, and to work in environments which are dangerous to human operators. They can also be used as sensors, equipped for artificial vision, touch, and temperature sensing. Many are now capable of simple decision-making without the intervention of the operator. If the robots are in human form, they are called *androids*. » automation

robotics (dance) » **street dance**

Robson, Dame Flora (McKenzie) (1902–84) British actress, born at South Shields, Durham. She first appeared in 1921, and became famous especially for her historical roles in plays and films, such as Queen Elizabeth in *Fire over England* (1931). She was made a Dame in 1960, and died at Brighton, East Sussex. » theatre

Rochdale 53°38N 2°09W, pop (1981) 97 942. Town in Rochdale borough, Greater Manchester, NW England; on the R Roch, 16 km/10 ml NE of Manchester; railway; textiles (especially cotton), engineering; Co-operative Society founded here in 1844. » Manchester, Greater

Roche limit The lowest orbit at which a satellite can withstand tides raised within it by its parent planet. French mathematician Edouard Roche (1820–83) studied rotating liquid masses, and noted in 1848 that, if a moon orbited close enough to its parent planet, the stresses would exceed the strength of rock, tearing the planet apart. This mechanism could explain the presence of rings around Saturn and Uranus. » planet; Saturn (astronomy); Uranus (astronomy)

Rochester (UK), ancient **Durobrivae** 51°24N 0°30E, pop (1981) 24 402. Town in the Medway Towns urban area and Rochester upon Medway district, Kent, SE England; W of Chatham; an important early settlement at a ford over the R Medway; railway: 12th-c cathedral; 11th-c castle; Gad's Hill nearby, the home of Charles Dickens. » Dickens; Kent

Rochester (Minnesota, USA) 44°01N 92°28W, pop (1980) 57 890. Seat of Olmsted County, SE Minnesota, USA, on the Zumbro R; railway; electrical equipment, medical supplies; home of the Mayo Clinic, established in 1889. » Mayo, Charles Horace; Minnesota

Rochester (New York, USA) 43°10N 77°37W, pop (1980) 241 741. Seat of Monroe county, W New York, USA; port on Genesee R, 10 km/6 ml from L Ontario; first settled, 1811; city status, 1834; airfield; railway; university (1850); optical and photographic instruments, machines and tools; International Museum of Photography, Rochester Museum, Memorial Art Gallery; Lilac Festival (May). » New York (state)

rochet [**roch**it] A white, full-length, linen robe. It is worn by bishops, especially of the Anglican Communion, on ceremonial occasions. » bishop; vestments [i]

rock A naturally occurring material which comprises the solid Earth. Rocks are an assemblage of minerals, and are classified according to origin. » igneous/metamorphic/sedimentary rock; petrology; Plate IV

rock ape » **Barbary ape**

rock art » **Palaeolithic/Paleolithic art**

rock crawler A secondarily wingless, mainly nocturnal insect found in cold habitats above the tree line and around glaciers; body poorly pigmented with a thin flexible cuticle. (Order: *Grylloblattaria*, c.13 species.) » insect [i]

rock crystal » **quartz**

rock dove A pigeon native to Europe and Asia; grey with metallic neck feathers; inhabits cliffs and fields; eats seeds, grass, and snails; nests on cliffs (or buildings). It is the ancestor of all domestic and town-dwelling pigeons. (*Columba livia*.) » pigeon

rock music A type of popular music, originally called **rock and roll**, which spread throughout the USA and Europe in the 1950s. It began as a basically simple musical style, dominated by a strong dance beat and by the use of the electric guitar. It developed out of country and western, and more particularly from rhythm and blues – a style which previously had been played almost exclusively by US Black artists. The term 'rock and roll' was popularized by Cleveland disc jockey Alan Freed, who was also the first person to play rhythm and blues music to a predominantly White radio audience. The music gained widespread popularity during the late 1950s, when major artists included Bill Haley (1925–81), Elvis Presley (1935–77), and Chuck Berry (1926–). Primarily aimed at and enjoyed by a young audience, it became an important symbol of teenage rebellion.

During the 1960s the format was expanded considerably by such artists as Bob Dylan (1941–) and Jimi Hendrix (1942–70), and by bands such as the Rolling Stones and the Beatles. Then and since, the music has taken on a variety of outside influences, and groups have frequently expanded on the basic rock instrumentation of electric guitars, electric bass, vocals, and drums. Over the period, rock music has diversified into a distinct series of subgenres – from 'hard rock', in the late 1960s and early 1970s, to 'punk rock' in the late 1970s – most of which have been characterized not only by musical differences but by their own associated features in dress, lifestyle, and (in the 1980s) video publicity. » Beatles, The; Berry; country and western; Dylan; Haley; Hendrix; pop music; Presley; punk rock; rhythm and blues; Rolling Stones

rock rabbit » **hyrax; pika**

rock salt » **halite**

Rockefeller, John D(avison) (1839–1937) US industrialist and philanthropist, born at Richford, New York. After high school he went into the business world, and showed a talent for organization. In 1875 he founded with his brother **William** (1841–1922) the Standard Oil Company, securing control of the US oil trade. In the late 19th-c his power came under strong public criticism. He withdrew from active business in 1897, and devoted the rest of his life to philanthropy. He gave over 500 million dollars in aid of medical research, universities, and churches, and established in 1913 the **Rockefeller Foundation** 'to promote the wellbeing of mankind'. He died at Ormond, Florida. His third son, **Nelson A(ldrich)** (1908–79), became Republican Governor of New York State (1958–73), sought the Republican presidential nomination in 1960, 1964, and 1968, and in 1974 was Vice-President 1974–7 under President Ford. His youngest son, **Winthrop** (1912–73), a racial moderate, became Republican Governor of Arkansas in 1966. » Ford, Gerald R; foundation, philanthropic; Republican Party

Rockefeller Center A complex of 14 skyscrapers commissioned by J D Rockefeller II (1874–1960) and built (1931–40) in Manhattan, New York City. The centre now consists of 21 buildings housing offices, restaurants, shops, cinemas, broadcasting stations, and the Radio City Music Hall. » New York City; Rockefeller

Rockefeller Foundation » **foundation, philanthropic**

rocket A self-propelling device in which the fuel substances needed to produce the propulsion are carried internally. The term most commonly refers to space vehicles, although it can also apply to distress rockets and fireworks. In addition, rockets are used to power missiles, and for supersonic and assisted-take-off aeroplane propulsion. Rockets work by burning fuel inside a combustion chamber. Both the fuel and the oxygen (*oxidant*) needed to burn it are carried inside the rocket itself. When the fuel is burnt, a large volume of hot gas is produced, which exerts great pressure on the inside surface. The upward pressure is much greater than the downward pressure, because the gases are allowed to escape through a nozzle at the bottom. The stronger pressure at the top results in an upward force (*thrust*) that makes the rocket rise. The force and the upward movement continue until all the fuel is exhausted. *Solid fuel* rockets commonly use a mixture of nitrocellulose and nitroglycerin as the fuel source. The more efficient *liquid fuel* rockets use kerosene (fuel) and liquid oxygen (oxidant). Other means of propulsion, such as nuclear furnaces, are being developed. No single rocket is powerful enough to lift itself into orbit. A space-launcher is made up of several rockets creating a multi-stage (*step*) rocket. Once the fuel for one stage is exhausted, that stage is dumped, and the next stage is ignited. The rocket launcher becomes progressively lighter and faster as it climbs into space. » launch vehicle [i]; oxygen

Rockford 42°16N 89°06W, pop (1980) 139 712. Seat of Winnebago County, N Illinois, USA, on the Rock R; railway; machine tools, vehicle parts; agricultural centre; Burpee Art Gallery. » Illinois

Rockhampton 23°22S 150°32E, pop (1981) 50 146. City in Queensland, Australia, on the Fitzroy R; railway; air link and hydrofoil service to Great Keppel I; centre of Australia's largest beef-producing area; to the W, area around Emerald, Anakie, Rubyvale, Sapphire, and Willows rich in gemstones; Rocky Round-up rodeo (Apr); cooeeing contest (Aug) at nearby Cooee Bay. » Queensland

Rockingham, Charles Watson Wentworth, 2nd Marquess of (1730–82) British statesman and Prime Minister (1765–6, 1782). Created Earl of Malton in 1750, he served as gentleman of the bedchamber to George II and George III. As leader of a prominent Whig opposition group, he was called upon to form a ministry in 1765. He repealed the Stamp Act, affecting the American colonies, then court intrigues caused his resignation. He opposed Britain's war against the colonists. His was the most consistent opposition Whig group to George III's government in the 1760s and 1770s, and leading spokesmen, such as Fox and Burke, were adherents. He became Prime Minister again in 1782, but died soon after taking office. » American Revolution; Burke, Edmund; Fox, Charles James; Stamp Act

rockrose A small evergreen shrub, mostly native to the Mediterranean region and parts of Asia; leaves opposite, lance-shaped to oblong; flowers 5-petalled, white, yellow, or red. Some species are grown in gardens. (Genus: *Helianthemum*, 100 species. Family: *Cistaceae*.) » evergreen plants; shrub

Rocky Mountain goat A wild goat native to the mountains of N America; back legs shorter than front legs; thick shaggy white coat and short backward curved horns; also known as **mountain goat**, **goat antelope**, or **antelope goat**. (*Oreamnos americanus*.) » goat

Rocky Mountain sheep » **bighorn**

Rocky Mountain spotted fever » **typhus fever**

Rocky Mountains or **Rockies** Major mountain system of W N America, extending from C New Mexico generally NNW through the USA, into W Canada and N Alaska and reaching the Bering Strait N of the Arctic Circle; about 4 800 km/3 000 ml long; forms the continental divide, separating the Pacific drainage from the Atlantic and Arctic; highest point in the USA Mt Elbert (4 399 m/14 432 ft), in Canada Mt Robson (3 954 m/12 972 ft); principal pass the South Pass (Wyoming), followed by the Oregon Trail; divided into the Southern, Middle, Northern, and Arctic sections; important source of mineral wealth; several national parks, including Rocky Mountain, Grand Teton, Yellowstone, Glacier (Montana), Banff, Jasper, Yoho, Kootenay, Glacier (British Columbia), Northern Yukon, Gates of the Arctic. » North America

Rococo (Fr *rocaille*, 'rock-work') In art history, the period following the late Baroque in European art and design. It flourished especially in France and S Germany c.1700–50, until superseded by the Neoclassical taste spreading from Rome. Whereas Baroque was dramatic and powerfully theatrical, Rococo sought effects of charm and delicacy on a small scale – surface effects rather than bold masses. It was therefore most successful as a style of interior decoration, exemplified in the designs of Pierre Lepautre (c.1648–1716), Gilles-Marie Oppenord (1672–1742), Nicolas Pineau (1684–1754), and Juste Aurèle Meissonier (c.1693–1750). The greatest Rococo painter was Watteau. » Baroque (art and architecture); Neoclassicism (art); Watteau

rodent A mammal of worldwide order *Rodentia* (3 suborders, 30 families, 1 702 species); successful in most environments; 40% of all living mammal species are rodents; eats a wide range of food; chisel-like upper and lower incisor teeth grow continuously, kept short by gnawing; suborders are *Myomorpha* (**mouse-like rodents**, 1 137 species), *Sciuromorpha* (**squirrel-like rodents**, 377 species), and *Hystricomorpha* (**porcupine-like rodents**, 188 species, sometimes called *Caviomorpha* or **cavy-like rodents**). » beaver; cavy; hamster; jerboa; jumping mouse; kangaroo rat; mole rat; mouse; pocket gopher; porcupine; squirrel

rodeo A US sport, consisting mainly of competitive riding and a range of skills which derive from cowboy ranching practices. The events include bronco riding with and without saddle, bull riding, steer wrestling, calf roping, and team roping. In bronco riding, for example, the cowboy must stay on a wild bucking horse for a set time holding with only one hand, points being awarded for style to the horse and rider.

Rodgers, Richard » **Hammerstein, Oscar**

Rodin, (René François) Auguste [**roh**dĩ] (1840–1917) French sculptor, born in Paris. He trained in Paris and Brussels, and began to produce sculptures which, with their varying surfaces and finishes, resembled the Impressionist painters' effect of light and shade. The great 'La Porte de l'enfer' (The Gate of Hell) was commissioned for the Musée des Arts Décoratifs in 1880, and during the next 30 years he was mainly engaged on the 186 figures for these bronze doors. Among his other works is 'Le Penseur' (1904, The Thinker), in front of the Panthéon in Paris. He died at Meudon, near Paris. » French art; Impressionism (art); Salon

Rodnina, Irina [rod**nee**na] (1949–) Russian figure skater, born in

Moscow. She won the pairs title at three Olympics – 1972 (with Alexei Ulanov), 1976, and 1980 (both with Alexandr Zaitsev) – and won four world titles with Ulanov (1969–72) and six with Zaitsev (1973–8). During the same years she won the corresponding European titles. She married Zaitsev in 1975, retired in 1980, and trained to be an astronaut. » ice skating

Rodrigo, Joaquín [ro**dree**goh] (1901–) Spanish composer, born at Sagunto. Although blind from the age of three, he studied music with Dukas in Paris (1927–33), and travelled widely before settling in Madrid in 1939. His best-known work is the *Concierto de Aranjuez* (1939) for guitar and orchestra, and he has composed similar concertos for other instruments, as well as songs and other pieces that display a genuine hispanicism. » Dukas; guitar

Rodrigues Island [roh**dree**gez] 19°45S 63°20E, pop (1983) 33 572. Island in the Indian Ocean, E of Mauritius; part of the Mascarene Is; a dependency of Mauritius; rises to 396 m/1 299 ft at Mt Limon; chief town, Port Mathurin; fishing, subsistence agriculture; labour supply to Mauritius. » Mauritius [i]

rods and cones Photoreceptor cells of the vertebrate retina, so called because of their shapes. Rods are sensitive to dim light (*scotopic*) and function at twilight. Cones are sensitive to bright light (*photopic*) and function in daylight. Nocturnal animals usually have more rods than cones. Many mammals have two types of cones, but humans and apes have three. » colour vision; eye [i]; retina

roe deer A small true deer native to Europe and Asia; the smallest European deer (shoulder height, 750 mm/30 in); short upright antlers with three tines; virtually no tail; white rump; inhabits open woodland edges. (*Capreolus capreolus*.) » antlers [i]; deer

Roentgen » **Röntgen**

Rogation Days In the Christian Church, the three days before Ascension Day, once observed with fasting, processions and supplications to God (*rogations*).

Rogers, Ginger » **Astaire, Fred**

Roget, Peter Mark [**roz**hay] (1779–1869) British scholar and physician, born in London. He worked as a physician in Manchester and London, and became professor of physiology at the Royal Institution (1833–6). He is best known for his *Thesaurus of English Words and Phrases* (1852), which reached a 28th edition in his lifetime. He died at W Malvern, Worcestershire. » English language

Röhm or **Roehm, Ernst** [rerm] (1887–1934) German soldier, politician and Nazi leader, born in Munich. He became an early supporter of Hitler, the organizer and commander of the stormtroopers ('Brownshirts'). His plans to increase the power of this force led to his execution on Hitler's orders, near Munich. » Hitler; Night of the Long Knives

role A part played by an actor. In social psychology, the term is extended to refer to the part played by an individual in a given set of social circumstances (eg the role of 'mother' or 'leader'). **Role-playing** is the active performance of lines of action in a particular social setting; also, the conscious adoption of such lines of action, in situations of pretence, deception, or simulation. Role-playing as simulation may be used as a training or therapeutic method for improving social skills of a professional (eg interviewing) or non-professional kind. It has also been employed as a research method, where subjects playing the role of themselves, a prescribed character, or 'everyman', overtly act out or passively imagine participation in a scenario. **Role-conflict** may arise when someone tries to play two roles governed by incompatible normative expectations – for example, a clash between work and family duties, such as when a policeman is required to arrest his own son. » status; social psychology

Rolfe, (Frederick William) Father, pseudonym **Baron Corvo** (1860–1913) British novelist, historian, and essayist, born in London. He converted to Roman Catholicism, studied at Oxford, Oscott, and the Scots College in Rome, but failed in his efforts to join the priesthood (his nominal 'fatherhood' was spurious). His earliest fiction was published in the *Yellow Book* in the late 1890s, but much of his work – an odd mixture of fiction, wish-fulfilment and autobiography – was not published until after his death. His best-known novel is *Hadrian the Seventh* (1904), the story of the rise to the papacy of a poor literary hack. He died in Venice. » novel

Rolland, Romain [rolã] (1866–1944) French author, born at Clamecy. He studied in Paris and Rome, and in 1910 became professor of the history of music at the Sorbonne. He resigned in 1912 to devote himself to writing, published several biographies and a 10-volume novel, *Jean-Christophe* (1904–12), and in 1915 was awarded the Nobel Prize for Literature. He lived in Switzerland until 1938, then moved to France, and died at Vézelay. » French literature; novel

roller A crow-like bird of the widespread Old World family *Coraciidae* (11 species); usually blue and brown; inhabits woodland or open country; eats insects and small vertebrates; nests in hole; somersaults in flight when displaying (hence its name). The name is also used for the **cuckoo-roller** (*Leptosomatidae*) and the **ground-roller** (*Brachypteraciidae*). It is also a breed of canary. » canary; crow; jay

roller skating A pastime first seen in Liège, Belgium, in 1760. The modern four-wheeled skate was introduced by the US inventor James L Plymton in 1863. As a sport it developed in the late 19th-c, and competitions exist as for ice skating: individual, pairs, dancing, and speed skating. » ice skating; street hockey; RR117

Rolling Stones, the British rock group, members **Mick Jagger** (1944–) vocals, **Keith Richard** (1944–) guitar, **Bill Wyman** (1941–) bass, **Charlie Watts** (1942–) drums, **Ron Wood** (1947–) guitar, former member **Brian Jones** (1944–69) guitar, one of the longest-running and most successful popular music groups to emerge in the 1960s. They first performed together in 1962. At first, they were very much in the shadow of the Beatles, but their less boyish, more rebellious style together with their more aggressive music soon won them a large following. Although their uninhibited life styles and overtly sexual lyrics often hit the headlines, it was the excellence of their compositions (usually by Jagger and Richard) that ensured their continuing success. Among their early hits were 'The Last Time' and 'Satisfaction'. » Beatles, The; blues; rock music

Rollo (c.860–c.932) Viking leader who secured from Charles III of France in 911 a large district on condition of being baptized and becoming Charles's vassal. This grant was the nucleus of the duchy of Normandy. » Normans; Vikings

Rolls, C(harles) S(tewart) (1877–1910) British motorist and aeronaut, born in London. Educated at Eton and Cambridge, from 1895 he experimented with the earliest motor cars, and combined with Henry Royce for their production. In 1906 he crossed the English Channel by balloon, and in 1910 made a double crossing by aeroplane. Soon afterwards, he died in a flying accident at Bournemouth, Dorset. » aeroplane; balloon; car [i]; Royce, Henry

Rolls-Royce A major British firm of car engine and aero-engine manufacturers. In the 1970s the firm was split into two separate companies, following financial problems caused by the high cost of aero-engine research and development. The aero-engine side of the business passed into British government ownership, whilst Rolls-Royce (Cars) remained a separate commercial enterprise. In 1987 the aero-engine business was returned by the government to private ownership as a fully commercial company. » engine; Rolls; Royce, Henry

ROM An acronym of **Read-Only Memory**, a type of computer memory, usually integrated circuits, which can only be read from; the data is fixed during the manufacture of the chip. ROM is used where the data does not have to be altered; the data also remains intact even if the the electrical power is removed. » EAROM; EPROM; PROM; RAM

Romains, Jules [romĩ], pseudonym of **Louis Farigoule** (1885–1972) French writer, born at Saint-Julien-Chapteuil. Educated at Paris, he became a teacher, but established his name with his poems *La Vie unanime* (1908), and brought about the Unanimist school, devoted to a belief in universal brotherhood and group consciousness. He became a full-time writer from 1919, and remained prominent in French literature, his best-known works being the comedy *Knock, ou le triomphe de la médecine* (1923, Dr Knock, or the triumph of medicine) and the 27-volume cycle of novels, *Les Hommes de bonne* *volonté* (1932–46, Men of Good Will), covering the early 20th-c era of French life. He died in Paris. » French literature; novel; poetry

Roman architecture A form of classical architecture in which the clear, expressive use of the column and horizontals by the Greeks was replaced by a plastic use of rounded forms such as the arch, dome, and vault. There is greater reliance on the wall, combined with a more decorative use of architectural orders. The development of concrete used in conjunction with brick, along with a great deal of engineering skill, allowed the construction of buildings such as the Pantheon, Rome (100–125), with a 43 m/141 ft dome, and the Colosseum, Rome (72–80). Domestic buildings included the *domus*, a single-storey urban house based around an atrium; the *insula*, a multi-storey urban tenement block; and the *villa*, an often luxurious rural residence that reaches its apogee in Hadrian's Villa, Tivoli (AD 123). Other typically Roman buildings include the triumphal arch, basilica palace, and the complicated planning of the thermae, or baths. » amphitheatre; atrium; basilica; Greek architecture; Neoclassicism (art architecture); orders of architecture [i]; Renaissance architecture; Romanesque architecture; triumphal arch; vault [i]

Roman art Historically the most important artistic tradition in the ancient world, if not in all Western history, which has seen a whole series of classical (ie Roman) revivals from the early Middle Ages down to the 18th-c. Roman artists owed a strong debt to Hellenistic Greek art, especially in painting and sculpture, and many classical Greek statues survive only as Roman copies. However, in portraiture, especially busts, and in reliefs (eg those on Trajan's column and on triumphal arches), Roman sculptors were highly original, and set standards that were keenly pursued from the Renaissance to the 18th-c. Not much painting has survived, but murals in Roman houses featured scenes from Homer and Ovid in landscape settings. » art; classical revival; Greek art; mosaic; Renaissance art

Roman Catholicism The doctrine, worship, and life of the Roman Catholic Church. A direct line of succession is claimed from the earliest Christian communities, centring on the city of Rome, where St Peter (claimed as the first bishop of Rome) was martyred and St Paul witnessed. After the conversion of the Emperor Constantine (4th-c), Roman bishops acquired something of the authority and power of the emperor. Surviving the fall of Rome in the 5th-c, the Church was the only effective agency of civilization in Europe, and after the 11th-c schism with the Byzantine or Eastern Church, it was the dominant force in the Western world, the Holy Roman Empire. The Protestant Reformation of the 16th-c inspired revival, and the need to restate doctrine in an unambiguous form and to purge the church and clergy of abuses and corruption was recognized. The most dramatic reforms were enacted by the two Vatican Councils of the 19th-c and 20th-c. The Second Vatican Council signalled a new era, with a new ecumenical spirit pervading the Church. Although the doctrines of the faith remained largely untouched, there was a new openness to other Christian denominations – indeed, other world religions. Great emphasis was placed on the Church as the 'people of God', with the laity being given a much more active part in liturgy (eg the Mass being said in the vernacular instead of Latin).

Doctrine is declared by the pope, or by a General Council with the approval of the pope, and is summarized in the Nicene Creed. Scripture is authoritative, and authoritatively interpreted by the *magisterium* or teaching office of the Church. The tradition of the Church is accepted as authoritative, special importance being attributed to the early church fathers and to the mediaeval scholastics, notably St Thomas Aquinas. Principal doctrines are similar to those of mainstream Protestant and Orthdox Churches – God as Trinity, creation, redemption, the person and work of Jesus Christ and the place of the Holy Spirit – the chief doctrinal differences being the role of the Church in salvation, and its sacramental theology. Modern liturgies reflect a cross-section of historical inheritance, cultural environment, and social factors. Ancient traditional practices such as the veneration of the Virgin Mary and the Saints, or the Stations of the Cross, are still regarded as valuable aids to devotion. At the other extreme, Roman Catholic priests in South America, preaching liberation theology, have assumed a political role, for which they have been rebuked by Rome.

The hierarchy of the Church includes cardinals, bishops, priests, and several minor orders. Many religious orders, male and female, exist within the Church. The vast and complex organization of the Church is controlled by the Vatican, an independent state in Rome which, under the direction of the pope, implements Church policy, and administers property and finance. In predominantly Catholic countries, the Church maintains a degree of political influence, and extends canon law into the realm of civil law, notably on moral issues (eg birth control). » Aquinas; Bible; bishop; cardinal (religion); Council of the Church; God; Holy Roman Empire; liturgy; Mary (mother of Jesus); Mass; Paul, St; Peter, St; pope; priest; Reformation, Catholic; sacrament; Stations of the Cross; theology; Trinity; Vatican Councils

Roman Curia (Lat *curia*, 'court') An organization in the Vatican (Rome) which administers the affairs of the Roman Catholic Church under the authority of the pope. It is comprised of congregations (administrative), tribunals (judicial), and offices (ministerial), all as defined in canon law. » pope; Roman Catholicism; Vatican City

roman fleuve [rohmã flerv] (Fr 'river-novel') A term used for a series of novels, linked by common characters or preoccupations. Examples are Zola's Rougon-Macquart series (1871–93), the seven parts of Proust's *A la recherche du temps perdu* (1913–27), Galsworthy's *Forsyte Saga* (1906–28), and Anthony Powell's 12-volume *Dance to the Music of Time* (1951–76). » Galsworthy; novel; Powell, Anthony; Proust, Marcel; Zola

Roman history **The Monarchy** (753–509 BC). Founded, according to tradition, in 753 BC, Rome was initially ruled by kings, of whom Romulus was the first and Tarquinius Superbus the seventh and last. Expelled in 509 BC because of his tyrannical ways, he left the Romans with a long-abiding hatred of monarchy.

The Republic (509–31 BC). Brought into being with the overthrow of the monarchy, the Republican system of government was designed to prevent a tyrant ever ruling Rome again. Executive power was entrusted to two annually elected officials (consuls); their advisory council, the Senate, an ex-officio body of magistrates, provided the necessary elements of experience and continuity. The system brought stability, and Rome grew rapidly from a small city-state into an empire. The Punic Wars brought the W Mediterranean under her control, while the campaigns against the rulers of the Hellenistic world added Macedon, Greece, Asia Minor, and the Levant. But the system which had served the city-state so well could not cope with the government of this Empire. The Republic perished at Actium in 31 BC after decades of civil war in which great warlords such as Caesar, Pompey, Antony, and Octavian fought for supreme power.

The Empire (31 BC–AD 476 in the W, AD 1453 in the E). Cobbled together out of the wreckage of the Republic, the Roman Empire was the creation of one man, Augustus. Pretending that he had restored the Republic, he studiously avoided titles that smacked of absolute power, calling himself 'princeps' or first citizen – a Republican term – and the name for the early Empire 'the Principate'. In reality, he and his successors were absolute monarchs; later titles make this clear – the Emperor being called 'dominus' (master), and the name for the later Empire 'the Dominate'. Abroad, too, Augustus' arrangements affected the nature of the Empire permanently – the unbridled expansionism of Republican days was abandoned, and territorial limits were set – the Rhine and Danube in Europe, the Euphrates in Asia. Subsequent modifications were few; Britain (AD 43), Dacia, and Arabia (both annexed by Trajan in 106) were the only significant later additions.

From the outset, the Rhine–Danube frontier was the hardest to hold, with the tribes across the rivers exerting a relentless pressure upon the Roman defences. Rome managed to contain this pressure for several centuries, but only at an increasing cost to herself. The area saw a steady military build-up and ultimately constant fighting. The foundation in the 3rd-c of a new imperial capital (Nicomedia) nearer this frontier shows how the Empire's centre of gravity had shifted from Rome and

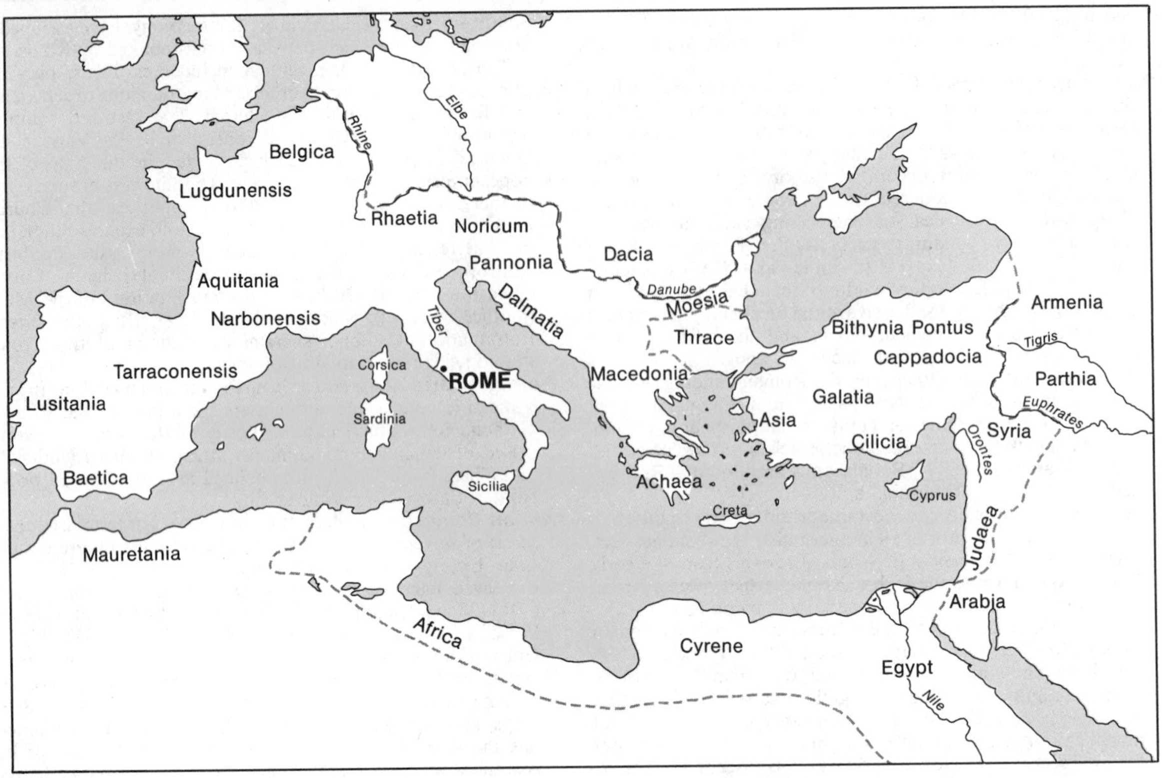

The Roman Empire in the 1st century AD

Italy to the N and E. This was the point where the very integrity of the Empire was threatened; and it was here that Rome's defences in the end were breached. In the 5th-c, hordes of trans-riverine tribesmen (eg Huns, Vandals, Visigoths, Ostrogoths) poured into the W provinces carrying all before them. In 476 with their deposition of the last Emperor, Romulus Augustulus, they marked symbolically their destruction of the W half of the Empire. The E provinces, however, proved more resilient; here the barbarian challenge was contained for another thousand years, until the E capital Constantinople fell to the Ottoman Turks in 1453. » Actium, Battle of; Augustus (Octavian); Bithynia; Britain, Roman; consul 1; Gallic Wars; Punic Wars; Senate, Roman

Roman Law The corpus of Roman Law starts with the primitive code, the XII Tables (450 BC), and ends with Justinian's complex codification (c.AD 530). In the intervening centuries Rome grew from a tiny city-state into a vast world empire and exchanged a Republican form of government for a monarchical one. Roman law reflects these changes: under the empire, the emperor himself gradually became the sole source of law, his pronouncements (*edicta*), written opinions on legal points (*rescripta*), and even instructions to his officials (*mandata*) all being legally binding. The collective name for these enactments is 'constitutions'. Older forms of law-making withered away, as the bodies formerly responsible (eg the people's assemblies (*comitia*) and the Senate) became obsolete or radically altered. » Justinian Code; Senate, Roman; Theodosian Code; Twelve Tables

Roman numerals The Roman symbols for numbers, which have a fixed value, and do not use the concept of place-value. The symbols generally used are I=1, V=5, X=10, L=50, C=100, D=500, and M=1 000 (the symbols L and D were later developments). In general, symbols were placed in decreasing order of size, eg XVI=16. A symbol may be repeated once, twice, or three times (eg XVIII=18), but not four times, this being avoided by altering the normal order of the symbols, so that 19=XIX not XVIIII. Some minor variations are found, eg today IIII is sometimes used on clock-faces instead of IV. » numeral; RR77

Roman religion The first Romans were farmers and lived in a world full of *numen*, a powerful spiritual force behind appearances waiting to be revealed, and *genius*, the spirit of an ancestor, or a locality. Etruscan and Italic deities were absorbed, and a priestly college was established, presided over

PRINCIPAL ROMAN GODS

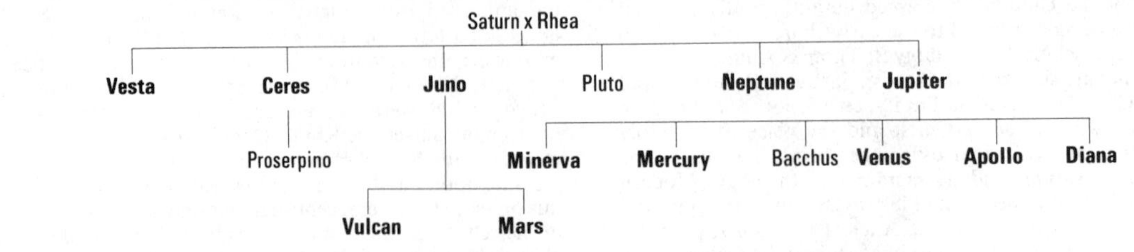

The 12 major gods of Olympus are shown in bold type. Bacchus in some accounts supplants Vesta. Pluto and Proserpino are gods of the Underworld

Chief Roman roads in Britain

by the *pontifex maximus*. By Cicero's time the diversity of cults had been organized into uniformity throughout most of Italy. Augustus took the title of *pontifex* for himself, and reaffirmed the ancient worship. The Romans believed that all peoples worshipped the same gods under different names (eg Mercury = Hermes), and so had no difficulty in absorbing Greek mythology, having nothing comparable themselves. After Augustus' death, the worship of the emperor became a religious duty, but increasingly exotic foreign cults flourished. When Constantine accepted Christianity in AD 312, the ancient Roman religion became 'paganism', ie the practices of country people. » Greek religion

Roman roads A network of usually straight roads radiating from ancient Rome. Built primarily for military purposes, the roads also served an important commercial function. Main routes were constructed on an earth footing with a layer of small stones in mortar above, on top of which was a hard filling surfaced with stone slabs. The Appian Way, built in the 3rd-c BC and linking Rome with present day Capua, was the first great Roman road. The Aurelian Way connected Rome with present day Pisa, while the Flaminian Way served as the main northern route. » Britain, Roman

romance (Mediaeval Lat *romanice* 'in the Romanic tongue') A literary genre which may be traced back to late Classical times, with Longus' *Daphnis and Chloe* and Apuleius' *Golden Ass* (both 2nd-c AD). The romance proper, as a tale (in verse or prose) of courtly love or pastoral idyll, flourished in late mediaeval and Renaissance Europe. There were three main sources: the Classical (Alexander, Troy, Thebes); Arthurian legend; and 'the matter of France' (Charlemagne and his court). The Renaissance romance drew also on pastoral sources, as in Sidney's *Arcadia* (1595). The romance was symbolically engulfed by the novel in Cervantes's *Don Quixote* (1605, 1615). » Apuleius; Arthur; chansons de geste; Charlemagne; novel; Sidney, Philip

Romance languages The languages which developed from the 'vulgar' or spoken form of Latin used throughout the Roman Empire. The major ones are Italian, French, Spanish, Portuguese, and Romanian, all of which are official languages in their respective states. There are also several non-standard varieties, such as Sardinian, Rhaetian (dialectal variants in N Italy and Switzerland), and Catalan, used mainly in NE Spain. Colonialism has dispersed the Romance languages throughout the world, so that over 700 million people now speak a Romance language or a creole based on one. French is spoken by c.60–70 million as a mother-tongue in France, Canada, Belgium, Switzerland, Luxemburg, Monaco, and many parts of Africa, Oceania, and the Americas, and is used as a second language by a further 200 million. Spanish is spoken by over 250 million people in Spain, most of the countries of C and S America, and by rapidly increasing numbers in the USA. Portuguese is spoken by c.160 million people, mainly in Brazil, and also in Portugal and parts of Africa. Italian is spoken by c.60 million in Italy and adjoining localities, as well as in parts of N Africa and the Americas. » creole; French/Italian/Latin/Portuguese/Spanish literature; Indo-European languages

Romanesque architecture The form of architecture prevalent in W Europe 10th–12th-c AD, characterized by the use of the round arch, clear plans and elevations and, typically, the two-tower facade. The use of rib vaults signified the introduction of Gothic architectural forms. Its greatest monuments are huge vaulted churches richly decorated with sculpture, such as at Santiago de Compostela and Durham. » arch [i]; facade; Gothic/Norman/Roman architecture; vault [i]

Romania, **Roumania**, or **Rumania**, official name **Republic of Romania**, Romanian **Republica România** pop (1990e) 23 265 000; area 237 500 sq km/91 675 sq ml. Republic in SE Europe, on the Balkan Peninsula and the lower Danube; divided into 41 counties (*judet*); bounded E by the Black Sea, S by Bulgaria, W by Yugoslavia and Hungary, and N and NE by Ukraine and Moldavia; capital, Bucharest; chief towns include Braşov, Constanţa, Iaşi, Timişoara, Cluj-Napoca; timezone GMT +2; population mainly Romanian (89%), with Hungarian and Gypsy minorities; official language, Romanian, with French widely spoken; chief religion, Eastern Orthodox Christianity (80%); unit of currency, the leu of 100 bani.

Physical description and climate. Carpathian Mts separate Old Romania from Transylvania, and form the heart of the country; E Carpathians between the N frontier and the Prahova Valley, an area of extensive forest cut by many passes; higher S Carpathians between the Prahova Valley and the Timiş-Cerna gorges; W Carpathians between the R Danube and the R Someş; highest peak, Negoiul (2 548 m/8 359 ft); Romanian Plain (S) includes the Bărăgan Plain (E), the richest arable area, and the Oltenian Plain (W), crossed by many rivers; c.3 500 glacial ponds, lakes, and coastal lagoons; over a quarter of the land forested; continental climate, with cold, snowy winters and warm summers; mildest area in winter along the Black Sea coast; plains of the N and E can suffer from drought; average annual rainfall, 1 000 mm/40 in (mountains), 400 mm/15.7 in (Danube delta).

History and government. Formed from the unification of Wallachia and Moldavia, 1862; monarchy created, 1866; joined the Allies in World War 1; Transylvania, Bessarabia, and Bucovina united with Romania, 1918; support given to Germany in World War 2; occupied by Soviet forces, 1944; monarchy abolished and People's Republic declared, 1947; Socialist Republic declared, 1965; increasingly independent of the USSR since the 1960s; relationships formed with China, and several Western countries; leading political force was the Romanian Communist Party, led by dictator Nicolae Ceaucescu; in December 1989 the violent repression of protest, resulting in the deaths of hundreds of demonstrators, sparked a popular uprising and the overthrow of the Ceaucescu regime. A provisional government led by dissidents promised free elections in 1990, but unrest and demonstrations continued.

Economy. Since World War 2, a gradual change from an agricultural to an industrial economy; mounting economic difficulties in the 1980s; state owns nearly 37% of farm land, mainly organized as collectives and state farms; wheat, maize, sugar beet, fruit, potatoes, vines; livestock; oil, natural gas, salt, iron ore, copper; iron and steel, metallurgy, engineering, chemicals, textiles, foodstuffs, electrical goods, electronics, machinery, rubber, timber, tourism. » Bucharest; Carpathian Mountains; Ceausescu; Moldavia and Wallachia; Transylvania; RR27 national holidays; RR59 political leaders

Romanian » **Romance languages**

Romanist The name given by art historians to those Dutch and Flemish artists who, in the 16th-c, travelled to Italy to see the works of the great Renaissance masters. Thus Jan Gossaert (called Mabuse) went to Italy in 1508, taking back to Antwerp the decorative details of the Renaissance and new subjects including the classical nude. » Flemish art; Gossaert; Renaissance art

romanization The use of the Roman alphabet to replace a language's writing system constructed on a different principle. This procedure has been very common in language planning, especially in countries where the native script is non-alphabetic in character, as in Chinese logographic writing or the Japanese katakana syllabary. Romanized versions also exist for several alphabetic systems, such as Arabic and Hindi. » alphabet [i]; graphology; logography; syllabary

Romanization In antiquity, the process whereby the subject peoples of W Europe adopted the language and customs of the Romans. At first involuntary, under the Empire it became a deliberate government policy. Roman-style towns were built in the less developed provinces, and the provincial aristocracy were encouraged to learn Latin and participate in local government. The prizes could be, in the first instance, the award of Roman citizenship and later even enrollment into the Roman Senate itself. » Britain, Roman; Senate, Roman

Romanovs The second (and last) Russian royal dynasty (1613–1917). The first Romanov tsar (Mikhail) was elected in 1613 after the Time of Troubles. The Romanovs ruled as absolute autocrats, allowing no constitutional or legal checks on their political power. The dynasty ended with the abdication of Nicholas II in February 1917, and his execution by Bolshevik guards in July 1918. » Alexander I; Catherine II; Nicholas I/II; Peter I; February Revolution; Revolution of 1905; Russian history; Russian Revolution; Time of Troubles

Romans, Letter to the A New Testament book, often considered the most significant of the works of the apostle Paul. Although Paul did not establish the Church in Rome, he wrote to it (perhaps c.55–8) to present his understanding of salvation for both Gentiles and Jews, and to warn against libertine and legalistic interpretations of the Christian message. Chapters 1–8 set out his understanding of justification and salvation; Chapters 9–11 address the problem of Israel's unbelief; Chapters 12–16 deal with Christian living and community relationships. » New Testament; Paul, St

Romanticism (art) In the visual arts, as in literature, an attitude of mind, rather than a style. Between c.1760 and c.1850 the range of subjects greatly expanded. Some were chosen for their heightened emotional qualities, such as the death-bed scenes by Greuze, David, and West, or horrific disasters, such as the 'Raft of the Medusa' (1819) by Géricault. Others are chosen for their exotic appeal, as with Delacroix's 'Algerian Women' (1834). Its features include: a cult of nostalgia, a yearning for 'long ago and far away'; Egyptian, Greek and mediaeval revivals in architecture and the decorative arts; and the treatment of lost causes: the Jacobites, the Huguenots, the Cavaliers. Leading romantics in Britain include Turner and Constable; in Germany, Caspar David Friedrich (1774–1840); in Spain, Goya. » Gothic revival; Nazarenes; Neoclassicism (art and architecture); Constable; David, Jacques Louis; Delacroix; Géricault; Goya; Turner, J M W; West, Benjamin

Romanticism (literature) A large-scale movement of the mind in the late 18th/early 19th-c, which affected the whole of human understanding and experience. The Renaissance made humanity the measure of the universe; Romanticism placed the individual at the centre of his/her own world. This was partly the work of philosophers, from the solipsist Berkeley and the sceptical Hume to Kant, with his dynamic model of the mind; but it was the imaginative writers of the time who effectively authorized and liberated the subjective impulse. Among the more important writers associated with Romanticism are, in England, Wordsworth, Coleridge, Blake, Keats, Shelley, and Byron; in Germany, Goethe and Schiller; in France, Rousseau and Hugo. But there are few writers who bear no trace of this profound revolution in thought and feeling, which is still discernible as one of the major tributaries of the modern age. » Blake, William; Coleridge; English/French/German literature; Goethe; Hugo; Kant; Keats; literature; Rousseau, Jean Jacques; Schiller; Shelley, Percy Bysshe; Wordsworth, William

Romanticism (music) Music particularly of the period c.1810–1910, in which subjective emotion is felt to take precedence over objective detachment, content over form, colour over line, and the lyrical and poetic over the architectonic. The Romantic period in music saw the growth of the modern symphony orchestra, an increased and more integral use of chromaticism, a general expansion of the inherited genres of opera, symphony, concerto, etc, and the emergence of new genres (the concert overture and symphonic poem) in which composers could express a response to literature and the other arts. German Lieder combined musical and literary Romanticism. National styles, based to some extent on a new awareness of a country's folk heritage, began to assert themselves, as in Czechoslovakia and Russia. The works of the major Romantic composers form the staple repertory of modern concert halls and opera houses. » classical music; Impressionism (music); Lied; programme music; rhapsody; symphonic poem; Beethoven; Berlioz; Chopin; Liszt; Mahler; Puccini; Schumann, Robert; Verdi; Wagner

Romany The language of the Gypsies, of Indo-Aryan origin. Dialects of Romany have taken on features of the languages with which they have come into contact in various parts of the world. Thus, before it became virtually extinct as a distinctive dialect in the second quarter of the 20th-c, Welsh Romany had adopted the distinctively Welsh sound written *ll*. » Gypsy; Indo-Aryan languages

Rome, Ital **Roma** 41°53N 12°30E, pop (1981) 2 840 259. Capital city of Italy, Lazio region, WC Italy; on the R Tiber, 20 km/12 ml from the Tyrrhenian Sea (E); on left bank are the Seven Hills of Rome – the Capitoline (50 m/164 ft), Quirinal (52 m/171 ft), Viminal (56 m/184 ft), Esquiline (53 m/174 ft),

ROME

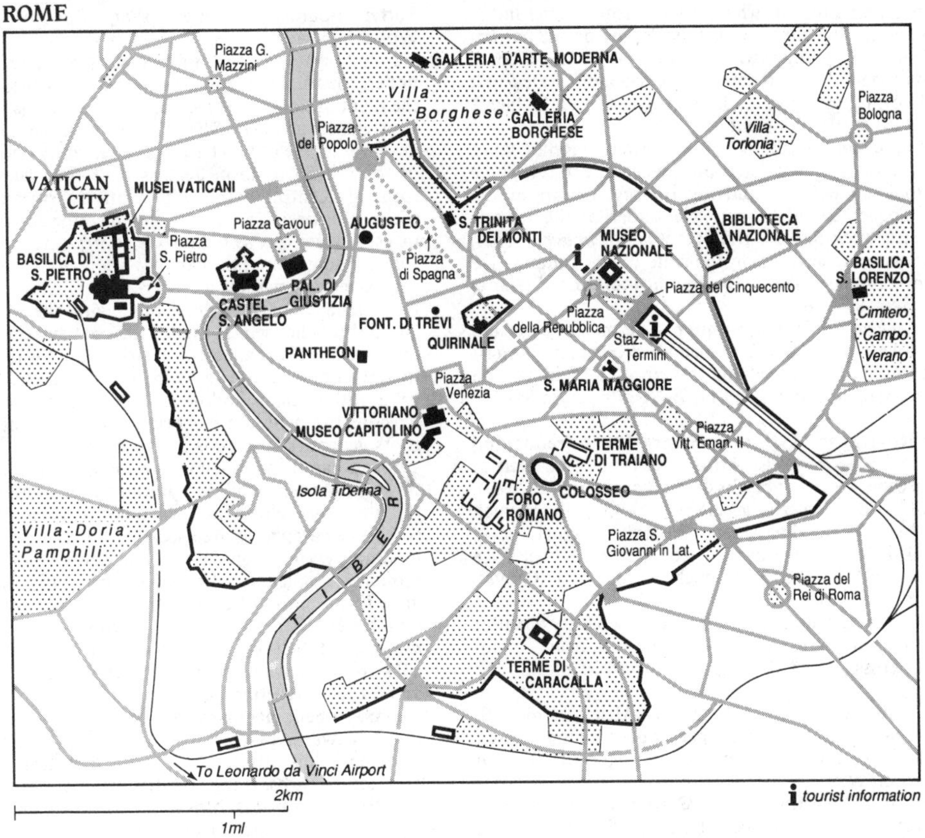

Palatine (51 m/167 ft), Aventine (46 m/151 ft), and Caelian (50 m/164 ft) – on which the ancient city was built during the 8th-c BC; centre of the Roman Empire; sacked by Germanic tribes, 5th-c; ecclesiastical centre from 6th-c; Vatican City on W bank; capital of unified Italy, 1971; airport; railway; metro; university (1303); important centre of fashion and film; headquarters of many cultural and research institutions; oil refining, chemicals, pharmaceuticals, fertilizers, iron and steel, glass, cement, engineering, textiles, brewing, foodstuffs; centre of Rome is a world heritage site; a major tourist city; Palazzo Venezia (15th-c), Forum Romanum, with relics of ancient Rome (Arch of Titus, Via Sacra, Curia, Arch of Septimius Severus), Colosseum (from AD 75), Baths of Caracalla (216), Arch of Constantine (312), Pantheon (27 BC), Trevi Fountain (1762), Galleria Borghese; several Renaissance palaces; numerous churches, notably St Peter's (in the Vatican), St John Lateran (Rome's cathedral), San Lorenzo and San Paolo outside the Walls, Santa Maria Maggiore; spring festival (Mar–Apr); numerous religious feasts and celebrations. » Capitoline Hill; Italy [i]; Lateran Treaty; Roman history [i]; St Peter's Basilica; Sistine Chapel; Terme; Vatican City

Rome, Treaties of (1957) » **European Community; EURATOM**

Rømer, Ole (Christensen) [**rer**mer] (1644–1710) Danish astronomer, born at Arhus, who used eclipses of Jupiter's satellites to make the first accurate determination of the velocity of light (1675). He died in Copenhagen. » Jupiter (astronomy); light

Rommel, Erwin (Johannes Eugen) (1891–1944) German field marshal, born at Heidenheim. Educated at Tübingen, he fought in World War 1, taught at Dresden Military Academy, and became an early Nazi sympathizer. He commanded Hitler's headquarters guard during the early occupations, and led a Panzer division during the 1940 invasion of France. He then commanded the Afrika Korps, where he achieved major successes. Eventually driven into retreat by a strongly reinforced 8th Army, he was withdrawn, a sick man, from N Africa, and appointed to an Army Corps command in France. Returning home wounded in 1944, he condoned the plot against Hitler's life. After its discovery, he committed suicide at Herrlingen. » El Alamein, Battle of; Hitler; World War 2

Romney, George [**rom**nee, **ruhm**nee] (1734–1802) British painter, born at Dalton-in-Furness, Lancashire. In 1757 he set up as a portrait painter, leaving his family and moving to London in 1762. Apart from two visits to France, and two years residence in Italy (1773–5), he stayed in Cavendish Square, where his reputation rivalled that of Reynolds. His many pictures of Lady Hamilton are particularly well known. He died at Kendal. » English art; Reynolds, Joshua

Romulus and Remus [**rom**yulus, **ree**mus] In Roman legend, the twin sons of Mars and the Vestal Virgin Rhea Silvia; an example of an invented myth, to explain the name of the city. They were thrown into the Tiber, which carried them to the Palatine, where they were suckled by a she-wolf. In building the wall of Rome, Remus made fun of the work and was killed by Romulus or one of his followers. Having founded Rome, Romulus was later carried off in a thunder-storm. » Roman history [i]

Romulus Augustulus (5th-c AD) The last Roman emperor of the West, deposed by Odoacer in 476. » Odoacer; Roman history [i]

roncey » **cob**

Ronda 36°46N 5°12W, pop (1981) 31 383. Picturesque town in Málaga province, Andalusia, S Spain, on R Guadalevin; railway; famous for its school of bullfighters; clothes, wine, leather, soap; Fiesta of La Reconquista (May), fiesta and fair (Sep). » Andalusia; Spain [i]

rondeau [ron**doh**] (Fr *rond* 'round') An Old French verse form of 13 or 15 (usually octosyllabic) lines, in three stanzas, using only two rhymes. It was popular in 16th-c France, and among the French Romantics (eg de Musset), and was imported into England in the late 19th-c (eg by Dobson, Swinburne). » French literature; poetry; verse

rondo A musical structure in which restatements of the initial theme are separated by contrasting episodes, eg on the pattern A–B–A–C–A–B–A, perhaps with an introduction and a coda. In the **sonata rondo**, the 'B' theme of this scheme is stated first in a related key, returning in the home key, and the 'C' theme may be replaced by development.

Ronsard, Pierre de [rõsah] (1524–85) French Renaissance poet, born at La Possonière. He trained as a page, but became deaf, and took up writing, studying for seven years at the Collège de Coqueret, and becoming a leader of the Pléiade group. His early works include *Odes* (1550) and *Amours* (1552), and he later wrote reflections on the state of the country. He died at Saint-Cosme-les-Tours. » French literature; Pléiade, La; poetry; Renaissance

röntgen or **roentgen** [**ront**guhn, **ront**juhn] The unit of exposure to ionizing radiation; symbol R; named after German physicist Wilhelm Röntgen. It is based on the amount of ionization produced in a standard volume of air by X-rays. » radiation; Röntgen

Röntgen or **Roentgen, Wilhelm Konrad von** [**rernt**guhn] (1845–1923) German physicist, born at Lennep. Educated at Zürich, he became professor of physics at Strasbourg (1876–9), Giessen (1879–88), Würzburg (1888–1900), and Munich (1900–20). In 1895 he discovered the electromagnetic rays which he called X-rays, for which he won the first Nobel Prize for Physics in 1901. He died in Munich. » rad; rem; X-rays

Röntgen rays » **X-rays**

rood screen An ornamental partition used to separate the altar and the choir from the nave. The name derives from Anglo-Saxon *rood*, 'cross, crucifix'. » chancel; choir; church [i]; nave

rook A crow native to Europe, Asia, and N Africa; black with pale bare patch on face; inhabits open country; omnivorous; forms dense nesting colonies in trees (*rookeries*). (*Corvus frugilegus*.) » crow

Roon, Albrecht (Theodor Emil), Graf von ('Count of') (1803–79) Prussian army officer, born at Pleushagen. He became War Minister (1859–73), and with Bismarck's support effectively reorganized the army, which helped make possible Prussian victories in the Danish, Austrian, and Franco-Prussian Wars of the 1860s and 1870s. He died in Berlin. » Austro-Prussian War; Bismarck; Franco-Prussian War

Roosevelt, Franklin D(elano), byname **FDR** (1882–1945) US Democratic statesman and 32nd President (1933–45), born at Hyde Park, New York. He became a lawyer (1907), a New York State Senator (1910–13), and Assistant Secretary of the Navy (1913–20), and was Democratic candidate for the vice-presidency in 1920, and Governor of New York (1928–32), although stricken with paralysis (polio) in 1921. He met the economic crisis with his 'New Deal' for national recovery (1933), and became the only president to be re-elected three times. He strove in vain to ward off war, modified the USA's neutrality to favour the Allies, and was brought in by Japan's action at Pearl Harbor (1941). He met with Churchill and Stalin at Teheran (1943) and Yalta (1945), but died at Warm Springs, Georgia, where he had long gone for treatment, three weeks before the German surrender. His wife, **Eleanor Roosevelt** (1884–1962), the niece of Theodore Roosevelt, later became chairman of the United Nations Commission on Human Rights (1947–51) and represented the USA at the General Assembly (1946–52). » Churchill, Winston; New Deal; Stalin; World War 2

Roosevelt, Theodore, byname **Teddy** (1858–1919) US Republican statesman and 26th President (1901–9), born in New York City. Educated at Harvard, he became leader of the New York legislature (1884). In 1898 he raised a volunteer cavalry ('Roosevelt's Roughriders') in the Cuban War, and came back to be Governor of New York State (1898–1900). Elected Vice-President in 1900, he became President on the death (by assassination) of McKinley, and was re-elected in 1904. An 'expansionist', he insisted on a strong navy, the regulation of trusts and monopolies, and introduced a 'Square Deal' policy for social reform. As Progressive candidate for the presidency in 1912, he was defeated by Wilson. He died at Oyster Bay, New York. » McKinley, William; Republican Party; Spanish-American War; Square Deal; Wilson, Woodrow

root (botany) The part of a plant's axis which usually lies underground, absorbing water and nutrients, and anchoring the plant in the soil; also commonly serving as a storage organ. It originates as the *radicle*, the embryonic root of the seed, and develops in one of two basic ways, either by repeated branching of the radicle to form a mass of fibrous **lateral roots** or by forming a central **taproot** with relatively few laterals. The tip of the root bears a cap, the *calyptra*, a continuously growing layer of cells which protect the root as it pushes through the soil. Immediately behind the calyptra is a region bearing **root hairs** – single-celled structures mainly responsible for the absorption of water from the soil. Behind this region the root may develop lateral branches which extend the root system. Like the stem, the root has a vascular system to conduct water and nutrients to and from it, but in roots the vascular tissue usually forms a solid rather than hollow cylinder which better resists the tensions that would otherwise uproot the plant. Unlike stems, roots generally lack buds and green tissue.

Roots can be modified in various ways to enhance or add to their functions. Swollen taproots act as storage organs; contractile roots help to pull rhizomes or corms deeper into the soil. **Pneumatophores** are specialized breathing roots developed in swampy, oxygen-poor ground. Roots which develop above ground are called **aerial roots**, and occur in many plants. They grow from stems or leaves, and absorb moisture direct from the atmosphere. Other types of aerial root include **buttress** or **prop roots**, which help support the stem or trunk, and **climbing** and **adhesive** roots, which help to elevate the plant. In epiphytes, the aerial roots are often green and capable of photosynthesis. A common phenomenon is the formation of symbiotic associations between plant roots and micro-organisms such as nitrogen-fixing bacteria and mycorrhizal fungi, which enhance the absorbing abilities of the roots. » epiphyte; mycorrhiza; photosynthesis; rhizoid; root nodule; stem (botany); symbiosis; vascular tissue

root (linguistics) The basic element (*morpheme*) of a word, which can occur on its own, and to which affixes can be added to give derived forms; also known as a **stem**. For example, from the root *kind*, we may derive *un-kind, kind-ly, kind-ness*, etc. In English, roots may be 'free', and occur on their own, such as *kind*; or they may be 'bound', and able to occur only in combination with affixes, such as *-duct* in *con-duct, ab-duct*. The root carries the core meaning of the word, and prefixes modify that meaning in regular ways. In addition, the suffixes carry grammatical information, marking the form's part of speech, as in *kind-ly* (adjective), *kind-ness* (noun). » affix; derivation

Root, Elihu (1845–1937) US statesman, born at Clinton, New York. Educated at New York, he became a lawyer, US Secretary of War (1899–1904), and Secretary of State (1905–9). He was awarded a Nobel Peace Prize in 1912 for his promotion of international arbitration. He died in New York City.

root nodule A small, tumour-like swelling on the roots of some plants caused by the invasion of benign micro-organisms which are able to fix atmospheric nitrogen into nitrates to the benefit of the host in return for sugars. An example is the nitrogen-fixing bacterium *Rhizobium*, associated with all members of the pea family (*Leguminosae*). » mycorrhiza; nitrate; pea [i]; root (botany)

rope A length of thick, twisted fibre used to secure objects together. The fibres are twisted for added strength, and can be natural (eg hemp, sisal, flax, jute, cotton) or synthetic (eg nylon, polyester). Synthetic fibre ropes are lighter and stronger, but they can be stretched more. Heavy ropes, such as those used to tie large ships to jetties, may have a diameter of up to 25 cm/10 in, though most are much thinner. Wire ropes are also used as cables on suspension bridges. » fibres

Roraima, Mount [ro**riy**ma] 5°12N 60°43W. Peak at the junction of the Brazil, Guyana, and Venezuela borders, South America; 442 km/275 ml SE of Ciudad Bolivar (Venezuela) in the Serra de Pacaraima; highest peak (2 875 m/9 432 ft) in the Guiana Highlands; a giant table mountain, total area 67 sq km/26 sq ml. » Guiana Highlands

Røros Mining town on the Glomma R in Norway; founded in 1644 after the discovery of large deposits of copper in the region; old miners' village, with unpainted timber houses; 18th-c church; a world heritage site. » Norway [i]

rorqual [**raw**kwuhl] A baleen whale of worldwide family *Balaenopteridae* (6 species); throat has 10–100 longitudinal furrows, allowing it to expand when feeding; small dorsal fin near tail; female larger than male; comprises **blue**, **sei**, **fin**, **minke**, **Bryde's** and **humpback** whales. » blue/humpback/sei whale; whale [i]

Rorschach, Hermann (1884–1922) Swiss psychiatrist and neurologist, born in Zürich. He devised a diagnostic procedure for mental disorders based upon the patients' interpretation of a series of standardized ink blots (the **Rorschach test**). His work received little attention until after his death, at Herisau, Switzerland. » projective tests; psychiatry

Rosa, Salvator (1615–73) Italian painter, born near Naples. He became famous at Rome for his talents as painter, etcher, actor, and poet; but he made powerful enemies by his satires, and withdrew to Florence for nine years. He then returned to Rome, where he died. He owes his reputation mainly to his landscapes of wild and savage scenes. » Italian art

Rosario [ros**a**rioh] 33°00S 60°40W, pop (1980) 875 623. Chief city in Santa Fe province, and third largest in Argentina; on the R Paraná, NW of Buenos Aires; Argentina's largest inland port, founded in 1725; airport; railway; university (1968); distribution centre and export outlet for local agricultural provinces; steel, machinery, cars, food processing; racecourse; golf club, boat club, aero club in the fashionable suburb of Fisherton; museums, cathedral, Municipal Palace (1896), Monument of the Flag (1957). » Argentina [i]

rosary A form of religious meditation, found in several religions, in which a sequence of prayers is recited using a string of beads or a knotted cord, each bead or knot representing one prayer in the sequence. In Christianity, it most commonly refers to the Rosary of the Blessed Virgin Mary, one of the most popular of Roman Catholic devotions. This is a sequence of one Our Father, ten Hail Marys, and one Glory Be to the Father (a *decade*), repeated fifteen times (in the full version) or five times (in the more commonly used shorter version), each decade being associated with a particular 'mystery' or meditation on an aspect of the life of Christ or the Virgin Mary. It probably dates from the 13th-c. » Jesus Christ; Mary (mother of Jesus); meditation; Roman Catholicism

Roscius, in full **Quintus Roscius Gallus** (c.134–62 BC) Roman comic actor, a slave by birth. He became the greatest comic actor in Rome, and was freed from slavery by the dictator, Sulla. He gave Cicero lessons in elocution, and was defended by him in a lawsuit. » Cicero; Sulla; theatre

Roscommon, Gaelic **Ros Comáin** pop (1981) 54 543; area 2 463 sq km/951 sq ml. County in Connacht province, WC Irish Republic; bounded E by R Shannon and watered by R Suck; capital, Roscommon (pop (1981) 1 673), 13th-c abbey and castle, formerly a wool town; agriculture, cattle; numerous lakes. » Irish Republic [i]

rose A genus of well-known shrubs or scrambling perennials, nearly all native to the N hemisphere. So-called climbing roses do not climb in a true sense, but grow up through other vegetation or similar supports, and are prevented from slipping back by the tough, often hooked, prickles on the stems. The leaves are pinnate, with three or (usually) more oval, toothed leaflets; they are semi-evergreen, retaining at least some leaves throughout the winter. The flowers of wild species are 5-petalled, flat or shallowly dish-shaped, white or yellow to red or purple, and often fragrant. Many garden roses have larger flowers with more numerous, less spreading petals, reaching an extreme in the tight, many-petalled blooms of cabbage roses. Cultivated forms also show a greater range of colours than wild plants. The orange, red or black fruit (*hip* or *hep*) consists of a fleshy receptacle expanded to enclose the dry achenes or true fruits within, the whole structure often being crowned with the persistent sepals. The hips are attractive to birds and animals, and are a rich source of vitamin C. The bright red growths resembling balls of thread often found on roses (called *robins' pincushions*) are galls caused by the gall-wasp *Cynips*.

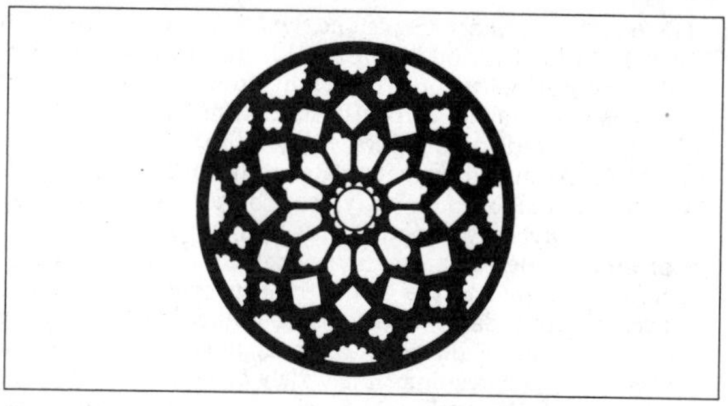

Rose or wheel window – Chartres cathedral

Prized for centuries for their beauty and as a source of perfume, roses are probably the world's most widely cultivated ornamental plants, with many wild species being taken directly into gardens or playing an important role in the development of garden forms. They are very hardy, tolerate most growing conditions, and provide a profusion of forms and colours. Exactly when they were first brought into cultivation is uncertain, but they were being grown in China and probably elsewhere c.5000 BC. Several distinct types of rose such as *floribundas* have been developed by horticulturalists, and there are now over 20 000 named cultivars, with several hundred more produced each year by the flourishing rose-breeding industry. (Genus: *Rosa*, 250 species. Family: *Rosaceae*.) » achene; attar; cultivar; evergreen plants; gall; perennial; pinnate; receptacle; sepal; shrub

Rose, Pete, properly **Peter (Edward)** (1942–) US baseball player, born in Cincinnati. He surpassed Ty Cobb's 57-year-old record of 4 191 base hits in 1985, and was the Most Valuable Player of the Year in 1973. In his career (1963–86), spent mainly with the Cincinatti Reds, he had a record 4 256 base hits. He was banned from baseball in 1989 after an investigation into alleged gambling offences. » baseball [i]

rose of Jericho A much-branched annual, growing to 15 cm/6 in, native to N Africa and W Asia; flowers small, white, cross-shaped. When the plant dies in the dry season, the spreading branches curve inwards, forming a basket-like ball which blows about like a tumbleweed, only expanding and releasing seeds from the pods when wetted by rain. (*Anastatica hierochuntica*. Family: *Cruciferae*.) » annual; tumbleweed

rose of Sharon A semi-evergreen shrub native to SE Europe and W Asia; rhizomatous; stems to 60 cm/2 ft, slender; leaves elliptical; flowers 7–8 cm/2¾–3 in diameter, 5-petalled, pale yellow with darker stamens. It is widely planted for ornament and ground cover. (*Hypericum calycinum*. Family: *Guttifereae*.) » evergreen plants; rhizome; Saint John's wort; shrub

rose window A round window with mullions or tracery radiating outwards from the centre. It is commonly associated with Gothic architecture, and is also known as a **wheel window**. » Gothic architecture; Gothic Revival; tracery [i]

Roseau, formerly **Charlotte Town** [roh**zoh**] 15°18N 61°23W, pop (1981) 20 000. Seaport and capital town of Dominica, Windward Is; on SW coast; cathedral (1841); trade in tropical fruit and vegetables; thermal springs nearby; Victoria Memorial Museum; badly damaged by hurricane, 1979. » Dominica

rosebay willow-herb An erect perennial species of willow-herb, growing to 120 cm/4 ft, native to Europe, Asia, and N America; creeping, spreading roots; leaves in whorls of three; flowers in long spikes, 2–3 cm/¾–1½ in diameter, with four narrow, dark purple sepals and four paler, spoon-shaped, notched petals, on a slender, purplish ovary-tube; capsule with numerous white-plumed seeds; also known as **fireweed**. It is sometimes cultivated for ornament, but is also an aggresive weed. (*Epilobium angustifolium*. Family: *Onagraceae*.) » perennial; sepal; willow-herb

Rosebery, Archibald Philip Primrose, 5th Earl of (1847–1929) British statesman and Liberal Prime Minister (1894–5), born in London. Educated at Eton and Oxford, he succeeded to the earldom in 1868, and after holding various educational and political posts, became Foreign Secretary

(1886, 1892–4) under Gladstone, whom he succeeded as Premier for a brief period before the Liberals lost the election of 1895. He was noted for his racehorse stables, and in his later years as a biographer of British statesmen. He died at Epsom, Surrey. » Gladstone; Liberal Party (UK)

rosella An Australian parrot, related to the budgerigar; inhabits woodland and open country; can be an agricultural pest. (Genus: *Platycercus*, 8 species.) » budgerigar; parrot

rosemary A dense, aromatic, evergreen shrub, growing to 2 m/6½ ft, native to the Mediterranean, typical of dry scrub; leaves narrow, dark green above, white beneath, margins inrolled; flowers pale blue, 2-lipped, upper slightly hooded, lower 3-lobed, spreading. It is widely cultivated for ornament and as a culinary herb. (*Rosmarinus officialis*. Family: *Labiatae*.) » evergreen plants; herb

Rosenberg, Julius (1918–53) and his wife **Ethel** (1915–53) US spies, born in New York City. They joined the Communist Party, and were part of a transatlantic spy ring uncovered after the trial of Klaus Fuchs in Britain. The husband was employed by the US army, and the wife's brother at the nuclear research station at Los Alamos. They were convicted of passing on atomic secrets through an intermediary to the Soviet vice-consul. They became the first US civilians to be executed for espionage, at Ossining (Sing Sing prison), New York. » Fuchs, Klaus

Roses, Wars of the (1455–85) A series of civil wars in England, which started during the weak monarchy of Henry VI; named from the emblems of the two rival branches of the House of Plantagenet, York (white rose) and Lancaster (red rose) – a symbolism which was propagated by the Tudor dynasty (1485–1603), which united the two roses. The wars began when Richard, Duke of York, claimed the protectorship of the crown after the King's mental breakdown (1453–4), and ended with Henry Tudor's defeat of Richard III at Bosworth (1485). The armies were small, and the warfare intermittent, although marked by brutal executions. The wars were not purely dynastic in origin, but were escalated by the gentry and by aristocratic feuds, notably between the Nevilles and the Percies, and by the unstable 'bastard feudal' system, in which relations among landed elites were increasingly based upon self-interest – a system that the Tudors sought to control. » Henry VI; Henry VII; Plantagenets; Richard III

Rosetta Stone A black basalt slab with a trilingual inscription in Greek and Egyptian hieroglyphic and demotic found in 1799 at Raschid, near Alexandria, on the Rosetta branch of the R Nile. Cross-correlation by Thomas Young and, particularly, Jean François Champollion allowed hieroglyphs to be deciphered for the first time, and provided the key to the Ancient Egyptian language. It is now in the British Museum. » Champollion; demotic script; hieroglyphics [i]; Young, Thomas

rosewood A high-quality wood scented like roses, because of the presence of aromatic gum. It is obtained from various trees of the genus *Dalbergia*, native to the tropics and subtropics, which have pinnate leaves and pea-flowers. (Family: *Leguminosae*.) » gum tree; pinnate; tree [i]

Rosh Hashanah [rosh ha**shah**na] The Jewish New Year (1 Tishri), which falls in September or October. During the New Year's Day service, a ram's horn is blown as a call to repentance and spiritual renewal. » Judaism

Rosicrucianism [rohzi**kroo**shuhnizm] An esoteric movement which spread across Europe in the early 17th-c. In 1614–15 two pamphlets appeared in Germany and were attributed to Christian Rosenkreutz (1378–1484), who claimed to possess occult powers based on scientific and alchemical knowledge he had brought from the East. He founded the Order of the Rosy Cross, and the pamphlets invited men of learning to join. No trace of the Order has been found, but many occult organizations claim Rosicrucian origins. » alchemy; mysticism; occultism

rosin A resin obtained as the residue from the distillation of turpentine, melting point c.120°C; also called **colophony**. Its colour varies from colourless to dark brown. It is used as a flux in soldering and as a lubricant. » resin; turpentine tree

Roskilde [**roh**skilduh] 55°39N 12°07E, pop (1981) 39 659. Port and ancient town at S end of Roskilde Fjord, Zealand, Denmark; capital of Denmark, 10th-c–1443; Peace of Roskilde (1658), by which Denmark lost land E of The Sound to Sweden; railway; university (1970); engineering, foodstuffs, distilling, tanning; triple-towered cathedral (12th-c); Viking Ships museum. » Denmark [i]; Sound, The

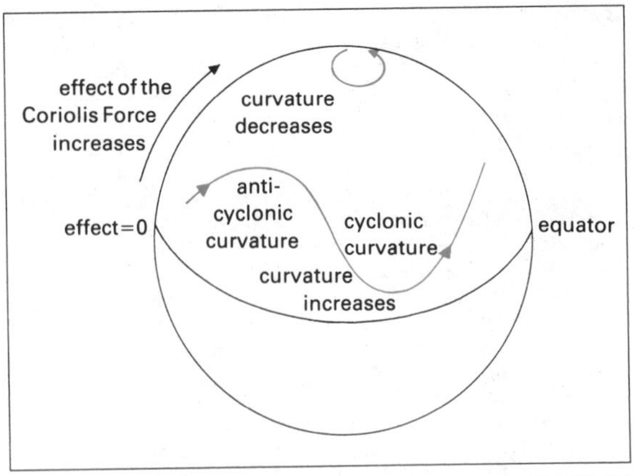

Rossby waves – The mechanism of development of high altitude westerly winds

Ross, Sir James Clark (1800–62) British polar explorer, born in London. He discovered the N magnetic pole in 1831, then commanded an expedition to the Antarctic seas (1839–43), where Ross Barrier, Sea, and Island are named after him. He was knighted in 1843, and died at Aylesbury, Buckinghamshire. » Antarctica [i]

Ross Dependency Land area 413 540 sq km/159 626 sq ml; permanent shelf ice area 336 770 sq km/129 993 sq ml. Antarctic territory administered by New Zealand (since 1923), including all the land between 160°E and 150°W and S of 60°S; no permanent inhabitants; scientific stations near L Vanda and at Scott Base on Ross I. » Antarctica [i]

Ross Sea Extension of the Pacific Ocean between Marie Byrd Land and Victoria Land in New Zealand's territory of Antarctica; S arm covered by the Ross Ice Shelf; McMurdo Sound (W) generally ice-free in late summer, an important base point for exploration; main islands, Roosevelt (E) and Ross (W); active volcano (Mt Erebus) on Ross I. » Antarctica [i]

Rossby waves Planetary-scale waves of westerly wind flow, found at high altitudes and based on the jet stream; named after the Swedish-American meteorologist C G Rossby (1898–1957). Occurring in both hemispheres, three to six waves complete the westerly circuit around the Earth. They result from a combination of the rotation of the Earth (planetary vorticity) and the variation with latitude of the Coriolis force, balanced by relative vorticity (the rotation of air associated with the clockwise spinning of an anticyclone and anticlockwise spinning of a depression or cyclone in the N hemisphere). In the N hemisphere a westerly moving wind, with zero initial vorticity, will be deflected northwards. As latitude increases, the relative vorticity becomes negative (*anticyclonic*), and the air is deflected back towards the Equator to a position where the vorticity becomes positive (*cyclonic*), and the air is deflected polewards once more. » anticyclone; Coriolis force; depression (meteorology) [i]; general circulation model; jet stream; wind [i]

Rossellini, Roberto (1906–77) Italian film director, born and died in Rome. His first independent film was *Roma, città aperta* (1945, Rome, Open City), made while it was still under German occupation, often with hidden cameras in a style which came to be known as 'neorealism', and followed by *Paisà* (1946, Paisan) and *Germania, anno zero* (1947, Germany, Year Zero). Later films on spiritual themes, and his liaison with Ingrid Bergman, were condemned by the Catholic Church in the USA, but another war-time story *Il generale della Rovere* (1959, General della Rovere) restored his popularity.

Rossetti, Christina (Georgina) (1830–94) British poet, born and died in London, the sister of D G Rossetti. A devout Anglican, and influenced by the Oxford Movement, she wrote mainly religious poetry, such as *Goblin Market and Other Poems* (1862). Her work displays the influence of the Pre-Raphaelite artistic movement, which her brother helped to found. » English literature; Oxford Movement; poetry; Rossetti, Dante Gabriel; Pre-Raphaelite Brotherhood

Rossetti, Dante Gabriel (1828–82) British poet and painter, born in London. He trained at the Royal Academy in London, and c.1850 helped to form the Pre-Raphaelite Brotherhood, which aimed to return to pre-Renaissance art forms involving vivid colour and detail. His early work was on religious themes, such as 'The Annunciation' (1850, Tate, London); his later manner became more secular, and more ornate in style. The death of his wife in 1862, and adverse criticism of his poetry, turned him into a recluse, but *Ballads and Sonnets* (1881) contains some of his best work. He died at Birchington-on-Sea, Kent. » English art; Pre-Raphaelite Brotherhood

Rossini, Gioacchino (Antonio) (1792–1868) Italian composer, born at Pesaro. He studied in Bologna, and began to write comic operas. Among his early successes were *Tancredi* (1813) and *L'Italiana in Algeri* (1813, the Italian Girl in Algiers), and in 1816 he produced his masterpiece, *Il Barbiere di Siviglia* (The Barber of Seville). As director of the Italian Theatre in Paris (1823), he adapted several of his works to French taste, and wrote *Guillaume Tell* (1829, William Tell). In 1836 he retired to Bologna and took charge of the Liceo, which he raised to a high position in the world of music. The revolutionary disturbances in 1847 drove him to Florence, and he returned in 1855 to Paris, where he died. His overtures in particular have continued to be highly popular items in concert programmes.

Rosslare, Gaelic **Ros Láir** [ros**lair**] 52°17N 6°23W, pop (1980e) 600. Port town in Wexford county, Leinster, SE Irish Republic; on St George's Channel, 8 km/5 ml SE of Wexford; ferry links with Fishguard and Milford Haven. » Wexford

Rostand, Edmond [rostã] (1868–1918) French poet and dramatist, born in Marseilles. After some early poetry, he achieved international fame with *Cyrano de Bergerac* (1897), the story of the nobleman with the enormous nose. This was followed by several other verse-plays, such as *L'Aiglon* (1900, The Eaglet) and *Chantecler* (1910). He died in Paris. » drama; French literature

Rostock or **Rostock-Warnemünde** 54°04N 12°09E, pop (1981) 236 011. Industrial port and capital of Rostock county, N Germany; at the mouth of R Warnow, on the Baltic Sea; founded, 12th-c; former Hanseatic League port; badly bombed in World War 2, rebuilt in the 1950s; chief cargo port of former East Germany; railway; rail ferry to Denmark; university (1419); shipyard, marine engineering, fish processing, electronics, navigation museum, 15th-c town hall. » Germany [i]; Hanseatic League

Rostov-na-Donu [ruh**stof** na duh**noo**], Eng **Rostov-on-Don** 47°15N 39°45E, pop (1989) 1 020 000. Port capital of Rostovskaya oblast, SE European Russia; on R Don, 46 km/29 ml from its entrance into the Sea of Azov; major grain-exporting centre in the 19th-c; access to the Volga–Don canal; airport; railway; university (1917); farm machinery, machine tools, aircraft, shipbuilding, clothing, leather, foodstuffs, wine. » Russia

Rostropovich, Mstislav (Leopoldovich) [rostruh**poh**vich] (1927–) Russian cellist and conductor, born at Baku. He studied at the Moscow Conservatory (1943–8), where he later became professor of cello (1956). In 1975, while in the USA, he and his wife decided not to return to the USSR; he then became musical director and conductor of the National Symphony Orchestra, Washington (1977). He formed a close friendship with Benjamin Britten, who wrote several cello works for him. He was made an honorary Knight Commander of the British Empire in 1987. » Britten; cello

Rota [**roh**ta] pop (1980) 1 261; area 85 sq km/33 sq ml. One of the three major islands in the N Mariana Is, W Pacific, 51 km/32 ml NE of Guam; length, 18 km/11 ml; airport; sugar cane, sugar refining; site of ancient stone columns. » Mariana Islands

Rotary International » service club

rotation » crop rotation

Roth, Henry (1906–) US novelist, born of Jewish parents in Tymenica, Austria-Hungary, and taken to New York City in 1907. He was educated at the City College there, and worked as a precision metal grinder in New York and Boston. Since 1946 he has lived in Maine and New Mexico. His only novel is *Call It Sleep* (1934), a classic treatment of Jewish immigrant life and childhood. » American literature; novel

Roth, Philip (1933–) US novelist, born at Newark, New Jersey, and educated at the University of Chicago. *Goodbye, Columbus* (1955) was a collection of short stories; *Letting Go* (1962) a novel about young Jewish intellectuals in various American locations. *Portnoy's Complaint* (1969) retains the background of contemporary American Jewish life for a story of its hero's failure in human relationships, emblematized in a compulsive desire to masturbate (the complaint of the title). Later novels record the history of a central character Nathan Zuckerman, from *My Life as a Man* (1974) to *The Anatomy Lesson* (1983). » American literature; novel

Rotherham [**roth**uhruhm] 53°26N 1°20W, pop (1981) 123 312. Town in Rotherham borough, South Yorkshire, N England; on the R Don, 9 km/5 ml NE of Sheffield; railway; coal, iron, steel, machinery, brassware, glass; late Gothic All Saints Church, Chantry Chapel of Our Lady (1383). » Yorkshire, South

Rothermere, Viscount » Harmsworth, Harold Sydney

Rothko, Mark (1903–70) US painter, born in Russia. He emigrated as a child and studied at Yale. During the 1940s he was influenced by Surrealism, but by the early 1950s he had evolved his own distinctive form of Abstract Expressionism, staining huge canvases with rectangular blocks of pure colour, creating a peaceful, meditative art very different from the busy patterns of Jackson Pollock and others. » abstract art; action painting; Pollock; Surrealism

Rothschild, Meyer Amschel [Ger **roht**shilt, Eng **roths**chiyld] (1743–1812) German financier, named from the 'Red Shield' signboard of his father's house, born and died in Frankfurt. He began as a moneylender, and became the financial adviser of the Landgrave of Hesse. The house transmitted money from the English government to Wellington in Spain, paid the British subsidies to Continental princes, and negotiated loans for Denmark (1804–12). His five sons continued the firm, establishing branches in other countries, and negotiated many of the great government loans of the 19th-c. » Napoleonic Wars

rotifer [**roh**tifer] A microscopic aquatic animal with an unsegmented body typically covered by a horny layer which may be thickened into plates; lacks a muscular body wall; swims by means of a ring of beating hair-like structures (cilia) that resembles a spinning wheel; contains c.1 800 species; also known as **wheel animalcules**. (Phylum: *Rotifera*.) » wheel animalcule

Rotorua [rohtoh**rooa**] 38°07S 176°17E, pop (1981) 48 314. Health resort in North Island, New Zealand; in a region of thermal springs, geysers, and boiling mud; Whakarewarewa (Maori village); Maori arts and crafts centre. » Maoris; New Zealand [i]

rotten borough The name given to British parliamentary boroughs before the Great Reform Act of 1832, which had few voters, had lost its original economic function, and was usually controlled by a landowner or by the Crown. Elections were rarely, if ever, contested. Examples were Gatton, Dunwich, and Old Sarum. Most rotten boroughs were disfranchised by the Reform Act of 1832. » Reform Acts

Rotterdam 51°55N 4°30E, pop (1984e) 1 025 466. Industrial city and chief port of the Netherlands, in South Holland province, W Netherlands; at the junction of the R Rotte with the Nieuwe Maas, 24 km/15 ml from the North Sea; major commercial centre of NW Europe since the 14th-c; Europort harbour area inaugurated, 1966; approach channel deepened in 1984; city centre almost completely destroyed by German bombing, 1940; railway; underground; university (1973); shipbuilding (largest shipyard in Europe), ship repairing, machinery, rolling stock, bicycles, engineering, oil refining, petrochemicals (largest plant on the Continent of Europe), foodstuffs, electronics, computers, clothing; birthplace of Erasmus; restored Groote Kerk, several museums; philharmonic orchestra. » Erasmus; Netherlands, The [i]

rottweiler [**rot**viyler] A German breed of dog, developed around the Alpine town of Rottweil to protect and herd cattle; agile, with heavy muscular body and neck; powerful muzzle and short soft ears; short black and tan coat; tail docked short; popular guard dogs; attracted adverse publicity in the late 1980s, following reports of several fatal attacks on children. » dog

Rouault, Georges (Henri) [**roo**oh] (1871–1958) French painter and engraver, born and died in Paris. He was apprenticed to a stained-glass designer in 1885, and retained that art's glowing colours, outlined with black, in his paintings of clowns, prostitutes, and Biblical characters. He joined the Fauves c.1904, and held his first one-man show in 1910. During the two World Wars he worked on a series of religious engravings, and also designed ballet sets and tapestries. » engraving; Fauvism; French art

Roubaix [roo**bay**] 50°42N 3°10E, pop (1982) 101 886. Industrial and commercial town in Nord department, NW France; on the Belgian border, 11 km/7 ml NE of Lille; chartered in 1469; centre of N France textile industry; textile machinery, clothing, carpets, plastics, rubber products; 15th-c Gothic Church of St-Martin.

Roubillac or **Roubiliac, Louis François** [**roo**beeyak] (1702 or 1705–62) French sculptor, born in Lyons. He studied in Paris, and c.1730 settled in London. His statue of Handel for Vauxhall Gardens (1738) first made him popular, and he completed statues of Newton, at Cambridge (1755), Shakespeare (1758, British Museum), and others. He died in London. » sculpture

Rouen, ancient **Rotomagus** [rooã] 49°27N 1°04E, pop (1982) 105 083. River port and capital of Seine-Maritime department, NW France; on right bank of R Seine, 86 km/53 ml NW of Paris; fifth largest port in France; former capital of Upper Normandy; scene of trial and burning of Joan of Arc, 1431; badly damaged in World War 2, but reconstructed largely as a Ville Musée (museum town); road and rail junction; university (1967); cotton, paper, petrochemicals, electronics, lubricants; birthplace of Flaubert; restored 13th–16th-c Gothic Cathedral of Notre-Dame; 14th-c Abbey Church of St-Ouen; Palais de Justice; Gros Horloge (clock tower). » Flaubert; Gothic architecture; Joan of Arc

Rouget de Lisle, Claude Joseph [roozhay duh **leel**] (1760–1836) French army officer, born at Lons-le-Saunier, and died at Choisy-le-Roi. He wrote and composed the *Marseillaise* when stationed in 1792 as captain of engineers at Strasbourg. Its original name was *Chant de guerre de l'armée du Rhin* (War Song of the Rhine Army), but it became known in Paris when it was sung by volunteers from Marseilles during the French Revolution.

Rough Riders The nickname for the First US Volunteer Cavalry Regiment, commanded during the Spanish-American War (1898) by Colonel Leonard Wood (1860–1927) and Lieutenant-Colonel Theodore Roosevelt. The Rough Riders' 'charge' up San Juan Hill in Cuba (1 Jul 1898) was actually carried out on foot. » Roosevelt, Theodore; Spanish-American War

roulette A casino game played with a spinning wheel and ball. The wheel is divided into 37 segments numbered 0–36, but not in numerical order (some wheels have a 38th segment numbered 00). All numbers are alternately either red or black except the 0. Punters bet, before the spin of the wheel, on the landing place of the ball after the wheel has stopped spinning. Bets take various forms. They can be on a single number, any two numbers, three numbers, and so on. Bets can also be placed as to whether the winning number will be odd or even, or red or black. » casino

Roumania » **Romania** [i]

rouncy » **cob**

round worm infestation A condition in which round worms (*nematodes*) live within the body of their hosts, many without causing disease. In humans the most common disease-inducing worms include (1) those that inhabit the intestine, such as ascaris, threadworms, whipworms, strongylodes, and hook worms, the commonest cause of anaemia in the tropics; (2) worms such as filaria that dwell in human tissues and are conveyed to humans by insect bites, producing such diseases as Bancroftian filariasis and river blindness; and (3) worms that cause disease in animals and are occasionally passed to humans, such as *Toxocara canis*, a common worm in dogs, which may affect children in close contact with affected puppies. » filariasis; hookworm infestation; nematode; river blindness; toxocariasis

rounders An outdoor bat-and-ball game from which baseball probably derived. Very popular in England, the first reference to rounders was in 1744. Each team consists of nine players, and the object, after hitting the ball, is to run around the outside of three posts before reaching the fourth and thus score a rounder. » baseball [i]

Roundheads » **Cavaliers**

roundworm » **nematode**

roup [roop] The name used for several diseases of poultry; one is characterized by swellings under the tail; another by the production of pus from the nostrils.

Rous, (Francis) Peyton [rows] (1879–1970) US pathologist, born in Baltimore, Maryland. He studied medicine at Johns Hopkins, then worked at the Rockefeller Institute, New York, to the age of 90, studying cancer. He devised culture methods for viruses and for cancerous cells; the **Rous chicken sarcoma**, which he discovered in 1911, remains the best-known example (as well as the first) of a cancer-producing virus. In 1966 he shared the Nobel Prize for Physiology or Medicine. He died in New York City. » cancer; virus

Rousseau, Henri [**roo**soh], byname **Le Douanier** (Fr 'The Customs Officer') (1844–1910) French primitive painter, born at Laval. He worked for many years as a minor customs official, hence his byname. Retiring in 1885, he spent his time painting and copying at the Louvre, and exhibited for several years at the Salon des Indépendants. He produced painstaking portraits, exotic imaginary landscapes, and dreams, such as 'Sleeping Gypsy' (1897, New York). He died in Paris. » French art; Salon

Rousseau, Jean Jacques [**roo**soh] (1712–78) French political philosopher, educationist, and essayist, born in Geneva, Switzerland. Largely self-taught, he carried on a variety of menial occupations, until after he moved to Paris in 1741, where he came to know Diderot and the *encyclopédistes*. In 1754 he wrote *Discours sur l'origine de l'inégalité parmi les hommes* (1755, Discourse on the Origin and Foundations of Inequality Amongst Men), emphasizing the natural goodness of human beings, and the corrupting influences of institutionalized life. He later moved to Luxembourg (1757), where he wrote his masterpiece, *Du contrat social* (1762, The Social Contract), a great influence on French revolutionary thought, introducing the slogan 'Liberty, Equality, Fraternity'. The same year he published his major work on education, *Emile*, in novel form, but its views on monarchy and governmental institutions forced him to flee to Swizerland, and then England, at the invitation of David Hume. There he wrote most of his *Confessions* (published posthumously, 1782). He returned to Paris in 1767, where he continued to write, but gradually became insane. He died at Ermenonville. » Diderot; Hume, David; French Revolution [i]

Rousseau, (Pierre Etienne) Théodore [**roo**soh] (1812–67) French landscape painter, born in Paris. He studied the old masters in the Louvre, and by 1833 had begun sketching in the Forest of Fontainebleau. During the 1840s he settled at Barbizon, where he worked with a group of other painters, and after 1849 his work became increasingly accepted. He died at Barbizon. » Barbizon School; French art

Routledge, George [**rut**lij] (1812–88) British publisher, born at Brampton, Cumberland. He went to London in 1833, and started up as a bookseller (1836) and publisher (1843), later taking his two brothers-in-law, W H and Frederick Warne, into partnership. He died in London.

Roux, (Pierre Paul) Emile [roo] (1853–1933) French bacteriologist, born at Confolens. He studied at Clermont-Ferrand, became assistant to Pasteur, and was appointed his successor (1905–18). In 1894 he helped to discover diphtheria antitoxin, and also worked on rabies and anthrax. He died in Paris. » diphtheria; Pasteur

Rovaniemi [rovan**yay**mee] 66°29N 25°40E, pop (1982) 31 363. Capital city of Lappi province, Finland; 160 km/99 ml N of Oulu, just S of the Arctic Circle; established, 1929; airfield; railway; river access to the Baltic; centre for timber trade; largely destroyed by fire (1944–5), and rebuilt by Alvar Aalto, who laid out the main streets in the design of a reindeer's antlers. » Aalto; Lapland

rove beetle An elongate, dark- or metallic-coloured beetle, usually with short, truncated wing cases; most are predators on other insects, some feed on fungal spores; common in leaf litter and damp habitats. (Order: *Coleoptera*. Family: *Staphylinidae*, c.30 000 species.) » beetle; devil's coach horse

rovings Loose assemblages of fibres produced at intermediate stages of the conversion of slivers (the untwisted strands produced by a combing machine) into yarns. Modern spinning methods often convert slivers directly into yarns. » combing; yarn

Rovno [**rov**nuh], Polish **Rowne**, Ger **Rowno** 50°39N 26°10E, pop (1983) 205 000. Capital city of Rovenskaya oblast, Ukraine, on R Uste; formerly in Poland; railway; machinery, metalwork, chemicals, flax, clothing; wooden Church of the Assumption (1756). » Ukraine

rowan A slender deciduous tree, growing to 20 m/65 ft, native to Europe; leaves pinnate with 5–8 pairs of toothed leaflets; flowers creamy, in large clusters; berries red, rarely yellow; also called **mountain ash**. It is often planted as a street or garden tree, together with several pink- or white-flowered species from Asia. (*Sorbus aucuparia*. Family: *Rosaceae*.) » deciduous plants; pinnate; tree [i]

Rowe, Nicholas [roh] (1674–1718) English poet and dramatist, born at Little Barford, Bedfordshire. Educated at Westminster, he became a lawyer, but from 1692 devoted himself to literature. Three of his plays became very popular: *Tamerlane* (1702), *The Fair Penitent* (1703), and *Jane Shore* (1714). The name of his character Lothario (in *The Fair Penitent*) is still used to describe a fashionable rake. He was the first to publish a critical edition of Shakespeare (1709–10). In 1715 he was appointed poet laureate and a surveyor of customs in London, where he died. » drama; English literature; poetry; Shakespeare [i]

rowing A sport or pastime in which a boat is propelled by oars as opposed to mechanical means. If there is only one rower with two oars it is known as *sculling*. Rowing involves two or more people, each rower having one oar. The sport dates from ancient times, but as an organized sport it can be traced to 1715, when the first rowing of the Doggetts Coat and Badge race took place on the R Thames. Famous races include the Oxford-Cambridge Boat Race, and the Diamond Sculls and Grand Challenge Cup, both contested at the Henley Royal Regatta each year. » Boat Race; Henley Royal Regatta; RR117

Rowlandson, Thomas (1756–1827) British caricaturist, born in London. He studied in London and Paris, then travelled widely in Britain, and became a specialist in humorous water-colours commenting on the social scene. Some of his best-known works are his illustrations to the 'Dr Syntax' series (1812–21), and 'The English Dance of Death' (1815–16). He died in London. » caricature; English art; watercolour

Rowley, Thomas [**roh**lee] » **Chatterton, Thomas**

Royal Academy of Arts A British academy founded in 1768 under royal patronage, with the aim of holding annual exhibitions (which are still held) to raise the status of artists, and to foster the development of a national school of history painting to rival the great schools of the continent. The Academy's first president was Sir Joshua Reynolds. Its premises are at Burlington House, London. » English art; Reynolds, Joshua

Royal Academy of Music A London conservatory founded in 1822, opened in 1823, and granted its royal charter in 1830. It moved to its present location in Marylebone in 1912. » conservatory

Royal Air Force (RAF) Britain's air force, established 1 April 1918, combining the existing forces of the Royal Flying Corps and the Royal Naval Air Service. Vital to Britain's survival in two World Wars, today the RAF comprises three Commands: Strike, Support, and RAF Germany, operating over 1 800 aircraft of which more than 500 are combat types. Responsibility for operating Britain's nuclear deterrent was transferred from the RAF's bomber squadrons to the Royal Navy's Polaris submarine force in 1969. » air force; Britain, Battle of; submarine

Royal and Ancient Golf Club of St Andrews (R & A) The ruling body of the game of golf in the eyes of most countries (the USA being a notable exception). Golf was played at St Andrews in the 16th-c, and the R & A was formed on 14 May 1754 when 22 noblemen formed themselves into the Society of St Andrews golfers. In 1834 the club adopted its present name. » golf

royal antelope A dwarf antelope native to W Africa; the smallest known antelope (shoulder height, 250 mm/10 in – so small that local people call it *king of the hares*, hence *royal*); reddish-brown; male with very short horns; female without horns; nocturnal. (*Neotragus pygmaeus*.) » antelope

royal assent A legal stage through which a bill has to pass in the UK before it becomes law. Because the legislature in the UK is the monarch-in-parliament, after a bill has passed through both Houses of Parliament, the monarch's assent is required in order that it may become law. This approval is a formality; it has never been withheld in modern times. » legislature; parliament

Royal Australian Air Force (RAAF) Australia's air force, established in 1921, formed from the wartime Australian Flying Corps. Poorly equipped with donated British government aircraft, it was under threat of being divided between the army and the navy until 1932. Its strength in the mid-1920s was 1 200 men and 128 aircraft, but in the late 1930s it was expanded and improved; by the mid-1980s, it had 22 000 personnel. The RAAF saw service in all theatres of World War 2. » air force

Royal Australian Navy (RAN) Australia's Navy, established in 1911, formed from the naval forces of the Australian colonies at Federation (1901). Based on the British Royal Navy, it had an early success in 1914 in sinking the German raider *Emden*, and saw action in the Atlantic, Mediterranean, and the Pacific. In the inter-war years, it was greatly reduced in size: by 1939, it had only 5 440 personnel; but by 1945 this figure had increased to 42 600. After the war, the RAN was reorganized around two aircraft carriers, but its Fleet Air Arm was disbanded. It saw action in E Asia and off Vietnam. By the mid-1980s it had 54 vessels and 17 000 personnel. » navy

Royal Ballet Britain's national ballet company, the inspiration of Dame Ninette de Valois. It gave its first performances in 1931, became Sadler's Wells Ballet and, in 1936, the Royal Ballet. De Valois also created a school (the Royal Ballet School), established a theatre base (Sadler's Wells, now Covent Garden) and a style of ballet based on the Russian training but adapted for British purposes. Its famous dancers have included Margot Fonteyn, Alicia Markova, and Anthony Dowell (now director of the company). » ballet; Valois, Ninette de

Royal British Legion An organization for all ex-servicemen and women, and serving members of HM Forces. Formed in 1921 as the British Legion, it was granted the Royal prefix in 1971. Its aim is to provide social and welfare services for its members and to perpetuate the memory of those who died in the service of their country; it provides poppies from its own factory for the Remembrance (or Poppy Day) Appeal each November. » American Legion; Remembrance Day

Royal College of Music A London conservatory founded by royal charter in 1883 and opened that year. It moved to its present location in Prince Consort Road in 1894. » conservatory

royal fern A perennial fern with thick rhizomes forming large clumps, native to wet or boggy places throughout temperate regions; fronds to 3 m/10 ft, bi-pinnate; fertile fronds with small upper leaflets bearing numerous brown sporangia. (*Osmunda regalis*. Family: *Osmundaceae*.) » fern; perennial; pinnate; rhizome; sporangium

royal garden parties In the UK, four summer gatherings held by the Queen, three in July in the grounds of Buckingham Palace, and the other a little later at Holyrood House, Scotland. Up to 10 000 people are invited to each party, to which formal or national dress must be worn.

Royal Greenwich Observatory The best-known observatory in the world, founded by Charles II of England in 1675 to improve navigation and time-keeping, and responsible for the operation of telescopes at the Roque de los Muchachos Observatory, Canary Is. Its role in the preparation of calendars, the Nautical Almanac, Astronomical Ephemeris, and time-keeping was of major importance until the mid-20th-c. Its transit circle has been used since 1851 for the accurate measurement of time; and the International Meridian Conference at Washington in 1884 agreed to take the axis of this telescope as the prime meridian of longitude. Its scientific activities moved in 1948 to Herstmonceux, Sussex, and the Old Greenwich Observatory is now a museum and planetarium. Its headquarters moved to Cambridge in 1990. » Greenwich Mean Time; observatory [i]

Royal Horticultural Society A society founded in the UK in 1804 'for the improvement of horticulture'; it received its royal charter in 1809. An experimental garden is maintained at Wisley, Surrey; shows and competitions, most notably the Chelsea Flower Show, are held annually. » horticulture

royal household In the UK, the collective term for those departments which serve members of the royal family in matters of day-to-day administration. In mediaeval times no distinction existed between the sovereign's ministers and personal servants; a survival of this earlier fusion of posts is to be found today in the titles of government Whips, such as Treasurer of the Household and Comptroller of the Household. » civil list

Royal Institution In the UK, a learned scientific society founded in 1799 by the physicist, Count Rumford. Its laboratories became Britain's first research centre, used in the 19th-c by Sir Humphry Davy and Michael Faraday. Lectures are still given at its headquarters in Albemarle Street, London, notably the Christmas lectures for young people. » Rumford, Benjamin Thompson

royal jelly A secretion produced by worker bees, fed to all bee larvae until the third day after hatching, and fed throughout larval development to those bees destined to become queens. It is a complex mixture of chemicals, claimed to have rejuvenating properties when used in cosmetics. » bee; larva

Royal Marines (RM) Britain's Marine force, which can trace its origin to the Lord High Admiral's Regiment first raised in 1664. The title *Royal Marines* was conferred in 1800. The first RM Commando units were raised in 1942. » Marines

Royal Mint The British government department responsible for manufacturing metal coins. The London mint probably dates from AD 825, and since the mid-16th-c it has enjoyed a legal monopoly of coinage. It is now situated in Llantrisant, S Wales.

Royal National Lifeboat Institution (RNLI) In the UK, a rescue organization manned by volunteers and financed by voluntary contributions, founded by Sir William Hillery (1771–1847) in 1824 as the Royal National Institution for the Preservation of Life from Shipwreck. The modern RNLI operates over 200 lifeboat stations and maintains over 250 active vessels. The offshore boats are powerful self-righting craft, carrying advanced safety equipment. » lifeboat

Royal Navy (RN) The naval branch of the British armed forces. A national English Navy is as old as Saxon times, but the Royal Navy as such originates in the time of Henry VIII, when a Navy Board and the title of Lord High Admiral were established. The primary instrument of British imperial expansion in the 18th-c and 19th-c, it reached the peak of its global power at the end of World War 2, when it had more than 500 warships. A fraction of that size today, the RN has been responsible for the operation of Britain's nuclear deterrent since 1969. » navy; nuclear weapons; warships [i]

Royal Observatory, Edinburgh An observatory at Edinburgh, Scotland, UK, founded in 1822. A pioneer of new techniques in astronomy, it is responsible for operating the UK telescopes at the Mauna Kea Observatory. » Mauna Kea Observatory; observatory [i]; telescope [i]

Royal Opera House The home of the Royal Ballet and the Royal Opera in Bow Street, London. Three successive buildings have occupied the site since the Theatre Royal opened there in 1732. The present building, by Edward Middleton Barry (1830–80), opened in 1858. » ballet; Covent Garden; opera

royal prerogative The set of powers, most of which are ill-defined, remaining within the preserve of the British monarch. These include the power to declare war, make treaties, appoint judges, pardon criminals and, most significantly, dissolve Parliament. In practice all these powers are taken on the advice of, and in effect made by, the Prime Minister and other government ministers. » monarchy

Royal Shakespeare Company An English theatre company based in Stratford-upon-Avon and London which has as a primary objective the regular production of Shakespeare's plays. It was developed out of the Shakespeare Memorial Theatre by Peter Hall between 1960 and 1968. Under his leadership and then that of Trevor Nunn, a major international reputation was established by the early 1970s. » Hall, Peter; theatre

Royal Society (RS) In the UK, a prestigious scientific institution – the oldest in the world to have enjoyed continuous existence. The inaugural meeting was held in Gresham College, London in 1666; Isaac Newton was its president 1703–27. » Newton, Isaac

Royal Society for Nature Conservation A British conservation society which co-ordinates the work of county naturalist trusts and urban wildlife groups. It was founded in 1912 as the Society for the Promotion of Nature Reserves. Together, the Society and naturalist trusts own or manage over 1 680 reserves (1987). » conservation (earth sciences); Nature Reserve

Royal Society for the Prevention of Cruelty to Animals » **RSPCA**

Royal Society for the Protection of Birds » **RSPB**

Royal Victorian Order (RVO) An order of knighthood instituted in 1896 by Queen Victoria, designed to reward distinguished service to the sovereign. There are five classes: Knights and Dames Grand Cross (GCVO), Knights and Dames Commanders (KCVO/DCVO), Commanders (CVO), Lieutenants (LVO), and Members (MVO). The motto is 'Victoria' and the ribbon blue with red and white edges. » decoration

Royce, Sir (Frederick) Henry (1863–1933) British engineer, born at Alwalton, Huntingdonshire. He began as a railway apprentice, but became interested in electricity and motor engineering, founding in Manchester (1884) the firm of Royce, Ltd. He made his first car in 1904, and his meeting with C S Rolls in that year led to the formation (1906) of Rolls-Royce, Ltd. He was created a baronet in 1930, and died at West Wittering, Sussex. » car [i]; jet engine [i]; Rolls

Rozeanu, Angelica [rozee**ah**noo], *née* **Adelstein** (1921–) Romanian table tennis player. She won 12 world titles between 1950 and 1956, including the singles title a record six times (1950–5), and was a member of the Romanian Corbillon Cup winning team (1950–1, 1953, 1955–6). She was made a Master of Sport, and appointed to the Romanian Olympic Commission. Upon her retirement in 1960, she emigrated to Israel. » table tennis

RR Lyrae variable A type of variable star in which the period of variation is rather precisely dependent on the luminosity of the star. This gives a key to finding the distance scale of the universe, because the observed period of an RR Lyrae of unknown distance indicates the absolute luminosity; by comparing this to the observed magnitude, the distance is inferred. » luminosity; magnitude; variable star

RSPB In the UK, an acronym for the **Royal Society for the Protection of Birds**, a society originally formed to protest against the killing of birds for their plumage. It is now one of the major conservation bodies, owning over 100 nature reserves. » bird [i]

RSPCA In the UK, an acronym for the **Royal Society for the Prevention of Cruelty to Animals**, the main animal welfare society, founded in 1824, supported by voluntary contributions. Its 230 inspectors investigate complaints, and where necessary institute legal proceedings. In the USA there are several animal societies. The oldest is the American Society for the Prevention of Cruelty to Animals (1866), but the Animal Protection Society of America (1968) has larger membership.

Ruapehu, Mount [rooa**pay**hoo] 39°18S 175°40E. Active volcano and highest peak on North Island, New Zealand; rises to 2 797 m/9 176 ft in Tongariro National Park; last eruption, 1945–6. » New Zealand [i]

rubber A resilient, elastic substance obtained from a variety of unrelated, latex-producing, tropical trees. These include **Ceará rubber** (*Manihot glaziovii*), **Panama rubber** (*Castilla elastica*), and indiarubber (*Ficus elastica*), but easily the most important source is **Parà rubber** (*Hevea braziliensis*), an evergreen tree native to Brazil. Raw rubber, or **caoutchouc**, is obtained from the milky latex exuded by the trees as a response to injury; exactly why they produce latex is not known. The latex is collected by making a series of spiral cuts halfway around the circumference of the trunk, severing the lactifers which run just beneath the bark, and allowing the fluid to flow down the cuts and collect in cups. The cuts heal quickly, and must be re-opened every day or so, these later cuts often yielding a greater quantity of latex than the initial ones. Alternatively, the cuts can be treated with a chemical which inhibits coagulation, prolonging the flow. A tree can yield 280 g/10 oz of latex before the flow stops. The tapping process begins when the trees are 5–7 years old, and continues throughout their lives (up to 30 years), with periodic breaks to allow the trees to recover. The alkaline latex is congealed using acid, pressed, and sometimes smoked, before undergoing various industrial treatments and manufacture into final products.

Initially, para rubber was collected solely from wild trees in Brazil, but from c.1900 they were introduced as plantation trees to other tropical countries, notably Malaysia, which has become the world's largest producer. *Synthetic rubbers*, made by the polymerization of isoprene or substituted butadienes, exceed natural rubber in the quantity used. *Styrene butadiene rubber* (SBR), containing c.25% styrene and 75% butadiene, is one of the most important forms in current use. » evergreen plants; indiarubber tree; isoprene [i]; latex; polymerization; tree [i]; vulcanization

rubber plant/tree » **indiarubber tree; rubber**

Rubbra, Edmund (1901–86) British composer, born in Northampton. He studied at Reading and London, and developed an interest in the polyphonic music of the 16th–17th-c. He wrote eleven symphonies, chamber, choral and orchestral music, songs, and solo instrumental works. He taught at Oxford (1947–68), and became professor of composition at the Guildhall School of Music (1961–74). He died at Chalfont St Peter, Buckinghamshire. » polyphony

rubella » **German measles**

Rubénisme A movement in French painting in the late 17th-c. There was a famous quarrel in the French Academy about which was more important – colour or design. The design party appealed to the example of Poussin (and were called *Poussinistes*); the colourists (who won) referred to Rubens. Among artists themselves, the greatest Rubéniste was Watteau. » French art; Rococo; Watteau

Rubens, (Peter Paul) [**roo**bnz] (1577–1640) Flemish painter, born at Siegen, Westphalia. Educated at Antwerp, he was intended for the law, but began to study art, travelling to Venice in 1600. He entered the service of the Duke of Mantua, and in 1605 was sent to Spain as a diplomat. There he executed many portraits and works on historical subjects. He then travelled in Italy, producing work much influenced by the Italian Renaissance, and in 1608 settled in Antwerp, becoming court painter to the Archduke Albert. His triptych 'Descent from the Cross' (1611–14) in Antwerp Cathedral is one of his early masterpieces. He became a prolific and renowned painter, and in 1622 was invited to France by Marie de Médicis, for whom he painted 21 large subjects on her life and regency (Louvre). In 1628 he was sent on a diplomatic mission to Philip IV of Spain, and there executed some 40 works. The following year he became envoy to Charles I of England, where his paintings included 'Peace and War' (National Gallery, London). He was knighted by both Charles I and Philip IV. In 1630 he retired to Steen, where he engaged in landscape painting, and died in Antwerp. » Baroque (art and architecture); Charles I (of England); Flemish art; Marie de Médicis; Renaissance

rubidium-strontium dating A method of radiometric dating for rocks more than 10 million years old. It uses the fact that the radioactive isotope ^{87}Rb decays with a known half-life to yield ^{87}Sr, and hence the amount of each isotope in a rock or mineral can be used to determine its age. » radiometric dating

Rubik's Cube A mathematical puzzle named after its inventor, Hungarian architect Ernó Rubik (1944–). A coloured cube is divided into nine other cubes, each of which will pivot. There are millions of combinations, but only one possible way of getting all six sides to form a different colour. Patented in 1975, it became a world craze in the late 1970s.

Rubinstein, Artur [**roo**binstiyn] (1887–1982) US pianist, born in Łódź, Poland. At the age of 12 he appeared in Berlin, and after further study began his career as a virtuoso, appearing in Paris, London, and the USA (1905–6). After World War 2 he lived in the USA, making frequent extensive concert tours. He died in Geneva. » piano

Rublyov or **Rublev** (c.1360–c.1430) Russian painter, a monk in the monasteries at Troitsky-Sergieva and at Andronnikov. He painted icons in the Cathedral of the Annunciation in the Kremlin, Moscow, and also murals, such as in the Cathedral of the Dormition at Vladimir and at Moscow. His icon of the Trinity represented as three angels (Tretyakov Gallery, Moscow) is considered his masterpiece. » icon (art/religion); Russian art

ruby A gem variety of corundum, coloured deep crimson to pale red by the presence of minor impurities of chromium. The best specimens come from Burma, Sri Lanka, and Thailand. » chromium; corundum; Plate V

rudbeckia A biennial or perennial, native to N America; large flower heads, characterized by the conspicuous conical receptacle in the centre, giving rise to the alternative name of **coneflower**; outer ray florets red, yellow, or orange. It is often grown as an ornamental. (Genus: *Rudbeckia*, 15 species. Family: *Compositae*.) » biennial; perennial; receptacle

rudd Freshwater fish widespread in European rivers and lakes, ranging E to the Caspian region; length up to 40 cm/16 in; greenish brown on back, sides yellow, fins reddish; feeds on invertebrates as well as on some plant material; popular with anglers. (*Scardinius erythrophthalmus*. Family: *Cyprinidae*.)

Rudolf I (1218–91) German King (1273–91), the founder of the Habsburg sovereign and imperial dynasty, born at Schloss Limburg, Breisgau. He increased his possessions by inheritance and marriage until he was the most powerful prince in Swabia. Chosen King by the electors, he was recognized by the Pope in 1274. He died at Speyer. » Habsburgs

Rudolf, Lake » **Turkana, Lake**

rue A small aromatic evergreen shrub with acrid scent and taste, native to the Balkans; leaves bluish-green, divided into wedge-shaped, slightly rounded segments; flowers with 4–5 rather dirty yellow petals curved up at the tips. It is cultivated as a culinary and medicinal herb. (*Ruta graveolens*. Family: *Rutaceae*.) » evergreen plants; herb; shrub

ruff A sandpiper native to Europe, Asia, and Africa; inhabits open country near water; breeding male with naked face and large ruff of feathers around neck; males display communally. The name is sometimes used for the male, with the female called **reeve**. (*Philomachus pugnax*.) » sandpiper

Rugby (UK) 52°23N 1°15W, pop (1981) 59 720. Town in Rugby district, Warwickshire, C England; on R Avon, 17 km/10 ml E of Coventry; famous boys' public school (1567) where by tradition the game of rugby football originated; railway; engineering, cement, light industry. » Arnold, Thomas; Warwickshire

Rugby (USA) 48°24N 100°00W, pop (1980) 3 335. City in Pierce County, North Dakota, USA; the geographical centre of N America. » North America; North Dakota

rugby football A team ball game played with an oval ball on a rectangular playing area. Rugby developed from the kicking game of football in 1823, when William Webb Ellis of Rugby school picked up the ball and ran with it. The *Rugby Football Union* (RFU) was formed in 1871. When the RFU refused permission for players with northern teams to receive 'broken time' payments for time off work to play rugby, the breakaway Northern Union was formed in 1895; and this became known as the *Rugby League*. Today, Union is regarded as the amateur game and League the professional game. The principal difference between the two games is the number of players per side; 15 in Union, 13 in League. The object is the same in both games, to score a try by grounding the ball in the opposing scoring area behind the goal line. Points scoring in both codes (League in brackets) is as follows: try 4 (4), conversion 2 (2), penalty 3 (2), dropped goal 3 (1). » football [i]; RR117

Ruggles, Carl (1876–1971) US composer, born at Marion, Massachusetts. He studied at Harvard, and conducted an orchestra at Winona, Minnesota, before moving to New York City in 1917. His orchestral piece, *Sun Treader* (1931) became well known in the 1960s, but his other works have been little played outside the USA. Also a painter, he died at Bennington, Vermont.

Ruhr, River [roor] River in Germany; rises N of Winterberg; flows W to the R Rhine at Duisburg; length 213 km/132 ml; navigable length 41 km/25 ml (head of navigation at Witten); its valley is an important mining and industrial area, cities include Essen, Bochum, Duisburg, Gelsenkirchen, Dortmund. » Germany [i]

Ruisdael » **Ruysdael**

Ruiz, Nevado del [rooees] 4°53N 75°22W. Active Andean volcanic peak in WC Colombia; rises to 5 399 m/17 713 ft in the Cordillera Central; 32 km/20 ml SE of Manizales; thermal springs, NW; erupted in 1985, causing flood and mudslide, with loss of many lives. » Andes; Colombia [i]

rum A spirit distilled either from sugar cane, freshly crushed, or from the fermentation of molasses, a by-product of the West Indian sugar cane industry. The British navy gave rum a special status in alcoholic beverages by providing a tot to all serving sailors. It is drunk wherever sugar cane is grown, but the most notable varieties come from the West Indies. » molasses

Rum Rebellion An uprising in Sydney which deposed the governor of New South Wales, Captain William Bligh (1808). Led by John Macarthur, a former army officer, and Major George Johnston, the Rebellion occurred because of personal antagonisms, and Bligh's attempt to end the use of rum as a currency. Bligh returned to England but was not reinstated as governor; Johnston was court-martialled and dismissed from the army; and Macarthur, on going to Britain, was forbidden to return to Australia until 1817. » Bligh

Rumania » **Romania** [i]

rumba A dance of Cuban origin which became popular as a ballroom dance in the USA and Europe in the 1930s. Its distinctive rhythm, often played on maracas or bongos, is the *tresillo*, a bar of eight quavers/eighth-notes divided 3 + 3 + 2. » bongos; maracas

Rumford, Benjamin Thompson, Count (1753–1814) Anglo-American administrator and scientist, born at Woburn, Massachusetts. He married in 1771, and joined the army, but left his family and fled to England in 1776, possibly because he was politically suspect. After the peace he was knighted, and in 1784 entered the service of Bavaria, where he carried out military, social, and economic reforms, for which he was made head of the Bavarian war department and count of the Holy Roman Empire. Always an enthusiastic amateur scientist, he first showed the relation between heat and work, a concept fundamental to modern physics. In 1799 he returned to London, and founded the Royal Institution. In 1802 he moved to Paris, and died at Auteuil.

ruminant A mammal of suborder *Ruminantia*, comprising the **traguloids** (chevrotains) and **pecorans** (other deer, giraffes, and Bovidae), and suborder *Tylopoda* (the camel family); an artiodactyl; many-chambered stomach breaks down coarse plant material; camels and chevrotains have three chambers; pecorans have four – the *rumen* (or *paunch*), *reticulum* (or *honeycomb bag*), *omasum* (*manyplies*, or *psalterium*), and *abomasum* (or *reed*); swallows much food quickly, then moves to a place of safety where it regurgitates mouthfuls (*cud*) from the omasum, chews them thoroughly, then reswallows; also known as a **cud-chewer**. » artiodactyl; Bovidae; Camelidae; chevrotain; deer; giraffe; mammal [i]

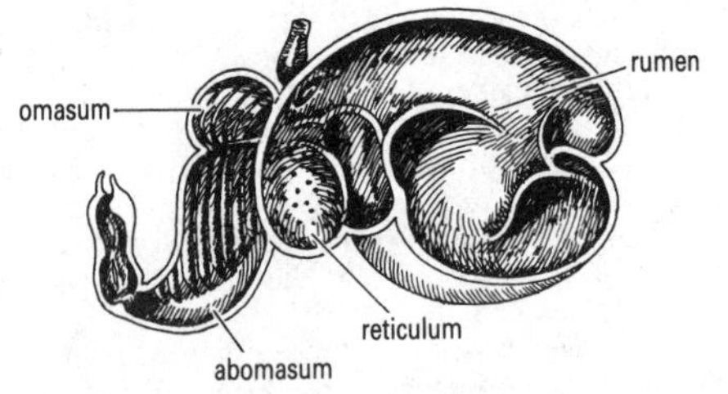

Ruminant – The four chambers of the pecoran stomach

rummy A popular domestic card game. Each player has seven cards, and the object is to form them into two hands, one of three cards and one of four (or one hand of seven) by taking and discarding cards from the pack. The hand obtained must be three (or four) cards of the same denomination, or a sequence of three (or four) cards of the same suit. Rummy is thought to have derived from *mah-jong*. A popular variation in the USA is **gin rummy**, whereby hands (of three or four) are laid face upwards and can be added to by any player during the game. Points are obtained for each card dropped according to its face value, and deducted according to which cards are left in the hand when one of the players wins the game by disposing of all his or her cards. » mah-jong; playing cards

Rump Parliament The members of the British Long Parliament who were left after Pride's Purge of conservative and moderate 'presbyterian' elements (Dec 1648). It numbered about 60, but by-elections brought it up to 125 by 1652. It abolished the monarchy and the House of Lords. When it fell out with the army, Cromwell dismissed it (Apr 1653). It was recalled in 1659 with the fall of the Protectorate, and dissolved itself in 1660. » Long Parliament; Pride, Thomas; Protectorate

Runcie, Robert (1921–) British Anglican churchman. He served in the Scots Guards during World War 2, was ordained in 1951, and was Bishop of St Albans for 10 years before becoming Archbishop of Canterbury (1980–91). He presided at the Lambeth Conference in 1987. » Church of England; Lambeth Conferences

Rundstedt, (Karl Rudolf) Gerd von [**runt**shtet] (1875–1953) German field marshal, born at Aschersleben. He served in World War 1, and in the early 1930s became military commander of Berlin. In 1939 he directed the attacks on Poland and France. Checked in the Ukraine in 1941, he was relieved of his command, but in 1942 was given a new command in France. He was recalled after the success of the 1944 Allied invasion, but returned to direct the Ardennes offensive. War crimes proceedings against him were dropped on the grounds of his ill health. He died at Hanover, Germany. » World War 2

Runeberg, Johan Ludvig [**roo**nuhberg] (1804–77) Finnish poet, writing in Swedish, born at Jakobstad. His first poems appeared in 1830, and he became known for his epic poems, notably *Elgskyttarne* (1832, The Moose Hunters) and *Hanna* (1836). His major work is the verse romance based on Scandinavian legend, *King Fjala* (1844). One of his poems became Finland's national anthem. He died at Borgå· » poetry; Swedish literature

runes The letters of the earliest Teutonic alphabet; widely known as the *futhark*, from the names of its first six symbols (*f*, *u*, *th*, *a*, *r*, *k*). Used mainly by the Scandinavians and the Anglo-Saxons, it comprised 24 basic symbols, though there was considerable regional variation both in the overall number of symbols and the symbol shapes used. Runes are preserved in c.4 000 inscriptions and a few manuscripts, dating from the 3rd-c AD. Their derivation is uncertain, but the letters show some resemblance to the Roman alphabet, and they may have developed through

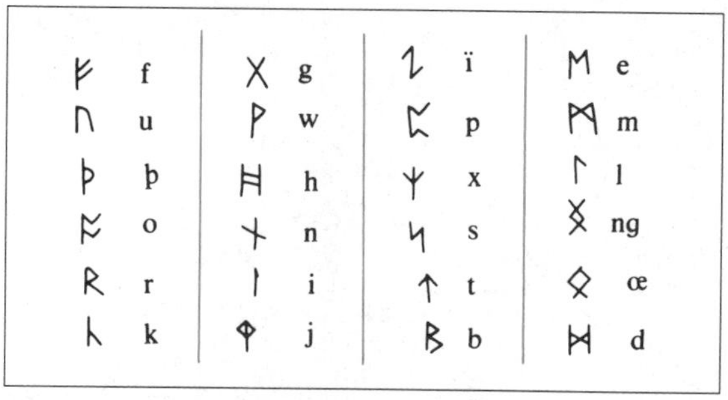

A version of the runic alphabet found in Britain

the need to adapt the Roman characters to the style of carving prevalent in N Europe at the time. » alphabet [i]; Anglo-Saxons; graphology

runner In botany, a lateral shoot which grows along the ground, rooting at the tip or at the nodes to form new plants. Typical of rosette plants, runners are often markedly different from the normal shoots. » stem; stolon

runner bean A twining perennial growing to 5 m/16 ft, native to tropical America; leaves with three broadly oval leaflets; pea-flowers scarlet or less commonly white, in stalked clusters from the leaf axils; pods up to 40 cm/15 in long, rough, containing large red, kidney-shaped seeds, veined like marble, purple-black. It is a common garden vegetable, widely cultivated for the edible young pods. Dwarf, non-climbing varieties are also grown. (*Phaseolus coccineus*. Family: *Leguminosae*.) » perennial; vegetable

Runnymede A meadow on the S bank of the R Thames, Surrey, SE England; 7 km/4 ml SE of Windsor, near Egham; here, or on Magna Carta Island in the river, King John signed the Magna Carta (1215); Commonwealth Air Forces war memorial (1953), Kennedy memorial; owned by the National Trust since 1931. » Magna Carta; Surrey

Runyon, (Alfred) Damon (1884–1946) US author, born at Manhattan, Kansas. After service in the Spanish-American War (1898), he became a journalist, then turned to poetry. He is best known for his short stories about underworld New York life. His collection *Guys and Dolls* (1932) was adapted for a musical revue (1950). From 1941 he worked as a film producer, and died in New York City. » American literature; poetry; short story

Rupert, Prince, byname **Rupert of the Rhine** (1619–82) Royalist commander in the English Civil War, born in Prague, the third son of the Elector Palatine Frederick V and Elizabeth, daughter of James I of England. A notable cavalry leader, he won several victories in the major battles of the war, but was defeated at Marston Moor (1644), and after his surrender of Bristol, was dismissed by Charles I. Banished by Parliament, he led the small Royalist fleet until it was routed by Blake (1650). He escaped to the West Indies, returning to Europe in 1653, and living in Germany until the Restoration. He died in London. » Blake, Robert; Charles I (of England); English Civil War

rupture » **hernia**

rush A densely tufted annual or evergreen perennial; cosmopolitan, but typically found in cold and wet places; leaves narrow, flat, channelled, or cylindrical and pointed; flowers with six perianth-segments, brownish, in dense heads, sometimes borne laterally below tip of stem. (Genus: *Juncus*, 300 species. Family: *Juncaceae*.) » annual; evergreen plants; perennial; perianth

Rush-Bagot Convention (1817) An agreement between the USA and Britain to demilitarize the Great Lakes by limiting the number, tonnage, and armament of ships on each side. The convention ended the threat of a Great Lakes arms race, but complete disarmament on the US/Canada border did not follow until decades later. The parties involved were acting US Secretary of State Robert Rush, and British minister to the USA Charles Bagot.

Rushdie, (Ahmad) Salman (1947–) Indian writer, born in Bombay of Muslim parents, and educated there and in England, at Rugby and Cambridge. He became widely known after the publication of his second novel, *Midnight's Children* (1981). *The Satanic Verses* (1988) caused worldwide controversy because of its treatment of Islam from a secular point of view, and in February 1989 he was forced to go into hiding because of a sentence of death passed on him by Ayatollah Khomeini of Iran. » Indian literature; Khomeini; novel

Rushmore, Mount 43°53N 103°28W. Mountain in W South Dakota, USA, in the Black Hills, SW of Rapid City; a national memorial; height 1 943 m/6 375 ft; famous for the gigantic sculptures of four past US presidents (Washington, Jefferson, Roosevelt, Lincoln); each head 18 m/60 ft high; constructed 1927–41 under the direction of Gutzon Borglum. » Borglum; South Dakota

Rusk, (David) Dean (1909–) US statesman, born in Cherokee Co, Georgia. Educated at Davidson College and Oxford, he became professor of government at Mills College, California (1934), and after war service held several government posts. In 1961 he became Secretary of State under Kennedy, and played a major role in the Cuban crisis of 1962. He retained the post under the Johnson administration, retiring in 1969. » Johnson, Lyndon B; Kennedy, John F

Ruska, Ernst (1906–88) German physicist, born at Heidelberg. He studied high voltage and vacuum methods at Munich and Berlin, and from 1928 worked on the development of the electron microscope. His transmission electron microscope achieved up to $10^6\times$, compared with $2000\times$ for a good optical microscope, and its commercial availability (from 1938 onwards) revolutionized biology. He was awarded the 1986 Nobel Prize for Physics, and died in Berlin. » electron microscope [i]

Ruskin, John (1819–1900) British author and art critic, born in London. Educated privately and at Oxford, he met Turner, and championed his painting in his first critical work, *Modern Painters* (1843–60). This book, along with *The Seven Lamps of Architecture* (1848) and *The Stones of Venice* (1851–3), made him the critic of the day, and his social criticism gave him the status of a moral guide or prophet. He became professor of fine art at Oxford in 1870, and founded several educational institutions. He died at Coniston, Lancashire. » Gothic revival; literary criticism; Turner, J M W

Russell, Bertrand (Arthur William), 3rd Earl (1872–1970) British philosopher and mathematician, born at Trelleck, Monmouthshire. He was educated privately and at Cambridge, where he became a fellow in 1895. Concerned to defend the objectivity of mathematics, he pointed out a contradiction in Frege's system, published his own *Principles of Mathematics* (1903), and collaborated with A N Whitehead in *Principia Mathematica* (1910–13). In 1907 he offered himself as a Liberal candidate, but was turned down for his 'free-thinking'. In 1916 his pacifism lost him his fellowship, and in 1918 he was six months in prison. From the 1920s he lived by lecturing and journalism, and became increasingly controversial. He visited the Soviet Union, was professor at Peking (1920–1), and started with his wife a progressive school near Petersfield (1927). He succeeded to his brother's title in 1931. The evils of fascism led him to renounce pacifism in 1939. Later works included *An Enquiry into Meaning and Truth* (1940) and *Human Knowledge* (1948). After 1949 he became a champion of nuclear disarmament, and engaged in unprecedented correspondence with several world leaders. Winner of the 1950 Nobel Prize for Literature, he was the single most important influence on 20th-c analytic philosophy. He died near Penrhyndeudraeth, Merioneth. » analytic philosophy; Frege; logic; Moore, G E; Whitehead

Russell, Henry Norris (1877–1957) US astronomer, born at Oyster Bay, New York. He was educated at Princeton, New Jersey, where he became director of the Observatory in 1908. Independently of Hertzsprung, he discovered the relationship between stellar absolute magnitude and spectral type. He died at Princeton. » Hertzsprung-Russell diagram [i]

Russell, Jack, properly **John** (1795–1883) British 'sporting parson', born at Dartmouth, Devon. Educated at Oxford, he became curate of Swymbridge near Barnstaple (1832–80), and master of foxhounds. A breed of terrier found in the West Country was named after him.

Russell (of Kingston Russell), John, 1st Earl (1792–1878) British statesman and Whig-Liberal Prime Minister (1846–52, 1865–6), born in London. Educated at Edinburgh, he became an MP in 1813. He was Home Secretary (1835–9) and Secretary for War (1839–41), and became Prime Minister after the Conservative Party split over the repeal of the Corn Laws (1846). In Aberdeen's coalition of 1852 he was Foreign Secretary and leader in the Commons. He lost popularity over alleged incompetent management of the Crimean War, and in 1855 he retired; but he became Foreign Secretary again in the second Palmerston administration (1859), and was made an earl in 1861. On Palmerston's death, he again became Premier, but resigned in 1866. He died at Richmond Park, Surrey. » Aberdeen, Earl of; Crimean War; Liberal Party (UK); Palmerston, Viscount; Whigs

Russell, Ken (1927–) British director, born in Southampton. In 1955 he made some documentary shorts which earned him a freelance assignment with BBC Television, for whom he produced experimental studies of Debussy, Isadora Duncan, Delius, and Richard Strauss, which gradually abandoned naturalism. He turned to feature films with *Women in Love* (1969), but continued with musically inspired themes in *The Music Lovers* (1971) and *Mahler* (1974). Other productions include *The Devils* (1971), *Savage Messiah* (1972), *Gothic* (1987), and *The Rainbow* (1989).

Russell, Lord William (1639–83) English Whig politician. Educated at Cambridge, he travelled in Europe, and at the Restoration became an MP. A supporter of Shaftesbury, and a leading member of the movement to exclude James II from the succession, he was arrested with others for participation in the Rye House Plot (1683), found guilty by a packed jury, and beheaded in London. » James II (of England); Rye House Plot; Shaftesbury, Earl; Whigs

Russell's viper A viper found from India to Java and on Komodo I; powerful venom; probably responsible for more human deaths from snakebite than any other species (mainly because it is common near habitation). (*Vipera russelli.*) » viper [i]

Russia, formerly (1917–91) the **Russian SFSR (Soviet Federal Socialist Republic)**, Russ **Rossiyskaya** pop (1990e) 147 400 000; area 17 075 400 sq km/6 591 100 sq ml. Republic occupying much of E Europe and N Asia; c.75% of the area of the former USSR, and over 50% of its population; bounded NW by Norway and Finland, W by Poland, SE by China, Mongolia, and Korea, N by the Arctic Ocean, and W and SW by the Atlantic Ocean and Caspian Sea; vast plains dominate the W half; Ural Mts separate the E European Plain (W) from the W Siberian Lowlands (E); E of the R Yenisey lies the C Siberian Plateau; N Siberian Plain further E; Caucasus, Tien Shan, and Pamir Ranges along the S frontier; Lena, Ob, Severnaya Dvina, Pechora, Yenisey, Indigirka, and Kolyma Rivers flow to the Arctic Ocean; Amur, Amgun, and rivers of the Kamchatka Peninsula flow to the Pacific Ocean; Caspian Sea basin includes the Volga and Ural Rivers; over 20 000 lakes, the largest being the Caspian Sea, L Taymyr, L Baikal; formed in 1917 from the remains of the Russian Empire as a socialist republic within the new Soviet Union; independence in 1991, following the break-up of the Soviet Union; capital, Moscow; chief cities, St Petersburg (Leningrad), Nizhny Novgorod (Gorky), Samara (Kuybyshev), Ekaterinburg (Sverdlovsk), Rostov-na-Donu, Volgograd, Novosibirsk, Chelyabinsk, Kazan, Omsk; oil, natural gas, coal, peat, gold, copper, platinum, zinc, tin, lead; metallurgy, machines, ships, vehicles, chemicals, textiles, timber; wheat, fruit, vegetables, tobacco, cotton, sugar beet. » Caspian Sea; Moscow; Siberia; Soviet Union [i]; Ural Mountains

Russian » **Russian literature; Slavic languages**

Russian art The art associated with Russia, which flourished under Byzantine influence down to the 18th-c, as seen in the 11th-c cathedral of Sta Sophia at Kiev, with its cupolas and mosaics by Greek artists. Since the 18th-c, W European influences have predominated. In the early 20th-c, Russian artists contributed to the abstract movement. » abstract art; Byzantine art; Constructivism; icon (art/religion); Pskov School

Russian blue A breed of domestic cat; *foreign short-haired* variety; thick blue-grey coat, each hair often with a silver tip; large thin ears and green eyes; also known as an **Archangel cat**. » cat

Russian Civil War A war which took place in Russia following the October 1917 Revolution. Anti-Bolshevik forces (Whites) led by tsarist generals mounted a series of military and political campaigns against the new Soviet regime, supported by the intervention of allied troops and the governments of Britain, France, the USA, and Japan. They were opposed by the Soviet Red Army, created by Trotsky, which successfully fought back against the Whites between 1918 and 1922. There were five main theatres of war: the Caucasus and S Russia; the Ukraine; the Baltic provinces; the Far North; and Siberia. After the end of World War 1 the military justification for allied intervention disappeared. The Red Army, which generally enjoyed more popular support than the Whites, gradually defeated the counter-revolutionary forces on all fronts, and established Soviet military and political power throughout the whole of Russia and its borderlands, with the exception of Poland, Finland, and the Baltic states, which received their independence. » Bolsheviks; Czech Legion; October Revolution; Russian Revolution; Trotsky; White Russians

Russian history There are five major periods of Russian history; the *Kievan* (9th–13th-c), *Mongol* (13th–15th-c), *Muscovite* (15th–17th-c), *Imperial* (18th–19th-c), and *Soviet* (20th-c). After the Mongol domination, the Moscow Grand Princes became rulers of an independent Muscovite state supported by the service-nobility (*dvoryanstvo*) and the Orthodox Church. During Peter I's reign the Russian Empire was established, stretching from Europe to the Pacific. In the Imperial period, the basis of the mainly agricultural economy was serfdom, half of the peasantry being owned by feudal landlords. After serfdom was abolished in 1861, the economy gradually began to industrialize along capitalist lines. Throughout the 19th-c a revolutionary movement constantly challenged the autocratic state. This, combined with increasing industrial and rural unrest led to the revolutions of 1905 and 1917, the collapse of the empire, and the formation of the first Soviet government. After the Civil War, the Union of Soviet Socialist Republics was founded in 1922. The mid-20th-c was dominated by the dictatorship of Stalin, which involved forced indus trialization and mass political terror. Stalin's excesses were later officially condemned, and a programme of economic and political restructuring (*perestroika*) introduced by President Gorbachev. By 1990, this process led to demands for independence from several Soviet republics, to the demise of the Communist Party of the Soviet Union, and (following the failed coup of 1991) to the break-up of the Soviet Union and its replacement by the Commonwealth of Independent States. » Bolsheviks; boyars; communism; Cossacks; Decembrists; duma; February Revolution; Gorbachev; kulaks; Mensheviks; October Revolution; Peter I; Revolution of 1905; Romanovs; Russian Civil War; Russia; Russo-Japanese War; Russo-Turkish Wars; Socialist-Revolutionary Party; Soviet Union [i]; Stalin; Time of Troubles; White Russians; zemstvo

Russian literature The development of Russian literature was delayed until the 18th-c. Before this time there was a rich and varied oral tradition of folk tales and *byliny* or epic songs, supplemented from the 16th-c by historically-based material. Some Western influence was relayed via Poland in the 17th-c, but it was French classicism which provided the real stimulus for the philologist Mikhail Lomonosov (1711–65), the poet Gavriil Derzhavin (1743–1816), the fables of Ivan Krylov (1769–1844), and the dramatist Aleksandr Griboedov (1795–1829). The greatest Russian writer, Aleksandr Pushkin (1799–1837), transcended all influences to become a major figure in both prose and verse; the Byronic novel in verse, *Evgeny Onegin* (1828), is his most characteristic work. The legacy of Pushkin has been divided between Romanticism and the Realism which has haunted Russian literature. The poet Mikhail Lermontov (1814–41) was drawn to both; as was the novelist Nikolai Gogol (1809–52), perceiving like Dickens the fantastic side of ordinary life. The novels of Ivan Turgenev (1818–83) and Ivan Goncharov (1812–91) reflected social problems, as was urged by the influential critics Vissarion Belinsky (1811–48) and Nikolai Chernyshevsky (1828–89). Meanwhile, poets such as Fyodor Tyuchev (1803–73) and Afanasi Fet (1820–92) ignored the Realist initiative, as did Nikolai Leskov (1831–95) with his stories of the exotic and grotesque.

The greatest of Russian novelists, Leo Tolstoy (1828–1910) and Fyodor Dostoyevsky (1821–81) evade these categorizations. Tolstoy's *War and Peace* (1863–9) and Dostoyevsky's *Crime and Punishment* (1866) simultaneously explore the materiality and the mystery of human experience. The stories and plays of Anton Chekhov (1860–1904) are also too subtle for simple classification. This century, the Symbolists Aleksandr Blok (1880–1921) and Andrei Bely (1880–1934), followed by the Acmeists Anna Akhmatova (1888–1966) and Osip Mandelstam (1891–1938), and the Futurists Vladimir Mayakovsky (1894–1930) and Viktor Khlebnikov (1885–1922), reclaimed the world of poetry: but post-revolutionary Russia has generally been hostile to such work, as it was to the poems and novels of Boris Pasternak (1890–1960). The official socialist Realism privileged the materialist fiction of Maxim Gorky (1868–1936) and Mikhail Sholokhov (1905–84). Much literature circulated unpublished (*samizdat*) or is published abroad (*tamizdat*) by such writers as Aleksandr Solzhenitsyn (1918–), Joseph Brodsky (1940–), and Irina Ratushinskaya. » Akhmatova; Chekhov; Dostoevsky; Gogol; Gorky, Maxim; Lermontov; Mayakovsky; Pasternak; Pushkin; Sholokhov; Solzhenitsyn; Tolstoy; Turgenev

Russian Orthodox Church A Church originating from missionary activity of the see of Constantinople of the Orthodox Church, with a community organized at Kiev in the 9th-c. In 988, Christianity was declared (by Vladimir) the official faith; in the 14th-c Moscow became the see of the metropolitan; and in the 15th-c the Church declared itself autonomous. It existed in a state of tension with the emperor, and after the Revolution of 1917, was separated from the state and suffered some persecution. Gaining some recognition as a result of support of the authorities in World War 2, it was largely controlled by government agencies. It reflected the Byzantine or Greek tradition until the 19th-c, when a new translation of the Bible was approved, and in the 20th-c there was some revival of interest on the part of the intelligentsia, conscious of the role the Church had played in Russian art and culture. The contemporary Russian Church retains fidelity in doctrine and liturgy to its Orthodox inheritance, but is also developing its national character. » Bible; Christianity; liturgy; Old Believers; Orthodox Church

Russian Revolution (1917) The revolution which overthrew the Russian imperialist regime and set up the first communist state. Mass demonstrations of revolutionary workers and soldiers in Petrograd led to the abdication of Nicholas II in February 1917. There followed a period of power-sharing between a provisional government and the Petrograd Soviet, known as 'dual power'. Lenin's Bolsheviks refused to collaborate, and in October led an insurgency of armed workers, soldiers, and sailors, seizing political power and establishing the first Soviet government. » Bolsheviks; Mensheviks; April Theses; February Revolution; July Days; October Revolution; Russian history; tsar

Russian wolfhound » borzoi

Russo-Finnish War War between the USSR and Finland during the winter of 1939–40 (the 'Winter War'). Soviet forces invaded Finland in order to secure Finnish territory from which to defend Leningrad against German attack. In spite of courageous Finnish resistance and early Russian bungling, Finland capitulated (Mar 1940) and was forced to cede territory to the Soviet Union. » World War 2

Russo-Japanese War (1904–5) War between the Russian Empire and Japan over rival territorial claims and imperial ambitions in N China. It was a series of military and naval disasters for Russia; it had little popular support, and was marked by ineffectual command and political confusion. The war ended in Japanese victory with the Treaty of Portsmouth (1905). » Russian history

Russo-Turkish Wars A series of wars between the Russian and Ottoman Empires from the 17th-c to the 19th-c, principally for domination of the Black Sea and adjacent regions. From the mid-18th-c they also involved national liberation struggles of the Slavonic and Orthodox peoples of the Balkans from Ottoman rule. As a result of the wars (the last in 1877–8), many areas gained their independence or were incorporated into the Russian Empire. » Ottoman Empire; Russian history

rust The product of corrosion, especially of iron-containing materials. It consists mainly of iron(III) oxide (Fe_2O_3) or hydrated forms. » corrosion

rust fungus A parasitic fungus that occurs as a thread-like network (*mycelium*) between cells of the host plant; includes genus *Puccinia*, over 4 000 species, some being parasites of commercial cereal crops. (Subdivision: *Basidiomycetes*. Order: *Uredinales*.) » Basidiomycetes; fungus; parasitology

Rutanzige, Lake » Edward, Lake

Ruth, Book of A book of the Hebrew Bible/Old Testament, presenting a popular story set in the time of Israel's tribal judges, but named after its central character, Ruth. Ruth's mother, Naomi, arranges a levirate marriage of Ruth to Boaz, the rich kinsman of Naomi's deceased husband, on their return to Judah from Moab; Ruth became the mother of Obed, grandfather of David. Usually dated c.5th–4th-c BC, it is significant for its liberal attitudes to non-Israelites and mixed marriages, since Ruth was a Moabitess. » David; Naomi; Old Testament

Ruth, Babe, byname of **George Herman Ruth** (1895–1948) US baseball star, born in Baltimore. He started his career as a pitcher with the Boston Red Sox in 1914, joined the New York Yankees in 1920, and hit a record 54 home runs in the season. He bettered the record to 60 in 1927, a figure which stood until 1961. In the 1926 World Series he became the first man to score three home runs in one game. When he retired in 1935 he had scored 714 home runs, a figure not bettered until 1974. Much sought after as a television personality after his retirement, he died in New York City. The Yankee Stadium is affectionately known as 'The House Babe Ruth built' because of the increased income he brought to the club during his career. The Babe Ruth Story was filmed in 1948. » baseball [i]

Rutherford (of Nelson), Ernest, 1st Baron (1871–1937) British physicist, a pioneer of subatomic physics, born near Nelson, New Zealand. Educated at Nelson and Christchurch, in 1895 he moved to Cambridge, and in 1898 became professor of physics at McGill, Canada, where with Frederick Soddy he proposed that radioactivity results from the disintegration of atoms (1903). In 1907 he became professor at Manchester, developing the modern conception of the atom. In 1919 he became professor at Cambridge and director of the Cavendish Laboratory. He won the Nobel Prize for Chemistry in 1908, was knighted in 1914, made a peer in 1931, and died at Cambridge. » atom; Bohr; radioactivity; Soddy

Rutherford, Dame Margaret (1892–1972) British theatre and film actress, born in London. She made her stage debut in 1925 at the Old Vic theatre, and gained fame as a character actress and comedienne, her gallery of eccentrics including 'Miss Prism' in *The Importance of Being Earnest* (stage 1939, film 1952) and 'Miss Whitchurch' in *The Happiest Days of Your Life* (stage 1948, film 1950). She also scored a success as Agatha Christie's 'Miss Marple' in a series of films from 1962. She was created a Dame in 1967, won an Oscar for her role in *The VIPs* in 1964, and died at Chalfont St Peter, Buckinghamshire.

Ruthwell Cross A runic stone cross at Ruthwell in the Scottish borders dating from the 7th-c. It is carved with scenes from the New Testament and stands 5 m/18 ft high. » runes [i]

rutile [**roo**tiyl, **roo**teel] A titanium dioxide (TiO_2) mineral, usually red-brown to black due to impurities of iron oxide, widespread in igneous and metamorphic rocks and in veins with quartz. It is a source of titanium, and also used as a gemstone. » gemstones; titanium

Rutland A former county in the UK, the smallest in England, since 1974 incorporated into Leicestershire. It has given its name to a reservoir, Rutland Water. » Leicestershire

Ruysdael, or **Ruïsdael, Jacob van** [**roys**dahl] (c.1628–82) Dutch landscape painter, born and died in Haarlem. He became a member of the Haarlem painters' guild in 1648, and c.1657 moved to Amsterdam, thereafter travelling in Holland

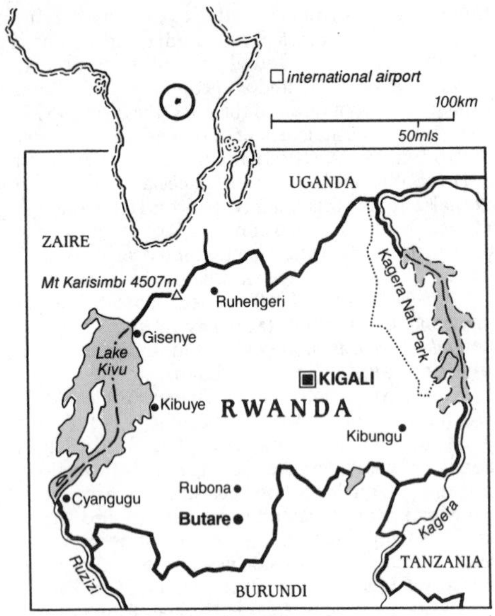

and Germany. His best works are country landscapes, and he also excelled in cloud effects, particularly in his seascapes. » Dutch art; landscape painting

Rwanda, official name **Republic of Rwanda** [roo**an**da] pop (1990e) 7 232 000; area 26 338 sq km/10 166 sq ml. Landlocked republic in C Africa, bounded N by Uganda, E by Tanzania, S by Burundi, and W by Zaire and L Kivu; capital, Kigali; timezone GMT +2; chief ethnic groups, Hutu (84%), Tutsi (14%); official languages, French, Kinyarwanda, with Kiswahili widely used in commerce; chief religions, Roman Catholicism (65%), local beliefs (25%); unit of currency, the Rwanda franc; at a relatively high altitude, highest point Karisimbi (4 507 m/14 787 ft) in the Virunga range; W third drains into L Kivu and then the R Congo, remainder drains towards the R Nile; many lakes; a highland tropical climate; two wet seasons (Oct–Dec, Mar–May); highest rainfall in the W, decreasing in the C uplands and to the N and E; average annual rainfall at Kigali, 1 000 mm/40 in; in the 16th-c the Tutsi tribe moved into the country and took over from the Hutu, forming a monarchy; German protectorate, 1899; mandated with Burundi to Belgium as the Territory of Ruanda-Urundi, 1919; United Nations Trust Territory administered by Belgium, after World War 2; unrest in 1959 led to a Hutu revolt and the overthrow of Tutsi rule; independence, 1962; military coup, 1973; return to civilian rule, 1980; further fighting, 1990; governed by a National Development Council of 70 members, a president, and a Council of Ministers; largely agricultural economy; coffee, tea, pyrethrum, maize, beans, livestock; cassiterite, wolfram, columbo-tantalite, beryl, amblygonite, reserves of methane; agricultural processing, beer, soft drinks, soap, furniture, plastic goods, textiles, cigarettes. » African history; Burundi [i]; Hutu and Tutsi; mandates; RR27 national holidays; RR59 political leaders

Ryan, Elizabeth (1892–1979) US lawn tennis player, born at Anaheim, California. She won 19 Wimbledon titles (12 doubles and 7 mixed doubles), a record which stood from 1934 until 1979, when it was surpassed by Billie Jean King. Six of her women's doubles titles were with Suzanne Lenglen (1899–1938). » tennis, lawn [i]

Ryan, (Lynn) Nolan (1947–) US baseball player, born at Refugio, Texas. He is regarded as one of the fastest pitchers ever seen in major league baseball, being once timed at 162.3 kph/100.9 mph. He started his career with the New York Mets in 1966, then played for the California Angels and Houston Astros. He has claimed more strikeouts (4 373) than any player in baseball history. His score of 383 strikeouts in 1973 is an all-time record. » baseball [i]

Ryazan [ryazan] 54°37N 39°43E, pop (1983) 483 000. Capital city of Ryazanskaya oblast, Russia; on R Oka, 192 km/119 ml SE of Moscow; founded, 1095; former capital of a principality; railway; cellulose, clothing, footwear, oil refining, chemicals. » Russia

Ryde 50°44N 1°10W, pop (1981) 19 843. Resort town in Medina district, I of Wight, S England; on NE coast of the island, 11 km/7 ml SW of Portsmouth; railway; ferry link with the mainland from Fishbourne to the W; transport equipment, tourism; Quarr Abbey (1132). » Wight, Isle of

Ryder Cup A golf tournament played every two years between professional male golfers from the USA and Europe. First played at Worcester, Massachusetts, in 1927, the Cup was named after English businessman Samuel Ryder (1859–1936), who suggested the idea of a regular international competition between the USA and Great Britain. The Great Britain team became a European team in 1979. » golf

rye A cereal resembling barley, but with longer, narrower ears. It succeeds on poor soils, and is cultivated in cold regions such as in N America and E Europe. It provides black bread, crispbreads, alcohol, and straw for hats and thatching. It is also planted for animal forage and, in the USA, for stabilizing soil. (*Secale cereale*. Family: *Gramineae*.) » barley; cereals; grass [i]

Rye House Plot An alleged plot by Whigs (Apr 1683) to murder Charles II of England and James, Duke of York, at Rye House near Hoddesdon, Hertfordshire; a counter-part to the alleged Popish Plot of 1678. It was foiled by the early departure of the royal pair from Newmarket. The conspirators were betrayed and captured; two of them, Algernon Sidney and William, Lord Russell, were executed. » Charles II (of England); Popish Plot; Sidney, Algernon

rye whisky/whiskey A whisky distilled from the fermentation of rye, popular in the S USA. Most other whiskies (but not bourbon) are made from barley. » rye; whisky

Rykov, Alexey Ivanovich (1881–1938) Russian revolutionary, Communist Party and government official, educated at Kazan University. He helped organize the October Revolution in Petrograd and was appointed People's Commissar for Internal Affairs in the first Soviet government. He held a number of senior government and party posts (1919–37), becoming a member of the Politburo (1919–29). In 1928 together with Bukharin and Tomsky, he led the 'right opposition' against Stalin's economic policies. In 1937 he was arrested for alleged anti-party activities, and shot some months later. » Bolsheviks; Bukharin; February/October Revolution; Stalin

Ryle, Gilbert (1900–76) British philosopher, born at Brighton, Sussex. Educated at Brighton and Oxford, where he was a tutor, he served in World War 2, then became Waynflete professor of metaphysical philosophy at Oxford (1945–68) and editor of *Mind* (1947–71). He was an influential defender of linguistic or 'ordinary language' philosophy, and is best-known for his book *The Concept of Mind* (1949) which argued against the mind/body dualism ('the ghost in the machine') proposed by Descartes. He died at Whitby, Yorkshire. » Descartes; dualism; linguistic philosophy

Ryle, Sir Martin (1918–84) British radio astronomer, born at Brighton, Sussex, the nephew of Gilbert Ryle. Educated at Oxford, he worked from 1945 on radio physics at the Cavendish Laboratory, Cambridge, becoming professor of radio astronomy (1959–82). His development of interferometers for radio astronomy enabled him to survey the most distant radio sources. In 1961 he challenged the generally accepted steady-state theory of the universe, and paved the way for renewed interest in the expanding-universe theory. He was knighted in 1966, appointed Astronomer Royal in 1972, and shared the Nobel Prize for Physics in 1974. » cosmology; Hoyle, Fred; interferometer; quasar; radio astronomy; radio galaxy; steady-state theory

Saar, River, Fr **Sarre** [zah] River in France and Germany; rises in the Vosges, flows N through NE France and NNW across the German border to the R Moselle just above Trier; length 240 km/150 ml; navigable length 120 km/75 ml; its valley is a noted wine area. » Vosges Mountains

Saarbrücken [**zah**brükn], Fr **Sarrebruck** 49°15N 6°58E, pop (1983) 190 100. Capital of Saarland province, Germany; on the R Saar, 62 km/38 ml SE of Trier; economic and cultural centre of Saarland; railway; university (1948); ironworks, metal products, coal, oil products, rubber, machine tools, electrical engineering, optical equipment; collegiate Church of St Arnual (13th–14th-c); noted for its trade fairs. » Germany [i]

Saarinen, Eero (1910–61) Finnish-US architect, born at Kirkkonummi, Finland. He went to the USA in 1923 with his architect father **(Gottlieb) Eliel** (1873–1950), studied sculpture in Paris (1929–30), and architecture at Yale (1930–4). His designs for Expressionist modern buildings include the Trans-World Airlines Kennedy Terminal, New York (1956–62). He died at Ann Arbor, Michigan. » architecture; Expressionism

Sabah [sa**bah**], formerly **North Borneo** pop (1980) 955 712; area 73 711 sq km/28 452 sq ml. State in E Malaysia, on the N tip of Borneo; bounded SW by Brunei, W by the South China Sea, E by the Sulu Sea, and S by Kalimantan (Indonesia); highest peak, Mt Kinabalu, 4 094 m/13 432 ft; watered by the R Kinabatangan; British protectorate, 1882; member of the Federation of Malaysia, 1963; capital, Kota Kinabalu; copper, oil, timber, copra, rice, rubber. » Borneo; Malaysia [i]

Sabbath or **Shabbat** (Heb 'cessation', 'rest') The seventh day of the week, which in Jewish belief is designated a day of rest and cessation from labour, beginning just before sunset on Fridays. The laws of Sabbath observance derive from a short ban found in the Pentateuch (*Ex* 20.8–11; 31.12–17) and from God's own rest in the Genesis creation account. Rabbinic regulations specify 39 forbidden activities, which are then further elaborated, but in more liberal Reform Judaism the Sabbath is mainly a day of worship. » Judaism; Pentateuch; rabbi

Sabin, A(lbert) B(ruce) [**say**bin] (1906–) US microbiologist, born at Białystok, Russia. He moved to the USA in 1921, and became a US citizen in 1930. He held posts at New York (1935) and Cincinnati (1939), where he became professor of paediatrics. He is best known for his research into a live virus as a polio vaccine, which works by causing a harmless infection of the intestinal tract, stimulating immunity to natural infection without causing disease. This has replaced the Salk vaccine, as it gives longer-lasting immunity, and is capable of being given orally. » poliomyelitis; Salk; vaccination; virus

Sabines [**sa**biynz] A people of ancient Italy, inhabiting the mountainous country NE of Rome. Often at war with the Romans, they were ultimately conquered and absorbed by them. » Romanization

sable An Asian marten with a thick and silky winter coat valuable to the fur trade (summer coat shorter and coarse); inhabits high forests, usually near streams. (*Martes zibellina.*) The fur of the **American pine marten** (*Martes americana*) is known as *American sable* or *Hudson Bay sable.* » marten

sable antelope A horse-like antelope native to Africa S of the Sahara; black with pale underparts (young are reddish-brown); long curved horns (length in male, over 1 m/3¼ ft); inhabits woodland. (*Hippotragus niger.*) » antelope

Sabra Palestinian refugee camp on the outskirts of Beirut, Lebanon; created following the evacuation of Palestinians from the city after the June 1982 Israeli attack; scene of a massacre of Palestinians by Christian Phalangists in September 1983. » Beirut

Sabratha Phoenician colony founded in the 8th-c BC on the NW coast of present-day Libya. The city was incorporated in Roman Africa in the 2nd-c BC. Now a world heritage site, the ruins of Sabratha include a reconstructed theatre facing the sea. » Phoenicia; Roman history [i]

sabretooth A fossil cat, often referred to as 'sabretooth tiger', but not closely related to the tiger; upper canine teeth enlarged, sabre-like, adapted for efficient stabbing action; jaw modified to give extra wide gape; body size up to that of lion; became extinct in the late Pleistocene epoch. (Family: *Felidae.* Genus: *Smilodon.*) » cat; fossil; Pleistocene epoch

saccades [sa**kaydz**] The jerky flicking of the eye from one point to another, in contrast with its slow drifts. They may be either voluntary (as in reading) or involuntary, and their study can provide important information about the nature of the reading process and other visual activities. » eye [i]

saccharin [**sak**arin] $C_7H_5NO_3S$, melting point 229°C. A white solid which has more than 400 times the sweetening power of sucrose. It is used as an artificial sweetener, normally as its sodium salt. Many people find that it leaves a bitter after-taste. » sucrose [i]

Sachs, Hans [zahks] (1494–1576) German poet and dramatist, born and died at Nuremberg. He was trained as a shoemaker, and 1511–16 travelled through Germany, practising his craft, and frequenting the schools of the Meistersingers ('master singers'). He wrote over 6 300 pieces, some celebrating the Reformation, others dealing with common life and manners in a vigorous, humorous style. He headed the Meistersingers of Nuremberg in 1554, and in that role was idealized in Wagner's opera. » German literature; poetry; Wagner

Sachs, Nelly (Leonie) (1891–1970) Swedish poet and dramatist, born in Berlin. Of Jewish descent, she fled from Germany in 1940, settled in Stockholm, and took Swedish nationality. Her best-known play is *Eli: Ein Mysterienspiel vom Leiden Israels* (1951, Eli: A Mystery Play of the Sufferings of Israel). She shared the Nobel Prize for Literature in 1966, and died in Stockholm. » Agnon; drama; Swedish literature

sackbut » **trombone**

Sackville, Thomas, 1st Earl of Dorset (1536–1608) English poet and statesman, born at Buckhurst, Sussex. He became a lawyer and entered parliament (1558), then collaborated with Thomas Norton (1532–84) in the tragedy *Gorboduc* (1561), the first English play in blank verse. Knighted in 1567, he later became a diplomat in Europe, Lord High Treasurer (1599), and an earl (1604). He died in London. » blank verse; English literature; poetry

Sackville-West, V(ictoria Mary), byname **Vita** (1892–1962) British poet and novelist, born at Knole, Kent. Her work expresses her closeness to the countryside where she lived, notably in the long poem, *The Land* (1926). Her best-known novels are *The Edwardians* (1930) and *All Passion Spent* (1931). In 1913 she married diplomat and critic **Harold (George) Nicolson** (1886–1968); *Passenger to Teheran* (1926) records their years in Persia. She died at Sissinghurst Castle, Kent. » English literature; novel; poetry

sacrament A Christian rite understood as an outward and visible sign of an internal and spiritual grace. Orthodox and Roman Catholic Churches recognize seven sacraments: baptism, confirmation, the Eucharist (Mass), penance, extreme unction, holy orders (ordination), and matrimony. Protestant

Churches recognize only baptism and the Eucharist (Communion) as sacraments. » anointing the sick; baptism; confirmation (religion); Eucharist; penance

Sacramento 38°35N 121°29W, pop (1980) 275 741. Capital of state and of Sacramento County, C California, USA, on the E bank of the Sacramento R; settled, 1839; expanded rapidly after gold discovered nearby, 1848; state capital, 1854; airport; railway; university (1947); food processing, high technology; major league team, Kings (basketball); Roman Corinthian State Capitol (1860) in Capitol Park; Crocker Art Gallery; Sutter's Fort (1840, now restored) contains a museum of Indian and pioneer relics. » California

Sacramento River Longest river in California, USA; rises in the Klamath Mts; flows 615 km/382 ml S to Suisin Bay; major tributaries the Pit, Feather, American; navigable as far as Red Bluff (412 km/256 ml) for small craft; Sacramento the principal port; joins with the San Joaquin to form the basis of the immense Central Valley Project for flood-control, irrigation, and hydroelectricity, using several dams and reservoirs. » California

sacred ibis An ibis native to Africa S of the Sahara, S Arabia, and Aldabra (formerly also Egypt); white with dark head and neck; soft dark plumes on tail; eats fish and insects; nests in tree or on ground. (*Threskiornis aethiopicus*.) » ibis

sacred scarab beetle A dung beetle that has specialized forelegs for forming dung into a ball and rolling it into an underground chamber for feeding larvae. (Order: *Coleoptera*. Family: *Scarabeidae*.) » dung beetle; larva; scarab [i]

sacrum A triangular-shaped bone at the lower end of the vertebral column, formed by fusion of the five sacral vertebrae. In humans standing upright, it lies almost horizontally, articulating with the two hip bones to complete the ring of bone known as the *pelvis*, and with the rest of the vertebral column at the fifth lumbar vertebra. The sacrum gives attachment to the muscles of the back. » pelvis; vertebral column; Plate XIII

Sadat, (Mohammed) Anwar El- [sa**dat**] (1918–81) Egyptian statesman and President (1970–81), born in the Tala district. He trained for the army in Cairo, and in 1952 was a member of the coup deposing King Farouk. After becoming President, he temporarily assumed the post of Prime Minister (1973–4), after which he sought settlement of the conflict with Israel. He met the Israeli Premier in Jerusalem (1977) and at Camp David, USA (1978), in which year he and Begin were jointly awarded the Nobel Peace Prize. Following criticism by other Arab statesmen and hard-line Muslims, he was assassinated in Cairo by extremists. » Arab-Israeli Wars; Begin; Farouk I; Islam; Nasser

saddle-bill stork » **jabiru**

saddleback A bird restricted to isolated pockets in New Zealand; dark with orange-brown band across back; long legs and tail; long curved bill; fold of skin on each cheek; weak flier; inhabits forests; eats insects; related to the huia. (*Creadion carunculatus*. Family: *Callaeidae*.) » huia

Sadducees [**sad**yooseez] A major party within Judaism (c.2nd-c BC–AD 70), the name probably deriving from the priest Zadok, whose descendants held priestly office from Solomon's times. They were mainly aristocrats, associated with the Jerusalem priesthood (with the high priest from among their number), and influential in Israel's political and economic life. Josephus suggests that they differed from the Pharisees by their denials of the legal force of oral traditions, of bodily resurrection, and of divine determinism. » Josephus; Judaism; Pharisees; Solomon (Old Testament); Zadokites

Sade, Marquis de [sahd], byname of **Donatien Alphonse François, Count of Sade** (1740–1814) French writer, born in Paris. He studied at Paris, served in the army, and was in 1772 condemned to death at Aix for his cruelty and sexual practices. He escaped, but was later imprisoned at Vincennes (1777) and in the Bastille (1784), where he wrote *Les 120 Journées de Sodome* (c.1784, The 120 Days of Sodom). After his release (1790), he wrote the licentious novels *Justine* (1791) and *La Philosophie dans le boudoir* (1793, Philosophy in the Bedroom). He died insane at Charenton, his name providing the language with the word 'sadism'. » French literature; novel; sado masochism

Sadler's Wells » **Royal Ballet**

Sado [**sah**doh] area 854 sq km/330 sq ml. Island in Chubu region, Japan; in the Sea of Japan, 48 km/30 ml W of Niigata, off N Honshu; 56 km/35 ml long, 19 km/12 ml wide; mountainous, with a central plain; rises to 1 173 m/3 848 ft (N); chief town and port, Ryotsu; farming, fishing, timber. » Japan [i]

sadomasochism Sexual behaviour in which gratification is based on the infliction (**sadism**) or receipt (**masochism**) of pain or humiliation. An example would be a couple in which one partner has heightened sexual arousal from beating his or her partner, while the other derives pleasure from the experience of being beaten.

Safavids A Persian dynasty (1501–1736) which laid down the foundations of the modern Iranian state. It made Shiism the official religion, and saw a flowering of the arts. » Shiites

safety film Also termed **non-flam**: photographic film with its emulsion coated on a cellulose triacetate or polyester base, which is slow burning and of low inflammability. The contrast is with the highly dangerous cellulose nitrate used before 1950. » film

safety lamp A device used by miners to detect explosive methane gas in mines ('firedamp'), invented in 1815 by Sir Humphry Davy. Any methane present would cause a change in the appearance of the flame, but a double layer of wire gauze surrounding it prevented the gas igniting. Flame lamps have now been almost entirely replaced by lamps powered by electricity. » Davy; firedamp; methane [i]

safflower An annual growing to 1 m/3¼ ft; leaves elliptical, finely spiny-toothed around the margin; flower heads thistle-like, up to 3 cm/1¼ in across, the florets bright red-orange. It is probably native to W Asia, but is no longer known in the wild. It has a long history of cultivation, formerly as a dye plant, but now mainly for the seeds which yield a useful oil. (*Carthamus tinctorius*. Family: *Compositae*.) » annual; dyestuff

saffron An autumn-flowering species of crocus, native to S Europe and Asia, with lilac flowers. The large, 3-branched, bright orange stigmas are a source of saffron, used as a food dye and as flavouring. (*Crocus sativus*. Family: *Iridaceae*.) » crocus; meadow saffron; stigma

saga (Old Norse 'saying') A mediaeval Icelandic or Scandinavian prose narrative, transcribed from oral tradition after 1100. There are several cycles. The term is also more generally used of any extended narrative, in fact or fiction: the Forsyte saga, the Watergate saga. » Icelandic/Norwegian literature

Sagan, Carl (Edward) [**say**gn] (1934–) US astronomer and writer, born in New York City. Educated at Chicago, he taught at Berkeley, Stanford, Harvard, and the Smithsonian Institution, becoming professor at Cornell in 1970. He has worked on the physics and chemistry of planetary atmospheres and surfaces, the origin of life on Earth, and the possibility of extraterrestrial life. Through such books as *Cosmic Connection* (1973) and his television programme, *Cosmos* (1980), he has done much to popularize astronomy and other aspects of science. » astronomy; Solar System

Sagan, Françoise [sah**gâ**], pseudonym of **Françoise Quoirez** (1935–) French novelist, born in Paris. Educated privately, at 18 she wrote the best-selling *Bonjour tristesse* (1954, Good Morning, Sadness). *Aimez-vous Brahms?* (Do You Like Brahms?) appeared in 1959. Her later novels and plays have had a mixed critical reception. » French literature; novel

Sagarmatha National park and world heritage area in Nepal; encompasses the peak of Mt Everest – Sagarmatha (Nepalese, 'whose head touches the sky') – and six other mountains over 7 000 m/23 000 ft; established to protect the flora and fauna of the area, and the culture of the Sherpas who inhabit the region. » Everest, Mount; Himalayas

sage An aromatic shrub growing to 0.5 m/1½ ft, native to S Europe; young stems square; leaves oblong, stalked, wrinkled, velvety, in opposite pairs; flowers 1–2 cm/0.4–0.8 in, purplish, 2-lipped, the upper lip hooded. It is widely cultivated as a culinary and medicinal herb. Purple-leaved and variegated forms are grown as ornamentals. (*Salvia officinalis*. Family: *Labiatae*.) » herb; salvia; shrub

sage grouse A grouse native to western N America; lives in drier areas than other grouse, inhabiting sagebrush plains; eats sagebrush leaves; males display at traditional sites (strutting grounds). *Centrocercus urophasianus.* » grouse

sagebrush The name applied to certain N American species of *Artemisia*, including **big sagebrush** (*Artemisia tridentata*), a much-branched aromatic shrub growing to 3 m/10 ft; leaves wedge-shaped, 3-toothed at the tips, silvery hairy; flower heads small, greenish, and inconspicuous; also called **sagebush**. The pollen is a common cause of hay fever during late summer. (Genus: *Artemisia*. Family: *Compositae*.) » hay fever; shrub

sagebush » **sagebrush**

Sagitta (Lat 'arrow') A small constellation in the Milky Way, near Cygnus. It includes a notable star cluster, M71. » constellation; Cygnus; Milky Way; star cluster

Sagittarius (Lat 'archer') [saji**tair**iuhs] A S constellation, containing bright 2nd and 3rd magnitude stars. It is an autumn sign of the zodiac, lying between Scorpius and Capricornus. Sagittarius lies in the direction of the centre of our Galaxy, though the view is obscured by intervening clouds of dust a few kiloparsecs away. Radio and infrared radiation from the Galactic centre can penetrate this dust, providing information on conditions there. » constellation; Galaxy; RR9

sago palm A small tree with large feathery leaves, native to SE Asia and the Pacific. The trunk contains large starch reserves to fuel a single great burst of flowering by the mature tree, after which it dies. Sago, a primary source of carbohydrate in the tropics, is obtained from the pith of trunks cut when the first flowers appear. (Genus: *Metroxylon*, 15 species. Family: *Palmae*.) » palm; starch

saguaro [suhg**wah**roh] The largest of the cacti, slow-growing, reaching 21 m/70 ft, with a thick stem and candelabra-like branches and white flowers; found only in Arizona, S California, and the Sonoran desert in Mexico. (*Carnegiea gigantea*. Family: *Cactaceae*.) » cactus [i]

Sagunto [sa**goon**toh], Arabic **Murviedro** (to 1877), ancient **Saguntum** 39°42N 0°18W, pop (1981) 54 759. Town in Valencia province, E Spain; on R Palancia, 25 km/15 ml N of Valencia; Costa del Azahar to the N; steel, fruit, linen, brandy; Roman theatre, fortress, Church of St Mary. » Costa del Azahar; Spain [i]; Valencia (Spain)

Sahara Desert (Arabic 'wilderness') Desert in N Africa; the largest desert in the world, area 7.7 million sq km/3 million sq ml; average width, 1 440 km/895 ml across N Africa from the Atlantic to the Libyan Desert, in which it continues unbroken to the Nile, and beyond that in the Nubian Desert to the Red Sea; covers parts of Morocco, Algeria, Tunisia, Libya, Egypt, Sudan, Chad, Niger, Mali, Mauritania, and Western Sahara; includes the Ahaggar and Tibesti Mts; parts of the Atlas Mts in the NW; areas of drift sand (*erg*), rock (*hamada*), or gravel and pebbles (*areg*); wind erosion intense; only small amounts of unpredictable rain, usually brief, heavy thunderstorms; scattered outlets of surface water at oases, where agriculture is possible; generally void of vegetation, apart from areas of stunted scrub; climate arid since the glacial epoch, when the region was relatively humid with a park savannah vegetation; camel caravans follow routes marked by oases; oil exploration near the Algeria–Libya frontier; phosphates in Morocco and Western Sahara; first crossed by Europeans in the 1820s. » Ahaggar Mountains; Atlas Mountains; desert; Tibesti Mountains

sahel A vegetation zone intermediate between desert and savannah conditions where rainfall is irregular and unpredictable. The vegetation is a transitional scrubland. The name is most commonly applied to the area S of the Sahara ('The Sahel'), including parts of Mauritania, Chad, Mali, Senegal, Burkina Faso, and Niger. The area frequently suffers from drought and famine. » desertification; drought; Sahara Desert; savannah

Said, Edward W [sa**eed**] (1935–) US-Palestinian professor and writer, born in Jerusalem. Educated in Cairo and at Princeton and Harvard, he joined the English department at Columbia, where he is now professor. He has become one of the major Palestinian spokesmen in the debate on the future of the Middle East, and took part in the 1988 gathering that declared the existence of an independent Palestinian state. » Palestine

saiga [**say**ga] A goat-antelope native to Asia; thick pale brown coat with longer hairs down throat; eyes protruding; nose

Head of saiga

grotesquely swollen with large downward-facing nostrils at tip; male with short yellow horns; inhabits cold steppelands. (*Saiga tatarica*.) » antelope

Saigon » **Ho Chi Minh City**

Sailer, Toni (Anton) [**zay**ler] (1935–) Austrian alpine skier, born at Kizbühel. In 1956, he became the first man to win all three Olympic skiing titles (downhill, slalom, giant slalom). He was the world combined champion in 1956 and 1958, and the world downhill and giant slalom champion in 1958. He later became an actor and singer, a hotel owner, and investor in textile business. » skiing

sailfish Large agile billfish widely distributed in open ocean surface waters; length up to 3.5 m/11½ ft; blue-grey above, underside silver; easily recognized by long tall dorsal fin; feeds on fish and squid; highly prized as excellent sport fish, and also taken commercially in some areas. (*Istiophorus platypterus*. Family: *Istiophoridae*.) » billfish

sailing A term used to describe the sport or pastime of travelling over water in a suitable craft. Sailing takes many forms. As a pastime, most use is made of small single- or double-sailed dinghies, often fitted with an outboard motor or auxiliary engine used when there is no wind; but large ocean-going yachts may be 25 m/80 ft or more in length. Several classes of racing yacht are recognized in Olympic and major international competitions. » Admiral's Cup; America's Cup

sailing rig » panel *p 1054*

Saimaa [**si**ymah] Lake system extending over the Finnish Lake Plateau, SE Finland; total area 4 400 sq km/1 700 sq ml; fifth largest lake system in Europe; timber floating; important communications system; L Saimaa area, 1 300 sq km/500 sq ml; maximum depth 100 m/325 ft; linked to an inlet of the Gulf of Finland by the Saimaa Canal (60 km/37 ml). » Finland [i]

sainfoin [**san**foyn] A perennial growing to 80 cm/30 in, possibly native to C Europe; leaves pinnate with 6–14 pairs of oblong-oval leaflets; pea-flowers bright pink veined with purple, up to 50 in each long-stalked, spike-like inflorescence arising from the leaf axils; pods 1-seeded, covered with a net-like pattern of ridges and tubercles. It is widely cultivated for fodder. (*Onobrychis viciifolia*. Family: *Leguminosae*.) » inflorescence [i]; perennial; pinnate

saint In Roman Catholic and Orthodox teaching, a man or woman recognized as being in heaven because of their special qualities. In the New Testament, all Christian believers are referred to as saints, but in the 2nd-c, veneration of saints (often martyrs) began, and individual saints were eventually looked to for intercession and devotion. The practice of veneration was forbidden by 16th-c Reformers, but continued in the Orthodox and Roman Catholic Churches. An elaborate procedure is required before canonization may proceed. » canonization; Orthodox Church; Reformation; Roman Catholicism

St Albans [**awl**bnz], Lat **Verulamium** 51°46N 0°21W, pop (1981) 77 187. Town in St Albans district, Hertfordshire, England; on R Ver, 40 km/25 ml NW of London; named after the first Christian martyr to be executed in Britain; Magna Carta

SAILING RIG

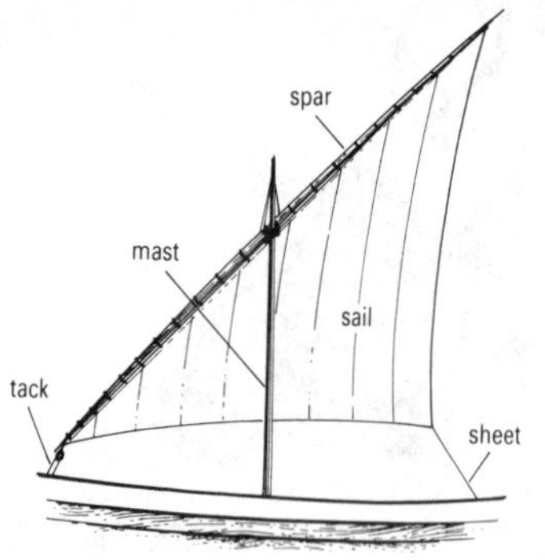

lateen rig

A large triangular sail is attached to a long tapering spar, resulting in an adaptable rig that can be secured at a variety of angles. Probably originating in Mesopotamia, it was adopted by the Egyptians, and later found throughout the Mediterranean. The Barbary Coast pirates of N Africa used it until the early 19th-c, and it can still sometimes be seen in Arab dhows.

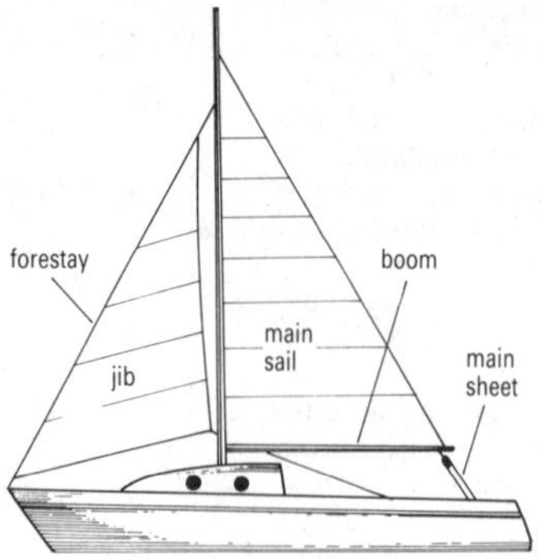

fore-and-aft rig

The sails are set in the fore-and-aft line, and are usually triangular, though sometimes quadrilateral. This rig is very much more efficient and manageable than the square rig, giving better performance to windward.

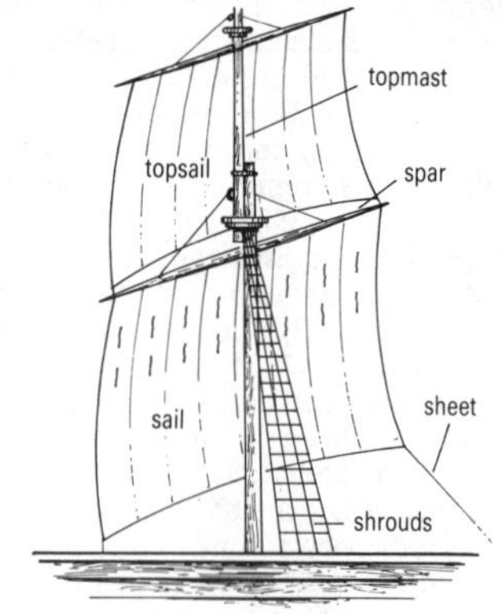

square rig

The sails are bent on to spars which are hung on the mast at the middle, thus usually making a square angle to the ship's fore-and-aft line.

drafted here; royal charter (1553); city status (1887); agricultural research station; railway; agricultural trade, microelectronics, printing; cathedral (1115, founded as Benedictine abbey, 793); Roman theatre; museum with Iron Age and Roman exhibits. » Britain, Roman; Hertfordshire; Magna Carta

St Andrews 56°20N 2°48W, pop(1981) 11 369. Town in NE Fife district, Fife, E Scotland; on S side of St Andrews Bay, 17 km/11 ml SE of Dundee; university (oldest in Scotland, founded 1412); textiles; tourism; St Andrews Royal and Ancient Golf Club, West Port (city gate, built 1589, restored 1843), remains of castle (1200) and cathedral (12th–13th-c); repertory theatre; arts centre; golf week (Apr); British Amateur Golf Championships (Jun). » Fife; Scotland [i]

St Anthony's fire » **ergotism**

St Anton am Arlberg 47°08N 9°52E. Winter sports resort in the Lechtal Alps (Arlberg massif), Vorarlberg, W Austria; cableway facilities on Valluga, Galzig, Brandkreuz, and Kapall; major skiing centre. » Lechtal Alps

St Bartholomew's Day Massacre (24 Aug 1572) The slaughter of French Huguenots in Paris, ordered by King Charles IX and connived at by the Queen Mother, Catherine de' Medici, to coincide with celebrations for the marriage of Marguerite de Valois and Henry of Navarre (18 Aug). An attempted assassination of the Huguenot leader Admiral Coligny failed (22 Aug), but mass butchery of Huguenots followed. » Catherine de' Medici; Charles IX; Huguenots

St Basil's Cathedral Part of the Historical Museum in Moscow. It was built (1555–61) as the Cathedral of the Intercession of the Virgin, but after 1588, when a chapel was added to house the remains of the ascetic Basil the Blessed, the present title was adopted. Eight chapels cluster round the principal church, and the assortment of spires and domes, together with the brightly painted exterior, create an exuberant, fairy-tale effect. » cathedral; Moscow

St Bernard The heaviest breed of dog (up to 100 kg/220 lb), developed at the Hospice of St Bernard in Switzerland to track people lost in the mountain snow; orange-brown and white; large with broad head, deep muzzle, pendulous ears; two forms: *smooth-haired* and *rough-haired*; also known as **Great Saint Bernard**. » dog

St Bernard's Passes Two transalpine frontier passes: the **Great Saint Bernard**, which crosses the Pennine Alps between Martigny in Switzerland and Aosta in Italy, and the **Little Saint Bernard**, which crosses the Graian Alps between Aosta and Bourg St Maurice in France. St Bernard of Menthon founded hospices in both passes in the 10th-c. » Alps; Bernard of Menthon

St Catharines 43°10N 79°15W, pop(1981) 124 018. Town in SE Ontario, SE Canada, S of Toronto; founded, 1784; railway; at entrance to Welland Ship Canal; university (1964); heart of Canada's fruit belt and major wine-growing region; light and heavy industry; Royal Canadian Henley Regatta (Aug); Niagara Grape and Wine Festival (Sept). » Ontario

St Christopher-Nevis » **St Kitts-Nevis**

St Croix [saynt **kroy**], formerly **Santa Cruz** pop(1980) 49 013; area 218 sq km/84 sq ml. Largest of the three main US Virgin Is, Lesser Antilles, Caribbean, 120 km/75 ml E of Puerto Rico; main towns, Christiansted (former capital of the Danish West Indies) and Frederiksted; tourism, oil refining, aluminium, textiles, pharmaceuticals, rum, fragrances. » Virgin Islands, United States

St Cyr, Ecole de [ay**kol** duh sã **seer**] A French military academy founded by Napoleon at Fontainebleau but transferred to St Cyr in 1808. The school was moved to Coetquidan in Brittany after World War 2, but retained the name of its former home. The buildings that it occupied at St Cyr were the former premises of a school for poor girls of good family established by Madame de Maintenon in 1687. » Napoleon I

St David's, Welsh **Tyddewi** 51°54N 5°16W, pop(1981) 1 800. Village in Preseli district, Dyfed, SW Wales, UK; 25 km/15 ml NW of Milford Haven on St Bride's Bay; episcopal seat; 12th-c cathedral honours the 6th-c Welsh patron saint, Dewi (David); mediaeval place of pilgrimage; smallest cathedral seat in UK. » Dyfed

St-Denis, Michel (Jacques Duchesne) [sĩ duh**nee**] (1897–1971) French theatre director, actor, and teacher, born at Beauvais. In 1931 he founded the Compagnie des Quinze, and directed numerous influential productions. When this company disbanded, he settled in England, founding with George Devine and others the London Theatre Studio (1936). His influence on British theatre continued with his work for the Old Vic (1947–52) and later with the Royal Shakespeare Company, where he became a director in 1962. He was appointed director of the Comédie de l'Est in 1952. He died in London. » Devine; Royal Shakespeare Company; theatre

St Denis, Ruth, originally **Ruth Dennis** (1879–1968) US dancer, choreographer, and teacher, born in Newark, New Jersey. She studied recitation, mime, and social dance before embarking on the development of an exotic form of modern dance, using oriental sources and mysticism. With Ted Shawn she started the Denishawn school and company, a training ground for the next generation of modern dancers including Doris Humphrey and Martha Graham. She died in Hollywood. » choreography; Graham, Martha; Humphrey, Doris; modern dance

St-Denis (France) [sĩ duh**nee**] 48°56N 2°21E, pop (1982) 91 275. Modern industrial town and railway centre in Seine-Saint-Denis department, NC France; N suburb of Paris; paints and varnishes, cars and aeronautical equipment; 12th-c Gothic Basilica of St-Denis, with tombs of several French monarchs. » Paris [i]

St Denis (Réunion) [sĩ duh**nee**] 20°52S 55°27E, pop (1982) 109 072. Capital of Réunion, on the N coast; airport; commerce, administration, tourism, agricultural trade. » Réunion

St Elias, Mount [ee**li**yas] 60°17N 140°55W. Mountain in St Elias Mts, on the Yukon–Alaska border, USA; rises to 5 489 m/18 008 ft; second highest peak in the USA. » United States of America [i]

St Elmo's fire A blue-green coloured electrical discharge which occurs during thunderstorm weather around the masts of ships, weather vanes, and aircraft wing tips. It is especially common in the Doldrums. » Doldrums; lightning; thunderstorm

St-Etienne [sĩ tay**tyen**] 45°27N 4°22E, pop (1982) 206 688. Manufacturing town and capital of Loire department, SW France; on the Central Plateau, 51 km/32 ml SW of Lyons; railway; university; school of mining (1816); food processing, electronics, firearms, chemicals; centre of metallurgical industry since 16th-c. » France [i]

Saint-Exupéry, Antoine (Marie Roger) de [sĩt eksyoo**puhree**] (1900–44) French airman and author, born in Lyons. A commercial and wartime pilot, his philosophy of 'heroic action' is found in such novels as *Vol de nuit* (1931, Night Flight). He is also known for his popular children's fable for adults, *Le Petit Prince* (1943, The Little Prince). He was declared missing after a flight to N Africa in World War 2. » French literature; novel

St Gallen [sankt **gal**uhn], Fr **St Gall** [sĩ **gal**] 47°25N 9°23E, pop (1980) 75 847. Ancient abbey town and capital of St Gallen canton, NE Switzerland; in a high valley in the Pre-Alps, 62 km/38 ml E of Zürich; developed around the abbey founded by St Gall, 7th-c; a world heritage site; university; commerce, textiles, engineering, tourism; cathedral (18th-c), Olma agriculture and milk industries fair, Spring Trade Fair (May). » Switzerland [i]

St George's 12°03N 61°45W, pop (1980e) 8 000. Port and capital town of Grenada, on SW coast; airport; founded as French settlement in 1650; port trade; tourism. » Grenada

St George's Channel Stretch of sea between the SE of Ireland (W) and Wales (E), connecting the Atlantic Ocean with the Irish Sea; at its narrowest between Carnsore Point (Ireland) and St David's Head (Wales), 74 km/46 ml across.

St Gotthard Pass [**got**hahd] 46°34N 8°31E. Mountain pass and tunnel (road and rail, 15 km/10 ml) between Andermatt and Airolo, over the St Gotthard massif in the Lepontine Alps, SC Switzerland; height, 2 108 m/6 916 ft; pass open between June and October; St Gotthard Hospice (14th-c). » Alps

St Helena 15°58S 5°43W; pop (1987) 5 644; area 122 sq km/47 sq ml. Volcanic island in the S Atlantic; a British territory, 1 920 km/1 200 ml from the SW coast of Africa; highest point, Diana's Peak (823 m/2 700 ft); discovered by the Portuguese on St Helena's feast day, 1502; annexed by the Dutch, 1633; annexed by the East India Company, 1659; Napoleon exiled here, 1815–21; Ascension and Tristan da Cunha made dependencies, 1922; port and capital, Jamestown; passenger and cargo services to the UK and S Africa; fish (mostly tuna), coffee, postage stamps; economy heavily subsidised by UK. » Ascension Island; Jamestown (St Helena); Napoleon I; Tristan da Cunha

St Helens 53°28N 2°44W, pop (1981) 114 822. Industrial town in St Helens borough, Merseyside, NW England; 18 km/11 ml E of Liverpool; railway; coal, engineering, textiles, glass. » Merseyside

St Helens, Mount 46°12N 122°12W. Volcano in SW Washington, USA, in the Cascade Range; rises to 2 549 m/8 363 ft; erupted 18 May 1980, causing damage amounting to $2.5 billion; a large area in the W states affected by volcanic ash; 100 people were killed and 276 homes destroyed. » volcano; Washington (state)

St Ives 50°12N 5°29W, pop (1981) 10 052. Resort town in Kerrier district, Cornwall, SW England; 12 km/7 ml NNE of Penzance; railway; tourism, water sports, fishing; festival of music and the arts (Sep). » Cornwall

St James's Palace Until the mid-19th-c, one of the principal royal palaces in London. Only parts of the original Tudor palace built for Henry VIII remain (notably the gatehouse and the chapel royal), and much of the building dates from the 18th-c. » Tudors

St John (Canada) 45°16N 66°03W, pop (1981) 80 521. Seaport in S New Brunswick, SE Canada, on Bay of Fundy at mouth of St John R; harbour ice-free all year; French fort, 1631–5; taken by British, 1758; many United Empire Loyalist immigrants after American Revolution; largely destroyed by fire, 1877; airfield; railway; shipbuilding, steel, pulp; Old Courthouse (1830), Trinity Church (rebuilt 1877), Chubb's Corner (1878), New Brunswick Museum, Martello Tower (1812), Fort Howe (1778); Reversing Falls (water falls in opposite directions over a rocky ledge according to the tide). » American Revolution; New Brunswick (Canada)

St John (US Virgin Is) pop (1980) 2 360; area 52 sq km/20 sq ml. Smallest of the three main US Virgin Is, Lesser Antilles, Caribbean, 8 km/5 ml E of St Thomas; contains the Virgin Is National Park, established in 1956, area 71 sq km/27 sq ml. » Virgin Islands, United States

St John's 47°34N 52°41W, pop (1981) 83 770. Capital of Newfoundland province, E Canada, SE of the island; Cabot landed here, 1497; British possession, 1583; held by the French, taken by the British 1762; airport; railway; university (1925); two cathedrals; shipbuilding, fish processing, timber; Signal Hill (where first wireless message received by Marconi, 1901), Colonial Building (1850). » Marconi; Newfoundland (Canada)

St John ambulance brigade A worldwide charitable organization that provides medical and nursing help to the aged, sick, and injured. It derives its inspiration from the Hospitallers, a military and religious order founded in the 11th-c (the Knights of Saint John of Jerusalem). » Hospitallers; nursing

St John's wort An annual and perennial, sometimes a shrub, native throughout temperate regions and tropical mountains; leaves gland-dotted, opposite or whorled, very narrow to oval; flowers often large and showy, yellow, 5-petalled with numerous stamens; fruit a capsule or berry. (Genus: *Hypericum*, 400 species. Family: *Guttifereae*.) » annual; perennial; rose of Sharon; shrub; stamen

Saint-Just, Louis (Antoine Léon Florelle) de [sĩ **zhüst**] (1767–94) French revolutionary, born at Decize. Educated at Soissons and Rheims, he studied law, and while in Paris began to write poetry and essays, notably *L'Esprit de la révolution* (1791, Spirit of the Revolution). He was elected to the National Convention (1792), attracted notice by his fierce tirades against the King, and as a devoted follower of Robespierre was sent on diplomatic and military missions. He joined the Committee of Public Safety (1793), contributing to the destruction of Danton and Hébert. He became President of the Convention (1794), and sponsored the radical Ventôse Laws, redistributing property to the poor. He was guillotined with Robespierre in the Thermidorian Reaction. » Danton; French Revolution [i]; Hébert; Robespierre

St Kilda 57°49S 8°34E. A group of small volcanic islands in the Atlantic Ocean, 160 km/62 ml W of Scotland; abandoned in 1930, having been inhabited for 2 000 years; cliffs (over 400 m/1 400 ft) colonized by over a million sea birds; a world heritage area. » Atlantic Ocean

St Kitts-Nevis or **St Christopher-Nevis**, official name **Federation of St Christopher and Nevis** pop (1990e) 44 100; area 269 sq km/104 sq ml. Independent state in the N Leeward Is, E Caribbean, c.360 km/225 ml SE of Puerto Rico; comprises the islands of St Christopher (St Kitts), Nevis, and Sombrero; divided into 14 parishes; capital, Basseterre; timezone GMT

−4; population mainly of African descent; official language, English; chief religion, Christianity; unit of currency, the East Caribbean dollar; St Kitts, length 37 km/23 ml, area 168 sq km/65 sq ml, mountain range rises to 1 156 m/3 793 ft at Mt Misery; Nevis, 3 km/1¾ ml SE, area 93 sq km/36 sq ml, dominated by a C peak rising to 985 m/3 232 ft; warm climate, average annual temperature 26°C, average annual rainfall 1 375 mm/54 in; low humidity; St Kitts the first British colony in the W Indies, 1623; control disputed between France and Britain, 17th–18th-c; ceded to Britain, 1783; St Kitts and Nevis united in 1882, along with Anguilla; state in association with the UK, 1967; separation of Anguilla, 1980; independence, 1983; British monarch is represented by a governor-general; governed by a prime minister and two legislative chambers, a 14-member National Assembly and an 8-member Nevis I Assembly; sugar and its products supply 60% of total exports; copra, cotton, electrical appliances, footwear, garments, tourism. » Anguilla; Basseterre; Charlestown; Leeward Islands (Caribbean); RR27 national holidays; RR59 political leaders

Saint Laurent, Yves (Henri Donat Mathieu) [sĩ loh**rã**] (1936–) French fashion designer, born in Oran, Algeria. He studied in Paris, graduating in modern languages, and was employed by Dior in 1955 after winning an International Wool Secretariat design competition. On Dior's death in 1957, he took over the house. In 1962 he opened his own house, and launched the first of his 160 Rive Gauche boutiques in 1966, selling ready-to-wear clothes, a trend which many other designers were to follow. » Dior; fashion

St Lawrence River, Fr **St Laurent** A principal river of N America, in E Canada, the chief outlet for the Great Lakes; issues from NE end of L Ontario and flows NE to the Gulf of St Lawrence N of the Gaspé Peninsula; forms part of border between Canada and USA; total length 1 197 km/744 ml; Thousand Islands rapids in Ontario used for hydroelectric power; several lakes along its course; major tourist area; tidal below Quebec, and increases gradually in width to c.145 km/90 ml; principal cities on its banks include Kingston, Montreal, Trois-Rivières, Quebec; formerly navigable for ocean-going vessels only as far as Montreal; St Lawrence Seaway (1955–9) between L Ontario and Montreal now allows passage to Great Lakes; often partly unnavigable in winter months. » Canada [i]; Great Lakes; St Lawrence Seaway

St Lawrence Seaway A system of canals, locks and dredged waterways providing a navigable channel from the Gulf of St Lawrence to the head of L Superior. In 1954 the Canadian and US governments co-operated on a project to establish a shipping lane 8 m/27 ft deep along the St Lawrence R; this was completed in 1959. The Welland Ship Canal is generally considered to be part of the present-day seaway. » canal; Welland Ship Canal

St Leger, Barry (1737–89) British army colonel. He fought in the American Revolution, and founded in 1776 his horse-racing stables at Doncaster. The St Leger race was named for him in 1778. » horse racing

St Leger » **Classics**

St-Lô, ancient **Briovera**, later **Laudus** [sĩ **loh**] 49°07N 1°05W, pop (1982) 24 792. Market town and capital of Manche department, NW France, 54 km/34 ml W of Caen; fortified by Charlemagne; almost completely destroyed in World War 2, but mediaeval part of town largely preserved; railway; horse breeding; 14th–15th-c Church of Notre-Dame (restored), Romanesque Church of Ste-Croix (restored). » Charlemagne

St-Louis (Senegal) [sĩ loo**ee**] 16°01N 16°30W, pop (1979) 96 594. Seaport capital of Saint-Louis region, Senegal; on a small island at the mouth of the R Sénégal, 177 km/110 ml NE of Dakar; built in 1658 on Sor I as a French trading company fort, and prospered with the slave trade; capital of French West Africa, 1895–1902; airfield; railway terminal; transportation point for surrounding area, fishing. » Senegal [i]

St Louis (USA) [saynt **loo**is] 38°37N 90°12W, pop (1980) 453 085. City and port in E Missouri, USA, on the Mississippi R; settled by the French, 1764; under Spanish control, 1770–1800; ceded to the USA, 1804; city status, 1822; railway; three universities (1818, 1853, 1960); largest city in the state; busiest inland port on the Mississippi; a major land transport hub; aircraft, spacecraft, machinery, metal and food products, chemicals, beer, fur trade, livestock, grain; major league teams, Cardinals (baseball), Cardinals (football), Blues (ice hockey); Gateway Arch (a giant steel arch on the river bank, 192 m/630 ft high, symbolizing the city as the gateway to the West); Art Museum, Science Centre, Missouri Botanical Garden, Goldenrod Showboat, Sports Hall of Fame; Ragtime and Jazz Festival (Jun), Veiled Prophet Fair (Jul). » Mississippi River; Missouri

St Lucia [**loo**sha, loo**see**a] pop (1990e) 151 000; area 616 sq km/238 sq ml. Second largest of the Windward Is, E Caribbean, 32 km/20 ml N of St Vincent; divided into 16 parishes; capital, Castries; chief towns, Vieux-Fort, Soufrière; timezone GMT −4; population mainly of African descent (90%); chief religion, Roman Catholicism; official language, English, with French patois widely spoken; unit of currency, the Eastern Caribbean dollar; length, 43 km/27 ml; maximum width, 23 km/14 ml; mountainous centre, rising to 950 m/3 117 ft at Mt Gimie; twin volcanic peaks of Gros and Petit Piton in SW; tropical climate; annual temperatures, 18–34°C; wet season (Jun–Dec); average annual rainfall, 1 500 mm/60 in (N coast), 4 000 mm/160 in (interior); reputedly visited by Columbus, 1502; disputed ownership between England and France, 17th–18th-c; British Crown Colony, 1814; independence, 1979; British monarch represented by a governor-general; 17-member House of Assembly, elected every five years, and an 11-member Senate; tourism the fastest-growing sector of the economy; bananas, cocoa, copra, citrus fruits, coconut oil; garments, textiles, electronic components, beverages, corrugated boxes, paper products, oil refining and transshipment. » Castries; Windward Islands; RR27 national holidays; RR60 political leaders

St-Malo [sĩ **mah**loh] 48°39N 2°00W, pop (1982) 46 000. Old port in Ille-et-Vilaine department, W France; at mouth of R Rance; badly damaged in World War 2; boatbuilding, fishing, electrical products, tourism; birthplace of Chateaubriand; tidal power station nearby. » Chateaubriand

St Mark's Cathedral A church constructed in 1063–71 on the site of a 9th-c shrine which housed the relics of St Mark, in Venice. It is built on a Byzantine Greek-cross plan, and is surmounted by five mosaic-covered domes. The richly decorated interior is faced with marble and mosaic. It became a cathedral in 1807. » Mark, St; Venice

St Michael and St George, the Most Distinguished Order of In the UK, an order of chivalry for those who have held high office or rendered distinguished service abroad; in practice most members belong to the diplomatic service. There are three classes: Knights and Dames Grand Cross (GCMG), Knights and Dames Commanders (KCMG/DCMG), and Companions (CMG). The motto is *Auspicium melioris aevi* (Lat 'a pledge of better times'), and the ribbon has equal stripes: blue, scarlet, blue. » decoration

St Moritz [sankt **mo**rits], Fr **Saint** [sĩ] **Moritz**, Romansch **San Murezzan** 46°30N 9°51E, pop (1980) 5 900. Resort town in Graubünden canton, SE Switzerland, in the Upper Engadine valley; altitude 1 853 m/6 079 ft; railway; spa; winter sports resort, home of the 1928 and 1948 Winter Olympics; facilities include a high ski-jump and the Cresta Run (bobsledding); Schiefer Turm. » Switzerland [i]

St-Nazaire [sĩ na**zair**] 47°17N 2°12W, pop (1982) 68 974. Seaport and industrial town in Loire-Atlantique department, W France; on right bank of R Loire at its mouth, 53 km/33 ml WNW of Nantes; thought to occupy site of Roman Carbilo; developed as deep-water port for Nantes in 19th-c; major debarkation port for American Expeditionary Force in World War 1; German submarine base in World War 2, in which the town was largely destroyed; shipbuilding, marine engineering, steel, fertilizers, brewing, food canning. » Nantes

St Paul 44°57N 93°06W, pop (1980) 270 230. Capital of state in Ramsey County, SE Minnesota, USA; a port on the Mississippi River E of its twin city Minneapolis; founded, 1838; capital of Minnesota Territory, 1849; city status, 1854; state capital, 1858; railway; university (1854); major industrial and commercial centre for a vast agricultural region; computers, electrical equipment, motor vehicles, chemicals, beer; State

Capitol, modelled after St Peter's in Rome, with the largest unsupported marble dome in the world; Winter Carnival (Feb), Festival of Nations (Apr). » Minneapolis; Minnesota

St Paul's Cathedral A Baroque cathedral on Ludgate Hill, London, built by Wren to replace the mediaeval cathedral destroyed by the Fire of London in 1666. It is surmounted by a central lantern dome which still dominates the C London skyline. » Fire of London; Wren, Christopher

St Peter's Basilica The largest Christian church, started in 1506 in Rome on the site of the 4th-c basilica built by Emperor Constantine. The present building was designed by Bramante on a Greek cross plan. This was adopted by successive architects, including Raphael and Michelangelo, but in 1660 Maderna was instructed to extend the nave, thereby changing the plan to that of a Latin cross. The immense dome, designed by Michelangelo and completed by Giacomo della Porta and Domenico Fontana, has a diameter of 42 m/137 ft. » Bramante; Constantine I (Emperor); Michelangelo; Raphael

St Petersburg (USA) 27°46N 82°39W, pop (1980) 238 647. Town in Pinellas County, W Florida, USA; a port on the tip of Pinellas Peninsula; settled, 1876; city status, 1903; airfield; railway; boatbuilding, trailers, air conditioners, electrical equipment, cement; trade in fruit and vegetables; major all-year tourist resort; large yacht basin. » Florida

St Petersburg (USSR) » **Leningrad**

St Pierre et Miquelon [sĩ **pyair** ay meeklõ] pop (1982) 6 041; area 240 sq km/93 sq ml. Two islands comprising a French overseas department in the N Atlantic Ocean, S of Newfoundland; main town, St Pierre; settled by Breton and Basque fishermen, 16th–17th-c; disputed between UK and France, 19th-c; confirmed as French territory, 1946; fishing, tourism. » Atlantic Ocean; France [i]

St-Quentin [sĩ kãtĩ] 49°51N 3°17E, pop (1982) 65 067. Industrial town in Aisne department, N France, on R Somme; railway; centre of woollen industry in Middle Ages; canal link to Belgium and N Germany; surrounded by battlefields throughout World War 1; chemicals, metalworks, electrical products, textiles; 12th–15th-c basilica, late-Gothic town hall, museum of entomology. » World War 1

Saint-Saëns, (Charles) Camille [sĩ **sãs**] (1835–1921) French composer and music critic, born in Paris. He began to compose at five, and studied at the Paris Conservatoire, writing his first symphony in 1853. He was a distinguished pianist and organist, and in 1871 helped to found the Société Nationale de Musique. He wrote four further symphonies; 13 operas, including his best-known, *Samson et Dalila* (1877); symphonic poems; piano, violin, and cello concertos; the popular *Carnival des animaux* (1886, Carnival of the Animals); church music, including his *Messe solennelle* (1855); chamber music; and songs. He died in Algiers.

St-Savin sur Gartempe, Church of [sĩ savĩ sür gah**tãmp**] An abbey church in St-Savin, W France; a world heritage monument. The original building, which was founded in 811 by Charlemagne over the tomb of the hermit St Savinus, was soon destroyed. The present building dates from the 11th-c, and is noted for its life-sized murals depicting biblical scenes. » Charlemagne

St-Simon, Claude Henri de Rouvroy, Comte de ('Count of') [sĩ see**mõ**] (1760–1825) French social reformer, the founder of French socialism, born in Paris. He served in the American War of Independence, and during the French Revolution was imprisoned as an aristocrat. His writing was a reaction against the savagery of the revolutionary period, and proclaimed a brotherhood of man in which science and technology would become a new spiritual authority, as in *Du système industriel* (1821, On the Industrial System) and *Nouveau christianisme* (1825, New Christianity). He died in Paris. » socialism

Saint-Simon, Louis de Rouvroy, Duke of [sĩ see**mõ**] (1675–1755) French writer, born in Paris. After some time in the army, he joined the court of Louis XIV, and from the 1690s kept a journal, published as his *Mémoires* (1752), giving impressions and descriptions of court life up to 1723. He died in Paris. » Louis XIV

St Swithin's Day The feast day of St Swithin (15 July), a former bishop of Winchester. According to a traditional rhyme, if it rains on St Swithin's Day it will rain for 40 days, and if it is dry, it will remain dry for 40 days.

St Thomas pop (1980) 44 218; area 72 sq km/28 sq ml. One of the three main US Virgin Is, Lesser Antilles, Caribbean, 64 km/40 ml N of St Croix; length, 21 km/13 ml; rises to 474 m/1 555 ft at Crown Mt; capital, Charlotte Amalie; airport; tourism, rum distilling; Coral World underwater observatory. » Virgin Islands, United States

St-Tropez [sĩ troh**pay**] 43°16N 6°39E. Fashionable resort on the Mediterranean coast, SE France, SW of Cannes; former small fishing port now frequented by yachtsmen, artists, and tourists. » Riviera

St Valentine's Day A day (14 Feb) on which special greetings cards (**valentine cards** or **valentines**) are sent, usually anonymously, to a person or people of the opposite sex to whom one feels attracted. There is a traditional English belief that birds choose their mates on this day.

St Vincent, official name **Saint Vincent and the Grenadines** pop (1990e) 115 000; land area 390 sq km/150 sq ml. Island group of the Windward Is, E Caribbean, 160 km/100 ml W of Barbados; divided into five parishes; capital, Kingstown; timezone GMT −4; population mainly of African descent; official language, English; chief religion, Protestantism; unit of currency, the East Caribbean dollar; comprises the island of St Vincent (length, 29 km/18 ml; width, 16 km/10 ml) and the N Grenadine Is; St Vincent volcanic in origin; highest peak Soufrière, active volcano (1 234 m/4 048 ft), most recent eruption 1979; tropical climate, average annual temperature 25°C, average annual rainfall 1 500 mm/60 in (coast), 3 800 mm/150 in (interior); visited by Columbus, 1498; British control, 1763; part of West Indies Federation, 1958–62; independence, 1979; British sovereign represented by a governor-general; a prime minister leads a 21-member House of Assembly, 15 of whom are elected; economy based on agriculture; bananas, arrowroot (world's largest producer), coconuts, nutmeg, mace, cocoa, sugar cane; food processing, cigarettes, textiles, beverages, furniture, tourism. » Grenadines, The; Kingstown; West Indies Federation; Windward Islands RR27 national holidays; RR60 political leaders

St Vincent, Cape, Port **Cabo de São Vicente** 37°01N 8°59W. Rocky headland 60 m/200 ft above sea-level on the Atlantic coast, Portugal; SW extremity of Portugal and of continental Europe; in the 12th-c a ship bearing the body of St Vincent came ashore here; scene of a British naval victory over the Spanish fleet in 1797. » Portugal [i]

St Vitus' dance » **chorea**

Sainte-Beuve, (Charles Augustin) [sĩt **berv**] (1804–69) French literary critic, born at Boulogne. Educated at Paris, he trained in medicine, then turned to writing. He produced several volumes of poetry, and in 1829 in the *Revue de Paris* began his *Causeries*, longer critical articles on French literature. His major works include several books of 'portraits' of literary contemporaries. His single novel, *Volupté*, appeared in 1835. In 1840 he became keeper of the Mazarin Library, and in 1848 professor of French literature at Liège. Nominated a Senator in 1865, his speeches in favour of liberty of thought earned him great popularity. He died in Paris. » Hugo; literary criticism

saintpaulia » **African violet**

Saints, the » **Clapham Sect**

Saipan [**siy**pan] pop (1980) 14 549; area 122 sq km/47 sq ml. Largest of the N Mariana Is, W Pacific, 240 km/150 ml NNE of Guam; length 23 km/14 ml; barrier reef protects a wide lagoon off the W coast; airport; tourism, copra, tropical fruit. » Mariana Islands, Commonwealth of the Northern

saithe [sayth] Commercially important codfish widely distributed in inshore waters of the N Atlantic; length up to 1.2 m/4 ft; dark green on back, sides and underside silvery grey; feeds on other fishes and crustaceans; popular with sea anglers; also called **coalfish**, **coley** or **pollock**. (*Pollachius virens*. Family: *Gadidae*.) » cod

Saka Era [**sah**ka] An era of dating in India calculated from AD 78. Possibly founded by Kaniska, it was certainly used early in the 2nd-c AD by Western Satraps, rulers in W India, and was also present in Sanskrit inscriptions in SE Asia. It has been used alongside Gregorian dates by the Indian Government since 1957. » satrapy; RR22

Sakai [**sa**kiy] 34°35N 135°28E, pop (1980) 810 106. City in Osaka prefecture, SC Honshu, Japan, on E shore of Osaka-wan Bay; formerly an important port, but harbour now silted up; university; chemicals, fertilizers, aluminium products, machinery. » Honshu

saké [**sa**kay] A Japanese rice wine, brewed in Japan for centuries, and very popular in winter. The drink has sweeter and drier varieties, and special, first, and second class grades. It is generally warmed in small bottles and drunk from small cups. Leaving your cup full means you have had enough. Saké is also presented to Shinto shrines, especially at New Year. » rice; shochu

Sakhalin, Jap **Karafuto** [saka**leen**] area 74 066 sq km/28 589 sq ml. Island in the Sea of Okhotsk, E Russia, separated from the Russian mainland (W) by the Tatar Strait, and from Japan (S) by La Pérouse Strait; length, 942 km/585 ml; maximum width, 160 km/100 ml; highest point 1 609 m/5 279 ft; first Russian visit, 1644; colonized by the Japanese, 18th-c; ceded to Russia in exchange for the Kuril Is, 1875; Japan gained control of S area, 1905; ceded to the USSR, 1945; two parallel mountain ranges run N–S; agriculture in the C and S; severe climate, annual mean temperature near freezing point; largely forested; oil, coal, timber, paper, dairy farming. » Russia

Sakharov, Andrei [**sa**karof] (1921–89) Russian physicist, born and educated in Moscow. In 1948 he joined the nuclear weapons research group, and is usually credited with a critical role in developing the Soviet hydrogen bomb. He became a full member of the Academy of Sciences in 1953. In 1958 he opposed nuclear weapon tests, thereafter supporting East–West co-operation and human rights, and in 1975 was awarded the Nobel Peace Prize. Exiled to Nizhni Novgorod in 1980 as a leading dissident, he lived under poor conditions until restored to favour in 1987. He was elected to the Congress of People's Deputies in 1989. » civil rights; hydrogen bomb [i]

Sakhmet or **Sekmet** [**sak**met] An ancient Egyptian goddess of Memphis, depicted with the head of a lioness; her name means 'powerful'. She is associated with savage cruelty, in particular towards the enemies of the Pharaoh. » Egyptian religion

saki [sa**kee**] A New World monkey; coat long, especially around face; tail long; broad mouth turns downwards at sides, producing a sad expression; lives in groups of up to 10 along river banks or forest edges. (Genus: *Pithecia*, 4 species.) » New World monkey

Saki » **Munro, H H**

Sakigake and Suisei project The first Japanese interplanetary spacecraft, launched to intercept Comet Halley. *Sakigake* ('forerunner') was launched (Jan 1985) as a test spacecraft for *Suisei* ('comet', launched Aug 1985). They were instrumented to measure solar wind interaction and the hydrogen cloud of the comet. They made highly successful encounters (11 and 8 Mar 1986 respectively) at substantially greater distances from the nucleus than other spacecraft in the 'Halley Armada' (VEGA and Giotto). They were built and operated by the Institute for Space and Astronautical Science. » Halley's comet; Space Organizations Worldwide

sal ammoniac [sal a**moh**niak] » **ammonium**

sal volatile [sal vuh**la**tilee] » **ammonium**

salad burnet » **burnet**

Saladin [**sal**adin], in full **Salah ed-din Yussuf ibn Ayub** (1137–93) Sultan of Egypt and Syria, the leader of the Muslims against the crusaders in Palestine, born at Tekrit, Mesopotamia. He entered the service of Nur ed-din, Emir of Syria, and on his death (1174) proclaimed himself Sultan, reduced Mesopotamia,.and received the homage of the Seljuk princes of Asia Minor. His remaining years were occupied in wars with the Christians, whom he defeated near Tiberias in 1187, recapturing almost all their fortified places in Syria. A further crusade, headed by the kings of France and England, captured Acre in 1191, and he was defeated. He died soon after at Damascus. » Crusades [i]; Islam

Salado, River, Span (**Río**) [sa**la**thoh] River forming part of a C Argentine system; rises as the Bermejo in W La Rioja province, flowing S then SE to join the R Colorado 240 km/149 ml W of Bahía Blanca; lower course sometimes called the Curacó; total length, 1 200 km/746 ml; this river must be distinguished from the **R Salado del Norte**, NC Argentina, which rises in the Andes, and flows 2 000 km/1 250 ml SE to the Paraná at Santa Fe. » Argentina [i]

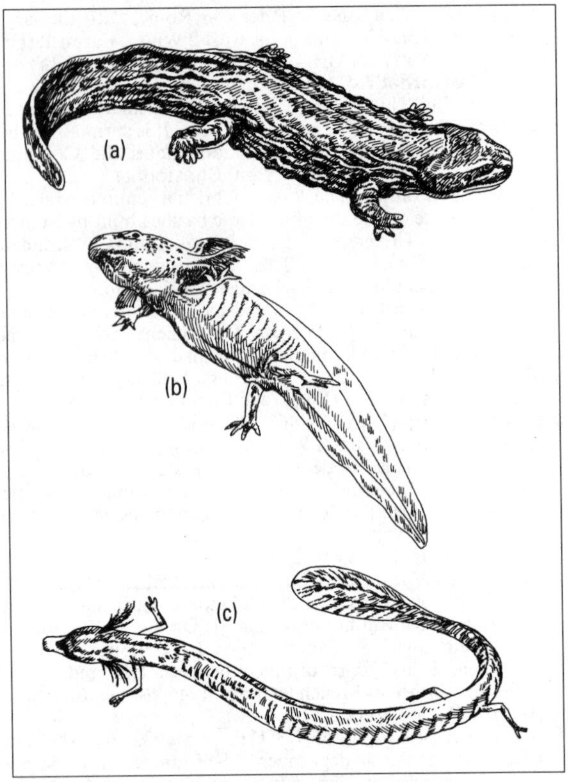

Salamanders – Hellbender (a), axolotl (b) and olm (c)

Salamanca [sala**mang**ka], ancient **Helmantica** or **Salmantica** 40°58N 5°39W, pop (1981) 167 131. Capital of Salamanca province, Castilla-León, W Spain; on R Tormes, 212 km/132 ml W of Madrid; scene of British victory over the French in the Peninsular War (1812); bishopric; railway; university (1940); agricultural centre, rubber products, wool, pharmaceuticals; House of Shells (15th-c), San Stefano monastery, old and new cathedrals; patronal festival (Jun), fair and fiesta (Sep). » Peninsular War; Spain [i]

salamander An amphibian widespread in the temperate N hemisphere and tropical S America; slim body with long tail; juveniles live in water, with feather-like gills and fin around tail; adults live mainly on dry land. (Order: *Urodela*, 358 species.) » amphibian; axolotl; fire salamander; hellbender; mudpuppy; newt; olm; siren

Salamis (ancient Cyprus) [**sa**lamis] The principal city of prehistoric and classical Cyprus, on the E coast 8 km/5 ml north of Famagusta, its mediaeval and modern successor. Founded c.1075 BC, it flourished particularly during the 8th–4th-c BC. Destroyed by earthquake in AD 332–42, it was rebuilt as the Christian city of Constantia, but permanently abandoned after the Arab raids in 647. » Cyprus [i]

Salamis (Greece) [**sa**lamis] or **Koulouri** 37°58N 23°30E, pop (1981) 20 437. Town in Attica department, Greece, on the W coast of Salamis I; to the E, scene of a decisive Greek naval victory over the Persians, 480 BC; local ferries; Navy Week (Jun–Jul). » Attica; Greece [i]; Persian Wars

Salang Tunnel and pass in the Hindu Kush, E Afghanistan; along the main supply route from Tadzhikistan to Kabul; focus of resistance activity by the Mujahadeen guerrillas against the Soviet troops and the Afghan Army during the occupation of Afghanistan (1979–89). » Afghanistan [i]; Hindu Kush; Mujahadeen

Salazar, António de Oliviera [sala**zah**] (1889–1970) Portuguese dictator (1932–68), born near Coimbra, where he studied law, and taught economics. In 1928 he became Minister of Finance, with extensive powers. As Premier, in 1932 he introduced a new, authoritarian regime, the *Estado Novo* ('New State'). He was also Minister of War (1936–44) and of Foreign Affairs (1936–47) during the delicate period of the Spanish Civil War. He retired in 1968, and died in Lisbon. » Spanish Civil War

Salcantay, Nevado [nay**vah**doh salkan**tiy**] 13°18S 72°35W. Andean peak in SC Peru, 72 km/45 ml WNW of Cuzco; highest point in the Cordillera Vilcabamba at 6 271 m/20 574 ft; Machu Picchu to the N. » Andes; Machu Picchu

Salchow, (Karl Emil Julius) Ulrich [**sal**kow] (1877–1949) Swedish figure skater. The first man to win an Olympic gold medal for this sport (1908), he was a record 10 times world champion (1901–11) and nine times European title holder between 1898 and 1913. He died in Stockholm. » ice skating

Sale (Australia) 38°06S 147°06E, pop (1983e) 13 820. City in SE Victoria, Australia; railway; supply centre for the Bass Strait oil fields; Omega Navigation Tower (427 m/1 400 ft), the highest building in Australia; oil and natural gas display; regional arts centre; tourism. » Victoria (Australia)

Sale (UK) 53°26N 2°19W, pop (1981) 57 933. Town in Trafford borough, Greater Manchester, NW England; 8 km/5 ml SW of Manchester; railway; engineering. » Manchester, Greater

Salem (Massachusetts) [**say**luhm] 42°31N 70°53W, pop (1980) 38 220. Seat of Essex County, NE Massachusetts, USA; residential suburb of Boston on Massachusetts Bay; settled, 1626; developed as port serving East Indies trade; 20 people executed as witches here, 1692; railway; birthplace of Nathaniel Hawthorne; Witch Museum, Salem Maritime National Historic Site, Pioneer Village. » Hawthorne; Massachusetts

Salem (Oregon) 44°56N 123°02W, pop (1980) 89 233. State capital in Marion County, NW Oregon, USA; on the Willamette R; founded by Methodist missionaries, 1841; capital of Oregon Territory, 1851; state capital, 1859; railway; university (1842); food processing, high technology equipment, metal goods. » Oregon

Salerno 40°40N 14°46E, pop (1981) 157 385. Industrial town and capital of Salerno province, Campania, Italy; 50 km/31 ml ESE of Naples, on a bay of the Tyrrhenian Sea; founded by the Romans, 197 BC; one of the earliest universities in Europe, a notable school of medicine (11th-c, closed 1812); scene of major World War 2 fighting, after Allied landing (1943); archbishopric; railway; new university (1970); milling, engineering, cement, textiles; cathedral (11th-c). » Italy [i]

Sales, St Francis of » **Francis of Sales, St**

sales tax A tax levied on goods sold, usually a percentage of the price. It is levied in the USA by most states, at differing rates, and on most products. The retail price quoted may include the sales tax element. » taxation; VAT

Salford [**sawl**fuhd] 53°30N 2°16W, pop (1981) 98 343. City in Salford borough, Greater Manchester, NW England; on the R Irwell and Manchester Ship Canal, W of Manchester; chartered in 1230; designated a city in 1926; university (1967); railway; docks for Manchester; textiles, electrical engineering, chemicals, clothing; Roman Catholic cathedral (1848); Peel Park Museum; art gallery. » Manchester, Greater

Salians » **Franks**

Salic Law In normal usage, a rule of succession to the throne barring women, and men whose royal descent is only through females. The principle was established in France from 1316, partly by ingeniously invoking the law-code of the Salian Franks, issued c.511 and given definitive form c.798 – Salic Law (Lat *Lex Salica*) in its original sense. » Franks

salicylic acid [salis**il**ik] A drug first prepared in 1838 from an extract of willow bark; its salt, sodium salicylate, was first used therapeutically for rheumatic pains and feverish cold in 1875. It was superseded in 1899 by the more potent acetylsalicylic acid (aspirin). » aspirin; willow

Salieri, Antonio [sal**yay**ree] (1750–1825) Italian composer, born in Verona. He arrived in Vienna at 16, and worked there for the rest of his life, becoming court composer (1774) and *Hofkapellmeister* (1788). He wrote over 40 operas, an oratorio, and masses, and became a famous rival of Mozart. He died in Vienna.

Salinger, J(erome) D(avid) (1919–) US author, born in New York City. He served in World War 2, then devoted himself to writing, especially in the *New Yorker* magazine. His fame rests on the novel *Catcher in the Rye* (1951), written in the idiom of a New York 16-year-old who has run away from school. Other books include *Nine Stories* (1953) and *Franny and Zooey* (1961). He has become a recluse in his later years. » American literature; novel

salinity The saltiness of sea water, ie the total amount of dissolved substances in sea water, usually reported in parts per thousand (‰), grams of solute per kilogram of sea water. The average salinity of ocean water is about 35 ‰. » salt

Salisbury » **Cecil, Robert**

Salisbury (Rhodesia) » **Harare**

Salisbury (UK) [**sawlz**bree], sometimes called **New Sarum** 51°05N 1°48W, pop (1981) 37 831. City in Wiltshire, S England; at the junction of the Avon, Nadder, Bourne, and Wylye Rivers, 34 km/21 ml NW of Southampton; Old Sarum (3 km/1¾ ml N), Iron Age hill fort, later the centre of settlement, but abandoned when New Sarum was founded in 1220 (though continued to return two members to parliament until the passing of the Reform Bill); Duke of Buckingham beheaded here in 1483, when Salisbury was the headquarters of Richard III; railway; engineering, tourism, agricultural trade; 13th-c cathedral, with the highest spire in Britain, contains one of four copies of the Magna Carta; Churches of St Thomas (15th-c), St Martin (13th–15th-c) and St Edmund (1407). » Magna Carta; Richard III; Wiltshire

Salisbury Plain A vast chalk plateau of open downs in Wiltshire, S England, rising to an average of 137 m/450 ft and covering some 77 700 ha/192 000 acres. Much of the area is now either under cultivation or used for army training, but it remains remarkable for a number of prehistoric sites, particularly Stonehenge. » Stonehenge

Salish [**say**lish] N American Indian groups, part of the Plateau Indian culture, who originally settled between the Rocky Mts and the Cascade Mts in present-day British Columbia, Washington, Idaho, and Montana. Today they are mostly settled on small reservations, working as farmers and labourers. They are also known as *interior Salish*, to distinguish them from the culturally different *coastal Salish*. » American Indians; Plateau Indians

saliva A secretory product of insect and terrestrial vertebrate salivary glands. In the latter it is a clear, often sticky solution of salts and proteins. It includes *mucin*, which binds food together and lubricates the throat to facilitate swallowing, and sometimes (eg in humans) the enzyme α-amylase (ptyalin), which aids starch digestion. Anti-coagulants are often present in the saliva of blood-sucking insects. » salivary glands

salivary glands Glands which secrete saliva, consisting of an excreting part (the *alveoli* or *acini*), and ducts which transport the saliva to the oral cavity. In humans there are three pairs of large glands and numerous small glands (in the palate, tongue, lips, and cheeks) which open directly onto the surface of the oral mucous membrane. The secretion of saliva is under the control of both the parasympathetic and sympathetic nervous systems. » nervous system; saliva

Salk, J(onas) E(dward) [saw(l)k] (1914–) US virologist, discoverer in 1953 of the first vaccine against poliomyelitis, born in New York City. He worked on an influenza vaccine at Michigan (1942–4), and later became director of virus research (1947–9) and professor (1949–54) at Pittsburgh. In 1953–4 he prepared inactivated poliomyelitis vaccine, given by injections, which (after some controversy) was successfully tested. He became a founding director of the Salk Institute, California, in 1975. » poliomyelitis; Sabin; vaccination

sallow Any of several species of willow with broad, greyish leaves, and catkins (the 'pussy willows' of hedgerows) appearing before the leaves. (Family: *Salicaceae*.) » willow

salmon Large anadromous (ascending rivers to breed) fish, widespread and locally common in the N Atlantic; length up to 1.5 m/5 ft; adults undertake extensive migrations at sea, feeding on a variety of fishes and crustaceans, returning to the headwaters of freshwater rivers to breed; greatly prized as game fish, and also taken commercially at sea; with the trouts and chars, comprise the very important family, *Salmonidae*. (*Salmo salar*.) » fish [i]; pink salmon; sockeye

salmonella A rod-shaped, typically motile bacterium that is a disease-causing agent of the human intestine. It can grow with or without oxygen, and includes the causative agents of typhoid and paratyphoid fever, as well as of bacterial dysentery and food poisoning. Acute vomiting and diarrhoea occur 12–24 hours after eating contaminated food. (Kingdom: *Monera*. Family: *Enterobacteriaceae*.) » bacteria [i]; food poisoning; intestine; typhoid fever

Salome [sa**loh**may] (1st-c) The traditional name of the daughter of Herodias. *Mark* 6.17–28 relates that she danced before Herod Antipas, and was offered a reward. At her mother's instigation, she was given the head of John the Baptist. The incident is not recorded in the historical account by Josephus, however. » Herod Antipas; John the Baptist; Josephus

Salon [salõ] In France, an exhibition of art by members of the French Royal Academy, originating in 1667 and held then in the *Salon d'Apollon* of the Louvre Palace, Paris; held annually since the time of the French Revolution. In the 19th-c the selection jury refused to hang many of the Impressionist and post-Impressionist painters, whose work was then shown (1863 and 1883) in the **Salon des Refusés**. The **Salon des Indépendents** is an annual art exhibition first held in Paris in 1884. In recent years, the term has come to be applied to other kinds of exhibition, such as the book-fair, **Salon du Livre**. » Impressionism (art)

Salonga [sa**long**ga] area 36 560 sq km/14 112 sq ml. National park in Zaire; a world heritage site; established in 1970; main rivers include the Salonga, Lomela, and Luilaka. » Zaire [i]

Salonica or **Salonika** [sa**lon**ika], Gr **Thessaloníki** 40°38N 22°58E, pop (1981) 706 180. Seaport and capital of Salonica department, Greece; second largest city of Greece; founded, 315 BC; capital of Roman Macedonia, 148 BC; held by Turkey, 1430–1912; base for Allied operations in World War 1; airport; railway; ferry to mainland and islands; university (1926); textiles, metal products, chemicals, cigarettes, agricultural trade, tourism; Arch of Galerius (297), 5th-c Basilica of Ayia Paraskevi, 9th-c Basilica of Ayios Dimitrios; carnival (Feb), Navy Week (Jun–Jul), international trade fair (Sep), song festival and film festival (Sep). » Greece [i]

Salote [sa**loh**tay] (1900–65) Queen of Tonga, who succeeded her father, King George Tupou II, in 1918. She is remembered in Britain for her colourful and engaging presence during her visit for the Coronation of Queen Elizabeth (1953). » Tonga

salp » **tunicate**

salsa A type of popular music of Cuban origin, taken to the E USA in the 1940s and 1950s, since when it has both merged with jazz and absorbed other influences, while retaining its distinctive rhythm. » jazz; pop music

salsify A plant, usually biennial, growing to 125 cm/50 in, native to the Mediterranean region; cylindrical taproot; leaves grass-like; flower-heads solitary, violet-purple, surrounded by about eight bracts; fruit with a large feathery parachute of hairs. It is widely grown for its edible fleshy root, and sometimes as an ornamental. (*Tragopogon porrifolius*. Family: *Compositae*.) » biennial; bract; root

salt An ionic compound derivable in principle from the reaction of an acid with a base. Most salts are solids at normal temperatures, and dissolve in water to release positive and negative ions (cations and anions). Common salt is sodium chloride (NaCl). » acid; base (chemistry)

SALT An acronym of **Strategic Arms Limitation Talks**, held between the USA and USSR. There have been two rounds of talks. The first began in Helsinki in 1969, designed to place a numerical limit on intercontinental nuclear weapons in the hope of slowing down the arms race. An agreement (SALT 1) was reached in 1974. After this there was a hardening of attitudes in the West against the intentions of the USSR, largely because of its refusal to allow on-site verification and its other international activities (eg the invasion of Afghanistan). In consequence, SALT 2 (1979) was not ratified by the US Senate, which felt it set dangerous precedents for SALT 3, and it was withdrawn. Both sides have, however, kept to the limitations set. There is little prospect for a SALT 3. » arms control

Salt Lake City 40°45N 111°53W, pop (1980) 163 033. State capital in Salt Lake County, N Utah, USA; on the Jordan R, near the S end of the Great Salt Lake; settled by Mormons, 1849; expanded as centre on route to California gold mines; world centre of the Mormon Church (60% of the population are Mormons); railway; university (1850); processing centre for irrigated agricultural region; aerospace components, electronic equipment, processed foods, agricultural chemicals; silver, lead, and copper smelting plants; major league team, Jazz (basketball); Temple Square, Trolley Square, Salt Lake Art Centre, Utah Museum of Fine Arts, Pioneer Memorial Museum, Hansen Planetarium, Utah Museum of Natural History; Utah Arts Festival (Jun). » Mormons; Utah

Salta 24°46S 65°28W, pop (1980) 260 323. Capital of Salta province, NW Argentina; on the R Arias, in the Lerma valley; altitude 1 190 m/3 904 ft; founded 1582; site of battle in which Spanish royalists were defeated (1813); airport; railway; university (1967); commercial and trade centre for extensive farming, timber, stock-raising, and mining area; cathedral contains venerated Christian images sent from Spain in 1592, and thought to have caused a miracle on 13 Sep 1692, when an earthquake ceased on their being carried through the streets; large parade held (Sep) in celebration of this event. » Argentina [i]

Saltillo [sal**tee**yoh] 25°30N 101°00W, pop (1980) 321 758. Resort capital of Coahuila state, N Mexico, 85 km/53 ml SW of Monterrey; altitude 1 609 m/5 279 ft; founded, 1575; railway; university (1867, refounded 1957); agricultural trade, textiles, ceramics, coal mining; cathedral (18th-c); fiestas (Oct). » Mexico [i]

saltpetre » **potassium**

saltwort A prickly, much-branched annual, native to the N hemisphere; stems red-striped; leaves narrow, very succulent, spine-tipped; flowers tiny, green. It is salt tolerant, growing on sandy shores. (*Salsola kali*. Family: *Chenopodiaceae*.) » annual

saluki [sa**loo**kee] The fastest breed of dog (speeds recorded up to 69 kph/43 mph), developed in Arabia to hunt in the desert with Bedouin; oldest of the greyhound group; resembles the greyhound, with long hair on ears, tail, and backs of legs (a smooth-haired form also exists); also known as the **Arabian hound** or **gazelle hound**. » dog; greyhound

Salut, Iles du [eel dü salü] Island archipelago c.13 km/8 ml off the coast of French Guiana, NE South America; includes Ile Royale, Ile Saint Joseph, and Ile du Diable (Devil's I); housed notorious French penal colonies from 1898 until 1940s; political prisoners on Devil's I included Alfred Dreyfus; hotel on Ile Royale is the warders' former mess hall. » Dreyfus; French Guiana [i]

Salvador [salva**daw**], also known as **Bahia** 12°58S 38°29W, pop (1980) 1 491 642. Port capital of Bahia state, NE Brazil, on the Atlantic coast SE of Recife; founded 1549, capital of Brazil until 1763; airfield; railway; university (1946); trade in sugar, tobacco, cocoa, gemstones; cigars, food processing, oil refining, petrochemicals, tourism; most of the city's 135 churches and the fortifications date from the 17th–18th-c; older parts of the upper city are a national monument and world heritage site; government palace, city library (1811), fort of Santo Antônio da Barra (1589); carnival (Nov–Jan). » Bahia; Brazil [i]

Salvador, El » **El Salvador** [i]

salvage Compensation paid to someone (the *salvor*) who saves maritime property (a ship or its cargo) from loss or damage. The service must be rendered at sea or in tidal waters. A salvor may claim an award in the courts, where he or she has acted voluntarily. Salvage may also be the subject of prior agreement between the salvor and the property owner. » Admiralty Court

salvarsan » **arsenicals**

Salvation Army A non-sectarian Christian organization founded in the East End of London by William Booth in 1865, dedicated to minister to the poor and needy. It retains a military-style structure and evangelical atmosphere, and its members, both men and women, wear distinctive uniform. It is now established in over 80 countries. » Booth, William; Christianity; evangelicalism

salvia A large genus of tropical and temperate annual or perennial herbs and shrubs; stems square; leaves in opposite pairs; flowers 2-lipped, the upper often hooded. The flower shape and colour are closely geared to pollinators. The New World species, pollinated by birds, typically are red, and have flowers with long straight tubes. In other species the flowers range from cream to red, mauve, or blue, are often curved, and are pollinated by long-tongued bees. Popular garden plants include the scarlet-flowered annual *Salvia splendens*. Some are aromatic herbs. (Genus: *Salvia*, 700 species. Family: *Labiatae*.) » annual; herb; perennial; pollination; sage

Salween, River [sal**ween**], Burmese **Nu Jiang** River in SE Asia, rising in SW China; flows generally S through Myanmar, forming part of Myanmar–Thailand border, to enter the Gulf of Martaban, an inlet of the Andaman Sea; because of rapids, navigable only to Kamamaung (120 km/75 ml from mouth); length 2 815 km/1 750 ml. » Andaman Sea; Burma [i]

Salyut ('Salute') space station The first-generation Soviet space station, capable of docking with the Soyuz crew ferry and Progress resupply vehicle; it provides 100 m^3/3 500 ft^3 of living space for up to five cosmonauts. Two versions have been flown in a programme spanning 1971 to the present, aimed at accumulating data on long-duration space-flight experience and biomedical experiments, Earth remote sensing, and micro-gravity science. The first station was flown in 1971, the last (Salyut 7) in 1982. The station's orbit eventually decays, with the vehicle re-entering the atmosphere and burning up. Crews have accumulated many hundred days of flight experience. A notably dangerous repair mission was undertaken to Salyut 7 in 1985, by V Dzhanibekov and V Savinykh, after the station seriously malfunctioned between crew occupancies. » Soviet space programme; Soyuz spacecraft

Salzburg [**zalts**boork] 47°25N 13°03E, pop (1981) 139 426. Capital of Salzburg state, C Austria; on the R Salzach; Old Town between the left bank of the river and the Mönchsberg ridge; railway; university (re-opened 1962); archbishopric; textiles, brewing, metallurgy; cathedral (1614–28), St Peter's Church (1130–43), Franciscan Church, Kollegienkirche (1694–1707), town hall (originally 1407); fortress of Hohensalzburg (1077) dominates the town; a focal point for the international tourist trade; birthplace of Mozart, a fame reflected in the Mozarteum (musical academy) and the Mozart Festival (Jan); Easter Festival, Salzburg Festival (Jul–Aug). » Austria [i]; Mozart

Salzburg Alps A division of the Eastern Alps along the Austro-German border S of Salzburg; highest peaks are the Hochkönig (2 938 m/9 639 ft) in Austria, and the Watzmann (2 713 m/8 901 ft) in Germany. » Alps

Salzkammergut [**zalts**kamergut] E Alpine region in C Austria; popular tourist area with many lakes; mountains include Dachstein and Totes Gebirge; towns include Gmunden, Hallstatt, Bad Aussee; name originally applied to a salt-mining area around Bad Ischl. » Austria [i]

Samaria [sam**air**ia] The site in C Palestine of the ancient capital of the N kingdom of the Hebrews, Israel. Destroyed by the Assyrians c.722 BC, Herod the Great rebuilt and enlarged it in the 20s BC. It remained a flourishing Greek-style city throughout the Roman period. It is now in the Israeli-occupied West Bank. » Assyria; Hellenization; West Bank

Samaritans 1 A sect of Jewish origin, living in Samaria, the N territory of Israel, who apparently were not deported in the Assyrian conquest of c.721 BC and who were in tension with the Jews of Judea during the rebuilding of Jerusalem after the return from exile and well into New Testament times. Jews criticized them for their mixed ancestry, their building of a rival temple on Mt Gerizim, and their schism from true Judaism. A small remnant survives today. » Judaism; Temple, Jerusalem 2 A group founded in London in 1953 by an Anglican priest, Chad Varah, providing a telephone counselling service to support those who are depressed or contemplating suicide. It is named after the 'Good Samaritan' in the parable of Jesus. In the UK, there are over 180 branches, operated by some 20 000 volunteers. A free, confidential, and anonymous service is offered for 24 hours a day.

Samarkand [samah**kant**] 39°40N 66°57E, pop (1989) 366 000. Capital city of Samarkandskaya oblast, Uzbekistan; a major industrial, scientific, and cultural centre situated in the fertile Zeravshan valley; Abbasid capital, 9th–10th-c; known as the city of Timur (1333–1405), after the Tatar conqueror; ruled by the Uzbeks, 16th–19th-c; airfield; railway; university (1933); solar research, fruit, wine, furniture, porcelain, clothing, foodstuffs, sheepskins, silk, cotton; Gur Amir mausoleum. » Abbasids; Gur Amir; Silk Road; Uzbekistan

samba A Brazilian dance which existed in various rural and urban forms, always accompanied by singing, before it was taken up as a ballroom dance in the 1930s. Lively, syncopated rhythms are a dominant feature.

Samhain [**sow**uhn] One of the Celtic quarterly feasts. It was celebrated on 1 November to mark the beginning of winter when, it was believed, the way to the 'other world' was opened and the dead could return to communicate with the living. There are many tales of mysterious happenings at Samhain. » Celts

samizdat (Russian *sam*, 'self' + *izdatelstvo*, 'publishing') Privately circulated editions of book-length and shorter texts not authorized for publication by the State censorship in the USSR, and usually reproduced from typescript. The publishing of such work abroad was known as *tamizdat* (Russian *tam*, 'there'). » publishing

Samos pop (1981) 31 629; area 476 sq km/184 sq ml. Wooded island in the E Aegean Sea, Greece, separated from W coast of Turkey by a strait only 2 km/1¼ ml wide; rises to 1 440 m/4 724 ft in the W; birthplace of Pythagoras; site of the Heraion; commerce, wine, tourism. » Greece [i]; Pythagoras

Samothrace, Gr **Samothráki** pop (1984e) 4 000; area 178 sq km/69 sq ml. Greek island in the NE Aegean Sea, 40 km/25 ml from the mainland; rises to 1 600 m/5 249 ft; noted for its sanctuary of the Great Gods, and for the 'Victory of Samothrace' sculpture (Louvre, Paris). » Aegean Sea; Greece [i]

Samoyed (anthropology) » **Nenets**

Samoyed (zoology) [**sam**oyed] An active spitz breed of dog, developed in Siberia; medium-sized with an extremely thick coat of straight pale hairs; tail carried over back only when alert, loosely curled. » dog; spitz

samphire A fleshy, much-branched perennial, growing to 30 cm/12 in, native to coastal areas of Europe, the Mediterranean, and the Black Sea; leaves divided into narrow linear segments, circular in cross-section; flowers yellowish, in umbels 3–6 cm/1¼–2½ in across. The fleshy leaves are sometimes made into a pickle. (*Crithmum maritimum*. Family: *Umbelliferae*.) » perennial; umbel

Samson (c.11th-c BC?) A legendary hero of the tribe of Dan, purportedly the last of Israel's tribal leaders ('judges') prior to Samuel and the establishment of the monarchy under Saul. Stories in *Jud* 13–16 tell of his great strength, his battles against the Philistines, his 20-year rule, and his fatal infatuation with Delilah. When she cut his hair, breaking his Nazirite vow, he lost his strength, and was held by the Philistines until his hair grew back and he pulled down their temple upon them. » Dan, tribe of; Delilah; Judges, Book of

Samudragupta [sam**ud**ragupta] (?–c.380) N Indian emperor, with a reputation as a warrior, poet, and musician. He epitomized the ideal king of the golden age of Hindu history. » Hinduism

Samuel (11th-c BC) (Heb probably 'name of God') In the Hebrew Bible/Old Testament, the last of the judges and first of the prophets, son of Elkanah and his wife Hannah; an Ephraimite who was dedicated to the priesthood as a child by a Nazirite vow. After the defeat of Israel and loss of the Ark of the Covenant to the Philistines, Samuel tried to keep the tribal confederation together, moving in a circuit among Israel's shrines. He presided, apparently reluctantly, over Saul's election as the first king of Israel, but later criticized Saul for assuming priestly prerogatives and disobeying divine instructions given to him. Samuel finally anointed David as Saul's successor, rather than Saul's own son, Jonathan. » Ark of the

Covenant; David; Jonathan; prophet; Samuel, Books of; Saul

Samuel, Books of Two books of the Old Testament, which were one in the Hebrew Bible and probably were also once combined with Kings; also called 1 and 2 Kings, in some Catholic versions. They present a narrative of Israel's history from the time of the prophet Samuel and Israel's first king Saul (1 *Sam*) to the story of David's accession and reign (2 *Sam*). They are probably a compilation from several, partially-overlapping sources, with a late editing after the Exile. » David; Deuteronomistic History; Kings, Book of; Old Testament; Samuel; Saul

Samuelsson, Bengt Ingemar (1934–) Swedish biochemist, born at Halmstad. He was educated at Stockholm, where he has been a professor and administrator since 1967. He shared the 1982 Nobel Prize for Physiology or Medicine for discoveries concerning prostaglandins and related substances. » prostaglandins

samurai [**sa**muriy] A Japanese warrior. Tokugawa Japan (1603–1868) had four hereditary classes: samurai, farmers, craftsmen, and merchants. (Outcasts were not part of this system.) Only samurai were allowed weapons, and they carried two swords. They had to serve their daimyo masters loyally and follow the warrior's code, Bushido; in return they received lodging and income. Samurai are often heroes in Japanese films. » bushido; daimyo; Meiji Restoration

San » **Khoisan**

San Andreas Fault A major fault in the Earth's crust running for about 950 km/600 ml through NW California to the Colorado Desert. It marks the boundary between the Pacific and American crustal plates, which are slipping past each other at an average rate of 1 cm/0.4 in a year. Sudden movements can cause earthquakes, the most notable of which devastated San Francisco in 1906. A serious movement also occurred in 1989. » earthquake; fault

San Andrés-Providencia [san an**drays** provee**then**sia] pop (1985) 36 515; area 44 sq km/17 sq ml. Administrative area of Colombia, comprising two small islands and seven groups of coral reefs and cays in the Caribbean; 480 km/300 ml N of Colombia; largest island, San Andrés; Providencia (also called Old Providence), 80 km/50 ml NNE of San Andrés; headquarters of pirate Henry Morgan in 17th-c; a duty-free zone; important international airline stopover; coconuts, vegetable oil, tourism. » Caribbean; Colombia [i]

San Antonio 29°25N 98°30W, pop (1980) 785 880. Seat of Bexar County, SC Texas, USA, on the San Antonio R; settled by the Spanish, 1718; captured by the Texans in the Texas Revolution, 1835; scene of the Mexican attack on the Alamo, 1836; five different flags flown during the city's history (Spain, Mexico, Republic of Texas, Confederate States of America, USA); airport; railway; two universities (1852, 1869); military aviation centre; industrial, trade, and financial centre for a large agricultural area; processed foods, aircraft, electronic equipment, building materials, chemicals, wood products, clothing, machinery; educational, artistic, and cultural centre; tourism; major league team, Spurs (basketball); the Alamo, Paseo del Rio (the Spanish Governor's palace), Museum of Art, Institute of Texan Cultures, Tower of the Americas (229 m/750 ft high); Fiesta San Antonio (Apr), Folklife Festival (Aug). » Alamo; Texas; Texas Revolution

San Bernardino 34°07N 117°19W, pop (1980) 117 490. Capital of San Bernardino County, California, USA, in the San Bernardino Valley; founded by Mormons, 1851; railway; university; Norton Air Force Base nearby; aerospace, steel; National Orange Show; museum. » California; Mormons

San Diego [san dee**ay**goh] 32°43N 117°09W, pop (1980) 875 538. Seaport capital of San Diego County, SW California, USA, on the E shore of San Diego Bay, just N of the Mexico border; first permanent White settlement in California; naval and marine base; airport; railway; four universities; shipbuilding, food processing, aerospace industries; cultural, convention, and research centre; tourism; major league teams, Padres (baseball), Chargers (football); early 19th-c adobe buildings in the Old Town district; tourism; San Diego de Alcalá mission (established 1769 by Junípero Serra and now restored), the first mission in California; Serra Museum; Cabrillo National Monument; aquatic park, zoo. » California

San Francisco 37°47N 122°25W, pop (1980) 678 974. City co-extensive with San Francisco County, W California, USA; bounded W by the Pacific Ocean, N by the Golden Gate, E by San Francisco Bay; built on a series of hills; connected to Marin county (N) by the Golden Gate Bridge and to Oakland (E) by the Transbay Bridge; Golden Gate Bridge is one of the longest single-span suspension bridges in the world (1 280 m/4 200 ft, excluding the approaches); mission and pueblo founded by the Spanish, 1776 (named Yerba Buena); Mexican control, 1821; taken by the US Navy, 1846; renamed San Francisco, 1848; grew rapidly after the discovery of gold nearby; from the 1860s developed as a commercial and fishing port; terminus of the first transcontinental railway, 1869; devastated by earthquake and fire, 1906; several areas seriously damaged by earthquake, 1989; tram (cable-car); railway; airport; four universities; financial and insurance centre of W coast; trade in fruit, cotton, mineral ores; fishing, textiles, printing, plastic and rubber products, shipbuilding, aircraft and missile parts; major tourist, cultural, and convention centre; major league teams, Giants (baseball), 49ers (football); largest Chinatown in the USA; Mission Dolores (1782), Cow Palace (shows, exhibitions, conventions, circuses), Museum of Art, Civic Centre complex at City Hall, Fisherman's Wharf, Nob Hill mansions; Alcatraz I in San Francisco Bay, site of the first lighthouse on the California coast and of a Federal prison (1934–63). » California; Golden Gate Bridge

San Joaquin River [san wa**keen**] River in C California, USA, in the S part of the Central Valley; rises in the Sierra Nevada; joins the Sacramento R just above Suisin Bay; 510 km/317 ml long; major tributaries the Fresno, Merced, Mariposa; connected with the Sacramento R in the Central Valley Project to increase irrigation, flood-control, and hydroelectricity. » California

San Jorge, Golfo [san **khor**khay], Eng **Gulf of St George** Broad inlet of the Atlantic in S Argentina; extends 135 km/84 ml N–S between Cabo Dos Bahías (N), where there is a penguin rookery, and Cabo Tres Puntas (S); 160 km/100 ml W–E; port of Comodoro Rivadavia on W shore. » Argentina [i]

San José (Costa Rica) [san ho**say**] 9°59N 84°04W, pop (1983e) 271 873. Capital city of Costa Rica, on the Pan-American Highway, in a broad fertile valley of the Meseta Central; altitude 1 150 m/3 773 ft; founded, 1737; capital, 1823; laid out in regular grid pattern; airport; railway; university (1940); coffee, tobacco, food processing, flowers, footwear, chemicals, electronics; cathedral, national theatre, national museum. » Costa Rica [i]

San José (USA) [san hoh**zay**] 37°10N 121°53W, pop (1980) 629 442. Capital of Santa Clara County, W California, USA, in the fertile Santa Clara Valley, at head of San Francisco Bay; first city in the state, 1777; state capital, 1849–51; railway; university; electronics, food processing, high technology, guided missiles. » California

San Juan [san **hwan**] 18°29N 66°08W, pop (1980) 434 849. Seaport capital of Puerto Rico, E Caribbean; on an island linked to the N coast of the mainland by a bridge; founded, 1510; airport; two universities (1912, 1950); cigars, tobacco, sugar, clothing, tourism; El Morro (1591, old Spanish fortress), cathedral (16th-c), Church of San José (16th-c), La Fortaleza (1533–40), Castillo de San Cristóbal (old fortress). » Puerto Rico [i]

San Lorenzo An early Olmec ceremonial centre in Veracruz province, Mexico. Occupied from c.1500 BC, it flourished c.1200–900 BC until succeeded by La Venta. On a partly artificial plateau c.50 m/160 ft high and 1.25 km/0.8 ml long stood c.200 houses with a population of c.1 000 sustained by maize agriculture, hunting, and fishing. The site is notable for its sculpture, which includes colossal basalt heads up to 2.3 m/8 ft high and 20 tonnes weight. » La Venta; Olmecs

San Luis Potosí [san loo**ees** poto**see**] 22°10N 101°00W, pop (1980) 406 630. Capital of San Luis Potosí state, NC Mexico, NNW of Mexico City; altitude 1 877 m/6 158 ft; founded as a Franciscan mission; seat of the Juárez government, 1863; railway; university (1826); refining of silver and arsenic, footwear, clothing; cathedral, Casa de la Cultura, Palacio de Gobierno (1770), Church of San Francisco. » Juárez; Mexico [i]

San Marino (city) 43°56N 12°26E, pop (1980) 4 623. Capital city of San Marino, C Italy, on Monte Titano; accessible only by road; surrounded by three enclosures of walls, including many gateways, towers, and ramparts; basilica, St Francis's Church, governor's palace. » San Marino (state)

San Marino (state) [san ma**ree**noh] pop (1990e) 23 000; area 61 sq km/23 sq ml. Landlocked republic in C Italy, S Europe, 20 km/12 ml from the Adriatic Sea; divided into nine castles (districts); the world's smallest republic; land boundaries, 34 km/21 ml; capital, San Marino; timezone GMT +1; chief religion, Roman Catholicism; official language, Italian; units of currency, the Italian lira and San Marino lira; ruggedly mountainous, centred on the limestone ridges of Monte Titano (793 m/2 602 ft) and the valley of the R Ausa; temperate climate, with cool winters and warm summers, 20–30°C; moderate rainfall throughout year, 880 mm/35 in; founded by a 4th-c Christian saint as a refuge against religious persecution; treaty of friendship with the Kingdom of Italy, preserving independence, 1862; governed by an elected 60-member unicameral parliament (the Great and General Council) and an 11-member Congress of State; wheat, grapes, cheese, livestock; postage stamps, tourism, textiles, pottery, chemicals, wine. » San Marino (city)

San Martín, José de [san mah**teen**] (1778–1850) S American patriot, born at Yapeyú, Argentina. He played a major role in winning independence from Spain for Argentina, Chile, and Peru. In 1817 he led an army across the Andes into Chile, defeating the Spanish at Chacubuco (1817) and Maipó (1818). He then captured Lima, and became Protector of Peru (1821), but resigned the following year after failing to reach an agreement with Bolívar, and died an exile in Boulogne, France. » Bolívar; Spanish-American Wars of Independence

San Miguel de Tucumán or **Tucumán** [san mee**gel** thay tookoo**man**] pop (1980) 496 914. Capital of Tucumán province, NW Argentina; on the R Salí; busiest city in N Argentina; founded 1565; many colonial buildings; site of defeat of Spanish royalists in 1812; two universities (1914, 1965); airport; railway; sugar refining, tourism; cathedral. » Argentina [i]

San Pedro Sula [**soo**la] 15°26N 88°01W, pop (1983e) 344 497. Industrial and commercial capital of Cortés department, NW Honduras; second largest city in Honduras, and one of the fastest-growing cities in Latin America; airport; railway; trade in bananas, coffee, sugar, timber; textiles, zinc roofing, furniture, cement, plastics, steel rolling. » Honduras [i]

San Salvador [san **sal**vadaw] 13°40N 89°18W, pop (1980) 425 119. Capital city of El Salvador, on the R Acelhuate; altitude, 680 m/2 230 ft; founded, 1525; destroyed by earthquake, 1854; capital, 1839; railway; food processing, textiles, commerce; cathedral; International Industrial Fair (Nov, every two years). » El Salvador [i]

San Salvador de Jujuy or **Jujuy** [san salva**thor** thay khoo**khooee**] 24°10S 65°48W, pop (1980) 124 487. Resort capital of Jujuy province, N Argentina; on the R Grande de Jujuy; founded 1565, and again in 1575, after destruction by Indians; hot springs at Termas de Reyes; airport; railway; agricultural, trade, mining, and timber centre; fishing, tourism, hydroelectricity; 18th-c cathedral, government house, Palacio de Tribunales. » Argentina [i]

San Sebastián Span [san sayvas**tyan**], Basque **Donostia** 43°17N 1°58W, pop (1981) 175 576. Fortified Basque seaport, fashionable resort, and capital of Guipúzcoa province, N Spain; on R Urumea, 469 km/291 ml N of Madrid; bishopric; airport; railway; seaport trade, fisheries, electronics, gloves, dairy produce; Church of St Mary (18th-c), Mount Urgel Park; Tamborada (Jan), Semana Grande (Aug). » Spain [i]

Sana [sa**nah**] 15°27N 44°12E, pop (1986) 427 150. Commercial centre and capital city of the Yemeni Republic, on a high plateau of the Arabian peninsula, altitude 2 170 m/7 119 ft; c.65 km/40 ml inland from Al Hudaydah, its port on the Red Sea; walled city, a world heritage site; university (1970); textiles, cement; Great Mosque, museum of S Arabian antiquities. » Yemen [i]

sanction In international law, penalties imposed by one state against another. Aside from war, two kinds of sanctions are recognized. *Retorsion* is a lawful act designed to injure another state, such as the withdrawal of economic aid. *Reprisals* are acts ordinarily illegal, but which are made lawful on account of a prior unlawful act committed by the other state. » international law; sentence

sand Grains of rock and mineral with sizes between 1/16 mm and 2 mm (0.0025–0.079 in), formed by the physical weathering of rocks, and composed of resistant minerals (usually quartz) not destroyed during weathering. Quartz-rich sand is used as an industrial source of silica for glassmaking and in cement. » quartz; sand dune; silica

Sand, George [sã], pseudonym of **Amandine Aurore Lucile Dudevant**, *née* **Dupin** (1804–76) French novelist, born in Paris. She left her husband (Baron Dudevant) and family in 1831, and returned to Paris to take up literature, becoming the companion of several poets, artists, philosophers, and politicians. After 1848 she settled at Nohant, where she spent the rest of her life in literary activity, varied by travel. Her first novel, *Indiana* (1832) was followed by over 100 books, the most successful being those describing rustic life, such as *François le Champi* (1848). She also wrote plays, autobiographical works (notably about her notorious affairs with de Musset and Chopin), and letters. » Chopin; French literature; Musset; novel

sand dollar A flattened, disk-like sea urchin found burrowing in soft sediments of shallow tropical and temperate seas; tubular feet arranged in a petal-like pattern on the upper body surface, serving a respiratory function. (Class: *Echinoidea*. Order: *Clypeasteroida*, c.130 species.) » sea urchin

sand dune A heaped accumulation of wind-driven sand with a shape determined by the speed and direction of the wind. Dunes slowly migrate with the wind direction, as sand particles are blown up the gentle slope and fall down the steep slope. They are characteristic of sandy deserts, such as the Sahara. » Sahara Desert; sand

sand hopper A semiterrestrial crustacean, with a flattened body, capable of vigorous jumping; often abundant along the sea shore, feeding on detritus; also known as **beach flea**. (Class: *Malacostraca*. Order: *Amphipoda*.) » crustacean

sand lizard A lizard of the family *Lacertidae*, native to Europe and W Asia; brown or green with small dark rings and two pale lines along back; inhabits heathland and sandy areas; eats mainly insects. (*Lacerta agilis*.) The name is also used for some other species in this family (eg of genus *Psammodromus*). » lizard [i]

sand spurrey A slender, sprawling annual or biennial, native to much of the temperate N hemisphere, especially on light, lime-free soils; narrow, opposite leaves; silver-brown leaf-like projections; flowers pink, 5-petalled. (*Spergula rubra*. Family: *Caryophyllaceae*.) » annual; biennial

sandalwood A hemiparasitic tree native to SE Asia; leaves opposite, oval; flowers rather inconspicuous, red, with 4-lobed bells. A fragrant timber is obtained from the white outer wood, used for carvings, incense, and joss sticks. Sandal oil is made from the yellow heartwood, and the roots are used for perfume and soap. (*Santalum album*. Family: *Santalaceae*.) » parasitic plant

Sanday, Edgar » **Faure, Edgar**

Sandburg, Carl (1878–1967) US poet, born at Galesburg, Illinois. He became a journalist, and began to write realistic and robust poems, reflecting industrial America. His books include *Cornhuskers* (1918) and *Good Morning, America* (1928). Interested in folksongs, he published a collection in *The American Songbag* (1927), and also wrote a vast *Life of Abraham Lincoln* (6 vols, 1926, 1939). He died at Flat Rock, North Carolina. » American literature; poetry

sanderling A pale sandpiper native to the N hemisphere; inhabits tundra and (in winter) coasts; eats minute crustaceans; follows edges of breaking waves on shore. (*Calidris alba*.) » sandpiper; *see illustration p 1064*

sandfly A small, hairy fly commonly found in moist, shady habitats; some feed by sucking blood of vertebrates, including humans; may act as carriers of diseases, such as leishmaniasis. (Order: *Diptera*. Families: *Psychodidae* and *Phlebotamidae*.) » fly; leishmaniasis

Sanderling

sandgrouse A bird native to Africa, Asia, and S Europe; resembles a plump pigeon; inhabits open country; eats seeds, shoots, and insects; males transport drinking water to chicks by saturating feathers on underparts. (Family: *Pteroclididae*, 16 species.) » grouse; pigeon

Sandino, Augusto César [san**dee**noh] (1895–1934) Nicaraguan revolutionary, born in Niquinohomo (or La Victoria), Nicaragua. He led guerrilla resistance to US occupation forces after 1926, and was later murdered, on the orders of Somoza, near Managua. The Nicaraguan revolutionaries of 1979 (later known as **Sandinistas**) took him as their principal hero. » Nicaragua [i]; Somoza

Sandown 50°39N 1°09W, pop (1981) 16 437 (with Shanklin). Town in South Wight district, I of Wight, S England; on Sandown Bay, S of Ryde and N of Shanklin; home of the poet Swinburne; railway; boatbuilding, electrical goods, tourism. » Swinburne; Wight, Isle of

sandpiper A wading bird, widespread, mostly native to the N hemisphere, migrating to the S during the N winter; long legs and bill; inhabits swamps or coasts; eats invertebrates and some berries. The name is sometimes restricted to only some species in this family. (Family: *Scolopacidae*, c.86 species.) » curlew; dunlin; godwit; knot; phalarope; redshank; ruff; sanderling [i]; snipe; stilt; turnstone; woodcock

sandstone A sedimentary rock composed of grains of sand (usually quartz) cemented together by a matrix, usually silica or calcium carbonate. It may be formed through deposition by water in marine or freshwater environments, or by wind action (as dunes). It is quarried as a building stone. » sand; sedimentary rock

Sandwich, John Montagu, 4th Earl of (1718–92) British politician, remembered as the inventor of *sandwiches*, which he devised in order to eat while playing around the clock at a gaming-table. He was First Lord of the Admiralty under both Henry Pelham and Lord North (1748–51, 1771–82), and was frequently attacked for corruption. He died in London. » North, Frederick; Pelham, Baron

Sandwich Island » **Efate**

Sangay [san**giy**] 2°00S 78°20W. Active Andean volcano, EC Ecuador; rises to 5 230 m/17 159 ft; Sangay National Park established in 1975; area 2 770 sq km/1 069 sq ml; a world heritage site. » Andes

Sanger, Frederick (1918–) British biochemist, born at Rendcombe, Gloucestershire. He studied in Cambridge, and worked there throughout his career, after 1951 at the Medical Research Council Unit. By the mid-1950s he secured a notable success by experimental work which revealed the full sequence of the 51 amino acids in insulin, for which he won the Nobel Prize for Chemistry in 1958. He then worked on the problems of the nucleic acids, and devised new methods to elucidate molecular structures for these also. His Nobel Prize for Chemistry in 1980 made him the first to win two such awards. » amino acid [i]; DNA [i]; genetics [i]; insulin

sangha [**suhng**ga] The community of *bhikkus* – those who have formally committed themselves to pursuing the Buddhist way of life and to living in accord with the set of rules known as the Patimokkha. It began with the first disciples of Buddha, and remains influential and widespread today. » Buddhism

Sanhedrin [san**hed**rin] (Gr 'council', also called by Josephus the *gerousia*, Gr 'senate') A Jewish council of elders meeting in Jerusalem, which during the Graeco-Roman period acquired internal administrative and judicial functions over Palestinian Jews, despite foreign domination. Convened by the high priest, its membership numbered 71, although local courts with this designation outside Jerusalem had fewer members (usually 23 or just 3) and more limited jurisdiction. After the fall of Jerusalem in AD 70, the Jerusalem Sanhedrin was effectively replaced by a new court of sages at Jabneh. » Jabneh; Judaism

sanicle A perennial growing to 60 cm/2 ft, native to woods in Europe, Asia, and Africa; leaves mostly basal, glossy and dark green, divided into 5–7 wedge-shaped lobes with toothed margins; flowers white or pink, in dense rounded umbels; fruit thickly covered with hooked bristles. (*Sanicula europaea*. Family: *Umbelliferae*.) » perennial; umbel

Sankara [**shan**kara] (?700–?750) Hindu philosopher and theologian, born in Kerala. The most famous exponent of Advaita (the Vedanta school of Hindu philosophy), he is the source of the main currents of modern Hindu thought. He died at Kedarnath. » Hinduism

Sankey, Ira David » **Moody, Dwight Lyman**

Sankt Gallen/Sankt Moritz » **St Gallen/St Moritz** (under **Saint**)

sans-culottes [sã kü**lot**] The French name for the mass of the working populace in French towns at the time of the Revolution, but more specifically applied to small-time Parisian shopkeepers, craftsmen, wage-earners, and unemployed who were politically active. Their demands for food controls and democratic government made them temporary allies of the Jacobins. » French Revolution [i]; Jacobins (French history)

Sans Souci [**sã** soo**see**] A Rococo palace built (1745–7) at Potsdam, Germany, for Frederick II of Prussia, who collaborated with his architect, Georg Wenzeslaus von Knobelsdorff (1699–1753), on its design. It has been preserved in its original state, and houses several picture galleries. » Potsdam; Rococo

sanseveria [sansi**vee**ria] » **mother-in-law's-tongue**

Sanskrit The name given to the early forms of Indo-Aryan, at c.1000 BC, in which the sacred Hindu texts known as the Vedas were written. Their grammatical form and pronunciation have been scrupulously preserved as a matter of religious observance. Sanskrit proved to be the key to the reconstruction of Indo-European in the 19th-c. » Indo-Aryan languages; Indo-European languages; reconstruction; Indian literature; Veda

Sanskrit literature » **Indian literature**

Sanskrit theatre/theater The classical Indian dramatic tradition which has a rich literature, written in Sanskrit, best exemplified by the plays of Bhasa, Sudraka, and Kalidasa. It was an aristocratic form of theatre with elaborate conventions governing all aspects of its stagecraft, recorded by Bharata around the 2nd-c BC. It had a history of over 1 000 years of performance, then declined after the Mohammedan invasion of N India in the 11th-c. Its influence is still strong in some of the traditional styles of dance and drama popular in modern India. » Indian theatre; Kutiyattam; Sanskrit; Yakshagana

Santa Ana (El Salvador) 14°00N 79°31W, pop (1980) 204 570. Capital city of Santa Ana department, NW El Salvador; 55 km/34 ml NW of San Salvador, on NE slopes of Santa Ana volcano; second largest city in the country; business centre of W El Salvador; railway; on the Pan-American Highway; coffee, sugar cane; cathedral, Church of El Calvario. » El Salvador [i]

Santa Ana (USA) 33°46N 117°52W, pop (1980) 203 713. Capital of Orange County, SW California, USA, on the Santa Ana R; founded, 1869; railway; aerospace, electronics, farm produce. » California

Santa Anna, Antonio López de (1797–1876) Mexican soldier, President (1833–6), and dictator (1839, 1841–5), born at Jalapa. Following the Texas revolt (1836), he defeated Texan forces at the Alamo, but was then routed at San Jacinto R, and imprisoned. He returned to power on two occasions (1846, 1853). An exile for many years, he was permitted to return to Mexico in 1872, and died in Mexico City. » Mexican War; Mexico [i]; Texas

Santa Barbara 34°25N 119°42W, pop (1980) 74 414. Resort

capital of Santa Barbara County, SW California, USA, on the Pacific Ocean; founded, 1782; railway; university (1891); oil, aerospace, electronics; tourism; Vandenburg air force base nearby; Santa Barbara Mission (established 1786, present building completed 1820); many buildings with Spanish architecture. » California

Santa Claus A name derived from *Sante Klaas*, a Dutch dialect form of St Nicholas, the patron saint of children, on whose feast day (6 Dec) presents were traditionally given to children. The English of New York took over from the Dutch the name and the present-giving custom, now transferred to Christmas Day. » Christmas

Santa Cruz or **Santa Cruz de la Sierra** 17°45S 63°14W, pop (1982) 376 917. City in Santa Cruz department, E Bolivia; country's second largest city; founded in 1561 by Spanish; airport (El Trompillo); railway; university (1880); oil refining, sugar cane, coffee, rice, tobacco, sugar refining; gas pipeline to Yacuiba; cathedral; carnival (before Lent). » Bolivia [i]

Santa Cruz de Tenerife [**san**ta **krooz** thay taynay**ree**fay] 28°28N 16°15W, pop (1981) 190 784. Seaport and capital of Santa Cruz de Tenerife province, Canary Is, on N coast of Tenerife I; airport; oil refinery, wine, tobacco, pharmaceuticals, beer, pottery, tourism, agricultural trade; carnival (Feb), Festival of Spain (Apr–May), spring festival (May), Fiesta of La Virgen del Carmen (Jul). » Canary Islands

Santa Fe (Argentina) [santa **fay**] 31°38S 60°43W, pop (1980) 287 240. River-port capital of Santa Fe province, NEC Argentina; at the mouth of the R Salado, and linked to the R Paraná by a short canal; founded 1573; airfield; railway; two universities (1919, 1959); rail, shipping, commercial, industrial, and agricultural centre; Jesuit La Merced Church (1660–1754), Casa de Gobierno, San Francisco Church (1680), Museo Histórico Provincial. » Argentina [i]

Santa Fe (USA) [santa **fay**] 35°41N 105°57W, pop (1980) 48 953. State capital in Santa Fe County, NC New Mexico, USA; at the foot of the Sangre de Cristo Mts; the oldest capital city in the USA; founded by the Spanish, 1609; centre of Spanish-Indian trade for over 200 years; after Mexican independence (1821), centre of trade with the USA; occupied by US troops, 1846; territorial capital, 1851; railway; administrative and tourist centre; noted for Indian wares; Palace of the Governors (1610), San Miguel Church (1636), Cathedral of St Francis, Museum of International Folk Art; Indian Market (Aug), Santa Fe Fiesta (Sept). » New Mexico; Santa Fe Trail

Santa Fe Trail A trading route from W Missouri through Kansas and Colorado to Santa Fe in New Mexico. The trail was pioneered by William Becknell in 1821, the year of Mexico's independence from Spanish rule. It remained a commercially important route for over 50 years, but declined after the Santa Fe railway was opened in 1880. » Santa Fe

Santa Marta [**san**ta **mah**ta] 11°18N 74°10W, pop (1985) 215 540. Caribbean port capital of Magdalena department, N Colombia; at mouth of R Manzanares; 96 km/60 ml E of Barranquilla, to which it is linked by bridge (1974); first town founded by the Conquistadores in Colombia (1525); Simón Bolívar died here (1830); airport; railway; oil terminal; trade in bananas, coffee, cocoa; leading seaside resort. » Bolívar; Colombia [i]

Santa Rosa de Copán » **Copán**

Santa Sophia » **Hagia Sophia**

Santander, Francisco de Paula [santan**dair**] (1792–1840) Colombian statesman, born at Rosario de Cúcuta, who took part in the Spanish-American Wars of Independence. He acted as Vice-President of Grancolombia (1821–7) during Bolívar's campaigns, and was President of New Granada (modern Colombia) in 1832–7. He died in Bogotá. » Bolívar; Colombia [i]; Spanish-American Wars of Independence

Santander [santan**dair**] 43°27N 3°51W, pop (1981) 180 328. Seaport, resort, and capital of Santander province, N Spain; 393 km/244 ml N of Madrid; bishopric; airport; railway; car ferries to Plymouth, Gijón; university (1972); paper, glass, soap, chemicals, brewing, textiles, shipbuilding, fish processing; royal palace, cathedral (13th-c), prehistory museum; Fiesta of Santiago (Jul–Aug), Semana Grande (Aug). » Spain [i]

Santarém (Brazil) [santa**rem**] 2°26S 54°41W, pop (1980) 102 181. River port in Pará state, N Brazil, at the junction of the Tapajós and Amazon Rivers; founded, 1661; third largest town on the Amazon; airfield; commerce, jute, gold, bauxite, timber, oil seed, textiles. » Amazon, River; Brazil [i]

Santarém (Portugal) [santa**rem**], ancient **Scalabis** or **Praesidium Julium** 39°12N 8°42W, pop (1981) 15 300. Walled capital of Santarém district, C Portugal, 69 km/43 ml NE of Lisbon; railway; olive oil, wine, fruit, tourism; Seminario (1676), Churches of Santa Clara (13th-c), Senhor da Graça, São João de Alporão, Torre das Cabeças; festival of São José (Mar), music festival (Apr), festival of flowers (May), agricultural show (Jun), food festival (Oct). » Portugal [i]

Santayana, George, originally **Jorge Augustín Nicolás Ruiz de Santayana** (1863–1952) US philosopher, poet, and novelist, born in Madrid. He moved to Boston in 1872, and was educated at Harvard, where he became professor of philosophy (1907–12), while retaining his Spanish nationality. His writing career began as a poet with *Sonnets and other Verses* (1894), but he later became known as a philosopher and stylist, in such works as *The Life of Reason* (5 vols, 1905–6), *Realms of Being* (4 vols, 1927–40), and his novel *The Last Puritan* (1935). He moved to Europe in 1912, stayed at Oxford during World War 1, then settled in Rome, where he died.

Santiago, **Gran Santiago**, or **Santiago de Chile** [santyah**goh**] 33°27S 70°38W, pop (1982) 4 039 287. Capital of Chile, crossed E–W by R Mapocho; founded, 1541; capital, 1818; often damaged by floods, fires, and earthquakes; commercial centre; over half Chile's manufacturing located here; airport (Pudahuel); airfield; railway; three universities (1738, 1888, 1947); cathedral; textiles, food processing, metals, shoes; Avenida O'Higgins (the Alameda) stretches for more than 3 km/1¾ ml, lined with ornamental gardens and statues; Santa Lucía Hill, site of first fort; Palacio de la Moneda, Parque O'Higgins, Parque Forestal; several museums and churches; conical hill of San Cristóbal to the NE, ascended by funicular railway. » Chile [i]

Santiago (de los Caballeros) [santyah**goh**] 19°30N 70°42W, pop (1982e) 394 237. Town in C Santiago province, Dominican Republic; second largest city in country; airfield; most important trading, distributing, and processing centre in N; in fertile Cibao agricultural region; cigarettes, pharmaceuticals, rum; scene of decisive battle of Dominican struggle for independence (1844); cathedral, fort. » Dominican Republic [i]

Santiago de Compostela [santyah**goh** thay kompos**tay**la], ancient **Campus Stellae**, Eng **Compostella** 42°52N 8°37W, pop (1981) 93 695. City in La Coruña province, Galicia, NW Spain, on R Sar; former capital of the Kingdom of Galicia; world-famous place of pilgrimage in the Middle Ages (shrine of St James); airport; railway; university (1501); the old town is a world heritage site; linen, paper, soap, brandy, silverwork; cathedral (11th–12th-c); Fiesta of Santiago Apostol (Jul). » Galicia; Spain [i]

Santiago de Cuba [santyah**goh** thay **koo**ba] 20°00N 75°49W, pop (1983e) 353 373. Seaport capital of Santiago de Cuba province, SE Cuba, on S coast; Cuba's second largest city; founded, 1514; formerly capital of the republic; scene of events in Spanish-American War of 1898, when town surrendered to US forces; scene of Castro's 1953 revolution; rail terminus; university (1947); trade in coffee, tobacco, sugar; cathedral (1528); Museum of Colonial Art; Festival de Caribe (Apr); carnival (Jul). » Castro; Cuba [i]

Santiago del Estero [santyah**goh** thel es**tay**roh] 27°48S 64°15W, pop (1980) 148 357. Capital of Santiago del Estero province, N Argentina; on the R Dulce; the oldest Argentinian town, founded in 1553 by settlers from Peru; university; railway; airfield; agricultural trade and lumbering centre; cathedral; Gothic Church of San Francisco (1590), Wagner Museum. » Argentina [i]

Santo Domingo, formerly **Ciudad Trujillo** 19°30N 70°42W, pop (1982e) 1 599 401. Capital city of Distrito Nacional, S Dominican Republic, on right bank of R Ozama; founded, 1496; airport; harbour; highway junction; university (1538); Renaissance cathedral (1514–40), Alcazar castle (1514). » Dominican Republic [i]

Santorini [santuh**reenee**], Gr **Santorin**, also **Thera** or **Thíra**

pop (1981) 7 083; area 75 sq km/29 sq ml. An island (ancient Thera) in the S Cyclades c.140 km/87 ml N of Crete. The last great eruption of its volcano (c.1470 BC), in an explosion four times more powerful than Krakatoa, has been held responsible (probably mistakenly) for the rapid decline of Minoan civilization. The excavated site displays notable wall paintings and 3-storeyed houses. » Cyclades; Greece [i]; Knossos; Minoan civilization; RR14

Santos [**san**tohs] 23°56S 46°22W, pop (1980) 410 933. Port in São Paulo state, SE Brazil; 63 km/39 ml SE of São Paulo and 5 km/3 ml from the Atlantic coast, on an island; founded in 1534; railway; the most important Brazilian port, handling over 40% of all imports, and about half of all exports; major industrial area around the oil refinery and hydroelectric plant at Cubatão, known locally as the Valley of Death because of chemical factory pollution; railway. » Brazil [i]

São Francisco, River (Port **Rio**) [fran**sees**koh] River in E Brazil; rises in the Serra de Canastra, flows NNE, NW, then ESE to enter the Atlantic 96 km/60 ml NE of Aracajú; length 2 900 km/1 800 ml; main route of access into the interior of E Brazil; hydroelectricity at several points. » Brazil [i]

São Paulo [sõw **pow**loh] 23°33S 46°39W, pop (1980) 7 032 547. Capital of São Paulo state, SE Brazil, on the R Tietê; founded by Jesuits 1554; airport (Congonhas); airfield; railway; three universities (1934, 1952, 1970); developed since the 19th-c to become the leading commercial and industrial centre in S America; fastest-growing S American city; pharmaceuticals, machine tools, furniture, steel, vehicles, chemicals, food processing; neo-Gothic cathedral, Museum of Art, Museum of Brazilian Art, Iparinga Monument, the Anhembi (one of world's largest exhibition halls), Butantan Institute (with snake farm). » Brazil [i]

São Tiago [**sõw tyah**goh] or **Santiago** 14°55N 23°31W; pop (1980) 145 923; area 991 sq km/382 sq ml. Largest island in Cape Verde, in the Sotavento group; rises to 1 320 m/4 331 ft at Antonia Peak; chief town, Praia; fine beaches at Gamboa, Prainha, Quebra-Canela; Ribeira Grande, 15th-c colonial capital; airport; coffee, sugar, oranges. » Cape Verde [i]; Praia

São Tomé and Príncipe, Port **São Tomé e Príncipe**, official name **Democratic Republic of São Tomé and Príncipe** [sõw to**may**, **preen**sipe] pop (1990e) 121 000; area 963 sq km/372 sq ml. Equatorial island republic in the Gulf of Guinea, off the coast of W Africa; comprises São Tomé, Príncipe, and several smaller islands; capital, São Tomé; timezone GMT +1; official language, Portuguese; unit of currency, the dobra; volcanic islands, heavily forested; São Tomé lies c.440 km/275 ml off the coast of N Gabon, area 845 sq km/326 sq ml, greatest height 2 024 m/6 640 ft; Príncipe lies c.200 km/124 ml off Gabon; tropical climate; average annual temperature 27°C (coast), 20°C (mountains); rainy season (Oct–May); annual average rainfall 500–1 000 mm/20–40 in; visited by the Portuguese, 1469–72; Portuguese colony, 1522; port of call on route to the East Indies; resistance to Portuguese rule led to riots in 1953, and the formation of an overseas liberation movement based in Gabon; independence, 1975; one-party state, with a president and a 40-member National People's Assembly; economy based on agriculture, employing c.70% of the population; cocoa, copra, palm kernels, coffee; restructuring of the economy announced in 1985, with greater involvement in agriculture, management, commerce, banking, and tourism. » Gabon [i]; Portugal [i]; RR27 national holidays; RR60 political leaders

Saône, River [sohn], ancient **Arar** River in E France rising in the Mts Faucilles (Vosges); flows SW then S to meet the R Rhône at Lyons; length 480 km/298 ml; linked by canal to the Loire, Seine, Marne, Meuse, Moselle, and Rhine. » France [i]

sapi-utan or **sapi-outan** » anoa

sapodilla plum » chicle

saponification The hydrolysis of a fat (glyceride) in a basic solution, yielding glycerol and the salt of the fatty acids. The reaction is an example of an ester hydrolysis. » fat; hydrolysis; soap

Sapor II » Shapur II

Sapper, pseudonym of **Herman Cyril McNeile** (1888–1937) British novelist, born at Bodmin, Cornwall. He trained as a soldier before achieving fame as the creator of 'Bulldog' Drummond, the aggressively patriotic hero of a series of thrillers written between 1920 and 1937, of which *The Final Count* (1926) is a typical example. » novel

The step pyramid at Saqqarah

sapphire A gem variety of corundum, coloured by the addition of minor amounts of impurity. It occurs in a variety of colours (except red, when it is termed *ruby*), but blue is the most valuable. » corundum; gemstones; ruby; Plate V

Sappho (c.610–c.580 BC) Greek poet, born in Lesbos. The greatest female poet of antiquity, she wrote lyrics unsurpassed for depth of feeling, passion, and grace. Only two of her odes are extant in full, but many fragments have been found in Egypt. She is said to have plunged into the sea from the Leucadian rock, because Phaon did not return her love, but this event seems to have no historical foundation. Tradition also represents her as exceptionally immoral, but this too has been disputed. » Greek literature; ode; poetry

Sapporo [sa**poh**roh] 43°05N 141°21E, pop (1980) 1 401 757. Capital of Hokkaido prefecture, WC Hokkaido, Japan; founded, 1871; railway; subway; university (1876); winter sports, timber, brewing, flour, agricultural machinery; Ainu museum; Snow Festival with snow sculpture (Jan–Feb); scene of 1972 Winter Olympics. » Hokkaido

saprophyte [**sap**ruhfiyt] A plant which feeds on the products of decay. It includes many fungi. A few flowering plants are saprophytic; they have reduced leaves, lack chlorophyll (and therefore cannot photosynthesize), and form symbiotic associations with mycorrhizal fungi which aid in the breakdown of dead tissue on which the plant feeds. » chlorophyll; fungus; mycorrhiza; photosynthesis; symbiosis

sapsucker A woodpecker, native to N America and the Caribbean; inhabits woodland; eats sap, insects, berries, and nuts; juvenile plumage differs from adult. (Genus: *Sphyrapicus*, 2 species.) » woodpecker

Saqqarah The large necropolis of Memphis in Egypt, where several pharaohs and many noble Egyptians were buried. The most famous surviving monument is the stepped pyramid of Zozer (c.2630 BC). Designed by Imhotep, it marked a radical advance in pyramid design. » Memphis (ancient Egypt); pyramid

sarabande A 16th-c dance of Spanish or Latin-American origin in triple time. In a different form and slower tempo it became a standard movement of the Baroque suite, where a long note on the second beat is a distinctive feature. » Baroque (music); suite

Saragossa [saragosa], Span **Zaragoza**, ancient **Salduba** 41°39N 0°53W, pop (1981) 590 750. Industrial city and capital of Saragossa province, Aragón, NEC Spain; on R Ebro, 325 km/202 ml NE of Madrid; scene of a long siege against the French in the Peninsular War (1808–9); archbishopric; airport; railway; university (1553); iron and steel, machinery, chemicals, textiles, soap, paper, foodstuffs, plastics, glass; El Pilar and La Seo cathedrals, 16th-c Exchange, Aljafarería Moorish palace; Fiesta of Our Lady of Pilar (Oct), spring festival (May). » Spain [i]

Sarah or **Sarai** (Heb 'princess') Biblical character, wife and half-sister of Abraham, who is portrayed (*Gen* 12–23) as having accompanied him from Ur to Canaan. On account of her beauty, she posed as Abraham's sister before Pharaoh in Egypt and Abimelech in Gerar, since their desire for her may have endangered her husband's life. Long barren, she is said to have eventually given birth to Isaac in her old age as God promised. Allegedly she died at age 127 in Kiriath-arba. » Abraham; Hagar; Isaac; Old Testament

Sarajevo [sarayayvoh] 43°52N 18°26E, pop (1981) 448 500. Capital of Bosnia and Herzegovina republic, Yugoslavia, on R Miljacka; governed by Austria, 1878–1918; scene of the assassination of Archduke Francis Ferdinand and his wife (28 Jun 1914); airport; railway; university (1946); vehicles, brewing, engineering, chemicals, carpets, tobacco; educational and cultural centre; site of 1984 Winter Olympic Games; old town, Husref Bey mosque, Imperial mosque, two cathedrals; Yugoslav Song Festival (Apr), International Festival of Military Music (Jun), slivovitz and wine fair (Oct). » Bosnia and Herzegovina; Yugoslavia [i]

Saransk [saransk] 54°12N 45°10E, pop (1983) 293 000. Capital city of Mordovskaya, C European Russia, on R Insar; founded as a fortress, 1641; railway; university (1957); foodstuffs, electrical engineering, machinery, chemicals, clothing; Church of John the Apostle (1693). » Russia

Sarapis » **Serapis**

Saratoga, Battle of (Oct 1777) One of the most important engagements of the US War of Independence. Actually fought near modern Schuylerville, New York, the battle brought the defeat of a large British army under John Burgoyne by American continental troops and militia under Horatio Gates. The outcome ended British plans to cut New England off from the rest of the states, and encouraged French intervention on the American side. » American Revolution; Burgoyne; Gates

Saratov [saratahf] 51°30N 45°55E, pop (1989) 905 000. River-port capital of Saratovskaya oblast, E European Russia, on R Volga; founded as a fortress, 1590; airport; railway; university (1909); oil refining, chemicals, clothing, leatherwork, precision instruments; Troitskii Cathedral (1689–95). » Russia

Sarawak [sarahwak] pop (1980) 1 235 553; area 124 449 sq km/48 037 sq ml. State in E Malaysia, on NW coast of Borneo; bounded S by Kalimantan (Indonesia), N by the South China Sea and NE by Brunei and Sabah; flat, narrow coastal strip, belt of foothills, and highly mountainous forested interior; highest peak, Mt Murud (2 423 m/7 949 ft); watered by the R Rajang; given by the Sultan of Brunei to James Brooke, the 'white raja' in 1841, and ruled by the Brooke family until World War 2; British protectorate, 1888; Crown Colony, 1946; capital, Kuching; oil, rice, sago, rubber, pepper, fishing; national park around Mt Mulu. » Borneo; Malaysia [i]

Sarcodina [sahkuhdiyna] A subphylum of protozoans, all of which possess some kind of pseudopodia; most are free-living in aquatic habitats or soil; cell body typically naked, sometimes with a shell (*test*); reproduces by splitting in two (binary fission); often produces resistant cysts to aid dispersal and avoid adverse conditions. » cyst (biology); phylum; pseudopodium; Protozoa; shell; systematics

sarcoidosis An uncommon, multi-system, chronic inflammatory disorder of unknown cause. The condition resembles tuberculosis, but no tuberculosis bacilli have ever been found, and the condition usually resolves spontaneously. » tuberculosis

sarcoma A malignant tumour in connective tissue, bone, or muscle. Sarcomas are much less common than are **carcinomas**, which arise from the lining tissues of the skin and internal organs. » cancer

Sardanapalus Legendary Assyrian king, notorious for his effeminacy and sensual lifestyle. He probably represents an amalgam of at least three Assyrian rulers, one of them being Assurbanipal. » Assurbanipal; Assyria

sardine » **pilchard**

Sardinia, Ital **Sardegna** pop (1981) 1 594 175; area 24 090 sq km/9 299 sq ml. Region and island of Italy; settled by Phoenicians; formed part of Kingdom of Sardinia, 18th-c; capital and chief port, Cagliari; main towns, Sassari, Carbonia, Oristano, Iglesias; length 272 km/169 ml; width 144 km/89 ml; second largest island in the Mediterranean; largely hilly, rising to 1 835 m/6 020 ft in the Monti del Gennargentu; well-wooded C and N; mineral-bearing SW; fertile alluvial plain of Campidano; corn, wine, olives, citrus fruits, vegetables, tobacco, pastoral farming; fishing, sea salt, mining (zinc, lead, manganese, coal), food processing, petrochemicals, tourism. » Cagliari; Corsica; Italy [i]; Sardinia, Kingdom of

Sardinia, Kingdom of An Italian kingdom created 1718–20 through the Duchy of Savoy's acquisition of Sardinia, in compensation for the loss of Sicily. Despite its name, the kingdom's heart remained Savoy/Piedmont. In the mid-19th-c, Sardinia/Piedmont emerged as the chief driving force behind the move towards Italian unity. In 1861, Victor Emmanuel (Vittorio Emanuele) II of Sardinia became the first King of Italy. » Risorgimento; Victor Emmanuel II

Sardinian » **Romance languages**

Sardis The capital of Lydia and the political centre of Asia Minor in the pre-Hellenistic period. A flourishing city in Roman imperial times, it contained one of the largest and richest Jewish communities in the entire empire. » Lydia; Roman history [i]

sardonyx [sahduhniks] A white and brown variety of onyx. » agate

Sardou, Victorien [sahdoo] (1831–1908) French dramatist, born and died in Paris. His first efforts were failures, but after his marriage he met the actress Virginie Brécourt, for whom he wrote several plays, and his work became widely known in Europe and the USA. His plays include *Les Pattes de monde* (1860, A Scrap of Paper), *La Tosca* (1887) on which Puccini's opera is based, and over 60 others, many written for Sarah Bernhardt. » Bernhardt; drama; French literature

Sargasso Sea [sahgasoh] Sluggish area of the Atlantic Ocean, between the Azores and the West Indies within the 'Horse Latitudes', about 30°N; a still sea, located at the centre of clockwise-moving warm surface currents, allowing great biological activity; abundance of surface gulfweed; breeding ground for eels which migrate to Europe. » Atlantic Ocean; Horse Latitudes

Sargent, John Singer (1856–1925) US painter, born in Florence. He studied at Florence and Paris, where he first gained recognition; but most of his work was done in England, where he became the most fashionable portrait painter of his age. He travelled much to the USA, where as well as portraits he worked on decorative paintings for public buildings, such as the 'Evolution of Religion' for Boston library. He died in London.

Sargent, Sir (Harold) Malcolm (Watts) (1895–1967) British conductor, born at Ashford, Kent. Originally an organist, he first appeared as a conductor when his *Impression on a Windy Day* was performed at a Promenade Concert in 1921. He conducted the Royal Choral Society from 1928, the Liverpool Philharmonic Orchestra (1942–8), and the BBC Symphony Orchestra (1950–7). From 1948 he was in charge of the London Promenade Concerts. His sense of occasion and unfailing panache won him great popularity at home and abroad. He was knighted in 1947, and died in London.

Sark, Fr **Sercq** pop (1978e) 600; area 4 sq km/1½ sq ml. Smallest of the four main Channel Islands, lying between Guernsey and the Cotentin Peninsula, France; consists of Great and Little Sark, connected by an isthmus; separate parliament (the Chief Pleas); Seigneurie of Sark established by Elizabeth I; ruler known as the Seigneur (male) or Dame (female); no cars allowed on the island. » Channel Islands [i]

Sarmatia [sahmaysha] In Roman times, the area to the N of the Black Sea and the middle and lower Danube occupied by the Sarmatians, a nomadic people closely related to the Scythians. Although never conquered by Rome, Sarmatia did not escape Roman control altogether: many Sarmatian chieftains were clients of Rome and ruled in her interest. » nomadism; Scythians

saros [sayros] The natural cycle over which sequences of lunar and solar eclipses repeat themselves. The period is 6 585.32 days (c.18 years): over this cycle the Earth, Sun, and Moon return to the same relative positions. An eclipse in one saros occurs about 8 hours later and 115° of longitude further West in the next cycle. This predictability was known to the Maya, and to the builders of Stonehenge. » eclipse

Saroyan, William [saroyan] (1908–81) US writer, born and died at Fresno, California. His first work, *The Daring Young*

Man on the Flying Trapeze (1934), a volume of short stories, was followed by a number of highly original novels, such as *The Human Comedy* (1943), and plays, such as *The Time of Your Life* (1939). After 1958 he lived mainly in Paris. » American literature; drama; novel

Sarpedon [sah**pee**duhn] In the *Iliad*, a son of Zeus, who led the Lycian troops on the Trojan side, and made an important speech on the duties of a warrior. He was killed by Patroclus, and carried off by Sleep and Death to Lycia. » Trojan War

Sarraute, Nathalie [sa**roht**], originally **Tcherniak** (1902–) French writer, born at Ivanovo, Russia. She moved to France as a child, and was educated at Paris and Oxford, becoming a lawyer and then a full-time writer. She was a leading exponent of the *nouveau roman*. Her books include *Tropismes* (1939, Tropisms), *Portrait d'un inconnu* (1947, Portrait of a Man Unknown), *Les Fruits d'or* (1963, The Golden Fruits), and *Entre la vie et la mort* (1968, Between Life and Death). She has also written plays and essays. » French literature; nouveau roman; novel

sarrusophone [sa**rooz**uhfohn] A musical instrument made of brass in various sizes, with a double reed. It was designed by a French bandmaster, W Sarrus, in 1856 as a substitute for oboes and bassoons in military bands, but enjoyed only brief success. » reed instrument

sarsaparilla A climbing, prickly perennial, native to tropical and subtropical regions; leaves leathery, 3-veined; flowers greenish or yellowish, six perianth-segments; berries red or black. The dried roots, especially of *Smilax America* species, yield a drug used to treat rheumatism. (Genus: *Smilax*, 350 species. Family: *Smilacaceae*.) » perennial; perianth

Sarto, Andrea del, originally **Vannucchi** (1486–1531) Italian painter, born and died in Florence, the son of a tailor (*sarto* 'tailor'). In 1509–14 he was engaged by the Servites to paint a series of frescoes for their church of the Annunciation, and a second series was next painted for the Recollets. Many of his most celebrated pictures are in Florence. » Florentine School; fresco; Italian art

Sartre, Jean-Paul [**sah**truh] (1905–80) French existentialist philosopher and writer, born and died in Paris. He taught philosophy at Le Havre, Paris, and Berlin, was imprisoned in Germany (1941), and after his release joined the resistance in Paris. In 1945 he emerged as the leading light of the left-bank intellectual life of Paris. His novels include the trilogy, *Les Chemins de la liberté* (1945–9, The Roads to Freedom), and he also wrote (especially after the war) a large number of plays, such as *Huis clos* (1944, In Camera/No Exit) and *Le Diable et le bon Dieu* (1951, Lucifer and the Lord). His philosophy is presented in *L'Etre et le néant* (1943, Being and Nothingness). In 1964 he published his autobiography *Les Mots* (Words), and was awarded (but declined) the Nobel Prize for Literature. In the later 1960s he became closely involved in opposition to US policies in Vietnam, and supported student rebellion in 1968. » de Beauvoir, Simone; existentialism; Flaubert; French literature; Heidegger; Vietnam War

SAS An acronym for **Special Air Service**, a British army unit specializing in clandestine and anti-terrorist operations. First formed in 1941 as a special commando unit to parachute behind enemy lines, the SAS (motto 'Who Dares Wins') was revived as a regular unit of the British Army in 1952 for special operations. Its work is highly secret, but it served with distinction during the Falklands campaign of 1982. » army

sashimi [sa**shee**mee] Japanese sliced raw fish, considered a delicacy, and served in many special restaurants. Popular are tuna, sea bream, flatfish, squid, octopus, and shellfish. They are eaten with a seasoning of soy sauce and *wasabi*, green mustard. Slices of raw fish on small portions of boiled seasoned rice are called *sushi*. » fugu; shoyu

Saskatchewan [sas**ka**chooan] pop (1981) 968 313; area 652 380 sq km/251 883 sq ml. Province in WC Canada; bounded S by the USA; fertile plain in S two-thirds; N third is in Canadian Shield; rises to 1 392 m/4 567 ft in the Cypress Hills (SW); many lakes, largest Athabasca (NW), Reindeer (NE), Wollaston (NE); several rivers; capital, Regina; other chief towns, Saskatoon, Moose Jaw, Prince Albert, Yorkton; wheat (about two-thirds of Canada's production), barley, cattle, dairy farming, oil, natural gas, potash (largest fields in the world), timber; important fur-trading region at end of 17th-c; Hudson's Bay Company land, acquired by Canada in 1870 to become part of Northwest Territories; railway arrived, 1882–3; land disputes led to Saskatchewan Rebellion, 1884; province of Canada, 1905; governed by a Lieutenant-Governor and an elected 64-member Legislative Assembly. » Canada [i]; Canadian Shield; Hudson's Bay Company; Regina

Saskatchewan River [sas**ka**chooan] River in S Canada, formed in Saskatchewan, 48 km/30 ml E of Prince Albert, by two headstreams which rise in the Rocky Mts of W Alberta; flows E into L Winnipeg; length 1 287 km/800 ml; the main early route to the Western plains and the mountains. » Canada [i]

Saskatoon [saska**toon**] 52°10N 106°40W, pop (1981) 154 210. Town in C Saskatchewan, SC Canada, on the S Saskatchewan R; settled in 1882 as a temperance colony; developed in early 1900s with settlers from the USA; airfield; railway; university (1907); centre of large grain-growing area; light and heavy industry, oil-related industries, meat packing, flour milling; the Western Development Museum, Memorial Art Gallery; Pioneer Days and Saskachimo Exposition (Jul). » Saskatchewan

Sasquatch » **Bigfoot**

sassaby » **topi**

sassafras [**sas**uhfras] A name applied to several different plants. True sassafras is a large shrub or tree, growing to 30 m/100 ft, native to eastern N America; aromatic foliage; inconspicuous greenish flowers; blue-grey, berry-like fruits. Oil of sassafras, chiefly a flavouring, is distilled from the bark, twigs, and roots. Infusion of the bark is medicinal. (*Sassafras albidum*. Family: *Lauraceae*.) » shrub; tree [i]

Sassanids The aggressive Persian dynasty that overthrew the Parthian Empire in AD 224 and became Rome's fiercest challenger in the E. They were driven from Mesopotamia by the Arabs in AD 636. » Parthians; Persian Empire

Sassari [**sas**aree] 40°43N 8°34E, pop (1981) 119 596. Capital town of Sassari province, Sardinia, Italy, 176 km/109 ml NNW of Cagliari; archbishopric; university (1562); centre of agricultural trade; cathedral (begun 12th-c); Cavalcata Sarda (traditional costumes) on feast of the Assumption. » Sardinia

Sassoon, Siegfried (Lorraine) [sa**soon**] (1886–1967) British poet and novelist, born at Brenchley, Kent. World War 1, in which he served, gave him a hatred of war, fiercely expressed in his *Counterattack* (1918) and *Satirical Poems* (1926). He also wrote several autobiographical works, such as *Memoirs of a Fox-Hunting Man* (1928). His later poetry became increasingly devotional, and he became a Catholic in 1957. He died at Heytesbury, Wiltshire. » English literature; poetry

SAT An abbreviation for **Scholastic Aptitude Test**, a general examination of verbal and mathematical skills not related to specific course work, taken in the USA by high-school pupils wishing to attend university. The test claims to be objective, but has been criticized for being culturally biased towards the middle class.

Satan » **Devil**

Satanism The worship of Satan or other figures of demonology. It may include the perversion of religious rituals (eg the black Mass), the practice of witchcraft, and other practices associated with the occult. There was a revival of Satanism in the 19th-c, and instances of it are still to be found. » Devil; occultism; witchcraft

satellite 1 A type of spacecraft intended to orbit the Earth or some other heavenly body. The first artificial satellite was Sputnik 1, launched by the USSR on 4 October 1957, and there are now more than 3 000 satellites orbiting the Earth for remote sensing, military surveillance, communications, and space astronomy. Russia is responsible for 65% of all launches; the USA, Japan, and Europe for the rest. Geostationary satellites orbit at c.36 000 km/22 500 ml above Earth, taking 24 hours to orbit, so they appear in almost the same part of our sky at all times. They are important for communications, especially satellite television, since fixed dishes can be used at ground stations. » satellite television; spacecraft **2** The 54 moons of the planets in our Solar System. Jupiter and Saturn have extensive systems. Ganymede (Jupiter) is the biggest, exceeding the size of Mercury and Pluto; Mars has the smallest known satellites. » Solar System

satellite DNA A particular type of DNA, characterized by unusual proportions of the base pairs. Short base pair sequences are repeated many times, and localized in the centromeric region of chromosomes. Its function is not fully known, but it is thought to be involved in the pairing and representation of the centromere regions at meiosis. » centromere; DNA [i]; meiosis [i]

satellite television Television transmission using super-high-frequency beam linkage by way of an artificial satellite followed in its elliptical terrestrial orbit; commenced in 1962 with Telstar. Shortly after, satellites in fixed geostationary orbit above the Equator were introduced, providing continuous communication without tracking. Initially this was between large ground stations, but in the 1970s direct broadcasting from satellite (DBS) was developed experimentally. Programmes were relayed at sufficient power to serve domestic TV receivers within a specific territory, known as the 'footprint', using small individual dish antennae of 60 cm diameter or less. Several commercial DBS services were provided in the USA during the 1980s, and in Europe from 1989. » dish; satellite; television

Sati or **Suttee** [suh**tee**] A custom which led Indian widows to burn themselves alive on husbands' funeral pyres. It was a voluntary act, but one often committed under pressure from the family, who sought prestige or property left to the wife. It was prohibited during Mughal times, and suppressed by the British in 1828.

Satie, Erik (Alfred Leslie) [sa**tee**] (1866–1925) French composer, born at Honfleur. He worked as a café pianist, and studied erratically in Paris, not beginning to compose seriously until after he was 40. He wrote ballets, lyric dramas, and whimsical pieces which were in violent revolt against musical orthodoxy, and which influenced Debussy, Ravel, and others. He died in Paris.

satin spar A fibrous, massive form of gypsum, used for ornamental carving. » gypsum

satinwood A deciduous tree growing to 25 m/10 ft, native to S India and Ceylon; leaves to 60 cm/2 ft, pinnate with 10–20 pairs of asymmetric leaflets; flowers 5-petalled, creamy-white, in clusters. It provides very hard, heavy, yellow wood, valued for its satin-like lustre. (*Chloroxylon swietenia*. Family: *Flindersiaceae*.) » deciduous plants; pinnate; tree [i]

satire A literary genre whose double derivation, from Latin *satura* 'mixture' and the parodic satyr play, underlines its complex form and motive. The motive includes the exposure of folly and the castigation of vice, with the Latin satirists Horace and Juvenal representing these two extremes. But satire is also both festive and fictive, and the works of Rabelais and Swift, the plays of Ben Jonson, and the novels of Dickens are much more than the sum of their moral exhortations. Satire has colonized all literary forms, and in doing so has tended to expose formal conventions themselves. This excess of consciousness explains the overlap between satire, parody, and irony. » Dickens; Horace; irony; Jonson; Juvenal; literature; parody; Rabelais; Swift

satisficing In economics, an alternative theory of the firm to the traditional view that a firm's aim is to maximize profits. Firms may have to settle for something less than the best possible outcome; for example, management may avoid risky (but very rewarding) ventures. The theory was proposed in 1959 by US economist H A Simon (1916–), who won the Nobel Prize for Economics in 1978. » profit

satrapy The chief territorial sub-division of the Achaemenid Empire, administered by a satrap (literally, 'a protector of the kingdom'). About 20 in number, the most westerly was Ionia and the most easterly Gandhara. » Achaemenids; Ionia

satsuma [sat**soo**ma] A citrus fruit; a variety of mandarin with an easily detachable rind. (*Citrus reticulata*. Family: *Rutaceae*.) » citrus; mandarin

Satu Mare [sa**too** ma**ray**] 47°48N 22°52E, pop (1983) 124 691. Resort town and capital of Satu Mare county, NW Romania, on R Someş; airfield; railway junction; tourism, grain, livestock, timber, wine trade, mining equipment, rolling stock, electric motors, textiles, food processing. » Romania [i]

saturated In chemistry, a term describing a hydrocarbon containing no multiple bonds. The name derives from the fact that these compounds contain the maximum amount of hydrogen for their carbon content. Alkanes are saturated hydrocarbons; alkenes and alkynes are **unsaturated**. » hydrocarbons

saturated fatty acids » **polyunsaturated fatty acids**

Saturn (astronomy) The sixth planet from the Sun, notable for its ring system – first seen by Galileo in 1610, and first identified by Huygens in 1656. It has nine major moons, including Titan, which alone has an atmosphere. Its main characteristics are: mass 5.69×10^{26} kg; mean density 0.69 g/cm^3; equatorial radius 60 000 km/37 000 ml; polar radius 49 000 km/30 000 ml; rotational period 10 h 40 m 30 sec; orbital period 29.5 years; inclination of equator 29°; mean distance from the Sun 9.54 AU. Like Jupiter, it is a hydrogen/helium planet with a presumed innermost core of rocky composition and several Earth masses, an outer core of metallic hydrogen and helium, a liquid mantle of hydrogen/helium, and an atmosphere about 1 000 km/600 ml deep. Also, like Jupiter, it is believed to have several cloud layers: solid ammonia (the highest), ammonium hydrosulphide, water ice, and water-ammonia. It is less colourful than Jupiter, and less vividly banded, possibly due to greater obscuration by ammonia clouds. It has less obvious discrete features such as vortices, but Voyager images do reveal definite structure within the bands of clouds.

The rings were observed by Voyager to have particle-size distribution ranging up to several metres. Their infrared signature suggests that they are made of water ice – possibly created by break-up of a moon whose orbit decayed inside the limit where tidal flexing exceeded the moon's material strength. The rings show a complex structure including several divisions and innumerable 'ringlets'. The moons, except Titan, are low in density, indicating that they are mainly composed of ices, but still with some 'rocky' material which comprises the core. All appear to be locked in synchronous orbits about Saturn. They have all been subject to meteoritic bombardment, and exhibit cratered surfaces. » Dione; Enceladus; Galileo; Huygens; Hyperion; Iapetus; Jupiter (astronomy); Mimas; Phoebe (astronomy); planet; Rhea; Solar System; Tethys; Titan; Voyager project [i]; Plate I

Saturn (mythology) or **Saturnus** A Roman god; either Etruscan in origin, or, as legend has it, a genuine importation of the Greek Cronus. At his festival (Saturnalia, 17 Dec) slaves had temporary liberty, and presents were exchanged. » Cronus

saturniid moth [sa**terneeid**] A moth of the family *Saturniidae*; large, with wingspan up to 300 mm/12 in; conspicuous eyespots and banded markings present on wings; pupal cocoons of some species used for production of silk; c.1 300 species, including the *atlas* and *emperor moths*. (Order: *Lepidoptera*.) » emperor moth; moth; pupa

satyagraha [satya**gra**hah] 'Truth-force', M K Gandhi's philosophy of non-violent resistance to evil. It was conceived in S Africa in response to laws discriminating against Asians (1906), and used in campaigns against British rule in India. The approach involved fasting, economic boycotts, hand-spinning, and hand-weaving. » civil disobedience; Gandhi; Non-Co-operation Movement

satyr In Greek mythology, a minor deity associated with Dionysus; usually depicted with goat-like ears, tail, and legs. Rural, wild and lustful, the satyrs were said to be the brothers of the nymphs. » Dionysus; nymph; satyriasis

satyriasis [satuh**riy**asis] Pathological exaggerated sexual drive or excitement in a male. Some individuals have an associated psychiatric disorder. Treatment has included behavioural approaches, psychoanalytic therapies, and the use of female hormones in extreme cases. The corresponding drive in females is known as **nymphomania**. » behaviour therapy; hormones; psychoanalysis

satyrid butterfly [sa**tee**rid] A group of butterflies now included in the family *Nymphalidae*; wings mostly brown or orange-black, with eyespots; adults generally shade-loving; caterpillars mostly feeding on grasses and sedges. (Order: *Lepidoptera*.) » butterfly; caterpillar

sauce A seasoned liquid served with or over a food; it may be hot or cold, savoury or sweet. Cold sauces may be formed from a mixture (eg vinaigrette), an emulsification (eg mayonnaise), or a purée (eg any fruit sauce). For hot sauces the liquid used may be stock, milk, or water, and the thickening agent may be a blend of melted butter and flour (as in the classic béchamel and velouté sauces), egg yolks and cream, a starch thickener (eg cornflour, arrowroot), butter (eg hollandaise), or, in 'new' cookery, a purée of vegetables. » flour

Saud » **Ibn Saud**

Saudi Arabia [sowdee araybia], official name **Kingdom of Saudi Arabia**, Arabic **Al-Mamlaka al-Arabiya as-Saudiya** pop (1990e) 14 131 000; area 2 331 000 sq km/899 766 sq ml. Arabic kingdom comprising about four-fifths of the Arabian Peninsula, divided into 14 provinces; bounded W by the Red Sea, NW by Jordan, N by Iraq, NE by Kuwait, E by the Arabian Gulf, Qatar, and the United Arab Emirates, SE and S by Oman, S by S Yemen, and SW by N Yemen; capital, Riyadh; chief towns, Jedda, Mecca, Medina, At Taif, Ad Dammam; timezone GMT +3; population mainly Arab (90%); official language, Arabic; chief religion, Islam; unit of currency, the riyal; Red Sea coastal plain bounded E by mountains; highlands in SW contain Jebel Abha, Saudi Arabia's highest peak (3 133 m/10 279 ft); Arabian Peninsula slopes gently N and E towards the oil-rich Al Hasa plain on the Arabian Gulf; interior comprises two extensive areas of sand desert, the Nafud (N) and the Great Sandy Desert (S); some large oases; salt flats numerous in E lowlands; large network of wadis drains NE; hot and dry climate, average temperatures 21°C (N), 26°C (S); day temperatures may rise to 50°C in the interior; night frosts common in N and highlands; Red Sea coast hot and humid; sparse mean annual rainfall, c.10 mm/0.4 in; famed as the birthplace of Islam, a centre of pilgrimage to the holy cities of Mecca, Medina, and Jedda; modern state founded by Ibn Saud who by 1932 united the four tribal provinces of Hejaz (NW), Asir (SW), Najd (C), and Al Hasa (E); governed as an absolute monarchy based on Islamic law and Arab Bedouin tradition; a king is head of state and prime minister, assisted by a 26-member Council of Ministers; oil discovered in the 1930s; now the world's leading oil exporter; reserves account for about a quarter of the world's known supply; rapidly developing construction industry; natural gas, steel, petrochemicals, fertilizers, refined oil products; large areas opened up for cultivation in 1980s; wheat, dairy produce, dates, grains, livestock, pilgrimage trade. » Islam; Jedda; Mecca; Medina; Riyadh; RR27 national holidays; RR60 political leaders

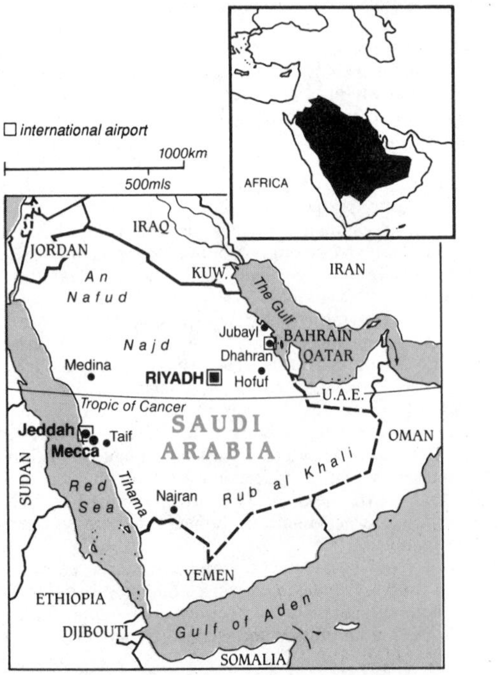

sauerkraut A popular German food, produced by layering alternately shredded white cabbage and salt in a wooden box. Air is expelled by placing a weight on top. The cabbage salt layers are left for 3–4 weeks to ferment. » cabbage

Saul [sawl] (11th-c BC) Old Testament king, the first to be elected by the Israelites. He conquered the Philistines, Ammonites, and Amalekites, became jealous of David, his son-in-law, and was ultimately at feud with the priestly class. At length Samuel secretly anointed David king. Saul fell in battle with the Philistines on Mt Gilboa. » David; Old Testament; Samuel

Saul of Tarsus » **Paul, St**

Sault Ste Marie [soo saynt maree], Fr [soh sĭt maree] 46°32N 84°20W, pop (1981) 82 697. Town in SC Ontario, S Canada, on N shore of St Mary's R, linking L Huron and L Superior; opposite Sault Ste Marie, Michigan, connected by an international bridge; fort, 1751, taken by the British, 1762; Soo canals link L Superior (183 m/600 ft) and L Huron (177 m/581 ft); airport; railway; steel, lumber, paper, agricultural trade, tourism. » Great Lakes; Ontario

Saurischia [sawriskia] The reptile-hipped dinosaurs; characterized by a forward-pointing pubis bone in the pelvic girdle, as in modern reptiles. They comprise two main groups: the *Theropoda*, including the two-legged flesh-eaters such as *Tyrannosaurus*; and the giant plant-eating forms belonging to the *Sauropodomorpha*, including *Diplodocus*. » Allosaurus; Coelurus; dinosaur [i]; Diplodocus; Tyrannosaurus rex

saury [sawree] Agile, slender-bodied fish, widespread and locally common in temperate ocean surface waters; head pointed or forming a narrow beak; feeds on other fishes and crustaceans; includes the Atlantic skipper, *Scomberesox saurus*; body length up to 45 cm/18 in. (Family: *Scomberosocidae*, 2 genera, 4 species.)

sausage A cylindrical portion of minced meat, usually blended with breadcrumbs and herbs, and enclosed in an edible casing. Originally, the casing came from prepared animal intestine; today it is made from edible carbohydrate polymers. Sausages may be wet (requiring cooking) or dry (ready to eat), as in frankfurters and salami respectively. » meat

sausage dog » **dachshund**

Saussure, Ferdinand de [sohsür] (1857–1913) Swiss linguist, born and died in Geneva, often described as the founder of modern linguistics. He taught historical linguistics at Paris (1881–91), and became professor of Indo-European linguistics and Sanskrit (1901–13) and then of general linguistics (1907–13) at Geneva. The work by which he is best known, the *Cours de linguistique générale* (1916, Course in General Linguistics) was compiled from the lecture notes of his students after his death. His focus on language as an 'underlying system' inspired a great deal of later semiology and structuralism. » diachrony; linguistics; structuralism

Savage, Michael Joseph (1872–1940) New Zealand statesman and Prime Minister (1935–40). Born in Australia, he came to New Zealand in 1907. An MP from 1919, he became leader of the Labour Party in 1933 and then Prime Minister. As leader of the first Labour government, he presided over a notable set of social reforms. He died in office. » New Zealand [i]

savannah The grassland region of the tropics and subtropics, located between areas of tropical rainforest and desert. The length of the arid season prevents widespread tree growth; the scattered trees which do exist, such as acacia and baobab, are adapted to reduced precipitation levels. Fires, both natural and as a result of human activity, help to promote and maintain grassland. » sahel; tropics

Savannah 32°05N 81°06W, pop (1980) 141 390. Seat of Chatham County, E Georgia, USA; port near the mouth of the Savannah R; founded, 1733; during the War of Independence, held by the British, 1778–82; captured by Sherman during the Civil War, 1864; airfield; railway; trade in tobacco, cotton, sugar, clay, woodpulp; chemicals, petroleum, rubber, plastics, paper products; fisheries; railway engineering; city's historic district designated a national historic landmark; St Patrick's Festival (Mar). » American Revolution/Civil War; Georgia

Save the Children Fund In the UK, the largest international children's charity, founded in 1919, and having as its president the Princess Royal. It is concerned with the rescue of children from disaster and the longer-term welfare of children in need.

Savery, Thomas (c.1650–1715) English engineer, born at Shilstone, Devon. He realized that a vacuum could be produced if a steam-filled vessel could be cooled so that the steam condensed, thus allowing the pressure of the atmosphere to act on the piston and do work. This was the first practical steam engine, and it was in use by c.1700. Unfortunately, it used steam at a high pressure for those times, and this proved to be a major difficulty in manufacturing the devices. He died in London. » steam engine

Savile, Jimmy (1926–) British television and radio personality, born in Leeds. A former miner, he achieved fame as a disc jockey. His flamboyant style contrasts with his other role as voluntary helper at Leeds Infirmary and elsewhere; he has used his nationwide prominence and popularity to raise huge sums of money for deserving causes. He was awarded the OBE in 1971.

saving The proportion of an individual's income that is not spent. The **marginal propensity to save** (MPS) is an economic concept measuring the proportion of a person's additional income that is saved. If MPS is low, marginal propensity to consume is high, helping to boost the economy through the 'multiplier' effect. In developing countries, too little saving is seen as one of the most urgent problems requiring solution. » developing countries

savings and loan associations » **building society**

Savonarola, Girolamo (1452–98) Italian religious and political reformer, born at Ferrara. He became a Dominican at Bologna in 1474, and after an initial failure, came to be recognized as an inspiring preacher. He became Vicar-General of the Dominicans in Tuscany in 1493, and his preaching began to point towards a political revolution as the means of restoring religion and morality. When a republic was established in Florence (1494), he became its guiding spirit, fostering a Christian commonwealth, with stringent laws governing the repression of vice and frivolity. In 1495 he was called to Rome to answer a charge of heresy. He disregarded the order, was excommunicated in 1497, and burned in Florence. » Christianity; Dominicans; humanism

savory Either of two related species with square stems, opposite paired leaves, and 2-lipped purplish or white flowers in whorls forming loose spikes. **Summer savory** (*Satureja hortensis*) is a slender, bushy annual native to the Mediterranean. **Winter savory** (*Satureja montana*) is a woody perennial native to S Europe. Both are grown as culinary herbs. (Genus: *Satureja*. Family: *Labiatae*.) » annual; herb; perennial

Savoy, House of Rulers of the duchy of Savoy, a transalpine area in present-day Switzerland and France, from the 11th-c to the 19th-c. Its heyday in European politics was from the mid-14th-c to the mid-15th-c; thereafter it was hemmed in by French and Spanish monarchies. It suffered in the Italian Wars of the 16th-c, the Thirty Years' War, and the Napoleonic Wars.

saw, musical A common handsaw used as a musical instrument by pressing it towards the thigh and drawing a violin bow across the straight edge. The pitch is controlled by the curve of the blade, and it is usually imbued with a heavy vibrato by movements of the hand or leg. » idiophone

saw-bill » **merganser**

Sawchuk, Terry, properly **Terrance (Gordon)** (1929–70) US ice hockey player, born in Winnipeg, Canada. One of the game's greatest goalminders, he started his career with the Detroit Red Wings in 1950, and later played for the Boston Bruins, Toronto Maple Leafs, Los Angeles Kings, and New York Rangers. He kept a clean sheet in a record 103 National Hockey League games, and appeared in 971 games 1950–70, a record for a goalminder. He was largely responsible for the crouched stance of goalminders subsequently adopted by other players. He died in New York City. » ice hockey

sawfish A very large and distinctive ray, with a greatly prolonged snout, armed on each side with a regular row of strong blunt teeth; the saw is used to delve in soft sediments for food; widespread in tropical seas, and may be common in shallow estuaries ranging into fresh water; largest species is *Pristis pectinata*; length up to 7.5 m/25 ft. (Family: *Pristidae*, 1 genus.) » ray

sawfly A wasp-like insect which lacks a constricted waist; egg-laying tube large, saw-like, and used for depositing eggs deep into plant tissues; larvae caterpillar-like, feeding on, or boring into, plant stems, leaves, or wood. (Order: *Hymenoptera*. Suborder: *Symphyta*.) » insect [i]; larva; wasp

Saxe, (Hermann) Maurice, Comte de ('Count of'), byname **Marshal de Saxe** (1696–1750) Marshal of France, born at Goslar, the illegitimate son of Augustus II, King of Poland, formerly Elector of Saxony. He served in the French army in the War of the Polish Succession (1733–8), and in the War of the Austrian Succession (1740–8) invaded Bohemia, taking Prague by storm. In 1744 Louis XV appointed him Commander in Flanders, where he won victories at Fontenoy (1745), Raucoux (1746), and Lauffeld (1747), and was promoted to Marshal of France. After the war he retired and died at Chambord. » Austrian Succession, War of the; Louis XV

Saxe-Coburg-Gotha The name of the British royal family, 1901–17. King Edward VII inherited it from his father, Prince Albert, the second son of the Duke of Saxe-Coburg-Gotha. The obviously Germanic name was abandoned during World War 1 as a means of asserting the 'Englishness' of royalty and playing down the extent of its German blood. » Edward VII

saxhorn A musical instrument, made from brass tubing, resembling a small tuba, with the mouthpiece set at right angles and an upright bell. It was patented in 1843 by French instrument-maker Adolphe Sax (1814–94), and manufactured in various sizes. Alto and tenor saxhorns are used today in brass bands, where they are known, rather confusingly, as tenor and baritone horns. » brass instrument [i]; tuba

saxifrage A large, varied genus of annuals or perennials, native to N temperate regions and S America, mainly in arctic or alpine regions, many showing adaptations to a water-poor environment; often tufted, domed, or creeping, with slightly fleshy leaves closely packed together and frequently encrusted with chalk deposits secreted by special glands; flowers in branched inflorescences or solitary, usually 5-petalled, white, yellow, through pink to purple; fruit a capsule. Many species are cultivated in gardens. (Genus: *Saxifraga*, 370 species. Family: *Saxifragaceae*.) » annual; inflorescence [i]; London pride; perennial

Saxo Grammaticus, byname **the Scholar** (c.1140–1206) Danish chronicler, born in Zealand. He was secretary to Archbishop Absalon of Lund, at whose request he wrote the *Gesta Danorum*, a Latin history of the Danes, in 16 books. The work is partly legendary and partly historical.

Saxons A Germanic people from the N German plain. With the Angles, they formed the bulk of the invaders who in the two centuries following the Roman withdrawal from Britain (409) conquered and colonized most of what became England. They were especially prominent in Essex, Sussex, and Wessex. » Anglo-Saxons; Wessex

Saxony A German ducal and electoral state which experienced many changes of fortune. Prominent from the 9th–11th-c, it was reduced by the Emperor Frederick I to two small areas on the R Elbe (1180–1422). Dynastic alliances enlarged the Saxon state on the Middle Elbe in the 15th-c. Frederick the Wise adopted Lutheranism (1524), establishing Saxony's Protestant leadership, and despite family divisions, it grew prosperous in the 16th-c. The reign of John George I (1611–56) marked its steady eclipse by Brandenburg, and new duchies (eg Hanover) were formed out of Lower Saxony. Under the Catholic elector Frederick Augustus (reigned 1694–1733), Saxony's prestige improved with the acquisition of the Polish crown, but his namesake became a client of Napoleon, only to lose two-fifths of his territory at the Congress of Vienna (1815). Saxony was merged in the North German Confederation (1866) and the German Reich (1871). » Germany [i]; Protestantism; Reich

saxophone A single-reed musical instrument, made of metal with a wide conical bore. It was patented in 1846 by French instrument-maker Adolphe Sax (1814–94), and made in a variety of sizes and pitches, the most frequently used being the alto and tenor instruments. These are usually joined by the soprano and baritone instruments to form the saxophone quartet; bass and contrabass sizes are also in use. A favourite in jazz and dance bands of the 20th-c, the saxophone has been used occasionally in orchestral music. » reed instrument; woodwind instrument [i]

Sayan Mountains [**sayan**] Mountain range mainly in S Siberian Russia, and extending into N Mongolia; E Sayan Mts stretch 1 090 km/677 ml SE from the lower R Yenisey, forming the boundary between Russia and Mongolia in the E; highest peak, Munku-Sardyk (3 491 m/11 453 ft); W Sayan Mts lie entirely within Russia, stretching 640 km/398 ml NE from the Altay Mts; gold, coal, graphite, silver, lead; lumbering, hunting, agriculture. » Russia

Sayers, Dorothy L(eigh) (1893–1957) British writer, born in Oxford. Educated at Oxford, she became a celebrated writer of detective stories. Beginning with *Clouds of Witness* (1926), she related the adventures of her hero Lord Peter Wimsey in various accurately observed milieux – such as advertising in *Murder Must Advertise* (1933) or bell-ringing in *The Nine Tailors* (1934). She then earned a reputation as a leading Christian apologist with her plays, radio broadcasts, and essays. She died at Witham, Essex. » detective story

scabbardfish » **ribbonfish**

scabies A harmless common itchy skin infestation with the itch-mite (*Sarcoptes scabei*), which buries below the skin surface. Superimposed streptococcal infection is common in the tropical countries. » itch; mite; streptococcus

scabious A perennial growing to 70 cm/27 in, native to Europe, W Asia, and N Africa; leaves pinnately lobed, in opposite pairs; flowers bluish-lilac, with five unequal petals, in heads 1.5–3.5 cm/0.6–1.4 in across. The flowers around the edge have much larger petals than those in the centre. It is cultivated along with other similar species for ornament. (*Scabiosa columbaria*. Family: *Dipsacaceae*.) » perennial; pinnate

Scafell or **Scawfell** [skawfel] 54°28N 3°12W. Mountain in Lake District of Cumbria, NW England; highest peak in England, rising to 977 m/3 205 ft in the Cumbrian Mts, W of Ambleside. » Lake District

scalar In mathematics, a physical quantity which can be represented by a real number, having magnitude but not direction, such as mass, time, and temperature. Any real number may be considered to be a scalar, in contrast with complex numbers, which may be considered to be vectors. » numbers; vector (mathematics)

Scalawags A derogatory term for White Southerners who co-operated with occupying forces during the era of Reconstruction following the American Civil War. Many Scalawags had never favoured secession, and some were principled opponents of slavery. » Carpetbaggers; Reconstruction

scale In music, the notes forming the basic vocabulary of a melodic or harmonic system, arranged in a succession of upward or downward steps. Since stepwise movement is common in most types of music, the practising of scales forms a basic part of an instrumentalist's training. Some of the more important scales in Western music are shown here, in each case with middle C as the starting note (*tonic*), but the placing of tones (T) and semitones (S) would be the same no matter what note the scale began on. » microtone; mode (music); pentatonic scale; serialism; temperament (music); tonality; tone 1

scale insect A plant-sucking bug; wingless adult females usually protected by a scale-like wax covering secreted over the body; males non-feeding, with one pair of wings; less than 8 mm/⅓ in long; newly hatched larvae (*crawlers*) dispersed by wind; c.4 000 species, including many pests of economically important plants. (Order: *Homoptera*. Family: *Coccidae*.) » bug (entomology); kermes; larva

scales Small bony or horny plates which form the body covering of fishes and reptiles. The scales covering the wings of some insects, such as butterflies and moths, are modified cuticular hairs.

Scaliger, Julius Caesar (1484–1558) Italian humanist scholar, born at Riva, Venice. He studied medicine at Padua, became a French citizen in 1528, and settled at Agen, where he wrote learned works on grammar, philosophy, botany, and zoology. His third son, **Joseph Justus** (1540–1609), became one of the most erudite scholars of his day, a classical linguist and historian, best known for his *Opus de emendatione temporum* (1583), a study of earlier methods of calculating time. Born at Agen, he studied in Paris, became a Protestant, and travelled widely in Europe, finally becoming professor at Leyden in 1593, where he died. » humanism; Renaissance

scallop A marine bivalve mollusc with unequal shell valves; lives unattached to a substrate, and is able to swim by clapping its valves together; margin of its mantle provided with a ring of tentacles and numerous eyes; fished commercially for human consumption. (Class: *Pelecypoda*. Order: *Ostreoida*.) » bivalve; mollusc

scaly anteater » **pangolin**

scaly-tailed squirrel A squirrel-like rodent; inhabits woodland in C Africa; not a true squirrel; base of tail with large scales on undersurface; six species resemble flying squirrels, with a membrane supported by long rod of cartilage projecting from each elbow. (Family: *Anomaluridae*, 7 species.) » flying squirrel; rodent; squirrel

scaly-weaver » **weaverbird**

scampi The Italian culinary term for large gulf shrimps or Dublin Bay prawns, usually fried in batter. » prawn

Scandinavian languages The languages of the N Germanic branch of Indo-European, including Norwegian (c.4½ million in Norway and the USA), Swedish (c.8½ million in Sweden, Finland, and the USA), Danish (c.5 million in Denmark, W Germany, and the USA), Icelandic (c.¼ million in Iceland and the USA), and Faroese (c.40 000 in the Faroe Is). These languages are mutually intelligible to varying degrees, though there are substantial differences between the *continental* varieties as a group (Swedish, Danish, Norwegian), and the *insular* varieties (Icelandic, Faroese). Their status as separate languages rests on the political independence of their speech communities. » Germanic languages; Indo-European languages; Scandinavian literature

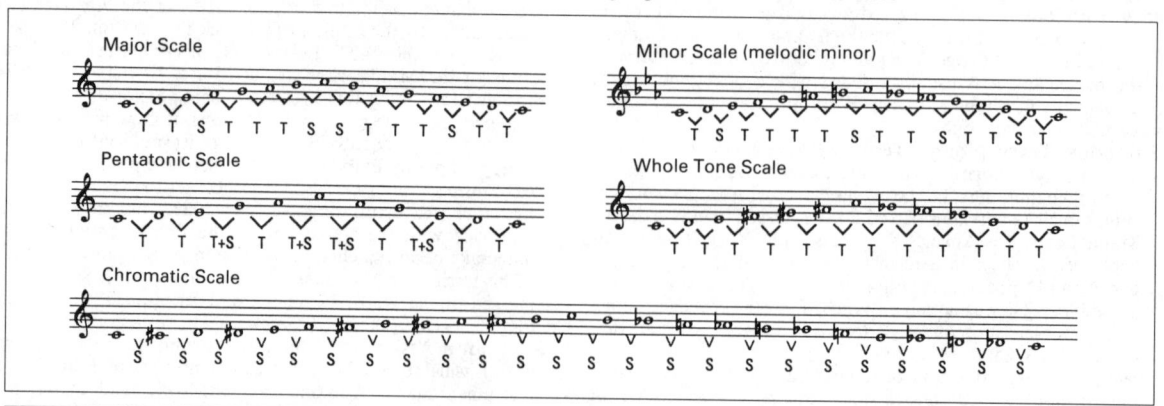

Musical scales

Scandinavian literature » **Danish/Icelandic/Norwegian/Swedish literature**

scanning The exploration of a picture area along a systematic series of lines, providing information in sequential form. In video, the camera image scanned by a set of horizontal lines is reproduced on the screen of a cathode ray tube in the same fashion. For TV broadcasting, two sets of interlaced alternate scanning lines are employed, giving a total picture coverage of 525 lines 30 times a second for American NTSC and 625 lines 25 times a second for European PAL. Optical scanning at a much slower rate is also employed for the transmission of facsimile documents and pictures over land lines, and for the electronic preparation of colour separations in graphic arts. » television

Scapa Flow The area of open water in the Orkney Is, Scotland, surrounded by the islands of Mainland, Hoy, Flotta, S Ronaldsay, and Burray. It was a British naval base in World Wars 1 and 2. In 1919 the German naval fleet was scuppered there.

scapegoat In ancient Jewish ritual (*Lev* 16), on the Day of Atonement and after the sacrifices of a bull and a goat as sin-offerings, a second goat (the 'scapegoat') was released into the wilderness 'to Azazel', possibly a desert demon, symbolizing how the people's sins were removed. The high priest cast lots to determine the respective fates of the two goats. Today the term is more generally applied to one who takes the blame for another. » Yom Kippur

Scaphopoda [skaf**op**uhda] » **tusk shell**

scapula A triangular bone on each side of the body over the upper part of the back (second to seventh ribs). With the clavicle it forms the *pectoral girdle*. Its only point of attachment with the axial skeleton is indirectly via the clavicle. It sits within a sea of muscles which connect it to the thorax, vertebral column, and upper limb. Its position on the chest wall therefore depends on the interplay of the activity of the various muscles attached to it. It moves in conjunction with the shoulder joint to increase the total range of movement of the upper limb. » bone; clavicle; Plate XIII

scarab The dung beetle, symbolic in ancient Egypt of resurrection and immortality. Amulets and stamp seals were often made in the shape of the beetle, and worn either in pendants or rings. » sacred scarab beetle

Scarborough [**skah**bruh] 54°17N 0°24W, pop (1981) 38 048. Coastal resort town in Scarborough district, North Yorkshire, N England; on the North Sea 25 km/15 ml N of Bridlington; a Roman signal station in the 4th-c; England's oldest spa town; railway; electrics, foodstuffs, fishing, tourism; 12th-c castle, museum of regional archaeology. » Yorkshire, North

Scarfe, Gerald (1936–) British cartoonist, born in London. His cartoons are based on extreme distortion in the tradition of Gillray (eg Mick Jagger's lips are drawn larger than the rest of his face), and have appeared in *Punch* since 1960, *Private Eye* since 1961, and elsewhere, especially the *Sunday Times* since 1967. He has also worked as a theatrical designer. » cartoon (art); Gillray

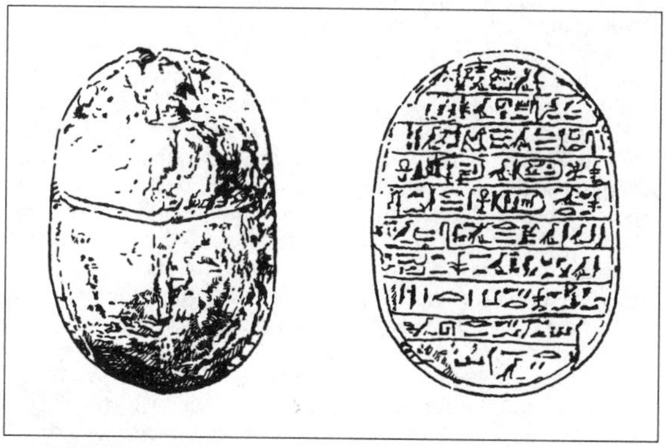

Scarab

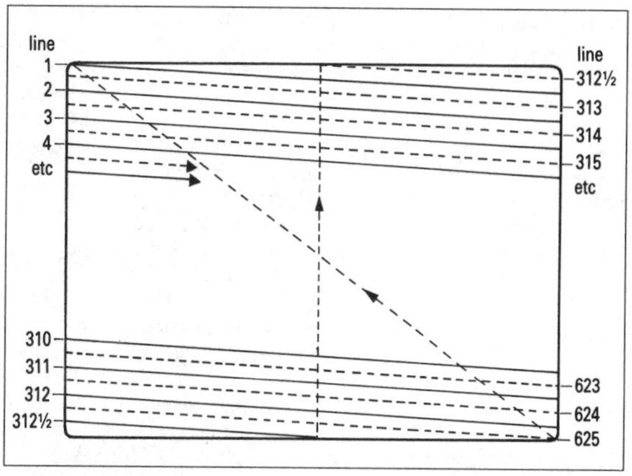

Interlaced scanning – In the system, 312½ lines (shown solid) are scanned from top to bottom in 1/50 sec. The interlacing lines (shown broken) are scanned in the next 1/50 sec to give a complete 625 line scan every 1/25 sec.

Scargill, Arthur (1938–) British trade unionist, born and educated in Leeds. He became president of the National Union of Mineworkers in 1982, and member of the Trades Union Congress General Council. He is primarily known for his strong defence of British miners through a socialist politics that has often brought his union into conflict with government, most particularly during the miners' strike of 1984–5. » socialism; trade union

Scarlatti, (Pietro) Alessandro (Gaspare) (1660–1725) Italian composer, born at Palermo, Sicily. He produced his first opera in Rome (1679), where he became *maestro di cappella* to Queen Cristina of Sweden. He was musical director at the court in Naples (1683–1702, 1709–25), and became a leading figure in Italian opera. He reputedly wrote over 100 operas, of which 40 survive complete, including *Tigrane* (1715). He also wrote 10 masses, c.700 cantatas, and oratorios, motets, and madrigals. He died at Naples.

Scarlatti, (Guiseppe) Domenico (1685–1757) Italian composer, born in Naples, the son of Alessandro Scarlatti. In Rome he was from 1711 *maestro di cappella* to the Queen of Poland, for whom he composed several operas, and he also served in Lisbon and Madrid. As choirmaster of St Peter's, Rome (1714–19), he wrote much church music. He was a skilled harpsichordist, and is mainly remembered for the 555 sonatas written for this instrument. He died in Madrid. » harpsichord; sonata

scarlet fever An acute infectious disease of children caused by haemolytic streptococcus, usually in the pharynx and tonsils, but also in the genital tract or in wounds. A sore throat is followed by a generalized red skin rash. It responds rapidly to antibiotics, but complications include middle-ear infection, rheumatic fever, and glomerulonephritis. » ear [i]; glomerulonephritis; rheumatic fever; streptococcus

scarlet pimpernel » **pimpernel**

Scarron, Paul [skarõ] (1610–60) French writer, born and died in Paris. During his 20s the onset of paralysis forced him to take up writing for a living, and he produced many sonnets, madrigals, songs, epistles, and satires. He is best known for his realistic novel, *Le Roman comique* (1651–7, The Comic Novel). In 1652 he married Françoise d'Aubigné (later, Madame de Maintenon). » French literature; madrigal; Maintenon, Madame de; novel; satire; sonnet

scattering In physics, the redirection of a beam of light or sound, or a stream of particles resulting from a collision. An approaching beam is directed on to a target material which scatters it into a detector. Scattering experiments are an important source of information in atomic, nuclear, particle, and solid state physics. » cross section; electron diffraction; neutron diffraction; Raman scattering; Rayleigh scattering; spectroscopy; X-ray diffraction

Scawfell » **Scafell**

scepticism/skepticism A philosophical tradition which casts doubt on the possibility of human knowledge. An extreme version, held by the followers of Pyrrho of Elis, maintains that one is never in a position to have justified beliefs about anything, including the truth of scepticism. Less extreme versions are directed at particular sources of knowledge, such as perception, memory, or reason. » Pyrrho

Schacht, (Horace Greely) Hjalmar [shahkht] (1877–1970) German financier, born at Tinglev. In 1923 he became president of the Reichsbank, and founded a new currency which ended the inflation of the mark. He was Minister of Economics (1934–7), but in 1939 was dismissed from his bank office for disagreeing with Hitler over rearmament expenditure. Interned by the Nazis, he was acquitted at Nuremberg. In 1953 he set up his own bank in Düsseldorf. He died in Munich. » Nazi Party

Schaffhausen [shaf**how**zn], Fr **Schaffhouse** 47°42N 8°38E, pop (1980) 34 250. Industrial town and capital of Schaffhausen canton, NE Switzerland; on the R Rhine, 37 km/23 ml N of Zürich; well-preserved mediaeval town; railway; engineering, iron and steel works, chemicals, aluminium smelting; falls and rapids nearby; Kastel Munot (1564–85), Minster (1087–1150). » Switzerland [i]

Scharnhorst, Gerhard Johann David von [**shahn**hawst] (1755–1813) Prussian general and military reformer, born at Bordenau, Hanover. He worked with Gneisenau to reform the Prussian army after its defeat by Napoleon, served as Chief-of-Staff to Blücher, and was fatally wounded fighting the French at Lützen, dying in Prague. » Blücher; Gneisenau; Prussia

Schawlow, Arthur (Leonard) [**shaw**loh] (1921–) US physicist, born at Mount Vernon, New York. Educated at Toronto and Columbia, New York, he worked at Bell Telephone Laboratories (1951–61), then became professor at Stanford. With his brother-in-law Charles Townes he devised the laser, although the first working model was made by Maiman in 1960. He shared the Nobel Prize for Physics in 1981. » laser [i]; Maiman; Townes

Scheel, Walter (1919–) West German statesman and President (1974–9), born in Solingen. After serving in the Luftwaffe in World War 2 he went into business, joined the Free Democratic Party (FDP), and was elected to the Bundestag in 1953. He was Minister for Economic Co-operation (1961–6) and Foreign Minister (1969–74), and in 1970 negotiated treaties with the USSR and Poland. » Germany [i]

scheelite [**shee**liyt] A mineral calcium tungstate ($CaWO_4$) occurring in hydrothermal veins and pegmatites. It is an important ore of tungsten. » tungsten; wolframite

Schelde or **Scheldt, River** [**skel**duh, skelt], Fr **Escaut** River rising in Aisne department, N France; flows N and NE through Belgium to Antwerp, then NW to meet the North Sea through two estuaries (East and West Schelde) in the Netherlands; length 435 km/270 ml; connected by canal to several other N European rivers.

Schelling, Friedrich (Wilhelm Joseph) von (1775–1854) German philosopher, born at Leonberg. Educated at Tübingen and Leipzig, he became professor at Jena (1798–1803), Würzburg (1803–8) and Erlangen (1820–7), and from 1806 was secretary of the Royal Academy at Munich. He moved to a chair at Berlin in 1841. His early work, influenced by Fichte and Kant, culminated in his *System des transzendentalen Idealismus* (1800, System of Transcendental Idealism), an important influence on Romanticism. He died at Bad Ragaz, Switzerland. » Fichte; idealism; Kant

scherzo [**skairt**soh] A lively musical piece, though not necessarily a 'joke', as the Italian name suggests. Haydn and Beethoven established it as an alternative to the minuet (whose metre and structure it took over) in the classical symphony, sonata, etc. » Beethoven; Haydn; minuet; trio **2**

Schiaparelli, Elsa [skyapa**rel**lee] (1890–1973) Italian fashion designer, born in Rome. After studying philosophy, she lived in the USA, but went to Paris in 1920. She designed and wore a sweater, as a result of which she received orders from a US store, which started her in business. Her designs were inventive and sensational, and she was noted for her use of colour, including 'shocking pink', and her original use of traditional fabrics. She featured zippers and buttons, and made outrageous hats. » fashion

Schiaparelli, Giovanni (Virginio) [skyapa**rel**lee] (1835–1910) Italian astronomer, born at Savigliano. He studied at Berlin and at Pulkova, Russia, and became director of Brera Observatory, Milan. He observed meteors and double stars, discovered the asteroid Hesperia, and termed vague linear features on Mars as 'canali' (1877). He died in Milan. » asteroids; double star; Lowell, Percival; Mars (astronomy); meteor

Schick Test A test of the susceptibility to diphtheria, in which a small amount of diphtheria toxin is injected into the skin. A localized reaction indicates susceptibility, when immunization may be desirable. The test is named after the Austrian paediatrician, Bela Schick (1877–1967). » diphtheria

Schiele, Egon [**shee**luh] (1890–1918) Austrian painter, born at Tulln. He studied at the Vienna Academy of Fine Arts in 1906, met Klimt in 1907, and developed a powerful form of Expressionism in which figures, often naked and emaciated and drawn with hard outlines, fill the canvas with awkward, anguished gestures. In 1912 he was arrested, and some of his work was destroyed by the police. He died in Vienna, a victim of the influenza epidemic. » Expressionism (art); Klimt; Sezession

Schiller, (Johann Christoph) Friedrich (von) (1759–1805) German dramatist, poet, and historian, born at Marbach. He attended a military academy, and became an army surgeon in Stuttgart, where he began to write *Sturm und Drang* verse and plays. The revolutionary appeal of his first play, *Die Räuber* (1781, The Robbers), made it an instant success. He later settled in Dresden, where his works included the poem *An die Freude* (Ode to Joy, later set to music by Beethoven in his choral symphony). He became professor of history at Jena in 1788. His last decade was highly productive, including the dramatic trilogy, *Wallenstein* (1796–9), the greatest German historical drama, *Maria Stuart* (1800), and *Wilhelm Tell* (1804). He died at Weimar. » drama; German literature; poetry; Sturm und Drang

Schinkel, Karl Friedrich (1781–1841) German architect, born at Neuruppin. He studied at Berlin and in Italy, became state architect of Prussia (1815), and director of public works (1830). He designed a wide range of buildings, in classical style, and introduced new streets and squares in Berlin. He also became known as a painter, illustrator, and furniture and stage designer. He died in Berlin.

schipperke [**ship**uhk] A breed of dog, developed in Belgium, used as a watchdog on barges; small, lively; erect pointed ears, pointed muzzle, no tail; thick, usually black, coat; also known as **little boatman**, **little captain**, or **little corporal**. » dog

schist [shist] A medium-grade regional metamorphic rock characterized by a foliated texture, resulting from the alignment and segregation of layers of mica minerals. » metamorphic rock; micas

schistosomiasis [skistohsuh**miy**asis] A common cause of illness in tropical countries, resulting from infestation with one of three species of the genus *Schistosoma*, a fluke; also known as **bilharziasis**. The flukes pass through the blood circulation, where they cause disease of the lungs, bladder, liver, and large bowel. Clinical features include pneumonia, blood in the urine, diarrhoea, liver and kidney failure, and involvement of the central nervous system. » blood fluke

schizophrenia A major psychiatric disorder characterized by an alteration of thinking and perception, including a loss of contact with reality. In addition there may be a basic change in personality and a loss of normal emotional responsiveness. Schizophrenic patients often feel that their unexpressed thoughts are known to others and can be influenced by external forces. Trivial events and objects take on inappropriately significant meaning. There may be considerable withdrawal. The causes are not fully understood, but there is a major genetic component and a well-established higher incidence in winter-born children. Brain damage, either at birth or subsequently, may produce a schizophrenia-like picture, and social stresses are thought to be of particular significance in the relapse of this condition. Management includes prevention (by minimizing social stresses), prophylactic drug treatment, treatment of acute illness (usually with anti-psychotic drugs), and skilful counselling concerning the impact of the illness for the sufferers, and rehabilitation. » abulia; catatonia; personality; psychosis

Schlegel, August Wilhelm von [**shlay**gl] (1767–1845) German poet and critic, born at Hanover. He studied theology at Göttingen, but soon turned to literature, settling in Jena, where (1798) he became professor of literature and fine art. He then lectured at Berlin (1801–4), and from 1818 until his death was professor of literature at Bonn. He is famous for his translations of Shakespeare and other authors, and for founding Sanskrit studies in Germany. A leading figure of the Romantic movement, he died in Bonn. His brother, **Karl Wilhelm Friedrich** (1772–1829), also born at Hanover, became the greatest critic produced by the German Romantics, editing with him the journal *Das Athenaeum*, and writing widely on comparative literature and philology. He died in Dresden. » comparative linguistics/literature; German literature; poetry; Romanticism (literature); Shakespeare [i]

Schleiermacher, Friedrich (Ernst Daniel) [**shliy**uhmahkhuh] (1768–1834) German theologian and philosopher, born at Breslau. Educated at Halle, he became a preacher in Berlin (1796), and a professor at Halle (1804–6) and Berlin (from 1810). He was a leader of the movement which led to the union in 1817 of the Lutheran and Reformed Churches in Prussia. His most important work is *Der christliche Glaube* (1821–2, The Christian Faith), and he also wrote on Christian ethics, a life of Jesus, sermons, and letters. Widely held to be the founder of modern Protestant theology, he died in Berlin. » Lutheranism; Protestantism; Reformed Churches; theology

Schlesinger, Arthur M(eier) Jnr (1917–) US historian, born at Columbus, Ohio, son of the historian **Arthur M(eier)** (1888–1965). He was educated at Harvard, where he became professor of history (1954–61) and special assistant to President Kennedy (1961–3). His publications include *The Age of Jackson* (1945) and *A Thousand Days: John F Kennedy in the White House* (1965), both Pulitzer prizewinners. He then became professor of humanities at New York (1966) and President of the American Institute of Arts and Letters (1981). » Kennedy, John F

Schlesinger, John (1926–) British actor and director, born in London. He directed art documentary films for television, and made his first feature film of contemporary social realism, *A Kind of Loving*, in 1962, followed by *Billy Liar* (1963). His interpretation of Hardy's *Far from the Madding Crowd* (1967), the downbeat urban *Midnight Cowboy* (1969), and the sensitive *Sunday, Bloody Sunday* (1971) showed his width of range. Later productions in the USA explored political responsibilities, such as *Day of the Locust* (1975), *Marathon Man* (1976), and *Yanks* (1979). Films of the 1980s include *Honky Tonk Freeway* (1980), *Believers* (1987), and *Madame Sousatka* (1989). He has also directed for stage and opera.

Schleswig [**shlez**vig] A heavy breed of horse, developed in Germany; height, 15½–16 hands/1.5–1.6 m/5–5¼ ft; usually pale brown with yellow mane; body long and deep; short powerful legs; also known as **Schleswig heavy draught**. » horse [i]

Schleswig-Holstein [**shles**vikh **hol**shtiyn] pop (1990) 2 594 606; area 15 721 sq km/6 068 sq ml. Northernmost province of Germany, bounded N by Denmark; includes the North Frisian Is; capital, Kiel; chief towns include Lübeck, Flensburg; coast includes an extensive swimming and sailing resort area; shipbuilding, machinery, foodstuffs, electrical engineering; focus of a dispute between Denmark and Prussia in the 19th-c, leading to war (1863) and annexation by Prussia (1866). » Frisian Islands; Germany [i]; Kiel; Prussia

Schlick, Moritz (1882–1936) German philosopher, one of the leaders of the 'Vienna Circle' of logical positivists, born in Berlin. He studied physics at Heidelberg, Lausanne, and Berlin, taught at Rostock and Kiel, and from 1922 was professor of inductive sciences at Vienna. An early exponent of Einstein's relativity theories, his major works include *Allgemeine Erkenntnislehre* (1918, General Theory of Knowledge) and *Fragen der Ethik* (1930, Problems of Ethics). He was shot down on the steps of the university by a deranged student. » logical positivism; Vienna Circle

Schlieffen, Alfred, Graf von ('Count of') [**shlee**fn] (1833–1913) Prussian field marshal, born in Berlin. He advocated the plan which bears his name (1895), on which German tactics were unsuccessfully based in World War 1. He envisaged a German breakthrough in Belgium and the defeat of France within six weeks by a major right-wheel flanking movement through Holland, cutting off Paris from the sea, holding off the Russians meanwhile with secondary forces. » World War 1

Schliemann, Heinrich [**shlee**man] (1822–90) German archaeologist, born at Neubukow. After a successful business career, he retired early to realize his ambition of finding the site of the Homeric poems by excavating the tell at Hisarlik in Asia Minor, the traditional site of Troy. From 1871 he discovered nine superimposed city sites, one containing a considerable treasure (found 1873) which he over-hastily identified as Priam's. He excavated several other Greek sites, and died in Naples. » Homer; shaft-graves; tell; Troy

schlieren photography [**shleer**uhn] A means of forming a photographic image of density variations in a transparent fluid. It relies on the refraction of incident light because of variations in the fluid density, and is used in the analysis of wind tunnel experiments to show the flow and pressure patterns round an object. » photography; refraction [i]

Schmidt, Helmut (Heinrich Waldemar) (1918–) West German statesman and Chancellor (1974–82), born in Hamburg. After service in World War 2, he studied at Hamburg, joined the Social Democratic Party in 1946, and became a member of the Bundestag in 1953. He was Minister of Defence (1969–72) and of Finance (1972–4), in which role he created a firm basis for Germany's continued economic growth. He succeeded Brandt as Chancellor in 1974, describing his aim as the 'political unification of Europe in partnership with the United States'. » Brandt, Willy; Germany [i]; Kohl

Schmidt telescope An astronomical instrument invented in 1932 by Estonian Bernhard Schmidt (1879–1935), which uses a correcting plate in the optical path to achieve distortion-free images over a wide field. Along with the Schmidt camera, it is used to make extensive sky surveys. » Cassegrain telescope

Schnauzer [**shnowt**ser] A German breed of dog; terrier-like with thick wiry coat; marked eyebrows, moustache, and beard; top of head flat, with short pendulous ears; three forms: **giant** (bred to herd sheep and cattle), **standard**, and **miniature** (both used as rat-catchers). » dog; terrier

Schneider Trophy A flying trophy for seaplanes presented by French armaments magnate Jacques Schneider in 1913. After being won outright by Great Britain in 1931 the contest ceased, but the races were revived in the 1980s.

Schnitzler, Arthur (1862–1931) Austrian dramatist and novelist, born and died in Vienna. He was a physician before he turned playwright, writing highly psychological, often strongly erotic short plays and novels. They include his one-act play cycles *Anatol* (1893) and *Reigen* (1900, filmed as *La Ronde*, 1950). » drama; German literature; novel

Schoenberg or **Schönberg, Arnold** [**shern**berg] (1874–1951) Austrian composer, born in Vienna. He was largely self-taught, and in his 20s lived by orchestrating operettas while composing such early works as the string sextet *Verklärte Nacht* (1899, Transfigured Night). His search for a personal musical style emerged in these works, which were not well received: his *Chamber Symphony* caused a riot at its first performance in 1907 through its abandonment of the traditional concept of tonality. He became known for his concept of 'twelve-note' or 'serial' music, used in most of his later works. At the end of World War 1 he taught in Vienna and Berlin, until exiled by the Nazi government in 1933. He settled in California, took US nationality in 1941, and died in Los Angeles. » atonality; serialism

scholastic aptitude test » SAT

scholasticism Philosophical speculation as it developed in cathedral-schools in W Europe 12th–14th-c AD. It is characterized by its use of philosophy in the service of Christianity, its use of ancient authorities such as Aristotle and St Augustine, and its dialectical method. » Aquinas; Augustine, St (of Hippo); dialectic

Schönbrunn Palace [**shern**brun] A Baroque palace in Vienna, designed (1696–1730) by Fischer von Erlach for Emperor Leopold I, and converted by Nikolaus Pacassi for Maria Theresa's use in the 1740s. Although the palace is used for state receptions, some rooms are open to the public. » Fischer von Erlach; Maria Theresa; Vienna

school (art) In art history, very broadly the art of one country (eg 'the French school') or more specifically one city (eg 'the Florentine school' or 'Avignon school'). Connoisseurs like to distinguish a master's autograph work from that of his followers or assistants by referring to the latter as 'school' works, and this type of classification has proved useful to the art trade. The term is, however, often used very imprecisely. » Avignon/Barbizon/Danube/Euston Road/Florentine/Fontainebleau/Hudson River/New York/Norwich/Paris/Pskov/Sienese/Utrecht/Venetian School

school (education) A place where learning can take place, usually classified according to whether it is for primary or secondary age pupils. The term can also denote a grouping of subjects, such as a humanities school, and in the USA can mean a university. » comprehensive/community/grammar/high/independent/infant/maintained/middle/nursery/open-plan/preparatory/public/ragged/secondary modern school; School of the Air; sixth-form college

School of the Air A two-way radio educational service for Australian children living in isolated areas; begun in South Australia in 1951 to supplement correspondence teaching and reduce feelings of isolation. The Aussat satellite (launched in 1985) was partly intended to improve the technical quality of broadcasts. » Open University

schooner A sailing vessel with more than one mast, each fore-and aft-rigged. The masts are usually of equal height, but when two-masted the forward one is often shorter. » ship [i]

Schopenhauer, Arthur [**shoh**pnhowuh] (1788–1860) German philosopher, born at Danzig. Educated at Göttingen and Berlin, he taught at Berlin (1820), where he boldly held his lectures at the same times as Hegel, whose ideas he rejected, but he failed to attract students. He then lived in retirement as a scholar at Frankfurt am Main, where he died. His chief work, *Die Welt als Wille und Vorstellung* (1819, The World as Will and Idea), emphasizes the central role of human will as the creative, primary factor in understanding. His conception of the will as a blind, irrational force led him to a rejection of Enlightenment doctrines and to pessimism. » Enlightenment

Schreiner, Olive (Emilie Albertina) [**shri**ynuh], pseudonym **Ralph Iron** (1855–1920) South African author, born at Wittebergen, Cape Colony. Largely self-educated, she went to England (1881–9), working as a governess, while she wrote her successful *The Story of an African Farm* (1883), the first sustained, imaginative work to come from Africa. In her later work she became a passionate propagandist for women's rights, pro-Boer loyalty, and pacifism, as in *Woman and Labour* (1911). She died in Cape Town. » African literature

Schrödinger, Erwin [**shroh**dinguh] (1887–1961) Austrian physicist, born and died in Vienna. He taught at Stuttgart, Breslau, Zürich, Berlin, Oxford (1933–8), and Dublin (1940–56), after which he retired to Vienna. He originated the study of wave mechanics as part of the quantum theory with his celebrated wave equation, for which he shared the Nobel Prize for Physics in 1933. » Dirac; quantum field theory; Schrödinger's equation; wave (physics) [i]

Schrödinger's equation A fundamental equation of quantum mechanics. It describes the evolution in space and time of the wavefunction of a quantum system, given the forces acting on it. For simple atoms, solutions obtained using approximation techniques give good agreement with experiments. » quantum mechanics; Schrödinger; wavefunction

Schubert, Franz (Peter) (1797–1828) Austrian composer, born in Vienna. At 11 he became a member of the chapel choir at the imperial court, and with little formal training began to compose. From 1817 he lived precariously as a composer and teacher, until his association with the operatic baritone, Johann Michael Vogl, with whom he founded the successful 'Schubertiads' – private and public accompanied recitals of his songs, which made them known throughout Vienna. His major works include the 'Trout' piano quintet (1819), his C major symphony (1825), and his B minor symphony (1822), known as the 'Unfinished'; but he is particularly remembered as the greatest exponent of German songs (*Lieder*), which number c.600. He also wrote a great deal of choral and chamber music. He died of typhoid in Vienna. » Lied

Schuman, Robert (1886–1963) French statesman and Prime Minister (1947–8), born in Luxembourg. He held several government posts after World War 2, and as Foreign Minister (1948–52) proposed the **Schuman plan** (1950) for pooling the coal and steel resources of W Europe. He was President of the EEC Assembly (1958–60), and died at Metz. » European Economic Community

Schumann, Clara (Josephine), *née* **Wieck** (1819–96) German pianist and composer, born in Leipzig. She gave her first concert at 11, and published four of her Polonaises the following year. Her compositions include chamber music, songs, and many piano works, including a concerto. She married Robert Schumann in 1840, and from 1878 was principal piano teacher in the Conservatory at Frankfurt-am-Main, where she died. » Schumann, Robert

Schumann, Elisabeth (1888–1952) US operatic soprano and Lieder singer, born at Merseburg, Germany. She made her debut in Hamburg in 1909, and in 1919 was engaged by Richard Strauss for the Vienna State Opera, later specializing in Lieder by such composers as Schubert and Strauss. She left Austria in 1936, settled in the USA, where she became a US citizen (1944), and died in New York City. » Lied; Strauss, Richard

Schumann, Robert (Alexander) (1810–56) German composer, born at Zwickau. He studied law at Leipzig, then turned to music, and particularly the piano, but after injuring a finger (1832) he gave up performing for writing and composing. He produced a large number of compositions, until 1840 almost all for the piano. He then married Clara, the daughter of his piano teacher, Friedrich Wieck, after much opposition from her father, and under her influence began to write orchestral works, notably his A minor piano concerto (1845) and four symphonies. He also wrote chamber music and a large number of songs (Lieder), in addition to his continuing piano compositions. In 1843 he was appointed professor at the new Leipzig Conservatory, but mental illness caused him soon to move to Dresden, and he died there in an asylum. » Lied; Schumann, Clara

Schuschnigg, Kurt von (1897–1977) Austrian statesman and Chancellor (1934–8), born at Riva. He served in World War 1, practised law, was elected a Christian Socialist Deputy (1927), and became Minister of Justice (1932) and of Education (1933). His attempt to prevent Hitler occupying Austria led to his imprisonment until 1945. He then lived in the USA, where he became professor of political science at St Louis (1948–67). He died near Innsbruck. » Austria [i]; World War 2

Schwann, Theodor [shvahn] (1810–82) German physiologist, born at Neuss. Educated at Berlin, he became professor of physiology at Louvain (1838) and Liège (1848). He discovered the enzyme pepsin, investigated muscle contraction, demonstrated the role of micro-organisms in putrefaction, and extended the cell theory from plants to animal tissues. He died at Cologne. » cell; pepsin

Schwarzenberg, Felix (Ludwig Johann Friedrich) [**shvahtz**uhnberg] (1800–52) Austrian statesman, born at Krummau. During the 1848 Revolution, he was made Prime Minister, and created a centralized, absolutist, imperial state. He then sought Russian military aid to suppress the Hungarian rebellion (1849), and demonstrated Austrian superiority over Prussia at the Olmütz Convention (1850). His bold initiatives temporarily restored Habsburg domination of European affairs. He died in Vienna. » Habsburgs; Prussia; Revolutions of 1848

Schwarzkopf, (Olga Maria) Elisabeth (Friederike) [**shvahts**kopf] (1915–) German soprano, born at Janotschin. She studied at Berlin, where she made her debut in 1938, and sang in the Vienna State Opera (1944–8) and at Covent Garden

(1949–52). She first specialized in coloratura roles and later appeared more as a lyric soprano, especially in recitals of Lieder. » coloratura; Lied

Schwarzschild, Karl [**shvahts**chilt] (1873–1916) German theoretical astrophysicist, who computed exact solutions of Einstein's field equations in general relativity – work which led directly to modern research on black holes. The **Schwarzschild radius** is the critical radius at which an object becomes a black hole if collapsed or compressed indefinitely. At this radius the escape velocity is the speed of light. Its value is 9 mm/0.35 in for Earth, 3 km/1.9 ml for the Sun. » black hole; general relativity; gravitational collapse

Schweitzer, Albert [**shviy**tsuh] (1875–1965) German medical missionary, theologian, musician, and philosopher, born at Kaysersberg. He studied at Strasbourg, Paris, and Berlin, and in 1896 made his famous decision that he would live for science and art until he was 30, and then devote his life to serving humanity. He became a curate at Strasbourg (1899), taught at the university (1902), and was appointed principal of the theological college (1903). His religious writing includes *Von Reimarus zu Wrede* (1906, trans The Quest of the Historical Jesus), and major works on St Paul. True to his vow, despite his international reputation in music and theology, he began to study medicine in 1905, and after qualifying (1913) set out with his newly-married wife to set up a hospital to fight leprosy and sleeping sickness at Lambaréné, French Equatorial Africa, where he remained for the rest of his life, apart from fund-raising visits and occasional lectures in Europe. He was awarded the Nobel Peace Prize in 1952. » leprosy; Paul, St; theology; trypanosomaisis

Schwerin [**shvay**reen] 53°37N 11°22E, pop (1982) 122 700. Capital of Schwerin county, N Germany; surrounded by 11 lakes, SW of Rostock; former capital of Mecklenburg state; railway; marine engineering, power cables, sewing machines, plastics, hydraulic products, pharmaceuticals, food processing, tourism; palace, 13th-c Gothic cathedral, art museum. » Germany [i]

Schwitters, Kurt [**shvit**ers] (1887–1948) German artist, born at Hanover. He studied at the Dresden Academy, and painted abstract pictures before joining the Dadaists. His best-known contribution to the movement was *Merz*, a name he gave to a form of collage using such everyday detritus as broken glass, tram tickets, and scraps of paper picked up in the street. From 1920 onwards he slowly built from bits and pieces of rubbish a three-dimensional construction which he called his *Merzbau*, and which filled the house before being destroyed in an air raid in 1943. In 1937 he fled to Norway, then in 1940 to England, where he died at Ambleside. » abstract art; collage; Dada

Schwyz [shveets] 47°02N 8°39E, pop (1980) 12 100. Capital town of Schwyz canton, C Switzerland, 35 km/22 ml E of Lucerne; the town and canton gave their name to the whole country; the flag of Schwyz (white cross on a red ground) has become the national flag; railway; tourism; Church of St Martin (18th-c), town hall (1642–3), museum. » Switzerland [i]

sciatica Pain in the distribution of the sciatic nerve, ie over the buttocks and the back of the leg as far as the foot. It is commonly due to pressure on the lumbosacral nerve roots of the sciatic nerve, resulting from the prolapse of an intervertebral disc. » nervous system; prolapsed intervertebral disc

science fiction Fiction that focuses on the technical possibilities and human effects of scientific advance. Mary Shelley's *Frankenstein* (1820) is a precursor, though the first novelist to explore this theme systematically is Jules Verne, with four novels (1863–73) including *20 000 Leagues under the Sea.* H G Wells brought more scientific rigour to his five novels at the end of the century, which include *The Time Machine* (1895) and *The First Men in the Moon* (1901). In 1926 there was the first publication of Hugo Gernsback's journal *Amazing Stories*, which established the popularity of 'SF' as a genre; but major authors, such as Ray Bradbury (eg *Fahrenheit 451*, 1954), Arthur C Clarke (eg *Childhood's End*, 1954), and Isaac Asimov (eg *Foundation Trilogy*, 1957–63), did not emerge until after World War 2. Other important works from this period are Walter M Miller's *A Canticle for Leibowitz* (1960), Frank Herbert's *Dune* (1965), and Kurt Vonnegut's *Slaughterhouse Five* (1969). There is now a 'new wave' of science fiction writers, including J G Ballard, Brian Aldiss, Michael Moorcock, and Thomas Disch; and a specialist sub-genre of computer SF, pioneered by William Gibson. » Asimov; Ballard; Bradbury, Ray; novel; Shelley, Mary; Verne; Vonnegut; Wells, H G

Science Museum A museum in S Kensington, London, housing the most important British collection of scientific and technological exhibits. The collection was separated from the Victoria and Albert Museum in 1909, and has since expanded. » museum; Victoria and Albert Museum

science park A concentration of scientific and high technology industries and businesses on one site. This allows individual businesses to co-operate and make use of products and ideas developed at the site. The term includes research parks established by universities to promote academic and business links in science, and technology parks designed for the commercial exploitation of high technology. Science parks began in the USA in the 1930s. In the UK the first were started in the late 1970s (eg the Cambridge Science Park).

scientology A movement on the fringe of Christianity, developed in the USA by L Ron Hubbard in the 1950s, which strives to open the mind of adherents to all great truths and to self-determination. Jesus is seen as one of several important teachers. The Church's scientific and religious claims have given rise to much controversy, as have its methods of financial management, and in the 1980s it defended several lawsuits in the USA. » Christianity; Hubbard

Scilly, Isles of [**sil**ee] pop (1987e) 1 900; area 16 sq km/6 sq ml. A group of c.140 islands and islets WSW of Land's End, Cornwall, SW England; administered by Duchy of Cornwall; includes the five inhabited islands of St Mary's (chief town Hugh Town), St Martin's, Tresco, St Agnes, Bryher; tourism, horticulture (early vegetables and flowers), agriculture; Bronze Age settlements. » Cornwall

scintillation counter A device for detecting the passage of charged particles, using materials such as sodium iodide, or special plastics which emit light (*scintillate*) when charged particles pass through them. The light pulses are recorded using photomultipliers. The technique is an important means of timing the passage of particles in particle physics experiments. » particle detectors

Scipio Aemilianus, also called **Scipio Africanus Minor** (185–129 BC) Roman statesman, general, and orator, famous primarily for the sack of Carthage in the Third Punic War (146 BC), the destruction of Numantia (133 BC), and his patronage of the arts. Members of the so-called 'Scipionic Circle' included the historian Polybius, the Stoic Panaetius, the poet Lucilius, and the playwright Terence. His opposition to the reforms of the Gracchi may have been the cause of his sudden death, possibly by poison. » Gracchi; Polybius; Punic Wars; Terence

Scipio Africanus Major, Publius Cornelius [**ski**pioh] (236–c.183 BC) Innovative Roman general of the Second Punic War, whose victory at Ilipa (206 BC) forced the Carthaginians out of Spain, and whose defeat of Hannibal at Zama (202 BC) broke the power of Carthage altogether. Honoured for this with the title 'Africanus', he remained in the forefront of affairs until forced into retirement by his political enemies of the 180s. » Hannibal; Punic Wars

scirocco » Sirocco

scissorbill » skimmer

scoliosis » vertebral column

scops owl A typical owl of widespread genus *Otus* (c.40 species); an Old World species, often called *scops owl*, with the New World species called **screech owl**; inhabits woodland or dry open country; eats insects (occasionally small birds). » owl

scorpion A terrestrial arthropod; body typically elongate, up to 180 mm/7 in long, including a long tail bearing a conspicuous terminal sting; venom of some forms dangerous to humans; most are nocturnal predators of other arthropods; c.1 200 species, mostly tropical in distribution. (Class: *Arachnida*. Order: *Scorpiones*.) » Arachnida; arthropod

scorpion fly A slender, winged insect that typically inhabits moist forests; mouthparts forming a long snout; feeding on nectar or preying on other insects; two pairs of similar, membraneous wings; male holds end of abdomen upturned, resembling the tail of a scorpion; larvae caterpillar-like. (Order: *Mecoptera*, c.450 species.) » insect [i]; larva; scorpion

scorpionfish Robust bottom-living marine fish with well-developed fin and body spines, frequently armed with venom glands; strong cryptic coloration; widespread in tropical to cool temperate seas; includes the W Atlantic *Scorpaena plumieri*, common on shallow reefs and hard bottoms; length up to 40 cm/16 in. (Family: *Scorpaenidae*, 11 genera.) » fish [i]

Scorpius (Lat 'scorpion') One of the few constellations that really does look like the object it is named for; often wrongly called 'Scorpio'. It is in the S sky, in a very rich part of the Milky Way, with many good clusters visible through binoculars, including Scorpius X-1, the first X-ray star discovered. It is an autumn sign of the zodiac, lying between Libra and Sagittarius. The brightest star is Antares, a huge supergiant some 300 times the Sun's diameter, near the end of its evolution. Distance: 130 parsecs. » constellation; Milky Way; star cluster; X-rays; RR9

scotch whisky A spirit distilled from malted barley, either *single malt*, the product of one distillery (c.40 varieties of Island, Highland, Lowland, and Speyside malts) or *blended* whiskies. Grain whisky, distilled from barley and maize in continuous stills, is now used as the base for much of the blended whisky. About 85% of the whisky made in Scotland is exported. » barley; maize; spirits; whisky

Scotland pop (1981) 5 130 735; area 78 742 sq km/30 394 sq ml (water 1 603 sq km/619 sq ml). Northern constituent part of the United Kingdom, comprising all mainland N of the borders (from Solway to Berwick) and the island groups of Outer and Inner Hebrides, Orkney, and Shetland; bounded W by the Atlantic and E by the North Sea; maximum length 441 km/274 ml, maximum width 248 km/154 ml; of 787 islands only c.60 exceed 8 sq km/3 sq ml; Scottish Gaelic known or used by c.80 000; divided into Southern Uplands (rising to 843 m/2 766 ft at Merrick), Central Lowlands (most densely populated area), and Northern Highlands (divided by the fault line following the Great Glen, and rising to 1 344 m/4 409 ft at Ben Nevis); W coast heavily indented; several wide estuaries on E coast, primarily Firths of Forth, Tay, and Moray; many freshwater lochs in the interior, largest Loch Lomond (70 sq km/27 sq ml) and deepest Loch Morar (310 m/1 020 ft); Roman attempts to limit incursions of N tribes marked by Antonine Wall and Hadrian's Wall; beginnings of unification, 9th-c; wars between England and Scotland in Middle Ages; Scottish

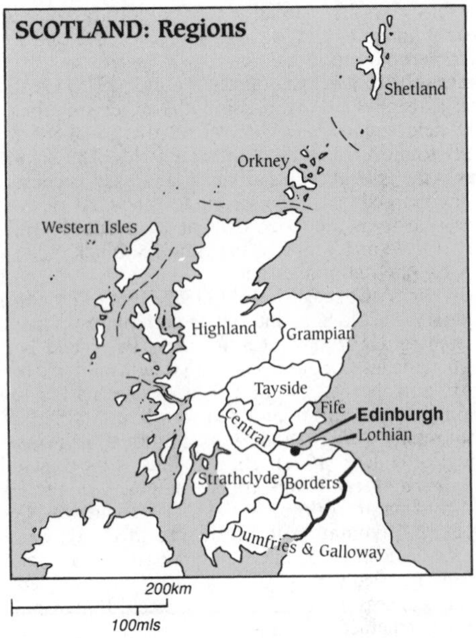

independence declared by Robert Bruce, recognized 1328; Stuart succession, 14th-c; crowns of Scotland and England united in 1603; parliaments united under Treaty of Union in 1707; unsuccessful Jacobite rebellions, 1715, 1745; devolution proposal rejected in 1979; capital, Edinburgh; other chief towns, Glasgow, Dundee, Aberdeen; since 1974, divided into 12 regions and 53 districts; industries mainly in C region, based on local coal, but all heavy industry declined through the 1980s, with closure of many pits; shipbuilding, steel, vehicles, whisky, oil services on E coast, textiles, agriculture and forestry, fishing and fish farming, tourism (especially in Highlands). » Bruce, Robert; Edinburgh; Gaelic; Kenneth I; Scottish Ballet/literature/National Party/reels; Stuarts; Union, Acts of; RR40

Scotland Yard, officially **New Scotland Yard** The headquarters of the Metropolitan Police at Westminster in London, although the title is often used to indicate the Criminal Investigation Department (CID). Its name derives from its original site by Great Scotland Yard.

Scott, Sir George Gilbert (1811–78) British architect, born at Gawcott, Buckinghamshire. He studied in London, and influenced by Pugin became the leading practical architect of the British Gothic revival, responsible for the building or restoration of many ecclesiastical and civil buildings, such as the Albert Memorial (1862–3), St Pancras Station and Hotel in London (1865), and Glasgow University (1865). He became professor of architecture at the Royal Academy in 1868, was knighted in 1872, and died in London. » Gothic architecture; Pugin

Scott, Paul (Mark) (1920–78) British novelist, born, educated, and died in London. He served with the Indian Army in India and Malaya (1943–6), then worked as a literary agent until 1960. His reputation is based on four novels collectively known as the *Raj Quartet* (1965–75) comprising *The Jewel in the Crown* (1965), *The Day of the Scorpion* (1968), *The Towers of Silence* (1971), and *A Division of the Spoils* (1975), in which he gave an exhaustive account of the British withdrawal from India. » English literature; novel

Scott, Sir Peter (Markham) (1909–89) British artist, ornithologist, and broadcaster, born in London. An Olympic sportsman (dinghy sailing), he served in the navy in World War 2. He began to exhibit his paintings of bird scenes in 1933, and after the war led several ornithological expeditions (Iceland, 1951, 1953; Australasia and the Pacific, 1956–7). His writing and television programmes helped to popularize natural history, and he received a knighthood in 1973. » ornithology

Scott, R(obert) F(alcon) (1868–1912) British Antarctic explorer, born near Devonport, Devon. He joined the navy in 1881, and commanded the National Antarctic Expedition (1900–4) which explored the Ross Sea area, and discovered King Edward VII Land. In 1910 he led a second expedition to the S Pole (17 Jan 1912), only to discover that the Norwegian expedition under Amundsen had beaten them by a month. All members of his party died, their bodies and diaries being found by a search party eight months later. He was posthumously knighted, and the Scott Polar Research Institute at Cambridge was founded in his memory. » Amundsen; Antarctica [i]; Oates, Lawrence

Scott, Ronnie (1927–) British jazz saxophonist and night club owner, born in London. After visiting New York as a member of the band aboard the *Queen Mary*, he returned to England and disseminated the modern bebop style. He has been a soloist in several great European jazz orchestras, as well as a leader in his own right. In 1959 he opened a jazz club in London's Soho district which has become an international landmark. » bebop; jazz; saxophone

Scott, Sir Walter (1771–1832) British novelist and poet, born in Edinburgh, Scotland. He attended school and university in Edinburgh, trained as a lawyer (1792), and began to write ballads in 1796, though his first major publication did not appear until 1802: *The Border Minstrelsy*. His ballads made him the most popular author of the day, and were followed by other romances, such as *The Lady of the Lake* (1810). He then turned to historical novels, which fall into three groups: those set in the background of Scottish history, from *Waverley* (1814) to *A Legend of Montrose* (1819); a group which takes up themes from the Middle Ages and Reformation times, from *Ivanhoe* (1819) to *The Talisman* (1825); and his remaining books, from *Woodstock* (1826) until his death. His last years were spent in immense labours for his publishers, much of it hack editorial work, in an attempt to recover from bankruptcy, following the collapse of his publishing ventures in 1826. His journal is an important record of this period of his life. Created a baronet in 1820, he died at Abbotsford, Roxburgh. » ballad; novel; Scottish literature

Scottish Ballet A company which began life as Western Theatre Ballet in Bristol in 1957, founded by Elizabeth West and Peter Darrell. In 1969 it divided into two: most dancers went to Scotland to form the Scottish Theatre Ballet, and some went to Manchester to form the Northern Ballet. Many new works have been created by Darrell such as *Tales of Hoffmann* (1972). » ballet; Scotland [i]

Scottish literature Scottish literature may be divided into that written in Gaelic, in Scots, and in English. Though there are some manuscripts from the 12th-c, little early Gaelic literature survives in Scotland, despite the claim by James Macpherson (1736–96) to have reconstructed the poems of the ancient bard Ossian: and there is hardly any trace of the great bardic families that preserved the oral tradition. It was not until the mid-18th-c that Alexander MacDonald published poetry in Gaelic, to be followed by few others; but Sorley Maclean (1911–) is a great Gaelic poet of the present century.

Scots or 'Lallans' (lowland) first survives in 13th-c minstrelsy, and in John Barbour's poem *The Bruce* (1375). The turn of the 15th–16th-c was a rich period, with James I's own *King's Quair*, Henryson's masterpiece *The Testament of Cresseid*, the *Wallace* by Henry the Minstrel, and the work of William Dunbar (c.1460–c.1520), and Gawain Douglas (c.1474–1522). The oral tradition lay behind the vernacular revival in the 18th-c with Allan Ramsey (c.1685–1758), Robert Fergusson (1750–74), and pre-eminently Robert Burns (1759–96). Several 19th-c writers, including James Hogg (1770–1835) and Robert Louis Stevenson (1850–94) wrote in both Scots and English; while Hugh MacDiarmid (C M Grieve, 1892–1978) has written some of the finest poetry of the 20th-c in this medium.

Literature in English dates from the union of the English and Scottish crowns in 1603. Notable early work is the poetry of William Drummond (1585–1649) and the translation of Rabelais by Sir Thomas Urquhart (1611–60). There was a flowering in the 18th-c with the poetry of James Thomson, the novels of Tobias Smollett (1721–71), the biography of James Boswell (1740–95), and the philosophy of David Hume and Adam Smith. Centrality was maintained in the 19th-c with the work of Sir Walter Scott (1771–1832), Thomas Carlyle (1795–1881), and Robert Louis Stevenson. This century Scotland has produced such novelists as Compton Mackenzie (1883–1972), Lewis Grassic Gibbon (1901–35), Neil Gunn (1891–1973), and Muriel Spark (1918–); and a number of distinguished poets, including W S Graham (1918–86), Edwin Morgan (1920–), Norman MacCaig (1910–), and Douglas Dunn (1942–). » Celtic/English literature; Boswell; Burns; Drummond; Dunbar; Dunn; Gibbon, Lewis Grassic; Henryson; Hogg, James; MacCaig; MacDiarmid; Mackenzie, Compton; Morgan, Edwin; Ossian; Ramsay, Allan; Scott, Walter; Smollett; Spark; Stevenson, Robert Louis

Scottish National Party (SNP) A political party formed in 1928 as the National Party of Scotland, which merged with the Scottish Party in 1933. It first won a seat at a by-election in 1945. Its greatest success was in the 1974 general election, when it took nearly a third of Scottish votes and won 11 seats. Since then its support has declined, although in 1988 it achieved a surprise victory in the Govan by-election. Its principal policy aim is independence for Scotland from the UK. » home rule; nationalism; Scotland [i]

Scottish reels A form of stepping dance performed to bagpipes and showing French aristocratic connections. It was originally performed in circles as in 'round reels' (such as threesome, foursome, fivesome, sixsome, and eightsome reels) and later in lines, 'longwise' forms. The feet are in balletic positions with the weight on the balls of the feet. Typical steps include the slip step, pas de basque, strathspey, and schottische. Men's costume is the kilt; women wear dresses with a tartan sash. » Scotland [i]; traditional dance

Scottish terrier A breed of dog; long body with very short legs; short erect tail; long head, with eyebrows, moustache, and beard; short erect ears; coat thick and wiry, almost reaching the ground; also known as **Scottie**. The coarser-haired form is called the **Aberdeen terrier**. » dog; terrier

Scottish universities » panel (*below*)

scouting The practice of teaching the young to become good citizens and leaders, based on the principles laid down by Robert Baden-Powell, founder of the Boy Scout movement in 1907. Scouts are taught to do duty to God, their country, and other people. The Scout Association operates in over 100 nations, and has over 14 million members, classified into *Cub Scouts* or *Wolf Cubs* (aged 8–11), *Scouts* (11–16), and *Venture Scouts* (16–29). Their motto is *Be prepared*. The corresponding association for girls, known as *Girl Scouts* or *Girl Guides*, was founded in 1910 by Baden-Powell and his sister, Agnes. In the UK, its three classes of membership are *Brownie Guides* (aged 7–10), *Guides* (10–16), and *Ranger Guides* (14–20); in the USA, the groups are *Brownies* (7–8), *Juniors* (9–11), *Cadettes* (12–14) and *Seniors* (15–17). There are around 7 million Guides throughout the world. » Baden-Powell

scrambling » moto-cross

scrambling circuit A circuit or device used to protect the security of voice, data, or video signals in communication systems. The original signal is coded by the scrambler before transmission, and reconstituted into its original form at the receiver. The technique prevents unauthorized personnel gaining access to the signals during transmission.

scramjet A special ramjet designed for operation at very high

SCOTTISH UNIVERSITIES

INSTITUTION	FOUNDED	CHARTERED
St Andrews	1411	1413
Glasgow	1451	1453
Aberdeen	1494	1496
Edinburgh	1582	1582
Strathclyde	1796 (as a college)	1964
Heriot Watt	1821 (as a college)	1966
Dundee	1881 (as a college)	1967
Stirling	1967	1967

speeds (c.6–25 times the speed of sound) where the performance of a conventional ramjet becomes impracticable. In principle, the engine is similar in operation to a conventional ramjet, but the gases flowing through the combustion chamber move at supersonic rather than subsonic speed. » jet engine [i]; ramjet

scrapie A progressive degenerative disease of the central nervous system of sheep and goats worldwide. Symptoms may not appear until two years after infection. There are two forms of the disease: in one, there is uncontrollable itching, the animal scraping itself against objects (hence the name); in the other, there is drowsiness, trembing of the head and neck, and paralysis of the legs. The animals usually die within six months of the first symptoms appearing. The causal agent is widely accepted as one of the slow or unconventional viruses. Some individuals show a genetic susceptibility to the disease. » bovine spongiform encephalopathy; virus

screamer A bird native to S America; large body, longish fleshy legs, small head, and chicken-like bill; angle of wing with sharp spur; found near water; eats water plants; swims and flies well; related to ducks and geese. (Family: *Anhimidae*, 3 species.) » duck; goose

scree Loose, angular fragments of rock debris, formed by the action of rain and frost, which accumulate on hill slopes; also termed *talus*.

screech owl » **scops owl**

screen The surface on which an image is displayed, reflective for front projection, translucent for back projection. Reflection characteristics should suit the viewing conditions: the picture on a diffuse matt white screen can be viewed over a wide angle, whereas a metallized or glass-beaded surface reflects much more light but only over a narrow angle. In the cinema theatre, the screen is perforated with a pattern of small holes so that sound from loudspeakers behind is not seriously attenuated. » back/front projection; television

screen-process printing A form of printing in which ink is forced through the mesh of a screen (originally – but less frequently today – made of silk). The image to be communicated is the uninked area of the printing substrate (normally paper), created by hand or photomechanical transfer on the screen. Screen-process is used for a wide range of commercial printed work in which large areas of solid colour are required, such as posters and showcards. It is also widely used in the decoration of fabrics. » printing [i]

screening A system which prevents the pick-up or transmission of stray electrical signals; also known as **shielding**. In coaxial cable links between aerials and televisions, the outer metal webbing screens the signal-carrying inner wire. Grids in the front of microwave ovens shield users from harmful microwaves. Conducting enclosures and meshes shield electrical signals. Enclosures of ferromagnetic material, typically iron, shield magnetic fields. A *Faraday cage* is an earthed wire mesh cage used for electrostatic screening. » electricity; electrostatics; magnetic field [i]; microwaves

screening tests Investigations that are carried out on apparently well persons in order to identify unrecognized disease. Screening is undertaken for a number of reasons. It may be done in epidemiological research to determine the incidence and prevalence of a disease. It may be carried out in order to protect the public, especially against communicable disease. *Prescriptive* screening is carried out solely for the benefit of the individual, to detect disease at an early stage in its development; included in this category are mammography surveys to detect carcinoma of the breast, regular cervical smears to detect cervical cancer, blood pressure measurement, chest radiography, and the biochemical analysis of blood. » blood test; cancer; epidemiology; radiography

screw pine A large genus of evergreen trees and shrubs, native to Old World tropics, superficially resembling palms; stems supported by aerial roots; leaves sword-shaped; flowers small, in a spadix protected by a sheathing spathe; fruit pineapple-shaped, starchy, in some species edible like breadfruit. (Genus: *Pandanus*, 600 species. Family: *Pandanaceae*.) » breadfruit; evergreen plants; palm; shrub; spadix; tree [i]

screwworm The larval stage of a fly found in N and S America. The larvae are parasitic on the tissues of mammals, including humans, excavating a cavity in the skin, and feeding on living and dead tissues. It can cause serious damage, and occasionally death. (Order: *Diptera*. Family: *Calliphoridae*.) » fly; larva

Scriabin, Aleksandr Nikolayevich [**skryah**bin] (1872–1915) Russian composer and pianist, born and died in Moscow. He studied at the Moscow Conservatory, and became professor of the pianoforte (1898–1904). His compositions include three symphonies, two tone poems, and 10 sonatas. After 1900 his involvement with theosophy influenced several of his compositions, such as *Prometheus* (1910), which was performed to the accompaniment of coloured lights. » theosophy

scribe In general, a writer of documents or copyist; more specifically, in post-exilic and pre-rabbinic Judaism, a class of experts on the Jewish law (the *sopherim*). Although Ezra was both a priest and a scribe, a class of lay Torah scholars eventually arose, who not only preserved and interpreted Biblical laws, but by New Testament times were also involved with courts of justice. Most were Pharisees. They were also attested in Judaism outside of Palestine. » Ezra; Judaism; Pharisees; rabbi; Torah

Scribner, Charles (1821–71) US publisher, born in New York City. Educated at Princeton, in 1846 he co-founded the New York publishing firm bearing his name. *Scribner's Magazine* dates from 1887. He died at Lucerne, Switzerland, his three sons continuing the business.

scrofula Tuberculosis of the lymph nodes of the neck, with abscess formation and ulceration of the overlying skin. Now a rare condition, it was formerly known as the 'King's evil', because of the popular belief that the sovereign's touch would cure it. » lymph; tuberculosis

scrub bird A bird native to Australia; small with strong legs, stout sharp bill, and broad fan-shaped tail; inhabits wet woodland; eats insects (occasionally small vertebrates); feeds on ground; seldom flies. (Family: *Atrichornithidae*, 2 species.)

scrub-fowl » **megapode**

scuba diving A form of underwater swimming with the aid of a self-contained underwater breathing apparatus (abbreviated as *scuba*), or *aqualung*. The first such device was developed by French naval officer Jacques Yves Cousteau and engineer Émil Gagnan in 1942. The Confédération Mondiale des Activités Subaquatique (World Underwater Federation) was founded in 1959. » Cousteau; skin diving; swimming

sculling » **rowing**

sculpin » **bullhead**

Sculptor A small S constellation, and one of the faintest, but including rich clouds of very faint galaxies. » constellation; galaxy; RR9

sculpture Traditionally, modelling in a soft material such as clay or wax, the result sometimes being cast in metal, or carving from some hard material such as stone or wood. In the 20th-c there has been much work done by joining together prefabricated pieces, a technique known as *assemblage*. Early Greek bronzes were cast from wooden models, using the 'lost wax' process, but most Renaissance and modern bronzes are cast from clay originals. An alternative process involves firing the clay model in a kiln, to produce a terracotta. Stone carving has been characterized by its greatest practitioners, notably Michelangelo, as a process of releasing from the block a formal idea conceived by the artist as already existing in the stone. Tools include saws, a variety of chisels, drills, and – for finishing – rasps and abrasives. Throughout history and in all cultures, sculpture has been coloured, but since the Renaissance the preference has been for displaying the natural surface of the material used. Marble, the most prestigious stone, has normally been given a high polish. » assemblage; bronze; cire perdue; maquette; Michelangelo; mobile; modelling **2**; relief sculpture; term (art); wood carving

scumbling A technique in painting whereby one colour is dragged or rubbed across another to give a rich, rough texture. Unlike a glaze, which is transparent, a scumble is opaque, and the effect depends upon allowing the underneath layer to show through in irregular patches. » glaze

scurvy A nutritional disorder which results from a lack of vitamin C. Bleeding occurs into the skin, around teeth and bones, and into the joints. » vitamins [i]

scurvy-grass A N temperate annual and perennial; leaves oval to kidney-shaped, fleshy, forming a rosette; flowers white, cross-shaped. The sharp-tasting leaves, rich in vitamin C, were used by 17th-c sailors to combat scurvy. (Genus: *Cochlearia*, 25 species. Family: *Cruciferae*.) » annual; perennial; scurvy; vitamins [i]

Scutari, Lake [skoo**tah**ree] , Albanian **Ligen i Shkodrës**, Serbo-Croatian **Skadarsko Jezero**, ancient **Lacus Labeatis** Lake in SW Yugoslavia and NW Albania; largest lake in the Balkans; town of Shkodër on SW shore; area 370 sq km/143 sq ml; underwater springs. » Albania [i]; Yugoslavia [i]

Scutum (Lat 'shield') A tiny S constellation in the Milky Way. » constellation; Milky Way; RR9

Scylla [**si**la] In Greek mythology, a sea-monster usually located in the Straits of Messina opposite to Charybdis. Originally a woman, she was changed by Circe or Amphitrite into a snake with six heads; in the *Odyssey* she snatched six men from Odysseus' ships. » Charybdis; Odysseus

Scyphozoa [siyfuh**zoh**a] A class of jellyfish with gastric tentacles derived from the stomach wall (*endoderm*) and 4-radial body symmetry; polyp stage of life cycle reduced or absent. (Phylum: *Cnidaria*.) » jellyfish [i]; polyp (marine biology)

Scythians [**si**thianz] In Graeco-Roman times a nomadic people of the Russian steppes who migrated to the area N of the Black Sea in the 8th-c BC, displacing the Cimmerians who previously lived there. They were well known to the Greeks, with whom they traded corn for luxury goods. » Cimmerians; nomadism; Pazyryk

SDI An acronym for **Strategic Defense Initiative**, the proposal first made by President Reagan in 1983 (dubbed by the press 'Star Wars') that the US should develop the technologies for a defensive layered 'shield' of weapons based primarily in space, able to shoot down incoming ballistic missiles. SDI has remained controversial because it seemed to overthrow the principle of 'mutual assured destruction' on which the idea of deterrence rested. Also the technologies it would need to perfect, such as directed energy, as well as being very difficult to achieve, might ultimately be used for offensive as well as defensive purposes. » homing overlay device; particle beam weapons

SDP » **Social Democratic Party**

sea A part of an ocean which is generally shallower and defined by somewhat loosely drawn boundaries related to the surrounding landmasses. *Epicontinental* seas, such as the North Sea and the China Sea, lie over part of a continental shelf. *Landlocked* seas, such as the Mediterranean, are isolated from the oceans except by narrow channels. Large inland lakes may also be called seas, such as the Caspian Sea and the Dead Sea. » continental margin

sea, law of the A branch of international law, which divides the sea into three zones. *Internal waters* include ports, rivers, lakes, and canals. *Territorial waters* include the width of sea adjacent to a coastal state, which legally belongs to that state. The width has traditionally been 3 ml (4.8 km), generally measured from the low water line, although many states now claim a greater width. Foreign ships have a right of innocent passage through territorial waters; this does not extend to foreign aircraft in the airspace above the waters. Outside the territorial waters are the *high seas*, which may be used freely by all shipping. Many states claim exclusive economic zones extending beyond territorial waters; for example, exclusive fishery rights extending for 200 miles are now claimed by most coastal states. » international law

sea anemone [a**nem**uhnee] A typically solitary, marine coelenterate with a cylindrical body attached at its base to a substrate, and bearing a circle of tentacles at the top around its mouth; some species form colonies; c.800 species known, from the inter-tidal zone to abyssal depths. (Phylum: *Cnidaria*. Order: *Actiniaria*.) » coelenterate

sea bass Large fish found in inshore waters along the Pacific coast of N America; length up to 1.8 m/6 ft; fished commercially in some areas, but especially popular amongst anglers; name also used for deep-bodied *Stereolepis gigas* (family: *Serranidae*); length up to 2 m/6½ ft. (*Cynoscion nobilis*. Family: *Scianidae*.) » fish [i]

sea bream Any of several deep-bodied fish widespread in tropical to temperate seas; includes European *Pagellus bogaraveo*, ranging from the Mediterranean to Norway; length up to 50 cm/20 in; head bluntly rounded; pinkish red, with a large dark spot above the pectoral fin; popular with anglers, and commercially fished in some areas; also called **porgy**. (Family: *Sparidae*.) » fish [i]

sea buckthorn A thorny, deciduous, suckering shrub, growing to 3 m/10 ft, native mainly to the coasts of Europe and Asia; leaves up to 8 cm/3 in, narrow, covered with minute silvery scales; flowers tiny, green, appearing before leaves; males and females on separate plants; berries bright orange. It is sometimes planted as a dune stabilizer. (*Hippophae rhamnoides*. Family: *Eleagnaceae*.) » deciduous plants; shrub

sea butterfly A planktonic marine snail, with a reduced or absent shell; found in open oceanic waters; feeds mainly on other invertebrates; possesses lateral fins used in active swimming; also known as a **pteropod**. (Class: *Gastropoda*. Order: *Gymnosomata*.) » gastropod; plankton; snail

sea canary » **beluga** (mammal)

sea cow A term used for any mammal of the order *Sirenia* (manatees and the dugong); formerly used also for the walrus and the hippopotamus. » dugong; manatee

sea cucumber A typically sausage-shaped, soft-bodied marine invertebrate (echinoderm); mouth at one end surrounded by up to 30 tentacles, anus at the other end; skin leathery, containing minute bony structures (ossicles); found on or in the sea bed, from shallow water to the deep sea. (Class: *Holothuroidea*.) » echinoderm [i]

sea duck » **diving duck**

sea eagle A fish-eating eagle of genus *Haliaeetus* (8 species), found on coasts. Other species of *Haliaeetus* (especially those found near freshwater) are called **fish eagles**, though they do eat other vertebrates as well as fish. » eagle

sea elephant » **elephant seal**

sea fan A branching form of coral found in colonies mostly in warm shallow waters around coral reefs; body supported by a skeleton formed from horny protein-like material; growth typically 2-dimensional, producing a fan-like colony. (Phylum: *Cnidaria*. Order: *Gorgonacea*.) » coral

sea-floor spreading The movement of oceanic crustal plates away from a central mid-oceanic ridge, where new crust is formed by basaltic igneous rock intruded into the fissures as the plates move apart. All the major ocean basins contain a mid-ocean ridge, and the age of the ocean floor increases away from its axis. » oceanic ridges; plate tectonics [i]

sea gooseberry » **ctenophore**

sea hare A herbivorous marine mollusc, typically found on seaweed in shallow water; shell small, more or less internal; can expel coloured ink from its mantle when irritated. (Class: *Gastropoda*. Order: *Anaspidacea*.) » herbivore; mollusc

sea holly A stiff perennial growing to 60 cm/2 ft, a coastal plant of sandy and shingle shores, native to Europe, N Africa, and SW Asia; holly-like leaves bluish-green, spiny-tipped; flowers bluish-white, in dense globular heads 1.5–3 cm/0.6–1.2 in across, surrounded by spiny bracts; fruit covered in hooked bristles. The young tops of the roots are sometimes eaten as a vegetable. (*Eryngium maritimum*. Family: *Umbelliferae*.) » bract; perennial

sea horse A distinctive small fish, widely distributed and usually found concealed amongst algae and other marine growths; body with segmented armour and slender prehensile tail, length 4–30 cm/1½–12 in; snout prolonged into a horse-like head; swims upright in water, using delicate membranous fins; feeds on small planktonic organisms. (Genus: *Hippocampus*. Family: *Syngnathidae*.) » fish [i]; *see illustration p 1082*

sea ice Ice formed from freezing sea water. At high latitudes in the Arctic and Antarctic, the temperature may drop low enough for sea water to freeze (on average, at −1.9°C). As ice forms, dissolved salts are excluded from the ice structure, increasing the salinity of the surround water, and producing sea ice with a lower salinity than the water from which it formed.

Sea horse

Eventually all of the salt is excluded from the sea ice, leaving fresh water ice. Icebergs are distinct from sea ice, and represent large pieces of glaciers which have broken off at the coast and drifted out to sea. » iceberg; salinity

sea lavender A perennial with a deep tap-root, native to salt marshes in Europe and N America. It has a much-branched flowering stem, bearing rows of numerous small, lilac, slightly papery flowers. It is very salt-tolerant, able to withstand periodic immersion by high tides. (*Limonium vulgare*. Family: *Plumbaginaceae*.) » perennial; root (botany)

sea leopard » **leopard seal**

sea lettuce A green seaweed in which the body (*thallus*) is sheet-like and only two cells thick; found on rocks in the inter-tidal zone and in estuaries. (*Ulva lactuca*. Class: *Chlorophyceae*. Order: *Ulvales*.) » seaweed

sea level datum » **Ordnance Datum**

sea lily » **crinoid**

sea mouse A marine annelid worm with a flattened body covered with bristles that conceal lines of dorsal scales; body oval shaped, bearing paddle-like lobes (*parapodia*) along both sides; found in shallow coastal waters. (Class: *Polychaeta*. Order: *Phyllodocida*.) » annelid; worm

sea otter A mammal native to N Pacific coasts; lives mostly in the water; thick insulating coat; broader body than freshwater otters; front feet small, not webbed; eats mainly shellfish; floats on its back with a stone on its chest, and breaks prey open on the stone. (*Enhydra lutris*. Family: *Mustelidae*.) » Mustelidae; otter

sea pen A type of coral found in colonies embedded in soft substrates on the sea bed; colony comprises a main axial individual (*polyp*) bearing secondary polyps on side branches; often supported by a horny skeleton. (Phylum: *Cnidaria*. Order: *Pennatulacea*.) » coral; polyp

Sea Peoples An assortment of marauders, probably from the Mycenaean world, who destroyed the Hittite empire in Anatolia c.1200 BC, and penetrated as far south as Egypt before being checked and dispersed. The Achaeans may have been among the invaders. » Achaeans; Hittites; Mycenaean civilization

sea perch Small deep-bodied fish found in fresh, brackish, and coastal marine waters of the W North Atlantic; length up to 35 cm/14 in; silver with greenish grey upper surface; valuable commercially, and a good sport fish for anglers. (*Morone americana*. Family: *Serranidae*.) » fish [i]

sea pie » **oystercatcher**

sea pink » **thrift**

sea robin » **gurnard**

sea slug A marine slug-like mollusc, often brightly coloured and of an elaborate shape, with various projections (papillae) along its body; shell absent; mostly carnivorous, but most species have a specialized diet. (Class: *Gastropoda*. Order: *Nudibranchia*.) » gastropod; mollusc; slug (biology)

sea snake A venomous snake of family *Hydrophiidae* (50 species), sometimes included in family *Elapidae*; inhabits warm coastal waters in the Pacific and Indian oceans; small head, thick body, tail flattened from side to side; eats fish and fish eggs; venom very powerful; most give birth to live young in the water, and spend entire life at sea. Species of genus *Laticauda* are called *sea kraits*; these lay eggs, and are often found on land. » krait; snake

sea spider A long-legged, small-bodied marine arthropod, found on the sea bed from the inter-tidal zone to deep sea; most are predators, sucking juices from soft-bodied prey such as sea anemones and seaweeds; contains c.1 000 species. (Subphylum: *Chelicerata*. Class: *Pycnogonida*.) » arthropod

sea squirt » **tunicate**

sea star » **starfish**

sea urchin A typically hollow, globular marine invertebrate (echinoderm); body formed by fused skeletal plates bearing moveable spines; anus usually on upper surface, mouth on lower surface; complex jaw apparatus known as 'Aristotle's lantern'; feeds by scavenging, grazing, or ingesting sediment; contains c.5 000 fossil and 950 living species, including sand dollars and heart urchins. (Phylum: *Echinodermata*. Class: *Echinoidea*.) » echinoderm [i]; heart urchin; sand dollar

Seaborg, Glenn T(heodore) (1912–) US nuclear chemist, born at Ishpeming, Michigan. He was educated in California, where he became professor of chemistry at Berkeley in 1945, and helped to discover the transuranic elements from neptunium (No. 93) to nobelium (No. 102). He shared the Nobel Prize for Chemistry in 1951. » chemical elements

sea-dog » **skimmer**

seagull » **gull**

seakale A perennial native to the Atlantic coasts of Europe; fleshy root; large, bluish, cabbage-like leaves; white, cross-shaped flowers. The forced, blanched shoots are eaten as a vegetable. (*Crambe maritima*. Family: *Cruciferae*.) » perennial; vegetable

seal (biology) A marine mammal of the family *Phocidae*, called the **true seal**, **earless seal**, or **hair seal** (19 species); has fur and a thick layer of blubber; no external ears; cannot turn rear flippers forwards; moves on land by shuffling body horizontally along the ground; in water swims with up and down strokes of hind flippers; group of young called a 'pod'. » common/crabeater/elephant/hooded/leopard seal; mammal [i]; sea-lion

seal (communication) A blob of wax, or other adhesive substance, bearing an impression, and attached to a document as evidence of its authenticity; also the engraved or carved object (the *matrix* or *die*) used to make the impression. The study of seals, which are found from the oldest times, is known as **sigillography**, and is particularly useful in historical studies as a means of identifying, dating, and validating documents. » wax

sea-lion A marine mammal of the family *Otariidae*, called **eared seals** (14 species); resembles the true seal, but has small external ears and, on land, turns long hind flippers forwards under its body, and moves rapidly with body raised from the ground; swims mainly using forelimbs; spends more time on land than true seals; some (**fur seals**) have a thick undercoat of soft fur, and have been hunted commercially. » seal

Sealyham terrier A breed of dog, developed in the 19th-c on the Sealyham estate, Haverfordwest, Wales, by John Owen Tucker Edwardes, who tried to breed the most vicious terrier possible; long body with short legs; short erect tail; long head with eyebrows, moustache, and beard; short pendulous ears; thick pale wiry coat. » dog; terrier

seance A meeting of one or more persons, generally with a spiritualist medium, for the purpose of contacting the deceased. A seance, sometimes referred to as a 'sitting', may involve apparent paranormal phenomena associated with mental mediumship, such as the medium supposedly receiving communications from deceased people, or the apparent control of the medium by an alleged spirit (a *spirit guide* or *control*). Seances may also involve physical mediumship, such as materializations, and some psychokinetic activity (raps, movement of objects, etc). They are also frequently associated with the fraudulent production of phenomena of this kind. » medium (parapsychology); psychokinesis; spiritualism

seaplane An aircraft capable of taking off and landing upon water using a specially shaped body or floats. Seaplanes were designed to take advantage of the sea as a runway, and developed from the earliest days as a small class of specialized aircraft. The most famous seaplanes were those that took part in the Schneider trophy races of the late 1920s and early 1930s, when the trophy was finally won by a British Supermarine S6B at a speed of 407 mph (655 kph). » aircraft [i]

Search for Extraterrestrial Intelligence (SETI) A NASA research programme, managed by Ames Research Center, aimed at using large radio telescopes to detect artificially-generated radio signals coming from interstellar space. The hypothesis that intelligent life may exist elsewhere in the galaxy is based on telescopic and spacecraft evidence that organic molecules are common in space, and on the hypothesis that planetary formation is a common by-product of star formation. The search is conducted in the quiet region of the electromagnetic spectrum – the 'microwave window' between 1 000 and 10 000 megahertz frequency. First proposed in 1959, 30 very limited searches have already been undertaken. The new programme, starting in 1989, is based on the increasing power of available radio telescopes and on advanced electronics able to search millions of frequency bands each second. » electromagnetic radiation [i]; NASA; telescope [i]; space exploration

Searle, Ronald (William Fordham) (1920–) British artist, born in Cambridge. He served in World War 2, and the drawings he made during his three years' imprisonment by the Japanese helped to establish his reputation as a serious artist. After the war he became widely known as the creator of the macabre schoolgirls of 'St Trinians'. He settled in France in 1961.

Sears Tower The national headquarters of Sears, Roebuck and Co in Chicago, Illinois; the tallest office building in the world. Built in 1970–4, it has 110 storeys and reaches a height of 443 m/1 454 ft. » Chicago

seascape painting A genre of painting which flourished in the Netherlands in the 17th-c, reflecting the importance of overseas trade for the Dutch economy. The greatest master of sea-painting was, however, Turner, whose great shipwrecks are among the highest achievements of 19th-c English art. » landscape painting; painting; Turner, J M W

seasickness » **travel sickness 1**

seasonal affective disorder A recurrent change in mood occurring at a particular time of year. Most commonly there is a pattern of repeated depressions during winter, for which treatment with bright lights at either end of the day has been shown to be effective. » depression (psychiatry)

Seaspeak A variety of English, developed in the 1980s, used for international communications at sea. It is restricted in its expressive capacity to a relatively small set of messages, and is intended to forestall difficulties and misunderstandings which might arise from the multiplicity of languages spoken by the world's sailors. » register

SEATO » **South East Asia Treaty Organization**

Seattle [**see**atl] 47°36N 122°20W, pop (1980) 493 846. Capital of King County, WC Washington, USA; on the E shore of Puget Sound; transportation, industrial, commercial, financial, and cultural centre of the Pacific NW; founded, 1851; developed rapidly as a seaport after the 1897 Alaskan gold rush and the opening of the Panama Canal; main port serving Alaska; airport; railway; monorail; two universities (1861, 1892); aircraft, shipbuilding, food canning; trade in grain, timber, fruit, fish; close to scenic and recreational areas; Space Needle, a tower 183 m/600 ft high with a revolving restaurant and observation deck; Seattle Art Museum; major league teams, Mariners (baseball), SuperSonics (basketball), Seahawks (football). » gold rush; Panama Canal; Washington (state)

seaweed A common name for any large marine alga belonging to the *Chlorophyceae* (green seaweeds), *Phaeophyceae* (brown seaweeds), and *Rhodophyceae* (red seaweeds). » algae; brown algae; Fucus; kelp; sea lettuce

sebaceous glands » **skin** [i]

Sebastian, St (?–288), feast day 20 January. Roman martyr, a native of Narbonne. He was a captain of the praetorian guard, and secretly a Christian. When his belief was discovered, Diocletian ordered his death by arrows; but the archers did not quite kill him, and he was nursed back to life. When he upbraided the tyrant for his cruelty, he was beaten to death with rods. » Christianity; Diocletian

Sebastiano del Piombo [**pyom**boh], originally **Sebastiano Luciano** (c.1485–1547) Venetian painter, called *del Piombo* ('of the Seal') from his appointment in 1523 as sealer of briefs to Pope Clement VII. He studied under Giovanni Bellini, and went to Rome c.1510, where he worked with Michelangelo. His masterpiece is the 'Raising of Lazarus' (1519, National Gallery, London). He died in Rome. » Bellini; Italian art; Michelangelo

Sebastopol [se**bas**tuhpol], Russ **Sevastopol** 44°36N 33°31E, pop (1983) 328 000. Port in Krymskaya (Crimean) oblast, Ukraine; on the SW shore of a peninsula separating the Sea of Azov from the Black Sea; founded, 1783; besieged by the British and French for nearly a year, in the Crimean War; rail terminus; naval base; seaside resort; health resorts nearby; bricks, tiles, food products, textiles, shoes. » Crimea; Crimean War; Ukraine

SECAM An acronym of **Séquentiel Couleur à Mémoire**, a coding system for colour television developed in France in the 1960s and later adopted in the USSR, Eastern Europe, and some Middle East countries. The two colour difference signals are not phase separated, but transmitted on alternate lines of the picture. A delay line in the receiver allows them to be combined at the final stage, although at some sacrifice of colour definition. » colour television [i]; NTSC; PAL

Secession, Right of A US constitutional doctrine that individual states enjoyed the right to leave (or secede from) the Federal Union. Espoused by the South before the Civil War, the doctrine was discredited during that conflict. » American Civil War

Secombe, Sir Harry » **Goons, The**

second Base SI unit of time; symbol s; defined as the duration of 9 192 631 770 periods of the radiation corresponding to the transition between the two hyperfine levels of the ground state of the caesium-133 atom. Formerly defined as 1/86 400 of the mean solar day, the atomic definition is now the basis of universal time. » time; units (scientific)

second-generation computers » **computer generations**

second messenger In physiology, a term used to describe intermediate factors (eg nucleotides, phospholipids, calcium ions) present within the cell wall or interior. When activated by a variety of neurotransmitters or hormones (the *first messengers*) they initiate a sequence of events leading ultimately to a cellular response (such as contraction, relaxation, secretion, or a change in electrical activity). » cell; hormones; neurotransmitter; receptors

second sight A Celtic folklore term for paranormal ability, most frequently used to refer to precognitive extrasensory perception abilities. Second sight is often regarded as an unwanted gift, as anyone possessing it does not have control over what they will 'see', and thus may obtain unpleasant information, such as concerning an impending illness or death. » extrasensory perception; paranormal

second-strike capability » **strategic capability**

Second World » **Three Worlds theory**

Second World War » **World War 2**

secondary education The phase of education following the primary stage, beginning in most countries at the age of 11 or 12. Usually the style of education moves towards more specialized work in key subjects, or fields of study taught by specialist teachers. Secondary education usually ends at some point between the age of 15 and 19, this varying in different countries, and culminates in most cases in some kind of public leaving examination or award. In some countries secondary education is not universally available. Its organization is also varied, sometimes within the same country, and may involve either a single secondary school or a break and a move to a senior school at the age of 14, 15, or 16. » high school; middle school; primary education

secondary emission The emission of electrons from the

surface of a material because of its bombardment with electrons. The emitted electrons have a spectrum of energies ranging up to that of the incident electrons. Metals emit fewer secondary electrons than insulators. The effect is exploited in photomultipliers. » Auger effect; electron; field emission; photoelectric effect; photomultiplier; sputtering; thermionics

secondary modern school A school in those parts of the UK which operate a selective system. Intake consists of those children who were not successful in gaining entry to a grammar school, or who did not wish to attend it. » comprehensive/grammar school

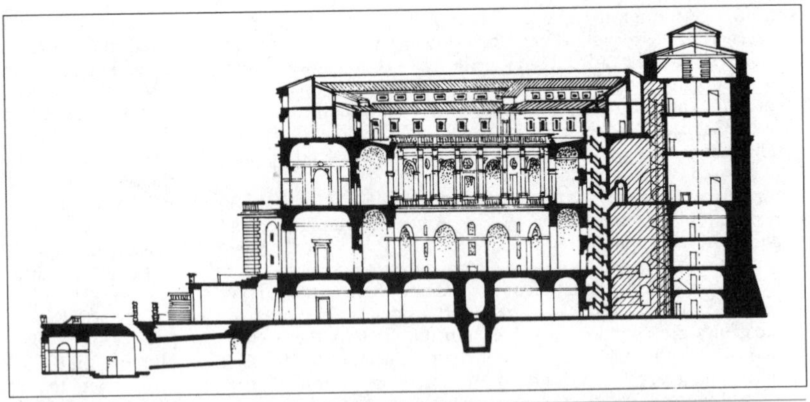

A section of the Palazzo Farnese, Caprarola (1559 onwards), architect G B da Vignola

secondary store » **auxiliary store**

secret service » **intelligence service**

Secretariat, UN » **United Nations**

secretary In its most widely used sense, a person who carries out general clerical duties in an office, such as typing and filing. In business, it refers to the legally required position of Company Secretary, whose responsibilities include ensuring that the company complies with the provisions of the Companies Acts (in the UK), and other regulations. In trade unions, it refers to the most senior full-time employee. In government, it is used for the person who administers a department of state, either the elected minister (the 'Secretary of State') or a permanent civil servant. In the USA, the Secretaries of State are the most senior officers of the Administration, appointed by the President.

secretary bird A large, ground-dwelling bird of prey, native to S Africa; long stilt-like legs; head with an untidy crest of long feathers (resembling pens held behind the ear of a secretary); inhabits grassland; eats small ground-living animals; walks up to 30 km/20 ml a day; soaring flight; nests in trees. (*Sagittarius serpentarius*. Family: *Sagittariidae*.) » bird of prey

secretary of state The title of most UK government ministers who preside over a department, as distinct from junior ministers. It has increasingly replaced the title of *minister*, although formally there is now little to distinguish them except that secretaries of state are normally in charge of larger departments. In the USA, the term refers to the head of the state department in charge of foreign affairs, a senior member of the administration.

secretion The process by which material is taken up (eg from the blood) or produced by a cell and expelled to serve a purpose elsewhere in the body. The term also refers to the specific substance (eg a hormone or neurotransmitter) expelled by the cell or organism. » cell

sect A separately organized group, usually religious, which rejects established religious or political authorities, and claims to adhere to the authentic elements of the wider tradition from which it has separated itself. It is distinctive and exclusive, claiming to possess true belief, correct ritual, and warranted standards of conduct. Membership is voluntary, but the sect accepts or rejects persons on the basis of some test of worthiness, and membership takes precedence over all other allegiances. » Arya Samaj; Christadelphians; Doukhobors; Druze; Mandaeans; Nichiren Buddhism; Ophites; religion

section An architectural drawing showing a building cut through a vertical plane, normally used to disclose the construction. » axonometric [i]

secular Christianity A mid-20th-c theology which acknowledged the secularization of W civilization and sought to present a 'religionless' Christianity, with the emphasis on human freedom and responsibility, and divine transcendence understood historically rather than metaphysically. » Bonhoeffer; Christianity; 'death of God' theology

securities A general term for financial assets, such as stocks, shares, and government bonds. It can also apply to any documents giving a title to property, or to 'claims on income' (as in the case of security for a bank loan). » bond; shares; stocks

Securities and Exchange Commission (SEC) A body set up in 1934 in the USA during the Great Depression to regulate and control the issue of shares by corporations. It ensures that statements about the stocks being sold are accurate, and generally regulates the way US stock markets operate. » shares; stocks

Securities and Investments Board (SIB) An agency set up in 1985 to regulate the activities of investment business in the UK. It has power, under the Financial Services Act (1986), to oversee the activities of various self-regulatory organizations which have been set up to control aspects of the UK's financial markets. These include the Investment Management Regulatory Board (IMRO), dealing with investment managers; the Financial Intermediaries, Managers and Brokers Regulatory Association (FIMBRA), covering independent life assurance and unit trust salesmen and brokers; the Life Assurance and Unit Trust Companies (LAUTRO); and the Securities Association, monitoring some 700 firms, including investment banks, provincial stockbrokers, and securities dealers. The SIB can subpoena documents and witnesses, and initiate prosecutions. It has no powers in relation to takeovers or insider dealing. » insider dealing; investment

Security Council » **United Nations**

sedatives Drugs used to calm anxious patients without actually causing sleep. However, many sedatives in larger doses can be used as sleeping agents. Phenobarbitone was previously the most commonly used sedative, but it has been replaced for this purpose by drugs such as the safer benzodiazepines (eg Valium and Librium). Sedatives used in the last century include bromides, chloral hydrate, and paraldehyde. » barbiturates; benzodiazepines; thalidomide

Seddon, Richard John, byname **King Dick** (1845–1906) New Zealand statesman and Prime Minister (1893–1906), born at Eccleston, Lancashire, UK. He settled in New Zealand in 1866, and entered parliament in 1879. As Prime Minister he led a Liberal party government remembered for its social legislation, such as introducing old age pensions. He died at sea, while returning to New Zealand from Australia. » New Zealand [i]

sedge A name applied to many members of the family *Cyperaceae*, but especially to two plants. *Carex* is a huge genus, found almost everywhere, but especially common in alpine and marshy, subarctic habitats, where it forms an important and characteristic part of the vegetation. It is mostly a rhizomatous perennial; tufts of grass-like leaves; stems triangular in cross-section; flowers tiny, lacking perianth; males and females usually in separate spikes which resemble those of grasses; characteristic fruit oval, 3-sided, beaked. (Genus: *Carex*, 1 500–2 000 species). *Cladium mariscus* is similar to *Carex*, but has keeled, saw-edged leaves, and is a dominant plant of fens and swamps throughout warmer regions. (Family: *Cyperaceae*.) » grass [i]; perennial; perianth; rhizome

sedimentary rock Consolidated deposits composed of material laid down by water, wind, ice, or gravity, or by chemical precipitation. They are generally classified into three groups: *Clastic rocks* are made up of fragments of pre-existing rocks or minerals, and bound together by a cementing medium which is formed after deposition, eg shales, sandstones, and conglomerates. *Organic rocks* are composed largely of the remains of living organisms, eg coal and fossiliferous limestone. *Inorganic rocks* are formed by chemical precipitation from supersaturated solutions, eg some limestones and evaporite deposits. » coal; conglomerate (mineralogy); evaporite deposits; limestone; sandstone; shale; stratigraphy

sedimentation The process of deposition of rock fragments suspended in water on to the floor of an ocean, sea, lake, or river floodplain. The unconsolidated sediment may become compacted, dewatered, and cemented together by processes collectively known as *diagenesis*, ultimately forming a sedimentary rock. » diagenesis; sedimentary rock

Seebeck effect » **thermoelectric effects**

seed The mature, fertilized ovule of a plant, containing the embryo and a food store to sustain the seedling during germination, enclosed within a protective coat, the *testa*. In gymnosperms the seeds lie exposed on the cone scales; in flowering plants they are protected within the ovary. Some seeds are very large and are produced in small numbers (eg the coconut); others are very small and are produced in prodigious numbers (eg the orchid). Seeds, aided by the fruit, offer a means of dispersal, and in annuals a means of surviving harsh seasons. Some seeds germinate immediately after dispersal, but others remain dormant until exposed to specific conditions, such as low temperatures or high light intensities. » flowering plants; fruit; germination; gymnosperms; nut; reproduction; seed plant

seed fern An extinct group of plants occurring as fossils from the Devonian to Triassic periods. They had fern-like fronds, but woody stems and seed-like structures reminiscent of seed plants. They were formerly considered potential ancestors (now discounted) of flowering plants, but are possibly ancestral to cycads and two fossil gymnosperm groups, *Bennettitales* and *Caytoniales*. (Order *Pteridospermales*.) » cycad; Devonian period; fern; flowering plants; fossil; gymnosperms; Triassic period

seed-leaf » **cotyledons**

seed plant Any plant reproducing by seeds. All flowering plants and gymnosperms are included. In some classifications these together form the Division *Spermatophyta*. » flowering plants; gymnosperms; seed

Seeger, Pete (1919–) US folk singer, songwriter, guitarist, and banjo player, born in New York City. He enrolled in Harvard in 1936, but left to travel the USA learning folk songs. He organized the Almanac Singers with Woody Guthrie in 1940, and toured with them until 1942. In 1949–52 and 1955–7 he led the Weavers, and had such folk hits as 'Good-night Irene' and 'On Top of Old Smokey'. Several of his songs became popular hits in the 1960s, such as 'If I Had a Hammer' and 'Where Have All the Flowers Gone?', and he co-wrote the lyrics for 'We Shall Overcome'. He is an activist on issues of ecology, politics, and individual liberties. » civil rights; folk music; Guthrie, Woody

Seghers, Hercules [saygers] (c.1589–c.1635) Dutch painter, born at Haarlem, and probably studied in Amsterdam. He was author of some of the grandest and most romantic mountain landscapes of the 17th-c (influencing Rembrandt, who collected his work), yet fewer than 15 pictures survive. Most of his works are original and powerful etchings, but even these are rare. He was last recorded in 1633 living at The Hague. » etching; landscape painting; Rembrandt

segmented worm » **annelid**

Segovia, Andrés [suhg**oh**via] (1894–1987) Spanish guitarist, born at Linares. Largely self-taught, he gave his first concert in 1909, and quickly gained an international reputation. Influenced by the Spanish nationalist composers, he evolved a revolutionary guitar technique permitting the performance of a wide range of music, and many modern composers composed works for him. He was created Marquis of Salobrena by royal decree (1981), and died in Madrid. » guitar

Segovia [suhg**oh**via] 40°57N 4°10W, pop (1981) 53 237. Capital of Segovia province, Castilla-León, NWC Spain, 87 km/54 ml NW of Madrid; altitude c.1 000 m/3 000 ft; bishopric; railway; wool, thread, pottery, cement, flour, fertilizers, rubber, chemicals; Roman aqueduct and old town, a world heritage site; cathedral (16th-c), Moorish citadel, El Parral monastery, Churches of St Martin and St Esteban. » Spain [i]

Segrè, Emilio (Gino) [**seg**ray] (1905–89) US physicist, born at Tivoli, Italy. He studied and taught in Rome, working under Fermi, and in 1936 became director of the physics laboratory at Palermo. Dismissed by the fascist regime in 1938, he settled in the USA, took US nationality (1944), and became professor of physics at Berkeley (1946–72). He shared the 1959 Nobel Physics Prize for discovering the antiproton. » antiproton

segregation The cultural, political, and typically geographical separation of one group of people from another. It is often based on perceived ethnic or racial divisions, an extreme example being apartheid (literally 'separateness') in S Africa, where physical segregation between Whites and Blacks is most apparent (eg in public transport, washrooms, housing, sport). It also characterized the period of Black slavery in the USA, generally being associated with the exploitation of poorer ethnic groups by a politically dominant elite. » apartheid; civil rights; Jim Crow Laws; racial discrimination

sei whale [say] A rorqual found in open oceans worldwide, except in polar regions; length, up to 20 m/65 ft; dark grey with white underparts; streamlined, with a flat head; eats minute crustaceans and some small fish. (*Balaenoptera borealis*.) » rorqual

Seiber, Mátyás [**ziy**buh] (1905–60) British composer, born in Budapest, Hungary. He studied at Budapest under Kodály, became professor of jazz (1928–33) at Frankfurt am Main, and in 1935 settled in Britain as a teacher. He gained only belated recognition as a composer, his works including chamber music, piano pieces, and songs. He was killed in a motor accident in South Africa. » Kodály

seiche [saysh] An oscillation or sloshing of water in a partially confined body of water such as a bay or estuary. The period of time required for the oscillation is determined by the physical size and shape of the basin. » estuary; wave (oceanography)

Seifert, Jaroslav [**say**fert] (1901–) Czech poet, born in Prague. His major works include *Postovni holub* (1929, The Carrier Pigeon), *Ruce Venusiny* (1936, The Hands of Venus) and *Zhasnete svetla* (1938, Put Out The Lights), and with his postwar volume *Prilba hliny* (1945, A Helmet of Earth) he was established as the national poet. He refused all compromise after the communist takeover in 1948, and was awarded the Nobel Prize for Literature in 1984. » Czech literature; poetry

Seikan Tunnel [**say**kan] A Japanese rail tunnel beneath the Tsugara Strait, linking Tappi Saki, Honshu, with Fukushima, Hokkaido; constructed 1972–88; length 54 km/34 ml.

Seine, River [sen] River in NC France, rising in the Langres plateau, 30 km/19 ml NW of Dijon; flows NW through the limestone Champagne Pouilleuse, W and S across the fertile dairy country of Brie, then NW past Paris and Rouen to Normandy; estuary discharges into the English Channel S of Cap de la Hève; length 776 km/482 ml; third longest river in France; several canal links to other major rivers. » France [i]; Paris [i]

seismic wave A shock wave propagated through the Earth as a result of an earthquake. There are four types of wave. *P* (compressional) and *S* (transverse) waves both have high frequency, and are transmitted through the Earth, but only *P* waves can travel through fluid zones. *L* waves are transverse, have low frequency, and are confined to the upper part of the crust. *Rayleigh* waves develop close to the epicentre, and are responsible for the rolling movement of the Earth's surface during an earthquake. » earthquake; seismology

seismic zone A belt of intense earthquake activity which occurs at the boundaries between crustal plates. » earthquake; plate tectonics [i]

seismograph The data collected by a **seismometer**, an instrument that records and measures the arrival of seismic waves from distant earthquakes, or from movement caused by explosions in the Earth's crust. » earthquake; seismic wave

seismology The study of earthquakes and the propagation of seismic waves through the Earth. By studying the velocity of seismic waves, the structure of the Earth and the discontinuities which define its core, mantle, and crust have been discovered. By using artificial explosions to generate shock waves, the structure of the underlying rocks can be determined, and applied to the exploration for oil and gas. » earthquake; seismic wave; seismograph

seismometer » **seismograph**

Sejanus, Lucius Aelius [suhjaynuhs] (?–31) Prefect of the Praetorian Guard (14–31), and all-powerful at Rome after the Emperor Tiberius's retirement to Capri (26). He systematically eliminated possible successors to Tiberius, such as Agrippina's sons, so that he himself might wield supreme power after Tiberius's death as regent for his young grandson Gemellus. His plans, however, were made known to Tiberius, and his fall from grace was sudden and spectacular. » Agrippina the Elder; Praetorian Guard; Tiberius

Sekmet » **Sakhmet**

Sekondi-Takoradi 4°59N 1°43W, pop(1982) 123 670. Major seaport and capital of Western region, S Ghana; on the Gulf of Guinea, 180 km/112 ml WSW of Accra; founded by the Dutch, 16th-c; Sekondi expanded after construction of railway to Tarkwa (1898–1903), and merged with Takoradi, 1946; important supply base during World War 2; railway repair, cigarettes, boatbuilding, foodstuffs, trade in minerals. » Ghana [i]

seladang » **gaur**

selaginella [seluhjinela] A large genus of mostly tropical spore-bearing plants related to clubmosses and quillworts; long, regularly branched stems with numerous small leaves in four ranks, either all alike or with the upper two small and the lower two larger and spreading; sporangia arranged in cone-like strobili. It is one of the few living members of the ancient Class *Lycopsida*. (Genus: *Selaginella*, 700 species. Family: *Selaginellaceae*.) » clubmoss; quillwort; sporangium; strobilus

Selangor [saylanggaw] pop(1980) 1 426 250; area 7 997 sq km/ 3 087 sq ml. State in W Peninsular Malaysia, on the Strait of Malacca; British protectorate, 1874; separated from federal territory of Wilayah Persekutuan, 1981; capital, Shah Alam; rubber, tin, commerce. » Malaysia [i]

Selcraig, Alexander » **Selkirk, Alexander**

Selden, John (1584–1654) English historian and antiquary, born near Worthing, Sussex. Educated at Oxford and London, he became a lawyer (1612), entered parliament in 1623, and in 1628 helped to draw up the Petition of Right, for which he was imprisoned until 1634. He entered the Long Parliament in 1640, but after the execution of Charles I, took little part in public matters, and died in London. His best-known book, *Table Talk*, was published after his death (1689). » English Civil War; Long Parliament

select committee Members of a legislature whose task is to inquire into matters that come within its competence, usually as prescribed by the legislature or government. Two main types may be distinguished: *ad hoc*, which normally ceases to exist when its task is completed; and *permanent* or *standing*, which normally lasts for an electoral term and which investigates particular policy areas or the actions of government departments. Select committees vary in their power and influence across political systems; membership is usually based on party composition in the legislature. An example is the Senate committee set up to investigate the Watergate affair. » legislature; Watergate

selection (Australian history) » **free selection**

selective dissemination of information (SDI) Systems responsible for matching particulars of new publications, etc, with the stated interests of potential recipients (*interest profiles*), and dispatching information to them. Usually computer-assisted, such systems permit the regular checking of new data against existing interest profiles.

selective school » **comprehensive school; grammar school**

Selene [seleenee] In Greek mythology, the goddess of the Moon. There seems to have been no cult among the Greeks, but the Moon was important in witchcraft. She was depicted as a charioteer (the head of one of her horses may be seen among the Elgin Marbles). » Artemis; Endymion; Phoebe (mythology)

selenium [suhleeniuhm] Se, element 34. A metalloid in the oxygen group, found as a minor constituent of sulphide ores, and mainly produced from the residue of copper refinement. Its chemistry is similar to that of sulphur, with main oxidation states −2, +2, +4, and +6. *Hydrogen selenide* (H_2Se) has a particularly obnoxious smell and is very toxic. Mainly important for its electrical properties, selenium can be used to convert light to electric current (in photocells) and alternating to direct current (in rectifiers). » chemical elements; metalloids

selenium cell An early photoconductive light-sensitive detector, consisting of a thin film of selenium between suitable electrodes. The conductivity of the selenium increases with the increasing intensity of light falling on it. » photoelectric cell; selenium; xerography [i]

Seleucids [seloosidz] The Greek dynasty descended from Alexander the Great's general, Seleucus. The main beneficiaries of Alexander's Persian conquests, initially the Seleucids ruled a vast empire stretching from Asia Minor to NW India. By the time Rome suppressed them in 63 BC, all that was left was their Syrian heartland. » Hellenistic Age; Persian Empire; Seleucus I Nicator

Seleucus I Nicator ('Conqueror') [silookuhs] (c.358–281 BC) Macedonian general of Alexander the Great, founder of the Seleucid dynasty. He rose from being satrap of Babylonia (321 BC) to being the ruler of an empire which stretched from Asia Minor to India. To hold his unwieldy empire together, he founded a new, more central capital at Antioch in N Syria (300 BC). » Alexander the Great; Antigonus I; Seleucids

self-determination A doctrine dating back to the 18th-c that cultural communities and national groupings have the right to determine their own destiny, including political independence and the right to self-rule. The principle that each nation has the right to fashion its own state is incorporated in the United Nations Charter, and is a major plank in anti-colonialism. » separatism; United Nations

self-heal A perennial, often purple- or bronze-tinged, native to the temperate N hemisphere and Australia; stems growing to 30 cm/12 in, square, erect or spreading; leaves oval, in opposite pairs; flowers 2-lipped, violet-blue, in crowded whorls forming a dense terminal spike. It is an old medicinal herb. (*Prunella vulgaris*. Family: *Labiatae*.) » herb; perennial

self-help group An organization formed by people with a common problem, or difficult situation, to enable them to help each other, such as Alcoholics Anonymous. Support is provided at meetings and by individual contacts, which are especially valuable for those (such as single parents) who are coping on their own. » Alcoholics Anonymous

self-regulatory organization (SRO) A body which manages its own affairs and has its own rules of conduct, eliminating the need for government legislation. Lloyd's and the London Stock Exchange are two such bodies. From time to time the government may threaten to introduce legislation to ensure public control, usually if some adverse event has taken place. These bodies then modify their own rules to guard against any repetition of the problem. » Lloyd's; Securities and Investments Board; stock exchange

Selfridge, Harry Gordon (1858–1947) British merchant, born at Ripon, Wisconsin, USA. Educated privately, he joined a trading firm in Chicago, and was made a junior partner in 1892. While visiting London in 1906, he bought a site in Oxford Street, and built upon it the large store which bears his name (opened 1909). He took British nationality in 1937, and died in London.

Seljuqs/Seljuks A family of Turkish mercenary soldiers that rose to prominence and conquered much of Asia Minor in the 11th–12th-c. They were converted to the Muslim faith, and became established as sultans in the area of present-day Syria and E Turkey. Their decline in the 13th-c was brought on by Mongol pressure from the E and their defeat at Kösedagh (1243). » Islam; Mongols

Selkirk or **Selcraig, Alexander** (1676–1721) Scottish sailor, born at Largo, Fife, whose story suggested that of Defoe's Robinson Crusoe. He joined the South Sea buccaneers, quarrelled with his captain, and at his own request was put ashore on Juan Fernández (1704). He lived there alone until 1709, when he was discovered and brought back to Britain. He returned to Largo in 1712. » Defoe

Sellafield, formerly **Windscale** 54°38N 3°30W. Nuclear power plant in Cumbria, NW England; on the Irish Sea coast, W of Gosforth; processes nuclear waste; nearby Calder Hall gas-cooled, moderated nuclear reactors, commercial operation 1956–9. » Cumbria; nuclear reactor [i]

Sellers, Peter » **Goons, The**

Selous Game Reserve [suh**loo**] A game reserve established upon the Rufiji R system, C Tanzania, in 1905; still largely unexplored; noted for the variety of its scenery and wildlife; a world heritage site. » Tanzania [i]

Selous mongoose » **meerkat**

selva The Portuguese term for the tropical rainforest of the Amazon Basin. Its use has been extended to cover similar vegetation types elsewhere. » rainforest

Selwyn-Lloyd, (John) Selwyn (Brooke), Baron (1904–78) British Conservative politician, born in the Wirral. Educated at Cambridge, he became a barrister and practised in Liverpool. He entered local government, served in World War 2, and became an MP in 1945. He was appointed Minister of State (1951), Supply (1954–5), and Defence (1955), Foreign Secretary (1955–60), defending Eden's policy on Suez, Chancellor of the Exchequer, introducing the 'pay pause' (1960–2), Lord Privy Seal and Leader of the House (1963–4), and Speaker of the House of Commons (1971–6). He was created a life peer in 1976, and died at Preston Crowmarsh, Oxfordshire. » Conservative Party; Eden

Selznick, David O(liver) (1902–65) US film producer, born in Pittsburgh. He founded his own company in 1937, which at its peak made *Gone with the Wind* (1939). Among the stars he created was Jennifer Jones, who also appeared in his last co-production *A Farewell to Arms* (1957), and to whom he was married from 1949 until his death in Hollywood.

semantics The study of the meaning-system of a language. The word *meaning* has itself many meanings, and semantic approaches vary widely. In one view, meaning is the relationship between language and the external world (*referential* or *denotative* meaning), and semantics enquires into the precise relationship between a word and the concept it stands for. In another, it involves the mental state of the speaker, as reflected in a range of personal and emotional overtones (*affective* or *connotative* meaning). In a third, it refers to the social context in which language is used, and from which it derives part of its significance (*contextual* meaning). In a fourth, it refers to the sense relations which link words and phrases, by which we know, for example, that some words have the 'same' meaning (eg *car*, *automobile*), some have 'opposite' meaning (eg *single*, *married*), and some have an 'included' meaning (eg *banana*, included within *fruit*). Within linguistics, it is useful to distinguish between *lexical* meaning (the 'dictionary meaning' of a word), and *structural* meaning, which a form derives from its position and function in the grammatical system of the language. » componential analysis; connotation; etymology; linguistics; synonym

semaphore A code and signalling apparatus for visual communication. It consists of one or two mechanically-operated arms attached to an upright post, or two hand-held flags at arm's length, which are moved in a vertical plane to a sequence of positions. Each position represents a different letter of the alphabet, numeral, or punctuation feature. The system was widely used in visual telegraphy, especially at sea, before the advent of electricity. Old-style railway signals are a simple form of semaphore, with a single arm having two positions to indicate 'stop' or 'go'. » sign; RR81

Semarang [sama**rahng**] 6°58S 110°29E, pop (1980) 646 590. Fishing port and capital of Java Tengah province, C Java, Indonesia; large Chinese population; airfield; railway; university (1960); shipbuilding, fishing, textiles, trade in coffee, sugar, rubber; Gedung Batu cave, Mudu war memorial, Klinteng Sam Poo Kong temple. » Java

Semele [**sem**ilee] In Greek mythology, the daughter of Cadmus, and mother by Zeus of Dionysus. She asked Zeus to appear in his glory before her, and was consumed in fire, but it made her son immortal. Semele is probably related to the Phrygian goddess Zemelo. » Dionysus

semen Yellow-white fluid ejaculated from the penis at orgasm. It consists of spermatozoa and secretions from the accessory sex glands (seminal vesicles, prostate, urethral, and bulbo-urethral glands). The secretions assist in the nourishment and motility of the spermatozoa. Fructose is their main source of energy, and prostaglandins facilitate their transport by increasing the motility of the uterus. » AIDS; artificial insemination; infertility; penis [i]; sperm bank

semi-diurnal tide A tidal cycle with two high and two low tides per lunar day; also known as a **semi-daily** tide. The two high tides are of nearly equal height, and the two low tides nearly equal. » tide

semi-opera A stage entertainment of the Restoration period with spoken dialogue, in which music played an incidental but substantial role, often in self-contained masques. Purcell's *The Fairy Queen* (1692) is an outstanding example. » masque; opera; Purcell, Henry

semi-precious stones » **gemstones**

semicircular canals » **vestibular apparatus**

semiconductor A substance whose electrical conductivity is between that of an insulator and a conductor at room temperature. The conductivity can be made to vary with temperature and the impurities in the semiconductor crystal. In **intrinsic** semiconductors, usually made from pure crystals of germanium or silicon, conductivity rises with temperature. The conductivity of **extrinsic** semiconductors depends on introducing impurities such as arsenic or phosphorus into intrinsic semiconductors – a process known as 'doping'. Typical semiconductor devices such as diodes and transistors each have a different arrangement of impurities in the crystal. » doping; electrical conduction; integrated circuit; resistivity; semiconductor diode; transistor; thyristor

semiconductor diode A simple diode consisting of a positive/negative junction made of a semiconductor material such as silicon. An electric current flows when a forward bias is applied to the junction; reverse bias produces only a small leakage current until breakdown voltage is reached. Semiconductor diodes are used to rectify alternating currents and as voltage limiters, and have replaced thermionic valve diodes in most applications. » diode; light-emitting diode; semiconductor; thermionic valve; zener diode

semiconductor laser A tiny infrared laser, crucial to optical fibre communications and compact disc players. A current flowing across the junction between two regions of semiconductor (eg gallium arsenide) doped in different ways causes electron transitions in the material. The device comprises a flat junction between two parallel mirrors and perpendicular to them. » laser [i]; optical fibres [i]; optoelectronics

Seminole [**sem**inohl] A Muskogean-speaking N American Indian group of SE USA, descended from Creeks who settled in Florida in the late 18th-c, many intermarrying with runaway Negro slaves. They fought Whites encroaching on their territory, eventually surrendering to US troops in the 1820s and 1830s, and moved to reservations in Oklahoma. Population c.5 000. » American Indians

semiology » **semiotics**

semiotics The study of signs, sign systems, and the social production of meaning, also known as **semiology**. It is a multi-disciplinary area of study, which derives from the pioneering work on language by the Swiss linguist Ferdinand de Saussure and the US philosopher C S Peirce. A fundamental notion is the arbitrary nature of communication systems (written and spoken language, gestures, dress, etc). Meaning is largely produced by relationships and differences between individual signs, organized in codes, rather than by simple reference to external reality. Although inherently unstable, such systems are regulated by convention, the source and purpose of which are found in a given culture. The field is often divided into three main branches: *syntax*, the study of how linguistic items can be transformed into other linguistic items; *semantics*, the study of meaning and reference; and *pragmatics*, the study of how context affects linguistic interpretation. » code; Peirce; pragmatics; Saussure; semantics; sign; syntax

Semipalatinsk [semipa**la**tinsk], formerly **Semipalatka** 50°26N 80°16E, pop (1983) 301 000. River-port capital of Semipalatinskaya oblast, Kazakhstan, on R Irtysh; founded as a fortress, 1718; airport; railway; wool textiles, clothing, footwear, foodstuffs, ship repairing, meat packing. » Kazakhstan

Semiramis [se**mi**ramis] In Greek mythology, the daughter of the goddess Derceto, who became queen of Assyria, being the wife of Onnes and then Ninus. Later she reigned alone, and founded many cities, including Nineveh and Babylon. She is probably based on historical Sammuramat (c.810–805 BC).

Semites A group of peoples found in SW Asia. In antiquity they included the Ammonites, Amorites, Assyrians, Babylonians, Canaanites, and Phoenicians; today the most prominent Semitic peoples are the Jews and the Arabs. » Assyria; Babylonia; Phoenicia

Semitic alphabets The writing systems of the Semitic languages spoken in the Middle East, in which only consonants are registered, the vowels being optionally marked by diacritics. The earliest known alphabet was North Semitic, developed in the 2nd-c BC in Palestine and Syria. This became the model for the Hebrew, Arabic, and Phoenician alphabets. » alphabet [i]; graphology

Semitic languages » **Afro-Asiatic languages**

semolina A heated solution of the flour of hard wheat. It is used to make pasta and milk puddings. » durum

Senanayake, Don Stephen [sena**niy**akay] (1884–1952) First Prime Minister of Sri Lanka (1947–52), born in Colombo. He was educated in Colombo and then worked on his father's rubber estate. Entering the Legislative Council in 1922, he founded the co-operative society movement in 1923, and was elected to the State Council in 1931 where he was Minister of Agriculture for 15 years. Following independence, he became Prime Minister, as well as Minister of Defence and External Affairs. He died after falling from his horse in Colombo. » Sri Lanka [i]

Senate The upper house of the US Congress, consisting of two Senators from each State (100 in all), chosen by the people to serve for six years; a third are chosen every two years. It has powers of 'advice and consent' on presidential treaties and appointments. Much of its work is done through committees rather than on the floor. It is presided over by the US Vice-President, who can cast the deciding vote if there is a tie. » Congress; House of Representatives

Senate, Roman An advisory body, first to the kings, then the consuls, finally the emperor. Initially composed of heads of families of the patrician class, by the end of the Republic it was made up of ex-magistrates, and its resolutions had come to have the force of law. » consul **1**; patricians; plebeians; Roman history [i]

Sendai [sen**diy**] 38°16N 140°52E, pop (1980) 664 868. Capital of Miyagi prefecture, NE Honshu, Japan, on W Ishinomaki-wan Bay; airport; railway; university (1907); commerce, food processing, pottery, metal products, textiles; base for tours to local hot springs and spas; Tanabata, or Star Festival (Aug). » Honshu

Sendero Luminoso [sen**dai**roh loomi**noh**soh] Literally, 'Shining Path'; a rural guerrilla movement of uncompromisingly revolutionary character, operating in the Peruvian C Andes (though capable, also, of mounting terrorist actions in cities) during the 1980s. » guerrilla; Peru [i]; terrorism

Seneca An Iroquois-speaking N American Indian group, who settled in present-day W New York State and E Ohio. A member of the Iroquois League, they expanded through warfare in the 17th-c, and supported the British during the American Revolution, which led to the destruction of their villages by US troops, and their settlement on reservations in 1797. Population c.4 600. » Iroquois Confederacy

Seneca, Lucius (or **Marcus**) **Annaeus**, byname **the Elder** (c.55 BC–AD c.40) Roman rhetorician, born at Córdoba, Spain. Besides a history of Rome, now lost, he wrote several works on oratory. Parts of his *Colores Controversiae* and *Suasoriae* have survived. » Latin literature; rhetoric

Seneca, Lucius Annaeus, byname **the Younger** (c.5 BC–AD 65) Roman philosopher, statesman, and author, born at Córdoba, Spain, the son of Seneca (the Elder). Banished to Corsica (41–9) by Claudius, on a charge of adultery, he was recalled by Agrippina, who entrusted him with the education of her son Nero. Made consul by Nero in 57, his high moral aims gradually incurred the Emperor's displeasure, and he withdrew from public life. Drawn into conspiracy, he was condemned, and committed suicide in Rome. The publication of his *Tenne Tragedies* in 1581 was important in the evolution of Elizabethan drama, which took from them the five-act division, as well as the horrors and the rhetoric. » Latin literature; Nero; rhetoric; Stoicism; tragedy

Senefelder, Aloys [**zay**nuhfelduh] (1771–1834) Bavarian inventor, born in Prague. He became an actor and playwright, and accidentally discovered the technique of lithography by using a grease pencil on limestone (1796). After various trials he opened an establishment of his own in Munich, where he died. » lithography

Senegal [senuh**gawl**], **Sénégal**, official name **Republic of Senegal**, Fr **République de Sénégal** pop (1990e) 7 277 000; area 196 840 sq km/75 980 sq ml. Country in W Africa, divided into 10 regions; bounded N by Mauritania, E by Mali, S by Guinea and Guinea-Bissau, and W by the Atlantic Ocean; surrounds the Gambia on three sides; capital, Dakar; chief towns, Thiès, Kaolack, Saint-Louis, Ziguinchor; timezone GMT; chief ethnic groups, Wolof (36%), Fulani (17.5%), Serer (16.5%); chief religions, Islam (75%), local beliefs (20%); official language, French; unit of currency, the franc CFA; most westerly country in Africa; coast characterized by dunes, mangrove forests, mudbanks; extensive low-lying basin of savannah and semi-desert vegetation to the N; seasonal streams drain to the R Sénégal; S rises to around 500 m/1 600 ft; tropical climate with a rainy season (Jun–Sep); high humidity levels and high night-time temperatures, especially on the coast; rainfall decreases from S (1 000–1 500 mm/40–60 in) to N (300–350 mm/12–14 in); average annual rainfall at Dakar, 541 mm/21 in; average temperature, 22–28°C; part of the Mali Empire, 14th–15th-c; French established a fort at Saint-Louis, 1659; incorporated as a territory within French West Africa, 1902; autonomous state within the French community, 1958; joined with French Sudan as independent Federation of Mali, 1959; withdrew in 1960 to become a separate independent republic; joined with The Gambia to form the Confederation of Senegambia, 1982–9; governed by a president (elected for a 5-year term), prime minister, cabinet, and 120-member National Assembly; economy mainly agricultural, employing c.75% of the workforce; groundnuts, cotton, sugar, millet, sorghum, manioc, maize, rice, livestock; phosphate, titanium, zirconium,

□ international airport

iron ore, gold, oil, natural gas, salt; fishing, timber, agricultural processing, textiles, chemicals, cement, footwear, shipbuilding and repairing, tourism. » Dakar; Gambia, The [i]; Mali [i]; Senegambia, Confederation of; RR27 national holidays; RR60 political leaders

Sénégal, River River in W Africa; rises in the Fouta Djallon massif (Guinea), and flows N and NW, forming the N frontier of Senegal with Mauritania; enters the Atlantic Ocean at Saint-Louis; upper course above Bafoulabé known as the R Bafing; navigable as far as Bafing at high water; length including the Bafing, 1 635 km/1 016 ml. » Senegal [i]

Senegambia, Confederation of An association between The Gambia and Senegal, begun in 1982, designed to integrate military, economic, communications, and foreign policies, and to establish joint institutions while preserving independence and sovereignty. It proved to be of limited value, and the association was ended by mutual agreement in 1989. » Gambia, The [i]; Senegal [i]

Senghor, Léopold Sédar (1906–) Senegalese statesman and first President (1960–), born in Senegal. He became a teacher, writer, and politician, a member of the French Constituent Assembly in 1945, the deputy for Senegal in the French National Assembly (1948–58), and President following his country's independence. He has won several literary awards as a poet. » Senegal [i]

senile dementia » **dementia**

senna A drug obtained from the pods and dried leaves of certain species of *Cassia*, a large group of trees and shrubs native to Africa and Arabia, and often cultivated elsewhere; it is one of the most widely grown species. A source of **Alexandrian senna** is *Cassia acutifolia*, a shrub growing to 90 cm/3 ft or more, native to Egypt, and from the Sudan to Nigeria; leaves with 3–7 pairs of oval leaflets; flowers 5-petalled, yellow veined with red in long clusters. (Genus: *Cassia*. Family: *Leguminosae*.) » shrub; tree [i]

Sennacherib [suh**na**kuhrib] (8th–7th-c BC) King of Assyria (704–681 BC), the son of Sargon II and grandfather of Assurbanipal. He was an able ruler, whose fame rests mainly on his conquest of Babylon (689 BC), and his rebuilding of Nineveh. He figures prominently in the Bible, because of his attack on Jerusalem. » Assurbanipal; Assyria; Esarhaddon; Nineveh

Sennett, Mack, originally **Michell Sinott** (1880–1960) US film producer, born at Richmond, Quebec. He worked in the theatre as a comic in burlesque companies, and from 1908 in silent films. He later formed his own company, and made hundreds of shorts, establishing a whole generation of players and a tradition of knockabout slapstick under the name of Keystone Komics (1912) and later the Sennett Bathing Beauties (1920). He was given a Special Academy Award in 1937 for his long contributions to film comedy. He died in Hollywood.

sensitive plant A perennial, prickly-stemmed herb, growing to 90 cm/3 ft, native to S America; a common weed in tropical areas, and in cooler climates often cultivated as a novelty in hothouses; leaves divided into narrow leaflets. It is exceedingly sensitive, exhibiting nastic movement, closing up at night. This response can also be triggered at greater speed by a shock stimulus such as a touch or shake. The exact mechanism is unknown, although signals passed through the phloem may cause changes in water potential in the cells of the leaflet stalk, or perhaps involve contractile proteins. The movement may be a means of reducing transpiration or a protective response to grazing animals. After a while the leaflets return to their original position. (*Mimosa pudica*. Family: *Leguminosae*.) » herb; nastic movement; perennial; phloem; transpiration

sentence In law, the decision of a court imposed on a person convicted of a crime, such as a fine, a period of imprisonment, a period of supervision, the death sentence, or an absolute discharge. Penal policy as reflected in sentences aims variously at deterrence, prevention of crime, punishment, and rehabilitation. » community service order; detention centre; parole; probation; youth custody centre

Seoul or **Sŏul** [sohl] 37°30N 127°00E, pop (1984) 9 501 413. Special city and capital of Korea, in the Han river valley; founded, 14th-c; called Hanyang until the 20th-c; seat of the Yi dynasty government 1392–1910; badly damaged in Korean War; airport (Kimpo); railway; 17 universities; engineering, textiles, tanning, food processing; Kyongbok-kung Palace (14th-c, rebuilt 1867), including National Museum and National Folk Museum; Ch'angdŏ-kung palace (1405, rebuilt 1611); Toksu-kung palace, including Museum of Modern Art; Chongmyo (ancestral tablets of Yi dynasty), Namdaemun (Great South Gate, reconstructed 1448), Pagoda Park, Seoul Grand Park, Seoul Land (Korean version of Disneyland); location of 1988 Olympic Games. » Korea [i]

sepal [**se**pl] One of the outermost whorl of flower parts, collectively termed the *calyx*. Usually green, free, or sometimes fused together, they protect the flower in bud. They sometimes assume other roles, such as becoming enlarged and brightly coloured, and acting as petals. » flower [i]; petal

separation, judicial An order granted by a court in England and Wales where either marriage partner presents a petition supported by one of the facts necessary for a divorce. The parties remain married, however. Parties to a marriage may live apart without a court order, though the formal order of separation means that neither party can be accused of desertion. » divorce

separation of powers A political doctrine, associated with the 18th-c philosopher Montesquieu, which argues that, to avoid tyranny, the three branches of government (legislature, executive, and judiciary) should be separated as far as possible, their relationships governed by checks and balances. The US Constitution is a practical example of an attempt at separation of powers. Parliamentary systems such as that of the UK do not have a complete separation, as the heads of the executive (ie government ministers) sit as members of the legislature. Nonetheless, most systems claim independence of the judiciary. » legislature; Lord Chancellor; Montesquieu

separatism The demand for separation by a particular group or area from the territorial and political sovereignty of the state of which they are a part. Examples of separatist movements are the Basques in Spain and the Tamils in Sri Lanka. Separatism is associated with claims for the right to self-determination, and is often connected with discrimination against minorities. » self-determination

sepek takraw (Malay 'kick', Thai 'rattan ball') A 3-a-side court game played on a badminton court with a ball made from the rattan palm. The ball is propelled over the centre net (which is lower than in badminton) by players using any part of the body other than their arms or hands. It is popular in SE Asia, particularly the Philippines, Malaysia, and Thailand. » badminton

Sephardim [se**fah**dim] Descendants of Jews who lived in Spain and Portugal before 1492, but who were then expelled for not accepting Christianity, and became refugees in N Africa, Turkey and Italy. Subsequently they migrated to N Europe and the Americas, where during the 16th–17th-c they kept distinct from other Jews (especially those from C Europe), considering themselves innately and culturally superior. They preserved their own rituals, customs, dialect (Ladino), and pronunciation of Hebrew. » Diaspora; Hebrew; Judaism

sepiolite » **meerschaum**

septicaemia/septicemia [septi**see**mia] The occurrence and multiplication of bacteria in the blood stream; more commonly known as **blood poisoning**. It is usually a serious complication of infection, by which sepsis is dispersed throughout the body. » blood

Septuagesima [sepchooa**je**sima] In the Western Christian Church, the third Sunday before Lent, apparently so called by analogy with Quadragesima and Quinquagesima (Latin *septuagesimus*, 'seventieth'); the 70th day before Easter. » Lent

Septuagint [**sep**tuajint] A translation into Greek of the Hebrew Bible, obtaining its name (meaning 'translation of the 70') from a legend in the *Letter of Aristeas* (2nd-c BC) about its composition as the work of 72 scholars, six from each of the twelve tribes of Israel. The translation was begun c.3rd-c BC to meet the need of Greek-speaking Jews in the Diaspora, but work progressed by several stages over about a century. It has a different order of books from that in the Hebrew canon, and contains some works not in that canon. When it was adopted by Christians as their preferred version of the Old Testament, it lost favour among the Jews. » Apocrypha, Old Testament; Bible; Diaspora; Old Testament

sequence (mathematics) In mathematics, an ordered set of numbers such that the *n*th term can always be written as a function of *n*. In an arithmetic sequence, where *a* is the first term and *d* the common difference, the *n*th term is $a+(n-1)d$. A **series** is the sum of the terms in a sequence. Thus the exponential series is $1+\frac{x}{1!}+\frac{x^2}{2!}+\frac{x^3}{3!}+\frac{x^4}{4!}\cdots$.
» arithmetic/geometric sequence

sequence (music) **1** From c.850 to c.1000, a non-Biblical Latin text added to a long portion of chant originally sung to one syllable at the end of the Alleluia; later, a similar syllabic chant specially composed. All but four sequences (they include the *Dies irae* of the Requiem Mass) were banned from the liturgy in the 16th-c, but the *Stabat Mater* was later admitted. » liturgy; plainchant **2** A musical phrase immediately repeated at a different pitch. The opening of Beethoven's Fifth Symphony furnishes a familiar example.

sequoia [sekwoya] » **coast redwood**

Sequoia (California) [sekwoya] National park in E California, USA, in the Sierra Nevada, E of Fresno; contains the enormous, ancient sequoia trees; area 1 631 sq km/630 sq ml. » California; coast redwood

Sequoia (US history) [sekwoyaa] or **Sequoyah** (c.1770–1843) Cherokee Indian leader, born at Taskigi, North Carolina. He was a major figure behind the decision of the Cherokee to adopt as much as possible of White culture, while retaining their own identity, and personally invented an alphabet for their language. He died in Mexico. » Cherokee; Indian Wars

seraphim [serafim] Heavenly beings mentioned in Jewish Scriptures only in the vision in *Isa* 6, where they are described as having six wings and being stationed above the throne of God, chanting refrains announcing the holiness of God. The origin of the term is uncertain. They are similar to the cherubim in *Ezek* 1. » cherubim; God

Serapis [seraypis, serapis] A compound deity, combining the names and aspects of two Egyptian gods, Osiris and Apis, to which were further added features of major Greek gods, such as Zeus and Dionysus. The god was introduced to Alexandria by Ptolemy I in an attempt to unite Greeks and Egyptians in common worship. » Apis; Osiris

Serbia [serbia], Serbo-Croatian **Srbija** pop (1981) 9 313 676; area 88 361 sq km/34 107 sq ml. Mountainous republic in Yugoslavia; bounded E by Romania and Bulgaria, N by Hungary, S by Macedonia, and W by Albania and other Yugoslav republics; land rises to the Dinaric Alps (W) and Stara Planina (E); Serbian state founded, 6th-c; overrun by Turks, 1389; kingdom, 1882; incorporated into Yugoslavia, including the autonomous regions of Vojvodina (N) and Kosovo (S), 1918; constituent republic, 1946; capital, Belgrade; chief towns include Niš, Priština, Prizren, Kragujevac, Leskovac; unrest in the 1980s in Kosovo between the Albanian majority and Serbian minority, causing many Serbs to leave the region; confrontation with Croatia over disputed border areas and status of Serbian minority, leading to civil war, 1991; wheat, maize, vines, livestock, coal, copper. » Belgrade; Yugoslavia [i]

serenade Originally, music to be played or sung in the evening, especially for courting. The term is now most widely applied to works for full or string orchestra in several movements, which are lighter in style and less ambitious than a symphony. » symphony

Serengeti [serengetee] area 14 763 sq km/5 698 sq ml. National park in N Tanzania; a world heritage site; established in 1951; average elevation c.1 500 m/5 000 ft; noted for its wildlife, especially wildebeeste, gazelle, zebra, impala, buffalo, topi, eland, kongoni, giraffe, elephant, hyena, and lion; famous for the mass migratory treks of the grass-eating animals and their predators. » Tanzania [i]

serfdom The condition of peasants lacking personal freedom, especially of movement and the disposal of property, and liable to uncertain or arbitrary obligations; an intermediate position between slavery and freedom. Post-mediaeval references to serfdom in W Europe normally have scant social reality; but in E Europe serfdom persisted – in Russia until 1861. » Black Death; ceorl; feudalism; villein

sergeant at arms In the UK, the officer of the House of Commons responsible for maintaining order and for internal administration. Appointed by the sovereign on the recommendation of the house, he also has certain ceremonial functions, particularly that of carrying the Speaker's mace in procession to the Chair at the beginning of the day's business. » Commons, House of

serialism A method of composing music in which a series (or 'row' or 'set') of different notes is used, in accordance with certain strict practices, as the basis of a whole work. The most common type is 12-note serialism, in which the 12 pitches of the chromatic scale are re-ordered to form one of a possible 479 001 600 different series. This can then be presented vertically as chords, or horizontally as melodic lines, or as a mixture of both; it can be used backwards (*retrograde*), or with the intervals inverted (*inversion*), or in both retrograde and inversion; it can also be transposed to any other pitch. Thus, 48 versions of a single series are possible, and these provide all the pitch material for the composition. Schoenberg arrived at 12-note serialism in 1923, as a means of structuring atonal music; his method was adopted, in very different ways, by his pupils Berg and Webern. Some later composers, notably Boulez, Nono, and Stockhausen, have applied serial methods to such other elements of composition as rhythm, dynamics, and articulation. » atonality; chromaticism; scale [i]; Berg; Boulez; Nono; Schoenberg; Stockhausen; Webern

seriema [seriema] A ground-dwelling bird, inhabiting grassland and scrub in the New World tropics; long legs and neck; tuft of feathers between eyes; poor flier; eats insects, small vertebrates, leaves, seeds, and fruit; also known as the **cariama**. (Family: *Cariamidae*, 2 species.)

series (mathematics) » **sequence** (mathematics)

serin » **canary**

serjeanty [sahjuhntee] or **sergeantry** The name for a wide range of tenures in mediaeval times, by which men held land on condition of performing some definite personal service, other than knight-service, to the superior lord. The services demanded were weighty or frivolous, but the distinction made in England between grand and petty serjeanties is an invention of legal antiquarians. » feudalism

Sermon on the Mount or **Plain** A great collection of Jesus' ethical teaching, depicted in *Matt* 5–7 as preached on a mountain early in Jesus' ministry, but in *Luke* 6.20–49 as on a 'plain'. Matthew's version is longer, and contains the Beatitudes, teaching about true adherence to God's law, instruction on love of enemies, the Lord's Prayer, admonitions about material anxieties, the Golden Rule, and exhortations to observe what is taught. » Beatitudes; Golden Rule; Jesus Christ; Lord's Prayer

serology A branch of medicine which specializes in the analysis of serum. It looks for evidence of infection, by the detection of antibodies or micro-organisms. » medicine; serum

serotine bat [seruhtiyn] A bat found from Europe to SE Asia and N Africa; brown with pale tips to the hairs; slow flying; eats mainly large moths and beetles. (*Eptesicus serotinus*. Family: *Vespertilionidae*.) » bat

serotonin [seruhtohnin] A widely distributed chemical substance (a monoamine), particularly found in the blood, brain, and certain cells of the gut; it is also known as **5-hydroxytryptamine (5-HT)**. It is synthesized from the amino acid *tryptophan*, plays an important part in haemostasis, and probably also acts as a neurotransmitter in the central nervous system. It is involved in sleep, emotional disposition (mood), prolactin secretion, and circadian rhythms. » amines; biological rhythm; haemostasis; neurotransmitter; paracrine

serow [seroh] A goat antelope, native to SE Asia; thick dark coat; long pointed ears and short, slightly curved, horns; two species: **mainland serow** (*Capricornis sumatrensis*) and **Japanese**, **Formosa**, or **Taiwanese serow** (*Capricornis crispus*). (Genus: *Capricornis*.) » antelope

Serpens (Lat 'serpent') A constellation in the N hemisphere. It is unique, because it is bisected (by Ophiuchus) into two distinct sections: **Caput** ('head') and **Cauda** ('body'). » constellation; Ophiuchus; RR9

serpent » snake

serpentine A hydrous magnesium silicate ($Mg_3Si_2O_5(OH)_4$) occurring in altered basic and ultrabasic igneous rocks by the decomposition of olivine and pyroxene. There are two main forms: *chrysotile* (an asbestos variety) and *antigorite*. It is soft, green to black, and used in decorative carving. » olivine; pyroxenes; talc

SERPS » pension

serpulid [serpyoolid] A tube-building bristleworm; reduced head, bearing a crown of gills; body retractable inside a calcareous tube; aperture closed by a flap (operculum); found in the inter-tidal zone in shallow waters. (Phylum: *Annelida*. Class: *Polychaeta*.) » bristleworm; calcium

sertão [sertõw] The remote underdeveloped backlands and semi-arid plateau of NE Brazil. It is a major area of drought (eg in the late 19th-c). There is a discontinuous vegetation cover of thorn scrub, as well as sandy saline soils and rock pavement. The economy is based on semi-nomadic subsistence cattle-rearing. » Brazil [i]; drought

serum The residue of any animal liquid after the separation and removal of the more solid components. It is specifically used to refer to human blood serum, which is a clear, yellowish fluid separated from clotted blood plasma. Serum with appropriate antibodies protects against specific diseases (eg typhoid, tetanus). » blood; serology

serum sickness The repeated injection of foreign protein (such as in immunization) or other antigenic substances sometimes gives rise to an acute severe reaction, consisting of fever, urticaria, arthritis, and abnormal amounts of protein in the urine (*proteinuria*). » arthritis; protein; urticaria

serval [servl] A nocturnal member of the cat family, native to S Africa; slender, with long neck and short tail; pale with small or large dark spots (small-spotted type formerly called **servaline cat**); occasionally black; solitary; inhabits savannah near streams; eats rodents, birds, and small antelopes. (*Felis serval*.) » Felidae

Servetus, Michael [servaytuhs] (1511–53) Spanish theologian and physician, born at Tudela. He studied law, worked largely in France and Switzerland, and in his theological writings denied the Trinity and the divinity of Christ. He escaped the Inquisition but was burnt by Calvin at Geneva for heresy. While studying medicine at Paris he discovered the pulmonary circulation of the blood. » blood; Calvin, John; Trinity

service club A group of men and women organized to perform volunteer community service. The first such club, for business and professional men, was formed in 1905 by US lawyer Paul Harris (1868–1947) in Chicago, Illinois, using the name *Rotary* (because the meetings took place at each member's office in turn). This grew into Rotary International, whose motto 'Service above Self' embodies the ideals of all service clubs, and which is now a worldwide organization. Women were admitted for the first time in 1987. *Kiwanis International* began in 1915 in Detroit, Michigan, and the *International Association of Lions Clubs* was formed in Dallas, Texas in 1917; there are many others. All sponsor a wide range of community projects. » club

service industry An industry which does not manufacture a product, but provides a service. It is a fast-growing sector in most Western nations, representing a higher proportion of gross domestic product and employment than the manufacturing industry. Activities range from banking and other financial services to tourism, hotels, and catering. The expression 'post-industrial society' refers to a situation where relatively few people are engaged in manufacturing. » gross domestic product

service tree The name given to two species of *Sorbus*, native to Europe, both deciduous trees with white flowers in large, flat clusters. The true service tree (*Sorbus domestica*) has pinnate leaves with 6–10 pairs of toothed leaflets, and reddish-brown berries 2–3 cm/¾–1¼ in, edible when over-ripe. The wild service tree or **chequerberry** (*Sorbus torminalis*) has lobed leaves and brown berries 1–2 cm/0.4–0.8 in, used for preserves and drinks. (Family: *Rosaceae*.) » deciduous plants; pinnate; tree [i]

Servile Wars The collective name for the official attempts to suppress the slave uprisings of the late 2nd-c and early 1st-c BC in Sicily and S Italy. The most serious was the revolt led by Spartacus, in which tens of thousands of slaves were involved. It took the Romans two years to suppress it (73–71 BC). » Spartacus

servo system A system controlled by a servomechanism: a high-power output device is controlled with a command signal from a low-input device. The servomotor corrects the difference between demanded output and actual output using feedback, which results in an amplification of effort. Power-assisted braking or steering are servo systems. » control engineering

sesame An annual growing to 60 cm/2 ft, probably native to SE Asia; leaves opposite and usually lobed below, alternate above; flowers c.3 cm/1¼ in long, white, usually marked with purple or yellow, solitary in the leaf axils; fruit an oblong capsule. It is cultivated in warmer countries for its seeds, which are used for baking and as a source of oil in margarine, soap manufacture, and cosmetics. (*Sesamum indicum*. Family: *Pedaliaceae*.) » annual

Sessions, Roger (Huntingdon) (1896–1985) US composer, born in New York City. Educated at Harvard and Yale, he lived in Europe (1925–33), then taught music in the USA at Princeton (1935–45, 1953–65) and Berkeley (1945–52). He later taught at the Juilliard School of Music in New York City. His compositions include nine symphonies, a violin concerto, piano and chamber music, and operatic works. He died at Princeton, New Jersey.

set In mathematics, a well-defined class of elements, ie a class where it is possible to tell exactly whether any one element does or does not belong to it. We can have the set of all even numbers, as every number is either even or not even, but we cannot have the set of all large numbers, as we do not know what is meant by 'large'. The **empty set** $\varnothing$ is the set with no elements. The **universal set** $\mathscr{E}$ or $\mathscr{U}$ is the set of all elements, and the complement A' of a set A is the set of all elements in $\mathscr{E}$ which are not in A. The **intersection** of two sets A and B (written $A \cap B$) is the set of all elements in both A and B. The **union** of two sets A and B (written $A \cup B$) is the set of all elements in either A or B or both. » Cantor; Venn diagram [i]

Set or **Seth** An ancient Egyptian god, depicted with the head of an animal with a long muzzle. The brother and enemy of Osiris, he was associated with evil forces and rebellion. » Osiris

set-aside policy An agricultural policy designed to reduce surplus production, by requiring the withdrawal of land from production in exchange for specific payments or guarantees. It has been used extensively in the USA, and is currently gaining support in Europe.

setter A long-haired sporting dog which belongs to one of several breeds performing the same function as a pointer; probably developed by breeding spaniels with pointers. » English/Gordon/Irish setter; pointer; spaniel; sporting dog

Settlement, Act of An important British statute of 1701 which determined the succession of the English throne after the death of Queen Anne and her heirs, if any. It excluded the Catholic Stuarts from the succession, which was to pass to the Electress Sophia of Hanover, descendant through the female line of James I. Future monarchs were to be communicant members of the Church of England, and were not permitted to leave the country without the consent of parliament. » Anne; Stuarts

Setúbal [setoobal] 38°30N 8°58W, pop (1981) 76 800. Industrial seaport and capital of Setúbal district, S Portugal; at the mouth of R Sado, 32 km/20 ml SE of Lisbon; railway; cement, car parts, domestic appliances, steel, ship repair, fish canning, salt, wine; Santiago fair (Jul). » Portugal [i]

Seurat, Georges (Pierre) [serrah] (1859–91) French artist, born and died in Paris. He studied and set up a studio in Paris, where he became known for such works as 'Une Baignade' (1883–4, Tate, London) and 'Sunday Afternoon on the Island of La Grande Jatte' (1884–6, Chicago), painted in a Divisionist style. His colour theories were influential, but his main achievement was the marrying of an Impressionist palette to classical composition. » Divisionism; French art; Impressionism (art)

Seven against Thebes In Greek legend, seven champions who attacked Thebes to deprive Eteocles of his kingship. They were led by his brother Polynices; the other six were Tydeus, Adrastus (or Eteoklos), Capaneus, Hippomedon, Parthenopaeus, and Amphiarus. They were defeated by another seven champions at the seven gates of Thebes; all were killed in battle, except for Amphiarus, whom the Earth swallowed alive, and Adrastus, who escaped. Later the sons of the Seven, the Epigoni, led by Adrastus, succeeded in destroying the city. » Creon; Eteocles; Polynices

Seven Days Battles (26 Jun–2 Jul 1862) The final conflict in the Peninsular Campaign during the American Civil War, fought below Richmond between the York and James Rivers. The battles began with a Southern offensive intended to drive the Union forces off the Peninsula, but ended with a Confederate withdrawal. » American Civil War; Peninsular Campaign

seven deadly sins The fundamental vices thought, in Christian tradition, to underlie all sinful actions. They are pride, covetousness, lust, envy, gluttony, anger, and sloth. » Christianity; sin

Seven Sisters » **Pleiades** (astronomy)

Seven Sleepers of Ephesus In mediaeval legend, seven persecuted Christians who fled into a cave at the time of the Emperor Decius (AD 250); they slept for 200 years, emerging in 447 at the time of Theodosius II. The story was thought to confirm the resurrection of Christ.

seven whistler » **whimbrel**

Seven Wise Men of Greece Seven men famed in antiquity for their wisdom. The lists vary, but Solon of Athens, Thales of Miletus, Bias of Priene, and Pittacus of Mytilene are common to all of them. These and all the others mentioned belonged to the period 620–550 BC. » Miletus

Seven Wonders of the Ancient World The most renowned man-made structures of the ancient world: the Pyramids of Egypt; the Hanging Gardens of Babylon; the Tomb of Mausolus at Halicarnassus; the Temple of Artemis at Ephesus; the Colossus of Rhodes; the Statue of Zeus at Olympia; and the Pharos of Alexandria. » Babylon; Colossus of Rhodes; Ephesus; Mausolus, Tomb of; Pharos of Alexandria; pyramid; Zeus, statue of

Seven Years' War (1756–63) A major European conflict rooted in the rivalry between Austria and Prussia and the imminent colonial struggle between Britain and France in the New World and the Far East. Hostilities in N America (1754) pre-dated the Diplomatic Revolution in Europe (1756), which created two opposing power blocs: Austria, France, Russia, Sweden, and Saxony against Prussia, Britain, and Portugal. British maritime superiority countered Franco-Spanish naval power, and prevented a French invasion. The European war, precipitated by Prussia's seizure of Saxony, was marked by many notable pitched land battles. Saved from total defeat when Russia switched sides, Frederick II of Prussia retained Silesia in 1763. » Elizabeth Petrovna; Frederick II (of Prussia); George II (of Great Britain); Granby; Louis XV; Montcalm; Maria Theresa; Paris, Treaties of **1**; Vendôme, Duke of; Villars, Duke of

severe combined immunodeficiency (SCI) A type of immune deficiency resulting from failure of the thymus to develop, and thus to produce lymphocytes, which are involved in the production of antibodies. Babies born with this condition have little ability to withstand infection, and rarely survive beyond infancy; but some success has been obtained with thymic transplantation. » immunity; thymus

Severini, Gino [sayvuh**ree**nee] (1883–1966) Italian artist, born at Cortona. He studied in Rome and Paris and signed the first Futurist manifesto in 1910. After 1914 he reverted to a more representational style, which he used in fresco and mosaic work, particularly in a number of Swiss and Italian churches. From 1940 onwards he adopted a decorative Cubist manner. He died in Paris. » Cubism; fresco; Futurism; Italian art

Severn, River River in SE Wales and W England; rises on Plynlimon, C Wales; flows NE and E to Shrewsbury, then SE and S through Worcester and Gloucester; wide estuary into the Bristol Channel; navigable to Gloucester; length 354 km/220 ml; known for the Severn bore (tidal wave c.2 m/6 ft); railway tunnel (completed 1885); **Severn Bridge**, suspension bridge carrying M4 motorway, links Aust in Somerset with Beachley on the Gwent border (988 m/3 240 ft); completed 1966. » Bristol Channel

Severnaya Zemlya [**say**vernaya zem**lya**], formerly **Zemlya Imperatora**, Eng **North Land** or **Nicholas II Land** area 37 001 sq km/14 282 sq ml. Uninhabited archipelago in the Arctic Ocean, N of the Taymyr Peninsula, Russia; separates the Laptev Sea (E) from the Kara Sea (W); glaciers on the larger islands. » Russia

Severus, Lucius Septimius (c.146–211) Roman emperor (193–211) and founder of the Severan dynasty (193–235), the first Roman emperor to be born in Africa (at Leptis Magna, of Romanized Punic stock). Declared emperor by the army in 193, he spent the early years of his reign securing his position against his rivals. Once established, he proved to be an able administrator, effecting many reforms, and showing a particularly close interest in the army and the law. His final years were spent in Britain, trying unsuccessfully to restore order in the N of the province. He died at Eboracum (York). » Britain, Roman; Leptis Magna

Sévigné, Madame de [**say**veenyay], *née* **Marie de Rabutin-Chantal** (1626–96) French writer, born in Paris. She was a member of French court society, and after the marriage of her daughter in 1669 she began a series of letters, lasting over 25 years, recounting the inner history of her time in great detail, and in a natural, colloquial style. She died at Grignan, the letters being published posthumously (1725).

Seville [se**vil**], Span **Sevilla**, ancient **Hispalis** 37°23N 6°00W, pop (1981) 653 833. River port and capital of Seville province, Andalusia, S Spain; on R Guadalquivir, 538 km/334 ml SW of Madrid; Moorish cultural centre, 8th–13th-c; trading centre with the Americas, 16th-c; archbishopric; airport; railway; university (1502); tourism, furniture, olives, agricultural machinery, chemicals; birthplace of Velásquez and Murillo; cathedral (15th-c), largest Gothic church in the world, with tomb of Columbus; Moorish citadel and Archivo de Indias, a world heritage site; Maria Luisa Park, fine arts museum, Pilate's House, Palace of St Telmo; Scipio's Roman settlement of Italica, 7 km/4 ml NW; April fair, Festival of Spain (autumn), Fiesta of La Virgen de los Reyes (Aug), St Miguel fair (Sep). » Andalusia; Columbus, Christopher; Giralda; Murillo; Spain [i]; Velásquez

Sèvres porcelain The French royal porcelain factory, founded c.1745 to produce soft and hard paste luxury porcelain. The early products included many beautiful figures in white unglazed 'biscuit' ware, but the factory's speciality became items with exquisitely painted vignettes against richly coloured plain grounds with elaborate gilding. » porcelain

Seward Peninsula Peninsula in Alaska, USA, separating Kotzebue Sound (N) and Norton Sound (S); the most W point of the N American continent. » Alaska

Sewell, Anna (1820–78) British novelist, born at Yarmouth, Norfolk. An invalid for most of her life, her *Black Beauty* (1877), the story of a horse, written as a plea for the more humane treatment of animals, is perhaps the most famous fictional work about horses. She died at Old Catton, Norfolk. » English literature; novel

sewellel » **mountain beaver**

sex chromosome A chromosome represented differently in the sexes, and responsible for the genetic determination of the sex of an individual. The sex carrying a homologous pair of sex chromosomes (XX) is *homogametic*; the sex with a dissimilar pair (XY) or unpaired (X) sex chromosome is *heterogametic*. All gametes of the homogametic sex carry one X-chromosome. Half of the gametes produced by the heterogametic sex carry an X-chromosome and the other half a Y-chromosome, or no sex chromosome at all. In humans, the female is the homogametic sex and the male is the heterogametic. » chromosome [i]; gamete; homology

sex hormones Steroid hormones produced and secreted mainly by the gonads, necessary for sexual development and the control of reproductive function. In humans the most important are certain androgens (testosterone and dihydrotestosterone) found predominantly in males, and progestogens (progesterone) and certain oestrogens (oestradiol, oestrone, and oestriol) found predominantly in females. They probably act on the brain to influence sexual and other behaviour. » androgens; gonad; hormones; oestrogens; progesterone; steroid [i]

sex therapy Treatment for sexual problems of psychological origin, which may arise as a result of a mental reaction to physical illness by the affected individual or partner, or to psychological attitudes themselves, either of which imperil normal sexual relations. An assessment of the individual or couple's problem is followed by simple counselling or, in the event of failure, by referral to specially trained sex therapists, who generally advise a graduated programme of tasks which the couple pursue at home. Emphasis is placed on the need for mutual understanding of each other's problems, and the need for mutual communication.

Sexagesima [seksa**je**sima] The second Sunday before Lent, apparently so called by analogy with Quadragesima and Quinquagesima (Latin *sexagesimus*, 'sixtieth'); the 60th day before Easter. » Lent

sexism A set of preconceived assumptions about the 'proper' roles, attitudes, and characteristics (especially physical) that men and women should have, typically working to the advantage of men over women; for example, the assumption that 'a woman's place is in the home', or that men are 'naturally aggressive'. Sexism can be identified by behaviour, speech, and the written word, and is criticized most strongly by feminists. » feminism; role

Sextans (Lat 'sextant') A very faint equatorial constellation between Leo and Hydra. » constellation; Hydra (astronomy); Leo; RR9

sextant An optical instrument for measuring angular distances; in particular, the elevation of the Sun above the horizon at noon, for determining latitude. The observer views the horizon through a telescope, and simultaneously (through a mirror attached to an arm on a graduated arc) the Sun. The mirror can be moved over the arc to produce a coincidence of the Sun-image and the horizon. For land use, an artificial horizon is provided by a pool of mercury; in aircraft, a bubble-level horizon is used. » latitude and longitude [i]

sexual problems » **dyspareunia; incest; masturbation; Oedipus complex; paedophilia; sadomasochism; satyriasis; transsexual; vaginismus; voyeurism**

sexually transmitted diseases » **AIDS; gonorrhoea; syphilis; venereal disease**

Seychelles [say**shelz**], official name **Republic of Seychelles** pop(1990e) 68 700; land area 453 sq km/175 sq ml. Island group in the SW Indian Ocean, N of Madagascar, comprising 115 islands scattered over 1 374 000 sq km/530 000 sq ml between 4° and 5°S; includes Mahé (153 sq km/59 sq ml), Praslin (38 sq km/15 sq ml), La Digue (10 sq km/4 sq ml); capital, Victoria (on Mahé); timezone GMT +4; population largely descended from 18th-c French colonists and their freed African slaves; chief languages, Creole, French, English; chief religion, Roman Catholicism (95%); islands fall into two main groups; a compact group of 41 mountainous islands rising steeply from the sea, highest point 906 m/2 972 ft on Mahé; steep forest-clad slopes drop down to coastal lowlands with a vegetation of grass and dense scrub; to the SW, a group of low-lying coralline islands and atolls; tropical climate, rainfall varying with altitude, higher on S sides of the islands; colonized by the French, 1768; captured by Britain, 1794; incorporated as a dependency of Mauritius, 1814; separate colony, 1903; independent republic within the Commonwealth, 1976; governed by a president, elected for a 5-year term, a Council of Ministers, and a 25-member unicameral National Assembly; fruit, vegetables, livestock, cinnamon, copra; expanding tourist industry; diversifying small industry; brewing, soap, plastics, furniture, cigarettes, soft drinks, steel fabricated goods, fishing. » Mauritius [i]; Victoria (Seychelles); RR27 national holidays; RR60 political leaders

Seyfert, Carl [**say**fert] (1911–60) US astronomer, who first drew attention (1943) to the existence of galaxies with brilliant nuclei. » galaxy; quasar

Seymour, Jane (c.1509–37) Third Queen of Henry VIII, the mother of Edward VI, and the sister of Protector Somerset. She was a lady-in-waiting to Henry's first two wives, and married him 11 days after the execution of Anne Boleyn. She died soon after the birth of her son, at Hampton Court, London. » Boleyn; Edward VI; Henry VIII (of England)

Sezession [set**ses**yohn] (Ger 'secession') The name adopted by a number of groups of modern artists in Germany between c.1890 and World War 1, who seceded from the orthodox academic bodies to form their own exhibiting societies. The Munich Sezession was founded in 1882, Vienna in 1897, Berlin in 1899. » Art Nouveau; Brücke, die; German art

Sfax [sfaks] 34°45N 10°43E, pop(1984) 231 911. Seaport and capital of Sfax governorate, E Tunisia, 240 km/150 ml SSE of Tunis; chief port and second largest city of Tunisia; built on the site of Roman and Phoenician settlements; occupied by Sicilians (12th-c) and Spaniards (16th-c); also a base for Barbary pirates; modern city built after 1895; airfield; railway; trade in esparto, oil, peanuts and dates; phosphate processing, textiles, fishing; museum of folk arts and traditions, archaeological museum; festival of music and popular arts (Jul). » Tunisia [i]

sfumato [sfoo**mah**toh] (Ital 'smoke') A term used in art history for the very soft tonal transitions achieved by such painters as Leonardo da Vinci and Correggio. This was a technical advance on the sharp outlines of 15th-c painting (eg Botticelli, Mantegna) and helped 16th-c masters to achieve a greater naturalism. » Correggio; Leonardo da Vinci

sgraffito or **graffito** A technique in art in which one colour is laid over another and a design scratched through. Mediaeval and Renaissance buildings were sometimes decorated with two layers of plaster – one white, one coloured – and scratched decoration applied. Mediaeval artists sometimes painted over gold leaf to achieve similar effects.

Shabbat » **sabbath**

Shabuoth or **Shavuot(h)** [sha**voo**-oth, -ot] The Jewish Feast of Weeks, observed in May or June (6 Sivan) in commemoration of God's giving of the Law to Moses on Mount Sinai (Exodus 19); also known as Pentecost. » Moses; RR23

Shackleton, Sir Ernest Henry (1874–1922) British explorer, born at Kilkee, Co Kildare, Ireland. He was a junior officer in Scott's National Antarctic Expedition (1901–3), and nearly reached the S Pole in his own expedition of 1909. In 1915 his ship *Endurance* was crushed in the ice, and he and five others made a perilous journey of 1 300 km/800 ml to bring relief for the crew. Knighted in 1909, he died at S Georgia during a fourth expedition. » Antarctica [i]; Scott, R F

shad Small herring-like fish native to the Atlantic seaboard of N America but now widespread on the Pacific coast also; adults live in coastal marine waters migrating into fresh water to breed; live in large schools feeding mainly on plankton; length up to 75 cm/30 in; silver with greenish-blue upper surface. (*Alosa sapidissima*. Family: *Clupeidae*.) » herring

shaddock A citrus fruit resembling grapefruit, 10–25 cm/4–10 in in diameter; globose or pear-shaped, with greenish-yellow rind and sweet pink or yellow pulp. It is grown mainly in the tropics. (*Citrus grandis*. Family: *Rutaceae*.) » citrus

shadow-mask tube A cathode-ray tube for the display of colour video images. Electron beams from three separate guns modulated by the red, green, and blue signals are deflected by the scanning system through holes in the shadow-mask plate to fall on minute phosphor dots of the appropriate colour comprising the screen. These dots glow according to the intensity of the beam reaching them and, being too small to be seen individually, appear as additive colour hues. In most tubes the phosphor dots are arranged as triads in delta formation, but vertical stripes in groups of three are also employed, when the shadow-mask plate becomes a grille. » cathode-ray tube; colour television [i]; *illustration p 1094*

shadow puppets Puppets which are manipulated in performance so as to cast a shadow on a screen. There are two major traditions in the world, marked by a difference in technique. In one, the sticks operating the two-dimensional figures are worked from below, as with Balinese and Javanese shadow theatre. In the other, the sticks are operated from behind, at right angles to the screen, and the puppets are pressed close to its surface, as with Chinese and Turkish shadow theatre. » puppetry

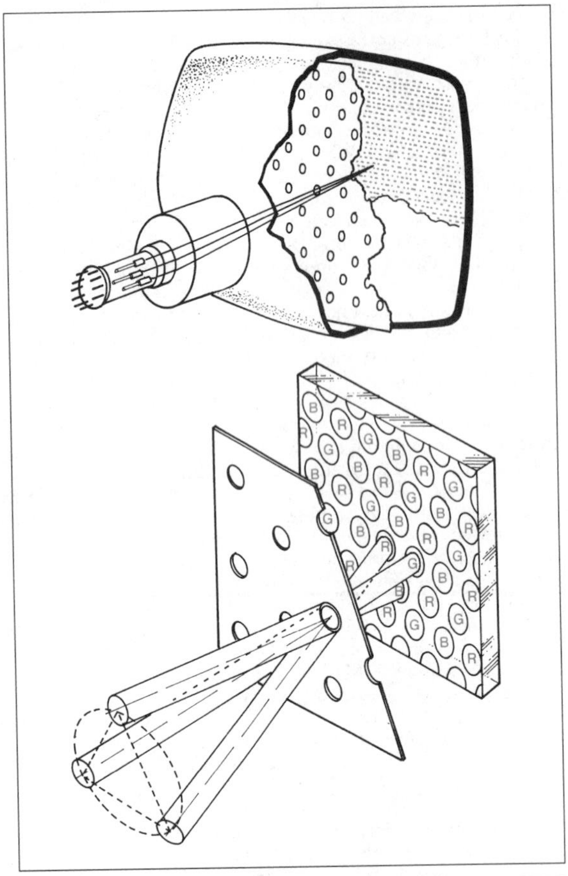

Shadow-mask tube – Modulated electron beams from three separate guns pass through holes in the mask plate to fall on the individual colour phosphor dots which comprise the screen. (Lower illustration a magnified detail)

Shadwell, Thomas (c.1642–92) English dramatist, born at Brandon, Norfolk. Educated at Cambridge, he became a lawyer, and found success with his first satirical comedy, *The Sullen Lovers* (1668), and such later 'comedies of manners' as *Epsom-Wells* (1672). He carried on a literary feud with Dryden, whom he satirized, and who attacked him in turn in *MacFlecknoe* (1682) and other poems. He succeeded Dryden as poet laureate in 1689, and died in London. » Dryden; English literature; satire

shaft graves Two groups of royal tombs at the W end of the citadel of Mycenae, Greece, the most notable discovered in 1876 by Heinrich Schliemann. They consist of six wooden-roofed, rock-cut, rectangular chambers c.4.5 m/15 ft by 6.4 m/21 ft, each with between two and five spectacular burials of the 16th-c BC, with gold death masks, jewellery, drinking vessels, and weapons. They were claimed (erroneously) by Schliemann as the graves of Homer's Agamemnon and Clytemnestra. » Homer; Mycenae; Schliemann

Shaftesbury, Anthony Ashley Cooper, 1st Earl of (1621–83) English statesman, born at Wimborne St Giles, Dorset. Educated at Oxford, he became a member of the Short Parliament (1640) and of the Barebones Parliament (1653), and was made one of Cromwell's Council of State, but from 1655 was in opposition. At the Restoration he became a baron and Chancellor of the Exchequer (1661–72), a member of the Cabal (1667), an earl (1672), and Lord Chancellor (1672–3). He was dismissed in 1673, and led the opposition to the succession of James, Duke of York (later James II). Charged with treason in 1681, he was acquitted, but fled to Holland in 1682, and died soon after in Amsterdam. » Barebones Parliament; Cabal; English Civil War; Restoration

Shaftesbury, Anthony Ashley Cooper, 3rd Earl of (1671–1713) English philosopher, born in London, the grandson of the 1st Earl of Shaftesbury. Educated in London and Winchester, he entered parliament in 1695, but ill health drove him from politics to literature. He is best-known for his essays, collected as *Characteristics of Men, Manners, Opinions, Times* (1711). He was one of the leading English deists, with a considerable influence in Europe. He succeeded to the earldom in 1699, and in 1711 moved to Naples, where he died. » deism

Shaftesbury, Anthony Ashley Cooper, 7th Earl of (1801–85) British factory reformer and philanthropist, born in London. Educated at Harrow and Oxford, he entered parliament in 1826, and became the main spokesman of the factory reform movement. He piloted successive factory acts (1847, 1859) through parliament, regulated conditions in the coal mines (1842), and provided lodging houses for the poor (1851). A leader of the evangelical movement within the Church of England, he succeeded to his earldom in 1851. He died at Folkestone, Kent. » evangelicalism

shag » **cormorant**

Shah Jahan [shah ja**han**] (1592–1666) Mughal Emperor of India (1628–58), born at Lahore. His reign saw two wars in the Deccan (1636, 1655), the subjugation of Bijapur and Golconda (1636), and attacks on the Uzbegs and Persians. A ruthless but able ruler, the magnificence of his court was unequalled. His buildings included the Taj Mahal, the tomb of his beloved third wife, **Mumtaz Mahal**. In 1658 he was held prisoner by his son Aurangzebe until his death, at Agra. » Aurangzebe; Mughal Empire; Taj Mahal

Shakers The popular name for members of the United Society for Believers in Christ's Second Appearing, founded in England under the leadership of Ann Lee (1736–87), a psychic visionary, who led them to America in 1774. They believe that Christ has appeared with Ann Lee. They are communitarian and pacifist, and their ecstatic dancing gave rise to their popular name. Their acceptance of strict celibacy has led to their virtual disappearance. » Christianity; millenarianism

Shakespeare, William (1564–1616) English dramatist and poet, the greatest English writer, born and died at Stratford-upon-Avon, Warwickshire, the son of **John Shakespeare**, a glover, and **Mary Arden**, of farming stock. Much uncertainty surrounds his early life. He was the eldest of three sons, and there were four daughters. He was educated at the local grammar school, and married **Anne Hathaway**, from a local farming family, in 1582, who bore him a daughter, Susanna, in 1583, and twins Hamnet and Judith in 1585. He moved to London, possibly in 1591, and became an actor. During 1592–4, when the theatres were closed for the plague, he wrote his poems 'Venus and Adonis' and 'The Rape of Lucrece'. His sonnets, known by 1598, though not published until 1609, fall into two groups: 1 to 126 are addressed to a fair young man, and 127 to 154 to a 'dark lady' who holds both the young man and the poet in thrall. Who these people are has provided an exercise in detection for numerous critics.

The first evidence of his association with the stage is in 1594, when he was acting with the Lord Chamberlain's company of players, later 'the King's men'. When the company built the Globe theatre S of the Thames in 1597, he became a partner, living modestly at a house in Silver St until c.1606, then moving near the Globe. He returned to Stratford c.1610, living as a country gentleman at his house, New Place. His will was made in March 1616, a few months before he died, and he was buried at Stratford.

An enormous amount of investigation of the authorship, text, and chronology of the plays marks the modern era of Shakespeare scholarship, including detailed studies of the age in which he lived, and of the Elizabethan stage. Authorship is still a controversial subject for certain plays, such as *Titus Andronicus*, *Two Noble Kinsmen*, *Henry VI*, part I, and his part in *Timon of Athens*, *Pericles*, and *Henry VIII*. This has involved detailed studies of the various editions of the plays, in particular the different quarto editions, and the first collected works, the First Folio of 1623. It is conventional to group the plays into early, middle, and late periods, and to distinguish comedies, tragedies, and histories, recognizing other groups that do

SHAKESPEARE: THE PLAYS

EARLY COMEDIES	WRITTEN	WELL-KNOWN CHARACTERS
The Comedy of Errors	1590–94	Antipholus, Dromio, Adriana
Love's Labour's Lost	1590–94	Armado, Berowne, Costard
The Two Gentlemen of Verona	1592–3	Proteus, Valentine, Julia, Sylvia
The Taming of the Shrew	1592	Petruchio, Katharina, Sly
HISTORIES		
Henry VI Part 1	1589–90	Henry, Talbot, Joan of Arc
Henry VI Part II	1590–91	Henry, Margaret, Jack Cade
Henry VI Part III	1590–91	Henry, Margaret, Richard of Gloucester
Richard III	1592–3	Richard, Margaret, Clarence, Anne
King John	1595–7	John, Constance, Arthur, Bastard
Richard II	1595	Richard, John of Gaunt, Bolingbroke
Henry IV Part I	1596	Henry, Hal, Hotspur, Falstaff
Henry IV Part II	1597	Henry, Hal, Falstaff, Mistress Quickly
Henry V	1599	Henry (formerly Hal), Pistol, Nym, Katherine
Henry VIII	1613	Henry, Katherine, Wolsey
MIDDLE COMEDIES		
A Midsummer Night's Dream	1595	Oberon, Titania, Puck, Bottom
The Merchant of Venice	1596–8	Bassanio, Portia, Shylock, Jessica
The Merry Wives of Windsor	1597	Falstaff, Mistress Quickly, Shallow
As You Like It	1599	Rosalind, Orlando, Touchstone, Jacques
Twelfth Night	1600–02	Orsino, Olivia, Viola, Malvolio, Feste, Sir Andrew Aguecheck
DARK COMEDIES		
Much Ado About Nothing	1598	Beatrice, Benedick, Dogberry, Verges
All's Well That Ends Well	1602–3	Bertram, Helena, Parolles
Measure for Measure	1604–5	Duke, Angelo, Isabella, Mariana
TRAGEDIES		
Romeo and Juliet	1595–6	Romeo, Juliet, Mercutio, the Nurse
Hamlet	1600–01	Hamlet, Ophelia, the Ghost, the Grave-Digger
Othello	1604	Othello, Desdemona, Iago, Cassio
King Lear	1605–6	Lear, Cordelia, the Fool, Kent, Edgar/Poor Tom
Macbeth	1605–6	Macbeth, Lady Macbeth, Banquo/Ghost, the Three Witches
GREEK AND ROMAN PLAYS		
Titus Andronicus	1590–94	Andronicus, Aaron, Lavinia
Julius Caesar	1599	Caesar, Brutus, Cassius, Antony
Troilus and Cressida	1601–2	Troilus, Cressida, Pandarus
Timon of Athens	1605–9	Timon, Apemantus
Antony and Cleopatra	1606–7	Antony, Cleopatra, Enobarbus
Coriolanus	1607–8	Coriolanus, Volumnia
LATE COMEDIES		
Pericles	1607–8	Pericles, Marina
Cymbeline	1609–10	Imogen, Iachimo
The Winter's Tale	1611	Leontes, Perdita, Florizel, Autolycus
The Tempest	1613	Prospero, Miranda, Ferdinand, Ariel, Caliban

not fall neatly into these categories. Details of these groups are shown in the panel. » Burbage; comedy; drama; English literature; poetry; tragedy

shale Sedimentary rock predominantly formed from consolidated and compacted clay deposits. It has a characteristic fissility along the bedding planes (ie it splits easily along closely-spaced parallel surfaces) because of the orientation of the platy clay minerals. Oil shale contains sufficient decayed organic matter that an oil can be extracted from it by destructive distillation. » clay minerals; sedimentary rock

Shalimar Gardens A celebrated garden designed by the Mughal emperor Jahangir for his wife, Nur Jahan, in 1616. The garden is laid out on four terraces by Dal Lake, in Kashmir, India. » Kashmir

shallot [sha**lot**] A variety of onion with clusters of small, oval bulbs, widely grown as a vegetable. » allium; onion

shaman A person thought to possess special powers to communicate with and influence the spirits by dissociating his soul from his body. The spirits assist him in performing his duties, which include discovering the cause of illness, famine, and any other misfortune, and prescribing an appropriate cure. Shamans are found among Siberian and Asian peoples; similar practitioners are found in many other religions, under other names.

shamisen A Japanese lute, with a long, slender neck and three silk or nylon strings which are plucked with an ivory plectrum. It is used principally to accompany singing. » lute; plectrum; string instrument 2 [i]

Shammai [**sham**iy] (c.1st-c BC–1st-c AD) A Jewish scholar and Pharisaic leader, apparently a native of Jerusalem, head of a famous school of Torah scholars, whose interpretation of the Law was often in conflict with the equally famous school led by Hillel. Relatively little is known of Shammai himself, except that his legal judgments were often considered severe and literalistic, compared to Hillel's. Both are often referred to in the Mishnah. » Hillel I; Judaism; Mishnah; Pharisees; Torah

shamrock The name applied to several different plants with leaves divided into three leaflets, including **wood sorrel** (*Oxalis acetosella*) and various species of **clover** (*Trifolium*). Although adopted as the national emblem of Ireland, and worn each year to commemorate St Patrick, its true botanical identity remains uncertain, although many regard **lesser trefoil** (*Trifolium dubium*) a likely candidate. It is a slender annual growing to 25 cm/10 in; flowers yellow, up to 15 clustered in tiny stalked heads up to 9 mm/0.35 in across, petals later turning dark brown; native to Europe, N Africa, and the W African islands (Macaronesia). (Family: *Leguminosae*.) » annual; clover; trefoil

Shan A Tai-speaking people, the second largest minority group in Burma, who ruled Burma during the 13th–16th-c. Buddhists, with a strong identity, they are mainly concentrated in Shan state, constituting half of its population of 3.1 million. Most are rice farmers. » Burma [i]; Tai

Shanghai 31°13N 121°25E; municipality pop (1982) 11 859 748; urban centre pop (1984e) 6 881 300; municipality area 5 800 sq km/2 239 sq ml. Port in E China, on the Yellow Sea, on Huangpu and Wusong Rivers; largest city in China; developed in the Yuan period as a cotton centre; trading centre in the 17th–18th-c; opened to foreign trade, 1842; two airports; two airfields; rail and sea links to other cities; university (1895) and several other higher education institutions; oil refining, shipbuilding, engineering, chemicals, pharmaceuticals, textiles, paper; People's Park, People's Square, Jade Buddha Temple (1882), Industrial Exhibition Hall, museum of natural history, Songjiang County Square Pagoda and Dragon Wall (11th-c), Longhua Temple (c.7th-c); Yu Yuan (Garden of Happiness), 1577, the basis for 'willow pattern' chinaware. » China [i]; Opium Wars; willow pattern

Shankar, Ravi (1920–) Indian sitar player, born at Varanasi. He took up a professional career as a player and composer in the 1940s and, through his foreign tours and recordings, has done much to make Indian classical music better known abroad. » sitar [i]

Shanklin » **Sandown**

Shannon, Gaelic **Rineanna** 52°42N 8°57W, pop (1981) 7 998. Town in Clare county, Munster, W Irish Republic; W of Limerick near R Shannon; duty-free airport; gateway to Ireland for transatlantic visitors; electronics; boat show rally (Jul). » Clare; Irish Republic [i]

Shannon, River River in the Irish Republic, rising in Cavan county, Ulster, and flowing c.385 km/240 ml SW through L Allen, L Ree, and L Derg to Limerick Bay; navigable for most of its length; hydroelectric power at Ardnacrusha. » Irish Republic [i]

SHAPE » **NATO**

Shapur or **Sapor II**, byname **the Great** (309–79) King of Persia (309–79), declared king at his birth by the Persian nobility, and who ruled with the help of regents until the age of 16. Under him the Sassanian Empire reached its zenith. He successfully challenged Roman control of the Middle East, forcing Jovian to cede five provinces to him (363), and establishing Persian control over Armenia. » Artaxerxes I; Jovian; Sassanids

sharecropping A US agricultural practice by which short-term tenants (usually Black) worked land for landlords (usually White) for a percentage of the crop raised. As much a means of labour and racial control as of economic production, sharecropping provided the economic basis of post-slavery White supremacy. » slave trade

sharefarming A form of tenure in which the landlord provides the land, fixed equipment, and often a proportion of the variable inputs, in exchange for an agreed proportion of the final crop. It is well-established in the USA and in many other countries. » tenure

shares Certificates of part ownership of a company, which represent equal amounts of money invested in the company. Companies limited by shares receive their funds from investors when they are first set up, and these funds are taken in exchange for share certificates. Each share represents a vote at a General Meeting of the company, and control of the company is in the hands of whoever owns more than 50% of the shares. A share also entitles the owner to a share of the profits, if enough has been made to declare a dividend. The capital invested to buy shares is called *risk capital*, because in the event of the company becoming insolvent, the shareholder could lose the money invested. » dividend; equity (economics); investment; preference shares; privatization

Shari'a The sacred law of Islam, embracing all aspects of a Muslim's life. The Shari'a has four sources: the *Qur'an* (Koran), the *sunna* or 'practice' of the Prophet Mohammed, *'ijma* or consensus of opinion, and *qiyas* or 'reasoning by analogy'. » Islam; Koran

Sharjah [**shah**ja] or **Shariqah** pop (1980) 159 000; area 2 600 sq km/1 004 sq ml. Third largest of the United Arab Emirates, NE of Dubai; capital, Ash Sharjah; offshore oil production began in 1974; natural gas, ship and vehicle repairing, cement, paper bags, steel products, paint. » United Arab Emirates [i]

shark Any of a large group of active predatory cartilaginous fishes belonging to 19 separate families: *Alopiidae* (thresher shark), *Carcharhinidae* (blue shark, white shark), *Cetorhinidae* (basking shark), *Chlamydoselachidae* (frilled shark), *Dalatiidae* (dwarf shark), *Echinorhinidae* (bramble shark), *Heterodontidae* (Port Jackson shark), *Hexanchidae* (cow shark), *Lamnidae* (mackerel shark), *Mitsukurinidae* (goblin shark), *Odontaspidae* (sand shark), *Orectolobidae* (wobbegong), *Oxynotidae*, *Pseudotriakidae*, *Rhincodontidae* (whale shark), *Scyliorhinidae* (dogfishes, catsharks), *Sphyrnidae* (hammerhead shark), *Squalidae* (dogfishes), *Triakidae* (leopard shark). » basking/blue/goblin/Greenland/hammerhead/mackerel/nurse/thresher/tiger/whale/white shark; cartilaginous fish; dogfish; tope

shark-sucker » **remora**

Sharp, Cecil (James) (1859–1924) British collector of folk songs and dances, born and died in London. Educated at Cambridge, he became a lawyer, then turned to music. He published several collections of British and US folk material, and in 1911 founded the Folk-Dance Society. » folk music

Sharpeville [**shahp**vil] 26°40S 27°52E, pop (1972e) 42 000. Black African township in Transvaal province, NE South Africa, S of Johannesburg; scene of the Sharpeville massacre (1960); centre of the Sharpeville Students National Resistance Movement. » apartheid; Sharpeville massacre; South Africa [i]

Sharpeville massacre (21 Mar 1960) A major incident in the Black African township of Sharpeville in Transvaal province, South Africa, when police opened fire on a crowd demonstrating against the laws restricting non-White movements and requiring non-Whites to carry identification (the *pass laws*); 69 people were killed and 180 wounded. The anti-pass law campaign had been called by both the African National Congress (ANC) and the rival Pan-African Congress (PAC). The massacre produced an international outcry, and made Black nationalism in South Africa increasingly radical. The ANC formed a fighting wing, the *Umkhonte We Sizwe* ('Spear of the Nation'), and both the ANC and PAC were banned. Later in the year South Africa became a republic, and was refused re-admission to the Commonwealth. » apartheid; Black Consciousness Movement; civil rights; Commonwealth, (British); South Africa [i]

Shastri, Lal (Bahadur) (1904–66) Indian statesman and Prime Minister (1964–6), born at Mughalsarai, Uttar Pradesh. He joined the independence movement at 16, and was often imprisoned by the British. He excelled as a Congress Party official, and in Nehru's Cabinet became Minister of Transport (1957), Commerce (1958), and Home Affairs (1960). He succeeded Nehru as Premier, but died of a heart attack in Tashkent, Uzbekistan, the day after signing a 'no war' agreement with Pakistan. » Indian National Congress; Nehru

Shatt al-Arab [**shat** al arab] Tidal river formed by the union of the Tigris and Euphrates Rivers, SE Iraq; flows 192 km/119 ml SE through marshland to enter the Arabian Gulf; part of the Iraq–Iran border in its lower course; wide delta, containing the world's largest date-palm groves; navigable for ocean-going vessels as far as Basra; international commission in 1935 gave control to Iraq, but disputes over navigational rights continued, and were one of the issues that led to the outbreak of the Gulf War. » Gulf War; Iraq [i]

Shavuot(h) » **Shabuoth**

Shaw, Anna Howard (1847–1919) US minister and feminist, born in Newcastle upon Tyne, UK. Her family migrated to the USA, and after a youth of considerable privation she studied at Albion College and Boston University. She became a Methodist minister, joined in the Women's Christian Temperance Union, and after striking up a friendship with Susan B Anthony became active in the women's suffrage movement. She became president of the National American Women's Suffrage Association in 1904, holding office until 1915, and died in Boston. » Anthony, Susan B; Methodism; women's liberation movement

Shaw, Artie, originally **Arthur Arshawsky** (1910–) Bandleader and clarinettist, born in New York City. He tried novel writing and numerous music jobs before he found success as leader of a swing band, notably with 'Begin the Beguine' (1938), 'Star Dust' (1940), and 'Moonglow' (1941). He rivalled Goodman as a clarinet soloist, playing orderly improvisations in a voluble tone. Notoriously, he married eight times, always to a well-known beauty, including actresses Lana Turner, Ava Gardner, and Evelyn Keyes. He quit music altogether in 1955. » clarinet; Goodman

Shaw, George Bernard (1856–1950) Irish dramatist, essayist, and pamphleteer, born in Dublin. In 1876 he left office-work in Ireland and moved to London. In 1882 he turned to socialism, joined the committee of the Fabian Society, and became known as a journalist, writing music and drama criticism, and publishing critical essays. He began to write plays in 1885, and among his early successes were *Arms and the Man* (1894), *Candida* (1897), and *The Devil's Disciple* (1897). There followed *Man and Superman* (1903), *Major Barbara* (1905), *The Doctor's Dilemma* (1906), and several others, displaying an increasing range of subject matter. Later plays include *Androcles and the Lion* (1912), a 'religious pantomime', and *Pygmalion* (1913), an 'anti-romantic' comedy (adapted as a musical play, *My Fair Lady*, in 1956, filmed in 1964). After World War 1 followed *Heartbreak House* (1919), *Back to Methuselah* (1921), and *Saint Joan* (1923). He wrote over 40 plays, and continued to write them even in his 90s. He was also passionately interested in the question of spelling reform, wrote most of his own work in shorthand, and left money in his will for the devising of a new English alphabet on phonetic principles (which came to be called 'Shavian'). In 1935 he was awarded the Nobel Prize for Literature. He died at Ayot St Lawrence, Hertfordshire. » drama; English/Irish literature; Fabian Society; socialism; spelling reform

Shaw, (Richard) Norman (1831–1912) British architect, born in Edinburgh, Scotland. He studied in London, where he practised, becoming a leader of the trend away from Victorian style back to traditional Georgian design, as in Swan House, Chelsea, New Scotland Yard (1888), and the Piccadilly Hotel (1905). He died in London. » Georgian Style

Shawnee Algonkin-speaking N American Indians who originally settled in Ohio, but who were pushed out of the area by the Iroquois. Defeated in 1794 by US forces at the Battle of Fallen Timbers, they were divided up into three sections and settled in Oklahoma. Population c.2 200. » American Indians; Iroquois

she-oak An evergreen, somewhat weeping tree, growing to 18 m/60 ft, native to SE Australia and Tasmania; slender, cylindrical, grooved and jointed stems and branches; leaves reduced to whorls of scales sheathing each joint; flowers also very reduced, males in spikes, females in clusters which resemble cones in fruit. The curious structure and reduction of the various organs are adaptations to the very dry conditions in which the tree grows. (*Casuarina stricta*. Family: *Casuarinaceae*.) » evergreen plants; tree [i]

shear modulus A measure of a material's resistance to twisting; symbol G, units Pa (pascal); also called the **modulus of rigidity** or **torsion modulus**. A higher G value means that the material is harder to twist. It is defined as shear stress divided by shear strain, and is applicable only to solids. For example, steel $G = .8 \times 10^{11}$ Pa. » mechanical properties of matter; strain; stress; torsion

shearwater A petrel with a long slender bill; plumage dark above, dark or pale beneath. Some species with long wings and tail are found over the open ocean, and fish in flight; species with shorter wings and tail fish while swimming near coasts. The name is also used for skimmers. » muttonbird; petrel; skimmer

sheathbill A white, pigeon-like shorebird, native to the Antarctic and sub-Antarctic; short, stout bill with horny cover at base; the only native Antarctic bird without webbed feet; flies reluctantly but well; eats shore animals and seaweed; often scavenges in penguin colonies. (Family: *Chionididae*, 2 species.) » pigeon

Sheba, Queen of [**shee**ba] (c.10th-c BC) Monarch mentioned in *1 Ki* 10 and *2 Chron* 9, perhaps from SW Arabia (modern Yemen), although placed by some in N Arabia, who is said to have journeyed to Jerusalem to test the wisdom of Solomon and exchange gifts, although this may imply a trade pact. The story depicts the splendour of Solomon's court. » Solomon (Old Testament)

sheep A grazing mammal of family *Bovidae*; may be classified as an antelope; eight species in genus *Ovis* (seven wild species and the domestic sheep, *Ovis aries*); male with large spiralling horns; female with small horns (females of some domestic breeds and the European mouflon are hornless); wild sheep have a coarse outer coat and a fleecy under-layer which grows only in winter; domesticated breeds have only the under-layer, which is thick and grows continuously (presumably as a result of selective breeding); mouflon domesticated 10 000–11 000 years ago in Middle East; male called a *ram* or *tup*, female a *ewe*, young a *lamb*. » antelope; aoudad; argali; bighorn; Bovidae; merino; mouflon

sheep-goat effect In parapsychology, an experimental effect in which those who accept the possibility of paranormal effects ('sheep') tend to produce better results under laboratory test conditions than those who do not ('goats'). » paranormal; parapsychology; psi

sheep ked A small, wingless fly that is an external parasite on sheep; feeds by sucking blood; a pest of economic importance that causes staining of the wool. (Order: *Diptera*. Family: *Hippoboscidae*.) » fly; parasitology

sheepdog Any working dog used to guard sheep from wild animals or to assist in herding; also any dog belonging to a breed formerly used for this purpose. » collie; dog; kelpie (zoology); non-sporting dog; Old English sheepdog; Shetland sheepdog; working dog

sheet lightning » **lightning**

Sheffield 53°23N 1°30W, pop(1981) 477 257, urban area (1987e) 532 300. City in South Yorkshire, N England; on the R Don; separated from Manchester to the W by the High Peak of Derbyshire; developed as a cutlery-manufacturing town in the early 18th-c and as a steel town in the 19th-c; city status in 1893; major rebuilding after World War 2 bombing; university (1905); railway; steels, engineering, tool-making, cutlery, silverware, glass, optical instruments; 12th-c cathedral Church of St Peter and St Paul; Mappin Art Gallery; Crucible Theatre; Abbeydale industrial hamlet; Cutlers' Hall (1832). » Hillsborough; Yorkshire, South

Sheffield plate An imitation silver plate made from copper sheet rolled between films of silver, discovered c.1742 by a Sheffield cutler, Thomas Boulsover (1706–88). This technique was exploited commercially by Matthew Boulton in Birmingham. » Boulton; silver plate

Sheffield Shield A silver trophy purchased from a donation of £150 by Lord Sheffield to promote Australian cricket. It has been the object of annual cricket competitions between the colonies (to 1900) and the states (after 1900) since 1892–3. New South Wales won the Shield 39 times to 1986. » cricket (sport) [i]

Shekinah [shek**iy**na] (Heb 'dwelling', 'residence') God's special 'presence' with his people, Israel; in rabbinic works, his immanence, often associated with particular locations where he consecrated a place or object, as with the burning bush at Sinai or the Tabernacle in the wilderness. The motifs of light and glory are frequently linked with it. Some later Jewish philosophers considered it a created entity or intermediary figure distinct from God. » God; rabbi; Tabernacle

Shelburne, William Petty Fitzmaurice, 2nd Earl of (1737–1805) British statesman and Prime Minister (1782–3), born in Dublin. Educated at Oxford, he entered parliament, succeeded to his earldom in 1761, became President of the Board of Trade (1763) and Secretary of State (1766). Made Premier on the death of Rockingham, he resigned when outvoted by the coalition between Fox and North. In 1784 he was made Marquis of Lansdowne, and died in London. » Fox, Charles James; North, Frederick; Rockingham, Marquess of

sheldgoose A S American goose of the genus *Chloephaga* (5 species); eats grass (4 species) or seaweed (the **kelp goose**, *Chloephaga hybrida*); nests on ground. (Subfamily: *Anatinae*. Tribe: *Tadornini*.) » goose

sheldrake » **shelduck**

shelduck A goose-like duck, native to the Old World (except the far N); eats grass, water weeds, and invertebrates; nests in burrows or holes; also known as a **sheldrake**. (Genus: *Tadorna*, 7 species. Subfamily: *Anatinae*. Tribe: *Tadornini*.) » duck; goose

shelf » **continental margin**

shell The mineralized outer covering of a variety of invertebrate animals, such as molluscs and brachiopods; usually containing a large amount of calcium. The calcareous shell of a bird's egg is a secondary egg membrane secreted by the genital duct of the mother bird. » brachiopod; calcium; egg; mollusc

shellac A resin generally obtained from a secretion from the insect *Tachardia lacca*. Solutions of shellac are used as varnishes and French polish. » resin

Shelley, Mary (Wollstonecraft), *née* **Godwin** (1797–1851) British writer, born and died in London. She eloped with Shelley in 1814, and married him two years later. She wrote several novels, notably *Frankenstein, or the Modern Prometheus* (1818), travel books and journals, and edited Shelley's poems and other works after his death (1823). » novel; Shelley, Percy Bysshe

Shelley, Percy Bysshe (1792–1822) British Romantic poet, born at Horsham, Sussex. He attended Eton and Oxford, but was expelled for his pamphlet, *The Necessity of Atheism* (1811). He married Harriet Westbrook in London, and settled in Keswick, where he was influenced by William Godwin, and wrote his revolutionary poem *Queen Mab* (1813). He formed a liaison with Godwin's daughter, Mary, with whom he eloped (1814) and later married. From 1818 he lived in Italy, touring with his family and friends. There he met Byron, and wrote the bulk of his poetry, including odes, lyrics, and the verse drama *Prometheus Unbound* (1818–19). During this tour, he was drowned near Leghorn. » Byron; English literature; Godwin, William; ode; poetry; Romanticism (literature)

shellfish An informal name for edible molluscs and crustaceans collectively; includes groups such as shrimps, crabs, lobsters, clams, bivalves, whelks, and mussels. » crustacean; mollusc

Shelter (National Campaign for the Homeless) In the UK, a charity founded in 1966 to provide help for the homeless and to campaign on their behalf. Its income comes principally from donations.

Sheltie » **Shetland pony; Shetland sheepdog**

Shem Biblical character, the eldest son of Noah, the brother of Ham and Japheth. He is said to have escaped the Flood with his father and brothers, and to have lived 600 years. His descendants are listed in *Gen* 10, where he is depicted as the legendary father of 'Semitic' peoples, meant to include the Hebrews. » Flood, the; Genesis, Book of; Noah

Shema [she**mah**] (Heb 'hear') A well-known ancient Jewish prayer, traced at least to the 2nd-c AD, incorporating the words of *Deut* 6.4–9, 11.13–21 and *Num* 15.37–41, and beginning 'Hear, O Israel: The Lord our God, the Lord is one'. It introduces the Jewish morning and evening prayers, preceding the Amidah and itself preceded by two benedictions. It may be recited in any language and affirms belief in the oneness of God. » Amidah; Judaism; mezuzah; tefillin

Shenandoah River River in West Virginia and Virginia, USA; formed at the junction of the North Fork and South Fork Rivers; flows 88 km/55 ml NE to meet the Potomac R near Harper's Ferry; Shenandoah National Park (775 sq km/300 sq ml). » Virginia

Shenyang, formerly **Mukden** 41°50N 123°26E, pop (1984e) 4 134 800. Capital of Liaoning province, NE China; largest industrial city in NE China; trading centre for nomads, 11th-c; capital of Manchu state, 1625; attacked by Japanese (1931), which led to the establishment of Manchukuo; occupied by Nationalists, 1945; taken by Communists, 1948; renamed, 1949; airfield; railway; university; electrical equipment, engineering, chemicals, textiles, food processing; Imperial Palace (1625–36), Dongling (tomb of Nurhachi, founder of Manchu state), Beiling (tomb of Nurhachi's son and heir, Abukai). » China [i]; Manchukuo

shepherd moons Small natural moons whose gravitational fields serve to confine narrow rings around some of the outer planets. For example, the 'F' Ring of Saturn discovered by Pioneer 11 is a ribbon c.100 km/60 ml wide; its 'braided' structure was observed by Voyager spacecraft, which also discovered moons Pandora and Prometheus near the ring edges. Uranus' Epsilon Ring is similarly bounded by Desdemona and Cordelia. Shepherd moons are believed to control other narrow rings around these planets, but they have not yet been discovered; analogously, small moons within the rings are believed responsible for gaps observed in the rings. » Pioneer programme; Saturn (astronomy); Uranus (astronomy); Voyager project [i]

Shepherd of Hermas A popular 2nd-c Christian work purportedly from Hermas, a Roman slave who was freed and became a merchant. The work is divided into visions, mandates, and similitudes (or parables), and is called 'The Shepherd' after the angel of repentance who appears in one of the visions. Its strong moral earnestness and stress on the need for penitence after baptism appealed to parts of the early Church, which for a time considered it 'inspired', but ultimately distinguished it from the New Testament canon. » baptism; canon **1**; Christianity

shepherd's purse A small annual weed, 3–40 cm/1¼–15 in, found almost everywhere; a rosette of oblong, lobed, or entire leaves and white, cross-shaped flowers; capsules heart-shaped, reminiscent of an old-style peasant's purse. (*Capsella bursa-pastoris*. Family: *Cruciferae*.) » annual

Shepparton 36°25S 145°26E, pop (1983e) 25 420. City in N Victoria, Australia, in the fertile Goulburn Valley; railway; grain, fruit, wool, wine, food processing; Arts Centre; International Village, featuring worldwide tourist information. » Victoria (Australia)

sherardizing A steel protection process named after English inventor Sherard Osborn Cowper-Coles (1866–1935). A steel object is heated in finely divided zinc dust to just below the melting point of the zinc. An amalgam forms, so that the outermost layer of the finished product is pure zinc, which grades into an adherent iron/zinc alloy. It is very corrosion resistant, and good for surface painting. » steel

Sheraton, Thomas (1751–1806) British cabinet maker, born at Stockton-on-Tees, Durham. He settled in London c.1790, wrote a *Cabinetmaker's Book* (1794), and produced a range of Neoclassical designs which had a wide influence on contemporary taste in furniture. He died in London. » Neoclassicism (art and architecture)

Sheridan, Philip H(enry) (1831–88) US general, born at Albany, New York. Educated at West Point, he commanded a Federal division at the beginning of the Civil War, and took part in many of the campaigns. In 1864 he was given command of the Army of the Shenandoah, turning the valley into a barren waste, and defeating General Lee. He had a further victory at Five Forks in 1865, and was active in the final battles which led to Lee's surrender. He died at Nonquitt, Massachusetts, never having lost a battle. » American Civil War; Lee, Robert E

Sheridan, Richard Brinsley (Butler) (1751–1816) Anglo-Irish dramatist, born in Dublin, Ireland. Educated at Harrow, he turned immediately to writing, and settled in London. In 1775 appeared the highly successful comedy of manners, *The Rivals*, and this was followed by several other comedies and farces, notably *School for Scandal* (1777). He became manager of Drury Lane Theatre in 1778, and a Whig MP in 1780. He died in London. » comedy; drama; English literature

Sherman, William Tecumseh (1820–91) US general, born at Lancaster, Ohio. Trained at West Point, he became a general in the Union army during the Civil War. His most famous campaign was in 1864, when he captured Atlanta, and commenced his famous 'March to the Sea', with 65 000 men, which divided the Confederate forces. After capturing Savannah, he moved N through the Carolinas, gaining further victories which helped to bring forward the Confederate surrender. He died in New York City. » American Civil War; Indian Wars

Sherpa A mountain people of Sikkim State and Nepal, India. Related to Tibetans, they share their culture and language. They are famous as mountain traders and porters in the Himalayas. Population c.80 000. » Nepal [i]; Sikkim

Sherrington, Sir Charles Scott (1857–1952) British physiologist, born in London. Educated at Cambridge and Berlin, he taught at London, where he became professor of pathology (1891–5), and was then professor of physiology at Liverpool (1895–1913) and Oxford (1913–35). His research on the nervous system constituted a landmark in modern physiology. Knighted in 1922, he shared the Nobel Prize for Physiology or Medicine in 1932. He died at Eastbourne, Sussex. » Adrian; nervous system

sherry A white wine (usually a blend of younger and older wines), fortified with brandy; named after Jerez de la Frontera in the Andalusian region of Spain, the centre of excellence for sherry. There are several types: *fino* is dry, light-coloured, of a high quality, and usually drunk young; *amontillado* is darker and moderately dry; *oloroso* is fuller and dark, the sweetest available. » brandy; wine

Sherwood Forest An area of heath and woodland, mainly in Nottinghamshire, UK, where mediaeval kings hunted deer. It is famed for being the home of Robin Hood. » Robin Hood

Shetland or **The Shetlands**, formerly **Zetland** pop (1981) 27 277; area 1 433 sq km/553 sq ml. Group of c.100 islands off coast of NE Scotland; 80 km/50 ml NE of Orkney Is; c.20 inhabited; chief islands, Mainland, Unst, Yell, Fetlar, Whalsay; low-lying, highest point Ronas Hill in N Mainland (450 m/1 476 ft); capital, Lerwick, on Mainland; annexed by Norway in 9th-c; annexed by Scotland, 1472; target of first German air-raid on Britain in World War 2 (Nov 1939); cattle and sheep raising, knitwear, fishing, oil services at Lerwick and Sandwick, oil terminal at Sullom Voe; small Shetland ponies, well-known for their strength and hardiness; several prehistoric remains, especially Staneydale Temple (W Mainland), Neolithic or early Bronze Age hall; Jarlshof (S Mainland), remains of three villages occupied from Bronze Age to Vikings; Mousa Broch (Iron Age, on Mousa). » Orkney; Scotland [i]; Three Age System

Shetland pony The strongest of all breeds of horse (can pull twice its own weight), developed on the Scottish Shetland and Orkney Is; height, 9 hands/0.9 m/3 ft; stocky, with short legs; long mane and tail; also known as **Sheltie** or **Shelty.** The taller and more slender **American Shetland pony** was developed in the USA from Shetland stock. » horse [i]

Shetland sheepdog A type of sheepdog developed in the Shetland Is, Scotland; resembles a small collie with a thick coat; also known as a **Sheltie**, or **Shelty**. » collie; sheepdog

shield A geological term for a large region of stable continental crust, usually Precambrian in age and forming the core of a continental land mass. It is predominantly composed of metamorphic and igneous rocks. » Baltic Shield; Canadian Shield; Precambrian era

shield bug A typically shield-shaped, true bug; adults mostly feed on plants, sometimes as predators; c.5 000 species, including some pests of economically important crops. (Order: *Heteroptera*. Family; *Pentatomidae*.) » bug (entomology)

shielding » **screening**

shifting cultivation A system of agriculture found in areas of tropical rainforest; also known as **swidden cultivation**. It is a response to loss of soil fertility and vegetation regeneration which occurs after a few years cultivation, forcing farmers to move to new areas. *Slash and burn* describes the method of vegetation clearance. In some regions people move on to completely new areas. Elsewhere they live in a permanent settlement and practise a form of land rotation known as *bush and fallow*, in which vegetation is allowed to regenerate in areas where soil fertility is exhausted. It is then recultivated. » rainforest

Shih Tzu [shee **tsoo**] A toy breed of dog of Tibetan or Chinese origin; similar to the Pekingese in shape; muzzle short but not flat; thick straight coat, especially on head, where hair cascades from top to cover eyes and ears. » dog; Pekingese

Shihchiachuang » **Shijiazhuang**

Shiites [**shee**iyts] Members of an Islamic religious movement prominent in Iran and Iraq. After the murder of Ali, the son-in-law and nephew of the Prophet Mohammed, his followers continued to support his claim to the Muslim caliphate and became known as *Shi'at* or *Shi'a Ali* ('partisans of Ali') or, more commonly, *Shi'is*, usually anglicized as *Shiites*. They believe that Ali and his followers were both temporal rulers and Imams. Today about 99 per cent of Iranians and 60 per cent of Iraqis are Shiites. The most important group is the 'Twelver' Shiites, who believe that there were twelve imams – Ali and his descendents – after the Prophet Mohammed, and that the twelfth did not die, but disappeared, and one day will return to bring justice to the world. Since the 16th-c, Twelver Shiism has been Iran's state religion. » Ali; imam; Islam; Ismailis; Sunnis

Shijiazhuang or **Shihchiachuang** [shijiah**jwang**] 38°04N 114°28E, pop (1984e) 1 127 800. Capital of Hebei province, N China; a major railway junction; mining (coal, iron ore, limestone, marble), cotton-growing, textiles, dyeing, printing; China's largest pharmaceutical plant; Longcang Temple stela (Sui dynasty), Zhuanlunzang pavilion (10th-c); to the N, 6th-c Buddhist monastery of Longxing Si, containing 10th-c bronze statue of Guanyin, Goddess of Mercy (22 m/72 ft high, with 42 arms). » Buddhism; China [i]

shikki [**shik**ee] Japanese lacquerware, also know as *nurimono*. Lac, a natural varnish from lacquer trees, is applied to wooden cups, trays, tables, and many other items. Hardwearing, a good insulator and shiny, it is well suited to traditional art and craft objects, though often expensive. It is still widely used in homes and restaurants for traditional food boxes, soup bowls, chopsticks, etc. » chopsticks; lacquer

Shikoku [shi**koh**koo] pop (1980) 4 163 000; area 18 795 sq km/7 255 sq ml. Smallest of the four main islands of Japan; S of Honshu and E of Kyushu; bounded N by the Seto Naikai Sea, S by the Pacific Ocean; subtropical climate; mountainous and wooded interior; chief towns, Matsuyama, Takamatsu; rice, wheat, tobacco, soya beans, orchards, copper, camphor. » Japan [i]

Shilluk An E Sudanic-speaking poeple living along the Nile S of Khartoum in the Sudan Republic. They are farmers, with many cattle, and organized into a kingdom under the *reth* or king, the prototype of the 'divine kingship' in ethnographic studies. Population c.500 000. » Nilotes; Sudan [i]

Shiloh [**shiy**loh] The site of an ancient city in C Palestine about 14 km/9 ml N of Bethel; noted as the central sanctuary of the tribes of Israel during the conquest and settlement of Palestine under the tribal judges. It also sheltered the Ark of the Covenant, and was thus a strong unifying force amongst the tribes. It was destroyed c.1050 BC, when the Ark was captured by the Philistines, and the priesthood then moved to Nob. » Ark of the Covenant; Judaism

Shiloh, Battle of (1862) An engagement in the American Civil War in NE Mississippi between Union forces under General Grant and Confederate forces under Albert Sidney Johnston (1803–62). Losses were heavy on both sides, with 13 000 Union and 11 000 Confederate casualties. » Grant, Ulysses S

shingles A condition arising from the re-activation of the chickenpox virus which lies latent in the ganglia of sensory somatic nerves; also known as **herpes zoster**. It causes pain and a blister-like (vesicular) rash over the segmental distribution of a sensory nerve. Common sites are the trunk, the cornea of the eye, and the adjacent skin above the eye. » chickenpox; nervous system; virus

Shinkansen [shingkan**sen**] The Japanese New Tokaido Line, a standard gauge line from Tokyo to Osaka for high speed trains (commonly known as 'bullet trains'), completed in 1964. The network is being extended to cover all main Honshu routes. It uses a fully computerized seat reservation system, like airlines.

It provides an excellent service, and has been commercially successful, unlike many of the old lines. » locomotive [i]; railway

Shinto [**shin**toh] The indigenous religion of Japan, so named in the 8th-c to distinguish it from Buddhism, from which it subsequently incorporated many features. It emerged from the nature-worship of Japanese folk religions, and this is reflected in ceremonies appealing to the mysterious powers of nature (*kami*) for benevolent treatment and protection. By the 8th-c divine origins were ascribed to the imperial family, and in time became the basis for State Shintoism and its loyalty and obedience to the Emperor. In the 19th-c it was divided into Shrine (*jinga*) Shinto and Sectarian (*kyoho*) Shinto, with the former regarded as a 'state cult' and the latter officially recognized as a religion but ineligible for state-support. In 1945, State Shinto lost its official status. » Buddhism; jinja

shinty A 12-a-side stick and ball game originating in Ireland more than 1 500 years ago, taken to Scotland, and now popular in the Scottish Highlands. The playing pitch is up to 155 m/170 yd long and 73 m/80 yd wide with two goals, known as *hails*, at each end. The object is to score goals by using the *caman* (stick) to propel the ball.

Shinwell, Baron Emmanuel, byname **Manny** (1884–1986) British Labour politician, born and died in London. A 'street-corner' socialist in Glasgow, he became an MP in 1922, held junior office in the interwar Labour governments, and in the postwar Labour government was Minister of Fuel and Power, nationalizing the mines (1946), Secretary of State for War (1947), and Minister of Defence (1950–1). Well known for his party political belligerence, in his later years he mellowed into a backbench 'elder statesman'. He was awarded a life peerage in 1970. » Labour Party; socialism

ship A sea-going vessel of considerable size. The Egyptians built river boats around 3000 BC, but at the time of Queen Hatshepsut (c.1500 BC) an expedition to E Africa was mounted using vessels of about 20 m/60 ft in length. These are the first sea-going ships of which there are reliable pictorial records; they were steered by oars over the stern. Great strides were made in ship design by the Phoenicians, who traded throughout the Mediterranean, but they left no pictorial records.

Greeks and Romans built galleys relying on oars for manoeuvrability and much of their propulsion, a square sail coming into use when the wind was favourable. Roman merchant vessels 28–56 m/90–180 ft long were propelled by a large square sail hung from a single mast, with a smaller sail mounted on a bowsprit to improve steering qualities; they were steered with two oars or sweeps mounted on the stern. Viking ships varied in length from 20 m/70 ft to 40 m/120 ft, were propelled by a large square-rigged sail and oars, and steered with a massive sweep hung over the starboard side well aft. By the 15th-c the Portuguese had developed the lateen-rigged caravel into a three- or four-masted ocean-going craft. Out of this grew the carrack, where lateen sails gradually gave way to square sails and the forecastle developed a pronounced overlap at the stem. The stern-mounted rudder appears to have come into general use at about this time.

In Europe, the square rig increased in complexity and refinement until the last decade of the 19th-c. US influence dates from 1845, with the clipper ship. Their ships were generally larger than the British, and very often faster. The ultimate refinement in sail came with the British-built tea clippers, such as the *Cutty Sark*. These ships were immediately made obsolescent by the opening of the Suez Canal (1869) because they could not navigate in this area of light and fickle winds.

In 1801 the first viable steamship, the *Charlotte Dundas*, was used as a tug on the Forth-Clyde canal. The first steamship to cross the Atlantic was the US-built *Savannah*, but she steamed for only 3½ days out of her 25-day passage, sailing for the rest of the time. The first continuous steam crossing of the Atlantic was achieved by the British-owned packet vessel, the 700-ton *Sirius*, in 1838. Brunel's *Great Britain* (1844) was the first screw-propelled, double-bottomed, iron-hulled transatlantic passenger ship. High pressure steam in 1860 heralded the end of the sailing ship's supremacy. Steam turbines were demonstrated at the Spithead Review in 1897, and powered the *Mauretania* when she took the Blue Riband in 1907. The diesel engine, patented in 1892, won ocean-going acceptance in the 5 000 gross ton *Selandia* in 1912; but these engines, though cheaper to run and occupying less space, could not provide the power nor the reliability needed for passenger vessels until the late 1970s. In 1968 the *Queen Elizabeth 2* was built with steam turbines, but in 1987 she was re-engined using diesel-electric propulsion, gaining power and speed with lower fuel costs. In 1988, only 2.8% of the world's ships were steam-powered, but this represented 16.8% of world tonnage.

Nuclear-fuelled vessels provide an alternative means of generating the heat to provide steam to drive turbines. This method is used in government vessels such as ice-breakers, aircraft carriers, and missile-carrying submarines, but it has proved to be uneconomical for merchant vessels. In the 1970s very large tankers were built, powered by steam turbines. When fully laden they displace 600 000 tons, but steam at a relatively modest speed of 15 knots. Future developments will see no great overall increase in ship size, but there will be faster container ships and many large cruise ships, all diesel-engined. » barque; brig; brigantine; bulker; caravel [i]; carrack; clipper ship; container ship; cutter; dredger; galleon; Gokstad ship; icebreaker; longship; obo; reefer; ro ro; sailing rig [i]; schooner; Ship of Cheops; Sutton Hoo ship burial; tanker; trawler; trireme [i]; warships [i]

ship money An English tax on maritime areas to support royal naval forces, abuse of which brought discredit to Charles I. The tax, dating from mediaeval times, had been collected without difficulty under James I. Charles I's extension of the tax to inland shires in 1635 caused opposition. The proposal to make it permanent in 1636 provoked refusals to pay by John Hampden and others; it was outlawed in 1641. » Charles I (of England); Hampden

Ship of Cheops An ancient Egyptian funeral ship found dismantled at Giza in 1954 in one of five boat pits (the last still unexcavated) around the Pyramid of Cheops (?–2566 BC). Perfectly preserved by airless conditions, it comprised 1 224 pieces of timber laid in 13 layers, together with ropes, baskets, and matting. Reconstructed, the ship measures 44 m/143 ft long with a beam of 6 m/19 ft. Carrying six pairs of oars 6.5–8.5 m/21–28 ft long, and a cabin amidships, it displaces 45 tonnes. » pyramid

Shipton, Eric (Earle) (1907–77) British mountaineer. He spent many years climbing in E and C Africa, and obtained much of his knowledge of the East during his terms as consul-general in Kashgar (1940–2, 1946–8) and Kunming (1949–51). Between 1933 and 1951 he either led or was member of five expeditions to Mt Everest, and helped pave the way for the successful Hunt-Hillary expedition of 1953. » Hillary; Hunt, John

shipworm A typically marine bivalve mollusc; body elongate, with reduced shell plates used to burrow into submerged wood such as ship hulls and pilings. (Class: *Pelecypoda*. Family: *Teredinidae*.) » bivalve; mollusc

Shiraz [shee**raz**] 29°38N 52°34E, pop (1983) 800 416. Capital city of Shiraz district, Fars, SW Iran; 184 km/114 ml ENE of Bushehr, its port on the Arabian Gulf; capital of Persia, 1750–79; fifth largest city in Iran; airfield; university (1945); noted for its wines, rugs, hand-woven textiles, silverwork, mosaics. » Iran [i]

shire The largest breed of horse, developed in England from war-horses used to carry knights in armour; used for farm work; height, 17–18 hands/1.7–1.8 m/5½–6 ft; black or brown and white; convex face; long legs with hair covering hooves. » horse [i]

Shiva [**shee**va] One of the three principal deities of the Hindu triad (*Trimurti*) – a god of contrasting features: creation and destruction, good and evil, fertility and asceticism. He is the original Lord of the Dance (*Nataraja*) and his principal symbolic representation is a phallic emblem denoting procreation. » Hinduism; Kali; lingam; Nataraja; Trimurti

Shkodër [**shkoh**duh], Ital **Scutari**, ancient **Scodra** 42°05N 19°30E, pop (1980) 66 500. Market town and capital of Shkodër district, NW Albania, between the R Drin and L Scutari; former capital of Albania; railway; ferrous metallurgy, food-

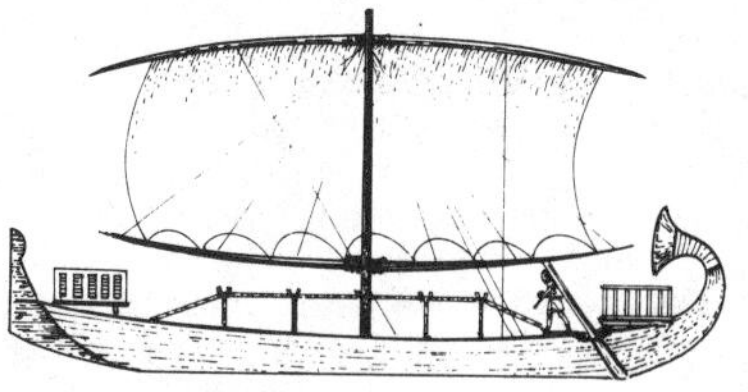

Egyptian ship, c. 1480 BC, length 21 m/70 ft

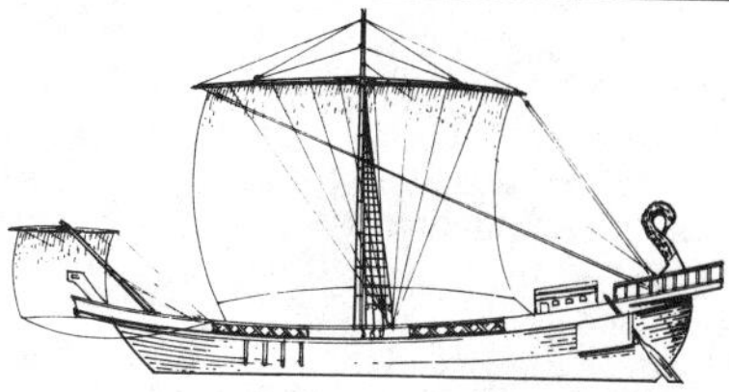

Roman merchantman, AD 200, length 27 m/90 ft

Viking longship, AD 800, length 24 m/80 ft

Portuguese carrack, 1490, length c. 24 m/80 ft

American clipper, *Flying Cloud*, 1851, length 64 m/209 ft

Great Britain, 1844, length 98 m/322 ft

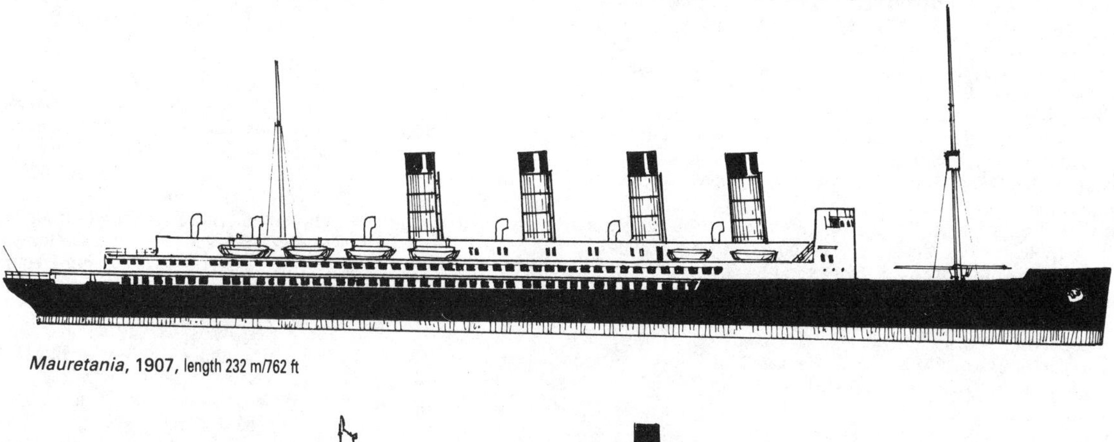

Mauretania, 1907, length 232 m/762 ft

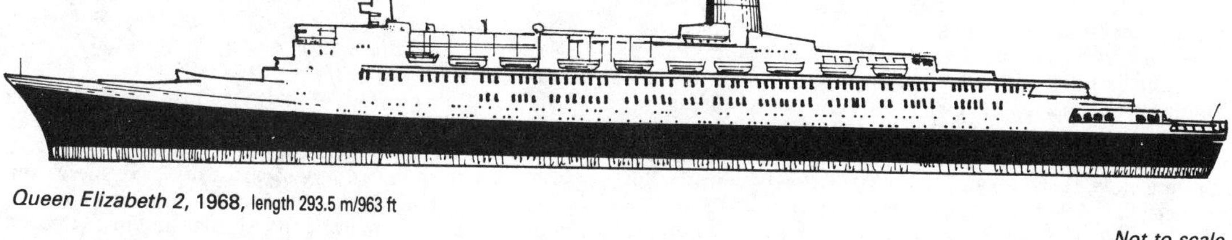

Queen Elizabeth 2, 1968, length 293.5 m/963 ft

Not to scale

Ships

stuffs, tobacco, cement, leather, wood products; 14th-c citadel, cathedral. » Albania [i]

shochu [**shoh**choo] Japanese alcoholic spirits, distilled from potatoes, colourless, but with a certain odour. It is cheaper than saké, and traditionally a rough drink for labourers and poor people. It was popularized in the 1980s as the basis for cocktails, and had an unexpected success with young, fashion-conscious Japanese. It is still drunk (cold) in cheap drinking places. » saké

shock A term used by the lay public to denote the psychological state of fear or grief that follows a sudden accident, calamity, or bereavement. Its medical use refers to a clinical state in which the blood pressure and circulation is insufficient to maintain the functioning of the brain or other organs. This may arise because of loss of blood, because of inadequate pumping of blood by the heart, or because the capacity of the blood vessels to hold a normal amount of blood is suddenly increased. Serious bleeding following trauma leads to shock because the normal response of blood vessels to contract after blood loss is unable to compensate for the loss of blood volume. Acute heart failure arising from a myocardial infarct may result in failure to maintain the necessary blood pressure. Septicaemia sometimes causes the abnormal dilation of blood vessels, and so lowers the blood pressure. » blood vessels [i]; myocardial infarction; septicaemia

shock therapy A term sometimes used as a synonym for electroconvulsive therapy, but also for electrosleep, in which a weak rhythmically-repeated pulse of unidirectional electric current is applied to the brain for the treatment of anxiety, insomnia, and a variety of other medical conditions with a psychological component (eg bronchial asthma and duodenal ulceration). Because the term is ambiguous, psychiatrists often recommend its avoidance. » electroconvulsive therapy; sleep

shock wave A moving, large-amplitude compression wave across which density, temperature, and pressure change abruptly. It is caused by a violent disturbance or supersonic motion. An explosion will produce a pressure shock wave in the surrounding air. A thunderclap is a shock wave caused by the rapid heating of air by lightning. A heavy impact on a solid will cause a stress shock wave. Shock waves cause a non-linear response in the medium. » Čerenkov radiation; sonic boom

Shockley, William B(radford) (1910–89) US physicist, born in London. Educated at the California Institute of Technology and Harvard, he began work with Bell Telephone Laboratories in 1936, and became professor of engineering at Stanford in 1963. In World War 2 he directed US research on antisubmarine warfare. In 1947 he helped to devise the point-contact transistor. He then devised the junction transistor, which heralded a revolution in radio, TV, and computer circuitry. He shared the Nobel Prize for Physics in 1956. » Bardeen; computer; electronics; transistor

shoddy Products made from reprocessed old wool. Strictly the term applies only to the loose fibre, but it is commonly used to describe the products made from shoddy. » wool

shoebill A large, grey, stork-like bird with a large head; bill extremely wide and deep, shaped like a broad shoe; inhabits marshes in C Africa; nocturnal; eats small vertebrates, molluscs, and carrion; also known as the **shoe-billed stork** or **whale-headed stork**. (*Balaeniceps rex*. Family: *Balaenicipidae*.) » stork

Shoemaker, Bill, properly **William Lee**, byname **The Shoe** (1931–) US jockey, born at Fabens, Texas. Only 4 ft 11 in/149.8 cm tall, and weighing 95 lb/43 kg, he has won more races than any other jockey – nearly 9 000 winners between 1949 and his retirement in 1989. In 1953 he rode a world record 485 winners in one season. » horse racing

shofar or **shophar** [**shoh**fah] A Hebrew term for a ram's horn, blown as a musical instrument; mentioned in the Bible as to be sounded particularly at the Jewish New Year (Rosh Hashana) and at the close of the Day of Atonement (Yom Kippur), but also used at war or for announcing important events. In modern times in Israel it has also been blown on Friday afternoons to announce the Sabbath. » Judaism; Sabbath

shogi A Japanese form of chess, believed to have originated in India. Played on a squared board, the pieces have different powers; the object is to checkmate the king. Each player has 20 pieces. » chess

Shogun [**shoh**guhn] A Japanese general, the head of a system of government which dates from 1192, when a military leader received the title *seii-tai-shogun* ('Barbarian Quelling Generalissimo') from the Emperor. Most important were the Tokugawa Shoguns (1603–1868), who ruled as military dictators, the Emperor remaining a figurehead, without power. The Shoguns' rule strictly regulated and controlled life down to the smallest detail. The system ended in 1868. » Meiji Restoration

Sholes, Christopher Latham [shohlz] (1819–90) US inventor, born at Mooresbury, Pennsylvania. A printer in his early years, he went on to develop the typewriter, being granted a number of patents (1868–71). He sold out to the Remington Arms Company, who perfected the invention and marketed it as the Remington typewriter. He died in Milwaukee, Wisconsin. » Remington

Sholokhov, Mikhail Aleksandrovich (1905–84) Russian novelist, born and died near Veshenskaya. After serving in the Red Army (1920), he became a writer, best known for his novel tetralogy *Tikhy Don* (1928–40, The Quiet Don), and other novels of Cossack life. He won the Nobel Prize for Literature in 1965. » novel; Russian literature

Shona A cluster of Bantu-speaking agricultural peoples of E Zimbabwe, who include the Manyika, Kalanga, and Haranga. A powerful state during the 13th–15th-c, with their capital at Great Zimbabwe, they resisted encroachment of White pioneers in the 1890s, but were ruthlessly suppressed. Their members dominate ZANU, the ruling party of Zimbabwe. Population c.5 million. » Bantu-speaking peoples; Great Zimbabwe; Zimbabwe [i]

shooting The use of firearms for pleasure, hunting, sport, or in battle. The first reference to the gun was in 1326, and it soon became the chief weapon of war. It developed as a sport in the 15th-c, the first shooting club being formed at Lucerne, Switzerland, in 1466. Competitive shooting takes many forms and uses different types of weapon. The most popular weapons are the standard pistol, small bore rifle, full bore rifle, air rifle, and air pistol. All events involve shooting at targets, either still or moving, as in clay pigeon shooting. In the UK, hunting for game is very popular among the aristocracy, particularly grouse shooting, which has a specifically defined season (12 Aug to 10 Dec). » biathlon; clay pigeon shooting; game bird; pistol; rifle; RR118

shooting star » **meteor**

shop stewards Workers appointed by their fellows within a trade union to represent them on matters relevant to their pay and conditions. In some instances the post is a full-time job, but often in very small firms, very little time will be spent in these matters. It is estimated that there are over 200 000 union representatives in the UK. » trade union

short story A prose fiction of not more than some 10 000 words. Beyond this lie the similarly imprecise categories 'long short story', 'novella', and 'short novel'. There are many rudimentary forms of short story, including myths, fables, legends, and parables; the mediaeval *fabliau* was a clear progenitor, and Boccaccio and Chaucer were masters of the art. But the modern short story began in the mid-19th-c with Edgar Allan Poe, and was confirmed as a major genre by Maupassant in France and Turgenev and Chekhov in Russia. Many important 20th-c writers have favoured the form on account of its concentration and atmospheric potential. » novel; novella; Chekhov; Faulkner; Fitzgerald, F Scott; Hemingway; James, Henry; Joyce, James; Kipling; Lawrence, D H; Mansfield, Katherine; Maupassant; Poe; Turgenev

Short Take-Off and Landing » **STOL**

shorthand A method of writing at speed to take verbatim records of speech, also known as **stenography**. Shorthand systems variously use symbols which are abbreviations of words (as in *speedwriting*), representations of speech sounds, or arbitrary symbols which the user has to memorize. It has been much used in commerce and industry, and in courts of law, for taking records of the proceedings of meetings, and for the dictation of correspondence. The use of shorthand was popular in Ancient Greece and Rome, came into fashion in England in

SHORTHAND

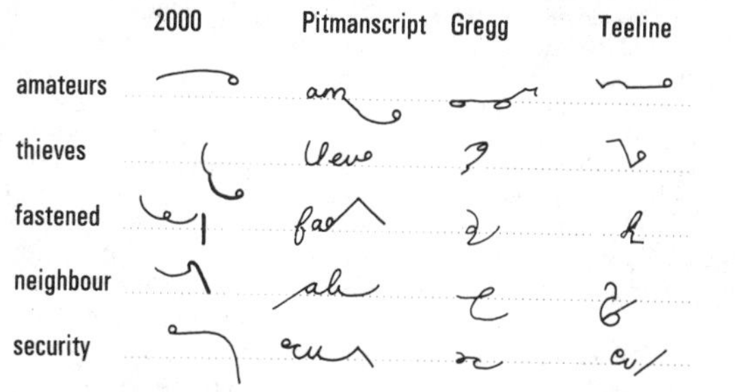

Five words transcribed in Pitman 2000, Pitmanscript, Gregg and – a relative newcomer – Teeline, a combination of shorthand and speed-writing that became increasingly popular in the 1980s.

the 16th-c, and was further popularized by the need for written commercial records with the advent of the Industrial Revolution. However, in recent years, its popularity has lessened with the advent of dictating machines permitting audio playback to the typist.

shorthorn A type of domestic cattle with short horns. In 18th-c England, Charles and Robert Colling improved the type, leading to such breeds as the **Durham** (the *shorthorn* of the American ranchers) and the **Teeswater**. In 19th-c England, Thomas Bates developed the **dairy shorthorn**. Other breeds are the **northern dairy shorthorn, whitebred shorthorn, beef shorthorn**, and the (often hornless) **Lincoln red**. » cattle

shortsightedness » **eye** [i]

Shoshoni N American Indians who once lived in California, Nevada, Utah, and Wyoming. Shoshoni were semi-nomadic hunter-gatherers; Wind River and N Shoshoni acquired horses and hunted the buffalo, culturally resembling Plains Indians. The Comanche split from the Wind River group and became feared raiders in the SW. Population c.9 000, mostly on reservations. » American Indians; Comanche; hunter-gatherers

Shostakovich, Dmitri Dimitriyevich [shosta**koh**vich] (1906–75) Russian composer, born in St Petersburg. He studied at the Conservatory there, and composed his first symphony in 1925. His music was at first highly successful, but his operas and ballets were later criticized by government and press for a failure to observe the principles of 'Soviet realism'. He was reinstated by his fifth symphony (1937), and subsequently composed prolifically in all forms. He wrote 15 symphonies; violin, piano, and cello concertos; chamber music; and choral works. He died in Moscow.

shot put An athletics field throwing event. The shot is a brass or iron sphere weighing 7.3 kg/16 lb for men and 3.6 kg/8 lb 13 oz for women. It is propelled, using only one hand, from a starting position under the chin. The thrower must not leave the 2.1 m/7 ft diameter throwing circle. In competition six throws are allowed. The current world record for men is 23.06 m/74 ft 8 in, achieved by Ulf Timmermann (East Germany, born 1 Nov 1962) on 22 May 1988 at Khania, Greece; for women it is 22.63 m/74 ft 3 in, achieved by Natalya Lisovskaya (USSR, born 16 Jul 1962) on 7 June 1987 in Moscow. » athletics

shotgun A smooth-bore weapon firing cartridges filled with small lead or steel pellets (*shot*), which spread in flight to broaden their destructive effects; widely used by farmers and sportsmen. Single-barrelled, pump-action, multiple-round shotguns have a military application for close-in defence. » firearms

shou » **red deer**

shoulder Commonly used to refer to the rounded region at the top of the arm passing towards the neck and upper back; more specifically, in anatomy, the articulation between the humerus and the the scapula. It is an extremely mobile joint, at the expense of some joint stability. When dislocation occurs, it tends to be a downward and forward movement of the humerus with respect to the scapula. » scapula

shovelboard » **shuffleboard**

shoveller/shoveler A dabbling duck, native to S America (1 species), S Africa (1 species), Australia and New Zealand (1 species), and the N hemisphere (1 species); nests in reed beds; also known as the **spoonbill**. (Genus: *Anas*, 4 species.) » dabbling duck

show jumping Horse jumping over a course containing a variety of strategically placed fences. Most competitions involve all competitors having one attempt at clearing the fences. Those who clear the fences and incur no penalty points are then involved in a 'jump-off' against the clock, where speed as well as accuracy is important. Points are incurred for knocking down a fence, or for refusing to jump a fence. » equestrianism

show trials Originally a series of trials held in Moscow in the late 1930s under Stalin. It refers to any political trial where the accused make a public confession of their 'crimes', although their guilt is often open to doubt. The process tries to justify political repression by allowing the state to point to the use of 'fair' procedures in dealing with opponents of the regime. » Stalinism

showboat A paddle-wheel river steamer complete with theatre and its own repertory company. They were mainly used along the Mississippi in the 19th-c.

shoyu [**shoh**yoo] Japanese soy sauce, made from soya beans, wheat, salt, and water, and traditionally sold in saké shops. It is dark brown in colour, with a different taste from Chinese soy sauce, added to many dishes as flavouring. Soya bean paste (*miso*) is used in many foods, such as *miso-shiru* (bean paste soup). » saké; sashimi; sukiyaki; tempura

Shrapnel, Henry (1761–1842) British artillery officer, who retired from active service as a lieutenant-general in 1825. In c.1793 he invented the shrapnel shell, an anti-personnel device which exploded while in flight, scattering lethal lead shot and other material.

Shreveport 32°31N 93°45W, pop (1980) 205 820. Seat of Caddo parish, NW Louisiana, USA, on the Red R; founded, 1837; developed rapidly after the discovery of oil, 1906; airfield; railway; university; major oil and natural gas centre; lumber and metal products, cotton, telephones, chemicals; Red River Revel (Oct). » Louisiana

shrew A widespread mammal of family *Soricidae* (246 species); an insectivore; mouse-like with a longer pointed snout and small eyes; ears often hidden in fur; often lives near water; some have a venomous bite. The name is also used for several other small mammals, and for the 15 species of African *elephant shrews* (Order: *Macroscelidea*). » insectivore; otter shrew; tree shrew

Shrewsbury [**shrooz**bree, **shrohz**bree], Anglo-Saxon **Scrobesbyrig** 52°43N 2°45W, pop (1981) 59 169. County town in Shrewsbury and Atcham district, Shropshire, WC England; on the R Severn, 63 km/39 ml NW of Birmingham; Roman city of Uriconium to the E; headquarters of Edward I during the struggle for Wales; site of Battle of Shrewsbury (1403); railway; engineering, agricultural trade, market gardening; Church of St Mary, abbey church, Rowley's mansion (1618), 11th-c castle; Shropshire and W Midland agricultural show (May), National Ploughing Championships (Oct). » Edward I; Shropshire

shrike A bird mainly of the Old World, especially Africa; strong bill with hooked tip; grasping, clawed feet; eats insects and small mammals; often hangs prey from thorns or twigs. The **red-backed shrike** (*Lanius collurio*) is also called the **butcherbird**. The name *shrike* is also used for many birds of other families. (Family: *Laniidae*, c.72 species.) » woodchat

shrimp An aquatic crustacean; females typically carry eggs on abdominal legs until ready to hatch into swimming larvae (*zoeae*); many species are of considerable economic importance as food; some are cultured commercially. (Class: *Malacostraca*. Order: *Decapoda*.) » mantis shrimp; prawn; tadpole shrimp

shrimp plant A bushy perennial growing to 1 m/3¼ ft, native to Mexico, named for the flower spikes which fancifully resemble crustacea; stems arching; leaves oval, in pairs; flowers hooded, white, almost hidden by broadly oval, overlapping pinkish bracts. (*Beloperone guttata*. Family: *Acanthaceae*.) » bract; crustacean; perennial

Shropshire, sometimes abbreviated **Salop**, pop (1987e) 396 500;

area 3490 sq km/1347 sq ml. County in WC England, divided into six districts; bounded W by Powys and Clwyd in Wales; drained by the R Severn; county town, Shrewsbury; chief towns include Telford, Oswestry, Wellington, Ludlow; agriculture (especially dairy farming, cattle, sheep, cereals), engineering; Ironbridge Gorge open-air museum. » England [i]; Ironbridge; Shrewsbury

Shrove Tuesday In the UK, the day before the beginning of Lent, so called because traditionally on that day Christians went to confession and were 'shriven' (absolved from their sins). Shrove Tuesday is often known as **Pancake Day** from the custom of making pancakes on that day. » Lent

shrub A woody perennial plant, usually differentiated from a tree by being smaller and having a trunk which produces branches at or near the base; but the distinction is far from clear-cut, and some large shrubs are essentially small trees. Many shrubs are very small, and woody only at the very base, and can easily be mistaken for herbs; but they do not die back to ground level in winter. » herb; tree [i]

shuffleboard A popular deck game played aboard ship. It is a larger version of the popular shove-halfpenny. Wooden discs, usually about 15 cm/6 in in diameter, are pushed along the deck with long-handled drivers and into a scoring area. It is also known as **shovelboard**.

Shultz, George P(ratt) (1920–) US educator and statesman, born in New York City. He studied at Princeton and the Massachusetts Institute of Technology, then taught at MIT and Chicago, where he became Dean of the Graduate School of Business. He was named Secretary of Labor by President Nixon (1969), and went on to hold a number of high governmental posts before returning to private life in 1974. In 1982 President Reagan made him Secretary of State, a post he retained for the rest of the Reagan presidency. » Nixon, Richard M; Reagan, Ronald

Shute, Nevil, originally **Nevil Shute Norway** (1899–1960) British writer, born at Ealing, Middlesex. Educated at Shrewsbury and Oxford, he became an aeronautical engineer, and began to write novels in 1926. After World War 2, he emigrated to Australia, which became the setting for most of his later books, notably *A Town Like Alice* (1949), and *On the Beach* (1957). He died in Melbourne. » novel

shuttle In spinning, a spindle-shaped device holding a bobbin, used to carry the crosswise threads (weft) through the lengthwise threads (warp) during weaving. Few modern weaving machines employ shuttles. » spinning

Shwe Dagon Pagoda An important Buddhist pilgrimage site in Rangoon, Burma. It consists of a magnificent gold-plated shrine (stupa) 98 m/326 ft high. Its tip is set with many thousands of diamonds, rubies, and sapphires. Tradition holds that the Shwe Dagon houses eight of the Buddha's hairs, and that a pagoda has occupied this site for over 2000 years. » Buddha; Rangoon

Shwezigon Pagoda A pagoda erected in the 11th-c near Pagan, Burma, as a reliquary shrine for a tooth and a bone of the Buddha. It is the centre of one of Burma's most popular yearly festivals. » Buddha

si-rex [**siy**reks] » **rex**

SI units » **units** (scientific)

sial The silica and alumina-rich upper part of the Earth's crust which makes up the bulk of the continents and overlies the sima. » alumina; Earth [i]; silica; sima

Sialkot [**syal**koht] 32°29N 74°35E, pop (1981) 296000. City in Punjab province, E Pakistan, E of the R Chenab; railway; rubber goods, ceramics, cutlery, surgical instruments; ancient fort, mausoleum of Sikh apostle Nanak. » Pakistan [i]

Siam » **Thailand** [i]

siamang [**siy**amang] A gibbon native to Malaya and Sumatra; the largest gibbon (armspan of 1.5 m/5 ft); long black coat; web of skin joining second and third toes; throat with large red balloon-like vocal sac (inflates just before calling). (*Hylobates syndactylus*.) » gibbon

Siamese cat A domestic cat of the *foreign short-haired* variety; many breeds, some called **Siamese** in Britain, **short-hair** in the USA; lean, with a triangular face and blue eyes; coat pale with darker 'points' (ie face, legs and tail); many named after the dark colour (eg *red point Siamese* or *red colorpoint short-hair*). » cat

Siamese twins A fault in embryological development in which identical twins are born physically joined together. The deformity ranges from one in which the twins may merely share one umbilical cord to one in which heads or trunks are joined together and cannot be separated. The name derives from the first twins in whom the condition was recognized, Chang and Eng (1811–74), born in Siam (modern Thailand). » embryology

Sian » **Xi'an**

Sian Ka'an [syan **kahn**] A reserve covering over 5000 sq km/1900 sq ml in the Yucatán Peninsula, Mexico; a world heritage area. In addition to the flora and fauna of the region, the reserve also protects 20 Maya archaeological sites and the way of life of c.800 descendants of the Maya Indians. » Mayas; Yucatán

Sibelius, Jean (Julius Christian) [si**bay**liuhs] (1865–1957) Finnish composer, born at Tavastehus. He turned from law to music, studying at the Helsinki Conservatory, Berlin, and Vienna. A passionate nationalist, he wrote a series of symphonic poems based on episodes in the Finnish epic *Kalevala*. From 1897 a state grant enabled him to devote himself entirely to composition, and his seven symphonies (he destroyed his eighth), symphonic poems – notably *Finlandia* (1899) – and violin concerto won great international as well as national popularity. He died at Järvenpää. » Kalevala

Siberia area c.7511000 sq km/2900000 sq ml. Vast geographic region of Asiatic Russia, comprising the N third of Asia; from the Ural Mts (W) to the Pacific Ocean (E), and from the Arctic Ocean (N) to the Kazakhstan steppes and the Chinese and Mongolian frontiers (S); Arctic islands include Severnaya Zemlya, New Siberian Is, Wrangel I; off the Pacific coast are Sakhalin and the Kuril Is; **W Siberian Lowlands** stretch over 1500 km/1000 ml from the Ural Mts (W) to the R Yenisey (E); **C Siberian Plateau** lies between the R Yenisey (W) and the R Lena (E); the **E Siberian Highlands**, including the Altay Mts, rise to 4506 m/14783 ft at Gora Belukha; c.155000 rivers, notably the Ob, Yenisey, Lena; extreme continental climate; average winter temperatures generally below −18°C; January temperatures in NE average −51°C; summer temperatures relatively high, average 15–18°C (Jul), in coldest winter areas; precipitation generally low; tundra extends c.320 km/200 ml inland along the Arctic coast; coal, timber, gold, iron, nickel, dairying, grain, cattle, reindeer, maize, sorghum, soya beans, hydroelectric power; chief cities (Novosibirsk, Omsk, Krasnoyarsk, Irkutsk, Khabarovsk, Vladivostok) lie on the Trans-Siberian Railway; used as a penal colony and place of exile for political prisoners; vast areas occupied by counter-revolutionary armies, after the 1917 Revolution, overthrown by Soviet forces in 1922; dramatic economic development under the 5-year plans, relying heavily on forced labour and population resettlement to establish mining, industrial, and agricultural installations. » Asia; Kamchatka; Kuznets Basin; Russia; Trans-Siberian Railway; tundra

Siberian argali » **argali**

Siberian husky A friendly medium-sized Arctic spitz breed of dog developed in Siberia; coat thick, soft, white with grey or tan; tail carried in single curve over back, or relaxed when at rest. » husky; spitz

Siberian Plateau, Central, Russ **Sredne Sibirskoye Ploskogorye** Upland region in E Siberian Russia, between the R Yenisey (W) and the R Lena (E); average height, 300–800 m/1000–2500 ft. » Siberia

Siberut [seebuh**root**] area 500 sq km/193 sq ml. Island 140 km/87 ml off the W coast of Sumatra, Indonesia; a nature and 'traditional use' reserve area protecting the dwarf gibbon, pig-tailed langur, Mentawi leaf monkey, and Mentawi macaque; air connections with Padang. » Indonesia [i]

Sibyl or **Sibylla** In Roman legend, a prophetess who uttered mysterious wisdom. Aeneas met the Cumaean Sibyl, who was inspired by Apollo and whose prophecies were written on leaves; she had been given a thousand years of life, and eventually shrank to a tiny creature hung up in a bottle. Later there were said to be ten Sibyls, and because of Virgil's Fourth

Eclogue, they became famous in Christian art, as in the Sistine Chapel. The **Sybilline Books** were nine books of prophecy offered by the Sybil to Tarquinus Priscus, who refused to pay her price; she destroyed three, and came again, with the same result; she destroyed three more, and then Tarquin bought the remainder for the price originally asked. » Apollo (mythology)

Sicilian Vespers The wholesale massacre of the French in Sicily which began the Sicilian revolt against Charles of Anjou, King of Naples-Sicily, and a war ending in 1302. It was so called because the first killings occurred during a riot in a church outside Palermo at vespers (evensong) on Easter Monday, 1282. » Angevins

Sicily, Ital **Sicilia** pop (1981) 4 906 878; area 25 706 sq km/9 922 sq ml. Largest and most populous island in the Mediterranean, separated from the mainland of Italy by the narrow Strait of Messina; length 288 km/179 ml; width 192 km/119 ml; settled by the Greeks, 8th-c BC; province of Rome, 3rd-c BC; Norman conquest, 11th-c; conquest by Aragon, 1284; Kingdom of the Two Sicilies, 1815; conquest by Garibaldi, 1860, and unification with Italy; capital, Palermo; chief towns, Trapani, Messina, Catania; mountainous, average height 450 m/1 450 ft; Monti Nebrodi (N) rise to nearly 2 000 m/6 500 ft; large earthquake zone on E coast, culminating in Mt Etna (3 323 m/10 902 ft), highest point; an under-developed area, with considerable poverty; intensive vegetable growing, fruit, wine in fertile coastal areas; arable and pastoral farming in dry interior; fishing, salt extraction, petrochemicals, food processing, potash, asphalt, marble, tourism. » Etna, Mount; Garibaldi; Italy [i]; Messina, Strait of; Palermo; Sicilian Vespers

Sickert, Walter (Richard) (1860–1942) British artist, born in Munich, Germany. After three years on the English stage, he turned to art, studying in London and Paris, where he met Degas, and used his techniques to illustrate music hall interiors and London life. The Camden Town Group (later the London Group) was formed under his leadership c.1910, and he became a major influence on later English painters. He died at Bath, Somerset. » Camden Town Group; Degas; English art

sickle cell disease An inherited chemical abnormality of haemoglobin (the red pigment contained within red blood cells), in which the red cells contain haemoglobin S instead of the normal haemoglobin A. As a result the cells become sickle-shaped in place of their normal biconcave circular form. Such cells are more fragile than normal; they do not survive as long in the circulation, and anaemia is common. Because of their shape, thrombosis occurs within the blood vessels, giving rise to multiple tissue infarcts. The disease is common in Africa. » haemoglobin; thrombosis

Siddons, Sarah, *née* **Kemble** (1755–1831) British actress, born at Brecon, Wales, the eldest child of Roger Kemble. She was a member of her father's theatre company from her earliest childhood, and in 1773 married her fellow actor, **William Siddons**. She gained a great reputation in the provinces, and after playing at Drury Lane in 1782 became the unquestioned queen of the stage, unmatched as a tragic actress. She retired in 1812, and died in London. » Kemble; theatre

side drum A shallow drum with a skin at each end, the upper one struck with a pair of wooden sticks, the lower fitted with 'snares' (strings of metal or gut) which, when engaged, give the tone a rasping edge. It is used in orchestras, dance bands, and military bands, and is worn slightly to one side when marching (hence the name). » drum; percussion [i]; tabor

sidereal day » day

sidereal time Time measured by considering the rotation of the Earth relative to the distant stars (rather than to the Sun, which is the basis of civil time). » solar time; time

sidewinder A snake which moves by pushing its head forward onto the ground, then winding the body forwards and sideways until it lies stretched out to one side; meanwhile the head is moved forward again. Repeating this behaviour allows the snake to move rapidly over soft sand. Sidewinding is used by several species, especially vipers (eg the horned viper), but no species uses it all the time. *Crotalus cerastes* (the N American horned rattlesnake) usually uses sidewinding, and is commonly called the **sidewinder**. » horned viper; rattlesnake; viper [i]

Sidewinder

Sidi bel Abbès [**si**dee bel **a**bes] 35°15N 0°39W, pop (1982) 165 266. Chief town of Sidi bel Abbès department, N Algeria, N Africa; 56 km/35 ml S of Oran; originally a walled town, and a military post under French occupation; headquarters of the French Foreign Legion until 1962; railway; cereals, wine, machinery. » Algeria [i]

Siding Spring Observatory An observatory in the Warrumbungle Mts of New South Wales, Australia, administered by the Australian National University. It is the site of the Anglo-Australian telescope and the new Australian National University telescopes. » observatory [i]; telescope [i]

Sidmouth (of Sidmouth), Henry Addington, 1st Viscount (1757–1844) British Tory statesman and Prime Minister (1801–4), born in London. Educated at Winchester and Oxford, he left law for politics, and became an MP in 1783. He was Speaker of the House (1789–1801) when, upon Pitt's resignation, he was invited to form a ministry. His administration negotiated the Peace of Amiens (1802), which held for barely a year. His government ended in 1804, when he was created a viscount. He later became Home Secretary under Liverpool (1812–21), unpopular for coercive measures such as the Six Acts of 1819. He died at Richmond, Surrey. » Liverpool, Earl of; Napoleonic Wars; Pitt (the Younger)

Sidney, Algernon (1622–83) English Whig politician, born at Penshurst, Kent. He became a cavalry officer in the English Civil War on the parliamentary side, and was wounded at Marston Moor (1644). In 1645 he entered parliament, and served as governor in several cities. An extreme Republican, he resented Cromwell's usurpation of power, and retired to Penshurst (1653–9). After the Restoration he lived on the Continent, but in 1677 was pardoned and returned to England. However, in 1683, he was implicated on very little evidence in the Rye House Plot, and beheaded in London. » English Civil War; Rye House Plot; Whigs

Sidney, Sir Philip (1554–86) English poet, born at Penshurst, Kent, and educated at Shrewsbury and Oxford. He gained Elizabeth I's displeasure when he advised her against a projected marriage plan, and in 1580 left the court. Knighted in 1583, he was sent to the Netherlands to assist in the struggle against Spain, and was fatally wounded at Zutphen. His literary work, written 1578–82, was not published until after his death. It includes the unfinished pastoral romance, *Arcadia*, the *Defence of Poesie*, and a sonnet cycle, *Astrophel and Stella*. » English literature; pastoral; poetry; sonnet

Sidon [**siy**dn] 33°32N 35°22E, pop (1980e) 24 740. Seaport capital of W Lebanon, on the Mediterranean Sea, 35 km/22 ml N of Tyre, at the centre of a well-watered coastal plain; founded in the third millennium BC; once noted for its glass and purple dyes; railway; oil refining; Crusader castle; ruins of Phoenician Temple of Echmoun nearby. » Lebanon [i]

Sielmann, Heinz [**zeel**man] (1917–) German naturalist and nature film photographer, born at Königsberg. He began to make films in 1938, and won the German Oscar for documentary films three years running (1953–5). He evolved techniques enabling him to film the inside of animal lairs and birds' nests, which revolutionized the study of animal behaviour.

siemens [seemuhnz] SI unit of electrical conductance; symbol S; defined as 1 divided by resistance as measured in ohms. » resistance; Siemens; units (scientific); RR70

Siemens, (Ernst) Werner von [zeemuhns] (1816–92) German engineer, born at Lenthe, Hanover. He joined the Prussian army, and in 1844 took charge of the artillery workshops at Berlin. He developed the telegraphic system in Prussia, devised several forms of galvanometer, and determined the electrical resistance of different substances. He founded a telegraph manufacturing firm in 1847, was ennobled in 1888, and died in Berlin. His three brothers were also involved in industry, notably **(Karl) Wilhelm** (1823–83, known as (Charles) William, upon moving to England in 1844), who invented a new steel-making technique in 1861. » blast furnace [i]; galvanometer; siemens; telegraphy

Siena [seeayna] 43°19N 11°19E, pop (1981) 61 989. Capital town of Siena province, Tuscany, C Italy; 70 km/43 ml S of Florence; founded by the Etruscans; centre of the Ghibelline faction and a rival of Florence, 12th-c; influential centre of mediaeval art; archbishopric; university (1240); major tourist city; cathedral (13th-c); town hall (13th-c) with tower, Torre del Mangia (14th-c); Palazzo Buonsignori (14th-c), Church of San Domenico (13th–14th-c), house of St Catherine; Palio parade and horse race (Jul–Aug). » Catherine of Siena, St; Ghibellines; Sienese School; Tuscany

Sienese School A school of art which flourished in Siena in the 14th-c and early 15th-c. Great artists included Duccio, Martini, and the Lorenzetti brothers. Sienese art is more charming and decorative than that of Florence, less dramatic, and has deep roots in the Gothic and Byzantine traditions. » Florentine School; International Gothic; Italian art; school (art); Siena; Duccio di Buoninsegna; Lorenzetti; Martini

Sienkiewicz, Henryk (Adam Alexander Pius) [shengkyay-vich] (1846–1916) Polish novelist, born near Luków. Educated at Warsaw, he travelled in the USA, and in the 1870s began to write articles, short stories, and novels. His major work was a war trilogy about 17th-c Poland, beginning with *Ogniem i mieczem* (1884, With Fire and Sword), but his most widely-known book is the story of Rome under Nero, *Quo Vadis?* (1896). He won the Nobel Prize for Literature in 1905, and died at Vevey, Switzerland. » Nero; novel; Polish literature

Sierra Club A US private, non-profit conservation organization. It was founded by the US naturalist and writer, John Muir (1838–1914) in 1892. » conservation (earth sciences)

Sierra Leone, official name **Republic of Sierra Leone** [syera leeohn] pop (1990e) 4 151 000; area 72 325 sq km/27 917 sq ml. Coastal republic in W Africa, divided into four provinces; bounded N by Guinea, SE by Liberia, and S by the Atlantic Ocean; capital, Freetown; chief towns, Bo, Sefadu, Makeni, Kenema, Lunsar; timezone GMT; population chiefly African (eg Mende, Temne); official language, English, with Krio widely spoken; chief religions, local beliefs (70%), Islam (25%); unit of currency, the leone; length, 322 km/200 ml; width 290 km/180 ml; low narrow coastal plain; W half rises to an average height of 500 m/1 600 ft in the Loma Mts; highest point, Loma Mansa (1 948 m/6 391 ft); Tingi Mts (SE) rise to 1 853 m/6 079 ft; equatorial climate, with a rainy season (May–Oct); highest rainfall on the coast; temperatures uniformly high throughout the year, c.27°C; average annual rainfall at Freetown, 3 436 mm/135 in; first visited by Portuguese navigators and British slave traders; land bought from local chiefs by English philanthropists who established settlements for freed slaves, 1780s; British Crown Colony, 1808; hinterland declared a British protectorate, 1896; independence, 1961; republic, 1971; governed by a president, cabinet, and 127-member parliament; mining is the most important sector of the economy; diamonds represent c.60% of exports; bauxite, gold, titanium, iron ore, columbium, limestone, salt, aluminium, chromite; over 70% of the population involved in subsistence agriculture, chiefly rice, coffee, cocoa, ginger, palm kernels, cassava, citrus fruits; food processing, soap, timber, furniture. » Freetown; slave trade; RR27 national holidays; RR60 political leaders

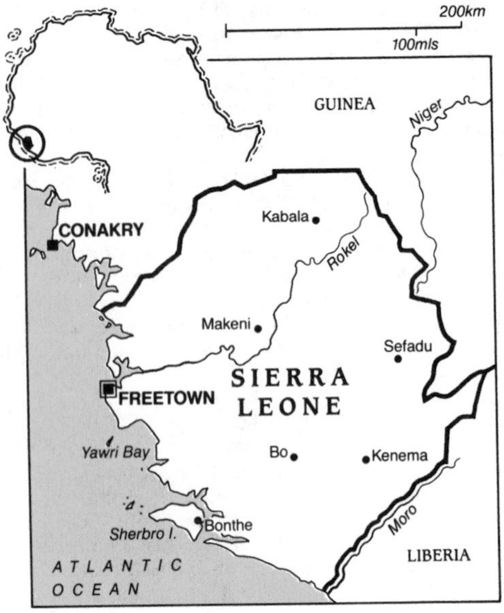

□ international airport

Sierra Nevada (Spain) [syera nayvahda] Mountain range in Andalusia, S Spain, rising to 3 478 m/11 411 ft at Mulhacén, the highest peak in continental Spain. » Spain [i]

Sierra Nevada (USA) [syera nuhvahda] Mountain range in W USA, mainly in E California; extends NW–SE for 725 km/450 ml between the Cascade and Coastal Ranges; highest point in the USA outside Alaska, Mt Whitney (4 418 m/14 495 ft); contains Yosemite, Sequoia and Kings Canyon national parks. » California

Sierra Nevada de Mérida [syera nayvahda thay mayreetha] Mountain range in W Venezuela; a spur of the Andes; length, 500 km/300 ml; width, 50–80 km/30–50 ml; rises to 5 007 m/16 427 ft at Pico Bolívar, highest peak in Venezuela; world's highest cable railway runs to Pico Espejo (4 765 m/15 633 ft). » Venezuela [i]

sievert [seevert] In radioactivity, the SI unit of dose equivalent, equal to absorbed dose multiplied by the relative biological effectiveness; symbol Sv; because it takes account of different radiations' ability to cause biological damage, Sv is used in radiation safety measurements. » radioactivity units [i]; units (scientific); RR70

Sièyes, Emmanuel Joseph, Comte ('Count'), byname **Abbé Sièyes** [syayes] (1748–1836) French cleric and political theorist, born at Fréjus. His pamphlet, *Qu'est-ce que le tiers-état?* (1789, What is the Third Estate?) stimulated bourgeois awareness and won him great popularity. He became a member of the National Convention, and later served on the Committee of Public Safety (1795) and in the Directory. In 1799, he helped to organize the revolution of 18th Brumaire, becoming a member of the Consulate. When Napoleon assumed supreme power, his authority waned, and he withdrew to his estates. He was exiled at the Restoration (1815), lived in Brussels until 1830, returning after the July Revolution to Paris, where he died. » French Revolution [i]; July Revolution; Napoleon I

sifaka [sifaka] A leaping lemur; long silky hair and long tail; variable in colour (usually white with dark patches); small gliding membranes from arms to sides of body; can leap 10 m/33 ft between trees; eats leaves. (Genus: *Propithecus*, 2 species.) » lemur

sigillography » **seal** (communication)

Sigiriya An ancient city in C Sri Lanka – also the rock which towers 180 m/600 ft above it; a world heritage site. The rock is surmounted by a palace built in the 5th-c by King Kasyapa I. Sigiriya is renowned not only for the grandeur of its ruins, but also for the frescoes adorning the W cliffs of the rock. » Sri Lanka [i]

Sigismund (Emperor) (1368–1437) Holy Roman Emperor (1433–7), the son of Charles IV. He became King of Hungary (1387), German King (1411), and King of Bohemia (1419). In 1396 he was defeated by the Ottoman Turks at Nicopolis, but later conquered Bosnia, Herzegovina, and Serbia. As Emperor, he induced the Pope to call the Council of Constance to end the Hussite schism (1414), but made no effort to uphold the safe conduct he had granted to John Huss, and permitted him to be burned. As a result, his succession in Bohemia was opposed by the Hussites. He died at Znojmo, Moravia. » Huss

sign Something that stands for something else, which it may or may not resemble, the relationship often being agreed by convention; for example, an arrow indicates direction, and greying hair the ageing process. In semiotics a sign comprises a *signifier* (its physical appearance, sound, etc) and a *signified* (the mental concept it evokes). Each sign's meaning is determined partly by its differential relationship with other signs in the same code, partly by its relationship with the thing it stands for. *Signification* is the process by which signs acquire meaning in a specific cultural context. » semiotics; symbol

sign language A communication system in which manual signs are used to express a corresponding range of meanings to those conveyed by spoken or written language. There are several different kinds of sign language. The most widely-used are those which have developed naturally in a deaf community, such as the American, British, French, and Swedish Sign Languages. Contrary to popular belief, such languages are not mutually intelligible, as they use different signs and rules of sentence structure. There are also several systems which have been devised by educators and linguists for working with language-handicapped populations, such as Seeing Essential English (1966), the Paget-Gorman Sign System (1951), and Cued Speech (1966). The study of sign languages has been traced back to the work of Abbé Charles Michel de l'Epée (1712–89), who in 1775 developed a sign language for use in a Paris school for the deaf. » American Sign Language; augmentative and alternative communication; dactylology; RR82

Signac, Paul [seen**yak**] (1863–1935) French artist, born and died in Paris. He exhibited in 1884 with the Impressionists, and was later involved in the Neoimpressionist movement. With Seurat he developed Divisionism (but using mosaic-like patches of pure colour rather than Seurat's pointillist dots), mainly in seascapes. In his writing he sought to establish a scientific basis for his theories. » Divisionism; French art; Impressionism (art); Seurat

signal detection theory An approach to the detection of physical signals, developed in communication engineering, but widely applied in experimental psychology. The theory holds that, when attempting to detect differences between sources of stimulation, responses are governed by two factors: the observer's sensitivity and the observer's decision criteria. It provides rigorous methods and mathematical tools for measuring both factors. » experimental psychology; psychophysics

Signorelli, Luca [seenyor**el**lee], also known as **Luca da Cortona** (c.1441–1523) Italian painter, born and died at Cortona. He painted many frescoes at Loreto, Rome, Florence, Siena, Cortona, and Orvieto, where the cathedral contains his greatest work, the frescoes of 'The Preaching of Anti-Christ' and 'Last Judgment' (1500–4). He was one of the painters summoned by the Pope in 1508 to adorn the Vatican, and dismissed to make way for Raphael. » fresco; Italian art; Raphael

Sigurd [**see**gerd] In Norse mythology, the son of Sigmund the Volsung, who kills Fafnir the dragon and wins Brunhild. He marries Gudrun, having forgotten Brunhild, and is killed by Gudrun's brother Gutthorn. Virtually the same story is told of **Siegfried** [**seeg**freed] in German legends. » Brunhild; Gudrun; Nibelungen

sika [**see**ka] A true deer native to E Asia (introduced in New Zealand and UK); brown (with pale spots in summer) with white rump; white spot halfway down rear leg; long antlers; can interbreed with the red deer to produce fertile offspring; also known as **Japanese deer**. (*Cervus nippon*.) » deer; red deer

Sikh Wars [seek] Two campaigns (1845–6, 1848–9) between the British and the Sikhs which led to the British conquest and annexation of the Punjab, NW India (Mar 1849).

Sikhism [**seek**izm] A religion founded by the Guru Nanak (1469–1539) in the Punjab area of N India. Under his leadership and that of his nine successors Sikhism prospered. It is called a religion of the gurus, and seeks union with God through worship and service. God is the true Guru, and his divine word has come to humanity through the ten historical gurus. The line ended in 1708, since when the Sikh community is called guru. The Adi Granth, their sacred scripture, is also called a guru. The Sikh understanding of life is closely related to Punjab identity. » Adi Granth; guru; Punjab (India); religion

Sikkim [**sik**im] pop (1981) 315 682; area 7 299 sq km/2 817 sq ml. State in NE India, in the E Himalayas; bounded W by Nepal, N by China, and E by China and Bhutan; ruled by Namgyal dynasty, 14th-c until 1975; part of British Empire, 1866–1947; protectorate of India, 1950; voted to become a state, 1975; capital, Gangtok; governed by a 32-member Assembly; Mt Kangchenjunga on Nepal border; inhabited mostly by Lepchas, Bhutias, and Nepalis; state religion, Mahayana Buddhism, but many of the population are Hindu; rice, maize, millet, cardamom, soybean, fruit, tea; cigarettes, copper, zinc, lead, watches, carpets, woodwork, silverwork. » India [i]

Sikorski, Władysław (Eugeniusz) (1881–1943) Polish general, statesman, and Prime Minister (1922–3), born in Galicia (part of modern Poland). Educated at Kraków and Lvóv, he fought in the Russian-Polish War (1920–1), became Commander-in-Chief (1921), and Premier. After Piłsudski's coup (1926) he retired and wrote military history in Paris. He returned to Poland in 1938, but on being refused a command, fled to France, becoming Commander of the Free Polish forces and from 1940 Premier of the Polish government in exile in London. He was killed in an air crash at Gibraltar. » Piłsudski; Poland [i]

Sikorsky, Igor (Ivan) (1889–1972) US aeronautical engineer, born in Kiev, Russia. Educated at St Petersburg and Kiev, he built and flew the first four-engined aeroplane (1913), then emigrated to the USA (1919), became a US citizen (1928), and founded the Sikorsky Aero Engineering Corporation (1923). He built several flying boats, and in 1939 produced the first successful helicopter. He died at Easton, Connecticut. » aeronautics; helicopter

silage A fodder made from grass, maize, or other leafy material and preserved in an air-tight tower-silo or silage pit. Initial fermentation creates organic and amino acids, which act as preservatives. Silage is fed mainly to beef and dairy cattle, but can be used by other ruminants. » fermentation

Silbury Hill An artificial chalk mound, 40 m/130 ft high, erected c.2700 BC near Avebury in S England. Probably prehistoric Europe's largest barrow, it has a base area of 2.2 ha/5.4 acres, a volume of 354 000 cu m/463 000 cu yd, and was an estimated 18 million man-hours in construction. Excavated by tunnelling in 1776, 1849, and 1968–70, it remains archaeologically enigmatic. » Avebury

Silchester Situated SW of Reading, UK, Silchester's ancient name was Calleva Atrebatum. One of the three main Belgic towns (*oppida*) of pre-Roman Britain, it was also a prosperous place in Roman times until its mysterious abandonment at an unknown date. » Britain, Roman

Sileni [siy**lee**nee] Followers of Dionysus, depicted with horse ears, tail, and legs, or as old men in need of support (*Papposileni*). They could give good advice to humans if caught. The name is a plural form of *Silenus*. » Silenus

silent film Before the use of sound film, motion pictures which relied entirely on visual performance, the words of any spoken dialogue appearing on the screen only as occasional sub-titles between picture scenes. But cinema presentation was far from silent, with musical accompaniment ranging from a large orchestra in major theatres down to continuous piano in smaller halls. » cinema; sound film

Silenus [siy**lee**nuhs] In Greek mythology, a demi-god, who fostered and educated Dionysus. He is represented as a festive old man, usually quite drunk.

Silesia [sileezha], Czech **Slezsko**, Polish **Śląsk**, Ger **Schlesien** Region of EC Europe on both banks of the R Oder in SW Poland, NC Czechoslovakia, and SE Germany; bounded S by Sudetes Mts; disputed area between Austria and Prussia, 17th–18th-c; divided into Upper and Lower Silesia, 1919; greater part granted to Poland, 1945; a largely industrial region, including the coal-mining and metal industries of Katowice and nearby cities. » Czechoslovakia [i]; Poland [i]

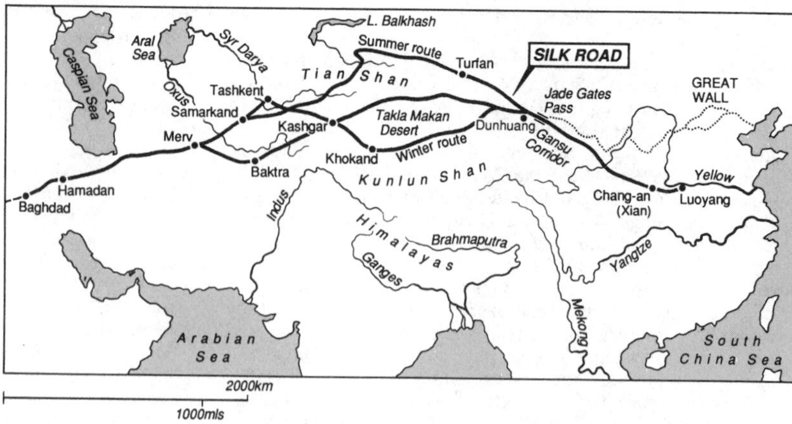

silhouette A technique of paper cut-out picture popularized by French finance minister Étienne de Silhouette (1709–67) and used for cheap miniature portraits until the rise of photography in the mid-19th-c. The term is often extended to cover any type of dark image against a light background, or light on dark, as in Greek vase-painting.

silica Silicon dioxide (SiO_2), the main constituent of the Earth's crust, occurring in nature as pure minerals or combined with other elements in silicate minerals. The crystalline forms of silica are quartz, tridymite, and cristobalite, which are progressively higher temperature phases, and the cryptocrystalline varieties termed chalcedony. Amorphous silica is found naturally in opal, and may be produced by the rapid cooling of molten silica; it is used in the production of glass and cement. » chalcedony; opal; quartz; sial; silicate minerals; sima

silicate minerals A group of minerals constituting about 95% of the Earth's crust, and containing silicon and oxygen combined with one or more other elements. Structurally they are all based on SiO_4, the tetrahedron, and most are complex polymeric structures of tetrahedra. They are classified according to the degree of polymerization, from silicates containing isolated SiO_4 groups (eg olivines, garnets) to rings (eg beryl) to chain silicates (eg pyroxenes (single chains) and amphiboles (double chains), sheets (eg micas, clays), and three-dimensional frameworks (eg quartz, feldspars)). » polymerization; silicon

silicon Si, element 14, melting point 1 410°C. A grey solid non-metal, the second most common element, 26% by weight, it is the second element in the carbon family, and likewise forms mainly covalent compounds, with a valence of 4. It does not occur uncombined in the Earth's crust, and is virtually always found combined with oxygen. In addition to a large number of minerals which are essentially SiO_2, it occurs in many alumino-silicates. Very pure silicon is widely used in electronic devices. It is also doped with controlled amounts of aluminium, phosphorus, and other elements to alter its conductivity. Silicates make up most of brick, stone, cement, and glass. » carbon; chemical elements; silicon carbide; silicone

silicon carbide SiC. A compound produced by fusing a mixture of carbon and silica; also known as **carborundum**. It has several crystalline modifications, all of which are high-melting and hard, and is used mainly as an abrasive. » carbon; silica

silicon chip A very small slice of silicon, a few millimetres square, on which many electronic circuits containing many components are built; also called an **integrated circuit**. Silicon chips are reliable and cheap to produce in large numbers (although the manufacturing process is very complex), and they are now used in computers, calculators, many modern programmed household appliances, and in most electronic applications. They have been a major factor in the microminiaturization of devices: a computer which once filled a large room can now be made on one small silicon chip. » computer; integrated circuit; microminiaturization; silicon

Silicon Valley Santa Clara County, W California, USA, between Palo Alto and San José; a world centre for electronics, computing, and database systems. » California; microelectronics; silicon

silicone An open-chain or cyclic polymer containing the repeating unit $-SiR_2-O-$. Odourless, colourless, insoluble in and unreactive with water, and having high flashpoints, silicones are used in high-temperature lubricants, hydraulic fluids, and varnishes. » polymerization; silicon

silicosis An industrial disease of such occupations as mining, stone dressing, sand blasting, and of the ceramics industry. It results from the inhalation of fine particles of silica which induce scarring of the lungs. » occupational diseases; silica

silk A very fine fibre obtained from the cocoons of silkworms. Japan and China (where silk production originated) provide most of the high-quality cultivated silk. The fabrics are renowned for their lustre, drape, and handle. » fibre; silkworm

silk-cotton tree » **kapok tree**

Silk Road Ancient trade route from E China to C Asia and Europe; from the 2nd-c AD, the best-known route ran from Xi'an through the Hexi Corridor to the E Mediterranean coast; during the Sui dynasty (581–618), a route further N ended at Istanbul; in exchange for silk, China received grapes, cotton, chestnuts, lucerne, and pomegranates; Chinese techniques for silkworm breeding, iron-smelting, paper-making, and irrigation spread W; the route also brought Buddhism to China. » Buddhism; China [i]; Hexi Corridor; silk

silk-screen » **screen-process printing**

silkworm The larva of the common silk moth, *Bombyx mori*, that spins the silk cocoon from which commercial silk is derived; larvae feed on mulberry leaves. The cocoon is unwound mechanically, after softening, and each may contain up to 3 km/2 ml of silk. The domesticated silkworm is no longer found in the wild. (Order: *Lepidoptera*. Family: *Bombycidae*.) » larva; moth; silk

silky-flycatcher » **flycatcher**

silky terrier A toy breed of dog developed from terriers (including the Yorkshire terrier) in Australia; short legs, erect ears; long, straight, silky, brown and blue-grey coat (hair 125–150 mm/5–6 in long). » non-sporting dog; Yorkshire terrier

sill A sheet-like body of igneous rock that has been intruded between layers of sedimentary rock, and shows a conformable relationship with the bedding planes. It is usually composed of medium-grained rock, typically dolerite. Examples include the Palisades Sill in New Jersey, USA, and the Whin Sill in N England. » dolerite; igneous rock; intrusive rock

Sillitoe, Alan [silitoh] (1928–) British novelist, born in Nottingham of working-class parents. Before serving in the RAF, he worked in a bicycle factory for several years. This produced the subject for his first and most popular novel, *Saturday Night, Sunday Morning* (1958). Later novels include *The Death of William Posters* (1965), *A Tree on Fire* (1967), and *A Start in Life* (1970). » English literature; novel

Sills, Beverly (1929–) US soprano, born in New York City. She made her operatic debut in Philadelphia in 1947, but did not attract wide notice until 1966, when she took the part of Cleopatra in Handel's *Giulio Cesare*. She was later highly successful in early 19th-c Italian roles. She was made director of the New York City Opera in 1979, and retired from the stage the following year. » opera

Silone, Ignazio [silohnay], pseudonym of **Secondo Tranquilli**

(1900–78) Italian novelist, born at Aquilo, and educated in Abruzzi and Rome. He was active in the struggle against fascism, and escaped to Switzerland in 1941, returning to Italy in 1944. *Fontamara* (1933) describes the interplay between the peasants of Abruzzi and their fascist governors. Later novels include *Pane e vino* (1937, Bread and Wine), and *Il seme sotto la neve* (1941, The Seed beneath the Snow). He died in Geneva. » fascism; Italian literature; novel

silt The aggregate of fine mineral particles produced by the erosion and weathering of rock, ranging in size from 0.0625–0.002 mm (0.0025–0.00008 in), a size range intermediate between that of clay and sand. Silt deposits are laid down by water, and may consolidate to form the sedimentary rock, siltstone. » clay; sand

Silurian period [siy**loo**rian] The third of the geological periods of the Palaeozoic era, extending from c.435 million to 408 million years ago. Marine fauna were generally similar to the Ordovician period, although graptolites became extinct and true-jawed fish evolved. The earliest land plants appeared. » geological time scale; Ordovician period; Palaeozoic era; RR16

Silvanus or **Sylvanus** [sil**vay**nuhs, sil**vah**nuhs] In Roman religion, the god of uncultivated land, especially woodland; he was therefore strange, and dangerous, like Pan. The name is possibly a synonym of Faunus. » Pan

silver Ag (Lat *argentum*), element 47, melting point 961°C. A lustrous transition metal, relatively rare, but occurring uncombined in nature, known and used since ancient times. It also occurs as a sulphide (Ag_2S), particularly along with those of other elements; a major source is the sludge from copper refinement. Of all elements, it is the best conductor of electricity. Long used extensively in coinage, it has now become too expensive for that purpose. Much used in jewellery and medals, it requires regular cleaning, as the surface becomes coated with Ag_2S. Its compounds, which normally show oxidation state +1 (especially AgBr), are used in photography; surfaces of AgBr, after activation by light, are easily reduced to Ag. » chemical elements; metal; sulphur; RR90

silver birch A slender, elegant, short-lived species of birch reaching 15–18 m/50–60 ft, with distinctive silvery-white bark. Native to Europe, usually in colder regions, it is often planted for ornament. (*Betula pendula*. Family: *Betulaceae*.) » birch

silver fir An evergreen conifer native to the temperate N hemisphere; foliage often silvery or bluish; needles leathery, leaving distinctive circular scars when shed; cones breaking up to release seeds when ripe. Widely grown for timber and as ornamentals, its resin yields Canada balsam. It is sensitive to polluted air, and does not thrive in or near industrial areas. (Genus: *Abies*, 50 species. Family: *Pinaceae*.) » conifer; evergreen plants; resin

silver fox » **red fox**

silver Persian » **chinchilla cat**

silver plate A term applied to goods made of silver of sterling standard, established by law in England in the 13th-c, when hallmarking was also introduced. It should not be confused with the various 19th-c techniques of *silver plating*, which involved a thin skin of sterling silver applied to base metal. » hallmarks [i]; Sheffield plate; silver

silverfish A tapering, primitively wingless insect covered with silvery white scales; tail 3-pronged; commonly found in houses; active at night, moves swiftly; feeds on a variety of plant and animal matter. (Order: *Thysanura*. Family: *Lepismatidae*.) » insect [i]

silverpoint A technique used by artists for drawing on paper, popular in the Renaissance, but afterwards superseded by the invention of the graphite pencil. The paper is coated with Chinese white paint and the drawing made with a slim metal point (silver, gold, copper, or lead). Leonardo da Vinci and Raphael made beautiful silverpoint drawings. » Leonardo da Vinci; pencil; Raphael

silverside Small slender-bodied fish widespread in inshore waters of temperate to tropical seas; body length typically 10–15 cm/4–6 in; often greenish above, with characteristic silver line along the side; eyes large; includes common E North Atlantic sand smelt, *Atherina presbyter*. (Family: *Atherinidae*, 8 genera.)

silverweed A creeping, rooting perennial native more or less throughout temperate regions; distinctive, pinnate leaves, densely clothed with silky, silvery hairs; flowers with an epicalyx and calyx, 5-petalled, yellow. (*Potentilla answerina*. Family: *Rosaceae*.) » epicalyx; perennial; pinnate; potentilla

Silves [**seel**vish] 37°11N 8°26W, pop (1981) 10 000. Town in the Algarve, S Portugal; on R Arade, 36 km/22 ml NE of Lagos; former Moorish capital; Moorish castle, cathedral (13th-c), Church of the Misericordia. » Algarve

sima [**siy**ma] The silica and magnesia-rich lower part of the crust which underlies the sial of the continents and forms the bulk of the oceanic crust. » Earth [i]; magnesium; sial; silica

Simenon, Georges (Joseph Christian) [**see**muhnõ] (1903–89) Belgian master of the crime novel, born at Liège. In Paris he became one of the most prolific authors of his day, writing several hundred novels under a variety of pseudonyms. He revolutionized detective fiction with his tough, morbidly psychological Inspector Maigret series, beginning in 1933. He died at Lausanne, Switzerland. » novel

Simeon Stylites, St [stiy**liy**teez] (387–459), feast day 5 January (W), 1 September (E). The earliest of the Christian ascetic 'pillar' saints. After living nine years in a Syrian monastery without leaving his cell, he became revered as a miracle-worker. To separate himself from the people, c.420 he established himself on top of a pillar c.20 m/70 ft high at Telanessa, near Antioch, where he spent the rest of his life preaching to crowds. He had many imitators, known as *stylites*.

Simeon, tribe of One of the 12 tribes of ancient Israel, purportedly descended from Jacob's second son by Leah. Its territory was in the S extremity of Palestine, S of Judah, into which it seems to have been nearly absorbed. » Israel, tribes of [i]; Jacob; Old Testament

Simien National park situated in a region of mountains and severe erosion in N Ethiopia; established in 1969 to protect threatened native species such as the lion-maned gelada baboon, and the Ethiopian ibex; a world heritage site. » Ethiopia [i]

simile » **metaphor**

Simla [**sim**la] 31°07N 77°09E. Hill station in Himachal Pradesh state, N India; NE of Chandigarh, to which it is linked by rail; altitude c.2 200 m/7 100 ft; established in 1819 as former summer capital of British India; grain, timber, handicrafts. » India [i]

Simnel, Lambert (c.1475–1535) English imposter, a joiner's son, who in 1487 was set up in Ireland, first as a son of Edward IV, and then as the Duke of Clarence's son, Edward, Earl of Warwick (1475–99), who was imprisoned in the Tower. Crowned at Dublin as 'Edward VI' (1487), he landed in Lancashire with 2 000 German mercenaries, and was defeated at Stoke, Nottinghamshire. He later made his peace with Henry VII, who employed him as a royal scullion and falconer. » Edward IV; Henry VII

Simon, Claude (Eugene Henri) [**see**mõ] (1913–) French novelist, born at Tananarive, Madagascar. He was educated at Paris, Oxford, and Cambridge, and later earned a living producing wine at Salses. His novels include *Le Vent* (1957, The Wind), *L'Herbe* (1958, The Grass), and *Le Palace* (1962, The Palace). » French literature; novel

Simon (of Stackpole Elidor), John (Allsebrook), 1st Viscount (1873–1954) British Liberal statesman and lawyer, born in Manchester. Educated at Edinburgh and Oxford, he entered parliament in 1906, and was knighted in 1910. He was Attorney-General (1913–15) and Home Secretary (1915–16), before resigning from the Cabinet for his opposition to conscription. Deserting the Liberals to form the Liberal National Party, he supported MacDonald's coalition governments and became Foreign Secretary (1931–5), Home Secretary in the Conservative government (1935–7), Chancellor of the Exchequer (1937–40), and Lord Chancellor in Churchill's wartime coalition (1940–5). Created viscount in 1940, he died in London. » Churchill, Winston; Liberal Party (UK); MacDonald, Ramsey

Simon Magus Eng **Simon the Magician** (1st-c) Practitioner of magic arts, who appears in Samaria c.37 well known for his sorceries. With Peter's condemnation of his offer to buy the gift of the Holy Ghost, and Simon's submission, the narrative of *Acts* (8.9–24) leaves him. Later Christian authors bring him to Rome and make him the author of heresies. » Acts of the Apostles; Peter, St

Simon Peter » **Peter, St**

simony [**sim**uhnee] The practice of giving or acquiring some sacred object, spiritual gift, or religious office for money, or carrying on a trade in such matters. The practice was most notorious in the mediaeval practice of trading in indulgences. » canon law; Holy Spirit; indulgences; Simon Magus

simple harmonic motion A periodic motion in which the restoring influence acting towards the rest position is proportional to the displacement from rest, as in a pendulum undergoing small swings. Simple harmonic motion is much easier to analyse than general periodic motion; the latter can be broken down into simple harmonic components. » Hooke's law; non-linear physics; periodic motion

Simplon Pass, Ital **Passa del Sempione** Mountain pass between Brig, Switzerland and Domodossola, Italy, over the S Bernese Alps; height, 2 006 m/6 581 ft; built on the orders of Napoleon, 1801–5; opening of the rail tunnel (20 km/12 ml) in 1906 has made the road route less important. » Bernese Alps

Simpson, Sir James Young (1811–70) British obstetrician, born at Bathgate, Scotland. He trained in Edinburgh, where he became professor of midwifery in 1840. He introduced chloroform as an anaesthetic, and was the first to use it as an anaesthetic in labour. He was created a baronet in 1866. » anaesthetics, general

Simpson, O(renthal) J(ames) (1947–) US footballer, born in San Francisco. He joined the Buffalo Bills in 1968, and led the League as top rusher four times (1972–76). He rushed for a record 2 002 yards in 1973, and in 1975 had a then record 25 touchdowns in one season. » football [i]

Simpson, Thomas (1710–61) British mathematician, born at Nuneaton, Warwickshire, where he was educated. He became professor of mathematics at Woolwich (1743), and published a long series of works (1737–57) on algebra, trigonometry, chance, and other topics. » algebra; trigonometry

Simpson Desert Desert in SE Northern Territory and SW Queensland, C Australia; mostly scrubland and sand dunes; area c.77 000 sq km/30 000 sq ml; first crossed in 1939 by Cecil Madigan; Queensland region contains a national park (c.5 550 sq km/2 150 sq ml). » Australia [i]

simulator A mechanical, electro-mechanical, or computer device for producing a realistic representation of an event or system. It is used where the real thing is very expensive and inaccessible, and to train operators (eg aircraft pilots) in safety. In an aircraft simulator, the visual and movement responses that a pilot would experience in flight are reproduced by computer graphics and mechanical movement of the simulated flight deck. Computers are also used to simulate complex phenomena where there are many variables, such as in atmospheric circulation studies. » computer

simultaneity » **special relativity** [i]

simultaneous equations Two or more equations that are true at the same time. Two simultaneous equations in two unknowns, such as $x+y=5$, $x-y=3$, in general have one pair of solutions, here $x=4$, $y=1$. However, they may have an infinite number of solutions, such as $x+2y=3$ and $2x+4y=6$, which are satisfied by all numbers of the form $x=k$, $y=\frac{1}{2}(3-k)$. They may also have no solutions, as with $x+2y=4$ and $x+2y=5$. Similarly, n equations in n unknowns may have one unique set of solutions, no solutions, or an infinite number of solutions. » equations

sin A religious term signifying purposeful disobedience to the known will of God or an action offensive to God. It is a factor in many religions, though it is represented in a a wide variety of ways. The Hebrew Bible represents sin as a constant element in the experience of Israel. There is an emphasis upon human responsibility for sin, and this is carried over into Christian doctrine, where it is joined with the idea of the inevitability of sin in the concept of original sin. » Bible; Christianity; God; grace; Judaism; original sin

Sinai [**siy**niy] pop (1976) 10 104; area 60 174 sq km/23 227 sq ml. Desert peninsula and governorate in NE Egypt; bounded by Israel and Gulf of Aqaba (E) and Egypt and Gulf of Suez (W); N coastal plain rises S to mountains reaching 2 637 m/8 651 ft at Mt Catherine, Egypt's highest point, and Mt Sinai, 2 286 m/7 500 ft; capital, El Arish; oil, manganese; some livestock and agriculture in irrigated areas; a battlefield since ancient times; taken by Israel, 1967; returned to Egypt following the peace agreement, 1984; tourist resorts in S include Sharm el Sheikh, Dahab, Ras Muhammad, Nuweiba. » Arab–Israeli Wars; Camp David Accords; Egypt [i]; Sinai, Mount

Sinai, Mount [**siy**niy] Mountain of uncertain location, traditionally placed among the granite mountains of the S Sinai peninsula, but sometimes located in Arabia E of the Gulf of Aqabah; also called **Horeb** in the Hebrew Bible. According to the Book of Exodus, this is where God revealed himself to Moses, and made a covenant with Israel by giving Moses the Ten Commandments on tablets of stone. » Moses; Sinai; Ten Commandments

Sinanthropus [sin**an**throhpuhs] » **Peking Man**

Sinatra, Frank, properly **Francis (Albert)** (1915–) US singer and actor, born at Hoboken, New Jersey. Now widely recognized as one of the greatest singers of popular songs, he began in the 1940s with riots among the teenage girls in his audiences. With the Tommy Dorsey orchestra (1940–2), his hit records included 'I'll Never Smile Again' and 'Without a Song', and he starred on radio and in movies, most notably *Anchors Aweigh* (1945). Then his appeal disappeared as suddenly as it had arrived. He was all but forgotten by 1953, when his memorable acting in the movie *From Here to Eternity* won awards and revived his career. Several choice roles in films followed, and his revival as an actor led to new opportunities as a singer. He produced his masterworks in a series of recordings (1956–65), especially the albums *For Swinging Lovers*, *Come Fly With Me*, and *That's Life*. His personal life has always proven noteworthy, with turbulent marriages to Ava Gardner and Mia Farrow, among others, and alleged Mafia connections. » song

Sinclair, Upton (Beall) (1878–1968) US novelist, born in Baltimore. Educated at New York and Columbia, he became a journalist, and found success with his novel exposing meat-packing conditions in Chicago, *The Jungle* (1906). Later novels, such as *Metropolis* (1908) and *King Coal* (1917), became increasingly moulded by his socialist beliefs. He died at Bound Brook, New Jersey. » American literature; Democratic Party; novel; socialism

Sind pop (1981) 19 029 000; area 140 914 sq km/54 393 sq ml. Province in SE Pakistan; bounded E and S by India and SW by the Arabian Sea; capital, Karachi; fertile, low-lying and generally flat land dissected by the R Indus; invaded by Alexander the Great, 325 BC; arrival of Islam, 8th-c; part of the Chandragupta Ganges Empire and the Delhi Empire; under British rule, 1843; autonomous province, 1937; province of Pakistan, 1947; agricultural economy; rice, cotton, barley, oilseed; irrigation from the Sukkur Barrage (N). » Pakistan [i]

sinfonietta An orchestral piece, usually in several movements but on a smaller scale, and normally for smaller forces, than a symphony; a well-known example is Janáček's *Sinfonietta* (1926). The term is also used for a chamber orchestra, such as the London Sinfonietta (founded 1968). » Janáček; symphony

Singapore, official name **Republic of Singapore** [singa**paw**] pop (1990e) 2 718 000; area 618 sq km/238 sq ml. Republic at the S tip of the Malay Peninsula, SE Asia; consists of the island of Singapore and about 50 adjacent islets; linked to Malaysia by a causeway across the Johore Strait; capital, Singapore City; timezone GMT +8; ethnic groups include Chinese (77%), Malay (15%); Chinese mainly Buddhists, Malays mainly Muslims; chief languages, English, Malay, Chinese, Tamil; unit of currency, the Singapore dollar of 100 cents; Singapore I, c.42 km/26 ml by 22 km/14 ml at its widest points; low-lying, rising to 177 m/581 ft at Bukit Timah; deep-water harbour

(SE); equatorial climate; high humidity; average annual rainfall, 2 438 mm/96 in; temperature 21–34°C; originally part of the Sumatran Sri Vijaya kingdom; leased by the British East India Company, on the advice of Sir Stamford Raffles, from the Sultan of Johore, 1819; Singapore, Malacca, and Penang incorporated as the Straits Settlements, 1826; British Crown Colony, 1867; occupied by the Japanese, 1942–5; self-government, 1959; part of the Federation of Malaya from 1963 until its establishment as an independent state in 1965; a prime minister, elected every four years, leads a single-chamber parliament of 81 members, elected for 4-year terms; major transshipment centre; oil refining, rubber, food processing, chemicals, electronics, ship repair, financial services, fishing. » Malaysia [i]; Raffles; Singapore City; RR27 national holidays; RR60 political leaders

Singapore City 1°20N 103°50E. Seaport capital of Singapore, on SE coast of Singapore I; one of the world's busiest ports; third largest oil refining centre; distribution base for many international companies; first container port in SE Asia, 1972; airport; railway; two universities (1953, 1964); Tiger Balm Gardens, St Andrew's Cathedral, Sultan Mosque, Monkey God Temple, Poh Toh Temple, Siang Lin-Si Temple, House of Jade, national museum, botanical gardens. » Singapore

Singer, Isaac (Bashevis) (1904–) US Yiddish writer, born in Radzymin, Poland. Educated in Warsaw, he emigrated to the USA in 1935, where he became a journalist and US citizen. He set his books among the Jews of Poland, Germany, and America. His novels include *The Family Moskat* (1950) and *The Magician of Lublin* (1960), and his short stories *Gimpel the Fool and Other Stories* (1957). Considered by many the last and greatest Yiddish writer, he was awarded the Nobel Prize for Literature in 1978. » American literature; novel; Yiddish

Singer, Isaac (Merrit) (1811–75) US inventor and manufacturer of sewing machines, born at Pittstown, New York. He became a machinist, patenting a rock drill (1839), a carving machine (1849), and at Boston (1852) an improved single-thread, chain-stitch sewing machine, incorporating some features of Howe's machine. His company quickly became the largest producer of sewing machines in the world. He retired to England in 1863, and died at Torquay, Devon. » Howe, Elias

singing One of the oldest of human activities, which, in the sense of inflected pitch, may well have preceded speech as a form of human communication. In Western art music, it has usually been allied to words (especially poetry), but this is by no means the case in many ethnic communities, or even in some Western folk traditions (eg Irish keening). The training of choirs was important in the mediaeval and Renaissance church, but it was with the development of opera in the 17th-c that the highly trained solo singer, especially the soprano and the castrato, came into prominence. Singing treatises of the period tend to concern themselves with matters of notation and vocal embellishments, and it was not until the 19th-c that teachers began to set down methods of voice production. The 20th-c has witnessed a reaction against a too scientific and 'cultured' approach to vocal training, and a return to more natural methods of voice production. » barbershop quartet; castrato; countertenor; song; tessitura

single-cell proteins » **novel proteins**

Single Integrated Operational Plan » **SIOP**

Singspiel [**zing**shpeel] A German opera with spoken dialogue. Mozart's *Die Zauberflöte* (The Magic Flute) is a famous example. » Mozart; opera

Sinhalese The dominant ethnic group (73%) of Sri Lanka, descended from N Indians who came to the area in the 5th-c BC. Predominantly Buddhist, they have an occupational caste system. Population c.10.4 million. » caste; Sri Lanka [i]

Sining » **Xining**

Sinitic languages » **Chinese**

Sinn Féin [shin **fayn**] (Gaelic 'Ourselves Alone') An Irish political party founded in 1900 by Arthur Griffith in support of Irish independence from Britain. By the end of World War 1 it had become the main Irish nationalist party. It formed a separate assembly from the UK parliament, and succeeded in creating the Irish Free State (1922). Following the Anglo-Irish Treaty, it split to form the two main Irish parties, and in 1970 it split again into official and provisional wings. It has remained active in Northern Ireland, and has close contacts with the Irish Republican Army. » Fianna Fáil; Fine Gael; IRA

Sino-Japanese Wars 1 (1894–5) A longstanding conflict between Chinese and Japanese interests in Korea, which resulted in war during the Ming period. China suffered a humiliating defeat, and by the Treaty of Shimonseki recognized Korean independence and ceded Taiwan, the Liaodong Peninsula, and the Pescadores to Japan. **2** (1937–45) The Sino-Japanese War proper broke out in 1937 with the Japanese invasion of Tianjin (Tientsin) and Beijing (Peking), but this was only the ultimate phase of Japan's territorial designs on China. Manchuria had already been occupied and a puppet state created in 1932. Nanjing was invaded in December 1937, and most of N China was soon under Japanese control. From December 1941, US intervention became the major factor in the Pacific War, which ended with Japan's surrender in 1945. » Manchukuo; United Fronts; World War 2

Sino-Tibetan languages A family of languages spoken in China, Tibet, and Burma. Alongside their similarities with each other, they display similarities with other neighbouring language groups, so their classification is tentative. There are some 300 languages in the family, the main ones being Tibetan, Burmese, and the eight major varieties of Chinese. » Chinese; Tibetan

Sinope [siy**noh**pee] The ninth natural satellite of Jupiter, discovered in 1914; distance from the planet 23 700 000 km/ 14 727 000 ml; diameter 40 km/25 ml. » Jupiter (astronomy); RR4

sinopia [see**noh**pia] (Ital 'red ochre') A term used not only for the reddish-brown pigment itself, but also for the underdrawings made by fresco painters using this substance. Modern conservation has brought to light the hidden *sinopie* underneath many Renaissance frescoes. » fresco; paint

sintering One of the techniques of powder metallurgy. Metal parts are made by forming a shape in metal powder and then holding it for several hours just below the melting point of the metal, or (if an alloy) at that of the higher melting component. It is an economical process for making small parts, and is necessary for metal which has so high a melting point that it cannot easily be cast. It can produce porous structures, advantageous in lubrication. » powder metallurgy

Sintra [**seen**tra], formerly **Cintra** 38°47N 9°25W, pop (1981) 20 000. Small resort town in Lisbon district, C Portugal, 12 km/7 ml N of Estoril; former summer residence of the Portuguese royal family; railway; agricultural centre, tourism; National Palace (14th–15th-c), Moorish castle, Pena palace; São Pedro fair (Jun). » Portugal [i]

sinus An air or blood-filled space within the head. The **air-filled sinuses** (the *paranasal sinuses*) all communicate with the nasal cavity, at the front of the face, and are lined with respiratory epithelium. Their purpose is to lighten the skull and also act as resonance chambers in the production of sounds. (A change in the quality of the voice during a cold results from these sinuses becoming infected, and filling with fluid, thus affecting their resonating properties). The **blood-filled sinuses** are generally found between the layers of the outer membrane which surrounds the brain (the *dura mater*), and drain venous blood from the brain to the internal jugular vein. » brain [i]; nose; sinusitis; skull

sinusitis Infection of the lining of one or more sinuses around the nose and in the bones of the face, which sometimes arises from infection of the upper respiratory passages (eg common cold, pharyngitis, tonsillitis). It results in severe pain over the sinus or headache with fever. » sinus

Sion (Jerusalem) [**ziy**uhn] » **Zion**

Sion (Switzerland) [syõ], Ger **Sitten** 46°14N 7°22E, pop (1980) 22 877. Capital town of Valais canton, SW Switzerland, 80 km/50 ml S of Bern; bishopric since the 6th-c; railway; market town for wine, fruit, and vegetables of the Rhône valley; brewing; former cathedral (10th–13th-c), 17th-c town hall, Church of Notre-Dame (12th–13th-c), bishop's fortress (1294); music festival (Jul–Aug). » Switzerland [i]

SIOP An acronym for **Single Integrated Operational Plan**, the all-embracing military plan, the subject of continual updating according to policy, for the deployment and use of US nuclear forces. » nuclear weapons

Sioux [soo] or **Dakota** A cluster of Siouan-speaking N American Indian groups belonging to the Plains Indian culture. Having moved from further N into present-day N and S Dakota, they acquired horses, fought wars against other Indian groups, and hunted the buffalo. They were later involved in clashes with advancing White settlers and prospectors, and were finally defeated at Wounded Knee (1890). Population c.48 000, mostly on reservations. » American Indians; Plains Indians

Sioux City [soo] 42°30N 96°24W, pop (1980) 82 003. Seat of Woodbury County, W Iowa, USA, at the junction of the Big Sioux and Missouri Rivers; railway; shipping and trade centre in agricultural region, with grain and hog markets; fertilizers, electric tools. » Iowa

Sioux Falls [soo] 43°33N 96°44W, pop (1980) 81 343. Seat of Minnehaha County, SE South Dakota, USA, on Big Sioux R; largest city in the state; established, 1857; city status, 1883; airfield; railway; industrial and commercial centre in a livestock farming region; meat processing; sandstone quarries. » South Dakota

siphon/syphon A means of transferring liquid from high to low levels using gravity. The siphon is a liquid-filled pipe with one end submerged in the upper volume of liquid, the other end in the lower volume. Fluid moves through the pipe under the influence of gravity at a rate proportional to the difference in liquid levels. » fluid mechanics; gravitation

Siphonaptera [siyfuhn**ap**tuhra] » **flea**

Sipuncula [si**punk**yoola] » **peanut worm**

Siqueiros, David Alfaro [si**kay**ros] (1896–1974) Mexican mural painter, born at Chihuahua. He helped to launch the review *El Machete* in Mexico City in 1922, and in 1930 was imprisoned for revolutionary activities. He was later expelled from the USA, and during the 1930s worked in S America. One of the principal figures in 20th-c Mexican mural painting, he was notable for his experiments with modern synthetic materials. He died at Cuernavaca. » Mexican art; Rivera, Diego

Siraj ud Daula, originally **Mirza Muhammad** [si**rahj** ud **dow**la] (c.1732–57) Ruler of Bengal under the nominal suzerainty of the Mughal Empire. He came into conflict with the British over their fortification of Calcutta, and marched on the city in 1756. The British surrender led to the infamous Black Hole, for which he was held responsible. Following the recapture of Calcutta, the British under Clive joined forces with his general, Mir Jafar, and defeated him at Plassey in 1857. He fled to Murshidabad, but was captured and executed. » Black Hole of Calcutta; Clive; Mughal Empire

siren A salamander native to SE North America; dark eel-like body; length, up to 900 mm/36 in; no hind legs; tiny front legs; feathery gills; spends life in muddy pools; burrows in mud during drought; covering of slime becomes dry and paper-like; can rest like this for two months. (Family: *Sirenidae*, 3 species.) » salamander [i]

Sirens In Greek mythology, deceitful creatures, half-woman and half-bird, who lured sailors to death by their singing. Odysseus was able to sail past their rocky island by stopping the ears of his crew with wax; and by having himself bound to the mast, was restrained when he heard their song. In later legends they drown themselves after this defeat. » Odysseus

Sirhan, Sirhan Bishara » **Kennedy, Robert F**

Sirius The brightest star in our sky, and sixth nearest; also known as the **Dog Star**. It has a faint companion star, which was the first white dwarf star to be recognized as such. » white dwarf

Sirocco/Scirocco A wind similar to the Khamsin in origin, blowing from the Sahara Desert. As it crosses the Mediterranean Sea it picks up moisture, and arrives in S Europe as a moist, oppressive, warm wind. » Khamsin; wind [i]

Sirte, Gulf of [**seer**tay], Arabic **Khalij Surt** Gulf in the Mediterranean Sea off the coast of N Libya, between Misratah (W) and Benghazi (E); access to the Gulf waters is an area of dispute between Libya and the USA. » Libya [i]

siskin A finch, found worldwide; eats seeds and insects. (Genus: *Carduelis*, 16 species, or *Serinus*, 2 species. Family: *Fringillidae*.) » finch

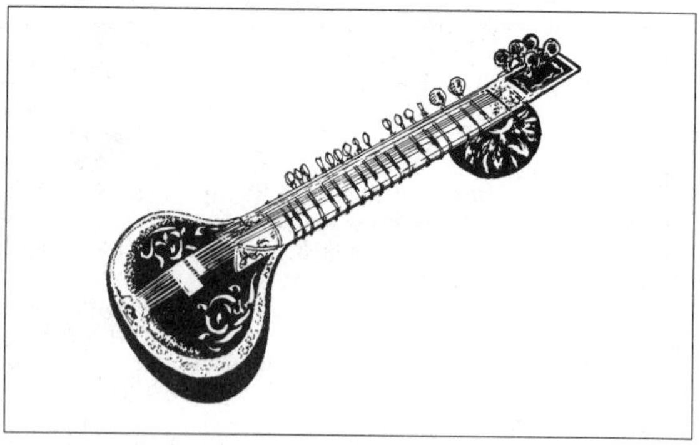

Sitar

Sisley, Alfred [**sees**lay] (1839–99) French Impressionist painter and etcher, who trained under Charles Gleyre (1806–74) in Paris. He painted landscapes almost exclusively, particularly in the valleys of the Seine, Loing, and Thames. He died at Moret-sur-Loing, France, his works beginning to sell only after his death. » Impressionism (art); landscape painting

Sistine Chapel [**sis**teen] A chapel in the Vatican, built in 1475–81 for Pope Sixtus IV. It is remarkable for a series of frescoes executed on its ceiling and altar wall by Michelangelo. It is the scene of papal elections, and is also the home of the Sistine Choir. » Michelangelo; Vatican City

Sisyphus [**sis**ifuhs] In Greek mythology, a Corinthian king who was a famous trickster; in one story he catches and binds Thanatos (Death). In the Underworld he was condemned to roll a large stone up a hill from which it always rolled down again.

sitar [si**tah**] A large Indian lute, with a gourd resonator and a long fretted neck. It originated in Persia in the Middle Ages. The modern concert sitar, used in Indian classical music, is about 122 cm/4 ft long, with usually seven strings plucked with a wire plectrum. In addition, about 12 sympathetic strings vibrate freely when the main strings are sounded. » lute; plectrum; string instrument 2 [i]

sitatunga [sita**tung**ga] A spiral-horned antelope native to Africa S of the Sahara; shaggy, slightly oily coat; brown with small white patches and lines; hooves long and splayed; inhabits wet areas; swims well; may hide under water with only nostrils showing. (*Tragelaphus spekei*.) » antelope

Sites of Special Scientific Interest (SSSIs) Areas designated by the Nature Conservancy Council for the purposes of conservation, including some of the UK's best examples of particular wildlife habitats, interesting geological or physiographical features, and habitats for rare plants and animals. In return for compensation, management agreements may be made between the council and site landowners to protect them. Nevertheless, many have been lost or damaged. » conservation (earth sciences); habitat loss; Nature Conservancy Council

Sithole, Rev Ndabaningi [si**toh**lay] (1920–) Zimbabwean clergyman and politician, born at Nyamandhlovu, Rhodesia. He began as a teacher, and after studying in the USA (1955–8) became a Congregationalist minister, and joined the National Democratic Party. He became President of the Zimbabwe African National Union (ZANU) in 1963. An advocate of violent resistance by Black African nationalists, he joined Mugabe in his struggle against Nkomo. After a period of detention in the 1960s, he was eclipsed by Mugabe, and later moved into a close political alliance with Bishop Muzorewa. » Mugabe; Muzorewa; Nkomo; Zimbabwe [i]

Sitka National monument on W Baranof I, SE Alaska, USA; Indian stockade, totem poles, Russian blockhouse; established, 1910; scene of last stand of Tlingit Indians against the Russians, 1804; town and naval base of Sitka nearby. » Alaska

Sitting Bull (1834–90) American Indian warrior, chief of the Dakota Sioux. He was a leader in the Sioux War of 1876–7, after which he escaped to Canada, but surrendered in 1881. After touring with Buffalo Bill's Wild West Show, he returned to his people, and was present in 1890 when the army suppressed the 'ghost dance' messianic religious movement. He was killed during the army's action. » Cody, William F; Indian Wars; Sioux

Sitwell, Dame Edith (1887–1964) British poet, born at Scarborough, Yorkshire, the sister of Osbert and Sacheverell Sitwell. She first attracted notice through editing an annual anthology of new poetry, *Wheels* (1916–21), and her own experimental poetry was controversially received with *Façade* (1922), which (with Walton's music) was given a stormy public reading in London. She became a Catholic in 1955, after which her works reflect a deeper religious symbolism, as in *The Outcasts* (1962). She was created a Dame in 1954, and died in London. » English literature; poetry; Sitwell, Osbert/Sacheverell; Walton, William

Sitwell, Sir Osbert (1892–1969) British author, born in London, the brother of Edith and Sacheverell Sitwell. Educated at Eton, he served in World War 1, began writing poetry, and acquired notoriety with his satirical novel of the Scarborough social scene, *Before the Bombardment* (1927). He is best known for his 5-volume autobiographical series, beginning with *Left Hand: Right Hand* (1944). He became a baronet in 1942, and died near Florence. » English literature; novel; satire; Sitwell, Edith/Sacheverell

Sitwell, Sir Sacheverell (1897–1988) British poet and art critic, born at Scarborough, Yorkshire, the brother of Edith and Osbert Sitwell. Educated at Eton, he served in the army, then travelled in Spain and Italy, where he began to write books on art and architecture, such as *Southern Baroque Art* (1924). His many volumes of poetry cover a period of over 30 years, from *The People's Palace* (1918) to *An Indian Summer* (1982). He became a baronet on the death of his brother, Osbert, in 1969, and died near Towcester, Northamptonshire. » English literature; poetry; Sitwell, Edith/Osbert

Sivaji [sheevajee] (c.1627–80) Founder of the Maratha Kingdom in W India, born at Shivner, Poona. He campaigned against the Mughals, and was enthroned as an independent ruler in 1674. Renowned as a military leader, social reformer, and advocate of religious tolerance, his last years were made difficult by internal problems and pressure from outside enemies. He died at Rajgarh. » Mughal Empire

Six Day War » Arab-Israeli Wars

Six, Les [lay **sees**] A group of composers united for about six years after 1917 to further the cause of modern French music. It comprised Germaine Tailleferre (1892–1983), Georges Auric, Louis Durey, Arthur Honegger, Darius Milhaud, and Francis Poulenc. » Auric; Durey; Honegger; Milhaud; Poulenc

sixth-form college A college in the UK for pupils over the age of 16 and up to 18 or 19, which often takes pupils from feeder schools catering for 11- to 16-year-olds. It specializes in A-level work, but other forms of examination and qualification may also be offered.

Sizewell Nuclear power station in Suffolk, E England; gas-cooled, graphite-moderated reactors came into operation in 1966; site of the first UK pressurized light-water-moderated and cooled reactor (**Sizewell B**). » nuclear reactor [i]; Suffolk

Sjælland [**shel**ahn] area 7514 sq km/2900 sq ml. Group of islands in Danish territorial waters, between Jutland and S Sweden; includes Zealand (Sjælland), Møn, Samsø, Amager, and Saltholm. » Denmark [i]; Zealand

Skagerrak [**ska**guhrak] Arm of the Atlantic Ocean linking the North Sea with the Baltic Sea by way of the Kattegat; bounded (N) by Norway and (S) by Denmark; main arm, Oslo Fjord; 240 km/150 ml long and 135 km/84 ml wide. » Atlantic Ocean

skaldic poetry (Old Norse *skald* 'poet') Poetry composed and recited by recognized individuals in Iceland and the Scandinavian countries between 800 and 1100. After this time, written versions made the *skald* redundant. » Icelandic/Norwegian literature; poetry

Skalkottas, Nikos [skal**ko**tas] (1904–49) Greek composer, born at Halkis. He studied at the Athens Conservatory and in Berlin, and then earned his living as an orchestral violinist in Athens. His works, dating mostly from 1935–45, show a complex use of serial techniques, and were not much performed until after his death, which occurred in Athens. » serialism

Skanda [**skahn**da] The Hindu god of War, the 'Attacker', who is also responsible for the demons who bring diseases.

Skanderbeg, byname of **George Castriota** or **Kastrioti** (1405–68) Albanian patriot. Carried away by Ottoman Turks at the age of seven, he was brought up a Muslim, and became a favourite commander of Sultan Murad II, who gave him his byname, a combination of *Iskander* ('Alexander') + the rank of Bey. In 1443 he changed sides, renounced Islam, and drove the Turks from Albania. For 20 years he maintained Albanian independence, but after his death, at Lezhë, opposition to the Turks collapsed. » Albania [i]; Islam

Skara Brae [**skah**ra **bray**] An exceptionally preserved Neolithic village of c.3100–2500 BC on the Bay of Skaill, Stromness, Scotland, exposed below sand dunes by storms in 1850. It supported a population of c.30–40, and comprises a tight cluster of nine squarish stone huts, turf-roofed, and with alleys between, furnished internally with stone-slabbed dressers, cupboards, box beds, hearths, water tanks, and latrines. » Three Age System

skate Any of several bottom-living rays of the family *Rajidae*; includes the large European species, *Raja batis*, found in deeper offshore waters from the Arctic to the Mediterranean; length up to 2.5 m/8 ft; upper surface greenish-brown with lighter patches; fished commercially along with other species such as the smaller thornback ray (*Raja clavata*), length up to 85 cm/34 in. » ray

skateboarding Riding on a single flexible board, longer and wider than the foot, fixed with four small wheels on the underside. It is possible to achieve speeds of over 100 kph/60 mph. It developed as an alternative to surfing, and became very popular in the USA during the 1960s and in the UK during the 1970s, where it regained popularity in 1988.

skating » ice hockey; ice skating; roller skating

Skegness 53°10N 0°21E, pop (1981) 16116. Resort town in E Lindsey dist, Lincolnshire, EC England; on the North Sea coast, 30 km/19 ml NE of Boston; railway; engineering, tourism; bird reserve just S of the town. » Lincolnshire

skeleton The hardened tissues forming the supporting framework of plants and animals. In vertebrates it usually refers to the assembly and arrangement of bones. The *appendicular* skeleton comprises the bones of the limbs and the pelvic and pectoral girdles, while the *axial* skeleton comprises the bones of the vertebral column, skull, ribs, and sternum. » bone; orthopaedics; osteopathy; Paget's disease; Plate XIII

Skeleton Coast area 16390 sq km/6326 sq ml. National park in NW Namibia; established in 1971; runs along the Atlantic Ocean coast between Walvis Bay and the Angolan frontier. » Namibia [i]

Skelton, John (c.1460–1529) English satirical poet. Educated at Cambridge, and perhaps also Oxford, he was court poet to Henry VII, and tutor to Prince Henry (VIII). He produced some translations and elegies in 1489, but became known for his satirical vernacular poetry, such as *Colyn Cloute* (1522). He died in London. » English literature; Henry VII; poetry; satire

skepticism » scepticism

sketch In art, a term with two meanings: **1** A rough preliminary drawing in which the artist tries out his ideas. **2** A drawing (in any medium, including paint) of a deliberately spontaneous and 'unfinished' appearance, but considered as an end in itself. Sketches of the first sort were normally destroyed by the artist on completion of the picture; but with the rise of collecting in the 16th-c they were sought after, which greatly encouraged the production of sketches of the second sort. » maquette; modello

sketchphone A system, linked to the telephone network, by which line drawings and sketches can be transmitted long distances to suitable receiving equipment. An electronic touch-sensitive screen sends sketches via a computer and the telephone line to a receiver. » telephone

Skiathos [**skee**athos] area 48 sq km/18 sq ml. Island of the N

Sporades, Greece, in the W Aegean Sea, 4 km/2½ ml from the mainland; chief town, Skiathos; a popular holiday resort. » Dodecanese; Greece [i]

Skiddaw 54°40N 3°08W. Mountain in the Lake District of Cumbria, NW England; rises to 928 m/3 045 ft E of Bassenthwaite. » Lake District

Skien [**shay**uhn] 59°14N 9°37E, pop (1983) 46 730. Ancient town and river-port capital of Telemark county, SE Norway; on the R Skiensalv; railway; copper, iron ore, heavy industry. » Norway [i]

skiffle A type of popular music of the 1950s in which the washboard provided a distinctive timbre. It emanated from the USA, but the best-known singer was the Scot, Lonnie Donegan (1931–).

skiing The art of propelling oneself along snow while standing on skis, and with the aid of poles, named from the Norwegian word *ski*, 'snow shoe'. Very popular as a pastime and as a sport, the earliest reference to skiing dates from c.2500 BC. Competitive skiing takes two forms. **Alpine skiing** consists of the downhill and slaloms (zig-zag courses through markers), which are races against the clock. **Nordic skiing** incorporates cross-country skiing, the biathlon, and ski jumping. Other forms include *ski-flying* (hang-gliding on skis) and *skijoring* (being towed behind a vehicle or horse), as well as several freestyle varieties. » biathlon; RR118

skimmer A bird inhabiting tropical freshwater and coasts in America, Africa, India, and SE Asia; related to the tern; lower bill longer and narrower than upper; catches fish by flying low with lower bill cutting water surface; also known as the **shearwater**, **sea-dog**, or **scissorbill**. (Family: *Rhynchopidae*, 3 species.) » shearwater; tern

skin The tough, pliable, waterproof covering of the body, blending with the mucous membranes of the mouth, nose, eyelids, and urogenital and anal openings. It is the largest single organ in the body – approximately 1.8 sq m/19.4 sq ft in the adult human and 1–2 mm/0.04–0.08 in thick. As well as a surface covering, it is also a sensory organ providing sensitivity to touch, pressure, changes in temperature, and painful stimuli. Its waterproofing function prevents fluid loss from the body, but it also has an absorptive function when certain drugs, vitamins, and hormones are applied to it in a suitable form. It is usually loosely applied to underlying tissues, so that it is easily displaced. When subjected to continuous friction, it responds by increasing the thickness of its superficial layers. When wounded, it responds by increased growth and repair.

Skin is composed of a superficial layer (the *epidermis*) and a deeper layer (the *dermis*). The epidermis consists of many cell layers, the deeper ones actively proliferating, with the cells produced gradually passing towards the surface (becoming keratinized as they do so), to be ultimately shed as the skin rubs against clothing and other surfaces. The epidermis contains many sensory nerve endings, but no blood vessels. It is firmly anchored to the underlying dermis by epidermal pegs and reciprocal projections from the dermis. The dermis is the deeper interlacing feltwork of collagen and elastic fibres containing blood and lymphatic vessels, nerves and sensory nerve endings, a small amount of fat, hair follicles, sweat and sebaceous glands, and smooth muscle. It is firmly anchored to the subcutaneous connective tissue.

Skin colour depends on the presence of pigment (*melanin*) and the vascularity of the dermis. In response to sunlight, skin increases its degree of pigmentation, making it appear darker. Some areas show a constant deeper pigmentation (the external genitalia, the perianal region, the armpit, and the areola of the breast. » acne; bruise; burn; dandruff; dermatitis; dermatology; erysipelas; impetigo; itch; keloid; keratin; mange; melanins; mole; prickly heat; psoriasis; tissue; urticaria; wart

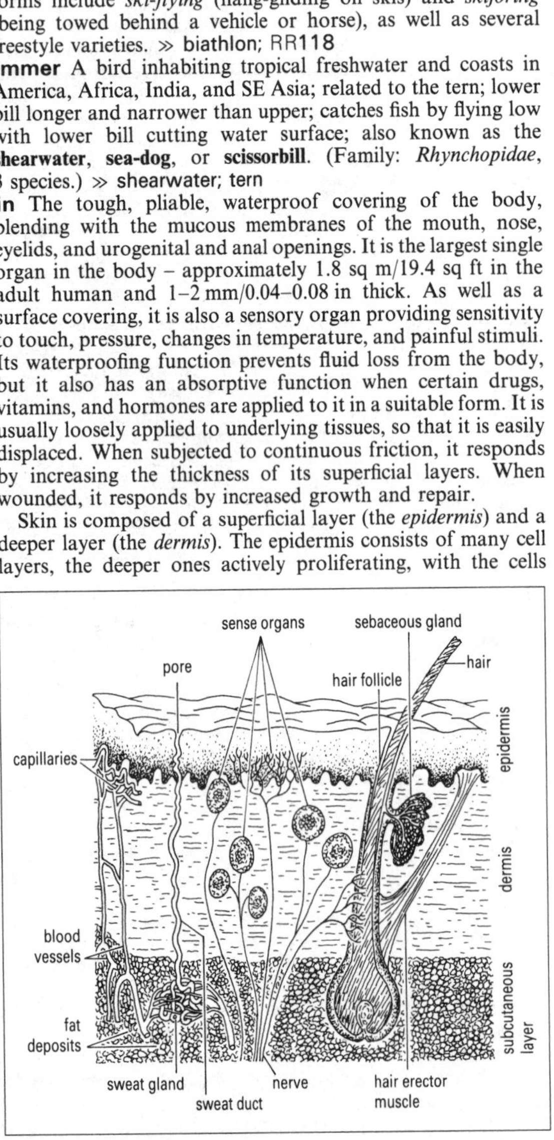

Magnified section through the skin of a mammal

skin cancer » **keratosis; melanoma**

skin-diving A form of underwater swimming, popularized in the 1930s. Until the advent of the scuba, skin-divers used only goggles, face mask, flippers, and a short breathing tube, or *snorkel*.

skin effect For alternating current, an effect whereby the bulk of the current is carried along the outer edge of the conductor; contrasts with direct current, where the current is spread evenly across the diameter of the conductor. It is caused by induced eddy currents in the core of the conductor, which oppose the applied current primarily in the interior. The skin effect is more noticeable at high frequencies. An implication is that carriers of high frequency current need only be hollow tubes instead of solid rods or wires. » alternating current; electrical conduction

skink A lizard of the family *Scincidae* (1 275 species), worldwide in tropical and temperate regions; usually with a long thin body and short legs (some species without legs); head often with large flat scales; tongue broad, rounded; many species burrow; most eat invertebrates; large species eat plants. » lizard [i]; slowworm

Skinner, B(urrhus) F(rederic) (1904–90) US psychologist, born at Susquehanna, Pennsylvania. He studied at Harvard, taught at the Universities of Minnesota and Indiana, returning to Harvard in 1948. A behaviourist, he is a proponent of operant conditioning and inventor of the *Skinner box* for facilitating experimental observations. His main scientific works include *The Behavior of Organisms* (1938) and *Verbal Behavior* (1957), but his social and political views have reached a wider public through *Walden Two* (1948) and *Beyond Freedom and Dignity* (1971). » behaviourism; conditioning

skipjack Small species of tuna fish widespread in offshore waters of tropical to temperate seas; locally abundant and very important in commercial tuna fisheries, as well as being excellent sport fish; body length up to about 1 m/3¼ ft; upper surface blue, sides silver with darker longitudinal banding. (*Katsuwonus pelamis*. Family: *Scombridae*.) » fish [i]

skipper A butterfly with relatively short wings and a large head and body; antennae often club-shaped, and widely separated at base; caterpillars commonly feed on grasses. (Order: *Lepidoptera*. Family: *Hesperiidae*, c.3 100 species.) » butterfly; caterpillar

Skiros [**skee**ros] pop (1981) 2 757; area 209 sq km/81 sq ml. Largest island of the N Dodecanese, Greece, in the Aegean Sea; length 36 km/22 ml; maximum width 14 km/9 ml; handicrafts, particularly hand-weaving and furniture; tourism. » Dodecanese; Greece [i]

skittles A game played in several different forms, all of which have the same objective: to knock down nine pins with a ball. The most popular forms are **alley skittles**, played in long alleys, and **table skittles**, played indoors and on a specially constructed table with a swivelled ball attached to a mast by means of a chain. The pins are much smaller than those used in ten-pin bowling, and are replaced on their spots manually (instead of mechanically, as in bowling). » bowling

Skopje [**skop**ye] or **Skoplje**, Turkish **Üsküp**, ancient **Scupi**

42°00N 21°28E, pop (1981) 506 547. Industrial capital of Macedonia republic, S Yugoslavia; on R Vardar, 320 km/200 ml SE of Belgrade; capital of Serbia, 14th-c; largely destroyed by earthquake, 1963; airport; railway; university (1949); flour, brewing, tobacco, cement, carpets; old town and bazaar, ethnographic museum, Daut Pasha Hammam (Turkish bathhouse, 1489), Mustapha Pasha mosque, museum of contemporary art; trade fair (Jun), international tobacco and machinery fair (Sep). » Macedonia; Yugoslavia [i]

Skorzeny, Otto [skawtzaynee] (1908–75) Austrian soldier, born in Vienna, noted for his commando-style operations in World War 2. He joined the Nazi Party in 1930, was mobilized into the SS, and fought in France, Serbia, and Russia (1939–43). He freed Mussolini from internment in a mountain hotel on the Gran Sasso Range (1943), abducted Horthy, the Regent of Hungary (1944), but failed to capture Tito. During the German counter-offensive in the Ardennes (1944), he carried out widespread sabotage behind Allied lines. He was tried at Nuremberg as a war criminal, but was acquitted (1947). He died in Madrid. » Horthy; Mussolini; Nuremberg Trials; Tito; World War 2

Skraelings [skraylingz] (Old Norse *skraelinga* 'pitiful wretch') The name given by the Vikings to the native peoples – principally Beothuk Indians and Inuit – they encountered in Greenland and N America. *Skraelingsland* was Labrador. » Vikings; Vínland

skua A large, gull-like seabird; widespread; usually dark plumage, fleshy band (*cere*) at base of bill; central tail feathers longest; chases other seabirds until they disgorge food; undertakes long migrations; also known as the **jaeger** or **bonxie**. (Family: *Stercorariidae*, 7 species.) » gull

skull The skeleton of the head and face, composed of many individual bones closely fitted together. It consists of a large cranial cavity, which encloses the brain; and the bones of the face, which complete the walls of the orbits (eye sockets), nasal cavity, and roof of the mouth. The lower jaw (*mandible*) may also be included as part of the skull. At birth and in the young child, the skull bones are separable, though with difficulty; with increasing age the joints between the bones may become ossified. In the young, this greater elasticity reduces the risk of fracture.

The skull articulates with the urer part of the vertebral column. The top of the skull is relatively smooth and rounded, while the underside is irregular, having many openings for the passage of nerves and vessels. It functions to protect the brain, to provide bony support for the openings of the digestive and respiratory tracts (mouth and nose respectively), and to house and protect the eyeballs (within the orbital cavities) and the organs of hearing and balance (within the temporal bone). The major bony parts (the number present is shown in parentheses) are the *frontal* (1), *parietal* (2), *occipital* (1), *temporal* (2), *maxillary* (2), *ethmoid* (1), and *zygomatic* (2) bones. » bone; brain [i]; cephalic index; jaw; joint; trepanning; Plate XII, XIII

skull-cap A very widespread perennial; stem square; leaves in opposite pairs; flowers 2-lipped, often with up-turned tube; calyx with distinctive helmet-shaped dorsal flange. Many species have brightly coloured flowers, and are cultivated for ornament. Others are medicinal, used for nerve tonics. (Genus: *Scutellaria*, 300 species. Family: *Labiatae*.) » perennial; sepal

skunk A mammal of family *Mustelidae*, native to the New World; long black and white coat; squirts foul-smelling fluid as defence; eats insects, vegetation, small vertebrates; nine species in genera *Mephitis* (**striped** and **hooded** skunks, or (in USA) **polecats**, **wood-pussies**, **essence pedlars**, **pikets**, or **PKs**), *Spilogale* (**spotted skunks**), and *Conepatus* (**hog-nosed skunks**). » Mustelidae; polecat

Skyamsen » **Thunderbird**

skydiving Falling from an aircraft and freefalling down to a height of 600 m/2 000 ft, when the parachute must be opened, before gliding to the ground. During the free fall, the parachutist can perform a wide range of stunts. In team events, members form different kinds of pattern by holding hands. The sport is often called simply **freefalling**. » parachuting

Skye Island in Highland region, W Scotland; second largest island of the Inner Hebrides, area 1 665 sq km/643 sq ml; separated from mainland (E) by the Sound of Sleat; Cuillin Hills in SW, rising to 1 008 m/3 307 ft at Sgurr Alasdair; much indented by sea lochs; chief towns, Portree, Broadford, Dunvegan; ferry links from Uig to Lochmaddy (North Uist) and Tarbert (Harris); also Armadale–Mallaig and Kyleakin–Kyle of Lochalsh; Dunvegan castle, Kilmuir croft museum, Clan Donald centre at Ardvasar, Dunsgiath castle, Skye water mill and black house (W of Dunvegan); crofting, fishing, sheep, cattle, tourism. » Hebrides; Scotland [i]

Skye terrier A small terrier developed in Britain; long body with very short legs and long tail; long straight coat reaching the ground; long hair on head (covering eyes), ears, and tail; may be aggressive to strangers. » dog; terrier

Skylab project The first US space station, launched on a Saturn V vehicle in May 1973, based on technology and equipment inherited from the Apollo Project. The laboratory/habitat was built within the empty third stage Saturn V fuel tank (prior to launch). It was operated in low Earth orbit for 171 days by three successive 3-man crews. The longest staytime in space was 84 days for the third crew. It was used for a variety of in-orbit experiments and for Earth observations. After the last crew completed its mission, the station was left unattended until atmospheric re-entry in July 1979. It was the source of worldwide attention during its final days because there were fears of debris impacting Earth's surface (some pieces were in fact recovered from the Australian desert). Notable also were the emergency repairs effected by the first crew, after the station's micrometeoroid and heat shield was torn off during the launch. » launch vehicle [i]; space station

skylark A lark native to the Old World N hemisphere; inhabits grassland, farmland, salt marshes, and sand dunes; sings during ascending and descending fluttering flight. (Genus: *Alauda*, 2 species.) » lark

skyscraper A multi-storey building of great height, typically using a steel frame and curtain wall construction, the floors being accessed via high-speed lifts. The term was first used in the USA at the end of the 19th-c. At 443 m/1454 ft, the Sears Tower, Chicago (1970–4), architects Skidmore Owings & Merrill, is currently the world's tallest building; but perhaps the most famous skyscrapers are those of the 1920s, such as the Empire State Building (1929–31), architects Shreve Lamb & Harmon, and the Chrysler Building (1928–30), architect William van Alen, both in New York City. » Chicago School (architecture); CN Tower; curtain wall; Sears Tower

Slade, Felix (1790–1868) British antiquary and art collector, born at Halsteads, Yorkshire. He bequeathed to the British Museum his engravings and Venetian glass, and founded art professorships at Oxford, Cambridge, and University College, London. The Slade School of Fine Art, London, is named after him.

slander A defamatory statement made in some transient form – sounds (not necessarily words) or gestures. The term is not recognized by all jurisdictions (eg in Scotland). » defamation; libel; tort

slash and burn cultivation » **shifting cultivation**

slate A fine-grained metamorphic rock having a perfect cleavage because of the parallel alignment of mica crystals. This is the result of directed stress during the low grade regional metamorphism of shale or mudstone. Split into thin sheets it is used for roofing, being durable and light. Well-known occurrences are in N Wales and the Vosges, France. » metamorphic rock; micas

slave-making ant A parasitic ant, the workers of which raid the nests of other ant species and carry off the pupae. These pupae are reared as slaves to feed their captors and care for the captors' larvae. (Order: *Hymenoptera*. Family: *Formicidae*.) » Amazon ant; ant; pupa

slave trade A trade in Africa which started in ancient times. Slaves were sent across the Sahara and were traded in the Mediterranean by Phoenicians; Graeco-Roman traders in the Red Sea and beyond traded slaves from E Africa to Egypt and the Middle East. These trades continued in mediaeval times, but the scale of the trade built up with the arrival of the Portuguese in Africa and the development of the labour-intensive plantation system in the W African islands of São

Tomé and Principe, Brazil, the Caribbean, the southern American colonies, and later the Indian Ocean islands, and South and East Africa. The Portuguese dominated the trade in the 16th-c, the Dutch in the early 17th-c, while the late 17th-c was a period of intense competition with the French, British, Danes, and Swedes joining the early practitioners. The trade reached its peak in the second half of the 18th-c, and from this period the E African slave trade became more significant, particularly during the period of Omani power up to the 1860s. The British abolished the slave trade in 1807, and the institution of slavery in 1833. They then instituted Royal Naval anti-slaver squadrons on the coasts of W and E Africa. There have been various estimates of the number of slaves removed from Africa, the most reliable figure being c.12.5 million between 1650 and 1850. Many other people must have lost their lives in the wars stimulated by the trade, and the total drain meant that at the very least the African population remained static for over two centuries. » slavery; Wilberforce

slavery A system of social inequality in which some people are treated as items of property belonging to other individuals or social groups. There have been different types and conditions of slavery. At one extreme, slaves might be worked to death, as in the Greek mining camps of the 5th-c and 4th-c BC. At the other, slaves were used less as chattels and more as servants, working in households, and to an extent even administering them and acting as tutors to young children. » American Civil War; social stratification; slave trade

Slavic or **Slavonic languages** The NE branch of the Indo-European languages, normally divided into *South Slavic* (eg Bulgarian), *West Slavic* (eg Polish), and *East Slavic* (eg Russian). All of the main languages have official status and a standard form. There are written records of Old Church Slavonic from the 9th-c, and its modern form, Church Slavonic, is used as a liturgical language in the Eastern Orthodox Church. The Baltic and Slavic languages between them have c.300 million mother-tongue speakers, more than half of whom speak Russian. Russian is spoken by c.150 million people as a mother-tongue, and by a further 270 million as a second language, throughout the republics of the former USSR. Polish is spoken by c.40 million in Poland and surrounding areas, as well as by emigrants in several parts of the world, such as the UK and USA. Serbo-Croatian is spoken in Yugoslavia and some adjacent areas by c.18 million. Czech is spoken in W Czechoslovakia by c.10 million. All the East Slavic languages, and some others, are still written in Cyrillic script. » Baltic/Indo-European languages; Cyrillic alphabet; Czechoslovak/Polish/Russian literature

Slavic religion An animistic religion, with themes from hunting, fishing, and agriculture, common to Slavic regions, being practised certainly up to the 14th-c, with traces surviving into the 20th-c. Local deities and supreme gods were worshipped, but there were no temple centres or any organized priestly caste. » animism; religion

Slavs The largest group of European peoples sharing a common ethnic and linguistic origin, consisting of Russians, Ukrainians, Byelorussians, Poles, Czechs, Slovaks, Bulgarians, Serbs, Croats, Montenegrins, and Macedonians. The ancient Slavs, inhabiting C and E Europe, were first mentioned in 2nd-c AD sources. After World War 2, most of the Slav nations were ruled by socialist governments. » Slavic languages; socialism

sleep An unconscious state where the subject shows little responsiveness to the external world. There are two phases of sleep which alternate throughout the night. In deep sleep, the brain activity (EEG) shows slow delta waves (**slow wave sleep**, or **SWS**). This is interrupted every 90 minutes or so by 30 minutes of **rapid eye movement** (**REM**) sleep. Here the muscles are completely relaxed, but the closed eyes show rapid movements. The brain activity is that of wakefulness, but the subject does not respond to stimuli. Dreaming occurs in REM sleep, and perhaps also in SWS. The sleep cycle is controlled by the reciprocal activity of nerve cells in the brain stem. Sleep is restorative. Growth hormone, which promotes cell division, is secreted during SWS. » brain [i]; electro-encephalogram

sleep-walking or **somnambulism** A state in which an individual rises from the bed and walks about for a variable period. It is unrelated to dream activity, and occurs particularly when an individual is subject to stress. It is most common in children, and in most cases stops by the time the child reaches puberty. There are few long-term consequences, and the most important component of management is ensuring that the sleep-walker has a safe environment (eg blocking off access to a flight of stairs). » sleep

sleeping sickness » **trypanosomiasis**

sleet A form of precipitation found in near-freezing surface air. In the UK the term is used for partially melted snow which reaches the ground, or a mixture of snow and rain. In the USA it describes raindrops which have frozen into ice pellets, and then partially thawed before reaching the ground. » precipitation; rainfall; snow

slepton » **supersymmetry**

slide A still picture transparency mounted for projection. Large slides 3¼ in square (82.5 mm), often hand-drawn, were used in magic lanterns, but the modern form is a colour photograph 36 × 24 mm in a standard mount 2 in square (50 mm). One of the most popular formats for amateur photography, slides are widely used as illustrations in educational and commercial presentations, in audio-visual shows, and as inserts in television news and current affairs programmes. » audio-visual aids; multi-vision

slide projector A projector which shows an enlarged image of a slide transparency on a screen. Up to 80 standard slides loaded in straight or circular feed trays can be automatically selected one at a time by remote control or signals from a magnetic tape. To avoid the brief dark interval between successive pictures, slide projectors are often used in pairs so that one image dissolves smoothly into the next; several pairs may be grouped for elaborate multi-image presentation. » projector [i]; slide

slide rat » **pika**

Sliema [**slee**ma] 35°55N 14°31E, pop (1983e) 20 116. Residential and resort town on N coast of main island of Malta, across Marsamxett Harbour from Valletta; largest town in Malta; casino, water-sports facilities, yacht repair yard; boat to Comino. » Malta [i]

Sligo (county) [**sli**ygoh], Gaelic **Sligeach** pop (1981) 55 474; area 1 795 sq km/693 sq ml. County in Connacht province, W Irish Republic; bounded N by the Atlantic Ocean; watered by R Moy; Ox Mts to the W; capital, Sligo; cattle, dairy farming, coal; associated with W B Yeats. » Irish Republic [i]; Sligo (town); Yeats

Sligo (town) [**sli**ygoh] 54°17N 8°28W, pop (1981) 18 002. Seaport capital of Sligo county, Connacht, W Irish Republic; at head of Sligo Bay where it meets R Garrogue; railway; technical college; fishing, textiles, food processing; megalithic stones at nearby Carrowmore; Yeats international summer school and language school; Gaelic cultural activities (summer). » Gaelic; Irish Republic [i]; megalith; Sligo (county); Yeats

Slim (of Yarralumia and of Bishopston), William (Joseph), 1st Viscount (1891–1970) British field marshal, born in Bristol, Gloucestershire. Educated at King Edward's School, Birmingham, he served during World War 1 in Gallipoli and Mesopotamia. In World War 2, his greatest achievement was to lead his reorganized forces, the famous 14th 'forgotten' army, to victory over the Japanese in Burma. He was Chief of the Imperial General Staff (1948–52) and a highly successful Governor-General of Australia (1953–60). Knighted in 1944, he became a viscount in 1960, and died in London. » World War 2

slime mould A primitive micro-organism resembling a fungus, but with an amoeba-like colony stage in its life cycle; some are cellular, some plasmodial (lacking walls between cells). (Class: *Myxomycota*.) » amoeba; clubroot; fungus

slipped disc » **prolapsed intervertebral disc**

slipper gloxinia » **gloxinia**

slippery elm A species of elm native to N America. The slippery inner bark contains a sticky juice used in medicines. (*Ulmus rubra*. Family: *Ulmaceae*.) » elm

Sloane, Sir Hans (1660–1753) British physician, born at Killyleagh, Co Down, Ireland. He studied in London and in France, and settled in London as a physician, but spent 1685–6 in Jamaica, collecting a herbarium of 800 species. His museum and library of 50 000 volumes and 3 560 manuscripts formed the nucleus of the British Museum. He died in London. » British Museum

sloe » **blackthorn**

sloop A single-masted, fore-and-aft rigged sailing vessel with only one headsail. In the 18th-c, the term was also used for any small naval vessel. In World War 2, it referred to an anti-submarine vessel superior to a corvette in speed and equipment. » corvette; ship [i]

sloth A South American mammal of family *Megalonychidae* (**two-toed sloths**, 2 species) or of family *Bradypodidae* (**three-toed sloths**, 3 species); two-toed sloths actually have two fingers (all sloths have three toes); an edentate; eats leaves; hangs upside down in trees using huge claws; round head, shaggy coat (which hides ears), no tail; grooves on hairs may contain blue-green algae which assist camouflage. » Edentata

sloth bear A bear native to S India and Sri Lanka; long black shaggy coat with pale snout and yellow crescent on chest; long front claws; can close nostrils; eats mainly bees and termites. (*Melursus ursinus*.) » bear

Slough [slow] 51°31N 0°36W, pop (1981) 97 389. Town in Slough district, Berkshire, S England; NE of Windsor, 30 km/18½ ml W of C London; railway; paints, pharmaceuticals, electronics, plastics, aircraft parts, vehicle parts, foodstuffs; London Heathrow airport nearby. » Berkshire

Slovak Republic or **Slovakia**, Czech **Slovensko** pop (1984) 5 108 817; area 49 035 sq km/18 927 sq ml. Republic in E Czechoslovakia; bounded N by Poland, E by Ukraine, S by Hungary, SW by Austria, and W by the Czech Republic; Tatra Mts in N, rising to 2 655 m/8 710 ft at Gerlachovsky; part of Great Moravia, 9th-c; part of Magyar Empire from 10th-c; province of Czechoslovakia, 1918; capital, Bratislava; chief towns include Košice, Banská Bystrica, Prešov; agricultural region, especially cereals, wine, fruit. » Czechoslovakia [i]

Slovenes A Slavonic people, numbering (1945) some 1 600 000 and concentrated in the NW corner of the Balkan peninsula; overwhelmingly Roman Catholic. Before 1918, they were subjects of the Habsburg Empire; they are now mainly citizens of Yugoslavia, though c.100 000 continue to inhabit Italy and c.80 000 Austria. » Habsburgs

Slovenia, Serbo-Croat **Slovenija** pop (1981) 1 891 864; area 20 251 sq km/7 817 sq ml. Mountainous republic in N Yugoslavia, bounded N by Austria, W by Italy, E by Hungary, and S by Croatia; capital, Ljubljana; chief towns include Maribor, Kranj, Celje; settled by Slovenians, 6th-c; later controlled by Slavs and Franks; part of the Austro-Hungarian Empire until 1918; people's republic, 1946; declaration of independence, 1990, opposed by central government; maize, wheat, sugar beet, potatoes, livestock, timber, lignite, textiles, vehicles, steel; coal, lead, mercury. » Yugoslavia [i]

slowworm A legless lizard, native to Europe, NW Africa, and SW Asia; grey or brown; female with darker line along side; long tail may be shed, but never grows back to full length; eats worms and slugs; also known as **blindworm** – a name additionally used for skinks of genus *Typhlosaurus*. (*Anguis fragilis*. Family: *Anguidae*.) » lizard [i]; skink

SLR » **reflex camera**

slug (biology) A terrestrial snail with an elongate body and usually a small external shell, or no shell at all; typically two pairs of tentacles on its head, the upper pair bearing the eyes; common in moist environments. (Class: *Gastropoda*. Subclass: *Pulmonata*.) » sea slug; snail

slug (physics) » RR71

slump » **depression** (economics); **recession**

Sluter, Claus or **Claes** (c.1350–c.1405) Flemish sculptor, born (probably) at Haarlem. He went to Dijon under the patronage of Philip the Bold of Burgundy, and died there. His chief works are the porch sculptures of the Carthusian house of Champmol near Dijon, and the tomb of Philip the Bold. » Flemish art; sculpture

smallpox A highly infectious viral disease. As a result of a World Health Organization programme including vaccination, smallpox was declared in 1979 to have been completely eradicated. The virus is now kept only in two designated laboratories outside the UK. » virus

smart bomb » **bomb**

smelt Slender-bodied marine and freshwater fish belonging to either the N hemisphere family *Osmeridae* or the Australasian family *Retropinnidae*; several species migrate into fresh water to breed; includes the European smelt, *Osmerus eperlanus* (length up to 30 cm/12 in), found in coastal waters and rivers from Biscay to Norway. » fish [i]

smelting Obtaining a metal from its ore by heating, using fuel which will simultaneously remove other components of the ore (such as the oxygen of oxides), and a flux to promote the removal of impurities. Copper was probably the first metal to be obtained from an ore, and tin, lead, and silver were also smelted in early times. Charcoal was the universal fuel and reducing agent until the use of coke in the 18th-c. Forced draughts were used in classical times, leading eventually to the blast furnace. There are many variants of the fuel combustion forms of smelting, and electrical methods are also employed, as in the case of aluminium. » Bessemer process; charcoal; coke; flux (technology); open-hearth process

Smetana, Bedřich [**sme**tana] (1824–84) Czech composer, born at Litomyšl. He studied in Prague, and in 1848 opened a music school with the financial support of Liszt. He conducted in Sweden (1856–9), and in Prague became conductor of the new National Theatre (1866). His compositions, intensely national in character, include nine operas, notably *Prodaná nevěsta* (1866, The Bartered Bride), and many chamber and orchestral works, including the series of symphonic poems *Má Vlast* (1874–9, My Country). Overwork destroyed his health, and in 1874 he became deaf, though he continued to compose until a mental breakdown in 1883. He died in Prague.

smew A small bird (a merganser), native to the N Old World; untidy crest on back of head; male white with black back and tail, black patch below eye and on back of head; female mainly brown; inhabits fresh or sheltered coastal waters. (*Mergus albellus*.) » merganser

Smiles, Samuel (1812–1904) British author and social reformer, born at Haddington, Berwickshire, Scotland. Educated at Edinburgh, he settled as a surgeon in Leeds, but left medicine for journalism, editing the *Leeds Times* (1838–42), and becoming involved in railway companies until 1866. His main work was a guide to self-improvement, *Self-Help* (1859), with its short lives of great men and the admonition 'Do thou likewise', but he wrote many biographical and moral books. He died in London. » biography; English literature; Golden Rule

Smith, Adam (1723–90) British economist and philosopher, born at Kirkcaldy, Fife, Scotland. Educated at Glasgow and Oxford, he became professor of logic at Glasgow (1751), but took up the chair of moral philosophy the following year. In 1776 he moved to London, where he published *An Inquiry into the Nature and Causes of the Wealth of Nations* (1776), the first major work of political economy. This examined in detail the consequences of economic freedom, such as division of labour, the function of markets, and the international implications of a *laissez-faire* economy. His appointment as commissioner of customs (1778) took him back to Edinburgh, where he died. » laissez-faire; political economy

Smith, Bessie (1894–1937) US blues singer, born at Chattanooga, Tennessee. Raised in poverty in the US South, she ran away as a teenager with Ma Rainey's Rabbit Foot Minstrels, a Black revue. She was a veteran of honky tonks, circuses, and tent shows by the time she recorded her first sides in New York in 1923. By the end of the year she had sold an astounding two million records. Known as the Empress of the Blues, her handsome, commanding presence made her as sensational on stage as did her imperious, bittersweet voice on record. By 1928, her success had waned, as popular taste swung to dance music. She died in a car accident in Mississippi. » blues; jazz

Smith, Dodie, pseudonym **C L Anthony** (1896–) British dramatist, novelist, and theatre producer. She started as an actress but turned to writing, producing such successful plays as *Dear Octopus* (1938). She is also known for her children's book *The Hundred and One Dalmations* (1956). » drama

Smith, Florence Margaret » **Smith, Stevie**

Smith, Frederick » **Birkenhead, Earl of**

Smith, Ian (Douglas) (1919–) Prime Minister of Rhodesia

(1964–79), born at Selukwe. Educated in Rhodesia and South Africa, he fought in World War 2, and became an MP in 1948. In 1961 he became a founder of the Rhodesian Front, dedicated to immediate independence without African majority rule. As Premier, in 1965 he unilaterally declared independence, which resulted in the imposition of increasingly severe economic sanctions. After an intensive guerrilla war, he created an 'internal settlement', and Muzorewa's caretaker government made him a member of the Transitional Executive Council of 1978–9 to prepare for the transfer of power. The internal settlement was overturned by the Lancaster House Agreement, and he was elected an MP under Mugabe's government. He continued to be a vigorous opponent of the one-party state. » Lancaster House Agreement; Mugabe; Muzorewa; Zimbabwe [i]

Smith, John (1580–1631) English adventurer, born at Willoughby, Lincolnshire. He fought in France and Hungary, where he was captured by the Turks, and sold as a slave. After escaping to Russia, he joined an expedition to colonize Virginia (1607), and was saved from death by Pocahontas. His energy in dealing with the Indians led to his being elected president of the colony (1608–9). He wrote valuable accounts of his travels, and died in London. » Pocahontas

Smith, Joseph (1805–44) US founder of the Mormons, born at Sharon, Vermont. He received his first 'call' as a prophet in 1820, was later told of a hidden gospel written on golden plates in 'reformed Egyptian', and on the night of 22 September 1827 the sacred records were delivered into his hands on a hill near Palmyra, New York. The *Book of Mormon* (1830) contained a history of America to the 5th-c of the Christian era, written by a prophet named Mormon, during which Christ is said to have appeared after his ascension and established his Church in the New World. Ordained priest by the angel Moroni, Smith was to be the instrument of the Church's re-establishment. Despite ridicule and hostility, the new 'Church of the Latter-day Saints' rapidly gained converts. He founded Nauvoo, Illinois in 1840, becoming mayor, and starting the practice of 'spiritual wives'. Violence followed his announcement as a candidate for the US presidency. He was imprisoned for conspiracy, and killed by a mob who broke into Carthage jail, where he and his brother Hyram were awaiting trial. » Jesus Christ; Mormons; prophet

Smith, Stevie, pseudonym of **Florence Margaret Smith** (1902–71) British writer, born at Hull, Yorkshire. Educated in London, she wrote novels, such as *Novel on Yellow Paper* (1936), but acquired a reputation principally as an eccentrically humorous poet on serious themes, illustrated by *Not Waving but Drowning* (1957). She died in London. » English literature; poetry

Smithfield An area just outside the walls of the City of London, in former times the scene of tournaments, trials, fairs, and cattle markets. The main London meat market has been located here since the mid-19th-c. » London [i]

Smithsonian Institution A foundation for the promotion of knowledge, endowed in 1826 by the English scientist James Smithson (1765–1829), established by Act of Congress in 1846, and opened in Washington, DC in 1855. It administers a number of art, history, and science museums, scientific research centres, and is the parent organization of several autonomous artistic and academic establishments. » National Gallery of Art

smog A form of air pollution with several sources. In Britain before the mid-20th-c, the smogs of industrial cities were a form of radiation fog, in which soot and smoke acted as condensation nuclei, and gases such as sulphur dioxide (SO_2) and carbon monoxide (CO) were unable to escape. Such a smog (Dec 1952) was responsible for the deaths of more than 4 000 people in London, which led to the Clean Air Act of 1956. At lower latitudes, photochemical smogs (*heat hazes*) occur. Emissions of hydrocarbons and oxides of nitrogen from industrial processes and vehicle exhausts react with sunlight. » acid rain [i]; fog; ozone; temperature inversion

smoke tree A deciduous shrub growing to c.3 m/10 ft, native to S Europe and Asia; leaves rounded, widest above the middle, turning bronzy-purple in autumn; flowers 4–6-petalled, tiny, purplish, eventually fading pink, in plume-like inflorescences, at a distance reminiscent of smoke. (*Cotinus cogyria*. Family: *Anacardiaceae*.) » deciduous plants; inflorescence [i]; shrub

smoked foods The preservation of food using the ancient method of exposing it over a period of time to wood smoke. The preservation is achieved partly through drying and partly through the effects of chemicals in the smoke. » food preservation

smoking The practice of inhaling the fumes from burning tobacco leaves, generally using cigarettes, cigars, or pipes, introduced into Europe from the Americas by early explorers. The practice is habit-forming, and is known to be a causative factor in the development of several diseases, notably lung cancer, throat cancer, and heart and respiratory conditions. The risk increases with the number of cigarettes smoked per day. In several countries, there have been anti-smoking advertising campaigns and a ban on the television advertising of tobacco products; cigarette packets and press advertisements also carry government health warnings. » nicotine; tobacco [i]

Smolensk [smuh**lensk**] 54°49N 32°04E, pop (1983) 321 000. River-port capital of Smolenskaya oblast, WC European Russia, on the upper Dnieper R; first mentioned, 9th-c; part of Russia, 1654; severely damaged in World War 2; railway; linen textiles, flax, fertilizers, engineering; Cathedral of the Assumption (12th-c). » Russia

Smollett, Tobias (George) (1721–71) British novelist, born at Cardross, Dunbartonshire, Scotland. Educated at Glasgow, he visited Cartagena in 1741, and settled in London as a surgeon in 1744. He turned to writing, achieving success with his first works, the picaresque novels *The Adventures of Roderick Random* (1748) and *The Adventures of Peregrine Pickle* (1751). He spent several years in journal editing, translating, and writing historical and travel works. He retired to Italy in 1768, and died near Leghorn, having just completed his masterpiece, *Humphry Clinker* (1771). » English literature; novel; picaresque novel

smooth snake A harmless European snake of family *Colubridae*; scales smooth, not ridged; side of head with dark horizontal line; inhabits dry heathland or open woodland; eats mainly lizards, also some small snakes and mammals. (*Coronella austriaca*.) » snake

smut fungus A fungus that is a parasite of plants, especially grasses, including cereals and sugar cane; fungus body (*mycelium*) grows within host tissues and forms masses of black, soot-like spores on the surface of the infected plant. (Subdivision: *Basidiomycetes*. Order: *Ustilaginales*.) » Basidiomycetes; fungus

Smuts, Jan (Christian) (1870–1950) South African general, statesman, and Prime Minister (1919–24, 1939–48), born at Malmesbury, Cape Colony. Educated at Cambridge, he became a lawyer, fought in the second Boer War (1899–1902), and entered the House of Assembly in 1907. He held several Cabinet posts, led campaigns against the Germans in South West Africa and Tanganyika, was a member of the Imperial War Cabinet in World War 1, and succeeded Botha as Premier. He was a significant figure at Versailles, and was instrumental in the founding of the League of Nations. As Minister of Justice under Hertzog, his coalition with the Nationalists in 1934 produced the United Party, and he became Premier again in 1939. He died near Pretoria. » Boer Wars; Botha, Louis; Hertzog; League of Nations

Smyrna » **Izmir**

Smythe, Pat(ricia), married name **Koechlin** (1928–) British show jumper, born in Switzerland. She won the European championship four times on *Flanagan* (1957, 1961–3), and in 1956 was the first woman to ride in the Olympic Games, winning a bronze medal in the team event. She won the Queen Elizabeth II Cup on *Mr Pollard* in 1958. She has ridden very little since her marriage in 1963. » equestrianism

snail A common name for many types of gastropod mollusc, but sometimes used more specifically for members of the subclass *Pulmonata*; predominantly terrestrial or freshwater forms; usually possess a spirally coiled external shell, without an operculum closing off the shell aperture; mantle cavity modified as a vascularized lung for air breathing; includes pond snails and garden snails. (Class: *Gastropoda.*) » abalone; conch; cone shell; gastropod; helmet shell; limpet; mollusc; murex; olive shell; periwinkle (marine biology); sea butterfly; shell; triton shell; wentletrap; whelk

snail kite A true kite found from Florida to S America; lives near freshwater marshes; eats only snails of genus *Pomacea*; upper bill long, slender and sickle-shaped, used for extracting snail from shell; also known as **everglades kite**. (*Rostrhamus sociabilis.*) » kite

snake A reptile believed to have evolved c.135 million years ago, either from burrowing lizards or from a group of swimming marine lizards; also known as **serpent**; c.2 400 living species, found worldwide except in very cold regions and on some islands; characterized by having separate jaw bones connected by ligaments; these bones can move apart, allowing prey much wider than the snake's head to be swallowed; eats animals (or eggs); cannot chew (swallows prey whole, digestive juices dissolving bones and teeth); long cylindrical scaly body; no limbs or eyelids; no obvious ears; skin moulted several times each year; internal organs modified to fit into the thin body; kidneys lie one behind the other, not side by side; left lung absent or small (except in pythons and boas); c.300 venomous species, which inject less than half their venom with each bite; more than 50 species dangerous to humans; 30–40 000 people die each year from snakebite. (Suborder: *Serpentes* or *Ophidia*. Order: *Squamata.*) » black/coral/flying/mangrove/sea/smooth/tree/vine/wart/whip snake; adder; asp; boa; boomslang; cobra; diamondback; krait; lizard [i]; mamba; python; reptile; taipan; viper [i]

snake bird » **darter** [i]

snake-necked turtle A side-necked turtle, native to S America and Australasia; very long slender neck; lives in or near freshwater; usually carnivorous; called *tortoise* in Australia; also known as **long-necked turtle**. (Family: *Chelidae*, 36 species.) » turtle (biology)

snake plant » **mother-in-law's-tongue**

Snake River River in NW USA; rises in NW Wyoming; flows through Idaho (via the Snake R Plain), along part of the Oregon–Idaho and Washington–Idaho borders, into Washington, joining the Columbia R near Pasco; length c.1 600 km/1 000 ml; major tributaries the Bruneau, Boise, Owyhee, Grande Ronde, Clearwater, Palouse; contains several gorges, the largest being Hell's Canyon; used for irrigation and hydroelectricity. » Hell's Canyon; United States of America [i]

snake's head » **fritillary** (botany)

snakefly A predatory insect characterized by an elongation of the thorax that produces a snake-like neck; adults have two pairs of similar wings with complex veins; usually found on or under bark; feeds on insects. (Order: *Neuroptera*. Family: *Raphidiidae.*) » insect [i]

snapdragon A short-lived, slightly bushy perennial, growing to 80 cm/30 in, native to Europe; lower leaves opposite, upper alternate; flowers strongly zygomorphic, the tube with two lips, the lower 3-lobed, with a projection (the *palate*) closing the tube and forming a landing platform for bumble-bees, the only insects with sufficient weight and strength to part the lips and reach the nectar within. The flowers of the wild plants are reddish-purple, with cultivars in a range of colours. It is cultivated as an ornamental annual. (*Antirrhinum majus*. Family: *Scrophulariaceae.*) » cultivar; perennial; zygomorphic flower

snapper Deep-bodied fish of the family *Lutjanidae* (4 genera, 300 species), widespread and locally common in tropical seas; name derives from the long conical front teeth and highly mobile jaws; some species are a valuable food fish; includes the common tropical Atlantic **grey snapper**, *Lutjanus griseus*. The name is also used for some of the large family *Sparidae*, with similar canine-like front teeth. » fish [i]

snapping turtle A reptile native to N and C America; large head which cannot be withdrawn into shell; strong hooked jaws; long tail; inhabits fresh water; eats animals that live in (or enter) water; two species: **snapping turtle** (*Chelydra serpentina*) and **alligator snapping turtle** (*Macroclemys temminckii*). (Family: *Chelydridae.*) » turtle (reptile)

snare drum A side drum to which snares (lengths of wire) are fitted. When engaged they touch the skin to give a rasping edge to the sound. » percussion [i]; side drum

Snead, Sam(uel) Jackson, byname **Slammin' Sam** (1912–) US golfer, born at Hot Springs, Virginia. He was the winner of a record 84 tournaments on the US Professional Golfers Association (PGA) Tour between 1936 and 1965. Professional since 1934, he is credited with 135 victories worldwide. He won the British Open in 1946, the US PGA Championship in 1942, 1949, and 1951, and the US Masters in 1949, 1952, and 1954. » golf

Snell's law » **refraction** [i]

Śniardwy [**shnyahd**vee] area 114 sq km/44 sq ml. Lake in Suwałki voivodship, NE Poland; largest lake in Poland; greatest depth 23 m/77 ft. » Poland [i]

snipe A sandpiper, found worldwide; mottled brown plumage; shortish legs and long straight bill; inhabits mainly marshes and mountain meadows; small groups called 'wisps'. (Genus: *Gallinago*, 17 species, or *Coenocorypha*, 1 species.) » sandpiper

snooker A popular indoor game played with cues on a standard English billiards table by 2 (sometimes 4) players. 22 balls are placed at specific positions on the table: one white, 15 reds, and six coloured balls (yellow, green, brown, blue, pink, and black). The object is to use the cue to hit the white ball to send ('pot') the other balls into any of six pockets around the table. The coloured balls have an ascending points value of 2–7, while each red is worth one point. After potting a red, the successful player must then attempt to pot a coloured ball, after which a further red is played; this sequence (known as a 'break') continues until a foul is played or a ball not potted. Reds stay in the pocket when potted. The colours return to the table when potted, unless there are no reds left; they must then be potted in ascending order, and stay off the table. The game ends when the black is finally potted; and the winner is the player with most points. Snooker was invented by army officers serving in the Devonshire Regiment in India in 1875, who developed it from Black Pool. The game was named by one of the officers, Neville Chamberlain. It is now one of the most popular television sports. » pyramids; RR118; Plate XV

Snorri Sturluson (1179–1241) Icelandic poet and historian. In 1215 he was elected supreme judge of the island, but after interfering with the domestic troubles of Norway, he incurred the ill-will of King Haakon, who had him murdered. His main

Snapdragon – Inset shows bee parting lips of flower

works were the *Prose Edda* and the *Heimskringla*, a series of sagas of the Norwegian kings down to 1177. » Icelandic literature; saga

snow A type of solid precipitation which forms at temperatures below the freezing point of water. At very cold temperatures, single ice crystals may fall as snow. At higher temperatures, ice crystals aggregate into geometrical forms called **snow flakes**. Close to freezing point, snow may turn to sleet as it begins to thaw. » precipitation; sleet; whiteout

Snow, C(harles) P(ercy), 1st Baron (1905–80) British novelist and physicist, born in Leicester. He was educated at Leicester and at Cambridge, where he became a fellow (1930–50) and a tutor (1935–45). He was the author of a cycle of successful novels portraying English life from 1920 onwards, starting with *Strangers and Brothers* (1940), and including *The Masters* (1951), *The New Men* (1954), and *Corridors of Power* (1964). His controversial *Two Cultures* (Rede lecture, 1959) discussed the dichotomy between science and literature and his belief in closer contact between them. He married the novelist Pamela Hansford Johnson in 1950, was knighted in 1957, became a life peer in 1964, and died in London. » English literature; Johnson, Pamela Hansford; novel

snow bunting A bird (a bunting) native to the northern N hemisphere; in winter white with black back; in summer brown head and back, white underparts; inhabits open stony country or (in winter) coasts; eats seeds and insects. (*Plectrophenax nivalis*.) » bunting

snow goose A goose native to N America and from E Siberia to Japan. There are two races: **greater** and **lesser**. The lesser has two colour phases, the darker being called the **blue goose**. (*Anser coerulescens*, sometimes described as 3 species.) » goose

snow leopard A rare big cat native to the mountains of SC Asia, living near the snow line; thick pale grey coat with dark rings (sometimes enclosing small spots); inhabits meadows, rocks, and (in winter) forests; eats goats, sheep, deer, smaller mammals, birds; also known as **ounce**. (*Panthera uncia*.) » Felidae

snow sheep » **bighorn**

snowball tree » **guelder rose**

Snowdon, 1st Earl of, originally **Anthony Armstrong-Jones** (1930–) British photographer and designer, who married Princess Margaret in 1960 (divorced 1978). A freelance photojournalist since 1951, he designed the Aviary of the London Zoo in 1965, and in recent years has devoted much effort to presenting the conditions of the handicapped, both in photographic studies and in television documentaries. » Margaret, Princess

Snowdon, Welsh **Yr Wyddfa** 53°04N 4°05W. Mountain with five peaks rising to 1 085 m/3 560 ft in Gwynedd, NW Wales, UK; highest peak in England and Wales; centre of Snowdonia National Park (area 2 188 sq km/845 sq ml, established 1951); tourism; rack railway from Llanberis to main peak. » Gwynedd

snowdrop A bulb often flowering in late winter, native to Europe and W Asia; leaves strap-shaped, very narrow, bluish-green; flowers on long stalks, solitary, drooping, white; three outer perianth-segments spreading; three inner smaller, with green spot at base of apical notch. (*Galanthus nivalis*. Family: *Amaryllidaceae*.) » bulb; perianth

snowshoe hare A nocturnal N American hare with a coat which is brown in summer, white in winter; inhabits coniferous forests; populations undergo large fluctuations in numbers over 8–10-year periods; also known as **snowshoe rabbit** or **varying hare**. (*Lepus americanus*.) » hare

Snowy Mountains Scheme A massive construction project in SE Australia carried out 1949–72, but first proposed in 1881. The object of the Scheme was to divert the Snowy R inland into the Murrumbidgee R to provide hydroelectricity and irrigation. It consists of 16 storage dams, 7 power stations, 80 km/50 ml of aqueducts, and 145 km/90 ml of tunnels. » irrigation

snowy owl A typical owl native to the northern N hemisphere; plumage mainly white; inhabits tundra, marshes, and Arctic islands; hunts during day; eats mammals and birds up to the size of Arctic hares and ducks; nests on ground. (*Nyctea scandiaca*.) » owl

snuff Any drug prepared as a fine powder which is administered by sniffing; it is absorbed through the nasal mucous membranes. More commonly snuff is synonymous with tobacco snuff, taken for its nicotine content. Tobacco snuff was used by some American Indian tribes and later adopted by Europeans. In the 17th-c, snuff-taking was adopted in parts of Asia where smoking was illegal. It reached the peak of popularity in the French court in the 18th-c, but its use was brought to an end by the French Revolution. Snuff is rarely used nowadays. » nicotine; tobacco [i]

Snyder, Gary (1930–) US poet, born in San Francisco. He studied Japanese and Chinese at Berkeley, and since 1965 has lived mainly in Japan, writing poems which bring together American and Eastern culture. Collections include *Myths and Texts* (1965), *The Back Country* (1967), and *Axe Handles* (1983). » American literature; poetry

Snyders, Frans (1579–1657) Dutch painter, born and died in Antwerp. He specialized in still life and animals, often assisting Rubens and other painters, and became court painter to the Governor of the Low Countries, for whom he painted some of his finest hunting scenes. » Dutch art; Rubens

Soane, Sir John (1753–1837) British architect, born at Goring, Oxfordshire. He trained in London, spent 1777–80 in Italy, held several government posts, and became professor of architecture at the Royal Academy (1806). His designs include the Bank of England (1792–1833, now rebuilt) and Dulwich College Art Gallery (1811–14). His house at Lincoln's Inn Fields has become a museum. He died in London.

soap The salt of a fatty acid, usually stearic (octadecanoic) or palmitic (hexadecanoic) acids. Commercial soaps for toilet use are usually the sodium or potassium salts; insoluble calcium soaps are used as lubricants. » napalm; palmitic acid; saponification; stearic acid

soapstone » **talc**

soapwort A perennial with creeping stolons and erect leafy stems, native to Europe and Asia; flowers 2.5 cm/1 in in diameter, fragrant; calyx tubular, often reddish; five petals, spreading, pale pink, each with two scales at the base. (*Saponaria officinalis*. Family: *Caryophyllaceae*.) » perennial; sepal; stolon

Sobers, Gary, properly **Sir Garfield (St Aubrun)** (1936–) West Indian cricketer, born in Barbados. A great all-rounder, he is the only man to score 8 000 Test runs and take 200 wickets. During his career (1953–74) he scored 28 315 runs in first-class cricket (average 54.87) and took 1 043 wickets (average 27.74). Against Pakistan at Kingston in 1958 he scored a Test cricket world record 365 not out. Playing for Nottinghamshire against Glamorgan at Swansea in 1968, he scored a record 36 runs in one over. He retired in 1974, and was knighted the following year. » cricket (sport) [i]

soccer » **football 1** [i]

soccerene » **buckminsterfullerene**

Sochi [sochee] 43°35N 39°46E, pop (1983) 304 000. Seaport in Krasnodarskiy kray, S European Russia; founded as a spa, 1910; stretches for over 30 km/19 ml along the E shore of the Black Sea; airport; railway; important holiday and health resort; fortress ruins (1838). » Russia

social action Activity taken by a group which is intended to achieve some reform or to promote a particular cause. As the term 'social' implies, the action is pursued through channels other than those of the formal government and political systems. Instead, action is carried out on a broader front designed, among other things, to build support and influence opinion among members of society. It is most commonly associated with radical politics. Contemporary examples include Greenpeace and the various groups involved in animal rights. » radicalism

Social and Liberal Democratic Party (SLDP) » **Liberal Party** (UK)

social anthropology » **anthropology**

social behaviourism A school of thought in social psychology which argues that all observable social action is in response to the hidden needs, desires, or beliefs of the deeper 'self'. These ideas were given particular prominence through the work of social psychologist George Herbert Mead (1863–1931). » pragmatism; social psychology

social cognition In psychology, the processes through which the social world is perceived, understood, and reasoned about. Theorists who write about these processes tend to stress the impact of thinking on social action. » prejudice

social contract or **social compact** The voluntary, unwritten agreement between a society's members to act in a mutually responsible manner, accepting the authority of the state which in turn guarantees and upholds certain moral principles. The philosophy maintains that greater efforts should be made to secure more equality for all sections of society. How far government should interfere with market forces to achieve this would be the subject of consensus within a nation. This philosophy was first propounded by Hobbes, Locke, and Rousseau, and has been an important feature of much liberal political theory in recent years. The concept was also seen in the UK in 1975, when the Labour government under Wilson arrived at a consensus with the Trades Union Council on the broad social and economic policies that the government should pursue. However, in 1978 no agreement could be reached, and the system lapsed. » Hobbes; Labour Party; Locke, John; Rousseau, Jean Jacques; trade union; Wilson, Harold

Social Darwinism A school of thought which developed within 19th-c sociology based on the belief that social evolution depended on society adapting most efficiently to its environment. The associated 'eugenics movement' argued that Western society had developed because of the superior abilities of Whites compared with other 'racial' groups. » eugenics; Galton; sociology

social democracy A section of the socialist movement which emerged in the late 19th-c after the break-up of the First International, and which advocates achieving social change through reformist rather than revolutionary means. Social democrats accept and work through existing state structures, although such movements may contain radical left-wing sections. Some political parties that have adopted the social democratic label in the latter part of the 20th-c are, however, moderate centrist parties. » International; reformism; Social Democratic Party; socialism

Social Democratic Party (SDP) A UK political party formed in 1981 by a 'gang of four', comprising David Owen (1938–), Shirley Williams (1930–), Roy Jenkins (1920–), and Bill Rogers (1928–). They broke away from the Labour Party primarily over disagreements on policy and the degree of influence exerted on party policy by the trade unions. Although espousing socialist principles, the party was a moderate centrist one. The SDP formed an electoral pact with the Liberals in 1981, but despite some early electoral successes failed to break the two-party 'mould' of British politics. It merged with the Liberal Party in 1988 becoming the **Social and Liberal Democratic Party**, although a rump, led by David Owen, continued in existence as the SDP until 1990. » Labour Party; Liberal Party (UK); Jenkins, Roy; Owen, David; Williams, Shirley

social engineering A term used (often critically) to describe the techniques dominant social groups may use to manipulate the subordinate population. It is typically applied to policies of government that lack democratic accountability; for example, many criticized the manipulative family planning programmes of the Indian government during the 1970s.

Social Gospel An early 20th-c movement in the USA concerned with the application of Christian principles to the social and political order in the service of the Kingdom of God. Among its most prominent leaders were Washington Gladden (1836–1918), Walter Rauschenbusch (1861–1918), and Shailer Matthews (1863–1941). » Christianity

social history History which concentrates upon the interaction of groups and upon the nature of social structures in the past. Once undervalued, both as a descriptive subject concerned with unearthing the minutiae of everyday life and as a less analytical appendage to economic history, social history has developed rapidly since the 1960s. It has incorporated social science method, particularly in analysing the importance of class and status in understanding the process of social change. While much social history has concentrated upon the history of the lower orders, usually neglected in political history, increasing attention has been paid since the early 1980s to the analysis of the middle classes and the aristocracy as social groups. The insights of social history have also begun to broaden the scope of political history, such that the distinction between the two disciplines has become blurred. » class; history; politics; social science; status

social medicine » **community medicine**

social mobility The way individuals or groups move from one status or class position to another, either higher ('upward' social mobility) or lower ('downward' social mobility), within the social hierarchy. It is typically measured in terms of movement across a range of pre-existing positions which enjoy unequal access to material and cultural 'goods'. One can improve one's access to such goods, and so be upwardly mobile in a number of ways, most importantly by education, marriage, or occupation. Entire social groups may also be mobile, by using their resources to enhance their position: for example, occupational groups may improve their status by 'professionalizing' their expertise. » social stratification; status

social mobilization Significant social change which leads individuals, families, and groups within society to a higher level of political consciousness, resulting in new political demands. The process can be illustrated by the movement from a rural to an industrial economy or from a colony to an independent state.

social movement Any significant social or political force which aims to bring about change, but which has only the minimum of organization and operates through self-generating and independent action, such as the women's movement. These movements have played a significant part in many important social and political changes. They sometimes produce more organized forms of action, in the form of political parties and pressure groups.

social psychology The study of the behaviour of groups of individuals. Social psychologists might record anything from fine-grained details of the body posture and gaze direction of an individual, in an attempt to understand non-verbal communication, to large-scale characteristics of crowd behaviour. They are also concerned with concepts that necessarily involve more than one individual, such as leadership, friendship, and persuasion. » prejudice; psychology; role

social realism A term current in art criticism since World War 2, referring to pictures which treat 'real life' subjects in a way that challenges the values of 'bourgeois' society. Courbet's 'Stonebreakers' (1849) may have been the first great social realist picture. In the 20th-c the term has been applied to the US Ashcan School, and in Europe to Italian artist Renato Guttoso (1912–87). » Ashcan School; Courbet; Realism; Socialist Realism

social science A general term designating a number of disciplines, such as sociology, economics, political science, and geography, which have explored various aspects of society – such as social structure, the market, power, and spatial relations – through methods which are conventionally understood to be 'scientific'. Research involves data collection and analysis in order to test hypotheses or models. Mathematical analyses are now commonplace in some areas, such as demography and social mobility studies. Nevertheless, there is still debate over whether these disciplines can be truly 'scientific', given that they are measuring patterns of human behaviour rather than the organic or inanimate material of the natural and physical sciences. » economics; geography; political science; sociology

social security **1** In the USA, a tax on wages and salaries imposed to pay for retirement benefits, disability insurance, and hospital insurance. The tax is an important part of all federal revenues (around 40%), and is the equivalent of British national insurance. » national insurance **2** In the UK, the provision of financial aid by the state to reduce poverty. It comprises a wide range of benefits (covering such matters as housing and family allowances) which are available to those in need.

social stratification A system of social inequality in which social groups occupy different positions (or *strata*) based on their unequal access to and ownership of material, political, and cultural (eg educational) resources. Social stratification is never a random process, but a product of economic and social relations that 'allocate' people to specific positions. » class; slavery

social studies A range of disciplines within the arts, humanities, and social sciences, including sociology, history, economics, and geography, whose principal concern is the study of various aspects of society. With the development of more sophisticated and scientific analyses, the term is less favoured today and more likely to be replaced by *social sciences*. » economics; geography; history; social science; sociology

social system The structured pattern of social relationships which together have a systemic character. A society has a social system inasmuch as change in some aspects of society will bring change in other parts. There have been different types of social system prevailing in different periods of history, such as feudalism, capitalism, and socialism. Sociologists have also distinguished 'traditional' from 'modern' social systems, but there is considerable debate over the exact meaning of these two terms. » capitalism; feudalism; socialism

social work Usually understood to refer to the occupational activities of the social-work profession, ie the provision of social services to the 'needy', including counselling, care, and the general administration of the benefits of the state. Social work has its origins in late 19th-c charitable organizations which provided assistance to hospital staff and helped distribute poor relief.

socialism A wide-ranging political doctrine which first emerged in Europe during industrialization in the 18th-c. Most socialists would agree that social and economic relationships play a major part in determining human possibilities, and that the unequal ownership of property under capitalism creates an unequal and conflictive society. The removal of private property or some means of counterbalancing its power, it is held, will produce a more equal society where individuals enjoy greater freedom and are able to realize their potential more fully. A socialist society will thus be more co-operative and fraternal. Possibly the major division within socialism is between those who believe that to bring it about revolution is necessary, and those who believe change can be achieved through reforms within the confines of democratic politics. There are also differences as to how far capitalist production needs to be eradicated to bring about a socialist society. » anarchism; Maoism; Marxism; Marxism-Leninism; New Left; reformism; revolution; social democracy; syndicalism

Socialist Labor Party The longest-lasting socialist party in the USA. It nominated its first presidential candidate in 1892 and has existed ever since. » socialism

Socialist Realism In literature and art, the official style of the former Soviet Union and of other socialist states, intended to appeal to the masses, and typically representing ordinary workers going about their mundane tasks. The Hungarian critic Georg Lukács was a major proponent, and Russian self-exile Andrei Sinyavsky (1925–) a noted antagonist. The novels of Mikhail Sholokhov may be cited, but few writers can exactly fulfil a prescription for what Trotsky called 'the literature of the future'. » literary criticism; Lukács; Realism; Sholokhov; social realism

Socialist Revolutionary (SR) Party A neo-populist revolutionary party in Russia, founded in 1902 and led by Victor Chernov (1873–1952). The SR's radical agrarian programme envisaged the uncompensated redistribution and 'socialization' of the land among a communally organized peasantry. Their 'fighting detachments' carried out a number of spectacular political assassinations between 1902 and 1918. In 1917 Chernov was minister of agriculture in the provisional government. » radicalism; Russian revolution

society » **class; consumer/post-industrial society**

Society Islands, Fr **Archipel de la Société** pop (1983) 152 129; area 1 535 sq km/592 sq ml. One of the five archipelagoes of French Polynesia, comprising the Windward Is (including Tahiti) and the Leeward Is; two clusters of volcanic and coral islands in a 720-km/450-ml chain stretching NW–SE; visited by Captain Cook in 1769, and named by him after the Royal Society; French protectorate, 1844; French colony, 1897; capital, Papeete (Tahiti); phosphates, copra, vanilla, mother-of-pearl. » Leeward Islands (French Polynesia); Windward Islands (Pacific)

Socinus, Laelius [sosiynuhs], originally **Lelio (Francesco Maria) Sozini** (1525–62) Italian Protestant reformer, born at Siena. He trained as a lawyer at Padua, then turned to Biblical studies. He travelled widely in Europe, settling in Zürich (1548), where he died. His anti-Trinitarian views were developed by his nephew **Faustus Socinus** (1539–1604) into a doctrine known as **Socinianism**. » Protestantism; Reformation; Trinity

sociobiology The integrated study of the biological basis of social behaviour, based on the assumption that all behaviour is adaptive. Emphasis is placed on social systems as ecological adaptations, and explanations are given in terms of evolutionary theory. » biology; ecology; evolution; sociology

sociogram » **sociometry**

sociolinguistics The study of the relationships between language and the society which uses it. The subject has a wide range, encompassing the analysis of all the varieties used in a community, and the contexts in which they are appropriate. This includes the use of standard and non-standard forms, and the attitudes towards them of different groups; the language of different social class and caste groups; the differences between male and female speech; and the character of multilingual societies, particularly the social functions assigned to the languages by bilingual members of the community. The subject sometimes includes such societally-based studies as dialectology and ethnolinguistics. » bilingualism; dialectology; diglossia; ethnolinguistics; linguistics; sociology; stylistics

sociology The study of patterned social behaviour which constitutes a social system or society, a term originally coined by French social theorist Auguste Comte. Sociologists explore the way in which social structures are continually modified as a result of social interaction, and thereby seek to explain the development of new institutions or new types of society. Modern sociology has a number of key theoretical approaches which try to account for social structure and social change. While they differ in very important respects, they all share the belief that they can 'get behind' the surface appearance of everyday life, to reveal its complexity and interest. Any aspect of society can be examined sociologically, but there have emerged certain areas of study that have gained most attention, such as crime, the family, gender, the media, science and technology, medicine, and systems of inequality. » Comte; ethnomethodology; Frankfurt School; social behaviourism; Social Darwinism; social studies; symbolic interactionism

sociometry A technique for mapping social networks. The networks are based on respondents ranking those people they find more and those less desirable; the technique can be used by psychologists to build a theory of association between people. A graphical representation of a network of social relationships is known as a **sociogram**. » psychiatry; social psychology

sockeye Species of salmon, widespread in the N Pacific Ocean and adjacent rivers; length up to 80 cm/32 in; feeds mainly on crustaceans during life at sea; migrates into fresh water to breed, the adults dying after spawning; an important commercial species along the American seaboard; also known as **red salmon**. (*Oncorhynchus nerka*. Family: *Salmonidae*.) » salmon

Socrates [sokrateez] (469–399 BC) Greek philosopher, born and died in Athens. Little is known of his early life. By Plato's account, he devoted his last 30 years to convincing the Athenians that their opinions about moral matters could not bear the weight of critical scrutiny. His technique, the so-called **Socratic method**, was to ask for definitions of such morally significant concepts as piety and justice, and to elicit contradictions from the responses, thus exposing the ignorance of the responder and motivating deeper enquiry into the concepts. His profession to know none of the answers himself is ironic: he most likely held the doctrines that human excellence is a kind of knowledge; thus, that all wrongdoing is based on ignorance; that no one desires bad things; and that it is worse to do injustice than to suffer it. He was tried on charges of impiety and corruption of the youth by zealous defenders of a restored democracy in Athens. Found guilty, he was put to death by drinking hemlock. His personality and his doctrines were immortalized in Plato's dialogues; his influence on Western philosophy is incalculable. » Plato

soda » **sodium**

soda bread A type of bread which uses bicarbonate to provide the necessary carbon dioxide. In contrast to yeast-risen bread, it is easier and quicker to prepare. » bicarbonate; bread

Soddy, Frederick (1877–1956) British radiochemist, born at Eastbourne, Sussex. Educated in Wales and at Oxford, he held posts at Montreal, Glasgow, Aberdeen, and Oxford, where he was professor of chemsistry (1919–36). In 1913 he discovered forms of the same element with identical chemical qualities but different atomic weights (*isotopes*), for which he won the Nobel Prize for Chemistry in 1921. He died at Brighton, Sussex. » isotopes

Södertälje [serdertelye], formerly **Tälje** 59°11N 17°39E, pop(1982) 79 794. Industrial town in Stockholm county, SE Sweden; suburb of Stockholm on the Södertälje Canal (1807–19); originally a Viking trading station set between L Mälar and the Baltic Sea. » Stockholm

sodium Na (Lat *natrium*), element 11, melting point 97.8°C. A very soft and reactive alkali metal, not found free in nature, but always in the form of one of its salts, in which it shows oxidation state +1. These occur in salt deposits, but **sodium chloride** (common salt, or NaCl) can also be extracted from ocean water, of which it makes up about 3.5%. The metal is obtained by electrolysis of molten NaCl, and is a very strong reducing agent, widely used in organic reactions and for the production of **sodium cyanide** (NaCN) and **sodium cyanamide** (Na_2CN_2), used in metallurgy and fertilizers. **Sodium carbonate** and **bicarbonate** (Na_2CO_3 and $NaHCO_3$), also called *washing soda* and *baking soda*, are important industrial chemicals, as is **sodium hydroxide** (NaOH), also called *caustic soda* or *lye*, used in soap making. » alkali; chemical elements; metal; reducing agent; salt; RR90

Sodom and Gomorrah [soduhm, guhmohra] Two of five 'cities of the plain' in ancient Palestine, perhaps now submerged under the S end of the Dead Sea or located to the SE of the Dead Sea. In *Gen* 18–19 they were legendary for their wickedness, especially their sexual perversity. The stories tell how Lot and his family were warned to flee from their home in Sodom just before the city was destroyed by 'brimstone and fire' as a divine judgment. » Genesis, Book of; Lot

Soekarno » **Sukarno**

Sofia [sofeea] Bulgarian **Sofiya**, Lat **Serdica**, 42°40N 23°18E, pop(1981) 1 070 358. Capital of Bulgaria since 1878, situated on a plateau in W Bulgaria; Roman town 1st–4th-c; under Byzantine rule 6th–9th-c; under Turkish rule 1382–1878; university (1888); airport (Vrazhdebna); railway; steel, machinery, electronics, food processing, chemicals; museums, theatre, opera house, observatory; Mausoleum of Georgi Dimitrov; Alexander Nevsky memorial cathedral; 4th-c St George Rotunda; 6th-c Church of St Sofia; Boyana Church; Sofia Musical Weeks (May–Jun); National Chorus Festival (May); international book fair. » Bulgaria [i]

soft-shelled turtle A reptile native to E USA, Africa, and S Asia; small shell covered by leathery skin (without horny plates); nostrils on end of narrow projection; three claws on each foot; inhabits freshwater (occasionally estuaries). (Family: *Trionychidae*. Order: *Chelonia*, 22 species.) The SE Asian *Carettochelys insculpta* (Family: *Carettochelyidae*) is called the **pig-nosed softshell turtle**. » turtle (biology)

softball A smaller version of baseball, played on a diamond-shaped pitch with sides measuring 60 ft (18.3 m). The object, as in baseball, is to score runs by completing a circuit of the diamond before being put out. The principal difference between the two sports is the pitching; in softball it is done underarm. Each side consists of nine players who take it in turn to bat. The pitcher attempts to get players out by forcing them to play a non-winning stroke. A game lasts for nine innings per team, and each innings lasts until a team has three players put out. Players can be put out while running between bases if tagged by a player with the ball. » baseball [i]; RR119

software In computing, a term used, in contrast to *hardware*, to include all the programs, manuals, instructions, and other material which can exist in written form and be used on computer systems. » firmware; hardware

Sogne Fjord [songnuh fyawd], Norwegian **Sognefjorden** Inlet of Norwegian Sea, Sogn og Fjordane county, W coast of Norway; extends E inland 204 km/127 ml; largest Norwegian fjord; average width, 5 km/3 ml; maximum depth, 1 245 m/4 085 ft. » fjord; Norway [i]

soil The top layer of the Earth's surface, comprising a mixture of fine weathered rock particles and organic matter. The finest particles form clay; the less fine, silt; and the coarsest, sand. Provided moisture is available, soils generally support vegetation, and provide a habitat for a wide range of soil flora and fauna. » soil profile/science

soil profile A vertical section through the soil revealing four basic soil horizons: the surface layer, or **topsoil**, which contains organic material; an **upper subsoil**, rich in nutrients but containing little organic matter; a **lower subsoil** of partly weathered mineral material; and the **bedrock** material from which the upper layers may have been derived. » soil; soil science

soil science The study of soil, its information, and its management as a medium for plant growth. It includes both the physical management of soil, through cultivation, drainage, and irrigation, and the chemical management of soil, through the control of nutrient status, acidity, and salinity. » agronomy; chernozem; humus; loam; pedology; soil; soil profile

soja » **soya bean**

Soka Gakkai (Jap 'value creating society') [sohka gakiy] An association of lay Buddhists of the Nichiren school, founded in Japan in 1930 by Tsunesaburo Makiguchi and Josei Toda. Claiming over 16 million followers, it is highly organized, and dedicated to the promotion of Nichiren beliefs. It sponsors its own political party and operates its own schools and a university. » Nichiren Buddhism

sol-fa, tonic » **tonic sol-fa**

solar cell A device for converting light directly into electrical power. It exploits the photovoltaic effect in junctions between semiconductor materials. Cells using single crystals of silicon are efficient (converting c.14% of incident energy to electricity) but expensive; other materials are cheaper, such as germanium arsenide and amorphous silicon. The cells are arranged in arrays in series and parallel to give the desired voltage and current. A single silicon cell, 10 cm/4 in in diameter, has an output voltage of about 0.6V and an output power of about 0.4W. Solar cells are used to provide electrical power in remote places, such as buoys and space satellites. » electricity; photovoltaic effect

solar constant The total radiation of all frequencies falling on the Earth from the Sun, as measured for an average Earth–Sun distance; symbol S, value 1 367 W/m^2 (watt per metre squared). It is found to vary by about 1% in a way which is related to sunspot activity. » electromagnetism; radiometry; Sun

solar day » **day**

solar flare A violent release of energy in the vicinity of an active region on the Sun, emitting energetic particles, X-rays, and radio waves. It causes notable auroral displays in our upper atmosphere. » aurora; Sun

solar power Energy radiating from the Sun, exploited in a number of ways to provide energy for heat and electricity generation. Solar panels or collectors (a black metal absorber) can be used to extract heat from the warmth of sunshine to heat water or air in pipes contained in or beneath the panels. In some arid countries, panels are used to power stills for evaporating saline water, condensing the vapour and collecting it as freshwater. Collectors can also be focused onto a small area of water to heat it, producing steam for electricity generation. The use of solar energy is constrained by the need for sufficient sunshine, the supply of which is unpredictable at temperate latitudes. However, in many developing countries it has great potential, especially as it is a renewable energy resource. By the early 1980s, solar collectors were producing energy equivalent to 0.01% of the world's total oil consumption. » alternative energy; energy; renewable resources

solar prominence Flamelike clouds of matter in the solar chromosphere, sometimes triggered by solar flares, reaching heights of 1 000 000 km/600 000 ml at extremes. They are visible using special instruments such as the coronagraph, or during a total eclipse. » chromosphere; eclipse; solar flare

Solar System The Sun and its associated, gravitationally bound, system of nine known planets, their 54 satellites, the c.3 000 asteroids, the comets, and interplanetary dust. The planets – Mercury, Venus, Earth, Mars (the four 'inner planets'), Jupiter, Saturn, Uranus, Neptune (the four outer 'gas giants') and Pluto – and asteroids orbit approximately in the plane of the Sun's equator, and rotate about the Sun in the same direction (counter-clockwise when viewed from a N polar direction). There is systematic variation in the character of the planets: the inner planets are comparatively small and dense, and are composed of high-temperature condensates (chiefly iron and metal silicates), while the four outer planets are much larger, and mainly composed of low-temperature condensates (chiefly gases and ices); Pluto is unique and poorly known. The asteroids also show systematic variation of properties with distance from the Sun. The comets – made of ices and dust – lie at greatest distance from the Sun in a shell known as the 'Oort Cloud', and are only tenuously bound gravitationally. The subject of intensive exploratory study by telescopes and spacecraft, much information has also been derived from the study of meteorites which originate from asteroids. It is thought that the planetary system was formed 4.6 thousand million years ago as a by-product of the Sun's formation, which resulted from the gravitational collapse of an accumulation of gas and dust in this region of the Milky Way galaxy. » asteroids; comet; Galaxy; interplanetary matter; Oort Cloud; planet; Sun; RR4

solar time Time measured by considering the rotation of the Earth relative to the Sun. **Mean solar time** is established by reference to the mean Sun, and was established as the fundamental measure of clock time before it was realized that the Earth has variable rotation. **Apparent solar time** is time shown by a sundial. The difference between the two can amount to 16.4 minutes (late October). » sidereal time; sundial; universal time

solar wind A stream of charged particles ('plasma') emanating from the upper atmosphere (corona) of the Sun and expanding continuously into the interplanetary medium with a velocity of 400–800 km/sec (250–500 ml/sec). Most of the flow appears to originate in the Sun's polar regions. The solar magnetic field is embedded in radially outflowing plasma, and due to the Sun's rotation forms a spiral pattern like a rotating garden water sprinkler. The plasma interacts dynamically with planetary environments as it flows by them, notably by shaping the magnetospheres of those planets with magnetic fields. It is a highly dynamic phenomenon, influenced by such factors as solar flares and X-ray bursts. » aurora; magnetosphere; Solar System; Sun

solder An alloy which will melt easily at a moderate temperature, and so provide a bond between two metal surfaces. It usually consists of tin and lead, when used for joining copper, brass, or iron with tin-plate. As distinct from welding, soldering only fills in interstices in the juxtaposed metals, and does not fuse into them. » alloy

soldier beetle An elongate beetle; wing cases usually parallel-sided; adults commonly found on flowers and vegetation; larvae typically predatory, found in soil, leaf litter, and under bark; adults feed on nectar, pollen, or as predators. (Order: *Coleoptera*. Family: *Cantharidae*, c.5 000 species.) » beetle; larva

sole Any of the flatfish in the family *Soleidae*, widespread in shallow continental shelf waters of tropical to temperate seas; includes the common European sole, or **Dover sole** (*Solea solea*), distributed from the Mediterranean to Norway; length up to 50 cm/20 in; both eyes on right side of body; very popular food fish, taken commercially mainly by trawl. The name is also used elsewhere for flatfish belonging to other families. » flatfish

Solemn League and Covenant An alliance between the English Parliament and the Scottish rebels against Charles I, agreed in September 1643. Parliament promised £30 000 a month to the Scots and the introduction of full Presbyterianism in England; the Scots agreed to provide an army to the hard-pressed parliamentarians to fight Charles. The pact facilitated parliamentary victory in the first Civil War, but Presbyterianism was never fully implemented. » English Civil War; Presbyterianism

solenodon [sohleenuhduhn] A mammal native to Cuba (*Solenodon cubanus*), and to Haiti and the Dominican Republic (*Solenodon paradoxurus*); an insectivore, resembling a very large shrew (length, up to 330 mm/13 in), with longer legs; has a venomous bite; inhabits forests; eats plants and small vertebrates. (Family: *Solenodontidae*, 2 species.) » insectivore; shrew

solenoid A coil of wire, usually cylindrical, partially surrounding a moveable iron core. When a current flows in the coil, a magnetic field is produced which makes the core move. A solenoid converts electrical energy into mechanical energy, as in operating a switch or circuit breaker. » electricity; magnetism

Solent, the A channel separating the I of Wight from mainland England; a major shipping route from Southampton; yacht racing. » Southampton; Wight, Isle of

solfeggio [solfejioh] » **solmization**

solicitor A lawyer whose responsibilities involve giving legal advice to clients. In order to practise, solicitors in the UK require a practising certificate from the appropriate Law Society. Solicitors have a right to appear for clients in the lower courts. Most are concerned with advice on criminal law, family law, landlord and tenant law, and debt disputes. » barrister; criminal law; debt; Law Society

Solicitor-General In the UK, one of the government's law officers, who is a member of the House of Commons and junior to the Attorney-General. There is also a Solicitor-General for Scotland, who holds a similar position. » Attorney-General

solid A dense form of matter characterized by its ability to transmit twisting forces and its inability to flow; virtually incompressible; tends to retain shape when stressed; described as rigid, the atoms generally not being free to move from point to point. Solids are divided into crystals, comprising ordered arrays of atoms; amorphous solids, which are disordered arrays; and polymers and rubbers, which comprise long chain-like molecules. » amorphous solid; ceramics; crystals; electron diffraction; ice; liquid crystals; melting point; neutron diffraction; phases of matter [i]; polymerization; solid-state physics; spin glass; sublimation (chemistry); X-ray diffraction

solid-state device A device in which an electric signal flows through a solid material rather than a vacuum. Most are made from solid semiconductor materials, such as transistors and thyristors. They are much smaller and lighter than the traditional vacuum tubes, use less power, last longer, are more dependable, and cost less. » electricity; semiconductor; transistor; thyristor

solid-state physics The study of all properties of matter in the solid state; a sub-branch of condensed matter physics, which includes liquids and solids. Traditionally it focuses on crystal structure, more recently embracing more complex systems such as alloys, ceramics, amorphous solids, and surfaces. » critical phenomena; electrical and magnetic properties of solids; electronic structure of solids; materials science; mechanical properties of matter; physics; solid; superconductivity; surface physics; thermal conduction; thin films

Solidarity An organization established in Poland (Sep 1980) as the National Committee of Solidarity (*Solidarność*) to co-ordinate the activities of the emerging independent trade union following protracted industrial unrest, notably in the Lenin shipyard in Gdańsk. Its first president was Lech Wałesa. It organized a number of strikes in early 1981 for improved wages and conditions, and became a force for major political reform. It attempted to seek reconciliation with the Polish government through proposing a council for national consensus, but suffered continuous harassment and was rendered largely ineffective by the declaration of martial law (Dec 1981) and by being made illegal. It remained underground, but came back into the political arena in mid-1988. Following its successes in the 1989 elections, Solidarity entered into a coalition government with the communists, with one of its members (Tadeusz

Mazowiecki) eventually becoming Prime Minister. » Poland [i]; trade union; Walesa

Solihull [**sol**eehuhl] 52°25N 1°45W, pop (1981) 94 613. Town in West Midlands, C England; a suburb of SE Birmingham; National Exhibition Centre; Birmingham airport nearby; railway; vehicles, packaging, machinery. » West Midlands

soliloquy A stage device whereby a character talks aloud but alone, as it were confiding in the audience. The soliloquies of Richard III and Hamlet are famous examples in Shakespeare. The soliloquy is unfashionable today; but there are similarities with the interior monologue or 'voice-over' in film. » drama; stream of consciousness

Solingen [**zoh**lingn] 51°10N 7°05E, pop (1983) 161 100. Industrial city in Dusseldorf district, Germany; in the Ruhr valley, 22 km/14 ml ESE of Düsseldorf; badly bombed in World War 2; cutlery, chemicals, petrochemicals, hardware. » Germany [i]

solipsism **1** The doctrine that I alone exist; claimed by critics of Descartes to be an unwelcome consequence of trying to infer an independent reality solely from my mental experiences. **2** *Methodological* solipsism maintains that psychology ought to study only those mental states, such as sensations, which do not imply the existence of something outside the mind. » Descartes; psychology

solitaire An extinct dodo-like bird. The name is also used for the **Hawaiian honeycreeper** (*Viridonia sagittirostris*) and New World thrushes of the genera *Myadestes* (7 species) and *Entomodestes* (2 species). » dodo; honeycreeper; thrush (bird)

soliton A moving, solitary, stable wave having a well-defined position and constant amplitude. In quantum theories, solitons appear to behave as particles having unusual attributes; they can be observed in water in shallow channels, such as tidal bore waves. » wave (physics) [i]

solmization A system for learning and recalling music by fitting syllables to pitches in a scale. The one used in Western music is attributed to Guido d'Arezzo (11th-c), who fitted the initial syllables of the first six lines of a Latin hymn to the notes of the hexachord to make *ut* (later changed to *do*), *re*, *mi*, *fa*, *sol*, *la*; *si* was added later. Textless singing exercises using these syllables are called *solfeggio*, in France *solfège*. » Guido d'Arezzo; tonic sol-fa

solo A card game which is a form of whist, and similar to bridge. Players have to declare how many tricks they will win before each game. Tricks are won as in whist. » bridge (recreation); whist

Solomon (Old Testament) (10th-c BC) Famous king of Israel, the second son of David and Bathsheba. His outwardly splendid reign (described in 1 *Ki* 1–11 and 2 *Chron* 1–10) saw the expansion of the kingdom and the building of the great Temple in Jerusalem. But high taxation and alliances with heathen courts bred discontent which later brought the disruption of the kingdom under his son Rehoboam. Solomon was credited with extraordinary wisdom, and became a legendary figure in Judaism, so that his name became attached to several Biblical and extra-canonical writings. » David; Proverbs, Book of; Solomon, Psalms of; Song of Solomon; Wisdom of Solomon

Solomon (music), professional name of **Solomon Cutner** (1902–88) English pianist, born in London. After appearing with great success as a child prodigy, he retired for further study, and won a high reputation as a performer of the works of Beethoven, Brahms, and some of the modern composers. He did not tour as extensively as most players, and was forced to retire through paralysis in 1965. » piano

Solomon, John (William) (1931–) British croquet player, educated at Charterhouse. He made his international debut against New Zealand in 1950 at age 19, and never missed an England Test Match between 1950 and 1973. He won a record 10 Open Croquet Championships (1953, 1956, 1959, 1961, 1963–8), the Men's Championship 10 times between 1951 and 1972, the Open Doubles Championship 10 times (all with Edmond Cotter) between 1954 and 1969, and the Mixed Doubles title once (with Freda Oddie) in 1954. He was winner of the President's Cup a record nine times. » croquet

Solomon, Psalms of A book of the Old Testament Pseudepigrapha, consisting of 18 psalms, probably written c.1st-c BC in response to the Roman occupation of Jerusalem. It expresses hopes for a Jewish state free of foreign domination, brought about by a messianic deliverer. It is traditionally considered the work of a Pharisee, but this is uncertain, and is significant for its expression of Jewish messianic expectations at this time. » messianism; psalmody; Pseudepigrapha; Solomon (Old Testament)

Solomon Islands pop (1990e) 319 000; land area 27 556 sq km/10 637 sq ml. Archipelago of several hundred islands in the SW Pacific Ocean, stretching c.1 400 km/870 ml between Papua New Guinea (NW) and Vanuatu (SE); capital, Honiara; chief towns, Gizu, Auki, Kirakira; timezone GMT +11; chief ethnic group, Melanesians (93%); chief religion, Christianity (95%); official language, English, with pidgin English widely spoken; unit of currency, the Solomon Island dollar of 100 cents; six main islands of Choiseul, Guadalcanal, Malaita, New Georgia, San Cristobal, Santa Isabel; the large islands have forested mountain ranges of mainly volcanic origin, deep narrow valleys, and coastal belts lined with coconut palms and ringed by reefs; highest point, Mt Makarakomburu (2 477 m/8 126 ft) on Guadalcanal, the largest island; equatorial climate; average temperature, 27°C; high humidity; average annual rainfall, c.3 500 mm/138 in; visited by the Spanish, 1568; S Solomon Is placed under British protection, 1893; outer islands added to the protectorate, 1899; scene of fierce fighting in World War 2; independence, 1978; British monarch is represented by a governor-general; prime minister leads a parliament of 38 members elected for four years; economy based on agriculture; forestry, livestock, fisheries, taro, rice, bananas, yams, copra, oil palm, rice; palm oil milling, fish processing, food processing, crafts. » Guadalcanal; Honiara; RR27 national holidays; RR60 political leaders

Solomon's seal A perennial growing to 80 cm/30 in, native to Europe and Asia; rhizomatous; stems arching; leaves 5–12 cm/2–4¾ in, oval, in two rows; flowers white, bell-shaped, hanging in clusters beneath the stem. (*Polygonatum multiflorum*. Family: *Liliaceae*.) » perennial; rhizome

Solomon Sea » **Coral Sea**

Solon (7th–6th-c BC) Athenian statesman, lawgiver, and poet. As chief archon, he enacted many economic, constitutional, and legal reforms, and paved the way for the development of democracy at Athens, and her emergence as a great trading state. Enslavement for debt was abolished, a new currency instituted, and citizenship granted to foreign craftsmen settling in Athens. Wealth rather than birth was made the criterion for participation in political life, and Draco's inhumane legal code was largely repealed. » archon; Draco (ancient Greece)

solstice An event when the Sun is at its furthest point from the Equator, resulting in the longest day and shortest night (the **summer solstice**) in one hemisphere and the shortest day and longest night (the **winter solstice**) in the other hemisphere. In the N hemisphere, the summer solstice is on 21 or 22 June and the winter solstice on 21 or 22 December. Solstices occur because the Earth's axis is inclined to the plane of its orbit around the Sun. » midnight sun

Solti, Sir Georg [**shol**tee] (1912–) British conductor, born in Budapest. World War 2 forced him to give up his post as conductor of the Budapest Opera, and he worked in Switzerland until 1946, when he became director at the Munich Staatsoper (until 1952) and later at Frankfurt (1952–61) and Covent Garden, London (1961–71). He later conducted the Chicago Symphony Orchestra and the London Philharmonic. He was granted an honorary knighthood in 1971, and took British nationality in 1972.

solubility The extent to which one substance dissolves in another. It is expressed as the mass/number of moles of a solute which will dissolve in a given volume/mass/number of moles of solvent. » mole (physics); solution

solution A uniform phase, generally liquid, containing more than one component. When one component is present in excess, it is called the **solvent**; minor components are called **solutes**. Many alloys are solid solutions, in which the various metal atoms are randomly dispersed through the structure. » alloy; solvent; titration

Solutrean [solyoo**tree**uhn] In European prehistory, a short division of the Upper Palaeolithic Age, named after the site at La Solutré, Saône et Loire, C France, discovered in 1866. Its finely-made, bifacial stone tools date to c.19000–18000 BC. » Three Age System

Solvay process or **ammonia-soda process** A technique for the production of sodium carbonate (an important industrial alkali), devised in 1865 by Belgian chemist Ernest Solvay (1838–1922), and improved by Ludwig Mond in 1870. Sodium chloride is treated with ammonia and then with carbon dioxide. This produces sodium bicarbonate (which is heated to give the desired sodium carbonate) and ammonium chloride, which is treated with lime to recover the ammonia for recycling. » Mond

solvent The main component of a solution. Water is often described as the 'universal solvent', but the term is often applied specifically to organic materials such as acetone and ethyl acetate, used in paints and adhesives. » solution

Solway Firth Inlet of the Irish Sea, separating Cumbria, England, from Dumfries and Galloway, Scotland; estuary of Esk and Eden Rivers; length c.65 km/40 ml; width at mouth, c.40 km/25 ml; noted for its salmon fisheries. » Irish Sea

Solzhenitsyn, Aleksandr (Isayevich) [solzhuh**nit**zin] (1918–) Russian writer, born at Kislovodsk. Educated at Rostov in mathematics and physics, he fought in World War 2, and was imprisoned (1945–53) for unfavourable comment on Stalin's conduct of the war. On his release, he became a teacher, and started to write. His first novel, *Odin den iz zhizni Ivana Denisovicha* (1962, One Day in the Life of Ivan Denisovich), set in a prison camp, was acclaimed both in the USSR and the West; but his subsequent denunciation of Soviet censorship led to the banning of his later, semi-autobiographical novels, *Rakovy korpus* (1968, Cancer Ward) and *V kruge pervom* (1968, The First Circle). He was expelled from the Soviet Writers' Union in 1969, and awarded the Nobel Prize for Literature in 1970 (received in 1974). His later books include *Arkhipelag Gulag* (1973–8, The Gulag Archipelago), a factual account of the Stalinist terror, for which he was arrested and exiled (1974). He now lives in the USA. » novel; Russian literature; Stalin

Somali A Cushitic-speaking people of Somalia and parts of Kenya, Ethiopia, and Djibouti. Roughly two-thirds are transhumant herders (the Samaal) living inland, with farmers and traders along the coast (the Saab). Divided into many traditionally autonomous groups, they have a powerful sense of cultural unity based largely on Islam and the Somali language. Population c.4 million. » Islam; Somalia; transhumance

Somalia [soh**mah**lia], official name **Somali Democratic Republic**, Arabic **Jamhuriyadda Dimugradiga Somaliya** pop (1990e) 7 555 000; area 686 803 sq km/265 106 sq ml. NE African republic, divided into 16 regions; bounded NW by Djibouti, W by Ethiopia, SW by Kenya, E by the Indian Ocean, and N by the Gulf of Aden; capital, Mogadishu; chief towns, Hargeysa, Berbera, Kismaayo; timezone GMT +3; chief ethnic group, Somali (85%); chief religion, Islam (Sunni); official language, Somali; unit of currency, the Somali shilling; occupies the E Horn of Africa, where a dry coastal plain broadens to the S, and rises inland to a plateau at nearly 1 000 m/3 300 ft; forested mountains on the Gulf of Aden coast rise to 2 416 m/7 926 ft at Mt Shimbiris; considerable variation in climate; Berbera (N coast), annual average rainfall 61 mm/2.4 in, average maximum daily temperatures 29–42°C; more rainfall (Apr–Sep) on E coast; Mogadishu annual average rainfall 490 mm/19.3 in, average daily maximum temperatures 28–32°C; serious and persistent threat of drought; settled by Muslims, 7th-c; Italian, French, and British interests after the opening of the Suez Canal, 1869; after World War 2, Somalia formed by the amalgamation of Italian and British protectorates; independence, 1960; from the 1960s, territorial conflict with Ethiopia (which has a large Somali population); military coup, 1969; governed by a president, a Council of Ministers, and a People's Assembly of 171 elected members and six appointed deputies; new constitution, 1991; NE region seceded as Somaliland

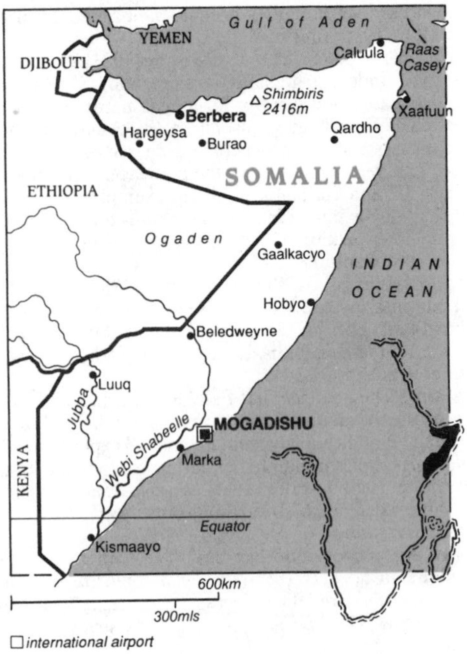

Republic, 1991; a largely nomadic people (70%) raising cattle, sheep, goats, camels; cultivation practised close to rivers; bananas, sugar, spices, cotton, rice, citrus fruits, maize, sorghum, oilseeds, tobacco; textiles, cigarettes, food processing, fishing; some tin, gypsum, uranium, iron ore; difficult communications within the country. » Ethiopia [i]; Mogadishu; RR27 national holidays; RR60 political leaders

somatomedins [sohmatoh**me**dinz] A group of related chemical substances (peptides), present in the plasma of vertebrates, which mediate the growth-promoting actions of somatotrophin (growth hormone). They are synthesized and released mainly by the liver into the blood, and stimulate protein synthesis and cell replication in individual tissues or organs. » growth hormone; liver; peptide; plasma (physiology)

somatostatin [sohmatoh**sta**tin] A chemical substance (a polypeptide) identified in the brain (hypothalamus), pancreas (D-cells in the islets of Langerhans), stomach (mucosal D-cells), and small and large intestines. It generally has an inhibitory action: *hypothalamic* somatostatin (a neurohormone) inhibits growth hormone and thyroid-stimulating hormone secretion from the front lobe of the pituitary; *pancreatic* somatostatin (a paracrine) inhibits insulin and glucagon release. » hypothalamus; paracrine; peptide

somatotrophin » growth hormone

Somers (of Evesham), John, 1st Baron [**suh**merz] (1651–1716) English Whig statesman, born in Worcester. Educated at Oxford, he became a lawyer (1676) and an MP (1689). He helped to draft the Declaration of Rights (1689), and after the Revolution of 1688 held several posts under William III, culminating as Lord Chancellor (1697). William's most trusted minister, he was the object of frequent attacks, which led to his impeachment (and acquittal) in 1701. He was President of the Privy Council under Anne (1708–14), and died at Brookmans, Hertfordshire. » Whigs; William III

Somerset [**suh**merset] pop (1987e) 452 300; area 3 451 sq km/ 1 332 sq ml. County of SW England, divided into five districts; bounded N by the Bristol Channel; uplands in the W include Exmoor and the Brendon and Quantock Hills; Mendip Hills in NE, Blackdown Hills in S; county town, Taunton; chief towns include Bridgwater and Yeovil; agriculture (especially dairy farming), tourism, light engineering, beverages (especially cider), footwear, food processing; Cheddar Gorge, Wookey Hole limestone caves. » England [i]; Exmoor; Taunton

Somme, Battle of the (1916) A major British offensive against German troops in NW France (1 Jul–19 Nov) which developed into the bloodiest battle in world history, with more than a million casualties. It was launched by British commander-in-chief, Douglas Haig. When the attack was abandoned, the Allies had advanced ten miles from previous positions. The battle formed part of the war of attrition on the Western Front. » Haig, Douglas; World War 1

Somme, River [som] River in N France, rising near St-Quentin; flows SW then NW and W to the English Channel near Saint-Valéry-sur-Somme; length 245 km/152 ml; linked by canals to the waterways of the industrial N; scene of some of the worst fighting in World War 1 (1916). » France [i]; Somme, Battle of the

somnambulism » **sleep-walking**

Somnath, Temple of [sumnaht] A famous Shiva temple in SW Gujarat, India. Its fabled wealth attracted the attention of Mahmud of Ghazni, who sacked it in 1024, removing its jewels together with (according to tradition) its wonderful gates. The event helped to create a tradition of Muslim intolerance and ferocity among N Indian Hindus. » Shiva

Somoza (García) Anastasio [somohsa] (1896–1956) Nicaraguan dictator, born at San Marcos, Nicaragua, and educated in the USA. As chief of the National Guard he established himself in supreme power in the early 1930s, and retained power until assassinated. His sons **Luis Somoza Debayle** (1923–67) and **Anastasio Somoza Debayle** (1925–80) continued dynastic control of Nicaragua until the 1979 revolution. » Nicaragua [i]

Son of Man A term found in Jewish and Christian literature, most strikingly in the New Testament Gospels as a frequent self-designation of Jesus. The term's significance is debated: in Aramaic it is an idiomatic reference to 'man' in general, and possibly also a circumlocution for 'I'; in *Dan* 7 it seems to depict the righteous ones who are exalted at the end of the age and given dominion; in 1 *Eno* 48 it apparently describes a heavenly messianic figure who will exercise judgment in the End times. » eschatology; Jesus Christ; Messiah

sonar An acronym of **sound navigation and ranging**, a means of detecting underwater vessels and objects, shoals of fish, and sea bed features. The device emits pulsed bursts of sound underwater and listens for reflected echoes (**active sonar**), or simply listens for and interprets the sounds a target, such as a submarine, may itself make (**passive sonar**). » submarine

sonata A musical composition, usually for keyboard (harpsichord, piano, organ) or for another instrument with keyboard. The main Baroque type, however, was the trio sonata for two solo instruments (usually violins) and continuo, exemplified in works by Corelli, Purcell, and Handel. These were normally in four or more movements, but the 550 or so keyboard sonatas of Domenico Scarlatti are nearly all single-movement works of a type much cultivated in Italy and Spain. The classical sonatas of Haydn, Mozart, and Beethoven are nearly all in three or four movements, with the first usually in what has become known as 'sonata form', and the last often a sonata rondo. This overall plan was adopted by many 19th–20th-c composers, including Schubert, Chopin, Brahms, Shostakovitch, and Prokofiev. Others (such as Liszt), have occasionally united the different movements into a single structure, or rejected the traditional form altogether. » Baroque (music); movement; rondo; Chopin; Corelli, Archangelo; Handel; Haydn; Liszt; Purcell, Henry; Scarlatti, Domenico

sonatina A sonata of modest proportions, often not difficult to play. » sonata

Sonderbund [**zon**derbund] A political and military league of seven Swiss Catholic cantons (Uri, Schwyz, Unterwalden, Zug, Fribourg, Lucerne, Valais), formed in 1845 to resist liberal plans for centralization. The 25-day Sonderbund War (1847) ended with the government's defeat of the Sonderbund, and the creation of a Federal State (1848). » Switzerland [i]

Sondheim, Stephen (Joshua) (1930–) US composer, born in New York City. He studied with Milton Babbitt and earned his first success with his lyrics for Bernstein's *West Side Story* (1957). His own highly successful musicals, including *A Funny Thing Happened on the Way to the Forum* (1962), *A Little Night Music* (1972), and *Sweeney Todd* (1979), have contributed immeasurably to the revival of the musical in America. » Babbitt, Milton; Bernstein, Leonard; musical

song Quite apart from liturgical song (for which a special nomenclature exists), folksong, popular music, and the indigenous music of non-Western cultures, there remains a vast corpus of song which defies any brief survey or classification. Mediaeval vernacular song, at least as it has reached us, was unaccompanied monody, sung mainly to courtly, amatory, sometimes religious texts. Renaissance song was largely polyphonic, reaching its highest point of development in the Italian and English madrigal. The earliest important repertories of solo song with notated accompaniment are from the early 17th-c – those of Monteverdi, and other Italian monodists, and the lute-songs of Dowland and his English contemporaries. The main type of small-scale solo vocal music of the Baroque period was the cantata, perfected by Alessandro Scarlatti and Handel. The development of the piano in the late 18th-c made possible the rich flowering of Romantic song, especially in Germany, while a special contribution of later composers (such as Mahler and Britten) has been the song cycle with orchestra. » aria; blues; cantata; chant; Eurovision Song Contest; flamenco; frottola; hymn; Lied; madrigal; Meistersinger; monody; pop music; singing; song cycle; troubadours; Dowland; Handel; Monteverdi; Scarlatti, Alessandro

song cycle A sequence of separate songs united by some common theme or narrative thread. The earliest was perhaps Beethoven's *An die ferne Geliebte* (To the Distant Beloved); later examples include Schubert's *Die Winterreise* (The Winter Journey), and Mahler's *Kindertotenlieder* (Songs on the Death of Children). » Britten; Lied; Mahler; song

Song dynasty also **Sung dynasty** (960–1279) A Chinese dynasty founded by Zhao Kuangying with its capital at Kaifeng. From the beginning it was threatened by the Khitan, who in 1125 conquered all N China, which they then ruled from Beijing (Peking). The Song court was re-established at Hangzhou (then called Linan), but the 'Southern Song dynasty' was destroyed by the Mongols, who had earlier overcome the Khitan. » China [i]

Song of Solomon, Song of Songs, or **Canticles** A book of the Hebrew Bible/Old Testament, probably a collection of love songs, although sometimes considered a single poem or drama. The absence of explicit religious content, and the presence of erotic allusions, caused some 2nd-c rabbis to question its canonical status, but allegorical religious interpretation made it acceptable in most Christian and Jewish circles. Although the poems may be quite ancient, the collection is usually dated c.3rd-c BC on linguistic grounds. » allegory; Old Testament; poetry; Solomon (Old Testament)

Song of the Three Young Men Part of the Old Testament Apocrypha, or in Catholic versions an extension of the Book of Daniel inserted between what would be 3.23 and 24 in other texts; one of several additions to Daniel found in Greek and Latin versions, but not in Hebrew. It tells of three Jewish captives in Babylon who are cast into a fiery furnace for refusing to worship an idol, and it presents a hymn of thanksgiving and praise that is today known as the *Benedicite* in Catholic worship. Its date is uncertain, but is often put c.2nd–1st-c BC. » Apocrypha, Old Testament; Azariah, Prayer of; Daniel, Book of

song thrush A thrush native to Europe (N Africa during winter) and NE Asia; similar to the mistle thrush, but wing feathers an even brown; inhabits woodland, hedgerows, and gardens; eats snails by breaking the shells against a rock (called its *anvil*). (*Turdus philomelos*.) » mistle thrush; thrush (bird)

Song Ziwen [sung dziwen], **Sung Tsu-wen** or **Soong, T V** (1894–1971) Chinese financier and diplomat, born in Shanghai. His sister Song Qinling (c.1892–1981) married Sun Yatsen, and through this Song became closely associated with the Nationalist Party. He provided the financial stability which made possible the 1926 Northern Expedition that reunited China under the Nationalists. A second sister, Sung Mei-ling (c.1899–) married Jiang Jieshi (Chiang Kai-shek) in 1927. Song served as Finance Minister of the new government until 1931. When the Nationalist government was overthrown in 1949, he moved to the USA, and died in San Francisco. » Guomindang; Jiang Jieshi; Sun Yatsen

songbird A bird of the passerine order, sub-order *Oscines*. This sub-order includes most birds renowned for their singing ability. » babbler; lark; passerine; sparrow; starling; sunbird; swallow; tanager; thickhead; thrush (bird); tit; treecreeper; wagtail; warbler; waxbill; waxwing; weaverbird; white-eye; whydah; wren

Songhai [**song**giy] A W African state which rose to power in the region formerly dominated by Mali in the second half of the 15th-c, commanding the trade routes of the Sahara, the great market at Timbuktu, and the area W to Senegal. It declined as a result of the Portuguese re-orientation of trade routes, and was attacked by Moroccan forces in the 1590s. Songhai peoples still control much of the Saharan caravan trade. Population c.1.4 million (1980 est). » African history; Berber; Mali [i]

sonic boom A pressure shock wave created by aircraft travelling at supersonic speeds. The shock wave is produced continually, and travels outwards from the aircraft. Where it meets the ground it is percieved as a loud bang. Its intensity at ground level depends on aircraft height, flight pattern, and weather, and may be sufficient to cause damage to buildings. » aerodynamics [i]; aircraft [i]; shock waves

sonnet (It *sonnetto* 'little song') A poem of 14 lines, usually in iambic pentameter, and with a structural balance between the first 8 lines (*octave*) and the last 6 (*sestet*). A variety of rhyme schemes may be employed. Introduced in 13th-c Italy, the sonnet has remained one of the most popular and adaptable of all poetic forms. » English/Italian literature; metre (literature); poetry; Shakespeare [i]

Sons of Liberty An organization in the American Revolution that provided popular leadership in the resistance movement against Britain. Composed mainly of artisans, small traders, and dissident intellectuals, it operated as an organized intercolonial group in 1765–6. Thereafter, the men who had taken part continued to provide popular leadership. The term was also used to describe all Americans involved in the revolutionary movement. » American Revolution

Soong, T V » **Song Ziwen**

sooty shearwater » **muttonbird**

Soper, Donald (Oliver), Baron (1903–) British Methodist minister, born in London. Widely known for his open-air speaking on London's Tower Hill, he became superintendent of the West London Mission in 1936, and has written many books on Christianity and social questions, and particularly on international issues from the pacifist angle. He was made a life peer in 1965. » Methodism; missions, Christian

sopherim » **scribe**

Sophia (1630–1714) Electress of Hanover, born in The Hague, the youngest daughter of Elizabeth Stuart (the daughter of James I of England) and Frederick Elector Palatine, also elected King of Bohemia (1618). In 1658 she married Ernest Augustus, Duke of Brunswick-Lüneburg, who became the first Elector of Hanover. She was the mother of George, Elector of Hanover, who became George I of Britain. Named in the Act of Settlement (1701) as the Protestant successor to the English crown after Anne, she died at Herrenhausen shortly before the Queen. » Anne; George I

Sophia Alexeyevna (1657–1704) Regent of Russia (1682–9), daughter of Tsar Alexey Mikhailovich and his first wife, Maria Miloslavskaya, born in Moscow. On the death of her brother, Tsar Fyodor Alexeyevich (1682), she opposed the accession of her half-brother, Peter (the future Peter the Great), and took advantage of a popular uprising in Moscow to press the candidature of her mentally deficient brother, Ivan. A compromise was reached whereby both Ivan (V) and Peter were proclaimed joint Tsars, with Sophia as Regent. Supported by leading boyars she became the *de facto* ruler of Russia. A faction of the nobility succeeded in removing her from power in 1689, and (apart from a failed attempt to regain power in 1698) she spent the rest of her life in a convent in Moscow. » boyars; Peter I

Sophists A collection of 5th-c BC Greek itinerant teachers of rhetoric, statecraft, and philosophy, the most influential of whom was Protagoras of Abdera. They are vividly portrayed in the dialogues of Plato, usually as dialectical opponents of Socrates. Their philosophical doctrines typically included the denial of a real world beyond the world of appearances, scepticism about the gods, and a belief in the perfectibility of humans. » Gorgias; Protagoras

Sophocles [**sof**uhkleez] (c.496–406 BC) Greek tragic dramatist, born at Colonus Hippius. He wrote 123 plays, of which only seven survive, all written after his victory over Aeschylus in a dramatic contest in 468 BC: *Ajax*, *Electra*, *Women of Trachis*, *Philoctetes*, and his three major plays *Oedipus Rex*, *Oedipus at Colonus*, and *Antigone*. He played an important part in Athenian public life, and assisted Pericles in the war against the Samians (440 BC). He died in Athens. » Aeschylus; drama; Greek literature; Pericles; tragedy

Sophonias [sofuh**ni**yas] » **Zephaniah, Book of**

Sopot [so**pot**], Ger **Zoppot** 54°27N 18°01E, pop (1983) 51 500. Resort town in Gdańsk voivodship, N Poland; between wooded slopes and the Bay of Gdańsk; part of the *Tri-City* with Gdańsk and Gdynia; railway; hydrotherapy treatment centre, open-air opera, racecourse; international song festival. » Poland [i]

Sopwith, Sir Thomas (Octave Murdoch) (1888–1989) British aircraft designer and sportsman, born in London. He won a prize for the longest flight across the English Channel in 1910, and founded the Sopwith Aviation Company in 1912, building many of the aircraft used in World War 1, such as the Sopwith Camel. Chairman of the Hawker Siddeley Group from 1935, and president from 1963, he was knighted in 1953. He died at Compton Manor, Hampshire. » aircraft [i]

sorbic acid A permitted food preservative which can inhibit the growth of moulds. Such preservatives are known as *antimycotic*. Sorbic acid is obtained from the unripe fruits of the mountain ash. » food preservation; rowan

Sorbonne » **Paris, University of**

sorcery » **witchcraft**

sorghum A cereal resembling maize in general appearance, but with dense heads of small grains. The most important is *Sorghum vulgare*, also called **kaffir corn** or **guinea corn**, cultivated as a staple food in much of Africa and parts of Asia, and in America and Australia for animal feed. One variety yields sugar in the same way as sugar cane. (Genus: *Sorghum*, 60 species. Family: *Gramineae*.) » cereals; grass [i]; maize; sugar cane

sororate » **levirate**

sorority » **fraternity and sorority**

sorrel Any of several species of dock, native to Europe, usually with spear-shaped, acid-tasting leaves used as vegetables or in salads. (Genus: *Rumex*. Family: *Polygonaceae*.) » dock

sorus A plant structure formed from a number of sporangia. It is usually associated with ferns, where they are arranged in distinctive patterns on the undersides of the fronds, but they are also found in some algae and fungi. The lid-like flap of tissue covering and protecting the sorus in some ferns is known as the **indusium**. » algae; fern; fungus; sporangium

Sosigenes of Alexandria [so**sij**uhneez] (1st-c BC) Astronomer and mathematician who advised Julius Caesar on calendar reform. He recommended a year of 365.25 days, and inserted an extra 67 days into the year 46 BC to bring the months back in register with the seasons. » Julian calendar

Sotheby, John [**suh**thuhbee] (1740–1807) British auctioneer and antiquarian, who founded at Covent Garden in 1744 the first sale room in Britain exclusively for books, manuscripts, and prints. He became a director of the firm (1780–1800), then known as Leigh and Sotheby, which was transferred to the Strand in 1803.

Sotho-Tswana A cluster of Sotho-speaking peoples of Botswana, Lesotho, the Transvaal, Orange Free State, and N Cape. The pre-colonial social organization of all these peoples was very similar, which distinguishes them from the other main S African group of Bantu-speakers, the Nguni. The main subgroupings are the various Tswana groups, traditionally independent chiefdoms; the S Sotho of Lesotho and the Orange Free State, who were united in a single political unit in the early 19th-c; and the Pedi and other N Sotho peoples of the N Transvaal. » Bophuthatswana; Botswana [i]; Lesotho [i]; Nguni; South Africa [i]

Soto, Fernando de » **de Soto, Fernando**

Soto [**soh**toh] » **Zen Buddhism**

Soufflot, Jacques Germain [**soo**floh] (1713–80) French architect, born at Irancy. In 1738 he was municipal architect at Lyons, and became the leading French Neoclassical designer, his major works being the Panthéon and the Ecole de Droit in Paris. He died in Paris. » Neoclassicism (art and architecture)

soul (music) A strongly emotional type of popular music which followed on from rhythm and blues in the 1960s, and drew on other types of pop music. It is associated primarily with Black US singers, such as Aretha Franklin (1942–). » pop music; gospel music; rhythm and blues

soul (religion) Usually, the principle of life, the ultimate identity of a person, or the immortal constituent of the self. The concept derives from Plato, for whom it was a metaphysical entity, ultimately incorruptible and eternal. In Christian thought, the concept became fused with the idea of the resurrection of the body. There are links with the concept of *atman* in Hindu and Buddhist thought. » atman; Christianity; mind; Plato; resurrection

Sŏul » **Seoul**

Soult, Nicolas Jean de Dieu [soolt] (1769–1851) French Marshal, born and died at Saint-Amans-La-Bastide. Created Marshal of France by Napoleon in 1804, he led the French armies in the Peninsular War (1808–14) until defeated at Toulouse (1814). A skilled opportunist, he turned Royalist after Napoleon's abdication, but joined him in the Hundred Days, acting as his Chief-of-Staff at Waterloo. Exiled until 1819, he was gradually restored to all his honours, and presided over three ministries of Louis Philippe (1832–4, 1839–40, 1840–7). » Hundred Days; Louis Philippe; Napoleon I; Peninsular War; Waterloo, Battle of

sound A wave motion comprising a sequence of pressure pulses passing through some medium, typically air. The source of sound is a mechanical oscillator in a medium, such as a vibrating guitar string or a loudspeaker cone in air. It can be detected aurally, or using microphones or transducers. The speed of sound in air is 332 m/s; in fresh water at 20°C, it is 1 482 m/s. » acoustics; aerodynamics [i]; phonon; reflection; sonar; sound intensity level [i]; supersonic; wave (physics) [i]

Sound, the, Danish **Øresund** Strait between Zealand I, Denmark, and S Sweden, connecting the Kattegat with the Baltic Sea; width of narrowest section, 6 km/4 ml. » Denmark [i]

sound barrier » **aerodynamics** [i]

sound film Cinema pictures with synchronized sound. In 1926, 16 inch gramophone discs running at 33 rpm (revolutions per minute) were linked to the film projector, but this was quickly replaced by integral sound-on-film systems. A photographic sound record is printed by the side of the picture as a continuous track in which sound modulations are represented by variations of either its density or its width. During projection the track passes a narrow illuminated slit, varying the transmitted light received by a photocell to produce electrical signals which are amplified to loudspeakers behind the screen. To record high frequencies it was necessary to increase the rate of projection from 16 to 24 frames a second. By 1930, sound film had become universal in cinemas, although the variable density system of modulation gradually disappeared. Improvements in the quality of photographic sound recording and reproduction have continued, with noise reduction, extended frequency range, and stereophonic presentation, and the use of digital sound representation is envisaged. » cinematography [i]; Movietone; projector [i]; silent film

sound intensity level Symbol L_I, units db (decibel); noise level relative to the faintest audible sound, which is rated as 0 db. It is related to sound intensity I, units W/m^2, the power per unit area of the sound wave. $L_I = 10 \log(I/I_o)$, where I_o is taken to be 10^{-12} W/m^2, the sound intensity corresponding to 0 db. A selection of typical sound intensity level equivalents is given in the panel. » decibel; sound

SOUND INTENSITY LEVEL

SOURCE	SOUND INTENSITY LEVEL (db)
jet aircraft	120
heavy machinery	90
busy street	70
conversation	50
whisper	20

sound law A regular series of changes in the sound system of a language, during a period of its history. The Great Vowel Shift in English, which took place around the end of the 14th-c, provides an example: the pronunciation of several vowels altered markedly in the direction of their modern forms. For example, Middle English *gōs* (pronounced with a vowel similar to that in *toast*) became Modern *goose*, and *gēs* (similar to the vowel in *lace*) became *geese*. In English, the nature of such changes can often be deduced from the spelling, which is less prone to change, and tends to preserve the values of an earlier period of pronunciation. » comparative linguistics

sound navigation and ranging » **sonar**

sound recording The conversion of sound into a storage medium from which it can later be reproduced. At first, the process was conducted entirely acoustically: sound signals were stored by direct mechanical conversion into grooves in a cylinder or disc, and reproduced using a phonograph or gramophone. In **digital recording**, which became dominant in the 1980s, the signal converted into corresponding electrical vibrations is sampled (up to 30 000 times a second), and the information represented and recorded numerically. With the compact disc, these digits are then directly decoded in the reproducing device, giving a recording that suffers no distortion as a result of the transmission process. Standard recording practice is to use a microphone array, the amplified electrical signal levels being balanced by recording engineers in a mixing console, and recorded digitally on a multi-track tape recorder. After dubbing and editing, copies are made from the master tape in several ways. For records, the tape drives an analogue disc-cutting machine acting on a lacquer-coated aluminium master; this leads to a nickel stamper from which multiple plastic pressings are made. For tapes, copies are made using a bank of cassette tape recorders. For digital compact discs, a laser inscribes a photoresist-coated master with a spiral track of pits and plateaux. » compact disc; digital recording; Dolby system; magnetic tape **1**; pick-up; stereophonic sound; tape recorder

sour cherry » **cherry**

sour sop A small evergreen tree, growing to c.5 m/16 ft, native to C America; leaves pinnate; flowers fleshy with six green and yellow petals; fruit 25 cm/10 in, heart-shaped, green, covered with fleshy spines, containing numerous seeds buried in white, fragrant pulp. It is widely cultivated in the tropics for the fruit, used for flavouring drinks. (*Annona muricata*. Family: *Annonaceae*.) » evergreen plants; pinnate; tree [i]

Sousa, John Philip [**soo**za] (1854–1932) US composer and bandmaster, born in Washington, DC. His early training as a conductor was gained with theatre orchestras, and in 1880 he led the US Marine Band. His own band, formed in 1892, won an international reputation, and he became known as the composer of over 100 rousing military marches, and the inventor of the sousaphone. He died at Reading, Pennsylvania. » sousaphone

sousaphone [**soo**zafohn] A musical instrument resembling a tuba, but with the tubing encircling the player's body. It was designed by John Philip Sousa to be played while marching, and was first made in 1898. » brass instrument [i]; Sousa; tuba

souslik [**soo**slik] or **suslik** [**suhs**lik] A squirrel native to Asia, Europe, and N America; coat may be striped or spotted; inhabits open country; lives in burrows; some species called *gophers*; also known as **ground squirrel**. (Genus: *Spermophilus*, 32 species.) » gopher; rodent; squirrel

Sousse [soos] 35°50N 10°38E, pop (1984) 83 509. Port and capital of Sousse governorate, NE Tunisia, 115 km/71 ml SSE of Tunis; founded by the Phoenicians, 9th-c BC; destroyed by the Vandals, AD 434; railway; tourism, crafts, clothing, ceramics, carpets; Mosque Zakak, the Great Mosque (850),

Hanafite Mosque, Ribat fortress (9th-c); festival of music and popular arts (Apr–May), Aoussou Festival (Jul–Aug). » Phoenicia; Tunisia [i]; Vandals

South Africa, official name **Republic of South Africa**, Afrikaans **Republiek van Suid-Afrika** pop (1990e) 30 797 000; area 1 233 404 sq km/476 094 sq ml. South African republic, divided into the four provinces of Cape, Natal, Orange Free State, Transvaal; bounded NW by Namibia, N by Botswana, NE by Zimbabwe, Mozambique, and Swaziland, E and SE by the Indian Ocean, and SW and W by the S Atlantic Ocean; Lesotho is landlocked within its borders; includes the independent homelands of Bophuthatswana, Ciskei, Transkei, and Venda; also the six non-independent national states of Gazankulu, Lebowa, QwaQwa, KwaZulu, KaNgwane, and KwaNdebele; administrative capital, Pretoria; judicial capital, Bloemfontein; legislative capital, Cape Town; largest city, Johannesburg; timezone GMT +2; population is 70% Black African, 18% White, 3% Asian, and 9% Coloured; most Whites and Coloureds and c.60% of Africans are Christian, c.60% of Asians are Hindu, and c.20% are Muslim; official languages, English and Afrikaans, with many African languages spoken; unit of currency, the rand of 100 cents.

Physical description. Occupies the S extremity of the African plateau, fringed by fold mountains and a lowland coastal margin to the W, E, and S; N interior comprises the Kalahari Basin, scrub grassland and arid desert, altitude 650–1 250 m/2 100–4 100 ft; peripheral highlands rise to over 1 200 m/3 900 ft; Great Escarpment rises E to 3 482 m/11 424 ft at Thabana Ntlenyana; Orange R flows W to meet the Atlantic, chief tributaries the Vaal and Caledon Rivers.

Climate. In the E, subtropical, with lush vegetation; water temperatures c.24°C (May–Aug) and 28°C (Oct–Feb); average monthly rainfall at Durban, 28 mm/1.1 in (Jul), 130 mm/5 in (Mar), annual average 1 101 mm/43 in; dry moistureless climate on W coast; annual average at Cape Town, 510 mm/20 in, average minimum daily temperatures 7°C (Jul), average maximum 26°C (Jan–Feb); desert region further N, annual average rainfall less than 30 mm/1.2 in.

History and government. Originally inhabited by Khoisan tribes; many Bantu tribes from the N after c.1000; Portuguese reached the Cape of Good Hope, late 15th-c; settled by Dutch, 1652; arrival of British, 1795; British annexation of the Cape, 1814; Great Trek by Boers NE across the Orange R to Natal, 1836; first Boer republic founded, 1839; Natal annexed by the British 1846, but the Boer republics of Transvaal (founded 1852) and Orange Free State (1854) were recognized; discovery of diamonds (1866) and gold (1886) led to rivalry between British and Boers; South African Wars, 1880–1, 1899–1902; Transvaal, Natal, Orange Free State, and Cape Province joined as the Union of South Africa, a dominion of the British Empire, 1910; sovereign state within the Commonwealth, 1931–61; independent republic, 1961; Botswana and Lesotho independence, 1966; Swaziland independence, 1968; independence granted by South Africa to Transkei (1976), Bophuthatswana (1977), Venda (1979), and Ciskei (1981), not recognized internationally; politics dominated by treatment of non-White majority; after 1948, the apartheid policy resulted in the development of separate political institutions for different racial groups; Africans were considered permanent citizens of the 'homelands' to which each tribal group was assigned; continuing racial violence and strikes led to the declaration of a state of emergency in 1986, and several countries imposed economic and cultural sanctions (especially in the field of sport); progressive dismantling of apartheid system by de Klerk from 1990; governed by a three-chamber legislature comprising a 178-member House of Assembly (for Whites), 166 elected for 5 years, an 85-member House of Representatives (for Coloureds), and a 45-member House of Delegates (for Asians); there is also a 60-member President's Council.

□ international airport

Economy. Industrial growth as a result of 19th-c gold and diamond discoveries; cheap African labour used for new products and technologies; grain, wool, sugar, tobacco, cotton, citrus fruit, dairy products, livestock, fishing; motor vehicles, machinery, chemicals, fertilizers, textiles, clothes, metal products, electronics, computers, tourism; gold (over half of the country's export income), diamonds, uranium, metallic ores, asbestos. » African history; apartheid; Bantu-speaking peoples; Bloemfontein; Boer Wars; Bophuthatswana; Cape Town; Ciskei; Great Trek; Johannesburg; Pretoria; Transkei; Venda; RR27 national holidays; RR60 political leaders

South African Native National Congress A nationalist organization founded in 1912 to promote the interests of educated African Christians in South Africa. At first imitative and gradualist, it later dropped the 'native' from its title. It went through a moribund period in the 1930s, but was revived in World War 2 under the leadership of Dr A B Xuma. After the war Oliver Tambo (1917–) and Nelson Mandela (1918–) organized its youth wing. It was active in the 1950s in leading opposition to the measures of the Afrikaner Nationalist government, but was banned in 1961 and Mandela sent to prison in 1964. Other members of its leadership went into exile. It remains the principal African opposition to White rule in South Africa. » African National Congress; Afrikaners; apartheid; Black Consciousness Movement; Mandela; nationalism

South America The fourth largest continent, extending c.7 500 km/5 000 ml from 12°25N to 56°S; area c.18 million sq km/7 million sq ml; linked to N America (NW) by the isthmus of Panama; bounded N by the Caribbean Sea, E by the Atlantic Ocean, and W by the Pacific Ocean; includes Argentina, Bolivia, Brazil, Chile, Colombia, Ecuador, Guyana, Paraguay, Peru, Suriname, Uruguay, and Venezuela; outlying islands include the Falkland Is, Galapagos Is, and Tierra del Fuego; the Andes run almost the full W length, rising to 6 969 m/22 834 ft at Aconcagua; largest lake, Titicaca; major river basins, the Orinoco, Paraná, and Amazon (containing the world's largest tropical rainforest); considerable evidence of early Indian kingdoms, notably the Incas, destroyed by Spanish and Portuguese invaders during the 16th-c; most countries achieved independence following war in the early 19th-c. » Amazon, River; American Indians; Andes; Incas; Spanish-American Wars of Independence

South Australia pop (1986) 1 393 800; area 984 000 sq km/380 000 sq ml. State in S Australia; established as a British Crown Colony 1836; became a state 1901; included most of Northern Territory 1863–1901; composed of seven statistical divisions; bordered S by the Great Australian Bight and the Southern Ocean; largely desert, notably the Great Victoria Desert and Nullarbor Plain; fertile land in the SE corner irrigated by the Murray R; coastline dissected by the Spencer and St Vincent Gulfs; dry salt lakes inland (Eyre, Torrens,

Gairdner, Frome); the Gawler Ranges in the S, Flinders and Mt Lofty Ranges in the E; highest point, Mt Woodroffe (1 440 m/4 724 ft); Murray R enters the ocean in the SE; Woomera Prohibited Area (weapons-testing range) extends across the Great Victoria Desert into Western Australia; 9 600 km/6 000 ml-long Dingo Fence protects S grazing sheep from wild dogs (possession of a dingo is illegal in this state); capital, Adelaide; principal towns Whyalla, Mount Gambier, Port Pirie, Port Augusta; wheat, barley, fruit, wool, meat, wine, oil refining, natural gas; copper, silver, lead mining; supplies 95% of world's opals; oranges and other citrus fruit in irrigated orchards along the Murray R; almost half of Australia's wine produced from the Barossa Valley N of Adelaide; state holidays Labour Day (Oct), Proclamation Day (Dec). » Adelaide; Australia [i]; dingo; Great Victoria Desert; Nullarbor Plain

South Bend 41°41N 86°15W, pop (1980) 109 727. Seat of St Joseph County, N Indiana, USA, on the St Joseph R; city status 1865; railway; aircraft equipment, motor vehicles, clothing, engineering; University of Notre Dame nearby. » Indiana

South Carolina pop (1987e) 3 425 000; area 80 580 sq km/31 113 sq ml. State in SE USA, divided into 46 counties; the 'Palmetto State'; settled by the French at Port Royal, 1562; included in the Carolina grant in 1663, but returned to the Crown in 1729; brought under American control after the battle of Guilford Courthouse, 1781; eighth of the original 13 states to ratify the Constitution, 1788; the first state to secede from the Union, 1860; Confederate forces attacked Fort Sumter 12 Apr 1861, starting the Civil War; slavery abolished, 1865; re-admitted to the Union, 1868; capital, Columbia; other chief cities Charleston, Greenville, Spartanburg; bounded E and SE by the Atlantic Ocean; rivers include the Pee Dee, Edisto, Savannah (forms most of Georgia border), Wateree, and Congaree, the latter two joining to form the Santee; Blue Ridge Mts in the extreme NW; highest point Mt Sassafras (1 085 m/3 560 ft); flat and (in the S) swampy coastland, cut by numerous rivers and creeks to form the Sea Islands, a major tourist centre; ground rises inland towards the rolling Piedmont, the agricultural and manufacturing centre; reservoirs at L Murray, L Marion, and L Moultrie; textiles and clothing, using the large cotton crop; lumber, chemicals, machinery, foodstuffs; tobacco, soybeans, poultry, cattle, dairy products, peaches, peanuts, sweet potatoes, corn; fishing. » American Civil War; Columbia; United States of America [i]; RR39

South China Sea area c.2 974 600 sq km/1 148 200 sq ml. W arm of the Pacific Ocean, bounded by Taiwan (N), the Philippines (E), Borneo (SE), and the SE Asian coast (NW, W, SW); subject to violent typhoons; main arms, Gulfs of Tongkin and Kompong; shallow in SE, c.60 m/200 ft; deep basin in NE, reaching 5 490 m/18 012 ft; numerous island groups and coral reefs; major fishing region. » Pacific Ocean

South Dakota [da**koh**ta] pop (1987e) 709 000; area 199 723 sq km/77 116 sq ml. State in NC USA, divided into 66 counties; the 'Coyote State'; part of the USA as a result of the Louisiana Purchase, 1803; included in Dakota Territory, 1861; population swelled when gold was discovered in the Black Hills, 1874; separated from North Dakota and became the 40th state of the Union, 1889; capital, Pierre; chief cities Sioux Falls, Rapid City, Aberdeen; crossed by the Missouri and Big Sioux Rivers; the Bois de Sioux and Minnesota Rivers form part of the E border; the Black Hills rise in the SW corner of the state; highest point Mt Harney Peak (2 207 m/7 241 ft); W of Missouri R is a semi-arid, treeless plain, one-third owned by Sioux Indians; severe erosion has formed the barren Bad Lands, where there are many ancient marine and land fossils; E of the R Missouri are rich, fertile plains; cattle, wheat, hogs, dairy products, corn, soybeans, oats; meat packing, food processing; town of Lead in the Black Hills is the nation's leading gold-mining centre; second largest gold and beryllium producer in the USA; Mt Rushmore (in the Black Hills); Indian reserves at Crow Creek, Rosebud, Pine Ridge, Cheyenne. » Louisiana Purchase; Pierre; Sioux; United States of America [i]; RR39

South Downs Way Long-distance footpath following the South Downs of East and West Sussex, S England; stretches from Eastbourne to Harting; length 129 km/80 ml. » Downs

South East Asia Treaty Organization (SEATO) An organization founded mainly to provide collective defence in the case of an attack by external aggressors against any one of the eight signatories to the treaty: Australia, France, New Zealand, Pakistan, the Philippines, Thailand, UK, and USA. A further purpose was economic cooperation. SEATO's headquarters is in Bangkok.

South Georgia 54°30S 37°00W; area c.3 750 sq km/1 450 sq ml. Barren, mountainous, snow-covered island in the S Atlantic, about 500 km/300 ml E of the Falkland Is; a British Dependent Territory administered from the Falkland Is; length, 160 km/100 ml; discovered by the London merchant De la Roche, 1675; landing by Captain Cook, 1775; British annexation, 1908 and 1917; invaded by Argentina and recaptured by Britain, April 1982; only village, Grytviken; research stations maintained here and on the neighbouring Bird I; sealing and whaling centre until 1965; burial place of Ernest Shackleton. » Cook, James; Falkland Islands [i]; Falklands War; Shackleton

South Glamorgan pop (1987e) 399 500; area 416 sq km/161 sq ml. County in S Wales, UK, divided into two districts; created in 1974; bounded S by the Bristol Channel; capital, Cardiff; agriculture (Vale of Glamorgan), steel, plastics, engineering, vehicle components, food processing; Welsh Folk Museum at Cardiff. » Wales [i]

South India, Church of A Church inaugurated in 1947 in Madras, India, from the merger of Anglicans, Methodists, and United Churches. It reflected a common desire for missionary and social work as well as worship, and tries in its organization to preserve the traditions of each of its constituent traditions. It is governed by a General Synod, with bishops, presbyters, and deacons, and significant lay participation. » Anglican Communion; ecumenism; Methodism; missions, Christian

South Island pop (1981) 852 748; area 153 978 sq km/59 435 sq ml. The larger and southernmost of the two main islands of New Zealand; separated from North Island by the Cook Strait, and from Stewart I (S) by the Foveaux Strait; fertile plains on coast give way to mountains; Southern Alps run through the centre, containing Mt Cook (3 764 m/12 349 ft), highest point in New Zealand; Westland to the W, a narrow forested strip; Canterbury Plain to the E, largest area of flat lowland; numerous bays and fjords to the SW; chief towns include Christchurch, Invercargill, Dunedin, Nelson; tobacco, hops, coal, cement, timber, greenstone, sheep, pottery, fruit, tourism. » New Zealand [i]

South Korea » **Korea** [i]

South Orkney Islands, Span **Orcadas del Sur** area 620 sq km/239 sq ml. Group of islands in the S Atlantic, NE of the Graham Peninsula; main islands Coronation, Signy, Laurie, Inaccessible; used by British and US whalers since 1821; barren and uninhabited, apart from scientific research; claimed by Argentina. » British Antarctic Territory

South Pacific Commission An organization set up in 1948 by Western states then exercising colonial rule in the S Pacific. The purpose was to advance the economic and social interests of the peoples under their control within a framework of regional co-operation. The S Pacific nations also joined, from the 1960s, as they became independent.

South Pacific Forum An organization founded in 1971 to provide a setting where the heads of government of independent and self-governing Pacific island states could meet to discuss their common political concerns with each other and with Australia and New Zealand.

South Pole » **Poles**

South Sandwich Islands 56°18–59°25S 26°15W. Group of small, uninhabited islands in the S Atlantic, c.720 km/450 ml SE of South Georgia; a British Dependent Territory administered from the Falkland Is; discovered by Captain Cook, 1775; annexed by Britain, 1908 and 1917. » Falklands Islands

South Sea Bubble A financial crisis in Britain (1720) arising out of speculation mania generated by Parliament's approval of the South Sea Company proposal to take over three-fifths of the National Debt. Many investors were ruined in the aftermath, but Robert Walpole's plan for stock transfer retrieved the situation and made his reputation. » shares; stocks; Walpole, Robert

South Shetland Islands area 4 622 sq km/1 784 sq ml. Group of mountainous islands in the S Atlantic, NW of the Graham Peninsula, c.880 km/550 ml SE of Cape Horn; main islands King George, Elephant, Clarence, Gibbs, Nelson, Livingston, Greenwich, Snow, Deception, Smith; discovered in 1819; occasionally used for scientific bases. » British Antarctic Territory

South West Africa People's Organization (SWAPO) A nationalist organization in Southwest Africa (Namibia), which opened a guerrilla campaign against South African rule in Namibia in 1969. South Africa had acquired the mandate to the German colony of South West Africa after World War 1, and had refused to hand it over to the United Nations trusteeship council after World War 2, attempting instead to integrate it into South Africa. The South Africans tried to create an internal settlement in Namibia, but without UN support. Frontline states and the Organization of African Unity gave their support to SWAPO, and Angola provided it with bases for its liberation movement. South Africa attempted to destabilize Angola by supporting a dissident movement, UNITA, within that state. The Angola regime was supported by Cuban forces. At the end of 1988, an international agreement was reached in Geneva linking arrangements for the future independence of Namibia with the withdrawal of Cuban troops from Angola, and the cessation of South African attacks on that country and its support for the UNITA rebels. » Angola [i]; mandates; Namibia [i]; Organization of African Unity

South Yorkshire » **Yorkshire, South**

Southampton, Henry Wriothesley, 3rd Earl of (1573–1624) English courtier, born at Cowdray, Sussex. He was known as a patron of poets, notably of Shakesepeare, who dedicated to him both *Venus and Adonis* (1593) and *The Rape of Lucrece* (1594). He became involved in the rebellion of Essex (1600), and was imprisoned, but released by James I. He died at Bergen-op-Zoom while in charge of English volunteers against Spain in the Netherlands. » Essex, Earl of; Shakespeare [i]

Southampton, Lat **Clausentum**, Anglo-Saxon **Hamwih** 50°55N 1°25W, pop (1981) 205 337. Port city in Southampton district, Hampshire, S England; on Southampton Water, at the mouth of the Test and Itchen Rivers; major UK port handling container traffic and passenger ships; four tides daily; site of both Roman and Saxon settlements; *Mayflower* set sail from here en route to N America in 1620; *Titanic* sailed from here on her disastrous maiden voyage (1912); city status (1964); university (1952); railway; ferries to the I of Wight and N Europe; marine engineering, petrochemicals, cables, electrical goods; St Michael's Church (1070); 15th-c Guildhall; 14th-c wool house now housing a maritime museum; *Mayflower* memorial. » Hampshire; Pilgrim Fathers

Southcott, Joanna (c.1750–1814) British religious fanatic, born in Dorset. In c.1792 she declared herself to be the woman in *Rev* 12 who would give birth to the second Prince of Peace. She went to London, where she obtained a great following, but died soon after the date of the supposed birth. Her followers, who believed she would rise again, were still to be found at the beginning of the 20th-c. » Revelation, Book of

Southend, properly **Southend-on-Sea** 51°33N 0°43E, pop (1987e) 162 500. Resort town co-extensive with Southend-on-Sea district, Essex, SE England; on the R Thames estuary, 57 km/35 ml E of London; famous pier, 2 km/1¼ ml long; railway; airfield; 12th-c Prittlewell Priory museum. » Essex

Southern Alps Mountain range in WC South Island, New Zealand; length c.320 km/200 ml NE–SW; contains New Zealand's highest peaks, Mt Cook (3 764 m/12 349 ft), Mt Tasman (3 497 m/11 472 ft), and Mt Dampier (3 440 m/11 286 ft); 19 named peaks exceed 3 000 m/10 000 ft; only two mountain passes (Haast Pass and Arthur's Pass) allow E–W travel; popular area for mountain-climbing and skiing. » New Zealand [i]; South Island

Southern Cross » **Crux**

Southern Ocean » **Antarctic Ocean**

southernwood An aromatic shrub growing to 1 m/1¼ ft; leaves finely divided with narrow thread-like lobes, grey-haired beneath; flower heads globular, 3–4 mm/0.12–0.16 in across; florets dull yellow. Of uncertain origin, it is widely grown as an ornamental. Its sweetly aromatic leaves are used for flavouring. (*Artemisia abrotanum.* Family: *Compositae*.) » shrub

Southey, Robert [**suh<u>th</u>ee**] (1774–1843) British poet and writer, born in Bristol. Educated at Westminster and Oxford, he left without a degree, studied law, and settled in Keswick, where he was associated with Wordsworth and Coleridge. Originally a radical in politics, his views mellowed, and in 1809 he began to contribute to the Tory *Quarterly Review*. Although made poet laureate in 1813, his poetry did not become as well known as his prose works, such as his life of Nelson, and his letters. He died at Keswick. » Coleridge; English literature; poetry; Wordsworth, William

Southport 53°39N 3°01W, pop (1981) 90 962. Coastal resort town in Sefton borough, Merseyside, NW England; on the Irish Sea, S of the R Ribble estuary, 25 km/15 ml N of Liverpool; the original 'garden city'; a notable golfing area (Birkdale); railway; chemicals, engineering; annual flower show. » Merseyside

Southwark [**suh<u>th</u>uhk**] 51°30N 0°06W, pop (1987e) 216 800. Borough of C Greater London, England; S of the R Thames; includes the suburbs of Bermondsey, Southwark, Camberwell; formerly famous for its inns and Elizabethan theatres (site of Globe Theatre); railway; 13th-c Southwark Cathedral, Dulwich College (1621), Guy's Hospital (1721), Imperial War Museum. » London [i]

Southwell, Robert (1561–95) English poet and martyr, born at Horsham, Norfolk. Educated at Douai and Rome, he became a Jesuit and was ordained in 1584. He travelled to England as a missionary in 1586, aiding persecuted Catholics, but was betrayed, tortured, and executed in London. Beatified in 1929, he is known for his devotional lyrics (eg 'The Burning Babe'), and for several prose treatises and epistles. » English literature; Jesuits; poetry; Reformation

Southwest Africa » **Namibia** [i]

Southwest Indians N American Indian groups living in the SW states of New Mexico, Utah, Colorado, and Texas, and in Mexico. Historically, some of the tribes came to the area from Middle America, such as the Pueblo (including the Hopi and Zuni), introducing many aspects of Middle American culture, while others migrated from the NE, such as the Athapascan-speaking Navajos and Apaches. Many prehistoric remains provide evidence of early settlement, dating back to possibly 10 000 years ago. Farming spread to the area from Mexico, and probably for more than 1 000 years many groups have been living in permanent settlements, growing crops and producing basketry, weavings, and other crafts. Contact with Whites since the 16th-c has been disruptive, and today most Indians are poor, depending for their survival on outside aid. The largest Indian groups in N America currently live in the area. » Apache; Hopi; Navajo; Pueblo; Zuni

Soutine, Chaim [**sooteen**] (1893–1943) Lithuanian artist, born at Smilovich. He studied at Vilna, and went to Paris in 1911, where he became known for his paintings of carcasses, and for his series of 'Choirboys' (1927). He died in Paris, and was later recognized as a leading Expressionist painter. » Expressionism

sovereign A British gold coin originally worth £1, but since the abolition of the gold standard, worth considerably more. Until recently, sovereigns were minted only on special occasions, but now they can be purchased, their price varying with the price of gold. New coins are called *Britannias.* » currency

sovereignty The capacity to determine conduct within the territory of a nation-state without external legal constraint. Sovereign powers may be exercised by a legislature, as in the UK. Where legal limits are placed upon the organs of government by the constitution, as in the USA, sovereignty is claimed to reside with the people.

soviet Originally, a workers' council established in Russia after the 1905 revolution. They re-appeared as workers' and soldiers' councils, important instruments of the 1917 revolution. Members of soviets were elected by popular vote, and lower soviets could not control higher ones. The highest was the Supreme Soviet, the legislative body of the USSR.

Soviet space programme A dominant element in the exploration of space after the launch of Sputnik in 1957. Its characteristic secrecy of activity has increasingly diminished in recent years as the programme has taken on an international emphasis. Its organizational separation into military and civil activities is less clear than in other countries. The civilian element has a complex organizational structure: launch activities, scientific spacecraft fabrication, and commercial activities are under the direction of the newly-created Glavkosmos Agency; traditional civilian co-operative scientific programmes are managed by the Intercosmos Council of the Soviet Academy of Sciences (ASUSSR), with its array of science and technology institutes. The Babakan Research and Test Centre of Glavkosmos appears to be analogous to the major NASA Center in the USA. ASUSSR is responsible for science strategy and experiment implementation; it includes the Institute for Space Research (IKI), the Vernadsky Institute for Geochemistry and Analytical Chemistry, and the Institute of Radioengineering and Electronics. ASUSSR's Intercosmos Council co-ordinates the international aspects of the programmes. For manned programmes, the Ministry of Health's Institute of Biomedical Problems is responsible for cosmonaut health and safety. The three principal launch sites (cosmodromes) are Tyuratam (or Baykonur), Plesetsk, and Kaputstin Yar; together these launch more than 100 spacecraft each year. There are three major deep space tracking stations: Yevpatoria (Crimea), Ussuriysk (Russian Far East), and a facility under construction in C Asia, supported also by stations in E Europe, Cuba, Africa, and Antarctica. The mission control centre is located in Kaliningrad (near Moscow), supported by facilities in Yevpatoria and Simeiz. » cosmonaut; Luna/Mars/Venera programme; Progress/Soyuz/Vostok spacecraft; Mir/Salyut space station; space exploration; Sputnik; VEGA project

Soviet Union, official name **Union of Soviet Socialist Republics (USSR)**, Russ **Soyuz Sovyetskikh Sotsialisticheskikh Republik** (Cyrillic alphabet, **CCCP**) pop (1989e) 287 800 000; area 22 402 076 sq km/8 647 201 sq ml. Former federation of 15 Union Republics which until its dissolution in December 1991 jointly formed the world's largest sovereign state; bounded W by Turkey, Romania, Hungary, Czechoslovakia, Poland, Lithuania, Latvia, Estonia, Finland, and Norway, and S by Iran, Afghanistan, China, Mongolia, and N Korea; capital, Moscow; timezones GMT +3 to +13; ethnic groups include Russian (52%), Ukrainian (16%), and over 100 other groups; official language, Russian; chief religion, Russian Orthodox (18%), with 70% atheist; unit of currency, the rouble of 100 kopeks; Union Republics usually known as **Soviet Socialist Republics (SSR)**; there were in addition 20 **Autonomous Soviet Socialist Republics (ASSR)**, and several smaller divisions (6 *krays*, 123 *oblasts*, 8 *autonomous oblasts*, 10 *autonomous okrugs*).

Physical description. Divided by the Ural Mts into European (W) and Asian (E) sectors; length of the Urals, 2 400 km/1 500 ml; narrow in the N, widening S into parallel ridges; highest peak, Narodnaya (1 894 m/6 214 ft); E European Plain in the W, largely below 300 m/1 000 ft, dissected by several major rivers, notably the S-flowing Dnestr, Dnieper, Don, Volga; steppelands of the W Siberian Lowlands in the E, drained by the N-flowing Ob, Yenisey, and Irtysh; C Siberian Plateau and N Siberian Plain further E; bordered S and E by a complex of fold mountains along the Chinese–Mongolian frontier and the Pacific seaboard; mountain systems occupied about a fifth of the total area; in C Asia, the Pamir, Tien Shan, and Altay ranges rise to over 5 000 m/16 000 ft; highest mountain, Communism Peak (7 495 m/24 590 ft) in the Pamirs; Caucasus Mts form a bridge between the Black Sea (W) and the Caspian Sea (E), and between Europe (N) and Asia (S); chief islands, Wrangel I and Sakhalin I.

Climate. Comprised about a sixth of the land area of the world, and thus had several different climatic regions, from polar (N) to sub-tropical (S); variable weather in N and C European Russia, winter temperatures increasingly severe in E and N; average temperatures at Moscow, −9.4°C (Jan), 18.3°C (Jul); average annual rainfall, 630 mm/24.8 in; winters also severe in S European Russia (Ukraine, Moldavia), but conditions drier in extreme SE, with mild winters along Black Sea coasts (the 'Russian Riviera'); winter temperatures much higher in the Caucasus Mts and Transcaucasia, with conditions almost tropical in the summer; rainfall well-distributed throughout the year (W); driest part was WC Asia (steppes and deserts of Kazakhstan, Uzbekistan, Turkmenistan), with warm to hot summers and cold winters; cold, dry winters in the mountains of C Asia (borders of Afghanistan and China); continental climate in Siberia, with very cold and prolonged winters, and short, often warm summers; average temperatures at Vladivostok, −14.4°C (Jan), 18.3°C (July); average annual rainfall, 599 mm/23.6 in.

History and government. Settled by many ethnic groups including the nomadic Slavs, Turks, and Bulgars, 3rd–7th-c; Moscow established as centre of political power in the N, 14th-c; Tatars expelled under Russia's first tsar, Ivan IV (the Terrible); internal disorder amongst a feudal nobility and constant warfare with border countries (eg Poland, Sweden) prevented Russian development until Tsar Peter I (the Great); under Catherine II (the Great) Russia became a great power, extending territory into S and E Asia; 1917 Revolution ended the monarchy, initiating a 5-year political struggle between Mensheviks and Bolsheviks; first Soviet government headed by Lenin; vigorous socialist reform begun by Stalin in the 1920s, including the collectivization of agriculture and rapid industri-

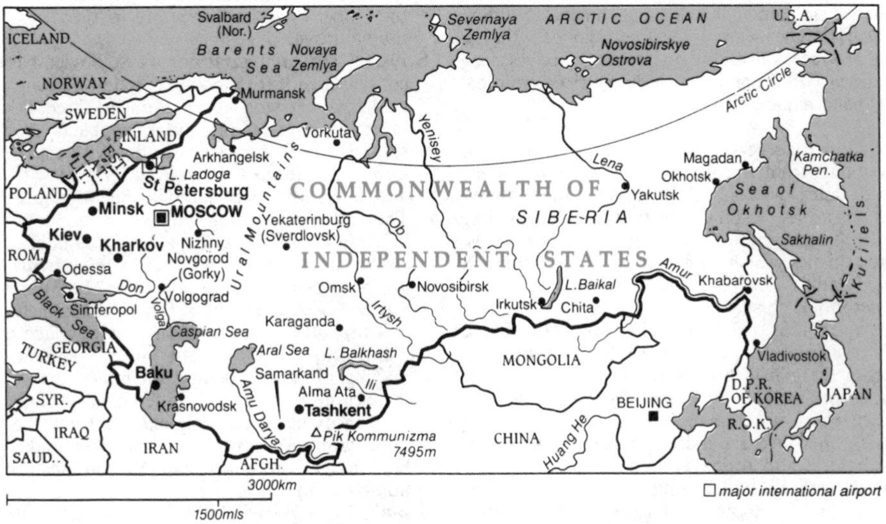

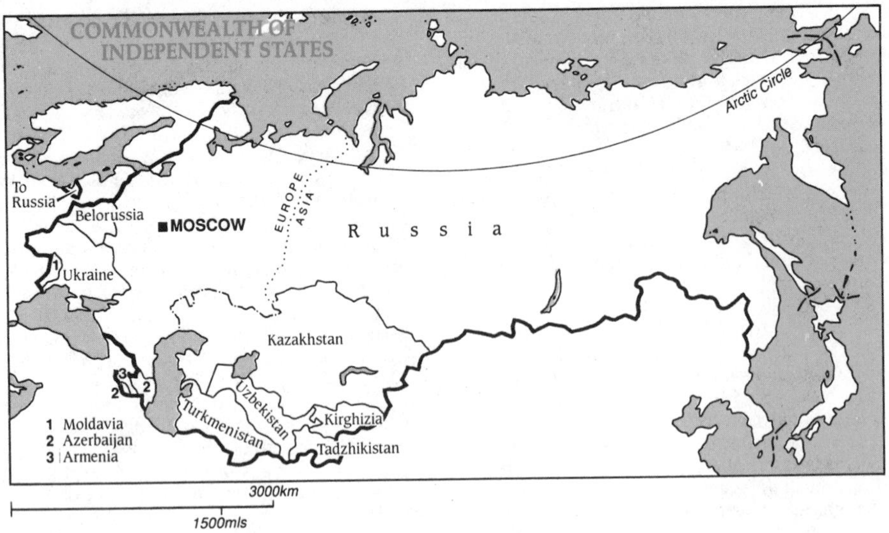

alization; territories extended in the W after World War 2, with a corridor of communist-dominated countries between USSR and W Europe; period of Cold War following World War 2; intervention to suppress Hungarian uprising (1956) and Czech programme of liberalization (1968); invasion of Afghanistan, 1979–88; series of disarmament agreements in 1980s, with new approach to international relations under Gorbachev (*glaznost*); constitutional reforms implemented in 1989 instituted a new Congress of the USSR People's Deputies, with 2 250 members; competition was introduced for some seats; the Congress elects from its ranks a 542-member Supreme Soviet, which acts as the effective legislature, and like the previous (larger) Supreme Soviet consists of the Council of the Union and the Council of Nationalities; the Republics have their own Supreme Soviets, Presidiums, and Council of Ministers; emergence of local independence movements in 1990, beginning in Lithuania, then in Estonia, Latvia, Moldavia, Georgia, and Ukraine.

Economy. After 1917, a system of centralized economic planning aimed to transform a pre-eminently agrarian, backward country with a primitive system of agriculture into an industrial state supported by intensive, mechanized collective farming; a series of 5-year plans in operation from the 1920s; wheat, oats, barley, rice, potatoes, cotton, sugar beet, flax, sunflowers, livestock fodder; world's leading producer of coal, oil, iron ore; natural gas, manganese, nickel, cobalt, chromium, uranium, copper, lead, zinc; vehicles, machinery, building materials, industrial chemicals, consumer goods, timber (world's leading producer), fishing; armaments, space research and development. » RR27 national holidays; RR64 political leaders; RR10 space exploration

sow » pig

sow thistle The name for several species of the genus *Sonchus*, annuals or perennials from Europe, Asia, and Africa; stems exuding a white latex when broken; leaves often spiny-margined, the stem leaves clasping with two rounded ear-like lobes at the base; large, yellow dandelion-like flower-heads. They are not true thistles, which tend to have stiffer and much sharper spines. (Genus: *Sonchus*. Family: *Compositae*.) » annual; latex; perennial; thistle

Soweto [soh**we**toh] 26°15S 27°52E, pop (1980) 864 000. Black African township in Transvaal province, NE South Africa; the name derives from the official title of South-West Township; linked by rail (5 km/3 ml) to industrial W Johannesburg; resistance to the teaching of Afrikaans in schools led to student riots in April 1976, when several hundred people were killed. » Afrikaans; apartheid; South Africa [i]

soya bean A bushy reddish-haired annual, growing to 2 m/ 6½ ft; leaves with three large oval leaflets; pea-flowers rather inconspicuous; violet, pink, or white, in small clusters in the leaf axils; pods up to 8 cm/3 in long, hairy; also called **soja** or **soy bean**. It is of unknown origin, but has a long history of cultivation in E Asia, and many varieties are now widely grown in both the Old and New World. The edible seeds (*soya beans*), which are rich in protein, are eaten as a vegetable and used in the production of artificial meat, to make flour, and to yield an oil employed in margarine and cooking oils. There are also numerous industrial uses, such as in enamels, paints, varnishes, lubricants, and rubber substitutes. The plants also provide a valuable food for livestock. (*Glycine max*. Family: *Leguminosae*.) » annual; vegetable

Soyinka, Wole, in full **Akinwande Oluwole Soyinka** (1934–) Nigerian writer, born near Abeokuta. Educated at Ibadan and Leeds, he became a play-reader at the Royal Court Theatre, where his first play, *The Invention* was performed in 1955. After returning to Ibadan in 1959, he founded two theatre companies, and built up a new Nigerian drama, in English but using the words, music, and dance of the traditional festivals. His writing is deeply concerned with the tension between old and new in modern Africa. His poetic collection *A Shuttle in the Crypt* (1972) appeared after his release in 1969 from two years political detention. His first novel, *The Interpreters* (1965), was called the first really modern African novel. He became professor of comparative literature at Ife in 1972, and was awarded the Nobel Prize for Literature in 1986. » African literature; drama; novel

Soyuz ('Union') spacecraft A Soviet basic space capsule, consisting of three modules (orbiter, descent, and instrumentation), and carrying a crew of one to three. It has been flown on several dozen missions, and is capable of precision targeting to soft-land in C Asia (contrasting with the US ocean-recovery technique). It has been used to ferry crew to and from Salyut and, later, Mir space stations with which docking takes place. The first flight was in 1967, when its pilot, V Komarov, was killed in a landing accident. Soyuz 19 docked with the Apollo spacecraft in Earth orbit after its rendezvous (Jul 1975). There was a notable launch accident (Sep 1983) in which the crew of Soyuz T-10A ejected to safety as the launch vehicle exploded. » Mir/Salyut space station; Soviet space programme

SP betting An illegal but popular system in Australia for making off-course betting on horse races. Up to the 1960s many hotels and barbers offered SP ('starting price') betting, but since that time, competition from the government-run Totalisator Agency Boards (TABS) and large-scale illegal bookmaking rings have made SP betting a thing of the past. » horse racing

Spaak, Paul Henri (1899–1972) Belgian statesman and Prime

Minister (1938–9, 1946, 1947–9), born in Brussels. He became the first socialist Premier, Foreign Minister with the government-in-exile during World War 2, and in 1946 President of the first General Assembly of the United Nations. After his later periods as Premier, he was again Foreign Minister (1954–7, 1961–8), in which role he became one of the founding fathers of the EEC, and Secretary-General of NATO (1957–61). He died in Brussels. » European Economic Community; NATO; United Nations

space exploration Imagined for centuries, the era began with the first artificial satellite (Sputnik, 1957) and the first manned flight (Gagarin, 1961), with subsequent rapidly evolving capabilities in Earth orbit and Solar System exploration (initiated by Mariner 2, 1962). It is an arena of intense international competition and, recently, co-operation. The utilitarian uses of space – communications and meteorology – are now taken for granted; astronomy and Earth remote-sensing capabilities provide a new perspective on the universe and our own planet. Solar System exploration has provided reconnaissance as far as Neptune, in-depth exploration of Mars and Venus, and detailed study of the Moon; the study of comets and asteroids is less advanced. Human activity has been demonstrated even to the point of crewed lunar landings (Apollo programme, 1969–72) and continuing space station occupancy (Salyut and Mir space stations), but remains dangerous and costly. Launch vehicle advances have achieved a re-usable crewed orbiter (US space shuttle), but inexpensive, reliable transportation is still in the future. The two dominant participants have been the USA and USSR, with the Europeans and Japanese becoming increasingly influential. Space physiological effects on humans are likely to limit the rate at which future exploration proceeds. » Apollo programme; astronaut; cosmonaut; launch vehicle [i]; Solar System; Space Organizations Worldwide; space station

space law A branch of international law which deals with rights in air space and outer space. Foreign aircraft have no right to fly over the territory or territorial waters of another state. In practice, states enter into bilateral agreements with other states whereby each grants the other rights in air space. The rules relating to aircraft do not apply to artificial satellites in outer space. The Outer Space Treaty of 1967 provides that outer space may be used by all states. » international law; sea, law of the

space mine A proposed munition of warfare in space; a spacecraft loaded with explosive which can be directed to detonate against a target spacecraft. » mine

Space Organizations Worldwide A state-consortium of organizations responsible for the space programmes of the spacefaring nations. It includes the *National Aeronautics and Space Administration* (NASA) in the USA; *Glavkosmos* (commercial) and *Intercosmos* (co-operative scientific) in Russia; the *European Space Agency* (ESA) of 13 countries; the *Centre Nationale d'Etudes Spatiales* (CNES) in France; the *British Space Centre* in the UK; and the *Institute of Space and Astronautical Science* (ISAS) and the *National Space Development Agency* (NASDA) in Japan. » European Space Agency; Helios project; Institute of Space and Astronautical Science of Japan; NASA; Soviet space programme; space exploration

space physiology and medicine The branch of medicine devoted to understanding the effects of space flight on human physiology and to assuring the health of astronauts. The observed effects of weightlessness include motion sickness, cardiovascular deconditioning, red blood cell mass loss, and bone mineral loss. Exercise, diet, biofeedback, and drug therapy have been used as countermeasures with some success. Radiation protection is a matter of concern for long-duration missions; and medical care during flights is also an issue. Long-duration flight experience has mainly been accumulated by the USSR on Salyut and Mir space stations. Longest flights (as of end 1987) are 84 days (US Skylab 4 crew) and 325 days (USSR Mir cosmonaut). The minimum round trip flight duration for a manned Mars mission would be about 1 year for a 2-week stay at the planet. » astronaut; cosmonaut; medicine; space station

space shuttle A re-usable crewed launch vehicle. The first-generation US shuttle became operational in 1982, managed by NASA's Johnson and Marshall Space Centers, while the USSR and European Space Agency versions were still under development. The US shuttle carries up to seven crew, and is capable of launching a 27 000 kg/60 000 lb payload into low Earth orbit; missions are up to 9 days duration. It comprises a delta-winged lifting body orbiter with main engines, a jettisonable external fuel tank, and two auxiliary solid rocket boosters. The fleet comprises four vehicles: *Columbia*, *Challenger*, *Discovery*, and *Atlantis*. It has been successfully used to launch numerous science and applications satellites and on-board experiments, and was used to carry the Spacelab module. The *Challenger* explosion on the 25th flight (26 Jan 1986) 73 sec after launch caused the loss of the crew. The first reflight took place in September 1988, and a replacement fourth orbiter is planned to be operational in 1992. » launch vehicle [i]; lifting body; spacecraft; Spacelab; RR11; *see illustration p 1136*

space station A long-lived crewed spacecraft in low Earth orbit; examples are US Skylab and USSR Mir. It is used for the accumulation of long-duration flight experience and related biomedical research, for astronomy, for Earth observations, and for microgravity experiments. Eventually, it will be used as a transportation node for human planetary missions. The NASA space station Freedom is scheduled for construction around 1996. » Mir/Salyut space station; Skylab project; space physiology and medicine

Space Telescope » **Hubble Space Telescope**

space-time A fundamental concept in the special and general theories of relativity. Einstein showed that a complete description of relative motion required equations including time as well as the three spatial dimensions. The form in which time is expressed gives it the mathematical property of a fourth coordinate, or dimension. Space-time is the single entity which unifies both space and time into a four-dimensional structure. In the general theory, Einstein showed that this 'fabric of the universe' becomes curved in the presence of matter, and this enabled him to give an elegant account of gravitation which has replaced Newton's theory. » Einstein; general relativity; Minkowski space; Newton, Isaac

spacecraft Vehicles designed to operate in the vacuum–weightlessness–high radiation environment of space; used to convey human crew, to acquire scientific data, to conduct utilitarian operations (eg telecommunications and synoptic weather observations), and to conduct research (eg microgravity experiments). The first spacecraft (Sputnik 1) was launched by the USSR in 1957 (4 Oct). They require highly reliable automated command and control, attitude stabilization, thermal control, radio telemetry, and data processing systems. Specialized spacecraft have been designed to be controllable on re-entry into the Earth's atmosphere (eg the NASA Space Shuttle), and to operate in atmospheres of other planets (eg Soviet Venera and US Pioneer atmospheric entry probes). » Explorer 1; Progress/Soyuz/Vostok spacecraft; space exploration; Space Organizations Worldwide; Sputnik

Spacelab A research facility flown in the cargo bay of the NASA space shuttle; designed, built, and financed by the European Space Agency. It had flown four times by the end of 1985. It consists of a pressurized experiment module for scientist-astronaut activities, and one or more pallets upon which telescopes and Earth remote-sensing experiments are mounted. » European Space Agency; NASA; space shuttle [i]

spadefoot toad A frog native to Europe, Asia, and N America; sharp projections (*spades*) on hind feet; burrows in dry sandy areas; breeds rapidly in temporary pools; in desert pools some tadpoles grow up to 180 mm/7 in long, and eat smaller tadpoles. (Family: *Pelobatidae*, 54 species.) » frog

spadix [**spay**diks] A specialized type of inflorescence in which the usually tiny flowers are crowded on a fleshy, cylindrical axis, generally enveloped by a large bract – the *spathe*. It is typical of, but not confined to, the arum family (*Araceae*). » arum lily; bract; inflorescence [i]

spaghetti Western A motion picture drama following the themes and settings of the American 'Western', but cheaply

The orbiter structure is divided into nine major sections: the forward fuselage, which consists of upper and lower sections that fit clamlike around a pressurized crew compartment; wings; midfuselage; payload bay doors; aft fuselage; forward reaction control system; vertical tail; orbital manoeuvring system/reaction control system pods; and body flap. The majority of the sections are constructed of conventional aluminium and protected by re-usable surface insulation. The forward fuselage structure is composed of 2024 aluminium alloy skin-stringer panels, frames and bulkheads. The crew compartment is supported within the forward fuselage at four attachment points, and is welded to create a pressure-tight vessel. The three-level compartment has a side hatch for normal passage, and hatches in the airlock to permit extravehicular and intravehicular activities. The side hatch can be jettisoned.

All measurements are given in feet, with metric equivalents in parentheses.

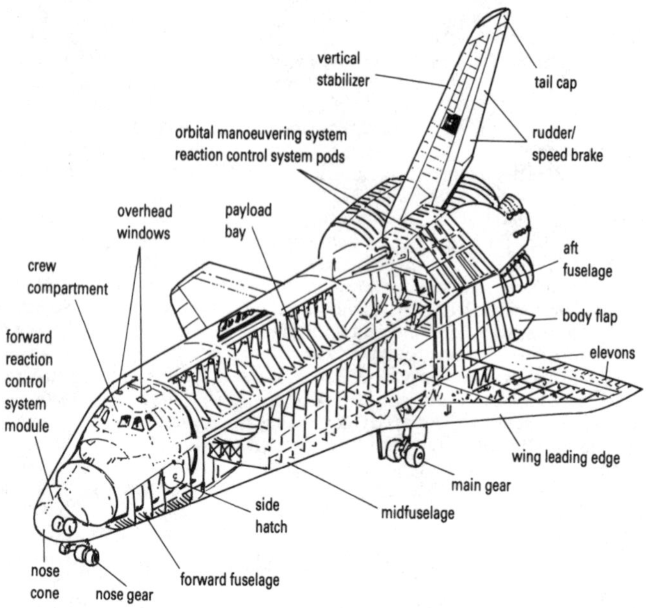

Minimum Ground Clearances	ft (m)
Body Flap	12.07 (3.7)
Main Gear Door	2.85 (0.87)
Nose Gear Door	2.95 (0.89)
Wing Tip	11.92 (3.6)

Orbiter weight in lb/kg (approximate)

Orbiter Vehicle (OV)	Total dry weight with three space shuttle main engines	Total dry weight without three space shuttle main engines
OV-102 Columbia	178 289/80 872	157 289/71 346
OV-103 Discovery	171 419/77 756	151 419/68 684
OV-104 Atlantis	171 205/77 659	151 205/68 587

Solid rocket booster weights in lb/kg (approximate)

1 300 000/590 000 each at launch (propellant weight 1 100 000/500 000 each). Inert weight 192 000/87 000 each.

External tank weight in lb/kg (approximate)

1 655 600/750 000 with propellants. Inert weight 66 000/30 000.

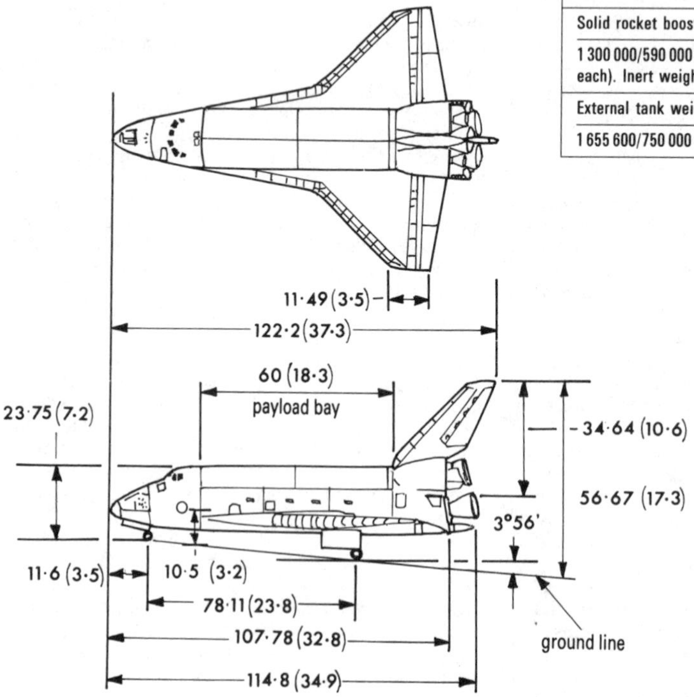

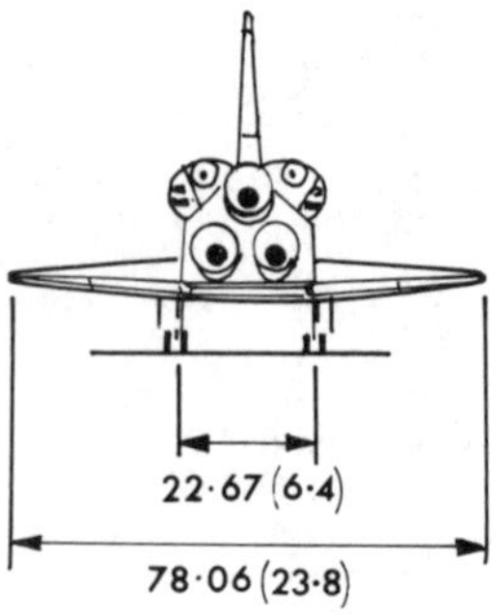

Space shuttle

produced by European companies on locations in Spain and Italy. The first of this genre was *A Fistful of Dollars* (1964, *Per un Pugno di Dollari*), a German-Spanish-Italian co-production directed by Sergio Leone and starring Clint Eastwood, both of whom repeated their success during the following 10 years. » cinema

Spain, Span **España**, official name **Kingdom of Spain**, Span **Reino de España**, ancient **Iberia**, Lat **Hispana** pop (1990e) 39 618 000; area of mainland 492 431 sq km/190 078 sq ml; total area 504 750 sq km/194 833 sq ml. Country in SW Europe, occupying four-fifths of the Iberian Peninsula, and including the Canary Is, Balearic Is, and several islands off the coast of N Africa, as well as the Presidios of Ceuta and Melilla in N Morocco; divided into 17 regions; mainland Spain situated between the Atlantic and the Mediterranean, bounded by France (N) across the Pyrenees and by Portugal (W); capital, Madrid; chief cities include Barcelona, Valencia, Seville, Saragossa, Málaga; timezone GMT + 1; official language, Spanish, with Catalan, Galician, and Basque also spoken in certain regions; chief religion, Roman Catholicism (99%); unit of currency, the peseta of 100 centimos.

Physical description and climate. Mostly a furrowed C plateau (the Meseta, average height 700 m/2 300 ft) crossed by mountains; Andalusian or Baetic Mts (SE) rise to 3 478 m/11 411 ft at Mulhacén; Pyrenees (N) rise to 3 404 m/11 168 ft at Pico de Aneto; rivers run E–W, notably the Tagus, Ebro, Guadiana, Miñho, Duero, Guadalquivir, Segura, and Júcar; continental climate in the Meseta, with hot summers, cold winters, low rainfall; high rainfall in the mountains, with deep winter snow; S Mediterranean coast has the warmest winter temperatures on the European mainland.

History and government. Early inhabitants included Iberians, Celts, Phoenicians, Greeks, and Romans; Muslim domination from the 8th-c; Christian reconquest completed by 1492; a monarchy since the unification of the Kingdoms of Castile, León, Aragón, and Navarre, largely achieved by 1572; 16th-c exploration of the New World, and the growth of the Spanish Empire; period of decline after the Revolt of the Netherlands in 1581, and the defeat of the Spanish Armada in 1588; War of the Spanish Succession, 1701–14; involved in the Peninsular War against Napoleon, 1808–14; war with the USA in 1898 led to the loss of Cuba, Puerto Rico, and remaining Pacific possessions; dictatorship under Primo de Rivera (1923–30), followed by exile of the King and establishment of the Second Republic (1931); military revolt headed by Franco in 1936 led

to civil war and a Fascist dictatorship; Prince Juan Carlos of Bourbon nominated to succeed Franco, 1969; acceded, 1975; governed by a bicameral parliament (*Cortes*) comprising a 350-member Congress of Deputies elected for four years and a 257-member Senate; since 1978 there has been a move towards local government autonomy with the creation of 17 self-governing regions.

Economy. A traditionally agricultural economy gradually being supplemented by varied industries; textiles, iron, steel, shipbuilding, electrical appliances, cars, cork, salt, wine, potash, forestry, fishing, tourism; iron, coal, lignite, sulphur, zinc, lead, wolfram, copper; wheat, rice, maize, barley, oats, hemp, flax, olives, oranges, lemons, almonds, pomegranates, bananas, apricots, grapes; a member of the EEC from 1986. » Bourbons; Castile; Cortes; Franco; Peninsular War; Revolt of the Netherlands; Spanish-American War; Spanish Armada/art/literature/Civil War; Spanish Succession, War of the; Thirty Years' War; RR27 national holidays; RR60 political leaders

spandrel A triangular space on the wall of a building, defined by the curve of an arch, a vertical line drawn up from the side of the arch, and a horizontal line through its apex. Particularly in 20th-c architecture, it refers to an infill panel below a window, often of a different material to the rest of the wall. » arch [i]

spaniel A sporting dog belonging to one of several breeds originally developed to assist hunters; bred to retrieve game, especially birds; usually small, affectionate, with long pendulous ears; now popular pets. » Brittany/cocker/English cocker/King Charles/springer spaniel; Maltese (zoology); retriever; sporting dog

Spanish » **Romance languages; Spanish literature**

Spanish-American War (1898) A brief conflict growing out of US intervention in the Cuban revolution for independence, effectively ended by the destruction of the Spanish fleet. The war resulted in Cuban independence under US suzerainty, and in US acquisition of Puerto Rico and the Philippines.

Spanish-American Wars of Independence (1810–26) Wars fought in S America, following Napoleon's invasion of Spain (1808): reformers in the major S American colonies set up semi-independent governments (1810), which were rejected both by royalists in the colonies and by the Spanish king, Ferdinand VII, when restored in 1814. The ensuing wars were fought in two main theatres: Venezuela, New Granada and Quito, where Simón Bolívar was the leading patriot general, and Argentina and Chile, from where General José de San Martín mounted an invasion of the Viceroyalty of Peru, still held by Spain (1820–1). The final liberation of Peru was effected in 1824 by Bolívar. The last Spanish garrisons in S America, at Callao (Peru) and on the island of Chiloé (Chile), surrendered to the patriots in 1826. » Bolívar; San Martín

Spanish Armada A fleet of 130 Spanish ships, commanded by Medina Sidonia, carrying 20 000 soldiers and 8 500 sailors, sent by Philip II of Spain to invade England in 1588. The invasion was in retaliation for English support of Protestant rebels in the Netherlands, the execution of Mary, Queen of Scots (1587), and raids on Spanish shipping, such as Drake's at Cádiz (1587); Philip's aim was to gain control of the English Channel. The fleet, hampered by orders to rendezvous with Spanish forces in the Netherlands, was routed by English attacks off Gravelines (28–29 Jul); 44 ships were lost in battles and during the flight home around Scotland and Ireland. Although a victory for the English, counter-armadas were unsuccessful, and the war lasted until 1604. » Drake; Elizabeth I; Philip II (of Spain)

Spanish art The art associated with Spain, which has flourished in the Peninsula since prehistoric times. The Roman occupation (218 BC–AD 414) saw extensive building, but most of this has perished. After the Muslim invasion of 711, Córdoba became the centre of an artistically splendid culture which exerted a deep influence on later Christian art. A recognizable national tradition began in the 9th-c with the Mozarabic style (ie the art of Spanish Christians under Muslim rule). From the 11th-c, richly decorated Romanesque cathedrals were built, such as at Santiago de Compostela. The great period in painting and sculpture began in the late 16th-c, when a powerfully emotional realism emerged in response to Counter-Reformation ideals. Major painters included El Greco, Velasquez, and Zurbarán; sculptors included Juan Martínez Montañés (1568–1649) and Alonso Cano (1601–67). The most important later masters were Goya and Picasso. » Islamic art; Goya; Greco, El; Picasso; Spain [i]; Velázquez; Zurbarán

Spanish bayonet A species of yucca often grown as an indoor novelty, resembling a short log which puts forth leaves when watered. (*Yucca aloifolia*. Family: *Agavaceae*.) » yucca

Spanish chestnut » **sweet chestnut**

Spanish Civil War (1936–9) The conflict between supporters and opponents of the Spanish Republic (1931–6). The 'Republicans' included moderates, socialists, communists, and Catalan and Basque regionalists and anarchists. The 'Nationalist' insurgents included monarchists, Carlists, conservative Catholics, and fascist Falangists. The armed forces were divided. Both sides attracted foreign assistance: the Republic from the USSR and the International Brigades; the Nationalists from fascist Italy and Nazi Germany. The Nationalist victory was due to the balance of foreign aid; to 'non-intervention' on the part of the Western democracies; and to greater internal unity, achieved under the leadership of General Franco.

The war took the course of a slow Nationalist advance. The Nationalists initially (Jul 1936) seized much of NW Spain and part of the SW, then (autumn 1936) advanced upon but failed to capture Madrid. They captured Málaga (Mar 1937) and the N coast (Mar–Oct 1937); advanced to the Mediterranean, cutting Republican Spain in two (Apr 1938); overran Catalonia (Dec 1938–Feb 1939); and finally occupied Madrid and SE Spain (Mar 1939). » Basques; Carlism; Catalonia; Falange; fascism; Franco; International Brigades; Spain [i]

Spanish fly A slender, metallic-green beetle which exudes acrid yellow fluid from its joints; larvae eat honey of ground-dwelling bees; wing cases formerly collected as a source of blistering agent (*cantharidin*) and as a counter-irritant; more popularly (but completely spuriously), used as an aphrodisiac, where its high toxicity has led to many cases of fatal poisoning. (Order: *Coleoptera*. Family: *Meloidae*.) » aphrodisiacs; beetle; larva

Spanish literature Spanish literature begins with the *Cantar de Mio Cid* (c.1140, Song of my Cid), one of the few popular epics to survive in written form. The 14th-c miscellany *Libro de buen amor* (The Book of Good Love) by Juan Ruiz is a more self-conscious work; but real sophistication had to await the absorption of classical and Italian influences in the 16th–17th-c. The mystical writings of St Teresa (1515–82) and St John of the Cross (1542–91) sounded a distinctive note, and Garcilaso de la Vega (1503–36) and Luis de León (1527–91) began the long tradition of Spanish love poetry, secular and religious. The Golden Age of Spanish literature continues with the satires of Francisco de Quevedo (1580–1645) and the numerous plays of Lope de Vega and Pedro Calderón (1600–81). But the greatest single work is Miguel de Cervantes' complex masterpiece *Don Quixote* (1605–15), an essential reference point in world fiction. Scientific and political thought occupied the 18th-c. A short-lived Romantic movement much influenced by Byron and Scott gave way to a rich Realist tradition in fiction, the most important writer being Benito Pérez Galdós (1843–1920), with over 80 novels on Spanish life and history. The 'Generation of '98', including Pio Baroja (1872–1956) and novelist and social critic Miguel de Unamuno (1864–1936) provided new perspectives; as did the poets Juan Ramón Jiménez (1881–1958; Nobel Prize, 1956) and Antonio Machado (1875–1939). Two other notable poets fell victims to Franco in the Spanish Civil War, Federico García Lorca (1899–1936) and Miguel Hernández (1910–42). Perhaps Spanish literature has not recovered since that time; but meanwhile a number of Spanish-American writers have become dominant figures in world literature. » Baroja; Calderón de la Barca; Cervantes; epic; Galdós; Jiménez; Latin-American literature; Lorca; picaresque novel; Realism; Romanticism; Spain [i]; Unamuno; Vega

Spanish Main The mainland area of Spanish S America, known until the 19th-c for its pirates. It extends from Panama to the Orinoco R estuary in Venezuela. » buccaneers

Spanish moss A plant (an epiphyte) related to pineapple, native to warm parts of America. The roots are present in the seedlings only; the mature plants are anchored by winding around tree branches and hanging in grey festoons. It is able to survive very dry conditions. The slender stems are covered with scaly hairs which absorb water directly from the atmosphere. Greenish, 3-petalled flowers are occasionally produced. It is used to stuff upholstery, hence its alternative name, **vegetable horsehair**. (*Tillandsia usneoides*. Family: *Bromeliaceae*.) » epiphyte; pineapple

Spanish Riding School A school of classical horsemanship situated in Vienna, founded in the late 16th-c. The school is famous for its Lipizzaner horses, bred especially for *haute école* ('high school') riding, and originally imported from Spain. » equestrianism; Lipizzaner

Spanish Succession, War of the (1701–13) A conflict fought in several theatres – the Netherlands, Germany, Spain, the Mediterranean, and the Atlantic – between the Grand Alliance (headed by Britain, the Dutch, and the Habsburg Emperor) and Louis XIV of France, supported by Spain. Hostilities arose after the death of the last Habsburg, Charles II; attempts to negotiate compromise Partition Treaties (1698, 1700) failed. The war was concluded by the Treaties of Utrecht. » Benbow; Charles II (of Spain); Eugene, Prince; Habsburgs; Leopold I (Emperor); Louis XIV; Marlborough, Duke of; Philip V; Queen Anne's War

Spanish Town 17°59N 76°58W, pop (1982) 89 097. Capital city of St Catherine parish, Middlesex county, S Jamaica; on the R Cobre, 18 km/11 ml W of Kingston; second largest city in Jamaica; capital, 1535–1872; railway; serves a rich agricultural area; cathedral (1655), ruins of the King's House (1762), court house (1819), folk museum, White Marl Arawak museum. » Jamaica [i]

Spark, Muriel (Sarah) (1918–) British writer, born in Edinburgh, Scotland. Educated in Edinburgh, she was editor of *Poetry Review* (1947–9), and published poetry, short stories, and critical biographies. She is best known for her novels, notably *Memento Mori* (1959), *The Prime of Miss Jean Brodie* (1961), and *The Driver's Seat* (1970). She now lives in Italy. » English literature; novel

spark ignition engine An internal combustion engine which initiates the combustion of its air/fuel mixture by means of a spark, usually generated by a sparking plug. This type of engine is most commonly found in motor cars. » four-stroke engine [i]; internal combustion engine

sparrow A small songbird, native to the Old World, with some introduced in the New World and Australasia; plumage usually brown/grey; inhabits open country and habitation. The name is also used for some buntings, accentors, and estrildid 'finches'. (Family: *Ploceidae*, c.37 species; but some authorities place the sparrow in a separate family *Passeridae*.) » accentor; bunting; finch; house sparrow; songbird

sparrow-weaver » **weaverbird**

sparrowhawk A hawk, native to the Old World, and to C and S America; inhabits scrub and woodland; eats birds, other small vertebrates, and insects. The name was formerly used for *Falco sparverius*, a New World falcon. (Genus: *Accipiter*, 24 species.) » falcon; hawk

Sparta (Greece) [**spah**ta], Gr **Spartí** 37°05N 22°25E, pop (1981) 14 388. Capital town of Lakonia department, S Greece; on the R Evrotas, 50 km/31 ml SW of Athens; refounded on an ancient site in 1834; trade in fruit and olive oil; carnival (Feb). » Greece [i]

Sparta (Greek history) One of the two leading city-states of ancient Greece, the other being Athens. Initially, Sparta's political and cultural development was entirely normal, but this situation changed with the revolt (c.650 BC) of Messenia, a territory crucial to her viability as a state. The need to suppress the revolt and prevent a similar recurrence led to a series of military and social reforms, traditionally associated with Lycurgus, which effectively arrested her development. While Athens went on to develop a radical democracy, acquire an overseas empire, and become a cultural pace-setter, militaristic Sparta remained backward, inward-looking, and utterly philistine. Her defeat of Athens in 404 BC put her centre stage, but she played her role so badly that the other city-states combined against her. Thebes delivered the final blow at Leuctra in 371 BC. » Greek history; Lycurgus; Messenia; Peloponnesian War; Thebes

Spartacists A left-wing revolutionary faction (the *Spartakusbund*), led by Rosa Luxemburg (1871–1919) and Karl Liebknecht (1871–1919) in 1917, which supported the Russian Revolution, and advocated ending the war and a German socialist revolution. Luxemburg and Liebknecht were murdered in disturbances during the period following the Kaiser's abdication in 1918. » left wing; Luxemburg; Russian Revolution

Spartacus (?–71 BC) Thracian-born slave and gladiator at Capua, who led the most serious slave uprising in the history of Rome (73–71 BC). With a huge army of slaves and dispossessed, he inflicted numerous defeats on the Roman armies sent against him, until defeated and killed by Crassus. His supporters were crucified wholesale, their bodies left hanging along the Appian Way to act as a deterrent to other would-be rebels. » Appian Way; Crassus; Pompey the Great; Servile Wars

Spartakiad Sporting games held every four years in the Soviet Union, until 1979 for nationals only. They were named after the ancient Greek city of Sparta, which placed great emphasis on physical fitness.

spastic » **cerebral palsy**

spathe A large sheathing bract which surrounds the specialized inflorescence called a *spadix*. The spathe is often brightly coloured. » bract; inflorescence [i]; spadix

spatial filtering » **optics** [i]

Speaker The officer who presides over a legislative chamber. The post originated in 14th-c England, where one member of the Commons was designated to speak to the king. In the UK, the Speaker presides over the House of Commons, maintains order, and interprets its rules and practice. He is a constituency MP elected by fellow members, but must sever his party connections and be entirely impartial. Most Commonwealth countries have similar officers, although seldom is the office so detached from party political affairs, and in some instances speakers are notably partisan. In the US House of Representatives, the Speaker is a leader of the majority party, and expected to assist in securing the passage of his party's legislation. » Commons, House of; House of Representatives

spear thistle A biennial thistle, growing to 150 cm/5 ft or more, native to Europe, W Asia, and N Africa; stems spiny-winged; leaves lobed, margins with long stout spines; flower-heads to 4 cm/1½ in across, reddish-purple; fruits with a parachute of feathery hairs aiding dispersal by the wind. It is believed to be the thistle adopted as the national emblem of Scotland. (*Cirsium vulgare*. Family: *Compositae*.) » biennial; thistle

spearmint » **mint**

Special Air Service » **SAS**

Special Drawing Rights (SDRs) Rights which can be exercised by members of the International Monetary Fund to draw on a pool of mixed currencies (US dollar, British pound, Japanese yen, French franc, German mark) set up by the Fund for use in emergencies. The facility is available to solve temporary balance of payments problems. » balance of payments; International Monetary Fund

special education The provision of education to children who have special educational needs. They may be pupils who suffer from some kind of physical or mental handicap, who have learning or emotional difficulties, or whose needs cannot otherwise be catered for within the normal provision. In many cases the pattern is to provide special schools, but the trend in some countries has been for such children to be taught in ordinary schools. » compensatory education; mainstreaming

special effects Trick shots in motion pictures, forming two main groups: those achieved entirely in front of the camera, and those in which the recorded image is modified. Among the former are the many ways in which the area photographed is extended, by scenes painted on glass or miniature sets built in perspective; scale models shot in slow motion represent trains, liners, and spaceships while animated models, shot frame-by-frame, bring fantastic creatures to life. A frequent need for image combination is to show live actors performing against a different background, which may be an actual distant location, a model, or even a drawing. An early technique was back-projection, now replaced by the more efficient reflex front projection. In another method the actors are shot against a large uniform blue backing, to be combined with the background later, using travelling mattes for film and chromakey for video. Two or more camera images must often be combined in dissolves, wipes, and split screen effects; in film all these need optical printing at the laboratory after photography, but in video they can be made directly, either during shooting or in videotape editing. Vision mixers provide vast scope for image manipulation effects which are completely beyond those possible on film. » blue-backing shot; chromakey; matte shot; reflex projection; travelling matte; wipe

Special Operations Executive (SOE) An organization set up with British War Cabinet approval in July 1940 in response to Churchill's directive to 'set Europe ablaze'; it later also operated in the Far East. It promoted and co-ordinated resistance activity in enemy-occupied territory until the end of World War 2. » Churchill, Winston; Maquis; World War 2

special relativity A system of mechanics applicable at high velocities (approaching the velocity of light) in the absence of gravitation; a generalization of Newtonian mechanics, due almost entirely to Albert Einstein (1905). Its fundamental postulates are that the velocity of light c is the same for all observers, no matter how they are moving; that the laws of physics are the same in all inertial frames; and that all such frames are equivalent. On this basis, no object may have a velocity in excess of the velocity of light; and two events which appear simultaneous to one observer need not be so for another. The system gives laws of mechanics which reproduce those of 'common sense' Newtonian mechanics at low velocities, and is well supported experimentally, especially in particle physics. Generalized special relativity, incorporating gravitation, is called **general relativity**.

The constancy of the velocity of light is supported experimentally (eg the Michelson–Morley experiment), and implied by Maxwell's equations of electromagnetism, which express the velocity of light in terms of simple fundamental electric and magnetic constants. Newtonian mechanics is impossible to reconcile with this, since it produces velocity addition rules (Illustrations (a) and (b) *p 1140*) which fail for light and Maxwell's equations. Einstein's solution (1905) was to insist that the velocity of light really is the same for all observers, and that the form of Maxwell's equations is the same for all. This then implied that the rules of mechanics needed to be rewritten. The new system of mechanics derived by Einstein is consistent only if old notions of basic quantities such as mass, energy, space, and time are modified; it also incorporates a velocity addition rule which accounts for the apparent paradox of Illustration (d).

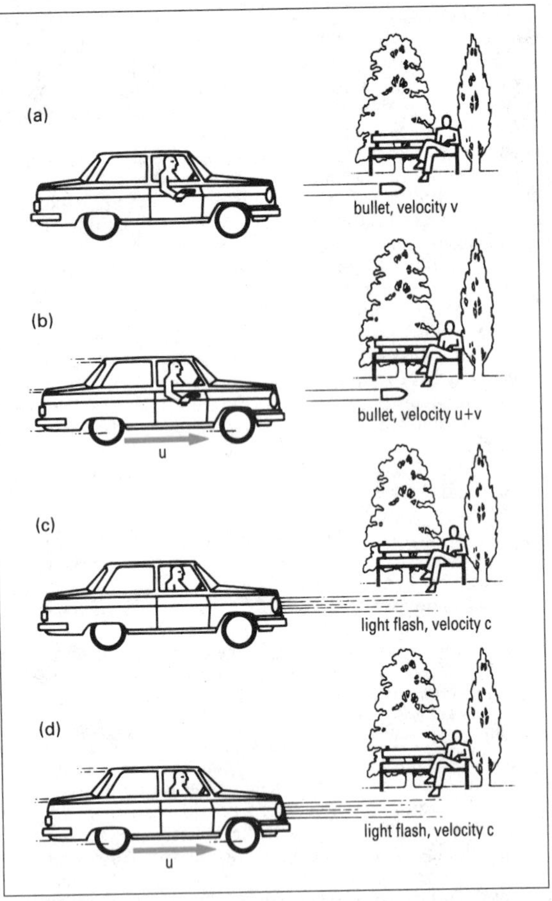

Special relativity – In (a) a bullet with velocity v is fired from a stationary car; in (b) a car is moving with velocity u, with a similar bullet fired in the same direction as the motion of the car; as seen by an observer, the bullet has velocity u+v. In (c) a flash of light sent by a stationary car is measured by an observer as c, the standard velocity of light; in (d) a flash of light is sent from a car moving at velocity u; the observer measures the velocity of the flash and finds that it too is c, not c+u. The velocity of light is always the same.

Special relativistic mechanics is fully supported by observation. » clock paradox; Einstein; Lorentz contraction; mass-energy relation; Michelson; Minkowski space; Newton, Isaac; tachyon; time dilation

speciality fibres Textile fibres obtained mainly from the goat and camel families, such as cashmere, mohair, vicuna, camel, alpaca, and angora (rabbit). They are relatively rare and expensive. » fibres

species A group of organisms, minerals, or other entities formally recognized as distinct from other groups. In biology, the species is a group of actually or potentially interbreeding natural populations, reproductively isolated from other similar groups such that exchange of genetic material cannot occur. Most species cannot interbreed with others; those that can, typically produce infertile offspring. This biological concept of the species cannot be applied to fossils, or to organisms that do not reproduce sexually. These species are defined on a comparative morphological basis. » fossil; morphology (biology); reproduction; systematics; taxonomy

specific dynamic action A transient rise in resting metabolic rate following the consumption of a meal. Also known as *diet-induced thermogenesis* or the *thermic* effect of food, its exact role in energy metabolism is poorly understood. » metabolism

specific gravity » **relative density**

specific heat capacity » **heat capacity**

specific performance In law, a court order directed to a person in breach of contract, ordering that he or she carry out the contract as agreed; known as a *specific implement* in Scottish law. The court may refuse to grant the order, as damages may be an adequate remedy. Specific performance is, however, a suitable remedy for a breach of contract to sell (or buy) land. » contract; damages

speckle interferometry A technique used in optical and infrared astronomy to produce high-resolution images. It processes numerous short exposures in a way which removes the effects of erratic motions (twinkling) caused by turbulence in the Earth's atmosphere. » astronomy

speckle pattern A granular image formed where a laser beam strikes an unpolished surface. It is a form of interference pattern present only with laser light – a consequence of laser light's unique (coherence) properties. » coherence; laser [i]

spectacled bear The only bear native to the S hemisphere; inhabits forests in W foothills of the Andes; small (shoulder height, 750 mm/30 in); dark with pale rings around eyes; builds platforms in trees from broken branches; eats mainly plants; also known as **Andean bear**. (*Tremarctos ornatus*.) » bear

spectacles A frame which supports lenses held in front of each eye, designed to correct abnormalities of refraction, such as long or short sight, and astigmatism (asymmetry of the cornea). Convex lenses help those who are long-sighted; concave lenses those who are short-sighted. *Bifocal* spectacles have lenses where the upper and lower parts have different curvatures, enabling the wearer to focus on distant and near objects respectively. » eye [i]

spectroscopy The study of energy levels in atoms or molecules, using absorbed or emitted electromagnetic radiation. Inner atomic electrons give spectra in the X-ray region; outer atomic electrons give visible light spectra; the rotation and vibration of molecules give infrared spectra; the precession of nuclear magnetic moments gives radio-wave spectra. Many types of spectroscopy exist, often used to identify the structure of an unknown substance or to detect the presence of known substances. » atomic spectra [i]; Auger effect; mass spectrometer; Mössbauer effect; nuclear magnetic resonance; photoemission spectroscopy; Raman scattering; resonant ionization spectroscopy; scattering; secondary emission; spectrum

spectrum The distribution of electromagnetic energy as a function of wavelength or frequency. A common example is the spectrum of white light dispersed by a prism to produce a rainbow of constituent colours; the rainbow is the spectrum of sunlight refracted through raindrops. For white light the colours are red, orange, yellow, green, blue, and violet in order of decreasing wavelength. All objects with temperatures above absolute zero emit electromagnetic radiation by virtue of their warmth alone; this *black body radiation* is emitted at progressively shorter wavelengths as temperature is increased. The universe (3 K) sends us microwaves; objects at room temperature (295 K) infrared rays; the Sun (6 000K) yellow light; and the solar corona (1 million K) X-rays. Individual atoms can emit and absorb radiation only at particular wavelengths corresponding to the transitions between energy levels in the atom. The spectrum of a given atom (or element) therefore consists of a series of emission or absorption lines. A familiar example is sodium, used in low pressure street lights, where almost all the energy emerges as a pair of lines in the yellow part of the spectrum. The device for displaying a spectrum is called a **spectrograph**. By analysing the spectrum of a substance, its chemical composition can be deduced. » atomic spectra [i]; dispersion; electromagnetic radiation [i]; light; optics [i]; spectroscopy; Plate X

speech pathology The study and treatment of all forms of clinically abnormal linguistic behaviour; also known as **(speech and) language pathology**. In several countries (eg the USA), speech pathologists are professionals concerned with the treatment of language-handicapped people; in others (eg the UK) the equivalent profession is that of speech therapist. » anomia; aphasia; apraxia; clinical linguistics; cluttering; dysarthria; dysgraphia; dyslexia; dysphonia; language; stuttering; voice disorder

speech therapy » **speech pathology**

speed (pharmacology) » **amphetamine**

speed (photography) A rating of the sensitivity of a photographic material on a recognized numerical scale, such as ASA or EI (in which doubling the sensitivity doubles the rating number), and DIN, the German national standard (where doubling sensitivity adds 3°). Both are combined on the International Standards scale in the form ISO 200/24°. » ASA rating; film

speed (physics) The rate of change of distance with time; symbol *v*, units m/s; a scalar quantity. Speed is the magnitude of velocity, but unlike velocity specifies no direction. » velocity

Speed, John (1552–1629) English antiquary and cartographer, born in Cheshire. He began as a tailor, but his considerable historical learning brought him patronage, and he was able to publish his 54 *Maps of England and Wales* (1608–10) and other works. » cartography

speed of light » **velocity of light**

speedometer An instrument fitted in a vehicle to show its speed. Usually a cable from the vehicle road-drive rotates a magnet, which induces an eddy current in a non-magnetic conductor attached to a pointer. The interaction of the permanent magnet and the induced fields turns the pointer against a restoring spring. » magnetism

speedway A form of motorcycle racing on machines with no brakes and only one gear. The most popular form is on an oval track, and involving four riders at one time. Other forms include *long track* racing and *ice speedway*. The sport originated in the USA in 1902. » motorcycle racing; RR119

speedwell An annual or perennial, some agricultural weeds, native to N temperate regions; stems creeping or erect; leaves opposite, lance-shaped or oval, often toothed; flowers solitary or in spikes, blue or white, with a short tube and four petals, upper largest, lower smallest. (Genus: *Veronica*, 300 species. Family: *Scrophulariaceae*.) » annual; perennial

Speenhamland system The most famous of many local expedients in Britain to improve the operation of the old poor laws at a time of crisis. The name was taken from the Berkshire parish whose magistrates in 1795 introduced scales of relief for labourers dependent both on the prevailing price of bread and the size of labourers' families. The principles spread to many S and E parishes in the early 19th-c. It was much criticized by political economists for encouraging the poor to breed! » Poor Laws

Speer, Albert (1905–81) German architect and Nazi government official, born at Mannheim. He joined the Nazi Party in 1931, became Hitler's chief architect in 1934, and Minister of Armaments in 1942. Always more concerned with technology and administration than ideology, he openly opposed Hitler in the final months of the war, and was the only Nazi leader at Nuremberg to admit responsibility for the regime's actions. He was imprisoned for 20 years in Spandau, Berlin, and after his release in 1966 became a writer. He died in London. » Hitler; Nazi Party

Speke, John Hanning (1827–64) British explorer, born at Bideford, Devon. He served in India, and in 1854 went with Burton to search for the equatorial lakes of Africa. They discovered L Tanganyika (1858), then Speke travelled on alone, finding the lake he named Victoria, and saw in it the headwaters of the Nile. Back in England, his claims to have discovered the source of the Nile were doubted, and so a second expedition set out (1860–3). On his return, his claims were again challenged, and he was about to defend his discovery when he was killed in a shooting accident near Corsham, Wiltshire. » Burton, Richard (Francis); Nile, River

speleology/spelaeology The scientific exploration and study of caves and other underground features, surveying their extent, physical history and structure, and natural history. When cave-exploring is taken up as a hobby, it is known as **spelunking** (US) or **potholing** (UK), where people descend through access points (potholes) to follow the course of underground rivers and streams. » RR13

spelling reform A movement to regularize a language's spelling system. In English, for example, the spelling system is widely perceived as being irregular, because of a relatively small but frequently used number of striking inconsistencies between sounds and letters. The irregularity was famously illustrated by George Bernard Shaw's mischievous spelling of *fish* as *ghoti* – *f* as in ***rough***, *i* as in ***women***, *sh* as in ***patient***! Such variations in spelling patterns (one sound represented by several letters or letter-sequences; one letter representing several sounds) result from the disparate historical sources of English words, which have at various periods been influenced by Anglo-Saxon, Old Norse, Latin, Norman French, and Greek, each with its own conflicting spelling conventions.

The retention of such disparity has largely resulted from the conservatism forced on the written language by the needs of the printing press for continuity in spelling practices. This has led to calls for reform of the spelling system – sometimes for the complete replacement of existing symbols (as in Shaw's proposal for a new alphabet), more usually for a 'standardizing system', in which the existing alphabet is used in a way which more consistently reflects the correspondence between sound and symbol. Several dozen proposals have been fully worked out in the course of the present century. The main aim is to ease reading and spelling problems for learners and users of the language. The vested interests of the publishing world, allied to general public tolerance and conservatism, have so far militated against the widespread adoption of any new standardizing system. » English language; i.t.a.

spelunking » **speleology**

Spence, Sir Basil (Urwin) (1907–76) British architect, born in Bombay, India. Educated at Edinburgh and London, he gradually emerged as the leading postwar British architect, with his fresh approach to new university buildings, the pavilion for the Festival of Britain (1951), and most famously the new Coventry Cathedral (1951), which boldly merged new and traditional structural methods. He was professor of architecture at Leeds (1955–6) and at the Royal Academy (1961–8). He was knighted in 1960, and died at Eye, Suffolk.

Spencer, Lady Diana » **Charles, Prince of Wales**

Spencer, Herbert (1820–1903) British evolutionary philosopher, born in Derby. He became a civil engineer for a railway in 1837, but engaged extensively in journalism. A firm (pre-Darwinian) believer in evolution, his main work is the 9-volume *System of Synthetic Philosophy* (1862–93), which brought together biology, psychology, sociology, and ethics. He was a leading advocate of 'Social Darwinism'. He died at Brighton, Sussex. » Darwin, Charles; Social Darwinism

Spencer, Sir Stanley (1891–1959) British artist, born at Cookham, Berkshire. He studied in London, then lived and worked mainly at Cookham. During 1926–33 he executed murals (using his war experiences) in the Oratory of All Souls, Burghclere. He produced many purely realistic landscapes, but his main works interpret the Bible in terms of everyday life, such as 'Resurrection: Port Glasgow' (1950, Tate, London). Knighted in 1959, he died at Taplow, Buckinghamshire. » English art

Spencer-Churchill, Baroness » **Churchill, Winston**

Spender, Sir Stephen (Harold) (1909–) British poet and critic, born in London. Educated at Oxford, he became in the 1930s one of the group of 'modern poets' with Auden and Day-Lewis. His many poetic works include *Poems from Spain* (1939), *Ruins and Visions* (1942), and *The Generous Days* (1971). His *Collected Poems, 1928–85* were published in 1985. He was co-editor of *Horizon* (1939–41) and *Encounter* (1953–67), and professor of English at London (1970–7). He was knighted in 1983. » Auden; Day-Lewis; English literature; poetry

Spengler, Oswald (1880–1936) German philosopher of history, born at Blankenburg. Educated at Halle, Munich, and Berlin, he taught mathematics before devoting himself entirely to the morbidly prophetic *Der Untergang des Abendlandes* (1918–22, 2 vols, The Decline of the West), which argues that all cultures are subject to the same cycle of growth and decay in accordance with predetermined 'historical destiny'. His views greatly encouraged the Nazis, though he never became one himself. He died in Munich. » Nazi Party

Spenser, Edmund (?1552–99) English poet, born in London. Educated at Merchant Taylors' and Cambridge, he obtained a place in Leicester's household, which led to a friendship with Sir Philip Sidney and a circle of wits (the *Areopagus*). His first original work was a sequence of pastoral poems, *The Shepheards Calendar* (1579). In 1580 he became secretary to the Lord Deputy in Ireland, and for his services was given Kilcolman Castle, Co Cork, where he settled in 1586. Here he began his major work, *The Faerie Queene*, using a 9-line verse pattern which later came to be called the 'Spenserian stanza'. The first three books, dedicated to Elizabeth I, were published in 1590, and the second three in 1596, but the poem was left unfinished at his death, in London. » Elizabeth I; English literature; pastoral; poetry; Renaissance; sonnet

sperm The male gamete of animals. It is typically a small motile cell which locates and penetrates the female gamete (*ovum*). It contains little cytoplasm. » cytoplasm; gamete; semen

sperm bank The storage of human sperm for long periods in a frozen state, with a view to future use in artificial insemination. In this way young men receiving treatment for malignant disease which may lead to sterility can preserve their procreative ability. Infertile couples may use stored donor spermatozoa, selected as being of above-average quality with regard to motility and numbers. » semen; sterilization **1**

sperm whale A toothed whale, widespread in tropical and temperate seas; eats mainly squid; bulbous head contains spermaceti organ; three species: **sperm whale** or **cachalot** (*Physeter catodon*), the largest toothed mammal (length up to 20 m/65 ft), grey-black, head up to one-third length of body; **pygmy sperm whale** (*Kogia breviceps*), length 3.4 m/11 ft, and **dwarf sperm whale** (*Kogia simus*), length 2.5 m/8 ft, both with head one-sixth length of body. (Family: *Physeteridae*.) » ambergris; spermaceti; whale [i]

spermaceti [sperma**see**tee] A waxy oil found in the head of sperm whales (almost 2 000 litres/440 UK galls/530 US galls per whale in *Physeter catodon*); solidifies in air; function unclear; formerly used as a lubricant, and in ointments and candles; name (mistakenly) means 'whale's sperm'. » sperm whale

Spey, River River in Highland and Grampian regions, NE Scotland; rises near Corrieyairack Pass, SSE of Fort Augustus; flows NE into Spey Bay, to the E of Lossiemouth; noted for its salmon fishing; length 171 km/106 ml; in lower reaches, the fastest-flowing river in Britain. » Scotland [i]

Speyer Cathedral [**shpi**yer] Romanesque cathedral founded by Conrad II (c.990–1039) in 1060 at Speyer, SW Germany. The church, which is noted for its royal tombs and crypt, has required reconstruction on several occasions, most recently after World War 2. It is a world heritage site. » Romanesque architecture

sphalerite A zinc sulphide (ZnS) mineral, also known as **zinc blende**. Colourless when pure, it often contains iron, which darkens its colour. It occurs in hydrothermal veins, usually associated with galena and silver minerals. It is the principal ore of zinc. » galena; iron; zinc

sphere In mathematics, the locus in space of all points equidistant from a fixed point (the centre). The distance of each point from the centre is the radius r of the sphere. The surface area of a sphere is $4\pi r^2$; the volume of a sphere is $\frac{4}{3}\pi r^3$. Archimedes discovered that the suface area of a sphere is equal to the curved surface area of the cylinder circumscribing the sphere, and asked that this should be commemorated on his tombstone. When Cicero was serving in Syracuse 200 years after the death of Archimedes, he discovered a tomb which he recognized as that of Archimedes, because it carried the diagram shown below. » Archimedes; geometry

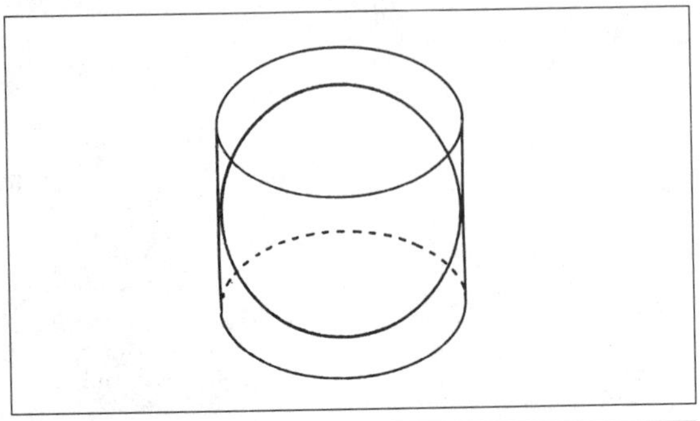

Cylinder circumscribing a sphere

sphinx [sfingks] In ancient Greece a mythological monster with a human head and a recumbent animal body (usually a lion's); sometimes it was winged and had female breasts. Originating in the east, probably Egypt, it is found throughout the Levant and E Mediterranean.

sphygmomanometer [sfigmuhma**no**mituh] A device for measuring blood pressure. An inflatable rubber cuff is used round a limb (usually the arm), and inflated until the pulse (heard through a stethoscope) can no longer be detected. The cuff is then slowly deflated until the sound of the pulse can be heard again. The first sound heard reflects the pressure of blood in the arteries as the heart actively contracts (*systole*). As the deflation of the cuff continues, a second sound is heard, reflecting the resting pressure (*diastole*) within the arteries. The pressure is read off either electronically or direct from a column of mercury. » blood pressure

Spica [**spi**yka] » **Virgo**

spice A pungent-tasting plant used to flavour or preserve food. The term is used particularly when referring to hard parts, such as dry fruits and seeds, but it can include parts such as flower buds. » allspice; caraway; cardamom; cinnamon; clove tree; coriander; cumin; fenugreek; ginger; herb; mace; nutmeg; pepper **2**

Spice Islands » **Moluccas**

spider A predatory, terrestrial arthropod; body divided into head (*prosoma*) and abdomen (*opisthosoma*) joined by slender waist; prosoma with 2–8 simple eyes, four pairs of slender legs, and a pair of fangs (*chelicerae*) used to inject poison into prey; opisthosoma bears respiratory organs (book lungs and tracheae) and usually three pairs of silk-spinning organs (*spinnerets*). Spider silk is used to make webs, traps, homes, and funnels, to wrap prey, and in dispersal, as small spiders on silk threads can be carried by the wind. (Class: *Arachnida*. Order: *Araneae*, c.35 000 species.) » Arachnida; arthropod; black widow/funnel-web/money/sun/trapdoor/water/wolf spider; orb weaver; tarantula

spider crab A slow-moving crab with a small slender body and long legs; leg span up to 4 m/13 ft in the giant species; body and appendages often covered with growths of seaweed, sponges, or hydroids for camouflage. (Class: *Malacostraca*. Order: *Decapoda*.) » crab; Hydrozoa

spider mite A small, reddish mite that sucks at the undersides of leaves and can cause great destruction of economically important crops, such as tomatoes and beans. (Order: *Acari*. Family: *Tetranychidae*.) » mite

spider monkey A New World monkey; slender with extremely long legs and tail; thumbs small or absent; may swing from trees using fingers as hooks, but usually walks along tops of branches. (Genus: *Ateles*, 4 species.) » New World monkey; woolly spider monkey

spider plant A fleshy-rooted perennial native to S Africa; leaves tufted, narrow, curved; inflorescence to 60 cm/2 ft, branched, bearing white flowers and tufts of leaves which root on contact with the soil, forming new plants. A cultivar with cream-striped leaves is widely grown as a house plant. (*Chlorophytum comosum*. Family: *Liliaceae*.) » cultivar; inflorescence [i]; perennial

spider wasp A slender, solitary wasp; long-legged adult females usually run over ground to catch spiders; these are paralysed, and an egg is laid on each spider, which is usually left in a burrow or cup-shaped nest made of mud. (Order: *Hymenoptera*. Family: *Pompilidae*.) » wasp

Spielberg, Steven (1947–) US film director, born in Cincinnati. He worked first in television, but achieved a blockbuster success with the monster film *Jaws* (1975), and followed this with science fiction in *Close Encounters of the Third Kind* (1977)

and *ET, The Extra-Terrestrial* (1982). Dazzling adventure stories, *Raiders of the Lost Ark* (1981) and *Indiana Jones and the Temple of Doom* (1984), were interspersed with the psychic themes of *Poltergeist* (1983) and *Gremlins* (1984). *The Color Purple* (1986) was a study of social problems in the US Deep South. He then joined with the Disney Studios to produce *Who Framed Roger Rabbit?* (1988), using an unusual combination of elaborately detailed animation characters in combination with live action.

spikelet A structure peculiar to the inflorescence of grasses, consisting of 1–several reduced flowers enclosed in a series of small bracts. The spikelets can be arranged in several ways to form the inflorescence. » bract; grass [i]; inflorescence [i]

Spillane, Mickey, properly **Frank Morrison Spillane** (1918–) US popular novelist, born in New York City. He wrote for pulp magazines to pay for his education, producing his first novel *I, the Jury* in 1947. His novels often feature the private detective, Mike Hammer. *Kiss Me Deadly* (1952) is a typical example of his work, in its representation of sadism, cheap sex, and casual violence. » detective story

spin A vector attribute of sub-atomic particles, having a precise meaning only in quantum theory, but modelled on classical mechanical spin; symbol *S*; units ($h/2\pi$), where *h* is Planck's constant (but usually values are stated with units omitted). It may thus be thought of as referring to a particle spinning on its axis, with a higher spin number corresponding to a faster rotation. In the quantum case, only certain values of spin are possible. Electrons and protons have spin ½; photons have spin 1. » angular momentum; boson; Dirac equation; fermions; magnetic moment; quantum mechanics; quantum numbers

spin glass A dilute mixture of a magnetic material in some other substance, often a metal (eg weak alloys of iron in gold, or manganese in copper), in which the magnetic component is randomly dispersed. It shows no long-range magnetic ordering, but is characterized by a sharp peak in magnetic susceptibility as temperature increases, which is thought to indicate a phase transition. » magnetic susceptibility; magnetism

spin resonance » **magnetic resonance**

spin statistics » **Bose-Einstein statistics; Fermi-Dirac statistics**

spina bifida [**spiy**na **bif**ida] A congenital defect of one or more vertebrae, in which the arch of a vertebra fails to develop. As a result the spinal cord is unprotected and may be damaged. It usually affects the lower back, and when severe may cause paralysis of the lower limbs. Antenatal diagnosis can be made by detecting an abnormal protein (alfa-foetoprotein) in amniotic fluid, or by ultrasonography. » congenital abnormality; prenatal diagnosis; vertebral column

spinach beet » **beet**

spinal cord That part of the vertebrate central nervous system contained within and protected by the vertebral column, continuous with the medulla oblongata of the brain. It is essentially a long thick cable formed by thousands of parallel-running axons surrounding a central H-shaped core of grey matter (*cell bodies*). It has a minute central canal (containing cerebrospinal fluid) which is continuous with the ventricles of the brain. In the human adult it is approximately 45 cm/18 in long, and extends down as far as the second lumbar vertebra. The end tapers to a pointed tip. The front (*ventral*) horns of the grey matter contain the cell bodies of the neurones that supply voluntary muscles; their axons form the ventral roots. The rear (*dorsal*) horns of the grey matter consist of cell bodies concerned with the processing of sensory information, which enters the spinal cord through the dorsal roots. Between the ventral and dorsal horns on each side, at certain levels, a lateral horn projects which contains the cell bodies of neurones of the sympathetic part of the autonomic nervous system. The peripheral white part of the spinal cord consists of axons arranged in tracts that convey information to or from the brainstem, or between different segments of the spinal cord. In humans, 31 pairs of spinal nerves arise from the spinal cord, formed from the ventral (motor) and dorsal (sensory) nerve roots. » nervous system; neurone [i]; poliomyelitis; vertebral column; Plate XIII

spindle tree A small deciduous tree or shrub, growing to 6 m/20 ft, native to Europe and W Asia; leaves narrowly oval, pointed, toothed; flowers in clusters of 3–8, greenish with four narrow petals; fruit a pink, 4-lobed capsule 1–1.5 cm/0.4–0.6 in, splitting to reveal seeds with fleshy orange arils. (*Euonymus europaeus*. Family: *Celastraceae*.) » aril; deciduous plants; shrub; tree [i]

spine » **vertebral column**

spinel The name given to a group of minerals which are double oxides of divalent and trivalent metals. Its principal members are *chromite* ($FeCr_2O_4$), the chief source of chromium, *magnetite* (Fe_3O_4), and *spinel* ($MgAl_2O_4$), which may be valuable as a gemstone, particularly when coloured red because of minor impurities. They occur as accessory minerals in igneous and metamorphic rocks. » chromium; gemstones

spinet A keyboard instrument resembling a harpsichord, but with a single set of strings running diagonally to the keyboard. It was particularly popular in 17th-c England. » harpsichord; keyboard instrument; virginals

spinifex A coarse, spiny-leaved grass, native to E Asia and Australasia. The spikelets have long, spiny bracts, and are massed to form globular heads which break off and act as tumbleweeds before breaking up. (Genus: *Spinifex*, 3 species. Family: *Gramineae*.) » bract; grass [i]; tumbleweed

spinning The conversion of fibres into yarns. Two main types of yarn were traditionally produced: in *woollen* yarns, the fibres are randomly arranged; in *worsted* types, the fibres lie parallel to the length of the yarn. New methods, such as friction and rotor spinning, are now very important and are far removed from the early hand methods using the distaff and, later, the spinning wheel. » carding; wool

Spinoza, Benedict de [spin**oh**za] (Heb **Baruch**) (1632–77) Dutch-Jewish philosopher and theologian, born in Amsterdam. His deep interest in optics, the new astronomy, and Cartesian philosophy made him unpopular, and he was expelled from the Jewish community in 1656. His major works include the *Tractatus Theologico-Politicus* (1670), which despite its anonymity made him famous, and his *Ethica* (published posthumously, 1677). In 1673 he refused the professorship of philosophy at Heidelberg, in order to keep his independence, and died a few years later in Amsterdam. » Descartes; dualism; materialism

spiny anteater » **echidna**

spiny lobster A lobster-like marine crustacean with a well-developed abdomen but without conspicuous pincers (*chelipeds*); antennae often very long; commonly exploited for food; known as **crawfish** in N America. (Class: *Malacostraca*. Order: *Decapoda*.) » crustacean; lobster

spiracle An external opening of the respiratory system of insects. The system comprises flexible tubes (*tracheae*) and air sacs that penetrate throughout the insect's body. Air enters the tracheae through 10 pairs of spiracles arranged along body segments. » insect [i]

spiraea/spirea [spiy**ree**a] A deciduous, sometimes suckering shrub, native to the temperate N hemisphere; leaves narrow to broadly oval, entire, toothed or lobed; flowers 5-petalled, white or pink, in dense clusters. It is a popular ornamental. (Genus: *Spiraea*, 100 species. Family: *Rosaceae*.) » deciduous plants; shrub; sucker

spirit An aqueous solution of ethanol (particularly one obtained by distillation) which may contain other solutes. » ethanol; solution

spirit control » **seance**

spiritism » **spiritualism**

spirits Alcoholic beverages produced by distilling ethanol from a fermentation of mash from various sources, such as barley for whisky, sugar cane for rum, and potatoes for vodka. Many are flavoured to give a distinct taste, such as by the use of the juniper berry for gin. Others are blended with wines to produce such drinks as port, a blend of brandy and wine. » brandy; gin; rum; vodka; whisky

spiritualism An organized religion which believes that spirits of the deceased survive bodily death and communicate with the living, usually via a medium by means of messages, or apparently paranormal physical effects. While many different cultures, past and present, believe in *spiritism* (the ability of spirits of the deceased to communicate with the living), spiritualism is primarily a Western religion, most commonly found in N America and in Europe, arising in the mid-1800s. It attempts to distinguish itself from other spiritist beliefs by taking a 'scientific' approach; spiritualists query whether communicating spirits are who they claim to be by posing questions which could only be answered by the spirit of the deceased and by the person asking the question. Spiritualists believe in God, and feel that through communications with the deceased they may come to better understand the laws of God. They welcome members from different religious faiths. Spiritualism is frequently criticized for having at least some members who use trickery to produce its phenomena. » medium (parapsychology)

spirochaete [**spi**yrohkeet] A motile, spiral-shaped bacterium. Some spirochaetes are free-living in aquatic habitats; others inhabit the intestinal tract and genital areas of animals. They include the causative agents of such diseases as syphilis and relapsing fever. (Kingdom: *Monera*. Family: *Spirochaetaceae*.) » bacteria [i]

Spirogyra [spiyruh**jiy**ra] A filament-like green alga found in freshwater; chloroplast a spiral, ribbon-like band extending along the cell; sexual reproduction involves conjugation between two filaments, and results in the formation of a resistant zygote. (Class: *Chlorophyceae*. Order: *Zygnematales*.) » algae; chloroplast; zygote

spiroplasm A motile, spiral-shaped mycoplasm, parasitic in insects and plants. It includes the causative agent of yellow disease in plants. (Kingdom: *Monera*. Class: *Mollicutes*.) » mycoplasma

spit A ridge of sand and gravel stretching out along a coastline, deposited by longshore drift and often forming a lagoon on the landward side. A spit which links an island to the mainland is termed a *tombolo*. » lagoon

Spitalfields An area in the East End of London, which flourished as a centre of silk-weaving from the late 17th-c (when Huguenot weavers settled there) until the late 19th-c. It lies on the site of a 12th-c spittle-house, or hospital, from which its name derives. » East End; Huguenots

Spitsbergen » **Svalbard**

spittlebug » **froghopper**

spitz [spits] (Ger *spitz*, 'pointed') A dog belonging to a group of breeds, characterized by a curled tail usually held over the back, pointed ears and muzzle, and (usually) a thick coat. » Alaskan malamute; basenji; corgi; dog; elkhound; husky; keeshond; Pomeranian; Samoyed (zoology)

Spitz, Mark (Andrew) (1950–) US swimmer, born at Modesto, California. He earned worldwide fame at the 1972 Olympics by winning seven gold medals, all in world record time. He also won two golds in the 1968 Games, and set a total of 26 world records between 1967 and 1972. He turned professional in 1972, and also appeared in several films. » swimming

spleen A soft, delicate, relatively mobile organ which is responsible for clearing the body of bacteria, protozoa, and non-living particles; the destruction of red blood cells; and the metabolism of iron, fats, and proteins. It is situated under cover of the rib-cage on the left side of the body towards the midline. It cannot normally be felt from outside unless enlarged to three times its normal size. It receives a large blood supply from the aorta. When distended, it acts as a reservoir from which blood can be returned to the general circulation when required. It can be ruptured by severe blows to the lower left part of the thoracic cage. Because of its large blood supply, it bleeds profusely, and therefore has to be removed quickly, otherwise the abdominal cavity soon fills with blood and death results. In adults, the loss of the spleen does not cause any ill effects. » blood; malaria; thorax; Plate XII

spleenwort A large and widespread genus of perennial ferns, found especially in the temperate N hemisphere; fronds entire, pinnate or bi-pinnate, often leathery; sori oval, oblong, or narrow. Some species are viviparous, budding tiny plantlets on the fronds which detach and form new plants. (Genus: *Asplenium*, 650 species. Family: *Polypodiaceae*.) » bird's-nest fern; fern; perennial; pinnate; sorus

Split Ital **Spalato** 43°31N 16°28E, pop (1981) 235 922. Seaport and city in W Croatia, Yugoslavia; largest town on the Yugoslav Adriatic coast; airport; railway; car ferries to Italy and Turkey; university (1974); shipyards, coal, fishing, tourism; Diocletian's palace (3rd-c), a world heritage site; cathedral; summer festival of drama and music (Jun–Aug), festival of light music (Jul). » Croatia; Yugoslavia [i]

Spock, Dr Benjamin (McLane) (1903–) US child-care expert, born at New Haven, Connecticut. Educated at Yale and Columbia, he practised paediatrics from 1933, and in 1946 published his best-selling *Common Sense Book of Baby and Child Care*. He became professor of paediatrics at Western Reserve (1955–67), specializing in psychoanalysis in child care. In 1968 he appealed successfully against a conviction under the anti-conscription law, and published *Dr Spock on Vietnam* (with M Zimmermann). He was a People's Party candidate for the US presidency in 1972 and the vice-presidency in 1976. » paediatrics

Spode, Josiah (1754–1827) British potter, born at Stoke-on-Trent, Staffordshire. He learned his trade in his father's workshops, and in 1770 founded a firm which manufactured pottery, porcelain, and stoneware. He became the foremost china manufacturer of his time, and was made potter to George III in 1806. After merging in 1833 with William Taylor Copeland (1797–1868), the firm also made numerous white imitation marble (*Parian*) figures. » porcelain; pottery; stoneware

Spohr, Louis, originally **Ludwig** (1784–1859) German composer, violinist, and conductor, born at Brunswick. Largely self-taught, he became court conductor at Kassel (1822–57), and is remembered chiefly as a composer for the violin, for which he wrote 17 concertos. He also composed nine symphonies, eleven operas, and other choral and chamber works. He died at Kassel.

spoils system The US practice of filling public offices on the basis of loyalty to the party in power: 'to the victors belong the spoils'. It was said to have originated with De Witt Clinton, governor of New York (1817–23). In common use during the 19th-c, it was in disrepute thereafter as a result of civil service reforms. » Albany Regency; Clinton, De Witt; mugwump

Spokane [spoh**kan**] 47°40N 117°24W, pop (1980) 171 300. Capital of Spokane County, E Washington, USA, on the Spokane R; founded, 1872; city status, 1891; university (1887); airfield; railway; commercial centre for inland farming, forestry, and mining areas (the 'Inland Empire'); art centre; museum; Episcopal and Roman Catholic Cathedrals. » Washington (state)

Spoleto [spo**lay**toh], Lat **Spoletium** 42°44N 12°44E, pop (1981) 20 000. Town in Perugia province, Umbria, C Italy, 96 km/60 ml NE of Rome; textiles, tourism; cathedral (11th-c), San Salvatore basilica (4th-c), Roman theatre, amphitheatre, bridge, triumphal arch; Festival of Two Worlds (music, drama, art, Jun–Jul). » Umbria

spondylosis [spondi**loh**sis] Degeneration of the vertebral bodies and of the joints between them. It especially affects the cervical and lumbar vertebrae, ie the spine in the neck and lower back. » vertebral column

sponge A multicellular animal with a body that lacks organization into tissues and organs; body perforated by a complex system of internal canals through which flagellate cells propel water; water typically enters body via pores (*ostia*), and leaves via larger pores (*oscula*); feeds by filtering food from water within the canal system; body often supported by a skeleton of mineralized tiny pointed structures (spicules) or organic fibres; mostly marine, found from inter-tidal zone to deep sea; sometimes freshwater. (Phylum: *Porifera*.) » flagellum

spontaneous generation The concept that life can arise spontaneously from non-living matter by natural processes without the intervention of supernatural powers; also known as **abiogenesis**. » life

spontaneous symmetry breaking In physical systems, the consequence of symmetry reducing in an unpredictable way as a system changes to one of lower energy. For example, when a ferromagnetic material such as iron is cooled to below its Curie temperature its atoms align, representing a state of reduced energy and symmetry. It is an important principle in particle physics, especially in the prediction of masses of W and Z particles in weak interaction theory. » Curie temperature; ferromagnetism; Glashow-Weinberg-Salam theory; symmetry

spoonbill An ibis-like bird, native to Old World (Genus: *Platalea*, 5 species) or C and S America (*Ajaia ajaja*); bill straight and broadly flattened at tip; eats aquatic animals and plants or insects. (Family: *Threskiornithidae*.) » ibis; shoveller

Spooner, William Archibald (1844–1930) British Anglican clergyman and educationalist, Dean (1876–89) and Warden (1903–24) of New College, Oxford. As an albino he suffered all his life from weak eyesight, but surmounted his disabilities with heroism, and earned a reputation for kindness. His name is forever associated with a nervous tendency to transpose initial letters or half-syllables in speech, the **spoonerism** (eg 'a half-warmed fish' for 'a half-formed wish').

spoonworm An unsegmented, soft-bodied marine worm; body cylindrical or sac-like, bearing an extendable tube (proboscis) used for food collection and respiration, and spines that assist in burrowing or anchorage. (Phylum: *Echiura*, c.140 species.) » worm

sporangium [spuh**ran**jiuhm] The organ in which spores are formed in certain types of plant. In algae and fungi they are unicellular; in bryophytes and ferns they are multicellular. » spore

spore A plant reproductive cell which is capable of developing into a new individual, either directly or after fusion with another spore. Spores typically function as a means of dispersal, and sometimes also as a resistant stage allowing the organism to survive periods of adverse conditions. A spore does not contain an embryo, and is thus distinct from a seed. » plant; reproduction; seed

sporophyte The asexual (spore-producing or *diploid*) generation in the life cycle of a plant, produced by the fusion of two haploid gametes. In ferns and flowering plants it is the dominant part of the life cycle, being more specialized than the gametophyte, and capable of surviving in a wider range of conditions. In bryophytes it is the minor generation, at least partly reliant on the gametophyte for survival. » alternation of generations; bryophyte; gamete; gametophyte; spore

Sporozoa [sporuh**zoh**a] A class of parasitic protozoans found in animal hosts. Reproduction typically involves an alternation between asexual (multiple fission) and sexual phases. Sexual reproduction results in the formation of resistant cysts containing infective stages. Several species cause serious diseases in humans and domesticated animals. (Phylum: *Apicomplexa*.) » cyst (biology); parasitology; Protozoa; reproduction

Sport Aid An international event, organized by Bob Geldof, which preceded the opening of the UN General Assembly's special session on Africa in 1986. Its aim was to publicize the problems of the continent, to raise money for famine relief, and to encourage governments to take appropriate action. More than 20 million people in 76 countries took part in sponsored sporting events, and £50 million was raised. » Geldof

sporting dog A dog belonging to a group of breeds developed to assist in field sports; includes pointers, setters, retrievers, spaniels (these four also called **gundogs**); used occasionally to include terriers and hounds. » dog; hound; pointer; retriever; setter; spaniel; terrier

Sports, Book of A statement by James I of England in 1618, declaring which sports could be legally performed on Sundays after divine services. It was re-issued in 1633 and declared from pulpits. It provoked refusals from tender consciences, deprivations from livings, and pamphleteer Prynne's remark, 'so many paces in the dance; so many paces to hell'. » James I (of England); Prynne

sports medicine The medical care of sportsmen and sportswomen. It involves the care and prevention of soft tissue injuries (eg strains and torn ligaments), injuries of overuse (eg inflammation in and around tendons as a result of rowing), fractures from accidents or from excessive walking, and trauma to the brain, as occurs in boxing. It is also concerned with methods of rehabilitation, the study of factors that improve performance, such as diet, training, and cardiorespiratory function, the effect of mechanical stresses, and the psychology of competition. The effects and detection of body-building drugs and other banned substances in professional sport is a growing aspect of the discipline.

spots (photography) » **luminaires**

sprain Injury to a joint without fracture or displacement of bones. It is usually the result of a twisting movement, in which muscle and tendon attachments are torn. » joint

sprat Small slender-bodied fish widespread and locally common in large shoals in coastal waters from Norway to the Mediterranean; length up to 15 cm/6 in; silver with upper surface green; support important commercial fisheries, being sold fresh or canned; young fish sold as whitebait. (*Sprattus sprattus*. Family: *Clupeidae*.) » brisling

spreadsheets Computer programs which allow data, numbers, or text to be entered and presented in a rectangular matrix. Data can be manipulated in a variety of different ways defined by the user; for example, columns or rows of numbers can be added, interchanged, or multiplied by constants. Spreadsheets provide a powerful and relatively simple means of analysing financial and other numeric data, and are widely used in the commercial world. » program, computer

spring tide An especially large tidal range occurring twice monthly, produced by the tidal forces of the Sun and Moon acting in conjunction. These maximum monthly tides occur during new and full moon. » neap tide; tide

springbok or **springbuck** A gazelle native to S Africa; reddish-brown with white rump and thick dark line along side; both sexes with short lyre-shaped horns with inturned tips; inhabits dry open country; may leap 3.5 m/11.5 ft into the air when alarmed. (*Antidorcas marsupialis*.) » gazelle [i]

springer spaniel A medium-sized spaniel with thick coat; ears shorter and more highly set than in cocker spaniels; two breeds, white and brown (or black) **English springer spaniel**, and older, shorter-eared, white and red-brown **Welsh spaniel** or **springer**. » cocker spaniel; spaniel

Springfield (Illinois) 39°48N 89°39W, pop (1980) 99 637. Capital of state in Sangamon County, C Illinois, USA; settled, 1818; city status, 1840; home and burial place of President Lincoln; railway; major commercial centre; electrical equipment, machinery, chemicals. » Illinois; Lincoln, Abraham

Springfield (Massachusetts) 42°06N 72°35W, pop (1980) 152 319. Seat of Hampden County, SW Massachusetts, USA, on the Connecticut R; railway; machinery, metal and paper products; game of basketball devised at Springfield College; Springfield Armoury (1794–1968), basketball hall of fame; Eastern States Expo (Sep). » Massachusetts

Springfield (Missouri) 37°13N 93°17W, pop (1980) 133 116. Seat of Greene County, SW Missouri, USA; established, 1829; railway; university; industrial, trade and shipping centre; dairy products, livestock, poultry, fruit; clothing, furniture, typewriters; tourist centre for Ozark Mts; Museum of the Ozarks. » Missouri; Ozark Mountains

springhaas [**spring**has] A nocturnal squirrel-like rodent, native to S Africa; superficially resembles a small kangaroo (length, less than 1 m/3¼ ft) with bushy black-tipped tail; inhabits open sandy country; digs burrows; also known as **springhare** or **jumping hare**. (*Pedetes capensis*. Family: *Pedetidae*.) » kangaroo; rodent; squirrel

Springsteen, Bruce (1949–) US rock singer, guitarist, and songwriter, born in New Jersey. In 1973, having travelled with obscure bands such as Doctor Zoom and the Sonic Boom, he signed with Columbia Records and released his first recording amid unprecedented hype, being featured on the front covers of both *Time* and *Newsweek* in the same week. In the event, his ascent to stardom was more gradual, and more merited. In 1976, he released a hit in 'Born to Run', a raucous song, roughly sung, with memorable, street-smart images in the lyric. Other hits with similar virtues followed, leading to his current position as one of the leading rock performers. » rock music

springtail A blind, primitively wingless insect often extremely abundant in soils or leaf litter; leaps by means of a forked spring organ folded up on underside of abdomen. (Order: *Collembola*, c.2 000 species.) » insect [i]

spruce An evergreen conifer native to the temperate N hemisphere, especially E Asia; leaves needle-like, leaving persistent, peg-like bases on shoot when shed; cones pendulous, ripe after one year. It is a widespread forestry tree, grown for timber and for its turpentine-yielding resin. (Genus: *Picea*, 50 species. Family: *Pinaceae*.) » conifer; evergreen plants; Norway spruce; resin

sprue » **malabsorption**

sprung rhythm A term invented by the poet Gerard Manley Hopkins (1844–89) to describe a rhythm founded on stress rather than syllable count. Novel in the late 19th-c, this in fact relates back to Old English alliterative verse. » English literature; Hopkins, Gerard Manley; metre (literature); poetry

spurge A large worldwide genus of diverse, latex-producing plants, annuals or perennials, sometimes shrubs. Some from arid regions look like cacti, having independently evolved similar adaptations to drought, and when not in flower can be distinguished from cacti only by the presence of latex. Its distinctive flower, called a *cyathium*, is in fact a condensed and reduced inflorescence represented by a single ovary (the female flower), several stamens (the male flowers), four large glands, and a ring of perianth-like, often brightly coloured bracts. (Genus: *Euphorbia*, 2 000 species. Family: *Euphorbiaceae*.) » annual; bract; cactus [i]; inflorescence [i]; latex; ovary; perennial; perianth; shrub; stamen

spurrey » **corn spurrey; sand spurrey**

Sputnik [**sput**nik] The world's first artificial satellite. Sputnik 1 was launched by the USSR (4 Oct 1957) from Tyuratam launch site; weight 84 kg/185 lb; battery powered; it transmitted a radio signal for 21 days. Sputnik 2 was launched in November 1957; weight 508 kg/1 120 lb; it carried the dog 'Laika', killed by injection after seven days of returning biomedical data. » Explorer 1; Soviet space programme

sputtering The ejection of atoms from the surface of a metal, caused by the impact of ions. It may be used to produce ultra-clean metal surfaces by knocking off contaminant atoms, or as a source of metal atoms in the vacuum deposition of thin metal films. Sputtering damages thermionic cathodes. » ion; thermionics; thin films

spy story A specialized form of fiction which centres on the hazards and excitements of espionage. Spying has a long history; there is a spy's guide in Chinese from the 6th-c BC, and a recognizable spy novel *Sa Kno* by the Chinese author Lo Kra-Chung (1260–1341). But the modern spy story begins with the works of William le Queux (1864–1927) and Erskine Childers (eg *The Riddle of the Sands*, 1903). Conrad contributed *The Secret Agent* (1907) to the genre, and two novels by John Buchan have become classics: *The Thirty-Nine Steps* (1915) and *Greenmantle* (1916). Between the wars Somerset Maugham, Eric Ambler, and Graham Greene wrote authentic and unsensational spy stories; then Ian Fleming's James Bond glamourized the enterprise in book and film. But the novels of John le Carré (eg *The Spy Who Came In From the Cold*, 1963) and Len Deighton (eg *Funeral in Berlin*, 1964) have returned to a more realistic not to say cynical presentation of espionage. » detective story; novel; Buchan; Childers; Fleming, Ian; Greene, Graham; Le Carré; Maugham

squall A sudden increase in wind speed. For at least one minute, minimum velocity must increase by at least 8 m/26 ft per second, and reach 11 m/36 ft per second before declining rapidly. » wind [i]

squall-line A narrow line of thunderstorms which may extend for hundreds of kilometres ahead of a cold front, though only a few kilometres wide. It is associated with thunderstorms, gale force winds, and a sudden drop in temperature. » cold front; thunderstorm; tornado; wind [i]

square cloth Any fabric in which the number of warp and weft threads per centimeter is approximately equal. Square cloths are more expensive to make than most fabrics, and are mainly used where a woven design has a square repeat sequence.

Square Deal The popular name for the domestic policies of US President Roosevelt, especially the enforcement of the Antitrust Acts. The term was coined by Roosevelt during a speaking tour in the summer of 1902. » Antitrust Acts; Roosevelt, Theodore

squark » **supersymmetry**

squash (botany) Any of several species of the cucumber family, native to America; all trailing or climbing vines with tendrils; large, yellow, funnel-shaped flowers; fruits of various shapes and colours. Cultivated for their fruits, they are divided into two types: **summer squashes**, derived from marrow, are eaten before becoming ripe and fibrous; **winter squashes**, derived from four species including marrow and pumpkin, are eaten ripe and can be stored through winter. (*Cucurbita maxima/mixta/moschata/pepo*. Family: *Cucurbitaceae*.) » cucumber; marrow (botany); pumpkin

squash rackets (UK) **/racquets** (US) A popular indoor racket-and-ball court game, usually called **squash**. It developed from rackets at Harrow school in 1817, but with a softer ball. It is played by two players on an enclosed court 32 ft (9.75 m) long by 21 ft (6.4 m) wide. Each hits the ball against a front wall alternately. The object is to play a winning shot by forcing your opponent to fail to return the ball. Popular as a means of keeping fit, it is a strenuous game which requires players to be in good physical condition. » rackets; RR119

squeak rabbit » **pika**

squid A carnivorous marine mollusc with a streamlined body bearing fins towards the back; shell reduced to an internal cartilaginous rod; eight arms and two tentacles around mouth, used to catch prey; active swimmers; found in coastal and oceanic waters. (Class: *Cephalopoda*. Order: *Teuthoidea*.) » cartilage; Cephalopoda [i]; mollusc

squill A perennial native to Europe, Asia, and S Africa; small bulb; narrow leaves; flowers star- or bell-shaped, sometimes drooping, blue or purple. **Spring squill** (*Scilla verna*) produces flowers and leaves in the spring; **autumn squill** (*Scilla autumnalis*) produces flowers later in the year, before the leaves appear. (Genus: *Scilla*, 80 species. Family: *Liliaceae*.) » bulb; perennial

squint A defect in the alignment of the eyes, most commonly affecting movement in the horizontal plane; also known as a **strabismus**. It is usually congenital in origin, and may be associated with an abnormality in focusing (*refractive error*). In adults, it arises from weakness of one or more of the muscles that move the eyeball, and occurs in several diseases. » diabetes mellitus; eye [i]; myasthenia gravis

squirrel A rodent of family *Sciuridae* (267 species), virtually worldwide except Australasia; fine fur and bushy tail; most eat seeds; range from small tree-dwelling squirrels to cat-sized ground-dwelling squirrels (including prairie dogs and marmots); ground squirrels live in extensive burrows, and may hibernate for up to 9 months. » chipmunk; flying squirrel; marmot; prairie dog; red squirrel; rodent; scaly-tailed squirrel; souslik

squirrel monkey A New World monkey; small, lively, with long black-tipped tail; white face with black tip to muzzle; coat short, greyish; inhabits woodland near riverbanks; troops may contain up to 100 individuals. (Genus: *Saimiri*, 2 species.) » New World monkey

squirting cucumber A roughly hairy, spreading or trailing perennial, native to the Mediterranean; leaves heart-shaped, slightly lobed; flowers yellow; fruit 2.5–5 cm/1–2 in long, oval. When the ripe fruit is touched or falls, the seeds and a watery liquid are forcibly ejected in a jet through the hole formed by the stalk. (*Ecballium elaterium*. Family: *Cucurbitaceae*.) » perennial

Sri-Jayawardenapura [sree jiyahwahdna**poo**ra] 6°55N 79°52E. Capital of Sri Lanka since 1983; located in an E suburb of Colombo. » Colombo; Sri Lanka [i]

Sri Lanka [sree **lang**ka], formerly **Ceylon**, official name **Democratic Socialist Republic of Sri Lanka** pop (1990e) 17 103 000; area 65 610 sq km/25 325 sq ml. Island state in the Indian Ocean, separated from the Indian sub-continent by the Palk Strait, but linked by a series of coral islands known as Adam's Bridge; divided into nine provinces; bounded by the Bay of Bengal (E) and the Gulf of Mannar (W); capital (since 1983), Sri-Jayawardenapura, a suburb of the former capital, Colombo; chief towns, Jaffna, Kandy, Galle; timezone GMT

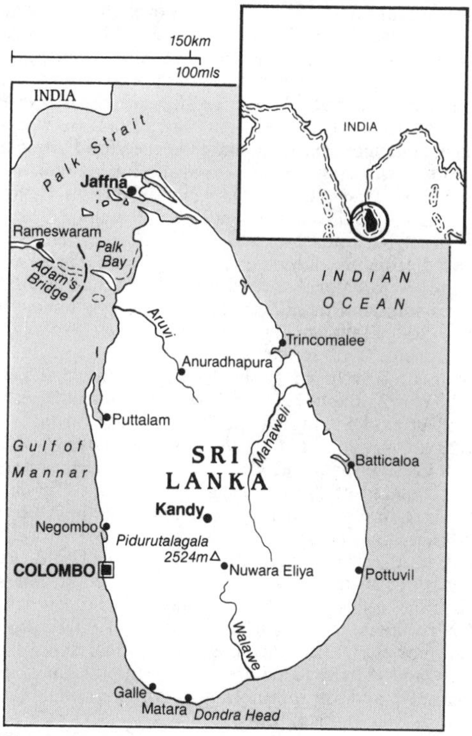

□ international airport

+5½; ethnic groups include Sinhalese (74%), Tamils (18%), Muslims (7%); official language, Sinhala; chief religions, Buddhism (69%), Hinduism (15%), Christianity (8%), Islam (8%); unit of currency, the Sri Lankan rupee of 100 cents; a pear-shaped island, 440 km/273 ml long, 220 km/137 ml wide; low-lying areas in N and S, surrounding SC uplands; highest peak, Pidurutalagala (2 524 m/8 281 ft); coastal plain fringed by sandy beaches and lagoons; N region generally arid in the dry season; nearly half the country is tropical monsoon forest or open woodland; high temperatures and humidity in the N plains; average daily temperatures at Trincomalee, 24–33°C; temperatures in the interior reduced by altitude; greatest rainfall on SW coast and in the mountains; visited by the Portuguese, 1505; taken by the Dutch, 1658; British occupation, 1796; British colony, 1802; Tamil labourers brought in from S India during colonial rule, to work on coffee and tea plantations; Dominion status, 1948; independent republic, 1972; governed by a president, elected for a 6-year term, and a 225-member National State Assembly, which sits for six years; acute political tension exists between the Buddhist Sinhalese majority and the Hindu Tamil minority, who wish to establish an independent state in the N and E; considerable increase in racial violence in the area during the 1980s; agriculture employs 46% of the labour force; rice, rubber, tea, coconuts, spices, sugar cane; timber, fishing; graphite, coal, precious and semi-precious stones; electricity produced largely by water power; textiles, chemicals, paper, rubber, tobacco, food processing, oil, wood, and metal products. » Colombo; Sri-Jayawardenapura; Tamil; RR27 national holidays; RR61 political leaders

Srinagar [**sree**nagah] 34°08N 74°50E, pop (1981) 520 000. Summer capital of Jammu-Kashmir state, N India, in the Vale of Kashmir, on R Jhelum; founded, 6th-c; capital status, 1948; airfield; shawls (cashmeres), silks, woollens, carpets; Buddhist ruins, mosque (1623). » Jammu-Kashmir

SS An acronym for **Schutzstaffel** ('protective squad'), a Nazi organization founded in 1925 as Hitler's personal bodyguard. From 1929 it was transformed and expanded by Himmler into an elite force. Within the Third Reich it became an independent organization, controlling a dominant repressive apparatus, and responsible for concentration camps and racial policy. It formed its own armed detachments, which after 1939 became the *Waffen* ('armed') SS. During World War 2 it became an alternative army, an autonomous power within the Third Reich, and the principal agent of racial extermination policy. » Himmler; Nazi Party; World War 2

stabilizers (economics) The factors in a modern economic system which help to keep the economy stable, avoiding the worst effects of trade cycle fluctuations. They mainly relate to fiscal policy, in that tax receipts will change with rises or falls in incomes (*automatic stabilizers*). The government can also help stabilize the economy with positive steps, such as public works to alleviate recession, and changes in tax rates. » fiscal policy

stabilizers (shipping) A device which limits rolling in a ship, usually in the form of moveable fins. They were first fitted successfully in the P & O liner *Chusan* in 1950. An older form fitted in the Italian liner *Conti de Savoia* in 1932 was claimed to be successful, but it was never fitted in other vessels.

Staël, Madame de [stahel], byname of **Anne Louise Germaine Necker, Baroness of Staël-Holstein** (1766–1817) French writer, born and died in Paris, the daughter of the financier, Necker. Both before and after the French Revolution, her *salon* became a centre of political discussion. In 1803 she was forced to leave Paris, and visited Weimar, Berlin, and Vienna, returning to France at intervals. She wrote novels, plays, essays, historical and critical works, and political memoirs, becoming known with her *Lettres* (1788, Letters) on Rousseau, and achieving European fame with her romantic novel, *Corinne* (1807). Her major work, *De L'Allemagne* (Germany), was published in London in 1813. » French literature; Necker; novel

staffage [sta**fahj**] In art history, French term referring to the small figures and animals which provide interest in a landscape. In the 17th-c it was common for a landscape painter to employ a specialist to add the staffage. » landscape painting

Stafford 52°48N 2°07W, pop (1981) 62 242. County town of Staffordshire, C England; railway; engineering, chemicals, electrical goods, footwear, timber; 11th-c castle, destroyed in the Civil War; Churches of St Mary and St Chad, 18th-c William Salt library, Shire Hall, Borough Hall, Guildhall; birthplace of Izaak Walton; Shugborough (6 km/4 ml E), the ancestral home of the Earls of Lichfield. » English Civil War; Staffordshire; Walton, Izaak

Staffordshire pop (1987e) 1 027 500; area 2 716 sq km/1 048 sq ml. County in C England, divided into nine districts; in the basin of the R Trent; county town, Stafford; chief towns include Stoke-on-Trent, Newcastle-under-Lyme, Burton-upon-Trent; agriculture, coal, pottery, brewing; Potteries, Vale of Trent, Cannock Chase. » England [i]; Potteries, the; Stafford; Wedgwood, Josiah

Staffordshire bull terrier A medium-sized terrier developed in Britain as a fighting dog or guard dog; thick-set muscular body with a short coat, broad head, long muzzle, soft ears. » terrier

stag beetle A large, dark-coloured beetle; males up to 66 mm/2½ in long, typically with large, antler-like processes on head, formed from mandibles; larvae fleshy, living in rotting wood; adults feed on liquids and sap. (Order: *Coleoptera*. Family: *Lucanidae*, c.1 200 species.) » beetle; larva

stag's horn fern A type of fern (an epiphyte), native to Australia. Its sterile fronds are rounded, and braced against the tree to form the mantle, giving anchorage and support. Its fertile fronds are long, branched like antlers, and bear numerous sporangia, giving a suede-like appearance to the underside. (*Platycerium bifurcatum*. Family: *Polypodiaceae*.) » epiphyte; fern; sporangium

stage That part of a theatre where the performance is presented. The relationship established between performers and audience by the position of the stage is of fundamental importance to any theatrical event. » apron/open/transverse stage; proscenium; theatre in the round

stagecoach A type of horse-drawn coach that appeared in the mid-17th-c offering carriage to the public on predetermined routes and stages, usually running between provincial towns and London. With the introduction by the Post Office of mail coaches in the 1780s, new standards of time-keeping and efficiency were forced upon the privately-owned stagecoach lines. The coming of the railways in the 1830s and 1840s quickly ended the dominating role of stagecoaches within public transport, although in some isolated parts of Britain their use continued until the 1870s. In the USA, the first mail stagecoaches ran between Boston and New York in 1784, but the main period of their use was from 1800 to 1840, by which time all the principal cities as far W as Pittsburgh were connected by several stagecoach lines. However, the stagecoach in the USA never achieved the importance that river travel did, and by 1850 with the coming of the railroad they ceased to be of importance, except in some isolated areas in the West.

stagflation An economic situation where there is no growth in the economy (it is stagnating), yet inflation is rising. In these situations, boosting economic activity might well increase inflation. Conversely, action to stem inflation might cause a recession. » inflation; recession

staghound » **deerhound**

stained glass Pieces of different coloured glass mounted in lead framing to form a pictorial image. It was introduced from Byzantine art for the windows of European buildings in the late 12th-c, and flourished most splendidly in Western Romanesque and Gothic churches. It remained popular throughout the mediaeval period, and was enthusiastically revived in the 19th-c (eg by Burne-Jones, Matisse, Rouault). In the Middle Ages the glass itself was often coloured by the addition of metal oxides during the glass-making process, or by the layering of coloured glass over uncoloured glass (*flashing*); but from the 16th-c the technique of painting in enamel on the glass became more common. » Burne-Jones; Byzantine art; Matisse; Rouault

stainless steels A group of steels which resist rusting and chemical attack through the addition of nickel and chromium. They are used to make utensils, cutlery, and chemical reaction vessels. » chromium; nickel; steel

Stakhanovism An economic system in the USSR designed to raise productivity through incentives. It was named after the first worker to receive an award, coalminer Alexei Grigorievich Stakhanov (1906–77), who in 1935 reorganized his team's workload to achieve major gains in production. The movement lasted only until 1939.

stalactites and stalagmites Icicle-like deposits of limestone formed by precipitation from slowly dripping water from the ceilings of caves. Stalactites grow from the ceiling, while stalagmites form on the floor and grow upwards at a rate of less than half a millimetre per year. » limestone

Stalin, Joseph, originally **Iosif Vissarionovich Dzhugashvili** (1879–1953) Georgian Marxist revolutionary and later virtual dictator of the USSR (1928–53), born at Gori, Georgia, the son of a cobbler and ex-serf. He was educated at Tiflis Orthodox Theological Seminary, from which he was expelled in 1899. After joining a Georgian Social Democratic organization (1898), he became active in the revolutionary underground, and was twice exiled to Siberia (1902, 1913). As a leading Bolshevik he played an active role in the October Revolution, and became People's Commissar for Nationalities in the first Soviet government and a member of the Communist Party Politburo. In 1922 he became General Secretary of the Party Central Committee, a post he held until his death, and also occupied other key positions which enabled him to build up enormous personal power in the party and government apparatus. After Lenin's death (1924) he pursued a policy of building 'socialism in one country', and gradually isolated and disgraced his political rivals, notably Trotsky. In 1928 he launched the campaign for the collectivization of agriculture during which millions of peasants perished, and the first five-year plan for the forced industrialization of the economy. Between 1934 and 1938 he inaugurated a massive purge of the party, government, armed forces, and intelligentsia in which millions of so-called 'enemies of the people' were imprisoned, exiled, or shot. In 1938 he signed the Non-Aggression Pact with Hitler which bought the Soviet Union two years respite from involvement in World War 2. After the German invasion (1941), the USSR became a member of the Grand Alliance, and Stalin, as war leader, assumed the title of Generalissimus. He took part in the conferences of Teheran, Yalta, and Potsdam which resulted in Soviet military and political control over the liberated countries of postwar E and C Europe. From 1945 until his death he resumed his repressive measures at home, and conducted foreign policies which contributed to the Cold War between the Soviet Union and the West. He died near Moscow, and his body was displayed in the Lenin Mausoleum. He was posthumously denounced by Khrushchev at the 20th Party Congress (1956) for crimes against the Party and for building a 'cult of personality'. Under Gorbachev many of Stalin's victims have been rehabilitated, and the whole phenomenon of 'Stalinism' officially condemned by the Soviet authorities. His body was removed from the mausoleum in 1961 and buried near the Kremlin. » Bolsheviks; Cold War; Gorbachev; Khrushchev; Lenin; October Revolution; Potsdam Conference; Russian Revolution; Stalinism; Teheran Conference; Trotsky; World War 2; Yalta Conference

Stalingrad, Battle of (1942–3) One of the great battles of World War 2, fought between Nazi German and Soviet troops in and around Stalingrad (now Volgograd) on the R Volga during the winter of 1942–3. After savage fighting, which cost 70 000 German lives, the German 6th army surrendered (Feb 1943), yielding 91 000 prisoners-of-war to the Russians. The battle is regarded as a major turning-point in the Allied victory over Germany. » World War 2

Stalinism A label used pejoratively outside the USSR to refer to the nature of the Soviet regime 1929–53. It refers to a monolithic system, tightly disciplined and bureaucratic, with the party hierarchy having a monopoly of political and economic power. It also encompasses the total subservience of society and culture to political ends, suppression of political opponents, and the promotion of an individual above the party. » communism; Stalin

stamen The male organ of a flower, consisting of a stalk-like filament bearing sac-like anthers containing pollen; collectively forming the *androecium* or third whorl of a flower. The number and arrangement is often diagnostic for plant families. » flower [i]; pollen [i]

Stamford 41°03N 73°32W, pop (1980) 102 453. City in Fairfield County, SW Connecticut, USA, on Long Island Sound; residential suburb for New York City; established, 1641; city status, 1893; railway; computers and electronic components, office equipment. » Connecticut; New York City

Stamitz, Johann (Wenzel Anton) (1717–57) Bohemian violinist and composer, born at Havlíčkův Brod. He became concert master at the Mannheim court in 1745, where he developed sonata form, and trained the orchestra to a level of perfection unrivalled in Europe. His works include 74 symphonies, several concertos, chamber music, and a mass. He died at Mannheim, having founded a school of symphonists which had a profound influence on Mozart. » Mozart; sonata

stammering » **stuttering**

Stamp Act A British Act passed in 1765 by the administration of George Grenville (1712–70), which levied a direct tax on all papers required in discharging official business in the American colonies. It was the first direct tax levied without the consent of the colonial assemblies, and it caused much discontent in the colonies, six of which petitioned against it. The Act was withdrawn by the Rockingham government in 1766. » American Revolution; Grenville, Baron; Rockingham; Townshend Acts

standard form In mathematics, a number in the form $A \times 10^n$, where $1 \leqslant A < 10$ and n is an integer, positive or negative. This form is useful for very large numbers, eg $3\,000\,000\,000 = 3 \times 10^9$ and very small numbers, eg $0.000\,000\,003 = 3 \times 10^{-9}$. » numbers

standard language The variety of a language which has greatest social and political prestige within a speech community. It cuts across regional differences in usage, and tends to have a levelling effect on regional variation on account of its social and political power-base. It functions as a linguistically 'neutral' norm for use in the media and education, and is the variety usually employed in religious, legal, and literary style. » sociolinguistics

standard of living The level of welfare achieved by a nation or group; usually measured in terms of food, clothing, housing, and other material benefits. There has been a considerable long-term rise in living standards in the West, particularly since 1945; but the same has not been true of the poorer developing nations. A simple measure for comparative purposes is gross national product per head of population. This shows a very fast rate of growth in W Europe and the USA, and a very wide gap between the richest nations and the poorest. » developing countries; gross domestic product

standard time The officially established local time adopted by a region or country, + or − so many hours from Greenwich Mean Time. The Earth can be divided into 24 time zones each based on sections of 15° of longitude. In each of these, standard time is calculated from the position of the Sun at a central point within the zone. In practice, to avoid unnecessary complications in countries which span more than 15° of longitude, zones may be larger. Some countries have more than one time zone; for example in the USA there are seven standard time zones and in continental Europe two (+1 hour and +2 hours from GMT). Zones differ generally by a whole hour, although there are a few cases of half-hour zones (eg South Australia). » Date Line; Greenwich Mean Time; RR17

standing crop » **biomass**

standing wave » **wave** (physics) [i]

Standish, Myles (c.1584–1656) English colonist, born probably at Ormskirk, Lancashire. After serving in the Netherlands, he sailed with the *Mayflower* in 1620, and became military head of the first American settlement at Plymouth, and treasurer of the colony (1644–9). He died at Duxbury, Massachusetts. » Mayflower

Stanford, Sir Charles (Villiers) (1852–1924) Irish composer, born in Dublin. Educated at Cambridge, Leipzig, and Berlin, he became organist at Trinity College (1872–93), professor in the Royal College of Music (1883), and professor of music at Cambridge (1887). He wrote several major choral works, six operas, seven symphonies, and a great deal of chamber music, songs, and English church music. Knighted in 1901, he died in London.

Stanhope, James, 1st Earl (1675–1721) British soldier and statesman, born in Paris. He entered parliament as a Whig in 1701, and commanded in Spain during the War of the Spanish Succession (1701–14). He was Secretary of State for Foreign Affairs under George I, and became his Chief Minister in 1717. He died in London. » George I; Spanish Succession, War of the; Whigs

Stanislaus Leszczynski [leshchinskee] (1677–1766) King of Poland (1704–9, 1733–5), born at Lemberg. After his election in 1704, under the influence of Charles XII of Sweden, he was driven out by Peter the Great. Re-elected in 1733, he lost the War of the Polish Succession, and formally abdicated in 1736, receiving the Duchies of Lorraine and Bar. He died at Lunéville. » Charles XII; Peter I

Stanislavsky (Konstantin Sergeyevitch), originally **Alexeyev** (1863–1938) Russian actor, theatre director, and teacher, born and died in Moscow. As a talented amateur actor, he co-founded in 1888 the Moscow Society of Art and Literature, and in 1898 helped to found the Moscow Arts Theatre. His work with this influential company, and his teaching on acting, proved to be a major contribution to 20th-c theatre. His system remains the basis of much Western actor-training and practice. » Moscow Art Theatre; Nemirovich-Danchenko; theatre

Stanisław II (August) Poniatowski (1732–98) Last King of Poland (1764–95), born at Wołczyn. He travelled to St Petersburg in 1757, and became a favourite of the future Empress, Catherine II. Through her influence he was elected King, but was unable to stop the partitions of Poland (1772, 1793). Despite the rebellion of Kosciusko, the country was partitioned again in 1795. He abdicated, and died in St Petersburg. » Catherine II: Kosciusko; Poland, Partitions of

Stanley, Sir Henry Morton (1841–1904) British explorer and journalist, born at Denbigh, Wales. In 1859 he went as cabin boy to New Orleans, where he was adopted by a merchant named Stanley. In 1867 he joined the *New York Herald*, and as its special correspondent he travelled to Abyssinia and Spain. In 1869 he was told to 'find Livingstone' in Africa. In 1871 he left Zanzibar for Tanganyika and encountered Livingstone at Ujiji. In 1874 Stanley led a second expedition which explored L Tanganyika, and traced the Congo to the sea. In 1879, on a third expedition, he founded the Congo Free State, and in 1887–9 a further expedition went to the aid of Emin Pasha in the Sudan. He became a British citizen in 1892, and an MP (1895–1900). Knighted in 1899, he died in London. » Livingstone

Stanley 51°45S 57°56W, pop (1980) 1 000. Port and capital of the Falkland Is, on the E coast of East Falkland; airport (Mt Pleasant), with links to the UK and to airstrips throughout the colony; whaling, wool trade, service industries. » Falkland Islands [i]

Stanley, Mount Mountain in the Ruwenzori range on the frontier between Zaire and Uganda; height of Margherita Peak 5 110 m/16 765 ft; highest point in Zaire and Uganda; first ascent, by the Duke of Abruzzi's expedition, 1906. » Ruwenzori Mountains

Stanley Cup An end-of-season ice hockey series between the winners of the two conferences in the National Hockey League (NHL) in the USA and Canada. It was first presented in 1893 by Lord Stanley of Preston, then Governor-General of Canada. » ice hockey

Stanleyville » **Kisangani**

Stannaries Former tin-mining districts of Cornwall, UK, lying within the lands of the Duchy of Cornwall. In ancient times the tin miners of the Stannaries held special privileges, including the right to send representatives to the Stannary Parliament and to administer their own courts. » Duchy of Cornwall; tin

Stanton, Elizabeth, *née* **Cady** (1815–1902) US feminist, born at Johnstown, New York. Educated at Troy (New York) Female Seminary, she involved herself in the anti-slavery and temperance movements, and in 1840 married the abolitionist Henry B Stanton. She was personally responsible for the emergence of women's suffrage as a public issue, but she regarded women's rights as a much larger problem. She died in New York City. » civil rights; slave trade; women's liberation movement

stapelia A perennial native to arid areas of tropical and S Africa, superficially resembling cacti, and similarly drought-adapted; fleshy, green stems swollen with water-storage tissue; leaves reduced to deciduous scales. The large carrion flowers, with five petals surrounding an inner, horned ring, are mottled red or maroon, and produce an overpowering smell of rotten meat. (Genus: *Stapelia*, 75 species. Family: *Asclepiadaceae*.) » cactus [i]; carrion flower; perennial

staphylococcus [stafilohkokuhs] A spherical bacterium c.1 micron in diameter, commonly occurring in clusters, and requiring oxygen for growth. It is found on the mucous membranes and skin of humans and other animals. It can cause superficial abscesses, and chronic to fatal systemic infections. (Kingdom: *Monera*. Family: *Micrococcaceae*.) » bacteria [i]; mucous membrane; skin [i]

Staples, The » **Farne Islands**

star A sphere of matter held together entirely by its own gravitational field, and generating energy by means of nuclear fusion reactions in its deep interior. The important distinguishing feature of a star is the presence of a natural nuclear reactor in its core, where the pressure of the overlying mass of material is sufficient to cause nuclear reactions, the principal one of which is the conversion of hydrogen to helium. About 0.5% of the mass becomes electromagnetic radiation. The minimum mass needed to make a star is probably 1/20th the mass of the Sun; the maximum about 70 times as great as the Sun. » binary/circumpolar/double/dwarf/giant/neutron/pulsating/variable star; electromagnetic radiation [i]; globular cluster; gravitation; pulsar; quasar; star cluster; supergiant; supernova

Star Chamber, Court of The royal prerogative court in Britain for hearing subjects' petitions and grievances, of uncertain date but increasingly prominent under the Tudors and early Stuarts. It consisted of privy councillors and two chief justices, who dealt swiftly and efficiently with cases, particularly those involving public order. Charles I used it against government opponents. It was abolished by the Long Parliament in 1641. » Long Parliament; Stuarts

star cluster A group of stars physically associated in space, held together by mutual gravitational attraction. Loosely packed, open clusters in a galactic plane contain a few hundred stars and are young. Dense, globular clusters are spherical, have millions of stars distributed in a halo around a galaxy, and are billions of years old. » galaxy; globular cluster; gravitation; star

star-of-Bethlehem A perennial with a small bulb, native to S Europe and the Mediterranean region; leaves narrow, grooved, with a white stripe down the centre; flowers 1.5–2 cm/0.6–0.8 in in diameter; six narrow petals, white with a green stripe on the back. (*Ornithogalum umbellatum*. Family: *Liliaceae*.) » bulb; perennial

Star of Bethlehem A star mentioned in *Matt* 2.1–12, depicted as heralding Jesus' birth and guiding magi from the East to the birthplace in Bethlehem. Although sometimes considered a comet (Halley's comet c.11 BC), a supernova, or a conjunction of Jupiter and Saturn in the constellation Pisces (c.7 BC), it is doubtful that these can explain the sustained presence or movement that is described. Legends about the births of Mithridates and Alexander Severus also allege the presence of special stars. » Jesus Christ; Magi

Star of David or **Magen David** ('Shield of David') A six-pointed star, consisting of two crossed equilateral triangles, which in the last two centuries has come to symbolize Judaism, although its use for this can be traced back at least to the 7th-c AD. It appears on Israel's national flag today as a blue design against white. It has also symbolized the Zionist movement, and a red version signifies the society in Israel that corresponds to the Red Cross. » David; Judaism; Red Cross; Zionism

star system The process of building up an individual leading actor or actress in motion pictures as an internationally recognized personality took root in Hollywood before 1920 and developed with the power of the major studios. These combined worldwide publicity with tight control of the artistes, who were their 'property' and their best guarantee of box-office success. » cinema

Star Wars » **SDI**

starch $(C_6H_{10}O_5)_n$. A carbohydrate; a condensation polymer of glucose, and isomeric with cellulose, found as a reserve material in living cells. Partial hydrolysis gives amylose (an oligomer) and maltose (a dimer). Its non-food uses include adhesives, pill filler, and paper sizing. » carbohydrate; condensation (chemistry); glucose [i]; hydrolysis

starfish A typically 5-armed, star-shaped marine invertebrate (echinoderm); arms merge gradually into a central body disc; more than five arms often present; most species omnivorous, feeding as scavengers or predators; can digest prey externally; contains c.1 500 living species, from inter-tidal zone to deep sea; also called **sea star**. (Phylum: *Echinodermata*. Subclass: *Asteroidea*.) » crown of thorns; echinoderm [i]

stargazer Heavy-bodied bottom-living marine fish of the family *Uranoscopidae* (3 genera); distinguished by a large vertical mouth and tiny eyes placed on top of a robust flattened head; fins well developed, gill cover bearing a strong poison spine; powerful electric organs located behind the eyes; widespread in tropical to temperate seas, typically living buried in soft sediments.

Stari Ras Former Serbian city located near the present-day town of Novi Pazar in Yugoslavia; a world heritage site. It became the first capital of independent Serbia in the 12th-c, but little now remains of the city save the 13th-c monastery of Sopocani, founded by King Uros I. » Serbia

starling A songbird, native to the Old World, with some introduced to the Americas; plumage often with metallic sheen, usually dark but sometimes colourful; inhabits woodland, open country; omnivorous; gregarious; flocks often a major nuisance on city buildings and large structures (eg the Forth Bridge, Scotland). The name is also used for the **military starling** (*Leistes militaris*), an American oriole. (Family: *Sturnidae*, 92 species.) » grackle; hill mynah; magpie; mynah; oriole; oxpecker; songbird

Starr, Ringo » **Beatles, The**

START An acronym of **Strategic Arms Reduction Talks**, held between the USA and USSR (Jun 1982–Dec 1983), then recessed indefinitely. They began because of NATO concern at the scale of Soviet land-based heavy missiles, but became bogged down in issues to do with the number of missiles versus their capability, and the inclusion by the US of the introduction of Cruise and Pershing missiles as a bargaining counter. Talks were resumed under the accord between President Reagan and General Secretary Gorbachev, and agreement was reached in 1991. » arms control; NATO

state (politics) A form of political association which in the main enjoys the unique right of being able to use legitimate coercion over a particular territory. The rights and duties of office holders of the state are set down in law, including constitutional law. Many regard it as the means for achieving national unity, and throughout history several writers have attributed a mission or wider purpose to the state over and above its individual parts. Liberals tend to see it simply as an expression of the views of individuals within society. Marxists, on the other hand, see the state as an instrument of class rule. In practice, it is difficult to define precisely what constitutes the state, unless it is simply seen as a set of public rules and offices, and there is considerable disagreement over what it is and should be. » nationalism

State Department The oldest department of the US government, established by the fourth Act of Congress (Jul 1789), responsible to the President for the conduct of foreign affairs. It is headed by a Secretary of State, and is regarded as the most senior department of government. » Congress

Staten Island [**stat**n] pop (1980) 352 121, area 153 sq km/59 sq ml. Borough of New York City, USA, co-extensive with Richmond County; an island separated from New Jersey by Kill van Kull and Arthur Kill Channels, and from Long Island by the Narrows; oil refining, shipbuilding, paper, printing; first settled in 1641; named by early Dutch settlers after the *Staaten* or States General of 17th-c Holland. » New York City

states' rights A US Constitutional doctrine that the separate states enjoy areas of self-control which cannot be breached by the federal government. The doctrine flourished among White Southerners between Reconstruction and the Civil Rights Movement, and amounted to a code term for White supremacy. » civil rights

static electricity Electric charge which does not flow. Objects can acquire a static charge by rubbing against one another (eg by combing hair or rubbing a balloon on a jumper), which transfers electrons from one object to the other. High voltages can be produced; a static build-up can cause dangerous sparks. » electricity; electrostatics; van de Graaff generator

statice [**stat**isee] A biennial native to the Mediterranean; leafy, winged stem; distinctive rosette of wavy-edged leaves; flowers papery, various colours, in one-sided spikes. It is often grown for the everlasting flowers used in dried decorations. (*Limonium sinuatum*. Family: *Plumbaginaceae*.) » biennial

Stations of the Cross A popular form of devotion in the Roman Catholic and some Anglican Churches. It consists of meditating on a series of 14 pictures or carvings recalling the passion of Christ from his condemnation to his burial. » Jesus Christ; Roman Catholicism

statistical linguistics » **mathematical linguistics**

statistical mechanics A branch of physics which provides a link between large-scale phenomena involving many atoms or molecules, and the microscopic properties and interactions of individual atoms and molecules. Observable macroscopic properties correspond to the combination of the average value of some attribute (eg velocity) for a single atom with the distribution of that attribute over the entire collection of particles. The subject is essential in understanding such domains as critical phenomena and the thermodynamic properties of solids. » Boltzmann constant; Brownian motion; kinetic theory of gases; many body theory; Maxwell–Boltzmann distribution; quantum statistical mechanics; statistics

statistics The branch of mathematics which deals with the collection and analysis of numerical data. From an analysis of the data, a statistician will produce numbers giving information. Numbers commonly found useful are those representative of a set of data – 'averages', such as mean, median, and mode, and those indicating variation in the data, describing the spread or dispersion, such as range and standard deviation. » chi-square test; correlation; mean; median; mode; probability of an event; variance; Galton; Gauss; Poisson

Statue of Liberty » **Liberty, Statue of**

status The social position a person occupies, and the rank or esteem it enjoys. Systems of social stratification may be based on a strong status order, as in traditional caste systems, or status may be just one dimension of a more complex social hierarchy. » caste; social stratification; Weber, Max

statute A particular law passed by the legislature, such as an act of Parliament. A statute has a short title by which it is generally known, eg the Housing Act (1985). » legislature; parliament

statute of limitations » **limitation of actions**

Stauffenburg, Claus, Graf von ('Count of') [**shtow**fnburg] (1907–44) German soldier, born at Jettingen. Initially welcoming the advent to power of Hitler, he quickly became alienated by Nazi brutality. He was a colonel on the German general staff in 1944, and placed the bomb in the unsuccessful attempt to assassinate Hitler at Rastenburg (20 Jul 1944). He was shot next day. » Hitler; Nazi Party

Stavanger [sta**vang**er] 58°58N 5°45E, pop (1983) 91 964. Seaport capital of Rogaland county, SW Norway; on a S branch of the Bokn Fjord, 304 km/189 ml WSW of Oslo; founded, c.8th-c; airport; rail terminus; important North Sea oil centre; oil refinery, fish-canning, shipyards, oil-rig construction; St Swithin's Cathedral (12th-c). » Norway [i]

Stavisky, (Serge) Alexandre (?1886–1934) French swindler, born in Kiev, Russia, who went to Paris in 1900 and was naturalized in 1914. He floated a series of fraudulent companies, and in 1933 was discovered to be handling bonds to the value of more than 500 million francs on behalf of the municipal pawnshop in Bayonne. He fled to Chamonix and probably committed suicide; but in the meantime the affair had revealed widespread corruption in the government, business, the judiciary, and the police, and precipitated the fall (1934) of Prime Minister Camille Chautemps (1885–1963).

steady state theory One of two rival theories of cosmology (the other is the Big Bang), proposed in 1948. It asserts that 'things are as they are because they were as they were'. The universe is infinitely old, and contains the same density of material (on average) at all points and at all times. In order to compensate for the observed expansion of the universe, it is thus necessary to postulate the continuous spontaneous creation of matter. From the mid-1960s this model fell out of favour. » Big Bang; cosmology

steam The vapour phase of water (H_2O); also called 'live steam', to distinguish it from 'dead steam', visible droplets of recondensed vapour. » water

steam engine An external combustion engine, in which the engine's working fluid (steam) is generated in a boiler outside the engine. The steam is brought into the engine by valves, and through its pressure and expansive properties a piston is made to oscillate within a cylinder. This oscillatory motion is then converted into rotary motion by means of a crankshaft mechanism. » engine; locomotive [i]

steamship » **ship** [i]

stearic acid [stee**ar**ik] $C_{17}H_{35}COOH$, IUPAC **octadecanoic acid**, melting point 71°C. A waxy solid, the commonest of the fatty acids obtained from the saponification of animal fat. It is used in soap and candle manufacture. » carboxylic acids; IUPAC; saponification

stearin(e) [**stee**arin] The name used to describe fats derived from stearic acid, and also for a mixture of stearic and palmitic acids used in candle manufacture. » fat; palmitic acid; stearic acid

steatite [**stee**uhtiyt] » **talc**

steel The chief alloy of iron, and the most used of all metals. It consists of iron hardened by the presence of a small proportion of carbon. It was made in small amounts in ancient times by heating cast-iron to reduce surface carbon, and was later made in crucibles in small quantities for tools. Large-scale manufacture for constructional purposes began with the Bessemer process (1856 onwards). Most steel used today is a simple carbon steel, but there exist many special steels formed by the addition of other metals, eg high alloy steels for tools, and stainless steel (with nickel and chromium). » alloy; Bessemer process; carbon; iron

Steel, David (Martin Scott) (1938–) British politician and Leader of the Liberal Party (1976–88), born at Kirkcaldy, Fife, Scotland, and educated in Kenya and at Edinburgh. He became an MP in 1965, sponsored a controversial Bill to reform the laws on abortion (1966–7), and was active in the anti-apartheid movement. He became Liberal Chief Whip (1970–5), before succeeding Jeremy Thorpe as Liberal leader. In 1981 he led the Party into an Alliance with the Social Democratic Party. Following successful merger negotiations between the two parties (1987–8), he was the last leader of the Liberal Party. He remains active in politics both as an MP and Party spokesman. » Liberal Party (UK); Thorpe

steel band An ensemble, native to Trinidad, consisting mainly of steel drums – tuned percussion instruments made from used oildrums. Some steel bands are highly accomplished at playing arrangements of Western classics, as well as W Indian music for Carnival and other community festivities. » percussion [i]

steel engraving In printmaking, a technique of engraving introduced in the 19th-c, in which steel plates were introduced to cope with the enormous demand for reproductions of popular pictures. These were harder and longer-lasting than the traditional copper plates; but they proved almost impossible to cut, so as an alternative copper plates were given a steel facing by the simple process of electrolysis. » electrolysis [i]; engraving

Steele, Sir Richard (1672–1729) English essayist, dramatist, and politician, born in Dublin, Ireland. Educated at Charterhouse and Oxford, he joined the army, but gave it up to become a writer. He wrote three successful comedies, and in 1707 became editor of *The London Gazette*. He is best known for the satirical, political, and moral essays which formed much of the content of the new periodicals *The Tatler* (1709–11), which he founded, and *The Spectator* (1711–12), which he co-founded with Addison. He supported the House of Hanover, and was rewarded by George I with the appointment of supervisor of Drury Lane Theatre, and a knighthood. In 1722 he retired to Carmarthen, Wales, where he died. » Addison, Joseph; drama; English literature; satire

Steen, Jan (Havickszoon) [stayn] (1626–79) Dutch painter, born and died at Leyden. He joined the Leyden guild of painters in 1648, lived in The Hague until 1654, then became a brewer at Delft, and an innkeeper at Leyden. His best works were genre pictures of social and domestic scenes depicting the everyday life of ordinary folk, as in 'The Music Lesson' (National Gallery, London). » Dutch art; genre painting

steenbok or **steinbok** A dwarf antelope native to Africa S of the Sahara; reddish-brown with white underparts; large ears with white insides; short vertical horns; inhabits grass or scrubland; when threatened, lies flat and relies on camouflage. (*Raphicerus campestris*.) » antelope

steeplechase 1 A form of national hunt horse racing in which the horses have to negotiate fixed fences normally between 3–4 ft (0.9–1.2 m) high. The first steeplechase was in Ireland in 1752, when Mr O'Callaghan and Mr Edmund Blake matched their horses to race over 4½ ml (7.2 km) across country between Buttevant Church and St Leger Church. The world's most famous steeplechase is the Grand National. » Grand National; horse racing **2** A track athletics event over 3 000 m. The competitors have to negotiate 24 hurdles and seven water jumps. Each obstacle is 3 ft (0.9 m) high. » athletics

Stefan, Josef (1835–93) Austrian physicist, born near Klagenfurt, Austria. He was educated at Vienna, where he spent his career. His work in experimental physics was wide-ranging, but his fame rests on his research on thermal radiation, begun in 1879. He found an experimental law describing radiant heat loss from a hot surface (**Stefan's law**), and used it to make the first satisfactory estimate of the Sun's surface temperature. Attempts by others to find a theoretical basis for Stefan's law led to major advances in physics, and eventually to Planck's quantum theory of 1900. He died in Vienna. » blackbody radiation; Planck; quantum theory; radiation

Stegodon [**steg**uhduhn] An extinct, elephant-like mammal known from the Pliocene epoch of India; upper tusks long and very closely placed together; lower tusks only vestiges; only two cheek teeth present at a time. (Order: *Proboscidea.*) » elephant; mammal [i]; Pliocene epoch

Stegosaurus [steguh**saw**ruhs] A large dinosaur attaining a length of 9 m/30 ft; characterized by two rows of plates along back from skull to tail; four-legged, but forelimbs shorter than hindlimbs; known from the Upper Jurassic period of Colorado. (Order: *Ornithischia.*) » dinosaur [i]; Jurassic period; Ornithischia

Steichen, Edward (Jean) (1879–1973) US photographer, born in Luxemburg, but taken to the USA as a child. After working in Europe, he joined Alfred Stieglitz in setting up the American Photo-Secession Group in 1902, and through their gallery in New York City exercised considerable influence in establishing photography as an acceptable form of modern art. He became director of photography at the New York Museum of Modern Art (1945–62), and died in Connecticut. » Stieglitz

Stein, Gertrude (1874–1946) US writer, born at Allegheny, Pennsylvania. She studied psychology and medicine in the USA, then settled in Paris, where she was absorbed into the world of experimental art and letters. Her main works include *Three Lives* (1908); *Tender Buttons* (1914), in which she tried to apply the theories of Cubist art to writing; and her most widely-read book, *The Autobiography of Alice B Toklas* (1933). She was revered as a critic in Paris, and her home became a salon for artists and writers between the two World Wars. She died in Paris. » American literature; Cubism; literary criticism

Stein, (Heinrich Friedrich) Karl, Baron von (1757–1831) Prussian statesman, born at Nassau. He studied law at Göttingen, and entered the service of Prussia in 1780, becoming Secretary for Trade (1804–7) and Chief Minister (1807–8), when he carried out important reforms in the army, economy, and both national and local government. In 1812 he went to St Petersburg, and built up the coalition against Napoleon. He was later adviser to Alexander I (1812–15), then retired to Kappenberg in Westphalia, where he died. » Alexander I; Napoleonic Wars; Prussia

Stein, Peter [shtiyn] (1937–) German theatre director, born in Berlin. From his very first production in 1967, he became established as a leading avant-garde director in Germany. Since 1970, he has been responsible for a remarkable series of collective creations at the Berlin Schaubuhne, where over a long rehearsal period the political and social context of a play is woven into an ensemble presentation. » theatre

Steinbeck, John (Ernst) [**stiyn**bek] (1902–68) US novelist, born at Salinas, California. He studied at Stanford, but did not take a degree, and worked as a labourer while writing. His first novel of repute was *Tortilla Flat* (1935), and soon after came his major work, *The Grapes of Wrath* (1939), a study of the poor in the face of disaster and threatened disintegration. Other books include *Of Mice and Men* (1937), *East of Eden* (1952), and the humorous *Cannery Row* (1945). He won the Nobel Prize for Literature in 1962, and died in New York City. » American literature; novel

steinbok » **steenbok**

Steiner, George (1929–) British critic and scholar, born in Paris, and educated there and at Chicago, Harvard, and Oxford. He worked at the Institute for Advanced Study at Princeton (1956–8), then taught at Cambridge and Geneva. He is one of the leading exponents of comparative literature in our time, his publications including *The Death of Tragedy* (1960), *Language and Silence* (1967), *After Babel* (1975), and *Antigones* (1984). » comparative literature; literary criticism

Steiner, Rudolf (1861–1925) Austrian social philosopher, the founder of anthroposophy, born at Kraljevec. He studied science and mathematics, and edited Goethe's scientific papers, before coming temporarily under the spell of the theosophists. In 1912 he propounded his own approach, establishing his first 'school of spiritual science', or 'Goetheanum', at Dornach in Switzerland. His aim was to integrate the psychological and the practical dimensions of life into an educational, ecological, and therapeutic basis for spiritual and physical development. Many schools and research institutions arose from his ideas, notably the **Rudolf Steiner Schools** for maladjusted and handicapped children, focusing on the development of the whole personality of the child. He died at Dornach. » eurhythmics; Goethe; theosophy

Steinway, Heinrich Engelhard [**stiyn**way], originally **Steinweg** [**stiyn**vekh] (1797–1871) US piano-maker, born at Wolfshagen, Germany. He fought at Waterloo, and in 1835 established a piano factory in Brunswick. In 1850 he transferred the business to the USA, where he introduced many innovations into the instrument, such as a cast-iron frame. He died in New York City. » piano

stele (plural **stelai**) [**stee**lee, **stee**liy] In ancient Greece, a carved or inscribed upright rectangular stone which could be used as a gravestone, a boundary marker on property, or a permanent display board for public laws and documents.

stellar evolution The sequence of events and changes covering the entire life cycle of a star. The principal stage of evolution is the nuclear burning of hydrogen to form helium, with a consequential release of energy. Eventually the hydrogen in the core is exhausted, and the star becomes a red giant. In the final stages of evolution there are several paths, depending on the mass of the star: the formation of a white dwarf (stars like our Sun), a neutron star (a few solar masses), or a supernova (tens of solar masses). » helium; hydrogen; neutron star; planetary nebula; protostar; red giant; supernova; white dwarf

stellar populations Groups of stars crudely classified by their age and location within a galaxy. **Population I** stars are young (up to about a thousand million years), found in spiral arms, whereas **Population II** are several thousand million years old, distributed throughout the galaxy. Even at a quite superficial level the two populations are readily distinguished: I has brilliant blue supergiants, whereas in II red giants and faint dwarf stars predominate. The chemical evolution of a galaxy means that the I stars are much richer in the heavier elements synthesized in stellar explosions than the ancient II stars, which formed before heavy elements were abundant. » chemical elements; dwarf star; red giant; star; supergiant

stem (botany) The main axis of a plant, usually but not always above ground, and bearing the buds, leaves, and reproductive organs. It is formed from the apical end of the embryonic axis lying above the cotyledons in the seed, developing into the *plumule* or embryonic shoot. This may form one or several stems, often branched to display the leaves to best advantage for photosynthesis. The stem contains a vascular system: this conducts water and nutrients from the roots to the leaves, and the products of photosynthesis from the leaves to all other parts of the plant. In woody species, the stem is strengthened with additional supporting tissues, and protected by bark and cork layers. Stems may show various modifications, and assume new or additional functions, sometimes taking over from other organs. Thus, runners and rhizomes are stems which grow horizontally above and below ground respectively, giving rise to new plants at intervals; bulbs, corms, and tubers are stems modified to form storage organs that live from one growing season to the next, initiating new growth each year; and the stems of cacti store water. Green stems can photosynthesize, functioning as leaves, and may even be flattened and leaf-like in appearance. Stems can also act as climbing organs, either the whole stem twining or the tips only being modified to form tendrils. » bulb; cactus [i]; corm; cotyledons; photosynthesis; rhizome; root (botany); runner; tuber; vascular tissue

stem (linguistics) » **root** (linguistics)

Sten gun The standard submachine-gun of the British Army from 1942 onwards. The gun was cheap, rugged, and manufactured in large quantities. Its name derives from its designers Stephard and Turpin, and the Enfield factory where it was made. » submachine-gun

Stendhal, pseudonym of **Marie Henri Beyle** (1783–1842) French writer, born at Grenoble. He was a soldier under Napoleon, settled in Paris in 1821, and after the 1830 Revolution was appointed consul at Trieste and Civitavecchia. He wrote biographies, critical works on music, art, and literature, and was best known for his novels, notably *Le Rouge et le noir*

(1831, The Red and the Black) and *La Chartreuse de Parme* (1839, The Charterhouse of Parma). He died in Paris. » French literature; novel

Stenmark, Ingemark (1956–) Swedish skier, born at Tärnaby, 100 miles S of the Arctic Circle. One of the greatest slalom/giant slalom racers, he won both events at the 1980 Olympics with a 3 in/8 cm metal plate in his ankle following an accident the previous year. Between 1974 and 1989 he won a record 86 World Cup races, including a record 13 in the 1979 season. Overall champion three times (1976–8), he won 15 slalom/giant slalom titles, and five world titles. He retired in 1989, and now lives in Monte Carlo. » skiing

Steno, Nicolaus Dan **Steensen, Niels** (1638–86) Danish anatomist and geologist, born in Copenhagen. Brought up a strict Lutheran, he studied anatomy in Amsterdam, where he discovered the duct of the parotid gland and explained the function of the ovaries. He settled in Florence in 1665, as physician to the duke, then became a Catholic, and in 1677 was made a bishop and apostolic vicar to N Germany. He was the first to explain the structure of the Earth's crust. He died at Schwerin, Germany. » fossil; ovary

stenography » **shorthand** [i]

stenotype » **palantype**

step dance A social and often competitive form of dance relying on rhythmically complex footwork using parts of the foot, heel, and toe beats, often performed in clogs. It has been maintained through folk festivals both as a social and an exhibition dance. The structure is part fixed and part improvized in performance. It is currently enjoying a major revival among young people. » traditional dance

stephanotis [stefuh**noh**tis] A twining, evergreen perennial, native to Madagascar; a clustered wax flower; stems to 3 m/10 ft or more; leaves glossy, oblong-elliptical; flowers in axillary clusters, tubular with five spreading lobes, white, strongly fragrant; also called **Madagascar jasmine**. (*Stephanotis floribunda.* Family: *Asclepiadaceae.*) » evergreen plants; perennial; wax plant

Stephen (c.1090–1154) Last Norman King of England (1135–54), the son of Stephen, Count of Blois, and Adela, the daughter of William the Conqueror. He had sworn to accept Henry I's daughter, Empress Matilda, as Queen, but seized the English crown and was recognized as Duke of Normandy on Henry's death in 1135. Though defeated and captured at the Battle of Lincoln (Feb 1141), he was released nine months later after Matilda's supporters had been routed at Winchester. But Matilda strengthened her grip on the West Country; David I of Scotland annexed the N English counties by 1141; and Matilda's husband, Count Geoffrey of Anjou, conquered Normandy by 1144–5. Stephen was also repeatedly challenged by baronial rebellions, and after 18 years of virtually continuous warfare, he was forced in 1153 to accept Matilda's son, the future Henry II, as his lawful successor. His reputation as the classic incompetent king of English mediaeval history is nevertheless undeserved. He was remarkably tenacious in seeking to uphold royal rights, and his war strategy was basically sound. His inability to defend the Norman Empire was due largely to the sheer weight of his military burdens, especially the major offensives of the Scots in the N and the Angevins in the S. He died at Dover. » Angevins; David I; Henry I/II; William I (of England)

Stephen I (c.975–1038), feast day 2 Sep. The first king of Hungary (997–1038). He formed Pannonia and Dacia into a regular kingdom, organized Christianity, and introduced many social and economic reforms. He received from the pope the title of 'Apostolic King' and, according to tradition, St Stephen's Crown, now a Hungarian national treasure. He died at Esztergom, and was canonized in 1083.

Stephen, St (1st-c AD) Feast day 26 Dec. According to the Book of Acts (Chapters 6–7), the first Christian martyr; also one of the seven chosen to manage the finances and alms of the early Church; possibly one of the Hellenists. He was charged by the Jewish authorities for speaking against the Temple and the Law, was tried by the Sanhedrin, and stoned to death by the crowds in Jerusalem. » Acts of the Apostles; Christianity; Hellenists; Sanhedrin

Stephenson, George (1781–1848) British inventor of the locomotive, born at Wylam, Northumberland. He worked in a colliery, received a rudimentary education at night school, and in 1812 became engine-wright at Killingworth. There he constructed his first locomotive (1814). His most famous engine, the 'Rocket', running at 58 km/36 ml an hour, was built in 1829. He worked as an engineer for several railway companies, and became a widely used consultant. He died near Chesterfield, Derbyshire. » engine; locomotive [i]

Stephenson, Robert (1803–59) British civil engineer, born at Willington Quay, Northumberland, the son of George Stephenson. Educated at Newcastle and Edinburgh, he assisted his father in surveying the Stockton and Darlington Railway, worked as a mining engineer in Colombia, and managed his father's locomotive engine-works at Newcastle. He attained independent fame through his tubular design for the Britannia bridge over the Menai Straits in Wales (1850), and for bridges at Conway, Montreal, Newcastle, and elsewhere. He became an MP in 1847, and died in London. » bridge (engineering) [i]; civil engineering; Stephenson, George

Stephenson, Sir William, byname **Intrepid** (1896–1989) Secret intelligence chief, born at Point Douglas, near Winnipeg, a Canadian of Scottish descent. Educated at Argyle High School, Winnipeg, he became involved in British secret intelligence through visits to Germany to buy steel in the early 1930s. His information on Enigma, the German cipher machine, led to MI6's acquisition of a prototype in 1939. In 1940 he was appointed British intelligence chief in N and S America, representing the interests of MI5, MI6, and Special Operations Executive. He died at Paget Parish, Bermuda. The novelist Ian Fleming, a member of his wartime staff, is said to have adopted Stephenson as the model for the character 'M' in the James Bond books. » Special Operations Executive; World War 2

steppe The extensive grassland, treeless region of Eurasia. It extends from the Ukraine through SE European and C Asian Russia to the Manchurian plains. Large areas of steppe are important for wheat growing (eg in the Ukraine). » pampa(s); prairie

steradian [stuh**ray**dian] SI unit of solid angle; symbol sr; an area drawn on the surface of a sphere equal to the square of the radius of the sphere subtends a solid angle of 1 steradian at the centre of the sphere; the total area of a sphere subtends a solid angle of 4π sr at the centre. » geometry; units (scientific)

stere » RR71

stereochemistry The study of the spatial relationships between atoms in molecules, especially the configuration of the atoms bonded to a central atom and the occurrence of geometrical and optical isomers. » chemistry; isomers; molecule

stereolithography » **lithography**

stereophonic sound The recording and transmission of sound which, when reproduced, appears to the listener to come from different directions and to reproduce a sound field similar to that where the sound was originally recorded. It normally uses two microphones, and two loudspeakers to reproduce the sound which has been recorded on two separate channels. Two-track stereo tape recordings appeared in 1954; the first single-groove, two-track stereo records were made in 1957; and FM stereo broadcasts began in 1961. » frequency modulation; sound recording

stereoscopic photography Also termed **3-D** (three-dimensional), the recording and presentation of paired images to give the viewer an impression of solidarity and depth. The basic system, developed from 1845, is to photograph the scene with two cameras whose lenses are 2½ in/65 mm apart, the normal separation of human eyes, and view the results in a device which allows each eye to see only its appropriate right- or left-eye record. Twin-lens cameras produce pairs of colour transparencies to be mounted for individual viewing, or shown to a large audience on two projectors each fitted with a polarizing filter orientated at right angles to the other. The two pictures are superimposed on a metallized screen, and the viewers wear spectacles with corresponding polarizing filters so that each eye sees only the correct image. 3-D cinematography is similarly based on recording right- and left-eye views, either on separate strips or side by side on one wide film. An early form of cinema presentation used anaglyph prints, but current practice for colour film is polarized projection and viewing. Holographic methods for both still and moving monochrome pictures are gaining in importance for scientific and technical applications. » anaglyph; holography; photography; polarizing filter

sterilization 1 A surgical operation to render the individual unable to conceive. In the male the simplest procedure is to divide each vas deferens where it emerges from the inguinal ring, a procedure known as *vasectomy*. In the female, obliteration of the Fallopian tubes is the simplest approach. In either case, access of sperm to the ova is blocked. » contraception; Fallopian tubes 2 » asepsis

sterling The name of the currency of Britain, usually used to distinguish the British pound from other currencies (*pound sterling*). The name derives from the Norman coin known as a *steorling*, which had a star on one face. The **sterling area** was the name given to countries which kept their reserves in sterling – mainly the British Commonwealth nations. Sterling is no longer a reserve currency, this role having been adopted by the US dollar. » currency; dollar

Stern, Otto (1888–1969) German-US physicist, born at Sohrau (now in Poland). He studied at Breslau and taught at several German universities before emigrating to the USA in 1933, and becoming professor of physics at the Carnegie Technical Institute at Pittsburgh (1933–45). In 1920 he carried out an experiment with Walter Gerlach (1889–1979), demonstrating that some atomic nuclei have a magnetic moment, which provided major evidence in favour of quantum theory. He was awarded the Nobel Prize for Physics in 1943, and died at Berkeley, California. » atom; quantum mechanics

Sternberg, Josef von, originally **Jonas Stern** (1894–1969) Austrian film director, born in Vienna. He worked in silent films in Hollywood in the 1920s as scriptwriter, cameraman, and director, but went to Germany to make his most famous film *Der blaue Engel* (1930, The Blue Angel) with Marlene Dietrich. This was followed by six more Hollywood features in which she starred, the last being *The Devil is a Woman* (1935); but his autocratic methods and aloof personality made him unpopular in the studios, and his later career was erratic. His last film *The Saga of Anatahan* (1953) was made in Japan. He died in Hollywood. » Dietrich

Sterne, Laurence (1713–68) British novelist, born at Clonmel, Co Tipperary, Ireland. Educated at Halifax and Cambridge, he was ordained in 1738, and appointed to a living in Yorkshire. In 1759 he wrote the first two volumes of his comic novel, *The Life and Opinions of Tristram Shandy*, which was very well received in London, and the remaining volumes appeared between 1761 and 1767. From 1762 he lived mainly abroad, for health reasons, publishing *A Sentimental Journey through France and Italy* in 1768. He died in London. » English literature; novel

sternum An elongated, almost flat bone lying in the midline of the front wall of the thorax; also known as the **breastbone**. It articulates with the clavicle (providing the only point of attachment of the upper limb and pectoral girdle to the axial skeleton) and the ribs, and overlies a large proportion of the heart, thereby affording it some protection. » bone; clavicle; respiration; thorax; Plate XIII

steroid Any of several natural products, including many hormones, bile acids, and the *sterols*, derived from the non-glyceride portion of fats, the best known of which is cholesterol. The molecule contains the cyclopentanoperhydrophenanthrene nucleus shown in the illustration. Steroids are

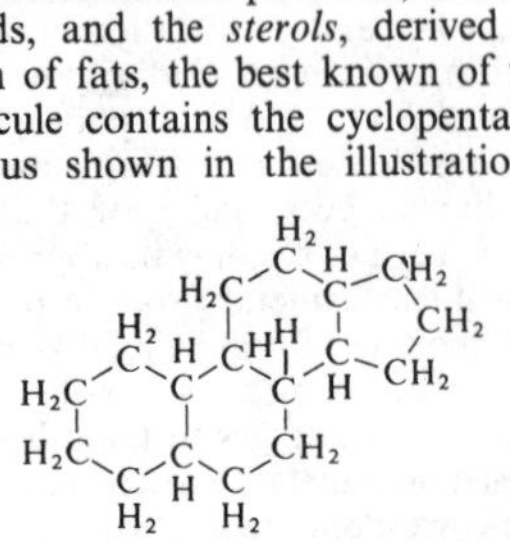

responsible for maintaining many vital functions, including sexual characteristics, salt and water balance, and muscle and bone mass. » anabolic steroids; androgens; cholesterol; corticosteroids; hormones; oestrogens; progesterone; testosterone

Stevenage [steevnij] 51°55N 0°14W, pop (1981) 74 523. Town in Stevenage district, Hertfordshire, SE England; 45 km/28 ml N of London; the first 'new town', 1946; railway; wide range of light industries. » Hertfordshire

Stevens, Wallace (1879–1955) US poet, born at Reading, Pennsylvania. Educated at Harvard, he became a journalist and lawyer, then joined an insurance company at Hartford, where he lived until his death. For many years he wrote abstruse and philosophical verse, but he was over 40 when his first volume, *Harmonium* (1923), was published. His *Collected Poems* appeared in 1954. He is now regarded as a major if idiosyncratic poet. » American literature; poetry

Stevenson, Adlai (Ewing) (1900–65) US Democratic politician, born in Los Angeles. Educated at Princeton, he became a lawyer, took part in several European missions for the State Department (1943–5), and was elected Governor of Illinois (1948). He helped to found the United Nations (1946), stood twice against Eisenhower as presidential candidate (1952, 1956), and was the US delegate to the UN in 1961–5. He died in London. » Eisenhower; United Nations

Stevenson, Robert Louis (Balfour) (1850–94) British writer, born in Edinburgh, Scotland. Educated at Edinburgh, he became a lawyer (1875), then turned to writing travel sketches, essays, and short stories for magazines. The romantic adventure story, *Treasure Island*, brought him fame in 1883, and entered him on a course of romantic fiction which included *Kidnapped* (1886), *The Strange Case of Dr Jekyll and Mr Hyde* (1886), *The Master of Ballantrae* (1889), and the unfinished *Weir of Hermiston* (1896), considered his masterpiece. In 1888 he settled for health reasons at Vailima, Samoa, where he died. » English/Scottish literature; novel

Stevenson screen A shelter for meteorological instruments, particularly thermometers, providing protection from solar radiation. It is a white, wooden box with louvred sides to give ventilation. The thermometers within the screen should be 1.25 m/4.1 ft above the ground to avoid strong temperature gradients at ground level, and to give comparability from screen to screen. It was invented by Thomas Stevenson (1818–87), the father of Robert Louis Stevenson. » meteorology; radiation

Stewart, Jackie, properly **John (Young)** (1939–) British motor racing driver, born at Milton, Dunbartonshire, Scotland. He started in 99 races, and won 27 world championship races between 1965 and 1973, a record until surpassed by Alain Prost in 1987. He was world champion in 1969 (driving a Matra), 1971, and 1973 (both Tyrrell). He retired at the end of 1973, and took up a career in broadcasting. He is also expert at clay pigeon shooting, and came close to Olympic selection. » motor racing; Prost

Stewart, James (Maitland) (1908–) US film actor, born at Indiana, Pennsylvania. He took a degree in architecture at Princeton, and started in films in 1935, establishing a character of honesty and integrity in *You Can't Take It With You* (1938), and the comedy *The Philadelphia Story* (1940), for which he won an Oscar. He served with distinction in the US Air Force during World War 2, and returned to make a series of outstanding Westerns (1950–5) and two successes for Hitchcock, *Rear Window* (1954) and *Vertigo* (1958). His later work continued to provide a wide range of character roles, including *Fools' Parade* (1971) and *Right of Way* (1982).

Stewart Island pop (1983e) 540; area 1 735 sq km/670 sq ml. Island of New Zealand, to the S of South Island, across the Foveaux Strait; highest point, Mt Anglem (977 m/3 205 ft); a refuge for animal and bird life; largely uninhabited; small settlement of Oban on Halfmoon Bay; accessible by plane or ferry from Bluff, S of Invercargill; fishing. » New Zealand [i]

Stewarts » **Stuarts**

stibine [stibeen] SbH_3. A highly poisonous gas formed by the reduction of antimony compounds. » antimony; Marsh test

stibnite An antimony sulphide (Sb_2S_3) mineral found in low-temperature hydrothermal veins, lead-grey in colour, often occurring as long prismatic crystals. It is the chief ore of antimony. » antimony

stick insect A large twig-like insect with an elongate body and legs; resemblance to twig enhanced by habit of swaying from side to side; up to 300 mm/12 in long; feeding on leaves; also known as **walking sticks**. (Order: *Phasmida*. Family: *Phasmatidae*, c.2 000 species.) » insect [i]

stickleback Small marine or freshwater fish of the family *Gasterosteidae* (5 genera), common throughout the N hemisphere; body typically elongate with a number of strong dorsal spines; mouth small and protruding; male builds nest, and guards developing eggs; includes the familiar and ubiquitous **3-spine stickleback** (*Gasterosteus aculeatus*), found in streams and lakes as well as shallow marine habitats; length up to 6 cm/2½ in. » fish [i]

Stieglitz, Alfred (1864–1946) US photographer, born at Hoboken, New Jersey, but studied in Berlin and worked in Europe during the 1880s. He founded the American Photo-Secession Group with Edward Steichen in 1902, and consistently influenced the development of creative photography as an art form through his magazine *Camera Work* (1903–17) and his gallery of modern art in New York City. His polemical writings and his own creative work continued until his death, in New York City. » Steichen

Stiernhielm, Georg [**steern**hyelm] (1598–1672) Swedish poet, born at Vika, and educated at Uppsala and in Germany. Ennobled by Gustavus Adolphus (1594–1632), he was the favourite court poet of Queen Christina. Besides much lyric poetry, he wrote a didactic allegorical poem *Hercules* (1647). Known as the father of Swedish poetry, he died in Stockholm. » poetry; Swedish literature

stifftail A diving duck, native to the New World, S Europe, Africa, W Asia, and Australasia; long, stiff, tail feathers; inhabits freshwater; mainly nocturnal. (Tribe: *Oxyurini*, especially Genus: *Oxyura*, 6 species. Subfamily: *Anatinae*.) » diving duck; duck

stigma In flowering plants, the part of the carpel receptive to pollen. Sticky secretions, corrugated surfaces, or hairs may help collect and retain pollen grains. Those of wind-pollinated flowers are often feathery, to increase the contact area, while those of insect-pollinated flowers are often borne on elongated styles which present the stigma in the appropriate position to pick up pollen from the insect's body. The stigma, and often the style, may through physiological means operate a complex compatibility system which accepts only pollen of the correct type. » carpel; flowering plants; pollination; style

stigmata Marks or wounds appearing on the human body, similar to those of the crucified Jesus. They may be temporary (related to ecstasy or revelation) or permanent, and are alleged to be a sign of miraculous participation in Christ's passion. » cross; Jesus Christ

stilbestrol/stilboestrol » **DES**

Stilicho, Flavius [**stil**ikoh] (?–408) Roman general, half-Roman, half-Vandal, who was virtual ruler of the W Roman Empire (395–408) under the feeble Emperor Honorius. His greatest achievements were his victories over Alaric and the Visigoths in N Italy at Pollentia (402) and Verona (403). » Alaric I; Honorius

still life In art, the representation of objects such as books, candles, cooking utensils, musical instruments, fruit, flowers, etc. Still life was painted in antiquity; in W Europe it flourished above all in the Netherlands in the 17th-c. Some still lifes are obviously symbolic; others seem to be demonstrations of painterly skill. » painting; vanitas

stilt A long-legged wading bird, especially *Himantopus himantopus* (from warm regions worldwide, with many names for different races); also the **banded** or **red-breasted stilt** (*Cladorhynchus leucocephala*), from Australia and New Zealand. (Family: *Recurvirostridae*, 2 species.) » sandpiper

Stilwell, Joseph Warren, byname **Vinegar Joe** (1883–1946) US soldier, born at Palatka, Florida. Educated at West Point, he fought in World War 1, and later became an authority on China. He was military attaché at the US embassy in Beijing (Peking) 1932–9, and in 1942 commanded US forces in China, Burma, and India. Recalled after a dispute with Jiang Jieshi (Chiang Kai-shek) in 1944, he commanded the US 10th army in the Pacific until the end of the war. He died in San Francisco. » World War 2

stimulants Drugs such as amphetamine which produce feelings of wakefulness, alertness, elation, and an increased capacity to concentrate. Caffeine is a mild stimulant. Contrary to popular belief, alcohol is not a stimulant. » amphetamine; caffeine; drug addiction

stimulated emission » **laser** [i]

stinging nettle A perennial with creeping rhizomes often forming large patches, native or introduced throughout temperate regions; leaves heart-shaped, toothed; flowers tiny, green, in drooping spikes; males and females on separate plants. The whole plant is covered in stinging hairs acting like hypodermic syringes, each with a bulbous base containing acid, and a brittle, needle-like tip. When touched, the tip pierces the skin and breaks off, while pressure on the base injects acid, causing a sting and subsequent rash. Wilting or cooking removes the ability to sting. The leaves are used as a vegetable and for tea; the stems yield tough fibres for cloth. (*Urtica dioica*. Family: *Urticaceae*.) » dead-nettle; perennial; rhizome

stingray Any of several bottom-living rays (families: *Dasyatidae*, *Potamotrygonidae*, *Urolophidae*) in which the tail is whip-like and armed with one or more sharp poison spines; includes the large European stingray, *Dasyatis pastinaca*, common in shallow inshore waters from the North Sea to the Mediterranean; body length up to 2.5 m/8 ft. » ray

stinkhorn The fruiting body of some fungi of the order *Phallales*; body initially phallus-like, with a white stem and swollen ovoid cap; cap dissolves into putrid slime, containing spores that are dispersed by flies attracted over great distances by the foetid odour. (Subdivision: *Basidiomycetes*.) » Basidiomycetes; fungus

stipendiary magistrate In England and Wales, a salaried and legally qualified magistrate. Such magistrates may sit alone when trying cases, unlike lay magistrates, and are found in London and other large towns. » justice of the peace

Stirling 56°07N 3°57W, pop (1981) 38 842. Capital of Central region, C Scotland, on S bank of R Forth, 34 km/21 ml NE of Glasgow; railway; university (1967); machinery, textiles, brick making, coachbuilding; Stirling castle (12th-c), former residence of Scottish kings; ruins of Cambuskenneth Abbey (1147), scene of Bruce's parliament (1326); Church of the Holy Rude (1414), MacRobert Arts Centre, Smith Art Gallery and Museum; Wallace Monument (1870), 2 km/1¼ ml NNE; Stirling Festival (May). » Bruce, Robert; Central (Scotland); Scotland [i]; Wallace, William

Stirling Range Mountain range in SW Western Australia; extends 64 km/40 ml parallel with SW coast; rises to 1 109 m/3 638 ft at Bluff Knoll. » Western Australia

stitchwort Either of two species of bluish-green perennials with brittle stems native to woodlands in Europe, N Africa, and Asia Minor; leaves paired, narrow, rather grass-like; flowers white, 5-petalled. The **greater stitchwort** (*Stellaria holostea*) has flowers 2–3 cm/¾–1½ in in diameter, petals divided to halfway. The **lesser stitchwort** (*Stellaria graminea*) has flowers 0.5–1.2 cm/0.2–0.5 in in diameter, with petals divided to more than halfway. (Genus: *Stellaria*. Family: *Caryophyllaceae*.) » perennial

stoat A mammal of family *Mustelidae*, native to Europe, Asia, and N America; in summer, resembles a large weasel (length, 500 mm/20 in) with black tip to tail; winter coat (*ermine*) white, with black tail tip; inhabits woodland and tundra; eats mainly rabbits. (*Mustela erminea*.) » Mustelidae; weasel

stochastic processes » **random processes**

stock An annual or perennial, growing to 80 cm/30 in, native to Europe and Asia; slightly woody stems; leaves greyish; flowers in spikes, purple, red or white, cross-shaped, often double in cultivars. It includes **garden stock** or **gilliflower** (*Matthiola incana*) and **night-scented stock** (*Matthiola bicornis*). (Genus: *Matthiola*, 55 species. Family: *Cruciferae*.) » annual; cultivar; perennial

stock-car racing A type of motor racing which takes different forms in the USA and UK. In the USA, highly supercharged production cars race around banked concreted tracks. In the UK, 'bangers' (old cars) race against each other on a round or oval track with the intention of being the last car still moving at the end of the race. Several 'rough' tactics amongst drivers are allowed, in the hope of eliminating a fellow driver. » motor racing

stock exchange A building where stocks, shares, and bonds are traded. The London Stock Exchange, located in the City of London near the Bank of England, deals in some 7 000 securities. Until 1986, business was carried out on 'the floor of the House', ie in the Stock Exchange itself. Individuals and institutions wishing to buy or sell securities would contact a stockbroker, who would place the order with a jobber (a trader on the floor). 27 October 1986 was the date of the 'Big Bang' when the distinction between brokers and jobbers was abolished, as were minimum commission scales; and a computerized system was introduced for share trading. Firms are now brokers/dealers; they may buy and sell on their own account as well as act as agents for others. The London Stock Exchange has some 5 000 individual members and over 300 member firms. Most capital cities in the West have a stock exchange, Wall Street in New York City being the largest. » shares; Stock Exchange Automated Quotations; stock market; stocks

Stock Exchange Automated Quotations (SEAQ) A system introduced in 1986 in the London Stock market for trading securities. It is a computerized market-making activity which enables member firms to buy and sell and quote prices for specific securities. The prices are therefore known to all continuously. » stock exchange

stock market The system of buying and selling stocks and shares; also, a building in which these transactions take place (the *stock exchange*). A stock market 'crash' refers to a situation when the prices of stocks fall dramatically, resulting in many bankruptcies. The most famous case was the Wall Street crash of 1929; a less dramatic crash also occurred in October 1987 in most world stock markets. » bear market; Dow Jones Index; equity (economics); stock exchange

Stockhausen, Karlheinz (1928–) German composer, born at Mödrath. He studied at Cologne and Bonn, joined the *musique concrète* group in Paris, and experimented with compositions based on electronic sounds. In 1953 he helped to found the electronic music studio at Cologne, and became director there in 1963. In 1971 he was appointed professor of composition at the Hochschule für Musik in Cologne. He has written orchestral, choral, and instrumental works, including some which combine electronic and normal sonorities, such as *Kontakte* (1960), and parts of a huge operatic cycle, *Licht* (Light). » electronic music

Stockholm 59°20N 18°03E, pop (1982) 649 587. Seaport and capital of Sweden; on a group of islands and the adjacent mainland, where L Mälar joins the Saltsjö, an arm of the Baltic Sea; largest city in Sweden; founded, 1255; important trading centre of the Hanseatic League; capital, 1436; bishopric; airport; railway; underground railway; university (1878); metalworking, engineering, textiles, foodstuffs, brewing, tourism; royal palace (18th-c), German church (17th-c), national museum, Drottningholm Palace (royal family residence). » Hanseatic League; Sweden [i]

Stockholm syndrome The unnatural close relationship that occasionally develops between a hostage of a criminal or terrorist and his or her captor. It was first described in a woman held hostage in a bank in Sweden who remained faithful to the thief during his imprisonment.

Stockport 53°25N 2°10W, pop (1981) 136 792. Town in Stockport borough, Greater Manchester, NW England; at junction of the Tame and Goyt Rivers which join to form the R Mersey, 10 km/6 ml SE of Manchester; railway; Manchester airport nearby; electronics, computers, aerospace, textiles (especially cotton), printing, engineering, foodstuffs. » Manchester, Greater

stocks A term which in general refers to financial assets. In accountancy, stocks are physical items held in storage, ie materials or goods for sale; in the USA, these are known as *inventories*. In business and finance, the term refers specifically to securities or documents having a value. These may be shares in a company or loans to governments or companies. The US expression 'common stock' refers to the British 'ordinary shares' of a company. » equity (economics); shares

Stockton, Earl of » Macmillan, Harold

Stockton 37°58N 121°17W, pop (1980) 149 779. Inland seaport and city in San Joaquin County, C California, USA; on a deep-water channel to the San Joaquin R; founded, 1847; railway; university (1851); food processing, marine engineering, agricultural trade. » California

Stockton-on-Tees 54°34N 1°19W, pop (1981) 87 223. Town in Stockton-on-Tees district, Cleveland, NE England; on the R Tees estuary; developed with the opening of the Stockton–Darlington railway in 1825; ship repairing, engineering, chemicals. » Cleveland (UK)

Stoicism A philosophical movement which flourished in Greece and Rome (300 BC–180 AD), founded by Zeno of Citium. It included such figures as Seneca, Epictetus, and Marcus Aurelius. Stoicism emphasized that all people are equally part of a law-governed physical nature; the ideal life is one of unperturbedness and duty to the dictates of this natural order. » Zeno of Citium

Stoke-on-Trent 53°00N 2°10W, pop (1987e) 246 700. Industrial city in Staffordshire, C England; part of the Potteries urban area; on the R Trent, 217 km/135 ml NW of London; an amalgam (1910) of the former Tunstall, Burslem, Hanley, Stoke-on-Trent, Fenton, and Longton municipal authorities; University of Keele (1962) nearby; railway; clayware (largest producer in the world), coal, steel, chemicals, engineering, rubber, paper; birthplace of Josiah Wedgwood and Arnold Bennett; Wedgwood museum at Barlaston (7 km/4 ml S). » Bennett, Arnold; ceramics; Staffordshire; Wedgwood, Josiah

Stoker, Bram, properly **Abraham** (1847–1912) Irish writer, born and educated in Dublin. He studied law and science, and partnered Henry Irving in running the Lyceum Theatre from 1878. Among several books, he is remembered for the classic horror tale *Dracula* (1897). He died in London. » Irving, Henry; novel

Stokes' law In physics, a law expressing the viscous drag force F acting on a spherical object of radius r moving with velocity v through a fluid of viscosity η as $F=6\pi\eta rv$; stated in 1845 by British physicist George Stokes (1819–1903). It determines the terminal velocity of small raindrops, or small bubbles in water. » drag; terminal velocity; viscosity

Stokowski, Leopold (Antonin Stanisław Bołesławawicz) [sto**kof**skee] (1882–1977) US conductor of Polish origin, born in London. He studied in London, and built up an international reputation as a conductor with orchestras of Philadelphia (1912–36), New York (1946–50), and Houston (1955–60). In 1962 he founded the American Symphony Orchestra in New York City. Also known for his music in Walt Disney's *Fantasia* (1940) and other films, he died at Nether Wallop, Hampshire. » Disney

STOL An acronym for a fixed-wing aircraft specially designed for **Short Take-Off and Landing**. These aircraft usually accomplish their function by special aerodynamic devices providing high lift. The ability to have short take-offs is highly dependent on the aircraft being able to perform well at low forward speeds, and until World War 2 this was not a major problem because of the generally low speeds employed. The War brought a need for slow-speed STOL observation aircraft, of which the Fieseler Fi 156 Storch was the most famous. » aerodynamics [i]; aircraft [i]; jet engine [i]

stolon A long shoot which bends under its own weight to the ground, and roots at the tip or at the nodes to form new plants. » runner; stem (botany)

Stolypin, Peter Arkadyevich [**stol**ipin] (1862–1911) Russian statesman and Prime Minister (1906–11), born in Dresden, educated at the University of St Petersburg. After service in the Ministry of the Interior (from 1884) he became Governor of Saratov province (1903–6), where he ruthlessly put down local peasant uprisings and helped to suppress the revolutionary upheavals of 1905. As Premier, he introduced a series of agrarian reforms, which had only limited success. In 1907 he suspended the Second Duma, and arbitrarily limited the franchise. He was assassinated in Kiev. » duma; Nicholas II; Revolution of 1905

stomach A digestive pouch between the oesophagus and the duodenum, which stores food, secretes gastric juice (that kills ingested bacteria and initiates protein digestion) and, by wave-like contractions, churns and releases its contents into the duodenum at a controlled rate. Its size and position in humans is related to body build, but varies within the same individual with posture (standing, lying down) and contents (empty, full). It is divided into the *cardiac* region around the cardiac orifice (where the oesophagus opens into the stomach), the *fundus* (the region above the level of the cardiac orifice), the *body*, and the *pylorus*, which opens into the duodenum at the *pyloric orifice*. Its most fixed parts are the cardiac and pyloric orifices, the latter remaining closed except for the periodic release of the stomach contents. » duodenum; gastric ulcer; gastritis; oesophagus; peptic ulcer; Plate XII

stomata In plants, pores concentrated on the lower leaf surface through which gases and water vapour enter and leave the leaf. They are bounded by *guard cells*, which bend when swollen with water and open the stoma, or straighten when dehydrated and close it, preventing further water loss from the leaf. » leaf [i]; lenticel; transpiration

Stone Age » Three Age System

stone carving » sculpture

stone circles Circular or near-circular rings of prehistoric standing stones found, particularly in Britain and Ireland, in the Late Neolithic and Early Bronze Age. About 900 examples survive, some as much as 400 m/1 300 ft in diameter. They most probably functioned as temples in which celestial events, the passing of the seasons, and the fertility of the land and people could be celebrated. » Avebury; megalith; Stonehenge; Three Age System

stone curlew » thick-knee

Stone Mountain Memorial A memorial carving on the exposed face of Stonewall Mountain in NW Georgia, USA. The work, which was completed in 1972, depicts Confederate leaders Jefferson Davis, Robert E Lee, and 'Stonewall' Jackson. It was executed by sculptors Gutzon Borglum, Augustus Lukeman, and Walter Kirtland Hancock, who worked on it in succession over a period of 50 years. » Confederate States of America; Davis, Jefferson; Jackson, Thomas Jonathon; Lee, Robert E

stone-plover » plover

stonebass » wreckfish

stonechat A thrush native to the Old World (except Australasia); male with dark head, white neck spots and pale reddish breast; inhabits open country; eats insects, grain, and berries; often perches on bush, fence, etc. (*Saxicola torquata*.) » thrush (bird)

stonecrop A large genus of succulents, mostly perennials, native to N temperate regions; leaves very narrow to almost circular, but always fleshy; flowers 5-petalled, starry, mainly white, yellow, or red. (Genus: *Sedum*, 300 species. Family: *Crassulaceae*.) » perennial; succulent

stonefish Grotesque fish found in shallow inshore waters of the Indo-Pacific region, especially around coral reefs; body strongly camouflaged in shape and colour; length 30–60 cm/12–24 in; dorsal fin armed with sharp poison spines that can inflict extremely painful stings. (Genus: *Synanceia*. Family: *Synanceiidae*.) » fish [i]

stonefly A primitive, winged insect typically found among stones along river banks; adults are poor fliers that run and hide when disturbed; larvae usually aquatic in running water. (Order: *Plecoptera*, c.2 000 species.) » insect [i]; larva

Stonehenge A prehistoric sanctuary near Amesbury, S England, 130 km/80 ml W of London; a world heritage site. In use c.3100–1100 BC, it was constructed in three phases: c.2800 BC, a low bank and ditch of earth c.110 m/360 ft in diameter; c.2100 BC, a double ring of 80 pillars of South Wales bluestone, apparently dismantled before completion; and c.2000 BC, the surviving monument, a 30 m/100 ft diameter lintelled circle and inner horseshoe of 80 dressed sarsen (sandstone) blocks, each weighing 20–50 tonnes. Alignment on the midsummer sunrise/midwinter sunset implies prehistoric use for seasonal festivals, but the association with the druids dates only from 1905, and has no historical basis. » Avebury; stone circles

stoneware A type of ceramic midway between pottery and porcelain, made of clay and a fusible stone. It is fired to a point where partial vitrification renders it impervious to liquids, but unlike porcelain it is seldom more than slightly translucent. » porcelain; pottery

stoolball An 11-a-side bat-and-ball game resembling cricket and rounders. The batter defends his wicket, a 1 ft (30 cm) square wooden board 4 ft 8 in (1.4 m) from the ground, which the underarm bowler attempts to hit. Runs are scored in a similar way to cricket. The bat is wooden, but similar in shape to a tennis racket. » cricket (sport) [i]; rounders

stop-go policy A government economic policy in which action taken to boost the economy (*go*) results in inflation or exchange rate problems. Action is then taken to cure these problems, which results in a slow-down of the economy (*stop*). The phrase was particularly applied to the incomes policies tried out in many countries without much success in the 1960s. » prices and incomes policy

Stopes, Marie (Charlotte Carmichael) (1880–1958) British pioneer advocate of birth control, suffragette, and palaeontologist, born in Edinburgh, Scotland. Educated at London and Munich, in 1904 she became the first female science lecturer at Manchester. Alarmed at the unscientific way in which men and women embarked upon married life, she wrote a number of books on the subject, of which *Married Love* (1918), in which birth control is mentioned, caused a storm of controversy. She later founded the first birth control clinic in N London (1921). The author of over 70 books, she died near Dorking, Surrey. » contraception; women's liberation movement

Stoppard, Tom, originally **Tom Straussler** (1937–) British dramatist, born at Zlín, Czechoslovakia. He lived in Singapore, moving with his family to England in 1946, where he was educated. In 1960 he went to London as a freelance journalist and theatre critic, and wrote radio plays. He made his name in 1967 with *Rosencrantz and Guildenstern are Dead*. Other plays include the philosophical satire *Jumpers* (1972), *Travesties* (1974), and the romantic comedy, *The Real Thing* (1982). He has also written a novel, *Lord Malquist and Mr Moon* (1966), short stories, television plays, and film scripts. His wife, **Miriam Stoppard** (1937–) is a doctor, writer, and popular broadcaster on physical health and child care. » drama; English literature; satire

storax An aromatic gum obtained by making incisions in the trunk of sweet gums (*Liquidambar*) and the storax tree (*Styrax offinale*), a small deciduous tree with drooping clusters of 3–6 white flowers, native to the Mediterranean region. » deciduous plants; sweet gum; tree [i]

Storey, David (Malcolm) (1933–) British novelist and playwright, born at Wakefield, Yorkshire, and educated at the Slade School of Fine Art, London. The action of *This Sporting Life* (1960), his first novel, is set in the world of rugby league, and the characters of his play *The Changing Room* (1972) are footballers. The play *Life Class* (1974), is set in an art college. Other novels, such as *Saville* (1976), use autobiographical material from his South Yorkshire mining county background, as does the play *In Celebration* (1969). » drama; English literature; novel

stork A large bird, native to warm regions worldwide; long legs, neck, and long stout bill; flies with neck and legs outstretched; inhabits forest, dry country, or water margins; eats invertebrates, small vertebrates, or carrion. The **white stork** (*Ciconia ciconia*) is the stork of fable, a summer visitor to Europe, which prefers to nest on buildings; its numbers in N Europe have diminished in the 20th-c. (Family: *Ciconiidae*, 17 species.) » Abdim's stork; adjutant; ibis; jabiru; marabou

storksbill An annual or perennial, native to temperate regions; leaves divided into two rows of leaflets; flowers white, pink, or purple; fruit with a long point resembling a bird's beak. Changes in humidity cause the beak of ripe fruits to twist and untwist like a corkscrew, helping to embed the seed in the soil. (Genus: *Erodium*, 90 species. Family: *Geraniaceae*.) » annual; perennial

storm An intense meteorological disturbance, categorized on the Beaufort scale as force 10 (storm) or force 11 (violent storm). Wind speeds range from 25–32 m per sec/55–72 ml per hour. » Beaufort Scale; thunderstorm; wind [i]; RR15

Storm, (Hans) Theodor Woldsen (1817–88) German writer, born at Husum. He became a lawyer (1864–80), wrote a volume of poems (1857), and became known for his novellas, notably *Der Schimmelreiter* (1888, The Rider on the White Horse). He died at Hademarschen. » German literature; novella

storm-cock » **mistle thrush**

storm petrel A petrel, worldwide, found at sea unless breeding; eats plankton snatched from sea surface; nests in burrows. Some (subfamily: *Oceanitinae*) 'walk' across the water surface in flight; others (subfamily: *Hydrobatinae*) swoop over the water. Many make long migrations. (Family: *Hydrobatidae*, 22 species.) » petrel

storm surge A localized rise in sea level produced by on-shore winds and reduced atmospheric pressure caused by large storms. Much of the flood damage produced by hurricanes, typhoons, and other major storms is the result of storm surge. Along the coasts of India and China these surges have resulted in death tolls of hundreds of thousands. One of the most devastating surges in recent history occurred in the North Sea during the winter of 1953, causing the sea level to rise more than 3 m/10 ft along the coast of the Netherlands.

Stormont A suburb of Belfast, N Ireland, in which are situated Parliament House (built in 1932 to house the parliament of N Ireland, and now the home of the N Ireland Assembly), Stormont House, and Stormont Castle. » Belfast

Stornoway 58°12N 6°23W, pop(1981) 8638. Port capital of Western Isles region, NW Scotland, on E coast of Lewis; airfield; fishing, oil supply services, tweeds, knitwear, tourism; An Lanntair art gallery, Museum Nan Eilean Steornabhagh. » Scotland [i]; Western Isles

Stoss [shtohs] or **Stozz, Veit** (c.1447–1533) German woodcarver and sculptor, born and died in Nuremberg. He worked mainly in Kraków (1477–96), where he carved the high altar of the Marienkirche. Back in Nuremberg, he worked for 30 years in various churches, including St Lorenz's, which contains his 'Annunciation'. » German art; sculpture

stout » **beer** [i]

Stowe, Harriet (Elizabeth) Beecher (1811–96) US novelist, born at Litchfield, Connecticut. She became a teacher, and in 1836 married the Rev C E Stowe, a professor of theology, with whom she settled at Brunswick, Maine. She became famous through her *Uncle Tom's Cabin* (1852), which immediately focused anti-slavery sentiment in the North. Her other novels include *Dred* (1856) and *The Minister's Wooing* (1859), and she also wrote essays and poems. She died at Hartford, Connecticut. » American Civil War; American literature; novel

Strabane [stra**ban**], Gaelic **An Srath Ban** 54°49N 7°27W, pop(1981) 10340. Market town in Tyrone, W Northern Ireland; on the Mourne and Finn Rivers, where they meet to form the R Foyle; Irish border town; textiles, engineering, salmon fishing. » Tyrone

strabismus » **squint**

Strabo ('squint-eyed') (c.60 BC–after AD 21) Greek geographer and historian, born at Amasia in Pontus. He seems to have spent his life in travel and study, visiting Greece and Egypt, and settling in Rome after AD 14. Only a few fragments remain of his 47-volume historical work, but his *Geographica* in 17 books has survived almost complete, and provides extensive observations on the Mediterranean area, as well as copious references to previous writers.

Strachey, (Giles) Lytton (1880–1932) British biographer, born in London. Educated at Cambridge, he lived in London, and became a member of the Bloomsbury group of writers and artists. He began his writing career as a critic, but turned to biography, creating a literary bombshell with his *Eminent Victorians* (1918), an impertinent challenge to the self-assured, monumental studies previously typical of this genre. Later works included *Queen Victoria* (1921) and *Elizabeth and Essex* (1928). He died near Hungerford, Berkshire. » biography; Bloomsbury group

Stradivari or **Stradivarius, Antonio** (c.1644–1737) Italian violin maker, born and died at Cremona. He experimented with the design of string instruments, and assisted by his two sons perfected the Cremona type of violin. It is thought that he made over a thousand violins, violas, and violoncellos between 1666 and his death; about 650 of these still exist. » violin

Strafford, Thomas Wentworth, 1st Earl of (1593–1641) English statesman, born in London. Educated at Cambridge, he was knighted in 1611, and in 1614 succeeded to his baronetcy, and entered parliament. He acted with the Opposition (1625–8), but after being appointed President of the North and Baron Wentworth (1628), he supported Charles I. In 1632 he became Lord Deputy of Ireland, where he imposed firm rule. In 1639 he became the King's principal adviser, and Earl of Strafford. His suppression of the rebellion in Scotland failed, and he was impeached by the Long Parliament. Despite a famous defence at Westminster, he was executed on Tower Hill. » Bishops' Wars; Charles I (of England); Long Parliament

straight line In geometry, a line such that, if P,Q,R are any three points on this line, the gradient of PQ is equal to the gradient of QR. In Cartesian geometry, the equation of a straight line can be written in the form $ax+by+c=0$. » Cartesian co-ordinates; geometry

strain The fractional change in the dimensions of some object subjected to stress, expressed as a number. For force acting along the axis of a rod, **linear strain** is the change in length divided by the original length. **Volume strain** is the fractional change in volume for an object pressured on all sides. **Shear strain** measures the effectiveness of a twisting force. » elastic hysteresis; mechanical properties of matter; stress (physics)

Straits Settlements The name given to the former British crown colony which consisted of Singapore, Malacca, the Dindings, Penang, and Province Wellesley. All became part of Malaysia in 1963, and Singapore became independent in 1965. » Malaysia [i]

strangeness In particle physics, an internal additive quantum number conserved in strong and electromagnetic interactions, but not in weak interactions; symbol S. It was introduced during the 1930s to explain 'strange' reactions observed in cosmic ray experiments. Strange quarks are those having strangeness $S=-1$; strange particles contain at least one strange quark. » particle physics; quantum numbers; quark

Strangford Lough Inlet of the North Channel, E Northern Ireland; separated from the sea (E) by the Ards peninsula; length, 27 km/17 ml; width, 6 km/4 ml; entrance c.1 km/¾ ml wide, 8 km/5 ml long; contains several islands. » Northern Ireland [i]

strangler fig » **fig**

Stranraer [stran**rah**] 54°54N 5°02W, pop(1981) 10873. Port capital of Wigtown district, Dumfries and Galloway, SW Scotland; at the head of Loch Ryan; railway; ferries to N Ireland; footwear, metal products, transport equipment; Wigtown district museum. » Dumfries and Galloway; Scotland [i]

Strasberg, Lee (1901–82) US theatre director, actor, and teacher, born at Budzanow, Austria. He became an actor in 1925, and gained a reputation with the Theatre Guild of New York. In 1931 he was involved in the formation of the Group Theatre, with which he worked as a teacher, evolving a technique (influenced by Stanislavsky) which became known everywhere as 'the method'. He exercised great influence as director of the Actors' Studio (1949–82), his pupils including Marlon Brando, Ann Bancroft, and Paul Newman. He died in New York City. » Actors' Studio; Group Theatre; Stanislavsky

Strasbourg [**straz**berg], Fr [straz**boor**], Ger **Strassburg** [**shtras**-boorkh], ancient **Argentoratum** 48°35N 7°42E, pop(1982) 252264. Industrial and commercial city, and capital of Bas-Rhin department, NE France; on the R Ill, W of its junction with the R Rhine; sixth largest city in France; important transportation centre and largest river port in France; part of a bishopric since 1003; free imperial city in 13th-c; ceded to France, 1697; taken by Germany, 1871; returned to France, 1918; railway junction; university (founded 1537); trade in minerals, building materials, petroleum products, grain; iron and steel, metalworking, engineering, furniture, foodstuffs, paper, textiles, tanning; seat of the Council of Europe, European Parliament, European Commission of Human Rights, and European Science Foundation; printing developed here by Gutenberg; tourist centre of Alsace; congress and conference centre; Gothic Cathedral of Notre-Dame (begun 1015, with noted 14th-c astronomical clock), Château des Rohan (1728–42), old town hall, Palais de l'Europe (1972–7), La Petite France (16th-c quarter of old Strasbourg); international music festival (Jun). » Alsace; Council of Europe; European Parliament; Gutenberg

Strategic Arms Limitation Treaty » **SALT**

Strategic Arms Reduction Talks » **START**

strategic capability The capability of states with long-range missiles or aircraft to make war or carry out reprisals. It is divided into a number of categories depending on the ability or otherwise of a state to respond to an attack, and whether it can destroy an adversary's strategic military installations or its civilian industries and cities. A **first-strike capability** defines the state's capacity to launch an initial attack. In a **pre-emptive strike**, the intention is to disarm an enemy by 'getting in first', thereby reducing or removing one's vulnerability to attack. A **second-strike capability** is the capacity to survive a first attack with sufficient resources intact to be able to inflict unacceptably high damage on an aggressor. Such a capability relies on having appropriate early warning systems of an attack, and the holding of missiles in underground silos and on submarines.

Strategic Defense Initiative » **SDI**

strategic studies The academic study of the military, political, economic, and technological factors which affect the relations between nations. As distinct from military science, which from ancient times has concerned itself with the deployment of personnel and material in war, strategic studies looks at the continuous process of military relations between nations in war and peace, and has risen to particular prominence in the age of nuclear weapons. » military science

Stratford-upon-Avon 52°12N 1°41W, pop (1981) 21 732. Town in Stratford-upon-Avon district, Warwickshire, C England; on the R Avon, 13 km/8 ml SW of Warwick; birthplace of William Shakespeare; railway; tourism, engineering, boatbuilding, textiles; Royal Shakespeare Theatre (season Apr–Jan); Shakespeare's birthplace; Anne Hathaway's Cottage; Holy Trinity Church (where Shakespeare and his wife are buried); Shakespeare's birthday and St George's Day (23 Apr); Mop Fair (12 Oct). » Shakespeare [i]; Warwickshire

Strathclyde [strath**kliyd**] pop (1981) 2 404 532; area 13 537 sq km/5 225 sq ml. Region in W and C Scotland, divided into 19 districts; bounded by the Atlantic Ocean (W); encloses the basin of the R Clyde; Highland area (N), including lochs, mountains, and islands; lower part of the Clyde contains Glasgow and Clydeside, industrial centre of Scotland containing c.50% of the country's population; part of the Southern Uplands to the S; capital, Glasgow; major towns include Paisley, Motherwell, Greenock, Airdrie, Dumbarton, Hamilton, Coatbridge, Kilmarnock; coal, engineering, shipbuilding, farming; tourism in the isles. » Arran; Clyde, River; Clydeside; Glasgow; Hebrides; Scotland [i]

stratification A geological term for the formation of layers in sedimentary rock in which breaks in the deposition or changes in the nature of the deposited material define visible bedding planes. The term is also used in describing sequences of lava flows. » lava; sedimentary rock; stratigraphy

stratigraphy A branch of geology concerned with the study of sequences of layers of rock, usually sedimentary. It aims to unravel changes in their depositional environment, and to correlate rocks of the same age in different places by their rock type and fossil content. » sedimentary rock

stratocumulus clouds Low layer clouds with a distinct cumulus or rounded shape; layers of cloud are rolled into rounded forms. They are white or grey in colour, and are found at c.500–2 000 m/1 600–6 500 ft. Cloud symbol: Sc. » cloud [i]; cumulus clouds; stratus clouds

stratosphere The layer of the Earth's atmosphere at a height of c.15–50 km/10–30 ml, separated from the troposphere below by the tropopause, and from the mesosphere above by the stratopause. A stable layer, unaffected by the weather, it has a gradually increasing temperature with height from about −50°C to around 0°C. It contains the ozone layer. » atmosphere [i]; mesosphere; ozone layer; troposphere

Stratton, Charles (Sherwood), byname **Tom Thumb** (1838–83) US midget showman, born at Bridgeport, Connecticut. He stopped growing at six months of age, and stayed 63 cm/25 in until his teens, eventually reaching 101 cm/40 in. Barnum displayed him in his museum from the age of five, under the name of General Tom Thumb, and he became famous throughout the USA and Europe. In 1863 his marriage to Lavinia Warren (1841–1919), also a midget, was widely publicized. He died at Middleboro, Massachusetts. » Barnum; dwarfism; theatre

stratus clouds The lowest layer of clouds in the atmosphere. They are composed of water droplets, and result in dull, overcast, and often drizzly conditions associated with the warm sector of a depression. They are found up to c.500 m/1 600 ft, above which other stratiform clouds (eg altostratus, nimbostratus clouds) form. » altostratus/cirrostratus/nimbostratus clouds; cloud [i]; depression (meteorology) [i]

Strauss, Johann (the Elder) (1804–49) Austrian violinist, conductor, and composer, born and died in Vienna. He founded with Josef Lanner the Viennese Waltz tradition, and toured widely in Europe with his own orchestra. He composed several marches, notably the *Radetzky* (1848), and numerous waltzes. His sons **Eduard** (1835–1916) and **Josef** (1827–70) were both conductors, and Josef and especially Johann became known as composers of waltzes. » Strauss, Johann (the Younger); waltz

Strauss, Johann (the Younger) (1825–99) Austrian violinist, conductor and composer, born and died in Vienna. He studied law, but turned to music, touring with his own orchestra. He wrote over 400 waltzes, notably *The Blue Danube* (1867) and *Tales from the Vienna Woods* (1868), as well as polkas, marches, several operettas, including *Die Fledermaus* (1874), and a favourite concert piece, *Perpetuum Mobile*. » waltz

Strauss, Richard (1864–1949) German composer, born in Munich. Educated at Munich and Berlin, he conducted at Meiningen, Munich, Weimar, Bayreuth, and Berlin. He is best known for his symphonic poems, such as *Till Eulenspiegels lustige Streiche* (1894–5, Till Eulenspiegel's Merry Pranks) and *Also sprach Zarathustra* (1895–6, Thus Spoke Zarathustra), and his operas, notably *Der Rosenkavalier* (1911) and *Ariadne auf Naxos* (1912, Ariadne on Naxos). He also wrote concertos, songs, and several small-scale orchestral works. He died at Garmisch-Partenkirchen. » symphonic poem

Stravinsky, Igor (Fyodorovich) (1882–1971) Russian-US composer, born near St Petersburg. He studied law, but turned to musical composition under Rimsky-Korsakov. He became famous with his music for the Diaghilev ballets *The Firebird* (1910), *Petrushka* (1911), and *The Rite of Spring* (1913). Essentially an experimenter, after World War 1 he devoted himself to Neoclassicism, as in his ballet *Pulcinella* (1920), based on Pergolesi, the opera-oratorio *Oedipus Rex* (1927), and the choral *Symphony of Psalms* (1930). He settled in France (1934) and finally in the USA, where he became a US citizen (1945). Other major compositions include the *Symphony in C major* (1940), the opera *The Rake's Progress* (1951), and such later works as *Requiem Canticles* (1966), in which he adopted serialism. He died in New York City. » Diaghilev; Neoclassicism (music); Rimsky-Korsakov; serialism

strawberry A perennial with arching runners rooting at nodes to form new plants, native to N and S America, Europe (N as far as Ireland), and Asia; leaves in a basal rosette, with three toothed leaflets; flowers 5-petalled, white; false fruit consisting of swollen, fleshy, red receptacle bearing brown, dry, achenes (the 'seeds') on the surface. The **wild strawberry** (*Fragaria vesca*) has fruits 2 cm/¾ in long. The **alpine strawberry** is a variety with few or no runners. The **garden strawberry** (*Fragaria × ananassa*) is a larger-fruited hybrid first raised in 18th-c France. The **hautbois strawberry** (*Fragaria moschata*) has purplish, musky fruits. (Genus: *Fragaria*, 15 species. Family: *Rosaceae*.) » achene; perennial; receptacle; runner

strawberry finch » **avadavat**

strawberry tree An evergreen shrub or small tree, native to the Mediterranean and W Europe north to Ireland; leaves reddish,

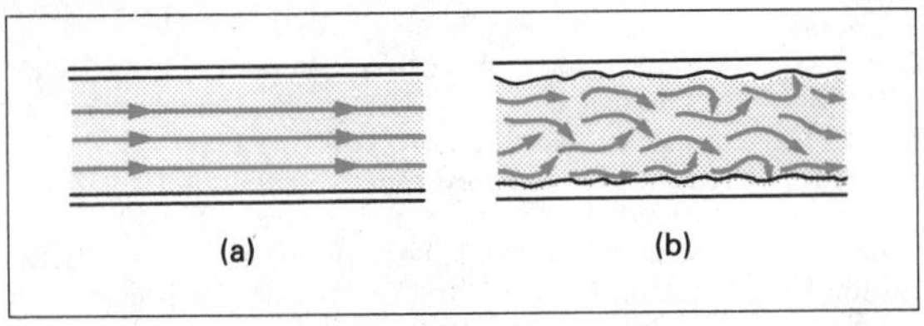

Streamlining – Streamline flow (a); turbulent flow (b)

leathery; flowers white, bell-shaped, in drooping clusters; fruits red, spherical, covered with soft warts. (*Arbutus unedo.* Family: *Ericaceae.*) » evergreen plants; shrub; tree [i]

stream of consciousness A term introduced by William James in his *Principles of Psychology* (1890) to describe the continuous, random activity of the mind. It has been adopted by writers and critics to refer to the techniques used to register this inner experience in writing. Notable early exponents were James Joyce, and Dorothy Richardson (1873–1957). » James, William; Joyce, James; novel

streaming Putting children into higher or lower groups according to their general ability, as opposed to teaching them in *mixed ability* (also known as 'heterogeneous' groups), or *mixed age* groups (also called 'vertical' or 'family' groups. If this is done on the basis of their competence in a particular subject, the process is known as *setting*. In the USA the equivalent term is *tracking*. » mainstreaming

streamlining A condition of fluid flow such that no turbulence occurs. Streamlining refers to the design of the shape of machinery or apparatus (eg automobiles, aircraft) so that turbulence is reduced to a minimum. It may also refer to the design of fixed structures which stand in an air or liquid stream where it is desired to reduce turbulence.

Streep, Meryl (Louise) (1949–) US actress, born at Baking Ridge, New Jersey. She studied at the Yale School of Drama, and played on Broadway before her film debut in *Julia* (1977). Since then she has provided a varied range of fine performances, gaining Academy Awards for *Kramer v Kramer* (1979) and *Sophie's Choice* (1982), and critical acclaim for *The French Lieutenant's Woman* (1981), *Out of Africa* (1985), and *Heartburn* (1986).

street dance Forms of competitive dance that started in the early 1970s among gangs of youths in New York, such as the Zulu Kings (showing African links) and the Rock Steady Crew. The dance movement known as 'King Tut' uses head and arm movements typical of Egyptian dance. **Break dancing** was part of the Bronx graffiti art and rapping culture. It aims to develop control and coordination to perform acrobatic and athletic feats either solo, with a partner, or in a group to demonstrate superiority over rival gangs. Dancers spin the body on the head, back, and hands, performing aerial dives and fast footwork. *The Turtle* and *The Beetle Crawl* are typical patterns. **Body popping** is a jerky articulation of isolated parts of the body creating a chain of movement that ripples, for example, in the *Wave*. In contrast there are also smooth gliding movements. References to birds or snakes are found. **Robotics** is a form where mime and puppet movements are important. A mechanical effect is created by tense muscles in a stiff body; the movements are small and sharp. » modern dance

street hockey A form of hockey played on roller skates, popular in the USA, and now becoming so in the UK. It is so named because children used to play on street corners, but it is now generally played on enclosed areas, such as playgrounds. » hockey [i]

Streicher, Julius [**striy**kher] (1885–1946) German journalist and politician, born at Fleinhausen. He was associated with Hitler in the early days of Nazism, taking part in the 1923 putsch. A ruthless persecutor of the Jews, he incited anti-Semitism through the newspaper *Der Stürmer*, which he founded and edited. He was hanged at Nuremberg as a war criminal. » Nazi Party

Streisand, Barbra, byname of **Barbara Joan Streisand** (1942–) US actress and singer, born in New York City. Starting as a nightclub singer, stage and television appearances brought her the lead in the Broadway show *Funny Girl*, which she repeated in the 1968 film version to win an Oscar. She has continued with a number of large-scale film comedies and musicals, often with theatrical backgrounds, notably *Hello, Dolly* (1969), and *A Star is Born* (1976), and she co-produced, directed, and acted in *Yentl* (1983).

strength » **tensile strength**

streptococcus A spherical to ovoid bacterium which occurs in chains. It tolerates oxygen, but does not use it in metabolism. Some species are useful in dairy fermentations; others are found in animal intestinal tracts and may be disease-causing. It includes the causative agents of scarlet fever and pneumonia. (Kingdom: *Monera.* Family: *Streptococcaceae.*) » bacteria [i]; metabolism

streptomycin [streptoh**miy**sin] An antibiotic discovered in 1944 which became the first clinically effective drug for the treatment of tuberculosis, and until 1952 was the only drug available for treating this disease. Side-effects occur quite frequently, most commonly deafness. Although drug resistance developed during its first years of use, it is still occasionally used in a cocktail of several drugs for treating tuberculosis. It is also used in the treatment of unusual infections not responsive to safer antibiotics, such as plague. » antibiotics; drug resistance; tuberculosis

Stresemann, Gustav [**shtray**zuhman] (1878–1929) German statesman, born in Berlin. Entering the Reichstag in 1907 as a National Liberal, he became leader of the Party, and later founded and led its successor, the German People's Party. He was Chancellor of the new German (Weimar) Republic in 1923, then Minister of Foreign Affairs (1923–9). He pursued a policy of conciliation, helped to negotiate the Locarno Pact (1925), and secured the entry of Germany into the League of Nations (1926). He shared the Nobel Peace Prize for 1926, and died in Berlin. » League of Nations; Locarno Pact

stress (physics) A force per unit area which acts on an object attempting to deform it. A force F applied along the axis of a bar of cross section A produces a **linear stress** of F/A, units Pa (pascal). Such a force is involved in attempts to pull apart layers of atoms (**tensile stress**) or to push them together (**compressive stress**). A twisting force causes **shear stress**, which tries to slide layers of atoms over one another. » elastic hysteresis; mechanical properties of matter; piezo-electric effect; strain

stress (psychology) In psychology, a situation where certain external circumstances (**stressors**) lead to a stereotyped non-specific response from a person (the **stress response**). Stressors may be physical (noise, heat) or psychological (bereavement, unemployment), but their effect depends on their interpretation by the recipient. The stress response, physiologically, consists of cortical desynchronization and release of stress hormones; behavioural symptoms include attentional selectivity, memory loss, and autonomic activity (eg sweating). Coping strategies include denial (denying that the stressing circumstances exist) and intellectualizing (giving a rational evaluation of the situation). » hormones; nervous system; physiology

strike (economics) A form of industrial action, where a group of workers stop work in protest at some action by their employer, or because of a failure of collective bargaining to achieve the desired results. An *official* strike is one which has been formally agreed by the members of the union, whereas an *unofficial* strike occurs where action has been taken by employees without the formal support of the union, as set out in its constitution. Since the passing of the Trade Union Act (1984), unions in the UK have to hold a secret ballot of members before strike action is formally declared. » industrial action; trade union

strike (geology) » **dip and strike**

Strindberg, (Johan) August (1849–1912) Swedish dramatist, born and died in Stockholm. Educated at Uppsala, he settled in Stockholm as a writer. He first achieved fame with the novel *Röda Rummet* (1879, The Red Room), followed by several plays. He travelled in France, Switzerland, and Denmark and published his *Giftas I* and *II* (1884–6), collections of short stories, which led to his recall to Sweden (1884) to stand trial for alleged blasphemy. His plays *Fadren* (1887, The Father)

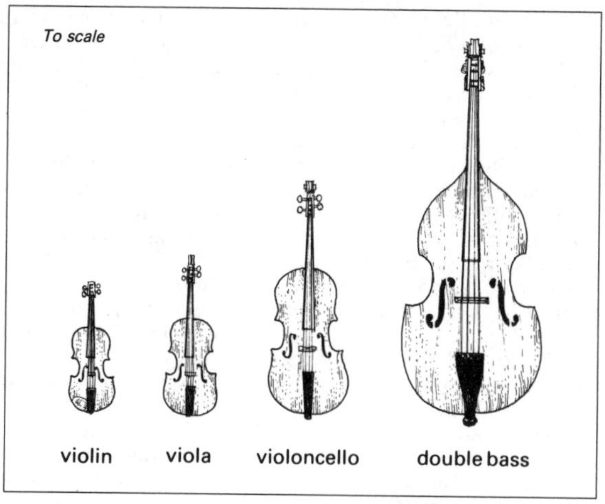

String instruments

and *Fröken Julie* (1888, Miss Julie) brought him to the forefront as the exponent of naturalistic drama. Later plays were more symbolic in form and religious in theme. His final 'chamber plays' were written for the *Intimate Theatre*, which he founded in 1907. » drama; Swedish literature

string instrument 1 bowed Musical instruments in which the sound is produced by drawing a bow across one or more taut strings. The number of strings and their tuning have varied, but the difficulty of bowing one inside string only without touching its neighbours, obviated to some extent by the use of a curved bridge, means that bowed instruments have usually had fewer strings than plucked ones, or rarely more than six. Gut, metal, and (more recently) nylon are the materials most often needed for the strings themselves. The bowed string instruments of the modern orchestra – violin, viola, cello, and double bass – all have four strings (some double basses have five). The strings can be plucked as well as bowed. » baryton; bow; cello; chordophone; crwth; double bass; hurdy-gurdy; kit; string quartet; viola; viola da gamba; violin **2 non-bowed** Musical instruments in which the sound is produced by plucking or striking one or more strings. Many are fitted with keyboards; others are played with sticks or hammers, or are plucked or strummed with fingers or plectra. The strings themselves are in some cases *stopped* (usually by pressure from the fingers of the player's left hand) to produce different pitches: others are played *open* (ie unstopped). In the former case, the fingerboard is often *fretted* (ie fitted with raised strips of metal, gut, or wood) to facilitate note-finding and to produce a clear sound. A large number of non-bowed string instruments are folk instruments, the only one commonly found in the modern orchestra being the harp. Bowed string instruments such as the violin may, however, be plucked as well. » aeolian harp; balalaika; banjo; bouzouki; chitarrone; chordophone; cimbalom; cittern; dulcimer; gittern; guitar; harp; Hawaiian guitar; keyboard instrument; kinnor; kithara [i]; koto; lute; lyre; mandolin; pipa; plectrum; psaltery; shamisen; sitar [i]; theorbo; ʿud; ukulele; zither

string quartet An ensemble of two violins, viola, and cello; also, a piece of music for such an ensemble. Since the 18th-c the string quartet has been regarded as the most satisfying medium for serious chamber music. The first important composer of string quartets was Haydn, who established the four-movement structure and wrote some of the earliest masterpieces in the form. The other Viennese masters, Mozart, Beethoven and Schubert, also cultivated it with particular distinction and originality; notable among later examples are those of Bartók and Shostakovitch. » Haydn; string instrument 1 [i]

stringy-bark » **gum tree**

strobilus [strohbiyluhs] A cone-shaped group of leaves or leaf-like structures bearing sporangia and found in spore-bearing vascular plants. In gymnosperms it has become the woody cone, and is still recognizable in some primitive flowering plants, such as magnolia. » gymnosperms; magnolia; sporangium

strobo-flash Photographic recording of a moving object by a series of very brief exposures at regular intervals, as by sequential electronic flash lighting during the open period of the camera shutter. In cinematography, strobe-lighting with electronic flash synchronized to the camera frame rate produces sharp images of fast-moving objects. » photography

stroboscope A device for producing a succession of short pulses of light, usually using light from a mercury arc lamp. The pulse frequency is variable, with several thousand flashes per second possible. In photography, it may be used to produce several images of a moving object in a single picture. » light; photography

Stroessner, Alfredo [strersnuh] (1912–) Paraguayan dictator, born at Encarnación, Paraguay. He took up a military career, fighting in the Chaco War, and became President in 1954. He was re-elected at regular intervals, but forced to stand down after a coup in 1989. » Chaco War; Paraguay [i]

Stroheim, Erich (Oswald) von [strohhiym] (1886–1957) Austrian film director and actor, born in Vienna. He served in the Austrian army, and held a variety of jobs before moving to the USA in 1914. His first success as film director was with *Blind Husbands* (1919), followed by the classic film *Greed* (1923). Later he returned to film acting, often playing the roles of German officers, as in *Desert Fox*. He died near Paris.

stroke A sudden interference with the blood supply to the brain which results in the death of nerve tissue followed by varying degrees of disability of speech, sight, understanding, or movement. It may be caused by the rupture of an artery, by the clotting of blood within an artery (*thrombosis*), or by an embolism. » aphasia; blood vessels [i]; cerebral haemorrhage; embolism

Strong, Roy (1935–) British art historian and museum director, born in London. Educated at Queen Mary College, London, and at the Warburg Institute, he became assistant keeper at the National Portrait Gallery, London, in 1959, and its director in 1967. He was director of the Victoria and Albert Museum (1974–87).

strong interaction The strong short-range force binding together protons and neutrons in atomic nuclei, and quarks in protons and neutrons; also called **strong nuclear force**. It is independent of and stronger than electromagnetic force, and governs nuclear fission, fusion, and alpha decay. The widely accepted theory of strong force is quantum chromodynamics. » alpha decay; baryon; forces of nature [i]; hadron; isospin; nuclear physics; particle physics; quantum chromodynamics; resonances

strong nuclear force » **strong interaction**

strontium Sr, element 38, melting point 769°C. A very reactive metal, very similar to calcium, and also an alkaline earth element. Not found uncombined, its main sources are the sulphate and the carbonate, $SrSO_4$ and $SrCO_3$. Its main importance is that it will replace calcium in most crystals, and this is particularly serious since one isotope, ^{90}Sr, is an important product of nuclear fission, with a half-life of 28 years. » calcium; chemical elements; metal; nuclear fission; RR90

structuralism A theory which attempts to define the general properties of cultural systems, including language, mythology, art, and social organization; the approach derives from the work of the Swiss linguist Ferdinand de Saussure (1857–1913) and the French anthropologist Claude Lévi-Strauss (1908–). The fundamental thesis is that individual terms or phenomena can be understood only in relationship to other elements of the same system, and that each system is built up using a limited set of contrasts or oppositions. Some structuralists believe that this reflects innate characteristics of the human mind, while others believe that the repetitive form taken by cultural structures has to do with the constraints imposed upon any medium of communication, which has to encode, decode, and transmit messages. The impact of structuralism on literary criticism has been especially significant, since by redefining the relationship between language and world as cultural rather than natural, structuralism undermines traditional conceptions of meaning, and (as Roland Barthes has shown) exposes the ideology built into our assumptions and values. » Barthes; deconstruction; empiricism; Lévi-Strauss; linguistics; Saussure; semiotics

structure plan A requirement of UK planning law. Each planning authority has to produce a structure plan which is approved by the Secretary of State for the Environment. It forms the basis for policies of development (eg land use, traffic management) in the authority's area. Development proposals for farming and forestry are not included. Once approved, a plan may be renewed after five years, but most last for longer.

Struve A distinguished astronomical dynasty. Friedrich Georg Wilhelm von Struve (1793–1864), born in Germany, became director of the Dorpat Observatory, Estonia, in 1818; his son, O W Struve (1819–1905) became director of Pulkova Observatory in 1861. The latter's elder son, K H Struve (1854–1920) became director of the Berlin Observatory in 1904, while his younger son, G W L Struve (1858–1920) became director of Kharkov Observatory in 1894. The latter's son, Otto (1897–1963) fought with the White Russian army, and emigrated to the USA in 1921, becoming a US citizen. He founded then directed the McDonald Observatory (1939–47), and became the first director of the US National Radio Astronomy Observatory (1959–62). Members of four generations of the family received the gold medal of the Royal Astronomical Society, a feat unique in the history of astronomy. » astronomy

strychnine A poisonous alkaloid present in members of the genus *Strychnos*, thorny trees or climbing shrubs with hook-like tendrils, native to the tropics. *Strychnos nux vomica* was introduced into Germany in the 16th-c as a rat poison (and is still used for this purpose). Although strychnine became widely used in medicine in the 18th-c, it has no justifiable clinical use. Accidental poisonings occasionally occur; death results from convulsions. Strychnine has been used by drug dealers to bulk out supplies of heroin, since both drugs are white powders which share a similar bitter taste. (Genus: *Strychnos*, 200 species. Family: *Loganiaceae*.) » alkaloids; curare; shrub; tree [i]

Stuart or **Stewart, Charles (Edward Louis Philip Casimir)**, bynames **the Young Pretender** and **Bonny Prince Charlie** (1720–88) Claimant to the British crown, born in Rome, the son of James Edward Stuart. Educated in Rome, he became the focus of Jacobite hopes. In 1744 he went to France to head the planned invasion of England, but after the defeat of the French fleet he was unable to leave for over a year. He landed with seven followers at Eriskay in the Hebrides (Jul 1745) and raised his father's standard. The clansmen flocked to him, Edinburgh surrendered, and he kept court at Holyrood. Victorious at Prestonpans, he invaded England, but turned back at Derby for lack of evident English support, and was routed by the Duke of Cumberland at Culloden Moor (1746). The rising was ruthlessly suppressed, and he was hunted for five months. With the help of Flora Macdonald he crossed from Benbecula to Portree, disguised as her maid. He landed in Brittany, then lived in France and Italy, where (after his father's death in 1766) he assumed the title of Charles III of Great Britain. He died in Rome. » Cumberland, William Augustus; Forty-five Rebellion; Jacobites; Macdonald, Flora; Stuarts

Stuart or **Stewart, James (Francis Edward)**, byname **the Old Pretender** (1688–1766) Claimant to the British throne, the only son of James II and VII and his second wife, Mary of Modena, born in London. As a baby he was conveyed to St Germain, and proclaimed successor on his father's death (1701). After failing to land in Scotland in 1708, he served with the French in the Low Countries. In 1715 he landed at Peterhead during the Jacobite rising, but left Scotland some weeks later. Thereafter he lived mainly in Rome, where he died. » Fifteen Rebellion; Jacobites; James II (of England); Stuarts

Stuart, John McDouall (1815–66) Australian explorer, born at Dysart, Fife, Scotland. He accompanied Captain Charles Sturt's expedition (1844–5), made six expeditions into the interior (1858–62), and in 1860 traversed Australia from S to N. Mt Stuart is named after him. » Sturt

Stuart (Australia) » **Alice Springs**

Stuarts, also spelled **Stewarts** A Scottish royal family, commencing with Robert II (reigned 1371–90), which succeeded to the English throne in 1603 with the accession of James VI and I, the cousin of Elizabeth I, and the great-grandson of Henry VIII's sister, Margaret. As English monarchs the family's fortunes were mixed. James I (1603–25) and Charles II (1649–85) were both successful politicians (although the second spent his first eleven years as king in exile). But Charles I (1625–49) and James II (1685–8) were not, and both lost their thrones. The Stuart line ended in 1714 with the death of Queen Anne, although pretenders laid claim to the throne and invaded Britain in support of their claims as late as 1745. » Anne; Charles I/II (of England); James I/II (of England); Mary II; Robert II; Stuart, Charles Edward; RR64

Stubai Alps [**shtoo**biy], Ger **Stubaier Alpen** Mountain range of the E Alps in Tirol state, W Austria, rising to 3 507 m/11 506 ft at Zuckerhütl; numerous glaciers. » Alps

Stubbs, George (1724–1806) British anatomist, painter, and engraver, born in Liverpool. He studied at York, and in 1754 travelled in Italy and Morocco. In 1766 he published his monumental *Anatomy of the Horse*, illustrated by his own engravings. He was best known for his sporting pictures, and excelled in painting horses. He died in London. » English art; engraving

stucco [**stu**koh] A good quality plaster often used in classical architecture for low relief ornamental carvings and mouldings. It is also employed as an inexpensive render which can replace or resemble stone. » gypsum

Studenica Monastery [**stoo**duhnitsa] The most notable of the Serbian monasteries, founded in 1183 near Uscé in present-day Yugoslavia. The complex, a world heritage site, includes several churches noted for their mediaeval frescoes. Those which decorate the Church of the Virgin prefigure developments in Western art generally associated with late 13th-c Italy. » fresco; Serbia

Students for a Democratic Society (SDS) A radical splinter group of the movement opposed to US involvement in Vietnam, founded at Columbia University, New York City, and advocating social disruption and violence. Although the movement spread to over 200 universities, it was subject to factionalism. Two of its members were given punitive sentences in the Chicago Conspiracy Trial of 1969. » Weathermen

study skills The ability to study effectively. Many schools and colleges offer courses in study skills. Topics covered usually include effective reading (how to skim, scan, slow down at important stages, make notes, use an index), information gathering and the proper use of library and resource centre facilities, revision techniques, and understanding one's own learning strategies.

stump-jump plough An Australian-designed plough (patented 1881) with shears that work independently of each other, allowing the cultivation of land with roots or large stones. Ordinary ploughs break under such conditions. The stump-jump plough was used to open up the mallee lands of SE Australia. » plough [i]

stupa [**stoo**pa] An Indian cairn or mound originally constructed over the ashes of an emperor or some other great person, such as the Buddha. Later they were used to house the ashes of Buddhist monks and holy relics. » Buddhism; pagoda

sturgeon Any of a group of large primitive fish found in fresh and marine waters of the N hemisphere; body elongate, armed with rows of heavy bony scales; head tapering, underside mouth with long barbels; tail asymmetrical, the upper lobe long; body length 1–5 m/3–16 ft; several species support important commercial fisheries; eggs sold as caviare. (Family: *Acipenseridae*, 4 genera, 25 species.) » beluga (fish); caviare

Sturluson, Snorri » **Snorri Sturluson**

Sturm und Drang [**shtoorm** unt **drang**] (Ger 'storm and stress') A revolutionary literary movement in late-18th-c Germany, which rejected classical values in favour of subjective feeling and artistic creativity. An important tributary of the Romantic movement, it influenced Goethe, Schiller, and Herder. » German literature; Goethe; Herder; Romanticism (literature); Schiller

Sturt, Charles (1795–1869) British explorer, born in Bengal, India. He went as an army captain to Australia, and headed three important expeditions (1828–45), discovering the Darling

(1828) and the lower Murray Rivers (1830). Blinded by hardship and exposure, he received in 1851 a pension from the first South Australian parliament. He died at Cheltenham, England. » Darling River

stuttering A disorder of fluency in the use of language; also called **stammering**. There is difficulty in controlling the rhythm and timing of speech, and a failure to communicate easily, rapidly, and continuously. Individual sounds may be abnormally repeated, lengthened, or fail to be released. Symptoms range from mild to severe. The cause is unknown, but several physiological, genetic, and psychological factors have been implicated. A large number of treatments are available (some of which, often advertised in the popular press, can make exaggerated claims for success). Approaches used in speech therapy include the teaching of new techniques of speech production (eg slowed speech), the use of acoustic devices to be worn by the stutterer to facilitate fluent speech, and the training of new attitudes to the task of becoming part of the everyday speech community. » cluttering; speech pathology

Stuttgart [**shtut**gaht] 48°47N 9°12E, pop (1983) 571 100. Capital of Baden-Württemberg province, Germany; on the R Neckar, 61 km/38 ml ESE of Karlsruhe; founded, 10th-c; former capital of the kingdom of Württemberg; former seat of the Reichstag National Assembly; badly bombed in World War 2; railway, airport; two universities (1967); notable mineral springs; cars, electrical equipment, paint, telecommunications, engineering, precision equipment, foodstuffs, textiles, paper, publishing; major fruit and wine area; birthplace of Hegel; castle (originally 13th-c, much rebuilt), palace (18th-c), St Leonard's Church (15th-c), Stiftskirche (12th-c), Liederhall; Spring Festival (Apr), Stuttgart Ballet Week (May), Lichterfest (Jul), Cannstatt Folk Festival (Sep). » Germany [i]; Hegel

Stuyvesant, Peter [**sti**yvuhsant] (1592–1672) Dutch administrator, born at Scherpenzeel. He became Governor of Curaçao, and from 1646 directed the New Netherland colony. He proved a vigorous but arbitrary ruler, a rigid sabbatarian, and an opponent of political and religious freedom, but did much for the commercial prosperity of New Amsterdam until his reluctant surrender to the English in 1664. He died near New York City. » New Netherland

stye A localized infection in a gland or around a hair follicle in the eyelid. It causes a small, painful swelling in the eyelid, and is best treated by an appropriate antibiotic. » eye [i]

style (botany) In flowering plants, the upper part of the carpel, separating the ovary and stigma. It may be elongated to better present the stigma to receive pollen. In more primitive flowers the styles (like the carpels) are generally separate; in more advanced flowers they are often fused. It sometimes persists after fertilization, and aids in seed dispersal, as with the plume-like styles of clematis, which catch the wind. » carpel; clematis; ovary; stigma

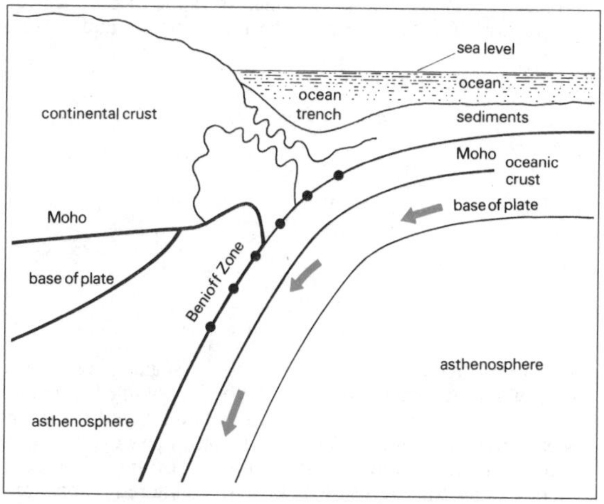

Subduction zone

stylistics The systematic study of style, using the principles and procedures of linguistics. 'Style' here includes a range of senses, from the features of language which identify an individual (as in 'Shakespeare's style') to those which identify major occupational groups within a community (as in 'legal style', 'scientific style'). Stylistic studies also encompass the social role a speaker or writer is playing (eg 'being a lawyer, preacher'), the particular medium of communication selected (eg public lecture, newspaper article), and the degree of social closeness or distance between the participants (leading to differing degrees of formality or casualness in usage). In all cases, stylistics focuses upon the *choices* that are available to the language user. **Literary stylistics**, accordingly, studies the linguistic choices made by authors in the various genres of literature (novel, short story, poetry, etc). In **stylometry** or **stylostatistics**, a quantitative analysis is made of a text, to determine its statistical structure. Such studies are particularly important in plotting historical changes in style, or in investigating questions of disputed authorship. » literary criticism; register; sociolinguistics

Stylites, Simeon » Simeon Stylites

stylometry » stylistics

stylops A small parasitic insect which uses bees or other insects as host; males with fan-like hindwings and reduced forewings; females typically larva-like and wingless. (Order: *Strepsiptera*. Family: *Stylopidae*.) » insect [i]; larva; parasitology

styrene C_6H_5–CH=CH_2, boiling point 145°C, *phenylethene* or *vinylbenzene*. A colourless liquid, which undergoes addition polymerization to a glassy resin called **polystyrene**. 'Expanded' polystyrene, made porous with trapped gas, is widely used as a thermally-insulating packing material. » polymerization; resin

styrene butadiene rubber » rubber

Styx [stiks] In Greek mythology, a principal river of the Underworld; the name means 'hateful'. It was so terrible that even the gods in Homer swore by it. It was also the name of a river in Arcadia, which passes through a gloomy gorge. » Charon (mythology); Hades

sub-atomic particles A general term for all particles smaller than atoms. It refers to electrons, protons, and neutrons, which directly constitute atoms, and to other particles including composite particles, resonances, and fundamental particles. They are classified by mass, spin, charge, and other properties. All sub-atomic particles are either bosons (force particles) or fermions (matter particles). » atom; boson; fermions; fundamental particles; particle physics; quasi-particles; resonances; soliton

subconscious » unconscious

subduction zone A region in which one crustal plate of the Earth is forced down (subducted) beneath another, and moves down into the mantle where it is eventually assimilated. Present-day subduction zones occur around the margins of the Pacific Ocean at the sites of deep ocean trenches, and are associated with earthquake and volcanic activity and the formation of island arcs such as Japan and the Aleutian Is. » earthquake; island arc; plate tectonics [i]

sublimation (chemistry) Passing directly from solid to vapour without an intermediate liquid phase. Substances which sublime at normal pressures include solid carbon dioxide ('dry ice') and iodine. » phases of matter [i]

sublimation (psychiatry) The psychological process in which unacceptable drives and behaviours are channelled unconsciously into socially acceptable patterns of behaviour. The benefits are both the unconscious avoidance of the anxiety associated with unacceptable actions, and the positive rewards associated with socially acceptable and valued behaviour. An example would be a young man with strong aggression who takes up competitive sports (eg football or the martial arts), and succeeds in these. Society approves of his sporting prowess and he avoids unacceptable aggressive actions.

subliminal advertising Advertising designed to be imperceptible to the conscious mind of audiences. It mostly involves split-second projections of brand names or commands ('Eat Popcorn'), screened in the cinema or on television, or sound messages at frequencies beyond the range of human hearing. In the late 1950s the alleged use of such 'sub-threshold effects' for commercial ends caused alarm in the USA and UK. In particular, Vance Packard's book, *The Hidden Persuaders*, brought the issue to the notice of an anxious general public. Subliminal advertising is now banned in most countries, though its actual extent and effectiveness is still disputed. » advertising; subliminal perception

subliminal perception Literally, perception that is below the threshold (of awareness). Clear evidence for subliminal perception comes from laboratory experiments where the presence of a briefly presented stimulus, which an observer is unable to report, can influence the speed of processing of subsequent stimuli. » consciousness; subliminal advertising

submachine-gun A small arm midway in size between a pistol and a rifle, capable of firing a burst of automatic fire. First developed practically around 1918, it was used extensively during World War 2 (the British Sten gun and German MP 38 being typical weapons), but it has been replaced in most modern armies by the assault rifle. » machine-gun; rifle; Sten gun

submarine A vessel capable of remaining submerged for a considerable period of time. Submarines as originally conceived were strictly speaking 'submersibles'; a World War 2 U-boat, for example, would typically have spent 85% of her time on the surface. The longest known submerged patrol was steamed in 1982–3 by HM Submarine *Warspite* lasting 111 days in the S Atlantic, during which she covered 30 804 nautical miles (57 085 km). Such endurance comes from the installation of a nuclear reactor which supplies the heat to produce steam for the turbines. Since the advent of nuclear-armed, submarine-launched ballistic missiles, such as Polaris, submarines have become the most powerfully armed and strategically important of all warships, playing two distinct roles. They can act as an attack vessel, armed with torpedoes and missiles to attack other ships (including other submarines) at sea; and they can act as a floating platform for long-range missiles. **Ballistic missile submarines** (SSBNs) carrying submarine-launched ballistic missiles (SLBMs), are now exclusively nuclear-powered, and are operated by the US, Russian, British, French, and Chinese navies. » ballistic missile; depth charge; sonar; torpedo; U-boat; warships [i]

submarine canyon An underwater canyon which typically cuts the continental margin, and may lead across the continental rise as far as the abyssal plains. These canyons serve as channels for the transport of shallow water sediments from the continental shelf to the deep sea. Turbidity currents are suspected as the most likely mechanisms for the transportation of these sediments. » canyon; turbidity current

Subotica [soobuhtitsa], Hungarian **Szabadka** 46°04N 19°41E, pop (1981) 154 611. Largest town in the autonomous province of Vojvodina, NW Serbia republic, Yugoslavia; railway; fruit trade, foodstuffs, chemicals; Palic health resort nearby; Duzijanca traditional harvest festival (Jul). » Serbia; Yugoslavia [i]

subpoena (Lat, 'under penalty') An order to a person to attend court to give evidence or produce relevant documents. Failure to comply with the order is a contempt of court. The term is not used in Scottish law. » contempt of court

subsistence agriculture A form of farming where the land provides most of the necessities of life – food, fuel, and shelter. Tools and other items which cannot be generated in this way are acquired through trading surplus commodities. » crofting

substance P A chemical substance (a peptide) found throughout the body, particularly high concentrations occurring in the gut, spinal cord, and brain. Its physiological role is unclear: it possibly acts as a neurotransmitter for neurones conveying sensory information from peripheral pain receptors to the central nervous system. » neurotransmitter; peptide

substitution reaction A chemical reaction in which one group in a molecule is replaced by another. A typical example is the formation of an alcohol from an alkyl halide: $OH^- + RCl \rightarrow ROH + Cl^-$. » chemical reaction

succession (botany) » **vegetation succession**

succinic acid [suhksinik] $HOOC\text{–}CH_2\text{–}CH_2\text{–}COOH$, IUPAC **butanedioic acid**, melting point 188°C. A colourless solid, occurring in sugar cane, and also formed during fermentation. Important derivatives include the cyclic anhydride, used in resins, and the imide, used as a disinfectant. » acid; sugar cane

Succoth » **Sukkoth**

succubus [suhkyubuhs] A malevolent female spirit supposed in mediaeval superstition to have intercourse with men in their sleep, the union resulting in the birth of demons, witches and deformed children. » incubus

succulent A plant in which the stems and leaves are fleshy and swollen with water-storage tissues; common in arid regions and other places where water is present, but not easily available. Succulents often have adaptations to reduce water-loss, such as thick, waxy cuticles and reduced or inrolled leaves. Examples are cacti, houseleeks, and many bromeliads. » bromeliad; cactus [i]; houseleek

Suchow » **Suzhou**

sucker A shoot growing from a root, usually at some distance from the parent and eventually developing its own root system and becoming independent of the parent plant. Many trees produce suckers freely, and can eventually form small groves in this way. » root (botany)

sucking fish » **remora**

Suckling, Sir John (1609–42) English poet and dramatist, born at Whitton, Middlesex. He studied at Cambridge, then lived splendidly at court, but involvement in political intrigue led him to flee the country, and he died (it is said by his own hand) in Paris. His plays (*Aglaura*, 1637) are austere, but his lyrics, taking something from Donne and Herbert, are among the finest in the language. They were published in *Fragmenta Aurea* (1646). » Donne; English literature; Herbert, George

Sucre, Antonio José de [sookray] (1793–1830) S American soldier-patriot, born at Cumaná, Venezuela. He was Bolívar's lieutenant, defeated the Spaniards at Ayacucho (1824), and became the first President (1826) of Bolivia. He resigned in 1828, took service with Colombia, and won the battle of Tarqui (1829) against Peru. He was assassinated at Berruecos, near Pasló. » Bolívar; Colombia [i]; Spanish-American Wars of Independence

Sucre [sookray], formerly **Chuquisaca** 19°05S 65°15W, pop (1982) 79 941. City in Oropeza province, SC Bolivia; altitude 2 705 m/8 875 ft; official judicial and legal capital of Bolivia, and capital of Chuquisaca region; founded 1538; revolutionary centre against Spain in 18th-c; airfield; railway; university (1624); oil refining, cement, agricultural centre; colonial Legislative Palace (where Declaration of Independence signed), Santo Domingo (Palace of Justice), 17th-c cathedral and museum, Churches of San Miguel and San Francisco. » Bolivia [i]

sucrose [sookrohs] $C_{12}H_{22}O_{11}$, the best-known sugar – a disaccharide made up of a glucose molecule joined to a fructose molecule. It is digested in the small intestine to produce equal proportions of the monosaccharides glucose and fructose,

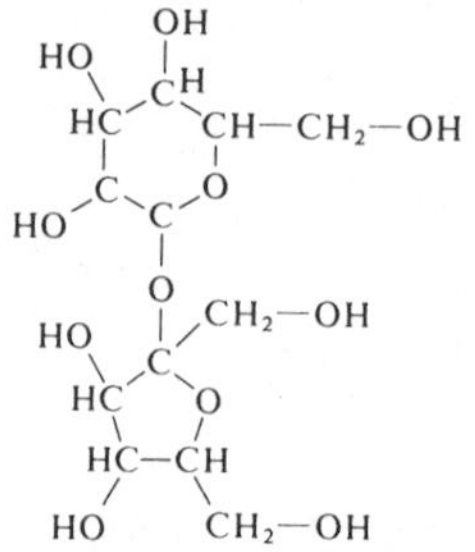

which are then absorbed. Sucrose is the sugar of table sugar, icing sugar, and castor sugar, and may be obtained from either sugar beet or sugar cane. Western diets derive c.17% of their energy from sucrose. Whilst expert committees disagree about a recommended value for daily intakes of sugar for adults, there is general agreement that for children exposure to frequent intakes of sugar predisposes to dental caries. » caries; disaccharide; sugar cane; sugars

Sudan [soo**dan**], official name **Democratic Republic of Sudan**, Arabic **Jamhuryat es-Sudan al-Democratia** pop (1990e) 24 423 000; area 2 504 530 sq km/966 749 sq ml. NE African republic, divided into seven regions; bounded N by Egypt, NW by Libya, W by Chad, SW by the Central African Republic, S by Zaire, SE by Uganda and Kenya, E by Ethiopia, and NE by the Red Sea; capital, Khartoum; chief towns, Port Sudan, Atbara, Kassala, Wadi Medani, Kosti; timezone GMT +2; chief ethnic groups, Nilotic, Negro, Nubian, Arab; chief religions, Islam (Sunni, 70%), local beliefs (20%); official language, Arabic; unit of currency, the Sudanese pound; largest country on the African continent, astride the middle reaches of the R Nile; E edge formed by the Nubian Highlands and an escarpment rising to over 2 000 m/6 500 ft on the Red Sea; Imatong Mts (S) rise to 3 187 m/10 456 ft at Kinyeti, highest point in Sudan; Dafur Massif in the W; White Nile flows N to meet the Blue Nile at Khartoum; desert conditions in NW, minimal annual rainfall 160 mm/6.3 in at Port Sudan, increasing S to 1 000 mm/40 in; in hottest months (Jul–Aug), temperature rarely falls below 24°C in the N; Christianized, 6th-c; Muslim conversion from 13th-c; Egyptian control of N Sudan, early 19th-c; Mahdi unified W and C tribes in a revolution, 1881; fall of Khartoum, 1885; combined British–Egyptian offensive in 1898, leading to a jointly administered condominium; independence, 1956; drought and N–S rivalry have contributed to years of instability and several coups; a transitional constitution of 1987 provided for a president, prime minister, Council of Ministers, and 264-member Legislative Assembly; constitution suspended after military coup, 1989; economy dominated by agriculture, employing over 75% of the people; large-scale irrigation schemes, fed by dams; major famines, especially 1984–5, 1990–1; commercial farming (N) and livestock farming (S); cotton, sugar, groundnuts, castor seeds, sorghum, wheat; gum arabic (80% of world supply); reserves of copper, lead, iron ore, chromite, manganese, gold, salt; food processing, sugar, textiles, soap, shoes, soft drinks, beer, paper products, cement; development hindered by poor transport system; the only main paved highway (Khartoum–Port Sudan) completed in 1980. » Khartoum; Mahdi; RR27 national holidays; RR61 political leaders

Sudbury 46°30N 81°01W, pop (1981) 91 829. Town in EC Ontario, S Canada; developed after arrival of railway, 1883; city, 1930; university (1960); mining (nickel, copper, cobalt, platinum, palladium), smelting, refining, pulp, paper, tourism, fishing, hunting; Numismatic Park. » Ontario

sudden infant death syndrome The sudden, unexpected death of an infant for which no adequate cause can be found on clinical or post-mortem examination; also known as **cot death**. Typically an apparently healthy infant is put to bed in the evening and is found to be dead in the night or early morning. Several causes may be responsible, but all remain speculative. Current theories include the cessation of breathing (*apnea*) as a result of an unusually prolonged spell of respiratory irregularity that to lesser degrees affects many newborn or immature infants; an exaggerated neural response to the drawing up of a small amount of stomach contents into the respiratory tract; obstruction to the airways as a result of temporary closure of the structures below the pharynx; increased vulnerability to toxins of respiratory bacteria that are normally harmless; and disturbance of body temperature control related to a cold environment or to excessive covering with bedding. » respiration

Sudeten or **Sudetenland** [soo**day**tuhnland] Mountainous territory on Polish–Czech border, comprising the Sudetic Mts rising to 1 603 m/5 259 ft at Sněžka; during World War 2, the name also applied to the parts of Bohemia and Moravia occupied by German-speaking people; invaded by Germany in 1938, and restored to Czechoslovakia in 1945. » Czechoslovakia [i]

Sue, Eugène [sü], pseudonym of **Marie Joseph Sue** (1804–57) French novelist, born in Paris. He served as surgeon in Spain (1823) and at Navarino Bay (1827) and wrote a vast number of Byronic novels idealizing the poor, such as *Les Mystères de Paris* (1843, The Mysteries of Paris), which was a major influence on Hugo. A republican deputy, he was driven into exile in 1851, and died at Annecy. » Byron; French literature; Hugo; novel

Suetonius, in full **Gaius Suetonius Tranquillus** (75–160) Roman biographer and antiquarian. He became Hadrian's secretary, a post he lost when he was compromised in a court intrigue. He then devoted himself to writing, his best-known work being *De vita Caesarum* (The Lives of the First Twelve Caesars), remarkable for its terseness, elegance, and impartiality. Only fragments survive of his other writings, on major Roman literary figures. » Hadrian; Latin literature

Suez [sooiz], Arabic **El Suweis** 29°59N 32°33E, pop (1976) 193 965. Seaport capital of Suez governorate, E Egypt; on Gulf of Suez, Red Sea, at S end of Suez Canal, 129 km/80 ml E of Cairo; railway; oil refining and storage, fertilizers, shipping services. » Egypt [i]; Suez Canal

Suez Canal Canal connecting the Mediterranean and Red Seas, in NE Egypt; built by Ferdinand de Lesseps, 1859–69; length

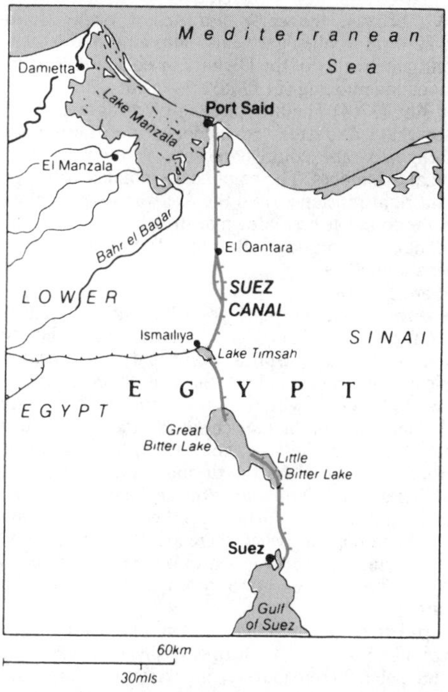

184 km/114 ml, including 11 km/7 ml of approaches to Suez (S end) and Port Said (N end); minimum width, 60 m/197 ft; minimum draught, 16 m/52 ft; passes through L Timsah, and the Great and Little Bitter Lakes; by 1882 Convention, open to vessels of any nation (except in wartime); controlled by British, 1882–1956; nationalized by Egypt, 1956; blocked by Egypt during war with Israel, 1967; re-opened, 1975; a major international waterway, and a substantial Egyptian economic asset. » Arab-Israeli Wars; Egypt [i]; Lesseps; Suez Crisis

Suez Crisis A political crisis focused on the Suez Canal in 1956. Intensive re-armament by Egypt, the Egyptian nationalization of the Suez Canal, and the establishment of a unified command with Jordan and Syria aimed at surrounding and eliminating Israel, led in October to a pre-emptive strike by Israel in Sinai. Following this attack, the UK and France asked both sides to withdraw from the Canal Zone and agree to temporary occupation. When this was rejected by Egypt, the British and French invaded, but had to withdraw following diplomatic action by the USA and USSR. Israel was also forced to relinquish the Sinai peninsula. There have been many allegations of collusion between Israel, France, and the UK. » Arab-Israeli Wars; Eden; Nasser

suffix » **affix**

Suffolk [**suhf**uhk] pop (1987e) 635 100; area 3 797 sq km/1 466 sq ml. County of E England, divided into seven districts; bounded E by the North Sea; county town, Ipswich; chief towns include Lowestoft, Felixstowe, Bury St Edmunds; engineering, fishing, high technology, agriculture (wheat, barley, sugar beet), food processing, horse breeding; Sizewell, Sutton Hoo ship burial. » England [i]; Ipswich; Sizewell; Sutton Hoo ship burial

Suffolk punch A heavy breed of horse developed in England; height, 16 hands/1.6 m/5¼ ft; plain brown; large powerful body with short, strong legs; traditionally a popular farm horse. » horse [i]

suffragettes Those women who identified with and were members of the late 19th-c movement in the UK and USA to secure voting rights for women. The vote was 'won' after the end of World War 1 in 1918, though it was limited to those women of 30 years of age or over. There were many men and women opponents of female suffrage, and in England it was not until 1929 that women over 21 achieved the right to vote. » Pankhurst; women's liberation movement

Sufism An Islamic mystical movement which represented a move away from the legalistic approach in Islam to a more personal relationship with God. The word comes from *suf* 'wool', because the early story-tellers from whom Sufism evolved wore woollen garments. Sufis aim to lose themselves in the ultimate reality of the Divinity by constant repetition of the *dhikr* or 'mentioning (of God)'. » Islam

Sugar Act (1764) The first piece in the programme of imperial reform that led to American independence. It attempted for the first time to raise colonial revenue without reference to the colonial assemblies. The colonials responded with protest, but not outright resistance, and the Act was sporadically enforced until the complete breakdown of British-American relations. » American Revolution; Boston Tea Party; Stamp Act; Townshend Acts

sugar beet » **beet**

sugar cane A bamboo-like grass but with soft canes 3–8 m/10–26 ft high, 3.5–5 cm/1½–2 in in diameter; white to yellowish-green, red, or purplish; cultivated in tropical and subtropical environments; long thought to be sterile, but now known to be fertile, with several vigorous high-yielding hybrids available. The cane is cut, chopped, and soaked in water to extract the sugar (*sucrose*), and the sugary solution is filtered, clarified, and dried. As the drying process develops, sucrose crystallizes out, leaving *molasses* behind. The raw sugar is brown, and can be further purified to yield white sugar. Contrary to popular belief, there are no nutritional differences between white and brown sugar. (*Saccharum officinarum*. Family: *Gramineae*.) » bamboo; grass [i]; molasses; sucrose [i]; sugars

sugar palm A tree growing to 12 m/40 ft, native to Malaysia; leaves 1–1.5 m/3¼–5 ft, feathery, silver beneath; also called **gomuti palm**. When mature, inflorescences form successively from the tip to the base of the trunk, which dies in corresponding stages. Sugar is obtained from the copious sap collected when the young inflorescences are cut. (*Arenga sacchifera*. Family: *Palmae*.) » inflorescence [i]; palm; tree [i]

sugars A group of sweet-tasting carbohydrates, chemically classified into single-unit (*monosaccharide*) and double-unit (*disaccharide*) types. Most people take *sugar* to mean sucrose; however, many other sugars are present in our diet, although not to the same levels as sucrose. These include lactose, the sugar of milk, and free glucose and fructose in fruits and honey. Free glucose is only half as sweet as sucrose, while free fructose is about 70% more sweet. » disaccharide; honey; sucrose [i]; sugar cane

Suicheng » **Liupanshui**

suicide The act of deliberate self-destruction. Up to 1961 in the UK, attempted suicide was considered to be a crime. Since then it has been accepted as a terminal symptom of a mental illness or abnormal mental state. It is a recognized complication of severe depressive illness or psychosis in which the individual suffers from inconsolable moods of despair, guilt, and self-blame. In other cases death results unintentionally from a conscious attempt to manipulate a situation, or from an impulse to obtain redress of circumstances which cause distress. Such individuals do not wish to die, but have misjudged the full effect of the act or of the lack of help. This especially applies to the act of self-poisoning. Fortunately the majority of persons who indulge in self-poisoning do not die, and usually live to regret their attempt. This act is sometimes referred to as **parasuicide**. In some societies, suicide in certain circumstances is socially acceptable (eg as an obligation following the death of a master or a spouse) and in ancient Greece and Rome, it was offered to the privileged as an alternative to execution. » depression (psychiatry); psychosis

suite In Baroque music, a set of dances, all in the same key, perhaps preceded by a prelude; the terms *partita* and *ordre* are also used. By c.1700 the standard dances were the allemande, courante, sarabande, and gigue, with additional dances (if any) placed between the last two. Since the 19th-c the term has been used for a sequence of separate but connected pieces (as in Holst's *The Planets*) and for an orchestral selection from an opera, ballet, or other long work. » Baroque (music); prelude

Sukarno or **Soekarno, (Ahmed)** (1902–70) Indonesian statesman and first President of Indonesia (1945–66), born in Surabaya, Java. He formed the Indonesia National Party in 1927, was imprisoned by the Dutch in Bandung (1929–31), and lived in exile until 1942, when he was made leader during the Japanese occupation. He became President when Indonesia was granted independence in 1945. His popularity waned as the country suffered increasing internal chaos and poverty, while his government laid themselves open to charges of corruption. An abortive communist coup (1965) led to student riots and a takeover by the army, his powers gradually devolving onto General Suharto. Sukarno finally retired in 1968, and died in Jakarta.

Sukhothai [sukuh**tiy**] 17°00N 99°51E. Ancient ruined city of Thailand, 440 km/273 ml N of Bangkok; founded in the mid-13th-c when the nation of Thailand came into being; former capital of the Thai-Khmer state; now a historical park. » Thailand [i]

sukiyaki [**soo**keeyakee] A Japanese beef dish. Traditionally Buddhism avoided meat, but Westerners introduced meat eating after 1868, and *sukiyaki* was an adaptation to Japanese taste. Thinly sliced beef is cooked with suet in an iron pan in the middle of the table. Sauce is added, made of *shoyu*, beaten raw egg, sugar, and *mirin* (a type of sweet saké). » saké; shoyu

Sukkoth or **Succoth** [**suh**k-ohth, -oht] The Jewish Feast of Tabernacles or Booths celebrated in September or October (15–21 Tishri) as a festival of thanksgiving. 'Booths' or light temporary shelters are constructed in homes or gardens and in synagogues, in memory of the huts or tents used by the Israelites in the desert after leaving Egypt (Exodus 13). » RR23

Sukkur [**suk**oor], also **Sakhar** 27°42N 68°54E, pop (1981) 193 000. City in Sind province, Pakistan; on E bank of R Indus, 360 km/224 ml NNE of Karachi; Sukkur (Lloyd) Barrage built

1928–32 (dam 58 m/190 ft high), with seven canals irrigating 18 million sq km/7 million sq ml; railway junction; textiles, vegetable oils, flour milling. » Pakistan [i]

Sulaiman or **Suleyman I**, byname **the Magnificent** (1494–1566) Ottoman Sultan (1520–66), who added to his dominions by conquest Belgrade, Budapest, Rhodes, Tabriz, Baghdad, Aden, and Algiers. His fleets dominated the Mediterranean, although he failed to capture Malta. His system of laws regulating land tenure earned him the name *Kanuni* ('lawgiver'), and he was a great patron of arts and architecture. He died during the siege of Szigeth in his war with Austria. » Ottoman Empire

Sulawesi [soola**way**see] Island in Indonesia, off E Borneo; mountainous and forested; rice, tuna, maize, kapok, copra; nickel, coal, asphalt, mica, sulphur, salt; divided into four provinces; **South Sulawesi**, formerly **South Celebes**, pop (1980) 442 302, area 27 686 sq km/10 687 sq ml, capital Ujung Pandang; **Central Sulawesi**, formerly **Central Celebes**, pop (1980) 1 289 639; area 69 726 sq km/26 914 sq ml, capital Palu; **South-East Sulawesi**, formerly **South-East Celebes**, pop (1980) 6 062 212, area 72 781 sq km/28 093 sq ml, capital Kendari; **North Sulawesi**, formerly **North Celebes**, pop (1980) 2 115 384, area 19 023 sq km/7 343 sq ml, capital Manado; includes the Sangir Is. » Indonesia [i]

Suleyman » **Sulaiman**

sulfur » **sulphur**

Sulla, Lucius Cornelius, byname **Felix** ('Lucky') (138–78 BC) Ruthless and enigmatic Roman politician of the late Republic, whose bitter feud with Marius, begun in Africa in 107 BC during the Jugurthine War, twice plunged Rome into civil war in the 80s BC. In 88 BC he chose to lead his army against the state rather than surrender to Marius his command of the war against Mithridates, and on returning to Rome (83 BC) used his forces to defeat the Marians and secure his own (illegal) position. Appointed 'Dictator' in 82 BC, he set about reforming the state, and enacted a number of measures to boost the authority of the Senate. These did not long survive his sudden retirement in 79 BC, but his reform of criminal jurisdiction lasted into the Empire. » Jugurtha; Marius; Mithridates VI Eupator

Sullivan, Sir Arthur (Seymour) (1842–1900) British composer, born and died in London. He studied in London and Leipzig, and became an organist in London. His association with the theatre started in 1867, and from 1871 he was known for his collaboration with W S Gilbert in such comic operas as *HMS Pinafore* (1878) and *The Pirates of Penzance* (1879). He also composed a grand opera, *Ivanhoe* (1891), cantatas, ballads, a *Te Deum*, and hymn tunes. He was knighted in 1883. » Gilbert, W S

Sullivan, Jim, properly **James** (1903–77) British rugby player, born in Cardiff, Wales. He played rugby union for Cardiff before joining Wigan rugby league club in 1921. He kicked a world record 2 859 goals, including a record 22 in one game (Wigan v Flimby & Fothergill, 1925). Player-coach of Wigan in 1932, he retired in 1946, and later became coach to Rochdale Hornets and St Helens. He died near Wigan. » rugby football

Sullivan, Louis (Henry) (1856–1924) US architect, born in Boston. He studied at Boston and Paris, and began to practise in Chicago with his partner, Dankmar Adler (1844–1900). His experimental, functional skeleton constructions of skyscrapers and office blocks, particularly the Gage building and stock exchange, Chicago, earned him the title 'Father of Modernism'. He died in Chicago.

Sully, Maximilien de Béthune, Duc de ('Duke of') [**sü**lee] (1560–1641) French Huguenot soldier, financier, and statesman who became Henry IV's Chief Minister, born at Rosny. He fought in the later stages of the Wars of Religion (1574–98) and was wounded at Ivry (1590). Instrumental in arranging Henry of Navarre's marriage to Maria de' Medici (1600), he became the King's trusted counsellor. His major achievement was the restoration of the economy after the civil wars. In 1606 he was created duke, but after Henry's assassination (1610) was forced to retire to his estates, where he died. » Huguenots; Religion, Wars of

Sully Prudhomme [**sü**lee prü**dom**], pseudonym of **René François Armand Prudhomme** (1839–1907) French poet, born in Paris. He studied science, then developed an interest in philosophy which underlies most of his poetical works. His early *Stances et poèmes* (1865) was widely praised, and among his later important works were the didactic poems *La Justice* (1878, Justice) and *Le Bonheur* (1888, Happiness). A leader of the Parnassian movement, which tried to restore elegance and control to poetry in reaction against Romanticism, he won the first Nobel Prize for Literature in 1901, and died in Paris. » French literature; poetry; Romanticism (literature)

sulphonamides/sulfonamides [suhl**fon**amiydz] The first drugs to be used for the prevention and cure of bacterial infections in humans; their introduction in the late 1930s resulted in a sharp decline in deaths from infectious diseases. The therapeutic value of prontosil (a dye), the first of many sulphonamides, was discovered in 1938 by Gerhard Domagk (1895–1964). Some resistance developed through overuse (eg the mass prophylactic use of sulfadiazine in military personnel during World War 2), and they were generally superseded by penicillin; but they are still important in the treatment of some infections. » antibiotics; penicillin

sulphur/sulfur S, element 16, a non-metal occurring in nature in yellow molecular crystals of S_8, also called **brimstone**. The molecular structure is that of a puckered ring. The solid melts at 113°C and boils at 440°C. The viscosity of liquid sulphur increases on heating, as the rings are converted to chains of indefinite length. Gaseous sulphur above the boiling point contains substantial S_2, analogous to O_2. Many other different forms have been identified. In addition to the free element, sulphur is also recovered from many sulphide ores. It shows a great variety of oxidation states, the most common being −2, +4, and +6, giving rise to compounds called **sulphides**, **sulphites**, and **sulphates**. By far the most important use is oxidation to sulphuric acid. » chemical elements; sulphuric acid

sulphur-bottom whale » **blue whale**

sulphuric acid H_2SO_4, boiling point 330°C. A strong dibasic acid, a colourless oily liquid, formerly known as *oil of vitriol* or simply *vitriol*. It is one of the most important industrial chemicals, produced by the catalytic oxidation of sulphur dioxide, itself produced by the oxidation of sulphur or by the roasting of sulphide ores. It is used in the production of almost all other acids, and in the manufacture of fertilizers, fabrics, dyestuffs, and detergents. » acid; oxidation; sulphur

sumac or **sumach** [**soo**mak] Any of several species of a genus which includes poison ivy and the turpentine tree, many causing skin damage or dermatitis. The best-known is **stag's horn sumac** (*Rhus typhina*), a suckering shrub native to N America; twigs velvety-hairy; leaves pinnate; flowers in conical clusters, males green, females reddish. (Genus: *Rhus*. Family: *Anacardiaceae*.) » dermatitis; pinnate; poison ivy; turpentine tree

Sumatra [soo**mah**tra], Indonesian **Sumatera** pop (1980) 28 016 100; area 473 606 sq km/182 812 sq ml. Island in W Indonesia, S of the Malay Peninsula; 1 760 km/1 094 ml long and 400 km/250 ml wide; fifth largest island in the world; includes the Riau archipelago (E) and the Mentawi Is (W); centre of Buddhist kingdom of Sri Vijaya, 7th–13th-c; visited by Marco Polo, 13th-c; separatist movement followed Indonesian independence, 1949; major cities include Medan, Jambi, Padang, Pekanbaru, Banda Aceh; Bukit Barisan range (W) rises to 3 805 m/12 483 ft at Gunung Kerinci; Batanghari, longest river in Sumatra; swamp and marshland in SE (a third of the island); oil, tin, bauxite, gold, natural gas; rubber, coffee, tea, pepper. » Indonesia [i]; Palembang

Sumer [**soo**mer] The name given to the part of Lower Mesopotamia between Babylon and the Persian Gulf. It is the place where the world's first urban civilization evolved; among the greatest of Sumerian city-states were Eridu, Ur, and Uruk. Surviving art forms date from c.2500 BC, and include the stone statues of Gudea and many coloured bas-reliefs. » Babylonian art; bas-relief; Eridu; Mesopotamia; Sumerian and Assyrian architecture; Ur; Uruk

Sumerian and Assyrian architecture One of the earliest instances of architecture, dating from the 4th millennium BC, located on the Euphrates delta on the Persian Gulf. It is characterized by the use of brick arches, domes, and vaults, typically decorated with a surface geometrical pattern of red, black, and brown mosaics, as at the ziggurat temple of Warka (c.2900–2340 BC). It was later adapted by the Assyrians in N Mesopotamia for buildings such as the vast 23-acre Palace of Saragon at Khorsabad (c.722–705 BC). » arch [i]; Persian architecture; Sumer; vault [i]; ziggurat [i]

summary trial In the UK, a trial in the magistrates' court or (in Scotland) the sheriff court (courts of *summary jurisdiction*). Many offences are classified as summary, and this almost always decides the venue. In practice, many indictable offences are also tried on a summary basis, because either the prosecution or defence seeks summary trial. In some cases the defendant charged with a summary offence may be tried before a jury (ie in the Crown Court, in England and Wales). A number of indictable offences, including murder and rape, must be tried in the Crown Court. Theft is an example of an indictable offence mostly tried in the magistrates' court or sheriff court. » Crown Court; indictment; jury; justice of the peace; stipendiary magistrate

summer cypress A bushy annual, growing to 1 m/3¼ ft or more, native to Europe and Asia; leaves very narrow, pale green; flowers tiny, green. The colour and habit are slightly reminiscent of cypress trees. Cultivars with leaves turning deep russet-red in autumn are sometimes called **burning bush**. (*Kochia scoparia*. Family: *Chenopodiaceae*). » annual; cultivar; cypress

summer-grape » grapevine

Summer Time » Daylight Saving Time

summit diplomacy A term first used in the 1950s for negotiations between heads of state and governments with the intention of resolving disagreements; also known as **summitry**. It was regarded as a means of circumnavigating what was viewed as less effective traditional diplomacy. Since the 1960s it has been applied to any special meeting between national leaders, usually following lengthy diplomatic negotiations, with a symbolic and formal content.

sumo wrestling A Japanese national sport steeped in history and tradition. Competition takes place in a 12 ft (3.66 m) diameter circle, the object being to force one's opponent out of the ring or to the ground. Sumo wrestlers are very large and eat vast amounts of food to increase their weight and body size. » wrestling

Sumy [soomee] 50°55N 34°49E, pop (1983) 248 000. Capital city of Sumskaya oblast, NE Ukraine, on R Psel; founded, 1652; airfield; railway; wool textiles, clothing, fertilizers, foodstuffs. » Ukraine

Sun The central object of our Solar System and the nearest star to the Earth. Its average distance from Earth is 150 million km/93 million ml, and on account of this proximity it is studied more than any other star. The source of its energy is nuclear reactions in the central core (temperature 15 million K, relative density 155) extending to a quarter of the solar radius and including half the mass. Our Sun is nearly 5 thousand million years old, and is about halfway through its expected life cycle. Every second it annihilates 5 million tonnes of matter, to release 39×10^{26} watts of energy. » solar constant/ flare/ prominence/time/wind; Solar System; sunspot; Plate I

sun bear The smallest bear (length, 1.3 m/4 ft), native to SE Asia; short black coat with pale snout and yellow crescent on chest; inhabits tropical forest; climbs well; eats honey, insects, small vertebrates, fruit; also known as **honey bear**, **Malay bear**, or **bruang**. (*Helarctos malayanus*.) » bear

Sun Dance An annual ceremony originally lasting from two to five days which grew up in the 1870s among the Plains Indians of N America. A trance was produced in the dancers through fixing their gaze upon the Sun. Others attached themselves to a sacred pole by skewers thrust through their chest muscles, and then pulled themselves outwards until the flesh gave way, thereby acquiring the gift of individual power. » Plains Indians

sun rose An evergreen shrub native to the Mediterranean region; leaves opposite, very narrow to oval or oblong; flowers large, white, or pink, with five distinctive crumpled petals. (Genus: *Cistus*, 20 species. Family: *Cistaceae*.) » evergreen plants; shrub

sun spider A long-legged, predatory arthropod found mostly in deserts and arid habitats; fangs (*chelicerae*) massive; other mouthparts (*pedipalps*) leg-like; first pair of legs slender, used as feelers; also known as **wind scorpions**. (Class: *Arachnida*. Order: *Solpugida*, c.900 species.) » Arachnida; arthropod

Sun Temple A richly sculptured Hindu temple built in the 13th-c at Konarak, Orissa, India. The temple itself represents seven horses pulling the splendid chariot of Surya, the Sun-god. It was known as the Black Pagoda to sailors of old, who navigated by it. » Hinduism

Sun-tzu (4th-c BC) Chinese general and military philosopher, a native of the state of Ch'i (modern Shantung). He was the author of *Ping-fa* (The Art of War), the first known military treatise, containing profound and still-relevant insights into the philosophy of human conflict. He moved to Wu, whose armies he led to great victories over the rival principalities of Ch'u, Ch'i, and Ch'in.

Sun Yixian or **Sun Yat-sen** [sun yat**sen**] (1866–1925) Founder and early leader of China's Nationalist Party, born in Xiangshan, Guangdong province. He was educated in Hawaii and in Hong Kong, where he trained as a doctor. Alarmed by the weakness and decay of China, he founded the Society for the Revival of China, and sprang to fame when, on a visit to London, he was kidnapped by the Chinese legation, and released through the intervention of the Foreign Office. He then helped to organize risings in S China. He returned to China after the 1911 Wuhan rising, realized that he would not be widely acceptable as President, and voluntarily handed over the office to Yuan Shikai. After the assassination of his follower, Sung Chiao-jen, civil war ensued (1913), and he set up a separate government at Guangzhou (Canton). He died in Beijing (Peking), widely accepted as the true leader of the nation. » Guomindang; Yuan Shikai

sunbird A small songbird, native to the Old World tropics and the Middle East; slender curved bill and tubular tongue; inhabits woodland (drab species) or open country (bright, often iridescent, species); eats nectar, fruit, and insects. Unrelated birds of the genus *Neodrepanis* (Family: *Philepittidae*) are called **false sunbirds** or **sunbird-asities**. (Family: *Nectariniidae*, 106 species.) » songbird

sunbittern A long-legged water bird, native to C and S America; slim head, sharp pointed bill, rounded wings and tail, mottled plumage; inhabits edges of streams in woodland; eats fish and water invertebrates. (*Eurypyga helias*. Family: *Eurypygidae*.)

sunburn Damage to the skin caused by strong sunlight, especially in people with fair complexions. Short exposure results in redness and itch. More prolonged exposure causes pain, swelling of the skin, and blistering, accompanied by fever, headache, and nausea. » heat stroke; keratosis; melanoma; ultraviolet radiation

Sunda Islands [**soon**da] Island group in Indonesia, comprising the **Greater Sunda Is** of Java, Sumatra, Borneo, and Sulawesi, with their small adjacent islands, and **Nusa Tenggara**, formerly the **Lesser Sunda Is** of Bali, Lombok, Sumba, Sumbawa, Flores, and Timor, with their small islands. » Indonesia [i]

Sundanese A people from the highlands of W Java, Indonesia, but now also living in other parts of Java and Sumatra. One of three main groups on the island, they converted to Islam in the 16th-c. They are culturally similar to other Javanese, but have a distinctive language. Population c.19 million. » Java

Sundarbans National park in India and Bangladesh; area c.10 000 sq km/3 900 sq ml; established in 1973 to protect the mangrove habitat of the Ganges delta and its wildlife, particularly India's largest surviving population of tigers; a world heritage site. » Ganges, River

Sunday The day of the week set aside by the Christian religion for divine worship, mainly in commemoration of Christ's resurrection. Already in New Testament times it replaced the Jewish Sabbath, when Paul and the Christians of Troas gathered on the first day of the week to 'break bread' (*Acts* 20), and it is called 'the Lord's day' (*Rev* 1). In 1971 the UK ratified the recommendation of the International Standardization

Organization that Monday replace Sunday as the first day of the week. » Christianity; Sabbath

Sunday School Classes for the religious education of children, usually linked to worship services, in Protestant Churches. They derive from the Sunday charity school, instituted in London in 1780, for the basic education of children of the poor. » Protestantism

Sunderland, formerly **Wearmouth** 54°55N 1°23W, pop (1981) 195 896. Port town in Sunderland borough, Tyne and Wear, NE England; at the mouth of the R Wear, 16 km/10 ml SE of Newcastle upon Tyne; site of monastery (674); railway; shipbuilding, ship repair, chemicals, glass, vehicles, coal trade; museum, art gallery. » Tyne and Wear

sundew A carnivorous plant, mostly a small perennial, native in most tropical and temperate regions, especially Australasia and S Africa; leaves spoon- or paddle-shaped, covered with long, red hairs; flowers 5-petalled, in slender spikes. The long hairs of the leaves are tentacle-like, being mobile and ending in a spherical gland which secretes a sticky substance. Insects attracted to the glistening drops are caught, and their struggles cause the surrounding hairs to bend inwards, preventing escape. The leaf itself may also bend over to enfold the prey. The glands then secrete enzymes, and the plant digests the prey before the leaf and hairs unfold. (Genus: *Drosera*, 100 species. Family: *Droseraceae*.) » carnivorous plant; enzyme; perennial

sundial A device for showing the passage of time by the shadow cast on a graduated scale by a *gnomon* (some solid object, such as a rod or triangular plate attached to the dial). The earliest-known sundial dates from c.300 BC. With the development of Greek mathematics very elaborate dials were made. The study revived in the Middle Ages: many types were devised, and the theory of dialling was much studied until dials were gradually outmoded by clocks in the 17th–18th-c. » nocturnal

Sundsvall [**suns**val] 62°22N 17°20E, pop (1982) 94 397. Seaport and commercial town in SE Västernorrland county, E Sweden, on the Gulf of Bothnia; important trading centre from the 6th-c; charter, 1624; railway; woodworking, papermaking, oil port. » Sweden [i]

sunfish Large and very distinctive fish widespread in open waters of tropical to temperate seas; body compressed, almost circular; length typically 1–2 m/3¼–6½ ft, but up to 4 m/13 ft; mouth small, teeth fused into a sharp beak; dorsal and anal fins tall, posteriorly positioned, tail fin absent; also called **trunkfish**. (*Mola mola*. Family: *Molidae*.)

sunflower A large annual growing to 3 m/10 ft, a native of N America; stem stout, usually unbranched, bearing broadly oval to heart-shaped leaves; usually a solitary drooping flower head up to 30 cm/12 in across; outer ray florets golden yellow. It is a popular garden ornamental. Several varieties are cultivated for the edible and rich oil-yielding seeds. (*Helianthus annuus*. Family: *Compositae*.) » annual

Sung dynasty » **Song dynasty**

Sung Tsu-wen » **Song Ziwen**

sungrabe » **finfoot**

Sunnis Members of an Islamic religious movement representing 'orthodoxy' in Islam, comprising about 80 per cent of all Muslims. They recognize the first four caliphs as following the right course (*rashidun*), and base their *sunnah* ('path' of the Prophet Mohammed) upon the Koran and the *hadith* or 'traditions' of the Prophet. They are organized into four legal schools which all enjoy equal standing. The other major Islamic group is made up of Shiites. » Islam; Shiites

sunscreen The use of barrier creams to reduce the penetration of ultraviolet rays to the skin. A number of substances are used, including para-aminobenzoic acid and zinc. » sunburn

sunspot An apparently dark region on the solar photosphere, the central part termed the *umbra*. Sunspots have a temperature of 4 000K, compared to 6 000K for the photosphere generally, so appear dark by contrast. They are caused by an intense magnetic field erupting from within the Sun, and follow a cycle of growth and decay over c.11 years. » photosphere; Sun; Zürich sunspot number

sunstroke » **heat stroke**

super-ego » **ego**

superbowl » **football 2** [i]; RR103

superconducting quantum interference device (SQUID) Rings of superconducting material employing Josephson junctions, used for the accurate measurement of minute magnetic fields. It relies on an interaction between the field under test and the current around a ring. It can be used to measure low temperatures and to monitor brain activity. » Josephson junction; magnetic field [i]; superconductivity

superconductivity The property of zero electrical resistance, accompanied by the expulsion of magnetic fields (the Meissner effect), exhibited by certain metals, alloys, and compounds when cooled to below some critical temperature, typically less than −260°C. Both effects must be present for true superconductivity. An electrical current established in a superconducting ring of material will continue indefinitely while the low temperature is maintained. A superconducting material subjected to a current larger than some critical current, or to a magnetic field larger than some critical field, will cease to be superconducting. Superconductivity was first observed by Dutch physicist Heike Kamerlingh Onnes in 1911, using mercury. High temperature superconductivity, for temperatures in excess of −250°C, was first observed in 1986 by Argentinian physicist Alex Müller (1943–) and German physicist Georg Bednorz (1950–), using a ceramic of copper oxide containing barium and lanthanum. Similar effects have been observed in other ceramics, some of which superconduct at temperatures greater than −180°C; but as yet no commercially useful high-temperature superconductor is available, because of low critical fields and currents plus the brittle nature of the material. Superconductors are currently used in large magnets, such as those required by nuclear magnetic resonance spectrometers and particle accelerators. » alloy; BCS theory; ceramics; cryogenics; electrical conduction; magnetic field [i]; Meissner effect; Josephson junction; resistance; superfluidity

supercooling The cooling of certain liquids, a condition which occurs in many processes, natural and industrial, below a temperature considered their freezing point. When this is done the condition is unstable, and the supercooled liquid will, if disturbed, change into the solid phase stable at that temperature. These supercooling conditions occur in the formation of ice crystals in clouds, the freezing of surface water in lakes, and freeze drying. The passage from supercooled water to ice is usually brought about by some nucleus, such as a dust particle. Certain substances can, however, persist in a supercooled state, notably glasses, which although to all intents and purposes permanent solids, are considered to be supercooled liquids. » glass 2 [i]

superfluidity The property of zero resistance to flow (ie zero viscosity), exhibited by liquid helium at temperatures below −271°C. Superfluid helium exhibits unusual properties, including the ability to creep out of a container apparently in defiance of gravity, and the inability to be set spinning in the way a solid object can. Superfluidity is an example of quantum behaviour directly observable on a large scale. » cryogenics; helium; superconductivity; viscosity

supergiant A rare type of star, very massive, and the most luminous known. Examples include Polaris, Betelgeuse (in Orion), and Canopus. They are 10–60 solar masses, 10 000 times brighter than the Sun, and thus visible at great distances. » star

supergravity A speculative quantum theory incorporating gravity, electromagnetic force, and nuclear force. It is a gauge theory based on supersymmetry, postulating gravitons and gravitinos as carriers of the gravitational force. Theoretically attractive, it lacks experimental support. » grand unified theories; supersymmetry

superheterodyne [sooper**het**uhruhdiyn] The most common technique used in radio reception. The incoming radio frequency signal is converted into a lower intermediate frequency by mixing it with a signal generated inside the receiver, called the *local oscillator*. This intermediate frequency is easier to amplify and manipulate than the initial radio frequencies. » frequency modulation; oscillation; radio

Superior, Lake Largest of the Great Lakes, and the largest freshwater lake in the world; part of US–Canadian boundary;

length 563 km/350 ml; breadth 257 km/160 ml; maximum depth 405 m/1 329 ft; area 82 103 sq km/31 692 sq ml, 35% in Canada; connected with L Huron (SE) via St Mary's R (the Soo canals); several islands, including Isle Royale (a US national park); transport of minerals (especially iron ore), grain. » Great Lakes

supernatural » **paranormal**

supernova A rare and spectacular explosion resulting in the destruction of a massive star. At the endpoint of stellar evolution, the hydrogen fuel in the star core has all been converted to helium. The star therefore cools, and contracts. This is a runaway process, because as the star shrinks, the gravitational force at the surface increases, resulting in an intensification of inwards forces. In stars of a few solar masses, the central core implodes in less than one second, and this triggers an instantaneous nuclear explosion of all the unprocessed material outside the core. At the centre a neutron star, pulsar, or black hole is the endpoint. The exploded atmosphere is blasted into space at about one-tenth the speed of light, and the remnant can be detected for hundreds of years on account of its radio emission. Light emision from it is temporarily 100 million times brighter than the Sun, and the star can be seen for up to two years. Well known examples are the supernova of 4 July 1054 (Crab Nebula), 1604 (seen by Kepler), and 1987 in the Large Magellanic Cloud. They are intrinsically rare; none have been sighted within our Milky Way since the invention of the telescope. » black hole; neutron star; pulsar; star; stellar evolution

superovulation syndrome A condition which occasionally results when infertile women are given human gonadotrophic hormone and/or the synthetic drug clomiphene to stimulate ovulation. Several ova may be simultaneously released and fertilized, with consequential multiple births. » gonadotrophin; pregnancy [i]

superoxide A compound containing the ion O_2^-, formed by the heavier alkali metals, instead of normal oxides. » alkali

superphosphates Fertilizers containing phosphate as the $H_2PO_4^{2-}$ ion. They are so called because, for a given weight, $Ca(H_2PO_4)_2$ contains more phosphorus than does $CaHPO_4$. » fertilizer; phosphate

superposition » **interference** [i]

Superrealism » **Photorealism**

supersonic In fluid mechanics, fluid flow which is faster than the velocity of sound in that fluid, either in the case of an object moving through the fluid, or a fluid moving around a stationary object. Supersonic aircraft fly faster than the speed of sound in air. » aerodynamics [i]; fluid mechanics; sound

superstrings A speculative quantum theory, embracing all the forces of nature, which may avoid the difficulties encountered by early unification schemes involving gravity; proposed by British physicist Michael Green and US physicist John Schwartz in 1984. It is based on a fundamental extended submicroscopic string in place of the usual point particle, plus supersymmetry. It is consistent only in ten dimensions, and has no experimental support. » forces of nature [i]; grand unified theories; supersymmetry

supersymmetry In particle physics, a symmetry relation linking particles of different spins. Theories incorporating supersymmetry predict particles that are partners to observed particles, having the same mass but different spin. No such supersymmetric partners (squark, slepton, photino, and others) have been observed. » superstrings; supergravity

supination A movement of the forearm in which the palm of the hand is brought to face forwards, so that the thumb is directed away from the body. In this position the radius and ulna lie parallel to each other. It is a much more powerful movement than pronation, and as most people are right-handed, this accounts for the right-hand thread on screws and other such phenomena. » arm; pronation

supply and demand An economic concept which states that the price of an article (or 'good') will move to the level where the quantity demanded by purchasers equals the quantity that suppliers are willing to sell. » demand; elasticity (economics); equilibrium; market forces

supply-side economics An economic theory that policy measures should be taken to boost the supply of goods and services, or output. It contrasts with the Keynesian view of economic management, with its emphasis on policies that would change aggregate demand. The theory was used to some extent in the USA and UK during the early 1980s. » supply and demand

supportive psychotherapy An approach in which an attempt is made to reinforce the patient's defences, thus allowing the suppression of disturbing psychological material. There is no attempt to probe emotional conflicts in any depth. The technique is used in situations where the symptoms are relatively trivial and therefore not meriting detailed investigation, or with patients who are too fragile to achieve greater insight without major and possibly permanent decompensation (psychological breakdown with the possible development of a psychosis). The technique emphasizes reassurance, counselling, re-education, persuasion and suggestion. It is often carried out by non-medical members of a psychiatric team, such as nursing staff. » psychosis; psychotherapy

supralittoral zone » **benthic environments**

suprarenal glands » **adrenal glands**

Suprematism A form of modern art based on four simple shapes: rectangle, circle, triangle and cross. This movement was started in Russia c.1913 by Kazimir Malevich (1878–1935), who demonstrated the aesthetic purity of it all by painting a white square on a white ground. » abstract art; Cubism; Minimal art; modern art

Supreme Court In the USA, the highest federal court established under the constitution, members of which are appointed by the President with the advice and consent of the Senate. In addition to its jurisdiction relating to appeals, the court also exercises oversight of the constitution through the power of judicial review of the acts of state, federal legislatures, and the executive. » Constitution of the United States

Supreme Headquarters Allied Expeditionary Force (SHAEF) A force formally established (13 Feb 1944) under US General Eisenhower, with British Air Chief Marshal Tedder as deputy supreme commander, to mount the Allied invasion of occupied Europe and strike at the heart of Germany. » D-Day; Eisenhower; Tedder; World War 2

Supreme Soviet » **soviet**

Surabaya [soora**bah**ya] or **Surabaja** 7°14S 112°45E, pop (1980) 1 556 255. Industrial seaport capital of Java Timor province, E Java, Indonesia, at mouth of R Kali Mas; Indonesia's second largest city; port facilities at Tanjung Perak; important trading centre since the 14th-c; airfield; railway; university (1954); naval base; oil refining, textiles, glass, footwear, tobacco, rubber. » Java

Surat [**soo**rat] 21°12N 72°55E, pop (1981) 913 000. Port in Gujarat, W India, on the Gulf of Cambay, 240 km/150 ml N of Bombay; rich trading centre of Mughal Empire, 17th–18th-c; first English trading post in India, 1612; headquarters of British East India Company until 1687; railway; university (1967); textiles, engineering; noted for its zari thread work and diamond cutting. » Gujarat

surface active agent » **surfactant**

surface physics The study of the electronic and structural properties of the surface of matter, ie the outermost layer of atoms. Surface properties are important in several domains, including catalysis, corrosion, the emission of electrons from surfaces, optical properties, and friction. Surface layers formed at the interface of two solids are also important, as in semiconductor devices. Experiments rely on such techniques as electron diffraction and field ion microscopy, using samples in ultrahigh vacuums. » field emission; molecular beam epitaxy; photoelectric effect; quantum Hall effect; rheology; secondary emission; solid-state physics; sputtering; surface tension [i]; thermionics; thin films; tribology; vacuum deposition

surface printing A term sometimes used for those techniques of printmaking which do not involve cutting, etching, or scraping the block or plate. The main techniques are lithography and monotype, but the term is sometimes extended to include screen-printing. » lithography; monotype; printing [i]; screen printing

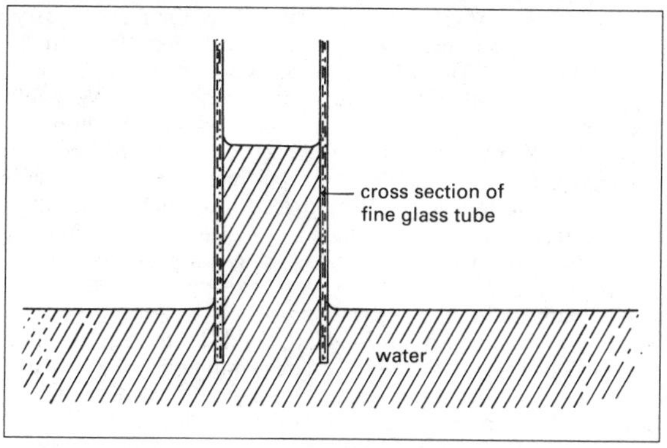

Water rises up a narrow pipe by capillarity, a surface tension effect which can be explained in terms of pressure differences across a curved air–liquid boundary. The curved liquid is called the meniscus.

surface structure » **deep structure**

surface tension A property of the surface of a liquid, which always seeks to achieve the minimum area, corresponding to the state of lowest energy. It is caused by the inward attraction of surface molecules. Surface tension γ is the energy needed to form the surface divided by the area of surface formed; units N/m. For water at 20°C in air, $\gamma = .073$ N/m. Because of surface tension, liquid surfaces appear elastic, as observed in bubbles and soap films. » capillarity

surfactant Any substance that strongly influences the surface properties of a material; also called a **surface active agent**. It is often applied to soaps and detergents, whose cleaning powers depend on the surfactant's ability to increase the spreading and wetting power of water. Surfactants are also important in lubrication and water repellent coatings. » surface tension [i]

surgeonfish Any of the family *Acanthuridae* of colourful deep-bodied fish widespread in tropical seas, especially in the Indo-Pacific; name refers to the sharp moveable spine on sides of tail which can be erected for defence; body length typically 10–40 cm/4–16 in; teeth specialized for scraping algae from coral surfaces; also called **tang**.

surgery The branch of medicine which treats diseases and conditions by operating on the patient. The use of the hands for the treatment of disease dates from prehistoric times. Trephining the skull to allow the escape of disease from the body was a very early procedure, and practised along with the splinting of fractures, the lancing of abscesses, and the application of pressure for bleeding. Obstacles to the development of surgery were pain, infection, and shock, which could not be controlled until the 20th-c. Consequently, early surgical operations were limited to near the surface of the body, such as hernia repair, removal of bladder stones, and amputation. With modern anaesthesia, all parts of the body have become accessible, beginning with the removal of the appendix for appendicitis, and leading to the repair of perforated peptic ulcers, the removal of part of the lungs for cancer, neurosurgery, the replacement of blocked blood vessels to the heart, and organ transplantation. The development of artificial parts of the body and their substitution for worn-out tissues such as the replacement of hip joints and the aorta is also a remarkable modern development. » asepsis; medicine; microsurgery; plastic surgery; trepanning

suricate » **meerkat**

Suriname, also **Surinam**, official name **Republic of Suriname** [**soo**rinam] pop (1990e) 411 000; area 163 265 sq km/63 020 sq ml. Republic in NE South America, divided into nine districts; bounded W by Guyana, E by French Guiana, and S by Brazil; capital, Paramaribo; timezone GMT −3½; chief ethnic groups, East Indians (37%), Creoles (31%), Javanese (15%); official language, Dutch, with Surinamese widely spoken; wide range of religious groups; unit of currency, the Suriname guilder; diverse natural regions, ranging from coastal lowland through savannah to mountainous upland; coastal strip mostly covered by swamp; highland interior (S) overgrown with dense tropical forest; tropically hot and humid, two rainy seasons (May–Jul, Nov–Jan); Paramaribo temperatures, 22–33°C; average monthly rainfall 310 mm/12.2 in (N), 67 mm/2.6 in (S); sighted by Columbus, 1498; first settled by the British, 1651; taken by the states of Zeeland, 1667; captured by the British, 1799; restored to the Netherlands, 1818; independent republic, 1975; emigration of c.40% of population to the Netherlands, following independence; military coup, 1980; 1987 constitution provides for a 51-member National Assembly elected for five years, and a president elected by the Assembly; lack of foreign exchange has hindered development of the economy, which is based on agriculture and mining; bauxite mining provides c.80% of export income; sugar cane, rice, citrus fruits, coffee, bananas, oil palms, cacao, fishing; vast timber resources. » Netherlands, The [i]; Paramaribo; RR27 national holidays; RR61 political leaders

Surrealism (Fr 'over' or 'intense' realism) An important movement in modern art and literature which flourished between the Wars, mainly in France. The first Surrealist manifesto of André Breton (1924) proposed the subversion of 19th-c Realism by the three related means of humour, dream, and counter-logic (the absurd). This initiative was taken up by many artists and writers, and the term is now used to describe the heightened or distorted perception and registration of reality, by whatever means. The basic idea was to free the artist from the demands of logic, and to penetrate beyond everyday consciousness to the 'super-reality' that lies behind. Freud's theory of the subconscious was appealed to, and many pictures by Dali, Magritte, and Tanguy seek to recreate the fantasy world of dreams. Objects are taken out of their normal context, their scale drastically changed, or they are represented as made of an inappropriate material, such as Dali's melting watches. Other leading Surrealists include Ernst, Chirico, and Arp, and its influence is clear in many works by Picasso and Klee. In literature, the movement is illustrated by the poetry of Aragon and Eluard, the plays of Ionesco and Beckett, and the novels of Genet and Burroughs. Luis Buñuel guaranteed its impact on the cinema. Advertising since c.1960 has been indebted to the images of Surrealism, usually rendered by trick photography. » absurdism; Dada; metaphysical painting; modern art; Realism; Aragon; Arp; Beckett; Breton, André; Buñuel; Chirico; Dali; Duchamp; Eluard; Ernst; Ionesco; Klee; Magritte; Picabia; Picasso; Tanguy

Surrey, Henry Howard, Earl of (c.1517–47) English courtier and poet, born at Hunsdon, Hertfordshire. In 1532 he ac-

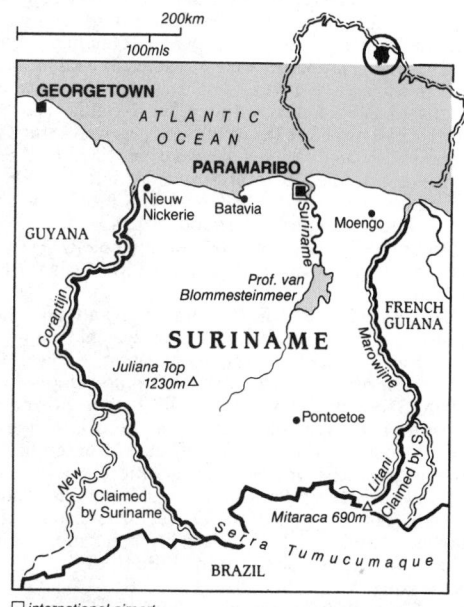

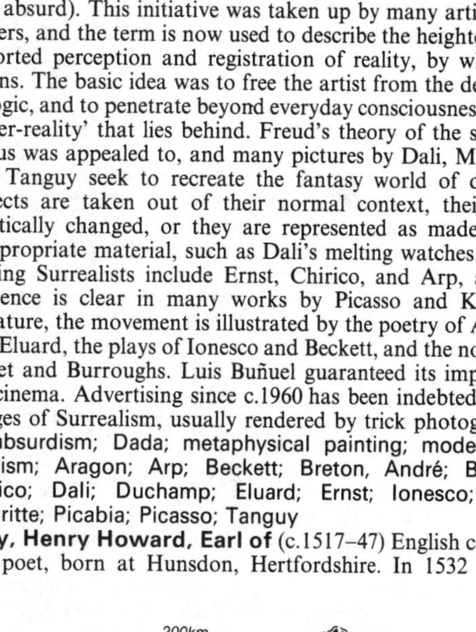

□ *international airport*

companied Henry VIII to France, was knighted in 1542, and served in Scotland, France, and Flanders. On his return in 1546, his enemies at court charged him with treason, and he was found guilty and beheaded. He is remembered for his love poetry, influenced by the Italian tradition, in which he pioneered the use of blank verse and the Elizabethan sonnet form. » blank verse; English literature; poetry; sonnet

Surrey pop (1987e) 1 000 400; area 1 679 sq km/648 sq ml. County in SE England, divided into 11 districts; partly in Greater London urban area; drained by the Thames, Mole, and Wey Rivers; crossed E–W by the North Downs, rising to 294 m/964 ft at Leith Hill; administrative centre, kingston-upon-Thames; chief towns include Guildford, Reigate, Leatherhead, Staines, Woking; largely residential; agriculture, light industry; Box Hill, Leith Hill, Runnymede, Royal Botanic Gardens (Kew), North Downs. » Downs; England [i]; Guildford

Surtees, John (1934–) British racing driver and motorcyclist, born at Westerham, Kent, the only man to win world titles on two and four wheels. He won the 350 cc motor cycling world title in 1958–60, and the 500 cc title in 1956, and 1958–60 (all on an MV Augusta). He then turned to car racing, and won the 1964 world title driving a Ferrari. He later became a racing car manufacturer. » motor cycle racing

Surtsey Island [**sert**see] area 1.9 sq km/0.7 sq ml. Volcanic island off S coast of Iceland; one of the Westman Is; erupted and formed in 1963; now a nature reserve. » Westman Islands

surveillance TV Closed circuit television with many security applications, from supervising customer areas in supermarkets to continuous remote monitoring of several unattended locations from a central office. Small monochrome cameras sensitive to low light levels are fitted with wide-angle lenses for maximum coverage from a fixed viewpoint or one which can be varied by remote control. A time-lapse videotape recorder may be operated frame-by-frame at specified intervals or triggered by a movement detector. » closed circuit television

surveying The accurate measurement and collection of data, such as relief, for a given area in order to make a map. It has traditionally been based on fieldwork, using equipment such as chains, plane tables, and theodolites, used to measure the distance, elevation, and angle of an object from an observation point. The use of aerial photographs and satellite imagery as a basis for mapping is increasing. **Geodetic surveying** is the measurement of the size and shape of the Earth, and the determination of the position of places on its surface. » aerial photography; benchmark; cartography; geodesy; map; remote sensing

Surveyor programme A series of robotic soft-lander missions to the Moon undertaken by NASA (May 1966–Jan 1968) in preparation for the manned Apollo landings. It was highly successful, with five of the seven spacecraft landing as planned. Surface material properties were measured at landing sites, and panoramic images returned. Chemistry measurements on later missions (5 and 6) demonstrated the basaltic character of Moon rocks long before the Apollo samples were returned. The camera and scoop of Surveyor 3 were recovered by Apollo 12 astronauts from the Ocean of Storms landing site. The series was managed and operated by NASA's Jet Propulsion Laboratory. » Apollo programme; Moon; NASA

Surya [**soor**ya] The Sun-god in Hindu mythology. He was the son of Indra, the pre-eminent god of the Rig-Veda. » Hinduism; Veda

Susa [**soo**za] The Greek name for **Shushan**, in antiquity, the main city of Elam and the capital of the Achaemenid empire under Darius I and his successors. It is the site of the world's best preserved ziggurat. » Elam; Persian Empire; ziggurat [i]

Susanna, Story of A book of the Old Testament Apocrypha, or Chapter 13 of the Book of Daniel in Catholic versions of the Bible; an addition to the Book of Daniel of uncertain date or provenance. It tells of how the beautiful Jewess Susanna is wrongfully accused in Babylon of adultery and is condemned to death, but is rescued by Daniel. The artful narrative commends lessons of Jewish morality and faith in God. » Apocrypha, Old Testament; Daniel, Book of

suslik » **souslik**

Suslov, Mikhail Andreyevich (1902–82) Soviet politician, born at Shakhovskoye. He joined the Communist Party in 1921, and was a member of the Central Committee from 1941 until his death. An ideologist of the Stalinist school, he became a ruthless and strongly doctrinaire administrator. Very different from Khrushchev in temperament and political outlook, he opposed Khrushchev's 'de-Stalinization' measures, economic reforms, and foreign policy, and was instrumental in unseating him in 1964. He died in Moscow. » Khrushchev; Stalin

suspension A mixture in which particles (of solid or liquid) are dispersed through another phase (liquid or gas) without dissolving in it. Suspensions are not indefinitely stable, and will eventually settle into separate phases. » colloid

Sussex Former county of England; divided into East Sussex and West Sussex in 1974, West Sussex gaining part of S Surrey. » Sussex, East; Sussex, West

Sussex, East pop (1987e) 698 000; area 1 795 sq km/693 sq ml. County of SE England, divided into seven districts; bounded S by the English Channel; South Downs parallel to the coast, part of the Weald to the N; drained by the R Ouse; county town Lewes; chief towns include Brighton, Eastbourne, Bexhill, Hastings; agriculture (cereals, fruit, vegetables), electronics, furniture, service industries; major tourist area on S coast; Beachy Head, Ashdown Forest, the Weald, Romney Marsh; castles at Bodiam, Hastings, Lewes, Pevensey; site of Battle of Hastings. » Downs; England [i]; Hastings, Battle of; Lewes; Weald, the

Sussex, Kingdom of A kingdom of the Anglo-Saxon heptarchy, situated between Kent and Wessex, and founded probably by c.500. After its reduction to a dependency of Mercia in the late 8th-c, it never regained the status of a kingdom, and was annexed to Wessex in the 9th-c. » Anglo-Saxons; Wessex

Sussex, West pop (1987e) 700 000; area 1 989 sq km/768 sq ml. County of S England, divided into seven districts; bounded S by the English Channel; drained by the Adur and Arun Rivers; South Downs run parallel to the coast; county town, Chichester; other major towns include Worthing, Crawley, Horsham; agriculture, horticulture, tourism, electronics, light engineering; the Weald, Arundel and Bamber castles, Petworth House, Goodwood. » Chichester; England [i]

Sutherland, Graham (Vivian) (1903–80) British artist, born and died in London. He studied at London, worked mainly as an etcher until 1930, then made his reputation as a painter of romantic, mainly abstract landscapes. He was an official war artist (1941–5), and later produced several memorable portraits, including 'Sir Winston Churchill' (1955). He also designed ceramics, posters, and textiles: his large tapestry, 'Christ in Majesty', was hung in the new Coventry Cathedral in 1962. » English art; etching; landscape painting

Sutherland, Dame Joan (1926–) Australian operatic soprano, born in Sydney. She made her debut at Sydney in 1947, came to London in 1951, and joined the Royal Opera, becoming resident soprano at Covent Garden. She gained international fame in 1959 with her roles in Donizetti's *Lucia di Lammermoor* and Handel's *Samson*. She has sung regularly in opera houses and concert halls all over the world, and in 1965 returned to Australia for a triumphant tour with her own company. In 1954 she married the conductor Richard Bonynge (1930–), and was made a Dame in 1979. » coloratura

Sutlej, River [**sut**lej] River of Asia; the longest of the five rivers of the Punjab; rises in Xizang region (Tibet), and flows NW as the Xiangquan He; enters India, meandering through the Himalayas, and flows SW to its confluence with the R Chenab E of Alipur; combined stream flows SW for 81 km/50 ml to meet the Indus; length 1 370 km/850 ml; used for irrigation and hydroelectric power, particularly at the Bhakara Dam, India. » Punjab (India, Pakistan)

Suttee » **Sati**

Sutton Hoo ship burial The grave of an Anglo-Saxon king, probably Raedwald of East Anglia (AD ?–624/5), discovered beneath a barrow on the R Deben near Woodbridge, E England, in 1939. Amidships in a 40-oar open rowing boat (4.25 m/14 ft in beam and 27 m/89 ft long) stood a wooden burial chamber containing silver plate, gold jewellery, and coins, weapons, and domestic equipment (now in the British Museum). It is the richest single archaeological find ever made in Britain. » Gokstad ship

Suva [**soo**va] 18°08S 178°25E, pop(1981) 68 178. Chief port and capital of Fiji, on SE coast of Viti Levu I; overlooked by Tholoisuva Forest Park; city since 1953; university (1968); copra processing, soap, edible oil, handicrafts, steel rolling mill, tourism. » Fiji; Viti Levu

Suwon [soo**wuhn**] or **Suweon** 37°16N 126°59E, pop(1984) 402 319. Industrial capital of Kyonggi province, NW Korea; 48 km/30 ml S of Seoul; subway from Seoul; agricultural college; reconstructed fortress walls and gates; Korean Folk Village nearby. » Korea [i]

Suzhou or **Suchow** [soo**joh**], formerly **Wuhsien** 31°21N 120°40E, pop(1984e) 695 500. Town in Jiangsu province, E China, on the banks of the Grand Canal; first settled c.1000 BC; capital, Kingdom of Wu, 518 BC; railway; silk, light industry, chemicals, electronics, handicrafts; over 150 ornamental gardens, including Canglang (Surging Wave) pavilion (c.1044), Shizilin (Lion Grove, 1350), and Wangshi Yuan (Garden of the Master of the Nets, 12th-c); Huqiu (Tiger Hill) artificial hill (height 36 m/118 ft), built by the King of Wu as a tomb for his father. » China [i]; Grand Canal

Svalbard [**sval**bahd] pop(1980e) 3 700; area 62 000 sq km/ 23 932 sq ml. Island group in the Arctic Ocean, c.650 km/ 400 ml N of the Norwegian mainland; four large and several smaller islands; chief islands, Spitsbergen, Nordaustlandet, Edgeøya, Barentsøya, Prins Karls Forland; discovered, 1596; formerly an important whaling centre; incorporated in Norway, 1925; administrative centre, Longyearbyen; coal, phosphate, asbestos, iron ore, galena, sphalerite, chalcopyrite, limestone dolerite, anhydrite. » Norway [i]

Svedberg, Theodor (1884–1971) Swedish physical chemist, born at Fleräng. He was educated at Uppsala, where he spent his whole career. In 1924 he described his ultracentrifuge, in which a solution can be spun at very high speed, and used it to develop methods for separating proteins. He won the Nobel Prize for Chemistry in 1926, and died at Órebro, Sweden. » biochemistry; centrifuge; protein

Sverdlovsk [sverd**lofsk**], known as **Ekaterinburg** or **Yekaterinburg** (to 1924, and 1991–) 56°52N 60°35E, pop(1989) 1 367 000. Industrial capital city of Sverdlovskaya oblast, E European Russia; in the E foothills of the Ural Mts, on R Iset; founded as a military stronghold and trading centre, 1821; airport; on the Trans-Siberian Railway; university (1920); iron ore, gold, copper; heavy engineering, metallurgy, gem cutting, clothing, textiles, tyres, fertilizers; Museum of Mineralogy. » Russia; Trans-Siberian Railway

Sveshtari tomb A 3rd-c BC tomb, located near the village of Sveshtari in N Bulgaria; a world heritage site. The tomb, which was discovered in 1982, is noted for the 10 caryatids and the frieze decorating the burial chamber. » caryatid; Thrace

Svevo, Italo [**zvay**voh], pseudonym of **Ettore Schmitz** (1861–1928) Italian novelist, born in Trieste. He worked as a bank clerk, then turned to writing, encouraged by James Joyce, who taught him English. He had a considerable success with *La Coscienza di Zeno* (1923, The Confessions of Zeno), a psychological study of inner conflicts. He died at Motta di Livenza. » Italian literature; Joyce, James; novel

Swabia A SW mediaeval German duchy, extending from the R Rhine in the W to the Alps in the S, Bavaria in the E, and Franconia in the N, containing the cities of Strasbourg, Constance, and Augsberg. The Peasants' War of 1524–5 began here, because landlords and peasants were at odds, imperial authority was increasing, and Lutheran doctrines were spreading. » Peasants' War

Swabian League An alliance of 22 imperial German cities, clerical lords, and princes, with a league of knights of Swabia (1488), to support the Holy Roman Empire and to check the threats of Wittelsbach, the dukes of Bavaria, and Swiss rebels against the Habsburgs. It was active in suppressing rebellions in 1523–5, but declined because of religious divisions caused by the Reformation. » Habsburgs; Holy Roman Empire; Reformation

Swahili A cluster of Bantu-speaking peoples of the coast and islands of E Africa, ethnically and culturally an amalgam of African groups and Arab immigrants entering the area continually since ancient times. By the 10th-c, they controlled the trade of E Africa and the Indian Ocean; from the 12th-c they built large and distinctive mosques, forts, and palaces; and by the 15th-c they were at the height of their power as a trading nation. The language Swahili probably replaced Arabic from about the 13th-c, and is today spoken by c.4 million as a lingua franca throughout E Africa. Population c.500 000. » African languages; Bantu-speaking peoples; lingua franca; Niger-Congo languages

swallow A small songbird, found worldwide; dark blue/green above, pale below; tail long, forked; inhabits open country near freshwater; eats small insects caught in flight; temperate populations migrate; nests in holes or mud nests on cliffs, buildings, etc. The name is also used for several unrelated birds. (Family: *Hirundinidae*, 57 species.) » martin; songbird

swallowtail butterfly A large, colourful butterfly in which hindwings are extended into slender tails; adults and larvae usually distasteful to predators. (Order: *Lepidoptera*. Family: *Papilionidae*.) » butterfly; larva

Swammerdam, Jan (1637–80) Dutch naturalist, born and died in Amsterdam. He trained in medicine, then turned to the study of insects, devising a classification which laid the foundations of entomology. He first observed red blood corpuscles (1658), and discovered the valves in the lymph vessels and the glands in Amphibia named after him. » blood; entomology

swamp A permanently flooded area of land with thick vegetation of reeds or trees. *Mangrove swamps* are common along river mouths in tropical and subtropical areas. In the Carboniferous period, marine swamps were common, and are the origin of present-day coal deposits. » Carboniferous period; coal; Everglades; mangrove

swamp cypress A deciduous or semi-evergreen conifer, native to the SE USA and Mexico; leaves awl-shaped, soft; also called **bald cypress**. In swampy ground the root system of *Taxodium distichum* produces woody, hollow 'knees', which project into the air and are believed to act as pneumatophores. (Genus: *Taxodium*, 3 species. Family: *Taxodiaceae*.) » conifer; cypress; deciduous/evergreen plants; pneumatophore

swamp hawk » **marsh harrier**

swan A large water bird of the duck family; found worldwide; usually white; neck very long; male called *cob*, female *pen*. (Tribe: *Anserini*. Genus: *Cygnus*, 10 species, and *Coscoroba*, 2 species. Subfamily: *Anserinae*.) » black swan; duck; mute swan; water-fowl

Swan Hill 35°23S 142°37E, pop(1983e) 9 110. Town in N Victoria, Australia, on the Murray R; railway; airfield; sheep farming, fruit growing, wine; Pioneer Settlement (open-air museum); Clockworld (collection of over 500 clocks and watches from the past 300 years). » Victoria (Australia)

Swan River Major watercourse of SW Australia; rises as the Avon R in the hills near Corrigin; flows past Perth, entering the Indian Ocean at Fremantle; receives the Helena and Canning Rivers; length (including the Avon) 386 km; the Swan River Settlement (1829) was the first colonial settlement in Western Australia; Swanland is a fertile region producing wheat, fruit, wine, wool, timber. » Perth (Australia)

Swanscombe skull The partial female skull of an archaic form of *Homo sapiens* found at Swanscombe near London in 1935–6. Its possible age is 250 000 years. » Homo [i]

Swansea, Welsh **Abertawe** 51°38N 3°57W, pop(1981) 175 172. Port city and county town in Swansea district, West Glamorgan, S Wales, UK; on the Bristol Channel at the mouth of the R Neath where it enters Swansea Bay; chartered, 1158–84; airfield; railway; university college (1920); national vehicle licensing centre; trade in coal, oil, ores; Norman castle, Royal Institution of South Wales (1835), Guildhall, industrial and maritime museum, marina; Swansea Music Festival (Oct). » West Glamorgan

swastika A symbol consisting of a cross with its four arms bent at right angles, either clockwise or anticlockwise. Found in ancient Hindu, Mexican, Buddhist, and other traditions, possibly representing the Sun, it is now politically and culturally tainted, since its appropriation by the Nazi party as its official emblem. The name derives from the Sanskrit 'svasti + ka', meaning a mystical cross used to denote good luck. » symbol; RR93

Swazi A Bantu-speaking agricultural and pastoral people living in Swaziland and adjoining parts of S Africa. They are one of the Nguni cluster of peoples, and were formed into a kingdom in the early 19th-c. Swaziland, independent since 1968, is governed by traditional Swazi institutions, with the king as head of state. Population c.1.2 million. » Bantu-speaking peoples; Nguni; Swaziland [i]

Swaziland, official name **Kingdom of Swaziland** [**swah**zeeland] pop (1990e) 770 000; area 17 363 sq km/6 702 sq ml. Constitutional monarchy in SE Africa, divided into four administrative districts; bounded N, W, S, and SE by South Africa, and NE by Mozambique; capital, Mbabane; timezone GMT +2; chief ethnic group, Swazi; chief religions, Christianity (57%), local beliefs; official languages, English (government business), Siswati; unit of currency, the lilangeni (plural, emalangeni);

small country, 192 km/119 ml N–S and 144 km/89 ml E–W; mountainous Highveld (W), highest point Emblembe (1 862 m/6 109 ft); more populated Middleveld (C), descending to 600–700 m/2 000–2 300 ft; rolling, bush-covered Lowveld (E), irrigated by river systems; humid, near temperate climate in the W, average annual rainfall 1 000–2 280 mm/40–90 in; subtropical and drier in the C; tropical in the W, with relatively little rain (500–890 mm/20–35 in, susceptible to drought); average annual temperature 15.6°C (W), 22.2°C (E); arrival of Swazi in the area, early 19th-c; boundaries with the Transvaal decided, and independence guaranteed, 1881; British agreed to Transvaal administration, 1894; British High Commission territory, 1903; independence as a constitutional monarchy, 1968; governed by a bicameral parliament consisting of a 50-member National Assembly and a 20-member Senate; the king chooses a cabinet and a prime minister to advise him; agriculture employs 70% of the population; maize, groundnuts, beans, sorghum, sweet potatoes, cotton, tobacco, pineapples, rice, sugar cane, citrus; several hydroelectric schemes; asbestos, iron ore, coal, wood products, sugar refining, canning, food and drink processing, textiles, cement, paper, chemicals, televisions. » Mbabane; Transvaal; RR27 national holidays; RR61 political leaders;

sweat A dilute solution of salts (mainly sodium chloride) and other small molecules (eg urea, lactic acid, and ammonia) actively secreted by sweat (*sudoriferous*) glands present in the skin of mammals. It provides a mechanism for the excretion of nitrogen. Evaporation from the skin surface involves heat loss; sweating is thus particularly important in humans with respect to temperature regulation. » homoiothermy; prickly heat

sweat lodge A rite of purification, spiritual and physical, widely found among N American Indians, especially among C and SW tribes. The leader conducts the participants into a specially constructed lodge, where they are seated around a mound of heated stones. Prayers and songs are offered as the leader pours heated water over the stones. It is believed that gods and spirits are present, prompting spontaneous individual and collective prayers. » American Indians

swede A biennial vegetable, related to rape, with a taproot and stem base forming a fleshy tuber. In its second (sometimes first) year, the tubers 'bolt', producing tall stems and numerous yellow cross-shaped flowers. (*Brassica napus*, variety *napobrassica*. Family: *Cruciferae*.) » biennial; brassica; rape (botany); root (botany); tuber; vegetable

Sweden, Swed **Sverige**, official name **Kingdom of Sweden**, Swed **Konungariket Sverige** pop (1990e) 8 529 000; area 411 479 sq km/158 830 sq ml. Kingdom of N Europe, occupying the E side of the Scandinavian peninsula, divided into 24 countries (*Län*); bounded E by Finland, the Gulf of Bothnia, and the Baltic Sea, SW by the Skagerrak and Kattegat, and W and NW by Norway; capital, Stockholm; chief towns, Gothenburg, Malmö, Uppsala, Norrköping, Västerås, Örebro; timezone GMT +1; population mainly of Teutonic descent; chief religion, Lutheran Protestantism (93%); unit of currency, the Swedish krona of 100 öre; large amount of inland water (9%), chief lakes being Vänern, Vättern, and Mälaren; many coastal islands, notably Gotland and Öland; c.57% forested; Kjölen Mts (W) form much of the boundary with Norway; highest peak, Kebnekaise (2 111 m/6 926 ft); several rivers flow SE towards the Gulf of Bothnia; many waterfalls; typically continental climate, with considerable range of temperature between summer and winter, except in the SW, where winters warmer; enclosed parts of Baltic Sea often freeze in winter; average

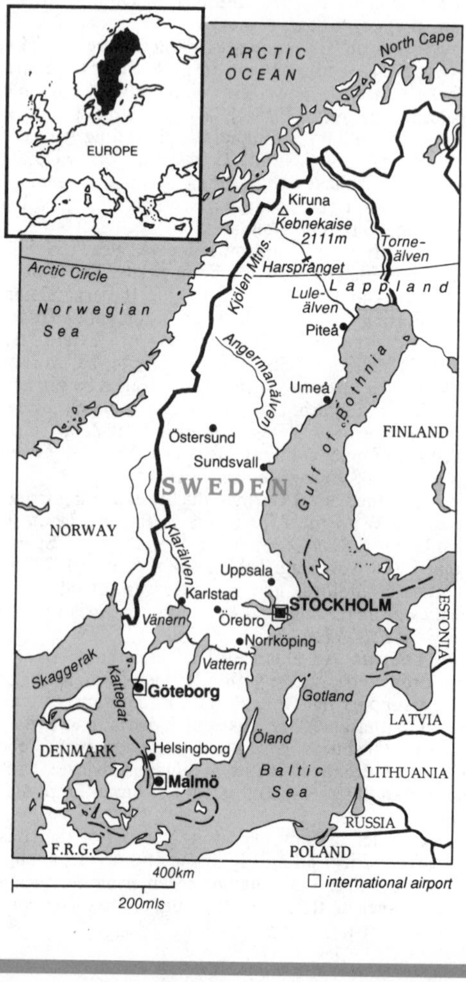

number of days with a mean temperature below freezing increases from 71 in Malmö to 120 in Stockholm and 184 at Haparanda near the Arctic Circle; formed from the union of the kingdoms of the Goths and Svears, 7th-c; Danes continued to rule in the extreme S (Skåne) until 1658; united with Denmark and Norway under Danish leadership, 1389; union ended in 1527, following revolt led by Gustavus Vasa; Sweden acquired Norway from Denmark (1814); union with Norway dissolved, 1905; a neutral country since 1814; a representative and parliamentary democracy, with a monarch as head of state; governed by a prime minister and single-chamber parliament (*Riksdag*) of 349 elected members; gradual shift in the economy from the traditional emphasis on raw materials (timber and iron ore) to advanced technology; transportation equipment, electronics, electrical equipment, chemicals, engineering, steelmaking, non-ferrous metals; hydroelectricity provides 70% of power; c.57% of Sweden forested; wheat, barley, oats, hay, sugar beet, peas, grain, cattle, fishing, tourism. » Gustavus Vasa; Kalmar Union; Stockholm; Swedish literature; RR27 national holidays; RR61 political leaders

Swedenborg, Emmanuel, originally **Swedberg** (1688–1772) Swedish mystic and scientist, born in Stockholm. Educated at Uppsala, he travelled in Europe, and on his return was appointed assessor in the college of mines. He wrote books on algebra, navigation, astronomy, and chemistry, and in 1734 published his monumental *Opera Philosophica et Mineralia* (Philosophical and Logical Works), a mixture of metallurgy and metaphysical speculation on the creation of the world. Curious dreams convinced him that he had direct access to the spiritual world. He communicated his spiritual explorations in *Heavenly Arcana* (1749–56), and spent the rest of his life in Amsterdam, Stockholm, and London, expounding his doctrines in such works as *The New Jerusalem* (1758). He died in London, and in 1787 his followers (known as Swedenborgians) formed the Church of the New Jerusalem. » New Jerusalem, Church of the; mysticism

Swedish » **Germanic/Scandinavian languages; Swedish literature**

Swedish literature The translation of the Bible by the brothers Petri (1526–41) provides the earliest work. Classical influences dominated the 17th-c, and English and French the 18th-c, until the Realistic poetry of Karl Bellman (1740–95) and Thomas Thorild (1759–1808). But Johan Kellgren (1751–95) is the greatest poet of his generation. The writing of Emanuel Swedenborg (1688–1772) ranged from science to mysticism. The verse dramas of Per Atterbom (1790–1835) brought Romanticism to Sweden, and epic works by the Finn Johan Runeberg (1804–77) were also popular. The novel took root by the mid-19th-c, with the versatile Karl Almqvist (1793–1866) and the early feminist Fredrika Bremer (1810–65). The obsessive themes of August Strindberg (1849–1912) produced both novels and plays. Poets Gustav Fröding (1860–1911) and Eric Karlfeldt (1864–1931) reacted in the 1890s against Naturalism. The early 20th-c brought the pessimistic novels of Hjalmar Söderberg (1869–1941) and the fantasy fiction of Hjalmar Bergman (1883–1931); also the adventurous poets Gunnar Ekelof (1907–68) and Harry Martinson (1904–78). Postwar literature has dwelt on spiritual impoverishment, with the documentary novel significantly popular (Per Sundman, 1922–). Meanwhile, following the example of Selma Lagerlöf (1858–1940; Nobel Prize, 1909), a number of Swedish writers such as Astrid Lindgren (1907–) and Tove Jansson (1914–) have written successful books for children. » Almqvist; Bergman, Hjalmar; Fröding; Lagerlöf; literature; Runeberg; Strindberg; Sweden [i]; Swedenborg

Sweet, Henry (1845–1912) British philologist, born in London. He became reader in phonetics at Oxford, where he pioneered Anglo-Saxon studies. His works include Old and Middle English texts, primers, and dictionaries, and a historical English grammar. He was the probable source for Professor Higgins in Shaw's *Pygmalion*. » comparative linguistics; English; phonetics; Shaw, George Bernard

sweet alyssum A low, bushy annual or perennial, native to the Mediterranean; leaves narrow; flowers very numerous, white or blue, cross-shaped. It is one of the most popular garden bedding plants, grown as a hardy annual, and often referred to simply as 'alyssum'. (*Lobularia maritima*. Family: *Cruciferae*.) » alyssum; annual; perennial

sweet bay An evergreen shrub or tree, growing to 20 m/65 ft, but often less, native to the Mediterranean; leathery leaves lance-shaped, wavy-edged; male and female flowers yellow, 4-lobed; berry black; often referred to simply as **bay**. It is the 'laurel' of poets and victors in classical times, and is now a popular pot herb. (*Laurus nobilis*. Family: *Lauraceae*.) » evergreen plants; herb; laurel; shrub; tree [i]

sweet briar » **eglantine**

sweet cherry » **cherry**

sweet chestnut A deciduous tree, growing to 30 m/100 ft, native to the Mediterranean and W Asia, and cultivated and naturalized elsewhere; leaves oblong, toothed, glossy; long catkins have green female flowers below yellow males; nuts shiny, brown, three enclosed in a densely spiny case; also called **Spanish chestnut**. The nuts are the familiar roast chesnuts. (*Castanea sativa*. Family: *Fagaceae*.) » deciduous plants; horse chestnut; tree [i]

sweet cicely A perennial growing to 2 m/6½ ft, smelling strongly of aniseed, native to Europe; leaves divided, leaflets with oval toothed segments, leaf stalks sheathing; flowers white, in umbels 1–5 cm/0.4–2 in across, petals unequal; also called **garden myrrh**. It is cultivated as a seasoning. (*Myrrhis odorata*. Family: *Umbelliferae*.) » perennial; umbel

sweet corn » **maize**

sweet gale » **bog myrtle**

sweet gum A deciduous tree native to N America, Asia Minor, and China; leaves 5-lobed, turning bright red in autumn; male and female flowers tiny, in separate, globular heads. It yields storax, a fragrant amber-coloured gum used in adhesives and perfumes. (*Liquidambar*, 6 species. Family: *Styracaceae*.) » deciduous plants; storax; tree [i]

sweet pea An annual climber, a native of S Italy and Sicily, but widely grown as an ornamental; stems broadly winged, growing to 2 m/6½ ft or more; leaves divided with two oblong-oval, fine-pointed leaflets and branched tendrils; flowers up to 3.5 cm/1½ in, sweetly scented, borne in the upper leaf axils. The wild plants are purple-flowered, but following many years of intensive plant breeding, cultivars now exist in a wide range or combination of colours. (*Lathyrus odoratus*. Family: *Leguminosae*.) » annual; climbing plant; cultivar

sweet potato A tuberous perennial with trailing or climbing stems; leaves oval to heart-shaped; flowers large, purple, funnel-shaped. Its origin is obscure. It is unknown in the wild, but numerous different strains are cultivated throughout warm regions as a staple food. The edible tubers, sometimes wrongly called *yams*, resemble large potatoes, but may have white, yellow, to red or purple, sweet-tasting flesh. (*Ipomaea batatas*. Family: *Convolvulaceae*.) » perennial; potato; tuber; yam

sweet sop » **custard apple**

sweet violet A species of violet lacking stems but with creeping stolons, native to Europe, Asia Minor, and N Africa. Its strongly-scented flowers are distilled for perfume and for flavourings. However, the scent rapidly becomes undetectable, because of the dulling effect on the nose of the chemical, iodine. (*Viola odorata*. Family: *Violaceae*.) » iodine; stolon; violet

sweet william A perennial, native to S Europe; leaves elliptical, in opposite pairs, sheathing stem; flowers in dense, compact head, epicalyx of four long scales, calyx cylindrical; five petals, dark red or pink, in garden forms also white, and often spotted or barred. (*Dianthus barbatus*. Family: *Caryophyllaceae*.) » epicalyx; perennial; pink; sepal

Sweyn [svayn] or **Swegn**, byname **Forkbeard** (?–1014) King of Denmark (987–1014) and England (1013–14), the son of Harold Blue-tooth, and the father of Canute. He first attacked England in 994, and had broken the back of English resistance by 1012. During his final campaign in 1013, he established mastery over the whole country and was recognized as King, while Ethelred the Unready withdrew to exile in Normandy. He died suddenly at Gainsborough, Lincolnshire. » Canute; Ethelred (the Unready)

swidden cultivation » **shifting cultivation**

swift A swallow-like bird of the worldwide family *Apodidae* (**true swifts**, 78 species) or the SE Asian *Hemiprocnidae* (**crested swifts**, 4 species); small feet; lands only on near-vertical surfaces; spends most of its life flying; eats insects caught in the air; may even copulate in flight. The name is also used for the **swift parakeet** (Family: *Psittacidae*). » parakeet; swallow; swiftlet

Swift, Jonathan (1667–1745) Anglo-Irish clergyman and satirist, born and died in Dublin. Educated at Dublin, he moved to England, where he became secretary to the diplomat, Sir William Temple. During a visit to Ireland, he was ordained in the Anglican Church (1695). He wrote several poems, then turned to prose satire, attacking religious dissension in *A Tale of a Tub* (1704), and produced a wide range of political and religious essays and pamphlets. He was made dean of St Patrick's, Dublin, in 1714, and afterwards visited London only twice. His world-famous satire, *Gulliver's Travels*, appeared in 1726, and in later years he wrote a great deal of light verse, and several essays on such topics as language and manners. » English literature; satire

swift moth A medium-to-large moth with wings typically rounded at tip; wings coupled in flight by overlapping lobe of forewing; females scatter eggs on vegetation; caterpillars feed on roots or in wood. (Order: *Lepidoptera*. Family: *Hepialidae*.) » caterpillar; moth

swiftlet A small **true swift**, native to the Indian Ocean, S Asia, and the W Pacific; nests in caves (or buildings). Some species use echolocation. Birds' nest soup is made from the saliva-rich nests of three species of the genus *Aerodramus*. (Tribe: *Collocaliini*, 15 species.) » swift

swimming The act of propelling oneself through water without any mechanical aids. One of the oldest pastimes, the earliest reference to it as a sport is in Japan in 36 BC. There are four strokes: the *breast stroke*, developed in the 16th-c, and the *front crawl* (freestyle), *backstroke*, and *butterfly*, developed in the 20th-c. In competitions there are also relays, involving four swimmers, and medley races, which are a combination of all four strokes. In major events the pool is normally 50 m/55 yd long and divided into eight lanes. Race lengths range from 50 m (55 yd) to 1 500 m (1 640 yd). » channel swimming; scuba diving; skin diving; RR119

Swinburne, Algernon Charles (1837–1909) British poet and critic, born and died in London. Educated at Eton and Oxford, he left without a degree, travelled in Europe, and became associated with the Pre-Raphaelite Brotherhood. He achieved success with his play *Atalanta in Calydon* (1865), and the first of his series of *Poems and Ballads* (1865) took the public by storm. Other works include *Songs before Sunrise* (1871), *Tristram of Lyonesse* (1882), and several critical studies. » English literature; literary criticism; poetry; Pre-Raphaelite Brotherhood

Swindon 51°34N 1°47W, pop (1981) 128 493. Old market town in Thamesdown district, Wiltshire, S England; 113 km/70 ml W of London; developed into a modern industrial town with the arrival of the Great Western Railway in the 19th-c; railway; railway engineering, vehicle parts, pharmaceuticals, electronics, clothing; Great Western Railway museum (1962); 9 km/5 ml E is the White Horse of Uffington. » Wiltshire

swine » pig

swine fever The name used for two highly contagious viral infections of pigs. An infection of the intestines is called *hog cholera*, and an infection of the lungs is called *swine plague*. » pig

Swiss cheese plant » monstera

Swiss Guards The papal police corps, originally instituted by Pope Julius II (reigned 1503–13) and recruited from the mercenaries of the cantons of the Swiss confederacy, whose reputation as infantrymen was established after their victories over the Burgundian calvary in 1476. Their dark blue, yellow, and red uniforms were designed by Michelangelo. » Julius II; Michelangelo; pope

Swiss lake dwellings Prehistoric settlements around the Swiss lakes, first identified in 1854 at Obermeilen, L Constance, by Swiss archaeologist Ferdinand Keller (1800–81), when abnormally low water revealed extensive timber piling. Over 200 comparable Neolithic sites preserved by waterlogging were subsequently revealed (1860–75). Thought by Keller to have been built on platforms over open water in the manner of the Pacific Is, the houses are now known merely to have been sited on the marshy lake edge. » Glastonbury lake village; Three Age System

Swithin or **Swithun, St** (?–862), feast day 15 July. English saint and divine, adviser to Egbert. In 852 he was made Bishop of Winchester, where he died. When in 971 the monks exhumed his body to bury it in the rebuilt cathedral, the removal, which was to have taken place on 15 July, is said to have been delayed by violent rains. Hence the current belief that if it rains on that day, it will rain for 40 days more. » Anglo-Saxons; Egbert

Switzerland, Fr **La Suisse**, Ger **Schweiz**, Ital **Svizzera**, ancient **Helvetia**, official name **Swiss Confederation**, Fr **Confédération Suisse**, Ger **Schweizerische Eidgenosseschaft**, Ital **Confederazione Svizzera** pop (1990e) 6 756 000; area 41 228 sq km/ 15 914 sq ml. Landlocked European republic, divided into 23 cantons (including six demicantons); bounded E by Liechtenstein and Austria, S by Italy, W by France, and N by Germany; federal capital, Bern; largest city, Zürich; chief towns, Lucerne, St Gallen, Lausanne, Basle, Geneva; timezone GMT +1; chief languages, German (65%), French (18%), Italian (12%), Romansch (1%); chief religions, Roman Catholicism, Protestantism; unit of currency, the Swiss franc of 100 centimes.

Physical description and climate. The Alps run roughly E–W in the S; highest peak, Dufourspitze (4 634 m/15 203 ft); Pre-Alps (NW) average 2 000 m/6 500 ft; Jura Mts run SW–NW; mean altitude of C plateau, 580 m/1 900 ft, fringed with great lakes; chief rivers, the Rhine, Rhône, Inn, and tributaries of the Po; c.3 000 sq km/1 160 sq ml of glaciers, notably the Aletsch; temperate climate, varying greatly with relief and altitude; warm summers, with considerable rainfall; winter temperatures average 0°C; average annual rainfall in C plateau, c.1 000 mm/ 40 in; average annual temperature 7–9°C; the Föhn, a warm wind, is noticeable in late winter and spring in the Alps.

History and government. Part of the Holy Roman Empire, 10th-c; Swiss Confederation created in 1291, when the cantons of Uri, Schwyz, and Unterwalden formed a defensive league; expanded during the 14th-c; centre of the Reformation, 16th-c; Swiss independence and neutrality recognized under the Treaty of Westphalia, 1648; conquered by Napoleon, who instituted the Helvetian Republic, 1798; organized as a confederation of 22 cantons, 1815; federal constitution, 1848; neutral in both World Wars; governed by a parliament comprising a 46-

member Council of States (*Ständerat*) and a 200-member National Council (*Nationalrat*), directly elected for four years; a president elected yearly.

Economy. Increased specialization and development in high-technology products; machinery, precision instruments, watches, drugs, chemicals, textiles; a major financial centre; headquarters of many international organizations; all-year tourist area; dairy farming, wheat, potatoes, sugar beet, grapes, apples. » Alps; Bern; Föhn wind; Napoleon I; Sonderbund; RR27 national holidays; RR62 political leaders

Sword-Brothers » **Livonian Knights**

sword dance A ceremonial form of dance. In Scotland individuals or groups perform jigs over crossed swords placed on the floor. In England the dancers are linked together by metal or wooden swords, and perform intertwining figures without breaking the circle. The dance ends with all swords locked in a knot or rose and the ritual decapitation of the leader. *Longsword* is a slow version found in S Yorkshire, and *Rapper* a fast form found in N Yorkshire. » traditional dance

swordfish Large, agile, and very distinctive fish found worldwide in temperate and warm temperate seas; length up to 5 m/16 ft; upper jaw prolonged into a flattened blade or 'sword', teeth absent; dorsal fin tall; feeds mainly on small fish and squid; exploited commercially in many areas. (*Ziphias gladius*. Family: *Xiphiidae*.) » fish [i]

swordtail Small colourful freshwater fish native to streams and swamps of C America; length up to c.12 cm/5 in; green with orange side stripe; lower edge of tail fin in male prolonged to form the 'sword'; a popular aquarium fish, with many varieties produced by selective breeding. (*Xiphophorus helleri*. Family: *Poeciliidae*.) » fish [i]

Sybaris [sibaris] An ancient Greek city under the toe of Italy whose citizens were notorious for their wealth and luxurious life-style – whence the term 'sybarite'. It was obliterated in 510 BC by the neighbouring town of Croton, and never re-founded. » Paestum

sycamore A spreading deciduous tree, growing to 35 m/115 ft, native to C and S Europe and W Asia; leaves 10–15 cm/4–6 in, palmately divided into five toothed lobes; flowers yellowish, lacking petals, in pendulous clusters; winged seeds fused in pairs. It is widely planted for shelter and ornament, seeding and spreading freely. (*Acer pseudoplatanus*. Family: *Aceraceae*.) » deciduous plants; maple; palmate; tree [i]

Sydenham's chorea Irregular, jerking, and unpredictable movements of the limbs, and sometimes of the whole body; girls are especially affected. The condition is related to streptococcal infection and rheumatic fever. It is named after English physician Thomas Sydenham (1624–89). » chorea; rheumatic fever; streptococcus

Sydney 33°55S 151°10E, pop (1986) 3 430 600. Port and state capital of New South Wales, Australia, on the shore of Port Jackson; largest city in Australia; Sydney statistical division comprises 44 municipalities and shires, total population 3 204 696; founded as the first British settlement, 1788; airport; railway; three universities (1850, 1949, 1964); two cathedrals; two major harbours (Sydney, Port Botany); commercial, cultural, and financial centre; shipbuilding, coal, electronics, oil refining, metal products, machinery, brewing, chemicals, paper, clothing, food processing; trade in wool, grain; Sydney Harbour Bridge (1932); Sydney Opera House on Bennelong Point peninsula; State Parliament House; national art gallery (1871); The Rocks (heritage area); Darling Harbour; Chinatown; National Maritime Museum; Festival of Sydney (Jan); Sydney Royal Easter Show; Sydney Cup Week (horse racing) (Apr). » Botany Bay; New South Wales; Sydney Harbour Bridge; Sydney Opera House

Sydney Harbour Bridge One of Australia's best-known landmarks, and the widest and heaviest arch bridge in the world, built 1923–32; length of main arch 503 m/1 651 ft; highest point 134 m/440 ft above sea-level. The bridge provides a rail and road link across the harbour. It was finally paid for by tolls in 1985. » bridge (engineering) [i]; New Guard; Sydney

Sydney Opera House Australia's best-known contemporary building. Its imaginative design came from an international competition, won in 1956 by the Danish architect Joern Utzon (1918–) in 1956. Because no building with its features had been built before, costs mounted enormously (from the original A $7.5 million), and in the political controversy Utzon resigned in 1966. The Opera House was completed in 1973. It had cost over A $100 million, much of this coming from a New South Wales government lottery. » Sydney

syenite A coarse-grained igneous rock containing feldspar and hornblende as essential minerals, with some biotite. » feldspar; hornblende; igneous rock

Sykes–Picot Agreement A secret agreement concluded in 1916 by diplomat Sir Mark Sykes (for Britain) and Georges Picot (for France) partitioning the Ottoman Empire after the war. France was to be the dominant power in Syria and Lebanon, and Britain in Transjordan, Iraq, and N Palestine. The rest of Palestine was to be under international control, and an Arab state was to be established. » Palestine

syllabary A writing system in which the basic units (*graphemes*) correspond to syllables, normally representing a sequence of consonant and vowel. An example is found in Japanese *kana*, where the graphemes correspond to such spoken sequences as *ka*, *ga*, and *no*. This system is modelled on the spoken language, Japanese being a language which has no consonant clusters. Consequently, borrowings from English are regularly restructured to break up any consonant clusters into strings of consonant + vowel, eg *spry* would typically appear as 'saparai'. » graphology

syllogism A deductive argument containing two premisses. *Categorical* syllogisms contain subject-predicate sentences, as in 'Some dogs are chihuahuas, All chihuahaus are small; therefore Some dogs are small'. *Hypothetical* syllogisms contain conditional sentences: 'If roses are red, then violets are blue, If violets are blue, then carnations are pink; therefore If roses are red, then carnations are pink'. » deduction; logic; premiss

Sylt [zilt, zült] Largest of the North Frisian Is, off the Schleswig-Holstein coast; area 99 sq km/38 sq ml; length 37 km/23 ml; popular summer resort. » Frisian Islands

Sylvanus » **Silvanus**

Sylvester II, originally **Gerbert of Aurillac** (c.940–1003) French Pope (999–1033), born at Aurillac. Renowned for his achievements in chemistry, mathematics, and philosophy, he is said to have introduced Arabic numerals and to have invented clocks. He became Abbot of Bobbio (982) and Archbishop of Ravenna (988), and as Pope, upheld the primacy of Rome against the separatist tendencies of the French Church. He died in Rome. » pope

symbiosis [simbiohsis] A general term for the living together of two dissimilar organisms. It is commonly used to describe all the different types of relationship between the members of two different and interacting species, including parasitism, mutualism, commensalism and inquilinism. It is sometimes used in a restricted sense for those mutualistic relationships in which each interacting species derives benefit from the association. » commensalism; inquilinism; mutualism; parasitology

symbol Something which, by convention, stands for something else. A symbol is a variety of sign, whose form and meaning are often arbitrary, and agreed upon by the community using it (eg black or white as the colour of mourning). With scientific symbols (such as in chemistry) that agreement is universal, formal, and fixed. However, most symbols, such as those using words themselves, are less rigidly constrained, allowing scope for differing interpretations. This is particularly so in literature, where writers often create their own symbols. » semiotics; sign

symbolic interactionism A sociological theory which explains patterns of behaviour according to the meanings and symbols that people share in everyday interaction. The theory was developed by the Chicago school of sociologists in the 1930s, and emphasizes that a mutual understanding between people depends on their continually monitoring, checking, and negotiating the meaning of what they say and how they behave. » ethnomethodology; sociology

symbolic logic » **logic**

Symbolism In general terms, the belief that ideas or emotions may be objectified in terms which make them communicable, whether in words, music, graphics or plastic forms. This belief may be traced back to Plato; it was elaborated by the Neoplatonists and by Swedenborg, and is clearly active in much Romantic poetry (especially Coleridge, Shelley, and Blake) and in the writings of Poe. The systematic invocation of a transcendental world in poetry was practised by several French poets in the mid-19th-c, who came to be known as Symbolists. Their influence on subsequent art, literature, and aesthetic theory has been far-reaching. The modern novel as well as poetry and drama is often heavily symbolic; the visual arts and the cinema likewise employ sophisticated 'coding' techniques. » English/French literature; Poe; poetry; Symbolists; Swedenborg

Symbolists A group of mid-19th-c French poets, including Baudelaire, Mallarmé, Verlaine, and Rimbaud. Their general aim was to invoke rather than to describe reality, by subliminal means. A Symbolist manifesto was published in 1886 by Jean Moréas (1856–1910), and the ideas were ably expounded by Arthur Symons in *The Symbolist Movement in Literature* (1899). In art, there was a reaction against Realism and Impressionism; leading artists included Denis, Puvis de Chavannes, and Redon. » French literature; Impressionism (literature); Nabis; Realism; Symbolism; Baudelaire; Denis, Maurice; Mallarmé; Puvis de Chavannes; Redon; Rimbaud; Verlaine

symmetry Any aspect of a system that is the same after some operation. For example, a square rotated by 90° is indistinguishable from the original, and so has symmetry under rotation by 90°. A circle is symmetric under any rotation about its centre. In physical systems, symmetry is related to conservation laws, and is expressed mathematically using group theory. » conservation laws; spontaneous symmetry breaking; supersymmetry

symmetry breaking » spontaneous symmetry breaking

Symonds, John Addington [simuhnz] (1840–93) British author and critic, born in Bristol. He was educated at Harrow and Oxford, where he became a fellow in 1862. His major work was *Renaissance in Italy* (7 vols, 1875–86), and he also wrote travel books, literary monographs, biographies, translations, and poetry. For health reasons, in 1877 he settled in Davos, Switzerland, and died in Rome. » literary criticism

Symons, Arthur (William) [simuhnz] (1865–1945) British critic and poet, born at Milford Haven, Pembrokeshire, Wales. He did much to familiarize the British with the literature of France and Italy, producing several translations, and in 1899 publishing the influential *The Symbolist Movement in Literature* (1899). He died at Wittersham, Kent. » literary criticism; Symbolism

sympathetic nervous system » autonomic nervous system

symphonic poem A single-movement orchestral work in which a composer seeks to express the emotional, pictorial, or narrative content of a poem, story, painting, etc. It was developed by Liszt from the programmatic concert overture and taken up by other Romantic composers, including Smetana, Franck, and Strauss. Strauss preferred the term *Tondichtung* ('tone poem'). » overture; programme music; Romanticism (music); Franck, César; Liszt; Smetana; Strauss, Richard

symphony An orchestral work originating in the 18th-c, although the term had been used earlier with different meanings. The classical symphony of Haydn, Mozart, Beethoven, and Schubert was mostly in four movements: a fast movement in sonata form; a slow movement; a minuet or scherzo; and a finale, often in sonata form like the first movement. In the 19th-c the structure was varied a good deal, and programmatic or descriptive intentions were often present, as in the five-movement *Symphonie fantastique* of Berlioz. The example of Beethoven's Ninth Symphony, which used solo singers and chorus, was followed by many composers, including Mahler. Sibelius's structural innovations led eventually to a single-movement symphony (No. 7, composed in 1924), while other composers (eg Shostakovich) have either modified the romantic structure to serve their expressive purposes or, like Stravinsky, sought to restore the older symphonic styles. » minuet; movement; programme music; scherzo; sinfonietta; symphonic poem; Beethoven; Haydn; Mahler; Mozart; Sibelius

Symplegades [sim**play**gadeez] In Greek mythology, the Clashing Rocks, situated at the entrance to the Black Sea, through which the *Argo* had to pass. » Argonauts

synagogue (Gr 'congregation', 'meeting') The local Jewish institution for instruction in the Torah and worship, but not infringing on the ritual or sacrificial roles of the Jerusalem priesthood. It was the local religious focal point of individual Jewish communities, both in Palestine and in cities of the Diaspora. Congregations were usually governed by a body of elders, who exercised certain disciplinary functions. While the term *synagogue* applied to the congregation, eventually it was also used of the buildings in which the people met, and in great cities such as Alexandria these could be quite elaborate. After the destruction of Jerusalem and the Temple in AD 70, the institution of the synagogue gained even greater importance as the major religious institution in Jewish life. Rabbis became leaders of synagogues in this later period. In Orthodox synagogues, men and women have traditionally separated; but in non-Orthodox synagogues, they now sit together. » Diaspora; elder 1; Judaism; rabbi; Torah

synapse [**siy**naps] The specialized junction between two neurones, present in the nervous system of all animals. Nerve impulses at the axon terminals of one neurone are transmitted across the junction either chemically (by neurotransmitters) or electrically (by local currents) to influence the excitability of the other neurone. » neurone [i]

sync pulse In motion pictures, signals linked to the camera frame rate recorded on the separate sound magnetic tape for subsequent matching to the picture. In a television signal, sync pulses are included at the end of every line and after each field period to ensure correct operation of transmission, recording, and receiving equipment. » field (photography)

synchrony » diachrony

synchrotron A machine for accelerating sub-atomic particles, usually protons or electrons. The particles are guided through an evacuated pipe in a circular path by magnets, accelerated by radiofrequency (rf) electric fields. In a large machine, each pulse of particles may make tens of thousands of revolutions, being accelerated at each pass through the rf source. Magnetic field and rf frequency increase in a synchronized way with increasing particle velocity to maintain a circular path. Machines vary in size up to several kilometres diameter. They are a major experimental tool in particle physics. » particle accelerators; synchrotron radiation

synchrotron radiation X-ray radiation emitted by charged particles travelling around a synchrotron. Accelerating electrical charges emit electromagnetic radiation, so by the same mechanism charged particles moving in a circle emit radiation. The technique is used for X-ray diffraction studies of materials, and for producing semiconductor chips using X-ray lithography. » bremsstrahlung; particle accelerators; synchrotron; X-ray diffraction

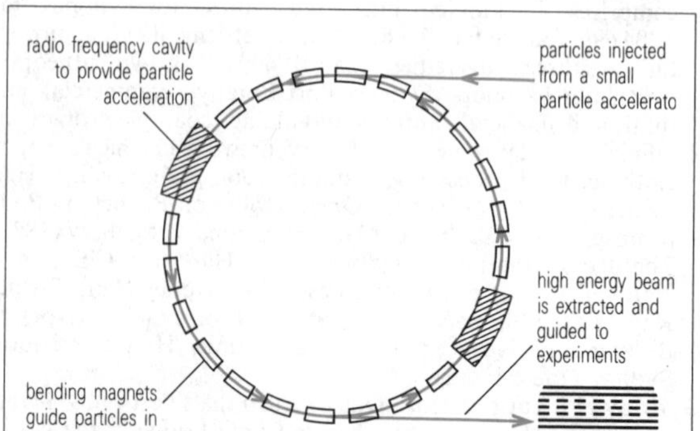

A synchrotron particle accelerator. The bending magnets may number a few hundred, and the complete machine may be several kilometres across. The particle beam travels inside an evacuated pipe, itself inside a tunnel.

syncline A geological fold structure in the form of a trough or inverted arch, produced by the downfolding of stratified rocks. It is the opposite of an anticline. » anticline; stratification

syncope [**sing**kuhpee] » **fainting**

syndicalism A revolutionary socialist doctrine that emphasized workers taking power by seizing the factories in which they worked; developed in the 1890s, and common in France, Italy, and Spain in the early 20th-c. The state was to be replaced by worker-controlled units of production. Often a general strike was advocated as part of the strategy. By 1914 it had lost its political force. The name, deriving from *syndicat* (Fr 'trade union'), has also been applied to various non-revolutionary doctrines supporting worker control. » anarchism; socialism

Synge, J(ohn) M(illington) [sing] (1871–1909) Irish dramatist, born near Dublin. Educated at Dublin, he studied music in Europe, then turned to writing. On the advice of Yeats, he settled among the people of the Aran Is, who provided the material for his plays, notably *The Playboy of the Western World* (1907). He had a profound influence on the next generation of Irish playwrights and was a director of the Abbey Theatre from 1904. He died in Dublin. » Abbey Theatre; drama; Irish literature; Yeats

synodic period The average time taken by a planet to return to the same position in its orbit relative to the Earth. For the Moon this is 29.53 days, the interval between successive new moons. » planet; Moon

synonym A word which is similar enough in meaning to another word for it to be usable as a substitute in some contexts, such as *illuminate* and *light*. An **antonym** is a word which has the opposite meaning to another, such as *light* and *dark*. A **hyponym** is a word whose meaning is included within that of another, such as *horse* and *animal*. The study of sense relations of this kind is part of the subject of semantics. » semantics

synoptic gospels A term applied to three New Testament Gospels (Matthew, Mark, Luke), so called because of the striking amount of common material that they contain. Most of Mark's Gospel, for example, is reproduced in Matthew and Luke, and the correspondence often extends to the order of passages and wording, although differences also exist. The precise way in which the works are interrelated is known as the 'synoptic problem', for which many competing solutions have been offered. John's Gospel presents a strikingly different portrayal of Jesus. » Gospels, canonical

synovitis Inflammation of the synovial membranes that enclose tendons or cover surfaces within and around the joints. It arises from persistent injury (eg from sports), or from bacterial or immunological inflammation, when it takes the form of arthritis. » arthritis; bursitis; joint; sports medicine; tendon

synroc [**sin**rok] An artificial ceramic material used to store high-level radioactive waste. The waste is added to mixed powdered metal oxides from which the ceramic is formed by heat and compression. Radioactive waste atoms displace some host atoms, and so are chemically bound into a material similar in type to natural ceramic. It is under development as an alternative to storage using glass. » ceramics; radioactivity

syntax The study of how the items of a language, independent of their semantics, can be combined or decomposed. A syntax for a language specifies a set of grammatical categories (such as, perhaps, *noun phrase* and *sentence*) and a set of rules which defines the ways in which larger items are built up from smaller units. » grammar; semantics

synthesizer An electronic apparatus for generating musical sounds, usually fitted with one or more keyboards and loudspeakers. One of the earliest and best known was developed in 1964 by Robert A Moog (1934–). Like many of those which followed, it could produce only one sound at a time, but since 1975 newer 'polyphonic' types have been developed, including digital ones based on microprocessors, which are not limited in this respect. » electrophone; keyboard instrument

synthetic chemistry The study of the preparation of chemical compounds. It is generally divided into organic and inorganic chemistry, and is particularly important in the pharmaceutical industry. » chemistry; pharmacology

synthetic elements In chemistry, isotopes (generally radioactive) made by nuclear reactions. All isotopes of all actinide elements are synthetic. » actinides; isotopes

synthetic language » **analytic language**

Synthetism A term sometimes used by art critics to refer to the Symbolist artists, to distinguish them from the Symbolist poets. It is also sometimes applied to the Nabis. » Nabis; Symbolists

syphilis A chronic infection caused by *Treponema pallidum*; a sexually transmitted disease in which a primary lesion (a *chancre*) appears on the genitalia or anus. This is followed in several weeks by a skin rash and features of generalized infection and fever. These features subside, and the condition may then remain latent for 10 or more years. Thereafter the heart, aorta, and brain may become affected, and meningitis, insanity, and aortic swellings (*aneurysms*) can develop. The course of the disease is variable, but unlike AIDS the causative organism is sensitive to penicillin treatment. » meningitis; penicillin; penis [i]; vagina; venereal disease

syphon » **siphon**

Syracuse (Italy) [**si**rakyooz], Ital **Siracusa** 37°04N 15°18E, pop (1981) 117 615. Seaport capital of Siracusa province, Sicily, Italy; 53 km/33 ml SSE of Catania; founded by Greek settlers, 734 BC; leading cultural centre, 5th-c BC; taken by the Romans, 212 BC; railway; food processing, petrochemicals; birthplace of Archimedes, Theocritus; cathedral (640), Greek theatre (5th-c BC), Roman amphitheatre, temples, aqueducts. » Archimedes; Sicily; Theocritus

Syracuse (USA) [**si**rakyooz] 43°03N 76°09W, pop (1980) 170 105. Seat of Onondaga County, C New York, USA; 19 km/12 ml S of W end of L Oneida; developed in association with salt works during the 1780s and later at the junction of the Erie and Oswego Canals; city status, 1847; airfield; railway; university (1870); electrical equipment. » New York (state)

Syria, Arabic **Suriya**, official name **Syrian Arab Republic**, Arabic **Al-Jumhuriyah al-Arabiyah as-Suriyah** pop (1990e) 12 028 000; area 185 180 sq km/71 479 sq ml. Republic in the Middle East, divided into 14 governorates (*mohofazats*); bounded W by the Mediterranean Sea and Lebanon, SW by Israel and Jordan, E by Iraq, and N by Turkey; capital, Damascus; chief towns, Aleppo, Homs, Hama, Latakia; timezone GMT +2; population mainly Arab (90%); official language, Arabic; chief religions, Islam (74% Sunni Muslim, 16% Alawite Druze and other sects), Christianity (10%); unit of currency, the Syrian pound; narrow Mediterranean coastal plain; Jabal al Nusayriyah mountain range rises to c.1 500 m/5 000 ft; steep drop (E) to Orontes R valley; Anti-Lebanon range (SW) rises to 2 814 m/9 232 ft at Mt Hermon; open steppe and desert to the

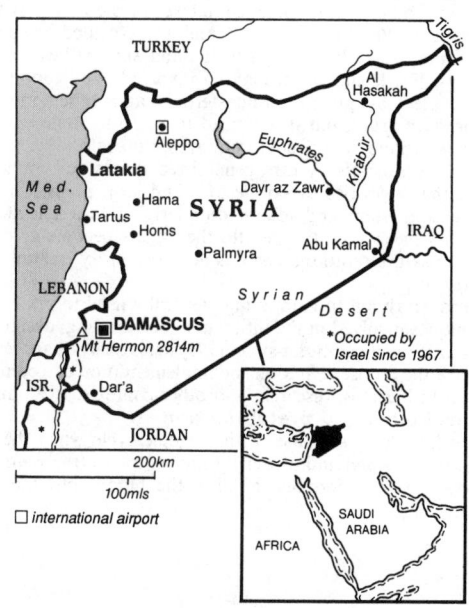

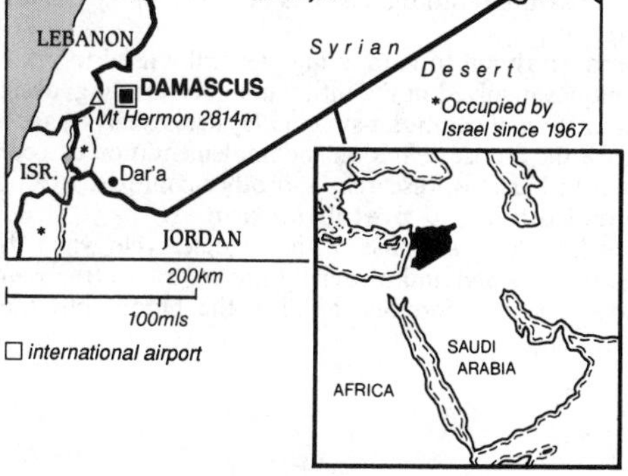

E; coastal Mediterranean climate, with hot, dry summers and mild, wet winters; desert or semi-desert climate in 60% of country, annual rainfall below 200 mm/8 in; *khamsin* wind causes temperatures to rise to 43–49°C; Damascus, mean annual rainfall 225 mm/9 in, average temperatures 7°C (Jan), 27°C (Jul); part of the Phoenician Empire; Islam introduced, 7th-c; conquered by Turks, 11th-c; scene of many Crusader battles in Middle Ages; part of Ottoman Empire, 1517; brief period of independence, 1920, then made a French mandate; independence, 1946; merged with Egypt and Yemen to form the United Arab Republic, 1958; re-established itself as independent state under present name, 1961; Golan Heights region seized by Israel, 1967; after outbreak of civil war in Lebanon (1975), Syrian troops sent to restore order, and are currently much involved in the region's power struggle; governed by a president, elected for a 7-year term; 250-member People's Council elected for a 4-year term; since 1974, oil has been the most important source of export revenue; cotton, phosphate, textiles, beverages, tobacco, cement, oil refining, food processing, tourism; cotton, wheat, barley, rice, olives, millet, sugarbeet, tobacco; fruit; cattle breeding, poultry; Euphrates dam project (begun 1978) presently supplies 97% of domestic electricity demand, and is intended to increase area of arable land by 6400 sq km/2500 sq ml. » Arab-Israeli Wars; Crusades [i]; Damascus; Islam; khamsin; Phoenicia; RR27 national holidays; RR62 political leaders

Syriac » **Aramaic**

syringa » **lilac; mock orange**

syrinx [siringks] The voice-producing organ of birds; situated in the windpipe where this divides into two. It has vibrating membranes, a reverberating capsule (*tympanum*), and various muscles. The structure and position of the syrinx has been used in bird classification to indicate the relationships of groups. » trachea

Syrinx [siringks] In Greek mythology, a nymph pursued by Pan. She called on the Earth to help, and so sank down into it and became a reed-bed. Pan cut some of the reeds, and made the panpipes. » Pan

systematics The classification of organisms into a hierarchical series of groups which emphasizes their presumed evolutionary interrelationships. The main categories of modern classifications are (in order of increasing generality) species, genus, family, order, class, phylum (animals), division (plants), and kingdom. » binomial nomenclature; genus; kingdom; species; phylum; taxonomy

systemic lupus erythematosus (SLE) [loopuhs erithuhmatohsuhs] A generalized disorder affecting connective tissue throughout the body, characterized by the presence of several auto-antibodies and immune complexes in the blood. It tends to affect 30–40-year-old females, and is aggravated by sunlight and some drugs. It causes arthritis and skin rashes, and the kidneys, heart, and brain may be involved. The condition is ameliorated by giving corticosteroids and other immunosuppressive drugs, but it may lead to death in some cases. » arthritis; connective tissue; immunosuppression

systemic sclerosis A rare generalized disease of connective tissue that gives rise to skin lesions and joint pains. The skin may become shiny and adhere to underlying tissues, leading to difficulty in opening the mouth; the fingers become cold, and develop skin ulceration. There is no satisfactory treatment. » joint; skin [i]

systems analysis In computing, generally used to refer to the techniques involved in the intimate understanding, design, and optimization of computer systems. **Systems analysts** are responsible for the precise definition and implementation of a computer system in business, research, and other contexts. » computer

systems building » **prefabrication**

systole [sistuhlee] A phase of the cardiac cycle when the atria (the *atrial systole*) and especially the ventricles (the *ventricular systole*) contract forcibly, ejecting the blood into the aorta (from the left ventricle) and pulmonary trunk (from the right ventricle). » diastole; heart [i]

syzygy [sizijee] An astronomical situation which occurs when the Sun, Earth, and Moon are roughly in a straight line. Eclipses are likely when the Moon is at syzygy. » eclipse

Szczecin [shchetseen], Ger **Stettin** 53°25N 14°32E, pop (1983) 389 200. Industrial river-port capital of Szczecin voivodship, NW Poland; on R Oder 60 km/37 ml from the Baltic Sea; largest Baltic trading port; urban status, 1243; member of the Hanseatic League, 1360; Prussian rule, 1720–1945; badly damaged in World War 2; ceded to Poland, 1945; contains area of Międzyodrze, 5 km/3 ml of docks, canals, and transshipment facilities; airfield; railway; maritime college; medical academy; technical university (1946); shipbuilding, yacht-building, synthetic fibres, cranes, iron, tools, deep-sea fishing, fish processing; St James's Cathedral, castle (16th-c), 13th–14th-c city walls. » Poland [i]

Szeged [seged] 46°16N 20°10E, pop (1981) 172 000. River-port capital of Csongrád county, S Hungary, on R Tisza; railway; university (1872, refounded 1921); biological centre of the Hungarian Academy of Sciences; railway; timber and salt trade, chemicals, hemp, salami, red pepper; cultural centre of the S Alföld; medicinal baths; castle (1242), votive church; open-air festival (Jul–Aug). » Hungary [i]

Székely [saykel] A Magyar-speaking people, numbering c.400 000, inhabiting the SE Transylvanian region of post-1918 Romania; generally believed to be of ethnically Turkic descent. In both the interwar and the contemporary periods, the position of the Székely has given rise to disputes between the Romanian and Hungarian states.

Székesfehérvár [saykeshfeheervah], Ger **Stuhlweissenburg**, ancient **Alba Regia** 47°15N 18°25E, pop (1984e) 109 000. Capital of Fejér county, WC Hungary; ancient capital of Hungarian kingdom; badly damaged in World War 2; market centre for tobacco, wine, fruit; light metal works; cathedral, episcopal palace, Garden of Ruins with remains of 11th-c royal cathedral. » Hungary [i]

Szell, George [zel] (1897–1970) US conductor and pianist, born in Budapest. Educated at Vienna, he made his debut as a conductor in Berlin (1914), and later conducted many of the world's major orchestras. He settled in the USA in 1939, and from 1946 was musical director and conductor of the symphony orchestra in Cleveland, where he died.

Szewinska, Irena [shuhvinska], *née* **Kirszenstein** (1946–) Polish athlete, born in St Petersburg, Russia. She established herself at the 1964 Olympics with a silver medal in the long jump, and a gold in Poland's relay squad. She set world records at 100 m and 200 m in 1965, won three gold medals at the European Championships in 1966, and took the Olympic 200 m title in 1968 in world record time. She later won bronze medals at the 1971 European Championships and the 1972 Olympics. She then stepped up to 400 m, and in 1976 won the Olympic title in a new world record 49.28 sec. She appeared in her fifth Olympics at Moscow in 1980. » athletics

Szilard, Leo [zilahd] (1898–1964) Hungarian-US physicist, born in Budapest, where he studied before moving successively to Berlin, Oxford, London, and (in 1938) the USA. Earlier than most physicists, he saw (in 1934) the possibility of large-scale energy generation by nuclear fission, and even patented the idea. He initiated the idea of an atomic bomb, and worked throughout World War 2 on this, and with Fermi on the first atomic pile. From 1946 he worked in biophysics at Chicago, and died at La Jolla, California. » atomic bomb; Fermi; nuclear fission

Szombathely [sombot-hay], Ger **Steinamanger**, ancient **Sabaria** 47°14N 16°38E, pop (1984e) 86 000. Capital of Vas county, W Hungary, on R Gyöngyös; bishopric; railway; chemicals, textiles, timber; cathedral, 14th-c Franciscan church, 17th-c Dominican church, Garden of Ruins with excavations of 4th-c imperial palace. » Hungary

T

T'ien-ching » Tianjin

Ta-t'ung » Datong

Tabari, Abu Jafar Mohammed Ben Jarir al- (839–923) Arab historian, born at Amol, Persia. He travelled throughout the Middle East collecting scholarly material, and wrote a major commentary on the Koran, and a history of the world from creation until the early 10th-c. His work provided a basis for later historical and religious studies. He died at Baghdad. » Koran

Tabarley, Eric (1931–) French yachtsman. He was twice winner of the single-handed trans-Atlantic race, in 1964 in *Pen Duick II*, and in 1976 in *Pen Duick VI*. » sailing

tabasco sauce A spicy red sauce rich in chillis and hot red peppers, originating in the Mexican state of Tabasco. It is made from the fruit of the plant *Capsicum frutescens*, and is used to flavour soups, stews, and other hot dishes. » sauce

Tabernacle A movable sanctuary or tent; in early Israelite religion, the shelter for the Ark of the Covenant during the desert wanderings and conquest of Canaan, eventually replaced by Solomon's Temple. Elaborate instructions for its construction and furnishing are given in the Book of Exodus, but many consider these to derive from a later priestly source. » Ark of the Covenant; Atonement, Day of; Holy of Holies; Temple, Jerusalem

Tabernacles, Feast of » **Sukkoth**

tablature A system of musical notation tailored to a particular instrument or group of instruments and indicating the keys, frets, etc to be used rather than the pitch to be sounded. German organ tablature used mainly letters in conjunction with rhythmic signs; lute tablatures used letters or numerals on lines representing the strings of the instrument. The only instruments for which tablature is normally used today are the ukulele and the guitar: the notation conveys a diagrammatic indication of finger-placings. » musical notation

Table Mountain 33°58S 18°25E. Mountain in SW Cape province, South Africa; height 1 086 m/3 563 ft; a flat-topped central massif flanked on either side by the Lion's Head and Devil's Peak; often shrouded in cloud, known as the 'Tablecloth'; Kirstenbosch national botanical gardens on E slopes; Cape Town at the foot. » Cape Town; South Africa [i]

table tennis An indoor bat-and-ball game played by two or four players on a table measuring 9 ft (2.75 m) by 5 ft (1.52 m). The centre of the table has a net 6 in (15.25 cm) high stretched across it. The ball must be hit over the net and into the opposing half of the table. The object is to force one's opponent to make an error and thus not return the ball successfully. In doubles, the players must hit the ball alternately and in order. The winner is the first to reach 21 points with at least a 2-point lead. The exact origins of the game are uncertain, but it is thought to have been first played in the 1880s. Known as *ping pong* in the early part of the 20th-c, it is very popular in China and Korea. » RR120

tabor A small double-headed side drum with snares, known from mediaeval times. It was often played with one stick, the player at the same time blowing a three-holed pipe to accompany dancing. » side drum

Tabriz [tab**reez**], ancient **Tauris** 38°05N 46°18E, pop (1983) 852 296. Capital city of Tabriz district, NW Iran; fourth largest city in Iran; often severely damaged by earthquakes; airport; railway; university (1949); industrial and commercial centre; carpets; ruined 15th-c Blue Mosque and citadel. » Iran [i]

Tachisme » **action painting**

tachometer An instrument for measuring the speed of rotation. There are many methods; a typical modern device rotates a magnet near a non-magnetic conductor, exerting a force through the field produced by eddy currents. » magnetism

tachyon [**tak**yon] A hypothetical elementary particle having imaginary mass (ie m^2 less than 0), and able to travel faster than the velocity of light without violating special relativity. Observable effects are predicted, but have not been seen. » particle physics; special relativity [i]

Tacitus, in full **Publius** or **Gaius Cornelius Tacitus** [tasituhs] (c.55–120) Roman historian. He studied rhetoric at Rome, became a praetor, and established a great reputation as an orator, becoming consul in 97. His major works are two historical studies, the 12-volume *Historiae* (Histories), of which only the first four books survive whole, and the *Annales* (Annals), of possibly 18 books, of which only eight have been completely preserved. His concise and vivid prose style was a major influence on later writers. » rhetoric; Latin literature

Tacoma [ta**koh**ma] 47°14N 122°26W, pop (1980) 158 501. Port capital of Pierce County, WC Washington, USA, on Commencement Bay; settled, 1868; city status, 1875; railway; university (1888); air force base; major NW Pacific container port exporting timber, fruit, tallow, agricultural machinery; boatbuilding, chemicals, food processing, metalwork, wood, paper products; state historical society; tourist centre; Chinese museums, Fort Nisqually, daffodil festival. » Washington (state)

tactical voting Casting one's vote in an election for a candidate with the best chance of defeating another candidate who would otherwise be the most likely to win. This generally occurs where the candidate of one's choice is highly unlikely to be successful, or where preventing a particular candidate from being elected is of greater importance. » franchise

Tadmur or **Tadmor**, Gr **Palmyra** 34°36N 38°15E, pop (1970) 12 705. Ancient city in Hims governorate, C Syria, a world heritage site; 208 km/129 ml NE of Damascus; financial capital of the E world, 1st–2nd-c; on ancient caravan route from Arabian Gulf to Mediterranean Sea; rail terminus; many examples of Hellenistic art and architecture; numerous temples, including Temple of Bêl; Monumental Arch; several tombs on hill slopes (E). » Hellenization; Syria [i]

tadpole The larva of an amphibian, especially a frog or toad; largest, 250 mm/10 in long; usually a short spherical body, feathery gills, large tail; most eat microscopic plants; with age, gills and tail shrink, legs appear, become carnivorous; also known as **pollywog**, **polliwog**, **pollywig**, **polliwig**, or **porwiggle** (from Old English *tade poll*, 'toad head', Middle English *pollwyggle*, 'head wiggle'). » amphibian; frog

tadpole shrimp A primitive freshwater crustacean found in temporary pools in arid regions; shield-shaped carapace covers head and thorax; abdomen slender, with many segments; feeds on detritus or as a predator; c.11 living species. (Class: *Branchiopoda*. Order: *Notostraca*.) » crustacean; shrimp

Tadzhikistan [tajikis**tahn**], Russ **Tadzhikskaya** pop (1989) 5 109 000; area 143 100 sq km/55 200 sq ml. Republic in SE Middle Asia, bounded S by Afghanistan and E by China; Tien Shan, Gissar-Alai, and Pamir ranges cover over 90% of the area; Communism Peak reaches 7 495 m/24 590 ft; R Amudarya flows E–W along the S border; largest lake, L Kara-Kul; became a Soviet Socialist Republic, 1929; declaration of independence, 1991; capital, Dushanbe; chief towns, Leninabad, Kurgan-Tyube, Kulyab; oil, natural gas, coal, lead, zinc, machinery, metalworking, chemicals, food processing; cotton, wheat, maize, vegetables, fruit; hot mineral springs and health resorts. » Soviet Union [i]

Taegu [tiy**goo**] 35°52N 128°36E, pop (1984) 2 012 039. Special city in SE Korea; largest inland city after Seoul; railway; university (1946); market town at centre of apple-growing area; textiles; Haeinsa temple (802) with the Tripitaka Koreana, a set of 80 000 wooden printing blocks engraved with Buddhist scripture (13th-c); Tonghwasa Temple nearby (17th-c). » Korea [i]

Taejon [tiy**jon**] 36°20N 127°26E, pop (1984) 842 429. Capital of Ch'ungch'ongnam province, C Korea; badly damaged in Korean War; railway; university (1952); agricultural centre; Yusong Hot Springs (W); Kyeryongsan national park (W). » Korea [i]

taekwondo A martial art developed in Korea by General Choi Hong Hi. It officially became part of Korean tradition and culture in 1955, and is now popular as a sport. The International Taekwondo Federation was founded in 1966. » martial arts

Taft, William Howard (1857–1930) US statesman and 27th President (1909–13), born at Cincinnati, Ohio. Educated at Yale, he became a lawyer, Solicitor-General (1890), the first civil governor of the Philippine Is (1901), and Secretary of War (1904–8). As President he secured an agreement with Canada that meant relatively free trade. From 1913 he was professor of law at Yale, and from 1921 Chief Justice. He died in Washington, DC. His son **Robert Alphonso** (1889–1953) became a US Senator (1938) and Republican leader (1939–53), but was defeated as presidential candidate on three occasions. » Republican Party

Taganrog [tagan**rok**] 47°14N 38°55E, pop (1983) 285 000. Seaport in Rostovskaya oblast, S European Russia; on NE shore of the Gulf of Taganrog of the Sea of Azov; founded as a fortress and naval base, 1698; rail terminus; metallurgy, machines, foodstuffs, shipyards, leatherwork; birthplace of Chekhov. » Chekhov; Russia

Tagore, Sir Rabindranath (1861–1941) Indian poet and philosopher, born and died in Calcutta. He is best known for his poetic works, notably *Gitanjali* (1910, Song Offering), and short stories, such as *Galpaguccha* (1912, A Bunch of Stories), but he also wrote plays and novels. In 1901 he founded near Bolpur the Santiniketan, a communal school to blend Eastern and Western philosophical and educational systems. He received the Nobel Prize for Literature in 1913, the first Asiatic to do so, and was knighted in 1915 – an honour which he resigned in 1919 as a protest against British policy in the Punjab. » Indian literature; poetry

Tagus, River [**tay**guhs], Span **Río Tajo**, Port **Tejo** River rising in the Sierra de Albarracin, Spain; flows 785 km/488 ml SW to the Portuguese border, which it follows for 44 km/27 ml; below Vila Franca de Xira, opens out into the Tagus estuary at Lisbon Bay; 229 sq km/88 sq ml of the estuary given reserve status in 1976; length, 1 007 km/626 ml; navigable, 212 km/132 ml to Abrantes. » Portugal [i]; Spain [i]

Tahiti, Fr **Archipel de Tahiti** Eng [ta**hee**tee], Fr [ta**ee**tee] 17°37S 149°27W; pop (1983e) 116 000; area 1 042 sq km/402 sq ml. Largest island of French Polynesia, S Pacific Ocean, belonging to the Windward group of the Society Is; length, 48 km/30 ml; French colony, 1880; capital, Papeete; rises to 2 237 m/7 339 ft in the volcanic peak of Mt Orohena; vanilla, coconuts, copra, sugar cane, tourism; home of Gauguin (1891–3). » French Polynesia; Papeete

tahr [tah] A S Asian goat antelope; thick coat except on head; short curved horns; inhabits steep, tree-covered hillsides; three species: **Himalayan tahr** (introduced in New Zealand), **Nilgiri tahr**, and **Arabian tahr**. (Genus: *Hemitragus*.) » antelope

Tai [tiy] National park in Guiglo and Sassandra departments, SW Côte d'Ivoire; area 3 300 sq km/1 300 sq ml; established in 1972; a world heritage site. » Côte d'Ivoire [i]

Tai, Mount [tiy], Chin **Taishan** The most revered of China's five sacred mountains, and a key geological, religious, and cultural site in Shandong province; a world heritage site. Evidence of settlement dates back 400 000 years, and the area is rich in fossils, medicinal plants, ancient ruins, and temples. » China [i]

Taif, At [at **tiyf**] 21°05N 40°27E, pop (1974) 204 857. Summer resort town in Mecca province, WC Saudi Arabia; 64 km/40 ml ESE of Mecca; on a high plateau at an altitude of 1 158 m/3 799 ft; the unofficial seat of government during the summer; airfield; centre of fruit-growing district (grapes, apricots, pomegranates); noted for its wine. » Saudi Arabia [i]

taiga A Russian term for the open coniferous forest zone intermediate between the boreal forest and tundra regions. Sometimes it is used synonymously with the term *boreal*, though in the taiga the vegetation canopy is more open, with occasional stands of deciduous trees. Open areas are usually poorly drained muskeg. » boreal forests; conifer; deciduous plants; muskeg; tundra

Tailang » **Mon**

tailorbird An Old World warbler, native to India and SE Asia; inhabits forest and cultivation; eats insects and nectar; nest formed by folding a large leaf and 'sewing' the edges together with separate stitches of wool, silk, or spider's web. (Genus: *Orthotomus*, 9 species.) » warbler

Taimyr, Lake » **Taymyr, Lake**

Tainan or **T'ai-nan** [tiy**nan**] 23°01N 120°14E, pop (1985e) 622 073. Independent municipality and oldest city in Taiwan, on SW coast of Taiwan I; capital, 1684–7; university (1971); agricultural trade, fish market, crafts; oldest Confucian temple in Taiwan (1665), Yi T'sai castle (1874). » Taiwan [i]

Taine, Hippolyte (Adolphe) [ten] (1828–93) French critic, historian, and positivist philosopher, born at Vouziers. Educated at Paris, he turned to writing, and made a reputation with his critical works, followed by several philosophical studies in which he attempted to explain moral qualities and artistic excellence in purely descriptive, quasi-scientific terms. His greatest work, *Les Origines de la France contemporaine* (1875–94, The Origins of Contemporary France) constituted a strong attack on the men and the motives of the Revolution. He died in Paris. » positivism

taipan [**tiy**pan] A venomous snake, native to NE Australia and New Guinea; one of the world's most deadly snakes; the largest Australian snake (length, up to 4 m/13 ft); aggressive (but rare); brown with paler head; eats mainly small mammals. (*Oxyuranus scutellatus*.) The Australian **fierce snake** (*Parademansia microlepidota*) is sometimes placed in genus *Oxyuranus* and called **desert taipan**. (Family: *Elapidae*.) » snake

Taipei or **Taibei**, also **T'ai-pei** [tiy**bay**] 25°05N 121°32E, pop (1982e) 2 300 000. Capital of Taiwan, at the NW end of the island; one of the fastest-growing cities in Asia; occupied by the Japanese, 1895–1945; seat of the Nationalist Government, 1949; airport; airfield; railway; three universities (1927, 1928, 1946); textiles, plastics, electronics, foodstuffs, shipbuilding, machinery, crafts; National Palace Museum, Chung Cheng Memorial Hall, Lung Shan (Dragon Mountain) Temple (1740, rebuilt several times). » Taiwan [i]

Taiping Rebellion (1851–65) A rebellion that spread all over S China, led by Hong Xiuquan (1822–64), a Hakka from Guangdong. Its programme, which aimed at ushering in a 'Heavenly Kingdom of Great Peace' (*Taiping tianguo*) was a mixture of religion and political reform. The rebels took Nanjing (Nanking) in 1853 and made it their capital, but internal strife, foreign intervention, and the Qing forces under Zeng Guofan (1811–72) eventually brought the downfall of the movement. » Qing dynasty

Tairov, Aleksandr Yakovlevich [taeerof], originally **Kornblit** (1885–1950) Russian theatre director and actor, born at Rovno. He acted in Kiev, Petersburg, Riga, and Simbirsk (1905–13), then directed at the Free Theatre in Moscow, before founding the Moscow Chamber Theatre with his wife in 1914. He remained director of this theatre until shortly before his death, pioneering a 'synthetic theatre' of abstract balletic movement which aspired to the emotional precision of music. His *Notes of a Director* appeared in 1921. He died in Moscow. » theatre

Taiwan [tiy**wan**], formerly **Formosa**, official name **Republic of China** pop (1990e) 20 220 000; area 36 000 sq km/13 896 sq ml. Island republic consisting of Taiwan I and several smaller islands; divided into 16 counties (*hsien*), c.130 km/80 ml off the

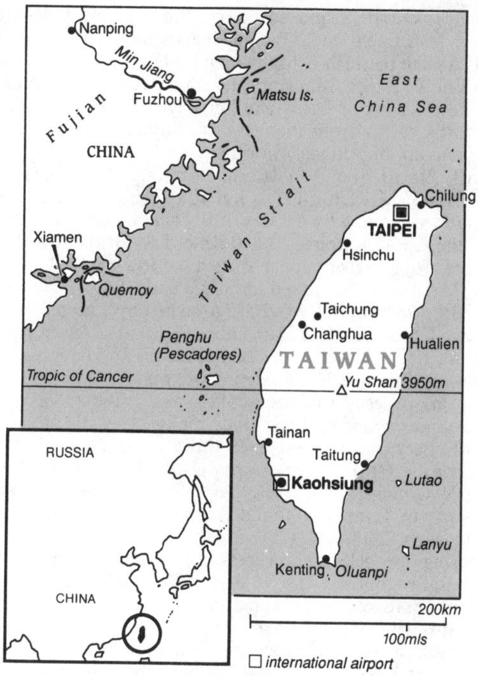

SE coast of China; separated from China (W) by the Taiwan Strait; bounded S by the South China Sea, N by the East China Sea, and E by the Pacific Ocean; capital, Taipei; timezone GMT +8; population mainly Han Chinese (98%); official language, Mandarin Chinese; several religions practised; unit of currency, the new Taiwan dollar; c.395 km/245 ml long, 100–145 km/60–90 ml wide; mountain range runs N–S, covering two-thirds of the island; highest peak, Yu Shan (3 997 m/13 113 ft); low-lying land mainly in the W; crossed by the Tropic of Cancer; tropical monsoon-type climate; annual rainfall generally over 2 000 mm/80 in; wettest period, summer (May–Sep); typhoons bring heavy rains (Jul–Sep); hot and humid summers; mild and short winters; average daily temperature at Taipei, 12–19°C (Jan), 24–33°C (Jul–Aug); monthly rainfall, 71 mm/2.8 in (Dec), 290 mm/11.4 in (Jun); visited by the Portuguese, 1590; conquered by Manchus, 17th-c; ceded to Japan, 1895; returned to China, 1945; Jiang Jieshi (Chiang Kai-shek) moved the Nationalist government here, 1949; governed by a president, who appoints a premier; the National Assembly has 920 members; parliament (*Yuan*) has 313 members; economy has changed from agriculture to industry since the 1950s; high technology, textiles, footwear, electronics, plastics, cement, furniture, consumer goods, iron and steel, petrochemicals, machinery, plywood, canned food; small deposits of coal, natural gas, limestone, marble, asbestos; sugar, bananas, pineapples, citrus fruits, vegetables, tea, fish. » Chinese; Jiang Jieshi; Guomindang; Taipei; RR27 national holidays; RR62 political leaders

Taiyuan [tiy**yooahn**] or **Yangku** 37°50N 112°30E, pop (1984e) 1 838 100. Capital of Shanxi province, NEC China; founded during W Zhou dynasty; development promoted by the West in late 19th-c; railway; coal, iron, steel, chemicals, textiles; Shanxi museum; c.25 km/15 ml SE, Jinci temples from the N Wei dynasty. » China [i]; Zhou dynasty

Taizé [**tay**zay] An ecumenical community founded near Lyons, France, by members of the French Reformed Church in 1940. Members observe a rule similar to most monastic orders, but dress as laymen. Their aim is the promotion of Christian unity, particularly between Protestants and Catholics. They provide a popular retreat and mission to the young. » ecumenism; monasticism; Reformed Churches; Roman Catholicism

Taizhong, also **T'ai-chung** [tiy**chung**] 24°09N 120°40E, pop (1982e) 636 406. Independent municipality and third largest city in Taiwan; economic, cultural, and commercial centre of C Taiwan; agricultural trade; designated an export processing zone. » Taiwan [i]

Taj Mahal [**tahj** ma**hahl**] A renowned monument to love constructed (1632–54) at Agra in Uttar Pradesh, India, as a mausoleum for Mumtaz Mahal, the favourite wife of Shah Jahan. Built of white marble and inlaid with semi-precious stones and mosaic work, it is a masterpiece of Mughal architecture, and a world heritage site. A huge central dome surrounded by four smaller domes surmounts the main structure, which is flanked by four slim minarets. The whole is mirrored in an ornamental pool. » Shah Jahan

takahe [**tak**ahee] A large, rare, flightless rail, native to New Zealand; green back, blue head, neck, and breast; stout red bill; inhabits high valleys in the Murchison Mts; eats coarse vegetation, especially snow-grass. (*Notornis mantelli*.) » rail

Talamanca Range–La Amistad Reserve A reserve on the Costa Rican border with Panama; area 50 000 sq km/19 000 sq ml; stretches from the Pacific to the Atlantic, encompassing a wide range of ecosystems, and providing a unique habitat for many species; a world heritage area. » Costa Rica [i]

talapoin [**tal**uhpoyn] The smallest Old World monkey, from W Africa; greenish with pale underparts; round head and long tail; partly webbed hands and feet; swims well; inhabits forest near water; also known as **pygmy guenon**. (*Miopithecus talapoin*.) » guenon; Old World monkey

Talbot, William Henry Fox (1800–77) British pioneer of photography, born at Melbury Abbas, Dorset. Educated at Harrow and Cambridge, he became an MP (1833), and in 1838 succeeded in making photographic prints on silver chloride paper, which he termed 'photogenic drawing', and later developed and patented the Calotype process. He died near Chippenham, Wiltshire. » Calotype; photography

talc A hydrous magnesium silicate mineral ($Mg_3Si_4O_{10}(OH)_2$), formed in metamorphic rocks as light-grey soft masses; also known as **steatite** or **soapstone**. It may be associated with serpentine. There are large deposits in Austria and India. It is used in cosmetics (talcum powder) and in the paper, paint, rubber, and textile industries. It may also be carved for ornaments. » magnesium; serpentine; silicate minerals

Talca [**tal**ka] 35°25S 71°39W, pop (1982) 134 721. Capital of Talca province, C Chile; S of Santiago; founded, 1692; destroyed by earthquake, 1742 and 1928, then completely rebuilt; Chilean independence declared here, 1818; railway; greatest wine-producing area in Chile; O'Higgins Museum. » Chile [i]

Talcahuano [talka-**hwan**oh] 36°40S 73°10W, pop (1982) 208 941. Port in Concepción province, C Chile; on a peninsula, 12 km/7 ml from Concepción; best harbour in Chile, containing main naval base and dry docks; railway; steel, using iron ore from N Chile. » Chile [i]

Taliesin [taliesin] (6th-c) Welsh bard, possibly mythical, known only from a collection of poems, *The Book of Taliesin*, written in the late 13th-c. His name is given in the 9th-c *Historia Britonum* of Nennius. » Nennius; poetry; Welsh literature

tallage A manorial obligation in the form of a tax, paid by villeins in Britain; also a tax paid on the ancient Demesne lands of the crown (ie recorded in the Domesday Book as royal lands in 1066), even if subsequently granted away as fiefs. It was frequently levied to pay for military campaigns before 1340, when Parliament abolished it, and substituted subsidies and aids. » Domesday Book

Tallahassee [tala**ha**see] (Muskogean 'town-old'), 30°27N 84°17W, pop (1980) 81 548. Capital of state in Leon County, NW Florida, USA; originally a settlement of Apalachee Indians; state capital, 1824; ordinance of secession from the Union adopted here, 1861; railway; two universities; government and trade centre; wood products, processed foods. » Florida

Talleyrand (-Périgord, Charles Maurice de) [talayrã] (1754–1838) French statesman, born and died in Paris. Educated for the Church, he was ordained (1779), appointed Bishop of Autun (1788), elected to the States General, and made President of the Assembly (1790). He lived in exile in England and the USA until after the fall of Robespierre. As Foreign Minister under the Directory (1797–1807), he helped to consolidate Napoleon's position as Consul (1802) and Emperor (1804); but alarmed by Napoleon's ambitions, he resigned in 1807, becoming leader of the anti-Napoleonic faction. He became Foreign Minister under Louis XVIII, representing France with great skill at the Congress of Vienna (1814–15). He then lived largely in retirement, but was Louis Philippe's chief adviser at the July Revolution, and was appointed French Ambassador to England (1830–4). » French Revolution [i]; July Revolution; Louis XVIII; Louis Philippe; Napoleon I

Tallien, Jean Lambert [tal**yĩ**] (1767–1820) French revolutionary politician, born and died in Paris. As President of the Convention (1794), he was denounced by Robespierre, but conspired with Barras and Fouché to bring about the former's downfall. He became a member of the Council of Five Hundred under the Directory (1795–9), and accompanied Napoleon to Egypt (1798). » Barras; Fouché; French Revolution [i]; Napoleon I; Robespierre

Tallinn, formerly Ger **Revel** or **Reval** (to 1917) [**ta**lin] 59°22N 24°48E, pop (1983) 454 000. Seaport capital of Estonia, on S coast of the Gulf of Finland; member of the Hanseatic League; taken by Russia, 1710; capital of independent Estonia, 1918–40; occupied by Germany in World War 2; airfield; railway; extensive military and naval installations; major transportation junction; electric motors, shipbuilding, superphosphates, shale gas; citadel (13th-c), former Governor's Palace (1767–73), Toomkirik (cathedral, 13th–15th-c). » Estonia; Hanseatic League

Tallis, Thomas (c.1505–85) English musician, 'the father of English cathedral music'. One of the greatest contrapuntists of the English School, an adaptation of his plainsong responses, and his setting of the Canticles in D Minor, are still in use. He wrote much church music, including a motet in 40 parts, *Spem in alium*. In 1575 Queen Elizabeth granted him, with Byrd, a monopoly for printing music and music paper in England. He died in London. » Byrd, William; counterpoint

Talmud [**tal**mud] (Heb 'study') An authoritative, influential compilation of rabbinic traditions and discussions about Jewish life and Law. After the Mishnah of Rabbi Judah was compiled (c.200), it became itself an object of study by Jewish scholars in Palestine and Babylon; their commentary on it (the *Gemara*), together with the Mishnah, constitutes the Talmud, of which there were two versions: the Jerusalem or Palestinian Talmud (c.4th-c) and the longer Babylonian Talmud (c.500). » Gemara; Judaism; Mishnah; Torah

talus » **scree**

tam-tam » **gong**

Tamale [tam**a**le] 9°26N 0°49W, pop (1982) 226 715. Capital of Northern region, Ghana; 430 km/267 ml N of Accra; airfield; educational centre; cotton, groundnuts, civil engineering. » Ghana [i]

tamandua [taman**doo**a] » **anteater**

tamaraw or **tamarau** » **water buffalo**

tamarin [**tam**arin] A marmoset of genus *Saguinus* (10 species); lower canine teeth longer than incisors; eats fruit and small animals; also known as **long-tusked marmoset**. The name is also used for *Leontopithecus rosalia* (**golden lion tamarin**, **golden marmoset**, or **lion-headed marmoset**). » marmoset

tamarisk A slender shrub or tree, native to the Mediterranean and Asia; deciduous small twigs with scaly leaves giving a feathery appearance; flowers in spikes, 4–5 petals, pink or white. It is salt tolerant, and often grows in sandy soils and near the sea. (Genus: *Tamarix*, 54 species. Family: *Tamaricaceae*.) » deciduous plants; manna; shrub; tree [i]

tambourine A small frame drum fitted with jingles, and covered on one side with parchment or plastic. It may be shaken, tapped with the fingertips, stroked with a moistened thumb, etc to produce various effects, mostly while accompanying dancing. » drum; membranophone

Tambov [tam**bof**] 52°44N 41°28E, pop (1983) 286 000. Capital city of Tambovskaya oblast, SC European Russia, on a tributary of the R Oka; founded as a fortress, 1636; airfield; railway; synthetic resins and plastics, clothing, engineering. » Russia

Tamil A Dravidian-speaking people of S India and Sri Lanka, living as traders and seafarers. Predominantly Hindu, they were instrumental in diffusing Indian culture to many parts of SE Asia in the 11th-c. Many migrated in the 19th-c as labourers to Fiji, W Indies, Mauritius, South Africa, and SE Asia. Tamil is now the major Dravidian language of S India, with written records dating from the 3rd-c BC. Population c.50 million. » Dravidian languages; Hinduism

Tamil Nadu [tamil **nah**doo], formerly **Madras** pop (1981) 48 297 456; area 130 069 sq km/50 207 sq ml. State in S India, bounded E and S by the Bay of Bengal; Sri Lanka to the S; part of the Chola Empire, 10th–13th-c; first British trading settlement, 1611; largely under British control by 1801; boundaries of Mysore state altered in 1956 and 1960; renamed Tamil Nadu, 1968; capital, Madras; governed by a 63-member Legislative Council and a 234-member Legislative Assembly; most S point, Cape Comorin; several hill ranges and rivers; population mainly Hindu (c.90%); rice, maize, pulses, millets, sugar cane, cotton, oilseed, tobacco, coffee, tea, rubber, pepper; coal, chromite, bauxite, limestone, manganese; textiles, tanning, machinery, tyres, forestry. » India [i]; Madras

Tammany Hall The most powerful of the four Democratic Party Committees in New York State; originally a club (the Society of Tammany) founded in 1789, which in the late 19th-c and early 20th-c was notorious for its political corruption. During the selection process for presidential candidates, it generally controls the votes of the other New York State representatives. » Democratic Party

Tammerfors » **Tampere**

Tammuz or **Thammuz** [**ta**muz] A Babylonian god of vegetation who was beloved by Ishtar (in Syria by Astarte). He returns from the dead and dies again each year. » Adonis; Ishtar

Tampa 27°57N 82°27W, pop (1980) 271 523. Seat of Hillsborough County, W Florida, USA; a port on the NE coast of Tampa Bay; developed around a military post, 1824; later a cigar-making centre, then a resort; airport; railway; university (1931); processing and shipping centre for citrus fruit and phosphates; brewing, printing and publishing, electrical equipment, food products (mainly shrimp), fabricated metals, chemicals, cigars; major league team, Buccaneers (football); David Falk and Tampa Theatres, Museum of Science and Industry, Tampa Museum, Busch Gardens; Gasparilla Invasion (Feb). » Florida

Tampere, Swedish **Tammerfors** [**tam**pere] 61°32N 23°45E, pop (1982) 167 211. City in Häme province, SW Finland; on the Tammerkoski rapids by L Näsijärvi, c.160 km/100 ml NNW of Helsinki; second largest city in Finland; established, 1779; developed as industrial centre in 19th-c; airfield; railway; boat trips to Virrat; university (1966); technological institute (1965); hydroelectricity; footwear, leather, textiles, metal, timber products; cathedral (20th-c); Theatre Summer (Aug). » Finland [i]

Tampico [tam**pee**koh] 22°18N 97°52W, pop (1980) 267 957. Seaport in Tamaulipas state, NE Mexico, on the Gulf of Mexico; airport; railway; oil refining, oil products, boatbuilding, timber, fishing, fish processing. » Mexico [i]

Tana, Lake, Amharic **Tana Hāyk** Lake in NWC Ethiopia; area 3 600 sq km/1 400 sq ml; altitude 1 829 m/6 001 ft; source of the Blue Nile; notable for its 40 monasteries on islands in the lake. » Blue Nile; Ethiopia [i]

Tanabata A Japanese festival (7 Jul, but in some places 7 Aug) dedicated to the two stars Vega and Altair – two lovers (according to an originally Chinese folk-tale) allowed to meet once a year on that night.

tanager [**tan**ajuh] A songbird, native to the New World tropics; plumage usually brightly coloured; wings short, rounded; usually inhabits woodland; eats fruit, insects, seeds, and nectar. (Family: *Thraupidae*, c.239 species.) » honeycreeper; magpie; songbird

Tananarive » **Antananarivo**

Tancred (c.1076–1112) Norman crusader, grandson of Robert Guiscard. He went on the First Crusade, distinguished himself in the sieges of Nicaea, Tarsus, Antioch, Jerusalem, and Ascalon, and was given the principality of Tiberias (1099). He also ruled at Edessa and Antioch, where he died. » Crusades [i]; Guiscard; Normans

tang » **surgeonfish**

Tang or **T'ang dynasty** (618–907) A Chinese dynasty founded by Li Yuan with its capital at Changan (present-day Xi'an). In 690 Wu Zetian, a former concubine of the second Emperor and the Empress of the third, became herself Emperor of China – the only woman ever to do so. In 755 the rebellion of An Lushan, a young general, though crushed, left the dynasty unable to control all its provinces as before, and there resulted a period of political disunity known as the Five Dynasties and Ten Kingdoms. The Tang dynasty is generally regarded as the golden age of Chinese poetry. » China [i]

Tanga [**tang**ga] 6°10S 35°40E, pop (1978) 103 409. Seaport capital of Tanga region, NE Tanzania; on the Indian Ocean opposite Pemba I; formerly the starting point for caravans heading into the interior; occupied by the British, 1916; Tanzania's second largest port; centre of an agricultural area; tourism, sisal, cocoa, clothing, seafoods, fruit, coconut oil, tea. » Tanzania [i]

Tanganyika, Lake [tangganyeeka] Freshwater lake in EC Africa; mostly along the Tanzania–Zaire frontier, with smaller sections within the Zambian (S) and Burundian (NW) frontiers; length, 645 km/400 ml NNW–SSE; the longest, deepest (over 1 400 m/4 600 ft) and second largest lake (after L Victoria) in Africa; second only to L Baikal (Russia) in depth; width, 25–80 km/15–50 ml; altitude, 772 m/2 533 ft; main ports are at Kigoma (Tanzania), Kalémié (Zaire), and Bujumbura (Burundi); European discovery in 1858 by John Speke and Richard Burton; small-scale naval warfare took place on the lake between British and German forces in 1915–16. » Africa; Speke

tangent A line (usually a straight line) which touches a curve at a point P with the same gradient as the curve at P. It is sometimes convenient to think of a tangent meeting a curve at two (or more) coincident points. The tangent to a circle at a point P is perpendicular to the radius of the circle through P. » geometry

tangerine A citrus fruit; a variety of mandarin with bright orange rind. (*Citrus reticulata*. Family: *Rutaceae*.) » citrus; mandarin

Tangier or **Tangiers** [tan**jeer(z)**], ancient **Tingis** 35°48N 5°45W, pop (1982) 266 346. Seaport capital of Nord-Ouest province, N Morocco; at W end of the Strait of Gibraltar, an important strategic position at entrance to the Mediterranean; held by the Vandals, Byzantines, and Arabs; occupied by the Portuguese in 1471, and later by the Spanish, English, and Moors; established as an international zone, 1923; Spanish occupation in World War 2; part of Morocco, 1959; free port status restored, 1962; airport; railway; university (1971); textiles, cigarettes, fishing, tourism; royal summer residence; kasbah fortress, Dar Shorfa Palace; Caves of Hercules on coast to the W. » Morocco [i]

Tangshan or **T'angshan** 39°37N 118°05E, pop (1984e) 1 366 100. City in E Hebei province, N China; ESE of Beijing (Peking); railway; coal mining, heavy industry. » China [i]

Tanguy, Yves [tãgee] (1900–55) French-US artist, born in Paris. Mainly self-taught, he began to paint in 1922, joining the Surrealists in 1926. He worked in Africa from 1930, and moved to the USA in 1939, where he became a US citizen. All his pictures are at the same time Surrealist and nonfigurative, being peopled with numerous small objects or organisms, whose meaning and identity, as in the landscape of another planet, is unknown. » Surrealism

Tanizaki, Junichiro [tanizakee] (1886–1965) Japanese novelist, born in Tokyo. He became known in the West only after the translation in 1957 of his long novel *Sasameyuki* (1943–8, The Makioka Sisters), a notable example of descriptive realism. Among his later novels are *Kagi* (1960, The Key) and *Futen rojin nikki* (1962, Diary of a Mad Old Man). He died in Yugawara. » Japanese literature; novel

tank An armoured fighting vehicle, typically equipped with tracks enabling it to manoeuvre across broken ground, and armed by a high velocity gun in a rotating turret. The first practical tanks were devised and used in action in 1916 by the British. In the years before 1939, they were developed into fast-moving, hard-hitting machines capable of independent action. This had a great impact on warfare, amply demonstrated by the success of the German Panzer divisions and the *blitzkrieg* concept (1939–42). Huge armoured battles continued to be fought on the E and W Fronts, and the tank emerged as the most important land weapon of World War 2. Even in the nuclear age, tanks and tank forces remain the most important part of a modern land force. The vehicles show a great deal of electronic sophistication, equipped with advanced night vision devices, laser range-finders, and fire control computers. » antitank gun/missile; armoured fighting vehicle; blitzkrieg; Panzer

tanker A vessel designed to carry liquid in bulk in a number of tanks, each of which is an integral part of the hull structure. The largest vessel ever built was the *Seawise Giant*, an oil tanker capable of carrying 564 739 tonnes deadweight. In 1988 the vessel with the largest gross tonnage was the Greek-registered oil tanker *Hellas Fos* of 254 076 gross tons and a deadweight capacity of 555 051 tonnes. » ship [i]

Tannaim [**tan**aeem] (Aramaic 'teachers', 'transmitters of oral tradition') Early sages and teachers of Judaism (mainly 10–220 AD) who were instrumental in the emerging rabbinic movement by their study of the Jewish Law (Torah) and formulation of the nucleus of the Mishnah and Midrashim. Followers of Hillel and Shammai are often considered the first Tannaim. » Hillel I; Judaism; Mishnah; rabbi; Shammai; Torah

Tannhäuser [**tan**hoyzer] The name of both a legendary German knight and a 13th-c minstrel, conflated in a popular ballad. It tells of a man who seeks forgiveness for a life of pleasure, but, being refused absolution by the Pope, returns to his former ways. The story is the subject of an opera by Richard Wagner, produced in 1845. » ballad; German literature

tanning The process of turning raw animal hide or skin into a permanent, durable, flexible form. Cleaned skin is soaked in solutions of vegetable extracts containing tannins (eg oak bark) or, since the 19th-c, chrome salts. » leather

tannins A mixture of derivatives of polyhydroxybenzoic acid from various plants, notably tea. They are water-soluble, with a bitter and astringent taste, and have long been used in the tanning of leather and in dyeing. » benzoic acid; tea

Tantalus [**tan**taluhs] In Greek mythology, a king of Sisyphos in Lydia, who committed terrible crimes. He stole the food of the gods, so becoming immortal, and served them his son Pelops in a dish. For this he was punished in the Underworld; he sits in a pool which recedes when he bends to drink, and the grapes over his head elude his grasp. » Pelops

tantra [**tan**tra] A type of Hindu or Buddhist ritual text, and the practice of its instruction. Tantras may include texts describing spells, magical formulas, mantras, meditative practices, and rituals to be performed. The practice of Tantra requires instruction by a guru. » Buddhism; guru; Hinduism; mantra

Tanzania, official name **United Republic of Tanzania** [tanza**neea**] pop (1990e) 24 403 000; area 939 652 sq km/362 706 sq ml. E African republic, divided into 22 regions; bounded S by Mozambique and Malawi, SW by Zambia, W by Zaire, NW by Burundi, Rwanda, and Uganda, N by Kenya, and E by the Indian Ocean; includes the islands of Zanzibar, Pemba, and Matia; capital, Dodoma; chief towns, Dar es Salaam, Zanzibar, Mwanza, Tanga, Arusha; timezone GMT +3; population mainly of Bantu origin; chief religion on the mainland, Christianity (35%); on Zanzibar, almost entirely Islam; official languages, English, Swahili; unit of currency, the Tanzanian shilling.

Physical description and climate. Largest E African country, just S of the Equator; coast fringed by long sandy beaches protected by coral reefs; rises towards a C plateau, average elevation 1 000 m/3 300 ft; high grasslands and mountain ranges, C and S; Rift Valley branches round L Victoria (N), where there are several high volcanic peaks, notably Mt Kilimanjaro (5 895 m/19 340 ft); extensive Serengeti plain to the W; E branch of the Rift Valley runs through C Tanzania from NE of L Victoria, containing several lakes; W branch runs S down the W side of L Victoria, and includes L Tanganyika and L Rukwa; hot, humid, tropical climate on coast and offshore islands; average temperatures c.23°C (Jun–Sep), 27°C (Dec–Mar); average annual rainfall over 1 000 mm/40 in; hot and dry on the C plateau, average annual

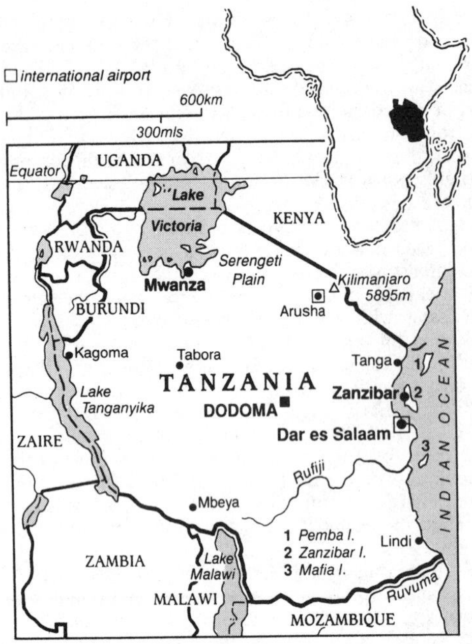

rainfall 250 mm/10 in; semi-temperate at altitudes above 1 500 m/5 000 ft; permanent snow on high peaks.

History and government. Early links with Arab, Indian, and Persian traders; Swahili culture developed, 10th–15th-c; Zanzibar capital of the Omani empire, 1840s; exploration of the interior by German missionaries and British explorers, mid-19th-c; Zanzibar a British protectorate, 1890; German East Africa established, 1891; British mandate to administer Tanganyika, 1919; first E African country to gain independence and become a member of the Commonwealth, 1961; republic with Julius Nyerere as President, 1962; Zanzibar given independence as a constitutional monarchy with the Sultan as head of state; Sultan overthrown in 1964, and Act of Union between Zanzibar and Tanganyika led to the United Republic of Tanzania; governed by a president, elected for a 5-year term, a cabinet, and a National Assembly of 243 members serving a 5-year term.

Economy. Largely based on agriculture; rice, sorghum, coffee, sugar, cloves (most of the world's market), coconuts, tobacco, cotton; reserves of iron, coal, tin, gypsum, salt, phosphate, gold, diamonds, oil; food processing, cotton, cement, cigarettes; tourism relating to Mt Kilimanjaro, beaches and reefs, national parks, and the five game reserves. » Dodoma; Nyerere; Rift Valley; Serengeti; Zanzibar (island); RR27 national holidays; RR62 political leaders

Taoism [**tow**izm] A translation of the Chinese terms for 'the school of the tao' and the 'Taoist religion'. The former refers to the philosophy of the classical Taoist texts of no earlier than the 4th–3rd-c BC: *The Lao Tzu* or *Tao te ching*, *The Chuang Tzu*, and *The Lieh Tzu*. *Tao* or 'the way' is central in both Confucianism and Taoism, with the former stressing the tao of humanity, and the latter the tao of nature, harmony with which ensures appropriate conduct. Expressions of mystical thought, they are concerned with the political order and practical life of the individual. Taoist religion developed later, and incorporated alchemy, divination, and magic. » Confucianism; Lao Zi

tape recorder Equipment for storing sound and other information on magnetic tape; also used to play back these recordings. The sound to be recorded is turned into an electrical signal by a microphone, and fed to the recording head. Magnetic tape passes over this head, and a record of the original sound is imprinted in magnetic signals on the tape. Electrical signals from a radio or other source can also be recorded on tape. Tape recorders are widely used in the recording and broadcasting industry, and in home entertainment. Portable tape recorders are popular with those who like to take their music with them. » magnetic tape 1; sound recording

tapestry A heavy decorative textile, hand-woven with multi-colour pictorial designs, and often of large size. Oriental in origin, tapestries were used for wall hangings, furniture, and floor coverings. Imitation tapestry fabrics are made on jacquard looms. The Middle Ages is the period of greatest renown for tapestry weaving, with France, Belgium, and Holland excelling at the craft. Some tapestries were not woven but were embroidered – the Bayeux Tapestry being a famous example. » Bayeux Tapestry

tapeworm A parasitic flatworm; adults commonly found in intestines of vertebrates; body typically comprises an attached head (*scolex*) and a chain of segments (*proglottids*) produced by budding; life cycle usually includes a larval stage found in a different intermediate host that is eaten by the final host. (Phylum: *Platyhelminthes*; class: *Cestoda*.) » flatworm; larva; parasitology; tapeworm infestation

tapeworm infestation A condition in which tapeworms (*cestodes*) live within the body of their hosts. The largest is *Taenia saginata* (beef tapeworm), which may be several metres in length. It does not cause significant disease in humans, but the knowledge of its presence may distress the patient. Other tapeworms include *Taenia solium*, which affects pigs and causes hydatid disease in humans, and smaller worms which affect dogs, cats, sheep, and fish. The fish tapeworm is common in Scandinavia, Africa, and Asia, and causes a form of anaemia similar to that arising from vitamin B_{12} deficiency. » hydatid disease; tapeworm; vitamins [i]

tapioca A starchy preparation derived from the root crop *cassava*. The flour of the cassava is low in protein, which is readily removed by washing in water. Tapioca is used in puddings and as a thickening agent in liquid food. » cassava

tapir [**tay**puh] A nocturnal mammal native to C and S America and SE Asia; resembles a small, smooth-skinned, hornless rhinoceros, with a short smooth coat, and a snout extended as a short trunk; the only perissodactyl with four toes on front feet; inhabits woodland; young with pale horizontal stripes and spots. (Family: *Tapiridae*, 4 species.) » perissodactyl [i]; rhinoceros

tar The liquid product of heating coal in the absence of air (**coal tar**). It contains many important substances, extractable by solvents or further distillation, and useful in the chemical industry (benzene, phenol, pyridine, etc). **Wood tar** is the first product of the destructive distillation of wood. Further distillation yields *creosote* and a variety of organic compounds depending on the wood; for example, resinous woods yield turpentine. The residue is *pitch*. » coal

Tara A prehistoric hillfort, 40 km/23 ml NW of Dublin, the supposed site of St Patrick's conversion of Lóegaire in the 5th-c AD, and the traditional seat of the kings of Ireland from pre-Christian times to the death of Maél Sechnaill II of Meath in 1022. Archaeologically its earthworks are poorly known, but for the Mound of the Hostages, a megalithic passage grave of the early 3rd millennium BC. » megalith; Patrick, St

tarantella A lively folkdance from S Italy, named after the town of Taranto. It was said to cure (or in some legends to be induced by) the bite of the tarantula. » tarantula

tarantula Any of the large hairy spiders of the family *Theraphosidae*; rather sluggish spiders with a strong bite which may be venomous; hairs can cause rash when handled. The name is also used for a large, hairy species of wolf spider (family: *Lycosidae*), found in Italy. (Order: *Araneae*.) » spider; wolf spider

Tarawa 1°30N 173°00E, pop (1985) 21 191. Capital town of Kiribati, on Tarawa atoll in the Gilbert Is, C Pacific Ocean; airport; copra, mother-of-pearl; scene of US–Japanese battle in 1943. » Kiribati

Tarbes [tahb], ancient **Bigorra** 43°15N 0°03E, pop (1982) 54 055. Industrial and commercial city, and capital of Hautes-Pyrénées department, S France; on left bank of R Adour, 37 km/23 ml ESE of Pau; originally a Roman settlement; ancient capital of province of Bigorre; road and rail junction; firearms, furniture, footwear, agricultural trade; 12th–14th-c cathedral, national stud farm (Les Haras, 1806), Jardin Mussey.

Tardigrada [tah**di**grada] » **water bear**

tare » **vetch**

targum [**tah**guhm] (Heb 'translation') An Aramaic translation of the Hebrew Scriptures or parts thereof, probably originally composed orally (c.1st-c BC) when the Torah was read aloud in the synagogues, since most Jews of the time understood Aramaic rather than Hebrew, but then written in the rabbinic period. The translations sometimes betray early rabbinic ideology. Best-known is the *Targum Onkelos*. » Aramaic; Bible; Judaism; Old Testament; rabbi; Torah

tariff A tax placed on goods imported into a country. Its aims are to prevent too many imports entering the country, and to raise revenues for a government. If tariffs become too strict, there will be a rise in smuggling. » free trade; protectionism

Tarim Basin Largest inland basin in China; area 530 000 sq km/205 000 sq ml; bounded by Kunlun and Altun Shan Ranges (S) and Tien Shan Range (N); desert and salt lakes in centre, including largest desert in China, Taklimakan Shamo (area 327 000 sq km/126 000 sq ml); rich in salt and non-ferrous metals; nuclear testing takes place in the region. » China [i]

Tarim He River in NW China, in N Tarim Basin; largest inland river in China; fed by glaciers and melting snow from the Tien Shan Mts (N); a frequently changing river course; length 2 179 km/1 354 ml. » China [i]

Tarkenton, Fran, properly **Francis** (1940–) US footballer, born at Richmond, Virginia. He played for the Minnesota Vikings and New York Giants (1961–78), and gained 47 003 yards passing, a National Football League record. His 3 686 passes completed is also a record. » football [i]

Tarlton or **Tarleton, Richard** (?–1588) English clown who first performed with Leicester's Men, but joined Queen Elizabeth's Men on the formation of that company in 1583. He became the most famous and skilful popular entertainer of his age, especially in the dramatic jigs which were a regular feature of the playhouses. » theatre

taro A perennial native to SE Asia; leaves large, oval, with long stalk attached near centre of blade; spathe pale yellow; also called **dasheen**. It is cultivated commercially in the tropics for its large corms, rich in easily digested starch suitable for invalids and infants. The corms must first be boiled to remove poisonous calcium oxalate crystals. (*Colocasia esculenta*. Family: *Araceae*.) » corm; perennial; spathe

tarpan A wild horse native to the steppes of SE Europe; thought to be a *plateau type* ancestor of modern domestic breeds; grey-brown with dark stripe along spine, occasionally with stripes on front legs; stiff, erect mane; wild tarpan hunted to extinction for food in 1879 (last captive individual died in 1919); subsequently tarpan-like horses were bred selectively to 'restore' the type. » horse [i]; Przewalski's horse

Tarpeia [tah**pee**a] According to a Roman legend, a Roman woman who betrayed the Capitol to the Sabines, in return for 'what they wore on their left arms' (meaning gold rings). In their disgust, they threw their shields on her and crushed her to death. » Sabines

tarpon Large fish widespread in open waters of the Atlantic Ocean, and greatly prized as a sport fish; length up to 2.4 m/8 ft; mouth oblique, lower jaw prolonged; dorsal fin small with long posterior fin ray; larvae live in shallow inshore waters and brackish marshes. (*Tarpon atlanticus*. Family: *Megalopidae*.)

Tarquinius Superbus (6th-c BC) Tyrannical king of Rome, possibly of Etruscan extraction, whose overthrow (510 BC) marked the end of monarchy at Rome, and the beginning of the Republic. Most of the details about his life are probably fictional. » Lucretia; Roman history [i]

tarragon An aromatic perennial growing to 120 cm/4 ft, native to Asia; leaves narrowly lance-shaped, the basal ones 3-lobed at the apex; flower heads globular, 3 mm/0.12 in across, yellowish, drooping in lax panicles. It is widely cultivated as a condiment, and for seasoning vinegar. (*Artemisia dracunculus*. Family: *Compositae*.) » perennial; panicle

Tarragona [tara**go**na], Lat **Tarraco** 41°05N 1°17E, pop (1981) 111 689. Port and capital of Tarragona province, Catalonia, NE Spain; 534 km/332 ml ENE of Madrid; archbishopric; airport; railway; agricultural trade, chemicals, vegetable oils; Roman aqueduct and amphitheatre, cathedral (12th–13th-c), archaeological museum; Fiesta of St Magin (Aug), Fiesta of Santa Tecia (Sep). » Catalonia; Spain [i]

tarsier [**tah**siuh] A nocturnal primate native to Indonesia and the Philippines; large eyes, long hind legs; long naked tail with tuft of hairs at the tip; leaps between branches; inhabits woodland. (Family: *Tarsiidae*, 3 species.) » primate (biology)

Tarski, Alfred (1902–83) Polish logician, born in Warsaw. He was educated at Warsaw, and taught there until 1939, when he moved to the USA, teaching at Berkeley, California, from 1942. He made pioneering contributions to the study of formal semantics, especially to the definition of 'truth', and to several branches of mathematics and mathematical logic. He died at Berkeley. » logic; semantics

Tarsus [**tah**suhs] 36°52N 34°52E, pop (1980) 121 074. Town in Içel province, S Turkey, on W bank of R Pamuk; important ancient city of Asia Minor; birthplace of St Paul; railway; agricultural trade centre. » Turkey [i]

tartan A fabric of a twill structure, made from variously coloured warp and weft yarns, using checkered designs which are almost always symmetrical. Tartans are mainly associated with the Scottish clans, in a tradition of dress dating from the 17th-c. » twill

Tartar » **Tatar**

tartaric acid [tah**ta**rik] IUPAC **2,3-dihydroxybutanedioic acid**, $C_4H_6O_6$. A compound with three stereo-isomers: a pair of mirror images, and one in which one half of the molecule is the mirror image of the other, called **meso-tartaric acid**. The isomer shown in the illustration, and its potassium and calcium salts, are found widely in plants. Potassium hydrogen tartrate is used as an acid in baking powder, and is called **cream of tartar**. **Tartar emetic** is a double salt of potassium and antimony. » isomers; IUPAC

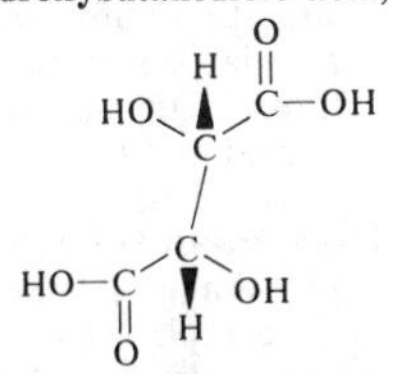

Tartarus [**tah**taruhs] In Greek mythology, the name of the part of the Underworld where those who offended the gods were punished. The Titans were thrust down there after their rebellion, and infamous criminals were tortured. » Ixion; Sisyphus; Tantalus

tartrazine An artificial yellow colouring permitted for use in foods. It has been associated with hypersensitivity reactions among urticaria sufferers and asthmatics. The prevalence of true tartrazine sensitivity is about 1 in 10 000, while the self-diagnosed sensitivity is 7%. » asthma; colouring agents; urticaria

Tarutao [tahruh**tow**] area 1 400 sq km/540 sq ml. Marine national park in Thailand; a group of 51 islands 30 km/19 ml off the W coast, near the Thailand–Malaysia frontier, N of the Langkawi Is. » Thailand [i]

Tashkent [tash**kent**] 41°16N 69°13E, pop (1989) 2 073 000. Capital city of Uzbekistan, in the foothills of the Tien Shan Mts; oldest city of C Asia, known in the 1st-c BC; taken by Russia, 1865; virtually rebuilt after earthquake damage, 1966; airport; railway; university (1920); solar research, chemicals, heavy engineering, clothing, footwear, textiles, cotton; venue for international conferences; Islamic centres of Kukeldash (c.17th-c) and Barakkhana (c.15th–16th-c). » Uzbekistan

Tasman, Abel Janszoon (1603–c.1659) Dutch navigator, born near Groningen. He was sent in quest of the 'Great South Land' by Antony Van Diemen (1593–1645), Governor-General of Batavia, and in 1642 discovered the area he named Van Diemen's Land (now Tasmania) and New Zealand, followed by Tonga and Fiji (1643). He made a second voyage (1644) to the Gulf of Carpentaria and the NW coast of Australia. » Tasmania

Tasman Sea [**taz**man] Part of the Pacific Ocean separating E Australia and Tasmania from New Zealand; linked to the Indian Ocean by the Bass Strait; shallow, narrow continental shelf off Australia, sinking to depths of 4 570 m/14 990 ft in the

Tasman abyssal plain; named for the Dutch explorer Abel Tasman. » abyssal plains; Pacific Ocean; Tasman

Tasmania, formerly **Van Diemen's Land** (to 1856) pop (1986) 449 100; area 67 800 sq km/26 200 sq ml. Island state of Australia, separated from the mainland by the Bass Strait; includes the main island of Tasmania, and several smaller islands, notably King I (1 099 sq km/424 sq ml), Flinders I (1 374 sq km/530 sq ml), Bruny I (362 sq km/140 sq ml); discovered by Abel Tasman, 1642; first European settlement, 1803 (a British dependency of New South Wales); Port Arthur was the largest penal colony in Australia; became a separate colony, 1825; now divided into four statistical divisions; the smallest of Australia's states; mountainous interior, with a Central Plateau rising to 1 617 m/5 305 ft at Mt Ossa; a temperate maritime climate influenced by the westerly 'Roaring Forties' winds; the most fertile regions along the NW and E coasts and along the river valleys; capital, Hobart; chief towns Devonport, Launceston, Burnie-Somerset, Queenstown, New Norfolk; sheep, cattle, pigs, cereals, apples, hogs, wood, paper, chemicals, machinery, textiles; mining of tin, copper, zinc, lead, silver, gold, coal; abundant hydroelectric power; first Aborigines to settle here crossed the land bridge now formed by the Bass Strait 25 000 years ago; tourism; Western Tasmania Wilderness National Parks; numerous unique plants and animals, notably the Tasmanian Tiger (now feared to be extinct) and the Tasmanian Devil, both carnivorous marsupials; state holidays Labour Day (Mar), Bank Holiday (Apr). » Australia [i]; Hobart; Tasman

Tasmanian devil An Australian carnivorous marsupial; the largest dasyure (length, up to 1.1 m/3.6 ft); bear-like in shape, with large powerful head and long bushy tail; dark with pale throat, pale patches on sides, pale muzzle; eats mainly carrion (including fur and bones), also kills snakes, birds, etc. (*Sarcophilus harrisii.*) » dasyure; marsupial [i]

Tasmanian tiger/wolf » **thylacine** [i]

TASS An acronym of **Telegrafnoe Agentsvo Sovetskovo Soyuza** (Telegraph Agency of the Soviet Union), the national news agency of the USSR, state-owned, with headquarters in Moscow. Established in 1935, TASS supplied the Western media with news of the USSR, and acted as a conduit for Western agencies supplying the Soviet media. » news agency

Tassili N'Ajjer [tasilee **na**jair] National park in E Algeria, N Africa; NE of the Ahaggar (Hoggar) Mts; area 1 000 sq km/386 sq ml; established in 1972; a sandstone plateau contains many prehistoric cave paintings of animals and people. » Ahaggar Mountains; Algeria [i]; Palaeolithic art

Tasso, Torquato (1544–95) Italian poet, born at Sorrento. He studied law and philosophy at Padua, where he published his first work, a romantic poem, *Rinaldo*. After joining the court of the Duke of Ferrara, he wrote his epic masterpiece on the capture of Jerusalem during the first crusade, *Gerusalemme Liberata* (1581, Jerusalem Liberated). He later rewrote his work, in response to criticisms, as *Gerusalemme Conquistata* (1593). He died in Rome, where he was to have been crowned as poet laureate. » epic; Italian literature; poetry; tragedy

taste buds Small sensory organs located on the tongue and palate, which recognize four primary tastes: sweet, sour, salt, and bitter. Some parts of the mouth are more sensitive to certain tastes; for example, the tip of the tongue is sensitive to salt and sweet stimuli, the back to bitter stimuli, and the edges to sour and salt. » tongue

tatami [ta**tah**mee] A Japanese mat, made of layers of rushes, edged with narrow strips of black cloth, the cloth pattern indicating the quality. Japanese-style rooms have floors consisting of thick matting. Tatami are standard size, equivalent to one sleeping space, and rooms are described as '6 mat, 8 mat' etc. Shoes are never worn on tatami. » futon

Tatar or **Tartar** A Turkic-speaking people living in Russia. Sunni Muslims since the 14th-c, they were a highly stratified mediaeval society. Traditionally farmers and pastoralists, in the 18th–19th-c, they became important as political agents, traders, teachers, and administrators in the Russian Empire. Population c.5 million.

Tate, (John Orley) Allen (1899–1979) US poet and critic, born at Winchester, Kentucky, and educated at Vanderbilt. His poetry was intellectual and allusive; volumes including *Mr Pope and Other Poems* (1928) and *A Winter Sea* (1945) are gathered in *Collected Poems* (1977). His critical stance was associated with the New Criticism. He died in Nashville, Tennessee. » American literature; poetry; New Criticism

Tate, Sir Henry (1819–99) British sugar magnate, art patron, and philanthopist, born at Chorley, Lancashire. He patented a method for cutting sugar cubes in 1872 and attained great wealth as a Liverpool sugar refiner. The Tate Gallery is named after him. » Tate Gallery

Tate, Nahum (1652–1715) Irish poet and dramatist, born in Dublin. Educated at Dublin, he moved to London, where his first play was staged in 1678. He is known for his 'improved' versions of Shakespeare's tragedies, substituting happy endings to suit the popular taste, and with Dryden's help he wrote a second part to that poet's *Absalom and Achitophel* (1682). He became poet laureate in 1692, and died in London. » Dryden; Irish literature; Shakespeare [i]

Tate Gallery A London gallery housing the nation's chief collection of British art and modern foreign art. It was opened in 1897 as a branch of the National Gallery, but became administratively autonomous in 1915, and fully independent in 1955. » London [i]; National Gallery; Tate, Henry

Tati, Jacques [ta**tee**], byname of **Jacques Tatischeff** (1908–1982) French actor and film producer, born at Pecq. He began in music-hall, and directed his first film in 1931. After *Jour de Fête* (1947, The Big Day), directed and written by himself, he made his reputation as the greatest film comedian of the postwar period, notably in *Les Vacances de Monsieur Hulot* (1953, Mr Hulot's Holiday) and *Mon Oncle* (1958, My Uncle), which won several awards. He died in Paris.

Tatra Mountains [**tah**tra], Czech **Tatry** Mountain group in C Carpathian Mts, comprising the High Tatra (*Vysoké Tatry*) and Low Tatra (*Nízké Tatry*); highest group of the Carpathians and of Czechoslovakia, rising to 2 655 m/8 710 ft at Gerlachovsky; High Tatra National Park, area 500 sq km/200 sq ml, established in 1948. » Carpathian Mountains

Tatum, Art, properly **Arthur** (1910–56) US jazz pianist, born at Toledo, Ohio. He learned violin and then piano at Cousino School for the Blind and the Toledo School of Music. By the time he arrived in New York in 1932, his technical skills astounded other musicians. He embellished the melodies of popular songs in ways that seemed to press the limits of dexterity, and which extended the harmonic bounds of jazz. An insatiable performer, he often (according to legend) played the piano continuously for 24 hours, pausing only to refill his whiskey glass. He died suddenly of uraemia in Los Angeles, California. » jazz; piano

Taung skull The million-year-old partial skull and brain cast of a young *Australopithecus africanus*, found at Taung, S Africa, in 1924. This was the first discovery of a creature seemingly intermediate between ape and man. » *Australopithecus*

Taunton 51°01N 3°06W, pop (1981) 48 863. County town in Taunton Deane district, Somerset, SW England; on the R Tone, in the Vale of Taunton Deane; founded in 705; rebellion of Perkin Warbeck ended here (1497); Duke of Monmouth crowned king here (1685); 12th-c castle hall, where Bloody Assizes held (1685); railway; cider, textiles, leather, optical instruments, light engineering; Somerset county museum. » Bloody Assizes; Monmouth, Duke of; Warbeck

Taupo, Lake [**tow**poh] area 606 sq km/234 sq ml. Lake in C North Island, New Zealand, filling an old volcanic crater; length 40 km/25 ml, width 27 km/17 ml; largest New Zealand lake; used as a reservoir, and also for fishing and water sports; town of Taupo in NE; location of a geothermal power scheme; thermal pools at Tokaanu. » New Zealand [i]

tauraco » **turaco**

Taurus (Lat 'bull') [**taw**ruhs] A prominent N constellation, including the Pleiades and the Crab Nebula. It is a spring sign of the zodiac, lying between Aries and Gemini. Its brightest star is the red giant, Aldebaran, one of the few stars where the diameter has been measured directly at about 45 times the Sun's diameter. Distance: 21 parsecs. » giant star; Pleiades

Taurus Mountains [**taw**ruhs], Turkish **Toros Dağlari** Mountain chain of S Turkey, extending in a curve from L Eğridir roughly parallel to the Mediterranean coast as far as the R Seyhan;

highest peak, Ala Dağlari (3 910 m/12 828 ft); its NW extension across the R Seyhan is called the **Anti-Taurus**; in the SE are the Cilician Gates, an important pass in ancient times; chromium, copper, silver, zinc, iron, arsenic. » Turkey [i]

tautology In philosophy, any sentence in propositional logic that is logically true, or true solely in virtue of its form, not its content. Thus, regardless of whether 'Mars is a city' is true or false, 'Either Mars is a city or it is not the case that Mars is a city' is a tautology. » logic

tautomerism [taw**tom**uhrizm] In chemistry, the existence of a rapidly established equilibrium between two isomers which differ only in the location of one or more hydrogen atoms. » isomers

Tavener, John (Kenneth) (1944–) British composer, born in London, where he studied at the Royal Academy of Music (1961–5). His music is predominantly religious, and includes the cantata *The Whale* (1966), *Ultimos ritos* (1972, Last Rites) for soloists, chorus, and orchestra, and a sacred opera *Therese* (1979). He was converted to the Russian Orthodox faith in 1976. » cantata

tawny owl A typical owl, native to Europe, Asia, and N Africa; mottled brown with black eyes and no ear tufts; inhabits woodland and habitation (occasionally open country); eats small vertebrates and insects. The name is also used for the **tawny fish owl** and **tawny-browed owl**. (*Strix aluco*.) » owl

tax-haven A country where tax rates are particularly low. Companies or individuals may choose to reside there to avoid paying high rates of tax in their own home country. The Isle of Man, the Channel Is, and some West Indian countries are current examples. » taxation

taxation The means by which a government raises money to finance its activities. *Direct* taxes are paid by individuals (eg income tax, national insurance contributions) and companies (eg corporation tax). *Indirect* taxes are those levied on goods and services (eg value-added tax, sales tax). The taxation rules frequently change, in response to government policy and needs, and changes are generally announced in a budget statement. In the past, tax has been levied on many things, including windows and jockeys. » black economy; budget; capital gains tax; capital transfer tax; corporation tax; covenant **1**; customs and excise; estate duty; excess profits tax; excise tax; fiscal drag; income tax; inheritance tax; progressive taxation; purchase tax; sales tax; tax-haven; turnover tax; VAT

Taxila [**tak**sila] The chief city of the Achaemenid satrapy of Gandhara, now a major archaeological site covering 65 sq km/25 sq ml in Punjab, Pakistan; a world heritage area. Excavations have revealed three distinct cities, the earliest dating from c.400 BC; the second was occupied successively by Bactrian Greeks, Scythians, Parthians, and Kushans; the third was founded c.130 and flourished for over five centuries. » Achaemenids; Punjab (Pakistan); satrapy

taxis [**tak**sis] A directed movement or orientation reaction of an organism to a stimulus. Taxis is usually used with a prefix to indicate the nature of the stimulus, for example *chemotaxis* (for a chemical stimulus), *phototaxis* (for a light stimulus), and *thermotaxis* (for a temperature stimulus). Movement towards the stimulus is a *positive* taxis, movement away from stimulus a *negative* taxis, so that an animal that moves towards the source of a light is 'positively phototactic'. » ethology; tropism

taxonomy The theory and practice of describing, naming, and classifying organisms. It is divided into *alpha taxonomy*, the description and designation of species typically on the basis of morphological characters; *beta taxonomy*, the arrangement of species into hierarchical systems of higher categories; and *gamma taxonomy*, the study of the evolutionary relationships between groups (*taxa*) and of variation within and between populations. » binomial nomenclature; morphology (biology); systematics

Tay, River Longest river in Scotland; length 192 km/119 ml; rises on Ben Lui in the Grampians; flows NE, E, then SE to enter the Firth of Tay, extending 40 km/25 ml ENE to the North Sea at Buddon Ness; crossed at Dundee by the two Tay Bridges (rail and road); noted for its salmon fishing. » Scotland [i]

Tay-Sachs disease A rare inherited disorder in which an abnormal accumulation of lipid occurs in the brain, causing mental deficiency and blindness in infancy. The condition is named after British ophthalmologist Warren Tay (1843–1927), who described cherry-red spots in the retinae of affected children, and US neurologist Bernard Sachs (1858–1944). » eye [i]; fat

Taylor, Elizabeth (Rosemond) (1932–) US film star, born in London. She moved with her family to Los Angeles in 1939, where she made her screen debut in 1942. As a child star she made several films, and was first seen as an adult in *The Father of the Bride* (1950). Her later films included *Cat on a Hot Tin Roof* (1958), *Butterfield 8* (1960, Academy Award), and *Cleopatra* (1962), which provided the background to her well-publicized romance with her co-star Richard Burton, with whom she made several films, including *Who's Afraid of Virginia Woolf?* (1966, Academy Award). Later films include *The Mirror Cracked* (1981) and Zeffirelli's *Young Toscanini* (1988). She has been married eight times, her husbands including the actor Michael Wilding, film producer Michael Todd, Richard Burton (twice), and US senator John Warner. » Burton, Richard (Jenkins)

Taylor, Frederick W(inslow) (1856–1915) US engineer, born and died in Philadelphia. He developed the concept of rational principles underlying not only engineering, but also engineering management. He discovered the process of heat treatment of high-speed steel (1898), but is better known for the development of time-and-motion study, which he established as an important management tool. He has claims to being the first ever 'efficiency expert'. » ergonomics

Taylor, Zachary (1784–1850) US general, statesman, and 12th President (1849–50), born at Montebello, Virginia. He joined the army in 1808, fought against the Indians, and in 1840 was given command of the army in the SW. In the Mexican War (1846–8) he captured Matamoros, and won a major victory at Buena Vista, though heavily outnumbered. He emerged from the war as a hero, and was given the Whig presidential nomination. The main issue of his presidency was the status of the new territories, and the extension of slavery there, but he died in Washington DC only 16 months after taking office. » Mexican War

Taymyr or **Taimyr, Lake** [tiy**mir**] (Russ **Ozero**) area 4 560 sq km/1 760 sq ml. Lake in N Siberian Russia, on the N Taymyr Peninsula; length, 250 km/155 ml; maximum depth, 26 m/85 ft; frozen over (Sep–Jun); coal deposits nearby. » Russia

Tayside pop (1981) 391 846; area 7 493 sq km/2 892 sq ml. Region in E Scotland, divided into three districts; bounded E by the Firth of Tay and the North Sea; Grampian Mts in the NW; Lowlands/Highlands boundary runs NE; drained by the Tay, Isla, Ericht, Earn, and South Esk Rivers; largest lochs, Rannoch, Tummel, Tay; capital, Dundee; major towns include Forfar, Arbroath, Montrose, Perth; farming, tourism. » Dundee; Scotland [i]

Tbilisi [tbi**lee**see], formerly **Tiflis** (to 1936) 41°43N 44°48E, pop (1989) 1 260 000. Capital city of Georgia; on the R Kura, between the Greater and Lesser Caucasus; founded, 5th-c; ancient trading point between Europe and India; airport; railway junction; university (1918); machinery, film making, printing, publishing, foodstuffs, wine, silk, electrical equipment, locomotives, plastics; ruins of Narikala (4th–17th-c), Anchiskhati Church (6th-c), Sioni Cathedral (6th–7th-c). » Georgia (republic)

Tchad » **Chad** [i]

Tchaikovsky or **Tschaikovsky, Piotr Ilyich** [chiy**kof**skee] (1840–93) Russian composer, born at Kamsko-Votkinsk. He began as a civil servant, joined the St Petersburg Conservatory in 1862, and moved to Moscow in 1865. There he became known for his operas, second symphony, and first piano concerto. After an unsuccessful marriage, he retired to the country to devote himself to composition, making occasional visits abroad, and died in St Petersburg. Among his greatest works are the ballets *Swan Lake* (1876–7), *The Sleeping Beauty* (1890), and *The Nutcracker* (1892), the last three of his six symphonies, two piano concertos, and several tone poems, notably *Romeo and Juliet* and *Italian Capriccio*.

Tchogha Zanbil The site in SW Iran of a religious centre built in the 13th-c BC by King Untash Napirisha; a world heritage site. The city comprises three palaces, five underground tombs, ten temples, and a ziggurat. For 600 years it was inhabited only by priests. » ziggurat [i]

Te Anau, Lake [tee **anow**] area 344 sq km/133 sq ml. Lake in SW South Island, New Zealand, on E edge of Fiordland national park; second largest lake in New Zealand, and largest on South I; length 61 km/38 ml; width 9.7 km/6 ml; glow-worm caves in the W; water sports. » New Zealand [i]

Te Kanawa, Dame Kiri [tay **kah**nawa] (1944–) New Zealand operatic soprano, born at Gisborne. After winning many awards in New Zealand and Australia she came to London, where she made her debut with the Royal Opera Company in 1970. She has since taken a wide range of leading roles, and in 1981 sang at the wedding of the Prince and Princess of Wales. She was made a Dame in 1982.

tea A small evergreen tree growing to c.4 m/13 ft in the wild, but only a small shrub in cultivation; leaves leathery, toothed and pointed; flowers 5-petalled, white, fragrant; native to Burma and Assam, but cultivated in China since early times, with Japan, India, and Sri Lanka now also major producers. Cultivated plants are pruned to encourage new growth. The shoot tips with the first two leaves are picked, allowed to wither, then rolled, fermented, and dried; when infused with boiling water they make the well-known beverage containing the stimulants tannin and caffeine. (*Camellia sinensis*. Family: *Theaceae*.) » camellia; evergreen plants; shrub; tree [i]

tea ceremony » **chanoyu**

Teacher of Righteousness The religious leader and founder of the Qumran community, probably in the mid-2nd-c BC; apparently a Zadokite priest who opposed the Hasmoneans, assuming the role of Jewish high priest, and who led his followers into exile near the Dead Sea. His identity is otherwise unknown, but this title is applied to him in the Damascus Document and various Qumran commentaries, because of his role in guiding the community in their interpretation of the Torah. » Maccabees; Qumran, community of; Torah; Zadokites

teak A large evergreen tree, growing to 45 m/150 ft, native to S India and SE Asia; leaves up to 45 cm/18 in, oval, opposite; flowers small, white, 5-lobed bells. It is a source of high-quality, durable, water-resistant timber. Extremely heavy, teak sinks in water unless thoroughly dried, so the trees are killed by having a girdle of bark cut near the base, and are left for up to two years before felling. (*Tectona grandis*. Family: *Verbenaceae*.) » evergreen plants; tree [i]

teal A small dabbling duck, found worldwide; eats water weeds and invertebrates. The name is also used for the perching ducks *Nettapus coromandelianus*, *Callonetta leucophrys*, and *Amazonetta brasiliensis*. (Genus: *Anas*, 16 species.) » dabbling duck; duck; perching duck

Teamsters' Union The **International Brotherhood of Teamsters, Chauffeurs, Warehousemen and Helpers of America**, the largest US labour union, with over 1½ million members. Founded in 1903, it was expelled from the AFL/CIO in 1957 for corruption, but was re-affiliated in 1987. It carries out a normal range of union activities on behalf of its members, and has considerable power in some industrial sectors. » American Federation of Labor – Congress of Industrial Organizations; trade union

Teapot Dome Scandal A US government scandal in the early 1920s involving the lease of land for oil exploration in California, and especially at Teapot Dome, Wyoming. The Attorney General was forced to resign, after refusing access to files. Following other resignations, criminal proceedings were introduced.

teasel A large, stiff and prickly biennial, growing to 2 m/6½ ft, native to Europe and the Mediterranean; stem angled; rosette leaves oblong to elliptical, dying after the first year; stem leaves narrower, paired, fused at base to form water-filled cups; flowers tiny, white or mauve, in heads the size and shape of an egg, surrounded by curved, prickly bracts. The heads of the cultivated **fuller's teasel** (subspecies *sativus*) have stiff bracts used for raising the nap on cloth; the bracts of the wild plant (subspecies *fullonum*) are too flexible. (*Dipsacus fullonum*. Family: *Dipsacaceae*.) » biennial; bract

Tebbit, Norman (Beresford) (1931–) British Conservative politician, born at Enfield, Greater London. Elected to parliament in 1970, he served in Margaret Thatcher's governments as Employment Secretary (1981–3), and Secretary for Trade and Industry (1983–5). His career was interrupted in 1984 when both he and his wife were badly hurt after the IRA bombing of the Grand Hotel at Brighton. In 1985 he became Chancellor of the Duchy of Lancaster and also Chairman of the Party. In 1987, there were open disagreements between him and Mrs Thatcher over the handling of the general election campaign, and shortly after the Conservative victory he retired to the backbenches. » Conservative Party; IRA; Thatcher

Technicolor The trademark of a colour cinematography process internationally dominant between 1935 and 1955. Shooting involved special three-strip cameras and multiple release prints by photo-mechanical dye-transfer. Even after the introduction of colour negative in 1953, dye-transfer printing continued to the mid-1970s. » cinematography [i]

technocracy A label describing a supposed shift in 'real' power from elected governments to technical experts. The term was in vogue in the 1930s and again in the 1960s when economic, social, and strategic defence planning was adopted in some Western industrial societies, and the role of experts in decision-making was enhanced. The 'end of ideology' was hailed in some quarters. » ideology

technology The use of tools, machines, materials, techniques, and sources of power to make work easier and more productive. Industrial technology began 200 years ago with the introduction of power-driven machines, the growth of factories, and the mass production of goods. Whereas science is concerned with understanding how and why things happen, technology deals with making things happen; it can be subdivided into many specializations, such as medical, military, and nuclear. Technology has helped people to gain control over nature, and so build a civilized world. Undesirable side-effects include increased pollution and loss of jobs as a result of automation. » automation; machine [i]

tectonics The study of the structure of the Earth's crust, particularly such processes as the movement of rocks during folding and faulting. » Earth [i]; orogeny; plate tectonics [i]

Tecumseh (c.1768–1813) American Indian chief of the Shawnees, who joined his brother, 'The Prophet', in a rising against the Whites. It was suppressed at Tippecanoe in 1811, and he passed into English service, commanding the Indian allies in the War of 1812. He fell fighting at the Thames in Canada. » Indian Wars; War of 1812

Tedder (of Glenguin), Arthur William, 1st Baron (1890–1967) British Marshal of the Royal Air Force, born at Glenguin, Stirlingshire, Scotland. During World War 2 he directed research and development at the Air Ministry, served as Commander-in-Chief (RAF) in the Middle East Air Force, moved on to the Mediterranean theatre (1943), and became Deputy Supreme Commander of the Allied Expeditionary Force under Eisenhower (1943–5). He was appointed Marshal of the RAF (1945), and created a baron (1946). He died at Banstead, Surrey. » air force; World War 2

Tees, River [teez] River of NE England; rises on Cross Fell, Cumbria and flows 128 km/79 ml SE through Durham, along the North Yorkshire border and into Cleveland where it develops into a broad estuary that meets the North Sea below Middlesbrough; passes through heavily industrialized **Teesside**; linked to R Tyne as part of UK's first regional water grid system supplying water to industrial NE; upper river valley known as **Teesdale**. » Tyne, River

Teesside Pop (1981) 382 690. Urban area surrounding the R Tees estuary in Cleveland, NE England; includes Stockton-on-Tees, Redcar, Thornaby, Middlesbrough; formed in 1967, and part of Cleveland since 1974; railway; airport (Middleton St George). » Cleveland (UK); Tees, River

teeth Small, bone-like structures of the jaws used for the biting and chewing of food. They are firmly anchored in the alveolar bone of the jaws, and project from the gums. The number,

THE APPROXIMATE TIMES OF ERUPTION AND SHEDDING OF THE VARIOUS TEETH IN HUMANS

	ERUPTION	SHED
MILK		
Incisor 1	6 months	6–7 years
Incisor 2	8 months	7–8 years
Canine 1	8 months	10–12 years
Molar 1	1 year	9–11 years
Molar 2	2 years	10–12 years
PERMANENT		
Incisor 1	7–8 years	
Incisor 2	8–9 years	
Canine	10–12 years	
Premolar 1	10–11 years	
Premolar 2	11–12 years	
Molar 1	6–7 years	
Molar 2	12 years	
Molar 3	17–21 years	

Note: The lower teeth usually appear before the upper equivalent teeth.

arrangement, and type of teeth varies between different animals. Some animals have two sets (eg most mammals); others have several rows which gradually move forwards as others are lost (eg sharks). Each tooth consists of a core of *pulp* surrounded by *dentine*, which is covered in its upper part by enamel and in its lower part by cement. The *crown* is the enamel-covered part that projects beyond the gums; it may have one or more projections called *cusps*. The surfaces of the crowns form the *occlusal surfaces*, which meet when the upper and lower teeth are brought together. The cement-covered part of the tooth is the *root*, and is firmly attached to the bone of the alveolar socket by the peridontal membrane. The teeth have a very rich blood and nerve supply.

In many mammals, different types of teeth can be identified: *incisors* for cutting, *canines* for cutting and tearing, and *premolars* and *molars* for grinding. In humans the first set of teeth (*deciduous* or *milk* teeth) usually appear between 6 and 24 months of age, there being 20 deciduous teeth in all (2 incisors, 1 canine, and 2 molars in each half jaw). These gradually become replaced (from about age 6) by the *permanent* teeth, with the addition of 3 more teeth in each half jaw giving a total complement of 32. The third molar is often referred to as the *wisdom* tooth, because of its time of eruption. Not all of the teeth may appear. » caries; dentistry; fluoridation of water; gums; jaw

tefillin [tef**ileen**] Jewish phylacteries or frontlets, consisting of two black leather cubes with leather straps, bound over the head and arm, and worn during Jewish morning prayers, except on sabbaths and festivals. The cubes contain scriptural texts (such as *Deut* 6.4–9, 11.13–21; *Ex* 13.1–16), and the explanation of their use is traced to Biblical commandments about the words of the Law being a 'sign upon your hand or frontlets between your eyes'. » Amidah; Judaism; Shema

Tegucigalpa [taygoosi**gal**pa] 14°05N 87°14W, pop (1983e) 532 519. Capital city of Honduras; founded as a mining camp, 1524; comprises two distinct towns, the almost flat Comayagüela and the hilly Tegucigalpa, separated by the R Choluteca; altitude 975 m/3 200 ft; capital, 1880; airport; university (1847); textiles, sugar, wood products, plastics, chemicals, metal and electrical products; some silver, lead, zinc mining; 18th-c cathedral, 18th-c Church of Virgen de los Dolores. » Honduras [i]

Teheran or **Tehran** [tair**ahn**] 35°44N 51°30E, pop (1983) 5 734 199. Capital city of Iran, in Teheran province, N Iran; altitude 1 200–1 700 m/4 000–5 500 ft; superseded Esfahan as capital of Persia, 1788; largely rebuilt after 1925; airport; road and rail junction; six universities (oldest, 1935); carpets, textiles, tanning, chemicals, glass, car assembly; Niavaran, Golestan, Marmar, Saadabad, and Baharstan Palaces; Shahyad Tower, symbol of modern Iran. » Iran [i]

Teheran Conference The first inter-allied conference of World War 2, attended by Stalin, Roosevelt, and Churchill in 1943. The subjects discussed were the co-ordination of Allied landings in France with the Soviet offensive against Germany, Russian entry in the war against Japan, and the establishment of a post-war international organization. Failure to agree on the future government of Poland foreshadowed the start of the Cold War. » Churchill, Winston; Cold War; Roosevelt, Franklin D; Stalin; Teheran; World War 2

Tehran » Teheran

Teilhard de Chardin, Pierre [**tay**yah duh **shah**dĩ] (1881–1955) French geologist, palaeontologist, Jesuit priest, and philosopher, born at Sarcenat. He lectured in pure science at the Jesuit College in Cairo, was ordained in 1911, and in 1918 became professor of geology at the Institut Catholique in Paris. He went on palaeontological expeditions in China and C Asia, but his unorthodox ideas led to a ban on his teaching and publishing. Nevertheless, his work in Cenozoic geology and palaeontology became known, and he was awarded academic distinctions. His major work, *Le Phénomène humain* (written 1938–40, The Phenomenon of Man) was posthumously published. Based on his scientific thinking, it argues that humanity is in a continuous process of evolution towards a perfect spiritual state. From 1951 he lived in the USA, and died in New York City. » Cenozoic era; geology; Jesuits; palaeontology

tektite A rounded, flat, and glassy meteorite ranging in diameter from submillimetre size up to c.10 cm/4 in. » meteorite

Tel Aviv-Yafo 32°05N 34°46E, pop (1982) 325 700. Twin cities in Tel Aviv district, W Israel, a commercial port on the Mediterranean Sea; Israel's largest conurbation; Tel Aviv founded in 1909 as a garden suburb of Jaffa, the most ancient port in Israel and today an artists' centre; former capital (to 1950) of Israel; airport; railway; two universities (1953, 1974); commercial centre (Israeli stock exchange), food processing, textiles, chemicals; Franciscan monastery of St Peter (1654). » Israel [i]

Tel el Amarna The ancient Akhetaten ('the horizon of Aten'), a short-lived Egyptian city on the E bank of the R Nile, c.250 km/150 ml S of Cairo. Founded c.1350 BC by the heretic pharoah Akhenaton as both a royal residence and administrative capital, it was abandoned on his death, and subsequently demolished. Notable finds are the cuneiform Amarna tablets, c.300 diplomatic documents discovered in 1887; and the celebrated painted bust of Akhenaten's queen, Nefertiti, found 1911–12 and now in Berlin. » Akhenaton; cuneiform [i]

Tel Quel [tel **kel**] A French journal of cultural criticism, founded in 1960 by French writer Philippe Sollers (1936–). It provided a platform for many radical interventions in the overlapping fields of art, literature, philosophy, politics, semiotics, and psychoanalysis by such writers as Barthes, Derrida, Foucault, Kristeva, and Todorov. It ceased publication in 1982. » French literature; literary criticism

telebanking A system which enables banking transactions to be carried out via a communications network. This could be over interactive cable television, with provision for the user to send signals to the bank, but is more commonly through a viewdata system or an interactive computer link. » cable television; teleshopping; viewdata

telecine Equipment for converting motion picture film to video for broadcast television or videotape recording. In the flying spot system, a continuously moving film is scanned by a spot of light generated on a cathode ray tube. The transmitted light is then converted to red, green, and blue signals by a beam-splitting optical system and three photo-multiplier tubes. Developments in digital scanning allow special effects to be introduced during transfer. » flying spot scanner; telerecording

telecommunications The transmission of data-carrying signals, often between two widely-separated points; it includes radio, telegraphy, telephones, television, and computer networks. Telecommunications in the modern sense began in the 19th-c: the Great Western Railway telegraph lines from Paddington to Slough, England, opened in 1843; telephones for commercial use were installed in Boston and Cambridge, Massachusetts, in 1877; radio telegraphy became a commercial success after Marconi founded the Wireless, Telegraph and Signal Co in London in 1897. During the 20th-c, first radio (from the 1920s) and then television (from the 1950s) became important for communication over distance. In 1962 the US Telstar 1 satellite was launched to relay communications signals; however, this had a low orbit, and so could be used for only a short part of each day. Now large numbers of *geostationary* satellites provide day-long international links for telephony and television transmissions, carried by high frequency radio waves (microwaves). The use of optical fibre links in telephone cables enables hundreds of simultaneous conversations to be transmitted. » Marconi; mobile communications; optical fibres [i]; radio; satellite; telegraphy; telephone; television

teleconferencing The connection of several locations by television links to provide continuous inter-communication of sound and sight. In some applications, the picture is presented as a rapidly changing series of stills, rather than in continuous motion, in order to reduce the bandwidth required in transmission. » television

telegraphy Communication at a distance of written, printed, or pictorial matter, by the transmission of electrical signals along wires. Modern examples of this are telex and fax. In **radiotelegraphy** the message is carried by radio waves rather then along a wire. » fax; radio; telecommunications; telephone; telex

telekinesis » **psychokinesis**

Telemachus [telemakuhs] In the *Odyssey*, the son of Odysseus and Penelope. He sets out to find his father, visiting Nestor and Menelaus. Later he helps Odysseus fight Penelope's suitors. » Odysseus

Telemann, Georg Philipp [tayluhman] (1681–1767) German composer, born at Magdeburg. Educated at Leipzig, he taught himself music by learning to play a wide range of instruments and studying the scores of the masters. He held several posts as *Kapellmeister*, notably at Frankfurt (1712–21), and became musical director of the Johanneum at Hamburg from 1721 until his death. A prolific composer, his works include church music, 46 passions, over 40 operas, oratorios, many songs, and a large body of instrumental music.

telemarketing A marketing system which uses the telephone, handling responses to advertisements which carry telephone numbers. The telephone operators receive calls, take orders, or arrange for brochures to be sent. It also involves making calls to prospective clients on behalf of marketing outlets, to generate leads, orders, or interest. » telephone

teleological ethics Any normative ethical theory which takes the goodness or badness of the consequences of an action as fundamental in determining whether it is right or wrong. Teleologists also typically provide a theory about what sorts of things are in fact good. They claim that an action is right if it produces at least as much goodness as any alternative. Egoists such as Hobbes maintain that one ought to produce maximum goodness for oneself. Utilitarians such as Mill insist that the right action must produce maximum goodness on balance for everyone affected, even if that requires choosing less goodness for oneself. » deontological ethics; egoism; Hobbes; Mill; utilitarianism

teleology A view which maintains, against mechanism, that some phenomena can be explained fully only by citing the functions they perform ('a function of the liver is to secrete bile') or the purposes for which the activity was undertaken ('Iago lied in order to provoke Othello'). Functional explanations need not imply conscious design. » mechanism

teleost [teleeuhst] Any of a large group of ray-finned fishes in which the tail is symmetrical, without an upturned body axis; comprises the great majority of extant species of true bony fishes, exhibiting rich diversity, and found in all marine and freshwater habitats. (*Actinopterygii*.) » bony fish; fish [i]

telephone A device for transmitting speech sounds over a distance. In 1876 Alexander Graham Bell was granted a patent to develop such an instrument, and his induction receiver, along with Thomas Edison's carbon transmitter, form the basis of the modern telephone. In the mouthpiece, a carbon microphone translates sound vibrations into a varied electric current which is relayed through wires to the receiver, where it is converted back into sound waves by a diaphragm and an electromagnet. Amplifiers (repeaters) placed at intervals along a line make long-distance telephoning possible, and vacuum-tube amplifiers with long-life expectancy make transatlantic cable-laying economically viable. Today, communications satellites and computerized call-routing systems transmit millions of simultaneous calls worldwide. » Bell, Alexander Graham; Edison; loudspeaker [i]; microphone [i]; telecommunications

telephoto lens A camera lens of long focal length but comparatively short overall dimensions, giving increased magnification for a limited angle of view. In 35 mm still cameras, focal lengths of 100 to 300 mm are usual, but for special purposes such as news work, sports and natural history 500 to 1 000 mm may be employed. » camera; lens

telerecording The transfer of a video programme to motion picture film. Since the interval between successive video frames is very short, a film camera with extremely rapid movement from one frame to the next is essential. Direct photography of a shadow-mask colour video display is not satisfactory, and a three-tube system is preferred, in which separate cathode-ray screens for the three colour components are optically combined in register when photographed on colour negative film. For high definition recordings, three colour separations can be recorded by electron beam as successive frames on black and white film, printed in combination to produce a colour negative. In another method, red, green, and blue laser beams modulated by the video information are combined by a rotating mirror optical system to scan colour negative film directly, exposing each frame as a series of fine horizontal lines. » cinematography [i]; telecine; video

telescope An optical instrument for producing magnified images of distant objects. Telescopes came into widespread use in Europe at the beginning of the 17th-c, but were probably known much earlier. The earliest devices were made c.1608 by Lippershey and Galileo. Astronomical telescopes produce an inverted image, but give a larger field of view and higher magnification than terrestrial (upright image) telescopes. **Refracting telescopes** use a lens to bring light rays to a focus, a technique first applied to astronomy by Galileo. In its modern form, with lenses corrected for chromatic aberration, this telescope is still in use, especially among amateurs. **Reflecting telescopes** use a mirror to bring the light rays to a focus, a technique first applied to astronomy by Newton, who recognized its merits in overcoming the false colours of lenses. Herschel developed techniques for casting large primary mirrors (1783). The largest telescopes today are all reflectors. For special purposes, such as photography, there may be a combination of mirror and lens, as in the Schmidt camera.

Radio telescopes collect and analyse cosmic radio emission from celestial sources. The basic type consists of a steerable, paraboloidal, collecting dish with a central detector connected to amplifiers. Radio-source structure can be displayed through an image analysis system to produce a picture similar to a photograph. A **radio interferometer** is a group of steerable antennae which send to a common receiver the interference responses characteristic of the source. Telescopes for other types of radiation (eg infrared, ultraviolet, X-rays) are also used, sometimes above the Earth's atmosphere. » altazimuth; aperture synthesis; binoculars; coelostat; coronagraph; electromagnetic radiation [i]; Galileo; Herschel; Newton, Isaac; Very Large Array; Australia/Cassegrain/Hubble Space/Maksutov/Newtonian/Schmidt/Space Telescope

Telescopium (Lat 'telescope') [teliskohpiuhm] A small S constellation delineated by Lacaille in honour of the astronomical telescope. » constellation; Lacaille

teleshopping A system for shopping from home, using a communications network such as a public videotex system; also called **on-line shopping**. A list of food and goods available to the shopper is displayed on the television screen, and these can be ordered directly over the communications link. » telebanking

Telesto [telestoh] The thirteenth natural satellite of Saturn, discovered in 1980; distance from the planet 295 000 km/183 000 ml; diameter 30 km/19 ml. » Saturn (astronomy); RR4

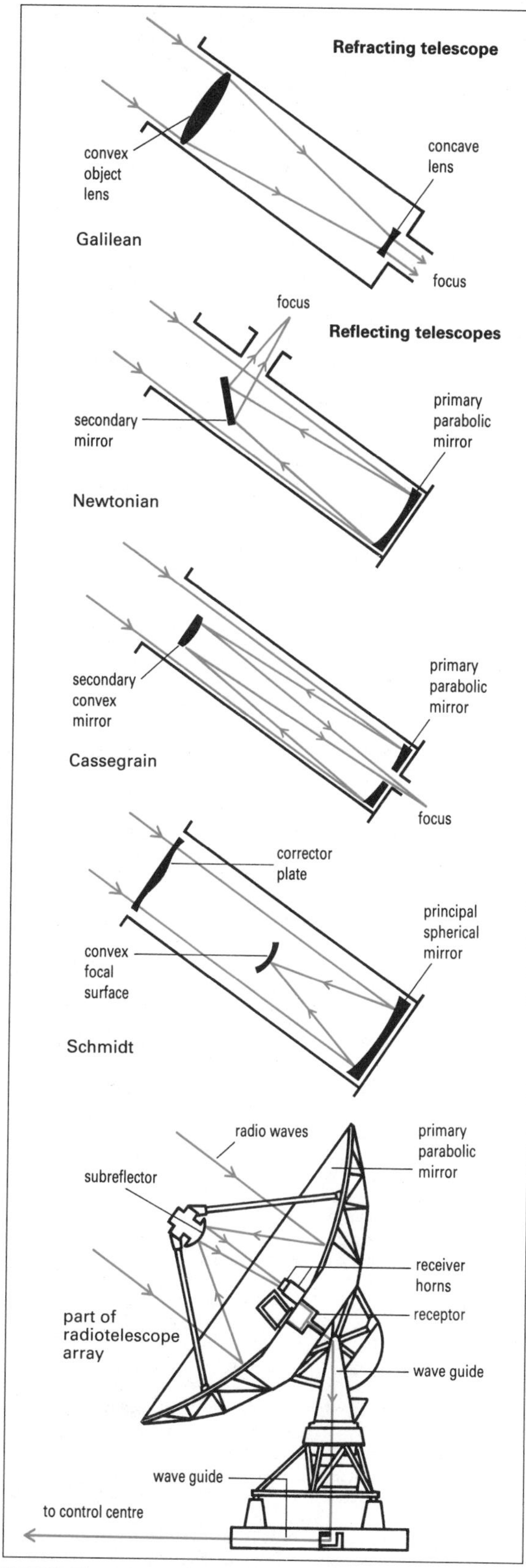

Telescope – Section through five types

teletext An information service of alpha-numerical data and simple diagrams transmitted as individual pages in digitally-coded form in the field-blanking intervals of a TV broadcast signal. The constantly-updated results, typically news headlines, football scores, weather maps, etc, can be displayed on any domestic receiver equipped with a decoder and page-selection keyboard. In the UK, the services Ceefax (BBC) and Oracle (IBA) were introduced in the 1970s. » Ceefax; field; Oracle; television; viewdata

television The transmission and reproduction of moving pictures and associated sound by electronic means. The image of a scene in a TV camera is analysed by scanning along a series of horizontal lines, the variations of brightness along each line being converted into a train of electrical signals for transmission or recording. At the receiver the picture is reconstituted on the fluorescent screen of a cathode-ray tube by an electron beam scanning a precisely similar pattern, the brightness of each point depending on the beam intensity controlled by the incoming signal. The number of scanning lines and the picture frequency vary in different systems, the American standard having 525 lines with 30 pictures per second (pps) and the European 625 lines at 25 pps. In both cases one complete picture, or frame, is scanned in two sets of alternate lines, termed *fields*, which are interlaced to reduce flicker in the receiver image. As scanning returns from the end of one line to the start of the next, there is a brief period without picture information, *horizontal blanking*; similarly after each completed field there is the vertical interval, *field blanking*, while scanning returns from bottom to top. Synchronizing pulses at precise time intervals are inserted in these periods to ensure correct scanning in the receiver. For terrestrial broadcasting the complete vision signal modulates a radio wave in one of the Ultra High Frequency (UHF) bands between 470 and 890 Mhz as a carrier, while the corresponding sound (audio) signal has its own carrier at a slightly higher frequency. High-definition TV systems with more than 1 000 scanning lines will be transmitted via satellite using the Super High Frequency (SHF) band, 11;7 to 12.5 GHz. » cable/high-definition/satellite television; camera; eidophor; frequency; MAC; MATV

television camera » **camera**

Telford, Thomas (1757–1834) British engineer, born at Westerkirk, Dumfries, Scotland. He began as a stonemason, taught himself architecture, and in 1787 became surveyor of public works for Shropshire. He planned the Ellesmere (1793–1805) and Caledonian (1803–23) canals, the road from London to Holyhead, with the Menai Suspension Bridge (1825), and built in all over 1 000 miles of road, 1 200 bridges, as well as harbours, docks, and other buildings. He died in London. » bridge (engineering) [i]; civil engineering

Telford 52°42N 2°28W. A new town in Shropshire, WC England, designated in 1963, comprising three previous urban areas: **Telford Dawley**, pop (1981) 28 662; **Telford North**, pop (1981) 53 165; **Telford South**, pop (1981) 23 354; on the R Severn SE of Shrewsbury, 55 km/34 ml NW of Birmingham; originally designated as Dawley New Town; railway; electronics, plastics, vehicles, metal products. » Shropshire

tell An Arabic 'mound' or 'hill', equivalent to Persian *tepe*, Turkish *hüyük*; in archaeological usage, an artificial mound formed through the long-term accumulation of mud brick from houses successively levelled and rebuilt. Most common in the Near East, Anatolia, and the Balkans, tells can stand 30 m/100 ft high, and yield evidence of occupation over several millennia. » Çatal Hüyük; Jericho

Tell, William Legendary Swiss patriot of Bürglen in Uri, a famous crossbow marksman, reputedly the saviour of his native district from the oppressions of Austria. According to tradition, he was compelled by the tyrannical Austrian governor to shoot an apple off his own son's head from a distance of 80 paces. Later, Tell slew the tyrant, and so initiated the movement which secured the independence of Switzerland. Similar tales are found in the folklore of many countries, and Tell's existence is disputed. His name first occurs in a chronicle of 1470. » Switzerland [i]

Teller, Edward (1908–) US nuclear physicist, born in Budapest, Hungary. Educated at Karlsruhe, Munich, Göttingen, and Copenhagen, he travelled to the USA in 1935, becoming a US citizen in 1941. He worked on the atomic bomb project (1941–6), and was professor at Chicago (1946), director of the new nuclear laboratories at Livermore, California (1958–60), and professor at Berkeley (from 1963). He was one of the architects of the crash programme to build and test (1952) the world's first hydrogen bomb. » atomic bomb; hydrogen bomb [i]

Tellus » **Gaea**

Telugu [teluhgoo] The Dravidian language associated particularly with the state of Andhra Pradesh in S India. It has some 50 million speakers. » Dravidian languages

Tema [tema] 5°41N 0°00W, pop (1982) 323 909. Seaport in Greater Accra region, S Ghana, E of Accra; railway; largest artificial harbour in Africa (1962); civil engineering, metal smelting, oil refining, chemicals. » Ghana [i]

tembadau » **banteng**

Tempe [tempee] 33°25N 111°56W, pop (1980) 106 743. Health resort in Maricopa County, SC Arizona, USA; settled, 1872; railway; university (1885); Fiesta Bowl (Jan). » Arizona

tempera A method of painting with powdered pigment mixed with egg-yolk, usually on specially prepared wooden panels. This water-based technique was normal in the Middle Ages, and was not generally superseded until oil painting became popular in the late 15th-c. » paint; oil painting; watercolour

temperament A tuning system for keyboard and fretted string instruments in which some of the 'pure' intervals of 'just intonation' (the tuning derived from the natural harmonic series) are made slightly larger or smaller (ie 'tempered') in order to accommodate polyphony and a wide range of modulation. In **equal temperament**, which became universally employed in the 19th-c, the octave is divided into 12 equal semitones, the only pure interval being the octave itself. Earlier tuning systems had sought various compromises between purity of interval, variety of key, and flexibility of modulation. » harmonic series [i]; scale [i]; tonality

temperance movement A response to the social evils caused by the alcoholism so widespread in the 18th-c and 19th-c. Temperance societies were organized first in the USA, then in Britain and Scandinavia. The original aim was to moderate drinking, but prohibition became the goal. Federal prohibition became a reality in the USA in 1919, but was repealed in 1933.

temperature Measurement related to heat flow between objects. Heat will be transferred between objects having different temperatures. It is measured using thermometers, thermocouples, and pyrometers, and is controlled using thermostats. The Kelvin temperature scale is used in physics (an SI unit), fixed by the triple point of water, 273.16 K. Other temperature scales include the Celsius (°C), also called Centigrade, Fahrenheit (°F) and Rankine (°R). » pyrometer; temperature inversion; thermocouple; thermodynamics; thermometer; RR79

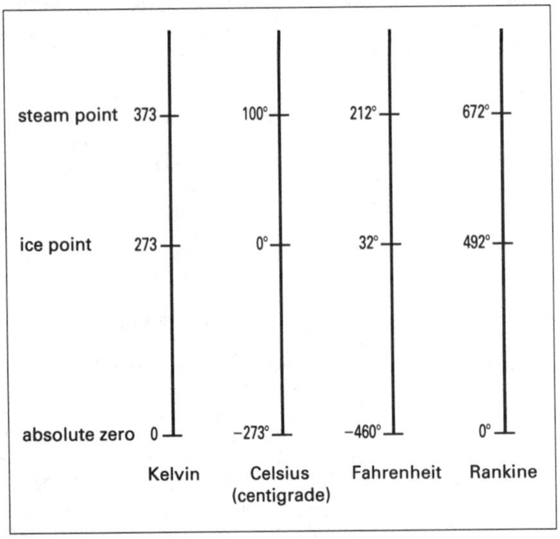

Temperature scales

temperature inversion A meteorological phenomenon which results when a layer of warm air traps cooler air below – the reverse of the normal state of affairs, where air temperature decreases with increasing altitude. A surface temperature inversion occurs when radiation fog develops. Inversions also occur at higher altitudes, such as when a warm air mass overrides a colder one along a warm front. Inversions may result in significant air pollution, as pollutants are trapped below the warm air until the inversion clears. » fog; front; smog; temperature [i]

Templars The Poor Knights of Christ and of the Temple of Solomon; an international religious-military order, whose members were subject to monastic vows. The order was founded c.1120 chiefly to protect pilgrims to the Holy Land; its name derives from the location of its headquarters – near the site of the Jewish Temple in Jerusalem. It developed into a great army, acquiring wealth and property, and was suppressed by Pope Clement V in 1312. » Crusades [i]; knight

temple A building in the ancient world used as a sanctuary for the gods. Temples had rather different functions from modern churches. They were not places where people gathered together indoors for communal worship; their main purpose was to provide, quite literally, a dwelling place for the gods. Thus all temples, whether big or small, were for the most part no more than a repository for the cult statue(s) of the god(s) to whom they had been dedicated. The dark, unlit room in which the statue(s) stood was called the *naos* (Greek) or *cella* (Latin); the main altar for sacrifice was outside the building. Thus most religious activity was external to the temple rather than inside it. Graeco-Roman temples were sometimes also used as a storage place for state treasures and important documents. The Parthenon at Athens not only housed the cult statue of Athena Parthenos; it also contained the national treasury. » Acropolis; Parthenon; Zeus, statue of

Temple A group of buildings, including the 12th-c Temple church, in Fleet St, London. They were established on land once owned by the Knights Templar, and have housed the offices of the Inner and Middle Temples for centuries. The 12th-c Temple in Paris was also Templar property. It later became a royal prison, and was demolished in 1811. » Inns of Court; London [i]; Templars

Temple, Jerusalem The central shrine of Jewish worship and its priesthood since its establishment under Solomon. It was first destroyed by Nebuchadrezzar in c.587 BC, but rebuilt later in the 6th-c BC after the return from exile. Extended on an elaborate scale by Herod the Great, beginning c.20 BC, it was barely renewed before its destruction under Titus during the Jewish revolt of AD 70. Still unrestored today, its site is now partly occupied by the Muslim mosque, the Dome of the Rock, built in the late 7th-c AD. » Herod the Great; Holy of Holies; Judaism; Solomon (Old Testament); Tabernacle

Temple, Shirley (1928–) US child film star, born at Santa Monica, California. During 1934–8 she appeared in more than 20 feature films, such as *Stand Up and Cheer* (1934) and *Bright Eyes* (1934), and was consistently the top US movie star. She appeared as a teenager in a few films in the 1940s without great success, but in her married status as Mrs S T Black she entered politics, and was US Ambassador to Ghana (1974–6).

Temple, Sir William (1628–99) English diplomat and essayist, born in London. Educated at Cambridge, he became a diplomat in 1655, was made Ambassador at The Hague, and negotiated the Triple Alliance (1668) against France. Made a baronet in 1666, in 1677 he helped to bring about the marriage of the Prince of Orange to the Princess Mary, daughter of James, Duke of York (later James II). After the revolution he declined a political post to devote himself to literature, living in retirement at Moor Park, Surrey, where he died. His essay style was a major influence on 18th-c writers, including Swift, who was his secretary. » Swift; William III

Temple, William (1881–1944) British Anglican churchman, born at Exeter. Educated at Rugby and Oxford, he was ordained in 1908, and became Bishop of Manchester (1921–9), Archbishop of York (1929–42), and Archbishop of Canterbury

(1942–4). An outspoken advocate of social reform, he crusaded against usury, slums, dishonesty, and the aberrations of the profit motive. He was also a leader in the reform of Church structures and in the ecumenical movement. He died at Westgate-on-Sea, Kent. » Church of England; ecumenism

Temple Bar A site at the junction of the Strand and Fleet St, London, where from 1301 a gateway marked the boundary of the Cities of London and Westminster. The original gateway was replaced in 1672 by one designed by Wren; in 1878 this was in turn replaced by a statue of a griffin. » London [i]; Wren, Christopher

Temple of Heaven A group of buildings in Beijing (Peking), in which the Emperors formerly conducted their devotions. The complex was laid out in 1406–20, and is regarded as a masterpiece of traditional Chinese architecture. » Beijing

Temple of the Tooth The Dalada Maligawa, an important Buddhist pilgrimage site in Kandy, Sri Lanka. The shrine was built to house one of the Buddha's teeth, which is believed to have been conveyed to Sri Lanka in 1590. » Buddha; Kandy

tempura [tem**pu**ra] A Japanese fritter, originating with the Portuguese in 16th-c Japan. Thinly sliced onions, green peppers, etc and small mushrooms, eggplants, prawns, etc are dipped in batter, and deep-fried in sunflower seed oil. They are served crisp, with diluted soy sauce mixed with grated radish to balance the oil. » shoyu

Ten Commandments or **Decalogue** The fundamental laws of the Jews; in the Bible, said to have been given to Moses on Mt Sinai. They describe the general religious and moral requirements for the Jewish people, and set the terms of God's covenant with them, although often phrased as universal principles. Slightly variant forms of the 'ethical' decalogue are found in *Ex* 20 and *Deut* 5, but a 'cultic' variant appears in *Ex* 34.14–26 (covering major Jewish feasts and offerings). A further tradition declares that God inscribed them on two tablets of stone which were then deposited in the Ark of the Covenant (*Deut* 9). The well-known 'ethical' decalogue contains the commands: (1) that the God of Israel shall be acknowledged as one and unique, (2) worship of images is prohibited, (3) misuse of the Lord's name is prohibited, (4) the Sabbath must be observed, (5) one's parents must be honoured, (6–10) murder, adultery, theft, false testimony, and coveting one's neighbour's goods are prohibited. This numbering varies, however, in some Jewish and Christian circles. » Ark of the Covenant; covenant; God; Sinai, Mount; Torah

Ten Lost Tribes of Israel Ten tribes of Israel taken captive by Assyria in 721 BC and merged (hence 'lost') with the Assyrians. They are alleged by British Israelites to be the ancestors of the British and American peoples, but this theory is largely discredited. » Israel, tribes of [i]

ten-pin bowling » **bowling**

Ten Years' War (1868–78) The name usually given to the unsuccessful Cuban insurrection against Spanish colonial rule. The rebels accepted their defeat in the Pact of Zanjón (Feb 1878). » Cuba [i]; Spain [i]

tenant farming A form of tenure where a farmer pays rent to a landlord for the use of a farm's land and buildings. Tenants usually own their own stock and working capital. In Britain tenants have security of tenure, and may pass their tenancy on to near relatives. » tenure

tench Freshwater fish native to slow rivers and lakes of Europe and W Asia, but now more widespread; length up to 60 cm/2 ft; body stout, fins rounded; mouth with pair of thin barbels; dark green to brown; fished commercially in some areas, and popular with anglers. (*Tinca tinca*. Family: *Cyprinidae*.) » fish [i]

tendon An extremely strong fibrous cord or sheet of connective tissue (bundles of collagen fibres), continuously attaching muscle to bone or cartilage. When tendon fibres pass across or around bony surfaces, they may develop either a surrounding (*synovial*) sheath or a (*sesamoid*) bone within them in order to reduce friction. Occasionally the sheath becomes inflamed (*tenosynovitis*), and movement may be painful. The two layers of the sheath may then be heard rubbing against one another, producing a creaking noise (*crepitus*). Sometimes a tendon may appear as a thin sheet of dense connective tissue, in which case it is known as an *aponeurosis*. » bone; cartilage; muscle [i]; synovitis; tissue

tendril An organ with which climbing plants attach themselves to supports; derived from modified leaves, branches, or inflorescences. Most tendrils coil around the support; others end in sticky, sucker-like pads; a few are negatively phototropic, and grow into dark cracks in the support. » climbing plant; inflorescence [i]; sucker; tropism

tenebrism In art history, the realistic and strongly-shadowed style adopted by certain Spanish and Neapolitan painters in the early 17th-c. The 'tenebristi' were not an organized group, but were all influenced by the dramatic style of Caravaggio. » Caravaggio; chiaroscuro

Tenerife » **Canary Islands**

Teng Hsiao-p'ing » **Deng Xiaoping**

Teniers, David (the Elder) [te**neers**] (1582–1649) Flemish Baroque genre painter, born and died in Antwerp, about whom little is known. His famous son, **David Teniers (the Younger)** (1610–90), was born in Antwerp, and in c.1647 settled in Brussels, where he died. He executed c.700 paintings, and is best known for his scenes of peasant life, in the tradition of Breughel. » Baroque (art and architecture); Breughel; Flemish art; genre painting

Tennant Creek 19°31S 134°15E, pop (1981) 3 118. Town in Northern Territory, Australia, between Darwin and Alice Springs; airfield; an important gold mining centre since the 1930s; also bismuth, copper, silver; 114 km/70 ml S are the Devil's Marbles, an outcrop of weathered round granite boulders in a scenic reserve; Goldrush festival in May. » Northern Territory

Tennessee pop (1987e) 4 855 000; area 109 149 sq km/42 144 sq ml. State in SEC USA, divided into 95 counties; the 'Volunteer State'; ceded by France, 1763; explored by Daniel Boone, 1769; temporary state of Franklin formed in 1784, after the War of Independence; Federal government created the Territory South of the Ohio (1790); admitted as the 16th state to the Union, 1796; seceded, 1861; the scene of many battles during the Civil War, including Shiloh, Chattanooga, Stone River; slavery abolished, 1865; re-admitted to the Union, 1866; Ku Klux Klan founded at Pulaski, 1866; capital, Nashville; other major cities Memphis, Knoxville, Chattanooga; Mississippi R follows the W border; Holston and French Broad Rivers form the Tennessee R; highest point Clingmans Dome (2 025 m/6 644 ft); in the E lie the Great Smoky Mts, Cumberland Plateau, narrow river valleys, and heavily forested foothills, which severely restrict farming; fertile 'bluegrass' country in the C, ideal for livestock and dairy farming; in the W is a rich floodplain where most of the state's cotton is grown; many lakes created by the Tennessee Valley Authority's damming of the Tennessee and Cumberland Rivers; tobacco, soybeans, hay, cotton; cattle and dairy products; chemicals, processed foods, textiles, electrical equipment; coal, cement; nation's largest producer of zinc and pyrites; several popular tourist areas. » American Civil War; Boone; Ku Klux Klan; Nashville; United States of America [i]; RR39

Tennessee River River in SE USA; formed near Knoxville, Tennessee, by the confluence of the French Broad and Holston Rivers; forms part of the Alabama–Mississippi border; flows into Kentucky to join the Ohio R at Paducah; length (including the French Broad) 1 398 km/869 ml; major tributaries the Little Tennessee, Clinch, Hiwasee, Elk, Duck; used for irrigation, flood-control, and hydroelectric power (the Tennessee Valley Authority, 1933). » United States of America [i]

Tennessee walking horse A breed of horse developed in the USA for riding; all descended from one stallion called *Black Allan*; height, 15–16 hands/1.5–1.6 m/5–5¼ ft; uniform colour; tail held erect at base; unusually smooth fast walk, unique to the breed. » horse [i]

Tenniel, Sir John [**ten**yel] (1820–1914) British artist, born in London. Self-trained, he became known as a *Punch* cartoonist (from 1851) and book illustrator, notably in his work for *Alice's Adventures in Wonderland* (1865) and *Through the Looking-glass* (1872). He was knighted in 1893, and died in London. » Carroll

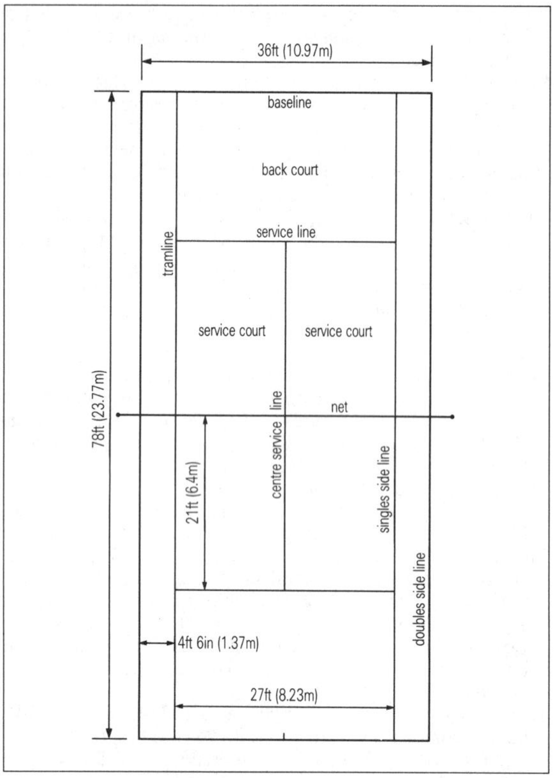

Tennis court – Dimensions

Tennis Court Oath (1789) An oath taken in a tennis court at Versailles by representatives of the Third Estate locked out of their assembly place. Declaring themselves to be the National Assembly, the deputies swore never to separate until a constitution was established for France. » French Revolution [i]

tennis elbow Pain in the external aspect of the elbow following repetitive trauma, such as may occur in playing tennis. It may possibly result from small tears in the muscles in the region. » elbow

tennis, lawn A racket-and-ball game for two or four players developed from real tennis. It is played on a rectangular court measuring 78 ft (23.77 m) long by 27 ft (8.23 m) wide for singles, or 36 ft (10.97 m) wide for doubles. A net 3 ft (0.9 m) high at the centre is stretched across the width of the court. Playing surface varies, and can be grass, clay, shale, concrete, wood, or other suitable man-made materials. The object is to play winning strokes by forcing one's opponent(s) to fail to return the ball successfully over the net. In doubles, players may hit the ball in any order, but must serve in rotation. The most famous lawn tennis championship is the All England Championships at Wimbledon each year. 'Field Tennis' was played in the 18th-c, but the game similar to the modern game was introduced by Major Walter Clopton Wingfield at a Christmas Party at Nantclywd, Wales, in 1873. His game was called *sphairistike.* » Davis Cup; paddle tennis; platform tennis; real tennis; Wightman Cup; RR120

Tennyson, Alfred, 1st Baron, byname **Alfred, Lord Tennyson** (1809–92) British poet, born at Somersby, Lincolnshire. Educated at Cambridge, he published his first poetry in 1830, but it was not well received; a revised volume in 1842 established his reputation. His major poetic achievement was the elegy mourning the death of his friend, Arthur Hallam, *In Memoriam* (1850); and in the same year he succeeded Wordsworth as poet laureate. In 1855 he wrote *Maud: a Monodrama*, and 1859–85 published a series of poems on the Arthurian theme, *Idylls of the King* (1859). In the 1870s he wrote several plays, and continued to write poetry until his death. He became a baron in 1884, and died at Aldworth, Surrey. » Arthur; English literature; poetry; Wordsworth, William

Tenochtitlan [te**nok**tit**lahn**] The island capital of L Texcoco, now beneath Mexico City, from which the Aztecs dominated Mexico from c.1344–5 to the Spanish Conquest in 1519. About 13 sq km/5 sq ml in area, it had c.60 000 houses and a population of c.200 000. » Aztecs

tenrec [**ten**rek] A mammal of family *Tenrecidae* (31 species), native to Madagascar; an insectivore; species can resemble hedgehogs, moonrats (but lack tails), shrews, or moles; female of the hedgehog-like **common tenrec** (*Tenrec ecaudatus*) has up to 29 nipples. » hedgehog; insectivore; moonrat; otter shrew; shrew

Tenrikyo (Jap 'teaching of heavenly truth') [ten**reek**yoh] A Japanese faith-healing movement founded by a female shaman Nakayama Miki (1798–1887). Her birthplace, Tenri, near the ancient capital of Nara, is the chief religious centre of this missionary sect. » faith healing; shaman

tensile strength The stretching stress at which a material breaks; symbol σ, units Pa (pascal). For metals this is greater when the metal is cold-worked or stretched into wires. For stresses slightly less than tensile strength, most materials undergo plastic deformation. For steel piano wire and cast iron, tensile strengths are 2×10^9 and 2×10^6 Pa, respectively. » fracture (physics); mechanical properties of matter

tenure A teacher's right to permanency of appointment, usually gained after successful completion of a probationary period. The concept became a contentious political issue in the UK when the government abolished it for university teachers appointed after the 1988 Education Bill had been introduced in Parliament.

Tenzing Norgay, byname **Sherpa Tenzing** (1914–86) Nepalese mountaineer, born at Tsa-chu near Makalu. He made his first climb as a porter with a British Everest expedition in 1935, and later climbed many of the Himalayan peaks. In 1953 he succeeded in reaching the Everest summit with Edmund Hillary, for which he was awarded the George Medal. He later became head of the Institute of Mountaineering at Darjeeling. » Everest, Mount; Hillary

Teotihuacán [tayo**tee**wuhkahn] A great Aztec city, 30 km/20 ml NE of Mexico City, flourishing c.450–650 with a population of c.125 000–200 000, but destroyed and burnt in c.700; a world heritage site. Fully urbanized, its N–S street grid covers 20 sq km/8 sq ml and contained 5 000 buildings. Major monuments include the 70 m/220 ft high Pyramid of the Sun, the Pyramid of the Moon, and the *Ciudadela* or royal palace, with its temple of Quetzalcoatl. » Aztecs; Tenochtitlan

tepal » **perianth**

teratorn A condor-like vulture with a wingspan exceeding 4 m/13 ft; the largest flying bird ever to have lived, now extinct; known from Pleistocene fossils from a Californian tar pit. (Genus: *Teratornia.*) » Pleistocene epoch; vulture

Terborch or **Terburg, Gerard** [ter**bawkh**] (1617–81) Dutch painter, born at Zwolle. He studied at Haarlem, and travelled widely in Europe, before settling at Deventer in 1654, where he became burgomaster. He worked mostly on a small scale, producing genre pictures and fashionable portraits, but is best known for his painting of the 'Peace of Munster' (1648, National Gallery, London). » Dutch art; genre painting

Terbrugghen, Hendrik (c.1588–1629) Dutch painter, born at Deventer. He studied at Utrecht, and was until c.1615 in Italy, where he came under the influence of Caravaggio. He excelled in chiaroscuro effects, and in the faithful representation of physiognomical details and drapery, as in his 'Jacob and Laban' (1627, National Gallery, London). He died at Utrecht. » Caravaggio; chiaroscuro; Dutch art

terebinth » **turpentine tree**

Terence (Publius Terentius Afer) (c.190–159 BC) Latin comic poet, born at Carthage, N Africa. He became the slave of a Roman senator, who gave him an education in Rome and freed him. His successful first play, *Andria* (166 BC, The Andrian Girl), introduced him to Roman society, where his chief patrons were Laclius and the younger Scipio. His surviving six comedies are Greek in origin and scene, directly based on

Menander. Many of his conventions were later used by European dramatists. » comedy; drama; Menander; poetry; Latin literature

Terengganu [terenggahnoo] pop (1980) 525 255; area 12 928 sq km/ 4 990 sq ml. State in NE Peninsular Malaysia; formerly a fief of Malacca and then of Johor, before coming under the rule of Thailand; ceded to Britain, 1909; capital, Kuala Terengganu; fishing, offshore oil. » Malaysia [i]

Teresa of Avila, St (1515–82), feast day 15 October. Spanish saint and mystic, born at Avila. She entered a Carmelite convent there in 1535, and became famous for her ascetic religious exercises and sanctity. In 1562 she re-established the ancient Carmelite rule, with additional observances. Her many writings include an autobiography, *The Way of Perfection*, and the mystical work, *The Interior Castle*. She died at Alba de Tormes, and was canonized in 1622. » Carmelites; mysticism

Teresa, Mother » **Theresa, Mother**

Teresa of Lisieux » **Theresa of Lisieux**

Tereshkova, Valentina [tereshkohva] (1937–) Russian cosmonaut and the first woman to fly in space, born at Maslennikovo. She worked in a textile factory, qualified as a sports parachutist, and entered training as a cosmonaut in 1962, becoming a solo crew member of the 3-day Vostok 6 flight launched on 16 June 1963. She was made a hero of the Soviet Union, and became a member of the Central Committee of the Soviet Communist Party in 1971. » cosmonaut; Soviet space programme; Vostok

term or **terminal figure** A sculptured head, or head and shoulders, on a pillar which tapers towards its base. Such figures have become popular as garden ornaments since the Renaissance. The term is very similar to a **herm**, so-called because in Greece the god Hermes was frequently represented in this way. » Hermes (mythology); sculpture

term bank A large computerized databank of terminology, cross-referenced for the same items in a range of languages. The provision of such resources has followed the 20th-c explosion in technical terminology, which has led to an urgent need to standardize usage between different languages, and to register and correlate differences where they exist. The European Community has its own version in the European Automatic Dictionary, on-line via Euronet.

Terme The national museum of Rome, containing one of the world's most important collections of Greek and Roman art. It is housed in the ancient Diocletian Baths. » Diocletian; museum

terminal velocity The greatest velocity an object will reach when allowed to fall through some fluid (usually air or water). Terminal velocity is attained when the resistive forces due to the medium, which increase with velocity, are equal and opposite to the accelerating force acting in the direction of motion. Its value depends on the fluid and on the object's shape, density, and surface roughness. » acceleration due to gravity; free fall; Stokes' law

Terminus The Roman god of boundary marks, where his statue or bust was sometimes placed. His stone on the Capitol was within the temple of Jupiter Optimus Maximus, but was not allowed to be covered in.

termite A small, social insect that constructs nests in rotten wood or makes earth mounds which may measure several metres across and contain millions of individuals: caste structure of colony well-developed; workers mostly sterile, blind, and with soft white cuticle (known as **white ants**); soldiers sterile, with large heads and strong jaws; adults (*imagos*) winged, reproductive forms with compound eyes; gut contains harmless bacteria enabling the digestion of cellulose in wood; c.2 000 species, causing great economic problems in the tropics, damaging timber buildings and crops. (Order: *Isoptera.*) » ant

tern A small, gull-like sea-bird, found worldwide; plumage usually pale with black cap and forked tail; head with partly erectile crest (**crested tern**) or smooth. Some species, such as **noddies** (**ternlets**) and **marsh terns**, are darker, often with wedge-shaped tails. (Family: *Laridae*, 42 species; some authors put the tern in a separate family, *Sternidae.*) » Arctic tern; gull; skimmer

terpene A class of natural products, also known as **essential oils**, based upon the oligomerization of isoprene, having formulae closely related to $(C_5H_8)_n$. Common examples, whose names show their origins, are pinene, limonene, menthol, and carotene. » essential oils; isoprene [i]; oligomer

Terpsichore [terpsikawree] In Greek mythology, one of the Muses, usually associated with dancing or lyric poetry. » Muses

Terra Australis Incognita ('The Unknown South Land') A supposed continent once thought to exist in the S Pacific in order to balance the Eurasian land-mass of the N hemisphere. First argued into being by ancient Greek thinkers, it provided a major stimulus for exploration until it was shown not to exist by James Cook on his second great voyage (1772–5). » Cook, James

terracotta Clay, modelled into sculpture or tiles and fired in a kiln, becoming hard and brittle but very permanent. Examples survive from ancient times and from all over the world. » sculpture; Xi'an

terrapin [terapin] A reptile of the family *Emydidae*, found in fresh or brackish water or on land; hind feet may be enlarged to assist with swimming; some species eat small animals when young, plants when adult; also known as **pond turtle**. The name is sometimes used only for some of the pond turtle species. (Order: *Chelonia.*) » box turtle; Chelonia [i]; reptile

terrier A small hardy domestic dog, bred for hunting (especially foxes); originally sent into burrows after prey; traditionally aggressive, tenacious, fearless; many modern breeds. » Airedale/Bedlington/Border/Boston/bull/Cairn/fox/Irish/Lakeland/Scottish/Sealyham/silky/Skye/Staffordshire bull/West Highland white/Yorkshire terrier; dandie dinmont; dog; Jack Russell; Schnauzer; sporting dog

Territorial Army A British reserve military force, first formed in 1908 by amalgamating the old volunteer and yeomanry regiments in a new force of part-time soldiers, each battalion of which was attached to a battalion of the regular army. The 'Terriers' (known as the Territorial Force to 1920, the Territorials thereafter) fought with distinction in the two world wars. They receive continuous training on a part-time basis, and are assigned to UK field forces prepared to be sent as a direct reinforcement to the British Army of the Rhine, or to act in home defence. » militia; yeomanry

territory In US history, political status prior to the attainment of statehood, held in two stages. In the first, an 'unorganized territory' was ruled by a judge; in the second, an 'organized' territory could elect its own legislature and non-voting delegate to Congress. Hawaii and Alaska were the last two places to have territorial status. » Ordinance of 1787

terrorism Coercive and violent behaviour undertaken to achieve or promote a particular political objective or cause, often involving the overthrow of established order. Terrorist activity is designed to induce fear through its indiscriminate, arbitrary, and unpredictable acts of violence, often against members of the population at large. It may be 'official', as under Stalin, or 'unofficial', as employed by various opposition or underground movements. Such movements are usually minority groups (such as the IRA) who feel there are no other means available to them of achieving their objectives. Terrorism may be confined to a specific territory or may have an international dimension, manifest in hijackings and hostage-taking. » Baader-Meinhof; IRA; PLO; Red Brigades

Terry, Dame (Alice) Ellen (1848–1928) British actress, born in Coventry, a member of a large family of actors. She appeared on stage at eight, from 1862 played in Bristol, and after a short-lived marriage and retirement, established herself as the leading Shakespearean actress in London, dominating the English and US theatre (1878–1902) in partnership with Henry Irving. In 1903 she went into theatre management, and toured and lectured widely. She was made a Dame in 1925, and died at Small Hythe, Kent. » Craig; Irving, Henry

Tertiaries Members of the Third Order of religious life. Normally, these are lay people striving after Christian perfection in life in the world under the guidance of a religious Order, such as the Franciscans or Dominicans. A **Regular Tertiary** is a member of a community bound by vows. » Christianity; Orders, Holy; monasticism

tertiary education Post-secondary education. It is often used to refer to further and higher education, but in the UK it can also refer to attendance at a **tertiary college**, which is a college for all those over 16 wishing to pursue academic or vocational courses. » further education

Tertiary period The earlier of the two geological periods of the Cenozoic era, extending from c.65 million to 2 million years ago. It is divided into five epochs; the Palaeocene, Eocene, Oligocene, Miocene, and Pliocene. Early Tertiary times are marked by great mountain-building episodes (Alps, Himalayas, Andes, Rockies) and the diversification of mammals. » Cenozoic era; geological time scale; orogeny; RR16

Tertullian, in full **Quintus Septimus Florens Tertullianus** (c.160–220) Christian theologian, born at Carthage. He lived for some time at Rome, was converted (c.196), and then returned to Carthage, where he died. His opposition to worldliness in the Church culminated in his becoming a leader of the Montanist sect (c.207). The first to produce major Christian works in Latin, he thus exercised a profound influence on the development of ecclesiastical language. He wrote books against heathens, Jews, and heretics, as well as several practical and ascetic treatises. » Christianity; Montanism; theology

Teruel [terooel], ancient **Turba** 40°22N 1°08W, pop(1981) 28 225. Capital of Teruel province, Aragón, EC Spain; on R Turia, 302 km/188 ml from Madrid; bishopric; railway; clothes, woollens, soap, leather, flour, wood products, foodstuffs; cathedral (16th-c), Los Arcos aqueduct, Church of St Peter; the town's Mudéjar architecture, a mixture of Christian and Islamic influences, is a world heritage site. » Aragón; Spain [i]

terza rima [**tert**sa **ree**ma] (Ital 'third rhyme') An Italian verse form, where the rhyme dovetails the three-line stanzas, ending with aba, beb, cdc, etc. It is used by Dante in the *Divina Commedia*, and also by Petrarch and Boccaccio, but has never been successfully employed in other languages. » Dante; metre (literature); poetry; rhyme

tesla SI unit of magnetic flux density; symbol T; defined as a magnetic flux of 1 weber per square metre; named after US inventor Nikola Tesla. » magnetic flux; Tesla; units (scientific); RR71

Tesla, Nikola (1856–1943) US inventor, born at Smiljan, Croatia (modern Yugoslavia). He studied at Graz, Prague, and Paris, emigrating to the USA in 1884. He left the Edison Works at Menlo Park to concentrate on his own inventions, which included improved dynamos, transformers, electric bulbs, and the high-frequency coil which now bears his name. He died in New York City. » magnetic flux; tesla

tessera » **mosaic**

tessitura [tessi**too**ra] That part of a vocal compass in which the most demanding passages in a piece of music are concentrated. An aria, operatic role, etc may be said to demand a high tessitura, without containing any exceptionally high notes. » singing

Test Act A British Act passed in 1673 by a parliament anxious to curb Catholic influence at Charles II's court. Every office holder had to take Oaths of Supremacy and Allegiance, and to take communion according to the rites of the Church of England. A declaration against transubstantiation also had to be made. The passage of the Act necessitated the resignation of the King's brother, James, Duke of York, as Lord High Admiral. The Act remained in force until 1828. » Catholic Emancipation; Charles II (of England); Church of England; transubstantiation

test-tube baby The lay term to indicate ***in vitro* fertilization and embryo replacement** (IVF). The procedure is indicated in infertility, notably when there is damage to the Fallopian tubes that is not amenable to repair, but it is also used for other causes of infertility. Such women are given drugs that stimulate ovulation. Several ova are then retrieved from the surface of the ovaries by a technique known as *laporoscopy* and placed in a suitable culture medium to which spermatozoa are added. About 40 hours later the ova are examined to confirm that fertilization has occurred, after which the fertilized egg (4–8 cells in size) is transferred to the uterus via the vagina and cervix. Successful pregnancy occurs in about 10–20% of cases. » Fallopian tubes; infertility; pregnancy [i]

testament literature A loose genre of writings found in the Old Testament Pseudepigrapha, stemming from post-exilic times, which purportedly gives the last words or 'testaments' of significant figures from Israel's history. Although often ethical in nature, testaments also include visions of the future. In their present form, some may reflect Christian and not just Jewish interests. Most notable are the *Testaments of the 12 Patriarchs*, the *Testament of Moses*, the *Testament of Adam*, and the *Testament of Job*. » Pseudepigrapha

testing » **achievement/criterion-referenced/norm-referenced/objective test; continuous assessment; SAT**

testis (plural **testes**) The essential reproductive gland (*gonad*) of male animals, producing spermatozoa; also known as the **testicle**. In vertebrates the testis also synthesizes and secretes sex hormones (androgens). In mammals (eg humans), there are usually two, lying suspended within the scrotum, oval and flattened in shape. Each testis is divided into a number of wedge-shaped small lobes, containing a convoluted seminiferous tube (from which the spermatozoa arise). The spermatozoa pass from this tube into a straight seminiferous tube, then into the rete testis and to the highly convoluted *epididymis* (a duct c.6 m/20 ft long in men). Between the seminiferous tubes are groups of glandular cells (the *interstitial cells of Leydig*) which produce *testosterone*, essential for the development and maintenenac of male sexual characteristics. » androgens; castration; gonad; penis [i]

testosterone [tes**tos**tuhrohn] The male sex hormone, produced in the testes, and responsible for the development of the primary sex organs, secondary sex characteristics (eg facial hair), and sexual behaviour. » hormones; oestrogens; steroid [i]; testis

tetanus A disease resulting from infection with *Clostridium tetani*, which exists in the soil and in the gut of humans and animals; also known as **lockjaw**. It especially affects farmers and gardeners. Infection enters the body through wounds in the skin caused by a nail or splinter. The bacteria produce a toxin which affects motor nerve cells in the spinal cord, and induces convulsions and muscle spasms. The disease can be prevented by active vaccination, and treated by antitoxin and penicillin. » nervous system; penicillin

Tethys [**tee**this] The third natural satellite of Saturn, discovered in 1684; distance from the planet 295 000 km/183 000 ml; diameter 1 050 km/650 ml; orbital period 1.888 days. » Saturn (astronomy); RR4

Tétouan or **Tetuán** [tay**twahn**] 35°34N 5°22W, pop(1982) 199 615. City in Nord-Ouest province, NE Morocco; 60 km/37 ml SE of Tangier; settled by Moorish exiles from Spain, 15th-c; captured by Spanish, 1860; airfield; textiles, leather, soap, tiles; trade in agriculture and livestock. » Morocco [i]

tetra Any of many small colourful freshwater fish, family *Characidae*, from S and C America; popular with aquarists; length typically 3–10 cm/1.2–4 in; body rather carp-like, but lacking barbels and with well-developed jaw teeth. » carp

tetra-ethyl lead $Pb(C_2H_5)_4$. An organometallic compound made by the reaction of lead chloride with a Grignard reagent, used as an additive to petrol to control 'knocking'. Its hazardous properties and those of its decomposition products are leading to its progressive disuse. » Grignard; knocking; lead; petrol

tetracyclines [tetra**siy**klinz] A class of antibiotics obtained from the bacteria *Streptomyces*, active against a broad spectrum of infections. The first to be produced was chlortetracycline (aureomycin, now superseded) in 1948. » antibiotics

Tetragrammaton » **Yahweh**

Tetzel, Johann (c.1465–1519) German monk, born at Pirna, Saxony. He became a Dominican in 1489, and was appointed in 1516 to preach an indulgence in favour of contributors to the building fund of St Peter's at Rome. This he did with great ostentation, thereby provoking the Wittenberg theses of Luther, and his own reply. He died at Leipzig. » Dominicans; indulgences; Luther; Reformation

Teutonic Knights Members of the Order of St Mary of the Germans, a religious-military order founded c.1190 and inspired by crusading ideals. By the 14th-c they controlled the E Baltic lands of the Livonian Knights, Prussia, and E Pomerania. The Order was dissolved in Germany in 1809, but re-established in Austria in 1834. » Crusades [i]; Livonian Knights; Prussia

tex » **count** (textiles)

Texas pop (1987e) 16 789 000; area 691 003 sq km/266 807 sq ml. State in SW USA, divided into 254 counties; the 'Lone Star State'; second largest state in the USA; first settled by the Spanish in the late 1600s; first American settlement, 1821; American rebellion after request for separate statehood turned down by Mexico, 1835; declared independence, defeated by Santa Ana at the Alamo, 1836; Mexican army then defeated by Sam Houston at San Jacinto, 1836; independence of Texas recognized; admitted to the Union as the 28th state, 1845; US–Mexican War, with Mexican defeats at Palo Alto and Resaca de la Palma; joined the Confederate states in the Civil War (the only state not to be overrun by Union troops); re-admitted to the Union, 1870; discovery of extensive oil deposits (1901) transformed the economy; capital, Austin; other major cities Houston, Dallas, San Antonio, El Paso, Fort Worth; bounded SE by the Gulf of Mexico, SW by Mexico; rivers include the Red, Sabine, Trinity, Brazos, Colorado; Rio Grande forms the state's entire international border with Mexico; Davis and Guadalupe Mts in the extreme W; highest point Guadalupe Peak (2 667 m/8 750 ft); much of the E hilly, forested country with cypress swamps, cotton and rice cultivation, extensive oil fields; Gulf coastal plains around Houston heavily industrialized; tourism and heavy industry in the drier S coastal region; intensive agriculture in the irrigated lower Rio Grande valley, producing citrus fruits and winter vegetables; richest agricultural land in the C and N (the Blackland prairies); SC plains and Edwards Plateau have vast wheat and cotton farms and cattle ranches; far N dry, barren, mountainous; nation's leading producer of oil and natural gas; chemicals, processed foods, machinery, fabricated metals; major producer of cattle, sheep, cotton; wheat, sorghum, dairy produce, rice, vegetables, fishing; large Spanish-speaking population. » Alamo; Austin; Dallas; Houston; Mexican War; Rio Grande; United States of America [i]; RR39

textlinguistics The study of the structure of linguistic texts (spoken or written), in which the texts are seen as having a specific communicative function, such as road signs, poems, or conversations. Analyses are made of the way the elements of a text cohere, and how its content is structured, from such points of view as grammar, vocabulary, pronunciation, and graphic layout. » discourse analysis; linguistics; stylistics

textual criticism A scholarly procedure devoted to establishing the authenticity and accuracy of literary texts; unlike other forms of criticism, not interpretive or evaluative in character. It involves the scrutiny of manuscripts where they exist, the collation of different readings (*recension*), and where evidence is incomplete or inconclusive, the practice of emendation. The method was first applied to Biblical texts in the 19th-c, but is now used even on the works of modern authors. » Bible; literary criticism; literature

Thabana-Ntlenyana, Mount [ta**ba**na uhntlen**ya**na] or **Mount Thadentsonyane** 29°28S 29°16E. Mountain in E Lesotho, in the Drakensberg Mts; highest peak in Lesotho, 3 482 m/11 424 ft, and also in Africa S of Mt Kilimanjaro. » Lesotho [i]

Thackeray, William Makepeace (1811–63) British novelist, born in Calcutta. Educated at Charterhouse and Cambridge, he left without taking a degree, and became a journalist. He first attracted attention with his work in *Punch* (1842), in which he exploited the view of society as seen by the butler ('Jeames's Diary') and the great theme of English snobbery. His major novels were all published as monthly serials: *Vanity Fair* (1847–8), *Pendennis* (1848), *Henry Esmond* (1852), and *The Newcomes* (1853–5). He travelled widely as a lecturer in Europe and the USA, and in 1860 became the first editor of *The Cornhill Magazine*, where much of his later work (now little read) appeared. He died in London. » English literature; novel

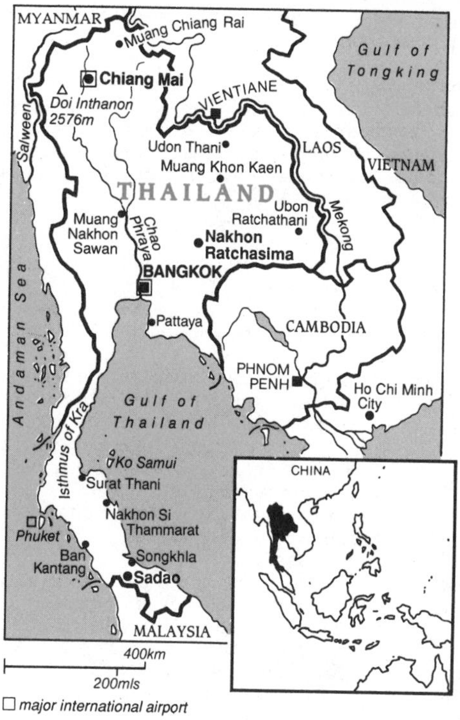

Thai The official language of Thailand, spoken by c.30 million people, with much dialectal variation. Its relationship with other language groups in neighbouring China and the Pacific is not clear. There is written evidence of the language from the 13th-c. » Thailand [i]

Thailand, Thai **Muang Thai**, formerly **Siam**, official name **Kingdom of Thailand** [**tiy**land] pop (1990e) 56 217 000; area 513 115 sq km/198 062 sq ml. Kingdom in SE Asia, divided into 72 provinces (*changwats*); situated N and W of the Gulf of Thailand and bounded W by the Andaman Sea, W and NW by Burma, NE and E by Laos, E by Cambodia, and S by Malaysia; capital, Bangkok; chief cities include Chiang Mai, Ban Hat Yai, Nakhon Ratchasima; timezone GMT +7; ethnic groups include Thai (75%), Chinese (14%); official language, Thai; chief religion, Buddhism; unit of currency, the baht; C agricultural region dominated by the floodplain of the Chao Praya R; NE plateau rises above 300 m/1 000 ft and covers a third of the country; mountainous N region rising to 2 595 m/8 514 ft at Doi Inthanon; narrow, low-lying S region separates the Andaman Sea from the Gulf of Thailand; covered in tropical rainforest; mangrove-forested islands off the coast; equatorial climate in the S; tropical monsoon climate in the N and C; evidence of Bronze Age communities, 4000 BC; Thai nation founded, 13th-c; only country in S and SE Asia to have escaped colonization by a European power; occupied by the Japanese in World War 2; king is head of state, advised by a 12-member Privy Council; military coup, 1991; 292-member National Legislative Assembly; plans for a new constitution; agriculture is the most important economic activity; rice, manioc, maize, bananas, pineapple, sugar cane, rubber, teak; textiles, electronics, cement, chemicals, food processing, tourism; tin (world's third largest supplier), tungsten (world's second largest supplier), manganese, antimony, lead, zinc, copper, natural gas. » Bangkok; Thai; RR27 national holidays; RR62 political leaders

thalamus » **diencephalon**

thalassaemia/thalassemia [thala**see**mia] An inherited disease in which there is impaired formation of normal haemoglobin-A, with resulting anaemia. The anaemia may be mild, or so severe that the likelihood of survival without blood transfusions is low. It occurs in SE Asia and in the Mediterranean area. » anaemia; haemoglobin

Thaleia » **Thalia**

Thales [**thay**leez] (c.620–c.555 BC) Greek natural philosopher, traditionally regarded as the first philosopher, born at Miletus. His mercantile journeys took him to Egypt and Babylon, where he acquired land-surveying and astronomical techniques, and is said to have predicted the solar eclipse in 585 BC. None of his writings survive, but Aristotle attributes to him the doctrine that water is the original substance from which all things are derived. » Aristotle

Thalia or **Thaleia** [tha**li**ya] In Greek mythology, the Muse of comedy and idyllic poetry. » Muses

thalidomide A sedative introduced in West Germany in 1956, in the UK in 1958, and subsequently in some other countries. It became widely used because of its particular safety (even massive overdoses are not lethal). However, it was recognized as a teratogen (causing congenital abnormalities) and withdrawn; approximately 20% of babies whose mothers had taken thalidomide during early pregnancy suffered absence of limbs or part of limbs. It has been estimated to be responsible for 10000 cases of deformity. Since this disaster, all drugs and other chemicals with which humans come into contact have been required to prove lack of teratogenic potential before they can be marketed. » sedatives

Thallophyta [tha**lo**fita] A collective name formerly used for all lower plant-like organisms that lack differentiation into root, stem, and leaf; sometimes treated as a subkingdom of plants comprising the eucaryotic algae and fungi; also known as **Thallobionta**. » algae; eucaryote; fungus; plant

thallus The body of a plant which is not differentiated into stem, leaves, and roots. It is usually flattened, and may also be branched. » leaf [i]; root (botany); stem (botany)

Thames, River [temz], Lat **Tamesis** River rising in the Cotswold Hills, SE Gloucestershire, England; flows 352 km/219 ml E and SE through Oxfordshire, Berkshire, Surrey, and Greater London; approaches the North Sea in a long, wide estuary between Essex (N) and Kent (S); navigable as far as London by large ships; chief tributaries, the Cherwell, Thame, Lea, Colne, Roding, Kennet, Mole, Wey, and Medway Rivers; upper part beyond Oxford often called R Isis; joined by Grand Union Canal near Brentford; known as the *Pool* by London Bridge; two embankments built at London, from Blackfriars Bridge to Westminster (1864) and from Westminster Bridge to Vauxhall (1866); Thames Conservancy Board established in 1857; administration of the river below Teddington given to the Port of London Authority in 1908; tidal barrier built across approach to London to reduce risk of floods (completed 1983). » London [i]

Thanet, Isle of Pop (1987e) 126900. Urban area in E Kent, SE England, originally an island; contains the towns of Margate, Broadstairs, and Ramsgate; railway. » Kent

Thanksgiving Day A day set apart for a public acknowledgement of God's goodness and mercy; in Canada the second Monday in October, and in the USA the fourth Thursday of November, both public holidays. The occasion dates from 1621, when the new American settlers celebrated their first harvest. It gradually spread throughout the USA, and has been observed nationally since 1863. In modern times, the day is especially important for family reunion.

Thant, U (1909–74) Burmese diplomat, born at Pantanaw. He was a teacher who took up government work when Burma became independent in 1948, becoming the country's United Nations representative in 1957. As Secretary-General of the UN (1962–71), he played a major diplomatic role during the Cuban crisis. He also formulated a plan to end the Congolese Civil War (1962) and mobilized a UN peace-keeping force in Cyprus (1964). He died in New York City. » Cuban Missile Crisis; United Nations

Thar Desert [tah] or **(Great) Indian Desert** area c.320000 sq km/125000 sq ml. Arid region in NW India and E Pakistan, S Asia; 800 km/500 ml long and 400 km/250 ml wide; between the Indus and the Sutlej Rivers (W) and the Aravalli Range (E); bounded S by the Rann of Kutch; crossed by irrigation canals in N and W, largest the Rajasthan Canal. » desert; India [i]; Pakistan [i]

Tharp, Twyla (1942–) US dancer, choreographer, and director, born at Portland, Indiana. She studied with Graham, Cunningham, and Paul Taylor (1930–), and danced with Taylor (1963–5). Since then she has choreographed and danced with her own group, and made new work for various other ballet and modern dance companies. Flippant, throwaway movement, and an amusing edge to her works, disguises meticulous structure and comment on current social issues, as in *Push Comes to Shove* (1976). » choreography; Cunningham; Graham, Martha; modern dance; postmodern dance

Thatcher, Margaret (Hilda) (1925–) British Conservative Prime Minister (1979–90), born at Grantham, Lincolnshire. Educated at Oxford, she worked as a research chemist. Following her marriage, she was called to the Bar in 1954. Elected to parliament in 1959, and after holding junior office, she became Minister of Education (1970–4). In 1975 she replaced Edward Heath as Leader of the Conservative Party to become the first woman party leader in British politics. Under her leadership, the Conservative Party moved towards a more 'right wing' position, and British politics and society became more polarized than at any other time since World War 2. Her government instituted the privatization of nationalized industries and national utilities, tried to institute a market in state-provided health care and education, and reduced the role of local government as a provider of services. She was elected for a third term of office in 1987, and by 1988 had become the longest serving premier of the 20th-c. She resigned (Nov 1990) as a result of the controversy which followed her opposition to full monetary and economic union with Europe. » Conservative Party; European Monetary System; Heath, Edward; right wing

Thatta monuments A group of monuments in Thatta, former capital of Sind in present-day Pakistan; a world heritage site. From 14th–18th-c the city flourished as a centre of Islamic arts. Its monuments include the 17th-c Great Mosque built by Shah Jahan, and graves in the 'City of Mausoleums', a vast necropolis covering 15 sq km/6 sq ml. » Islam; Shah Jahan; Sind

theatre/theater Derived from the Greek for 'seeing place', the term originally signified the area occupied by spectators. It now describes the whole building and the social art form it houses. Since the Renaissance, scenic illusion has played a dominant role in the history of Western theatre, as is evident in the development of the proscenium. However, throughout the 20th-c, with film and television appropriating this pictorial tradition, theatre has rediscovered the efficacy of open stages, emblematic staging, and the direct presentational styles of such popular forms as *commedia dell' arte*, boulevard theatre, or mummers' plays. In this respect, for modern Western theatre the influence of the ancient and sophisticated traditions of, for example, Chinese, Indian, and Japanese theatre has been strong. » Actors' Studio; Berliner Ensemble; Broadway; Comédie Française, La; *commedia dell' arte*; English Stage Company; Fringe, the; Habima; masque; Meiningen Players; music hall; Provincetown Players; Royal Shakespeare Company; stage; theatre in the round; Theatre Workshop; Abbey / Globe / Group / Indian / legitimate / Living / Moscow Art/Open/patent theatre/theater

theatre/theater in the round A theatre in which the auditorium surrounds a central stage and both performer and audience share the same acoustic space. Also known as an **arena stage**, the form demands that the actors project in all directions simultaneously. » open stage; theatre

Theatre Workshop An English theatre company founded in Manchester by Joan Littlewood in 1945. From 1953 onwards it was based in London at the Theatre Royal, Stratford East, and is best remembered for its vigorous ensemble acting exemplified by such shows as *The Hostage* and *Oh, What a Lovely War*. » Littlewood; theatre

Thebe [**thee**bee] A tiny natural satellite of Jupiter, discovered in 1979 by Voyager 2; distance from the planet 222000 km/138000 ml; diameter 100 km/60 ml. » Jupiter (astronomy); Voyager project [i]; RR4

Thebes [theebz] **1** The ancient capital of Upper Egypt, and the location of many magnificent pharaonic temples and tombs, such as Tutankhamen's; a world heritage site. It was situated on the R Nile, where the town of Luxor now stands – a major tourist centre from as far back as Roman times. » Luxor; pharaoh Tutankhamen **2** In ancient Greece, the most powerful city-state in Boeotia. Although prominent in Greek legend (the Oedipus cycle is based there), in historical times it was rarely able to rival Athens and Sparta. Only under the brilliant Epaminondas in the 370s BC did it succeed briefly in being the leading power in Greece. It is now the capital town of Boeotia department, SE Greece, 52 km/32 ml NNW of Athens; pop (1981) 18 712, a market town for a rich agricultural region. » Boeotia; Epaminondas

theft The dishonest taking of property belonging to another person, with the intention of permanently depriving that person of the property. Borrowing is not theft, but it may sometimes be the subject of another criminal sanction: the taking of a motor-car without the owner's consent is a criminal offence. » criminal law; robbery

thegn [thayn] (Old English 'one who serves') In Anglo-Saxon England, a member of the noble class. Until the Norman Conquest, thegns were indispensable to effective royal control of the localities. From 1066, most of them lost lands, status, and political influence to Norman barons and knights. Some even entered the service of the Byzantine emperor. » Anglo-Saxons; Byzantine Empire; ceorl; Norman Conquest

theine [**thee**in] » **caffeine**

theism Belief in a single divine being, transcendent and personal, who created the world and, although involved with and related to the creation, is distinct from it. It is a feature of Jewish and Islamic as well as Christian faith, and is contrasted with both deism and pantheism. » agnosticism; atheism; deism; God; pantheism

theme park An entertainment centre based on a particular theme, the most popular being wildlife parks. Many are also amusement parks. The first theme park was Disneyland, at Anaheim, California, opened in 1955, based on the Walt Disney cartoon characters.

Themis [**the**mis] In Greek mythology, the goddess of established law and justice (really a personification). As a consort of Zeus, she is the mother of the Horae and the Moerae. » Horae; Moerae

Themistocles [the**mis**tuhkleez] (c.523–c.458 BC) Athenian general, visionary politician, and hero of Salamis. By persuading the Athenians to develop Peiraeus as a port (493 BC), and to use their rich silver deposits to build a fleet (483 BC), he not only made possible their great naval victory at Salamis (480 BC), but also laid the foundations of their maritime empire. He fell from favour c.470 BC, and was ostracized. After many adventures, he served the Persian king in Asia Minor as the Governor of Magnesia and two other cities. » Delian League; Persian Wars; Salamis; ostracism

Theocritus [thee**ok**rituhs] (c.310–250 BC) Greek pastoral poet, born (probably) at Syracuse. He was brought up in Cos, and lived for a time at the court of Ptolemy Philadelphus in Alexandria. About 30 of his poems survive, though the authenticity of some have been disputed. His short poems dealing with pastoral subjects, and representing a single scene, came to be called 'idylls' (*eidullia*). Tennyson was deeply influenced by him, as were the pastoral poets of the Renaissance. » Greek literature; pastoral; poetry; Tennyson

theodicy [thee**od**uhsee] The defence and vindication of God, defined as both omnipotent and good in the light of evil in the world. The term was first used by Leibniz in 1710. » God; Leibniz

theodolite An optical surveying instrument for measuring vertical or (more importantly) horizontal angles. It is a small telescope, with cross wires, movable over horizontal and vertical graduated circular scales. It is usually seen mounted on a stable tripod. » surveying

Theodora (c.500–47) Byzantine empress (527–47), an actress, dancer, and prostitute who became mistress, then wife, of Justinian (522). A woman of great intelligence and courage, she played a major backstage role throughout his long and distinguished reign, and probably saved his throne during the Nika riots by her intervention (532). » Justinian

Theodorakis, Mikis (1925–) Greek composer, born in Khios. He studied at the Paris Conservatoire, and in 1959 his ballet *Antigone* was produced at Covent Garden. On his return to Greece, he became intensely critical of the Greek musical and artistic establishment. When the right-wing government took power in 1967, he was imprisoned and his music banned; but he was released in 1970, after worldwide appeals. His prolific musical output includes oratorios, ballets, song cycles, and music for film scores, the best known of which was *Zorba the Greek* (1965).

Theodore of Mopsuestia (c.350–428) Christian theologian, born in Antioch, and made Bishop of Mopsuestia in Cilicia in 392. He wrote commentaries (mostly now lost) on almost all the books of Scripture. As the teacher of Nestorius, he was perhaps the founder of Nestorianism, and his views on the Incarnation were condemned by the fifth ecumenical council in 553. » allegory; Christianity; heresy; Incarnation; Nestorians

Theodoric or **Theoderic**, byname **the Great** (?–526) King of the Ostrogoths (471–526), who invaded Italy in 489, defeating the barbarian ruler, Odoacer. His long reign secured for Italy tranquillity and prosperity, the Goths and the Romans continuing as distinct nations, each with its own tribunals and laws. He established his capital at Ravenna, where he died. » Odoacer; Ostrogoths

Theodosian Code [theeuh**doh**shan] A codification of the law promulgated throughout the Roman Empire in 438 by the Emperor Theodosius II (401–50). Its sixteen books summarized all the laws that had been enacted since the beginning of the reign of Constantine the Great (312). » Justinian Code; Roman Law

Theodosius I, byname **the Great** (c.346–95) Roman emperor of the East (379–95). Made emperor because of his military abilities, he solved the long-standing Gothic problem by allowing the Goths to settle S of the Danube as allies of Rome. His title comes from his vigorous championship of orthodox Christianity. » Theodosius II

Theodosius II (401–50) Roman emperor (408–50), the grandson of Theodosius I and, like him, a staunch champion of orthodox Christianity. He is chiefly remembered for his codification of the Roman law. » Theodosian Code

theology Literally, the science of the divine, or of discourse about God. In Christianity, it is understood as the systematic critical clarification of the historical beliefs of the Church. It has been divided into **natural theology**, ie that which can be known about God from nature or by reason alone, and **revealed theology**, that which can only be known through the self-disclosure of God. » Christianity; God; revelation

Theophrastus [theeuh**fras**tuhs] (c.372–286 BC) Greek philosopher, born at Eresus, Lesbos. At Athens he studied under Plato, becoming the close friend of Aristotle, and head of the Peripatetic school after Aristotle's death. He was responsible for preserving many of Aristotle's works, along with many fragments of the Presocratics. » Aristotle; Presocratics

theorbo [thee**aw**boh] A large lute with six strings above a fretted fingerboard, and seven or eight additional bass strings which are not stopped and have a separate pegbox. It was widely used in the 17th-c as a continuo instrument. » chitarrone; continuo; lute; string instrument **2** [i]

theorem A proposition proved by logical deduction from one or more initial premises. Although geometrical theorems are the most widely known, theorems exist in all branches of mathematics. A theorem which has already been proved and is then used towards the proof of another theorem is known as a **lemma**. If the theorem is 'statement p implies statement q', the **converse** is 'statement q implies statement p'. The converse of a theorem is not always true. For example, if two triangles are congruent, they are equal in area, but two triangles that are equal in area are not necessarily congruent. » arithmetic; algebra; calculus, fundamental theorem of; congruence

theosophy [thee**os**uhfee] Any system of philosophical or theological thought based on the direct and immediate experience of the divine. It has been used to describe any developed system of mystical thought and practice, and especially the principles of the Theosophical Society founded in 1875 by Madame Blavatsky (1831–91) and H S Olcott (1832–1907) at New York. » Blavatsky

Thera [**thee**ra] » Santorini

Therapsida [thuh**rap**sida] An order of fossil reptiles including the direct ancestors of the mammals; known mainly from the Permian and Triassic periods; many with well-differentiated dentitions; some with a secondary palate, and mammal-like limbs, but only one middle ear bone. (Subclass: *Synapsida*.) » Dicynodon; Permian period; reptile; Triassic period

Theravada [thera**vah**da] The form of Buddhism commonly found in S Asia (Sri Lanka, Burma, Thailand, Cambodia, and Laos). Its doctrines remain essentially as they were in the 3rd-c BC, and it is generally distinguished from the later Mahayana Buddhism in its rejection of the theory of bodhisattvas. » bodhisattva; Buddhism; Mahayana

Theresa (of Calcutta), Mother, originally **Agnes Gonxha Bojaxhiu** (1910–) Christian missionary in India, born in Yugoslavia. She went to India in 1928, and taught at a convent school in Calcutta, taking her final vows in 1937. She became principal of the school, but in 1948 left the convent to work alone in the slums. After medical training in Paris, she opened her first school for destitute children in Calcutta. She was gradually joined by other nuns, and her House for the Dying was opened in 1952. Her sisterhood, the Missionaries of Charity, started in 1950, and in 1957 she started work with lepers and in many disaster areas of the world. She was awarded the Pope John XXIII Peace Prize in 1971, and the Nobel Peace Prize in 1979. » leprosy; missions, Christian

Theresa of Lisieux, originally **(Marie Françoise) Thérèse Martin**, bynames **The Little Flower, St Theresa of the Child Jesus** (1873–97) French saint, born at Alençon. An intensely religious child, she entered the Carmelite convent of Lisieux in Normandy at the age of 15, where she remained until her death from tuberculosis nine years later. During her last years she wrote an account of her life which was published posthumously as the *Histoire d'une âme* (1898, Story of a Soul), showing how the most ordinary person can attain sainthood by following her 'little way' of simple, childlike Christianity. She was canonized in 1925, and in 1947 associated with Joan of Arc as patron saint of France. » Carmelites; Christianity; Joan of Arc; monasticism

therm » British thermal unit

thermae [**ther**miy] The elaborate public bathing complexes that were a standard feature of urban life under the Roman Empire. Functioning very much as community centres, the larger thermal establishments contained far more than changing rooms and hot and cold baths. Among other facilities on offer there might be exercise grounds (*palaestrae*), clubrooms, lecture theatres, and libraries. » Romanization

thermal conduction The transfer of heat through a substance without bulk movement of the substance; thermal conductivity symbol k, units W/(m.K) (watt per metre-kelvin). Heat transfer is through poor conductors via the thermal vibrations of atoms. Metals are good conductors, and transfer heat via conduction electrons in the free electron gas. They typically conduct heat a thousand times better than non-metals such as glass or wood. » convection; electronic structure of solids; heat; phonon; thermal insulation

thermal efficiency In thermodynamics, the ratio of useful work derived from a heat engine to the heat absorbed by it; symbol e, a number between 0 and 1. It represents a theoretical maximum possible efficiency. For car engines, $e = 0.5$; for coal-fired power stations, $e = 0.4$ (approximate values). » Carnot engine; heat engine; thermodynamics

thermal equilibrium In thermodynamics, a characteristic of two systems when heat ceases to flow between them. Quantities such as pressure and temperature, which are monitors of thermal variations, cease to change. For example, a cup of coffee allowed to reach thermal equilibrium will be the same temperature as the surrounding room, and the same temperature throughout the coffee. » equilibrium; heat; thermodynamics

thermal expansion The increase in size observed in most materials when heated. The expansion results from the increased thermal motion of atoms. The change in the length of a solid rod equals the product of its starting length, the change in temperature, and α, the coefficient of expansion. For copper, $\alpha = 1.7 \times 10^{-5}/°C$. » Boyle; heat

thermal insulation Shielding whose function is to reduce heat flow. Heat loss by conduction is stemmed using layers of material having low thermal conductivity. Loss by convection is reduced by preventing the movement of fluids around the object. Loss by heat radiation is reduced using reflective coatings. » screening; thermal conduction

thermal noise In electronic circuits, a background signal due to thermal effects which partially masks the true signal. It is caused by the random thermal motion of conduction electrons in resistive components, and decreases with reduced temperature and resistance. It is one source of audio amplifier hiss. » electronics; resistance

thermal printer A type of printer which generally uses thermally sensitive paper and produces characters using a set of electrically heated wires. Although thermal printers are relatively inexpensive, the special paper they use is not. » printer, computer

thermic lance A torch-like cutting device for resistant steel and alloys, which depends on the fact that iron will burn in oxygen. A main nozzle for a jet of oxygen has a subsidiary nozzle for acetylene, which serves only to pre-heat the metal to the temperature at which it will begin to burn in the stream of oxygen. Thereafter the oxygen stream is sufficient to maintain the burning of the steel. » alloy; iron; steel

Thermidor The *coup d'état* of 16–27 July 1794 (8–9 Thermidor Year II), when Robespierre and his Jacobin supporters were overthrown, ending the most radical phase of the French Revolution. Among the instigators of Thermidor were such former Jacobins as Joseph Fouché and Paul Barras who, with members of the Convention, set about dismantling the machinery of the Reign of Terror. » Barras; Fouché; French Republican calendar; Jacobins (French History); Robespierre

thermionic valve An electronic device (an *electron tube*) containing two or more electrodes, which are used to regulate the flow of electrons in an electric current. A heated cathode emits electrons which are attracted to a positively-biased anode, and the electron flow is controlled by varying the voltage on intermediate electrodes called *control grids*. The simplest type is the diode used in rectifying circuits. Thermionic valves were used in all types of electronic circuit, but have now largely been replaced by semiconductor devices such as the transistor. » anode; diode; rectifier; semiconductor; transistor

thermionics The study of the processes involved in thermionic emission, ie the emission of electrons from a metal surface caused by applying heat to that surface. Normally such electrons would return to the metal, but in devices such as thermionic valves and electron guns they are drawn away by a positively charged anode to give a useful beam of electrons. The effect was discovered by Thomas Edison in 1883. » Edison; electron; electronic structure of solids; field emission; photoelectric effect; secondary emission; thermionic valve

thermistor A temperature sensor constructed from semiconductor material whose electrical resistance falls rapidly as the temperature rises. It is used in electronic circuits measuring or controlling temperature, and in time-delay circuits. » electricity; resistance; semiconductor

thermite A mixture of aluminium and iron oxide which, if ignited, undergoes a fierce chemical reaction producing a high temperature (c.2 400°C) and yielding molten iron (or other metal if another oxide is used). The process was devised in 1895 by German chemist Hans Goldschmidt (1861–1923). It is useful for the preparation of intractable metals, or in welding, and has been used for incendiary bombs. » aluminium; bomb; iron

thermochemistry The study of the energy changes accompanying chemical reactions. These changes are precisely defined for precisely defined reactants and products. They are widely used in determining the energy value of foods. » chemistry

thermocline The depth in the ocean where temperature decreases rapidly. In many ocean areas, including all of the tropics, a permanent thermocline begins at approximately 100 m/325 ft depth. This is just below the surface layer mixed by the wind, where sea surface temperatures may range as high as 28°C. The thermocline may extend to depths of 1 000 m/3 250 ft or more, where temperatures may be as low as 2°C. In some ocean areas, such as the N Atlantic, seasonal warming may produce a shallow 'seasonal thermocline' above the deeper permanent thermocline. » temperature [i]

thermocouple A type of thermometer that allows the direct electronic monitoring of temperature. A temperature-dependent potential difference exists across the junction between two different metals (the *contact potential*). If one such junction is placed in the sample, and the other held at constant temperature, the potential difference between the two junctions is a measure of the sample temperature. » contact potential; thermoelectric effects; thermometer

thermodynamics The study of heat and heat-related phenomena, based on four fundamental laws.

Zeroth Law If two systems are in thermodynamic equilibrium with a third, they will be in thermodynamic equilibrium with one another. For example, two objects left to stand a while in a still room will be the same temperature as the room and therefore as each other.

First Law The sum of the energy changes occurring in some isolated process is zero, which is equivalent to the statement that total energy is conserved. For example, a battery may be used to raise the temperature of some water electrically, in which case chemical energy from the battery is converted into heat; but the total energy of the complete system before and after the circuit is switched on is the same.

Second Law A law giving direction to thermodynamic processes in time, and in so doing forbids some which would otherwise be allowed by the First Law. It may be expressed in several equivalent ways. **1** No heat engine can have a thermal efficiency of 100%, ie it is impossible to convert heat totally into mechanical work; for example, car engines and power stations can never be 100% efficient, no matter how well they are built. **2** No process may have as its only outcome the transfer of heat from a cold object to a hot one; for example, a refrigerator requires power to make an object at room temperature cold, whereas a cold object will warm up to room temperature on its own. **3** A system will always finish in the state which can be realized in the greatest number of ways; for example, a drop of ink in water will finish up dispersed evenly through the water since this corresponds to the greatest number of arrangements of ink and water atoms. **4** For a closed system, entropy is either constant or increasing.

Third Law Absolute zero can never be reached.

Before the 19th-c, it was generally assumed that heat was a material substance, termed *caloric*. Hot objects were thought to contain more caloric than cold ones, and an object's supply of caloric was limited. The modern conception, that heat is a form of energy, and that heat flow is energy transfer, was originally due to the Anglo-American scientist Count Rumford in 1798. Conservation of energy was first understood by French physicist Sadi Carnot in 1830, British physicist James Joule in 1843, and others. Joule used a system of falling weights to drive paddles immersed in water, thereby raising its temperature and establishing the equivalence of mechanical energy and heat (1845). The idea that all forms of energy are equivalent comes from German physicist Hermann von Helmholtz. British physicist Lord Kelvin proposed the absolute thermodynamic temperature scale (1845), which now bears his name. The second law of thermodynamics is due to him (1851) and German physicist Rudolf Clausius (1850). Kelvin developed the notion that mechanical energy gradually dissipates into heat energy, an idea developed by Clausius into the concept of entropy. Classical thermodynamics, which is independent of the microscopic detail of systems, stems largely from their work. Expressing the thermodynamic properties of systems on the assumption that they are composed of large numbers of distinct atoms is termed *statistical mechanics*. » absolute zero; blackbody radiation; Carnot; Clausius; energy; entropy; heat; heat capacity; heat engine; Helmholtz; ideal gas; internal energy; Joule; Joule-Thompson effect; Kelvin; kinetic theory of gases; Rumford; statistical mechanics; temperature [i]; thermal equilibrium; thermometer

thermoelectric effects A general expression for temperature-dependent electrical properties of matter. Thermocouples use a potential difference resulting from the difference in temperature between two junctions of dissimilar metals (the *Seebeck effect*, discovered in 1821 by German physicist Thomas Seebeck 1770–1831). The *Peltier effect* (discovered in 1834 by French physicist Jean Peltier (1785–1845) is the reverse of the Seebeck effect, and may be used to make refrigerators having no moving parts, essentially by operating a thermocouple in reverse. » contact potential; thermocouple

thermogenesis » **specific dynamic action**

thermography A detection technique which converts invisible heat energy into a visible picture. Objects radiate varying amounts of infrared (IR) heat energy, depending on their temperature. Inside a thermograph, a solid-state detector 'sees' the IR, even in the dark or smoke. TV-style pictures show temperatures by variations in brightness or colour. » solid-state device; Plates XI, XIII

thermohaline circulation Marine circulation caused by differences in the temperature and salinity of sea water. These differences are caused by heating or cooling, evaporation or precipitation, and freezing or thawing, and result in density differences in surface sea water. An increase in salinity or a decrease in temperature produces an increase in density, and conversely a decrease in salinity or an increase in temperature produces a decrease in density. Though the density differences appear small (1.02–1.07 g/cm^3), they produce a vertical circulation. When the density of surface water is greater than that of the water below it, it sinks, pushing less dense water aside, until it reaches a level where the water below is denser. Here it spreads laterally. The result is an ocean made up of layers of water with the most dense on the bottom and those of progressively lower densities lying above. The oceans for the most part are vertically stratified in this manner. The water layers having characteristic temperatures and salinities are known as *water masses* or *water types*.

The thermohaline circulation differs from the wind-driven surface water circulation pattern, which is arranged in latitudinal belts following climatic zones. The well-mixed surface layer and the thermocline zone are the zones which experience the greatest changes in physical properties. Below the base of the main ocean thermocline (about 1 000 m/325 ft), variations in physical properties tend to be much smaller. This deep thermohaline circulation is almost completely unconnected with the surface circulation except around Antarctica, where the Antarctic Circumpolar Current extends from the surface to the bottom and forms the main link between the three major ocean basins. In fact, most deep water masses are formed at high latitudes, the bottom waters of all oceans coming from the Antarctic. » current (oceanography); thermocline

thermoluminescence dating A method of dating ancient pottery by measuring the energy accumulated in the crystal lattice of its inclusions of quartz, through the breakdown over time of naturally occurring uranium. The technique is now increasingly extended to burnt flint, calcite, and sediments. » archaeology; quartz; uranium

thermometer A device for measuring temperature. In household alcohol and mercury thermometers, heat causes the liquid in a reservoir to expand, forcing some of the liquid up a graduated tube. The graduations are fixed by calibration against known markers of chosen temperature scale. The first reliable mercury-in-glass thermometer was invented by German physicist Gabriel Fahrenheit in 1714. » Fahrenheit; pyrometer; temperature [i]; thermocouple

thermonuclear bomb » **hydrogen bomb** [i]

thermoplastic A class of resin which softens and hardens reversibly on heating and cooling any number of times. » plastics; resin

Thermopylae [ther**mo**pilee] A pass between mountains and sea in central Greece. The failure of the Greeks to hold it in 480 BC enabled the Persians to invade Attica, capture Athens, and sack the Acropolis. » Acropolis; Persian Wars

thermoset A class of resin which sets irreversibly on heating. Examples include epoxy resins such as 'araldite'. » epoxy resin [i]; plastics; polymerization

thermosphere The upper atmospheric layer above the mesopause (c.80 km/50 ml, separating the mesosphere from the thermosphere) in which atmospheric densities are very low. The lower part is composed mainly of nitrogen (N_2) and oxygen in molecular (O_2) and atomic (O) forms, whereas above 200 km/125 ml atomic oxygen predominates over N_2 and N. Temperatures increase with altitude because of the absorption of ultraviolet radiation by atomic oxygen. The term **ionosphere** is also used for the atmosphere above 80 km/50 ml. » atmosphere [i]; ionosphere; mesosphere

Theseus [**thee**syoos] A legendary king and national hero of Athens, who features in the story of Oedipus, Procrustes, the Argonauts, and others. With Ariadne's help he killed the Minotaur; he conquered the Amazons, and married their queen, Hippolyta; later, he married Phaedra. » Ariadne; Hippolytus; Minotaur; Phaedra

Thessalonians, Letters to the New Testament writings of Paul to the church he founded in the capital of the Roman province of Macedonia, although his authorship of the second letter is disputed. In the first letter (perhaps c.50 AD), he defends his earlier ministry in Thessalonica against Jewish propaganda, appears gratified at their perseverance despite persecution, and instructs them about ethical matters and Christ's second coming. The second letter is similar, but emphasizes the persecution of the community, and tries to dampen a fanaticism based on the belief that the Day of the Lord had already arrived, leading to idleness. » New Testament; Paul, St; Pauline Letters; parousia

Thessaloníki [thesalo**nee**kee] » **Salonica**

Thessaly, Gr **Thessalía** [**the**salee] pop (1981) 695 654; area 14 037 sq km/5 418 sq ml. Fertile agricultural region of E Greece, bounded W by the Pindhos Mts, and E by the Aegean Sea; annexed by Greece, 1881; capital, Larisa; famed in ancient times for its horses; major cereal region in Greece. » Greece [i]

Thetis [**the**tis] In Greek mythology, a nereid destined to bear a son greater than his father. This was the secret known to Prometheus. She was married to Peleus, and was the mother of Achilles. » Achilles; nereid; Peleus; Prometheus

thiamine A water soluble vitamin (B_1) which acts as an enzyme co-factor in the oxidation of glucose. A deficiency leads to beriberi, a disease once common especially in SE Asia, where polished rice, low in vitamin B_1, was the staple food. Thiamine is more rapidly degraded in the cooking process when the medium is alkaline; thus, the use of soda in the boiling of vegetables reduces thiamine levels. » beriberi; enzyme; glucose [i]; vitamins [i]

thiazole [**thi**yazohl] C_3H_3NS, boiling point 117°C. A five-membered ring compound; a colourless liquid, the basis for a range of dyestuffs. This ring system occurs in vitamin B_1 (*thiamine*). » ring; vitamins [i]

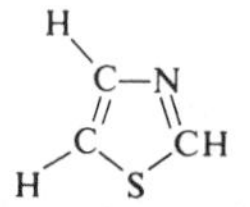

thick-knee A plover-like bird, wide-spread; legs with swollen ankles (not knees!); plumage mottled; eyes large, yellow; inhabits dry pebbled areas or water margins; eats invertebrates; mainly nocturnal; also known as the **stone curlew**, **stone plover**, **Norfolk plover**, **dikkop**, **willaroo**, or **goggle-eye**. (Family: *Burhinidae*, 9 species.) » plover

thickhead A songbird, native to E India, SE Asia, and Australia; rounded head and strong bill, inhabits forest and scrubland; eats insects; relatively inactive and unafraid of humans; also known as the **whistler**. (Family: *Pachycephalidae*, 46 species.) » songbird

Thiers, (Louis) Adolphe [tyair] (1797–1877) French statesman, historian, and first President of the Third Republic (1871–3), born in Marseilles. Educated at Aix, he became a lawyer and journalist. He held several posts in the government of Louis Philippe, and was twice Prime Minister (1836, 1839). He supported Napoleon in 1848, but was arrested and banished at the *coup d'état* of 1851, only to re-enter the Chamber in 1863 as a critic of Napoleon's policies. After the collapse of the Second Empire he became chief of the executive power in the provisional government, suppressed the Paris Commune, and was elected President. Defeated by a coalition of monarchists, he resigned in 1873. He died at St Germain-en-Laye. His most ambitious literary work was the 20-volume *L'histoire du consulat et de l'empire* (1845–62, History of the Consulate and the Empire). » Charles X (of France); Commune of Paris; July Revolution; Louis Philippe; Napoleon III

Thiès [tyes] 14°49N 16°52W, pop (1979) 126 886. Capital of Thiès region, Senegal, 55 km/34 ml E of Dakar; airfield; railway junction; African cultural and craft centre noted for its tapestries; aluminium, cotton, phosphates, cement, asbestos. » Senegal [i]

Thimphu [**thim**poo] or **Thimbu**, also **Tashi Chho Dzong** 27°32N 89°43E; pop (1980e) town, 9 301; district 76 647. Official capital of Bhutan, C Asia, on R Raidak; founded 1581; fortified town, a major monastery; capital since 1962; air strip; rice, wheat, maize, timber; Tashi Chho Dzong castle. » Bhutan [i]

thin films Fine layers of material formed by deposition on some substrate, varying in thickness from single atom layers, about 10^{-10} m, to 10^{-6} m. They are used as samples in analytic techniques such as transmission electron microscopy and neutron diffraction. The materials in a thin film configuration can have structures distinct from those in the bulk state, and the structure of the film material can be controlled by the production method. A number of novel effects (such as the quantum Hall effect) are observed in thin films, often because the electrons are constrained to move in a plane. Commercial uses include reflective coatings on compact discs, anti-reflective coatings on lenses, and the production of electronic components and integrated circuits. They are formed using a variety of techniques, such as vacuum deposition, molecular beam epitaxy, electroplating, and others. » molecular beam epitaxy; quantum Hall effect; solid-state physics; sputtering; surface physics; vacuum deposition

Thingvellir [theeng**vet**lir] 64°15N 21°06W. National shrine of Iceland, 52 km/32 ml E of Reykjavík at the N end of Thingvalla Water; the Icelandic *Althing*, oldest parliament in the world, was founded here in 930; focal point of the country until 1880; a national cemetery. » Iceland [i]

Thíra [**thee**ra] » **Santorini**

third-generation computers » **computer generations**

third stream A type of music which aims to combine the styles of Western art music with those of jazz or various ethnic traditions. Among composers associated with it are André Hodeir (1921–), John Lewis (1920–), and Günther Schuller (1925–). » jazz

Third World » **Three Worlds theory**

Thirteen Colonies The American provinces that revolted against British rule and declared independence in 1776. From N to S they were New Hampshire, Massachusetts, Rhode Island, Connecticut, New York, New Jersey, Pennsylvania, Delaware, Maryland, Virginia, N Carolina, S Carolina, and Georgia. Fourteen states actually declared independence, because Vermont separated from New York at the same time. In imperial terms the Thirteen Colonies had been less important to British statesmen than the sugar-producing islands of the W Indies. » American Revolution

thirty-eighth parallel The boundary line proposed for the partition of Korea at the Potsdam Conference in 1945, after the defeat of Japan (who had annexed Korea in 1910). In 1948 the Democratic People's Republic of North Korea was proclaimed (but not recognized by the Western powers). Since the Korean War, the 38th parallel again forms the line of division between North and South Korea. » Korea [i]; Korea, North [i]; Korean War

Thirty-nine Articles A set of doctrinal formulations for the Church of England, issued after several earlier efforts under Elizabeth I in 1563 (but without Article 29 about 'eating the body', in order to appease the Romanists), and finally adopted as a whole by the Convocation of 1571. They do not comprise a creed, but rather a general Anglican view on a series of contentious matters in order to maintain the unity of the Anglican churches and Anglican Communion. Some articles are ambiguous in wording, but they are generally opposed to both extreme Romanist and extreme Anabaptist views. They concern matters such as the presence of Christ in the Eucharist, the authority of Scriptures and the Councils, and the doctrine of predestination. Church of England clergy have been required since 1865 to affirm these principles in general terms. » Anabaptists; Anglican Communion; Church of England; Roman Catholicism

Thirty Tyrants The Spartan-backed clique which seized power in Athens towards the end of the Peloponnesian War (404 BC), overthrew the democracy, and instituted a reign of terror. They were overthrown in 403 BC and the democracy restored. » Peloponnesian War; Sparta (Greek history)

Thirty Years' War (1618–48) A complex phase, specifically German in origin, of a long and intermittent power struggle between the kings of France and the Habsburg rulers of the Holy Roman Empire and Spain (1491–1715). The background was complicated by the developing confrontation between militant Calvinism and re-invigorated, post-Tridentine Catholicism; also by the underlying constitutional conflict between the Holy Roman Emperor and the German princes, illustrated in the Bohemian Revolt (1618). With the Elector Frederick V's defeat (1620) and intervention by other powers (eg Sweden, Transylvania, Denmark, France), the conflict intensified, spreading to other theatres. Isolated as Spain collapsed, the Emperor opened negotiations (1643–8) which ended the German war, at the Peace of Westphalia. » Calvinism; Habsburgs; Holy Roman Empire; Roman Catholicism; Trent, Council of

thistle The name applied to several spiny plants of the daisy family, *Compositae*, many belonging to the genera *Cirsium* and *Carduus*. All have leaves with spiny margins, flower heads often almost globular, solitary or in clusters, surrounded by overlapping, usually spine-tipped bracts; florets reddish, purple, or white. (Family: *Compositae*.) » bract; daisy

Thistle, The Most Ancient and Most Noble Order of the A Scottish order of chivalry, probably instituted by James III of Scotland. There are 16 members under the sovereign (though royal knights may be additional to this number). The motto of the order is *Nemo me impune lacessit* (Lat 'No-one provokes me with impunity'); the ribbon is green. » decoration; James III

Thomas, St (1st-c AD), feast day 21 Dec. A disciple of Jesus, listed as one of the twelve apostles in the Gospels, but most prominent in John's Gospel where he is also called Didymus ('the Twin'), and where he is portrayed as doubting the resurrection until he touches the wounds of the risen Christ (*John* 20). Early church traditions describe him subsequently as a missionary to the Parthians or a martyr in India. Many later apocryphal works bear his name, such as the *Gospel of Thomas*, *Acts of Thomas*, and *Apocalypse of Thomas*. He is the patron saint of Portugal. » apostle; Jesus Christ

Thomas, Dylan (Marlais) (1914–53) British poet, born in Swansea, Wales. He worked as a journalist, and established himself with the publication of *Eighteen Poems* in 1934. He married Caitlin Macnamara in 1936, and published *Twenty-Five Poems* the same year. His *Collected Poems* appeared in 1952, and he then produced the radio 'play for voices', *Under Milk Wood* (1954). He also wrote an unfinished novel, *Adventures in the Skin Trade* (1955), and several collections of short stories, many of which were written originally for radio. He became an alcoholic in later years, and died in New York City during a lecture tour. » poetry; Welsh literature

Thomas, (Philip) Edward (1878–1917) British poet and critic, born in London. Educated at St Paul's and Oxford, he became a hack writer of reviews, critical studies, and topographical works. Not until 1914, encouraged by Robert Frost, did he realize his potential as a poet, writing most of his work during active service between 1915 and his death at Arras, France. » English literature; Frost; poetry

Thomas, Sir George (Alan) (1881–1972) British badminton player, born in Istanbul, Turkey. He was the winner of a record 21 All-England titles between 1903 and 1928, including the singles title four times (1920–3). In 1934 he was elected president of the International Badminton Federation, a post he held for 21 years, and in 1939 presented a Cup (the 'Thomas Cup') to be contested by national teams. He represented England for 27 years at badminton, was also an international at lawn tennis and chess, and was twice British chess champion. » badminton

Thomas, R(onald) S(tuart) (1913–) British poet, born in Cardiff, Wales. Educated at the University of Wales, he was ordained in 1936 and became a rector in the Church of Wales (1942–78). His collections include *Poetry for Supper* (1958), *The Bread of Truth* (1963), and *Laboratories of the Spirit* (1975). » poetry; Welsh literature

Thomas à Becket » **Becket, Thomas à**

Thomas à Kempis » **Kempis, Thomas à**

Thomas Aquinas, St » **Aquinas, St Thomas**

Thomism [**toh**mizm] In Christian philosophical theology, the name given to the doctrines of Thomas Aquinas, and to later schools claiming descent from him. » Aquinas; Christianity

Thompson, Colonel John T(alafierro) (1860–1940) US inventor, who in 1918 originated the Thompson gun, one of the world's first effective sub-machine guns. The 'Tommy Gun' became infamous as a favourite weapon of the gangsters of prohibition America, and as the M1 was widely used by Allied forces in World War 2. » sub-machine gun

Thompson, Daley (Francis Morgan) (1958–) British athlete, born in London, the son of a Nigerian father and a Scottish mother. An outstanding decathlete, his first major honour was in the 1978 Commonwealth Games, which he retained in 1982 and 1986. He was world champion (1983), European champion (1982, 1986), and Olympic champion (1980, 1984), injury preventing a third successive Olympic title in 1988, when he finished fourth. He broke the world record four times between 1980 and 1984. » athletics

Thompson, Francis (1859–1907) British poet, born at Preston, Lancashire. He studied for the priesthood, turned to medicine, but failed to graduate. He was rescued from poverty, ill health, and opium addiction by Wilfrid and Alice Meynell, to whom he had sent some poems for Meynell's magazine *Merry England*. His later work was mainly religious in theme; it includes the well-known *The Hound of Heaven*. He died in London. » English literature; poetry

Thomsen, Christian » **Three Age System**

Thomson, James (1700–48) British poet, born at Ednam, Roxburgh, Scotland. Educated at Edinburgh for the ministry, he abandoned his studies and turned to writing in London (1725). He is best known for his four-part work, *The Seasons* (1730), the first major nature poem in English; his ode 'Rule, Britannia', from *Alfred, a Masque* (1740); and the Spenserian allegory, *The Castle of Indolence* (1748). He died at Richmond, Surrey. » English literature; poetry; Spenser

Thomson, Sir J(oseph) J(ohn) (1856–1940) British physicist, born near Manchester. He was educated at Cambridge, where he became professor of experimental physics in 1884. He showed in 1897 that cathode rays were rapidly-moving particles, and by measuring their speed and specific charge deduced that these 'corpuscles' (electrons) must be nearly 2 000 times smaller in mass than the lightest known atomic particle, the hydrogen ion. He received the Nobel Prize for Physics in 1906, was knighted in 1908, and made the Cavendish Laboratory a major research institution. He died at Cambridge. » nuclear physics

Thomson (of Fleet), Roy (Herbert), 1st Baron (1894–1976) British newspaper and television magnate, born in Toronto, Canada. He held a variety of jobs, and became prosperous after setting up his own radio transmitter at North Bay (1931), founding what later became the NBC network. He started other radio stations, and bought many Canadian and US newspapers. He settled in Edinburgh on acquiring his first British paper, *The Scotsman* (1952), bought the Kemsley newspapers in 1959 (including the *Sunday Times*, to which he added the first colour supplement in 1962), and in 1966 took over *The Times*. Other business interests included Scottish Television and North Sea oil. He was created a peer in 1964, and died in London.

Thomson, Virgil (1896–89) US composer and critic, born in Kansas City. He studied at Harvard and Paris, and was influenced by *Les Six*. He is best known for his operas with libretti by Gertrude Stein, *Four Saints in Three Acts* (1934) and *The Mother of Us All* (1947). He also wrote symphonies, ballets, and choral, chamber, and film music. He was music critic of the *New York Herald Tribune* (1940–54). He died in New York City. » *Six, Les*; Stein, Gertrude

Thomson, Sir William » **Kelvin (Lord)**

Thor In Norse mythology, the god of Thunder, son of Odin and Frigga; also known as the Hurler. His hammer is called Miolnir. In the stories, much is made of his appetite for food and drink. He is the strongest of the gods, and protects them. At Ragnarok he will fight with the Midgard-Serpent, kill it, and then die. » Germanic religion; Ragnarok

thorax That part of the body between the neck and the abdomen enclosed by the thoracic part of the vertebral column, the ribs, and the sternum, and separated from the abdomen by the diaphragm; also known as the **thoracic cage** or **chest**. Roughly cone-shaped, it surrounds and protects the lungs, heart, and great vessels, and also contains the oesophagus, thymus gland, and part of the thyroid gland. It provides support against the elastic pull of the lungs, which would otherwise collapse. The thorax is able to change its shape (and thus volume) by moving its bony parts with respect to each other, as well as by contracting the diaphragm. The breast sits on the upper part of the front of the thorax. » diaphragm; rib; sternum; vertebral column

Thoreau, Henry David [tho**roh**] (1817–62) US essayist and poet, born and died at Concord, Massachusetts. Educated at Harvard in 1837, he taught for a while, and c.1839 began his walks and studies of nature which became his major occupation. In 1845 he built himself a shanty in the woods by Walden Pond, near Concord, where his writings included *Walden, or Life in the Woods* (1854). He supported himself by general jobs, and occasionally lectured and wrote for magazines. After his death, several books were published, based on his daily journal (from 1835) of his walks and observations, such as *Summer* (1884) and *Winter* (1887). » American literature; poetry

thorn apple An evil-smelling annual weed throughout most of the N hemisphere; up to 1 m/3¼ ft high; leaves coarsely toothed; flowers trumpet-shaped, white to blue; fruit a spiny, ovoid capsule containing poisonous seeds; also called **jimson weed**, possibly after Jamestown, Virginia, the site of early records of its narcotic effects on humans. (*Datura stramonium*. Family: *Solanaceae*.) » annual; narcotics

thornbill An Australian warbler, native to Australia and New Guinea; inhabits woodland, scrub, and savannah; eats insects and seeds; also known as the **thornbill warbler**. The name is also used for eight species of hummingbird. (Genus: *Acanthiza*, 12 species. Family: *Acanthizidae*.) » hummingbird; warbler

Thorndike, Dame (Agnes) Sybil (1882–1976) British actress, born at Gainsborough, Lincolnshire. She trained as a pianist, but turned to the stage, making her debut in 1904, and joining a repertory company in Manchester. In 1924 she played the title role in the first English performance of Shaw's *Saint Joan*, and during World War 2 was a notable member of the Old Vic Company. She married the actor **Lewis Casson** (1875–1969) in 1908, and was made a Dame in 1931. She died in London. » theatre

Thornhill, Sir James (1675–1734) English Baroque painter, born at Melcombe Regis, Dorset. He executed paintings for the dome of St Paul's, Blenheim, Hampton Court, and Greenwich Hospital, and founded a drawing school, where Hogarth (who became his son-in-law) was one of his pupils. In 1718 he was made history painter to the king. Knighted in 1720, he became an MP in 1722, and died at Thornhill, Dorset. » Baroque (art and architecture); English art; Hogarth

thorny devil » **Moloch** (reptile)

thoroughbred The fastest breed of horse (over 65 kph/40 mph), developed in England for racing; height, 16 hands/1.6 m/5¼ ft; elegant, athletic, highly-strung; all descended from three Arab stallions of the early 18th-c – the *Darley Arabian*, the *Godolphin Arabian*, and the *Byerley Turk*; also known as **English thoroughbred** or **racehorse**. » Arab horse; falabella; horse [i]

Thorpe, (John) Jeremy (1929–) British Liberal politician. Educated at Eton and Oxford, he became a barrister in 1954, and an MP in 1959. Elected Leader of the Liberal Party in 1967, he resigned the leadership in 1976 following a series of allegations of a previous homosexual relationship with a Mr Norman Scott. In 1979, shortly after losing his seat in the General Election, he was acquitted of charges of conspiracy and incitement to murder Mr Scott. » Liberal Party (UK)

Thorvaldsen, Bertel (c.1768–1844) Danish Neoclassical sculptor, born and died in Copenhagen. He studied at Copenhagen and Rome, working in both places. His best-known pieces include 'Christ and the Twelve Apostles', the reliefs 'Night and Morning', the 'Dying Lion' at Lucerne, and the Cambridge statue of Byron. All the works in his possession he bequeathed, with the bulk of his fortune, to his country. » Neoclassicism (art); sculpture

Thoth [**thohth, toht**] An ancient Egyptian Moon-god, sometimes depicted with the head of an ibis, sometimes as a baboon. He wears a crown showing the Moon's disc. The god of words, magic, and scribes; in the Underworld he records the souls of the dead. He is usually identified with Hermes.

Thothmes III » **Thutmose III**

thought experiment In physics, an experiment visualized but not performed because it is too difficult, but which nonetheless may demonstrate important principles; also called a **gedanken-experiment**. The classic example is Einstein's analysis of experiments performed in free-falling or accelerating lifts to demonstrate the equivalence principle. » Einstein; equivalence principle

Thousand, Expedition of the (1860) A military campaign led by Garibaldi, originally involving 1 146 men, which formed a crucial stage in the Italian Risorgimento. Sailing from Genoa, they arrived in Sicily, and quickly defeated Neapolitan forces. Assisted by a local popular rising, they seized Sicily, crossed to the mainland, and four months later had liberated the Kingdom of Naples. » Garibaldi; Risorgimento

Thrace, Gr **Thráki** [thrays] pop (1981) 345 220; area 8 578 sq km/3 311 sq ml. NE region of Greece, bounded N by Bulgaria, E by Turkey, and S by the Aegean Sea; in classical times, part of an area associated with the worship of Dionysius; area now divided between Turkey, Greece, and Bulgaria; capital, Komotini; region of fertile plains, producing corn, wine, rice, and tobacco. » Dionysius; Greece [i]

threadfin Any of the tropical marine and estuarine fish in the family *Polynemidae* (3 genera); long free pectoral fin rays which serve in part as sensitive feelers, and from which they derive their name; body length may reach over 1.5 m/5 ft; several are valuable food fish. » fish [i]

Three Age System The chronological division of Old World prehistory into three successive ages of **Stone**, **Bronze**, and **Iron**. Rooted in classical ideas about the past taken up by such Renaissance scholars as the naturalist Michele Mercati (1541–93), the scheme owes its archaeological exploitation to the Dane, Christian Jürgensen Thomsen (1788–1865), who adopted it in 1819 to classify the collections of the new National Museum in Copenhagen. It became widely influential a generation later with the English publication of Thomsen's *Ledetraad til Nordisk Oldkyndighed* (1836, A Guide to Northern Antiquities), and his pupil Jens Worsaae's *Danmarks Oldtid* (1843, The Primaeval Antiquities of Denmark). The subdivision of the Stone Age into the **Palaeolithic** (**Old Stone Age**), characterized by chipped stone, and the **Neolithic** (**New Stone Age**), characterized by polished stone tools, stems from the English archaeologist Sir John Lubbock's *Prehistoric Times* (1865). The term **Mesolithic** (**Middle Stone Age**), covering the five millennia following the end of the last glaciation, was also coined in the 1860s, though **Chalcolithic** for the **Copper** or earliest Bronze Age belongs to more recent times. » Acheulian; Aurignacian; archaeology; Beaker culture; Gravettian; Kurgan culture; La Tène; Magdalenian; Maglemosian; Mousterian; Natufian; Solutrian

three-D (3-D) films » **stereoscopic photography**

Three Emperors' League (Ger *Dreikaiserbund*) An entente (1873, renewed 1881 and 1884) between Emperors William I of Germany, Francis Joseph of Austria-Hungary, and Alexander II of Russia. It was designed by Bismarck to protect Germany by isolating France and stabilizing SE Europe. Largely superseded by the Dual Alliance (1879) of Germany and Austria-Hungary, it lapsed in 1887. » Bismarck

Three Worlds theory A theory that sees the world as being divided into three main blocs of countries, defined by their economic status. These are the developed capitalist economies (the **First World**), the developed communist countries (the **Second World**), and underdeveloped countries (the **Third World**), covering most of Latin America and recently independent African and Asian states. The Third World countries tend to adopt a position of neutrality, thereby dividing the world politically in three. The large number and diversity of Third World nations makes an adequate definition impossible: the concept includes the oil-rich countries alongside the poorest countries. Some (including the United Nations) recognize a 'Fourth World', of the 25 poorest nations. » capitalism; communism; developing countries

thresher shark Large and very distinctive surface-living shark, widespread in tropical to temperate seas; easily recognized by the remarkably long upper lobe of tail fin which may exceed half its body length; tail lobe used to round up shoals of fish by thrashing the water surface; body length up to 6 m/20 ft. (*Alopias vulpinus*. Family: *Alopiidae*.) » fish [i]; shark

threshold In psychology, the physically measured value of stimulation at which an observer's response changes from one category to another. The smallest amount of stimulation required for detection is the **absolute** threshold; the smallest detectable difference between sources of stimulation is the **difference** threshold. » acuity

thrift A densely tufted perennial, woody at base, native to Europe; leaves grass-like, bluish green; flowers pink, scented, in long-stalked, hemispherical heads; also called **sea pink**. It is a mainly coastal plant, occasionally found inland. (*Armeria maritima*. Family: *Plumbaginaceae*.) » perennial

thrip A minute insect in which the wings, when present, are slender with a long fringe of hairs; mouthparts specialized for piercing and sucking; feeds on plant juices, fungi, pollen, and body juices of insects. (Order: *Thysanoptera*, c.5 000 species.) » insect [i]

Throckmorton, Sir Nicholas (1515–71) English diplomat. He fought at Pinkie (1547), was knighted in 1547, and became Ambassador to France and Scotland. In 1569 he was imprisoned for promoting the scheme to marry Mary, Queen of Scots, to the Duke of Norfolk, but soon released. He died in London. His daughter, **Elizabeth**, married Sir Walter Raleigh. His nephew, **Francis** (1554–84) was executed for planning a conspiracy to overthrow Elizabeth I. » Elizabeth I; Mary, Queen of Scots

thrombophlebitis » **phlebitis**

thrombosis The formation of a blood clot within a blood vessel, resulting in a partial or complete blockage. Its basis is the formation of the protein, fibrin, which is formed from a soluble precursor, fibrinogen. Fibrin forms a mesh in which platelets and red blood cells are trapped, and produces a plug to the flow of blood. The conversion of fibrinogen to fibrin is activated by a complex series of enzymes which include 13 coagulation factors and requires calcium ions. The process is initiated by contact of the blood with damaged blood vessels and tissues. Thrombosis may occur within any artery or vein in the body. » blood vessels [i]

thrush (bird) A medium-sized songbird, widespread, inhabiting diverse regions from tropical rain forests to deserts; often feeds on ground; eats fruit and invertebrates. Some species are called **chats**. (Family: *Turdidae*, c.300 species.) » blackbird; bluebird; chat; fieldfare; mistle thrush; nightingale; ouzel; redstart; redwing; robin; solitaire; song thrush; songbird; stonechat; wheatear; whinchat

thrush (disease) » **candidiasis**

Thucydides [thyoo**sid**ideez] **1** (c.460–c.400 BC) Athenian aristocratic historian of the Peloponnesian War. Though scrupulously accurate in his narrative of events, he is not altogether unprejudiced. Exiled for 20 years by the democracy for military incompetence in the N Aegean (424 BC), he is consistently critical of the democratic system and its leaders in the war years. » Peloponnesian War **2** (5th-c BC) Athenian politician, son-in-law of Cimon, and leader of the opposition to Pericles until ostracized in 443 BC. He was probably a relative of Thucydides, the historian. » Cimon; ostracism; Pericles

Thuggee [**thuh**gee] An Indian cult which combined robbery and ritual murder (usually by strangling) in the name of Kali (the Hindu goddess of destruction). Under British Governor-General Lord Bentinck (1833–5), and his agent Captain William Sleeman, vigorous steps were taken to eradicate the problem. » Hinduism; Kali

thuja » **arbor vitae**

Thule [**thyoo**lee] 77°30N 69°29W. Eskimo settlement in NW Greenland; on coast of Hayes Halvø peninsula; founded as a Danish trading post in 1910; Danish–US airforce base nearby; scientific installations; name also given by the ancients to the most northerly land of Europe, an island described c.310 BC by the Greek navigator, Pytheas. » Greenland [i]

Thumb, Tom » **Stratton, Charles**

Thummim » **Urim and Thummim**

Thun, Fr **Thoune** [toon] 46°46N 7°38E, pop (1980) 36 891. Town in Bern canton, Switzerland, on the R Aare near L Thun; gateway to the Bernese Oberland; railway junction; engineering, watches, cheese; castle (1191). » Switzerland [i]

Thunder Bay 48°27N 89°12W, pop (1981) 112 486. Resort and port in S Ontario, S Canada, on NW shore of L Superior; created in 1970 by the union of Fort William and Port Arthur; airfield; railway; university (1965); grain storage and shipping point; shipbuilding, paper, pulp, vehicles; Centennial Park. » Ontario; Superior, Lake

Thunderbird or **Skyamsen** A totem figure in NW American Indian religion. Lightning flashes from its eye and it feeds on killer whales. The chief of the Thunderbirds was Golden Eagle (Keneun). » American Indians

thunderstorm A storm of heavy rain, thunder, and lightning which occurs when cumulonimbus clouds develop in unstable, humid conditions. As air rises, condensation releases latent heat, and this increases the available energy, reinforcing the rising tendency of the air. Above the level at which condensation occurs, supercooled water droplets coalesce to form precipitation-sized droplets. As rain falls, instability decreases, the cloud ceases to grow, and precipitation soon stops. However, a series of cumulonimbus clouds may allow storms to continue. During a thunderstorm, an electric charge builds up at the base of the cloud, and when large enough, is discharged in the form of lightning. Thunderstorms are often associated with the passage of a cold front during a depression, and with intense heating and moisture availability at low latitudes. » cloud [i]; cumulonimbus clouds; lightning; rainfall; storm

Thurber, James (Grover) (1894–1961) US writer and cartoonist, born at Columbus, Ohio. Educated at Ohio State, he left without taking a degree, and became a journalist, making his reputation on the staff of *The New Yorker* from 1927. His drawings first appeared in his book *Is Sex Necessary?* (1929), and there are several anthologies of his work, such as *Thurber's Dogs* (1955) and the posthumous *Vintage Thurber* (1963). He died in New York City.

Thuringia A historic area of Germany, including the Harz Mts and Thuringian forest, a march or frontier region against the Slavs. Controlled by various dynasties, from the 10th-c Dukes of Saxony to the House of Wettin (1265), it was divided between Saxony, Hesse-Kassel, and others from 1485–1920, and is now a province within united Germany. » Germany

Thuringian Forest, Ger **Thüringer Wald** Region of forest land covering about two-thirds of the county of Suhl in S Germany between the Weisse Elster (E) and R Werra (W); formerly included in the German state of Thuringia, becoming part of East Germany in 1945; popular tourist region; winter sports resort at Oberhof. » Germany [i]

Thurso 58°35N 3°32W, pop (1981) 8 896. Port town in Caithness district, Highland region, N Scotland; on N coast, at head of R Thurso, 30 km/19 ml NW of Wick; N terminus of railway system; car ferry service to Orkney from Scrabster; St Peter's Church (17th-c), Thurso Folk Museum. » Highland; Scotland [i]

Thutmose III, also **Thothmes** or **Tuthmosis** (?–1450 BC) Egyptian pharaoh (c.1504–1450 BC), one of the greatest of Egyptian rulers, who re-established Egyptian control over Syria and Nubia, and ornamented his kingdom with revenues from these conquests. He built the temple of Amon at Karnak, and erected many obelisks, including 'Cleopatra's Needle'. In the early

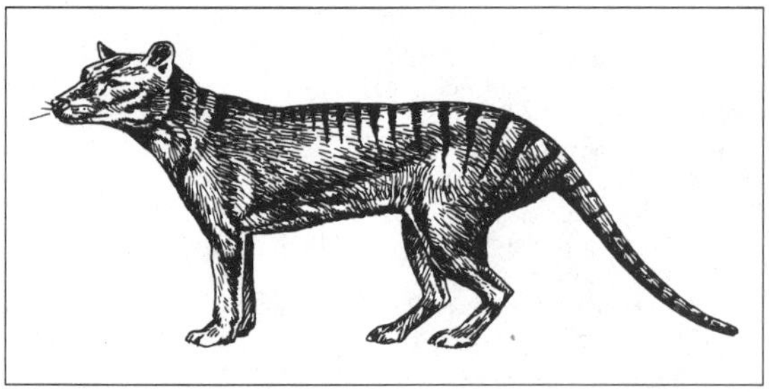

Thylacine

years of his reign, power lay in the hands of Hatshepsut, the sister/wife of Thutmose II.

Thyestes [thiyesteez] In Greek mythology, a son of Pelops, who inherited the curse upon that house. His brother Atreus set before him a dish made of the flesh of Thyestes' children. Later, he became the father of Aegisthus. » Aegisthus; Atreus; Pelops

thylacine [**thiy**lasiyn] An Australian marsupial, probably extinct since the 1930s; length, up to 1.6 m/5¼ ft; dog-like, with long thick tail; sandy brown with dark vertical stripes over back and hindquarters; could sit upright on hind legs and tail like a kangaroo; female with short backward-facing pouch covering four teats; when last known, was nocturnal in the Tasmanian mountains; ate wallabies, smaller marsupials, birds, and (since European settlement) sheep; also known as the **Tasmanian wolf** or **tiger**. (Family: *Thylacinidae*.) » marsupial [i]

thyme A small spreading aromatic shrub, often only a few cm high, native to Europe and Asia; leaves small, narrow, in opposite pairs; flowers 2-lipped, usually pink or mauve, in crowded whorls forming spikes or heads. It is widely cultivated as a culinary herb, with variegated forms as ornamentals. It is a large genus, with numerous narrowly-defined species and hybrids, many with distinctive scents and tastes. The best-known are **common thyme** (*Thymus vulgaris*), **lemon thyme** (*Thymus citriodora*), and **carroway thyme** (*Thymus herba-barona*). (Genus: *Thymus*, c.400 species. Family: *Labiatae*.) » herb; shrub

thymine [**thiy**meen] $C_5H_6N_2O_2$. One of the pyrimidine bases in

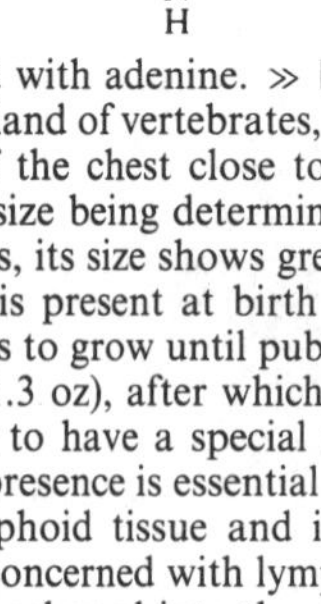

DNA, usually paired with adenine. » DNA [i]; pyrimidines

thymus A lymphoid gland of vertebrates, which in mammals lies in the upper part of the chest close to the great vessels and heart, its shape and size being determined by the surrounding structures. In humans, its size shows great individual variation at any given age; it is present at birth (average weight 13 g/0.5 oz), and continues to grow until puberty (average weight in the adolescent 37 g/1.3 oz), after which it gradually regresses. The thymus appears to have a special relation to cells of the vascular system. Its presence is essential in the newborn for the development of lymphoid tissue and immunological competence. In adults it is concerned with lymphocyte production, of which only a few are released into the circulation, the remainder being destroyed within the gland itself. In early life, precursor cells migrate from bone marrow into the thymus, where they mature to become T-lymphocytes (*T-cells*) responsible for cellular immunity. » gland; lymphocyte; lymphoid tissue; severe combined immunodeficiency

thyratron An electronic valve filled with a gas (usually mercury vapour or an inert gas) at low pressure. It is used for switching, and as a controlled rectifier in applications such as welding. Such valves are now being replaced by semiconductor devices. » gas **1**; rectifier; semiconductor; thyristor

thyristor A semiconductor device that acts as a switch; also called a **silicon-controlled rectifier**. A flow of current can be initiated by a signal, and the current then becomes independent of the signal. This flow will stop only if the voltage across the thyristor is reversed. Thyristors are replacing gas-filled electronic valves. » rectifier; semiconductor; solid-state device; thyratron

thyrocalcitonin » **calcitonin**

thyroid gland An endocrine gland of vertebrates situated in the region of the neck, overlying the lower part of the larynx and the upper part of the trachea. Because of its attachment to the larynx, it moves upward on swallowing. In humans its size varies with age, sex, and general nutrition, increasing slightly in women during menstruation and pregnancy. The thyroid secretes thyroid hormone and calcitonin (from C-cells). Unlike other endocrine glands, it maintains a large store of hormone. » cretinism; goitre; hormones; hyperthyroidism; larynx; myxoedema

thyroid hormone A collective term for iodine-containing amine hormones secreted from vertebrate thyroid glands. In humans and other mammals, the principle hormones are thyroxine (T_4) and trilodothyronine (T_3), which have important roles in foetal development and throughout life in the control of metabolism. Their synthesis and release is controlled by *thyroid-stimulating hormone* (TSH), a glycoprotein hormone produced in the front lobe of the pituitary gland of vertebrates, also known as *thyrotrophin*. In amphibian tadpoles, thyroid hormone is essential for metamorphosis. » amines; cretinism; dwarfism; hormones; hyperthyroidism; hypothyroidism; myxoedema; pituitary gland; thyroid gland

thyrotrophin » **thyroid hormone**

Thysanoptera [thiysan**op**tuhra] » **thrip**

Tiahuanaco [teea**hwa**nakoh] An ancient urban and ceremonial settlement covering 4 sq km/1.5 sq ml near the S end of L Titicaca, Bolivia. At an altitude of 3 842 m/12 600 ft, it was occupied c.1500 BC–AD 1200, flourishing particularly c.500–1000 AD with a population of c.30 000. The ceremonial core, covering 50 ha/125 acres, is notable for the Akapana, a stone platform-mound 200 m/660 ft square and 15 m/50 ft high.

Tiananmen Square The largest public square in the world, covering 40 ha/98 acres and lying before the gate to the Imperial Palace in C Beijing (Peking). It was here that the People's Republic was proclaimed in September 1949. In June 1989, it was the scene of mass protests by students and others against the Chinese government, crushed by troops of the Chinese Army with an undisclosed number of dead. » Beijing; Forbidden City

tiang » **topi**

Tianjin, **Tientsin**, or **T'ien-ching** [tien**jin**] 39°08N 117°12E; municipality pop (1982) 7 764 141; urban centre pop (1984e) 5 312 100; municipality area 4 000 sq km/1 500 sq ml. Port city in E China; 50 km/31 ml W of Bo Hai Gulf on Hai He R; on Grand Canal; China's largest artificial harbour, built during Japanese occupation (1937–45), completed 1952; founded in Warring States period (403–221 BC); developed in Middle Ages as a grain port; attacked by British and French in 1860; badly damaged by earthquake, 1976; airport; railway; two universities; designated a special economic zone; iron and steel, consumer goods, carpets; Tianjin Art Museum, Industrial Exhibition Hall, many European-style buildings and Victorian mansions. » China [i]; Grand Canal

Tiber, River [**tiy**ber], Ital **Tevere**, ancient **Tiberis** Second longest river of Italy, rising in the Etruscan Apennines on Monte Fumaiolo; length 405 km/252 ml; flows S and SSW past Rome to enter the Tyrrhenian Sea near Ostia; two mouths, the Fiumara (silted up) and the Fiumicino, kept navigable by canalization. » Italy [i]

Tiberias [tiy**bee**rias], Hebrew **Tevarya** 32°48N 35°32E, pop (1982e) 29 000. Holiday resort town in Northern district, N Israel, on W shore of L Tiberias; named after the Roman emperor, Tiberius; medicinal hot springs known since ancient times; one of the four holy cities of the Jews; Jewish settlement re-established in 1922; Monastery of St Peter. » Israel [i]

Tiberias, Lake or **Sea of Galilee**, Hebrew **Yam Kinneret**, ancient

Sea of Chinnereth area 166 sq km/64 sq ml. Lake in Northern district, NE Israel, in the Jordan valley; 210 m/689 ft below sea-level; length 22.5 km/14 ml; width 12 km/7½ ml; maximum depth 46 m/150 ft; fed and drained by the R Jordan; Israel's largest reservoir, with water piped as far as the Negev; many centres around the lake of historic and scriptural interest, especially connected with the life of Jesus; first kibbutz founded to the S in 1909. » Israel [i]; Jesus Christ; kibbutz; Negev

Tiberius, properly **Tiberius Julius Caesar Augustus** (42 BC–AD 37) Roman emperor (14–37), the son of Livia, and stepson and successor of the Emperor Augustus. Deeply conservative by nature, he was content to continue Augustus' policies and simply consolidate his achievements. Despite the soundness of his administration and foreign policy, politically his reign was a disaster. While the suspicious death of his heir Germanicus (19), followed by the excesses of his chief henchman, the praetorian prefect Sejanus, made him unpopular, the reign of terror that followed Sejanus' downfall (31) made him an object of universal loathing. Few mourned when he died on Capri, the island retreat that had been his home since 26. » Agrippina the Elder; Germanicus; Livia; Roman history [i]; Sejanus

Tibesti Mountains [teebestee] Mountain range in NC Africa, largely in NW Chad, partly in Libya and Sudan; area 100 000 sq km/38 600 sq ml, length 480 km/300 ml; highest mountain group in Sahara; highest peak, Emi Koussi (3 415 m/11 204 ft); spectacular rock formations created by wind erosion. » Chad [i]; Sahara Desert

Tibet » **Xizang**

Tibet Plateau or **Qinghai-Tibet Plateau**, Chinese **Xizang Gaoyuan** Plateau in W and SW China; includes Xizang, Qinghai, W Sichuan, and SW Gansu; average altitude, 4 000 m/13 000 ft, highest plateau in the world ('the roof of the world'); area 2.3 million sq km/0.9 million sq ml; bounded S by the Himalayas, N by Kunlun Shan and Qilian Shan Ranges, W by Karakoram Range, and E by Hengduan Shan Range; several internal ranges separate basins, valleys, and lakes; source of many rivers of E, SE, and S Asia, including the Yangtze, Yellow, Mekong, Salween, Indus, Brahmaputra, and Tarim; major farming region in S, with warm, humid climate; C and N are cold and dry, with ice and snow for 6 months each year; uplift continues at over 10 mm/0.4 in per year. » China [i]; Xizang

Tibetan One of the major languages in the Sino-Tibetan group. During the recent occupation of Tibet by China, Chinese has been promoted officially at the expense of Tibetan, but there are probably 3–4 million speakers. Written records, mainly to do with the Buddhist religion, date from the 8th-c AD. » Sino-Tibetan languages

Tibetan art The art associated with Tibet, which for a thousand years has reflected the intense spirituality and mysticism of Lamaism. Wall-paintings and banners, Buddhist sculpture in stone, wood, metal, and ivory, as well as tombs and stupas, were produced by anonymous craftsmen following age-old rules. » Chinese art; Indian art; Lamaism

tibia » **leg**

Tibullus (c.54–19 BC) Latin poet, considered by Quintilian to be the greatest elegaic writer. He fought in Aquitania, but withdrew from military life and became a member of a literary circle in Rome. The heroine of his first book of love poetry was the wife of an officer absent on service in Cilicia; of his second, a fashionable courtesan. The other works under his name are probably by several authors. » poetry; Latin literature

tic An involuntary non-rhythmic motor movement or vocal production which serves no apparent purpose. It may occur as the result of a neurological lesion, and most famously in Giles de la Tourette syndrome, where the patient may suddenly utter a sound like a bark, or swear without provocation or intention to do so. » coprolalia

tick A large mite specialized as a blood-feeding, external parasite of terrestrial vertebrates; fangs modified for cutting skin; cuticle typically elastic, stretching to accommodate blood meal; can transmit diseases of humans and domesticated animals. (Order: *Acari*. Family: *Ixodidae*.) » mite

tickbird » **oxpecker**

ticket of leave A pass issued to convicts in Australia as a reward for good behaviour; it was a form of parole which could be issued after 4, 6, or 8 years depending on whether the sentence was for 7, 14 years, or life, respectively. About 30% of convicts received tickets of leave by 1840. » transportation

tidal wave The extremely long-period waves driven by the forces producing the tides. The term is often popularly but incorrectly used to refer to tsunami waves, which are not related to tides. » tide; tsunami; wave (oceanography)

tide The regular, periodic rise and fall of the surface of the sea. The tides are produced by differences in gravitational forces acting on different points on the Earth's surface, and affect all bodies of water to some extent. These so-called tidal forces are produced primarily by the Sun and Moon. The Sun's tidal forces are only about half as strong as those of the Moon, due to the Sun's greater distance from the Earth. The position of the Sun, Moon, and other celestial bodies with respect to the Earth produces variations in the timing and magnitude of the tides. » bore; diurnal/mixed/semi-diurnal/spring tide; gravitation; tidal wave

Tien Shan or **Tyan Shan** Mountain range in C Asia, on border of Russia and China; separates Tarim (N) and Dzungarian (S) Basins; contains glaciers up to 70 km/40 ml long; length, 2 500 km/1 500 ml; passes at Shengli Daban and Qijiaojing; higher in W, rising to 7 439 m/24 406 ft at Tomur (Pobedy) peak; contains rich deposits of coal, rock salt, and metals; dense forests on N slopes; mainly grassland in S. » China [i]; Tarim Basin

Tientsin » **Tianjin**

Tiepolo, Giovanni Battista [tyaypuhloh] (1696–1770) Italian artist, born in Venice. The last of the great Venetian painters, he became renowned as a decorator of buildings throughout Europe. Examples of his work can be found in the ceiling paintings of the Würzburg and Madrid palaces, where his imaginary skies are filled with floating, gesticulating Baroque figures, apparently unbounded by the structure of the buildings. He died in Madrid. » Baroque (art and architecture); Italian art; Venetian School

Tiergarten A park covering 255 ha/630 acres in W Berlin, Germany. Originally a royal hunting ground, it was landscaped in the 18th-c and opened to the public. The park was re-established, after being severely damaged during World War 2 and the bitter winter that followed, when many trees were cut for fuel. » Berlin, West

Tierra del Fuego [tyera thel fwaygoh] pop (1980) 29 392; area 73 746 sq km/28 473 sq ml. Island group at the extreme S of South America; E side (about one third) belongs to Argentina (National Territory), remainder belongs to Chile; boundary agreed in 1881; bounded by the Magellan Strait (N), Atlantic Ocean (E), Pacific Ocean (W), and Beagle Channel (S); highest point Monte Darwin (2 438 m/7 999 ft); Cape Horn southernmost point; discovered by Magellan 1520; capital (Argentina) Ushuaia, southernmost town in the world; capital (on Chile mainland) Punta Arenas; sheep, timber, fishing, oil, natural gas; dispute over islands at E end of Beagle Channel, resolved 1985 in favour of Chile. » Argentina [i]; Chile [i]; Magellan

tiger A member of the cat family native to S and SE Asia; reddish brown with dark vertical stripes (occasional individuals almost white with pale stripes and blue eyes); inhabits diverse habitats, often near water; swims well; hunts by sight and sound; eats mainly large mammals; several subspecies: **Bengal**, **Indochinese**, **Chinese**, **Sumatran**, **Siberian** (the largest known cat), and possibly extinct **Caspian**, **Bali**, and **Javan** tigers. (*Panthera tigris*.) » Felidae; liger

tiger beetle An active, brightly-coloured beetle found in open, sunny habitats; larvae typically live in burrows; both larvae and adults feed mainly on small insects. (Order: *Coleoptera*. Family: *Carabidae*.) » beetle; larva

tiger cat A common name sometimes used for medium-sized spotted wild cats (eg ocelot, margay, serval, and C American *little spotted cat*). The name is also used for a domestic cat with tabby coloration. » wild cat

tiger fish Large predatory freshwater fish with strong fang-like teeth, widespread in rivers and lakes of Africa; length up to 1.8 m/6 ft; powerful and much prized as a sport fish. The name is also used for several fish in other families that are predatory with strong teeth, or have conspicuous striped coloration. (Genus: *Hydrocynus*. Family: *Characidae*.) » fish [i]

tiger heron » **heron**

tiger moth A medium-sized, typically colourful moth; caterpillar larvae usually hairy, known as **woolly bears**; may be important pests causing damage to tree foliage; many produce sound using a vibrating organ on side of body. (Order: *Lepidoptera*. Family: *Arctiidae*.) » caterpillar; cinnabar (entomology); moth

tiger shark Large and very dangerous shark widely distributed in tropical and warm temperate seas; length up to 5 m/16 ft; grey to brown, with darker vertical stripes and patches, the pattern becoming indistinct in large specimens. (*Galeocerda cuvier*. Family: *Carcharhinidae*.) » shark

tigon [**tiy**guhn] » **liger**

Tigray or **Tigre** [**tee**gray] pop (1984e) 2 409 700; area 65 900 sq km/25 437 sq ml. Region in NE Ethiopia; mountainous W half, with peaks including Mokada (2 295 m/7 529 ft); low-lying E half, with large section below sea-level at centre of Danakil Depression; capital, Mekele; one of the areas most severely affected by the drought in the 1980s, and a centre of resistance to the government; Tigre people are Semitic-speaking, mostly nomadic herders in the N, agriculturalists in the S. » Afro-Asiatic languages; Ethiopia [i]

tigrillo » **ocelot**

Tigris, River [**tiy**gris], Arabic **Shatt Dijla**, Turkish **Dicle** River in SE Turkey and Iraq; rises in EC Turkey, and flows generally SE through Iraq; joins the Euphrates 64 km/40 ml NW of Basra to form the Shatt al-Arab; length 1 850 km/1 150 ml; navigable to Baghdad for shallow-draft vessels; several dams used for flood control and irrigation; ancient transportation route, with several ancient cities along its banks, eg Nineveh, Seleucia, Ashur, Calah. » Iraq [i]; Shatt al-Arab

Tijuana [tee**hwah**na] 32°32N 117°02W, pop (1980) 461 257. Border town in NW Baja California Norte, NW Mexico; on the Pacific Ocean at the frontier with California, USA; airfield; resort town with casinos and nightclubs; horse racing, dog racing, bullfights. » Mexico [i]

Tikal [tee**kahl**] An ancient Mayan city in the Petén rainforest of N Guatemala, settled by 250 BC, at its peak in the 7th–8th-c AD, but abruptly abandoned c.900. In area 16 sq km/6 sq ml, it contained an estimated 3 000 buildings with a population of c.20–30 000. Monuments include palaces, plazas, ten reservoirs, and six temple pyramids, the largest 70 m/229 ft high. It is a world heritage site. » Mayas

Tilburg [**til**berkh] 51°31N 5°06E, pop (1984e) 221 684. Industrial city in North Brabant province, S Netherlands; on the Wilhelmina Canal, 54 km/34 ml SE of Rotterdam; railway; woollens, metalworking; major business and cultural centre in the S; capital of Dutch Catholicism. » Netherlands, The [i]

Tilbury 51°28N 0°23E, pop (1981) 11 468. Port town in Grays-Tilbury urban area, Thurrock district, Essex, SE England; on the R Thames estuary, E of London; railway; major port and docks for London and the SE. » Essex

till or **boulder clay** A geological term for sediment or drift consisting of an unstratified and unsorted deposit of clay, sand, gravel, and boulders left behind after the retreat of glaciers and ice-sheets. **Tillite** is till which has consolidated into solid rock. » glaciation; moraine; stratification

Till Eulenspiegel » **Eulenspiegel, Till**

Tillett, Benjamin (1860–1943) British trade union leader, born in Bristol. He worked as a brickmaker, bootmaker, and sailor, and achieved prominence as leader of the great dockers' strike (1889), and of the transport workers' strike in London (1911). He became a Labour MP (1917–24, 1929–31), and died in London. » trade union

Tilley, Vesta, professional name of **Lady de Frece**, *née* **Matilda Alice Powles** (1864–1952) British music-hall entertainer, born in Worcester. She first appeared as 'The Great Little Tilley', aged four, in Nottingham, adopted her professional name, and became a celebrated male impersonator. Her many popular songs included *Burlington Bertie* and *Following in Father's Footsteps*. She retired in 1920, and died in London. » music hall; theatre

Tillich, Paul (Johannes) (1886–1965) German Protestant theologian, born at Starzeddel, Prussia. He became a Lutheran pastor (1912), and held professorships at Marburg, Dresden, Leipzig, and Frankfurt. Dismissed by the Nazis in 1933, he moved to the USA, where he became a US citizen (1940), and taught at the Union Theological Seminary, New York (1933–56), Harvard (1956–62), and Chicago (1962–5), where he died. His major work was *Systematic Theology* (1953–63, 3 vols). » existentialism; theology

Tilly, Johann Tskerlaes, Graf von ('Count of') (1559–1632) Flemish soldier, born at Tilly, Brabant. He successfully commanded the forces of the Catholic League in the Thirty Years' War, gaining decisive victories at the White Mountain and Prague (1620). Created a count of the Holy Roman Empire, he defeated Denmark at Lütter (1626). His destruction of Magdeburg (1631) branded him a brutal soldier, and he was routed by Gustavus Adolphus at Breitenfeld in Saxony (1631). He was fatally wounded crossing into Bavaria and died at Ingolstadt. » Gustavus II; Thirty Years' War

timber line The boundary above which trees occur but do not achieve full growth. Between the timber line and the tree line, the trees are stunted and dwarfed.

timber wolf » **wolf**

timbre The sound quality of a voice or musical instrument, which depends on the prominence or otherwise of upper harmonics (partials) in the notes produced. The timbre of a flute or recorder, for example, is weak in upper harmonics compared with that of the much brighter violin or trumpet. The 'clanging' sound of a bell results from the number and strength of upper partials which are not concordant with the fundamental. » harmonic

Timbuktu [timbuhk**too**], Fr **Tombouctou** 16°49N 2°59W, pop (1976) 20 483. Town in Gao region, N Mali, 690 km/429 ml NE of Bamako; settled in the 11th-c; a chief centre of Muslim learning; declined after conquest by Morocco, 16th-c; taken by the French, 1893; airfield; adjoining town of Kabara serves as a port on the R Niger; tourism, salt, power plant; Djinguereber Mosque (13th-c), Sankore Mosque (14th-c), Sidi Yahya Mosque (15th-c). » Mali [i]

time That which distinguishes sequential events from simultaneous events; symbol t, units s (second); the fourth dimension, in addition to the three spatial dimensions. It allows the assignment of cause and effect, and according to our perception the assignment of past, present, and future. In Newtonian mechanics, time is absolute, meaning that a second as measured by one observer is the same as a second measured by any other observer in the universe. Relativity explains that this view of the nature of time is false. In thermodynamic systems, the directionality of time derives from entropy. » clock parodox; day; Daylight Saving Time; ephemeris/sidereal/solar/standard/universal time; entropy; general relativity; light year; month; Newtonian mechanics; second; space-time; special relativity [i]; time dilation

time and motion study The technique of job analysis to discover how tasks are actually carried out; more usually known now as *work study* or *industrial engineering*. Its aim is to find the most efficient way of performing a task, both in terms of time and effort, in order to raise productivity. When used as a basis for wage negotiations, it can lead to industrial disputes. » productivity

time code A series of digitally coded signals appearing sequentially on the magnetic tape of a video or audio recording, and sometimes on film, to provide specific identification for each frame in editing and post-production. In its simplest form it denotes Hours, Minutes, Seconds and Frames, which may be selected as 24, 25 or 30 per second. » tape recorder

time dilation The slowing of time for objects moving at velocities close to the velocity of light, as perceived by a stationary observer. If observer A watches the clock held by observer B as B moves past, A will see B's clock as running slowly. In turn, B will see A's clock as running slowly. The symmetry is consistent with the principle that no observer is 'more at rest' than any other. Time dilation is observed in particle physics where moving unstable particles appear to decay more slowly than identical stationary particles. » particle physics; special relativity [i]; velocity

time-lapse photography A series of photographs taken at regular intervals from the same viewpoint to record the development of a subject, for example, plant growth, cloud formation, metallic corrosion, or traffic flow. When filmed as successive single frames, subsequent projection at normal speed provides a rapid presentation of slow changes. A similar technique is available in video cameras. » photography

Time of Troubles A period of intense social and political turmoil in Russia (1598–1613), involving a series of successive crises, civil war, famines, Cossack and peasant revolts, foreign invasions, and widespread material destruction. The period ended with a national uprising against the invading Poles, and the election of the first Romanov tsar. » Cossacks; Romanovs; Russian history; tsar

time-sharing (computing) A means of providing simultaneous access by several users to the same computer. Each user, in turn, is assigned full use of the central processing unit for a very small duration, making it appear that each user has continuous access. » real-time computing

time-sharing (leisure) The joint ownership of holiday accommodation by a consortium. Depending upon the number of shares acquired, each share holder is entitled to a specific period of holiday. A register of time-share owners exists, enabling them to exchange their accommodation for another during their holiday entitlement period.

Times Square A public square in Manhattan, New York City, situated at the junction of Broadway, 42nd Street, and 7th Avenue, and at the centre of the city's theatre district. It takes its name from the Times Tower, built in 1904 to house the offices of the *New York Times*. » Broadway; New York City

Timgad The former Roman city of Thaugadi in NE Algeria; a world heritage site. Founded by the Emperor Trajan in AD 100, and abandoned after the 5th-c, it is a noted example of Roman planning. The site has been extensively restored, and archaeological work still continues. » Holy Roman Empire; Trajan

Timişoara, Magyar **Temesvár** [timuhsh**wah**ra] 45°45N 21°15E, pop (1983) 303 499. Capital of Timiş county, W Romania, on the Bega Canal; ceded to Romania, 1919; violent suppression of a pro-Hungarian demonstration there in December 1989, with many civilians killed, sparked a more general uprising against the Ceaucescu regime; railway; university (1962); technical university (1920); fine arts academy; electrical engineering, textiles, chemicals, pharmaceuticals, food processing, footwear, metal; two cathedrals; Hunyadi Castle (15th-c). » Romania [i]

Timor [**tee**maw] pop (1980) 1 382 207; area 33 912 sq km/13 090 sq ml. Mountainous island in SE Asia, in the Sunda group, NW of Australia; divided between Portugal and Holland, 1859; **West Timor** (former Dutch Timor) included in Indonesia at independence, administered as part of the province of Nusa Tenggara Timur; capital, Kupang; coffee, coconuts; former Portuguese territory of **East Timor** declared itself independent as the Democratic Republic of East Timor, 1975; invaded by Indonesian forces and annexed, the claim not recognized by the United Nations; now administered by Indonesia as the province of Timor Timur; area 14 874 sq km/5 741 sq ml; pop (1980) 555 350; independence movement established by Fretilin continues to be active; capital, Dili; maize, coffee. » Indonesia [i]; Sunda Islands

Timor Sea [**tee**maw] Part of the Pacific Ocean, SE of Timor, Indonesia, and NW of Northern Territory, Australia; lies over a wide continental shelf, with depths down to 110 m/360 ft, but deepens off Timor. » Pacific Ocean

Timoshenko, Semyon Konstantinovich (1895–1970) Russian general, born at Furmanka, the Ukraine. He joined the Tsarist army in 1915, and in the revolution took part in the defence of Tsaritsyn. In 1940 he smashed Finnish resistance during the Russo-Finnish War, then commanded in the Ukraine, but failed to stop the German advance (1942). He also served as People's Commissar of Defence, improving the system of army training. He retired in 1960, and died in Moscow. » Russo-Finnish War; World War 2

Timothy, Letters to Two of the Pastoral Letters in the New Testament, for which Pauline authorship is often disputed today. Both letters are purportedly addressed to Paul's close companion Timothy (*Acts* 16.1; *1 Thess* 3.2), but mostly concern questions of church order and discipline, and problems with false teachers who seemingly were spreading gnostic and Jewish speculations. The second letter, however, does make several references to Paul's personal experiences and circumstances. » Gnosticism; New Testament; Pastoral Letters; Pauline Letters

timpani [**tim**panee] (singular **timpano**) Drums made from large copper bowls (hence the English name **kettledrum**), with heads of calfskin or plastic, which can be tuned to various pitches by means of hand-screws or, in modern instruments, pedals. They are normally played with two felt-headed sticks, but other types may be specified. As military instruments, two timpani were carried on horseback at either side of the rider. Since the 17th-c they have been regular members of the orchestral percussion section. » drum; percussion [i]

Timur, byname **Timur Lenk** (Turk 'Timur the Lame'), English **Tamerlane** or **Tamburlaine** (1336–1405) Tatar conqueror, born near Samarkand. In 1369 he ascended the throne of Samarkand, subdued nearly all Persia, Georgia, and the Tatar empire, and conquered all the states between the Indus and the lower Ganges (1398). He won Damascus and Syria from the Mameluke sovereigns of Egypt, then defeated the Turks at Angora (1402), taking Sultan Bajazet prisoner. He died while marching to conquer China. » Bajazet I

tin Sn (Lat *stannum*), element 50, melting point 232°C. A white metal in the carbon group of elements, occurring in nature mainly as the oxide (SnO_2), and isolated by reduction with carbon. The metal forms a very strongly adhering oxide coat, and is therefore not corroded easily. Tin is used as a plating for other metals because of its corrosion resistance. Tin compounds are less widely used than the metal. Common oxidation states of tin are +2 and +4. » chemical elements; corrosion; metal; oxide; RR90

Tin Pan Alley A nickname coined c.1900 for the popular music-publishing centre of New York City situated on 28th Street and 6th Avenue, and later near 49th Street. » New York City

tinamou [**tin**amoo] A partridge-like bird, native to the New World tropics; inhabits woodland, scrub, or grassland; eats plant material, insects, and (occasionally) mice; eggs incubated by male. (Family: *Tinamidae*, c.50 species.) » partridge

Tinbergen, Jan (1903–) Dutch economist, born in The Hague, and educated at Leyden. His major contribution was the econometric modelling of cyclical movements in socio-economic growth. He was director of the Central Planning Bureau in the Netherlands, and also worked with developing countries. In 1969 he shared the first Nobel Prize for Economics. » econometrics; Frisch, Ragnar

Tinbergen, Nikolaas (1907–88) Dutch ethologist, born in The Hague. He graduated in zoology at Leyden, and later taught there, and from 1947 at Oxford. His major concern was with the patterns of animal behaviour in nature, showing that many are stereotyped. His research covered several species, in relation to camouflage, learning behaviour, courtship, and aggression, and he also studied autism in children. He shared the Nobel Prize for Physiology or Medicine in 1973. » ethology; Lorenz

Tindale, William » **Tyndale, William**

tineid moth [**tin**eeid] A small, drab moth of the family *Tineidae*; caterpillars mainly feed on dried organic matter; c.3 500 species, including the clothes moths, which cause damage to carpets and clothes, and other pests of stored products. (Order: *Lepidoptera*.) » caterpillar; clothes moth; moth

Tinian [**tin**ian] pop (1980) 866; area 101 sq km/39 sq ml. One of the N Mariana Is, W Pacific, 5 km/3 ml SW of Saipan; length 18 km/11 ml; four long runways built by the USA during World War 2; plaque commemorates the launching of the Hiroshima bombing mission in 1945; site of ancient stone columns. » Mariana Islands, Commonwealth of the Northern

tinnitus [**tin**ituhs] A ringing or hissing sound heard within the ear, which may arise from almost any disorder of the ear or its nerve supply. When the cause is simple, such as excessive wax in the external ear, the condition is easily remedied; in other cases, the disorder is usually intractable. » ear [i]

tinplate A thin steel sheet coated with tin by dipping or electrolytic deposition. It is used for light robust containers and protective constructions. First tried out in the late 17th-c, it was not used to any extent until the invention of canning in the early 19th-c, since when it has attained world-wide industrial importance. » electrolysis [i]; tin

Tintoretto, byname of **Jacopo Robusti** (1518–94) The greatest of the late Venetian painters, born (probably) in Venice, the son of a dyer or *tintore*. Except for visits to Mantua (1580, 1590–3), he lived all his life in Venice. His major works include 'The Last Supper' (1547, Venice), 'The Last Judgment' (c.1560, Venice) and the 'Paradiso', famous for its great size (1588, Venice). From 1564 he was employed in decorating the Albergo, and the Halls of the Scuola of San Rocco and its church, which contains a vast iconographical scheme from the Old and New Testaments, including the 'Crucifixion' (1565) and 'Annunciation' (1583–7). » Italian art; Michelangelo; Titian; Venetian School

Tipasa A village on the N coast of Algeria, standing on the ruins of the ancient city of Tipasa; a world heritage site. The original settlement, founded in the 5th-c BC, passed through many hands, from Phoenician to Roman, before it was abandoned in the 5th-c. » Algeria [i]; Phoenicia; Holy Roman Empire

Tipperary, Gaelic **Thiobrad Árann** [tipuh**rai**ree] County in Munster province, SC Irish Republic; divided into **North Riding** (pop (1981) 58 984; area 1 996 sq km/770 sq ml) and **South Riding** (pop (1981) 76 277; area 2 258 sq km/872 sq ml); watered by R Suir; Silvermine Mts (N), Galty Mts (S), Slieve Ardagh Hills (W); capital, Clonmel; rich dairy-farming area; centre for horse and greyhound breeding; festival of Irish and modern music and dance at Tipperary town (Jun). » Clonmel; Irish Republic [i]

Tippett, Sir Michael (Kemp) (1905–) British composer, born in London. He studied at the Royal College of Music, and became director of music at Morley College (1940–51). His oratorio, *A Child of our Time* (1941), reflecting the problems of the 1930s and 1940s, won him wide recognition. A convinced pacifist, he was imprisoned as a conscientious objector during World War 2. He scored a considerable success with his operas *The Midsummer Marriage* (1952) and *King Priam* (1961), and among his other works are four symphonies, a piano concerto, and string quartets. He was knighted in 1966.

Tippoo Sahib or **Tipú Sultán** [**ti**poo suhl**tahn**] (1749–99) Sultan of Mysore (1782–99), born at Devanhalli, the son of Haidar Ali. He continued his father's policy of opposing British rule, and in 1789 invaded the British-protected state of Travancore. In the ensuing war (1790–2) he was defeated by Cornwallis and had to cede half his kingdom. After recommencing hostilities in 1799, he was killed during the siege of Seringapatam. » Cornwallis; Haidar Ali

Tiranë [tee**rah**nuh], Ital **Tirana** 41°20N 19°50E, pop (1980) 194 000. Capital town of Albania and of Tiranë district; in a valley in the foothills of the Kruja-Dajti Mts, 40 km/25 ml from the Adriatic Sea; founded by Turks in the early 17th-c; made capital in 1920; residential area built by the Italians (1939–43); industrial area to the W; university (1957); railway; airport (Rinas); textiles, foodstuffs, footwear, metalworking, ceramics, glass, engineering, wood products, distilling, building materials, furniture; coal mines nearby. » Albania [i]

Tiresias [tiy**re**zias] In Greek mythology, a blind Theban prophet, who takes a prominent part in Sophocles' plays about Oedipus and Antigone. Later legends account for his wisdom by saying that he had experienced the life of both sexes. » Sophocles

Tirol or **Tyrol** [ti**rohl**] pop (1981) 586 139; area 12 647 sq km/ 4 882 sq ml. Federal state of W Austria, bounded by W Germany to the N and Italy to the S; drained by the R Inn; lakes include the Achensee, Walchsee, Tristacher See, Schwarzsee; capital, Innsbruck; hydroelectric power (Zillertal, Kaunertal), agriculture, forestry, powder metallurgy, diesel engines, vehicles, optical instruments; leading state for tourism, especially winter sports (eg at Kitzbühel). » Austria [i]; Bavarian Alps; Innsbruck

Tirol Alps » **Bavarian Alps**

Tirpitz, Alfred (Friedrich) von (1849–1930) German admiral, born at Küstrin. He joined the Prussian navy in 1865, was ennobled in 1900, and rose to be Lord High Admiral (1911). As Secretary of State for the imperial navy (1897–1916), he raised a fleet to challenge British supremacy of the seas, and acted as its commander 1914–16. He advocated unrestricted submarine warfare, and resigned when this policy was opposed. He later sat in the Reichstag, then retired to Ebenhausen, where he died. » World War 1

Tirso de Molina [**teer**soh day muh**lee**na], pseudonym of **Gabriel Téllez** (c.1571–1648) Spanish dramatist, born in Madrid. Educated at Alcalá, he became prior of the monastery of Soria. A disciple of his contemporary, Lope de Vega, he wrote many comedies and religious plays, but is best known for his treatment of the Don Juan legend in *El burlador de Sevilla* (1635, The Seducer of Seville). He died at Soria. » drama; Spanish literature; Vega, Lope de

Tirthankara (Sanskrit, 'ford-maker') [teer**tuhng**kara] A title used by Jains of the 24 great heroes of their tradition who, by their teaching and example, taught them the way to cross the stream from the bondage of physical existence to freedom from rebirth. They are also called *Jina*, 'conqueror', from which Jains take their name. » Jainism

Tiruchchirappalli [tiroochira**pah**lee] or **Trichinopoly** [trikuh**no**-**puh**lee] 10°45N 78°45E, pop (1981) 608 000. City in Tamil Nadu, S India, on the Kaveri R; airfield; railway; educational, religious, and commercial centre, noted for its gold, silver, and brass working; fort, shrine of Sringam, monument to Shiva. » Tamil Nadu

Tiryns [**tee**rinz] An ancient Greek town in the Argolid near Mycenae, famous for the remains of its fortified Bronze Age palace. Large parts of its Cyclopean walls still stand. » Argolid; Mycenae

Tissot, James Joseph Jacques [**tee**soh] (1836–1902) French painter, born at Nantes. He trained in Paris, where he was influenced by Degas, then in the 1870s settled in London, painting highly accomplished scenes of Victorian life. As a result of a visit to Palestine in 1886, he produced a series of the life of Christ in watercolour. » Degas; French art; watercolour

tissue A group or layer of similarly specialized cells, or cells and associated fibres, which have specific functions. Most animals are composed of some or all of the following types of tissue. **Epithelial** tissue consists of cells only, and covers all internal and external surfaces. **Connective** tissue (eg fat) consists of cells and fibres, and tends to have a passive role, supporting or joining the more functionally active tissues. **Skeletal** tissue (eg bone, cartilage) is modified connective tissue, in which the cells and fibres lie in a rigid matrix. **Muscular** tissue consists of fibres arranged in particular patterns, and is responsible for producing movements at joints (*skeletal muscle*), peristaltic contractions of the alimentary tract (*smooth muscle*), and the regular beating of the heart (*cardiac muscle*). **Nervous** tissue is composed of cells, some of which have long nerve tracts, specialized to convey and transmit information from one part of the body to another. » cellulitis; connective tissue; Marfan's syndrome; muscle [i]; neurone [i]; skeleton

tissue fluid » **interstitial fluid**

Tisza, River, Czech **Tisa**, Russian **Tissa** [**ti**sa] Longest tributary of the R Danube in E Europe; rises in the W Ukrainian Carpathian Mts and flows S into the Great Plain of Hungary, where it is used for irrigation and hydroelectricity; major land reclamation schemes along its course; enters the Danube SW of Belgrade; length 962 km/598 ml; navigable for 780 km/485 ml. » Hungary [i]

tit A small, lively, acrobatic songbird, native to the N hemisphere and Africa; inhabits woodland and habitation; in the wild, eats insects and seeds; also known as the **titmouse** or **typical tit**; includes the **chickadees** of N America. The name is also used for the **long-tailed tit** (Family: *Aegithalidae*), the **penduline tit** (Family: *Remizidae*), and numerous other birds of diverse groups. (Family: *Paridae*, 46 species.) » bluetit; coal/crested/great/long-tailed tit; chickadee; songbird

Titan (astronomy) Saturn's largest satellite, discovered in 1655;

distance from the planet 1 222 000 km/759 000 ml; diameter 5 150 km/3 200 ml; orbital period 15.945 days. It is the second largest moon in the Solar System, and the only satellite with a substantial atmosphere, principally composed of nitrogen and methane. It was approached closely by Voyager 1, but global haze cover prevented observation of the surface. » Saturn (astronomy); Voyager project [i]; RR4

Titan (mythology) [**tiy**tn] In Greek mythology, a member of the older generation of gods, the children of Uranus and Gaia. After Zeus and the Olympians took power, the Titans made war on them; but they were defeated and imprisoned in Tartarus. One or two, notably Prometheus, helped Zeus. The Titans may represent memories of pre-Greek Mediterranean gods. » Cronus; Greek gods [i]; Hyperion (mythology); Iapetus (mythology); Mnemosyne; Oceanus; Phoebe (mythology); Prometheus; Rhea (mythology)

Titania (astronomy) The largest satellite of Uranus, discovered in 1787 by Herschel; distance from the planet 436 000 km/271 000 ml; diameter 1 600 km/1 000 ml. It has an icy, cratered surface, with extensive scarps. » Herschel; Uranus (astronomy); RR4

Titania (mythology) In Greek mythology, a female Titan, identified with the Moon. In Shakespeare's *A Midsummer Night's Dream* she is the queen of the fairies, who is tricked into falling in love with Bottom the Weaver. » fairies; Oberon; Titan

Titanic [tiy**tan**ik] White Star Line's 46 329 gross tons passenger liner, which collided with an iceberg in the N Atlantic on her maiden voyage in April 1912. Lifeboat capacity was inadequate, and just over 700 people were saved, whilst 1 500 went down with the ship. The vessel was rediscovered in 1985, explored, and photographed on the sea bed. As she was found to be broken into two unequal pieces, each severely damaged, it is unlikely that she will ever be raised. The task is not impossible, but it would be prohibitively expensive.

titanium Ti, element 22, melting point 1 660°C. A lustrous, white metal, with a relatively low density of 4.5 g/cm^3. It is found widely distributed in nature, never uncombined, and usually as an oxide (TiO_2). The metal, produced by magnesium reduction, is used in some alloys, especially for aircraft. Its compounds usually show oxidation states +3 and +4. The dioxide is a particularly important white pigment in paints. » alloy; chemical elements; metal; RR90

titanothere [tiy**tan**uhtheer] A medium- to large-sized, plant-eating mammal; known as fossils from the early Tertiary period of N America and E Asia; some stood 2.5 m/8 ft at the shoulder; often with paired nasal horns; includes Brontotherium. (Order: *Perissodactyla.*) » Brontotherium; herbivore; mammal [i]; Tertiary period

tithes Offerings of a proportion (literally 'the tenth part') of one's property or produce to God, often given to the priesthood of temples; customary among peoples since ancient times. In Jewish Law, instructions regarding tithes were listed in *Lev* 27, and were subsequently elaborated in the Talmud. Taxes of this description were used to support Christian clergy in Europe from mediaeval times, and in England from the 10th-c, until greater secularization after the Reformation brought increased opposition. Civil tithes were replaced in England by a rent charge in 1836, and even this was abolished in 1936. » Church of England; Reformation; Talmud

titi or **tee-tee** [**tee**tee] A New World monkey of genus *Callicebus* (3 species); thick coat and long tail; moves slowly; characteristically crouches on a branch with all four feet together, tail hanging vertically. The name is also used for short-tusked marmosets of genus *Callithrix* (3 species). » marmoset; New World monkey

Titian, in full **Tiziano Vecellio** [**tish**an] (c.1490–1576) Venetian painter, born at Pieve di Cadore. Trained in the studio of Giovanni Bellini, he assisted Giorgione with the paintings on the Fondaco dei Tedeschi (1508). His early paintings display Giorgione's influence, and his own revolutionary style is not apparent until after c.1516, in such works as the 'Assumption of the Virgin' (1516–18, Venice). For the Duke of Ferrara he painted three great mythological subjects, 'Feast of Venus' (c.1515–18), 'Bacchanal' (c.1518, both Prado, Madrid), and the richly-coloured 'Bacchus and Ariadne' (c.1523, National Gallery, London). From 1530, he also painted many pictures for Emperor Charles V, and this period includes his 'Ecce Homo' (1543, Vienna). He later executed a series of works on mythological scenes for Philip of Spain, and in his last years painted several religious and mythological subjects, such as 'The Fall of Man' (c.1570, Madrid) and 'Christ Crowned with Thorns' (c.1570, Munich). He died in Venice. » Bellini; Giorgione; Italian art; Venetian School

TITLE EQUIVALENTS BETWEEN DIFFERENT LANGUAGES

ENGLAND	FRANCE	HOLY ROMAN EMPIRE (Germany)	ITALY	SPAIN
king	roi	Kaiser	re	rey
prince	duc	Herzog	duca	duque
duke	prince	Pfalzgraf	principe	principe
marquess	marquis	Markgraf	marchese	marques
earl	comte	Landgraf	conde	conde
viscount	vicomte		visconte	vizconde
baronet				

Titicaca, Lake (Span **Lago**) [teetee**ka**ka] Lake in SE Peru and W Bolivia; largest lake in S America (area 8 289 sq km/3 199 sq ml) and highest large lake in world (3 812 m/12 506 ft); major transportation artery between Peru and Bolivia; length 177 km/110 ml; width 56 km/35 ml; maximum depth 475 m/1 558 ft; two parts, L Chucuito and L Uinamarca, connected by Strait of Tiquina; steamers run from Guaqui (Bolivia) to Puno (Peru); mining centre, Matilde, on NE shore; hunting and fishing resort; base for Bolivian Yacht Club; contains 36 islands, including Titicaca and Coati with archaeological remains; on SW shore is Copacabana, a place of recreation for the Royal Inca family, famous for its sanctuary and 17th-c temple (Franciscan monastery) with statue of Virgin de Copacabana (1576), place of pilgrimage; ruins of ancient centre of Tiahuanaco empire nearby. » Bolivia [i]; Incas

Titius-Bode law » **Bode's law**

title » **panel** (above)

titmouse » **tit**

Tito [**tee**toh], byname **Marshal Tito**, originally **Josip Broz** (1892–1980) Yugoslav statesman and President (1953–80), born near Klanjec. In World War 1 he served with the Austro-Hungarian army, was taken prisoner by the Russians, and became a communist. He was imprisoned for conspiring against the regime in Yugoslavia (1928–9), and became Secretary of the Communist Party in 1937. In 1941 he organized partisan forces against the Axis conquerors, and after the war became the country's first communist Prime Minister (1945), consolidating his position with the presidency in 1953. He broke with Stalin and the Cominform in 1948, developing Yugoslavia's independent style of communism ('Titoism'), and played a leading role in the association of nonaligned countries. He died at Ljubljana. » Axis Powers; Chetniks; communism

Titograd [**tee**tohgrad], formerly **Podgorica** (to 1948) 42°28N 19°17E, pop (1981) 132 290. Capital of Montenegro republic, Yugoslavia; on R Morava, N of L Scutari; badly damaged in World War 2; named after Marshal Tito; airfield; railway; university (1973); aluminium, metalwork, furniture, tobacco; birthplace of Diocletian. » Diocletian; Montenegro; Tito; Yugoslavia [i]

titration A technique for finding the volume of one solution chemically equivalent to a given volume of another, usually by adding the first solution slowly until equivalence is reached. This can be detected by the addition of a small amount of an indicator material. » solution

Titus, properly **Titus Flavius Vespasianus** (39–81) Roman emperor (79–81), the elder son and successor of Vespasian. Popular with the Romans for his generosity, charm, and military prowess, he is execrated in Jewish tradition for his destruction of Jerusalem (70) and suppression of the Jewish Revolt. His brief reign was marred by many natural calamities, notably the eruption of Vesuvius (79). He completed the

Colosseum, begun by his father. » Pompeii; Vesuvius

Titus, St (1st-c), feast day 6 February (W), 23 August (E). In the New Testament, a Gentile companion of the apostle Paul, not mentioned in *Acts*, but referred to in *Gal* 2 and 2 *Cor* 8.6. Ecclesiastical tradition makes him the first Bishop of Crete. The purported Letter of Paul to Titus gives advice on the way the churches there should be organized. » New Testament; Paul, St; Titus, Letter to

Titus, Letter to One of the Pastoral Letters in the New Testament, for which Pauline authorship is usually disputed today. The letter addresses problems of church order and false (gnostic?) teachers, with specific instructions about the importance of sound doctrine, the selection of elders and bishops, family and social relationships, and submission to rulers and authorities. » Gnosticism; New Testament; Pastoral Letters; Pauline Letters

Tiv An agricultural people of C Nigeria, living along the Benue R. Egalitarian and lacking chiefdoms, they are organized around kinship ties. Much of their traditional culture is still intact, and they have expanded into neighbouring groups. They speak a Niger-Congo language. Population c.1.8 million. » Niger-Congo languages; Nigeria [i]

Tlaloc [tla**lok**] The Aztec god of rain, to whom children were sacrificed in time of drought. The features of his face are formed of serpents, representing the lightning. » Aztecs

Tlapanek » Hokan languages

Tlemcen [tlem**sen**], ancient **Pomaria** 34°53N 1°21W, pop (1982) 220 884. Chief town of Tlemcen department, NW Algeria, N Africa; 113 km/70 ml SW of Oran; capital of major Moroccan dynasties (12th–16th-c); despite French occupation from 1842, a well-preserved Muslim culture; railway; agriculture, carpets; leather, olive oil, tourism; Almovarid Great Mosque (1135), Grand Mosque, Museum of Bel Hassane. » Algeria [i]; Almoravids

Tlingit A N American Indian group of the Pacific NW coast (from Prince William Sound to S Alaska), who lived mainly by fishing and hunting. They are famed for their art, including Chilkat blankets woven from cedar bark and goat hair, and subtly coloured wood sculptures. Population (including the Haida) c.7 500. » American Indians; Northwest Coast Indians

TNT The abbreviation for **trinitrotoluene**, $C_7H_5N_3O_6$. A high explosive made by the nitration of toluene with nitric and sulphuric acids; a solid melting at 82°C. Used for filling shells and bombs, it is one of the most effective and easiest to handle of the military high explosives. » explosives

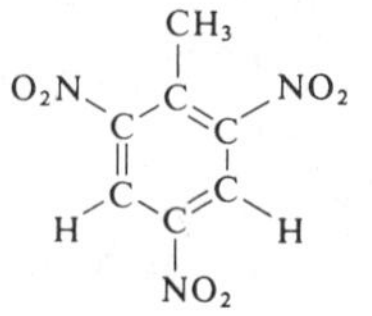

toad » frog

toadfish Robust bottom-living fish of the family *Batrachoididae* (6 genera), found in inshore waters of tropical to temperate seas; body typically elongate, tapering to a small tail, dorsal and anal fins long; eyes placed on top of flattened head, mouth large with strong teeth; some species have powerful poison spines. » frogfish

toadflax An annual or perennial, native to the N hemisphere, especially the Mediterranean region; leaves opposite, alternate or whorled; flowers in a variety of colour combinations, strongly zygomorphic; tube spurred and 2-lipped, the lower lip 3-lobed with a projection (the *palate*) closing the tube, so that pollinators must part the lips to reach nectar held in the spur. (Genus: *Linaria*, 150 species. Family: *Scrophulariaceae*.) » annual; perennial; pollination; zygomorphic flower

toadstool An informal name for many typically umbrella-shaped fungal fruiting bodies, especially those that are poisonous or inedible. » fungus

Toamasina, also **Tamatave** 18°10S 49°23E, pop (1978e) 59 100. Port on the E coast of Madagascar, on the Indian Ocean, 367 km/228 ml NE of Antananarivo; Madagascar's main port, and a popular tourist resort; airfield; railway; surrounded by sugar-cane plantations; Ivoloina Gardens nearby. » Madagascar [i]

tobacco An annual or shrubby perennial, native to warm parts of New World and Australasia; large leaves; tubular flowers, greenish, yellow, pink, or reddish. The dried, slightly fermented leaves of various species, principally *Nicotiana tabaccum*, are used for smoking, chewing, and snuff, and contain the powerful alkaloid *nicotine* which is both poisonous and addictive. (Genus: *Nicotiana*, 66 species. Family: *Solanaceae*.) » alkaloids; annual; nicotine; perennial; shrub; smoking

Tobacco plant

Tobago [tuh**bay**goh] pop (1980) 39 500; area 300 sq km/116 sq ml. Island in the West Indies; part of the Republic of Trinidad and Tobago; chief town, Scarborough; united with Trinidad in 1889; airport; luxury hotel-conference centre at Rocky Point; tourist complex at Minster Point. » Trinidad and Tobago

Tobey, Mark (1890–1976) US painter, born at Centerville, Wisconsin. He visited Europe and the Near East (1925–7) and lived in England (1931–8), for a while being resident artist at Dartington Hall. After a visit to the Far East in 1934, he developed his personal kind of abstract painting, his 'white writing' based on the patterns of Chinese calligraphy. He died in Basle. » abstract art

Tobit or **Tobias, Book of** [**toh**bit] A book of the Old Testament Apocrypha, or deuterocanonical book in Catholic Bibles; named after its hero, Tobit, written perhaps c.3rd–2nd-c BC by an unknown author. This popular legend is set in 8th-c BC Nineveh, from where Tobit's son (Tobias) is sent to Media, accompanied by the angel Raphael, to reclaim money deposited there by his father. He also learns magic formulas to heal his father's blindness and to exorcize a demon from his future wife, Sarah. The characters exemplify aspects of Jewish piety. » Apocrypha, Old Testament; Judaism

tobogganing » bobsledding

Tobruk or **Tubruq** [tu**bruk**] 32°06N 23°56E, pop (1979) 34 200. Seaport in Darnah province, N Libya, on the Mediterranean coastline; occupied by the Italians, 1911; important battle site in World War 2; taken by Australians (Jan 1941), then changed hands several times until finally taken by the British (late 1942); naval ship repair. » Libya [i]; Rommel

Toby jug A pottery jug in the form of a seated figure, usually a stout man smoking a pipe and wearing a tricorn hat which forms the pouring lip. Such jugs seem to have been introduced by Ralph Wood (1715–72) and his son working in Burslem, Staffordshire, in the second half of the 18th-c. » pottery

Toc H A Christian fellowship founded in 1915 as a club for British soldiers serving in Belgium. Its name derives from its location in Talbot House (named after Lt Gilbert Talbot (1891–1915)), the initials of which were 'pronounced' by army signallers as 'Toc H'. The club is non-sectarian, and now engages in a wide range of social work in the English-speaking world. » Christianity

tocopherol A naturally-occurring E-vitamin, which functions as an anti-oxidant, inhibiting rancidity in oils rich in polyunsaturated fatty acids. It is widely distributed in foods, but its highest levels are found in vegetable oils. In the body, it serves the same function, preserving the integrity of membranes rich in the polyunsaturated fatty acids. Vitamin E deficiency in humans is unknown. » antioxidants; polyunsaturated fatty acids; vitamins [i]

Tocqueville, Alexis (Charles Henri Maurice Clérel) de, [**tok**veel] (1805–59) French historian and political scientist, born at Verneuil, He became a lawyer (1825), and in 1831 went to the USA to report on the prison system. On his return, he published a penetrating political study, *De la Démocratie en Amerique* (1835, Democracy in America), which gave him a European reputation. He became a member of the Chamber of Deputies in 1839, and in 1849 was Vice-President of the Assembly and briefly Minister of Foreign Affairs. After Louis Napoleon's coup, he retired to his estate, where he wrote the first volume of *L'Ancien Régime et la Révolution* (1856, The Old Regime and the Revolution). He died at Cannes before it could be completed. » Napoleon III

todai [toh**diy**] The Japanese abbreviation of *Tokyo Daigaku*, Tokyo University, founded in 1877, an amalgamation of older institutions. It is Japan's leading 'national' (ie state) university. Entrance is strictly on merit, by examination. Many *Todai* graduates go into large companies or government ministries. » university

Todd, Mike, properly **Michael Todd**, originally **Avrom Hirsch Goldbogen** (1909–58) US showman, born in Minneapolis. In 1927 he went to Hollywood as a soundproofing expert, staged a real 'Flame Dance' spectacle at the Chicago World Fair (1933), and produced plays, musical comedies, and films, including a jazz version of Gilbert and Sullivan, *The Hot Mikado* (1939). He sponsored the 'TODD-AO' wide-screen process, used for his greatest film, *Around the World in Eighty Days* (1956, Academy Award). He married his third wife, Elizabeth Taylor, in 1957 and was killed the next year in an aircrash over New Mexico. » Taylor, Elizabeth

Todi, Jacopone da (c.1230–1306) Italian religious poet, born at Todi in Spoleto. He practised as an advocate, was converted in 1268, became a Franciscan in 1278, and was imprisoned (1298–1303) for satirizing Pope Boniface VIII. To him is ascribed the authorship of the *Stabat Mater*, and other Latin hymns; and he wrote *laudi spirituali* ('spiritual praises'), important in the development of Italian drama. He died at Collazzone. » Italian literature; poetry; satire

tog A unit for measuring the 'warmth' rating in bedding textiles. The tog rating is a measure of thermal resistance: the higher the value, the better its performance.

Togliatti » **Tolyatti**

Togo, Heihachiro, Koshaku ('Marquess') (1847–1934) Japanese admiral, born at Kagoshima. He trained at Greenwich, served against China (1894), and as commander during the war with Russia (1904–5), bombarded Port Arthur, and defeated the Russian fleet at Tsushima (1905). He was ennobled in 1907, and died in Tokyo. » Russo-Japanese War

Togo, official name **Republic of Togo**, Fr **République Togolaise** [**toh**goh] pop (1990e) 3 764 000; area 56 600 sq km/21 848 sq ml. Republic in W Africa, divided into five regions; bounded W by Ghana, N by Burkina Faso, and E by Benin; capital, Lomé; chief towns include Sokodé, Palimé, Atakpamé; timezone GMT; chief ethnic groups, Hamitic (N) and Ewe (S); official language, French, with many local languages spoken; chief religions, local beliefs (70%), Christianity (20%); unit of currency, the franc CFA; land rises from the lagoon coast of the Gulf of Guinea, past low-lying plains to the Atakora Mts running NE–SW in the N; highest peak, Pic Baumann (986 m/3 235 ft); flat plains in NW; tropical climate; rain throughout year in S; one rainy season in N (Jul–Sep); average annual rainfall at Lomé, 875 mm/34 in; formerly part of the Kingdom of Togoland; German protectorate, 1884–1914; mandate of the League of Nations in 1922, divided between France (French Togo) and Britain (part of British Gold Coast); trusteeships of the United Nations, 1946; French Togo became an autonomous republic within the French Union, 1956;

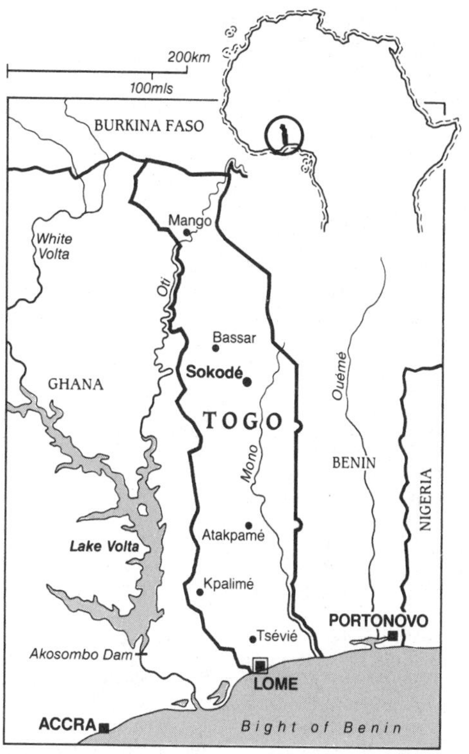

□ international airport

British Togoland voted to join the Gold Coast (Ghana), 1957; independence, 1960; military coups, 1963, 1967; return to civilian rule, 1980; governed by a president, a cabinet, and a 77-member National Assembly, elected for five years; largely agricultural economy; coffee, cocoa, cotton, cassava, maize, rice, timber; phosphates, bauxite, limestone, iron ore, marble; cement, steel, oil refining, food processing, crafts, textiles, beverages. » Ghana [i]; Lomé; mandates; RR27 national holidays; RR63 political leaders

Tojo, Hideki [**toh**joh] (1885–1948) Japanese general, statesman, and Prime Minister (1941–4), born in Tokyo. He attended military college, became military attaché in Germany (1919), served in Manchuria as Chief-of-Staff (1937–40), and during World War 2 was Minister of War (1940–1) and Premier. Arrested in 1945, he attempted to commit suicide, but was hanged as a war criminal in Tokyo. » World War 2

Tok Pisin [tok **pi**zhin] An English-based pidgin, spoken by c.750 000 people in Papua New Guinea, and heavily influenced by local Papuan languages. It is now spoken by some as a mother-tongue, and has thus become a creole. » creole; pidgin

tokamak [**to**kamak] A machine used in nuclear fusion research. A complex system of magnetic fields confines the plasma of reactive charged particles in a hollow torus-shaped chamber, where it is then heated to temperatures in excess of 10^8°C. » Joint European Torus; nuclear fusion; plasma (physics)

tokay gecko [**toh**kay **ge**koh] A large gecko (length, almost 300 mm/12 in), native to India and SE Asia; mottled coloration; nocturnal; eats insects and small vertebrates; common in houses; male calls 'gekk-ho' loudly (all geckos named after this call); also known as **common gecko**. (*Gekko gekko*.) » gecko

Tokelau, formerly **Union Islands** [tohkuh**low**] 8–10°S 171–173°W; pop (1981) 1 572; area 10.1 sq km/3.9 sq ml. Island territory under New Zealand administration, consisting of three small atolls (Atafu, Nukunonu, Fakaofo) in the S Pacific Ocean, c.3 500 km/2 200 ml NNE of New Zealand; chief settlement, Nukunonu; timezone GMT −11; ethnic group, Polynesian; chief languages, Tokelauan, English; inhabitants are citizens of New Zealand; Western Samoa and New Zealand currencies in use; each atoll consists of low-lying, scrub-covered, reef-bound islets encircling a lagoon; hot and humid climate, tempered by trade winds; British protectorate in 1877; annexed in 1916, and included with the Gilbert and Ellice Islands Colony; returned to separate status in 1925, under administrative control of New Zealand, but substantially self-governing at local level; copra, coconuts, breadfruit, pawpaw, bananas, pigs, fowl; principal revenue earners are copra, stamps, souvenir coins, and handicrafts. » New Zealand [i]

token economy A system whereby residents or members of an institution (eg psychiatric hospital, school, custody centre) can earn *tokens* in exchange for socially approved or co-operative behaviour. They then use the tokens to 'buy' chosen goods or privileges. » behaviour modification

tokonama [tohkoh**nah**ma] A Japanese alcove, in Japanese-style houses the place for scroll painting, flower arrangement, and art objects, especially at New Year. At home or in a restaurant the most honoured place for the guest is next to the tokonama.

Tokugawa, Ieyasu [tokoo**gah**wa] (1542–1616) The third of the three great historical unifiers of Japan, after Nobunaga and Hideyoshi, a noble from E Japan. He took power after the Battle of Sekigahara (1600), and founded the Tokugawa shogunate (1603–1868). He completed Edo Castle (the present Tokyo Imperial Palace) as his headquarters, and instituted an all-pervading centralized control of Japanese life, whose effects are still felt. His mausoleum is at Nikko. » daimyo; Hideyoshi; Meiji Restoration; Nobunaga; Shogun

Tokyo 35°40N 139°45E, pop (1987) 11 720 000 (metropolitan district). Seaport capital of Japan, Kanto region, E Honshu; on N shore of Tokyo-wan bay, on R Sumida; founded as village of Edo, 12th-c; headquarters of the Tokugawa shogunate, 1603; imperial capital, 1868; severe earthquake damage, 1923; heavily bombed in World War 2; airport; railway; over 100 universities; shipbuilding, engineering, chemicals, textiles, electrical goods, vehicles; major problems of atmospheric pollution and traffic congestion; Tokyo Tower (1958), tallest metal tower in the world; Ginza shopping district, Idemitsu art gallery, 17th-c Imperial Palace, Meiji Shrine, Asakusa Kannon temple (645); Disneyland (1983), 10 km/6 ml SE. » Japan [i]; Meiji Shrine; Shogun

Toledo (USA) [tuh**lee**doh] 41°39N 83°33W, pop (1980) 354 635. Seat of Lucas County, NW Ohio, USA; port at the mouth of the Maumee R, at the W end of L Erie; formed by the union of two settlements, 1833; involved in the 'Toledo War' (1835–6), a boundary dispute between Ohio and Michigan; railway; university (1872); vehicles, glass and fabricated metal products, machinery, oil products; trade in coal and grain; one of the country's largest rail centres; Museum of Art, Zoological Gardens, Crosby Gardens, Fort Meigs State Memorial, Bluebird Passenger Train. » Ohio

Toledo (Spain) [to**lay**do], Lat **Toletum** 39°50N 4°02W, pop (1981) 57 769. Capital of Toledo province, Castilla-La Mancha, Spain; on R Tagus, 71 km/44 ml SSW of Madrid; former capital of Visigothic kingdom of Castile and of Spain; railway; tourism, metalwork, silk, artwork, confectionery; noted for its swords and knives; Moorish citadel, cathedral (13th–17th-c), El Greco's house, Churches of St Thomas and St Romanus, Santa Cruz museum; archbishop is primate of Roman Catholic province of Spain; old city is a world heritage site; Fiesta of Olivio (Apr–May), fiesta and fair (Aug). » Greco, El; Spain [i]; Visigoths

tolerance In medicine, a diminishing effect when certain drugs are given continuously. Several mechanisms are responsible, which include a change in the wall of the cell membranes that bind the drug, or a change in the way the drug is degraded in the body. *Immunological tolerance* represents the inherent or acquired failure of the immune system to distinguish between the self and a foreign protein or organ graft. » immunity; pharmacology; transplantation

Tolkien, J(ohn) R(onald) R(euel) (1892–1973) British philologist and writer, born in Bloemfontein, South Africa. He was educated in Birmingham and at Oxford, where he became professor of Anglo-Saxon (1925–45) and of English language and literature (1945–59). His interest in language and saga led to his books about a fantasy world in which the beings have their own language and mythology, notably *The Hobbit* (1937), *The Lord of the Rings* (3 vols, 1954–5), and *The Silmarillion* (1977). He died at Bournemouth, Hampshire. » comparative linguistics; English literature

Tolpuddle martyrs Agricultural labourers at Tolpuddle, Dorset, who were organized in 1833 into a trade union by a Methodist local preacher, George Loveless (1796–1874), convicted of taking illegal oaths, and transported. The action provoked substantial protests, and the labourers were eventually pardoned. » trade union

Tolstoy, Count Leo Nikolayevich (1828–1910) Russian writer, moralist, and mystic, one of the world's greatest novelists, born at Yasnaya Polyana, Tula province. Educated privately and at Kazan, he left university without a degree, joined the army in 1851, and began a literary career, becoming known for his short stories. After fighting in the Crimean War, he left the army, travelled abroad, and in 1862 married **Sophie Andreyevna Behrs**, who bore him 13 children. He settled on his Volga estate, where he wrote his epic story of Russia during the Napoleonic Wars, *Voyna i Mir* (1865–9, War and Peace), followed by *Anna Karenina* (1875–7). He then experienced a spiritual crisis which culminated in such works as *Ispoved* (written 1879, A Confession) and *V chyom moya vera* (1883, What I Believe). He made over his fortune to his wife and lived poorly as a peasant under her roof. Leaving home secretly, he died of pneumonia some days later at Astopovo railway station. His doctrines founded a sect, and Yasnaya Polyana became a place of pilgrimage. » Christianity; novel; Russian literature

Toltecs [**tol**teks] A people (or peoples) who controlled most of C Mexico between c.AD 900 and AD 1150; the last such dominant culture prior to the Aztecs. Their capital was at Tula, 80 km/50 ml N of Mexico City. The most impressive Toltec ruins are at Chichen Itzá in Yucatán, where a branch of the culture survived beyond the fall of its C Mexican hegemony. » Chichén Itzá; Mexico [i]

Toluca or **Toluca de Lerdo** [to**loo**ka] 19°17N 99°39W, pop (1980) 357 071. Capital of México state, C Mexico, 66 km/41 ml W of Mexico City; altitude 2 675 m/8 776 ft; founded, 1535; university (1956); textiles, pottery, food processing; Churches of Tercer Orden and Vera Cruz, Convent of Carmen, Museo de Bellas Artes, Palacio de Gobierno, Museo del Arte Popular. » Mexico [i]

toluene [**tol**yooeen] $C_6H_5CH_3$, IUPAC **methylbenzene**, boiling point 111°C. A colourless liquid with a characteristic odour, widely used as an organic solvent, being substantially less toxic than benzene. It is obtained from coal tar, and is the starting point for many organic syntheses. » picric acid; TNT [i]

Tolyatti or **Togliatti**, formerly **Stavropol** (to 1964) 53°32N 49°24E, pop (1989) 630 000. Town in Kuybyshevskaya oblast, Russia, on the Kuybyshev reservoir; founded, 1738; relocated in the mid-1950s when it was flooded by the reservoir of the nearby hydroelectric power plant; rail terminus; synthetic rubber, fertilizers, machinery, foodstuffs. » Russia

Tom Thumb » **Stratton, Charles**

tom-tom A cylindrical, double-headed, high-pitched drum, played with sticks in sets of two or more in Western dance bands and jazz groups. » drum

Tomar [tu**mah**] 39°36N 8°25W, pop (1981) 13 800. Town in Santarém district, C Portugal, on R Nabão; railway; textiles, paper, cork, distilling; Convent of Christ, a world heritage site; Church of São João Baptista; festival of the Tabuleiros (Jul, even-numbered years). » Portugal [i]

tomatillo An annual native to tropical America; flowers bright yellow with dark basal spots; berry 5 cm/2 in, yellow to purple, often bursting through the bladdery calyx. It is a locally important food crop. (*Physalis ixocarpa*. Family: *Solanaceae*.) » annual; physalis; sepal

tomato A bushy annual native to Pacific S America, but now cultivated on a commercial scale throughout the world; leaves pinnate with toothed or lobed leaflets; flowers in short sprays (*trusses*), yellow, with five reflexed petals; berry bright red, fleshy, edible; originally called **love apple** and regarded as an aphrodisiac. The plants are resistant to pests such as greenfly, probably as a result of naturally produced chemicals in the sap. (*Lycopersicon esculentum*. Family: *Solanaceae*.) » annual; aphrodisiacs; pinnate

Tombaugh, Clyde W(illiam) [**tom**bow] (1906–) US astronomer, born at Streator, Illinois. He discovered the planet Pluto at the Lowell Observatory in 1930 as a result of a systematic search in the constellation Gemini. » Gemini; Pluto (astronomy)

tombolo [**tom**buhloh] » **spit**

Tommy gun » **submachine gun; Thompson, John T**

tomography A technique using X-rays or ultrasound in which a clear image of structures in a single plane of body tissues at a particular depth is achieved. » ultrasound; X-rays

Tomsk 56°30N 85°05E, pop (1983) 459 000. River-port capital of Tomskaya oblast, WC Siberian Russia, on R Tom; founded, 1604; major Siberian trade centre until bypassed by the Trans-Siberian railway in the 1890s; airfield; railway; university (1888); machinery, metalworking, chemicals, pharmaceuticals. » Russia; Trans-Siberian Railway

tomtit » **bluetit; great tit**

ton » RR71

tonality The property of music which is written 'in a key', ie with a particular pitch as a point of aural reference (usually firmly established at the beginning and end) towards which other key centres gravitate. The theoretical corner-stones of tonality are the diatonic major and minor scales, in which pitches are related to a tonic, or key-note, so that the intervals between any two degrees of the scale remain the same whichever note serves as the tonic. Tonality admits only two modes (major and minor), but each of these may be expressed in 12 possible keys, related to each other in a kind of hierarchical system based on the number of diatonic notes they have in common. Tonality gradually replaced modality in the 16th–17th-c, and served as the main structural basis for musical work of the next 250 years. It became threatened in the late 19th-c when the level of chromaticism (ie the use of notes foreign to the diatonic scale) began to weaken the aural perception of a tonic, and in the 20th-c several alternatives to tonality were proposed. » atonality; bitonality; chord; chromaticism; diatonicism; harmony; mode (music); pantonality; polytonality; scale [i]; serialism

tone In music, **1** the interval (equal to two semitones) between, for example, the first two notes of a diatonic scale, or *doh* and *ray* in tonic sol-fa. » scale [i] **2** The timbre of a voice or instrument. » timbre **3** US usage for *note* (pitch) in such contexts as '12-tone music', 'tone cluster', and 'tone row'. » note cluster

Tone, (Theobald) Wolfe (1763–98) Irish nationalist, born in Dublin. Educated at Dublin, he was called to the Bar in 1789, acted as secretary of the Catholic Committee, helped to organize the United Irishmen, and had to flee to the USA and to France (1795). He induced France to invade Ireland on two occasions, and was captured during the second expedition. He was condemned to be hanged, but committed suicide in Dublin. » nationalism

tone cluster » **note-cluster; tone 3**

tone language A language in which the pitch level (*tone*) carried by a word is an essential signal of its meaning. In one variety of Chinese, for example, the word *ma* means 'mother' with a level tone, and *horse* with a falling-rising tone. » prosody

tone poem » **symphonic poem**

Tonga, formerly **Friendly Islands** pop (1990e) 96 300; area 646 sq km/249 sq ml. Island group in the SW Pacific Ocean, 2 250 km/1 400 ml NE of New Zealand; capital, Nuku'alofa; timezone GMT +13; population mainly Tongans (98%); chief religion, Christianity; official language, English; unit of currency, the pa'anga; consists of 169 islands, 36 inhabited, divided into three main groups (coral formations of Ha'apai and Tongatapu-Eua, mountainous Vava'u); largest island is Tongatapu, with two-thirds of the population, area 260 sq km/100 sq ml; W islands mainly volcanic, some still active, height 500–1 000 m/1 600–3 200 ft; highest point, extinct volcano of Kao (1 014 m/3 327 ft); semi-tropical climate; average annual temperature at Tongatapu, 23°C, average annual rainfall 1 750 mm/69 in; occasional hurricanes in summer months; British protectorate in 1899, under its own monarchy; independence, 1970; governed by a sovereign, Privy Council, and a unicameral Legislative Assembly of cabinet members, nobles, and elected people's representatives; economy largely based on agriculture; copra, coconuts, bananas, watermelons, yams, taro, cassava, groundnuts, rice, maize, tobacco, sugar cane; tourism and cottage handicrafts are small but growing industries. » Nuku'alofa; RR27 national holidays; RR63 political leaders

Tongariro [tonggareeroo] 39°08S 175°42E; area 765 sq km/295 sq ml. Active volcano rising to 1 968 m/6 457 ft in Tongariro national park in CSW North Island, New Zealand; contains the active volcanoes of Ruapehu and Ngauruhoe; winter skiing resort; many historical Maori sites; established in 1894. » New Zealand [i]

Tongeren [**tong**uhruhn], Fr **Tongres** 50°47N 5°28E, pop (1982) 29 765. Rural market town in S Limburg province, Belgium, on R Jeker; oldest town in Belgium, founded 1st-c AD; basilica of Our Lady. » Belgium [i]

Tongkin or **Tonking, Gulf of** [tong**king**] Gulf in Indo-China, situated E of Vietnam and W of Hainan I, China; an inlet of the South China Sea.

Tongres [tõgruh] » **Tongeren**

tongue A highly mobile, muscular structure vital for the digestive functions of chewing, taste, and swallowing. In humans it is also important in speech, being essential for the production of all vowels and most consonants. It consists of a free front part within the mouth (horizontal at rest), containing numerous taste buds, and a more fixed back part in the oropharynx, which has accumulations of lymphoid tissue associated with it (the *lingual tonsil*). The two parts are separated by a V-shaped furrow on the upper surface, with its apex directed backwards. A pit at the apex marks the site of origin of the thyroglossal duct (which gives rise to the thyroid gland). The upper surface (*dorsum*) of the front part is covered with various types of *papillae*, most of which are studded with taste buds. The mucous membrane covering the tongue is continuous with that of the floor of the mouth and the oropharynx. The muscles of the tongue are grouped into those which change its shape (the *intrinsic* muscles) and those which change its position within the mouth (the *extrinsic* muscles). » mouth; pharynx; tonsils

tongue worm A simple, worm-like arthropod that lives as an internal parasite in the lungs and nasal passages of reptiles, birds, and mammals; feeds on blood. (Subphylum: *Pentastomida*, c.55 species.) » arthropod; parasitology; worm

tonic sol-fa A system of musical notation devised by John Curwen, who based it on the solmization system of Guido d'Arezzo, anglicizing the pitch names to *doh*, *ray*, *me*, *fah*, *soh*, *la*, *te*. These could be abbreviated to their initial letters, and furnished with other signs to indicate note-lengths, rests, and octave transposition. An ability to read the notation requires training in sol-fa, which is gained through singing exercises in the schoolroom with the help of a scale-chart, or 'modulator'. » scale [i]; solmization

toning Chemically converting a black and white photograph to another colour. Examples include changing the black metallic silver of the image to silver sulphide for sepia tones, or to iron or copper compounds for blue or red-brown respectively. A wide range of other hues can be obtained by bleaching the silver image and redeveloping with colour couplers. » colour photography; couplers

Tonkin Gulf Resolution (1964) A resolution adopted by the US Congress after alleged attacks by N Vietnamese torpedo boats on US destroyers in the Gulf of Tonkin. It empowered the president to take 'all necessary steps, including the use of armed force' to assist a member of the Southeast Asia Treaty Organization seeking aid 'in defense of its freedom'. It became the legal underpinning for the US position during the Vietnam War. » Southeast Asia Treaty Organization; Vietnam War

Tonlé Sap [**ton**lay **sap**], Eng **Great Lake** Freshwater lake in WC Cambodia, in a depression on the Cambodian Plain, where it acts as a natural flood reservoir; area 2 850 sq km/1 100 sq ml during the dry season; linked to the Mekong R by the Tonlé Sap R, confluence at Phnom Penh; seasonal reversal of the river, flowing towards the Mekong in the dry season, and away from it in the wet season; height raised by c.9 m/29 ft and area almost tripled during the wet season; important communications route; fishing. » Cambodia [i]

tonnage and poundage British mediaeval customs duties: tonnage was collected on tuns of imported wine; poundage at a rate of 3*d*. per £ of the value of imports. From the reign of Henry V, Parliament granted the taxes for life to monarchs, with the exception of Charles I in 1625 (who collected them anyway). They were incorporated into the civil list in 1697. » civil list

tonne » **kilogram**

tonsillitis Acute or chronic inflammation of the tonsils, usually due to infection with streptococci. The condition usually responds to treatment with antibiotics. Removal of the tonsils (*tonsillectomy*) is now rarely required, and only when the tonsils are greatly enlarged and the infection deep-seated. » streptococcus; tonsils

tonsils Accumulations of lymphoid tissue found at the entrance to the respiratory and digestive tracts. Four such regions can be identified on each side of the body. The **palatine** tonsils (also referred to simply as 'the tonsils') are found at the entrance to the oropharynx. The **lingual** tonsils are under the epithelium of the back part of the tongue (again in the proximity of the oropharynx). The **tubal** tonsils are in the nasopharynx, associated with the opening of the auditory tube. The **pharyngeal** tonsils are situated close to the base of the skull above the auditory tube behind the nasal cavity; they are also known as the *adenoids*. The four pairs of tonsils form a protective ring of tissue whose primary function is to combat airborn infections entering the body. » adenoids; lymphoid tissue; pharynx; quinsy; tonsillitis

tonsure The shaving of all or part of the head, to denote clerical or monastic status. It is still compulsory for certain monks and priests. » monasticism

Tooke, John Horne, originally **John Horne** (1736–1812) British radical politician, born and died in London. Educated at Eton and Cambridge, he became a lawyer, and in 1760 a vicar. In 1771 he formed the Constitutional Society, supporting the American colonists and parliamentary reform. His spirited opposition to an enclosure bill procured him the favour of the rich Mr Tooke of Purley in Surrey, which led to his new surname and *The Diversions of Purley* (1786), written while in prison for supporting the American cause. He was tried for high treason in 1794, acquitted, and became an MP in 1801. » American Revolution; Wilkes

tools Any implement which is used to carry out a task. Early man made the first axes by sharpening flint. Stone tools were replaced around 4000 BC by metal tools, which were used to build instruments and simple machines. The Industrial Revolution saw the introduction of machine tools, and mass production of goods became a possibility. Modern tools are now available for any task, often powered by electricity, and varying enormously in size, from the vast grabs used in the building industry to the sensitive handling tools used in the nuclear industry. » machine [i]; machine tools

tooth » **teeth** [i]

toothwort A parasitic perennial, native to Europe and Asia; stem white; flowers tinged dull purple, forming a one-sided spike. It closely resembles the broomrapes, but is parasitic on roots of trees and shrubs, especially elm and hazel. (*Lathraea sqaumaria*. Family: *Scrophulariaceae*.) » broomrape; parasitic plant; perennial

Toowoomba 27°35S 151°54E, pop (1981) 63 401. City in Queensland, Australia, 130 km/80 ml W of Brisbane; airfield; railway; commercial centre for the rich agricultural Darling Downs area; trading in meat, wool, wheat, dairy produce; engineering, food processing, iron, clothing, agricultural machinery; Early Settlers Museum; St Matthew's Church (1859); Carnival of Flowers (Sep). » Queensland

top-down processing » **bottom up/top-down processing**

top minnow » **killifish**

topaz An aluminium silicate mineral ($Al_2SiO_4(OH,F)_2$), occurring in acid igneous rocks, pegmatites, and veins, with a colour range including colourless, yellow, and blue. It may be used as a gemstone. » aluminium; gemstones; silicate minerals

tope [tohp] Slender-bodied grey shark common in inshore waters of the E North Atlantic; related species found around Australia; length up to c.2 m/6½ ft; feeds mainly on bottom-living fish. (*Galeorhinus galeus*. Family: *Carcharhinidae*.) » shark

Topeka [tuh**pee**ka] 39°03N 95°40W, pop (1980) 115 266. Capital of state in Shawnee County, E Kansas, USA, on Kansas R; settled by anti-slavery colonists, 1854; capital, 1861; railway; university (1865); marketing and processing centre for agricultural products, particularly cattle and wheat; railway engineering; important centre for psychiatric research and therapy. » Kansas

topi [**toh**pee] An African ox-antelope with a long face; lyre-shaped horns ringed with ridges; coat with large dark patches on rich chestnut red; inhabits grassland; fastest of all hoofed mammals (over 70 kph/40 mph); also known as **bastard hartebeest**, **sassaby**, **tsessebi**, **tiang**, **tiangs damalisc**, or **korrigum**. (*Damaliscus lunatus*.) » antelope

topography The study of the physical characteristics of the Earth's surface (eg relief, soils, vegetation). A topographical map portrays information such as elevation and gradient through the use of symbols and special shading to show contours and spot heights. » map

topology A generalization of geometry which studies the properties of shapes and space that are independent of distance. The usual map of the London Underground is an example of a topological diagram, for it shows the lines joining various stations, yet is not to scale. Topology has been developed very widely this century, and can perhaps now best be described as the study of continuity. » geometry; Möbius strip [i]; Plate XIII

tor A mound of weathered, well-jointed, resistant bare rocks. The rock is usually crystalline, and is exposed when surrounding and overlying rocks are stripped away by agents of erosion, such as frost action and chemical weathering. Examples include the granite tors of Dartmoor, UK. Similar features in the tropics are known as **kopjes**. » crystals; erosion

Torah [**toh**ra] (Heb 'instruction') The Jewish Law, most narrowly considered the Priestly Code found in the Pentateuch and said to have been given to Moses by God. The term was also often applied to the Pentateuch as a whole; and as the importance of the Prophets and Writings grew, it was sometimes used to describe them all as divinely revealed instructions and traditions. This written Torah was eventually supplemented in Pharisaic and rabbinic tradition by the Oral Torah, not a fixed revelation but an elucidation and application of the Written Torah by sages of various periods. » Judaism; Mishnah; Old Testament; Pentateuch; rabbi

Torbay 50°28N 3°30W, pop (1987e) 117 700. Urban area in Devon, SW England, formed in 1968; includes the resort towns of Torquay, Paignton, and Brixham; railway; tourism, horticulture, electronics. » Devon

Tories The British political party which emerged in 1679–80 as the group opposed to the exclusion of James, Duke of York, from succession to the throne. The name was taken from 17th-c Irish outlaws who plundered and killed English settlers. The party developed after the Glorious Revolution of 1688 as the supporters of the divine right of monarchy, and had particular support from the country squirearchy and most sections of the Anglican church. It opposed religious toleration for Catholics and Dissenters. The Tories enjoyed periods of power in the reign of Queen Anne, but the party went into decline after the Hanoverian succession, when some of its supporters became Jacobites. It is generally agreed to have revived under the younger Pitt as the leading opposition to French Revolutionary ideology in the 1790s, and Lord Liverpool became the first prime minister to acknowledge the title 'Tory' in the early 19th-c. Toryism developed into Conservatism under Peel, but survived as a nickname for the Conservatives. » Conservative Party; Liverpool, Lord; Peel; Whigs

torii [**toh**ree] A Shinto gateway in Japan, the traditional arch at the entrance to the sacred grounds of Shinto shrines, generally orange-red in colour, but sometimes unpainted, giving the name of the deity. At shrines of the harvest god, or the fox deity (*Inari*), those wanting good fortune may donate torii with their names. A famous torii is found on the Inland Sea off Miyajima. » RR93

tormentil [**taw**mntil] Any of various species of *Potentilla*, with 4-petalled, yellow flowers. (Genus: *Potentilla*. Family: *Rosaceae*.) » potentilla

tornado A column of air rotating rapidly (up to 100 m per sec/c.225 ml per hour) around a very low pressure centre. Over the Great Plains of the USA they may develop from squall-line thunderstorms, and are common in spring and early summer. The mechanism of formation is not fully understood, but they are associated with low pressure systems, and resemble a dark funnel extending from the cloud base to the ground. Although short-lived, lasting 1–2 hours and usually only a few hundred metres in diameter, they can be very destructive in restricted areas. A tornado is also known as a 'twister' in the USA. » squall-line; water-spout; whirlwind

Tornio, River, Swed **Torne älv** River in N and NE Sweden; issues from L Torneträsk in NW Sweden; flows SE and S, forming part of the Swedish–Finnish border in its lower course; enters the Gulf of Bothnia at Tornio; length 566 km/352 ml. » Sweden [i]

Toronto 43°42N 79°25W, pop (1981) 599 217; (metropolitan area) 2 998 947. Capital of Ontario province, SE Canada, on N shore of L Ontario, at the mouth of the Don R; second largest city in Canada; French fort, 1749; occupied by the British, 1759; settled by United Empire Loyalist migrants from the American Revolution, 1793, named York; capital of Upper Canada, 1796; city and modern name, 1834; capital of Ontario, 1867; ice-free harbour (Apr–Nov); two airports; railway; subway; two universities (1827, 1959); leading commercial and cultural centre; diverse industries, such as meat packing, petroleum and metal products, machinery, clothing, food processing, publishing, trade in coal and grain; major league teams, Blue Jays (baseball), Maple Leafs (ice hockey); several theatres, ballet, Toronto Symphony Orchestra; O'Keefe Centre, home of the Canadian Opera Company; Art Gallery of Ontario, Sigmund Samuel Canadiana Gallery; Osgoode Hall (1828); old City Hall (1891–9) with 91 m/298 ft-high clocktower; Fort York (1793, restored 1934); Ontario Centennial Centre of Science and Technology; Canadian National Exhibition, Horse Show, and Dog Show (Aug–Sep), Royal Agricultural Winter Fair (Nov). » American Revolution; C N Tower; Ontario

torpedo A munition of naval warfare, in essence a guided underwater missile, equipped with a motor to propel it through the water and an explosive charge fused to detonate on impact with its target. The first practical torpedo dates from the middle of the 19th-c. In modern warfare, guided torpedoes are a key anti-submarine weapon, equipped with sonar-seeking heads which identify and track underwater sounds, and computerized systems to guide them towards the source of noise. » missile, guided; sonar; submarine

torpedo ray » **electric ray**

Torquay [taw**kee**] 50°28N 3°30W, pop (1981) 57 491. Resort town in Torbay district, Devon, SW England; 30 km/19 ml S of Exeter; centre for recreational sailing; railway; Torr Abbey (12th-c), Kent's Cavern; regatta (Aug). » Devon

torque In mechanics, the ability of a force to cause rotation. Torque equals the product of the force with the perpendicular distance between the rotation axis and the line of action of the force; symbol Γ; units Nm. » mechanics; moment [i]

Torquemada, Tomás de [tawkay**mah**da] (1420–98) First Inquisitor-General of Spain, born at Valladolid. He was Dominican prior at Segovia (1452–74), and persuaded Ferdinand and Isabella to ask the Pope to sanction the institution of the 'Holy Office' of the Inquisition. As Grand Inquisitor from 1483, he displayed great cruelty, and was responsible for an estimated 2 000 burnings. He died at Avila. » Ferdinand (of Castile); Inquisition

torr Unit of pressure; symbol torr; named after Italian physicist Evangelista Torricelli; originally defined as the pressure equal to a column of mercury 1 millimetre high; 1 torr = 133.3 Pa (pascal, SI unit); still commonly used in vacuum physics. » pascal; Torricelli; units (scientific); vacuum

Torrens, Lake Salt lake in SC South Australia, W of the Flinders Ranges; 240 km/150 ml long; 65 km/40 ml wide; area 5 775 sq km/2 229 sq ml. » South Australia

Torreón [toray**ohn**] 25°34N 103°25W, pop (1980) 363 886. Town in Coahuila state, N Mexico, on the R Nazas; railway; cotton, wheat. » Mexico [i]

Torres Strait Channel between the Coral Sea (E) and the Arafura Sea (W), to the N of Cape York, Queensland, Australia; c.130 km/80 ml wide; discovered by Spanish explorer Luis Vaez de Torres, 1606; contains **Torres Strait Islands**, which may be remains of a land bridge linking Asia and Australia; annexed by Queensland in 19th-c; inhabited by Polynesians, Melanesians, Aborigines, pop (1981) 6 131; pearl culture, fishing; much emigration to Australia. » Queensland

Torricelli, Evangelista [toree**chel**lee] (1608–47) Italian physicist and mathematician, born at Faenza. He went in 1627 to Rome, where he devoted himself to mathematics, became Galileo's amanuensis (1641), and succeeded him as professor at the Florentine Academy. He discovered the effect of atmospheric pressure on water in a suction pump, and gave the first description of a barometer, or 'torricellian tube'. He died at Florence. » barometer; Galileo; torr

Tórshavn, also **Thorshavn** [**tors**-hown] 62°02N 6°47W, pop (1981) 11 618. Seaport capital of the Faeroe Is; on SE coast of Strømø I; commerce and fishing. » Faeroe Islands

torsion The application of twisting force. *Torsional forces* cause shear strain. *Torsion pendulums* rely on a flat disc suspended horizontally by a wire attached centrally, so that the disc twists first one way then the other. *Torsion balances* measure forces by detecting the degree of twist. » pendulum; shear modulus; torque [i]

tort A wrong actionable in the civil courts. The usual remedies are damages and/or an injunction. In some instances, the tort may be 'waived', and the defendant required to account for profits gained through the wrong. Individual torts include negligence, trespass, and nuisance. Inducing a breach of contract is also a tort, though breach of contract, another civil wrong, is not so classified. *Delict* is the analogous term in Scottish law. » contract; court of law; damages; injunction; negligence; nuisance

Tortelier, Paul [taw**tel**yay] (1914–90) French cellist, born in Paris, where he studied at the Conservatoire and made his debut (1931). Before World War 2 he played in orchestras in Monte Carlo and Boston, and then achieved worldwide recognition as one of the leading soloists on his instrument. His

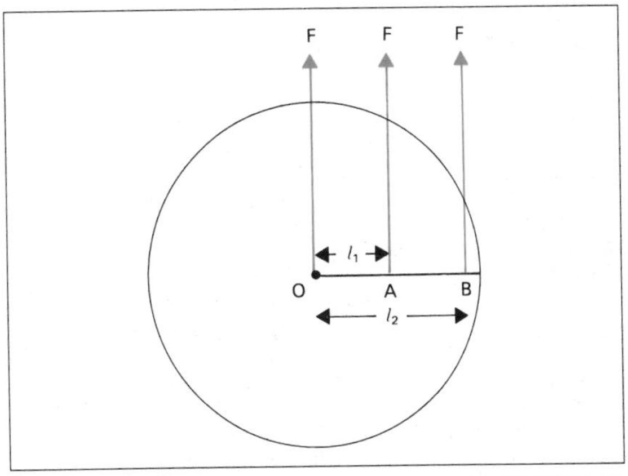

Torque – Force F acting through a fixed centre O will not cause the disc to rotate, whereas the force applied at points A and B will. Applied at point B, a given force produces torque $\Gamma = Fl_2$ larger than the torque Fl_1 at A. A force applied at the outer edge of a disc thus sets the disc spinning more rapidly than the same force applied closer to the centre.

son **Yan Pascal** (1947–) and daughter **Maria de la Pau** (1950–) are highly gifted players of the violin and piano respectively. » cello

tortoise A land-dwelling reptile of order *Chelonia*; feet short, round, with short claws; toes not webbed; used especially for 41 species of family *Testudinidae*; native to tropical and subtropical regions (except Australasia); usually vegetarian. » Chelonia [i]; Galapagos giant tortoise [i]; reptile; turtle (biology)

tortoise beetle A flattened beetle in which the sides of the body are expanded to give a tortoiseshell-like appearance; larvae feed on plants and typically conceal themselves beneath faeces and cast skins. (Order: *Coleoptera*. Family: *Chrysomelidae*.) » beetle; larva

tortoiseshell butterfly A colourful butterfly; wings reddish with dark patches, and with blue patches on both wings or on hindwings; forelegs reduced, non-functional; eggs ribbed; caterpillars with spikes. (Order: *Lepidoptera*. Family: *Nymphalidae*.) » butterfly; caterpillar

tortoiseshell cat A British short-haired domestic cat; mottled coat of black, dark red, and light red (with no white); difficult to produce; almost always female (males rare and sterile); also known as **calimanco cat** or **clouded tiger**. The name (often shortened to **tortie**) is also used for other breeds with mottled markings. » cat

Toruń, Ger **Thorn** [to**roon**] 53°01N 18°35E, pop (1983) 182 400. Industrial river port and capital of Toruń voivodship, NC Poland, on R Vistula; railway; university (1945); synthetic fibres, electronics, wool, fertilizer; birthplace of Copernicus; Church of St John (13th-c), palace of the bishops of Kuyawy (1693), castle (13th-c), ethnographical museum, burghers' manor (15th-c); annual Polish theatre festival. » Copernicus; Poland [i]

Torvill, Jayne (1957–) and **Christopher Dean** (1958–) British figure skaters, both from Nottingham. They were world ice dance champions 1981–4, and Olympic champions in 1984. Their highly acclaimed performances included an interpretation of music from Ravel's *Bolero*, and the musical, *Barnum*, which was choreographed by British actor Michael Crawford. They retired from competitive skating in 1984, and turned professional. » ice skating

Toscanini, Arturo [toskan**ee**nee] (1867–1957) Italian conductor, born at Parma. He studied cello at Parma and Milan, and while playing at Rio de Janeiro in 1886 was suddenly called upon to replace the conductor, presenting a triumphant performance of *Aida*. He later conducted at La Scala, Milan (1898–1908), the Metropolitan Opera House, New York (1908–15), the New York Philharmonic (1926–36), the Bayreuth (1930–1) and Salzburg (1934–7) festivals, and brought into being the National Broadcasting Orchestra of America (1937–53). He died in New York City.

Tosefta or **Tosephta** [toh**sef**ta] (Aramaic 'supplement') A large collection of rabbinic, extra-Mishnaic traditions and discussions which expand and supplement the teachings of the Mishnah, but usually considered of lesser authority. The material is arranged topically, with headings similar to those of the Mishnah. In its present form, it was perhaps compiled c.4th–5th-c AD, but some of the traditions were much earlier. » Mishnah; rabbi; Talmud

total art » **Gesamtkunstwerk**

totalitarianism In its modern form, a political concept first used to describe the USSR's communist regime and Italy and Germany's fascist regimes during the period between the two World Wars. It is difficult to distinguish empirically from related concepts such as authoritarianism and dictatorship, but certain common features can be identified. These relate to the use of power and the means of government employed by the leadership, which claims exclusive rights to govern, usually on behalf of the party and its ideology. Furthermore, all aspects of social, political, industrial, military, and economic life are controlled or permeated by the state apparatus. Political opposition is suppressed, and decision-making is highly centralized. » authoritarianism; communism; dictator; fascism

Totalizator A method of placing bets at horse race or greyhound meetings, commonly known as the **Tote**. All money invested is returned to winning punters, less expenses and taxes. Totalizator betting was first tried at Newmarket and Carlisle on 2 July 1928.

totem pole An elaborately carved pole about 20 m/65 ft high, erected in front of houses, made by Pacific NW Coast American Indians. The tradition dates back to the mid-19th-c, when huge trees were cut down. A symbol of prestige, lacking any religious meaning, many contained crests or life histories of the men who commissioned them. » Northwest Coast Indians

toucan A largish bird with an enormous bill, native to the New World tropics; brightly coloured; bare coloured skin around eye; long tail; inhabits woodland; eats seeds, fruit, invertebrates, and small vertebrates. (Family: *Ramphastidae*, 42 species.)

touch-me-not » **balsam**

toughness A measure of a material's resistance to the propagation of cracks. A material is tough if it is difficult to tear or shatter. Glass is brittle because of the presence of many tiny cracks, but fibre glass is tough, since embedding glass fibres in resin prevents the spread of cracks. » mechanical properties of matter

Toulon [toolõ], Lat **Tilio Martius** 43°10N 5°55E, pop (1982) 181 405. Fortified naval port and capital of Var department, SE France; on Mediterranean Sea, 70 km/43 ml SE of Marseille; most important naval port in France; major naval station in World War 1; French fleet scuttled here in 1942, to prevent German capture; railway; episcopal see; shipbuilding, oil refining, armaments, chemicals, textiles; Gothic Cathedral of Ste-Marie-Majeure (11th–12th-c), naval museum, opera house, zoo. » Gothic architecture; World War 2

Toulouse [too**looz**], ancient **Tolosa** 43°37N 1°27E, pop (1982) 354 289. Capital of Haute-Garonne department, S France; on R Garonne and Canal du Midi, 213 km/132 ml SE of Bordeaux; capital of former province of Languedoc; fourth largest city in France; road and rail junction; archbishopric; university (1229); Catholic Institute of Toulouse (1877); cultural and economic centre of S France; electronics, aircraft, armaments, textiles, chemicals; Church of St-Sernin (11th–12th-c), Gothic Church of the Jacobins (1216), Cathedral of St-Etienne (11th–17th-c), observatory, botanical gardens; known as the 'red city' because of its numerous brick buildings. » Languedoc

Toulouse-Lautrec (-Monfa), Henri (Marie Raymonde) de, [too**looz** loh**trek**] (1864–1901) French painter and lithographer, born at Albi. Physically frail, at the age of 14 he broke both his legs, which then ceased to grow. From 1882 he studied in Paris and in 1884 settled in Montmartre, where he painted and drew the cabaret stars, prostitutes, barmaids, clowns, and actors of that society, as in 'The Bar' (1898, Zürich) and 'At the Moulin Rouge' (1892, Chicago). He also depicted fashionable society, such as 'At the Races' (1899), and produced several portraits. His alcoholism brought a complete breakdown, forcing him into a sanatorium (1899); he recovered to resume his hectic life until his death at Malromé. Over 600 of his works are in the Musée Lautrec at Albi. » French art; lithography

Tour de France The world's most gruelling bicycle race, first held in 1903. Riders have to cover approximately 4 800 km/3 000 ml of French countryside during a three-week period each July. About 10 million people watch the race each year. » cycling

touraco » **turaco**

Touraine [too**ren**] Former province in C France, now occupying the department of Indre-et-Loire and part of Vienne; became part of France, 1641; known for its Huguenot silk-weaving trade; chief town, Tours. » Huguenots; Tours

tourmaline A complex borosilicate mineral containing sodium, calcium, iron, magnesium, and other metals, found in igneous and metamorphic rocks. It forms hard, dense, prismatic crystals, and may be used as a gemstone. » gemstones; silicate minerals

Tournai, Flemish **Doornik**, ancient **Tornacum** 49°52N 5°24E, pop (1982) 67 576. Administrative and cultural town in W Hainaut province, Belgium, on the R Scheldt, 22 km/14 ml E of

Lille; bishopric; second oldest town in Belgium, founded 275 AD; railway; cement, machinery, foodstuffs, textiles (especially carpets), tourism; cathedral (11th–12th-c, restored 19th-c). » Belgium [i]

Tourneur, Cyril [toorner] (c.1575–1626) English dramatist. He published several poems, but is known for his two plays, *The Revenger's Tragedy* (1607, sometimes assigned to Webster or Middleton), and *The Atheist's Tragedy* (1611). He died at Kinsale, Co Cork, on returning from an expedition to Cadiz. » drama; English literature; tragedy

Tours [toor], ancient **Caesarodunum** or **Turoni** 47°22N 0°40E, pop (1982) 136 483. Industrial and commercial city, and capital of Indre-et-Loire department, WC France; between Loire and Cher Rivers, 206 km/128 ml SW of Paris; episcopal see, 3rd-c; grew up around tomb of St Martin (died in 397), becoming a place of pilgrimage and centre of healing; Huguenot silk industry in 15th–16th-c; airport; road and rail junction; university (1970); metallurgy, plastics, electronics, wine, tourism; birthplace of Balzac; 12th–16th-c Cathedral of St-Gatien, several silk museums, museum of Touraine wines, art museum. » Balzac; Huguenots; Martin, St; Touraine

Toussaint L'Ouverture, originally **François Dominique Toussaint** [toosĩ loovertür] (1746–1803) Black revolutionary leader, born a slave in Saint Domingue (Haiti, from 1804). In 1791, he joined the insurgents, and by 1797 was effective ruler of the former colony. He drove out British and Spanish expeditions, restored order, and aimed at independence. Napoleon sent a new expedition to Saint Domingue, and proclaimed the re-establishment of slavery. Toussaint was eventually arrested, and died in a French prison. His surname comes from his bravery in once making a breach in the ranks of the enemy. » Haiti; Napoleon I

Tower Bridge The easternmost bridge on the R Thames, London. The bridge can open to allow large ships in and out of the Pool of London. It was designed by Sir Horace Jones (1819–87) and Sir John Wolfe Barry (1836–1918), and opened in 1894. » bridge (engineering) [i]; London [i]; Thames, River

Tower of London A palace-fortress started by the Normans in the 11th-c. From the 15th-c to the 18th-c the Tower was notorious as a state prison. It is now Britain's most popular tourist attraction, and the depository of the royal coronation regalia. » crown jewels; London [i]; Normans

town gas » **gas 2** [i]

town hall clock » **moschatel** [i]

Townes, Charles H(ard) (1915–) US physicist, born at Greenville, S Carolina. He worked at Bell Telephone Laboratories, taught at Columbia, and became professor of physics at the Massachusetts Institute of Technology (1961–7), and at California (1967). He shared the 1964 Nobel Prize for Physics for his work on the development of the maser, and later the laser. » laser [i]; maser

Townshend (of Rainham), Charles, 2nd Viscount (1674–1738) English Whig statesman, born and died at Raynham, Norfolk. Educated at Eton and Cambridge, he succeeded his father as viscount (1687), was made Secretary of State by George I (1714–16, 1721–30), and became a leading figure in the Whig ministry with his brother-in-law, Robert Walpole. After a resignation engineered by Walpole, he became known as 'turnip Townshend' for his interest in agricultural improvement, and his proposal to use turnips in crop rotation. » crop rotation; George I; Walpole, Robert; Whigs

Townshend Acts (1767) Taxes imposed by the British Parliament on five categories of goods imported into the American colonies, after successful colonial resistance to the Stamp Act (1765). The Townshend Taxes likewise met resistance, and four categories were repealed in 1770. The fifth, on tea, remained in effect until the Boston Tea Party. The Acts are named after British Chancellor of the Exchequer, Charles Townshend (1725–67), who sponsored them. » American Revolution; Stamp Act

Townsville 19°13S 146°48E, pop (1986) 103 700. Industrial port and resort in Queensland, Australia, on Cleveland Bay; founded 1864; largest city in tropical Australia; headquarters of the Great Barrier Reef Marine Park Authority and the Australian Institute of Marine Science; airport; railway; university (1970); army and air-force bases; copper, lead, nickel, cobalt and silver mining, food processing, engineering; trade in beef, wool, sugar; Townsville Pacific Festival (Jun); Magnetic I a tourist centre. » Great Barrier Reef; Queensland

toxaemia of pregnancy » **eclampsia**

toxic shock syndrome A sudden collapse with shock and falling blood pressure, which results from toxins released into the blood stream by infection with staphylococci. A rare occurrence, it has been mainly associated with the use by women of superabsorbent tampons, the infection originating in the vagina. » shock; staphylococcus

toxicology The study of the adverse effects of chemicals on living systems. Toxicology allows prediction of the risks likely to be associated with a particular chemical or drug. The modern science was founded in the 19th-c by French chemist Mathieu Orfila (1787–1853).

toxin A poison produced by a micro-organism which causes certain diseases or disorders. Botulinum toxin from the bacteria *Clostridium botulinum* is one of the most powerful, deadly toxins known. Toxins from *Salmonella typhi* cause typhoid fever; *Pasteurella pestis* cause bubonic plague; *Shigella dysenteriae* cause dysentery. Toxins can also be secreted by plants and animals. » aflatoxin; botulism; toxicology

toxocariasis [toksohkariyasis] Infection with the ova of *Toxocara canis* (carried by dogs), which may be eaten especially by children and migrate throughout the body. They cause allergic features such as asthma, and sometimes also a lesion of the eye. » allergy

toxoplasmosis [toksohplazmohsis] Infection with the protozoa *Toxoplasma gondi*. It is often harmless, but may be transmitted by an infected mother to the foetus, leading to congenital toxoplasmosis, with involvement of the brain, eyes, heart, and lungs. » Protozoa

toy dog » **non-sporting dog**

Toynbee, Arnold (Joseph) (1889–1975) British historian, born in London. Educated at Winchester and Oxford, he served in the Foreign Office in both World Wars, and attended the Paris peace conferences (1919 and 1946). He was professor of modern Greek and Byzantine history at London (1919–24) and director of the Royal Institute of International Affairs, London (1925–55). His major work was the 10-volume *History of the World* (1934–54). He died at York. » Paris, Treaties of

Toynbee Hall The first university settlement (institutions through which universities provide support to deprived inner city communities), founded in E London in 1885. It was named after the social reformer and economist Arnold Toynbee (1852–83), who dedicated himself to improving the quality of life of the urban poor. » London [i]; university

trabeated construction » **post and lintel** [i]

trace elements » **nutrients**

tracer bullet A bullet containing a charge of chemical compound (such as phosphorous) which glows brightly as it flies through the air, indicating in darkness or through the fog of war the 'trace' of the bullet's path, and thus its efficacy in reaching the target.

tracery The ornamental stone pattern work used in the upper part of a window, screen, panel, or other building element. It is usually associated with Gothic architecture, although the term was first used in 17th-c England. There are two main types: the simpler **plate tracery**, giving emphasis to the spaces in between, and the more complicated **bar tracery**, used extensively in Gothic churches. Various stylistic sub-divisions include geometrical, intersecting, panel, and reticulated. » Gothic architecture; Gothic Revival; *see illustration p 1222*

trachea [trakeea] A tube connecting the larynx with the principal bronchi; also known as the **windpipe**. It has an external fibrous membrane which encloses hoops of cartilage (open at the back) that prevent the trachea from collapsing. During breathing the trachea stretches longitudinally (up to 2 cm/0.8 in). In the human adult it is 9–15 cm/3.5–6 in long. In cases of respiratory distress the trachea can be surgically opened between the cartilage rings within the lower part of the neck to provide a passage for air (*tracheostomy*); however, care must be taken to avoid the thyroid gland which overlies the

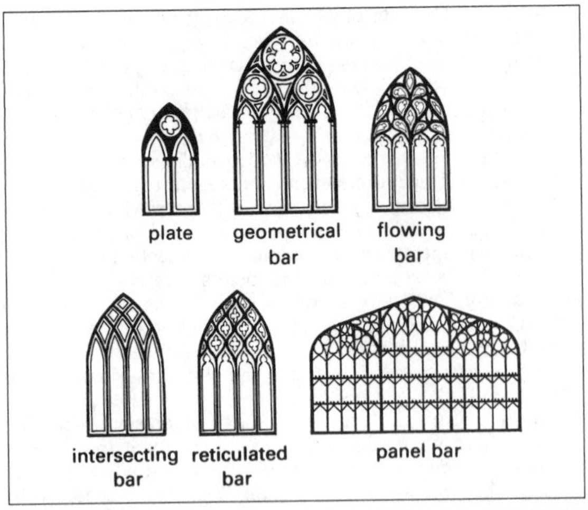

Tracery in windows

second to fourth cartilage rings. » bronchi; cartilage; croup; larynx; respiration; Plate XII

trachoma [tra**koh**ma] Infection with a *Chlamydia* bacterium that affects the eyes, leading to conjunctivitis and blindness. Vast numbers of people living in the tropics and subtropics are affected. » blindness; chlamydia; conjunctivitis; eye [i]

Tractarianism » **Oxford Movement**

tractor A self-propelled vehicle found on farms or similar places of work, and normally used for towing and powering various agricultural machines. Tractors do not usually have a frame or springs, but use the engine and transmission housing to provide structural rigidity, with the tyres to provide cushioning.

Tracy, Spencer (Bonadventure) (1900–67) US actor, born in Milwaukee. He trained in New York City, and played on Broadway before his film debut in *Up the River* (1930). His reputation increased with Academy Awards for *Captains Courageous* (1937) and *Boys' Town* (1938), and he was regarded as Hollywood's best actor of the 1940s and 1950s, playing opposite Katharine Hepburn in nine outstanding comedies from *Woman of the Year* (1942) to *Pat and Mike* (1952), and in such varied productions as *Bad Day at Black Rock* (1955) and *Judgment at Nuremberg* (1961). He died from a heart attack in Los Angeles just after the completion of his last film, *Guess Who's Coming to Dinner*.

trade association » **employers' association**

trade cycle The pattern of changing levels of activity in an economy over a period of time. It is seen most clearly in the way growth rates and unemployment levels vary from year to year. High points of activity are *booms*, and low spots are *recessions* or *slumps*. Economists have identified a typical trade cycle as lasting seven or eight years, but much longer trends have also been identified. The major problem for governments is how to even out economic activity and maintain continuous growth. » recession

trade rat » **pack rat**

trade union An association of people, often in the same type of business, trade, or profession, who have joined together to protect their interests and improve their pay and working conditions. The trade union movement developed in the early years of the 19th-c, growing rapidly after the repeal of the Combination Acts (declaring unions illegal) in 1824–5. The Grand National Consolidated Trade Union claimed a million members. In 1834, six Dorset labourers were sentenced to transportation to Australia for attempting to press for higher wages; these have become famous as the 'Tolpuddle Martyrs'. Since then, unions have played an important role in industrial relations. They have developed in all Western nations over the last 150 years. In the UK there are almost 100 such bodies, half of them supporting the Labour Party. They are often organized into branches, with local 'shop' representation in the form of a shop steward. The Transport and General Workers Union (TGWU) is Britain's largest trade union, with c.1.4 million members drawn from many industries and trades. » American Federation of Labor – Congress of Industrial Organizations; Australian Council of Trade Unions; industrial action; International Conference of Free Trade Unions; shop stewards; Teamsters' Union; Trades Union Congress; World Federation of Trade Unions

trade winds Winds blowing from areas of high pressure, centred on the Tropics of Cancer (23.5°N) and Capricorn (23.5°S), towards the Intertropical Convergence Zone at the Equator. In the N hemisphere the trade winds blow from the NE, whereas in the S hemisphere they blow from the SE. The winds blow stronger over the oceans than over land. » general circulation model; intertropical convergence zone; wind [i]

trademark A symbol placed on an article to show that it has been made by a certain company. When the mark is registered, its unauthorized use is illegal. It is an important marketing device, aimed at creating a strong brand image for a product. In the USA, trademarks often include the sign ®, signifying that the mark has been registered.

Trades Union Congress (TUC) A voluntary association of trade unions in the UK, founded in 1868. It meets annually in September to decide policy, and representation at the Conference is based on one delegate per 5 000 members. Very large unions therefore have considerable voting power – 'the block vote'. There are over 80 affiliated unions, representing some 10 million individual union members. The role of the TUC is to develop systematic relations with the government and the Confederation of British Industry, to represent the interests of its members on national councils and commissions, and to help settle disputes between members. It also has representation on the Council of ACAS. There is a separate Scottish Trades Union Congress. » ACAS; Confederation of British Industry; trade union

tradescantia A succulent perennial with jointed, often trailing stems, native to the New World; leaves alternate, oval, stalkless; flowers 3-petalled, often white or blue, in small terminal clusters; named after John Tradescant the younger, botanist and gardener to Charles I of England. Several species and cultivars, especially those with variegated leaves, are grown as house plants. (Genus: *Tradescantia*, 60 species. Family: *Commelinaceae*.) » cultivar; perennial; succulent; wandering jew/sailor

traditional dance Traditional dances occur worldwide, and could be illustrated from every nation. There are two main forms: *ceremonial* dances are performed at particular times of the year and in a performer/audience context; *social* dances are performed at any time of the year, and are participatory and recreational in context.

England The main forms of ceremonial dance are Morris and sword, although hobby horse and horn dances also exist. Regional differences are evident, but all involve visits from one place to another with the purpose of bringing good luck, and contain some kind of disguise which should not be broken. Its origins are uncertain, but similarities with other rituals can be traced world-wide and back to pre-Christian times. Social forms are country dancing and step dancing. The dances of 16th-c country folk are generally seen as the first examples of this informal and neighbourly dance style. Lines, circles, and square sets are common patterns, and the steps are based on simple walking and skipping. Cecil Sharp was the most influential figure in the revival of interest in traditional dances at the beginning of the 20th-c and in the establishment of the English Folk Song and Dance Society, which promotes social dancing, research, and publications. Much debate exists about the value of preserving older forms or allowing the folk tradition to evolve. Morris, for example, was formerly danced only by men but is now frequently performed by women too. Recently there has been a growth of annual folk festivals.

Ireland Early forms of traditional dance share the European history of country and court dance. Jigs and reels are typical, resembling English and Scottish stepping. The competitive high stepping form is a creation of the 20th-c. Arms are held stiffly to the sides; the body is erect; there is rapid, complex rhythmic use of the feet; and the knees are sharply lifted.

Scotland The main form is social dancing, but with the elegance of the French court. The indigenous dance is the reel. Country dances progress in two long lines, in male/female couples. There are also square dances such as the quadrille, and circle dances such as the Circassian circle. The dances take place to traditional tunes, formerly played on the fiddle, and now also on the accordion. They are promoted by the Royal Scottish Country Dance Society.

Wales There are few traces of traditional dance, as little popular dancing survived religious disapproval. There are some reels and country dances similar to England and Scotland. However, the Eisteddfod, an international folk festival, is held in July each year, and here dances from many nations can be seen. » country/maypole/Morris/step/sword dance; Scottish reels

Trafalgar, Battle of (1805) The most famous naval engagement of the Napoleonic Wars, which destroyed Napoleon's hopes of invading England and established British naval supremacy for a century. Fought off Cape Trafalgar, Spain, between the British and Franco-Spanish fleets, the English triumph was marred by the death of Nelson at the moment of victory. » Napoleonic Wars; Nelson, Horatio

tragedy A play which presents the occurrence and the effects of a great misfortune suffered by an individual, and reverberating in society. Earlier, this required a great person as protagonist, but modern writers have attempted to confer tragic status on ordinary people. The fundamental purpose of tragedy (reminding us of its origins in religious ritual) was claimed by Aristotle to be the 'awakening of pity and fear', of a sense of wonder and awe at human potential, including the potential for suffering; it makes or implies an assertion of human value in the face of a hostile universe.

Not all cultures have produced tragedy; indeed, it has only three great 'moments' in Western history – in ancient Greece, in early 17th-c England, and in later 17th-c France. Elizabethan tragedy began with very simple materials, in the 'revenge' tradition deriving from the Roman dramatist Seneca; but Marlowe's *Dr Faustus* (c.1590) already shows a man facing the heights and depths of his own nature, while Shakespeare's greatest tragedies (*Hamlet*, *Othello*, *King Lear*, *Macbeth*; 1600–6) take us through suffering and madness to the very brink of being, where the 'bare forked animal' struggles for meaning on the 'sterile promontory' of this world. In France, the tragedies of Corneille (*Le Cid*, 1636) and more especially Racine (*Andromaque*, 1667; *Phèdre*, 1677) reincarnated with their grave alexandrines the severe beauty of Greek drama. Since this time tragic vision and utterance have been complicated (some would say denied) by the mass misfortunes and partial consolations of the modern world; see the complementary arguments in Nietzche's *Birth of Tragedy* (1872) and George Steiner's *Death of Tragedy* (1961). But plays such as Arthur Miller's *Death of a Salesman* (1949) are tragedies for our time; and one should not overlook the tragic dimension achieved by film. » Aeschylus; Aristotle; comedy; Corneille; drama; Greek literature; Racine; Shakespeare [i]; tragi-comedy

tragi-comedy A form of drama which allows the mixture of tragic and comic elements. Decried by Neoclassical critics, it was defended by Dr Johnson in his *Preface to Shakespeare* (1765) as 'exhibiting the true state of sublunary nature'. Much modern drama (for example, Beckett's *Waiting for Godot*, 1953) exploits ambiguous and incongruous emotions in the spirit of tragi-comedy. » Beckett; comedy; Johnson, Samuel; Shakespeare [i]; tragedy

tragopan A pheasant, native to SE Asia; inhabits woodland; nests in tree. (Genus: *Tragopan*, 5 species.) » pheasant

Traherne, Thomas [tra**hern**] (c.1636–74) English mystical writer, born at Hereford. Educated at Oxford, he was ordained rector at Credenhill. The manuscripts of his *Poetical Works* (1903) and *Centuries of Meditations* (1908) were discovered by chance on a London street bookstall in 1896. He died at Teddington, Greater London. » English literature; poetry

Trajan, properly **Marcus Ulpius Trajanus** [**tray**jan] (c.53–117) Roman emperor (98–117), selected as successor by the aged Nerva for his military skills. He was the first emperor after Augustus to expand the Roman Empire significantly. The wealth from Dacia's gold mines enabled him to launch an ambitious building programme, especially in Rome, where he constructed a new forum, library, and aqueduct. A sensitive but firm ruler, he was one of Rome's most popular emperors. » Dacia; Hadrian

Tralee [tra**lee**], Gaelic **Tráighlí** 52°16N 9°42W, pop(1981) 17 035. Capital of Kerry county, Munster, SW Irish Republic; NE of Slieve Mish Mts; connected to the Atlantic Ocean by a canal; railway; technical college; agricultural trade, bacon-curing, tourism; St Patrick's Week festival (Mar); Rose of Tralee festival (Sep), with street dancing and singing. » Irish Republic [i]; Kerry

tram A passenger vehicle normally propelled by an electric motor fed from overhead lines, designed to run on rails set into public roads. The tram is still a major means of transport in many European cities, but in the UK the only remaining service is to be found in Blackpool, where it has the status of a tourist attraction. In general, the improvement of road surfaces through the abandonment of cobbles and the improvement of self-contained motor transport has meant that the tram has been unable to compete without subsidy. » electricity; trolley bus

trampolining The art of performing acrobatics on a spring canvas sheet stretched across a frame, first used at the turn of the 20th-c as a circus attraction. The name derives from Spanish *trampolín* 'springboard'. It was developed into a sport following the design of a prototype modern trampoline by American diving and tumbling champion George Nissen in 1936.

tranquillizer » **benzodiazepines**

Trans-Siberian Railway An important rail route extending across Siberia, originally between terminals at Chelyabinsk in the Urals and Vladivostok on the Pacific. It was constructed 1891–1905, with an extension around L Baykal completed in 1917. The line, which has played a major role in the development of Siberia, is now largely electrified; the journey from Moscow to Vladivostok (9 311 km/5 786 ml) takes seven days. » Siberia

transactional analysis A method of psychotherapy in which the parent, child, or adult component of any interaction is analysed in addition to considering the unconscious pattern of a patient's actions. The purpose is to unravel emotional problems and to highlight the specific strategies an individual uses in social communication. The technique was developed by Canadian psychiatrist Eric Berne (1910–70) in the mid-1950s, in his view as a way of more quickly attaining treatment objectives compared with traditional psychoanalysis. » psychoanalysis; psychotherapy

Transalpine Gaul » **Gaul**

Transcaucasia Region extending S from the Greater Caucasus to the Turkish and Iranian frontiers, between the Black Sea (W) and the Caspian Sea (E); comprises the republics of Georgia, Azerbaijan, and Armenia, which 1922–36 formed the Transcaucasian SFSR; chief towns include Kutaisi, Batumi, Tbilisi, Kirovabad, Baku. » Caucasus Mountains

transcellular fluid A component of extracellular fluid, separated from the rest of the fluid by a layer of cells (eg an epithelium). Important examples are cerebrospinal fluid, the fluids inside the eye, the synovial fluid of joints, and the contents of the gastro-intestinal tract. » extracellular fluid

transcendental meditation A meditation technique taught by Maharishi Mahesh Yogi, based in large part on Hindu meditation. It has been widely practised in the West since the 1960s, when he 'converted' the Beatles. Its practitioners are taught to meditate for twenty minutes twice a day as a means of reducing stress and achieving relaxation. » Beatles, The; maharishi

transcendentalism In general, any philosophical theory (especially Kant's) which maintains that there are things beyond experience that condition the way we experience. In particular, the term applies to a movement in 19th-c New England headed by Emerson and Thoreau, which rejected Calvinism and exalted individual conscience, autonomy, and imagination. » Emerson; Kant; Thoreau

Transdanubia, Hungarian **Dunántúl** Geographical region in Hungary, lying W of the R Danube and extending to the Hungarian Alps and S to the R Drava; occupies a third of Hungary; hilly and fertile region, noted for livestock and wine production. » Hungary [i]

transducer Any device which converts one form of energy into another. A microphone is an acoustic transducer, converting sound waves into electrical signals. Electromechanical transducers convert electrical signals into mechanical oscillations, as in piezo-electric ultrasound generators. » loudspeaker [i]; microphone [i]; turbine; ultrasound

transept The part of a cruciform-planned church that projects out at right angles to the main body of the building, usually between nave and chancel. » chancel; choir; church [i]; nave

transfer (of training) The effect of performing one task on the subsequent performance of another. Performance on the subsequent task may be improved, in comparison with a control group (**positive transfer**); or it may be inhibited (**negative transfer**). It is important to take account of unwanted transfer effects in the design of experiments involving several different treatments of the same subjects. » control group; learning

transfer pricing The price charged when an article is passed from one part or department of a company to another. There are difficulties when the transfer is across national frontiers, as in the case of multinational companies, since the company may avoid taxes in one country by artificially fixing the price. » transnational corporations

transference (psychiatry) The unconscious attachment of feelings originally associated with significant early figures in one's life (eg parents) to others (particularly to the psychotherapist). In psychotherapy this allows for the exploration of a patient's early difficulties which have remained unresolved. The term was coined by Freud in 1895. » Freud, Sigmund; psychotherapy

transformational grammar » **generative grammar**

transformer A device which transfers an alternating current (AC) from one circuit to one or more other circuits, usually with a change of voltage. It is usually used for converting the high voltage from AC power supplies to the normal domestic supply voltage. » electricity

transhumance The transfer of livestock, usually cattle and sheep, between winter and summer pastures. It is characteristic of some mountainous regions, where whole families may move, with their flocks, up to the high altitude pastures. It may also occur in arctic regions, where livestock are moved to more northerly pastures for the summer. » livestock farming

transistor A solid-state device, made by joining semiconductors with different electrical characteristics, which can be used as an amplifier or a rectifier. Small, robust, and safe (since they need low voltage), transistors have replaced thermionic valves in television, radio, and computers, and have revolutionized the construction of electronic circuits. » electronics; rectifier; semiconductor; solid-state device; thermionic valve

transit circle » **meridian circle**

transit instrument An astronomical instrument for observing the passage of a body over the meridian of the observer. The earliest was developed in 1689 by Danish astronomer Olaus Roemer (1644–1710). Generally, a telescope is mounted on a fixed horizontal axis so as to sweep the meridian in a vertical plane. It is used for such purposes as correcting clocks, by recording a fixed local time (eg noon) by observation. Since the difference in time between noon at some place and noon at Greenwich is a measure of its longitude, the instrument can also be used as a means of determining longitude. » latitude and longitude [i]; telescope [i]

transit time In nutrition, the time taken for an ingested marker to move along a specified region of the gut. Whole gut transit time measures mouth to anus velocity. Velocities may also be measured separately through the small and large bowels.

transition In genetics, a type of mutation caused by the substitution in DNA or RNA of one purine by the other, or of one pyrimidine by the other. It is brought about by mutagens such as nitrous acid, hydroxylamine, and the base analogues. » DNA [i]; RNA; transversion

transition elements Chemical elements in which an incomplete electron shell other than the valence level is being filled. They are all metals, and include the elements with atomic numbers 21 (scandium) to 29 (copper) and their groups. They have similar chemistries, and most show oxidation states +2 and +3 commonly. They typically form coloured, paramagnetic compounds and a large range of co-ordination compounds. » chemical elements; metal; vanadium; RR90

transition state In a chemical reaction, an unstable arrangement of atoms characteristic of the highest energy through which the atoms must pass during the reaction. » chemical reaction

Transkei [tranz**kiy**] pop (1987e) 2 832 000; area 42 200 sq km/16 300 sq ml. Independent Black homeland in SE South Africa; between the Kei and Mtamvuna Rivers on the Indian Ocean; capital, Umtata; traditional territory of the Xhosa; self-government, 1963; granted independence by South Africa (not recognized internationally), 1976; forestry, livestock, maize, sorghum, coffee, tea, sugar cane; over 372 000 people are commuters or migrant workers in South Africa. » apartheid; South Africa [i]; Xhosa

translation The conversion of one language into another; often used specifically with reference to written texts, as opposed to the **interpretation** of spoken language. There are various types of translation: **word-for-word translation**, in which each word is found an equivalent, carrying over the grammatical and lexical features of the original, often makes little sense, because it breaks the structural rules of the target language; for example, Welsh *Mae hi yn bwrw hen wragedd a ffynn* would translate as 'Is she in rain old women and sticks'. **Literal translation** adheres to the linguistic structure of the original, but transposes it into the appropriate grammatical conventions of the target language; the above example would give 'She is raining old women and sticks'. **Free translation** translates the 'sense' of the text, relaxing the shackles of strict linguistic equivalence, and seeks an idiomatic equivalent for the Welsh expression, giving something like 'It is raining cats and dogs'. » back translation; semantics

transliteration The written representation of a word in the closest corresponding characters of a different language. The process is commonly seen at work in loan-words, as in the Welsh *miwsig* from 'music', *bws* from 'bus'.

translocation In genetics, the transfer of a segment of one chromosome to another. Translocations are frequently reciprocal. » chromosome [i]

transmembrane potential » **membrane potential**

transmission The system fitted to an engine that transmits the power generated by the engine to the point at which it is required. Normally this system is composed of mechanical components such as gears, shafts, clutches, and chains, but other methods using hydraulic and electrical means can also be used. » clutch; engine; gear

transmutation In nuclear physics, the conversion of one nuclide to another, either by natural radioactive decay or by collision with other nuclei or particles. Loosely, one element can thus be transmuted into another. Alchemy failed, since it attempted to manipulate only chemical properties, not the nucleus, which is what controls the element's type. » alchemy; nuclear physics; nuclide

transnational corporations Large corporate enterprises whose activities spread across a number of nations, via subsidiaries, holding companies, etc; sometimes used interchangeably with **multinational corporations**. It also implies that these firms have no obvious 'national' economy with which they are most closely associated. Hence, at times, these corporations may act in ways which appear to go against the interests of their 'home' economy, such as closing some factories as part of a global restructuring programme. » economics

transpiration The loss of water vapour from a plant. It mainly occurs from leaves via the stomata, which partially control the process by opening and closing in response to humidity changes in the air. The process cools and prevents damage to the leaves in hot weather, and helps draw water up from the roots to other parts of the plant. » leaf [i]; stomata

transplantation The transfer of an organ or tissue from one person to another. Unless the recipient is an identical twin, such a graft sets up an immunological reaction of variable severity which may destroy the transplanted tissue. This reaction results from the introduction of foreign protein to the recipient. It may be partially or completely controlled by the use of immunosuppressive drugs, and is less severe in closely related persons. Tissues that have been transplanted successfully are bone marrow, undertaken for leukaemia, and the kidney and heart, carried out for severe kidney and heart failure. Tissue for transplantation may be obtained from living donors or from suitable cadavers. The cornea in front of the eye may also be transplanted, but is a special case as it does not set up any immunological reaction in the host. Corneas can be stored in banks, and used to treat blindness when this results from damage to the front of the eyes. » bone marrow; cornea; heart [i]; kidneys; immunosuppression

transportation Sentence of banishment from England for those convicted of certain offences, introduced in 1597. Increasingly large numbers of English convicts were shipped to N America in the 17th-c and 18th-c as the number of crimes for which transportation could be applied was greatly expanded; but in 1788, after the US War of Independence, the inflow was stopped. As a result, the British government turned their attention to Australia, and from the first British settlement (1788) to 1820, convicts were the largest single group in the population; 162 000 convicts (137 000 males and 25 000 females) were transported to Australia from 1788 to 1868, mainly in New South Wales (1788–1840), Van Dieman's Land, (1803–52) and Western Australia (1850–68). Most of the convicts were young, poorly-educated urban-dwellers convicted of some form of theft. A number of those who arrived before 1820 became wealthy; others, especially those at Port Arthur or Norfolk I, lived and died under a savage and inhuman rule. But the typical fate of most convicts was assignment to private service, usually with a conditional pardon or ticket of leave which amounted to freedom in Australia but not permission to return to Britain. » penal settlements; ticket of leave

transposing instrument A musical instrument which sounds at a higher or lower pitch than that at which its music is notated. There are various practical and historical reasons for this, the main one being to regularize the fingering of wind instruments, so that a player can change from one size (and pitch) of an instrument to another, without having to adopt a different fingering system. In the modern orchestra the main transposing instruments are as follows (sound level above/below written pitch is shown in parentheses): piccolo (one octave above), cor anglais (a perfect 5th below), clarinet in A (a minor 3rd below), clarinet in B♭ (a major 2nd below), horn in F (a perfect 5th below), trumpet in B♭ (a major 2nd below), celesta (one octave above), and double bass (one octave below).

Transputer A one-chip computer developed in the UK by Inmos Ltd, which has been designed specifically to allow parallel processing involving large numbers of Transputers working together. This technique can provide very fast, powerful computers, and systems have been designed which include more than 1 000 Transputers. A special language, OCCAM, has been developed for the Transputer. » parallel processing

transsexual A person who has changed behaviour, physical appearance, and body (by surgery and/or the consumption of hormones) to that of the opposite sex. It is a form of gender alteration in which anatomically normal individuals realize that they are physically normal, but wish to convert to the opposite sex. » gender

transubstantiation The Roman Catholic doctrine of the Eucharist (Mass), affirming the belief that the bread and wine used in the sacrament are converted into the body and blood of Christ, who is therefore truly present. The doctrine, rejected by 16th-c Reformers, was reaffirmed by the Council of Trent. » consubstantiation; Counter-Reformation; Eucharist; Mass; Roman Catholicism; Trent, Council of

transuranic elements [tranzyoo**ran**ik] » **actinides**

Transvaal [tranz**vahl**] pop (1985) 7 532 179; area 262 499 sq km/101 325 sq ml. Province in South Africa, bounded N by the Limpopo R following the frontier with Botswana and Zimbabwe; Transvaal Drakensberg Mts in the SE; capital, Pretoria; chief towns include Johannesburg, Krugersdorp, Vereeniging; settled by the Boers after the Great Trek of 1831; independence, 1852, recognized by Britain; known as the South African Republic; annexed by Britain, 1877; Boer rebellion in 1880–1 led to restoration of the republic; annexed as a British colony, 1900; self-government, 1906; joined Union of South Africa, 1910; gold, diamonds, iron, oil, engineering, hydroelectricity, grain, tobacco, clothing, forestry; the most prosperous province in the country. » Boer Wars; Great Trek; Pretoria; South Africa [i]

transverse stage An open stage in a theatre positioned in the middle of the auditorium but stretching from wall to wall, dividing the audience into two groups facing each other across the acting area. » open stage

transverse wave » **wave** (physics) [i]

transvestism The recurrent practice, in heterosexual men, of dressing as a woman, normally for sexual excitement. It usually begins in adolescence, and is generally carried out only in private.

Transylvania [transil**vay**nia], Magyar **Erdély**, Ger **Siebenbürgen** Geographical region and province of N and C Romania, separated from Wallachia and Moldavia by the Carpathian Mts; a former Hungarian principality that became part of the Austro-Hungarian Empire; incorporated into Romania, 1918; part of the region ceded to Hungary by Hitler in World War 2; chief towns, Cluj-Napoca and Braşov. » Romania [i]

Transylvania Company An American land company organized in 1775. It bought the site of original White settlements in Kentucky from the Indians, in defiance of British policy that all lands in the W belonged to the Crown. The company collapsed during the American Revolution. » Indian Wars

Transylvanian Alps or **Southern Carpathian Mountains**, Romanian **Carpatii Meridionali** Mountain range in C Romania; a S branch of the E European Carpathian Mts; highest peak, Negoiul (2 548 m/8 359 ft); includes the national park of Retezat, area 130 sq km/50 sq ml, established in 1935. » Carpathian Mountains

trap shooting » **clay pigeon shooting**

trapdoor spider A spider that lives in a silk-lined tube constructed in a burrow in the ground, closed off by a silk lid; passing insects are attacked and pulled into the tube with great speed; found in Africa, the Americas, and Australia. (Order: *Araneae*.) » spider

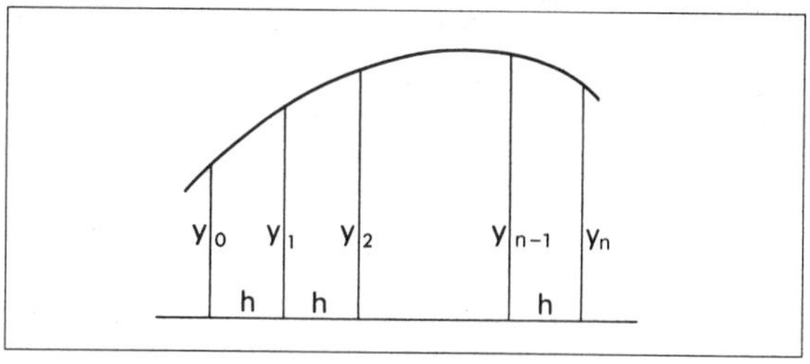

The trapezium rule

trapezium rule In mathematics, an approximate method for finding the value of an integral. Regarding the integral as the area of a region between a curve and the x-axis, this region is divided into n trapezia, width h, each of which has area $\frac{1}{2}h(y_r+y_{r+1})$. The area of the whole region is $\frac{1}{2}h\,[y_0+2(y_1+y_2+\ldots)+y_n]$. » integral calculus [i]

Trappists The popular name of the Cistercians of the More Strict Observance, centred on the monastery of La Trappe, France, until 1892. The Order continues throughout the world, devoted to divine office, and noted for its austerity, (eg perpetual silence, and abstention from meat, fish, and eggs). » Cistercians; monasticism

Trás-os-Montes ('beyond the mountains') [**traz** uzh **mõ**tesh] area 10 784 sq km/4 163 sq ml. Mountain area and former region of NE Portugal, bounded N and E by Spain; population concentrated in the fertile valleys, growing grapes and fruit; sheep and goats graze on the bare upland plateaux. » Portugal [i]

Traun, Lake [trown], Ger **Traunsee** or **Gmundner See** Lake in Reutte district, Tirol, C Austria; area 24.5 km/15 ml; length 12 km/7 ml; width 3 km/1¾ ml; maximum depth 191 m/627 ft; summer resorts include Gmunden, Traunkirchen, Ebensee, Rindbach; water sports. » Austria [i]; Tirol

travel sickness **1** Nausea and vomiting induced by the motion of ships, cars, and aeroplanes in a proportion of healthy individuals. The motion disturbs the function of the semicircular canals in the inner ear, and causes a reflex stimulation of the vomiting centre in the brain stem. Psychological factors and fear of sickness play a part in some people. » ear [i] **2** A short attack of diarrhoea commonly affecting those who visit foreign and developing countries. It sometimes arises from genuine food poisoning, but it may also stem from the acquisition in the gut of otherwise harmless (non-pathogenic) bacteria to which the traveller is not accustomed. » diarrhoea

travelator » **escalator**

traveller's tree An evergreen tree somewhat resembling a palm, native to Madagascar, and widely cultivated in the tropics; leaves grow to 3 m/10 ft, in two ranks, giving a fan-like appearance. The sheathing stalks form the trunk, and collect considerable quantities of drinkable water. (*Ravenala madagascariensis*. Family: *Strelitziaceae*.) » evergreen plants; palm; tree [i]

travelling matte An image combination process in cinematography for superimposing foreground action on a separately photographed background scene by printing at the laboratory. A matte, a strip of film with opaque silhouettes of the foreground, is used to reserve this area when printing the background, and the foreground action is inserted into this space at a second printing using a complementary matte. In video special effects, a corresponding result is obtained by 'keying'. » matte shot; special effects

Traven, B [**tray**vuhn], pseudonym of **Benick Traven Torsvan** (1890–1969) US author of *The Treasure of the Sierra Madre* (1935), on which the celebrated film by John Huston is based. Little is known about his background, but he was probably born in Chicago of Swedish (or German) parents, and lived in Mexico during the 1930s and later. Most of his novels were first published in Germany, such as *The Death Ship* (1926), and *The Rebellion of the Hanged* (1936). He died in Mexico City. » Huston; novel

Travers, Ben(jamin) (1886–1980) British playwright, born in London. He became famous for the farces which played in the Aldwych Theatre, London, continuously from 1922 until 1933. His later work was not so successful, although he was still writing in his nineties, and his last play, *The Bed Before Yesterday* was first produced in 1975. » theatre

travertine A type of limestone formed by precipitation from springs or streams rich in dissolved calcium carbonate. When porous and spongy in appearance, it may be termed *calc tufa*. It is extensively mined in Tuscany, Italy, and used as a paving stone. » limestone

trawler A vessel designed to drag a large bag-shaped net along or near the bottom of the sea to catch fish. Modern trawlers equipped with echo-sounder fish finders and refrigeration to preserve their catch may be as big as 4000 gross tons. » ship [i]

treacle A product obtained from molasses, used to sweeten and darken cakes and puddings. During the refining process, the molasses darkens from a richly golden syrup to a black treacle, also known as *blackstrap molasses* in the USA. » molasses; sugar cane

treason The crime of failing to pay proper allegiance to a government or monarch. In the USA, treason is defined in Article III, section (3) of the Constitution. In the UK the law on treason is governed by the Treason Act (1351), and comprises a number of unlawful activities, including compassing the monarch's death (conspiring or inciting to kill the monarch) and levying war against the monarch in his or her realm (insurrection). Disloyalty is essential to the crime – the person who commits treason must owe allegience to the Crown. This includes British subjects, but persons other than British subjects may owe this allegience. An alien who has accepted the protection of the Crown may commit treason. » alien

treasury In business and accounting, the function of managing finance, especially its provision and use. It includes the provision of capital, borrowing, the short-term deposit of surplus funds, and foreign exchange dealing. In UK government terms, the **Treasury** is the name of the department responsible for managing the nation's finances, headed by the Chancellor of the Exchequer, who is responsible to the Prime Minister (the First Lord of the Treasury). It operates through the central bank to manage the government's monetary policy. In the USA, it is known as the **Department of Treasury**, and elsewhere usually as the **Ministry of Finance**.

treasury bills Bills sold at a discount over a three-month period by the Bank of England on behalf of the government. The bills are issued to discount houses at below their face value, and are redeemed at face value, the difference (as a percentage) being the *discount rate*. These bills are frequently used by the government as a form of short-term borrowing. » discount houses

treaty ports Chinese ports opened to foreign trade after the Opium Wars in the mid-19th-c. The Treaty of Nanjing (Nanking) in 1842 opened Canton, Amoy (Xiamen), Fuzhou, Ningbo, and Shanghai (for 80 years previously Canton had been the only open port), and the Treaty of Tianjin (Tientsin) in 1858 opened a further ten ports, including Nanjing, Hankou, and Swatow (Shantou). » Opium Wars

Trebizond Turkish **Trabzon** A city on the Black Sea coast of present-day Turkey, former capital of the Christian empire (1204–1461), founded by Alexius Comnenus. It was the outpost of Greek culture in Asia Minor until the Greek defeat by the Turks in 1922. » Alexius Comnenus

tree A large, perennial plant with a single, woody, self-supporting stem (the *trunk* or *bole*) extending to a considerable height above the ground before branching to form the leafy crown. Trees exhibit a wide variety of shapes, from very narrow, columnar forms to wide-spreading ones, and may be evergreen or deciduous. They occur in many different plant families. Dicotyledonous and gymnosperm trees grow in height by extension of the shoots, and in girth by the addition of internal tissue layers; monocotyledonous trees achieve their full girth as seedlings, and subsequently increase in height only. A few other groups, such as the so-called tree-ferns, produce arborescent or tree-like forms. » deciduous plants; dicotyledons; evergreen plants; gymnosperms; monocotyledons; perennial; shrub; tree fern

Tree, Sir Henry (Draper) Beerbohm (1853–1917) British actor-manager, born and died in London. After a commercial education in Germany, he became an actor, took over the Haymarket theatre (1887), and built His Majesty's theatre (1897), where he rivalled Irving's productions at the Lyceum. He founded the Royal Academy of Dramatic Art in 1904, and scored a great success with the first production of Shaw's *Pygmalion* in 1914. » Irving, Henry; theatre

tree duck » **whistling duck**

tree fern The name applied to members of two fern families in which the woody rhizome forms a trunk-like stem reaching 25 m/80 ft, and is covered with the scars of old frond-bases, the current fronds forming a crown. It is native to much of the tropics and subtropics, and is the characteristic plant of various regions. The very slender, superficially palm-like habit makes it a popular ornamental. (Families: *Cyatheaceae*, *Dicksoniaceae*.) » fern; rhizome

tree frog A frog adapted to live in trees; flat with sucker-like discs on fingers and toes; two families: **true tree frogs** (*Hylidae*, 637 species), and **Old World tree frogs** (*Rhacophoridaea*, 184 species). The name is also used for some frogs in other families. » frog

tree kangaroo A kangaroo of genus *Dendrolagus* (7 species); hind legs not longer than front legs; hands and feet with long claws; hair on neck grows forwards and sheds water when head held low; inhabits rain forests; may jump to ground from heights of 18 m/60 ft; eats leaves and fruit. » kangaroo

tree of heaven A fast-growing deciduous tree to

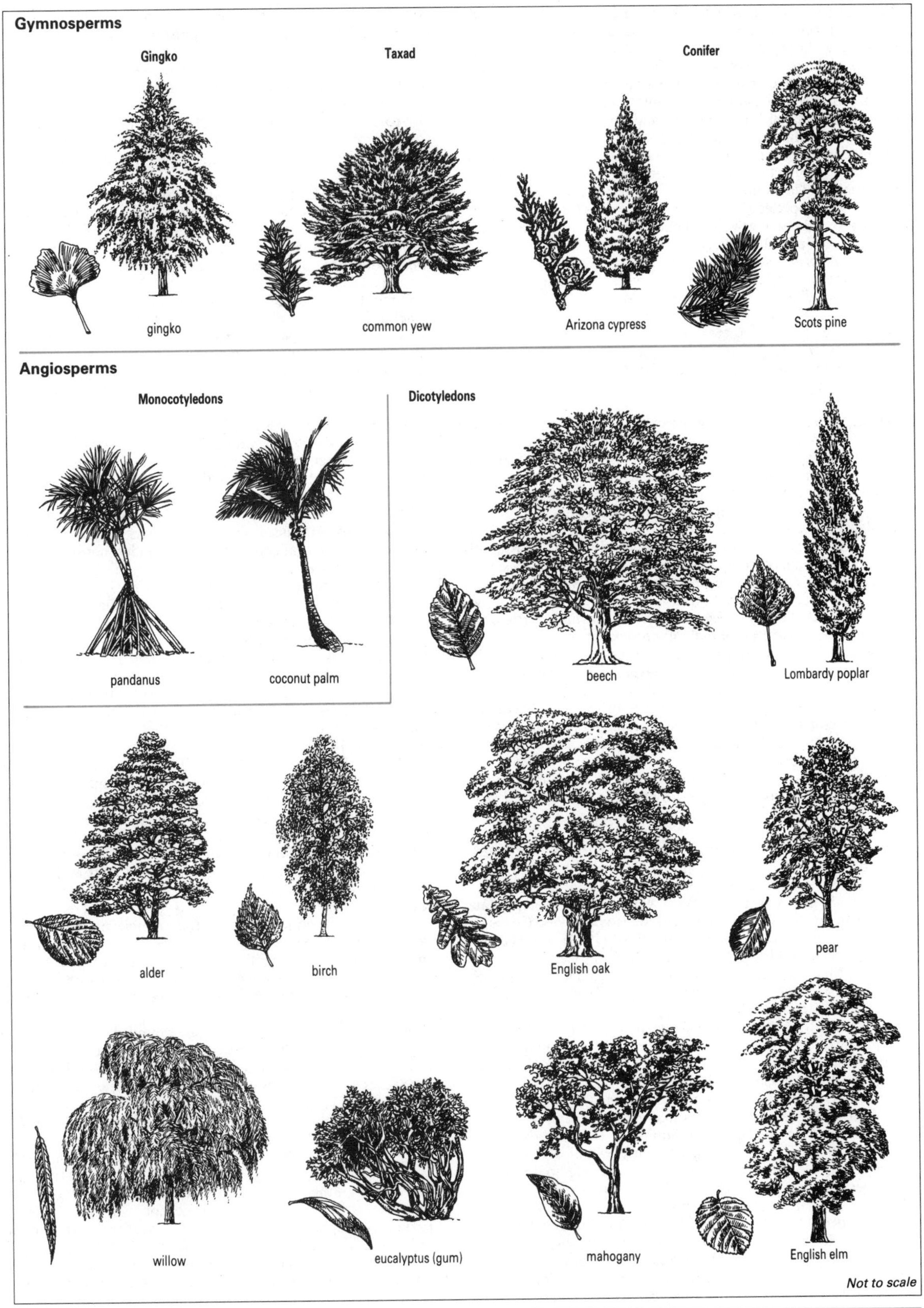
Gymnosperms
Gingko
Taxad
Conifer
gingko
common yew
Arizona cypress
Scots pine
Angiosperms
Monocotyledons
Dicotyledons
pandanus
coconut palm
beech
Lombardy poplar
alder
birch
English oak
pear
willow
eucalyptus (gum)
mahogany
English elm
Not to scale

Trees

20–30 m/65–100 ft, native to China, and widely planted elsewhere for ornament, shade, and as a soil stabilizer; leaves pinnate, with 13–25, 2–4-toothed leaflets, red when young; flowers in large clusters, starry, greenish-white, strong-smelling; fruit with an elongated wing. (*Ailanthus altissima*. Family: *Simaroubaceae*.) » deciduous plants; pinnate; tree [i]

tree shrew A small SE Asian mammal, rodent-like with a long tail and long thin shrew-like muzzle; tail bushy or with tufted tip; lives in trees and on ground; eats insects and fruit; formerly classified as insectivores or as primates; resembles ancestral mammals of 220 million years ago. (Order: *Scandentia*. Family: *Tupaiidae*, 16 species.) » insectivore; primate (biology); shrew

tree snake Any snake which spends much of its life in trees., The term is applied to many unrelated species, but within the family *Colubridae* some species of genus *Boiga* may be called **brown tree snakes**, and species of *Dendrelaphis* may be called **green tree snakes**. » snake; vine snake

treecreeper Either of two families of songbirds of the N hemisphere: the US **creeper** (*Certhiidae*, 6 species); and the **Australian treecreeper** (*Climacteridae*, 6 species), native to Australia and New Guinea; inhabits woodland; eats insects caught on trees and (Australian treecreepers) on ground. » songbird

treehopper A small, hopping insect that feeds by sucking the sap of trees and shrubs; nymphs often gregarious; many produce honeydew and are attended by ants; c.2 500 species, mainly in warm dry regions. (Order: *Homoptera*. Family: *Membracidae*.) » insect [i]; nymph (entomology)

trefoil Either of two groups of plants belonging to the pea-family. *Leguminosae* is a yellow-flowered species of clovers (genus *Trifolium*). Genus *Lotus* is a widely distributed group of annual or perennial herbs, occurring in Europe, Asia, Africa, N America, and Australia; leaves divided into five leaflets; pea-like flowers, small, often yellow or reddish-coloured; pods long, many-seeded. (Family: *Leguminosae*.) » annual; birdsfoot-trefoil; clover; herb; perennial; shamrock

Trematoda [tremuh**toh**da] A class of parasitic flatworms; body flattened and covered with a horny layer (cuticle); one or more attachment organs present; gut well developed, often with large intestinal cavity for storing and digesting food, and without an anus; contains c.8 000 species, including the monogenetic and digenetic flukes. (Phylum: *Platyhelminthes*.) » flatworm; fluke; parasitology

Tremiti Islands (Ital **Isole**) area 3 sq km/1.16 sq ml. Rocky limestone archipelago in Puglia, S Italy, in the Adriatic Sea; chief islands, San Domino, San Nicola, Caprara; popular area for scuba diving. » Italy [i]

Trenchard (of Wolfeton), Hugh Montague, 1st Viscount (1873–1956) British Marshal of the RAF, born at Taunton, Somerset. He joined the army in 1893, served in India, South Africa, and West Africa, and developed an interest in aviation. He commanded the Royal Flying Corps in World War 1, helped to establish the RAF (1918), and became the first Chief of Air Staff (1918–29). As Commissioner of the London Metropolitan Police (1931–5), he founded the police college at Hendon. He became a peer in 1930, and died in London. » Royal Air Force

Trent, Council of (1545–63) A Council of the Roman Catholic Church, held at Trento, Italy. It was called to combat Protestantism and to reform the discipline of the Church, and as such spear-headed the Counter-Reformation by clarifying many points of doctrine and practice. » Councils of the Church; Counter-Reformation; Protestantism; Roman Catholicism

Trent, River River rising S of Biddulph in N Staffordshire, C England; flows 275 km/171 ml SE, then E and NE through Derbyshire, Nottinghamshire, and Humberside to meet the Humber estuary near Whitton; linked by canal to many Midland industrial towns. » England [i]

Trent Affair (1861) An incident between the USA and Britain in which the USS *San Jacinto* removed two officials of the Confederate States from the British ship *Trent*. The issue provoked considerable British anger until the Confederate officials were released by the American Secretary of State. » American Civil War

Trento, Ger **Trent** 46°04N 11°08E, pop (1981) 99 179. Capital town of Trento province, Trentino-Alto Adige, N Italy, on t left bank of the R Adige; archbishopric; railway; electric goods, chemicals, cement, wine; cathedral (11th–12th-c), Ca tello del Buon Consiglio, Church of Santa Maria Maggio (16th-c), where the Council of Trent met. » Councils of t Church; Italy [i]

Trenton 40°14N 74°46W, pop (1980) 92 124. State capital New Jersey in Mercer County, W New Jersey, USA, on the bank of the Delaware R; settled by English Quakers in t 1670s; city status, 1792; scene of a British defeat by Geor Washington, 1776; monument (47 m/154 ft) marks the batt site; railway; manufactured steel, machinery, ceramics; researc and development centre; State House complex; William Tre House. » New Jersey; Washington, George

trepanning One of the earliest surgical operations: the remov of a rectangle or disc of bone from the vault of the sku commonly to alleviate pressure on the brain caused by sku fracture; also known as **trephination**. Prehistoric instances a known from Europe, the Pacific, N and S America (notably skull from Cuzco with seven healed holes), Africa, and Asi The instrument involved (now called a *trephine*) is still com monly used in neurosurgical operations. » palaeopatholog skull; surgery

trephination » **trepanning**

Tretyakov Gallery [tretya**koff**] One of the world's largest a galleries, located in Moscow, and housing exhibits of Russia painting and sculpture from the 11th-c to the present. Th museum building was designed by Viktor M Vasnetso (1848–1926) and erected in 1901–2; the gallery passed into sta ownership in 1918. Because of lack of space to house the 50 0C exhibits, a new gallery is presently under construction. » Moscow; museum

Trevelyan, G(eorge) M(acaulay) (1876–1962) British his torian, born at Welcombe, Warwickshire. Educated at Harro and Cambridge, he served in World War 1, and becam professor of modern history at Cambridge (1927–40). He best-known as a pioneer social historian. His *English Soci History* (1944) was a companion volume to his *History England* (1926). He died at Cambridge. His father, **George Ott** (1838–1928) was a statesman and historian, the biographer c Lord Macaulay.

Trèves » **Trier**

Trevithick, Richard (1771–1833) British engineer and inven tor, born at Illogan, Cornwall. He became a mining engineer a Penzance, and 1796–1801 invented a steam carriage, which ra between Camborne and Tuckingmill, and which in 1803 wa run from Leather Lane to Paddington by Oxford Street. H later went to Peru and Costa Rica (1816–27), where his engine were introduced into the silver mines. He died at Dartforc Kent. » steam engine

triads The Western name given to Chinese secret societie (because of the importance of the triangle in the initiatio ceremonies). These societies are very old, and mystical i origin, but in modern times the branches of the societie outside China helped greatly in the struggle to establish th Republic. The societies are reputed to be involved in organize crime.

triangle (mathematics) A plane figure bounded by three straigh lines (*sides*). If all three are equal, the triangle is said to b *equilateral*; if two are equal, it is said to be *isosceles*. The sum o the angles of a triangle was proved by the Greeks to be equal t two right angles. If the largest angle in a triangle is less than right angle, the triangle is called *scalene*; if the largest angle i greater than a right angle the triangle is *obtuse-angled*; if th largest angle is a right angle, the triangle is called *right-anglea* and the subject of Pythagoras' theorem. A spherical triangle i one drawn on the surface of a sphere, much used in navigation In such a triangle, the angle-sum is not two right angles; i particular, a spherical triangle with two vertices on the equato and one at a pole can have an angle sum of three right angles » congruent triangles; Pythagoras' theorem [i]

triangle (music) A musical instrument of great antiquity, made from a steel rod in the form of a triangle, with one corner lef open, and struck with a short metal beater to produce a high silvery sound of indefinite pitch. » percussion [i]

Triangulum (Lat 'triangle') A small prominent N constellation between Aries and Andromeda. It includes the notable spiral galaxy M33. It should not be confused with the prominent and appropriately named S constellation **Triangulum Australe** ('southern triangle'). » constellation; RR9

Trianon, Grand/Petit » **Versailles**

Triassic period [triyasik] The earliest of the periods of the Mesozoic era, extending from c.248 million to 213 million years ago. It was characterized by the first appearance of dinosaurs and small mammals. Plant life was mainly primitive gymnosperms, with ferns and conifers dominant. » dinosaur [i]; geological time scale; Mesozoic era; RR16

triathlon A three-part sporting event consisting of sea swimming (3.8 km/2.4 ml), cycling (180 km/112 ml), and marathon running (42.2 km/26.2 ml). The events take place in sequence on a single occasion.

tribe A term sometimes used to describe ethnic minorities which formerly enjoyed political autonomy, but which have been incorporated into a nation state. In practice, it is usually applied only to such groupings in Third World countries, and its use carries a denigrating implication that the 'tribe' is backward, and that its political aspirations, if any, are illegitimate. » Three Worlds Theory

tribes of Israel » **Israel, tribes of** [i]

tribology [triy**bol**uhjee] The study of phenomena involving the sliding of one surface over another. It includes friction, lubrication, and wear. » friction; rheology; surface physics

tribunal An official body exercising functions of a judicial nature. In the UK, tribunals frequently deal with matters where the citizen is in conflict with a government department. They tend to be specialized, governing such issues as employment rights, mental health, and taxation. The proceedings of a tribunal may be subject to judicial review. » judicial review

tribunes In late Republican Rome, ten annually elected officials whose function was to defend the lives and property of ordinary citizens. The office was part of the 'cursus honorum', coming between the quaestorship and praetorship. » consul **1**; cursus honorum; praetors

Triceratops [**triy**suhratops] The largest ceratopsian dinosaur, known from the Cretaceous period of N America; heavily built, reaching 9 m/30 ft in length; four-legged; bony frill at back of skull relatively short; paired nasal horns above eyes well developed; plant-eating; probably lived in herds. (Order: *Ornithischia*.) » Cretaceous period; dinosaur [i]; herbivore; Ornithischia

Trichina [tri**kiy**na] A small roundworm, parasitic in the small human intestine; infection usually results from eating raw or undercooked pork. (*Trichinella spiralis*. Phylum: *Nematoda*.) » intestine; nematode; parasitology

Trichinopoly [trikuh**nop**uhlee] » **Tiruchchirappalli**

trichomoniasis [trikuhmuh**niy**asis] Infestation of the mucous membrane of the vagina with a flagellated protozoa. It causes irritation and vaginal discharge, and may be passed to the male urethra during sexual contact. » Protozoa; vagina

trick or treat » **Hallowe'en**

Trident missile The US Navy's third-generation submarine-launched ballistic missile (SLBM) system, following on from the earlier Polaris and Poseidon missiles. The first version, Trident C-4, became operational in 1980. The larger Trident D-5 was scheduled to enter service with the US Navy in 1989, and the British Royal Navy in the mid-1990s. The missile has a very long range (11 000 km/7 000 ml, and carries up to 14 individually targettable re-entry vehicles (MIRVs). A stellar-inertial navigation system gives it accuracy equivalent to its land-based counterparts, even though it is launched from a moving platform. » ballistic missile; MIRV; Polaris missile; submarine

Trier, Fr **Trèves**, Eng **Treves** [treevz], ancient **Augusta Treverorum** [treer] 49°45N 6°39E, pop (1983) 94 700. River-port capital of Trier district, Germany; on the R Moselle near the Luxembourg border; one of Germany's oldest towns; bishopric since the 4th-c; railway; university (1970); Roman Catholic Theological College; centre of wine production and trade; birthplace of Marx; Porta Nigra (2nd-c), cathedral (4th-c, 11th–12th-c), and Roman basilica, world heritage sites. » Germany [i]; Marx

Trieste [tree-**est**], Ital [tree-**es**tay] 45°39N 13°47E, pop (1981) 252 369. Seaport and capital town of Trieste province, Friuli-Venezia Giulia, NE Italy, on the Adriatic coast; largest port in the Adriatic; capital of Free Territory of Trieste, established by the United Nations in 1947, divided in 1954 between Italy and Yugoslavia; airport; railway; university (1938); shipbuilding and repairing, oil refining, spirits and liqueurs; town hall (1874), Cathedral of San Giusto (14th-c), Church of Sant'Antonio (1849), castle (15th–18th-c); International Trade Fair (Jun–Jul). » Italy [i]

triggerfish Deep-bodied fish with a spiny first dorsal fin; large front spine, locked in upright position by a second smaller spine, and serving to wedge the fish in rock crevices away from predators; body strongly compressed, teeth well-developed, pelvic fins absent. (Family: *Balistidae*, 5 genera.) » fish [i]

Triglav [**tree**glaf] 46°21N 13°50E. Mountain in NW Slovenia republic, Yugoslavia; highest peak in the Julian Alps and in Yugoslavia, rising to 2 863 m/9 393 ft. » Julian Alps; Slovenia; Yugoslavia [i]

triglyceride The chemical compound found in most dietary fats and most of the storage fat in adipose tissue. A glycerol molecule ($C_3H_8O_3$) combines with three fatty acids, mostly of chain length 14–20. » polyunsaturated fatty acids

trigonometry The branch of mathematics mainly concerned with relating the sides and angles of a triangle, based on triangles being similar if they have one right angle and one other angle equal. The **trigonometric functions** can be defined as the ratio of sides of a right-angled triangle, the commonest being

$$\text{sine} = \frac{\text{opposite}}{\text{hypotenuse}}, \quad \text{cosine} = \frac{\text{adjacent}}{\text{hypotenuse}}, \quad \text{tangent} = \frac{\text{opposite}}{\text{adjacent}}.$$

The most useful results for triangles that do not contain a right angle are the sine formula

$$\frac{a}{\sin A} = \frac{b}{\sin B} = \frac{c}{\sin C}$$

and the cosine formula $a^2 = b^2 + c^2 - 2bc \cos A$. » angle; function (mathematics) [i]; triangle (mathematics)

Trikhonís, Lake [treekho**nees**] area 96 513 sq km/37 254 sq ml. Largest lake in Greece, 16 km/10 ml NNE of Missolonghi; length 19 km/12 ml; width 4.8 km/3 ml. » Greece [i]

Trilling, Lionel (1905–75) US author and critic, born and died in New York City. He was educated at Columbia University, where he taught from 1931, becoming professor of English in 1948. He wrote studies on Matthew Arnold (1939) and E M Forster (1948), and many books of critical essays, such as *The Liberal Imagination* (1950) and *Sincerity and Authenticity* (1972). » literary criticism

trilobite An extinct primitive marine arthropod, characterized by two grooves along its body producing a tri-lobed appearance; diverse and widespread from the Cambrian to the Permian periods; ranged from minute to 1 m/3 ft long; mostly living on sea bottom; sometimes planktonic. (Phylum: *Arthropoda*. Class: *Trilobita*, c.4 000 species.) » arthropod; Cambrian period; Permian period; RR16

trimaran [**triy**maran] A vessel with a narrow hull and large outriggers or floats giving the appearance of a three-hulled craft. The design gives great stability, thus permitting a large sail area which produces relatively high speed. It is mainly used for yachts. » catamaran; yacht [i]

Trimurti (Sanskrit, 'having three forms') [tri**moor**tee] The Hindu triad, manifesting the cosmic functions of the Supreme Being, as represented by Brahma, Vishnu, and Shiva. Brahma is the balance between the opposing principles of preservation and destruction, symbolized by Vishnu and Shiva respectively. » Brahma; Hinduism; Shiva; Vishnu

Trincomalee or **Trinkomali** [tringkuhma**lee**] 8°44N 81°13E, pop (1981) 44 313. Seaport capital of Trincomalee district, Sri Lanka; 257 km/160 ml NE of Colombo on Koddiyar Bay, at the mouth of the R Mahaweli; one of the earliest Tamil settlements; taken by the British, 1795; principal British naval base during World War 2 after the fall of Singapore; notable deep-water harbour; exports dried fish and coconuts; ruins of Temple of a Thousand Columns (3rd-c BC), Hindu temple, Fort Fredrick. » Sri Lanka [i]

Trinidad and Tobago, official name **Republic of Trinidad and Tobago** pop (1990e) 1 233 000; area 5 128 sq km/1 979 sq ml. Southernmost islands of the Lesser Antilles chain, SE Caribbean, just off the S American mainland; capital, Port of Spain; chief towns, San Fernando, Arima, Scarborough; timezone GMT −4; population mainly of East Indian or African descent; official language, English; chief religions, Roman Catholicism (34%), Hinduism (25%); unit of currency, the Trinidad and Tobago dollar; island of Trinidad (4 828 sq km/ 1 864 sq ml) roughly rectangular in shape; separated from Venezuela (S) by the 11 km/7 ml-wide Gulf of Paria; crossed by three mountain ranges; N range includes El Cerro del Aripo (940 m/3 084 ft); remainder of the land low-lying, with large areas of mangrove swamps along coasts; Tobago lies 30 km/19 ml NE (area 300 sq km/116 sq ml); Main Ridge extends along most of the island, rising to 576 m/1 890 ft; tropical climate, annual average temperature of 29°C; average rainfall, 1 270 mm/50 in (W), 3 048 mm/120 in (NE); visited by Columbus, 1498; Trinidad settled by Spain, 16th-c; ceded to Britain, 1802; Tobago a British colony, 1814; joint British Crown Colony, 1899; independent member of the Commonwealth, 1962; republic, 1976; governed by a president (elected for a 5-year term) and bicameral parliament, comprising a 31-member Senate and a 36-member House of Representatives; economy based on the oil and gas industry; industrial complex on W coast of Trinidad includes a steel mill, ammonia plants, and facilities for producing methanol and urea; cement, oil refining, petrochemicals, asphalt, processing of sugar, cocoa, coffee, fruit; main tourist centre on Tobago. » Antilles; Caribbean; West Indies; RR27 national holidays; RR63 political leaders

trinitrotoluene [triyniytrohtolyooeen] » **TNT** [i]

Trinity A distinctively Christian doctrine that God exists in three persons, Father, Son, and Holy Spirit. The unity of God is maintained by insisting that the three persons or modes of existence of God are of one substance. The doctrine arose in the early Church because strictly monotheistic Jews nevertheless affirmed the divinity of Christ (the Son) and the presence of God in the Church through the Holy Spirit. The functions of the persons of the Trinity, and the relationship between them, has been the subject of much controversy (eg the split between Eastern and Western Churches on the *Filioque* clause), but the trinitarian concept is reflected in most Christian worship. » Christianity; Filioque; God; Holy Spirit; Jesus Christ

Trinity House The lighthouse authority for England and Wales, the Channel Islands, and Gibraltar. It is one of the principal pilotage authorities, and also supervises the maintainance of navigation marks carried out by local harbour authorities. Its pilotage role is undergoing a fundamental change, with control being gradually devolved to local port management.

Trinity Sunday In the Christian Church, the Sunday after Whitsunday, observed in honour of the Trinity. » Trinity; Whitsunday

trio 1 An ensemble of three singers or instrumentalists, or a piece of music for such an ensemble. The string trio is normally composed of violin, viola, and cello; in the piano trio, a piano replaces the viola. Haydn, Mozart, and Beethoven are among those who wrote for both these ensembles. » chamber music **2** The central section of a minuet or scherzo, which in the earliest examples often employed a three-part texture. » minuet; scherzo

triode An electronic valve having three electrodes; a positive anode, an electron-emitting cathode, and a negatively-biased control grid. A triode can be used as an amplifier or oscillator. » anode; oscillator; diode; thermionic valve

tripack Originally a combination of three photographic emulsion layers coated on two or three supports to produce colour separation negatives by a single exposure in the camera. It is now entirely replaced by **integral tripack** having the three emulsions on a single base. » integral tripack

tripe The stomach of ruminants, used as food – both the rumen (*plain tripe*) and the reticulum (*honeycomb tripe*). In France and the UK it is traditionally stewed with onions, vegetables and herbs, although the recipes differ. » ruminant [i]

Triple Alliance, War of the or **Paraguayan War** (1864–70) devastating war fought by Paraguay against the combined forces of Brazil, Argentina and Uruguay (the Triple Alliance) and provoked by the ambitions of the Paraguayan dictator Francisco Solano López (1826–70). The eventual victory of the Allies (most of the troops were provided by Brazil) was achieved at the cost of reducing the male population of Paraguay by nine-tenths. » Paraguay [i]

Triple Crown A term used in many sports to describe the winning of three major events. In British horse racing it is the Derby, 2 000 Guineas, and St Leger; in US racing, the Preakness Stakes, Kentucky Derby, and Belmont Stakes. In British Rugby Union it is the beating of the other three Home countries in the International Championship. » horse racing; rugby football

Triple Entente A series of agreements between Britain and France (1904) and Britain and Russia (1907) initially to resolve outstanding colonial differences. It aligned Britain to France and Russia, who had concluded a military alliance in 1893–4. In 1914, the Triple Entente became a military alliance.

triple glazing Three layers of glass separated by air spaces to give improved thermal or acoustic insulation. As with double glazing, the spaces may be permanently sealed or openable, the former being the most common and efficient. The insulation from triple glazing is significantly greater than from double glazing. » double glazing; thermal insulation

triple jump An athletics field event, which takes place in the same area as the long jump. Competitors, after completing their run-up, must take off and hop on the same foot. The second phase is a step onto the other foot, followed by a jump. The rules which govern the measuring and number of jumps are the same as for the long jump. The event was previously called the *hop, step, and jump*. The current world record is 17.97 m/58 ft 11 in, achieved by William Banks (USA, born 1 Mar 1956) on 16 June 1985 at Indianapolis, USA. » athletics; long jump

Tripoli (Lebanon) [tripuhlee], Arabic **Trablous**, Gr **Tripolis**, ancient **Oea** 34°27N 35°50E, pop (1980e) 175 000. Seaport capital of Tripoli division, NW Lebanon; second largest city in Lebanon; trade centre for N Lebanon and NW Syria; mostly occupied by Sunni Muslims; two Palestinian refugee camps nearby; railway; port trade, oil refining; Tower of the Lion, 12th-c Crusader Castle of St Gilles, 13th-c Mamelukes' Grand Mosque. » Lebanon [i]; Sunnis

Tripoli (Libya), Arabic **Tarabulus** or **Tarabulus al-Gharb**, ancient **Oea** 32°54N 13°11E, pop (1982) 980 000. Seaport capital of Libya; on the Mediterranean coast, 345 km/214 ml SSW of Malta; founded by the Phoenicians, and later developed by the Romans; important Axis base in World War 2; bombed (1941–2) and occupied by the British (1943); bombed by US Air Force in response to alleged terrorist activities, 1986; airport; railway; university (1973); olive oil, fruit, fish, textiles; arch of Marcus Aurelius (1st-c BC); old city partly surrounded by Byzantine and mediaeval walls. » Axis Powers; Libya [i]

Tripolitania [tripolitaynia] Region of N Africa, lying between Tunis and Cyrenaica; former province of W Libya; under Turkish control from the 16th-c until 1911; under Italian control until 1943; British control until 1952. » Libya [i]

triptych » **altarpiece**

Tripura [tripoora] pop (1981) 2 060 189; area 10 477 sq km/ 4 044 sq ml. State in E India, bounded N, W and S by Bangladesh; became a state of India, 1949; status changed to union territory, 1956; reverted to a state, 1972; capital, Agartala; governed by a 60-member Legislative Assembly; mostly hilly and forested; tribal shifting cultivation gradually being replaced by modern farming methods; rice, wheat, tea, cotton, jute, oilseed, sugar cane; food processing, steel, handicrafts. » India [i]

trireme [triyreem] A Mediterranean war galley of Greek origin propelled by three banks of oars. Speeds of up to nine knots are claimed for short distances. It was fitted with a square sail for use with a favourable wind, and also a strong projection fixed to the bow below the waterline, used to ram other ships. » bireme; ship [i]

Tristan da Cunha [**tri**stan da **kun**ya] 37°15S 12°30W; pop (1982) 324; area 98 sq km/38 sq ml. Small volcanic island in the S Atlantic, about midway between S Africa and S America; volcanic cone rises to 2 060 m/6 758 ft; three uninhabited islands nearby; inhabitants are the descendants of a British garrison established in 1816 during Napoleon's exile in St Helena; became a dependency of St Helena, 1922; chief settlement, Edinburgh; islanders evacuated in 1961 after a volcanic eruption, but returned in 1963; fishing (crayfish), crafts, postage stamps. » Napoleon I; St Helena

Trireme

Tristram or **Tristan** [**tris**tram] In the Arthurian legends, a knight who was sent to woo Iseult (Isolde) on behalf of his uncle, King Mark of Cornwall. He fell in love with her himself, then fled to Brittany, where he married Iseult of the White Hands. » Arthur

tritium [**tri**tiuhm] A heavy isotope of hydrogen, in which the nucleus comprises one proton and two neutrons rather than a single proton (as for common hydrogen). It is radioactive, with a half-life of 12.3 years. It does not occur naturally, but is formed in nuclear reactions, and is an important ingredient of nuclear fusion reactions and hydrogen bombs. » deuterium; hydrogen; isotopes; nuclear fusion

Triton (astronomy) The principal natural satellite of Neptune, discovered in 1846; distance from the planet 355 000 km/221 000 ml; diameter 2 720 km/1 690 ml. Uniquely, for a large moon, its orbit is retrograde about Neptune. The encounter by Voyager 2 (Aug 1989) showed it has a thin atmosphere of nitrogen, with a surface pressure of 10 microbar. There is a darker pinkish hemisphere and a lighter bluish-white hemisphere, both with a complex geological history including impacts, flooding, melting, faulting, and collapse. There is some evidence of current nitrogen volcanism. » Neptune (astronomy); retrograde motion; Voyager project [i]; RR4

Triton (mythology) [**triy**tn] In Greek mythology, the son of Poseidon and Amphitrite. He is depicted in art as a fish from the waist down, and blowing a conch-shell. The beings of similar form (mermen) who serve Poseidon are often referred to as Tritons.

triton shell [**triy**tn] A large marine snail found in the Indo-Pacific region; one of the world's largest snails, length up to 36 cm/14 in; shells used as ceremonial trumpets by Pacific islanders. (Class: *Gastropoda*. Order: *Mesogastropoda*.) » gastropod; snail

triumphal arch A free-standing gateway of purely aesthetic and symbolic function, usually monumental in proportion, built of stone, and with ornate surface decoration. It was first used in Rome in the 2nd-c BC, but the most famous example is the Arc de Triomphe de l'Étoile, Paris (1806–35), architect J F Chalgrin. » arch [i]; Roman architecture

triumvirate Literally, 'a group of three men'; in ancient Rome **1** the name given to any publicly appointed administrative board of three; **2** the name commonly, though incorrectly, applied to the unofficial coalition between Caesar, Pompey, and Crassus in 60 BC; **3** the name given to the joint rule from 43 BC of Antony, Octavian, and Lepidus. » Roman history [i]

Trivandrum or **Trivandram** [tri**van**druhm] 8°31N 77°00E, pop (1981) 520 000. Capital of Kerala state, SW India; 1 255 km/780 ml SSE of Bombay, on the Malabar coast; airfield; railway; university (1937); commercial and cultural centre; textiles, soap, copra, coir ropes; noted for its wood and ivory carving; early 18th-c temple to Vishnu. » Kerala

Trobriand Islander A Melanesian people of the scattered Trobriand Is, off New Guinea; cultivators and famous for their ceremonial gift exchange system, the *kula*. They were studied by Malinowski from 1915, and their way of life described in several monographs, including *Argonauts of the Western Pacific* (1922). Population c.17 000. » Malinowski; Melanesia

trogon [**troh**guhn] A bird native to the New World tropics, Africa, and SE Asia; plumage soft, brightly-coloured; tail long; inhabits woodland; eats insects, spiders, fruit, and (occasionally) small vertebrates. (Family: *Trogonidae*, c.40 species.) » quetzal

Troilus [**troh**iluhs, **troy**luhs] In Greek legend, a prince of Troy, the son of Priam and Hecuba, who was killed by Achilles. In mediaeval stories, he is the lover of Cressida. » Cressida; Pandarus

Trojan asteroids Asteroids which have orbits very similar to Jupiter, positioned 60° ahead or behind the planet, where they are trapped in a stable configuration. About 230 are known. They are named after the heroes of the *Iliad*. » asteroids; Jupiter (astronomy)

Trojan Horse A huge wooden horse left behind on the beach by the Greeks, who had pretended to give up the siege of Troy. Told by Sinon that it was an offering to Athena, the Trojans broke down their city wall to bring it inside. At night, warriors emerged and captured the city. » Trojan War

Trojan War In Greek legend, the 10-year conflict between the Greeks and Trojans, which began when Paris carried off Helen, the wife of Menelaus, and ended in the sacking of Troy. The story was the subject of Homer's *Iliad*, and is tentatively dated on the basis of archaeology to c.1260 BC. » Achilles; Agamemnon; Menelaus; Odysseus; Patroclus; Sarpedon; Trojan Horse; Troy

troll [trohl] In early Scandinavian mythology a huge ogre, in later tradition a mischievous dwarf, the guardian of treasure, inhabiting caves and mountains and skilled with his hands. » mythology

trolley bus A type of bus popular in the UK until the 1960s, using an electric motor rather than an internal combustion engine as its motive power. Electricity was provided by overhead cables, with the electricity being conducted from the wires by means of trailing wiper arms. The trolley bus differed from the tram in not running on tracks. » electricity; tram

Trollope, Anthony (1815–82) British novelist, born and died in London. He joined the Post Office in 1834, working as a clerk, becoming in 1841 postal surveyor in Ireland, where he began to write. His first novel in the Barsetshire series, *The Warden*, appeared in 1855, and was followed by such successful books as *Barchester Towers* (1857), *Framley Parsonage* (1861), and *The Last Chronicle of Barset* (1867). A political series of novels followed, including *Phineas Finn* (1869) and *The Eustace Diamonds* (1873). Among his later novels were *The Way We Live Now* (1875) and *Mr Scarborough's Family* (1883). » English literature; novel

trombone A musical instrument made from brass tubing, mainly cylindrical, which expands to a bell at one end and is fitted with a cup-shaped mouthpiece at the other. A slide is used to vary the length, and therefore the fundamental pitch, of the instrument, which is made in various sizes. Its history dates back to the 15th-c; until c.1700 it was known as the *sackbut*. It was much used in the 17–18th-c for church music and for supernatural scenes in opera, and in the 19th-c it became a regular member of the symphony orchestra. Trombones are prominent also in jazz groups, and in brass, dance, and military bands. » brass instrument [i]

Tromp, Maarten (Harpertzoon) (1598–1653) Dutch Admiral, born at Briel. In 1639 he defeated a superior Spanish fleet off Gravelines, and won the Battle of the Downs later that year. Knighted by Louis XIII of France (1640) and by Charles I of England (1642), he then fought the French pirates based on Dunkirk, while his encounter with Blake in 1652 started the first Anglo-Dutch War. Victorious off Dover, he was defeated by a superior English fleet off Portland, and finally off Terhejide, near Schevingen, where he was killed. His son, **Cornelis (Maartenzoon)** (1629–91) was a Lieutenant-Admiral in the later Anglo-Dutch Wars. » Blake, Robert; Charles I (of England); Dutch Wars; Louis XIII

trompe l'oeil [trõp **ler**ee] (Fr 'deceive the eye') A painting which may have little aesthetic value, but which is cleverly designed to trick the spectator into thinking the objects represented are really there. According to Pliny, the ancient Greek painter Zeuxis painted grapes which birds tried to peck. » illusionism; Naturalism (art); Zeuxis

Tromsø [**trom**ser] 69°42N 19°00E, pop (1983) 47 316. Seaport capital of Troms county, N Norway; on a small island between South Kvaløy and the mainland; founded, 13th-c; charter, 1794; largest town in N Norway; base for expeditions to the Arctic; bishopric; university (1972); fishing, fish processing, sealing; observatory for the study of the aurora borealis; Tromsdalen church (1975), Tromsø museum. » Norway [i]

Trondheim [**trond**hiym], formerly **Nidaros**, later Ger **Trondhjem**, **Drontheim** 63°36N 10°23E, pop (1983) 134 665. Seaport and capital of Sør-Trøndelag county, C Norway, at the mouth of the R Nidelv (Nea), on S shore of Trondheim Fjord; former capital of Norway during the Viking period; occupied by the Germans, 1940–5; bishopric; airport; railway; university (1968); shipbuilding, fishing, trade in timber; cathedral (1066–93), royal palace (18th-c), Church of Our Lady (13th-c). » Norway [i]; Vikings

Troödos Mountains [**troh**uhthos] Mountain range in C Cyprus; rises to 1 951 m/6 4001 ft at Mt Olympus, highest peak on the island. » Cyprus [i]

Troon 55°32N 4°40W, pop (1981) 14 233. Town and golf resort in Kyle and Carrick district, Strathclyde, W Scotland; at N end of Ayr Bay, 9 km/6 ml N of Ayr; railway; boatbuilding. » Scotland [i]; Strathclyde

Trooping the Colour In the UK, originally the display of the regimental standard to the troops; now usually taken to refer to the annual ceremony on Horse Guards Parade, London, when the Queen reviews one of the seven regiments of her personal guard and its flag, or 'colour' is paraded before her. The ceremony takes place to mark the Queen's official birthday, in June.

tropic bird A marine bird, native to tropical seas world-wide; plumage white or pink with black line through eye; wings slender, pointed; central tail feathers very long (may be longer than body); catches fish and squid by plunging into water; on land, is unable to stand. (Family: *Phaethontidae*, 3 species.)

tropical rainforest » **rainforest**

tropical year The time taken for the Earth to complete one revolution round the Sun relative to the vernal equinox: 365.24219 mean solar days. » equinox

tropics A climatic zone located between the Tropics of Cancer (23.5°N) and Capricorn (23.5°S). The N tropic is so called because the Sun at the summer solstice (when it is vertically over that tropic) enters the zodiacal sign of Cancer; the S tropic is named for a similar reason. A number of different climates are recognized, based on the seasonal distribution of precipitation; there is no satisfactory single definition. Temperatures are generally high, such as a mean monthly temperature greater than 20°C/68°F. In the *humid* tropics mean annual rainfall is above 2 000 mm/c.80 in, and only one month of the year has less than 50 mm/c.2 in. Rainforest is the characteristic vegetation. In a tropical *wet-dry* climate, there is greater seasonality; mean annual rainfall is greater than 1 000 mm/c.40 in, with at least five wet months, each receiving more than 50 mm/c.2 in. Savannah is the characteristic vegetation. » rainforest; savannah; zodiac [i]

tropism [**troh**pizm] A plant response by directional movement towards (positive) or away from (negative) a sustained external stimulus. It is attained by unequal growth of the sides of the organ stimulated by growth hormones. **Phototropism** is a response to light; **geotropism** to gravity; and **chemotropism** to chemicals. » auxins; growth hormone; nastic movement

troposphere The lowest layer of the Earth's atmosphere, within which the weather is active because of the continual motion of the air and a steadily decreasing temperature with height. The upper boundary of the troposphere (the *tropopause*) is located at a temperature inversion: warmer air in the stratosphere overlies the troposphere, and effectively forms a barrier to convection. The height of the tropopause is correlated with sea level temperature, season, and daily changes in surface pressure; it is at c.8–16 km/5–10 ml, generally higher at the Equator than at the Poles, and also higher at the Poles in summer than in winter. » atmosphere [i]; convection; insolation; solar radiation; stratosphere

Trotsky, Leon, pseudonym of **Lev Davidovich Bronstein** (1879–1940) Russian Jewish revolutionary, born at Yanovka, the Ukraine. Educated in Odessa, in 1898 he was arrested as a Marxist and exiled to Siberia. He escaped in 1902, joined Lenin in London, and in the abortive 1905 Revolution was President of the St Petersburg Soviet. He then worked as a revolutionary journalist in the West, returning to Russia in 1917, when he joined the Bolsheviks and played a major role in the October Revolution. In the Civil War he was Commissar for War, and created the Red Army. After Lenin's death (1924) his influence began to decline; he was ousted from the Party by Stalin, who opposed his theory of 'permanent revolution', exiled to C Asia (1927), and expelled from the Soviet Union (1929). He continued to agitate as an exile, and was sentenced to death in his absence by a Soviet court in 1937. He finally found asylum in Mexico, where he was assassinated by one of Stalin's agents. » Bolsheviks; Lenin; October Revolution; Revolution of 1905; Russian Revolution; Stalin; Trotskyism

Trotskyism A development of Marxist thought by Leon Trotsky. Essentially a theory of permanent revolution, Trotskyism stressed the internationalism of socialism, avoided co-existence, and encouraged revolutionary movements abroad; this conflicted with Stalin's ideas of 'socialism in one country'. Trotskyism has since inspired other extreme left-wing revolutionary movements but they are factionally divided, and have little support ouside some Western capitalist states. » communism; Marxism-Leninism; Stalinism; Trotsky

troubadours [**troo**badoor] (Provençal, 'inventor') Court poet-musicians (some known by name, such as Guillaume d'Acquitaine) who flourished in the S of France 1100–1350. They wrote (in the S dialect *langue d'oc*) mainly love poems, and had an important influence on the development of the European lyric. They included Bernart de Ventadorn (c.1130–90) and Arnaut Daniel (c.1150–c.1200). Their equivalent in the N (writing in the N dialect *langue d'oil*) were the **trouvères**, who also wrote *chansons de geste*. Among the best known were Blondel de Nesle (12th-c) and Adam de la Halle (c.1250–88). » Blondel; chansons de geste; French literature; poetry

trout Any of several species of the family *Salmonidae*, existing in two forms: the **brown trout**, confined to fresh water, and the migratory and much larger **sea trout**; includes the European trout, *Salmo trutta*, found in marine and adjacent freshwaters from Norway to the Mediterranean, Black Sea, and Caspian Sea; an excellent food fish, very popular with anglers, and also farmed commercially. » salmon

trouvères » **troubadours**

Trowbridge [**troh**brij] 51°20N 2°13W, pop (1981) 27 476. County town in West Wiltshire district, Wiltshire, S England; 12 km/7 ml SE of Bath; railway; foodstuffs; brewing, clothing, printing, dairy products. » Wiltshire

Troy, Turkish **Truva**, ancient **Troy** or **Ilium** Ancient ruined city in

Çanakkale province, W Turkey; the archaeological site lies S of the Dardanelles, near Hisarlik; in Greek legend it was beseiged by a confederation of Greek armies for 10 years (Trojan War), as recounted by Homer in the *Iliad*; from the Stone Age to Roman times, over a period of 4 000 years, the city was rebuilt on the same site nine times; excavated by Heinrich Schliemann in the 1870s, the occupation level known as Troy VIIa is thought to be the city of the Greek legend. » Homer; Schliemann; Trojan War; Turkey [i]

Troyes, ancient **Augustobona Tricassium** [trwah] 48°19N 4°03E, pop (1982) 64 769. Capital city of Aube department, NEC France; on channel of the R Seine, 150 km/93 ml SE of Paris; bishopric, 4th-c; capital of old province of Champagne; railway; centre of hosiery trade; textiles, machinery, foodstuffs; Cathedral of St-Peter and St-Paul (13th–16th-c), Church of St-Urbain (13th-c), Church of Ste-Madeleine (16th-c), former Abbey of St-Loup, with famous library, Musée des Beaux-Arts, hosiery museum. » Champagne-Ardenne

Trucial States The former name of the United Arab Emirates of Abu Dhabi, Ajman, Dubai, Fujairah, Ras al Khaimah, Sharja, and Umm al Qaiwain on the Persian Gulf and Gulf of Oman. The name derives from a truce signed between the ruling sheiks and Great Britain in 1820. In 1892 they accepted British protection. » United Arab Emirates [i]

Trudeau, Pierre (Elliott) (1919–) Canadian statesman and Liberal Prime Minister (1968–79, 1980–4), born in Montreal. Educated at Montreal, Harvard, and London, he became a lawyer, helped to found the political magazine *Cité Libre* (1950), and was professor of law at Montreal (1961–5). Elected an MP in 1965, he became Minister of Justice (1967) and an outspoken critic of Québecois separatism. His term of office as Prime Minister saw the October (1970) Crisis in Quebec, the introduction of the Official Languages Act, federalist victory during the Quebec Referendum (1980), and the introduction of Canada's constitution (1982). He resigned as leader of the Liberal Party and from public life in 1984. » Canada [i]

Truffaut, François (1932–1984) French film critic and director, born in Paris. His first career, as a critic from 1953, led to his 'auteur' concept of film-making. In 1959 he made his first feature as director/actor/co-scriptwriter, *Les Quatre Cents Coups* (The 400 Blows), effectively launching the French 'Nouvelle Vague' movement, followed by *Tirez sur le Pianiste* (1960, Shoot the Pianist), *Jules et Jim* (1962), and *Fahrenheit 451* (1966), in all of which he was also co-scriptwriter. He continued actively at work throughout the 1970s, notably with *La Nuit américaine* (1972, Day for Night), for which he received an Oscar. He returned from colour photography to his first love of black and white in his final film *Vivement Dimanche* (1983, Lively Sunday). He died at Neuilly-sur-Seine. » auteur theory; Nouvelle Vague

truffle The underground fruiting body of fungi belonging to the genus *Tuber*; often found in soils under beech woods; may be fleshy or waxy; remains closed and has no active dispersal mechanism for spores; much sought after as a delicacy. (Subdivision: *Ascomycetes*. Order: *Tuberales*.) » Ascomycetes; fungus

Trujillo [troo**heel**yoh] 8°06S 79°00W, pop (1981) 354 557. Capital of La Libertad department, NW Peru; founded by Pizarro, 1536; airfield; railway; university (1824); cathedral, several convents, monasteries, and colonial churches. » Peru [i]

Trujillo (Molina), Rafael Leonidas [troo**heel**yoh] (1891–1961) Dictator of the Dominican Republic from 1930 until his assassination in Santo Domingo, a city he had renamed Ciudad Trujillo. Born in San Cristóbal, Dominican Republic, he rose to prominence as commander of the police. His regime was both highly repressive and highly corrupt.

Truk pop (1980) 37 742; area 127 sq km/49 sq ml. One of the Federated States of Micronesia, W Pacific, comprising 11 high volcanic islands in the Truk lagoon and numerous outlying atolls; capital, Moen; more than 60 ships of the Japanese wartime fleet lie sunk at various depths in the lagoon, one of the largest in the world. » Micronesia, Federated States of

Truman, Harry S (1884–1972) US Democratic statesman and 33rd President (1945–53), born at Lamar, Missouri. Elected to the Senate in 1934, he was chairman of a special committee investigating defence, Vice-President (1944), and President on the death of Roosevelt, being re-elected in 1948 in a surprise victory over Dewey. His decisions included the dropping of the first atom bomb on Japan, the postwar loan to Britain, and the sending of US troops to South Korea. He promoted the policy of giving military and economic aid to countries threatened by communist interference (the **Truman Doctrine**). At home, he introduced a 'Fair Deal' of economic reform. He died in Kansas City, Missouri. » Democratic Party; Fair Deal

trumpet A musical instrument made from cylindrical brass (or other metal) tubing, fitted with a cup-shaped mouthpiece, and widening at the other end to a flared bell. It was traditionally used for signalling, and since the 17th-c as an orchestral and solo instrument. Until the 19th-c it was restricted to the notes of the harmonic series, many trumpeters of Bach's time specializing in the high 'clarino' register. The fundamental pitch could be altered by fitting 'crooks' (pieces of tubing) of various lengths; since about 1830, trumpets have been fitted with valves to perform the same function more easily. The modern trumpet has three valves and is a transposing instrument pitched in B♭. » brass instrument [i]; harmonic series [i]; transposing instrument

trumpet creeper » **trumpet vine**

trumpet vine A deciduous climber native to E Asia and eastern N America; stems clinging by aerial roots; leaves pinnate; flowers orange-scarlet, trumpet-shaped with five unequal lobes; also called a **trumpet creeper**. It is a popular ornamental. (Genus: *Campsis*, 2 species. Family: *Bignoniaceae*.) » climbing plant; deciduous plants; pinnate

trumpeter A plump, ground-living bird, native to tropical S America; plumage mainly black with short tail; neck slender and legs long; flies reluctantly; inhabits rain forests; eats fruit and insects. (Family: *Psophiidae*, 3 species.)

trunkfish Small and very bizarre fish whose body is encased in rigid and often ornate case-like armour of small polygonal plates; includes *Lactophrys trigonus*, found around reefs and sea grass beds of the W Atlantic; length up to 40 cm/16 in; fins small and membranous, eyes prominent. (Family: *Ostracontidae*.) » sunfish

Truro 50°16N 5°03W, pop (1981) 18 557. County town in Carrick district, Cornwall, SW England; on R Truro, 20 km/12 ml SW of St Austell; Royal Institution of Cornwall; railway; foodstuffs, engineering, seaweed fertilizer, pottery; cathedral (1880–1910), Pendennis Castle (1543). » Cornwall

trust An arrangement whereby a person (*the trustee*) holds property for the benefit of another (*the beneficiary*). The terms of the settlement or will creating the trust are binding on the trustees. Some trusts are created by operation of law. A trustee in breach of trust is liable for the damage suffered. » equity

Trust Territory A non-self-governing area, the administration of which is supervised by the United Nations under Article 75, established after World War 2. The origins of the system lay in the need to administer colonial territories taken from powers defeated in World War 1. Trusteeship Agreements are entered into between the administering country, whose task is to prepare the people for independence and encourage the develoment of human rights, and the United Nations. Most such areas are now independent, with the exception of a small number of Pacific islands. » United Nations

Trusteeship » **Trust Territory**

Trusteeship Council » **United Nations**

Truth, Sojourner (c.1797–1883) US abolitionist, born into slavery in New York State. She escaped just before slavery ended there in 1827, and settled in New York City, involving herself in the religious enthusiasms of the day until 1843, when she became a travelling preacher. She joined the abolitionist movement and became an effective anti-slavery speaker. She eventually settled in Battle Creek, Michigan but remained active in the causes of Black and women's rights until her death. » slave trade; women's liberation movement

Truth or Consequences, or **Truth or C.**, formerly **Hot Springs** (to 1950) 33°08N 107°16W, pop (1980) 5 219. Town in Sierra County, SW New Mexico, USA, on the Rio Grande; the new name was adopted by a citizens' vote, following the offer made by the presenter of a famous radio programme that if the town adopted the name of his show he would hold a yearly fiesta with the programme presented from there. » New Mexico

trypanosomiasis [tripanuhsuh**miy**asis] Any of several diseases caused by infection with one of the trypanosomes that live on the skin of rodents, armadilloes, and domestic animals. *African trypanosomiasis* is widely distributed in Africa, and is transmitted to humans by bites from tsetse flies; it is also known as **sleeping sickness**. Fever may be severe and prolonged, and the liver, spleen, lungs, and heart may be involved; drowsiness and coma can occur. *American trypanosomiasis* is transmitted by blood-sucking bugs, and occurs widely in S and C America; also known as **Chagas' disease**, after the Brazilian physician Carlos Chagas (1879–1934). Young children are commonly affected with fever, enlargement of lymph nodes, and involvement of the brain and heart. » bug (entomology); Protozoa

Tsai T'ien » **Zai Tian**

tsaine » **banteng**

Tsaochuang » **Zaozhuang**

tsar Derived from the Lat. *Caesar*, this was the title used by the rulers of Russia from 1547 to 1721. It remained in common use until the Revolution (1917), although the official title of the ruler from 1721 until 1917 was Emperor.

Tsavo [tsah**voh**] National park in SE Kenya, established in 1948; area 20 800 sq km/8 000 sq ml; home of many African herd animals, as well as of the lion, hippopotamus, and rhinoceros. » Kenya [i]

Tschaikovsky » **Tchaikovsky**

Tselinograd, formerly **Akmolinsk** (to 1961) 51°10N 71°30E, pop (1983) 253 000. Capital town of Tselinograd oblast, Kazakhstan, on R Ishim; founded as a fortress, 1830; airport; railway junction; agricultural machinery, ceramics, foodstuffs, clothing. » Kazakhstan

Tseng Kuo-fan » **Zeng Guofan**

tsessebi » **topi**

tsetse fly [**tet**see] A small biting fly found in tropical Africa; mouthparts form a needle-like proboscis; feeds on blood of vertebrates; of great medical and veterinary importance as the carrier of sleeping sickness (in humans) and nagana (in cattle); serious epidemics in the early 20th-c, and recurrent outbreaks since; a major impediment to the use of horses and draught oxen in the early European exploration of Africa. (Order: *Diptera*. Family: *Glossinidae*.) » fly; trypanosomiasis

Tsinan » **Jinan**

Tsingtao » **Qingdao**

Tsiolkovsky, Konstantin (Eduardovich) [tseeol**kof**skee] (1857–1935) Russian physicist and rocketry pioneer, born at Izhevsk, Ryazan, Tsarist Russia. Self-educated, and handicapped by deafness, his visionary ideas on the use of rockets for space exploration were published in 1903. From 1911 he developed the basic theory of rocketry, and also multi-stage rocket technology (1929). Much earlier (1881), unaware of Maxwell's work, he independently developed the kinetic theory of gases. He died in Moscow. » Goddard; Maxwell, James Clerk; rocket; spaceflight

tsunami Long-period ocean waves produced by movements of the sea floor associated with earthquakes, volcanic explosions, or landslides. Tsunami waves may cross entire ocean basins at speeds as great as 800 km/500 ml per hour, and strike coastal regions with devastating force. Thousands of lives have been lost in regions of the Pacific subject to destructive tsunamis, which may reach heights in excess of 30 m/100 ft. They are also referred to as *seismic sea waves*, and in popular (but not technical oceanographic) use as *tidal waves*. » tidal wave; wave (oceanography); RR14

Tsvetayeva, Marina Ivanova [tsve**tiy**uhva], married name **Efron** (1892–1941) Russian poet, born in Moscow. Strongly anti-Bolshevik, she was allowed to emigrate in 1922, and wrote and published most of her poetry abroad, such as *Vyorsty* (1922, Miles), and *Posle Rossii 1922–25* (1928, After Russia). She returned to the USSR in 1939. After the execution of her husband and the arrest of her daughter, she committed suicide in Yelabuga. » poetry; Russian literature

Tswana » **Sotho-Tswana**

Tuamotu Archipelago [tow**moh**too] 135–143°W 14–23°S; pop (1977) 8 537; area 826 sq km/319 sq ml. Island group of French Polynesia, E of the Society Is; consists of two parallel ranges of 78 atolls; largest group of coral atolls in the world; chief islands include Rangiroa, Hao, Fakarava; area used for nuclear testing by the French since 1962. » French Polynesia

Tuareg [**twah**reg] A Berber pastoral people of the C Sahara and the N Sahel zone of W Africa. A traditionally highly stratified feudal society, in the past they were caravan traders and feared raiders. Many died during the severe drought of the 1970s. Population c.900 000. » Berber; pastoralism

tuatara [tooa**tah**ra] A rare lizard-like reptile, native to islands off the coast of New Zealand; the only remaining member of the order *Rhyncocephalia*; primitive in form (resembling extinct species); green or orange-brown; length, up to 650 mm/26 in; male with crest of tooth-like spines along back; nocturnal; digs burrow or shares burrow of a nesting petrel; eats invertebrates, small vertebrates, birds' eggs. (*Sphenodon punctatus*.) » lizard [i]; reptile

Tuatha de Danann [**too**aha day **don**an] A race of wise beings who came to Ireland c.1500 BC, and became the ancient gods of the Irish; the name means 'the people of the goddess Danu'. They were conquered by the Milesians, and retreated into tumuli near the R Boyne. » Dagda, the; Danu

tuba A musical instrument made from brass tubing curved elliptically, with usually four valves, a mouthpiece set at right angles, and a wide bell pointing upwards. It is the largest and lowest in pitch of all brass instruments, and succeeded the ophicleide as the bass of the orchestral brass section in the mid-19th-c. It is made in various sizes, some of which are known by other names. » brass instrument [i]; euphonium; saxhorn; sousaphone

tubenose A marine bird found worldwide; musk-like odour; nostrils long and tubular on long, grooved, hooked bill; also known as **petrel**. Its stomach contains oil which is used to feed its young, or which may be vomited as a defence. The order includes albatrosses, fulmars, shearwaters, and various petrels. (Order: *Procellariiformes*, or *Tubinares*.) » albatross; fulmar; petrel; shearwater

tuber An underground organ storing food for the next season's growth. **Stem** tubers are distinguished by the presence of buds or 'eyes'; **root** tubers bear no buds. » root (botany); stem (botany)

tuberculosis (TB) A disease almost always caused in humans by infection with *Mycobacterium tuberculosis*. Although diminishing in frequency, it still remains one of the most important infections in the world. The organisms enter the body via the respiratory or the gastro-intestinal tract. The disease follows one of several courses. Entry of the organism into the body is not always followed by a feeling of illness, and primary TB may be revealed only on a chest X-ray as a small lesion in the lungs and enlarged lymph nodes, which later mostly become calcified. In rare cases the primary infection may spread locally, or enter the blood stream and produce widespread TB (*miliary tuberculosis*). More often, clinical TB develops months or years after the primary infection, and is often due to re-infection. Any organ in the body may be affected, but pulmonary TB with fever, cough, sputum, and haemoptysis is the most common. The outlook of patients with TB has been transformed with the development of specific anti-tuberculous antibiotics. » BCG; haemoptysis; Koch, Robert; lungs; lupus vulgaris; Mantoux test; scrofula

Tubifex [**tyoo**bifeks] A freshwater annelid worm, found part buried in mud on river beds in low oxygen conditions; red in colour because of haemoglobin in blood; feeds by extracting organic material from mud; commonly used to feed aquarium fishes. (Class: *Oligochaeta*. Order: *Haplotaxida*.) » annelid; haemoglobin

Tübingen [**tü**binguhn] 48°32N 9°04E, pop (1983) 74 700. Capital of Tübingen district, Germany; on R Neckar, 27 km/17 ml S of Stuttgart; railway; university (1477); publishing, paper, textiles, machinery. » Germany [i]

Tubman, Harriet (c.1820–1913) US abolitionist and rescuer of slaves, born in Dorchester Co, Maryland. She escaped from slavery in Maryland (1849), and from then until the Civil War she was active on the slave escape route (the 'Underground Railroad'), making a number of dangerous trips into the South.

She acquired fame among abolitionists, and counselled John Brown before his attempt to launch a slave insurrection in 1859. During the Civil War she was a Northern spy and scout, but was denied a federal pension until 1897. She died at Auburn, New York. » American Civil War; slave trade

Tubruq » **Tobruk**

Tubuai Islands [too**bwiy**] or **Austral Islands**, Fr **Iles Tubuai** pop (1983) 6 283; area 137 sq km/53 sq ml. Volcanic island group of French Polynesia, 528 km/328 ml S of the Society Is; comprises a 1 300 km/800 ml chain of volcanic islands and reefs; chief islands, Rimatara, Rurutu, Tubuai, Raivaevae, Rapa; chief settlement, Mataura (Tubuai); coffee, copra. » French Polynesia

tubular bells A set of metal tubes tuned to different pitches and suspended in a large frame. They are struck with a short mallet to produce bell sounds in orchestral and operatic music. » percussion [i]

TUC » **Trades Union Congress**

Tucana (Lat 'toucan') [too**kah**na] A faint S constellation, which includes the prominent Small Magellanic Cloud and the notable globular cluster 47 Tuc. » constellation; globular cluster; Magellanic Clouds

Tuchachevski, Mikhail Nicolaevich [tuka**chef**skee] (1893–1937) Marshal of the Soviet Union, and from 1926 Chief-of-Staff of the Red Army, which he was influential in transforming from a peasant army into a modern, mechanized force. His vigour and independence made him suspect to Stalin, and in 1937 he was executed, an early victim of the great purge which decimated the Red Army's officer corps. » Red Army; Stalin

Tucson [**too**son] 32°13N 110°58W, pop (1980) 330 537. Seat of Pima County, SE Arizona, USA, on the Santa Cruz R; the Spanish founded the Presidio of San Augustín de Tuguison in 1776 near the site of the San Xavier del Brac Indian Mission (1700); ceded to the USA, 1853; city status, 1883; state capital, 1867–77; airport; railway; university (1885); electronic, optical and research industries; processing and distributing centre for cotton, livestock, and nearby mines; major tourist and health resort; Davis-Monthan Air Force Base nearby; Tucson Festival (Apr). » Arizona

Tucumán » **San Miguel de Tucumán**

Tudor, Owen » **Henry VII**

Tudors A N Wales gentry family, one of whose scions married a Plantagenet in the early 15th-c. Elevated to the peerage in the mid-15th-c, they ruled England from 1485 to 1603. The dynasty began when Henry, 2nd earl of Richmond and son of Margaret Beaufort (a Lancastrian claimant to the crown) overthrew Richard III in 1485. It ended with the death of Elizabeth I in 1603. » Edward VI; Elizabeth I; Henry VII; Henry VIII; Mary I; RR64

tuff » **pyroclastic rock**

tug of war An athletic event of strength involving two teams who pull against each other from opposite ends of a long thick rope. A team normally consists of eight members. With sheer strength and determination they have to pull their opponents over a predetermined mark. Ancient Chinese and Egyptians participated in similar events. The first rules were drawn up by the New York Athletic Club in 1879. It was part of the Olympic programme 1900–28.

tui [**too**ee] A honeyeater native to the New Zealand area; dark plumage with small knot of white feathers on throat, and collar of delicate white filaments; inhabits forest and habitation; eats insects, fruit, and nectar; also known as the **parson bird**. (*Prosthemadera novaeseelandiae*.) » honeyeater

Tuileries [**twee**luhree(z)] Formal gardens laid out in the 17th-c by Le Nôtre in Paris. They are all that remain of the former Tuileries Palace built for Catherine Medici in the 16th-c, and destroyed by fire in 1871. » Le Nôtre; Paris [i]

Tula (Mexico) [**too**la] An ancient Meso-American city, c.65 km/40 ml NW of Mexico City, from which the Toltecs dominated C Mexico c.900–1150 AD. It was 14 sq km/5½ sq ml in area and at its height had a population of c.30–40 000. It developed from c.750 AD, and was destroyed c.1168. Within its overall grid of houses and courtyards lies a central plaza containing temple pyramids, colonnaded meeting halls, and a ballcourt. » Mesoamerican ballgame; Toltecs

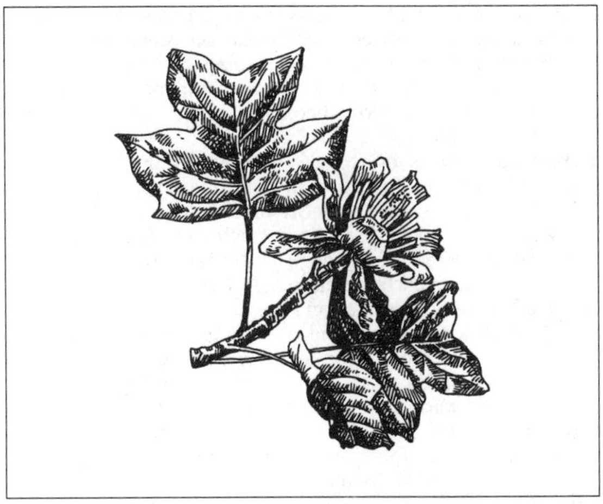

Tulip tree – Flower and leaves

Tula (Russia) [**too**la] 54°11N 37°38E, pop (1989) 540 000. Industrial capital town of Tulskaya oblast, NC European Russia; on R Upa, 193 km/120 ml S of Moscow; Imperial Small Arms Factory founded here by Peter the Great, 1712; railway; airfield; metallurgy, machinery, chemicals, biscuits; Uspenskii Cathedral (1762–4). » Peter I; Russia

tulip A bulb native to Europe and Asia, especially the steppe regions with cold winters and hot dry summers; stems erect; leaves narrow to oval, sometimes wavy; flowers, solitary, occasionally 2–6, in a variety of shapes and colours but usually large and showy, with six rounded or pointed, in some forms fringed perianth-segments or tepals. A popular ornamental for centuries, a huge industry is built around the several thousand named cultivars, especially in Holland, the country foremost in breeding tulips. (Genus: *Tulipa*, 100 species. Family: *Liliaceae*.) » bulb; cultivar; perianth

tulip tree A deciduous tree reaching 35 m/115 ft, native to N America; leaves 4-lobed with a squared apex; flowers with six greenish yellow petals, resembling the tulip in size and shape, hence the name. It is a valuable timber tree, known commercially as **Canary** or **American whitewood**. (*Liriodendron tulipifera*. Family: *Magnoliaceae*.) » deciduous plants; tree [i]; tulip

Tull, Jethro (1674–1741) English agriculturist, born at Basildon, Berkshire. Educated at Oxford, he became a lawyer, but turned to farming. He introduced several new farming methods, including the invention of a seed drill which planted seeds in rows (1701). He died near Hungerford, Berkshire. » agriculture

Tullamore, Gaelic **Tulach Mhór** [tuhla**maw**] 53°16N 7°30W, pop (1981) 8 724. Capital of Offaly county, Leinster, C Irish Republic; road junction on the Grand Canal, W of Dublin; railway; agricultural trade, spinning, distilling; abbey nearby at Durrow founded by St Columba. » Irish Republic [i]; Offaly

Tulsa [**tuhl**sa] 36°10N 95°55W, pop (1980) 360 919. Seat of Tulsa County, NE Oklahoma, USA; port on the Arkansas R; settled as a Creek Indian village in the 1830s; developed in the 1880s with the coming of the railway; airport; university (1894); major national centre of the petroleum industry; oil refining, petrochemicals, aerospace industry, metal goods; Gilcrease Institute of Art; May Festival, Great Labour Day Raft Race. » Oklahoma

tumbleweed The name given to various bushy plants which, at the end of the growing season, break off at ground level and are blown and rolled considerable distances by the wind, simultaneously scattering their seeds. They are mainly found in dry, open country most suitable for this method of dispersal. » rose of Jericho; spinifex

tumour A swelling of any kind in any part of the body. The term is often used to refer to a **neoplasm** (a benign or malignant new growth); but swellings caused by infection or by the growth of a cyst are also often referred to as tumours. » abscess; cancer; cyst; polyp

tuna Any of several large fast-swimming predatory fish (especially the *Thunnus* species) found in surface ocean waters; belong with the mackerels to the family *Scombridae*; body characteristically spindle-shaped and adapted for power and speed; many are heavily exploited commercially. » albacore; bonito; yellowfin tuna

Tunbridge Wells or **Royal Tunbridge Wells** 51°08N 0°16E, pop (1981) 58 141. Spa town in Tunbridge Wells district, Kent, SE England; 50 km/31 ml SE of London; iron-rich springs discovered in 1606; fashionable health resort in 17th–18th-c; 'Royal' since 1909, a legacy of visits made by Queen Victoria; railway; light industry, printing. » Kent

tundra The treeless vegetation zone found polewards of the taiga of N America, Europe, and Asia. Often underlain by permafrost, the vegetation is dominated by mosses, lichens, herbaceous perennials, dwarf shrubs, and grasses. The growing season is short, but warm enough for snow to melt and the active layer of permafrost to thaw. The resulting boggy depressions provide breeding ground for mosquitoes. » grass [i]; lichen; moss; muskeg; perennial; permafrost; shrub; taiga

tungsten W (Ger *wolfram*), element 74, density 20 g/cm^3, melting point 3 410°C. A grey metal, difficult to work, occurring mainly with other elements in oxide ores, from which it can be recovered by carbon reduction. The metal is extensively used for lamp filaments, because of its high melting point and general lack of reactivity. Compounds mainly show the oxidation states +4 and +6. *Tungsten carbide* (WC), is very hard, and is used in cutting and grinding tools. » chemical elements; metal; RR90

Tungurahua [toongoo**rah**wa] 1°26S 78°26W. Andean volcano in C Ecuador; 30 km/19 ml SE of Ambato; rises to 5 016 m/16 456 ft; spa town of Baños at N foot; dormant, though emits vapours from time to time; erupted in 1886, devastating Baños. » Andes

Tunguska event An explosion of enormous force low in the atmosphere over the Siberian wilderness area of Tunguska R valley (30 Jun 1908). This naturally occurring event is thought to have resulted from the impact of a small comet nucleus or asteroid. Equivalent to about a 2-megaton atomic bomb explosion, it levelled 3 000 sq km/1 200 sq ml of forest. No meteoritic debris was recovered, suggesting that the impactor was of low strength and perhaps made of volatile materials. » asteroids; comet; Meteor Crater; meteor; meteorite

Tunguska, River River in N Russia; comprises three tributaries of the R Yenisey, known as the Lower, Stony, and Upper Tunguska; greatest length, 3 200 km/2 000 ml. » Russia; Yenisey, River

tunicate [**tyoo**nikuht] A marine invertebrate chordate; may be solitary or in colonies, base attached or free swimming; adult body enclosed in leathery tunic (*test*); water drawn into a branchial sac via an inhalant siphon; food particles then trapped by mucus and water expelled from an exhalant siphon; larval stage possesses a notochord, dorsal nerve cord, and posterior tail; c.1 250 species, including sea squirts, salps, and larvaceans. (Phylum: *Chordata*. Subphylum: *Tunicata*.) » Chordata; larva; notochord

tuning fork A two-pronged metal instrument, invented in 1711 by English trumpeter John Shore (c.1662–1752), which is made to vibrate and then pressed down on a wooden surface to produce a note (virtually free from upper harmonics) to which voices or instruments can adjust their pitch. » idiophone; temperament

Tunis [**tyoo**nis] 36°50N 10°13E, pop (1984) 556 654. Seaport capital of Tunisia, 240 km/150 ml from Sicily; in a strategic position on the Mediterranean; Phoenician origin, later dominated by Carthage; capital status, 1236; captured by Turks, 1533; gained notoriety as a pirate base; occupied by French, 1881; airport; railway; university (1960); chemicals, textiles, tourism; Great Mosque of Zitouna (9th-c), Dar Ben Abdullah (19th-c house), Museum of Islamic Art, Palace of Dar Hussein, Dar Beb Abdallah Museum, Dar Lasram Museum, Bardo National Museum; Medina of Tunis is a world heritage site; film festival of Carthage (Oct). » Phoenicia; Tunisia [i]

Tunisia, official name **Republic of Tunisia**, Arabic **Al Djoumhouria Attunusia** [tyoo**ni**zia] pop (1990e) 8 182 000; area 164 150 sq km/63 362 sq ml. N African republic, divided into 18 governorates (*gouvernorats*); bounded W by Algeria, SE by Libya, and NE and N by the Mediterranean; capital, Tunis; chief towns, Bizerte, Sousse, Sfax; timezone GMT +1; population mainly Arabic (98%); chief religion, Islam (98%); official language, Arabic, but French widely spoken; unit of currency, the dinar of 1 000 millimes; Atlas Mts (NW) rise to 1 544 m/5 065 ft at Chambi; C depression runs W–E, containing several saline lakes; dry, sandy upland to the S; Mediterranean climate on coast, with hot, dry summers and wet winters; daily maximum 14–33°C; average annual rainfall at Tunis, 420 mm/17 in, over twice this level in the Atlas Mts; further S, rainfall decreases and temperatures can be extreme; variously ruled by Phoenicians, Carthaginians, Romans, Byzantines, Arabs, Spanish, and Turks; French protectorate, 1883; independence, 1956; monarchy abolished and republic declared, 1957; 141-member National Assembly, elected every five years; a president, also elected for five years, appoints a prime minister and cabinet; agriculture employs 50% of the population,

but of declining importance; world's fourth largest producer of olive oil; wheat, barley, henna, almonds, cork, citrus fruits, dates, grapes, vegetables; livestock, fishing, sugar refining, oil refining, cement, tyres, textiles, carpets, food processing, paper, tourism; world's fifth largest producer of phosphates; oil, iron ore, lead, zinc; also reserves of gold, barite, fluorspar. » Atlas Mountains; Tunis; RR27 national holidays; RR63 political leaders

Tunja [**toon**kha] 5°33N 73°23W, pop (1985) 93 159. Capital of Boyacá department, EC Colombia; in arid mountainous area, altitude 2 819 m/9 249 ft; university (1953); one of the oldest cities in Colombia, seat of the Zipa (one of the two Chibcha kings); refounded as a Spanish city, 1539; decisive battle of Boyacá fought 16 km/10 ml to the S, 1818; Church of Santo Domingo (begun 1594), Santa Clara Chapel (1580), Parque Bosque de la Republica, Casa del Fundador Suárez Rendón (1540–3, now a museum). » Colombia [i]

tunnel An artifical underground passage constructed for a variety of purposes, such as roads, railways, canals, mining, or conducting water. Tunnels are constructed either by cutting away the material above and then covering the tunnel over (the *cut and cover* method), or by driving through the ground using hand tools, a tunnelling shield, or rock drills as appropriate. In soft ground, some form of tunnel lining is required, and this is put in place either as the tunnel advances or immediately afterwards. The longest tunnel in the world is the Delaware Aqueduct in New York (169 km/105 ml), which is used for water supply.

tunnel diode A heavily doped semiconductor junction diode, with a very thin junction region. Breakdown occurs at very low reverse voltages, and there is no region of high reverse resistance. It has a negative resistance over part of its operating region, and is used in high frequency amplifiers and oscillators. » diode; doping; oscillator; resistance; semiconductor

tunnelling » **quantum tunnelling**

tunny » **tuna**

Tuonela [**too**uhnayla] In the Finnish poem *Kalevala*, the name of a dark river in the Far North, which borders the Other World. To visit Tuonela is the object of the shaman in his trance, when he tries to accompany the spirits of the dead. » Kalevala

tup » **sheep**

Tupamaros [toopa**mah**ros] An Uruguayan urban guerrilla movement founded by Raúl Sendic in 1963, named after the 18th-c Peruvian Indian rebel, Túpac Amaru. The movement was suppressed by the military-controlled government of 1972–85. » Uruguay [i]

tupelo [**tyoo**puhloh] A deciduous tree native to the swamps of eastern N America; leaves turning bright scarlet in autumn; inconspicuous flowers, small, greenish; males and females on separate trees; edible fruit 1–2 cm/0.4–0.8 in, oval, blue-black; also called **black gum** and **pepperidge**. It is cultivated mainly for ornament. (*Nyssa sylvatica*. Family: *Nyssaceae*.) » deciduous plants; tree [i]

Tupolev, Andrei (Nikolaevich) [**too**puhlef] (1888–1972) Russian aircraft designer, born at Pustomezovo. From 1922, headed the design office of the central aerohydrodynamics institute in Moscow, producing over 100 types of aircraft, and in 1955 he built the first Soviet civil jet, the Tu-104. In 1968 he completed the first test flight of a supersonic passenger aircraft, the Tu-144. He died in Moscow. » aircraft [i]; jet engine [i]

Tupungato, Cerro [tupun**gah**toh] 33°22S 69°50W. Mountain on the border between Argentina and Chile, rising to 6 800 m/22 309 ft; c.80 km/50 ml SSE of Cerro Aconcagua. » Andes

tur » **goat**

turaco [**toor**akoh] A large African bird, inhabiting woodland and dry scrub; eats fruit and insects; tail long; head usually with crest; also known as the **touraco**, **tauraco**, (in S Africa) **lourie** or **loerie**, and (in W Africa) **plantain-eater**. The woodland species are brightly-coloured (some colours produced by pigments being found only in this family); the scrubland species (also called **go-away birds**) are duller. (Family: *Musophagidae*, 24 species.)

turbidity current A current composed of sediment particles suspended in water that may flow down slope underwater at a velocity measured in tens of knots. It is thought to be an important agent in transporting shallow marine sediments to the deep sea, carving out a submarine canyon in the process. As these turbidity currents lose speed on the low gradients of the continental rise and abyssal plains, they leave sedimentary deposits known as *turbidities*. » current (oceanography); submarine canyon

turbine A balanced wheel having at its rim a large number of small radiating blades of aerofoil cross section. When an axial flow of fluid is made to pass over the blades, the turbine rotates about its shaft. The shaft's rotation can then be used for useful external work. If the fluid is steam, the engine is called a **steam turbine**; if water, a **water turbine**. In a **turbo-jet** aircraft, the gas turbine engine is arranged so that the thrust is derived directly from the rearward expulsion of exhaust gases. In a **turbo-prop** aircraft, the exhaust gases drive a turbine fixed to a propeller; the use of the propeller increases the efficiency of propulsion at low speeds over that of a jet. » aerodynamics [i]; engine; gas turbine; jet engine [i]

turbo-jet; turbo-prop » **turbine**

turbot European flatfish widespread on gravel bottoms of inshore waters of the E North Atlantic; length up to 1 m/3¼ ft; light brown with darker spots and patches; feeds mainly on small fishes; excellent food fish taken commercially by trawl and line; also popular with sea anglers. (*Scophthalmus maximus*. Family: *Scophthalmidae*.) » flatfish

turbulence In fluid flow, a flow in which pressure and velocity change constantly and erratically. Common examples are wind and water swirling around obstructions. Flow along pipes becomes turbulent at sufficiently high flow rates. » chaos; fluid mechanics; Reynolds' number

Turenne, Henri de la Tour d'Auvergne, Vicomte de ('Viscount of') [**tü**ren] (1611–75) French Marshal, born at Sedan, son of the Protestant Duc de Bouillon, and grandson of William the Silent. He learned soldiering from his uncles, the Princes of Orange, and in the Thirty Years' War fought with distinction for the armies of the Protestant alliance. He captured Breisach (1638) and Turin (1640), and for the conquest of Roussillon from the Spaniards (1642) was made Marshal of France (1643). In the civil wars of the Frondes, he joined the *frondeurs* at first, but then switched sides; his campaigning (1652–3) saved the young King Louis XIV and Mazarin's government. In the Franco-Spanish war he conquered much of the Spanish Netherlands after defeating Condé at the Battle of the Dunes (1658). He won lasting fame for his campaigns in the United Provinces during the Dutch War (1672–5), but advancing along the Rhine he was killed at Sasbach. » Condé; Dutch Wars; Frondes; Louis XIV; Mazarin; Thirty Years' War

Turgenev, Ivan (Sergeyevich) [toor**gay**nef] (1818–83) Russian novelist, born in Orel province. Educated at St Petersburg and Berlin, he joined the Russian civil service in 1841, but in 1843 abandoned this to take up literature. His first studies of peasant life, *A Sportsman's Sketches* (1852), made his reputation, but earned governmental ill favour. He was banished for two years to his country estates, and then lived mainly in Germany and France. His greatest novel, *Fathers and Sons* (1862), was badly received in Russia, but a particular success in England. He also wrote poetry, plays, short stories, and tales of the supernatural. He died near Paris. » drama; novel; Russian literature

Turgot, Anne Robert Jacques [**toor**goh] (1727–81) French economist and statesman, born and died in Paris. Educated at the seminary of Saint-Sulpice, he renounced the Church for the law, and became a magistrate in the Parlement of Paris and was promoted to Intendant at Limoges (1761–74), where he carried out reforms. Here he published his best-known work, *Refléxions sur la formation et la distribution des richesses* (1766, Reflections on the Formation and Distribution of Wealth). Appointed Comptroller-General of finance by Louis XVI (1774), he embarked on a comprehensive scheme of national economic reform, but the opposition of the privileged classes to his Six Edicts led to his overthrow (1776), and he died forgotten, his reforms abandoned. » Louis XVI; Parlement

Turin [tyoo**rin**], Ital **Torino**, ancient **Augusta Taurinorum** 45°04N 7°40E, pop (1981) 1 117 154. Capital city of Turin province, Piedmont, NW Italy, on left bank of R Po; founded by the Taurini; Roman colony under Augustus; capital of Kingdom of Sardinia, 1720; centre of the 19th-c Risorgimento; first capital of the Kingdom of Italy until 1865; airport; railway; archbishopric; university (1404); iron, steel, cars, machinery, rolling stock, underwater defence systems, textiles, vermouths, confectionery, printing and publishing; Porta Palatina (Roman city gate), cathedral (15th-c), Palazzo Reale (1646–58), Palazzo Carignano (1680), Palazzo Madama (1718–20); carnival (Feb), International Motor Show and Industrial Vehicle Show in alternate years. » Italy [i]; Piedmont; Risorgimento

Turing, Alan (Mathison) (1912–54) British mathematician, born in London. Educated at Cambridge and Princeton, he worked in cryptography during World War 2, then joined the National Physical Laboratory (1945) and the computing laboratory at Manchester (1948). He provided a precise mathematical characterization of computability, and introduced the theoretical notion of an idealized computer (since called a **Turing machine**), laying the foundation for the field of artificial intelligence. He committed suicide at Wilmslow, Cheshire. » artificial intelligence

Turkana, Lake [toor**kah**na], formerly **Lake Rudolf** (to 1979) area 6 405 sq km/2 472 sq ml. Lake in NW Kenya and Ethiopia, E Africa, 400 km/250 ml N of Nairobi; N extremity extends into Ethiopia; length 290 km/180 ml; width 56 km/35 ml; depth c.70 m/230 ft; important area for fossil hominid finds; shrinking because of high evaporation, and becoming increasingly saline; European discovery in 1888, named after the crown prince of Austria. » Kenya [i]; Leakey

turkey A large pheasant-like bird, native to C and S North America; head naked; male with pendulous fold of skin at base of bill, and prominent spur on each leg; inhabits mixed woodland; omnivorous; plumage dark, mottled (domestic populations paler); domesticated in 16th-c. (Family: *Meleagrididae*, 2 species.) » pheasant

Turkey, Turkish **Türkiye**, official name **Republic of Turkey**, Turkish **Türkiye Cumhuriyeti** pop (1990e) 56 940 000; area 779 452 sq km/300 868 sq ml. Republic lying partly in Europe and partly in Asia, divided into 67 provinces; W area (Thrace) bounded by the Aegean Sea and Greece, N by Bulgaria and the Black Sea, E area (Anatolia) by Georgia, Armenia, and Iran, and S by Iraq, Syria, and the Mediterranean Sea; capital, Ankara; chief cities, Istanbul, Izmir, Adana, Bursa, Gaziantep; timezone GMT +3; chief ethnic groups, Turkish (85%) and Kurd (12%); official language, Turkish; chief religion, Islam; unit of currency, the Turkish lira.

Physical description and climate. Turkish Straits (Dardanelles, Sea of Marmara, Bosporus) connect the Black Sea (NE) and Mediterranean Sea (SW); mountainous, average height 1 100 m/3 700 ft; ranges extend W–E along the N and S coasts of Anatolia; average altitude of high C plateau, 1 000–2 000 m/3 300–6 600 ft; Taurus Mts cover the entire S part of Anatolia; highest region is E Anatolia, highest peak Mt Ararat (5 165 m/16 945 ft); width of alluvial coastal plains, 20–30 km/12–19 ml; chief rivers the Kizil Irmak, Sakarya, Seyhan; typically Mediterranean climate on Aegean and Mediterranean coasts, with hot, dry summers and warm, wet winters; temperatures at Istanbul, 5°C (Jan), 23°C (Jul), average annual rainfall, 723 mm/28 in; low rainfall on the interior plateau, with cold winters; summers warm or hot with occasional thunderstorms.

History and government. Seljuk sultanate replaced by the Ottoman in NW Asia Minor, 13th-c; Turkish invasion of Europe, first in the Balkans (1375); fall of Constantinople, 1453; empire at its peak under Sulaiman the Magnificent, 16th-c; Turks pressed back by Russians and Austrians, 17th-c; Turkey regarded by Britain as a bulwark against Russian expansion, 19th-c; following alleged Armenian massacres, Britain abandoned support of Turkey; Young Turks seized power, 1908; Balkan War, 1912–13; allied with Germany during World War 1; republic followed Young Turk revolution, led by Kemal Atatürk, 1923; policy of westernization and economic development; neutral throughout most of World War 2, then sided with Allies; military coups, 1960, 1980; strained relations with Greece, and invasion of Cyprus, 1974; constitution provides for a single-chamber, 450-member National Assembly; a president appointed by the Assembly holds office for seven years, appointing a prime minister and a Council of Ministers.

□ international airport

Economy. Agriculture employs over 60% of the workforce; cotton, tobacco, cereals, figs, silk, olive oil, dried fruits, nuts; mohair, wool, hides; chrome, coal, lignite, copper concentrate, sulphur, oil; food processing, textiles, iron and steel, cement, leather goods, glass, ceramics, tourism; many Turks find work in Europe, especially Germany. » Ankara; Atatürk; Cyprus [i]; Istanbul; Ottoman Empire; Seljuks; Sulaiman; Young Turks; RR27 national holidays; RR63 political leaders

Turkish » **Altaic**

Turkish cat A breed of long-haired domestic cat from the area around L Van, Turkey; thick white coat with reddish-brown markings on head and reddish-brown tail; enjoys swimming; also known as **Van cat** or **swimming cat**. » cat

Turkmenia [terk**men**ia], formerly **Turkmenistan** or **Turkmen SSR**, Russ **Turkmenskaya** pop (1989) 3 534 000; area 488 100 sq km/188 400 sq ml. Republic in SW Middle Asia; bounded S by Iran and Afghanistan, and W by the Caspian Sea; c.80% occupied by the Kara-Kum desert; people live mainly around oases; chief river, the Amudarya; proclaimed a Soviet Socialist Republic, 1924; moves towards independence, 1990–1; capital, Ashkhabad; chief towns, Chardzhou, Mary, Krasnovodsk, Nebit-Dag; oil refining, chemicals, food processing, rugs, machinery; cotton, silk; noted for Turkoman horses and Karakul sheep. » Kara-Kum; Soviet Union [i]

Turks and Caicos Islands [**kay**kuhs] pop (1980) 7 413; area 500 sq km/200 sq ml. Two island groups comprising c.30 islands and cays forming the SE archipelago of the Bahamas chain, W Atlantic Ocean; 920 km/570 ml SE of Miami; capital, Grand Turk; timezone GMT −5; population mainly of African descent; chief religion, Christianity; official language, English; unit of currency, the US dollar; Turks Is and Caicos Is separated by 35 km/22 ml; only six of the islands are inhabited; subtropical climate; average annual rainfall on Grand Turk, 525 mm/21 in; temperatures 24–27°C (winter), 29–32°C (summer); occasional hurricanes; visited by the Spanish, 1512; linked formally to the Bahamas, 1765; transferred to Jamaica, 1848; British Crown Colony, 1972; internal self-government, 1976; British sovereign represented by a governor, who presides over an 8-member Council; corn, beans, fishing, fish-processing; tourism is a rapidly expanding industry. » Caicos Islands

Turku, Swedish **Åbo** [**too**rkoo] 60°27N 22°15E, pop (1982) 163 484. Seaport and capital of Turku-Pori province, SW Finland; on R Aurajoki near its mouth on the Gulf of Bothnia; third largest city in Finland; established, 11th-c; capital of Finland until 1812; peace between Sweden and Russia signed here, 1743; airport; railway; ferries to Sweden and Åland Is; two universities (Swedish 1918, Finnish 1920); shipbuilding, engineering, foodstuffs, textiles; Rantasipi Congress Centre; music festival (Aug). » Finland [i]

turmeric [**ter**muhrik] A perennial native to India, related to ginger and East Indian arrowroot; rhizomatous; stem to c.1 m/3¼ ft; flowers with a yellow lip, borne in a dense spike with white and pink bracts. It is cultivated for the fleshy, aromatic rhizomes, ground to provide the distinctive smell and colour of curry powder. It also produces a yellow dye. (*Curcuma longa.* Family: *Zingiberaceae.*) » arrowroot; bract; ginger; perennial; rhizome

Turner, J(oseph) M(allord) W(illiam) (1775–1851) British landscape artist and watercolourist, born in London. After little formal education, he entered the Royal Academy at 14, and soon began to exhibit. He travelled widely in Britain, making architectural drawings in the cathedral cities, and spent three years in collaboration with Girtin producing watercolours. He then took to oils, his early works including 'Frosty Morning' (1813) and 'Crossing the Brook' (1815). After his first visit to Italy (1819), his work showed several literary influences, as in 'Ulysses deriding Polyphemus' (1829); his second visit (1829) marks the begining of his last great artistic period, including 'The Fighting Téméraire' (1839) and 'Rain, Steam and Speed' (1844); all in the National Gallery, London. He led a secretive private life, never married, and died in London. » English art; Girtin; Impressionism (art); landscape painting

Turner, Nat (1800–31) US slave insurrectionary, born in Southampton Co, Virginia. He learned to read, and in 1831 made plans for a slave uprising. Leading a force of eight, he succeeded in killing 51 Whites, but the revolt quickly collapsed. Captured after six weeks in hiding, he was hanged at Jerusalem, Virginia. » slave trade

turnip An annual or biennial vegetable, 1 m/3¼ ft high; bright green, deeply-lobed leaves; yellow, cross-shaped flowers. The cultivated turnip (subspecies *rapa*) has an edible tuberous taproot, and is widely grown as a vegetable and for fodder. The wild turnip (subspecies *moestris*) lacks a swollen taproot. (*Brassica rapa*. Family: *Cruciferae*.) » annual; biennial; brassica; root (botany); vegetable

turnover tax A tax levied at several stages in the progression from materials to finished goods, or when certain services are provided. For example, a miller pays turnover tax on wheat from the farmer; the baker pays it on the flour; and the customer pays it on the bread. Unlike value-added tax, there is no credit for tax paid at earlier stages. » VAT

turnpike A gate across a road to stop the passage of vehicles or persons until a toll is paid. The roads were known as *turnpike roads*, and were common during the 18th–19th-c. The tolls collected were used both for the upkeep of the road and as profit for the shareholders.

turnstone Either of two species of sandpiper, genus *Arenaria*: the **ruddy turnstone** (*Arenaria interpres*), found world-wide on coasts; also the **black turnstone** (*Arenaria melanocephala*), found on the W coast of N America; turns stones and seaweed with short bill, seeking invertebrates; also eats carrion. » sandpiper

turpentine tree A deciduous shrub or small tree, growing to 10 m/30 ft, native to the Mediterranean region and SW Asia; leaves leathery, pinnate with 3–9 leaflets; flowers tiny, in axillary plumes; fruits coral-red; also called **terebinth**. It produces a resin which yields turpentine. (*Pistacia terebinthus*. Family: *Anacardiaceae*.) » deciduous plants; pinnate; shrub; sumac; tree [i]

Turpin, Dick, byname of **Richard Turpin** (1705–39) English robber, born at Hempstead, Essex. He was a butcher's apprentice, smuggler, housebreaker, highwayman, and horse thief. He entered into partnership with Tom King, and was hanged at York for the murder of an Epping keeper. His ride to York belongs (if to any one) to 'Swift John Nevison', who in 1676 is said to have robbed a sailor at Gadshill at 4 am, and to have established an 'alibi' by reaching York at 7.45 pm.

turquoise A hydrated aluminium phosphate mineral formed by the surface alteration of aluminium-rich rock, with bright-blue to green-blue masses or veins, opaque with a waxy lustre. It is valued as a semi-precious stone. » aluminium; gemstones

turtle (biology) A reptile of order *Chelonia*; in the USA, includes all species; in the UK, only the marine species with the legs modified as paddles (**sea turtles**, 7 species in families *Chelonidae* and *Dermochelyidae*); sea turtles spend almost their entire life at sea, coming ashore only to bask or lay eggs in the sand of beaches. » green/hawksbill/leatherback/snake-necked/snapping/soft-shelled turtle; Chelonia [i]; matamata [i]; reptile; terrapin

turtle (computing) An electromechanical computer drawing device; precise movements of the turtle are transmitted to the computer. The device, which is used in LOGO and some other languages, predates but is rather similar to the mouse. » mouse (computing)

turtle dove A dove native to Europe, W Asia, and N Africa; eye with dark ring; breast pink, wing feathers with reddish edges; patch of black and white lines on neck; inhabits woodland and heaths. (*Streptopelia turtur*.) » dove

Tuscan order The simplest of the five main orders of classical architecture, probably derived from Etruscan-type temples. It closely resembles the Doric order, but with a plain base, shaft, and entablature. » column; Doric order; entablature; Greek architecture; orders of architecture [i]; Roman architecture

Tuscany, Ital **Toscana** pop (1981) 3 581 051; area 22 989 sq km/ 8 874 sq ml. Region of Italy; capital, Florence; chief towns, Pisa, Siena, Lucca, Leghorn; mountainous with fertile valleys and marshy coastal plain; industry mainly in the Arno valley; iron, lignite, mercury, marble; engineering, shipbuilding, pharmaceuticals, glass, crystal, textiles, craftwork; important agricultural area; market gardening, flowers; home of Chianti wine; tourism focused on traditional centres of art, notably Florence, Siena, Pisa. » Florence; Italy [i]

Tusculum [**tuhs**kyooluhm] Originally an independent Latin town in the mountains SE of Rome, by the late Republic it had become a fashionable country retreat for wealthy Romans. Both Cicero and Lucullus had villas there. » Cicero; Latium; Lucullus

tusk shell A marine, bottom-living mollusc found partly embedded in sediment from shallow water to abyssal depths; body bilaterally symmetrical, within a curved, tubular shell open at both ends; foot protrusible, often used for burrowing; head poorly developed, but with a tube (proboscis) for catching protozoan prey. (Class: *Scaphopoda*.) » mollusc

Tussaud, Marie [tü**soh**], Eng [tuh**sawd**], *née* **Grosholtz** (1761–1850) French modeller in wax, born at Strasbourg. She was apprenticed to her uncle, Dr Curtius, in Paris and inherited his wax museums after his death. After the revolution, she attended the guillotine to take death masks from the severed heads. She toured Britain with her life-size portrait waxworks, and in 1835 set up a permanent exhibition in Baker St, London. It was burnt down in 1925, and re-opened in Marylebone Rd in 1928. The exhibition still contains her own handiwork, notably of Marie Antoinette, Napoleon, and Burke and Hare in the Chamber of Horrors. She died in London. » wax

tussock moth A medium-sized moth in which the proboscis is usually absent; wings often white with darker markings; caterpillars often brightly coloured and hairy; hairs commonly woven into walls of pupal cocoon. (Order: *Lepidoptera*. Family: *Lymantriidae*.) » caterpillar; gypsy moth; moth; pupa

Tutankhamen (14th-c BC) Egyptian pharaoh of the 18th dynasty (1361–1352), the undistinguished son-in-law of the heretic pharaoh, Akhenaton. He came to the throne at the age of 12, and is famous only for his magnificent tomb at Thebes, which was discovered intact in 1922 by Lord Carnarvon and Howard Carter. » Akhenaton

Tuthmosis III » **Thutmose III**

Tutsi » **Hutu and Tutsi**

Tutuola, Amos [tutu**oh**la] (1920–) Nigerian novelist, born at Abeokuta. He is celebrated in the West as the author of *The Palm-Wine Drinkard* (1952), a transcription in pidgin English prose of an oral tale of his own invention. Later novels in the same manner include *My Life in the Bush of Ghosts* (1954) and *The Brave African Huntress* (1958). » African literature; pidgin; Yoruba

Tuvalu, formerly **Ellice Is** (to 1976) [toova**loo**] 5–11°S 176–180°E; pop (1990e) 9 100; area 26 sq km/10 sq ml. Island group in the SW Pacific, 1 050 km/650 ml N of Fiji; capital, Funafuti; timezone GMT +12; chief ethnic group, Polynesian; chief languages, Tuvaluan, English; chief religion, Christianity; unit of currency, the Australian dollar; comprises nine low-lying coral atolls, running NW–SE in a chain 580 km/360 ml long; hot and humid climate; average annual temperature, 30°C; average annual rainfall, 3 535 mm/139 in; invaded by Samoans, 16th-c; British protectorate, as the Ellice Is, 1892; administered as a colony jointly with the Gilbert Is (now Kiribati), 1915; separate constitution, following 1974 referendum; independence, 1978; British monarch represented by a governor-general; governed by a prime minister, cabinet, and unicameral 12-member parliament; copra, tropical fruit, fishing, crafts, postage stamps. » Funafuti; Kiribati; RR63 political leaders

Twain, Mark, pseudonym of **Samuel Langhorne Clemens** (1835–1910) US writer, born at Florida, Missouri. A printer first, and then a Mississippi pilot, he adopted his pen name from a well-known call of the man sounding the river in shallow places ('mark twain' meaning 'by the mark two fathoms'). In 1867 he visited France, Italy, and Palestine, gathering material for his *Innocents Abroad* (1869), which established his reputation as a humorist. His two masterpieces, *Tom Sawyer* (1876) and *Huckleberry Finn* (1884), drawn from his own boyhood experiences, are firmly established among the world's classics; other favourites are *A Tramp Abroad* (1880) and *A Connecticut Yankee in King Arthur's Court* (1889). Widely known as a lecturer, he developed a great popular following. In his later years, financial speculations led to his bankruptcy. He died at Redding, Connecticut. » American literature; novel

twayblade An orchid native to cool and arctic regions of Europe and Asia; stem with one pair of broad, oval leaves; flowers green with a yellowish 2-lobed lip. Any insect visiting the flower triggers an explosion of sticky liquid which sets in 2–3 seconds, glueing the pollinia to the insect's head. (*Listera ovata.* Family: *Orchidaceae.*) » orchid [i]; pollination

tweed A coarse, heavy, wool, outerwear fabric, first made in S Scotland, manufactured in several distinctive weave patterns. Often mistakenly associated with the R Tweed, the name originates from 'tweel', a Scottish word for twill fabrics. Its manufacture in the I of Harris was developed c.1850 by Lady Dunmore, who encouraged its use amongst the British aristocracy. Traditional tweeds have a 'country' look, but modern designs are often multi-coloured and lighter weight, and more suitable for ladies' wear. » twill

Tweed, River River in SE Scotland and NE England, rises in SW Borders region at Tweed's Well; flows generally E, forming part of the border between England and Scotland; enters the North Sea at Berwick-upon-Tweed; length, 155 km/96 ml.

Twelfth Day In the Christian church, Epiphany (6 Jan), the twelfth day after Christmas. **Twelfth Night** is the evening of 5 January, traditionally a time of festivity.

Twelve, the » **apostle**

Twelve Tables Drawn up by a commission of ten men in 451–450 BC, the first attempt by the Romans to codify their laws. Produced under pressure from the plebeians, their publication (on twelve tablets) was intended to curb the power of the patricians. Although the original tablets themselves do not survive, quotations from them in ancient authors indicate that they contained rulings from all branches of the law as it existed at that time. » plebeians; patricians; Roman Law

twelve-tone music Music based on the 12 notes of the chromatic scale arranged in a predetermined order. » serialism; tone **3**

Twenty-one Demands A series of demands presented by Japan to China in 1915, which included recognition of Japanese control of Manchuria, Shandong, Inner Mongolia, SE China and the Yangzi Valley; imposition of Japanese advisers in the Chinese administration; and compulsory purchase of 50% of its munitions from Japan. President Yuan Shikai accepted them as the basis of a treaty, but the resulting popular patriotic protest movement gave impetus to the rise of Chinese nationalism. » Yuan Shikai

twilight The interval of time shortly after sunset or just before sunrise. **Civil twilight** begins or ends when the Sun is 6° below the local horizon; **nautical twilight** 12° below the horizon, and **astronomical twilight** 18° below the horizon.

twilight sleep Originally, the use of morphine and hyoscine to induce tranquility and reduce the pain during uterine contractions in labour. This drug regime is now rarely employed. » labour; morphine

twill A type of woven fabric characterized by a pattern of diagonal lines. Many variations are possible, such as *herringbone* twills, where the pattern zigzags across the cloth. Twill weaves produce strong, hard-wearing fabrics, often employed in sports and work-wear situations. » denim; tartan

twin paradox » **clock paradox**

twinning The linking of two towns or cities in different countries, so that they may have a 'special relationship' and foster cultural exchanges. For example, Edinburgh, Scotland is twinned with Munich, Germany (1954); Nice, France (1958); Florence, Italy (1964); Dunedin, New Zealand (1974); San Diego, USA (1977); Vancouver, Canada (1977); and Xian, China (1985).

twins A pair of offspring produced at the same birth. **Fraternal** (or *dizygotic*) twins are derived from two separate fertilized eggs. **Identical** (or *monozygotic*) twins are derived from a single fertilized egg, and are thus genetically identical. » pregnancy [i]; zygote

twist The winding together of fibres, which gives added strength to yarns. The twist level affects other factors than strength, including stretch and softness. » yarn

twitch grass » **couch grass**

two-stroke engine A practical engine cycle with one in two strokes of the piston being the power stroke. This type of engine is frequently used to drive light motorcycles. » Carnot cycle; engine; motorcycle

Two Thousand Guineas » **Classics**

Tyan Shan » **Tien Shan**

Tyche [**tiy**kee, **too**kay] The Greek goddess of chance or luck, prominent in the Hellenistic period. She is depicted as blind, or, with a wall, as the luck of a city. » Fortuna; Hellenistic Age

Tyler, John (1790–1862) US statesman and 10th President (1841–5), born in Charles City Co, Virginia. He became a lawyer, member of the state legislature (1811–16), Governor of Virginia (1825–7), and a Senator (1827–36). Elected Vice-President in 1840, he became President on the death of Harrison in 1841, only a month after his inauguration. His administration was marked by the annexation of Texas. He later remained active in politics, adhering to the Confederate cause until his death, at Richmond, Virginia. » Confederate States of America; Harrison, William Henry

Tyler, Wat (?–1381) English leader of the Peasants' Revolt (1381). The rebels of Kent, after taking Rochester Castle, chose him as captain, and marched to Canterbury and London. At the Smithfield conference with Richard II blows were exchanged, and Tyler was wounded by the Mayor of London, William Walworth. He was taken to St Bartholomew's Hospital, where Walworth had him dragged out and beheaded. » Peasants' Revolt; Richard II

Tynan, Kenneth (1927–80) British theatre critic, born in Birmingham. He read English at Oxford, where he became deeply involved in the theatre. As drama critic for several publications, notably *The Observer* (1954–63), he was one of the first to champion John Osborne and the other new playwrights of the time. He became literary manager of the National Theatre (1963–9), an editor in films and television, and achieved further fame with his controversial revue *Oh, Calcutta!* (1969). » theatre

Tyndale or **Tindale, William** (?–1536) English translator of the Bible, born (probably) at Slymbridge in Gloucestershire. Educated at Oxford, he became a chaplain and tutor, sympathetic to humanist learning. In 1524 he went to Hamburg and Wittenberg, and in 1525 to Cologne, where he completed his translation of the English New Testament. In 1531 he went to Antwerp, where he continued to work on an Old Testament translation, but before it was finished he was seized, accused of heresy, imprisoned, and executed at Vilvorde, Belgium. » Bible; humanism

Tyne, River [tiyn] River of NE England; formed by confluence of North Tyne and South Tyne, NW of Hexham, Northumberland; flows 48 km/30 ml E across Kielder Moor and through Tyne and Wear to meet the North Sea between Tynemouth and South Shields; South Tyne rises on Cross Fell, E Cumbria; North Tyne rises in the Cheviot Hills, and is dammed to form Kielder Water reservoir; linked to R Tees as part of regional water grid system; navigable 13 km/8 ml above Newcastle; serves the industrial towns of Newcastle, Jarrow, Gateshead, Wallsend, and South Shields. » Kielder Water; Tees, River

Tyne and Wear [weer] pop (1987e) 1 135 800; area 540 sq km/208 sq ml. Former county of NE England, created in 1974, divided into five boroughs; bounded E by the North Sea; drained by the Tyne and Wear Rivers; administrative centre, Newcastle upon Tyne; chief towns include Gateshead, Jarrow, Wallsend, Sunderland; a highly industrialized area, especially since the Industrial Revolution; suffered serious decline following the Great Depression, especially in shipbuilding; now designated a special development area, with considerable diversification of industries; shipbuilding, engineering, coal mining, chemicals; metropolitan council abolished in 1986. » Great Depression; England [i]; Industrial Revolution; Newcastle (UK); Tyne, River

Tyneside pop (1981) 782 410. Urban area in Tyne and Wear, NE England; includes Newcastle upon Tyne, Gateshead, Jarrow, Felling, Hebburn, Newburn, Longbenton–Killingworth, Wallsend, and North and South Shields; airport (Woolsington); railway. » Tyne and Wear

Type A/Type B personality A personality dimension identified by US cardiologists Meyer Friedman (1910–) and Ray Rosenman (1920–). Type A individuals are competitive, aggressive, and hostile towards others, over-committed to work, fast-thinking, and fast-talking. They hate waiting, feel a sense of time urgency, and often do more than one task at once. Type B individuals' characteristics are opposite to those of type A. The type A personality has been associated with coronary heart disease. » personality

typhoid fever An infectious disease caused by *Salmonella typhi*, also known as **enteric fever**. The disease spreads by way of infected water, milk, or food, or by carriers of the disease employed in food preparation. Diagnosis is by blood culture. It was formerly a serious infection, with a swinging temperature, drowsiness, diarrhoea, and abdominal rash, progressing to delirium and coma within a few weeks. The condition is now readily treated with antibiotics. Immunization is desirable for those who travel to parts of the world where the infection is endemic. » immunization; paratyphoid fever; salmonella

typhoon » **hurricane**

typhus fever Any of several illnesses caused by infection with a strain of *Rickettsia*; also known as **spotted fever**. Louse-borne typhus is caused by *Rickettsia prowazeki* and is common in overcrowded conditions. Flea-borne typhus is caused by *Rickettsia mooneri*; it is milder than the louse-borne disease, which is a severe illness with headache, prostration, and a measles-like rash. Tick-borne typhus fever (*Rocky mountain spotted fever*) is caused by *Rickettsia rickettsii*, and occurs in the USA and S America; it is similar in its clinical course to the louse-borne disorder. Several other species cause similar infections in South Africa, Australia, and India. A specific serological test, the Weil-Felix reaction, is the basis of diagnosis. The infections respond to the appropriate antibiotic. » flea; louse; tick; rickettsia

typical owl » **owl**

typography The design of letterforms for use as typefaces, and of typeset documents. Typefaces are designed for a multitude of purposes (eg books, newspapers, stationery, handbills) and for use on various kinds of typesetting equipment, in both print and non-print media (such as film and television). Typographers, selecting the typeface most suited to the job in hand, will not be over-concerned with origin and original purpose, as long as the face meets their immediate needs. Thus Times New Roman, cut in 1932 for the redesigned *Times*, was swiftly picked up for use in a bible, then equipped by its makers with a wide range of mathematical characters for the setting of academic journals, and is now the most popular typeface for bookwork. The choice of typeface is important because the right face can convey the appropriate style or mood, or refer in its design to the appropriate historical period; also because some faces are economical of space where others are profligate with it when correctly used; and because particular jobs may require special mathematical, linguistic, or scientific characters only available in certain faces. However, many typefaces are in copyright, and cannot be copied for use on equipment other than that of their owners, so the designer is limited both by the range of typefaces available on each piece of typesetting equipment and also by the typefaces offered by each firm of typesetters. » copyright; graphic design

Tyr [teer] The Norse god of battle, who guards the other gods. He was the only one brave enough to place his hand in the mouth of the Fenris wolf as a pledge. When the wolf realized that it was caught, it bit off the hand.

tyramine A chemical compound derived from the amino acid tyrosine, which occurs in foods such as cheese and wine, sometimes in large quantities. Normally tyramine is degraded by the enzyme monoamine oxidase (MAO). If MAO is reduced, as occurs with certain antidepressants, tyramine accumulates, leading to an elevation in blood pressure. Migraine headaches may be associated with excess amine production aggravated by a high intake of tyramine. » antidepressants; migraine

Tyrannosaurus rex [tiranuh**saw**ruhs reks] The largest terrestrial, flesh-eating animal of all time; known from the Cretaceous period; a dinosaur reaching 12 m/40 ft in length; skull massive with short, deep jaws bearing dagger-like teeth; tail heavy and muscular; forelimbs tiny, each with only two fingers; slow-moving, with a top speed of about 4 kph/2.5 mph; probably a scavenger rather than an active hunter. (Order: *Saurischia*.) » Cretaceous period; dinosaur [i]; Saurischia

tyrant In Greek city-states of the 7th-c and 6th-c BC, a neutral term, possibly of Lydian origin, simply describing an absolute ruler who had seized power illegally. Only later (5th-c BC) did it acquire its present meaning – a cruel and oppressive ruler. » Greek history; Lydia

Tyre, Arabic **Sour** [tiyr] 33°12N 35°11E, pop (1980e) 14 000. Mediterranean fishing port, SW Lebanon; railway; ancient city was the most important commercial centre in the E Mediterranean, noted for silk, glass, and Tyrean purple dye; excavations since 1947 have uncovered remains of Crusader, Arab, Byzantine, and Graeco-Roman cities; several Roman remains, including one of the largest hippodromes of the Roman period; a world heritage site. » Lebanon [i]

tyre/tire A circular cushion fixed to the rim of a wheel, which absorbs variations in the road surface, so providing an easier ride to the vehicle. Most tyres are *pneumatic*, being flexible tubes stiffened by high-pressure air. Depending upon the type of tyre, this pneumatic stiffening may or may not be provided by a thin inner tube. The tyre is composed of the *tread*, which comes into contact with the road surface, and the *body* or *carcase*. Most tyres are made of a combination of rubber compounded with other chemicals and fabric, usually nylon or polyester. The inventor of the pneumatic tyre was Robert William Thomson, who patented a design for application to coaches in 1845. In spite of this, solid rubber tyres were used extensively until 1888, when John Boyd Dunlop successfully applied the pneumatic tyre to the bicycle, and tyres assumed a recognizably modern form. » aquaplaning; bicycle; Dunlop; Michelin

Tyrol » **Tirol**

Tyrone [tiy**rohn**], Gaelic **Tir Eoghain** pop (1981) 143 884; area 3 136 sq km/1 210 sq ml. County in W Northern Ireland, consisting of four districts; bounded E by Lough Neagh, and NW and S by the Republic of Ireland along the R Foyle; hilly, with the Sperrin Mts rising (N) to 683 m/2 241 ft at Mt Sawel; county town, Omagh; other chief towns, Dungannon, Cookstown, Strabane; oats, potatoes, flax, turnips, sheep, cattle. » Northern Ireland [i]; Omagh

Tyrrhenian Sea [tiy**ree**nian] Arm of the Mediterranean Sea; bounded by the Italian Peninsula, Sicily, Sardinia, and Corsica; major ports, Naples and Palermo. » Mediterranean Sea

Tyson, Mike, properly **Michael (Gerald)** (1966–) US boxer, born in New York City. The National Golden Gloves heavyweight champion in 1984, he turned professional the following year. A lethal puncher, 15 of his first 25 opponents were knocked out in the first round. He beat Trevor Berbick (1952–) for the World Boxing Council version of the world heavyweight title in 1986 to become the youngest heavyweight champion (20 yr 145 days), and added the World Boxing Association title in 1987, when he beat James Smith (1954–). Later that year he became the first undisputed champion since 1978, when he beat Tony Tucker (1958–). » boxing [i]

Tyumen [tyoo**mayn**] 57°11N 65°29E, pop (1983) 397 000. Capital city of Tyumenskaya oblast, SW Siberian Russia, on R Nitsa; founded, 1585; first settled Russian town E of the Ural Mts; formerly an important centre of trade with China; railway junction; university; cotton textiles, clothing, machine tools and instruments, oil refining. » Russia

Tz'u Hsi » **Ci Xi**

Tzu-po » **Zibo**

U

U and non-U Terms coined by English linguist Alan Ross (1907–) in an effort to capture the essentials of class-based variation in English usage. Though a gross distinction, both socially and linguistically, it does highlight an important intersection of social class and language use in British English. Markers of **upper-class** (U) and **non-upper-class** (non-U) usage can be features of pronunciation and grammar, styles of greeting in correspondence, and (most prolifically) vocabulary, such as U *luncheon* and *pudding* for non-U *dinner* and *sweet*. The contentiousness of the notion becomes apparent on considering the intermediate gradations in usage which go unremarked – the third term *lunch* for most people of professional status, and the use of *pudding* by non-U speakers from many dialectal backgrounds. » class

U-boat An abbreviation of *Unterseeboat* (Ger 'submarine'). The German Navy launched large-scale submarine offensives in both World Wars, and each time the U-boats came close to victory. » submarine

U-matic The trade name for the first helical-scan videotape cassette recorder introduced by Sony in 1970, initially for the professional non-broadcast market. It uses ¾ inch tape (19 mm) at a speed of 9.53 cm/sec in a large cassette 221 × 140 × 32 mm with a playing time of up to one hour. It is widely used for all forms of industrial video production, and its extended high-band form, known as BVU or U-format SP, can provide the quality required for broadcast television standards. » videotape recorder

Ubangi, River, Fr **Oubangui** [oo**bang**gee] Major tributary of R Zaire (Congo), in N and WC Africa; follows frontier between Central African Republic and Zaire to join R Zaire 97 km/60 ml SW of Mbandaka; length 1 060 km/660 ml; including longest headstream (R Uele), 2 250 km/1 400 ml. » Zaire, River

Ucayali, River [ookiya**lee**] River in E Peru; one of the Amazon's main headstreams, formed by the union of the Apurímac and Urubamba Rivers; flows c.1 600 km/1 000 ml N, joining the R Marañón to form the Amazon 88 km/55 ml SSW of Iquitos; navigable by small craft. » Amazon, River; Peru [i]

Uccello, Paolo [oo**chel**loh], originally **Paolo di Dono** (1397–1475) Florentine painter, born at Pratovecchio. He trained under Ghiberti, worked in Venice as a mosaicist (1425–31), then settled in Florence, where he applied the principles of perspective to his paintings. In 'The Flood' (1447–8, Florence), his use of perspective and foreshortening gives a sternly realistic effect. He died in Florence. » Florentine School; Italian art; mosaic

'ud An Arabian lute, known since the 7th-c, with usually five courses of strings, played with a plectrum or with the fingers of both hands. It is the ancestor of the European lute. » lute; plectrum; string instrument **2** [i]

udad » **aoudad**

Udall, Nicholas (1504–56) English dramatist, born in Southampton. Educated at Winchester and Oxford, he became (c.1534) headmaster of Eton. His dismissal in 1541 for indecent offences did not affect his standing at the court, and he was appointed prebendary of Windsor. He made many classical translations, but is chiefly remembered as the author of the first major comedy in English, *Ralph Roister Doister* (c.1563, published 1567). He died in London. » comedy; drama; English literature

Udine [**oo**deenay] 46°04N 13°14E, pop (1981) 102 021. Industrial town and capital of Udine province, Friuli-Venezia Giulia, NE Italy, 61 km/38 ml NW of Trieste; suffered severe bombing in World War 2; archbishopric; railway; textiles, leather, chemicals; castle (16th-c), cathedral, town hall (15th-c). » Italy [i]

UEFA (Union of European Football Associations) A football organization founded in 1954 by the representatives of the association football governing bodies of 30 European nations, and now consisting of 34 members. UEFA is responsible for organizing the three major European club tournaments: the Champions' Cup, the Cup Winners' Cup, and the UEFA Cup. They also run their own European Championship, a World Cup style of competition for national teams. » football [i]

Ufa [oo**fa**] 54°45N 55°58E, pop (1989) 1 083 000. Capital city of Baskirskaya, E European Russia; in the Ural Mts, on the R Ufa, at its confluence with the Dema and Zilim Rivers; founded as a fortress, 1586; airport; railway; university (1957); clothing, cotton textiles, oil refining, chemicals. » Russia

Uffizi [oo**feet**see] A museum in Florence, Italy, housing one of the world's greatest collections of works by Italian masters. The Renaissance palace, designed by Vasari in 1560, was opened to the public by the Medici family in the 17th-c. » Medici; museum; Vasari

Uganda, official name **Republic of Uganda** [yoo**gan**da] pop (1990e) 16 928 000; area 238 461 sq km/92 046 sq ml. E African republic, divided into 10 provinces; bounded S by Rwanda, L Victoria, and Tanzania, E by Kenya, N by Sudan, and W by Zaire; capital, Kampala; chief towns, Jinja, Mbale, Tororo, Soroti; timezone GMT +3; chief ethnic group, Ganda; chief religion, Christianity (66%); official language, English, with Luganda and Swahili widely used; unit of currency, the Uganda shilling; landlocked country, mainly plateau, height 900–1 000 m/3 000–3 250 ft; dry savannah or semi-desert in the N; population concentrated in the fertile L Victoria basin; W Rift Valley runs along Uganda's frontier with Zaire; Mt Stanley massif straddles the frontier, including Margherita Peak (5 110 m/16 765 ft), highest point in Uganda and Zaire; main lakes include Victoria (SE), George (SW), Edward (SW), Albert (W), Kwania (C), Kyoga (C), and Bisina (formerly L Salisbury, E); the two main rivers are upper reaches of the R Nile, the Victoria Nile and the Albert Nile; highest rainfall along the shores of L Victoria and in the mountains to the W and SW, exceeds 1 500 mm/60 in; daily temperatures at Entebbe, 24–28°C; C and NE areas receive under 1 000 mm/40 in annually; visited by Arab traders in the 1830s; explored by Speke in the 1860s and Stanley in the 1870s; granted to the British East Africa Company, 1888; Kingdom of Buganda became a British protectorate, 1893; other territory included by 1903; independence, 1962; Dr Milton Obote assumed all powers, 1966; coup led by General Idi Amin Dada, 1971; reacting to Amin's repressive regime, Tanzanian troops and Ugandan exiles marched on Kampala, overthrowing the government, 1979; further coup in 1985; parliament normally consists of 126 members; governed by a National Resistance Council which is part-elected and part-appointed by the president; a cabinet appointed by the Council is led by a prime minister; agriculture is the main economic activity; coffee, cotton, tea, tobacco, sugar, maize, millet, yams, sorghum, groundnuts, livestock, fishing; textiles, fertilizers, food processing, plywood, brewing; tungsten, copper, tin, beryl, phosphate, limestone. » Albert Nile; Amin; Kampala; Nile, River; Speke; Stanley; Victoria Nile; RR27 national holidays; RR63 political leaders

Uganda Martyrs A group of 22 African youths, converted to Roman Catholicism, killed for their faith in Uganda between 1885 and 1887. Canonized in 1964, they were among many

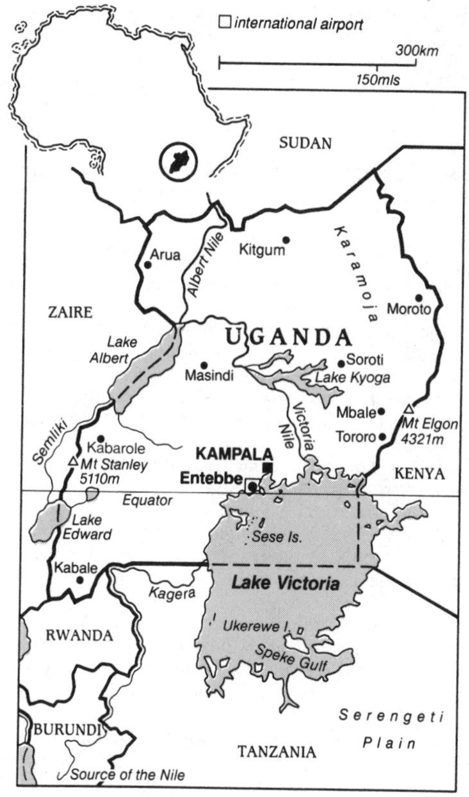

Christians put to death in that period of persecution. » canonization; Roman Catholicism

Ugarit A flourishing Canaanite city on the coast of N Syria opposite Cyprus, which in the late Bronze Age (c.1450–1200 BC) enjoyed wide contacts with the Egyptians, the Hittites, and the Mycenaeans. It was destroyed by the Sea Peoples c.1200 BC. » Canaan; Sea Peoples

Uhland, (Johann) Ludwig [oolant] (1787–1862) German lyric poet, born, educated, and died at Tübingen. He studied law, and was active in politics, becoming a liberal deputy for Tübingen at the assemblies of Württemberg (1819) and Frankfurt (1848). His 1815 collection of poems contained many popular ballads reflecting his interest in folklore and mediaeval studies. » ballad; German literature; poetry

UHT-milk An acronym of **ultra-high-temperature** milk; milk heated to a temperature of 132°C for one second, and subsequently packed in an air-tight container. It will then have a shelf life of 6 months at room temperature. » milk; pasteurization

Uighurs [weegoorz] One of China's national minorities, now numbering over 6 million and for the most part settled in Xinjiang. They are a people of Turkik origin who emerged as an independent force as early as the 7th-c. They developed their own script, and practised a religion which was a form of Manicheism. » Manicheism

Ujung Pandang, formerly **Makassar** or **Macassar** (to 1973) [oojoong pandang] 5°09S 119°28E, pop (1980) 434 766. Seaport capital of Sulawesi Selatan province, Indonesia; in SW corner of Sulawesi I; important trade centre of E Indonesia, established by the Dutch in 1607; free port, 1848; airfield; university (1956); coffee, rubber, copra, resin, spices. » Sulawesi

ukiyo-e (Jap 'pictures of the floating world') In Japanese painting and printmaking, a movement that flourished in the 16th–19th-c. Favourite themes included theatrical subjects, actors, prostitutes, and landscapes. The coloured woodcuts of Hokusai and Hiroshige influenced 19th-c French artists. » Hiroshige; Hokusai; Japanese art

Ukraine, Russ **Ukrainskaya** pop (1983) 50 461 000; area 603 700 sq km/233 028 sq ml. Republic in SE Europe, bounded W by Poland, Czechoslovakia, Hungary, and Romania, and S by the Black Sea; generally a plain with high elevations in the W, S and SE; Ukrainian Carpathians (W) rise to 2 061 m/6 762 ft at Mt Goveria; chief rivers, the Dnieper, Dnestr, Severskiy Donets, Prut; many reservoirs and lakes; gradually became part of Russia, 17th–18th-c; declared independence, 1918; became a Soviet Socialist Republic, 1922; declaration of independence, 1991; capital, Kiev; chief towns, Kharkov, Donetsk, Odessa, Dnepropetrovsk, Lvov, Zaporozhye, Krivoy Rog; contains the Donets coalfield (area 25 900 sq km/10 000 sq ml); iron ore, metallurgy, machinery, fertilizers, fibres, synthetic resins, plastics, dyes, rubber products, food processing, natural gas, oil refining; major Soviet grain exporting republic; wheat, sugar beet, sunflower, cotton, flax, tobacco, soya, hops, fruit, vegetables. » Cossacks; Kiev; Soviet Union [i]

ukulele [yookuh**lay**lee] A Hawaiian musical instrument, resembling a small guitar, with four gut or nylon strings that are strummed with the fingernails and fingertips. Since the 1920s it has been a favourite instrument in the USA for popular music, especially as an accompaniment to a solo singer. » guitar; string instrument 2 [i]; tablature

Ulaanbaatar [oolahn **bah**taw], formerly **Ulan Bator**, **Urga** (to 1924) 47°54N 106°52E, pop (1988) 500 000. Capital of Mongolia, in Selenge county, C Mongolia, surrounded by the Khenti Mts; founded as Urga in 1639, centre of Lamaistic religion in Mongolia; trading centre on caravan routes between Russia and China, 18th-c; capital, 1921; university (1942); meat processing, carpets, brewing, wood processing, veterinary medicine, mining, foodstuffs. » Mongolia

Ulan-Ude [oo**lan** oo**de**], formerly **Verkhneudinsk** (to 1934) 51°45N 107°40E, pop (1983) 321 000. Capital city of Buryatskaya, SE Siberian Russia; on R Selenga, 75 km/47 ml E of L Baikal; founded, 1666; airfield; railway junction; meat processing, machinery, metalwork, boat-building, woodwork; Odigitrievskii Cathedral (1741–85). » Russia

Ulanova, Galina (Sergeyevna) [oo**lah**nuhva] (1910–) Russian ballerina, born in St Petersburg. She studied at the Maryinski Theatre School, and made her debut at the Kirov Theatre in St Petersburg in 1928. She became the leading ballerina of the Soviet Union and was four times a Stalin prizewinner. She has appeared in several films made by the Moscow State Ballet Company and in 1957 was awarded the Lenin prize. She gave her final performance in 1962, and became ballet mistress at the Kirov. » ballet

Ulbricht, Walter [**ul**brikht] (1893–1973) East German communist statesman, born in Leipzig. At first a cabinetmaker, he entered politics in 1912, and in 1928 became communist deputy for Potsdam. He left Germany on Hitler's rise in 1933, spending most of his exile in the Soviet Union. In 1945 he returned as head of the German Communist Party, and became Deputy Premier of the German Democratic Republic and General Secretary of the Party in 1950. He was largely responsible for the 'sovietization' of East Germany, and built the Berlin wall in 1961. He retired in 1971, and died in East Berlin. » communism; Germany [i]

ulcer A break in the surface of the skin or mucous membrane, which may be acute in onset and short-lived or persistent. In the skin, infection is a common cause or complication, and inadequate blood supply is often a contributory factor. Ulcers may also occur in the mouth, oesophagus, and gastro-intestinal tract, in which trauma or other factors are responsible. » duodenal/gastric/peptic ulcer

Uleaborg » **Oulu**

Ulfilas or **Wulfila** [**ul**feelas] (c.311–83) Gothic translator of the Bible. Consecrated a missionary bishop to his fellow countrymen by Eusebius of Nicomedia in 341, after seven years' labour he was forced to migrate with his converts across the Danube. He devised the Gothic alphabet, and carried out the first translation of the Bible into a Germanic language. He died in Constantinople. » Bible; Gothic

Ullapool 57°54N 5°10W, pop (1981) 1 146. Port town in Ross and Cromarty district, Highland region, NW Scotland; on E shore of Loch Broom; ferry service to Stornoway, I of Lewis;

tourist resort; fishing, fish processing; Ullapool museum. » Highland; Scotland [i]

Ullswater Lake in the Lake District of Cumbria, NW England; SW of Penrith; second largest lake in England; length 12 km/7 ml; width 1 km/¾ ml; depth 64 m/210 ft. » Lake District

Ulm [oolm] 48°24N 10°00E, pop (1983) 99 400. Industrial and commercial city in Baden-Württemberg province, Germany; on R Danube, 72 km/45 ml SE of Stuttgart; scene of Napoleon's defeat of Austria, 1805; railway; university (1967); cars, transport equipment, electrical engineering, textiles, leatherwork; birthplace of Einstein; Gothic Minster (1377–1529), with the world's highest spire (161 m/528 ft). » Einstein; Germany [i]; Gothic architecture; Napoleonic Wars

ulna » **arm**

Ulster [**uhl**ster] pop (1981) 230 159; area 8 012 sq km/3 093 sq ml. Province in the Irish Republic, comprising counties of Cavan, Donegal, and Monaghan; Donegal separated by part of Connacht, lying W of N Ireland; Cavan and Monaghan lie to the S of N Ireland; chief towns include Donegal, Letterkenny, Cavan, and Monaghan; a former kingdom; land confiscated by the English Crown, and distributed to Protestant English and Scots settlers in the 17th-c; partitioned in 1921 into the present-day division. » Irish Republic [i]; Northern Ireland [i]

Ultra A British security classification (the very highest) given during World War 2 to intelligence gathered from the breaking of the key German military codes used with their 'Enigma' encryption device. 'Ultra' intelligence was available to the British high command from the outset of the war, and was of crucial importance during the Battle of Britain and the Battle of the Atlantic. » cryptography

Ultramontanism [uhltramon**tay**nizm] Literally, 'beyond the mountains'; a movement, deriving from France, asserting the centralization of the authority and power of the Roman Catholic Church in Rome and the Pope. It gained impetus after the French Revolution (1789), and reached its high point with the First Vatican Council (1870) and the declaration of papal infallibility. » French Revolution [i]; infallibility; pope; Roman Catholicism; Vatican Councils

ultrasound Sound of a frequency greater than 20 000 Hz; inaudible to humans, but certain animals such as dogs and bats can hear some ultrasonic signals. Pulses of very high frequency sound are reflected back to different extents by different materials (eg the tissues of the human body). If such a 'sonar' device is connected to a computer, accurate representations of the structure of the material can be made (in the medical case, with relatively little danger of injury to the patient). Ultrasound is therefore widely used in medical scanning (eg in the examination of a foetus) and also in engineering (eg detecting cracks in railway lines). It is produced and detected using high-frequency transducers. The study of ultrasound is **ultrasonics**. » sonar; sound; transducer

ultraviolet astronomy The detection and analysis of radiation from celestial sources in the wavelength range 50–320 nm. The hottest stars emit most of their radiation in this waveband, which is accessible only from rockets and satellites. Extensive spectrographic studies of active galaxies and quasars, as well as of stars and the interstellar medium, have been carried out using the International Ultraviolet Explorer (a UK–NASA–European Space Agency satellite) in the 120–300 nm range. » astronomy; spectroscopy; ultraviolet radiation

ultraviolet radiation Electromagnetic radiation of wavelength a little shorter than visible light, between 3.9×10^{-7} m and 10^{-8} m; discovered in 1801 by German physicist Johann Ritter (1776–1810). Invisible to the naked eye, it causes fluorescence in some substances. It is produced by electron transitions in atoms, such as in mercury discharge lamps. Ultraviolet radiation from the Sun causes tanning of the skin. » electromagnetic radiation [i]; fluorescence

Uluru [ooloo**roo**] National park in Northern Territory, C Australia; area c.1 325 sq km/500 sq ml; contains the Olgas, a series of steep-sided rock domes, and Ayers Rock; an area of continuing cultural and religious significance to the Aboriginal people; a world heritage site. » Aborigines; Ayers Rock; Northern Territory

Ulyanovsk, formerly **Simbirsk** (to 1924) [ul**ya**nufsk] 54°19N 48°22E, pop (1989) 625 000. River-port capital of Ulyanovskaya oblast, European Russia; founded as a fortress, 1648; airfield; railway; machinery, metalworking, leatherwork, footwear, vodka; birthplace of Lenin; renamed after his family name, Ulyanov; Palace of Books (1847). » Lenin; Russia

Ulysses » **Odysseus**

Ulysses project A joint ESA-NASA space exploration mission to observe the Sun and solar wind from a high solar latitude perspective. It requires the spacecraft to fly on a trajectory which passes over the poles of the Sun, and requires a boost from Jupiter's gravity field. The spacecraft was launched using the NASA shuttle in Oct 1990, and sent first to Jupiter, where its trajectory will be bent steeply out of the ecliptic to return over the Sun at a distance of about 1 Astronomical Unit. It is powered by a radioisotope thermo-electric generator. Originally named the 'International Solar Polar Mission', it was planned as a two-spacecraft mission, before the cancellation of the NASA spacecraft. It is managed by ESA's Space Research and Technology Centre and by NASA's Jet Propulsion Laboratory. » European Space Agency; NASA; radioisotope thermo-electric generator; Sun

Umayyads [oo**mi**yadz] A Damascus-based dynasty, founded by the Muslim general Muawiya ibn Abi-Sufyan, which ruled until 750. It replaced the era of the four Medina-based caliphs, of whom the last, Ali, was murdered in 661. » Abbasids; Ali

umbel A type of inflorescence, typical of the carrot family (*Umbelliferae*), in which all the flower-stalks arise from the top of the stem, the outermost stalks longest, giving a flat-topped, umbrella-shaped cluster of flowers. » carrot; inflorescence [i]

Umberto I (1844–1900) King of Italy (1878–1900), born at Turin. He fought in the war against Austria (1866), and as King brought Italy into the Triple Alliance with Germany and Austria (1882). He supported Italian colonialism in Africa, but his popularity declined after Italy's defeat by the Ethiopians at Adowa in 1896. He was assassinated at Monza. » Adowa, Battle of

Umberto II (1904–83) Last King of Italy (1946), born at Racconigi. He succeeded to the throne after the abdication of his father, Victor Emmanuel III, but himself abdicated a month later, after a national referendum had declared for a republic. He left Italy, and in 1947 he and his descendants were banished from Italy. He then lived in Portugal, and died in Geneva. » Italy [i]

umbilical cord A solid flexible cord which connects the developing foetus of some mammals (eg humans and dogs) to the maternal placenta within the uterus. When first formed, it is comparatively short, but increases in length as the foetus and amniotic cavity enlarge (the average length in humans is 60 cm/24 in.) It allows the foetus to float freely in the fluid of the uterus (the *amniotic cavity*) and to obtain nutrition from the placenta, as well as to eliminate waste products, by the flow and return of blood through the vessels within it. At birth it is severed close to the infant's front abdominal wall, leaving a scar (the *umbilicus* or *navel*). » placenta (anatomy); uterus [i]

umbra » **sunspot**

umbrella bird A large cotinga; males with dark plumage and umbrella-like crest covering head and bill; breast with inflatable air sac and pendant feathered fold of skin; call is like a bull bellowing. (Genus: *Cephalopterus*, 3 species.) » cotinga

Umbria pop (1981) 807 552; area 8 456 sq km/3 264 sq ml. Region of C Italy; capital, Perugia; chief towns, Foligno and Terni; L Trasimeno, largest lake in the Italian peninsula; prosperous farming region (corn, olives, wine, sugar beet, tobacco, market gardening, sheep farming); industry around Terni, Narni, and Foligno (chemicals, metalworking); textiles and crafts in Perugia and Spoleto; Umbrian school of painting during the Renaissance (eg Raphael). » Italian art; Italy [i]; Perugia

Umbriel The fourth largest satellite of Uranus, discovered in 1851, distance from the planet 266 000 km/165 000 ml; diameter 1 100 km/700 ml. » Ariel; Uranus (astronomy)

Umeå [**ü**mayaw] 63°50N 20°15E, pop (1982) 82 925. Seaport and capital of Västerbotten county, N Sweden; on the Gulf of

Bothnia at the mouth of the R Ume älv; seat of the Provincial Appeal Court; railway; university (1963); woodworking. » Sweden [i]

Umm al Qaiwain [oom al kiywiyn] pop (1983e) 14 300; area 750 sq km/290 sq ml. Member state of the United Arab Emirates, between Sharjah and Ras al Khaimah; capital, Umm al Qaiwain; fishing, light industry; agriculture concentrated in the fertile enclave of Falaj al Mualla. » United Arab Emirates [i]

Ummayyad Mosque [oomiyad] The great mosque at Damascus in Syria built (705–15) on the site of a Christian church to John the Baptist, and believed to incorporate the reliquary shrine of the saint's head. » John the Baptist

Un-American Activities Committee A committee of the House of Representatives established in 1938 to consider the loyalty of federal government employees. Supposedly concerned with identifying communists, it was notorious for harassing individuals whose political opinions offended committee members. Its name was later changed to the International Security Committee, and it was abolished in 1975. » House of Representatives

Unamuno (y Jugo), Miguel de [oonamoonoh] (1864–1936) Spanish philosopher and author, born at Bilbao. Educated at Bilbao and Madrid, he became professor of Greek at Salamanca (1892), and a writer of mystic philosophy, historical studies, essays, travel books, and austere poetry. His main philosophical work is *Del sentimiento trágico de la vida en los hombres y en los pueblos* (1913, The Tragic Sense of Life in Men and Peoples). He was exiled as a republican in 1924, but reinstated in 1931. He died at Salamanca. » Spanish literature

uncertainty principle » **Heisenberg uncertainty principle**

unconscious When used psychoanalytically, the collection of feelings, drives, memories, and emotional conflicts which individuals are not aware of, but which influence their mental processes and behaviour, such as in dreams and slips of the tongue indicating true feelings. In contrast, the **subconscious** is used colloquially to describe memories about which an individual is only dimly aware, but which can be recalled if focused upon. » psychoanalysis

underground A complete railway system designed to operate underground in tunnels or tubes, also known as the **tube**, **subway**, or **metro**. Traction is supplied almost exclusively by electric motor. Undergrounds are usually built where the provision of normal surface or overhead railways is not possible, usually because of congestion or other environmental considerations. Due to their high cost of construction, undergrounds are normally used only for passenger traffic within large cities. The first practical underground railway was the City and South London Railway, which opened for traffic in 1890. The idea rapidly spread around the world thereafter. » Plate XIV; railway

Underground Railroad A network of safe houses, hiding places, and routes to aid escaped American slaves to reach freedom in the N or Canada. Never formally organized, it was active as early as 1786, but was most widespread and active after 1830. One of the major means of resistance to slavery, estimates suggest that it helped at least 50 000 runaways. » slavery

underpainting In art, preliminary layers of paint, often monochrome, establishing the balance of light and shade in a picture before the application of coloured glazes and impasto. This method was normal for most painters until the late 19th-c. » glaze; impasto

underpopulation » **overpopulation**

underwing moth A moth with rather narrow wings; at rest, hindwings concealed beneath usually drab forewings; during flight hindwings revealed, often with flashes of bright colours. (Order: *Lepidoptera*. Family: *Noctuidae*.) » moth

underwriter In business and insurance, a person or company that guarantees payment if a certain event should occur. In the case of share issues, an underwriter guarantees to buy all shares not taken up. In insurance, payment is guaranteed in the event of a loss. » insurance; Lloyd's

Undset, Sigrid [unset] (1882–1949) Norwegian novelist, born at Kalundborg, Denmark. She worked in an office for 10 years, and after her marriage turned to writing. Her major novels were *Kristin Lavransdatter* (1920–2), a 14th-c trilogy, followed by the series *Olav Audunssön* (4 vols, 1925–7). She became a Catholic in 1924, which influenced her later work, most of which had contemporary settings. She won the Nobel Prize for Literature in 1928, and died at Lillehammer, Norway. » Norwegian literature; novel

undue influence In law, improper pressure used by one person upon another, in relation to some transaction. A gift (or contract) may be set aside where there has been undue influence applied by the donee (or one contracting party) to the donor (or other contracting party). Certain relationships (eg between solicitor and client, religious leader and follower) carry the presumption of undue influence, so that the burden of disproof lies on the stronger party. » contract

undulant fever » **brucellosis**

UNESCO An acronym of the **United Nations Educational, Scientific and Cultural Organization**, founded in 1946 with the objective of contributing to peace and security by promoting collaboration among nations through education, science, and culture. It has a general conference, executive board, and secretariat, with headquarters in Paris. In the mid-1980s, there emerged serious concern among the non-communist industrialized countries over the organization's administrative inefficiency and its allegedly inappropriate political aims. In consequence the USA left in 1985, which had a major impact on UNESCO's finances. The UK and Singapore subsequently withdrew.

Ungaretti, Giuseppe [ungarettee] (1888–1970) Italian poet, born in Alexandria, Egypt. He studied at Paris, and fought in the Italian army in World War 1, where he began to write poetry, published as *Il porto sepolto* (1916, The Buried Port). He became professor of Italian literature at São Paulo, Brazil (1936–42) and at Rome (1942–58). His poems, characterized by symbolism, compressed imagery, and modern verse structure, became the foundation of the *hermetic* movement (from *ermetico* 'obscure', a term used by a critic of his work). He died in Milan. » hermetic; Italian literature; poetry

Ungaro, Emanuel (Maffeolti) [ungaroh] (1933–) French fashion designer, born in Aix-en-Provence of Italian parents. He trained to join the family tailoring business, but went instead to Paris in 1955, where he worked for a small tailoring firm, and later joined Balenciaga. In 1965 he opened his own house, with Sonia Knapp designing his fabrics. Initially featuring rigid lines, his styles later softened. In 1968 he produced his first ready-to-wear lines. » Balenciaga; fashion

Ungava-Quebec Crater » **Chubb Crater**

ungulate A mammal in which toes end in hooves rather than claws; includes *artiodactyls* (**even-toed ungulates**) and *perissodactyls* (**odd-toed ungulates**); also the **primitive ungulates** (elephant, hyrax, aardvark); usually large and herbivorous. » artiodactyl; herbivore; mammal [i]; perissodactyl [i]

unicameral system A legislature which has only one chamber. This uncommon system tends to be found in countries with relatively small populations, where there would be problems in maintaining a dual system of representation. New Zealand, Israel, and Denmark are examples. » bicameral system

unicorn A fabulous creature, a horse with a single horn on its forehead; probably based on stories of the rhinoceros. In mediaeval legend it could be captured only by a virgin putting its head in her lap.

Unidad Popular [oonida popoolar] Literally, 'People's Unity'; a coalition of six left-wing political parties in Chile (Communists, Socialists, Radicals, and three minor groups) formed to support the presidential candidacy and government (1970–3) of Dr Salvador Allende. » Allende; Chile

Unification Church A religious movement founded by the Reverend Sun Myung Moon in 1954 in Korea, known popularly as the 'Moonies'. Its teachings are based on Moon's book *Divine Principle*, which contains a special interpretion of the Bible, and on revelations he is said to have received from God. The purpose of creation was to establish a perfect family, but the Fall frustrated its realization until its fulfilment in Rev and Mrs Moon. Its most important ritual is the mass weddings conducted by Rev Moon, and there is weekly re-dedication. The Church has extensive commercial interests, and some of its activities have generated public hostility. » religion

uniformitarianism In geology, the principle that geological processes controlling the evolution of the Earth's crust were of the same kind throughout geological time as they are today. First formulated by British geologist James Hutton, it contrasts with the earlier theory of **catastrophism**, which postulated that the history of the Earth has to be explained by events radically different from anything going on at the present day. » geology; Hutton, James

Uniformity, Acts of A series of acts passed by the British Parliament in 1549, 1552, 1559, and 1662. They sought to impose religious uniformity by requiring the use of the Church of England liturgy as contained in the Book of Common Prayer (various editions, 1549–1662). The act of 1552 penalized Catholic recusants; that of 1662 excluded dissenting Protestant clergy. » Book of Common Prayer

union (economics) » **trade union**

union (mathematics) » **set**

Union, Acts of The Acts which joined England in legislative union with Scotland (1707) and Ireland (1800). The 1707 Act brought 45 Scottish MPs to join the new House of Commons of Great Britain, and 16 peers became members of the House of Lords. The Scottish legal system remained separate. The 1800 Act created the United Kingdom of Great Britain and Ireland, which came into effect in 1801, and lasted until 1922. This was brought about after the collapse of the Irish rebellion (1798) in order to increase British security in the French wars. The Irish parliament was abolished; 100 Irish MPs were added to the UK House of Commons, and 32 Peers to the Lords. The Churches of England and Ireland were united. » United Kingdom [i]

Union Islands » **Tokelau**

Union Movement A party formed by Sir Oswald Mosley in 1948 as a successor to his New Party (1931) and the British Union of Fascists (1932). It put up a handful of candidates 1959–66, failing to secure a significant number of votes. The party's main plank was opposition to immigration, but it also included a call to unite Europe into a vast market to buy and sell from Africa. Mosley gave up the leadership in 1966, and the movement went into decline, dying out by the end of the 1960s. » fascism; Mosley

Union of European Football Associations » **UEFA**

Union of Soviet Socialist Republics » **Soviet Union** [i]

Uniramia [yooni**ray**mia] A group of arthropods characterized by their 1-branched (*uniramous*) limbs, and by jaws that bite transversely at the tip; comprises the insects (*Insecta*), centipedes (*Chilopoda*), millipedes (*Diplopoda*), and velvet worms (*Onychophora*); sometimes treated as a separate phylum at the arthropodan level of organization. » arthropod; centipede; insect [i]; millipede; systematics; velvet worm

unit trust A form of investment. The trust buys shares in a number of companies, and offers the public an opportunity to buy a unit of the portfolio. It is a means of spreading risk. There are over 1 000 unit trusts in the UK, catering for the general investor and for special situations. » investment

Unitarians A religious group which, although in many ways akin to Christianity, rejects the doctrines of the Trinity and the divinity of Christ. As an organized group, it dates back to the Anabaptists at the time of the Reformation. » Anabaptists; Jesus Christ; Reformation; Trinity

United Arab Emirates, Arabic **Ittihad al-Imarat al-Arabiyah**, formerly **Trucial States** pop (1990e) 1 903 000; area 83 600 sq km/ 32 300 sq ml. Federation comprising seven internally self-governing emirates, EC Arabian Peninsula, bounded N by the Arabian Gulf, E by Oman, S and W by Saudi Arabia, and NW by Qatar; capital, Abu Dhabi; timezone GMT +4; population 19% Emirian, 23% other Arabs, 50% S Asian; official language, Arabic; chief religion, Islam; unit of currency, the dirham; located along the S shore (Trucial Coast) of the Arabian Gulf; Al Fujairah has a coastline along the Gulf of Oman; salt marshes predominate on the coast; barren desert and gravel plain inland; Hajar Mts in Al Fujairah rise to over 1 000 m/3 000 ft; hot climate with limited rainfall; winter temperatures average 21°C, with high humidity (70%+); less humid in summer, maximum temperatures rising to 45°C; sandstorms common; mean annual rainfall, Abu Dhabi 32 mm/1¼ in; peace treaty with Britain signed by rulers of the Trucial States, 1820; new state formed by six emirates, 1971; Ras al Khaimah joined, 1972; governed by a Supreme Council comprising the hereditary rulers of the seven emirates; an important commercial and trading centre; economy based on oil and gas, Abu Dhabi the major producer, followed by Dubai; iron and steel, petrochemicals, construction, ship repairing, tourism, fishing, light industry; saline water supplies have restricted agriculture to the oases and the irrigated valleys of the Hajar Mts; vegetables, fruits, dates, dairy farming. » Abu Dhabi; Ajman; Dubai; Fujairah, Al; Ras al Khaimah; Sharjah; Umm al Qaiwain; RR27 national holidays; RR63 political leaders

United Church of Christ A Christian denomination formed in the USA in 1961 (after 20 years of negotiations) by the union of the Congregational and Christian Churches with the Evangelical and Reformed Church. Envisioned as an ecumenical Protestant Church, it allows for variation in local organization and in the interpretation of doctrine, but continues to reflect its Reformed theological background. » Congregationalism; Reformed Churches

United Fronts Two political movements in China in the late 1930s, which promoted co-operation between the Communist and National Parties in the face of Japanese aggression. In Dec 1936, the Xi'an incident ended with an anti-Japanese alliance between the two Parties, and after the outbreak of the Sino-Japanese War (1937) the Communist Party initiated a second united front. Clashes between Nationalist and Communist forces made it an uneasy alliance from the start, and by 1941 it had virtually disintegrated, although efforts were made to revive it in 1943. » Xi'an incident

United Gold Coast Convention A nationalist party formed in the Gold Coast (later, Ghana) in 1947. Kwame Nkrumah became Secretary General in 1948, but it was soon apparent that he was at odds with the leadership, since he desired to promote a more radical approach. In 1949 he formed the Convention People's Party, which led Ghana to independence in 1957. » nationalism; Nkrumah

United Irishmen, Society of A society formed in Belfast in 1791 by Protestant lawyer Wolfe Tone, which supported the French Revolution and espoused both religious equality and parliamentary reform. Its early support was primarily located in Ulster. As agitation increased, so United Irishmen became increasingly associated with support for Catholicism. The Society was instrumental in organizing French support for the

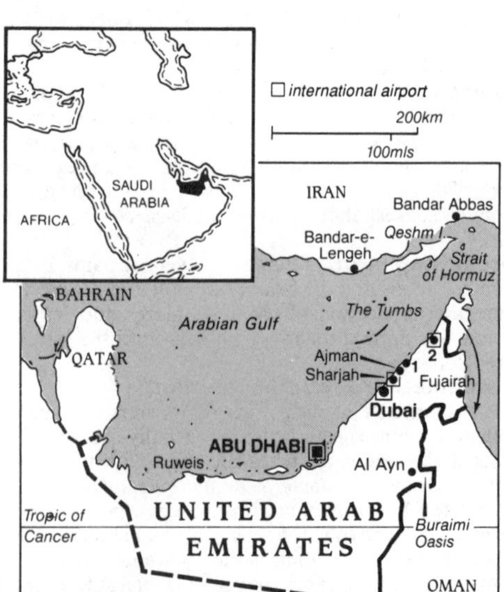

□ *major international airport*

unsuccessful Irish rebellion of 1798, and afterwards went into decline. » French Revolution [i]; Tone

United Kingdom (UK), also **United Kingdom of Great Britain and Northern Ireland** or **Great Britain** pop (1990e) 57 384 000; area 244 755 sq km/94 475 sq ml. Kingdom of W Europe, comprising the kingdoms of England and Scotland, the principality of Wales, and Northern Ireland; population 81.5% English, 9.6% Scottish, 2.4% Irish, 1.9% Welsh, and 2% West Indian, Asian, and African; official language, English, with Welsh and Gaelic spoken by minorities; chief religion, Christianity; unit of currency, the pound sterling of 100 pence; Wales was effectively joined to England in 1301, Scotland in 1603, and Ireland in 1801 (the United Kingdom of Great Britain and Ireland); present name dates from 1922, following the establishment of the Irish Free State; a kingdom with a monarch as head of state; governed by a bicameral parliament, comprising an elected 650-member House of Commons, and a House of Lords with hereditary peers, life peers, Anglican bishops, and law lords; a Cabinet is appointed by the Prime Minister. » England [i]; Northern Ireland [i]; Scotland [i]; Wales [i]; RR27 national holidays; RR64 political leaders; *see illustration p 487*

United Kingdom Atomic Energy Authority An authority set up by the Atomic Energy Authority Act in 1954, which has prime responsibility for research and the development of nuclear power in the UK on behalf of the government. It conducts research into new reactor systems, including safety and environmental issues, and provides support for the UK nuclear industry. » International Atomic Energy Agency; nuclear reactor [i]

United Nations (UN) An organization formed to maintain world peace and foster international co-operation, formally established on 24 October 1945 with 51 founder countries. The UN Charter, which was drafted during the war by the USA, UK, and USSR, remains virtually unaltered despite the growth in membership and activities. There are six 'principal organs'. The **General Assembly** is the plenary body which controls much of the UN's work, supervises the subsidiary organs, sets priorities, and debates major issues of international affairs. The 15-member **Security Council** is dominated by the five permanent members (China, France, UK, Russia, and USA) who each have the power of veto over any resolutions; the remaining ten are elected for two-year periods. The primary role of the Council is to maintain international peace and security; its decisions, unlike those of the General Assembly, are binding on all other members. It is empowered to order mandatory sanctions, call for ceasefires, and establish peacekeeping forces (these forces were awarded the Nobel Peace Prize in 1988). The use of the veto has prevented it from intervening in a number of disputes, such as Vietnam. The **Secretariat**, under the Secretary-General, employs some 16 000 at the UN's headquarters in New York City and 50 000 worldwide. The staff are answerable only to the UN, not national governments, and are engaged in considerable diplomatic work. The Secretary-General is often a significant person in international diplomacy and is able to take independent initiatives. The **International Court of Justice** consists of 15 judges appointed by the Council and the Assembly. As only states can bring issues before it, its jurisdiction depends on the consent of the states who are a party to a dispute. It also offers advisory opinions to various organs of the UN. The **Economic and Social Council** is elected by the General Assembly; it supervises the work of various committees, commissions, and expert bodies in the economic and social area, and co-ordinates the work of UN specialized agencies. The **Trusteeship Council** oversees the transition of Trust territories to self-government.

In addition to the organs established under the Charter, there is a range of subsidiary agencies, many with their own constitutions and membership, and some pre-dating the UN. The main agencies are the **Food and Agriculture Organization**, the **Intergovernmental Maritime Consultative Organization**, the **International Atomic Energy Authority**, the **International Bank for Reconstruction and Development** ('World Bank'), the **International Civil Aviation Organization**, the **International Development Association**, the **International Finance Corporation**, the **International Fund for Agricultural Development**, the **International Labour Organization**, the **International Monetary Fund**, the **United Nations Educational, Scientific and Cultural Organization**, the **Universal Postal Union**, the **International Telecommunication Union**, the **World Meterological Organization**, and the **World Health Organization**.

The UN had 161 members in 1991. It is generally seen as a forum where states pursue their national interest, rather than as an institution of world government, but it is not without considerable impact. » International Bank for Reconstruction and Development; International Monetary Fund; UNESCO; United Nations Conference on Trade and Development; RR36, 37, 65

United Nations Agencies » **United Nations**

United Nations Conference on Trade and Development (UNCTAD) An organ of the UN, established by the 1964 General Assembly, which meets irregularly to consider ways of increasing international trade and promoting economic development. Its executive board meets annually. It provides the main forum through which underdeveloped countries can put their views to the major economic powers. » United Nations

United Nations Economic, Scientific and Cultural Organization » **UNESCO**

United Provinces of the Netherlands Seven sovereign states of the Dutch Republic (Holland, Zeeland, Gelderland, Utrecht, Friesland, Groningen and Overyssel), roughly comprising the present kingdom of the Netherlands, but originally part of the Burgundian lands until they achieved independence from the Spanish crown (1568–1648). The republic declined in the 18th-c, collapsing during the Revolutionary Wars (1795). » Burgundy; French Revolutionary Wars; Netherlands, Austrian and Spanish

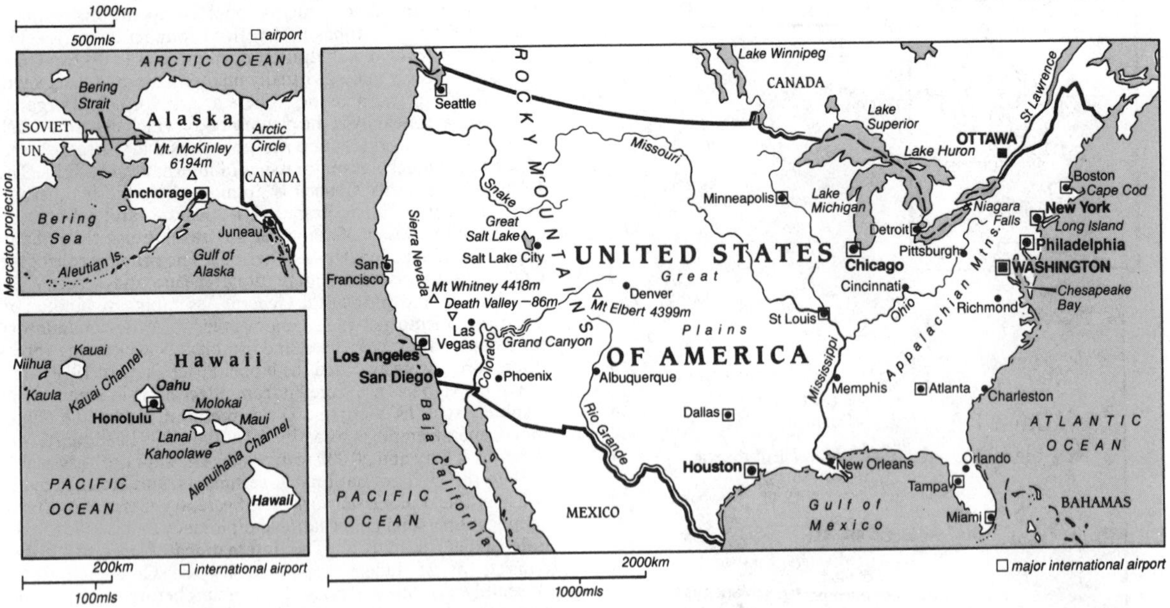

United Service Organizations (USO) Founded in the USA in 1941, it is an association of agencies, such as the YMCA, the YWCA, and the Salvation Army, whose aims are to care for the recreational needs of the Armed Forces. » Young Men's Christian Association

United States military academies Federal training institutions for people who want to become officers in the US armed forces. The **United States Air Force (USAF) Academy** was formed by Act of Congress in 1948, and is located near Colorado Springs, USA. The **United States Military Academy** was founded in 1802, and is now at West Point on the Hudson R, New York State. The **United States Naval Academy** was founded in 1845, and is at Annapolis, Maryland. In each of these institutions, there are about 4 400 officer cadets in training; women have been admitted since 1976. The **United States Coast Guard (USCG) Academy** was founded in 1876, and has been located at New London, Connecticut since 1936. This has a complement of 850 male and female cadets. » air force; army; coastguard; navy

United States of America (USA), also called **United States**, and often **America** pop (1990e) 251 394 000; area 9 160 454 sq km/ 3 535 935 sq ml. A federal republic of North America; fourth largest country in the world; includes the detached states of Alaska and Hawaii; timezones GMT −5 (E coast) to −8 (Pacific Coast), Alaska GMT −9, Hawaii GMT −10; capital Washington; chief cities include New York, Chicago, Los Angeles, Philadelphia, Detroit, Houston; ethnic groups 86.2% of European origin (including 6.2% Hispanic), 11% Black, 1.6% Asian and Pacific, 0.7% American Indian, Eskimo, and Aleut; religion mainly Christianity (70%); official language English, with a sizeable Spanish-speaking minority; currency is the US dollar of 100 cents; national holiday 4 July (Independence Day).

Physical description. The E Atlantic coastal plain is backed by the Appalachian Mts from the Great Lakes to Alabama, a series of parallel ranges including the Allegheny, Blue Ridge, and Catskill Mts. To the S, the plain broadens out towards the Gulf of Mexico and into the Florida peninsula. To the W, the Gulf Plains stretch N to meet the higher Great Plains from which they are separated by the Ozark Mts. Further W, the Rocky Mts rise to over 4 500 m/14 750 ft (highest point Mt McKinley, Alaska, 6 194 m/20 321 ft). The lowest point is in Death Valley (−86 m/−282 ft). Drainage N is into the St Lawrence R or the Great Lakes. In the E, the Hudson, Delaware, Potomac, and other rivers flow E to the Atlantic Ocean. The central plains are drained by the great Red River–Missouri–Mississippi River system and by other rivers flowing into the Gulf of Mexico. In the W, the main rivers are the Columbia and Colorado.

Climate. US climate varies from conditions found in hot tropical deserts (in the SW) to those typical of Arctic continental regions. Most regions are affected by westerly depressions that can bring cloud, rain, and changeable weather. Rainfall is heaviest in the Pacific NW, lightest in the SW. In the Great Plains, wide temperature variation is the result of cold air from the Arctic as well as warm tropical air from the Gulf of Mexico. On the W coast the influence of the Pacific Ocean results in a smaller range of temperatures between summer and winter. On the E coast there is a gradual increase in winter temperatures southwards. The states bordering the Gulf of Mexico are subject to hurricanes and tornadoes moving NW from the Caribbean.

History and government. First settled by 'Indian' groups who migrated from Asia across the Bering land-bridge over 25 000 years ago, the country was explored by the Norse (9th-c) and by the Spanish (16th-c), who settled in Florida and Mexico. In the 17th-c, there were settlements by the British, French, Dutch, Germans, and Swedish. Many Black Africans were introduced as slaves to work on the plantations. In the following century, British control grew throughout the area. A revolt of the English-speaking colonies in the War of Independence (1775–83) led to the creation of the United States of America, which then lay between the Great Lakes, the Mississippi, and Florida. George Washington was its first president. Louisiana was sold to the USA by France in 1803 (the Louisiana Purchase) and the westward movement of settlers began. Florida was ceded by Spain in 1819, and further Spanish states joined the Union between 1821 and 1853. In 1860–1, 11 Southern states left the Union over the slavery issue, and formed the Confederacy; the Civil War (1861–5) ended in victory for the North, and the Southern states later rejoined the Union. In 1867 Alaska was purchased from Russia, and the Hawaiian Is were annexed in 1898 (both admitted as states in 1959). Several other islands are formally associated with the USA, such as Puerto Rico, American Samoa, and Guam.

In the 19th-c, millions of immigrants arrived from Europe and the Far East, many of them refugees, leading to the description of the USA as the 'melting pot' of nations. More recently, large numbers of Spanish-speaking people have arrived mainly from Mexico and the West Indies. In the 20th-c the USA has become the chief industrial nation in the world, with vast mineral and agricultural resources, a highly diversified economy, and an advanced system of communica-

tions and transportation. It was a leader in the space exploration programme of the 1970s. In recent years, large increases in consumption have led to an unfavourable balance of trade, and the need to reduce public spending.

The USA entered World War 1 on the side of the Allies in 1917, and again in World War 2 after the Japanese attack on Pearl Harbor in 1941. Since then, the country has emerged as the chief world power opposed to Communism, a policy which led to major military involvements in Korea and Vietnam. The campaign for Black civil rights developed here in the 1960s, accompanied by much civil disturbance. The Congress consists of two bodies: a 435-member House of Representatives elected for 2-year terms, and a 100-member Senate elected for 6-year terms. A president, who is elected every four years by a college of state representatives, appoints an executive cabinet responsible to Congress. The USA is divided into 50 federal states and the District of Columbia, each state having its own two-body legislature and governor. » American Civil War/Indians/Revolution; civil rights; Congress; federalism; Indian Wars; Washington (DC); World War 1/2; RR10 space programme; RR19 distances between cities; RR38 list of states; RR65 list of presidents

United States Trust Territory of the Pacific Islands 1–22°N 142–172°E; pop (1980) 116974; area 1779 sq km/687 sq ml. Group of more than 2000 islands in the W Pacific Ocean, N of Papua New Guinea; until 1990 comprised the Commonwealth of the N Mariana Is, Federated States of Micronesia, Republic of Belau, and the Marshall Is; population mostly Micronesian, with some Polynesian; official language, English; islands mainly of volcanic origin, few rising above 120 m/400 ft; administered by Japan in the inter-war years; placed under UN trusteeship, 1947; Commonwealth of the N Mariana Is established in political union with the USA, 1975; each of the other territories negotiating a status of free association with the USA; trust status ended for all except Belau, 1990; economy based on agriculture, fisheries, tourism; coconuts, sugar cane, cassava, yams, copra, fish processing. » Belau; Mariana Islands, Commonwealth of the Northern; Micronesia, Federated States of; Marshall Islands; Pacific Ocean

unities In literature, the dimensions of time, place, and action, requiring a play to consist of one plot unfolding in one place within one day. Neoclassical critics made into strict rules what had been offered as guidelines in Aristotle's *Poetics*. Dr Johnson rejected the unities in his *Preface to Shakespeare* (1765). » Aristotle; classicism; drama; Johnson, Samuel; Neoclassicism (art)

units (scientific) Most quantities in science are expressed using the International System of units, abbreviated to **SI units**, introduced in 1960 by the General Conference on Weights and Measures. The most fundamental are called **base units**: the metre, kilogram, second, ampere, kelvin, candela, and mole. There are two so-called **supplementary units**: the radian and steradian. All quantities of interest can be expressed in terms of these units. Certain combinations which appear often are called **derived units** and have special names, eg the newton, which is defined as $m.kg/s^2$. Many other units exist, either for historical reasons or because they are more convenient in some special application than the corresponding SI unit; examples are the parsec, a length unit used in astronomy, and calories, which are used in measurements of the energy content of food. Other systems of units have been used: these include the old FPS British system, based on foot, pound, and second; the CGS system, based on centimetre, gram, and second; and the MKSA system, based on metre, kilogram, second, and ampere. SI units are an extension of MKSA units. » natural units; RR70

Universal Postal Union » United Nations

universal time The precise system of time measurement used for all practical purposes. Formerly based on *mean solar time*, it has since 1972 been based on *international atomic time*, a uniform time derived from the frequencies of selected transitions within atoms. It is now identical to Greenwich Mean Time. » Greenwich Mean Time; solar time

universalism The religious belief that all people will be saved. It implies rejection of the traditional Christian belief in hell. A feature of much contemporary Protestant theology, it is motivated by moral doubts concerning eternal punishment, and by a recognition of the validity of other non-Christian world faiths. » Christianity; hell; predestination; Protestantism

universals Alleged metaphysical entities such as redness, betweenness, and running, referred to by adjectives, prepositions, and verbs; they are claimed not to be individuals, because universals are repeatable while individuals are not. Platonists and realists claim that universals really exist; conceptualists say they exist only in minds; nominalists deny their existence. » conceptualism; metaphysics; nominalism; Platonism; realism

universe In modern astronomy, the totality of all that is in the cosmos and that can affect us by means of physical forces. The definition excludes anything that is in principle undetectable physically, such as regions of spacetime that were, are, or will be irreversibly cut off from our own spacetime. » Big Bang; inflationary universe; microwave background radiation; Olbers' paradox

university An institution of higher education which offers study at degree level. Courses may be taken leading to bachelor, master, or doctoral level. It is less vocational in nature than a polytechnic, but vocational courses can be followed, leading to qualifications in such professions as medicine, teaching, engineering, and the law, sometimes in conjunction with professional bodies. Research is given a high priority. » Cambridge [i] /London [i] /Open/Oxford [i] /Paris University; degree (education); Ivy League [i]; New/Red-brick/Scottish universities [i]; Todai

univocalic A written composition that makes use of only one vowel, in all its words. The opening couplet from a 16-line poem by C C Bombaugh, written in 1890, illustrates the nature of the task: 'No monk too good to rob, or cog, or plot./No fool so gross to bolt Scotch collops hot...' » lipogram

Unknown Soldier or **Warrior** An unnamed soldier, taken as representative of all those who died in World War 1, whose grave is a memorial to all war dead. Several countries have such a memorial: in France beneath the Arc de Triomphe; in the UK in Westminster Abbey; in the USA in Arlington National Cemetery (the Unknown Soldier). » World War 1

Unleavened Bread, Feast of » Passover

Unter den Linden [**un**tuh den **lin**dn] A boulevard running between Mark-Engels Platz and the Brandenburg Gate, in the heart of present-day E Berlin, Germany. Formerly a stately avenue lined with linden trees and historic buildings, much of its character was destroyed during World War 2. » Berlin, East

Untersee » Zeller See

untouchables » caste

Up-Helly-Aa [uhp heli **ah**] A festival held annually in Lerwick in the Shetland Islands, UK, on the last Thursday in January, ending in the burning of a replica Viking longboat.

Upanishads [oo**pan**ishadz] The last section of the Hindu scriptures (the Veda), composed in Sanskrit between 800 and 400 BC. The name, meaning 'to sit near', refers to the secret transmission of these teachings by gurus. » Hinduism; Indian literature; Veda

upas tree [**yoo**puhs] An evergreen tree native to Malaysia; leaves oblong; flowers tiny, green, in globose heads. The milky latex is used to make a powerful arrow-poison. In the 18th-c, misunderstanding led to the belief that poisonous emanations from the tree killed all life for miles around. (*Antiaris toxicaria*. Family: *Moraceae*.) » evergreen plants; latex; tree [i]

Updike, John (Hoyer) (1932–) US writer, born at Shillington, Pennsylvania. Educated at Harvard and Oxford, he wrote poetry, stories, and criticism for the *New Yorker* magazine from 1955. His novels, exploring human relationships in contemporary US society, include *Rabbit, Run* (1960), *Couples* (1968), *Rabbit is Rich* (1981, Pulitzer Prize), and *The Witches of Eastwick* (1984), and he has published several collections of short stories, selected in *Forty Stories* (1987). » American literature; novel; short story

Uppsala [**up**sala] 59°55N 17°38E, pop (1982) 149 333. Capital city of Uppsala county, E Sweden, 64 km/40 ml NNW of Stockholm; archbishopric; railway; educational centre, with university (1477) and many other academic institutions; engineering, pharmaceuticals, printing; cathedral (13th–15th-c), with tombs of Gustavus Vasa and other kings; castle (16th-c). » Gustavus I; Sweden [i]

Ur The early home of the Jewish patriarch Abraham, Ur was an ancient Sumerian city-state lying to the SE of Babylon. It was at its zenith in the third millennium BC, when twice it became the capital of Sumer. Destroyed by Elam c.2000 BC, the city recovered but never attained its former greatness. It was finally abandoned in the 4th-c BC. » Abraham; Elam; Sumer

uraemia/uremia A rise in the concentration of urea in the blood, one of the first chemical abnormalities to be detected in kidney failure. The term now encompasses all the many chemical abnormalities that occur in the blood in the course of kidney failure. » blood; kidney failure

Ural Mountains [**yoo**ral(z)] or **The Urals**, Russ **Uralskiy Khrebet** Mountain range in Russia, forming the traditional boundary between Europe and Asia, and separating the E European Plain (W) from the W Siberian Lowlands (E); extends 1 750 km/1 100 ml S from Novaya Zemlya in the Arctic Ocean to the N Kazakhstan border; low, parallel N–S ridges, generally 200–1 000 m/700–3 300 ft high; N Urals contain the highest peak, Mt Narodnaya (1 894 m/6 214 ft); C Urals form a plateau, crossed by several transport routes, including the Trans-Siberian Railway; S Urals consist of several parallel ranges, reaching a maximum width of 150–200 km/100–125 ml; heavily forested; rich mineral deposits; oil, iron ore, coal, copper, manganese, gold, aluminium, potash, bauxite, asbestos, zinc, lead, silver, nickel, gemstones; industrialized area in the S; cities include Magnitogorsk, Ekaterinburg (Sverdlovsk). » Russia; Trans-Siberian Railway

Uralic languages A family of languages descended from an ancestor spoken in the region of the N Ural Mts over 7 000 years ago. Although some have been written since the 13th-c, Uralic languages are now in decline, largely because of the propagation of Russian in their place. The major languages are Finnish, Estonian, and Lapp, with an isolated member, Magyar, in Hungary. Numerous minor languages, all with less than 30 000 speakers each, are scattered through N Russia. » Lapp; Magyar; Slavic languages

Urania [yoo**ray**nia] In Greek mythology, the Muse of astronomy. » Muses

uraninite » pitchblende

uranium U, element 92, density 19 g/cm^3, melting point 1 132°C. The heaviest of the naturally occurring elements, it has no stable isotopes, but the commonest (^{238}U) has a half-life of more than 10^9 years. Once used as a yellow glass pigment, uranium compounds are now almost exclusively used for conversion to plutonium in nuclear fuel applications. » chemical elements; nuclear reactor [i]; plutonium; RR90

uranium-lead dating A method of radiometric dating for old rocks, using the fact that the radioactive isotope ^{238}U decays with a known half-life to give ^{206}Pb, and another isotope of uranium ^{235}U decays to give ^{207}Pb. The amount of each isotope in a rock can be used to determine its absolute age. » radiometric dating

Uranus (astronomy) [**yoo**ranuhs, yoo**ray**nuhs] The seventh planet from the Sun, discovered by Herschel in 1781; a smaller 'gas giant' than Jupiter or Saturn, and a near twin to Neptune. It is accompanied by five principal moons and a unique ring system. It has the following characteristics: mass 8.7×10^{25} kg; radius 25 900 km/16 000 ml; mean density 1.18 g/cm^3; rotational period 84.01 years; orbital period 17.3 hours; eccentricity of orbit 0.047; inclination of equator 82°; mean distance from the Sun 2.87×10^9 km. Composed mainly of hydrogen and helium, like Jupiter and Saturn, Uranus has a larger percentage of ammonia and methane. Its interior lacks sharp compositional boundaries, but has a rock-rich core, ice-rich mantle, and deep atmosphere. Its low temperature allows condensation of methane clouds (methane gas in the upper atmosphere absorbs red light and accounts for the planet's greenish hue), with ammonia and water clouds also likely at lower levels.

It is highly unusual in having a rotation axis tilted, so that the poles lie almost in the ecliptic, and its equatorial plane with rings and moons lies almost perpendicular to the ecliptic. It was observed at close range for the first time by Voyager 1 in 1986. Little contrast was observed in the clouds, which do show evidence of a banded structure. There is no significant internal heat souce; the circulation is driven primarily by an unusual distribution of solar heat input and by rapid rotation. The temperatures at the poles and the equator are similar, indicating some dynamical means of redistributing heat deposited at the poles. Voyager discovered one new ring to add to the nine discrete rings already observed telescopically. The rings are very dark, narrow, widely separated, and slightly eccentric. There are five major moons (Miranda, Ariel, Umbriel, Titania, Oberon) in synchronous rotation; ten small moons were discovered by Voyager. » ammonia; methane [i]; planet; shepherd moons; Solar System; Voyager project [i]; RR4

Uranus (mythology) or **Ouranus** [**yoo**ranuhs, yoo**ray**nuhs] In Greek mythology, the earliest sky-god, who was the father of the Titans. A very abstract figure, not the subject of worship or of art, he was displaced by Cronus. He is equivalent to Roman *Caelus*, 'the heavens'. » Titan (mythology)

Urartu A state which flourished from the 9th-c to the 7th-c BC in the mountains of E Turkey around L Van. Abutting onto the territory of the Assyrians, then at the height of their power, Urartu was often engaged in hostilities with them. » Assyria

Urban II, originally **Odo of Lagery** (1042–99) French Pope (1088–99), born at Châtillon-sur-Marne. He became a monk at Cluny, and was made Cardinal Bishop of Ostia in 1078. As Pope, he introduced ecclesiastical reforms, drove foreign armies from Italy, and launched the first Crusade. He died in Rome, and was beatified in 1881. » Crusades; pope

urbanization The demographic process whereby an increasing proportion of the population of a region or country live in urban areas, particularly a country's largest urban settlement. It is characterisitic of economically advancing nations, where it is occurring at a much faster rate than it did historically in the developed (Western) world. Urbanization is linked to industrialization. Large urban areas did of course exist before the Industrial Revolution (eg in Asia). » city; demography; urban

Urdu » **Indo-Aryan languages**

urea [yooreea] $H_2N–CO–NH_2$, melting point 135°C. A colourless solid, manufactured by heating ammonia and carbon dioxide under pressure: $2NH_3 + CO_2 \rightarrow H_2NCONH_2 + H_2O$; also called **carbamide**. Although excreted in the urine of mammals, it is used as an animal feed additive as well as a fertilizer. It is the starting material for urea resins. » ammonia; resin; urea formaldehyde resin; urine

urea formaldehyde resin A plastic made by the co-polymerization of urea with formaldehyde. Its main outlets are in adhesives, and as a thermosetting resin for moulding. It is also used for plastic foam formation. » formaldehyde; polymerization; resin; urea

urethritis Inflammation of the urethra, caused by one of several organisms such as *Gonococcus* and *Chlamydia*. The symptoms include a burning sensation on passing urine, and frequency of urination. » urinary system

Urey, Harold C(layton) (1893–1981) US chemist and pioneer in the study of the Solar System, born at Walkerton, Indiana. Educated at Montana, California, and Copenhagen, he taught at Baltimore (1924–9), Columbia (1929–45), and Chicago (1945–58), and was director of war research, Atomic Bomb Project, Columbia (1940–5). In 1932 he isolated heavy water and discovered deuterium, for which he won the Nobel Prize for Chemistry in 1934. His work on lunar and planetary formation laid the scientific foundation for the space age exploration of the Solar System. He died at La Jolla, California. » deuterium; Solar System; space exploration

Urfé, Honoré d' [ürfay] (1568–1625) French writer, born in Marseilles. He fought in the religious wars of France and later settled in Savoy. He was the author of the pastoral romance, *Astrée* (1610–27), regarded as the first French novel. He was killed at Villefranche-sur-mer during the war between Savoy and Genoa. » French literature; novel; pastoral

uric acid [yoorik] An acid derived from purine, $C_5H_4N_4O_3$; like urea, used by animals as a means of excreting nitrogen. Deposits of crystals of uric acid and its salts cause pain in gout and rheumatism. » purines; urine

Urim and Thummim [oorim, thuhmim] Objects of uncertain description, kept in the breastplate and vestments of the Israelite high priest. They were apparently used to discern God's answer to 'yes'-or-'no' questions put to him, and served either as gemstones catching the light (if *urim* means 'lights') or as flat markers used in casting lots (if *urim* means 'curse' and *thummim* means 'perfect'). » Judaism; oracle

urinary stones The formation of calculi within the kidney substance and pelvis, ureter, and bladder. They commonly consist of salts of calcium, magnesium, ammonium phosphate, carbonate, and oxalate. Factors predisposing to their formation include working in hot climates, high dietary calcium and oxalate intake, and familial factors. Uric acid stones are found in gout, and cystine stones in a rare metabolic disease, cystinuria. » calculi; kidneys

urinary system The physiological system involved in the production, storage, and excretion of urine. In mammals it consists of a pair of kidneys each connected to a muscular sac (the *bladder*) by a narrow fibromuscular tube (the *ureter*); a single *urethra* leaves the bladder to the exterior. Urine produced by the kidneys is temporarily stored in the bladder, then expelled via the urethra. » bladder; kidneys; penis [i]; pyelonephritis; urine

urine A liquid or semi-solid solution produced by the kidneys in vertebrates (eg humans), Malpighian tubules in some invertebrates (eg insects), and nephridia in most invertebrates (eg annelids, molluscs). It consists of water, the end-products of metabolism (eg urea, uric acid, hydrogen ions), dietary constituents taken in excess (eg salts, vitamins), and foreign substances (eg drugs), or their derivatives. The volume and composition of urine is species-, diet-, and environment-specific, as well as being influenced by the state of health and the degree of physical activity. The expulsion of urine from the bladder is often referred to as *micturition*. » diuretics; haematuria; kidneys; urinary system

Urnes Stave Church [oornuhs] A 12th-c church constructed of wooden staves in Urnes, Sogn og Fjordane county, Norway. The church, considered to be the finest of its kind, is a world heritage monument. » Norway [i]

Ursa Major [ersa mayja] (Lat 'great bear') A huge and conspicuous constellation, containing the asterism The Plough. It is mentioned extensively in literature from the earliest times, and is the one constellation that most people in the N hemisphere can locate without difficulty. A modest (20 cm) telescope will show double stars, spiral galaxies, and a notable planetary nebula in this general area. » asterism; constellation; Plough, the; Polaris; RR9

Ursa Minor (Lat 'little bear') The constellation around the N celestial pole. Its brightest star is Polaris. » constellation; Polaris; RR9

Ursulines Worldwide congregations of sisters engaged in the education of girls. The principal and oldest congregation was founded in 1535 by St Angela Merici as the Company of St Ursula, after the 4th-c legendary saint and martyr. » nun

urticaria [ertikairia] A skin rash due to the release of histamine from mast and other cells, resulting in the formation of weals and blisters in the skin; also known as **nettle rash** or **hives**. The commonest form results from allergy. » histamine; skin [i]

Uruguay, official name **Oriental Republic of Uruguay, República Oriental del Uruguay** pop (1990e) 3 033 000; area 176 215 sq km/ 68 018 sq ml. Republic in E South America, divided into 19 departments; bordered E by the Atlantic Ocean, N by Brazil, and W by the R Uruguay and Argentina; capital, Montevideo; chief towns include Salto, Paysandú, Mercedes; timezone GMT −3; population mainly European (90%); chief religion, Roman Catholicism (66%); official language, Spanish; unit of currency, the nuevo peso of 100 centésimos; grass-covered

plains (S) rise N to a high sandy plateau; R Negro flows SW to meet the R Uruguay on the Argentine frontier; temperate climate with warm summers and mild winters; average temperature at Montevideo, 16°C; average annual rainfall, 978 mm/38 in; originally occupied by Charrúas Indians; visited by the Spanish, 1515; part of the Spanish Viceroyalty of Río de la Plata, 1726; province of Brazil, 1814–25; independence, 1828; unrest caused by Tupamaro guerrillas in late 1960s and early 1970s; military rule until 1985; a president is advised by a Council of Ministers, and a bicameral legislature consists of a 30-member Senate and a 99-member Chamber of Deputies, both elected for five years; economy traditionally based on livestock and agriculture; meat, wool, hides, maize, wheat, sorghum, rice, citrus fruit, potatoes, vegetable oils; fishing, food processing and packing, cement, chemicals, textiles, leather, steel, light engineering. » Montevideo; Tupamaros; RR27 national holidays; RR65 political leaders

Uruguay, River Span (**Río**), Port **Rio Uruguai** S American river; rises in S Brazil and flows W, SW, and S along the Brazil–Argentina and Uruguay–Argentina borders, joining the R Paraná above Buenos Aires to form the R Plate; length c.1 600 km/1 000 ml; navigable only in its lower course; main ports, Concepción del Uruguay (Argentina) and Paysandu (Uruguay). » Argentina [i]

Uruk One of the greatest city-states of Sumer, lying to the NW of Ur. The home of the legendary Gilgamesh, it is also the site of the earliest writing ever found. Although it came under the domination of Ur c.2100 BC, it outlasted its powerful neighbour, surviving well into the Parthian period (3rd-c AD). » Sumer; Ur

Ürümqi [urumchee], **Urumchi**, or **Wu-lu-k'o-mu-shi** 43°43N 87°38E, pop (1984e) 1 147 300. Capital of Xinjiang autonomous region, NW China; airfield; railway; eight universities; two medical schools; agricultural college (1952); steel, oil, chemicals, textiles, farm machinery; headquarters of Communists in 1930s and 1940s. » China [i]

urus [yooruhs] » **aurochs**

US Marines or **US Marine Corps** World-famous fighting force, created by Congress in 1798, which served with distinction in the Pacific in World War 2 and during the Korean and Vietnam Wars. Marines are traditionally known as 'leathernecks', from the leather collars on the early uniforms. » Marines

US War of Independence » **American Revolution**

USA » **United States of America** [i]

Usborne, Mount 51°35S 58°57W. Mountain on the island of East Falkland, c.65 km/40 ml W of Stanley; highest point in the Falkland Is, rising to 705 m/2 313 ft. » Falkland Islands [i]

Usher » **Ussher**

Uspallata [uspayahta] 32°50S 70°04W. Pass in the Andes between Mendoza (Argentina) and Santiago (Chile); at the foot of Aconcagua; rises to 3 900 m/12 795 ft; statue of Christ of the Andes erected in 1904 to commemorate peaceful boundary settlements. » Andes

Ussher or **Usher, James** (1581–1656) Irish divine, born in Dublin. Educated at Dublin, he was ordained in 1601 and became professor of divinity (1607–21), Bishop of Meath (1620), and Archbishop of Armagh (1625). He settled in England after 1640, and though loyal to the throne was treated with favour by Cromwell. His major work was the *Annales Veteris et Novi Testamenti* (1650–4, Annals of the Old and New Testament), which gave a long-accepted chronology of Scripture, and fixed the Creation at 4004 BC. He died at Reigate, Surrey. » Bible; Cromwell, Oliver

USSR » **Soviet Union** [i]

Ust-Kamenogorsk [oostkamyinuhgawsk] 50°00N 82°36E, pop (1983) 296 000. River-port capital of Vostochno Kazakhstanskaya oblast, Kazakhstan, on R Irtysh; founded as a fortress, 1720; airfield; railway; machinery, metallurgy; zinc, copper, lead. » Kazakhstan

Ustinov, Sir Peter (Alexander) [yustinof] (1921–) British actor and playwright, born in London, the son of White Russian parents. He first appeared on the stage in 1938, and after army service in World War 2, worked in films as an actor, writer, and producer, and in broadcasting as a satirical comedian. A prolific playwright, his works include *The Love of Four Colonels* (1951), *Romanoff and Juliet* (1956), and *Overheard* (1981). He has made over 50 films, and in recent years has established a considerable reputation as a raconteur.

Ustinov [oosteenof], formerly **Izhevsk** 56°49N 53°11E, pop (1983) 594 000. Capital city of Udmurtskaya, Russia; founded, 1760; airfield; railway; university; cultural and educational centre; metalworking, machine building, paper, foodstuffs. » Russia

Usumacinta, River Span **Río** [oosoomaseenta] River in Guatemala and Mexico, formed by the meeting of the Pasión and Chixoy Rivers on the border; follows a winding course NW to enter the Gulf of Mexico at Frontera; length (with the Chixoy, which rises in Guatemala) c.965 km/600 ml; navigable for 480 km/300 ml. » Guatemala; Mexico

Utah [yootaw] pop (1987e) 1 680 000; area 219 880 sq km/84 899 sq ml. State in W USA, divided into 29 counties; the 'Beehive State'; first White exploration by the Spanish, 1540; acquired by the USA through the Treaty of Guadalupe Hidalgo, 1848; arrival of the Mormons, 1847; Utah Territory organized, 1850; several petitions for statehood denied because of the Mormons' practice of polygamy; antagonism between Mormon Church and Federal law over this issue led to the 'Utah War', 1857–8; joined the Union as the 45th state, 1896; capital, Salt Lake City; other chief cities Provo and Ogden; rivers include the Colorado and Green; contains the Great Salt Lake in the NW, the largest salt-water lake in the country (2 590 sq km/1 000 sq ml); L Utah is a freshwater lake S of Great Salt Lake; the Wasatch Range, part of the Rocky Mts, runs N–S through the state; the Uinta Mts in the NE; highest point Kings Peak (4 123 m/13 527 ft); mountainous and sparsely inhabited E region dissected by deep canyons; major cities (containing four-fifths of the population) lie along W foothills of the Wasatch Range; the Great Basin further W; the arid Great Salt Lake Desert in the NW; cattle, sheep, poultry, hay, wheat, barley, sugar-beets; copper, petroleum, coal; aerospace research, machinery, transportation equipment, electronic components, fabricated metals, processed foods; tourism (Arches, Bryce Canyon, Glen Canyon National Recreation Area, Zion National Park). » Guadalupe Hidalgo, Treaty of; Mormons; Salt Lake City; United States of America [i]; RR39

Utamaro, (Kitigawa) (1753–1806) Japanese painter and master of the colour print, born and trained at Edo (modern Tokyo). He came to specialize in portraits of court ladies, in which the gracefulness of face, figure, and flowing robes was depicted in a precisely detailed style which brought him great contemporary success. He also painted flowers, birds and fish, and carried the technique of the *ukiyo-e* to its highest artistic level. » Japanese art; ukiyo-e

uterine tubes » **Fallopian tubes**

uterus A pear-shaped, thick-walled muscular organ of females which projects upwards and forwards above the bladder from the upper part of the vagina; also known as the **womb**. It consists of a *fundus* (the region of the body above the level of entrance of the Fallopian tubes), a *body*, and the *cervix* (separated from the body by a slight narrowing). The lower end of the cervix is surrounded by the upper part of the vagina. At birth the uterus is mainly an abdominal organ, the cervix being relatively large and not distinct from the body. It grows slowly until just before puberty, when its growth is rapid for a time. In old age the uterine wall becomes harder than in the younger woman. The pregnant uterus increases rapidly in size and weight as it rises into the abdomen. In the human female, the non-pregnant uterus is c.7.5 cm/3 in in length and weighs 40 gm/1.4 oz. During pregnancy it increases in size to become c.20 cm/8 in in length and can weigh as much as 1 kg/2.2 lb by the eighth month. Immediately after child-birth it contracts, so that by the end of the eighth week it is back to its normal size (this process is known as *involution*). If implantation does not follow ovulation, the superficial layers of the inner lining of the uterus are shed in response to hormonal changes. » Caesarian section; cervix; dilation and

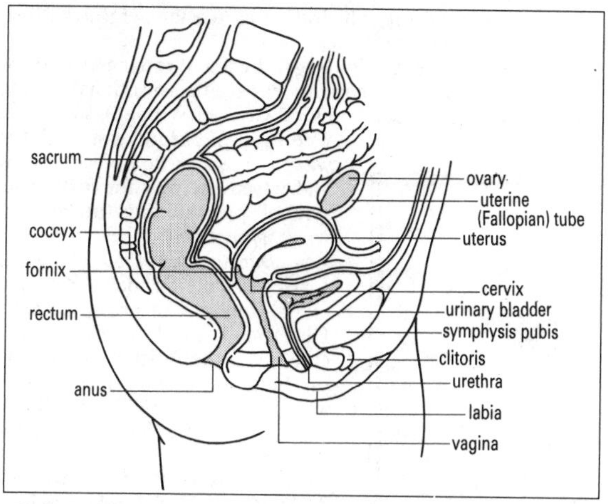

Main female organs of reproduction and surrounding structures

curettage; Fallopian tubes; gynaecology; hysterectomy; menstruation; vagina

Uther Pendragon [yoothuh pen**dra**gn] In the Arthurian legends, a king of Britain, who was the father of King Arthur by Ygerna, the wife of Duke Gorlois of Cornwall. » Arthur

Utica [**yoo**tika] 43°06N 75°14W, pop(1980) 75 632. Seat of Oneida County, C New York, USA, on the Mohawk R; railway; Munson-Williams-Proctor Institute (art); Utica Eisteddfod; dairy farming, textiles. » New York (state)

utilitarianism A teleological ethical theory which maintains that one ought always to act so as to maximize welfare. *Act* utilitarians such as Bentham enjoin us always to choose that action, of the available alternatives, which will produce the most welfare on balance for all people affected. *Rule* utilitarians (Hume, at times) enjoin us to follow those rules, general conformity to which would produce more welfare than alternative rules. An act utilitarian would claim that one ought not to keep a promise if keeping it would be harmful, whereas a rule utilitarian might claim that the promise should be kept because keeping it conforms to a rule, general conformity to which is maximally valuable. » Bentham; Hume, David; teleological ethics

Utopia (Gr 'nowhere') A name for a fictional republic, invented by Sir Thomas More in *Utopia* (1516); hence, any imaginary (and by implication, unattainable) ideal state. Later works include Samuel Butler's *Erewhon* (= Nowhere), 1872; William Morris's *News from Nowhere* (1891); and Aldous Huxley's *Island* (1962). The term **dystopia** refers to the reverse, a nightmare state such as Orwell's *Nineteen Eighty Four* (1948). » English literature; More, Thomas; novel; utopianism

utopianism A general term to describe a political philosophy distinguished by its belief in an ideal future state of global social harmony. Its supporters work to establish the basis for the utopia of the future. It has taken many forms, such as Owenism, anarchism, and other radical forms of social collectivism. » Owen, Robert; political science; Utopia

Utrecht, Lat **Trajectum ad Rhenum** [yoo**trekt**], Dutch [**oo**trekht] 52°06N 5°07E, pop(1984e) 501 357. Capital of Utrecht province, W Netherlands; on R Kromme Rijn and the Amsterdam–Rhine Canal, 32 km/20 ml SSE of Amsterdam; NE end of the Randstad conurbation; political and cultural centre; Union of Utrecht (1579); Treaties of Utrecht (1713–14); archbishopric; railway; university (1634); steel rolling, machinery, building materials, pharmaceuticals, chemicals, fertilizers, electrical products, foodstuffs, textiles, furniture, tourism; Cathedral of St Michael (1254), Maliebaan (1636), Paushuize (1523, Pope's House), several museums and old churches; centre for trade fairs. » Netherlands, The [i]

Utrecht School A group of Dutch painters who went to Rome early in the 17th-c and were deeply influenced by Caravaggio. The most important were Dirck van Baburen (c.1595–1624), Gerard van Honthorst (1590–1656), and Hendrik Terbrugghen (1588–1629). » Carravaggio; Honthorst; school (art); Terbrugghen; Utrecht

Utrecht, Treaties of (1713–14) The peace settlement ending the War of the Spanish Succession, a series of agreements between France, Spain, and the Grand Alliance powers, including the Treaties of Rastadt and Baden. The Bourbons made considerable concessions in terms of territory and dynastic claims, but Louis XIV's grandson, Philip V, retained the throne of Spain. » Philip V; Spanish Succession, War of the

Utrillo, Maurice [oo**tree**loh] (1883–1955) French painter, born in Paris. Despite acute alcoholism, he was a prolific artist, producing picture-postcard views of the streets of Paris, particularly old Montmartre. He died at Le Vésinet. » French art

Uttar Pradesh [**oo**tar pra**daysh**] pop(1981) 110 858 019; area 294 413 sq km/113 643 sq ml. State in NC India, bounded N by Nepal and China; known as the Bengal Presidency until 1833, then divided into provinces of Agra and Oudh; under one administration, 1877; called United Provinces of Agra and Oudh, 1902; renamed as United Provinces, 1935; adopted present name in 1950; capital, Lucknow; governed by a 108-member Legislative Council and a 426-member Legislative Assembly; official language, Hindi; crossed by several rivers and canals; largest producer of foodgrains in India; sugar, edible oils, textiles, leather, paper, chemicals, handloom weaving; coal, copper, limestone, bauxite, silica, phosphorite, pyrophyllite. » India [i]

Uttley, Alison (1884–1976) British author of children's stories, born on a farm in Derbyshire. Educated at Manchester, she was widowed in 1930, and turned to writing to support herself and her young son. *The Country Child* (1931) was followed by a series of books, mainly for children, which revealed her knowledge of the countryside. Many were in the Beatrix Potter tradition, featuring much-loved characters such as Little Grey Rabbit and Sam Pig. » Potter, Beatrix

uvula The conical, midline muscular structure of the soft palate, of variable length in humans (5–20 mm/0.2–0.8 in). It is elevated in swallowing, and is occasionally used in the production of speech sounds (eg the French 'uvular r'). » palate

Uxmal [oosh**mahl**] An ancient Mayan city, 80 km/50 ml S of Merida in the Yucatan peninsula, Mexico. Covering 60 ha/160 acres, it flourished c.600–1000 AD, and was finally abandoned c.1450. Its ceremonial buildings are a notable feature – particularly the Temple of the Magician on its huge pyramid, and the so-called Governor's Palace, erected on a triple terrace. » Mayas

Uzbekistan [uzbeki**stahn**], Russ **Uzbekskaya** pop(1989) 19 905 000; area 447 400 sq km/172 696 sq ml. Republic in C and N Middle Asia, bounded S by Afghanistan and NW by the Aral Sea; large area occupied by the Kyzyl-Kum desert; chief rivers, the Amudarya, Syr-Darya, Chirchik; proclaimed a Soviet Socialist Republic, 1924; declaration of independence, 1991; capital, Tashkent; chief towns, Samarkand, Andizhan, Namangan; coal, oil, oil refining, metallurgy, fertilizers, machinery, cotton, silk, food processing; intensive cultivation with the aid of irrigation; third largest cotton-growing area in the world. » Soviet Union [i]; Tashkent

V

V-1 The abbreviation of *Vergeltungswaffe-1* (Ger 'revenge weapon 1'); small, winged, pilotless aircraft powered by a pulse jet motor, developed by the Luftwaffe. They carried a tonne of high explosive several hundred miles at a speed of c.800 kph/500 mph, slow enough for some to be intercepted by gunfire and high speed aircraft. Between 1944 and 1945, 5 823 were launched against Britain. From the noise of their motors, they were also known as **buzz-bombs**. » bomb; Luftwaffe; V-2

V-2 The abbreviation of *Vergeltungswaffe-2* (Ger 'revenge weapon 2'); a guided ballistic missile developed by the German army, which began rocket experiments under the direction of Wernher von Braun in 1937. Because of its very high speed, it could not be intercepted by gun or aircraft. It was unstoppable, but wildly inaccurate. Between September 1944 and March 1945, 1 054 fell on Britain. » ballistic missile; Braun, Wernher von; V-1

V-effect » **alienation-effect**

Vaal River [vahl] River in South Africa; length 1 200 km/750 ml; a major tributary of the Orange R which it joins SW of Kimberley; rises in SE Transvaal, close to the Swaziland frontier; flows W and then SW along the border between Transvaal and Orange Free State; dammed at Bloemhof. » South Africa [i]

Vaasa, Swedish **Vasa**, formerly **Nikolainkaupunki** 63°06N 21°38E, pop (1982) 54 249. Seaport and capital of Vaasa province, SW Finland; on the Gulf of Bothnia, 352 km/219 ml NW of Helsinki; established, 1606; destroyed by fire, 1852; rebuilt on present site c.1860; airfield; railway; shortest ferry route between Finland and Sweden; ship repairing, metal products, textiles; Vaasa Festival (Jun), Stundars Feast (Jul). » Finland [i]

Vac [vats] 47°49N 19°10E, pop (1984e) 36 000. River port and summer resort town in Pest county, NC Hungary; on R Danube, 32 km/20 ml N of Budapest; bishopric; railway; textiles, footwear, cement, distilling, tools; cathedral, triumphal arch. » Hungary [i]

vaccination A medical procedure which derives its name from *vaccinia*, the virus responsible for cowpox, used by Jenner in 1795 to protect against smallpox. This represented the first type of immunization ever carried out. Today, the term is used in a more general sense, equivalent to *immunization*. » immunization; Jenner

vacuum Any space in which no matter is present. In the laboratory, near vacuum is achieved by pumping out air from an enclosed chamber. Vacua of between 10^{-4} and 10^{-10} Pa are needed in many experiments if results are not to be affected by unwanted gas atoms. Many physics experiments and standard techniques are only possible due to modern high vacuum technology. A perfect vacuum can never be attained; the closest is interstellar space. » physics; vacuum deposition

vacuum deposition A technique for producing thin films of materials. Atoms of a material are evolved from a heated source in the vacuum chamber, and allowed to strike the surface of the substrate to be coated. The technique is used to provide the aluminium coating on compact discs; and printed circuit boards are made by depositing a metal film through a mask. » compact disc; thin films; vacuum

vacuum technology A technology which produces and uses pressures from a thousand to one million million times less than the atmosphere. Thin coatings (metal or non-metal) are made by evaporation in a vacuum, and used in optical instruments or the electronics industry. The technology is used to provide vacuums inside television tubes, X-ray tubes, particle accelerators, and for dehydration at low temperatures ('freeze drying'). » vacuum

Vadim, Roger, originally **Roger Vadim Plemiannikov** (1928–) French film director, born in Paris. His sensational *Et Dieu Créa la Femme* (1956, And God Created Woman), starring his wife Brigitte Bardot as a sex-kitten, was a massive box-office success, and paved the way for further sex-symbol presentations of his later wives, Annette Stroyberg in *Les Liasions Dangereuses* (1959, Dangerous Liaisons), Jane Fonda in *Barbarella* (1968), and his mistress, Catherine Deneuve in *La Vice et La Vertue* (1962, Vice and Virtue). His later US productions, *Night Games* (1979) and *Surprise Party* (1983), did not arouse the same degree of interest. » Bardot

Vaduz 47°08N 9°32E, pop (1983e) 4 927. Capital of Liechtenstein, in the R Rhine valley; metalworking, engineering, tourism, agricultural trade; 12th-c castle (rebuilt, 20th-c), Red House, Prince's picture gallery, state art collection, postal museum. » Liechtenstein

vagina A variable-sized passage, open at its lower end, which communicates at its upper end with the cavity of the uterus. At its lower end the vagina opens into the pudendal cleft between the *labia minora*. In virgins the opening is partly closed by a thin crescent-fold (the *hymen*). In the human female the vagina is directed upwards and backwards making an angle of 90° with the axis of the cervix. » candidiasis; cervix; gonorrhoea; syphilis; trichomoniasis; uterus [i]; venereal disease

vaginismus A spasm of the muscles surrounding the entry of the vagina, preventing entry of the penis (or an inanimate object). This can be treated by counselling, which includes educational explanation concerning sexual intercourse, combined with the use of behavioural techniques which are successful in most cases. » dyspareunia

vagus [vayguhs] The tenth cranial nerve, arising from the medulla oblongata. It descends in the neck supplying the muscles of the larynx and pharynx, and then passes through the thorax into the abdomen. In the thorax it supplies the oesophagus, trachea, lungs, heart, and great vessels, while in the abdomen it supplies the stomach, the small and part of the large intestine, the pancreas, and the liver. The vagus carries out a wide range of regulatory functions, for example decreasing heart rate and stimulating gastric acid secretion. » acetylcholine; medulla oblongata; nervous system

Váh, River River in E Czechoslovakia, rising on slopes of the Low Tatra as two headstreams; flows S to meet R Danube at Komárno; length 392 km/244 ml. » Czechoslovakia [i]

Vakhtangov, Evgeny Bagrationovich [vakh**tang**of] (1883–1923) Russian theatre director, actor, and teacher, born at Vladikavkaz, Armenia. He became an actor with The Moscow Art Theatre in 1911, and from 1920 was head of the Third Studio, which after 1926 became the Vakhtangov Theatre. In all aspects of his work he made a synthesis of Stanislavsky's and Meyerhold's methods, stressing the expressiveness of the actor. His concept of 'fantastic realism' informed his finest and most influential productions, notably Anski's *The Dybbuk*, staged for the Habima Theatre in 1922. He died in Moscow at the height of his career. » Habima; Meyerhold; Moscow Art Theatre; Stanislavsky; theatre

Valcamonica A world heritage site in Lombardy, N Italy, where 130 000 rock engravings dating from the 7th-c BC to the 1st-c AD have been excavated. The carvings have proved to be an important record for reconstructing the economic and cultural life of the period. » Lombardy

valence [**vay**luhns] The combining power of an atom expressed either as (1) the **covalence**, or net number of bonds an atom makes, weighting double bonds as two, etc, or (2) the **electrovalence**, essentially equivalent to the oxidation state. Valence electrons are those furthest from the nucleus of an atom which are involved in chemical change. » atom; chemical bond; VSEPR

Valencia (Spain) [va**len**sia], Span [va**len**thia] pop (1981) 3 646 778; area 23 260 sq km/8 978 sq ml. Autonomous region of E Spain, occupying a narrow coastal area from the Ebro delta to R Segura; a former Moorish kingdom, under Spanish rule from 1238; C plateau cut by several rivers; includes tourist resorts on the Costa Blanca and Costa del Azahar; chief town, Valencia, pop (1981) 751 734, on R Turia; third largest city in Spain; archbishopric; airport; railway; car ferries to Balearics and Canary Is; university (1500); tourism, wine, fruit, chemicals, shipyards, textiles, vehicles, ironwork, silk; ceramics museum, fine arts museum, Serranos military towers (14th-c), cathedral (13th–15th-c); Fiesta of La Virgen de los Desamparados (May), St James fair (Jul). » Costa Blanca; Costa del Azahar; El Cid; Spain [i]

Valencia (Venezuela) [va**len**sia] 10°11N 67°59W, pop (1981) 616 177. Capital of Carabobo state, N Venezuela; on R Cabriales, 5 km/3 ml from L Valencia; third largest city in Venezuela; railway; university (1852); noted for its oranges; agricultural trade; cathedral (18th-c). » Venezuela [i]

valentine (card) » **St Valentine's Day**

Valentino, byname of Valentino Garavani (1933–) Italian fashion designer, born in Rome. He studied fashion in Milan and Paris, then worked for Dessès and Laroche in Paris. He opened his own house in Rome in 1959, but achieved worldwide recognition with his 1962 show in Florence. » fashion

Valentino, Rudolph [valuhn**tee**noh] (1895–1926) US film actor, born at Castellaneta, Italy. He studied agriculture, but emigrated to the USA in 1913, and first appeared on stage as a dancer. In 1919 he made his screen debut in *The Four Horsemen of the Apocalypse*, and his performances in *The Sheikh* (1921), *Blood and Sand* (1922), and other silent film dramas made him the leading 'screen lover' of the 1920s. He died suddenly in New York City, at the height of his fame, and his funeral resembled that of a popular ruler.

Valera, Eamon de » **de Valera, Eamon**

valerian A perennial herb native to Europe, Asia. Valerian (*Valeriana officinalis*) has pinnate leaves; toothed leaflets; flowers 5 mm/0.2 in diameter, pink, in dense terminal heads; the corolla tube 5-lobed, pouched at base; fruits with a parachute of feathery hairs. The related and similar **red valerian** (*Centranthus ruber*) has undivided, oval leaves and red or white spurred flowers. (Family: *Valerianaceae*.) » herb; perennial; pinnate

Valéry, (Ambroise) Paul (Toussaint Jules) [val**ay**ree] (1871–1945) French poet and critic, born at Sète. He settled in Paris in 1892 and after writing a great deal of poetry relapsed into a 20 years' silence, taken up with mathematics and philosophical speculations, later published as *Cahiers* (29 vols, 1957–60). He emerged in 1917 with a new Symbolist poetic outlook and technique in *La Jeune Parque* (1917, The Young Fate) and *Charmes* (1922). He died in Paris. » French literature; literary criticism; poetry; Symbolism

Valetta » **Valletta**

Valhalla [val**hal**a] In Norse mythology, a great hall built by Odin to house warriors who die bravely in battle. Every night they get drunk, and every day fight to the death and rise again. After this intensive training they will form an army to help the gods in the Last Battle. » Germanic religion; Odin; Ragnarok

Valium » **benzodiazepines**

Valkyries [val**kee**reez, **val**kireez] In Norse and German mythology, the Maidens of Odin, who were also called Choosers of the Slain. They rode out with the Wild Hunt, or appeared as swans, in order to collect warriors killed in battle for Valhalla. » Odin; Valhalla

Valladolid [valyado**leeth**] 41°38N 4°43W, pop (1981) 330 242. Capital of Valladolid province, Castilla-León, NWC Spain; on R Pisuerga, 193 km/120 ml NE of Madrid; archbishopric; airport; railway; university (1346); vehicles, cement, ironwork, flour, leather goods; Columbus died here; cathedral (16th-c), Cervantes museum, Santa Cruz College; International Film Week (Apr), fair and fiesta (Sep), Festival of Spain (Oct–Nov). » Columbus, Christopher; Spain [i]

Valle d'Aosta [**val**ay da**os**ta], Fr **Val d'Aoste** pop (1981) 112 353; area 3 263 sq km/1 259 sq ml. Autonomous region of Italy, bounded W by France and N by Switzerland; tourism, winegrowing, livestock; population mostly French-speaking; an important valley since ancient times, being the access route to the Great and Little St Bernard Passes through the Alps. » Alps; Italy [i]

Vallée de Mai [**val**ay duh **me**] Nature reserve on Praslin I in the Seychelles; a world heritage area. It is noted as the unique habitat of the coco-de-mer palm: 4 000 trees, many of them over 800 years old, grow in the reserve. » Seychelles

Valles Marineris A vast, complex system of interconnected canyons stretching for c.4 000 km/2 500 ml around Mars; located just S of the equator, and extending from near the summit of a region of extensive volcanism ('Tharsis') to the E until it merges with a region characterized as 'chaotic' terrain. Generally the canyons are over 3 km/1½ ml deep and over 100 km/60 ml wide; in the central section they are over 7 km/4 ml deep and 600 km/350 ml wide. There are giant landslides in places along their steep walls. They were discovered by Mariner 9 orbiter in 1972, and studied in detail by Viking orbiters. » Mariner programme; Mars (astronomy); Viking project

Valletta or **Valetta** [**val**eta] 35°54N 14°32E, pop (1983e) 14 040. Capital of Malta, on a peninsula between the Grand Harbour and the Marsamxett Harbour; a world heritage site; founded by the Knights of St John, 1566; airport (Luqa); university (1769); dockyards, yachting centre, transshipment centre, tourism; Palace of the Grand Masters, St John's co-cathedral (16th-c), National Museum of Fine Arts. » Malta [i]

valley An elongated trough in the Earth's surface, most commonly formed by the erosional action of rivers over a long period of time. It may also be carved out by glaciers, in which case they are U-shaped rather than (as in river valleys) V-shaped. Extensional movements of the Earth's crust may produce large rift valleys by faulting. » glacier; rift valley [i]; river [i]

Valley Forge State park in Chester County, Pennsylvania, USA, 7 km/4 ml SE of Phoenixville, on the R Schuylkill; winter headquarters of George Washington, 1777–8; renowned for the endurance and loyalty shown by the troops during the severe winter. » American Revolution; Pennsylvania; Washington, George

Valley of the Kings A remote limestone wadi on the W bank of the R Nile at Luxor, 650 km/400 ml S of Cairo: its Arabic name is *Wadi Biban el Moluk* ('The Valley of the Gates of the Kings'). Cut into its walls are the tombs of the Egyptian kings of the New Kingdom (XVIII–XX Dynasties, 1550–1070 BC), their families, and retainers. Those of Rameses VI, Horemheb, Amenhotep II, Tuthmosis III, Seti I, and Tutankhamun are of particular note. » Egyptian history, Ancient [i]; Luxor; pharaoh

Valois [**val**wa] A ruling dynasty of France from the accession of Philip VI, Count of Valois (1328) to the death of Henry III (1589). The succession was maintained in the direct male line from the 14th-c until Louis XII of the Orleans branch assumed the crown (1498). The last three Valois kings – Francis II (1559–60), Charles IX (1560–74), and Henry III (1574–89) – were all childless. » Charles IX (of France); Henry III (of France); Louis XII; Orleans, House of; Philip VI

Valois, Dame Ninette de, originally **Edris Stannus** [**val**wah] (1898–) British dancer, born at Blessington, Co Wicklow, Ireland. She first appeared in pantomime at the Lyceum in 1914, and made a European tour with Diaghilev (1923–5). She became director of ballet at the Abbey Theatre, Dublin, and in 1931 founded the Sadler's Wells Ballet, continuing as its artistic director until 1963. She is regarded as the pioneer of British ballet, both in her own choreography – such as *The Rake's Progress* (1935) and *Checkmate* (1937) – and in the development of a school and two major companies. She was created a Dame in 1951. » ballet; Diaghilev; Royal Ballet

Valparaíso [valpara**ee**soh] 33°03S 71°07W, pop (1982) 266 577.

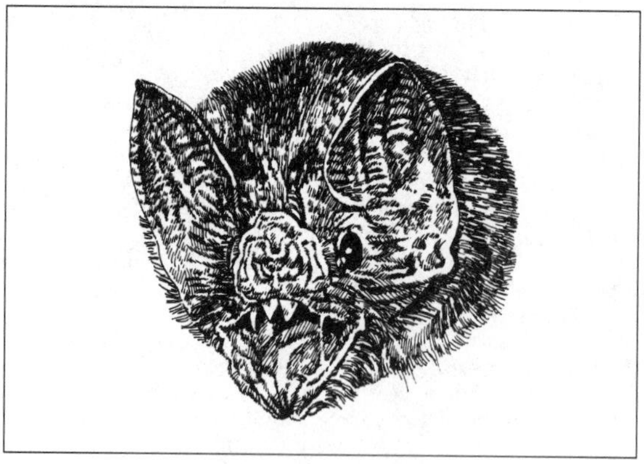

Vampire bat

Port and capital of Valparaíso province, C Chile; Chile's main port and a major commercial centre; lower and upper areas, connected by winding roads and funicular railways; founded, 1536; most old buildings destroyed by earthquakes; railway; cathedral; Naval Academy; two universities (1926, 1928); chemicals, textiles, sugar, clothing, vegetable oils; lift runs from the Plaza Aduana to the Paseo Veintiuno de Mayo terrace on Cerro Artillería, giving panoramic view; firework display on the bay at New Year. » Chile [i]; Viña del Mar

value-added The value which is added to the materials and components bought in by a company. It is the sum of wages, interest payments, depreciation, and profits.

value-added tax » **VAT**

valve » **thermionic valve**

vampire In Slavic folklore a dead person of either sex who cannot rest in the grave, but rises at night to prey on and suck the blood of the living (the bite of a vampire turning the victim also into a vampire). Vampires are repelled by crucifixes, garlic, and daylight, and can be destroyed by being beheaded or pierced through the heart with a wooden stake. Bram Stoker's *Dracula* (1897) popularized the myth. » folklore

vampire bat A bat of family *Desmodontidae*, native to the New World tropics; sharp pointed incisor teeth; no tail; flies low over ground; drinks blood; lands near resting animal and walks to it using wings and legs; may trim hair or feathers with teeth; makes shallow incision with incisors (prey usually not disturbed) and laps blood; tongue has grooves to carry blood to mouth; bat's saliva prevents blood clotting, and wound may bleed for eight hours; feeding may take two hours; at least 20 ml of blood drunk per night. There are three species: the **common** or **great vampire** (*Desmodus rotundus*), the **white-winged vampire** (*Diaemus youngi*), and the **hairy-legged vampire** (*Diphylla ecaudata*). Bats of the family *Megadermatidae*, and some species of *Phyllostomidae*, are called **false vampires** (they do not drink blood). » bat

van Allen, James (Alfred) (1914–) US physicist and pioneer in space physics, born at Mt Pleasant, Iowa. Educated at Iowa (Wesleyan College and University), he became director of high altitude research at Johns Hopkins in 1946, where he was involved in the launching of the USA's first satellite, Explorer I (1958), and professor of physics at Iowa in 1951. Using data from satellite observations, he showed the existence of two zones of radiation around the Earth. » Explorer I; magnetosphere; van Allen radiation belts

van Allen radiation belts Two rings of high-energy-charged particles surrounding the Earth, probably originating in the Sun and trapped by the Earth's magnetic field. The lower, more energetic belt is at c.300 km/185 ml from the Earth's surface; the outer belt at c.16 000 km/10 000 ml. They were discovered in 1958 by US physicist James van Allen from satellite data. » geomagnetic field; magnetosphere; van Allen

van Buren, Martin (1782–1862) US statesman and eighth President (1837–41), born and died at Kinderhook, New York. He became a lawyer, state Attorney-General (1816), Senator (1821), Governor of New York (1828), Secretary of State (1829), and Vice-President (1832). In 1824 he was a member of the group which founded the Democratic Party. Arriving in office during the financial panic of 1837, his measure introducing a treasury independent of private banks created opposition, and he was overwhelmingly defeated by the Whigs in 1840. In 1848 he ran unsuccessfully for President as the Free Soil candidate, in opposition to the spread of slavery. » Democratic Party; slavery; Whigs

van de Graaff, Robert (Jemison) (1901–67) US physicist, born at Tuscaloosa, Alabama. An engineering graduate, he studied physics at the Sorbonne and Oxford, where he constructed an improved type of electrostatic generator (later called the **van de Graaf generator**). At the Massachusetts Institute of Technology, he developed this into the **van de Graaf accelerator**, which became a major tool of atomic and nuclear physicists. » particle accelerators; van de Graaff generator

van de Graaff generator A machine for producing high electrostatic potential differences, invented by US physicist Robert van de Graaff in 1931. An electric charge deposited by electrical discharge onto a moving rubber loop is transported to the interior of a hollow metal dome, where it is transferred to the dome and stored. Potential differences of several million volts may be obtained. The device provided an early type of particle accelerator. » corona discharge; static electricity; van de Graaff

van de Velde, Henri [van duh **vel**duh] (1863–1957) Belgian architect, born at Antwerp. He began as a painter before pioneering the modern functional style of architecture. He established the famous Weimar School of Arts and Crafts (1906) from which developed the Bauhaus. Gropius was his pupil. » Art Nouveau; Bauhaus; Gropius

van de Velde, Willem (the Elder) (c.1611–93) Dutch marine painter, born at Leyden. He came to England in 1657, and painted large pictures of sea battles in Indian ink and black paint for Charles II and James II. His son, **Willem (the Younger)** (1633–1707), also born at Leyden, followed his father to England, and became court painter to Charles II in 1674. A second son, **Adriaen** (1636–72), was a landscape painter. » Dutch art

van der Goes, Hugo [khoos] (c.1440–82) Flemish painter, born (probably) at Ghent. Dean of the painters' guild at Ghent (1473–5), he then entered the monastery of the Rode Klooster, Brussels, but continued to paint. His works include the large Portinari altarpiece in the Uffizi, Florence. » altarpiece; Flemish art

van der Post, Sir Laurens (Jan) [van duh **post**] (1906–) South African writer, born at Philippolis. He served with the commandos during World War 2, and on his return to South Africa made several voyages of exploration to the interior. He has written novels, but is best known for his books in the mixed genres of travel, anthropology, and metaphysical speculation. These include *Venture to the Interior* (1951) and *The Lost World of the Kalahari* (1958). The influence of Jung is pervasive in his work. » African literature; Jung; novel

van der Waals, Johannes Diderik [van duh **vahlz**] (1837–1923) Dutch physicist, born at Leyden. Professor of physics at Amsterdam (1877–1908), he extended the classical 'ideal' gas laws (of Boyle and Charles) to describe the behaviour of real gases, deriving the **van der Waals equation of state** in 1873. This work led others to liquefy a range of common gases, and also provided new basic concepts for physical chemistry. He was awarded the Nobel Prize for Physics in 1910, and died in Amsterdam. » gas 1; gas laws; van der Waals interaction

van der Waals forces [van duh **vahlz**] Weak attractive forces which apply between molecules of all kinds. They are strongest between polarizable molecules, generally those containing atoms of high atomic number or having multiple bonds. » molecule; van der Waals

van der Waals interaction [van duh **vahlz**] A weak electrostatic interaction between neutral atoms that decreases with distance r between atoms as r^{-6}; discovered by Dutch physicist Johannes van der Waals in 1873. It results from the electric dipoles on atoms, which are either permanent or temporarily induced. It is responsible for the liquefaction of helium and other noble gases. » electric dipole moment; noble gases; van der Waals

Van Diemen's Land » **Tasmania**

van Dyck, Sir Anthony [van **diyk**] (1599–1641) Flemish painter, one of the great masters of portraiture, born at Antwerp. He worked under Rubens, who greatly influenced his style, visited England in 1620, and from 1621 travelled widely in Italy, where he painted portraits and religious subjects. By 1627 he was back in Antwerp, and in 1632 went to London, where he was knighted by Charles I, and made painter-in-ordinary. His work greatly influenced the British school of portraiture in the 18th-c, and left a thoroughly romantic glimpse of the Stuart monarchy, in his paintings of the royal family and most of the notables at the time. He died in London. » Flemish art; Rubens; Stuarts

van Eyck, Jan [van **iyk**] (?–1441) Flemish painter, born (possibly) at Maaseik or Maastricht. He worked for John of Bavaria at The Hague (1422–4), and from 1425 for Philip Duke of Burgundy, mainly at Bruges. The first and greatest master of the new realistic approach to painting in the 15th-c Netherlands, his skill is well-attested by the highly-finished 'Arnolfini Wedding Portrait' (1434, National Gallery, London). He died at Bruges. » Flemish art

van Gogh, Vincent (Willem) [hokh], Br Eng [gof], US Eng [goh] (1853–90) Dutch painter, born at Groot-Zundert. At 16 he worked in an art dealer's, then became a teacher, and an evangelist at Le Borinage (1878–80). In 1881 he went to Brussels to study art, and settled at The Hague, where he produced his early drawings and watercolours. At Nuenen he painted his first masterpiece, a domestic scene of peasant poverty, 'The Potato Eaters' (1885, Amsterdam). He then studied in Paris (1886–8), where he developed his individual style of brushwork and a more colourful palette. At Arles, the Provençal landscape gave him many of his best subjects, such as 'Sunflowers' (1888, Tate, London) and 'The Bridge' (1888, Cologne). He showed increasing signs of mental disturbance (after a quarrel with Gauguin, he cut off part of his own ear), and was placed in an asylum at St Rémy (1889–90). He then stayed at Auvers-sur-Oise, where at the scene of his last painting, 'Cornfields with Flight of Birds' (Amsterdam), he shot himself, and died two days later. One of the pioneers of Expressionism, he used colour primarily for its emotive appeal, and profoundly influenced the Fauves and other experimenters of 20th-c art. » Dutch art; Expressionism; Fauvism; Gauguin; watercolour

Van, Lake, Turkish **Van Gölü** area 3 173 sq km/1 225 sq ml. Salt lake in mountainous E Anatolia, Turkey; largest lake in the country; length, 120 km/75 ml; width, 80 km/50 ml; ferry service; salt extraction, fishing; home of the ancient Armenian civilization. » Armenia (Turkey); Turkey [i]

van Meegeren, Han or **Henricus** [van **may**guhruhn] (1889–1947) Dutch artist and forger, born at Deventer. In 1945 he was accused of selling art treasures to the Germans. To clear himself, he confessed to having forged the pictures, and also the famous 'Supper at Emmaus', which had been 'discovered' in 1937, and was widely accepted to be by Vermeer. In 1947 he was imprisoned, and died a few weeks later.

van't Hoff, Jacobus Henricus » **Hoff, Jacobus Henricus van't**

van Vleck, John (Hasbrouck) (1899–1980) US physicist, born at Middletown, Connecticut. He was educated mainly at Harvard, where he returned to teach in 1934. He founded the modern theory of magnetism based on quantum theory, and also devised theories of magnetic behaviour in crystals. He shared the Nobel Prize for Physics in 1977, and died at Cambridge, Massachusetts. » crystals; magnetism; quantum mechanics

vanadium [van**ay**dium] V, element 23, density 6.1 g/cm^3, melting point 1 890°C. A transition metal, not occurring free in nature, and often replacing phosphorus as an impurity in phosphate rocks. The main uses for the metal are in steel production, usually in combination with chromium. Its compounds show many colours and oxidation states, +2, +3, +4, and +5 all being easily prepared. The stability of the +5 state accounts for its interchangeability with phosphorus. » chemical elements; phosphorus; transition elements; RR90

Vanbrugh, Sir John (1664–1726) English playwright and Baroque architect, born and died in London. He became a leading spirit in society life, scored a success with his comedies *The Relapse* (1696) and *The Provok'd Wife* (1697), and became a theatre manager with Congreve. As architect, he designed Castle Howard, Yorkshire in 1702. He became comptroller of royal works in 1714, and was knighted the same year. » Baroque (art and architecture); Congreve

Vance, Cyrus R(oberts) (1917–) US lawyer and statesman, born at Clarksburg, West Virginia. He studied at Yale and served in the navy, before entering private law practice. He held a number of government posts, and served as Secretary of State under President Carter, resigning in 1980 over the handling of the crisis when US diplomats were being held hostage in Iran. » Carter, Jimmy

Vancouver 49°13N 123°06W, pop (1981) 414 281; (Greater Vancouver) 1 310 600. Seaport in SW British Columbia, SW Canada, opposite Vancouver I, between Burrard Inlet (N) and Fraser R (S); third largest city in Canada; settled c.1875, named Granville; reached by railway, 1886; city and modern name, 1886; airport; railway; two universities (1908, 1963); shipbuilding, fishing, oil refining, distilling, brewing, timber, trucks and trailers, machinery, tourism; major league team, Vancouver Canucks (ice hockey); Lipsett Indian Museum in Hastings Park; Stanley Park, with zoo, aquarium, and totem poles; art gallery; Lions Gate Bridge (longest bridge in the Commonwealth); Chinatown, second largest Chinese community in N America; Pacific National Exhibition (Aug). » British Columbia

Vancouver, George (c.1758–98) British navigator and explorer, born at King's Lynn, Norfolk. He sailed with Cook on his second and third voyages and, promoted captain (1794), did survey work in Australia, New Zealand, and the W coast of N America, sailing round the island later named after him (1795). He died at Richmond, Surrey. » Cook, James

Vandals A Germanic people, originally perhaps from the Baltic area, who settled in the Danube valley in the 4th-c. Pushed W by the Huns, they invaded Gaul (406), crossed into Spain, conquered Roman Africa (429–39), and sacked Rome (455). The Byzantine general Belisarius reconquered N Africa in 533–4. » Belisarius; Gaul; Huns; Roman history [i]

Vanderbilt, Cornelius (1794–1877) US financier, born on Staten I, New York. At 16 he bought a boat, and ferried passengers and goods; by 40 he had become the owner of steamers running to Boston and up the Hudson. In 1849, during the gold rush, he established a route to California; and during the Crimean War, a line of steamships to Le Havre. At 70 he became a railroad financier. He endowed Vanderbilt University at Nashville, Tennessee, and died in New York City.

Vanderbilt, Harold S(tirling) (1884–1970) US industrialist, born at Oakdale, New York. He developed the current scoring system for contract bridge while playing aboard the SS *Finland* in 1925 on a journey from Los Angeles to Havannah. » bridge (recreation)

Vane, Sir Henry (1613–62) English statesman, born at Hadlow, Kent. Educated at Westminster and Oxford, he travelled in Europe, became a Puritan, and sailed for New England (1635), where he was Governor of Massachusetts; but his advocacy of toleration lost him popularity, and he returned in 1637. He entered parliament, became joint Treasurer of the Navy, and was knighted (1640). He helped to impeach Strafford, promoted the Solemn League and Covenant, and was a strong supporter of the parliamentary cause in the Civil War. During the Commonwealth he was appointed one of the Council of State (1649–53), but he opposed Cromwell's becoming Lord Protector in 1653, and retired from politics. On Cromwell's death he returned to public life (1659), opposed the Restoration, and was imprisoned and executed. » Cromwell, Oliver; English Civil War; Protectorate; Solemn League and Covenant; Strafford

Vänern, Lake [**ve**nern] area 5 585 sq km/2 156 sq ml. Lake in SW Sweden; length, 146 km/91 ml; maximum depth, 98 m/321 ft; largest lake in Sweden; chief towns on its banks, Karlstad, Vänersborg, Lidköping, Mariestad. » Sweden [i]

vanilla An evergreen climbing orchid, native to C America. The large green flowers are followed by slender pods up to 15 cm/6 in long, which turn black when dried and contain the essence *vanillin*, used as flavouring. (*Vanilla planifolia*. Family: *Orchidaceae*.) » climbing plant; evergreen plants; orchid [i]

vanitas A type of still-life picture, produced mainly in Leyden in the 17th-c, in which symbolic objects such as skulls, hourglasses, and old books are arranged to remind us that life is short and uncertain. The name comes from the Bible (*Eccles* 1. 2): *vanitas vanitatum* ('vanity of vanities'). » still life

Vannes [van], ancient **Dariorigum** 47°40N 2°47W, pop (1982) 45 397. Port and capital of Morbihan department, NW France; on Gulf of Morbihan, 107 km/66 ml WNW of Nantes; railway; animal feedstuffs, chicken and turkey processing, textiles, shipbuilding, petfoods; picturesque Old Town, Château Gaillard (Brittany's first parliament building), Cathedral of St-Pierre (13th–19th-c). » Brittany

Vanua Levu [vanooa layvoo] area 5 556 sq km/2 145 sq ml. Mountainous volcanic island in SW Pacific Ocean; second largest of the Fiji Is, 32 km/20 ml NE of Viti Levu; length 176 km/109 ml; chief town, Labasa; coconut plantations; sugar, copra, gold, tourism; Great Sea Reef the third longest barrier reef in the world. » Fiji

Vanuatu [vanooahtoo], formerly **New Hebrides**, official name **Republic of Vanuatu** pop (1990e) 147 000; area 14 763 sq km/ 5 698 sq ml. An irregular Y-shaped island chain in the SW Pacific Ocean, 400 km/250 ml NE of New Caledonia; 12 islands and 60 islets, the largest being Espiritu Santo (3 947 sq km/ 1 523 sq ml), Malekula (2 024 sq km/781 sq ml), and Efate (985 sq km/380 sq ml); capital, Vila (on Efate); timezone GMT +11; population mainly Melanesian (95%); chief religion, Roman Catholicism; national language, Bislama; official languages, English, French; unit of currency, the vatu; mainly volcanic and rugged, with raised coral beaches fringed by reefs; highest peak (on Espiritu Santo) rises to 1 888 m/6 194 ft; several active volcanoes; densely forested, with narrow strips of cultivated land on coast; tropical climate, with a hot and rainy season (Nov–Apr) when cyclones may occur; annual temperatures at Vila, 16–33°C, average annual rainfall 2 310 mm/ 91 in; visited by the Portuguese, 1606; under Anglo-French administration as the condominium of the New Hebrides, 1906; independence as the Republic of Vanuatu, 1980; governed by a president, prime minister, and cabinet, and a representative 46-member Assembly; agriculture includes yams, breadfruit, taro, manioc, bananas, copra, cocoa, coffee, cattle, pigs; manganese, fish processing, foodstuffs, crafts; tourism rapidly increasing, especially from cruise ships. » Melanesia; Pacific Ocean; Vila; RR27 national holidays; RR66 political leaders

vapour pressure The pressure exerted by the gas (vapour) surrounding a solid or liquid. A solid or liquid is always surrounded by a vapour of the same substance in equilibrium with it. For example, at room temperature, the vapour pressure of water is c.0.2% of atmospheric pressure. Vapour pressure increases with temperature. » boiling point; condensation (physics); humidity

Varanasi » **Benares**

Vargas, Getúlio (Dornelles) (1883–1954) President of Brazil (1930–45, 1951–4), born at São Borja. He was elected a Federal deputy in 1923, and in 1930 seized power by revolution. His government did much to unify Brazil. From 1937, when he dissolved congress and suppressed all political parties and trade unions, he governed as a mild dictator. In 1945 he was ousted by popular clamour for a democratic constitution, but under this was voted back to office (1950). Four years later, in the face of mounting opposition, he committed suicide in Rio de Janeiro. » Brazil [i]

variable star Any star with a luminosity that is not constant as a function of time. The variation can be regular or irregular. Stars may vary in their apparent magnitude for several reasons. In an *eclipsing binary*, the pair of stars periodically eclipse, as seen from the Earth, and the apparent magnitude of the pair falls when one member is concealed from view. Also, many stars *pulsate*, and the change in size and surface temperature leads to a consequential change in luminosity. The principal types are Cepheid variables, RR Lyrae stars, and the long-period Mira variables. » Cepheid variable; Mira Ceti Mira; RR Lyrae variable; star

variance In mathematics, a measure of the spread or dispersion from the mean of a set of scores. If m_x is the mean of the scores $x_1, x_2, x_3, \ldots x_n$, the variance s_x^2 is given by $\frac{1}{n}\sum_{i=1}^{n}(x_i - m_x)^2$. The standard deviation is the square root of the variance. The **covariance** s_{xy} of a sample of n pairs of scores $(x_i y_i)$ is $\frac{1}{n}\sum_{i=1}^{n}(x_i - m_x)(y_i - m_y)$. This measures the association between the two variables x and y. » correlation

variations (music) A type of musical composition in which a theme is presented a number of times in different guises or with fresh embellishments. The theme itself may be the composer's own (eg Haydn's *Variations in F minor* for piano), or someone else's (eg Brahm's *Variations on a Theme of Paganini*), or a folksong (eg Delius's *Brigg Fair*). Elgar's *Enigma Variations* (on an original theme) are musical portraits of himself and friends 'pictured within'. » chaconne; partita; passacaglia; rhapsody

varicose veins Distended veins which result from obstruction to the flow of blood within them or incompetence of their valves. They may occur anywhere in the body, but the veins in the legs are most often affected. Prolonged standing and familial factors contribute to their development. When severe, they lead to pain and swelling of the affected leg, which may develop skin ulceration. » phlebitis; vein

Varna, also **Stalin** (1949–56), Lat **Odessus** 43°13N 27°56E, pop (1981) 293 950. Resort and capital of Varna province, E Bulgaria; in a bay of the Black Sea, 469 km/291 ml E of Sofia; site of Hungarian defeat by the Turks (1444); third largest town and largest harbour in Bulgaria; airport; railway; shipbuilding, chemical industry, power production, food processing, tourism; Roman thermae and baths; gold hoard (3500–3000 BC) discovered in the Varna necropolis (1972); museums, theatre, art gallery, opera house; Summer International Music Festival. » Bulgaria [i]

varnish A liquid which dries to a hard protective transparent or decorative film, consisting of a solution of gums in oil with a thinner such as turpentine. *Spirit varnishes* have resins (such as, notably, shellac) dissolved in alcohol (industrial or methylated spirit). Modern varieties have polymers such as polyurethane in solvents. The ancient Japanese and Chinese lacquers consisted simply of the exudation of certain trees, with colours added. » polymerization; resin

varnish tree » **lacquer tree**

Varro, Marcus Terentius (116–27 BC) Roman scholar and author, born at Reate. Educated at Athens, he fought under Pompey, and in the Civil War was legate in Spain. Pardoned by Caesar, he was appointed public librarian (47 BC), but under the second triumvirate Antony placed his name on the list of the proscribed. His property was restored by Augustus. He wrote over 600 books, covering a wide range of subject matter; only his work on agriculture and part of his book on Latin survive. » Antonius; Augustus; Caesar; Latin literature

varve dating A method of dating the ages of Pleistocene shales, by counting the layers (*varves*) found in the fine lake sediments deposited by the water flowing from glaciers. The layered arrangement arises from the alternation of fine and coarser material from winter to summer. » Pleistocene epoch; shale; stratification

varying hare » **snowshoe hare**

Vasa (Finland) » **Vaasa**

Vasa (Swedish history) A royal dynasty that provided all Swedish monarchs from 1523 to 1818, with only two exceptions. It was founded by Gustavus I (reigned 1523–60), who led the country's conversion to the Lutheran Reformation and ousted foreign powers. Great military leaders Gustavus II Adolphus (reigned 1611–32) and Charles XII (reigned 1682–1718) made Sweden into a major European power before the latter's defeat by the Russians at Poltava (1709). » Charles XII; Gustavus I; Gustavus II; Luther, Martin

Vasarely, Viktor [vazaraylee] (1908–) Hungarian painter, born at Pecs. He began as a medical student in Budapest before studying art (1928–9) at the 'Budapest Bauhaus' (the Mühely Academy), moving to Paris in 1930. His particular kind of geometrical-abstract painting, which he began to practise c.1947, pioneered the visually disturbing effects that were later called Op Art. He has also experimented with Kinetic Art. » Bauhaus; kinetic art; Op Art

Vasari, Giorgio [vazahree] (1511–74) Italian art historian, born at Arezzo. He studied under Andrea del Sarto, and lived mostly at Florence and Rome. He was an architect and painter, best known for his design of the Uffizi in Florence, but today his fame rests on his *Le Vite de' più eccellenti architetti, pittori, e scultori italiani* (1550, The Lives of the Most Eminent Italian Architects, Painters, and Sculptors), which remains the major source of information on its subject. » Renaissance; Sarto; Uffizi

vascular plant Any plant possessing xylem and phloem, distinct conducting tissues which together make up the vascular system; they include flowering plants, gymnosperms, ferns, clubmosses, and horsetails, and in some classifications form the Division *Tracheophyta*. Additional differences between vascular plants and the non-vascular bryophytes and algae are the presence of stomata, and the sporophyte as the dominant generation. The lack of fossil links between tracheophytes and the mosses and algae is cited as evidence that these groups evolved separately. » alternation of generations; clubmoss; flowering plants; gymnosperms; horsetail; phloem; sporophyte; stomata; vascular tissue; xylem

vascular tissue The conducting tissues, both xylem and phloem, which transport water, minerals, and sap through a plant, and help provide internal support. It forms thin strands called *vascular bundles*, with xylem to the inside and phloem to the outside, separated by a cambium layer which provides for secondary growth of the conducting tissues. These bundles are scattered throughout the stem or arranged in a ring. In trees and shrubs the bundles eventually join to form a band. » cambium; graft (botany) [i]; phloem; shrub; tree [i]; xylem

vasectomy » **sterilization 1**

vasoactive intestinal polypeptide (VIP) A chemical substance (a 28-amino-acid polypeptide) first discovered in pig intestine and later found in other mammals. It is thought to be a NANC type of neurotransmitter regulating blood flow, glandular and intestinal secretions, and smooth muscle relaxation (especially in the airways). It is present in high concentration in the human penis, where it might be involved in erection. » NANC; peptide

vasopressin » **antidiuretic hormone**

vassal A freeman who had acknowledged the lordship of a superior by giving homage and swearing fealty, normally in return for a fief. Obligations existed on both sides. The lord's default, especially in giving protection, rendered the relationship void, as did the disobedient vassal's withholding of military assistance and general support. » feudalism

VAT (value-added tax) An indirect tax levied upon certain products or services as a percentage of their value. The customer pays the tax on top of the basic price. In the UK, VAT was introduced in 1973 as a replacement for purchase tax. » customs and excise; sales tax

Vatican City, Ital **Stato della Città del Vaticano** pop c.1 000; area 44 ha/109 acres. Papal sovereign state in Rome, on the W bank of the R Tiber; created in 1929 by the Lateran Treaty; timezone GMT + 1; includes St Peter's, the Vatican Palace and Museum, several buildings in Rome, and the Pope's summer villa at Castel Gandolfo; three entrances, in the care of the Pontifical Swiss Guard ('The Bronze Doors', at the end of the right-hand colonnade; the Arch of Charlemagne, or 'Arch of the Bells'; and the Via di Porta Angelica); contains several great museums and works of art; the city issues its own stamps and coinage. » Lateran Treaty; pope; St Peter's Basilica; Sistine Chapel; RR67

Vatican Councils Two councils of the Roman Catholic Church. The **First** (1869–70) was called by Pope Pius IX to deal with doctrine, discipline and canon law, foreign missions, and the relationship between Church and state. It is best remembered for the decree on papal infallibility and the triumph of the Ultramontanists. The **Second** (1962–5) was called by Pope John XXIII, with the task of renewing religious life and bringing up-to-date the belief, structure, and discipline of the Church (*aggiornamento*). Its reforms in liturgy and its ecumenical tendencies have had far-reaching effects throughout the Christian world. » aggiornamento; canon law; Council of the Church; ecumenism; John XXIII; liturgy; Pius IX; Roman Catholicism; Ultramontanism

Vättern, Lake [vetern], also **Vetter** or **Wetter** area 1 912 sq km/ 738 sq ml. Lake in S Sweden, E of L Vänern; extends 130 km/81 ml from Askersund (N) to Jönköping (S); maximum width 30 km/19 ml; Sweden's second largest lake; connected with the Baltic by the Göta Canal. » Sweden [i]

Vauban, Sebastien le Prestre de [vohbã] (1633–1707) French soldier and military engineer, born at Saint Léger. After serving in the Frondes (1651), he joined the government forces in 1653, and by 1658 was chief engineer under Turenne, serving with him at the siege of Lille (1667). He brought about a revolution in siege warfare and fortification; he directed siege operations throughout Louis XIV's campaigns, and surrounded the kingdom with a cordon of fortresses (1667–88). Created Marshal of France in 1703, he died in Paris. » Frondes; Louis XIV; Turenne

vaudeville In the USA, a variety show tradition stemming from the family entertainments created by Tony Pastor from 1881 onwards. In France, the term was originally used for the dumb shows with songs of the Paris fairs, and later for the light satirical songs popular in 18th-c theatres. The 'vaudeville finale', in which each character sang a verse in turn, was used in comic operas such as Mozart's *Die Entführung aus dem Serail* (The Seraglio). » music hall; opera; theatre

Vaughan, Henry (1622–95) Welsh religious poet, born at Newton-by-Usk, Breconshire. Educated at Oxford and London, he became a doctor, and settled near Brecon. His best-known works are the pious meditations, *Silex Scintillans* (1650) and the prose devotions *The Mount of Olives* (1652). He also published elegies, translations, and other pieces, all within the tradition of metaphysical poetry. » English literature; metaphysical poetry

Vaughan Williams, Ralph (1872–1958) British composer, born at Down Ampney, Gloucestershire. He studied at Cambridge, London, Berlin, and Paris, and developed a national style of music which derived from English choral tradition, especially of the Tudor period, and folksong. Notable in his early orchestral music is the *Fantasia on a Theme of Tallis* (1910) for strings. He composed nine symphonies, the ballet *Job* (1930), the opera *The Pilgrim's Progress* (1948–9) and numerous choral works. He also wrote for the stage, as in his music for *The Wasps* (1909), and for films, such as *Scott of the Antarctic* (1948), and composed many songs and hymns. He died in London.

vault An arched covering over any building; usually built of stone or brick, and sometimes imitated in wood or plaster. Various configurations exist, including the barrel, cross, domical, fan, and rib vaults. » arch [i]; Gothic architecture/ Revival; Perpendicular style; Roman architecture

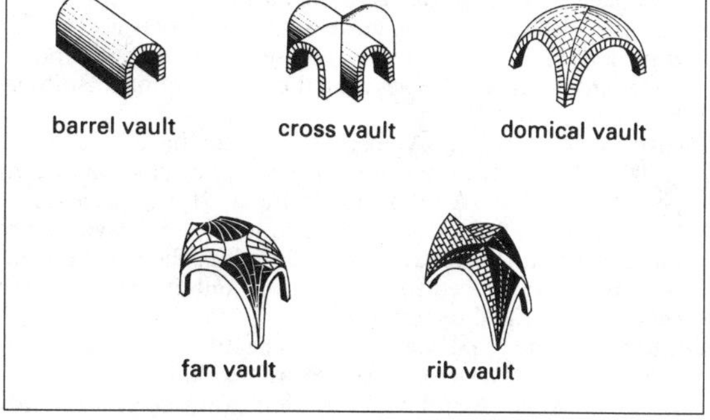

Types of vault

Vavilov, Nikolai Ivanovich (1887–1943) Russian plant geneticist, born in Moscow. In 1930 he was appointed by Lenin to direct Soviet agricultural research, and especially to harness it to the needs of production. He established 400 institutes, and built up a collection of 26 000 varieties of wheat. His principle of diversity postulated that the region of greatest diversity represents a plant's origin. His reputation was challenged by Lysenko, who denounced him at a genetics conference in 1937, and gradually usurped his position. Vavilov was arrested as a 'British spy' in 1940, and is thought to have died in a Siberian concentration camp. » genetics [i]; Lysenko

VDU An acronym of **visual display unit**, the screen attached to a computer. Most VDUs are based on cathode-ray-tube technology similar to that used in television sets, and both single colour and full colour versions are used. An increasing number of VDUs are being based on liquid crystal displays, particularly in portable computer applications. » cathode-ray tube; liquid crystals

vector (mathematics) In mathematics, a quantity having magnitude and direction. Vector quantities include position (showing the position of one point relative to another), displacement (the distance in a certain direction), velocity, acceleration, force, and momentum. They contrast with the *scalar* quantities of distance, time, mass, energy, etc, which have magnitude only. Vectors can also be defined in a more abstract form, as an ordered set of numbers subject to certain laws of composition. This set will often be displayed as the entries in a matrix, eg $\begin{pmatrix}3\\4\end{pmatrix}$ or (3 4). Addition of two vectors is then defined by

$$\begin{pmatrix}a\\b\end{pmatrix}+\begin{pmatrix}c\\d\end{pmatrix}=\begin{pmatrix}a+c\\b+d\end{pmatrix}.$$

The number of entries is called the *dimension* of the vector, and vectors so defined can have any number of dimensions. » matrix; scalar

vector (medicine) An organism, commonly an arthropod, which acts as an intermediary agent in transferring a pathogenic micro-organism from one host to another. Examples are ticks in typhus fever, mosquitoes in yellow fever and malaria, and sandflies in leishmaniasis. » arthropod

vector potential » **magnetic vector potential**

Veda [**vay**da] The 'sacred knowledge' of the Hindus, dating from c.1500 BC, contained in the four collections called the *Vedas*, the *Brahmanas* appended to them, and the *Aranyakas* and *Upanishads* which serve as an epilogue or conclusion. Originally the Veda consisted of the Rig-veda (sacred songs or hymns of praise), Sama-veda (melodies and chants used by priests during sacrifices), and Yajur-veda (sacrificial formulae); to which was later added the Athara-veda (spells, charms, and exorcistic chants). The Aranyakas and Upanishads deny that ritual sacrifice is the only means to liberation, and introduce monistic doctrine. They were eventually understood as the fulfilment of Vedic aspirations, and are called the *Vedanta* ('the end of the Veda'). » Brahmanas; Hinduism; Indian literature; monism; Upanishads; Vedanta

Vedanta A system of mediaeval Indian thought expressed in commentaries on the *Brahma Sutras*, which in turn were inspired by the *Upanishads*. Shankara (AD 788–820) founded Advaita Vedanta, whose most distinctive doctrines are that *Brahman* (Holy Power) and *atman* (self) are identical, and that the world of separate selves is an illusion. » atman; Brahman; Hinduism; Upanishads

Vedic Age [**vay**dik] A period in the history of India (1500–600 BC) which began with the migration of Indo-European tribes (Indo-Aryans) to N India. It was a period of transition from nomadic pastoralism to settled village communities, with cattle the major form of wealth. There was religious worship of personified forces of nature and abstract divinities, centred on a ritual of sacrifice.

veduta [vay**doo**ta] (Ital 'view') In art, a painting of a place, usually a city. Canaletto's views of Venice are well-known, especially in England, as they were bought by 18th-c Grand Tourists rather as we might buy coloured postcards today, and can be seen in most galleries and country houses. » landscape painting

Vega [**vay**ga] » **Lyra**

Vega (Carpio), Lope (Félix) de [**vay**ga] (1562–1635) Spanish dramatist and poet, born and died in Madrid. Educated at Alcalá, he served in the Armada (1588), and became secretary to the Duke of Alba (1590) and Duke of Sessa (1605). He first made his mark as a ballad writer, and after 1588 produced a wide range of historical and contemporary dramas – about 2 000 plays and dramatic pieces, of which over 400 still survive. He joined a religious order in 1610. » ballad; drama; poetry; Spanish literature

VEGA project [**vay**ga] A highly successful Soviet mission to Venus and Comet Halley undertaken 1984–6; the name is an acronym based on the Russian equivalents for 'Venus' and 'Halley'. Two spacecraft each deployed a lander and a balloon at Venus (Jun 1985), then used a Venus gravity assist to fly on to intercept Comet Halley (6 and 9 Mar 1986), Vega 2 passing within 8 900 km/5 530 ml of its nucleus. The mission carried an ambitious science payload, highly international in scope; all elements of the mission were boldly undertaken in public view, and proved to be highly successful. The balloons were deployed at 54 km/34 ml altitude and tracked for two days by an international network of antennas, including NASA's Deep Space Network (DSN) – a notable example of international co-operation. Likewise for the Halley flyby, the VEGA Project supplied optical navigation data, and DSN supplied radio tracking inputs to the European Space Agency's Giotto Project. This provided the first close-up view of the comet's nucleus, and the first measurements of gas and dust properties. The spacecraft were severely battered by the 75 km–50 ml/sec impact of Halley dust, becoming non-operational. » Halley's comet; Soviet space programme; Venus (astronomy)

vegan » **vegetarianism**

vegemite The copyright brand name for a popular Australian spread for sliced bread. First produced in 1923 under the name 'Parwill', vegemite is a concentrated yeast based on vegetable extract. » yeast

vegetable In a broad sense, anything of or concerning plants; but commonly referring to a plant or its parts, other than fruits and seeds, used for food. The term is often qualified by reference to the particular parts eaten, (eg leaf vegetable, root vegetable). A number of foods often called vegetables are actually fruits, such as the tomato. » aubergine; brassica; cabbage; carrot; celery; courgette; fruit; globe artichoke; kohlrabi; leek; legume; lentil; lettuce; marrow (botany); onion; pulse (botany); radish; runner bean; seakale; soya bean; swede; turnip

vegetable horsehair » **Spanish moss**

vegetarianism The practice of eating a diet devoid of meat. People who follow a diet containing animal protein from dairy products and eggs are known as **ovo-lacto-vegetarians**. Those who shun all animal foods are known as **vegans**. People become vegetarians for a variety of ethical, ecological, and religious reasons. The vegetarian diet may be healthier than that of the omnivore, since it is likely to contain less fat and more fibre. There are few nutritional disadvantages in being vegetarian, the only possible problem being in the low levels and low availability of iron in vegetable foods. Veganism, however, does pose problems, with low dietary intakes of available calcium, iron, and zinc, and little or no dietary intake of vitamin B_{12}, which is never found in plants. Vegans overcome the latter problem by taking vitamin B_{12} tablets, or by eating fermented foods where the bacteria provide the B_{12}. » diet; omnivore; vitamins [i]

vegetation succession The sequential development of plant communities occupying one site over a period of time. For example, a pond is gradually colonized by floating aquatic vegetation. With the infilling of sediments the water becomes shallower, and rooted plants (eg reeds and sedges) become established. Eventually the pond dries out, and shrubs and trees colonize the site. » climax vegetation

vegetative reproduction Any means by which a plant reproduces itself without forming seeds or spores. In single-celled algae and fungi, it is achieved by simple cell division. Many bryophytes produce detachable buds called *gemmae*. Higher plants, especially flowering plants, may increase by a variety of means, such as bulbils, tubers, stolons, and runners. Fragments of stems or roots may break off and grow into new plants, as in many perennial weeds. Some plants, including fern species, bud off small plantlets along the edges of their leaves or in the leaf axils, a process called *vivipary*. Some species (eg blackberries) reproduce entirely in one or more of these ways, never producing viable seeds. All new plants produced by these means are *clones*, ie with a genetic make-up identical to that of the parent. A successful plant can thus produce offspring equally well-adapted to similar conditions. The process is also used in horticulture, allowing mass production of plants with desirable traits which might be lost in breeding. » algae; bryophyte; bulbil; fern; fungus; runner; stolon; tuber

vein A vessel usually conveying deoxygenated blood from tissues back to the heart. *Deep* veins accompany arteries; *superficial* veins lie in the subcutaneous tissue, and often appear as blue channels just below the skin (eg at the wrist and on the forearm). Blood flow in veins is slower and at a lower pressure than in arteries; consequently veins are often larger and their walls are thinner. When empty, veins collapse. In most veins valves are present, formed by endothelial folds strengthened by fibrous and elastic tissue. The valves are arranged to prevent flow back to the periphery, and so help to support a column of blood in veins where there is an upward flow (eg the veins of the legs). Incompetence of the valves in leg veins leads to varicose veins, which can become painful and require surgical removal. » artery; circulation; epithelium; phlebitis; varicose veins

Vejle [**viy**luh] 55°43N 9°30E, pop (1981) 43 300. Seaport and manufacturing town, capital of Vejle county, E Jutland, Denmark, at head of Vejle Fjord; railway; engineering, foodstuffs; 13th-c St Nicholas's Church; 14 km/9 ml NW is Jelling, with 10th-c burial mounds of King Gorm and Queen Thyra. » Denmark [i]

Vela (Lat 'sails') [**vee**la] A S constellation whose four brightest stars form a near quadrilateral. It includes the small faint constellation, Pyxis ('mariner's compass'), the Vela pulsar, which emits optical flashes and spins 11 times per second. » constellation; pulsar; RR9

Velázquez, Diego (Rodríguez de Silva) [vay**las**keth] (1599–1660) Spanish painter, born in Seville. He studied in Seville, where he set up his own studio in 1618. His early works were domestic genre pieces, of which 'Old Woman Cooking Eggs' (1618, Edinburgh) is typical. He moved to Madrid in 1823, and on the advice of Rubens, visited Italy (1629–31), which transformed his sombre, naturalistic style into a more colourful approach, influenced by Titian. He then devoted himself to court portraits, executing several of the royal family and other personalities. He is best known for his three late masterpieces, 'Las Meninas' (1655, Maids of Honour; Madrid), 'Las Hilanderas' (c.1657, The Tapestry Weavers; Madrid), and 'Venus and Cupid', known as the 'Rokeby Venus' (c.1658, National Gallery, London). Knighted in 1659, he died in Madrid. » bodegone; Rubens; Spanish art; Titian

veld(t) The undulating plateau grassland of S Africa, primarily in Zimbabwe and the Republic of South Africa. It can be divided into the **high veld** (>1 500 m/c.5 000 ft), **middle veld** (900–1 500 m/c.3 000–5 000 ft) and **low veld** (<900 m/c.3 000 ft). The nature of the veld also changes from bush veld to grass veld or sand veld. » grass [i]

Veliko Tŭrnovo [**ve**likuh **toor**nuhvuh] 43°04N 25°39E, pop (1981e) 65 000. Capital of Veliko Tŭrnovo province, NEC Bulgaria; on the R Yantra, 241 km/150 ml NE of Sofia; airport; railway; capital of the second Bulgarian kingdom (1187–1393); Tsarevets Hill with its fortress walls, patriarch's palace, royal palace and defensive tower, Forty Martyrs Church (1230), Renaissance museum. » Bulgaria [i]

Velingrad 42°01N 23°59E, pop (1981e) 25 000. Spa town in Pazardzhik province, S Bulgaria, in the Rhodope Mts; a well-known therapeutic centre, with 70 thermal springs; railway. » Bulgaria [i]

vellum » **parchment**

velocity For **linear motion**, the rate of change of distance with time in a given direction; velocity *v*, units m/s. For **rotational motion**, it is the rate of change of angle with time; angular velocity *ω*, units radian/s. Both are vector quantities. » acceleration; mechanics; momentum; speed (physics); vector (mathematics); velocity of light

velocity of light A universal constant, the same value for all observers and all types of electromagnetic radiation; symbol *c*, value 2.998×10^8 m/s. First determined in 1676 by Danish scientist Olaf Rømer (1644–1710) using astronomical observations, it is expressed in electromagnetic quantities via Maxwell's equations. » light; Maxwell, James Clerk; special relativity [i]

velvet worm A primitive terrestrial arthropod; body cylindrical, segmented, length up to 150 mm/6 in; head with a pair of antennae and a pair of jaws; legs lobe-like; c.70 species, mostly nocturnal and feeding on small invertebrates. (Phylum: *Arthropoda*. Subphylum: *Onychophora*.) » arthropod; Peripatus

Venda [**ven**da] pop (1987e) 516 000; area 6 500 sq km/2 509 sq ml. Independent Black homeland in NE South Africa; close to the Zimbabwe frontier; self-government, 1973; granted independence by South Africa (not recognized internationally), 1979; capital, Thohoyandou; traditional territory of the Vhavenda; sisal, tea, coffee; reserves of coal, magnesite, copper, corundum, lead, graphite, phosphate; over 60 000 people commute to work or are migrant workers in South Africa. » apartheid; South Africa [i]

Vendée, Wars of the [vã**day**] French counter-revolutionary insurrections in the W provinces against the central government in Paris. The brutal rising in La Vendée (1793), when priests and nobles encouraged the conservative peasantry to rebel against the Convention's conscription and anticlerical policies, was a precedent for other provincial revolts in 1795, 1799, 1815, and 1832. » French Revolution [i]

Vendôme, Louis Joseph, Duc de ('Duke of') [vã**dohm**] (1654–1712) French general, born in Paris, the great-grandson of Henry IV. He fought in the Dutch campaign of 1672, and in the War of the Grand Alliance (1689–97). He commanded in Italy and Flanders during the War of the Spanish Succession (1701–14), was victorious at Cassano (1705) and Calcinato (1706), but defeated at Oudenarde by Marlborough (1708), and recalled after the loss of Lille. Sent to Spain in 1710 to aid Philip V, he recaptured Madrid, defeated the English at Brihuega and the Austrians at Villaviciosa, but died soon after at Vinaroz. » Spanish Succession, War of the

Venera Programme [vuh**nair**a] A highly successful evolutionary series of Soviet space missions to Venus 1961–83 (plus VEGA landers and balloons of 1985). Its highlights include: the first successful atmospheric entry probe (Venera 4, 1967); the first complete descent to the surface (Venera 5, 1969); the first science measurements on the surface (Venera 7, 1970); the first TV pictures from the surface (Venera 9, 1975); the first chemical analysis of the soil (Venera 13, 1981); the first high resolution images of the surface from orbit using radar to penetrate clouds (Venera 15/16, 1983); and the first balloons deployed and tracked in the atmosphere (VEGA, 1985). » Magellan Project; Soviet space programme; VEGA project; Venus (astronomy)

venereal disease (VD) A range of infectious diseases usually transmitted by sexual contact and occasionally in other ways. There is no specific treatment for AIDS or hepatitis B virus infection. Syphilis, gonorrhoea, and chancroid are treated with appropriate antibiotics. » AIDS; chancroid; gonorrhoea; hepatitis; syphilis

Venetian School The art associated with Venice, beginning with the building of the Basilica of St Mark in the 11th-c, with its rich mosaics and proud Byzantine domes. Painting developed from the 14th-c onwards and became one of the greatest traditions in Renaissance Europe. Leading masters included Bellini, Giorgione, Titian, Veronese, and Tintoretto. In contrast to Florence, Venice fostered a painterly and atmospheric approach based on colour and tone rather than on outline. The Baroque period saw the building of magnificent churches such as Sta Maria della Salute, and the 18th-c saw a final flowering in painting, with G B Tiepolo, Canaletto and Guardi. » Florentine school; Italian art; school (art); Bellini; Canaletto; Giorgione; Guardi; Tiepolo; Tintoretto; Titian; Veronese

Venezuela [venuhzwayla], official name **Republic of Venezuela**, Span **República de Venezuela** pop (1990e) 19 735 000; area 912 050 sq km/352 051 sq ml. Most northerly country in S America; divided into 20 states, two territories and one federal district; bounded N by the Caribbean, S by Brazil, E by Guyana, SW and W by Colombia; capital, Caracas; chief towns, Maracaibo and Ciudad Guayana; timezone GMT −4; chief ethnic groups, mestizo (67%), European (21%); official language, Spanish; chief religion, Roman Catholicism (96%); unit of currency, the bolívar of 100 céntimos; Guiana Highlands (SE) cover over half the country; Venezuelan Highlands in the W and along the coast, reaching heights of over 5 000 m/16 000 ft; lowlands around L Maracaibo and in the valley of the Orinoco R, which crosses the country S–NE; generally hot and humid climate; one rainy season (Apr–Oct); annual temperatures at Caracas, 13–27°C, monthly rainfall 10–109 mm/0.4–4.3 in; rainfall on coast increases to 1 000 mm/40 in in the E, and in the Highlands to 1 500 mm/60 in; originally inhabited by Caribs and Arawaks; seen by Columbus, 1498; Spanish settlers, 1520; frequent revolts against Spanish colonial rule; independence movement under Bolívar, leading to the establishment of the State of Gran Colombia (Colombia, Ecuador, Venezuela), 1821; independent republic, 1830; governed by an elected two-chamber National Congress, comprising a Senate and a 196-member Chamber of Deputies; a president is advised by a Council of Ministers; largely an agricultural country until the 1920s, when the development of oil from Maracaibo transformed the economy; over 90% of export revenue now derived from oil; iron ore, natural gas, aluminium, gold, nickel, iron, copper, manganese; cement, steel, chemicals, food, shipbuilding, vehicles; 20% of the land is under cultivation; coffee, cocoa, maize, tobacco, sugar; dairy and beef cattle. » Bolívar; Caracas; Gran Colombia; RR27 national holidays; RR66 political leaders

□ international airport

Venice, Ital **Venezia**, Lat **Venetia** 45°26N 12°20E, pop (1981) 346 146. Seaport capital of Venice province, Venetia, NE Italy, on the Gulf of Venice, at the head of the Adriatic Sea; 4 km/2½ ml from the Italian mainland in a salt-water lagoon, separated from the Adriatic by narrow spits of land; built on 118 small islands, and crossed by numerous canals, notably the Grand Canal, the main traffic artery; the houses and palaces are built on piles; connects with the mainland by a road and rail causeway, and by ferries; patriarch-archbishopric; airport; railway; commerce, lace, textiles, glass, crafts; a major tourist area; St Mark's Cathedral (11th-c) and Campanile (99 m/325 ft-high bell-tower, rebuilt 1905–12), Doge's Palace (14th–15th-c), Bridge of Sighs (c.1595), Church of Saints John and Paul (14th-c); Venetian Carnival (Feb–Mar), Gondola Race (Sep), Festival of Modern Art (Sep); fresh anxiety in the 1980s over the risk to the city from flooding and pollution; Venice and the lagoon are world heritage sites. » Bridge of Sighs; Doge's Palace; Italy [i]; Rialto Bridge; St Mark's Cathedral

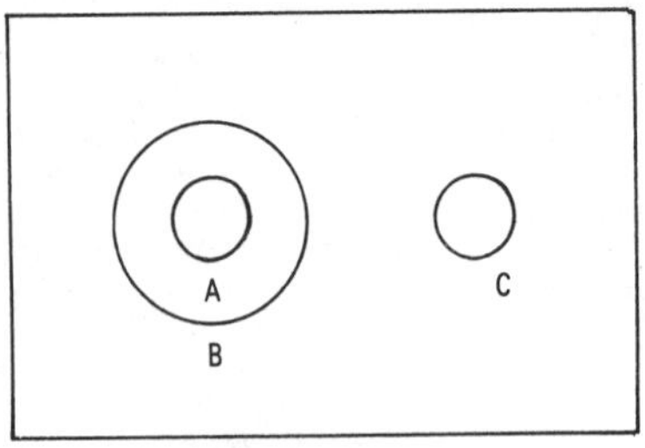

Venn diagram

Venn diagram In mathematics, a diagram illustrating the relations between sets, devised by the English logician, John Venn (1834–1923). For example, the diagram shows that Set *A* is a subset of *B*, and *B* does not contain any elements of *C*, ie *B* and *C* are disjoint. » set; union

ventricles 1 The chambers of the heart which eject blood into the pulmonary trunk (right ventricle) or the aorta (left ventricle). » heart [i] **2** The spaces within the brain where cerebrospinal fluid (CSF) is produced. There are four ventricles (the remains of the original hollow part of the neural tube of the embryo), below which a central canal extends into the spinal cord. Apertures in the system allow CSF to escape into the subarachnoid space. Any blockage or acute narrowing traps CSF within the ventricles, leading eventually to their enlargement (*hydrocephalus*). » brain [i]; cerebrospinal fluid; hydrocephalus; skull

Ventris, Michael (George Francis) (1922–1956) British linguist, born at Wheathampstead, Hertfordshire. As a teenager he heard Arthur Evans lecture on the undeciphered Minoan scripts found on tablets excavated at palace sites in Crete (Linear B), and determined to solve the puzzle. Although an architect by training, after World War 2 he devoted much of his time to analysis of the texts, and in 1952 announced that the language of Linear B was early Greek, a conclusion later confirmed by other scholars. He was killed in a car accident near Hatfield, Hertfordshire. » comparative linguistics; Evans, Arthur; Linear B

Venturi tube A device for measuring the amount of fluid flowing in a tube; named after the Italian physicist Giovanni Battista Venturi (1746–1822). The tube is constricted to form a throat, and pressure is measured on either side, the pressure difference indicating the rate of flow. Devices of this kind are used in engine carburettors. » Bernoulli's principle; fluid mechanics

Venus (astronomy) The second planet from the Sun, attaining the greatest brilliancy in the night sky, outshining all the stars, hence its poetic names the 'morning/evening star'. There are no natural satellites. It has the following characteristics: mass 4.87×10^{27} g; radius 6 051 km/3 760 ml; mean density 5.2g/cm^3; equatorial gravity 887 cm/s^2; rotational period 243 days (retrograde); orbital period 224.7 days; obliquity 3; orbital eccentricity 0.007; mean distance from the Sun 108.2×10^6 km. It approaches nearer to the Earth than any other planet, and is a near twin to Earth in size and density, but with a radically different atmosphere of mainly carbon dioxide, 100 times denser than our own, and with surface temperatures near 460°C. It is completely shrouded in clouds and haze layers of sulphuric acid composition. The thick atmosphere and cloud cover create a greenhouse effect that maintains high temperatures, even though clouds reflect a large fraction of incident sunlight. There is no observable magnetic field. The surface characterized by radar telescopes and by orbital radar observations (Pioneer Venus Orbiter and Veneras 15 and 16) is about 70% rolling plains, 10% highlands, and 20% lowland. The highlands, possibly volcanic in origin, are continental in size and reach a maximum elevation of 11 km/6¾ ml above the mean. There are relatively few impact craters because of the thick atmosphere. Even after 25 years of exploratory space missions to Venus, major questions remain about the planet's structure and history. » greenhouse effect; Magellan project; Mariner/Pioneer/Venera programme; planet; Solar System

Venus (mythology) Originally an obscure Italian deity of the vegetable garden, she was identified with Aphrodite, and, as a Roman goddess, took over the latter's mythology and attributes. » Aphrodite; Cupid; Psyche

Venus's fly trap A small carnivorous perennial, native only to the pine barrens of SE USA; leaves forming a rosette; flowers white, 5-petalled, in slender spikes up to 15 cm/6 in high. Each leaf is divided into a lower, winged portion and an upper portion (the trap) formed by two hemisperical lobes each bearing three trigger hairs and fringed with teeth. Stimulation of these hairs by an insect causes the lobes to snap shut, the teeth crossing to trap the prey. When the lobes are tightly squeezed together, red glands on the inner surface secrete enzymes, and the plant digests the prey before the leaf re-opens. (*Dionaea muscipula*. Family: *Droseraceae*.) » carnivorous plant; enzyme; perennial

Venus's girdle A ribbon-like comb jelly; body flattened; main tentacles reduced; secondary tentacles present in grooves near mouth. (Phylum: *Ctenophora*.) » ctenophore

Veracruz [vayra**kroos**] 19°11N 96°10W, pop (1980) 305 456. Seaport in Veracruz state, E Mexico, on the Gulf of Mexico; site of Cortés landing, 1519; airport; railway; principal port of entry for Mexico; textiles, chemicals, iron and steel, soap, sisal, trade in coffee, vanilla, tobacco; Palacio Municipal (17th-c), Castle of San Juan de Ulúa (1565), Baluarte de Santiago fort, city museum. » Mexico [i]

verbena » **lemon verbena; vervain**

Verde, Cape » **Cap Vert**

Verdi, Giuseppe (Fortunino Francesco) [**ver**dee] (1813–1901) Italian composer, born at Le Roncole, Parma. After studying at Milan, he began to write operas, achieving his first major success with *Nabucco* (1842). *Rigoletto* (1851), *Il Trovatore* (1853), and *La Traviata* (1853) established him as the leading Italian operatic composer of the day. His spectacular *Aida* was commissioned for the new opera house in Cairo, built in celebration of the Suez Canal (1871). Apart from the *Requiem* (1874), there was then a lull in output until, in his old age, he produced *Otello* (1887) and *Falstaff* (1893). He died in Milan. » opera

verdigris [**ver**digree] Basic copper carbonate, approximately $Cu_3(CO_3)_2(OH)_2$, formed in the atmospheric corrosion of copper surfaces. It is green in colour. » copper; corrosion

Vereeniging, Peace of (1902) The peace treaty which ended the Boer War, signed at Pretoria. The Boers won three important concessions: an amnesty for those who had risen in revolt within the Cape Colony; a promise that the British would deny the franchise to Africans until after the Boer republics were returned to representative government; and additional financial support for reconstruction. The Peace ensured that there would be no significant change in the political relationship of Whites and Blacks in South Africa. » Boer Wars

Vergil » **Virgil**

Vergina [vair**jee**na] Ancient Aigai, Greece, the first capital of Macedonia. It is notable archaeologically for the excavation in 1977 of the reputed grave of Philip of Macedon, the father of Alexander the Great. Below a burial mound 110 m/360 ft diameter and 14 m/46 ft high lay a spectacular vaulted tomb with a painted stucco facade; finds included weapons, armour, drinking vessels, furniture, and a gold casket holding cremated bones and a gold wreath of acorns and oak leaves. » Macedon; Philip II (of Macedon)

verificationism A philosophical position, held by the logical positivists, which claims that synthetic propositions are meaningful only if their truth or falsity can be determined, in principle, by empirical observation (eg 'The number of stars in

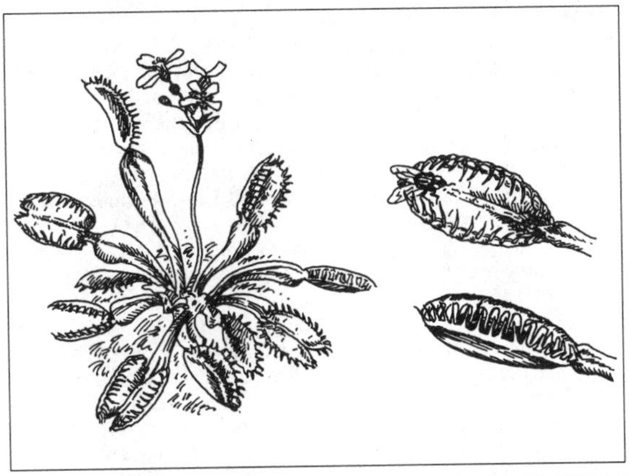

Venus's fly trap

the universe is even'). Verificationists typically assert that propositions such as 'God exists' and 'Murder is wrong' are meaningless. » analytic-synthetic distinction; Ayer; logical positivism

Verlaine, Paul (Marie) [ver**len**] (1844–96) French poet, born at Metz. Educated in Paris, he joined the civil service, but mixed with the leading Parnassian writers, and achieved success with his second book of poetry, *Fêtes galantes* (1869). In 1872 he left his family to travel with the young poet Rimbaud, but their friendship ended in Brussels (1873) when Verlaine, drunk and desolate at Rimbaud's intention to leave, shot him in the wrist. While in prison for two years, he wrote *Romances sans paroles* (1874, Songs Without Words). He became a Catholic, then taught French in England, where he wrote *Sagesse* (1881, Wisdom). In 1877 he returned to France, where he wrote critical studies, notably *Les Poètes maudits* (1884), short stories, and sacred and profane verse. He died in Paris. » French literature; Parnassians; poetry; Rimbaud

Vermeer, Jan (1632–75) Dutch painter, born and died at Delft. He married in 1653, and that year was admitted master painter to the guild of St Luke, which he served as headman. He gained some recognition in his lifetime in Holland, but he made little effort to sell; as a result, his art was forgotten until 19th-c researchers re-established his reputation. He painted small, detailed domestic interiors, notable for their use of perspective and treatment of the various tones of daylight. Forty of his paintings are known, among them the 'Allegory of Painting' (c.1665, Vienna) and 'Woman reading a Letter' (c.1662, Amsterdam). » Dutch art; van Meegeren

vermiculite A group of clay minerals formed by the alteration of micas. They consist of porous and flaky particles which expand about 20 times their volume when heated, producing low-density, thermally-insulating, and inert material used in plaster, insulation, and packing material, and as a medium for raising plants from seeds. » clay minerals; micas

vermilion » **mercury**

Vermont [ver**mont**] pop (1987e) 548 000, area 24 899 sq km/ 9 614 sq ml. New England state in NE USA, divided into 14 counties; the 'Green Mountain State'; explored by Champlain, 1609; first settlement established at Fort Dummer, 1724; 14th state admitted to the Union, 1791; capital, Montpelier; largest town, Burlington; the Green Mts run N–S through the C; rivers drain W from the mountains into L Champlain which forms much of the W border, and E into the Connecticut R which forms much of the E border; highest point Mt Mansfield (1 339 m/4 393 ft); forestry and timber products, arable farming, grazing, dairy products, maple syrup, marble and granite. » Champlain; Montpelier; United States of America [i] RR39

vermouth A fortified red or white wine. Pure alcohol is used for the fortification, up to the same alcohol level as sherry, and various herbs and spices are added for flavour. Martini is a popular cocktail of gin (or vodka) and vermouth. » sherry; wine

vernal equinox » **equinox**

Verne, Jules (1828–1905) French novelist, born at Nantes. He studied law at Paris, then turned to literature. From 1848 he wrote opera libretti, then in 1863 he developed a new vein in fiction, exaggerating and anticipating the possibilities of science. His best-known books are *Voyage au centre de la terre* (1864, Journey to the Centre of the Earth), *Vingt mille lieues sous les mers* (1870, Twenty Thousand Leagues under the Sea), and *Le Tour du monde en quatre-vingts jours* (1873, Around the World in Eighty Days). He died at Amiens. Several successful films have been made from his novels. » novel; science fiction

Vernon, Edward (1684–1757) British admiral. He joined the navy in 1700, and also became an MP (1727–41). In 1739, during the War of Jenkins' Ear, he was sent to harry the Spaniards in the Antilles, and his capture of Portobello made him a national hero. During the Jacobite rebellion of 1745 his masterly dispositions in the Channel successfully kept the standby Gallic reinforcements in their ports. He was nicknamed 'Old Grog', from his grogram coat, and in 1740 ordered the dilution of navy rum with water, the mixture being thereafter known as 'grog'. » Forty-five Rebellion; Jenkins' Ear, War of

Verona [ve**roh**na] 45°26N 11°00E, pop (1981) 265 932. Capital town of Verona province, Venetia, N Italy, on the R Adige; important communications centre; railway; agricultural market centre; textiles, paper, furniture, tourism; many Roman and mediaeval remains; cathedral (12th-c), Church of San Giorgio in Braida (16th-c), Castel Vecchio (1354–5), Church of San Zeno Maggiore (11th–12th-c); operatic festival in the Roman amphitheatre (Jul–Aug). » Italy [i]

Veronese, Paolo, byname of **Paolo Caliari** [vayruh**nay**zay] (c.1528–88) The greatest of the Venetian decorative painters, born at Verona. He worked at Verona and Mantua, then settled in Venice (1555), where he came to rank with Titian and Tintoretto. The Church of San Sebastiano in Venice contains many pictures of the period before his visit to Rome (1560). His major paintings include 'The Marriage Feast at Cana' (Louvre), 'The Adoration of the Magi' (1573, National Gallery, London), and 'Feast in the House of the Levi' (1573, Venice), which brought him before the Inquisition for trivializing religious subjects. He died at Venice. » Italian art; Tintoretto; Titian; Venetian School

Verrazano-Narrows Bridge A major steel suspension bridge across the entrance to New York Harbor; constructed in 1959–64; length of main span 1 298 m/4 260 ft; named after the Italian explorer, Giovanni da Verrazano (1485–1528). » bridge (engineering) [i]; New York City

Verrocchio, Andrea del, byname of **Andrea del Cione** [ver**ok**-keeoh] (c.1435–88) Florentine sculptor, painter, and goldsmith, born in Florence. Of the paintings ascribed to him, only the 'Baptism' in the Uffizi is certain, and this was completed by Leonardo da Vinci, whom he taught. He is best known for his magnificent equestrian statue of Colleoni at Venice, where he died. » Italian art; Leonardo da Vinci; Uffizi

verruca [vuh**roo**ka] » **wart**

Versailles [ver**siy**] A chateau built for Louis XIII at the village of Versailles, 23 km/14 ml SW of Paris in the 17th-c, and transformed under Louis XIV to create a palace, unequalled in its display of wealth, in which to house the entire court. Later extensions were the Grand Trianon (a smaller residence in the palace grounds) and the Petit Trianon (added by Louis XV). The palace was ransacked during the French Revolution, but has been restored to its original state, and is now a world heritage site. It has been the scene of several peace treaties, notably at the end of the American War of Independence (1783), the Franco-Prussian War (1871), and World War 1 (1919). » chateau; Le Brun; Le Nôtre; Louis XIV; Versailles, Treaty of

Versailles, Treaty of A peace treaty drawn up in 1919 between Germany and the Allied powers at Paris. Of the 434 articles, the most controversial was article 231 assigning to Germany and her allies responsibility for causing World War 1, and establishing liability for reparation payments. Germany lost all overseas colonies, and considerable territory to Poland in the E. The Rhineland was demilitarized and occupied by Allied troops, and German armed forces were strictly limited. » Paris Peace Conference; World War 1

verse A single line of poetry, a stanza, or poetry in general (English verse). *Versification* refers to the technical characteristics of a given poetic form, and also to the exploitation of these by a given poet. » metre (literature); poetry

Vert, Cap » **Cap Vert**

vertebra » **vertebral column**

vertebral column The backbone of all vertebrates: a series of bony elements (*vertebrae*) separated by *intervertebral discs*, and held together by ligaments and muscles. The amount of movement between adjacent vertebrae is small, but when added together the vertebral column is extremely mobile. In the majority of vertebrates, the column lies horizontally, being supported by hind- and fore- limbs. In humans, however, it is held erect and supported by the hindlimbs only. It carries and supports the thorax, and gives attachment to many muscles; it surrounds and protects the spinal cord from mechanical trauma; it acts as a shock absorber (by virtue of its curvatures and the presence of the invertebral discs); and it can transmit forces from one part of the body to another. In humans, it is 72–75 cm/28–30 in long (c.40% of an individual's height) and consists of seven cervical, twelve thoracic, five lumbar, five fused sacral, and four fused coccygeal vertebrae. At birth it presents a single C-shaped curvature (concave forward) which acquires secondary curvatures in the opposite direction in both the lumbar and cervical regions. The cervical curvature develops in order to keep the head erect, while the lumbar curvature is associated with the development of standing and walking.

The intervertebral disc is responsible for c.25 % of the length of the vertebral column. Each disc consists of a central gelatinous core surrounded by rings of fibrous tissue. During the course of the day the discs gradually lose water and become thinner; consequently at the end of the day an individual is not as tall as first thing in the morning (the difference may be as large as 2 cm/0.8 in. Similarly, with increasing age the discs also lose water, so that an individual's height may decrease in later life.

The mobility of the vertebral column is determined and controlled by the interplay between the geometry of the bony elements and the arrangement of the soft tissue elements (disc, ligaments, and muscles). An abnormal sideways bending of the vertebral column (*scoliosis*) may be present in as many as 15 % of the population, but is of clinical significance in only 0.5 %; it is more common in females than in males. In the majority of cases the underlying cause of the scoliosis is unknown, but factors include weakness of the back muscles and disease of the spine. » ankylosing spondilitis; coccyx; epidural anaesthesia; lumbago; lumbar puncture; orthopaedics; prolapsed invertebral disc; skeleton; spina bifida; spinal cord; spondilosis; Plate XIII

Vertebrata » **Chordata**

vertical integration A business situation where a company expands by buying up its suppliers or its customers, thus controlling all the processes of production, from raw materials through to the sale of the final product. The advantages for a company are that, since it owns its suppliers or customers, the profits made by them are kept in the firm. In addition, owning suppliers should ensure delivery of the materials and components they produce, and owning customers guarantees a market for the firm's products. The major disadvantage is that management may not have expertise in all stages. An example of vertical integration is the oil industry, where all stages can be owned, from oil wells, through tankers and refineries, to petrol stations.

Vertical Take-Off and Landing » **VTOL**

Verulamium [veryoo**lay**miuhm] A Belgic town in Roman Britain which stood on the site of present-day St Albans. Completely destroyed in the Revolt of Boadicea (Boudicca) in AD 60, it was later rebuilt and became a focal point for the Romanization of the province. » Britain, Roman

vervain A tough-stemmed perennial, growing to 60 cm/2 ft, native to Europe, Asia, and N Africa; leaves opposite, pinnately lobed; flowers 4 mm/0.16 in, lilac, in slender spikes. (*Verbena officinalis*. Family: *Verbenaceae*.) » perennial; pinnate

vervet monkey A guenon native to Africa S of the Sahara; yellow-brown with a black face surrounded by white whiskers; inhabits grassland near trees; adult male with blue scrotum; many geographical variations, including the *grass monkey*, *grivet monkey*, and *green monkey*. (*Cercopithecus aethiops*.) » guenon

Verwoerd, Hendrik (Frensch) [fer**voort**] (1901–66) South African statesman and Prime Minister (1958–66), born in Amsterdam, the Netherlands. He was educated at Stellenbosch, where he became professor of applied psychology (1927) and sociology (1933), and edited the nationalist *Die Transvaler* (1938–48). Elected Senator in 1948, he became Minister of Native Affairs (1950) and Premier. His administration was marked by the highly controversial policy of apartheid, an attempt on his life (1960), and the establishment of South Africa as a Republic (1962). He was assassinated in Cape Town. » apartheid; South Africa [i]

Very, Edward Wilson [**vee**ree] (1847–1910) US ordnance expert and inventor. He served in the US Navy (1867–85), became an admiral, and in 1877 invented chemical flares ('Very Lights') for signalling at night.

Very Large Array The world's most elaborate full synthesis radio telescope at Socorro, New Mexico, consisting of 27 antennae arranged on rail tracks forming a Y. It is used to investigate the structure of gaseous nebulas in our Galaxy, and of remote radio galaxies and quasars. » aperture synthesis; Galaxy; National Radio Astronomy Observatory; telescope [i]

very large scale integration (VLSI) A technique of manufacturing integrated circuits with a very high number of individual components. It is usually defined to refer to integrated circuits containing more than 100 000 components in one chip. » chip; integrated circuit

Vesalius, Andreas [vuh**zay**liuhs] Flemish **Andries van Wesel** (1514–64) Belgian anatomist, born in Brussels. He was educated at Louvain, Padua, and Paris, and became professor at Padua, Bologna, and Basle. His major work was the *De humani corporis fabrica libri septem* (1543, The Seven Books on the Structure of the Human Body), which greatly advanced the science of anatomy with its detailed descriptions and drawings. He was sentenced to death by the Inquisition for his new approach, involving dissection of the human body, but the sentence was commuted to a pilgrimage to Jerusalem. On his return from this journey, he died at Zante, in Greece. » anatomy

Vespasian [ves**pay**zhuhn] properly **Titus Flavius Vespasianus** (9–79) Roman emperor (69–79), and founder of the Flavian dynasty (69–96). Declared emperor by the troops in the East, where he was engaged in putting down the Jewish Revolt, he ended the civil wars that had been raging since Nero's overthrow, put the state on a sound financial footing, and restored discipline to the army. Among his many lavish building projects was the Colosseum. He was succeeded by his son, Titus. » Domitian; Nero; Titus

Vespers The evening hour of the divine office of the Western Church. In monastic, cathedral, and collegiate churches in the Roman Catholic Church it is sung daily between 3 and 6 pm. » liturgy; Roman Catholicism

Vespucci, Amerigo [ves**poo**chee] (1454–1512) Italian explorer, born in Florence. He promoted a voyage to the New World in the track of Columbus, sailed with its commander (1499), and explored the coast of Venezuela. In 1505 he was naturalized in Spain, and from 1508 was pilot-major of the kingdom. He died at Seville. His name was given to America through an inaccurate account of his travels published in Lorraine (1507), in which he is represented as having discovered and reached the mainland in 1497. » Columbus, Christopher

Vesta (astronomy) The fourth asteroid discovered (1807). It is one of the very few that can ever be seen with the unaided eye, mainly on account of its high reflectivity. » asteroids

Vesta (mythology) Roman goddess of the hearth. Her sacred fire, and a shrine containing sacred objects, were kept in a round building, and tended by the Vestal Virgins. » Hestia

Vestal Virgins In ancient Rome, the aristocratic, virgin priestesses of Vesta, the goddess of the hearth. They tended the sacred flame which burned perpetually in the Temple of Vesta near the forum. » forum; temple

Vesterålen or **Vesteraalen** [**ves**teroluhn] Island group in the Norwegian Sea, off the NW coast of Norway, WSW of Narvik, just N of the Lofoten group; principal islands Hinnøy, Langøya, Andøya, Hadseløy; fishing, fish processing. » Norway [i]

vestibular apparatus The part of the internal ear concerned with balance, consisting of a series of spaces and tubes within the temporal bone of the skull. It contains the *saccule* and *utricle*, which convey information regarding head position by responding to linear and tilting movements, and three *semicircular canals*, which convey information about rotatory and angular movements of the head. Hair-like processes project into a jelly-like mass containing numerous crystalline bodies (the *otoliths*). Under the influence of gravity the otoliths move and stimulate the hair cells, thereby conveying information regarding head position. The nerve impulses generated by the hair cells enter the brain through the vestibulo-cochlear nerve, and evoke reflex movements of the eyes, trunk, and limbs, as well as the conscious sensation of head movement. » cochlea; ear [i]

vestigial organ [ves**tij**ial] A degenerate or imperfectly formed organ that has been reduced in structure or functional significance during the course of evolution or development. The human appendix and the wings of an ostrich are regarded as vestigial structures. » morphology (biology)

vestments Special and distinctive garments worn by clergy in the worship and liturgy of the Christian Church. » liturgy; mitre; pallium; *see illustration p 1266*

Vestris, Madame, byname of **Lucia Elizabeth Vestris** or **Mathews**, *née* **Bartolozzi** (1797–1856) British actress, born and died in London. At 16 she married the dancer Armand Vestris (1787–1825), but they separated two years later, and she went on the stage in Paris. She appeared at Drury Lane in 1820, becoming famous in a wide range of roles. She was lessee of the Olympic Theatre for nine years, and later managed Covent Garden and the Lyceum. In 1838 she married the comedian, Charles James Mathews (1803–78). » theatre

Vesuvius [vuh**soo**viuhs], Ital **Vesuvio** 40°49N 14°26E. Active volcano in Campania, S Italy, 15 km/9 ml SE of Naples; height 1 277 m/4 190 ft; crater circumference, 1 400 m/4 593 ft, depth 216 m/709 ft; first recorded eruption AD 79, overwhelming Pompeii, Herculaneum, and Stabiae; eruptions at long intervals until 1631, more regular activity since; last eruption, 1944; fruit and vines grow on lower slopes. » Pompeii; volcano

vetch A large group of annuals and perennials, often climbing or scrambling, native to N temperate regions and S America; also called **tare**; leaves pinnate with 2–many, often narrow leaflets, usually terminating in a tendril, which is sometimes branched; pea-flowers solitary or in small or long spike-like inflorescences arising from the leaf axils; pods flattened, splitting lengthwise into two valves. It is generally of little economic importance, and is sometimes an agricultural pest. One form of common vetch (*Vicia sativa*), a purple-flowered annual native to Europe, N Africa, and parts of Asia, is widely cultivated for animal forage. (Genus: *Vicia*, 140 species. Family: *Leguminosae*.) » annual; inflorescence [i]; perennial; pinnate; tendril

Veterans' Day A public holiday in the USA (Nov 11), held to honour veterans of all wars; originally instituted as Armistice Day after World War 1, by which name it was known until 1954. » Armistice Day

veterinary science The science concerned with the diseases of animals, especially their treatment or their avoidance. It is applied primarily to domesticated animals, or to captive animals in zoos. » bovine spongiform encephalopathy; scrapie

Vézelay church [vayzuh**lay**] The 12th-c abbey church of St Madeleine, a world heritage monument at Vézelay, E France. It is noted both as a masterpiece of Romanesque architecture and as the start of one of the main pilgrimage routes to Santiago de Compostela in Spain. » Romanesque architecture

Vézère Valley [vay**zair**] A stretch of the Vézère R valley in S France, of great archaeological importance; a world heritage

RELIGIOUS VESTMENTS

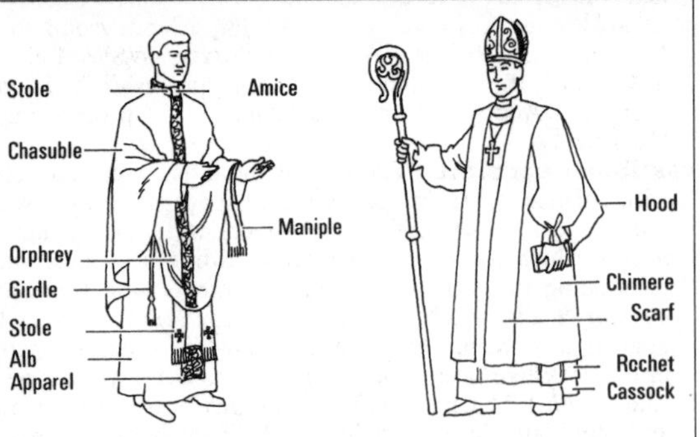

alb A long white garment reaching to the ankles; derived from an ancient tunic.
amice A linen square worn round the back to protect the other vestments; formerly a neckcloth.
apparels Ornamental panels at the foot of the alb, front and back, and on the amice.
cassock The long black gown worn under other vestments; formerly, the daily working costume of the clergy.
chasuble Outer sleeveless vestment worn by a priest or bishop when celebrating Holy Communion; derived from the commonest outdoor garment of classical times.
chimere Worn by bishops over the rochet; of black or scarlet, open in front.
cope In the pre-Christian era, a long cloak; now a costly embroidered vestment, semi-circular in shape, worn by bishops and priests on special occasions.
cotta Similar to the surplice, but shorter, especially in the sleeves; sometimes used by clergy and servers in place of the surplice.
hood Worn by clergy at choir offices; a mediaeval head-dress, now worn hanging down the back; denotes a university degree.
maniple Worn over the left arm by bishops, priests, and deacons at the Eucharist; originally a napkin.
orphreys The embroidered strips, customarily cross-shaped, on a chasuble.
rochet Worn by bishops, similar to an alb, but used without girdle or apparels.
stole Once a napkin or towel carried by servants on the left shoulder; now folded and narrow, worn over both shoulders.
surplice Of white linen, reaching to the knees; worn by choir and servers as well as clergy.

site. Its yield of flint tools and fossilized remains has been formative in the modern understanding of the Old Stone Age. The grottoes are also noted for their wall paintings and engravings. » Three Age System

VHS (Video Home Service) The trade name for a videotape cassette recorder introduced in 1976 by JVC/Matsushita for the domestic market, and widely adopted by other manufacturers. It uses ½ in (12.7 mm) tape at a speed of 2.34 cm/sec in a cassette 189 × 104 × 25 mm. It has a playing time of up to 4 hours, and has proved to be the most internationally popular home VTR system. A smaller cassette (VHS-C) is used for camcorders. **Super-VHS** is an improved version with separate luminance and chrominance signals, using metal particle tape to give higher picture definition and colour quality. » videotape recorder

Viaud, Louis Marie Julien [vee**oh**] » **Loti, Pierre**

Viborg [**vee**bor] 56°28N 9°25E, pop (1981) 28 659. Ancient city and capital of Viborg county, NC Jutland, Denmark; railway; engineering, distilling, textiles; 12th-c Gothic cathedral (restored 1864–76). » Denmark [i]

vibraphone A musical instrument resembling a xylophone, but with metal bars and resonators that are fitted with electrically operated vanes. These rapidly open and close to produce a vibrating, tremolo effect, but the mechanism may be switched off if required. The instrument is usually played with soft beaters, and since the 1920s has frequently been used in jazz, dance, and orchestral music. » percussion [i]; xylophone

vibration » **oscillation**

vibrio A straight or curved, rod-shaped bacterium, typically with flagella at one end. It can grow in the presence or absence of oxygen, and is found in aquatic environments and animal intestines. It includes the causative agent of cholera. (Kingdom: *Monera*. Family: *Vibrionaceae*.) » bacteria [i]; cholera

viburnum » **guelder rose**

vicar (Lat *vicarius*, 'substitute') Literally, one who takes the place of another; for example, the pope is said to be the Vicar of Christ. In Anglican Churches, the term applies technically to the priest acting for the rector, but is widely used for any parish priest or minister. » Church of England

Vicente, Gil [vee**sen**tay] (c.1470–c.1537) Portuguese dramatist and poet. He accompanied the court, writing many plays and entertainments in both Spanish and Portuguese. He wrote on religious, national, and social themes, as well as farces, and pastoral and romantic plays, all with great lyricism and a predominantly comical spirit. » drama; poetry; Portuguese literature

Vicenza, ancient **Vicetia** [vee**chen**tsa] 45°33N 11°33E, pop (1981) 114 598. Capital town of Vicenza province, Venetia, NE Italy; 35 km/22 ml NW of Padua; railway junction; textiles, carpets, iron and steel; home of Palladio; Basilica Palladiana (1549–1614), Teatro Olimpico, Rotonda, cathedral (15th-c). » Italy [i]; Palladio

Vichy [**vee**shee] The informal name of the French political regime between 1940 and 1945; officially the **French State (l'État Français)**. Established at the spa town of Vichy following Germany's defeat of France (1940), its head of state was Marshal Philippe Pétain and its other dominant political figure Pierre Laval, Prime Minister from 1942. Although a client regime of Germany, Vichy succeeded in maintaining a degree of autonomy. » Laval, Pierre; Pétain; World War 2

Vickers test » **hardness**

Vicksburg 32°21N 90°53W, pop (1980) 25 434. Seat of Warren County, W Mississippi, USA; port on the Mississippi R; settled, 1791; captured by Union forces during the Civil War (1863) after a long siege – the 'Vicksburg Campaign' gave control of the Mississippi to the North, splitting the Confederacy on a N–S axis; national cemetery nearby, where c.13 000 unknown Union troops are buried, brought from all over the South; railway; important processing and shipping centre for cotton, timber, and livestock area; lumber products, machinery, mobile homes, chemicals, fertilizers, food products; headquarters of US Mississippi River Commission. » American Civil War; Mississippi

Vicky, pseudonym of **Victor Weisz** (1913–66) British political cartoonist, born in Berlin. He emigrated to Britain in 1935, worked with several newspapers, and established himself as the leading left-wing political cartoonist of the period. His collections include *Vicky's World* (1959).

Vico, Giambattista [**vee**koh] (1668–1744) Italian historical philosopher, born and died at Naples. He studied law, but devoted himself to literature, history, and philosophy, becoming in 1699 professor of rhetoric at Naples. In his *Scienza Nuova* (1725, New Science), now recognized as a landmark in European intellectual history, he attempted to systematize the humanities into a single human science in a cyclical theory of the growth and decline of societies. Though his historicist philosophy of history was largely neglected in the 18th-c, it undoubtedly influenced many later scholars, including Goethe and Marx. » Goethe; Marx

Victor Emmanuel II (1820–78) First King of Italy (1861–78), born at Turin. As King of Sardinia from 1849, he appointed Cavour as his Chief Minister (1852). He fought against Austria (1859), winning victories at Montebello, Magenta, and Solferino, and gaining Lombardy. In 1860 Modena, Parma, the Romagna, and Tuscany were peacefully annexed, Sicily and Naples were added by Garibaldi, and Savoy and Nice were ceded to France. Proclaimed King at Turin, he fought on the side of Prussia in the Austro-Prussian War (1866), and after the fall of the French Empire (1870) he entered and annexed Rome, where he later died. » Austro-Prussian War; Cavour; Garibaldi; Italy [i]; Risorgimento

Victor Emmanuel III (1869–1947) King of Italy (1900–46), born at Naples. He initially ruled as a constitutional monarch, but defied parliamentary majorities by bringing Italy into World War 1 on the side of the Allies in 1915, and in 1922 when he offered Mussolini the premiership. The fascist government then reduced him to a figurehead. He played an important part in effecting Mussolini's fall (1943), but was irremediably tarnished by his association with fascism. Having relinquished power to his son, he abdicated in 1946, and died at Alexandria. » fascism; Mussolini

Victoria, in full **Alexandrina Victoria** (1819–1901) Queen of Great Britain (1837–1901) and (from 1876) Empress of India, born in London, the only child of George III's fourth son, Edward, and Victoria Maria Louisa of Saxe-Coburg, sister of Leopold, King of the Belgians. Taught by Lord Melbourne, her first Prime Minister, she had a clear grasp of constitutional principles and the scope of her own prerogative, which she resolutely exercised in 1839 by setting aside the precedent which decreed dismissal of the current ladies of the bedchamber, thus causing Peel not to take up office as Prime Minister. In 1840 she married Prince Albert of Saxe-Coburg and Gotha, and had four sons and five daughters. Strongly influenced by her husband, with whom she worked in closest harmony, after his death (1861) she went into lengthy seclusion, neglecting many duties, which brought her unpopularity and motivated a republican movement. But with her recognition as Empress of India, and the celebratory golden (1887) and diamond (1897) jubilees, she rose high in her subjects' favour, and increased the prestige of the monarchy. She had strong preferences for certain Prime Ministers (notably Melbourne and Disraeli) over others (notably Peel and Gladstone), but following the advice of Albert did not press these beyond the bounds of constitutional propriety. At various points in her long reign she exercised some influence over foreign affairs, and the marriages of her children had important diplomatic, as well as dynastic implications in Europe. She died at Cowes, Isle of Wight, and was succeeded by her son as Edward VII. » Albert, Prince; Disraeli; Gladstone; Melbourne, Viscount; Peel

Victoria, Tomás Luis de or **Vittoria, Tommaso Ludovico da** (c.1548–1611) Spanish composer, born at Avila. He studied music in Rome, and at Loyola's Collegium Germanicum was appointed chaplain and (in 1573) choirmaster. In 1578 he was made chaplain at San Girolamo della Carità, and c.1585 returned to Spain as chaplain to the widowed Empress Maria in Madrid, where he was choirmaster until his death. He wrote only religious music, his 180 works including several books of motets and over 20 masses.

Victoria (Australia) pop (1986) 4 207 700; area 227 600 sq km/ 87 900 sq ml. State in SE Australia; visited by Captain Cook, 1770; Melbourne settled, 1835; separated from New South Wales, 1851; gold discovered Ballarat, 1851; now comprises 12 statistical divisions; bordered S by the Bass Strait and SW by the Southern Ocean; second smallest state; E is the Great Dividing Range, known in this region as the Australian Alps; highest point Mt Bogong (1 986 m/6 516 ft); about 36% of the land occupied by forest; SW region known as Gippsland; several inland lakes, mostly very saline; irrigation storages include L Eildon on the Goulburn R and L Hume on the Murray; contains 25% of the Australian population concentrated into 3% of the land; capital, Melbourne; principal towns, Geelong and Ballarat; produces about a fifth of Australia's agricultural output of wheat, oats, barley, maize, tobacco, hops, fodder crops, citrus fruits, grapes, apples, vegetables, wool, hides, mutton, lamb, dairy products; timber, coal mining (Latrobe Valley one of the world's largest deposits of brown coal), motor parts; oil and natural gas fields in the Gippsland Basin and Bass Strait; state holiday Labour Day (Mar). » Australia [i]; Cook, James; Melbourne

Victoria (Canada) 48°25N 123°22W, pop (1981) 64 379. Capital of British Columbia province, W Canada, at SE end of Vancouver I, on the Juan de Fuca Strait; founded as fur-trading post, 1843; provincial capital, 1866; airfield; railway; university (1963); shipbuilding, timber, fish canning, computer software, tourism; Parliament Buildings (1893–7), Empress Hotel (1906–8), Thunderbird Park (unique collection of totem poles), Butchart Gardens. » British Columbia

Victoria (Seychelles) 4°37S 55°28E, pop (1985e) 23 000. Seaport capital of the Seychelles, Indian Ocean; situated on the NE coast of Mahé I; trade in copra, vanilla, cinnamon, tortoise-shell, guano. » Seychelles

Victoria, Lake area 69 500 sq km/26 827 sq ml. Lake in E Africa, bounded S by Tanzania, NW by Uganda, and NE by Kenya; largest lake on the African continent; altitude 1 300 m/4 265 ft; 400 km/250 ml long; 240 km/150 ml wide; contains several islands, notably the Sese archipelago; level raised by the Owen Falls Dam, 1954; main lakeside ports, Kisumu (Kenya) and Mwanza (Tanzania); European discovery by John Speke, 1858; extensively explored by Stanley, 1875; originally called Ukewere, renamed in honour of Queen Victoria. » Africa; Speke

Victoria and Albert Museum A museum of fine and applied arts, opened in London in 1852 as the Museum of Manufactures, and later renamed the Museum of Ornamental Art. Articles bought from the Great Exhibition (1851) formed the core of the original display. In 1899, when Queen Victoria laid the foundation stone of the present building, she requested that it be renamed the Victoria and Albert. » Great Exhibition; museum

Victoria Cross (VC) In the UK, the highest military decoration, instituted by Queen Victoria in 1856 and awarded 'for conspicuous bravery in the face of the enemy'. Since 1902 it can be conferred posthumously; in 1920 women became eligible, but no woman has received it. The medal is inscribed 'For valour'; the ribbon is crimson. » decoration

Victoria Desert » **Great Victoria Desert**

Victoria Falls, indigenous name **Mosi oa Tunya** ('the smoke that thunders') Waterfalls on the Zambezi R, on the Zambia–Zimbabwe frontier, SC Africa; height, 61–108 m/200–354 ft; width, 1 688 m/5 538 ft; comprises five main falls (Eastern Cataract, Rainbow Falls, Devil's Cataract, Horseshoe Falls, Main Falls); European discovery by Livingstone, 1855; named after Queen Victoria; facing towns of Livingstone (Zambia) and Victoria Falls (Zimbabwe); major tourist attraction. » Livingstone, David; Zambezi, River

Victoria Island Island in Northwest Territories, Canada, in the Arctic Ocean; area 217 290 sq km/83 874 sq ml; 515 km/320 ml long; 274–595 km/170–370 ml wide; deeply indented; discovered 1838; named for Queen Victoria; sparse population. » Northwest Territories

Victoria Nile Upper reach of River Nile in NW Uganda; flows generally NW from the N end of L Victoria to enter L Kyoga, then in a NW arc into the Kabalega national park, passing the Kabalega (Murchison) Falls; ends in a swampy delta at the NE end of L Albert; length 420 km/260 ml. » Nile, River

Victoria Peak 22°18N 114°08E. Principal peak on Hong Kong Island, SE Asia; height, 554 m/1 818 ft; named after Queen Victoria; Peak Tramway (opened 1888) takes tourists to the summit for notable views of the city and harbour. » Hong Kong [i]

***Victory*, HMS** Nelson's flagship at the battle of Trafalgar (1805). Originally laid down in 1759, but not completed until 1778, she was the seventh vessel in the Royal Navy to bear the name. She is now in permanent dry dock, but still flies the white ensign as flagship to the commander-in-chief, Portsmouth. » Nelson, Horatio

vicuña [**vikyoona**] A wild member of the camel family, native to high grassland in the C Andes; resembles a llama, but smaller, more slender, and more graceful; produces the finest wool in the world; the only living artiodactyl in which the lower incisor teeth grow continuously. (*Vicugna vicugna*.) » alpaca; artiodactyl; Camelidae; llama

Vidal, Gore [**vidal**] (1925–) US writer, born at West Point, New York. He served in the army, then published his first novel, *Williwaw* (1946), drawing on his wartime experiences. His many novels include several satirical comedies, such as *Myra*

Breckenridge (1968) and *Duluth* (1983), and the historical trilogy, *Burr* (1974), *1876* (1976), and *Lincoln* (1984). His fictional history of America reaches the 20th-c with *Empire* (1987). He has also written short stories, plays (eg *Visit to a Small Planet*, 1956), film scripts, and essays. » American literature; novel; satire; short story

video Strictly, that part of the television signal which carries the picture information, as distinct from the audio signal carrying the sound; but by extension the term has become generally accepted to cover the electronic recording and reproduction of combined picture and sound, especially in its non-broadcast application. As a noun, a 'video' is an abbreviation for a videotape recorder, a videotape cassette, or the recorded programme itself. » videotape recorder

video disc A reproduction medium in which both picture and sound are recorded as an extremely fine spiral track on a flat circular disc. A series of pits in a reflective surface is optically scanned with a helium-neon laser, and the reflected beam read by a photo-diode to produce the signal. A 30 cm diameter disc can contain an hour's programme, and by recording exactly two fields per rotation throughout the spiral, single-frame still pictures can be shown. Unlike videotape, access from one part of the programme to another can be very rapid. » videotape

video games » **electronic games**

videogram A complete programme recorded as a videotape cassette or video disc for distribution by sale or hire. » video disc; videotape

videotape A high quality magnetic coating on a flexible polyester base for recording and reproducing video signals. The original formulae using dispersions of ferric oxide were improved by the addition of cobalt; further developments with chrome dioxide, metal-particle dispersions, and metal-evaporated coatings allowed increased information packing on narrower and thinner strips. Videotape has been made in widths of 2 in (50.8 mm, now obsolete), 1 in (25.4 mm), ¾ in (19 mm), ½ in (12.7 mm), 8 mm, and ¼ in (6.3 mm); the latter two widths are used for domestic applications. Overall thickness has been reduced from 30–35 μm to 13–16 μm, and metal-evaporated types are as thin as 10 μm. » videotape recorder

videotape recorder (VTR) A device for recording the picture and sound signals from a television camera on magnetic tape. To obtain a writing speed sufficient for the very high frequencies of a television signal, the recording head must travel rapidly across the moving magnetic tape. In early VTR machines, tape 2 inches wide ran at 15 inches per second past a rotating drum with four heads, producing quadruplex transverse tracks across its width; sound and control signals were recorded longitudinally on the two edges. This became the standard in television broadcasting from 1956 to the 1980s. Modern VTRs use narrower tape with helical scanning, each diagonal track recording a single TV field, with audio and control on the edges. The first helical-scan system meeting broadcast TV standards was the C format with 1 inch tape running from reel to reel; but for the less critical home video market cheaper and more convenient handling was needed. The easily-loaded cassettes of the U-matic system provided this, rapidly followed by several other systems, including Betamax and VHS, all incompatible; U-matic was preferred for professional production and VHS for domestic use. In the 1980s two more helical systems for high-quality production and broadcast were introduced, Betacam in 1981 and M-II in 1986; both use ½ inch tape with component recording of the luminance and compressed chrominance signals on separate adjacent tracks. In 1987–8, digital recording on videotape (DVTR) became available in the D1 and D2 formats, and soon after, the first digital recorders using solid-state storage chips. » Betacam; Betamax; D1 and D2 formats; helical scan [i]; U-matic; VHS; videotape

videowall A rectangular grouping of a number of separate video monitor screens, from 3 × 3 units upwards. They can be programmed for the display of individual single, multiple, or combination images with a sound track from videotape or disc recordings. » video

Vidor, King (1894–1982) US film director, born at Galveston, Texas. He went to Hollywood in 1915, and took a variety of jobs in the studios. His first feature film was *The Turn in the Road* (1919), followed by the silent classics *The Big Parade* (1925) and *The Crowd* (1928). With the coming of sound he made *Hallelujah* (1929) with an all-Black cast, and over the next 30 years his work included such varied productions as *Northwest Passage* (1940), an Italian co-production of *War and Peace* (1956), and the big screen epic *Solomon and Sheba* (1959). He died at Paso Robles, California.

Vienna, Ger **Wien** 48°13N 16°22E, pop (1981) 1 531 346. Capital city and a state of Austria; at the foot of the Wienerwald on the R Danube; C area surrounded by the monumental buildings and gardens of the Ringstrasse, developed 1859–88; badly damaged in World War 2, and occupied by the Allies (1945–55); to the NE extends a circuit of inner suburban districts; UNO-City, conference and office complex (opened 1979), with the offices of the United Nations agencies based in Vienna; archbishopric; university of technology (1815); university (1873–84); Spanish Riding School; refugees arriving in Austria are initially housed at the Traiskirchen camp amidst the Panonian vineyards near the city; metal products, precision instruments, electrical goods, engines, gearboxes, textiles, furniture; major tourist city, with several theatres, museums, concert halls, parks; associations with many composers in 18th–19th-c; Gothic St Stephen's Cathedral, St Peter's Church, Baroque Schottenkirche (12th-c, rebuilt 1638–48), former Bohemian Court Chancery, Gothic Church of Maria am Gestade, Romanesque Ruprechtskirche (12th–13th-c), Franciscan church (1603–11), Maria Theresa monument (1887), Palais Trautson (High Baroque architecture), Neo-Gothic town hall (1872–83), Baroque Palace of Schönbrunn, Opera House, Burgtheater; International Trade Fair (spring, autumn). » Albertina; Austria [i]; Danube, River; Schönbrunn Palace

Vienna, Congress of (1814–15) A European assembly convened at the instigation of the four victorious Powers to redefine the territorial map of Europe after the defeat of Napoleon. The negotiators were concerned to create a balance of power and to avoid alienating any major state; they incurred posterity's criticism for ignoring nationalism and perpetuating autocracy. » nationalism; Napoleonic Wars

Vienna Circle A philosophical discussion group founded in Vienna in the early 1920s by Schlick and invigorated in the late 1920s by Carnap. It rapidly became an international focus for logical positivism, disintegrating in the 1930s with the rise of Naziism. Its affiliates included Gödel, Wittgenstein, and Popper. » Carnap; logical positivism; Schlick

Vientiane [vyentyan], Lao **Viangchan** 17°59N 102°38E, pop (1979e) 90 000. Capital city of Laos, SE Asia; port on R Mekong, close to the Thailand frontier (W); airport; university (1958); brewing, textiles, cigarettes, detergents, matches, timber products; maize, rice, livestock; national museum, national library; Nam Ngum Dam (N), That Luang Temple (16th-c). » Laos [i]

Viet Cong or **Vietcong** ('Vietnamese communists') The name given by the Saigon government in 1959 to all the guerrilla forces that fought the South Vietnamese government during the Vietnam War. In 1960 they formed the National Liberation Front, whose demands included the withdrawal of all foreign troops and the overthrow of the government in South Vietnam. » Vietnam War

Viet Minh or **Vietminh** The abbreviation of **Vietnam Doc Lap Dong Minh** ('League for the Independence of Vietnam'), a politico-military organization formed by Ho Chi-minh in 1941. It included nationalists and communists, and aimed at liberating Vietnam from the Japanese and gaining independence from France. In 1945 it formed a government in Hanoi, and its army defeated the French at Dien Bien Phu in 1954. » Ho Chi-minh; Vietnam War

Vietnam, official name **Socialist Republic of Vietnam**, Vietnamese **Cong Hoa Xa Hoi Chu Nghia Viet Nam** pop (1990e) 66 128 000; area 329 566 sq km/127 212 sq ml. Independent socialist state in Indo-China, divided into three autonomous cities and 36 provinces; bounded E by the South China Sea, W by Laos and Cambodia, and N by China; capital, Hanoi; chief

cities, Ho Chi Minh (Saigon), Haiphong, Da Nang; timezone GMT +7; chief ethnic group, Vietnamese; chief religions, Confucianism, Buddhism, Taoism, Roman Catholicism; official language, Vietnamese; unit of currency, the dông.

Physical description and climate. Occupies a narrow strip along the coast of the Gulf of Tongking and the South China Sea; broader at the Mekong R delta (S) and along the Red R valley (N); highest peak, Fan si Pan (3 143 m/10 311 ft); limestone plateau in the S stretches W into Cambodia; tropical monsoon-type climate, dominated by S–SE winds (May–Sep) and N–NE winds (Oct–Apr); average annual rainfall, 1 000 mm/40 in (lowlands), 2 500 mm/100 in (uplands); high humidity in rainy season; temperatures high in the S, cooler in the N (Oct–Apr).

History and government. Under the influence of China for many centuries; regions of Tongking (N), Annam (C), and Cochin-China (S) united as Vietnamese Empire, 1802; French interest in the area from mid-19th-c; French protectorates established in Cochin-China (1867), and in Annam and Tongking (1884); formed the French Indo-Chinese Union with Cambodia and Laos, 1887; occupied by the Japanese in World War 2; communist Viet-Minh League under Ho Chi-minh formed after the War, not recognized by France; Indo-Chinese War, resulting in French withdrawal, 1946–54; 1954 armistice divided the country between the communist 'Democratic Republic' in the N and the 'State' of Vietnam in the S; civil war led to US intervention on the side of South Vietnam, 1965; fall of Saigon, 1975; reunification as the Socialist Republic of Vietnam, 1976; governed by a prime minister and a two-chamber legislature, comprising a 496-member National Assembly, elected every five years, and a 15-member Council of State, appointed by the Assembly; large numbers of refugees tried to find homes in the W in the late 1970s; Chinese invasion of Vietnam in 1979 greatly increased the number attempting to leave the country by sea; these 'Boat People' have presented non-communist countries with a continuing problem.

Economy. Over 70% of the workforce employed in agriculture; rice, maize, sorghum, beans, sugar, sweet potatoes, tea, coffee, rubber, tobacco, groundnuts, fishing, forestry; wood and rubber products, textiles, paper, fertilizers, glass, cement, food processing, light engineering; coal, tin, zinc, offshore oil; Vietnam War brought depopulation of the countryside, and considerable destruction of forest and farmland; towns overcrowded with refugees have since contributed to the economic problems, as have natural disasters caused by typhoons and flooding. >> boat people; Hanoi; Ho Chi-minh; Vietnam War; RR27 national holidays; RR66 political leaders

Vietnam War The war between communist North Vietnam and non-communist South Vietnam, also known as the *First* and *Second Indo-Chinese Wars*. The first began in 1946 after the breakdown of negotiations between France and the Viet Minh under Ho Chi-minh, and ended with the defeat of the French at Dien Bien Phu in 1954. The subsequent Geneva settlement left North Vietnam under communist rule, and the South ruled first by the emperor Bas Dai (until 1955) and then by Ngo Dinh Diem's dictatorial regime. (The elections planned at Geneva never took place.) From 1961, US aid and numbers of 'military advisers' increased considerably. From 1964, US aircraft bombarded the North, and by 1968 over 500 000 US troops were involved. These troops were withdrawn in 1973, and hostilities ceased in 1975, when the North's victory was completed with the capture of Saigon (renamed Ho Chi Minh City). >> My Lai incident; Viet Cong; Viet Minh; Vietnam [i]

Vietnamese An Austro-Asiatic language, spoken in Vietnam, Laos, and Cambodia by over 50 million people. 1 000 years of political and linguistic domination by China (until the 10th-c AD) has resulted in little being known of early Vietnamese, and there are no known early writings. A Latin-based alphabet, called *Quoc-ngu* (national language) was introduced in the 17th-c. >> Austro-Asiatic languages; Vietnam [i]

viewdata An interactive information service using a telephone link between the user and a central computer, eg PRESTEL, run by British Telecom in the UK. It can be used for home banking, armchair shopping, ticket ordering, and other such functions. The service is different from *teletext*, which is a non-interactive system transmitted along with television signals. >> acoustic coupler; PRESTEL; teletext

Vignola, Giacomo (Barozzi) da [veen**yo**la] (1507–73) Italian architect, born at Vignola. He studied at Bologna, and in Rome designed the Villa di Papa Giulio for Pope Julius III and the Church of the Gesú, which had a great influence on French and Italian church architecture. He died in Rome.

Vigny, Alfred Victor, Comte de ('Count of') [**vee**nyee] (1797–1863) French Romantic writer, born at Loches. He served in the army (1814–28), then turned to writing. His best-known works include the historical novel, *Cinq-Mars* (1826), a volume of exhortatory tales, *Stello* (1832), and the Romantic drama, *Chatterton* (1835). Several other works, including his journal and the philosophical poems, *Les Destinées* (1864, Destinies), were published after his death, in Paris. >> drama; French literature; novel; poetry; Romanticism (literature)

Vigo [**vee**goh] 42°12N 8°41W, pop (1981) 258 724. Naval and commercial port in Pontevedra province, Galicia, NW Spain; Spain's chief port for transatlantic traffic; airport; boat services to the Canary Is; shipbuilding, metallurgy; watersports; Castle of St Sebastian, Castro Castle; El Carmen fiesta (Jul), Pilgrimage to Monte de Santa Tecia (Aug). >> Galicia; Spain [i]

Viking project The first successful landing mission to Mars (Jul 1976), planned to search for evidence of life on Mars, and consisting of two highly instrumented orbiter-lander spacecraft. It was launched on Titan-Centaur vehicles in 1975, with the first landing (20 Jul 1976) on Chryse Planitia and the second (3 Sep 1976) on Utopia Planitia. Although evidence for life was not found, data from other lander and orbiter experiments have provided the basis for continuing intensive research on Martian evolution and climate. Orbiters and landers continued to return imaging and other data for several years after the primary project was completed. The project was managed by NASA's Langley Research Center, and operated from the Jet Propulsion Laboratory. >> Mars (astronomy); NASA; RR10

Vikings Raiders, traders, and settlers from Norway, Sweden, and Denmark, who between the late 8th-c and the mid-11th-c conquered and colonized large parts of Britain, Normandy, and Russia; attacked Spain, Morocco, and Italy; traded with Byzantium, Persia, and India; discovered and occupied Iceland

and Greenland; and reached the coast of N America. As seaborne raiders they gained a deserved reputation for brutality and destructiveness, but as merchants and settlers they played an influential and positive role in the development of mediaeval Europe. Their earliest overseas setttlements were in the Orkney and Shetland Is, which remained united to the Norwegian crown until 1472. » Canute; Danelaw; Germanic religion; Normans; Rollo; Vínland

Vila, also **Port-Vila** [**vee**la] 17°45S 168°18E, pop(1979) 14 801. Port and capital town of Vanuatu, on the SW coast of Efate I; airport; meat canning, agricultural trade. » Vanuatu

Vila Real [**vee**la ray**ahl**] 41°17N 7°48W, pop(1981) 13 300. Capital of Vila Real district, N Portugal; on R Corgo, 116 km/72 ml ENE of Oporto; airfield; port wine, pottery, tanning, textiles; Mateus Rosé produced nearby; cathedral, Church of São Pedro (16th-c), Mateus House, Roman sanctuary of Panoias 7 km/4 ml SE. » Portugal [i]

Villa, Francisco, byname **Pancho**, originally **Doroteo Arangol** [**vee**yah] (1877–1923) Mexican revolutionary, born near San Juan del Río, Durango. He followed a variety of modest occupations until the Mexican Revolution made him famous as a military commander. In a fierce struggle for control of the revolution, he was defeated by Venustiano Carranza, and withdrew to his strongholds in N Mexico, eventually making peace with the government (1920). He was murdered at Parral. » Mexico [i]

Villa-Lobos, Heitor [veela **loh**bush] (1887–1959) Brazilian composer and conductor, born and died in Rio de Janeiro. He studied at Rio, and travelled widely in Brazil, collecting material on folk music. His many compositions include twelve symphonies, as well as operas, large-scale symphonic poems, concerti, and ballets. He is also known for the nine suites *Bachianas Brasileiras* (1930–45), in which he treats Brazilian-style melodies in the manner of Bach. In 1932 he became director of musical education for Brazil.

Villahermosa [**veel**ya-air**moh**sa] 18°00N 92°53W, pop(1980) 250 903. River-port capital of Tabasco state, SE Mexico, on the R Grijalva; university (1958); agricultural trade, distilling, sugar refining; Centro de Investigaciones de las Culturas Olmecas; Mayan brick-built ruins of Comacalco to the NW. » Mexico [i]

Villars, Claude Louis Hector, Duke of [**vee**lah] (1653–1734) French marshal under Louis XIV, born at Moulins. He fought in the third Dutch War (1672–8), and in the War of the Spanish Succession (1701–14) inflicted heavy losses on Marlborough at Malplaquet (1709). In 1711 he headed the last army France could raise, and defeated the British and Dutch at Denain (1712). He later became the principal adviser on military affairs, and fought again in his 80s at the outbreak of the War of the Polish Succession (1733–8). He died at Turin. » Marlborough, Duke of; Spanish Succession, War of the

Villehardouin, Geoffroi de [veelah**dwĩ**] (c.1160–c.1213) French mediaeval chronicler. He took part in the Fourth Crusade, and described the events from 1198 to 1207, including the capture and sack of Constantinople in 1204. » Crusades [i]

villein [**vi**layn] In mediaeval England, a legally unfree peasant or serf; tied to the manor; liable to arbitrary obligations, including labour services on the lord's estate (demesne); denied control over goods and property; and wholly bound to the lord's jurisdiction. In practice, custom often mitigated the main disabilities. Underlying economic forces (notably the underpopulation caused by the Black Death), rather than the Peasants' Revolt, effectively ended villeinage in the 15th-c. » Black Death; feudalism; manor; Peasants' Revolt; serfdom

Villeneuve, Pierre (Charles Jean Baptiste Sylvestre) de [**veel**nerv] (1763–1806) French admiral, born at Valensoles. He commanded the rear division of the French navy at the Battle of the Nile, and in 1805 was in charge of the French fleet at Trafalgar, where he was taken prisoner. Released in 1806, during his return journey to Paris to face Napoleon, he committed suicide at Rennes. » Aboukir Bay, Battle of; Napoleonic Wars; Trafalgar, Battle of

Villiers de L'Isle Adam, Count (Philippe) Auguste (Mathias) [**veel**yay duh leel a**dã**] (1840–89) French writer, born at St-Brieuc. He wrote many poems, short stories (eg *Contes Cruels*, 1883, Cruel Tales), novels (eg *Isis*, 1862), and plays (eg *La Révolte*, 1870, The Revolt). The elements of intense idealism and refined excess in his work link him to both the Symbolists and the Decadents. A Catholic aristocrat, he lived for a while with the monks of Solesmes, and died in Paris. » Decadents; French literature; Symbolism

Villon, François, pseudonym of **François de Montcorbier** [**vee**yõ] (1431–?) French poet, born in Paris. While at university in Paris, he had to flee after fatally wounding a priest in a street brawl (1455). He joined a criminal organization, the 'Brotherhood of the Coquille', and wrote some of his ballades in its secret jargon. Pardoned in 1456, he returned to Paris and there wrote *Le Lais* (The Legacy, also known as *Le Petit Testament*), followed by his long poetic sequence, *Le Grand Testament* (1461). Throughout this period, he is known to have taken part in several crimes, and in 1463 received a death sentence, commuted to banishment. He left Paris, and nothing further is known of him. » ballad; French literature; poetry

Vilnius, formerly **Wilno** (1920–39) [**veel**niuhs] 54°40N 25°19E, pop(1989) 582 000. Capital city of Lithuania, on R Vilnya; one of the largest industrial centres of the Baltic region; formerly part of Poland; ceded to Russia, 1795; occupied by Germany in World War 2; airport; railway junction; university (1579); machinery, metalworking, chemicals, foodstuffs, textiles; cathedral (1777–1801), Gediminas Castle. » Lithuania

Vimy Ridge An escarpment 8 km/5 ml NE of Arras (Pas-de-Calais), a strongly held part of the German defence line on the Western Front in World War 1. It was successfully stormed during the Battle of Arras by the Canadian Corps of the British 1st Army (1917). This feat of arms had great symbolic significance in establishing Canada's identity as an independent nation. » World War 1

Viña del Mar [**veen**ya t͟hel **mah**] 33°02S 71°35W, pop(1982) 290 014. Seaside town in Valparaíso province, C Chile; 9 km/5 ml from Valparaíso city; residential suburb and popular S American resort; Sporting Club, with racecourse and playing fields; Granadilla Golf Club, casino, sports stadium, Tranque Sausalito (artificial lake), Salinas golf course, Cerro Castillo (presidential summer palace), Quinta Vergara (gallery), Teatro Municipal; festival of El Roto (Jan); international musical festival (Feb). » Chile [i]; Valparaíso

Vincent de Beauvais Lat **Vincentius Bellovacensis** [vĩsã duh boh**vay**] (c.1190–c.1264) French Dominican and encyclopedist, who gathered together, under the patronage of Louis IX, the entire knowledge of the Middle Ages in his *Speculum Majus* (Great Mirror). Its three parts, on natural, doctrinal, and historical subjects, were supplemented by a section on morals in the 14th-c, by an unknown author. » Louis IX

Vincent de Paul, St (c.1580–1660), feast day 27 September. French priest and philanthropist, born at Pouy. Ordained in 1600, he was captured by corsairs in 1605, and sold into slavery at Tunis, but after persuading his master to return to the Christian faith, escaped to France in 1607. He formed associations for helping the sick, became almoner-general of the galleys (1619), and in 1625 founded the Congregation of Priests of the Missions (or 'Lazarists', from their priory of St Lazare) and (1634) the Sisterhood of Charity. He died in Paris, and was canonized in 1737. » Lazarists; missions, Christian

Vincentians » **Lazarists**

Vinci, Leonardo da » **Leonardo da Vinci**

vine » **climbing plant; grapevine**

vine snake A tree snake of family *Colubridae*; name used especially for New World species of genus *Oxybelis* and S Asian species of genus *Dryophis*; green or brown with pointed snout; length, up to 2 m/6½ ft, but thickness only 10–15 mm/0.4–0.6 in; resembles forest vines; eats juvenile birds and lizards. » tree snake

vinegar A sour liquid used as a food preservative or domestic flavour enhancer. It derives from the oxidization of alcohol by bacteria, the ethanol being converted to acetic acid. There is a wide range of vinegars, with different colours and aromas, determined by the source of the alcohol used, eg red wine, white wine, cider, malt. » ethanol; food preservation

vinegar eel A small roundworm, length 1–2 mm/ 0.039–0.0788 in, found in fermenting vinegar; feeds on yeasts. (Phylum: *Nematoda*.) » nematode; vinegar; yeast

Vingt, les [lay vĩ] A group of 20 modern painters, including Ensor, founded in Brussels in 1884. For ten years they held exhibitions where pictures by leading Post-Impressionists such as Seurat, Gauguin, Cézanne, and van Gogh were shown. » modern art; Post-Impressionism; Ensor

vingt-et-un » **pontoon**

Vinland [**veen**land] A generalized Norse name meaning 'Berry' or 'Vine Land', applied to the E coast of N America from the time of its first sighting by the Viking Leif Eriksson c.AD 985. Though the 'Vinland Map', purportedly of the 1440s, is a 20th-c forgery, accounts of the Norse discovery of America in Icelandic sagas are confirmed by archaeological evidence. » L'Anse aux Meadows; Leif Eriksson; Skraelings; Vikings

Vinson Massif Highest peak in Antarctica, rising to 5 140 m/ 16 863 ft in the Ellsworth Mts. » Antarctica [i]

vinyl An important organic chemical grouping ($CH_2=CH-$). The double bond lends itself to polymerization, so that many types of polymer are based on it, their nature depending on the substituents. » polyvinylacetate; polyvinylchloride

viola A bowed string instrument, in all essential respects like a violin but slightly larger and tuned a 5th lower. » string instrument **1** [i]; string quartet; violin

viola da gamba Strictly speaking, any member of the viol family – bowed string instruments held upright on the knees, or between the legs, of the player; more generally, the bass instrument of that family, loosely resembling a cello but with sloping shoulders, a flat back, six strings, and a fretted fingerboard like a guitar's. » cello; string instrument **1** [i]

violet An annual and perennial native to most temperate regions, many being alpine species; leaves often heart-shaped; zygomorphic flowers 5-petalled with a backward projecting spur, blue, yellow, white, or these colours combined, sometimes fragrant. It includes the species commonly known as **pansies**. (*Viola*, 500 species. Family: *Violaceae*.) » annual; dog violet; heartsease; pansy; perennial; sweet violet; zygomorphic flower

violin The most widespread of all bowed string instruments, and one of the most important instruments in Western music since the 17th-c. The four-string violin was developed in the 16th-c from earlier three-string types, and reached its highest point of perfection between 1650 and 1730 in the hands of Stradivari and the Amati and Guarneri families. Later modifications have included the lengthening of the fingerboard, and the provision of a chin rest; steel and nylon have largely replaced gut as the main material for the strings. The other regular members of the violin family are the viola, cello, and double bass. » kinnor; kit; string instrument **1** [i]; string quartet; viola; Guarneri; Stradivari

Viollet-Le-Duc, Eugène (Emmanuel) [**vyo**hlay luh **dük**] (1814–79) French architect and archaeologist, born in Paris. He studied in France and Italy, and in 1840 directed the restoration of Ste Chapelle, Paris. His other restorations included the cathedrals of Notre Dame, Amiens, and Laon, and the Château de Pierrefonds. He died at Lausanne, Switzerland.

violoncello » **cello**

viper A venomous snake of family *Viperidae* (187 species), worldwide except Australia; most give birth to live young; thick body; head usually triangular, broad (due to poison glands and associated muscles at sides); fangs attached to front of upper jaw, folding flat against roof of mouth; venom destroys blood cells and vessels, and causes internal bleeding. » asp; Gaboon/horned/Russell's viper; pit viper [i]; snake

viper's bugloss [**byoo**glos] A stout, erect, bristly biennial, growing to c.1 m/3¼ ft, native to Europe and W Asia; leaves 15 cm/6 in, lance-shaped to oblong, rough; a large panicle formed by the basal stalked inflorescence of numerous coiled cymes, with flowers all on one side; flowers funnel-shaped, pink in bud, opening blue. (*Echium vulgare*. Family: *Boraginaceae*.) » biennial; inflorescence [i]; panicle

Virgil or **Vergil**, in full **Publius Vergilius Maro** (70–19 BC) The greatest Latin poet, born at Andes, near Mantua. He studied rhetoric and philosophy in Rome, and became one of the endowed court poets who gathered round the minister and patron, Maecenas. His *Eclogues* (37 BC) were received with great enthusiasm. Soon afterwards he withdrew to Campania, where he wrote the *Georgics*, or *Art of Husbandry* (36–29 BC), and for the rest of his life worked at the request of the Emperor on the *Aeneid*. When this was almost completed, he travelled in Greece and Asia, but fell ill, and died at Brundisium. » Aeneas; epic; Latin literature; Maecenas; pastoral; poetry; rhetoric; Theocritus

Virgin Birth » **Immaculate Conception**

Virgin Islands, British pop (1987) 12 197; area 153 sq km/ 59 sq ml. Island group at the NW end of the Lesser Antilles chain, E Caribbean; c.80 km/50 ml E of Puerto Rico; British dependent territory; capital, Road Town (on Tortola I); timezone GMT −4; population mainly of African or mixed descent; official language, English; chief religion, Protestantism; unit of currency, the US dollar; comprises four large islands (Tortola, Virgin Gorda, Anegada, Jost Van Dyke) and over 30 islets and cays; only 16 islands inhabited; highest point, Sage Mt (540 m/1 772 ft) on Tortola I; sub-tropical climate; temperatures 17–28°C (winter), 26–31°C (summer); average annual rainfall, 1 270 mm/50 in; Tortola colonized by British planters, 1666; constitutional government, 1774; part of the Leeward Is, 1872; separate Crown Colony, 1956; governor represents the British sovereign; 6-member Executive Council and a Legislative Council of 11 members; over 50% of national income from tourism; construction, rum, paint, gravel and stone extraction, livestock, coconuts, sugar cane, fruit and vegetables, fish. » Antilles; Leeward Islands (Caribbean); Road Town

Virgin Islands, United States, official name **Virgin Islands of the United States**, formerly **Danish West Indies** (to 1917) pop (1989e) 107 000; area 342 sq km/132 sq ml. A group of more than 50 islands in the S and W of the Virgin Is group, Lesser Antilles, Caribbean Sea, 64 km/40 ml E of Puerto Rico; capital, Charlotte Amalie; timezone GMT −4; official language, English; chief religion, Protestantism; unit of currency, the US dollar; three main inhabited islands, St Croix, St Thomas, St John; volcanic origin; highest peak, Crown Mt (474 m/1 555 ft) on St Thomas; average temperature 21–29°C (Dec–Mar), 24–31°C (Jun–Sep); low humidity; Denmark colonized St Thomas and St John in 1671, and bought St Croix from France in 1733; purchased by the USA, 1917; now an unincorporated territory of the USA; a governor serves a 4-year term, with an elected 15-member unicameral legislature; chief industry is tourism; St Croix industries include oil and alumina refining, clocks and watches, textiles, rum, fragrances, pharmaceuticals, vegetables, fruit, sorghum. » Charlotte Amalie; St Croix; St John (US Virgin Is); St Thomas

virginals A keyboard instrument with a mechanism similar to that of the harpsichord, but with strings set at right angles to the keys (as in the clavichord). No fully convincing explanation of the name has been advanced. The instrument was widely used from the 15th-c to the 17th-c, when it was superseded by the spinet. » clavichord; harpsichord; keyboard instrument; spinet

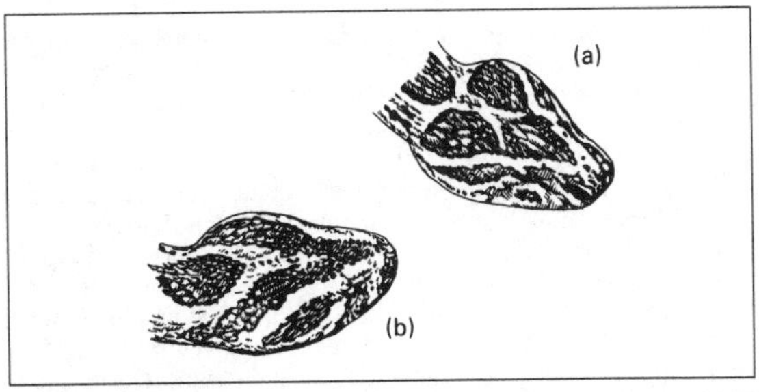

Viper heads showing the 'V' marking – Palestinian viper (a); Russell's viper (b)

Virginia pop (1987e) 5 904 000; area 105 582 sq km/40 767 sq ml. State in E USA, divided into 95 counties and 41 independent cities; 'Old Dominion'; bounded E by Maryland, Chesapeake Bay, and the Atlantic Ocean; first permanent British settlement in America (at Jamestown, 1607); named after Elizabeth I (the 'Virgin Queen'); one of the first colonies to move for independence; scene of the British surrender at Yorktown, 1781; tenth of the original 13 states to ratify the Constitution, 1788; scene of several major battles in the Civil War (Richmond was the Confederacy capital); re-admitted to the Union, 1870; capital, Richmond; other major cities Norfolk, Virginia Beach, Newport News; Potomac R follows the Maryland state border; Rappahannock, York, and James Rivers cross the state to Chesapeake Bay; Blue Ridge Mts in the W; highest point Mt Rogers (1 743 m/5 718 ft); flat and swampy coastal area (the Tidewater region); to the W, land rises into the rolling, fertile Piedmont, interrupted further W by the Blue Ridge Mts; W of these lies a series of beautiful valleys (the Valley of Virginia), notably the Shenandoah; tobacco (chief agricultural crop), dairy produce, cattle, hay, corn, peanuts, sweet potatoes, apples; chemicals, tobacco products (Richmond), electrical equipment, ships (on the shores of Hampton Roads channel); coal mining (in the SW); scenic mountains, valleys, and shores, as well as the area's history, make tourism a major state industry. » American Civil War; Richmond (USA); United States of America [i]; RR39

Virginia Beach 36°51N 75°59W, pop (1980) 262 199. Independent city, SE Virginia, USA, on the Atlantic Ocean; a major summer resort; naval air station; railway; Cape Henry Memorial (site of English landing in 1607); Marine Science Museum. » Virginia

Virginia creeper Either of two species of very similar deciduous climbers with sucker-bearing tendrils, tiny green flowers, and bright red autumn foliage, both widely grown as ornamentals. *Parthenocissus quinquefolia*, native to eastern N America, has palmate leaves with five pointed leaflets; *Parthenocissus tricuspidata* native to China and Japan, has 3-lobed leaves. (Family: *Vitaceae*.) » climbing plant; deciduous plants; palmate; sucker; tendril

Virginia Resolutions » **Kentucky and Virginia Resolutions**

Virgo (Lat 'virgin') A large N constellation, which contains an abundance of faint galaxies as well as the first quasar to be recognized as such, 3C 273, and one of the very largest galaxies known, M87. Its brightest star is Spica, a close binary. It is a summer sign of the zodiac, lying between Leo and Libra. » binary star; constellation; galaxy; quasar; RR9

viroid A fragment of infectious nucleic acid that resembles a virus; typically consisting of a small loop of ribonucleic acid not enclosed within a protein shell (*capsid*). It includes the causative agents of some plant diseases, such as hop stunt. » RNA; virus

virtual image » **optics** [i]

virtual particle A term used to describe any particle appearing as an intermediary in a sub-atomic particle reaction. Virtual particles borrow energy according to the Heisenberg uncertainty principle, and in so doing temporarily violate the mass-energy conservation law. For example, an electron and a positron may interact via a virtual photon – an unphysical photon which has borrowed energy to become temporarily heavy. No virtual particle is directly observable, but they are needed to describe particle reactions in quantum field theory. » Feynman diagrams [i]; Heisenberg uncertainty principle; particle physics; quantum field theory

Virunga [vi**rung**ga] National park in the Kivu region of NW Zaire; environments include marshy deltas, savannah, volcanic landscapes, and snow-covered mountains; noted for its wild mammals, particularly its gorilla colonies; a world heritage site. » Zaire [i]

virus The smallest infectious particle, 10–300 nm in diameter. Viruses infect other micro-organisms such as bacteria, fungi, and algae, as well as higher plants and animals. The genetic material of each virus is present as a molecule of either ribonucleic acid or deoxyribonucleic acid, encased inside a protein shell (*capsid*). Complex viruses have an outer envelope surrounding the capsid. Viruses replicate only in living cells, their nucleic acid directing the host cell to synthesize material required for producing more virus. Virus particles can survive in a dried, crystalline, and metabolically inert state. The study of viruses is known as **virology**. » DNA [i]; RNA; viroid; Plate XIII

Visayan Islands [vi**si**yan] area 61 991 sq km/23 928 sq ml. Island group in the C Philippines; N of Mindanao I, S of Luzon I; bounded by the Sulu Sea (W) and Philippine Sea (E); chief islands include Cebu, Bohol, Panay, Leyte, Samar, Negros, Masbate; sugar, coconuts. » Philippines [i]

viscacha [vis**ka**cha] A cavy-like rodent from S America; resembles a large chinchilla; lives among rocks or in burrows; four species in genera *Lagostomus* (**plains viscacha**) and *Lagidium* (**mountain viscacha**, **mountain chinchilla**, or **rock squirrel**). (Family: *Chinchillidae*.) » cavy; chinchilla; rodent

Visconti, Count Luchino (1906–76) Italian stage and film director, born in Milan. An early interest in music and the theatre led him to stage designing and the production of opera and ballet. A short spell as assistant to Renoir turned his attention to the cinema. His first film, *Ossessione* (1942, Obsession), took Italy by storm, with its strict realism and concern with social problems. Later films included *La Terra Trema* (1947, The Earth Trembles), *Il Gattopardo* (1963, The Leopard), and *Morte a Venezia* (1971, Death in Venice).

viscose The solution of cellulose from which regenerated cellulose fibre (rayon) is produced. Discovered in 1892, the viscose process is still the basis of most rayon manufacturing. » cellulose; rayon

viscosity [vis**kos**itee] A measure of a fluid's reluctance to flow, corresponding to internal friction in the fluid as one portion of the fluid seeks to slide over another; symbol η, units Pa.s (pascal.second), but a more common unit is poise, P (1P = 0.1 Pa.s). It is defined as the ratio of shear stress to the rate of change of shear strain. For water, $\eta = 0.01$ P; for castor oil, $\eta = 9.86$ P. η is also called the **absolute** or **dynamic viscosity**. The quantity η divided by fluid density is the **kinematic viscosity**. » fluid mechanics; friction; Reynolds' number; rheology

viscount (Lat *vice-comes* 'deputy of a duke') In the UK, the fourth highest title of honour in the peerage, or the courtesy title of the eldest son of an earl or a marquess. » peerage; titles [i]

Vishinsky, Andrei » **Vyshinsky, Andrei**

Vishnu [**vish**noo] A major Hindu deity, second in the triad (*Trimurti*) of gods manifesting the cosmic functions of the Supreme Being. The preserver of the universe and the embodiment of goodness and mercy, he is believed to have assumed visible form in nine descents (*avataras*): three in non-human form, one in hybrid form, and five in human form, of which his appearances as Rama and Krishna are the most important. » avatar; Hinduism; Krishna; Trimurti

visibles » **invisibles**

Visigoths A Germanic people, forming one of the two great Gothic tribes, who fled from the Huns in 376 into the Roman Empire, and eventually founded the Visigothic kingdom, embracing at its height in the 7th-c Portugal, virtually all Spain, and part of S Gaul. It was extinguished by the Arab conquest of 711. » Gaul; Goths; Huns

vision The process by which organisms form an internal representation of the external environment on the basis of the pattern of light available to them. The crucial requirement is for a light-sensitive receptor. Higher animals have many such *photoreceptors* (about 230 million in each eye in humans) making up a photoreceptive suface, the *retina*. For anything more than crude light detection, an *image* is essential; this constitutes an orderly representation on the retina of the spatial array of objects in the environment. Information from the retina passes up the one million fibres of the optic nerve to the occipital cortex, the first of many brain regions devoted to vision. The way in which the brain encodes basic visual features such as colour, edges, and movement is becoming increasingly understood, but very little is known of how these features are interpreted to enable us to recognize objects. » acuity; brain [i]; colour vision; constancy; eye [i]; Gestalt psychology; illusion

THE MAIN TYPES OF VITAMIN

FAT SOLUBLE VITAMINS

VITAMIN	CHEMICAL NAME	PRECURSOR	MAIN SYMPTOM OF DEFICIENCY	DIETARY SOURCE
A	retinol	β-carotene	xerophthalmia (eye disease)	*retinol:* milk, butter, cheese, egg yolk, liver and fatty fish *carotene:* green vegetables, yellow and red fruits and vegetables, especially carrots
D	cholecalciferol	UV-activated 7-dehydro-cholesterol	rickets, osteomalacia	fatty fish, margarine, and some fortified milks
K	phytomenadione		haemorrhagic problems	green leafy vegetables and liver
E	tocopherols		multiple effects	vegetable oils

WATER SOLUBLE VITAMINS

VITAMIN	CHEMICAL NAME	MAIN SYMPTOM OF DEFICIENCY	DIETARY SOURCE
C	ascorbic acid	scurvy	citrus fruits, potatoes, green leafy vegetables
B-vitamins			
B_1	thiamine	beri-beri	seeds and grains; widely distributed
B_2	riboflavin	failure to thrive	liver, milk, cheese, yeast
–	nicotinic acid	pellagra	meat, fish, cereals, pulses
B_6	pyridoxine	dermatitis; neurological disorders	cereals, liver, meat, fruits, leafy vegetables
B_{12}	cyanocobalamin	anaemia	meat, milk, liver
–	folic acid	anaemia	liver, green vegetables
–	pantothenic acid	dermatitis	widespread
–	biotin	dermatitis	liver, kidney, yeast extracts

vision mixer Equipment used in video production for the selection of programme material from several sources – multiple cameras, telecine, slide scanner, videotape recorder – with facilities for transition effects between scenes and for image combination at the time of shooting and in post-production editing. The term also refers to the technician who operates the equipment under the director or editor.

Vistula, River, Polish **Wisła** [**vist**yoola] Longest river in Poland; rises in the Carpathians in SW Poland and flows NE, N, and NW for 1 047 km/651 ml to meet the Baltic Sea at Gdańsk; navigable for 941 km/585 ml; linked by canal to E and W Europe; dammed at Goczałkowice. » Poland [i]

visual display unit » **VDU**

vitalism The doctrine, held by Bergson and Driesch, which maintains that the living functions of a biological organism cannot be accounted for in terms of the chemical or physical processes of its non-living parts. Thus every living organism has an immaterial life force, which may or may not be capable of existing apart from the physical organism. » Bergson; Driesch; mechanism

vitamins Organic substance present in minute quantities in natural foods that are essential for health, classified as either *water soluble* or *fat soluble*. When absent from the diet or present in insufficient amounts, they result in specific abnormalities, due to the derangement of particular metabolic processes. » animal protein factor; antivitamin factors; ascorbic acid; biotin; cyanocobalamin; folic acid; megavitamin therapy; pyridoxine; retinol; riboflavin; tocopherol; vegetarianism

Vitebsk [**vee**tyepsk] 55°10N 30°14E, pop (1983) 324 000. River-port capital of Vitebskaya oblast, NE Belorussia, on R Zapadnaya Dvina; founded, 11th-c; airfield; railway; agricultural trade, wool textiles, footwear, machine tools. » Belorussia

Viti Levu [**vee**tee **lay**voo] area 10 429 sq km/4 026 sq ml. Largest and most important island of Fiji, SW Pacific Ocean, separated from Vanua Levu, 32 km/20 ml NE, by the Koro Sea; length 144 km/89 ml; width 104 km/65 ml; mountainous interior, rising to 1 324 m/4 344 ft at Tomaniivi (Mt Victoria); lower reaches of main rivers provide fertile alluvial flats; capital, Suva; airport; gold mining, sugar milling, tourism; experimental irrigated rice projects near Suva; Tholoisuva Forest Park. » Fiji

Vitosha or **Vitosa** [**vee**tosha] 42°40N 23°15E. W Bulgaria's largest ski resort, 20 km/12 ml E of Sofia; altitude 1 810 m/5 938 ft; notable skiing facilities. » Bulgaria [i]

vitrification » **glass** [i]

vitriol » **sulphuric acid**

Vitruvius, in full **Marcus Vitruvius Pollio** [vit**roo**viuhs] (1st-c AD) Roman architect and military engineer. He was in the service of Augustus, and wrote the 10-volume *De Architectura* (On Architecture), the only Roman treatise on architecture still extant. » Augustus

Vittoria, Span **Vitoria** [vee**toh**ria] 42°51N 2°40W, pop (1981) 192 773. Basque capital of Álava province, N Spain, 351 km/218 ml N of Madrid; scene of French defeat in the Peninsular War (1813); bishopric; airport; railway; vehicles, steel, electronics, explosives, arms, machinery, furniture, sugar refining; Church of St Peter, old and new cathedrals; Fiesta of St Prudence (Apr), La Virgen Blanca fair (Aug), pilgrimage to Olarizu (Sep), autumn music festival. » Basque Provinces; Peninsular War; Spain [i]

Vittoria, Tommaso Ludovico da » **Victoria, Tomás Luis de**

Vittorino da Feltre, originally **Vittorino dei Ramboldini** [veet-tuh**ree**noh da **fel**truh] (c.1378–1446) Italian educationist, born at Feltre. He studied and taught at Padua, and in 1423 was summoned to Mantua as tutor to the children of the Marchese Gonzaga. There he founded a school for both rich and poor children (1425), in which he devised new methods of instruction, introducing a wide curriculum, and integrating the development of mind and body through the study of the Classics and Christianity. He died at Mantua. » education

Vivaldi, Antonio (Lucio) [viv**al**dee] (1678–1741) Venetian

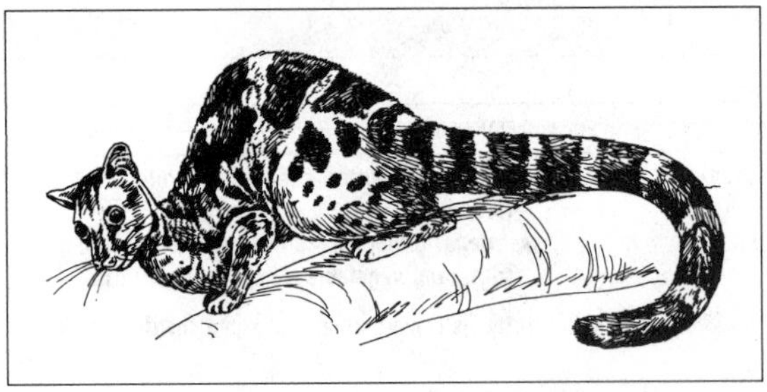

Viverridae – Banded linsang

violinist and composer, born at Venice. He was ordained in 1703, but gave up officiating, and was attached to the Conservatory of the Ospedale della Pietà at Venice (1703–40). The twelve concertos of *L'Estro Armonico* (1712) gave him a European reputation; *The Four Seasons* (1725), an early example of programme music, proved highly popular; and he wrote many operas, sacred music, and over 450 concertos. He died in Vienna.

Vivekananda [vivay**kan**anda], also called **Narendranath Datta** (1862–1902) Hindu philosopher, born and died in Calcutta. Educated in a Western-style university, he first joined the Brahmo Samaj, attracted by its policy of social reform. Later, he met Ramakrishna and became his leading disciple, establishing the headquarters of the Ramakrishna Order at Belur Math on the Ganges, near Calcutta. He attempted to combine Indian spirituality with Western materialism, and became the main force behind the Vedanta movement in the West. » Brahmo Samaj; Ramakrishna

Viverridae [viveridee] A family of small to medium-sized carnivores native to the S Old World; 72 species; long thin body, long tail, pointed muzzle, short legs; coat often spotted or banded; most secrete pungent fluid from glands near tail; inhabit woodland or dense undergrowth; eat small vertebrates, invertebrates, eggs, fruit, carrion. » binturong; carnivore [i]; civet; fossa; genet; ichneumon (mammal); linsang; meerkat; mongoose

Vivés, Juan Luis or **Ludovicus Vives** [**vee**vays] (1492–1540) Spanish philosopher and humanist, born at Valencia. He studied at Paris but, disliking scholasticism, went to Louvain, where he became professor of humanities (1519). He dedicated his edition of St Augustine's *Civitas Dei* to Henry VIII, who summoned him to England in 1523 as tutor to Princess Mary. His writings include *Adversus Pseudodialecticos* (1570, Against the Pseudo-Dialecticians), and several other works on educational theory and practice. Imprisoned in 1527 for opposing Henry's divorce, he then lived mostly at Bruges, where he died. » Henry VIII

viviparity [vivi**par**itee] In animals, the production of live young rather than eggs. The embryos grow within the mother's body, which provides nourishment via a placenta or similar structure. Viviparity occurs in placental mammals and some other animals. In plants, it refers to the production of seeds that germinate within the fruit while still attached to the parent plant. » placenta (anatomy); reproduction

vivisection The practice of dissecting live animals for experimental purposes. The research includes experiments which look for the effects of new drugs, food additives, cosmetics, and a wide range of chemicals on the body tissue and behaviour of such animals as guinea pigs, rabbits, rats, and monkeys, as an alternative to using human subjects. Such research is now strictly controlled by legislation in most Western nations, but nonetheless provokes considerable public opposition in some countries, including the use of violence against scientists and research organizations by animal rights extremists.

Vlaanderen [**vlan**duhruhn] » **Flanders**

Vladimir (Svyatoslavich) I, byname **the Great** (?–1015), feast day 15 Jul. Grand Prince of Kiev (c.978–1015). One of ancient Russia's most illustrious rulers, he consolidated the state, and led victorious campaigns against the Viatichi, Lithuanians, and Bulgars. Under his rule the economy and culture of Kievan Russia generally flourished. In 988 he was converted to Christianity, and adopted the Greek Orthodox rite from Byzantium as the official religion of Russia. After his death, Kievan Russia was torn apart by dynastic rivalries among his 12 sons. He was later canonized. » Russian history

Vladivostok [vladee**vos**tok], 43°10N 131°53E, pop (1989) 648 000. Seaport capital of Primorskiy kray, Russia, on the Sea of Japan; chief Russian port on the Pacific Ocean (kept open in winter by ice-breakers); base for fishing and whaling fleets; founded, 1860; terminus of the Trans-Siberian Railway; university (1920); naval base; shipbuilding and repairing, precision instruments, foodstuffs, building materials. » Russia; Trans-Siberian Railway

Vlaminck, Maurice de [**vla**mĩk] (1876–1958) French artist, born in Paris. He was largely self-taught, worked with Derain, and came to be influenced by van Gogh. By 1905 he was one of the leaders of the Fauves, using typically brilliant colour, then painted more realist landscapes under the influence of Cézanne (1908–14), and later developed a more sombre Expressionism. He died at Rueil-la-Gadelière. » Cézanne; Derain; Expressionism; Fauvism; French art; van Gogh

Vlissingen » **Flushing**

Vlorë or **Vlora** [**vlo**ruh], Ital **Valona**, ancient **Aulon** 40°27N 19°30E, pop (1980) 58 000. Seaport and capital of Vlorë district, SW Albania, on the Bay of Vlorë, 112 km/69 ml SW of Tiranë; a 5th-c bishopric; independence proclaimed here in 1912; railway; well-protected harbour; fishing, olive oil processing. » Albania [i]

VLSI » **very large scale integration**

Vltava, River [**vuhl**tava], Ger **Moldau** River in W Czechoslovakia, formed in the Bohemian Forest by the junction of two headstreams; flows SE and N to meet the R Elbe near Melnik; length 427 km/265 ml; navigable for c.80 km/50 ml; major source of hydroelectricity. » Czechoslovakia [i]

VOA » **Voice of America**

vocal cords Two muscular folds in the larynx, behind the Adam's apple. They are very flexible, and are brought together to impede the airflow during speech, when they vibrate and produce voice, used in the articulation of vowels and many consonants. They are also used to vary the pitch of the voice (generally, the faster the vibration, the higher the pitch) and are also involved in the production of several distinctive tones of voice. When they are completely open, the air flows freely, as in whispering and the pronunciation of 'h'. » electrolaryngography; intonation; larynx

vocational education Education which is aimed at the preparation of students for their present or future employment. Often undertaken in colleges of further education, it can also take place on the job in the workplace itself. A wide range of vocational qualifications is usually available, some from chartered award-giving institutions, others from professional organizations. In addition, pre-vocational education is available for pupils of school age who wish to acquire work experience and explore the nature of different careers before making their choice. » access course; further education; polytechnic

vodka A colourless spirit produced from potatoes, the national drink of Poland and Russia. It is almost tasteless, and is thus used in many mixed drinks, such as the 'Bloody Mary' (vodka and tomato juice). It is best served chilled. » spirits

Vogel, Hans-Jochen [**voh**gl] (1926–) German politician, successor to Helmut Schmidt as leader of the Social Democratic Party (SPD) and the Party's nominee for the chancellorship of West Germany. A former Minister of Housing and Town Planning (1972–4) and Minister of Justice (1974–81), he also served briefly as governing mayor of West Berlin (1981). » Germany [i]; Schmidt, Helmut

Voice of America (VOA) The external broadcasting service of the US Information Agency, founded in 1942. In the late 1980s, the VOA was broadcasting world-wide in English and 45 other languages (including nine to the USSR) from five stations in the USA, and a number of overseas relay stations. » broadcasting

Volans (Lat 'flying fish') [**voh**lanz] A tiny and inconspicuous S constellation near the Large Magellanic Cloud. » constellation; Magellanic Clouds; RR9

volcano A vent or fissure in the Earth's crust where molten lava is erupted onto the surface. The shape of a volcano depends on the composition of the lava. Lower-temperature, viscous, silica-rich lava forms steep-sided cones interbedded with ash, such as Mt Fuji, Japan. Less viscous, silica-poor, basaltic lavas form gentle slopes, as found in Iceland. Most volcanoes are confined to the zones along boundaries between crustal plates, and are closely associated with earthquakes, as in the circum-Pacific 'ring of fire'; but there are notable exceptions, such as the Hawaiian Is, which have formed on a 'hot spot' in the Earth's crust. The scientific study of volcanoes is known as **vulcanology**. » earthquake; igneous rock; lava; plate tectonics [i]; RR14

Volcano Islands Group of Japanese islands in the W Pacific Ocean; includes Iwo Jima, Kita Iwo, and Minami Iwo; administered by the USA, 1945–68; returned to Japan in 1968; sulphur, sugar. » Iwo Jima; Japan [i]

Volcanus » **Vulcan** (mythology)

vole A mouse-like rodent native to Asia, Europe, and N America; most species with large head, blunt snout, and short tail; eats grasses, seeds and insects; population numbers rise and fall drastically every few years; closely related to lemmings. (Tribe: *Microtini*, 96 species.) » lemming; mouse (zoology); rodent; water vole

Volga, River, ancient **Rha** Longest river of Europe, in C European Russia; rises in the Valdai Hills, and flows generally SE to enter the Caspian Sea, forming a broad delta below Astrakhan; length, 3 531 km/2 194 ml; principal navigable waterway in Russia; linked by canal to the Baltic, White Sea, Sea of Azov, and Black Sea; many reservoirs on its course; important source of hydroelectric power and irrigation. » Russia

Volgograd [**vol**guhgrat], formerly **Tsaritsyn** (to 1925), **Stalingrad** (1925–61) 48°45N 44°30E, pop (1989) 999 000. Capital city of Volgogradskaya oblast, SE European Russia, on R Volga; E terminus of the Volga–Don Canal; founded, 16th-c; largely destroyed in World War 2; airport; railway; aluminium, oil, oil refining, clothing, footwear, leatherwork, tractors, foodstuffs. » Mamaev Kurgan; Russia

volleyball An indoor court game, played by two teams of 6-a-side. Players hit the ball with their hands or arms over a raised net in the hope of forcing an error, and thus score points. Invented in 1895 by William G Morgan at the Holyoke YMCA, Massachussetts, it was originally known as *mintonette*. » RR122

Volsungasaga [**vol**sunga**sah**ga] A 13th-c German epic deriving in part from the Norse *Edda*. It tells the story of the dynasty of the Volsungs, which is linked to that of the Nibelungs. » Edda; German literature; Nibelungen

volt SI unit of electrical potential difference; symbol V; named after Italian physicist Alessandro Volta; if the power dissipated between two points along a wire carrying a current of 1 amp is 1 watt, then the potential difference between the two points equals 1 volt. » potential difference; units (scientific); Volta; RR71

Volta, Alessandro (Giuseppe Antonio Anastasio), Count [**vol**ta] (1745–1827) Italian physicist, born and died at Como. He was professor of natural philosophy at Pavia (1774–1804), where he experimented on current electricity, and invented an electric battery which gave the first reliable supply of electricity. His name is given to the unit of electric potential, the volt. » electricity

Volta, River River in Ghana, formed by junction of Black Volta and White Volta Rivers as they enter L Volta; flows S to enter the Gulf of Guinea at Ada; dammed at Akosombo to form L Volta (area 8 500 sq km/3 300 sq ml); Volta River Scheme designed to supply power, improve navigation, and help develop bauxite deposits; length including L Volta c.480 km/300 ml. » Ghana [i]

voltage » **potential difference**

Voltaire, pseudonym of **François Marie Arouet** [vol**tair**] (1694–1778) French writer, the embodiment of the 18th-c Enlightenment, born in Paris. Educated by the Jesuits in Paris, he studied law, then turned to writing. For lampooning the Duc d'Orléans he was imprisoned in the Bastille (1717–18), where he rewrote his tragedy *Oedipe*. This brought him fame, but he gained enemies at court, and was forced to go into exile in England (1726–9). Back in France, he wrote plays, poetry, historical and scientific treatises, and his *Lettres philosophiques* (1734). He regained favour at court, becoming royal historiographer, then moved to Berlin at the invitation of Frederick the Great (1750–3). In 1755 he settled near Geneva, where he wrote the satirical short story, *Candide* (1759). From 1762 he produced a range of antireligious writings and the *Dictionnaire philosophique* (1764). In 1778, he returned as a celebrity to Paris, but died soon after his arrival. » drama; Enlightenment; French literature; satire; tragedy

voltmeter An instrument used for measuring potential difference or electromotive force between points in a circuit. Most voltmeters consist of an ammeter connected in line with a high resistance, and calibrated in volts. The current flowing is proportional to the potential difference, although the presence of the measuring instrument reduces the potential difference. » electricity

Voluntary Service Overseas (VSO) A British charity founded in 1958 to send skilled volunteers to work for two-year periods in developing countries. The host government provides a living allowance and accommodation; VSO provides the briefing, airfare, and a grant. » Peace Corps

Volvox A freshwater green alga commonly occurring in spherical colonies (*coenobia*) of more than 500 cells; cells flagellate, usually containing a single cup-shaped chloroplast. (Class: *Chlorophyceae*. Order: *Volvocales*.) » chloroplast; flagellum; green algae

von Euler, Ulf (Svante) (1905–83) Swedish physiologist, born, educated, worked, and died in Stockholm. In 1970 he shared the Nobel Prize for Physiology or Medicine for his isolation and identification of noradrenaline as a sympathetic nervous system transmitter. » Axelrod; Katz; neurotransmitter; noradrenaline

Vonnegut, Kurt, Jr [**von**uhguht] (1922–) US novelist, born in Indianapolis and educated at Cornell. After serving with the US Air Force in World War 2, he studied anthropology at Chicago. His novels are satirical fantasies, usually cast in the form of science fiction, as in *Player Piano* (1952) and *Cat's Cradle* (1963). He is best known for *Slaughterhouse-Five* (1969). » novel; science fiction

voodoo The popular religion of Haiti, also found in the West Indies and parts of S America. A blending of Roman Catholicism with W African religion, its followers attend both the church and the voodoo temple, where a voodoo priest or priestess leads a ritual invoking of the spirits of the voodoo world through magical diagrams, songs, and prayer. The spirits possess the members in trance. » Haiti; magic; Roman Catholicism

Voortrekkers » **Afrikaners; Great Trek**

Voronezh [vuh**ron**yesh] 51°40N 39°10E, pop (1989) 887 000. River-port capital of Voronezhskaya oblast, EC European Russia, on R Voronezh; founded as a fortress, 1586; airport; railway; university (1918); agricultural trade, excavators, synthetic rubber, foodstuffs, atomic power generation. » Russia

Voroshilov, Kliment Yefremovich [voruh**shee**luhf] (1881–1969) Soviet Marshal, statesman, and President (1953–60), born near Dniepropetrovsk. He joined the Russian Social Democratic Labour Party in 1903, but political agitation soon brought about his exile to Siberia, where he remained a fugitive until 1914. He played a military rather than a political role in the 1917 Revolution, and as Commissar for Defence (1925–40) was responsible for the modernization of the Red Army. He was removed from office after the failure to prevent the German siege of Leningrad, but stayed active in the party, and became head of state after Stalin's death. He died in Moscow. » Red Army; Russian Revolution; Stalin; World War 2

Voroshilovgrad [vuhruh**shi**luhfgrat], formerly **Lugansk** (to 1935, 1958–70) 48°35N 39°20E, pop (1983) 485 000. Capital city of Voroshilovgradskaya oblast, E Ukraine, on a tributary of R Severskiy Donets; founded, 1795; airfield; railway; iron and steel; wool textiles, leatherwork, footwear, mining equipment. » Ukraine

Vorster, John, originally **Balthazar Johannes Vorster** (1915–83)

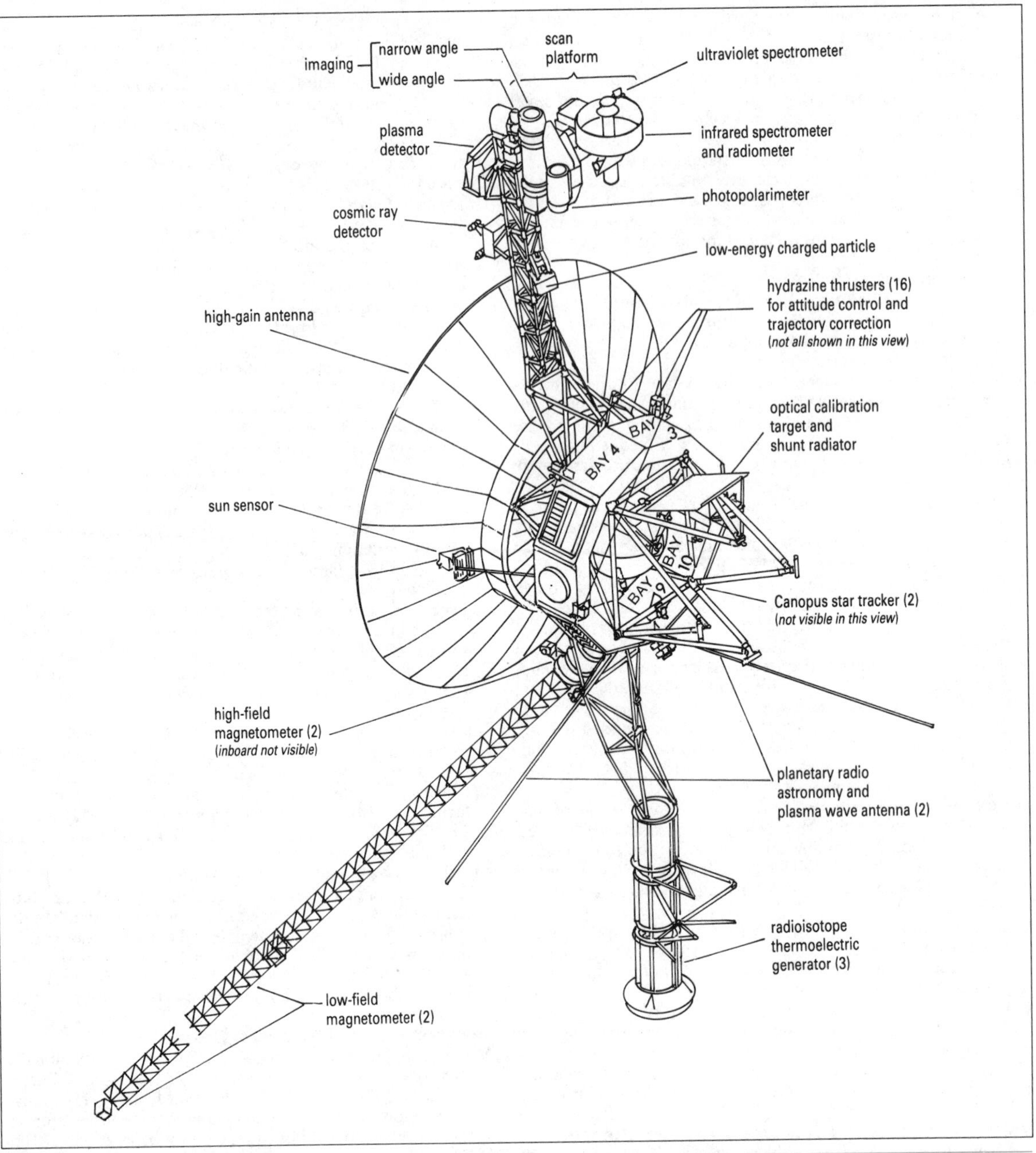

Voyager spacecraft (shown without thermal blankets, for clarity), giving the locations of most of the external science and engineering instrumentation

South African statesman, Prime Minister (1966–78), and President (1978–9), born at Jamestown. Educated at Stellenbosch, he became a lawyer, and joined an extreme Afrikaner movement. In 1953 he became a Nationalist MP, and was Minister of Justice under Verwoerd (1961), whom he succeeded, maintaining the policy of apartheid. In 1978, after a scandal over the misappropriation of government funds, he resigned for health reasons, and was elected President, but stood down from this position nine months later when an investigating Commission found him jointly responsible. He died in Cape Town. » apartheid; South Africa [i]; Verwoerd

vortex A rotational form of fluid flow. Lines of flow are curved, and may even form closed loops. Examples of vortices are whirlpools, tornadoes, and the circulating eddies caused by obstructions in rivers. » fluid mechanics

Vorticism A modern art movement started in England in 1913, partly inspired by the Futurists. Leading members included Wyndham Lewis (1884–1957), C R W Nevinson (1889–1946), and Henri Gaudier-Brzeska (1891–1915). Two issues were published of a journal, *Blast* (1914), and an exhibition was held (1915), after which the movement petered out. » Cubism; Futurism; modern art; Lewis, Wyndham

Vortigern (5th-c) Semi-legendary British King who, according to Bede, recruited Germanic mercenaries led by Hengist and Horsa to help fight off the Picts after the final withdrawal of the Roman administration from Britain (409). Tradition has it that the revolt of these troops opened the way for the Germanic conquests and settlements in England. » Angles; Bede; Jutes; Picts; Saxons

Vosges Mountains [vohzh], ancient **Vosegus** area 7 425 sq km/

2 866 sq ml. Range of hills in NE France near the Franco-German frontier; separated from the Jura (S) by the Belfort Gap; thickly-wooded hills, several rivers descending to the Rhine and the Central Plateau; highest point, Ballon de Guebwiller (1 423 m/4 669 ft); length, 250 km/155 ml; skiing and rock climbing. » Jura Mountains

Vostok 78°27S 106°51E. Russian scientific station in Antarctica; lowest temperature ever recorded on Earth (−88.3°C) measured here; South Geomagnetic Pole (1985) nearby. » Antarctica [i]

Vostok ('East') **spacecraft** [**vos**tok] The first generation of Soviet crewed spacecraft, carrying a single member. Vostok 1 took the first human into space (12 Apr 1961) – Yuri Gagarin, who orbited Earth once on a flight of 118 min. Crew were recovered over land after ejection from the capsule at 7 000 m/23 000 ft altitude after re-entry. The last Vostok flight carried Valentina Tereshkova, the first woman to fly in space (Vostok 6, 16 Jun 1963). **Voskhod** ('Sunrise') was an intermediate-generation Soviet crewed spacecraft following Vostok and preceding Soyuz; it made only two flights, in 1964 and 1965. » Gagarin; Soviet space programme; spacecraft; Tereshkova

voting » **franchise** (politics)

voucher scheme A scheme for giving parents a voucher equivalent in value to the average cost of a child's education, which they are then entitled to spend at a school of their choice. This may be either a local authority school or a private fee-paying school, where they might have to top up the fee. The system has been tried on an experimental basis in the USA, and is favoured by some politicians in the UK. » education; open enrolment

vowel One of the two main categories of speech sound (the other being *consonant*). Phonetically, a vowel is a sound produced when the air flows freely through the mouth without constriction from the pharynx, tongue, or lips; it may also flow partly through the nose (a *nasal vowel*). Vowel quality is determined by the shape of the lips and the position of the tongue. Phonologically, a vowel is defined by its function in the structure of a syllable: it forms the nucleus of the syllable, and (unlike a consonant) can stand alone (as in such words as *I* and *a* in English). » consonant; phonetics; phonology

Voyager project A multiple outer-planet flyby mission undertaken by NASA to make the first detailed exploration beyond Mars, and designed to take advantage of a rare (every 175 years) celestial alignment of Jupiter, Saturn, Uranus, and Neptune. Twin spacecraft in the Mariner series were launched on Titan-Centaur vehicles in 1977. They flew through the Jovian system (Mar, Jul 1979) and, with a boost from Jupiter's gravity, flew on to Saturn (encounters Nov 1980, Aug 1981). Following the Saturn flyby, Voyager 1's trajectory is taking it upward out of the ecliptic; Voyager 2 used Saturn's gravity to fly on to the historic encounters with Uranus (Jan 1986) and Neptune (Aug 1989). The spacecraft, powered by radioisotope thermo-electric generators, were built and are operated by NASA's Jet Propulsion Laboratory. They may send back data about the outermost reaches of the Solar System until well into the 21st-c. » Deep Space Network; NASA; Neptune (astronomy); radioisotope thermo-electric generator; Solar System

voyeurism A repeated tendency to observe others engaging in intimate, including sexual, behaviour. Sexual excitement often occurs in anticipation of the voyeuristic act, which may be accompanied by masturbation. » masturbation

Voznesensky, Andrei Andreievich [vozhnuh**shen**skee] (1933–) Russian poet, born in Moscow. Educated as an architect, he published his first two collections *Mozaika* and *Parabola* in 1960. His best-known volume *Antimiry* (Antiworlds) appeared in 1964, and the more difficult poems of *Soblazn* (Temptation) in 1979. The rock musical *Avos*, based on one of his poems, was produced in Moscow in 1981. » Russian literature

VSEPR The acronym of **valence shell electron pair repulsion**, a simple but effective method for predicting the configuration of bonded atoms about a central one in terms of the pairs of valence electrons on the central atom. For example, water, where the oxygen atom has two bonds and two lone pairs, has four pairs, and is thus an essentially tetrahedral arrangement, resulting in an H–O–H angle of less than 110°, while O=C=O, with no lone pairs on C, is linear. » atom; valence

VSO » **Voluntary Service Overseas**

VTOL An acronym for a fixed-wing aircraft specially designed for **Vertical Take-Off and Landing**. The most successful aircraft of this type is the Hawker Siddeley Harrier, which can deflect the thrust from its jet engine from the vertical to the horizontal whilst in flight. Since the early 1950s the USA has built a series of propeller-driven aircraft of various configurations, some of which stood on their tails and took off vertically, such as the Convair XFY-1. » aerodynamics [i]; aircraft [i]; jet engine [i]

Vuillard, (Jean) Edouard [vwee**yah**] (1868–1940) French painter and printmaker, born at Cuiseaux. One of the later Impressionists, a member of *Les Nabis*, he was influenced by Gauguin and the vogue for Japanese painting. He executed mainly flower pieces and simple interiors, painted with a great sense of light and colour. Also known for his textiles, wallpapers, and decorative work in public buildings, he died at La Baule. » French art; Gauguin; Impressionism (art); Intimisme; Nabis

Vulcan (astronomy) A hypothetical planet inside the orbit of Mercury. » Mercury (astronomy)

Vulcan (mythology), also **Vulcanus** or **Volcanus** The Roman god of fire, especially destructive fire and volcanic activity, sometimes called Mulciber. He was identified with Greek Hephaestus, and later given his attributes, such as metal-working. » Hephaestus

vulcanite or **ebonite** A hard black material made by the vulcanization of rubber with a high proportion of sulphur (2:1). It was important as an insulator before the coming of modern synthetics. » rubber; vulcanization

vulcanization The modification of the properties of rubber by chemical treatment, originally and still mainly (except for certain synthetic rubbers) with sulphur. Other chemicals may speed the vulcanization process or serve as extenders. The technique, which originated with Charles Goodyear in 1839, improves tensile strength, elasticity, and abrasion resistance. » Goodyear; rubber; vulcanite

vulcanology » **volcano**

Vulgate [**vuhl**gayt] The Latin translation of the Christian Bible, originating with Jerome (c.405), who attempted to provide an authoritative alternative to the confusing array of Old Latin versions in his day. From c.7th-c, it emerged in Western Christianity as the favourite Latin version (*vulgate* meaning the 'common' edition), but was itself revised and corrupted through the centuries. In 1546 the Council of Trent recognized it as the official Latin text of the Roman Catholic Church. » Bible; Jerome, St; Roman Catholicism

Vulpecula (Lat 'fox') [vuhl**pek**yula] A small N constellation in the Milky Way. » constellation; Milky Way; RR9

vulture A bird of prey specialized to feed on carrion; head often lacking long feathers. There are two groups. **Old World vultures** (Family: *Accipitridae*, 14 species) evolved over 20 million years ago; formerly world-wide but now absent from the Americas; no sense of smell. **New World** or **cathartid** vultures (Family: *Cathartidae*, 7 species) evolved more recently; formerly present in the Old World but now restricted to the Americas. » bird of prey; condor; griffon; lammergeier

Vygotsky, Lev Semenovich (1896–1934) Russian psychologist, born at Gomel, Belorussia. Originally a teacher and literary scholar with interests in creativity, he took up a scientific post at the Institute of Psychology in Moscow in 1924. He examined contemporary psychology, notably behaviourism and introspectionism, attempting to establish a Marxist view that thought originates in interactions, which themselves are influenced by social history. His writings, such as *Thought and Language* (1934–62) and *Mind in Society* (1978), have had a major influence on Soviet and (since the 1960s) Western psychology. » dialectical psychology; Marxism

Vyshinsky, Andrei Yanuaryevich [vi**shin**skee] (1883–1954) Russian jurist and politician, born in Odessa. He studied law at Moscow, joined the Communist Party in 1920, and became professor of criminal law and Attorney-General (1923–5). He was the public prosecutor at the state trials (1936–8) which removed Stalin's rivals, and later became the Soviet delegate to the United Nations (1945–9, 1953–4), and Foreign Minister (1949–53). He died in New York City. » Stalin

W

W particle A particle that carries weak nuclear force; symbol W; mass 81 GeV; charge +1 (W^+) or −1 (W^-); spin 1; decays to an electron or muon plus neutrino. Predicted by the Glashow-Weinberg-Salam theory, it was discovered in 1983 in proton-antiproton collisions at the European Organization for Nuclear Research (CERN). » boson; fundamental particles; Glashow-Weinberg-Salam theory; weak interaction

Wabash River [**waw**bash] River in Ohio, Indiana, and Illinois, USA; rises in W Ohio; flows 764 km/475 ml across Indiana to meet the Ohio R SW of Evansville. » United States of America [i]

Wace, Robert [ways] (12th-c) Anglo-Norman poet, born in Jersey, Channel Is. He studied in Paris, and was a canon of Bayeux (1160–70). He wrote several verse lives of the saints, a Norman-French version of Geoffrey of Monmouth's *Historia Regum Britanniae*, entitled the *Roman de Brut* (1155), and the *Roman de Rou* (1160–74), an epic of the exploits of the Dukes of Normandy. » French literature; Geoffrey of Monmouth; poetry

Waco [**way**koh] 31°33N 97°09W, pop (1980) 101 261. Seat of McLennan County, C Texas, USA, on the Brazos R; named after an Indian tribe; founded, 1849; airfield; railway; university (1845); trading, shipping, and industrial centre in the heart of the Blacklands; tyres, glass, paper; Texas Ranger Hall of Fame. » Texas

Waddington, C(onrad) H(al) (1905–75) British embryologist and geneticist, born at Evesham, Worcestershire. Educated at Cambridge, he studied palaeontology, then biology, and became professor of animal genetics at Edinburgh (1947–70). He introduced important concepts into evolutionary theory, envisaging a mechanism by which Lamarckianism could be incorporated into orthodox Darwinian genetics. He also helped to popularize science in such general books as *The Ethical Animal* (1960). He died in Edinburgh. » Darwin, Charles; genetics [i]; Lamarck

wadi A desert ravine or steep-sided gorge formed during flash floods, but generally containing water only during rainy seasons.

Wafd The name of the Egyptian nationalist party which sent a delegation under the nationalist leader Saad Zaghlul to the British High Commissioner in 1919; the word means 'delegation'. The *New Wafd* became Egypt's official opposition party in 1984, but was replaced as such in 1987 by an alliance headed by the Muslim Brotherhood. » Muslim Brotherhood

Wagga Wagga 35°07S 147°24E, pop (1981) 36 837. Town in New South Wales, Australia; at the centre of a rich agricultural area W of Canberra; railway; airfield. » New South Wales

Wagner, (Wilhelm) Richard [**vah**gner] (1813–83) German composer, born at Leipzig. Educated at Dresden and Leipzig, his early efforts at composition were unsuccessful, and in Paris (1839–42), he made a living by journalism and hack operatic arrangements. His *Rienzi* (1842) was a great success at Dresden, and he was appointed *Kapellmeister*, but his next operas, including *Tannhäuser* (1845), were failures. Deeply implicated in the revolutionary movement, he fled from Saxony (1848), moving to Paris and Zürich. The poem of the Ring cycle was finished in 1852, and in 1853 he began to write *Das Rheingold* (The Rhinegold), followed by *Die Walküre* (1856, The Valkyrie) and Part I of *Siegfried* (1857). In 1861 he was allowed to return to Germany, but still lacked recognition and support, and had to flee from Vienna to avoid imprisonment for debt. In 1864 he was saved from ruin by the eccentric young King of Bavaria, Ludwig II, who became a fanatical admirer of his work, and offered him every facility at Munich. His first wife, Minna, having died in 1866, Wagner then married Cosima von Bülow, the wife of his musical director, after her divorce. To fulfil his ambition to give a complete performance of the *Ring* (*Walküre, Siegfried, Götterdämmerung*, with *Rheingold* as introduction), he started the now famous theatre at Bayreuth, which opened in 1876. *Parsifal*, his last opera, was staged in 1882, a year before his sudden death from a heart attack, in Venice. His son, **Siegfried** (1869–1930) was director of the Bayreuth theatre from 1909. His grandson, **Wieland** (1917–66), took over the directorship in 1951, and revolutionized the production of the operas, stressing their universality as opposed to their purely German significance. Wieland's brother, **Wolfgang** (1919–) has been artistic director at Bayreuth since 1966. » leitmotif; opera

wagtail A small, ground-dwelling songbird, found world-wide; plumage usually bold, black-and-white, yellow, or green (dull species are called **pipits**); long tail which wags vertically; inhabits open country; eats mainly insects. The name is also used for two New World flycatchers and one fantail. (Family: *Motacillidae*, 48 species.) » fantail; flycatcher; pipit; songbird

Wahhabis [**wa**habeez] An Islamic movement which derives from Muhammad ibn Abd al-Wahhab, a religious reformer from Uyaina near Riyadh, and Muhammad ibn Saud, the ancestor of the present rulers of Saudi Arabia. The alliance was to lead to the unification in the 18th-c of most of the peninsula under the Saudi banner. The modern reunification of the Kingdom was carried out 1902–32 by King Abd al-Aziz, otherwise known as 'Ibn Saud'. Arabs call the followers of Abd al-Wahhab *muwahhidun* or 'unitarians' rather than *Wahhabis*, which is an anglicism. The movement maintains that legal decisions must be based exclusively on the Koran and the *Sunna*. The original Wahhabis banned music, dancing, poetry, silk, gold, and jewellery, and in the 20th-c, the *ikhwan* ('brotherhood') have attacked the telephone, radio, and television as innovations not sanctioned by God. » Ibn Saud; Islam; Saudi Arabia [i]

Waikato, River [wiy**ka**toh] River in North Island, New Zealand; length 425 km/264 ml from its source, the Upper Waikato R; longest river in New Zealand; rises in L Taupo then flows NW to enter the Tasman Sea S of Manukau Harbour; source of hydroelectric power. » New Zealand [i]

Waikiki Beach [wiykee**kee**] Resort beach in SE Honolulu on the Pacific island of Oahu, Hawaii state, USA; surfing popular on the reef; concerts and hula shows featured at the Kapiolani Park. » Hawaii (state)

Wain, John (Barrington) (1925–) British novelist and critic, born at Stoke-on-Trent, Staffordshire. Educated at Oxford, he lectured in English at Reading (1947–55) before becoming a freelance author. His novels include *Hurry on Down* (1953) and *The Contenders* (1958), and he has also written poetry, associated with the Movement, such as *Weep Before God* (1961). He was professor of poetry at Oxford (1973–8). » Angry Young Men; English literature; novel; poetry

Waitangi Day [wiy**tang**i] The national day of New Zealand (6 Feb), commemorating the Treaty of Waitangi made between Britain and the Maori chiefs in 1840. » Maoris, Waitangi, Treaty of

Waitangi, Treaty of A compact signed by Maori representatives and Governor William Hobson at Waitangi (6 Feb 1840) on the occasion of the British annexation of New Zealand. The legal force of the Treaty, and the obligations it imposed of protecting Maori interests in land, were subsequently denied by a settler-controlled government and judiciary, but this interpretation was reversed in the 1980s. » New Zealand [i]

Waite, Terry, properly **Terence (Hardy)** (1939–) Adviser to the Archbishop of Canterbury on Anglican Communion Affairs since 1980. As the Archbishop's special envoy, he was particularly involved in negotiations to secure the release of hostages held in the Middle East; between 1982 and the end of 1986, 14 hostages were freed through his intercession. He was himself kidnapped in Beirut in January 1987 while involved in secret negotiations to win the release of hostages held in Lebanon; he was released on 18 November 1991. » Anglican Communion

Waitz, Grete, *née* **Andersen** [viyts] (1953–) Norwegian athlete, born in Oslo. Formerly a track champion at 3 000 m, at which she set world records in 1975 and 1976, she has since developed into the world's leading female road athlete. The world marathon champion in 1983, and the Olympic silver medallist in 1984, she has four times set world best times for the marathon. She won the London Marathon in 1983 and 1986, and the New York marathon a record nine times between 1978 and 1988. She has also been the women's cross-country champion five times (1978–81, 1983). » athletics

Wajda, Andrzej [**viy**duh] (1926–) Polish film director, born at Suwalki. He studied art at Krakow, then enrolled in the Lodz film school (1950). His first feature film, *Pokolenie* (1954, A Generation), dealt with the effects of the war on disillusioned Polish youth. He is best known outside Poland for *Czlowiek z marmary* (1977, Man of Marble), dealing with the Stalinist era, and *Czlowiek z zelaza* (1981, Man of Iron), which uses film actually made during the rise of the Solidarity trade union. His films range from romantic comedy to epic, including literary adaptations, such as of *Crime and Punishment* (1984), and he has also worked in television and the theatre. » Solidarity

Wake Islands 19°18N 166°36E; pop (1981) 1 600; area 10 sq km/ 4 sq ml. Horseshoe-shaped coral atoll enclosing three islands in C Pacific Ocean, 1 200 km/750 ml N of Kwajalein, Marshall Is; annexed by USA, 1898; seaplane base opened, 1935; important for trans-Pacific air flights; under control of US Air Force since 1972. » Pacific Ocean

Wakefield, Edward Gibbon (1796–1862) British colonial statesman, born in London. Sentenced for abduction in 1827, he wrote in prison *A Letter from Sydney* (1829), which outlined his theory of colonization, expanded in several other books. He influenced the South Australian Association (1836) and formed in 1837 the New Zealand Association. He emigrated to New Zealand in 1853, and died in Wellington. » Wakefield settlements

Wakefield 53°42N 1°29W, pop (1981) 75 838. Administrative centre of West Yorkshire, N England; on the R Calder, 13 km/8 ml S of Leeds; a woollen centre since the 16th-c; railway; textiles, chemicals, mining machinery, machine tools; site of Battle of Wakefield (1460) in Wars of the Roses. » Roses, Wars of the; Yorkshire, West

Wakefield settlements Settlements of British migrants founded and organized according to Edward Gibbon Wakefield's (1796–1862) ideas of 'systematic colonization'. He proposed (1829) that the revenue from the sale of crown land should be used to finance the migration of suitable workers and their families. The aim was to maintain traditional standards of order and refinement by transplanting a cross-section of English society, and restricting land ownership to the wealthy. The settlements were Adelaide, in Australia; and Wellington, Wanganui, New Plymouth, Nelson, Otago, and Canterbury in New Zealand.

Walachia » **Moldavia and Wallachia**

Walburga » **Walpurga**

Walcott, Derek (1930–) West Indian poet and dramatist, born in St Lucia and educated at the University of the West Indies, Jamaica. He has lived mostly in Trinidad, where he founded the Trinidad Theatre Workshop in 1959. He produced three early but assured volumes, *In A Green Night* (1962), *The Castaway* (1965), and *The Gulf* (1969). His *Collected Poems* was published in 1986. » Caribbean literature; drama; poetry

Waldenses or **Waldensians** A small Christian community originating in a reform movement initiated by Peter Waldo at Lyons, France, in the 12th-c. They rejected the authority of the pope, prayers for the dead, and veneration of the saints. Excommunicated and persecuted, they survived through the Middle Ages. After the Reformation, as Protestants, they continued mainly in N Italy, with missions in S America. » Protestantism; Reformation

Waldheim, Kurt [**valt**hiym] (1918–) Austrian statesman and President (1986–), born near Vienna. He served on the Russian front, but was wounded and discharged (1942), then studied at Vienna, and entered the Austrian foreign service (1945). He became Minister and subsequently Ambassador to Canada (1955–60), Director of Political Affairs at the Ministry (1960–4), Austrian representative at the United Nations (1964–8, 1970–1), Foreign Minister (1968–70), and UN Secretary-General (1972–81). His presidential candidature was controversial, because of claims that he had lied about his wartime activities, and been involved in anti-Jewish and other atrocities, but he denied the allegations, and despite international pressure, continued with his campaign. » Austria [i]; United Nations

Waler A breed of horse, developed in the 19th-c in Australia, especially New South Wales (hence the name); a riding horse, developed by cross-breeding various imported breeds; strong with good stamina. » horse [i]

Wales, Welsh **Cymru** [**kuhm**ree] pop (1987e) 2 836 200; area 20 761 sq km/8 014 sq ml. Principality on the W coast of the UK, since 1974 divided into eight counties; bounded E by England, W by St George's Channel, N by the Irish Sea, and S by the Bristol Channel; includes the island of Anglesey off the NW coast; nearly 20% of the population speak Welsh, mainly in the N; capital, Cardiff; chief towns include Swansea, Newport, Merthyr Tydfil, Bangor, Wrexham; rises to 1 085 m/3 560 ft at Snowdon in the Snowdonia range (NW); also, Cambrian Mts (C), Brecon Beacons (S); drained by the Severn, Clwyd, Dee, Conwy, Dovey, Taff, Teifi, Tawe, Towy, Usk, and Wye Rivers; industrialized S valleys and coastal plain, based on local coal; tourism in N and NW, with seaside resorts and mountains; ferries to Ireland at Holyhead, Fishguard; important source of water for England; slate, lead, steel, engineering, oil refining, fishing, forestry, sheep, dairy products; much light industry in recent decades, following Great Depression and reduction in coal and steel industries; Royal Mint at Llantrisant; Anglo-Saxon invaders of Britain drove the Brythonic Celts into Wales, calling them *Waelisc*, 'foreign'; Offa's Dyke as frontier from the Dee to the Wye, 8th-c; Rhodri Mawr united Wales against Saxons, Norse, and Danes, 9th-c; Edward I of England established authority over Wales, building several castles, 12th–13th-c; Edward I's son created first Prince of Wales (1301); 14th-c revolt under Owen Glendower;

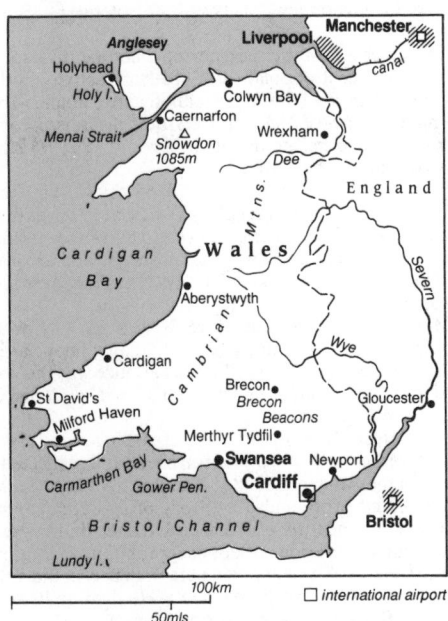

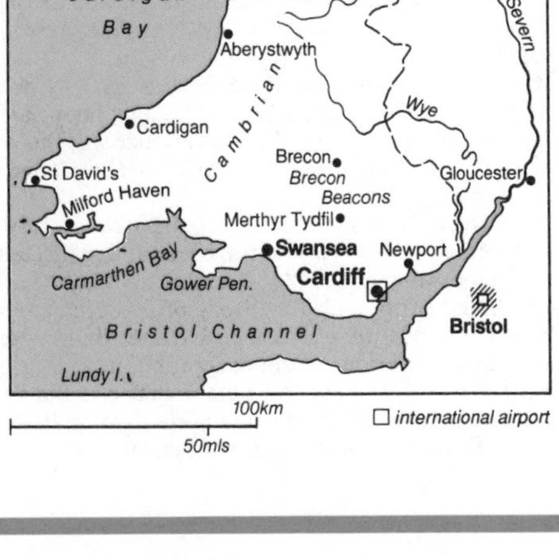

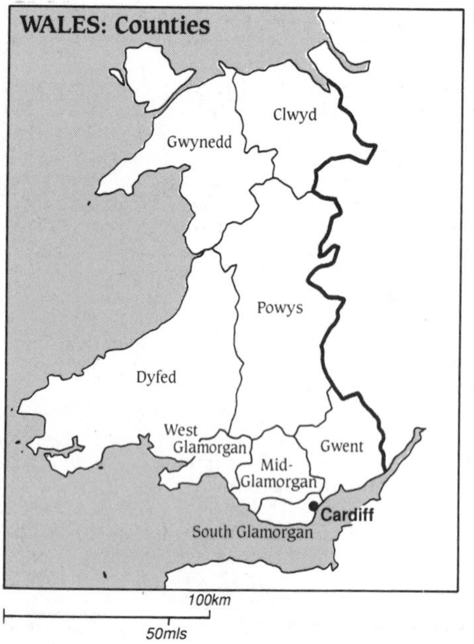

politically united with England at Act of Union, 1535; centre of Nonconformist religion since 18th-c; University of Wales, 1893, with constituent colleges; political nationalist movement (Plaid Cymru), returned first MP in 1966; Welsh television channel; 1979 referendum opposed devolution; national day, 1 March (St David's Day). » Cardiff; Clwyd; Dyfed; Edward I; Glendower, Owen; Gwent; Gwynedd; Mid Glamorgan; Nonconformists; Offa's Dyke; Plaid Cymru; Powys; Snowdon; South Glamorgan; Welsh; West Glamorgan; RR41

Wałesa, Lech [vawensa] (1943–) Polish trade unionist, born at Popowo. A former Gdansk shipyard worker, he became leader of the independent trade union, *Solidarity*, which openly challenged the Polish government's economic and social policies. He held negotiations with the leading figures in the Church and State, but was detained by the authorities when martial law was declared in 1981. He was released in 1982, and was awarded the Nobel Peace Prize in 1983. He has continued to be a prominent figure in Polish politics, and was much involved in the negotiations which led to Solidarity being involved in government in 1989. » Poland [i]; Solidarity; trade union

walking Either a leisurely pursuit, or a competitive sport. *Fell walking* is the most popular form of leisure activity in the UK. As a sport, both road and track walking are popular. The rules governing the use of the feet are strict: the raised foot must touch the ground before the other leaves it. » RR122

walking stick » **stick insect**

wall-flower A perennial reaching 20–60 cm/8–24 in, native to the E Mediterranean; stem slightly woody at base; leaves lance-shaped, crowded on stem; flowers yellow to orange-red, fragrant. Cultivars have a wide colour range and are grown as biennials. (*Cheiranthus cheiri.* Family: *Cruciferae.*) » biennial; cultivar; perennial

Wall Street A street in Manhattan, New York City, where the New York Stock Exchange and other major financial institutions are located. The road follows what once was the walled N boundary of the original Dutch colony. » New York City

wallaby » **kangaroo**

Wallace, Alfred Russel (1823–1913) British naturalist, born at Usk, Monmouthshire. He travelled and collected plant samples in the Amazon (1848–52) and the Malay Archipelago (1854–62), and propounded a theory of evolution by natural selection, independently of Darwin. He contributed greatly to the scientific foundations of zoogeography, including his proposal for the evolutionary distinction between the fauna of Australia and Asia ('Wallace's line'). He died at Broadstone, Dorset. » Darwin, Charles; zoogeography

Wallace, (Richard Horatio) Edgar (1875–1932) British writer, born in London. He served in the army in South Africa, where he later (1899) became a journalist, and in 1905 published his first success, the adventure story *The Four Just Men.* He wrote over 170 novels and plays, and is best remembered for his crime novels, such as *The Clue of the Twisted Candle.* A film scriptwriter in his later years, he died in Hollywood. » novel

Wallace, Lewis, byname **Lew** (1827–1905) US writer and soldier, born at Brookville, Indiana. He served in the Mexican War and the Civil War, became a lawyer, and was Governor of New Mexico (1878–81) and Minister to Turkey (1881–5). He was author of the successful religious novel *Ben Hur* (1880), which has twice formed the subject of a spectacular film (1927, 1959). He died at Crawfordsville, Indiana. » novel

Wallace, William (?–1305) Scottish knight and champion of the independence of Scotland, born probably at Elderslie, near Paisley. He routed the English army at Stirling (1297), and took control of the government of Scotland as 'Guardian', but was defeated by Edward I at Falkirk (1298). He was eventually captured near Glasgow (1305), and was hanged, drawn, and quartered at Smithfield, London. Many legends collected around him due to his immense popular appeal as a national figure resisting foreign oppression. » Edward I

Wallachia [wolaykia] » **Moldavia and Wallachia**

wallaroo A kangaroo with a shaggy coat and naked muzzle; two species: the solitary **wallaroo**, **Euro**, or **hill kangaroo** (*Macropus robustus*) from rocky hill regions, and the **antilopine wallaroo** (*Macropus antilopinus*), which occurs in groups ('mobs') on N Australian grassland. » kangaroo

wallcreeper A nuthatch-like bird, native to S Europe and Asia; blue-grey with broad red and white wings; bill long, slender, curved; inhabits rocky areas of high mountains; eats insects and spiders. (*Tichodroma muraria.* Family: *Tichodromadidae.*) » nuthatch

Wallenstein or **Waldstein, Albrecht (Wenzel Eusebius), Herzog von** ('Duke of') [woluhnstiyn], Ger [valuhnshtiyn] (1583–1634) Bohemian general, born at Hermanice. During the Thirty Years' War he became Commander of the Imperial armies and won a series of victories (1625–9), gaining the titles of the Duke of Mecklenburg and 'General of the Baltic and Oceanic Seas'. His ambition led to his dismissal in 1630, but he was reinstated to defend the Empire against Swedish attack. He recovered Bohemia, but was defeated by Gustavus Adolphus at Lützen (1632), and was again dismissed. His intrigues led to an Imperial proclamation of treason, resulting in his assassination at Eger by Irish mercenaries. » Gustavus II; Thirty Years' War

Waller, Edmund (1606–87) English poet, born at Coleshill, Buckinghamshire. Educated at Eton and Cambridge, he became an MP in 1621, and was a member of the Long Parliament in 1640. In 1643 he plunged into a conspiracy ('Waller's plot') against parliament, was arrested, and banished. He lived mostly in France, returning to England in 1651. His collected poems were published in 1645. He died at Beaconsfield, Buckinghamshire. » English Civil War; English literature; poetry

Waller, Fats (Thomas) (1904–43) US jazz pianist, organist, singer, and songwriter, born in New York City. He performed with such ebullience, frequently parodying songs and styles, that it was sometimes hard for his audiences to see him as more than a buffoon. He was, for all that, a brilliant piano player in the stride tradition and a great, natural songwriter, as seen in such hits as 'Ain't Misbehavin' (1929) and 'Keepin' Out of Mischief Now' (1932). He is rumoured to have written many more standards, among them 'Sunny Side of the Street', and then sold the rights for quick cash. He died of pneumonia on his way to Kansas City from Los Angeles, while entertaining soldiers at training camps. » jazz; piano

walleye Large freshwater fish related to the zander, found in rivers and lakes of E North America; length up to 90 cm/3 ft; feeds mainly on small fishes and crustaceans; an excellent food fish and sport fish. (*Stizostedion vitreum.* Family: *Percidae.*) » zander

Wallis, Sir Barnes (Neville) (1887–1979) British aeronautical engineer and inventor. He trained as a marine engineer, and became a designer in the airship department of Vickers, where he designed the R 100. His many successes include the design of the Wellington bomber, the bombs which destroyed the German warship Tirpitz and V-rocket sites, and the 'bouncing bombs' which destroyed the Mohne and Eder dams. He later became chief of aeronautical research at the British Aircraft Corporation, Weybridge (1945–71), and in the 1950s designed the first swing-wing aircraft. He was knighted in 1968. » aeronautics; aircraft [i]; airship

Wallis, John (1616–1703) English mathematician, born at Ashford, Kent. Educated at Cambridge, he took orders, but in 1649 became professor of geometry at Oxford. His *Arithmetica Infinitorum* (1655, The Arithmetic of Infinitesimals) anticipated calculus and the binomial theorem; and he also wrote on proportion, mechanics, grammar, logic, decipherment, theology, and the teaching of the deaf. He died at Oxford. » calculus

Wallis and Futuna Islands, official name **Territory of the Wallis and Futuna Islands** pop (1982) 11 943; area 274 sq km/106 sq ml. Island group in the SC Pacific Ocean, NE of Fiji; a French overseas territory comprising the Wallis Is and the Hooru Is, 230 km/140 ml apart; capital, Matu Utu on Uvéa; chief ethnic group, Polynesian; chief religion, Roman Catholicism; unit of currency, the franc; Wallis Is (area 159 sq km/61 sq ml) include Uvéa, rising to 145 m/476 ft at Mt Lulu, ringed by low-lying coral reefs; Hooru Is (115 sq km/44 sq ml) include Futuna and Alofi, mountainous and volcanic; Futuna rises to 765 m/2 510 ft at Mt Puke; Alofi is uninhabited; warm and damp climate, with a cyclone season (Oct–Mar); French protectorate, 1842; overseas territory of France, 1961; governed by an administrator, assisted by an elected 20-member Territorial Assembly; subsistence farming, fishing, copra, yams, taro roots, bananas, timber. » France [i]; Pacific Ocean

Wallonia French-speaking region of S Belgium; c.3.5 million Walloons (36% of Belgian population); dividing line with Flanders to the N; many towns renowned for their art treasures (Tournai, Huy, Namur, Liège); steel, engineering. » Belgium [i]; Fleming and Walloon

Walloon » **Fleming and Walloon**

walnut A deciduous, spreading tree, growing to 30 m/100 ft, native to the Balkans, and widely planted and naturalized elsewhere; leaves pinnate with 7–9 pairs of elliptical leaflets; male flowers in catkins on old wood, females in clusters on new wood; fruit 4–5 cm/1½–2 in, smooth, green. The wrinkled woody seed is the familiar walnut. (*Juglans regia*. Family: *Juglandaceae*.) » deciduous plants; nut; pinnate; tree [i]

Walpole, Sir Hugh (Seymour) (1884–1941) British novelist, born in Auckland, New Zealand. Educated at Cambridge, he became a teacher, then an author. His many novels were very popular during his lifetime, and include *The Secret City* (1919), *The Cathedral* (1922), and the 4-volume family saga, *The Herries Chronicle* (1930–3). Knighted in 1937, he died near Keswick, Cumberland. » novel

Walpole, Sir Robert (1676–1745) English statesman and leading minister (1721–42) of George I and George II, born at Houghton, Norfolk. Educated at Eton and Cambridge, he became a Whig MP in 1701, and was made Secretary for War (1708) and Treasurer of the Navy (1710). Sent to the Tower for alleged corruption during the Tory government (1712), he was recalled by George I, and made a Privy Councillor and (1715) Chancellor of the Exchequer. After the collapse of the South Sea Scheme, he again became Chancellor (1721), and was widely recognized as 'prime minister', a title (unknown to the Constitution) which he hotly repudiated. A shrewd manipulator of men, he took trouble to consult backbench MPs, and followed policies of low taxation designed to win their favour. He was regarded as indispensible by both George I and George II. His popularity began to wane in the 1730s over the Excise Scheme and also over his determination to avoid foreign wars. He did not fully recover from the outbreak of a war he had opposed in 1739, and resigned in 1742. His period in office is widely held to have increased the influence of the House of Commons in the Constitution. He was created Earl of Orford, and died in London. » George I/II (of Great Britain); South Sea Bubble

Walpurga, Walpurgis, or **Walburga, St** [val**poor**ga] (c.710–c.777), feast day 25 February. English abbess and missionary, born in Wessex. A Benedictine nun at Wimbourne monastery, Dorset, she travelled with her brother Willibald to Germany, and became Abbess of Heidenheim, where she died. **Walpurgis night** (30 Apr) is so called from a confusion of the day when her relics were moved to Eichstätt (1 May) and the popular superstitions regarding the flight of witches on that night. » Benedictines; monasticism

walrus A marine mammal of family **Odobenidae**; resembles a large sea-lion with a broad bristly snout; canine teeth enormous, forming tusks; skin with little hair; inhabits coastal Arctic waters; eats mainly clams. (*Odobenus rosmarus*.) » sea-lion

Walsingham, Sir Francis (c.1530–90) English statesman, born at Chislehurst, Kent. He studied at Cambridge, became a diplomat, and was made a Secretary of State to Elizabeth I (1573–90), a member of the Privy Council, and knighted. A Puritan sympathizer, and a strong opponent of the Catholics, he developed a complex system of espionage at home and abroad, enabling him to reveal the plots of Throckmorton and Babington against the Queen, and was one of the commissioners to try Mary at Fotheringay. In his last months he increasingly took up religious meditation, and died in London. » Babington; Elizabeth I; Mary, Queen of Scots; Puritanism; Throckmorton

Walter, Bruno, originally **Bruno Walter Schlesinger** [**val**tuh] (1876–1962) German conductor, born in Berlin. He conducted at Cologne, Hamburg, and Vienna, directed the Munich Opera (1913–22) and the Berlin Opera (1925–9), and conducted at Leipzig (1929–33). On fleeing from the Nazis in 1933 he settled in the USA, where he conducted the New York Philharmonic and other orchestras, and also conducted at the Metropolitan Opera. He died at Beverly Hills, California.

Walter, Hubert (c.1140–1205) English churchman and statesman. He became Bishop of Salisbury (1189), and accompanied Richard I on the Third Crusade (1190–3). Appointed Archbishop of Canterbury in 1193, he played key roles in raising the ransom to secure Richard's release from captivity, and in containing the rebellion of the King's brother, John. At the end of 1193, he became justiciar of England, and was responsible for all the business of government until his resignation in 1198. On John's accession (1199), he became Chancellor, and was consulted on important matters of state. He died at Teynham, Kent. » Crusades [i]; John; justiciar; Richard I

Walter, John (1739–1812) British printer and newspaper publisher, born in London. In 1784 he acquired a printing office in Blackfriars, London, nucleus of the later Printing House Square buildings, and in 1785 founded *The Daily Universal Register* newspaper, which in 1788 was renamed *The Times*. He died at Teddington, Middlesex. His son, **John Walter II** (1776–1847) managed the paper from 1802–47, and was in turn succeeded by **John Walter III** (1818–94). » newspaper

Walther von der Vogelweide [**vahl**ter fon duh **foh**guhlviyduh] (c.1170–1230) German lyric poet. In 1190–98 he was in high favour at the court of Austria, and was later at Mainz and Magdeburg. In 1204 he outshone his rivals in the great contest at the Wartburg. He first sided with the Guelphs, but made friends with the victorious Hohenstaufen, Frederick II, who gave him a small estate. » Guelphs

Walton, Izaak (1593–1683) English writer, born in Stafford. In 1621 he settled in London as an ironmonger, but left the city for Staffordshire during the Civil War, and after the Restoration lived in Winchester, where he died. Best known for his treatise on fishing and country life, *The Compleat Angler* (1653), he also wrote several biographies. » English Civil War; English literature

Walton, Sir William (Turner) (1902–83) British composer, born at Oldham, Lancashire. Educated at Oxford, where he wrote his first compositions, he became known through his instrumental setting of poems by Edith Sitwell, *Façade* (1923). His works include two symphonies, concertos for violin, viola, and cello, the biblical cantata *Belshazzar's Feast* (1931), and the opera *Troilus and Cressida* (1954). He is also known for his film music, notably for Olivier's *Henry V*, *Hamlet*, and *Richard III*. He was knighted in 1951, and died in Ischia, Italy. » Sitwell, Edith

waltz A dance in triple time which supplanted the minuet and the *Deutsche* (German Dance) to become the most popular ballroom dance in 19th-c Europe – despite the initial shock caused by the requirement that the man should grasp his female partner at the waist. Austrian composer and violinist Joseph Lanner (1801–43) and the Strauss family established the style in Vienna, its most distinctive musical feature being an accompaniment of a low note on the first beat, and a repeated chord in the inner parts on the second and third. The modern waltz uses a slower tempo. » Strauss, Johann (the Elder)

Walvis Bay, Afrikaans **Walvisbaai** [**wol**vis] 22°59S 14°31E, pop (1980e) 25 000. Seaport in WC Namibia; on the Atlantic Ocean coast, 275 km/171 ml WSW of Windhoek; Walvis Bay enclave (area 1 128 sq km/435 sq ml) administered by South Africa as part of Cape Province; annexed by the Dutch, 1792; taken by Britain, 1878; incorporated into Cape Colony, 1884; remaining a South African enclave after Namibian independence; airfield; railway terminus; handles most of Namibia's trade; fishing. » Namibia [i]; South Africa [i]

wampum Beads used as a form of exchange, mnemonic devices, and guarantees of promises by certain Iroquois-speaking N American Indian groups, and later in trade with Europeans. They were made of bits of seashells cut, drilled, and strung into belts or strands. » Iroquois

wandering jew A species of tradescantia with variegated leaves. It is a popular house plant. (*Tradescantia fluminensis*. Family: *Commelinaceae*.) » tradescantia

Wandering Jew A character in Christian legend who taunted Christ as he carried his cross, and was condemned to wander the Earth until the end of the world or until Christ's second coming. Various Jews, notably Ahasuerus of Hamburg in 1602, have been identified with the character. » Jesus Christ

wandering sailor A species of tradescantia, with leaves maroon on undersides. It is a popular house plant. (*Tradescantia blossfeldiana*. Family: *Commelinaceae*.) » tradescantia

Wang Jingwei [wang jing**way**] (1883–1944) Chinese associate of the revolutionary and Nationalist leader Sun Yixian (Sun Yat-sen), born in Guangzhou (Canton). He studied in Japan, where he joined Sun's revolutionary party, and from 1917 became his personal assistant. In 1927 he was appointed head of the new Nationalist government at Wuhan, and in 1932 became titular head of the Nationalist Party. In 1938, after the outbreak of war with Japan, Wang offered to co-operate with the Japanese, and in 1940 he became head of a puppet regime ruling the occupied areas. He died at Nagoya, Japan. » Guomindang; Jiang Jieshi; Sun Yixian

Wanganui, River [wanga**nooee**] River in W North Island, New Zealand; rises NW of L Taupo, then flows S to enter the Tasman Sea 195 km/121 ml N of Wellington; length 290 km/180 ml; longest navigable river in New Zealand; paddle-boats visit a local winery; town of Wanganui near the mouth, pop (1988e) 41 000, an outdoor resort area and agricultural centre. » New Zealand [i]

Wankel engine [**vang**kuhl] A particular form of internal combustion engine whose piston rotates about a horizontal axis in a specially shaped combustion chamber, rather than oscillating within a cylinder, as in a conventional internal combustion engine. Although not the only type of rotary piston engine, the Wankel engine has been mass-produced for use in motor cars, and is the best-known example. Particular problems related to sealing and reliability have been overcome, but to date it has not achieved widespread application. It is named after its designer, German engineer Felix Wankel (1902–). » internal combustion engine

wapiti [**wop**itee] » **red deer**

war A military conflict between two states, or, in the case of civil war, between different groups within a state. International war is subject to international law, and wars can be either lawful or unlawful. There have been a series of treaties since the 18th-c covering the conduct of war, largely designed to prevent 'unnecessary suffering', or action that has no military advantage. The use of more overtly ideological wars and modern weapons have made it more difficult to regulate the conduct of war (eg greater difficulty in protecting civilians from aerial bombardment). Today the main source of international law on war or the use of force is the United Nations Charter, notably article 2(4). Distinctions are also now drawn between **conventional warfare**, which does not involve the use of nuclear weapons, **nuclear warfare**, **chemical warfare**, and **biological warfare**. A **guerrilla war** is conducted by non-regular forces, often avoiding direct engagement, designed to make a state ungovernable prior to a seizure of power. » biological/chemical warfare; nuclear weapons

War of 1812 (1812–14) A war between Britain and the USA, declared by the latter on the basis of British conduct towards neutral US shipping during the Napoleonic Wars. Expectations of conquest were also important. Fought at sea, along the Canadian border, in Chesapeake Bay, and on the lower Mississippi, it brought the British capture and burning of Washington, DC, and the bombardment of Baltimore. US victories in several sea duels and at New Orleans (fought after the Treaty of Ghent had restored peace) became central elements in the US military self-image.

War of Independence, US » **American Revolution**

War of the Pacific (1879–83) A war fought by Chile with Peru and Bolivia (in alliance since 1873) and arising out of Chilean grievances in the Atacama desert, then Bolivian-held. Chile won command of the sea in the early months of the war, and sent large expeditions to Peru, occupying the capital, Lima (Jan 1881). Peace treaties with Peru (1883) and Bolivia (1904) gave Chile large territorial gains. » Bolivia [i]; Chile [i]; Peru [i]

Warbeck, Perkin (c.1474–99) Flemish impostor, pretender to the English throne, born at Tournai, Flanders. In 1492 he appeared at the court of the Duchess of Burgundy, sister of Edward IV of England, and professed to be Richard, Duke of York, the younger of Edward's two sons who were murdered in the Tower. He made an ineffectual landing in Kent (1495), then landed in Cornwall (1497), but was captured at Beaulieu, Hampshire. Imprisoned in the Tower, he was executed after trying to escape. » Edward IV

warble fly A small, robust fly; larvae live as parasites under the skin of mammals, feeding on fluids exuding from tissues, and causing swellings (*warbles*) under the skin; c.60 species, some important as pests of domesticated animals. (Order: *Diptera*. Family: *Oestridae*.) » fly; larva

warbler A songbird of the families *Sylviidae* (**Old World warblers**, 350 species), *Parulidae* (**American warblers** or **wood warblers**, 114 species), *Acanthizidae* (**Australian warblers**, 65 species), or *Maluridae* (**Australian wren-warblers**, 26 species). The name is also used for the **warbler-finch** (one of Darwin's finches). » blackcap; Darwin's finches; gnatcatcher; redstart; reed warbler; tailorbird; thornbill; whitethroat; wren

Ward, Artemus » **Browne, Charles Farrar**

Ward, Dame Barbara (Mary), Baroness Jackson of Lodsworth (1914–81) British journalist, economist, and conservationist, born in York. Educated at Oxford, she became foreign editor of *The Economist*, and was a prolific and popular writer on politics, economics, and ecology. Her books included *The International Share Out* (1936), *Spaceship Earth* (1966), and *Only One Earth* (1972). She was created a dame in 1974, and became a life peer in 1976. » ecology

warfarin » **anticoagulants**

Warhol, Andy, originally **Andrew Warhola** (?1926–87) US artist and film-maker, born at Pittsburgh, Pennsylvania. He studied art in New York City, and worked as a commercial designer before becoming a pioneer in 1961 of Pop Art, with his brightly-coloured exact reproductions of familiar everyday objects such as the famous soup-can label. His first films, such as the 3-hour silent observation of a sleeping man, *Sleep* (1963), developed into technically more complex work, though still without plot, notably *Chelsea Girls* (1967). In 1968 he was seriously injured in a shooting, and control of his films passed to others. In 1969 he founded the fashion journal, *Interview*. In the 1960s he also turned to music, founding a rock revue called

The Exploding Plastic Inevitable (1966–7). He died in New York City. » Pop Art

Warlock, Peter, pseudonym of **Philip Arnold Heseltine** (1894–1930) British musicologist and composer, born and died in London. Largely self-taught, in 1920 he founded *The Sackbut*, a spirited musical periodical. His works include the song cycle *The Curlew* (1920–2), the orchestral suite *Capriol* (1926), many songs, often in the Elizabethan manner, and choral works.

warlords Chinese provincial military rulers who engaged in a bitter power struggle and civil war after the death of President Yuan Shikai in 1916. They were eventually subdued by the Northern Expedition of Jiang Jieshi (Chiang Kai-shek) in 1927. » Yuan Shikai

warm bloodedness » homoiothermy

Warner, Jack (1892–1978) US film producer, born at London, Ontario. He was the youngest of the four Warner Brothers (Harry, Albert, Sam, Jack) who after a period in film exhibition and distribution, moved into production and set up studios in 1923. Warners were the first to introduce sound into their films, and the success of *The Jazz Singer* (1927) led to great expansion in both cinema ownership and studio resources, until the US Anti-Trust Laws in the 1950s forced them to dispose of their theatres. Jack had always been the one most directly concerned with actual film creation, and he continued to supervise major productions such as *My Fair Lady* (1964) and *Camelot* (1967), but when he became the last surviving brother, he sold his interest and the name to the Canadian company Seven Arts. He died in Los Angeles.

warranty » condition

Warren, Earl (1891–1974) US politician and jurist, born in Los Angeles. He studied at Berkeley, and became a lawyer. An active Republican, he rose through minor state offices to be Governor of California, and became Chief Justice in 1954. During his time in office, the Supreme Court adopted a strongly liberal policy, most notably on civil rights. He was responsible for the epochal decision in *Brown v. Board of Education of Topeka, Kansas* (1954), outlawing school segregation, and was chairman of the federal commission that investigated the assassination of President Kennedy. He died in Washington, DC. » civil rights; Kennedy, John F

Warren, Robert Penn (1905–89) US writer, born at Guthrie, Kentucky. Educated at Vanderbilt, Berkeley, Yale, and Oxford, he became professor of English at Louisiana, Minnesota, and Yale, and established an international reputation with his novel, *All the King's Men* (1943, filmed 1949). He wrote several other novels, short stories, and volumes of poetry. » American literature; novel

Warrington 53°24N 2°37W, pop (1981) 82 522. Town in Warrington district, Cheshire, NWC England; on the R Mersey, 25 km/15 ml SW of Manchester; designated a 'new town' in 1968; railway; engineering, brewing, tanning, wire, chemicals, soap. » Cheshire

Warsaw, Polish **Warszawa**, Ger **Warschau**, Russ **Varshava** 52°15N 21°00E, pop (1983) 1 641 400. River-port capital of Poland, on R Vistula, on the Mazovian plain; city centre is a world heritage site; established, 13th-c; capital of the Duchy of Mazovia, 1413; capital of Poland, 1596; occupied by Germany in both World Wars; Jewish ghetto established in 1940, with uprising and death of most residents in 1943; largely destroyed in World War 2; post-war reconstruction of the mediaeval old town followed the pre-war street pattern; airport; railway; Polish Academy of Sciences; two universities (1818, 1945); steel, metallurgy, machinery, electrical engineering, clothing, food processing, pharmaceuticals, printing; restored 14th-c Cathedral of St John, royal castle, Adam Mickiewicz museum of literature, Łazienkowski Palace; international book fair (May), folk fair (May), modern music festival (Sep), international Chopin piano competitions (every 5 years), jazz festival (Oct). » Poland [i]

Warsaw Pact The countries which signed the East European Mutual Assistance Treaty in Warsaw in 1955: Albania, Bulgaria, Czechoslovakia, East Germany, Hungary, Poland, Romania, and the USSR. Albania withdrew in 1968. The pact established a unified military command for the armed forces of all the signatories. All members were committed to giving immediate assistance to any other party attacked in Europe. It was a communist response, in part, to the formation of NATO by the West, and was formally dissolved in 1991. » NATO

warships Vessels designed for use in wartime. Navies of the world still employ a vast range of warships, but the use of highly sophisticated guided-missile weaponry has made their roles less easily defined than those of the World War 2 period. The role of minesweepers has changed subtly to 'mine countermeasure', whereas the traditional aircraft carrier is still common, although probably at the limit of development. The US navy has recommissioned battleships, whilst the USSR has redesigned and revived the battle-cruiser. Modern submarines remain submerged for over three months when necessary, and can perform a diversity of roles. The term *cruiser* is now used mainly for guided-missile vessels packing awesome fire power. The role of the destroyer is mainly offensive in the hunter-killer context, whereas frigates are mainly general purpose defensive vessels. » aircraft carrier; battle cruiser; battleship; corvette; cruiser; destroyer; frigate; ironclad; Jane; landing craft; minesweeper; ship [i]; submarine; *see illustration p 1284*

wart A small benign overgrowth in the outer layer of the skin, arising from a virus infection; also known as a **verruca**. It is common in children, and unpredictable in occurrence, recurrence, and spontaneous disappearance. » skin [i]; virus

wart snake A snake of family *Acrochordidae* (2 species), found from India to Australia; specialized for life in freshwater (almost helpless on land); rough scales produce a 'warty' skin; also known as **water snake**. Some experts include these species in the family *Colubridae*, and call the 37 species of rough-skinned Asian snakes in this family **wart snakes**. » snake

warthog A wild pig native to Africa S of the Sahara; sparse covering of shaggy hair, especially on shoulders; face broad, flattened, with four wart-like knobs of thickened skin; large curved tusks; inhabits open country. (*Phacochoerus aethiopicus*.) » pig

Warwick, Richard Neville, Earl of, byname **the Kingmaker** (1428–71) English soldier and politician, who exercised great power during the first phase of the Wars of the Roses. Created Earl of Warwick in 1450, he championed the Yorkist cause. In 1460 he defeated and captured Henry VI at Northampton, had his cousin, Edward of York, proclaimed King as Edward IV (1461), and then destroyed the Lancastrian army at Towton. When Edward tried to assert his independence, Warwick joined the Lancastrians, forced the King to flee to Holland, and restored Henry VI to the throne (1470). He was defeated and killed by Edward IV at the Battle of Barnet. » Edward IV; Henry VI; Roses, Wars of the

Warwick [worik] 52°17N 1°34W, pop (1981) 21 990. County town in Warwick district, Warwickshire, C England; on the N bank of the R Avon, 15 km/9 ml SW of Coventry; founded in 914 and partly destroyed by fire in 1694; university (1965); railway; agriculture, engineering, carpets, tourism; 14th-c Warwick Castle, Lord Leycester hospital (1383). » Warwickshire

Warwickshire pop (1987e) 484 200; area 1 981 sq km/765 sq ml. County of C England, divided into five districts; drained by R Avon; county town, Warwick; chief towns include Nuneaton, Royal Leamington Spa, Rugby, Stratford-upon-Avon; agriculture, tourism, engineering, textiles; castles at Kenilworth and Warwick; Shakespeare industry at Stratford. » England [i]; Shakespeare [i]; Warwick

Wasa A four-masted Swedish warship of 1628 which foundered on her maiden voyage due to poor stability, with a loss of 50 personnel. She was salvaged in 1961 and preserved in dry dock in Stockholm. She is the best surviving example of a 17th-c ship. » Mary Rose

Wash, the Shallow inlet of the North Sea on E coast of England; between Norfolk (S) and Lincolnshire (W and N); receives the Welland, Witham, Nene, and Ouse Rivers; bounded by a low marshy coast. » Fens, the

Washington, Booker T(aliaferro) (1856–1915) US Black leader and educationist, born a slave in Franklin Co, Virginia. After emancipation (1865), he was educated at Hampton Institute, Virginia, and Washington DC, then became a teacher, writer, and speaker on Black problems. In 1881 he was

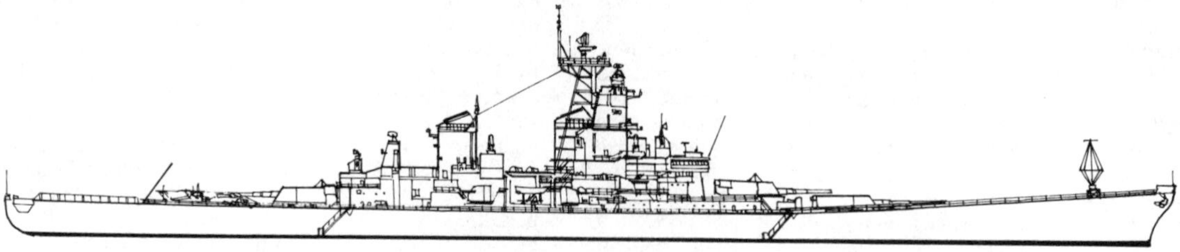

US battleship *New Jersey*, length 270 m/887 ft

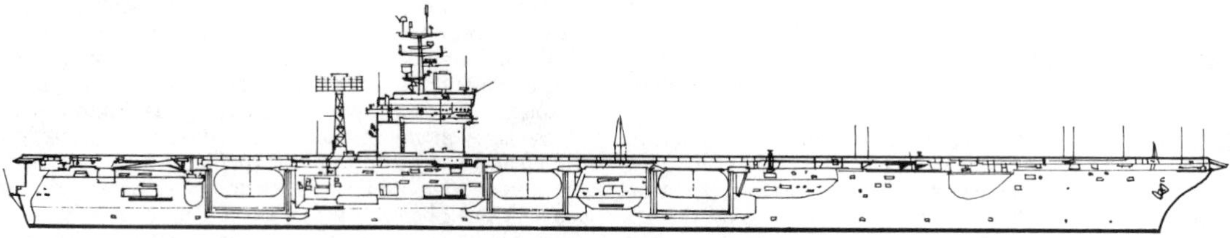

US nuclear-fuelled aircraft carrier *Nimitz*, length 322 m/1090 ft

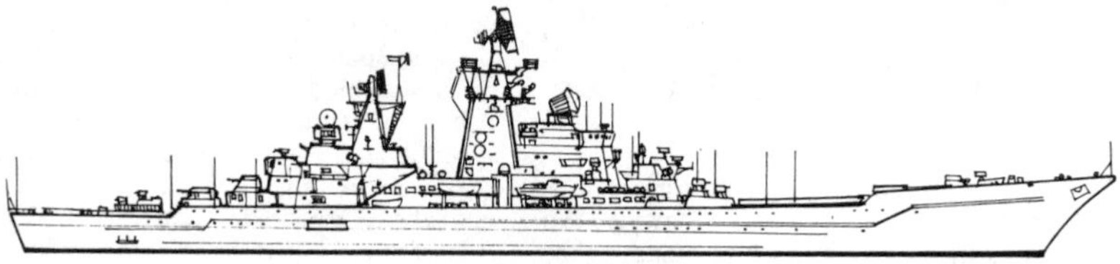

Soviet battle cruiser, Kirov class, length 191 m/626 ft

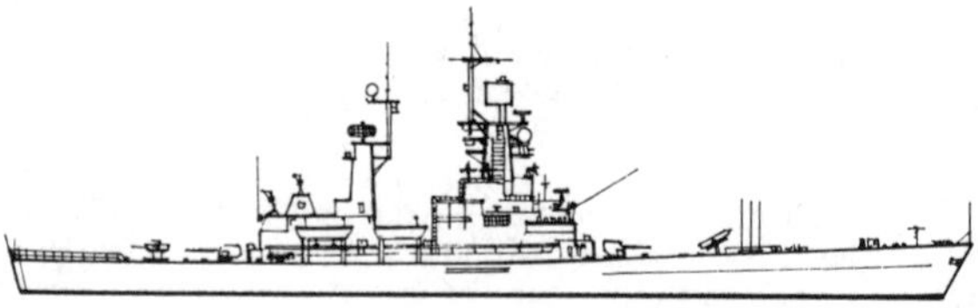

US guided-missile cruiser *Virginia*, length 178 m/558 ft

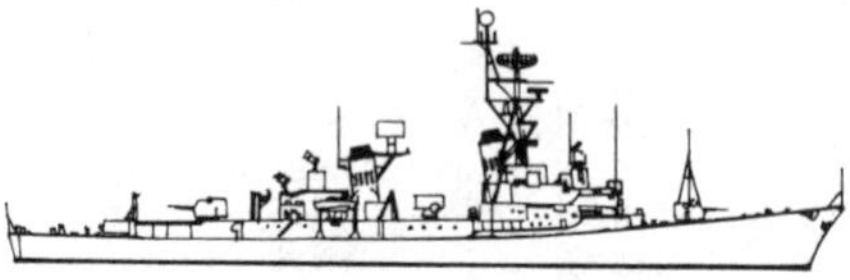

US destroyer *Waddell*, length 133 m/437 ft

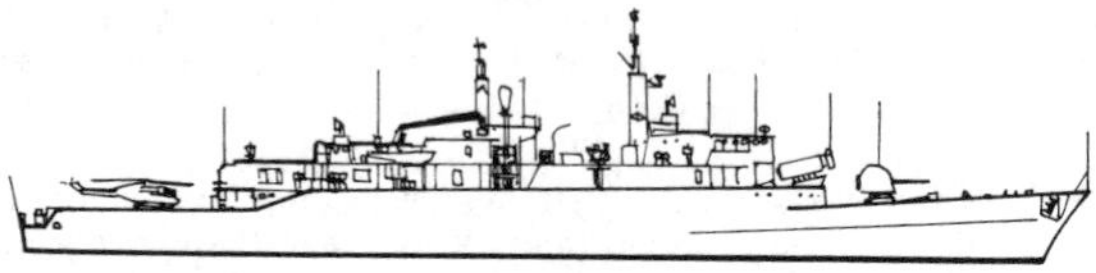

UK frigate *Alacrity*, length 110 m/384 ft

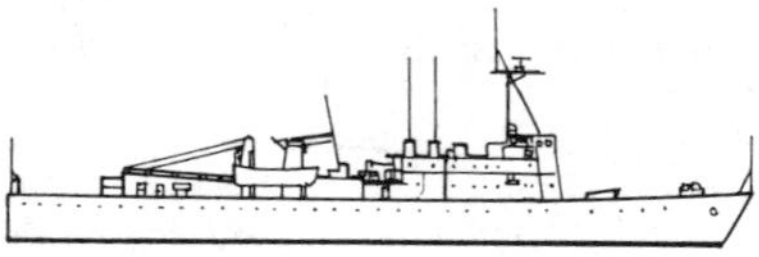

UK minelayer *Abdiel*, length 39 m/127 ft

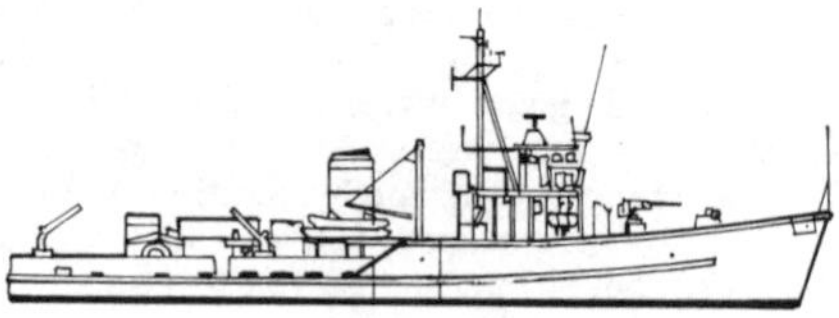

UK minesweeper *Wilton*, length 46 m/153 ft

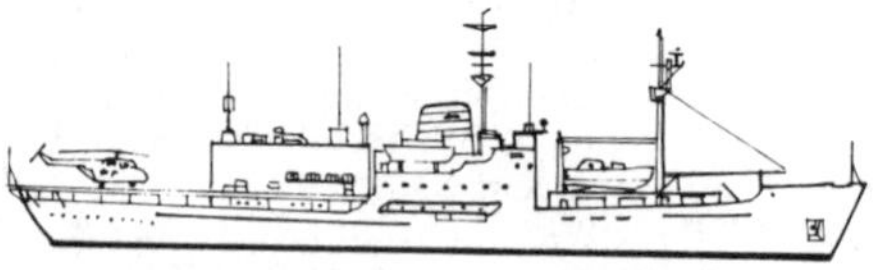

UK patrol vessel *Endurance*, length 93 m/305 ft

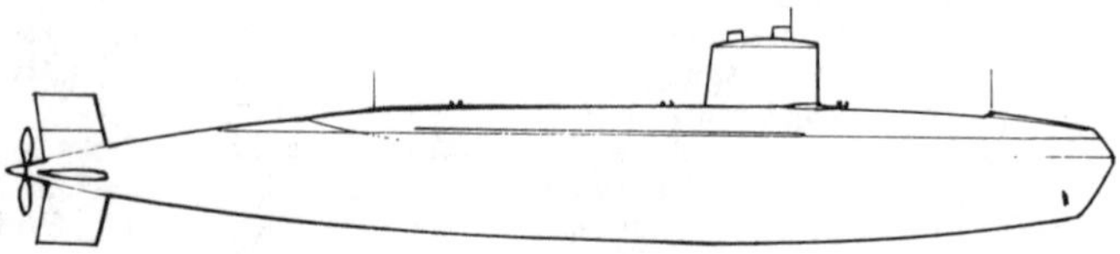

UK nuclear-fuelled submarine, Resolution class, length 130 m/425 ft

Lengths to the nearest whole number

Warships

appointed principal of the newly-opened Tuskegee Institute, Alabama, and built it up into a major centre of Black education. He was the foremost Black leader in late 19th-c USA, winning White support by his acceptance of the separation of Blacks and Whites. He was strongly criticized by W E B du Bois, and his policies were repudiated by the 20th-c civil rights movement. He died at Tuskegee. >> civil rights; du Bois

Washington, George (1732–99) Commander of American forces and first President of the USA, born at Bridges Creek, Virginia. He had an informal education, worked as a surveyor, and first fought in the campaigns of the French and Indian War (1754–63). He then managed the family estate at Mount Vernon, Virginia, becoming active in politics, and represented Virginia in the first (1774) and second (1775) Continental Congresses. He was given command of the American forces, where he displayed great powers as a strategist and leader of men. Following reverses in the New York area, he retreated through New Jersey, inflicting notable defeats on the enemy at Trenton and Princeton (1777). He suffered defeats at Brandywine and Germantown, but held his army together through the winter of 1777–8 at Valley Forge. After the alliance with France (1778), he forced the surrender of Cornwallis at Yorktown in 1781. He then retired to Mount Vernon, and sought to secure a strong government by constitutional means. In 1787 he presided over the Constitutional Convention, and became President, remaining neutral while political parties were formed, but eventually joining the Federalist Party. He retired in 1797, and died at Mount Vernon. >> American Revolution; Constitutional Convention; Continental Congress; Cornwallis; Mount Vernon

Washington (state) pop (1987e) 4 538 000; area 176 473 sq km/68 139 sq ml. State in NW USA, divided into 39 counties; the 'Evergreen State'; first settled in the late 18th-c, part of Oregon Territory, a prosperous fur-trading area; Britain and the USA quarrelled over the region until the international boundary was fixed by treaty to lie along the 49th parallel, 1846; became a territory, 1853; joined the Union as the 42nd state, 1889; after arrival of the railway (1887), developed through lumbering and fishing; Seattle an important outfitting point during the Alaskan gold rush, 1897–9; capital, Olympia; major cities Seattle, Tacoma, Edmonds, Bellingham; bounded N by Canada (British Columbia), NW by the Strait of Juan de Fuca, W by the Pacific Ocean; rivers include the Columbia, Snake, Okanogan, Sanpoil, Yakima; Olympic Peninsula with the Olympic Mts in the NW (Mt Olympus 2 428 m/7 966 ft); Puget Sound to the E, extending c.160 km/100 ml inland, with numerous bays and islands; Cascade Range runs N–S through the middle of the state; mountainous and forested country in the W; dry and arid land in the E; highest point Mt Rainier (4 395 m/14 419 ft); Mt Saint Helens volcano in the S (erupted May 1980); North Cascades National Park; apples (nation's largest crop), wheat, livestock, dairy produce; aircraft, aerospace, oil refining, food processing; mining (wide range of minerals); major tourist area; substantial Indian population and several reservations. >> Olympia (USA); St Helens, Mount; Seattle; United States of America [i]; RR39

Washington (DC) 38°54N 77°02W, pop (1980) 638 333. Capital of the USA, co-extensive with the District of Columbia; situated between Maryland and Virginia, on the E bank of the Potomac R, at its junction with the Anacostia R; the US legislative, administrative, and judicial centre: the Federal Government provides most of the city's employment; site chosen in 1790 by George Washington, planned by Pierre L'Enfant; occupied by the Federal Government, 1800; sacked and burned by the British, 1814; centre of government, justice, and law enforcement; two airports (Washington National, Dulles); railway; five universities; major league teams, Bullets (basketball), Capitals (ice hockey), Redskins (football). >> Capitol; Gallaudet College; Library of Congress; Lincoln Memorial; National Gallery of Art; Smithsonian Institution; Washington Monument; White House

Washington Monument A marble column in honour of George Washington, designed by Robert Mills (1781–1855) and erected (1848–84) in Washington, DC. The tower, which is 169 m/555 ft high, incorporates many blocks of stone bearing inscriptions from the states, foreign governments, or organizations who donated them. >> Washington, George

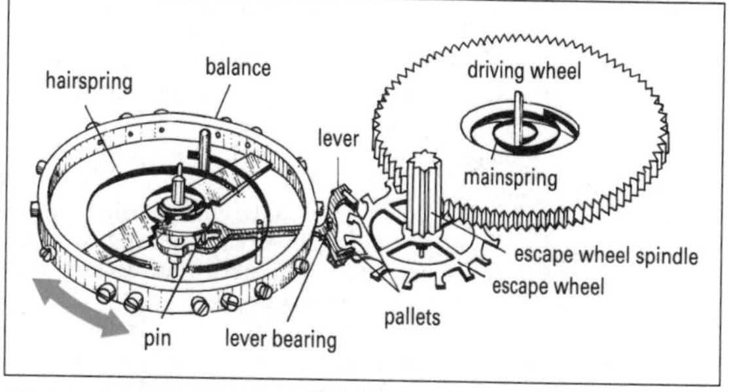

Watch – Drive mechanism (lever escapement)

wasp The common name of several different types of solitary and social insects of the order *Hymenoptera*, including spider wasps, digger wasps, ichneumons, woodwasps, potter wasps, gall wasps, and hornets. Social wasps (mainly in the family *Vespidae*) are usually banded black and yellow; females inflict painful stings; some produce nests of paper-like material; larvae fed on masticated paste of arthropod prey. Solitary wasps usually provision their nest with paralysed prey to feed the larvae. >> digger/gall/potter/spider wasp; hornet; ichneumon (insect); larva; woodwasp; Plate IX

waste disposal The disposal of waste from domestic, industrial, and agricultural sources; a major environmental concern. Methods commonly used include burial in landfill sites and at sea, incineration (sometimes for power generation), and the production of refuse-derived fuel pellets which can be used as an energy source. Care is needed with the disposal of toxic and hazardous substances to ensure that pollution of water, air, and land is avoided, and to prevent the build-up of methane, an inflammable gas. It is possible to recover this landfill gas as an energy source. An alternative to the disposal of some waste is recycling (eg of paper and glass). >> biogas; hazardous substances; pollution; radioactive waste; recycling

watch A small timepiece for wear or in the pocket. Watches have been made ever since the invention of the mainspring (c.1500) made portable clocks possible. Like clocks they needed a means of maintaining a constant speed as the mainspring ran down. The earliest means was the *fusee* (a cord wound round a conical barrel). From c.1670 the spring-maintained balance became general. In recent times electrical movements have been much used, a small battery replacing the mainspring as a source of energy. Timing methods include a tiny, electrically driven tuning fork, and the vibration of a quartz crystal. Sometimes the traditional analogue display (by rotation of hands) is replaced by a digital display using a liquid crystal display (LCD) face. >> clock [i]; liquid crystals

water H_2O. The commonest molecular compound on Earth; a liquid, freezing to ice at 0°C and boiling to steam at 100°C. It covers about 75% of the Earth's surface, and dissolves almost everything to some extent. It is essential to life, and occurs in all living organisms. It is strongly hydrogen-bonded in the liquid phase, and co-ordinates to dissolved ions. Unusually, the solid is less dense than the liquid; this results in ice floating on ponds, and accounts for the destructiveness of continued freezing and thawing. Water containing substantial concentrations of calcium and magnesium ions is called 'hard', and is 'softened' by replacing these ions with sodium or potassium, which do not form insoluble products with soaps. >> hydrate; ice

water avens >> avens

water bear A microscopic animal possibly related to the arthropods; body short, bearing four pairs of stumpy legs usually armed with claws; mouthparts elongated for piercing; c.400 species, found in surface water films on mosses, lichens, algae, plant litter, and soil. (Phylum: *Tardigrada*.) >> arthropod

water beetle A dark, shiny beetle up to 40 mm/1½ in long; silvery in appearance underwater because of air layer trapped on the underside of body and wing cases; larvae feed on snails; adults usually plant feeders; c.2 000 species, abundant in the tropics. (Order: *Coleoptera*. Family: *Hydrophilidae*.) » beetle; larva

water boatman A predatory aquatic bug that swims upside-down in water, using its paddle-like hindlegs; forelegs used to grasp prey; c.200 species, distributed world-wide. (Order: *Heteroptera*. Family: *Notonectidae*.) » bug (entomology)

water buck A grazing antelope native to Africa S of the Sahara; large with shaggy brown or grey coat; male with long erect horns ringed with ridges; inhabits savannah and woodland near water; two forms: **common waterbuck** and **defassa waterbuck**. (*Kobus ellipsiprymnus*.) » antelope

water buffalo A SE Asian member of the cattle family; lives near water; often wallows; closely related to the anoa; two species: *Bubalis bubalis* (**Asian water buffalo**, **wild water buffalo**, **Asiatic buffalo**, **carabao**, or **arni** – widely domesticated), and *Bubalis mindorensis* (**tamaraw** or **tamarau**). » anoa; Bovidae

water chestnut A free-floating aquatic annual, native to warm parts of Europe, Asia, and Africa, and introduced elsewhere; roots green; leaves in rosettes, blade rhomboid, stalk with an air chamber; flowers white, 4-petalled; fruits woody, triangular with 2–4 spiny horns. Fast-growing, it forms thick, floating mats which can block waterways. The fruit, rich in starch and fat, forms a staple food in much of Asia. The water chestnuts sold in Europe are often storage organs of the sedge *Cyperus esculentus*. (*Trapa natans*. Family: *Trapaceae*.) » annual; sedge

water-crowfoot An aquatic species of buttercup, growing in still or slow-moving water. Its leaves are of two kinds, either or both of which may be present, depending on the species: *submerged leaves* are finely divided and filamentous; *floating* leaves are circular or lobed. The predominantly white flowers project above the water. (*Ranunculus subgenus Batrachium*, c.30 species. Family: *Ranunculaceae*.) » buttercup

water deer A deer native to China and Korea (introduced in UK and France); the only true deer without antlers; canine teeth of male form long downward-pointing tusks; inhabits marshland; eats water plants; also known as **Chinese water deer**. (*Hydropotes inermis*.) » antlers [i]; deer

water fern » **azolla**

water flea A small aquatic crustacean; characterized by a jerky swimming motion using large antennae for propulsion; body short; head free; trunk enclosed by a bivalved carapace; often reproduces by parthenogenesis; c.450 species, most in freshwater but a few marine. (Class: *Branchiopoda*. Order: *Cladocera*.) » crustacean; parthenogenesis

water-fowl Aquatic birds, especially ducks, geese, and swans; also known as **wildfowl**. The name *waterfowl* is often used for populations kept in captivity; *wildfowl* for wild birds, especially those hunted. Some other water birds (eg waders) may also be included. » duck; swan

water gas A gas produced by passing steam over hot coke to give hydrogen and carbon monoxide: $H_2O + C \rightarrow CO + H_2$. This process yields a gas of high energy content, but it is endothermic, and is thus often made concurrently with producer gas, so that the reaction is spontaneous. The resulting 'semiwater gas' has, of course, a lower energy content. » coke; gas 2 [i]; producer gas

water glass A concentrated aqueous solution of sodium silicate (Na_2SiO_3), which sets to a hard, transparent layer, and is used as a waterproofing agent and a preservative. » silica; sodium

water-hole A frequency band considered most suitable for any contact by extraterrestrials with Earth. Still relatively free of radio signals (though satellite communication is now permitted on parts of the band), the waterhole is so called because it includes the emission frequency of H_2O. » radio

water hyacinth A free-floating perennial aquatic plant, native to S America, and introduced elsewhere; roots purple; leaves in rosettes, blade circular, stalk inflated and bladder-like; flowers c.4 cm/1½ in long, funnel-shaped, violet, in short dense inflorescence. It grows and spreads rapidly, blocks waterways, reservoirs, etc, and is probably the world's most troublesome aquatic weed. (*Eichhornia speciosa*. Family: *Pontederiaceae*.) » inflorescence [i]

water lily An aquatic perennial found in still or very slow-moving water in many parts of the world; large, floating, or slightly emergent leaves and flowers; leaves heart-shaped or rounded; flowers bowl-shaped with numerous petals and stamens. (Family: *Nymphaeaceae*.) » perennial; Queen Victoria water lily; stamen

water louse A freshwater crustacean found in stagnant or slow-flowing water containing rotting plants; abdominal segments fused; adult females carry developing young in brood pouch on underside of thorax; feeds on decaying vegetation. (Class: *Malacostraca*. Order: *Isopoda*.) » crustacean

water-melon A trailing vine with tendrils, native to the Mediterranean, Africa, and tropical Asia; leaves deeply palmately-lobed; male and female flowers yellow, c.3 cm/1½ in in diameter, funnel-shaped; fruit up to 60 cm/2 ft long, ovoid, rind dark green, leathery; black seeds embedded in red flesh. It is cultivated for fruit. (*Citrullus lanatus*. Family: *Cucurbitaceae*.) » palmate; tendril

water milfoil A submerged aquatic perennial, found almost everywhere; stems rooted or free-floating, leaves feathery, in whorls; flowers small, in slender spikes above water, reddish or yellowish, males 4-petalled, females without petals. Some species are used as aquarium plants. (Genus: *Myriophyllum*, 45 species. Family: *Halagoraceae*.) » perennial

water moccasin » **cottonmouth**

water opossum » **yapok**

water polo Developed in Britain in 1869, and played by teams of 7-a-side in a swimming pool. The object is to score goals by propelling the ball into the opposing team's goal at the end of the pool. It was originally known as 'football in water'. » football [i]; polo; RR122

water rat A term used generally for many unrelated rats which inhabit the edge of water bodies; some species modified to a semi-aquatic life style, with webbed hind feet and waterproof fur. The name is sometimes used for the water vole. » muskrat; rat; water vole

water scorpion An aquatic bug that lives submerged, breathing through a tubular tail that reaches the surface; lies in wait for prey, which is grasped with forelegs; c.200 species, found in still or slow-moving waters. (Order: *Heteroptera*. Family: *Nepidae*.) » bug (entomology)

water snake » **grass snake; wart snake**

water spider The only spider that lives permanently submerged; builds a bell-shaped retreat which it fills with air carried down on hindlegs; breathing by means of air film over body surface; feeds mainly on crustaceans; bite venomous, causing vomiting and fever. (Order: *Araneae*. Family: *Agelenidae*.) » crustacean; spider

water-spout The marine equivalent of a tornado; a rapidly rotating funnel of air which extends from the cloud base to the water surface, picking up water. Condensation also occurs within the vortex. When a water-spout reaches land, its water content is rapidly released. » tornado; whirlwind

water table The surface below which the ground is saturated with water. The position of the water table varies with the topography and amount of rainfall; where it intersects the surface, springs are formed. » groundwater; hydrology

water turkey » **darter** [i]

water vole A vole of genus *Arvicola*; three species: *Arvicola richardsoni* of NW North America, *Arvicola sapidus* from Europe, and *Arvicola terrestris* from Europe and Asia; most individuals burrow into banks of streams and ponds, but some live away from water; also known as **bank vole**. » vole

watercolour Any form of painting in which the pigment is mixed with a water-soluble medium such as gum arabic. Watercolour was used in ancient Egypt and China, and mediaeval manuscripts were illuminated with water-based paint. However, gouache and tempera are not regarded as 'pure' watercolour, which relies on transparent washes on special heavy paper, usually white or light-tinted. The great masters of 'pure' watercolour were all English, including Girtin, Cotman, and Turner. » gouache; medium (art); paint; tempera; Cotman; Girtin; Turner, J M W

watercress A semi-aquatic perennial, native to Europe and Asia; hollow stems creeping, rooting; leaves pinnate; flowers small, white, cross-shaped. It has been cultivated since the 19th-c as a vitamin C-rich salad plant. Its peppery tasting leaves stay green in the autumn. (*Nasturtium officinale*. Family: *Cruciferae*.) » perennial; pinnate; vitamins [i]

Waterford (county), Gaelic **Phort Láirge** pop (1981) 88 591; area 1 839 sq km/710 sq ml. County in Munster province, S Irish Republic; bounded S by Atlantic Ocean, with coastal inlets at Youghal, Dungarvan, Tramore, and Waterford; Knockmealdown Mts in the W; watered by Suir and Barrow Rivers; apple growing, cattle, glass making; popular resorts such as Tramore on S coast. » Irish Republic [i]; Waterford (city)

Waterford 52°15N 7°06W, pop (1981) 39 636. Seaport, county borough, and capital of Co Waterford, Munster, S Irish Republic; on R Suir at its mouth on Waterford harbour; railway; technical college; shipyards, food processing, footwear, paper, glass and crystal; remains of city walls, cathedral (1793), Blackfriars priory (1226); light opera festival (Sep). » Irish Republic [i]; Waterford (county)

Watergate (1972–4) A political scandal that led to the first resignation of a president in US history (Richard Nixon, in office 1968–74). The actual 'Watergate' is a hotel and office complex in Washington, DC, where the Democratic Party had its headquarters. During the presidential campaign of 1972, a team of burglars was caught inside Democratic headquarters, and their connections were traced to the White House and to the Committee to Re-elect the President. Investigations by the Washington Post, a grand jury, and two special prosecutors revealed that high officials who were very close to President Nixon were implicated, and that Nixon himself was aware of illegal measures to cover up that implication. A number of officials were eventually imprisoned. Nixon himself left office when it became clear that he was likely to be impeached and removed. » Irangate; Nixon, Richard M

Waterhouse, Alfred (1830–1905) British architect, born in Liverpool. He studied at Manchester, where he designed the town hall and assize courts, then in London built the romanesque Natural History Museum (1873–81). He also designed many educational buildings, and from his great use of redbrick came the name 'redbrick university'. He died at Yattendon, Berkshire.

Waterloo, Battle of (1815) The final defeat of Napoleon, ending the French Wars and the Emperor's last bid for power in the Hundred Days. A hard-fought battle, in which Blucher's Prussian force arrived at the climax to support Wellington's mixed Allied force; a number of crucial blunders by the French contributed to their defeat. » Blücher; Hundred Days; Napoleon I; Napoleonic Wars; Wellington, Duke of

Waterloo Cup » **bowls; coursing**

Watling Street » **Roman roads** [i]

Watson, James (Dewey) (1928–) US geneticist, born in Chicago. Educated at Chicago and Indiana, he worked in Copenhagen and then Cambridge, where with Crick and Wilkins he helped to discover the molecular structure of DNA, for which he shared the 1962 Nobel Prize for Physiology or Medicine. He became professor of biology at Harvard in 1961, and director of a molecular biology research centre at Long Island, New York in 1968. » DNA [i]

Watson, John B(roadus) (1878–1958) US psychologist, born at Greenville, South Carolina. Educated at Chicago, he became professor of psychology at Johns Hopkins (1908–20), where he established an animal research laboratory, and became known for his behaviourist approach, which he later applied to human behaviour. In 1921 he entered advertising, and wrote several general books on psychology. He died in New York City. » behaviourism

Watson, Tom, properly **Thomas (Sturges)** (1949–) US golfer, born in Kansas City, Missouri. He turned professional in 1971, and has since won 32 tournaments on the US tour, with career winnings second only to Jack Nicklaus. He has won the British Open five times (1975, 1977, 1980, 1982–3), the US Open (1982), and the Masters (1977, 1981). » golf; Nicklaus

watt SI unit of power; symbol W; named after British inventor James Watt; the production of 1 joule of energy per second corresponds to a power of 1 watt; commonly used as **kilowatts** (kW, 10^3 W) or **megawatts** (MW, 10^6 W). » kilowatt-hour; power; units (scientific); Watt; RR71

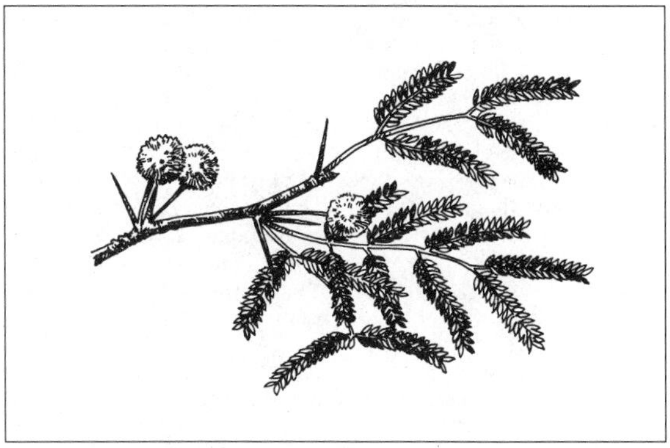

Wattle – Leaves, flower and thorn

Watt, James (1736–1819) British inventor, born at Greenock, Renfrewshire, Scotland. He went to Glasgow in 1754 to learn the trade of a mathematical-instrument maker, and there, after a year in London, he set up in business. He was employed on surveys for several canals, improved harbours and rivers, and by 1759 was studying steam as a motive force. In 1763–4, in the course of repairing a working model of the Newcomen engine, he hit upon the expedient of the separate condenser. After other improvements, he went into partnership with Matthew Boulton (1728–1809), and the new engine was manufactured at Birmingham in 1774. Several other inventions followed, including the design of a steam locomotive (1784). The term *horse-power* was first used by him, and the metric unit of power is named after him. He retired in 1800, and died near Birmingham. » Industrial Revolution; steam engine; watt

Watteau, (Jean) Antoine [**va**toh] (1684–1721) French Rococo painter, born at Valenciennes. In 1702 he went to study in Paris, where he worked as a scene painter and a copyist. His early canvases were mostly military scenes, but it was the mythological 'L'Embarquement pour l'île de Cythère' (1717, Embarkation for the island of Cythera) which won him membership of the Academy. He is also known for his 'Fêtes galantes' (scenes of gallantry), quasi-pastoral idylls in court dress which became fashionable in high society. He died at Nogent-sur-Marne. » French art; Rococo

wattle A large group of mainly trees or shrubs, native to many tropical and subtropical areas, but notably Australia where (together with the eucalypts) they form the dominant tree vegetation. The leaves are divided into numerous tiny leaflets or, in many species, reduced in the adult form to a flattened leaf-stalk (*phyllode*) resembling a leaf-blade. The flowers are mostly yellow, very small but numerous, in rounded or catkin-like clusters. Many species are planted as shade trees and for ornament. The foliage may be used as fodder for livestock. Many are useful timber trees, producing very hard tough wood. The bark and pods are employed for tanning. Some yield gum arabic. Several species are widely cultivated for stabilizing sandy soils. Commonly cultivated species include the **blue-leaved wattle** (*Acacia cyanophylla*) from W Australia, a small tree growing to 10 m/30 ft; leaf stalks bluish-green, up to 30 cm/12 in long, often pendulous; flowers in heads to 1.5 cm/0.6 in across, arranged in long leafy clusters; pods brown, constricted between the seeds. Also common is the **silver wattle** (*Acacia dealbata*) from SE Australia and Tasmania, a tree growing to 30 m/100 ft; leaves finely divided with 20–50 pairs of narrow leaflets, silvery-white when young; flowers deep yellow, fragrant, in rounded heads. It is the 'mimosa' of florists. (Genus: *Acacia*, 1 200 species. Family: *Leguminosae*.) » gum arabic/tree; shrub; tree [i]

wattle and daub A framework of interlaced twigs and rods plastered with mud or clay. The walls of timber-framed houses were often made of wattle and daub. If protected from the weather by good overhanging eaves to the roof, these walls can last for hundreds of years.

wattmeter An instrument for measuring electric power. Many types are used, the most common being the *electrodynamic* wattmeter which depends on the interaction of fields in two sets of coils. The *thermal* wattmeter depends on the heating effect of the current, and the *electrostatic* wattmeter is employed for calibration and standardization purposes. » electricity; watt

Watts, George Frederick (1817–1904) British painter, born in London. He studied in London, and first attracted notice by his cartoon of 'Caractacus' (1843) in the competition for murals for the new Houses of Parliament. He became known for his penetrating portraits of notabilities, 150 of which he presented to the National Portrait Gallery in 1904. He also executed some sculpture, notably 'Physical Energy' in Kensington Gardens, London. He died at Compton, Surrey. » cartoon (art); English art

Watts Towers A group of sculptures incorporating metal, stone, cement, tiles, glass, and waste materials, in the Watts district of Los Angeles, California. The towers were completed in 1954, having been constructed over a period of 35 years by Simon Rodin (1879–1965). » Los Angeles

Waugh, Evelyn (Arthur St John) [waw] (1903–66) English writer, born in London. Educated at Oxford, he quickly established a reputation with such social satirical novels as *Decline and Fall* (1928), *Vile Bodies* (1930), and *Scoop* (1938). He became a Catholic in 1930, and his later books display a more serious attitude, as seen in the religious theme of *Brideshead Revisited* (1945), and his war trilogy, beginning with *Men at Arms* (1952). He died near Taunton, Somerset. His son **Auberon** (1939–) became a novelist and journalist, known for his diary in the satirical magazine *Private Eye* and for many critical reviews and essays. » English literature; novel; satire

wave (oceanography) In oceanography, a disturbance moving under or along the surface of the water. Most ocean surface waves are generated by the wind blowing over the surface of the sea, imparting energy to the water. The speed with which these waves travel is determined by their wavelength and/or the depth of the water through which they are moving. The height of wind-generated ocean surface waves is determined by the wind *velocity*, the length of time the wind blows over the water (*duration*), and the distance it blows over the water (*fetch*). Waves can be transmitted over thousands of miles of ocean, often losing little energy until they break upon a shore. » bore; seiche; tidal wave; tide; tsunami; wind [i]

wave (physics) » **wave motion**

wave motion A disturbance from equilibrium which propagates in time from one place to another. Many phenomena are governed by waves, such as electromagnetic waves, quantum matter waves for electrons, seismic waves, and vibration. **Longitudinal waves** occur when the displacement is in the same direction as the wave propagation (eg sound waves). **Transverse waves** correspond to a displacement perpendicular to the direction of wave propagation (eg ripples on water). **Standing waves** (also called **stationary waves**) result from interference between waves travelling in opposite directions (eg on a guitar string, where waves run along the string, reflected from end to end). For standing waves, the ratio of the instantaneous value of displacement at one point to that at another does not change. **Periodic waves** (ie waves produced by some regular repeating motion) are described by amplitude A, frequency f or period T, and wavelength λ (see illustration); wave velocity $v=f\lambda$ m/s. **Sine waves** may be expressed as $y=A\sin 2\pi(ft-x/\lambda)$. Complicated periodic waves can be expressed as sums of sine waves using Fourier analysis. » amplitude; diffraction; Doppler effect; frequency; Huygens' principle; interference; phase; polarization; quantum mechanics; wavelength

wave-particle duality The principle that sub-atomic particles also exhibit wave-like properties, whereas electromagnetic waves also exhibit particle-like properties. The former can be illustrated by interference as observed in electron and neutron diffraction; the latter in the Compton and photoelectric effects. » interference [i]; photoelectric effect; quantum mechanics; wave (physics) [i]

Wave Rock Unique rock formation in SC Western Australia, near the town of Hyden; estimated to be 2 700 million years old; wave-shaped granite formation eroded by water and wind. » Western Australia

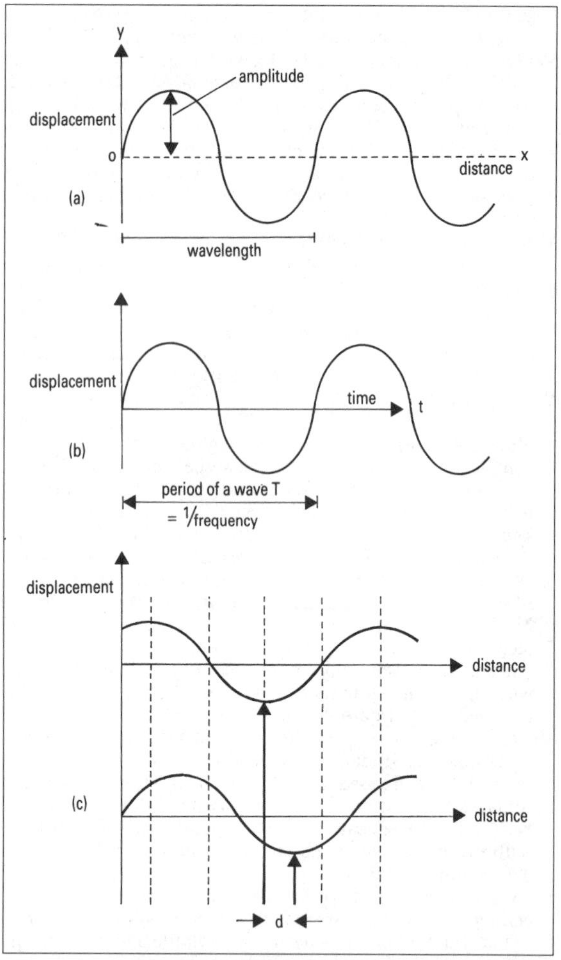

Wave – Sine wave at a fixed time, displaying amplitude and wavelength (a); sine wave at a fixed position, displaying period T (b); two sine waves out of phase ie one leads the other, with a phase difference ϕ given by $\phi=2\pi d/\lambda$ (c).

wavefunction A wave expression containing all possible information about a quantum system, such as electrons in atoms. The square of wavefunction is related to the outcome of physical observation. Variation of wavefuction in space and time is described by Schrödinger's equation. » quantum mechanics; Schrödinger's equation; wave (physics) [i]

wavelength The distance between two successive crests of a wave along the direction of propagation; symbol λ, units m (metres). The wavelength of light is 390–780 nm; the wavelength of sound, 16 mm–16 m. » wave (physics) [i]

Wavell, Archibald Percival, 1st Earl (1883–1950) British field marshal, born at Winchester, Hampshire. Educated at Winchester and Sandhurst, he served in South Africa and India, became Allenby's Chief-of-Staff in Palestine, and in 1939 was given the Middle East Command. He defeated the Italians in N Africa, but failed against Rommel, and in 1941 was transferred to India, where he became Viceroy (1943). He was made field marshal and viscount (1943), earl (1947), Constable of the Tower (1948), and Lord-Lieutenant of London (1949), where he died. » Allenby; Rommel; World War 2

wavenumber » **wavelength**

wax A substance of a firm but plastic solid consistency, with a low coefficient of friction, and water-repellant. There are two main kinds. *Mineral* waxes, notably paraffin wax, are hydrocarbons of high molecular weight with a micro-crystalline structure. *Plant* and *animal* waxes are esters of fatty acids, which fulfil a mainly protective function (as *beeswax* in the honeycomb). There are also synthetic organic substances of the same general chemical composition as these natural waxes. Beeswax has a long history as a preferred material for candles and polishes, and (since it can be finely worked sculpturally) as a medium for modelling, such as in wax museums and anatomical models. » carboxylic acids; hydrocarbons; paraffin wax

wax flower » **wax plant**

wax moth A small moth that feeds on the wax and combs of honeybees. It fills the tunnels inside the hive with silk. (Order: *Lepidoptera*. Family: *Pyralidae*.) » honeybee; moth

wax plant An evergreen climbing perennial, reaching 6 m/20 ft or more, native to Australia; leaves elliptical, glossy and rather fleshy; flowers in drooping heads, fragrant, 5-petalled, waxy-white with red centre; also called **wax flower**. (*Hoya carnosa*. Family: *Asclepiadaceae*.) » climbing plant; evergreen plants; perennial; stephanotis

waxbill A songbird of the weaver-finch family (17 species); native to Africa, Arabia, and S Asia to N Australia (introduced elsewhere); inhabits open woodland and scrub; eats seeds and insects. The name is sometimes used for the entire family. » avadavat; finch; songbird; weaver-finch; zebra finch

waxwing A songbird of the N hemisphere; grey-brown with black tail; head with crest; some individuals with red, wax-like tips to some wing feathers; inhabits woodland and gardens; eats berries and insects. (Family: *Bombicillidae*, 3 species.) » songbird

wayfaring tree A deciduous, star-shaped, hairy shrub or small tree, growing to 6 m/20 ft, native to Europe, typically a plant of chalk soils; leaves ovoid, toothed, rough-textured; flowers 5-petalled, white, in rounded clusters 6–10 cm/2½–4 in across; fruit berry-like, red becoming black when ripe. (*Viburnum lantana*. Family: *Caprifoliaceae*.) » deciduous plants; shrub; tree [i]

Wayland In Norse, German, and Old English legends, a clever inventor, known as Wayland the Smith. He is lame, having been maimed by King Nidud. Many heroes carry swords made by him; his 'Smithy' is a dolmen on the Berkshire Downs, UK.

Wayne, John, originally **Marion Michael Morrison**, byname **Duke** (1907–79) US film actor, born at Winterset, Iowa. After a succession of small parts in low-budget films and serials, he achieved stardom as the Ringo Kid in *Stagecoach* (1939). He went on to make over 80 films, typically starring as a tough but warm-hearted gunfighter or lawman. He specialized in Westerns, and was awarded an Oscar for his role in *True Grit* (1969). He died in Los Angeles.

weak interaction The feeble short-range force responsible for radioactive beta decay, characterized by the presence of a particle called the neutrino; also known as **weak nuclear force**. It is mediated by W and Z particles. Weak force is the only force exhibiting a handedness. » beta decay; CP violation; Glashow-Weinberg-Salam theory; neutrino; parity (physics); particle physics

weak nuclear force » **weak interaction**

Weald, the [weeld] Area in Kent, Surrey, and Sussex, SE England, between North and South Downs; fertile agricultural area; fruit, vegetables, hops, sheep; former extensive woodlands, providing charcoal for iron industry in Middle Ages; often refers strictly to area in Kent SW of the greensand ridge from Hythe through Ashford to Westerham. » Downs

weasel A small carnivorous mammal with a long thin body, short legs, and small head; tail usually half length of body; brown with pale underparts (may be all white in winter). The name is also used for the **North African striped weasel** (*Poecilictis libyca*), **African striped weasel** (*Poecilogale albinucha*), and **Patagonian weasel** (*Lyncodon patagonicus*). (Genus: *Mustela*, 9 species. Family: *Mustelidae*.) » carnivore [i]; Mustelidae

weather The atmospheric processes operating at a location at a particular time: for example, day-to-day conditions of temperature, precipitation, atmospheric pressure, and wind; the scientific study of weather is *meteorology*. A location's range of weather conditions is determined by its climate. Weather differs from climate in that it is concerned with short-term meteorological events, whereas climate encompasses all the weather characteristics of a place, and is concerned with the long-term behaviour of atmospheric processes. **Weather forecasting** is the prediction of future weather conditions, and is usually restricted to the immediate future (up to 3 days or so, but with decreasing confidence up to 10 days). The degree of success in forecasting is dependent on location; some regions (eg NW Europe) experience complex weather patterns, others (eg desert regions) experience more consistent weather patterns. » climate; meteorology; weather satellite

weather balloon » **radiosonde balloon**

weather satellite A satellite used to record global weather patterns. As a platform for remote sensing instruments, measurements are made of atmospheric energy fluxes, atmospheric and surface temperatures, cloud cover, and amounts of water vapour. Weather satellites are generally in polar, near-polar, or geostationary orbit. In polar orbit (eg METEOSAT) they are c.500–1 500 km/300–900 ml above the Earth, and their paths cross the Equator at approximately 90°, with each orbit crossing over or near to the Poles about every 90 minutes. Geostationary satellites (eg GEOS) remain in the same position relative to the Earth at all times, at an altitude of about 35 400 km/22 000 ml. Satellite observations allow access to remote areas of the Earth for which surface meteorological data are lacking. » meteorology; remote sensing; weather

Weathermen A highly radical US splinter group of Students for a Democratic Society which advocated spreading chaos by bombing campaigns, out of which would emerge a new brotherhood of man. More than 4 000 bomb incidents occurred between 1969–70, although all twelve members charged in 1970 with conspiracy to commit bombings were freed by the Supreme Court due to the inadmissibility of wire-tapping evidence. » Students for a Democratic Society

weaver » **weaverbird**

weaver-finch A finch-like bird, also known as the **estrildid finch** or (sometimes) the **waxbill**; native to the Old World tropics; eats grass seeds, fruit, and insects. (Family: *Estrildidae*, c.130 species.) » finch; waxbill; whydah

weaverbird A finch-like songbird, also known as **weaver**. The family includes the **true weaver**, **buffalo-weaver**, **sparrow-weaver**, and **scaly-weaver**. Many (not all) species weave nests suspended from branches. The group sometimes includes **weaver-finches**. » finch; grosbeak; quelea; songbird; whydah

weaving An ancient craft in which fabric is produced by interlacing warp (lengthwise) and weft (crosswise) threads on machines called *looms*. Hand looms are known from very early times. They developed little until the Industrial Revolution, when the flying shuttle was invented by John Kay, in association with Richard Arkwright, in 1733, followed later in the century by Cartwright's power loom. Today's modern weaving machines have dispensed with shuttles; 'bullets', 'rapiers', water jets, and air jets now carry the weft across the warp, with 1 000 picks per minute being possible on some machines. » Arkwright; Cartwright; spinning

Webb, James E(dwin) (1906–) US official and administrator of NASA during its programme to land a man on the Moon, born at Tally Ho, North Carolina. He became head of Bureau of the Budget under President Truman (1946–9) and later his Under-Secretary of State (1949–52). He was chosen by President Kennedy in 1961 to create in NASA an agency capable of successfully undertaking the Apollo Project, and retired from NASA in 1968, a year before the Apollo 11 landing. » Apollo project; NASA

Webb, Sidney (James) (1859–1947) and **(Martha) Beatrice**, *née* **Potter** (1858–1943) British social reformers, historians, and economists, married in 1892. Sidney was born and educated in London, became a lawyer, and joined the Fabian Society, where he wrote many powerful tracts. Beatrice was born near Gloucester, and became involved with the social problems of the time. After their marriage they began a joint life of service to socialism and trade unionism, publishing their classic *History of Trade Unionism* (1894), *English Local Government* (1906–29, 9 vols), and other works. They also started the *New Statesman* (1913). Sidney became an MP (1922), President of the Board of Trade (1924), Dominions and Colonial Secretary (1929–30), and Colonial Secretary (1930–1), and was created a baron in 1929. They both died at Liphook, Hampshire. » Fabian Society; socialism

Webber, Andrew Lloyd » **Lloyd Webber, Andrew**

weber [**vay**ber] SI unit of magnetic flux; symbol Wb; named after German scientist Wilhelm Weber (1804–91); defined as the amount of flux which, when allowed to decrease steadily to zero in 1 second, will produce 1 volt of electromotive force in the loop of wire through which the flux passes. » magnetic flux; units (scientific); RR71

Weber, Carl Maria (Friedrich) von [**vay**ber] (1786–1826) German composer and pianist, born near Lübeck. Nurtured by his family for music, he began to compose, and became conductor of the opera at Breslau (1804). In 1813 he settled in Prague as opera *Kapellmeister*, and about 1816 was invited by the King of Saxony to direct the German opera at Dresden. He is known as the founder of German romantic opera, notably in *Der Freischütz* (1821, The Freeshooter), *Euryanthe* (1823), and *Oberon* (1826), and he also wrote several orchestral works, piano, chamber, and church music, and many songs. He died in London.

Weber, Ernst Heinrich [**vay**ber] (1795–1878) German physiologist, born in Wittenberg. He became professor of anatomy (1818) and of physiology (1840) at Leipzig, where he devised a method of determining the sensitivity of the skin, introducing the concept of the 'just noticeable difference'. His findings were expressed mathematically by Fechner (the **Weber-Fechner Law** of the increase of stimuli). He died at Leipzig. » Fechner

Weber, Max [**vay**ber] (1864–1920) German economist, born at Erfuer. Educated at Heidelberg and Berlin, he held posts at Berlin (1893), Freiburg (1894), Heidelberg (1897), and Munich (1919). His best-known work is *Die protestantische Ethik und der Geist des Kapitalismus* (1904, The Protestant Ethic and the Spirit of Capitalism), which was a major influence on sociological theory. He helped to draft the constitution for the Weimar Republic (1919), and died soon after in Munich. » Protestant ethic; Weimar Republic

Webern, Anton (Friedrich Wilhelm) von [**vay**bern] (1883–1945) Austrian composer, born in Vienna. He studied under Schoenberg, and became one of his first musical disciples, making wide use of twelve-tone techniques, which led to several hostile demonstrations when his works were first performed. For a while he worked as a conductor and tutor in various cities, before settling in Mödling in 1918. His works, which include a symphony, cantatas, several short orchestral pieces, chamber music, a concerto for nine instruments, and songs, have profoundly influenced many later composers. The Nazis banned his music, and he worked as a proofreader during World War 2. He was accidentally shot dead by a US soldier near Salzburg. » Schoenberg; twelve-tone music

webspinner A small, slender insect commonly found in tropical forests, inhabiting extensive galleries or tunnels of silk constructed under bark, and in soil, litter, or moss. (Order: *Embioptera*, c.200 species.) » insect [i]

Webster, John (c.1580–c.1625) English Elizabethan dramatist. Little is known of him, though he is supposed to have been at one time clerk of St Andrews, Holborn. He collaborated with several other writers, especially Dekker, but is best known for his two tragedies, *The White Devil* (1612) and *The Duchess of Malfi* (1623). » Dekker; drama; English literature; Lamb, Charles; tragedy

Webster, Noah (1758–1843) US lexicographer, born at Hartford, Connecticut. Educated at Yale, he became a lawyer, but preferred teaching, and achieved fame with the first part (later known as 'Webster's Spelling Book') of *A Grammatical Institute of the English Language* (1783). Political articles and pamphlets, lecturing, and journalism occupied him until 1798, when he retired to a literary life at New Haven, Connecticut, where he died. He is best known for his *American Dictionary of the English Language* (1828). » dictionary; English

Webster–Ashburton Treaty (1842) An agreement between Britain and the USA which established the present-day boundary between NE USA and Canada. Among specific issues were disputed territory between Maine and New Brunswick and at the N end of Lake Champlain, navigation rights on the St John's R, and control of the Mesabi iron deposits. The treaty also established provisions for joint US/British action against the African slave trade. The parties involved were US secretary of state Daniel Webster and Alexander Baring, Baron Ashburton.

Weddell Sea Arm of the Atlantic Ocean, SE of Argentina; bounded by the Antarctic Peninsula (W), Coats Land (E), and S Orkney and Sandwich Is (N); ice shelves cover the S extent; named after James Weddell (1787–1834), who claimed to have discovered the sea in 1823. » Atlantic Ocean

Wedekind, Frank [**vay**duhkint] (1864–1918) German dramatist, born at Hanover. He worked in business and journalism, before becoming a cabaret performer, playwright, and producer. He is best known for his unconventional tragedies, in which he anticipated the Theatre of the Absurd: *Erdgeist* (1895, Earth Spirit), *Frühlings Erwachen* (1891, The Awakening of Spring), and *Die Büchse der Pandora* (1903, Pandora's Box). He died in Munich. » absurdism; drama; German literature; tragedy

Wedgwood, Dame Cicely Veronica (1910–) British historian, born at Stocksfield, Northumberland. Educated at Oxford, she became a specialist in 17th-c history, writing such biographies as *Oliver Cromwell* (1939) and *William the Silent* (1944), and several general works, such as *The Thirty Years' War* (1938). She was created a Dame in 1968.

Wedgwood, Josiah (1730–95) English potter, born at Burslem, Staffordshire. He worked in the family pottery business, became a partner in a Staffordshire firm (1754), and began to devise his own ware. He emulated antique models, producing an unglazed blue jasper ware, with raised designs in white, and a black basalt ware (**Wedgwood ware**). In 1759, he opened a factory at Burslem, and a decade later, one near Hanley, which he called 'Etruria'. From c.1768–80 he was in partnership with Thomas Bentley (1730–80), who introduced advanced marketing techniques to the firm. His concern over social welfare led him to build a village for his workmen at Etruria, where he died. » pottery

Weeks, Feast of » **Shabuoth**

Weelkes, Thomas (c.1575–1623) English madrigal composer. He became organist at Winchester College (1597) and Chichester Cathedral (1602). Nearly 100 of his madrigals have survived, as well as some instrumental music, and fragments of his sacred music. He died in London. » madrigal

weeping willow Any of several species of willow, all making quite large trees, with the smaller branches pendulous, often reaching the ground. Many are ornamentals, and arose in cultivation. One of the most common is **golden weeping willow**, *Salix × chrysocoma*. (Family: *Salicaceae*.) » willow

weever Bottom-dwelling fish with powerful poison spines on first dorsal fin and gill covers; eyes large and placed on top of head, mouth oblique; typically lives partly buried in sandy bottoms feeding on small fishes and crustaceans. (Genus: *Trachinus*. Family: *Trachinidae*.) » fish [i]

weevil A robust beetle with a characteristic snout on the front of the head; wing cases often sculptured and toughened; antennae club-like, with elbow joint; c.60 000 species, including many important pests such as the grain weevil and cotton boll weevil. (Order: *Coleoptera*. Family: *Curculionidae*.) » beetle; boll weevil

Wegener, Alfred (Lothar) [**vay**guhner] (1880–1930) German explorer and geophysicist, born in Berlin. He was professor of meterology at Hamburg (1919), and of geophysics and

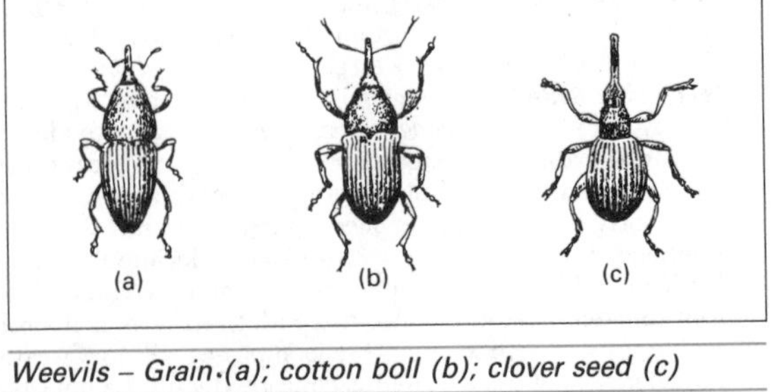

Weevils – Grain (a); cotton boll (b); clover seed (c)

meteorology at Graz (1924). His theory of continental drift is named after him (**Wegener's hypothesis**), and is the subject of his main publications. He died in Greenland on his fourth expedition there. » continental drift

Weigel, Helene [**vi**ygl] (1900–71) German actress-manager, born in Austria. She married Bertolt Brecht in 1929, and became a leading exponent of his work, particularly in *Die Mutter* (1932, The Mother), and *Mutter Courage und ihre Kinder* (1949, Mother Courage and her Children). She took control of the Berliner Ensemble after Brecht's death in 1956, and was instrumental in furthering his influence through the international tours she managed. » Berliner Ensemble; Brecht

weigela [wiy**je**la] A small deciduous shrub native to E Asia; leaves opposite, oval, finely toothed; flowers trumpet-shaped, 5-lobed, pink or crimson, in clusters. It is widely grown as an ornamental. (Genus: *Weigela*, 12 species. Family: *Caprifoliaceae*.) » deciduous plants; shrub

weight The downwards force on an object due to the gravitational attraction of the Earth; symbol G, units N (newton); distinct from mass. The weight of an object of mass 1 kg is 9.81 N, using $G = mg$, where m is mass and g is acceleration due to gravity, $g = 9.81$ m/s^2. Weight decreases with altitude. » acceleration due to gravity; force; mass

weight for height A measure used in nutrition studies to enable the weight of people to be compared. Direct comparisons of weight are invalid, since a six-foot person will weigh more than a five-foot person; thus weights are usually adjusted to correct for height. The most commonly used method is to divide weight in kilograms by the square of height in metres, yielding a figure known as the **body mass index**.

weightlifting A test of strength by lifting weights attached to both ends of a metal pole (*barbell*). Weightlifting formed part of the Ancient Olympic Games, and in the 19th-c was a popular attraction at many of the leading circuses. It was introduced as a sport c.1850, and held its first world championship in 1891. Competitors have to make two successful lifts: the *snatch*, taking the bar directly above the head, and the *clean and jerk*, taking the bar onto the chest then above the head with outstretched arms. The aggregate weight of the two lifts gives a lifter's total, and competitors gradually increase the weight attempted for their next lifts. Another form of weightlifting is *powerlifting* which calls for sheer strength as opposed to technique. This takes three forms: the *squat*, *dead lift*, and *bench press*. Weight training is increasingly popular amongst keep-fit enthusiasts, as well as top sportsmen and sports women. » RR122

Weil, Simone [vayl] (1909–43) French philosophical writer and mystic, born in Paris. She taught philosophy in several schools, interspersing this with periods of manual labour to experience the working-class life. In 1936 she served in the Republican forces in the Spanish Civil War. In 1941 she settled in Marseilles, where she developed a deep mystical feeling for the Catholic faith, yet a profound reluctance to join an organized religion. She escaped to the USA in 1942 and worked for the Free French in London, before her death at Ashford, Kent. Her posthumously published works include *La Pesanteur et la Grâce* (1946, Gravity and Grace) and *Attente de Dieu* (1950, Waiting for God).

Weil's disease [viyl] An infectious disease caused by *Leptospira icterohaemorrhagiae*, commonly carried by rodents; also known as **leptospirosis**. People bathing in canals or stagnant fresh water pools may be affected by the organism penetrating the skin through cuts or abrasions. Associated with muscle pain and jaundice, the condition carries a mortality of c.20%. It is named after German physician Adolf Weil (1848–1916), who described the syndrome clinically in 1886. » infection; jaundice

Weill, Kurt [viyl] (1900–50) German composer, born at Dessau. He studied and worked at Berlin, became a composer of instrumental works, then collaborated with Brecht, achieving fame with *Die Dreigroschenoper* (1928, The Threepenny Opera). A refugee from the Nazis, he settled in the USA in 1934. In all his works, he was influenced by the idioms of jazz, but his later operas and musical comedies, all of which contain an element of social criticism, did not repeat the success of the first. He died in New York City. » Brecht

Weimar [**viy**mah] 50°59N 11°20E, pop (1981) 63 725. City in Weimar district, S Germany, on R Ilm; railway; colleges of technology, music, and architecture; farm machinery, chemicals; associations with Schiller, Goethe, Liszt; former concentration camp of Buchenwald nearby; Goethe National Museum, Liszt Museum, observatory, Weimar Castle, Belvedere Castle (18th-c). » Germany [i]; Goethe; Liszt; Schiller; Weimar Republic

Weimar Republic The name by which the German federal republic of 1919–33 is known. In 1919 a National Constituent Assembly met at Weimar, on the R Elbe, and drew up a constitution for the new republic. The government moved from Weimar to Berlin in 1920. In 1933, two months after becoming Chancellor, Hitler passed an Enabling Act suspending the Weimar constitution. » Hitler; Weimar

Weinberg Salam theory » **Glashow-Weinberg-Salam theory**

Weinberger, Caspar (Willard) [**wiyn**berguh] (1917–) US politician. A former lawyer, he was state finance director of California during Ronald Reagan's governorship (1968–9). He served in the Nixon and Ford administrations, then became Secretary of Defense after Reagan's election victory in 1980. He resigned his office in 1987, and returned to private life. » Ford, Gerald R; Nixon, Richard M; Reagan

Weissmuller, Johnny, properly **(Peter) John**, originally **Jonas** [**wiyz**muhler] (1904–1984) US swimmer, born at Freidorf, Romania. His family emigrated to the USA in 1908. In 1922 he made history by becoming the first person to swim 100 m in under one minute. He won the 100 m freestyle at the 1924 and 1928 Olympics. After turning professional in 1932, he became a swimsuit model for a clothing firm, and starred in 12 Tarzan films between 1932 and 1948. He died at Acapulco, Mexico. » swimming

Weizmann, Chaim (Azriel) [**viyts**man] (1874–1952) Jewish statesman and President of Israel (1949–52), born near Pinsk, Russia. He studied in Germany and Switzerland, then lectured on chemistry at Geneva and Manchester. He helped to secure the Balfour Declaration of 1917, and became President of the Zionist Organization (1920–30, 1935–46), and of the Jewish Agency (from 1929). He played a major role in the establishment of the state of Israel (1948), and was its first President. He died at Rehovot, Israel. » Balfour; Israel [i]; Zionism

weld A biennial, native to Europe, W Asia, and N Africa; leaves narrow, wavy; first year rosette dense; stem in second year growing to 1.5 m/5 ft; flowers small, yellowish, in long spike, 4-petalled, three petals divided into three or more lobes; fruit a 3-lobed capsule; also called **dyer's rocket**. It was once cultivated as a source of bright yellow dye. (*Reseda luteola*. Family: *Resedaceae*.) » biennial; dyestuff

Welensky, Sir Roy (1907–) Rhodesian statesman, born in Salisbury, Southern Rhodesia. A railway worker and trade unionist, he was elected to the Legislative Council of Northern Rhodesia in 1938, knighted in 1953, and from 1956 to its break-up in 1963 was Prime Minister of the Federation of Rhodesia and Nyasaland. His handling of the constitutional crisis in 1959 aroused much controversy. » Zimbabwe [i]

welfare economics An economic theory devoted to studying how best to distribute the gross national product and a nation's wealth among the competing claimants, and the extent of interference with market forces by the government. The major work in this area was by Arthur Pigou (1877–1959), professor of political economy at Cambridge until 1944. » gross domestic product

welfare state A system of government whereby the state assumes responsibility for protecting and promoting the welfare of its citizens in such areas as health, income maintenance, unemployment, and pensions. Although earlier origins can be found, the development of modern welfare states was significantly influenced by the Beveridge Report of 1944, and a comprehensive system was established in the UK following World War 2, funded out of national insurance contributions and taxation. Such systems may be universal in coverage or subject to some form of means testing. In recent years concern has been expressed about the proportion of the budget consumed by welfare services, with those on the political right claiming that welfare provision decreases self-reliance and freedom of choice. » Beveridge

Welland Ship Canal Canal in Ontario, E Canada, linking L Erie and L Ontario, bypassing Niagara Falls; first canal opened 1829; modern canal, 1932; length 61 km/38 ml; can be used by vessels up to 223 m/732 ft in length. » Great Lakes; St Lawrence Seaway

Welles, (George) Orson (1915–85) US film director and actor, born in Kenosha, Wisconsin. He made his acting debut in Dublin (1931), then returned to the USA where he became a radio producer (1934), and founded the Mercury Theatre (1937). In 1938 his radio production of Wells's *War of the Worlds* was so realistic that it caused panic. In 1941, he wrote, produced, directed, and acted in the film *Citizen Kane*, a revolutionary landmark in cinema technique, and this was followed by *The Magnificent Ambersons* (1942). He played a variety of memorable stage and film roles, the most celebrated being that of 'Harry Lime' in *The Third Man* (1949). He died in Los Angeles.

Wellesley, Arthur » **Wellington, 1st Duke of**

Wellesley (of Norragh), Richard (Colley), 1st Marquis (1760–1842) British administrator, born at Dangan, Co Meath, Ireland. He became an MP (1784), a Lord of the Treasury (1786), a marquis (1799), and Governor-General of India (1797–1805). Under his administration British rule in India became supreme: the influence of France was extinguished, and the power of the princes reduced by the crushing of Tippoo Sahib (1799) and the Marathas (1803). After his return to England, he became Ambassador to Madrid (1805), Foreign Minister (1809), and Lord-Lieutenant of Ireland (1821, 1833). He died in London. » Tippoo Sahib

Wellesz, Egon (Joseph) [veles] (1885–1974) Austrian composer and musicologist, born in Vienna. He studied under Schoenberg, and subsequently became professor of musical history at Vienna (1930–8). Exiled from Austria by the Nazis, he became a research fellow then lecturer and reader in music (1944–56) at Oxford, where he died. His works include six operas, nine symphonies, and much choral and chamber music. » Schoenberg

Wellington, Arthur Wellesley, 1st Duke of (1769–1852) British general, statesman, and Prime Minister (1828–30), born in Dublin, Ireland. He joined the army in 1787, was sent to India with his regiment, and there defeated Tippoo Sahib, became Governor of Mysore, and broke the power of the Marathas. Knighted in 1804, he became an MP (1806), and Irish Secretary (1807). He defeated the Danes during the Copenhagen expedition (1807), and in the Peninsular War drove the French out of Portugal and Spain, gaining victories at Talavera (1809), Salamanca (1812), and Toulouse (1814). For his role in this campaign he was given many honours, and created Duke of Wellington. After Napoleon's escape from Elba, he routed the French at Waterloo. He supported Liverpool's government, and joined it as Master-General of the Ordnance (1818). He also became Constable of the Tower (1826) and army Commander-in-Chief (1827). His period as Prime Minister significantly weakened the Tory Party, which split over the question of Catholic emancipation, and was further weakened by disagreements over trade and reform. Wellington's opposition to parliamentary reform brought down his government, which was succeeded by the Whigs. He was Foreign Secretary under Peel (1834–5), retired from public life in 1846, and died at Walmer Castle, Kent. » Liverpool, Lord; Napoleonic Wars; Peel; Peninsular War; Tories; Waterloo, Battle of; Whigs

Wellington 41°17S 174°47E, pop (1988e) 325 200. Capital city and seat of government of New Zealand, on S coast of North Island; founded, 1840; capital, 1865; airport; railway; ferry to South Island; university (1897); vehicles, footwear, chemicals, soap, metal products, trade in dairy produce, meat; Government Building, Parliament Buildings (1922, 1980), General Assembly Library (1897), War Memorial Museum, St Paul's Cathedral (1866), Michael Fowler Centre, national art gallery, national museum. » New Zealand [i]

wellingtonia » **mammoth tree**

Wells, H(erbert) G(eorge) (1866–1946) British author, born at Bromley, Kent. He was apprenticed to a draper, tried teaching, studied biology in London, then made his mark in journalism and literature. He played a vital part in disseminating the progressive ideas which characterized the first part of the 20th-c. He achieved fame with scientific fantasies such as *The Time Machine* (1895) and *War of the Worlds* (1898), and wrote a range of comic social novels which proved highly popular, notably *Kipps* (1905) and *The History of Mr Polly* (1910). A member of the Fabian Society, he was often engaged in public controversy, and wrote several socio-political works dealing with the role of science and the need for world peace, such as *The Outline of History* (1920) and *The Work, Wealth and Happiness of Mankind* (1932). He died in London. » English literature; Fabian Society; novel; science fiction

wels Large nocturnal freshwater catfish found in large rivers and lakes of E Europe; length up to 3 m/10 ft; body devoid of scales, mouth with long barbels, anal fin long; feeds on fish and other aquatic vertebrates; fished commercially in some areas using traps and lines, and also farmed. (*Silurus glanis*. Family: *Siluridae*.) » catfish

Welsh The Celtic language spoken in Wales, assigned equal status with English in all legal and administrative affairs. Of all the extant Celtic languages, Welsh enjoys the most vibrant literary scene, which continues a tradition dating from the epic poem *Taliesin* (c.6th-c), and the prose tales of the *Mabinogi*, preserved in mediaeval manuscripts recording an oral tradition many centuries older. Its high point is the annual, week-long, high-culture festival, the National Eisteddfod, which has become the focal point of Welsh identity for many. A development of equal importance, particularly for the majority who have no commitment to high culture, is the establishment of a Welsh-language television channel, which has broadened the range of information and entertainment sources in the media. There are about 500 000 speakers of Welsh, though their numbers have declined by an average of about 5% every decade since 1900. » Celtic languages; Welsh literature

Welsh corgi » **corgi**

Welsh literature The *cynfeirdd* or early poets produced a rich literature in Welsh from the late 6th-c, many poems being attributed to Aneurin and Taliesin from that period. This poetry survives in the 'Four Books of Wales', dating from the 12th–14th-c, which also contain the eleven mediaeval prose tales comprising the *Mabinogion*, a conscious synthesis of Arthurian and native materials. The mediaeval court poets (or *Gogynfeirdd*) constituted the bardic schools, and drew up the rules of Welsh versification, while Dafydd ap Gwilym (flourished 1340–70) developed the simpler *cwyddau* or lyrical code. The first formal Eisteddfod was held in the 15th-c; and the Bible was translated into Welsh by 1588. From this point the anglicization of Welsh culture led to a gradual decline. The last great work in Welsh was Elis Wyn's prose *Gweledigaethea y Bardd Cwsc* (1704, Visions of the Sleeping Bard). There was still a vigorous tradition of ballad and folk-song, and religious fervour occasioned a revival in the 18th-c, with the lyrics of Williams Pantycelyn (1717–91) and many fine Methodist hymns, although Methodism inhibited the development of prose fiction. Antiquarian interest also played its part, inspired by Lewis Morris (1701–65), although 19th-c poets such as John Blackwell (1797–1840) and John Ceiriog Hughes (1832–87) tended to avoid the traditional metres. A 20th-c revival has been prompted by the example of Sir John Morris-Jones (1864–1929); and besides the Bangor School including Thomas Jones and T H Parry-Williams, there have been several popular poets, not least William Evans (1882–1968). Meanwhile, many Welsh writers have contributed to English literature, including the three Powys brothers (John Cowper, 1872–1964; Llewelyn, 1884–1939, Theodore Francis, 1875–1953), and the poets Dylan Thomas (1914–53) and R S Thomas (1913–). » Aneurin; bard; Celtic/English literature; Taliesin; Thomas, Dylan; Thomas, R S; Welsh

Welsh Nationalist Party » **Plaid Cymru**

Welsh pony A breed of horse divided by size and appearance: Section A (**Welsh mountain pony**), height up to

12 hands/1.2 m/4 ft; Section B (resembling Section A but 12–13½ hands/1.2–1.4 m/4–4½ ft high; Section C (resembling a small Welsh cob, up to 13½ hands/1.4 m/5 ft high; Section D is the **Welsh cob**. The **American Welsh pony** in the USA is a breed descended from Welsh animals. » cob; horse [i]

Welsh poppy A perennial growing to 60 cm/2 ft, native to W Europe, an isolated, westernmost species of an otherwise Asian genus; leaves pale green, divided into lobed segments; flowers 5–7 cm/2–2¾ in diameter, 4-petalled; fruit an elliptical capsule; producing yellow latex. (*Mecanopsis cambrica*. Family: *Papaveraceae*.) » latex; perennial; poppy

welwitschia [wel**wi**chia] A peculiar gymnosperm found only in the deserts of SW Africa, where most of the moisture comes from sea fogs. Its turnip-like stem produces just two strap-shaped leaves several metres long, which grow throughout the plant's life of over a century, becoming torn and ragged. (*Welwitschia mirabilis*. Family: *Gnetaceae*.) » gymnosperms

Welwyn Garden City [**wel**in] 51°48N 0°13W, pop (1981) 41 102. Town in Hatfield district, Hertfordshire, SE England; 10 km/6 ml NE of St Albans; founded in 1919 by Ebenezer Howard; designated a 'new town' in 1948; railway; chemicals, plastics, pharmaceuticals, food processing. » Hertfordshire; Howard, Ebenezer

Wembley Stadium One of the most famous football stadiums in the world, built at Wembley in NE London in 1923. It has a capacity of 100 000. » football [i]; London [i]

Wenceslaus or **Wenceslas, St**, byname **Good King Wenceslas** (c.903–35), feast day 28 September. Duke and patron of Bohemia, born at Stochov. He received a Christian education, and after the death of his father (c.924) encouraged Christianity in Bohemia, against the wishes of his mother. Probably at her instigation, and because he had put his duchy under the protection of Germany, he was murdered by his brother Boleslaw. He became the patron saint of Bohemia and Czechoslovakia. » Christianity

wentletrap A marine snail from the Indo-Pacific region; usually colourless shell with a highly sculptured surface and regularly spaced ribs. (Class: *Gastropoda*. Order: *Mesogastropoda*.) » gastropod; snail

Wentworth, Thomas » **Strafford, Earl of**

Wentworth, W(illiam) C(harles) (1793–1872) Australian landowner and politician, born on Norfolk I. He took part in the expedition which explored the Blue Mts in 1813, then studied at Cambridge, and became a lawyer. He was a staunch protagonist of self-government for Australia, which he made the policy of his newspaper *The Australian* (established 1824), and he was elected to the Legislative Council in 1842. He retired to England in 1862, and died at Wimborne, Dorset. » Australia [i]

Wenzel, Hanni [**ven**suhl] (1956–) Liechtenstein alpine skier, born at Staubirnen, Germany. At the 1980 Olympics she won the gold medal in the slalom and giant slalom, and the silver in the downhill. Her total of four Olympic gold medals (including a bronze in 1976) is a record for any skier. She was combined world champion and overall World Cup winner in 1980. » skiing

Werfel, Franz [**ver**fuhl] (1890–1945) Austrian-Jewish writer, born in Prague, Czechoslovakia. He lived in Vienna until 1938, when he moved to France, and then to the USA. He wrote poems and plays, but is best known for his novels, notably the epic *Die vierzig Tage des Musa Dagh* (1933, The Forty Days of Musa Dagh) and the story of the Lourdes visionary, *Das Lied von Bernadette* (1941, The Song of Bernadette). He died in Hollywood. » German literature; novel

Wergeland, Hendrik Arnold [**ver**guhland] (1808–45) Norwegian poet, dramatist, and patriot, born at Kristiansand. He is best known for his poetry, notably his Creation epic, *Skabelsen, mennesket, og messias* (1830, Creation, humanity, and desire), and for such narrative poems as *Den Engelske lods* (1844, The English pilot). A leader of the cause of Norwegian nationalism, he became Norway's national poet. He died at Christiania. » epic; Norwegian literature; poetry

Wesak [**we**sahk] A Buddhist festival held in May to celebrate the birth, enlightenment and death of the Buddha. » Buddha; Buddhism

Weser, River [**vay**zer], ancient **Visurgis** Major river in Germany, formed by the confluence of the Werra and Fulda Rivers at Münden in Lower Saxony; flows generally N to the North Sea forming an estuary at Wesermünde; length 440 km/273 ml; connected to the Rhine and Elbe by the Mittelland Canal. » Germany [i]; Mittelland Canal

Wesker, Arnold (1932–) British dramatist, born in London. His Jewish family background and his varied attempts at earning a living (having left school at 14) are important ingredients of his plays. The Kahn family trilogy, *Chicken Soup with Barley*, *Roots*, and *I'm Talking about Jerusalem* (1959–60), echo the march of events, pre- and post-World War 2, in a left-wing family. Later plays include *The Kitchen* (1959), *Chips with Everything* (1962), *The Friends* (1970), and *Caritas* (1981). » Centre 42; drama; English literature

Wesley, John (1703–91) British evangelist and founder of Methodism, born at Epworth, Lincolnshire. Educated at Charterhouse and Oxford, he was ordained deacon (1725) and priest (1728), and in 1726 became a fellow at Oxford and lecturer in Greek. Influenced by the spiritual writings of William Law, he became leader of a small group which had gathered round his brother **Charles** (1707–88), nicknamed the Methodists, a name later adopted by John for the adherents of the great evangelical movement which was its outgrowth. On their father's death, the brothers went as missionaries to Georgia (1735–8), but the mission proved a failure. In 1738, at a meeting in London, during the reading of Luther's preface to the epistle to the Romans, he experienced an assurance of salvation which convinced him that he must bring the same assurance to others; but his zeal alarmed most of the parish clergy, who closed their pulpits against him. This drove him into the open air at Bristol (1739), where he founded the first Methodist chapel, and then the Foundry at Moorfields, London, which became his headquarters. His life was frequently in danger, but he outlived all persecution, and the itineraries of his old age were triumphal processions throughout the country. He was a prolific writer, producing grammars, histories, biographies, collections of hymns, his own sermons and journals, and a magazine. He died in London. » evangelicalism; Law, William; Methodism; Whitefield, George

Wesley, Samuel (1766–1837) British organist and composer, born in Bristol, son of Charles Wesley. One of the most famous organists of his day, he was an ardent enthusiast of J S Bach. Though a Roman Catholic (to the displeasure of his father and uncle), he wrote also for the Anglican liturgy, leaving a number of fine motets and anthems, including *In Exitu Israel*. » Bach, Johann Sebastian; Wesley, John

Wessex A kingdom of the Anglo-Saxon heptarchy, with its main centres at Winchester and Hamwic (Southampton). Under Alfred, Wessex – by then incorporating Kent and Sussex – was the only English kingdom to withstand the onslaughts of the Vikings. Alfred's successors reconquered the Danelaw, and had united all England under a single monarchy by 954. » Alfred; Anglo-Saxons; Mercia; Vikings

West, Benjamin (1738–1820) American painter, born at Springfield, Pennsylvania. He was sent on a sponsored visit to Italy, and on his return journey was induced to settle in London (1763). George III was his patron for 40 years. The representation of modern instead of classical costume in his best-known picture 'The Death of General Wolfe' (c.1771) was an innovation in English historical painting. He died in London. » George III

West, Mae (1892–1980) US actress, born in New York City. A child performer, she spent some years in vaudeville and on Broadway before her first film *Night After Night* (1932). Throughout the 1930s a series of racy comedies, often with her own dialogue-script, exploited her voluptuousness and sexual badinage, although under much pressure from censorship. She subsequently returned to the stage and nightclubs, but made two late character appearances in *Myra Breckinridge* (1970) and *Sextette* (1978), before her death from a stroke in Los Angeles. Her name was given to an airman's pneumatic life-jacket which, when inflated, was considered to give the wearer the generous bosom for which she herself was noted. » theatre; vaudeville

West, Nathanael, pseudonym of **Nathan Wallenstein Weinstein** (1903–40) US novelist, born and educated in New York City. After associating with Surrealist writers in Paris during the mid-1920s, he returned to New York and wrote four short fantasy novels, of which the best known are *Miss Lonelyhearts* (1933) and *The Day of the Locust* (1939). The latter is a satire on Hollywood, where he had worked as a scriptwriter. He died in a road accident near El Centro, California. » American literature; novel; Surrealism

West, Dame Rebecca, pseudonym of **Cicily Isabel Andrews**, *née* **Fairfield** (1892–1983) British novelist and critic, born and died in London. Educated in Edinburgh, she was for a short time on the stage, but turned to journalism. She is best known for her studies arising out of the Nuremberg war trials: *The Meaning of Treason* (1947) and *A Train of Powder* (1955). Her novels include *The Judge* (1922), *The Thinking Reed* (1936), and *The Birds Fall Down* (1966). She was created a Dame in 1959. » English literature; novel; Nuremberg Trials

West Bank Region of the Middle East W of the R Jordan and the Dead Sea; comprises the Jordanian governorates of Jerusalem, Hebron, and Nablus; part of the former mandate of Palestine, administered by Jordan 1949–67; seized by Israel in the 1967 War, and remains under Israeli occupation, administered as the district of Judea-Samaria; area includes Old (East) Jerusalem, as well as Bethlehem, Jericho, Hebron, and Nablus; a focus of territorial aspirations by the Palestine Liberation Organization; scene of an uprising (*intifada*) against the Israelis since early 1988, during which time schools and many shops have been closed; Palestinian sources claim that Israeli troops have killed 393 Palestinians (Dec 1989) attempting to control the uprising. » Arab–Israeli Wars; East Bank; Israel [i]; Jordan [i]; PLO

West Bengal [benggawl] pop (1981) 54 485 560; area 87 853 sq km/ 33 911 sq ml. State in NE India, bounded NW by Nepal, E by Bangladesh, and S by the Bay of Bengal; crossed by many rivers; created in 1947, when the former province of Bengal was divided between the new state of West Bengal and the Muslim majority districts of East Bengal (now Bangladesh); capital, Calcutta; governed by a 295-member Legislative Assembly; rice, foodgrains, oilseed, jute; coal, aluminium, steel, fertilizer; extensive rail network. » Calcutta; India [i]

West Glamorgan pop (1987e) 363 200; area 817 sq km/ 315 sq ml. County in S Wales, UK, divided into four districts; created in 1974; bounded S by the Bristol Channel; county town, Swansea; other chief towns, Neath, Port Talbot; steel, coal, tinplate, aluminium, chemicals, tourism; Gower Peninsula nearby. » Swansea; Wales [i]; RR41

West Highland Way Long-distance footpath in Scotland; stretching from Milngavie near Glasgow to Fort William; length 158 km/98 ml; opened in 1980. » Scotland [i]

West Highland white terrier A small muscular terrier developed in Scotland; thick coat of straight white hair; rounded head; short, pointed, erect ears. » terrier

West Indies Federation (1958–1962) An unsuccessful attempt to establish a single government for the English-speaking West Indies. After the Federation failed, the countries of the English-speaking Caribbean slowly gained their independence. » Caribbean Sea

West Irian » **Irian Jaya**

West Midlands pop (1987e) 2 624 300; area 899 sq km/ 559 sq ml. Former county of C England, divided into seven boroughs; administrative centre, Birmingham; other chief towns include Wolverhampton, West Bromwich, Coventry, Walsall; vehicles, aircraft, engineering; metropolitan council abolished in 1986. » Birmingham; England [i]

West Point A US military academy founded by Act of Congress in 1802 at the West Point military station on the Hudson R in the state of New York. » New York (state)

West Sussex » **Sussex, West**

West Virginia pop (1987e) 1 897 000; area 62 758 sq km/ 24 232 sq ml. State in E USA, divided into 55 counties; the 'Mountain State'; part of Virginia until the Civil War, when the area remained loyal to the Union, and split from Confederate East Virginia, 1861; 35th state admitted to the Union as West Virginia, 1863; capital, Charleston; other chief cities Huntington, Wheeling, Parkersburg, Morgantown; Ohio R follows the Ohio state border, with several tributaries; Potomac R forms part of the N border; Allegheny Mts dominate the E; highest point Mt Spruce Knob (1 481 m/4 859 ft); a rugged, hilly state, most of which is in the Allegheny Plateau; 65% forested; some cattle, dairy products, apples, eggs, corn, tobacco; nation's leading producer of bituminous coal; major producer of natural gas; also stone, cement, salt, oil; glass, chemicals, metals, machinery; both summer and winter tourism. » American Civil War; Charleston (West Virginia); United States of America [i]; Virginia; RR39

westerlies The prevailing winds found at mid-latitudes, between 30° and 60°N and S of the Equator. In the N hemisphere the prevailing direction is from the SW; in the S hemisphere it is from the NW. Westerlies in the S hemisphere are stronger because there is a smaller land mass, and are known as the **Roaring Forties**, from the latitudes at which they occur. » general circulation model; wind [i]

Western A novel or film concerned with the opening up and civilizing of the American West; an epic theme featuring hunters and trackers, cowboys and Indians, stagecoach and railroad, the cavalry, lawmen, the California goldrush, women, horses, and dogs. Fenimore Cooper established a model in *The Pioneers* (1823), basing his Leatherstocking on the exploits of Daniel Boone. Davy Crockett and Kit Carson were similarly fictionalized; and journalist E Z C Judson (1828–86; pseudonym Ned Buntline) promoted Buffalo Bill Cody to mythic status as 'the *beau ideal* of the plains' in dime novels (from 1860), for which Prentiss Ingraham (1843–1904) later wrote over 200 Buffalo Bill stories. Cody's Wild West Show (from 1882) was a by-product. The railroad robbery by Butch Cassidy and his Wild Bunch in 1900 occasioned Edwin S Porter's film *The Great Train Robbery* (1903), beginning the great tradition of Western films, such as *Stagecoach* (1939), *High Noon* (1952), *Shane* (1953), and *Butch Cassidy and the Sundance Kid* (1969). The Western film has drawn on 20th-c Western fiction by such writers as Zane Grey (1875–1939), and C E Mulford, creator of Hopalong Cassidy. » American literature; cinema; Cooper, James Fennimore; epic

Western Australia pop (1986) 1 496 100; area 2 525 500 sq km/ 975 000 sq ml. State in W Australia; Dutchman Dirk Hartog landed here in 1616, and Englishman William Dampier in 1688; Britain's first non-convict settlement on the Swan R, 1829; governed at first by New South Wales; separate colony, 1890; now comprises nine statistical divisions; bounded S by the Great Australian Bight, W by the Indian Ocean and N by the Timor Sea; a third of the total area of Australia; over 90% occupied by the Great Plateau (mean altitude 600 m/2 000 ft above sea-level); highest point, Mt Meharry (1 245 m/4 085 ft); Great Sandy Desert, Gibson Desert, Great Victoria Desert, Nullarbor Plain in the E; near the border with Northern Territory is Wolf Crater, the world's second largest meteorite crater; many dry salt lakes in the interior (notably L Lefroy and L McLeod); several archipelagoes off the coast; principal rivers the Swan, Avon, Blackwood, Gascoyne, Drysdale, Murchison, Ashburton, Fitzroy; capital, Perth; principal towns, Port Hedland, Busselton, Albany, Kalgoorlie, Carnarvon; fishing, forestry, wheat, sheep, wine, agricultural machinery; gold, iron ore, nickel, uranium, bauxite, mineral sands, superphosphates, oil and natural gas; state holidays Labour Day (Mar), Foundation Day (Jun). » Australia [i]; Perth (Australia)

Western European Union An organization of W European nations, founded in 1955 to co-ordinate defence and other policies, replacing the defunct European Defence Community; its members include Belgium, France, Italy, Luxembourg, the Netherlands, the UK, and Germany. It contains a Council of Ministers, a representative assembly in the Consultative Assembly of the Council of Europe, and a Standing Armaments Committee which works in co-operation with NATO. » Council of Europe; European Community; European Defence Community; NATO

Western Isles pop (1981) 31 884; area 2 898 sq km/1 119 sq ml. Administrative region in Scotland; group of islands off the W coast (Outer Hebrides), separated from the mainland by the Minch and Little Minch; bounded W by the Atlantic Ocean;

main islands, Lewis, North Uist, Benbecula, South Uist, Barra; c.210 km/130 ml N–S; capital, Stornoway, on Lewis; fishing, cattle, sheep, Harris tweed; name often used to refer to both Inner and Outer Hebrides. » Hebrides; Lewis with Harris; Scotland [i]; Stornoway

Western Reserve Territory in NW Ohio successfully claimed by the state of Connecticut in 1786, during the final settlement of interstate boundary disputes that dated from the colonial era. Connecticut's claim thereafter was to simple ownership, not to jurisdiction. » Connecticut

Western Sahara pop (1990e) 186 000; area 252 126 sq km/ 97 321 sq ml. Former Spanish province in NW Africa, between Morocco (N) and Mauritania (S) and bounded NE by Algeria; chief town, Layoun, pop (1982) 96 784; desert area, rich in phosphates; partitioned by Morocco and Mauritania after its Spanish status ended in 1975; withdrawal of Mauritania, 1979; now administered by Morocco; named the **Democratic Saharan Republic** by the independence movement, *Frente Polisario*, which has set up a 'government in exile'; Saharan guerrillas operating from within Algeria. » Mauritania [i]; Morocco [i]

Western Samoa, official name **The Independent State of Western Samoa** [sa**moh**a] pop (1989e) 163 000; area 2 842 sq km/ 1 097 sq ml. Territory in the SW Pacific Ocean, 2 600 km/ 1 600 ml NE of Auckland, New Zealand; divided into 24 districts; comprises two large and seven smaller islands, four of which are inhabited (Upolu, Savai'i, Apolima, Manono); capital, Apia; timezone GMT − 11; chief ethnic group, Polynesian; official languages, Samoan, English; chief religion, Christianity; unit of currency, the Western Samoan dollar (tala) of 100 cents; formed from ranges of extinct volcanoes, rising to 1 829 m/6 001 ft on Savai'i; many dormant volcanoes (last activity, 1905–11); thick tropical vegetation; several coral reefs along coast; tropical climate; rainy season (Dec–Apr); average annual temperatures, 22–30°C; average annual rainfall, 2 775 mm/109 in; hurricanes occur; visited by the Dutch, 1772; 1889 commission divided Samoa between Germany (which acquired Western Samoa) and the USA (which acquired Tutuila and adjacent small islands, now known as American Samoa); New Zealand granted a League of Nations mandate for Samoa, 1919; UN Trust Territory under New Zealand, 1946; independence, 1962; governed by a monarch as head of state, a prime minister, and a 47-member Legislative Assembly elected for three years; largely agricultural subsistence economy; taro, yams, breadfruit, pawpaws; coconuts, cocoa, bananas; tourism increasing; internal transportation system depends largely on roads and ferries; charter air service operates between the two main islands. » American Samoa; Apia; mandates; Trust Territory; RR27 national holidays; RR66 political leaders

Western Wall The only surviving part of the Second Temple of Jerusalem and, as such, the most sacred of Jewish sites. Traditionally a place of prayer and lamentation during the dispersion of the Jews, it was formerly often referred to as the 'Wailing Wall'. » Temple, Jerusalem; Judaism

Westland area 1 175 sq km/454 sq ml. National park, E South Island, New Zealand; joins the Mt Cook National Park along the main divide of the Southern Alps; glaciers, mountains, lakes, forest; established in 1961; a world heritage site. » Southern Alps

Westman Islands, Icelandic **Vestmannaeyjar** pop (1983) 4 743. Group of 15 islands and 30 reefs off the S coast of Iceland; includes the volcanic island of Heimaey which erupted in 1973; island of Surtsey was formed during eruptions in 1963–6; fish processing. » Iceland [i]; Surtsey Island

Westmeath, Gaelic **na h-Iarmhidhe** [west**meeth**] pop (1981) 61 523; area 1 764 sq km/681 sq ml. County in Leinster province, C Irish Republic; bounded on SW by R Shannon; crossed by the Royal Canal; capital, Mullingar; cattle, agriculture. » Irish Republic [i]; Mullingar

Westminster Abbey The collegiate church of St Peter in Westminster, London. There was probably a monastic settlement on this site from the 8th-c. The first recorded abbey church, consecrated in 1065, was replaced from 1245 by the present building in early English Gothic style. The monastery was dissolved in 1540. Westminster Abbey has a special importance in English history, serving as a coronation church and national shrine, with many memorials to those who have shaped the country's history and culture. » London [i]

Westminster Assembly A body of clerics (120) and laymen (30) convened by the English Long Parliament in 1643 to arrange a religious settlement to replace the Church of England. Dominated by Presbyterians, it produced a directory of public worship to replace the Prayer Book, and the Westminster Confession of Faith. Its influence declined when the power of the army, which favoured toleration, increased after 1648. » Church of England; Long Parliament; Presbyterianism

Westminster, City of 51°30N 0°09W, pop (1987e) 173 400. Borough of C Greater London, England; N of the R Thames; includes Hyde Park, St James's Park, Green Park and the suburbs of Paddington, Westminster, and Marylebone; administrative centre of the UK; Statutes of Westminster (1275, 1285, 1290) laid the foundations of English law; includes the major tourist area from Westminster Bridge through Trafalgar Square to the West End. » Big Ben; Buckingham Palace; Downing Street; Hyde/St James's Park; Houses of Parliament; National/National Portrait/Tate Gallery; St James's Palace; Westminster Abbey; Whitehall

Westminster Confession of Faith The main Presbyterian Confession of Faith, adopted by the Westminster Assembly, England, in 1643. It sets forth the main doctrines of the Christian faith from a Calvinistic perspective, and became the major confessional influence among Reformed Churches of the English-speaking world. » confession **1**; Calvinism; Reformed Churches

Westminster, Palace of » **Houses of Parliament**

Westminster, Statutes of Part of a comprehensive legislative programme undertaken by Edward I to reform English law and administration. The first Statute (1275) was concerned mainly with criminal matters, notably compulsory trial by jury; the second (1285) covered many fields of law, and facilitated the creation of entailed estates; the third (1290) protected lords' feudal incidents. » Edward I; feudalism

Westmorland Former county of NW England; part of Cumbria since 1974.

Westphalia A NW German principality, first settled by Saxons c.700, given to the Archbishop of Cologne (1180), and later forming part of the Lower Rhine-Westphalian Circle of the Empire (1512). In 1803–6 it was divided between Brandenburg-Prussia and neighbouring states. Although the name was coined for Napoleon's satellite kingdom (1807), the princes regained possession (1814–15). » Holy Roman Empire; Napoleon I

wet rot A type of timber decay caused by the cellar fungus, *Coniophora puteana*; found only in wood with a high moisture content. » fungus

'wets' and 'dries' Terms coined in the early 1980s to describe the political stances of members of the Thatcher administration in the UK. Initially a derogatory label, 'wets' – those with less radical views than the Prime Minister – were often concerned over the social consequences of certain government policies. 'Dries' were firm supporters of such policies. » Thatcher

Wexford (county), Gaelic **Loch Garman** pop (1981) 99 081; area 2 352 sq km/908 sq ml. County in Leinster province, SE Irish Republic; bounded by St George's Channel and Atlantic Ocean with bays at Wexford, Waterford, and Bannow; Wicklow Mts (N), Blackstairs Mts (W); watered by R Barrow and R Slaney; capital, Wexford; main seaport, Rosslare; rich farmland (cattle) and resort area. » Irish Republic [i]; Wexford (town)

Wexford (town) 52°20N 6°27W, pop (1981) 15 364. Capital of Wexford county, Leinster, Irish Republic; at mouth of R Slaney where it meets Wexford harbour; railway; machinery, motor vehicles, brewing, cheese, textiles; opera festival (Oct). » Wexford (county)

Weyden, Rogier van der [**viy**dn] (c.1400–64) Flemish religious painter, born at Tournai. He studied in Tournai, and by 1436 was official painter to the city of Brussels. He executed many portraits and altarpieces, and among his best-known works are the 'Descent from the Cross' (c.1435–40, Madrid) and the 'Last Judgment' altarpiece (c.1450, Beaune). He died in Brussels. » altarpiece; Flemish art

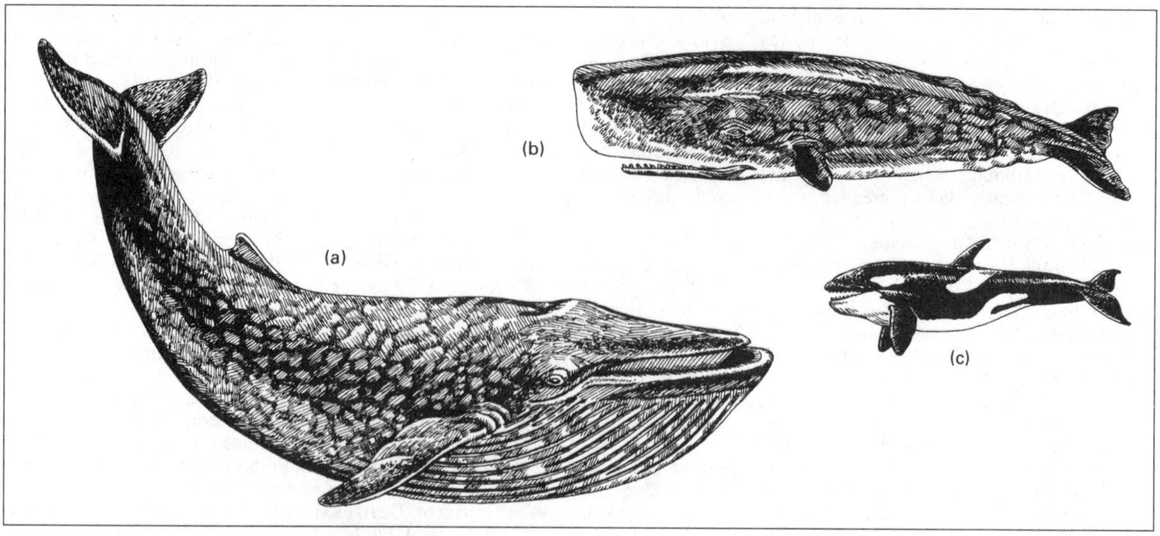

Whales – Blue whale (a); sperm whale (b); killer whale (c)

whale An aquatic mammal of worldwide order *Cetacea* (79 species); evolved from four-legged land mammals; spends entire life in water; resembles fish in shape (although tail blades – *flukes* – are horizontal, not vertical); breathes air through opening(s) on top of head; has insulating layer of oily blubber under skin; two major groups: **toothed whales** (5 families with 69 species, including the sperm whale, killer whale, dolphin, and porpoise); eat mainly fish and squid; locate prey using sonar; single breathing opening; larger **baleen whales** (3 families with 10 species, including rorquals, grey whales, and right whales); sieve plankton using baleen plates; double breathing openings; once hunted extensively. » blue/killer/pilot/right/sperm whale; baleen [i]; bottlenose; dolphin; grampus; mammal [i]; narwhal; rorqual

whale-headed stork » **shoebill**

whale shark The largest of all fishes, widely distributed in surface waters of tropical seas; length up to 18 m/60 ft; weight up to 20 tonnes; feeds mainly on small planktonic organisms. (*Rhincodon typus*. Family: *Rhincodontidae*.) » plankton; shark

whalebone » **baleen** [i]

whaling The hunting of whales for oil, meat, and blubber, which has resulted in a serious decline in whale populations and the near-extinction of several species. Whaling began in the 10th-c in the Bay of Biscay, but in the last two centuries it has been concentrated in Arctic and Antarctic waters. Overexploitation reached a peak in the Arctic in the 1930s, and in the Antarctic in the 1960s. The International Whaling Commission, set up in 1946, exists to regulate the industry, but overfishing has continued. A moratorium on commercial whaling was to begin in 1985, but not all countries have agreed to it, and several have used loopholes, which allow the killing of whales for research, in order to continue whaling. » whale [i]

Wharton, Edith (Newbold), *née* **Jones** (?1861–1937) US novelist, born in New York City. Educated privately and in Europe, she published her first stories, *The Greater Inclination*, in 1899. She wrote mainly about upper-class New York society, and is best known for her novels, *The House of Mirth* (1905), *Ethan Frome* (1911), and *The Age of Innocence* (1920, Pulitzer Prize). After 1907 she lived mainly in France, where she died. » American literature; novel

wheat A cereal second only to rice in importance, originating in the Middle East but cultivated throughout temperate regions of the world; its inflorescence is a dense, cylindrical head. There are numerous species and cultivars with different growth properties and yielding different qualities of flour, such as bread wheat (*Triticum aestivum*) and **durum** (*Triticum durum*) from which macaroni is made. Wheat is the only cereal suitable for making bread, because of the presence of the elastic protein gluten. (Genus: *Triticum*, 20 species. Family: *Gramineae*.) » bread; cereals; cultivar; durum; gluten; grass [i]; inflorescence [i]; oats

wheatear A thrush native to the N hemisphere and S Africa; inhabits open country, especially dry stony areas; eats insects and seeds. The name is a corruption of 'white arse' (after white rump). (Genus: *Oenanthe*, 20 species.) » thrush (bird)

Wheatstone, Sir Charles (1802–75) British physicist, born in Gloucester. He became professor of experimental philosophy at London (1834), known for his experiments in sound. He invented the concertina (1829), took out a patent for an electric telegraph (1837), explained the principle of the stereoscope (1838), and invented a sound magnifier for which he introduced the term *microphone*. **Wheatstone's Bridge**, a device for the comparison of electrical resistances, was brought to notice (though not invented) by him. Knighted in 1868, he died in Paris. » microphone [i]; resistance

wheel One of the most important innovations in human material culture, allowing continuous rotary motion, and the continuous conversion of rotary motion into linear motion, and vice versa. The earliest wheels are found c.3500 BC; the earliest with spokes c.2000 BC. The first were sections of tree trunks, but later types were built up of planks joined and cut to shape. Other improvements were the separate axle, the reinforced hub, which could be lubricated, and the tyre, which strengthened the rim.

wheel animalcule » **rotifer**

wheel window » **rose window** [i]

Wheeler, Sir (Robert Eric) Mortimer (1890–1976) British archaeologist, born in Glasgow, Scotland. Educated at Bradford and London, he became Director of the National Museum of Wales (1920), and Keeper of the London Museum (1926–44). He carried out notable excavations in Britain at Verulamium (St Albans) and Maiden Castle, and from 1944–7 was Director-General of Archaeology in India. He then held a chair at the Institute of Archaeology in London (1948–55). Knighted in 1952, he was well known for spirited popular accounts of his subject, in books and on television. He died at Leatherhead, Surrey. » archaeology; Maiden Castle

whelk A marine snail with a spirally coiled external shell; aperture closed off by a chitinous covering (*operculum*) once head and body are drawn inside; single gill present in mantle cavity; most species are carnivores or scavengers. (Class: *Gastropoda*. Order: *Neogastropoda*.) » chitin; gastropod; snail

whidah » **whydah**

Whig Party (USA) One of two major US political parties during the decades prior to the Civil War. The name was adopted in 1834 to signify opposition to 'King' Andrew Jackson (president, 1829–37). The Whigs stood for greater governmental intervention in the economy than did the Democrats, who followed Jackson, but both parties agreed on the necessity of keeping the slavery issue out of politics. The Whigs collapsed in 1854, precisely because the slavery issue could no longer be contained. » Jackson, Andrew; slave trade

Whigs (UK) A British political party which emerged in 1679–80 as the group agitating for the exclusion of James, Duke of York, on the grounds of his Catholicism. The name was probably a contraction of 'Whiggamores' – militant Scottish Presbyterians. The party benefited from the political changes of the Revolution of 1688 and, during its long period of dominance in British politics after 1714, drew much strength from defending 'the principles of 1688', which included limited monarchy and the importance of parliament. Whiggery is better seen as a general set of beliefs along these lines, rather than as a unified party. Most of its leaders were great landowners who used political patronage to create family-based groupings in parliament. The party was supported by many in the moneyed and commercial classes, and by Nonconformists who looked to the Whigs (usually mistakenly) to provide religious toleration. Whig fortunes waned in the late 18th-c, and Whigs became leading members of the new Liberal party from the mid-19th-c. » Liberal Party (UK); Nonconformists; parliament; Presbyterianism; Tories

whimbrel A curlew (*Numenius phaeopus*) which breeds in the N hemisphere on tundra and moors; migrates to muddy and sandy shores in the S hemisphere; striped head; eats insects, berries, and shore invertebrates, especially crabs; also known as the **seven whistler**. *Numenius minutus*, found from Asia to Australasia, is sometimes called the **little whimbrel**. » curlew

whinchat A bird of the thrush family, native to Europe, N Africa, and W Asia; mottled above, pale beneath, with light 'eyebrow' line; inhabits moors and grassland. (*Saxicola rubetra*; other species of *Saxicola* also sometimes called whinchats.) » thrush (bird)

whip A party official in a legislative chamber responsible for ensuring that members attend and vote in accordance with party policy; the name derives from the jargon of hunting, a 'whipper in'. Success will depend upon the extent of party cohesiveness and discipline that can be exercised. In the UK, the term is also the title of a weekly document detailing forthcoming parliamentary business.

whip-poor-will A N American bird (a goatsucker, *Caprimulgus vociferus*); inhabits open woodland. *Caprimulgus noctitherus* is sometimes called the **Puerto Rican whip-poor-will**. » goatsucker

whip scorpion A nocturnal, predatory arthropod; body scorpion-like, up to 75 mm/3 in long, ending in a long whip-like tail; feeds on insects and small amphibians; c.85 species, usually found under stones and bark in the tropics and subtropics. (Class: *Arachnida*. Order: *Uropygi*.) » Arachnida; arthropod; scorpion

whip snake Any long thin snake resembling a whip. In the family *Colubridae* the name is used especially for some species of the genus *Coluber* (from Europe and N America) and N American species in the genus *Masticophis*. » snake

whipbird An Australian babbler; plumage dark, soft; tail long; bill sharp; head with crest; lives near ground in woodland and scrub; eats insects and spiders; nests in dense undergrowth. (Genus: *Psophodes*, 2 species.) » babbler

whippet A small slender breed of dog developed in Britain by cross-breeding small greyhounds with terriers; resembles greyhound but slightly deeper body; occasionally used for racing or hunting rabbits. » greyhound; terrier

whirligig A dark, shiny beetle that lives in groups on the surface of ponds; fast-moving, typically swimming in small circles using paddle-like middle and hind legs; eyes divided for vision above and below water surface; feeds on insects at water surface. (Order: *Coleoptera*. Family: *Gyrinidae*.) » beetle

whirlwind A column of air rotating rapidly around a localized centre of low pressure. It is caused by local surface heating, which results in instability and convectional uprising. » tornado; water-spout

whisk fern A group of only 10 living species plus various fossil forms, considered the most primitive of vascular plants and the possible ancestors to the ferns. They are epiphytic or grow in rock crevices, and have rhizoids but no true roots. The slender, green stems are regularly forked and have a primitive, poorly defined vascular tissue. Leaf-like appendages are tiny, the fertile ones bearing spores. Fossil forms date mainly from the Devonian period, the most famous being *Rhynia*. (Class: *Psilophyta*.) » Devonian period; epiphyte; fern; fossil; rhizoid; spore; vascular tissue

whiskey » **whisky**

Whiskey Rebellion (1794) An insurrection of farmers in W Pennsylvania, USA, against the excise tax imposed by the federal government on whiskey, which they made in large quantities from their crops of grain. The rebellion was suppressed by government forces led by Henry Lee (1756–1818) and Alexander Hamilton (1757–1804). » Hamilton, Alexander

whisky (Ireland/US **whiskey**) A spirit distilled from fermented grain, such as barley, rye, or wheat; the main spirit produced and consumed in Ireland and Scotland. Whiskies can be single malt, a product of a single distillate, or a blend of several batches, often from several different distilleries. » bourbon; rye whisky; Scotch whisky

whist A non-gambling card game, normally played with four people in pairs. Each player receives 13 cards, and the object is to win more tricks than the opposing pair. Trumps are decided before each game, and at **whist drives** trumps are normally played in the following order; hearts, clubs, diamonds, spades. A round of 'no trumps' is also common. » bridge (recreation); Jones, Henry

whistler (botany) » **thickhead**

whistler (zoology) » **mountain beaver**

Whistler, James (Abbott) McNeill (1834–1903) US artist, born at Lowell, Massachusetts. He studied for the army, then left the USA to take up art in Paris, and later in London, where his work was controversially received. He is best known for his evening scenes ('nocturnes'), such as 'Old Battersea Bridge' (c.1872–5, Tate, London), and for the famous portrait of his mother (1871–2, Louvre). He also became known for his etchings and lithographs, especially those dealing with the London riverside. He died in London. » etching

Whistler, Rex (1905–44) British artist. He studied at London, and excelled in the rendering of 18th-c life, ornament, and architecture, particulary in book illustration, murals, and designs for the theatre and ballet. Fine examples of his work are preserved at Plas Newydd, Anglesey. He was killed in World War 2. » English art

whistling duck A small, slender duck, widespread in the tropics; dives for food; feeds at night; eats invertebrates and plant material; some species nest in hollow trees; also known as **tree duck**. (Tribe: *Dendrocygnini*, 8 species.) » duck

Whitby, Synod of A meeting in Britain in 663 when, before Oswiu king of Northumbria, the differences in organization between Roman and Celtic Christianity were debated. Roman concepts of church order prevailed, with the result that the two Christian traditions in Britain were eventually united in their acceptance of the authority and practices of Rome. » Christianity; Northumbria

White, Gilbert (1720–93) English clergyman and naturalist, born at Selborne, Hampshire. He was educated at Oxford, where he became a fellow, was ordained in 1751, and from 1755 lived uneventfully as curate at Selborne, where he died. His *Natural History and Antiquities of Selborne* (1789) has become an English classic: an inspirational naturalist's handbook, it has never been out of print.

White, Patrick (Victor Martindale) (1912–90) Australian author, born in London. His youth was spent partly in Australia, and partly at Cheltenham and Cambridge, where he was educated. His first novel, *Happy Valley*, appeared in 1939, and after service in World War 2, he returned to Australia, where he wrote several novels, short stories, and plays, achieving international success with *The Tree of Man* (1954). He won the Nobel Prize for Literature in 1973. » Australian literature; novel

White, T(erence) H(anbury) (1906–64) British novelist, born in Bombay, India, and educated at Cheltenham and

Cambridge. With the exception of the largely autobiographical *The Goshawk* (1951), his best work was in the form of legend and fantasy, especially his sequence of novels about King Arthur, *The Once and Future King* (1958), beginning with *The Sword in the Stone* (1937). He died at Piraeus, Greece. » English literature; novel

white ant » **termite**

White Australia Policy The unofficial national policy of Australia from 1901 to the late 1960s, designed to exclude non-European migrants; it was particularly aimed at Asians, Pacific Islanders, and Africans who, it was feared, might come to dominate Europeans. The trade union movement supported the policy on the grounds that it excluded workers who might undermine union wage rates. In the 1950s and 1960s, the Colombo Plan (1950) brought Asian students to Australia, and their presence helped to reduce racial prejudice in the major urban areas. In the late 1960s, the policy was progressively dismantled, and race was replaced as a basis for admission by other criteria such as educational and technical qualifications. » Dictation Test

white bryony A perennial with a large, white, tuber-like base, native to Europe, W Asia, and N Africa; stems long, slender, climbing by tendrils; leaves palmately 3–5-lobed, toothed; flowers greenish-white, 5-petalled, males 12–18 mm/0.45–0.7 in diameter, females smaller, on separate plants; berry 5–8 mm/0.2–0.3 in diameter, changing from green through white and orange to red. (*Bryonia dioica*. Family: *Cucurbitaceae*.) » palmate; perennial; tendril; tuber

White Canons » **Premonstratensians**

white cedar A species of *arbor vitae*, native to eastern N America, which provides white or yellowish timber. (*Thuja occidentalis*. Family: *Cupressaceae*.) » arbor vitae

white currant » **red currant**

white dwarf A small, dim star in the final stages of its evolution. The masses of known white dwarfs do not exceed 1.4 solar masses. They are defunct stars, collapsed to about the diameter of the Earth, at which stage they stabilize, with their electrons forming a degenerate gas, the pressure of which is sufficient to balance gravitational force. » stellar evolution

white-eye A small songbird, native to Old World tropical regions; white ring around eye; tongue-tip brush-like; inhabits woodland edges and scrub; eats soft fruit, nectar, insects, and spiders. The name is also used for some pochards. (Family: *Zosteropidae*, c.85 species.) » pochard; songbird

White Friars » **Carmelites**

White Horse, Vale of the A site in Oxfordshire, England, of a stylized representation of a horse carved on the chalk hillside, probably during the Iron Age. Perhaps originally a cult object for the local Celtic tribe, the Belgae, it has inspired many imitations. » Celts; Three Age System

White House The official residence of the US president, situated on Pennsylvania Avenue in Washington, DC. The 132-room Neoclassical mansion was built (1793–1801) from the designs of James Hoban (1762–1831) who also supervised its reconstruction (1814–29) after it was burnt down by the British in 1814. Major restoration work was carried out in 1948–52 after the building was discovered to be in danger of collapse. » Neoclassicism (art and architecture); Washington (DC)

White Nile or **Bahr El Ablad** Upper reach of R Nile in S and E Sudan; a continuation of the Albert Nile, which crosses into SE Sudan from NE Uganda at Nimule; flows generally N to Khartoum, where it is joined from the E by the Blue Nile, forming the R Nile proper; length 1 900 km/1 180 ml. » Nile, River

white paper In the UK, a government publication setting out its policy and legislative intentions in a specific area, such as the annual Expenditure White Paper. Depending upon the area in question, different degrees of scope exist for consultation and discussion before the proposals are put into effect. » green paper

White Plains 41°02N 73°46W, pop (1980) 46 999. Seat of Westchester County, SE New York, USA; Miller Hill Restoration, Washington's headquarters; Provincial Congress ratified the Declaration of Independence here (Jul 1776); scene of the Battle of White Plains (Oct 1776). » American Revolution; New York (state)

White Russia » **Belorussian SSR**

White Russians The name collectively given to counter-revolutionary forces led by ex-tsarist officers, which fought unsuccessfully against the Bolshevik Red Army during the Russian Civil War (1918–22). The Whites were supported by the military intervention of British, American, French, and Japanese troops; when these withdrew, White resistance to the Red Army collapsed. » Bolsheviks; Russian history

White Sands An area of white gypsum sand dunes in S New Mexico, USA, designated a national monument in 1933. It is surrounded by a missile testing range. The first nuclear explosion took place here in July 1945. » atomic bomb; New Mexico

White Sea, Russian **Beloye More** area c.95 000 sq km/ 36 670 sq ml. Arm of the Arctic Ocean and inlet of the Barents Sea, NW European Russia; port of Belmorsk connected to St Petersburg on the Baltic by a 225 km/140 ml-long canal system, completed in 1933; ice-breakers keep some sea channels open in winter; herring and cod fishing. » Arctic Ocean

white shark Large and extremely aggressive shark, considered the most dangerous of all sharks; widespread in tropical to temperate seas, mostly in open waters but occasionally inshore; length up to 6 m/20 ft; grey to brown above, underside white; teeth large and finely serrated; feeds on a variety of fish and on other sharks, dolphins, and seals; many attacks on humans are by white sharks. (*Carcharodon carcharias*. Family: *Lamnidae*.)

white whale » **beluga** (mammal)

whitebait Small silvery fish found abundantly in shallow coastal waters and estuaries; includes the S African *Atherina breviceps*, and in the N Atlantic the small first-year herrings, *Clupea harengus*, and young sprats, *Sprattus sprattus*. » herring; sprat

whitebeam A spreading, deciduous tree or shrub, native to Europe; leaves oval, shallowly lobed or toothed, white-woolly beneath; flowers white, in clusters; berries red. Cultivars with white-flecked berries and purple twigs are common street trees. (*Sorbus aria*. Family: *Rosaceae*.) » cultivar; deciduous plants; shrub; tree [i]

Whitefield, George (1714–70) British Methodist evangelist, born in Gloucester. Associated with the Wesleys at Oxford, he became an enthusiastic evangelist. He founded no distinct sect, but many of his adherents followed the Countess of Huntingdon in Wales, and formed the Calvinistic Methodists. The Countess appointed him her chaplain, and built and endowed many chapels for him. He made several visits to America, where he played an important role in the Great Awakening. He died near Boston, Massachusetts. » Calvinism; Great Awakening; Huntingdon, Countess of; Methodism; Wesley, John

whitefish Any of a small group of fresh and brackish water fishes widespread in lakes and large rivers of the N hemisphere; some populations are migratory, others remain in fresh water; species include the vendace, cisco, and houting. (Genus: *Coregonus*. Family: *Salmonidae*.) » fish [i]

whitefly A small, sap-sucking bug; adults active fliers; bodies and wings covered with a waxy, white powder; immature stages immobile, typically found on underside of leaves; commonly produces honeydew, and attended by ants. (Order: *Homoptera*. Family: *Aleyrodidae*, c.1 200 species.) » bug (entomology)

Whitehall A wide thoroughfare lying between Parliament and Trafalgar Squares in London, and by association the offices of central government which line it. All that remains of the Palace of Whitehall, from which the street takes its name, is the 17th-c banqueting house designed by Inigo Jones. » Jones, Inigo; London [i]

Whitehead, A(lfred) N(orth) (1861–1947) British mathematician and Idealist philosopher, born at Ramsgate. He was educated at Sherborne and Cambridge, where he was senior lecturer in mathematics until 1910. He then taught at London (1910–14), becoming professor of applied mathematics at Imperial College (1914–24), and was then professor of philosophy at Harvard (1924–37). He collaborated with his former pupil, Bertrand Russell, in writing the *Principia Mathematica*

(1910–13). Other more popular works include *Adventures of Ideas* (1933) and *Modes of Thought* (1938). He died at Cambridge, Massachusetts. » idealism; Russell, Bertrand

Whitehorse 60°41N 135°08W, pop (1981) 17 742. Capital of Yukon territory, NW Canada; on the R Lewes, 145 km/90 ml E of the Alaskan border; founded during Klondike gold rush, 1900; mining, fur-trapping, tourism. » Yukon

Whitelaw, William (Stephen Ian), 1st Viscount (1918–) British Conservative politician. Educated at Winchester and Cambridge, he served in World War 2, and became an MP in 1955. After a number of junior posts, and several years as Chief Whip (1964–70, he became Leader of the House of Commons (1970–2), Secretary of State for Northern Ireland (1972–3) and for Employment (1973–4), and Home Secretary (1979–83). Made a viscount in 1983, he was Leader of the House of Lords until 1988. » Conservative Party

whiteout A condition which occurs when there is a scattering of light between the base of low cloud and a bright snow surface, making it difficult to locate the horizon. The term is also used for blizzard conditions in which it is difficult to determine direction. » snow

whitethroat Either of two species of Old World warbler, native to Europe, Africa, and S Asia: the **whitethroat** (*Silvia communis*); and the **lesser whitethroat** (*Silvia curruca*), which includes **small** and **Hume's whitethroats**); inhabits open woodland; eats insects and fruit. (Genus: *Silvia*.) » warbler

Whitgift, John (c.1530–1604) English prelate, born at Grimsby, Lincolnshire. Educated at Cambridge, he was ordained in 1560, and rose to be Dean of Lincoln (1571), Bishop of Worcester (1577), Archbishop of Canterbury (1583), and Privy Councillor (1586). He attended Queen Elizabeth in her last moments, and crowned James I. He was a champion of conformity, and vindicated the Anglican position against the Puritans. He died in London. » Church of England; Elizabeth I; Puritanism

whiting European codfish widely distributed in shallow shelf waters from N Norway to the Black Sea; length up to 70 cm/28 in. (*Merlangius merlangus*. Family: *Gadidae*.) The name is also used for a popular food and game fish of the W North Atlantic. (*Menticirrhus saxatilis*. Family *Sciaenidae*.) » cod

Whiting, John (1917–63) British dramatist. He studied at London, and became an actor before emerging as a dramatist, with such early plays as *Saint's Day* (1951) and *A Penny for a Song* (1956). His best-known work was *The Devils* (1961), a dramatization of Huxley's *The Devils of Loudon*. » drama; English literature

Whitlam, (Edward) Gough (1916–) Australian statesman and Labor Prime Minister (1972–5). Educated at Sydney, he became a lawyer, an MP (1952), and leader of the Australian Labor Party (1967). As Prime Minister he ended conscription and relaxed the policy on non-White immigrants. He was dismissed by the Governor-General after the opposition blocked his money bills in the upper house of the Senate – the first time that the crown had so acted against an elected Prime Minister. He resigned as an MP in 1978 to take up a university appointment at Canberra. » Australian Labor Party

Whitman, Walt (1819–92) US poet, born at West Hills, Long Island, New York. He worked in offices, and as a teacher, then turned to journalism. His major poetic work was *Leaves of Grass* (1855), originally a small folio of 95 pages, which grew in the eight succeeding editions to over 400 pages. During the Civil War he became a volunteer nurse in the hospitals of the Northern army – an experience which forms much of the subject matter of his later prose works, notably *Democratic Vistas* (1871) and *Specimen Days & Collect* (1882–3). After the war he received a government clerkship, and in 1873 left Washington for Camden, New Jersey, where he lived until his death. » American Civil War; American literature; poetry

Whitney, Eli (1765–1825) US inventor, born at Westborough, Massachusetts. Educated at Yale, he became a teacher, but then came to reside on a cotton plantation and devised the cotton-gin (patented in 1793). In 1798 he got a government contract for the manufacture of firearms, and made a fortune in this business, developing a new system of mass-production. He died at New Haven, Connecticut. » cotton [i]; firearms

Whitsunday or **Whit Sunday** In the Christian Church, the seventh Sunday after Easter, commemorating the day of Pentecost. The name Whit ('white') Sunday derives from the white robes traditionally worn by those baptized on this day. » Pentecost

Whittier, John Greenleaf (1807–92) US Quaker poet and abolitionist, born near Haverhill, Massachusetts. Largely self-educated, he embarked on a career as a writer and journalist, publishing a collection of poems and stories, *Legends of New England*, in 1831. In 1840, he settled at Amesbury, where he devoted himself to the cause of emancipation. His later works include *In War Time* (1864) and *At Sundown* (1892). In his day considered second only to Longfellow, he died at Hampton Falls, Massachusetts. » American literature; Longfellow; poetry; slave trade

Whittington, Richard, byname **Dick** (c.1358–1423) English merchant, supposed to have been the youngest son of Sir William Whittington of Pauntley in Gloucestershire, on whose death he set out at 13 for London, where he found work as an apprentice. He became an alderman and sheriff, and in 1397 Lord Mayor of London. The legend of his cat is an accepted part of English folklore.

Whittle, Sir Frank (1907–) British inventor and aviator, born at Coventry, Warwickshire. Educated at Cambridge, he joined the RAF and began research on the problems of jet propulsion. He successfully developed the jet engine for aircraft (1941), and became government technical adviser on engine design (1946–8). He was knighted in 1948. » aeroplane; jet engine [i]; turbine

Whitworth, Kathy, properly **Kathrynne (Ann)** (1939–) US golfer, born at Monahans, Texas. The most successful woman golfer of all time, she has won 88 tournaments on the US Women's circuit, including all the women's 'Majors' except the US Open. She turned professional in 1958, and won the US Ladies Professional Golf Association Championship four times: 1967, 1971, 1975, 1982. She was the leading money winner eight times between 1965 and 1973. » golf

WHO » **United Nations**

whooping cough A highly infectious disease which results from *Bordetella pertussis*, mainly affecting children; also known as **pertussis**. Upper respiratory catarrh is followed by a series of short sharp coughs followed by a deep inspiration (the 'whoop'). Diagnosis is by swabs from the nasopharynx, and the bacteriological culture of the causative micro-organism. The condition carries a high mortality in infants, and active immunization is highly desirable. » immunization

whooping crane A crane native to N America; breeds in Canada; migrates to Gulf of Mexico; plumage white; face red; extremely rare (only 18 birds known in 1969). (*Grus americana*.) » crane

whortleberry » **bilberry; cowberry**

whydah [**wid**uh] A songbird of genus *Vidua* (8 species), with uncertain relationships, treated variously as a weaver-finch or weaverbird, and sometimes put in a separate family (*Viduidae*); finch-like; male with very long tail; lays eggs in nests of (other) weaver-finches; young reared by 'foster' parents; also known as **whidah** or **widow finch**. Some species are called **combassous**, **indigo birds**, or **indigo finches**. The name (as well as **widow bird**) is also used for some weaverbirds of the genus *Euplectes*. » finch; songbird; weaverbird; weaver-finch

Whymper, Edward (1840–1911) British wood-engraver and mountaineer, born in London. He was trained as an artist on wood, but became better known for his mountaineering than for his book illustrations. During 1860–9 he conquered several hitherto unscaled peaks of the Alps, including the Matterhorn (1865), and later travelled in Greenland, the Andes, and Canada. He died at Chamonix, France.

Wichita [**wich**itaw] 37°42N 97°20W, pop (1980) 279 272. Seat of Sedgwick County, S Kansas, USA, on the Arkansas R; settled, 1864; named after an Indian tribe; city status, 1871; largest city in Kansas; airport; railway; two universities (1892, 1898); chief commercial and industrial centre in S Kansas; aircraft, chemical and petroleum products, railway engineering, food processing (grain and meat); Cow Town (1870s replica); Wichita River Festival (May). » Kansas

WIDE-SCREEN CINEMA: SCREEN PROPORTIONS (ASPECT RATIOS)

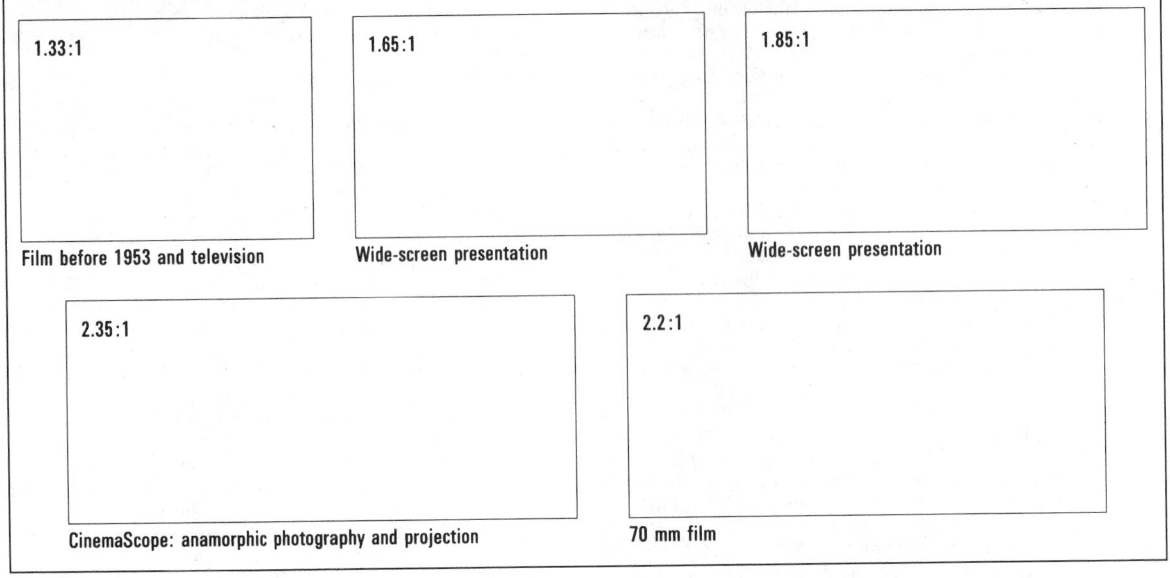

Wicklow, Gaelic **Cill Mhantáin**, byname **The Garden of Ireland** pop (1981) 87 449; area 2 025 sq km/782 sq ml. County in Leinster province, E Irish Republic; bounded E by Irish Sea; watered by Slaney, Liffey, and Avoca Rivers; Wicklow Mts (W); capital, Wicklow (pop 1981, 5 341); agriculture; resort towns (eg Bray). » Irish Republic [i]

wide-screen cinema For more than 50 years the proportions of the cinema screen were comparatively square, 4 × 3, aspect ratio (AR) 1.33:1. But following public interest in Cinerama, 20th-Century Fox in 1953 introduced CinemaScope, whose double-width format, 2.35:1. proved popular. Enlarged screens were installed in many theatres, but in some there was insufficient proscenium width, and in these the screen height was reduced to give a wide-screen appearance with AR between 1.65:1 and 1.85:1. Several systems using film gauges wider than 35 mm were tried, but of these only 70 mm prints, AR 2.2:1, have continued. The IMAX and OPTIMAX systems, using a very large frame on 70 mm, provide the widest screen presentation, but can be seen at only about 100 purpose-built theatres throughout the world. All regular feature films are now wide-screen, but television has retained the former 4 × 3 proportion, so there is some loss of picture when they are shown in video. High-definition television in the 1990s will adopt a wider format, probably 16 × 9, AR 1.78:1. » cinema; Cinerama; CinemaScope; screen

widgeon » **wigeon**

Widor, Charles Marie (Jean Albert) (1844–1937) French composer, born at Lyons. He was organist at Lyons and (1870) at St Sulpice, Paris, and became professor of organ (1890) and composition (1896) at the Paris Conservatoire. He composed ten symphonies for the organ, as well as a ballet, chamber music, and other orchestral works.

widow bird/finch » **whydah**

Wieland, Christoph Martin [**vee**lant] (1733–1813) German writer, born near Biberach. After several early devotional works, he made the first German translation of Shakespeare (1762–6), and wrote a number of popular romances, notably *Agathon* (1766–7). After holding a professorship at Erfurt, he was called to Weimar to train the grand-duchess's sons, where he lived until his death. During this time he translated many classical authors, and wrote his best-known work, the heroic poem *Oberon* (1780). » German literature; poetry

Wieliczka salt mine [vye**lit**ska] A salt mine in S Poland which has been worked for over 500 years, and which is still in operation; a world heritage site. Apart from its antiquity and immense size, the mine is noted for its museum of salt mining techniques and equipment, and for its subterranean architecture and sculptures. » Poland [i]; salt

Wien, Wilhelm [veen] (1864–1928) German physicist, born at Gaffken, E Prussia. Educated at Göttingen and Berlin, he worked as assistant to Helmholtz, and later was professor at Würzburg (1900–20) and then at Munich. In the early 1890s he studied thermal radiation, and by 1896 had developed **Wien's formula** describing the distribution of energy in a radiation spectrum as a function of wavelength and temperature. The formula fails for long wavelengths, and it was this failure which inspired Planck to devise the quantum theory which revolutionized physics in 1900. Wien was awarded the Nobel Prize for Physics in 1911. He died in Munich. » Helmholtz; Planck; quantum mechanics; radiation

Wien [veen] » **Vienna**

Wiener, Norbert [**wee**nuh] (1894–1964) US mathematical logician, the founder of cybernetics, born at Columbia, Missouri. A child prodigy, he entered university at 11, studied at Harvard, Cornell, Cambridge, and Göttingen, and became professor of mathematics at the Massachusetts Institute of Technology (1932). During World War 2 he worked on guided missiles, and his study of the handling of information by electronic devices, based on the feedback principle, encouraged comparison between these and human mental processes in *Cybernetics* (1948) and other works. He died in Stockholm. » cybernetics

Wies pilgrimage church [vees] An 18th-c church in Wies, S Germany, founded in 1330 to house a miraculously weeping statue of Jesus, and soon the centre of a religious cult. The present building, a masterpiece of Bavarian religious Baroque, was designed by Dominikus Zimmermann (1685–1766); it is a world heritage site. » Baroque (art and architecture); Jesus Christ

Wiesbaden [**veez**bahdn] 50°05N 8°15E, pop (1983) 272 600. Capital city of Hesse province, Germany; on the R Rhine, 32 km/20 ml W of Frankfurt am Main; railway; chemicals, cement, hydraulics, tools; popular health resort; a traditional wine centre, most of the large German Sekt (sparkling wine) cellars are in this area. » Germany [i]; wine

Wigan 53°33N 2°38W, pop (1981) 88 901. Town in Wigan borough, Greater Manchester, NW England; 27 km/17 ml NE of Liverpool, on R Douglas and the Leeds–Liverpool Canal; a borough since 1246; railway; engineering, cotton, foodstuffs, packaging; Wigan Pier, now a museum, made famous by George Orwell, in *The Road to Wigan Pier* (1932). » Manchester, Greater; Orwell

wigeon or **widgeon** A dabbling duck of genus *Anas*: the **European wigeon** (*Anas penelope*), from Eurasia and N Africa (some reach N America); the **North American wigeon** or **baldpate** (*Anas americana*), some of which reach Europe; and the **Chiloë wigeon** (*Anas sibilatrix*), from S America. » dabbling duck

Wight, Isle of, Lat **Vectis** pop (1987e) 126 900; area 381 sq km/ 147 sq ml. Island county off the S coast of England, divided into two districts; in the mouth of Southampton Water, separated from Hampshire by the Solent and Spithead; an irregular range of chalk hills running E–W ends at the imposing cliffs of the vertical sandstone Needles near Alum Bay; drained by the R Medina; county town, Newport; chief towns include Cowes, Ryde, Sandown, Shanklin, Ventnor; ferry services from Portsmouth, Southampton, Lymington; tourism, agriculture, hovercraft and boat building, electronics; yachting (especially Cowes Regatta Week); Osborne House. » England [i]; Newport (Isle of Wight)

Wightman Cup An annual lawn tennis competition involving professional women's teams from the USA and UK. It was first held in 1923, and named after the former US player Hazel Wightman (*née* Hotchkiss) (1886–1974). » tennis, lawn [i]

Wigman, Mary, originally **Marie Wiegmann** (1886–1973) German dancer, choreographer, and teacher, born at Hanover. Her career as Germany's most famous modern dancer began after World War 1, when she toured extensively and opened a school in Dresden in 1920. She created numerous solo and group dances which typified German expressionist dancing. Her activities were reduced during World War 2, but in 1945 she started work again in Leipzig and Berlin. Through her schools and teaching and her highly dramatic performances she provided the focus for the development of a performance form of European modern dance. She died in Berlin. » choreography; modern dance

Wilberforce, William (1759–1833) British politician, evangelist, and philanthropist, born in Hull, Yorkshire. Educated at Cambridge, he became an MP (1780), and in 1788 began the movement which resulted in the abolition of the slave trade in the British West Indies in 1807. He next sought to secure the abolition of all slaves, but declining health compelled him in 1825 to retire from parliament. He died in London, one month before the Slavery Abolition Act was passed in parliament. A lifelong friend of the Younger Pitt, he was like him a strong opponent of reformers in the 1790s. His evangelical beliefs led him to urge the aristocracy to practise 'real Christianity', and to give a moral lead to the poor. » evangelicalism; Pitt (the Younger); slave trade

Wilbye, John (1574–1638) English madrigal composer, born at Diss, Norfolk. He was a farmer, who became a household musician at Hengrave Hall (1593–1628), then at Colchester, Essex. He is known for only 66 madrigals, but these are renowned for his careful setting of literary texts, and for several translations of Italian poems. He died at Colchester. » madrigal

wild boar A wild ancestor of the domestic pig, native to Europe, NW Africa, and S Asia; thick dark hair; male with tusks; domesticated in SE Asia 5–10 000 years ago. (*Sus scrofa*.) » pig

wild cat A member of the cat family, found from N Europe to Africa and India; ancestor of the domestic cat, but larger, with a shorter, thicker tail; inhabits forest, scrubland, and open country; eats small rodents and birds. The name is also used for any member of the family other than the domestic cat. (*Felis silvestris*.) » cat; Felidae

wild cherry » **gean**

wild ox » **aurochs**

Wilde, Oscar (Fingal O'Flahertie Wills) (1854–1900) Irish writer, born in Dublin. Educated at Dublin and Oxford, he established himself among the social and literary circles in London, was celebrated for his wit and flamboyant manner, and became a leading member of the 'art for art's sake' movement. His early work included his *Poems* (1881), the novel *The Picture of Dorian Gray* (1891), and several comic plays, notably *Lady Windermere's Fan* (1892) and *The Importance of being Earnest* (1895). *The Ballad of Reading Gaol* (1898) and *De Profundis* (1905) reveal the effect of two years' hard labour for homosexual practices revealed during his abortive libel action (1895) against the Marquis of Queensberry, who had objected to Wilde's association with his son. He died an exile in Paris, having adopted the name of **Sebastian Melmoth**. » art for art's sake; drama; English/Irish literature; novel; poetry

wildebeest [**wil**duhbeest, **vil**duhbeest] An African grazing antelope; sturdy, with a large convex face; short horns spread sideways with upturned tips; long mane; long fringe of hairs along throat; tail almost reaching ground; inhabits grassland; two species: *Connochaetes taurinusa* (**blue wildebeest** or **brindled gnu** – includes **Cookson's wildebeest** and **white-bearded wildebeest**), and *Connochaetes gnou* (**black wildebeest** or **white-tailed gnu**); also known as **gnu**. » antelope

Wilder, Billy, originally **Samuel Wilder** (1906–) US film director and scriptwriter, born in Vienna. He wrote for several German films from 1929, but as a Jew was forced to leave in 1933, and moved to Hollywood, working initially as a screenwriter. He started as a director in 1942 with *The Major and the Minor*, and continued for some 40 years with a wide variety of productions, which he often co-produced and scripted, including *The Lost Weekend* (1945), for which he won an Oscar, *Sunset Boulevard* (1955), and *The Apartment* (1960), another Award winner. Many of his later productions were in Europe, such as *The Private Life of Sherlock Holmes* (1970) in England and *Fedora* (1978) in Germany.

Wilder, Thornton (Niven) (1897–1976) US writer, born at Madison, Wisconsin. Educated at Yale, he studied in Rome, and taught literature at Chicago (1930–7). His first novel, *The Cabala* (1926), was followed by the very successful *The Bridge of San Luis Rey* (1927), and the plays *Our Town* (1938) and *The Skin of Our Teeth* (1942), which all won Pulitzer Prizes. His later plays included *The Matchmaker* (1954), the basis of the musical *Hello Dolly* (1964). He died at Hamden, Connecticut. » American literature; novel

Wilderness Campaign 1 (1864) An indecisive conflict in the American Civil War between the Union army under General Grant and the Confederate army under General Lee, fought in the Wilderness area of Virginia. It was the first test of Grant's strategy of relentless pressure on Lee, regardless of his own losses. » Grant, Ulysses S; Lee, Robert E **2** (1755) The term **Battle of the Wilderness** is also used for a conflict in Western Pennsylvania, in which Indians and French troops decimated a larger British army under General Edward Braddock. Washington, who commanded the American auxiliaries, emerged from that fight with a considerable military reputation. » Washington, George

Wilderness Road The early route across the S Appalachian Mts, from the Holston R through Cumberland Gap to Boonesborough on the Kentucky R. It was constructed in 1775 by a party led by Daniel Boone under the sponsorship of Richard Henderson, founder of the Transylvania Company. » Appalachian Mountains; Boone

wildfowl » **water-fowl**

wildlife refuge An area set aside for the protection and conservation of wildlife (eg Serengeti National Park, Tanzania, and Australia's Great Barrier Reef). Ideally it should be a wilderness area large enough to sustain its plant and animal population. With increased global pressure for land, wildlife refuges may also need to serve a purpose; for example, the Indonesian government has foregone timber revenues from a new rainforest park in Sulawesi, but in doing so has protected the catchment area of rice farmers downstream of the reserve. » endangered species; National Park; Nature Reserve

Wilfrid or **Wilfrith, St** (634–709), feast day 12 October. English monk and bishop, born in Northumbria. He trained at Lindisfarne, and upheld the replacement of Celtic by Roman religious practices at the Synod of Whitby (664). As Bishop of York (c.665), he was involved in controversy over the organization of the Church in Britain, and was the first churchman to appeal to Rome to settle the issue. He died at Oundle, Mercia. » Anglo-Saxons; Lindisfarne; monasticism

Wilhelmina (Helena Pauline Maria) (1880–1962) Queen of the Netherlands (1890–1948), born at The Hague. She succeeded her father William III at the age of 10, her mother acting as Regent until 1898. An upholder of constitutional monarchy, she especially won the admiration of her people during World War 2. Though compelled to seek refuge in Britain, she steadfastly encouraged Dutch resistance to the German occupation. In 1948, she abdicated in favour of her daughter **Juliana**, and assumed the title of Princess of the Netherlands. She died at Het Loo, Netherlands. » Juliana

wili [**vee**lee] In Slavic folklore the spirit of a betrothed maiden who has died before her wedding-day. Wilis nightly haunt highways, compelling any passing youth to dance with them until he drops dead. The tradition was recorded by Heinrich Heine and used in the ballet *Giselle* by Théophile Gautier. » folklore

Wilkes, John (1727–97) British politician and journalist, born and died in London. He studied at Leyden, and became an MP (1757), and attacked the ministry in his weekly journal, *North Briton* (1762–3). He was imprisoned, released, then expelled from the house for libel. Re-elected on several occasions, and repeatedly expelled, he came to be seen as a champion of liberty, and an upholder of press freedom. In 1774 he became Lord Mayor of London, and in the same year finally gained admission to parliament, where he remained until his retirement in 1790.

Wilkes Land Area of Antarctica between Queen Mary Land (W) and Terre Adélie, lying mostly between 105° and 135° E; includes the Australian scientific station at Casey (established 1961). » Antarctica [i]

Wilkie, Sir David (1785–1841) British painter, born at Cults, Fife, Scotland. He studied at Edinburgh and London, where he settled after the success of his 'Pitlessie Fair' (1804) and 'The Village Politicians' (1806). His fame mainly rests on his genre painting, but he also painted portraits, and in his later years sought to emulate the richness of colouring of the old masters, choosing more elevated subjects. In 1830 he was made painter-in-ordinary to the king, was knighted in 1835, and died on his voyage home from a tour in the Middle East. » genre painting

Wilkins, Sir George (Hubert) (1888–1958) Australian polar explorer, born at Mt Bryan East. He was part of an expedition to the Arctic (1913–18), then flew from England to Australia (1919), explored the Antarctic with Shackleton (1920–2), and made a pioneer flight from Alaska to Spitsbergen over polar ice (1928). In 1931 he failed to reach the N Pole in the submarine *Nautilus*. Knighted in 1928, he died at Framingham, Massachusetts. » Poles; Shackleton

Wilkins, Maurice (Hugh Frederick) (1916–) British biophysicist, born at Pongaroa, New Zealand. Educated at Birmingham and Cambridge, he carried out wartime research into uranium isotope separation in California, then joined the Medical Research Council's Biophysics Research Unit at King's College London in 1946, becoming deputy-director (1955) and director (1970–2). With Crick and Watson he shared the Nobel Prize for Physiology or Medicine in 1962 for work on the structure of DNA. » biophysics; DNA [i]

Wilkinson, Sir Geoffrey (1921–) British inorganic chemist, born at Todmorden, Yorkshire. He was educated at Imperial College, London, where he returned in 1956 after war work in Canada and the USA. While at Harvard in 1952, he showed that ferrocene has a molecule with an iron atom sandwiched between two carbon rings; since then, thousands of such *metallocenes* have been made and studied. He shared the Nobel Prize for Chemistry in 1973. » catalysis; chemistry

will (law) A document in which a person sets out the way in which his or her property (the *estate*) is to be distributed to beneficiaries after death. In order to be valid, a will must comply with certain requirements: for example, it must be signed in the presence of two witnesses, both of whom are present at the same time. A will may be challenged on various grounds, including the ground that it has not been properly executed. A dependant (eg a spouse) can expect to receive reasonable financial provision under a will, and can apply to the court if this is not provided. If a person dies without making a will (dies *intestate*), statutory rules in some jurisdictions govern the distribution of property. » probate

will (philosophy) » **free will**

will o' the wisp » **ignis fatuus**

Willandra Lakes A world heritage area covering c.6 000 sq km/ 2 300 sq ml in the Murray R Basin in New South Wales, Australia. The region contains an extensive system of Pleistocene freshwater lake sites, and provides a remarkable 'fossil landscape', generally unmodified since the end of the Pleistocene ice age. Certain archaeological discoveries made here have been dated at 30 000–40 000 years BC. » Murray River; Pleistocene epoch

willaroo » **thick-knee**

Willemstad [**vil**uhmstaht] 12°12N 68°56W, pop (1983e) 50 000. Capital town of the Netherlands Antilles, on SW coast of Curaçao I; established by the Dutch as a trading centre, mid-17th-c; airport; free port; oil refining (handling Venezuelan oil), ship repair, tourism. » Netherlands Antilles [i]

Willendorf A prehistoric site near Krems, lower Austria, with Gravettian occupation dated c.32–28 000 BC. It is celebrated for the 'Willendorf Venus', a large-bellied, heavy-breasted limestone statuette, 11 cm/4⅜ in high, its limbs under-emphasized but the buttocks enlarged. Painted with red ochre, it presumably served as a fertility or house goddess. » Gravettian

William I Ger **Wilhelm** (Emperor) (1797–1888) King of Prussia (1861–88) and first German Emperor (1871–88), born and died in Berlin, the second son of Frederick William III. His use of force during the 1848 revolution made him unpopular, and he was forced to leave Prussia temporarily for London. As King, he consolidated the throne and strengthened the army: Bismarck was placed at the head of the ministry, with Roon, the author of the new army system, as War Minister. He was victorious against Denmark (1864), Austria (1866), and France (1871), when he was proclaimed Emperor. The rapid rise of socialism in Germany led to severe repressive measures, and he survived several attempts at assassination. He died in Berlin. » Bismarck; Roon; Prussia; socialism

William I (of England), byname **the Conqueror** (c.1028–87) Duke of Normandy (1035–87) and the first Norman King of England (1066–87), the illegitimate son of Duke Robert of Normandy. Edward the Confessor, who had been brought up in Normandy, most probably designated him as future King of England in 1051. When Harold Godwin, despite an apparent oath to uphold William's claims, took the throne as Harold II, William invaded with the support of the papacy, defeated and killed Harold at the Battle of Hastings, and was crowned King on Christmas Day 1066. The key to effective control was military conquest backed up by aristocratic colonization, so that by the time of Domesday Book (1086), the leaders of Anglo-Saxon society S of the Tees had been almost entirely replaced by a new ruling class of Normans, Bretons, and Flemings, who were closely tied to William by feudal bonds. He died near Paris, while defending Normandy's S border. » Anglo-Saxons; Domesday Book; Edgar the Atheling; Edward the Confessor; Harold II; Hereward; Norman Conquest

William I (of the Netherlands), **Prince of Orange**, byname **William the Silent** (1533–84) First of the hereditary stadholders of the United Provinces of the Netherlands (1572–84), born at Dillenburg, Nassau. He joined the aristocratic protest to the oppressive policies of Philip II of Spain, and in 1568 took up arms against the Spanish crown. After initial reverses, he began the recovery of the coastal towns with the help of the Sea Beggars, and became stadholder of the Northern provinces, united in the Union of Utrecht (1579). He was assassinated at Delft by a Spanish agent. His byname comes from his ability to keep secret Henry II's scheme to massacre all the Protestants of France and the Netherlands, confided to him when he was a French hostage in 1559. » Henry II (of France); Philip II (of Spain); United Provinces of the Netherlands

William I (of Scotland), byname **the Lion** (c.1142–1214) King of Scots (1165–1214), the brother and successor of Malcolm IV. In 1173–4 he invaded Northumberland during the rebellion against Henry II, but was captured at Alnwick, and by the Treaty of Falaise (1174) recognized Henry as the feudal superior of Scotland. Despite his difficulties with England, he made Scotland a much stronger kingdom, and in 1192 Celestine III declared the Scottish Church free of all external authority save the pope's. William died at Stirling. » David I; Henry II (of England)

William II Ger **Wilhelm** (Emperor) (1859–1941) German Emperor and King of Prussia (1888–1918), born at Potsdam, the eldest son of Frederick (II) and Victoria (the daughter of Britain's Queen Victoria), and grandson of William I. He dismissed Bismarck (1890), and began a long period of personal rule, displaying a bellicose attitude in international affairs. He pledged full support to Austria-Hungary after the assassination of the Archduke Franz Ferdinand at Sarajevo (1914), but then made strenuous efforts to prevent an escalation of the resulting international crisis. During the war he became a mere figurehead, and when the German armies collapsed, and US President Wilson refused to negotiate while he remained in power, he abdicated and fled the country. He settled at Doorn, in the Netherlands, living as a country gentleman until his death. » Bismarck; Jameson raid; Wilson, Woodrow; World War 1

William II (of England), byname **Rufus** (c.1056–1100) King (1087–1100), the second surviving son of William the Conqueror. His main goal was the recovery of Normandy from his elder brother Robert Curthose, and from 1096, when Robert relinquished the struggle and departed on the First Crusade, William ruled the duchy as *de facto* duke. He also led expeditions to Wales (1095, 1097); conquered Carlisle and the surrounding district (1092); and after the death of Malcolm Canmore, exercised a controlling influence over Scottish affairs. Contemporaries condemned his government of England as arbitrary and ruthless. He exploited his rights over the Church and the nobility beyond the limits of custom, and quarrelled with Anselm, Archbishop of Canterbury. His personal conduct outraged the moral standards of the time, for he was most likely a homosexual. He was killed by an arrow while hunting in the New Forest. It has been supposed that he was murdered on the orders of his younger brother, who succeeded him as Henry I, but his death was almost certainly accidental. » Anselm, St; Crusades [i]; Henry I (of England); Malcolm III; William I (of England)

William III (of Great Britain), byname **William of Orange** (1650–1702) Stadholder of the United Provinces (1672–1702) and King of Great Britain (1689–1702), born at The Hague, the son of William II of Orange by Mary, the eldest daughter of Charles I of England. In 1677 he married his cousin, **Mary** (1662–94), the daughter of James II by Anne Hyde. Invited to redress the grievances of the country, he landed at Torbay in 1688 with an English and Dutch army, and forced James II to flee. William and Mary were proclaimed rulers early the following year. He defeated James's supporters at Killiecrankie (1689) and at the Boyne (1690), then concentrated on the War of the Grand Alliance against France (1689–97), in which he was finally successful. In later years, he had to withstand much parliamentary opposition to his proposals, and there were many assassination plots. He died in London, childless, the crown passing to Mary's sister, Anne. » Grand Alliance, War of the; James II (of England)

William IV (of Great Britain), byname **The Sailor King** (1765–1837) King of Great Britain and Ireland, and King of Hanover (1830–7), born in London, the third son of George III. He entered the navy in 1779, saw service in the USA and the West Indies, became Admiral in 1811, and Lord High Admiral in 1827–8. His elder brother having died, he succeeded George IV in 1830. Widely believed to have Whig leanings to his accession, he developed Tory sympathies, and did much to obstruct the passing of the first Reform Act (1832). He was the last monarch to use prerogative powers to dismiss a ministry with a parliamentary majority when he sacked Melbourne in 1834 and invited the Tories to form a government. He died at Windsor, Berkshire, and was succeeded by his niece, Victoria. » Melbourne, Viscount; Reform Acts; Tories; Whigs

William of Malmesbury (c.1090–c.1143) English chronicler and Benedictine monk, the librarian of Malmesbury Abbey, Wiltshire. The emphasis he placed on the importance of documentary material and non-written sources, including architectural and other kinds of visual evidence, gives him a key place in the development of historical method. His main works are: *Gesta Regum Anglorum*, a general history of England from the coming of the Anglo-Saxons; *Gesta Pontificum Anglorum*, an ecclesiastical history of England from the Conversion; and *Historia Novella*, a contemporary narrative of English affairs from c.1125 to 1142. » Anglo-Saxons; Benedictines

William of Tyre (c.1130–86) Chronicler and churchman, born in Palestine of French parents. Educated at Paris and Bologna, he entered the service of the Kings of Jerusalem, and was appointed Archbishop of Tyre in 1175. His main work, *Historia rerum in partibus transmarinis gestarum* (History of Deeds in Foreign Parts), deals with the history of Palestine from 614 to 1184, and is especially valuable to the historian of the 12th-c Crusades. » Crusades [i]

William of Wykeham or **Wickham** (1324–1404) English churchman and statesman, born at Wickham, Hampshire, the son perhaps of a serf, who rose to become the chief adviser of Edward III. He was appointed Keeper of the Privy Seal (1363), Bishop of Winchester (1367), and was twice Chancellor of England (1367–71, 1389–91). He founded New College, Oxford, and Winchester College, both of which were fully established by the 1390s. He died at Bishops Waltham, Hampshire. » Edward III

Williams, Betty » **Corrigan, Mairead**

Williams, (George) Emlyn (1905–87) British playwright and actor, born at Mostyn, Flintshire, Wales. Educated at Oxford, he joined a repertory company in 1927, and achieved success as a dramatist with *A Murder has been Arranged* (1930) and the psychological thriller, *Night Must Fall* (1935). He appeared in many London and Broadway productions, featured in several films, and gave widely acclaimed readings from the works of Dickens, Dylan Thomas, and Saki. He died in London.

Williams, John (Christopher) (1942–) Australian guitarist, born in Melbourne and resident in England since 1952. He studied with Segovia, and made his professional debut in 1958. He has since taught at colleges in London and Manchester. His musical sympathies are wide-ranging; several classical composers have written works for him, and he founded a rock group known as Sky. » guitar; Segovia

Williams, J(ohn) P(eter) R(hys) (1949–) British rugby player, born at Bridgend, Mid Glamorgan, Wales. He was an excellent tennis player as a junior, representing Wales. He trained in medicine, and played rugby for the London Welsh, Bridgend, Wales, and the British Lions. He is the most capped Welshman, with 55 appearances, and the world's most capped fullback (54). » rugby football

Williams, Roger (c.1604–83) English colonist who founded Rhode Island, born in London. Educated at Charterhouse and Cambridge, he took Anglican orders, became an extreme Puritan, and emigrated to New England in 1630. He refused to join the congregation at Boston, and moved to Salem, where he was persecuted and banished. He then purchased lands from the Indians, and founded the city of Providence (1636), allowing full religious toleration. In 1643 and 1651 he came to England to procure a charter for his colony, became its president (1654–8), and died at Providence. » Puritanism; Rhode Island

Williams, Shirley (Viven Teresa), *née* **Brittain** (1930–) British politician. A former journalist, and Secretary of the Fabian Society (1960–4), she became a Labour MP in 1964. After many junior positions, she was Secretary of State for Prices and Consumer Protection (1974–6), and for Education and Science (1976–9). She lost her seat in 1979, became a co-founder of the Social Democratic Party in 1981, and the Party's first elected MP later that year. She lost her seat in the 1983 general election, but remained as the SDP's President (1982–7). She supported the merger between the SDP and the Liberal Party. » Labour/Liberal Party (UK); Social Democratic Party

Williams, Tennessee, pseudonym of **Thomas Lanier Williams** (1911–83) US dramatist, born at Columbus, Mississippi. Educated at Columbia, St Louis, and Iowa, he worked at a wide range of theatrical jobs until he achieved success with *The Glass Menagerie* (1944). His later plays, almost all set in the Deep South against a background of decadence and degradation, include *A Streetcar Named Desire* (1947, Pulitzer Prize), *Cat on* *a Hot Tin Roof* (1955, Pulitzer Prize), *Suddenly Last Summer* (1958), and *Night of the Iguana* (1961). He also wrote short stories, essays, poetry, memoirs, and two novels. He died in New York City. » American literature; drama

Williams, William Carlos (1883–1963) US poet and novelist, born and died at Rutherford, New Jersey. Educated in Geneva and at the University of Pennsylvania, he became a doctor. He developed a distinctly American style for his shorter lyrics, which commanded attention from *Spring and All* (1923), and were collected in two volumes (1950, 1951). He adapted this for his 'personal epic', *Paterson* (1946–51). He also wrote plays, essays, a trilogy of novels, and criticism, including *In The American Grain* (1925). » American literature; novel; poetry

Williamsburg 37°17N 76°43W, pop(1980) 9870. Independent city and capital of James City County, SE Virginia, USA, between the York and James Rivers; settled, 1633 (as Middle Plantation, renamed 1699); state capital, 1699–1780; Colonial Williamsburg is a major building restoration scheme; College of William and Mary (1693). » Virginia; William III

Williamson, Henry (1895–1977) British writer, born in Bedfordshire. He served in World War 1, became a journalist, then turned to farming in Norfolk. He wrote several semi-autobiographical novels, including his long series *A Chronicle of Ancient Sunlight* (1951–69), but is best known for his classic nature stories, such as *Tarka the Otter* (1927). He died in Berkshire. » novel

Williamson, Malcolm (Benjamin Graham Christopher) (1931–) British composer, born in Sydney, Australia. He came to England in 1953, and began his career as a solo pianist and organist. His compositions include the operas *Our Man in Havana* (1963) and *The Red Sea* (1972), several works for television and films, ballets, orchestral, vocal, choral, and piano music, and 'cassations', often involving the audience. He was made Master of the Queen's Musick in 1975.

willow A large genus of mostly N temperate deciduous trees and shrubs; leaves oval or lance-shaped; flowers in separate male and female catkins; seeds plumed with silky hairs for wind dispersal. Willows show a wide range of form, from low, creeping arctic species to large trees, many growing in or near water. They are a source of withies for basket-work and cricket bats. The bark contains salicin, an original source of aspirin. Some species are ornamental, with brightly-coloured winter twigs. Numerous natural hybrids are known. (Genus: *Salix*, 500 species. Family: *Salicaceae*.) » aspirin; deciduous plants; osier; sallow; shrub; tree [i]; weeping willow

willow-herb A somewhat variable genus of mostly perennials, native throughout temperate and arctic regions; narrow to lance-shaped leaves in pairs; flowers with four rose, purple, sometimes white petals on top of a long, cylindrical, purplish ovary; fruit a capsule containing numerous white-plumed seeds. (Genus: *Epilobium*, 215 species. Family: *Onagraceae*.) » ovary; perennial; rosebay willow-herb

willow pattern A decorative scene used on pottery table wares, showing a Chinese landscape, with figures, buildings, and a bridge, carried out in blue transfer printing on white. It was first engraved by Thomas Minton for Thomas Turner at Caughley c.1780, and subsequently widely copied by many factories. » Minton ceramics

Wills, Helen (Newington), married names **Moody** and **Roark** (1905–) US lawn tennis player, born at Berkeley, California. A great baseline player, she won the Wimbledon singles title eight times in nine attempts (1927–30, 1932–3, 1935, 1938). Between 1927 and 1932 she won all the major singles championships (except the Australian) without losing a set. In all, she won 31 Grand Slam events. » tennis, lawn [i]

Willstätter, Richard [vilshtetuh] (1872–1942) German organic chemist, born at Karlsruhe. He studied at Munich, and became professor at Zürich (1905–12). He did notable work on natural product chemistry, especially on plant pigments (for which he won the Nobel Prize for Chemistry in 1915) and on medicinal chemicals, and he developed effective gas masks in World War 1. He became professor at Munich in 1916, but increasing anti-Semitism made his position difficult, and he resigned his chair in 1925 in protest. The rise of Nazi power forced him to flee, and he reached Switzerland in 1939. He died at Locarno. » organic chemistry

Wilmington (Delaware) 39°45N 75°33W, pop(1980) 70195. Seat of New Castle County, N Delaware, USA; a port at the confluence of Brandywine Creek, the Christina R, and the Delaware R; founded by the Swedes as Fort Christina, 1638; taken by the British and renamed Willington, 1731; renamed Wilmington, 1739; city status, 1832; largest city in the state; airfield; railway; chemicals ('the chemical capital of the world'), explosives, automobiles; shipyards, railway engineering; home of several large corporations; State House complex, Winterthur Museum, Hagley Museum. » Delaware

Wilmington (North Carolina) 34°14N 77°55W, pop(1980) 44000. Seat of New Hanover County, SE North Carolina, USA, a port on the Cape Fear R; first armed resistance to the Stamp Act, 1765; headquarters of British troops under Cornwallis, 1781; the last Confederate port to close in the Civil War; Wilmington College (1947); the state's largest port; airfield; railway; metal and wood products, textiles, clothing, boilers, fertilizers; Azalea Festival (Apr). » American Revolution; North Carolina; Stamp Act

Wilmot Proviso (1846) A motion introduced in the US Congress by David Wilmot (Democrat, Pennsylvania) to forbid the expansion of slavery into territory acquired during the Mexican War. It passed the House of Representatives but not the Senate, where the South and the North had equal strength. The debate was a major step in the politicization of the slavery issue. » Mexican War; slave trade

Wilson, Sir Angus (Frank Johnstone) (1913–91) British writer, born at Bexhill, E Sussex. Educated at Westminster and Oxford, he began writing in 1946 and rapidy established a reputation with his short stories, *The Wrong Set* (1949). His works include the novels *Hemlock and After* (1952), *Anglo-Saxon Attitudes* (1956), and *The Old Man at the Zoo* (1961), the play *The Mulberry Bush* (1955), and two volumes of short stories. He was professor of English literature at East Anglia (1966–78), was knighted in 1980, and moved to France. His *Collected Stories* were published in 1987. » English literature; novel; short story

Wilson, C(harles) T(homson) R(ees) (1869–1959) British pioneer of atomic and nuclear physics, born at Glencorse, Midlothian, Scotland. He was educated at Manchester and Cambridge, where he became professor of natural philosophy (1925–34). Noted for his study of atmospheric electricity, his major achievement was to devise the cloud chamber method for observing the track of alpha-particles and electrons, enabling the interaction of atomic particles to be followed. In 1927 he shared with Compton the Nobel Prize for Physics, and died at Carlops, Peeblesshire. » cloud chamber; Compton, Arthur

Wilson, Edmund (1895–1972) US literary and social critic, born at Red Bank, New Jersey. Educated at Princeton, he became journalist, associate editor of the *New Republic* (1926–31), and book critic of the *New Yorker*. An early critical success was his study of the Symbolist movement, *Axel's Castle* (1931). He was a prolific and wide-ranging author, producing several studies on aesthetic, social, and political themes, as well as verse, plays, travel books, and historical works. He died at Talcottville, New York. » literary criticism; Symbolism

Wilson, Edward (Osborne) (1929–) US biologist, born at Birmingham, Alabama, where he graduated in biology. He studied at Harvard, where he joined the faculty in 1956. His early work was in entomology, but his conclusions (eg on the behaviour of competing populations of different species) were extended to other species including the human, notably in his book *Sociobiology: the New Synthesis* (1975) which virtually founded the subject of sociobiology, and stimulated much discussion and some contention. » sociobiology

Wilson (of Rievaulx), (James) Harold, Baron (1916–) British Labour statesman and Prime Minister (1964–70, 1974–6), born in Huddersfield. He was educated at Oxford, where he became a lecturer in economics in 1937. An MP in 1945, he was President of the Board of Trade (1947–51), and the principal Opposition spokesman on economic affairs. An able and hard-hitting debater, in 1963 he succeeded Gaitskell as Leader of the Labour Party, becoming Prime Minister in 1964. His economic plans were badly affected by a balance of payments crisis, leading to severe restrictive measures. He was also faced with the problem of Rhodesian independence, opposition to Britain's proposed entry into the Common Market, and an increasing conflict between the two wings of the Labour Party. Following his third general election victory, he resigned suddenly as Labour leader in 1976. Knighted in 1976, he became a life peer in 1983. » European Economic Community; Gaitskell; Labour Party; prices and incomes policy

Wilson (of Libya and of Stowlangtoft), Henry Maitland, 1st Baron (1881–1964) British field marshal, born in London. Educated at Eton and Sandhurst, he fought in South Africa and in World War 1, and at the outbreak of World War 2 was appointed Commander of British troops in Egypt. He led the initial British advance in Libya (1940–1) and the unsuccessful Greek campaign (1941), and became Commander-in-Chief Middle East (1943) and Supreme Allied Commander in the Mediterranean theatre (1944). He headed the British Joint Staff Mission in Washington (1945–7), and was raised to the peerage in 1946. He died at Chilton, Buckinghamshire. » World War 2

Wilson, Richard (1714–82) British landscape painter, born at Penygroes, Montgomeryshire, Wales. He began as a portrait painter, but after a visit to Italy (1752–6) turned to landscapes. In London in 1760 he exhibited his 'Niobe', and was recognized as one of the leading painters of his time. In 1776 he became librarian to the Royal Academy. He died at Llanberis, Caernarvonshire. » landscape painting

Wilson, (Thomas) Woodrow (1856–1924) US statesman and 28th President (1913–21), born at Staunton, Virginia. Educated at Princeton and Johns Hopkins, he became a lawyer and university professor, president of Princeton, and Governor of New Jersey (1911). Elected Democratic President in 1912 and 1916, his administration saw the prohibition and women's suffrage amendments to the constitution, America's participation in World War 1, his peace plan proposals (the 'Fourteen Points'), and his championship of the League of Nations. His health declined after the Senate's rejection of the Treaty of Versailles, and he died in Washington, DC. » Democratic Party; Fourteen Points; League of Nations; World War 1

Wiltshire pop (1987e) 550 900; area 3 481 sq km/1 344 sq ml. County of S England, divided into five districts; chalk downland of Salisbury Plain at the centre of the county; drained by the Avon and Kennet Rivers; county town, Trowbridge; chief towns include Salisbury, Swindon, Chippenham; agriculture, engineering, clothing, brewing; many ancient prehistoric remains, such as Stonehenge, Avebury, Silbury Hill; Marlborough Downs, Savernake Forest, Longleat House, Wilton House. » Avebury; England [i]; Salisbury Plain; Silbury Hill; Stonehenge; Trowbridge

Wimbledon Residential district in Merton borough, S Greater London, England; Wimbledon Common; headquarters of the All England Tennis Club; annual lawn tennis championships (Jun–Jul). » London [i]; tennis, lawn [i]; RR120

Winchester, Lat **Venta Belgarum**, Anglo-Saxon **Wintanceaster** 51°04N 1°19W, pop (1981) 35 664. City and county town in Winchester district, Hampshire, S England; on the R Itchen, 105 km/65 ml SW of London; Roman settlement the fifth largest in Britain; capital of Wessex in 519, and capital of England in 827; William the Conqueror crowned here as well as in London; *Domesday Book* compiled here; from the 14th-c the city declined into a small provincial town; railway; engineering; burial place of St Swithin; Gothic cathedral (1079–93), longest in the world; Winchester College (1382), oldest public school in England; 12th-c St Cross Hospital; 13th-c castle hall, containing a mediaeval 'replica' of Arthur's Round Table; Southern Cathedrals' Festival (Jul). » Arthur; Domesday Book; Hampshire; Swithin, St; William I (of England)

Winchester disk A small solid rotatable disk, coated with magnetizable material, used as a computer storage medium for microcomputers. The disk is housed in a hermetically sealed unit, and is rotated rapidly while in use. In comparison with floppy disks of similar size, a Winchester disk can store considerably more data (typically 10 to 100 megabytes), and since it rotates much more rapidly than floppy disks, data can be written to and read from the disk more rapidly. » access time; byte; hard disk; magnetic disk

Winckelmann, Johann (Joachim) (1717–68) German archaeologist and art historian, born at Stendal, Prussia. Educated at Halle and Jena in theology and medicine, in 1748 he turned to the history of art, and became librarian to a cardinal in Rome (1755). His works include the pioneering study, *Geschichte der Kunst des Alterthums* (1764, History of the Art of Antiquity), and in 1763 he became superintendent of Roman antiquities. He was murdered at Trieste.

wind The movement of air along the pressure gradient from areas of high to lower pressure; one of the basic elements of weather. Pressure gradients develop through the unequal cooling or heating of a layer of atmosphere. The steeper the gradient, the stronger the wind. Wind direction is also determined by the Coriolis force and by surface friction. The Coriolis force opposes the force of the pressure gradient and, at high altitudes where the frictional effect of the Earth's surface is absent, exactly balances the pressure gradient, producing a geostrophic wind. In the N hemisphere the Coriolis force deflects wind to the right, and in the S hemisphere to the left. At low altitudes, the frictional force of the Earth's surface reduces the influence of the Coriolis force, diverting the wind towards the centre of the low pressure area. As one of the basic elements of weather, there are many local names for different winds. » anabatic wind; anemometer [i]; Beaufort scale; Coriolis force [i]; Föhn/Foehn wind; general circulation model; geostrophic wind; Harmattan; isobar; jet stream; katabatic wind; Khamsin; Mistral; Sirocco; squall; trade winds; westerlies

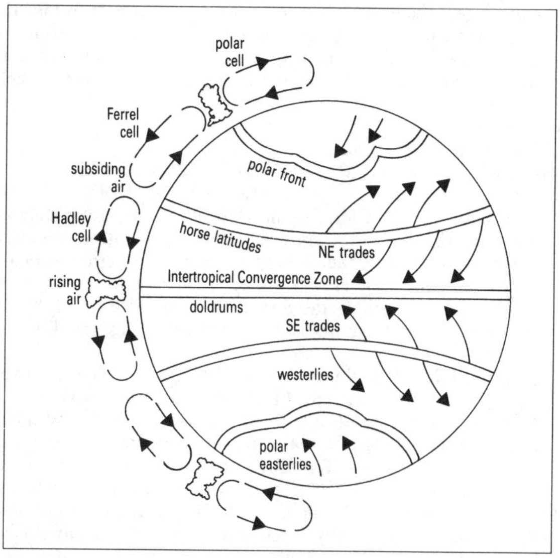

The three cell general circulation model of the atmosphere

wind chill An effect of wind decreasing the apparent temperature felt by a human body. Strong winds increase the heat loss from exposed flesh, and so at low temperatures may induce hypothermia at a higher air temperature than would occur in calm conditions. The wind chill equivalent temperature relates air temperature to wind speed. For example an air temperature of −18°C/0°F with no wind would be equivalent to −38°C/−36°F at 7 m/23 ft per second. » bioclimatology; hypothermia

wind instrument » **aerophone**

wind scorpion » **sun spider**

wind shear A meteorological term applied to the rate of change of wind velocity. As it changes with height it is known as the *vertical* wind shear. The amount of shear depends on the temperature structure of the air. » wind [i]

wind tunnel » **aerodynamics** [i]

Windermere 54°23N 2°54W, pop (1981) 7956. Lakeside resort town in South Lakeland district, Cumbria, NW England; 11 km/7 ml NW of Kendal, on L Windermere; railway; major tourist centre; 15th-c Church of St Martin; Rydal Mount (10 km/6 ml NW), Wordsworth's home from 1813 to 1850; Brantwood, home of Ruskin. » Cumbria; Lake District; Ruskin; Wordsworth, William

Windermere, Lake Largest lake in England, in the Lake District of Cumbria, NW England; extending 18 km/11 ml S from Ambleside; linked to Morecambe Bay by the R Leven; largest island, Belle Isle; remains of 13th-c chapel on Ladyholme. » Lake District; Windermere

Windhoek [**vint**huk] 22°34S 17°06E, pop (1981e) 105 000. Capital of Namibia, 1 450 km/900 ml N of Cape Town, South Africa; altitude, 1 650 m/5 413 ft; occupied by South African forces, 1915; capital of German South-West Africa, 1922; airport; railway; administration, meat canning, diamonds, copper, sheepskins (karakul); cathedral. » Namibia [i]

windmill A mill worked by the action of wind on sails. Windmills have been used principally for grinding corn, cleansing (*fulling*) cloth, and for drainage. There are three types: *post mills*, where the mill itself revolves on a central post to face the wind, and *tower mills* (built of brick) and *smock mills* (built of timber), where only the cap revolves. Windmills were in common use until the end of the 19th-c, when they were largely superseded by the advent of steam power.

windpipe » trachea

Windscale » Sellafield

Windsor, Duke and Duchess of » Edward VIII

Windsor (Canada) 42°18N 83°00W, pop (1981) 192 083. Town in S Ontario, SE Canada, on Detroit R, opposite Detroit; founded 1835; rapid industrial growth in 19th-c; railway; university (1857); vehicles, food processing, pharmaceuticals, paints, salt, distilling; Hiram Walker Historical Museum; Point Pelee National Park to the S (area 15.5 sq km/6 sq ml, established 1918), notable for birds and butterflies. » Detroit; Ontario

Windsor (UK) 51°30N 0°38W, pop (1981) 31 544. Town linked with Eton in Windsor and Maidenhead district, Berkshire, S England; W of London, on R Thames; railway; Windsor Castle, Eton College (1440); Royal Windsor Horse Show (May); horse-racing at Royal Ascot (Jun); Eton wall game on St Andrew's Day (30 Nov). » Berkshire; Windsor Castle

Windsor, House of The name of the British royal family since 1917. This unequivocally English name resulted from a Declaration by George V, a member of the House of Saxe-Coburg-Gotha. It was felt that a Germanic surname for the British monarchy was inappropriate, especially during a war against Germany. » English history; George V

Windsor Castle The largest of England's castles, situated on the R Thames at Windsor, Berkshire. It was founded by William I and first used as a royal residence by Henry I. The process of converting Windsor from a fortress into a palace began in the 16th-c. The castle stands on the edge of Windsor Great Park, formerly a royal hunting ground. » Windsor

Windward Islands (Caribbean) Island group of the Lesser Antilles in the Caribbean Sea; S of the Leeward Is, from Martinique (N) to Grenada (S), excluding Trinidad and Tobago; so called because of their exposure to the prevailing NE trade winds; formerly the name of a British colony comprising Dominica, St Lucia, St Vincent, and Grenada. » Antilles; Leeward Islands (Caribbean)

Windward Islands (French Polynesia), Fr **Iles du Vent** pop (1981e) 107 000. Island group of the Society Is, French Polynesia; comprises Tahiti, Moorea, and the smaller Mehetia, Tetiaroa, and Tubuai Manu Is; capital, Papeete; coconuts, tourism. » Papeete; Society Islands; Tahiti

wine The alcoholic beverage produced from the fermentation of grapes or other fruits. The alcohol content varies from 7% to 13%, but is usually 12%, the point at which fermentation stops. A wine's taste is determined by the type of grape used, the soil in which it is grown, and the local climate. It may be white, red, or rosé, dry or sweet, still or sparkling. White wine can be made from red (or black) grapes as well as white (or green): the final colour depends on whether the skins are left to ferment with the juice. Sweet wine is taken from the vat before fermentation has finished, while some sugar remains; dry wine is left to ferment until all the sugar has been converted to alcohol. Sparkling wine is produced by bottling it before the fermentation process is completed, so that fermentation continues in the bottle. Fermentation is stopped by the addition of alcohol (eg brandy) to produce fortified wines (eg sherry and port).

Known since ancient times, viniculture was taken to Italy by the Greeks, and by the Romans to Gaul (modern France). France has long been regarded as the producer of the greatest wines, in Bordeaux (claret) and Burgundy. France and Italy are the leading growers and producers, with Spain and Germany also traditional winemaking centres. The 20th-c has seen the development of vineyards in the New World, and in the 1980s other European countries (eg Bulgaria) began to produce large quantities of wine for export. Following the devastation of European vineyards by the phylloxera insect in the 19th-c, most grapes in Europe are grown on cuttings grafted on to American root stock (which is resistant to phylloxera). In California and Australia, winemaking has developed as an industry; all processes, from the delivery of the grape to the packing of filled bottles for transportation, can be carried out in factory surroundings, to produce all qualities of wine from basic to excellent. » alcohol; fermentation; grapevine; phylloxera

Wingate, Orde (Charles) (1903–44) British general, born at Naini Tal, India. Educated at Charterhouse and Woolwich, he was commissioned in 1922, and served in the Sudan (1928–33) and Palestine (1936–9), where he helped create a Jewish defence force. In the Burma theatre (1942) he organized the Chindits – specially trained jungle-fighters who were supplied by air, and thrust far behind the enemy lines. He was killed in a plane crash in Burma. » Chindits; World War 2

Winkler, Hans-Günther [**ving**kler] (1926–) West German show jumper, born at Wuppertal-Barmen, Westphalia. He is the only man to have won five Olympic gold medals at show jumping: the team golds in 1956, 1960, 1964, and 1972, and the individual title on *Halla* in 1956. On the same horse he won the individual world title in 1954 and 1955. He made his German international debut in Spain in 1952, and later became team captain. » equestrianism

Winnipeg 49°53N 97°10W, pop (1981) 564 473. Capital of Manitoba province, C Canada, on the Red R where it meets the Assiniboine R; established 1738 as Fort Rouge; fur-trading post, 1806; modern name, 1873; expansion after arrival of railway, 1881; severely damaged by flood, 1950; airport; university (1967); meat packing, fur trading, textiles, machinery, aircraft parts; major league team, Winnipeg Jets (ice hockey); railway memorial; Centennial Arts Centre (concert hall, planetarium, museum), Civic Auditorium (home of Winnipeg Symphony Orchestra), Art Gallery, Royal Winnipeg Ballet; Festival du Voyageur (Feb); Folklorama (Aug). » Manitoba

Winnipeg, Lake Lake in SC Manitoba province, S Canada, 64 km/40 ml NNE of Winnipeg; length 386 km/240 ml; breadth 88 km/55 ml; area 24 390 sq km/9 414 sq ml; drained N into Hudson Bay by the Nelson R; a remnant of the glacial L Agassiz. » Manitoba

Winnipesaukee, Lake [winipuh**saw**kee] Largest lake in New Hampshire, NE USA; a popular resort area N of Concord; area 184 sq km/71 sq ml. » New Hampshire

Winston-Salem 36°06N 80°15W, pop (1980) 131 885. Seat of Forsyth County, NC North Carolina, USA; Winston founded in 1849, Salem in 1766; towns united, 1913; Wake Forest University (1834); railway; the nation's chief tobacco manufacturer; textiles, furniture; Old Salem. » North Carolina

winter aconite A tuberous perennial, native to S Europe, and a popular garden ornamental. It flowers very early in spring. A ring of divided bracts forms a ruff below the bright yellow cup-shaped flower; the leaves appear after flowering. (*Eranthus hyemalis*. Family: *Ranunculaceae*.) » bract; perennial; tuber

Winter Palace » Hermitage

Winter War » Russo-Finnish War

wintergreen A family of small evergreen perennials, native to N temperate and arctic regions; rhizomatous; leaves oval;

flowers drooping, bell-shaped, 5-petalled, pink or white. Genus *Pyrola* (20 species) has alternate leaves and flowers in slender spikes; *Orthilia secunda* has alternate leaves and flowers in 1-sided spikes; *Moneses uniflora* has opposite leaves and solitary flowers. (Family: *Pyrolaceae*.) » evergreen plants; perennial; rhizome

Winterhalter, Franz Xaver (1806–73) German painter, born at Menzenschwand. He studied in Freiburg and Munich, and was appointed court painter to Grand Duke Leopold of Baden. In 1834 he went to Paris, where he became the fashionable artist of his day, painting many royal figures, such as Napoleon III and Queen Victoria. He died at Frankfurt am Main. » German art

Winterthur [vintertoor] 47°30N 8°45E, pop (1980) 86 758. Town in Zürich canton, Switzerland; near the R Töss in the Pre-Alpine region, NE of Zürich; railway junction; engineering, transport equipment, textiles; town hall (18th–19th-c). » Switzerland [i]

Winthrop, John (1588–1649) English colonist, born at Groton, Suffolk. Educated at Cambridge, he became a lawyer, and in 1629 was appointed Governor of Massachusetts colony. He was re-elected Governor, with brief intervals, during his life, and had more influence probably than anyone else in forming the political institutions of the Northern states of America. He died in Boston. » Massachusetts

wipe (photography) A transition effect in motion pictures or video in which one scene is gradually replaced by the next at a boundary line moving across the picture area, sharply defined ('hard-edge') or diffuse ('soft-edge'). An expanding or contracting circular outline is termed an **iris wipe**. » special effects

wire service » **news agency**

wireworm » **click beetle**

Wisconsin [wiskonsin] pop (1987e) 4 807 000; area 145 431 sq km/ 56 153 sq ml. State in N USA, divided into 72 counties; the 'Badger State'; first settled by French traders, 1670; surrendered to the British, 1763; ceded to the USA, 1783 (part of the Northwest Territory); Territory of Wisconsin formed, 1836; 30th state to join the Union, 1848; bounded N by L Superior and L Michigan, E by L Michigan; capital, Madison; other major cities Milwaukee, Green Bay, Racine; rivers include the Mississippi (part of the W border), Menominee (part of the E border), and Wisconsin; L Winnebago lies to the E; c.26 000 sq km/ 10 000 sq ml of L Michigan lie within the state boundary; highest point Timms Hill (595 m/1 952 ft); glaciated terrain in the N and W, largely forested; over 8 500 lakes; timber products, dairy products, paper, metal products, machinery, food processing, electrical equipment, transport equipment, grain, vegetables, brewing; produces more milk, butter, and cheese than any other state; over a third of the nation's cheese production; heavy industry in the Milwaukee area. » Madison; Michigan, Lake; United States of America [i]; RR39

Wisdom, Book of » **Wisdom of Solomon**

wisdom literature In the Hebrew Bible, a group of writings, usually including Proverbs, Ecclesiastes, the Song of Songs, and Job, although the influence of wisdom may also be found in other Biblical stories (eg Esther) and in some of the Psalms. Amongst the Apocrypha, it also includes Ecclesiasticus and the Wisdom of Solomon. The literature is usually traced to a special class of sages in Israel who sought to draw lessons for life from general human experience rather than from revealed religious truths, although in fact their humanistic observations were often integrated with a belief in Yahweh and his law. » Ecclesiastes/Ecclesiasticus/Job/Proverbs, Book of; Old Testament; Solomon (Old Testament); Wisdom of Solomon

Wisdom of Jesus, the Son of Sirach » **Ecclesiasticus, Book of**

Wisdom of Solomon or **Book of Wisdom** A book of the Old Testament Apocrypha, or deuterocanonical work in the Catholic Bible, purportedly from Solomon, but usually attributed to an unknown Alexandrian Jew c.1st-c BC. Like other Jewish wisdom literature, it praises the figure of Wisdom above ungodliness, but is a mixture of poetry and philosophical prose rather than short aphorisms. The follies of idolatry are emphasized, and reinforced by examples from the Exodus of the contrasting fates of the faithful Israelites and idolatrous Egyptians. » Apocrypha, Old Testament; Solomon (Old Testament)

Wise Men » **Magi**

Wiseman, Nicholas (Patrick Stephen) (1802–65) British Roman Catholic churchman, born at Seville, Spain. He was brought up at Waterford and Ushaw, entered the English College at Rome, was ordained in 1825, and became rector of the College in 1828. His appointment as the first Archbishop of Westminster and a cardinal (1850) called forth a storm of religious excitement, which led to the passing of the Ecclesiastical Titles Assumption Act. One of his best-known works was the historical novel, *Fabiola* (1854). He died in London. » Roman Catholicism

wisent [veezuhnt] » **bison**

Wishart, George (c.1513–46) Scottish reformer and martyr, born at Pitarrow, Kincardineshire. In 1538 he was a schoolmaster in Montrose, where he incurred a charge of heresy for teaching the Greek New Testament. He then spent several years on the continent, returning to Scotland in 1543. He preached the Lutheran doctrine in several towns, and was arrested and burned at St Andrews. One of his converts was John Knox. » Beaton, David; Knox, John; Lutheranism

wisteria A deciduous climbing shrub from E Asia and N America; leaves pinnate with oval-oblong leaflets; pea-flowers fragrant, lilac, violet, or white, in long pendulous clusters. It is often grown for ornament, and can reach a considerable age, developing thick, gnarled stems. Commonly grown species include *Wisteria sinensis*, native to China with lilac-mauve flowers, and *Wisteria floribunda* from Japan, with blue-purple flowers. (Genus: *Wisteria*, 6 species. Family: *Leguminosae*.) » climbing plant; deciduous plants; pinnate; shrub

witan or **witenagemot** (Old English 'meeting of wise men') The council of the Anglo-Saxon kings, once regarded as the first English 'parliament'. It was not a popular assembly imposing constitutional restraints on kingship, but in essence an informal advisory body of great men. It nevertheless upheld the convention that kings should take into account the views of important subjects. » Anglo-Saxons; parliament

witch hazel A deciduous shrub or small tree, native to E Asia and eastern N America; flowers in short-stalked clusters, each with four long strap-shaped yellow petals, usually appearing before oval leaves. The bark yields an astringent lotion; the twigs are often used in dowsing. (Genus: *Hamamelis*, 6 species. Family: *Hamamelidaceae*.) » deciduous plants; dowsing; shrub; tree [i]

witchcraft The alleged possession and exercise of magical or psychic powers, especially involving the manipulation of natural objects or events; often called *black magic* if harmful to people, *white magic* if helpful. In Africa, the power of witches is said to be innate, and people may not even know that they are witches. In Europe the Christian Church began persecuting witches in the 14th-c, alleging that witches consciously made a pact with Satan. The persecution later spread to America, and by the end of the 17th-c c.200 000 people had been executed. Contemporary witchcraft in the West sees itself as an alternative religion, celebrating gods drawn from various European pre-Christian religions, and exercising its magical powers in beneficial ways. » magic; Salem (Massachusetts); voodoo

Witt, Katerina (1965–) East German figure skater, born at Karl-Marx-Stadt. The East German champion in 1982, she won the first of six successive European titles in 1983, was world champion in 1984–5 and 1987–8, and Olympic champion in 1984 and 1988. » ice skating

Wittenberg [vitnberk] 51°53N 12°39E, pop (1981) 53 874. Town in Wittenberg district, EC Germany; on R Elbe, SW of Berlin; associated with the beginning of the Reformation, 1517; part of Prussia, 1814; railway; university (1817); chemical plants; 16th-c Augustinian monastery where Luther lived; Schlosskirche, to the doors of which Luther nailed his 95 theses. » Germany [i]; Luther; Reformation

Wittgenstein, Ludwig (Josef Johann) [vitgenshtiyn] (1889–1951) Austrian philosopher, born in Vienna. He studied engineering at Berlin and Manchester, then became interested in mathematical logic, which he studied under Russell (1912–13). While serving in the Austrian army in World War 1, he wrote the *Tractatus Logico-philosophicus* (1921), in which he argued that an adequate account of language must recognize that any sentence is a picture of the fact it represents, and that any thought is a sentence. In 1929 he began lecturing at Cambridge, submitting the *Tractatus* as his doctoral dissertation. He worked at a hospital in London during World War 2, returned to Cambridge afterwards, and resigned his chair in 1947. Between 1936 and 1949 he worked on the *Philosophische Untersuchungen* (1953, Philosophical Investigations), in which he rejected the doctrines of the *Tractatus*, claiming that linguistic meaning is a function of the *use* to which expressions are put, or the 'language games' in which they play a role. He became a naturalized British subject in 1938, and died at Cambridge. » Russell, Bertrand

Witwatersrand or **The Rand** [witwawterzrand], Afrikaans [vuhtvahtersrant] ('white water's reef) Region centred on a ridge of gold-bearing rock in S Transvaal province, South Africa; length 100 km/60 ml; width 40 km/25 ml; Johannesburg located near its centre; the power house of the South African economy, with many Black townships nearby providing a reserve of labour; gold discovered in 1886 (produces over half the world's supply). » South Africa [i]; Transvaal

woad A biennial or perennial with numerous yellow, cross-shaped flowers and pendulous, oblong, flattened, purplish capsules. It has been cultivated since ancient times, but is now reduced to an occasional cornfield weed. The blue dye used by Ancient Britons (and still produced until the 19th-c) is made by exposing part-dried, crushed leaves to the air. (*Isatis tinctoria.* Family: *Cruciferae.*) » biennial; perennial

Wöhler, Friedrich [voeler] (1800–82) German chemist, born near Frankfurt. Educated at Heidelberg, he taught at Berlin and Kassel, then became professor of chemistry at Göttingen (1836), where he died. He isolated aluminium (1827) and beryllium (1828), and discovered calcium carbide, from which he obtained acetylene. His synthesis of urea from ammonium cyanate in 1828 was a turning point for organic chemistry. » aluminium; beryllium; organic chemistry

Wodehouse, Sir P(elham) G(renville) [wudhows] (1881–1975) British novelist, born at Guildford, Surrey. Educated in London, he worked in a bank, then became a freelance writer. He wrote school stories, made his name with *Piccadilly Jim* (1918), and established his reputation with the creation of Bertie Wooster and his 'gentleman's gentleman' Jeeves. A prolific writer, he produced a succession of novels, short stories, sketches, and librettos. During World War 2 he was interned in Germany. He then lived in the USA, and became a US citizen in 1955. Knighted in 1975, he died at Southampton, New York. » English literature; novel

Woden » **Odin**

Wojtyla, Karol Jozef » **John Paul II**

Wolds Way Long-distance footpath stretching from Hull to Filey, N England; links with the Cleveland Way; length 115 km/71 ml.

wolf A member of the dog family; two species: the **grey** (or **timber**) wolf (*Canis lupus*), the largest wild dog and ancestor of the domestic dog, native to forests throughout the temperate N hemisphere (distribution now patchy); and the rare **red wolf** (*Canis rufus*) of E USA. The name is sometimes used for the coyote and less closely-related dogs, such as the S American **maned wolf** (*Chrysocyon brachyurus*) and the **Falkland Island wolf** (*Dusicyon australis*). » Canidae; coyote; dog

Wolf, Hugo (Philipp Jakob) [volf] (1860–1903) Austrian composer, born at Windischgraz. He studied at the Vienna Conservatoire, then earned a living by teaching, conducting, and music criticism. From 1888 he composed c.300 songs, settings of poems by Goethe and others, and wrote an opera, *Der Corregidor* (1895), and other works. For the most part he lived in poverty, became insane in 1897, and died in the asylum at Steinhof, near Vienna.

Wolf-Ferrari, Ermanno [volf fuhrahree] (1876–1948) Italian composer, born and died in Venice. Sent to Rome to study painting, he turned to music, and studied in Munich, returning to Venice in 1899. He became an operatic composer, his best-known works being *I quattro rusteghi* (1906, The School for Fathers) and *Il segreto di Susanna* (1909, Susanna's Secret). He also composed choral and chamber works, and music for organ and piano.

wolf fish Large blenny-like fish found in moderately deep and colder waters of the N Atlantic; length up to 1.2 m/4 ft; head robust, teeth strong and pointed; body tapers to small tail fin, dorsal and anal fins long; feeds mainly on echinoderms, crustaceans, and molluscs. (*Anarhichas lupus.* Family: *Anarhichadidae.*) » blenny

wolf spider A medium-to-large, hairy spider that runs over the ground to capture prey; some burrow or make funnel-shaped webs. (Order: *Araneae.* Family: *Lycosidae*, c.3000 species.) » spider

Wolfe, Charles (1791–1823) Irish poet, born in Dublin. Educated at Winchester and Dublin, he is remembered for his poem 'The Burial of Sir John Moore', which appeared anonymously in 1817 and at once caught the admiration of the public. He was ordained in 1817, and became rector of Donoughmore. He died at Queenstown, Co Cork. » Moore, John; poetry

Wolfe, James (1727–59) British soldier, born at Westerham, Kent. Commissioned in 1741, he fought against the Jacobites in Scotland (1745–6), and was sent to Canada during the Seven Years' War (1756–63). In 1758 he was prominent in the capture of Louisburg, and commanded in the famous capture of Quebec (1759), where he was killed. » Abraham, Plains of; Seven Years' War; Montcalm

Wolfe, Thomas (Clayton) (1900–38) US novelist, born at Asheville, North Carolina. Educated at North Carolina and Harvard, he wrote several plays, but found success with novels, notably *Look Homeward, Angel* (1929) and *Of Time and the River* (1935). He died in Baltimore. » American literature; novel

Wolfenden, Baron John Frederick (1906–85) British educationist, born at Halifax, Yorkshire. He was educated at Wakefield and Oxford, where he became a fellow (1929), and was then headmaster at Uppingham (1934) and Shrewsbury (1944), and Vice-Chancellor of Reading University (1950). He was best known for his government investigation of homosexuality and prostitution (the **Wolfenden Report**, 1957). Knighted in 1956, he became a life peer in 1974, and died at Guildford, Surrey. » education

Wölfflin, Heinrich [verlflin] (1864–1945) Swiss art historian, born at Winterthur. He studied under Jacob Burckhardt, whom he succeeded as professor of art history at Basle in 1893. He was one of the founders of modern art history, pioneering the 'scientific' method of formal analysis based on the systematic comparison of works of art in terms of contrasting stylistic features. His approach is expounded in three books: *Renaissance and Baroque* (1888), *Classic Art* (1899), and *Principles of Art History* (1915). » Burckhardt

wolfhound » **borzoi; Irish wolfhound**

wolfia A tiny floating freshwater herb related to duckweed, consisting only of a minute green thallus 0.5–1 mm/0.02–0.04 in across, with a budding pouch from which new plants are produced. Flowers, one male and one female, concealed in a cavity, are often absent. It is the smallest flowering plant in the world. (*Wolfia arrhiza.* Family: *Lemnaceae.*) » duckweed; flowering plants; herb; thallus

Wolfit, Sir Donald (1902–68) British actor-manager, born at Newark, Nottinghamshire. He began his stage career in 1920, formed his own company in 1937, and became known for his Shakespeare performances. During the Battle of Britain (1940) he instituted the first London season of 'Lunchtime Shakespeare'. He also appeared in several films and on television, and was knighted in 1957. » theatre

wolfram [wulfram] » **tungsten**

Wolfram von Eschenbach [volfram fon eshuhnbakh] (c.1170–c.1220) German poet, born near Anspach, Bavaria. He was a Bavarian knight who served at many courts, writing love songs and other works, He is best known for his epic *Parzival* (c.1200–10), which introduced the theme of the Holy Grail into German literature, and from which Wagner derived the libretto of his *Parsifal.* » German literature; poetry; Wagner

wolframite An iron manganese tungstate mineral ($(Fe,Mn)WO_4$), found in pegmatites and hydrothermal veins as

Wombat

tabular crystals or brown masses. It is the principal ore of tungsten. » scheelite; tungsten

Wolfsburg [**volfs**boork] 52°27N 10°49E, pop (1983) 124 000. City in Lüneburg district, West Germany; 24 km/15 ml NE of Brunswick, on the Mittelland and Elbe Branch Canals; founded, 1938; railway; vehicles, machinery, tools; known as the 'Volkswagen town' (site of car factory). » Germany, West [i]

Wolfson, Sir Isaac (1897–) British businessman, born in Glasgow, Scotland. He became managing director of Great Universal Stores in 1934, and is now honorary life president. In 1955 he set up the Wolfson Foundation for the advancement of health, education, and youth activities in the UK and the Commonwealth. He was made a baronet in 1962, and is active in Jewish causes. His son, **Leonard** (1927–), is a life peer. » foundations, philanthropic

Wollongong [wuluhn**gong**] 34°25S 150°52E, pop (1986) 237 600. Urban centre in SE New South Wales, Australia, extending 48 km/30 ml along the coast; includes the towns of Wollongong, Bulli, and Port Kembla; railway; university (1975); steel, coal, dairy farming. » New South Wales

Wollstonecraft (Godwin), Mary (1759–97) Anglo-Irish feminist, born in London. After working as a teacher and governess, she became a translator and literary adviser. In 1792 she wrote *Vindication of the Rights of Woman*, advocating equality of the sexes. She was in Paris during the French Revolution. A first marriage having broken up, she married William Godwin in 1797, and died in London soon after giving birth to a daughter, Mary (later, Mary Shelley). » Godwin, William

Wolof A W Atlantic-speaking agricultural people of Senegal and Gambia, traditionally grouped into a state with elaborate hierarchical distinctions. They developed a powerful empire (14th–16th-c), were involved in the European slave trade, and later worked in factories and on European trading vessels. Population c.2.3 million.

Wolpe, Joseph [**vol**pay] (1915–) South African psychiatrist, born in Johannesburg. He trained at the University of Witwatersrand, and later worked at Temple University, Florida. From animal experiments, he concluded that behaviour was environmentally conditioned. He published *Psychotherapy by Reciprocal Inhibition* (1958) and was co-author of *Behavioural Therapy Techniques* (1966), with which he founded the field of behavioural therapy, widely used in the treatment of neurotic disorders. » behaviour therapy; neurosis

Wolseley, Garnet Joseph, 1st Viscount [**wulz**lee] (1833–1913) British field marshal, born at Golden Bridge, Co Dublin, Ireland. He joined the army in 1852, and served in the Burmese War (1852–3), the Crimea (where he lost an eye), the Indian Mutiny (1857), and the Chinese War (1860). He put down the Red River rebellion (1870) in Canada, and commanded in the Ashanti War (1873). After other posts in India, Cyprus, South Africa, and Egypt, he led the attempted rescue of General Gordon at Khartoum. He became a baron (1882) and, after the Sudan campaign (1884–5), a viscount. As army Commander-in-Chief (1895–1901), he carried out several reforms, and mobilized forces for the Boer War (1899–1902). The author of several military works, he died at Mentone, France. » African history; Gordon; Red River Rebellion

Wolsey, Thomas (c.1475–1530) English cardinal and statesman, born at Ipswich, Suffolk. Educated at Oxford, he was ordained in 1498, appointed chaplain to Henry VII in 1507, and became Dean of Lincoln. Under Henry VIII, he became Bishop of Lincoln, Archbishop of York (1514), and a cardinal (1515). Made Lord Chancellor (1515–29), he pursued legal and administrative reforms. He was Henry VIII's leading adviser, in charge of the day-to-day running of government. He aimed to make England a major power in Europe, and also had ambitions to become Pope, but his policy of supporting first Emperor Charles V (1523) then Francis I of France (1528) in the Habsburg–Valois conflict was unsuccessful, and high taxation caused much resentment. When he failed to persuade the Pope to grant Henry's divorce, he was impeached and his property forfeited. Arrested on a charge of high treason, he died while travelling to London. » Habsburgs; Henry VIII; Valois

Wolverhampton [wulvuh**hamp**tn] 52°36N 2°08W, pop (1981) 254 561. Town in West Midlands, C England; in the industrial 'Black Country', 20 km/12 ml NW of Birmingham; named after Wulfruna (sister of Edgar II) who endowed the first collegiate church here in 994; railway; metal products, locks and keys, engineering, chemicals, bicycles; 15th-c Church of St Peter. » West Midlands

wolverine A mammal of family *Mustelidae*, native to the N forests and tundra of Scandinavia, Asia, and N America; stocky (length, 1 m/3¼ ft), pointed muzzle, bushy tail; dark brown, often pale on face and sides; eats mainly small mammals; also known as **glutton**. (*Gulo gulo*.) » Mustelidae

womb » uterus [i]

wombat A nocturnal Australian marsupial; length, up to 1.25 m/4 ft; bear-like, with a stout body, very small tail; round head, blunt muzzle with a large nose pad; pouch of female opens backwards; digs burrows; eats coarse grasses. (Family: *Vombatidae*, 3 species.) » marsupial [i]

Women's Institutes, National Federation of (WI) A woman's voluntary organization, started in Canada in 1897 by Adelaide Hoodles to provide classes in domestic science and home-making. The WI spread to Britain in 1915, and to other Commonwealth countries. There are now some 9 200 institutes in England and Wales (but none in Scotland, which has its own Scottish Women's Rural Institutes).

women's liberation movement A broad cultural and political movement initiated by women to improve their social position by freeing themselves from the constraints and disadvantages of a society said to be dominated by men. 'Women's lib' has very strong roots in the USA and Europe, and has been 'politicized' especially by radical feminists who claim the continued existence of 'patriarchy' (ie male dominance) in capitalist societies; the origins of women's liberation can be traced back to the French Revolution (1789). » feminism; women's studies

Women's Royal Voluntary Service (WRVS) In the UK, an organization founded in 1938 (designated Royal in 1966), made up of unpaid helpers who do community work. During World War 2 they helped mitigate the social disruptions of wartime; in peacetime their role is to supplement the social services. They pioneered the first home help scheme (1944), and run the meals on wheels service for the housebound elderly, as well as providing voluntary workers for day centres, hospitals, playgroups, prison visiting, and rural transport.

women's services Military organizations in which women enlist for non-combatant duty. In Britain, there are separate corps for army, navy, and air force. The **Women's Royal Army Corps (WRAC)** was founded in 1949, directly succeeding the Auxiliary Territorial Service (ATS) within which large numbers of women had served during World War 2. British women had served during World War 1 in the **Women's Auxiliary Army Corps (WAAC)** formed in 1917. The **Women's Royal Naval Service (WRNS)**, popularly known as 'the Wrens', was first formed in 1917. The **Women's Royal Air Force (WRAF)** was formed in 1918, and later became known as the **Women's Auxiliary Air Force (WAAF)**. In the USA, the **Women's Army Corps (WAC)** was established in 1948, and was dissolved in 1978.

women's studies The study of the history and contemporary role of girls and women. More available in further and higher education than in schools, it is favoured by feminist groups, who feel that girls and women are disadvantaged and that the nature of this disadvantage is often not mentioned in education. » feminism; gender; women's liberation movement

wood The bulk of the tissue making up the trunk and branches of trees and shrubs, consisting of *xylem*. Its exact composition varies between species, affecting properties of the timber produced. For commercial purposes, it is divided into two types: **softwoods**, derived from gymnosperms, and **hardwoods**, which have a less regular grain and are derived from flowering plants. The terms are misleading, as some softwoods are very hard and durable. » flowering plants; gymnosperms; shrub; tree [i]; vascular tissue; xylem

Wood, Sir Henry (Joseph) (1869–1944) British conductor, born in London. He studied music at London, became an organist, and in 1895 helped to found the Promenade Concerts which he conducted annually until his death. He composed operettas and an oratorio, but his international reputation was gained as a conductor, first at the Queen's Hall, London, and then at the Albert Hall. Knighted in 1911, he died at Hitchin, Hertfordshire.

Wood, Mrs Henry, *née* **Ellen Price** (1814–87) British novelist, born at Worcester. She wrote a series of melodramatic novels, of which *East Lynne* (1861) was a longstanding success. In 1867 she acquired the monthly *Argosy*, and her novels went on appearing in it long after her death, in London. » novel

wood alcohol » **methanol**

wood avens » **avens**

wood block A percussion instrument (also known as a **Chinese block**) in the form of a hollowed rectangular or spherical block of wood, with one or more slits in the surface, which is struck with a wooden stick. Often grouped in four or five different sizes, they are frequently used in jazz and orchestral music. » percussion [i]

Wood Buffalo National park in N Alberta and S Northwest Territories, C Canada; includes part of Buffalo L and L Claire and part of the Caribou and Birch Mts; Great Canadian Oil Sands to the S; area 44 807 sq km/17 295 sq ml; established in 1922; noted for its herds of bison; a world heritage site. » bison; Canada [i]

wood carving A form of sculpture found since remote prehistoric times. Wood has provided an accessible, easily-worked, and durable material. The Egyptians coated their wooden statues with stucco and painted them, a technique also used in mediaeval church art. Extraordinary heights of naturalism were reached by 15th-c sculptors in Germany, notably Veit Stoss (1447–1533), Adam Krafft (c.1455–c.1508), and Tilman Riemenschneider (1460–1531), and by Gibbons in 17th-c England. Wood has proved a popular material with 20th-c sculptors, whether abstract or figurative. » abstract art; figurative art; sculpture; stucco; Gibbons, Grinling; Hepworth; Stoss

wood engraving A method of printmaking from wooden blocks, which differs from woodcut in that the end rather than the side of the block is used and the wood must be very hard. The design is engraved in the wood with a burin, producing fine lines. » burin; engraving; woodcut

wood-hoopoe » **hoopoe**

wood-ibis » **ibis**

wood lily A perennial native to woodland in eastern N America; rhizomatous; three leaves, in a single whorl near top of stem; flower solitary, terminal; three sepals, green; three petals, white turning pink. It is cultivated together with related species for ornament. (*Trillium grandiflorum*. Family: *Trilliaceae*.) » perennial; rhizome

wood mouse » **fieldmouse**

wood ox » **anoa**

wood pigeon A pigeon native to Europe, N Africa, and W Asia; plumage dark grey with white patch on neck; inhabits woodland, cultivation, and habitation; also known as **ringdove**. (*Columba palumbus*.) » pigeon

wood rat » **pack rat**

wood sorrel A perennial native to Europe and temperate Asia; leaves with three heart-shaped leaflets, acid-tasting; flowers long-stalked, 1–1.6 cm/0.4–0.6 in, funnel-shaped, white or lilac. It is very shade tolerant. (*Oxalis acetosella*. Family: *Oxalidaceae*.) » oxalis; perennial

wood warbler » **warbler**

woodbine » **honeysuckle**

woodchat A shrike native to Europe, Africa, and W Asia; top of head and neck chestnut brown; breast white; inhabits woodland and scrub; eats insects and small birds; also known as **woodchat shrike**. (*Lanius senator*.) » shrike

woodchuck A marmot native to N America; large (length, 800 mm/31.5 in), aggressive; may dig a den in woodland for the winter months; also known as **groundhog** (*Marmota monax*.) » marmot

woodcock A short-legged sandpiper, native to the Old World and eastern N America; mottled brown; bill long, straight, held downward during flight; inhabits woodland; eats earthworms and insect larvae. (Genus: *Scolopax*, 6 species.) » sandpiper

woodcreeper A bird native to the New World tropics; tail stiffened as in woodpeckers; many shapes of bill; inhabits woodland; eats insects, frogs, and snakes; also known as a **woodhewer**. (Family: *Dendrocolaptidae*, 47 species; sometimes placed in the family *Furnariidae*.) » woodpecker

woodcut One of the simplest and oldest methods of relief-printing. The design is gouged into the smooth surface of a block of wood, and sticky ink rolled over the top. The cut-away areas print as white patches, the rest as solid black. It therefore lends itself to crude, forceful designs with simple shapes and sharp contrasts. » relief printing; wood engraving

Woodhenge Prehistoric site in Wiltshire, S England; 3 km/1¾ ml NE of Stonehenge, near Amesbury; discovered by aerial reconnaissance in 1926. Little visible above ground, it apparently consisted of a number of concentric ovals of wooden pillars oriented for the same ritualistic forms as were in use at Stonehenge. » Stonehenge

woodhewer » **woodcreeper**

Woodland culture A generic term for the Indian culture of the E USA as far W as the Great Plains, c.700 BC–AD 1500. Characterized archaeologically by burial mounds, cord-impressed pottery, and tobacco smoking, its main traditions are *Adena-Hopewell* (c.700 BC–AD 400), centred on S Ohio with only rudimentary horticulture, and *Mississippian* (c.700–1500 AD), agriculturally stronger, with an emphasis on maize, beans, squash, and the use of bows and arrows for hunting. » American Indians; Cahokia; Hopewell

woodlouse A terrestrial crustacean found under stones, in litter and soil; abdominal limbs modified for aerial breathing and for reproduction; thoracic legs adapted for walking; some species able to roll into a protective ball. (Order: *Isopoda*, c.3 500 species.) » crustacean; louse

woodmouse » **fieldmouse**

woodpecker A bird of the family *Picidae* (198 species), inhabiting woodland; clings to tree trunks; tail stiff and presses against tree for support (except in small **piculets** (subfamily: *Picumninae*, 27 species) and **wrynecks**); eats insects, fruit, nuts, young birds, and (**sapsuckers**) sap. » sapsucker; woodcreeper; wryneck; yellowhammer

woodrush A tufted perennial, sometimes with stolons, found almost everywhere; leaves grass-like, fringed with long, colourless hairs; flowers with six perianth-segments, brownish, in terminal heads. (Genus: *Luzula*, 80 species. Family: *Juncaceae*.) » perennial; perianth; stolon

Woodward, R(obert) B(urns) (1917–79) US chemist, born in Boston, Massachusetts. Educated at the Massachusetts Institute of Technology, he taught at Harvard, becoming professor of science (1960–79), and director of the Woodward Research Institute at Basle (1963). He won the 1965 Nobel Prize for Chemistry for his syntheses of complex organic substances, including quinine, cholesterol, and chlorophyll. He died in Cambridge, Massachusetts.

woodwasp A wasp with a large egg-laying tube, and no waist separating thorax and abdomen. Some are small and parasitic (Family: *Orussidae*), laying eggs on the larvae of wood-boring beetles; others (Family: *Siricidae*) are large, and have larvae that feed on timber. (Order: *Hymenoptera*.) » beetle; larva; parasitology; wasp

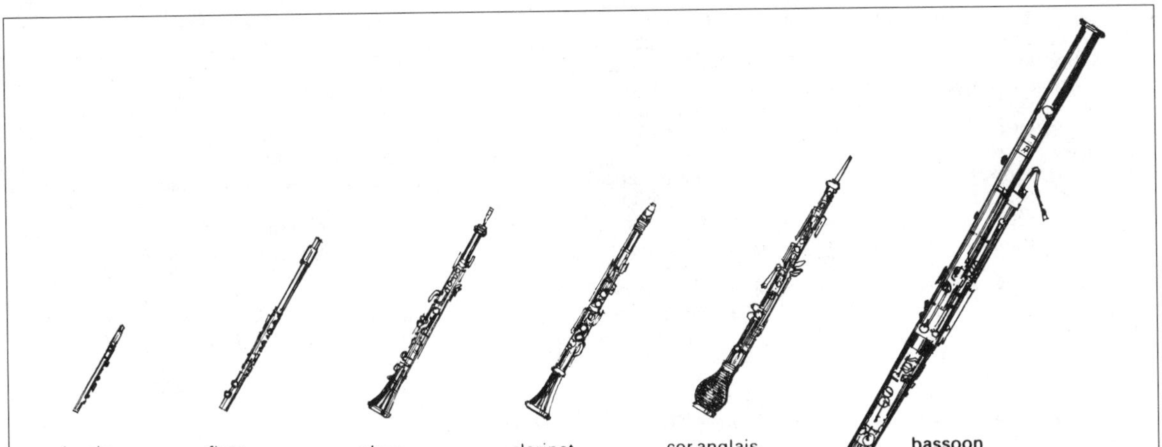

Woodwind instruments

woodwind instrument A musical instrument made principally from wood (or, in the case of the saxophone and some flutes, from metal), in which a column of air is activated by the player blowing across a mouth-hole (as in the flute or piccolo), through a duct (as in the recorder), or against a single or double reed (as in the bassoon, cor anglais, oboe, and clarinet). » aerophone; Bartolozzi sounds; bassoon; clarinet; cor anglais; cornett; didgeridoo; fife; flageolet; flute; oboe; ocarina; panpipes; piccolo; recorder; reed instrument

woodworm » **furniture beetle**

woody nightshade A scrambling woody perennial, native to Europe, Asia, and N Africa; leaves oval with 1–4 deep lobes or leaflets at the base; flowers like those of the related potato, with five purple petals, curving backwards, and a cone of yellow stamens; berries oval, green turning yellow and finally red when ripe, mildly poisonous; also called **bittersweet**. (*Solanum dulcamara*. Family: *Solanaceae*.) » perennial; potato; stamen

Wookey Hole Limestone caves near the village of Wookey in Sedgemoor district, Somerset, SW England; on the SW slopes of the Mendip Hills near the R Axe, 22 km/14 ml SE of Weston-super-Mare; prehistoric tools found in the caves. » Somerset

wool The fibre obtained from the fleeces of sheep. There are many qualities of wool, from fine soft wools obtained from the merino sheep of Australia, South Africa, and Argentina to coarse fibres which come from sheep in the cooler climates of New Zealand, Europe, and N America. Medium quality wools are used in clothing, including knitwear of the Shetland type; coarse wools are used mainly for carpets and other furnishings. » merino; shoddy

Woolf, (Adeline) Virginia (1882–1941) British novelist, born in London. Educated privately, in 1912 she married **Leonard (Sidney) Woolf** (1880–1969), with whom she set up the Hogarth Press (1917). A leading member of the Bloomsbury Group, she made a major contribution to the development of the novel, in such works as *Mrs Dalloway* (1925), *To the Lighthouse* (1927), and *The Waves* (1931), noted for their impressionistic style, a development of the stream-of-consciousness technique. She also wrote biographies and critical essays. After mental illness, she committed suicide near her home at Rodmell, Sussex. Publication of her *Diary* (5 vols, 1977–84) and *Letters* (6 vols, 1975–80) has further enhanced her reputation. » English literature; novel; stream of consciousness

Woolley, Sir (Charles) Leonard (1880–1960) British archaeologist, born and died in London. Educated at Leatherhead and Oxford, he carried out excavations at Carchemish, Al'Ubaid, and Tell el-Amarna. He subsequently directed the important excavations (1922–34) at Ur in Mesopotamia, revealing in 1926 spectacular discoveries of gold and lapis lazuli in the royal tombs. He was knighted in 1935, and wrote several popular accounts of his work, notably *Digging up the Past* (1930). » archaeology; Ur

woolly bear » **carpet beetle; tiger moth**

woolly monkey A New World monkey; large round head, long grasping tail; short dense woolly coat; plain dark colour; eats fruit and some insects; if food plentiful, will eat until abdomen markedly swollen; also known as **barrigudo**. (Genus: *Lagothrix*, 2 species.) » New World monkey; woolly spider monkey

woolly rhinoceros An extinct rhinoceros, once native to Europe and N Asia; length, 3.5 m/11 ft; thick coat of long hair; snout with two horns; in old males, front horn could be 1 m/3 ft long; hunted by humans in Europe 30 000 years ago. (*Coelodonta antiquitatis*.) » rhinoceros

woolly spider monkey A rare New World monkey, resembling the spider monkey in having long limbs and tail, but having a thick woolly coat like the woolly monkey; thumb minute; naked face is red, especially when excited. (*Brachyteles arachnoides*.) » New World/spider/woolly monkey

woolsack A large red cushion filled with wool that the Lord Chancellor sits on in the UK House of Lords. It is said to represent the authority of the Lord Chancellor who presides over the proceedings of the House. » Lords, House of

Woolworth, F(rank) W(infield) (1852–1919) US merchant, born at Rodman, New York. He was a farm worker until becoming a shop assistant in 1873. In 1879 he opened a store in Utica, New York, for five-cent goods only; this failed, but a second store, in Lancaster, Pennsylvania, selling also ten-cent goods, was successful. He then built a chain of similar stores, setting up the F W Woolworth Company in 1905. At the time of his death the company controlled over 1000 stores from their headquarters in the Woolworth building, New York City. His stores came to Britain in 1910.

Wootton (of Abinger), Baroness Barbara Frances (1897–1988) British social scientist, born at Cambridge. She was educated at Cambridge, where she became a lecturer in economics, and was director of studies (1927–44) and professor in social studies (1948–52) at London. A frequent royal commissioner and London magistrate, she is best known for her work, *Testament for Social Science* (1950), in which she attempted to assimilate the social to the natural sciences. Created a life peer in 1958, she died in London.

Worcester Anglo-Saxon **Wigorna Ceaster** [**wus**ter] 52°11N 2°13W, pop(1981) 74 790. County town of Hereford and Worcester, WC England; on the R Severn, 38 km/24 ml SW of Birmingham; founded c.680 AD; site of Cromwell victory in Civil War; Royal Worcester Porcelain Co established here in 1862; railway; sauce, engineering, furniture, vehicle parts, porcelain, gloves; 14th-c cathedral; 11th-c Commandery founded by St Wulfstan; 18th-c Guildhall; Dyson Perrins Museum; Three Choirs Festival in rotation with Hereford and Gloucester (Sep). » English Civil War; Hereford and Worcester

Worcester porcelain Porcelain made at a factory in Worcester, England, founded in 1751 by John Wall (1708–76), and still manufacturing porcelain. The factory produced many useful wares especially in blue and white, but is noted for its lavishly enamelled and gilded pieces of the late 18th-c, and its Regency porcelain painted with flowers and figure subjects. » porcelain; Regency Style

word class A group of words which share several grammatical properties, such as the same kind of inflection or position in sentence structure; also known as **part of speech**. For example, the class of *nouns* consists of such words as *cat* and *table*, which have plurals in *-s*, can be preceded by the definite article, *the*, and can be used as subject and object in a sentence (*the cat/table looked nice*, *I see the cat/table*). The grouping of words into classes was first carried out by the Greeks, and the main classes (noun, verb, etc) have since been universally used in language description. » conversion (linguistics); derivation

word processor A computer program or computer system which allows the operator to enter text from a keyboard into a computer and to view it on the computer screen. Text can be readily manipulated in a large number of ways – to change the format, correct errors, make additions to existing text, etc – and can be printed by a device attached to the computer. The information produced by the computer can also be distributed on other media, such as floppy disks. Word processors are very widely used, and are replacing manual typewriters in many applications. » printer, computer; program, computer

Worde, Wynkyn de (?–?1535) London printer, born in Holland or in Alsace. He was a pupil of Caxton, and in 1491 succeeded to his stock-in-trade. He made great improvements in printing and typecutting, and was the first in England to use italic type. » Caxton; printing [i]

Wordsworth, Dorothy (1771–1855) William Wordsworth's sister, and lifetime companion, born at Cockermouth, Cumberland. Her *Journals* show a keen sensibility and acute observation of nature, which served both Wordsworth and Coleridge in their poems. In 1829 she suffered a breakdown from which she never fully recovered, and died at Rydal, Cumberland. » Coleridge; Wordsworth, William

Wordsworth, William (1770–1850) British poet, born at Cockermouth, Cumberland. Educated at Hawkshead in the Lake District and Cambridge, he went on a walking tour through France and Switzerland (1790). Back in France in 1790, he developed republican sentiments, and had an affair with a French girl, Annette Vallon, by whom he had a daughter. He returned to England at the outbreak of the war (1793), and after an unsettled period set up house at Racedown, Dorset, with his sister, Dorothy. There he discovered his true vocation, that of the poet exploring the lives of humble folk living in close contact with nature. After moving to Alfoxden, Somerset (1797), he wrote with Coleridge the *Lyrical Ballads* (1798), the first manifesto of the new Romantic poetry, which opened with Coleridge's *Ancient Mariner* and concluded with Wordworth's *Tintern Abbey*. After a year in Germany, he moved to Dove Cottage, Grasmere, married **Mary Hutchinson** in 1802, and wrote much of his best work, including his poetic autobiography, *The Prelude* (1805, published posthumously in 1850), and two books of poems (1807). Critics are inclined to mark the decline of his powers after this remarkable outpouring. He succeeded Southey as poet laureate in 1843, and died at Rydal Mount. » Coleridge; English literature; poetry; Romanticism (literature); Wordsworth, Dorothy

work The product of force and distance; symbol W, units J (joule). Applying a force F to an object over a distance d means work $W = Fd$ is done, equal to the object's increase in kinetic energy. The rate of doing work is *power*. » force; kinetic energy; power

work-hardening An alteration in the properties of a metal by repeated hammering, rolling, or other forming processes. The nature of the change depends on the initial crystal structure of the metal. The process may be deleterious, in producing brittleness, or advantageous, in increasing strength. The effects of work-hardening may be relieved by annealing. » annealing; metal

work study » **time and motion study**

work-to-rule » **industrial action**

workfunction The minimum energy which must be supplied to extract an electron from a solid; symbol Φ, units J (joule), or more often eV (electronvolt). It is a measure of how tightly electrons are bound to a material. For example, for copper, $\Phi = 4.4$ eV. » contact potential; electron; photoelectric effect

workhouse A building used for accommodation, and often employment, of the unemployed poor in Britain. Many workhouses had been built by groups (unions) of parishes in the 18th-c, but the workhouse gained special notoriety after the Poor Law Amendment Act (1834), when the policy was to build more workhouses, and place as many able-bodied paupers as possible in them. Here conditions were to be 'less eligible' than those which lowly-paid but independent labourers could experience. This workhouse policy was much criticized by radicals and reformers, who unearthed many 'workhouse scandals'. » Poor Laws

working dog A category of domestic dog, used for breeds developed to assist humans in non-sporting activities (eg sheepdogs, guard dogs, huskies); sometimes classed with *non-sporting dogs*. » dog; husky; non-sporting dog; sheepdog

Working Men's Clubs and Institutes Union In the UK, clubs that provide education and recreation for working men; originally founded as an alternative to the public house. The Union was created in 1862, the inspiration of the Rev Henry Solly; initially the clubs did not serve alcohol, but now provide it at a lower price than in public houses, which helps to contribute to the popularity. There are now over 2 400 such clubs.

works council » **industrial democracy**

Works Projects Administration (1935–43) A US federal agency established under President F. D. Roosevelt to combat unemployment during the Great Depression. Originally called the **Works Progress Administration**, it built transportation facilities, parks, and buildings. Some 8 500 000 people were employed during its history, including artists and writers as well as manual workers. » Great Depression; Roosevelt, Franklin D

World Bank » **International Bank for Reconstruction and Development**

World Council of Churches An inter-denominational Council of Churches, formed in Amsterdam in 1948. Originating in the ecumenical movement of the early 20th-c, its main task is to seek the unity of the Church. It comprises most of the main-line Christian denominations with the exception of the Roman Catholic Church, with which, however, it keeps close contact. Its headquarters is in Geneva, and its ruling body, a representative Assembly, meets every six or seven years. » Christianity; ecumenism

World Court » **International Court of Justice**

World Cup A term used to describe an international sporting competition. The soccer World Cup is the best known, and was first contested in Uruguay in 1930 for the Jules Rimet Trophy. In recent years other sports such as skiing, athletics, rugby league, rugby union, and cricket have inaugurated World Cup competitions. » football [i]

World Federation of Trade Unions (WFTU) An association of world trade union federations, set up in 1945. The democratic unions of W Europe and N America broke away in 1949, after a squabble with communist members. In the 1980s it contained some 55 affiliated national trade union federations, mainly from E Europe, dominated by the USSR. Its headquarters is in Prague. » International Confederation of Free Trade Unions

World Health Organization (WHO) A specialized agency formed in 1948 within the United Nations to advance international co-operation for the improvement in health of peoples in all countries. It is primarily concerned with the control of epidemic diseases, vaccination and other programmes, worldwide sanitation, and water supplies. It also acts as a clearing house for information on such topics as drugs, nuclear hazards, and cancer research. » medicine; United Nations

world heritage site A site (natural or cultural) recognized by the international community (in the shape of the World

Heritage Convention founded by the General Conference of UNESCO in 1972) as possessing universal value, and thus coming under a collective responsibility. A country nominates a site to the Convention, and a decision on whether to include it in the world heritage list is made by an international 21-member committee. In 1989 there were 110 states party to the convention, and 317 sites on the list. » conservation; environment; UNESCO

World Meteorological Organization » **United Nations**

World Series » **baseball** [i]

World Trade Center A complex of buildings occupying 6.5 ha/16 acres in Manhattan, New York City. Its two 110-storey skyscrapers were the world's tallest buildings from their completion in 1973, until topped by the Sears Tower a year later. » New York City

World War 1 (1914–18) A war whose origins lay in the reaction of other great powers to the ambitions of the German Empire after 1871. The resulting political tensions divided Europe into two camps, the Triple Alliance and the Triple Entente. The assassination of the heir to the Habsburg throne, Franz Ferdinand, at Sarajevo in Bosnia (28 Jun 1914), triggered the war. Austria declared war on Serbia (28 Jul); Russia mobilised in support of Serbia (29–30 Jul); and Germany declared war on Russia (1 Aug), and on France (3 Aug). The German invasion of neutral Belgium (4 Aug) brought the British into the war on the French side. Japan joined Britain, France, and Russia under the terms of an agreement with Britain (1902, 1911), and Italy joined the Allies in May 1915. Turkey allied with Germany (Nov 1914), and they were joined by Bulgaria (Oct 1915).

Military campaigning centred on France and Belgium in W Europe, and on Poland and W Russia in E Europe. The British Expeditionary Force and French army prevented the Germans, at the first battle of Ypres, from reaching the Channel ports. By the end of 1914, a static defence line had been established from the Belgian coast to Switzerland. The Allies attempted to break the stalemate by a campaign in Gallipoli (Apr 1915–Jan 1916), but failed. On the E and SE fronts, the Central Powers occupied Poland and most of Lithuania, and Serbia was invaded. For three years, an Allied army was involved in a Macedonian campaign, and there was also fighting in Mesopotamia against Turkey. Naval competition had played a crucial role in heightening tension before 1914, but in the event, the great battle fleets of Germany and Britain did not play an important part in the war. The only significant naval encounter, at Jutland in 1916, proved indecisive.

The Allies organized a large offensive for the W front in 1916, but were forestalled by the Germans, who attacked France at Verdun (Feb–Jul). To relieve the situation, the Battle of the Somme was launched, but proved indecisive. The Germans then unleashed unrestricted submarine warfare (Jan 1917) to cripple Britain economically before the USA could come to her aid. The USA declared war (2 Apr 1917) when British food stocks were perilously low, and the German submarine menace was finally overcome by the use of convoys. Tanks were used effectively by the Allies at the Battle of Cambrai (1917). In the spring of 1918, the Germans launched a major attack in the W, but were driven back, with the USA providing an increasing number of much-needed troops. By September, the German army was in full retreat, and signified its intention to sue for peace on the basis of President Wilson's Fourteen Points. By November, when the armistice was signed, the Allies had recaptured E Belgium and nearly all French territory. Military victories in Palestine and Mesopotamia resulted in a Turkish armistice (31 Oct 1918).

Estimated combatant war losses were: British Empire, just under 1 million: France, nearly 1.4 million; Italy, nearly ½ million; Russia, 1.7 million; USA, 115 000; Germany 1.8 million; Austria-Hungary 1.2 million, and Turkey 325 000. About double these numbers were wounded. » ANZAC; Central Powers; Fourteen Points; Gallipoli campaign; Marne/Passchendaele/Somme/Vimy Ridge/Ypres, Battle of; Paris Peace Conference **1**; reparations; Triple Entente; Versailles, Treaty of; Allenby; Beatty; Bethmann-Hollweg; Byng, Julian; Foch; French, John; Haig; Hindenburg, Pual von; Jellicoe; Joffre; Lloyd-George; Ludendorff; Pershing; Schlieffen; Tirpitz; William II (Emperor); Wilson, Woodrow

World War 2 (1939–45) A war whose origins lay in three different conflicts which merged after 1941: Germany's desire for European expansion; Japan's struggle against China; and a resulting conflict between Japanese ambitions and US interests in the Pacific. The origins of the war in Europe lay in German unwillingness to accept the frontiers laid down in 1919 by the Treaty of Versailles. After the German invasion of Czechoslovakia (Mar 1939), Britain and France pledged support to Poland. Germany concluded an alliance with Russia (Aug 1939), and then invaded Poland (1 Sep). Britain and France declared war on Germany (3 Sep), but could not prevent Poland from being overrun in four weeks. For six months there was a period of 'phoney war', when little fighting took place, but the Germans then occupied Norway and Denmark (Apr 1940), and Belgium and Holland were invaded (10 May). A combination of German tank warfare and air power brought about the surrender of Holland in four days, Belgium in three weeks, and France in seven weeks. There followed the Battle of Britain, in which Germany tried to win air supremacy over Britain, but failed. As a result, the planned invasion of Britain was postponed, and never subsequently took place. Germany launched submarine attacks against British supply routes, but then moved E and invaded Greece and Yugoslavia (Apr 1941). British military efforts were concentrated against Italy in the Mediterranean and N Africa. After early reverses for Italy, Rommel was sent to N Africa with the Afrika Corps to reinforce Italian military strength, and campaigning continued here for three years until Allied troops finally ejected German and Italian forces in mid-1943, invaded Sicily and then Italy itself, and forced Italy to make a separate peace (3 Sep 1943).

In June 1941, Germany invaded her ally Russia along a 2 000 mile front, and German armies advanced in three formations: to the outskirts of Leningrad in the N, towards Moscow in the centre, and to the Volga R in the S. After spectacular early successes, the Germans were held up by bitter Russian resistance, and by heavy winter snows and Arctic temperatures, for which they were completely unprepared. From November 1942 they were gradually driven back. Leningrad was under siege for nearly 2½ years (until Jan 1944), and about a third of its population died from starvation and disease. The Germans were finally driven out of Russia (Aug 1944). A second front was launched against Germany by the Allies (Jun 1944), through the invasion of Normandy, and Paris was liberated (25 Aug). Despite German use of flying bombs and rockets against British bases, the Allies advanced into Germany (Feb 1945) and linked with the Russians on the R Elbe (28 Apr). The Germans surrendered unconditionally at Rheims (7 May 1945).

In the Far East, Japan's desire for expansion led to her attack on Pearl Harbor and other British and US bases (7 Dec 1941), and the USA declared war against Japan the next day. In reply Japan's allies, Germany and Italy, declared war on the USA (11 Dec). Within four months, Japan controlled SE Asia and Burma. Not until June 1942 did naval victories in the Pacific stem the advance, and Japanese troops defended their positions grimly. Bitter fighting continued until 1945, when, with Japan on the retreat, the USA dropped two atomic bombs on Hiroshima and Nagasaki (6 and 9 Aug). Japan then surrendered (14 Aug).

Casualty figures are not easy to obtain accurately, but approximately 3 million Russians were killed in action, 3 million died as prisoners-of-war, 8 million people died in occupied Russia, and about 3 million in unoccupied Russia. Germany suffered 3¼ million military casualities, around 6 million total casualties, and lost a million prisoners of war. Japan suffered just over 2 million military casualties and just over ¼ million civilian deaths. France lost a total of ½ million dead, and Britain and her Commonwealth just over 600 000. The USA suffered just over 300 000 casualties. It is also estimated that in the course of the German occupation of a large part of Europe, about 6 million Jews were murdered in extermination and labour camps. » Afrika Corps; Allies; Anschluss; appeasement; Atlantic Charter; Atlantic Wall; Axis Powers; blitzkrieg; Chindits; D-Day; Desert Rats; Free

French; Gestapo; Holocaust; Home Guard; kamikaze; Lebensraum; Lend-Lease Agreement; Maginot Line; Munich Agreement; Normandy Campaign; North African Campaign; Nuremberg Trials; Pearl Harbor; Special Operations Executive; SS; Atlantic/Britain/Bulge, the/El Alamein/Plate, River/Stalingrad, Battle of; Casablanca/Paris Peace **2**/ Potsdam/Teheran/Yalta Conference; Anders; Alanbrook; Alexander (of Tunis); Auchinleck; Badoglio; Blamey; Bock; Bradley, Omar; Churchill, Winston; Dowding; Eisenhower; Goebbels; Goering; Himmler; Hitler; Horrocks; Jodl; Keitel; Kesselring; MacArthur; Mannerheim; Montgomery; Mountbatten, Louis; Mussolini; Nimitz; Patton; Pétain; Quisling; Raeder; Ribbentrop; Rommel; Roosevelt, Franklin D; Rundstedt; Slim; Stalin; Stilwell; Tedder; Timoshenko; Tojo; Wavell; Wilson, Henry Maitland; Wingate; Zhukov

World Wide Fund for Nature An international voluntary organization, founded in 1961 as the World Wildlife Fund, with its headquarters in Switzerland; International President, the Duke of Edinburgh. It aims to create awareness of the need for conservation of endangered wild animals, plants, and places, and promote the wise use of the world's natural resources. Examples include its campaigns to save the tiger, gorilla, and panda. It changed to its present name in 1988. » International Union for the Conservation of Nature and Natural Resources

World Wildlife Fund » **World Wide Fund for Nature**

World's View 20°30S 28°30E. The grave of Cecil John Rhodes in Matabeleland South province, Zimbabwe, 40 km/25 ml SW of Bulawayo. » Rhodes; Zimbabwe [i]

worm The common name for a wide range of long-bodied, legless invertebrate animals. » acornworm; annelid; arrow worm; beardworm; earthworm; fanworm; flatworm; guinea worm; horsehair worm; leech; lugworm; nematode; parchment worm; peanut worm; ragworm; ribbon worm; spoonworm; tapeworm; tongue worm

worm lizard » **amphisbaena**

Worms [vorms], ancient **Borbetomagus**, Eng [wermz] 49°38N 8°23E, pop (1983) 73 000. River port in Rheinhessen-Pfalz district, Germany; on R Rhine, 16 km/10 ml NNW of Mannheim; one of the oldest towns in Germany; capital of kingdom of Burgundy, 5th-c; scene of many Imperial Diets; badly bombed in World War 2; railway; sheeting and foils, chemicals; centre of the wine trade (notably for Liebfraumilch); cathedral (11th–12th-c). » Burgundy; Diet, Imperial; Germany [i]; Worms, Diet of

Worms, Diet of Meetings of the estates of the German empire in 1521 and 1545, which sealed the religious fate of 16th-c Germany. At the first, Luther was condemned, following papal declarations of heresy and excommunication (1520, 1521); at the second, an attempt to heal the religious divisions between Catholics and Lutherans failed amidst suspicion of papal intentions. » Lutheranism; Roman Catholicism; Worms

wormwood An aromatic perennial growing to 90 cm/3 ft, native to Europe and Asia, and often introduced elsewhere; leaves deeply cut, silvery on both sides with a covering of silky hairs; flower heads numerous, yellow, up to 3 mm/0.12 in across, drooping in a dense panicle. It is cultivated as a flavouring, and also used in the preparation of absinthe liqueur. (*Artemisia absinthium*. Family: *Compositae*.) » panicle; perennial

Wörther See [**vurt**er zay] Lake in SE Austria, W of Klagenfurt; area 18.8 sq km/7.2 sq ml; length 4 km/2½ ml; width 1.5 km/ 0.9 ml; maximum depth 86 m/282 ft; popular for water sports; chief lakeside town, Velden; fashionable resort, Kärnten. » Austria [i]

Worthing 50°48N 0°23W, pop (1987e) 97 400. Resort town coextensive with Worthing district, West Sussex, S England; 17 km/10 ml W of Brighton; once a fishing village, it developed into a fashionable coastal resort after its discovery by Princess Amelia, daughter of George III; railway; electronics, engineering, plastics, furniture, horticulture; Cissbury Ring (2 km/ 1¼ ml N), 3rd-c fort and Neolithic flint mines. » Sussex, West; Three Age System

Wotan » **Odin**

Wounded Knee The site in S Dakota of the final defeat of Sioux Indians (29 Dec 1890). The 'battle' was in fact a massacre by US troops, suppressing ceremonies inspired by the Paiute Indian religious leader Wovoka. » Indian Wars

woundwort An annual or perennial, found almost everywhere; square stems erect; leaves in opposite pairs; flowers 2-lipped, usually white to pink or purple with darker spots, in whorls. It had an old herbal use in salves for treating cuts; the hairy-leaved species was also used as lint. Some species produce edible tubers. (Genus: *Stachys*, 300 species. Family: *Labiatae*.) » annual; herb; perennial; tuber

Wouwermans, Philips [**vow**vuhmans] (1619–68) Dutch painter of battle and hunting scenes, born and died at Haarlem. His pictures are mostly small landscapes, with several figures in energetic action. His cavalry skirmishes, with a white horse generally in the foreground, were especially characteristic and popular. He had two brothers, also painters, **Peter** (1623–82) and **Jan** (1629–66), who chose similar subjects. » Dutch art

wrack » **Fucus**

Wrangel, Ferdinand Petrovitch, Baron von [**vrang**guhl] (1794–1870) Russian explorer, born at Pskov. He travelled in Arctic waters and on Siberian coasts, and made valuable surveys and observations. The island he nearly reached in 1821 was sighted in 1849, and named after him in 1867. Governor of Russian lands in Alaska (1829–35) and Naval Minister (1855–7), he retired in 1864, and died at Tartu.

Wrangel, Pyotr Nikolayevich, Baron [**vrang**guhl] (1878–1928) Russian army officer and Commander of White Russian forces during the Civil War, born at Aleksandrovsk, Lithuania, and educated at the St Petersburg Mining Institute. He entered military service in 1904 and commanded a cavalry corps during World War 1. In the Civil War, he commanded cavalry divisions and the Volunteer Army in the Ukraine, and in 1920 became Commander-in-Chief of the White armies in the S. After the Red Army victory, he fled to Turkey with the remnants of his troops. He died in Brussels, and was buried in Belgrade. » Russian Civil War; White Russians

Wrangel Island [**vran**gil], Russ **Ostrov Vrangelya** area 5 180 sq km/2 000 sq ml. Tundra-covered island in the W Chukchi Sea, near the NE extremity of Asia; length, 120 km/75 ml; width, 72 km/45 ml; rises to 1 097 m/3 599 ft; named after F P Wrangel (Vrangel), a 19th-c Russian navigator; ceded to Russia, 1924; government Arctic station and trading post; small settlements of Chukchi and Eskimo.

wrasse [ras] Any of a large group of mostly small colourful fishes widespread in tropical to temperate seas; length typically 10–30 cm/4–12 in; includes the European **ballan wrasse** (*Labrus bergylta*) and **cuckoo wrasse** (*Labrus mixtus*), found mainly around rocky coasts feeding on crustaceans and molluscs. (Family: *Labridae*, 15 genera.). » fish [i]

wreckfish Large heavy-bodied fish found mainly in the tropical Atlantic; length up to 2 m/6½ ft; also called **stonebass**. (*Polyprion americanus*. Family: *Serranidae*.) » fish [i]

wren A small songbird of the New World family *Troglodytidae* (**wrens**, c.65 species, one extending to the N Old World); name also used for *Maluridae* **Australian wrens/wren-warblers**, 26 species, including the **fairy** or **blue wrens**, **grasswrens**, and **emu-wrens**); *Xenicidae*, sometimes called *Acanthisittidae* (**New Zealand wrens**, 3 species); and for many small birds of other families. » emu wren; goldcrest; rifleman; songbird; warbler

Wren, Sir Christopher (1632–1723) English architect, born at East Knoyle, Wiltshire. Educated at Westminster and Oxford, in 1657 he became professor of astronomy at Gresham College, London, and in 1661 professor of astronomy at Oxford. After the Great Fire of London (1666), he drew designs for rebuilding the whole city, but his scheme was never implemented. In 1669 he designed the new St Paul's and many other churches and public buildings in London, such as the Royal Exchange and Greenwich Observatory. Knighted in 1672, he held posts at Windsor Castle and Westminster Abbey, and became an MP (1687). He died in London, and is buried in St Paul's. » architecture

Wren, P(ercival) C(hristopher) (1885–1941) British popular novelist, born in Devon. In the course of an adventurous early life he joined the French Foreign Legion, and this provided him with the background of several novels of adventure, notably *Beau Geste* (1924) and *Beau Sabreur* (1928). » English literature; novel

wren babbler A small babbler, found from India to SE Asia; inhabits woodland; eats mainly insects, some snails, possibly seeds. (Tribe: *Pomatorhinini*, 22 species.) » babbler

wren-warbler » **emu wren; warbler**

wrestling The sport of one man fighting against another, but without the use of fists. In most cases the object is to fell your opponent to the ground. Wrestling was contested at the Ancient Olympic Games. Many forms exist, the most popular amateur forms being *freestyle* and *Graeco-Roman*. In the latter, holds below the waist and the use of the legs are prohibited. Other forms include *Sambo*, which originated in Russia; *Sumo*, the national sport of Japan; British variations *Cumberland and Westmoreland* and *Devon and Cornwall*; *Kushti*, the national style of wrestling in Iran; *Glima*, practised in Iceland; *Schwingen*, practised in Switzerland; and *Yagli*, the national sport of Turkey. Female wrestling has also developed in recent years: women do not compete at championship level, but do take part in professional bouts. » judo; sumo wrestling; RR122

Wrexham [**rek**suhm] 53°03N 3°00W, pop (1981) 40928. Market centre in Wrexham Maelor district, Clwyd, NE Wales, UK; 20 km/12 ml SW of Chester; railway; coal, electronics, bricks, pharmaceuticals, food processing, metal goods; cathedral; 15th-c Church of St Giles. » Clwyd

Wright, Frank Lloyd (1867–1959) US architect, born at Richland Center, Wisconsin. He studied civil engineering at Wisconsin, where the collapse of a newly-built wing led him to apply engineering principles to architecture. He became known for his low-built, prairie-style residences, but soon launched out into more controversial designs, and is regarded as the leading designer of modern private dwellings, planned in conformity with the natural features of the land. Among his larger works are the Imperial Hotel in Tokyo and the Guggenheim Museum of Art in New York City. An innovator in the field of open planning, he died at Phoenix, Arizona. » architecture

Wright, Judith (1915–) Australian poet, born near Armidale, New South Wales. Educated at Sydney, she worked in educational administration in Queensland. She is valued for the broad sympathies of *The Moving Image* (1946), in which she was one of the first White writers to recognize aboriginal claims, and the personal lyrics of *Woman to Man* (1950). Her *Collected Poems* appeared in 1971. » Aborigines; Australian literature; poetry

Wright brothers US aviation pioneers: **Orville** (1871–1948), born and died at Dayton, Ohio, and his brother **Wilbur** (1867–1912), born near Millville, Indiana. They were the first to fly in a heavier-than-air machine (17 Dec 1903), at Kitty Hawk, North Carolina. Encouraged by this, they abandoned their cycle business and formed an aircraft production company (1909), of which Wilbur was president until his death, at Dayton. In 1915 Orville sold his interests in the company in order to devote himself to aeronautical research. » aeronautics; aircraft [i]

Wright, Peter » **intelligence service**

Wright, Richard (1908–60) US Black novelist, born at Natchez, Mississippi. Brought up in Memphis, he lived in Chicago (1928–45), and became a member of the Communist Party (1932–44). His disenchantment with this experience is the subject of *The God That Failed* (1950). He is most widely known for *Native Son* (1940), the first substantial novel of US Black revolt, and for his autobiography *Black Boy* (1945). Three other novels, including *The Outsider* (1953), were written after his move to Paris, where he died. » American literature; novel

wrist A region of the upper limb between the forearm and the hand, consisting of eight *carpal* bones arranged in two rows, one of which articulates with the radius and the other with the metacarpals. The two rows make an arch forming part of a tunnel (the *carpal tunnel*), which transmits nearly all the structures entering the hand (eg the long flexor tendons to the digits and the median nerve). Inflammation within the tunnel may cause compression of the median nerve (*carpal tunnel syndrome*) resulting in weakness of some of the thumb muscles, and loss of some sensation over the fingers. Similar symptoms may occur during the latter stages of pregnancy, when enlargement of the sheaths associated with the tendons compress the median nerve. The symptoms subside when the inflammation or swelling goes. » arm; hand

writing systems » **alphabet [i]; cuneiform [i]; epigraphy; graphology; hieroglyphics [i]; ideography; logography; pictography [i]; syllabary**

Wrocław [**vrots**waf], Ger **Breslau** 51°05N 17°00E, pop (1983) 631 500. River-port capital of Wrocław voivodship, W Poland, on R Oder; capital of lower Silesia; founded, 10th-c; first Polish publications printed here, 1745; badly damaged in World War 2; airport; railway junction; technical university (1945); shipyards, metallurgy, railway carriages, electronics, chemicals, clothes; pantomime theatre established by Henryk Tomaszewski; cathedral (13th-c), Church of St Mary Magdalene (13th–14th-c), national museum; international student theatre festivals, oratorio and cantata festival, festival of jazz. » Poland [i]

wrought iron A form of iron, of very low carbon content, once much used for forging, but now mostly replaced by steel. Pig-iron is melted with some addition of iron oxide to reduce the carbon content. As the iron becomes purer, the melting point rises and the iron becomes less fluid. It is worked around, and lumps are taken out of the furnace and hammered to remove slag, some of which remains as fibrous inclusions. Wrought iron is tougher than cast iron. Famous wrought iron structures were the SS *Great Britain* (1856) and the Eiffel Tower (1889). It is not much used now, except for decorative purposes. » carbon; cast iron

wrybill A small plover, native to New Zealand; bill straight when seen from side, but tip bends to right; inhabits river beds and sand flats; feeds by pointing head to right and sifting insects from surface of mud with bill. (*Anarhynchus frontalis*.) » plover

wryneck A short-billed, uncharacteristic woodpecker, native to Europe, Asia, and Africa; mottled brown; inhabits woodland and savannah; often feeds on ground; eats mainly ants; nests in holes of other woodpeckers. (Genus: *Jynx*, 2 species. Subfamily: *Jynginae*.) » woodpecker

Wu, Chien-Shiung (1912–) Chinese-US experimental physicist, born in Shanghai. Educated in China, and at Berkeley (from 1936), she became a staff member at Columbia, New York, in 1946. Her research has been in particle physics, notably her confirmation that some physical processes (such as beta particle emission) are not identical in a mirror-image system. » particle physics

Wu-lu-k'o-mu-shi » **Ürümqi**

Wu Peifu or Wu P'ei-fu [woo pay**foo**] (1874–1939) Major figure in the warlord struggles of China (1916–27), born in Shandong province. He joined the new army created by Yuan Shikai, and after Yuan's death (1916), when Duan Qirui sought to reunite China by force and in dependence on Japan, Wu and other N generals refused Duan's orders. In the civil war which followed, he was unable to sustain his government of national unity (1923). He died in Japanese-occupied Beijing (Peking). » Duan Qirui; warlords; Yuan Shikai

Wu Yue, Eng **The Five Holy Mountains** [**woo** yoo**ay**] Collective name for five mountains in China, regarded in Chinese legend as the gathering places of the gods; Tai Shan in Shandong province (1 545 m/5 069 ft), Hua Shan in Shaanxi province (2 154 m/7 067 ft), Song Shan in Henan province (1 512 m/4 961 ft), Heng Shan in Hunan province (1 290 m/4 232 ft), and Heng Shan in Shanxi province (2016 m/6 614 ft). » China [i]

Wuhan, Han-kow, or **Han-kou** 30°35N 114°19E, pop (1984e) 3 337 500. Inland port and capital of Hubei province, EC China; at confluence of Han Shui and Yangtze Rivers; union (1950) of three municipalities of Wuchang, Hankou, Hanyang; commercial centre of C China; airfield; railway; Wuhan university (1913); Central China Engineering Institute; iron, steel, fertilizer, limestone, machine tools, cotton, fisheries; Guiyuan Buddhist Temple (c.1600), now a museum; Changjiang Bridge (first modern bridge to cross the Yangtze R, 1957); Red Hill Park in Wuchang, with Yuan dynasty pagoda (1307–15). » China [i]; Yuan dynasty

Wuhsien » **Suzhou**

Wulfila » **Ulfilas**

Wundt, Wilhelm (Max) [vunt] (1832–1920) German physiologist and psychologist, born at Neckarau. He taught at Heidelberg and Zürich, then became professor of physiology at Leipzig (1875). A distinguished experimental psychologist, he wrote on the nerves and the senses, and the relations between physiology and psychology. He died at Grossbothen, Germany.

Wuppertal [**vu**pertahl] 51°15N 7°10E, pop (1983) 386 000. Industrial city in Düsseldorf district, Germany; on R Wupper in the Ruhr valley, 26 km/16 ml ENE of Düsseldorf; includes the former towns of Barmen, Elberfeld, and Vohwinkel; university (1972); textiles, brewing, plastics, electronics, packaging, lime, metalworking. » Germany [i]; Ruhr, River

Würzburg [**vürts**boork] 49°48N 9°57E, pop (1983) 129 500. Industrial city in Unterfranken district, Germany; on R Main, 96 km/60 ml ESE of Frankfurt am Main; railway; university (1582); engineering, chemicals, machine tools; centre of wine production and trade in Franconia; cathedral (11th–13th-c), St Mary's chapel (1377–1479), Old Main bridge (1473–1543), Marienberg (fortress, 13th-c); Würzburg Residence (episcopal palace built by Balthasar Neumann, 1719–44), a world heritage site. » Germany [i]; Neumann, Balthasar

Wyatt, James (1746–1813) British architect, born at Burton Constable, Staffordshire. He visited Italy for several years, and achieved fame with his Neoclassical design for the London Pantheon (1772). He became surveyor to the Board of Works (1796), restored several cathedrals, and designed many country houses. His best-known work is the Gothic revival Fonthill Abbey (1796–1807), which largely collapsed in the 1820s. He died near Marlborough, Wiltshire. » Gothic architecture

Wyatt, Sir Thomas (1503–42) English courtier and poet, born at Allington, Kent. Educated at Cambridge, he was warmly received at court, knighted (1536), made high sheriff of Kent (1537), and went on several diplomatic missions. In 1557 his poems, published in *Tottel's Miscellany*, helped to introduce the Italian sonnet and other forms into English literature. He died at Sherborne, Dorset. » English literature; poetry; sonnet

Wycherley, William [**wich**uhlee] (c.1640–1716) English dramatist, born at Clive, Shropshire. He studied at France and Oxford, became a lawyer, then lived as a courtier and turned to writing. He wrote several satirical comedies, notably *The Country Wife* (1675) and *The Plain Dealer* (1677), both based on plays by Molière. He was imprisoned for debt, but was finally given a pension by James II, and died in London. » comedy; drama; English literature; Molière; satire

Wycliffe or **Wicliffe, John** [**wik**lif] (c.1330–84) English religious reformer, born near Richmond, Yorkshire. He was educated at Oxford, where he taught philosophy, then entered the Church, becoming rector of Lutterworth, Leicestershire in 1374. He was sent to Bruges to treat with ambassadors from the Pope about ecclesiastical abuses, but his views were found unacceptable, and he was prosecuted. He then attacked the Church hierarchy, priestly powers, and the doctrine of transubstantiation, wrote many popular tracts in English (as opposed to Latin), and issued the first English translation of the Bible. His opinions were condemned, and he was forced to retire to Lutterworth, where he wrote prolifically until his death. The characteristic of his teaching was its insistence on inward religion in opposition to the formalism of the time. His followers were known as 'Lollards', and the influence of his teaching was widespread in England, in many respects anticipating the Reformation. » Bible; Lollards; Reformation; transubstantiation

Wye, River **1** River rising on Plynlimon, C Wales; flows 208 km/129 ml SE and E through Powys, Hereford, and along the Gwent–Gloucestershire border to meet the R Severn estuary S of Chepstow; notable for its valley scenery; fishing. **2** River rising in Buckinghamshire, SC England; flows 15 km/9 ml SE to meet the R Thames at Bourne End. **3** River rising near Buxton in Derbyshire, C England; flows 32 km/20 ml SE to join the R Derwent at Rowsley. » England [i]

Wyler, William (1902–81) US film director, born at Mulhouse, Alsace (then in Germany). He emigrated to the USA in 1922, where he worked on many sides of film-making before becoming a director of Western shorts and low budget productions. In 1935 his association with the producer Sam Goldwyn resulted in several successes, including the Oscar-winning *Mrs Miniver* (1942) and *The Best Years of Our Lives* (1946). His later productions covered a wide field, including *Friendly Persuasion* (1956), *Ben Hur* (1959) for which he won another Academy Award, and *Funny Girl* (1968). He died at Beverley Hills, California.

Wyndham, John, pseudonym of **John Wyndham Parkes Lucas Beynon Harris** (1903–69) British science-fiction writer, born at Knowle, Warwickshire. He worked at a variety of jobs, then in the late 1920s began to write science-fiction tales for popular magazines, achieving fame with his first novel, *The Day of the Triffids* (1951). His other books include *The Kraken Wakes* (1953), *The Chrysalids* (1955), and *The Midwich Cuckoos* (1957), as well as collections of short stories, such as *The Seeds of Time* (1969). He died in London. » novel; science fiction; short story

Wynkyn de Worde » **Worde, Wynkyn de**

Wyoming [wiy**oh**ming] pop (1987e) 490 000; area 253 315 sq km/97 809 sq ml. State in W USA, divided into 23 counties; the 'Equality State'; most of the region acquired by the USA from France in the Louisiana Purchase, 1803; Spain, Britain, and the Republic of Texas all laid claims to other parts; total American jurisdiction 1848; Wyoming Territory established, 1868; major growth after the arrival of the railway, 1868; first territory or state to adopt women's suffrage, 1869; admitted to the Union as the 44th state, 1890; conflicts between cattle and sheep ranchers in the 1890s; contains the Wind River Indian reservation; capital, Cheyenne; Casper the other chief city; a sparsely populated state; rivers include the Snake, Yellowstone, Green, N Platte; Wind River Range in the W, Absaroka Range, Teton Mts, Bighorn Mts in the N; all form part of the Rocky Mts (largely forested); highest point Gannett Peak (4 201 m/13 782 ft); eroded 'badlands' in the extreme NE; higher tablelands in the SE; in the SW, South Pass the natural gateway through the Rocky Mts; ranching and farming on the fertile Great Plains (E); cattle, sheep, sugar-beets, dairy produce, wool, hay, barley; an important mining state; oil, natural gas, sodium salts, uranium, coal, gold, silver, iron, copper; very little manufacturing (petroleum products, timber, food processing); major tourist area (hunting, fishing, rodeos); two national parks at Grand Teton and Yellowstone. » Cheyenne; Louisiana Purchase; Rocky Mountains; United States of America [i]; Yellowstone; RR39

WYSIWYG [**wi**seewig] An acronym of **what you see is what you get**, used to refer to those computer systems, usually word processors or desk-top publishing systems, where the display on the screen exactly mimics the final result produced by the printer. » desk-top publishing; word processor

Wyss, Johann Rudolf [vees] (1781–1830) Swiss writer, born and died at Berne. He is best known for his completion and editing of *Der Schweizerische Robinson* (1812–13, The Swiss Family Robinson), written by his father, **Johann David Wyss**. He collected Swiss tales and folklore, and was professor of philosophy at Berne from 1806. » folklore; novel

Wyszyński, Stefan [vi**shin**ski] (1901–81) Polish cardinal, born at Zuzela. Educated at Włocławek and Lublin, he was ordained in 1924, and became Bishop of Lublin (1946), Archbishop of Warsaw and Gniezno (1948), and a cardinal (1952). Following his indictment of the communist campaign against the Church, he was imprisoned (1953). Freed in 1956, he agreed to a reconciliation between Church and state under the Gomułka regime, but relations remained uneasy. He died in Warsaw. » communism; Gomułka

wytch elm » **elm**

X

X-ray astronomy A general term for the study of the X-rays from cosmic sources. It needs satellite-borne instruments, because X-rays do not penetrate our atmosphere. Sources studied include the Crab Nebula, binary stars in which transfer of mass is taking place, and active galactic nuclei. » astronomy; X-rays

X-ray diffraction An interference effect in which atoms in a material scatter X-rays to give a pattern of spots or concentric rings. These may be detected photographically, and their position and intensity can be used to determine the material's structure. The technique was discovered by German physicist Max von Laue in 1912. » diffraction [i]; solid; synchrotron radiation; X-rays

X-ray laser A source of X-rays produced by laser action. They can be produced from cylindrical arrays of wires mounted around a nuclear explosive device, powered by the explosion. The alternative relies on exciting inner electrons of certain heavy atoms using ultraviolet lasers. The technique is experimental only. » laser [i]; X-rays

X-rays Invisible electromagnetic radiation having a much shorter wavelength than light, between 10^{-8} and 3×10^{-11} metres; discovered by German physicist Wilhelm Röntgen in 1895, and originally called **Röntgen rays**. They are produced by the transitions of electrons in the inner levels of excited atoms, or by the rapid deceleration of charged particles. A common means of production is by firing electrons into a copper target. X-rays are useful in medicine, since different components of the body absorb X-rays to a different extent, but enough radiation passes through the body to register on a photograhic plate beyond. » atomic spectra [i]; bremsstrahlung; electromagnetic radiation [i]; exposure; synchrotron radiation; X-ray astronomy/diffraction/laser

X–Y plotter A form of pen recorder where one or more pens can be placed anywhere on the drawing surface. This allows complicated drawings and text to be produced. » computer graphics

Xanthophyceae [zanthoh**fi**ysee-ee] » **yellow-green algae**

Xavier, St Francis » **Francis Xavier, St**

Xenakis, Iannis [ze**nah**kees] (1922–) Greek composer, born at Braila, Romania. He studied engineering in Athens and worked as an architect for Le Corbusier in Paris. He did not turn to musical composition until 1954, with *Metastasis* for orchestra, and went on to develop a highly complex style which incorporated mathematical concepts of chance and probability (so-called *stochastic music*), as well as electronic techniques. His works are mainly instrumental and orchestral. » electronic music; Corbusier, Le

xenoglossia [zenuh**glo**sia] » **glossolalia**

xenon [**ze**non] Xe, element 54, boiling point −107°C. The fifth of the noble gases recovered from the atmosphere, of which it makes up only 0.000009%. Like the other noble gases, it is used in gas discharge tubes. It forms the most extensive range of compounds of any noble gas, showing oxidation states of +2, +4, +6, and +8. Its fluorides, especially XeF_2, are used as fluoridating agents. » chemical elements; fluoride; noble gases; RR90

Xenophanes [ze**no**faneez] (c.570–c.480 BC) Greek philosopher, born at Colophon, Ionia. He travelled extensively, perhaps spending considerable time in Sicily. He attacked traditional Greek conceptions of the gods, arguing against anthropomorphism and polytheism. » anthropomorphism; polytheism

Xenophon [**ze**nuhfuhn] (c.435–354 BC) Greek historian, essayist, and soldier, born and died at Attica. A friend and pupil of Socrates, in 401 he served with a group of 10 000 Greek mercenaries under Persian Prince Cyrus, who was fighting against his brother, the King of Persia. After Cyrus was killed, the Greeks were isolated over 1500 km/900 ml from home. Xenophon was elected leader, and the group successfully fought their way back to the Black Sea. This heroic feat formed the basis of his major work, *Anabasis Kyrou* (The Expedition of Cyrus). » Socrates

xenopus [**zen**uhpuhs] » **clawed toad**

xerographic printer In computing, a printer which uses electrostatic techniques to provide text and/or graphics. Most photocopiers are of this type. Laser printers generally use this basic technology, which has the advantage of being silent, and capable of very high quality reproduction. » printer, computer; xerography [i]

xerography [ze**ro**grafee] The most widely used method of photocopying, first devised in the late 1930s by US physicist Chester F Carlson, but not developed commercially until the 1950s. A photoconductive surface is charged and exposed to the image to be copied; the charge is lost except in the image areas. The secondary image so produced is developed with a charged pigment which is transferred to copy paper and fixed by heat. Using this technique, it is possible to print on both sides of the paper, vary the size of the original image, and (since the 1970s) reproduce coloured images. The name derives from the Greek words meaning 'dry writing'. » electrostatics; photoconductivity; photocopying

Xerxes I [**zerk**seez] (c.519–465 BC) Achaemenid king of Persia (485–465 BC), the son of Darius I. He is remembered in the West mainly for the failure of his forces against the Greeks in the Second Persian War at Salamis, Plataea, and Mycale. » Darius I; Persian Wars

X400 One of a series of standards, denoted by X codes, recommended by the CCITT (Comité Consultatif International de Téléphonie et de Télégraphie), covering the attachment of various terminals to public data networks. X400 is a message-handling system standard. It should enable dissimilar equipment, such as telex, word-processors and computers, to handle electronic mail. » electronic mail; telegraphy; word processor

Xhosa [**koh**sa] A cluster of Bantu-speaking peoples of the Transkei and Ciskei, South Africa, including the Ngqika, Gcaleka, and others who fled from Zulu armies in the early 1800s. They are mixed farmers, although many work today as migrant labourers, and are settled permanently in urban centres. Xhosa is the most widely spoken African language in

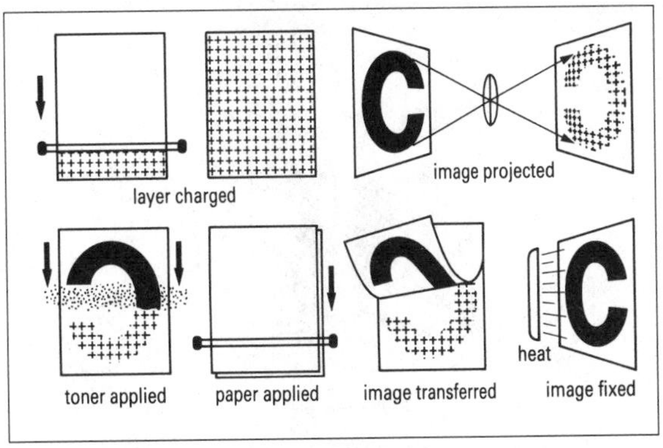

Stages in the xerographic process

South Africa. Population c.5.5 million. » Bantu-speaking peoples; click language; Nguni

Xi'an or **Sian** [shee**ahn**], formerly **Changan**, **Siking** 34°16N 108°54E, pop (1984e) 2 276 500. Capital of Shaanxi province, C China; first capital of feudal China; many pagodas from Tang dynasty; airport; railway; university (1937); tourism, heavy industry, cotton, food processing, chemicals, electrical equipment, fertilizers; Ming Dynasty Drum Tower, 14th-c Bell Tower, Banpo Neolithic village (10 km/6 ml E); tumulus of Emperor Qin Shihuangdi (30 km/18 ml E); terracotta warriors of Emperor Qin, discovered 1974; Big Wild Goose pagoda (652); Great Mosque (742); Hua Qing hot springs, scene of the Xi'an incident (1936); Zhaoling, tomb of Tang Emperor Tia Zong. » China [i]; Qin dynasty; Qin Shihuangdi Mausoleum; Tang dynasty; Xi'an incident

Xi'an incident In Dec 1936 Jiang Jieshi (Chiang Kai-shek) was held hostage in Xi'an by one of his own commanders, the 'young marshal' Zhang Xueliang, who demanded an anti-Japanese united front. He was released only on the intervention of Zhou Enlai (Chou En-lai). A united front of communist and nationalist forces resulted. » Chiang Kai-shek; Chou En-lai; United Fronts; Xi'an

Xiamen, **Hsia-men**, or **Amoy** [shah**men**] 24°26N 118°07E, pop (1984e) 532 600. Subtropical port city in Fujian province, SE China; on island in Taiwan Strait at mouth of Jiulong R; connected to mainland by 5 km/3 ml-long causeway (1949); first settled during S Song dynasty (1127–1279); made an open port, 1842; designated a special economic zone, 1981; new harbour; airfield; railway; university (1921); electronics, food products, textiles, building materials; centre of growing unofficial trade between China and Taiwan; 5 km/3 ml E, 10th-c Nanputo Temple; Overseas Chinese Museum. » China [i]; Opium Wars; Taiwan [i]

Xingu [**sheeng**goo] National park in NE Mato Grosso state, WC Brazil; crossed by branches of the Xingu R (length c.1 980 km/1 230 ml), a S tributary of the Amazon; created in 1961 by the Vilas Boas brothers to protect the Indian tribes, but in recent years it has suffered from property developers, and new roads now threaten the continued existence of the tribes living there. » Brazil [i]

Xinhua The national news agency of the People's Republic of China, with headquarters in Beijing (Peking). Established as the communist Red China News Agency in 1929, and renamed *Hsin Hua* in 1937 (Xinhua since 1979), it is sometimes known nowadays as the New China News Agency. » news agency

Xining [shee**ning**], **Hsining**, or **Sining** 36°35N 101°55E, pop (1984e) 576 400. Capital of Qinghai province, WC China; NW of Lanzhou; airfield; railway; chemicals, metal, leather. » China [i]

Xizang [shit**sang**] or **Tibet** pop (1986) 2 030 000; area 1 221 600 sq km/471 538 sq ml. Autonomous region in SW China; S and W border includes Bhutan, India, and Nepal; in the Tibet Plateau, average altitude 4 000 m/13 000 ft; Himalayas in the S, on borders with India, Nepal, and Bhutan, rising to 8 848 m/29 028 ft at Mt Everest; Kunlun Shan range in the N; major farming area in S valleys; several rivers and lakes (largest salt-water lake, Nam Co, NW of Lhasa); capital, Lhasa; wheat, peas, rapeseed; sheep, yak and goat raising, forestry, medicinal musk, caterpillar fungus, textiles; mining of chromium, iron, copper, lead, zinc, borax, salt, mica, gypsum; dominated by Buddhist lamas since 7th-c AD until departure of Dalai Lama into exile (1959); conquered by Mongols, 1279–1368; controlled by Manchus, 18th-c; Chinese rule restored in 1951, and full control asserted after revolt in 1959; most monasteries and temples now closed or officially declared historical monuments, but many people still worship daily; thought to be fewer than 1 000 lamas in Xizang, compared to almost 110 000 monks in 2 500 monasteries prior to 1959. » Buddhism; China [i]; Dalai Lama; Manchu; Tibet Plateau

xylem [**ziy**luhm] A tissue composed of several types of conducting cells and supporting fibres which transports water and minerals up from the roots to all other parts of a plant. Located in the vascular bundles, the cells die when mature. They form the 'wood' of woody plants. » vascular tissue; wood

xylenes [**ziy**leenz] $C_6H_4(CH_3)_2$. A mixture of three isomers of dimethylbenzene, all of which occur in coal tar, and all of which boil at c.140°C. The mixture is used as a solvent, especially in preparations for microscopy, and as a starting material for the production of phthalic acids for polymers. » coal tar; isomers

xylophone A percussion instrument known in various forms since the 14th-c. The modern orchestral instrument has two rows of wooden bars arranged like a piano keyboard, with a compass of 3½–4 octaves. These are mounted over tubular resonators and played with hard wooden sticks. » marimba; percussion [i]

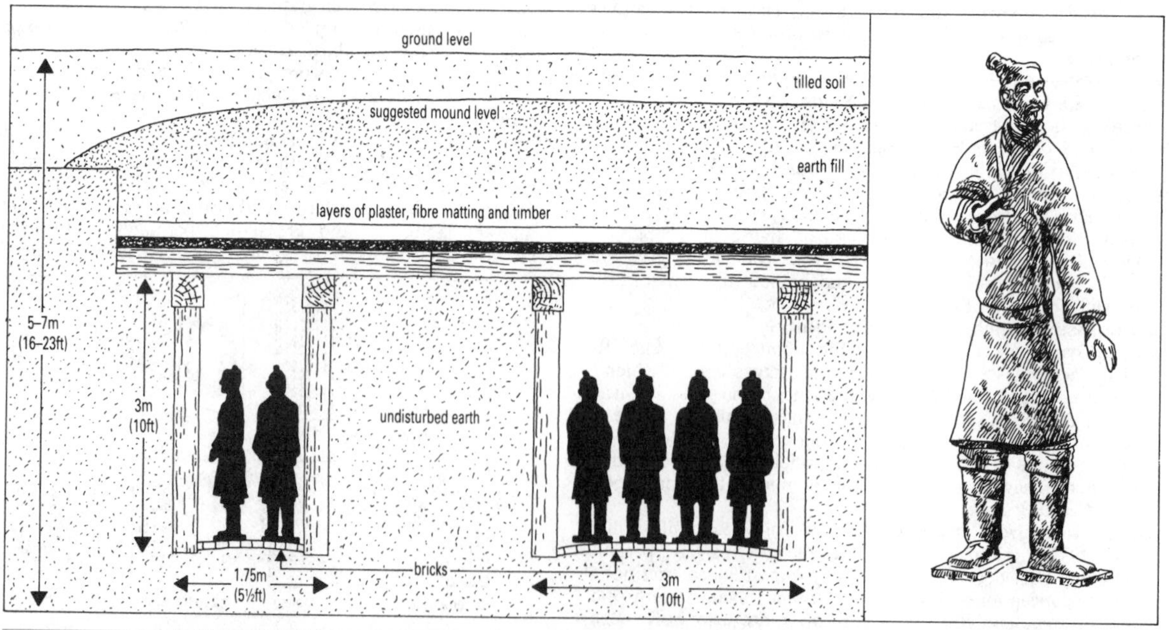

Xi'an – Cross section to show the method of burial for the terracotta warriors. The inset illustration shows one warrior (a standing crossbowman) in detail.

yacht A sailing or power-driven vessel used for the pleasure of the owner, derived from the Dutch *jacht*, a small, fast vessel. Charles II received one as a gift from the Dutch at the conclusion of his exile in Holland in 1660. The first known yacht race was between Charles II and his brother James in 1661 from Greenwich to Gravesend and back. Yachting increased steadily in popularity throughout the 19th-c, and received a great boost from the continuing interest of Edward Prince of Wales and other royals. The biggest growth period has been since 1960 throughout the developed world. » America's Cup; sailing

Yahweh [**yah**way] or **YHWH** The name of the God of Israel, perhaps deriving from Israel's experiences at Sinai, although also found in Biblical stories of the patriarchs. The name is usually taken to mean 'He is/will be', 'He comes to be/creates', or 'He causes to fall'. The unvocalized YHWH (known as the **Tetragrammaton**) is considered by Jews too sacred to pronounce aloud, except by the high priest in the Holy of Holies on the Day of Atonement, and is usually replaced orally by Adonai ('Lord') when it is read from the Bible. Christians erroneously vocalized it as Jehovah. » Bible; Elohim; God; Holy of Holies; Jehovah

yak A member of the cattle family, native to the high Tibetan Plateau; thick shaggy brown coat; white muzzle; widely spread upturned horns; domesticated yak highly-strung and stubborn; females crossbred with male domestic cattle or zebu; hybrid offspring (a *dzo*) economically important as draught animals, but males are sterile. (*Bos mutus*; domestic form sometimes called *Bos grunniens*.) » Bovidae; cattle; ox; zebu

Yakshagana [jakshah**gah**na] A literary and theatrical tradition of Karnataka, on the W coast of India. Developed from the conventions of Sanskrit theatre, it has been influenced greatly by Kannada literature. It lacks the intricate language of hand-gestures and eye-gestures of the classical stage, but has evolved a distinctive system of symbolic make-up and costuming. » Sanskrit theatre

yakuza [**ya**kooza] A Japanese gangster. Like the Sicilian Mafia, its Western equivalent, Japanese organized crime has a long history. Gangsters belong to recognized groups (*boryokudan*). Often tattooed, gangsters cultivate a samurai-like loyalty and are proud of their traditions. Like the Mafia, they are widely involved in such activities as gambling, extortion, racketeering, and the 'protection' of pachinko halls. » pachinko; samurai

Yakut A Turkic-speaking Mongoloid people of NE Siberia, and the main group in the area. Despite the severe climate, they are sedentary cattle and reindeer herders, and fishermen, and are now fully assimilated to the Russian way of life. They call themselves *Sakha*. Population c.328 000 (1979). » Siberia

Yale University » Ivy League [i]

Yalow, Rosalyn (Sussman) (1912–) US medical physicist, born in New York City. Educated there and at Illinois, she joined the Veterans Administration Hospital in New York City in 1947. In the 1950s she devised the technique of radioimmunoassay, whereby even minute amounts of a hormone can be measured accurately. She shared the Nobel Prize for Physiology or Medicine in 1977. » endocrine glands; hormones; radioimmunoassay

INTERNATIONAL RACING YACHT CLASSES

CLASS	CREW	TYPE OF CRAFT
Finn	1	Centre board dinghy
Flying Dutchman	2	Centre board dinghy
International 470	2	Centre board dinghy
International Soling	3	Keel boat
International Star	2	Keel boat
International Tornado	2	Catamaran
Windglider	1	Single board

Yalta Conference A meeting at Yalta, in the Crimea, during World War 2 (4–11 Feb 1945), between Churchill, Stalin, and Roosevelt. Among matters agreed were the disarmament and partition of Germany, the Russo-Polish frontier, the establishment of the United Nations, and the composition of the Polish government. In a secret protocol it was also agreed that Russia would declare war on Japan after the war with Germany ended. » Churchill, Winston; Curzon Line; reparations; Roosevelt, Franklin D; Stalin; World War 2

Yalu, River [ya**loo**] River forming the N border between North Korea and NE China; rises in the Changbai Shan range; flows S, W, then SW to form most of the border between North Korea and China; flows into Korea Bay; length 790 km/490 ml. » Korea, North [i]

yam A tuberous perennial, native to tropical and subtropical regions; climbing aerial stems annual, twining; leaves often heart-shaped; flowers small, white or greenish, in axillary clusters. Some 60 species are important food plants, especially in SE Asia, W Africa, and S America, where they are cultivated for the starchy tubers weighing up to 9 kg/20 lb and propagated like potatoes. In recent years some species have become important as a source of a steroid-type chemical used in oral contraceptives. (Genus: *Dioscorea*. Family: *Dioscoriaceae*.) » perennial; steroid [i]; sweet potato; tuber

Yamagata, Prince Aritomo (1838–1922) Japanese general, statesman, and Prime Minister (1890–1, 1898–1900), born at Hagi. He was adviser to the Emperor, War Minister (1873), and Chief-of-Staff (1878). His modernization of the military system led to the defeat of China (1894–5) and Russia (1904–5), and the emergence of Japan as a significant force in world politics. He died in Tokyo.

Yamamoto, Yohji [yama**moh**toh] (1943–) Japanese fashion designer, born in Tokyo. He studied at Pawat Kaio University, then helped his mother with her dress shop. He started his own company in 1972, producing his first collection in Tokyo in 1976. After some time in Paris he opened a new headquarters in London in 1987. He designs loose, functional clothes for men and women, featuring a great deal of black, which conceal rather than emphasize the body. » fashion

Yamashita, Yashiro (1957–) Japanese judo fighter, born at Kyushu. He won nine consecutive Japanese titles (1977–85), the Olympic open class gold medal (1984), and four world titles: 1979, 1981, 1983 (over 95 kg class), and 1981 (open class). He retired in 1985 after 203 consecutive bouts without defeat from 1977. He was 5 ft 11 in/180.3 cm tall, and weighed 280 lb/127 kg. » judo

Yamoussoukro [yamoo**soo**kroh] 6°49N 5°17W, pop (1983) 70 000. Capital of Côte d'Ivoire, in Bouaké department; agricultural trade, fishing, forestry, perfumes; weekend resort town, NW of Abidjan; presidential residence. » Abidjan; Côte d'Ivoire [i]

Yamuna or **Jumna, River** [**yah**muna] River of NW India; rises in the Himalayas of N Uttar Pradesh; flows SW to Delhi, then generally SE to join the R Ganges; length 1 370 km/850 ml; confluence with the Ganges is one of the most sacred Hindu places; Taj Mahal at Agra on its banks. » Ganges, River; Hinduism; India [i]

Yang, Chen Ning (1922–) US physicist, born in Hofei, China. He gained a scholarship to Chicago in 1945, was professor at the Institute for Advanced Studies, Princeton (1955–65), and then at New York State University Center. He specialized in particle physics, and with T-D Lee disproved the established physical principle known as the parity law, for which they shared the 1957 Nobel Prize for Physics. » Lee, Tsung-Dao; parity (physics)

Yangchow » **Yangzhou**

Yangku » **Taiyuan**

Yangon » **Rangoon**

Yangtze River [**yang**ksee] or **Yangtse-kiang**, also **Chang Jiang** Longest river in China and third longest in the world; length c.6 300 km/3 900 ml; rises in the Tanggula Shan range; flows E as the Tongtian He, then S as the Jinsha Jiang, becoming the Yangtze after Yibin in S Sichuan; flows NE through the Sichuan basin, a series of gorges, and across the Hubei plain to enter the E China Sea at Shanghai; drainage area, over 1 800 000 sq km/694 800 sq ml; provides c.40% of China's electricity; Gezhouba Dam near Yichang one of the largest in the world; major transportation artery between E and W China, navigable for over 940 km/580 ml; bridges at Chongqing, Wuhan, and Nanjing facilitate N–S communication; densely populated river basin contains about a quarter of China's cultivated land; numerous mineral deposits. » China [i]

Yangzhou or **Yangchow** [yang**joh**] 32°25N 119°26E, pop (1984e) 382 200. City in Jiangsu province, E China, on Yangtze and Hua Rivers; first settled during Spring and Autumn Period (770–476 BC); major communications centre after building of Grand Canal, 6th-c AD; largest multiple-purpose water control project in China (1961–75); artistic centre for crafts, lacquerware screens, jade carving and printing; Fajing Si (Tang dynasty temple), museum. » China [i]; Grand Canal

Yao (of Africa) A cluster of agricultural Bantu-speaking peoples of Tanzania, Malawi, and Mozambique, organized into many small chiefdoms. They were famous 19th-c traders between the Arab-dominated coast and inland. Because of the slave trade they clashed with European colonial powers. The majority are Muslims. Population c.1 million. » Bantu-speaking peoples

Yao (of China and SE Asia) A mountain village people of SE Asia, dispersed and culturally diverse. Most are farmers who trade with people from the lowlands, although in China some are wet-rice cultivators. Population 1.2 million in China, 5 000 in Thailand, and 370 000 in Vietnam and Laos.

Yaoundé or **Yaundé** [yao**on**day] 3°51N 11°31E, pop (1984) 552 000. Capital of Cameroon, W Africa; 210 km/130 ml E of Douala; established as military post by Germans in 1899; occupied by Belgian colonial troops, 1915; capital of French Cameroon, 1921; airport; railway to the coast (Douala); university (1962); football stadium (1972); tourism, sugar refining, cigarettes, oil refining. » Cameroon [i]

Yap pop (1980) 8 172; area 119 sq km/46 sq ml. One of the Federated States of Micronesia, W Pacific; comprises the four large islands of Yap, Gagil-Tomil, Map, and Rumung, with some 130 outer islands; airport; capital, Colonia; copra, tropical fruit. » Micronesia, Federated States of

yapok [ya**pok**] A marsupial native to C and S America; slender with long legs, pointed head, long naked tail; inhabits freshwater; the only truly semiaquatic marsupial; hind feet webbed; female has watertight backward opening pouch; eats fish and large crustaceans; also known as **water opossum**. (*Chironectes minimus*. Family: *Didelphidae*.) » marsupial [i]; opossum

yarn The spun thread from which woven, knitted, and other fabrics are manufactured. Yarns vary widely in their properties, depending upon fibre content, count, and the spinning process used. » bulked yarn; count (textiles); twist

Yaroslavl [yaruh**slafl**] 57°34N 39°52E, pop (1989) 633 000. River-port capital of Yaroslavskaya oblast, E European Russia; oldest town on the R Volga, founded c.1024; railway; university (1971); textiles, synthetic rubber, tyres, lorries, diesel engines, chemicals, leather, tobacco, oil refining; Spaso-Preobrazhenski Monastery (12th-c). » Russia

yarrow A perennial growing to 60 cm/2 ft, native to Europe and W Asia, but now widely introduced elsewhere; leaves lance-shaped in outline, finely divided; flower heads numerous, in dense, flat-topped clusters; five outer ray florets, white or sometimes pink; also called **milfoil**. It was formerly employed extensively in herbal medicine. (*Achillea millefolium*. Family: *Compositae*.) » herb; perennial

Yates, Dornford, pseudonym of **Cecil William Mercer** (1885–1960) British novelist, born in London. Educated at Harrow and Oxford, he achieved great popularity with an entertaining series of fanciful escapist adventure fiction, such as *Berry and Co* (1921). » novel

Yavneh [yavne] » **Jabneh**

yawl » **ketch** [i]

yaws An infectious disease of tropical regions caused by the bacterium *Treponema pertenue*, transmitted by direct close contact with an infected person. The disease is largely confined to eruptions in the skin. Later the deep tissues and bones may be invaded, giving rise to deformities and scarring. » bacteria [i]

Yayoi In Japanese archaeology, the period c.300 BC–AD 300 that follows Jomon and precedes Kofun. Notable features are rice cultivation, irrigation, and the increasing use of bronze for weapons and tools. The name derives from the characteristically simple pottery of the period, first identified at Yayoi, Tokyo, in 1884. » Jomon; Kofun

yeast A fungus that can occur as single cells; typically reproduces by budding or by fission; used in fermentation processes in the brewing and baking industries. (Subdivision: *Ascomycetes*. Order: *Endomycetales*.) » Ascomycetes; fungus

Yeats, William Butler (1865–1939) Irish poet and dramatist, born near Dublin. Educated in London and Dublin, he became an art student, then turned to writing. In 1888 he published *The Wanderings of Oisin*, a long narrative poem that established his reputation. *The Celtic Twilight*, a book of peasant legends, appeared in 1893. His three most popular plays were *The Countess Cathleen* (1892), *The Land of Heart's Desire* (1894), and *Cathleen ni Houlihan* (1903), and he wrote several others for the Abbey Theatre, which he helped to found in 1904. He adopted a more direct style with *Responsibilities* (1914), which also marks a switch to contemporary subjects. Many of his best-known poems appeared in *The Tower* (1928), *The Winding Stair* (1929), and *A Full Moon in March* (1935). He won the Nobel Prize for Literature in 1923, and was a senator of the Irish Free State (1922–8). He died at Roquebrune, France. His *Collected Poems* were published in 1950. » Abbey Theatre; drama; Irish literature; poetry

yellow bird's nest A plant native to N temperate regions; a rhizomatous saprophyte; whole plant waxy, yellowish-white, completely lacking chlorophyll; stems 8–30 cm/3–12 in, slightly fleshy; leaves scale-like, clasping stem; flowers 1–1.5 cm/0.4–0.6 in, bell-shaped, 4–5 petalled. (*Monotropa hypopitys*. Family: *Monotropaceae*.) » chlorophyll; rhizome; saprophyte

yellow fever An infection caused by a virus which infests monkeys and is transmitted to humans from them by mosquitoes. It is often a mild short-lived feverish illness, but may become severe with jaundice, liver failure, and kidney failure, and lead to death. There is an effective vaccine against it. It occurs in Africa and S America. » virus

yellow-green algae Aquatic algae containing the photosynthetic pigments chlorophyll *a* and *c*, and various carotenoids which produce the yellow-green colour of the chloroplasts; vary in form from single cells to filaments; produce motile spores (*zoospores*) with a hairy forward-pointing and a naked backward-pointing flagellum. (Class: *Xanthophyceae*.) » algae; chloroplast; flagellum; photosynthesis

Yellow River, **Huang Ho** or **Huang He** Second longest river in China; length 5 464 km/3 395 ml; rises in Bayan Har Shan Range, WC China; flows NW through Inner Mongolia, then generally E or NE across the country to enter the Bo Hai Gulf; series of gorges in upper reaches, used for hydroelectricity; flooding formerly a major problem, now increasingly controlled by dykes; several conservancy projects on upper and middle reaches. » China [i]

Yellow Sea, Chinese **Hwang Hai** Inlet of the Pacific Ocean, bounded by China (N, W) and by N and S Korea (E); maximum width c.650 km/400 ml; maximum depth c.150 m/500 ft; named for its colour, because of the silt brought down by its rivers. » Pacific Ocean

yellow wood A large genus of evergreen conifers found in the mountains of warm temperate and tropical regions of the S hemisphere; leaves variable, scaly, needle-like or large and flat; single-seeded cone becoming fleshy, brightly coloured, edible. They are important forest trees, especially in Australasia, yielding valuable timber. (Genus: *Podocarpus*, 100 species. Family: *Pinaceae*.) » conifer; evergreen plants

yellowfin tuna Species of tuna fish widespread in surface waters of tropical and warm temperate seas; length up to 2 m/6½ ft; golden band along side of body, dorsal and anal fins yellow; feeds on surface fishes such as flying fish and skippers as well as on squid and crustaceans; heavily exploited commercially. (*Thunnus albacares*. Family: *Scombridae*.) » tuna

yellowhammer (Ger *ammer*, 'bunting') A bird (a bunting), native to NW regions of the Old World; black and yellow streaked plumage with chestnut rump; inhabits grass and farmland; eats seeds and insects; also known as the **yellow bunting**. The name is used in the USA for the woodpecker, *Colaptes auratus*. (*Emberiza citronella*.) » bunting; woodpecker

Yellowknife 62°30N 114°29W, pop (1981) 10 500. Capital of Northwest Territories, N Canada, on NW shore of Great Slave Lake at mouth of Yellowknife R; founded, 1935; capital, 1967; gold mining. » Northwest Territories

Yellowstone Largest US national park, and the world's first, mainly in NW Wyoming; contains over 3 000 hot springs and geysers, including Old Faithful, a geyser that spurts water at regular intervals; Yellowstone and Jackson Lakes; highest point Electric Peak (3 350 m/10 991 ft); area 8 992 sq km/3 472 sq ml. » National Park; Wyoming

Yeltsin, Boris Nikolayevich (1931–) Russian politician, born in Sverdlovsk (Yekaterinburg). He was appointed Moscow party chief in 1985, and a member of the politburo in 1986, but was demoted for his blunt criticism of party conservatives. Elected to the new Congress of USSR People's Deputies in 1989, he developed a high profile, and in 1990 was elected President of the Russian Federation. He gained international acclaim for his public opposition to the attempted coup in 1991, and has since played a leading role in Soviet politics. » Gorbachev; Russia

Yemen, official name **Republic of Yemen**, pop (1990e) 11 546 000; area 531 570 sq km/205 186 sq ml. Republic formed in May 1990 from the merging of North and South Yemen; political capital, Sana; commercial capital, Aden; governed by a 308-member House of Representatives; a 5-member Presidential Council holds office during a 30-month transitional period, leading to elections; both the rial (N Yemen) and the dinar (S Yemen) are acceptable currencies. (*Information about the two former countries is given below under separate headings, pending the availability of official statistics for the new state.*)

Yemen, North or **Yemen**, official name **Yemen Arab Republic**, Arabic **Al-Jamhuriya al-Arabiya al-Yamaniya** pop (1989e) 8 834 000; area 195 000 sq km/75 270 sq ml. Former republic occupying the SW corner of the Arabian peninsula, bounded W by the Red Sea, N by Saudi Arabia, and S by South Yemen; divided into 10 provinces; capital, Sana; chief towns, Taizz, Al Hudaydah; timezone GMT +3; chief religion, Islam; official language, Arabic; unit of currency, the riyal; narrow desert plain rises abruptly to mountains at 3 000–3 500 m/10 000–11 500 ft; dry and arid Rub al Khali to the E; hot and humid on coastal strip (W), average annual temperature 29°C; milder in highlands; winters can be cold; average annual rainfall, 380–500 mm/15–20 in, decreasing E to less than 120 mm/5 in; Turkish occupation (1872–1918), followed by rule of the Hamid al-Din dynasty until the revolution of 1962; fighting between royalists and republicans continued until 1967, when republican regime recognized; border clashes with South Yemen in 1970s; governed by a Consultative Council of 159 members, which elected a president and appointed a cabinet of c.20 ministers; agriculture employs c.75% of the labour force; millet, wheat, barley, pulses, fruit, vegetables; cotton has overtaken coffee as the chief cash crop; irrigation schemes likely to increase the area under cultivation; Qat, a narcotic leaf, now a major enterprise; textiles, cement, aluminium products, soft drinks, handicrafts, oil, salt. » Sana; RR27 national holidays; RR66 political leaders

Yemen, South, official name **The People's Democratic Republic of Yemen**, Arabic **Jumhurijah al-Yemen al-Dimuqratiyah al-Sha'abijah** pop (1989e) 2 406 000; area 336 570 sq km/129 916 sq ml. Former republic on the SW coast of the Arabian peninsula, divided into six governorates; bounded NW by North Yemen, N by Saudi Arabia, E by Oman, and S by the Gulf of Aden; capital, Aden; chief towns, Al Mukalla, Ash Shaykh Uthman; timezone GMT +3; population mainly Arab; official language, Arabic; chief religion, Islam; unit of currency, the dinar; includes islands of Socotra, Perim, Kamaran; flat, narrow coastal plain, backed by mountains rising to almost 2 500 m/8 200 ft; to the N, plateau merges with the gravel plains and sand wastes of the Rub al Khali basin; hot climate all year, with maximum temperatures over 40°C (Jul–Aug); very high humidity; average temperatures at Aden, 24°C (Jan), 32°C (Jul), average annual rainfall 46 mm/1.8 in; fishing port of Aden occupied by Britain, 1839; British protectorate, 1937; part of Federation of South Arabia, 1963; overrun by the National Liberation Front, British troops withdrawn, and republic proclaimed, 1967; border disputes with Oman and South Yemen in 1970s; governed by a 111-member Supreme People's Council, elected from the ruling Yemen Socialist Party, and a president; economy based on agriculture and light industry; millet, sorghum, dates, cotton, wheat, barley; fishing, oil refining. » Aden; RR27 national holidays; RR66 political leaders

Yenisey or **Yenisei, River** [yenisay] River in C Siberian Russia; rises in the E Sayanskiy Khrebet, and flows generally N to enter the Kara Sea via a long estuary; length, 3 487 km/2 167 ml; navigable for five months on the upper river course, three months on the lower course; forms W boundary of the C Siberian Plateau; coal, non-ferrous metals, hydroelectric power. » Russia

yeoman A person in late mediaeval England qualified, by holding freehold worth 40 shillings or more, to serve on juries and vote for knights of the shire. In the early modern period, the name is used for the better-off freeholders or tenant-farmers who were often dominant in village life and administration as churchwardens, constables, and overseers of the poor.

yeomanry A historic military expression, revived in Britain during the Napoleonic period for volunteer units of cavalry, organized on a county-by-county basis. In 1908, yeomanry regiments were absorbed by the Territorials. » Territorial Army

Yeomen of the Guard The oldest of the four corps of the

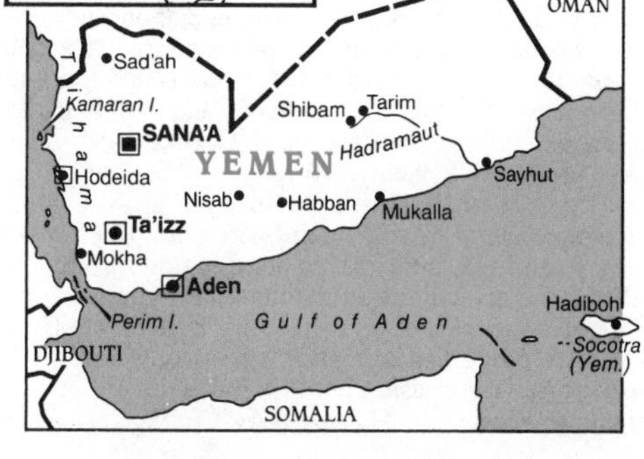

sovereign's personal bodyguard, known also as Beefeaters, supposedly in tribute to their healthy appearance. They are called out for special duties only, when they wear their basically Tudor uniforms. The same uniforms are worn by the Yeomen Warders of the Tower of London, whose original duty was to guard the Tower, but who now attend the gates and act as guides to the tourists. » Tower of London

Yerevan, also **Erivan** [yere**van**] 40°10N 44°31E, pop (1989) 1 199 000. Capital city of Armenia; on R Razdan, 15 km/9 ml from the Turkish frontier; altitude of highest part, 1 042 m/3 419 ft; one of the world's most ancient cities; ceded to Russia, 1828; airfield; railway; university; vodka, wine, textiles, chemicals, foodstuffs, tourism; ruins of a 16th-c Turkish fortress; badly damaged by earthquake, 1988. » Armenia

Yesenin, Sergei [ye**say**nin] (1895–1925) Russian poet, born at Konstantino (now Yesenino) to a peasant family. He left home at 17 and gained literary success with his first volume *Radunitsa* (1916, Mourning for the Dead). He was four times married (his third wife was Isadora Duncan), and his suicide in St Petersburg prompted a wave of imitative suicides in Russia. » Duncan, Isadora; poetry; Russian literature

yeti A supposed ape-like creature said to live at the edge of the snow-line in high valleys of the Himalayan Mts; generally described as large, covered in brown hair, and walking upright like a human; first reported in 1889; footprints of length 15–30 cm/6–12 in have been photographed, but various expeditions have failed to find it; also known as **abominable snowman, meti, temu, kang-mi, mirka, mi-go, sogpu**, or **shukpa**. » ape; Bigfoot; hominid

Yevtushenko, Yevegeny (Aleksandrovich) (1933–) Russian poet, born at Zima. He moved to Moscow in 1944, where he studied at the Gorky Institute of Literature. His early poetry, such as *The Third Snow* (1955), made him a spokesman for the young post-Stalin generation. His long narrative poem *Stantsiya Zima* (1956, Zima Junction), considering issues raised by the death of Stalin, prompted criticism, as did his *Babi Yar* (1962) which attacked anti-Semitism. In 1960 he began to travel abroad to give readings of his poetry. His first major stage piece, *Under the Skin of the Statue of Liberty*, was a huge success in 1972. He has also written a novel and other prose works, and engaged in acting and photography. » Babi Yar; poetry; Russian literature; Stalin

yew A small evergreen tree or shrub, native to the western N hemisphere; leaves narrow, flattened, spreading in two horizontal rows; seed surrounded by a scarlet, fleshy aril. The foliage and seeds are highly poisonous, but the aril is edible, though insipid. Many were traditionally planted in walled churchyards to prevent farm stock from eating them. Popular for topiary and mazes, they were once the source of the finest longbows. (Genus: *Taxus*, 10 species. Family: *Taxaceae*.) » aril; evergreen plants; shrub; tree [i]

Yggdrasil [**ig**drasil] In Norse mythology, a giant ash, the World-Tree, which supports the sky, holds the different realms of gods and men in its branches, and has its roots in the Underworld. » Asgard; Midgard; Norns

Yiddish A language used by E European Jews, developed from Old High German in the 9th-c, and written using the Hebrew alphabet. It flourished as a medium of literature in the 19th-c and in the first part of the 20th-c, but its literary use has diminished following the establishment of Hebrew as the official language of Israel. » Aleichem; Germanic languages; Hebrew

yield The interest paid on a stock, share, or bond in relation to its current market value, in percentage terms. If a company pays a dividend of 20p a share, before tax is deducted, and the share price is 400p, then the dividend yield is 5%. If the share price rises to 500p, then the yield becomes 4%. These are termed 'gross yields', being before tax. » dividend

yield point » **plastic deformation**

yield stress The lowest stretching stress at which a material undergoes an irreversible plastic deformation, producing what is called a 'permanent set' in the material; symbol σ_y, units Pa (pascal). For copper, $\sigma_y = 4 \times 10^7$ Pa; for steel, 4×10^8 Pa. » mechanical properties of matter; stress (physics)

yin and yang Two basic contrary forces in ancient Chinese thought, elaborated in Han dynasty Confucianism. Yang is associated with male, heat, light, heaven, creation, dominance; yin with female, cold, dark, earth, sustenance, passivity. Yin and yang forces are alleged to exist in most things, and operate cyclically to produce change. » Confucianism

Yin-hsien » **Ningbo**

Yinchuan or **Yinch'uan** 38°30N 106°19E, pop (1984e) 383 300. Capital of Ningxia autonomous region, N China; NE of Lanzhou; airfield; commercial centre; coal mining, wool, centre of agricultural trade; Muslims are a third of the population. » China [i]

Yippies A term referring to members of the Youth International Party that was established in the USA during the mid-1960s by young, highly-educated middle-class radicals who sought to create an 'alternative' American culture based on non-possessive values. They received considerable attention from the law enforcement agencies because of their alleged belief in 'free love' and use of drugs.

ylang-ylang [eelang **ee**lang] An evergreen tree growing to 25 m/80 ft, native to Malaysia and the Phillipines, and cultivated elsewhere; leaves up to 20 cm/8 in long, elliptical, arranged in two rows; flowers 10 cm/4 in diameter, 6-petalled, dull yellow, fragrant. Ylang-ylang or macassar oil from the flowers is used in perfumes. (*Cananga odorata*. Family: *Annonaceae*.) » evergreen plants; oil (botany); tree [i]

YMCA An acronym for **Young Men's Christian Association**, a charity founded in London in 1844 to promote the spiritual, social, and physical welfare of boys and young men. The YMCA developed rapidly in many countries, notably the USA; in the 1980s it was active in over 90 countries, with around 100 000 centres and 23 million people participating in its activities. » YWCA

Ynys Môn [**uh**nis **mohn**], Eng **Anglesey** area 715 sq km/276 sq ml. Island district of Gwynedd, NW Wales, UK; separated from Arfon by Menai Straits, spanned by two bridges; chief towns, Holyhead, Beaumaris, Amlwch, Llangefni, Menai Bridge; linked to Holy I by an embankment; ferry link from Holyhead to Dun Laoghaire and Dublin, Ireland; agriculture, aluminium, sheep rearing, marine engineering, tourism. » Gwynedd; Holyhead; Llangefni; Menai Straits

yobiko [yoh**bee**koh] A Japanese crammer's school. Educational qualifications are important in Japan for getting such jobs as in a large company, or a government office. Applicants must be university graduates. Starting at primary school, many pupils therefore have extra classes in the evenings and/or at weekends.

yoga In Indian religious tradition, any of various physical and contemplative techniques designed to free the superior, conscious element in a person from involvement with the inferior material world. More narrowly, Yoga is a school of Hindu philosophy which seeks to explain and justify the practices of yogin discipline. » Hinduism

yogurt or **yoghurt** A product, originating in the Balkans, obtained by fermenting milk with the bacteria *Lactobacillus bulgaricus* and *Streptococcus acidophilus*. This process produces lactic acid from lactose present in the milk. Yogurt may be made from full-fat, low-fat, or skimmed milk, and various sweetenings and flavourings may be added. » fermentation; lactose; milk

Yogyakarta [yahgya**kah**ta] or **Yogya** 7°48S 110°24E, pop (1980) 342 267. Capital of Yogyakarta special territory, SC Java, Indonesia; cultural centre of Java; airfield; railway; two universities (1945, 1949); textiles, leather, railway workshops, silverwork, crafts; sultan's palace (18th-c), Soino Budoyo museum, ancient temples of Borobudur and Prambanan. » Java

Yokohama [yohkoh**hah**ma] 35°28N 139°28E, pop (1980) 2 773 674. Port capital of Kanagawa prefecture, C Honshu, Japan; on W shore of Tokyo-wan Bay, SW of Tokyo; fourth largest city in Japan, handling 30% of foreign trade; first port to be opened to foreign trade, 1858; linked to Tokyo by first Japanese railway, 1872; largely destroyed by earthquake in 1923, and by bombing in 1945; railway; two universities (1949); shipbuilding, oil refining, engineering, chemicals, glass, furniture, clothes, trade in silk, rayon, fish; Sankei en Park (19th-c), Silk Museum; Port Festival (May), Black Ships' Festival (Jul). » Honshu; Tokyo

Yom Kippur [**yohm** ki**poor**, **yom ki**pur] The Day of Atonement, a Jewish holy day (10 Tishri) coming at the end of ten days of penitence which begin on Rosh Hashanah; a day devoted to fasting, prayer and repentance for past sins. » Judaism

Yom Kippur War » **Arab-Israeli Wars**

Yomeimon Gate [yoh**may**muhn] A structure built in the 17th-c at the entrance to the inner courtyard of the Toshogu shrine at Nikko, Japan. The gateway is covered with such a profusion of carving, lacquerwork, and gilding that its nickname, 'Higurashimon' (Twilight Gate), implies one could admire it until nightfall.

Yonge, Charlotte M(ary) [yung] (1823–1901) British novelist, born and died at Otterbourne, Hampshire. She achieved a great popular success with her *Heir of Redclyffe* (1853), and in all she published some 120 volumes of fiction, High Church in tone, which helped to spread the Oxford Movement. She also published children's books, historical works, translated a great deal, and edited a magazine for girls, *The Monthly Packet*. » novel; Oxford Movement

yoni [**yoh**nee] » **lingam**

Yonkers 40°56N 73°54W, pop (1980) 195 351. Town in Westchester County, SE New York, USA; a residential suburb on the Hudson R, at the N edge of Greater New York c.24 km/15 ml N of the city centre; named after the courtesy title ('Jonkheer') given to the early Dutch settler Adriaen van der Donck; railway; retailing; St Andrews golf course (first course in the USA), Hudson R Museum, Sherwood House. » New York (state)

York, ancient **Eboracum** 53°58N 1°05W, pop (1981) 99 910. City in North Yorkshire, N England; Roman settlement founded in AD 71 as capital of the Roman province of Britannia; thereafter a royal and religious centre, capital of Anglo-Saxon Northumbria; captured by the Danes (867), known as Jorvik; Archbishop of York bears the title Primate of England; expanded rapidly in the 19th-c as a railway centre; university (1963); railway; foodstuffs, chocolate, glass, railway coaches, scientific instruments, tourism; 14th-c city walls; York Minster (12th–15th-c), south transept badly damaged by fire in 1984, since restored; National Railway Museum; Castle Museum; Jorvik Viking Centre (1984); York Festival (Jun). » Britain, Roman; Danelaw; Yorkshire, North

York, Duke of In the UK, a title often given to the second son of the sovereign, such as Albert Frederick (later George VI), the second son of George V, and Andrew, the second son of Queen Elizabeth. » titles [i]

York, House of The younger branch of the Plantegenet dynasty, founded by Edmund of Langley, the fourth son of Edward III and first Duke of York (1385–1402), whence came three kings of England: Edward IV (1461–83), who usurped the Lancastrian king Henry VI; Edward V (1483); and Richard III (1483–5) killed at Bosworth Field, and succeeded by Henry VII, first of the Tudors. » Edward IV/V; Lancaster, House of; Plantagenets; Richard III; Roses, Wars of the

Yorkshire, North pop (1987e) 705 700; area 8 309 sq km/3 207 sq ml. County in N England, created in 1974, consisting of six districts; largest county in England, from Lancashire (W) to the North Sea (E); Pennines in the W; Vale of York, North Yorkshire Moors, Cleveland Hills in the E; R Ouse flows SE; county town, Northallerton; other chief towns Harrogate, Scarborough, Whitby, York; agriculture (cereals, dairy farming, sheep), electrical and mechanical equipment, footwear, clothing, vehicles, plastics, foodstuffs, tourism; Fylingdales radar station, Rievaulx Abbey, Yorkshire Dales national park, Castle Howard, York Minster, Fountains Abbey. » England [i]; Fountains Abbey; York

Yorkshire, South pop (1987e) 1 295 600; area 1 560 sq km/602 sq ml. Area of N England, created in 1974, divided into four metropolitan borough councils: Sheffield, Rotherham, Doncaster, Barnsley; agriculture (sheep, arable, dairy farming), coal, steel, engineering. » England [i]; Sheffield

Yorkshire, West pop (1987e) 2 052 400; area 2 039 sq km/787 sq ml. Former county of N England, divided into five boroughs; drained by the Aire and Calder Rivers; administrative centre, Wakefield; chief towns include Leeds, Bradford, Huddersfield, Halifax; metropolitan council abolished in 1986; wool textiles, coal, engineering, machinery, machine tools; Ilkley Moor, Haworth Parsonage (home of the Brontes), Peak District National Park. » Brontë, Anne/Charlotte/Emily; England [i]; Wakefield

Yorkshire coach horse » **Cleveland bay**

Yorkshire Dales National park in North Yorkshire and Cumbria, England; area 1 761 sq km/680 sq ml; established in 1954; limestone scenery (eg Kilnsey Crag, Gordale Crag, Malham Cove), popular with potholers and fell walkers; three main peaks of Ingleborough, Whernside, Pen-y-Ghent; Bolton Abbey (Wharfedale), Roman fort at Bainbridge. » Cumbria; Yorkshire, North

Yorkshire terrier A British toy terrier; very small, with long fine brown and blue-grey hair; coat reaches ground; head with large erect ears and very long hair; owners sometimes tie ribbons on its head. » non-sporting dog; terrier

Yorktown 37°14N 76°30W. Seat of York County, SE Virginia, USA, at the mouth of the York R; settled, 1631; now in Colonial National Historical Park; Revolutionary troops under Washington and Rochambeau besieged British forces under Cornwallis here in 1781, until the latter surrendered; also besieged during the Civil War by Union forces under McClellan, 1862. » American Civil War/Revolution; Virginia

Yorktown Campaign (30 Aug–19 Oct 1781) The final campaign of the US War of Independence, ending with the entrapment at Yorktown, Virginia, of the British army under Lord Cornwallis by troops under Washington and a French fleet under Admiral de Grasse (1722–88). The defeat destroyed the political will on the English side to continue the war. It brought the fall of Lord North, Prime Minister since 1770, and opened the way for peace negotiations. » American Revolution; Cornwallis; Washington, George

Yoruba [**yo**ruhba] A cluster of Kwa-speaking peoples of SW Nigeria and Benin, mostly organized in culturally similar but politically autonomous kingdoms, each ruled by a king who is both political and religious head. Their dominant state in the 17th–18th-c was the kingdom of Oyo, which broke up in the early 19th-c. They are highly urbanized, Ibadan being the largest pre-colonial city in Black Africa, and are famed for their art. Traditional religion still flourishes, although many are Muslims and Christians. Population c.16.5 million. » African history/languages; Benin [i]; Nigeria [i]

Yosemite [yoh**sem**uhtee] ('grizzly bear') National park in E California, USA, in the Sierra Nevada, E of San Francisco; 11 km/7 ml-long valley full of natural granite monoliths and waterfalls; rises to 3 990 m/13 090 ft in Mt Lyell; Half Dome Mt, El Capitan, Mariposa Grove; drained by the Merced R; Yosemite Falls (highest in N America); area 3 083 sq km/1 189 sq ml. » California

Yoshkar Ola, also **Ioshkar Ola** [yushkahru**la**] 56°38N 47°52E, pop (1983) 223 000. Capital city of Mariyskaya, EC European Russia, on R Kokshaga; founded, 1578; railway; pharmaceuticals, foodstuffs, agricultural machinery. » Russia

Young, Arthur (1741–1820) British agricultural and travel writer, born and died in London. He spent most of his life at Bradfield, Suffolk, where he rented a small farm, and carried out many agricultural experiments. In 1793 he became secretary to the Board of Agriculture. In his writings, he helped to elevate agriculture to a science, founding and editing the monthly *Annals of Agriculture* in 1784. » agriculture

Young, Brigham (1801–77) US Mormon leader, born at Whitingham, Vermont. Converted in 1832, he became one of the twelve apostles of the Church in 1835, and its president upon the death of Joseph Smith in 1844. After the Mormons were driven from Nauvoo, he led them to Utah (1847), where they founded Salt Lake City. He was appointed Governor of Utah in 1850, but was replaced in 1857 when an army was sent to establish federal law in the territory. He died at Salt Lake City, leaving 17 wives and 56 children. » Mormons; Salt Lake City; Smith, Joseph

Young, Cy, properly **Denton True Young** (1967–1955) US baseball player, born at Gilmore, Ohio. One of the first of baseball's greats, he made his senior debut in 1890 and played until 1911. During his career he played 906 games, pitched in 706 complete games, and won 511 games, all records. He died at Newcomerstown, Ohio. » baseball [i]

Young, Thomas (1773–1829) British physicist, physician, and

Egyptologist, born at Milverton, Somerset. He studied medicine at London, Edinburgh, Göttingen and Cambridge, then devoted himself to research, becoming professor of natural philosophy to the Royal Institution (1801). He established the wave theory of light, and made a fundamental contribution to the deciphering of the inscriptions on the Rosetta Stone. He died in London. » light; Rosetta Stone

Young Ireland An Irish protest movement, founded in 1840, which produced *The Nation* magazine, arguing for repeal of the Act of Union. It set up an Irish Confederation in 1847, which returned several nationalists to Parliament, and an unsuccessful Young Ireland rising took place in Tipperary in 1848. » nationalism; O'Connell; Union, Acts of

Young Italy An Italian patriotic organization which played an important role in the early stages of the Risorgimento, founded in Marseilles (1833) by Mazzini. Designed to arouse Italian national feeling and ultimately seize power, by 1833 it possessed 60 000 members, and had committees in all leading Italian cities. It played a significant part in the revolutions of 1848. » Mazzini; Risorgimento

Young Men's Christian Association » YMCA

Young Men/Women's Hebrew Association (YMHA/YWHA) In the USA, an organization to promote health, social activities, and Jewish culture. The first YMHA was founded in 1854, and the first independent YWHA in 1902. » Judaism

Young's modulus Linear stress divided by linear strain, a constant for a given material; symbol E, units Pa (pascal); also called the **modulus of elasticity** or the **elastic modulus**; named after British physicist Thomas Young. A high Young's modulus means that material is stiffer. For steel, $E = 2 \times 10^{11}$ Pa; for wood, E is about 0.1×10^{11} along the grain. » elasticity; Hooke's law; mechanical properties of matter; strain; stress (physics); Young, Thomas

Young Turks The modernizing and westernizing reformers in the early 20th-c Ottoman Empire. With the support of disaffected army elements under Enver Pasha, they rebelled against Sultan Abd-ul-Hamid II in 1908, and deposed him in 1909. The Young Turk revolution helped precipitate Austria-Hungary's occupation of Bosnia-Herzegovina (1908), the somewhat similar Greek officers' revolt of 1909, the Italian attack on Libya (1911), and the Balkan Wars (1912–13). » Enver Pasha; Ottoman Empire

Young Women's Christian Association » YWCA

Younghusband, Sir Francis (Edward) (1863–1942) British explorer, born at Murree, India. He joined the army in 1882, explored Manchuria (1886), and discovered the route from Kashgar into India via the Mustagh Pass. In 1902 he went on the expedition which opened up Tibet to the Western world. British resident in Kashmir (1906–9), he wrote much on India and C Asia, and founded the World Congress of Faiths in 1936. He died at Lytchett Minster, Dorset.

Yourcenar, Marguerite [yersuhnah], pseudonym of **Marguerite de Crayencour** (1903–87) French novelist, born in Brussels, Belgium. The daughter of a member of the French aristocracy, she was educated privately and spent her childhood travelling in Europe. In 1937 she left France for the USA, where she continued to live, taking dual US-French nationality. She is best known for her historical novel *Mémoires d'Hadrien* (1951), and for being the first woman to be elected to the Académie Française. She died at Northeast Harbor, Maine. » French literature; novel

youth custody centre An institution in the UK where offenders not less than 15 years of age nor more than 21 can be detained following sentence. Detention in these centres replaces borstal training and imprisonment. » detention centre; probation; sentence

Youth Hostels Association (YHA) » International Youth Hostel Association

Youth International Party » Yippies

Ypres [eepruh], Flemish **Ieper** 50°51N 2°53E, pop (1982) 18 161. Town in West Flanders province, W Belgium, close to the French border; long associated with the cloth trade; devastated in World War 1; Menin Gate (Menenpoort) memorial, graveyards, and Garden of Peace provide a place of pilgrimage; railway; textiles, textile machinery, foodstuffs, tourism; cloth hall (13th-c), St Martin's Cathedral; Festival of the Cats (May). » Belgium [i]; Ypres, Battles of

Ypres, Battles of [eepruh] **1** (Oct–Nov 1914) In World War 1, the halting of a German offensive to outflank the British Expeditionary Force. It left Ypres (Belgium) and its salient dominated on three sides by German-occupied heights. » World War 1 **2** (Apr–May 1915) A series of German attacks, using poison gas (chlorine) for the first time in warfare. It forced the British to shorten their defence line in the Ypres salient. » chlorine **3** (Jul–Nov 1917) » Passchendaele, Battle of

Yrigoyen, Hipólito [eerigohzhen] (1852–1933) President of Argentina (1916–22, 1928–30), born in Buenos Aires. He became principal leader of the Unión Cívica Radical (Radical Party) from 1896, and mounted a successful attack on the dominant conservative governments of the time, ushering in a period of Radical dominance. His second presidential term was ended by a military coup. » Argentina; Radical Party (Argentina)

yttrium [yitreeuhm] Y, element 39, density 4.5 g/cm^3, melting point 1 522°C. A relatively rare element occurring in ores of the lanthanide elements, many of whose properties it shares. Its compounds have interesting electrical and magnetic properties. It is a constituent of many superconducting ceramics, eg $YBa_2Cu_3O_7$. » chemical elements; lanthanides; superconductivity; RR90

Yu Shan [yoo **shan**], Eng **Mount Morrison** Highest peak on Taiwan, and the highest in NE Asia; in the island's C range; height 3 997 m/13 113 ft. » Taiwan [i]

Yuan dynasty (1279–1368) A Chinese dynasty founded by Kublai Khan, who completed the conquest of the Southern Song, and built a new capital (Marco Polo's 'Cambaluc') at Beijing (Peking). The Chinese never accepted their foreign rulers, and after Kublai's death in 1307 Mongol power rapidly declined. Civil war between Mongol princes broke out in 1328, and the dynasty was eventually overthrown by a Chinese uprising led by Zhu Yuanzhang. » Kublai Khan

Yuan Shikai or **Yuan Shih-k'ai** [yooan shikiy] (1859–1916) Chinese statesman and soldier, born in Honan province, the first President of the Republic established in 1912. He was careful to remain neutral during the Boxer Rebellion, from which he thus emerged with his army intact and with the gratitude of the foreign powers. On the death of his patron, the Empress Dowager Ci Xi (1908), he was removed from influence, but recalled after the successful Wuhan nationalist rising (1911). As President, he lost support by procuring the murder of the parliamentary leader of the Nationalists and making war on them, accepting Japan's Twenty-One Demands of 1915, and proclaiming himself Emperor (1915). Forced to abdicate, the humiliation may have hastened his death. » Boxer Rising; Ci Xi; Hundred Days of Reform; Qing dynasty; Twenty-one Demands; Zai Tian

Yucatán [ukatahn] pop (1980) 1 034 648; area 38 402 sq km/ 14 823 sq ml. State in SE Mexico, on the N Yucatán peninsula, bounded N by the Gulf of Mexico; a third covered by forests; savannah vegetation in drier NW; capital, Mérida; grain, tropical fruit, sisal, fishing, timber, sea salt, textiles, tobacco, brewing, tourism; numerous Mayan ruins, including Chichén Itzá and Uxmal; the name also often given to the whole peninsula, including the states of Quintana Roo and Campeche. » Chichén Itzá; Mayas; Mexico [i]; Palenque; Uxmal

yucca An evergreen plant native to the USA, Mexico, and the Caribbean; somewhat palm-like in appearance, trunk short, thick; leaves sword-shaped; flowers night-scented, white, bell-shaped and hanging, in a large pyramidal inflorescence. It forms a symbiotic association with a small moth, which lays eggs in the ovary then deliberately presses a ball of pollen onto the stigma of the flower to ensure fertilization and production of seeds, some of which form food for its larvae. Several species are grown as ornamentals. (Genus: *Yucca*, 40 species. Family: *Agavaceae*.) » Adam's needle; evergreen plants; inflorescence [i]; pollen [i]; Spanish bayonet; symbiosis

Yugoslavia [yoogohs**lah**via] or **Jugoslavia**, official name **Socialist Federal Republic of Yugoslavia**, Serbo-Croatian **Socijalistička Federativna Republika Jugoslavija** pop (1990e) 23 860 000;

area 256 409 sq km/98 974 sq ml. Communist state of six constituent federal republics in the Balkan peninsula of SE Europe; bounded W by the Adriatic Sea, NNW by Italy, N by Austria and Hungary, E by Romania and Bulgaria, SW by Albania, and S by Greece; capital, Belgrade; chief towns include Zagreb, Skopje, Sarajevo, Ljubljana; timezone GMT +2; chief ethnic groups, Serbs (36%), Croats (20%); chief religions, Serbian Orthodox (41%), Roman Catholicism (32%); unit of currency, the dinar of 100 paras; dominated in the N by the Danube, Drava, Tisza, and Sava Rivers, with fertile plains (NE); Julian and Karawanken Alps rise (N) to 2 863 m/9 393 ft at Triglav; Adriatic fringed by the Dinaric Alps; ranges in the S cut by deep river valleys; several great lakes (S); Mediterranean climate on Adriatic coast; continental climate in the N and NE; rain throughout the year, with summer maximum in the N; colder upland climate, with winter snow; Serbs, Croats, and Slovenes united under one monarch, 1918; country renamed Yugoslavia, 1929; civil war between Serbian royalists (Chetniks), Croatian nationalists, and Communists; occupied by Germans during World War 2; Federal People's Republic established under Tito, 1945; revised constitution in 1974 instituted a rotating leadership, with the prime minister elected annually; governed by a bicameral Federal Assembly, elected every four years, comprising a 220-delegate Federal Chamber and an 88-member Chamber of Republics and Provinces; following a break with the USSR in 1948, the country follows an independent form of communism and a general policy of nonalignment; at the end of the 1980s political disagreement between the federal republics increased; in an attempt to preserve Yugoslavian unity the government announced plans to rewrite the federal constitution to allow a multi-party system with direct elections; ethnic unrest in Serbia (Kosovo) and Croatia placed further strains on the federal system; Slovenia unilateral declaration of independence in 1990, followed by Macedonian and Croatian declarations in 1991, considered illegal by central government; confrontation between Croatia and Serb-dominated National Army developed into civil war, 1991; industrial base extended since World War 2; machine tools, chemicals, textiles, food processing, wood and metal products, oil refining; increased agricultural output, especially wheat, maize, sugar beet, livestock; wine, forestry, fishing; rapidly growing tourist industry. » Belgrade; Bosnia and Herzegovina; communism; Croatia; Macedonia; Montenegro; Serbia; Slovenia; Tito; RR27 national holidays; RR66 political leaders

Yukawa, Hideki (1907–81) Japanese physicist, born in Tokyo. Educated at Kyoto and Osaka, he became professor of theoretical physics at Kyoto (1939–50), visiting professor in the USA (1948–53), and director of the Research Institute for Fundamental Physics at Kyoto (1953–70). In 1935 he predicted the existence of the meson, and for his work in nuclear physics won the Nobel Physics Prize in 1949. He died in Kyoto. » meson

Yukon [**yoo**kon] pop (1981) 22 135; area 483 450 sq km/186 660 sq ml. Territory in NW Canada; boundary includes Alaska (W), Mackenzie Bay and Beaufort Sea (N); area of plateaux and mountain ranges, rising to 5 950 m/19 521 ft at Mt Logan; Selwyn Mts in the E; tundra in N; drained by the Yukon R and tributaries (S), Peel and Porcupine Rivers (N); several lakes; capital, Whitehorse; other towns include Watson Lake, Dawson City; minerals (gold, silver, zinc, lead, copper), hydroelectric power; Hudson's Bay Company fur-trading post, 1842; gold prospectors from 1873; district of Northwest Territories, 1895; separate territory when Klondike gold rush at its height, 1898; governed by a 5-member Executive Council appointed from a 16-member elected Legislative Assembly. » Canada [i]; gold rush; Hudson's Bay Company; Logan, Mount; tundra; Whitehorse

Yukon River Major river in N America, in Yukon territory and Alaska; rises in the Rocky Mts, flows generally NW then W and SW through C Alaska, veering NW to enter the Bering Sea in a wide delta near Alakanuk; length to the head of the longest headstream (the Nisutlin) 3 185 km/1 979 ml; navigable to Dawson for large vessels; widens in NE Alaska into the Yukon Flats (15–30 km/10–20 ml wide for c.320 km/200 ml); ice-bound most of the year (Oct–Jun); a major transportation route during the Klondike gold rush (1897–8). » Alaska; Yukon

Yunnan » **Kunming**

Yurak » **Nenets**

YWCA An acronym for **Young Women's Christian Association**, a charity formed in London in 1877 by the joining of a prayer union and a home for nurses travelling to and from the Crimean War (both established 1855). The movement spread to the USA in 1866, and a world organization was set up in 1892; it is now active in over 80 countries. » YMCA

Z

Z particle A particle that carries weak nuclear force; symbol Z; mass 94 GeV; charge zero; spin 1; decays to an electron plus positron, or a muon plus antimuon; Predicted by the Glashow-Weinberg-Salam theory, it was discovered in 1983 in proton-antiproton collisions at the European Organization for Nuclear Research (CERN). » boson; fundamental particles; Glashow-Weinberg-Salam theory

Zabaleta, Nicanor [thabalayta] (1907–) Spanish harpist, born at San Sebastian. He studied in Madrid and Paris, where he made his debut in 1925. He has been influential in popularizing the harp's solo repertory, and several composers have written works for him. » harp

Zabrze, Ger **Hindenburg** [zabuhzhe] 50°18N 18°47E, pop (1983) 196 500. Mining and industrial city in Katowice voivodship, S Poland, W of Katowice; second largest city in upper Silesian industrial region; railway; coal mining, iron and steel, mining machinery. » Poland [i]

Zacharias » **Zechariah, Book of**

Zacynthus, Gr **Zákinthos**, ancient **Zante** [zakinthuhs] pop (1981) 30 014; area 406 sq km/157 sq ml. Third largest of the Ionian Is, W Greece; length 40 km/25 ml; capital, Zacynthus; devastated by earthquakes in 1953; rugged W coast, hilly E coast, fertile C plain; currants, tourism. » Greece [i]; Ionian Islands

Zadar [zadah], Ital **Zara** 44°07N 15°14E, pop (1981) 116 174. Seaport and resort town in Croatia republic, W Yugoslavia, on the Adriatic; airfield; railway; car ferries to Ancona (Italy); conquered by Venice, 1000; passed to Austria, 1797; enclave of Italy, 1920–47; tourism, maraschino liqueur, glass, cigarettes; many Venetian buildings, Franciscan friary, cathedral, Roman remains at nearby Nin; summer festival of music. » Croatia; Yugoslavia [i]

Zadkine, Ossip (1890–1967) French sculptor, born at Smolensk, Russia. He studied in London and Paris, and developed an individual Cubist style, making effective use of the play of light on concave surfaces, as in 'The Three Musicians' (1926) and 'Destroyed City' (1952). During World War 2, his Jewish background caused him to flee to the USA, where he became an art teacher. He returned to France after the war, and died in Paris. » Cubism

Zadokites [zayduhkiyts] Descendants of Zadok, a priest apparently of Aaronic lineage and of the family of Eleazar, who opposed the conspiracy of Abiathar against Solomon and was appointed high priest, serving in Solomon's temple. His family continued to hold this office until Jerusalem fell in 587 BC, and again later in the Second Temple period until the office became a political appointment of the occupying power under Antiochus IV (c.171 BC). The Qumran community continued to look for a renewal of the Zadokite priesthood, and described its own priestly members in these terms. Some derive 'Sadducees' from Zadokites. » Aaron; Qumran, community of; Sadducees; Solomon (Old Testament); Teacher of Righteousness

Zagreb [zagreb], Ger **Agram**, Hungarian **Zágráb**, ancient **Andautonia** 45°48N 15°58E, pop (1981) 1 174 512. Capital city of Croatia republic, NW Yugoslavia, on R Sava; second largest city in Yugoslavia; Croat cultural centre; airport; railway; university (1669); electrical equipment, paper, textiles, carpets, light engineering; St Mark's Church, cathedral, ethnographical museum; trade fairs (Apr, Sep), tourism congress (Apr), international folk festival (Jul), Zagreb music and drama evenings (Jul–Sep). » Croatia; Yugoslavia [i]

Zagros Mountains [zagros] Major mountain system of W Iran, extending c.1 770 km/1 100 ml from the Turkish–Soviet frontier SE along the Arabian Gulf; highest point, Mt Sabalan (4 811 m/15 784 ft); large basins (NW), including L Urmia; series of parallel ridges separated by deep valleys (C); bare rock and sand dunes (SE); major oil fields lie along W foothills; crossed by the Trans-Iranian railway. » Iran [i]

Zai Tian or **Tsai T'ien**, reign-title **Guang Xu** or **Kuang Hsu)** [dziy tyen] (1871–1908) Ninth Emperor of the Qing dynasty (1875–1908), who remained largely under the control of the Empress Dowager Ci Xi (Tz'u Hsi). In 1898, after the defeat of China by Japan (1894–5), he was determined to reform and strengthen China, and threatened to abdicate if not given full authority. He issued a series of reforming edicts; but his attempts to gain power precipitated a coup, after which he was confined to his palace until his mysterious death one day before the death of the Empress Dowager. » Ci Xi; Hundred Days of Reform; Kang Yuwei; Qing dynasty

Zaire or **Zaïre** [zaheer], official name **Republic of Zaire**, Fr **République du Zaïre**, formerly **Congo Free State** (1885–1908), **Belgian Congo** (1908–60), **Democratic Republic of the Congo** (1960–71) pop (1990e) 34 138 000; area 2 343 950 sq km/904 765 sq ml. C African republic, divided into nine regions; bounded W by the Congo and the Atlantic Ocean, SW by Angola, SE by Zambia, E by Tanzania, Burundi, Rwanda, and Uganda, NE by Sudan, and N and NW by the Central African Republic; capital, Kinshasa; chief towns, Lubumbashi, Kisangani, Mbuji-Mayi; timezone GMT +1 (W), +2 (E); over 200 ethnic groups, mainly of Bantu origin; chief religions, Christianity (over 70%); official language, French; unit of currency, the zaïre of 100 makuta.

Physical description and climate. Land rises E from a low-lying basin to a densely-forested plateau; bounded E by volcanic mountains marking the W edge of the Great Rift Valley; Ruwenzori Mts (NE) on Ugandan frontier rise to 5 110 m/16 765 ft in the Mt Stanley massif; Mitumbar Mts further S; chain of lakes in the Rift Valley, including Albert, Edward, Kivu, and Tanganyika; narrow strip of land follows R Zaire (Congo) to the Atlantic Ocean (43 km/27 ml coastline);

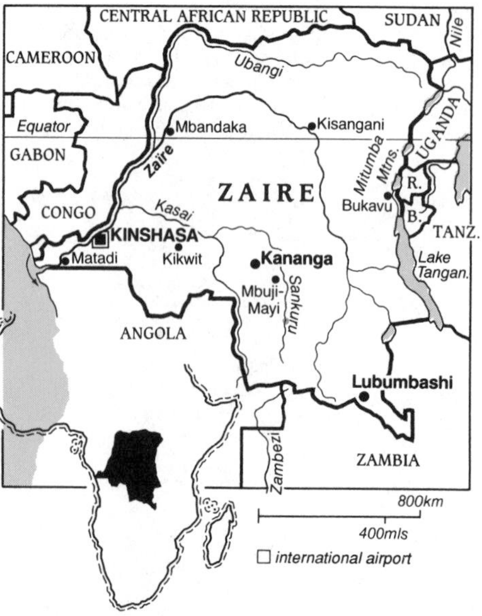

crossed by the Equator; hot and humid climate; average annual rainfall at Kisangani, 1 700 mm/67 in; average maximum daily temperatures 28–31°C.

History and government. Visited by the Portuguese, 1482; expeditions of Stanley, 1874–7; claimed by King Leopold II of Belgium, recognized in 1895 at the Berlin Conference; Congo Free State ceded to the state in 1907 and renamed the Belgian Congo; independence, 1960; mineral-rich Katanga (later, Shaba) province claimed independence, leading to civil war; UN peace-keeping force present until 1964; renamed Zaire, 1971; further conflict, 1977–8; a one-party state, governed by a president, elected for seven years, a 27-member National Executive Council, and a National Legislative Council of 210 members elected every five years; ultimate power lies with the Popular Movement of the Revolution, whose higher policy-making body is an 80-member Central Committee.

Economy. Nearly 80% of the population involved in subsistence farming; livestock, maize, yams, cassava, rice, beans, fruit; cash crops include cotton, sugar, oil palm products, quinquina, coffee, tea, cocoa; extensive mineral reserves; world's biggest producer of cobalt, industrial diamonds, copper; other reserves include tin, manganese, zinc, columbium, tantalum, cement, gold, silver, iron ore, rare-earth metals, offshore oil; textiles, cotton, wood products, tobacco processing, vegetable oil, chemicals, cement; major source of hydroelectricity. » Kinshasa; Rift Valley; Stanley, Henry Morton; RR27 national holidays; RR67 political leaders

Zaire, River, formerly **River Congo** River in C and W Africa; length c.4 670 km/2 900 ml, second longest in Africa; rises as the R Lualaba, which drains L Deleommune (S Zaire), and flows N, crossing the Equator SE of Kisangani, where it becomes known as R Zaire; flows NW in an arc across C Africa, then SW, with Congolese and Zairian capitals of Brazzaville and Kinshasa on opposite banks; makes a narrow trench in the Crystal Mts into the extreme W of Zaire, then enters the Atlantic Ocean SSE of Pointe-Noire; affected by ocean tide for 100 km/60 ml upstream; hydroelectricity from several dams; first European discovery of river mouth by Portuguese explorer, Diogo Cão, 1482; its extent appreciated only in the 19th-c, with explorations by Stanley, Livingstone, and others. » Congo [i]; Livingstone, David; Stanley, Henry Morton; Zaire [i]

zakat The alms tax obligatory on all Muslims, and the third of the five 'pillars' of Islam. Traditionally, it consisted of a 2.5% annual levy on income and capital.

Zakopane [zakuh**pa**ne] 49°17N 19°54E, pop (1983) 29 700. Chief town and winter sports resort in the High Tatra Mts, S Poland, S of Kraków; altitude 800–900 m/2 600–3 000 ft; railway; health resort, mountaineering; autumn festival, international festival of highland folklore (Sep). » Poland [i]

Zambezi expedition An official British expedition (1858–64), led by David Livingstone, to investigate the potentiality of the R Zambezi for steamship communication with the interior of Africa, in order to promote the destruction of the slave trade, its replacement by 'legitimate' commerce, and the extension of missionary activity in the region. The expedition was a failure: the Zambezi was found to be non-navigable, Livingstone's relations with his associates were difficult and helped to thwart the scientific objectives, and the earliest missionary endeavours met with disaster. » African history; Livingstone, David; slave trade

Zambezi [zam**bee**zee] or **Zambesi, River**, Port **Zambeze** River in SE Africa, flowing through Angola, Zimbabwe, Zambia, Namibia, and Mozambique; one of Africa's major rivers, length c.2 700 km/1 700 ml; rises in NW Zambia, and flows in a large 'S' shape generally SE; forms the Zambia–Namibia border (the Caprivi Strip); on the Zimbabwe–Zambia border are the Victoria Falls, L Kariba, and Kariba Dam; enters the Mozambique Channel as a marshy delta 210 km/130 ml NE of Beira; its middle course explored by Livingstone in the early 1850s. » Africa; Kariba Dam; Zambezi expedition

Zambia, official name **Republic of Zambia**, formerly **Northern Rhodesia** (to 1964) [**zam**bia] pop (1990e) 8 456 000; area 752 613 sq km/290 509 sq ml. S African republic, divided into eight provinces: bounded W by Angola, S by Namibia, SE by Zimbabwe and Mozambique, E by Malawi, NE by Tanzania, and NW by Zaire; capital, Lusaka; chief towns include Ndola, Kitwe, Kabwe, Livingstone; timezone GMT +2; chief ethnic group, Bantu (99%); chief religions, Christianity (over 50%), local beliefs; official language, English, with local languages widely spoken; unit of currency, the kwacha of 100 ngwee; high plateau, altitude 1 000–1 400 m/3 300–4 600 ft; highest point, 2 067 m/6 781 ft, SE of Mbala; Zambezi R rises in the N; warm-temperate climate on upland plateau; rainy season (Oct–Mar); average annual rainfall at Lusaka, 840 mm/33 in; maximum average daily temperatures, 23–35°C; tropical climate in lower river valleys; European influence followed Livingstone's discovery of the Victoria Falls, 1855; administered by the British South Africa Company under Rhodes; Northern and Southern Rhodesia declared a British sphere of influence, 1888; became Northern Rhodesia, 1911; British protectorate, 1924; joined with Southern Rhodesia and Nyasaland as the Federation of Rhodesia and Nyasaland, 1953; Federation dissolved, 1963; independence in 1964, with Kenneth Kaunda as first president; governed by a 125-member National Assembly serving 5-year terms, a president, chairman of cabinet, and Council of Ministers; economy based on copper and cobalt, which provide over half the national income; gold, lead, silver, zinc; maize, sugar, cassava, millet, sorghum, pulses, groundnuts, cotton; tobacco, cattle, copper wire, cement, fertilizer, explosives, vehicle assembly, sugar refining, food processing, textiles, glassware, tyres, bricks, brewing, oil refining. » Copperbelt; Kaunda; Livingstone, David; Lusaka; Rhodes; Zambezi, River; RR27 national holidays; RR67 political leaders

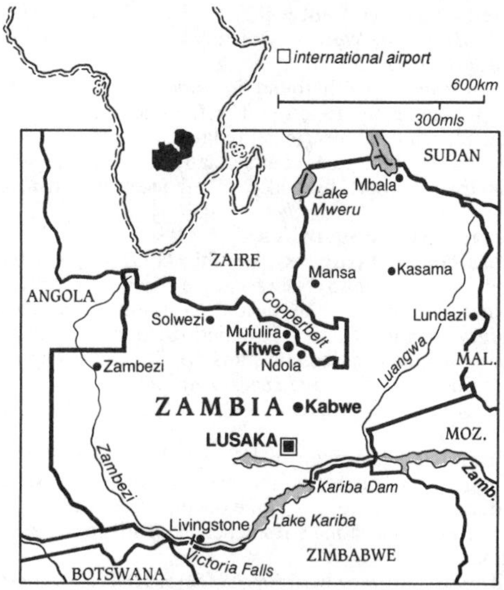

Zamboanga or **Zamboanga City** [sambo**hang**ga] 6°55N 122°05E, pop (1980) 343 722. Seaport in Zamboanga Del Sur province, W Mindanao, Philippines; founded, 1635; airfield; timber, copra, brass, tourism; Fort Pilar (17th-c); Bale Zamboanga Festival (Feb). » Philippines [i]

Zamenhof, L(azarus) L(udwig) [**za**muhnof] (1859–1917) Polish physician and oculist, the inventor of Esperanto, born at Białystok, Russian Empire. His aims were to promote international tolerance and world peace, which he hoped to achieve through the use of an artificial language. His textbook, *Lingvo Internacia* was published in 1887 under the pseudonym of 'Doktoro Esperanto'. He withdrew as leader of the Esperanto movement in 1912, and died in Warsaw. » artificial/auxiliary language; Esperanto

Zamyatin, Evgeny Ivanovich [zam**ya**tin] (1884–1937) Russian novelist and short-story writer, born in Lebedya, and educated at St Petersburg. He was exiled in 1905 after joining the Bolshevik Party, and again in 1911, but on each occasion soon returned to Russia. In 1921 he was a founder member of the Modernist group, the Serapion Brothers, and was briefly imprisoned by the Soviets in 1922. In 1932 he travelled to Paris, where he remained until his death. He is best known for the novel *My* (1920, We). » Bolsheviks; Modernism; Russian literature; Utopia

zander Freshwater fish found in large rivers and lakes of E Europe; length up to c.1 m/3¼ ft; greenish grey on back, underside white; a voracious predator, feeding on a variety of other fishes; exploited commercially in some regions, and popular as a sport fish; also called **pikeperch**. (*Stizostedion lucioperca*. Family: *Percidae*.) » fish [i]

Zante [**zan**tay] » **Zacynthus**

Zanuck, Darryl F(rancis) [**za**nuhk] (1902–79) US film producer, born at Wahoo, Nebraska. He became a scriptwriter for Warner Brothers in 1924, and co-founder of Twentieth-Century Pictures (later Twentieth-Century Fox) in 1933. Among his many successful films are *The Jazz Singer* (1927), *Little Caesar* (1930), *The Longest Day* (1962), and *The Sound of Music* (1965). He retired in 1971, and died at Palm Springs, California.

Zanzibar (city) [**zan**zibah] 6°10S 39°12E, pop (1978) 110 669. Capital of Zanzibar I, Tanzania, on the W coast; airfield; cigarettes, cloves, clove oil, lime oil, crafts; Beit El Ajaib palace (1833), Dr Livingstone's residence. » Tanzania [i]; Zanzibar (island)

Zanzibar (island) [**zan**zibah] pop (1985e) 571 000; area 1 660 sq km/641 sq ml. Island region of Tanzania, including several offshore islands, such as Tumbatu (NW) and Kwale (SW); separated from the mainland by the 40 km/25 ml-wide Zanzibar Channel; length, 85 km/53 ml; width, 39 km/24 ml; highest point, 118 m/387 ft; capital, Zanzibar; populated by Bantu peoples (from the mainland), Shiraz Persians, and Arabs; largely Islamic since the 10th-c; developed under Omani Arab rule into the commercial centre of the W Indian Ocean, 17th-c; now a world centre of clove production; annexed by Germany, 1885; exchanged for Heligoland in 1890, with Britain establishing a protectorate; independence, 1963; ruling Sultanate overthrown in 1964, and the People's Republic of Zanzibar created; joined with Tanganyika, Zanzibar, and Pemba to form the United Republic of Tanganyika and Zanzibar, later the United Republic of Tanzania. » African history; Tanzania [i]; Zanzibar (city)

Zaozhuang or **Tsaochuang** [jow**zhwang**] 34°53N 117°38E, pop (1984e) 1 570 300. City in Shandong province, E China; S of Jinan; railway; in major coal-mining area.

Zapata, Emiliano [sa**pah**ta] (1879–1919) Mexican revolutionary, born at Anencuilio, Morelos. He became a sharecropper and local leader, and after the onset of the Mexican Revolution, he mounted a land distribution programme in areas under his control. Along with Pancho Villa, he fought the Carranza government, and was eventually lured to his death at the Chinameca hacienda. » Mexico [i]; Villa

Zaporozhye, formerly **Aleksandrovsk** [zapuh**rozh**ye] 47°50N 35°10E, pop (1989) 884 000. River-port capital of Zaporozhskaya oblast, Ukraine, on R Dnieper; founded as a fortress, 1770; airfield; railway; major industrial and energy-producing centre; iron and steel, aluminium, cars, clothing, foodstuffs, hydroelectric power. » Ukraine

Zapotecs A Precolumbian Middle American Indian civilization of S Mexico (300 BC–AD 300), influenced by Olmec culture. It was centred on Monte Alban, a ceremonial site located on a high ridge in the Valley of Oaxaca. » American Indians; Olmecs

Zaria [**za**ria] 11°01N 7°44E, pop (1981e) 306 200. Town in Kaduna state, SW Nigeria, 145 km/90 ml SW of Kano; founded, 16th-c; airfield; railway junction; university (1962); engineering, tanning, printing, textiles, trade in sugar, groundnuts, cotton. » Nigeria [i]

Zarqa [**zah**ka] 32°04N 36°05E, pop (1983e) 215 000. Industrial town in Amman governorate, East Bank, N Jordan; site of major industrialization programme; large phosphate reserves nearby; airfield; railway; oil refining, tanneries, thermal centre. » Jordan [i]

zarzuela [thah**thway**la] A type of popular Spanish opera with spoken dialogue. The name derives from the palace near Madrid (now the king's residence) where the genre was first staged in the 17th-c. » opera

Zatopek, Emil [**za**tuhpek] (1922–) Czech athlete, born at Kopřivnice. After many successes in Czech track events, he won the 10 000 m title at the London Olympics in 1948. In the succeeding four years he showed himself to be the greatest long-distance runner of his time by breaking 13 world records and winning the 5 000 m, 10 000 m, and the Marathon at the 1952 Olympics. His wife **Dana** (*née* **Ingrova**, born on the same day as her husband, 19 Sep 1922)) won the Olympic javelin title in 1952. » athletics

Zealand, Danish **Sjælland**, Ger **Seeland** pop (1976e) 1 987 549; area 7 016 sq km/2 708 sq ml. Largest of the islands of Denmark, main island of the Sjælland group; bounded by the Kattegat (N, NW) and Great Belt (W); separated from Sweden by The Sound; length 128 km/80 ml; rises to 126 m/413 ft; chief towns Copenhagen, Roskilde, Helsingør; major agricultural area. » Denmark [i]; Sjælland

Zealots A militant Jewish sect which came into prominence in Palestine in the 1st-c AD. Its aim was to cast off the Roman yoke, using violence if necessary. It was disapproved of by the more traditional Pharisees and Sadducees. » Pharisees; Sadducees

zebra An African wild horse; stocky with bold black and white stripes and stubby mane; 3 species: *Equus grevyi* (**Grevy's zebra**, **imperial zebra**, or **hippotigris**) with narrow stripes; *Equus zebra* (**mountain zebra**) with loose flap of skin on throat, and short crosswise stripes on top of hindquarters (2 subspecies: **mountain zebra** and **Hartmann's mountain zebra**); and *Equus burchelli* (**common zebra**, **plains zebra** or **Burchell's zebra**) with variable markings (3 subspecies: **Grant's or Böhm's zebra**, **Selous's zebra**, and **Damaraland** or **Chapman's zebra**). » horse [i]; quagga

zebra finch A small waxbill, native to Australia and neighbouring islands; male with vertical black and white stripes on face; inhabits woodland and dry open country; eats seeds and insects; occurs in large flocks; makes domed nest from twigs and grass; kept widely as a cage bird. (*Poephila guttata*.) » waxbill

zebra fish Small colourful fish locally common in shallow inshore waters and estuaries of the Indian Ocean and W Pacific; length up to 30 cm/1 ft; grey to silver with dark horizontal banding; a good aquarium fish, also exploited as a food fish in Japan. (*Therapon jarbua*. Family: *Theraponidae*.) » fish [i]

zebrass An animal resulting from the mating of a male zebra and a female ass. » ass; zebra

zebu [**zee**boo] S Asian domestic cattle (introduced elsewhere); usually pale with upturned horns; fatty hump on shoulders; heavy hanging skin along throat; pendulous ears; traditionally considered sacred in India; more resistant to tropical diseases than European breeds; also known as **Brahman cattle** or **humped cattle**. (*Bos taurus*, sometimes called *Bos indicus*.) » Bovidae; cattle; yak

Zebulun [**zeb**yooluhn] One of the twelve tribes of ancient Israel, purportedly descended from the sixth son of Jacob by Leah. Its territory was in N Israel, a fertile part of later 'Galilee' between the sea of Galilee and the Mediterranean coast, but buffered on each side by other tribes; to the S it was bounded by the tribes of Issachar and Manasseh. » Israel, tribes of [i]; Jacob; Old Testament

Zechariah or **Zacharias, Book of** [zeka**ri**ya] One of twelve so-called 'minor' prophetic writings of the Hebrew Bible/Old Testament, attributed to Zechariah, writing c.520–518 BC after returning to Jerusalem from exile. It presents visions of the building of Jerusalem's Temple and of a new messianic age. Chapters 9–14, however, are often considered the work of later hands (c.3rd–5th-c BC), when the Temple rebuilding was no longer in view and when increasing disillusionment gave rise to stronger hopes for the future vindication of Israel. » Haggai, Book of; messianism; Old Testament; Temple, Jerusalem

Zeebrugge [**zee**bruguh] 51°20N 3°12E. Belgian ferry port, the scene of a major shipping disaster in March 1987, when the Townsend Thoresen ferry, *Herald of Free Enterprise*, foundered just outside the harbour, with the loss of 193 lives. The accident resulted from the main car deck doors having been left open to the sea. An official inquiry held four crew members and the ferry's operators to have been at fault in events leading to the capsize, and several recommendations to ensure future safety were made.

Zeeland [**zay**lant] pop (1984e) 355 500; land area 1 786 sq km/ 689 sq ml. Province in West Netherlands, bounded on the S by Belgium and on the W by the North Sea, in the estuary area of the Rhine, Maas and Schelde Rivers; capital, Middelburg; chief towns, Flushing, Breskens, Terneuzen; arable farming, fishing; entire area has been reclaimed from the sea by artificial dykes, and is mostly below sea-level; 'Delta Plan' intended to prevent a recurrence of the disastrous flooding of 1953, with sea and river dykes being strengthened and raised. » Netherlands, The [i]

Zeeman, Erik Christopher (1925–) British mathematician. Educated at Christ's Hospital and Cambridge, he became professor of mathematics at Warwick University in 1964. Early work developing topology and catastrophe theory produced many applications to physics, social sciences, and economics. » catastrophe theory; topology

Zeeman effect The splitting of atomic spectral lines when light-emitting atoms are subjected to strong magnetic fields; discovered in 1897 by Dutch physicist Pieter Zeeman. It results from the interaction of the outermost atomic electron with the field, so that what was a single spectral line without the field becomes two or more lines whose frequency spacing depends on the field strength. It is a consequence of the quantum nature of electrons in atoms. Important in understanding atomic structure, historically it supported the idea of electron spin. » atomic spectra [i]; Faraday effect; magnetic field [i]; spin; Zeeman, Pieter

Zeeman, Pieter (1865–1943) Dutch physicist, born at Zonnemaire. He studied and lectured at Leiden, and became professor of physics at Amsterdam (1900). An authority on magneto-optics, in 1902 he shared with Lorentz the Nobel Prize for Physics. He died in Amsterdam. » light; Lorentz; Zeeman effect

Zeffirelli, Franco (1923–) Italian stage, opera, and film director, born in Florence. He began his career as an actor and designer (1945–51), and during the 1950s produced many operas in Italy and abroad. His stage productions include *Romeo and Juliet* at the Old Vic (1960) and *Who's Afraid of Virginia Woolf* in Paris (1964). He has also filmed spectacular versions of *The Taming of the Shrew* (1966), *Romeo and Juliet* (1968), and the television *Jesus of Nazareth* (1977). Later productions include *Young Toscanini* (1988), and film versions of the operas *La Traviata* (1983) and *Otello* (1986).

Zeiss, Carl [tsiys] (1816–88) German optician, born at Weimar. In 1846 he established a factory at Jena which became noted for the production of lenses, microscopes, and other optical instruments. He died at Jena. » lens; microscope; optics [i]

Zeller See [**tsel**er zay] or **Untersee** [**un**terzay] Lake in N Austria, N of the Grossglockner; an arm of the Bodensee (L Constance) to which it is connected by the R Rhine; area 4.3 sq km/ 2¾ sq ml; length 4 km/2½ ml; width 1.5 km/0.9 ml; maximum depth 68 m/223 ft; resorts of Zell am See, Saalbach, and Kaprun have combined to form the 'Europa Sport Region'. » Austria [i]

zemstvo An organ of rural local self-government established in Russia following the emancipation of the serfs (1861). The zemstvos consisted of elected councillors, paid officials, and professional employees responsible for such matters as local education, health care, sanitation, and public welfare. Their activities were, however, severely curtailed by the bureaucratic and financial constraints imposed by central government. » duma; Russian history

Zen Buddhism [zen **bud**izm] A meditation school of Buddhism introduced into Japan by monks returning from China in the 12th-c. It originated in India, spreading to China, where it incorporated elements of Taoism. Zen stresses the personal experience of enlightenment based on a simple life lived close to nature, and upon methods of meditation which avoid complicated rituals and abstruse thought. In Japan, there are two main Zen bodies: Rinzai, introduced by Eisai (1141–1214), and Soto, introduced by Dogen (1200–53). Rinzai seeks spontaneous enlightenment, while Soto teaches a form of meditation in which enlightenment is a more gradual process. » Buddhism; Ch'an; meditation; Taoism

zener diode [**zee**nuh **diy**ohd] A semiconductor junction diode which produces a sharply increased reverse current when the reverse bias voltage reaches a certain value; named after US physicist Clarence Zener (1905–). This effect can occur at low reverse voltages of less than 6 volts. It is repeatable and reversible, and used in voltage stabilization circuits. » semiconductor diode

Zeng Guofan or **Tseng Kuo-fan** [**dzeng** gwoh**fan**] (1811–72) Chinese statesman, soldier, and philosopher, born in Hunan province. When ordered in 1852 to raise a militia against the Taiping rebels, he built a force as committed to Confucianism as the rebels were to their form of Christianity. His successes led to his appointment as Governor-General of the Nanjing (Nanking) area (1860); Nanjing was besieged, and recovered from the rebels in 1864. He died at Nanjing. » Confucianism; Taiping Rebellion

zenith » **nadir**

Zeno of Citium (c.336–c.265 BC) Greek philosopher, the founder of the Stoic school, born at Citium, Cyprus. He went to Athens c.315 BC, where he attended Plato's Academy and other philosophical schools, then opened his own school at the *Stoa poikile* ('painted porch'), from which the name of his philosophy derives. He committed suicide in Athens. » Stoicism

Zeno of Elea (c.490–c.420 BC) Greek philosopher, a native of Elea, Italy. A favourite disciple of Parmenides, he became known for a series of paradoxes, many of which denied the possibility of spatial division or motion. The best-known is 'Achilles and the Tortoise', whose conclusion is that no matter how fast Achilles runs, he cannot overtake a tortoise, if the tortoise has a head start. The rigour and dialectical nature of his arguments influenced Socrates' philosophical technique. » Parmenides; Socrates

zeolites [**zee**uhliyts] A group of hydrous aluminosilicate minerals containing sodium, potassium, calcium, and barium, and formed by the alteration of feldspars. They are characterized by open framework structures into which gases, ions, and molecules can easily diffuse, and hence they are used as molecular sieves and ion exchangers for water softening. They are also important catalysts for organic reactions. » feldspar; silicate minerals

Zephaniah, Book of [zefa**niy**a] One of twelve so-called 'minor' prophetic writings of the Hebrew Bible/Old Testament, attributed to Zephaniah, son of Cushi and descendant of Hezekiah, active in Josiah's reign (7th-c BC), but unknown apart from this work. It strongly denounces influences from heathen cults on Jewish religion, presumably preparing for Josiah's reforms, and proclaims God's judgment on Israel's enemies, but consolation for the remnant in Jerusalem who loyally await the 'Day of the Lord'. The mediaeval Latin hymn, *Dies irae*, was inspired by Zephaniah's account of the coming day of wrath. » Josiah; Old Testament; prophet

Zeppelin, Ferdinand (Adolf August Heinrich) Graf von (Count of) (1838–1917) German army officer, born at Constance. He served in the Franco-Prussian War, and in 1897–1900 constructed his first airship, setting up a factory for their construction at Freidrichshafen. Over 100 'zeppelins' were used in World War 1. He died near Berlin. » airship

Zermatt [**zer**mat] 46°01N 7°45E, pop (1981) 3 500. Fashionable skiing resort and popular mountaineering centre in the Pennine Alps, Valais canton, S Switzerland; Matterhorn rises to the SW. » Switzerland [i]

zero grazing A feeding system where freshly cut grass is fed to cattle, which are confined to a building, yard, or paddock, rather than being allowed to graze freely where the grass is growing. Zero grazing reduces wastage caused by fouling, poaching, and selective grazing. » dairy farming; intensive farming

zero point energy In quantum mechanics, the minimum non-zero energy of a quantum state. It is the residual energy that exists even as the temperature is reduced towards absolute zero;

a consequence of the uncertainty principle. » Heisenberg uncertainty principle; quantum mechanics

Zeus [zyoos] In Greek mythology, the supreme god, equivalent to Jupiter. He is usually depicted with thunderbolt and eagle, and associated with the oak-tree. Many conflicting myths have arisen from his prominence in local cults; in later Greek religion, he is almost a monotheistic concept. » aegis; Cronus; Jupiter (mythology); Prometheus

Zeus, statue of [zyoos] A colossal statue, wrought in ivory and gold over a core of wood, located in the Temple of Zeus at Olympia. It was one of the foremost works of the great Athenian sculptor, Phidias. » Olympia; Seven Wonders of the Ancient World; temple

Zeuxis [**zyook**sis] (5th-c BC) Greek painter, born at Heraclea. He excelled in the representation of natural objects. According to legend, his painting of a bunch of grapes was so realistic that birds tried to eat the fruit. » Greek art

Zhang Guotao or **Chang Kuo-T'ao** [jang gwoh**tow**] (1897–1979) Founding member of the Chinese Communist Party, born in Jiangxi province. As a student he played a part in the May Fourth Movement of 1919, and in 1921 joined the new Chinese Communist Party, rising to prominence as a labour leader. He played a leading role in the Nanchang Mutiny (1927). He opposed the elevation of Mao Zedong (Mao Tse-tung) as leader of the Party, but his army was destroyed by Muslim forces in the NW. He defected to the Nationalists in 1938. When the Chinese Communist Party won national power in 1949, he moved to Hong Kong. He died in Toronto. » communism; Mao Zedong; May Fourth Movement

Zhdanov, formerly **Mariupol** (to 1948) 47°05N 37°34E, pop (1983) 516 000. Seaport in Donetskaya oblast, Ukraine; at the mouth of the R Kalmius, on the Sea of Azov; founded, 18th-c; airfield; railway; noted mud-bath resort; coal trade, iron and steel, chemicals, fertilizers, metallurgical equipment, fishing. » Ukraine

Zhengzhou [jeng**joh**], **Chengchow**, or **Cheng-hsien** 34°35N 113°38E, pop (1984e) 1 551 600. Capital of Henan province, NC China; major market and transportation centre first settled before 1000 BC; modern settlement since arrival of railway, 1898; airfield; railway junction; textiles, food processing, light engineering; Henan provincial museum. » China [i]

Zhenjiang or **Chinkiang** [jenjiang] 32°08N 119°30E, pop (1984e) 397 300. River port in Jiangsu province, E China, at confluence of Yangtze R and Grand Canal; founded, 545 BC; railway; metallurgy, machinery, automobiles, ship-building, electronics, textiles, pharmaceuticals, chemicals; scenic area ('Three Hills of the Capital Gateway'); Fahaizdong (Monk Cave) and Bailongdong (White Dragon Cave); Jinshan Temple (4th-c); monastery, numerous temples, pavilions, and inscribed stone tablets on Jiao Shen (E); Dujinglou (Pavilion for Choosing Prospective Sons-in-Law), Shijianshi (Testing Swords Stone). » China [i]; Grand Canal

Zhitomir, also **Jitomir** [zhitomyir] 50°18N 28°40E, pop (1983) 264 000. Capital city of Zhitomirskaya oblast, WC Ukraine; on R Teterev, 165 km/102 ml W of Kiev; founded, 9th-c; railway junction; agricultural trade, machinery, metalworking, flax, clothing, footwear. » Ukraine

Zhou dynasty A Chinese dynasty founded between 1122 and 1027 BC. Accounts of its origins are a mixture of history and legend. It is traditionally held to have been founded by King Wu, who overthrew the last tyrannical ruler of the Shang dynasty, Zhouxin. Its capital was at Hao (near Xi'an) until 771 BC, and at Luoyi (near Luoyang) until its occupation by the Win in 256 BC. A form of feudal monarchy, the Zhou saw the first flowering of Chinese historical, philosophical, and literary writing, and the establishment of the culture that has endured to the present. » China [i]

Zhou Enlai or **Chou En-Lai** [**joh** enliy] (1898–1975) One of the leaders of the Communist Party of China, and Prime Minister of the Chinese People's Republic from its inception in 1949 until his death. In 1927 he became a member of the Politburo of the Communist Party of China, and in 1932 he was appointed to succeed Mao Zedong (Mao Tse-tung) as political commissar of the Red Army, but after 1935, following Mao's elevation, he served him faithfully, becoming the Party's chief negotiator and diplomat. As Minister of Foreign Affairs (and concurrently Prime Minister) he vastly increased China's international influence. Perhaps his greatest triumph of mediation was in the Cultural Revolution in China, when he worked to preserve national unity and the survival of government against the forces of anarchy. He died in Beijing (Peking). » Comintern; communism; Cultural Revolution; Jiang Jieshi; Mao Zedong; May Fourth Movement; Xi'an incident

Zhoukoudian [johkoh**dyan**] A village 55 km/34 ml SW of Beijing (Peking), where fossil remains of *Homo erectus* were discovered during the 1920s; a world heritage site. A wealth of other items have also been unearthed, and are displayed in an archaeological complex. » *Homo* [i]

Zhu De or **Chu Teh** [joo **de**] (1886–1976) One of the founders of the Chinese Red Army, born in Sichuan province, closely associated throughout his later career with Mao Zedong (Mao Tse-tung). He took part in the Nanchang Mutiny (1927), his defeated troops joining with those of Mao to found the Jiangxi Soviet. There, he and Mao evolved the idea of 'people's war', beating off attacks by vastly superior Nationalist forces until finally driven out in 1934. The Red Army then undertook the Long March, in which Zhu De was the leading commander. He died in Beijing (Peking). » communism; Long March; Mao Zedong

Zhu Jiang or **Chu-kiang**, Eng **Pearl River** [joo **jeeang**] River in S China formed by confluence of Xi Jiang, Bei Jiang, and Dong Jiang Rivers; forms wide estuary between Hong Kong and Macao, S of Guangzhou (Canton), flowing into the S China Sea; lengths, Xi Jiang 2 197 km/1 365 ml (taken as length of the Zhu Jiang itself), Bei Jiang 468 km/291 ml, Dong Jiang 523 km/325 ml; densely populated, fertile river valley; navigable as far as Wuzhou for large vessels. » China [i]

Zhukov, Giorgiy Konstantinovich (1896–1974) Soviet Marshal, born at Strelkovka. He joined the Red Army in 1918, commanded Soviet tanks in Outer Mongolia (1939), and became army Chief-of-Staff (1941). He lifted the siege of Moscow, and in 1943 his counter-offensive was successful at Stalingrad. In 1944–5 he captured Warsaw, conquered Berlin, and accepted the German surrender. After the war he was Commander of the Russian zone of Germany, and became Minister of Defence (1955), but was dismissed by Khrushchev in 1957. » Khrushchev; Stalingrad, Battle of; World War 2

Zia Ul-Haq, Muhammad [**zee**a ul **hak**] (1924–88) Pakistani general and President (1978–88), born near Jullundhur, Punjab. He served in Burma, Malaya, and Indonesia in World War 2, and in the wars with India (1965, 1971), rising rapidly to become general and army Chief-of-Staff (1976). He led a bloodless coup in 1977, imposed martial law, banned political activity, and introduced an Islamic code of law. Despite international protest, he sanctioned the hanging of former President Bhutto in 1979. He was killed in an aeroplane crash near Bahawalpur. » Bhutto; Pakistan [i]

Ziaur Rahman [zeea**oor** rah**mahn**] (1935–81) Bangladeshi soldier and President (1977–81). He played an important part in the emergence of the state of Bangladesh. Appointed chief of army staff after the assassination of Mujibur Rahman (1975), he became the dominant figure within the military. His government was of a military character, even after the presidential election of 1978 which confirmed his position. He survived many attempted coups, but was finally assassinated in Dhaka. » Bangladesh [i]; Rahman

Zibo [tsi**boh**] or **Tzu-po** 36°51N 118°01E, pop (1984e) 2 280 500. City in Shandong province, E China; E of Jinan; railway; coal mining, machinery, chemicals, electrical equipment. » China [i]

zidovudine » **AZT**

Ziegfeld, Florenz [**zeeg**feld] (1869–1932) US theatre manager, born in Chicago. He devised and perfected the American revue spectacle, based on the *Folies Bergères*. His *Follies of 1907* was the first of an annual series that continued until 1931 and made his name synonymous with extravagent theatrical production. He also produced a wide range of other musical shows, such as *Show Boat* (1927) and *Bitter Sweet* (1929). He died in Hollywood. » musical comedy; theatre

Ziegler, Karl (1898–1973) German chemist, born at Helsa.

The ziggurat at Ur

Educated at Marburg, he taught at Heidelberg and Halle, and in 1943 was appointed director of the Max Planck Carbon Research Institute at Mülheim. With Italian chemist Giulio Natta (1903–79) he was awarded the 1963 Nobel Prize for his research into long-chain polymers leading to new developments in industrial materials, such as polypropylene. He died at Mülheim. » polymerization

ziggurat A temple tower, in the shape of a mountain, found throughout ancient Sumeria and the adjacent region of Elam. It consisted of a high, pyramidal mound, constructed in stages and surmounted by a shrine. Access to the shrine was by a series of external stairways or ramps. Good examples come from Eridu, Ur, Uruk, and Choga Zanbil near Susa. » Elam; Sumer

Zillertal Alps [tsi**l**ertal], Ger **Zillertaler Alpen**, Ital **Alpi Aurine** Mountain range in the E Alps of N Italy and the S Tirol of Austria; extends from the Birnlücke in the E to the Brenner in the W; the highest peak is Hochfeiler (3 510 m/11 516 ft). » Alps

Zimbabwe [zim**bab**way], official name **Republic of Zimbabwe**, formerly **Southern Rhodesia** (to 1979) pop (1990e) 9 370 000; area 391 090 sq km/150 961 sq ml. Landlocked S African republic, divided into eight provinces; bounded S by South Africa, SW by Botswana, NW by Zambia, and NE, E, and SE by Mozambique; capital, Harare; chief towns include Bulawayo, Gweru, Mutare; timezone GMT +2; chief ethnic groups, Bantu (97%), mainly Shona and Ndebele; chief religions, Christianity and local beliefs; official language, English; unit of currency, the Zimbabwe dollar.

Physical description and climate. High plateau country, altitude 900–1 200 m/3 000–3 900 ft; 'Highveld' runs SW–NE, 1 200–1 500 m/3 900–5 000 ft; relief dips towards the Zambezi (N) and Limpopo (S) Rivers; mountains on E frontier rise to 2 592 m/8 504 ft at Mt Inyangani; generally subtropical climate, strongly influenced by altitude; warm and dry in the lowlands, with annual rainfall 400–600 mm/16–24 in; mountains receive 1 500–2 000 mm/60–80 in; average maximum daily temperatures at Harare, 21–29°C.

History and government. A mediaeval Bantu kingdom (12th–16th-c), with capital at Great Zimbabwe; visited by Livingstone in the 1850s; Southern Rhodesia under British influence in the 1880s as the British South Africa Company under Cecil Rhodes; divided into Northern and Southern Rhodesia, 1911; Southern Rhodesia became a self-governing British colony, 1923; Northern and Southern Rhodesia and Nyasaland formed a multi-racial federation, 1953; independence of Nyasaland and Northern Rhodesia, 1963; opposition to the independence of Southern Rhodesia under African rule resulted in a Unilateral Declaration of Independence (UDI) by the White-dominated government, 1965; economic sanctions and internal guerrilla activity forced the government to negotiate with the main African groups, the Zimbabwe African People's Union (ZAPU), led by Joshua Nkomo, the Zimbabwe African National Union (ZANU), led by Robert Mugabe, and the United African National Council (UANC), led by Bishop Abel Muzorewa; power eventually transferred to the African majority; independence as Zimbabwe in 1980, with Robert Mugabe as first prime minister; bicameral legislature replaced in 1990 by a new single-chamber parliament, the House of Assembly, with 150 members (120 elected); an executive president combines posts of head of state and head of government.

Economy. Agriculture involves 70% of the population; maize, sorghum, millet, rice, cassava, vegetables, tobacco, coffee, cotton, tea, groundnuts, wheat, sugar cane; cattle, pigs, poultry, forestry; rich mineral resources include gold, asbestos, nickel, coal, copper, chrome ore, iron ore, tin, silver, cobalt; iron, steel, foodstuffs, drink, tobacco, textiles, clothing, footwear, wood, furniture, paper; tourism to the national parks. » Harare; Livingstone, David; Mugabe; Muzorewa; Nkomo; Rhodes; Zimbabwe, Great; RR27 national holidays; RR67 political leaders

Zimbabwe African National Union » **Patriotic Front**

Zimbabwe African People's Union » **Patriotic Front**

Zimbabwe, Great Stone ruins covering an area of 25 ha/62 acres in SE Zimbabwe; a world heritage site. The site was probably occupied from the 4th-c, and the ruins themselves, which consist of a hilltop stronghold with dwellings below, date from the 8th-c onwards. The term *zimbabwe* is Bantu for 'stone houses'. » Zimbabwe [i]

Zimmer® walking frame A self-standing metal frame consisting of two double legs joined together by a bar in front; the name derives from the US orthopaedic company which manufactures it. It is used to assist walking by elderly persons, or those with pain or weakness in the legs. » orthopaedics

zinc Zn, element 30, density 7 g/cm^3, melting point 420°C. An active, silvery-blue metal, never occurring uncombined, but found in many minerals, especially as a sulphide. It may be recovered by roasting in air to give an oxide which is then reduced by carbon. It has been used from earliest times as an alloy with copper (*brass*), which is both stronger and less readily corroded than copper. It owes its corrosion resistance to an adherent oxide coating, and is used as a plating to protect iron (*galvanizing*). It is also used in primary batteries as an anode. In nearly all of its compounds, it has oxidation state +2. **Zinc oxide** (ZnO) is used as a pigment, filler, and mild antiseptic in cosmetics, pharmaceuticals, paints, and plastics. **Zinc sulphide** (ZnS) is used in luminous screens. » alloy; brass; chemical elements; metal; RR90

zinc blende » **sphalerite**

Zinder [**zin**der] 13°46N 8°58E, pop (1983) 82 800. Capital of Zinder department, SEC Niger, W Africa, 725 km/450 ml E of Niamey; on an important trade route to Kano (Nigeria); occupied by the French, 1899; colonial capital until the 1920s;

airfield; tanning, food processing, power plant; market centre; Sultan's Palace (1860). » Niger [i]

Zinjanthropus [zinjanthruhpuhs] The former name of *Australopithecus boisei.* » *Australopithecus*

zinnia An annual, perennial or small shrub, distributed from S USA to S America, but predominantly Mexican; leaves in opposite pairs or whorled; chrysanthemum-like flower-heads, showy. Several are popular garden ornamentals. (Genus: *Zinnia*, 22 species. Family: *Compositae*.) » annual; chrysanthemum; perennial; shrub

Zinoviev, Grigoriy Yevseyevich [zinovyef], originally **G Ye Radomyslskiy** (1883–1936) Russian Jewish revolutionary and politician, born in Kherson province, the Ukraine, and educated at Berne University. In 1924 he was made a member of the ruling Politburo, but because of opposition to Stalin's policies was expelled from the Party (1926). Reinstated in 1928, he was again expelled in 1932, and in 1935 was arrested after the assassination of Kirov. Charged with organizing terrorist activities, he was executed following the first of Stalin's Great Purge trials in Moscow. The so-called **Zinoviev letter** urging British Communists to incite revolution in Britain contributed to the downfall of the Labour government in the 1924 general elections. » Bolsheviks; Kirov, Sergey Mironovich; Lenin; October Revolution; Stalin

Zinzendorf, Nicolaus Ludwig, Graf von (Count of) (1700–60) German religious leader, born at Dresden. Educated at Wittenburg, he held a government post at Dresden. He invited the persecuted Moravians to his estates, and there founded for them the colony of *Herrnhut* ('the Lord's keeping'). His zeal led to conflict with the government, and he was exiled from Saxony in 1736. Ordained at Tübingen (1734), he became Bishop of the Moravian Brethren, wrote over 100 books, and died at Herrnhut. » Moravian Brethren

Zion or **Sion** [ziyon] (Heb probably 'fortress' or 'rock') Term used in the Old Testament and Jewish literature in various ways: for one of the hills in Jerusalem; for the mount on which the Temple was built; for the Temple itself; and symbolically for Jerusalem or even Israel as a whole. Today 'Mount Zion' usually denotes the SW hill in Jerusalem just S of the city wall. » Temple, Jerusalem; Zionism

Zionism The movement which sought to recover for the Jewish people its historic Palestinian homeland (the *Eretz Israel*) after centuries of dispersion. The modern movement arose in the late 19th-c with plans for Jewish colonization of Palestine, and under Theodor Herzl also developed a political programme to obtain sovereign state rights over the territory. Gaining support after World War 1, its objectives were supported by the British Balfour Declaration in 1917, as long as rights for non-Jews in Palestine were not impaired. After World War 2, the establishment of the Jewish state in 1948 received United Nations support. Zionism is still active, as a movement encouraging diaspora Jews to immigrate to and take an interest in the Jewish state. » Herzl; Israel [i]; messianism; Zion

zircon A zirconium silicate ($ZrSiO_4$) mineral commonly occurring in very small amounts in a wide variety of rocks. It is very hard, with a high refractive index, and is used as a gemstone. It is the principal source of zirconium. » gemstones

Ziska or **Žižka, John** [zhishka] (c.1370–1424) Bohemian Hussite leader, born at Trocznov. He fought against the Poles, Turks, and French, and soon after the murder of Huss, became Chamberlain to King Wenceslas. During the Civil War he was chosen leader of the popular party, captured Prague (1421), and erected the fortress of Tabor, his party coming to be called Taborites. Having lost both his eyes in battles, he continued to lead his troops in a series of victories, compelling Emperor Sigismund to offer the Hussites religious liberty, but he died at Przibislav before the war was over. » Huss; Sigismund (Emperor)

zither An Alpine musical instrument consisting of a box strung with five fretted and about 30 open (unfretted) strings. The fretted strings are stopped by the fingers of the left hand and plucked with a plectrum worn on the right thumb; the right-hand fingers pluck the open strings. The name is also used as a generic term for a variety of instruments consisting of a string bearer with or without a separate resonator – in other words, a simple chordophone. » chordophone; dulcimer; plectrum; string instrument 2 [i]

Zlatni Pyasăci [zlatnee pyasatsee], Eng **Golden Sands** 43°16N 28°00E. Beach resort on the Black Sea in Varna province, E Bulgaria; 17 km/10 ml NE of Varna; centre for international conferences and hydrotherapy treatment. » Black Sea; Bulgaria [i]

zodiac A zone of fixed stars, approximately 16 degrees in width, which marks the apparent courses of the Sun, Moon, and planets (apart from Pluto) about the Earth. Early astronomers projected patterns on to this area of sky, creating 12 groupings or constellations. It is important to distinguish between constellations – rather ill-defined star groups of variable size – and *signs*, an idealized version occupying equal 30 degree segments. The *sidereal* zodiac moves relative to the position of the Sun at the (northern) spring equinox. The *tropical* zodiac simply takes the equinoxial position as a starting point, irrespective of the underlying constellation. Only rarely do these two zodiacs coincide. On the 21st of each month (approximately) the Sun appears to change sign in the tropical zodiac, from Aries through Taurus, Gemini, Cancer, Leo, Virgo, Libra, Scorpio, Sagittarius, Capricorn, Aquarius and Pisces. The disposition of the planets within the signs of the zodiac furnishes important information to the astrologer. » astrology; constellation; equinox

zodiacal light A permanent glow of light, readily visible in the tropics after sunset as a cone of light extending from the horizon; also known as **gegenschein**. It is sunlight reflected from dust in interplanetary space. » interplanetary matter

Zoffany, John or **Johann** (1734–1810) London portrait painter, born at Frankfurt am Main, Germany. After studying art in Rome, he settled in London c.1758, securing royal patronage. His speciality was the conversation piece. He later lived in Florence (1772–9) and India (1783–90). He died at Strand, Middlesex. » conversation piece; English art

Signs of the zodiac

Zog I [zohg] (1895–1961) Albanian Prime Minister (1922–4), President (1925–8), and King (1928–39), born at Burgajet. Educated in Istanbul, he became leader of the nationalist party, and formed a republican government in 1922. Forced into exile in 1924, he returned with the assistance of Yugoslavia, and became President, proclaiming himself King in 1928. After Albania was overrun by the Italians (1939), he fled to Britain, and later lived in Egypt and France. He formally abdicated in 1946, and died at Suresnes, France. » Albania [i]

Zohar [**zoh**hah] The main text of the Jewish Kabbalah. Discovered in Spain in the late 13th-c, it was said to be the mystical teachings of Rabbi Simeon bar Yochai and his followers, who lived in Palestine in the 2nd–3rd-c. There have always been doubts about its authenticity, but Kabbalistic tradition accepts it as genuine. » Judaism; Kabbalah

zokor » **mole rat**

Zola, Emile (1840–1902) French novelist, born in Paris. He became a clerk and journalist, then began to write short stories, beginning with *Contes à Ninon* (1864). After his first major novel, *Thérèse Raquin* (1867), he began the long series called *Les Rougon-Macquart*, a sequence of 20 books described in the subtitle as 'the natural and social history of a family under the Second Empire'. The series contains such acclaimed studies as *Nana* (1880), *Germinal* (1885), and *La Terre* (1887, Earth), and *La Bête humaine* (1890, The Beast in Man). In 1898 he espoused the cause of Dreyfus in his open letter *J'accuse*, and was sentenced to imprisonment (1898), but escaped to England, and was given a great welcome on his return after Dreyfus had been cleared. He died in Paris. » Dreyfus; French literature; novel

Zollverein [**tsol**veriyn] A German customs union, based on the enlarged Prussia of 1814, and officially constituted in 1834. It comprised all of Germany save the Austrian Empire, Hanover, Brunswick, Oldenburg, and three N maritime states: a total of 17 states embracing 26 million people. It represented an important stage in the German unification process. » customs union; Prussia

zone plate In optics, a form of flat lens comprising alternating dark and transparent rings. Interference between light emerging from various transparent rings produces focusing. The zone plates of appropriate material are useful as lenses for microwaves and X-rays, for which glass lenses are useless. » interference [i]; lens; optics [i]

zoogeography [zohuhji**o**grafee] The study of the past and present geographical distributions of animals and animal communities. Hypotheses which explain these distribution patterns include dispersal (by migration or accidental transport) and separation by vicariance events (the formation of natural barriers to the spread of animals, especially by geological forces such as the spreading of the plates of the Earth's crust). » biogeography; phytogeography; zoology

zoology The branch of biology dealing with the study of animals. It includes their anatomy, behaviour, ecology, evolution, genetics, and physiology. » biological sciences; palaeozoology

zoom A visual effect in motion pictures or video, enlarging or diminishing the image as though rapidly approaching or receding. Originally made by actual camera movement, it is now provided by a **zoom lens** whose focal length, and hence its magnification, can be continuously varied. The range can be as much as 10:1, so that a single lens can function as wide-angle and telephoto. Zoom lenses are now standard for all video cameras, and are widely used in cinematography; they are sometimes fitted to portable projectors to give variable magnification for different screen sizes and distances. » camera; lens

zooplankton » **plankton**

zoosemiotics [zohsemee**o**tiks] The science of animal communication. Combining semiotics and ethology, this interdisciplinary field seeks to understand the many complex systems of meaning employed by animals. It includes the study of acoustic, visual, and chemical systems of communication, in such domains as bird call, bee-dancing, marine echolocation, cat and dog facial expressions, primate cries, and grasshopper signals. The term was coined in 1963 by the US linguist Thomas A Sebeok (1920–). » bee dancing; ethology; semiotics

zorilla [thor**ee**lya] An African mammal of family *Mustelidae*; long coat and long brush-like tail; black with white markings on face, long white stripes along body; superficially resembles the skunk, and may squirt foul-smelling fluid; also known as **striped polecat**. (*Ictonyx striatus*) » Mustelidae; polecat; skunk

Zorn, Anders (Leonard) (1860–1920) Swedish etcher, sculptor, and painter, born and died at Mora. He studied at Stockholm, travelled widely, returning to Mora in 1896. His paintings deal mainly with Swedish peasant life. He achieved European fame as an etcher, known for his series of nudes, and for his portraits. » etching

Zoroaster (Gr form of **Zarathushtra**) (6th-c BC) Iranian prophet and founder of the ancient Parsee religion which bears his name. He had visions of Ahura Mazda, which led him to preach against polytheism. He appears as a historical person only in the earliest portion of the Avesta. As the centre of a group of chieftains, he carried on a struggle for the establishment of a holy agricultural state against Turanian and Vedic aggressors. » Ahura Mazda; Avesta; polytheism; prophet; Zoroastrianism

Zoroastrianism The worship of a supreme God, Ahura Mazda, in Iran during the first millennium BC. Rites of worship were performed by priests (*Magi*), and there was a body of scriptures called *Avesta*, the earliest part of which was formed of hymns attributed to a religious teacher, Zoroaster. The expansion of Islam forced Zoroastrianism out of Persia, and today it is practised by Parsees. » Ahriman; Ahura Mazda; Avesta; Parseeism; Zoroaster

Zorrilla y Moral, José [thor**ee**lya ee mor**al**] (1817–93) Spanish poet, born at Valladolid. He studied law at Toledo and Valladolid, then devoted himself to literature in Madrid, where he died. He wrote many plays based on national legend, notably *Don Juan Tenorio* (1844), performed annually on All Saints' Day in Spanish-speaking countries. » poetry; Spanish literature

Zörs [tsurs] 47°09N 10°12E. Winter sports resort village in the Lechtal Alps, Vorarlberg, W Austria; altitude 1 720 m/5 643 ft; chairlift facilities on the Seekopf, Nördlicher, Trittkopf, and Krabachjoch mountains. » Lechtal Alps

Zouaves A body of troops in the French army, first raised from Algerian tribes in 1830, who dressed in flamboyant Moorish costume. During the American Civil War, several 'Zouave' style volunteer regiments were raised on the US side. » American Civil War

Zrenjanin [**zren**yanin], formerly **Veliki Beckerek** or **Petrovgrad** 45°22N 20°23E, pop(1981) 139 300. River-port city in the autonomous province of Vojvodina, N Serbia republic, Yugoslavia, on R Begej; railway; foodstuffs, canning, machinery. » Serbia; Yugoslavia [i]

Zsigmondy, Richard (Adolf) [**zhig**mondee] (1865–1929) Austrian chemist, born in Vienna. Educated at Munich, he carried out research at Berlin, taught at Graz, and became professor at Göttingen (1908–29), where he died. He was a pioneer of colloid chemistry, gaining the Nobel Prize for chemistry in 1925. In 1903 he introduced the ultramicroscope. » colloid

Zuccarelli, Francesco [zukah**ray**lee] (1702–88) Italian painter, born at Pitigliano, Tuscany. He trained at Florence and Rome, and was active at Florence, but worked mainly in Venice after 1732. His pastoral landscapes, populated by shepherds and maidens and painted in a soft Rococo style, were very popular, especially in England, where he worked 1752–62 and 1765–71. He died in Florence. » Italian art; landscape painting; Rococo

Zuccari or **Zuccaro, Taddeo** [tsu**kah**ree] (1529–66) Italian painter, born at Vado. Largely self-taught, he executed several frescoes and easel pieces, especially for the Farnese family. He died in Rome. His brother **Federigo** (c.1543–1609) painted portraits and frescoes, visited England, and became an influential art theorist. He died at Ancona. The two brothers were leaders of the Roman late Mannerist school. » fresco; Italian art; Mannerism

zucchini [zuk**ee**nee] » **courgette**

Zuckerman, Solly, Baron (1904–) British zoologist, born in

Cape Town, South Africa. He came to Oxford in 1934, became professor of anatomy at Birmingham (1946–68), and chief scientific adviser to the British government (1964–71). He carried out extensive research into primates, publishing such classic works as *The Social Life of Monkeys and Apes* (1932). He was made a life peer in 1971. » primate (biology)

Zug [tsug] 47°10N 8°31E, pop (1980) 21 609. Capital of Zug canton, C Switzerland; at NE end of Zuger Zee, 24 km/15 ml S of Zürich; railway junction; noted for its local kirsch; metallurgy, textiles; Gothic church (15th–16th-c). » Gothic architecture; Switzerland [i]

Zugspitze [**tsuk**shpitsuh] 47°25N 11°00E. Mountain in Germany, rising to 2 962 m/9 718 ft on the Wettersteingebirge of the Bavarian Alps, near the Austro-German border; highest point in Germany; hotel near the summit is one of Europe's highest atmospheric sampling stations. » Bavarian Alps

Zuider Zee [**zi**yder **zee**] Former shallow inlet of the North Sea in W Netherlands, divided since the 1920s into the outer Waddenzee (Wadden Sea) and the inner Ijsselmeer, which has been partially reclaimed as polder land. » Afsluitdijk Sea Dam; Netherlands, The [i]

Zukofsky, Louis [zoo**kof**skee] (1904–78) US poet, born and brought up in New York City. A leading experimentalist after Pound, his poems first appeared in *An Objectivist Anthology* (1932). Later works experimented with sound and typography. Two volumes of *All: The Collected Short Poems* (1965, 1967) exhibit his precision and frugality, which have been very influential. He published his *Autobiography* in 1970, and died at Port Jefferson, New York. » American literature; poetry; Pound

Zulu A Bantu-speaking agricultural and cattle people of Natal, South Africa; one of the Nguni group. They closely resemble the Xhosa both culturally and linguistically. The Zulu were formed into a kingdom in the early 19th-c, and became a formidable fighting force, dispersing many of the other peoples of S Africa far afield; but they were conquered by the Boers and British, and much of their territory annexed. They have retained a strong self-identity, and are organized politically into the modern Inkatha movement under their leader Chief Gatsha Buthulezi. Their territory, greatly contracted, became one of the 'Homelands' of modern South Africa: Kwazulu. Population c.6 million. » African history/languages; Afrikaners; Nguni; Xhosa

Zuni A N American Indian group of the American SW, living in New Mexico and Arizona; one of the Pueblo peoples, closely resembling the Hopi and Pueblo. A peaceful agricultural people, they were defeated by the Spanish in the 17th-c. Many are assimilated to US culture, although certain traditions are still intact. Population c.7 300. » Pueblo; Southwest Indians

Zurbarán, Francisco de [thoorba**ran**] (1598–1664) Spanish religious painter, born at Fuente de Cantos. He spent most of his life at Seville, where his best-known work, an altarpiece, is to be found. Apart from a few portraits and still-life studies, his main subjects were monastic and historical, and he came to be called the 'Spanish Caravaggio'. He died in Madrid. » altarpiece; Caravaggio; Spanish art

Zürich [**zoo**rikh], Ger [**tsü**reekh] 47°22N 8°32E, pop (1980) 369 522. Financial centre and capital of Zürich canton, N Switzerland; on R Limmat, at NW end of L Zurich, 96 km/60 ml NE of Bern; largest city in Switzerland; joined Swiss Confederation, 1351; important centre in the Reformation and Counter-Reformation; airport (Kloten); railway; university (1833); banking, finance, commerce, engineering, electrical products, textiles, tourism; Grossmünster (11th–14th-c), Fraumünster (13th-c, restored), town hall (17th-c), St Peter's Church (13th-c); International June Festival Weeks. » Reformation; Switzerland [i]

Zürich sunspot number A rather arbitrary index for describing the total numbers of sunspots and sunspot groups. It is of value, because it has been estimated since the mid-18th-c, and therefore gives an excellent longitudinal data series which shows phenomena such as the 11-year solar cycle effectively. » sunspot

Zweig, Arnold [tsviyk] (1887–1968) German-Jewish author, born at Glogua. His writing is socialistic in outlook, and coloured by his interest in Zionism, which led him to seek refuge in Palestine when exiled by the Nazis in 1934. He is best known for his pacifist novel, *Der Streit um den Sergeanten Grischa* (1928, The Case of Sergeant Grischa). He died in Berlin. » German literature; novel; Zionism

Zweig, Stefan [tsviyk] (1881–1942) Austrian writer, born in Vienna. He became known as a poet and translator, then as a biographer, short-story writer, and novelist, his work being characterized by his psychological insight into character. His best-known work was his set of historical portraits, *Sternstunden der Menschheit* (1928, The Tide of Fortune). He emigrated to London in 1934, and acquired British nationality, later moving to the USA and Brazil, where he committed suicide. » German literature; novel; poetry; short story

Zwickau [**tsvi**kow] 50°43N 12°30E, pop (1982) 120 852. Mining and industrial city in Zwickau district, SE Germany; on R Mulde, SW of Karl Marx Stadt; a free imperial city (1290–1323); railway; motor vehicles, chemicals, coal mining; birthplace of Schumann. » Germany [i]; Schumann, Robert

Zwicky, Fritz [**zvi**kee] (1898–1974) Swiss astronomer, born at Varna, Bulgaria. Educated in Zürich, he took a position at the California Institute of Technology in 1925. He researched extensively into galaxies and interstellar matter, and produced the standard catalogue on compact galaxies. In 1934 he predicted the existence of neutron stars and black holes. He died at Pasadena, California. » black hole; galaxy; interstellar molecule; neutron star

Zwingli, Huldreich [**tsving**lee] or **Ulrich** Lat **Ulricus Zuinglius** (1484–1531) Swiss Protestant reformer, born at Wildhaus. Educated at Berne, Vienna, and Basle, he was ordained in 1506, and became a chaplain to the Swiss mercenaries. In 1518, elected preacher in the Zürich minster, he opposed the selling of indulgences, and espoused the Reformed doctrines, obtaining the support of the civil authorities. In 1524 he split with Luther over the question of the Eucharist, rejecting every form of corporeal presence. War between the cantons followed, and he was killed in an attack on Zürich. » Eucharist; indulgences; Luther; Protestantism; Reformation

zwitterion [**tsvi**teriyuhn] A molecule containing both a positive and a negative charge simultaneously. It is the predominant form of an amino acid in solution, eg glycine NH_2–CH_2–COOH becomes $^+NH_3$–CH_2–COO^-. » amino acid [i]

Zwolle [**zvol**uh] 52°31N 6°06E, pop (1984e) 87 340. Capital city of Overijssel province, E Netherlands; on the Zwarte Water, which opens into the Ijsselmeer (NW); railway; canal junction; major cattle market; vehicles, machinery, foodstuffs, textiles, timber, leatherwork, chemicals, publishing, printing; St Michaelskerk (15th-c). » Netherlands, The [i]

Zworykin, Vladimir (Kosma) [**tsvo**rikin] (1889–1982) US physicist, born at Murom, Russia. Educated at Petrograd and Pittsburgh, he emigrated to the USA in 1919, and became a US citizen in 1924. He joined the Radio Corporation (1929), becoming director of electronic research (1934) and vice-president (1947). In 1923–4 he patented an all-electronic television system using a scanned camera-tube (the *iconoscope*), in 1929 demonstrated a cathode-ray display (the *kinescope*), and in later years contributed to the development of colour television and the electron microscope. He died at Princeton, New Jersey. » electron microscope [i]; television

zygomorphic flower A flower which is bilaterally symmetrical, so that it can be divided into equal halves in one plane only. It is often found in the more advanced plant families. » flower [i]

zygote [**zi**ygoht] The fertilized egg of a plant or animal, formed by the fusion of male (*sperm*) and female (*ovum*) gametes. It is usually diploid (possessing a double chromosome set), having received a haploid chromosome set from each gamete. » chromosome [i]; fertilization; gamete; twins

This section illustrates the varied uses of colour in the physical, natural, and social world. Its images include the computational displays of the Solar System and video screen, the communicative systems of humans and animals, and the imaginative forms of art and graphic design.

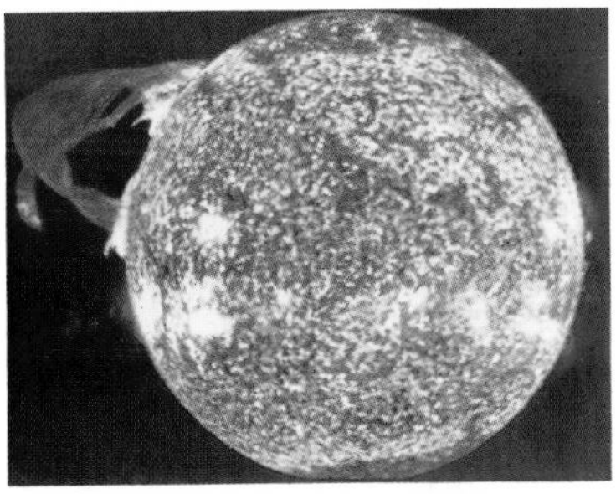

The solar disc

The Skylab photograph (above) shows a large loop prominence of gas. In the ultraviolet image (right), the faintest regions are red; brighter regions are yellow, blue, lilac, and white. » Sun

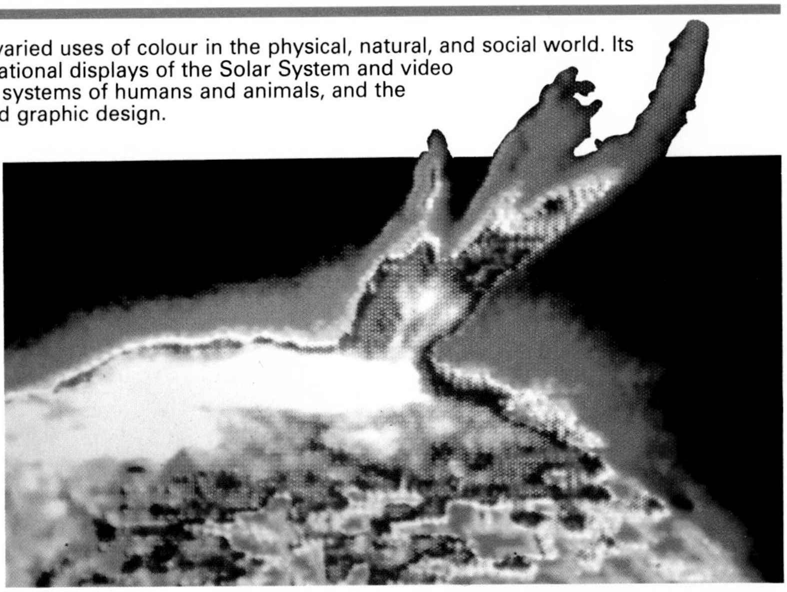

False-colour ultraviolet image of an eruptive prominence on the Sun

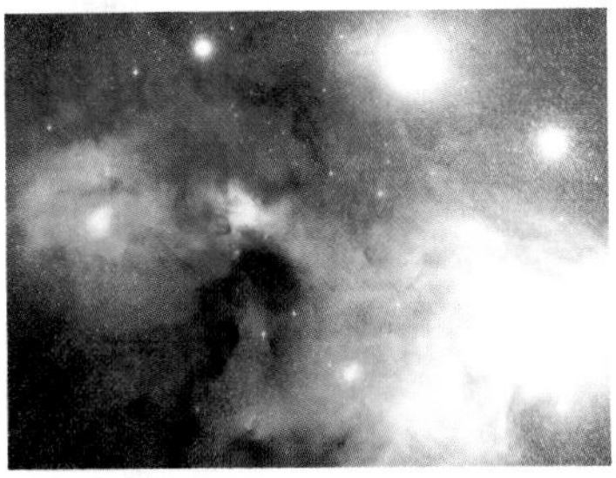

False-colour image of Rho Ophiuchi

In false-colour imaging, true colours are altered using special film, filters, or computer enhancement, so that physical features become more distinguishable.

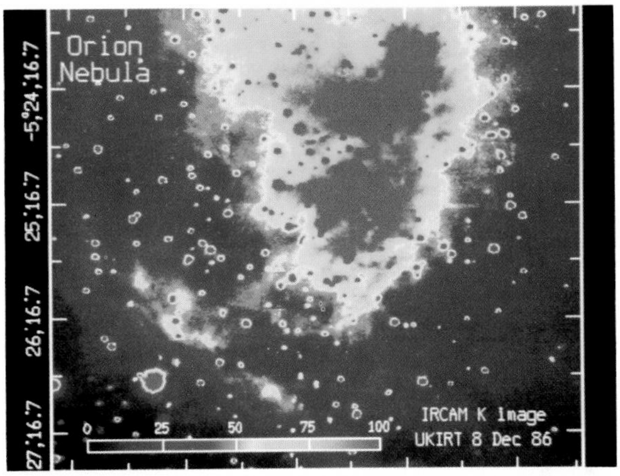

False-colour image of the Orion Nebula

The rings of Saturn

Saturn and its rings

The Voyager 1 image has been colour-enhanced to increase the visibility of the different bands of clouds in the N hemisphere. The blue band above the rings is the North Equatorial Belt. » Saturn

Satellites now routinely transmit photographs of the Earth's weather, climate, geology, landscape, and habitation. Colour-imaging is essential in order to appreciate the complex patterns involved. » satellite **2**

The Earth from space

Imaging the Earth
A false-colour image of the whole Earth, showing Africa, most of Europe and the Middle East, and part of South America. Land is shown in red, ocean in blue, and cloud in yellow.

The ozone hole
A satellite image of Antarctica, taken in the 1980's clearly shows the emerging 'hole' in the ozone layer (the dark patch in the centre, over Antarctica). » ozone layer

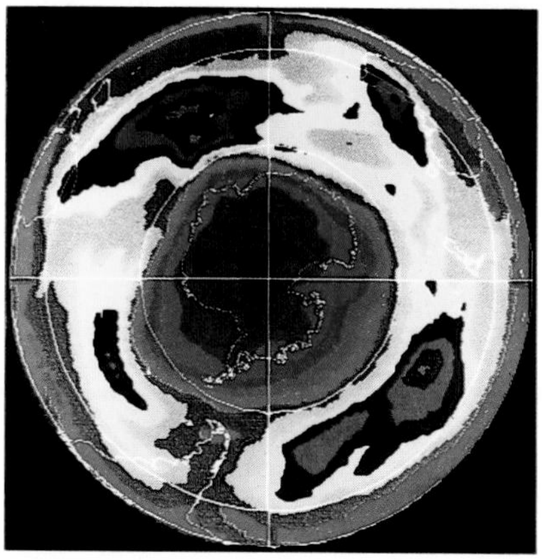

Ozone depletion over Antarctica

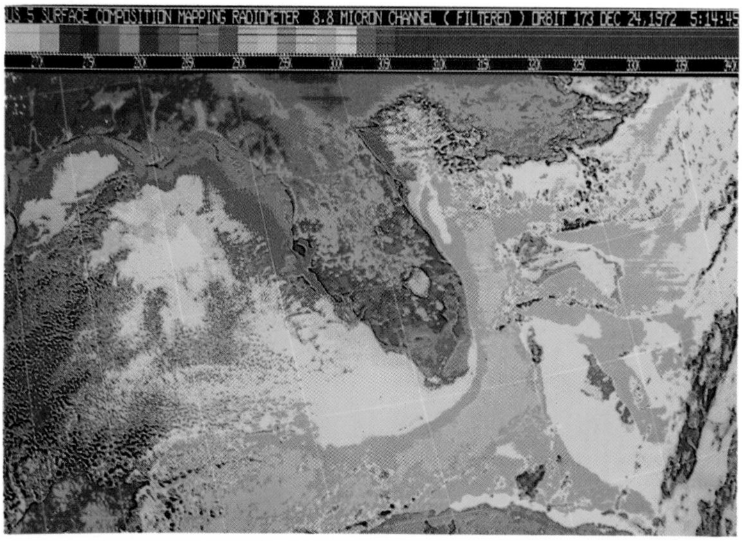

Caribbean heat waves
A thermal map of Florida, Cuba, and the Gulf Stream, generated by the Nimbus 5 satellite shows the warmest areas (notably the Gulf Stream) coloured pink, and the coolest areas coloured dark blue. Thermal infrared surveys monitor geothermal energy emitted in areas of volcanic or hot-spring activity, solar energy absorbed and re-emitted by the surface, and thermal energy generated by power stations and other constructions. » thermography

Thermal imaging of the Caribbean

Brazilian forests
Landsat infrared images of rainforest at Rondonia, W Brazil, where 'slash and burn' farmers were being relocated in the 1970s. Dense vegetation appears red; deforested areas appear blue/white. Settlements can be seen branching off from the main road, which runs left to right. The pictures clearly show the extensive deforestation over a five-year period. » rainforest

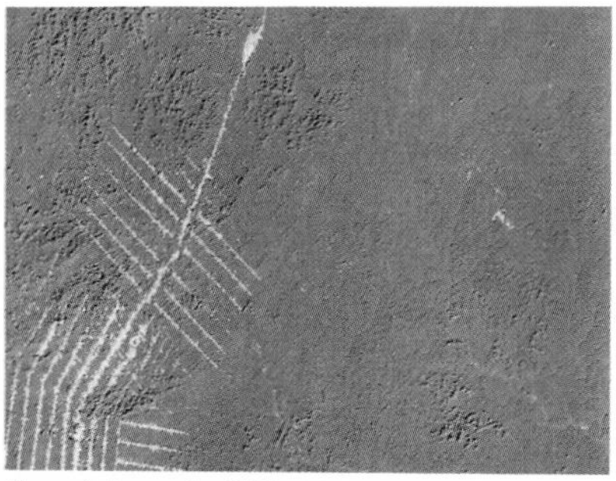

The rainforest in 1976

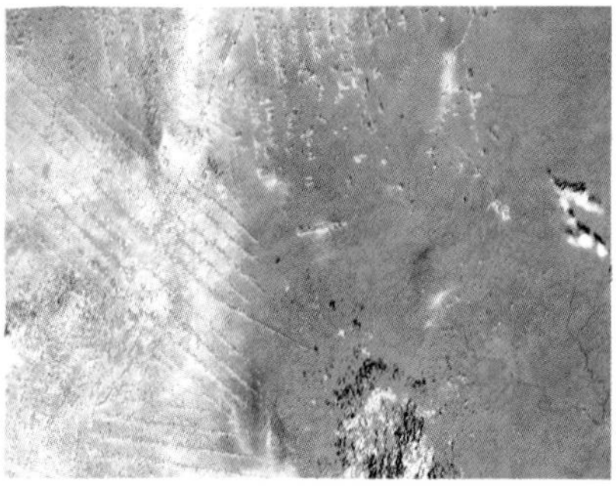

The rainforest in 1981

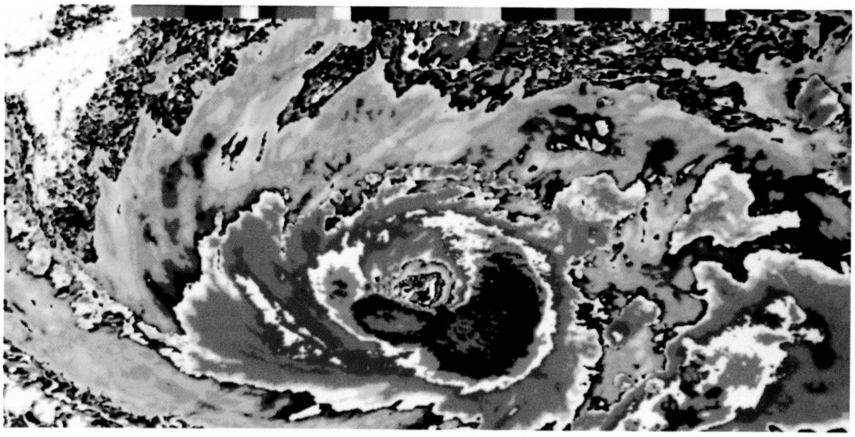

Hurricane Alicia crossing the Caribbean

Hurricane Monitoring
A satellite image of Hurricane Alicia, taken with an infrared scanner. The image records the temperature distribution across the spiralling hurricane in degrees kelvin. The circular feature at the centre is the eye of the hurricane, where the temperature is higher. » hurricane; kelvin

True-colour aerial photography

Complementary images
These photographs are of the same area of farmland and developed forestry in limestone uplands. The bluish tinge of the newly ploughed fields indicates that the soil is wet. Water shows up strongly as deep blue-black. Vegetation of different types and at different stages of growth shows up more clearly on the infrared photograph. » infrared photography

False-colour infrared photography

Map generation by radar
Radar signals are sent from an orbiting satellite to be translated by computer into the image shown here. Different heights are coded by different colours. The highest land is red, the lowest blue.

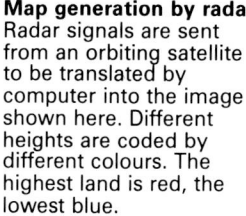

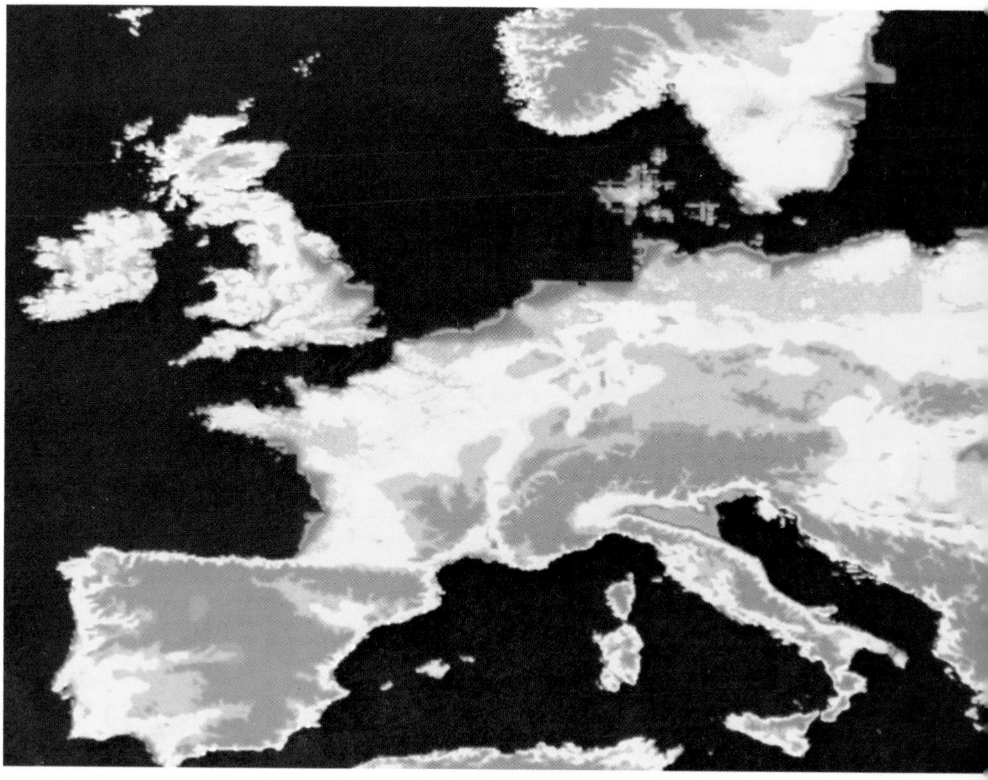

Height map of Europe, from radar information

Mineralogists rely greatly on colour to differentiate types of rock. In most cases, the distinctive colours are determined by the chemistry of the metals within the rocks.

Malachite

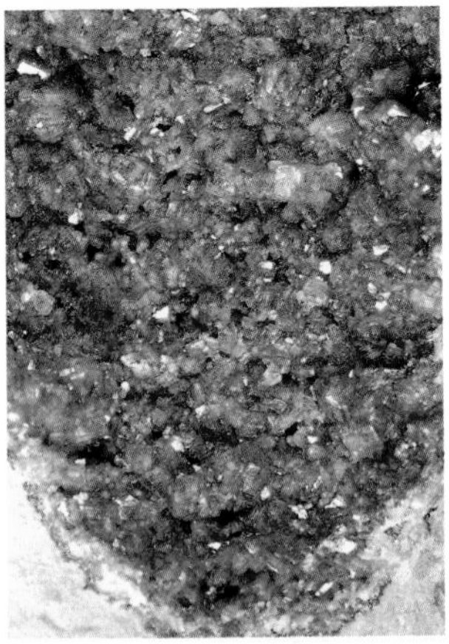

Cobaltocalcite

Rhodochrosite

Colour Sources
Most of the rocks illustrated on this page derive bright colours from their constituent metals: azurite and malachite contain copper; cobaltocalcite contains cobalt; rhodochrosite contains manganese; garnet contains chromium; fluorite contains calcium. In the case of lapis lazuli, the colour is related not to the chemistry but to various electrons in certain atomic positions. » rock

Azurite

Garnet, variety Uvarovite

Fluorite

The colours of natural rocks, such as those illustrated on this page, have always provided inspiration for the creation of decorative objects. Fluorite and lapis lazuli are but two of the many stones found in jewellery, architecture, and a wide range of ceremonial and ritualistic ornaments.

Lapis lazuli

A vase made at the end of the 19th century of fluorite from the 'Blue John' mine, near Castleton, Derbyshire

Gold crystals, from Ballarat, Australia

Jewels and gems
Coloured stones and metals, prized for their rarity or beauty, have been used for house ornamentation and personal adornment throughout history and across cultures. The raw material is invariably shaped, using chemical, physical, or mechanical means, to yield a product which has a pleasing aesthetic form.

Nephrite carving (mutton fat jade)

The uniqueness of gold
The colour and malleability of gold led to its rapid use in jewellery, following its discovery in the Middle East in the fourth millennium BC. No other natural rock could be shaped into such a wide range of intricate forms. Its classic natural colour can be given a variety of hues, when alloyed with other metals, a feature much exploited in modern times. » gold

Ruby in its rock matrix

Garnet, variety Almandine, in its rock matrix

Sapphire crystal

Emerald in its rock matrix

Gemstones
The rarest and most valuable gemstones are the *precious stones*, chiefly the diamonds, rubies, emeralds, and sapphires. In addition, there are the many kinds of *semi-precious stones*, such as garnet, jade, turquoise, opal, and amethyst. » gemstones

Opal, from White Cliffs, Australia

Amethyst and agate bowl, from South America

Black and white varieties of opal

Gold brooch with pearls and amethyst, from Scotland

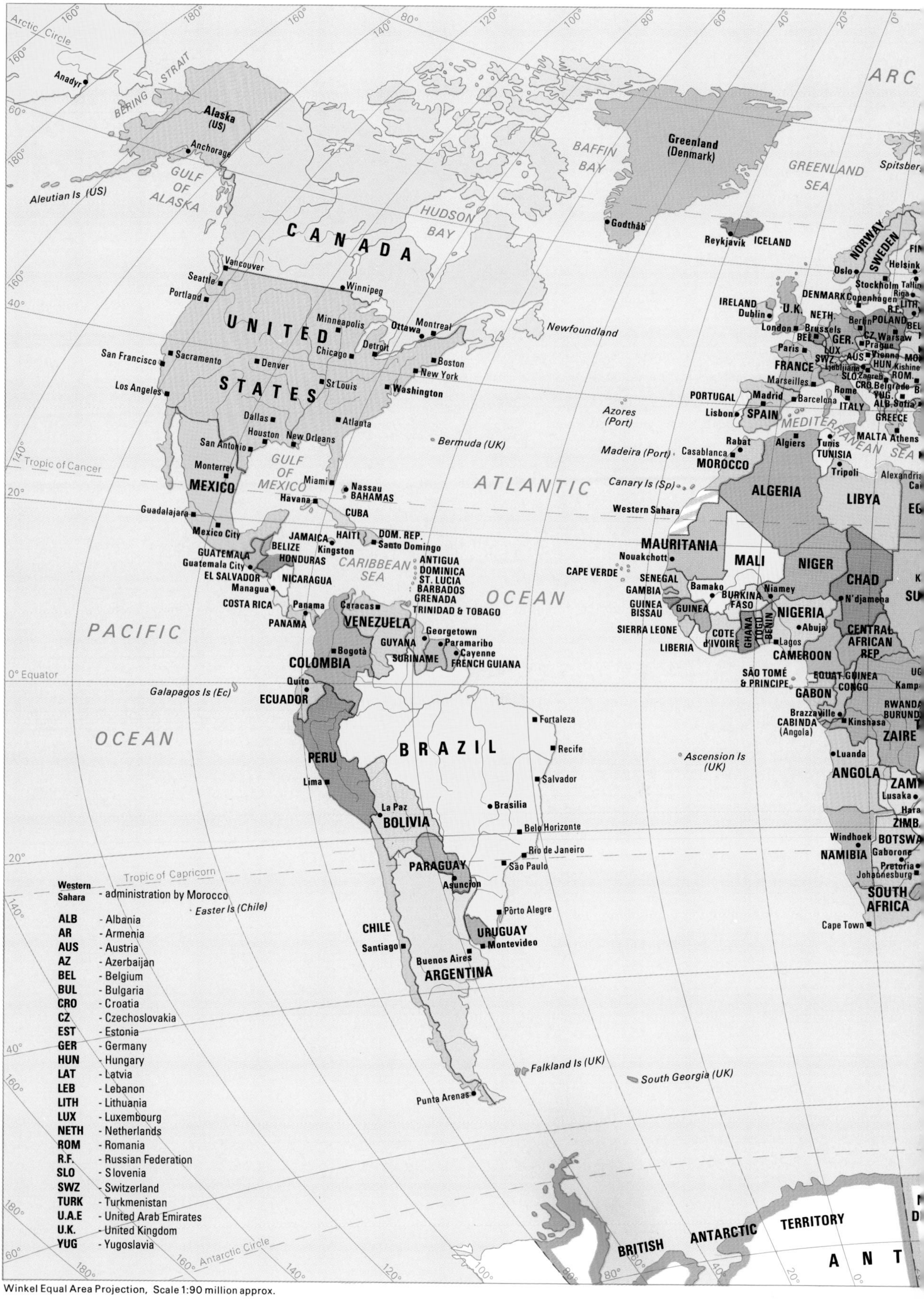

Winkel Equal Area Projection, Scale 1:90 million approx.

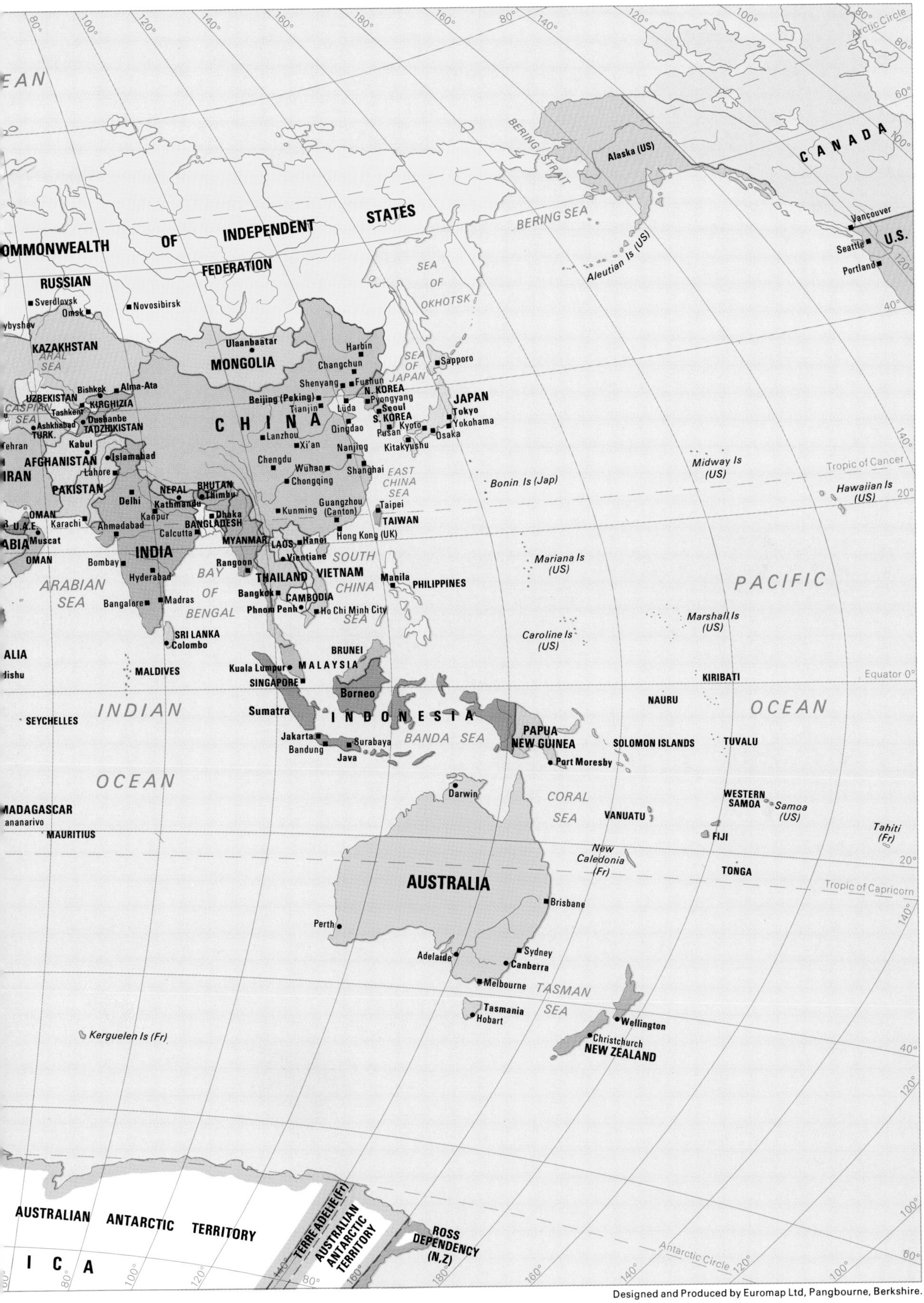
COMMONWEALTH OF INDEPENDENT STATES
RUSSIAN FEDERATION
CANADA
Alaska (US)
U.S.
BERING STRAIT
BERING SEA
Aleutian Is (US)
Vancouver
Seattle
Portland
SEA OF OKHOTSK
SEA OF JAPAN
Sverdlovsk
Omsk
Novosibirsk
KAZAKHSTAN
ARAL SEA
MONGOLIA
Ulaanbaatar
Harbin
Changchun
Shenyang
Fushun
Sapporo
JAPAN
Tokyo
Yokohama
Osaka
Kyoto
Kitakyushu
N. KOREA
Pyongyang
Seoul
S. KOREA
Pusan
Beijing (Peking)
Tianjin
Lüda
Qingdao
CHINA
Lanzhou
Xi'an
Nanjing
Shanghai
Chengdu
Wuhan
Chongqing
EAST CHINA SEA
Guangzhou (Canton)
Kunming
Taipei
TAIWAN
Hong Kong (UK)
UZBEKISTAN
Bishkek
Alma-Ata
KIRGHIZIA
Tashkent
CASPIAN SEA
Ashkhabad
TURK.
Dushanbe
TADZHIKISTAN
Tehran
Kabul
AFGHANISTAN
Islamabad
Lahore
IRAN
PAKISTAN
NEPAL
BHUTAN
Thimbu
Kathmandu
Delhi
Kanpur
Dhaka
BANGLADESH
Calcutta
OMAN
U.A.E.
Karachi
Ahmadabad
Muscat
INDIA
MYANMAR
LAOS
Hanoi
Vientiane
Rangoon
Bombay
Hyderabad
ARABIAN SEA
BAY OF BENGAL
THAILAND
VIETNAM
SOUTH CHINA SEA
Manila
PHILIPPINES
Bangkok
CAMBODIA
Phnom Penh
Ho Chi Minh City
Bangalore
Madras
SRI LANKA
Colombo
MALDIVES
BRUNEI
Kuala Lumpur
MALAYSIA
SINGAPORE
Borneo
Sumatra
INDONESIA
Jakarta
Bandung
Surabaya
Java
BANDA SEA
PAPUA NEW GUINEA
Port Moresby
SOLOMON ISLANDS
TUVALU
Bonin Is (Jap)
Midway Is (US)
Tropic of Cancer
Hawaiian Is (US)
Mariana Is (US)
PACIFIC OCEAN
Marshall Is (US)
Caroline Is (US)
KIRIBATI
Equator 0°
NAURU
INDIAN OCEAN
SEYCHELLES
MADAGASCAR
MAURITIUS
Darwin
CORAL SEA
VANUATU
WESTERN SAMOA
Samoa (US)
FIJI
Tahiti (Fr)
New Caledonia (Fr)
TONGA
Tropic of Capricorn
AUSTRALIA
Brisbane
Perth
Sydney
Adelaide
Canberra
Melbourne
TASMAN SEA
Tasmania
Hobart
Wellington
Christchurch
NEW ZEALAND
Kerguelen Is (Fr)
AUSTRALIAN ANTARCTIC TERRITORY
TERRE ADELIE (Fr)
AUSTRALIAN ANTARCTIC TERRITORY
ROSS DEPENDENCY (N.Z)
Antarctic Circle
Arctic Circle
Designed and Produced by Euromap Ltd, Pangbourne, Berkshire.

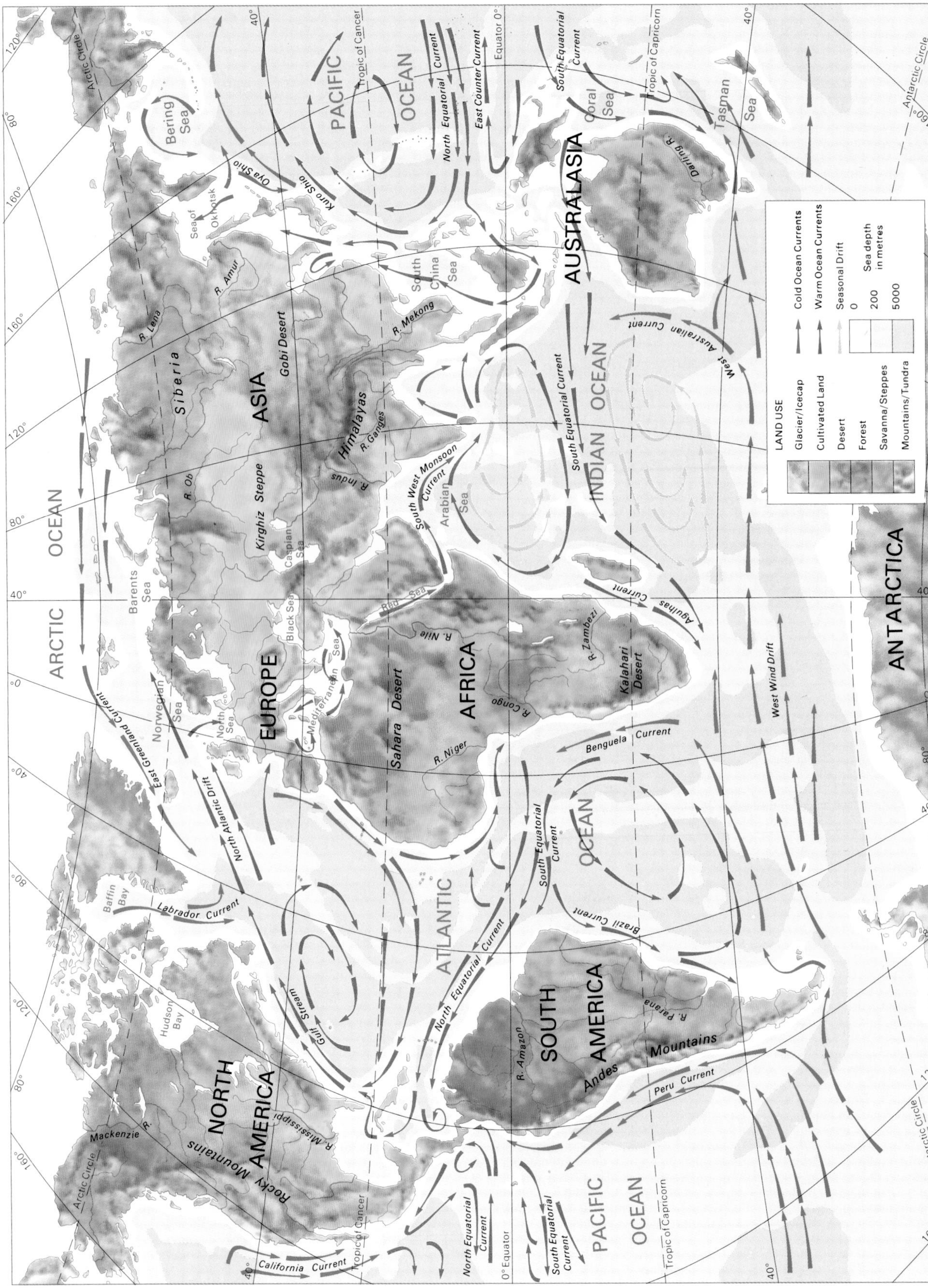

Designed and Produced by Euromap Ltd, Pangbourne, Berkshire

Arrow-poison frog

Warning
The arrow-poison frog and the paper wasp both have bold, colourful markings which tell other animals to keep their distance. Yellow is commonly used for this purpose (and not only by the animal kingdom — see Plate XV). » frog; wasp

Paper wasp

Butterfly fish

Protection
Many animals gain protection through the use of colour to confuse predators. Both the male Io moth and the butterfly fish, or angelfish, have 'eyes' which help to break up their outline, A similar reason may explain the bold black and white stripes of the zebra. » angelfish; moth

Male Io moth, showing eye spots

Concealment
The coffee bean caterpillar and camouflaged crab illustrate the use of colour for concealment. The colours enable the animal to blend into the natural background, providing a means of protection. » caterpillar; crab

Camouflaged crab

Male blue grouse

Attraction
The blue grouse and the frigate bird are examples of the way colour is used to attract another member of the species, in order to mate. During courtship, male frigate birds inflate their throat pouch until it appears like a large red balloon. » frigate bird; grouse

Coffee bean caterpillar

Galapagos frigate bird

Colour is apparent in the pure colours of light, as well as in the coloured pigments obtained from natural objects, such as rocks and plants, used in making paint, ink, and other materials.

The visible spectrum
When white light is passed through a prism, it splits up so that we see all the colours of the visible spectrum.
This range of pure colours can be seen in a rainbow. » prism; spectrum

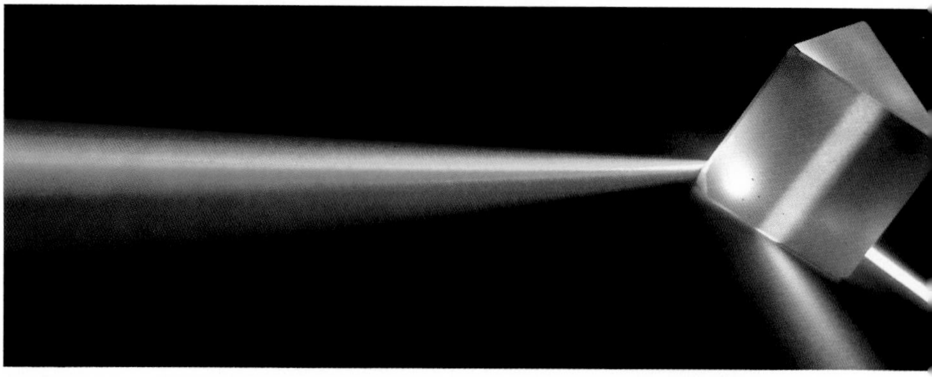

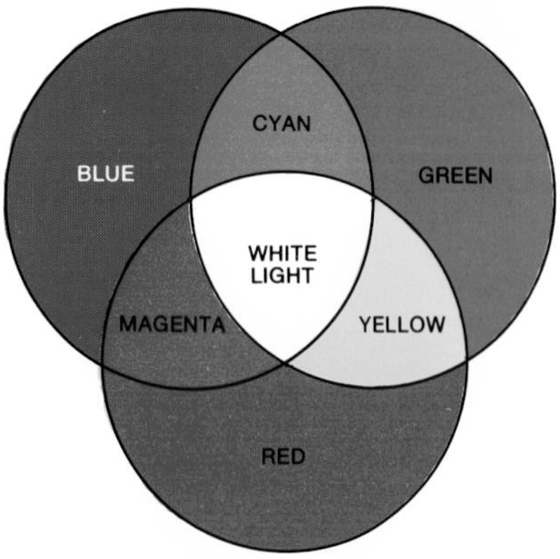

Primary colours of light

Primary colours
The three primary colours of light (shown left) are red, green and blue. They are known as 'additive' primaries, because they produce white light when added together.
The combination of two additive colours produces the 'subtractive' (or 'secondary') colours of magenta, cyan, and yellow. When two subtractive colours are mixed together, they produce the additive primaries (shown right).
A mixture of all three subtractive colours produces black.

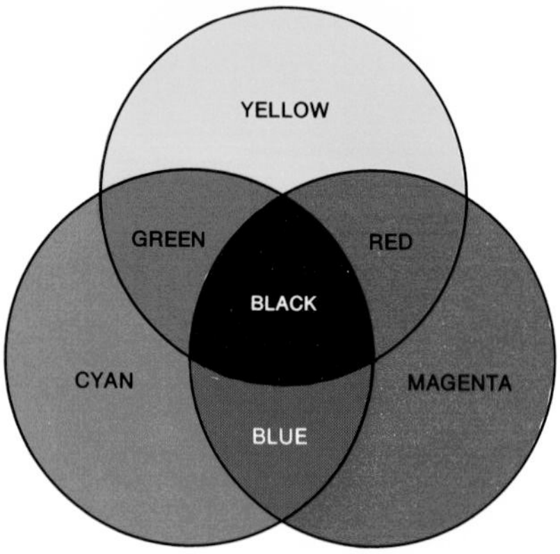

Primary colours of paint

Yellow printer negative

Magenta printer negative

Cyan printer negative

Black printer negative

Yellow proof

Magenta proof

Cyan proof

Black proof

Yellow proof

Yellow+magenta

Yellow+magenta+cyan

Yellow+magenta+cyan +black

Colour separation
A colour picture is printed by breaking down the original into the three basic colours — magenta, cyan, and yellow — plus black.
Four pieces of film are made, one for each colour (the 'four-colour process').
The illustration shows the effect of photographing an original picture four times through different colour filters, giving a separation negative for each colour (top line).
A blue filter gives a yellow negative (column 1), green gives magenta (column 2), red gives cyan (column 3), and a special filter gives black (column 4).
The process of combining the positive images is shown along the bottom line. » colour filter; printing

No single-page selection of paintings could hope to illustrate the range and depth of colour in art; equally, no colour section claiming to present the functions of colour dare omit such an essential topic. The present selection focuses on the way artists have used colour in an unexpected way, as in the yellow, purple, and green of the reflection (Monet), the stipple of colour on the sheep's fleece (Hunt), and the atmospheric effects of flat, bright colours (Gauguin). » art

Monet: 'Poplars on the Epte'

Detail of 'Poplars on the Epte'

Detail of 'Our English coasts'

William Holman Hunt: 'Our English coasts'

Picasso: 'Mother and child'

An example from the artist's 'blue period'

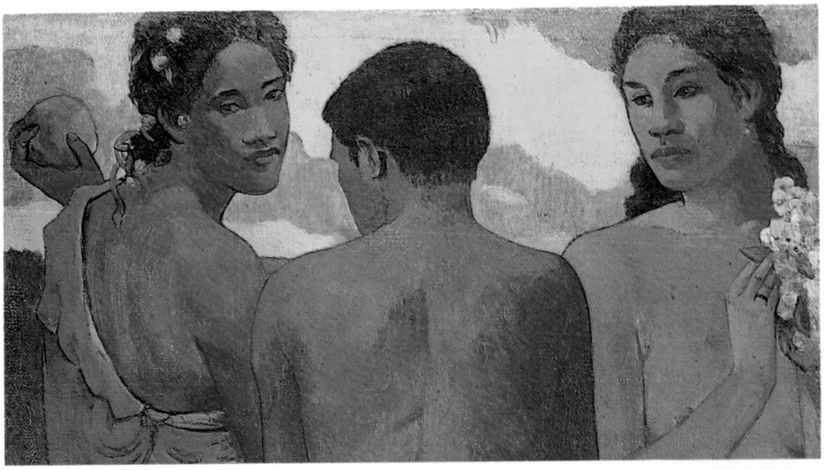

Gauguin: 'Three Tahitians'

William Gear: 'Autumn landscape'

Mondrian: 'Composition with grey, red, yellow, and blue'

Anatomical drawings have always relied on colour for the clear portrayal of body structures and functions. Similarly, colour displays are an essential feature of modern imaging techniques.

Muscles and internal organs

1 Parietal bone of the skull
2 Occipital bone of the skull
3 Humerus
4 Ilium
5 Trapezius muscle
6 Deltoid muscle
7 Triceps muscles (the biceps, at the front of the arm, cannot be seen from this view)
8 Latissimus dorsi muscle
9 Gluteus maximus muscle
10 Kidney
11 Trachea
12 Lungs
13 Heart
14 Liver (only a small part of the liver can be seen in this illustration)
15 Stomach
16 Spleen
17 Colon
18 Small intestine
19 Appendix
20 Bladder

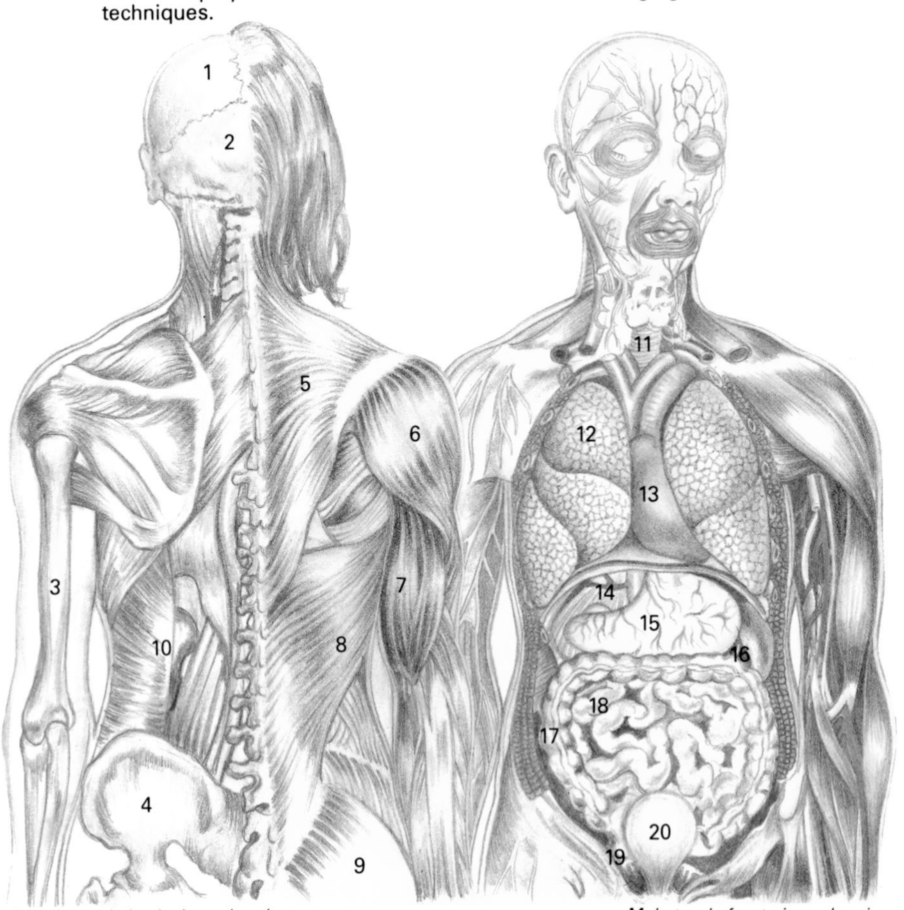

Female trunk, back view, showing main musculature

Male trunk, front view, showing main internal organs

Body thermography

A thermograph of a naked man, woman, and 8-year-old boy, seen from the front (the three images on the left) and the back (the three images on the right). The colour-coding represents the temperature of the skin: the colours range from white (the hottest parts) through red, orange, green, and blue to purple (the coolest parts). The hot V-shaped white area on the boy's back is typical of young children. The man has a bald spot, as can be seen from the loss of heat from the top of his head (the red and yellow patches in the fourth image from the left).

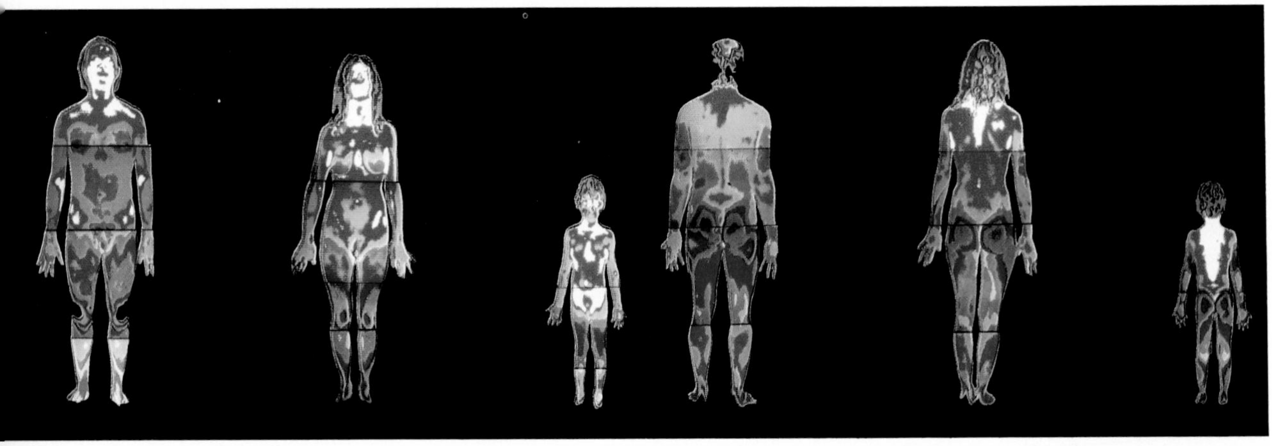

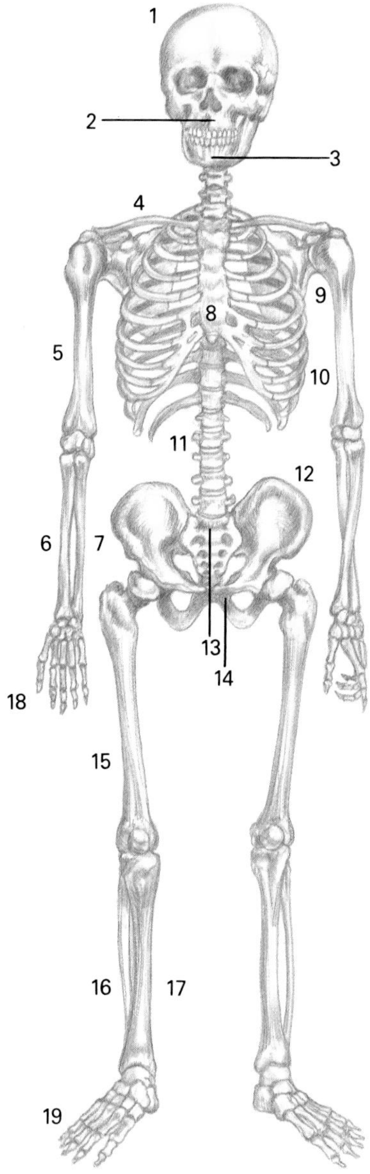

The human skeleton
The bones of the skeleton are often divided into two groups: the axial skeleton comprises the bones of the vertebral column, skull, ribs, and sternum; and the appendicular skeleton comprises the remainder.

1 Skull, displaying the frontal bone, and the front parts of the parietal and temporal bones
2 Maxilla
3 Mandible
4 Clavicle
5 Humerus
6 Radius
7 Ulna
8 Sternum
9 Scapula (obscured in this view by the upper ribs)
10 Ribs
11 Vertebral column, displaying (from above to below) cervical, thoracic, lumbar, sacral, and coccygeal vertebrae
12 Ilium
13 Sacrum
14 Coccyx
15 Femur
16 Fibula
17 Tibia
18 Bones of the hand, comprising the five metacarpals, the three phalanges in each finger, and the two phalanges in the thumb
19 Bones of the foot, comprising the seven tarsals, the five metatarsals, the two phalanges in the big toe, and the three phalanges in the other toes

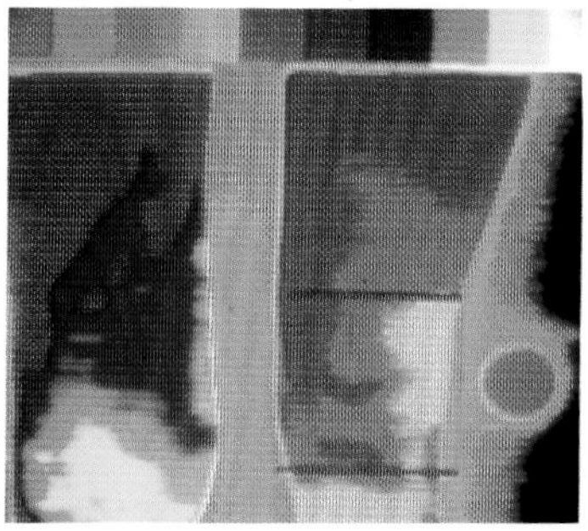

Thermographic diagnosis
A thermogram of a person's knees, seen from behind. The colour coding runs in one-degree steps from blue (= cold) to white (= hot). There is evidence of arthritis in the left knee, which in places is five degrees hotter than right. » arthritis; thermography

The AIDS virus
A false-colour scanning electron micrograph of Human Immunodeficiency Virus (HIV), here coloured orange. The virus is budding away from the plasma membrane (coloured blue) of an infected T-lymphocyte, a key cell in the human immune system. » AIDS; lymphocyte; virus

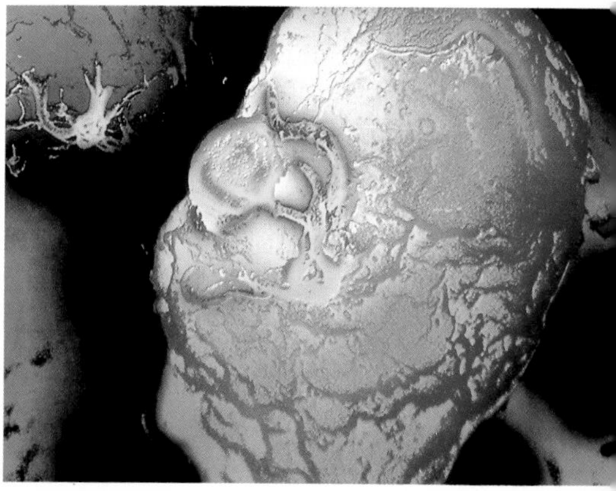

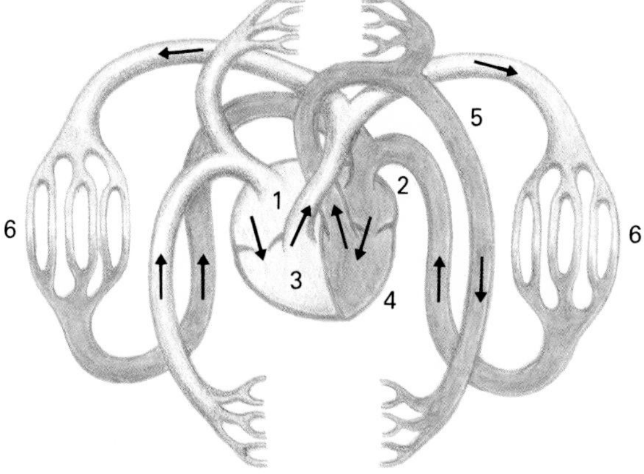

The cardio-pulmonary system
Colour provides a convenient means of showing the difference between blood which is oxygenated (coloured red) and blood which is de-oxygenated (coloured blue), in its path around the body. The vessels at the top of the diagram lead to the head and arms; those at the bottom lead to the liver, kidneys, intestines, and legs.

1 Right atrium
2 Left atrium
3 Right ventricle
4 Left ventricle
5 Aorta
6 Lung

The functional use of colour is profoundly illustrated in the variety of signs, signals, and symbols used in the codes and conventions of human visual communication.

The London Underground
Colour is essential in displaying the structure of any complex system of transportation. In an underground railway system, the colours, once established, are used as valuable guidance features in their own right, being more readily visible at a distance on notice-boards and in corridors.

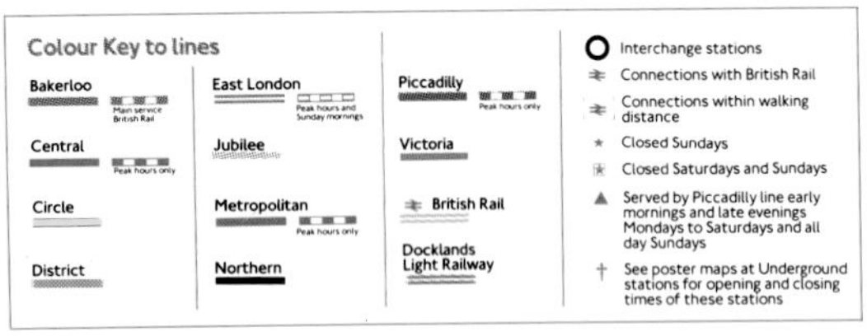

England expects that every man will do his duty
Lord Nelson's famous signal was sent at the Battle of Trafalgar (1805), using the marine flag code devised by Sir Home Popham in 1803. Each flag combination relates to a separate word in the Admiralty code book. 'Duty' was not listed in the book, so it had to be spelled out. » Nelson, Horatio

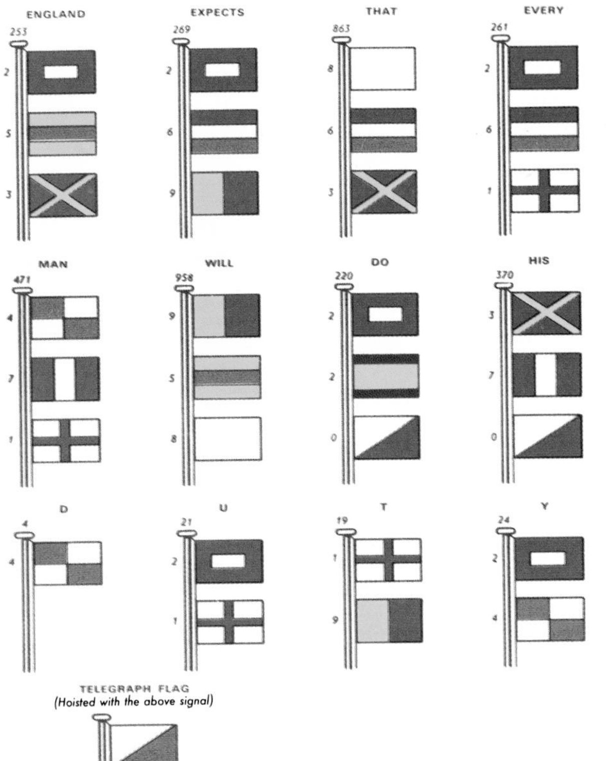

The signal displayed on the masthead

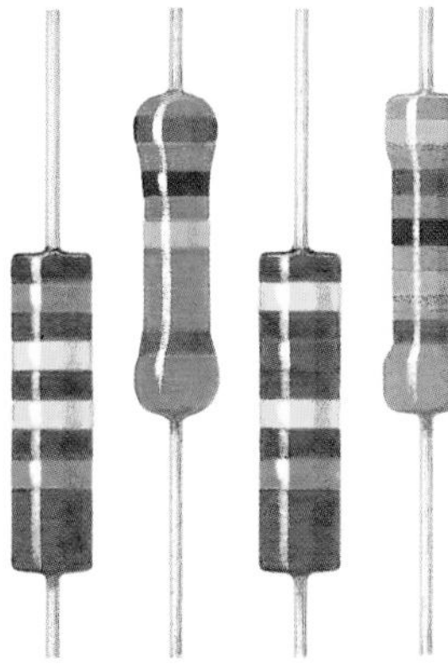

Colour-coded resistors

Electrical components
Resistors and other electrical components are often colour-coded to enable values to be read off in a convenient and economical way. International standards have been devised to ensure consistency, each colour representing a number (black-0, brown-1, red-2, orange-3, yellow-4, green-5, blue-6, purple-7, grey-8, white-9). A sequence of red-green-blue, for example, would indicate a resistance of 256 ohms. » resistor

No smoking — *Pedestrians prohibited* — *Caution: risk of ionizing radiation* — *Caution: risk of electric shock*

Road signs
Different kinds of road sign are distinguished by their dominant background colour. Danger signs are in red; warning signs are in yellow; directional signs in blue.

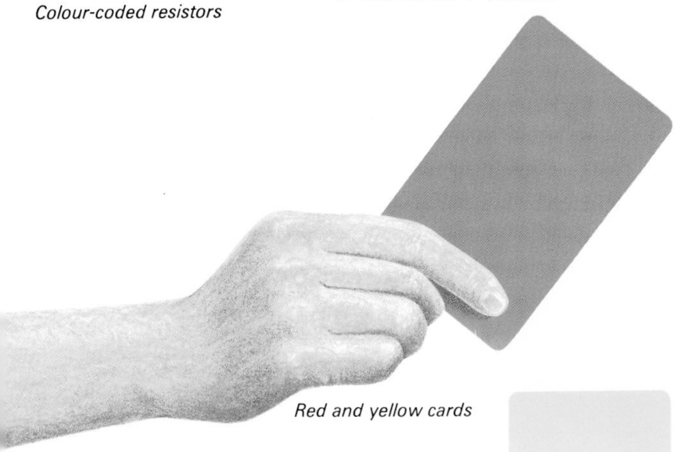

Red and yellow cards

Football codes
Yellow and red turn up again in sport, as a way of avoiding linguistic problems of communication. In football, since 1970, the referee shows a yellow warning card to a player who has committed a serious foul. If there is a second serious foul, the red card is shown, and the player is sent off. » football

Racing colours
Colour is used in many sports as a means of identification — whether of countries, teams, or individual affiliations. In horse racing, the livery worn by the jockey is an important identifier, especially when the race contains many riders.

Armed forces
A country's armed forces, police, traffic wardens, and other law enforcement agencies provide one of the most widely recognized examples of the identifying use of colour. The names of the colours involved may even enter the language as a whole, as in the case of 'navy blue'.

United Nations troops in their distinctive blue berets; United Nations flag below

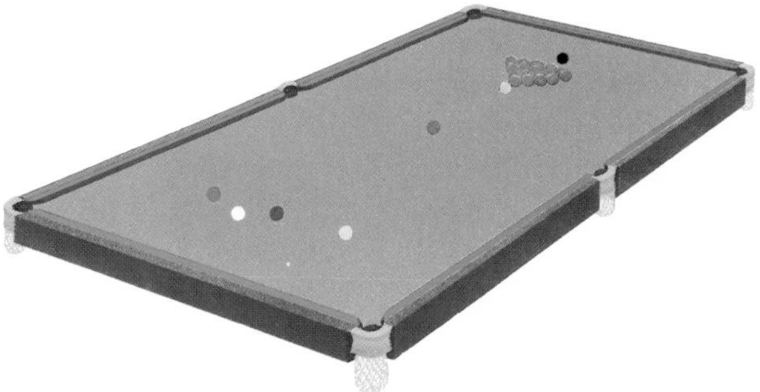

Snooker table before play begins

Colour values
Snooker, pool, and billiards are examples of games where differently coloured components have been assigned fixed values. In snooker, points are awarded when a ball is potted, as follows: red-1, yellow-2, green-3, brown-4, blue-5, pink-6, black-7. Curiously, the term 'coloured' has come to be used for all the score balls except red. » snooker.

The combined use of colour, movement and sound identify the modern world of computer graphics — a world which now ranges from experimental research, space simulations, and industrial designs to feature films, television advertising, and video games.

In science, computer graphics have achieved notable reputations in mathematics and astronomy, and especially in space exploration, where the imaginative images devised by NASA to illustrate the path of their Voyager space probe were widely acclaimed. One of the most valuable uses of the technique is in simulation — using a computer to predict the behaviour of a model of a physical system, such as an aircraft, an electronic circuit, a tidal barrage, or a nuclear reactor. Another is the way patterns can be shown in arrays of complex data, especially on television, where such techniques are nowadays routine in weather forecasting, political election programmes, sporting record reviews, and displays of business trends. The artistic use of the technique, both in the motion picture industry (in science fiction epics and large-scale cartoons) and in the fine arts, is an application whose potential has still to be fully explored. »computer art

A range of computer graphics displays

A home video game

Video games

Probably the most familiar of all computer graphic applications, video games have rapidly developed since the use of the first black-and-white table-tennis game ('Pong') in the 1970s, and the first monochrome versions of 'Space Invaders'. The bright, full-colour dynamic displays now in universal use have attracted millions, and in some cases have brought to light a new form of addiction. »electronic games

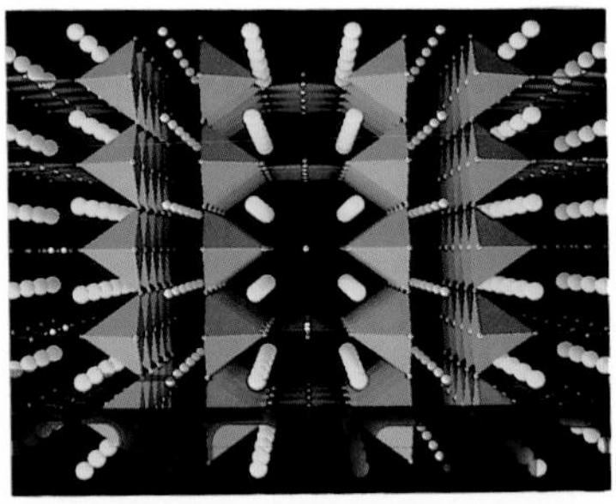

Superconductor crystal structure

Modelling molecules

Computer graphics representations of two structures: (right) the DNA molecule, showing its double helix structure; (above right) the crystal structure of one of the new generation of high-temperature superconductors, yttrium-barium-copper oxide (oxygen atoms are in the red, yttrium atoms in light blue, and barium atoms in yellow. »DNA; superconductivity

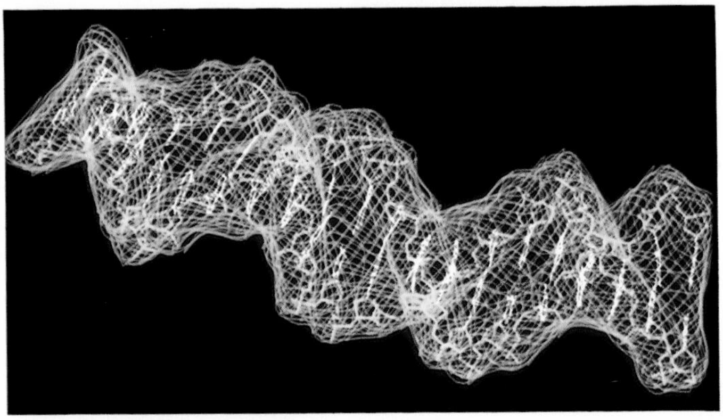

The double helix

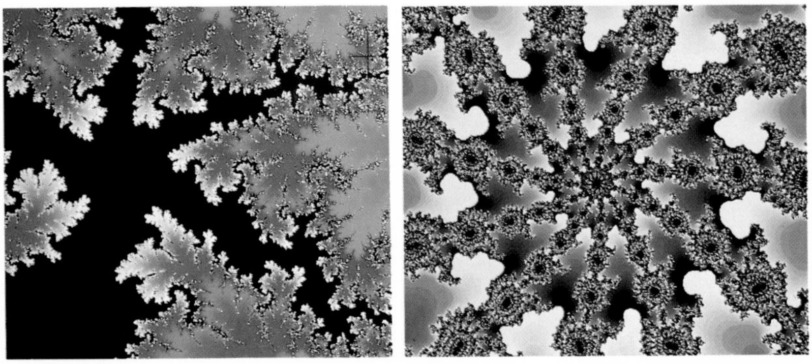

Detail of fractal patterns

Fractal geometry

Fractal geometry is the mathematical study of forms having a fractional dimension. Fractal patterns demonstrate the presence of order in apparently highly irregular systems, and rely very much on colour for their presentation. These computer graphic representations display details from a series of complex numbers known as the Mandelbrot Set, plotted from complex number co-ordinates. »fractals; numbers

READY REFERENCE

INDEX

THE EARTH IN SPACE

SPACE EXPLORATION

EARTH: GENERAL DATA

TIMES AND DISTANCES

NATIONS OF THE WORLD

POLITICAL LEADERS 1900–1990

MEASUREMENT

COMMUNICATION SYSTEMS

NAMES AND TITLES

COMPETITIVE SPORTS AND GAMES

COMMON ABBREVIATIONS

THE EARTH IN SPACE

PLANETARY DATA

Planet	Distance from sun (million km/ml): Maximum		Minimum		Sidereal period	Axial rotation (equatorial)	Diameter (equatorial) km	ml
Mercury	69.4	43.0	46.8	29.0	88 d	58 d 16 h	4878	3031
Venus	109.0	67.6	107.6	66.7	224.7 d	243 d	12104	7521
Earth	152.6	94.6	147.4	91.4	365.26 [1]	23 h 56 m	12756	7927
Mars	249.2	154.5	207.3	128.5	687 d	24 h 37 m 23 s	6794	4222
Jupiter	817.4	506.8	741.6	459.8	11.86 y	9 h 50 m 30 s	142800	88700
Saturn	1512	937.6	1346	834.6	29.46 y	10 h 14 m	120000	74600
Uranus	3011	1867	2740	1699	84.01 y	16–28 h [2]	52000	32300
Neptune	4543	2817	4466	2769	164.79 y	18–20 h [2]	48400	30000
Pluto	7364	4566	4461	2766	247.7 y	6 d 9 h	1145	711

[1] 365 d 5 h 48 m 46 s [2] Different latitudes rotate at different speeds. y: years d: days h: hours m: minutes s: seconds km: kilometres ml: miles

PLANETARY SATELLITES

	Year discovered	Distance from planet km	ml	Diameter km	ml
Earth					
Moon	–	384000	238000	3476	2155
Mars					
Phobos	1877	938000	583000	27	17
Deimos	1877	2346000	1458000	15	9
Jupiter					
Metis	1979	128000	79000	40	25
Adrastea	1979	129000	80000	24	15
Amalthea	1892	181000	112000	270	168
Thebe	1979	222000	138000	100	60
Io	1610	422000	262000	3650	5850
Europa	1610	671000	417000	3400	1925
Ganymede	1610	1070000	665000	5260	3270
Callisto	1610	1883000	1170000	4800	3000
Leda	1974	11110000	6904000	20	12
Himalia	1904	11480000	7134000	180	110
Lysithea	1938	11720000	7283000	40	25
Elara	1905	11740000	7295000	80	50
Ananke	1951	21200000	13174000	30	19
Carme	1938	22600000	14044000	40	25
Pasiphae	1908	23500000	14603000	50	30
Sinope	1914	23700000	14727000	40	25
Saturn					
Atlas	1980	138000	86000	40	25
1980 S27	1980	139000	86000	100	60
1980 S26	1980	142000	88000	100	60
Epimetheus	1980	151000	94000	140	90

	Year discovered	Distance from planet km	ml	Diameter km	ml
Janus	1980	151000	94000	200	120
Mimas	1789	186000	116000	390	240
Enceladus	1789	238000	148000	500	310
Calypso	1980	295000	183000	30	19
Telesto	1980	295000	183000	24	15
Tethys	1684	295000	183000	1050	650
Dione	1684	377000	234000	1120	700
Dione B	1982	378000	235000	15	9
Rhea	1672	527000	327000	1530	950
Titan	1655	1222000	759000	5150	3200
Hyperion	1848	1481000	920000	400	250
Iapetus	1671	3560000	2212000	1440	900
Phoebe	1898	12950000	8047000	160	100
Uranus					
Miranda	1948	130000	81000	400	250
Ariel	1851	191000	119000	1300	800
Umbriel	1851	266000	165000	1100	700
Titania	1787	436000	271000	1600	1000
Oberon	1787	583000	362000	1600	1000

A further ten satellites at distances from 50000–86000 km, and with diameters 15–170 km, were discovered in 1986.

	Year discovered	Distance from planet km	ml	Diameter km	ml
Neptune					
Triton	1846	355000	221000	3800	2400
Nereid	1949	5510000	3424000	300	190
Pluto					
Charon	1978	20000000	12500000	1000	620

THE NEAREST STARS

Star	Distance (light years)
Proxima Centauri	4.24
Alpha Centauri A	4.34
Alpha Centauri B	4.34
Barnard's Star	5.97
Wolf 359 (CN Leonis)	7.80
Lalande 21185	8.19
UV Ceti A	8.55
UV Ceti B	8.55
Sirius A	8.67
Sirius B	8.67
Ross 154	9.52
Ross 248 (HH Andromedae)	10.37
Epsilon Eridani	10.63
Ross 128 (FI Virginis)	10.79
L 789–6	11.12
GX Andromedae	11.22
GQ Andromedae	11.22
61 Cygnus A	11.22
61 Cygnus B	11.22
HD 173739	11.25
Epsilon Indi	11.25
Tau Ceti	11.41

STARS OF THE FIRST MAGNITUDE

Star	Proper name	Magnitude	Distance (l y)[1]
Alpha Canis Majoris	Sirius	−1.47	8.7
Alpha Carinae	Canopus	−0.71	98
Alpha Boötis	Arcturus	−0.06	36
Alpha Centauri	Rigil Kentaurus	+0.01	4.3
Alpha Lyrae	Vega	0.03	26
Alpha Aurigae	Capella	0.05	45
Beta Orionis	Rigel	0.14	815
Alpha Canis Minoris	Procyon	0.34	11
Alpha Orionis	Betelgeuse	0.41	520
Alpha Eridani	Achernar	0.49	118
Beta Centauri	Hadar	0.61	490
Alpha Aquilae	Altair	0.75	16
Alpha Tauri	Aldebaran	0.78	68
Alpha Virginis	Spica	0.91	220
Alpha Scorpii	Antares	0.92	520
Alpha Piscis Austrini	Fomalhaut	1.15	23
Beta Geminorum	Pollux	1.16	35
Alpha Cygni	Deneb	1.26	1 600
Beta Crucis	Mimosa	1.28	490
Alpha Leonis	Regulus	1.33	85
Alpha Crucis	Acrux	1.39	370

[1] l y = light years.

ANNUAL METEOR SHOWERS

Name	Dates	Star region
Quadrantids	1–6 January	Beta Boötis
Lyrids	19–22 April	Nu Herculis
Eta Aquarids	1–8 May	Eta Aquarii
Delta Aquarids	15 July–10 August	Delta Aquarii
Perseids	27 July–17 August	Eta Persei
Orionids	15–25 October	Nu Orionis
Leonids	14–20 November	Zeta Leonis
Andromedids	26 November–4 December	Gamma Andromedae
Geminids	9–13 December	Castor
Ursids	20–22 December	Kocab

TOTAL AND ANNULAR SOLAR ECLIPSES 1990–1999

Date	Extent of eclipse	Visible from parts of[1]
15 January 1991	Annular[2]	S Pacific, New Zealand, S Australia
11 July 1991	Total	Mid-Pacific, C & S America
4–5 January 1992	Annular	N American coast, Mid-Pacific
30 June 1992	Total	S American coast, S Atlantic Ocean
10 May 1994	Annular	Mid-Pacific, N America, N Africa
3 November 1994	Total	Indian Ocean, S Atlantic, S America, Mid-Pacific
29 April 1995	Annular	S Pacific, S America
24 October 1995	Total	Middle East, S Asia, S Pacific
9 March 1997	Total	C & N Asia, Arctic
26 February 1998	Total	Mid-Pacific, C America, N Atlantic
22 August 1998	Annular	Indonesia, S Pacific, Indian Ocean
16 February 1999	Annular	Indian Ocean, Australia
11 August 1999	Total	N Atlantic, N Europe, Middle East, N India

[1] The eclipse begins in the first country named. [2] In an annular eclipse a ring-shaped part of the sun remains visible.

PROPER NAMES OF STARS DESIGNATED 'ALPHA' IN EACH CONSTELLATION

Name	Constellation
Achernar	Eridanus
Acrux	Crux
Acubens	Cancer
Al Giedi	Capricornus
Al Rijil	Centaurus
Aldebaran	Taurus
Alderamin	Cepheus
Alkes	Crater
Alkhiba	Corvus
Alnair	Grus
Alphard	Hydra
Alphekka	Corona Borealis
Alpheratz	Andromeda
Altair	Aquila
Ankaa	Phoenix
Antares	Scorpius
Arcturus	Boötes
Arneb	Lepus
Atria	Triangulum Australe
Betelgeuse	Orion (Alpha)
Canopus	Carina
Capella	Auriga
Castor	Gemini (Alpha)
Choo	Ara
Cor Caroli	Canes Venatici
Deneb	Cygnus
Diadem	Coma Berenices
Dubhe	Ursa Major
Fomalhaut	Piscis Austrinus
Hamal	Aries
Kaïtain	Pisces
Kitalpha	Equuleus
Markab	Pegasus
Men	Lupus
Menkar	Cetus
Mirphak	Perseus
Phakt	Columba
Polaris	Ursa Minor
Praecipua	Leo Minor
Procyon	Canis Minor
Rasalgethi	Hercules
Rasalhague	Ophiuchus
Rasalmothallah	Triangulum
Regulus	Leo
Rukbat	Sagittarius
Sadalmelik	Aquarius
Shedir	Cassiopeia
Sirius	Canis Major
Spica	Virgo
Svalocin	Delphinus
Thuban	Draco
Unukalhai	Serpens
Vega	Lyra
Zubenelgenubi	Libra

THE NEAR SIDE OF THE MOON

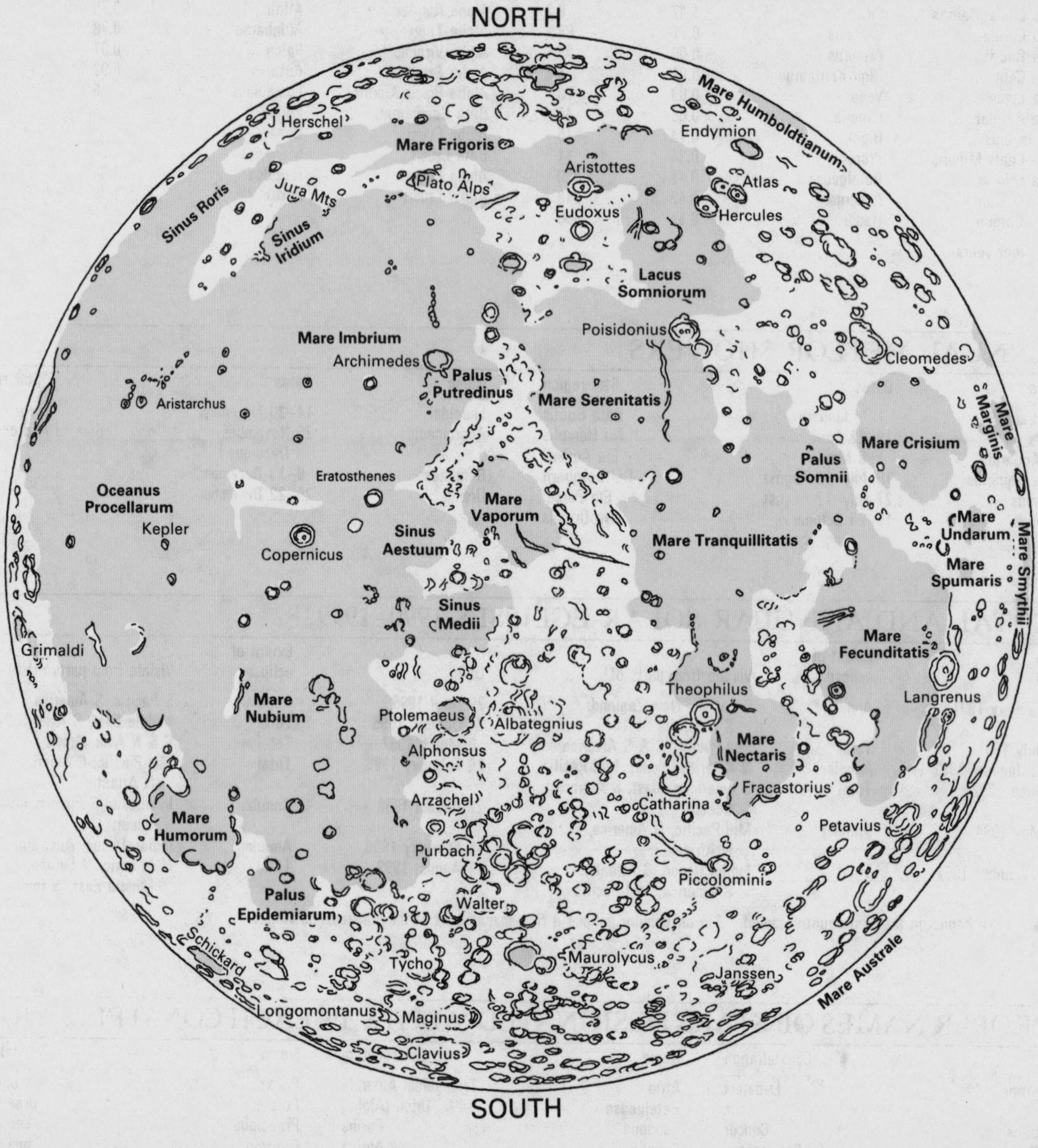

THE LUNAR 'SEAS'

Latin name	English name	Latin name	English name	Latin name	English name
Lacus Somniorum	Lake of Dreams	Mare Moscoviense	Moscow Sea	Oceanus Procellarum	Ocean of Storms
Mare Australe	Southern Sea	Mare Nectaris	Sea of Nectar	Palus Epidemiarum	Marsh of Epidemics
Mare Crisium	Sea of Crises	Mare Nubium	Sea of Clouds	Palus Putredinis	Marsh of Decay
Mare Fecunditatis	Sea of Fertility	Mare Orientale	Eastern Sea	Palus Somnii	Marsh of Sleep
Mare Frigoris	Sea of Cold	Mare Serenitatis	Sea of Serenity	Sinus Adstuum	Bay of Heats
Mare Humboldtianum	Humboldt's Sea	Mare Smythii	Smyth's Sea	Sinus Iridum	Bay of Rainbows
Mare Humorum	Sea of Humours	Mare Spumans	Foaming Sea	Sinus Medii	Central Bay
Mare Imbrium	Sea of Showers	Mare Tranquillitatis	Sea of Tranquillity	Sinus Roris	Bay of Dew
Mare Ingenii	Sea of Geniuses	Mare Undarum	Sea of Waves		
Mare Marginis	Marginal Sea	Mare Vaporum	Sea of Vapours		

THE FAR SIDE OF THE MOON

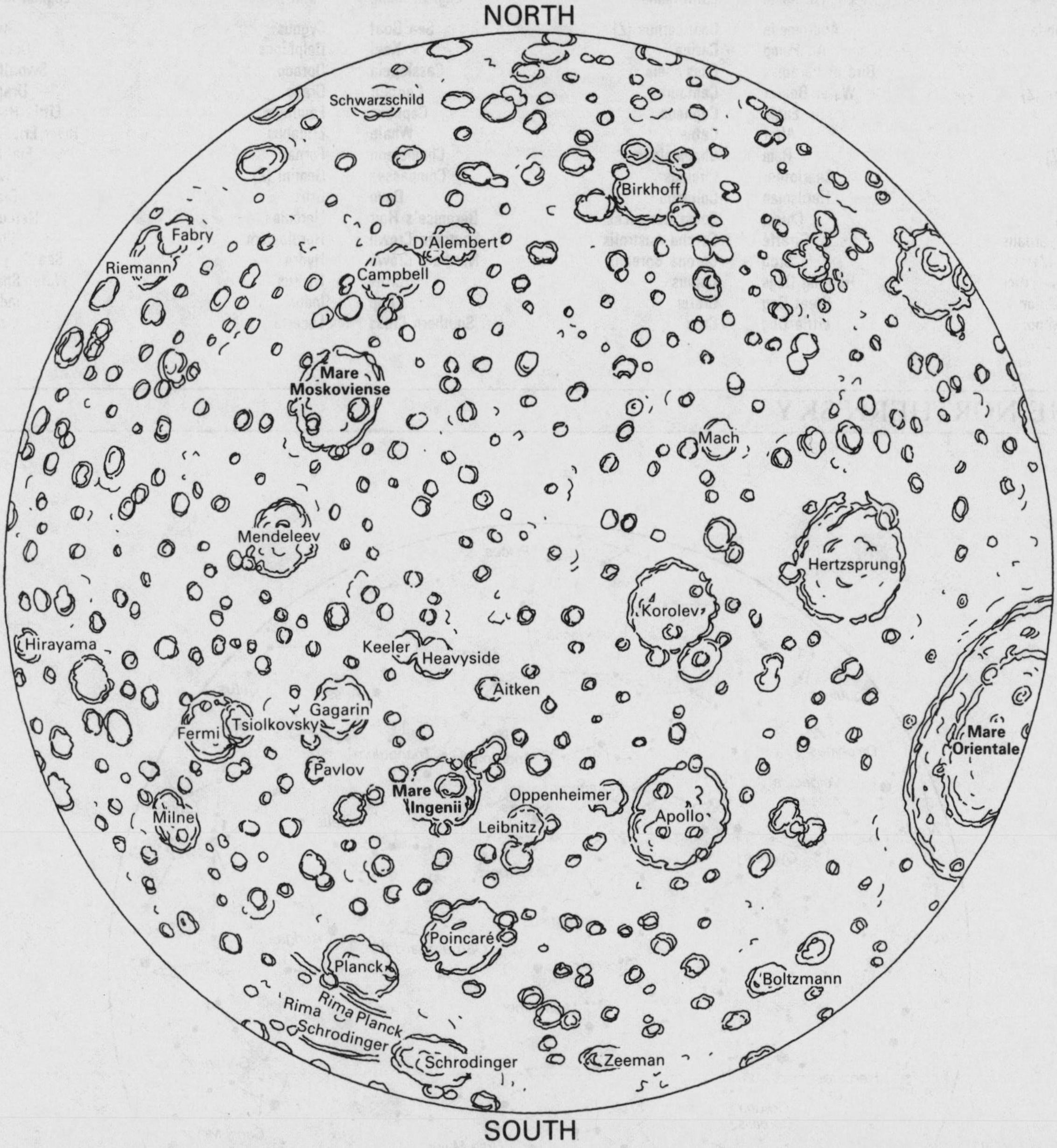

LUNAR ECLIPSES 1990–2000

Date	Percentage eclipsed	Time of mid-eclipse	Where visible
9 February 1990	Total	19.13	Africa, Asia, Australia, Europe
6 August 1990	Partial	14.12	Australia, SE Asia, Pacific
21 December 1991	Partial	10.34	Pacific, N America (W Coast), Japan, Australia
15 June 1992	Partial	04.58	N, C and S America, W Africa
9–10 December 1992	Total	23.45	Africa, Europe, Middle East, part of S. America
4 June 1993	Total	13.02	Pacific, Australia, SE Asia
29 November 1993	Total	06.26	N and S America
25 May 1994	Partial	03.32	C and S America, part of N America, W Africa
15 April 1995	Partial	12.19	Pacific, Australia, SE Asia
4 April 1996	Total	00.11	Africa, SE Europe, S America
27 September 1996	Total	02.55	C and S America, part of N America, W Africa
24 March 1997	Partial	04.41	C and S America, part of N America, W Africa
16 September 1997	Total	18.47	S Africa, E Africa, Australia
28 July 1999	Partial	11.34	Pacific, Australia, SE Asia
21 January 2000	Total	04.45	N America, part of S America, SW Europe, W Africa
16 July 2000	Total	13.57	Pacific, Australia, SE Asia

THE CONSTELLATIONS

Latin name	English name
Andromeda	Andromeda
Antlia	Air Pump
Apus	Bird of Paradise
Aquarius (Z)	Water Bearer
Aquila	Eagle
Ara	Altar
Aries (Z)	Ram
Auriga	Charioteer
Boötes	Herdsman
Caelum	Chisel
Camelopardalis	Giraffe
Cancer (Z)	Crab
Canes Venatici	Hunting Dogs
Canis Major	Great Dog
Canis Minor	Little Dog
Capricornus (Z)	Sea Goat
Carina	Keel
Cassiopeia	Cassiopeia
Centaurus	Centaur
Cepheus	Cepheus
Cetus	Whale
Chamaeleon	Chameleon
Circinus	Compasses
Columba	Dove
Coma Berenices	Berenice's Hair
Corona Australis	Southern Crown
Corona Borealis	Northern Crown
Corvus	Crow
Crater	Cup
Crux	Southern Cross
Cygnus	Swan
Delphinus	Dolphin
Dorado	Swordfish
Draco	Dragon
Equuleus	Little Horse
Eridanus	River Eridanus
Fornax	Furnace
Gemini (Z)	Twins
Grus	Crane
Hercules	Hercules
Horologium	Clock
Hydra	Sea Serpent
Hydrus	Water Snake
Indus	Indian
Lacerta	Lizard

THE NORTHERN SKY

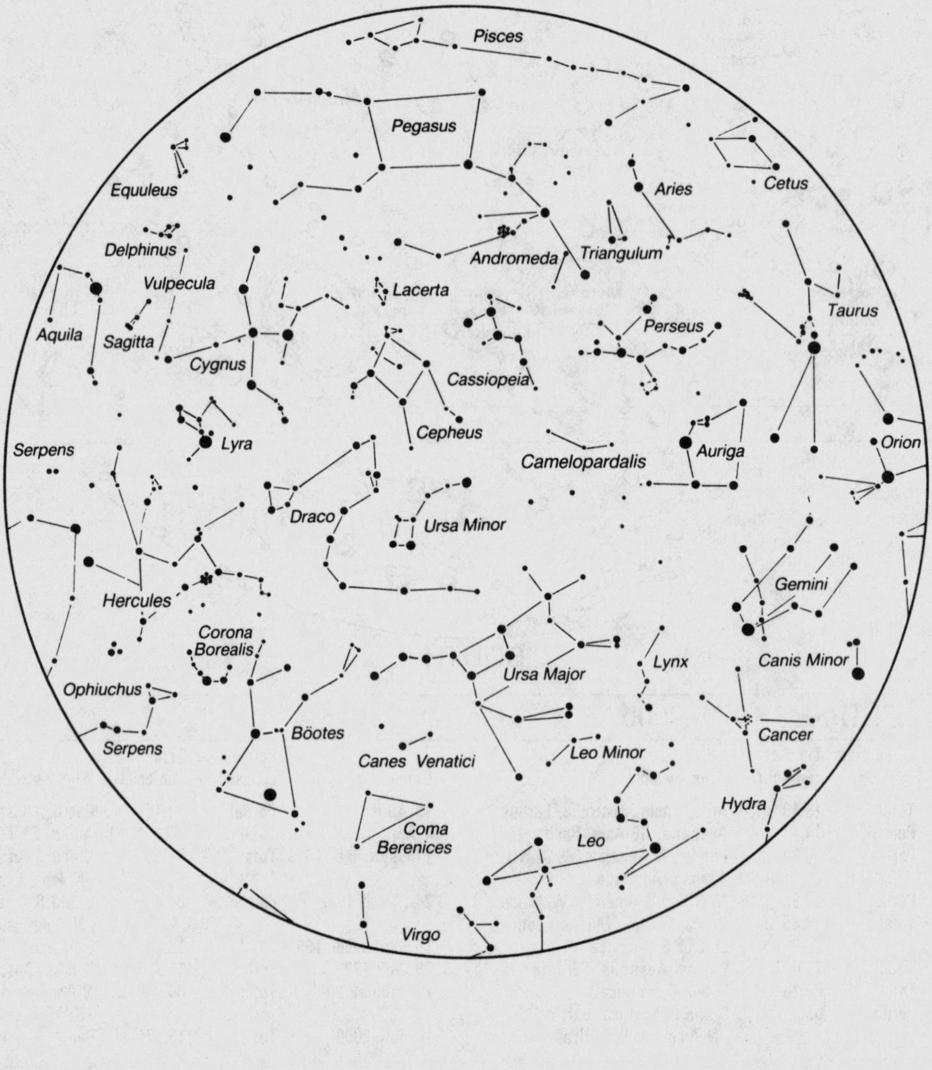

Latin name	English name	Latin name	English name	Latin name	English name
Leo (Z)	Lion	Pavo	Peacock	Serpens	Serpent
Leo Minor	Little Lion	Pegasus	Winged Horse	Sextans	Sextant
Lepus	Hare	Perseus	Perseus	Taurus (Z)	Bull
Libra (Z)	Scales	Phoenix	Phoenix	Telescopium	Telescope
Lupus	Wolf	Pictor	Easel	Triangulum	Triangle
Lynx	Lynx	Pisces (Z)	Fishes	Triangulum Australe	Southern Triangle
Lyra	Harp	Piscis Austrinus	Southern Fish	Tucana	Toucan
Mensa	Table	Puppis	Ship's Stern	Ursa Major	Great Bear
Microscopium	Microscope	Pyxis	Mariner's Compass	Ursa Minor	Little Bear
Monoceros	Unicorn	Reticulum	Net	Vela	Sails
Musca	Fly	Sagitta	Arrow	Virgo (Z)	Virgin
Norma	Level	Sagittarius (Z)	Archer	Volans	Flying Fish
Octans	Octant	Scorpius (Z)	Scorpion	Vulpecula	Fox
Ophiuchus	Serpent Bearer	Sculptor	Sculptor		
Orion	Orion	Scutum	Shield	Z: Found on the Zodiac	

THE SOUTHERN SKY

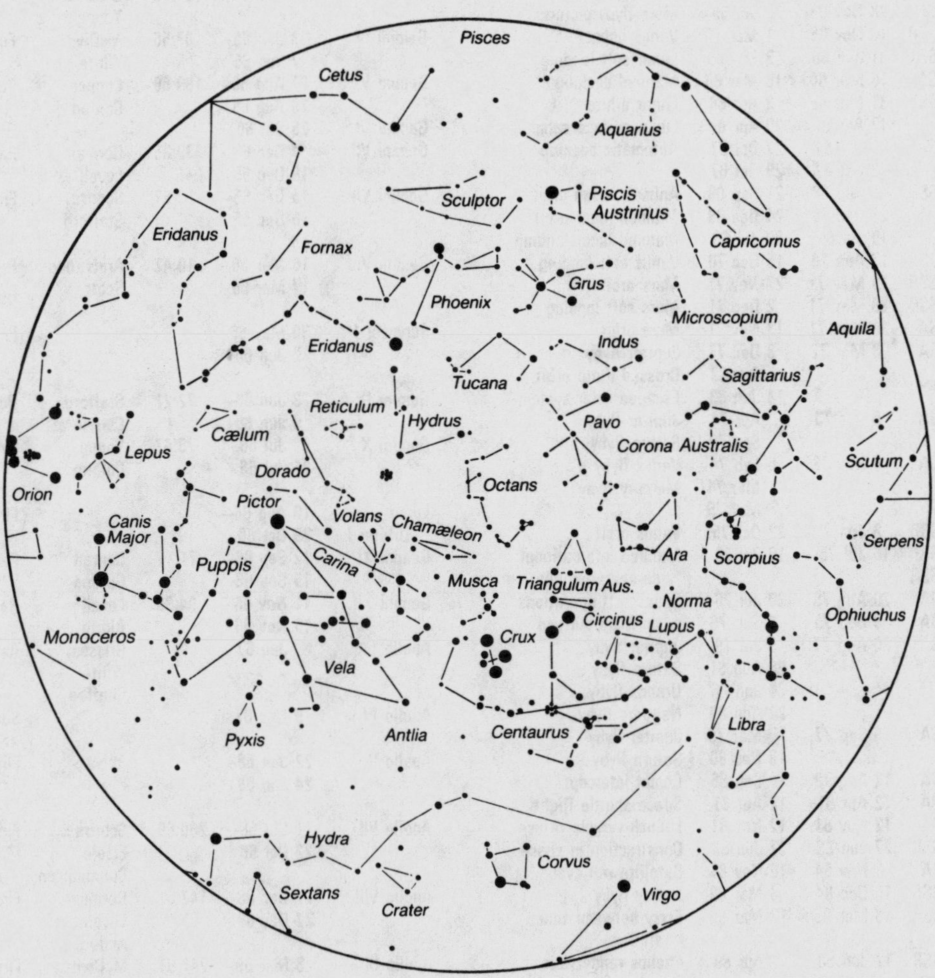

SPACE EXPLORATION

MAJOR SPACE 'FIRSTS'

Mission	USA/ USSR	Launch date	Event date	Event description
Sputnik 1	USSR	4 Oct 57	4 Oct 57	Earth satellite
Sputnik 2	USSR	3 Nov 57	3 Nov 57	Biosatellite
Explorer 1	USA	1 Feb 58	1 Feb 58	Discovered radiation belt (Van Allen)
Luna 1	USSR	2 Jan 59	2 Jan 59	Escaped earth gravity
Vanguard 2	USA	17 Feb 59	17 Feb 59	Earth photo
Luna 2	USSR	12 Sep 59	14 Sep 59	Lunar impact
Luna 3	USSR	4 Oct 59	7 Oct 59	Lunar photo (dark side)
TIROS 1	USA	1 Apr 60	1 Apr 60	Weather satellite
Transit 1B	USA	13 Apr 60	13 Apr 60	Navigation satellite
ECHO 1	USA	12 Aug 60	12 Aug 60	Communications satellite
Sputnik 5	USSR	19 Aug 60	20 Aug 60	Orbited animals
Vostok 1	USSR	12 Apr 61	12 Apr 61	Manned orbital flight
Mariner 2	USA	26 Aug 62	14 Dec 62	Venus flyby
Mars 1	USSR	1 Nov 62	6 Jun 63	Mars flyby
Vostok 6	USSR	16 Jun 63	16 Jun 63	Woman in orbit
Mariner 4	USA	28 Nov 64	15 Jul 65	Mars flyby pictures
Venera 3	USSR	16 Nov 65	1 Mar 66	Venus impact
Luna 9	USSR	31 Jan 66	3 Feb 66	Lunar soft landing
Gemini 8	USA	16 Mar 66	16 Mar 66	Manned docking
Luna 10	USSR	31 Mar 66	3 Apr 66	Lunar orbiter
Surveyor 3	USA	17 Apr 67	20 Apr 67	Lunar surface sampler
Cosmos 186/ 188	USA	22 Oct 67– 28 Oct 67	27 Oct 67– 29 Oct 67	Automatic docking
Zond 5	USSR	14 Sep 68	21 Sep 68	Animals moon orbit
Apollo 8	USA	21 Dec 68	24 Dec 68	Manned lunar orbit
Apollo 11	USA	16 Jul 69	20 Jul 69	Manned lunar landing
Venera 7	USSR	17 Aug 70	15 Dec 70	Venus soft landing
Mars 2	USSR	19 May 71	27 Nov 71	Mars orbit
Mars 3	USSR	28 May 71	2 Dec 71	Mars soft landing
Mariner 9	USA	30 May 71	13 Nov 71	Mars orbit
Pioneer 10	USA	3 Mar 72	3 Dec 73	Jupiter flyby
			Apr 83	Crossed Pluto orbit
			14 Jun 83	Escaped solar system
Pioneer 11	USA	6 Apr 73	Apr 74	Jupiter flyby
			Sep 79	Saturn flyby
Mariner 10	USA	3 Nov 73	5 Feb 74	Venus flyby
			Mar 74/ Mar 75	Mercury flyby
Venera 9	USSR	8 Jun 75	22 Oct 75	Venus orbit
Apollo/Soyuz	USA/ USSR	15 Jul 75	17 Jul 75	Manned international co-operative mission
Viking 1	USA	20 Aug 75	20 Jul 76	Spacecraft operations on Mars surface
Viking 2	USA	9 Sep 75	3 Sep 76	
Voyager 2	USA	20 Aug 77	9 Jul 79	Jupiter flyby
			26 Aug 81	Saturn flyby
			24 Jan 86	Uranus flyby
			24 Aug 89	Neptune flyby
Voyager 1	USA	5 Sep 77	5 Mar 79	Jupiter flyby
			13 Nov 80	Saturn flyby
ISEE-C	USA	12 Aug 78	Sep 85	Comet intercept
STS-1	USA	12 Apr 81	12 Apr 81	Space shuttle flight
STS-2	USA	12 Nov 81	12 Nov 81	Launch vehicle re-use
Soyuz T-9	USSR	27 Jun 83	27 Jun 83	Construction in space
STS 51-A	USA	8 Nov 84	16 Nov 84	Satellite retrieval
Vega 1	USSR	15 Dec 84	6 Mar 85	Halley flyby
Soyuz T-15	USSR	13 Mar 86	13 Mar 86	Ferry between space stations
Phobos 2	USSR	12 Jan 88	Apr 89	Phobos rendezvous

NASA MAJOR LAUNCHES

Mission	Launch	Duration (h:min)	Crew	Comment
Mercury (Freedom 7)	5 May 61	00:15	Shepard	First US manned suborbital flight
Liberty Bell 7	21 Jul 61	00:16	Grissom	Suborbital flight
Mercury (Friendship 7)	20 Feb 62	04:55	Glenn	First US manned orbital flight
Aurora 7	24 May 62	04:56	Carpenter	Orbital flight; manual reentry
Sigma 7	3 Oct 62	09:13	Schirra	6 orbits
Mercury (Faith 7)	15 May 62– 16 May 62	34:20	Cooper	22 orbits; last Mercury flight
Ranger VII	28 Jul 64– 31 Jul 64	68:36		First close-up TV pictures of lunar surface
Gemini II	19 Jan 65			Unmanned suborbital test flight
Gemini III	23 Mar 65	04:53	Grissom Young	First manned Gemini flight
Gemini IV	3 Jun 65– 7 Jun 65	97:56	McDivitt White	First spacewalk (by White, 36 min)
Gemini V	21 Aug 65– 29 Aug 65	190:56	Cooper Conrad	Simulated rendezvous manoeuvres
Gemini VI	25 Oct 65			Orbit not achieved
Gemini VII	4 Dec 65– 18 Dec 65	330:35	Borman Lovell	Part of mission without spacesuits
Gemini VII-A	15 Dec 65– 16 Dec 65	25:51	Schirra Stafford	First space rendezvous (with Gemini VII)
Gemini VIII	16 Mar 66– 17 Mar 66	10:42	Armstrong Scott	Rendezvous/docking with Agena target vehicle
Surveyor I	30 May 66– 2 Jun 66			First soft lunar landing, Ocean of Storms
Gemini IX-A	3 Jun 66– 6 Jun 66	72:21	Stafford Cernan	Docking not achieved
Gemini X	18 Jul 66– 21 Jul 66	70:47	Young Collins	First docked vehicle manoeuvres and spacewalks
Lunar Orbiter I	10 Aug 66– 29 Oct 66			First US craft to orbit moon
Gemini XI	12 Sep 66– 15 Sep 66	71:17	Conrad Gordon	Rendezvous/docking and spacewalks
Gemini XII	11 Nov 66– 15 Nov 66	94:35	Lovell Aldrin	Rendezvous/docking and spacewalks
Apollo I	Jan 67		Grissom White Chaffee	Astronauts killed in command module at launch site
Apollo IV	9 Nov 67			Successful launch of unmanned module
Apollo V	22 Jan 68– 24 Jan 68			Flight test of lunar module in earth orbit
Apollo VII	11 Oct 68– 22 Oct 68	260:09	Schirra Eisele Cunningham	First manned Apollo flight in earth orbit
Apollo VIII	21 Dec 68– 27 Dec 68	147:01	Borman Lovell Anders	First manned orbit of moon (10 orbits)
Apollo IX	3 Mar 69– 13 Mar 69	241:01	McDivitt Scott Schweickart	First manned lunar module flight in earth orbit

NASA MAJOR LAUNCHES (cont.)

Mission	Launch	Duration (h:min)	Crew	Comment
Apollo X	18 May 69–26 May 69	192:03	Stafford, Young, Cernan	First lunar module orbit of moon
Apollo XI	16 Jul 69–24 Jul 69	195:18	Armstrong*, Aldrin*, Collins	First men on moon 20 Jul, Sea of Tranquillity
Apollo 12	14 Nov 69–24 Nov 69	244:36	Conrad*, Bean*, Gordon	Moon landing, 19 Nov, Ocean of Storms
Apollo 13	11 Apr 70–17 Apr 70	142:54	Lovell, Swigert, Haise	Mission aborted, ruptured oxygen tank
Apollo 14	31 Jan 71–9 Feb 71 9 Feb 71	216:02	Shepard*, Mitchell*, Roosa	Moon landing 5 Feb, Fra Mauro area
Apollo 15	26 Jul 71–7 Aug 71	295:12	Scott*, Irwin*, Worden	Moon landing, 30 Jul, Hadley Rille; Lunar Roving Vehicle used
Apollo 16	16 Apr 72–27 Apr 72	265:51	Young*, Duke*, Mattingly	Moon landing, 20 Apr, Descartes
Apollo 17	7 Dec 72–19 Dec 72	301:52	Cernan*, Schmitt*, Evans	Longest Apollo mission, 11 Dec, Taurus-Littrow
Apollo-Soyuz (Test project)	15 Jul 75–24 Jul 75	217:28	Stafford, Brand, Slayton	Rendezvous/docking with Soyuz 19 (cf. facing page)

*Astronauts who landed on the moon; the remaining astronaut was the pilot of the command module.

SHUTTLE FLIGHTS 1981–9

Flight/Name	Launch	Landing	Commander/Pilot/Number of other crew
STS-1 (C)	12 Apr 81	14 Apr 81	Young/Crippen/none
STS-2 (C)	12 Nov 81	14 Nov 81	Engle/Truly/none
STS-3 (C)	22 Mar 82	30 Mar 82	Lousma/Fullerton/none
STS-4 (C)	27 Jun 82	4 Jul 82	Mattingly/Hartsfield/none
STS-5 (C)	11 Nov 82	16 Nov 82	Brand/Overmyer/2
STS-6 (Ch)	4 Apr 83	9 Apr 83	Weitz/Bobko/2
STS-7 (Ch)	18 Jun 83	24 Jun 83	Crippen/Hauck/3
STS-8 (Ch)	30 Aug 83	5 Sep 83	Truly/Brandenstein/3
STS-9 (C)	28 Nov 83	8 Dec 83	Young/Shaw/4
STS 41-B (Ch)	3 Feb 84	11 Feb 84	Brand/Gibson/3
STS 41-C (Ch)	6 Apr 84	13 Apr 84	Crippen/Scobee/3
STS 41-D (D)	30 Aug 84	5 Sept 84	Hartsfield/Coats/4
STS 41-G (Ch)	5 Oct 84	13 Oct 84	Crippen/McBride/5
STS 51-A (D)	8 Nov 84	16 Nov 84	Hauck/Walker/3
STS 51-C (D)	24 Jan 85	27 Jan 85	Mattingly/Shriver/3
STS 51-D (D)	12 Apr 85	19 Apr 85	Bobko/Williams/5
STS 51-B (Ch)	29 Apr 85	6 May 85	Overmyer/Gregory/5
STS 51-G (D)	17 Jun 85	24 Jun 85	Brandenstein/Creighton/5
STS 51-F (Ch)	29 Jul 85	6 Aug 85	Fullerton/Bridges/5
STS 51-I (D)	27 Aug 85	3 Sep 85	Engle/Covey/3
STS 51-J (A)	3 Oct 85	7 Oct 85	Bobko/Grabe/3
STS 61-A (Ch)	30 Oct 85	6 Nov 85	Hartsfield/Nagel/6
STS 61-B (A)	26 Nov 85	3 Dec 85	Shaw/O'Connor/5
STS 61-C (C)	12 Jan 86	18 Jan 86	Gibson/Bolden/5
STS 51-L (Ch)	28 Jan 86	exploded	Scobee/Smith/5
STS 26 (D)	29 Sept 88	3 Oct 88	Hauck/Covey/3
STS 27 (A)	2 Dec 88	6 Dec 88	Gibson/Gardner/3
STS 30 (A)	4 May 89	8 May 89	Walker/Grase/3

A Atlantis Ch Challenger C Columbia D Discovery

SKYLAB MISSIONS

Mission	Launch	Splashdown	Crew
1	14 May 73	–	Unmanned
2	25 May 73	22 Jun 73	Conrad, Kerwin, Weitz
3	28 Jul 73	25 Sep 73	Bean, Garriott, Lousma
4	16 Nov 73	8 Feb 74	Carr, Gibson, Pogue

MAJOR USSR MANNED LAUNCHES

Mission	Launch	Duration (h:min)	Crew	Comment
Vostok 1	12 Apr 61	01:48	Gagarin	First earth orbit
Vostok 2	6 Aug 61	25:18	Titov	Earth orbits
Vostok 3	11 Aug 62	94:22	Nikolayev	First dual mission
Vostok 6	16 Jun 63	70:50	Tereshkova	First female flight
Voshkod 1	12 Oct 64	24:17	Komarov, Feoktistov, Yegorov	Crew operated in 'shirt-sleeve' environment
Voshkod 2	18 Mar 65	26:02	Belyayev, Leonov	First spacewalk
Soyuz 1	23 Apr 67	27:00	Komarov	Cosmonaut killed
Soyuz 4	14 Jan 69	71:14	Shatalov	Spacecraft docked for 4 h; two cosmonauts transfer to Soyuz 4
Soyuz 5	15 Jan 69	72:46	Volynov, Khrunov, Yeliseyev	
Soyuz 6	11 Oct 69	118:42	Shonin, Kubasov	First mission with multiple crews
Soyuz 10	22 Apr 71	48:00	Shatalov, Yeliseyev, Rukavishnikov	Docked with Salyut 1 space station
Soyuz 11	6 Jun 71	552:00	Dobrovolsky, Volkov, Patsayev	Docked with Salyut 1; crew killed on return journey
Soyuz 14	4 Jul 74	16 days	Popovich, Artyukhin	Docked with Salyut 3
Soyuz 17	9 Jan 75	30 days	Gubarev, Grechko	Docked with Salyut 4
Soyuz 19 (Apollo-Soyuz Test Project)	15 Jul 75	6 days	Kubasov, Leonov	First international space mission with USA; ≫ p60 crew transfer
Soyuz 24	7 Feb 77	18 days	Gorbatko, Glazkov	Docked with Salyut 5
Soyuz 26	10 Dec 77	96 days	Romanenko, Grechko	First prime crew Salyut 6
Soyuz 27	10 Jan 78	6 days	Dzhanibekov, Makarov	First visiting crew to Salyut 6
Soyuz 28	2 Mar 78	8 days	Gubarev, Remek	Second visiting crew to Salyut 6
Soyuz 29	15 Jun 78	140 days	Kovalenok, Ivanchenko	Second prime crew of Salyut 6
Soyuz 32	25 Feb 79	175 days	Lyakhov, Ryumin	Third prime crew of Salyut 6
Soyuz T-4	12 Mar 81	75 days	Kovalenok, Savinykh	Last prime crew of Salyut 6
Soyuz 40	14 May 81	8 days	Popov, Prunariu	Last visiting crew to Salyut 6
Soyuz T-5	14 May 82	211 days	Berezovoy, Ledebev	Salyut 7 in orbit
Soyuz T-10	8 Feb 84	237 days	Kizim, Atkov, Solovyev	Longest manned space flight

EARTH: GENERAL DATA

There are no universally agreed estimates of the natural phenomena given in this section. Surveys make use of different criteria for identifying natural boundaries, and use different techniques of measurement. The sizes of continents, oceans, seas, deserts, and rivers are particularly subject to variation.

Age 4500000000 years (accurate to within a very small percentage of possible error)
Area 509600000 sq km/197000000 sq ml
Mass 5976 × 10^{27} grams

Land surface 148000000 sq km/57000000 sq ml (c.29% of total area)
Water surface 361600000 sq km/140000000 sq ml (c.71% of total area)
Circumference at equator 40076 km/24902 ml
Circumference of meridian 40000 km/24860 ml

CONTINENTS

Name	Area sq km	sq ml	Lowest point below sea level	m	ft	Highest elevation	m	ft
Africa	30293000	11696000 (20.2%)	Lake Assal, Djibouti	156	512	Mt Kilimanjaro, Tanzania	5895	19340
Antarctica	13975000	5396000 (9.3%)	Bently subglacial trench	2538	8327	Vinson Massif	5140	16864
Asia	44493000	17179000 (29.6%)	Dead Sea, Israel/Jordan	400	1312	Mt Everest, China-Nepal	8848	29028
Oceania	8945000	3454000 (6%)	Lake Eyre, S Australia	15	49	Puncak Jaya (Ngga Pulu)	5030	16500
Europe*	10245000	3956000 (6.8%)	Caspian Sea	29	94	Mt Elbrus, Russia	5642	18510
North America	24454000	9442000 (16.3%)	Death Valley, California	86	282	Mt McKinley, Alaska	6194	20320
South America	17838000	6887000 (11.9%)	Peninsular Valdez, Argentina	40	131	Aconcagua, Argentina	6960	22831

*Including western USSR.

OCEANS

Name	Area sq km	sq ml		Greatest depth	m	ft	Average depth	m	ft
Arctic	13986000	5400000	(3%)	Eurasia Basin	5122	16804	Arctic	1330	4300
Atlantic	82217000	31700000	(24%)	Puerto Rico Trench	8648	28372	Atlantic	3700	12100
Indian	73426000	28350000	(20%)	Java Trench	7725	25344	Indian	3900	12800
Pacific	181300000	70000000	(46%)	Mariana Trench	11040	36220	Pacific	4300	14100

LARGEST ISLANDS

Name	Area* sq km	sq ml
Australia	7892300	3046500
Greenland	2131600	823800
New Guinea	790000	305000
Borneo	737000	285000
Madagascar	587000	227600
Baffin	507000	196000
Sumatra	425000	164900
Honshu (Hondo)	228000	88000
Great Britain	219000	84400
Victoria, Canada	217300	83900
Ellesmere, Canada	196000	75800
Celebes	174000	67400
South I, New Zealand	151000	58200
Java	129000	50000
North I, New Zealand	114000	44200
Newfoundland	109000	42000
Cuba	105000	40500
Luzon	105000	40400
Iceland	103000	39700
Mindanao	94600	36500
Novaya Zemlya (two islands)	90600	35000
Ireland	84100	32500
Hokkaido	78500	30300
Hispaniola	77200	29800
Sakhalin	75100	29000
Tierra del Fuego	71200	27500
Tasmania	67900	26200

*Areas are rounded to the nearest three significant digits.

LARGEST SEAS

Name	Area* sq km	sq ml
Coral Sea	4791000	1850200
Arabian Sea	3863000	1492000
S China (Nan) Sea	3685000	1423000
Mediterranean Sea	2516000	971000
Bering Sea	2304000	890000
Bay of Bengal	2172000	839000
Sea of Okhotsk	1590000	614000
Gulf of Mexico	1543000	596000
Gulf of Guinea	1533000	592000
Barents Sea	1405000	542000
Norwegian Sea	1383000	534000
Gulf of Alaska	1327000	512000
Hudson Bay	1232000	476000
Greenland Sea	1205000	465000
Arafura Sea	1037000	400000
Philippine Sea	1036000	400000
Sea of Japan	978000	378000
E Siberian Sea	901000	348000
Kara Sea	883000	341000
E China Sea	664000	256000
Andaman Sea	565000	218000
North Sea	520000	201000
Black Sea	508000	196000
Red Sea	453000	175000
Baltic Sea	414000	160000
Arabian Gulf	238000	92200
St Lawrence Gulf	238300	92000

Oceans are excluded.
*Areas are rounded to the nearest 1000 sq km/sq ml.

LARGEST LAKES

Name/Location	Area* sq km	sq ml
Caspian Sea, Iran/Russia	371000	143240[1]
Superior, USA/Canada	82260	31760[2]
Aral Sea, Kazakhstan	64500	24900[1]
Victoria, E Africa	62940	24300
Huron, USA/Canada	59580	23000[2]
Michigan, USA	58020	22400
Tanganyika, E Africa	32000	12350
Baikal, Russia	31500	12160
Great Bear, Canada	31330	12100
Great Slave, Canada	28570	11030
Erie, USA/Canada	25710	9920[2]
Winnipeg, Canada	24390	9420
Malawi/Nyasa, E Africa	22490	8680
Balkhash, Kazakhstan	17–22000	6500–8500[1]
Ontario, Canada	19270	7440[2]
Ladoga, Russia	18130	7000
Chad, W Africa	10–26000	4–10000
Maracaibo, Venezuela	13010	5020[3]
Patos, Brazil	10140	3920[3]
Onega, Russia	9800	3800
Rudolf, E Africa	9100	3500
Eyre, Australia	8800	3400[3]
Titicaca, Peru	8300	3200

[1] salt lakes
[2] average of areas given by Canada and USA
[3] salt lagoons
*Areas are given to the nearest 10 sq km/sq ml.
The Caspian and Aral Seas, being entirely surrounded by land, are classified as lakes.

HIGHEST MOUNTAINS

Name	Height* m	ft	Location
Everest	8850	29030	China-Nepal
K2	8610	28250	Kashmir-Jammu
Kangchenjunga	8590	28170	India-Nepal
Lhotse	8500	27890	China-Nepal
Kangchenjunga S Peak	8470	27800	India-Nepal
Makalu I	8470	27800	China-Nepal
Kangchenjunga W Peak	8420	27620	India-Nepal
Llotse E Peak	8380	27500	China-Nepal
Dhaulagiri	8170	26810	Nepal
Cho Oyu	8150	26750	China-Nepal
Manaslu	8130	26660	Nepal
Nanga Parbat	8130	26660	Kashmir-Jammu
Annapurna I	8080	26500	Nepal
Gasherbrum I	8070	26470	Kashmir-Jammu
Broad-highest	8050	26400	Kashmir-Jammu
Gasherbrum II	8030	26360	Kashmir-Jammu
Gosainthan	8010	26290	China
Broad-middle	8000	26250	Kashmir-Jammu
Gasherbrum III	7950	26090	Kashmir-Jammu
Annapurna II	7940	26040	Nepal
Nanda Devi	7820	25660	India
Rakaposhi	7790	25560	Kashmir
Kamet	7760	25450	India
Ulugh Muztagh	7720	25340	Tibet
Tirich Mir	7690	25230	Pakistan
Muz Tag Ata	7550	24760	China
Communism Peak	7490	24590	Tadzhikistan
Pobedy Peak	7440	24410	China-Kirghizia
Aconcagua	6960	22830	Argentina
Ojos del Salado	6910	22660	Argentina-Chile

*Heights are given to the nearest 10 m/ft.

LARGEST DESERTS

Name/Location	Area sq km	sq ml
Sahara, N Africa	8600000	3320000
Arabian, SW Asia	2330000	900000
Gobi, Mongolia and NE China	1166000	450000
Patagonian, Argentina	673000	260000
Great Victoria, SW Australia	647000	250000
Great Basin, SW USA	492000	190000
Chihuahuan, Mexico	450000	175000
Great Sandy, NW Australia	400000	150000
Sonoran, SW USA	310000	120000
Kyzyl-Kum, Kazakhstan, Uzbekistan	300000	115000
Takla Makan, N China	270000	105000
Kalahari, SW Africa	260000	100000
Kara-Kum, Turkmenia	260000	100000
Kavir, Iran	260000	100000
Syrian, Saudi Arabia/Jordan/Syria/Iraq	260000	100000
Nubian, Sudan	260000	100000
Thar, India/Pakistan	200000	77000
Ust'-Urt, Kazakhstan, Uzbekistan	160000	62000
Bet-Pak-Dala, Kazakhstan	155000	60000
Simpson, C Australia	145000	56000
Dzungaria, China	142000	55000
Atacama, Chile	140000	54000
Namib, SE Africa	134000	52000
Sturt, SE Australia	130000	50000
Bolson de Mapimi, Mexico	130000	50000
Ordos, China	130000	50000
Alashan, China	116000	45000

Desert areas are very approximate, because clear physical boundaries may not occur.

LONGEST RIVERS

Name	Outflow	Length* km	ml
Nile-Kagera-Ruvuvu-Ruvusu-Luvironza	Mediterranean Sea (Egypt)	6690	4160
Amazon-Ucayali-Tambo-Ene-Apurimac	Atlantic Ocean (Brazil)	6570	4080
Mississippi-Missouri-Jefferson-Beaverhead-Red Rock	Gulf of Mexico (USA)	6020	3740
Chang Jiang (Yangtze)	E China Sea (China)	5980	3720
Yenisey-Angara-Selenga-Ider	Kara Sea (Russia)	5870	3650
Amur-Argun-Kerulen	Tartar Strait (Russia)	5780	3590
Ob-Irtysh	Gulf of Ob, Kara Sea (Russia)	5410	3360
Plata-Parana-Grande	Atlantic Ocean (Argentina/Uruguay)	4880	3030
Huang Ho (Yellow)	Yellow Sea (China)	4840	3010
Congo (Zaire)-Lualaba	Atlantic Ocean (Angola-Zaire)	4630	2880
Lena	Laptev Sea (Russia)	4400	2730
Mackenzie-Slave-Peace-Finlay	Beaufort Sea (Canada)	4240	2630
Mekong	S China Sea (Vietnam)	4180	2600
Niger	Gulf of Guinea (Nigeria)	4100	2550

*Lengths are given to the nearest 10 km/ml, and include the river plus tributaries comprising the longest watercourse.

HIGHEST WATERFALLS

Name	Height m	ft	Location
Angel (upper fall)	807	2648	Venezuela
Itatinga	628	2060	Brazil
Cuquenan	610	2000	Guyana-Venezuela
Ormeli	563	1847	Norway
Tysse	533	1749	Norway
Pilao	524	1719	Brazil
Ribbon	491	1612	USA
Vestre Mardola	468	1535	Norway
Roraima	457?	1500?	Guyana
Cleve-Garth	450?	1476?	New Zealand

Distances are given for individual leaps.

DEEPEST CAVES

Name/Location	Depth m	ft
Jean Bernard, France	1494	4900
Snezhnaya, Russia	1340	4397
Puertas de Illamina, Spain	1338	4390
Pierre-Saint-Martin, France	1321	4334
Sistema Huautla, Mexico	1240	4067
Berger, France	1198	3930
Vqerdi, Spain	1195	3921
Dachstein-Mammuthöhle, Austria	1174	3852
Zitu, Spain	1139	3737
Badalona, Spain	1130	3707
Batmanhöhle, Austria	1105	3626
Schneeloch, Austria	1101	3612
G E S Malaga, Spain	1070	3510
Lamprechtsofen, Austria	1024	3360

MAJOR VOLCANOES

Name	Height m	Height ft	Major eruptions (years)	Last eruption (year)
Aconcagua (Argentina)	6 960	22 831	extinct	
Ararat (Turkey)	5 198	18 350	extinct	Holocene
Awu (Sangihe Is)	1 327	4 355	1711, 1856, 1892	1968
Bezymianny (Russia)	2 800	9 186	1955–6	1984
Coseguina (Nicaragua)	847	1 598	1835	1835
El Chichón (Mexico)	1 349	4 430	1982	1982
Erebus (Antarctica)	4 023	13 200	1947, 1972	1986
Etna (Italy)	3 236	10 625	122, 1169, 1329, 1536, 1669, 1928, 1964, 1971	1986
Fuji (Japan)	3 776	12 388	1707	1707
Galunggung (Java)	2 180	7 155	1822, 1918	1982
Hekla (Iceland)	1 491	4 920	1693, 1845, 1947–8, 1970	1981
Helgafell (Iceland)	215	706	1973	1973
Jurullo (Mexico)	1 330	4 255	1759–74	1774
Katmai (Alaska)	2 298	7 540	1912, 1920, 1921	1331
Kilauea (Hawaii)	1 247	4 100	1823–1924, 1952, 1955, 1960, 1967–8, 1968–74, 1983–7	1988
Kilimanjaro (Tanzania)	5 930	19 450	extinct	Pleistocene
Klyuchevskoy (Russia)	4 850	15 910	1700–1966, 1984	1985
Krakatoa (Sumatra)	818	2 685	1680, 1883, 1927, 1952–3, 1969	1980
La Soufrière (St Vincent)	1 232	4 048	1718, 1812, 1902, 1971–2	1979
Laki (Iceland)	500	1 642	1783	1784
Lamington (Papua New Guinea)	1 780	5 844	1951	1956

Name	Height m	Height ft	Major eruptions (years)	Last eruption (year)
Lassen Peak (USA)	3 186	10 453	1914–5	192
Mauna Loa (Hawaii)	4 172	13 685	1859, 1880, 1887, 1919, 1950	198
Mayon (Philippines)	2 462	8 084	1616, 1766, 1814, 1897, 1968	197
Nyamuragira (Zaire)	3 056	10 026	1921–38, 1971, 1980	198
Paricutin (Mexico)	3 188	10 460	1943–52	195
Pelée, Mont (Martinique)	1 397	4 584	1902, 1929–32	193
Popocatepetl (Mexico)	5 483	17 990	1920	194
Rainier, Mt (USA)	4 392	14 416	1st-c BC, 1820	188
Ruapehu (New Zealand)	2 796	9 175	1945, 1953, 1969, 1975	198
St Helens, Mt (USA)	2 549	8 364	1800, 1831, 1835, 1842–3, 1857, 1980–	198
Santorini/Thira (Greece)	1 315?	4 316?	1470 BC, 197 BC, AD 46, 1570–3, 1707–11, 1866–70	195
Stromboli (Italy)	931	3 055	1768, 1882, 1889, 1907, 1930, 1936, 1941, 1950, 1952	198
Surtsey (Iceland)	174	570	1963–7	196
Taal (Philippines)	1 448	4 752	1911, 1965, 1969	197
Tambora (Sumbawa)	2 868	9 410	1815	188
Tarawera (New Zealand)	1 149	3 770	1886	197
Vesuvius (Italy)	1 289	4 230	79, 472, 1036, 1631, 1779, 1906	194
Vulcano (Italy)	502	1 650	antiquity, 1444, 1730–40, 1786, 1873, 1888–90	189

MAJOR EARTHQUAKES

All magnitudes on the Richter scale.

Location	Year	Magnitude	Deaths
San Francisco	1989	6.9	100
Armenia	1988	7.0	25 000
Mexico City	1985	8.1	7 200
N Yemen	1982	6.0	2 800
S Italy	1980	7.2	4 500
El Asnam (Algeria)	1980	7.3	5 000
NE Iran	1978	7.7	25 000
Tangshan (China)	1976	8.2	242 000
Guatemala City	1976	7.5	22 778
Kashmir	1974	6.3	5 200
Managua (Nicaragua)	1972	6.2	5 000
S Iran	1972	6.9	5 000
Chimbote (Peru)	1970	7.7	66 000
NE Iran	1968	7.4	11 600
Anchorage (USA)	1964	8.5	131
NW Iran	1962	7.1	12 000
Agadir (Morocco)	1960	5.8	12 000
Erzincan (Turkey)	1939	7.9	23 000
Chillan (Chile)	1939	7.8	30 000
Quetta (India)	1935	7.5	60 000
Gansu (China)	1932	7.6	70 000
Nan-shan (China)	1927	8.3	200 000
Kanto (Japan)	1923	8.3	143 000
Gansu (China)	1920	8.6	180 000
Avezzano (Italy)	1915	7.5	30 000
Messina (Italy)	1908	7.5	120 000
Valparaiso (Chile)	1906	8.6	20 000
San Francisco (USA)	1906	8.3	500
Ecuador/Colombia	1868	*	70 000
Calabria (Italy)	1783	*	50 000
Lisbon (Portugal)	1755	*	70 000
Calcutta (India)	1737	*	300 000
Hokkaido (Japan)	1730	*	137 000
Catania (Italy)	1693	*	60 000
Caucasia	1667	*	80 000
Shensi (China)	1556	*	830 000
Chihli (China)	1290	*	100 000
Silicia (Asia Minor)	1268	*	60 000
Corinth (Greece)	856	*	45 000
Antioch (Turkey)	526	*	250 000

*Magnitude not available.

MAJOR TSUNAMIS

Location of source	Year	Height m	Height ft	Location of deaths/damage	Deaths
Sea of Japan	1983	15	49	Japan, Korea	107
Indonesia	1979	10	32	Indonesia	187
Celebes Sea	1976	30	98	Philippine Is	5 000
Alaska	1964	32	105	Alaska, Aleutian Is, California	122
Chile	1960	25	82	Chile, Hawaii, Japan	1 260
Aleutian Is	1957	16	52	Hawaii, Japan	0
Kamchatka	1952	18.4	60	Kamchatka, Kuril Is, Hawaii	many
Aleutian Is	1946	32	105	Aleutian Is, Hawaii, California	165
Nankaido (Japan)	1946	6.1	20	Japan	1 997
Kii (Japan)	1944	7.5	25	Japan	998
Sanriku (Japan)	1933	28.2	93	Japan, Hawaii	3 000
E Kamchatka	1923	20	66	Kamchatka, Hawaii	3
S Kuril Is	1918	12	39	Kuril Is, Russia, Japan, Hawaii	23
Sanriku (Japan)	1896	30	98	Japan	27 122
Sunda Strait	1883	35	115	Java, Sumatra	36 000
Chile	1877	23	75	Chile, Hawaii	many
Chile	1868	21	69	Chile, Hawaii	25 000
Hawaii Is	1868	20	66	Hawaii Is	81
Japan	1854	6	20	Japan	3 000
Flores Sea	1800	24	79	Indonesia	4–500
Ariake Sea	1792	9	30	Japan	9 745
Italy	1783	?	?	Italy	30 000
Ryukyu Is	1771	12	39	Ryukyu Is	11 941
Portugal	1775	16	52	W Europe, Morocco, W Indies	60 000
Peru	1746	24	79	Peru	5 000
Japan	1741	9	30	Japan	1 000 +
SE Kamchatka	1737	30	98	Kamchatka, Kuril Is	?
Peru	1724	24	79	Peru	?
Japan	1707	11.5	38	Japan	30 000
W Indies	1692	?	?	Jamaica	2 000
Banda Is	1629	15	49	Indonesia	?
Sanriku (Japan)	1611	25	82	Japan	5 000
Japan	1605	?	?	Japan	4 000
Kii (Japan)	1498	?	?	Japan	5 000

EARTHQUAKE SEVERITY

lodified Mercalli intensity scale (1956 Revision)

ntensity alue	Description
	Not felt; marginal and long-period effects of large earthquakes.
	Felt by persons at rest, on upper floors or favourably placed.
	Felt indoors; hanging objects swing; vibration like passing of light trucks; duration estimated; may not be recognized as an earthquake.
/	Hanging objects swing; vibration like passing of heavy trucks, or sensation of a jolt like a heavy ball striking the walls; standing cars rock; windows, dishes, doors rattle; glasses clink; crockery clashes; in the upper range of IV, wooden walls and frames creak.
	Felt outdoors; direction estimated; sleepers wakened; liquids disturbed, some spilled; small unstable objects displaced or upset; doors swing, close, open; shutters, pictures move; pendulum clocks stop, start, change rate.
I	Felt by all; many frightened and run outdoors; persons walk unsteadily; windows, dishes, glassware break; knickknacks, books, etc, fall off shelves; pictures off walls; furniture moves or overturns; weak plaster and masonry D crack; small bells ring (church, school); trees, bushes shake visibly, or heard to rustle.
II	Difficult to stand; noticed by drivers; hanging objects quiver; furniture breaks; damage to masonry D, including cracks; weak chimneys broken at roof line; fall of plaster, loose bricks, stones, tiles, cornices, also unbraced parapets and architectural ornaments; some cracks in masonry C; waves on ponds, water turbid with mud; small slides and caving in along sand or gravel banks; large bells ring; concrete irrigation ditches damaged.
/III	Steering of cars affected; damage to masonry C and partial collapse; some damage to masonry B; none to masonry A; fall of stucco and some masonry walls; twisting, fall of chimneys, factory stacks, monuments, towers, elevated tanks; frame houses move on foundations if not bolted down; loose panel walls thrown out; decayed piling broken off; branches broken from trees; changes in flow or temperature of springs and wells; cracks in wet ground and on steep slopes.
IX	General panic; masonry D destroyed; masonry C heavily damaged, sometimes with complete collapse; masonry B seriously damaged; general damage to foundations; frame structures, if not bolted, shift off foundations; frames racked; serious damage to reservoirs; underground pipes break; conspicuous cracks in ground; in alluviated areas sand and mud ejected, earthquake fountains, sand craters.
X	Most masonry and frame structures destroyed with their foundations; some well-built wooden structures and bridges destroyed; serious damage to dams, dikes, embankments; large landslides; water thrown on banks of canals, rivers, lakes, etc; sand and mud shifted horizontally on beaches and flat land; rails bent slightly.
XI	Rails bent greatly; underground pipelines completely out of service.
XII	Damage nearly total; large rock masses displaced; lines of sight and level distorted; objects thrown into the air.

Note
Masonry A. Good workmanship, mortar and design; reinforced, especially laterally, and bound together by using steel, concrete etc; designed to resist lateral forces.
Masonry B. Good workmanship and mortar; reinforced, but not designed in detail to resist lateral forces.
Masonry C. Ordinary workmanship and mortar; no extreme weakness like failing to tie in at corners, but neither reinforced nor designed against horizontal forces.
Masonry D. Weak materials, such as adobe; poor mortar; low standards of workmanship; weak horizontally.

WIND FORCE AND SEA DISTURBANCE

Beaufort number	Wind speed m/sec	kph	mph	Wind name	Observable wind characteristics	Sea disturbance number	Average wave ht. m	ft	Observable sea characteristics
0	1	<1	<1	Calm	Smoke rises vertically	0	0	0	Sea like a mirror
1	1	1–5	1–3	Light air	Wind direction shown by smoke drift, but not by wind vanes	0	0	0	Ripples like scales, without foam crests
2	2	6–11	4–7	Light breeze	Wind felt on face; leaves rustle; vanes moved by wind	1	0.3	0–1	More definite wavelets, but crests do not break
3	4	12–19	8–12	Gentle breeze	Leaves and small twigs in constant motion; wind extends light flag	2	0.3–0.6	1–2	Large wavelets; crests beginning to break; scattered white horses
4	7	20–28	13–18	Moderate	Raises dust, loose paper; small branches moved	3	0.6–1.2	2–4	Small waves becoming longer; fairly frequent white horses
5	10	29–38	19–24	Fresh	Small trees in leaf begin to sway; crested wavelets on inland waters	4	1.2–2.4	4–8	Moderate waves with a more definite long form; many white horses; some spray possible
6	12	39–49	25–31	Strong	Large branches in motion; difficult to use umbrellas; whistling heard in telegraph wires	5	2.4–4	8–13	Large waves forming; more extensive white foam crests; some spray probable
7	15	50–61	32–38	Near gale	Whole trees in motion; inconvenience walking against wind	6	4–6	13–20	Sea heaps up; streaks of white foam blown along
8	18	62–74	39–46	Gale	Breaks twigs off trees; impedes progress	6	4–6	13–20	Moderately high waves of greater length; well-marked streaks of foam
9	20	75–88	47–54	Strong gale	Slight structural damage occurs	6	4–6	13–20	High waves; dense streaks of foam; sea begins to roll; spray affects visibility
10	26	89–102	55–63	Storm	Trees uprooted; considerable damage occurs	7	6–9	20–30	Very high waves with long overhanging crests; dense streaks of foam blown along; generally white appearance of surface; heavy rolling
11	30	103–17	64–72	Violent storm	Widespread damage	8	9–14	30–45	Exceptionally high waves; long white patches of foam; poor visibility; ships lost to view behind waves
12–17	⩾33	⩾118	⩾73	Hurricane		9	14	>45	Air filled with foam and spray; sea completely white; very poor visibility

GEOLOGICAL TIME SCALE

Eon	Era	Period	Epoch	Million years before present	Geological events	Sea life	Land life
Phanerozoic	Cenozoic	Quaternary	Holocene	0.01	Glaciers recede. Sea level rises. Climate becomes more equable.	As now.	Forests flourish again. Humans acquire agriculture and technology.
			Pleistocene	2.0	Widespread glaciers melt periodically causing seas to rise and fall.	As now.	Many plant forms perish. Small mammals abundant. Primitive humans established.
		Tertiary	Pliocene	5.1	Continents and oceans adopting their present form. Present climatic distribution established. Ice caps develop.	Giant sharks extinct. Many fish varieties.	Some plants and mammals die out. Primates flourish.
			Miocene	24.6	Seas recede further. European and Asian land masses join. Heavy rain causes massive erosion. Red Sea opens.	Bony fish common. Giant sharks.	Grasses widespread. Grazing mammals become common.
			Oligocene	38.0	Seas recede. Extensive movements of earth's crust produce new mountains (eg Alpine-Himalayan chain).	Crabs, mussels, and snails evolve.	Forests diminish. Grasses appear. Pachyderms, canines and felines develop.
			Eocene	54.9	Mountain formation continues. Glaciers common in high mountain ranges. Greenland separates. Australia separates.	Whales adapt to sea.	Large tropical jungles. Primitive forms of modern mammals established.
			Paleocene	65	Widespread subsidence of land. Seas advance again. Considerable volcanic activity. Europe emerges.	Many reptiles become extinct.	Flowering plants widespread. First primates. Giant reptiles extinct.
	Mesozoic	Cretaceous	Late Early	97.5 144	Swamps widespread. Massive alluvial deposition. Continuing limestone formation. S America separates from Africa. India, Africa and Antarctica separate.	Turtles, rays, and now-common fish appear.	Flowering plants established. Dinosaurs become extinct.
		Jurassic	Malm Dogger Lias	163 188 213	Seas advance. Much river formation. High mountains eroded. Limestone formation. N America separates from Africa. Central Atlantic begins to open.	Reptiles dominant.	Early flowers. Dinosaurs dominant. Mammals still primitive. First birds.
		Triassic	Late Middle Early	231 243 248	Desert conditions widespread. Hot climate gradually becomes warm and wet. Break up of Gondwanaland into continents.	Icthyosaurs, flying fish, and crustaceans appear.	Ferns and conifers thrive. First mammals, dinosaurs, and flies.
	Paleozoic	Permian	Late Early	258 286	Some sea areas cut off to form lakes. Earth movements form mountains. Glaciation in southern hemisphere.	Some shelled fish become extinct.	Deciduous plants. Reptiles dominant. Many insect varieties.
		Carboniferous	Pennsylvanian Mississippian	320 360	Sea-beds rise to form new land areas. Enormous swamps. Partly-rotted vegetation forms coal.	Amphibians and sharks abundant.	Extensive evergreen forests. Reptiles breed on land. Some insects develop wings.
		Devonian	Late Middle Early	374 387 408	Collision of continents causing mountain formation (Appalachians, Caledonides and Urals). Sea deeper but narrower. Climatic zones forming. Iapetus ocean closed.	Fish abundant. Primitive sharks. First amphibians.	Leafy plants. Some invertebrates adapt to land. First insects.
		Silurian	Pridoli Ludlow Wenlock Llandovery	414 421 428 438	New mountain ranges form. Sea level varies periodically. Extensive shallow sea over the Sahara.	Large vertebrates.	First leafless land plants.
		Ordovician	Ashgill Caradoc Llandeilo Llanvirn Arenig Tremadoc	448 458 468 478 488 505	Shore lines still quite variable. Increasing sedimentation. Europe and N America moving together.	First vertebrates. Coral reefs develop.	None.
		Cambrian	Merioneth St David's Caerfai	525 540 590	Much volcanic activity, and long periods of marine sedimentation.	Shelled invertebrates. Trilobites.	None.
Proterozoic	Precambrian	Vendian		650	Shallow seas advance and retreat over land areas. Atmosphere uniformly warm.	Seaweed. Algae and invertebrates.	None.
		Riphean	Late Middle Early	 900 1300	Intense deformation and metamorphism.	Earliest marine life and fossils.	None.
		Early Proterozoic		1600 2500	Shallow shelf seas. Formation of carbonate sediments and 'red beds'.	First appearance of stromatolites.	None.
Archaean		Archaean (Azoic)		4600	Banded iron formations. Formation of the earth's crust and oceans.	None.	None.

TIMES AND DISTANCES

INTERNATIONAL TIME DIFFERENCES

The time zones of the world are conventionally measured from longitude 0 at Greenwich Observatory (Greenwich Mean Time, GMT).

Each 15° of longitude east of this point is one hour ahead of GMT (eg when it is 2 pm in London it is 3 pm or later in time zones to the east). Hours ahead of GMT are shown by a plus sign, eg +3, +4/8.

Each 15° west of this point is one hour behind GMT (2 pm in London would be 1 pm or earlier in time zones to the west). Hours behind GMT are shown by a minus sign, eg −3, −4/8.

Some countries adopt time zones that vary from standard time. Also, during the summer, several countries adopt Daylight Saving Time (or Summer Time), which is one hour ahead of the times shown below.

» Date Line, Daylight Saving Time.

Afghanistan	+4
Albania	+1
Algeria	0
Angola	+1
Antigua	−4
Argentina	−3
Australia	+8/10
Austria	+1
Bahamas	−5
Bahrain	+3
Bangladesh	+6
Barbados	−4
Belgium	+1
Belize	−6
Benin	+1
Bermuda	−4
Bolivia	−4
Botswana	+2
Brazil	−2/5
Brunei	+8
Bulgaria	+2
Burkina Faso	0
Burundi	+2
Cambodia	+7
Cameroon	+1
Canada	−3/9
Cape Verde	−1
Central African Republic	+1
Chad	+1
Chile	−4
China	+8
Colombia	−5
Comoros	+3
Congo	+1
Costa Rica	−6
Côte d'Ivoire	0
Cuba	−5
Cyprus	+2
Czechoslovakia	+1
Denmark	+1
Djibouti	+3
Dominica	−4
Dominican Republic	−4
Ecuador	−5
Egypt	+2
El Salvador	−6
Equatorial Guinea	+1
Estonia	+3
Ethiopia	+3
Falkland Is	−3
Fiji	+12
Finland	+2
France	+1
Gabon	+1
Gambia, The	0
Germany	+1
Ghana	0
Gibraltar	+1
Greece	+2
Greenland	−3
Grenada	−4
Guatemala	−6
Guinea	0
Guinea-Bissau	0
Guyana	−3
Haiti	−5
Honduras	−6
Hong Kong	+8
Hungary	+1
Iceland	0
India	+5
Indonesia	+7/9
Iran	+3
Iraq	+3
Ireland	0
Israel	+2
Italy	+1
Jamaica	−5
Japan	+9
Jordan	+2
Kenya	+3
Kiribati	+12
Korea, North	+9
Korea, South	+9
Kuwait	+3
Laos	+7
Latvia	+3
Lebanon	+2
Lesotho	+2
Liberia	0
Libya	+1
Liechtenstein	+1
Lithuania	+3
Luxembourg	+1
Madagascar	+3
Malawi	+2
Malaysia	+8
Maldives	+5
Mali	0
Malta	+1
Mauritania	0
Mauritius	+4
Mexico	−6/8
Monaco	+1
Morocco	0
Mozambique	+2
Myanmar (Burma)	+6½
Namibia	+2
Nauru	+12
Nepal	+5
Netherlands	+1
New Zealand	+12
Nicaragua	−6
Niger	+1
Nigeria	+1
Norway	+1
Oman	+4
Pakistan	+5
Panama	−5
Papua New Guinea	+10
Paraguay	−3/4
Peru	−5
Philippines	+8
Poland	+1
Portugal	0
Qatar	+3
Romania	+2
Russia	+3/13
Rwanda	+2
St Christopher and Nevis	−4
St Lucia	−4
St Vincent	−4
Samoa	−11
San Marino	+1
Sao Tomé	0
Saudi Arabia	+3
Senegal	0
Seychelles	+4
Sierra Leone	0
Singapore	+8
Solomon Is	+11
Somalia	+3
South Africa	+2
Spain	+1
Sri Lanka	+5
Sudan	+2
Suriname	−3
Swaziland	+2
Sweden	+1
Switzerland	+1
Syria	+2
Taiwan	+8
Tanzania	+3
Thailand	+7
Togo	0
Tonga	+13
Trinidad and Tobago	−4
Tunisia	+1
Turkey	+3
Tuvalu	+12
Uganda	+3
United Arab Emirates	+4
UK	0
Uruguay	−3
USA*	−5/11
Vanuatu	+11
Venezuela	−4
Vietnam	+7
Yemen	+3
Yugoslavia	+1
Zaire	+1/2
Zambia	+2
Zimbabwe	+2

*For US State Time Zones, see RR38–9

INTERNATIONAL TIME ZONES

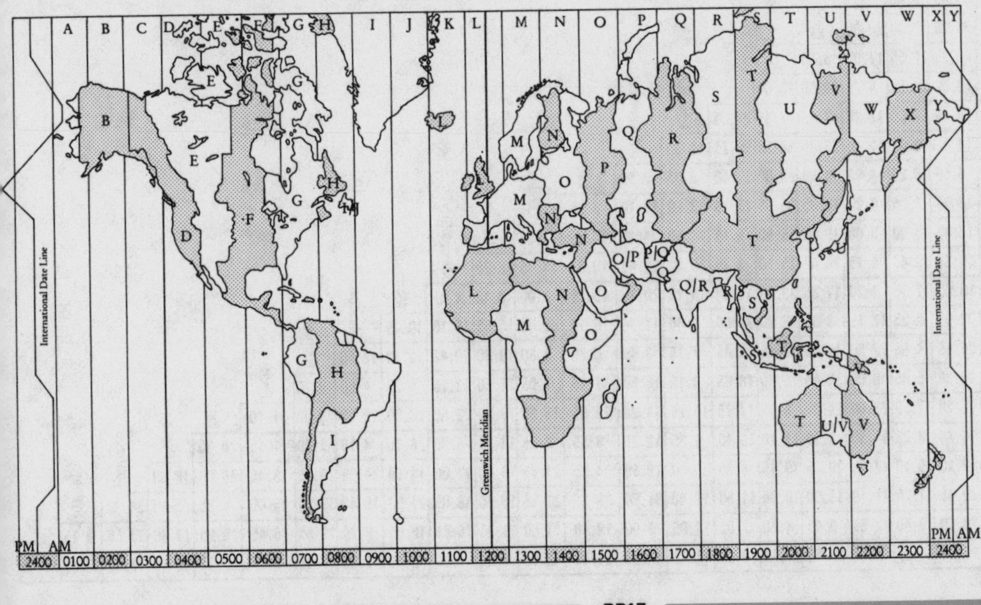

World times at 12 noon GMT
Some countries have adopted half-hour time zones which are indicated on the map as a combination of two coded zones. For example, it is 1730 hours in India at 1200 GMT. The standard times shown are subject to variation in certain countries where Daylight Saving/Summer Time operates for part of the year.

AIR DISTANCES

Air distances between some major cities, given in statute miles. To convert to kilometres, multiply number given by 1.6093.

*Shortest route.

	Amsterdam	Anchorage	Beijing	Buenos Aires	Cairo	Chicago	Delhi	Hong Kong	Honolulu	Istanbul	Johannesburg	Lagos	London	Los Angeles	Mexico City	Montreal	Moscow	Nairobi	Paris	Perth	Rome	Santiago	Sydney	Tokyo
Anchorage	4475																							
Beijing	6566	4756																						
Buenos Aires	7153	8329	12000																					
Cairo	2042	6059	6685	7468																				
Chicago	4109	28	7599	5587	6135																			
Delhi	3985	8925	2368	8340	2753	8119																		
Hong Kong	5926	5063	1235	3124	5098	7827	2345																	
Honolulu	8368	2780	6778	8693	9439	4246	7888	5543																
Istanbul	1373	6024	4763	7783	764	5502	2833	5998	9547															
Johannesburg	5606	1042	10108	5725	4012	8705	6765	6728	12892	4776														
Lagos	3161	7587	8030	4832	2443	7065	5196	7541	10367	3207	2854													
London	217	4472	5054	6985	2187	3956	4169	5979	7252	1552	5640	3115												
Los Angeles	5559	2333	6349	6140	7589	1746	8717	7231	2553	6994	10443	7716	5442											
Mexico City	5724	3751	7912	4592	7730	1687	9806	8794	4116	7255	10070	7343	5703	1563										
Montreal	3422	3100	7557	5640	5431	737	7421	8564	4923	4795	8322	5595	3252	2482	2307									
Moscow	1338	4291	3604	8382	1790	5500	2698	4839	8802	1089	6280	4462	1550	6992	6700	4393								
Nairobi	4148	8714	8888	7427	2203	8177	4956	7301	11498	2967	1809	2377	4246	9688	9949	7498	3951							
Paris	261	4683	5108	6892	1995	4140	4089	5987	7463	1394	5422	2922	220	5633	5714	3434	1540	4031						
Perth	9118	8368	4987	9734	7766	11281	5013	3752	7115	7846	5564	10209	9246	9535	11098	12402	8355	7373	12587					
Rome	809	5258	5306	6931	1329	4828	3679	5773	8150	852	4802	2497	898	6340	6601	5431	1478	3349	688	8309				
Santiago	7714	7919	13622	710	8029	5328	12715	3733	8147	10109	5738	6042	8568	5594	4168	5551	10118	7547	461	15129	7548			
Sydney	1039	8522	5689	7760	9196	9324	6495	4586	5078	9883	7601	11700	10565	7498	9061	9980	9425	9410	10150	2037	10149	13092		
Tokyo	6006*	3443	1313	13100	6362	6286	3656	1807	3831	5757	8535	9130*	6218	5451	7014	6913	4668	8565	6208*	4925	6146	11049	4640	
Washington	3854	3430	7930	6097	5859	590	7841	8385	4822	5347	8199	5472	3672	2294	1871	493	4884	7918	3843	11829	4495	5061	9792	6763

FLYING TIMES

Approximate flying times between some major cities. Timings quoted (in hours and minutes) are for 'flying time' only. In many cases in order to travel between two points chosen, it is necessary to change aircraft one or more times. Time between flights has not been included.

	Amsterdam	Anchorage	Beijing	Buenos Aires	Cairo	Chicago	Delhi	Hong Kong	Honolulu	Istanbul	Johannesburg	Lagos	London	Los Angeles	Mexico City	Montreal	Moscow	Nairobi	Paris	Perth	Rome	Santiago	Sydney	Tokyo
Anchorage	9.00																							
Beijing	16.50	11.45																						
Buenos Aires	17.45	10.48	28.31																					
Cairo	4.20	13.20	13.15	20.40																				
Chicago	8.35	5.44	15.15	15.40	18.40																			
Delhi	8.15	16.50	6.40	26.20	7.00	20.05																		
Hong Kong	15.15	11.40	3.00	29.35	10.55	17.05	6.05																	
Honolulu	16.42	5.45	10.55	19.00	22.50	9.25	16.50	13.05																
Istanbul	3.15	12.15	15.40	18.45	2.00	12.20	7.35	17.35	21.05															
Johannesburg	13.15	19.50	20.10	12.30	8.55	21.40	23.45	14.55	30.25	16.30														
Lagos	6.40	14.55	22.35	9.55	8.20	14.55	14.55	22.30	23.40	8.05	6.55													
London	1.05	8.30	18.05	16.35	5.35	8.30	10.35	16.05	17.15	3.50	13.10	6.25												
Los Angeles	11.15	6.13	15.25	13.45	21.00	5.00	19.30	15.50	5.15	14.50	24.10	17.25	11.00											
Mexico City	12.27	10.49	18.45	10.25	16.47	5.15	20.42	19.10	8.35	15.42	25.42	19.07	14.35	3.20										
Montreal	7.40	7.91	27.30	16.00	12.35	2.20	17.35	23.05	12.50	10.15	20.10	13.25	7.00	6.40	4.45									
Moscow	3.15	12.15	8.40	22.05	5.25	12.15	7.35	18.00	21.00	4.40	13.30	10.10	3.45	14.45	18.10	10.45								
Nairobi	8.15	17.00	16.00	24.55	4.55	17.00	10.45	12.45	25.45	7.15	3.45	6.20	8.30	19.30	20.42	15.30	12.50							
Paris	1.10	9.00	16.35	15.35	5.05	9.00	10.45	16.40	18.05	3.10	15.50	7.45	1.05	12.50	13.25	6.25	4.00	9.20						
Perth	20.35	17.25	11.15	25.20	17.10	23.00	9.30	8.15	17.25	15.25	14.20	25.55	19.30	19.30	22.50	26.30	19.40	23.00	21.40					
Rome	2.20	12.00	16.10	14.40	3.25	11.35	8.50	15.10	19.13	2.35	12.25	6.55	2.25	14.35	5.35	8.10	4.10	7.20	1.55	20.00				
Santiago	20.50	19.13	22.34	2.10	25.10	17.15	29.05	19.15	8.35	21.00	19.55	24.25	21.55	16.00	12.00	14.50	24.05	29.05	19.45	26.00	18.50			
Sydney	23.05	16.35	16.15	20.45	17.20	21.10	13.50	10.35	11.50	18.40	31.50	28.35	21.55	18.10	18.05	24.50	19.40	31.35	25.05	4.35	23.50	24.30		
Tokyo	11.40	7.20	3.50	28.30	19.40	12.55	9.45	4.20	7.05	14.05	25.00	18.40	11.50	11.55	16.25	18.55	9.25	19.55	16.45	10.05	17.40	27.55	9.15	
Washington	8.55	7.25	25.50	11.00	14.20	1.45	20.10	24.15	10.55	11.25	21.20	14.45	8.10	5.25	7.50	2.50	12.30	17.10	9.25	22.45	12.40	17.40	23.35	12.40

US AIR DISTANCES

These air distances between US cities are given in statute miles. To convert to kilometres, multiply number given by 1.6093.

	Atlanta	Boston	Chicago	Dallas	Denver	Detroit	Houston	Kansas City	Los Angeles	Miami	Minneapolis	New Orleans	New York	Oklahoma City	Omaha	Philadelphia	Phoenix	Pittsburgh	Portland	St Louis	Salt Lake City	San Antonio	San Francisco	Seattle
ston	946																							
icago	606	867																						
llas	721	1555	798																					
enver	1208	1767	901	654																				
etroit	595	632	235	982	1135																			
ouston	689	1603	925	217	864	1095																		
ansas City	681	1254	403	460	543	630	643																	
s Angeles	1946	2611	1745	1246	849	1979	1379	1363																
iami	595	1258	1197	1110	1716	1146	964	1239	2342															
inneapolis	906	1124	334	853	693	528	1046	394	1536	1501														
ew Orleans	425	1367	837	437	1067	936	305	690	1671	674	1040													
ew York	760	187	740	1383	1638	509	1417	1113	2475	1090	1028	1182												
klahoma City	761	1505	693	181	500	911	395	312	1187	1223	694	567	1345											
maha	821	1282	416	585	485	651	793	152	1330	1393	282	841	1155	418										
hiladelphia	665	281	678	1294	1569	453	1324	1039	2401	1013	980	1094	94	1268	1094									
hoenix	1587	2300	1440	879	589	1681	1015	1043	370	1972	1270	1301	2143	833	1037	2082								
ttsburgh	526	496	412	1061	1302	201	1124	769	2136	1013	726	918	340	1010	821	267	1814							
ortland	2172	2537	1739	1637	985	1959	1834	1492	834	2700	1426	2050	2454	1484	1368	2411	1009	2148						
t Louis	484	1046	258	546	781	440	667	229	1592	1068	448	604	892	462	342	813	1262	553	1708					
alt Lake City	1589	2105	1249	1010	381	1489	1204	919	590	2088	991	1428	1989	865	839	1932	507	1659	630	1156				
an Antonio	875	1764	1041	247	793	1215	191	697	1210	1143	1097	495	1587	407	824	1502	843	1277	1714	786	1086			
an Francisco	2139	2704	1846	1476	956	2079	1636	1498	337	2585	1589	1911	2586	1383	1433	2521	651	2253	550	1735	599	1482		
eattle	2182	2496	1720	1670	1019	1932	1874	1489	954	2725	1399	2087	2421	1520	1368	2383	1109	2124	132	1709	689	1775	678	
ashington DC	532	414	590	1163	1464	385	1189	927	2288	919	909	969	229	1158	1000	136	1956	184	2339	696	1839	1361	2419	2307

UK ROAD DISTANCES

Road distances between British centres are given in statute miles, using routes recommended by the Automobile Association based on the quickest travelling time. To convert to kilometres, multiply number given by 1.6093.

	Aberdeen	Birmingham	Bristol	Cambridge	Cardiff	Dover	Edinburgh	Exeter	Glasgow	Holyhead	Hull	Leeds	Liverpool	Manchester	Newcastle	Norwich	Nottingham	Oxford	Penzance	Plymouth	Shrewsbury	Southampton	Stranraer	York
irmingham	430																							
ristol	511	85																						
ambridge	468	101	156																					
ardiff	532	107	45	191																				
over	591	202	198	121	234																			
dinburgh	130	293	373	337	395	457																		
xeter	584	157	81	233	119	248	446																	
lasgow	149	291	372	349	393	490	45	444																
olyhead	457	151	232	246	209	347	325	305	319															
ull	361	136	227	157	246	278	229	297	245	215														
eeds	336	115	216	143	236	265	205	288	215	163	59													
iverpool	361	98	178	195	200	295	222	250	220	104	126	72												
Manchester	354	88	167	153	188	283	218	239	214	123	97	43	34											
Newcastle	239	198	291	224	311	348	107	361	150	260	121	91	170	141										
Norwich	501	161	217	62	252	167	365	295	379	309	153	173	232	183	258									
Nottingham	402	59	151	82	170	202	268	222	281	174	92	73	107	71	156	123								
Oxford	497	63	74	82	109	148	361	152	354	218	188	171	164	153	253	144	104							
Penzance	696	272	195	346	232	362	561	112	559	419	411	401	366	355	477	407	336	265						
Plymouth	624	199	125	275	164	290	488	45	486	347	341	328	294	281	410	336	265	193	78					
Shrewsbury	412	48	128	142	110	243	276	201	272	104	164	116	64	69	216	205	85	113	315	242				
Southampton	571	128	75	133	123	155	437	114	436	296	253	235	241	227	319	192	171	67	227	155	190			
Stranraer	241	307	386	361	406	503	130	457	88	332	259	232	234	226	164	393	295	371	572	502	287	447		
York	325	128	221	153	241	274	191	291	208	190	38	24	100	71	83	185	86	185	406	340	144	252	228	
London	543	118	119	60	155	77	405	170	402	263	215	196	210	199	280	115	128	56	283	215	162	76	419	209

INTERNATIONAL E-ROAD NETWORK ('Euroroutes')

Reference and intermediate roads (class A roads) have two-digit numbers; branch, link, and connecting roads (class B roads, not listed here), have three-digit numbers.

North-South orientated reference roads have two-digit odd numbers ending in the figure 5, and increasing from west to east. East-West orientated roads have two-digit even numbers ending in the figure 0, and increasing from north to south.

Intermediate roads have two-digit odd numbers (for N-S roads) or two-dig even numbers (for E-W roads) falling within the numbers of the referen roads between which they are located.

Only a selection of the towns and cities linked by E-roads are given on th page.

[···] indicates a sea crossing.

West-East orientation

Reference roads

E10 Narvik — Kiruna — Luleå
E20 Shannon — Dublin ··· Liverpool — Hull ··· Esbjerg — Nyborg ··· Korsør-Køge — Copenhagen ··· Malmö — Stockholm ··· Tallin — St Petersburg
E30 Cork — Rosslare ··· Fishguard — London — Felixstowe ··· Hook of Holland — Utrecht — Hanover — Berlin — Warsaw — Smolensk — Moscow
E40 Calais — Brussels — Aachen — Cologne — Dresden — Krakow — Kiev — Rostov na Donu
E50 Brest — Paris — Metz — Nurenberg — Prague — Mukačevo
E60 Brest — Tours — Besançon — Basle — Innsbruck — Vienna — Budapest — Bucharest — Constanţa
E70 La Coruña — Bilbao — Bordeaux — Lyon — Torino — Verona — Trieste — Zagreb — Belgrade — Bucharest — Varna
E80 Lisbon — Coimbra — Salamanca — Pau — Toulouse — Nice — Genoa — Rome — Pescara ··· Dubrovnik — Sofia — Istanbul — Erzincan — Iran
E90 Lisbon — Madrid — Barcelona ··· Mazara del Vallo — Messina — Reggio di Calabria — Brindisi ··· Igoumenitsa — Thessaloniki — Gelibolu ··· Lapseki — Ankara — Iraq

Intermediate roads

E06 Olderfjord—Kirkenes
E12 Mo i Rana — Umeå ··· Vaasa — Helsinki
E14 Trondheim—Sundsvall
E16 Londonderry — Belfast ··· Glasgow — Edinburgh
E18 Craigavon — Larne ··· Stranraer — Newcastle ··· Stavanger — Oslo — Stockholm — Kappelskär ··· Mariehamn ··· Turku — Helsinki — Leningrad
E22 Holyhead — Manchester — Immingham ··· Amsterdam — Hamburg — Sassnitz ··· Trelleborg — Norrköping
E24 Birmingham—Ipswich
E26 Hamburg—Berlin
E28 Berlin—Gdańsk
E32 Colchester—Harwich
E34 Antwerp—Bad Oeynhausen
E36 Berlin—Legnica
E42 Dunkirk—Aschaffenburg
E44 Le Havre — Luxembourg — Giessen
E46 Cherbourg—Liège
E48 Schweinfurt—Prague
E52 Strasbourg—Salzburg
E54 Paris—Basle—Munich
E56 Nurenberg—Sattledt
E58 Vienna—Bratislava
E62 Nantes—Geneva—Tortona
E64 Turin—Brescia
E66 Fortezza—Székesfehérvár
E68 Szeged—Braşov
E72 Bordeaux—Toulouse
E74 Nice—Alessandria
E76 Migliarino—Florence
E78 Grosseto—Fano
E82 Porto—Tordesillas
E84 Keşan—Silivri
E86 Krystalopigi—Yefira
E88 Ankara—Refahiye
E92 Igoumenitsa—Volos
E94 Corinth—Athens
E96 Izmir—Sivrihisar
E98 Topbogazi—Syria

North-South orientation

Reference roads

E05 Greenock — Birmingham — Southampton ··· Le Havre — Paris — Bordeaux — Madrid — Algeciras
E15 Inverness — Edinburgh — London — Dover ··· Calais — Paris — Lyon — Barcelona — Algeciras
E25 Hook of Holland — Luxembourg — Strasbourg — Basle — Geneva — Turin — Genoa
E35 Amsterdam — Cologne — Basle — Milan — Rome
E45 Gothenburg ··· Frederikshavn — Hamburg — Munich — Innsbruck — Bologna — Rome — Naples — Villa S Giovanni ··· Messina — Gela
E55 Kemi-Tornio — Stockholm — Helsingborg ··· Helsingør — Copenhagen — Gedser ··· Rostock — Berlin — Prague — Salzburg — Rimini — Brindisi ··· Igoumenitsa — Kalamata
E65 Malmö — Ystad ··· Świnoujście — Prague — Zagreb — Dubrovnik — Bitolj — Antirrion ··· Rion — Kalamata ··· Kissamos — Chania
E75 Karasjok — Helsinki ··· Gdańsk — Budapest — Belgrade — Athens ··· Chania — Sitia
E85 Černovcy — Bucharest — Alexandropouli
E95 St Petersburg—Moscow—Yalta

Intermediate roads

E01 Larne — Dublin — Rosslare ··· La Coruña — Lisbon — Seville
E03 Cherbourg—La Rochelle
E07 Pau—Zaragoza
E09 Orléans—Barcelona
E11 Vierzon—Montpellier
E13 Doncaster—London
E17 Antwerp—Beaune
E19 Amsterdam—Brussels—Paris
E21 Metz—Geneva
E23 Metz—Lausanne
E27 Belfort—Aosta
E29 Cologne—Sarreguemines
E31 Rotterdam—Ludwigshafen
E33 Parma—La Spezie
E37 Bremen—Cologne
E39 Kristiansand—Aalborg
E41 Dortmund—Altdorf
E43 Würzburg—Bellinzona
E47 Nordkap — Oslo — Copenhagen — Rødby ··· Puttgarden — Lübeck
E49 Magdeburg—Vienna
E51 Berlin—Nurenberg
E53 Plzeň—Munich
E57 Sattledt—Ljubljana
E59 Prague—Zagreb
E61 Klagenfurt—Rijeka
E63 Sodankylä — Naantali ··· Stockholm — Gothenburg
E67 Warsaw—Prague
E69 Tromsø—Tornio
E71 Košice—Budapest—Split
E73 Budapest—Metković
E77 Gdańsk—Budapest
E79 Oradea — Calafat ··· Vidín — Thessaloniki
E81 Halmeu—Piteşti
E83 Bjala—Sofia
E87 Tulcea — Eceabat ··· Çanakkale — Antalya
E89 Gerede—Ankara
E91 Toprakkale—Syria
E93 Orel—Odessa
E97 Trabzon—Aşkale
E99 Doğubeyazit—Ş Urfa

EUROPEAN ROAD DISTANCES

Road distances between some cities, given in kilometres.
To convert to statute miles, multiply number given by 0.6214

	Athens	Barcelona	Brussels	Calais	Cherbourg	Cologne	Copenhagen	Geneva	Gibraltar	Hamburg	Hook of Holland	Lisbon	Lyons	Madrid	Marseilles	Milan	Munich	Paris	Rome	Stockholm
arcelona	3313																			
russels	2963	1318																		
alais	3175	1326	204																	
herbourg	3339	1294	583	460																
ologne	2762	1498	206	409	785															
openhagen	3276	2218	966	1136	1545	760														
eneva	2610	803	677	747	853	1662	1418													
ibraltar	4485	1172	2256	2224	2047	2436	3196	1975												
amburg	2977	2018	597	714	1115	460	460	1118	2897											
ook of Holland	3030	1490	172	330	731	269	269	895	2428	550										
isbon	4532	1304	2084	2052	1827	2290	2971	1936	676	2671	2280									
yons	2753	645	690	739	789	714	1458	158	1817	1159	863	1778								
adrid	3949	636	1558	1550	1347	1764	2498	1439	698	2198	1730	668	1281							
Marseilles	2865	521	1011	1059	1101	1035	1778	425	1693	1479	1183	1762	320	1157						
Milan	2282	1014	925	1077	1209	911	1537	328	2185	1238	1098	2250	328	1724	618					
Munich	2179	1365	747	977	1160	583	1104	591	2565	805	851	2507	724	2010	1109	331				
Paris	3000	1033	285	280	340	465	1176	513	1971	877	457	1799	471	1273	792	856	821			
Rome	817	1460	1511	1662	1794	1497	2050	995	2631	1751	1683	2700	1048	2097	1011	586	946	1476		
Stockholm	3927	2868	1616	1786	2196	1403	650	2068	3886	949	1500	3231	2108	3188	2428	2187	1754	1827	2707	
Vienna	1991	1802	1175	1381	1588	937	1455	1019	2974	1155	1205	2935	1157	2409	1363	898	428	1249	1209	2105

MAP OF EUROPE

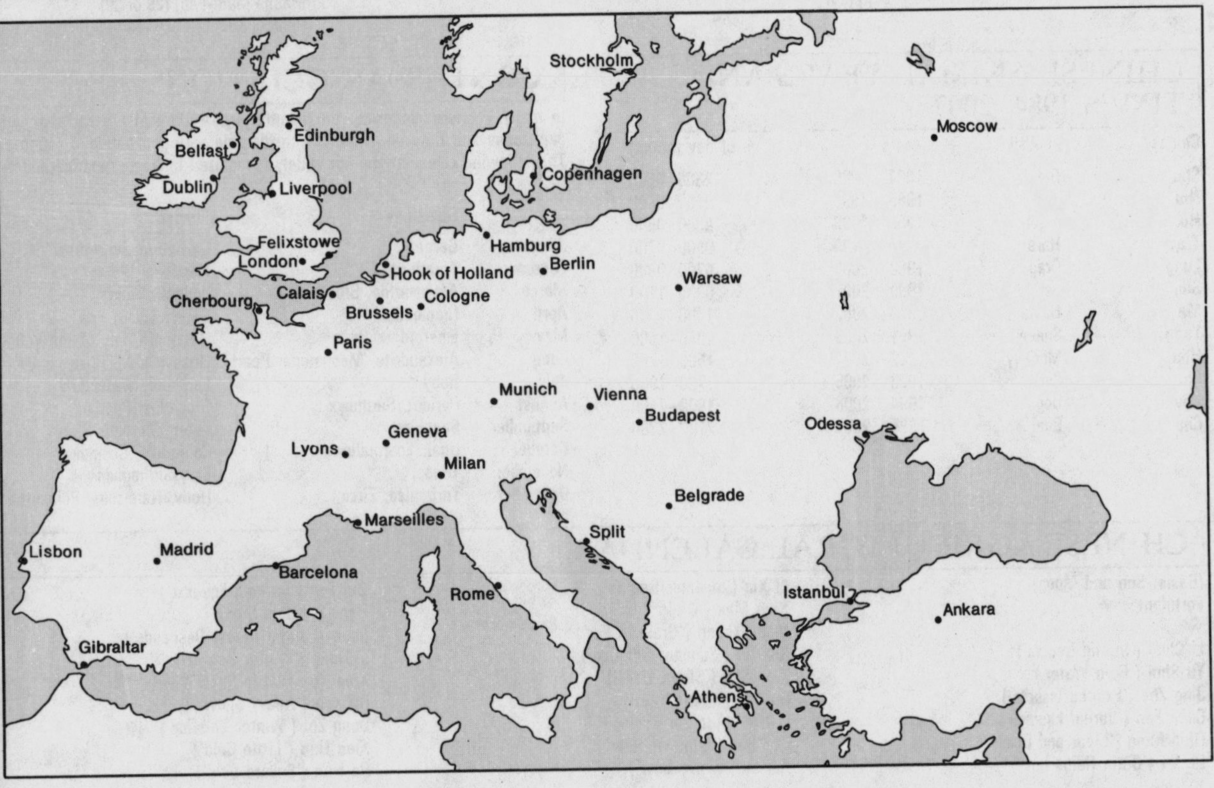

YEAR EQUIVALENTS

Jewish[1] (AM)		Islamic[2] (H)		Hindu[3] (SE)	
5750	(30 Sep 1989—19 Sep 1990)	1410	(4 Aug 1989—23 Jul 1990)	1911	(22 Mar 1989—21 Mar 1990)
5751	(20 Sep 1990— 8 Sep 1991)	1411	(24 Jul 1990—12 Jul 1991)	1912	(22 Mar 1990—21 Mar 1991)
5752	(9 Sep 1991—27 Sep 1992)	1412	(13 Jul 1991— 1 Jul 1992)	1913	(22 Mar 1991—20 Mar 1992)
5753	(28 Sep 1992—15 Sep 1993)	1413	(2 Jul 1992—20 Jun 1993)	1914	(21 Mar 1992—21 Mar 1993)
5754	(16 Sep 1993— 5 Sep 1994)	1414	(21 Jun 1993— 9 Jun 1994)	1915	(22 Mar 1993—21 Mar 1994)
5755	(6 Sep 1994—24 Sep 1995)	1415	(10 Jun 1994—30 May 1995)	1916	(22 Mar 1994—21 Mar 1995)
5756	(25 Sep 1995—13 Sep 1996)	1416	(31 May 1995—18 May 1996)	1917	(22 Mar 1995—20 Mar 1996)
5757	(14 Sep 1996— 1 Oct 1997)	1417	(19 May 1996— 8 May 1997)	1918	(21 Mar 1996—21 Mar 1997)
5758	(2 Oct 1997—20 Sep 1998)	1418	(9 May 1997—27 Apr 1998)	1919	(22 Mar 1997—21 Mar 1998)
5759	(21 Sep 1998—10 Sep 1999)	1419	(28 Apr 1998—16 Apr 1999)	1920	(22 Mar 1998—21 Mar 1999)
5760	(11 Sep 1999—29 Sep 2000)	1420	(17 Apr 1999— 5 Apr 2000)	1921	(22 Mar 1999—21 Mar 2000)

Gregorian equivalents are given in parentheses and are AD (= Anno Domini).

[1] Calculated from 3761 BC, said to be the year of the creation of the world. AM = Anno Mundi.

[2] Calculated from AD 622, the year in which the Prophet went from Mecca to Medina. H = Hegira.

[3] Calculated from AD 78, the beginning of the Saka era (SE), used alongside Gregorian dates in Government of India publications since 22 Mar 1957. Other importar Hindu eras include: Vikrama era (58 BC), Kalacuri era (AD 248), Gupta era (AD 320), and Harsa era (AD 606).

MONTH EQUIVALENTS

Gregorian equivalents to other calendars are given in parentheses; the figures refer to the number of solar days in each month.

Gregorian	Jewish	Islamic	Hindu
(Basis: Sun)	(Basis: Moon)	(Basis: Moon)	(Basis: Moon)
January (31)	Tishri (Sep–Oct) (30)	Muharram (Sep–Oct) (30)	Caitra (Mar–Apr) (29 or 30)
February (28 or 29)	Heshvan (Oct–Nov) (29 or 30)	Safar (Oct–Nov) (29)	Vaisakha (Apr–May) (29 or 30)
March (31)	Kislev (Nov–Dec) (29 or 30)	Rabi I (Nov–Dec) (30)	Jyaistha (May–Jun) (29 or 30)
April (30)	Tevet (Dec–Jan) (29)	Rabi II (Dec–Jan) (29)	Asadha (Jun–Jul) (29 or 30)
May (31)	Shevat (Jan–Feb) (30)	Jumada I (Jan–Feb) (30)	Dvitiya Asadha (*certain leap years*)
June (30)	Adar (Feb–Mar) (29 or 30)	Jumada II (Feb–Mar) (29)	Sravana (Jul–Aug) (29 or 30)
July (31)	Adar Sheni *leap years only*	Rajab (Mar–Apr) (30)	Dvitiya Sravana (*certain leap years*)
August (31)	Nisan (Mar–Apr) (30)	Shaban (Apr–May) (29)	Bhadrapada (Aug–Sep) (29 or 30)
September (30)	Iyar (Apr–May) (29)	Ramadan (May–Jun) (30)	Asvina (Sep–Oct) (29 or 30)
October (31)	Sivan (May–Jun) (30)	Shawwal (Jun–Jul) (29)	Karttika (Oct–Nov) (29 or 30)
November (30)	Tammuz (Jun–Jul) (29)	Dhu al-Qadah (Jul–Aug) (30)	Margasirsa (Nov–Dec) (29 or 30)
December (31)	Av (Jul–Aug) (30)	Dhu al-Hijjah (Aug–Sep) (29 or 30)	Pausa (Dec–Jan) (29 or 30)
	Elul (Aug–Sep) (29)		Magha (Jan–Feb) (29 or 30)
			Phalguna (Feb–Mar) (29 or 30)

CHINESE ANIMAL YEARS AND TIMES 1984–2007

Chinese	English	Years		Time of day (hours)
Shu	Rat	1984	1996	2300–0100
Niu	Ox	1985	1997	0100–0300
Hu	Tiger	1986	1998	0300–0500
T'u	Hare	1987	1999	0500–0700
Lung	Dragon	1988	2000	0700–0900
She	Serpent	1989	2001	0900–1100
Ma	Horse	1990	2002	1100–1300
Yang	Sheep	1991	2003	1300–1500
Hou	Monkey	1992	2004	1500–1700
Chi	Cock	1993	2005	1700–1900
Kou	Dog	1994	2006	1900–2100
Chu	Boar	1995	2007	2100–2300

MONTHS: ASSOCIATIONS

In many Western countries, the months are traditionally associated with gemstones and flowers. There is considerable variation between countries. The following combinations are widely recognized in North America and the UK.

	Gemstone	Flower
January	Garnet	Carnation, Snowdrop
February	Amethyst	Primrose, Violet
March	Aquamarine, Bloodstone	Jonquil, Violet
April	Diamond	Daisy, Sweet Pea
May	Emerald	Hawthorn, Lily of the Valley
June	Alexandrite, Moonstone, Pearl	Honeysuckle, Rose
July	Ruby	Larkspur, Water Lily
August	Peridot, Sardonyx	Gladiolus, Poppy
September	Sapphire	Aster, Morning Glory
October	Opal, Tourmaline	Calendula, Cosmos
November	Topaz	Chrysanthemum
December	Turquoise, Zircon	Holly, Narcissus, Poinsettia

CHINESE AGRICULTURAL CALENDAR

(Basis: Sun and Moon)
Fortnight

Li Chun ('Spring Begins')
Yu Shui ('Rain Water')
Jing Zhe ('Excited Insects')
Chun Fen ('Vernal Equinox')
Qing Ming ('Clear and Bright')
Gu Yu ('Grain Rains')
Li Xia ('Summer Begins')
Xiao Man ('Grain Fills')
Mang Zhong ('Grain in Ear')
Xia Zhi ('Summer Solstice')
Xiao Shu ('Slight Heat')
Da Shu ('Great Heat')
Li Qiu ('Autumn Begins')
Chu Shu ('Limit of Heat')
Bai Lu ('White Dew')
Qui Fen ('Autumn Equinox')
Han Lu ('Cold Dew')
Shuang Jiang ('Frost Descends')
Li Dong ('Winter Begins')
Xiao Xue ('Little Snow')
Da Xue ('Heavy Snow')
Dong Zhi ('Winter Solstice')
Xiao Han ('Little Cold')
Da Han ('Severe Cold')

MOVABLE CHRISTIAN FEASTS, 1990–2000

ear	Ash Wednesday	Easter	Ascension	Whit Sunday	Sundays after Trinity	First Sunday in Advent	Trinity Sunday	Corpus Christi
990	28 Feb	15 Apr	24 May	3 Jun	24	2 Dec	10 Jun	14 Jun
991	13 Feb	31 Mar	9 May	19 May	26	1 Dec	26 May	30 May
992	4 Mar	19 Apr	28 May	7 Jun	23	29 Nov	14 Jun	18 Jun
993	24 Feb	11 Apr	20 May	30 May	24	28 Nov	6 Jun	10 Jun
994	16 Feb	3 Apr	12 May	22 May	25	27 Nov	29 May	2 Jun
995	1 Mar	16 Apr	25 May	4 Jun	24	3 Dec	11 Jun	15 Jun
996	21 Feb	7 Apr	16 May	26 May	25	1 Dec	2 Jun	6 Jun
997	12 Feb	30 Mar	8 May	18 May	26	30 Nov	25 May	29 May
998	25 Feb	12 Apr	21 May	31 May	24	29 Nov	7 Jun	11 Jun
999	17 Feb	4 Apr	13 May	23 May	25	28 Nov	30 May	3 Jun
000	8 Mar	23 Apr	1 Jun	11 Jun	23	3 Dec	18 Jun	22 Jun

sh Wednesday, the first day of Lent, can fall at the earliest on 4 February and at the latest on 10 March.

alm (Passion) Sunday is the Sunday before Easter; Good Friday is the Friday before Easter; Holy Saturday (often referred to as Easter Saturday) is the Saturday efore Easter; Easter Saturday, in traditional usage, is the Saturday following Easter.

aster Day can fall at the earliest on 22 March and at the latest on 25 April. Ascension Day can fall at the earliest on 30 April and at the latest on 3 June. /hit Sunday can fall at the earliest on 10 May and at the latest on 13 June. There are not less than 22 and not more than 27 Sundays after Trinity. The first unday of Advent is the Sunday nearest to 30 November.

MAJOR IMMOVABLE CHRISTIAN FEASTS

or Saints' Days, *see* RR28–9.

an 1	Solemnity of Mary, Mother of God
an 6	Epiphany
an 7	Christmas Day (*Eastern Orthodox*)[1]
an 11	Baptism of Jesus
an 25	Conversion of Apostle Paul
eb 2	Presentation of Jesus (*Candlemas Day*)
eb 22	The Chair of Peter, Apostle
Mar 25	Annunciation of the Virgin Mary
un 24	Birth of John the Baptist
ug 6	Transfiguration
ug 15	Assumption of the Virgin Mary
ug 22	Queenship of Mary
ep 8	Birthday of the Virgin Mary
ep 14	Exaltation of the Holy Cross
ct 2	Guardian Angels
Nov 1	All Saints
Nov 2	All Souls
Nov 9	Dedication of the Lateran Basilica
Nov 21	Presentation of the Virgin Mary
Dec 8	Immaculate Conception
Dec 25	Christmas Day
Dec 28	Holy Innocents

[1] Fixed feasts in the Julian Calendar fall 13 days later than the Gregorian Calendar date.

MAJOR HINDU FESTIVALS

S = Sukla, 'waxing fortnight'.
K = Krishna 'waning fortnight'.

Caitra S 9	Ramanavami (Birthday of Lord Rama)
Asadha S 2	Rathayatra (Pilgrimage of the Chariot at Jagannath)
Sravana S 11–15	Jhulanayatra ('Swinging the Lord Krishna')
Sravana S 15	Rakshabandhana ('Tying on lucky threads')
Bhadrapada K 8	Janamashtami (Birthday of Lord Krishna)
Asvina S 7–10	Durga-puja (Homage to Goddess Durga) (*Bengal*)
Asvina S 1–10	Navaratri (Festival of 'nine nights')
Asvina S 15	Lakshmi-puja (Homage to Goddess Lakshmi)
Asvina K 15	Diwali, Dipavali ('String of Lights')
Kartikka S 15	Guru Nanak Jananti (Birthday of Guru Nanak)
Magha K 5	Sarasvati-puja (Homage to Goddess Sarasvati)
Magha K 13	Maha-sivaratri (Great Night of Lord Shiva)
Phalguna S 14	Holi (Festival of Fire)
Phalguna S 15	Dolayatra (Swing Festival) (*Bengal*)

MAJOR JEWISH FESTIVALS

For Gregorian calendar equivalents, *see* RR22.

1–2 Tishri	Rosh Hashana (New Year)
3 Tishri	Tzom Gedaliahu (Fast of Gedaliah)
10 Tishri	Yom Kippur (Day of Atonement)
15–21 Tishri	Sukkoth (Feast of Tabernacles)
22 Tishri	Shemini Atzeret (8th Day of the Solemn Assembly
23 Tishri	Simhat Torah (Rejoicing of the Law)
25 Kislev–2–3 Tevet	Hanukkah (Feast of Dedication)
10 Tevet	Asara be-Tevet (Fast of 10th Tevet)
13 Adar	Taanit Esther (Fast of Esther)
14–15 Adar	Purim (Feast of Lots)
15–22 Nisan	Pesach (Passover)
5 Iyar	Israel Independence Day
6–7 Sivan	Shavuoth (Feast of Weeks)
17 Tammuz	Shiva Asar be-Tammuz (Fast of 17th Tammuz)
9 Av	Tisha be-Av (Fast of 9th Av)

MAJOR ISLAMIC FESTIVALS

1 Muharram	New Year's Day; starts on the day which celebrates Mohammed's departure from Mecca to Medina in AD 622.
12 Rabi I	Birthday of Mohammed (Mawlid al-Nabi) AD 572; celebrated throughout month of Rabi I.
27 Rajab	'Night of Ascent' (Laylat al-Mi'raj) of Mohammed to Heaven.
1 Ramadan	Beginning of month of fasting during daylight hours.
27 Ramadan	'Night of Power' (Laylat al-Qadr); sending down of the Koran to Mohammed.
1 Shawwal	'Feast of breaking the Fast' ('Id al-Fitr); marks the end of Ramadan.
8–13 Dhu-l-Hijja	Annual pilgrimage ceremonies at and around Mecca; month during which the great pilgrimage (Hajj) should be made.
10 Dhu-l-Hijja	Feast of the Sacrifice ('Id al-Adha).

MAJOR JAPANESE FESTIVALS

Public holidays in Japan are listed on RR26. In addition, the following festivals should be noted;

1–3 Jan	Oshogatsu (New Year)
3 Mar	Ohinamatsuri (Doll's *or* Girls' Festival)
5 May	Tango no Sekku (Boys' Festival)
7 Jul	Hoshi matsuri *or* Tanabata (Star Festival)
13–31 Jul	Obon (Buddhist All Souls)

NATIONAL HOLIDAYS

The first part of each listing gives the holidays that occur on fixed dates (though it should be noted that holidays often vary according to local circumstances and the day of the week on which they fall). Most dates are accompanied by an indication of the purpose of the day eg Independence = Independence Day; dates which have no gloss are either fixed dates within the Christian calendar (for which see below) or bank holidays.

The second part of the listing gives holidays that vary, usually depending on religious factors. The most common of these are given in abbreviated form (see list below).

A number in brackets such as (*Independence*) (*2*) refers to the number of days devoted to the holiday.

The listings do not include holidays that affect only certain parts of a country, half-day holidays, or Sundays.

The following abbreviations are used for variable religious feast-days (*see further* RR23) :

A Ascension Thursday
Ad Id-ul-Adha (also found with other spellings — especially Eid-ul-Adha; various names relating to this occasion are used in different countries, such as Tabaski, Id el-Kebir, Hari Raja Haji)
Ar Arafa
As Ashora (found with various spellings)
C Carnival (immediately before Christian Lent, unless specified)
CC Corpus Christi
D Diwali, Deepavali
EM Easter Monday
ER End of Ramadan (known generally as Id/Eid-ul-Fitr, but various names relating to this occasion are used in different countries, such as Karite, Hari Raja Puasa)
ES Easter Sunday
GF Good Friday
HS Holy Saturday
HT Holy Thursday
NY New Year
PB Prophet's Birthday (known generally as Maulid-al-Nabi in various forms and spellings)
R First day of Ramadan
WM Whit Monday

The following fixed dates are shown without gloss:

Jan 1 New Year's Day
Jan 6 Epiphany
May 1 Labour Day (often known by a different name, such as Workers' Day)
Aug 15 Assumption of Our Lady
Nov 1 All Saints' Day
Nov 2 All Souls' Day
Dec 8 Immaculate Conception
Dec 24 Christmas Eve
Dec 25 Christmas Day
Dec 26 Boxing Day/St Stephen's Day
Dec 31 New Year's Eve

Afghanistan Apr 27 (Sawr Revolution), May 1, Aug 19 (Independence); Ad(3), Ar, As, ER(3), NY (Hindu), PB, R

Albania Jan 1, 11 (Republic), May 1, Nov 28 (Independence), 29 (Liberation)

Algeria Jan 1, May 1, Jun 19 (Righting), Jul 5 (Independence), Nov 1 (Revolution); Ad, As, ER, NY (Muslim), PB

Andorra Jan 1, 6, Mar 19 (St Joseph), May 1, Jun 24 (St John), Aug 15, Sep 8 (Our Lady of Meritxell), Nov 1, 4 (St Charles), Dec 8, 25, 26; A, C, CC, EM, GF, WM

Angola Jan 1, Feb 4 (Commencement of the Armed Struggle), May 1, Sep 17 (National Hero), Nov 11 (Independence), Dec 10 (MPLA Foundation), 25 (Family)

Argentina Jan 1, May 1, 25 (National), Jun 10 (Malvinas Islands Memorial), 20 (Flag), Jul 9 (Independence), Aug 17 (Death of General San Martin), Oct 12 (Columbus), Dec 8, 25, 31; GF, HT

Australia Jan 1, Apr 25 (Anzac), Dec 25, 26 (*except South Australia*); Australia (Jan), EM, GF, HS; *additional days vary between states*

Austria Jan 1, 6, May 1, Aug 15, Oct 26 (National), Nov 1, Dec 8, 24, 25, 26; A, CC, EM, WM

Bahamas Jan 1, Jul 10 (Independence), Dec 25, 26; EM, GF, WM; Labour (Jun), Emancipation (Aug), Discovery (Oct)

Bahrain Jan 1, Dec 16 (National); Ad(3), As(2), ER(3), NY (Muslim), PB

Bangladesh Feb 21 (Shaheed), Mar 26 (Independence), May 1, Jul 1, Nov 7 (National Revolution), Dec 16 (Victory), 25, 31; Ad(3), ER(3), NY (Bengali), NY (Muslim), PB, Jumat-ul-Wida (May), Shab-e-Barat (Apr), Buddah Purnima (Apr/May), Shab-I-Qadr (May), Jumat-ul-Wida (May), Durga Puza (Oct)

Barbados Jan 1, Nov 30 (Independence), Dec 25, 26; EM, GF, WM, Kadooment (Aug), May Holiday, United Nations (Oct)

Belgium Jan 1, May 1, Jul 21 (National), Aug 15, Nov 1, 11 (Armistice), Dec 25; A, EM, WM; May, Aug, Nov Bank Holidays; Regional Holiday (Jul *in N*, Sep *in S*)

Belize Jan 1, Mar 9 (Baron Bliss), May 1, 24 (Commonwealth), Sep 10 (National), 21 (Independence), Oct 12 (Columbus), Nov 19 (Garifuna Settlement), Dec 25, 26; EM, GF, HS

Benin Jan 1, 16 (Martyrs), Apr 1 (Youth), May 1, Oct 26 (Armed Forces), Nov 30 (National), Dec 25, 31 (Feed Yourself); Ad, ER

Bhutan May 2 (Birthday of Jigme Dorji Wangchuk), Jun 2 (Coronation of Fourth Hereditary King), Jul 21 (First Sermon of Lord Buddha, Death of Jigme Dorji Wangchuk), Nov 11–13 (Birthday of HM Jigme Singye Wangchuk), Dec 17 (National)

Bolivia Jan 1, May 1, Aug 6 (Independence), Nov 1, Dec 25; C(2), CC, GF

Botswana Jan 1, 2, Sep 30 (Botswana), Dec 25, 26; A, EM, GF, HS, President's Day (Jul); Jul, Oct Public Holidays

Brazil Jan 1, Apr 21 (Independence Hero Tiradentes), May 1, Sep 7 (Independence), Oct 12, Nov 2 (Memorial), 15 (Proclamation of the Republic), Dec 25; C(2), CC, GF, HS, HT

Brunei Jan 1, Feb 23 (National), May 31 (Royal Brunei Malay Regiment), Jul 15 (Sultan's Birthday), Dec 25; Ad, ER(2), GF, NY (Chinese), NY (Muslim), PB, R, Meraj (Mar–Apr), Revelation of the Koran (May)

Bulgaria Jan 1, May 1(2), 24 (Slav Literature, Bulgarian Education and Culture), Sep 9 (National) (2), Nov 7 (October Revolution)

Burkina Faso Jan 1, 3 (1966 Revolution), May 1, Aug 4, 15, Nov 1, Dec 25; A, Ad, EM, ER, PB, WM

Burma Jan 4 (Independence), Feb 12 (Union), Mar 2 (Peasants), 27 (Resistance), Apr 1, May 1, Jul 19 (Martyrs), Oct 1, Dec 25; NY (Burmese), Thingyan (Apr)(4), End of Buddhist Lent (Oct), Full Moon days

Burundi Jan 1, May 1, Jul 1 (Independence), Aug 15, Sep 18 (Victory of Uprona), Nov 1, Dec 25; A

Cameroon Jan 1, Feb 11 (Youth), May 1, 20 (National), Aug 15, Dec 25; A, Ad, ER, GF

Canada Jan 1, Jul 1 (Canada) (*except Newfoundland*), Nov 11 (Remembrance) Dec 25, 26; EM, GF, Labour (Sep), Thanksgiving (Oct), Victoria (May); *additional days vary between states*

Cape Verde Is Jan 1, 20 (National Heroes), Mar 8 (Women), May 1, Jun 1 (Children), Sep 12 (National), Dec 24, 25; GF

Central African Republic Jan 1, Mar 29 (Death of President Boganda), May 1, Jun 1 (Mothers), Aug 13 (Independence), 15, Sep 1 (Arrival of the Military Committee for National Recovery), Nov 1, Dec 1 (Republic), 25; A, EM, WM

NATIONAL HOLIDAYS (cont.)

had Jan 1, May 1, 25 (Liberation of Africa), Jun 7 (Liberation), Aug 11 (Independence), Nov 1, 28 (Republic), Dec 25; Ad, EM, ER, PB

hile Jan 1, May 1, 21 (Battle of Iquique), Jun 29 (Sts Peter and Paul), Aug 15, Sep 11 (National Liberation), 18 (Independence), 19 (Armed Forces), Oct 12 (Day of the Race), Nov 1, Dec 8, 25, 31; GF, HS

hina Jan 1, May 1, Oct 1 (National) (2); Spring Festival (4) (Jan/Feb)

olombia Jan 1, 6, May 1, Jun 29 (Saints Peter and Paul), Jul 20 (Independence), Aug 7 (National), 15, Oct 12 (Columbus), Nov 1, 15 (Independence of Cartagena), Dec 8, 25, 30, 31; A, CC, GF, HT, St Joseph (Mar), Sacred Heart (Jun)

ongo Jan 1, Mar 18 (Day of the Supreme Sacrifice), May 1, Jul 31 (Revolution), Aug 13–15 (The Three Glorious Days), Nov 1 (Day of the Dead), Dec 25 (Children), 31 (Foundation of the Party and People's Republic)

osta Rica Jan 1, Mar 19 (St Joseph), Apr 11 (National Heroes), May 1, Jun 29 (Saints Peter and Paul), Jul 25 (Annexation of Guanacaste), Aug 2 (Our Lady of the Angels), 15 (Mothers), Sep 15 (Independence), Oct 12 (Day of the Race), Dec 8, 25; CC, GF, HS, HT

ôte d'Ivoire Jan 1, May 1, Aug 15, Nov 1, Dec 7 (Independence), 24, 25, 31; A, Ad, EM, ER, GF, WM

uba Jan 1 (Day of Liberation), May 1, Jul 25 (National Rebellion) (2), Oct 10 (Beginning of the Independence Wars)

yprus Jan 1, 6, Mar 25 (Greek Independence), May 1, Oct 28 (Greek National), 29 (Turkish National), Dec 25, 26; Ad, EM, ER, GF, HS, PB

zechoslovakia Jan 1, 2, May 1, 9 (Anniversary of Liberation), Dec 24, 25, 26, 31; EM

enmark Jan 1, Jun 5 (Constitution), Dec 24, 25, 26; A, EM, GF, HT, WM, General Prayer (Apr/May)

jibouti Jan 1, May 1, Jun 27 (Independence)(2), Dec 25; Ad(2), ER(2), NY (Muslim), PB, Al-Isra Wal-Mira'age (Mar–Apr)

ominica Jan 1, May 1, Nov 3 (Independence), 4 (Community Service), Dec 25, 26; C(2), EM, GF, WM, August Monday

ominican Republic Jan 1, 6, 21 (Our Lady of Altagracia), 26 (Duarte), Feb 27 (Independence), May 1, Aug 16 (Restoration of the Republic), Sep 24 (Our Lady of Mercy), Dec 25; CC, GF

cuador Jan 1, May 1, 24 (Independence Battle), Jun 30, Jul 24 (Bolivar), Aug 10 (Independence), Oct 9 (Independence of Guayaquil), 12 (Columbus), Nov 2, 3 (Independence of Cuenca), Dec 6 (Foundation of Quito), 25, 31; C(2), GF, HT

gypt Jan 7 (Eastern Orthodox Christmas), Apr 25 (Sinai Liberation), May 1, Jun 18 (Evacuation), Jul 1, 23 (Revolution Anniversary), Oct 6 (Armed Forces); Ad(2), Ar, ER(2), NY (Muslim), PB, Palm Sunday and Easter Sunday (Eastern Orthodox), Sham El-Nessim (Apr–May)

El Salvador Jan 1, May 1, Jun 29, 30, Sep 15 (Independence), Oct 12 (Columbus), Nov 2, 5 (First Cry of Independence), Dec 24, 25, 30, 31; GF, HT, Ash Wednesday, San Salvador(4)

England & Wales Jan 1, Dec 25, 26; EM, GF, Early May, Late May and Summer (Aug) Bank Holidays

Equatorial Guinea Jan 1, May 1, Jun 5 (President's Birthday), Aug 3 (Armed Forces), Oct 12 (Independence), Dec 10 (Human Rights), 25; CC, GF, Constitution (Aug)

Ethiopia Jan 7 (Ethiopian Christmas), 19 (Ethiopian Epiphany), Mar 2 (Victory of Adwa), Apr 6 (Patriots), May 1, Sep 12 (Revolution), 27 (Finding of the True Cross); Ad, ER, NY (Ethiopian, Sep), PB, Ethiopian Good Friday and Easter

Fiji Jan 1, Oct 12 (Fiji), Dec 25, 26; D, EM, GF, HS, PB, August Bank Holiday, Queen's Birthday (Jun), Prince Charles' Birthday (Nov)

Finland Jan 1, May 1, Oct 31 (All Saints Observance), Nov 1, Dec 6 (Independence), 24, 25, 26, 31; A, EM, GF, Midsummer Eve and Day (Jun), Twelfthtide (Jan), Whitsuntide (May–Jun)

France Jan 1, May 1, 8 (Armistice), Jul 14 (Bastille), Aug 14 (Assumption Eve), 15, Oct 31 (All Saints Eve), Nov 1, 11 (Armistice), Dec 24, 25, 31; A, EM, GF, HS, WM, Ascension Eve, Whit Holiday Eve, Law of 20 Dec 1906, Law of 23 Dec 1904

Gabon Jan 1, Mar 12 (Anniversary of Renewal), May 1, Aug 17 (Independence), Nov 1, Dec 25; Ad, EM, ER, WM

Gambia Jan 1, Feb 1 (Senegambia), 18 (Independence), May 1, Aug 15 (St Mary), Dec 25; Ad, As, ER(2), GF, PB

German Federal Republic Jan 1, May 1, Jun 17 (National), Oct 3 (Unity), Dec 24, 25, 26; A, EM, GF, WM, Day of Penance (Nov)

Ghana Jan 1, Mar 6 (Independence), May 1, Jun 4 (June 4 Revolution), Jul 1 (Republic), Dec 25, 26, 31 (Revolution); EM, GF, HS

Greece Jan 1, 6, Mar 25 (National), May 1, Aug 15, Oct 28 (National), Dec 25, 26; GF, EM, WM, Monday in Lent

Grenada Jan 1–2, Feb 7 (Independence), May 1, Aug 3–4 (Emancipation), Oct 25 (Thanksgiving), Dec 25, 26; CC, EM, GF, WM

Guatemala Jan 1, May 1, Jun 30 (Army Day), Jul 1, Sep 15 (Independence), Oct 12 (Day of the Race), 20 (1944 Revolution), Nov 1, Dec 24, 25, 31; GF, HS, HT

Guinea Jan 1, Apr 3 (Second Republic), May 1, Aug 15, Oct 2 (Independence), Nov 1 (Army), Dec 25; Ad, EM, ER, PB

Guinea-Bissau Jan 1, 20 (National Heroes), Feb 8 (BNG Anniversary and Monetary Reform) Mar 8 (Women), May 1, Aug 3 (Martyrs of Colonialism), Sep 12 (National), 24 (Establishment of the Republic), Nov 14 (Readjustment), Dec 25

Guyana Jan 1, Feb 23 (Republic), May 1, Aug 1 (Freedom), Dec 25, 26; Ad, D, EM, GF, PB, Phagwah (Mar), Caribbean (Jul)

Haiti Jan 1 (Independence), 2 (Ancestry), Apr 14 (Americas), May 1, Aug 15, Oct 17 (Dessalines), 24 (United Nations), Nov 1, 2, 18 (Vertières), Dec 5 (Discovery), 25; A, C, CC, GF

Honduras Jan 1, Apr 14 (Pan American), May 1, Sep 15 (Independence), Oct 3 (Francisco Morazán's Birthday), 12 (America's Discovery), 21 (Armed Forces), Dec 25, 31; GF, HT

Hungary Jan 1, Apr 4 (Liberation Day), May 1, Aug 20 (Constitution), Nov 7 (October Socialist Revolution), Dec 25, 26; EM

Iceland Jan 1, May 1, Jun 17 (Independence), Dec 25, 26; A, EM, GF, HT, WM, First Day of Summer, August Holiday Monday

India Jan 1 (*some states*), 26 (Republic), May 1 (*some states*), Jun 30, Aug 15 (Independence), Oct 2 (Mahatma Ghandi's Birthday), Dec 25, 31; NY (Parsi, Aug, *some states*)

Indonesia Jan 1, Aug 17 (Independence), Dec 25; A, Ad, ER(2), GF, NY (Icaka, Mar), NY (Muslim), PB, Ascension of the Prophet (Mar/Apr), Waisak (May)

Iran Feb 11 (Revolution), Mar 20 (Oil), 21 (Now Rooz)(4), Apr 1 (Islamic Republic), 2 (13th of Farvardin), Jun 5 (15th Khordad Uprising); Ad, As, ER, PB, Prophet's Mission (Apr), Birth of the Twelfth Imam (Apr/May), Martyrdom of Imam Ali (May), Death of Imam Jaffar Sadegh (Jun/Jul), Birth of Imam Reza (Jul), Id-E-Ghadir (Aug), Death of the Prophet and Martyrdom of Imam Hassan (Oct/Nov)

Iraq Jan 1, 6 (Army Day), Feb 8 (8th February Revolution), Mar 21 (Spring Day), May 1, Jul 14 (14th July Revolution), 17 (17th July Revolution); Ad(4), As, ER(3), NY (Muslim), PB

Ireland Jan 1, Mar 17 (St Patrick), Dec 25, 26; EM, GF, June Holiday, August Holiday, October Holiday, Christmas Holiday

Israel Jan 1, May 14 (Independence Day); NY (Jewish, Sep/Oct), Purim (Mar), First Day of Passover (Apr), Last Day of Passover (Apr), Pentecost (Jun), Fast of Av (Aug), Day of Atonement (Oct), Feast of Tabernacles (Sep/Oct)(2)

NATIONAL HOLIDAYS (cont.)

Italy Jan 1, 6, Apr 25 (Liberation), May 1, Aug 14 (Mid-August Holiday)(2), Nov 1, Dec 8, 25, 26; EM

Jamaica Jan 1, May 23 (Labour), Aug 5 (Independence), Oct 20 (National Heroes), Dec 25, 26; Ash Wednesday, EM, GF

Japan Jan 1, 2, 3, 15 (Adults), Feb 11 (National Founding), Mar 21 (Vernal Equinox), Apr 29 (Emperor's Birthday), May 3 (Constitution Memorial), 5 (Children), Sep 15 (Respect for the Aged), 23 (Autumn Equinox), Oct 10 (Health-Sports), Nov 3 (Culture), 23 (Labour Thanksgiving)

Jordan Jan 1, May 1, 25 (Independence), Jun 10 (Great Arab Revolt and Army), Aug 11 (Accession of King Hussein), Nov 14 (King Hussein's Birthday), Dec 25; Ad(4), R, ER(4), NY (Muslim), PB

Kenya Jan 1, May 1, Jun 1 (Madaraka), Oct 20 (Kenyatta), Dec 12 (Independence), 25, 26; EM, GF, ER(3)

Kiribati Jan 1, Jul 12 (Independence)(3), Dec 25, 26; GF, HS, EM, Youth (Aug)

Korea, South Jan 1–3, Mar 1 (Independence Movement), 10 (Labour), Apr 5 (Arbor), May 5 (Children), Jun 6 (Memorial), Jul 17 (Constitution), Aug 15 (Liberation), Oct 1 (Armed Forces), 3 (National Foundation), 9 (Korean Alphabet), Dec 25; NY (Chinese, Jan/Feb), Lord Buddha's Birthday (May), Moon Festival (Sep/Oct)

Kuwait Jan 1, Feb 25 (National)(3); Ad(3), ER(3), NY (Muslim), PB, Ascension of the Prophet (Mar/Apr), Standing on Mt Arafat (Aug)

Lebanon Jan 1, Feb 9 (St Maron), May 1, Aug 15, Nov 1, 22 (Independence), Dec 25; Ad(3), As, EM, GF, ER(3), NY (Muslim), PB

Lesotho Jan 1, Mar 12 (Moshoeshoe's Day), 21 (National Tree Planting), May 2 (King's Birthday), Oct 4 (Independence), Dec 25, 26; A, EM, GF, Family (Jul), National Sports (Oct)

Liberia Jan 1, Feb 11 (Armed Forces), Mar 15 (J J Roberts), Apr 12 (Redemption), May 14 (National Unification), Jul 26 (Independence), Aug 24 (National Flag), Nov 29 (President Tubman's Birthday), Dec 25; Decoration (Mar), National Fast and Prayer (Apr), Thanksgiving (Nov)

Libya Mar 2 (Declaration of Establishment of Authority of People), 8 (National), 28 (Evacuation of British troops), Jun 11 (Evacuation of US troops), Jul 23 (National), Sep 1 (National), Oct 7 (Evacuation of Italian Fascists); Ad(4), ER(3), PB

Liechtenstein Jan 1, 6, Feb 2 (Candlemas), Mar 19 (St Joseph), May 1, Aug 15, Nov 1, Dec 8, 24, 25, 26, 31; A, C, CC, EM, GF, WM

Luxembourg Jan 1, May 1, Jun 23 (National), Aug 15, Nov 1, 2, Dec 25, 26, 31; A, EM, WM, Shrove Monday

Madagascar Jan 1, Mar 29 (Memorial), May 1, Jun 26 (Independence), Aug 15, Nov 1, Dec 25, 30 (National); A, EM, GF, WM

Malawi Jan 1, Mar 3 (Martyrs), May 14 (Kamuzu), Jul 6 (Republic), Oct 17 (Mothers), Dec 22 (Tree Planting), 25, 26 EM, GF, HS

Malaysia Jan 1 (*some states*), May 1, Jun 3 (Head of State's Birthday), Aug 31 (National), Dec 25; Ad, D (*most states*), ER(2), NY (Chinese, Jan/Feb, *most states*), NY (Muslim), PB, Wesak (*most states*); *several local festivals*

Maldives Jan 1, Jul 26 (Independence)(2), Nov 11 (Republic) (2); Ad(4), ER(3), NY (Muslim), PB, R(2), Huravee (Feb), Martyrs (Apr), National (Oct/Nov)(2)

Mali Jan 1, 20 (Army), May 1, 25 (Africa), Sep 22 (National), Nov 19 (Liberation), Dec 25; Ad, ER, PB, Prophet's Baptism (Nov)

Malta Jan 1, Mar 31 (National), May 1, Aug 15, Dec 13 (Republic), 25; GF

Mauritania Jan 1, May 1, 25 (Africa), Jul 10 (Armed Forces), Nov 28 (Independence); Ad, ER, NY (Muslim), PB

Mauritius Jan 1, 2, Mar 12 (Independence), May 1, Nov 1, Dec 25; Ad, D, ER, PB, Chinese Spring Festival (Feb)

Mexico Jan 1, Feb 5 (Constitution), Mar 21 (Juárez' Birthday), May 1, 5 (Puebla Battle), Sep 1 (Presidential Report), 16 (Independence), Oct 12 (Columbus), Nov 2, 20 (Mexican Revolution), Dec 12 (Our Lady of Guadaloupe), 25, 31; HT, GF

Monaco Jan 1, 27 (St Devote), May 1, 8 (Armistice, 1945), Jul 14 (National), Aug 15, Sep 3 (Liberation), Nov 1, 11 (Armistice, 1918), 19 (Prince of Monaco), Dec 8, 25; EM, WM

Mongolia Jan 1, 2, Mar 8 (International Women), May 1, Jul 10 (People's Revolution)(3), Nov 7 (October Revolution)

Morocco Jan 1, Mar 3 (Throne), May 1, 23 (Fête Nationale), Jul 9 (Youth), Aug 14 (Oued-ed-Dahab), Nov 6 (Al-Massira Day), 18 (Independence); Ad(2), ER(2), NY (Muslim), PB

Mozambique Jan 1, Feb 3 (Heroes), Apr 7 (Mozambican Women), May 1, Jun 25 (Independence), Sep 7 (Victory), 25 (Armed Forces), Dec 25

Nauru Jan 1, 31 (Independence), May 17 (Constitution), Jul 1 (Takeover), Oct 27 (Angam), Dec 25, 26; EM, GF, Easter Tuesday

Nepal Jan 11 (King Prithvi Memorial), Feb 19 (Late King Tribhuvan Memorial and Democracy), Nov 8 (Queen's Birthday), Dec 16 (King Mahendra Memorial and Constitution), 29 (King's Birthday); NY (Sinhala/Tamil, Apr), Maha Shivarata (Feb/Mar)

Netherlands Jan 1, Apr 30 (Queen's Birthday), May 5 (Liberation), Dec 25, 26; A, EM, GF, WM

New Zealand Jan 1, 2, Feb 6 (Waitangi), Apr 25 (Anzac), Dec 25, 26; EM, GF, Queen's Birthday (Jun), Labour (Oct)

Nicaragua Jan 1, May 1, Jul 19 (Sandinista Revolution), Sep 14 (Battle of San Jacinto), 15 (Independence), Dec 8, 25; GF, HT

Niger Jan 1, Apr 15 (Assumption of Power by Supreme Military Council), May 1, Aug 3 (Independence), Dec 18 (National), 25; Ad, ER, PB

Nigeria Jan 1, May 1, Oct 1 (National), Dec 25, 26; Ad(2), EM, ER(2), GF, PB

Northern Ireland Jan 1, Mar 17 (St Patrick, *not general*), Dec 25, 26, 29; GF, EM, Early May, Late May, July Bank Holiday, Summer Bank Holiday (Aug)

Norway Jan 1, May 1, 17 (Constitution), Dec 25, 26; A, EM, GF, HT, WM

Oman Nov 18 (National)(2), Dec 31; Ad(5), ER(4), NY (Muslim), PB, Lailat al-Miraj (Mar/Apr)

Pakistan Mar 23 (Pakistan), May 1, Jul 1, Aug 14 (Independence), Sep 6 (Defence of Pakistan), 11 (Death of Quaid-e-Azam), Nov 9 (Iqbal), Dec 25 (Christmas/Birthday of Quaid-e-Azam), 31; Ad(3), As(2), ER(3), PB, R

Panama Jan 1, 9 (National Mourning), May 1, Oct 11 (Revolution), 12 (Dia de la Hispanidad), Nov 3 (Independence from Colombia), 4 (Flag), 28 (Independence from Spain), Dec 8 (Mothers), 25; C(2), GF

Papua New Guinea Jan 1, Aug 15 (National Constitution), Sep 16 (Independence), Dec 25, 26; EM, GF, HS, Queen's Birthday (Jun), Remembrance (Jul)

Paraguay Jan 1, Feb 3 (St Blás), Mar 1 (Heroes), May 1, 14 (National Flag), 15 (Independence), Jun 12 (Peace with Bolivia), Aug 15, 25 (Constitution), Sep 29 (Battle of Boqueron Day), Oct 12 (Day of the Race), Nov 1, Dec 8, 25, 31; CC, GF, HT

Peru Jan 1, May 1, Jun 29 (Sts Peter and Paul), 30, Jul 28 (Independence)(2), Aug 30 (St Rose of Lima), Oct 8 (Combat of Angamos), Nov 1, Dec 8, 25, 31; GF, HT

Philippines Jan 1, May 1, Jun 12 (Independence), Jul 4 (Philippine-American Friendship), Nov 1, 30 (National Heroes), Dec 25, 30 (Rizal), 31; GF, HT

Poland Jan 1, May 1, Jul 22 (National Liberation), Nov 1, Dec 25, 26; CC, EM

NATIONAL HOLIDAYS (cont.)

Portugal Jan 1, Apr 25 (Liberty), May 1, Jun 10 (Portugal), Aug 15, Oct 5 (Republic), Nov 1, Dec 1 (Independence Restoration), Dec 8, 24, 25; C, CC, GF

Qatar Sep 3 (Independence), Dec 31; Ad(4), ER(4)

Romania Jan 1, 2, May 1(2), Aug 23 (National)

Russia Jan 1, Mar 8 (Women), May 1(2), 9 (Victory), Oct 7 (Constitution), Nov 7 (October Revolution)(2) (*former Soviet Union*)

Rwanda Jan 1, 28 (Democracy), May 1, Jul 1 (Independence), 5 (Peace), Aug 1 (Harvest), 15, Sep 25 (Referendum), Oct 26 (Armed Forces), Nov 1, Dec 25; A, EM, WM

Saint Christopher and Nevis Jan 1, Sep 19 (Independence), Dec 25, 26, 31; EM, GF, WM, Labour (May), Queen's Birthday (Jun), August Monday

Saint Lucia Jan 1, 2, Feb 22 (Independence), May 1, Dec 13 (Saint Lucia), Dec 25, 26; C, CC, EM, GF, WM, Emancipation (Aug), Thanksgiving (Oct)

Saint Vincent and the Grenadines Jan 1, 22 (Discovery), Oct 27 (Independence), Dec 25, 26; C (Jul), EM, GF, WM, Labour (May), Caricom (Jul), Emancipation (Aug)

São Tomé and Principe Jan 1, Feb 3 (Liberty Heroes), May 1, Jul 12 (National Independence), Sep 6 (Armed Forces), 30 (Agricultural Reform), Dec 21 (Power of the People), 25 (Family)

Saudi Arabia Sep 23 (National); Ad(7), ER(4)

Scotland Jan 1, 2, Dec 25, 26; GF, Early May, Late May, Summer Bank Holiday (Aug)

Senegal Jan 1, Feb 1 (Senegambia), Apr 4 (National), May 1, Aug 15, Nov 1, Dec 25; Ad, EM, ER, NY (Muslim), PB, WM

Seychelles Jan 1, 2, May 1, Jun 5 (Liberation), 29 (Independence), Aug 15, Nov 1, Dec 8, 25; CC, GF, HS

Sierra Leone Jan 1, Apr 19 (Republic), Dec 25, 26; Ad, EM, ER, GF, PB

Singapore Jan 1, May 1, Aug 9 (National), Dec 25; Ad, D, ER, GF, NY (Chinese, Jan/Feb)(2), Vesak

Solomon Islands Jan 1, Jul 7 (Independence), Dec 25, 26; EM, GF, HS, WM, Queen's Birthday (Jun)

Somalia Jan 1, May 1, Jun 26 (Independence), Jul 1 (Union), Oct 21 (Revolution)(2); Ad(2), ER(2), PB

South Africa Jan 1, Apr 6 (Founders), May 31 (Republic), Oct 10 (Kruger), Dec 16 (Vow), 25, 26; A, GF, Family (Mar/Apr)

Spain Jan 1, 6, Mar 19 (*most areas*), May 1, Aug 15, Oct 12 (Hispanity), Nov 1, Dec 6 (Constitution), 8, 25; CC, GF, HS, HT

Sri Lanka Jan 14 (Tamil Thai Pongal), Feb 4 (Independence), May 1, 22 (National Heroes), Jun 30, Dec 25, 31; Ad, D, ER, GF, NY (Sinhala/Tamil, Apr), PB, Maha Sivarathri (Feb/Mar), Full Moon (*monthly*)

Sudan Jan 1 (Independence), Mar 3 (Unity), Apr 6 (Revolution), Dec 25; Ad(5), ER(5), NY (Muslim), PB, Sham al-Naseem (Apr/May)

Suriname Jan 1, Feb 25 (Revolution), May 1, Jul 1 (Freedom), Nov 25 (Independence), Dec 25, 26; EM, ER, GF, Holi (Mar)

Swaziland Jan 1, Apr 25 (National Flag), Jul 22 (King's Birthday), Sep 6 (Independence), Oct 24 (United Nations), Dec 25, 26; A, EM, GF, Commonwealth (Mar)

Sweden Jan 1, 6, May 1, Nov 1 (All Saints), Dec 24, 25, 26, 31; A, EM, GF, WM, Midsummer Eve and Day (Jun)

Switzerland Jan 1, Aug 1 (National), Aug 15 (*many cantons*), Nov 1 (*many cantons*), Dec 24, 25, 26; A, CC (*many cantons*), EM, GF, WM; *several local holidays*

Syria Jan 1, Mar 8 (Revolution), Apr 17 (Evacuation) May 1, 6 (Martyrs), Jul 23 (Egyptian Revolution), Sep 1 (Libyan Unity), Oct 6 (Liberation), Dec 25; Ad(3), ER(4), ES, NY (Muslim), PB

Taiwan Jan 1, 2, 3, Mar 29 (Youth), Apr 5 (Ching Ming), Jul 1, Sep 28 (Birthday of Confucius), Oct 10 (National), 25 (Taiwan Restoration), 31 (Birthday of Chiang Kai-Shek), Nov 12 (Birthday of Dr Sun Yat Sen), Dec 25 (Constitution); NY (Chinese, Jan/Feb)(3), Dragon Boat Festival (Jun), Mid-Autumn Festival (Sep/Oct)

Tanzania Jan 1, 12 (Zanzibar Revolution), Feb 5 (Chama Cha Mapinduzi and Arusha Declaration), May 1, Jul 7 (Saba Saba Peasants), Dec 9 (Independence/Republic), 25; Ad, EM, ER(2), GF, PB

Thailand Jan 1, Apr 6 (Chakri), 13 (Songkran), May 1, 5 (Coronation), Jul 1 (Mid-Year), Aug 12 (Queen's Birthday), Oct 23 (King Chulalongkorn), Dec 5 (King's Birthday), 10 (Constitution), 31; ER, Makha Bucha (Feb), Visakha Bucha (May), Buddhist Lent (Jul)

Togo Jan 1, 13 (Liberation), 24 (Economic Liberation), Apr 24 (Victory), 27 (National), May 1, Aug 15, Nov 1, Dec 25; A, Ad, ER

Tonga Jan 1, Apr 25 (Anzac), May 5 (Birthday of Crown Prince Tupouto'a), Jun 4 (Emancipation), Jul 4 (Birthday and Coronation of King Taufa'ahau Tupou IV), Nov 4 (Constitution), Dec 4 (King Tupou I), 25, 26; EM, GF

Trinidad and Tobago Jan 1, Jun 19 (Labour), Aug 1 (Discovery), 31 (Independence), Sep 24 (Republic), Dec 25, 26; CC, EM, GF, WM

Tunisia Jan 1, 18 (Revolution), Mar 20 (Independence), Apr 9 (Martyrs), May 1, Jun 1 (Victory), 2 (Youth), Jul 25 (Republic), Aug 3 (President's Birthday), 13 (Women), Sep 3 (Sep 3 1934), Oct 15 (Evacuation); Ad(2), ER(2), NY (Muslim), PB

Turkey Jan 1, Apr 23 (National Sovereignty and Children), May 19 (Youth and Sports), Aug 30 (Victory), Oct 29 (Republic); Ad(4), ER(3)

Uganda Jan 1, Apr 1 (Liberation), May 1, Oct 9 (Independence), Dec 25, 26; EM, ER, GF, HS

UK *see* **England & Wales**; **Northern Ireland**; **Scotland**

United Arab Emirates Jan 1, Aug 6 (Accession of Ruler), Dec 2 (National)(2); Ad(3), ER(4), NY (Muslim), PB, Lailat al-Miraj (Mar/Apr)

USA Jan 1, Jul 4 (Independence), Oct 12 (Columbus Day)(*not all states*), Nov 11 (Veterans), Dec 25; Martin Luther King's Birthday (Jan, *not all states*); Washington's Birthday (Feb), Memorial (May), Labor (1st Mon in Sep), Columbus (Oct), Thanksgiving (last Thurs of Nov); *much local variation*

Uruguay Jan 1, Apr 19 (Landing of the 33 Orientales), May 1, 18 (Las Piedras Battle), Jun 19 (Artigas), Jul 18 (Constitution), Aug 25 (Independence), Oct 12 (Columbus), Nov 2, Dec 25; C(2), GF, HT, Monday—Wednesday of Holy Week

Vanuatu Jan 1, Mar 5 (Chiefs), May 1, Jul 30 (Independence), Aug 15, Dec 25, 26; A, EM, GF, Constitution (Oct), Unity (Nov)

Venezuela Jan 1, 6, Mar 19 (St Joseph), Apr 19 (Constitution), May 1, Jun 24 (Battle of Carabobo), 29 (Saints Peter and Paul), Jul 5 (Independence), 24 (Bolivar), Aug 15, Oct 12 (Columbus), Nov 1, Dec 8, 25; A, C(2), CC, GF, HT

Vietnam Jan 1, May 1, Sep 2 (Independence)

Western Samoa Jan 1, 2, Apr 25 (Anzac), Jun 1 (Independence) (3), Oct 12 (Lotu-o-Tamai), Dec 25, 26; EM, GF, HS

Yemen People's Democratic Republic Jan 1, Mar 8 (Women), May 1, Jun 22 (Corrective Move), Sep 26 (Revolution, *N area*), Oct 14 (Revolution), Nov 30 (Independence); Ad(3), ER(2), NY (Muslim), PB

Yugoslavia Jan 1, 2, May 1(2), Jul 4 (Fighters), Nov 29 (Republic)(3); People's Uprising (Jul)

Zaire Jan 1, 4 (Martyrs of Independence), May 1, 20 (Mouvement Populaire de la Revolution), Jun 24 (Anniversary of Currency, Promulgation, Constitution and Day of Fishers), 30 (Independence), Aug 1 (Parents), Oct 14 (Founder/Youth), 27 (Country's Change of Name), Nov 17 (Armed Forces), 24 (New Regime), Dec 25

Zambia Jan 1, May 1, 25 (Africa Freedom), Oct 24 (Independence), Dec 25; GF, HS, Youth (Mar), Heroes (Jul), Unity (Jul), Farmers (Aug)

Zimbabwe Jan 1, Apr 18 (Independence), 19 (Defence Forces), May 1, 25 (Africa), Aug 11 (Heroes)(2), Dec 25, 26; EM, GF

SAINTS' DAYS

The official recognition of Saints, and the choice of a Saint's Day, varies greatly between different branches of Christianity, calendars and localities. Only major variations are included below, using the following abbreviations:

C Coptic *G* Greek
E Eastern *W* Western

January
1 Basil (*E*), Fulgentius, Telemachus
2 Basil and Gregory of Nazianzus (*W*), Macarius of Alexandria, Seraphim of Sarov
3 Geneviève
4 Angela of Foligno
5 Simeon Stylites (*W*)
7 Cedda, Lucian of Antioch (*W*), Raymond of Penyafort
8 Atticus (*E*), Gudule, Severinus
9 Hadrian the African
10 Agatho, Marcian
12 Ailred, Benedict Biscop
13 Hilary of Poitiers
14 Kentigern
15 Macarius of Egypt, Maurus, Paul of Thebes
16 Honoratus
17 Antony of Egypt
19 Wulfstan
20 Euthymius, Fabian, Sebastian
21 Agnes, Fructuosus, Maximus (*E*), Meinrad
22 Timothy (*G*), Vincent
23 Ildefonsus
24 Babylas (*W*), Francis de Sales
25 Gregory of Nazianzus (*E*)
26 Paula, Timothy and Titus, Xenophon (*E*)
27 Angela Merici
28 Ephraem Syrus (*E*), Paulinus of Nola, Thomas Aquinas
29 Gildas
31 John Bosco, Marcella

February
1 Bride, Pionius
3 Anskar, Blaise (*W*), Werburga, Simeon (*E*)
4 Gilbert of Sempringham, Isidore of Pelusium, Phileas
5 Agatha, Avitus
6 Dorothy, Paul Miki and companions, Vedast
8 Theodore (*G*), Jerome Emiliani
9 Teilo
10 Scholastica
11 Benedict of Aniane, Blaise (*E*), Caedmon, Gregory II
12 Meletius
13 Agabus (*W*), Catherine dei Ricci, Priscilla (*E*)
14 Cyril and Methodius (*W*), Valentine (*W*)
16 Flavian (*E*), Pamphilus (*E*), Valentine (*G*)
18 Bernadette (*France*), Colman, Flavian (*W*), Leo I (*E*)
20 Wulfric
21 Peter Damian
23 Polycarp
25 Ethelbert, Tarasius, Walburga
26 Alexander (*W*), Porphyrius
27 Leander
28 Oswald of York

March
1 David
2 Chad, Simplicius
3 Ailred
4 Casimir
6 Chrodegang
7 Perpetua and Felicity
8 Felix, John of God, Pontius
9 Frances of Rome, Gregory of Nyssa, Pacian
10 John Ogilvie, Macarius of Jerusalem, Simplicius
11 Constantine, Oengus, Sophronius
12 Gregory (the Great)
13 Nicephorus
14 Benedict (*E*)
15 Clement Hofbauer
17 Gertrude, Joseph of Arimathea (*W*), Patrick
18 Anselm of Lucca, Cyril of Jerusalem, Edward
19 Joseph
20 Cuthbert, John of Parma, Martin of Braga
21 Serapion of Thmuis
22 Catherine of Sweden, Nicholas of Flüe
23 Turibius de Mongrovejo
30 John Climacus

April
1 Hugh of Grenoble, Mary of Egypt (*E*), Melito
2 Francis of Paola, Mary of Egypt (*W*)
3 Richard of Chichester
4 Isidore of Seville
5 Juliana of Liège, Vincent Ferrer
7 Hegesippus, John Baptist de la Salle
8 Agabus (*E*)
10 Fulbert
11 Gemma Galgani, Guthlac, Stanislaus
12 Julius I, Zeno
13 Martin I
15 Aristarchus, Pudus (*E*), Trophimus of Ephesus
17 Agapetus (*E*), Stephen Harding
18 Mme Acarie
19 Alphege, Leo IX
21 Anastasius (*E*), Anselm, Beuno, Januarius (*E*)
22 Alexander (*C*)
23 George
24 Egbert, Fidelis of Sigmaringen, Mellitus
25 Mark, Phaebadius
27 Zita
28 Peter Chanel, Vitalis and Valeria
29 Catherine of Siena, Hugh of Cluny, Peter Martyr, Robert
30 James (the Great) (*E*), Pius V

May
1 Asaph, Joseph the Worker, Walburga
2 Athanasius
3 Phillip and James (the Less) (*W*)
4 Gotthard
5 Hilary of Arles
7 John of Beverley
8 John (*E*), Peter of Tarantaise
10 Antoninus, Comgall, John of Avila, Simon (*E*)
11 Cyril and Methodius (*E*), Mamertus
12 Epiphanius, Nereus and Achilleus, Pancras
14 Matthias (*W*)
16 Brendan, John of Nepomuk, Simon Stock
17 Robert Bellarmine, Paschal Baylon
18 John I
19 Dunstan, Ivo, Pudens (*W*), Pudentiana (*W*)
20 Bernardino of Siena
21 Helena (*E*)
22 Rita of Cascia
23 Ivo of Chartres
24 Vincent of Lérins
25 Aldhelm, Bede, Gregory VII, Mary Magdalene de Pazzi
26 Philip Neri, Quadratus
27 Augustine of Canterbury
30 Joan of Arc

June
1 Justin Martyr, Pamphilus
2 Erasmus, Marcellinus and Peter, Nicephorus (*G*), Pothinus
3 Charles Lwanga and companions, Clotilde, Kevin
4 Optatus, Petrock
5 Boniface
6 Martha (*E*), Norbert
7 Paul of Constantinople (*W*), Willibald
8 William of York
9 Columba, Cyril of Alexandria (*E*), Ephraem (*W*)
11 Barnabas, Bartholomew (*E*)
12 Leo III
13 Anthony of Padua
15 Orsisius, Vitus
17 Alban, Botulph
19 Gervasius and Protasius, Jude (*E*), Romuald
20 Alban
21 Alban of Mainz, Aloysius Gonzaga
22 John Fisher and Thomas More, Niceta, Pantaenus (*C*), Paulinus of Nola
23 Etheldreda
24 Birth of John the Baptist
25 Prosper of Aquitaine
27 Cyril of Alexandria (*W*), Ladislaus
28 Irenaeus
29 Peter and Paul
30 First Martyrs of the Church of Rome

July
1 Cosmas and Damian (*E*), Oliver Plunket
3 Anatolius, Thomas
4 Andrew of Crete (*E*), Elizabeth of Portugal, Ulrich
5 Anthony Zaccaria
6 Maria Goretti
7 Palladius, Pantaenus
8 Kilian, Aquila and Prisca (*W*)
11 Benedict (*W*), Pius I
12 John Gualbert, Veronica
13 Henry II, Mildred, Silas
14 Camillus of Lellis, Deusdedit, Nicholas of the Holy Mountain (*E*)
15 Bonaventure, Jacob of Nisibis, Swithin, Vladimir
16 Eustathius, Our Lady of Mt Carmel
17 Ennodius, Leo IV, Marcellina, Margaret (*E*), Scillitan Martyrs
18 Arnulf, Philastrius
19 Macrina, Symmachus
20 Aurelius, Margaret (*W*)
21 Lawrence of Brindisi, Praxedes
22 Mary Magdalene
23 Apollinaris, Bridget of Sweden
25 Anne and Joachim (*E*), Christopher, James (the Great) (*W*)
26 Anne and Joachim (*W*)
27 Pantaleon
28 Innocent I, Samson, Victor I
29 Lupus, Martha (*W*), Olave
30 Peter Chrysologus, Silas (*G*)
31 Giovanni Colombini, Germanus, Joseph of Arimathea (*E*), Ignatius of Loyola

August
1 Alphonsus Liguori, Ethelwold
2 Eusebius of Vercelli, Stephen I

SAINTS' DAYS (cont.)

Jean-Baptiste Vianney
Hormisdas
Cajetan, Sixtus II and companions
Dominic
Matthias (*G*)
Laurence, Oswald of Northumbria
Clare, Susanna
Maximus (*W*), Pontian and Hippolytus, Radegunde
Maximilian Kolbe
Arnulf, Tarsicius
Roch, Simplicianus, Stephen of Hungary
Hyacinth
John Eudes, Sebaldus
Bernard, Oswin, Philibert
Jane Frances de Chantal, Pius X
Rose of Lima, Sidonius Apollinaris
Bartholomew (*W*), Ouen
Joseph Calasanctius, Louis IX, Menas of Constantinople
Blessed Dominic of the Mother of God, Zephyrinus
Caesarius, Monica
Augustine of Hippo
Beheading of John the Baptist, Sabina
Pammachius
Aidan, Paulinus of Trier

ptember

Giles, Simeon Stylites (*E*)
John the Faster (*E*)
Gregory (the Great)
Babylas (*E*), Boniface I
Zacharias (*E*)
Peter Claver, Sergius of Antioch
Finnian, Nicholas of Tolentino, Pulcheria
Deiniol, Ethelburga, Paphnutius
John Chrysostom (*W*)
Catherine of Genoa, Our Lady of Sorrows
Cornelius, Cyprian of Carthage, Euphemia, Ninian
Robert Bellarmine, Hildegard, Lambert, Satyrus
Januarius (*W*), Theodore of Tarsus
Agapetus or Eustace (*W*)
Matthew (*W*)
Adamnan, Linus
Sergius of Rostov
Cosmas and Damian (*W*), Cyprian of Carthage, John (*E*)

27 Frumentius (*W*), Vincent de Paul
28 Exuperius, Wenceslaus
29 Michael (*Michaelmas Day*), Gabriel and Raphael
30 Jerome, Otto

October

1 Remigius, Romanos, Teresa of the Child Jesus
2 Leodegar (Leger)
3 Teresa of Lisieux, Thomas de Cantilupe
4 Ammon, Francis of Assisi, Petronius
6 Bruno, Thomas (*G*)
9 Demetrius (*W*), Denis and companions, Dionysius of Paris, James (the Less) (*E*), John Leonardi
10 Francis Borgia, Paulinus of York
11 Atticus (*E*), Bruno (*d. 965*), Nectarius
12 Wilfrid
13 Edward the Confessor
14 Callistus I, Cosmas Melodus (*E*)
15 Lucian of Antioch (*E*), Teresa of Avila
16 Gall, Hedwig, Lullus, Margaret Mary Alacoque
17 Ignatius of Antioch, Victor
18 Luke
19 John de Bréboeuf and Isaac Jogues and companions, Paul of the Cross, Peter of Alcántara
21 Hilarion, Ursula
22 Abercius
23 John of Capistrano, James
24 Anthony Claret
25 Crispin and Crispinian, Forty Martyrs of England and Wales, Gaudentius
26 Demetrius (*E*)
28 Firmilian (*E*), Simon and Jude
30 Serapion of Antioch
31 Wolfgang

November

1 All Saints, Cosmas and Damian (*E*)
2 Eustace (*E*), Victorinus
3 Hubert, Malachy, Martin de Porres, Pirminius, Winifred
4 Charles Borromeo, Vitalis and Agricola
5 Elizabeth (*W*)
6 Illtyd, Leonard, Paul of Constantinople (*E*)
7 Willibrord
8 Elizabeth (*E*), Willehad
9 Simeon Metaphrastes (*E*)
10 Justus, Leo I (*W*)
11 Martin of Tours (*W*), Menas of Egypt, Theodore of Studios
12 Josaphat, Martin of Tours (*E*), Nilus the Ascetic
13 Abbo, John Chrysostom (*E*), Nicholas I
14 Dubricius, Gregory Palamas (*E*)
15 Albert the Great, Machutus
16 Edmund of Abingdon, Eucherius, Gertrude (the Great), Margaret of Scotland, Matthew (*E*)
17 Elizabeth of Hungary, Gregory Thaumaturgus, Gregory of Tours, Hugh of Lincoln
18 Odo, Romanus
19 Mechthild, Nerses
20 Edmund the Martyr
21 Gelasius
22 Cecilia
23 Amphilochius, Clement I (*W*), Columban, Felicity, Gregory of Agrigentum
25 Clement I (*E*), Mercurius, Mesrob
26 Siricius
27 Barlam and Josaphat
28 Simeon Metaphrastes
29 Cuthbert Mayne
30 Andrew, Frumentius (*G*)

December

1 Eligius
2 Chromatius
3 Francis Xavier
4 Barbara, John Damascene, Osmund
5 Clement of Alexandria, Sabas
6 Nicholas
7 Ambrose
10 Miltiades
11 Damasus, Daniel
12 Jane Frances de Chantal, Spyridon (*E*), Vicelin
13 Lucy, Odilia
14 John of the Cross, Spyridon (*W*)
16 Eusebius
18 Frumentius (*C*)
20 Ignatius of Antioch (*G*)
21 Peter Canisius, Thomas
22 Anastasia (*E*), Chrysogonus (*E*)
23 John of Kanty
26 Stephen (*W*)
27 John (*W*), Fabiola, Stephen (*E*)
29 Thomas à Becket, Trophimus of Arles
31 Sylvester

WEDDING ANNIVERSARIES

many Western countries, different wedding anniversaries have become ssociated with gifts of different materials. There is some variation between untries.

1st	Cotton	10th	Tin	35th	Coral
2nd	Paper	11th	Steel	40th	Ruby
3rd	Leather	12th	Silk, Linen	45th	Sapphire
4th	Fruit, Flowers	13th	Lace	50th	Gold
5th	Wood	14th	Ivory	55th	Emerald
6th	Sugar	15th	Crystal	60th	Diamond
7th	Copper, Wool	20th	China	70th	Platinum
8th	Bronze, Pottery	25th	Silver		
9th	Pottery, Willow	30th	Pearl		

THE SEASONS

N Hemisphere	S Hemisphere	Duration
Spring	Autumn	From vernal/autumnal equinox (c.21 Mar) to summer/winter solstice (c.21 Jun)
Summer	Winter	From summer/winter solstice (c.21 Jun) to autumnal/spring equinox (c.23 Sept)
Autumn	Spring	From autumnal/spring equinox (c.23 Sept) to winter/summer solstice (c.21 Dec)
Winter	Summer	From winter/summer solstice (c.21 Dec) to vernal/autumnal equinox (c.21 Mar)

PERPETUAL CALENDAR 1801–2000

The calendar for each year is given under the corresponding letter below.

1801	I	1821	C	1841	K	1861	E	1881	M	1901	E	1921	M	1941	G	1961	A	1981	
1802	K	1822	E	1842	M	1862	G	1882	A	1902	G	1922	A	1942	I	1962	C	1982	
1803	M	1823	G	1843	A	1863	I	1883	C	1903	I	1923	C	1943	K	1963	E	1983	
1804	B	1824	J	1844	D	1864	L	1884	F	1904	L	1924	F	1944	N	1964	H	1984	
1805	E	1825	M	1845	G	1865	A	1885	I	1905	A	1925	I	1945	C	1965	K	1985	
1806	G	1826	A	1846	I	1866	C	1886	K	1906	C	1926	K	1946	E	1966	M	1986	
1807	I	1827	C	1847	K	1867	E	1887	M	1907	E	1927	M	1947	G	1967	A	1987	
1808	L	1828	F	1848	N	1868	H	1888	B	1908	H	1928	B	1948	J	1968	D	1988	
1809	A	1829	I	1849	C	1869	K	1889	E	1909	K	1929	E	1949	M	1969	G	1989	
1810	C	1830	K	1850	E	1870	M	1890	G	1910	M	1930	G	1950	A	1970	I	1990	
1811	E	1831	M	1851	G	1871	A	1891	I	1911	A	1931	I	1951	C	1971	K	1991	
1812	H	1832	B	1852	J	1872	D	1892	L	1912	D	1932	L	1952	F	1972	N	1992	
1813	K	1833	E	1853	M	1873	G	1893	A	1913	G	1933	A	1953	I	1973	C	1993	
1814	M	1834	G	1854	A	1874	I	1894	C	1914	I	1934	C	1954	K	1974	E	1994	
1815	A	1835	I	1855	C	1875	K	1895	E	1915	K	1935	E	1955	M	1975	G	1995	
1816	D	1836	L	1856	F	1876	N	1896	H	1916	N	1936	H	1956	B	1976	J	1996	
1817	G	1837	A	1857	I	1877	C	1897	K	1917	C	1937	K	1957	E	1977	M	1997	
1818	I	1838	C	1858	K	1878	E	1898	M	1918	E	1938	M	1958	G	1978	A	1998	
1819	K	1839	E	1859	M	1879	G	1899	A	1919	G	1939	A	1959	I	1979	C	1999	
1820	N	1840	H	1860	B	1880	J	1900	C	1920	J	1940	D	1960	L	1980	F	2000	

A

January

S	M	T	W	T	F	S
1	2	3	4	5	6	7
8	9	10	11	12	13	14
15	16	17	18	19	20	21
22	23	24	25	26	27	28
29	30	31				

February

S	M	T	W	T	F	S
			1	2	3	4
5	6	7	8	9	10	11
12	13	14	15	16	17	18
19	20	21	22	23	24	25
26	27	28				

March

S	M	T	W	T	F	S
			1	2	3	4
5	6	7	8	9	10	11
12	13	14	15	16	17	18
19	20	21	22	23	24	25
26	27	28	29	30	31	

April

S	M	T	W	T	F	S
						1
2	3	4	5	6	7	8
9	10	11	12	13	14	15
16	17	18	19	20	21	22
23	24	25	26	27	28	29
30						

May

	1	2	3	4	5	6
7	8	9	10	11	12	13
14	15	16	17	18	19	20
21	22	23	24	25	26	27
28	29	30	31			

June

				1	2	3
4	5	6	7	8	9	10
11	12	13	14	15	16	17
18	19	20	21	22	23	24
25	26	27	28	29	30	

July

						1
2	3	4	5	6	7	8
9	10	11	12	13	14	15
16	17	18	19	20	21	22
23	24	25	26	27	28	29
30	31					

August

		1	2	3	4	5
6	7	8	9	10	11	12
13	14	15	16	17	18	19
20	21	22	23	24	25	26
27	28	29	30	31		

September

					1	2
3	4	5	6	7	8	9
10	11	12	13	14	15	16
17	18	19	20	21	22	23
24	25	26	27	28	29	30

October

1	2	3	4	5	6	7
8	9	10	11	12	13	14
15	16	17	18	19	20	21
22	23	24	25	26	27	28
29	30	31				

November

			1	2	3	4
5	6	7	8	9	10	11
12	13	14	15	16	17	18
19	20	21	22	23	24	25
26	27	28	29	30		

December

					1	2
3	4	5	6	7	8	9
10	11	12	13	14	15	16
17	18	19	20	21	22	23
24	25	26	27	28	29	30
31						

B (leap year)

January

S	M	T	W	T	F	S
1	2	3	4	5	6	7
8	9	10	11	12	13	14
15	16	17	18	19	20	21
22	23	24	25	26	27	28
29	30	31				

February

S	M	T	W	T	F	S
			1	2	3	4
5	6	7	8	9	10	11
12	13	14	15	16	17	18
19	20	21	22	23	24	25
26	27	28	29			

March

S	M	T	W	T	F	S
				1	2	3
4	5	6	7	8	9	10
11	12	13	14	15	16	17
18	19	20	21	22	23	24
25	26	27	28	29	30	31

April

S	M	T	W	T	F
1	2	3	4	5	6
8	9	10	11	12	13
15	16	17	18	19	20
22	23	24	25	26	27
29	30				

May

		1	2	3	4	5
6	7	8	9	10	11	12
13	14	15	16	17	18	19
20	21	22	23	24	25	26
27	28	29	30	31		

June

					1	2
3	4	5	6	7	8	9
10	11	12	13	14	15	16
17	18	19	20	21	22	23
24	25	26	27	28	29	30

July

1	2	3	4	5	6	7
8	9	10	11	12	13	14
15	16	17	18	19	20	21
22	23	24	25	26	27	28
29	30	31				

August

			1	2	3
5	6	7	8	9	10
12	13	14	15	16	17
19	20	21	22	23	24
26	27	28	29	30	31

September

						1
2	3	4	5	6	7	8
9	10	11	12	13	14	15
16	17	18	19	20	21	22
23	24	25	26	27	28	29
30						

October

	1	2	3	4	5	6
7	8	9	10	11	12	13
14	15	16	17	18	19	20
21	22	23	24	25	26	27
28	29	30	31			

November

				1	2	3
4	5	6	7	8	9	10
11	12	13	14	15	16	17
18	19	20	21	22	23	24
25	26	27	28	29	30	

December

2	3	4	5	6	7
9	10	11	12	13	14
16	17	18	19	20	21
23	24	25	26	27	28
30	31				

C

January

S	M	T	W	T	F	S
	1	2	3	4	5	6
7	8	9	10	11	12	13
14	15	16	17	18	19	20
21	22	23	24	25	26	27
28	29	30	31			

February

S	M	T	W	T	F	S
				1	2	3
4	5	6	7	8	9	10
11	12	13	14	15	16	17
18	19	20	21	22	23	24
25	26	27	28			

March

S	M	T	W	T	F	S
				1	2	3
4	5	6	7	8	9	10
11	12	13	14	15	16	17
18	19	20	21	22	23	24
25	26	27	28	29	30	31

April

S	M	T	W	T	F	S
1	2	3	4	5	6	7
8	9	10	11	12	13	14
15	16	17	18	19	20	21
22	23	24	25	26	27	28
29	30					

May

		1	2	3	4	5
6	7	8	9	10	11	12
13	14	15	16	17	18	19
20	21	22	23	24	25	26
27	28	29	30	31		

June

					1	2
3	4	5	6	7	8	9
10	11	12	13	14	15	16
17	18	19	20	21	22	23
24	25	26	27	28	29	30

July

1	2	3	4	5	6	7
8	9	10	11	12	13	14
15	16	17	18	19	20	21
22	23	24	25	26	27	28
29	30	31				

August

			1	2	3	4
5	6	7	8	9	10	11
12	13	14	15	16	17	18
19	20	21	22	23	24	25
26	27	28	29	30	31	

September

						1
2	3	4	5	6	7	8
9	10	11	12	13	14	15
16	17	18	19	20	21	22
23	24	25	26	27	28	29
30						

October

	1	2	3	4	5	6
7	8	9	10	11	12	13
14	15	16	17	18	19	20
21	22	23	24	25	26	27
28	29	30	31			

November

				1	2	3
4	5	6	7	8	9	10
11	12	13	14	15	16	17
18	19	20	21	22	23	24
25	26	27	28	29	30	

December

						1
2	3	4	5	6	7	8
9	10	11	12	13	14	15
16	17	18	19	20	21	22
23	24	25	26	27	28	29
30	31					

D (leap year)

January

S	M	T	W	T	F	S
	1	2	3	4	5	6
7	8	9	10	11	12	13
14	15	16	17	18	19	20
21	22	23	24	25	26	27
28	29	30	31			

February

S	M	T	W	T	F	S
				1	2	3
4	5	6	7	8	9	10
11	12	13	14	15	16	17
18	19	20	21	22	23	24
25	26	27	28	29		

March

S	M	T	W	T	F	S
					1	2
3	4	5	6	7	8	9
10	11	12	13	14	15	16
17	18	19	20	21	22	23
24	25	26	27	28	29	30
31						

April

S	M	T	W	T	F
	1	2	3	4	5
7	8	9	10	11	12
14	15	16	17	18	19
21	22	23	24	25	26
28	29	30			

May

			1	2	3	4
5	6	7	8	9	10	11
12	13	14	15	16	17	18
19	20	21	22	23	24	25
26	27	28	29	30	31	

June

						1
2	3	4	5	6	7	8
9	10	11	12	13	14	15
16	17	18	19	20	21	22
23	24	25	26	27	28	29
30						

July

	1	2	3	4	5	6
7	8	9	10	11	12	13
14	15	16	17	18	19	20
21	22	23	24	25	26	27
28	29	30	31			

August

				1	2
4	5	6	7	8	9
11	12	13	14	15	16
18	19	20	21	22	23
25	26	27	28	29	30

September

1	2	3	4	5	6	7
8	9	10	11	12	13	14
15	16	17	18	19	20	21
22	23	24	25	26	27	28
29	30					

October

		1	2	3	4	5
6	7	8	9	10	11	12
13	14	15	16	17	18	19
20	21	22	23	24	25	26
27	28	29	30	31		

November

					1	2
3	4	5	6	7	8	9
10	11	12	13	14	15	16
17	18	19	20	21	22	23
24	25	26	27	28	29	30

December

1	2	3	4	5	6
8	9	10	11	12	13
15	16	17	18	19	20
22	23	24	25	26	27
29	30	31			

E

January

S	M	T	W	T	F	S
		1	2	3	4	5
6	7	8	9	10	11	12
13	14	15	16	17	18	19
20	21	22	23	24	25	26
27	28	29	30	31		

February

S	M	T	W	T	F	S
					1	2
3	4	5	6	7	8	9
10	11	12	13	14	15	16
17	18	19	20	21	22	23
24	25	26	27	28		

March

S	M	T	W	T	F	S
					1	2
3	4	5	6	7	8	9
10	11	12	13	14	15	16
17	18	19	20	21	22	23
24	25	26	27	28	29	30
31						

April

S	M	T	W	T	F	S
	1	2	3	4	5	6
7	8	9	10	11	12	13
14	15	16	17	18	19	20
21	22	23	24	25	26	27
28	29	30				

May

			1	2	3	4
5	6	7	8	9	10	11
12	13	14	15	16	17	18
19	20	21	22	23	24	25
26	27	28	29	30	31	

June

						1
2	3	4	5	6	7	8
9	10	11	12	13	14	15
16	17	18	19	20	21	22
23	24	25	26	27	28	29
30						

July

	1	2	3	4	5	6
7	8	9	10	11	12	13
14	15	16	17	18	19	20
21	22	23	24	25	26	27
28	29	30	31			

August

				1	2	3
4	5	6	7	8	9	10
11	12	13	14	15	16	17
18	19	20	21	22	23	24
25	26	27	28	29	30	31

September

1	2	3	4	5	6	7
8	9	10	11	12	13	14
15	16	17	18	19	20	21
22	23	24	25	26	27	28
29	30					

October

		1	2	3	4	5
6	7	8	9	10	11	12
13	14	15	16	17	18	19
20	21	22	23	24	25	26
27	28	29	30	31		

November

					1	2
3	4	5	6	7	8	9
10	11	12	13	14	15	16
17	18	19	20	21	22	23
24	25	26	27	28	29	30

December

1	2	3	4	5	6	7
8	9	10	11	12	13	14
15	16	17	18	19	20	21
22	23	24	25	26	27	28
29	30	31				

F (leap year)

January

S	M	T	W	T	F	S
		1	2	3	4	5
6	7	8	9	10	11	12
13	14	15	16	17	18	19
20	21	22	23	24	25	26
27	28	29	30	31		

February

S	M	T	W	T	F	S
					1	2
3	4	5	6	7	8	9
10	11	12	13	14	15	16
17	18	19	20	21	22	23
24	25	26	27	28	29	

March

S	M	T	W	T	F	S
						1
2	3	4	5	6	7	8
9	10	11	12	13	14	15
16	17	18	19	20	21	22
23	24	25	26	27	28	29
30	31					

April

S	M	T	W	T	F
		1	2	3	4
6	7	8	9	10	11
13	14	15	16	17	18
20	21	22	23	24	25
27	28	29	30		

May

				1	2	3
4	5	6	7	8	9	10
11	12	13	14	15	16	17
18	19	20	21	22	23	24
25	26	27	28	29	30	31

June

1	2	3	4	5	6	7
8	9	10	11	12	13	14
15	16	17	18	19	20	21
22	23	24	25	26	27	28
29	30					

July

		1	2	3	4	5
6	7	8	9	10	11	12
13	14	15	16	17	18	19
20	21	22	23	24	25	26
27	28	29	30	31		

August

					1
3	4	5	6	7	8
10	11	12	13	14	15
17	18	19	20	21	22
24	25	26	27	28	29
31					

September

	1	2	3	4	5	6
7	8	9	10	11	12	13
14	15	16	17	18	19	20
21	22	23	24	25	26	27
28	29	30				

October

			1	2	3	4
5	6	7	8	9	10	11
12	13	14	15	16	17	18
19	20	21	22	23	24	25
26	27	28	29	30	31	

November

						1
2	3	4	5	6	7	8
9	10	11	12	13	14	15
16	17	18	19	20	21	22
23	24	25	26	27	28	29
30						

December

	1	2	3	4	5
7	8	9	10	11	12
14	15	16	17	18	19
21	22	23	24	25	26
28	29	30	31		

PERPETUAL CALENDAR 1801–2000 (cont.)

January

S	M	T	W	T	F	S
			1	2	3	4
5	6	7	8	9	10	11
12	13	14	15	16	17	18
19	20	21	22	23	24	25
26	27	28	29	30	31	

February

S	M	T	W	T	F	S
						1
2	3	4	5	6	7	8
9	10	11	12	13	14	15
16	17	18	19	20	21	22
23	24	25	26	27	28	

March

S	M	T	W	T	F	S
						1
2	3	4	5	6	7	8
9	10	11	12	13	14	15
16	17	18	19	20	21	22
23	24	25	26	27	28	29
30	31					

April

S	M	T	W	T	F	S
		1	2	3	4	5
6	7	8	9	10	11	12
13	14	15	16	17	18	19
20	21	22	23	24	25	26
27	28	29	30			

May

S	M	T	W	T	F	S
				1	2	3
4	5	6	7	8	9	10
11	12	13	14	15	16	17
18	19	20	21	22	23	24
25	26	27	28	29	30	31

June

S	M	T	W	T	F	S
1	2	3	4	5	6	7
8	9	10	11	12	13	14
15	16	17	18	19	20	21
22	23	24	25	26	27	28
29	30					

July

S	M	T	W	T	F	S
		1	2	3	4	5
6	7	8	9	10	11	12
13	14	15	16	17	18	19
20	21	22	23	24	25	26
27	28	29	30	31		

August

S	M	T	W	T	F	S
					1	2
3	4	5	6	7	8	9
10	11	12	13	14	15	16
17	18	19	20	21	22	23
24	25	26	27	28	29	30
31						

September

S	M	T	W	T	F	S
	1	2	3	4	5	6
7	8	9	10	11	12	13
14	15	16	17	18	19	20
21	22	23	24	25	26	27
28	29	30				

October

S	M	T	W	T	F	S
			1	2	3	4
5	6	7	8	9	10	11
12	13	14	15	16	17	18
19	20	21	22	23	24	25
26	27	28	29	30	31	

November

S	M	T	W	T	F	S
						1
2	3	4	5	6	7	8
9	10	11	12	13	14	15
16	17	18	19	20	21	22
23	24	25	26	27	28	29
30						

December

S	M	T	W	T	F	S
	1	2	3	4	5	6
7	8	9	10	11	12	13
14	15	16	17	18	19	20
21	22	23	24	25	26	27
28	29	30	31			

H (leap year)

January

S	M	T	W	T	F	S
			1	2	3	4
5	6	7	8	9	10	11
12	13	14	15	16	17	18
19	20	21	22	23	24	25
26	27	28	29	30	31	

February

S	M	T	W	T	F	S
						1
2	3	4	5	6	7	8
9	10	11	12	13	14	15
16	17	18	19	20	21	22
23	24	25	26	27	28	29

March

S	M	T	W	T	F	S
1	2	3	4	5	6	7
8	9	10	11	12	13	14
15	16	17	18	19	20	21
22	23	24	25	26	27	28
29	30	31				

April

S	M	T	W	T	F	S
			1	2	3	4
5	6	7	8	9	10	11
12	13	14	15	16	17	18
19	20	21	22	23	24	25
26	27	28	29	30		

May

S	M	T	W	T	F	S
					1	2
3	4	5	6	7	8	9
10	11	12	13	14	15	16
17	18	19	20	21	22	23
24	25	26	27	28	29	30
31						

June

S	M	T	W	T	F	S
	1	2	3	4	5	6
7	8	9	10	11	12	13
14	15	16	17	18	19	20
21	22	23	24	25	26	27
28	29	30				

July

S	M	T	W	T	F	S
			1	2	3	4
5	6	7	8	9	10	11
12	13	14	15	16	17	18
19	20	21	22	23	24	25
26	27	28	29	30	31	

August

S	M	T	W	T	F	S
						1
2	3	4	5	6	7	8
9	10	11	12	13	14	15
16	17	18	19	20	21	22
23	24	25	26	27	28	29
30	31					

September

S	M	T	W	T	F	S
		1	2	3	4	5
6	7	8	9	10	11	12
13	14	15	16	17	18	19
20	21	22	23	24	25	26
27	28	29	30			

October

S	M	T	W	T	F	S
				1	2	3
4	5	6	7	8	9	10
11	12	13	14	15	16	17
18	19	20	21	22	23	24
25	26	27	28	29	30	31

November

S	M	T	W	T	F	S
1	2	3	4	5	6	7
8	9	10	11	12	13	14
15	16	17	18	19	20	21
22	23	24	25	26	27	28
29	30					

December

S	M	T	W	T	F	S
		1	2	3	4	5
6	7	8	9	10	11	12
13	14	15	16	17	18	19
20	21	22	23	24	25	26
27	28	29	30	31		

January

S	M	T	W	T	F	S
				1	2	3
4	5	6	7	8	9	10
11	12	13	14	15	16	17
18	19	20	21	22	23	24
25	26	27	28	29	30	31

February

S	M	T	W	T	F	S
1	2	3	4	5	6	7
8	9	10	11	12	13	14
15	16	17	18	19	20	21
22	23	24	25	26	27	28

March

S	M	T	W	T	F	S
1	2	3	4	5	6	7
8	9	10	11	12	13	14
15	16	17	18	19	20	21
22	23	24	25	26	27	28
29	30	31				

April

S	M	T	W	T	F	S
			1	2	3	4
5	6	7	8	9	10	11
12	13	14	15	16	17	18
19	20	21	22	23	24	25
26	27	28	29	30		

May

S	M	T	W	T	F	S
					1	2
3	4	5	6	7	8	9
10	11	12	13	14	15	16
17	18	19	20	21	22	23
24	25	26	27	28	29	30
31						

June

S	M	T	W	T	F	S
	1	2	3	4	5	6
7	8	9	10	11	12	13
14	15	16	17	18	19	20
21	22	23	24	25	26	27
28	29	30				

July

S	M	T	W	T	F	S
			1	2	3	4
5	6	7	8	9	10	11
12	13	14	15	16	17	18
19	20	21	22	23	24	25
26	27	28	29	30	31	

August

S	M	T	W	T	F	S
						1
2	3	4	5	6	7	8
9	10	11	12	13	14	15
16	17	18	19	20	21	22
23	24	25	26	27	28	29
30	31					

September

S	M	T	W	T	F	S
		1	2	3	4	5
6	7	8	9	10	11	12
13	14	15	16	17	18	19
20	21	22	23	24	25	26
27	28	29	30			

October

S	M	T	W	T	F	S
				1	2	3
4	5	6	7	8	9	10
11	12	13	14	15	16	17
18	19	20	21	22	23	24
25	26	27	28	29	30	31

November

S	M	T	W	T	F	S
1	2	3	4	5	6	7
8	9	10	11	12	13	14
15	16	17	18	19	20	21
22	23	24	25	26	27	28
29	30					

December

S	M	T	W	T	F	S
		1	2	3	4	5
6	7	8	9	10	11	12
13	14	15	16	17	18	19
20	21	22	23	24	25	26
27	28	29	30	31		

J (leap year)

January

S	M	T	W	T	F	S
				1	2	3
4	5	6	7	8	9	10
11	12	13	14	15	16	17
18	19	20	21	22	23	24
25	26	27	28	29	30	31

February

S	M	T	W	T	F	S
1	2	3	4	5	6	7
8	9	10	11	12	13	14
15	16	17	18	19	20	21
22	23	24	25	26	27	28
29						

March

S	M	T	W	T	F	S
	1	2	3	4	5	6
7	8	9	10	11	12	13
14	15	16	17	18	19	20
21	22	23	24	25	26	27
28	29	30	31			

April

S	M	T	W	T	F	S
				1	2	3
4	5	6	7	8	9	10
11	12	13	14	15	16	17
18	19	20	21	22	23	24
25	26	27	28	29	30	

May

S	M	T	W	T	F	S
						1
2	3	4	5	6	7	8
9	10	11	12	13	14	15
16	17	18	19	20	21	22
23	24	25	26	27	28	29
30	31					

June

S	M	T	W	T	F	S
		1	2	3	4	5
6	7	8	9	10	11	12
13	14	15	16	17	18	19
20	21	22	23	24	25	26
27	28	29	30			

July

S	M	T	W	T	F	S
				1	2	3
4	5	6	7	8	9	10
11	12	13	14	15	16	17
18	19	20	21	22	23	24
25	26	27	28	29	30	31

August

S	M	T	W	T	F	S
1	2	3	4	5	6	7
8	9	10	11	12	13	14
15	16	17	18	19	20	21
22	23	24	25	26	27	28
29	30	31				

September

S	M	T	W	T	F	S
			1	2	3	4
5	6	7	8	9	10	11
12	13	14	15	16	17	18
19	20	21	22	23	24	25
26	27	28	29	30		

October

S	M	T	W	T	F	S
					1	2
3	4	5	6	7	8	9
10	11	12	13	14	15	16
17	18	19	20	21	22	23
24	25	26	27	28	29	30
31						

November

S	M	T	W	T	F	S
	1	2	3	4	5	6
7	8	9	10	11	12	13
14	15	16	17	18	19	20
21	22	23	24	25	26	27
28	29	30				

December

S	M	T	W	T	F	S
			1	2	3	4
5	6	7	8	9	10	11
12	13	14	15	16	17	18
19	20	21	22	23	24	25
26	27	28	29	30	31	

K

January

S	M	T	W	T	F	S
					1	2
3	4	5	6	7	8	9
10	11	12	13	14	15	16
17	18	19	20	21	22	23
24	25	26	27	28	29	30
31						

February

S	M	T	W	T	F	S
	1	2	3	4	5	6
7	8	9	10	11	12	13
14	15	16	17	18	19	20
21	22	23	24	25	26	27
28						

March

S	M	T	W	T	F	S
	1	2	3	4	5	6
7	8	9	10	11	12	13
14	15	16	17	18	19	20
21	22	23	24	25	26	27
28	29	30	31			

April

S	M	T	W	T	F	S
				1	2	3
4	5	6	7	8	9	10
11	12	13	14	15	16	17
18	19	20	21	22	23	24
25	26	27	28	29	30	

May

S	M	T	W	T	F	S
						1
2	3	4	5	6	7	8
9	10	11	12	13	14	15
16	17	18	19	20	21	22
23	24	25	26	27	28	29
30	31					

June

S	M	T	W	T	F	S
		1	2	3	4	5
6	7	8	9	10	11	12
13	14	15	16	17	18	19
20	21	22	23	24	25	26
27	28	29	30			

July

S	M	T	W	T	F	S
				1	2	3
4	5	6	7	8	9	10
11	12	13	14	15	16	17
18	19	20	21	22	23	24
25	26	27	28	29	30	31

August

S	M	T	W	T	F	S
1	2	3	4	5	6	7
8	9	10	11	12	13	14
15	16	17	18	19	20	21
22	23	24	25	26	27	28
29	30	31				

September

S	M	T	W	T	F	S
			1	2	3	4
5	6	7	8	9	10	11
12	13	14	15	16	17	18
19	20	21	22	23	24	25
26	27	28	29	30		

October

S	M	T	W	T	F	S
					1	2
3	4	5	6	7	8	9
10	11	12	13	14	15	16
17	18	19	20	21	22	23
24	25	26	27	28	29	30
31						

November

S	M	T	W	T	F	S
	1	2	3	4	5	6
7	8	9	10	11	12	13
14	15	16	17	18	19	20
21	22	23	24	25	26	27
28	29	30				

December

S	M	T	W	T	F	S
			1	2	3	4
5	6	7	8	9	10	11
12	13	14	15	16	17	18
19	20	21	22	23	24	25
26	27	28	29	30	31	

L (leap year)

January

S	M	T	W	T	F	S
					1	2
3	4	5	6	7	8	9
10	11	12	13	14	15	16
17	18	19	20	21	22	23
24	25	26	27	28	29	30
31						

February

S	M	T	W	T	F	S
	1	2	3	4	5	6
7	8	9	10	11	12	13
14	15	16	17	18	19	20
21	22	23	24	25	26	27
28	29					

March

S	M	T	W	T	F	S
		1	2	3	4	5
6	7	8	9	10	11	12
13	14	15	16	17	18	19
20	21	22	23	24	25	26
27	28	29	30	31		

April

S	M	T	W	T	F	S
					1	2
3	4	5	6	7	8	9
10	11	12	13	14	15	16
17	18	19	20	21	22	23
24	25	26	27	28	29	30

May

S	M	T	W	T	F	S
1	2	3	4	5	6	7
8	9	10	11	12	13	14
15	16	17	18	19	20	21
22	23	24	25	26	27	28
29	30	31				

June

S	M	T	W	T	F	S
			1	2	3	4
5	6	7	8	9	10	11
12	13	14	15	16	17	18
19	20	21	22	23	24	25
26	27	28	29	30		

July

S	M	T	W	T	F	S
					1	2
3	4	5	6	7	8	9
10	11	12	13	14	15	16
17	18	19	20	21	22	23
24	25	26	27	28	29	30
31						

August

S	M	T	W	T	F	S
	1	2	3	4	5	6
7	8	9	10	11	12	13
14	15	16	17	18	19	20
21	22	23	24	25	26	27
28	29	30	31			

September

S	M	T	W	T	F	S
				1	2	3
4	5	6	7	8	9	10
11	12	13	14	15	16	17
18	19	20	21	22	23	24
25	26	27	28	29	30	

October

S	M	T	W	T	F	S
						1
2	3	4	5	6	7	8
9	10	11	12	13	14	15
16	17	18	19	20	21	22
23	24	25	26	27	28	29
30	31					

November

S	M	T	W	T	F	S
		1	2	3	4	5
6	7	8	9	10	11	12
13	14	15	16	17	18	19
20	21	22	23	24	25	26
27	28	29	30			

December

S	M	T	W	T	F	S
				1	2	3
4	5	6	7	8	9	10
11	12	13	14	15	16	17
18	19	20	21	22	23	24
25	26	27	28	29	30	31

M

January

S	M	T	W	T	F	S
						1
2	3	4	5	6	7	8
9	10	11	12	13	14	15
16	17	18	19	20	21	22
23	24	25	26	27	28	29
30	31					

February

S	M	T	W	T	F	S
		1	2	3	4	5
6	7	8	9	10	11	12
13	14	15	16	17	18	19
20	21	22	23	24	25	26
27	28					

March

S	M	T	W	T	F	S
		1	2	3	4	5
6	7	8	9	10	11	12
13	14	15	16	17	18	19
20	21	22	23	24	25	26
27	28	29	30	31		

April

S	M	T	W	T	F	S
					1	2
3	4	5	6	7	8	9
10	11	12	13	14	15	16
17	18	19	20	21	22	23
24	25	26	27	28	29	30

May

S	M	T	W	T	F	S
1	2	3	4	5	6	7
8	9	10	11	12	13	14
15	16	17	18	19	20	21
22	23	24	25	26	27	28
29	30	31				

June

S	M	T	W	T	F	S
			1	2	3	4
5	6	7	8	9	10	11
12	13	14	15	16	17	18
19	20	21	22	23	24	25
26	27	28	29	30		

July

S	M	T	W	T	F	S
					1	2
3	4	5	6	7	8	9
10	11	12	13	14	15	16
17	18	19	20	21	22	23
24	25	26	27	28	29	30
31						

August

S	M	T	W	T	F	S
	1	2	3	4	5	6
7	8	9	10	11	12	13
14	15	16	17	18	19	20
21	22	23	24	25	26	27
28	29	30	31			

September

S	M	T	W	T	F	S
				1	2	3
4	5	6	7	8	9	10
11	12	13	14	15	16	17
18	19	20	21	22	23	24
25	26	27	28	29	30	

October

S	M	T	W	T	F	S
						1
2	3	4	5	6	7	8
9	10	11	12	13	14	15
16	17	18	19	20	21	22
23	24	25	26	27	28	29
30	31					

November

S	M	T	W	T	F	S
		1	2	3	4	5
6	7	8	9	10	11	12
13	14	15	16	17	18	19
20	21	22	23	24	25	26
27	28	29	30			

December

S	M	T	W	T	F	S
				1	2	3
4	5	6	7	8	9	10
11	12	13	14	15	16	17
18	19	20	21	22	23	24
25	26	27	28	29	30	31

N (leap year)

January

S	M	T	W	T	F	S
						1
2	3	4	5	6	7	8
9	10	11	12	13	14	15
16	17	18	19	20	21	22
23	24	25	26	27	28	29
30	31					

February

S	M	T	W	T	F	S
		1	2	3	4	5
6	7	8	9	10	11	12
13	14	15	16	17	18	19
20	21	22	23	24	25	26
27	28	29				

March

S	M	T	W	T	F	S
			1	2	3	4
5	6	7	8	9	10	11
12	13	14	15	16	17	18
19	20	21	22	23	24	25
26	27	28	29	30	31	

April

S	M	T	W	T	F	S
						1
2	3	4	5	6	7	8
9	10	11	12	13	14	15
16	17	18	19	20	21	22
23	24	25	26	27	28	29
30						

May

S	M	T	W	T	F	S
	1	2	3	4	5	6
7	8	9	10	11	12	13
14	15	16	17	18	19	20
21	22	23	24	25	26	27
28	29	30	31			

June

S	M	T	W	T	F	S
				1	2	3
4	5	6	7	8	9	10
11	12	13	14	15	16	17
18	19	20	21	22	23	24
25	26	27	28	29	30	

July

S	M	T	W	T	F	S
						1
2	3	4	5	6	7	8
9	10	11	12	13	14	15
16	17	18	19	20	21	22
23	24	25	26	27	28	29
30	31					

August

S	M	T	W	T	F	S
		1	2	3	4	5
6	7	8	9	10	11	12
13	14	15	16	17	18	19
20	21	22	23	24	25	26
27	28	29	30	31		

September

S	M	T	W	T	F	S
					1	2
3	4	5	6	7	8	9
10	11	12	13	14	15	16
17	18	19	20	21	22	23
24	25	26	27	28	29	30

October

S	M	T	W	T	F	S
1	2	3	4	5	6	7
8	9	10	11	12	13	14
15	16	17	18	19	20	21
22	23	24	25	26	27	28
29	30	31				

November

S	M	T	W	T	F	S
			1	2	3	4
5	6	7	8	9	10	11
12	13	14	15	16	17	18
19	20	21	22	23	24	25
26	27	28	29	30		

December

S	M	T	W	T	F	S
					1	2
3	4	5	6	7	8	9
10	11	12	13	14	15	16
17	18	19	20	21	22	23
24	25	26	27	28	29	30
31						

NATIONS OF THE WORLD

GENERAL DATA

For detailed information about each country, see the entries and maps located alphabetically in the main body of the encyclopedia. All countries are also shown on the political map of the world in the colour section, Plates VI–VII

In the case of countries that do not use the Roman alphabet (such as the Arabic countries), there is variation in the spelling of names and currencies, depending on the system of transliteration used.

Where more than one language is shown within a country, the status of th languages may not be equal. Some languages have a 'semi-official' status, o are used for a restricted set of purposes, such as trade or tourism.

Population census estimates are for 1990 or later.

English name	Local name	Official name (in English)	Capital (English name in parentheses)	Official language(s)	Currency	Populatio
Afghanistan	Afghānestān	Republic of Afghanistan	Kābul	Dari, Pushtu	1 Afghani (Af) = 100 puls	15592000
Albania	Shqīpëri	Republic of Albania	Tiranë (Tirana)	Albanian	1 Lek (L) = 100 qintars	326200
Algeria	Al-Jazā'ir (Arabic) Algérie (French)	Democratic and Popular Republic of Algeria	El Djazair (Algiers)	Arabic	1 Algerian Dinar (AD, DA) = 100 centimes	2470000
Andorra	Andorra	Principality of Andorra; the Valleys of Andorra	Andorra La Vella	Catalan, French	French Franc, Spanish Peseta	5100
Angola	Angola	People's Republic of Angola	Luanda	Portuguese	1 New Kwanza (kw, kz) = 100 lweis	1000200
Antigua and Barbuda	Antigua and Barbuda	Antigua and Barbuda	St John's	English	1 East Caribbean Dollar (EC$) = 100 cents	8060
Argentina	Argentina	Argentine Republic	Buenos Aires	Spanish	1 Austral (₳) = 1000 pesos	3288000
Australia	Australia	Commonwealth of Australia	Canberra	English	1 Australian Dollar ($A) = 100 cents	1707300
Austria	Österreich	Republic of Austria	Vienna	German	1 Schilling (S, Sch) = 100 Groschen	762300
Bahamas	Bahamas	Commonwealth of the Bahamas	Nassau	English	1 Bahamian Dollar (BA$, B$) = 100 cents	25300
Bahrain	Al-Baḥrayn	State of Bahrain	Al-Manāmah (Manama)	Arabic	1 Bahrain Dinar (BD) = 1000 fils	50300
Bangladesh	Bangladesh	People's Republic of Bangladesh	Dhaka (Dacca)	Bengali	1 Taka (TK) = 100 poisha	10799214
Barbados	Barbados	Barbados	Bridgetown	English	1 Barbados Dollar (Bds$) = 100 cents	25700
Belgium	Belgique (French) België (Flemish)	Kingdom of Belgium	Bruxelles (Brussels)	Flemish, French, German	1 Belgian Franc (BFr) = 100 centimes	995800
Belize	Belize	Belize	Belmopan	English	1 Belize Dollar (Bz$) = 100 cents	18900
Benin	Bénin	Republic of Benin	Porto-Novo	French	1 CFA Franc (CFAFr) = 100 centimes	474100
Bhutan	Druk-Yul	Kingdom of Bhutan	Thimbu/Thimphu	Dzongkha	1 Ngultrum (Nu) = 100 chetrum	144200
Bolivia	Bolivia	Republic of Bolivia	La Paz/Sucre	Spanish Aymara, Quechua	1 Boliviano (Bs) = 100 centavos	732200
Botswana	Botswana	Republic of Botswana	Gaborone	English, seTswana	1 Pula (P, Pu) = 100 thebes	129500
Brazil	Brasil	Federative Republic of Brazil	Brasília	Portuguese	1 Cruzeiro (Cr$) = 100 centavos	15036800
Brunei	Brunei	State of Brunei, Abode of Peace	Bandar Seri Begawan	Malay, English	1 Brunei Dollar (Br$) = 100 cents	25900
Bulgaria	Bălgarija	Republic of Bulgaria	Sofija (Sofia)	Bulgarian	1 Lev (Lv) = 100 stotinki	899700
Burkina Faso	Burkina Faso	Burkina Faso	Ouagadougou	French	1 CFA Franc (CFAFr) = 100 centimes	877600
Burma *see* Myanmar						
Burundi	Burundi	Republic of Burundi	Bujumbura	French, (Ki) Rundi	1 Burundi Franc (BuFr, FBu) = 100 centimes	545000
Cambodia	Cambodia	State of Cambodia	Phnum Pénh (Phnom Penh)	Khmer	1 Riel (CRl) = 100 sen	859200
Cameroon	Cameroun	Republic of Cameroon	Yaoundé	English, French	1 CFA Franc (CFAFr) = 100 centimes	1190000
Canada	Canada	Canada	Ottawa	English, French	1 Canadian Dollar (C$, Can$) = 100 cents	2662000
Cape Verde	Cabo Verde	Republic of Cape Verde	Praia	Portuguese	1 Escudo (CVEsc) = 100 centavos	339000
Central African Republic	République Centrafricaine	Central African Republic	Bangui	French	1 CFA Franc (CFAFr) = 100 centimes	287500
Chad	Tchad	Republic of Chad	N'Djamena	Arabic, French	1 CFA Franc (CFAFr) = 100 centimes	567800
Chile	Chile	Republic of Chile	Santiago	Spanish	1 Chilean Peso (Ch$) = 100 centavos	1317300

nglish name	Local name	Official name (in English)	Capital (English name in parentheses)	Official language(s)	Currency	Population
hina	Zhonghua	People's Republic of China	Beijing/Peking	Mandarin Chinese	1 Renminbi Yuan (RMBY, $, Y) = 10 jiao = 100 fen	1133682501
olombia	Colombia	Republic of Colombia	Bogotá	Spanish	1 Colombian Peso (Col$) = 100 centavos	32978000
omoros	Comores	Federal Islamic Republic of the Comoros	Moroni	Arabic, French	1 Comorian Franc (CFr) = 100 centimes	463000
ongo	Congo	Republic of Congo	Brazzaville	French	1 CFA Franc (CFAFr) = 100 centimes	2326000
osta Rica	Costa Rica	Republic of Costa Rica	San José	Spanish	1 Costa Rican Colón (CR₡) = 100 céntimos	3015000
ôte d'Ivoire (Ivory Coast)	Côte d'Ivoire	Republic of Côte d'Ivoire	Abidjan/ Yamoussoukro	French	1 CFA Franc (CFAFr) = 100 centimes	12657000
uba	Cuba	Republic of Cuba	La Habana (Havana)	Spanish	1 Cuban Peso (Cub$) = 100 centavos	10603000
yprus	Kipros (Greek) Kibris (Turkish)	Republic of Cyprus	Levkosia (Nicosia)	Greek, Turkish	1 Cyprus Pound (£C) = 100 cents	568000
zechoslovakia	Československo	Czech and Slovak Federative Republic	Praha (Prague)	Czech, Slovak	1 Koruna (Kčs) = 100 haler	15664000
enmark	Danmark	Kingdom of Denmark	København (Copenhagen)	Danish	1 Danish Krone (Dkr) = 100 øre	5139000
jibouti	Djibouti	Republic of Djibouti	Djibouti	Arabic, French	1 Djibouti Franc (DF, DjFr) = 100 centimes	530000
ominica	Dominica	Commonwealth of Dominica	Roseau	English	1 East Caribbean Dollar (EC$) = 100 cents	82200
ominican Republic	República Dominicana	Dominican Republic	Santo Domingo	Spanish	1 Dominican Peso (RD$, DR$) = 100 centavos	7170000
cuador	Ecuador	Republic of Ecuador	Quito	Spanish	1 Sucre (Su, S/.) = 100 centavos	10780000
gypt	Misr	Arab Republic of Egypt	Al-Qāhirah (Cairo)	Arabic	1 Egyptian Pound (E£, LE) = 100 piastres	53170000
l Salvador	El Salvador	Republic of El Salvador	San Salvador	Spanish	1 Colón (ES₡) = 100 centavos	5220000
quatorial Guinea	Guinea Ecuatorial	Republic of Equatorial Guinea	Malabo	Spanish	1 CFA Franc (CFAFr) = 100 centimes	350000
stonia	Eesti (Estonian) Estonskaya (Russian)	Republic of Estonia	Tallinn	Estonian, Russian	1 Rouble (R) = 100 kopecks (new currency planned: kroon)	1600000
thiopia	Ityopiya	People's Democratic Republic of Ethiopia	Adis Abeba (Addis Ababa)	Amharic	1 Ethiopian Birr (Br) = 100 cents	50340000
iji	Fiji	Sovereign Democratic Republic of Fiji	Suva	English	1 Fiji Dollar (F$) = 100 cents	740000
inland	Suomi (Finnish) Finland (Swedish)	Republic of Finland	Helsinki Helsingfors (Swedish)	Finnish, Swedish	1 Markka (FMk) = 100 penni	4978000
rance	France	French Republic	Paris	French	1 French Franc (Fr) = 100 centimes	56647000
abon	Gabon	Gabonese Republic	Libreville	French	1 CFA Franc (CFAFr) = 100 centimes	1170000
ambia, The	Gambia	Republic of the Gambia	Banjul	English	1 Dalasi (D, Di) = 100 butut	860000
ermany	Bundesrepublik Deutschland	Federal Republic of Germany	Berlin	German	1 Deutsche Mark (DM) = 100 Pfennige	79112831
hana	Ghana	Republic of Ghana	Accra	English	1 Cedi (₵) = 100 pesewas	15020000
reece	Ellás	Hellenic Republic	Athínai (Athens)	Greek	1 Drachma (Dr) = 100 leptae	10038000
reenland	Grønland (Danish) Kalaallit Nunaat	Greenland	Nuuk (Godthåb)	Danish, Greenlandic	1 Danish Krone (DKr) = 100 øre	55900
renada	Grenada	Grenada	St George's	English	1 East Caribbean Dollar (EC$) = 100 cents	101000
uatemala	Guatemala	Republic of Guatemala	Guatemala City	Spanish	1 Quetzal (Q) = 100 centavos	9197000
uinea	Guinée	Republic of Guinea	Conakry	French	1 Guinean Franc (GFr) = 100 cauris	6876000
uinea-Bissau	Guiné-Bissau	Republic of Guinea-Bissau	Bissau	Portuguese	1 Guinea-Bissau Peso (GBP, PG) = 100 centavos	973000
uyana	Guyana	Co-operative Republic of Guyana	Georgetown	English	1 Guyana Dollar (G$) = 100 cents	756000
Haiti	Haïti	Republic of Haiti	Port-au-Prince	French	1 Gourde (G, Gde) = 100 centimes	5862000
Holland *see* Netherlands, The						
Honduras	Honduras	Republic of Honduras	Tegucigalpa	Spanish	1 Lempira (L, La) = 100 centavos	4674000
Hong Kong	Hsiang Kang (Chinese) Hong Kong (English)	Hong Kong	*none*	English, Chinese	1 Hong Kong Dollar (HK$) = 100 cents	5841000
Hungary	Magyarország	Republic of Hungary	Budapest	Hungarian	1 Forint (Ft) = 100 fillér	10437000
celand	Ísland	Republic of Iceland	Reykjavik	Icelandic	1 Króna (IKr, ISK) = 100 aurar	254000
ndia	Bhārat (Hindi)	Republic of India	New Delhi	Hindi, English	1 Indian Rupee (Re, Rs) = 100 paisa	843930861 (91)
ndonesia	Indonesia	Republic of Indonesia	Jakarta	Bahasa Indonesia	1 Rupiah (Rp) = 100 sen	180763000
ran	Īrān	Islamic Republic of Iran	Tehrān (Tehran)	Farsi	1 Iranian Rial (Rls, RI) = 100 dinars	56293000
raq	Al-ʿIrāq	Republic of Iraq	Baghdād (Baghdad)	Arabic	1 Iraqi Dinar (ID) = 1000 fils	17754000

English name	Local name	Official name (in English)	Capital (English name in parentheses)	Official language(s)	Currency	Populatio
Ireland	Eire (Gaelic) Ireland (English)	Ireland	Baile Átha Cliath (Dublin)	Irish, English	1 Irish Pound/Punt (I£, IR£) = 100 new pence	350900
Israel	Yisra'el (Hebrew) Isrā'īl (Arabic)	State of Israel	Yerushalayim (Jerusalem)	Hebrew, Arabic	1 New Israeli Shekel (NIS) = 100 agorot	482200
Italy	Italia	Italian Republic	Roma (Rome)	Italian	1 Italian Lira (L, Lit) = 100 centesimi	5751200
Ivory Coast *see* Côte d'Ivoire						
Jamaica	Jamaica	Jamaica	Kingston	English	1 Jamaican Dollar (J$) = 100 cents	239100
Japan	Nihon	Japan	Tōkyō (Tokyo)	Japanese	1 Yen (Y,¥) = 100 sen	12369200
Jordan	Al'Urdunn	Hashemite Kingdom of Jordan	'Ammān (Amman)	Arabic	1 Jordan Dinar = 1000 fils	316900
Jugoslavia *see* Yugoslavia						
Kampuchea *see* Cambodia						
Kenya	Kenya	Republic of Kenya	Nairobi	(Ki) Swahili, English	1 Kenyan shilling (KSh) = 100 cents	2487200
Kiribati	Kiribati	Republic of Kiribati	Bairiki	English	1 Australian Dollar ($A) = 100 cents	7110
Korea, North	Chosōn Minjujuŭi In'min Konghwaguk	Democratic People's Republic of Korea	P'yŏngyang (Pyongyang)	Korean	1 Won (NKW) = 100 chon	2293700
Korea, South	Taehan-Min'guk	Republic of Korea	Sŏul (Seoul)	Korean	1 Won (W) = 100 chon	4279500
Kuwait	Al-Kuwayt	State of Kuwait	Al-Kuwayt (Kuwait City)	Arabic	1 Kuwaiti Dinar (KD) = 1000 fils	201400
Laos	Lao	Lao People's Democratic Republic	Viangchan (Vientiane)	Lao	1 Kip (Kp) = 100 at	402400
Latvia	Latvija (Latvian) Latviskaya (Russian)	Republic of Latvia	Riga	Latvian, Russian	1 Rouble (R) = 100 kopecks (new currency planned: lat)	270000
Lebanon	Al-Lubnān	Republic of Lebanon	Bayrūt (Beirut)	Arabic	1 Lebanese Pound/Livre (LL, £L) = 100 piastres	296500
Lesotho	Lesoto	Kingdom of Lesotho	Maseru	English, (se)Sotho	1 Loti (*plural* Maloti) (M, LSM) = 100 lisente	176000
Liberia	Liberia	Republic of Liberia	Monrovia	English	1 Liberian Dollar (L$) = 100 cents	259500
Libya	Lībiyā	Socialist People's Libyan Arab Jamahiriya	Tarābulus (Tripoli)	Arabic	1 Libyan Dinar (LD) = 1000 dirhams	420600
Liechtenstein	Liechtenstein	Principality of Liechtenstein	Vaduz	German	1 Swiss Franc (SFr, SwF) = 100 centimes	2870
Lithuania	Lietuva (Lithuanian) Litovskaya (Russian)	Republic of Lithuania	Vilnius	Lithuanian, Russian	1 Rouble (R) = 100 kopecks (new currency planned: litas)	370000
Luxembourg	Lëtzebuerg (Letz.) Luxembourg (Fr.) Luxemburg (Ger.)	Grand Duchy of Luxembourg	Luxembourg	French, German, Letzebuergesch	1 Luxembourg Franc (LFr) = 100 centimes	37900
Madagascar	Madagasikara	Democratic Republic of Madagascar	Antananarivo	Malagasy, French	1 Madagascar Franc (FMG, MgFr) = 100 centimes	1198000
Malawi	Malaŵi (Chewa) Malawi (English)	Republic of Malaŵi	Lilongwe	(chi)Chewa, English	1 Kwacha (MK) = 100 tambala	883000
Malaysia	Malaysia	Malaysia	Kuala Lumpur	Malay	1 Malaysian Dollar/Ringgit (M$) = 100 cents	1788600
Maldives	Maldives Divehi Jumhuriya	Republic of Maldives	Male	Divehi	1 Rufiyaa (MRf, Rf) = 100 laaris	21400
Mali	Mali	Republic of Mali	Bamako	French	1 CFA Franc (CFAFr) = 100 centimes	815000
Malta	Malta	Republic of Malta	Valletta	English, Maltese	1 Maltese Lira (LM) = 100 cents	35300
Mauritania	Mauritanie (French) Mūrītāniyā (Arabic)	Islamic Republic of Mauritania	Nouakchott	Arabic	1 Ouguiya (U, UM) = 5 khoums	199000
Mauritius	Mauritius	Mauritius	Port Louis	English	1 Mauritian Rupee (MR, MauRe) = 100 cents	108000
Mexico	México	United Mexican States	Ciudad de México (Mexico City)	Spanish	1 Mexican Peso (Mex$) = 100 centavos	8188500
Monaco	Monaco	Principality of Monaco	Monaco	French	1 French Franc (F) = 100 centimes	2930
Mongolia	Mongol Ard Uls	Mongolian People's Republic	Ulaanbaatar (Ulan Bator)	Khalka	1 Tugrik (Tug) = 100 möngö	211600
Morocco	Al-Magrib	Kingdom of Morocco	Rabat	Arabic	1 Dirham (DH) = 100 centimes	2511300
Mozambique	Moçambique	Republic of Mozambique	Maputo	Portuguese	1 Metical (Mt, MZM) = 100 centavos	1569600
Myanmar	Myanma Naingngandaw Pyidaungsu	Union of Myanmar	Rangoon	Burmese	1 Kyat (K) = 100 pyas	4167500
Namibia	Namibia	Republic of Namibia	Windhoek	Afrikaans, English	1 South African Rand (R)=100 cents	130000
Nauru	Naeoro (Nauruan) Nauru (English)	Republic of Nauru	Yaren District	Nauruan, English	1 Australian Dollar ($A) = 100 cents	900
Nepal	Nepāl	Kingdom of Nepal	Kathmandu	Nepali	1 Nepalese Rupee (NRp, NRs) = 100 paise/pice	1891000
Netherlands, The	Nederland	Kingdom of the Netherlands	Amsterdam/ 's-Gravenhage (The Hague)	Dutch	1 Dutch Guilder (Gld)/Florin (f) = 100 cents	1493400

English name	Local name	Official name (in English)	Capital (English name in parentheses)	Official language(s)	Currency	Population
New Zealand	New Zealand Aotearoa (Maori)	New Zealand	Wellington	English, Maori	1 New Zealand Dollar ($NZ) = 100 cents	3389000
Nicaragua	Nicaragua	Republic of Nicaragua	Managua	Spanish	1 New Córdoba (C$) = 100 centavos	3871000
Niger	Niger	Republic of Niger	Niamey	French	1 CFA Franc (CFAFr) = 100 centimes	7779000
Nigeria	Nigeria	Federal Republic of Nigeria	Lagos	English	1 Naira (N, ₦) = 100 kobo	119812000
Norway	Norge	Kingdom of Norway	Oslo	Norwegian	1 Norwegian Krone (NKr) = 100 øre	4246000
Oman	'Umān	Sultanate of Oman	Masqaṭ (Muscat)	Arabic	1 Rial Omani (RO) = 1000 baizas	1468000
Pakistan	Pākistān	Islamic Republic of Pakistan	Islāmābād (Islamabad)	Urdu	1 Pakistan Rupee (PRs, Rp) = 100 paisa	122600000
Panama	Panamá	Republic of Panama	Panamá (Panama City)	Spanish	1 Balboa (B, Ba) = 100 cents	2418000
Papua New Guinea	Papua New Guinea	Independent State of Papua New Guinea	Port Moresby	English, Tok Pisin, Hi-i Motu	1 Kina (K) = 100 toea	3671900
Paraguay	Paraguay	Republic of Paraguay	Asunción	Spanish	1 Guaraní (G/) = 100 céntimos	4279000
Peru	Perú	Republic of Peru	Lima	Spanish, Quechua	1 New Sol = 100 centavos	22332000
Philippines	Filipinas	Republic of the Philippines	Manila	English, Pilipino	1 Philippine peso (PP, –P) = 100 centavos	61480000
Poland	Polska	Polish Republic	Warszawa (Warsaw)	Polish	1 Złoty (Zl) = 100 groszy	38070000
Portugal	Portugal	Republic of Portugal	Lisboa (Lisbon)	Portuguese	1 Escudo (Esc) = 100 centavos	10388000
Puerto Rico	Puerto Rico	Commonwealth of Puerto Rico	San Juan	Spanish, English	1 US Dollar (US$) = 100 cents	3336000
Qatar	Qaṭar	State of Qatar	Ad-Dawḥah (Doha)	Arabic	1 Qatar Riyal (QR) = 100 dirhams	445000
Romania	România	Republic of Romania	Bucureşti (Bucharest)	Romanian	1 Leu (*plural* lei) = 100 bani	23265000
Russia	Rossiyskaya	Russian Federation	Moskva (Moscow)	Russian	1 Rouble (R) = 100 kopecks	147400000
Rwanda	Rwanda	Republic of Rwanda	Kigali	(Kinya) Rwanda, French	1 Rwanda Franc (RF) = 100 centimes	7232000
Saint Kitts and Nevis	Saint Christopher/Kitts and Nevis	Federation of Saint Christopher and Nevis	Basseterre	English	1 East Caribbean Dollar (EC) = 100 cents	44100
Saint Lucia	Saint Lucia	Saint Lucia	Castries	English	1 East Caribbean Dollar (EC$) = 100 cents	151000
Saint Vincent and the Grenadines	Saint Vincent and the Grenadines	Saint Vincent and the Grenadines	Kingstown	English	1 East Caribbean Dollar (EC$) = 100 cents	115000
San Marino	San Marino	Most Serene Republic of San Marino	San Marino	Italian	1 Italian Lira (L, Lit) = 100 centesimi	23000
São Tomé and Príncipe	São Tomé e Príncipe	Democratic Republic of São Tomé and Príncipe	São Tomé	Portuguese	1 Dobra (Db) = 100 centimos	121000
Saudi Arabia	Al-'Arabīyah as Sa'ūdīyah	Kingdom of Saudi Arabia	Ar-Riyāḍ (Riyadh)	Arabic	1 Saudi Arabian Riyal (SAR, SRls) = 100 halalah	14131000
Senegal	Sénégal	Republic of Senegal	Dakar	French	1 CFA Franc (CFAFr) = 100 centimes	7277000
Seychelles	Seychelles	Republic of Seychelles	Victoria	Creole French, English, French	1 Seychelles Rupee (SR) = 100 cents	68700
Sierra Leone	Sierra Leone	Republic of Sierra Leone	Freetown	English	1 Leone (Le) = 100 cents	4151000
Singapore	Singapore	Republic of Singapore	Singapore	Chinese, English, Malay, Tamil	1 Singapore Dollar/Ringgit (S$) = 100 cents	2718000
Solomon Islands	Solomon Islands	Solomon Islands	Honiara	English	1 Solomon Islands Dollar (SI$) = 100 cents	319000
Somalia	Somaliya	Somali Democratic Republic	Muqdisho (Mogadishu)	Arabic, Somali	1 Somali Shilling (SoSh) = 100 cents	7555000
South Africa	South Africa (English) Suid-Afrika (Afrikaans)	Republic of South Africa	Pretoria/Cape Town	Afrikaans, English	1 Rand (R) = 100 cents	30797000
Spain	España	Kingdom of Spain	Madrid	Spanish	1 Peseta (Pta, Pa) = 100 céntimos	39618000
Sri Lanka	Sri Lanka	Democratic Socialist Republic of Sri Lanka	Colombo/Sri Jayawardenapura	Sinhala, Tamil	1 Sri Lanka Rupee (SLR, SLRs) = 100 cents	17103000
Sudan	As-Sūdān	Republic of the Sudan	Al-Kharṭūm (Khartoum)	Arabic	1 Sudanese pound (LSd, £S) = 100 piastres	24423000
Suriname	Suriname	Republic of Suriname	Paramaribo	Dutch	1 Suriname Guilder/Florin (SGld, F) = 100 cents	411000
Swaziland	Swaziland	Kingdom of Swaziland	Mbabane	English, (si)Swati	1 Lilangeni (*plural* Emalangeni) (Li, E) = 100 cents	770000
Sweden	Sverige	Kingdom of Sweden	Stockholm	Swedish	1 Swedish Krona (Skr) = 100 øre	8529000
Switzerland	Schweiz (German) Suisse (French) Svizzera (Italian)	Swiss Confederation	Bern (Berne)	French, German, Italian, Romansch	1 Swiss Franc (SFr, SwF) = 100 centimes	6756000
Syria	As-Sūrīyah	Syrian Arab Republic	Dimashq (Damascus)	Arabic	1 Syrian pound (LS, Syr£) = 100 piastres	12028000
Taiwan	T'aiwan	Republic of China	T'aipei (Taipei)	Mandarin Chinese	1 New Taiwan Dollar (NT$) = 100 cents	20220000
Tanzania	Tanzania	United Republic of Tanzania	Dar es Salaam	(ki)Swahili, English	1 Tanzanian Shilling (TSh) = 100 cents	24403000

English name	Local name	Official name (in English)	Capital (English name in parentheses)	Official language(s)	Currency	Population
Thailand	Muang Thai	Kingdom of Thailand	Krung Thep (Bangkok)	Thai	1 Baht (B) = 100 satang	56217000
Togo	Togo	Republic of Togo	Lomé	French	1 CFA Franc (CFAFr) = 100 centimes	3764000
Tonga	Tonga	Kingdom of Tonga	Nuku'alofa	English, Tongan	1 Pa'anga/Tongan Dollar (T$) = 100 seniti	96300
Trinidad and Tobago	Trinidad and Tobago	Republic of Trinidad and Tobago	Port of Spain	English	1 Trinidad and Tobago Dollar (TT$) = 100 cents	1233000
Tunisia	Tunis (Arabic) Tunisie (French)	Republic of Tunisia	Tunis	Arabic	1 Tunisian Dinar (TD, D) = 1000 millémes	8182000
Turkey	Türkiye	Republic of Turkey	Ankara	Turkish	1 Turkish Lira (TL) = 100 Kurus	56940000
Tuvalu	Tuvalu	Tuvalu	Fongafale (on Funafuti)	English	1 Australian Dollar = 100 cents	9100
Uganda	Uganda	Republic of Uganda	Kampala	English	1 Uganda Shilling = 100 cents	16928000
USSR *see* Russia						
United Arab Emirates	Ittiḥād al-Imārāt al-'Arabīyah	United Arab Emirates	Abū Ẓaby (Abu Dhabi)	Arabic	1 Dirham (DH) = 100 fils	1903000
United Kingdom	United Kingdom/ (Great) Britain	United Kingdom of Great Britain and Northern Ireland	London	English	1 Pound Sterling (£) = 100 new pence	57384000
United States of America	United States of America (USA)	United States of America	Washington, DC	English	1 US Dollar ($, US$) = 100 cents	251394000
Uruguay	Uruguay	Oriental Republic of Uruguay	Montevideo	Spanish	1 Uruguayan New Peso (NUr$, UrugN$) = 100 centésimos	3033000
Vanuata	Vanuatu	Republic of Vanuatu	Vila	English, French, Bislama	1 Vatu (VT) = 100 centimes	147000
Venezuela	Venezuela	Republic of Venezuela	Caracas	Spanish	1 Bolívar (B) = 100 céntimos	19735000
Vietnam	Viêt-nam	Socialist Republic of Vietnam	Ha-noi (Hanoi)	Vietnamese	1 Dông = 10 hao = 100 xu	66128000
Western Samoa	Western Samoa (English) Samoa i Sisifo (Samoan)	Independent State of Western Samoa	Apia	English, Samoan	1 Tala (WS$) = 100 sene	186000
Yemen	Al-Yaman	Republic of Yemen	Sana/Aden	Arabic	1 Yemeni Riyal (YR, YRl) = 100 fils; 1 Yemeni Dinar (YD) = 1000 fils	11546000
Yugoslavia	Jugoslavija	Socialist Federal Republic of Yugoslavia	Beograd (Belgrade)	Macedonian, Serbo-Croat, Slovene	1 Yugoslav Dinar (D, Din) = 100 paras	23860000
Zaire	Zaïre	Republic of Zaire	Kinshasa	French	1 Zaïre (Z) = 100 makuta (*sing.* likuta)	34138000
Zambia	Zambia	Republic of Zambia	Lusaka	English	1 Kwacha (K) = 100 ngwee	8456000
Zimbabwe	Zimbabwe	Republic of Zimbabwe	Harare	English	1 Zimbabwe Dollar (Z$) = 100 cents	9370000

UNITED NATIONS MEMBERSHIP

Grouped according to year of entry.

1945 Argentina, Australia, Belgium, Belorussian SSR, Bolivia, Brazil, Canada, Chile, China (Taiwan) (to 1971), Colombia, Costa Rica, Cuba, Czechoslavakia, Denmark, Dominican Republic, Ecuador, Egypt, El Salvador, Ethiopia, France, Greece, Guatemala, Haiti, Honduras, India, Iran, Iraq, Lebanon, Liberia, Luxembourg, Mexico, Netherlands, New Zealand, Nicaragua, Norway, Panama, Paraguay, Peru, Philippines, Poland, Saudi Arabia, South Africa, Syria, Turkey, Ukranian SSR, USSR, UK, USA, Uruguay, Venezuala, Yugoslavia
1946 Afghanistan, Iceland, Sweden, Thailand
1947 Pakistan, Yemen (N)
1948 Burma
1949 Israel
1950 Indonesia
1955 Albania, Austria, Bulgaria, Kampuchea, (formerly Cambodia), Sri Lanka (formerly Ceylon), Finland, Hungary, Ireland, Italy, Jordan, Laos, Libya, Nepal, Portugal, Romania, Spain
1956 Japan, Morocco, Sudan, Tunisia
1957 Ghana, Malaya (Malaysia, 1963)
1958 Guinea
1960 Benin (formerly Dahomey), Burkina Faso (formerly Upper Volta), Cameroon, Central African Republic, Chad, Congo, Ivory Coast (Côte d'Ivoire), Cyprus, Gabon, Madagascar, Mali, Niger, Nigeria, Senegal, Somalia, Togo, Zaïre
1961 Mauritania, Mongolia, Sierra Leone, Tanganyika (within Tanzania, 1964)
1962 Algeria, Burundi, Jamaica, Rwanda, Trinidad and Tobago, Uganda
1963 Kenya, Kuwait, Zanzibar (within Tanzania, 1964)
1964 Malawi, Malta,Tanzania, Zambia
1965 Maldives, Singapore, The Gambia
1966 Barbados, Botswana, Guyana, Lesotho
1967 Yemen (S)
1968 Equatorial Guinea, Mauritius, Swaziland
1970 Fiji
1971 Bahrain, Bhutan, China (Peoples' Republic), Oman, Qatar, United Arab Emirates
1973 Bahamas, German Democratic Republic, German Federal Republic
1974 Bangladesh, Grenada, Guinea-Bissau
1975 Cape Verde, Comoros, Mozambique, Papua New Guinea, São Tomé and Principe, Suriname
1976 Angola, Seychelles, Western Samoa
1977 Djibouti, Vietnam
1978 Dominica, Solomon Islands
1979 St Lucia
1980 St Vincent and the Grenadines, Zimbabwe
1981 Antigua and Barbuda, Belize, Vanuatu
1983 St Christopher and Nevis
1984 Brunei
1990 Liechtenstein, Namibia, Yemen (formerly N Yemen and S Yemen)
1991 Estonia, Federated States of Micronesia, Latvia, Lithuania, Marshall Islands, N Korea, S Korea

SPECIALIZED AGENCIES OF THE UNITED NATIONS

bbreviated rm	Full title	Area of concern
.O	International Labour Organization	Social justice
AO	Food and Agriculture	Improvement of the production and distribution of agricultural products
NESCO	United Nations Educational, Scientific and Cultural Organization	Stimulation of popular education and the spread of culture
:AO	International Civil Aviation Organization	Encouragement of safety measures in international flight
RD	International Bank for Reconstruction and Development	Aid of development through investment
MF	International Monetary Fund	Promotion of international monetary co-operation
PU	Universal Postal Union	Uniting members within a single postal territory
VHO	World Health Organization	Promotion of the highest standards of health for all people
TU	International Telecommunication Union	Allocation of frequencies and regulation of procedures
VMO	World Meteorological Organization	Standardization and utilization of meteorological observations
FC	International Finance Corporation	Promotion of the international flow of private capital
MCO	Inter-governmental Maritime Consultative Organization	The co-ordination of safety at sea
DA	International Development Association	Credit on special terms to provide assistance for less developed countries
VIPO	World Intellectual Property Organization	Protection of copyright, designs, inventions etc
FAD	International Fund for Agricultural Development	Increase of food production in developing countries by the generation of grants or loans

WORLD POPULATION ESTIMATES

ate (AD)	Millions	Date (AD)	Millions	Date (AD)	Millions
1	200	1900	1625	1970	3700
1000	275	1920	1860	1980	4450
1250	375	1930	2070	1985	4845
1500	420	1940	2295	1990	5246
1700	615	1950	2500	2000	6100
1800	900	1960	3050	2050	11000

stimates for 2000 and 2050 are United Nations 'medium' estimates. They hould be compared with the 'low' estimates for these years of 5400 and 500, and 'high' estimates of 7000 and 13500, respectively.

AUSTRALIAN STATES

Name	Area sq km	sq ml	State Capital
Australian Capital Territory	2400	930	Canberra
New South Wales	801 400	309 400	Sydney
Northern Territory	1 346 200	519 800	Darwin
Queensland	1 727 200	666 900	Brisbane
South Australia	984 000	379 900	Adelaide
Tasmania	67 800	26 200	Hobart
Victoria	227 600	87 900	Melbourne
Western Australia	2 525 500	975 000	Perth

CANADIAN PROVINCES

Name	Area sq km	sq ml	Provincial Capital
Alberta	661 190	255 285	Edmonton
British Columbia	947 800	365 945	Victoria
Manitoba	649 950	250 945	Winnipeg
New Brunswick	73 440	28 355	Fredericton
Newfoundland	405 720	156 648	St John's
Northwest Territories	3 426 320	1 322 902	Yellowknife
Nova Scotia	55 490	21 424	Halifax
Ontario	1 068 580	412 578	Toronto
Prince Edward Islands	5 660	2 185	Charlottetown
Quebec	1 540 680	594 856	Quebec City
Saskatchewan	652 380	251 883	Regina
Yukon Territory	483 450	186 660	Whitehorse

SOUTH AFRICAN STATES

Name	Area sq km	sq ml	State Capital
Cape Province (Kaapprovinsie)	641 379	247 636	Cape Town
Natal	91 355	35 272	Pietermaritzburg
Orange Free State (Oranje Vrystaat)	127 993	49 418	Bloemfontein
Transvaal	262 499	101 351	Pretoria
Black States within South Africa			
Republics			
Bophuthatswana	44 000	17 000	Mmabatho
Ciskei	7 700	3 000	Zwelitsha
Transkei	42 200	16 300	Umtata
Venda	6 500	2 500	Thohoyandou
Other states			
Gazankulu	6 561	2 533	Giyani
KaNgwane	3 823	1 476	Nyamasane
KwaNdebele	2 860	1 100	Siyabuswa
KwaZulu	30 151	11 642	Uluni
Lebowa	22 503	8 688	Lebowakgomo
Qwaqwa	502	194	Phuthaditjhaba

AMERICAN STATES

Population: estimates are for 1987 (US Bureau of the Census)

Time Zones Two sets of figures indicate that different zones operate in a state. The second figure refers to Summer Time (April–October, approximately).

2 Aleutian/Hawaii Standard Time
3 Alaska Standard Time
4 Pacific Standard Time
5 Mountain Standard Time
6 Central Standard Time
7 Eastern Standard Time

Alabama (AL)
Pop 3 894 025 *Time Zone* 7/8
Nickname Camellia State, Heart of Dixie
Inhabitant Alabamian
Area 133 911 sq km/51 705 sq ml
Capital Montgomery
Bird Yellowhammer *Fish* Tarpon
Flower Camellia *Tree* Southern Pine

Alaska (AK)
Pop 525 000 *Time Zone* 3/4
Nickname Mainland State, The Last Frontier
Inhabitant Alaskan
Area 1 518 748 sq km/586 412 sq ml
Capital Juneau
Bird Willow Ptarmigan *Fish* King Salmon
Flower Forget-me-not
Gemstone Jade *Tree* Sitka Spruce

Arizona (AZ)
Pop 3 386 000 *Time Zone* 5
Nickname Apache State, Grand Canyon State
Inhabitant Arizonan
Area 295 249 sq km/114 000 sq ml
Capital Phoenix
Bird Cactus Wren *Flower* Giant Cactus
Gemstone Turquoise *Tree* Paloverde

Arkansas (AR)
Pop 2 388 000 *Time Zone* 6/7
Nickname Bear State, Land of Opportunity
Inhabitant Arkansan
Area 137 403 sq km/53 187 sq ml
Capital Little Rock
Bird Mockingbird *Flower* Apple Blossom
Gemstone Diamond *Tree* Pine

California (CA)
Pop 27 663 000 *Time Zone* 4/5
Nickname Golden State
Inhabitant Californian
Area 411 033 sq km/158 706 sq ml
Capital Sacramento
Animal California Grizzly Bear
Bird California Valley Quail
Fish South Fork Golden Trout
Flower Golden Poppy
Tree California Redwood

Colorado (CO)
Pop 3 296 000 *Time Zone* 5/6
Nickname Centennial State
Inhabitant Coloradan
Area 269 585 sq km/104 091 sq ml
Capital Denver
Animal Rocky Mountain Bighorn Sheep
Bird Lark Bunting *Flower* Columbine
Gemstone Aquamarine *Tree* Blue Spruce

Connecticut (CT)
Pop 3 211 000 *Time Zone* 7/8
Nickname Nutmeg State, Constitution State
Inhabitant Nutmegger
Area 12 996 sq km/5 018 sq ml
Capital Hartford
Bird American Robin *Flower* Mountain Laurel
Gemstone Garnet *Tree* White Oak

Delaware (DE)
Pop 644 000 *Time Zone* 7/8
Nickname Diamond State, First State
Inhabitant Delawarean
Area 5 296 sq km/2 045 sq ml
Capital Dover
Bird Blue Hen Chicken *Flower* Peach Blossom
Tree American Holly

District of Columbia (DC)
Pop 622 000 *Time Zone* 7/8
Inhabitant Washingtonian
Area 173.5 sq km/67 sq ml
Capital Washington
Bird Woodthrush *Flower* American Beauty Rose
Tree Scarlet Oak

Florida (FL)
Pop 12 023 000 *Time Zone* 6/7, 7/8
Nickname Everglade State, Sunshine State
Inhabitant Floridian
Area 151 934 sq km/58 664 sq ml
Capital Tallahassee
Bird Mockingbird *Flower* Orange Blossom
Gemstone Agatized Coral *Tree* Sabal Palm

Georgia (GA)
Pop 6 222 000 *Time Zone* 7/8
Nickname Empire State of the South, Peach State
Inhabitant Georgian
Area 152 571 sq km/58 910 sq ml
Capital Atlanta
Bird Brown Thrasher *Flower* Cherokee Rose
Tree Live Oak

Hawaii (HI)
Pop 1 083 000 *Time Zone* 2
Nickname Aloha State
Inhabitant Hawaiian
Area 16 759 sq km/6 471 sq ml
Capital Honolulu
Bird Nene *Flower* Hibiscus *Tree* Kukui

Idaho (ID)
Pop 998 000 *Time Zone* 4/5, 5/6
Nickname Gem State
Inhabitant Idahoan
Area 216 422 sq km/83 564 sq ml
Capital Boise
Bird Mountain Bluebird *Flower* Syringa
Gemstone Idaho Star Garnet
Tree Western White Pine

Illinois (IL)
Pop 11 582 000 *Time Zone* 6/7
Nickname Prairie State, Land of Lincoln
Inhabitant Illinoisan
Area 145 928 sq km/56 345 sq ml
Capital Springfield
Bird Cardinal *Flower* Butterfly Violet
Tree White Oak

Indiana (IN)
Pop 5 531 000 *Time Zone* 6/7, 7/8 (Daylight Saving Time not observed everywhere)
Nickname Hoosier State
Inhabitant Hoosier
Area 93 715.5 sq km/36 185 sq ml
Capital Indianapolis
Bird Cardinal *Flower* Peony
Tree Tulip Tree

Iowa (IA)
Pop 2 834 000 *Time Zone* 6/7
Nickname Hawkeye State, Corn State
Inhabitant Iowan
Area 145 747 sq km/56 275 sq ml
Capital Des Moines
Bird Eastern Goldfinch *Flower* Wild Rose
Tree Oak

Kansas (KS)
Pop 2 476 000 *Time Zone* 5/6, 6/7
Nickname Sunflower State, Jayhawker State
Inhabitant Kansan
Area 213 089 sq km/82 277 sq ml
Capital Topeka
Animal Bison *Bird* Western Meadowlark
Flower Native Sunflower *Tree* Cottonwood

Kentucky (KY)
Pop 3 727 000 *Time Zone* 6/7, 7/8
Nickname Bluegrass State
Inhabitant Kentuckian
Area 104 658 sq km/40 410 sq ml
Capital Frankfort
Bird Cardinal *Flower* Goldenrod
Tree Kentucky Coffee Tree

Louisiana (LA)
Pop 4 461 000 *Time Zone* 6/7
Nickname Pelican State, Sugar State, Creole State
Inhabitant Louisianian
Area 123 673 sq km/47 752 sq ml
Capital Baton Rouge
Bird Eastern Brown Pelican *Flower* Magnolia
Tree Bald Cypress

Maine (ME)
Pop 1 187 000 *Time Zone* 7/8
Nickname Pine Tree State
Inhabitant Downeaster
Area 86 153 sq km/33 265 sq ml
Capital Augusta
Bird Chickadee *Flower* White Pine Cone and Tassel *Gemstone* Tourmaline
Tree Eastern White Pine

Maryland (MD)
Pop 4 535 000 *Time Zone* 7/8
Nickname Old Line State, Free State
Inhabitant Marylander
Area 27 090 sq km/10 460 sq ml
Capital Annapolis
Bird Baltimore Oriole *Fish* Striped Bass
Flower Black-eyed Susan *Tree* White Oak

Massachusetts (MA)
Pop 5 855 000 *Time Zone* 7/8
Nickname Bay State, Old Colony
Inhabitant Bay Stater
Area 21 455 sq km/8 284 sq ml
Capital Boston
Bird Chickadee *Flower* Mayflower
Tree American Elm

Michigan (MI)
Pop 9 200 000 *Time Zone* 6/7, 7/8
Nickname Wolverine State, Great Lake State
Inhabitant Michigander
Area 151 579 sq km/58 527 sq ml
Capital Lansing
Bird Robin *Fish* Trout
Flower Apple Blossom *Gemstone* Chlorastrolik
Tree White Pine

Minnesota (MN)
Pop 4 246 000 *Time Zone* 6/7
Nickname Gopher State, North Star State
Inhabitant Minnesotan
Area 218 593 sq km/84 402 sq ml
Capital St. Paul
Bird Loon *Fish* Walleye
Flower Moccasin Flower
Gemstone Lake Superior Agate
Tree Red Pine

Mississippi (MS)
Pop 2 625 000 *Time Zone* 6/7
Nickname Magnolia State
Inhabitant Mississippian
Area 123 510 sq km/47 689 sq ml
Capital Jackson
Bird Mockingbird *Flower* Magnolia
Tree Magnolia

AMERICAN STATES (cont.)

Missouri (MO)
Pop 5 103 000 *Time Zone* 6/7
Nickname Bullion State, Show Me State
Inhabitant Missourian
Area 180 508 sq km/69 697 sq ml
Capital Jefferson City
Bird Bluebird *Flower* Hawthorn
Tree Dogwood

Montana (MT)
Pop 809 000 *Time Zone* 5/6
Nickname Treasure State, Big Sky Country
Inhabitant Montanan
Area 380 834 sq km/147 046 sq ml
Capital Helena
Bird Western Meadowlark *Flower* Bitterroot
Gemstone Sapphire, Agate
Tree Ponderosa Pine

Nebraska (NE)
Pop 1 594 000 *Time Zone* 5/6, 6/7
Nickname Cornhusker State, Beef State
Inhabitant Nebraskan
Area 200 342 sq km/77 355 sq ml
Bird Western Meadowlark *Flower* Goldenrod
Gemstone Blue Agate *Tree* Cottonwood

Nevada (NV)
Pop 1 007 000 *Time Zone* 4/5
Nickname Silver State, Sagebrush State
Inhabitant Nevadan
Area 286 341 sq km/110 561 sq ml
Capital Carson City
Bird Mountain Bluebird *Flower* Sagebrush
Tree Single-leaf Piñon

New Hampshire (NH)
Pop 1 057 000 *Time Zone* 7/8
Nickname Granite State
Inhabitant New Hampshirite
Area 24 032 sq km/9 279 sq ml
Capital Concord
Bird Purple Finch *Flower* Purple Lilac
Tree White Birch

New Jersey (NJ)
Pop 7 672 000 *Time Zone* 7/8
Nickname Garden State
Inhabitant New Jerseyite
Area 20 167 sq km/7 787 sq ml
Capital Trenton
Bird Eastern Goldfinch *Flower* Purple Violet
Tree Red Oak

New Mexico (NM)
Pop 1 500 000 *Time Zone* 5/6
Nickname Sunshine State, Land of Enchantment
Inhabitant New Mexican
Area 314 914 sq km/121 593 sq ml
Capital Santa Fe
Animal Black Bear *Bird* Roadrunner
Fish Cutthroat Trout *Flower* Yucca
Gemstone Turquoise *Tree* Piñon

New York (NY)
Pop 17 825 000 *Time Zone* 7/8
Nickname Empire State
Inhabitant New Yorker
Area 127 185 sq km/49 108 sq ml
Capital Albany
Bird Bluebird *Flower* Rose
Gemstone Garnet *Tree* Sugar Maple

North Carolina (NC)
Pop 6 413 000 *Time Zone* 7/8
Nickname Old North State, Tar Heel State
Inhabitant North Carolinian
Area 136 407 sq km/52 699 sq ml
Capital Raleigh
Animal Grey Squirrel *Bird* Cardinal
Fish Channel Bass *Flower* Dogwood
Gemstone Emerald *Tree* Longleaf Pine

North Dakota (ND)
Pop 672 000 *Time Zone* 5/6, 6/7
Nickname Flickertail State, Sioux State
Inhabitant North Dakotan
Area 180 180 sq km/69 567 sq ml
Capital Bismarck
Bird Western Meadowlark *Fish* Northern Pike
Flower Wild Prairie Rose
Gemstone Teredo petrified wood
Tree American Elm

Ohio (OH)
Pop 10 784 000 *Time Zone* 7/8
Nickname Buckeye State
Inhabitant Ohioan
Area 107 040 sq km/41 330 sq ml
Capital Columbus
Bird Cardinal *Flower* Scarlet Carnation
Tree Buckeye

Oklahoma (OK)
Pop 3 272 000 *Time Zone* 6/7
Nickname Sooner State
Inhabitant Oklahoman
Area 181 083 sq km/69 919 sq ml
Capital Oklahoma City
Bird Scissor-tailed Flycatcher
Flower Mistletoe *Tree* Redbud

Oregon (OR)
Pop 2 724 000 *Time Zone* 4/5
Nickname Sunset State, Beaver State
Inhabitant Oregonian
Area 251 409 sq km/97 073 sq ml
Capital Salem
Animal Beaver *Bird* Western Meadowlark
Fish Chinook Salmon *Flower* Oregon Grape
Gemstone Thunder Egg *Tree* Douglas Fir

Pennsylvania (PA)
Pop 11 936 000 *Time Zone* 7/8
Nickname Keystone State
Inhabitant Pennsylvanian
Area 117 343 sq km/45 308 sq ml
Capital Harrisburg
Animal Whitetail Deer *Bird* Ruffed Grouse
Flower Mountain Laurel *Tree* Hemlock

Rhode Island (RI)
Pop 986 000 *Time Zone* 7/8
Nickname Little Rhody, Plantation State
Inhabitant Rhode Islander
Area 3 139 sq km/1 212 sq ml
Capital Providence
Bird Rhode Island Red *Flower* Violet
Tree Red Maple

South Carolina (SC)
Pop 3 425 000 *Time Zone* 7/8
Nickname Palmetto State
Inhabitant South Carolinian
Area 80 579 sq km/31 113 sq ml
Capital Columbia
Animal Whitetail Deer *Bird* Carolina Wren
Fish Striped Bass *Flower* Yellow Jessamine
Tree Cabbage Palmetto

South Dakota (SD)
Pop 709 000 *Time Zone* 5/6, 6/7
Nickname Sunshine State, Coyote State
Inhabitant South Dakotan
Area 199 723 sq km/77 116 sq ml
Capital Pierre
Animal Coyote *Bird* Ring-necked Pheasant
Flower Pasque *Gemstone* Fairburn Agate
Tree Black Hills Spruce

Tennessee (TN)
Pop 4 855 000 *Time Zone* 6/7, 7/8
Nickname Volunteer State
Inhabitant Tennessean
Area 109 149 sq km/42 144 sq ml
Capital Nashville
Animal Raccoon *Bird* Mockingbird
Flower Iris *Gemstone* Pearl *Tree* Tulip Poplar

Texas (TX)
Pop 16 789 000 *Time Zone* 5/6, 6/7
Nickname Lone Star State
Inhabitant Texan
Area 691 003 sq km/266 807 sq ml
Capital Austin
Bird Mockingbird *Flower* Bluebonnet
Gemstone Topaz *Tree* Pecan

Utah (UT)
Pop 1 680 000 *Time Zone* 5/6
Nickname Mormon State, Beehive State
Inhabitant Utahn
Area 219 880 sq km/84 899 sq ml
Capital Salt Lake City
Bird Sea Gull *Flower* Sego Lily
Gemstone Topaz *Tree* Blue Spruce

Vermont (VT)
Pop 548 000 *Time Zone* 7/8
Nickname Green Mountain State
Inhabitant Vermonter
Area 24 899 sq km/9 614 sq ml
Capital Montpelier
Animal Morgan Horse *Bird* Hermit Thrush
Flower Red Clover *Tree* Sugar Maple

Virginia (VA)
Pop 5 904 000 *Time Zone* 7/8
Nickname Old Dominion State, Mother of Presidents
Inhabitant Virginian
Area 105 582 sq km/40 767 sq ml
Capital Richmond
Bird Cardinal *Flower* Dogwood
Tree Flowering Dogwood

Washington (WA)
Pop 4 538 000 *Time Zone* 4/5
Nickname Evergreen State, Chinook State
Inhabitant Washingtonian
Area 176 473 sq km/68 139 sq ml
Capital Olympia
Bird Willow Goldfinch *Fish* Steelhead Trout
Flower Western Rhododendron
Gemstone Petrified Wood
Tree Western Hemlock

West Virginia (WV)
Pop 1 897 000 *Time Zone* 7/8
Nickname Panhandle State, Mountain State
Inhabitant West Virginian
Area 62 758 sq km/24 232 sq ml
Capital Charleston
Animal Black Bear *Bird* Cardinal
Flower Big Rhododendron *Tree* Sugar Maple

Wisconsin (WI)
Pop 4 807 000 *Time Zone* 6/7
Nickname Badger State, America's Dairyland
Inhabitant Wisconsinite
Area 145 431 sq km/56 153 sq ml
Capital Madison
Animal Badger, Whitetail Deer *Bird* Robin
Fish Muskellunge *Flower* Wood Violet
Tree Sugar Maple

Wyoming (WY)
Pop 490 000 *Time Zone* 5/6
Nickname Equality State
Inhabitant Wyomingite
Area 253 315 sq km/97 809 sq ml
Capital Cheyenne
Bird Meadowlark *Flower* Indian Paintbrush
Gemstone Jade *Tree* Cottonwood

COUNTIES OF ENGLAND

County	Area sq km	Area sq ml	Population (1987 est.)	Admin. centre
Avon*	1346	520	951200	Bristol
Bedfordshire	1235	477	525900	Bedford
Berkshire	1259	486	740600	Reading
Buckinghamshire	1883	727	621300	Aylesbury
Cambridgeshire	3409	1316	642400	Cambridge
Cheshire	2328	899	951900	Chester
Cleveland*	583	225	554500	Middlesbrough
Cornwall	3564	1376	453100	Truro
Cumbria*	6810	2629	486900	Carlisle
Derbyshire	2631	1016	918700	Matlock
Devon	6711	2591	1010000	Exeter
Dorset	2654	1025	648600	Dorchester
Durham	2436	941	598700	Durham
Essex	3672	1418	1521800	Chelmsford
Gloucestershire	2643	1020	522200	Gloucester
Greater London*	1579	610	6770400	—
Greater Manchester*	1287	497	2580100	—
Hampshire	3777	1458	1537000	Winchester
Hereford and Worcester*	3926	1516	665100	Worcester
Hertfordshire	1634	631	986800	Hertford
Humberside*	3512	1356	846500	Hull
Isle of Wight	381	147	126900	Newport
Kent	3731	1441	1510500	Maidstone
Lancashire	3063	1183	1381300	Preston
Leicestershire	2553	986	879400	Leicester
Lincolnshire	5915	2284	574600	Lincoln
Merseyside*+	652	252	1456800	Liverpool
Norfolk	5368	2073	736200	Norwich
Northamptonshire	2367	914	561800	Northampton
Northumberland	5032	1943	300900	Newcastle upon Tyne
Nottinghamshire	2164	836	1007800	Nottingham
Oxfordshire	2608	1007	578000	Oxford
Shropshire	3490	1347	396500	Shrewsbury
Somerset	3451	1332	452300	Taunton
Staffordshire	2716	1049	1027500	Stafford
Suffolk	3797	1466	635100	Ipswich
Surrey	1679	648	1000400	Kingston upon Thames
Sussex, East	1795	693	698000	Lewes
Sussex, West	1989	768	700000	Chichester
Tyne and Wear*+	540	208	1135800	Newcastle
Warwickshire	1981	765	484200	Warwick
West Midlands*+	899	347	2624300	Birmingham
Wiltshire	3481	1344	550900	Trowbridge
Yorkshire, North	8309	3208	705700	Northallerton
Yorkshire, South	1560	602	1295600	Barnsley
Yorkshire, West+	2039	787	2052400	Wakefield

*New counties in 1974 were formed as follows:

Avon: parts of Somerset and Gloucestershire
Cleveland: parts of Durham and Yorkshire
Cumbria: Cumberland, Westmoreland, parts of Lancashire and Yorkshire
Greater London: London and most of Middlesex
Greater Manchester: parts of Lancashire, Cheshire and Yorkshire
Hereford and Worcester: Hereford, most of Worcestershire
Humberside: parts of Yorkshire and Lincolnshire
Merseyside: parts of Lancashire and Cheshire
West Midlands: parts of Staffordshire, Warwickshire and Worcestershire
Tyne and Wear: parts of Northumberland and Durham

+County status abolished in 1986

REGIONS OF SCOTLAND

Region	Area sq km	Area sq ml	Population (1987 est.)	Admin. centre	Former counties	New districts
Borders	4672	1804	102141	Newton St Boswells	Berwick, Peebles, Roxburgh, Selkirk, part of Midlothian	Berwickshire, Ettrick & Lauderdale, Roxburgh, Tweeddale
Central	2631	1016	272077	Stirling	Clackmannan, most of Stirling parts of Perth and W Lothian	Clackmannan, Falkirk, Stirling
Dumfries & Galloway	6370	2459	147036	Dumfries	Dumfries, Kirkcudbright, Wigtown	Annandale & Eskdale, Nithsdale, Stewartry, Wigtown
Fife	1307	505	344590	Glenrothes	Fife	Dunfermline, NE Fife, Kirkcaldy
Grampian	8704	3361	502863	Aberdeen	Aberdeen, Banff, Kincardine, most of Moray	Aberdeen, Banff & Buchan, Gordon, Kincardine & Deeside, Moray
Highland	25391	9804	200608	Inverness	Caithness, Inverness, Nairn, Ross & Cromarty, Sutherland, parts of Argyll and Moray	Badenoch & Strathspey, Caithness, Inverness, Lochaber, Nairn, Ross & Cromarty, Sutherland, Skye & Lochalsh
Lothian	1755	678	743700	Edinburgh	E Lothian, Midlothian, W Lothian	Edinburgh, E Lothian, Midlothian, W Lothian
Strathclyde	13537	5227	2332537	Glasgow	Ayre, Bute, Dunbarton, Lanark, Renfrew, most of Argyll, part of Stirling	Argyll & Bute, Bearsden & Milngavie, Clydebank, Clydesdale, Cumnock & Doon Valley, Cunninghame, Cumbernauld & Kilsyth, Dunbarton, E Kilbride, Eastwood, Glasgow, Hamilton, Inverclyde, Kilmarnock & Loudoun, Kyle & Carrick, Monklands, Motherwell, Renfrew, Strathkelvin
Tayside	7493	2893	393762	Dundee	Angus, Kinross, most of Perth	Angus, Dundee, Kinross, Perth
Orkney Is	976	377	19338	Kirkwall		
Shetland Is	1433	553	2427	Lerwick		

COUNTIES OF WALES

County	Area sq km	Area sq ml	Population (1987 est.)	Admin. centre	Former counties	New districts
Clwyd	2426	937	402800	Mold	Flint, most of Denbigh	Alyn & Deeside, Colwyn, Delyn, Glyndwr, Rhuddlan, Wrexham Maelor
Dyfed	5768	2227	343200	Carmarthen	Camarthen, Cardigan, Pembroke	Camarthen, Ceredigion, Dinefwr, Llanelli, Preseli, South Pembrokeshire
Gwent	1376	531	443100	Cwmbrǎn	Most of Monmouth, part of Brecon	Blaenau Gwent, Islwyn, Monmouth, Newport, Torfaen
Gwynedd	3869	1494	236300	Caernarvon	Anglesey, Caernarvon, Merioneth, part of Denbigh	Aberconwy, Arfon, Dwyfor, Meirionydd, Ynys Mŏn (Anglesey)
Powys	5077	1960	113300	Llandrindod Wells	Montgomery, Radnor, most of Brecon	Brecknock, Montgomery, Radnor
Mid Glamorgan	1018	393	543700	Cardiff	Parts of Glamorgan, Brecon, and Monmouth	Cynon Valley, Merthyr Tydfil, Ogwen, Rhondda, Rhymney Valley, Taff-Ely
S Glamorgan	416	161	399500	Cardiff	Parts of Glamorgan and Monmouth	Cardiff, Vale of Glamorgan
W Glamorgan	817	315	363200	Swansea	Part of Glamorgan	Afan, Lliw Valley, Neath, Swansea

DISTRICTS OF NORTHERN IRELAND

District	Area sq km	Area sq ml	Population (1987 est.)	Admin. centre	Formerly part of
Antrim	563	217	46600	Antrim	Antrim
Ards	369	142	63600	Newtownards	Down
Armagh	672	259	50700	Armagh	Armagh
Ballymena	638	246	56100	Ballymena	Antrim
Ballymoney	419	162	23800	Ballymoney	Antrim
Banbridge	444	171	32000	Banbridge	Down
Belfast	140	54	303800	—	Antrim
Carrickfergus	87	34	29300	Carrickfergus	Antrim
Castlereagh	85	33	57900	Belfast	Antrim, Down
Coleraine	485	187	47700	Coleraine	Antrim
Cookstown	623	240	27700	Cookstown	Tyrone
Craigavon	382	147	76600	Craigavon	Antrim, Down, Armagh
Down	646	249	56400	Downpatrick	Down
Dungannon	779	301	43900	Dungannon	Armagh, Tyrone
Fermanagh	1876	715	50300	Enniskillen	Fermanagh
Larne	338	131	28700	Larne	Antrim
Limavady	587	227	29600	Limavady	Londonderry
Lisburn	444	171	92900	Lisburn	Antrim, Down
Londonderry	382	147	97500	—	Londonderry
Magherafelt	573	221	33300	Magherafelt	Londonderry
Moyle	495	191	15200	Ballycastle	Antrim
Newry & Mourne	895	346	87100	Newry	Armagh, Down
Newtownabbey	152	59	72300	Newtownabbey	Antrim
North Down	73	28	70700	Bangor	Down
Omagh	1129	436	45800	Omagh	Tyrone
Strabane	870	336	35700	Strabane	Tyrone

OTHER BRITISH ISLANDS

Name	Area sq km	Area sq ml	Population (1986)	Admin. centre
Channel Is				
Alderney	8	3	2000	St Anne's
Guernsey	63	24	54380	St Peter Port
Jersey	116	45	80212	St Helier
Sark	4	2	604	
Isle of Man	572	221	64282	Douglas

COUNTIES OF IRELAND

County	Area sq km	Area sq ml	Population (1981)	Admin. centre
Carlow	896	346	39820	Carlow
Cavan	1891	730	53855	Cavan
Clare	3188	1231	87567	Ennis
Cork	7459	2880	402465	Cork
Donegal	4830	1865	125112	Lifford
Dublin	922	356	1003164	Dublin
Galway	5939	2293	172018	Galway
Kerry	4701	1815	122770	Tralee
Kildare	1694	654	104122	Naas
Kilkenny	2062	796	70806	Kilkenny
Laoighis (Leix)	1720	664	51171	Portlaoise
Leitrim	1526	589	27609	Carrick
Limerick	2686	1037	161661	Limerick
Longford	1044	403	31140	Longford
Louth	821	317	88514	Dundalk
Mayo	5398	2084	114766	Castlebar
Meath	2339	903	95419	Trim
Monaghan	1290	498	51192	Monaghan
Offaly	1997	771	58312	Tullamore
Roscommon	2463	951	54543	Roscommon
Sligo	1795	693	55474	Sligo
Tipperary	4254	1642	135261	Clonmel
Waterford	1839	710	88591	Waterford
Westmeath	1764	681	61523	Mullingar
Wexford	2352	908	99081	Wexford
Wicklow	2025	782	87449	Wicklow

POLITICAL RULERS & LEADERS 1900–91

Countries and organizations are listed alphabetically. Rulers are named chronologically since 1900 or (for new nations) since independence. For the major English-speaking nations, relevant details are also given of pre-20th-century rulers, along with a note of any political affiliation.

The list does not distinguish successive terms of office by a single ruler.

There is no universally agreed way of transliterating proper names in non-Roman alphabets; variations from the spellings given are therefore to be expected, especially in the case of Arabic rulers.

Minor variations in the titles adopted by Chiefs of State, or in the name of an administration, are not given; these occur most notably in countries under military rule.

Listings complete to December 1991.

AFGHANISTAN

Afghan Empire

Monarch

1881–1901 Abdur Rahman Khan
1901–19 Habibullah Khan
1919–29 Inayatullah Khan
1929 Habibullah Ghazi
1929–33 Nadir Shah
1933–73 Zahir Shah

Republic of Afghanistan

Prime Minister

1973–8 Mohammad Daoud Khan

Democratic Republic of Afghanistan Revolutionary Council

President

1978–9 Nur Mohammad Taraki
1979 Hafizullah Amin

Soviet Invasion
1979–86 Babrak Karmal
1986–7 Haji Mohammad Chamkani *Acting President*
1987– Mohammad Najibullah

General Secretary

1978–86 *As President*
1986– Mohammad Najibullah

Prime Minister

1929–46 Sardar Mohammad Hashim Khan
1946–53 Shah Mahmoud Khan Ghazi
1953–63 Mohammad Daoud
1963–5 Mohammad Yousef
1965–7 Mohammad Hashim Maiwandwal
1967–71 Nour Ahmad Etemadi
1972–3 Mohammad Mousa Shafiq

Prime Minister (cont.)

1973–9 *As President*
1979–81 Babrak Karmal
1981–8 Sultan Ali Keshtmand

Republic of Afghanistan from 1987
1988–9 Mohammad Hasan Sharq
1989–90 Sultan Ali Keshtmand
1990– Fazl Haq Khaleqiar

ALBANIA

Monarch

1928–39 Zog I (Ahmed Zogu)
1939–44 *Italian rule*

People's Socialist Republic

President

1944–85 Enver Hoxha
1985–91 Ramiz Alia
1991– Fatos Nano (*Provisional*)

Prime Minister

1914 Turhan Pashë Permëti
1914 Esad Toptani
1914–18 Abdullah Rushdi
1918–20 Turhan Pashë Permëti
1920 Sulejman Deluina
1920–1 Iljaz Bej Vrioni
1921 Pandeli Evangeli
1921 Xhafer Ypi
1921–2 Omer Vrioni
1922–4 Ahmed Zogu
1924 Iljaz Bej Vrioni
1924–5 Fan Noli
1925–8 Ahmed Zogu
1928–30 Koço Kota
1930–5 Pandeli Evangeli
1935–6 Mehdi Frashëri
1936–9 Koço Kota
1939–41 Shefqet Verlaci
1941–3 Mustafa Merlika-Kruja
1943 Eqrem Libohova
1943 Maliq Bushati
1943 Eqrem Libohova
1943 *Provisional Executive Committee* (Ibrahim Biçakçlu)
1943 *Council of Regents* (Mehdi Frashëri)
1943–4 Rexhep Mitrovica
1944 Fiori Dine
1944–54 Enver Hoxha
1954–81 Mehmed Shehu
1981–91 Adil Carcani

Republic of Albania
1991 Ylli Bufi
1991– Vilson Ahmeti

ALGERIA

President

1962–5 Ahmed Ben Bella
1965–78 Houari Boumedienne
1978– Chadli Benjedid

ANGOLA

President

1975–9 Antonio Agostinho Neto
1979– José Eduardo dos Santos

ANTIGUA AND BARBUDA

Prime Minister

1981– Vere Cornwall Bird

ARGENTINA

President

1898–1904 Julio Argentino Roca
1904–6 Manuel Quintana
1906–10 José Figueroa Alcorta
1910–14 Roque Sáenz Peña
1914–16 Victorino de la Plaza
1916–22 Hipólito Yrigoyen
1922–8 Marcelo T de Alvear
1928–30 Hipólito Yrigoyen
1930–2 José Félix Uriburu
1932–8 Augustin Pedro Justo
1938–40 Roberto M Ortiz
1940–3 Ramón S Castillo
1943–4 Pedro P Ramírez
1944–6 Edelmiro J Farrell
1946–55 Juan Perón
1955–8 Eduardo Lonardi
1958–62 Arturo Frondizi
1962–3 José María Guido
1963–6 Arturo Illia
1966–70 Juan Carlos Onganía
1970–1 Roberto Marcelo Levingston
1971–3 Alejandro Agustin Lanusse
1973 Héctor J Cámpora
1973–4 Juan Perón
1974–6 Martínez de Perón
1976–81 *Military Junta* (Jorge Rafaél Videla)
1981 *Military Junta* (Roberto Eduardo Viola)
1981–2 *Military Junta* (Leopoldo Galtieri)
1982–3 Reynaldo Bignone
1983–8 Raúl Alfonsín
1988– Carlos Menem

AUSTRALIA

Chief of State: British monarch, represented by Governor General

Prime Minister

1901–3 Edmund Barton *Prot*
1903–4 Alfred Deakin *Prot*
1904 John Christian Watson *Lab*
1904–5 George Houston Reid *Free*
1905–8 Alfred Deakin *Prot*
1908–9 Andrew Fisher *Lab*

AUSTRALIA (cont.)

Prime Minister (cont.)

1909–10 Alfred Deakin *Fusion*
1910–13 Andrew Fisher *Lab*
1913–14 Joseph Cook *Lib*
1914–15 Andrew Fisher *Lab*
1915–17 William Morris Hughes *Nat Lab*
1917–23 William Morris Hughes *Nat*
1923–9 Stanley Melbourne Bruce *Nat*
1929–32 James Henry Scullin *Lab*
1932–9 Joseph Aloysius Lyons *Un*
1939 Earle Christmas Page *Co*
1939–41 Robert Gordon Menzies *Un*
1941 Arthur William Fadden *Co*
1941–5 John Joseph Curtin *Lab*
1945 Francis Michael Forde *Lab*
1945–9 Joseph Benedict Chifley *Lab*
1949–66 Robert Gordon Menzies *Lib*
1966–7 Harold Edward Holt *Lib*
1967–8 John McEwen *Co*
1968–71 John Grey Gorton *Lib*
1971–2 William McMahon *Lib*
1972–5 Edward Gough Whitlam *Lab*
1975–83 John Malcolm Fraser *Lib*
1983–91 Robert James Lee Hawke *Lab*
1991– Paul Keating *Lab*

Co *Country*
Free *Free Trade*
Lab *Labor*
Lib *Liberal*
Nat *Nationalist*
Nat Lab *National Labor*
Prot *Protectionist*
Un *United*

AUSTRIA

President

1918–20 Karl Sätz
1920–8 Michael Hainisch
1928–38 Wilhelm Miklas
1938–45 *German rule*
1945–50 Karl Renner
1950–7 Theodor Körner
1957–65 Adolf Schärf
1965–74 Franz Jonas
1974–86 Rudolf Kirchsläger
1986– Kurt Waldheim

Chancellor

1918–20 Karl Renner
1920–1 Michael Mayr
1921–2 Johann Schober
1922 Walter Breisky
1922 Johann Schober
1922–4 Ignaz Seipel
1924–6 Rudolph Ramek
1926–9 Ignaz Seipel
1929–30 Ernst Streeruwitz
1930 Johann Schober
1930 Carl Vaugoin
1930–1 Otto Ender
1931–2 Karl Buresch
1932–4 Engelbert Dollfus
1934–8 Kurt von Schuschnigg
1938–45 *German rule*
1945 Karl Renner
1945–53 Leopold Figl
1953–61 Julius Raab
1961–4 Alfons Gorbach

Chancellor (cont.)

1964–70 Josef Klaus
1970–83 Bruno Kreisky
1983–6 Fred Sinowatz
1986– Franz Vranitzky

THE BAHAMAS

Chief of State: British monarch, represented by Governor General

Prime Minister

1973– Lynden O Pindling

BAHRAIN

Emir

1971– Isa Bin Salman Al-Khalifa

Prime Minister

1971– Khalifa Bin Salman Al-Khalifa

BANGLADESH

President

1971–2 Sayed Nazrul Islam *Acting*
1972 Mujibur Rahman
1972–3 Abu Saeed Chowdhury
1974–5 Mohammadullah
1975 Mujibur Rahman
1975 Khondaker Mushtaq Ahmad
1975–7 Abu Saadat Mohammad Sayem
1977–81 Zia Ur-Rahman
1981–2 Abdus Sattar
1982–3 Abdul Fazal Mohammad Ahsanuddin Chowdhury
1983–90 Hossain Mohammad Ershad
1990–1 Shehabuddin Ahmed
1991– Abdur Rahman Biswas

Prime Minister

1971–2 Tajuddin Ahmed
1972–5 Mujibur Rahman
1975 Mohammad Monsur Ali
1975–9 *Martial Law*
1979–82 Mohammad Azizur Rahman
1982–4 *Martial Law*
1984–5 Ataur Rahman Khan
1986–88 Mizanur Rahman Chowdhury
1988–89 Moudud Ahmed
1989–91 Kazi Zafar Ahmed
1991– Khaleda Zia

BARBADOS

Prime Minister

1966–76 Errol Walton Barrow
1976–85 JMG (Tom) Adams
1985–6 H Bernard St John
1986–7 Errol Walton Barrow
1987– L Erskine Sandiford

BELGIUM

Monarch

1865–1909 Leopold II
1909–34 Albert I
1934–50 Leopold III
1950– Baudoin I

Prime Minister

1899–1907 Paul de Smet de Nayer
1907–8 Jules de Trooz
1908–11 Frans Schollaert
1911–18 Charles de Broqueville
1918 Gerhard Cooreman
1918–20 Léon Delacroix
1920–1 Henri Carton de Wiart
1921–5 Georges Theunis
1925 Alois van de Vyvere
1925–6 Prosper Poullet
1926–31 Henri Jaspar
1931–2 Jules Renkin
1932–4 Charles de Broqueville
1934–5 Georges Theunis
1935–7 Paul van Zeeland
1937–8 Paul Émile Janson
1938–9 Paul Henri Spaak
1939–45 Hubert Pierlot
1945–6 Achille van Acker
1946 Paul Spaak
1946 Achille van Acker
1946–7 Camille Huysmans
1947–9 Paul Spaak
1949–50 Gaston Eyskens
1950 Jean Pierre Duvieusart
1950–2 Joseph Pholien
1952–4 Jean van Houtte
1954–8 Achille van Acker
1958–61 Gaston Eyskens
1961–5 Théodore Lefèvre
1965–6 Pierre Harmel
1966–8 Paul Vanden Boeynants
1968–72 Gaston Eyskens
1973–4 Edmond Leburton
1974–8 Léo Tindemans
1978 Paul Vanden Boeynants
1979–81 Wilfried Martens
1981 Marc Eyskens
1981– Wilfried Martens

BELIZE

Chief of State: British Monarch, represented by Governor General

Prime Minister

1981–4 George Cadle Price
1985–9 Manuel Esquivel
1989– George Cadle Price

BENIN

President

Dahomey

1960–3 Hubert Coutoucou Maga
1963–4 Christophe Soglo
1964–5 Sourou Migan Apithy
1965 Justin Tométin Ahomadegbé
1965 Tairou Congacou
1965–7 Christophe Soglo
1967–8 Alphonse Amadou Alley
1968–9 Émile Derlin Zinsou
1969–70 *Presidential Committee* (Maurice Kouandete)
1970–2 (Hubert Coutoucou Maga)
1972–5 Mathieu Kerekou

People's Republic of Benin

1975–90 Mathieu (*from 1980* Ahmed) Kerekou

Republic of Benin

1990– Ahmed Kerekou

BENIN (cont.)

Prime Minister

1958–9 Sourou Migan Apithy
1959–60 Hubert Coutoucou Maga
1960–4 *As President*
1964–5 Justin Tométin Ahomadegbé
1965–7 *As President*
1967–8 Maurice Kouandete
1968–90 *As President*

Republic of Benin
1990– Nicephore Soglo

BHUTAN

Monarch (Druk Gyalpo)

1907–26 Uggyen Wangchuk
1926–52 Jigme Wangchuk
1952–72 Jigme Dorji Wangchuk
1972– Jigme Singye Wangchuk

BOLIVIA

President

1899–1904 José Manual Pando
1904–9 Ismael Montes
1909–13 Heliodoro Villazón
1913–17 Ismael Montes
1917–20 José N Gutiérrez Guerra
1920–5 Bautista Saavedra
1925–6 José Cabina Villanueva
1926–30 Hernando Siles
1930 Roberto Hinojusa *President of Revolutionaries*
1930–1 Carlos Blanco Galindo
1931–4 Daniel Salamanca
1934–6 José Luis Tejado Sorzano
1936–7 David Toro
1937–9 Germán Busch
1939 Carlos Quintanilla
1940–3 Enrique Peñaranda y del Castillo
1943–6 Gualberto Villaroel
1946 Nestor Guillen
1946–7 Tomas Monje Gutiérrez
1947–9 Enrique Hertzog
1949 Mamerto Urriolagoitía
1951–2 Hugo Ballivián
1952 Hernán Siles Suazo
1952–6 Victor Paz Estenssoro
1956–60 Hernán Siles Suazo
1960–4 Victor Paz Estenssoro
1964–5 René Barrientos Ortuño
1965–6 René Barrientos Ortuño *and* Alfredo Ovando Candía
1966 Alfredo Ovando Candía
1966–9 René Barrientos Ortuño
1969 Luis Adolfo Siles Salinas
1969–70 Alfredo Ovando Candía
1970 Rogelio Mirando
1970–1 Juan José Torres Gonzales
1971–8 Hugo Banzer Suárez
1978 Juan Pereda Asbún
1978–9 *Military Junta* (David Padilla Arericiba)
1979 Walter Guevara Arze
1979–80 Lydia Gueiler Tejada
1980–1 *Military Junta* (Luis García Meza)
1981–2 *Military Junta* (Celso Torrelio Villa)

President (cont.)

1982 Guido Vildoso Calderón
1982–5 Hernán Siles Suazo
1985–9 Victor Paz Estenssoro
1989 Jaime Paz Zamora

BOTSWANA

President

1966–80 Seretse Khama
1980– Quett Masire

BRAZIL

President

1898–1902 Manuel Ferraz de Campos Sales
1902–6 Francisco de Paula Rodrigues Alves
1906–9 Alfonso Pena
1909–10 Nilo Peçanha
1910–14 Hermes Rodrigues da Fonseca
1914–18 Venceslau Brás Pereira Gomes
1918–19 Francisco de Paula Rodrigues Alves
1919–22 Epitácio Pessoa
1922–6 Artur da Silva Bernardes
1926–30 Washington Luís Pereira de Sousa
1930–45 Getúlio Dorneles Vargas
1945–51 Eurico Gaspar Dutra
1951–4 Getúlio Dorneles Vargas
1954–5 João Café Filho
1955 Carlos Coimbra da Luz
1955–6 Nereu de Oliveira Ramos
1956–61 Juscelino Kubitschek de Oliveira
1961 Jânio da Silva Quadros
1961–3 João Belchior Marques Goulart
1963 Pascoal Ranieri Mazilli
1963–4 João Belchior Marques Goulart
1964 Pascoal Ranieri Mazilli
1964–7 Humberto de Alencar Castelo Branco
1967–9 Artur da Costa e Silva
1969–74 Emílio Garrastazu Médici
1974–9 Ernesto Geisel
1979–85 João Baptista de Oliveira Figueiredo
1985–90 José Sarney
1990– Fernando Collor de Mello

BRUNEI

Monarch (Sultan)

1967– Muda Hassanal Bolkiah Muizzadin Waddaulah

BULGARIA

Monarch

1887–1908 Ferdinand *Prince*
1908–18 Ferdinand I
1918–43 Boris III
1943–6 Simeon II

President

1946–7 Vasil Kolarov
1947–50 Mincho Naichev
1950–8 Georgi Damianov
1958–64 Dimitro Ganev
1964–71 Georgi Traikov
1971–89 Todor Zhivkov
1989–90 Petar Mladenov
1990– Zhelyu Zhelev

Premier

1946–9 Georgi Dimitrov
1949–50 Vasil Kolarov
1950–6 Vulko Chervenkov
1956–62 Anton Yugov
1962–71 Todor Zhivkov
1971–81 Stanko Todorov
1981–86 Grisha Filipov
1986–90 Georgy Atanasov
1990 Andrei Lukanov
1990 Ginio Ganev
1990–1 Dimitar Popov
1991– Philip Dimitrov

First Secretary

1946–53 Vulko Chervenkov
1953–89 Todor Zhivkov
1989–90 Petar Mladenov
1990– Alexander Lilov

BURKINA FASO

President

Upper Volta
1960–6 Maurice Yaméogo
1966–80 Sangoulé Lamizana
1980 Saye Zerbo

People's Salvation Council
1982–3 Jean-Baptiste Ouedraugo *Chairman*

National Revolutionary Council
1983–4 Thomas Sankara *Chairman*

Burkina Faso
1984–7 Thomas Sankara *Chairman*
1987– Blaise Compaoré

BURMA (Union of Myanmar)

President

1948–52 Sao Shwe Thaik
1952–7 Agga Maha Thiri Thudhamma Ba U
1957–62 U Wing Maung
1962 Sama Duwa Sinwa Nawng

Revolutionary Council
1962–74 Ne Win

State Council
1974–81 Ne Win
1981–8 U San Yu
1988 U Sein Lwin
1988 Maung Maung
1988– Saw Maung

Prime Minister

1947–56 Thakin Nu
1956–7 U Ba Swe
1957–8 U Nu
1958–60 Ne Win
1960–2 U Nu
1962–74 Ne Win
1974–7 U Sein Win
1977–8 U Maung Maung Ka
1988 U Tun Tin
1988– Saw Maung

BURUNDI

Monarch

1962–6 Mwambutsa IV
1966 Ntare V

President

1966–77 Michel Micombero
1977–87 Jean-Baptiste Bagaza
1987– *Military Junta* (Pierre Buyoya)

CAMBODIA (Kampuchea)

Monarch

1941–55 Norodom Sihanouk II
1955–60 Norodom Suramarit

Chief of State

1960–70 Prince Norodom Sihanouk

Khmer Republic
1970–2 Cheng Heng *Acting Chief of State*
1972–5 Lon Nol
1975–6 Prince Norodom Sihanouk
1976–81 Khieu Samphan
1981– Heng Samrin

Government in exile

President

1970–5 Prince Norodom Sihanouk
1982– Prince Norodom Sihanouk

Prime Minister

1945–6 Son Ngoc Thanh
1946–8 Prince Monireth
1948–9 Son Ngoc Thanh
1949–51 Prince Monipong
1951 Son Ngoc Thanh
1951–2 Huy Kanthoul
1952–3 Norodom Sihanouk II
1953 Samdech Penn Nouth
1953–4 Chan Nak
1954–5 Leng Ngeth
1955–6 Prince Norodom Sihanouk
1956 Oum Chheang Sun
1956 Prince Norodom Sihanouk
1956 Khim Tit
1956 Prince Norodom Sihanouk
1956 Sam Yun
1956–7 Prince Norodom Sihanouk
1957–8 Sim Var
1958 Ek Yi Oun
1958 Samdech Penn Nouth *Acting Prime Minister*
1958 Sim Var
1958–60 Prince Norodom Sihanouk
1960–1 Pho Proung
1961 Samdech Penn Nouth
1961–3 Prince Norodom Sihanouk
1963–6 Prince Norodom Kantol
1966–7 Lon Nol
1967–8 Prince Norodom Sihanouk
1968–9 Samdech Penn Nouth
1969–72 Lon Nol

Prime Minister (cont.)

Khmer Republic (1970)
1972 Sisovath Sivik Matak
1972 Son Ngoc Thanh
1972–3 Hang Thun Hak
1973 In Tam
1973–5 Long Boret
1975–6 Samdech Penn Nouth
1976–9 Pol Pot
1979–81 Khieu Samphan
1981–5 Chan Si
1985– Hun Sen

Government in exile
1970–3 Samdech Penn Nouth
1982– Son Sann

CAMEROON

President

1960–82 Ahmadun Ahidjo
1982– Paul Biya

Prime Minister

1991– Sadou Hayatou

CANADA

Chief of State: British monarch, represented by Governor General

Prime Minister

1867–73 John A MacDonald *Con*
1873–8 Alexander Mackenzie *Lib*
1878–91 John A MacDonald *Con*
1891–2 John J C Abbot *Con*
1892–4 John S D Thompson *Con*
1894–6 Mackenzie Bowell *Con*
1896 Charles Tupper *Con*
1896–1911 Wilfrid Laurier *Lib*
1911–17 Robert Borden *Con*
1917–20 Robert Borden *Con*
1920–1 Arthur Meighen *Con*
1921–6 William Lyon Mackenzie King *Lib*
1926 Arthur Meighen *Con*
1926–30 William Lyon Mackenzie King *Lib*
1930–5 Richard Bedford Bennett *Con*
1935–48 William Lyon Mackenzie King *Lib*
1948–57 Louis St Laurent *Lib*
1957–63 John George Diefenbaker *Con*
1963–8 Lester Bowles Pearson *Lib*
1968–79 Pierre Elliott Trudeau *Lib*
1979–80 Joseph Clark *Con*
1980–4 Pierre Elliott Trudeau *Lib*
1984 John Turner *Lib*
1984– Brian Mulroney *Con*

Con *Conservative*
Lib *Liberal*

CAPE VERDE

President

1975–91 Aristides Pereira
1991– Antonio Mascarenhas Monteiro

Prime Minister

1975– Pedro Pires

CENTRAL AFRICAN REPUBLIC

President

1960–6 David Dacko
1966–79 Jean-Bédel Bokassa (*from 1977, Emperor Bokassa I*)
1979–81 David Dacko
1981– André Kolingba

Prime Minister

1991– Edouard Frank

CHAD

President

1960–75 François Tombalbaye
1975–9 *Supreme Military Council* (Félix Malloum)
1979 Goukouni Oueddi
1979 Mohammed Shawwa
1979–82 Goukouni Oueddi
1982–90 Hissène Habré
1990– Idriss Déby (*Interim*)

Prime Minister

1991– Jean Alingue Bawoyeu

CHILE

President

1900–1 Federico Errázuriz Echaurren
1901 Aníbal Zañartu *Vice President*
1901–3 Germán Riesco
1903 Ramón Barros Luco *Vice President*
1903–6 Germán Riesco
1906–10 Pedro Montt
1910 Ismael Tocornal *Vice President*
1910 Elías Fernández Albano *Vice President*
1910 Emiliano Figueroa Larraín *Vice President*
1910–15 Ramón Barros Luco
1915–20 Juan Luis Sanfuentes
1920–4 Arturo Alessandri
1924–5 *Military Juntas*
1925 Arturo Alessandri
1925 Luis Barros Borgoño *Vice President*
1925–27 Emiliano Figueroa
1927–31 Carlos Ibáñez
1931 Pedro Opaso Letelier *Vice President*
1931 Juan Esteban Montero *Vice President*
1931 Manuel Trucco Franzani *Vice President*
1931–2 Juan Estaban Montero
1932 *Military Juntas*
1932 Carlos G Dávila *Provisional President*
1932 Bartolomé Blanche *Provisional President*
1932 Abraham Oyanedel *Vice President*
1932 8 Arturo Alessandri Palma
1938–41 Pedro Aguirre Cerda
1941–2 Jerónimo Méndez Arancibia *Vice President*
1942–6 Juan Antonio Ríos Morales
1946–52 Gabriel González Videla
1952–8 Carlos Ibáñez del Campo
1958–64 Jorge Alessandri Rodríguez
1964–70 Eduardo Frei Montalva
1970–3 Salvador Allende Gossens
1973–90 Augusto Pinochet Ugarte
1990– Patricio Aylwin Azócar

CHINA

Emperor

1875–1908 Kuang-hsü
1908–12 Hsüan-T'ung

President

1912 Sun Yat-sen
1912–16 Yüan Shih-k'ai
1916–17 Li Yuan-hung
1917–18 Feng Kuo-chang
1918–22 Hsü Shih-ch'ang
1921–5 Sun Yat-sen *Canton Administration*
1922–3 Li Yuan-hung
1923–4 Ts'ao K'un
1924–6 Tuan Ch'i-jui
1926–7 *Civil Disorder*
1927–8 Chang Tso-lin
1928–31 Chiang Kai-shek
1931–2 Ch'eng Ming-hsu *Acting President*
1932–43 Lin Sen
1940–4 Wang Ching-wei *in Japanese-occupied territory*
1943–9 Chiang Kai-shek
1945–9 *Civil War*
1949 Li Tsung-jen

People's Republic of China

1949–59 Mao Zedong (Mao Tse-tung)
1959–68 Liu Shaoqi
1968–75 Dong Biwu
1975–6 Zhu De
1976–8 Sung Qingling
1978–83 Ye Jianying
1983–8 Li Xiannian (Li Hsien-nien)
1988– Yang Shangkun

Prime Minister

1901–3 Jung-lu
1903–11 Prince Ch'ing
1912 Lu Cheng-hsiang
1912–13 Chao Ping-chiin
1913–14 Sun Pao'chi
1914–16 *no Prime Minister*
1916–17 Chang-hsün
1917 Tuan Ch'i-jui
1918–19 Ch'ien Neng-hsün
1919 Kung Hsin-chan
1919–20 Chin Yün-p'eng
1920 Sa Chen-ping
1920–1 Chin Yün-p'eng
1921–2 Liang Shihi
1922 Yen Hui-ching
1922 Chow Tzu-ch'i
1922 Yen Hui-ching
1922 Wang Ch'ung-hui
1922–3 Wang Ta-hsieh
1923 Chang Shao-ts'êng
1923–4 Kao Ling-wei
1924 Jun Pao-ch'i
1924 Ku Wei-chiin
1924 Yen Hui-ch'ing
1924–5 Huang Fu
1925 Tuan Ch'i-jui
1925–6 Hsu Shih-ying
1926 Chia Teh-yao
1926 Hu Wei-te
1926 Yen Hui-ch'ing
1926 Tu Hsi-kuei
1926–7 Ku Wei-chün
1927 *Civil Disorder*

Prime Minister (cont.)

1927 *Executive Council*
1927–9 P'an Fu
1928–30 T'an Yen-kai
1930 Sung Tzu-wen *Acting Prime Minister*
1930 Wang Ching-wei
1930–1 Chiang Kai-shek
1931–2 Sun Fo
1932–5 Wang Ching-wei
1935–7 Chiang Kai-shek
1937–8 Wang Ch'ung-hui *Acting Prime Minister*
1938–9 K'ung Hsiang-hsi
1939–44 Chiang Kai-shek
1944–7 Sung Tzu-wen
1945–9 *Civil War*
1947–8 Chang Ch'ün
1948 Wong Wen-hao
1948–9 Sun Fo
1949 Ho Ying-ch'in
1949 Yen Hsi-shan
1949–76 Zhou Enlai (Chou En-lai)
1976–80 Hua Guofeng
1980–7 Zhao Ziyang (Chao Tzu-yang)
1987– Li Peng

Communist Party

Chairman

1935–76 Mao Zedong
1976–81 Hua Guofeng
1981–2 Hu Yaobang

General Secretary

1982–7 Hu Yaobang
1987–9 Zhao Ziyang (Chao Tzu-yang)
1989– Jiang Zemin

COLOMBIA

President

1900–4 José Manuel Marroquín *Vice President*
1904–9 Rafael Reyes
1909–10 Ramón González Valencia
1910–14 Carlos E Restrepo
1914–18 José Vicente Concha
1918–21 Marco Fidel Suárez
1921–2 Jorge Holguín *President Designate*
1922–6 Pedro Nel Ospina
1926–30 Miguel Abadía Méndez
1930–4 Enrique Olaya Herrera
1934–8 Alfonso López
1938–42 Eduardo Santos
1942 Alfonso López
1945–6 Alberto Lleras Camargo *President Designate*
1946–50 Mariano Ospina Pérez
1950–3 Laureano Gómez
1953–7 Gustavo Rojas Pinilla
1957 *Military Junta*
1958–62 Alberto Lleras Camargo
1962–6 Guillermo León Valencia
1966–70 Carlos Lleras Restrepo
1970–4 Misael Pastrana Borrero
1974–8 Alfonso López Michelsen
1978–82 Julio César Turbay Ayala
1982–6 Belisario Betancur
1986–90 Virgilio Barco Vargas
1990– César Gaviria Trujillo

COMMONWEALTH

Secretary General

1965–75 Arnold Smith
1975–90 Shridath S Ramphal
1990– Emeka Anyaoku

COMOROS

President

1976–78 Ali Soilih
1978–89 Ahmed Abdallah Abderemane
1989– Said Mohammed Djohar

CONGO

President

1960–3 Abbé Fulbert Youlou
1963–8 Alphonse Massemba-Debat
1968 Marien Ngouabi
1968 Alphonse Massemba-Debat
1968–9 Alfred Raoul
1969–77 Marien Ngouabi
1977–9 Joachim Yhomby Opango
1979– Denis Sassou-Nguesso

COSTA RICA

President

1894–1902 Rafael Yglesias y Castro
1902–6 Ascención Esquivel Ibarra
1906–10 Cleto González Víquez
1910–12 Ricardo Jiménez Oreamuno
1912–14 Cleto González Víquez
1914–17 Alfredo González Flores
1917–19 Federico Tinoco Granados
1919 Julio Acosta García
1919–20 Juan Bautista Quiros
1920–4 Julio Acosta García
1924–8 Ricardo Jiménez Oreamuno
1928–32 Cleto González Víquez
1932–6 Ricardo Jiménez Oreamuno
1936–40 León Cortés Castro
1940–4 Rafael Ángel Calderón Guardia
1944–8 Teodoro Picado Michalski
1948 Santos Léon Herrera
1948–9 *Civil Junta* (José Figueres Ferrer)
1949–52 Otilio Ulate Blanco
1952–3 Alberto Oreamuno Flores
1953–8 José Figueres Ferrer
1958–62 Mario Echandi Jiménez
1962–6 Francisco José Orlich Bolmarcich
1966–70 José Joaquín Trejos Fernández
1970–4 José Figueres Ferrer
1974–8 Daniel Oduber Quirós
1978–82 Rodrigo Carazo Odio
1982–6 Luis Alberto Monge Álvarez
1986–90 Oscar Arias Sánchez
1990– Rafael Angel Calderón

CÔTE D'IVOIRE

President

1960– Félix Houphouët-Boigny

Prime Minister

1990– Alassane Ouattara

CUBA

President

1902–6	Tomas Estrada Palma
1906–9	*US rule*
1909–13	José Miguel Gómez
1913–21	Mario García Menocal
1921–5	Alfredo Zayas y Alfonso
1925–33	Gerardo Machado y Morales
1933	Carlos Manuel de Céspedes
1933–4	Ramón Grau San Martín
1934–5	Carlos Mendieta
1935–6	José A Barnet y Vinagres
1936	Miguel Mariano Gómez y Arias
1936–40	Federico Laredo Bru
1940–4	Fulgencio Batista
1944–8	Ramón Grau San Martín
1948–52	Carlos Prío Socarrás
1952–9	Fulgencio Batista
1959	Manuel Urrutia
1959–76	Osvaldo Dorticós Torrado
1959–76	Fidel Castro Ruz *Prime Minister and First Secretary*
1976–	Fidel Castro Ruz *President*

CYPRUS

President

1960–77	Archbishop Makarios
1977–88	Spyros Kyprianou
1988–	Georgios Vassiliou

CZECHOSLOVAKIA

President

1918–35	Tomáš Garrigue Masaryk
1935–8	Edvard Beneš
1938–9	Emil Hácha

Occupation

1938–45	Edvard Beneš *Provisional President*
1939–45	Emil Hácha *State President*
1939–45	Jozef Tiso *Slovak Republic President*

Post-war

1945–8	Edvard Beneš
1948–53	Klement Gottwald
1953–7	Antonín Zápotocký
1957–68	Antonín Novotný
1968–75	Ludvík Svoboda
1975–89	Gustáv Husák
1989–	Vaclav Havel

Prime Minister

1918–19	Karel Kramář
1919–20	Vlastimil Tusar
1920–1	Jan Černý
1921–2	Edvard Beneš
1922–6	Antonin Švehla
1926	Jan Černý
1926–9	Antonin Švehla
1929–32	František Udržal
1932–5	Jan Malypetr
1935–8	Milan Hodža
1938	Jan Syrový
1938–9	Rudolf Beran
1940–5	Jan Šrámek *in exile*
1945–6	Zdeněk Fierlinger
1946–8	Klement Gottwald

Prime Minister (cont.)

1948–53	Antonin Zápotocký
1953–63	Viliam Široký
1963–8	Josef Lenárt
1968–70	Oldřich Černik
1970–88	Lubomír Štrougal
1988–9	Ladislav Adamec
1989–	Marian Calfa

First Secretary

1948–52	Rudolf Slánsky
1953–68	Antonín Novotný
1968–9	Alexander Dubček
1969–87	Gustáv Husák
1987–9	Mílos Jakes
1989	Karel Urbanek
1989–	Ladislav Adamec

DENMARK

Monarch

1863–1906	Christian IX
1906–12	Frederik VIII
1912–47	Christian X
1947–72	Frederik IX
1972–	Margrethe II

Prime Minister

1900–1	H Sehested
1901–5	J H Deuntzer
1905–8	J C Christensen
1908–9	N Neergaard
1909	L Holstein-Ledreborg
1909–10	C Th Zahle
1910–13	Klaus Berntsen
1913–20	C Th Zahle
1920	Otto Liebe
1920	M P Friis
1920–4	N Neergaard
1924–6	Thorvald Stauning
1926–9	Th Madsen-Mygdal
1929–42	Thorvald Stauning
1942	Wilhelm Buhl
1942–3	Erik Scavenius
1943–5	*No government*
1945	Wilhelm Buhl
1945–7	Knud Kristensen
1947–50	Hans Hedtoft
1950–3	Erik Eriksen
1953–5	Hans Hedtoft
1955–60	Hans Christian Hansen
1960–2	Viggo Kampmann
1962–8	Jens Otto Krag
1968–71	Hilmar Baunsgaard
1971–2	Jens Otto Krag
1972–3	Anker Jorgensen
1973–5	Poul Hartling
1975–82	Anker Jorgensen
1982–	Poul Schlüter

DJIBOUTI

President

1977–	Hassan Gouled Aptidon

Prime Minister

1977–8	Abdallah Mohammed Kamil
1978–	Barkat Gourad Hamadou

DOMINICA

President

1977	Frederick E Degazon
1978–9	Louis Cods-Lartigue *Interim President*
1979–80	Lenner Armour *Acting President*
1980–4	Aurelius Marie
1984–	Clarence Augustus Seignoret

Prime Minister

1978–9	Patrick Roland John
1979–80	Oliver Seraphine
1980–	Mary Eugenia Charles

DOMINICAN REPUBLIC

President

1899–1902	Juan Isidro Jiménez
1902–3	Horacio Vásquez
1903	Alejandro Wos y Gil
1903–4	Juan Isidro Jiménez
1904–6	Carlos Morales
1906–11	Ramon Cáceres
1911–12	Eladio Victoria
1912–13	Adolfo Nouel y Bobadilla
1913–14	José Bordas y Valdés
1914	Ramon Báez
1914–16	Juan Isidro Jiménez
1916–22	*US occupation* (Francisco Henríquez y Carrajal)
1922–4	(Juan Batista Vicini Burgos)
1924–30	Horacio Vásquez
1930	Rafael Estrella Urena
1930–8	Rafael Leónidas Trujillo y Molina
1938–40	Jacinto Bienvenudo Peynado
1940–2	Manuel de Jesus Troncoso de la Concha
1942–52	Rafael Leónidas Trujillo y Molina
1952–60	Hector Bienvenido Trujillo
1960–2	Joaquín Videla Balaguer
1962	Rafael Bonnelly
1962	*Military Junta* (Huberto Bogaert)
1962–3	Rafael Bonnelly
1963	Juan Bosch Gavino
1963	*Military Junta* (Emilio de los Santos)
1963–5	Donald Reid Cabral
1965	*Civil War*
1965	Elias Wessin y Wessin
1965	Antonio Imbert Barreras
1965	Francisco Caamaño Deñó
1965–6	Héctor García Godoy Cáceres
1966–78	Joaquín Videla Balaguer
1978–82	Antonio Guzmán Fernández
1982–6	Salvador Jorge Blanco
1986–	Joaquín Videla Balaguer

ECUADOR

President

1895–1901	Eloy Alfaro
1901–5	Leónides Plaza Gutiérrez
1905–6	Lizardo García
1906–11	Eloy Alfaro
1911	Emilio Estrada
1911–12	Carlos Freile Zaldumbide
1912–16	Leónides Plaza Gutiérrez

ECUADOR (cont.)

President (cont.)

1916–20 Alfredo Baquerizo Moreno
1920–4 José Luis Tamayo
1924–5 Gonzálo S de Córdova
1925–6 *Military Juntas*
1926–31 Isidro Ayora
1931 Luis A Larrea Alba
1932–3 Juan de Dios Martínez Mera
1933–4 Abelardo Montalvo
1934–5 José María Velasco Ibarra
1935 Antonio Pons
1935–7 Federico Páez
1937–8 Alberto Enriquez Gallo
1938 Manuel María Borrero
1938–9 Aurelio Mosquera Narváez
1939–40 Julio Enrique Moreno
1940–4 Carlos Alberto Arroya del Río
1944–7 José María Velasco Ibarra
1947 Carlos Mancheno
1947–8 Carlos Julio Arosemena Tola
1948–52 Galo Plaza Lasso
1952–6 José María Velasco Ibarra
1956–60 Camilo Ponce Enríquez
1960–1 José María Velasco Ibarra
1961–3 Carlos Julio Arosemena Monroy
1963–6 *Military Junta*
1966 Clemente Yerovi Indaburu
1966–8 Otto Arosemena Gómez
1968–72 José María Velasco Ibarra
1972–6 Guillermo Rodríguez Lara
1976–9 *Military Junta*
1979–81 Jaime Roldós Aguilera
1981–4 Oswaldo Hurtado Larrea
1984–8 León Febres Cordero
1988– Rodrigo Borja Cevallos

EGYPT

Kingdom of Egypt

Monarch

1922–36 Fouad I
1936–7 Farouk *Trusteeship*
1937–52 Farouk I

Republic of Egypt

President

1952–4 Mohammed Naguib
1954–70 Gamal Abdel Nasser
1970–81 Mohammed Anwar El-Sadat
1981– Mohammed Hosni Mubarak

Prime Minister

1895–1908 Mustafa Fahmy
1908–10 Butros Ghali
1910–14 Mohammed Said
1914–19 Hussein Rushdi
1919 Mohammed Said
1919–20 Yousuf Wahba
1920–1 Mohammed Tewfiq Nazim
1921 Adli Yegen
1922 Abdel Khaliq Tharwat
1922–3 Mohammed Tewfiq Nazim
1923–4 Yehia Ibrahim
1924 Saad Zaghloul
1924–6 Ahmed Zaywan
1926–7 Adli Yegen
1927–8 Abdel Khaliq Tharwat
1928 Mustafa An-Nahass

Prime Minister (cont.)

1928–9 Mohammed Mahmoud
1929–30 Adli Yegen
1930 Mustafa An-Nahass
1930–3 Ismail Sidqi
1933–4 Abdel Fattah Yahya
1934–6 Mohammed Tewfiq Nazim
1936 Ali Maher
1936–7 Mustafa An-Nahass
1937–9 Mohammed Mahmoud
1939–40 Ali Maher
1940 Hassan Sabri
1940–2 Hussein Sirry
1942–4 Mustafa An-Nahass
1944–5 Ahmed Maher
1945–6 Mahmoud Fahmy El-Nuqrashi
1946 Ismail Sidqi
1946–8 Mahmoud Fahmy El-Nuqrashi
1948–9 Ibrahim Abdel Hadi
1949–50 Hussein Sirry
1950–2 Mustafa An-Nahass
1952 Ali Maher
1952 Najib El-Hilali
1952 Hussein Sirry
1952 Najib El-Hilali
1952 Ali Maher

Republic of Egypt

1952–4 Mohammed Najib
1954 Gamal Abdel Nasser
1954 Mohammed Najib
1954–62 Gamal Abdel Nasser
1958–61 *United Arab Republic*
1962–5 Ali Sabri
1965–6 Zakariya Mohyi Ed-Din
1966–7 Mohammed Sidqi Soliman
1967–70 Gamal Abdel Nasser
1970–2 Mahmoud Fawzi
1972–3 Aziz Sidki
1973–4 Anwar El-Sadat
1974–5 Abdel Aziz Hijazy
1975–8 Mamdouh Salem
1978–80 Mustafa Khalil
1980–1 Anwar El-Sadat
1981–2 Hosni Mubarak
1982–4 Fouad Monyi Ed-Din
1984 Kamal Hassan Ali
1985–6 Ali Lotfi
1986– Atif Sidqi

EL SALVADOR

President

1899–1903 Tomás Regalado
1903–7 Pedro José Escalon
1907–11 Fernando Figueroa
1911–13 Manuel Enrique Araujo
1913–14 Carlos Meléndez *President Designate*
1914–15 Alfonso Quiñónez Molina *President Designate*
1915–18 Carlos Meléndez
1918–19 Alfonso Quiñónez Molina *Vice President*
1919–23 Jorge Meléndez
1923–7 Alfonso Quiñónez Molina
1927–31 Pio Romero Bosque
1931 Arturo Araujo
1931 *Military Administration*
1931–4 Maximiliano H Martinez *Vice President*
1934–5 Andrés I Menéndez *Provisional President*

President (cont.)

1935–44 Maximiliano H Martinez
1944 Andrés I Menéndez *Vice President*
1944–5 Osmin Aguirre y Salinas *Provisional President*
1945–8 Salvador Castaneda Castro
1948–50 *Revolutionary Council*
1950–6 Oscar Osorio
1956–60 José María Lemus
1960–1 *Military Junta*
1961–2 *Civil-Military Administration*
1962 Rodolfo Eusebio Cordón *Provisional President*
1962–7 Julio Adalberto Rivera
1967–72 Fidel Sánchez Hernández
1972–7 Arturo Armando Molina
1977–9 Carlos Humberto Romero
1979–82 *Military Juntas*
1982–4 *Government of National Unanimity* (Alvaro Magaña)
1984–9 José Napoleón Duarte
1989– Alfredo Cristiani

EQUATORIAL GUINEA

President

1968–79 Francisco Macias Nguema
1979– Teodoro Obiang Nguema Mbasogo

ESTONIA

President

1991– Arnold Rüütel

ETHIOPIA

Monarch

1889–1911 Menelik II
1911–16 Lij Iyasu (Joshua)
1916–28 Zawditu
1928–74 Haile Selassie *Emperor from 1930*

Provisional Military Administrative Council

Chairman

1974–7 Teferi Benti
1977–87 Mengistu Haile Mariam

People's Democratic Republic

President

1987–91 Mengistu Haile Mariam
1991– Meles Zenawi

EUROPEAN COMMUNITY (EC) COMMISSION

President

1967–70 Jean Rey
1970–2 Franco M Malfatti
1972–3 Sicco L Mansholt
1973–7 Francois-Xavier Ortoli
1977–81 Roy Jenkins
1981–5 Gaston Thorn
1985– Jacques Delors

FIJI

Chief of State: British monarch, represented by Governor General

Prime Minister

1970–87	Kamisese Mara
1987	Timoci Bavadra

Interim Administration

Governor General

1987	Penaia Ganilau
1987	*Military administration* (Sitiveni Rabuka)

Republic

Chairman

1987	Sitiveni Rabuka

President

1987–	Penaia Ganilau

Prime Minister

1987–	Kamisese Mara

FINLAND

President

1919–25	Kaarlo Juho Ståhlberg
1925–31	Lauri Kristian Relander
1931–7	Pehr Evind Svinhufvud
1937–40	Kyösti Kallio
1940–4	Risto Ryti
1944–6	Carl Gustaf Mannerheim
1946–56	Juho Kusti Paasikivi
1956–81	Urho Kekkonen
1982–	Mauno Koivisto

Prime Minister

1917–18	Pehr Evind Svinhufvud
1918	Juho Kusti Pasaikivi
1918–19	Lauri Johannes Ingman
1919	Kaarlo Castrén
1919–20	Juho Vennola
1920–1	Rafael Erich
1921–2	Juho Vennola
1922	Aino Kaarlo Cajander
1922–4	Kyösti Kallio
1924	Aino Kaarlo Cajander
1924–5	Lauri Johannes Ingman
1925	Antti Agaton Tulenheimo
1925–6	Kyösti Kallio
1926–7	Väinö Tanner
1927–8	Juho Emil Sunila
1928–9	Oskari Mantere
1929–30	Kyösti Kallio
1930–1	Pehr Evind Svinhufvud
1931–2	Juho Emil Sunila
1932–6	Toivo Kivimäki
1936–7	Kyösti Kallio
1937–9	Aino Kaarlo Cajander
1939–41	Risto Ryti
1941–3	Johann Rangell
1943–4	Edwin Linkomies
1944	Andreas Hackzell
1944	Urho Jonas Castrén
1944–5	Juho Kusti Paasikivi

Prime Minister (cont.)

1946–8	Mauno Pekkala
1948–50	Karl August Fagerholm
1950–3	Urho Kekkonen
1953–4	Sakari Tuomioja
1954	Ralf Törngren
1954–6	Urho Kekkonen
1956–7	Karl August Fagerholm
1957	Väinö Johannes Sukselainen
1957–8	Rainer von Fieandt
1958	Reino Iisakki Kuuskoski
1958–9	Karl August Fagerholm
1959–61	Väinö Johannes Sukselainen
1961–2	Martti Miettunen
1962–3	Ahti Karjalainen
1963–4	Reino Ragnar Lehto
1964–6	Johannes Virolainen
1966–8	Rafael Paasio
1968–70	Mauno Koivisto
1970	Teuvo Ensio Aura
1970–1	Ahti Karjalainen
1971–2	Teuvo Ensio Aura
1972	Rafael Paasio
1972–5	Kalevi Sorsa
1975	Keijo Antero Liinamaa
1975–7	Martti Miettunen
1977–9	Kalevi Sorsa
1979–82	Mauno Koivisto
1982–87	Kalevi Sorsa
1987–91	Harri Holkeri
1991–	Esko Aho

FRANCE

President

Third Republic

1899–1906	Emile Loubet
1906–13	Armand Fallières
1913–20	Raymond Poincaré
1920	Paul Deschanel
1920–4	Alexandre Millerand
1924–31	Gaston Doumergue
1931–2	Paul Doumer
1932–40	Albert Lebrun

Fourth Republic

1947–54	Vincent Auriol
1954–8	René Coty

Fifth Republic

1958–69	Charles de Gaulle
1969–74	Georges Pompidou
1974–81	Valéry Giscard d'Estaing
1981–	François Mitterrand

Prime Minister

Third Republic

1899–1902	Pierre Waldeck-Rousseau
1902–5	Emile Combes
1905–6	Maurice Rouvier
1906	Jean Sarrien
1906–9	Georges Clemenceau
1909–11	Aristide Briand
1911	Ernest Monis
1911–12	Joseph Caillaux
1912–13	Raymond Poincaré
1913	Aristide Briand
1913	Louis Barthou
1913–14	Gaston Doumergue
1914	Alexandre Ribot
1914–15	René Viviani

Prime Minister (cont.)

1915–17	Aristide Briand
1917	Alexandre Ribot
1917	Paul Painlevé
1917–20	Georges Clemenceau
1920	Alexandre Millerand
1920–1	Georges Leygues
1921–2	Aristide Briand
1922–4	Raymond Poincaré
1924	Frédéric François-Marsal
1924–5	Edouard Herriot
1925	Paul Painlevé
1925–6	Aristide Briand
1926	Edouard Herriot
1926–9	Raymond Poincaré
1929	Aristide Briand
1929–30	André Tardieu
1930	Camille Chautemps
1930	André Tardieu
1930–1	Théodore Steeg
1931–2	Pierre Laval
1932	André Tardieu
1932	Edouard Herriot
1932–3	Joseph Paul-Boncour
1933	Edouard Daladier
1933	Albert Sarrault
1933–4	Camille Chautemps
1934	Edouard Daladier
1934	Gaston Doumergue
1934–5	Pierre-Etienne Flandin
1935	Fernand Bouisson
1935–6	Pierre Laval
1936	Albert Sarrault
1936–7	Léon Blum
1937–8	Camille Chautemps
1938	Léon Blum
1938–40	Edouard Daladier
1940	Paul Reynaud
1940	Philippe Pétain

Vichy Government

1940–4	Philippe Pétain

Provisional Government of the French Republic

1944–6	Charles de Gaulle
1946	Félix Gouin
1946	Georges Bidault

Fourth Republic

1946 7	Léon Blum
1947	Paul Ramadier
1947–8	Robert Schuman
1948	André Marie
1948	Robert Schuman
1948–9	Henri Queuille
1949–50	Georges Bidault
1950	Henri Queuille
1950–1	René Pleven
1951	Henri Queuille
1951–2	René Pleven
1952	Edgar Faure
1952–3	Antoine Pinay
1953	René Mayer
1953–4	Joseph Laniel
1954–5	Pierre Mendès-France
1955–6	Edgar Faure
1956–7	Guy Mollet
1957	Maurice Bourgès-Maunoury
1957–8	Félix Gaillard
1958	Pierre Pflimin
1958–9	Charles de Gaulle

FRANCE (cont.)

Prime Minister (cont.)

Fifth Republic

1959–62 Michel Debré
1962–8 Georges Pompidou
1968–9 Maurice Couve de Murville
1969–72 Jacques Chaban Delmas
1972–4 Pierre Mesmer
1974–6 Jacques Chirac
1976–81 Raymond Barre
1981–4 Pierre Mauroy
1984–6 Laurent Fabius
1986–8 Jacques Chirac
1988–91 Michel Rocard
1991– Edith Cresson

GABON

President

1960–7 Léon M'ba
1967– Omar (Bernard-Albert, *to 1973*) Bongo

Prime Minister

1960–75 *As President*
1975–90 Léon Mébiame (Mébiane)
1990– Casimir Oyé Mba

THE GAMBIA

President

1965– Dawda Kairaba Jawara

GERMANY

German Democratic Republic (East Germany)
President

1949–60 Wilhelm Pieck

Chairman of the Council of State

1960–73 Walter Ernst Karl Ulbricht
1973–6 Willi Stoph
1976–89 Erich Honecker
1989 Egon Krenz
1989–90 Gregor Gysi
General Secretary as Chairman

Premier

1949–64 Otto Grotewohl
1964–73 Willi Stoph
1973–6 Horst Sindermann
1976–89 Willi Stoph
1989–90 Hans Modrow
1990 Lothar de Maizière

German Federal Republic (West Germany)
President

1949–59 Theodor Heuss
1959–69 Heinrich Lübke
1969–74 Gustav Heinemann
1974–9 Walter Scheel
1979–84 Karl Carstens
1984–90 Richard von Weizsäcker

Chancellor

1949–63 Konrad Adenauer
1963–6 Ludwig Erhard
1966–9 Kurt Georg Kiesinger
1969–74 Willy Brandt
1974–82 Helmut Schmidt
1982–90 Helmut Kohl

Germany
President

1990– Richard von Weizsäcker

Chancellor

1990– Helmut Kohl

GHANA

President

1960–6 Kwame Nkrumah

National Liberation Council

Chairman

1966–9 Joseph Arthur Ankrah
1969 Akwasi Amankwa Afrifa
1969–70 *Presidential Committee*

President

1970–2 Edward Akufo-Addo

Chairman

1972–8 *National Redemption Council* (Ignatius Kuti Acheampong)
1978–9 *Supreme Military Council* (Fred W Akuffo)
1979 *Armed Forces Revolutionary Council* (Jerry John Rawlings)

President

1979–81 Hilla Limann

Provisional National Defence Council

Chairman

1981– Jerry John Rawlings

Prime Minister

1960–9 *As President*
1969–72 Kufi Abrefa Busia
1972–8 *As President*
1978– *No Prime Minister*

GREECE

Monarch

1863–1913 George I
1913–17 Constantine I
1917–20 Alexander
1920–2 Constantine I
1922–3 George II
1923–4 Paul Koundouriotis *Regent*

Republic

President

1924–6 Paul Koundouriotis
1926 Theodore Pangalos
1926–9 Paul Koundouriotis
1929–35 Alexander T Zaïmis

Monarch

1935 George Kondylis *Regent*
1935–47 George II
1947–64 Paul
1964–7 Constantine II
1967–73 *Military Junta*
1973 George Papadopoulos *Regent*

Republic

President

1973 George Papadopoulos
1973–4 Phaedon Gizikis
1974–5 Michael Stasinopoulos
1975–80 Constantine Tsatsos
1980–5 Constantine Karamanlis
1985–90 Christos Sartzetakis
1990– Constantine Karamanlis

Prime Minister

1899–1901 George Theotokis
1901–2 Alexander T Zaïmis
1902–3 Theodore Diligiannis
1903 George Theotokis
1903 Demetrius G Rallis
1903–4 George Theotokis
1904–5 Theodore Deligiannis
1905 Demetrius G Rallis
1905–9 George Theotokis
1909 Demetrius G Rallis
1909–10 Kyriakoulis P Mavromichalis
1910 Stephen N Dragoumis
1910–15 Eleftherios K Venizelos
1915 Demetrius P Gounaris
1915 Eleftherios K Venizelos
1915 Alexander T Zaïmis
1915–16 Stephen Skouloudis
1916 Alexander T Zaïmis
1916 Nicholas P Kalogeropoulos
1916–17 Spyridon Lambros
1917 Alexander T Zaïmis
1917–20 Eleftherios K Venizelos
1920–1 Demetrius G Rallis
1921 Nicholas P Kalogeropoulos
1921–2 Demetrius P Gounaris
1922 Nicholas Stratos
1922 Peter E Protopapadakis
1922 Nicholas Triandaphyllakos
1922 Sotirios Krokidas
1922 Alexander T Zaïmis
1922–3 Stylianos Gonatas
1924 Eleftherios Venizelos
1924 George Kaphandaris
1924 Alexander Papanastasiou
1924 Themistocles Sophoulis
1924–5 Andreas Michalakopoulos
1925–6 Alexander N Chatzikyriakos
1926 Theodore Pangalos
1926 Athanasius Eftaxias
1926 George Kondylis
1926–8 Alexander T Zaïmis
1928–32 Eleftherios K Venizelos
1932 Alexander Papanastasiou
1932 Eleftherios K Venizelos

GREECE (cont.)

rime Minister (cont.)

932–3	Panagiotis Tsaldaris
933	Eleftherios K Venizelos
933	Nicholas Plastiras
933	Alexander Othonaos
933–5	Panagiotis Tsaldaris
935	George Kondylis
935–6	Constantine Demertzis
936–41	John Metaxas
941	Alexander Koryzis
941	*Chairman of Ministers* George II
941	*German Occupation* Emmanuel Tsouderos
941–2	George Tsolakoglou
942–3	Constantine Logothetopoulos
943–4	John Rallis

overnment in exile

941–4	Emmanuel Tsouderos
944	Sophocles Venizelos
944–5	George Papandreou

ost-war

945	Nicholas Plastiras
945	Peter Voulgaris
945	Damaskinos, Archbishop of Athens
945	Panagiotis Kanellopoulos
945–6	Themistocles Sophoulis
946	Panagiotis Politzas
946–7	Constantine Tsaldaris
947	Demetrius Maximos
947	Constantine Tsaldaris
947–9	Themistocles Sophoulis
949–50	Alexander Diomedes
950	John Theotokis
950	Sophocles Venizelos
950	Nicholas Plastiras
1950–1	Sophocles Venizelos
1951	Nicholas Plastiras
1952	Demetrius Kiusopoulos
1952–5	Alexander Papagos
1955	Stephen C Stefanopoulos
1955–8	Constantine Karamanlis
1958	Constantine Georgakopoulos
1958–61	Constantine Karamanlis
1961	Constantine Dovas
1961–3	Constantine Karamanlis
1963	Panagiotis Pipinellis
1963	Stylianos Mavromichalis
1963	George Papandreou
1963–4	John Paraskevopoulos
1964–5	George Papandreou
1965	George Athanasiadis-Novas
1965	Elias Tsirimokos
1965–6	Stephen C Stefanopoulos
1966–7	John Paraskevopoulos
1967	Panagiotis Kanellopoulos
1967–74	*Military Junta*
1967	Constantine Kollias
1967–73	George Papadopoulos
1973	Spyridon Markezinis
1973–4	Adamantios Androutsopoulos
1974–80	Constantine Karamanlis
1980–1	George Rallis
1981–9	Andreas Papandreou
1989	Tzannis Tzannetakis
1989–90	Xenofon Zolotas
1990–	Konstantinos Mitsotakis

GRENADA

Chief of State: British monarch, represented by Governor General

Prime Minister

1974–9	Eric M Gairy
1979–83	Maurice Bishop
1983–4	Nicholas Braithwaite *Chairman of Interim Council*
1984–9	Herbert A Blaize
1989–90	Ben Jones (*Acting*)
1990–	Nicholas Braithwaite

GUATEMALA

President

1898–1920	Manuel Estrada Cabrera
1920–2	Carlos Herrera y Luna
1922–6	José María Orellana
1926–30	Lázaro Chacón
1930	Baudillo Palma
1930–1	Manuel María Orellana
1931	José María Reyna Andrade
1931–44	Jorge Ubico Castañeda
1944	Federico Ponce Vaidez
1944–5	Jacobo Arbenz Guzmán
1945–51	Juan José Arévalo
1951–4	Jacobo Arbenz Guzmán
1954	*Military Junta* (Carlos Díaz)
1954	Elfego J Monzón
1954–7	Carlos Castillo Armas
1957	*Military Junta* (Oscar Mendoza Azurdia)
1957	Luis Arturo González López
1957–8	*Military Junta* (Guillermo Flores Avendaño)
1958–63	Miguel Ydígoras Fuentes
1963–6	*Military Junta* (Enrique Peralta Azurdia)
1966–70	Julio César Méndez Montenegro
1970–4	Carlos Araña Osorio
1974–8	Kyell Eugenio Laugerua García
1978–82	Romeo Lucas García
1982	Angel Aníbal Guevara
1982–3	Efraín Rios Montt
1983–6	Oscar Humberto Mejía Victores
1986–91	Marco Vinicio Cerezo Arévalo
1991–	Jorge Serrano Elias

GUINEA

President

1961–84	Ahmed Sékou Touré
1984–	Lansana Conté

Prime Minister

1958–72	Ahmed Sékou Touré
1972–84	Louis Lansana Beavogui
1984–5	Diarra Traore
1985–	*None*

GUINEA-BISSAU

President

1974–80	Luis de Almeida Cabral
1980–4	*Revolutionary Council* (João Bernardo Vieira)
1984–	João Bernardo Vieira

GUYANA

President

1970	Edward A Luckhoo
1970–80	Arthur Chung
1980–5	Linden Forbes Sampson Burnham
1985–	Hugh Desmond Hoyte

Prime Minister

1966–85	Linden Forbes Sampson Burnham
1985–	Hamilton Green

HAITI

President

1896–1902	P A Tirésias Simon Lam
1902	Boisrond Canal
1902–8	Alexis Nord
1908–11	Antoine Simon
1911–12	Michel Cincinnatus Leconte
1912–13	Tancrède Auguste
1913–14	Michael Oreste
1914	Oreste Zamor
1914–15	Joseph Davilmare Théodore
1915	Jean Velbrun-Guillaume
1915–22	Philippe Sudre Dartiguenave
1922–30	Joseph Louis Bornó
1930	Étienne Roy
1930–41	Sténio Joseph Vincent
1941–6	Élie Lescot
1946	*Military Junta* (Frank Lavaud)
1946–50	Dumarsais Estimé
1950	*Military Junta* (Frank Lavaud)
1950–6	Paul E Magloire
1956–7	François Sylvain
1957	*Military Junta*
1957	Léon Cantave
1957	Daniel Fignolé
1957	Antoine Kebreau
1957–71	François Duvalier ('Papa Doc')
1971–86	Jean-Claude Duvalier ('Baby Doc')
1986–8	Henri Namphy
1988	Leslie Manigat
1988	Henri Namphy
1988–90	Prosper Avril
1990	Ertha Pascal-Trouillot (*Interim*)
1990–1	Jean-Bertrand Aristide
1991–	*Military junta*

HONDURAS

President

1900–3	Terencio Sierra
1903	Juan Angel Arias
1903–7	Manuel Bonilla Chirinos
1907–11	Miguel R Dávila
1912–15	Manuel Bonilla Chirinos
1915–20	Francisco Bertrand
1920–4	Rafael López Gutiérrez
1924–5	Vicente Tosta Carrasco
1925–8	Miguel Paz Barahona
1929–32	Vicente Mejía Clindres
1932–49	Tiburcio Carías Andino
1949–54	Juan Manuel Gálvez

Head of State

1954–6	Julio Lozano Diaz
1956–7	*Military Junta*

President

1958–63	José Ramón Villeda Morales

HONDURAS (cont.)

Head of State

1963–5 Oswaldo López Arellano

President

1965–71 Oswaldo López Arellano
1971–2 Ramón Ernesto Cruz

Head of State

1972–5 Oswaldo López Arellano
1975–8 Juan Alberto Melgar Castro
1978–82 Policarpo Paz García

President

1982–6 Roberto Suazo Córdova
1986–9 José Azcona Hoyo
1989– Rafael Callejas

HUNGARY

Monarch

1900–16 Franz Josef I
1916–18 Charles IV

President

1919 Mihály Károlyi
1919 *Revolutionary Governing Council* (Sándor Garbai)
1920–44 Miklós Horthy *Regent*
1944–5 *Provisional National Assembly*
1946–8 Zoltán Tildy
1948–50 Árpád Szakasits
1950–2 Sándor Rónai
1952–67 István Dobi
1967–87 Pál Losonczi
1987–8 Károly Németh
1988–9 Bruno Ferenc Straub
1989–90 Mátyás Szűrös
1990– Árpád Göncz

Premier

1899–1903 Kálmán Széll
1903 Károly Khuen-Hédervráry
1903–5 István Tisza
1905–6 Géza Fejérváry
1906–10 Sándor Wekerle
1910–12 Károly Kuen Hédervráry
1912–13 László Lukács
1913–17 István Tisza
1917 Móric Esterházy
1917–18 Sándor Wekerle
1918–19 Mihály Károlyi
1919 Dénes Berinkey
1919 *Revolutionary Governing Council*
1919 Gyula Peidl
1919 István Friedrich
1919–20 Károly Huszár
1920 Sándor Simonyi-Semadam
1920–1 Pál Teleki
1921–31 István Bethlen
1931–2 Gyula Károlyi
1932–6 Gyula Gömbös
1936–8 Kálman Darányi
1938–9 Béla Imrédy
1939–41 Pál Teleki
1941–2 László Bárdossy

Premier (cont.)

1942–4 Miklós Kállay
1944 Döme Sztójay
1944 Géza Lakatos
1944 Ferenc Szálasi
1944–5 *Provisional National Assembly* (Béla Miklós Dálnoki)
1945–6 Zoltán Tildy
1946–7 Ferenc Nagy
1947–8 Lajos Dinnyés
1948–52 István Dobi
1952–3 Mátyás Rákosi
1953–5 Imre Nagy
1955–6 András Hegedüs
1956 Imre Nagy
1956–8 János Kádár
1958–61 Ferenc Münnich
1961–5 János Kádár
1965–7 Gyula Kállai
1967–75 Jenö Fock
1975–87 György Lázár
1987–8 Károly Grosz
1988–90 Miklós Németh
1990– József Antall

First Secretary

1949–56 Mátyás Rákosi
1956 Ernö Gerö
1956–88 János Kádár
1988– Károly Grosz

ICELAND

President

1944–52 Sveinn Björnsson
1952–68 Ásgeir Ásgeirsson
1968–80 Kristján Eldjárn
1980– Vigdís Finnbogadóttir

Prime Minister

1900–1 C Goos
1901–4 P A Alberti
1904–9 Hannes Hafstein
1909–11 Björn Jónsson
1911–12 Kristján Jónsson
1912–14 Hannes Hafstein
1914–15 Sigurður Eggerz
1915–17 Einar Arnórsson
1917–22 Jón Magnússon
1922–4 Sigurður Eggerz
1924–6 Jón Magnússon
1926–7 Jon Þorláksson
1927–32 Tryggvi Þórhallsson
1932–4 Ásgeir Ásgeirsson
1934–42 Hermann Jónasson
1942 Ólafur Thors
1942–4 Björn Þórðarsson
1944–7 Ólafur Thors
1947–9 Stefán Jóhann Stefánsson
1949–50 Ólafur Thors
1950–3 Steingrímur Steinþórsson
1953–6 Ólafur Thors
1956–8 Hermann Jónasson
1958–9 Emil Jónsson
1959–61 Ólafur Thors
1961 Bjarni Benediktsson
1961–3 Ólafur Thors
1963–70 Bjarni Benediktsson
1970–1 Jóhann Hafstein
1971–4 Ólafur Jóhannesson

Prime Minister (cont.)

1974–8 Geir Hallgrímsson
1978–9 Ólafur Jóhannesson
1979 Benedikt Gröndal
1980–3 Gunnar Thoroddsen
1983–7 Steingrímur Hermannsson
1987–8 Thorsteinn Pálsson
1988–91 Steingrímur Hermannsson
1991– Davíd Oddsson

INDIA

President

1950–62 Rajendra Prasad
1962–7 Sarvepalli Radhakrishnan
1967–9 Zakir Husain
1969 Varahagiri Venkatagiri *Acting President*
1969 Mohammed Hidayatullah *Acting President*
1969–74 Varahagiri Venkatagiri
1974–7 Fakhruddin Ali Ahmed
1977 B D Jatti *Acting President*
1977–82 Neelam Sanjiva Reddy
1982–7 Giani Zail Singh
1987– Ramaswami Venkataraman

Prime Minister

1947–64 Jawaharlal Nehru
1964 Gulzari Lal Nanda *Acting Prime Minister*
1964–6 Lal Bahadur Shastri
1966 Gulzari Lal Nanda *Acting Prime Minister*
1966–77 Indira Gandhi
1977–9 Morarji Desai
1979–80 Charan Singh
1980–4 Indira Gandhi
1984–9 Rajiv Gandhi
1989–90 Vishwanath Pratap Singh
1990–91 Chandra Shekhar
1991– P V Narasimha Rao

INDONESIA

President

1945–9 Ahmed Sukarno

Republic

1949–66 Ahmed Sukarno
1966– T N J Suharto

Prime Minister

1945 R A A Wiranatakusumah
1945–7 Sutan Sjahrir
1947–8 Amir Sjarifuddin
1948 Mohammed Hatta
1948–9 Sjarifuddin Prawiraranegara
1949 Susanto Tirtoprodjo
1949 Mohammed Hatta
1950 Dr Halim
1950–1 Mohammed Natsir
1951–2 Sukiman Wirjosandjojo
1952–3 Dr Wilopo
1953–5 Ali Sastroamidjojo
1955–6 Burhanuddin Harahap
1956–7 Ali Sastroamidjojo
1957–9 Raden Haji Djuanda Kurtawidjaja
1959–63 Ahmed Sukarno
1963–6 S E Subandrio
1966– *No Prime Minister*

IRAN (Persia)

Shah

1896–1907 Muzaffar Ad-Din
1907–9 Mohammed Ali
1909–25 Ahmad Mirza
1925–41 Mohammed Reza Khan
1941–79 Mohammed Reza Pahlavi

Republic

Leader of the Islamic Revolution

1979–89 Ruhollah Khomeini
1989– Sayed Ali Khamenei

President

1980–1 Abolhassan Bani-Sadr
1981 Mohammed Ali Rajai
1981–9 Sayed Ali Khamenei
1989– Hashemi Rafsanjani

Prime Minister

1979 Shahpur Bakhtiar
1979–80 Mehdi Bazargan
1980–1 Mohammed Ali Rajai
1981 Mohammed Javad Bahonar
1981 Mohammed Reza Mahdavi-Kani
1981–9 Mir Hossein Moussavi

IRAQ

Monarch

1921–33 Faisal I
1933–9 Ghazi I
1939–58 Faisal II
(*Regent, 1939–53,* Abdul Illah)

Republic

Commander of the National Forces

1958–63 Abdul Karim Qassem

Head of Council of State

1958–63 Mohammed Najib Ar-Rubai

President

1963–6 Abdus Salaam Mohammed Arif
1966–8 Abdur Rahman Mohammed Arif
1968–79 Said Ahmad Hassan Al-Bakr
1979– Saddam Hussein At-Takriti

IRELAND

Governor General

1922–7 Timothy Michael Healy
1927–32 James McNeill
1932–6 Donald Buckley

President

1938–45 Douglas Hyde
1945–59 Sean Thomas O'Kelly
1959–73 Eamon de Valera
1973–4 Erskine H Childers
1974–6 Carroll Daly
1976–90 Patrick J Hillery
1990– Mary Robinson

Prime Minister

1919–21 Eamon de Valera
1922 Arthur Griffiths
1922–32 William Cosgrave
1932–48 Eamon de Valera
1948–51 John Aloysius Costello
1951–4 Eamon de Valera
1954–7 John Aloysius Costello
1957–9 Eamon de Valera
1959–66 Sean Lemass
1966–73 John Lynch
1973–7 Liam Cosgrave
1977–9 John Lynch
1979–82 Charles Haughey
1982–7 Garret FitzGerald
1987– Charles Haughey

ISRAEL

President

1948–52 Chaim Weizmann
1952–63 Itzhak Ben-Zvi
1963–73 Zalman Shazar
1973–8 Ephraim Katzair
1978–83 Yitzhak Navon
1983– Chaim Herzog

Prime Minister

1948–53 David Ben Gurion
1954–5 Moshe Sharett
1955–63 David Ben Gurion
1963–9 Levi Eshkol
1969–74 Golda Meir
1974–7 Itzhak Rabin
1977–83 Menachem Begin
1983–4 Yitzhak Shamir
1984–8 Shimon Peres
1988– Yitzhak Shamir

ITALY

Kingdom of Italy

Monarch

1900–46 Victor Emmanuel III

Italian Republic

President

1946–8 Enrico de Nicola
1948–55 Luigi Einaudi
1955–62 Giovanni Gronchi
1962–4 Antonio Segni
1964–71 Giuseppe Saragat
1971–8 Giovanni Leone
1978–85 Alessandro Pertini
1985– Francesco Cossiga

Kingdom of Italy

Prime Minister

1900–1 Giuseppe Saracco
1901–3 Giuseppe Zanardelli
1903–5 Giovanni Giolitti
1905–6 Alessandro Fortis
1906 Sydney Sonnino
1906–9 Giovanni Giolitti
1909–10 Sydney Sonnino
1910–11 Luigi Luzzatti
1911–14 Giovanni Giolitti
1914–16 Antonio Salandra

Prime Minister (cont.)

1916–17 Paolo Boselli
1917–19 Vittorio Emmanuele Orlando
1919–20 Francesco Saverio Nitti
1920–1 Giovanni Giolitti
1921–2 Ivanoe Bonomi
1922 Luigi Facta
1922–43 Benito Mussolini
1943–4 Pietro Badoglio
1944–5 Ivanoe Bonomi
1945 Ferrucio Parri
1945 Alcide de Gasperi

Italian Republic

1946–53 Alcide De Gasperi
1953–4 Giuseppe Pella
1954 Amintore Fanfani
1954–5 Mario Scelba
1955–7 Antonio Segni
1957–8 Adone Zoli
1958–9 Amintore Fanfani
1959–60 Antonio Segni
1960 Fernando Tambroni
1960–3 Amintore Fanfani
1963 Giovanni Leone
1963–8 Aldo Moro
1968 Giovanni Leone
1968–70 Mariano Rumor
1970–2 Emilio Colombo
1972–4 Giulio Andreotti
1974–6 Aldo Moro
1976–8 Giulio Andreotti
1979–80 Francisco Cossiga
1980–1 Arnaldo Forlani
1981–2 Giovanni Spadolini
1982–3 Amintore Fanfani
1983–7 Bettino Craxi
1987 Amintore Fanfani
1987–8 Giovanni Goria
1988–9 Ciriaco de Mita
1989– Giulio Andreotti

JAMAICA

Chief of State: British monarch, represented by Governor General

Prime Minister

1962–7 William Alexander Bustamante
1967 Donald Burns Sangster
1967–72 Hugh Lawson Shearer
1972–80 Michael Norman Manley
1980–9 Edward Phillip George Seaga
1989– Michael Norman Manley

JAPAN

Chief of State (Emperor)

1867–1912 Mutsuhito (Meiji)
1912–26 Yoshihito (Taishō)
1926–89 Hirohito (Shōwa)
1989– Akihito (Heisei)

Prime Minister

1900–1 Hirobumi Itō
1901–6 Tarō Katsura
1906–8 Kimmochi Saionji
1908–11 Tarō Katsura
1911–12 Kimmochi Saionji
1912–13 Tarō Katsura
1913–14 Gonnohyōe Yamamoto

JAPAN (cont.)

Prime Minister (cont.)

1914–16 Shigenobu Ōkuma
1916–18 Masatake Terauchi
1918–21 Takashi Hara
1921–2 Korekiyo Takahashi
1922–3 Tomosaburō Katō
1923–4 Gonnohyōe Yamamoto
1924 Keigo Kiyoura
1924–6 Takaaki Katō
1926–7 Reijirō Wakatsuki
1927–9 Giichi Tanaka
1929–31 Osachi Hamaguchi
1931 Reijirō Wakatsuki
1931–2 Tsuyoshi Inukai
1932–4 Makoto Saitō
1934–6 Keisuke Okada
1936–7 Kōki Hirota
1937 Senjūrō Hayashi
1937–9 Fumimaro Konoe
1939 Kiichirō Hiranuma
1939–40 Nobuyuki Abe
1940 Mitsumasa Yonai
1940–1 Fumimaro Konoe
1941–4 Hideki Tōjō
1944–5 Kuniaki Koiso
1945 Kantarō Suzuki
1945 Naruhiko Higashikuni
1945–6 Kijūrō Shidehara
1946–7 Shigeru Yoshida
1947–8 Tetsu Katayama
1948 Hitoshi Ashida
1948–54 Shigeru Yoshida
1954–6 Ichirō Hatoyama
1956–7 Tanzan Ishibashi
1957–60 Nobusuke Kishi
1960–4 Hayato Ikeda
1964–72 Eisaku Satō
1972–4 Kakuei Tanaka
1974–6 Takeo Miki
1976–8 Takeo Fukuda
1978–80 Masayoshi Ōhira
1980–2 Zenkō Suzuki
1982–7 Yasuhiro Nakasone
1987–9 Noburu Takeshita
1989 Sasuke Uno
1989– Toshiki Kaifu

JORDAN

Monarch

1921–51 Abdallah Bin Hussein
1951–2 Talal I
1952– Hussein II

Prime Minister

1921 Rashid Tali
1921 Muzhir Ar-Raslan
1921–3 Rida Ar-Riqabi
1923 Muzhir Ar-Raslan
1923–4 Hassan Khalid
1924–33 Rida Ar-Riqabi
1933–8 Ibrahim Hashim
1939–45 Taufiq Abul-Huda
1945–8 Ibrahim Hashim
1948–50 Taufiq Abul-Huda
1950 Said Al-Mufti
1950–1 Samir Ar-Rifai
1951–3 Taufiq Abul-Huda
1953–4 Fauzi Al-Mulqi

Prime Minister (cont.)

1954–5 Taufiq Abul-Huda
1955 Said Al-Mufti
1955 Hazza Al-Majali
1955–6 Ibrahim Hashim
1956 Samir Ar-Rifai
1956 Said Al-Mufti
1956 Ibrahim Hashim
1956–7 Suleiman Nabulsi
1957 Hussein Fakhri Al-Khalidi
1957–8 Ibrahim Hashim
1958 Nuri Pasha Al-Said
1958–9 Samir Ar-Rifai
1959–60 Hazza Al-Majali
1960–2 Bahjat Talhuni
1962–3 Wasfi At-Tall
1963 Samir Ar-Rifai
1963–4 Sharif Hussein Bin Nasir
1964 Bahjat Talhuni
1965–7 Wasfi At-Tall
1967 Sharif Hussein Bin Nasir
1967 Saad Jumaa
1967–9 Bahjat Talhuni
1969 Abdul Munem Rifai
1969–70 Bahjat Talhuni
1970 Abdul Munem Rifai
1970 *Military Junta* (Mohammed Daud)
1970 Mohamed Ahmed Tuqan
1970–1 Wasfi At-Tall
1971–3 Ahmad Lozi
1973–6 Zaid Rifai
1976–9 Mudar Badran
1979–80 Sherif Abdul Hamid Sharaf
1980 Kassem Rimawi
1980–4 Mudar Badran
1984–5 Ahmad Ubayat
1985–9 Zaid Ar-Rifai
1989 Sharif Zaid Bin Shaker
1989–91 Mudar Badran
1991 Taher Al-Masri
1991– Sharif Zaid Bin Shaker

KENYA

President

1963–78 Mzee Jomo Kenyatta
1978– Daniel Arap Moi

KIRIBATI

President

1979–91 Ieremia T Tabai
1991– Teatao Teannaki

DEMOCRATIC PEOPLE'S REPUBLIC OF KOREA (North Korea)

President

1948–57 Kim Doo-bong
1957–72 Choi Yong-kun
1972– Kim Il-sung

Prime Minister

1948–76 Kim Il-sung
1976–7 Park Sung-chul

Prime Minister (cont.)

1977–84 Li Jong-ok
1984–6 Kang Song-san
1986–8 Yi Kun-mo
1988– Yon Hyong-muk

REPUBLIC OF KOREA (South Korea)

President

1948–60 Syngman Rhee
1960 Ho Chong *Acting President*
1960 Kwak Sang-hun *Acting President*
1960 Ho Chong *Acting President*
1960–3 Yun Po-sun
1963–79 Park Chung-hee
1979–80 Choi Kyu-hah
1980 Park Choong-hoon *Acting President*
1980–8 Chun Doo-hwan
1988– Roh Tae-woo

Prime Minister

1948–50 Lee Pom-sok
1950 Shin Song-mo *Acting Prime Minister*
1950–1 John M Chang
1951–2 Ho Chong *Acting Prime Minister*
1952 Lee Yun-yong *Acting Prime Minister*
1952 Chang Taek-sang
1952–4 Paik Too-chin
1954–6 Pyon Yong-tae
1956–60 Syngman Rhee
1960 Ho Chong
1960–1 John M Chang
1961 Chang To-yong
1961–2 Song Yo-chan
1962–3 Kim Hyun-chul
1963–4 Choe Tu-son
1964–70 Chung Il-kwon
1970–1 Paik Too-chin
1971–5 Kim Jong-pil
1975–9 Choi Kyu-hah
1979–80 Shin Hyun-hwak
1980 Park Choong-hoon *Acting Prime Ministe*
1980–2 Nam Duck-woo
1982 Yoo Chang-soon
1982–3 Kim Sang-hyup
1983–5 Chin Lee-chong
1985–8 Lho Shin-yong
1988 Lee Hyun-jae
1988–90 Kang Young-hoon
1990–1 Ro Jai-bong
1991– Chung Won-shik

KUWAIT

Emir

Family name: Al-Sabah
1896–1915 Mubarak
1915–17 Jaber II
1917–21 Salem Al-Mubarak
1921–50 Ahmed Al-Jaber
1950–65 Abdallah Al-Salem
1965–77 Sabah Al-Salem
1978– Jaber Al-Ahmed Al-Jaber

Prime Minister

1962–3 Abdallah Al-Salem
1963–5 Sabah Al-Salem
1965–78 Jaber Al-Ahmed Al-Jaber
1978– Saad Al-Abdallah Al-Salem

LAOS

Monarch

1904–59 Sisavang Vong
1959–75 Savang Vatthana

Lao People's Republic

President

1975–87 Souphanouvong
1987–91 Phoumi Vongvichit
1991– Kaysone Phomvihane

Prime Minister

1951–4 Souvanna Phouma
1954–5 Katay Don Sasorith
1956–8 Souvanna Phouma
1958–9 Phoui Sahanikone
1959–60 Sunthone Patthamavong
1960 Kou Abhay
1960 Somsanith
1960 Souvana Phouma
1960 Sunthone Patthamavong
1960 Quinim Pholsena
1960–2 Boun Oum Na Champassac
1962–75 Souvanna Phouma

Lao People's Democratic Republic
1975–91 Kaysone Phomvihane
1991– Khamtay Siphandon

LATVIA

President

1991– Anatolijs Gorbunovs

LEBANON

President

1943–52 Bishara Al-Khoury
1952–8 Camille Shamoun
1958–64 Fouad Shehab
1964–70 Charle Hilo
1970–6 Suleiman Frenjieh
1976–82 Elias Sarkis
1982 Bashir Gemayel
1982–8 Amin Gemayel
1988–9 *No President*
1989 Rene Muawad
1989– Elias Hrawi

Prime Minister

1943 Riad Solh
1943–4 Henry Pharaon
1944–5 Riad Solh
1945 Abdul Hamid Karame
1945–6 Sami Solh
1946 Saadi Munla
1946–51 Riad Solh
1951 Hussein Oweini
1951–2 Abdullah Yafi
1952 Sami Solh
1952 Nazem Accari
1952 Saeb Salam
1952 Fouad Chehab
1952–3 Khaled Chehab
1953 Saeb Salam
1953–5 Abdullah Yafi
1955 Sami Solh
1955–6 Rashid Karami

Prime Minister (cont.)

1956 Abdullah Yafi
1956–8 Sami Solh
1958–60 Rashid Karami
1960 Ahmad Daouq
1960–1 Saeb Salam
1961–4 Rashid Karami
1964–5 Hussein Oweini
1965–6 Rashid Karami
1966 Abdullah Yafi
1966–8 Rashid Karami
1968–9 Abdullah Yafi
1969–70 Rashid Karami
1970–3 Saeb Salam
1973 Amin al-Hafez
1973–4 Takieddine Solh
1974–5 Rashid Solh
1975 Noureddin Rifai
1975–6 Rashid Karami
1976–80 Selim Hoss
1980 Takieddine Solh
1980–4 Chafiq al-Wazan
1984–8 Rashid Karami
1988–90 Michel Aoun/Selim al-Hoss
1990 Selim al-Hoss
1990– Umar Karami

LESOTHO

Monarch

1966–90 Moshoeshoe II
1990– Letsie III

Prime Minister

1966–86 Leabua Jonathan

Chairman of Military Council

1986–91 Justin Metsing Lekhanya
1991– Elias Tutsoane Ramaema

LIBERIA

President

1900–4 Garretson Wilmot Gibson
1904–12 Arthur Barclay
1912–20 Daniel Edward Howard
1920–30 Charles Dunbar Burgess King
1930–43 Edwin J Barclay
1943–71 William V S Tubman
1971–80 William Richard Tolbert

People's Redemption Council

Chairman

1980–6 Samuel K Doe

President

1986–90 Samuel K Doe
1990– Amos Sawyer (*Acting*)

LIBYA

Monarch

1951–69 Mohammed Idris Al-Mahdi Al-Senussi

Revolutionary Command Council

Chairman

1969–77 Muammar Al-Gadhafi (Qadhafi)

General Secretariat

Secretary General

1977–9 Muammar Al-Gadhafi
1979–84 Abdul Ati Al-Ubaidi
1984–6 Mohammed Az-Zaruq Rajab
1986–90 Omar Al-Muntasir
1990– Abu Zaid Omar Dourda

Leader of the Revolution

1969– Muammar Al-Gadhafi

LIECHTENSTEIN

Prince

1858–1929 Johann II
1929–38 Franz von Paula
1938–89 Franz Josef II
1989– Hans Adam II

Prime Minister

1928–45 Franz Josef Hoop
1945–62 Alexander Friek
1962–70 Gérard Batliner
1970–4 Alfred J Hilbe
1974–8 Walter Kieber
1978– Hans Brunhart

LITHUANIA

President

1991– Vytautas Lansbergis

LUXEMBOURG

Grand Dukes and Duchesses

1905–12 William IV
1912–19 Marie Adelaide
1919–64 Charlotte *in exile 1940–4*
1964– Jean

Prime Minister

1915 Mathias Mongenast
1915–16 Hubert Loutsch
1916–17 Victor Thorn
1917–18 Léon Kaufmann
1918–25 Emil Reuter
1925–6 Pierre Prum
1926–37 Joseph Bech
1937–53 Pierre Dupong *in exile 1940–4*
1953–8 Joseph Bech
1958 Pierre Frieden
1959–69 Pierre Werner
1969–79 Gaston Thorn
1979–84 Pierre Werner
1984– Jacques Santer

MADAGASCAR

President

1960–72 Philibert Tsiranana
1972–5 Gabriel Ramanantsoa
1975 Richard Ratsimandrava
1975 Gilles Andriamahazo
1975– Didier Ratsiraka

Prime Minister

1960–75 *As President*
1975–6 Joël Rakotomala
1976–7 Justin Rakotoriaina

MADAGASCAR (cont.)

Prime Minister (cont.)

1977–88 Désiré Rakotoarijaona
1988–91 Victor Ramahatra
1991– Guy Willy Razanamasy

MALAWI

President

1966– Hastings Kamuzu Banda

MALAYSIA

Chief of State (Yang di-Pertuan Agong)

1957–63 Abdul Rahman
1963–5 Syed Putra Jamalullah
1965–70 Ismail Nasiruddin Shah
1970–5 Abdul Halim Muadzam Shah
1975–9 Yahya Petra Ibrahim
1979–84 Haji Ahmad Shah Al-Mustain Billah
1984–9 Mahmood Iskandar
1989– Azlan Muhibuddin Shah

Prime Minister

Malaya
1957–63 Abdul Rahman Putra Al-Haj

Malaysia
1963–70 Abdul Rahman Putra Al-Haj
1970–6 Abdul Razak bin Hussein
1976–9 Haji Hussein bin Onn
1979– Mahathir bin Mohamad

MALDIVES

Monarch (Sultan)

1954–68 Mohammed Farid Didi

Republic

President

1968–78 Ibrahim Nasir
1978– Maumoon Abdul Gayoom

MALI

President

1960–8 Modibo Keita
1969–91 Moussa Traoré
1991– *Military junta* (Amadou Touré)

Prime Minister

1986–88 Mamadou Dembelé
1988–91 *No Prime Minister*
1991– Soumana Sacko

MALTA

President

1974–6 Anthony Mamo
1976–81 Anton Buttigieg
1982–7 Agatha Barbara
1987–9 Paul Xuereb *Acting President*
1989– Vincent Tabore

Prime Minister

1962–71 G Borg Olivier
1971–84 Dom Mintoff
1984–7 Carmelo Mifsud Bonnici
1987– Edward Fenech Adami

MAURITANIA

President

1961–78 Mokhtar Ould Daddah
1979 Mustapha Ould Mohammed Salek
1979–80 Mohammed Mahmoud Ould Ahmed Louly
1980–4 Mohammed Khouna Ould Haydalla
1984– Moaouia Ould Sidi Mohammed Taya

MAURITIUS

Chief of State: British monarch, represented by Governor General

Prime Minister

1968–82 Seewoosagur Ramgoolam
1982– Anerood Jugnauth

MEXICO

President

1876–1911 Porfirio Diaz
1911 Francisco León de la Barra
1911–13 Francisco I Madero
1913–14 Victoriano Huerta
1914 Francisco Carvajal
1914 Venustiano Carranza
1914–15 Eulalio Gutiérrez *Provisional President*
1915 Roque González Garza *Provisional President*
1915 Francisco Lagos Chazaro *Provisional President*
1917–20 Venustiano Carranza
1920 Adolfo de la Huerta
1920–4 Alvaro Obregón
1924–8 Plutarco Elías Calles
1928–30 Emilio Portes Gil
1930–2 Pascual Ortíz Rubio
1932–4 Abelardo L. Rodríguez
1934–40 Lazaro Cardenas
1940–6 Manuel Avila Camacho
1946–52 Miguel Alemán
1952–8 Adolfo Ruiz Cortines
1958–64 Adolfo López Mateos
1964–70 Gustavo Díaz Ordaz
1970–6 Luis Echeverría
1976–82 José López Portillo
1982–8 Miguel de la Madrid Hurtado
1988– Carlos Salinas de Gortari

MONACO

Head of State

1889–1922 Albert
1922–49 Louis II
1949– Rainier III

MONGOLIA

Prime Minister

1924–8 Tserendorji
1928–32 Amor
1932–6 Gendun
1936–8 Amor

Prime Minister (cont.)

1939–52 Korloghiin Choibalsan
1952–74 Yumsjhagiin Tsedenbal

Chairman of the Praesidium

1948–53 Gonchighlin Bumatsende
1954–72 Jamsarangiin Sambu
1972–4 Sonomyn Luvsan
1974–84 Yumsjhagiin Tsedenbal
1984– Jambyn Batmunkh

President

1990– Punsalmaagiyn Ochirbat

Premier

1974–84 Jambyn Batmunkh
1984–90 Dumaagiyn Sodnom
1990– Dashiyn Byambasuren

MOROCCO

Monarch

1927–61 Mohammed V
1961– Hassan II

Prime Minister

1955–8 Si Mohammed Bekkai
1958 Ahmad Balfrej
1958–60 Abdullah Ibrahim
1960–3 *As Monarch*
1963–5 Ahmad Bahnini
1965–7 *As Monarch*
1967–9 Moulay Ahmed Laraki
1969–71 Mohammed Ben Hima
1971–2 Mohammed Karim Lamrani
1972–9 Ahmed Othman
1979–83 Maati Bouabid
1983–6 Mohammed Karim Lamrani
1986– Izz Id-Dien Laraki

MOZAMBIQUE

President

1975–86 Samora Moïses Machel
1986– Joaquim Alberto Chissanó

Prime Minister

1986– Mario da Graça Machungo

NAMIBIA

President

1990– Sam Nujoma

Prime Minister

1990– Hage Geingob

NAURU

President

1968–86 Hammer de Robürt
1986 Kennan Adeang
1986–9 Hammer de Robürt
1989 Kenas Aroi
1989– Bernard Dowiyogo

NEPAL

Monarch

1881–1911 Prithvi Bir Bikram Shah
1911–55 Tribhuvan Bir Bikram Shah
1956–72 Mahendra Bir Bikram Shah
1972– Birenda Bir Bikram Shah Deva

Prime Minister

1901–29 Chandra Sham Sher Jang Bahadur Rana
1929–31 Bhim Cham Sham Sher Jang Bahadur Rana
1931–45 Juddha Sham Sher Rana
1945–8 Padma Sham Sher Jang Bahadur Rana
1948–51 Mohan Sham Sher Jang Bahadur Rana
1951–2 Matrika Prasad Koirala
1952–3 Tribhuvan Bir Bikram Shah
1953–5 Matrika Prasad Koirala
1955–6 Mahendra Bir Bikram Shah
1956–7 Tanka Prasad Acharya
1957–9 *King also Prime Minister*
1959–60 Sri Bishawa Prasad Koirala
1960–3 *No Prime Minister*
1963–5 Tulsi Giri
1965–9 Surya Bahadur Thapa
1969–70 Kirti Nidhi Bista
1970–1 *King also Prime Minister*
1971–3 Kirti Nidhi Bista
1973–5 Nagendra Prasad Rijal
1975–7 Tulsi Giri
1977–9 Kirti Nidhi Bista
1979–83 Surya Bahadur Thapa
1983–6 Lokendra Bahadur Chand
1986–90 Marich Man Singh Shrestha
1990 Lokendra Bahadur Chand
1990–1 Krishna Prasad Bhattarai
1991– Girija Prasad Koirala

NETHERLANDS

Monarch

1898–1948 Wilhelmina
1948–80 Juliana
1980– Beatrix

Prime Minister

1897–1901 Nicholas G Pierson
1901–5 Abraham Kuyper
1905–8 Theodoor H de Meester
1908–13 Theodorus Heemskerk
1913–18 Pieter W A Cort van der Linden
1918–25 Charles J M Ruys de Beerenbrouck
1925–6 Hendrikus Colijn
1926 Dirk J de Geer
1926–33 Charles JM Ruys de Beerenbrouck
1933–9 Hendrikus Colijn
1939–40 Dirk J de Geer
1940–5 Pieter S Gerbrandy *in exile*
1945–6 Willem Schemerhorn/Willem Drees
1946–8 Louis J M Beel
1948–51 Willem Drees/Josephus R H van Schaik
1951–8 Willem Drees
1958–9 Louis J M Beel
1959–63 Jan E de Quay
1963–5 Victor G M Marijnen
1965–6 Joseph M L T Cals
1966–7 Jelle Zijlstra
1967–71 Petrus J S de Jong
1971–3 Barend W Biesheuvel
1973–7 Joop M Den Uyl
1977–82 Andreas A M van Agt
1982– Ruud F M Lubbers

NEW ZEALAND

Chief of State: British monarch, represented by Governor General

Prime Minister

1856 Henry Sewell
1856 William Fox
1856–61 Edward William Stafford
1861–2 William Fox
1862–3 Alfred Domett
1863–4 Frederick Whitaker
1864–5 Frederick Aloysius Weld
1865–9 Edward William Stafford
1869–72 William Fox
1872 Edward William Stafford
1873 William Fox
1873–5 Julius Vogel
1875–6 Daniel Pollen
1876 Julius Vogel
1876–7 Harry Albert Atkinson
1877–9 George Grey
1879–82 John Hall
1882–3 Frederick Whitaker
1883–4 Harry Albert Atkinson
1884 Robert Stout
1884 Harry Albert Atkinson
1884–7 Robert Stout
1887–91 Harry Albert Atkinson
1891–3 John Ballance
1893–1906 Richard John Seddon *Lib*
1906 William Hall-Jones *Lib*
1906–12 Joseph George Ward *Lib/Nat*
1912 Thomas Mackenzie *Nat*
1912–25 William Ferguson Massey *Ref*
1925 Frencis Henry Dillon Bell *Ref*
1925–8 Joseph Gordon Coates *Ref*
1928–30 Joseph George Ward *Lib/Nat*
1930–5 George William Forbes *Un*
1935–40 Michael Joseph Savage *Lab*
1940–9 Peter Fraser *Lab*
1949–57 Sidney George Holland *Nat*
1957 Keith Jacka Holyoake *Nat*
1957–60 Walter Nash *Lab*
1960–72 Keith Jacka Holyoake *Nat*
1972 John Ross Marshall *Nat*
1972–4 Norman Eric Kirk *Lab*
1974–5 Wallace Edward Rowling *Lab*
1975–84 Robert David Muldoon *Nat*
1984–89 David Russell Lange *Lab*
1989–90 Geoffrey Palmer *Lab*
1990 Mike Moore *Lab*
1990– James Brendan Bolger *Nat*

Lab Labour
Lib Liberal
Nat National
Ref Reform
Un United

NICARAGUA

President

1893–1909 José Santos Zelaya
1909–10 José Madriz
1910–11 José Dolores Estrada
1911 Juan José Estrada
1911–17 Adolfo Díaz
1912 Luis Mena *rival President*
1917–21 Emiliano Chamorro Vargas
1921–3 Riego Manuel Chamorro
1923–4 Martínez Bartolo
1925–6 Carlos Solórzano

President (cont.)

1926 Emiliano Chamorro Vargas
1926–8 Adolfo Díaz
1926 Juan Bautista Sacasa *rival President*
1928–32 José Marcia Moncada
1933–6 Juan Bautista Sacasa
1936 Carlos Brenes Jarquin
1937–47 Anastasio Somoza García
1947 Leonardo Argüello
1947 Benjamin Lascayo Sacasa
1947–50 Victor Manuel Román y Reyes
1950–6 Anastasio Somoza García
1956–63 Luis Somoza Debayle
1963–6 René Schick Gutiérrez
1966–7 Lorenzo Guerrero Gutiérrez
1967–72 Anastasio Somoza Debayle
1972–4 *Triumvirate*
1974–9 Anastasio Somoza Debayle
1979–84 *Government Junta of National Reconstruction*
1984–90 Daniel Ortega Saavedra
1990 Violeta Chamorro *President elect*

NIGER

President

1960–74 Hamani Diori
1974–87 Seyni Kountché
1987– Ali Saibou

Prime Minister

1990–1 Aliou Mahamidou
1991– Amadou Chef-fou

NIGERIA

President

1960–6 Nnamdi Azikiwe

Prime Minister

1960–6 Abubakar Tafawa Balewa

Military Government

1966 J T U Aguiyi-Ironsi
1966–75 Yakuba Gowon
1975–6 Murtala R Mohamed
1976–9 Olusegun Obasanjo

President

1979–83 Alhaji Shehu Shagari

Military Government

1983–4 Mohammadu Buhari
1985– Ibrahim B Babangida

NORWAY

Monarch

1872–1905 Oscar II *union with Sweden*
1905–57 Haakon VII
1957–91 Olav V
1991– Harald V

Prime Minister

1898–1902 Johannes Steen
1902–3 Otto Albert Blehr
1903–5 George Francis Hagerup
1905–7 Christian Michelsen

NORWAY (cont.)

Prime Minister (cont.)

1907–8	Jørgen Løvland
1908–10	Gunnar Knudsen
1910–12	Wollert Konow
1912–13	Jens Bratlie
1913–20	Gunnar Knudsen
1920–1	Otto Bahr Halvorsen
1921–3	Otto Albert Blehr
1923	Otto Bahr Halvorsen
1923–4	Abraham Berge
1924–6	Johan Ludwig Mowinckel
1926–8	Ivar Lykke
1928	Christopher Hornsrud
1928–31	Johan Ludwig Mowinckel
1931–2	Peder L Kolstad
1932–3	Jens Hundseid
1933–5	Johan Ludwig Mowinckel
1935–45	Johan Nygaardsvold
1945–51	Einar Gerhardsen
1951–5	Oscar Torp
1955–63	Einar Gerhardsen
1963	John Lyng
1963–5	Einar Gerhardsen
1965–71	Per Borten
1971–2	Trygve Bratteli
1972–3	Lars Korvald
1973–6	Trygve Bratteli
1976–81	Odvar Nordli
1981	Gro Harlem Brundtland
1981–6	Kåre Willoch
1986–9	Gro Harlem Brundtland
1989–90	Jan P Syse
1990–	Gro Harlem Brundtland

OMAN

Sultan

1888–1913	Faisal Bin Turki
1913–32	Taimur Bin Faisal
1932–70	Said Bin Taimur
1970–	Qabous Bin Said

PAKISTAN

President

1956–8	Iskander Mirza
1958–69	Mohammad Ayoub Khan
1969–71	Agha Mohammad Yahya Khan
1971–3	Zulfikar Ali Bhutto
1973–8	Fazal Elahi Chawdry
1978–88	Mohammad Zia Ul-Haq
1988–	Gulam Ishaq Khan

Prime Minister

1947–51	Liaqat Ali Khan
1951–3	Khawaja Nazimuddin
1953–5	Mohammad Ali
1955–6	Chawdry Mohammad Ali
1956–7	Hussein Shahid Suhrawardi
1957	Ismail Chundrigar
1957–8	Malik Feroz Khan Noon
1958	Mohammad Ayoub Khan
1958–73	*No Prime Minister*
1973–7	Zulfikar Ali Bhutto
1977–85	*No Prime Minister*
1985–88	Mohammad Khan Junejo

Prime Minister (cont.)

1988	Mohammad Aslam Khan Khattak
1988–90	Benazir Bhutto
1990	Ghulam Mustafa Jatoi
1990–	Nawaz Sharif

PANAMA

President

1904–8	Manuel Amador Guerrero
1908–10	José Domingo de Obaldia
1910	Federico Boyd
1910	Carlos Antonio Mendoza
1910–12	Pablo Arosemena
1912	Rodolfo Chiari
1912–16	Belisario Porras
1916–18	Ramón Maximiliano Valdés
1918	Pedro Antonio Diaz
1918	Cirilo Luis Urriola
1918–20	Belisario Porras
1920	Ernesto T Lefevre
1920–4	Belisario Porras
1924–8	Rodolfo Chiari
1928	Tomás Gabriel Duque
1928–31	Florencio Harmodio Arosemena
1931	Harmodio Arias
1931–2	Ricardo Joaquín Alfaro
1932–6	Harmodio Arias
1936–9	Juan Demóstenes Arosemena
1939	Ezequiel Fernández Jaén
1939–40	Augusto Samuel Boyd
1940–1	Arnulfo Arias Madrid
1941	Ernesto Jaén Guardia
1941	José Pezet
1941–5	Ricardo Adolfo de la Guardia
1945–8	Enrique Adolfo Jiménez Brin
1948–9	Domingo Diaz Arosemena
1949	Daniel Chanis
1949	Roberto Francisco Chiari
1949–51	Arnulfo Arias Madrid
1951–2	Alcibiades Arosemena
1952–5	José Antonio Remón
1955	José Ramón Guizado
1955–6	Ricardo Manuel Arias Espinosa
1956–60	Ernesto de la Guardia
1960–4	Roberto Francisco Chiari
1964–8	Marco A Robles
1968	Arnulfo Arias Madrid
1968	*Military Junta*
1968–9	Omar Torrijos Herrera
1969–78	Demetrio Basilio Lakas
1978–82	Aristides Royo
1982–4	Ricardo de la Esoriella
1984	Jorge Enrique Illueca Sibauste
1984–5	Nicolás Ardito Barletta
1985–8	Eric Arturo Delvalle
1988–9	Manuel Solís Palma
1989–	Guillermo Endara Gallimany

PAPUA NEW GUINEA

Prime Minister

1975–80	Michael T Somare
1980–2	Julius Chan
1982–5	Michael T Somare
1985–8	Paias Wingti
1988–	Rabbie Namiliu

PARAGUAY

President

1898–1902	Emilio Azeval
1902	Hector Carvallo
1902–4	Juan Antonio Escurra
1904–5	Juan Gaona
1905–6	Cecilio Baez
1906–8	Benigno Ferreira
1908–10	Emiliano Gonzáles Navero
1910–11	Manuel Gondra
1911	Albino Jara
1911	Liberato Marcial Rojas
1912	Pedro Peña
1912	Emiliano González Navero
1912–16	Eduardo Schaerer
1916–19	Manuel Franco
1919–20	José P Montero
1920–1	Manuel Gondra
1921	Félix Paiva
1921–3	Eusebio Ayala
1923–4	Eligio Ayala
1924	Luis Alberto Riart
1924–8	Eligio Ayala
1928–31	José Particio Guggiari
1931–2	Emiliano González Navero
1932	José Particio Guggiari
1932–6	Eusebio Ayala
1936–7	Rafael Franco
1937–9	Félix Paiva
1939–40	José Félix Estigarribia
1940–8	Higino Moríñigo
1948	Juan Manuel Frutos
1948–9	Juan Natalicio González
1949	Raimundo Rolón
1949	Felipe Molas López
1949–54	Federico Chaves
1954	Tomás Romero Pareira
1954–89	Alfredo Stroessner
1989	Andres Rodríguez

PERU

President

1899–1903	Eduardo López de Romaña
1903–4	Manuel Candamo
1904	Serapio Calderón
1904–8	José Pardo y Barreda
1908–12	Augusto B Leguía
1912–14	Guillermo Billinghurst
1914–15	Oscar R Benavides
1915–19	José Pardo y Barreda
1919–30	Augusto B Leguía
1930	Manuel Ponce
1930–1	Luis M Sánchez Cerro
1931	Leoncio Elías
1931	Gustavo A Jiménez
1931	David Samanez Ocampo
1931–3	Luis M Sánchez Cerro
1933–9	Oscar R Benavides
1939–45	Manuel Prado
1945–8	José Luis Bustamante y Rivero
1948–56	Manuel A Odría
1956–62	Manuel Prado
1962–3	*Military Junta*
1963–8	Fernando Belaúnde Terry
1968–75	*Military Junta* (Juan Velasco Alvarado)
1975–80	*Military Junta* (Francisco Morales Bermúdez)
1980–5	Fernando Belaúnde Terry
1985–90	Alan García Pérez
1990–	Alberto Keinya Fujimori

PHILIPPINES

President

Commonwealth
1935–44 Manuel L Quezon

Japanese Occupation
1943–4 José P Laurel

Commonwealth
1944–6 Sergio Osmeña

First Republic
1946–8 Manuel A Roxas
1948–53 Elpidio Quirino
1953–7 Ramon Magsaysay
1957–61 Carlos P Garcia
1961–5 Diosdado Macapagal
1965–72 Ferdinand E Marcos

Martial Law
1972–81 Ferdinand E Marcos

New Republic
1981–6 Ferdinand E Marcos
1986– Corazon C Aquino

POLAND

Chief of State

1945–7 Bolesław Bierut *Acting President*
1947–52 Bolesław Bierut
1952–64 Aleksander Zawadzki
1964–8 Edward Ochab
1968–70 Marian Spychalski
1970–2 Józef Cyrankiewicz
1972–85 Henryk Jabłonski
1985–90 Wojciech Jaruzelski *President 1989*
1990– Lech Walesa *President*

Premier

1947–52 Józef Cyrankiewicz
1952–4 Bolesław Bierut
1954–70 Józef Cyrankiewicz
1970–80 Piotr Jaroszewicz
1980 Edward Babiuch
1980–1 Józef Pinkowski
1981–5 Wojciech Jaruzelski
1985–8 Zbigniew Messner
1988–9 Mieczyslaw Rakowski
1989 Czeslaw Kiszczak
1989–91 Tadeusz Mazowiecki
1991 Jan Krzysztof Bielecki
1991– Jan Olszewski

First Secretary

1945–8 Władysław Gomułka
1948–56 Bolesław Bierut
1956 Edward Ochab
1956–70 Władysław Gomułka
1970–80 Edward Gierek
1980–1 Stanisław Kania
1981–9 Wojciech Jaruzelski
1989–90 Mieczyslaw Rakowski

PORTUGAL

President

1st Republic
1910–11 Teófilo Braga
1911–15 Manuel José de Arriaga

President (cont.)

1915 Teófilo Braga
1915–17 Bernardino Machado
1917–18 Sidónio Pais
1918–19 João do Canto e Castro
1919–23 António José de Almeida
1923–5 Manuel Teixeira Gomes
1925–6 Bernardino Machado

New State
1926 *Military Junta* (José Mendes Cabeçadas)
1926 *Military Junta* (Manuel de Oliveira Gomes da Costa)
1926–51 António Oscar Fragoso Carmona
1951–8 Francisco Craveiro Lopes
1958–74 Américo de Deus Tomás

2nd Republic
1974 *Military Junta* (António Spínola)
1974–6 *Military Junta* (Francisco da Costa Gomes)

3rd Republic
1976–86 António dos Santos Ramalho Eanes
1986– Mario Soares

Prime Minister

1932–68 António de Oliveira Salazar
1968–74 Marcelo Caetano
1974 Adelino da Palma Carlos
1974–5 Vasco Gonçalves
1975–6 José Pinheiro de Azevedo
1976–8 Mário Soares
1978 Alfredo Nobre da Costa
1978–9 Carlos Alberto de Mota Pinto
1979 Maria de Lurdes Pintasilgo
1980–1 Francisco de Sá Carneiro
1981–3 Francisco Pinto Balsemão
1983–5 Mário Soares
1985– Aníbal Cavaço Silva

QATAR

Emir

Family name: Al-Thani
1971–2 Ahmad Bin Ali
1972– Khalifah Bin Hamad

ROMANIA

Monarch

1881–1914 Carol I
1914–27 Ferdinand I
1927–30 Michael *Prince*
1930–40 Carol II
1940–7 Michael I

Republic

President

1947–8 Mihai Sadoveanu *Interim*
1948–52 Constantin I Parhon
1952–8 Petru Groza
1958–61 Ion Georghe Maurer
1961–5 Georghe Gheorghiu-Dej
1965–7 Chivu Stoica
1967–89 Nicolae Ceaușescu
1989– Ion Iliescu

General Secretary

1955–65 Georghe Gheorghiu-Dej
1965–89 Nicolae Ceaușescu

Prime Minister

1900–1 Petre P Carp
1901–6 Dimitrie A Sturdza
1906–7 Gheorge Grigore Cantacuzino
1907–9 Dimitrie A Sturdza
1909 Ionel Brătianu
1909–10 Mihai Pherekyde
1910–11 Ionel Brătianu
1911–12 Petre P Carp
1912–14 Titu Maiorescu
1914–18 Ionel Brătianu
1918 Alexandru Averescu
1918 Alexandru Marghiloman
1918 Constantin Coandă
1918 Ionel Brătianu
1919 Artur Văitoianu
1919–20 Alexandru Vaida-Voevod
1920–1 Alexandru Averescu
1921–2 Take Ionescu
1922–6 Ionel Brătianu
1926–7 Alexandru Averescu
1927 Ionel Brătianu
1927–8 Vintila I C Brătianu
1928–30 Juliu Maniu
1930 Gheorghe C Mironescu
1930 Juliu Maniu
1930–1 Gheorghe C Mironescu
1931–2 Nicolae Iorga
1932 Alexandru Vaida-Voevod
1932–3 Juliu Maniu
1933 Alexandru Vaida-Voevod
1933 Ion G Duca
1933–4 Constantin Angelescu
1934–7 Gheorghe Tătărescu
1937 Octavian Goga
1937–9 Miron Cristea
1939 Armand Călinescu
1939 Gheorghe Argeșanu
1939 Constantine Argetoianu
1939–40 Gheorghe Tătărescu
1940 Ion Gigurtu
1940–4 Ion Antonescu
1944 Constantin Sănătescu
1944–5 Nicolas Rădescu
1945–52 Petru Groza
1952–5 Gheorghe Gheorghiu-Dej
1955–61 Chivu Stoica
1961–74 Ion Gheorghe Maurer
1974–80 Manea Mănescu
1980–3 Ilie Verdet
1983–9 Constantin Dăscălescu
1989–91 Petre Roman
1991– Theodor Stolojan

RUSSIA

President

1991– Boris Yeltsin

RWANDA

President

1962–73 Grégoire Kayibanda
1973– Juvénal Habyarimana

SAINT CHRISTOPHER AND NEVIS

Chief of State: British monarch, represented by Governor General

Prime Minister

1983– Kennedy A Simmonds

SAINT LUCIA

Chief of State: British monarch, represented by Governor General

Prime Minister

1979 John Compton
1979–81 Allan Louisy
1981–3 Winston Francis Cenac
1983– John Compton

SAINT VINCENT AND THE GRENADINES

Chief of State: British monarch, represented by Governor General

Prime Minister

1979–84 Milton Cato
1984– James Fitz Allan Mitchell

SÃO TOMÉ AND PRINCIPE

President

1975–91 Manuel Pinto da Costa
1991– Miguel Trovoada

SAUDI ARABIA

Monarch

Family name: Al-Saud
1932–53 Abdulaziz Bin Abdur-Rahman
1953–64 Saud Bin Abdulaziz
1964–75 Faisal Bin Abdulaziz
1975–82 Khalid Bin Abdulaziz
1982– Fahd Bin Abdulaziz

SENEGAL

President

1960–80 Léopold Sédar Senghor
1981– Abdou Diouf

Prime Minister

1991– Habib Thiam

SEYCHELLES

President

1976–7 James R Mancham
1977– France-Albert René

SIERRA LEONE

President

1971 Christopher Okero Cole
1971–85 Siaka Stevens
1985 Joseph Saidu Momoh

Prime Minister

Commonwealth
1961–4 Milton Margai
1964–7 Albert Michael Margai
1967 Siaka Stevens
1967 David Lansana
1967 Ambrose Genda
1967–8 *National Reformation Council* (Andrew Saxon-Smith)
1968 John Bangura
1968–71 Siaka Stevens

Republic
1971–5 Sorie Ibrahim Koroma
1975–8 Christian Alusine Kamara Taylor
1978– *No Prime Minister*

SINGAPORE

President (Yang di-Pertuan Negara)

1959–70 Yusof bin Ishak
1970–81 Benjamin Henry Sheares
1981–5 Chengara Veetil Devan Nair
1985– Wee Kim Wee

Prime Minister

1959–90 Lee Kuan Yew
1990– Goh Chok Tong

SOLOMON ISLANDS

Chief of State: British monarch, represented by Governor General

Prime Minister

1978–82 Peter Kenilorea
1982–4 Solomon Mamaloni
1984–6 Peter Kenilorea
1986–9 Ezekiel Alebua
1989– Solomon Mamaloni

SOMALIA

President

1961–7 Aden Abdallah Osman
1967–9 Abdirashid Ali Shermarke

Supreme Revolutionary Council
1969–80 Mohammed Siad Barre

Republic
1980–91 Mohammed Siad Barre
1991– Ali Mahdi Mohammed

Prime Minister

1961–4 Abdirashid Ali Shermarke
1964–7 Abdirizak Haji Hussein
1967–9 Mohammed Haji Ibrahim Egal
1987–90 Mohammed Ali Samater
1990–91 Mohammed Hawadie Madar
1991– Umar Arteh Ghalib

SOUTH AFRICA

Governor General

1910–14 Herbert, Viscount Gladstone
1914–20 Sydney, Earl Buxton

Governor General (cont.)

1920–4 Arthur, Duke of Connaught
1924–31 Alexander, Earl of Athlone
1931–7 George Herbert Hyde Villiers
1937–43 Patrick Duncan
1943–5 Nicolaas Jacobus de Wet
1945–51 Gideon Brand Van Zyl
1951–9 Ernest George Jansen
1959 Lucas Cornelius Steyn
1959–61 Charles Robberts Swart

Republic

President

1961–7 Charles Robberts Swart
1967 Theophilus Ebenhaezer Dönges
1967–8 Jozua François Nandé
1968–75 Jacobus Johannes Fouché
1975–8 Nicolaas Diederichs
1978–9 Balthazar Johannes Vorster
1979–84 Marais Viljoen
1984–89 Pieter Willem Botha
1989– Frederik Willem de Klerk

Prime Minister

1910–19 Louis Botha *SAf*
1919–24 Jan Christiaan Smuts *SAf*
1924–39 James Barry Munnick Hertzog *Nat*
1939–48 Jan Christiaan Smuts *Un*
1948–54 Daniel François Malan *Nat*
1954–8 Johannes Gerardus Strijdom *Nat*
1958–66 Hendrik Frensch Verwoerd *Nat*
1966–78 Balthazar Johannes Vorster *Nat*
1978–84 Pieter Willem Botha *Nat*
1984– *No Prime Minister*

Nat National
SAf South African Party
Un United

SPAIN

Monarch

1886–1931 Alfonso XIII

Second Republic

President

1931–6 Niceto Alcalá Zamora y Torres
1936 Diego Martínez Barrio *Acting President*

Civil War
1936–9 Manuel Azaña y Díez
1936–9 Miguel Cabanellas Ferrer

Nationalist Government

Chief of State

1936–75 Francisco Franco Bahamonde

Monarch

1975– Juan Carlos I

Prime Minister

1900–1 Marcelo de Azcárraga y Palmero
1901–2 Práxedes Mateo Sagasta
1902–3 Francisco Silvela y Le-Vielleuze
1903 Raimundo Fernández Villaverde

SPAIN (cont.)

me Minister (cont.)

03–4 Antonio Maura y Montaner
04–5 Marcelo de Azcárraga y Palmero
05 Raimundo Fernández Villaverde
05 Eugenio Montero Ríos
05–6 Segismundo Moret y Prendergast
06 José López Domínguez
06 Segismundo Moret y Prendergast
06–7 Antonio Aguilar y Correa
07–9 Antonio Maura y Montaner
09–10 Segismundo Moret y Prendergast
10–12 José Canalejas y Méndez
12 Álvaro Figueroa y Torres
12–13 Manuel García Prieto
13–15 Eduardo Dato y Iradier
15–17 Álvaro Figueroa y Torres
17 Manuel García Prieto
17 Eduardo Dato y Iradier
17–18 Manuel García Prieto
18 Antonio Maura y Montaner
18 Manuel García Prieto
18–19 Álvaro Figueroa y Torres
19 Antonio Maura y Montaner
19 Joaquín Sánchez de Toca
19–20 Manuel Allendesalazar
20–1 Eduardo Dato y Iradier
21 Gabino Bugallal Araujo *Acting Prime Minister*
21 Manuel Allendesalazar
21–2 Antonio Maura y Montaner
22 José Sánchez Guerra y Martínez
22–3 Manuel García Prieto
23–30 Miguel Primo de Rivera y Oraneja
30–1 Dámaso Berenguer y Fusté
31 Juan Bautista Aznar-Cabañas
31 Niceto Alcalá Zamora y Torres
31–3 Manuel Azaña y Díez
33 Alejandro Lerroux y García
33 Diego Martínez Barrio
33–4 Alejandro Lerroux y García
34 Ricardo Samper Ibáñez
34–5 Alejandro Lerroux y García
35 Joaquín Chapaprieta y Terragosa
35–6 Manuel Portela Valladares
36 Manuel Azaña y Díez
36 Santiago Casares Quiroga
36 Diego Martínez Barrio
36 José Giral y Pereyra
36–7 Francisco Largo Caballero
37–9 Juan Negrín

hairman of the Council of Ministers

939–73 Francisco Franco Bahamonde

ime Minister

973 Torcuato Fernández Miranda y Hevía *Acting Prime Minister*
973–6 Carlos Arias Navarro
976–81 Adolfo Suárez
981–2 Calvo Sotelo
982– Felipe González

SRI LANKA

resident

972–8 William Gopallawa
978–89 Junius Richard Jayawardene
989– Ranasinghe Premadasa

Prime Minister

Ceylon

1947–52 Don Stephen Senanayake
1952–3 Dudley Shelton Senanayake
1953–6 John Kutewala
1956–9 Solomon West Ridgeway Dias Bandaranaike
1960 Dudley Shelton Senanayake
1960–5 Sirimavo Ratwatte Dias Bandaranaike
1965–70 Dudley Shelton Senanayake

Sri Lanka

1970–7 Sirimavo Bandaranaike
1977–89 Ranasinghe Premadasa
1989– D B Wijetunge

THE SUDAN

Chief of State

1956–8 *Council of State*
1958–64 Ibrahim Abboud
1964–5 *Council of Sovereignty*
1965–9 Ismail Al-Azhari
1969–85 Jaafar Mohammed Nimeiri *President from 1971*

Transitional Military Council

Chairman

1985–6 Abd Al-Rahman Siwar Al-Dahab

Supreme Council

Chairman

1986–9 Ahmad Al-Mirghani
1989– *As Prime Minister*

Prime Minister

1955–6 Ismail Al-Azhari
1956–8 Abdullah Khalil
1958–64 *As President*
1964–5 Serr Al-Khatim Al-Khalifa
1965–6 Mohammed Ahmed Mahjoub
1966–7 Sadiq Al-Mahdi
1967–9 Mohammed Ahmed Mahjoub
1969 Babiker Awadalla
1969–76 *As President*
1976–7 Rashid Al-Tahir Bakr
1977–85 *As President*
1985–6 *Transitional Millitary Council* (Al-Jazuli Dafallah)
1986–9 Sadiq Al-Mahdi *Military Council, Prime Minister*
1989– Omar Hassan Ahmed al-Bashir

SURINAME

President

1975–80 J H E Ferrier
1980–2 Henk Chin-a-Sen
1982–8 L F Ramdat-Musier *Acting President*
1988–90 Ramsewak Shankar
1990–1 Johan Kraag
1991– Ronald Venetiaan

National Military Council

Chairman

1980– Desi Bouterse

Prime Minister

1975–80 Henk Arron
1980 Henk Chin-a-Sen
1980–2 *No Prime Minister*
1982–3 Henry Weyhorst
1983–4 Errol Alibux
1984–6 Wim Udenhout
1986–7 Pretaapnarian Radbakishun
1987–8 Jules Wijdenbosch
1988– Henk Arron

SWAZILAND

Monarch

1967–82 Sobhuza II *Chief since 1921*
1983 Dzeliwe *Queen Regent*
1983–6 Ntombi *Queen Regent*
1986– Mswati III

Prime Minister

1967–78 Prince Makhosini
1978–9 Prince Maphevu Dlamini
1979–83 Prince Mbandla Dlamini
1983–6 Prince Bhekimpi Dlamini
1986–9 Sotsha Dlamini
1989– Obed Dlamini *Acting Prime Minister*

SWEDEN

Monarch

1872–1907 Oskar II
1907–50 Gustav V
1950–73 Gustav VI Adolf
1973– Carl XVI Gustaf

Prime Minister

1900–2 Fredrik von Otter
1902–5 Erik Gustaf Boström
1905 Johan Ramstedt
1905 Christian Lundeberg
1905–6 Karl Staaf
1906–11 Arvid Lindman
1911–14 Karl Staaf
1914–17 Hjalmar Hammarskjöld
1917 Carl Swartz
1917–20 Nils Edén
1920 Hjalmar Branting
1920–1 Louis de Geer
1921 Oscar von Sydow
1921–3 Hjalmar Branting
1923–4 Ernst Trygger
1924–5 Hjalmar Branting
1925–6 Rickard Sandler
1926–8 Carl Gustaf Ekman
1928–30 Arvid Lindman
1930–2 Carl Gustaf Ekman
1932 Felix Hamrin
1932–6 Per Albin Hansson
1936 Axel Pehrsson-Branstorp
1936–46 Per Albin Hansson
1946–69 Tage Erlander
1969–76 Olof Palme
1976–8 Thorbjörn Fälldin
1978–9 Ola Ullsten
1979–82 Thorbjörn Fälldin
1982–6 Olof Palme
1986–91 Ingvar Carlsson
1991– Carl Bildt

SWITZERLAND

President

1900 Walter Hauser
1901 Ernst Brenner
1902 Joseph Zemp
1903 Adolf Deucher
1904 Robert Comtesse
1905 Marc-Emile Ruchet
1906 Ludwig Forrer
1907 Eduard Müller
1908 Ernst Brenner
1909 Adolf Deucher
1910 Robert Comtesse
1911 Marc-Emile Ruchet
1912 Ludwig Forrer
1913 Eduard Müller
1914 Arthur Hoffmann
1915 Guiseppe Motta
1916 Camille Decoppet
1917 Edmund Schulthess
1918 Felix Calonder
1919 Gustave Ador
1920 Giuseppe Motta
1921 Edmund Schulthess
1922 Robert Haab
1923 Karl Scheurer
1924 Ernest Chuard
1925 Jean-Marie Musy
1926 Heinrich Häberlin
1927 Giuseppe Motta
1928 Edmund Schulthess
1929 Robert Haab
1930 Jean-Marie Musy
1931 Heinrich Häberlin
1932 Giuseppe Motta
1933 Edmund Schulthess
1934 Marcel Pilet-Golaz
1935 Rudolf Minger
1936 Albert Meyer
1937 Giuseppe Motta
1938 Johannes Baumann
1939 Philipp Etter
1940 Marcel Pilet-Golaz
1941 Ernst Wetter
1942 Philipp Etter
1943 Enrico Celio
1944 Walter Stampfli
1945 Eduard von Steiger
1946 Karl Kobelt
1947 Philipp Etter
1948 Enrico Celio
1949 Ernst Nobs
1950 Max Petitpierre
1951 Eduard von Steiger
1952 Karl Kobelt
1953 Philipp Etter
1954 Rodolphe Rubattel
1955 Max Petitpierre
1956 Markus Feldmann
1957 Hans Streuli
1958 Thomas Holenstein
1959 Paul Chaudet
1960 Max Petitpierre
1961 Friedrich Wahlen
1962 Paul Chaudet
1963 Willy Spühler
1964 Ludwig von Moos
1965 Hans Peter Tschudi
1966 Hans Schaffner
1967 Roger Bonvin
1968 Willy Spühler
1969 Ludwig von Moos

President (cont.)

1970 Hans Peter Tschudi
1971 Rudolf Gnägi
1972 Nello Celio
1973 Roger Bonvin
1974 Ernst Brugger
1975 Pierre Graber
1976 Rudolf Gnägi
1977 Kurt Furgler
1978 Willi Ritschard
1979 Hans Hürlimann
1980 Georges-André Chevallaz
1981 Kurt Furgler
1982 Fritz Honegger
1983 Pierre Aubert
1984 Leon Schlumpf
1985 Kurt Furgler
1986 Alphons Egli
1987 Pierre Aubert
1988 Otto Stich
1989 Jean-Pascal Delamuraz
1990 Arnold Koller
1991 Flavio Cotti

SYRIA

President

1943–9 Shukri Al-Quwwatli
1949 Husni Az-Zaim
1949–51 Hashim Al-Atasi
1951–4 Adib Shishaqli
1954–5 Hashim Al-Atasi
1955–8 Shukri Al-Quwwatli
1958–61 *Part of United Arab Republic*
1961–3 Nazim Al-Qudsi
1963 Luai Al-Atassi
1963–6 Amin Al-Hafiz
1966–70 Nureddin Al-Atassi
1970–1 Ahmad Al-Khatib
1971– Hafez Al Assad

Prime Minister

1946–8 Jamil Mardam Bey
1948–9 Khalid Al-Azm
1949 Husni Az-Zaim
1949 Muhsi Al-Barazi
1949 Hashim Al-Atassi
1949 Nazim Al-Qudsi
1949–50 Khalid Al-Azm
1950–1 Nazim Al-Qudsi
1951 Khalid Al-Azm
1951 Hassan Al-Hakim
1951 Maruf Ad-Dawalibi
1951–3 Fauzi As-Salu
1953–4 Adib Shishaqli
1954 Shewqet Shuqair
1954 Sabri Al-Asali
1954 Said Al-Ghazzi
1954–5 Faris Al-Khuri
1955 Sabri Al-Asali
1955–6 Said Al-Ghazzi
1956–8 Sabri Al-Asali
1958–61 *Part of United Arab Republic*
1961 Abd Al-Hamid As-Sarraj
1961 Mamun Kuzbari
1961 Izzat An-Nuss
1961–2 Maruf Ad-Dawalibi
1962 Bashir Azmah
1962–3 Khalid Al-Azm
1963 Salah Ad-Din Al-Bitaar
1963 Sami Al-Jundi

Prime Minister (cont.)

1963 Salah Ad-Din Al-Bitaar
1963–4 Amin Al-Hafez
1964 Salah Ad-Din Al-Bitaar
1964–5 Amin Al-Hafez
1965 Yousif Zeayen
1966 Salah Ad-Din Al-Bitaar
1966–8 Yousif Zeayen
1968–70 Nureddin Al-Atassi *Acting Prime Minister*
1970–1 Hafez Al-Assad
1971–2 Abdel Rahman Khleifawi
1972–6 Mahmoud Bin Saleh Al-Ayoubi
1976–8 Abdul Rahman Khleifawi
1978–80 Mohammed Ali Al-Halabi
1980–7 Abdel Rauof Al-Kasm
1987– Mahmoud Zubi

TAIWAN

President

1950–75 Chiang Kai-shek
1975–8 Yen Chia-kan
1978–87 Chiang Ching-kuo
1987– Lee Teng-hui

President of Executive Council

1950–4 Ch'eng Ch'eng
1954–8 O K Yui
1958–63 Ch'eng Ch'eng
1963–72 Yen Chia-ken
1972–8 Chiang Ching-kuo
1978–84 Sun Yun-suan
1984–9 Yu Kuo-hwa
1989–90 Lee Huan
1990– Hau Pei-tsun

TANZANIA

President

1964–85 Julius Kambarage Nyerere
1985– Ali Hassan Mwinyi

Prime Minister

1964–72 Rashid M Kawawa *Vice President*
1972–7 Rashid M Kawawa
1977–80 Edward M Sokoine
1980–3 Cleopa D Msuya
1983–4 Edward M Sokoine
1984–5 Salim A Salim
1985–90 Joseph S Warioba
1990– John Malecela

THAILAND

Monarch

1868–1910 Chulalongkorn, Rama V
1910–25 Rama VI
1925–35 Rama VII
1935–9 Rama VIII (Ananda Mahidol)
1939–46 Nai Pridi Phanomyong *Regent*
1946– Rama IX (Rangsit of Chainat *Regent 1946–5*

THAILAND (cont.)

rime Minister

932–3 Phraya Manopakom
933–8 Phraya Phahon Phonphahuyasena
938–44 Luang Phibun Songgram
945 Thawi Bunyaket
945–6 Mom Rachawongse Seni Pramoj
946 Nai Khuang Aphaiwong
946 Nai Pridi Phanomyong
946–7 Luang Thamrong Nawasawat
947–8 Nai Khuang Aphaiwong
948–57 Luang Phibun Songgram
957 Sarit Thanarat
957 Nai Pote Sarasin
957–8 Thanom Kittikatchom
958–63 Sarit Thanarat
963–73 Thanom Kittikatchom
973–5 Sanya Dharmasaki
975–6 Mom Rachawongse Kukrit Pramoj
976 Seni Pramoj
976–7 Thanin Kraivichien
977–80 Kriangsak Chammanard
980–7 Prem Tinsulanonda
987–91 Chatichai Choonhavan

ational Peace-Keeping Assembly
991– Anand Panyarachun (*Junta*)

TOGO

resident

960–3 Sylvanus Olympio
963–7 Nicolas Grunitzky
967–91 Gnassingbe Eyadema
991– Koukou Koffigoh

TONGA

onarch

893–1918 George Tupou II
918–65 Salote Tupou III
965– Taufa'ahau Tupou IV

rime Minister

970– Fatafehi Tu'ipelehake

TRINIDAD AND TOBAGO

resident

976–87 Ellis Emmanuel Clarke
987– Noor Hassanali

remier

956–62 Eric Williams

rime Minister

962–81 Eric Williams
981–6 George Chambers
986– Arthur Napoleon Raymond Robinson

TUNISIA

ey

943–57 Muhammad VIII

President

1957–87 Habib Bourguiba
1987– Zine Al-Abidine Bin Ali

Prime Minister

1956–7 Habib Bourguiba
1957–69 *No Prime Minister*
1969–70 Bahi Ladgham
1970–80 Hadi Nouira
1980–6 Mohammed Mezali
1986–7 Rashid Sfar
1987 Zine Al-Abidine Bin Ali
1987–9 Hadi Baccouche
1989– Hamed Karoui

TURKEY

Sultan of the Ottoman Empire

1876–1909 Abdülhamit
1909–18 Mehmet Reşat
1918–22 Mehmet Vahideddin

Turkish Republic

President

1923–38 Mustafa Kemal Atatürk
1938–50 İsmet İnönü
1950–60 Celâl Bayar
1961–6 Cemal Gürsel
1966–73 Cevdet Sunay
1973–80 Fahri S Korutürk
1982–9 Kenan Evren
1989– Turgut Özal

TUVALU

Chief of State: British monarch, represented by Governor General

Prime Minister

1978–81 Toalipi Lauti
1981–9 Tomasi Puapua
1989– Bikenibeu Paeniu

UGANDA

President

1962–6 Edward Muteesa II
1967–71 Apollo Milton Obote
1971–9 Idi Amin
1979 Yusuf Kironde Lule
1979–80 Godfrey Lukongwa Binaisa
1981–5 Apollo Milton Obote
1985–6 *Military Council* (Tito Okello Lutwa)
1986– Yoweri Kaguta Museveni

Prime Minister

1962–71 Apollo Milton Obote
1971–81 *No Prime Minister*
1981–5 Eric Otema Alimadi
1985 Paulo Muwanga
1985–6 Abraham N Waliggo
1986–91 Samson B Kisekka
1991– George Cosmas Adyebo

UNITED ARAB EMIRATES

President

1971– Zayed Bin Sultan Al-Nahyan

Prime Minister

1971–9 Maktoum Bin Rashid Al-Maktoum
1979–90 Rashid Bin Said Al-Maktoum
1990– Maktoum Bin Rashid Al-Maktoum

ABU DHABI
Tribe: Al Bu Falah *or* Al Nahyan (Bani Yas)
Family name: Al-Nahyan

Shaikh

1855–1909 Zayed
1909–12 Tahnoun
1912–22 Hamdan
1922–6 Sultan
1926–8 Saqr
1928–66 Shakhbout
1966– Zayed

AJMAN
Tribe: Al Bu Kharayban (Naim)
Family name: Al-Nuaimi

Shaikh

1900–10 Abdel-Aziz
1910–28 Humaid
1928–81 Rashid
1981– Humaid

DUBAI
Tribe: Al Bu Flasah (Bani Yas)
Family name: Al-Maktoum

Shaikh

1894–1906 Maktoum
1906–12 Butti
1912–58 Said
1958–90 Rashid
1990– Maktoum

FUJAIRAH
Tribe: Sharqiyyin
Family name: Al-Sharqi

Shaikh

1952–75 Mohammed
1975– Hamad

RAS AL-KHAIMAH
Tribe: Huwalah
Family name: Al-Qasimi

Shaikh

1921–48 Sultan
1948 Saqr

SHARJAH
Tribe: Huwalah
Family name: Al-Qasimi

Shaikh

1883–1914 Saqr
1914–24 Khaled
1924–51 Sultan
1951–65 Saqr
1965–72 Khaled
1972–87 Sultan
1987 Abdel-Aziz
1987– Sultan

UNITED ARAB EMIRATES (cont.)

UMM AL-QAIWAIN
Tribe: Al-Ali
Family name: Al-Mualla

Shaikh

1873–1904 Ahmad
1904–22 Rashid
1922–3 Abdullah
1923–9 Hamad
1929–81 Ahmad
1981– Rashid

UNION OF SOVIET SOCIALIST REPUBLICS

President

1917 Leo Borisovich Kamenev
1917–19 Yakov Mikhailovich Sverlov
1919–46 Mikhail Ivanovich Kalinin
1946–53 Nikolai Shvernik
1953–60 Klimentiy Voroshilov
1960–4 Leonid Brezhnev
1964–5 Anastas Mikoyan
1965–77 Nikolai Podgorny
1977–82 Leonid Brezhnev
1982–3 Vasily Kuznetsov *Acting President*
1983–4 Yuri Andropov
1984 Vasily Kuznetsov *Acting President*
1984–5 Konstantin Chernenko
1985 Vasily Kuznetsov *Acting President*
1985–8 Andrei Gromyko
1988–90 Mikhail Gorbachev

Executive President

1990–91 Mikhail Gorbachev

Chairman (Prime Minister)

Council of Ministers
1917 Georgy Evgenyevich Lvov
1917 Aleksandr Fyodorovich Kerensky

Council of People's Commissars
1917–24 Vladimir Ilyich Lenin
1924–30 Aleksei Ivanovich Rykov
1930–41 Vyacheslav Mikhailovich Molotov
1941–53 Josef Stalin

Council of Ministers
1953–5 Georgiy Malenkov
1955–8 Nikolai Bulganin
1958–64 Nikita Khrushchev
1964–80 Alexei Kosygin
1980–5 Nikolai Tikhonov
1985–90 Nikolai Ryzhkov
1990–1 Yuri Maslyukov (*Acting*)
1991 Valentin Pavlov

General Secretary

1922–53 Josef Stalin
1953 Georgiy Malenkov
1953–64 Nikita Khrushchev
1964–82 Leonid Brezhnev
1982–4 Yuri Andropov
1984–5 Konstantin Chernenko
1985–91 Mikhail Gorbachev

UNITED KINGDOM

Monarch

West Saxon Kings
802–39 Egbert
839–58 Æthelwulf
858–60 Æthelbald
860–5 Æthelbert
866–71 Æthelred
871–99 Alfred
899–924 Edward (the Elder)
924–39 Athelstan
939–46 Edmund
946–55 Edred
955–9 Edwy
959–75 Edgar
975–8 Edward (the Martyr)
978–1016 Æthelred (the Unready)
1016 Edmund (Ironside)

Danish Kings
1016–35 Cnut (Canute)
1035–7 Harold *Regent*
1037–40 Harold I (Harefoot)
1040–2 Harthacnut
1042–66 Edward (the Confessor)
1066 Harold II

House of Normandy
1066–87 William I (the Conqueror)
1087–1100 William II (Rufus)
1100–35 Henry I

House of Blois
1135–54 Stephen

House of Plantagenet
1154–89 Henry II
1189–99 Richard I (Cœur de Lion)
1199–1216 John
1216–72 Henry III
1272–1307 Edward I
1307–27 Edward II
1327–77 Edward III
1377–99 Richard II

House of Lancaster
1399–1413 Henry IV
1413–22 Henry V
1422–61 Henry VI

House of York
1461–70 Edward IV

House of Lancaster
1470–1 Henry VI

House of York
1471–83 Edward IV
1483 Edward V
1483–5 Richard III

House of Tudor
1485–1509 Henry VII
1509–47 Henry VIII
1547–53 Edward VI
1553–8 Mary I
1558–1603 Elizabeth I

House of Stuart
1603–25 James I (VI of Scotland)
1625–49 Charles I

Monarch (cont.)

Commonwealth and Protectorate
1649–53 *Council of State*
1653–8 Oliver Cromwell *Lord Protector*
1658–9 Richard Cromwell *Lord Protector*

House of Stuart (restored)
1660–85 Charles II
1685–8 James II
1689–94 William III (*jointly with* Mary II)
1694–1702 William III (*alone*)
1702–14 Anne

House of Hanover
1714–27 George I
1727–60 George II
1760–1820 George III
1820–30 George IV
1830–7 William IV
1837–1901 Victoria

House of Saxe-Coburg
1901–10 Edward VII

House of Windsor
1910–36 George V
1936 Edward VIII
1936–52 George VI
1952– Elizabeth II
see illustration p 487

Prime Minister

1721–42 Robert Walpole *Whig*
1742–3 Earl of Wilmington (Spencer Compton) *Whig*
1743–54 Henry Pelham *Whig*
1754–6 Duke of Newcastle (Thomas Pelham-Holles) *Whig*
1756–7 Duke of Devonshire (William Cavendish) *Whig*
1757–62 Duke of Newcastle *Whig*
1762–3 Earl of Bute (John Stuart) *Tory*
1763–5 George Grenville *Whig*
1765–6 Marquess of Rockingham (Charles Watson Wentworth) *Whig*
1766–7 Earl of Chatham (William Pitt the Elder) *Whig*
1767–70 Duke of Grafton (Augustus Henry Fitzroy) *Whig*
1770–82 Lord North (Frederick North) *Tory*
1782 Marquess of Rockingham *Whig*
1782–3 Earl of Shelburne (William Petty-Fitzmaurice) *Whig*
1783 Duke of Portland (William Henry Cavendish) *Coal*
1783–1801 William Pitt *Tory*
1801–4 Henry Addington *Tory*
1804–6 William Pitt *Tory*
1806–7 Lord Grenville (William Wyndham) *Whig*
1807–9 Duke of Portland *Tory*
1809–12 Spencer Perceval *Tory*
1812–27 Earl of Liverpool (Robert Banks Jenkinson) *Tory*
1827 George Canning *Tory*
1827–8 Viscount Goderich (Frederick John Robinson) *Tory*
1828–30 Duke of Wellington (Arthur Wellesley) *Tory*
1830–4 Earl Grey (Charles Grey) *Whig*
1834 Viscount Melbourne (William Lamb) *Whig*
1834–5 Robert Peel *Con*
1835–41 Viscount Melbourne *Whig*

UNITED KINGDOM (cont.)

Prime Minister (cont.)

1841–6	Robert Peel *Con*
1846–52	Lord John Russell *Lib*
1852	Earl of Derby (Edward George Stanley) *Con*
1852–5	Lord Aberdeen (George Hamilton-Gordon) *Peelite*
1855–8	Viscount Palmerston (Henry John Temple) *Lib*
1858–9	Earl of Derby *Con*
1859–65	Viscount Palmerston *Lib*
1865–6	Lord John Russell *Lib*
1866–8	Earl of Derby *Con*
1868	Benjamin Disraeli *Con*
1868–74	William Ewart Gladstone *Lib*
1874–80	Benjamin Disraeli *Con*
1880–5	William Ewart Gladstone *Lib*
1885–6	Marquess of Salisbury (Robert Gascoyne-Cecil) *Con*
1886	William Ewart Gladstone *Lib*
1886–92	Marquess of Salisbury *Con*
1892–4	William Ewart Gladstone *Lib*
1894–5	Earl of Rosebery (Archibald Philip Primrose) *Lib*
1895–1902	Marquess of Salisbury *Con*
1902–5	Arthur James Balfour *Con*
1905–8	Henry Campbell-Bannerman *Lib*
1908–15	Herbert Henry Asquith *Lib*
1915–16	Herbert Henry Asquith *Coal*
1916–22	David Lloyd George *Coal*
1922–3	Andrew Bonar Law *Con*
1923–4	Stanley Baldwin *Con*
1924	James Ramsay MacDonald *Lab*
1924–9	Stanley Baldwin *Con*
1929–31	James Ramsay MacDonald *Lab*
1931–5	James Ramsay MacDonald *Nat*
1935–7	Stanley Baldwin *Nat*
1937–40	Arthur Neville Chamberlain *Nat*
1940–5	Winston Churchill *Coal*
1945–51	Clement Attlee *Lab*
1951–5	Winston Churchill *Con*
1955–7	Anthony Eden *Con*
1957–63	Harold Macmillan *Con*
1963–4	Alec Douglas-Home *Con*
1964–70	Harold Wilson *Lab*
1970–4	Edward Heath *Con*
1974–6	Harold Wilson *Lab*
1976–9	James Callaghan *Lab*
1979–90	Margaret Thatcher *Con*
1990–	John Major *Con*

Coal *Coalition*
Con *Conservative*
Lab *Labour*
Lib *Liberal*
Nat *Nationalist*

UNITED NATIONS

Secretary General

1946–53	Trygve Lie *Norway*
1953–61	Dag Hammarskjöld *Sweden*
1962–71	U Thant *Burma*
1971–81	Kurt Waldheim *Austria*
1982–92	Javier Pérez de Cuéllar *Peru*
1992–	Boutros Ghalí *Egypt*

UNITED STATES OF AMERICA

President

Vice President in parentheses

1789–97	George Washington (1st) (John Adams)
1797–1801	John Adams (2nd) *Fed* (Thomas Jefferson)
1801–9	Thomas Jefferson (3rd) *Dem-Rep* (Aaron Burr, 1801–5) (George Clinton, 1805–9)
1809–17	James Madison (4th) *Dem-Rep* (George Clinton, 1809–12) *no Vice President 1812–13* (Elbridge Gerry, 1813–14) *no Vice President 1814–17*
1817–25	James Monroe (5th) *Dem-Rep* (Daniel D Tompkins)
1825–9	John Quincy Adams (6th) *Dem-Rep* (John C Calhoun)
1829–37	Andrew Jackson (7th) *Dem* (John C Calhoun, 1829–32) *no Vice President 1832–3* (Martin van Buren, 1833–7)
1837–41	Martin van Buren (8th) *Dem* (Richard M Johnson)
1841	William Henry Harrison (9th) *Whig* (John Tyler)
1841–5	John Tyler (10th) *Whig* *no Vice President*
1845–9	James Knox Polk (11th) *Dem* (George M Dallas)
1849–50	Zachary Taylor (12th) *Whig* (Millard Fillmore)
1850–3	Millard Fillmore (13th) *Whig* *no Vice President*
1853–7	Franklin Pierce (14th) *Dem* (William R King, 1853) *no Vice President 1853–7*
1857–61	James Buchanan (15th) *Dem* (John C Breckinridge)
1861–5	Abraham Lincoln (16th) *Rep* (Hannibal Hamlin, 1861–5) (Andrew Johnson, 1865)
1865–9	Andrew Johnson (17th) *Dem-Nat* *no Vice President*
1869–77	Ulysses Simpson Grant (18th) *Rep* (Schuyler Colfax, 1869–73) (Henry Wilson, 1873–5) *no Vice President 1875–7*
1877–81	Rutherford Birchard Hayes (19th) *Rep* (William A Wheeler)
1881	James Abram Garfield (20th) *Rep* (Chester A Arthur)
1881–5	Chester Alan Arthur (21st) *Rep* *no Vice President*
1885–9	Grover Cleveland (22nd) *Dem* (Thomas A Hendricks, 1885) *no Vice President 1885–9*
1889–93	Benjamine Harrison (23rd) *Rep* (Levi P Morton)
1893–7	Grover Cleveland (24th) *Dem* (Adlai E Stevenson)
1897–1901	William McKinley (25th) *Rep* (Garret A Hobart, 1897–9) *no Vice President 1899–1901* (Theodore Roosevelt, 1901)
1901–9	Theodore Roosevelt (26th) *Rep* *no Vice President 1901–5* (Charles W Fairbanks, 1905–9)

President (cont.)

1909–13	William Howard Taft (27th) *Rep* (James S Sherman, 1909–12) *no Vice President 1912–13*
1913–21	Woodrow Wilson (28th) *Dem* (Thomas R Marshall)
1921–3	Warren Gamaliel Harding (29th) *Rep* (Calvin Coolidge)
1923–9	Calvin Coolidge (30th) *Rep* *no Vice President 1923–5* (Charles G Dawes, 1925–9)
1929–33	Herbert Clark Hoover (31st) *Rep* (Charles Curtis)
1933–45	Franklin Delano Roosevelt (32nd) *Dem* (John N Garner, 1933–41) (Henry A Wallace, 1941–5) (Harry S Truman, 1945)
1945–53	Harry S Truman (33rd) *Dem* *no Vice President 1945–9* (Alben W Barkley, 1949–53)
1953–61	Dwight David Eisenhower (34th) *Rep* (Richard M Nixon)
1961–3	John Fitzgerald Kennedy (35th) *Dem* (Lyndon B Johnson)
1963–9	Lyndon Baines Johnson (36th) *Dem* *no Vice President 1963–5* (Hubert H Humphrey, 1965–9)
1969–74	Richard Milhous Nixon (37th) *Rep* (Spiro T Agnew, 1969–73) *no Vice President 1973, Oct–Dec* (Gerald R Ford, 1973–4)
1974–7	Gerald Rudolph Ford (38th) *Rep* *no Vice President 1974, Aug–Dec* (Nelson A Rockefeller, 1974–7)
1977–81	Jimmy Carter (39th) *Dem* (Walter F Mondale)
1981–9	Ronald Wilson Reagan (40th) *Rep* (George H W Bush)
1989–	George Herbert Walker Bush (41st) *Rep* (J Danforth Quayle)

Dem *Democrat*
Fed *Federalist*
Nat *National Union*
Rep *Republican*

URUGUAY

President

1899–1903	Juan Lindolfo Cuestas
1903–7	José Batlle y Ordóñez
1907–11	Claudio Williman
1911–15	José Batlle y Ordóñez
1915–19	Feliciano Viera
1919–23	Baltasar Brum
1923–7	José Serrato
1927–31	Juan Capisteguy
1931–8	Gabriel Terra
1938–43	Alfredo Baldomir
1943–7	Juan José de Amézaga
1947	Tomás Berreta
1947–51	Luis Batlle Berres
1951–5	Andrés Martínez Trueba

National Government Council (1955–67)

1955–6	Luis Batlle Berres
1956–7	Alberto F Zubiría
1957–8	Alberto Lezama
1958–9	Carlos L Fischer
1959–60	Martín R Etchegoyen

URUGUAY (cont.)

President (cont.)

1960–1 Benito Nardone
1961–2 Eduardo Víctor Haedo
1962–3 Faustino Harrison
1963–4 Daniel Fernández Crespo
1964–5 Luis Giannattasio
1965–6 Washington Beltrán
1966–7 Alberto Heber Usher
1967 Oscar Daniel Gestido
1967–72 Jorge Pacheco Areco
1972–6 Juan María Bordaberry Arocena
1976–81 Aparicio Méndez
1981–4 Gregorio Conrado Álvarez Armelino
1984–90 Julio María Sanguinetti Cairolo
1990 Luis Alberto Lacalle Herrera

VANUATU

President

1980–9 George Sokomanu (*formerly* Kalkoa)
1989– Fred Timakata

Prime Minister

1980–91 Walter Lini
1991– Donald Kalpokas

VENEZUELA

President

1899–1908 Cipriano Castro
1908–36 Juan Vicente Gomez
1936–41 Eleazar Lopez Contreras
1941–5 Isaias Medina Angarita
1945–7 *Military Junta* (Romulo Betancourt)
1947–8 Romulo Gallegos
1948–50 *Military Junta* (Carlos Delgado Chalbaud)
1950–9 *Military Junta* (Marcos Perez Jimenez)
1959–64 Romulo Betancourt
1964–9 Raul Leoni
1969–74 Rafael Caldera Rodriguez
1974–9 Carlos Andres Perez
1979–84 Luis Herrera Campins
1984–9 Jaime Lusinchi
1989– Carlos Andres Perez

VIETNAM

Democratic Republic of Vietnam

President

1945–69 Ho Chi Minh
1969–76 Ton Duc Thang

State of Vietnam
1949–55 Bao Dai

Republic of Vietnam
1955–63 Ngo Dinh Diem
1963–4 Duong Van Minh
1964 Nguyen Khanh
1964–5 Phan Khac Suu

President (cont.)

1965–75 Nguyen Van Thieu
1975 Tran Van Huong
1975 Duong Van Minh
1975–6 *Provisional Revolutionary Government* (Huynh Tan Phat)

Socialist Republic of Vietnam
1976–80 Ton Duc Thang
1980–1 Nguyen Hun Tho *Acting President*
1981–7 Truongh Chinh
1987– Vo Chi Cong

Democratic Republic of Vietnam

Prime Minister

1955–76 Pham Van Dong

State of Vietnam
1949–50 Nguyen Van Xuan
1950 Nguyen Phan Long
1950–2 Tran Van Huu
1952 Tran Van Huong
1952–3 Nguyen Van Tam
1953–4 Buu Loc
1954–5 Ngo Dinh Diem

Republic of Vietnam
1955–63 Ngo Dinh Diem
1963–4 Nguyen Ngoc Tho
1964 Nguyen Khan
1964–5 Tran Van Huong
1965 Phan Huy Quat
1965–7 Nguyen Cao Ky
1967–8 Nguyen Van Loc
1968–9 Tran Van Huong
1969–75 Tran Thien Khiem
1975 Nguyen Ba Can
1975–6 Vu Van Mau

Socialist Republic of Vietnam

Premier

1976–87 Pham Van Dong
1987–8 Pham Hung
1988 Vo Van Kiet *Acting Premier*
1988–91 Do Muoi
1991– Vo Van Kiet

General Secretary

1960–80 Le Duan
1986 Truong Chinh
1986–91 Nguyen Van Linh
1991– Do Muoi

WESTERN SAMOA

President

1962–3 Tupua Tamesehe Mea'ole Mallietoa Tanumafili II *joint Presidents*
1963– Mallietoa Tanumafili II

Prime Minister

1962–70 Fiame Mata'afa Faumuina Mulinu'u II
1970–6 Tupua Tamasese Leolofi IV
1976–82 Tupuola Taisi Efi
1982 Va'ai Kolone
1982 Tupuola Taisi Efi
1982–6 Tofilau Eti
1986–8 Va'ai Kolone
1988– Tafilau Eti Alesana

YEMEN

Yemen Arab Republic (North Yemen)

Monarch (Imam)

1918–48 Yahya Mohammed Bin Mohammed
1948–62 Ahmed Bin Yahya
1962–70 Mohammed Bin Ahmed

1962 Civil War

President

1962–7 Abdullah Al-Sallal
1967–74 Abdur Rahman Al-Iriani
1974–7 *Military Command Council* (Ibrahim Al-Hamadi)
1977–8 Ahmed Bin Hussein Al-Ghashmi
1978–90 Ali Abdullah Saleh

Prime Minister

1964 Hamud Al-Jaifi
1965 Hassan Al-Amri
1965 Ahmed Mohammed Numan
1965 *As President*
1965–6 Hassan Al-Amri
1966–7 *As President*
1967 Muhsin Al-Aini
1967–9 Hassan Al-Amri
1969–70 Abd Allah Kurshumi
1970–1 Muhsin Al-Aini
1971 Abdel Salam Sabra *Acting Prime Minister*
1971 Ahmed Mohammed Numan
1971 Hassan Al-Amri
1971–2 Muhsin Al-Aini
1972–4 Qadi Abdullah Al-Hijri
1974 Hassan Makki
1974–5 Muhsin Al-Aini
1975 Abdel Latif Deifallah *Acting Prime Minister*
1975–90 Abdel-Aziz Abdel-Ghani

People's Democratic Republic of Yemen (South Yemen)

President

1967–9 Qahtan Mohammed Al-Shaabi
1969–78 Salim Ali Rubai
1978 Ali Nasir Mohammed Husani
1978–80 Abdel Fattah Ismail
1980–6 Ali Nasir Mohammed Husani
1986–90 Haidar Abu Bakr Al-Attas

Prime Minister

1969 Faisal Abd Al-Latif Al-Shaabi
1969–71 Mohammed Ali Haithem
1971–85 Ali Nasir Mohammed Husani
1985–6 Haidar Abu Bakr Al-Attas
1986–90 Yasin Said Numan

Republic of Yemen

President

1990– Ali Abdullah Saleh

Prime Minister

1990– Haidar Abu Bakr Al-Attas

YUGOSLAVIA

Monarch

1921–34 Aleksandar II
1934–45 Petar II *in exile, 1941–*

YUGOSLAVIA (cont.)

Republic

National Assembly

Chairman

1945–53 Ivan Ribar

President

1953–80 Josip Broz Tito

Collective Presidency

1980 Lazar Koliševski
1980–1 Cvijetin Mijatović
1981–2 Serghei Kraigher
1982–3 Petar Stambolić
1983–4 Mika Spiljak
1984–5 Veselin Đuranović
1985–6 Radovan Vlajković
1986–7 Sinan Hasani
1987–8 Lazar Mojsov
1988–9 Raif Dizdarević
1989–90 Janez Drnovsek
1990–1 Borisav Jovic
1991–2 Stipe Mesic

Prime Minister

1929–32 Pear Živkovic
1932 Vojislav Marinković
1932–4 Milan Srškić
1934 Nikola Uzunović
1934–5 Bogoljub Jevtić
1935–9 Milan Stojadinović
1939–41 Dragiša Cvetković
1941 Dušan Simović

Government in exile

1942 Slobodan Jovanović
1943 Miloš Trifunović
1943–4 Božidar Purić
1944–5 Ivan Šubašić
1945 Drago Marušić

Home government

1941–4 Milan Nedić
1943–63 Josip Broz Tito

Prime Minister (cont.)

1963–7 Petar Stambolić
1967–9 Mika Špiljak
1969–71 Mitja Ribičič
1971–7 Džemal Bijedić
1977–82 Veselin Đuranović
1982–6 Milka Planinc
1986–9 Branko Mikulić
1989– Ante Marković

Communist Party

First Secretary

1937–52 Josip Broz Tito

League of Communists

1952–80 Josip Broz Tito

League of Communists Central Committee

President

1979–80 Stevan Doronjski *Acting President*
1980–1 Lazar Mojsov
1981–2 Dušan Dragosavac
1982–3 Mitja Ribičič
1983–4 Dragoslav Marković
1984–5 Ali Šukrija
1985–6 Vidoje Žarkovic
1986–7 Milanko Renovica
1987–8 Boško Krunić
1988–9 Stipe Suvar
1989–90 Milan Pancevski
1990– Miomir Grbovic

ZAÏRE

President

1960–5 Joseph Kasavubu
1965– Mobuto Sese Seko (*formerly* Joseph Mobutu)

Prime Minister

1960 Patrice Lumumba
1960 Joseph Ileo
1960–1 *College of Commissioners*
1961 Joseph Ileo

Prime Minister (cont.)

1961–4 Cyrille Adoula
1964–5 Moïse Tshombe
1965 Evariste Kimba
1965–6 Mulamba Nyungu wa Kadima
1966–77 *As President*
1977–80 Mpinga Kasenga
1980 Bo-Boliko Lokonga Monse Mihambu
1980–1 Nguza Karl I Bond
1981–3 Nsinga Udjuu
1983–6 Kengo wa Dondo
1986–8 *No Prime Minister*
1988 Sambura Pida Nbagui
1988–9 Kengo wa Dondo
1989–91 Lunda Bululu
1991 Mulumba Lukeji
1991 Etienne Tshisekedi
1991– Bernardin Mungul Diaka

ZAMBIA

President

1964–91 Kenneth Kaunda
1991– Frederick Chiluba

Prime Minister

1964–73 Kenneth Kaunda
1973–5 Mainza Chona
1975–7 Elijah Mudenda
1977–8 Mainza Chona
1978–81 Daniel Lisulu
1981–5 Nalumino Mundia
1985–9 Kebby Musokotwane
1989– Malimba Masheke

ZIMBABWE

President

1980–7 Canaan Sodindo Banana
1987– Robert Gabriel Mugabe

Prime Minister

1980– Robert Gabriel Mugabe

POPES

Antipopes are given in brackets

until *c.*64 Peter
*c.*64–*c.*76 Linus
*c.*76–*c.*90 Anacletus
*c.*90–*c.*99 Clement I
*c.*99–*c.*105 Evaristus
*c.*105–*c.*117 Alexander I
*c.*117–*c.*127 Sixtus I
*c.*127–*c.*137 Telesphorus
*c.*137–*c.*140 Hyginus
*c.*140–*c.*154 Pius I
*c.*154–*c.*166 Anicetus
*c.*166–*c.*175 Soter
175–89 Eleutherius
189–98 Victor I
198–217 Zephyrinus
217–22 Callistus I
[217–*c.*235 Hippolytus]
222–30 Urban I
230–5 Pontian
235–6 Anterus
236–50 Fabian
251–3 Cornelius
[251–*c.*258 Novatian]
251–4 Lucius I
254–7 Stephen I
257–8 Sixtus II
259–68 Dionysius
269–74 Felix I
275–83 Eutychianus
283–96 Caius
296–304 Marcellinus
308–9 Marcellus I
310 Eusebius
311–314 Miltiades
314–35 Sylvester I
336 Mark
337–52 Julius I
352–66 Liberius
[355–65 Felix II]
366–84 Damasus I
[366–7 Ursinus]
384–99 Siricius
399–401 Anastasius I
402–17 Innocent I
417–18 Zosimus
418–22 Boniface I
[418–19 Eulalius]
422–32 Celestine I
432–40 Sixtus III
440–61 Leo I
461–8 Hilarus
468–83 Simplicius
483–92 Felix III (II)
492–6 Gelasius I
496–8 Anastasius II
498–514 Symmachus
[498, 501–5 Laurentius]
514–23 Hormisdas
523–6 John I
526–30 Felix IV (III)
530–2 Boniface II
[530 Dioscorus]

POPES (cont.)

533–5	John II
535–6	Agapetus I
536–7	Silverius
537–55	Vigilius
556–61	Pelagius I
561–74	John III
575–9	Benedict I
579–90	Pelagius II
590–604	Gregory I
604–6	Sabinianus
607	Boniface III
608–15	Boniface IV
615–18	Deusdedit *or* Adeodatus I
619–25	Boniface V
625–38	Honorius I
640	Severinus
640–2	John IV
642–9	Theodore I
649–55	Martin I
654–7	Eugenius I[1]
657–72	Vitalian
672–6	Adeodatus II
676–8	Donus
678–81	Agatho
682–3	Leo II
684–5	Benedict II
685–6	John V
686–7	Cono
[687	Theodore]
[687–92	Paschal]
687–701	Sergius I
701–5	John VI
705–7	John VII
708	Sisinnius
708–15	Constantine
715–31	Gregory II
731–41	Gregory III
741–52	Zacharias
752	Stephen II (*not consecrated*)
752–7	Stephen II (III)
757–67	Paul I
[767–9	Constantine II]
[768	Philip]
768–72	Stephen III (IV)
772–95	Hadrian I
795–816	Leo III
816–17	Stephen IV (V)
817–24	Paschal I
824–7	Eugenius II
827	Valentine
827–44	Gregory IV
[844	John]
844–7	Sergius II
847–55	Leo IV
855–8	Benedict III
[855	Anastasius Bibliothecarius]
858–67	Nicholas I
867–72	Hadrian II
872–82	John VIII
882–4	Marinus I
884–5	Hadrian III
885–91	Stephen V (VI)
891–6	Formosus
896	Boniface VI
896–7	Stephen VI (VII)
897	Romanus
897	Theodore II
898–900	John IX
900–3	Benedict IV
903	Leo V
[903–4	Christopher]
904–11	Sergius III
911–13	Anastasius III
913–14	Lando
914–28	John X
928	Leo VI
928–31	Stephen VII (VIII)
931–5	John XI
936–9	Leo VII
939–42	Stephen IX
942–6	Marinus II
946–55	Agapetus II
955–64	John XII
963–5	Leo VIII
964–6	Benedict V
965–72	John XIII
973–4	Benedict VI
[974, 984–5	Boniface VII]
974–83	Benedict VII
983–4	John XIV
985–96	John XV
996–9	Gregory V
[997–8	John XVI]
999–1003	Sylvester II
1003	John XVII
1004–9	John XVIII
1009–12	Sergius IV
1012–24	Benedict VIII
[1012	Gregory]
1024–32	John XIX
1032–44	Benedict IX
1045	Sylvester III
1045	Benedict IX (*second reign*)
1045–6	Gregory VI
1046–7	Clement II
1047–8	Benedict IX (*third reign*)
1048	Damasus II
1048–54	Leo IX
1055–7	Victor II
1057–8	Stephen IX (X)
[1058–9	Benedict X]
1059–61	Nicholas II
1061–73	Alexander II
[1061–72	Honorius II]
1073–85	Gregory VII
[1080, 1084–1100	Clement III]
1086–7	Victor III
1088–99	Urban II
1099–1118	Paschal II
[1100–2	Theodoric]
1102	Albert]
[1105–11	Sylvester IV]
1118–19	Gelasius II
[1118–21	Gregory VIII]
1119–24	Callistus II
1124–30	Honorius II
[1124	Celestine II]
1130–43	Innocent II
[1130–8	Anacletus II]
[1138	Victor IV][2]
1143–4	Celestine II
1144–5	Lucius II
1145–53	Eugenius III
1153–4	Anastasius IV
1154–9	Hadrian IV
1159–81	Alexander III
[1159–64	Victor IV][2]
[1164–8	Paschal III]
[1168–78	Callistus III]
[1179–80	Innocent III]
1181–5	Lucius III
1185–7	Urban III
1187	Gregory VIII
1187–91	Clement III
1191–8	Celestine III
1198–1216	Innocent III
1216–27	Honorius III
1227–41	Gregory IX
1241	Celestine IV
1243–54	Innocent IV
1254–61	Alexander IV
1261–4	Urban IV
1265–8	Clement IV
1271–6	Gregory X
1276	Innocent V
1276	Hadrian V
1276–7	John XXI[3]
1277–80	Nicholas III
1281–5	Martin IV
1285–7	Honorius IV
1288–92	Nicholas IV
1294	Celestine V
1294–1303	Boniface VIII
1303–4	Benedict XI
1305–14	Clement V
1316–34	John XXII
[1328–30	Nicholas V]
1334–42	Benedict XII
1342–52	Clement VI
1352–62	Innocent VI
1362–70	Urban V
1370–8	Gregory XI
1378–89	Urban VI
[1378–94	Clement VII]
1389–1404	Boniface IX
[1394–1423	Benedict XIII]
1404–6	Innocent VII
1406–15	Gregory XII
[1409–10	Alexander V]
[1410–15	John XXIII]
1417–31	Martin V
[1423–9	Clement VIII]
[1425–30	Benedict XIV]
1431–47	Eugenius IV
[1439–49	Felix V]
1447–55	Nicholas V
1455–8	Callistus III
1458–64	Pius II
1464–71	Paul II
1471–84	Sixtus IV
1484–92	Innocent VIII
1492–1503	Alexander VI
1503	Pius III
1503–13	Julius II
1513–21	Leo X
1522–3	Hadrian VI
1523–34	Clement VII
1534–49	Paul III
1550–5	Julius III
1555	Marcellus II
1555–9	Paul IV
1559–65	Pius IV
1566–72	Pius V
1572–85	Gregory XIII
1585–90	Sixtus V
1590	Urban VII
1590–1	Gregory XIV
1591	Innocent IX

[1] Elected during the banishment of Martin I

[2] Different individuals

[3] There was no John XX

POPES (cont.)

1592–1605	Clement VIII	1700–21	Clement XI	1846–78	Pius IX
1605	Leo XI	1721–4	Innocent XIII	1878–1903	Leo XIII
1605–21	Paul V	1724–30	Benedict XIII	1903–14	Pius X
1621–3	Gregory XV	1730–40	Clement XII	1914–22	Benedict XV
1623–44	Urban VIII	1740–58	Benedict XIV	1922–39	Pius XI
1644–55	Innocent X	1758–69	Clement XIII	1939–58	Pius XII
1655–67	Alexander VII	1769–74	Clement XIV	1958–63	John XXIII
1667–9	Clement IX	1775–99	Pius VI	1963–78	Paul VI
1670–6	Clement X	1800–23	Pius VII	1978	John Paul I
1676–89	Innocent XI	1823–9	Leo XII	1978–	John Paul II
1689–91	Alexander VIII	1829–30	Pius VIII		
1691–1700	Innocent XII	1831–46	Gregory XVI		

1989: REVOLUTIONARY YEAR

15 January	Czechoslovakia: pro-democracy demonstration in Prague attacked by police.
19 January	USSR: defence cuts announced.
20 January	USSR: nuclear cuts announced for Eastern Europe.
20 January	USA: President Bush sworn in.
29 January	Hungary: statement by radical Communist Party member Imre Pozsgay, that the events of 1956 were not a counter-revolution, but a "popular uprising".
3 February	Paraguay: President Stroessner deposed by the army.
6 February	Poland: Solidarity begins official talks with the government.
15 February	Afghanistan: withdrawal of Soviet army completed.
22 February	Czechoslovakia: Dissident author Vaclav Havel jailed for nine months.
14 April	USSR: demonstrators shot in Tbilisi; Georgian leadership resigns.
17 April	Poland: ban on Solidarity lifted.
20 April	China: student demonstration broken up by police in Beijing (Peking).
25 April	USSR: hardliners purged from Central Committee.
27 April	China: major demonstration in Tiananmen Square, Beijing.
20–22 May	China: army halted by large numbers of demonstrators.
26 May	China: purge of moderates from government.
30 May	China: statue of Democracy and Freedom erected in Tiananmen Square.
2 June	China: army moves against demonstrators.
3 June	Iran: death of Ayatollah Khomeini.
4 June	China: army crushes student demonstrators, with undisclosed number of dead.
4 June	Poland: free elections promised.
17 June	Hungary: body of Imre Nagy disinterred and reburied in Budapest.
21 August	Czechoslovakia: demonstration to mark 21 years since crushing of the Prague Spring.
23 August	USSR: human chain formed across Estonia, Latvia, and Lithuania, on 50th anniversary of Soviet annexation.
24 August	Poland: Solidarity prime minister elected, Tadeusz Mazowiecki.
10 September	Hungary: border opened with Austria, allowing thousands of East Germans to leave for the West.
19 September	Hungary: free elections promised.
3 October	East Germany: closes border, as thousands more leave for the West.
9 October	East Germany: large demonstrations in Leipzig.
15 October	South Africa: release of Walter Sisulu and several other political prisoners.
18 October	East Germany: resignation of Erich Honecker, replaced by Egon Krenz.
19 October	UK: formal ending of hostilities with Argentina.
26 October	USSR: Gorbachev speech endorses developments in Eastern Europe.
31 October	East Germany: half a million demonstrators in Leipzig.
1 November	East Germany: border reopened to Czechoslovakia.
3 November	East Germany: East Germans permitted to travel across Czechoslovakia into West Germany without special formalities.
9 November	East Germany: opening of the Berlin Wall.
10 November	Bulgaria: Todor Zhivkov deposed.
14 November	Namibia: elections won by South West Africa People's Organization.
17 November	Czechoslovakia: major demonstration in Prague, violently put down by police.
19 November	East Germany: visit of West German Chancellor Kohl.
21 November	Czechoslovakia: meeting between Prime Minister Ladislav Adamec and leaders of the demonstration.
24 November	Czechoslovakia: resignation of Communist Party leadership.
30 November	Czechoslovakia: Communist Party gives up its leading role.
1 December	Vatican City: meeting between the Pope and President Gorbachev.
3 December	Mediterranean: meeting between Presidents Bush and Gorbachev; announcement of the end of the Cold War.
4 December	USSR: formal condemnation of 1968 invasion of Czechoslovakia.
6 December	East Germany: resignation of Egon Krenz.
7 December	Czechoslovakia: resignation of Adamec.
10 December	Czechoslovakia: non-communist government appointed.
11 December	Bulgaria: free elections promised.
14 December	South Africa: talks between President de Klerk and Nelson Mandela.
14 December	Chile: dictatorship ended with the election of Patricio Aylwin as President.
17 December	Romania: many demonstrators killed in Timisoara.
17 December	Brazil: first President elected for nearly 30 years, Fernando Collor de Mello.
20 December	Panama: invasion by USA; General Noriega deposed.
21 December	Romania: major demonstration in Bucharest, with criticism of President Nicolae Ceausescu.
22 December	Romania: Ceausescu deposed.
25 December	Romania: execution of Ceausescu and his wife, Elena.
28 December	Czechoslovakia: election of Alexander Dubcek as Chairman of the Czech parliament.
29 December	Czechoslovakia: election of Vaclav Havel as President.

MEASUREMENT

SI CONVERSION FACTORS

This table gives the conversion factors for many British and other units which are still in common use, showing their equivalents in terms of the International System of Units (SI). The column labelled 'SI equivalent' gives the SI value of one unit of the type named in the first column, eg 1 calorie is 4.189 joules. The column labelled 'Reciprocal' allows conversion the other way, eg 1 joule is 0.239 calories. (All values are to three decima places.) As a second example, 1 dyne is $10\mu N = 10 \times 10^{-6}$ N $= 10^{-5}$ N so 1 newton is $0.1 \times 10^{+6} = 10^{5}$ dyne. Finally, 1 torr is 0.133 kPa = 0.133×10^{3} Pa; so 1 Pa is 7.501×10^{-3} torr.

Unit name	Symbol	Quantity	SI equivalent	Unit	Reciproca
acre		area	0.405	hm^2	2.471
ångström*⁺	Å	length	0.1	nm	10
astronomical unit*	AU	length	0.150	Tm	6.684
atomic mass unit*	amu	mass	1.661×10^{-27}	kg	6.022×10^{26}
bar*⁺	bar	pressure	0.1	MPa	10
barn⁺	b	area	100	fm^2	0.01
barrel (US) = 42 US gal	bbl	volume	0.159	m^3	6.290
British thermal unit*	Btu	energy	1.055	kJ	0.948
calorie*	cal	energy	4.187	J	0.239
cubic foot	ft^3	volume	0.028	m^3	35.315
cubic inch	in^3	volume	16.387	cm^3	0.061
cubic yard	yd^3	volume	0.765	m^3	1.308
curie*⁺	Ci	activity of radionuclide	37	GBq	0.027
degree = 1/90 rt angle	°	plane angle	$\pi/180$	rad	57.296
degree Celsius*	°C	temperature	1	K	1
degree Centigrade*	°C	temperature	1	K	1
degree Fahrenheit*	°F	temperature	5/9	K	1.8
degree Rankine	°R	temperature	5/9	K	1.8
dyne	dyn	force	10	µN	0.1
electronvolt*	eV	energy	0.160	αJ	6.241
erg	erg	energy	0.1	µJ	10
fathom (6 ft)		length	1.829	m	0.547
fermi		length	1	fm	1
foot	ft	length	30.48	cm	0.033
foot persecond	$ft\ s^{-1}$	velocity	{ 0.305 1.097	$m\ s^{-1}$ $km\ h^{-1}$	3.281 0.911
gallon (UK)⁺	gal	volume	4.546	dm^3	0.220
gallon (US)⁺ = 231 in^3	gal	volume	3.785	dm^3	0.264
gallon (UK) per mile		consumption	2.825	$dm^3\ km^{-1}$	0.354
gauss	Gs, G	magnetic flux density	100	µT	0.01
grade = 0.01 rt angle		plane angle	$\pi/200$	rad	63.662
grain	gr	mass	0.065	g	15.432
hectare⁺	ha	area	1	hm^2	1
horsepower*	hp	power	0.746	kW	1.341
inch	in	length	2.54	cm	0.394
kilogram-force	kgf	force	9.807	N	0.102
knot⁺		velocity	1.852	$km\ h^{-1}$	0.540
light year*	l.y.	length	9.461×10^{15}	m	1.057×10^{-16}
litre*	l	volume	1	dm^3	1
Mach number*	Ma	velocity	1193.3	km h	8.380×10^{-4}
maxwell	Mx	magnetic flux	10	nWb	0.1
metric carat		mass	0.2	g	5
micron*	µ	length	1	µm	1
mile (nautical)⁺		length	1.852	km	0.540
mile (statute)		length	1.609	km	0.621
mile per hour (mph)	$mile\ h^{-1}$	velocity	1.609	$km\ h^{-1}$	0.621
minute = (1/60)°	′	plane angle	$\pi/10800$	rad	3437.75
oersted	Oe	magnetic field strength	$1/(4\pi)$	$kA\ m^{-1}$	4π
ounce (avoirdupois)	oz	mass	28.349	g	0.035
ounce (troy) = 480 gr		mass	31.103	g	0.032
parsec*	pc	length	30857	Tm	0.0000324
phot	ph	illuminance	10	klx	0.1
pint (UK)	pt	volume	0.568	dm^3	1.760
poise*	p	viscosity	0.1	Pa s	10
pound	lb	mass	0.454	kg	2.205
pound-force	lbf	force	4.448	N	0.225
pound-force/in⁻²		pressure	6.895	kPa	0.145

SI CONVERSION FACTORS (cont.)

Unit name	Symbol	Quantity	SI equivalent	Unit	Reciprocal
poundal	pdl	force	0.138	N	7.233
pounds per square inch	psi	pressure	6.895×10^3	K Pa	0.145
rad*+	rad	absorbed dose	0.01	Gy	100
rem*+	rem	dose equivalent	0.01	Sv	100
right angle = $\pi/2$ rad		plane angle	1.571	rad	0.637
röntgen+	R	exposure	0.258	$mC\ kg^{-1}$	3.876
second = (1/60)′	″	plane angle	$\pi/648$	mrad	206.265
slug		mass	14.594	kg	0.068
solar mass	M	mass	1.989×10^{30}	kg	5.028×10^{-31}
square foot	ft^2	area	9.290	dm^2	0.108
square inch	in^2	area	6.452	cm^2	0.155
square mile (statute)		area	2.590	km^2	0.386
square yard	yd^2	area	0.836	m^2	1.196
standard atmosphere	atm	pressure	0.101	MPa	9.869
stere	st	volume	1	m^3	1
stilb	sb	luminance	10	$kcd\ m^{-2}$	0.1
stokes	St	viscosity	1	$cm^2\ s^{-1}$	1
therm = 10^5 Btu		energy	0.105	GJ	9.478
ton = 2240 lb		mass	1.016	Mg	0.984
ton-force	tonf	force	9.964	kN	0.100
ton-force/in^{-2}		pressure	15.444	MPa	0.065
tonne	t	mass	1	Mg	1
torr* / mmHg	torr	pressure	0.133	kPa	7.501
X unit		length	0.100	pm	10
yard	yd	length	0.915	m	1.094

*See also main text entry.
+ In temporary use with SI.

SI PREFIXES

Factor	Prefix	Symbol	Factor	Prefix	Symbol	Factor	Prefix	Symbol	Factor	Prefix	Symbol
10^{18}	exa	E	10^6	mega	M	10^{-1}	deci	d	10^{-9}	nano	n
10^{15}	peta	P	10^3	kilo	k	10^{-2}	centi	c	10^{-12}	pico	p
10^{12}	tera	T	10^2	hecto	h	10^{-3}	milli	m	10^{-15}	femto	f
10^9	giga	G	10^1	deca	da	10^{-6}	micro	μ	10^{-18}	atto	a

COMMON MEASURES

Metric units

Length		Imperial equiv.
	1 millimetre	0.03937 in
10 mm	1 centimetre	0.39 in
10 cm	1 decimetre	3.94 in
100 cm	1 metre	39.37 in
1000 m	1 kilometre	0.62 mile
Area		**Imperial equiv.**
	1 square millimetre	0.0016 sq in
	1 square centimetre	0.155 sq in
100 sq cm	1 square decimetre	15.5 sq in
10000 sq cm	1 square metre	10.76 sq ft
10000 sq m	1 hectare	2.47 acres
Volume		**Imperial equiv.**
	1 cubic centimetre	0.016 cu in
1000 cu cm	1 cubic decimetre	61.024 cu in
1000 cu dm	1 cubic metre	35.31 cu ft
		1.308 cu yds
Liquid volume		
	1 litre	1.76 pints
100 litres	1 hectolitre	22 gallons
Weight		**Imperial equiv.**
	1 gram	0.035 oz
1000 g	1 kilogram	2.2046 lb
1000 kg	1 tonne	0.0842 ton

Imperial units

Length		Metric equiv.
	1 inch	2.54 cm
12 in	1 foot	30.48 cm
3 ft	1 yard	0.9144 m
1760 yd	1 mile	1.6093 km
Area		**Metric equiv.**
	1 square inch	6.45 sq cm
144 sq in	1 square foot	$0.0929\ m^2$
9 sq ft	1 square yard	$0.836\ m^2$
4840 sq yd	1 acre	0.405 ha
640 acres	1 square mile	259 ha
Volume		**Metric equiv.**
	1 cubic inch	$16.3871\ cm^3$
1728 cu in	1 cubic foot	$0.028\ m^3$
27 cu ft	1 cubic yard	$0.765\ m^3$
Liquid volume		
	1 pint	0.57 litre
2 pints	1 quart	1.14 litres
4 quarts	1 gallon	4.55 litres
Weight		**Metric equiv.**
	1 ounce	28.3495 g
16 oz	1 pound	0.4536 kg
14 lb	1 stone	6.35 kg
8 stones	1 hundredweight	50.8 kg
20 cwt	1 ton	1.016 tonnes

CONVERSION FACTORS

Imperial to metric

Length			Multiply by
inches	→	millimetres	25.4
inches	→	centimetres	2.54
feet	→	metres	0.3048
yards	→	metres	0.9144
statute miles	→	kilometres	1.6093
nautical miles	→	kilometres	1.852
Area			**Multiply by**
square inches	→	square centimetres	6.4516
square feet	→	square metres	0.0929
square yards	→	square metres	0.8361
acres	→	hectares	0.4047
square miles	→	square kilometres	2.5899
Volume			**Multiply by**
cubic inches	→	cubic centimetres	16.3871
cubic feet	→	cubic metres	0.0283
cubic yards	→	cubic metres	0.7646
Capacity			**Multiply by**
UK fluid ounces	→	litres	0.0284
US fluid ounces	→	litres	0.0296
UK pints	→	litres	0.5682
US pints	→	litres	0.4732
UK gallons	→	litres	4.546
US gallons	→	litres	3.7854
Weight			**Multiply by**
ounces (avoirdupois)	→	grams	28.3495
ounces (troy)	→	grams	31.1035
pounds	→	kilograms	0.4536
tons (long)	→	tonnes	1.016

Metric to imperial

Length			Multiply by
millimetres	→	inches	0.0394
centimetres	→	inches	0.3937
metres	→	feet	3.2808
metres	→	yards	1.0936
kilometres	→	statute miles	0.6214
kilometres	→	nautical miles	0.54
Area			**Multiply by**
square centimetres	→	square inches	0.155
square metres	→	square feet	10.764
square metres	→	square yards	1.196
hectares	→	acres	2.471
square kilometres	→	square miles	0.386
Volume			**Multiply by**
cubic centimetres	→	cubic inches	0.061
cubic metres	→	cubic feet	35.315
cubic metres	→	cubic yards	1.308
Capacity			**Multiply by**
litres	→	UK fluid ounces	35.1961
litres	→	US fluid ounces	33.8150
litres	→	UK pints	1.7598
litres	→	US pints	2.1134
litres	→	UK gallons	0.2199
litres	→	US gallons	0.2642
Weight			**Multiply by**
grams	→	ounces (avoirdupois)	0.0353
grams	→	ounces (troy)	0.0322
kilograms	→	pounds	2.2046
tonnes	→	tons (long)	0.9842

CONVERSION TABLES: LENGTH

in	cm	in	cm
⅛	0.3	16	40.6
¼	0.6	17	43.2
⅜	1	18	45.7
½	1.3	19	48.3
⅝	1.6	20	50.8
¾	1.9	21	53.3
⅞	2.2	22	55.9
1	2.5	23	58.4
2	5.1	24	61
3	7.6	25	63.5
4	10.2	26	66
5	12.7	27	68.6
6	15.2	28	71.1
7	17.8	29	73.7
8	20.3	30	76.2
9	22.9	40	101.6
10	25.4	50	127
11	27.9	60	152.4
12	30.5	70	177.8
13	33	80	203.2
14	35.6	90	228.6
15	38.1	100	254

cm	in	cm	in
1	0.39	24	9.45
2	0.79	25	9.84
3	1.18	26	10.24
4	1.57	27	10.63
5	1.97	28	11.02
6	2.36	29	11.42
7	2.76	30	11.81
8	3.15	31	12.2
9	3.54	32	12.6
10	3.94	33	12.99
11	4.33	34	13.39
12	4.72	35	13.78
13	5.12	36	14.17
14	5.51	37	14.57
15	5.91	38	14.96
16	6.3	39	15.35
17	6.69	40	15.75
18	7.09	50	19.69
19	7.48	60	23.62
20	7.87	70	27.56
21	8.27	80	31.5
22	8.66	90	35.43
23	9.06	100	39.37

Exact conversions
1 in = 2.540 cm   1 cm = 0.3937 in

in	mm	mm	in
⅛	3.2	1	0.04
¼	6.4	2	0.08
⅜	9.5	3	0.12
½	12.7	4	0.16
⅝	15.9	5	0.2
¾	19	6	0.24
⅞	22.2	7	0.28
1	25.4	8	0.31
2	50.8	9	0.35
3	76.2	10	0.39
4	101.6	11	0.43
5	127	12	0.47
6	152.4	13	0.51
7	177.8	14	0.55
8	203.2	15	0.59
9	228.6	16	0.63
10	254	17	0.67
11	279.4	18	0.71
12	304.8	19	0.75
13	330.2	20	0.79
14	355.6	25	0.98
15	381	50	1.97
		100	3.94

Exact conversions
1 in = 25.40 mm   1 mm = 0.0394 in

CONVERSION TABLES: LENGTH (cont.)

ft	m	m	ft
1	0.3	1	3.3
2	0.6	2	6.6
3	0.9	3	9.8
4	1.2	4	13.1
5	1.5	5	16.4
6	1.8	6	19.7
7	2.1	7	23.0
8	2.4	8	26.2
9	2.7	9	29.5
10	3.0	10	32.8
15	4.6	15	49.2
20	6.1	20	65.5
25	7.6	25	82.0
30	9.1	30	98.4
35	10.7	35	114.8
40	12.2	40	131.2
45	13.7	45	147.6
50	15.2	50	164.0
75	22.9	75	246.1
100	30.5	100	328.1
200	61.0	200	656.2
300	91.4	300	984.3
400	121.9	400	1312.3
500	152.4	500	1640.4
600	182.9	600	1968.5
700	213.4	700	2296.6
800	243.8	800	2624.7
900	274.3	900	2952.8
1000	304.8	1000	3280.8
1500	457.2	1500	4921.3
2000	609.6	2000	6561.7
2500	762.0	2500	8202.1
3000	914.4	3000	9842.5
3500	1066.8	3500	11482.9
4000	1219.2	4000	13123.4
5000	1524.0	5000	16404.2
10000	3048.0	10000	32808.4

Exact conversions
1 ft = 0.3048 m   1 m = 3.2808 ft

yd	m	m	yd
1	0.9	1	1.1
2	1.8	2	2.2
3	2.7	3	3.3
4	3.7	4	4.4
5	4.6	5	5.5
6	5.5	6	6.6
7	6.4	7	7.7
8	7.3	8	8.7
9	8.2	9	9.8
10	9.1	10	10.9
15	13.7	15	16.4
20	18.3	20	21.9
25	22.9	25	27.3
30	27.4	30	32.8
35	32.0	35	38.3
40	36.6	40	43.7
45	41.1	45	49.2
50	45.7	50	54.7
75	68.6	75	82.0
100	91.4	100	109.4
200	182.9	200	218.7
220	201.2	220	240.6
300	274.3	300	328.1
400	365.8	400	437.4
440	402.3	440	481.2
500	457.2	500	546.8
600	548.6	600	656.2
700	640.1	700	765.5
800	731.5	800	874.9
880	804.7	880	962.4
900	823.0	900	984.2
1000	914.4	1000	1093.6
1500	1371.6	1500	1640.4
2000	1828.8	2000	2187.2
2500	2286.0	2500	2734.0
5000	4572.0	5000	5468.1
10000	9144.0	10000	10936.1

Exact conversions
1 yd = 0.9144 m   1 m = 1.0936 yd

ml*	km	km	ml*
1	1.6	1	0.6
2	3.2	2	1.2
3	4.8	3	1.9
4	6.4	4	2.5
5	8.0	5	3.1
6	9.7	6	3.7
7	11.3	7	4.3
8	12.9	8	5.0
9	14.5	9	5.6
10	16.1	10	6.2
15	24.1	15	9.3
20	32.2	20	12.4
25	40.2	25	15.5
30	48.3	30	18.6
35	56.3	35	21.7
40	64.4	40	24.9
45	72.4	45	28.0
50	80.5	50	31.1
55	88.5	55	34.2
60	96.6	60	37.3
65	104.6	65	40.4
70	112.7	70	43.5
75	120.7	75	46.6
80	128.7	80	49.7
85	136.8	85	52.8
90	144.8	90	55.9
95	152.9	95	59.0
100	160.9	100	62.1
200	321.9	200	124.3
300	482.8	300	186.4
400	643.7	400	248.5
500	804.7	500	310.7
750	1207.0	750	466.0
1000	1609.3	1000	621.4
2500	4023.4	2500	1553.4
5000	8046.7	5000	3106.9

*Statute miles
Exact conversions
1 ml = 1.6093 km   1 km = 0.6214 ml

CONVERSION TABLES: AREA

sq in	sq cm	sq cm	sq in
1	6.45	1	0.16
2	12.90	2	0.31
3	19.35	3	0.47
4	25.81	4	0.62
5	32.26	5	0.78
6	38.71	6	0.93
7	45.16	7	1.09
8	51.61	8	1.24
9	58.06	9	1.40
10	64.52	10	1.55
11	70.97	11	1.71
12	77.42	12	1.86
13	83.87	13	2.02
14	90.32	14	2.17
15	96.77	15	2.33
16	103.23	16	2.48
17	109.68	17	2.64
18	116.13	18	2.79
19	122.58	19	2.95
20	129.03	20	3.10
25	161.29	25	3.88
50	322.58	50	7.75
75	483.87	75	11.63
100	645.16	100	15.50
125	806.45	125	19.38
150	967.74	150	23.25

Exact conversions
1 in^2 = 6.4516 cm^2 1 cm^2 = 0.155 in^2

sq ft	sq m	sq m	sq ft
1	0.09	1	10.8
2	0.19	2	21.5
3	0.28	3	32.3
4	0.37	4	43.1
5	0.46	5	53.8
6	0.56	6	64.6
7	0.65	7	75.3
8	0.74	8	86.1
9	0.84	9	96.9
10	0.93	10	107.6
11	1.02	11	118.4
12	1.11	12	129.2
13	1.21	13	139.9
14	1.30	14	150.7
15	1.39	15	161.5
16	1.49	16	172.2
17	1.58	17	183
18	1.67	18	193.8
19	1.77	19	204.5
20	1.86	20	215.3
25	2.32	25	269.1
50	4.65	50	538.2
75	6.97	75	807.3
100	9.29	100	1076.4
250	23.23	250	2691
500	46.45	500	5382
750	69.68	750	8072.9
1000	92.90	1000	10763.9

Exact conversions
1 ft^2 = 0.0929 m^2 1 m^2 = 10.7639 ft^2

acre	hectares	hectares	acre
1	0.40	1	2.5
2	0.81	2	4.9
3	1.21	3	7.4
4	1.62	4	9.9
5	2.02	5	12.4
6	2.43	6	14.8
7	2.83	7	17.3
8	3.24	8	19.8
9	3.64	9	22.2
10	4.05	10	24.7
11	4.45	11	27.2
12	4.86	12	29.7
13	5.26	13	32.1
14	5.67	14	34.6
15	6.07	15	37.1
16	6.47	16	39.5
17	6.88	17	42
18	7.28	18	44.5
19	7.69	19	46.9
20	8.09	20	49.4
25	10.12	25	61.8
50	20.23	50	123.6
75	30.35	75	185.3
100	40.47	100	247.1
250	101.17	250	617.8
500	202.34	500	1 235.5
750	303.51	750	1853.3
1000	404.69	1000	2471.1
1500	607.03	1500	3706.6

Exact conversions
1 acre = 0.4047 hectare
1 hectare = 2.471 acres

CONVERSION TABLES: AREA (cont.)

sq ml*	sq km	sq km	sq ml*	sq ml*	sq km	sq km	sq ml*	sq ml*	sq km	sq km	sq ml*
1	2.6	1	0.39	18	46.6	18	6.95	300	777.0	300	115.83
2	5.2	2	0.77	19	49.2	19	7.34	400	1036.0	400	154.44
3	7.8	3	1.16	20	51.8	20	7.72	500	1295.0	500	193.05
4	10.4	4	1.54	21	54.4	21	8.11	600	1554.0	600	231.66
5	12.9	5	1.93	22	57.0	22	8.49	700	1813.0	700	270.27
6	15.5	6	2.32	23	59.6	23	8.88	800	2072.0	800	308.88
7	18.1	7	2.70	24	62.2	24	9.27	900	2331.0	900	347.49
8	20.7	8	3.09	25	64.7	25	9.65	1000	2590.0	1000	386.1
9	23.3	9	3.47	30	77.7	30	11.58	1500	3885.0	1500	579.2
10	25.9	10	3.86	40	103.6	40	15.44	2000	5180.0	2000	772.2
11	28.5	11	4.25	50	129.5	50	19.31	2500	6475.0	2500	965.3
12	31.1	12	4.63	60	155.4	60	23.17	3000	7770.0	3000	1158.3
13	33.7	13	5.02	70	181.3	70	27.03	3500	9065.0	3500	1351.4
14	36.3	14	5.41	80	207.2	80	30.89	4000	10360.0	4000	1544.4
15	38.8	15	5.79	90	233.1	90	34.75	5000	12950.0	5000	1930.5
16	41.4	16	6.18	100	259.0	100	38.61	7500	19424.9	7500	2895.8
17	44.0	17	6.56	200	518.0	200	77.22	10000	25899.9	10000	3861.0

*Statute miles

Exact conversions

1 sq ml = 2.589999 sq km 1 sq km = 0.3861 sq ml

CONVERSION TABLES: VOLUME

cu in	cu cm	cu cm	cu in	cu ft	cu m	cu m	cu ft	cu yd	cu m	cu m	cu yd
1	16.39	1	0.61	1	0.03	1	35.3	1	0.76	1	1.31
2	32.77	2	1.22	2	0.06	2	70.6	2	1.53	2	2.62
3	49.16	3	1.83	3	0.08	3	105.9	3	2.29	3	3.92
4	65.55	4	2.44	4	0.11	4	141.3	4	3.06	4	5.23
5	81.93	5	3.05	5	0.14	5	176.6	5	3.82	5	6.54
6	93.32	6	3.66	6	0.17	6	211.9	6	4.59	6	7.85
7	114.71	7	4.27	7	0.20	7	247.2	7	5.35	7	9.16
8	131.10	8	4.88	8	0.23	8	282.5	8	6.12	8	10.46
9	147.48	9	5.49	9	0.25	9	317.8	9	6.88	9	11.77
10	163.87	10	6.10	10	0.28	10	353.1	10	7.65	10	13.08
11	180.26	11	6.71	11	0.31	11	388.5	11	8.41	11	14.39
12	196.64	12	7.32	12	0.34	12	423.8	12	9.17	12	15.70
13	213.03	13	7.93	13	0.37	13	459.1	13	9.94	13	17.00
14	229.42	14	8.54	14	0.40	14	494.4	14	10.70	14	18.31
15	245.81	15	9.15	15	0.42	15	529.7	15	11.47	15	19.62
20	327.74	20	12.20	20	0.57	20	706.3	20	15.29	20	26.16
50	819.35	50	30.50	50	1.41	50	1765.7	50	38.23	50	65.40
100	1638.71	100	61.00	100	2.83	100	3531.5	100	76.46	100	130.80

Exact conversions

1 in^3 = 16.3871 cm^3 1 cm^3 = 0.0610 in^3

Exact conversions

1 ft^3 = 0.0283 m^3 1 m^3 = 35.3147 ft^3

Exact conversions

1 yd^3 = 0.7646 m^3 1 m^3 = 1.3080 yd^3

CONVERSION TABLES: CAPACITY

Liquid measure

UK fluid ounces	litres	US fluid ounces	litres	litres	UK fluid ounces	US fluid ounces	UK pints	litres	US pints	litres	litres	UK pints	US pints
1	0.0284	1	0.0296	1	35.2	33.8	1	0.57	1	0.47	1	1.76	2.11
2	0.0568	2	0.0592	2	70.4	67.6	2	1.14	2	0.95	2	3.52	4.23
3	0.0852	3	0.0888	3	105.6	101.4	3	1.70	3	1.42	3	5.28	6.34
4	0.114	4	0.118	4	140.8	135.3	4	2.27	4	1.89	4	7.04	8.45
5	0.142	5	0.148	5	176.0	169.1	5	2.84	5	2.37	5	8.80	10.57
6	0.170	6	0.178	6	211.2	202.9	6	3.41	6	2.84	6	10.56	12.68
7	0.199	7	0.207	7	246.4	236.7	7	3.98	7	3.31	7	12.32	14.79
8	0.227	8	0.237	8	281.6	270.5	8	4.55	8	3.78	8	14.08	16.91
9	0.256	9	0.266	9	316.8	304.3	9	5.11	9	4.26	9	15.84	19.02
10	0.284	10	0.296	10	352.0	338.1	10	5.68	10	4.73	10	17.60	21.13
11	0.312	11	0.326	11	387.2	372.0	11	6.25	11	5.20	11	19.36	23.25
12	0.341	12	0.355	12	422.4	405.8	12	6.82	12	5.68	12	21.12	25.36
13	0.369	13	0.385	13	457.5	439.6	13	7.38	13	6.15	13	22.88	27.47
14	0.397	14	0.414	14	492.7	473.4	14	7.95	14	6.62	14	24.64	29.59
15	0.426	15	0.444	15	527.9	507.2	15	8.52	15	7.10	15	26.40	31.70
20	0.568	20	0.592	20	703.9	676.3	20	11.36	20	9.46	20	35.20	105.67
50	1.42	50	1.48	50	1759.8	1690.7	50	28.41	50	23.66	50	87.99	211.34
100	2.84	100	2.96	100	3519.6	3381.5	100	56.82	100	47.32	100	175.98	422.68

Exact conversions

1 fl oz = 0.0284 l 1 fl oz = 0.0296 l 1 l = 35.1961 UK fl oz 1 l = 33.8140 US fl oz

Exact conversions

1 UK pt = 0.5682 l 1 US pt = 0.4732 l 1 l = 1.7598 UK pt, 2.1134 US pt

1 UK pt = 1.20 US pt 1 US pt = 0.83 UK pt 1 US cup = 8 fl oz

CONVERSION TABLES: CAPACITY (cont.)

UK gallons	litres
1	4.55
2	9.09
3	13.64
4	18.18
5	22.73
6	27.28
7	31.82
8	36.37
9	40.91
10	45.46
11	50.01
12	54.55
13	59.10
14	63.64
15	68.19
16	72.74
17	77.28
18	81.83
19	86.37
20	90.92
21	95.47
22	100.01
23	104.56
24	109.10
25	113.65
50	227.30
75	340.96
100	454.61

Exact conversion
1 UK gall = 4.546 l

US gallons	litres
1	3.78
2	7.57
3	11.36
4	15.14
5	18.93
6	22.71
7	26.50
8	30.28
9	34.07
10	37.85
11	41.64
12	45.42
13	49.21
14	52.99
15	56.78
16	60.57
17	64.35
18	68.14
19	71.92
20	75.71
21	79.49
22	83.28
23	87.06
24	90.85
25	94.63
50	189.27
75	283.90
100	378.54

Exact conversion
1 US gall = 3.7854 l

litres	UK gallons	US gallons
1	0.22	0.26
2	0.44	0.53
3	0.66	0.79
4	0.88	1.06
5	1.10	1.32
6	1.32	1.58
7	1.54	1.85
8	1.76	2.11
9	1.98	2.38
10	2.20	2.64
11	2.42	2.91
12	2.64	3.17
13	2.86	3.43
14	3.08	3.70
15	3.30	3.96
16	3.52	4.23
17	3.74	4.49
18	3.96	4.76
19	4.18	5.02
20	4.40	5.28
21	4.62	5.55
22	4.84	5.81
23	5.06	6.08
24	5.28	6.34
25	5.50	6.60
50	11.00	13.20
75	16.50	19.81
100	22.00	26.42

Exact conversions
1 l = 0.220 UK gall
1 l = 0.2642 US gall

UK gall	US gall	UK gall	US gall	UK gall	US gall
1	1.2	7	8.4	13	15.6
2	2.4	8	9.6	14	16.8
3	3.6	9	10.8	15	18
4	4.8	10	12	20	24
5	6	11	13.2	25	30
6	7.2	12	14.4	50	60

Exact conversion
1 UK gall = 1.200929 US gall

US gall	UK gall	US gall	UK gall	US gall	UK gall
1	0.8	9	7.5	17	14.1
2	1.7	10	8.3	18	15
3	2.5	11	9.2	19	15.8
4	3.3	12	10	20	16.6
5	4.2	13	10.8	25	20.8
6	5	14	11.7	50	41.6
7	5.8	15	12.5	75	62.4
8	6.7	16	13.3	100	83.3

Exact conversion
1 US gall = 0.832688 UK gall

Petrol consumption
Use UK table and US table independently.

per UK gall		per litre	
ml	km	ml	km
30	48	6.6	10.61
35	56	7.7	12.38
40	64	8.8	14.15
45	72	9.9	15.92
50	80	11	17.69

per US gall		per litre	
ml	km	ml	km
30	48	7.9	12.78
35	56	9.3	14.91
40	64	10.6	17.04
45	72	11.9	19.17
50	80	13.2	21.30

Other liquid capacity measures

UK quarts	litres
1	1.14
2	2.27
3	3.41
4	4.55
5	5.68
10	11.36

Exact conversion
1 UK quart = 1.1365 l

US quarts	litres
1	0.95
2	1.89
3	2.84
4	3.78
5	4.73
10	9.46

Exact conversion
1 US quart = 0.9463 l

litres	UK quarts	US quarts
1	0.88	1.06
2	1.76	2.11
3	2.64	3.17
4	3.52	4.23
5	4.40	5.28
10	8.80	10.57

Exact conversions
1 l = 0.8799 UK quart
1 l = 1.0567 US quarts

cu in	litres
1	0.016
2	0.033
3	0.049
4	0.066
5	0.082
10	0.164

Exact conversion
1 in^3 = 0.0164 l

cu ft	litres
1	28.3
2	56.6
3	84.9
4	113.3
5	141.6
10	283.1

Exact conversion
1 ft^3 = 28.3161 l

litres	cu in	cu ft
1	61	0.03
2	122	0.07
3	183	0.11
4	244	0.14
5	305	0.18
10	610	0.35

Exact conversions
1 l = 61.0255 in^3 = 0.0353 ft^3

Dry capacity measures

UK bushels	cu m	litres
1	0.037	36.4
2	0.074	72.7
3	0.111	109.1
4	0.148	145.5
5	0.184	181.8
10	0.369	363.7

Exact conversions
1 UK bushel = 0.0369 m^3
1 UK bushel = 36.3677 l

US bushels	cu m	litres
1	0.035	35.2
2	0.071	70.5
3	0.106	105.7
4	0.141	140.9
5	0.175	176.2
10	0.353	352.4

Exact conversions
1 US bushel = 0.9353 m^3
1 US bushel = 35.2381 l

UK pecks	litres
1	9.1
2	18.2
3	27.3
4	36.4
5	45.5
10	90.9

Exact conversion
1 UK pk = 9.0919 l

US pecks	litres
1	8.8
2	17.6
3	26.4
4	35.2
5	44
10	88.1

Exact conversion
1 US pk = 8.8095 l

litres	UK pecks	US pecks
1	0.110	0.113
2	0.220	0.226
3	0.330	0.339
4	0.440	0.454
5	0.550	0.567
10	1.100	1.135

Exact conversions
1 l = 0.1100 UK pk
1 l = 0.1135 US pk

cu m	UK bushels	US bushels
1	27.5	28.4
2	55.0	56.7
3	82.5	85.1
4	110	113
5	137	142
10	275	284

Exact conversions
1 m^3 = 27.4962 UK bu
1 m^3 = 28.3776 US bu

litres	UK bushels	US bushels
1	0.027	0.028
2	0.055	0.057
3	0.082	0.085
4	0.110	0.114
5	0.137	0.142
10	0.275	0.284

Exact conversions
1 l = 0.0275 UK bu
1 l = 0.0284 US bu

US quarts	cu m	litres
1	1101	1.1
2	2202	2.2
3	3304	3.3
4	4405	4.4
5	5506	5.5
10	11012	11

Exact conversions
1 US qt = 1101.2209 cm^3
1 US qt = 1.1012 l

US pints	cu m	litres
1	551	0.55
2	1101	1.10
3	1652	1.65
4	2202	2.20
5	2753	2.75
10	5506	5.51

Exact conversions
1 US pt = 550.6105 cm^3
1 US pt = 0.5506 l

CONVERSION TABLES: WEIGHT

ounces*	grams
1	28.3
2	56.7
3	85
4	113.4
5	141.7
6	170.1
7	198.4
8	226.8
9	255.1
10	283.5
11	311.7
12	340.2
13	368.5
14	396.9
15	425.2
16	453.6

*avoirdupois

Exact conversion
1 oz (avdp) = 28.3495 g

grams	ounces*
1	0.04
2	0.07
3	0.11
4	0.14
5	0.18
6	0.21
7	0.25
8	0.28
9	0.32
10	0.35
20	0.71
30	1.06
40	1.41
50	1.76
60	2.12
70	2.47
80	2.82
90	3.18
100	3.53

Exact conversion
1 g = 0.0353 oz (avdp)

pounds	kilograms
1	0.45
2	0.91
3	1.36
4	1.81
5	2.27
6	2.72
7	3.18
8	3.63
9	4.08
10	4.54
11	4.99
12	5.44
13	5.90
14	6.35
15	6.80
16	7.26
17	7.71
18	8.16

Exact conversion
1 lb = 0.454 kg

pounds	kilograms
19	8.62
20	9.07
25	11.34
30	13.61
35	15.88
40	18.14
45	20.41
50	22.68
60	27.24
70	31.78
80	36.32
90	40.86
100	45.36
200	90.72
250	113.40
500	226.80
750	340.19
1000	453.59

Exact conversion
1 kg = 2.205 lb

kilograms	pounds
1	2.2
2	4.4
3	6.6
4	8.8
5	11
6	13.2
7	15.4
8	17.6
9	19.8
10	22
11	24.3
12	26.5
13	28.7
14	30.9
15	33.1
16	35.3
17	37.5
18	39.7

kilograms	pounds
19	41.9
20	44.1
25	55.1
30	66.1
35	77.2
40	88.2
45	99.2
50	110.2
60	132.3
70	154.4
80	176.4
90	198.5
100	220.5
200	440.9
250	551.2
500	1102.3
750	1653.5
1000	2204.6

Hundredweights: long, UK 112 lb; short, US 100 lb

UK cwt	kilograms
1	50.8
2	102
3	152
4	203
5	254
10	508
15	762
20	1016
50	2540
75	3810
100	5080

Exact conversions
1 UK cwt = 50.8023 kg

US cwt	kilograms
1	45.4
2	90.7
3	136
4	181
5	227
10	454
15	680
20	907
50	2268
75	3402
100	4536

Exact conversion
1 US cwt = 45.3592 kg

UK cwt	US cwt
1	1.12
2	2.24
3	3.36
4	4.48
5	5.6
10	11.2
15	16.8
20	22.4
50	56
75	84
100	102

Exact conversion
1 UK cwt = 1.1199 US cwt

Tons: long, UK 2240 lb; short, US 2000 lb

UK tons	tonnes
1	1.02
2	2.03
3	3.05
4	4.06
5	5.08
10	10.16
15	15.24
20	20.32
50	50.80
75	76.20
100	101.61

Exact conversion
1 UK ton = 1.0160 tonnes

US tons	tonnes
1	0.91
2	1.81
3	2.72
4	3.63
5	4.54
10	9.07
15	13.61
20	18.14
50	45.36
75	68.04
100	90.72

Exact conversion
1 US ton = 0.9072 tonne

UK tons	US tons
1	1.12
2	2.24
3	3.36
4	4.48
5	5.6
10	11.2
15	16.8
20	22.4
50	56
75	84
100	102

Exact conversion
1 UK ton = 1.1199 US tons

kilograms	UK cwt	US cwt
1	0.0197	0.022
2	0.039	0.044
3	0.059	0.066
4	0.079	0.088
5	0.098	0.11
10	0.197	0.22
15	0.295	0.33
20	0.394	1.44
50	0.985	1.10
75	1.477	1.65
100	1.970	2.20

Exact conversions
1 kg = 0.0197 UK cwt
= 0.0220 US cwt

US cwt	UK cwt
1	0.89
2	1.79
3	2.68
4	3.57
5	4.46
10	8.93
15	13.39
20	17.86
50	44.64
75	66.96
100	89.29

Exact conversion
1 US cwt = 0.8929 UK cwt

tonnes	UK tons	US tons
1	0.98	1.10
2	1.97	2.20
3	2.95	3.30
4	3.94	4.40
5	4.92	5.50
10	9.84	11.02
15	14.76	16.53
20	19.68	22.05
50	49.21	55.11
75	73.82	82.67
100	98.42	110.23

Exact conversions
1 tonne = 0.9842 UK ton
= 1.1023 US tons

US tons	UK tons
1	0.89
2	1.79
3	2.68
4	3.57
5	4.46
10	8.93
15	13.39
20	17.86
50	44.64
75	66.96
100	89.29

Exact conversion
1 US ton = 0.8929 UK ton

stones	pounds	stones	pounds
1	14	11	154
2	28	12	168
3	42	13	182
4	56	14	196
5	70	15	210
6	84	16	224
7	98	17	238
8	112	18	252
9	126	19	266
10	140	20	280

Exact conversions
1 st = 14 lb
1 lb = 0.07 st

stones	kilograms
1	6.35
2	12.70
3	19.05
4	25.40
5	31.75
6	38.10
7	44.45
8	50.80
9	57.15
10	63.50

Exact conversions
1 st = 6.350 kg
1 kg = 0.1575 st

CONVERSION TABLE: TYRE PRESSURES

lb per sq in	kg per sq cm	lb per sq in	kg per sq cm
10	0.7	26	1.8
15	1.1	28	2
20	1.4	30	2.1
24	1.7	40	2.8

NUMERICAL EQUIVALENTS

Arabic	Roman	Greek	Binary Numbers
1	I	α'	1
2	II	β'	10
3	III	γ'	11
4	IV	δ'	100
5	V	ε'	101
6	VI	ς'	110
7	VII	ζ'	111
8	VIII	η'	1000
9	IX	θ'	1001
10	X	ι'	1010
11	XI	ια'	1011
12	XII	ιβ'	1100
13	XIII	ιγ'	1101
14	XIV	ιδ'	1110
15	XV	ιε'	1111
16	XVI	ις'	10000
17	XVII	ιζ'	10001
18	XVIII	ιη'	10010
19	XIX	ιθ'	10011
20	XX	κ'	10100
30	XXX	λ'	11110
40	XL	μ'	101000
50	L	ν'	110010
60	LX	ξ'	111100
70	LXX	ο'	1000110
80	LXXX	π'	1010000
90	XC	,ο'	1011010
100	C	ρ'	1100100
200	CC	σ'	11001000
300	CCC	τ'	100101100
400	CD	υ'	110010000
500	D	φ'	111110100
1 000	M	,α	1111101000
5 000	V̄	,ε	1001110001000
10 000	X̄	,ι	10011100010000
100 000	C̄	,ρ	11000011010100000

Fraction	Decimal	Fraction	Decimal
1/2	0.5000	9/11	0.8181
1/3	0.3333	10/11	0.9090
2/3	0.6667	1/12	0.8333
1/4	0.2500	5/12	0.4167
3/4	0.7500	7/12	0.5833
1/5	0.2000	11/12	0.9167
2/5	0.4000	1/16	0.0625
3/5	0.6000	3/16	0.1875
4/5	0.8000	5/16	0.3125
1/6	0.1667	7/16	0.4375
5/6	0.8333	9/16	0.5625
1/7	0.1429	11/16	0.6875
2/7	0.2857	13/16	0.8125
3/7	0.4286	15/16	0.9375
4/7	0.5714	1/20	0.0500
5/7	0.7143	3/20	0.1500
6/7	0.8571	7/20	0.3500
1/8	0.1250	9/20	0.4500
3/8	0.3750	11/20	0.5500
5/8	0.6250	13/20	0.6500
7/8	0.8750	17/20	0.8500
1/9	0.1111	19/20	0.9500
2/9	0.2222	1/32	0.0312
4/9	0.4444	3/32	0.9375
5/9	0.5555	5/32	0.1562
7/9	0.7778	7/32	0.2187
8/9	0.8889	9/32	0.2812
1/10	0.1000	11/32	0.3437
3/10	0.3000	13/32	0.4062
7/10	0.7000	15/32	0.4687
9/10	0.9000	17/32	0.5312
1/11	0.0909	19/32	0.5937
2/11	0.1818	21/32	0.6562
3/11	0.2727	23/32	0.7187
4/11	0.3636	25/32	0.7812
5/11	0.4545	27/32	0.8437
6/11	0.5454	29/32	0.9062
7/11	0.6363	31/32	0.9687
8/11	0.7272		

%	Decimal	Fraction	%	Decimal	Fraction
1	0.01	1/100	30	0.30	3/10
2	0.02	1/50	31	0.31	31/100
3	0.03	3/100	32	0.32	8/25
4	0.04	1/25	33	0.33	33/100
5	0.05	1/20	33⅓	0.333	1/3
6	0.06	3/50	34	0.34	17/50
7	0.07	7/100	35	0.35	7/20
8	0.08	2/25	36	0.36	9/25
8⅓	0.089	1/12	37	0.37	37/100
9	0.09	9/100	38	0.38	19/50
10	0.10	1/10	39	0.39	39/100
11	0.11	11/100	40	0.40	2/5
12	0.12	3/25	41	0.41	41/100
12½	0.125	1/8	42	0.42	21/50
13	0.13	13/100	43	0.43	43/100
14	0.14	7/50	44	0.44	11/25
15	0.15	3/20	45	0.45	9/20
16	0.16	4/25	46	0.46	23/50
16⅔	0.167	1/6	47	0.47	47/100
17	0.17	17/100	48	0.48	12/25
18	0.18	9/50	49	0.49	49/100
19	0.19	19/100	50	0.50	1/2
20	0.20	1/5	55	0.55	11/20
21	0.21	21/100	60	0.60	3/5
22	0.22	11/50	65	0.65	13/20
23	0.23	23/100	70	0.70	7/10
24	0.24	6/25	75	0.75	3/4
25	0.25	1/4	80	0.80	4/5
26	0.26	13/50	85	0.85	17/20
27	0.27	27/100	90	0.90	9/10
28	0.28	7/25	95	0.95	19/20
29	0.29	29/100	100	1.00	1

MULTIPLICATION TABLE

	2	3	4	5	6	7	8	9	10	11	12	13	14	15	16	17	18	19	20	21	22	23	24	25
2	4	6	8	10	12	14	16	18	20	22	24	26	28	30	32	34	36	38	40	42	44	46	48	50
3	6	9	12	15	18	21	24	27	30	33	36	39	42	45	48	51	54	57	60	63	66	69	72	75
4	8	12	16	20	24	28	32	36	40	44	48	52	56	60	64	68	72	76	80	84	88	92	96	100
5	10	15	20	25	30	35	40	45	50	55	60	65	70	75	80	85	90	95	100	105	110	115	120	125
6	12	18	24	30	36	42	48	54	60	66	72	78	84	90	96	102	108	114	120	126	132	138	144	150
7	14	21	28	35	42	49	56	63	70	77	84	91	98	105	112	119	126	133	140	147	154	161	168	175
8	16	24	32	40	48	56	64	72	80	88	96	104	112	120	128	136	144	152	160	168	176	184	192	200
9	18	27	36	45	54	63	72	81	90	99	108	117	126	135	144	153	162	171	180	189	198	207	216	225
10	20	30	40	50	60	70	80	90	100	110	120	130	140	150	160	170	180	190	200	210	220	230	240	250
11	22	33	44	55	66	77	88	99	110	121	132	143	154	165	176	187	198	209	220	231	242	253	264	275
12	24	36	48	60	72	84	96	108	120	132	144	156	168	180	192	204	216	228	240	252	264	276	288	300
13	26	39	52	65	78	91	104	117	130	143	156	169	182	195	208	221	234	247	260	273	286	299	312	325
14	28	42	56	70	84	98	112	126	140	154	168	182	196	210	224	238	252	266	280	294	308	322	336	350
15	30	45	60	75	90	105	120	135	150	165	180	195	210	225	240	255	270	285	300	315	330	345	360	375
16	32	48	64	80	96	112	128	144	160	176	192	208	224	240	256	272	288	304	320	336	352	368	384	400
17	34	51	68	85	102	119	136	153	170	187	204	221	238	255	272	289	306	323	340	357	374	391	408	425
18	36	54	72	90	108	126	144	162	180	198	216	234	252	270	288	306	324	342	360	378	396	414	432	450
19	38	57	76	95	114	133	152	171	190	209	228	247	266	285	304	323	342	361	380	399	418	437	456	475
20	40	60	80	100	120	140	160	180	200	220	240	260	280	300	320	340	360	380	400	420	440	460	480	500
21	42	63	84	105	126	147	168	189	210	231	252	273	294	315	336	357	378	399	420	441	462	483	504	525
22	44	66	88	110	132	154	176	198	220	242	264	286	308	330	352	374	396	418	440	462	484	506	528	550
23	46	69	92	115	138	161	184	207	230	253	276	299	322	345	368	391	414	437	460	483	506	529	552	575
24	48	72	96	120	144	168	192	216	240	264	288	312	336	360	384	408	432	456	480	504	528	552	576	600
25	50	75	100	125	150	175	200	225	250	275	300	325	350	375	400	425	450	475	500	525	550	575	600	625

SQUARES AND ROOTS

No.	Square	Cube	Square root	Cube root
1	1	1	1.000	1.000
2	4	8	1.414	1.260
3	9	27	1.732	1.442
4	16	64	2.000	1.587
5	25	125	2.236	1.710
6	36	216	2.449	1.817
7	49	343	2.646	1.913
8	64	512	2.828	2.000
9	81	729	3.000	2.080
10	100	1 000	3.162	2.154
11	121	1 331	3.317	2.224
12	144	1 728	3.464	2.289
13	169	2 197	3.606	2.351
14	196	2 744	3.742	2.410
15	225	3 375	3.873	2.466
16	256	4 096	4.000	2.520
17	289	4 913	4.123	2.571
18	324	5 832	4.243	2.621
19	361	6 859	4.359	2.668
20	400	8 000	4.472	2.714
25	625	15 625	5.000	2.924
30	900	27 000	5.477	3.107
40	1 600	64 000	6.325	3.420
50	2 500	125 000	7.071	3.684

PHYSICAL CONSTANTS

1986 recommended values of the main fundamental physical constants of physics and chemistry, based on a least-squares adjustment with 17 degrees of freedom. The digits in parentheses are the one-standard-deviation uncertainty in the last digits of the given value. (After Cohen and Taylor, 1987.)

Quantity	Symbol	Value	Units	Relative uncertainty (ppm)
Universal constants				
speed of light in vacuum	c	299792458	$\mathrm{m\,s^{-1}}$	(exact)
permeability of vacuum	μ_0	$4\pi \times 10^{-7}$	$\mathrm{N\,A^{-2}}$	(exact)
		$= 12.566370614\ldots$	$10^{-7}\,\mathrm{N\,A^{-2}}$	
permittivity of vacuum, $1/\mu_0 c^2$	ε_0	8.854187817...	$10^{-12}\,\mathrm{F\,m^{-1}}$	(exact)
Newtonian constant of gravitation	G	6.67259(85)	$10^{-11}\,\mathrm{m^3\,kg^{-1}\,s^{-2}}$	128
Planck constant	h	6.6260755(40)	$10^{-34}\,\mathrm{J\,s}$	0.60
$h/2\pi$	$\hbar$	1.05457266(63)	$10^{-34}\,\mathrm{J\,s}$	0.60
Electromagnetic constants				
elementary charge	e	1.60217733(49)	$10^{-19}\,\mathrm{C}$	0.30
	e/h	2.41798836(72)	$10^{14}\,\mathrm{A\,J^{-1}}$	0.30
magnetic flux quantum, $h/2e$	Φ_0	2.06783461(61)	$10^{-15}\,\mathrm{Wb}$	0.30
Josephson frequency-voltage quotient	$2e/h$	4.8359767(14)	$10^{14}\,\mathrm{Hz\,V^{-1}}$	0.30
Bohr magneton, $e\hbar/2m_e$	μ_B	9.2740154(31)	$10^{-24}\,\mathrm{J\,T^{-1}}$	0.34
nuclear magneton, $e\hbar/2m_p$	μ_N	5.0507866(17)	$10^{-27}\,\mathrm{J\,T^{-1}}$	0.34
Atomic constants				
fine-structure constant, $\mu_0 ce^2/2h$	α	7.29735308(33)	10^{-3}	0.045
	α^{-1}	137.0359895(61)		0.045
Rydberg constant, $m_e c\alpha^2/2h$	R_∞	10973731.534(13)	$\mathrm{m^{-1}}$	0.0012
Bohr radius, $\alpha/4\pi R_\infty$	a_0	0.529177249(24)	$10^{-10}\,\mathrm{m}$	0.045
quantum of circulation	$h/2m_e$	3.63694807(33)	$10^{-4}\,\mathrm{m^2\,s^{-1}}$	0.089
	h/m_e	7.27389614(65)	$10^{-4}\,\mathrm{m^2\,s^{-1}}$	0.089
Electron				
electron mass	m_e	9.1093897(54)	$10^{-31}\,\mathrm{kg}$	0.59
		5.48579903(13)	$10^{-4}\,\mathrm{u}$	0.023
electron-muon mass ratio	m_e/m_μ	4.83633218(71)	10^{-3}	0.15
electron-proton mass ratio	m_e/m_p	5.44617013(11)	10^{-4}	0.020
electron specific charge	$-e/m_e$	−1.75881962(53)	$10^{11}\,\mathrm{C\,kg^{-1}}$	0.30
Compton wavelength, $h/m_e c$	λ_C	2.42631058(22)	$10^{-12}\,\mathrm{m}$	0.089
$\lambda_C/2\pi = \alpha a_0 = \alpha^2/4\pi R_\infty$	$\bar{\lambda}_C$	3.86159323(35)	$10^{-13}\,\mathrm{m}$	0.089
classical electron radius, $\alpha^2 a_0$	r_e	2.81794092(38)	$10^{-15}\,\mathrm{m}$	0.13
electron magnetic moment	μ_e	928.47701(31)	$10^{-26}\,\mathrm{J\,T^{-1}}$	0.34
electron g factor, $2(1+a_e)$	g_e	2.002319304386(20)		1×10^{-5}
electron-proton magnetic moment ratio	μ_e/μ_p	658.2106881(66)		0.010
Muon				
muon mass	m_μ	1.8835327(11)	$10^{-28}\,\mathrm{kg}$	0.61
		0.113428913(17)	u	0.15
muon magnetic moment	μ_μ	4.4904514(15)	$10^{-26}\,\mathrm{J\,T^{-1}}$	0.33
muon g factor, $2(1+a_\mu)$	g_μ	2.002331846(17)		0.0084
muon-proton magnetic moment ratio	μ_μ/μ_p	3.18334547(47)		0.15
Proton				
proton mass	m_p	1.6726231(10)	$10^{-27}\,\mathrm{kg}$	0.59
		1.007276470(12)	u	0.012
proton Compton wavelength, $h/m_p c$	$\lambda_{C,p}$	1.32141002(12)	$10^{-15}\,\mathrm{m}$	0.089
$\lambda_{C,p}/2\pi$	$\bar{\lambda}_{C,p}$	2.10308937(19)	$10^{-16}\,\mathrm{m}$	0.089
proton magnetic moment	μ_p	1.41060761(47)	$10^{-26}\,\mathrm{J\,T^{-1}}$	0.34
in Bohr magnetons	μ_p/μ_B	1.521032202(15)	10^{-3}	0.010
in nuclear magnetons	μ_p/μ_N	2.792847386(63)		0.023
proton gyromagnetic ratio	γ_p	26752.2128(81)	$10^4\,\mathrm{s^{-1}\,T^{-1}}$	0.30
	$\gamma_p/2\pi$	42.577469(13)	$\mathrm{MHz\,T^{-1}}$	0.30
uncorrected (H_2O, sph., 25°C)	γ'_p	26751.5255(81)	$10^4\,\mathrm{s^{-1}\,T^{-1}}$	0.30
	$\gamma'_p/2\pi$	42.576375(13)	$\mathrm{MHz\,T^{-1}}$	0.30
Neutron				
neutron mass	m_n	1.6749286(10)	$10^{-27}\,\mathrm{kg}$	0.59
		1.008664904(14)	u	0.014
neutron Compton wavelength, $h/m_n c$	$\lambda_{C,n}$	1.31959110(12)	$10^{-15}\,\mathrm{m}$	0.089
$\lambda_{C,n}/2\pi$	$\bar{\lambda}_{C,n}$	2.10019445(19)	$10^{-16}\,\mathrm{m}$	0.089
Physico-chemical constants				
Avogadro constant	N_A, L	6.0221367(36)	$10^{23}\,\mathrm{mol^{-1}}$	0.59
atomic mass constant $m_u = \frac{1}{12}m(^{12}\mathrm{C})$	m_u	1.6605402(10)	$10^{-27}\,\mathrm{kg}$	0.59
Faraday constant, $N_A e$	F	96485.309(29)	$\mathrm{C\,mol^{-1}}$	0.30
molar gas constant	R	8.314510(70)	$\mathrm{J\,mol^{-1}\,K^{-1}}$	8.4
Boltzmann constant, R/N_A	k	1.380658(12)	$10^{-23}\,\mathrm{J\,K^{-1}}$	8.5
molar volume (ideal gas), RT/p; $T = 273.15\,\mathrm{K}$, $p = 101\,325\,\mathrm{Pa}$	V_m	0.02241410(19)	$\mathrm{m^3\,mol^{-1}}$	8.4
Stefan-Boltzmann constant, $(\pi^2/60)\,k^4/\hbar^3c^2$	σ	5.67051(19)	$10^{-8}\,\mathrm{W\,m^{-2}\,K^{-4}}$	34
first radiation constant, $2\pi hc^2$	c_1	3.7417749(22)	$10^{-16}\,\mathrm{W\,m^2}$	0.60
second radiation constant, hc/k	c_2	0.01438769(12)	$\mathrm{m\,K}$	8.4

TEMPERATURE CONVERSION

Degrees Fahrenheit (F) → Degrees Celsius (Centigrade) (C)

°F	°C	°F	°C	°F	°C	°F	°C
1	−17.2	54	12.2	107	41.7	160	71.1
2	−16.7	55	12.8	108	42.2	161	71.7
3	−16.1	56	13.3	109	42.8	162	72.2
4	−15.5	57	13.9	110	43.3	163	72.8
5	−15.0	58	14.4	111	43.9	164	73.3
6	−14.4	59	15.0	112	44.4	165	73.9
7	−13.9	60	15.5	113	45.0	166	74.4
8	−13.3	61	16.1	114	45.5	167	75.0
9	−12.8	62	16.7	115	46.1	168	75.5
10	−12.2	63	17.2	116	46.7	169	76.1
11	−11.6	64	17.8	117	47.2	170	76.7
12	−11.1	65	18.3	118	47.8	171	77.2
13	−10.5	66	18.9	119	48.3	172	77.8
14	−10.0	67	19.4	120	48.9	173	78.3
15	−9.4	68	20.0	121	49.4	174	78.9
16	−8.9	69	20.5	122	50.0	175	79.4
17	−8.3	70	21.1	123	50.5	176	80.0
18	−7.8	71	21.7	124	51.1	177	80.5
19	−7.2	72	22.2	125	51.7	178	81.1
20	−6.7	73	22.8	126	52.2	179	81.7
21	−6.1	74	23.3	127	52.8	180	82.2
22	−5.5	75	23.9	128	53.3	181	82.8
23	−5.0	76	24.4	129	53.9	182	83.3
24	−4.4	77	25.0	130	54.4	183	83.9
25	−3.9	78	25.5	131	55.0	184	84.4
26	−3.3	79	26.1	132	55.5	185	85.0
27	−2.8	80	26.7	133	56.1	186	85.5
28	−2.2	81	27.2	134	56.7	187	86.1
29	−1.7	82	27.8	135	57.2	188	86.7
30	−1.1	83	28.3	136	57.8	189	87.2
31	−0.5	84	28.9	137	58.3	190	87.8
32	0	85	29.4	138	58.9	191	88.3
33	0.5	86	30.0	139	59.4	192	88.8
34	1.1	87	30.5	140	60.0	193	89.4
35	1.7	88	31.1	141	60.5	194	90.0
36	2.2	89	31.7	142	61.1	195	90.5
37	2.8	90	32.2	143	61.7	196	91.1
38	3.3	91	32.8	144	62.2	197	91.7
39	3.9	92	33.3	145	62.8	198	92.2
40	4.4	93	33.9	146	63.3	199	92.8
41	5.0	94	34.4	147	63.9	200	93.3
42	5.5	95	35.0	148	64.4	201	93.9
43	6.1	96	35.5	149	65.0	202	94.4
44	6.7	97	36.1	150	65.5	203	95.0
45	7.2	98	36.7	151	66.1	204	95.5
46	7.8	99	37.2	152	66.7	205	96.1
47	8.3	100	37.8	153	67.2	206	96.7
48	8.9	101	38.3	154	67.8	207	97.2
49	9.4	102	38.9	155	68.3	208	97.8
50	10.0	103	39.4	156	68.9	209	98.3
51	10.5	104	40.0	157	69.4	210	98.9
52	11.1	105	40.5	158	70.0	211	99.4
53	11.7	106	41.1	159	70.5	212	100.0

Degrees Celsius (Centigrade) (C) → Degrees Fahrenheit (F)

°C	°F	°C	°F
1	33.8	51	123.8
2	35.6	52	125.6
3	37.4	53	127.4
4	39.2	54	129.2
5	41.0	55	131.0
6	42.8	56	132.8
7	44.6	57	134.6
8	46.4	58	136.4
9	48.2	59	138.2
10	50.0	60	140.0
11	51.8	61	141.8
12	53.6	62	143.6
13	55.4	63	145.4
14	57.2	64	147.2
15	59.0	65	149.0
16	60.8	66	150.8
17	62.6	67	152.6
18	64.4	68	154.4
19	66.2	69	156.2
20	68.0	70	158.0
21	69.8	71	159.8
22	71.6	72	161.6
23	73.4	73	163.4
24	75.2	74	165.2
25	77.0	75	167.0
26	78.8	76	168.8
27	80.6	77	170.6
28	82.4	78	172.4
29	84.2	79	174.2
30	86.0	80	176.0
31	87.8	81	177.8
32	89.6	82	179.6
33	91.4	83	181.4
34	93.2	84	183.2
35	95.0	85	185.0
36	96.8	86	186.8
37	98.6	87	188.6
38	100.4	88	190.4
39	102.2	89	192.2
40	104.0	90	194.0
41	105.8	91	195.8
42	107.6	92	197.6
43	109.4	93	199.4
44	111.2	94	201.2
45	113.0	95	203.0
46	114.8	96	204.8
47	116.6	97	206.6
48	118.4	98	208.4
49	120.2	99	210.2
50	122.0	100	212.0

CONVERSION TABLES

To convert	To	Equation
°Fahrenheit	°Celsius	−32, ×5, ÷9
°Fahrenheit	°Rankine	+459.67
°Fahrenheit	°Réaumur	−32, ×4, ÷9
°Celsius	°Fahrenheit	×9, ÷5, +32
°Celsius	Kelvin	+273.15
°Celsius	°Réaumur	×4, ÷5
Kelvin	°Celsius	−273.15
°Rankine	°Fahrenheit	−459.67
°Réaumur	°Fahrenheit	×9, ÷4, +32
°Réaumur	°Celsius	×5, ÷4

Carry out operations in sequence.

OVEN TEMPERATURES

Gas Mark	Electricity °C	°F	Rating
½	120	250	slow
1	140	275	
2	150	300	
3	170	325	
4	180	350	moderate
5	190	375	
6	200	400	hot
7	220	425	
8	230	450	very hot
9	260	500	

INTERNATIONAL CLOTHING SIZES

Size equivalents are approximate, and may display some variation between manufacturers.

Women's suits/dresses

UK	USA	UK/ Continent
8	6	36
10	8	38
12	10	40
14	12	42
16	14	44
18	16	46
20	18	48
22	20	50
24	22	52

Men's suits and overcoats

UK/USA	Continental
36	46
38	48
40	50
42	52
44	54
46	56

Men's shirts

UK/USA	UK/ Continent
12	30–31
12½	32
13	33
13½	34–35
14	36
14½	37
15	38
15½	39–40
16	41
16½	42
17	43
17½	44–45

Women's hosiery

UK/USA	UK/ Continent
8	0
8½	1
9	2
9½	3
10	4
10½	5

Men's socks

UK/USA	UK/ Continent
9½	38–39
10	39–40
10½	40–41
11	41–42
11½	42–43

Adults' shoes

UK	USA (ladies)	UK/ Continent
4	5½	37
4½	6	38
5	6½	38
5½	7	39
6	7½	39
6½	8	40
7	8½	41
7½	8½	42
8	9½	42
8½	9½	43
9	10½	43
9½	10½	44
10	11½	44
10½	11½	45
11	12	46

Children's shoes

UK/USA	UK/ Continent
0	15
1	17
2	18
3	19
4	20
5	22
6	23
7	24
8	25
8½	26
9	27
10	28
11	29
12	30
13	32

INTERNATIONAL PATTERN SIZES

Young junior/teenage

Size	Bust cm	Bust in	Waist cm	Waist in	Hip cm	Hip in	Back waist length cm	Back waist length in
5/6	71	28	56	22	79	31	34.5	13½
7/8	74	29	58	23	81	32	35.5	14
9/10	78	30½	61	24	85	33½	37	14½
11/12	81	32	64	25	89	35	38	15
13/14	85	33½	66	26	93	36½	39	15⅜
15/16	89	35	69	27	97	38	40	15¾

Misses

Size	Bust cm	Bust in	Waist cm	Waist in	Hip cm	Hip in	Back waist length cm	Back waist length in
6	78	30½	58	23	83	32½	39.5	15½
8	80	31½	61	24	85	33½	40	15¾
10	83	32½	64	25	88	34½	40.5	16
12	87	34	67	26½	92	36	41.5	16¼
14	92	36	71	28	97	38	42	16½
16	97	38	76	30	102	40	42.5	16¾
18	102	40	81	32	107	42	43	17
20	107	42	87	34	112	44	44	17¼

Half-size

Size	Bust cm	Bust in	Waist cm	Waist in	Hip cm	Hip in	Back waist length cm	Back waist length in
10½	84	33	69	27	89	35	38	15
12½	89	35	74	29	94	37	39	15¼
14½	94	37	79	31	99	39	39.5	15½
16½	99	39	84	33	104	41	40	15¾
18½	104	41	89	35	109	43	40.5	15⅞
20½	109	43	96	37½	116	45½	40.5	16
22½	114	45	102	40	122	48	41	16⅛
24½	119	47	108	42½	128	50½	41.5	16¼

Women's

Size	Bust cm	Bust in	Waist cm	Waist in	Hip cm	Hip in	Back waist length cm	Back waist length in
38	107	42	89	35	112	44	44	17¼
40	112	44	94	37	117	46	44	17⅜
42	117	46	99	39	122	48	44.5	17½
44	122	48	105	41½	127	50	45	17⅝
46	127	50	112	44	132	52	45	17¾
48	132	52	118	46½	137	54	45.5	17⅞
50	137	54	124	49	142	56	46	18

INTERNATIONAL PAPER SIZES

A series

	mm	in
A0	841 × 1189	33.11 × 46.81
A1	594 × 841	23.39 × 33.1
A2	420 × 594	16.54 × 23.39
A3	297 × 420	11.69 × 16.54
A4	210 × 297	8.27 × 11.69
A5	148 × 210	5.83 × 8.27
A6	105 × 148	4.13 × 5.83
A7	74 × 105	2.91 × 4.13
A8	52 × 74	2.05 × 2.91
A9	37 × 52	1.46 × 2.05
A10	26 × 37	1.02 × 1.46

B series

	mm	in
B0	1000 × 1414	39.37 × 55.67
B1	707 × 1000	27.83 × 39.37
B2	500 × 707	19.68 × 27.83
B3	353 × 500	13.90 × 19.68
B4	250 × 353	9.84 × 13.90
B5	176 × 250	6.93 × 9.84
B6	125 × 176	4.92 × 6.93
B7	88 × 125	3.46 × 4.92
B8	62 × 88	2.44 × 3.46
B9	44 × 62	1.73 × 2.44
B10	31 × 44	1.22 × 1.73

C series

	mm	in
C0	917 × 1297	36.00 × 51.20
C1	648 × 917	25.60 × 36.00
C2	458 × 648	18.00 × 25.60
C3	324 × 458	12.80 × 18.00
C4	229 × 324	9.00 × 12.80
C5	162 × 229	6.40 × 9.00
C6	114 × 162	4.50 × 6.40
C7	81 × 114	3.20 × 4.50
DL	110 × 220	4.33 × 8.66
C7/6	81 × 162	3.19 × 6.38

All sizes in these series have sides in the proportion of $1 : \sqrt{2}$.
A series is used for writing paper, books and magazines.
B series for posters.
C series for envelopes.

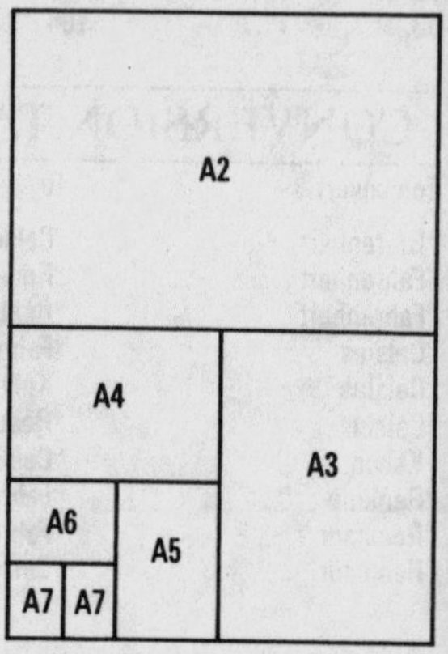

COMMUNICATION SYSTEMS

ALPHABETS

There is no agreement over the use of a single transliteration system in the case of Arabic, Hebrew, and Russian. The equivalents given below are widely used; but several other possibilities can be found.

ARABIC

Letter	Name	Transliteration
ا	'alif	'
ب	ba	b
ت	ta	t
ث	tha	th
ج	jim	j
ح	ha	h
خ	kha	kh
د	dal	d
ذ	dha	th
ر	ra	r
ز	za	z
س	sin	s
ش	shin	sh
ص	sad	s
ض	dad	d
ط	ta	t
ظ	za	z
ع	'ain	'
غ	ghain	gh
ف	fa	f
ق	qaf	q
ك	kaf	k
ل	lam	l
م	mim	m
ن	nun	n
ه	ha	h
و	waw	w
ي	ya	y

RUSSIAN

Letter	Transliteration
А а	a
Б б	b
В в	v
Г г	g
Д д	d
Е е	e
Ж ж	ž, zh
З з	z
И и	i
Й й	j
К к	k
Л л	l
М м	m
Н н	n
О о	o
П п	p
Р р	r
С с	s
Т т	t
У у	u
Ф ф	f
Х х	h, kh, ch
Ц ц	c, ts
Ч ч	č, ch
Ш ш	š, sh
Щ щ	šč, shch
Ъ ъ	″
Ы ы	y
Ь ь	
Э э	è
Ю ю	ju, yu
Я я	ja, ya

GERMAN

Letter	Transliteration
A a	a
Ä ä	ae
B b	b
C c	c
D d	d
E e	e
F f	f
G g	g
H h	h
I i	i
J j	j
K k	k
L l	l
M m	m
N n	n
O o	o
Ö ö	oe
P p	p
Q q	q
R r	r
S ſ s	s
T t	t
U u	u
Ü ü	ue
V v	v
W w	w
X x	x
Y y	y
Z z	z

HEBREW

Letter	Name	Transliteration
א	'aleph	'
ב	beth	b
ג	gimel	g
ד	daleth	d
ה	he	h
ו	waw	w
ז	zayin	z
ח	heth	h
ט	teth	t
י	yodh	y, j
ךכ	kaph	k
ל	lamedh	l
םמ	mem	m
ןנ	nun	n
ס	samekh	s
ע	'ayin	'
ףפ	pe	p, f
ץצ	saddhe	s
ק	qoph	q
ר	resh	r
שׁ	shin	sh, ś
שׂ	śin	ś
ת	taw	t

GREEK

Letter	Name	Transliteration
Α α	alpha	a
Β β	beta	b
Γ γ	gamma	g
Δ δ	delta	d
Ε ε	epsilon	e
Ζ ζ	zeta	z
Η η	eta	e, ē
Θ θ	theta	th
Ι ι	iota	i
Κ κ	kappa	k
Λ λ	lambda	l
Μ μ	mu	m
Ν ν	nu	n
Ξ ξ	xi	x
Ο ο	omicron	o
Π π	pi	p
Ρ ρ	rho	r
Σ σ,ς	sigma	s
Τ τ	tau	t
Υ υ	upsilon	y
Φ φ	phi	ph
Χ χ	chi	ch, kh
Ψ ψ	psi	ps
Ω ω	omega	o, ō

Semaphore	Letters	Morse	Braille
	A	•—	⠁
	B	—•••	⠃
	C	—•—•	⠉
	D	—••	⠙
	E	•	⠑
	F	••—•	⠋
	G	——•	⠛
	H	••••	⠓
	I	••	⠊
	J	•———	⠚
	K	—•—	⠅
	L	•—••	⠇
	M	——	⠍
	N	—•	⠝
	O	———	⠕
	P	•——•	⠏
	Q	——•—	⠟
	R	•—•	⠗
	S	•••	⠎
	T	—	⠞
	U	••—	⠥
	V	•••—	⠧
	W	•——	⠺
	X	—••—	⠭
	Y	—•——	⠽
	Z	——••	⠵

NATO ALPHABET

Letter	Code name	Pronunciation
A	Alpha	AL-FAH
B	Bravo	BRAH-VOH
C	Charlie	CHAR-LEE
D	Delta	DELL-TAH
E	Echo	ECK-OH
F	Foxtrot	FOKS-TROT
G	Golf	GOLF
H	Hotel	HOH-TELL
I	India	IN-DEE-AH
J	Juliet	JEW-LEE-ETT
K	Kilo	KEY-LOH
L	Lima	LEE-MAH
M	Mike	MIKE
N	November	NO-VEM-BER
O	Oscar	OSS-CAH
P	Papa	PAH-PAH
Q	Quebec	KEY-BECK
R	Romeo	ROW-ME-OH
S	Sierra	SEE-AIR-RAH
T	Tango	TAN-GO
U	Uniform	YOU-NEE-FORM
V	Victor	VIK-TAH
W	Whiskey	WISS-KEY
X	Xray	ECKS-RAY
Y	Yankee	YANG-KEY
Z	Zulu	ZOO-LOO

DEAF FINGERSPELLING

British

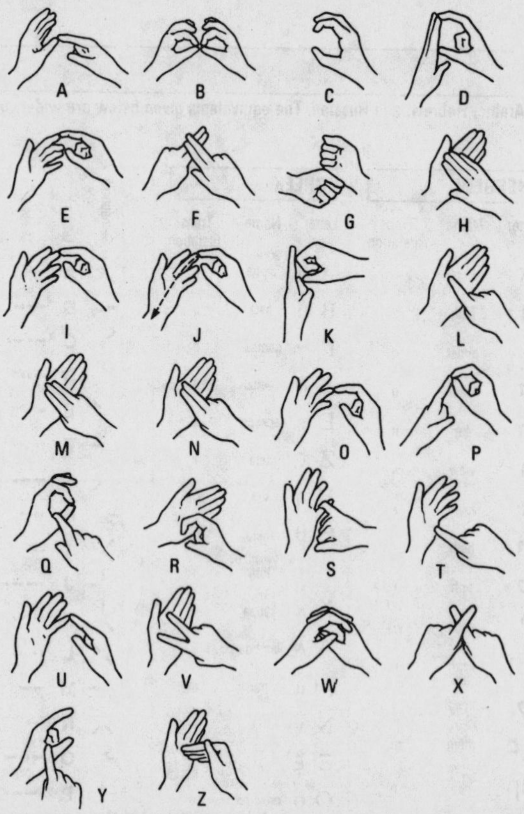

American

TYPEFACES

The typefaces shown are modern versions of the main groups under which most typefaces may be classified. The dates indicating the introduction of each group are approximate.

Gothic
ABCDEFGHIJKLMNOPQRSTUVWXYZ
abcdefghijklmnopqrstuvwxyz
15 & 7pt Old English Text (c.1450)

Venetian
ABCDEFGHIJKLMNOPQRSTUVWXYZ
abcdefghijklmnopqrstuvwxyz
15 & 7pt Centaur (c.1470)

Old Face
ABCDEFGHIJKLMNOPQRSTUVWXYZ
abcdefghijklmnopqrstuvwxyz
15 & 7pt Caslon Old Face (c.1495)

Transitional
ABCDEFGHIJKLMNOPQRSTUVWXYZ
abcdefghijklmnopqrstuvwxyz
15 & 7pt Baskerville (c.1761)

Modern
ABCDEFGHIJKLMNOPQRSTUVWXYZ
abcdefghijklmnopqrstuvwxyz
15 & 7pt Bodoni (c.1765)

Sans Serif
ABCDEFGHIJKLMNOPQRSTUVWXYZ
abcdefghijklmnopqrstuvwxyz
15 & 7pt Univers (c.1816)

Egyptian
ABCDEFGHIJKLMNOPQRSTUVWXYZ
abcdefghijklmnopqrstuvwxyz
12 & 7pt Rockwell (c.1830)

Old Style
ABCDEFGHIJKLMNOPQRSTUVWXYZ
abcdefghijklmnopqrstuvwxyz
15 & 7pt Goudy Old Style (c.1850)

Newspaper
ABCDEFGHIJKLMNOPQRSTUVWXYZ
abcdefghijklmnopqrstuvwxyz
12pt Century Bold & Century Roman (c.1890)

Contemporary
ABCDEFGHIJKLMNOPQRSTUVWXYZ
abcdefghijklmnopqrstuvwxyz
12 & 7pt Times New Roman (c.1932)

LANGUAGES: NUMBER OF SPEAKERS

anguage families

stimates of the numbers of speakers in the main language families f the world in the early 1980s. The list includes Japanese and orean, which are not clearly related to any other languages.

ain language families	
ndo-European	2 000 000 000
ino-Tibetan	1 040 000 000
iger-Congo	260 000 000
fro-Asiatic	230 000 000
ustronesian	200 000 000
ravidian	140 000 000
apanese	120 000 000
ltaic	90 000 000
ustro-Asiatic	60 000 000
orean	60 000 000
ai	50 000 000
ilo-Saharan	30 000 000
merindian (North, Central, South America)	25 000 000
ralic	23 000 000
liao-Yao	7 000 000
aucasian	6 000 000
ndo-Pacific	3 000 000
hoisan	50 000
ustralian aborigine	50 000
aleosiberian	25 000

Specific languages

The first column gives estimates (in millions) for mother-tongue speakers of the 20 most widely used languages. The second column gives estimates of the total population of all countries where the language has official or semi-official status; these totals are often over-estimates, as only a minority of people in countries where a second language is recognized may actually be fluent in it.

Mother-tongue speakers		Official language populations	
1 Chinese	1 000	1 English	1 400
2 English	350	2 Chinese	1 000
3 Spanish	250	3 Hindi	700
4 Hindi	200	4 Spanish	280
5 Arabic	150	5 Russian	270
6 Bengali	150	6 French	220
7 Russian	150	7 Arabic	170
8 Portuguese	135	8 Portuguese	160
9 Japanese	120	9 Malay	160
10 German	100	10 Bengali	150
11 French	70	11 Japanese	120
12 Panjabi	70	12 German	100
13 Javanese	65	13 Urdu	85
14 Bihari	65	14 Italian	60
15 Italian	60	15 Korean	60
16 Korean	60	16 Vietnamese	60
17 Telugu	55	17 Persian	55
18 Tamil	55	18 Tagalog	50
19 Marathi	50	19 Thai	50
20 Vietnamese	50	20 Turkish	50

SPEAKERS OF ENGLISH

he first column gives figures for countries where English is used as a mother-ongue or first language. (A question-mark indicates that no agreed estimates re available.) The second column gives total population figures (mainly 1985 estimates) for countries where English has official or semi-official status as a medium of communication. These totals are likely to bear little correlation with the real use of English in the area.

ountry	First language speakers of English	Country population
nguilla	10 000 –	10 000
ntigua and Barbuda	100 000	100 000
ustralia	14 000 000	15 000 000 +
ahamas	250 000	250 000
angladesh	?	92 600 000 +
arbados	250 000 +	250 000 +
elize	100 000 +	150 000 +
ermuda	50 000 +	50 000 +
hutan	?	1 200 000 +
otswana		1 000 000 –
runei		200 000 +
ameroon		8 000 000 +
anada	17 000 000 +	24 000 000 +
ominica	50 000 +	100 000 –
iji		600 000 +
hana		12 000 000
ibraltar		30 000 +
renada	100 000 +	100 000 +
uyana	900 000 +	900 000
ong Kong	?	6 000 000 –
ndia	?	700 000 000 +
rish Republic	3 300 000	3 300 000
amaica	2 300 000	2 300 000
Kenya		17 000 000
Kiribati		60 000 +
Lesotho		1 400 000
Liberia		2 000 000
Malawi		6 400 000
Malaysia (East)		14 300 000
Malta		350 000
Mauritius		1 000 000
Montserrat	15 000	15 000
Namibia		1 000 000
Nauru		8 000 +
Nepal	?	15 800 000 +
New Zealand	3 000 000	3 200 000
Nigeria	?	90 000 000 +
Pakistan	?	87 100 000 +
Papua New Guinea		3 500 000
Philippines		50 000 000
St Christopher and Nevis	60 000	60 000
St Lucia	?	100 000 +
St Vincent and the Grenadines	100 000 +	100 000 +
Senegambia		600 000
Seychelles		60 000
Sierra Leone		3 600 000
Singapore	?	2 500 000
Solomon Islands		200 000 +
South Africa	2 000 000 +	30 000 000
Sri Lanka	?	15 200 000 +
Suriname		395 000
Swaziland		600 000
Tanzania		18 500 000
Tonga		100 000 +
Trinidad and Tobago	1 200 000	1 200 000
Tuvalu		8 000 +
Uganda		13 000 000
UK	56 000 000 +	57 000 000
US	215 000 000	230 000 000 +
US territories in Pacific		300 000 –
Vanuatu		100 000
Western Samoa		150 000 +
Zambia		6 000 000
Zimbabwe	200 000 +	7 600 000
Other British territories	30 000 +	30 000 +
TOTALS	316 015 000 +	1 606 920 000 +

INTERNATIONAL CAR INDEX MARKS

A	Austria
ADN	former Yemen PDR
AFG	Afghanistan
AL	Albania
AND	Andorra
AUS	Australia*
B	Belgium
BD	Bangladesh*
BDS	Barbados*
BG	Bulgaria
BH	Belize
BR	Brazil
BRN	Bahrain
BRU	Brunei*
BS	Bahamas*
BUR	Myanmar (Burma)
C	Cuba
CDN	Canada
CH	Switzerland
CI	Côte d'Ivoire
CL	Sri Lanka*
CO	Colombia
CR	Costa Rica
CS	Czechoslovakia
CY	Cyprus*
D	Germany
DDR	former E Germany
DK	Denmark
DOM	Dominican Republic
DY	Benin
DZ	Algeria
E	Spain
EAK	Kenya*
EAT	Tanzania*
EAU	Uganda*
EAZ	Tanzania*
EC	Ecuador
ES	El Salvador
ET	Egypt
ETH	Ethiopia
F	France
FJI	Fiji*
FL	Liechtenstein
FR	Faroe Is
GB	UK*
GBA	Alderney*
GBG	Guernsey*
GBJ	Jersey*
GBM	Isle of Man*
GBZ	Gibraltar
GCA	Guatemala
GH	Ghana
GR	Greece
GUY	Guyana*
H	Hungary
HK	Hong Kong*
HKJ	Jordan
I	Italy
IL	Israel
IND	India*
IR	Iran
IRL	Ireland*
IRQ	Iraq
IS	Iceland
J	Japan*
JA	Jamaica*
K	Kampuchea
KWT	Kuwait
L	Luxembourg
LAO	Lao PDR
LAR	Libya
LB	Liberia
LS	Lesotho*
M	Malta*
MA	Morocco
MAL	Malaysia*
MC	Monaco
MEX	Mexico
MS	Mauritius*
MW	Malawi*
N	Norway
NA	Netherlands Antilles
NIC	Nicaragua
NL	Netherlands
NZ	New Zealand*
P	Portugal
PA	Panama
PAK	Pakistan*
PE	Peru
PL	Poland
PNG	Papua New Guinea*
PY	Paraguay
RA	Argentina
RB	Botswana*
RC	Taiwan
RCA	Central African Republic
RCB	Congo
RCH	Chile
RH	Haiti
RI	Indonesia*
RIM	Mauritania
RL	Lebanon
RM	Madagascar
RMM	Mali
RN	Niger
RO	Romania
ROK	Korea, Republic of
ROU	Uruguay
RP	Philippines
RSM	San Marino
RU	Burundi
RWA	Rwanda
S	Sweden
SD	Swaziland*
SF	Finland
SGP	Singapore*
SME	Suriname*
SN	Senegal
SU	former USSR
SWA	Namibia*
SY	Seychelles*
SYR	Syria
T	Thailand*
TG	Togo
TN	Tunisia
TR	Turkey
TT	Trinidad and Tobago*
USA	USA
V	Vatican City
VN	Vietnam
WAG	Gambia
WAL	Sierra Leone
WAN	Nigeria
WD	Dominica*
WG	Grenada*
WL	St Lucia*
WS	W Samoa
WV	St Vincent and the Grenadines*
YU	Yugoslavia
YV	Venezuela
Z	Zambia*
ZA	South Africa*
ZRE	Zaire
ZW	Zimbabwe*

*In countries so marked, the rule of the road is drive on the left; in other countries drive on the right.

BRITISH CAR INDEX MARKS

AA	Bournemouth
AB	Worcester
AC	Coventry
AD	Gloucester
AE	Bristol
AF	Truro
AG	Hull
AH	Norwich
AJ	Middlesbrough
AK	Sheffield
AL	Nottingham
AM	Swindon
AN	Reading
AO	Carlisle
AP	Brighton
AR	Chelmsford
AS	Inverness
AT	Hull
AU	Nottingham
AV	Peterborough
AW	Shrewsbury
AX	Cardiff
AY	Leicester
BA	Manchester
BB	Newcastle upon Tyne
BC	Leicester
BD	Northampton
BE	Lincoln
BF	Stoke-on-Trent
BG	Liverpool
BH	Luton
BJ	Ipswich
BK	Portsmouth
BL	Reading
BM	Luton
BN	Manchester
BO	Cardiff
BP	Portsmouth
BR	Newcastle upon Tyne
BS	Inverness
BT	Leeds
BU	Manchester
BV	Preston
BW	Oxford
BX	Haverfordwest
BY	London NW
CA	Chester
CB	Manchester
CC	Bangor
CD	Brighton
CE	Peterborough
CF	Reading
CG	Bournemouth
CH	Nottingham
CJ	Gloucester
CK	Preston
CL	Norwich
CM	Liverpool
CN	Newcastle upon Tyne
CO	Exeter
CP	Huddersfield
CR	Portsmouth
CS	Glasgow
CT	Lincoln
CU	Newcastle upon Tyne
CV	Truro
CW	Preston
CX	Huddersfield
CY	Swansea
DA	Birmingham
DB	Manchester
DC	Middlesbrough
DD	Gloucester
DE	Haverfordwest
DF	Gloucester
DG	Gloucester
DH	Dudley
DJ	Liverpool
DK	Manchester
DL	Portsmouth
DM	Chester
DN	Leeds
DO	Lincoln
DP	Reading
DR	Exeter
DS	Glasgow
DT	Sheffield
DU	Coventry
DV	Exeter
DW	Cardiff
DX	Ipswich
DY	Brighton
EA	Dudley
EB	Peterborough
EC	Preston
ED	Liverpool
EE	Lincoln
EF	Middlesbrough
EG	Peterborough
EH	Stoke-on-Trent
EJ	Haverfordwest
EK	Liverpool
EL	Bournemouth
EM	Liverpool
EN	Manchester
EO	Preston
EP	Swansea
ER	Peterborough
ES	Dundee
ET	Sheffield
EU	Bristol
EV	Chelmsford
EW	Peterborough
EX	Norwich
EY	Bangor
FA	Stoke-on-Trent
FB	Bristol
FC	Oxford
FD	Dudley
FE	Lincoln
FF	Bangor
FG	Brighton
FH	Gloucester
FJ	Exeter
FK	Dudley
FL	Peterborough
FM	Chester
FN	Maidstone
FO	Gloucester
FP	Leicester
FR	Preston
FS	Edinburgh
FT	Newcastle upon Tyne
FU	Lincoln
FV	Preston
FW	Lincoln
FX	Bournemouth
FY	Liverpool
GA	Glasgow
GB	Glasgow
GC	London SW
GD	Glasgow
GE	Glasgow
GF	London SW
GG	Glasgow
GH	London SW
GJ	London SW
GK	London SW
GL	Truro
GM	Reading
GN	London SW
GO	London SW
GP	London SW
GR	Newcastle upon Tyne
GS	Luton
GT	London SW
GU	London SE
GV	Ipswich
GW	London SE
GX	London SE
GY	London SE
HA	Dudley
HB	Cardiff
HC	Brighton
HD	Huddersfield
HE	Sheffield
HF	Liverpool
HG	Preston
HH	Carlisle
HJ	Chelmsford
HK	Chelmsford
HL	Sheffield
HM	London (Central)
HN	Middlesbrough
HO	Bournemouth
HP	Coventry
HR	Swindon
HS	Glasgow

BRITISH CAR INDEX MARKS (cont.)

HT	Bristol
HU	Bristol
HV	London (Central)
HW	Bristol
HX	London (Central)
HY	Bristol
JA	Manchester
JB	Reading
JC	Bangor
JD	London (Central)
JE	Peterborough
JF	Leicester
JG	Maidstone
JH	Reading
JJ	Maidstone
JK	Brighton
JL	Lincoln
JM	Reading
JN	Chelmsford
JO	Oxford
JP	Liverpool
JR	Newcastle upon Tyne
JS	Inverness
JT	Bournemouth
JU	Leicester
JV	Lincoln
JW	Birmingham
JX	Huddersfield
JY	Exeter
KA	Liverpool
KB	Liverpool
KC	Liverpool
KD	Liverpool
KE	Maidstone
KF	Liverpool
KG	Cardiff
KH	Hull
KJ	Maidstone
KK	Maidstone
KL	Maidstone
KM	Maidstone
KN	Maidstone
KO	Maidstone
KP	Maidstone
KR	Maidstone
KS	Edinburgh
KT	Maidstone
KU	Sheffield
KV	Coventry
KW	Sheffield
KX	Luton
KY	Sheffield
LA	London NW
LB	London NW
LC	London NW
LD	London NW
LE	London NW
LF	London NW
LG	Chester
LH	London NW
LJ	Bournemouth
LK	London NW
LL	London NW
LM	London NW
LN	London NW
LO	London NW
LP	London NW
LR	London NW
LS	Edinburgh
LT	London NW
LU	London NW
LV	Liverpool
LW	London NW
LX	London NW
LY	London NW
MA	Chester
MB	Chester
MC	London NE
MD	London NE
ME	London NE
MF	London NE
MG	London NE
MH	London NE
MJ	Luton
MK	London NE
ML	London NE
MM	London NE
MN	*(not used)*
MO	Reading
MP	London NE
MR	Swindon
MS	Edinburgh
MT	London NE
MU	London NE
MV	London SE
MW	Swindon
MX	London SE
MY	London SE
NA	Manchester
NB	Manchester
NC	Manchester
ND	Manchester
NE	Manchester
NF	Manchester
NG	Norwich
NH	Northampton
NJ	Brighton
NK	Luton
NL	Newcastle upon Tyne
NM	Luton
NN	Nottingham
NO	Chelmsford
NP	Worcester
NR	Leicester
NS	Glasgow
NT	Shrewsbury
NU	Nottingham
NV	Northampton
NW	Leeds
NX	Dudley
NY	Cardiff
OA	Birmingham
OB	Birmingham
OC	Birmingham
OD	Exeter
OE	Birmingham
OF	Birmingham
OG	Birmingham
OH	Birmingham
OJ	Birmingham
OK	Birmingham
OL	Birmingham
OM	Birmingham
ON	Birmingham
OO	Chelmsford
OP	Birmingham
OR	Portsmouth
OS	Glasgow
OT	Portsmouth
OU	Bristol
OV	Birmingham
OW	Portsmouth
OX	Birmingham
OY	London NW
PA	Guildford
PB	Guildford
PC	Guildford
PD	Guildford
PE	Guildford
PF	Guildford
PG	Guildford
PH	Guildford
PJ	Guildford
PK	Guildford
PL	Guildford
PM	Guildford
PN	Brighton
PO	Portsmouth
PP	Luton
PR	Bournemouth
PS	Aberdeen
PT	Newcastle upon Tyne
PU	Chelmsford
PV	Ipswich
PW	Norwich
PX	Portsmouth
PY	Middlesbrough
RA	Nottingham
RB	Nottingham
RC	Nottingham
RD	Reading
RE	Stoke-on-Trent
RF	Stoke-on-Trent
RG	Newcastle upon Tyne
RH	Hull
RJ	Manchester
RK	London NW
RL	Truro
RM	Carlisle
RN	Preston
RO	Luton
RP	Northampton
RR	Nottingham
RS	Aberdeen
RT	Ipswich
RU	Bournemouth
RV	Portsmouth
RW	Coventry
RX	Reading
RY	Leicester
SA	Aberdeen
SB	Glasgow
SC	Edinburgh
SCY	Truro (Isles of Scilly)
SD	Glasgow
SE	Aberdeen
SF	Edinburgh
SG	Edinburgh
SH	Edinburgh
SJ	Glasgow
SK	Inverness
SL	Dundee
SM	Glasgow
SN	Dundee
SO	Aberdeen
SP	Dundee
SR	Dundee
SS	Aberdeen
ST	Inverness
SU	Glasgow
SV	Spare
SW	Glasgow
SX	Edinburgh
SY	*Spare*
TA	Exeter
TB	Liverpool
TC	Bristol
TD	Manchester
TE	Manchester
TF	Reading
TG	Cardiff
TH	Swansea
TJ	Liverpool
TK	Exeter
TL	Lincoln
TM	Luton
TN	Newcastle upon Tyne
TO	Nottingham
TP	Portsmouth
TR	Portsmouth
TS	Dundee
TT	Exeter
TU	Chester
TV	Nottingham
TW	Chelmsford
TX	Cardiff
TY	Newcastle upon Tyne
UA	Leeds
UB	Leeds
UC	London (Central)
UD	Oxford
UE	Dudley
UF	Brighton
UG	Leeds
UH	Cardiff
UJ	Shrewsbury
UK	Birmingham
UL	London (Central)
UM	Leeds
UN	Exeter
UO	Exeter
UP	Newcastle upon Tyne
UR	Luton
US	Glasgow
UT	Leicester
UU	London (Central)
UV	London (Central)
UW	London (Central)
UX	Shrewsbury
UY	Worcester
VA	Peterborough
VB	Maidstone
VC	Coventry
VD	*Series withdrawn*
VE	Peterborough
VF	Norwich
VG	Norwich
VH	Huddersfield
VJ	Gloucester
VK	Newcastle upon Tyne
VL	Lincoln
VM	Manchester
VN	Middlesbrough
VO	Nottingham
VP	Birmingham
VR	Manchester
VS	Luton
VT	Stoke-on-Trent
VU	Manchester
VV	Northampton
VW	Chelmsford
VX	Chelmsford
VY	Leeds
WA	Sheffield
WB	Sheffield
WC	Chelmsford
WD	Dudley
WE	Sheffield
WF	Sheffield
WG	Sheffield
WH	Manchester
WJ	Sheffield
WK	Coventry
WL	Oxford
WM	Liverpool
WN	Swansea
WO	Cardiff
WP	Worcester
WR	Leeds
WS	Bristol
WT	Leeds
WU	Leeds
WV	Brighton
WW	Leeds
WX	Leeds
WY	Leeds
YA	Taunton
YB	Taunton
YC	Taunton
YD	Taunton
YE	London (Central)
YF	London (Central)
YG	Leeds
YH	London (Central)
YJ	Brighton
YK	London (Central)
YL	London (Central)
YM	London (Central)
YN	London (Central)
YO	London (Central)
YP	London (Central)
YR	London (Central)
YS	Glasgow
YT	London (Central)
YU	London (Central)
YV	London (Central)
YW	London (Central)
YX	London (Central)
YY	London (Central)

AIRCRAFT REGISTRATION CODES

These codes are painted on all aircraft showing their country of registration

AN	Nicaragua
AP	Pakistan
A2	Botswana
A6	United Arab Emirates
A7	Qatar
A9C	Bahrain
A40	Oman
B	China
C	Canada
CC	Chile
CCCP	former USSR
CN	Morocco
CP	Bolivia
CR, CS	Portugal
CU	Cuba
CX	Uruguay
C2	Nauru
C5	The Gambia
C6	Bahamas
C9	Mozambique
D	German Federal Republic
DM	former German Democratic Republic
DQ	Fiji
D2	Angola
D6	Comoros
EC	Spain
EI, EJ	Ireland
EL	Liberia
EP	Iran
ET	Ethiopa
F	France
F-H4	Vanuatu
G	United Kingdom
HA	Hungary
HB	Switzerland
HC	Ecuador
HH	Haiti
HI	Dominican Republic
HK	Colombia
HL	Korea, South
HP	Panama
HR	Honduras
HS	Thailand
HZ	Saudi Arabia
H4	Solomon Islands
I	Italy
JA	Japan
JY	Jordan
J5	Guinea Bissau
LN	Norway
LQ, LV	Argentina
LX	Luxembourg
LZ	Bulgaria
N	USA
OB	Peru
OD	Lebanon
OE	Austria
OH	Finland
OK	Czechoslovakia
OO	Belgium
OY	Denmark
PH	Netherlands
PJ	Netherland Antilles
PK	Indonesia
PP, PT	Brazil
PZ	Suriname
P2	Papua New Guinea
RDPL	Laos
RP	Philippines
SE	Sweden
SP	Poland
ST	Sudan
SU	Egypt
SX	Greece
S2	Bangladesh
S7	Seychelles
TC	Turkey
TF	Iceland
TG	Guatemala
TI	Costa Rica
TJ	Cameroon
TL	Central African Republic
TN	Congo
TR	Gabon
TS	Tunisia
TT	Chad
TU	Ivory Coast
TY	Benin
VH	Australia
VP-H	Belize
VQ-G	Grenada
VQ-L	St Lucia
VR-B	Bermuda
VR-C	Cayman Islands
VR-G	Gibraltar
VR-H	Hong Kong
VR-U	Brunei
VT	India
XA, XB, XC	Mexico
XT	Burkina Faso
XY, XZ	Myanmar (Burma)
YA	Afghanistan
YI	Iraq
YK	Syria
YR	Romania
YS	El Salvador
YU	Yugoslavia
YV	Venezuela
ZA	Albania
ZK, ZL, ZM	New Zealand
ZP	Paraguay
ZS, ZU	South Africa
ZT	Namibia
ZW, ZY	Zimbabwe
3B	Mauritius
3D	Swaziland
3X	Guinea
4R	Sri Lanka
4W	former Yemen Arab Republic
4X	Israel
5A	Libya
5B	Cyprus
5H	Tanzania
5N	Nigeria
5R	Madagascar
5T	Mauritania
5U	Niger
5V	Togo
5X	Uganda
5Y	Kenya
6O	Somalia
6V, 6W	Senegal
6Y	Jamaica
7O	former Yemen PDR
7Q-Y	Malawi
7T	Algeria
8P	Barbados
8R	Guyana
9G	Ghana
9H	Malta
9J	Zambia
9K	Kuwait
9L	Sierra Leone
9M	Malaysia
9N	Nepal
9Q	Zaire
9U	Burundi
9V	Singapore
9XR	Rwanda
9Y	Trinidad and Tobago

AIRLINE DESIGNATORS

Code	Airline	Country
AA	American Airlines	USA
AC	Air Canada	Canada
AE	Air Europe	UK
AF	Air France	France
AH	Air Algerie	Algeria
AI	Air India	India
AN	Ansett Airlines	Australia
AQ	Aloha Airlines	Hawaii
AR	Aerolineas Argentinas	Argentina
AS	Alaska Airlines	USA
AT	Royal Air Maroc	Morocco
AW	Air Niger	Niger
AY	Finnair	Finland
AZ	Alitalia	Italy
BA	British Airways	UK
BB	Sansa	Costa Rica
BD	British Midland Airways	UK
BG	Bangladesh Biman	Bangladesh
BH	Augusta Airways	Australia
BI	Royal Brunei Airlines	Brunei
BJ	Safe Air	New Zealand
BN	Braniff International Airways	USA
BO	Bouraq Indonesia Airlines	Indonesia
BP	Air Botswana	Botswana
BT	Ansett NT	Australia
BU	Braathens SAFE	Norway
BY	Britannia Airways	UK
CA	CAAC (Civil Aviation Administration of China)	China
CI	China Airlines	Taiwan
CM	COPA (Compania Panamena de Aviación)	Panama
CO	Continental Airlines	USA
CO	Air Micronesia	Mariana Is
CP	Canadian Airlines International	Canada
CQ	Aerolineas Federal Argentina	Argentina
CU	Cubana	Cuba
CX	Cathay Pacific Airways	Hong Kong
CY	Cyprus Airways	Cyprus
CZ	Celtic Air	Ireland
DA	Dan-Air Services	UK
DJ	Air Djibouti	Djibouti
DO	Dominicana de Aviación	Dominican Republic
DS	Air Senegal	Senegal

AIRLINE DESIGNATORS (cont.)

Code	Airline	Country
DT	TAAG Angola Airlines	Angola
DX	Danair	Denmark
DY	Alyemda-Democratic Yemen Airlines	former Republic of Yemen
EA	Eastern Airlines	USA
EI	Aer Lingus	Ireland
EK	Emirates	United Arab Emirates
ER	Air Togo	Togo
ET	Ethiopian Airlines	Ethiopia
EW	East-West Airlines	Australia
EX	Eagle Airways	New Zealand
FG	Bakhtar Afgan Airlines	Afghanistan
FI	Icelandair	Iceland
FJ	Air Pacific	Fiji
FO	Western New South Wales Airlines	Australia
FR	Ryanair (Dublin)	Ireland
GC	Lina Congo	Congo
GE	Guernsey Airlines	Channel Is
GH	Ghana Airways	Ghana
GI	Air Guinee	Guinea
GL	Gronlandsfly	Greenland
GN	Air Gabon	Gabon
GR	Aurigny Air Services	Channel Is
GT	GB Air	Gibraltar
GY	Guyana Airways Corporation	Guyana
HA	Hawaiian Airlines	USA
HH	Somali Airlines	Somalia
HM	Air Seychelles	Seychelles
HR	Friendly Islands Airways	Tonga
HT	Air Tchad	Chad
HV	Transavia Airlines	Netherlands
IA	Iraqi Airways	Iraq
IB	Iberia	Spain
IC	Indian Airlines	India
IE	Solomon Islands Airways	Solomon Is
II	Janair	USA
IP	Airlines of Tasmania	Australia
IR	Iranair	Iran
IY	Yemenia Yemen Airways	former Yemen Arab Republic
JE	Manx Airlines	Isle of Man
JG	Swedair	Sweden
JL	Japan Airlines	Japan
JM	Air Jamaica	Jamaica
JP	Trans Continental Airlines	USA
JQ	Trans Jamaica Airlines	Jamaica
JS	Chosonminhang Korean Airways	DPR Korea
JU	JAT Jugoslovenski Aerotransport	Yugoslavia
JY	Jersey European Airways	Channel Is
KC	Cook Islands International	Australia
KE	Korean Air	Rep. of Korea
KL	KLM	Netherlands
KM	Air Malta	Malta
KP	Air Cape	South Africa
KQ	Kenya Airways	Kenya
KU	Kuwait Airways	Kuwait
KV	Transkei Airways	South Africa
KY	Waterwings Airways	New Zealand
LA	Lan-Chile	Chile
LC	Loganair	UK
LE	Magnum Airlines	South Africa
LF	Linjeflyg	Sweden
LG	Luxair	Luxembourg
LH	Lufthansa	FRG
LJ	Sierra Leone Airlines	Sierra Leone
LL	Bell-Air	New Zealand
LN	Jamahiriya Libyan Arab Airlines	Libya
LO	LOT Polish Airlines	Poland
LU	Theron Airways	South Africa
LY	El Al Israel Airlines	Israel
MB	Midstate Airlines	Australia
MD	Air Madagascar	Madagascar
ME	Middle East Airlines	Lebanon
MK	Air Mauritius	Mauritius
MN	Commercial Airways	South Africa
MR	Air Mauritanie	Mauritania
MS	Egyptair	Egypt
MV	Ansett WA	Australia
MY	Air Mali	Mali
NB	National Airlines	South Africa
NH	All Nippon Airways	Japan
NJ	Namakwaland Lugdiens	South Africa
NL	Air Liberia	Liberia
NM	Mount Cook Airlines	New Zealand
NN	Air Martinique	Martinique
NO	Aus-Air	Australia
NR	Norontair	Canada
NU	Southwest Airlines	Japan
NV	Northwest Territorial Airways	Canada
NW	Northwest Airlines	USA
NX	Nationair	Canada
NZ	Air New Zealand	New Zealand
OA	Olympic Airways	Greece
OG	Air Guadeloupe	French W Indies
OK	CSA (Ceskoslovenske Aerolinie)	Czechoslovakia
OM	Air Mongol	Mongolian P R
ON	Air Nauru	Australia
OO	Sky West Airlines	Australia
OP	Air Panama Internacional	Panama
OR	Air Comores	Comoros
OS	Austrian Airlines	Austria
PA	Pan American World Airways	USA
PB	Air Burundi	Burundi
PC	Fiji Air	Fiji
PK	Pakistan International Airlines	Pakistan
PL	Aeroperu	Peru
PR	Philippine Airlines	Philippines
PS	Pacific Southwest Airlines	USA
PU	PLUNA (Primeras Lineas Uruguayas de Navegación Aerea)	Uruguay
PX	Air Niugini	Papua New Guinea
PY	Surinam Airways	Suriname
PZ	LAP (Lineas Aereas Paraguayas)	Paraguay
QB	Quebecair	Canada
QC	Air Zaire	Zaire
QF	Qantas Airways	Australia
QL	Lesotho Airways	Lesotho
QM	Air Malawi	Malawi
QN	Air Queensland	Australia
QU	Uganda Airlines	Uganda
QV	Lao Aviation	Lao PDR
QX	Horizon Airlines	USA
QY	Aero Virgin Islands	Virgin Is
QZ	Zambia Airways	Zambia
RA	Royal Nepal Airlines	Nepal
RB	Syrian Arab Airlines	Syria
RG	Varig	Brazil
RJ	Royal Jordanian	Jordan
RK	Air Afrique	Côte d'Ivoire
RL	Aeronica	Nicaragua
RN	Royal Air Inter	Morocco
RO	Tarom	Romania
RR	Royal Air Force	UK
RY	Air Rwanda	Rwanda
SA	South African Airways	South Africa
SD	Sudan Airways	Sudan
SH	SAHSA (Servicio Aero de Honduras)	Honduras
SJ	Southern Air	New Zealand
SK	SAS (Scandinavian Airlines)	Sweden
SM	Air Ecosse	UK
SN	Sabena	Belgium
SQ	Singapore Airlines	Singapore
SR	Swissair	Switzerland
SU	Aeroflot	Russia
SV	Saudia	Saudi Arabia
SW	Namib Air	Namibia
TC	Air Tanzania	Tanzania
TE	Air New Zealand – International	New Zealand
TH	Thai Airways	Thailand
TK	THY Turkish Airlines	Turkey
TM	LAM (Linhas Aereas de Moçambique)	
TN	Australian Airlines	Australia
TP	TAP Air Portugal	Portugal
TS	Transports Aeriens du Benin	Benin
TU	Tunis Air	Tunisia
TW	TWA (Trans World Airlines)	USA
TX	TAN (Transportes Aereos Nacionales)	Honduras
UA	United Airlines	USA
UB	Burma Airways	Myanmar (Burma)
UK	Air UK	UK
UL	Air Lanka	Sri Lanka
UM	Air Zimbabwe	Zimbabwe
UN	Eastern Australia Airlines	Australia
UP	Bahamasair	Bahamas
UQ	London European Airways	UK
UU	Réunion Air Service	Réunion
UY	Cameroon Airlines	Cameroon
VA	VIASA (Venezolana Internacional de Aviación)	Venezuela
VE	Avensa	Venezuela
VH	Air Burkina	Burkina Faso
VN	Hang Khong Vietnam	Vietnam
VO	Tyrolean Airways	Austria
VR	Transportes Aereos de Cabo Verde	Cape Verde Is
VS	Virgin Atlantic Airways	UK
VT	Air Tahiti	Tahiti
VU	Air Ivoire	Côte d'Ivoire
VX	ACES (Aerolineas Centrales de Colombia)	Colombia
WC	Wild Coast Air	South Africa
WI	Rottnest Airlines	Australia
WJ	Labrador Airways	Canada
WN	Southwest Airlines	USA
WT	Nigeria Airways	Nigeria
WX	Air NSW	Australia
WY	Oman Aviation Services	Oman
XX	Aereonaves del Peru	Peru
YK	Cyprus Turkish Airlines	Cyprus
YN	Air Creebec	Canada
YU	Dominair	Dominican Republic
YZ	Linhas Aereas da Guiné Bissau	Guiné Bissau
ZB	Monarch Airlines	UK
ZC	Royal Swazi National Airways	Swaziland
ZH	Ecuato Guineana de Aviación	Equatorial Guinea
ZP	Virgin Air	Virgin Is
ZQ	Ansett New Zealand	New Zealand
ZX	Air BC	Canada

INTERNATIONAL DIRECT DIALLING CODES

This table gives the international telephone direct dialling codes for most countries.

It is not always possible to dial internationally from every country to every other country, and there are sometimes restrictions and special numbers within a country, for which it is necessary to consult the local telephone directory.

Dialling procedure is as follows:
(a) Dial out, using the access code of the country from which you are making the call; you may need to wait for a dialling tone or announcement (shown by + in the table below).
(b) Then dial the code of the country you are calling, followed by any area or city code, and the subscriber number. (When making an international call, it is usually necessary to omit any initial 0 or 9 of an area/city code.)

Country	Dialling out code	Dialling in code
Afghanistan	none	93
Albania	none	355
Algeria	00+	213
Angola	none	244
Antigua and Barbuda	011	1 809 46
Argentina	00	54
Australia	0011	61
Austria	00	43
Bahamas	011	1 809
Bahrain	0	973
Bangladesh	00	880
Barbados	011	1 809
Belgium	00+	32
Belize	none	501
Benin	none	229
Bermuda	011	1 809 29
Bolivia	none	591
Botswana	none	267
Brazil	00	55
Brunei	00	673
Bulgaria	00	359
Burkina Faso	00	226
Cameroon	00	237
Canada	011	1
Chile	00	56
China	none	86
Colombia	90	57
Congo	00	242
Costa Rica	00	506
Côte d'Ivoire	00	225
Cuba	none	53
Cyprus	00	357
Czechoslovakia	00	42
Denmark	009	45
Djibouti	none	253
Dominica	none	1 809 449
Dominican Republic	none	1 809
Ecuador	none	593
Egypt	00	20
El Salvador	0	503
Ethiopia	none	251
Fiji	none	679
Finland	990	358
France	19+	33
Gabon	00	241
Gambia	none	220
Germany (former East)	06	37
Germany (former West)	00	49
Ghana	none	233
Gibraltar	00	350
Greece	00	30
Greenland	none	299
Grenada	none	1 809 440
Guatemala	00	502
Guyana	none	592
Haiti	none	509
Honduras	00	504
Hong Kong	001	852
Hungary	00+	36
Iceland	90	354
India	900	91
Indonesia	00	62
Iran	00	98
Iraq	00	964
Ireland	16	353
Israel	00	972
Italy	00	39
Jamaica	none	1 809
Japan	001	81
Jordan	0	962
Kenya	000	254
Korea, South	001	82
Kuwait	00	965
Laos	none	856
Lebanon	00	961
Lesotho	00	266
Liberia	00	231
Libya	00	218
Liechtenstein	00	41 75
Luxembourg	00	352
Madagascar	none	261
Malawi	101	265
Malaysia	00	60
Maldives	none	960
Malta	00	356
Mauritius	none	230
Mexico	98	52
Monaco	19+	33 93
Morocco	00	212
Mozambique	none	258
Myanmar (Burma)	none	95
Namibia	091	264
Nauru	none	674
Nepal	none	977
Netherlands	09+	31
New Zealand	00	64
Nicaragua	none	505
Niger	none	227
Nigeria	009	234
Norway	095	47
Oman	00	968
Pakistan	00	92
Panama	00	507
Papua New Guinea	31	675
Paraguay	none	595
Peru	00	51
Philippines	00	63
Poland	00	48
Portugal	00	351
Puerto Rico	135	1 809
Qatar	0	974
Romania	none	40
Rwanda	none	250
St Christopher and Nevis	00+	1 809 465
St Lucia	none	1 809 45
St Vincent and the Grenadines	none	1 809 45
Samoa, American	none	684
Samoa, Western	none	685
San Marino	00	39 541
Saudi Arabia	00	966
Senegal	00	221
Seychelles	0	248
Sierra Leone	none	232
Singapore	005	65
Solomon Is	00	677
Somalia	none	252
South Africa	09	27
Spain	07+	34
Sri Lanka	00	94
Sudan	none	249
Suriname	001	597
Swaziland	0992	268
Sweden	009	46
Switzerland	00	41
Syria	00	963
Taiwan	002	886
Tanzania	none	255
Thailand	001	66
Togo	none	228
Tonga	none	676
Trinidad and Tobago	01	1 809
Tunisia	00	216
Turkey	9+9	90
Uganda	none	256
United Arab Emirates	00	971
UK	010	44
USA	011	1
Uruguay	00	598
former USSR	810	7
Vanuatu	none	678
Venezuela	00	58
Yemen	00	967 and 969
Yugoslavia	99	38
Zaïre	none	243
Zambia	00	260
Zimbabwe	110	263

SOME SATELLITES IN GEOSTATIONARY ORBIT

Communications

Business

BS 1	1980
BS 2	1981
BS 3	1982
BS 4	1984
BS 5	1988

International

Intelsat 2 F-2	1967
Intelsat 2 F-3	1967
Intelsat 2 F-4	1967
Intelsat 3 F-2	1968
Intelsat 3 F-3	1969
Intelsat 3 F-4	1969
Intelsat 3 F-6	1970
Intelsat 3 F-7	1970
Intelsat 4 F-1	1975
Intelsat 4 F-2	1971
Intelsat 4 F-3	1971
Intelsat 4 F-4	1972
Intelsat 4 F-5	1972
Intelsat 4 F-7	1973
Intelsat 4 F-8	1974
Intelsat 4A F-1	1975
Intelsat 4A F-2	1976
Intelsat 4A F-3	1978
Intelsat 4A F-4	1977
Intelsat 4A F-6	1978
Intelsat 5 F-1	1981
Intelsat 5 F-2	1980
Intelsat 5 F-3	1981
Intelsat 5 F-4	1982
Intelsat 5 F-5	1982
Intelsat 5 F-6	1983
Intelsat 5 F-7	1983
Intelsat 5 F-8	1984
Intelsat 5 F-9	1984
Intelsat 5A F-10	1985
Intelsat 5A F-11	1985
Intelsat 5A F-12	1985
Intelsat 5A F-13	1988
Intelsat 5A F-15	1989
Intelsat 6 F-2	1989

Arabian

Arabsat 1A	1985
Arabsat 1B	1985

Australian

Aussat 1	1985
Aussat 2	1985
Aussat 3	1987

Brazilian

Brasilsat 1	1985
Brasilsat 2	1986

Canadian

Anik	1978
Anik 1	1972
Anik 2	1973
Anik 3	1975
Anik C1	1985
Anik C2	1983
Anik C3	1982
Anik D1	1982
Anik D2	1984
Telesat 1	1972
Telesat 2	1973
Telesat 3	1975
Telesat 4	1978
Telesat 5	1982
Telesat 6	1982
Telesat 7	1983
Telesat 8	1984
Telesat 9	1985

Chinese

China 15	1984
China 18	1986
China 22	1988
China 25	1988
China 26	1990

European

Astra 1A	1988
ECS 1	1983
ECS 2	1984
ECS 4	1987
ECS 5	1988
ESA GEOS 2	1978
Marcopolo 1	1989
Olympus	1989

French

TDF 1	1988
Telecom 1A	1984
Telecom 1B	1985
Telecom 1C	1988

French/German

Symphonie 1	1974
Symphonie 2	1975

German

DFS-Kopernicus 1	1989
TV-Sat 1	1987
TV-Sat 2	1989

Indian

Apple	1981
Insat 1A	1982
Insat 1B	1983
Insat 1C	1988

Indonesian

Palapa 1	1976
Palapa 2	1977
Palapa 3	1983
Palapa 5	1987

Italian

Sirio 1	1977

Japanese

Ayama 1	1979
Ayama 2	1980
CS-2A	1983
CS-2B	1983
CS-3A	1988
CS-3B	1988
ECS 1	1979
ECS 2	1980
ETS 2	1977
ETS 3	1982
ETS 5	1987
JCSat 1	1989
JCSat 2	1990
Sakura 2A	1983
Sakura 2B	1983
Sakura 3A	1988
Sakura 3B	1988
Superbird 1	1989

Mexican

Morelos 1	1985
Morelos 2	1985

Pan-American

Panamsat (PAS 1)	1988

Soviet

Cosmos 1888	1987
Cosmos 1894	1987
Cosmos 1897	1987
Cosmos 1940	1988
Cosmos 1961	1988
Cosmos 2054	1989
Ekran 1	1976
Ekran 2	1977
Ekran 3	1979
Ekran 4	1979
Ekran 5	1980
Ekran 6	1980
Ekran 7	1981
Ekran 8	1982
Ekran 9	1982
Ekran 10	1983
Ekran 11	1983
Ekran 12	1984
Ekran 13	1984
Ekran 14	1985
Ekran 15	1986
Ekran 16	1987
Ekran 17	1987
Ekran 18	1988
Ekran 19	1988
Gorizont 1	1978
Gorizont 2	1979
Gorizont 3	1979
Gorizont 4	1980
Gorizont 5	1982
Gorizont 6	1982
Gorizont 7	1983
Gorizont 8	1983
Gorizont 9	1984
Gorizont 10	1984
Gorizont 11	1985
Gorizont 12	1986
Gorizont 13	1986
Gorizont 14	1987
Gorizont 15	1988
Gorizont 16	1988
Gorizont 17	1989
Gorizont 18	1989
Gorizont 19	1989
Raduga 1	1975
Raduga 2	1976
Raduga 3	1977
Raduga 4	1978
Raduga 5	1979
Raduga 6	1980
Raduga 7	1980
Raduga 8	1981
Raduga 9	1981
Raduga 10	1981
Raduga 11	1982
Raduga 12	1983
Raduga 13	1983
Raduga 14	1984
Raduga 15	1984
Raduga 16	1985
Raduga 17	1985
Raduga 18	1986
Raduga 19	1986
Raduga 20	1987
Raduga 21	1987
Raduga 22	1988
Raduga 23	1989
Raduga	1989
Raduga	1989

Swedish

Tele-X	1989

US

ASC 1	1985
Comstar 1A	1976
Comstar 1B	1976
Comstar 1C	1978
Comstar 1D	1981
Early Bird	1965
Galaxy 1	1983
Galaxy 2	1983
Galaxy 3	1984
Gstar 1	1985
Gstar 2	1986
Gstar 3	1988
Intelsat 1 F-1	1965
Leasat 1	1984
Leasat 2	1984
Leasat 3	1985
Leasat 4	1985
Leasat 5	1990
LES 6	1968
LES 8	1976
LES 9	1976
RCA Satcom 1	1975
RCA Satcom 2	1976
RCA Satcom 3	1979
RCA Satcom 3R	1981
RCA Satcom 4	1982
RCA Satcom 5	1982
RCA Satcom 6	1983
RCA Satcom 7	1983
RCA Satcom K1	1986
RCA Satcom K2	1985
TDRS 1	1983
TDRS 3	1988
TDRS 4	1989
Telstar 3A	1983
Telstar 3C	1983
Telstar 3D	1985
Westar 1	1974
Westar 2	1974
Westar 3	1979
Westar 4	1982
Westar 5	1982

Maritime Communications

Marecs 1	1981
Marecs 2	1984
Marisat 1	1976
Marisat 2	1976
Marisat 3	1976

Meteorology

Japanese

GMS 1	1977
GMS 2	1981
GMS 3	1984
GMS 4	1989
Himawari 1	1977
Himawari 2	1981
Himawari 3	1984

European

Meteosat 1	1977
Meteosat 2	1981
Meteosat P2	1988
MOP 1	1989

US

GOES 1	1975
GOES 2	1977
GOES 3	1978
GOES 4	1980
GOES 5	1981
GOES 6	1983
GOES 7	1987
SMS 1	1974
SMS 2	1975
SMS 3	1975

Military Communications

NATO 1	1970
NATO 2	1971
NATO 3A	1976
NATO 3B	1977
NATO 3C	1978
NATO 3D	1984

UK

Skynet 1A	1969
Skynet 2A	1974
Skynet 2B	1974
Skynet 4A	1990
Skynet 4B	1988

US

DSCS 1	1971
DSCS 2	1971
DSCS 3	1973
DSCS 4	1973
DSCS 5	1975
DSCS 6	1975
DSCS 7	1977
DSCS 8	1977
DSCS 11	1978
DSCS 12	1978
DSCS 13	1979
DSCS 14	1979
DSCS 15	1982
DSCS 16	1982
DSCS TYPE 3	1985
Fleetsatcom 1	1978
Fleetsatcom 2	1979
Fleetsatcom 3	1980
Fleetsatcom 4	1980
Fleetsatcom 5	1981
Fleetsatcom 7	1986
Fleetsatcom 8	1989
IMEWS	1987
IMEWS 1	1970
IMEWS 2	1971
IMEWS 3	1972
IMEWS 4	1973
IMEWS 5	1975
IMEWS 6	1976
IMEWS 7	1977
IMEWS 8	1978
IMEWS 9	1979
IMEWS 10	1979
IMEWS 11	1981
IMEWS 12	1981
IMEWS 13	1982
Tactical comsat	1969
USA 7	1984
USA 11	1985
USA 12	1985
USA 20	1986
USA 28	1987
USA 48	1989

Research

IUE 1978 Ultra-violet Obs

TABLE OF ELEMENTS

Atomic weights are taken from the 1983 list of the International Union of Pure and Applied Chemistry.

For radioactive elements, the mass number of the most stable isotope is given in square brackets.

Elements for which there is an entry in the main part of the encyclopedia are preceded by ●. ≫ atomic weight.

Symbol	Element	Atomic No.	Weight
Ac	actinium	89	[227]
●Ag	silver	47	107.8682
●Al	aluminium	13	26.98154
Am	americium	95	[243]
●Ar	argon	18	39.948
●As	arsenic	33	74.9216
At	astatine	85	[210]
●Au	gold	79	196.9665
●B	boron	5	10.811
●Ba	barium	56	137.33
●Be	beryllium	4	9.01218
●Bi	bismuth	83	208.9804
Bk	berkelium	97	[247]
●Br	bromine	35	79.904
●C	carbon	6	12.011
●Ca	calcium	20	40.078
●Cd	cadmium	48	112.41
Ce	cerium	58	140.12
Cf	californium	98	[251]
●Cl	chlorine	17	35.453
Cm	curium	96	[249]
●Co	cobalt	27	58.9332
●Cr	chromium	24	51.9961
●Cs	cesium/ caesium	55	132.9054
●Cu	copper	29	63.546
Dy	dysprosium	66	162.50
Er	erbium	68	167.26
Es	einsteinium	99	[252]
Eu	europium	63	151.96
●F	fluorine	9	18.998403
●Fe	iron	26	55.847
Fm	fermium	100	[257]
Fr	francium	87	[223]
●Ga	gallium	31	69.723
Gd	gadolinium	64	157.25
●Ge	germanium	32	72.59
●H	hydrogen	1	1.00794
●He	helium	2	4.002602
Hf	hafnium	72	178.49
●Hg	mercury	80	200.59
Ho	holmium	67	164.9304
●I	iodine	53	126.9045
In	indium	49	114.82
Ir	iridium	77	192.22
●K	potassium	19	39.0983
●Kr	krypton	36	83.80
La	lanthanum	57	138.9055
●Li	lithium	3	6.941
Lu	lutetium	71	174.967
Lw	lawrencium	103	[260]
Md	mendelevium	101	[258]
●Mg	magnesium	12	24.305
●Mn	manganese	25	54.9380
●Mo	molybdenum	42	95.94
●N	nitrogen	7	14.0067
●Na	sodium	11	22.98977
Nb	niobium	41	92.9064
Nd	neodymium	60	144.24
●Ne	neon	10	20.179
●Ni	nickel	28	58.69
No	nobelium	102	[259]
Np	neptunium	93	[237]
●O	oxygen	8	15.9994
Os	osmium	76	190.2
●P	phosphorus	15	30.97376
Pa	protactinium	91	[231]
●Pb	lead	82	207.2
Pd	palladium	46	106.42
Pm	promethium	61	[145]
Po	polonium	84	[209
Pr	praseodymium	59	140.9077
●Pt	platinum	78	195.08
●Pu	plutonium	94	[244
●Ra	radium	88	[226
Rb	rubidium	37	85.4678
Re	rhenium	75	186.207
Rh	rhodium	45	102.9055
●Rn	radon	86	[222
Ru	ruthenium	44	101.07
●S	sulphur/sulfur	16	32.066
●Sb	antimony	51	121.75
Sc	scandium	21	44.95591
●Se	selenium	34	78.96
●Si	silicon	14	28.0855
Sm	samarium	62	150.36
●Sn	tin	50	118.710
●Sr	strontium	38	87.62
Ta	tantalum	73	180.9479
Tb	terbium	65	158.9254
Tc	technetium	43	[99]
Te	tellurium	52	127.60
Th	thorium	90	232.0381
●Ti	titanium	22	47.88
Tl	thallium	81	204.383
Tm	thulium	69	168.9342
●U	uranium	92	238.0289
Une	unnilennium	109	[266]
Unh	unnilhexium	106	[263]
Unp	unnilpentium	105	[262]
Unq	unnilquadium	104	[261]
Uns	unnilseptium	107	[262]
●V	vanadium	23	50.9415
●W	tungsten	74	183.85
●Xe	xenon	54	131.29
●Y	yttrium	39	88.9059
Yb	ytterbium	70	173.04
●Zn	zinc	30	65.39
Zr	zirconium	40	91.224

MATHEMATICAL SIGNS AND SYMBOLS

+	plus; positive; underestimate
−	minus; negative; overestimate
±	plus or minus; positive or negative; degree of accuracy
∓	minus or plus; negative or positive
×	multiplies (colloq. 'times') (6 × 4)
·	multiplies (colloq. 'times') (6.4); scalar product of two vectors (A·B)
÷	divided by (6 ÷ 4)
/	divided by; ratio of (6/4)
—	divided by; ratio of ($\frac{6}{4}$)
=	equals
≠, ≠	not equal to
≡	identical with
≢, ≢	not identical with
:	ratio of (6:4); scalar product of two tensors (Y:Z)
::	proportionately equals (1:2::2:4)
≈	approximately equal to; equivalent to; similar to
>	greater than
≫	much greater than
≯	not greater than
<	less than
≪	much less than
≮	not less than
⩾, ≧, ⋝	equal to or greater than
⩽, ≦, ⋜	equal to or less than
∝	directly proportional to
( )	parentheses
[ ]	brackets
{ }	braces
—	vinculum: division ($\overline{a-b}$); chord of circle or length of line ($\overline{AB}$); arithmetic mean ($\overline{X}$)
∞	infinity
→	approaches the limit
√	square root
∛, ∜	cube root, fourth root, etc.
!	factorial (4! = 4 × 3 × 2 × 1)
%	percent
′	prime; minute(s) of arc; foot/feet
″	double prime; second(s) of arc; inch(es)
⌒	arc of circle
°	degree of arc
∠, ∠s	angle(s)
≚	equiangular
⊥	perpendicular
∥	parallel
○, ⓢ	circle(s)
△, △s	triangle(s)
□	square
▭	rectangle
▱	parallelogram
≅	congruent to
∴	therefore
∵	because
≞	measured by
Δ	increment
∑	summation
∫	integral sign
∇	del: differential operator
∪	union
∩	interaction

MUSICAL SYMBOLS, TERMS AND ABBREVIATIONS

SYMBOLS

The staff or stave

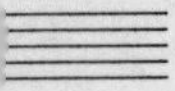

staff / stave; additional ('leger') lines are added above or below as required

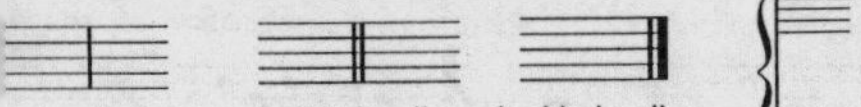

bar-line | double bar-line | double bar-line (conclusion) | brace, joining staves; read staves simultaneously

Clefs

These are in common use (the note Middle C is shown in each case):

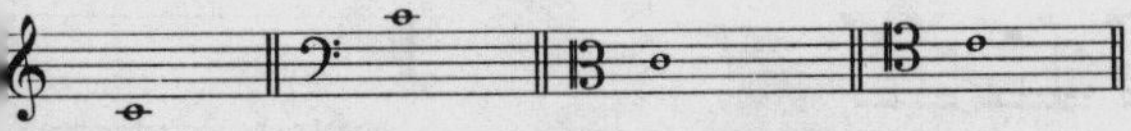

treble(G) clef | bass (F) clef | alto or viola (C) clef | tenor (C) clef

In older music the C clef is found on any of the five lines of the staff

Accidentals

- ♯ sharp, raising the pitch of a note by a semitone
- × double sharp, raising the pitch of a note by two semitones
- ♭ flat, lowering the pitch of a note by a semitone
- ♭♭ double flat, lowering the pitch of a note by two semitones
- ♮ natural, cancelling the effect of a previous accidental

Note lengths

- (or) breve (double whole note)
- semibreve (whole note)
- minim (half-note)
- crotchet (quarter-note)
- quaver (eighth-note)
- semiquaver (1/16 note)
- demisemiquaver (1/32 note)
- hemidemisemiquaver (1/64 note)

chord: two or more notes sounded simultaneously

Ties (⌒, ⌣) are used to combine the lengths of two or more notes of the same pitch; dots are used to extend the length of a note by one-half, eg:

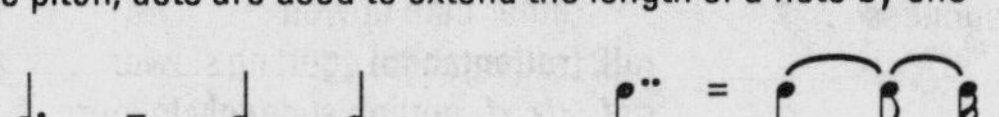

Beams are often used to group together quavers (eighth-notes) or shorter notes into larger units, eg:

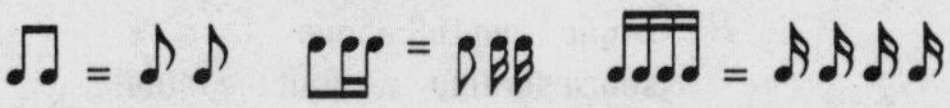

Time signatures

The lower figure indicates the unit of measurement, the upper figure the number of these units in a bar, eg:

- $\frac{2}{2}$ (or ₵) two minims (half-notes) or their equivalent in a bar
- $\frac{4}{4}$ (or C) four crotchets (quarter-notes) or their equivalent in a bar
- $\frac{3}{8}$ three quavers (eighth-notes) or their equivalent in a bar
- $\frac{9}{16}$ nine semiquavers (1/16-notes) or their equivalent in a bar

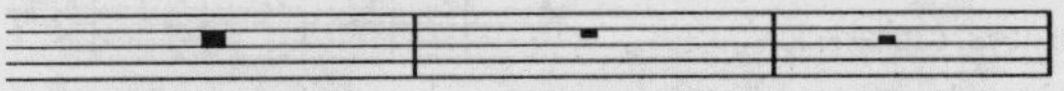

breve (double whole) | semibreve (whole), or whole bar | minim (half)

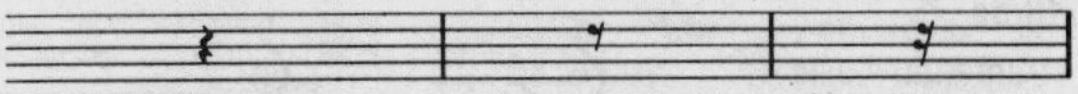

crotchet (quarter) | quaver (eighth) | semiquaver (1/16)

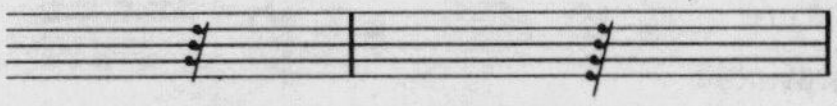

demisemiquaver (1/32) | hemidemisemiquaver (1/64)

A dot placed after a rest increases its length by one-half

Articulation and expression

staccato: the notes to be short and detached

staccatissimo: a more pronounced and accented staccato

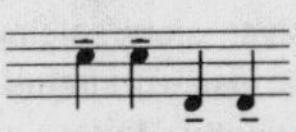

non legato: the notes to be detached but not staccato

slur: the notes to be played legato, or smoothly

pause, fermata: the note to be sounded beyond its written value at the discretion of the performer

accent: the note to be stressed

crescendo: becoming louder

decrescendo, diminuendo: becoming quieter

♩ = 84 placed at the beginning of a piece or section, an indication of the tempo (eg 84 crotchet beats per minute); often preceded by 'M.M.' (Metronom Maelzel)

Ornaments

arpeggio: the notes of a chord sounded in rapid succession, usually beginning with the lowest

acciaccatura, grace note: sounded lightly and rapidly in advance of the main note

appoggiatura: ornamental note, stressed and usually taking at least half the value of the main note

mordent ('lower' mordent): sounding approximately 

pralltriller, inverted (or 'upper') mordent: sounding approximately 

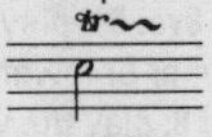

trill, shake: the rapid and continuous alternation of the written note and the note immediately above it

turn: sounding (depending on tempo and context) approximately  or  or 

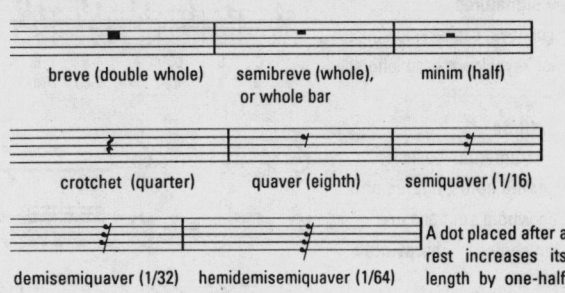

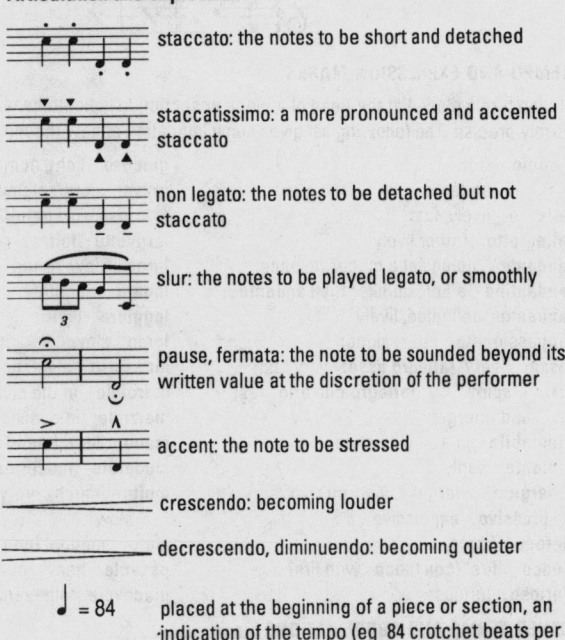

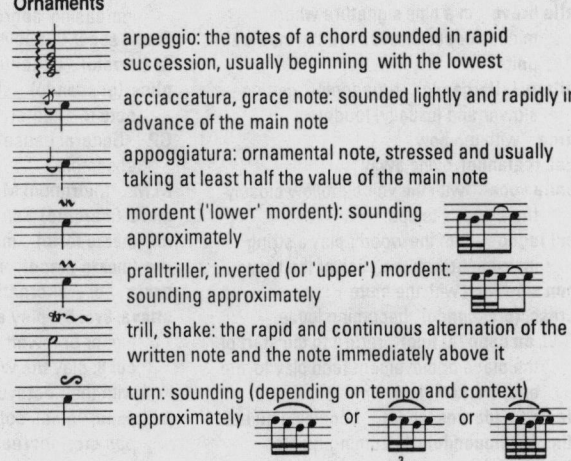

MUSICAL SYMBOLS, TERMS AND ABBREVIATIONS (cont.)

Key signatures
(Major keys: capital letters; minor keys; lower-case letters)

Repetition
In instrumental music repeated notes, figures and even whole sections are often shown in abbreviated form, eg:

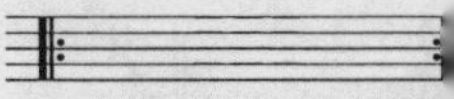

repeat signs, indicating that the passage between them is to be performed twice

TEMPO AND EXPRESSION MARKS

Italian terms placed at the head of a piece or section to indicate its tempo and general expression have changed in meaning over the years and are rarely precise. The following list gives some indication of how the more common terms are generally understood today.

adagio slow
agitato agitated
allegro lively, fast
allegretto rather lively
andante 'going'; at a moderate pace
andantino a little quicker than **andante**
animate animated, lively
appassionato impassioned
assai 'very' (**allegro assai** very fast)
brio 'spirit', 'fire' (**allegro con brio** fast and energetic)
cantabile in a singing style
dolente sadly
energico energetic, vigorous
espressivo expressive
feroce fierce
fuoco 'fire' (**con fuoco** with fire)
furioso furious
giocoso light, humorous
grave slow, solemn
grazioso graceful
larghetto fairly slow
largo slow, broad
legato smoothly
leggiero light
lento slow
maestoso majestic
marciale in the style of a march
marziale in a military style
meno 'less' (**meno mosso** slower)
moderato moderate, at a moderate pace
molto 'much', 'very' (**molto lento** very slow)
moto 'motion' (**con moto** quickly)
pesante heavy, ponderous
piacevole pleasant, agreeable
piu 'more' (**piu mosso** faster)
poco 'little' (**poco adagio** rather slowly)
presto very fast
prestissimo faster than **presto**
quasi 'as if', 'almost' (eg **andante, quasi allegretto**)
risoluto resolute, in a determined manner
scherzando in a jocular style
semplice simple, in an unforced style
sotto voce extremely quiet
strepitoso loud, noisy, boisterous
tanto, troppo 'so much', 'too much' (**allegro non tanto** fast, but not very fast; **lento ma non troppo** slow, but not becoming too slow)
veloce rapid
vivace lively, very fast
vivo vigorous, brisk

OTHER TERMS AND ABBREVIATIONS

This section lists only those symbols and terms that might be found in a musical score. For other musical terms, see the entries in the alphabetical section.

a tempo in time (ie reverting to the original speed)
accel., accelerando getting gradually faster
alla breve in a time signature where minims or semibreves are the metrical units
allarg. (allargando) broadening, getting slower and (usually) louder
arco with the bow
cal. (calando) dying away
colla voce 'with the voice'; follow closely the singer's tempo
col legno 'with the wood'; play a string instrument with the stick of the bow
con sordino with the mute
cresc. (crescendo) becoming louder
D.C., da capo (al fine) return to the start of the piece or movement (and play to the end, marked **Fine**)
decresc. (decrescendo) becoming quieter
dim. (diminuendo) becoming quieter
dol. (dolce) sweetly
D.S. dal segno return to and repeat from the sign (usually 𝄋)
f* (forte)** loud; ***ff* (fortissimo), *fff etc: increasing degrees of loudness
Fine see **D.C.** above
***fz* (forzato)** accented
gliss. (glissando) slide quickly from one note to another
GP 'General pause'; a rest for the whole ensemble
M.M. Metronom Maelzel
marc. (marcato) stressed, accented
***mf* (mezzo forte)** moderately loud
***mp* (mezzo piano)** moderately quiet
ossia 'or', 'alternatively'
ottava, 8va, 8 play a passage an octave higher or lower; **coll `ottava, col 8va, col 8:** play the written notes together with their octaves
p* (piano)** quiet, soft; ***pp* (pianissimo), *ppp etc: increasing (but imprecise) degrees of softness
ped. depress the sustaining ('loud') pedal on a piano; release indicated by *
pizz. (pizzicato) 'plucked ' with the finger, rather than bowed
rall. (rallentando) getting slower
rinf., *rfz, rf* getting suddenly louder
rit. ritard. (ritardando) getting slower
rubato with a freedom of tempo, but not impairing the overall flow of the music
segno see **D.S** above
senza sordino without the mute
***sf, sfz* (sforzando, sforzato)** strongly accented
simile play in the same manner as before
smorz. (smorzando) fading away
sost. (sostenuto) sustained
stacc. (staccato) short and detached
string. (stringendo) getting much faster
ten. (tenuto) linger slightly on the note
tre corde see **una corda** below
una corda depress the 'soft' pedal on the piano; release indicated by **tre corde**
V.S. (volti subito) turn the page quickly

RELIGIOUS SYMBOLS

The Trinity

Equilateral triangle · Triangle in circle · Circle within triangle · Trefoil · Triquetra · Triquetra and circle · Interwoven circles

God the Father

All-seeing eye · Hand of God · Hand of God · Lamb of God · Fish · Dove descending · Sevenfold flame

Old Testament

Seven branch candlestick The Menorah · Abraham · The Ten Commandments · Pentateuch (The Law) · Doorposts and lintel (Passover) · Twelve tribes of Israel · Star of David

Crosses

Aiguisée · Avellane · Barbée · Trefly · Canterbury · Celtic · Cercelée · Cross crosslet

Crux ansata · Entrailed · Fleurée · Globical · Graded (Calvary) · Greek · Iona · Jerusalem

Latin · Maltese · Millvine · Papal · Patée · Patée formée · Patonce · Patriarchal (or Lorraine) · Pommel or Pommée

Potent · Raguly or Ragulée · Russian Orthodox · St Andrew's (Saltire) · St Peter's · Tau (St Anthony's)

Monograms

IHC (Latin form) (from Gk IHCOYC 'Jesus') · Chi Rho (from Gk XPICTOC 'Christ')

The Church Year

Advent · Christmas · Epiphany · Lent · Maundy Thursday · Good Friday · Easter Day · Ascension · Pentecost

Other symbols

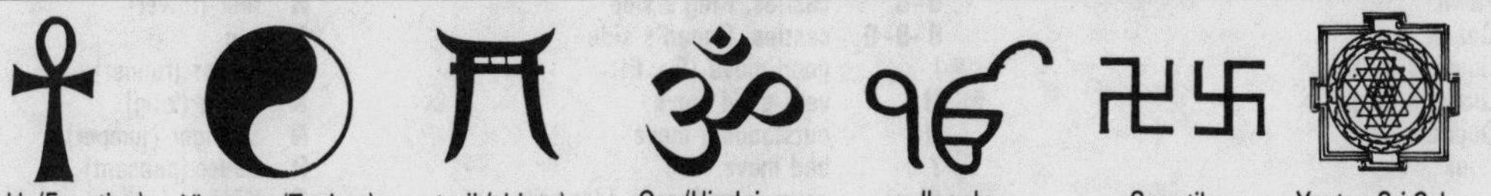

Ankh (Egyptian) · Yin-yang (Taoism) symbol of harmony · torii (shinto) · Om (Hinduism, Buddhism, Jainism; sacred syllable) · Ik-onkar (Sikhism; symbol of God) · Swastika · Yantra: Sri Cakra (wheel of fortune)

SYMBOLS IN GENERAL USE

&,	ampersand (*and*)
&c.	et cetera
@	at; per (in costs)
×	by (measuring dimensions (3 × 4)
£	pound
$	dollar (also peso, escudo, etc. in certain countries)
¢	cent (also centavo, etc. in certain countries)
©	copyright
®	registered
¶	new paragraph
§	new section
″	ditto
*	born (in genealogy)
†	died
*	hypothetical or unacceptable form (in linguistics)
☠	poison; danger
♂, □	male
♀, ○	female
✠	bishop's name follows
☎	telephone number follows
☜☞	this way
✂, ✂····	cut here

In astronomy

●	new moon
☽	moon, first quarter
○	full moon
☾	moon, last quarter

In meteorology

- cold front (in meteorology)
- warm front
- stationary front
- occluded front

In cards

♥	hearts
♦	diamonds
♠	spades
♣	clubs

CLOTHES CARE

- Do not iron
- Can be ironed with *cool* iron (up to 110°C)
- Can be ironed with *warm* iron (up to 150°C)
- Can be ironed with *hot* iron (up to 200°C)
- Hand wash only
- 60 — Can be washed in a washing machine. The number shows the most effective washing temperature (in °C)
- 60 — Reduced (medium) washing conditions
- 60 — Much reduced (minimum) washing conditions (for wool products)
- Do not wash
- Can be tumble dried (one dot within the circle means a low temperature setting; two dots for higher temperatures)
- Do not tumble dry
- Do not dry clean
- Ⓐ Dry cleanable (letter indicates which solvents can be used) A: all solvents
- Ⓕ Dry cleanable F: white spirit and solvent 11 can be used
- Ⓟ Dry cleanable P: perchloroethylene (tetrachloroethylene), white spirit, solvent 113 and solvent 11 can be used
- Ⓟ Dry cleanable, if special care taken
- Cl Chlorine bleach may be used with care
- Do not use chlorine bleach

CHESS NOTATION

QR QN QB Q K KB KN KR

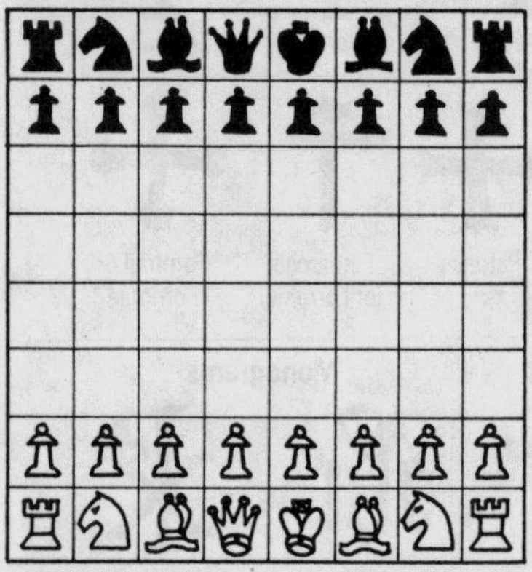

QR QN QB Q K KB KN KR

The opening position

Black

QR1 QR8	**QN1** QN8	**QB1** QB8	**Q1** Q8	**K1** K8	**KB1** KB8	**KN1** KN8	**KR1** KR8
QR2 QR7	**QN2** QN7	**QB2** QB7	**Q2** Q7	**K2** K7	**KB2** KB7	**KN2** KN7	**KR2** KR7
QR3 QR6	**QN3** QN6	**QB3** QB6	**Q3** Q6	**K3** K6	**KB3** KB6	**KN3** KN6	**KR3** KR6
QR4 QR5	**QN4** QN5	**QB4** QB5	**Q4** Q5	**K4** K5	**KB4** KB5	**KN4** KN5	**KR4** KR5
QR5 QR4	**QN5** QN4	**QB5** QB4	**Q5** Q4	**K5** K4	**KB5** KB4	**KN5** KN4	**KN5** KR4
QR6 QR3	**QN6** QN3	**QB6** QB3	**Q6** Q3	**K6** K3	**KB6** KB3	**KN6** KN3	**KR6** KR3
QR7 QR2	**QN7** QN2	**QB7** QB2	**Q7** Q2	**K7** K2	**KB7** KB2	**KN7** KN2	**KR7** KR2
QR8 QR1	**QN8** QN1	**QB8** QB1	**Q8** Q1	**K8** K1	**KB8** KB1	**KN8** KN1	**KR8** KR1

White

Descriptive notation
Each file is named by the piece on the first rank; ranks are numbered 1–8 away from the player.

Black

a8	b8	c8	d8	e8	f8	g8	h8
a7	b7	c7	d7	e7	f7	g7	h7
a6	b6	c6	d6	e6	f6	g6	h6
a5	b5	c5	d5	e5	f5	g5	h5
a4	b4	c4	d4	e4	f4	g4	h4
a3	b3	c3	d3	e3	f3	g3	h3
a2	b2	c2	d2	e2	f2	g2	h2
a1	b1	c1	d1	e1	f1	g1	h1

White

Algebraic notation
Each square is named by a combination of file letter and rank number.

Abbreviations

B	Bishop
K	King
KB	King's bishop
KN	King's knight
KR	King's rook
N	Knight
P	Pawn
Q	Queen
QB	Queen's bishop
QN	Queen's knight
QR	Queen's rook
R	Rook

x	captures (Q × P = Queen takes Pawn)
—	moves to (Q—KB4)
ch	check (R—QB3 ch)
dis ch	discovered check
dbl ch	double check
e.p.	en passant
mate	checkmate
0–0	castles, King's side
0–0–0	castles, Queen's side
!	good move (P × R!)
!!	very good move
!!!	outstanding move
?	bad move
!?	good or bad move (depends on response of the other player)

Chess pieces in other languages

French

B	fou (fool)
K	roi (king)
N	cavalier (horseman)
P	pion (pawn)
Q	dame, reine (lady), queen)
R	tour (tower)

German

B	Läufer (runner)
K	König (king)
N	Springer (jumper)
P	Bauer (peasant)
Q	Königin (queen)
R	Turm (tower)

LIBRARY CLASSIFICATION

The Dewey decimal system

The initial subdivisions of the ten major areas of the Dewey system are shown below. Fiction and biography are excluded from the classification.

000	**Generalities**
010	Bibliographies and catalogues
020	Library science
030	General encyclopedic works
040	(Unassigned)
050	General periodicals
060	General organizations
070	Newspapers and journalism
080	General collections
090	Manuscripts and book rarities
100	**Philosophy and related**
110	Ontology and methodology
120	Knowledge, cause, purpose, man
130	Pseudo- and parapsychology
140	Specific philosophic viewpoints
150	Psychology
160	Logic
170	Ethics (moral philosophy)
180	Ancient, medieval, Oriental philosophies
190	Modern Western philosophy
200	**Religion**
210	Natural religion
220	Bible
230	Christian doctrinal theology
240	Christian moral and devotional theology
250	Christian pastoral, parochial, etc.
260	Christian social and ecclesiastical theology
270	History and geography of Christian Church
280	Christian denominations and sects
290	Other religions and comparative religion
300	**The social sciences**
310	Statistical method and statistics
320	Political science
330	Economics
340	Law
350	Public administration
360	Welfare and association
370	Education
380	Commerce
390	Customs and folklore
400	**Language**
410	Linguistics and non-verbal language
420	English and Anglo-Saxon
430	Germanic languages
440	French, Provençal, Catalan
450	Italian, Romanian, etc.
460	Spanish and Portuguese
470	Italic languages
480	Classical and Greek
490	Other languages
500	**Pure sciences**
510	Mathematics
520	Astronomy and allied sciences
530	Physics
540	Chemistry and allied sciences
550	Earth sciences
560	Paleontology
570	Anthropological and biological sciences
580	Botanical sciences
590	Zoological sciences
600	**Technology (applied science)**
610	Medical sciences
620	Engineering and allied operations
630	Agriculture and agricultural industries
640	Domestic arts and sciences
650	Business and related enterprises
660	Chemical technology, etc.
670	Manufactures
680	Assembled and final products
690	Buildings
700	**The arts**
710	Civic and landscape art
720	Architecture
730	Sculpture and the plastic arts
740	Drawing and decorative arts
750	Painting and paintings
760	Graphic arts
770	Photography and photographs
780	Music
790	Recreation (recreational arts)
800	**Literature and rhetoric**
810	American literature in English
820	English and Anglo-Saxon literature
830	Germanic languages literature
840	French, Provençal, Catalan literature
850	Italian and Romanian literature
860	Spanish and Portuguese literature
870	Italic languages literature
880	Classical and Greek literature
890	Literature of other languages
900	**General geography and history, etc.**
910	General geography
920	General biography and genealogy
930	General history of ancient world
940	General history of modern Europe
950	General history of modern Asia
960	General history of modern Africa
970	General history of North America
980	General history of South America
990	General history of rest of world

The Library of Congress System

A	**General Works**
AE	Encyclopedias
AG	General reference books
AI	Indexes
AM	Museums
AN	Newspapers
AP	Periodicals
AS	Societies
AY	Yearbooks, annuals
AZ	Scholarship and learning
B	**Philosophy and Religion**
BC	Logic
BD	Metaphysics
BF	Psychology
BH	Aesthetics
BJ	Ethics
BL	Religion
BM	Judaism
BP	Oriental religions
BR	Christianity
BS	Bible
BT	Christian doctrine
BV	Practical Christianity
BX	Collections and sermons
C	**Historical Sciences**
CB	History of civilisation
CC	Archaeology
CD	Archives, diplomatics
CE	Chronology
CJ	Numismatics
CR	Heraldry
CS	Genealogy
CT	Biography, collections
D-F	**History and Topography**
D	World history, The World Wars
DA	Great Britain, excepting Scotland
DB	Austria-Hungary
DC	France
DD	Germany
DE	Classical antiquity
DF	Greece
DG	Italy
DH	Belgium
DJ	Holland
DK	Russia
DL	Scandinavia
DP	Spain and Portugal
DQ	Switzerland
DR	Turkey, Balkans
DS	Asia
DT	Africa
DU	Australia, Oceania
DX	Gypsies
E-F	America, Canada
G	**Geography, Anthropology**
GA	Mathematical geography
GB	Physical geography
GC	Oceanography
GF	Anthropogeography
GN	Anthropology
GR	Folklore
GT	Manners and customs
GV	Sports and pastimes
H	**Social Sciences, Economics**
HA	Statistics
HB	Economics
HC	Economic history and conditions
HD	Economic history, land industry and labour
HE	Transport, communication
HF	Commerce
HG	Finance
HJ	Finance, public
HM	Sociology
HN	Social history
HQ	Family, marriage, woman
HS	Associations
HT	Communities, classes
HV	Social pathology
HX	Socialism, communism
J	**Political Science**
JA	General works
JC	The State
JF	Constitutional history and description
JK-JL	American
JN	European
JQ	Asian, African, Australian
JS	Local government
JV	Colonization
JX	International law
K	**Law**
L	**Education**
LA	History of education
LB	Theory and practice
LC	Special forms
LD-LJ	Universities and colleges
M	**Music**
MA	Musical scores
ML	Literature of music
MT	Musical instruction
N	**Fine Arts**
NA	Architecture
NB	Sculpture
NC	Graphic arts
ND	Painting
NE	Engraving
NK	Decoration and ornament
O	**Prose Fiction**, alphabetically arranged by names of authors
P	**Language and Literature**
PA	Greek and Latin
PB	Celtic and Gaelic
PC	Romance languages
PD-PF	Teutonic languages
PG	Slavic languages and literatures
PH	Finno-Ugrian languages and literatures
PJ-PL	Oriental languages and literatures
PM	Hyperborean, Indian, and artificial languages and literatures
PN	General literature
PQ	French, Italian, Spanish literature
PR	English literature
PS	American literature
PT	German, Scandinavian literatures
Q	**Science**
QA	Mathematics
QB	Astronomy
QC	Physics
QD	Chemistry *See also* TP, Chemical Technology
QE	Geology
QH	Natural history
QK	Botany *See also* S, Agriculture
QL	Zoology *See also* SF, Farm animals
QM	Human anatomy
QP	Physiology
QR	Bacteriology
R	**Medicine**
RA	Public health
RB	Pathology
RC	Practice of medicine
RC	Surgery
RE	Ophthalmology
RF	Otology, rhinology, laryngology
RG	Gynecology
RJ	Pediatrics
RK	Dentistry
RL	Dermatology
RM	Therapeutics
RS	Materia medica
RT	Nursing
RX	Homeopathy
S	**Agriculture**
SB	Field crops, horticulture *See also* QK, Botany
SD	Forestry
SF	Farm animals, veterinary medicine
SH	Fish and angling
SK	Hunting sports
T	**Technology**
TA	General and civil engineering
TC	Hydraulic engineering
TD	Municipal and sanitary engineering
	Transport engineering
TE	Roads
TF	Railways
TG	Bridges, roofs
TH	Building construction
TJ	Mechanical engineering
TK	Electrical engineering *See also* QC, Physics
TL	Automobile engineering
TN	Mineral industries
TP	Chemical technology *See also* QD, Chemistry
TR	Photography
TS	Manufactures
TT	Trades
TX	Domestic science
U	**Military Science**
V	**Naval Science**
Z	**Bibliography**

NAMES AND TITLES

FIRST NAME PREFERENCES

Boys, England and Wales

	1920s		1950s		1960s		1970s		1980s
1	John	1	David	1	Paul	1	Stephen	1	Andrew
2	William	2	John	2	David	2	Mark	2	David
3	George	3	Peter	3	Andrew	3	Paul	3	Daniel
4	James	4	Michael	4	Stephen	4	Andrew	4	Christopher
5	Ronald	5	Alan	5	Mark	5	David	5	Stephen
6	Robert	6	Robert	6	Michael	6	Richard	6	Matthew
7	Kenneth	7	Stephen	7	Ian	7	Matthew	7	Paul
8	Frederick	8	Paul	8	Gary	8	Daniel	8	James
9	Thomas	9	Brian	9	Robert	9	Christopher	9	Mark
10	Albert	10	Graham	10	Richard	10	Darren	10	Michael
11	Eric	11	Philip	11	Peter	11	Michael	11	Adam
12	Edward	12	Anthony	12	John	12	James	12	Richard
13	Arthur	13	Colin	13	Anthony	13	Robert	13	Darren
14	Charles	14	Christopher	14	Christopher	14	Simon	14	Robert
15	Leslie	15	Geoffrey	15	Darren	15	Jason	15	Lee

Girls, England and Wales

	1920s		1950s		1960s		1970s		1980s
1	Joan	1	Susan	1	Trac(e)y	1	Claire	1	Sarah
2	Mary	2	Linda	2	Deborah	2	Sarah	2	Emma
3	Joyce	3	Christine	3	Julie	3	Nicola	3	Claire
4	Margaret	4	Margaret	4	Karen	4	Emma	4	Kelly
5	Dorothy	5	Carol	5	Susan	5	Joanne	5	Rebecca
6	Doris	6	Jennifer	6	Alison	6	Helen	6	Gemma
7	Kathleen	7	Janet	7	Jacqueline	7	Rachel	7	Rachel
8	Irene	8	Patricia	8	Helen	8	Lisa	8	Lisa
9	Betty	9	Barbara	9	Amanda	9	Rebecca		Victoria
10	Eileen	10	Ann	10	Sharon	10	Karen	10	Laura
11	Doreen	11	Sandra	11	Sarah		Michelle	11	Catherine
12	Lilian	12	Pamela	12	Joanne	12	Victoria	12	Nicola
	Vera		Pauline	13	Jane	13	Catherine	13	Michelle
14	Jean	14	Jean	14	Catherine	14	Amanda	14	Joanne
15	Marjorie	15	Jacqueline	15	Angela	15	Trac(e)y	15	Lindsay

Boys, USA

	1920s		1950s		1970s		1980s (*white*)		1980s (*non-white*)
1	Robert	1	Robert	1	Michael	1	Michael	1	Michael
2	John	2	Michael	2	Robert	2	Christopher	2	Christopher
3	William	3	James	3	David	3	Matthew	3	James
4	James	4	John	4	James	4	David	4	Jason
5	Charles	5	David	5	John	5	Jason	5	Robert
6	Richard	6	William	6	Jeffrey	6	Daniel	6	Anthony
7	George	7	Thomas	7	Steven	7	Robert	7	Brandon
8	Donald	8	Richard	8	Christopher	8	Eric	8	Kevin
9	Joseph	9	Gary	9	Brian	9	Brian	9	David
10	Edward	10	Charles	10	Mark	10	Joseph	10	Charles
11	Thomas	11	Ronald	11	William	11	Ryan	11	Aaron
12	David	12	Dennis	12	Eric	12	James		Brian
13	Frank	13	Steven	13	Kevin	13	Steven		Eric
14	Harold	14	Kenneth	14	Scott	14	John	14	John
15	Arthur	15	Joseph	15	Joseph	15	Jeffrey	15	Darryl

Girls, USA

	1920s		1950s		1970s		1980s (*white*)		1980s (*non-white*)
1	Mary	1	Linda	1	Michelle	1	Jennifer	1	Tiffany
2	Barbara	2	Mary	2	Jennifer	2	Sarah	2	Crystal
3	Dorothy	3	Patricia	3	Kimberly	3	Nicole	3	Ebony
4	Betty	4	Susan	4	Lisa	4	Jessica	4	Erica
5	Ruth	5	Deborah	5	Tracy	5	Katherine	5	Lakisha
6	Margaret	6	Kathleen	6	Kelly	6	Stephanie	6	Latoya
7	Helen	7	Barbara	7	Nicole	7	Elizabeth	7	Nicole
8	Elizabeth	8	Nancy	8	Angela	8	Amanda	8	Candice
9	Jean	9	Sharon	9	Pamela	9	Melissa	9	Danielle
10	Ann(e)	10	Karen	10	Christine	10	Lindsay	10	Brandi
11	Patricia	11	Carol(e)	11	Dawn	11	Rebecca	11	Jennifer
12	Shirley	12	Sandra	12	Amy	12	Lisa	12	Angela
13	Virginia	13	Diane	13	Deborah	13	Rachel	13	April
14	Nancy	14	Catherine	14	Karen	14	Lauren	14	Kimberly
15	Joan	15	Christine	15	Julie	15	Andrea	15	Stephanie

FIRST NAME MEANINGS

ne meanings of the most popular first names listed on the facing page are given below, along with a few other well-known names.

ame Original meaning

aron high mountain (*Hebrew*)
dam redness (*Hebrew*)
lan ?rock, noble (*Celtic*)
lbert noble bright (*Germanic*)
lexander defender of men (*Greek*)
lison *French diminutive of* Alice; of noble kind
manda fit to be loved (*Latin*)
my loved (*French*)
ndrea *female form of* Andrew
ndrew manly (*Greek*)
ngela messenger, angel (*Greek*)
nn(e) *English form of* Hannah
nthony *Roman family name*
pril name of the month
rthur ?bear, stone (*Celtic*)
arbara strange, foreign (*Greek*)
arry spear, javelin (*Celtic*)
eatrice bringer of joy (*Latin*)
enjamin son of my right hand (*Hebrew*)
ernard bear + brave (*Germanic*)
eth *pet form of* Elizabeth
etty *pet form of* Elizabeth
ill/Billy *pet form of* William
ob *pet form of* Robert
randi *variant of* Brandy, *from the common noun*
randon *place name*; broom-covered hill (*Germanic*)
rian ?hill (?*Celtic*)
andice *meaning unknown*
arl man, husbandman (*Germanic*)
arol(e) *forms of* Caroline, *Italian female form of* Charles
atherine ?pure (*Greek*)
harles man, husbandman (*Germanic*)
hristine *French form of* Christina *ultimately from* Christian; anointed
hristopher carrier of Christ (*Greek*)
laire bright, shining (*Latin*)
olin *form of* Nicholas
raig rock (*Celtic*)
rystal *female use of the common noun*
aniel God is my judge (*Hebrew*)
anielle *female form of* Daniel
arren *Irish surname*
arryl *surname; uncertain origin*
avid ?beloved, friend (*Hebrew*)
awn *female use of the common noun*
ean *surname*; valley *or* leader
eborah bee (*Hebrew*)
ennis of Dionysus (*Greek*), *the god of wine*
erek *form of* Theodoric; ruler of the people (*Germanic*)
Diane *French form of* Diana; divine (*Latin*)
Donald world mighty (*Gaelic*)
Donna lady (*Latin*)
Doreen *from* Dora, *a short form of* Dorothy; gift of God
Doris woman from Doris (*Greek*)
Dorothy gift of God (*Greek*)
Ebony *female use of the common noun*
Edward property guardian (*Germanic*)
Eileen *Irish form of* ?Helen
Elizabeth oath/perfection of God (*Hebrew*)

Name Original meaning

Emily *Roman family name*
Emma all-embracing (*Germanic*)
Eric ruler of all (*Norse*)
Erica *female form of* Eric
Eugenie *French form of* Eugene; well-born (*Greek*)
Frank *pet form of* Francis; Frenchman
Frederick peaceful ruler (*Germanic*)
Gail *pet form of* Abigail; father rejoices (*Hebrew*)
Gareth gentle (*Welsh*)
Gary *US place name*
Gavin *Scottish form of* Gawain; hawk + white (*Welsh*)
Gemma gem (*Italian*)
Geoffrey ?peace (*Germanic*)
George husbandman, farmer (*Greek*)
Graham *Germanic place name*
Hannah grace, favour (*Hebrew*)
Harold army power/ruler (*Germanic*)
Harry *pet form of* Henry; home ruler (*Germanic*)
Hayley *English place name*; hay-meadow
Heather *plant name*
Helen bright/shining one (*Greek*)
Ian *modern Scottish form of* John
Irene peace (*Greek*)
Jacqueline *French female form of* Jacques (James)
James *Latin form of* Jacob; one who takes by the heel (*Hebrew*)
Jane *from Latin* Johanna, *female form of* John
Janet *diminutive form of* Jane
Jason *form of* Joshua; Jehovah is salvation (*Hebrew*)
Jeffrey *US spelling of* Geoffrey
Jean *French form of* Johanna, *from* John
Jennifer fair/white + yielding/smooth (*Celtic*)
Jeremy *English form of* Jeremiah; Jehova exalts (*Hebrew*)
Jessica he beholds (*Hebrew*)
Joan *contracted form of* Johanna, *from* John
Joanne *French form of* Johanna, *from* John
John Jehovah has been gracious (*Hebrew*)
Jonathan Jehovah's gift (*Hebrew*)
Joseph Jehovah adds (*Hebrew*)
Joyce ?joyful (?*Latin*)
Julie *French female form of Latin* Julius; descended from Jove
Karen *Danish form of* Katarina (Catherine)
Katherine *US spelling of* Catherine
Kathleen *English form of Irish* Caitlin (*from* Catharine)
Kelly *Irish surname*; warlike one
Kenneth *English form of Gaelic*; fair one *or* fire-sprung
Kerry *Irish place name*
Kevin handsome at birth (*Irish*)
Kimberly *South African place name*
Lakisha La + ?Aisha; woman (*Arabic*)
Latoya La + *form of* Tonya (Antonia)
Laura bay, laurel (*Latin*)
Lauren *diminutive of* Laura
Lee *Germanic place name*; wood, clearing
Leslie *Scottish place name*

Name Original meaning

Lilian lily (*Italian*)
Linda serpent (symbol of wisdom) (*Germanic*)
Lindsay *Scottish place name*
Lisa *pet form of* Elizabeth
Margaret pearl (*Greek*)
Marjorie *from* Marguerite, *French form of* Margaret
Mark *English form of* Marcus, *from* Mars, *god of war*
Martin *from* Mars, *god of war* (*Latin*)
Mary *Greek form of* Miriam (*Hebrew*); *unknown meaning*
Matthew gift of the Lord (*Hebrew*)
Melissa bee (*Greek*)
Michael like the Lord (*Hebrew*)
Michelle *English spelling of French* Michèle, *from* Michael
Nancy *pet form of* Ann
Natalie birthday of the Lord (*Latin*)
Neil champion (*Irish*)
Nicholas victory people (*Greek*)
Nicola *Italian female form of* Nicholas
Nicole *French female form of* Nicholas
Pamela ?all honey (*Greek*)
Patricia noble (*Latin*)
Paul small (*Latin*)
Pauline *French female form of* Paul
Peter stone, rock (*Greek*)
Philip fond of horses (*Greek*)
Rachel ewe (*Hebrew*)
Rebecca ?noose (*Hebrew*)
Richard strong ruler (*Germanic*)
Robert fame bright (*Germanic*)
Ronald counsel + power (*Germanic*)
Ruth ?companion (*Hebrew*)
Ryan *Irish surname*
Sally *pet form of* Sarah
Samantha *female form of* Samuel; heard/name of God (*Hebrew*)
Sandra *pet form from* Alexandra
Sarah princess (*Hebrew*)
Scott *surname*; from Scotland
Sharon the plain (*Hebrew*)
Shaun *English spelling of Irish* Sean, *from* John
Shirley bright clearing (*Germanic*)
Simon *form of* Simeon; listening attentively (*Hebrew*)
Stephanie *French female form of* Stephen
Stephen crown (*Greek*)
Stuart steward (*Germanic*)
Susan *short form of* Susannah; lily (*Hebrew*)
Teresa woman of Theresia (*Greek*)
Thomas twin (*Hebrew*)
Tiffany manifestation of God (*Greek*)
Timothy honouring God (*Greek*)
Trac(e)y *?pet form of* Teresa
Vera faith (*Slavic*)
Victoria victory (*Latin*)
Vincent conquer (*Latin*)
Virginia maiden (*Latin*)
Walter ruling people (*Germanic*)
Wayne *surname*; wagon-maker
William will + helmet (*Germanic*)
Zoë life (*Greek*)

FORMS OF ADDRESS

In the formulae given below, *F* stands for forename and *S* for surname.

- ☐ Very formal ceremonial styles for closing letters are now seldom used: 'Yours faithfully' is assumed below, unless otherwise indicated.
- ☐ Forms of spoken address are given only where a special style is followed.
- ☐ Holders of courtesy titles are addressed according to their rank, but without 'The', 'The Right Hon.' or 'The Most Hon.'.
- ☐ Ranks in the armed forces, and ecclesiastical and ambassadorial ranks, precede titles in the peerage, eg 'Colonel the Earl of ——' or 'The Rev the Marquess of ——'.
- ☐ Although the correct forms of address are given below for members of the Royal Family, it is more normal practice for letters to be addressed to their private secretary, equerry, or lady-in-waiting.
- ☐ More detailed information about forms of address is to be found in Debrett's *Correct Form* and Black's *Titles and Forms of Address*.

Ambassadors (foreign)
Address on envelope: 'His/Her Excellency the Ambassador of ——' or 'His/Her Excellency the —— Ambassador'. (The wife of an ambassador is not entitled to the style 'Her Excellency'.) *Begin:* 'Your Excellency'. (Within the letter, refer to 'Your Excellency' once, thereafter as 'you'.) *Close:* 'I have the honour to be, Sir/Madam (or according to rank), Your Excellency's obedient servant'. *Spoken address:* 'Your Excellency' at least once, and then 'Sir' or 'Madam' by name.

Archbishop (Anglican communion)
Address on envelope: 'The Most Reverend the Lord Archbishop of ——'. (The Archbishops of Canterbury and York are Privy Counsellors, and should be addressed as 'The Most Reverend and Right Hon. the Lord Archbishop of ——'.) *Begin:* 'Dear Archbishop' or 'My Lord Archbishop'. *Spoken address:* 'Your Grace'. *Begin an official speech:* 'My Lord Archbishop'.

Archbishop (Roman Catholic)
Address on envelope: 'His Grace the Archbishop of ——'. *Begin:* 'My Lord Archbishop'. *Close:* 'I remain, Your Grace, Yours faithfully' or 'Yours faithfully'. *Spoken address:* 'Your Grace'.

Archdeacon
Address on envelope: 'The Venerable the Archdeacon of ——'. *Begin:* 'Dear Archdeacon' or 'Venerable Sir'. *Spoken address:* 'Archdeacon'. *Begin an official speech:* 'Venerable Sir'.

Baron
Address on envelope: 'The Right Hon. the Lord ——'. *Begin:* 'My Lord'. *Spoken address:* 'My Lord'.

Baron's wife (Baroness)
Address on envelope: 'The Right Hon. the Lady [S——]'. *Begin:* 'Dear Madam'. *Spoken address:* 'Madam'.

Baroness (in her own right)
Address on envelope: either as for Baron's wife, or 'The Right Hon. the Baroness [S——]'. Otherwise, as for Baron's wife.

Baronet
Address on envelope: 'Sir [F—— S——], Bt'. *Begin:* 'Dear Sir'. *Spoken address:* 'Sir [F——]'.

Baronet's wife
Address on envelope: 'Lady [S——]'. If she has the title 'Lady' by courtesy, 'Lady [F—— S——]'. If she has the courtesy style 'The Hon.', this precedes 'Lady'. *Begin:* 'Dear Madam'. *Spoken address:* 'Madam'.

Bishop (Anglican communion)
Address on envelope: 'The Right Reverend the Lord Bishop of ——'. (The Bishop of London is a Privy Counsellor, so is addressed as 'The Right Rev and Right Hon. the Lord Bishop of London'. The Bishop of Meath is styled 'The Most Reverend'.) *Begin:* 'Dear Bishop' or 'My Lord'. *Spoken address:* 'Bishop'. *Begin an official speech:* 'My Lord'.

Bishop (Episcopal Church in Scotland)
Address on envelope: 'The Right Reverend [F—— S——], Bishop of ——'. Otherwise as for a bishop of the Anglican communion. The bishop who holds the position of Primus is addressed as 'The Most Reverend the Primus'. *Begin:* 'Dear Primus'. *Spoken address:* 'Primus'.

Bishop (Roman Catholic)
Address on envelope: 'His Lordship the Bishop of ——' or 'The Right Reverend [F—— S——], Bishop of ——'. In Ireland, 'The Most Reverend' is used instead of 'The Right Reverend'. If an auxiliary bishop, address as 'The Right Reverend [F—— S——], Auxiliary Bishop of ——'. *Begin:* 'My Lord' or (more rarely) 'My Lord Bishop'. *Close:* 'I remain, my Lord' or (more rarely), 'my Lord Bishop'. Yours faithfully', or simply 'Yours faithfully'. *Spoken address:* 'My Lord' or (more rarely) 'My Lord Bishop'.

Cabinet Minister *see* Secretary of State

Canon (Anglican communion)
Address on envelope: 'The Reverend Canon [F—— S——]'. *Begin:* 'Dear Canon' or 'Dear Canon [*S*——]'. *Spoken address:* 'Canon' or 'Canon [S——]'.

Canon (Roman Catholic)
Address on envelope: 'The Very Reverend Canon [F—— S——]'. *Begin:* 'Very Reverend Sir'. *Spoken address:* 'Canon [*S*——]'.

Cardinal
Address on envelope: 'His eminence Cardinal [S——]'. If an archbishop, 'His Eminence the Cardinal Archbishop of ——'. *Begin:* 'Your Eminence' or (more rarely) 'My Lord Cardinal'. *Close:* 'I remain, Your Eminence (or 'My Lord Cardinal'), Yours faithfully'. *Spoken:* 'Your Eminence'.

Clergy (Anglican communion)
Address on envelope: 'The Reverend [F—— S——]'. *Begin:* 'Dear Sir' or 'Dear Mr [S——]'.

Clergy (Roman Catholic)
Address on envelope: 'The Reverend [F—— S——]'. If a member of a religious order, the initials of the order should be added after the name. *Begin:* 'Dear Reverend Father'.

Clergy (Other churches)
Address on envelope: 'The Reverend [F—— S——]'. *Begin:* 'Dear Sir/Madam' or 'Dear Mr/Mrs etc. [S——]'.

Countess
Address on envelope: 'The Right Hon. the Countess of ——'. *Begin:* 'Dear Madam'. *Spoken address:* 'Madam'.

Dean (Anglican)
Address on envelope: 'The Very Reverend the Dean of ——'. *Begin:* 'Dear Dean' or 'Very Reverend Sir'. *Spoken address:* 'Dean'. *Begin an official speech:* 'Very Reverend Sir'.

Doctor
Physicians, anaesthetists, pathologists and radiologists are addressed as 'Doctor'. Surgeons, whether they hold the degree of Doctor of Medicine or not, are known as 'Mr/Mrs'. In England and Wales, obstetricians and gynaecologists are addressed as 'Mr/Mrs', but in Scotland, Ireland and elsewhere as 'Doctor'. In addressing a letter to the holder of a doctorate, the initials DD, MD, etc. are placed after the ordinary form of address, eg 'The Rev John Smith, DD', the 'Rev Dr Smith' and 'Dr John Brown' are also used.

Dowager
Address on envelope: On the marriage of a peer or baronet, the widow of the previous holder of the title becomes 'Dowager' and is addressed 'The Right Hon. the Dowager Countess of ——', 'The Right Hon. the Dowager Lady ——', etc. If there is already a Dowager still living, she retains this title, the later widow being addressed 'The Most Hon. [F——], Marchioness of ——', 'The Right Hon. [F——], Lady ——', etc. However, many Dowagers prefer the style which includes their Christian names to that including the title Dowager. *Begin,* etc. as for a peer's wife.

Duchess
Address on envelope: 'Her Grace the Duchess of ——'. *Begin:* 'Dear Madam'. *Spoken address:* 'Your Grace'. (For Royal Duchess, *see* Princess.)

Duke
Address on envelope: 'His Grace the Duke of ——'. *Begin:* 'My Lord Duke'. *Spoken address:* 'Your Grace'. (For Royal Duke, *see* Prince.)

Earl
Address on envelope: 'The Right Hon. the Earl of ——'. *Begin:* 'My Lord'. *Spoken address:* 'My Lord'. (For Earl's wife, *see* Countess.)

Governor of a colony or **Governor-General**
Address on envelope: 'His Excellency [ordinary designation], Governor(-General) of ——'. (The Governor-General of Canada has the rank of 'Right Honourable', which he retains for life.) The wife of a Governor-General is styled 'Her Excellency' within the country her husband administers.

FORMS OF ADDRESS (cont.)

Begin: according to rank. Close: 'I have the honour to be, Sir (or 'My Lord', if a peer), Your Excellency's obedient servant'. *Spoken address:* 'Your Excellency'.

Judge, High Court
Address on envelope: if a man, 'The Hon. Mr Justice [S——]'; if a woman, 'The Hon. Mrs Justice [S——]'. *Begin:* 'Dear Sir/Madam'; if on judicial matters, 'My Lord/Lady'. *Spoken address:* 'Sir/Madam'; only on the bench or when dealing with judicial matters should a High Court Judge be addressed as 'My Lord/Lady' or referred to as 'Your Lordship/Ladyship'.

Judge, Circuit
Address on envelope: 'His/Her Honour Judge [S——]'. If a Knight, 'His Honour Judge Sir [F—— S——]'. *Begin:* 'Dear Sir/Madam'. *Spoken address:* 'Sir/Madam'; address as 'Your Honour' only when on the bench or dealing with judicial matters.

Justice of the Peace (England and Wales)
When on the bench, refer to and address as 'Your Worship'; otherwise according to rank. The letters 'JP' may be added after the person's name in addressing a letter, if desired.

Knight Bachelor
As Baronet, except that 'Bt' is omitted. Knight of the Bath, of St Michael and St George, etc. *Address on envelope:* 'Sir [F—— S——], with the initials 'GCB', KCB', etc. added. *Begin:* 'Dear Sir'.

Knight's wife
As Baronet's wife, or according to rank.

Lady Mayoress
Address on envelope: 'The Lady Mayoress of ——'. *Begin:* 'My Lady Mayoress'. *Spoken address:* '(My) Lady Mayoress'.

Lord Mayor
Address on envelope: The Lord Mayors of London, York, Belfast, Cardiff, Dublin and also Melbourne, Sydney, Adelaide, Perth, Brisbane and Hobart are styled 'The Right Hon. the Lord Mayor of ——'. Other Lord Mayors are styled 'The Right Worshipful the Lord Mayor of ——'. *Begin:* 'My Lord Mayor', even if the holder of the office is a woman. *Spoken address:* '(My) Lord Mayor'.

Marchioness
Address on envelope: 'The Most Hon. the Marchioness of ——'. *Begin:* 'Dear Madam'. *Spoken address:* 'Madam'.

Marquess
Address on envelope: 'The Most Hon. the Marquess of ——'. *Begin:* 'My Lord'. *Spoken address:* 'My Lord'.

Mayor
Address on envelope: 'The Worshipful the Mayor of ——'; in the case of cities and certain towns, 'The Right Worshipful'. *Begin:* 'Mr Mayor'. *Spoken address:* 'Mr Mayor'.

Mayoress
Address on envelope: 'The Mayoress of ——'. *Begin:* 'Madam Mayoress' is traditional, but some now prefer 'Madam Mayor'. *Spoken address:* 'Mayoress' (or 'Madam Mayor').

Member of Parliament
Address on envelope: Add 'MP' to the usual form of address. *Begin:* according to rank.

Monsignor
Address on envelope: 'The Reverend Monsignor [F—— S——]'. If a canon, 'The Very Reverend Monsignor (Canon) [F—— S——]'. *Begin:* 'Reverend Sir'. *Spoken address:* 'Monsignor [S——]'.

Officers in the Armed Forces
Address on envelope: The professional rank is prefixed to any other rank, eg 'Admiral the Right Hon. the Earl of ——', 'Lieut.-Col. Sir [F—— S——], KCB'. Officers below the rank of Rear-Admiral, and Marshal of the Royal Air Force, are entitled to 'RN' (or 'Royal Navy') and 'RAF' respectively after their name. Army officers of the rank of Colonel or below may follow their name with the name of their regiment or corps (which may be abbreviated). Officers in the women's services add 'WRNS', 'WRAF', 'WRAC'. *Begin:* according to social rank.

Officers (retired and former)
Address on envelope: Officers above the rank of Lieutenant (in the Royal Navy), Captain (in the Army) and Flight Lieutenant may continue to use and be addressed by their armed forces rank after being placed on the retired list. The word 'retired' (or in an abbreviated form) should not normally be placed after the person's name. Former officers in the women's services do not normally continue to use their ranks.

Pope
Address on envelope: 'His Holiness, the Pope'. *Begin:* 'Your Holiness' or 'Most Holy Father'. *Close:* if a Roman Catholic, 'I have the honour to be your Holiness's most devoted and obedient child' (or 'most humble child'); if not Roman Catholic, 'I have the honour to be (or 'remain') Your Holiness's obedient servant'. *Spoken address:* 'Your Holiness'.

Prime Minister
Address on envelope: according to rank. The Prime Minister is a Privy Counsellor (see separate entry) and the letter should be addressed accordingly. *Begin,* etc. according to rank.

Prince
Address on envelope: If a Duke, 'His Royal Highness the Duke of ——'; if not a Duke, 'His Royal Highness the Prince [F——]', if a child of the sovereign; otherwise 'His Royal Highness Prince [F——] of [Kent or Gloucester]'. *Begin:* 'Sir'. Refer to as 'Your Royal Highness'. *Close:* 'I have the honour to remain (or be), Sir, Your Royal Highness's most humble and obedient servant'. *Spoken address:* 'Your Royal Highness' once, thereafter 'Sir'.

Princess
Address on envelope: If a Duchess, 'Her Royal Highness the Duchess of ——'; if not a Duchess, the daughter of a sovereign is addressed as 'Her Royal Highness the Princess [F——]', followed by any title she holds by marriage. 'The' is omitted in addressing a princess who is not the daughter of a sovereign. A Princess by marriage is addressed 'HRH Princess [husband's F——] of ——'. *Begin:* 'Madam'. Refer to as 'Your Royal Highness'. *Close:* as for Prince, substituting 'Madam' for 'Sir'. *Spoken address:* 'Your Royal Highness' once, thereafter 'Ma'am'.

Privy Counsellor
Address on envelope: If a peer, 'The Right Hon. the Earl of ——, PC'; if not a peer, 'The Right Hon. [F—— S——]', without the 'PC'. *Begin,* etc. according to rank.

Professor
Address on envelope: 'Professor [F—— S——]'; the styles 'Professor Lord [S——]' and 'Professor Sir [F—— S——]' are often used, but are deprecated by some people. If the professor is in holy orders, 'The Reverend Professor'. *Begin:* 'Dear Sir/Madam', or according to rank. *Spoken address:* according to rank.

Queen
Address on envelope: 'Her Majesty the Queen'. *Begin:* 'Madam, with my humble duty'. Refer to as 'Your Majesty'. *Close:* 'I have the honour to remain (or 'be'), Madam, Your Majesty's most humble and obedient servant'. *Spoken address:* 'Your Majesty' once, thereafter 'Ma'am'. *Begin an official speech:* 'May it please Your Majesty'.

Rabbi
Address on envelope: 'Rabbi [initial and S——]' or, if a doctor, 'Rabbi Doctor [initial and S——]'. *Begin:* 'Dear Sir'. *Spoken address:* 'Rabbi [S——]' or '[Doctor S——]'.

Secretary of State
Address on envelope: 'The Right Hon. [F—— S——], MP, Secretary of State for ——', or 'The Secretary of State for ——'. Otherwise according to rank.

Viscount
Address on envelope: 'The Right Hon. the Viscount ——'. *Begin:* 'My Lord'. *Spoken address:* 'My Lord'.

Viscountess
Address on envelope: 'The Right Hon. the Viscountess ——'. *Begin:* 'Dear Madam'. *Spoken address:* 'Madam'.

NOBEL PRIZES 1971–91

Year	Peace	Literature	Economic Science	Chemistry	Physics	Physiology/Medicine	Year
1971	Willy Brandt	Pablo Neruda	Simon Kuznets	Gerhard Herzberg	Dennis Gabor	Earl W Sutherland	1971
1972	*none*	Heinrich Böll	John R Hicks Kenneth J Arrow	Stanford Moore William H Stein Christian B Anfinsen	John Bardeen Leon N Cooper John R Schrieffer	Gerald M Edelman Rodney R Porter	1972
1973	Henry A Kissinger Le Duc Tho (*declined*)	Patrick White	Wassily Leontief	Ernst Otto Fischer Geoffrey Wilkinson	Leo Esaki Ivar Giaever Brian D Josephson	Konrad Lorenz Nikolaas Tinbergen Karl von Frisch	1973
1974	Sean MacBride Sato Eisaku	Eyvind Johnson Harry Martinson	Gunnar Myrdal Friedrich A von Hayek	Paul J Flory	Martin Ryle Antony Hewish	Albert Claude George Emil Palade Christian de Duve	1974
1975	Andrei D Sakharov	Eugenio Montale	Leonid V Kantorovich Tjalling C Koopmans	John W Cornforth Vladimir Prelog	Aage N Bohr Ben R Mottelson L James Rainwater	David Baltimore Renato Dulbecco Howard M Temin	1975
1976	Mairead Corrigan Betty Williams	Saul Bellow	Milton Friedman	William N Lipscomb	Burton Richter Samuel Chao Chung Ting	Baruch S Blumberg Daniel C Gajdusek	1976
1977	Amnesty International	Vicente Aleixandre	James E Meade Bertil Ohlin	Ilya Prigogine	Philip W Anderson Nevill F Mott John H van Vleck	Rosalyn S Yalow Roger C L Guillemin Andrew V Schally	1977
1978	Menachem Begin Anwar al-Sadat	Isaac B Singer	Herbert A Simon	Peter Mitchell	Pjotr L Kapitza Arno A Penzias Robert W Wilson	Werner Arber Daniel Nathans Hamilton O Smith	1978
1979	Mother Teresa	Odysseus Elytis	Arthur Lewis Theodore W Schultz	Herbert C Brown George Wittig	Steven Weinberg Sheldon L Glashow Abdus Salam	Allan M Cormack Godfrey N Hounsfield	1979
1980	Adolfo Pérez Esquivel	Czesław Miłosz	Lawrence R Klein	Paul Berg Walter Gilbert Frederick Sanger	James W Cronin Val L Fitch	Baruj Benacerraf George D Snell Jean Dausset	1980
1981	Office of the UN High Commissioner for Refugees	Elias Canetti	James Tobin	Kenichi Fukui Roald Hoffman	Nicolaas Bloembergen Arthur L Schawlow Kai M Siegbahn	Roger W Sperry David H Hubel Torsten N Wiesel	1981
1982	Alfonso García Robles Alva Myrdal	Gabriel García Márquez	George J Stigler	Aaron Klug	Kenneth G Wilson	Sune K Bergström Bengt I Samuelsson John R Vane	1982
1983	Lech Walesa	William Golding	Gerard Debreu	Henry Taube	Subrahmanyan Chandrasekhar William A Fowler	Barbara McClintock	1983
1984	Desmond Tutu	Jaroslav Seifert	Richard Stone	Robert B Merrifield	Carlo Rubbia Simon van der Meer	Niels K Jerne Georges J F Köhler César Milstein	1984
1985	International Physicians for the Prevention of Nuclear War	Claude Simon	Franco Modigliani	Herbert Hauptman Jerome Karle	Klaus von Klitzing	Joseph L Goldstein Michael S Brown	1985
1986	Elie Wiesel	Wole Soyinka	James M Buchanan	Dudley R Herschbach Yuan Tseh Lee John C Polanyi	Gerd Binnig Heinrich Rohrer Ernst Ruska	Stanley Cohen Rita Levi-Montalcini	1986
1987	Oscar Arias Sánchez	Joseph Brodsky	Robert M Solow	Charles Pedersen Donald Cram Jean-Marie Lehn	George Bednorz Alex Müller	Susumu Tonegawa	1987
1988	UN Peacekeeping Forces	Naguib Mahfouz	Maurice Allais	Johann Deisenhofer Robert Huber Hartmut Michel	Leon Lederman Melvin Schwartz Jack Steinberger	James Black Gertrude Elion George Hitchings	1988
1989	Tenzin Ciyatso (Dalai Lama)	Camilo José Cela	Trygve Haavelmo	Sydney Altman Thomas Cech	Hans Dehmelt Wolfgang Paul Norman Ramsay	J Michael Bishop Harold E Varmus	1989
1990	Mikhail Gorbachev	Octavio Paz	Harry M Markovitz Merton Miller William Sharpe	Elias James Corey	Jerome Friedman Henry Kendall Richard Taylor	Joseph E Murray E Donnall Thomas	1990
1991	Aung Sun Suu Kyi	Nadine Gordimer	Ronald Coase	Richard R Ernst	Pierre-Gilles de Gennes	Erwin Neher Bert Sakmann	1991

POETS LAUREATE

1617 Ben Jonson*
1638 Sir William Davenant*
1668 John Dryden
1689 Thomas Shadwell
1692 Nahum Tate
1715 Nicholas Rowe
1718 Laurence Eusden
1730 Colley Cibber
1757 William Whitehead
1785 Thomas Warton
1790 Henry Pye
1813 Robert Southey
1843 William Wordsworth
1850 Alfred, Lord Tennyson
1896 Alfred Austin
1913 Robert Bridges
1930 John Masefield
1968 Cecil Day Lewis
1972 Sir John Betjeman
1984 Ted Hughes

*The post was not officially established until 1668.

MOTION PICTURE ACADEMY AWARDS

	Best film	Best actor	Best actress
1979	*Kramer vs Kramer* (Robert Beaton)	Dustin Hoffman *Kramer vs Kramer*	Sally Field *Norma Rae*
1980	*Ordinary People* (Robert Redford)	Robert de Niro *Raging Bull*	Sissy Spacek *Coal Miner's Daughter*
1981	*Chariots of Fire* (Hugh Hudson)	Henry Fonda *On Golden Pond*	Katharine Hepburn *On Golden Pond*
1982	*Gandhi* (Richard Attenborough)	Ben Kingsley *Gandhi*	Meryl Streep *Sophie's Choice*
1983	*Terms of Endearment* (James L Brooks)	Robert Duval *Tender Mercies*	Shirley MacLaine *Terms of Endearment*
1984	*Amadeus* (Milos Forman)	F Murray Abraham *Amadeus*	Sally Field *Places in the Heart*
1985	*Out of Africa* (Sydney Pollack)	William Hurt *Kiss of the Spider Woman*	Geraldine Page *The Trip to Bountiful*
1986	*Platoon* (Oliver Stone)	Paul Newman *The Color of Money*	Marlee Matlin *Children of a Lesser God*
1987	*The Last Emperor* (Bernardo Bertolucci)	Michael Douglas *Wall Street*	Cher *Moonstruck*
1988	*Rain Man* (Barry Levinson)	Dustin Hoffman *Rain Man*	Jody Foster *The Accused*
1989	*Driving Miss Daisy* (Bruce Beresford)	Daniel Day Lewis *My Left Foot*	Jessica Tandy *Driving Miss Daisy*
1990	*Dances with Wolves* (Kevin Kostner)	Jeremy Irons *Reversal of Fortune*	Kathy Bates *Misery*

PATRON SAINTS OF OCCUPATIONS

Accountants	Matthew
Actors	Genesius, Vitus
Advertisers	Bernadino of Siena
Architects	Thomas (Apostle)
Artists	Luke, Angelico
Astronauts	Joseph (Cupertino)
Astronomers	Dominic
Athletes	Sebastian
Authors	Francis de Sales
Aviators	Our Lady of Loreto
Bakers	Honoratus
Bankers	Bernardino (Feltre)
Barbers	Cosmas and Damian
Blacksmiths	Eligius
Bookkeepers	Matthew
Book trade	John of God
Brewers	Amand, Wenceslaus
Builders	Barbara, Thomas (Apostle)
Butchers	Luke
Carpenters	Joseph
Chemists	Cosmas and Damian
Comedians	Vitus
Cooks	Lawrence, Martha
Dancers	Vitus
Dentists	Apollonia
Doctors	Cosmas and Damian, Luke
Editors	Francis de Sales
Farmers	Isidore
Firemen	Florian
Fishermen	Andrew, Peter
Florists	Dorothy, Thérèse of Lisieux
Gardeners	Adam, Fiacre
Glassworkers	Luke, Lucy
Gravediggers	Joseph (Arimathea)
Grocers	Michael
Hotelkeepers	Amand, Julian the Hospitaler
Housewives	Martha
Jewellers	Eligius
Journalists	Francis de Sales
Labourers	James, John Bosco
Lawyers	Ivo, Thomas More
Librarians	Jerome, Catherine of Alexandria
Merchants	Francis of Assisi
Messengers	Gabriel
Metalworkers	Eligius
Midwives	Raymond Nonnatus
Miners	Anne, Barbara
Motorists	Christopher
Musicians	Cecilia, Gregory the Great
Nurses	Camillus de Lellis, John of God
Philosophers	Thomas Aquinas, Catherine of Alexandria
Poets	Cecilia, David
Policemen	Michael
Postal workers	Gabriel
Priests	Jean-Baptiste Vianney
Printers	John of God
Prisoners	Leonard
Radio workers	Gabriel
Sailors	Christopher, Erasmus, Francis of Paola
Scholars	Thomas Aquinas
Scientists	Albert the Great
Sculptors	Luke, Louis
Secretaries	Genesius
Servants	Martha, Zita
Shoemakers	Crispin, Crispinian
Singers	Cecilia, Gregory
Soldiers	George, Joan of Arc, Martin of Tours, Sebastian
Students	Thomas Aquinas
Surgeons	Luke, Cosmas and Damian
Tailors	Homobonus
Tax collectors	Matthew
Taxi drivers	Fiacre
Teachers	Gregory the Great, John Baptist de la Salle
Theologians	Augustine, Alphonsus Liguori, Thomas Aquinas
Television workers	Gabriel
Undertakers	Dismas, Joseph of Arimathea
Waiters	Martha
Writers	Lucy

LITERARY PRIZES

Booker Prize (UK)

1971 V S Naipaul *In a Free State*
1972 John Berger *G*
1973 J G Farrell *The Siege of Krishnapur*
1974 Nadine Gordiner *The Conservationist*; Stanley Middleton *Holiday*
1975 Ruth Prawer Jhabvala *Heat and Dust*
1976 David Storey *Saville*
1977 Paul Scott *Staying On*
1978 Iris Murdoch *The Sea, The Sea*
1979 Penelope Fitzgerald *Offshore*
1980 William Golding *Rites of Passage*
1981 Salman Rushdie *Midnight's Children*
1982 Thomas Keneally *Schindler's Ark*
1983 J M Coetzee *Life and Times of Michael K*
1984 Anita Brookner *Hotel du Lac*
1985 Keri Hulme *The Bone People*
1986 Kingsley Amis *The Old Devils*
1987 Penelope Lively *Moon Tiger*
1988 Peter Carey *Oscar and Lucinda*
1989 Kazuo Ishiguro *The Remains of the Day*
1990 A S Byatt *Possession*
1991 Ben Okri *The Famished Road*

Prix Goncourt (France)

1971 Jacques Laurent *Les Bêtises*
1972 Jean Carrière *L'Epervier de Maheux*
1973 Jacques Chessex *L'Ogre*
1974 Pascal Lainé *La Dentellière*
1975 Emile Ajar *La Vie devant soi*
1976 Patrick Grainville *Les Flamboyants*
1977 Didier Decoin *John L'Enfer*
1978 Patrick Modiano *Rue des boutiques obscures*
1979 Antonine Maillet *Pelagie-la-Charrette*
1980 Yves Navarre *Le Jardin d'acclimation*
1981 Lucien Bodard *Anne Marie*
1982 Dominique Fernandez *Dans la Main de l'ange*
1983 Frederick Tristan *Les Égares*
1984 Marguerite Duras *L'Amant*
1985 Yann Queffelec *Les Noces barbares*
1986 Michel Host *Valet de Nuit*
1987 Tahar ben Jalloun *La Nuit sacrée*
1988 Erik Orsenna *L'Exposition coloniale*
1989 Jean Vautrin *Un Grand Pas Vers le Bon Dieu*
1990 Jean Rouaud *Les Champs d'Honneur*
1991 Pierre Combescot *Les Filles du Calvaire*

Pulitzer Prize in Letters (USA)

1972 Wallace Stegner *Angle of Repose*
1973 Eudora Welty *The Optimist's Daughter*
1975 Michael Shaara *The Killer Angels*
1976 Saul Bellow *Humboldt's Gift*
1978 James Alan McPherson *Elbow Room*
1979 John Cheever *The Stories of John Cheever*
1980 Norman Mailer *The Executioner's Song*
1981 John Kennedy Toole *A Confederacy of Dunces*
1982 John Updike *Rabbit is Rich*
1983 Alice Walker *The Color Purple*
1984 William Kennedy *Ironweed*
1985 Alison Lurie *Foreign Affairs*
1986 Larry McMurtry *Lonesome Dove*
1987 Peter Taylor *A Summons to Memphis*
1988 Toni Morrison *Beloved*
1989 Anne Tyler *Breathing Lessons*
1990 Oscar Hijuelos *The Mambo Kings Play Songs of Love*

COMPETITIVE SPORTS AND GAMES

OLYMPIC GAMES

First Modern Olympic Games took place in 1896, founded by Frenchman Baron de Coubertin; held every four years; women first competed in 1900; first separate Winter Games celebration in 1924.

Venues

Summer Games	Winter Games
1896 Athens, Greece	—
1900 Paris, France	—
1904 St Louis, USA	—
1908 London, UK	—
1912 Stockholm, Sweden	—
1920 Antwerp, Belgium	
1924 Paris, France	Chamonix, France
1928 Amsterdam, Holland	St Moritz, Switzerland
1932 Los Angeles, USA	Lake Placid, New York, USA
1936 Berlin, Germany	Garmisch-Partenkirchen, Germany
1948 London, UK	St Moritz, Switzerland
1952 Helsinki, Finland	Oslo, Norway
1956 Melbourne, Australia	Cortina, Italy
1960 Rome, Italy	Squaw Valley, California, USA
1964 Tokyo, Japan	Innsbruck, Austria
1968 Mexico City, Mexico	Grenoble, France
1972 Munich, West Germany	Sapporo, Japan
1976 Montreal, Canada	Innsbruck, Austria
1980 Moscow, USSR	Lake Placid, New York, USA
1984 Los Angeles, USA	Sarajevo, Yugoslavia
1988 Seoul, South Korea	Calgary, Canada
1992 Barcelona, Spain	Albertville, France
1996 Atlanta, USA	

Olympic games were also held in 1906 to commemorate the 10th anniversary of the birth of the Modern Games.

The 1956 equestrian events were held at Stockholm, Sweden, due to quarantine laws in Australia.

Leading Medal Winners

Summer Games	Gold	Silver	Bronze	Total
1 USA	746	560	475	1781
2 USSR	395	323	299	1017
3 Great Britain	173	222	206	601
4 West Germany*	157	207	207	571
5 France	153	167	177	497
6 Sweden	131	139	169	439
7 East Germany	153	129	127	409
8 Italy	147	121	124	392
9 Hungary	124	112	136	372
10 Finland	97	75	110	282

Winter Games	Gold	Silver	Bronze	Total
1 USSR	79	57	59	195
2 Norway	54	60	54	168
3 USA	42	47	34	123
4 East Germany	39	36	35	110
5 Finland	33	43	34	110
6 Austria	28	38	32	98
7 Sweden	36	25	31	92
8 West Germany*	26	26	23	75
9 Switzerland	23	25	25	73
10 Canada	14	12	18	44

*Includes medals won as Germany 1896–1964.

	Gold	Silver	Bronze	Total
Summer	118	159	149	426
Winter	17	15	12	44

West and East Germany competed as two nations from 1968.

COMMONWEALTH GAMES

First held as the British Empire Games in 1930; take place every four years and between Olympic celebrations; became the British Empire and Commonwealth Games in 1954; the current title adopted in 1970.

Venues

1930 Hamilton, Canada
1934 London, England
1938 Sydney, Australia
1950 Auckland, New Zealand
1954 Vancouver, Canada
1958 Cardiff, Wales
1962 Perth, Australia
1966 Kingston, Jamaica
1970 Edinburgh, Scotland
1974 Christchurch, New Zealand
1978 Edmonton, Canada
1982 Brisbane, Australia
1986 Edinburgh, Scotland
1990 Auckland, New Zealand
1994 Victoria, Canada

Leading Medal Winners (including 1990)

Nation	Gold	Silver	Bronze	Total
1 England	420	368	368	1 156
2 Australia	397	374	382	1 153
3 Canada	287	301	299	887
4 New Zealand	94	121	161	376
5 Scotland	56	74	109	239
6 South Africa	60	44	47	151
7 Wales	32	39	60	131
8 Kenya	35	24	33	92
9 India	37	36	31	104
10 Northern Ireland	15	20	34	69

AEROBATICS

World Championships
First held in 1960 and every two years since then except 1974.

Recent winners (Men)

1968 Erwin Bloske (East Germany)
1970 Igor Egorov (USSR)
1972 Charlie Hillard (USA)
1976 Vikto Letsko (USSR)
1978 Ivan Tucek (Czechoslovakia)
1980 Leo Loudenslager (USA)
1982 Viktor Smolin (USSR)
1984 Petr Jirmus (Czechoslovakia)
1986 Petr Jirmus (Czechoslovakia)

Recent winners (Women)

1968 Madelyne Delcroix (France)
1970 Svetlana Savitskaya (USSR)
1972 Mary Gaffaney (USA)
1976 Lidia Leonova (USSR)
1978 Valentina Yaikova (USSR)
1980 Betty Stewart (USA)
1982 Betty Stewart (USA)
1984 Khalide Makagonova (USSR)
1986 Liubov Nemkova (USSR)

AMERICAN FOOTBALL

Superbowl
First held in 1967; takes place each January; an end-of-season meeting between the champions of the two major US leagues, the National Football Conference (NFC) and the American Football Conference (AFC).

Recent winners

1982 San Francisco 49ers (NFC)
1983 Washington Redskins (NFC)
1984 Los Angeles Raiders (AFC)
1985 San Francisco 49ers (NFC)
1986 Chicago Bears (NFC)
1987 New York Giants (NFC)
1988 Washington Redskins (NFC)
1989 San Francisco 49ers (NFC)
1990 San Francisco 49ers (NFC)
1991 New York Giants (NFC)
1992 Washington Redskins (NFC)

Most wins: (4), Pittsburgh Steelers 1975–6, 1979–80; (4) San Francisco 49ers 1982, 1985, 1989–90

ANGLING

World Fresh Water Championship
First held in 1957; takes place annually.

Recent winners (Individual)

1979 Gerard Heulard (France)
1980 Wolf-Rüdiger Kremkus (West Germany)
1981 David Thomas (England)
1982 Kevin Ashurst (England)
1983 Wolf-Rüdiger Kremkus (West Germany)
1984 Bobby Smithers (Ireland)
1985 David Roper (England)
1986 Lud Wever (Holland)
1987 Clive Branson (Wales)
1988 Jean-Pierre Fouquet (France)
1989 Tom Pickering (England)

Recent winners (Team)

1979 France
1980 West Germany
1981 France
1982 Holland
1983 Belgium
1984 Luxembourg
1985 England
1986 Italy
1987 England
1988 England
1989 Wales

Most wins: Individual (3), Robert Tesse (France) 1959–60, 1965. Team (11), France, 1959, 1963–4, 1966, 1968, 1972, 1974–5, 1978–9, 1981.

World Fly Fishing Championship
First held in 1981; takes place annually.

Winners (Individual)

1981 C. Wittkamp (Holland)
1982 Viktor Diez y Diez (Spain)
1983 Segismondo Fernandez (Spain)
1984 Tony Pawson (England)
1985 Leslaw Frasik (Poland)
1986 Slivoj Svoboda (Czechoslovakia)
1987 Brian Leadbetter (England)
1988 John Pawson (England)
1989 Wladyslaw Trzebuinia (Poland)

Winners (Team)

1981 Holland
1982 Italy
1983 Italy
1984 Italy
1985 Poland
1986 Italy
1987 England
1988 England
1989 Poland

Most wins: Individual (no-one has won more than one title). Team (4), Italy, as above.

ARCHERY

World Championships
First held in 1931; took place annually until 1959; since then, every two years.

Recent winners
Individual (Men)

1969 Hardy Ward (USA)
1971 John Williams (USA)
1973 Vikto Sidoruk (USSR)
1975 Darrell Pace (USA)
1977 Richard McKinney (USA)
1979 Darrell Pace (USA)
1981 Kysti Laasonen (Finland)
1983 Richard McKinney (USA)
1985 Richard McKinney (USA)
1987 Vladimir Yesheyev (USSR)
1989 Stanislav Zabrodsky (USSR)

Recent winners
Team (Men)

1969 USA
1971 USA
1973 USA
1975 USA
1977 USA
1979 USA
1981 USA
1983 USA
1985 South Korea
1987 South Korea
1989 USSR

Most wins: Individual (4), Hans Deutgen (Sweden) 1947–50. Team (14), USA 1957–83.

Recent winners
Individual (Women)

1969 Dorothy Lidstone (Canada)
1971 Emma Gapchenko (USSR)
1973 Linda Myers (USA)
1975 Zebiniso Rustamova (USSR)
1977 Luann Ryon (USA)
1979 Jin-Ho Kim (South Korea)
1981 Natalia Butuzova (USSR)
1983 Jin-Ho Kim (South Korea)
1985 Irina Soldatova (USSR)
1987 Ma Xiagjun (China)
1989 Soo Nyung-Kim (South Korea)

Recent winners
Team (Women)

1969 USSR
1971 Poland
1973 USSR
1975 USSR
1977 USA
1979 South Korea
1981 USSR
1983 South Korea
1985 USSR
1987 USSR
1989 South Korea

Most wins: Individual (7), Janina Kurkowska (Poland) 1931–4, 1936, 1939, 1947. Team (8), USA 1952, 1957–9, 1961, 1963, 1965, 1977.

ASSOCIATION FOOTBALL

FIFA World Cup
Association Football's premier event; first contested for the Jules Rimet Trophy in 1930; Brazil won it outright after winning for the third time in 1970; since then teams have competed for the FIFA (*Féderation Internationale de Football Association*) World Cup; held every four years.

Post-war winners

1950 Uruguay
1954 West Germany
1958 Brazil
1962 Brazil
1966 England
1970 Brazil
1974 West Germany
1978 Argentina
1982 Italy
1986 Argentina
1990 Germany

Most wins: (3), Brazil, as above; (3) Italy, 1934, 1938, 1982.

European Championship
Held every four years since 1960; qualifying group matches held over the two years preceding the final.

Winners

1960 USSR
1964 Spain
1968 Italy
1972 West Germany
1976 Czechoslovakia

ASSOCIATION FOOTBALL (cont.)

1980 West Germany
1984 France
1988 Holland

Most wins: (2), West Germany, as above.

South American Championship

First held in 1916, for South American national sides; discontinued in 1967, but revived eight years later; now played every two years.

Recent winners

1956 Uruguay·
1957 Argentina
1959* Argentina
1959* Uruguay
1963 Bolivia
1967 Uruguay
1975 Peru
1979 Paraguay
1983 Uruguay
1987 Uruguay
1989 Brazil

*There were two tournaments in 1959.

Most wins: (13), Uruguay, 1916–17, 1920, 1923–4, 1926, 1935, 1942, 1956, 1959, 1967, 1983, 1987

European Champions Cup

The leading club competition in Europe; open to the League champions of countries affiliated to UEFA (Union of European Football Associations); commonly known as the 'European Cup'; inaugurated in the 1955–6 season; played annually.

Recent winners

1981 Liverpool (England)
1982 Aston Villa (England)
1983 SV Hamburg (West Germany)
1984 Liverpool (England)
1985 Juventus (Italy)
1986 Steaua Bucharest (Romania)
1987 FC Porto (Portugal)
1988 PSV Eindhoven (Holland)
1989 AC Milan (Italy)
1990 AC Milan (Italy)
1991 Red Star Belgrade (Yugoslavia)

Most wins: (6), Real Madrid (Spain), 1956–60, 1966.

Football Association Challenge Cup

The world's oldest club knockout competition (the 'FA cup'), held annually; first contested in the 1871–2 season; first final at the Kennington Oval on 16 March 1872; first winners were The Wanderers.

Recent winners

1981 Tottenham Hotspur
1982 Tottenham Hotspur
1983 Manchester United
1984 Everton
1985 Manchester United
1986 Liverpool
1987 Coventry City
1988 Wimbledon
1989 Liverpool
1990 Manchester United
1991 Tottenham Hotspur

Most wins: (7), Aston Villa, 1887, 1895, 1897, 1905, 1913, 1920, 1957. Tottenham Hotspur, 1901, 1921, 1961–2, 1967, 1981–2.

Football League

The oldest league in the world, and regarded as the toughest; founded in 1888; consists of four divisions; the current complement of 92 teams achieved in 1950.

Recent winners

1981–2 Liverpool
1982–3 Liverpool
1983–4 Liverpool
1984–5 Everton
1985–6 Liverpool
1986–7 Everton
1987–8 Liverpool
1988–9 Arsenal
1989–90 Liverpool
1990–91 Arsenal

Most wins: (17), Liverpool, 1901, 1906, 1922–3, 1947, 1964, 1966, 1973, 1976–7, 1979–80, 1982–4, 1986, 1988.

ATHLETICS

World Championships

First held in Helsinki, Finland in 1983; take place every four years; Tokyo, Japan in 1991.

Event	Winners (Men)
1987	
100 m	Ben Johnson (Canada)
200 m	Calvin Smith (USA)
400 m	Thomas Schoenlebe (East Germany)
800 m	Billy Konchellah (Kenya)
1500 m	Abdi Bile (Somalia)
5000 m	Said Aouita (Morocco)
10000 m	Paul Kipkoech (Kenya)
Marathon	Douglas Waikihuru (Kenya)
3000 m steeplechase	Francesco Panetta (Italy)
110 m hurdles	Greg Foster (USA)
400 m hurdles	Ed Moses (USA)
20 km walk	Maurizio Damilano (Italy)
50 km walk	Hartwig Gauder (East Germany)
4 × 100 m relay	USA
4 × 400 m relay	USA
High jump	Patrik Sjoeberg (Sweden)
Long jump	Carl Lewis (USA)
Triple jump	Khristo Markov (Bulgaria)
Pole vault	Sergey Bubka (USSR)
Shot	Werner Gunthoer (Switzerland)
Discus	Jurgen Schult (East Germany)
Hammer	Sergey Litvinov (USSR)
Javelin	Seppo Raty (Finland)
Decathlon	Torsten Voss (East Germany)
1991	
100 m	Carl Lewis (USA)
200 m	Michael Johnson (USA)
400 m	Antonio Pettigrew (USA)
800 m	Billy Konchellah (Kenya)
1500 m	Noureddine Morceli (Algeria)
5000 m	Yobes Ondieki (Kenya)
10000 m	Moses Tanui (Kenya)
Marathon	Hiromi Taniguchi (Japan)
110 m hurdles	Greg Foster (USA)
400 m hurdles	Samuel Matete (Zambia)
3000 m steeplechase	Moses Kiptanui (Kenya)
20 km walk	Maurizio Damilano (Italy)
50 km walk	Alexandr Potashov (USSR)
4 × 100 m relay	USA
4 × 400 m relay	Great Britain
High jump	Charles Austin (USA)
Long jump	Mike Powell (USA)
Pole vault	Sergey Bubka (USSR)
Triple jump	Kenny Harrison (USA)
Shot	Werner Gunthor (Switzerland)
Discus	Lars Riedel (Germany)
Javelin	Kimmo Kinnunen (Finland)
Hammer	Yuriy Sedykh (USSR)
Decathlon	Dan O'Brien (USA)

Event	Winners (Women)
1987	
100 m	Silke Gladisch (East Germany)
200 m	Silke Gladisch (East Germany)
400 metres	Olga Bryzgina (USSR)
800 m	Sigrun Wodars (East Germany)
1500 m	Tatyana Samolenko (USSR)
3000 m	Tatyana Samolenko (USSR)
Marathon	Rosa Mota (Portugal)
100 m hurdles	Ginka Zagorcheva (Bulgaria)
400 m hurdles	Sabine Busche (East Germany)
10 km walk	Irinia Strakhova (USSR)
4 × 100 m relay	USA
4 × 400 m relay	East Germany
High jump	Stefka Kostadinova (Bulgaria)
Long jump	Jackie Joyner-Kersee (USA)
Shot	Natalya Lisovskaya (USSR)
Discus	Martina Hellman (*née* Opitz) (East Germany)
Javelin	Fatima Whitbread (UK)
Heptathlon	Jackie Joyner-Kersee (USA)
1991	
100 m	Katrin Krabbe (Germany)
200 m	Katrin Krabbe (Germany)
400 m	Marie-Jose Perec (France)
800 m	Lilia Nurutdinova (USSR)
1500 m	Hassiba Boulmerka (Algeria)
3000 m	Tatyana Dorovskikh (USSR)
10000 m	Liz McColgan (Great Britain)
Marathon	Wanda Panfil (Poland)
100 m hurdles	Lyudmila Narozhilenko (USSR)
400 m hurdles	Tatyana Ledovskaya (USSR)
10 km walk	Alina Ivanova (USSR)
4 × 100 m relay	Jamaica

ATHLETICS (cont.)

4 × 400 m relay	USSR
High jump	Heike Henkel (Germany)
Long jump	Jackie Joyner-Kersee (USA)
Shot	Huang Zhihong (China)
Discus	Tsvetanka Khristova (Bulgaria)
Javelin	Xu Demei (China)
Heptathlon	Sabine Braun (Germany)

AUSTRALIAN RULES FOOTBALL

Australian Football League

The top prize is the annual VFL Premiership Trophy; first contested in 1897 and won by Essendon. Known as the Victoria Football League until 1987.

Recent winners

1981 Carlton
1982 Carlton
1983 Hawthorn
1984 Essendon
1985 Essendon
1986 Hawthorn
1987 Carlton
1988 Hawthorn
1989 Hawthorn
1990 Collingwood
1991 Hawthorn

Most wins: (15), Carlton, 1906–8, 1914–15, 1938, 1945, 1947, 1968, 1970, 1972, 1979, 1981–2, 1987.

BADMINTON

World Championships

First held in 1977; initially took place every three years; since 1983 every two years.

Singles winners (Men)

1980 Rudy Hartono (Indonesia)
1983 Icuk Sugiarto (Indonesia)
1985 Han Jian (China)
1987 Yang Yang (China)
1989 Yang Yang (China)
1991 Zhao Jianhua (China)

Singles winners (Women)

1980 Wiharjo Verawatay (Indonesia)
1983 Li Lingwei (China)
1985 Han Aiping (China)
1987 Han Aiping (China)
1989 Li Lingwei (China)
1991 Tang Jiuhong (China)

Most titles: (4), Park Joo Bong (South Korea), men's doubles 1985, 1991, mixed doubles 1989, 1991.

Thomas Cup

An international team event for men's teams; inaugurated 1949, now held every two years.

Recent winners

1967 Malaysia
1970 Indonesia
1973 Indonesia
1976 Indonesia
1979 Indonesia
1982 China
1984 Indonesia
1986 China
1988 China
1990 China

Most wins: (8), Indonesia, 1958–61, 1964, 1970–9, 1984.

Uber Cup

An international event for women's teams; first held in 1957; now held every two years.

Recent winners

1966 Japan
1969 Japan
1972 Japan
1975 Indonesia
1978 Japan
1981 Japan
1984 China
1986 China
1988 China
1990 China

Most wins: (5), Japan, as above.

All-England Championship

Badminton's premier event prior to the inauguration of the World Championships; first held in 1899.

Recent winners
Singles (Men)

1982 Morten Frost (Denmark)
1983 Luan Jin (China)
1984 Morten Frost (Denmark)
1985 Zhao Jianhua (China)
1986 Morten Frost (Denmark)
1987 Morten Frost (Denmark)
1988 Ib Frederikson (Denmark)
1989 Yang Yang (China)
1990 Zhao Jianhua (China)
1991 Ardi Wiranata (Indonesia)

Recent winners
Singles (Women)

1982 Zang Ailing (China)
1983 Zang Ailing (China)
1984 Li Lingwei (China)
1985 Han Aiping (China)
1986 Yun-Ja Kim (Korea)
1987 Kirsten Larsen (Denmark)
1988 Gu Jiaming (China)
1989 Li Lingwei (China)
1990 Susi Susanti (Indonesia)
1991 Susi Susanti (Indonesia)

Most titles: (21: 4 singles, 9 men's doubles, 8 mixed doubles), George Thomas (England) 1903–28.

BASEBALL

World Series

First held in 1903; takes place each October, the best of seven matches; professional Baseball's leading event, the end-of-season meeting between the winners of the two Major Baseball leagues in the USA, the National League (NL) and American League (AL).

Recent winners

1981 Los Angeles Dodgers (NL)
1982 St Louis Cardinals (NL)
1983 Baltimore Orioles (AL)
1984 Detroit Tigers (AL)
1985 Kansas City Royals (AL)
1986 New York Mets (NL)
1987 Minnesota Twins (AL)
1988 Los Angeles Dodgers (NL)
1989 Oakland Athletics (AL)
1990 Cincinnati Reds (NL)
1991 Minnesota Twins (NL)

Most wins: (22), New York Yankees, 1923, 1927–8, 1932, 1936–9, 1941, 1943, 1947, 1949–53, 1956, 1958, 1961–2, 1977–8.

World Amateur Championship

Instituted in 1938; since 1974 held every two years.

Recent winners

1973 Cuba & USA (*shared*)
1974 USA
1976 Cuba
1978 Cuba
1980 Cuba
1982 South Korea
1984 Cuba
1986 Cuba
1988 Cuba
1990 Cuba

Most wins: (20), Cuba, 1939–40, 1942–43, 1950, 1952–3, 1961, 1969–73, 1976–80, 1984–86, 1988, 1990.

BASKETBALL

World Championship

First held 1950 for men, 1953 for women; takes place every four years.

Winners (Men)

1954 USA
1959 Brazil
1963 Brazil
1967 USSR
1970 Yugoslavia
1974 USSR
1978 Yugoslavia
1982 USSR
1986 USA
1990 Yugoslavia

Most wins: (3), USSR and Yugoslavia, as above.

Winners (Women)

1957 USA
1959 USSR
1964 USSR
1967 USSR
1971 USSR
1975 USSR
1979 USA
1983 USSR
1987 USA
1991 USA

Most wins: (6), USSR, as above.

National Basketball Association Championship

First held in 1947; the major competition in professional basketball in the USA, end-of-season

BASKETBALL (cont.)

NBA Play-off involving the champion teams from the Eastern (EC) Conference and Western Conference (WC).

Recent winners

1981 Boston Celtics (EC)
1982 Los Angeles Lakers (WC)
1983 Philadelphia 76ers (EC)
1984 Boston Celtics (EC)
1985 Los Angeles Lakers (WC)
1986 Boston Celtics (EC)
1987 Los Angeles Lakers (WC)
1988 Los Angeles Lakers (WC)
1989 Detroit Pistons (EC)
1990 Detroit Pistons (EC)
1991 Chicago Bulls (EC)

Most wins: (16), Boston Celtics, 1957, 1959–66, 1968–9, 1974, 1976, 1981, 1984, 1986.

BIATHLON

World Championships
First held in 1958; take place annually; the Olympic champion is the automatic world champion in Olympic years; women's championship first held in 1984.

Recent winners
Individual (Men)

10 km (15 km since 1988)
1979 Frank Ullrich (East Germany)
1980 Frank Ullrich (East Germany)
1981 Frank Ullrich (East Germany)
1982 Eirik Kvalfoss (Norway)
1983 Eirik Kvalfoss (Norway)
1984 Eirik Kvalfoss (Norway)
1985 Frank-Peter Rötsch (East Germany)
1986 Valeriy Medvetsev (USSR)
1987 Frank-Peter Rötsch (East Germany)
1988 Frank-Peter Rötsch (East Germany)
1989 Frank Luck (East Germany)

20 km
1979 Klaus Siebert (East Germany)
1980 Anatoliy Alyabyev (USSR)
1981 Heikki Ikola (Finland)
1982 Frank Ullrich (East Germany)
1983 Frank Ullrich (East Germany)
1984 Peter Angerer (West Germany)
1985 Yuriy Kashkarov (USSR)
1986 Valeriy Medvetsev (USSR)
1987 Frank-Peter Rötsch (East Germany)
1988 Frank-Peter Rötsch (East Germany)
1989 Eric Kralfoss (Norway)

Most individual titles: (6), Frank Ullrich (East Germany), as above plus 1978 10 km.

Recent winners
Individual (Women)

5 km (7.5 km since 1988)
1984 Venera Chernyshova (USSR)
1985 Sanna Gronlid (Norway)
1986 Kaya Parva (USSR)
1987 Yelena Golovina (USSR)
1988 Petra Schaaf
1989 Anna Elvebakk

10 km (15 km since 1988)
1984 Venera Chernyshova (USSR)
1985 Kaya Parva (USSR)
1986 Eva Korpela (Sweden)
1987 Sanna Gronlid (Norway)
1988 Anna Elvebakk
1989 Petra Schaaf

3 × 5 km relay (3 × 7.5 km since 1989)
1984 USSR
1985 USSR
1986 USSR
1987 USSR
1988 USSR
1989 USSR

BILLIARDS

World Professional Championship
First held in 1870, organized on a challenge basis; became a knockout event in 1909; discontinued in 1934; revived in 1951 as a challenge system; reverted to a knockout event in 1980.

Recent winners

1982 Rex Williams (England)
1983 Rex Williams (England)
1984 Mark Wildman (England)
1985 Ray Edmonds (England)
1986 Robbie Foldvari (Australia)
1987 Norman Dagley (England)
1988 Norman Dagley (England)
1989 Mike Russell (England)
1990 *not held*
1991 Mike Russell (England)

Most wins: (knockout) (6), Tom Newman (England), 1921–2, 1924–7. (challenge) (8), John Roberts, Jnr (England), 1870–85.

BOBSLEIGHING AND TOBOGGANING

World Championships
First held in 1930 (four-man) and in 1931 (two-man); Olympic champions automatically become world champions.

Recent winners (Two-man)

1980 Erich Schärer/Josef Benz (Switzerland)
1981 Bernhard Germeshausen/Hans-Jürgen Gerhardt (East Germany)
1982 Erich Schärer/Josef Benz (Switzerland)
1983 Ralf Pichler/Urs Leuthold (Switzerland)
1984 Wolfgang Hoppe/Dietmar Schauerhammer (East Germany)
1985 Wolfgang Hoppe/Dietmar Schauerhammer (East Germany)
1986 Wolfgang Hoppe/Dietmar Schauerhammer (East Germany)
1987 Ralf Pichler/Celest Poltera (Switzerland)
1988 Janis Kipurs/Vladimir Kozlov (USSR)
1989 Wolfgang Hoppe/Bogdan Musiol (East Germany)
1990 Gustav Weder/Bruno Gerber (Switzerland)

Recent winners (Four-man)

1980 East Germany
1981 East Germany
1982 Switzerland
1983 Switzerland
1984 East Germany
1985 East Germany
1986 Switzerland
1987 Switzerland
1988 Switzerland
1989 Switzerland
1990 Switzerland

Most wins: (Two-man) (8), Eugenio Monti (Italy) 1957–61, 1963, 1966, 1968. (Four-man) (14), Switzerland, 1939, 1947, 1954–5, 1957, 1971, 1973, 1975, 1982–3, 1986–9.

Luge World Championships
First held in 1955; annually until 1981, then every two years; up to 1980 the Olympic champions were also world champions if the event was included in the Olympic programme.

Recent winners
Men's single-seater

1976 Detlef Günther (East Germany)
1977 Hans Rinn (East Germany)
1978 Paul Hildgartner (Italy)
1979 Detlef Günther (East Germany)
1980 Bernhard Glass (East Germany)
1981 Sergey Danilin (USSR)
1983 Miroslav Zajonc (Canada)
1985 Michael Walter (East Germany)
1987 Markus Prock (Austria)
1989 George Hack (West Germany)

Most wins: (3), Thomas Köhler (East Germany), 1962, 1964, 1967.

Recent winners
Women's single-seater

1976 Margrit Schumann (East Germany)
1977 Margrit Schumann (East Germany)
1978 Vera Sosulya (USSR)
1979 Melitta Sollmann (East Germany)
1980 Vera Sosulya (USSR)
1981 Melitta Sollman (East Germany)
1983 Steffi Martin (East Germany)
1985 Steffi Martin (East Germany)
1987 Cerstin Schmidt (East Germany)
1989 Susi Erdmann (East Germany)

Most wins: (5), Margrit Schumann (East Germany), 1973–7.

BOWLS

World Championships
Instituted for men in 1966 and for women in 1969; held every four years.

Men's Singles

1966 David Bryant (England)
1972 Malwyn Evans (Wales)
1976 Doug Watson (South Africa)
1980 David Bryant (England)
1984 Peter Bellis (New Zealand)
1988 David Bryant (England)

Men's Pairs

1966 Australia
1972 Hong Kong
1976 South Africa
1980 Australia
1984 USA
1988 New Zealand

Men's Triples

1966 Australia
1972 USA
1976 South Africa
1980 England

BOWLS (cont.)

1984 Ireland
1988 New Zealand

Men's Fours

1966 New Zealand
1972 England
1976 South Africa
1980 Hong Kong
1984 England
1988 Ireland

Leonard Trophy
Team award, given to the nation with the best overall performances in the men's world championship.

Winners

1966 Australia
1972 Scotland
1976 South Africa
1980 England
1984 Scotland
1988 England

Most wins: (6), David Bryant (singles as above, plus Triples and Team 1980, 1988).

Women's Singles

1969 Gladys Doyle (Papua New Guinea)
1973 Elsie Wilke (New Zealand)
1977 Elsie Wilke (New Zealand)
1981 Norma Shaw (England)
1985 Merle Richardson (Australia)
1988* Janet Ackland (Wales)

Women's Pairs

1969 South Africa
1973 Australia
1977 Hong Kong
1981 Ireland
1985 Australia
1988* Ireland

Women's Triples

1969 South Africa
1973 New Zealand
1977 Wales
1981 Hong Kong
1985 Australia
1988* Australia

Women's Fours

1969 South Africa
1973 New Zealand
1977 Australia
1981 England
1985 Scotland
1988* Australia

Women's Team

1969 South Africa
1973 New Zealand
1977 Australia
1981 England
1985 Australia
1988* England

Most wins: (3), Merle Richardson (Fours 1977; Singles and Pairs 1985).
*The women's event was advanced to Dec 1988 (Australia)

World Indoor Championships
First held in 1979; take place annually.

Winners

1981 David Bryant (England)
1982 John Watson (Scotland)
1983 Bob Sutherland (Scotland)
1984 Jim Baker (Ireland)
1985 Terry Sullivan (Wales)
1986 Tony Allcock (England)
1987 Tony Allcock (England
1988 Hugh Duff (Scotland)
1989 Richard Coursie (Scotland)
1990 John Price (Wales)
1991 Richard Coursie (Scotland)

Most wins: (3), David Bryant (England).

Waterloo Handicap
First held in 1907 and annually at Blackpool's Waterloo Hotel; the premier event of Crown Green Bowling.

Recent winners

1981 Roy Nicholson
1982 Dennis Mercer
1983 Stan Frith
1984 Steve Ellis
1985 Tommy Johnstone
1986 Brian Duncan
1987 Brian Duncan
1988 Ingham Gregory
1989 Brian Duncan
1990 John Bancroft
1991 John Eccles

Most wins: (4), Brian Duncan.

BOXING

World Heavyweight Champions
The first world heavyweight champion under Queensbury Rules with gloves was James J. Corbett in 1892.

Champions since 1978	Recognizing Body
1978 Muhammad Ali (USA)	WBA
1978 Larry Holmes (USA)	WBC
1979 John Tate (USA)	WBA
1980 Mike Weaver (USA)	WBA
1982 Mike Dokes (USA)	WBA
1983 Gerry Coetzee (South Africa)	WBA
1984 Larry Holmes (USA)	IBF
1984 Tim Witherspoon (USA)	WBC
1984 Pinklon Thomas (USA)	WBC
1984 Greg Page (USA)	WBA
1985 Michael Spinks (USA)	IBF
1985 Tony Tubbs (USA)	WBA
1986 Tim Witherspoon (USA)	WBA
1986 Trevor Berbick (Canada)	WBC
1986 Mike Tyson (USA)	WBC
1986 James Smith (USA)	WBA
1987 Tony Tucker (USA)	IBF
1987 Mike Tyson (USA)	WBA/WBC
1987 Mike Tyson (USA)	UND
1989 Francesco Damiani (Italy)	WBO
1989 Mike Tyson (USA)	WBA/WBC/IBF
1990 James (Buster) Douglas (USA)	WBA/WBC/IBF
1991 Evander Holyfield (USA)	WBA/WBC/IBF
Ray Mercer (USA)	WBO

UND = Undisputed Champion
WBC = World Boxing Council
WBA = World Boxing Association
IBF = International Boxing Federation
WBO = World Boxing Organization

CANOEING

Olympic Games
The most prestigious competition in the canoeing calendar, included at every Olympic celebration since 1936; the Blue Riband event in the men's competition is the Kayak Singles over 1000 metres, and in the women's the Kayak Singles over 500 metres.

Single kayak (Men)

1936 Gregor Hradetzky (Austria)
1948 Gert Fredriksson (Sweden)
1952 Gert Fredriksson (Sweden)
1956 Gert Fredriksson (Sweden)
1960 Erik Hansen (Denmark)
1964 Rolf Peterson (Sweden)
1968 Mihaly Hesz (Hungary)
1972 Aleksandr Shaparenko (USSR)
1976 Rüdiger Helm (East Germany)
1980 Rüdiger Helm (East Germany)
1984 Alan Thompson (New Zealand)
1988 Greg Barton (USA)

Single kayak (Women)

1948 Keren Hoff (Denmark)
1952 Sylvi Saimo (Finland)
1956 Elisaveta Dementyeva (USSR)
1960 Antonina Seredina (USSR)
1964 Lyudmila Khvedosyuk (USSR)
1968 Lyudmila Pinayeva (USSR)
1972 Yulia Ryabchinskaya (USSR)
1976 Carola Zirzow (East Germany)
1980 Birgit Fischer (East Germany)
1984 Agneta Andersson (Sweden)
1988 Vania Guecheva (USSR)

Most wins: Men (3), Gert Fredriksson as above. No woman has won more than one title.

CHESS

World Champions
World Champions have been recognized since 1886; first women's champion recognized in 1927.

Post-war champions (Men)

1948–57 Mikhail Botvinnik (USSR)
1957–8 Vassiliy Smyslov (USSR)
1958–60 Mikhail Botvinnik (USSR)
1960–1 Mikhail Tal (USSR)
1961–3 Mikhail Botvinnik (USSR)
1963–9 Tigran Petrosian (USSR)
1969–72 Boris Spassky (USSR)
1972–5 Bobby Fischer (USA)
1975–85 Anatoliy Karpov (USSR)
1985– Gary Kasparov (USSR)

Longest reigning champion: 27 years, Emanuel Lasker (Germany) 1894–1921.

Champions (Women)

1927–44 Vera Menchik-Stevenson (UK)
1950–3 Lyudmila Rudenko (USSR)
1953–6 Elizaveta Bykova (USSR)
1956–8 Olga Rubtsova (USSR)
1958–62 Elizaveta Bykova (USSR)
1962–78 Nona Gaprindashvili (USSR)
1978– Maya Chiburdanidze (USSR)

Longest reigning champion: 17 years, Vera Menchik-Stevenson (UK), as above.

CONTRACT BRIDGE

World Team Championship
The game's biggest championship; men's contest (The Bermuda Bowl) first held in 1951, and now takes place every two years; women's contest (The Venice Cup) first held in 1974, and since 1985 is concurrent with the men's event.

Recent winners (Men)

1973 Italy
1974 Italy
1975 Italy
1976 USA
1977 USA
1979 USA
1981 USA
1983 USA
1985 USA
1987 USA
1989 Brazil

Most wins: (13), Italy, 1957–9, 1961–3, 1965–7, 1969, 1973–5.

Recent winners (Women)

1974 USA
1976 USA
1978 USA
1981 UK
1983 not held
1985 UK
1987 Italy
1989 United States

Most wins: (4), USA, as above.

World Team Olympiad
First held in 1960; since then, every four years.

Winners (Men)

1960 France
1964 Italy
1968 Italy
1972 Italy
1976 Brazil
1980 France
1984 Poland
1988 USA

Winners (Women)

1960 United Arab Emirates
1964 UK
1968 Sweden
1972 Italy
1976 USA
1980 USA
1984 USA
1988 Denmark

Most wins: Men (3), Italy, as above; women (3), USA, as above.

CRICKET

World Cup
First played in England in 1975; held every four years; the 1987 competition was the first to be played outside England, in India and Pakistan.

Winners

1975 West Indies
1979 West Indies
1983 India
1987 Australia

County Championship
The oldest cricket competition in the world; first won by Sussex in 1827; not officially recognized until 1890, when a proper points system was introduced.

Recent winners

1981 Nottinghamshire
1982 Middlesex
1983 Essex
1984 Essex
1985 Middlesex
1986 Essex
1987 Nottinghamshire
1988 Worcestershire
1989 Worcestershire
1990 Middlesex
1991 Essex

Most outright wins: (29), Yorkshire, 1893, 1896, 1898, 1900–2, 1905, 1908, 1912, 1919, 1922–5, 1931–3, 1935, 1937–9, 1946, 1959–60, 1962–3, 1966–8.

Refuge Assurance League
First held in 1969; known as the John Player League until 1987.

Recent winners

1981 Essex
1982 Sussex
1983 Yorkshire
1984 Essex
1985 Essex
1986 Hampshire
1987 Worcestershire
1988 Worcestershire
1989 Lancashire
1990 Derbyshire
1991 Nottinghamshire

Most wins: (3), Kent, 1972–3, 1976; Essex, as above; Lancashire 1969–70, 1989.

NatWest Bank Trophy
First held in 1963; known as the Gillette Cup until 1981.

Recent winners

1981 Derbyshire
1982 Surrey
1983 Somerset
1984 Middlesex
1985 Essex
1986 Sussex
1987 Nottinghamshire
1988 Middlesex
1989 Warwickshire
1990 Lancashire
1991 Hampshire

Most wins: (5), Lancashire, 1970–2, 1975, 1990.

Benson and Hedges Cup
First held in 1972.

Recent winners

1981 Somerset
1982 Somerset
1983 Middlesex
1984 Lancashire
1985 Leicestershire
1986 Middlesex
1987 Yorkshire
1988 Hampshire
1989 Nottinghamshire
1990 Lancashire
1991 Worcestershire

Most wins: (3), Kent, 1973, 1976, 1978; Leicestershire, 1972, 1975, 1985.

Sheffield Shield
Australia's leading domestic competition; contested inter-state since 1891–2.

Recent winners

1982 South Australia
1983 New South Wales
1984 Western Australia
1985 New South Wales
1986 New South Wales
1987 Western Australia
1988 Western Australia
1989 Western Australia
1990 Western Australia
1991 Victoria

Most wins: 39, New South Wales, 1896–7, 1900, 1902–7, 1909, 1911–12, 1914, 1920–1, 1923, 1926, 1929, 1932–3, 1938, 1940, 1949–50, 1952, 1954–62, 1965–6, 1983, 1985–6.

CROQUET

McRobertson Shield
Croquet's leading tournament; held spasmodically since 1925; contested by teams from Great Britain, New Zealand and Australia.

Winners

1925 Great Britain
1928 Australia
1930 Australia
1935 Australia
1937 Great Britain
1950 New Zealand
1956 Great Britain
1963 Great Britain
1969 Great Britain
1974 Great Britain
1979 New Zealand
1982 Great Britain
1986 New Zealand

Most wins: (7), Great Britain, as above.

CROSS COUNTRY RUNNING

World Championships
First international championship held in 1903, but only included runners from England, Ireland, Scotland and Wales; recognized as an official world championship from 1973; first women's race in 1967.

Recent winners
Individual (Men)

1982 Mohamed Kedir (Ethiopia)
1983 Bekele Debele (Ethiopia)
1984 Carlos Lopes (Portugal)
1985 Carlos Lopes (Portugal)
1986 John Ngugi (Kenya)
1987 John Ngugi (Kenya)
1988 John Ngugi (Kenya)
1989 John Ngugi (Kenya)
1990 Khalid Skah (Morocco)
1991 Khalid Skah (Morocco)

CROSS COUNTRY RUNNING (cont.)

Recent winners (Team)

1982 Ethiopia
1983 Ethiopia
1984 Ethiopia
1985 Ethiopia
1986 Kenya
1987 Kenya
1988 Kenya
1989 Kenya
1990 Kenya
1991 Kenya

Most wins: Individual (4), Jack Holden (England), 1933–5, 1939; Alain Mimoun (France), 1949, 1952, 1954, 1956; Gaston Roelants (Belgium), 1962, 1967, 1969, 1972. John Ngugi, as above. Team (44), England, between 1903 and 1980

Recent winners Individual (Women)

1982 Maricica Puica (Romania)
1983 Greta Waitz (Norway)
1984 Maricica Puica (Romania)
1985 Zola Budd (England)
1986 Zola Budd (England)
1987 Annette Sergent (France)
1988 Ingrid Kristiansen (Norway)
1989 Annette Sergent (France)
1990 Lynn Jennings (USA)
1991 Lynn Jennings (USA)

Recent winners Team (Women)

1982 USSR
1983 USA
1984 USA
1985 USA
1986 England
1987 USA
1988 USSR
1989 USSR
1990 USSR
1991 Ethiopia and Kenya (tied)

Most wins: Individual (5), Doris Brown (USA), 1967–71; Greta Waitz (Norway), 1978–81, 1983. Team (8), USA, 1968–9, 1975, 1979, 1983–5, 1987.

CURLING

World Championships
First men's championship held in 1959; first women's championship in 1979; takes place annually.

Recent winners (Men)

1979 Norway
1980 Canada
1981 Switzerland
1982 Canada
1983 Canada
1984 Norway
1985 Canada
1986 Canada
1987 Canada
1988 Norway
1989 Canada

Recent winners (Women)

1979 Switzerland
1980 Canada
1981 Sweden
1982 Denmark
1983 Switzerland
1984 Canada
1985 Canada
1986 Canada
1987 Canada
1988 West Germany
1989 Canada

Most wins: Men (19), Canada, 1959–64, 1966, 1968–72, 1980, 1982–3, 1985–7, 1989. Women (6), Canada, as above.

CYCLING

Tour de France
World's premier cycling event; first held in 1903.

Recent winners

1981 Bernard Hinault (France)
1982 Bernard Hinault (France)
1983 Laurent Fignon (France)
1984 Laurent Fignon (France)
1985 Bernard Hinault (France)
1986 Greg LeMond (USA)
1987 Stephen Roche (Ireland)
1988 Pedro Delgado (Spain)
1989 Greg LeMond (USA)
1990 Greg LeMond (USA)
1991 Miguel Indurain (Spain)

Most wins: (5), Jacques Anquetil (France), 1957, 1961–4; Eddy Merckx (Belgium), 1969–72, 1974; Bernard Hinault (France), 1978–9, 1981–2, 1985.

World Road Race Championships
Men's race first held in 1927; first women's race in 1958; takes place annually.

Recent winners (Professional Men)

1981 Freddy Maertens (Belgium)
1982 Giuseppe Saroni (Italy)
1983 Greg LeMond (USA)
1984 Claude Criquielion (Belgium)
1985 Joop Zoetemelk (Holland)
1986 Moreno Argentin (Italy)
1987 Stephen Roche (Ireland)
1988 Maurizio Fondriest (Italy)
1989 Greg LeMond (USA)
1990 Rudy Dhaemens (Belgium)
1991 Gianni Bugno (Italy)

Recent winners (Women)

1981 Ute Enzenauer (West Germany)
1982 Mandy Jones (Great Britain)
1983 Marianne Berglund (Sweden)
1984 *not held*
1985 Jeannie Longo (France)
1986 Jeannie Longo (France)
1987 Jeannie Longo (France)
1988 Jeannie Longo (France)
1989 Jeannie Longo (France)
1990 Catherine Marsal (France)
1991 Leontein van Moorsel (Netherlands)

Most wins: Men (3), Alfredo Binda (Italy), 1927, 1930, 1932; Rik Van Steenbergen (Belgium), 1949, 1956–7; Eddy Merckx (Belgium), 1967, 1971, 1974. Women (5), Jeannie Longo, as above.

CYCLO-CROSS

World Championships
First held in 1950 as an open event; separate professional and amateur events since 1967.

Recent winners (Professional)

1980 Roland Liboton (Belgium)
1981 Johannes Stamsnijder (Holland)
1982 Roland Liboton (Belgium)
1983 Roland Liboton (Belgium)
1984 Roland Liboton (Belgium)
1985 Klaus-Peter Thaler (West Germany)
1986 Albert Zweifel (Switzerland)
1987 Klaus-Peter Thaler (West Germany)
1988 Pascal Richard (Switzerland)
1989 Danny De Bie (Belgium)
1990 Hank Baars

Recent winners (Amateur)

1980 Fritz Saladin (Switzerland)
1981 Milos Fisera (Czechoslovakia)
1982 Milos Fisera (Czechoslovakia)
1983 Radomir Simunek (Czechoslovakia)
1984 Radomir Simunek (Czechoslovakia)
1985 Mike Kluge (West Germany)
1986 Vito di Tano (Italy)
1987 Mike Kluge (West Germany)
1988 Karol Camrola (Czechoslovakia)
1989 Ondrej Glaja (Czechoslovakia)
1990 Andreas Buesser

Most wins: Professional (7), Eric de Vlaeminck (Belgium), 1966, 1968–73. Amateur (5), Robert Vermiere (Belgium), 1970–1, 1974–5, 1977.

DARTS

World Professional Championship
First held at Nottingham in 1978.

Winners

1979 John Lowe (England)
1980 Eric Bristow (England)
1981 Eric Bristow (England)
1982 Jocky Wilson (Scotland)
1983 Keith Deller (England)
1984 Eric Bristow (England)
1985 Eric Bristow (England)
1986 Eric Bristow (England)
1987 John Lowe (England)
1988 Bob Anderson (England)
1989 Jocky Wilson (Scotland)
1990 Phil Taylor (England)
1991 Dennis Priestley (England)

Most wins: (5), Eric Bristow, as above.

World Cup
A team competition first held at Wembley in 1977; takes place every two years.

Winners (Team)

1979 England
1981 England
1983 England
1985 England
1987 England
1989 England
1991 England

Winners (Individual)

1979 Nicky Virachkul (USA)
1981 John Lowe (England)
1983 Eric Bristow (England)

DARTS (cont.)

1985 Eric Bristow (England)
1987 Eric Bristow (England)
1989 Eric Bristow (England)
1991 John Lowe (England)

Most wins: Team (6), England, as above. Individual (3), Eric Bristow (England), as above.

DRAUGHTS

World Championship
Held on a challenge basis; the champion since 1979 has been Dr M Tinsley (USA); he has defended the title five times.

British Open Championship
The leading championship in Britain; first held in 1926; now takes place every two years.

Recent winners

1970 I Edwards (Great Britain)
1972 G Davies (Great Britain)
1974 J McGill (Great Britain)
1976 A Huggins (Great Britain)
1978 J McGill (Great Britain)
1980 T Watson (Great Britain)
1982 T Watson (Great Britain)
1984 A Long (USA)
1986 H Delvin (Great Britain)
1988 DE Oldbury (Great Britain)

EQUESTRIAN EVENTS

World Championships
Show Jumping championships first held in 1953 (for men) and 1965 (for women); since 1978 they have competed together and on equal terms; team competition introduced in 1978; Three Day Event and Dressage championships introduced in 1966; all three now held every four years.

Winners
Show Jumping (Men)

1953 Francisco Goyoago (Spain)
1954 Hans-Günter Winkler (West Germany)
1955 Hans-Günter Winkler (West Germany)
1956 Raimondo D'Inzeo (Italy)
1960 Raimondo D'Inzeo (Italy)
1966 Pierre d'Oriola (France)
1970 David Broome (Great Britain)
1974 Hartwig Steenken (West Germany)

Winners
Show Jumping (Women)

1965 Marion Coakes (Great Britain)
1970 Janou Lefèbvre (France)
1974 Janou Tissot (*née* Lefèbvre) (France)

Winners (Individual)

1982 Norbert Koof (West Germany)
1986 Gail Greenough (Canada)
1990 Eric Navet (France)

Winners (Team)

1982 France
1986 USA
1990 France

Winners
Three Day Event (Individual)

1970 Mary Gordon-Watson (Great Britain)
1974 Bruce Davidson (USA)
1978 Bruce Davidson (USA)
1982 Lucinda Green (Great Britain)
1986 Virginia Leng (Great Britain)
1990 Blyth Tait (New Zealand)

Winners (Team)

1970 Great Britain
1974 USA
1978 Canada
1982 Great Britain
1986 Great Britain
1990 New Zealand

Winners
Dressage (Individual)

1970 Yelene Petouchkova (USSR)
1974 Reiner Klimke (West Germany)
1978 Christine Stückelberger (Switzerland)
1982 Reiner Klimke (West Germany)
1986 Anne Grethe Jensen (Denmark)
1990 Nicole Uphoff (West Germany)

Winners
Dressage (Team)

1970 USSR
1974 West Germany
1978 West Germany
1982 West Germany
1986 West Germany
1990 West Germany

FENCING

World Championships
Held annually since 1921 (between 1921–35, known as European Championships); not held in Olympic years.

Recent winners
Foil (Men) Individual

1975 Christian Noel (France)
1977 Alexander Romankov (USSR)
1978 Didier Flament (France)
1979 Alexander Romankov (USSR)
1981 Vladimir Smirnov (USSR)
1982 Alexander Romankov (USSR)
1983 Alexander Romankov (USSR)
1985 Mauro Numa (Italy)
1986 Andrea Borella (Italy)
1987 Mathias Gey (West Germany)
1989 Alexandr Koch (West Germany)

Recent winners
Foil (Team)

1975 France
1977 West Germany
1978 Poland
1979 USSR
1981 USSR
1982 USSR
1983 West Germany
1985 Italy
1986 Italy
1987 USSR
1989 USSR

Most wins: Individual (5), Alexander Romankov (USSR), 1974, 1977, 1979, 1982–3. Team (15), USSR (between 1959–89).

Recent winners
Foil (Women) Individual

1975 Ecaterina Stahl (Romania)
1977 Valentina Sidorova (USSR)
1978 Valentina Sidorova (USSR)
1979 Cornelia Hanisch (West Germany)
1981 Cornelia Hanisch (West Germany)
1982 Naila Giliazova (USSR)
1983 Dorina Vaccaroni (Italy)
1985 Cornelia Hanisch (West Germany)
1986 Anja Fichtel (West Germany)
1987 Elisabeta Tufan (Romania)
1989 Olga Velitchko (USSR)

Recent winners
Foil (Team)

1975 USSR
1977 USSR
1978 USSR
1979 USSR
1981 USSR
1982 Italy
1983 Italy
1985 West Germany
1986 USSR
1987 Hungary
1989 West Germany

Most wins: Individual (3), Helène Mayer (Germany), 1929, 1931, 1937; Ilona Elek (Hungary, 1934–5, 1951; Ellen Müller-Preiss (Austria), 1947, 1949, 1950 (*shared*); Cornelia Hanisch, as above. Team (15), USSR (between 1956–86).

Recent winners
Epee (Individual)

1975 Alexander Pusch (West Germany)
1977 Johan Harmenberg (Sweden)
1978 Alexander Pusch (West Germany)
1979 Philippe Riboud (France)
1981 Zoltan Szekely (Hungary)
1982 Jenö Pap (Hungary)
1983 Ellmar Bormann (West Germany)
1985 Philippe Boisse (France)
1986 Philippe Riboud (France)
1987 Volker Fischer (West Germany)
1989 Manuel Pereira (Spain)

Recent winners
Epee (Team)

1975 Sweden
1977 Sweden
1978 Hungary
1979 USSR
1981 USSR
1982 France
1983 France
1985 West Germany
1986 West Germany
1987 West Germany
1989 Italy

Most wins: Individual (3), Georges Buchard (France), 1927, 1931, 1933; Alexei Nikanchikov (USSR), 1966–7, 1970. Team (11), Italy (between 1931–58); France (between 1934–89).

Recent winners
Epee (Women) (Individual)

1989 Anja Straub (Switzerland)

Recent winners
Epee (Women) (Team)

1989 Hungary

Recent winners
Sabre (Individual)

1975 Vladimir Nazlimov (USSR)
1977 Pal Gerevich (Hungary)
1978 Viktor Krovopuskov (USSR)

FENCING (cont.)

1979 Vladimir Nazlimov (USSR)
1981 Mariusz Wodke (Poland)
1982 Viktor Krovopuskov (USSR)
1983 Vasiliy Etropolski (Bulgaria)
1985 György Nebald (Hungary)
1986 Sergey Mindirgassov (USSR)
1987 Jean-François Lamour (France)
1989 Grigory Kirienko (USSR)

Recent winners
Sabre (Team)

1975 USSR
1977 USSR
1978 Hungary
1979 USSR
1981 Hungary
1982 Hungary
1983 USSR
1985 USSR
1986 USSR
1987 USSR
1989 USSR

Most wins: Individual (3), Aladar Gerevich (Hungary), 1935, 1951, 1955; Jerzy Pawlowski (Poland) 1957, 1965–6; Yakov Rylsky (USSR), 1958, 1961, 1963. Team (17), Hungary (between 1930–82).

GAELIC FOOTBALL

All-Ireland Championship
First held 1887; takes place in Dublin on the third Sunday in September each year.

Recent winners

1979 Kerry
1980 Kerry
1981 Kerry
1982 Offaly
1983 Dublin
1984 Kerry
1985 Kerry
1986 Kerry
1987 Meath
1988 Meath
1989 Cork

Most wins: (30), Kerry, 1903–4, 1909, 1913–14, 1924, 1926, 1929–32, 1937, 1939–41, 1946, 1953, 1955, 1959, 1962, 1969–70, 1975, 1978–81, 1984–6.

GLIDING

World Championships
First held in 1937; current classes are Open, Standard and 15 metres; the Open class is the principal event, held every two years until 1978 and again since 1981.

Recent winners

1968 Harro Wödl (Austria)
1970 George Moffat (USA)
1972 Göran Ax (Sweden)
1974 George Moffat (USA)
1976 George Lee (Great Britain)
1978 George Lee (Great Britain)
1981 George Lee (Great Britain)
1983 Ingo Renner (Australia)
1985 Ingo Renner (Australia)
1987 Ingo Renner (Australia)
1989 Robin May (Great Britain)

Most wins: (3), George Lee, as above; Ingo Renner, as above.

GOLF

British Open
First held at Prestwick in 1860, and won by Willie Park; takes place annually; regarded as the world's leading golf tournament.

Recent winners

1981 Bill Rogers (USA)
1982 Tom Watson (USA)
1983 Tom Watson (USA)
1984 Severiano Ballesteros (Spain)
1985 Sandy Lyle (Great Britain)
1986 Greg Norman (Australia)
1987 Nick Faldo (Great Britain)
1988 Severiano Ballesteros (Spain)
1989 Mark Calcavecchia (USA)
1990 Nick Faldo (Great Britain)
1991 Ian Baker-Finch (Australia)

Most wins: (6), Harry Vardon (Great Britain), 1896, 1898–9, 1903, 1911, 1914.

United States Open
First held at Newport, Rhode Island in 1895, and won by Horace Rawlins; takes place annually.

Recent winners

1981 David Graham (Australia)
1982 Tom Watson (USA)
1983 Larry Nelson (USA)
1984 Fuzzy Zoeller (USA)
1985 Andy North (USA)
1986 Ray Floyd (USA)
1987 Scott Simpson (USA)
1988 Curtis Strange (USA)
1989 Curtis Strange (USA)
1990 Hale Irwin (USA)
1991 Payne Stewart (USA)

Most wins: (4), Willie Anderson (USA), 1901, 1903–5; Bobby Jones (USA), 1923, 1926, 1929–30; Ben Hogan (USA), 1948, 1950–1, 1953; Jack Nicklaus (USA), 1962, 1967, 1972, 1980.

US Masters
First held in 1934; takes place at the Augusta National course in Georgia every April.

Recent winners

1981 Tom Watson (USA)
1982 Craig Stadler (USA)
1983 Severiano Ballesteros (Spain)
1984 Ben Crenshaw (USA)
1985 Bernhard Langer (West Germany)
1986 Jack Nicklaus (USA)
1987 Larry Mize (USA)
1988 Sandy Lyle (Great Britain)
1989 Nick Faldo (Great Britain)
1990 Nick Faldo (Great Britain)
1991 Ian Woosnam (Great Britain)

Most wins: (6), Jack Nicklaus (USA), 1963, 1965–6, 1972, 1975, 1986.

United States PGA Championship
The last of the season's four 'Majors'; first held in 1916, and a match-play event until 1958; takes place annually.

Recent winners

1981 Larry Nelson (USA)
1982 Ray Floyd (USA)
1983 Hal Sutton (USA)
1984 Lee Trevino (USA)
1985 Hubert Green (USA)
1986 Bob Tway (USA)
1987 Larry Nelson (USA)
1988 Jeff Sluman (USA)
1989 Payne Stewart (USA)
1990 Wayne Grady (USA)
1991 John Daly (USA)

Most wins: (5), Walter Hagen (USA), 1921, 1924–7; Jack Nicklaus (USA), 1963, 1971, 1973, 1975, 1980.

Ryder Cup
The leading international team tournament; first held at Worcester, Massachusetts in 1927; takes place every two years between teams from the USA and Europe (Great Britain 1927–71; Great Britain and Ireland 1973–7).

Recent winners

1971	USA	18½–13½
1973	USA	19–13
1975	USA	21–11
1977	USA	12½–7½
1979	USA	17–11
1981	USA	18½–9½
1983	USA	14½–13½
1985	Europe	16½–11½
1987	Europe	15–13
1989	Drawn	14–14
1991	USA	15–13

Wins: (22), USA, 1927, 1931, 1935–7, 1947–55, 1959–67, 1971–83, 1991. (3), Great Britain, 1929, 1933, 1957. (2), Europe, 1985, 1987. (2), Drawn, 1969, 1989.

GREYHOUND RACING

Greyhound Derby
The top race of the British season, first held in 1927; run at the White City every year (except 1940) until its closure in 1985; since then all races run at Wimbledon.

Recent winners

1979 Sarah's Bunny
1980 Indian Joe
1981 Parkdown Jet
1982 Laurie's Panther
1983 I'm Slippy
1984 Whisper Wishes
1985 Pagan Swallow
1986 Tico
1987 Signal Spark
1988 Hit the Lid
1989 Lartigue Note

Most wins: (2), Mick the Miller, 1929–30; Patricia's Hope, 1972–3.

GYMNASTICS

World Championships
First held in 1903; took place every four years, 1922–78; since 1979, every two years.

Recent winners
Individual (Men)

1966 Mikhail Voronin (USSR)
1970 Eizo Kenmotsu (Japan)

GYMNASTICS (cont.)

1974 Shigeru Kasamatsu (Japan)
1978 Nikolai Adrianov (USSR)
1979 Aleksandr Ditiatin (USSR)
1981 Yuri Korolev (USSR)
1983 Dmitri Belozerchev (USSR)
1985 Yuri Korolev (USSR)
1987 Dmitri Belozerchev (USSR)
1989 Igor Korobichensky (USSR)
1991 Vitaly Scherbo (USSR)

Recent winners
Team (Men)

1966 Japan
1970 Japan
1974 Japan
1978 Japan
1979 USSR
1981 USSR
1983 China
1985 USSR
1987 USSR
1989 USSR
1991 USSR

Most wins: Individual (2), Marco Torrès (France), 1909, 1913; Peter Sumi (Yugoslavia), 1922, 1926; Yuri Korolev and Dmitri Belozerchev, as above. Team (8), USSR, as above, plus 1954, 1958, 1979.

Recent winners
Individual (Women)

1966 Vera Caslavska (Czechoslovakia)
1970 Ludmila Tourischeva (USSR)
1974 Ludmila Tourischeva (USSR)
1978 Yelena Mukhina (USSR)
1979 Nelli Kim (USSR)
1981 Olga Bitcherova (USSR)
1983 Natalia Yurchenko (USSR)
1985 Yelena Shoushounova (USSR) and Oksana Omeliantchuk (USSR)
1987 Aurelia Dobre (Romania)
1989 Svetlana Boginskaya
1991 Kim Zmeskal (USA)

Recent winners
Team (Women)

1966 Czechoslovakia
1970 USSR
1974 USSR
1978 USSR
1979 Romania
1981 USSR
1983 USSR
1985 USSR
1987 Romania
1989 USSR
1991 USSR

Most wins: Individual (2), Vlasta Dekanová (Czechoslovakia), 1934, 1938; Larissa Latynina (USSR), 1958, 1962, Vera Caslavska and Ludmila Tourischeva, as above. Team (10), USSR, as above plus 1954, 1958.

HANDBALL

World Championships
First men's championships held in 1938, both indoors and outdoors (latter discontinued in 1966); first women's outdoor championships in 1949, (discontinued in 1960); first women's indoor championships in 1957.

Winners
Indoors (Men)

1938 Germany
1954 Sweden
1958 Sweden
1961 Romania
1964 Romania
1967 Czechoslovakia
1970 Romania
1974 Romania
1978 West Germany
1982 USSR
1986 Yugoslavia

Winners
Outdoors (Men)

1938 Germany
1948 Sweden
1952 West Germany
1955 West Germany
1959 East/West Germany (*combined*)
1963 East Germany
1966 West Germany

Most wins: Indoors (4), Romania. Outdoors (4), West Germany (including 1 as combined East/ West German team).

Winners
Indoors (Women)

1957 Czechoslovakia
1962 Romania
1965 Hungary
1971 East Germany
1973 Yugoslavia
1975 East Germany
1979 East Germany
1982 USSR
1986 USSR

Winners
Outdoors (Women)

1949 Hungary
1956 Romania
1960 Romania

Most wins: Indoors (3), East Germany, as above. Outdoors (2), Romania, as above.

HANG GLIDING

World Championships
First held officially in 1976; since 1979, take place every two years.

Winners
Individual (Class 1)

1976 Christian Steinbach (Austria)
1979 Josef Guggenmose (West Germany)
1981 Pepe Lopez (Brazil)
1983 Steve Moyes (Australia)
1985 John Pendry (Great Britain)
1987 Rich Duncan (Australia)
1989 Robert Whittall (Great Britain)

Winners (Team)

1976 Austria
1979 France
1981 Great Britain
1983 Australia
1985 Great Britain
1987 Australia
1989 Great Britain

Most wins: Individual, no person has won more than one title. Team (3), Great Britain, as above.

HOCKEY

World Cup
Men's tournament first held in 1971, and every four years since 1978; women's tournament first held in 1974, and now takes place every three years.

Winners (Men)

1973 Netherlands
1975 India
1978 Pakistan
1982 Pakistan
1986 Australia
1990 Netherlands

Most wins: (3), Pakistan, as above, plus 1971, 1978.

Winners (Women)

1976 West Germany
1978 Netherlands
1981 West Germany
1983 Netherlands
1986 Netherlands
1989 Netherlands

Most wins: (5), Netherlands, as above, plus 1974.

Olympic Games
Regarded as hockey's leading competition; first held in 1908; included at every celebration since 1928; women's competition first held in 1980.

Post-war winners (Men)

1948 India
1952 India
1956 India
1960 Pakistan
1964 India
1968 Pakistan
1972 West Germany
1976 New Zealand
1980 India
1984 Pakistan
1988 Great Britain

Winners (Women)

1980 Zimbabwe
1984 Netherlands
1988 Australia

Most wins: Men (8), India, 1928, 1932, 1936, 1948, 1952, 1956, 1964, 1980. Women, no nation has won the title more than once.

HORSE RACING

The Derby
The 'Blue Riband' of the Turf; run at Epsom over 1½ miles; first run in 1780.

Recent winners

Horse (Jockey)
1981 Shergar (Walter Swinburn)
1982 Golden Fleece (Pat Eddery)
1983 Teenoso (Lester Piggott)
1984 Secreto (Christy Roche)
1985 Slip Anchor (Steve Cauthen)
1986 Shahrastani (Walter Swinburn)
1987 Reference Point (Steve Cauthen)
1988 Kahyasi (Ray Cochrane)
1989 Nashwan (Willie Carson)
1990 Quest for Fame (Pat Eddery)
1991 Generous (Alan Munro)

Most wins: Jockey (9), Lester Piggott, 1954, 1957, 1960, 1968, 1970, 1972, 1976–7, 1983.

HORSE RACING (cont.)

The Oaks

Raced at Epsom over 1½ miles; for fillies only; first run in 1779.

Recent winners

Horse (Jockey)
1981 Blue Wind (Lester Piggott)
1982 Time Charter (Billy Newnes)
1983 Sun Princess (Willy Carson)
1984 Circus Plume (Lester Piggott)
1985 Oh So Sharp (Steve Cauthen)
1986 Midway Lady (Ray Cochrane)
1987 Unite (Walter Swinburn)
1988 Diminuendo (Steve Cauthen)
1989 Aliysa (Walter Swinburn)
1990 Salsabil (Willie Carson)
1991 Jet Ski Lady (Christy Roche)

Most wins: Jockey (9), Frank Buckle, 1797–9, 1802–3, 1805, 1817–18, 1923.

One Thousand Guineas

Run over 1 mile at Newmarket; for fillies only; first run in 1814.

Recent winners

Horse (Jockey)
1981 Fairy Footsteps (Lester Piggott)
1982 On The House (John Reid)
1983 Ma Biche (Freddy Head)
1984 Pebbles (Philip Robinson)
1985 Oh So Sharp (Steve Cauthen)
1986 Midway Lady (Ray Cochrane)
1987 Miesque (Freddy Head)
1988 Ravinella (Gary Moore)
1989 Musical Bliss (Walter Swinburn)
1990 Salsabil (Willie Carson)
1991 Shadayid (Willie Carson)

Most wins: Jockey (7), George Fordham, 1859, 1861, 1865, 1868–9, 1881, 1883.

Two Thousand Guineas

Run at Newmarket over 1 mile; first run in 1809.

Recent winners

Horse (Jockey)
1981 To-Agori-Mou (Greville Starkey)
1982 Zino (Freddy Head)
1983 Lomond (Pat Eddery)
1984 El Gran Senor (Pat Eddery)
1985 Shadeed (Lester Piggott)
1986 Dancing Brave (Greville Starkey)
1987 Don't Forget Me (Willie Carson)
1988 Doyoun (Walter Swinburn)
1989 Nashwan (Willie Carson)
1990 Tirol (Michael Kinane)
1991 Mystiko (Michael Roberts)

Most wins: Jockey (9), Jem Robinson, 1825, 1828, 1831, 1833–6, 1847–8.

St Leger

The oldest of the five English classics; first run in 1776; raced at Doncaster annually over 1 mile 6 furlongs 127 yards.

Recent winners

Horse (Jockey)
1981 Cut Above (Joe Mercer)
1982 Touching Wood (Paul Cook)
1983 Sun Princess (Willie Carson)
1984 Commanche Run (Lester Piggott)
1985 Oh So Sharp (Steve Cauthen)
1986 Moon Madness (Pat Eddery)
1987 Reference Point (Steve Cauthen)
1988 Minster Son (Willie Carson)
1989 Michelozzo (Steve Cauthen)
1990 Snurge (Richard Quinn)
1991 Toulon (Pat Eddery)

Most wins: Jockey (9), Bill Scott, 1821, 1825, 1828–9, 1838–41, 1846.

Grand National

Steeplechasing's most famous race; first run at Maghull in 1836; at Aintree since 1839; war-time races at Gatwick 1916–18.

Recent winners

Horse (Jockey)
1981 Aldaniti (Bob Champion)
1982 Grittar (Mr Dick Saunders)
1983 Corbiere (Ben De Haan)
1984 Hallo Dandy (Neale Doughty)
1985 Last Suspect (Hywel Davies)
1986 West Tip (Richard Dunwoody)
1987 Maori Venture (Steve Knight)
1988 Rhyme 'N' Reason (Brendan Powell)
1989 Little Polveir (Jimmy Frost)
1990 Mr Frisk (Marcus Armytage)
1991 Seagram (Nigel Howke)

● 'Mr' denotes that the jockey is an amateur rider.

Most wins: Jockey (5), George Stevens, 1856, 1863–4, 1869–70. Horse (3), Red Rum 1973–4, 1977.

Prix de l'Arc de Triomphe

The leading end of season race in Europe; raced over 2400 metres at Longchamp; first run in 1920.

Recent winners

Horse (Jockey)
1981 Gold River (Gary Moore)
1982 Akiyda (Yves Saint-Martin)
1983 All Along (Walter Swinburn)
1984 Sagace (Yves Saint-Martin)
1985 Rainbow Quest (Pat Eddery)
1986 Dancing Brave (Pat Eddery)
1987 Trempolino (Pat Eddery)
1988 Tony Bin (John Reid)
1989 Caroll House (Michael Kinane)
1990 Caroll House (Michael Kinane)
1991 Suave Dancer (Cash Asmussen)

Most wins: Jockey (4), Jacko Doyasbère, 1942, 1944, 1950–1; Freddy Head, 1966, 1972, 1976, 1979; Yves Saint-Martin, 1970, 1974, 1982, 1984; Pat Eddery, as above. Horse (2), Ksar, 1921–2; Motrico, 1930, 1932; Corrida, 1936–7; Tantième, 1950–1; Ribot, 1955–6; Alleged 1977–8.

HURLING

All-Ireland Championship

First contested in 1887; played on the first Sunday in September each year.

Recent winners

1979 Kilkenny
1980 Galway
1981 Offaly
1982 Kilkenny
1983 Kilkenny
1984 Cork
1985 Offaly
1986 Cork
1987 Galway
1988 Galway
1989 Tipperary

Most wins: (26), Cork, 1890, 1892–4, 1902–3, 1919, 1926, 1928–9, 1931, 1941–4, 1946, 1952–4, 1966, 1970, 1976–8, 1984, 1986.

ICE HOCKEY

World Championship

First held in 1930; takes place annually (except 1980); up to 1968 Olympic champions also regarded as world champions.

Recent winners

1981 USSR
1982 USSR
1983 USSR
1984 USSR
1985 Czechoslovakia
1986 USSR
1987 Sweden
1988 USSR
1989 USSR
1990 USSR
1991 Sweden

Most wins: (24), USSR, 1954, 1956, 1963–71, 1973–5, 1978–9, 1981–4, 1986, 1988–90.

Stanley Cup

The most sought-after trophy at club level; the end-of-season meeting between the winners of the two conferences in the National Hockey League in the USA and Canada.

Recent winners

1981 New York Islanders
1982 New York Islanders
1983 New York Islanders
1984 Edmonton Oilers
1985 Edmonton Oilers
1986 Montreal Canadiens
1987 Edmonton Oilers
1988 Edmonton Oilers
1989 Calgary Flames
1990 Edmonton Oilers
1991 Pittsburgh Pirates

Most wins: (23), Montreal Canadiens, 1916, 1924, 1930–1, 1944, 1946, 1953, 1956–60, 1965–6, 1968–9, 1971, 1973, 1976–9, 1986.

ICE SKATING

World Championships

First men's championships in 1896; first women's event in 1906; pairs first contested in 1908; Ice Dance officially recognized in 1952.

Recent winners (Men)

1982 Scott Hamilton (USA)
1983 Scott Hamilton (USA)
1984 Scott Hamilton (USA)
1985 Alexander Fadeyev (USSR)
1986 Brian Boitano (USA)
1987 Brian Orser (Canada)
1988 Brian Boitano (USA)
1989 Kurt Browning (Canada)
1990 Kurt Browning (Canada)
1991 Kurt Browning (Canada)

Most wins: (10), Ulrich Salchow (Sweden), 1901–5, 1907–11.

ICE SKATING (cont.)

Recent winners (Women)

1982 Elaine Zayak (USA)
1983 Rosalynn Sumners (USA)
1984 Katarina Witt (East Germany)
1985 Katarina Witt (East Germany)
1986 Debbie Thomas (USA)
1987 Katarina Witt (East Germany)
1988 Katarina Witt (East Germany)
1989 Midori Ito (Japan)
1990 Jill Trenany (USA)
1991 Kristi Yamaguchi (USA)

Most wins: (10), Sonja Henie (Norway), 1927–36.

Recent winners (Pairs)

1982 Tassilo Thierbach/Sabine Baess (East Germany)
1983 Oleg Vasiliev/Yelena Valova (USSR)
1984 Paul Martini/Barbara Underhill (Canada)
1985 Oleg Vasiliev/Yelena Valova (USSR)
1986 Sergey Grinkov/Yekaterina Gordeeva (USSR)
1987 Sergey Grinkov/Yekaterina Gordeeva (USSR)
1988 Oleg Vasiliev/Yelena Valorva (USSR)
1989 Sergey Grinkov/Yekaterina Gordeeva (USSR)
1990 Sergey Grinkov/Yekaterina Gordeeva (USSR)
1991 Artur Dmitriev/Natalya Mishkutienko (USSR)

Most wins: (10), Irina Rodnina (USSR), 1969–72 (with Aleksey Ulanov), 1973–8 (with Aleksander Zaitsev).

Recent winners (Ice Dance)

1982 Christopher Dean/Jayne Torvill (Great Britain)
1983 Christopher Dean/Jayne Torvill (Great Britain)
1984 Christopher Dean/Jayne Torvill (Great Britain)
1985 Andrey Bukin/Natalya Bestemianova (USSR)
1986 Andrey Bukin/Natalya Bestemianova (USSR)
1987 Andrey Bukin/Natalya Bestemianova (USSR)
1988 Andrey Bukin/Natalya Bestemianova (USSR)
1989 Sergey Ponomarenko/Marina Klimova (USSR)
1990 Sergey Ponomarenko/Marina Klimova (USSR)
1991 Alexandr Zhulin/Maia Usova (USSR)

Most wins: (6), Aleksander Gorshkov and Lyudmila Pakhomova (USSR), 1970–4, 1976.

JUDO

World Championships
First held in 1956, now contested every two years; current weight categories established in 1979; women's championship instituted in 1980.

Recent winners
Open Class (Men)

1979 Sumio Endo (Japan)
1981 Yasuhiro Yamashita (Japan)
1983 Hitoshi Saito (Japan)
1985 Yoshimi Masaki (Japan)
1987 Noayo Ogawa (Japan)
1989 Noayo Ogawa (Japan)

Recent winners
Over 95 kg (Men)

1979 Yasuhiro Yamashita (Japan)
1981 Yasuhiro Yamashita (Japan)
1983 Yasuhiro Yamashita (Japan)
1985 Yung-Chul Cho (Korea)
1987 Grigori Vertichev (USSR)
1989 Noayo Ogawa (Japan)

Recent winners
Under 95 kg (Men)

1979 Tengiz Khubuluri (USSR)
1981 Tenzig Khubuluri (USSR)
1983 Valeriy Divisenko (USSR)
1985 Hitoshi Sugai (Japan)
1987 Hitoshi Sugai (Japan)
1989 Koba Kurtanidze (Japan)

Recent winners
Under 86 kg (Men)

1979 Detlef Ultsch (East Germany)
1981 Bernard Tchoullouyan (France)
1983 Detlef Ultsch (East Germany)
1985 Peter Seisenbacher (Austria)
1987 Fabien Canu (France)
1989 Fabien Canu (France)

Recent winners
Under 78 kg (Men)

1979 Shozo Fujii (Japan)
1981 Neil Adams (Great Britain)
1983 Nobutoshi Hikage (Japan)
1985 Nobutoshi Hikage (Japan)
1987 Hirotaka Okada (Japan)
1989 Byung-ju Kim (South Korea)

Recent winners
Under 71 kg (Men)

1979 Kyoto Katsuki (Japan)
1981 Chon-Hak Park (Korea)
1983 Kidetoshi Nakanishi (Japan)
1985 Byeong-Keun Ahn (Korea)
1987 Mike Swain (USA)
1989 Toshitiko Koga (Japan)

Recent winners
Under 65 kg (Men)

1979 Nikolai Soludkhin (USSR)
1981 Katsuhiko Kashiwazaki (Japan)
1983 Nikolai Soludkhin (USSR)
1985 Yuriy Sokolov (USSR)
1987 Yosuke Yamamoto (Japan)
1989 Drago Becanovic (Yugoslavia)

Recent winners
Under 60 kg (Men)

1979 Thierry Ray (France)
1981 Yasuhiko Moriwaki (Japan)
1983 Khazret Tletseri (USSR)
1985 Shinji Hosokawa (Japan)
1987 Kim Jae-Yup (South Korea)
1989 Amiran Totikashvili (USSR)

Most titles: (4), Yashiro Yamashita (Japan), 1981 (Open), 1979, 1981, 1983 (over 95 kg); Shozo Fujii (Japan), 1971, 1973, 1975 (under 80 kg), 1979 (under 78 kg).

Recent winners
Open (Women)

1980 Ingrid Berghmans (Belgium)
1982 Ingrid Berghmans (Belgium)
1984 Ingrid Berghmans (Belgium)
1986 Ingrid Berghmans (Belgium)
1987 Fenglian Gao (China)
1989 Estela Rodriguez (Cuba)

Recent winners
Over 72 kg (Women)

1980 Margarita de Cal (Italy)
1982 Natalina Lupino (France)
1984 Maria-Teresa Motta (Italy)
1986 Fenglian Gao (China)
1987 Fenglian Gao (China)
1989 Fenglian Gao (China)

Recent winners
Under 72 kg (Women)

1980 Jocelyne Triadou (France)
1982 Barbara Classen (West Germany)
1984 Ingrid Berghmans (Belgium)
1986 Irene de Kok (Netherlands)
1987 Irene de Kok (Netherlands)
1989 Ingrid Berghmans (Belgium)

Recent winners
Under 66 kg (Women)

1980 Edith Simon (Austria)
1982 Brigitte Deydier (France)
1986 Brigitte Deydier (France)
1987 Alexandra Schreiber (West Germany)
1989 Emanuela Pieraniozzi (Italy)

Recent winners
Under 61 kg (Women)

1980 Anita Staps (Netherlands)
1982 Martine Rothier (France)
1984 Natasha Hernandez (Venezuela)
1986 Diane Bell (Great Britain)
1987 Diane Bell (Great Britain)
1989 Catherina Fleury (France)

Recent winners
Under 56 kg (Women)

1980 Gerda Winklbauer (Austria)
1982 Béatrice Rodriguez (France)
1984 Ann-Maria Burns (USA)
1986 Ann Hughes (Great Britain)
1987 Catherine Arnaud (France)
1989 Catherine Arnaud (France)

Recent winners
Under 52 kg (Women)

1980 Edith Hrovat (Austria)
1982 Loretta Doyle (Great Britain)
1984 Kaori Yamaguchi (Japan)
1986 Dominique Brun (France)
1987 Sharon Rendle (Great Britain)
1989 Sharon Rendle (Great Britain)

Recent winners
Under 48 kg (Women)

1980 Jane Bridge (Great Britain)
1982 Karen Briggs (Great Britain)
1984 Karen Briggs (Great Britain)
1986 Karen Briggs (Great Britain)
1987 Z Li (China)
1989 Karen Briggs (Great Britain)

Most titles: (6), Ingrid Berghmans (Belgium), 1980, 1982, 1984, 1986 (Open), 1984, 1989 (both under 72 kg).

KARATE

World Championships
First held in Tokyo 1970; taken place every two years since 1980, when women first competed; there is a team competition plus individual competitions at Kumite (seven weight categories for men and three for women) and Kata.

KARATE (cont.)

Team winners

1970 Japan
1972 France
1975 Great Britain
1977 Holland
1980 Spain
1982 Great Britain
1984 Great Britain
1986 Great Britain
1988 Great Britain

Most wins: (4), Great Britain, as above.

LACROSSE

World Championships
First held for men in 1967; for women in 1969; taken place every four years since 1974; since 1982 the women's event has been called the World Cup.

Winners (Men)

1967 USA
1974 USA
1978 Canada
1982 USA
1986 USA

Most wins: (4), USA, as above.

Winners (Women)

1969 Great Britain
1974 USA
1978 Canada
1982 USA
1986 Australia

Most wins: (2), USA, as above.

Iroquois Cup
The sport's best known trophy; contested by English club sides annually since 1890.

Recent winners

1979 Cheadle
1980 South Manchester
1981 Cheadle
1982 Sheffield University
1983 Sheffield University
1984 Cheadle
1985 Cheadle
1986 Heaton Mersey
1987 Stockport
1988 Mellor
1989 Stockport

Most wins: (17), Stockport, 1897–1901, 1903, 1905, 1911–13, 1923–4, 1926, 1928, 1934, 1987, 1989.

MODERN PENTATHLON

World Championships
Held annually since 1949 with the exception of Olympic years, when the Olympic champions automatically become world champions.

Recent winners (Individual)

1979 Robert Nieman (USA)
1980 Anatoliy Starostin (USSR)
1981 Janusz Pyciak-Peciak (Poland)
1982 Daniele Masala (Italy)
1983 Anatoliy Starostin (USSR)
1984 Daniele Masala (Italy)
1985 Attila Mizser (Hungary)
1986 Carlo Massullo (Italy)
1987 Joel Bouzou (France)
1988 Janos Martinek (Hungary)
1989 Laszlo Fabien (Hungary)

Recent winners (Team)

1979 USA
1980 USSR
1981 Poland
1982 USSR
1983 USSR
1984 Italy
1985 USSR
1986 Italy
1987 Hungary
1988 Hungary
1989 Hungary

Most wins: Individual (6), Andras Balczo (Hungary), 1963, 1965–9, 1972. Team (16), USSR, 1956–9, 1961–2, 1964, 1969, 1971–4, 1980, 1982–3, 1985.

MOTOR CYCLING

World Championships
First organized in 1949; current titles for 500 cc, 250 cc, 125 cc, 80 cc and Sidecar; Formula One and Endurance world championships also held annually; the most prestigious title is the 500 cc category.

Recent winners (500 cc)

1981 Marco Lucchinelli (Italy)
1982 Franco Uncini (Italy)
1983 Freddie Spencer (USA)
1984 Eddie Lawson (USA)
1985 Freddie Spencer (USA)
1986 Eddie Lawson (USA)
1987 Wayne Gardner (Australia)
1988 Eddie Lawson (USA)
1989 Eddie Lawson (USA)
1990 Wayne Rainey (USA)
1991 Wayne Rainey (USA)

Most wins: (8), Giacomo Agostini (Italy), 1966–72, 1975.

Most world titles: (15), Giacomo Agostini, 500 cc as above, 350 cc 1968–74.

Isle of Man TT Races
The most famous of all motor cycle races; take place each June; first held 1907; principal race is the Senior TT.

Recent winners (Senior TT)

1981 Mick Grant (Great Britain)
1982 Norman Brown (Great Britain)
1983 Rob McElnea (Great Britain)
1984 Rob McElnea (Great Britain)
1985 Joey Dunlop (Ireland)
1986 Roger Burnett (Great Britain)
1987 Joey Dunlop (Ireland)
1988 Joey Dunlop (Ireland)
1989 Steve Hislop (Great Britain)
1990 Carl Fogarty (Great Britain)
1991 Steve Hislop (Great Britain)

Most Senior TT wins: (7), Mike Hailwood (Great Britain), 1961, 1963–7, 1979.

MOTOR RACING

World Championship
A Formula One drivers' world championship instituted in 1950; constructor's championship instituted in 1958.

Recent winners

1981 Nelson Piquet (Brazil) *Brabham*
1982 Keke Rosberg (Finland) *Williams*
1983 Nelson Piquet (Brazil) *Brabham*
1984 Niki Lauda (Austria) *McLaren*
1985 Alain Prost (France) *McLaren*
1986 Alain Prost (France) *McLaren*
1987 Nelson Piquet (Brazil) *Williams*
1988 Ayrton Senna (Brazil) *McLaren*
1989 Alain Prost (France) *McLaren*
1990 Ayrton Senna (Brazil) *McLaren*
1991 Ayrton Senna (Brazil) *McLaren*

Most wins: Driver (5), Juan Manuel Fangio (Argentina), 1951, 1954–7. Constructor (8), Ferrari, 1964, 1975–7, 1979, 1982–3.

Le Mans 24-Hour Race
The greatest of all endurance races; first held in 1923.

Recent winners

1981 Jacky Ickx (Belgium)
Derek Bell (Great Britain)
1982 Jacky Ickx (Belgium)
Derek Bell (Great Britain)
1983 Vern Schuppan (Austria)
Al Holbert (USA)
Hurley Haywood (USA)
1984 Klaus Ludwig (West Germany)
Henri Pescarolo (France)
1985 Klaus Ludwig (West Germany)
'John Winter'* (West Germany)
Paolo Barilla (Italy)
1986 Hans Stück (West Germany)
Derek Bell (Great Britain)
Al Holbert (USA)
1987 Hans Stück (West Germany)
Derek Bell (Great Britain)
Al Holbert (USA)
1988 Jan Lammers (Netherlands)
Johnny Dumfries (Great Britain)
Andy Wallace (Great Britain)
1989 Jochen Mass (West Germany)
Manuel Reuter (West Germany)
Stanley Dickens (Sweden)
1990 John Neilsen (Denmark)
Price Cobb (USA)
Martin Brundle (Great Britain)
1991 Volker Weidler (Germany)
Johnny Herbert (Great Britain)
Bertrand Gachot (Belgium)

*pseudonym

Most wins: (6), Jacky Ickx (Belgium), 1969, 1975–7, 1981–2.

Indianapolis 500
First held in 1911; raced over the Indianapolis Raceway as part of the Memorial Day celebrations at the end of May each year.

Recent winners

1981 Bobby Unser (USA)
1982 Gordon Johncock (USA)
1983 Tom Sneva (USA)
1984 Rick Mears (USA)
1985 Danny Sullivan (USA)

MOTOR RACING (cont.)

1986 Bobby Rahal (USA)
1987 Al Unser (USA)
1988 Rick Mears (USA)
1989 Emerson Fittipaldi (Brazil)
1990 Arie Luyendyk (Netherlands)
1991 Rick Mears (USA)

Most wins: (4), A J Foyt (USA), 1961, 1964, 1967, 1977; Al Unser (USA), 1970–1, 1978, 1987; Rick Mears (USA), 1979, 1984, 1988, 1991.

Monte Carlo Rally
The world's leading Rally; first held in 1911.

Recent winners

1980 Walter Röhrl (West Germany)
1981 Jean Ragnotti (France)
1982 Walter Röhrl (West Germany)
1983 Walter Röhrl (West Germany)
1984 Walter Röhrl (West Germany)
1985 Ari Vatanen (Finland)
1986 Henri Toivonen (Finland)
1987 Miki Biasion (Italy)
1988 Bruno Saby (France)
1989 Miki Biasion (Italy)
1990 Didier Auriol (France)
1991 Carlos Sainz (Spain)
1992 Didier Auriol (France)

Most wins: (4), Sandro Munari (Italy), 1972, 1975–7; Walter Röhrl (West Germany), as above.

NETBALL

World Championships
First held in 1963, then every four years.

Winners

1963 Australia
1967 New Zealand
1971 Australia
1975 Australia
1979 Australia, New Zealand, Trinidad & Tobago (*shared*)
1983 Australia
1987 New Zealand

Most wins: (5), Australia, as above.

ORIENTEERING

World Championships
First held in 1966; takes place every two years (to 1978, and since 1979).

Winners
Individual (Men)

1966 Age Hadler (Norway)
1968 Karl Johansson (Sweden)
1970 Stig Berge (Norway)
1972 Age Hadler (Norway)
1974 Bernt Frilen (Sweden)
1976 Egil Johansen (Norway)
1978 Egil Johansen (Norway)
1979 Oyvin Thon (Norway)
1981 Oyvin Thon (Norway)
1983 Morten Berglia (Norway)
1985 Kari Sallinen (Finland)
1987 Kent Olsson (Sweden)
1989 Peter Thoresen (Norway)

Winners
Individual (Women)

1966 Ulla Lindqvist (Sweden)
1968 Ulla Lindqvist (Sweden)
1970 Ingrid Hadler (Norway)
1972 Sarolta Monspart (Finland)
1974 Mona Norgaard (Denmark)
1976 Lia Veijalainen (Finland)
1978 Anne Berit Eid (Norway)
1979 Outi Bergonstrom (Finland)
1981 Annichen Kringstad (Norway)
1983 Annichen Kringstad Svensson (Norway)
1985 Annichen Kringstad Svensson (Norway)
1987 Arja Hannus (Sweden)
1989 Marita Skogum (Sweden)

Most wins: Men (2), Age Hadler (Norway), Egil Johansen (Norway), Oyvin Thon (Norway), as above. Women (3), Annichen Kringstad (Norway), as above.

Winners
Relay (Men)

1966 Sweden
1968 Sweden
1970 Norway
1972 Sweden
1974 Sweden
1976 Sweden
1978 Norway
1979 Sweden
1981 Norway
1983 Norway
1985 Norway
1987 Norway
1989 Norway

Winners
Relay (Women)

1966 Sweden
1968 Norway
1970 Sweden
1972 Finland
1974 Sweden
1976 Sweden
1978 Finland
1979 Finland
1981 Sweden
1983 Sweden
1985 Sweden
1987 Norway
1989 Sweden

Most wins: Men (7), Norway, as above. Women (8), Sweden, as above.

POLO

Cowdray Park Gold Cup
First held in 1956, replacing the Champion Cup; the British Open Championship for club sides; so named because played at Cowdray Park, Sussex.

Recent winners

1979 Songhai
1980 Stowell Park
1981 Falcons
1982 Southfield
1983 Falcons
1984 Southfield
1985 Maple Leafs
1986 Tramontona
1987 Tramontona
1988 Tramontona
1989 Giscours

Most wins: (5), Stowell Park, 1973–4, 1976, 1978, 1980.

POWERBOAT RACING

World Championships
Instituted in 1982; held in many categories, with Formula One and Formula Two being the principal competitions; Formula One discontinued in 1986; Formula Two became known as Formula Grand Prix.

Winners
Formula One

1982 Roger Jenkins (Great Britain)
1983 Renato Molinari (Italy)
1984 Renato Molinari (Italy)
1985 Bob Spalding (Great Britain)
1986 Gene Thibodaux (USA)
Discontinued

Most wins: (2), Renato Molinari (Italy), as above.

Winners
Formula Two/Formula Grand Prix

1982 Michael Werner (West Germany)
1983 Michael Werner (West Germany)
1984 John Hill (Great Britain)
1985 John Hill (Great Britain)
1986 Jonathan Jones (Great Britain) and Buck Thornton (USA) (*shared*)
1987 Bill Seebold (USA)
1988 Chris Bush (USA)
1989 Jonathan Jones (Great Britain)

Most wins: (2), Michael Werner (West Germany); John Hill (Great Britain), as above.

RACKETS

World Championship
Organized on a challenge basis, the first champion in 1820 was Robert Mackay (Great Britain).

Recent winners

1929–37 Charles Williams (Great Britain)
1937–47 Donald Milford (Great Britain)
1947–54 James Dear (Great Britain)
1954–72 Geoffrey Atkins (Great Britain)
1972–73 William Surtees (USA)
1973–74 Howard Angus (Great Britain)
1975–81 William Surtees (USA)
1981–84 John Prenn (Great Britain)
1984–86 William Boone (Great Britain)
1986– John Prenn (Great Britain)

Longest reigning champion: 18 years, Geoffrey Atkins, as above.

REAL TENNIS

World Championship
Organized on a challenge basis; the first world champion was M Clerge (France) c. 1740, regarded as the first world champion of any sport.

Recent winners

1916–28 Fred Covey (Great Britain)
1928–55 Pierre Etchebaster (France)
1955–57 James Dear (Great Britain)
1957–59 Albert Johnson (Great Britain)
1959–69 Northrup Knox (USA)

REAL TENNIS (cont.)

1969–72 Pete Bostwick (USA)
1972–75 Jimmy Bostwick (USA)
1976–81 Howard Angus (Great Britain)
1981–87 Chris Ronaldson (Great Britain)
1987– Wayne Davies (Australia)

Longest reigning champion: 33 years, Edmond Barre (France), 1829–62.

ROLLER SKATING

World Championships
Figure skating world championships were first organized in 1947.

Recent winners (Men Combined)

1979 Michael Butzke (East Germany)
1980 Michael Butzke (East Germany)
1981 Michael Butzke (East Germany)
1982 Michael Butzke (East Germany)
1983 Joachim Helmle (West Germany)
1984 Michele Biserni (Italy)
1985 Michele Biserni (Italy)
1986 Michele Tolomini (Italy)
1987 Kevin Carroll (USA)
1988 Sandro Guerra (Italy)
1989 Sandro Guerra (Italy)

Most wins: (5), Karl-Heinz Losch (West Germany), 1958–9, 1961–2, 1966.

Recent winners (Women Combined)

1979 Petre Schneider (West Germany)
1980 Petre Schneider (West Germany)
1981 Petre Schneider (West Germany)
1982 Claudia Bruppacher (West Germany)
1983 Claudia Bruppacher (West Germany)
1984 Claudia Bruppacher (West Germany)
1985 Chiara Sartori (Italy)
1986 Chiara Sartori (Italy)
1987 Chiara Sartori (Italy)
1988 Rafaela De Vinaccio (Italy)
1989 Rafaela De Vinaccio (Italy)

Most wins: (4), Astrid Bader (West Germany), 1965–8.

Recent winners (Pairs)

1979 Ray Chapatta/Karen Mejia (USA)
1980 Paul Price/Tina Kniesley (USA)
1981 Paul Price/Tina Kniesley (USA)
1982 Paul Price/Tina Kniesley (USA)
1983 John Arishita/Tammy Jeru (USA)
1984 John Arishita/Tammy Jeru (USA)
1985 John Arishita/Tammy Jeru (USA)
1986 John Arishita/Tammy Jeru (USA)
1987 Fabio Trevisani/Monica Mezzardi (Italy)
1988 Fabio Trevisani/Monica Mezzardi (Italy)
1989 David De Motte/Nicky Armstrong (USA)

Most wins: (4), Dieter Fingerle (West Germany), 1959, 1965–7; John Arishita and Tammy Jeru (USA), as above.

Recent winners (Dance)

1979 Dan Littel/Florence Arsenault (USA)
1980 Torsten Carels/Gabriele Achenback (East Germany)
1981 Mark Howard/Cindy Smith (USA)
1982 Mark Howard/Cindy Smith (USA)
1983 David Golub/Angela Famiano (USA)
1984 David Golub/Angela Famiano (USA)
1985 Martin Hauss/Andrea Steudte (West Germany)
1986 Scott Myers/Anna Danks (USA)
1987 Rob Ferendo/Lori Walsh (USA)
1988 Peter Wulf/Michela Mitzlaf (West Germany)
1989 Greg Goody/Jodee Viola (USA)

Most wins: (3), Jane Puracchio (USA), 1973, 1975–6; Dan Littel and Florence Arsenault (USA), 1977–9.

ROWING

World Championships
First held for men in 1962 and for women in 1974; Olympic champions assume the role of world champion in Olympic years; principal events are the single sculls.

Recent winners
Single Sculls (Men)

1981 Peter-Michael Kolbe (West Germany)
1982 Rudiger Reiche (East Germany)
1983 Peter-Michael Kolbe (West Germany)
1984 Perrti Karppinen (Finland)
1985 Perrti Karppinen (Finland)
1986 Peter-Michael Kolbe (West Germany)
1987 Thomas Lange (East Germany)
1988 Thomas Lange (East Germany)
1989 Thomas Lange (East Germany)
1990 Yuri Janson (USSR)
1991 Thomas Lange (Germany)

Most wins: (4), Peter-Michael Kolbe (West Germany), 1975, 1978, 1981, 1983; Perrti Karppinen (Finland), 1979, 1980, 1984, 1985; Thomas Lange (Germany), as above.

Recent winners
Sculls (Women)

1981 Sanda Toma (Romania)
1982 Irina Fetissova (USSR)
1983 Jutta Hampe (East Germany)
1984 Valeria Racila (Romania)
1985 Cornelia Linse (East Germany)
1986 Jutta Hampe (East Germany)
1987 Magdelena Georgieva (Bulgaria)
1988 Jutta Behrendt (East Germany)
1989 Elisabeta Lipa (Romania)
1990 Brigit Peter (East Germany)
1991 Silke Laumann (Canada)

Most wins: (5), Christine Hahn (*née* Scheiblich) (East Germany), 1974–8.

The Boat Race
An annual contest between the crews from the Oxford and Cambridge University rowing clubs; first contested in 1829; the current course is from Putney to Mortlake.

Recent winners

1981 Oxford
1982 Oxford
1983 Oxford
1984 Oxford
1985 Oxford
1986 Cambridge
1987 Oxford
1988 Oxford
1989 Oxford
1990 Oxford
1991 Oxford

Wins: 69, Cambridge; 67, Oxford; 1 dead-heat (1877).

Diamond Sculls
Highlight of Henley Royal Regatta held every July; first contested in 1884.

Recent winners

1981 Chris Baillieu (Great Britain)
1982 Chris Baillieu (Great Britain)
1983 Steve Redgrave (Great Britain)
1984 Chris Baillieu (Great Britain)
1985 Steve Redgrave (Great Britain)
1986 Bjarne Eltang (Denmark)
1987 Peter-Michael Kolbe (West Germany)
1988 Hamish McGlashan (Australia)
1989 Vaclav Chalupa (Czechoslovakia)
1990 Eric Verdonk (New Zealand)
1991 Wim van Belleghem (Belgium)

Most wins: (6), Stuart Mackenzie (Great Britain), 1957–62. Guy Nickalls (Great Britain), 1881–91, 1983–4.

RUGBY LEAGUE

Challenge Cup Final
First contested in 1897 and won by Batley; first final at Wembley Stadium in 1929.

Recent winners

1981 Widnes
1982 Hull
1983 Featherstone Rovers
1984 Widnes
1985 Wigan
1986 Castleford
1987 Halifax
1988 Wigan
1989 Wigan
1990 Wigan
1991 Wigan

Most wins: (12), Wigan, 1924, 1929, 1948, 1951, 1958–9, 1965, plus as above.

Premiership Trophy
End-of-season knockout competition involving the top eight teams in the first division; first contested at the end of the 1974–5 season.

Recent winners

1981 Hull Kingston Rovers
1982 Widnes
1983 Widnes
1984 Hull Kingston Rovers
1985 St Helens
1986 Warrington
1987 Wigan
1988 Widnes
1989 Widnes
1990 Widnes
1991 Hull

Most wins: (6), Widnes, 1980, plus as above.

Regal Trophy
A knockout competition, first held in 1971–2. Formerly known as the John Player Special Trophy, it adopted its current style in 1989–90.

Recent winners

1982 Hull
1983 Wigan
1984 Leeds
1985 Hull Kingston Rovers
1986 Wigan
1987 Wigan
1988 St Helens
1989 Wigan
1990 Wigan
1991 Wigan

Most wins: (6), Wigan, as above.

RUGBY UNION

World Cup
The first Rugby Union World Cup was staged in 1987; New Zealand were crowned the first champions after beating France in the final. Australia beat England in the final of the second competition, in 1991.

International Championship
A round robin competition involving England, Ireland, Scotland, Wales and France; first contested in 1884.

Recent winners

1982 Ireland
1983 France and Ireland
1984 Scotland
1985 Ireland
1986 France and Scotland
1987 France
1988 France and Wales
1989 France
1990 Scotland
1991 England

Most outright wins: (21), Wales, 1893, 1900, 1902, 1905, 1908–9, 1911, 1922, 1931, 1936, 1950, 1952, 1956, 1965–6, 1969, 1971, 1975–6, 1978–9.

County Championship
First held in 1889.

Recent winners

1982 Lancashire
1983 Gloucestershire
1984 Gloucestershire
1985 Middlesex
1986 Warwickshire
1987 Yorkshire
1988 Lancashire
1989 Durham
1990 Lancashire
1991 Cornwall

Most wins: (15) Gloucestershire, 1910, 1913, 1920–2, 1930–2, 1937, 1972, 1974–6, 1983–4.

Pilkington Cup
An annual knockout competition for English Club sides; first held in the 1971–2 season. Known as the John Player Special Cup until 1988.

Recent winners

1982 Gloucester and Moseley (*shared*)
1983 Bristol
1984 Bath
1985 Bath
1986 Bath
1987 Bath
1988 Harlequins
1989 Bath
1990 Bath
1991 Harlequins

Most wins: (6), Bath, as above.

Schweppes Welsh Cup
The knockout tournament for Welsh clubs; first held in 1971–2.

Recent winners

1982 Cardiff
1983 Pontypool
1984 Cardiff
1985 Llanelli
1986 Cardiff
1987 Cardiff
1988 Llanelli
1989 Neath
1990 Neath
1991 Llanelli

Most wins: (7), Llanelli, 1973–6, 1985, 1988, 1991.

SHOOTING

Olympic Games
The Olympic competition is the highlight of the shooting calendar; winners in all categories since 1980 are given below.

Free Pistol (Men)

1980 Aleksander Melentyev (USSR)
1984 Xu Haifeng (China)
1988 Sorin Babil (Romania)

Rapid Fire Pistol (Men)

1980 Corneliu Ion (Romania)
1984 Takeo Kamachi (Japan)
1988 Afanasi Kouzmine (USSR)

Small Bore Rifle (Three Position) (Men)

1980 Viktor Vlasov (USSR)
1984 Malcolm Cooper (Great Britain)
1988 Malcolm Cooper (Great Britain)

Running Game Target (Men)

1980 Igor Sokolov (USSR)
1984 Li Yuwei (China)
1988 Tor Heiestad (Norway)

Trap (Men)

1980 Luciano Giovanetti (Italy)
1984 Luciano Giovanetti (Italy)
1988 Dmitri Monakov (USSR)

Skeet (Men)

1980 Hans Rasmussen (Denmark)
1984 Matthew Dryke (USA)
1988 Axel Wegner (East Germany)

Small Bore Rifle (Prone) (Men)

1980 Karoly Varga (Hungary)
1984 Edward Etzel (USA)
1988 Miroslav Varga (Czechoslovakia)

Air Rifle (Men)

1984 Philippe Heberle (France)
1988 Goran Maksimovic (Yugoslavia)

Air Pistol (Men)

1988 Tariou Kiriakov (USSR)

Sport Pistol (Women)

1984 Linda Thom (Canada)
1988 Nino Saloukvadze (USSR)

Air Rifle (Women)

1984 Pat Spurgin (USA)
1988 Irina Chilova (USSR)

Small Bore Rifle (Women)

1984 Wu Xiaoxuan (China)
1988 Silvia Sperber (West Germany)

Air Pistol (Women)

1988 Jasna Sekuric (Yugoslavia)

SKIING

World Cup
A season-long competition first organized in 1967; champions are declared in downhill, slalom, giant slalom and super-giant slalom, as well as the overall champion; points are obtained for performances in each category.

Recent overall winners (Men)

1982 Phil Mahre (USA)
1983 Phil Mahre (USA)
1984 Pirmin Zurbriggen (Switzerland)
1985 Marc Girardelli (Luxembourg)
1986 Marc Girardelli (Luxembourg)
1987 Pirmin Zurbriggen (Switzerland)
1988 Pirmin Zurbriggen (Switzerland)
1989 Marc Girardelli (Luxembourg)
1990 Helmut Hochflehner (Austria)
1991 Franz Heinzer (Switzerland)

Recent overall winners (Women)

1982 Erika Hess (Switzerland)
1983 Tamara McKinney (USA)
1984 Erika Hess (Switzerland)
1985 Michela Figini (Switzerland)
1986 Maria Walliser (Switzerland)
1987 Maria Walliser (Switzerland)
1988 Michela Figini (Switzerland)
1989 Vreni Schneider (Switzerland)
1990 Katrin Gutensohn-Knopf (West Germany)
1991 Chantal Bournissen (Switzerland)

Most wins: Men (4), Gustavo Thoeni (Italy), 1971–3, 1975. Women (6), Annemarie Moser-Pröll (Austria), 1971–5, 1979.

SNOOKER

World Professional Championship
Instituted in the 1926–7 season; a knockout competition open to professional players who are members of the World Professional Billiards and Snooker Association; played at the Crucible Theatre, Sheffield.

Recent winners

1981 Steve Davis (England)
1982 Alex Higgins (Ireland)
1983 Steve Davis (England)
1984 Steve Davis (England)
1985 Dennis Taylor (Ireland)
1986 Joe Johnson (England)
1987 Steve Davis (England)
1988 Steve Davis (England)
1989 Steve Davis (England)
1990 Stephen Hendry (Scotland)
1991 John Parrott (England)

Most wins: (15), Joe Davis (England), 1927–40, 1946.

World Doubles
First played in 1982.

Winners

1982 Steve Davis (England)
Tony Meo (England)
1983 Steve Davis (England)
Tony Meo (England)
1984 Alex Higgins (Ireland)
Jimmy White (England)
1985 Steve Davis (England)
Tony Meo (England)

SNOOKER (cont.)

1986 Steve Davis (England)
Tony Meo (England)
1987 Mike Hallett (England)
Stephen Hendry (Scotland)
Discontinued

Most wins: (4), Steve Davis and Tony Meo (England), as above.

World Team Championship
Also known as the World Cup; first held in 1979.

Winners

1979 Wales
1980 Wales
1981 England
1982 Canada
1983 England
1984 *not held*
1985 Ireland
1986 Ireland 'A'
1987 Ireland 'A'
1988 England
1989 England
1990 Canada

Most wins: (4), England, as above.

World Amateur Championship
First held in 1963; originally took place every two years, but annual since 1984.

Recent winners

1976 Doug Mountjoy (Wales)
1978 Cliff Wilson (Wales)
1980 Jimmy White (England)
1982 Terry Parson (Wales)
1984 O. B. Agrawal (India)
1985 Paul Mifsud (Malta)
1986 Paul Mifsud (Malta)
1987 Darren, Morgan (Wales)
1988 James Wattana (Thailand)
1989 Ken Doherty (Republic of Ireland)
1990 Steven O'Connor (Republic of Ireland)

Most wins: (2), Gary Owen (England), 1963, 1966; Ray Edmonds (England), 1972, 1974; Paul Mifsud, as above.

SOFTBALL

World Championships
First held for women in 1965 and for men the following year; now held every four years.

Winners (Men)

1966 USA
1968 USA
1972 Canada
1976 Canada, New Zealand & USA (*shared*)
1980 USA
1984 New Zealand
1988 USA

Most wins: (5), USA, as above.

Winners (Women)

1965 Australia
1970 Japan
1974 USA
1978 USA
1982 New Zealand
1986 USA

Most wins: (3), USA, as above.

SPEEDWAY

World Championships
Individual championships inaugurated in 1936; team championship instituted in 1960; first official pairs world championship in 1970 (threes from 1991).

Recent winners

1981 Bruce Penhall (USA)
1982 Bruce Penhall (USA)
1983 Egon Muller (West Germany)
1984 Erik Gundersen (Denmark)
1985 Erik Gundersen (Denmark)
1986 Hans Nielsen (Denmark)
1987 Hans Nielsen (Denmark)
1988 Erik Gundersen (Denmark)
1989 Hans Nielsen (Denmark)
1990 Per Jonsson (Sweden)
1991 Jan Pedersen (Denmark)

Most wins: (6), Ivan Mauger (New Zealand), 1968–70, 1972, 1977, 1979.

Recent winners (Pairs)

1981 Bruce Penhall/Bobby Schwartz (USA)
1982 Dennis Sigalos/Bobby Schwartz (USA)
1983 Kenny Carter/Peter Collins (England)
1984 Peter Collins/Chris Morton (England)
1985 Erik Gunderson/Tommy Knudsen (Denmark)
1986 Erik Gundersen/Hans Nielsen (Denmark)
1987 Erik Gundersen/Hans Nielsen (Denmark)
1988 Erik Gundersen/Hans Nielsen (Denmark)
1989 Erik Gundersen/Hans Nielsen (Denmark)
1990 Hans Nielsen/Jan Pedersen (Denmark)
1991 Hans Nielsen/Jan Pedersen/ Tommy Knudsen (Denmark)

Most wins: (6), Hans Nielsen, as above.

Recent winners (Team)

1981 Denmark
1982 USA
1983 Denmark
1984 Denmark
1985 Denmark
1986 Denmark
1987 Denmark
1988 Denmark
1989 England
1990 USA
1991 Denmark

Most wins: (9), Great Britain/England, 1968, 1971–5, 1977, 1980, 1989.

SQUASH

World Open Championship
First held in 1976; takes place annually for men, every two years for women.

Winners (Men)

1981 Jahangir Khan (Pakistan)
1982 Jahangir Khan (Pakistan)
1983 Jahangir Khan (Pakistan)
1984 Jahangir Khan (Pakistan)
1985 Jahangir Khan (Pakistan)
1986 Ross Norman (New Zealand)
1987 Jansher Khan (Pakistan)
1988 Jahangir Khan (Pakistan)
1989 Jansher Khan (Pakistan)
1990 Jansher Khan (Pakistan)
1991 Rodney Martin (Australia)

Most wins: (6), Jahangir Khan (Pakistan), as above.

Winners (Women)

1979 Heather McKay (Australia)
1981 Rhonda Thorne (Australia)
1983 Vicky Cardwell (Australia)
1985 Sue Devoy (New Zealand)
1987 Sue Devoy (New Zealand)
1989 Martine Le Moignan (Great Britain)
1991 Sue Devoy (New Zealand)

Most wins: (3), Sue Devoy (New Zealand), as above.

SURFING

World Professional Championship
A season-long series of Grand Prix events; first held in 1970.

Recent winners (Men)

1979 Mark Richards (Australia)
1980 Mark Richards (Australia)
1981 Mark Richards (Australia)
1982 *Season changed to encompass 1982–3*
1983 Mark Richards (Australia)
1984 Tom Carroll (Australia)
1985 Tom Carroll (Australia)
1986 Tommy Curren (USA)
1987 Damien Hardman (Australia)
1988 Barton Lynch (Australia)
1989 Martin Potter (Great Britain)

Recent winners (Women)

1979 Margo Oberg (Hawaii)
1980 Lyne Boyer (Hawaii)
1981 Margo Oberg (Hawaii)
1982 *not held*
1983 Margo Oberg (Hawaii)
1984 Kim Mearig (USA)
1985 Frieda Zamba (USA)
1986 Frieda Zamba (USA)
1987 Wendy Botha (South Africa)
1988 Freida Zamba (USA)
1989 Wendy Botha (South Africa)

Most wins: Men (5), Mark Richards (Australia), 1975, 1979–83. Women (3), Margo Oberg (Hawaii), Freida Zamba (USA), as above.

SWIMMING AND DIVING

World Championships
First held in 1973 and again in 1975; since 1978 take place every four years; the complete list of 1990 champions is given below.

1990 World Champions (Men)

50 metres freestyle	Tom Jager (USA)
100 metres freestyle	Matt Biondi (USA)
200 metres freestyle	Giorgio Lamberti (Italy)
400 metres freestyle	Joerg Hoffmann (Germany)
1500 metres freestyle	Joerg Hoffmann (Germany)

SWIMMING AND DIVING (cont.)

100 metres backstroke	Jeff Rouse (USA)
200 metres backstroke	Martin Lopez-Zubero (Spain)
100 metres breaststroke	Norbert Rosza (Hungary)
200 metres breaststroke	Mike Barrowman (USA)
100 metres butterfly	Anthony Nesty (Suriname)
200 metres butterfly	Melvin Stewart (USA)
200 metres individual medley	Tamas Darnyi (Hungary)
400 metres individual medley	Tamas Darnyi (Hungary)
4×100 metres freestyle medley	USA
4×200 metres freestyle medley	Germany
4×100 metres medley relay	USA
1 m springboard diving	Edwin Jongejans (Netherlands)
Platform diving	Sun Shuwei (China)

1990 World Champions (Women)

50 metres freestyle	Zhuang Yong (China)
100 metres freestyle	Nicola Haislett (USA)
200 metres freestyle	Hayley Lewis (Australia)
400 metres freestyle	Janet Evans (USA)
800 metres freestyle	Janet Evans (USA)
100 metres backstroke	Krisztina Egerszegi (Hungary)
200 metres backstroke	Krisztina Egerszegi (Hungary)
100 metres breaststroke	Linley Frame (Australia)
200 metres breaststroke	Elena Volkova (USSR)
100 metres butterfly	Qian Hong (China)
200 metres butterfly	Summer Sanders (USA)
200 metres individual medley	Lin Li (China)
400 metres individual medley	Lin Li (China)
4×100 metres freestyle relay	USA
4×200 metres freestyle relay	Germany
4×100 metres medley relay	USA
1 m springboard diving	Gao Min (China)
Platform diving	Fu Mingxia (China)
Synchronized swimming	
Solo	Silvie Frechette (Canada)
Duet	USA
Team	USA

TABLE TENNIS

World Championships
First held in 1926 and every two years since 1957.

Recent winners
Swaythling Cup (Men's Team)

1971 China
1973 Sweden
1975 China
1977 China
1979 Hungary
1981 China
1983 China
1985 China
1987 China
1989 Sweden
1991 Sweden

Recent winners
Corbillon Cup (Women's Team)

1971 Japan
1973 South Korea
1975 China
1977 China
1979 China
1981 China
1983 China
1985 China
1987 China
1989 China
1991 Korea

Most wins: Swaythling Cup (12), Hungary, 1926, 1928–31, 1933 (twice), 1935, 1938, 1949, 1952, 1979. Corbillon Cup (9), China, 1965, 1975, 1977, 1979, 1981, 1983, 1985, 1987, 1989.

Recent winners
Men's Singles

1971 Stellan Bengtsson (Sweden)
1973 Hsi En-Ting (China)
1975 Istvan Jonyer (Hungary)
1977 Mitsuru Kohno (Japan)
1979 Seiji Ono (Japan)
1981 Guo Yuehua (China)
1983 Guo Yuehua (China)
1985 Jiang Jialiang (China)
1987 Jiang Jialiang (China)
1989 Jan-Ove Waldner (Sweden)
1991 Jorgen Persson (Sweden)

Most wins: (5), Viktor Barna (Hungary), 1930, 1932–5.

Recent winners
Women's singles

1971 Lin Hui-Ching (China)
1973 Hu Yu-Lan (China)
1975 Pak Yung-Sun (North Korea)
1977 Pak Yung-Sun (North Korea)
1979 Ge Xinai (China)
1981 Ting Ling (China)
1983 Cao Yanhua (China)
1985 Cao Yanhua (China)
1987 He Zhili (China)
1989 Qiao Hong (China)
1991 Deng Yaping (China)

Most wins: (6), Angelica Rozeanu (Romania), 1950–55.

Recent winners
Men's Doubles

1971 Istvan Jonyer/Tiber Klampar (Hungary)
1973 Stellan Bengtsson/Kjell Johansson (Sweden)
1975 Gabor Gergely/Istvan Jonyer (Hungary)
1977 Li Zhenshi/Liang Geliang (China)
1979 Dragutin Surbek/Anton Stipancic (Yugoslavia)
1981 Cai Zhenhua/Li Zhenshi (China)
1983 Dragutin Surbek/Zoran Kalinic (Yugoslavia)
1985 Mikael Applegren/Ulf Carlsson (Sweden)
1987 Chen Longcan/Wei Quinguang (China)
1989 Joerg Rosskopf/Stefen Fetzner (West Germany)
1991 Peter Karlson/Thomas von Scheele (Sweden)

Most wins: (8), Viktor Barna (Hungary/England), 1929–33 (won two titles 1933), 1935, 1939.

Recent winners
Women's Doubles

1971 Cheng Min-Chih/Lin Hui-Ching (China)
1973 Maria Alexandru (Romania)/Miho Hamada (Japan)
1975 Maria Alexandru (Romania)/Shoko Takashima (Japan)
1977 Pak Yong Ok (North Korea)/Yang Yin (China)
1979 Zhang Li/Zhang Deying (China)
1981 Zhang Deying/Cao Yanhua (China)
1983 Shen Jianping/Dai Lili (China)
1985 Dai Lili/Geng Lijuan (China)
1987 Yang Young-Ja/Hyun Jung-Hwa (Korea)
1989 Quio Hong/Deng Yaping (China)
1991 Chen Zhie/Gao Jun (China)

Most wins: (7), Maria Mednyanszky (Hungary), 1928, 1930–5.

Recent winners
Mixed Doubles

1971 Chang Shih-Ling/Lin Hui-Ching (China)
1973 Liang Geliang/Li Li (China)
1975 Stanislav Gomozkov/Anna Ferdman (USSR)
1977 Jacques Secretin/Claude Bergeret (France)
1979 Liang Geliang/Ge Xinai (China)
1981 Xie Saike/Huang Junqun (China)
1983 Guo Yuehua/Ni Xialian (China)
1985 Cai Zhenua/Cao Yanhua (China)
1987 Hui Jun/Geng Lijuan (China)
1989 Yoo Nam-Kyu/Hyun Jung-Hwa (South Korea)
1991 Wang Tao/Lin Wei (China)

Most wins: (6), Maria Mednyanszky (Hungary), 1927–8, 1930–1, 1933 (two titles).

TENNIS (LAWN)

Wimbledon Championships
The All-England Championships at Wimbledon are Lawn Tennis's most prestigious championships; first held in 1877.

Recent winners
Men's Singles

1981 John McEnroe (USA)
1982 Jimmy Connors (USA)

TENNIS (LAWN) (cont.)

1983 John McEnroe (USA)
1984 John McEnroe (USA)
1985 Boris Becker (West Germany)
1986 Boris Becker (West Germany)
1987 Pat Cash (Australia)
1988 Stefan Edberg (Sweden)
1989 Boris Becker (West Germany)
1990 Stefan Edberg (Sweden)
1991 Michael Stich (Germany)

Most wins: (7), William Renshaw (Great Britain), 1881–6, 1889.

Recent winners
Women's Singles

1981 Chris Evert-Lloyd (USA)
1982 Martina Navratilova (USA)
1983 Martina Navratilova (USA)
1984 Martina Navratilova (USA)
1985 Martina Navratilova (USA)
1986 Martina Navratilova (USA)
1987 Martina Navratilova (USA)
1988 Steffi Graf (West Germany)
1989 Steffi Graf (West Germany)
1990 Martina Navratilova (USA)
1991 Steffi Graf (Germany)

Most wins: (9), Martina Navratilova (Czechoslovakia/USA), 1978, 1979, plus as above.

Recent winners
Men's Doubles

1981 Peter Fleming/John McEnroe (USA)
1982 Peter McNamara/Paul McNamee (Australia)
1983 Peter Fleming/John McEnroe (USA)
1984 Peter Fleming/John McEnroe (USA)
1985 Heinz Gunthardt (Switzerland)/Balazs Taroczy (Hungary)
1986 Joakim Nystrom/Mats Wilander (Sweden)
1987 Ken Flach/Robert Seguso (USA)
1988 Ken Flach/Robert Seguso (USA)
1989 John Fitzgerald (Australia)/Anders Jarryd (Sweden)
1990 Rick Leach/Jim Pugh (USA)
1991 John Fitzgerald (Australia) Anders Jarryd (Sweden)

Most wins: (8), Lawrence Doherty/Reg Doherty (Great Britain), 1897–1901, 1903–5.

Recent winners
Women's Doubles

1981 Martina Navratilova/Pam Shriver (USA)
1982 Martina Navratilova/Pam Shriver (USA)
1983 Martina Navratilova/Pam Shriver (USA)
1984 Martina Navratilova/Pam Shriver (USA)
1985 Kathy Jordan/Elizabeth Smylie (Aus)
1986 Martina Navratilova/Pam Shriver (USA)
1987 Claudia Kohde-Kilsch (West Germany)/Helena Sukova (Czechoslovakia)
1988 Steffi Graf (West Germany)/Gabriela Sabatini (Argentina)
1989 Jan Novotna/Helena Sukova (Czechoslovakia)
1990 Jan Novotna/Helena Sukova (Czechoslovakia)
1991 Larissa Sarchenko/Natalya Zvereva (USSR)

Most wins: (12), Elizabeth Ryan (USA), 1914, 1919–23, 1925–7, 1930, 1933–4.

Recent winners
Mixed Doubles

1981 Betty Stove (Holland)/Frew McMillan (South Africa)
1982 Anne Smith (USA)/Kevin Curren (South Africa)
1983 Wendy Turnbull (Australia)/John Lloyd (Great Britain)
1984 Wendy Turnbull (Australia)/John Lloyd (Great Britain)
1985 Martina Navratilova (USA) Paul McNamee (Australia)
1986 Kathy Jordan/Ken Flach (USA)
1987 Jo Durie/Jeremy Bates (Great Britain)
1988 Sherwood Stewart/Zina Garrison (USA)
1989 Jim Pugh (USA)/Jan Novotna (Czechoslovakia)
1990 Rick Leach/Zina Garrison (USA)
1991 John Fitzgerald/Elizabeth Smylie (Australia)

Most wins: (7), Elizabeth Ryan (USA), 1919, 1921, 1923, 1927–8, 1930, 1932.

United States Open

First held in 1891 as the United States Championship; became the United States Open in 1968.

Recent winners
Men's Singles

1981 John McEnroe (USA)
1982 Jimmy Connors (USA)
1983 Jimmy Connors (USA)
1984 John McEnroe (USA)
1985 Ivan Lendl (Czechoslovakia)
1986 Ivan Lendl (Czechoslovakia)
1987 Ivan Lendl (Czechoslovakia)
1988 Mats Wilander (Sweden)
1989 Boris Becker (West Germany)
1990 Pete Sampras (USA)
1991 Stefan Edberg (Sweden)

Recent winners
Women's Singles

1981 Tracy Austin (USA)
1982 Chris Evert-Lloyd (USA)
1983 Martina Navratilova (USA)
1984 Martina Navratilova (USA)
1985 Hana Mandlikova (Czechoslovakia)
1986 Martina Navratilova (USA)
1987 Martina Navratilova (USA)
1988 Steffi Graf (West Germany)
1989 Steffi Graf (West Germany)
1990 Gabriela Sabatini (Argentina)
1991 Monica Seles (Yugoslavia)

Most wins: Men (7), Richard Sears (USA), 1881–7; Bill Larned (USA), 1901–2, 1907–11; Bill Tilden (USA), 1920–5, 1929. Women (7), Molla Mallory (*née* Bjurstedt) (USA), 1915–16, 1918, 1920–2, 1926; Helen Wills-Moody (USA), 1923–5, 1927–9, 1931.

Davis Cup

International team competition organized on a knockout basis; first held in 1900; contested on a challenge basis until 1972.

Recent winners

1981 USA
1982 USA
1983 Australia
1984 Sweden
1985 Sweden
1986 Australia
1987 Sweden
1988 West Germany
1989 West Germany
1990 USA
1991 France

Most wins: (29), USA, 1900, 1902, 1913, 1920–6, 1937–8, 1946–9, 1954, 1958, 1963, 1968–72, 1978–9, 1981–2, 1990.

TENPIN BOWLING

World Championships

First held in 1923 by the International Bowling Association; since 1954 organized by the Fédération Internationale des Quillieurs (FIQ); since 1963, when women first competed, held every four years.

Recent winners
Individual (Men)

1954 Göska Algeskog (Sweden)
1955 Nils Bäckström (Sweden)
1958 Kaarlo Asukas (Finland)
1960 Tito Reynolds (Mexico)
1963 Les Zikes (USA)
1967 David Pond (Great Britain)
1971 Ed Luther (USA)
1975 Bud Staudt (USA)
1979 Ollie Ongtawco (Philippines)
1983 Armando Marino (Colombia)
1987 Rolland Patrick (France)

Recent winners
Individual (Women)

1963 Helen Shablis (USA)
1967 Helen Weston (USA)
1971 Ashie Gonzales (Puerto Rico)
1975 Annedore Haefker (West Germany)
1979 Lita de la Roas (Philippines)
1983 Lena Sulkanen (Sweden)
1987 Edda Piccini (Italy)

Most wins: No one has won more than one title.

TRAMPOLINING

World Championships

First held in 1964 and annually until 1968; since then, every two years.

Recent winners
Individual (Men)

1970 Wayne Miller (USA)
1972 Paul Luxon (Great Britain)
1974 Richard Tison (France)
1976 Richard Tison (France)/Yevgeni Yanes (USSR) (*shared*)
1978 Yevgeni Yanes (USSR)
1980 Stewart Matthews (Great Britain)
1982 Carl Furrer (Great Britain)
1984 Lionel Pioline (France)
1986 Lionel Pioline (France)
1988 Vadim Krasnoshapka (USSR)

Most wins: (2), David Jacobs (USA), 1967–8; Wayne Miller (USA), 1966, 1970; Richard Tison (France) as above; Yevgeni Yanes (USSR) as above; Lionel Pioline (France) as above.

Recent winners
Individual (Women)

1970 Renee Ransom (USA)
1972 Alexandra Nicholson (USA)
1974 Alexandra Nicholson (USA)
1976 Svetlana Levina (USSR)
1978 Tatyana Anisimova (USSR)
1980 Ruth Keller (Switzerland)
1982 Ruth Keller (Switzerland)
1984 Sue Shotton (Great Britain)

TRAMPOLINING (cont.)

1986 Tatyana Lushina (USSR)
1988 Khoperia Roussoudan (USSR)

Most wins: (5), Judy Wills (USA), 1964–8.

TUG OF WAR

World Championships
Instituted in 1975, held yearly apart from 1979–84; contested at 560 kg from 1982.

Winners

	720 kg	640 kg	560 kg
1975	England	England	
1976	England	England	–
1977	England	Wales	–
1978	England	England	–
1980	England	England	–
1982	England	Ireland	Switzerland
1984	Ireland	Ireland	England
1985	Switzerland	Switzerland	Switzerland
1986	Ireland	Ireland	England
1988	Republic of Ireland	England	England
			Catchweight
			1984 England

Most titles: (16), England, as above.

VOLLEYBALL

World Championships
Inaugurated in 1949; first women's championships in 1952; now held every four years, but Olympic champions are also world champions in Olympic years.

Recent winners (Men)

1970 East Germany
1972 Japan
1974 Poland
1976 Poland
1978 USSR
1980 USSR
1982 USSR
1984 USA
1986 USA
1988 USA

Recent winners (Women)

1970 USSR
1972 USSR
1974 Japan
1976 Japan
1978 Cuba
1980 USSR
1982 China
1984 China
1986 China
1988 USSR

Most wins: Men (9), USSR, 1949, 1952, 1960, 1962, 1964, 1968, 1978, 1980, 1982. Women (8), USSR, 1952, 1956, 1960, 1968, 1970, 1972, 1980, 1988.

WALKING

Lugano Trophy
The principal Road Walking trophy; contested every two years by men's national teams; first held in 1961.

Recent winners

1973 East Germany
1975 USSR
1977 Mexico
1979 Mexico
1981 Italy
1983 USSR
1985 East Germany
1987 USSR
1989 USSR
1991 Italy

Most wins: (5), East Germany, 1965, 1967, 1970, 1973, 1985.

Eschborn Cup
The women's equivalent of the Lugano Trophy; first held in 1979; takes place every two years.

Winners

1981 USSR
1983 China
1985 China
1987 USSR
1989 USSR
1991 USSR

Most wins: (4), USSR, as above.

WATER POLO

World Championship
First held in 1973, and every four years since 1978; included in the World Swimming Championships; first women's event in 1986.

Winners (Men)

1973 Hungary
1975 USSR
1978 Italy
1982 USSR
1986 Yugoslavia

Winners (Women)

1986 Australia

Most wins: Men (2), USSR, as above.

World Cup
Inaugurated in 1979 and held every two years.

Winners

1979 Hungary
1981 USSR
1983 USSR
1985 West Germany
1987 Yugoslavia
1989 Yugoslavia

Most wins: (2), USSR, Yugoslavia, as above.

WATER SKIING

World Championships
First held in 1949; take place every two years; competitions for Slalom, Tricks, Jumps, and the Overall Individual title.

Recent winners
Overall (Men)

1971 George Athans (Canada)
1973 George Athans (Canada)
1975 Carlos Suarez (Venezuela)
1977 Mike Hazelwood (Great Britain)
1979 Joel McClintock (Canada)
1981 Sammy Duvall (USA)
1983 Sammy Duvall (USA)
1985 Sammy Duvall (USA)
1987 Sammy Duvall (USA)
1989 Patrice Martin (France)
1991 Patrice Martin (France)

Most wins: (4), Sammy Duvall (USA), as above.

Recent winners
Overall (Women)

1971 Christy Weir (USA)
1973 Lisa St John (USA)
1975 Liz Allan-Shetter (USA)
1977 Cindy Todd (USA)
1979 Cindy Todd (USA)
1981 Karin Roberge (USA)
1983 Ana-Maria Carrasco (Venezuela)
1985 Karen Neville (Australia)
1987 Deena Brush (USA)
1989 Deena Mapple (née Brush) (USA)
1991 Karen Neville (Australia)

Most wins: (3), Willa McGuire (*née* Worthington) (USA), 1949–50, 1955; Liz Allan-Shetter (USA), 1965, 1969 and as above.

WEIGHTLIFTING

World Championships
First held in 1898; 11 weight divisions; the most prestigious is the 110 kg-plus category (formerly known as Super Heavyweight); Olympic champions are automatically world champions in Olympic years.

Recent champions (110 kg)

1981 Anatoliy Pisarenko (USSR)
1982 Anatoliy Pisarenko (USSR)
1983 Anatoliy Pisarenko (USSR)
1984 Dean Lukin (Australia)
1985 Antonio Krastev (Bulgaria)
1986 Antonio Krastev (Bulgaria)
1987 Aleksander Kurlovich (USSR)
1988 Aleksander Kurlovich (USSR)
1989 Aleksander Kurlovich (USSR)
1990 Leonid Taranenko (USSR)
1991 Aleksander Kurlovich (USSR)

Most titles (all categories): (8), John Davies (USA), 82.5 kg 1938; 82.5 + kg 1946–50; 90 + kg 1951–2; Tommy Kono (USA), 67.5 kg 1952; 75 kg 1953, 1957–9; 82.5 kg 1954–6; Vasiliy Alexseyev (USSR), 110 + kg 1970–7.

WRESTLING

World Championships
Graeco-Roman world championships first held in 1921; first freestyle championships in 1951; each style contests 10 weight divisions, the heaviest being the 130 kg (formerly over 100 kg) category; Olympic champions become world champions in Olympic years.

WRESTLING (cont.)

Recent winners (Super-heavyweight/over 100 kg)
Freestyle

1981 Salman Khasimikov (USSR)
1982 Salman Khasimikov (USSR)
1983 Salman Khasimikov (USSR)
1984 Bruce Baumgartner (USA)
1985 David Gobedzhishvilli (USSR)
1986 Bruce Baumgartner (USA)
1987 Khadartsv Aslam (USSR)
1988 David Gobedzhishvilli (USSR)
1989 Ali Reiza Soleimani (Iran)
1990 David Gobedzhishvilli (USSR)
1991 Andreas Schroder (Germany)

Graeco-Roman

1981 Refik Memisevic (Yugoslavia)
1982 Nikolai Denev (Bulgaria)
1983 Jevgeniy Artiochin (USSR)
1984 Jeffrey Blatnick (USA)
1985 Igor Rostozotskiy (USSR)
1986 Thomas Johansson (Sweden)
1987 Igor Rostozotskiy (USSR)
1988 Alexsander Karoline (USSR)
1989 Alexsander Karoline (USSR)
1990 Alexsander Karoline (USSR)
1991 Alexsander Karoline (USSR)

Most titles (all weight divisions): Freestyle (10), Aleksander Medved (USSR), 90 kg 1962–4, 1966; 100 kg 1967–8, Over 100 kg 1969–72. Greco-Roman (7), Nikolai Balboshin (USSR), 100 kg 1973–4, 1976, 1978–9; Over 100 kg 1971, 1977; Valeriy Rezantsev (USSR), 90 kg 1970–6.

YACHTING

America's Cup
One of sport's famous trophies; first won by the schooner Magic in 1870; now held approximately every four years, when challengers compete in a series of races to find which of them races against the holder; all 25 winners up to 1983 were from the United States.

Post-war winners

Winning Yacht (Skipper)
1958 *Columbia* (USA) (Briggs Cunningham)
1962 *Weatherly* (USA) (Emil Mosbacher)
1964 *Constellation* (USA) (Bob Bavier)
1967 *Intrepid* (USA) (Emil Mosbacher)
1970 *Intrepid* (USA) (Bill Ficker)
1974 *Courageous* (USA) (Ted Hood)
1977 *Courageous* (USA) (Ted Turner)
1980 *Freedom* (USA) (Dennis Conner)
1983 *Australia II* (Australia) (John Bertrand)
1987 *Stars & Stripes* (USA) (Dennis Conner)
1988 *Stars & Stripes* (USA) (Dennis Conner)*

* *Stars and Stripes* won a special challenge match but on appeal the race was awarded *New Zealand* skippered by David Barnes. However, after much legal wrangling the cup was retained by *Stars & Stripes*.

Most wins: (Skipper) (3), Charlie Barr (USA), 1899, 1901, 1903; Harold Vanderbilt (USA), 1930, 1934, 1937.

Admiral's Cup
A two-yearly series of races in the English Channel, around Fastnet rock and at Cowes; four national teams of three boats per team; first held in 1957.

Recent winners

1969 USA
1971 Great Britain
1973 West Germany
1975 Great Britain
1977 Great Britain
1979 Australia
1981 Great Britain
1983 West Germany
1985 West Germany
1987 New Zealand
1989 Great Britain
1991 France

Most wins: (9), Great Britain, 1957, 1959, 1963, 1965, 1971, 1975, 1977, 1981, 1989.

GOVERNING BODIES IN SPORT: ABBREVIATIONS

AAA	Amateur Athletic Association
AAU	Amateur Athletic Union (USA)
ACU	Auto Cycle Union
AIBA	International Amateur Boxing Federation
ASA	Amateur Swimming Association
BDO	British Darts Organisation
FA	Football Association
FEI	International Equestrian Federation
FIA	International Automobile Association
FIAC	International Amateur Cycling Federation
FIBA	International Basketball Federation
FIBT	International Bobsleigh and Tobogganing Federation
FIC	International Canoeing Federation
FIDE	International Chess Federation
FIE	International Fencing Federation
FIFA	International Football Association Federation
FIG	International Gymnastic Federation
FIH	International Hockey Federation
FILA	International Amateur Wrestling Federation
FIM	International Motorcycling Federation
FINA	International Amateur Swimming Federation
FIQ	International Bowling Federation
FIRA	International Amateur Rugby Federation
FIS	International Ski Federation
FIT	International Trampoline Federation
FITA	International Archery Federation
FIVB	International Volleyball Federation
GAA	Gaelic Athletic Association
IAAF	International Amateur Athletic Federation
IBA	International Baseball Federation
IBF	International Badminton Federation
	International Boxing Federation
IBSF	International Billiards and Snooker Federation
ICF	International Curling Federation
IHF	International Handball Federation
IIHF	International Ice Hockey Federation
IJF	International Judo Federation
IOC	International Olympic Committee
IRFB	International Rugby Football Board
ISRF	International Squash Rackets Federation
ISU	International Skating Union
ITF	International Tennis Federation
ITTF	International Table Tennis Federation
IWF	International Weightlifting Federation
IWSF	International Water Ski Federation
IYRU	International Yacht Racing Union
LPGA	Ladies Professional Golfers Association
LTA	Lawn Tennis Association
MCC	Marylebone Cricket Club
NBA	International Basketball Federation (USA)
NBL	International Basketball League (USA)
NCAA	National Collegiate Athletic Association (USA)
NFL	National Football League (USA)
NHL	National Hockey League (USA)
PGA	Professional Golfers' Association
RFU	Rugby Football Union
RL	Rugby League
TCCB	Test and County Cricket Board
UEFA	Union of European Football Associations
UIPMB	International Union of Modern Pentathlon and Biathlon
UIT	International Shooting Union
USGA	United States Golf Association
USPGA	United States Professional Golfers' Association
WBA	World Boxing Association
WBC	World Boxing Council
WBO	World Boxing Organisation
WPBSA	World Professional Billiards and Snooker Association
WWSU	World Water Skiing Union

COMMON ABBREVIATIONS

This section includes all the abbreviations used in the body of the *Cambridge Encyclopedia*, along with a number of related notions in widespread contemporary use.

A

AA Alcoholics Anonymous
AA Automobile Association
AA(A) anti-aircraft (artillery)
AAA Amateur Athletics Association
AAA American Automobile Association
ABA Amateur Boxing Association
ABC American Broadcasting Association
ABC Australian Broadcasting Corporation
ABM antiballistic missile
ABTA Association of British Travel Agents
AC alternating current
ACAS Advisory, Conciliation, and Arbitration Service
ACLU American Civil Liberties Union
ACT Australian Capital Territory
ACTH adrenocorticotrophic hormone
ACTU Australian Council of Trade Unions
AD anno Domini (in the year of Our Lord)
A-D analog-to-digital (in computing)
ADH antidiuretic hormone
ADP adenosine diphosphate
AEA Atomic Energy Authority (UK)
AEC Atomic Energy Commission (USA)
AFC American Football Conference
AFL/CIO American Federation of Labor-Congress of Industrial Organizations
AFP Agence France Presse
AFV armoured fighting vehicle
AGM annual general meeting
AGR advanced gas-cooled reactor
AH anno Hegirae (in the year of Hegira)
AHF anti-haemophilic factor
AI artificial intelligence
AID artificial insemination by donor
AIDS Acquired Immune Deficiency Syndrome
AIF Australian Imperial Force
AIH artificial insemination by husband
ALCM air-launched cruise missile
ALGOL Algorithmic Language
ALP Australian Labor Party
ALU arithmetic and logic unit
AM amplitude modulation
AMA American Medical Association
amu atomic mass unit
ANC African National Congress
ANS autonomic nervous system
ANSI American National Standards Institute
ANZAC Australian and New Zealand Army Corps
ANZUS Australia, New Zealand and the United States
AOB any other business
AONB Area of Outstanding Natural Beauty
AP Associated Press
APEX Association of Professional, Executive, Clerical, and Computer Staff
APL A Programming Language
APR annual percentage rate
APRA Alianza Popular Revolutionaria Americana (American Popular Revolutionary Alliance)
AR aspect ratio
ARCIC Anglican Roman Catholic International Commission
A/S Advanced/Supplementary
ASA American Standards Association
ASCII American Standards Code for Information Interchange
ASDIC Admiralty Submarine Detection Investigation Committee
ASEAN Association of South-East Asian Nations
ASL American Sign Language
ASLEF Associated Society of Locomotive Engineers and Firemen
ASLIB Association of Special Libraries and Information Bureaux
ASM air-to-surface missile
ASPCA American Society for the Prevention of Cruelty to Animals
ASSR Autonomous Soviet Socialist Republic
ASTMS Association of Scientific, Technical, and Managerial Staffs
ATP adenosine triphosphate
ATS Auxiliary Territorial Service
ATV Associated Television
AU astronomical unit
AV audio-visual
AWACS Airborne Warning and Control System
AWU Australian Workers' Union

B

BAFTA British Academy of Film and Television Arts
BALPA British Airline Pilots' Association
B&W black and white
BASIC Beginners All-purpose Symbolic Instruction Code
BASIC (English) British American Scientific International Commercial
BBC British Broadcasting Association
BC before Christ
BCD binary coded decimal
BCG bacille (bacillus) Calmette Guérin
BCS Bardeen, Cooper & Schrieffer (theory)
BEF British Expeditionary Force
BEV Black English Vernacular
BHP Broken Hill Proprietary Company
BIA Bureau of Indian Affairs
BIS Bank for International Settlements
BLAISE British Library Automated Information Service
BMA British Medical Association
BOSS Bureau of State Security (South Africa)
BP blood pressure
BSE bovine spongiform encephalopathy
BSI British Standards Institution
BST British Summer Time
btu British thermal unit
BUF British Union of Fascists
BUPA British United Provident Association

C

CAB Citizen's Advice Bureau
CACM Central American Common Market
CAD computer aided design
CAI computer aided instruction
CAL computer aided learning
CAM computer aided manufacture
CAP Common Agricultural Policy
CARICOM Caribbean Community
CARIFTA Caribbean Free Trade Area
CATV cable television
CB citizen's band (radio)
CBE Commander of the (Order of the) British Empire
CBI Confederation of British Industry
CCD charge-coupled device
CCK cholecystokinin-pancreozymin
CCR camera cassette recorder
CCTV closed circuit television
CD Civil Defence
CDROM compact disc read-only memory
CDU Christian Democratic Union
CENTO Central Treaty Organization
CERN Organisation Européene pour la Recherche Nucléaire (formerly, Conseil Européen pour la Recherche Nucléaire)

ABBREVIATIONS (cont.)

CGS	centimetre-gram-second
CGT	capital gains tax
CGT	Confédération Générale du Travail
CH	Companion of Honour
CHAPS	Clearing House Automated Clearance System
CHIPS	Clearing House Interbank Payments System
CIA	Central Intelligence Agency
CID	Criminal Investigation Department
CIO	Congress of Industrial Organizations
CM	Congregation of the Mission
CMG	Companion of (the Order of) St Michael & St George
CNAA	Council for National Academic Awards
CND	Campaign for Nuclear Disarmament
CNES	Centre National d'Espace
CNS	central nervous system
COBOL	Common Business Oriented Language
COMAL	Common Algorithmic Language
COMECON	Council for Mutual Economic Assistance
CORE	Congress of Racial Equality
CP	Congregation of the Passion
CPI	Consumer Price Index
CP/M	control program monitor
CPR	cardio-pulmonary resuscitation
CPU	central processing unit
CRO	cathode-ray oscilloscope
CRT	cathode-ray tube
CSE	Certificate of Secondary Education
CSF	cerebrospinal fluid
CSIRO	Commonwealth Scientific and Industrial Research Organization
CSO	colour separation overlay
CTT	capital transfer tax
CV	cultivar
CVO	Commander of the Royal Victorian Order
CVS	chorionic villus sampling
CWA	County Women's Association
CWS	Co-operation Wholesale Society

D

D-A	digital-to-analog
DALR	dry adiabatic lapse rate
D&C	dilation and curettage
DBE	Dame Commander of the (Order of the) British Empire
DBMS	database management system
DBS	direct broadcasting from satellite
dc	direct current
DCF	discounted cash flow
DCMG	Dame Commander Grand Cross of (the Order of) St Michael and St George
DCVO	Dame Commander of the Royal Victorian Order
DDT	dichloro-diphenyl-trichloroethane
DES	Department of Education and Science
DES	diethylstilboestrol
DFC	Distinguished Flying Cross
DHA	District Health Authority
DIA	Defense Intelligence Agency
DLP	Democratic Labor Party (Australia)
DMSO	dimethyl sulphoxide
DNA	deoxyribonucleic acid
DOS	Disk Operating System
DSN	Deep Space Network
DSO	Distinguished Service Order
DST	daylight saving time
DTP	desk top publishing

E

EAC	European Atomic Commission
EARUM	electrically alterable read-only memory
EBCDIC	Extended Binary-Coded Decimal Interchange Code
EBU	European Boxing Union
EBU	European Broadcasting Union
EC	European Community
ECA	European Commission on Agriculture
ECF	extracellular fluid
ECG	electrocardiograph
ECM	European Common Market
ECO	European Coal Organization
ECOSOC	Economic and Social Council (of the United Nations)
ECOWAS	Economic Community of West African States
ECSC	European Coal and Steel Community
ECT	elctroconvulsive therapy
ECTG	European Channel Tunnel Group
ECU	European Currency Unit
EDC	European Defence Community
EDF	European Development Fund
EDVAC	Electronic Discrete Variable Automatic Computer
EEC	European Economic Community
EEG	electroencephalography
EEOC	Equal Employment Opportunity Commission
EFA	European Fighter Aircraft
EFC	European Forestry Commission
EFTA	European Free Trade Association
EGF	epidermal growth factor
EI	Exposure Index
ELDO	European Launcher Development Organization
ELF	Eritrea Liberation Front
emf	electromotive force
EMS	European Monetary System
emu	electromagnetic units
ENIAC	Electronic Numeral Indicator and Calculator
EOKA	Ethniki Organosis Kipriakou Agonos (Mational Organization of Cypriot Struggle)
EP	European Parliament
EPA	Environmental Protection Agency
EPR	Einstein-Podolsky-Rosen (paradox)
EPR	electron paramagnetic resonance
EPROM	electronically programmable read-only memory
ERNIE	Electronic Random Number Indicator Equipment
ERW	enhanced radiation weapon
ESA	Environmentally Sensitive Area
ESA	European Space Agency
ESC	electronic stills camera
ESCU	European Space Operations Centre
ESO	European Southern Observatory
ESP	extra-sensory perception
ESRO	European Space Research Organization
ESTEC	European Space Research and Technology Centre
ETU	Electricians Trade Union
EUFA	European Union Football Associations
EURATOM	European Atomic Energy Community

F

FA	Football Association
FAA	Federal Aviation Administration
FAO	Food and Agriculture Organization
FBI	Federal Bureau of Investigation
FCA	Farm Credit Administration
FCC	Federal Communications Commission
FDIC	Federal Deposit Insurance Corporation
FIFA	Fédération Internationale de Football Association (International Association Football Federation)
FIMBRA	Financial Intermediaries, Managers and Brokers Regulatory Association
FLN	Front de Liberation Nationale
fm	frequency modulation
FORTRAN	Formula Translation
FPS	foot-pound-second
FRELIMO	Frente de Libertação de Moçambique
FSH	follicle-stimulating hormone
FTC	Federal Trade Commission

G

GAR	Grand Army of the Republic
GATT	General Agreement on Tariffs and Trade
GBE	Knight/Dame Grand Cross of (the Order of the) British Empire
GC	George Cross
GCC	Gulf Co-operation Council
GCE	General Certificate of Education
GCHQ	Government Communications Headquarters

ABBREVIATIONS (cont.)

GCMG Knight/Dame Grand Cross of (the Order of) St Michael and St George
GCSE General Certificate of Secondary Education
GCVO Knight/Dame Grand Cross of the Royal Victorian Order
GDI gross domestic income
GDP gross domestic product
GEO geosynchronous Earth orbit
GESP generalized extra-sensory perception
GH growth hormone
GLC gas-liquid chromatography
GLCM ground-launched cruise missile
GM George Medal
GMC General Medical Council
GMT Greenwich Mean Time
GNP gross national product
GnRH gonadotrophin-releasing hormone
GP General Practitioner
GPSS General Purpose System Simulator
GUTS grand unified theories

H

HCG human chorionic gonadotrophin
HE His/Her Excellency
HEP hydro-electric power
HF high frequency
HGV heavy goods vehicle
HIH His/Her Imperial Highness
HIM His/Her Imperial Majesty
HLA human leucocyte antigen
HM His/Her Majesty
HMG His/Her Majesty's Government
HMI His/Her Majesty's Inspectorate
HMO Health Maintenance Organization
HMS His/Her Majesty's Ship/Service
HMSO His/Her Majesty's Stationery Office
HNC Higher National Certificate
HND Higher National Diploma
hp horsepower
HR House of Representatives
HRH His/Her Royal Highness

I

IAEA International Atomic Energy Agency
IBRD International Bank for Reconstruction and Development
IC integrated circuit
ICAO International Civil Aviation Organization
ICFTU International Confederation of Free Trade Unions
ICI Imperial Chemical Industries
IDA International Development Agency
IFAD International Fund for Agricultural Development
IFC International Finance Corporation
ILO International Labour Organization
IMCO Intergovernmental Maritime Consultative Organization
IMF International Monetary Fund
INLA Irish National Liberation Army
INRI Iesus Nazarenus Rex Iudeorum (Jesus of Nazareth, King of the Jews)
IPA International Phonetic Alphabet
IQ intelligence quotient
IR infrared
IRA Irish Republican Army
IRB Irish Republican Brotherhood
IRBM intermediate-range ballistic missile
ISBN International Standard Book Number
ISO International Organization for Standardization
ISSN International Standard Serial Number
ita International Teaching Alphabet
ITCZ intertropical convergence zone
ITN Independent Television News
ITT International Telephone and Telegraph Corporation
ITU International Telecommunication Union
ITV Independent Television
IUCN International Union for the Conservation of Nature and Natural Resources
IUD intra-uterine device
IUPAC International Union of Pure and Applied Chemistry
IUPAP International Union of Pure and Applied Physics
IVF in vitro fertilization
IVR International Vehicle Registration
IWW Industrial Workers of the World

J

JP Justice of the Peace
JET Joint European Torus

K

KADU Kenya African Democratic Union
KANU Kenya African National Union
KB Knight Bachelor; Knight of the Bath
KBE Knight Commander of the (Order of the) British Empire
KC King's Counsel
KCB Knight Commander of the Bath
KCMG Knight Commander Grand Cross of (the Order of) St Michael and St George
KCVO Knight Commander of the Royal Victorian Order
KG Knight of the Order of the Garter
KGB Komitet Gosudarstvennoye Bezhopaznosti (Committee of State Security)
KKK Ku Klux Klan
KMT Kuomintang
kpc kiloparsec
KT Knight of the Thistle

L

LAFTA Latin-American Free Trade Association
LAN local area network
LAUTRO Life Assurance and Unit Trust Companies
LCD liquid crystal display
LDC less developed country
LEA Local Education Authority
LED light-emitting diode
LEO low Earth orbit
LFA Less Favoured Area
LH luteinizing hormone
LHRH luteinizing-hormone-releasing hormone
LIFFE London International Financial Futures Exchange
LISP List Processing
LMS London Missionary Society
LPG liquefied petroleum gas
LSD lysergic acid diethylamide
LSI large-scale integration
LVO Lieutenant of the Royal Victorian Order

M

MAC Multiplexed Analog Component
MAO monoamine oxidase
MATV Master Antenna Television
MBE Member of the Order of the British Empire
MCA Monetary Compensation Amount
MCC Marylebone Cricket Club
MDMA methylenedioxymethamphetamine
ME myalgic encephalomyelitis
MH Medal of Honor
MHD magnetohydrodynamics
MICR magnetic ink character recognition
Mired micro reciprocal degrees
MIRV multiple independently targetted re-entry vehicle
MKSA metre-kilogram-second-ampere
MLR minimum lending rate
mmf magnetomotive force
MMI man-machine interaction
MOH Medal of Honor
Mpc megaparsec
MPS marginal propensity to save
MPTP methylphenyltetrahydropyridine
MRA Moral Rearmament
MSC Manpower Services Commission
MSG monosodium glutamate
MSH melanocyte-stimulating hormone
MVD Ministerstvo Vnutrennykh Del (Ministry for Internal Affairs)
MVO Member of the Royal Victorian Order

ABBREVIATIONS (cont.)

N

NAACP National Association for the Advancement of Colored People
NANC non-adrenergic, non-cholinergic
NASA National Aeronautics and Space Administration
NASDA National Space Development Agency
NATO North Atlantic Treaty Organization
NDE near-death experience
NEDC National Economic Development Office
NEP New Economic Policy
NF National Front
NFC National Football Conference
NGC New General Catalogue
NGF nerve growth factor
NHL National Hockey League
NHS National Health Service
NIH National Institutes of Health
NKVD Narodnyi Komissariat Vnutrennikh Del (People's Commissariat of Internal Affairs)
NLRB National Labor Relations Board
NMR nuclear magnetic resonance
NOW National Organization for Women
NPT Non-Proliferation Treaty
NRA National Recovery Administration
NRAO National Radio Astronomy Observatory
NSF National Science Foundation
NSPCC National Society for the Prevention of Cruelty to Children
NTSC National Television System Commission
NUM National Union of Mineworkers
NUT National Union of Teachers
NVC non-verbal communication

O

OAPEC Organization of Arab Petroleum Exporting Countries
OAS Organisation de l'Armée Secrète (Secret Army Organization)
OAS Organization of American States
OAU Organization of African Unity
OB Order of the Bath
OB outside broadcast
OBE Officer of the (Order of the) British Empire
OCarm Order of the Brothers of the Blessed Virgin Mary of Mount Carmel
OCart Order of Carthusians
OCR optical character recognition/reader
OCSO Order of the Reformed Cistercians of the Strict Observance
OD ordnance datum
ODC Order of Discalced Carmelites
ODECA Organizacion de Estados Centro Americanos (Organization of Central American States)
OECD Organization for Economic Co-operation and Development
OEEC Organization for European Economic Co-operation
OEM Original Equipment Manufacturer
OFM Order of Friars Minor
OFMCap Order of Friars Minor Capuchin
OFMConv Order of Friars Minor Conventual
OGPU Otdelenie Gosudarstvenni Politcheskoi Upravi (Special Government Political Administration)
OM Order of Merit
OMCap Order of Friars Minor of St Francis Capuccinorum
OOBE out-of-the-body experience
OP Order of Preachers
OPEC Organization of Petroleum Exporting Countries
OSA Order of the Hermit Friars of St Augustine
OSB Order of St Benedict
OSFC Order of Friars Minor of St Francis Capuccinorum
OTC over-the-counter (stocks and shares, drugs)
OTEC ocean thermal energy conversion
OU Open University
OXFAM Oxford Committee for Famine Relief

P

PAC Pan-African Congress
PAC political action committee
PAL phase alternation line
PAYE pay as you earn
pc parsec
PC personal computer
PC Poor Clares
PCP phenylcyclohexylpiperidine
PDGF platelet-derived growth factor
PDR precision depth recorder
PEN International Association of Poets, Playwrights, Editors, Essayists, and Novelists
PEP Political and Economic Planning
PF Patriotic Front
PGA Professional Golfers' Association
PH Purple Heart
PIN personal identification number
PK psychokinesis
PKU phenylketonuria
PLA People's Liberation Army
plc public limited company
PLO Palestine Liberation Organization
PM of F Presidential Medal of Freedom
PNLM Palestine National Liberation Movement
POW prisoner of war
PPI plan position indicator
PR proportional representation
PRO Public Record Office
PRO public relations officer
PROM programmable read-only memory
PSBR public sector borrowing requirement
PTA parent-teacher association
PTFE polytetrafluorethylene
PVA polyvinyl acetate
PVC polyvinyl chloride
PWA Public Works Administration
PWR pressurized-water reactor
PYO pick-your-own

Q

QC Queen's Counsel
QCD quantum chromodynamics
QED quantum electrodynamics

R

RA Royal Academy
R&A Royal & Ancient Golf Club of St Andrews
RAAF Royal Australian Air Force
RADA Royal Academy of Dramatic Art
RAF Royal Air Force
RAM random access memory
RAM Royal Academy of Music
RAN Royal Australian Navy
RDA recommended daily allowance
REM rapid eye movement
RGB red, green and blue (colour television)
RHA Regional Health Authority
RISC reduced interaction set computer
RKKA Rabochekrest'yanshi Krasny (Red Army of Workers and Peasants)
RM Royal Marines
rms root-mean-square
RN Royal Navy
RNA ribonucleic acid
RNLI Royal National Lifeboat Institution
ROM read only memory
RP received pronunciation
RPI retail price index
rpm revolutions per minute
rpm resale price maintenance
RS Royal Society
RSPB Royal Society for the Protection of Birds
RSPCA Royal Society for the Prevention of Cruelty to Animals
RTG radio-isotope thermo-electric generator
RVO Royal Victorian Order

S

SA Sturm Abteilung (Storm Troopers)
SALR saturated adiabatic lapse rate

ABBREVIATIONS (cont.)

SALT	Strategic Arms Limitation Talks
SAS	Special Air Service
SBR	styrene butadiene rubber
SCID	severe combined immuno-deficiency
SCLC	Southern Christian Leadership Conference
SDI	selective dissemination of information
SDI	strategic defense initiative
SDP	Social Democratic Party
SDR	special drawing rights
SDS	Students for a Democratic Society
SDU	Social Democratic Union
SEAQ	Stock Exchange Automated Quotations
SEATO	South East Asia Treaty Organization
SEC	Securities and Exchange Commission
SECAM	Séquence Electronique Couleur avec Mémoire (Electronic Colour Sequence with Memory)
SERPS	State Earnings Related Pension Scheme
SHAEF	Supreme Headquarters Allied Expeditionary Force
SHAPE	Supreme Headquarters Allied Powers, Europe
SHF	super high frequency
SI	Système International (International System)
SIB	Securities and Investments Board
SIOP	Single Integrated Operation Plan
SJ	Society of Jesus
SLBN	submarine-launched ballistic missile
SLCM	sea-launched cruise missile
SLDP	Social and Liberal Democratic Party
SLE	systemic lupus erythematosus
SLR	single lens reflex
SNCC	Student Non-Violent Co-ordinating Committee
SNOBOL	String-Oriented Symbolic Language
SNP	Scottish National Party
SOCist	Cistercians of Common Observance
SOE	Special Operations Executive
SONAR	sound navigation and ranging
SP	starting price
SQUID	superconducting quantum interference device
SR	Socialist Revolutionaries
SRO	self-regulatory organization
SS	Schutzstaffel (Protective Squad)
SSR	Soviet Socialist Republic
SSSI	Site of Special Scientific Interest
START	Strategic Arms Reduction Talks
STOL	short take-off and landing
SWAPO	South West Africa People's Organization
SWS	slow wave sleep

T

TAB	Totalisator Agency Board
TARDIS	Time and Relative Dimensions in Space
TASS	Telegrafnoe Agentsvo Sovetskovo Soyuza (Telegraph Agency of the Soviet Union)
TCDD	tetrachlorodibenzo-p-dioxin
TEFL	Teaching English as a Foreign Language
TESL	Teaching English as a Second Language
TGWU	Transport and General Workers Union
TNT	trinitrotoluene
TSB	Trustee Savings Bank
TT	Tourist Trophy
TTL	through the lens
TUC	Trades Union Congress
TV	television
TVA	Tennessee Valley Authority

U

UAE	United Arab Emirates
UAP	United Australia Party
UCAR	Union of Central African Republics
UCCA	University Central Council on Admissions
UDA	Ulster Defence Association
DI	Unilateral Declaration of Independence
FA	Union of European Football Association
[illegible]	unidentified flying object
UHF	ultra high frequency
UHT	ultra high temperature
UK	United Kingdom
UN	United Nations
UNCTAD	United Nations Conference on Trade and Development
UNDC	United Nations Disarmament Commission
UNDP	United Nations Development Programme
UNEP	United Nations Environment Programme
UNESCO	United Nations Economic, Scientific, and Cultural Organization
UNFAO	United Nations Food and Agriculture Organization
UNGA	United Nations General Assembly
UNHCR	United Nations High Commission for Refugees
UNHRC	United Nations Human Rights Commission
UNICEF	United Nations International Children's Emergency Fund
UNIDO	United Nations Industrial Development Organization
UNO	United Nations Organization
UNRWA	United Nations Relief and Works Agency for Palestine Refugees in the Near East
UNSC	United Nations Security Council
UNSG	United Nations Secretary General
UNTT	United Nations Trust Territory
UPU	Universal Postal Union
USA	United States of America
USAF	United States Air Force
USCG	United States Coast Guard
USIS	United States Information Service
USSR	Union of Soviet Socialist Republics

V

VA	Veterans Administration
VAT	value-added tax
VC	Victoria Cross
VCR	video cassette recorder
VD	venereal disease
VDU	visual display unit
VHF	very high frequency
VHS	Video Home Service
VIP	vasoactive intestinal polypeptide
VLF	very low frequency
VLSI	very large scale interpretation
VOA	Voice of America
VSEPR	valence shell electron pair repulsion
VSO	Voluntary Service Overseas
VTOL	vertical take-off and landing
VTR	video tape recorder

W

WAAC	Women's Auxiliary Army Corps
WAAF	Women's Auxiliary Air Force
WAC	Women's Army Corps
WASP	White Anglo-Saxon Protestant
WBA	World Boxing Association
WBC	World Boxing Council
WCC	World Council of Churches
WEA	Workers' Educational Association
WFTU	World Federation of Trade Unions
WHO	World Health Organization
WI	(National Federation of) Women's Institutes
WIPO	World Intellectual Property Organization
WMO	World Meteorological Organization
WPA	Work Projects Administration
WRAC	Women's Royal Army Corps
WRAF	Women's Royal Air Force
WRNS	Women's Royal Naval Service
WRVS	Women's Royal Voluntary Service
WVS	Women's Voluntary Service
WWF	World Wildlife Fund

Y

YHA	Youth Hostels Association
YMCA	Young Men's Christian Association
YMHA	Young Men's Hebrew Association
YWCA	Young Women's Christian Association
YWHA	Young Women's Hebrew Association

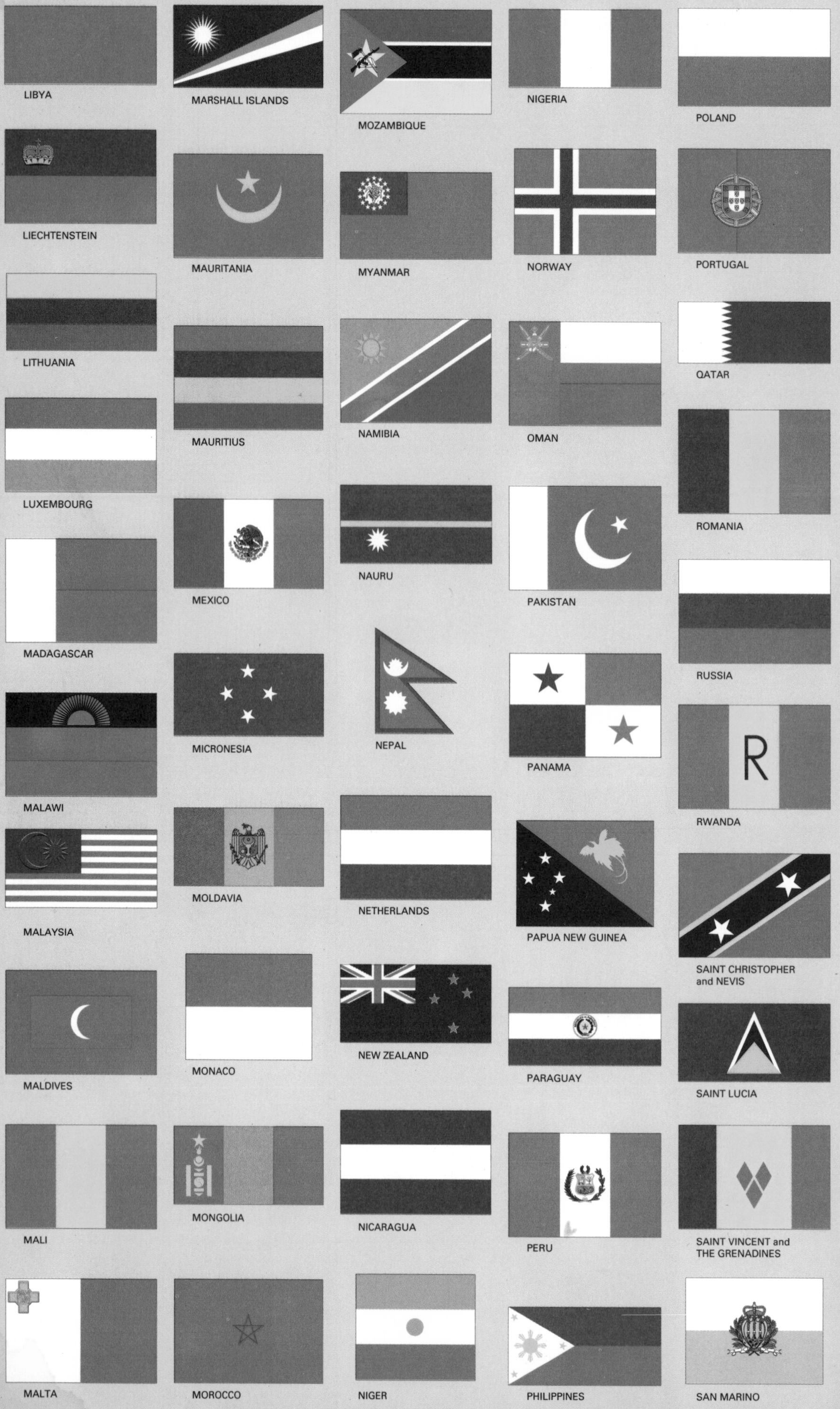
LIBYA
LIECHTENSTEIN
LITHUANIA
LUXEMBOURG
MADAGASCAR
MALAWI
MALAYSIA
MALDIVES
MALI
MALTA
MARSHALL ISLANDS
MAURITANIA
MAURITIUS
MEXICO
MICRONESIA
MOLDAVIA
MONACO
MONGOLIA
MOROCCO
MOZAMBIQUE
MYANMAR
NAMIBIA
NAURU
NEPAL
NETHERLANDS
NEW ZEALAND
NICARAGUA
NIGER
NIGERIA
NORWAY
OMAN
PAKISTAN
PANAMA
PAPUA NEW GUINEA
PARAGUAY
PERU
PHILIPPINES
POLAND
PORTUGAL
QATAR
ROMANIA
RUSSIA
RWANDA
SAINT CHRISTOPHER and NEVIS
SAINT LUCIA
SAINT VINCENT and THE GRENADINES
SAN MARINO